PETERSON'S® GRADUATE & PROFESSIONAL PROGRAMS

AN OVERVIEW

2017

PETERSON'S®

PETERSON'S®

About Peterson's®

Peterson's®, a Nelnet company, has been your trusted educational publisher for over 50 years. It's a milestone we're quite proud of, as we continue to offer the most accurate, dependable, high-quality education content in the field, providing you with everything you need to succeed. No matter where you are on your academic or professional path, you can rely on Peterson's publications and its online information at **www.petersons.com** for the most up-to-date education exploration data, expert test-prep tools, and the highest quality career success resources—everything you need to achieve your educational goals.

For more information, contact Peterson's Publishing, 3 Columbia Circle, Suite 205, Albany, NY 12203-5158; 800-338-3282 Ext. 54229; or find us on the World Wide Web at www.petersonsbooks.com.

ISSN 1093-8443
ISBN: 978-0-7689-4092-3

Printed in the United States of America

10 9 8 7 6 5 4 3 2 1 19 18 17

Fifty-first Edition

CONTENTS

A Note from the Peterson's Editors

The six volumes of Peterson's *Graduate and Professional Programs*, the only annually updated reference work of its kind, provide wideranging information on the graduate and professional programs offered by accredited colleges and universities in the United States, U.S. territories, and Canada and by those institutions outside the United States that are accredited by U.S. accrediting bodies. Nearly 36,000 individual academic and professional programs at more than 2,200 institutions are listed. Peterson's *Graduate and Professional Programs* have been used for more than forty years by prospective graduate and professional students, placement counselors, faculty advisers, and all others interested in postbaccalaureate education.

Graduate & Professional Programs: An Overview contains information on institutions as a whole, while the other books in the series are devoted to specific academic and professional fields:

Graduate Programs in the Humanities, Arts & Social Sciences
Graduate Programs in the Biological/Biomedical Sciences & Health-Related Medical Professions
Graduate Programs in the Physical Sciences, Mathematics, Agricultural Sciences, the Environment & Natural Resources
Graduate Programs in Engineering & Applied Sciences
Graduate Programs in Business, Education, Information Studies, Law & Social Work

The books may be used individually or as a set. For example, if you have chosen a field of study but do not know what institution you want to attend or if you have a college or university in mind but have not chosen an academic field of study, it is best to begin with the Overview guide.

Graduate & Professional Programs: An Overview presents several directories to help you identify programs of study that might interest you; you can then research those programs further in the other books in the series by using the Directory of Graduate and Professional Programs by Field, which lists 500 fields and gives the names of those institutions that offer graduate degree programs in each.

For geographical or financial reasons, you may be interested in attending a particular institution and will want to know what it has to offer. You should turn to the Directory of Institutions and Their Offerings, which lists the degree programs available at each institution. As in the Directory of Graduate and Professional Programs by Field, the level of degrees offered is also indicated.

All books in the series include advice on graduate education, including topics such as admissions tests, financial aid, and accreditation. **The Graduate Adviser** includes two essays and information about accreditation. The first essay, "The Admissions Process," discusses general admission requirements, admission tests, factors to consider when selecting a graduate school or program, when and how to apply, and how admission decisions are made. Special information for international students and tips for minority students are also included. The second essay, "Financial Support," is an overview of the broad range of support available at the graduate level. Fellowships, scholarships, and grants; assistantships and internships; federal and private loan programs, as well as Federal Work-Study; and the GI bill are detailed. This essay concludes with advice on applying for need-based financial aid. "Accreditation and Accrediting Agencies" gives information on accreditation and its purpose and lists institutional accrediting agencies first and then specialized accrediting agencies relevant to each volume's specific fields of study.

With information on more than 44,000 graduate programs in more than 500 disciplines, Peterson's *Graduate and Professional Programs* give you all the information you need about the programs that are of interest to you in three formats: **Profiles** (capsule summaries of basic information), **Displays** (information that an institution or program wants to emphasize), and **Close-Ups** (written by administrators, with more expansive information than the **Profiles**, emphasizing different aspects of the programs). By using these various formats of program information, coupled with **Appendixes** and **Indexes** covering directories and subject areas for all six books, you will find that these guides provide the most comprehensive, accurate, and up-to-date graduate study information available.

Peterson's publishes a full line of resources with information you need to guide you through the graduate admissions process. Peterson's publications can be found at college libraries and career centers and your local bookstore or library—or visit us on the Web at www.petersonsbooks.com. Peterson's books are now also available as ebooks.

Colleges and universities will be pleased to know that Peterson's helped you in your selection. Admissions staff members are more than happy to answer questions, address specific problems, and help in any way they can. The editors at Peterson's wish you great success in your graduate program search!

NOTICE: Certain portions of or information contained in this book have been submitted and paid for by the educational institution identified, and such institutions take full responsibility for the accuracy, timeliness, completeness, and functionality of such contents. Such portions or information include (i) each display ad that comprises a half page of information covering a single educational institution or program and (ii) each two-page description of a graduate school or program that appears in the "Close-Ups of Institutions Offering Graduate and Professional Work" section on pages 863–916.

THE GRADUATE ADVISER

The Admissions Process

Generalizations about graduate admissions practices are not always helpful because each institution has its own set of guidelines and procedures. Nevertheless, some broad statements can be made about the admissions process that may help you plan your strategy.

Factors Involved in Selecting a Graduate School or Program

Selecting a graduate school and a specific program of study is a complex matter. Quality of the faculty; program and course offerings; the nature, size, and location of the institution; admission requirements; cost; and the availability of financial assistance are among the many factors that affect one's choice of institution. Other considerations are job placement and achievements of the program's graduates and the institution's resources, such as libraries, laboratories, and computer facilities. If you are to make the best possible choice, you need to learn as much as you can about the schools and programs you are considering before you apply.

The following steps may help you narrow your choices.

- Talk to alumni of the programs or institutions you are considering to get their impressions of how well they were prepared for work in their fields of study.
- Remember that graduate school requirements change, so be sure to get the most up-to-date information possible.
- Talk to department faculty members and the graduate adviser at your undergraduate institution. They often have information about programs of study at other institutions.
- Visit the websites of the graduate schools in which you are interested to request a graduate catalog. Contact the department chair in your chosen field of study for additional information about the department and the field.
- Visit as many campuses as possible. Call ahead for an appointment with the graduate adviser in your field of interest and be sure to check out the facilities and talk to students.

General Requirements

Graduate schools and departments have requirements that applicants for admission must meet. Typically, these requirements include undergraduate transcripts (which provide information about undergraduate grade point average and course work applied toward a major), admission test scores, and letters of recommendation. Most graduate programs also ask for an essay or personal statement that describes your personal reasons for seeking graduate study. In some fields, such as art and music, portfolios or auditions may be required in addition to other evidence of talent. Some institutions require that the applicant have an undergraduate degree in the same subject as the intended graduate major.

Most institutions evaluate each applicant on the basis of the applicant's total record, and the weight accorded any given factor varies widely from institution to institution and from program to program.

The Application Process

You should begin the application process at least one year before you expect to begin your graduate study. Find out the application deadline for each institution (many are provided in the **Profile** section of this guide). Go to the institution's website and find out if you can apply online. If not, request a paper application form. Fill out this form thoroughly and neatly. Assume that the school needs all the information it is requesting and that the admissions officer will be sensitive to the neatness and overall quality of what you submit. Do not supply more information than the school requires.

The institution may ask at least one question that will require a three- or four-paragraph answer. Compose your response on the assumption that the admissions officer is interested in both what you think and how you express yourself. Keep your statement brief and to the point, but, at the same time, include all pertinent information about your past experiences and your educational goals. Individual statements vary greatly in style and content, which helps admissions officers differentiate among applicants. Many graduate departments give considerable weight to the statement in making their admissions decisions, so be sure to take the time to prepare a thoughtful and concise statement.

If recommendations are a part of the admissions requirements, carefully choose the individuals you ask to write them. It is generally best to ask current or former professors to write the recommendations, provided they are able to attest to your intellectual ability and motivation for doing the work required of a graduate student. It is advisable to provide stamped, preaddressed envelopes to people being asked to submit recommendations on your behalf.

Completed applications, including references, transcripts, and admission test scores, should be received at the institution by the specified date.

Be advised that institutions do not usually make admissions decisions until all materials have been received. Enclose a self-addressed postcard with your application, requesting confirmation of receipt. Allow at least ten days for the return of the postcard before making further inquiries.

If you plan to apply for financial support, it is imperative that you file your application early.

ADMISSION TESTS

The major testing program used in graduate admissions is the Graduate Record Examinations (GRE®) testing program, sponsored by the GRE Board and administered by Educational Testing Service, Princeton, New Jersey.

The Graduate Record Examinations testing program consists of a General Test and eight Subject Tests. The General Test measures critical thinking, verbal reasoning, quantitative reasoning, and analytical writing skills. It is offered as an Internet-based test (iBT) in the United States, Canada, and many other countries.

The GRE® revised General Test's questions were designed to reflect the kind of thinking that students need to do in graduate or business school and demonstrate that students are indeed ready for graduate-level work.

- **Verbal Reasoning**—Measures ability to analyze and evaluate written material and synthesize information obtained from it, analyze relationships among component parts of sentences, and recognize relationships among words and concepts.
- **Quantitative Reasoning**—Measures problem-solving ability, focusing on basic concepts of arithmetic, algebra, geometry, and data analysis.
- **Analytical Writing**—Measures critical thinking and analytical writing skills, specifically the ability to articulate and support complex ideas clearly and effectively.

The computer-delivered GRE® revised General Test is offered year-round at Prometric™ test centers and on specific dates at testing locations outside of the Prometric test center network. Appointments are scheduled on a first-come, first-served basis. The GRE® revised General Test is also offered as a paper-based test three times a year in areas where computer-based testing is not available.

You can take the computer-delivered GRE® revised General Test once every twenty-one days, up to five times within any continuous rolling twelve-month period (365 days)—even if you canceled your scores on a previously taken test. You may take the paper-delivered GRE® revised General Test as often as it is offered.

Three scores are reported on the revised General Test:

1. A **Verbal Reasoning score** is reported on a 130–170 score scale, in 1-point increments.
2. A **Quantitative Reasoning score** is reported on a 130–170 score scale, in 1-point increments.
3. An **Analytical Writing score** is reported on a 0–6 score level, in half-point increments.

The GRE® Subject Tests measure achievement and assume undergraduate majors or extensive background in the following eight disciplines:

- Biochemistry, Cell and Molecular Biology
- Biology
- Chemistry
- Computer Science
- Literature in English
- Mathematics
- Physics
- Psychology

The Subject Tests are available three times per year as paper-based administrations around the world. Testing time is approximately 2 hours and 50 minutes. You can obtain more information about the GRE® by visiting the ETS website at www.ets.org or consulting the *GRE® Information and Registration Bulletin*. The *Bulletin* can be obtained at many undergraduate colleges. You can also download it from the ETS website or obtain it by contacting Graduate Record Examinations, Educational Testing Service, P.O. Box 6000, Princeton, NJ 08541-6000; phone: 609-771-7670.

If you expect to apply for admission to a program that requires any of the GRE® tests, you should select a test date well in advance of the application deadline. Scores on the computer-based General Test are reported within ten to fifteen days; scores on the paper-based Subject Tests are reported within six weeks.

Another testing program, the Miller Analogies Test® (MAT®), is administered at more than 500 Controlled Testing Centers, licensed by Harcourt Assessment, Inc., in the United States, Canada, and other countries. The MAT® computer-based test is now available. Testing time is 60 minutes. The test consists of 120 partial analogies. You can obtain the *Candidate Information Booklet,* which contains a list of test centers and instructions for taking the test, from http://www.milleranalogies.com or by calling 800-328-5999 (toll-free).

Check the specific requirements of the programs to which you are applying.

How Admission Decisions Are Made

The program you apply to is directly involved in the admissions process. Although the final decision is usually made by the graduate dean (or an associate) or the faculty admissions committee, recommendations from faculty members in your intended field are important. At some institutions, an interview is incorporated into the decision process.

A Special Note for International Students

In addition to the steps already described, there are some special considerations for international students who intend to apply for graduate study in the United States. All graduate schools require an indication of competence in English. The purpose of the Test of English as a Foreign Language (TOEFL®) is to evaluate the English proficiency of people who are nonnative speakers of English and want to study at colleges and universities where English is the language of instruction. The TOEFL® is administered by Educational Testing Service (ETS) under the general direction of a policy board established by the College Board and the Graduate Record Examinations Board.

The TOEFL® iBT assesses the four basic language skills: listening, reading, writing, and speaking. It was administered for the first time in September 2005, and ETS continues to introduce the TOEFL® iBT in selected cities. The Internet-based test is administered at secure, official test centers. The testing time is approximately 4 hours. Because the TOEFL® iBT includes a speaking section, the Test of Spoken English (TSE) is no longer needed.

The TOEFL® is also offered in the paper-based format in areas of the world where Internet-based testing is not available. The paper-based TOEFL® consists of three sections—listening comprehension, structure and written expression, and reading comprehension. The testing time is approximately 3 hours. The Test of Written English (TWE®) is also given. The TWE® is a 30-minute essay that measures the examinee's ability to compose in English. Examinees receive a TWE® score separate from their TOEFL® score. The *Information Bulletin* contains information on local fees and registration procedures.

The TOEFL® paper-based test (TOEFL® PBT) began being phased out in mid-2012. For those who may have taken the TOEFL® PBT, scores remain valid for two years after the test date. The Test of Written English (TWE®) is also given. The TWE® is a 30-minute essay that measures the examinee's ability to compose in English. Examinees receive a TWE® score separate from their TOEFL® score. The Information Bulletin contains information on local fees and registration procedures.

Additional information and registration materials are available from TOEFL® Services, Educational Testing Service, P.O. Box 6151, Princeton, New Jersey 08541-6151. Phone: 609-771-7100. Website: www.toefl.org.

International students should apply especially early because of the number of steps required to complete the admissions process. Furthermore, many United States graduate schools have a limited number of spaces for international students, and many more students apply than the schools can accommodate.

International students may find financial assistance from institutions very limited. The U.S. government requires international applicants to submit a certification of support, which is a statement attesting to the applicant's financial resources. In addition, international students *must* have health insurance coverage.

Tips for Minority Students

Indicators of a university's values in terms of diversity are found both in its recruitment programs and its resources directed to student success. Important questions: Does the institution vigorously recruit minorities for its graduate programs? Is there funding available to help with the costs associated with visiting the school? Are minorities represented in the institution's brochures or website or on their faculty rolls? What campus-based resources or services (including assistance in locating housing or career counseling and placement) are available? Is funding available to members of underrepresented groups?

At the program level, it is particularly important for minority students to investigate the "climate" of a program under consideration. How many minority students are enrolled and how many have graduated? What opportunities are there to work with diverse faculty and mentors whose research interests match yours? How are conflicts resolved or concerns addressed? How interested are faculty in building strong and supportive relations with students? "Climate" concerns should be addressed by posing questions to various individuals, including faculty members, current students, and alumni.

Information is also available through various organizations, such as the Hispanic Association of Colleges & Universities (HACU), and publications such as *Diverse Issues in Higher Education* and *Hispanic Outlook* magazine. There are also books devoted to this topic, such as *The Multicultural Student's Guide to Colleges* by Robert Mitchell.

Financial Support

The range of financial support at the graduate level is very broad. The following descriptions will give you a general idea of what you might expect and what will be expected of you as a financial support recipient.

Fellowships, Scholarships, and Grants

These are usually outright awards of a few hundred to many thousands of dollars with no service to the institution required in return. Fellowships and scholarships are usually awarded on the basis of merit and are highly competitive. Grants are made on the basis of financial need or special talent in a field of study. Many fellowships, scholarships, and grants not only cover tuition, fees, and supplies but also include stipends for living expenses with allowances for dependents. However, the terms of each should be examined because some do not permit recipients to supplement their income with outside work. Fellowships, scholarships, and grants may vary in the number of years for which they are awarded.

In addition to the availability of these funds at the university or program level, many excellent fellowship programs are available at the national level and may be applied for before and during enrollment in a graduate program. A listing of many of these programs can be found at the Council of Graduate Schools' website: http://www.cgsnet.org. There is a wealth of information in the "Programs" and "Awards" sections.

Assistantships and Internships

Many graduate students receive financial support through assistantships, particularly involving teaching or research duties. It is important to recognize that such appointments should not be viewed simply as employment relationships but rather should constitute an integral and important part of a student's graduate education. As such, the appointments should be accompanied by strong faculty mentoring and increasingly responsible apprenticeship experiences. The specific nature of these appointments in a given program should be considered in selecting that graduate program.

TEACHING ASSISTANTSHIPS

These usually provide a salary and full or partial tuition remission and may also provide health benefits. Unlike fellowships, scholarships, and grants, which require no service to the institution, teaching assistantships require recipients to provide the institution with a specific amount of undergraduate teaching, ideally related to the student's field of study. Some teaching assistants are limited to grading papers, compiling bibliographies, taking notes, or monitoring laboratories. At some graduate schools, teaching assistants must carry lighter course loads than regular full-time students.

RESEARCH ASSISTANTSHIPS

These are very similar to teaching assistantships in the manner in which financial assistance is provided. The difference is that recipients are given basic research assignments in their disciplines rather than teaching responsibilities. The work required is normally related to the student's field of study; in most instances, the assistantship supports the student's thesis or dissertation research.

ADMINISTRATIVE INTERNSHIPS

These are similar to assistantships in application of financial assistance funds, but the student is given an assignment on a part-time basis, usually as a special assistant with one of the university's administrative offices. The assignment may not necessarily be directly related to the recipient's discipline.

RESIDENCE HALL AND COUNSELING ASSISTANTSHIPS

These assistantships are frequently assigned to graduate students in psychology, counseling, and social work, but they may be offered to students in other disciplines, especially if the student has worked in this capacity during his or her undergraduate years. Duties can vary from being available in a dean's office for a specific number of hours for consultation with undergraduates to living in campus residences and being responsible for both counseling and administrative tasks or advising student activity groups. Residence hall assistantships often include a room and board allowance and, in some cases, tuition assistance and stipends. Contact the Housing and Student Life Office for more information.

Health Insurance

The availability and affordability of health insurance is an important issue and one that should be considered in an applicant's choice of institution and program. While often included with assistantships and fellowships, this is not always the case and, even if provided, the benefits may be limited. It is important to note that the U.S. government requires international students to have health insurance.

The GI Bill

This provides financial assistance for students who are veterans of the United States armed forces. If you are a veteran, contact your local Veterans Administration office to determine your eligibility and to get full details about benefits. There are a number of programs that offer educational benefits to current military enlistees. Some states have tuition assistance programs for members of the National Guard. Contact the VA office at the college for more information.

Federal Work-Study Program (FWS)

Employment is another way some students finance their graduate studies. The federally funded Federal Work-Study Program provides eligible students with employment opportunities, usually in public and private nonprofit organizations. Federal funds pay up to 75 percent of the wages, with the remainder paid by the employing agency. FWS is available to graduate students who demonstrate financial need. Not all schools have these funds, and some only award them to undergraduates. Each school sets its application deadline and workstudy earnings limits. Wages vary and are related to the type of work done. You must file the Free Application for Federal Student Aid (FAFSA) to be eligible for this program.

Loans

Many graduate students borrow to finance their graduate programs when other sources of assistance (which do not have to be repaid) prove insufficient. You should always read and understand the terms of any loan program before submitting your application.

FEDERAL DIRECT LOANS

Federal Direct Loans. The Federal Direct Loan Program offers a variable-fixed interest rate loan to graduate students with the Department of Education acting as the lender. Students receive a new rate with each new loan, but that rate is fixed for the life of the loan. Beginning with loans made on or after July 1, 2013, the interest rate for loans made each July 1st to June 30th period are determined based on the last 10-year Treasury note auction prior to June 1st of that year, plus an added percentage. The interest rate can be no higher than 9.5%.

Beginning July 1, 2012, the Federal Direct Loan for graduate students is an unsubsidized loan. Under the *unsubsidized* program, the grad borrower pays the interest on the loan from the day proceeds are issued and is responsible for paying interest during all periods. If the borrower chooses not to pay the interest while in school, or during the grace periods, deferment, or forbearance, the interest accrues and will be capitalized.

Graduate students may borrow up to $20,500 per year through the Direct Loan Program, up to a cumulative maximum of $138,500, including undergraduate borrowing. No more than $65,000 of the $138,500 can be from subsidized loans, including loans the grad borrower may have received for periods of enrollment that began before July 1, 2012, or for prior undergraduate borrowing. You may borrow up to the cost of attendance at the school in which you are enrolled or will attend, minus estimated financial assistance from other federal, state, and private sources, up to a maximum of $20,500. Grad borrowers who reach the aggregate loan limit over the course of their education cannot receive additional loans; however, if they repay some of their loans to bring the outstanding balance below the aggregate limit, they could be eligible to borrow again, up to that limit.

For Unsubsidized loans first disbursed on or after July 1, 2015, and before July 1, 2016, the interest rate was 5.84%. For those first disbursed on or after July 1, 2016, and before July 1, 2017, the interest rate is 5.31%.

A fee is deducted from the loan proceeds upon disbursement. Loans with a first disbursement on or after July 1, 2010 but before July 1, 2012, have a borrower origination fee of 1 percent. For loans disbursed after July 1, 2012, these fee deductions no longer apply. The Budget Control Act of 2011, signed into law on August 2, 2011, eliminated Direct Subsidized Loan eligibility for graduate and professional students for periods of enrollment beginning on or after July 1, 2012, and terminated the authority of the Department of Education to offer most repayment incentives to Direct Loan borrowers for loans disbursed on or after July 1, 2012.

Under the *subsidized* Federal Direct Loan Program, repayment begins six months after your last date of enrollment on at least a half-time basis. Under the *unsubsidized* program, repayment of interest begins within thirty days from disbursement of the loan proceeds, and repayment of the principal begins six months after your last enrollment on at least a half-time basis. Some borrowers may choose to defer interest payments while they are in school. The accrued interest is added to the loan balance when the borrower begins repayment. There are several repayment options.

Federal Perkins Loans. The Federal Perkins Loan is available to students demonstrating financial need and is administered directly by the school. Not all schools have these funds, and some may award them to undergraduates only. Eligibility is determined from the information you provide on the FAFSA. The school will notify you of your eligibility.

Eligible graduate students may borrow up to $8,000 per year, up to a maximum of $60,000, including undergraduate borrowing (even if your previous Perkins Loans have been repaid). The interest rate for Federal Perkins Loans is 5 percent, and no interest accrues while you remain in school at least half-time. Students who are attending less than half-time need to check with their school to determine the length of their grace period. There are no guarantee, loan, or disbursement fees. Repayment begins nine months after your last date of enrollment on at least a half-time basis and may extend over a maximum of ten years with no prepayment penalty.

Federal Direct Graduate PLUS Loans. Effective July 1, 2006, graduate and professional students are eligible for Graduate PLUS loans. This program allows students to borrow up to the cost of attendance, less any other aid received. These loans have a fixed interest rate, and interest begins to accrue at the time of disbursement. Beginning with loans made on or after July 1, 2013, the interest rate for loans made each July 1st to June 30th period are determined based on the last 10-year Treasury note auction prior to June 1st of that year. The interest rate can be no higher than 10.5%. The PLUS loans do involve a credit check; a PLUS borrower may obtain a loan with a cosigner if his or her credit is not good enough. Grad PLUS loans may be deferred while a student is in school and for the six months following a drop below half-time enrollment. For more information, you should contact a representative in your college's financial aid office.

Deferring Your Federal Loan Repayments. If you borrowed under the Federal Direct Loan Program, Federal Direct PLUS Loan Program, or the Federal Perkins Loan Program for previous undergraduate or graduate study, your payments may be deferred when you return to graduate school, depending on when you borrowed and under which program.

There are other deferment options available if you are temporarily unable to repay your loan. Information about these deferments is provided at your entrance and exit interviews. If you believe you are eligible for a deferment of your loan payments, you must contact your lender or loan servicer to request a deferment. The deferment must be filed prior to the time your payment is due, and it must be re-filed when it expires if you remain eligible for deferment at that time.

SUPPLEMENTAL (PRIVATE) LOANS

Many lending institutions offer supplemental loan programs and other financing plans, such as the ones described here, to students seeking additional assistance in meeting their education expenses. Some loan programs target all types of graduate students; others are designed specifically for business, law, or medical students. In addition, you can use private loans not specifically designed for education to help finance your graduate degree.

If you are considering borrowing through a supplemental or private loan program, you should carefully consider the terms and be sure to read the fine print. Check with the program sponsor for the most current terms that will be applicable to the amounts you intend to borrow for graduate study. Most supplemental loan programs for graduate study offer unsubsidized, credit-based loans. In general, a credit-ready borrower is one who has a satisfactory credit history or no credit history at all. A creditworthy borrower generally must pass a credit test to be eligible to borrow or act as a cosigner for the loan funds.

Many supplemental loan programs have minimum and maximum annual loan limits. Some offer amounts equal to the cost of attendance minus any other aid you will receive for graduate study. If you are planning to borrow for several years of graduate study, consider whether there is a cumulative or aggregate limit on the amount you may borrow. Often this cumulative or aggregate limit will include any amounts you borrowed and have not repaid for undergraduate or previous graduate study.

The combination of the annual interest rate, loan fees, and the repayment terms you choose will determine how much you will repay over time. Compare these features in combination before you decide which loan program to use. Some loans offer interest rates that are adjusted monthly, quarterly, or annually. Some offer interest rates that are lower during the in-school, grace, and deferment periods and then increase when you begin repayment. Some programs include a loan origination fee, which is usually deducted from the principal amount you receive when the loan is disbursed and must be repaid along with the interest and other principal when you graduate, withdraw from school, or drop below half-time study. Sometimes the loan fees are reduced if you borrow with a qualified cosigner. Some programs allow you to defer interest and/or principal payments while you are enrolled in graduate school. Many programs allow you to capitalize your interest payments; the interest due on your loan is added to the outstanding balance of your loan, so you don't have to repay immediately, but this increases the amount you owe. Other programs allow you to pay the interest as you go, which reduces the amount you later have to repay. The private loan market is very competitive, and your financial aid office can help you evaluate these programs.

Applying for Need-Based Financial Aid

Schools that award federal and institutional financial assistance based on need will require you to complete the FAFSA and, in some cases, an institutional financial aid application.

If you are applying for federal student assistance, you **must** complete the FAFSA. A service of the U.S. Department of Education, the FAFSA is free to all applicants. Most applicants apply online at www.fafsa.ed.gov. Paper applications are available at the financial aid office of your local college.

After your FAFSA information has been processed, you will receive a Student Aid Report (SAR). If you provided an e-mail address on the FAFSA, this will be sent to you electronically; otherwise, it will be mailed to your home address.

Follow the instructions on the SAR if you need to correct information reported on your original application. If your situation changes after you file your FAFSA, contact your financial aid officer to discuss amending your information. You can also appeal your financial aid award if you have extenuating circumstances.

If you would like more information on federal student financial aid, visit the FAFSA website or download the most recent version of *Funding Education Beyond High School: The Guide to Federal Student Aid* at http://studentaid.ed.gov/students/publications/student_guide/index.html. This guide is also available in Spanish.

The U.S. Department of Education also has a toll-free number for questions concerning federal student aid programs. The number is 1-800-4-FED AID (1-800-433-3243). If you are hearing impaired, call toll-free, 1-800-730-8913.

Summary

Remember that these are generalized statements about financial assistance at the graduate level. Because each institution allots its aid differently, you should communicate directly with the school and the specific department of interest to you. It is not unusual, for example, to find that an endowment vested within a specific department supports one or more fellowships. You may fit its requirements and specifications precisely.

Accreditation and Accrediting Agencies

Colleges and universities in the United States, and their individual academic and professional programs, are accredited by nongovernmental agencies concerned with monitoring the quality of education in this country. Agencies with both regional and national jurisdictions grant accreditation to institutions as a whole, while specialized bodies acting on a nationwide basis—often national professional associations—grant accreditation to departments and programs in specific fields.

Institutional and specialized accrediting agencies share the same basic concerns: the purpose an academic unit—whether university or program—has set for itself and how well it fulfills that purpose, the adequacy of its financial and other resources, the quality of its academic offerings, and the level of services it provides. Agencies that grant institutional accreditation take a broader view, of course, and examine university-wide or college-wide services with which a specialized agency may not concern itself.

Both types of agencies follow the same general procedures when considering an application for accreditation. The academic unit prepares a self-evaluation, focusing on the concerns mentioned above and usually including an assessment of both its strengths and weaknesses; a team of representatives of the accrediting body reviews this evaluation, visits the campus, and makes its own report; and finally, the accrediting body makes a decision on the application. Often, even when accreditation is granted, the agency makes a recommendation regarding how the institution or program can improve. All institutions and programs are also reviewed every few years to determine whether they continue to meet established standards; if they do not, they may lose their accreditation.

Accrediting agencies themselves are reviewed and evaluated periodically by the U.S. Department of Education and the Council for Higher Education Accreditation (CHEA). Recognized agencies adhere to certain standards and practices, and their authority in matters of accreditation is widely accepted in the educational community.

This does not mean, however, that accreditation is a simple matter, either for schools wishing to become accredited or for students deciding where to apply. Indeed, in certain fields the very meaning and methods of accreditation are the subject of a good deal of debate. For their part, those applying to graduate school should be aware of the safeguards provided by regional accreditation, especially in terms of degree acceptance and institutional longevity. Beyond this, applicants should understand the role that specialized accreditation plays in their field, as this varies considerably from one discipline to another. In certain professional fields, it is necessary to have graduated from a program that is accredited in order to be eligible for a license to practice, and in some fields the federal government also makes this a hiring requirement. In other disciplines, however, accreditation is not as essential, and there can be excellent programs that are not accredited. In fact, some programs choose not to seek accreditation, although most do.

Institutions and programs that present themselves for accreditation are sometimes granted the status of candidate for accreditation, or what is known as "preaccreditation." This may happen, for example, when an academic unit is too new to have met all the requirements for accreditation. Such status signifies initial recognition and indicates that the school or program in question is working to fulfill all requirements; it does not, however, guarantee that accreditation will be granted.

Institutional Accrediting Agencies—Regional

MIDDLE STATES ASSOCIATION OF COLLEGES AND SCHOOLS

Accredits institutions in Delaware, District of Columbia, Maryland, New Jersey, New York, Pennsylvania, Puerto Rico, and the Virgin Islands.

Dr. Elizabeth Sibolski, President
Middle States Commission on Higher Education
3624 Market Street, Second Floor West
Philadelphia, Pennsylvania 19104
Phone: 267-284-5000
Fax: 215-662-5501
E-mail: info@msche.org
Website: www.msche.org

NEW ENGLAND ASSOCIATION OF SCHOOLS AND COLLEGES

Accredits institutions in Connecticut, Maine, Massachusetts, New Hampshire, Rhode Island, and Vermont.

Dr. Barbara E. Brittingham, President/Director
Commission on Institutions of Higher Education
3 Burlington Woods Drive, Suite 100
Burlington, Massachusetts 01803-4531
Phone: 855-886-3272 or 781-425-7714
Fax: 781-425-1001
E-mail: cihe@neasc.org
Website: http://cihe.neasc.org

THE HIGHER LEARNING COMMISSION

Accredits institutions in Arizona, Arkansas, Colorado, Illinois, Indiana, Iowa, Kansas, Michigan, Minnesota, Missouri, Nebraska, New Mexico, North Dakota, Ohio, Oklahoma, South Dakota, West Virginia, Wisconsin, and Wyoming.

Dr. Barbara Gellman-Danley, President
The Higher Learning Commission
230 South LaSalle Street, Suite 7-500
Chicago, Illinois 60604-1413
Phone: 800-621-7440 or 312-263-0456
Fax: 312-263-7462
E-mail: info@hlcommission.org
Website: www.hlcommission.org

NORTHWEST COMMISSION ON COLLEGES AND UNIVERSITIES

Accredits institutions in Alaska, Idaho, Montana, Nevada, Oregon, Utah, and Washington.

Dr. Sandra E. Elman, President
8060 165th Avenue, NE, Suite 100
Redmond, Washington 98052
Phone: 425-558-4224
Fax: 425-376-0596
E-mail: selman@nwccu.org
Website: www.nwccu.org

SOUTHERN ASSOCIATION OF COLLEGES AND SCHOOLS

Accredits institutions in Alabama, Florida, Georgia, Kentucky, Louisiana, Mississippi, North Carolina, South Carolina, Tennessee, Texas, and Virginia.

Dr. Belle S. Wheelan, President
Commission on Colleges
1866 Southern Lane
Decatur, Georgia 30033-4097
Phone: 404-679-4500 Ext. 4504
Fax: 404-679-4558
E-mail: questions@sacscoc.org
Website: www.sacscoc.org

WESTERN ASSOCIATION OF SCHOOLS AND COLLEGES

Accredits institutions in California, Guam, and Hawaii.

Dr. Mary Ellen Petrisko, President
Accrediting Commission for Senior Colleges and Universities
985 Atlantic Avenue, Suite 100
Alameda, California 94501
Phone: 510-748-9001
Fax: 510-748-9797
E-mail: wasc@wascsenior.org
Website: http://www.wascsenior.org/

Institutional Accrediting Agencies—Other

ACCREDITING COUNCIL FOR INDEPENDENT COLLEGES AND SCHOOLS
Anthony S. Bieda, Executive in Charge
750 First Street, NE, Suite 980
Washington, DC 20002-4241
Phone: 202-336-6780
Fax: 202-842-2593
E-mail: info@acics.org
Website: www.acics.org

DISTANCE EDUCATION AND ACCREDITING COMMISSION (DEAC)
Accrediting Commission
Leah Matthews, Executive Director
1101 17th Street, NW, Suite 808
Washington, DC 20036-4704
Phone: 202-234-5100
Fax: 202-332-1386
E-mail: info@deac.org
Website: www.deac.org

Specialized Accrediting Agencies

ACUPUNCTURE AND ORIENTAL MEDICINE
Mark S. McKenzie, LAc MsOM DiplOM, Executive Director
Accreditation Commission for Acupuncture and Oriental Medicine
8941 Aztec Drive
Eden Prairie, Minnesota 55347
Phone: 952-212-2434
Fax: 301-313-0912
E-mail: coordinator@acaom.org
Website: www.acaom.org

ALLIED HEALTH
Kathleen Megivern, Executive Director
Commission on Accreditation of Allied Health Education Programs (CAAHEP)
25400 US Hwy 19 North, Suite 158
Clearwater, Florida 33763
Phone: 727-210-2350
Fax: 727-210-2354
E-mail: mail@caahep.org
Website: www.caahep.org

ART AND DESIGN
Karen P. Moynahan, Executive Director
National Association of Schools of Art and Design (NASAD)
Commission on Accreditation
11250 Roger Bacon Drive, Suite 21
Reston, Virginia 20190-5248
Phone: 703-437-0700
Fax: 703-437-6312
E-mail: info@arts-accredit.org
Website: http://nasad.arts-accredit.org

ATHLETIC TRAINING EDUCATION
Micki Cuppett, Executive Director
Commission on Accreditation of Athletic Training Education (CAATE)
6850 Austin Center Blvd., Suite 100
Austin, Texas 78731-3184
Phone: 512-733-9700
E-mail: micki@caate.net
Website: www.caate.net

AUDIOLOGY EDUCATION
Doris Gordon, Executive Director
Accreditation Commission for Audiology Education (ACAE)
11480 Commerce Park Drive, Suite 220
Reston, Virginia 20191
Phone: 202-986-9550
Fax: 202-986-9500
E-mail: info@acaeaccred.org
Website: www.acaeaccred.org

AVIATION
Dr. Gary J. Northam, Executive Director
Aviation Accreditation Board International (AABI)
3410 Skyway Drive
Auburn, Alabama 36830
Phone: 334-844-2431
Fax: 334-844-2432
E-mail: bayenva@auburn.edu
Website: www.aabi.aero

BUSINESS
Robert D. Reid, Executive Vice President and Chief Accreditation Officer
AACSB International—The Association to Advance Collegiate Schools of Business
777 South Harbour Island Boulevard, Suite 750
Tampa, Florida 33602
Phone: 813-769-6500
Fax: 813-769-6559
E-mail: bob@aacsb.edu
Website: www.aacsb.edu

BUSINESS EDUCATION
Dennis N. Gash, President and Chief Executive Officer
International Assembly for Collegiate Business Education (IACBE)
11257 Strang Line Road
Lenexa, Kansas 66215
Phone: 913-631-3009
Fax: 913-631-9154
E-mail:iacbe@iacbe.org
Website: www.iacbe.org

CHIROPRACTIC
Craig S. Little, President
Council on Chiropractic Education (CCE)
Commission on Accreditation
8049 North 85th Way
Scottsdale, Arizona 85258-4321
Phone: 480-443-8877 or 888-443-3506
Fax: 480-483-7333
E-mail: cce@cce-usa.org
Website: www.cce-usa.org

CLINICAL LABORATORY SCIENCES
Dianne M. Cearlock, Ph.D., Chief Executive Officer
National Accrediting Agency for Clinical Laboratory Sciences
5600 North River Road, Suite 720
Rosemont, Illinois 60018-5119
Phone: 773-714-8880 or 847-939-3597
Fax: 773-714-8886
E-mail: info@naacls.org
Website: www.naacls.org

CLINICAL PASTORAL EDUCATION
Trace Haythorn, Executive Director
Association for Clinical Pastoral Education, Inc.
1549 Clairmont Road, Suite 103
Decatur, Georgia 30033-4611
Phone: 404-320-1472
Fax: 404-320-0849
E-mail: acpe@acpe.edu
Website: www.acpe.edu

DANCE
Karen P. Moynahan, Executive Director
National Association of Schools of Dance (NASD)
Commission on Accreditation
11250 Roger Bacon Drive, Suite 21
Reston, Virginia 20190-5248
Phone: 703-437-0700
Fax: 703-437-6312
E-mail: info@arts-accredit.org
Website: http://nasd.arts-accredit.org

DENTISTRY
Dr. Sherin Tooks, Director
Commission on Dental Accreditation
American Dental Association
211 East Chicago Avenue, Suite 1900
Chicago, Illinois 60611
Phone: 312-440-4643 or 800-621-8099
E-mail: accreditation@ada.org
Website: www.ada.org

DIETETICS AND NUTRITION
Mary B. Gregoire, Ph.D., Executive Director; RD, FADA, FAND
Academy of Nutrition and Dietetics
Accreditation Council for Education in Nutrition and Dietetics (ACEND)
120 South Riverside Plaza, Suite 2000
Chicago, Illinois 60606-6995
Phone: 800-877-1600 Ext. 5400 or 312-899-0040
Fax: 312-899-4817
E-mail: acend@eatright.org
Website: www.eatright.org/ACEND

EDUCATION PREPARATION
Christopher Koch, President
Council for the Accreditation of Education Preparation (CAEP)
1140 19th Street NW, Suite 400
Washington, DC 20036
Phone: 202-223-0077
Fax: 202-296-6620
E-mail: caep@caepnet.org
Website: www.caepnet.org

ENGINEERING
Michael Milligan, Ph.D., PE, Executive Director
Accreditation Board for Engineering and Technology, Inc. (ABET)
415 North Charles Street
Baltimore, Maryland 21201
Phone: 410-347-7700
E-mail: accreditation@abet.org
Website: www.abet.org

FORENSIC SCIENCES
Nancy J. Jackson, Director of Development and Accreditation
American Academy of Forensic Sciences (AAFS)
Forensic Science Education Program Accreditation Commission (FEPAC)
410 North 21st Street
Colorado Springs, Colorado 80904
Phone: 719-636-1100
Fax: 719-636-1993
E-mail: njackson@aafs.org
Website: www.fepac-edu.org

FORESTRY
Carol L. Redelsheimer
Director of Science and Education
Society of American Foresters
5400 Grosvenor Lane
Bethesda, Maryland 20814-2198
Phone: 301-897-8720 or 866-897-8720
Fax: 301-897-3690
E-mail: redelsheimerc@safnet.org
Website: www.safnet.org

HEALTHCARE MANAGEMENT
Commission on Accreditation of Healthcare Management Education (CAHME)
Anthony Stanowski, President and CEO
1700 Rockville Pike
Suite 400
Rockville, Maryland 20852
Phone: 301-998-6101
E-mail: info@cahme.org
Website: www.cahme.org

HEALTH INFORMATICS AND HEALTH MANAGEMENT
Claire Dixon-Lee, Executive Director
Commission on Accreditation for Health Informatics and Information Management Education (CAHIIM)
233 North Michigan Avenue, 21st Floor
Chicago, Illinois 60601-5800
Phone: 312-233-1100
Fax: 312-233-1948
E-mail:E-mail: claire.dixon-lee@cahiim.org
Website: www.cahiim.org

HUMAN SERVICE EDUCATION
Dr. Elaine Green, President
Council for Standards in Human Service Education (CSHSE)
3337 Duke Street
Alexandria, Virginia 22314
Phone: 571-257-3959
E-mail: info@cshse.org
Web: http://www.cshse.org

INTERIOR DESIGN
Holly Mattson, Executive Director
Council for Interior Design Accreditation
206 Grandview Avenue, Suite 350
Grand Rapids, Michigan 49503-4014
Phone: 616-458-0400
Fax: 616-458-0460
E-mail: info@accredit-id.org
Website: www.accredit-id.org

JOURNALISM AND MASS COMMUNICATIONS
Susanne Shaw, Executive Director
Accrediting Council on Education in Journalism and Mass Communications (ACEJMC)
School of Journalism
Stauffer-Flint Hall
University of Kansas
1435 Jayhawk Boulevard
Lawrence, Kansas 66045-7575
Phone: 785-864-3973
Fax: 785-864-5225
E-mail: sshaw@ku.edu
Website: http://www2.ku.edu/~acejmc/

LANDSCAPE ARCHITECTURE
Kristopher D. Pritchard, Executive Director
Landscape Architectural Accreditation Board (LAAB)
American Society of Landscape Architects (ASLA)
636 Eye Street, NW
Washington, DC 20001-3736
Phone: 202-216-2359
Fax: 202-898-1185
E-mail: info@asla.org
Website: www.asla.org

LAW
Barry Currier, Managing Director of Accreditation & Legal Education
American Bar Association
321 North Clark Street, 21st Floor
Chicago, Illinois 60654
Phone: 312-988-6738
Fax: 312-988-5681
E-mail: legaled@americanbar.org
Website: http://www.americanbar.org/groups/legal_education/resources/accreditation.html

LIBRARY
Karen O'Brien, Director
Office for Accreditation
American Library Association
50 East Huron Street
Chicago, Illinois 60611-2795
Phone: 312-280-2432
Fax: 312-280-2433
E-mail: accred@ala.org
Website: www.ala.org/accreditation/

MARRIAGE AND FAMILY THERAPY
Tanya A. Tamarkin, Director of Educational Affairs
Commission on Accreditation for Marriage and Family Therapy Education (COAMFTE)
American Association for Marriage and Family Therapy
112 South Alfred Street
Alexandria, Virginia 22314-3061
Phone: 703-838-9808
Fax: 703-838-9805
E-mail: coa@aamft.org
Website: www.aamft.org

MEDICAL ILLUSTRATION
Kathleen Megivern, Executive Director
Commission on Accreditation of Allied Health Education Programs (CAAHEP)
1361 Park Street
Clearwater, Florida 33756
Phone: 727-210-2350
Fax: 727-210-2354
E-mail: mail@caahep.org
Website: www.caahep.org

MEDICINE
Liaison Committee on Medical Education (LCME)
Robert B. Hash, M.D., LCME Secretary
American Medical Association
Council on Medical Education
330 North Wabash Avenue, Suite 39300
Chicago, Illinois 60611-5885
Phone: 312-464-4933
E-mail: lcme@aamc.org
Website: www.ama-assn.org

Liaison Committee on Medical Education (LCME)
Heather Lent, M.A., Director
Accreditation Services
Association of American Medical Colleges
655 K Street, NW
Washington, DC 20001-2399
Phone: 202-828-0596
E-mail: lcme@aamc.org
Website: www.lcme.org

MUSIC
Karen P. Moynahan, Executive Director
National Association of Schools of Music (NASM)
Commission on Accreditation
11250 Roger Bacon Drive, Suite 21
Reston, Virginia 20190-5248
Phone: 703-437-0700
Fax: 703-437-6312
E-mail: info@arts-accredit.org
Website: http://nasm.arts-accredit.org/

NATUROPATHIC MEDICINE
Daniel Seitz, J.D., Ed.D., Executive Director
Council on Naturopathic Medical Education
P.O. Box 178
Great Barrington, Massachusetts 01230
Phone: 413-528-8877
E-mail: www.cnme.org/contact.html
Website: www.cnme.org

NURSE ANESTHESIA
Francis R.Gerbasi, Ph.D., CRNA, COA Executive Director
Council on Accreditation of Nurse Anesthesia Educational Programs (CoA-NAEP)
American Association of Nurse Anesthetists
222 South Prospect Avenue, Suite 304
Park Ridge, Illinois 60068-4010
Phone: 847-655-1160
Fax: 847-692-7137
E-mail: accreditation@coa.us.com
Website: http://home.coa.us.com

NURSE EDUCATION
Jennifer L. Butlin, Executive Director
Commission on Collegiate Nursing Education (CCNE)
One Dupont Circle, NW, Suite 530
Washington, DC 20036-1120
Phone: 202-887-6791
Fax: 202-887-8476
E-mail: jbutlin@aacn.nche.edu
Website: www.aacn.nche.edu/accreditation

Marsal P. Stoll, Chief Executive Officer
Accreditation Commission for Education in Nursing (ACEN)
3343 Peachtree Road, NE, Suite 850
Atlanta, Georgia 30326
Phone: 404-975-5000
Fax: 404-975-5020
E-mail: mstoll@acenursing.org
Website: www.acenursing.org

NURSE MIDWIFERY
Heather L. Maurer, M.A., Executive Director
Accreditation Commission for Midwifery Education (ACME)
American College of Nurse-Midwives
8403 Colesville Road, Suite 1550
Silver Spring, Maryland 20910
Phone: 240-485-1800
Fax: 240-485-1818
E-mail: info@acnm.org
Website: www.midwife.org/Program-Accreditation

NURSE PRACTITIONER
Gay Johnson, CEO
National Association of Nurse Practitioners in Women's Health
Council on Accreditation
505 C Street, NE
Washington, DC 20002
Phone: 202-543-9693 Ext. 1
Fax: 202-543-9858
E-mail: info@npwh.org
Website: www.npwh.org

NURSING
Marsal P. Stoll, Chief Executive Director
Accreditation Commission for Education in Nursing (ACEN)
3343 Peachtree Road, NE, Suite 850
Atlanta, Georgia 30326
Phone: 404-975-5000
Fax: 404-975-5020
E-mail: info@acenursing.org
Website: www.acenursing.org

OCCUPATIONAL THERAPY
Heather Stagliano, DHSc, OTR/L, Executive Director
The American Occupational Therapy Association, Inc.
4720 Montgomery Lane, Suite 200
Bethesda, Maryland 20814-3449
Phone: 301-652-6611 Ext. 2682
TDD: 800-377-8555
Fax: 240-762-5150
E-mail: accred@aota.org
Website: www.aoteonline.org

OPTOMETRY
Joyce L. Urbeck, Administrative Director
Accreditation Council on Optometric Education (ACOE)
American Optometric Association
243 North Lindbergh Boulevard
St. Louis, Missouri 63141-7881
Phone: 314-991-4100, Ext. 4246
Fax: 314-991-4101
E-mail: accredit@aoa.org
Website: www.theacoe.org

OSTEOPATHIC MEDICINE
Director, Department of Accreditation
Commission on Osteopathic College Accreditation (COCA)
American Osteopathic Association
142 East Ontario Street
Chicago, Illinois 60611
Phone: 312-202-8048
Fax: 312-202-8202
E-mail: predoc@osteopathic.org
Website: www.aoacoca.org

PHARMACY
Peter H. Vlasses, PharmD, Executive Director
Accreditation Council for Pharmacy Education
135 South LaSalle Street, Suite 4100
Chicago, Illinois 60603-4810
Phone: 312-664-3575
Fax: 312-664-4652
E-mail: csinfo@acpe-accredit.org
Website: www.acpe-accredit.org

PHYSICAL THERAPY
Sandra Wise, Senior Director
Commission on Accreditation in Physical Therapy Education (CAPTE)
American Physical Therapy Association (APTA)
1111 North Fairfax Street
Alexandria, Virginia 22314-1488
Phone: 703-706-3245
Fax: 703-706-3387
E-mail: accreditation@apta.org
Website: www.capteonline.org

PHYSICIAN ASSISTANT STUDIES
Sharon L. Luke, Executive Director
Accredittion Review Commission on Education for the Physician Assistant, Inc. (ARC-PA)
12000 Findley Road, Suite 150
Johns Creek, Georgia 30097
Phone: 770-476-1224
Fax: 770-476-1738
E-mail: arc-pa@arc-pa.org
Website: www.arc-pa.org

PLANNING
Ms. Shonagh Merits, Executive Director
American Institute of Certified Planners/Association of Collegiate Schools of Planning/American Planning Association
Planning Accreditation Board (PAB)
2334 West Lawrence Avenue, Suite 209
Chicago, Illinois 60625
Phone: 773-334-7200
E-mail: smerits@planningaccreditationboard.org
Website: www.planningaccreditationboard.org

PODIATRIC MEDICINE
Alan R. Tinkleman, M.P.A., Executive Director
Council on Podiatric Medical Education (CPME)
American Podiatric Medical Association (APMA)
9312 Old Georgetown Road
Bethesda, Maryland 20814-1621
Phone: 301-581-9200
Fax: 301-571-4903
Website: www.cpme.org

PSYCHOLOGY AND COUNSELING
Jacqueline Remondet Wall, CEO of the Accrediting Unit,
Office of Program Consultation and Accreditation
American Psychological Association
750 First Street, NE
Washington, DC 20002-4202
Phone: 202-336-5979 or 800-374-2721
TDD/TTY: 202-336-6123
Fax: 202-336-5978
E-mail: apaaccred@apa.org
Website: www.apa.org/ed/accreditation

Carol L. Bobby, Ph.D., Executive Director
Council for Accreditation of Counseling and Related Educational Programs (CACREP)
1001 North Fairfax Street, Suite 510
Alexandria, Virginia 22314
Phone: 703-535-5990
Fax: 703-739-6209
E-mail: cacrep@cacrep.org
Website: www.cacrep.org

Richard M. McFall, Executive Director
Psychological Clinical Science Accreditation System (PCSAS)
1101 East Tenth Street
IU Psychology Building
Bloomington, Indiana 47405-7007
Phone: 812-856-2570
Fax: 812-322-5545
E-mail: rmmcfall@pcsas.org
Website: www.pcsas.org

PUBLIC HEALTH
Laura Rasar King, M.P.H., MCHES, Executive Director
Council on Education for Public Health
1010 Wayne Avenue, Suite 220
Silver Spring, Maryland 20910
Phone: 202-789-1050
Fax: 202-789-1895
E-mail: Lking@ceph.org
Website: www.ceph.org

PUBLIC POLICY, AFFAIRS AND ADMINISTRATION
Crystal Calarusse, Chief Accreditation Officer
Commission on Peer Review and Accreditation
Network of Schools of Public Policy, Affairs, and Administration
(NASPAA-COPRA)
1029 Vermont Avenue, NW, Suite 1100
Washington, DC 20005
Phone: 202-628-8965
Fax: 202-626-4978
E-mail: copra@naspaa.org
Website: www.naspaa.org

RADIOLOGIC TECHNOLOGY
Leslie Winter, Chief Executive Officer Joint Review Committee on Education in Radiologic Technology (JRCERT)
20 North Wacker Drive, Suite 2850
Chicago, Illinois 60606-3182
Phone: 312-704-5300
Fax: 312-704-5304
E-mail: mail@jrcert.org
Web: www.jrcert.org

REHABILITATION EDUCATION
Frank Lane, Ph.D., Executive Director
Council on Rehabilitation Education (CORE)
Commission on Standards and Accreditation
1699 Woodfield Road, Suite 300
Schaumburg, Illinois 60173
Phone: 847-944-1345
Fax: 847-944-1346
E-mail: flane@core-rehab.org
Website: www.core-rehab.org

RESPIRATORY CARE
Thomas Smalling, Executive Director
Commission on Accreditation for Respiratory Care (CoARC)
1248 Harwood Road
Bedford, Texas 76021-4244
Phone: 817-283-2835
Fax: 817-354-8519
E-mail: tom@coarc.com
Website: www.coarc.com

SOCIAL WORK
Dr. Stacey Borasky, Director of Accreditation
Office of Social Work Accreditation
Council on Social Work Education
1701 Duke Street, Suite 200
Alexandria, Virginia 22314
Phone: 703-683-8080
Fax: 703-519-2078
E-mail: info@cswe.org
Website: www.cswe.org

SPEECH-LANGUAGE PATHOLOGY AND AUDIOLOGY
Patrima L. Tice, Accreditation Executive Director
American Speech-Language-Hearing Association
Council on Academic Accreditation in Audiology and Speech-Language Pathology
2200 Research Boulevard #310
Rockville, Maryland 20850-3289
Phone: 301-296-5700
Fax: 301-296-8750
E-mail: accreditation@asha.org
Website: http://caa.asha.org

TEACHER EDUCATION
Christopher A. Koch, President
National Council for Accreditation of Teacher Education (NCATE)
Teacher Education Accreditation Council (TEAC)
1140 19th Street, Suite 400
Washington, DC 20036
Phone: 202-223-0077
Fax: 202-296-6620
E-mail: caep@caepnet.org
Website: www.ncate.org

TECHNOLOGY
Michale S. McComis, Ed.D., Executive Director
Accrediting Commission of Career Schools and Colleges
2101 Wilson Boulevard, Suite 302
Arlington, Virginia 22201
Phone: 703-247-4212
Fax: 703-247-4533
E-mail: mccomis@accsc.org
Website: www.accsc.org

TECHNOLOGY, MANAGEMENT, AND APPLIED ENGINEERING
Kelly Schild, Director of Accreditation
The Association of Technology, Management, and Applied Engineering (ATMAE)
275 N. York Street, Suite 401
Elmhurst, Illinois 60126
Phone: 630-433-4514
Fax: 630-563-9181
E-mail: Kelly@atmae.org
Website: www.atmae.org

THEATER
Karen P. Moynahan, Executive Director
National Association of Schools of Theatre Commission on Accreditation
11250 Roger Bacon Drive, Suite 21
Reston, Virginia 20190
Phone: 703-437-0700
Fax: 703-437-6312
E-mail: info@arts-accredit.org
Website: http://nast.arts-accredit.org/

THEOLOGY
Dr. Bernard Fryshman, Executive VP
Emeritus and Interim Executive Director
Association of Advanced Rabbinical and Talmudic Schools (AARTS)
Accreditation Commission
11 Broadway, Suite 405
New York, New York 10004
Phone: 212-363-1991
Fax: 212-533-5335
E-mail: k.sharfman.aarts@gmail.com

Daniel O. Aleshire, Executive Director
Association of Theological Schools in the United States and Canada (ATS)
Commission on Accrediting
10 Summit Park Drive
Pittsburgh, Pennsylvania 15275
Phone: 412-788-6505
Fax: 412-788-6510
E-mail: ats@ats.edu
Website: www.ats.edu

Dr. Timothy Eaton, Interim President
Transnational Association of Christian Colleges and Schools (TRACS)
Accreditation Commission
15935 Forest Road
Forest, Virginia 24551
Phone: 434-525-9539
Fax: 434-525-9538
E-mail: info@tracs.org
Website: www.tracs.org

VETERINARY MEDICINE
Dr. Karen Brandt, Director of Education and Research
American Veterinary Medical Association (AVMA)
Council on Education
1931 North Meacham Road, Suite 100
Schaumburg, Illinois 60173-4360
Phone: 847-925-8070 Ext. 6674
Fax: 847-285-5732
E-mail: info@avma.org
Website: www.avma.org

How to Use This Guide

As you identify the particular programs and institutions that interest you, you can use both the ***Graduate & Professional Programs: An Overview*** volume and the specialized volumes to obtain detailed information--***Graduate & Professional Programs: An Overview*** for information on the institutions overall and the specialized volumes for details about the individual graduate units and their degree programs.

Directory of Graduate and Professional Programs by Field

This directory lists the more than 500 fields covered in ***Peterson's Graduate and Professional Programs***, with an alphabetical listing of each of the institutions offering graduate or professional work in that field. Institutions in the United States and U.S. territories and those in Canada, Mexico, Europe, and Africa that are accredited by U.S. accrediting bodies are included. The directory enables readers who are interested in a particular academic area to quickly identify the colleges and universities that they might wish to attend. In each field, degree levels are given if an institution provided the information in response to *Peterson's Annual Survey of Graduate and Professional Institutions.* An *M* indicates that a master's degree program is offered; a *D* indicates that a doctoral program is offered; and an *O* signifies that other advanced degrees (e.g., certificates and specialist degrees) are offered. If no degree is listed, the school offers a degree in a subdiscipline of the field, not in the field itself.

All of the programs listed in this directory are profiled, and many are described in detail in **Close-Ups** or **Displays** in the specialized volumes. These **Displays** and **Close-Ups** are indicated in the directory listings by an asterisk, and their page numbers may be found by consulting the indexes of the specialized volumes. The **Profiles, Displays**, and **Close-Ups Index** at the back of this book indicate the institutions that chose to place a **Close-Up** or a **Display** in this volume.

Directory of Institutions and Their Offerings

This directory contains information identical to that in the **Directory of Graduate and Professional Programs by Field** but conversely presented. Accredited institutions in the United States and U.S. territories and those in Canada, Mexico, Europe, and Africa that are accredited by U.S. accrediting bodies are given here, with an alphabetical listing of which programs they offer out of the selected fields that are covered in the guides. The directory will be of value to readers who are interested in the range of programs at particular institutions, as well as those who wish to compare programs and degree levels. The degree levels are shown if the institution provided information in response to *Peterson's Annual Survey of Graduate and Professional Institutions*; the degree levels included are master's, doctorate, and other advanced degrees (e.g., certificates and specialist degrees), included as *M, D,* and *O,* respectively.

All of the programs listed in this directory are profiled, and many are described in detail in **Close-Ups** or outlined briefly in **Displays** in the specialized volumes. A note at the end of each institution's listing refers the reader to the specific page number if a **Display** or **Close-Up** appears in this book. If there is such information in the specialized volumes, an asterisk appears in the column that lists the degree level offered. The reader should then refer to the **Profiles, Displays, and Close-Ups Index** in the appropriate volume.

Profiles of Institutions Offering Graduate and Professional Work

This section presents profiles of accredited colleges and universities in the United States and U.S. territories and those in Canada, Mexico, Europe, and Africa that are accredited by U.S. accrediting bodies. Together with the other sections of this book, it is both a basic reference source and a foundation for the specialized volumes of ***Peterson's Graduate and Professional Programs***. (The specialized volumes provide descriptions of graduate programs in the humanities, arts, and social sciences; the biological/biomedical sciences and health-related medical professions; the physical sciences, mathematics, agricultural sciences, the environment, and natural resources; engineering and applied sciences; and business, education, information studies, law, and social work, respectively.) The profiles in this section include the data on graduate and professional units that were submitted in 2016 by each institution in response to *Peterson's Annual Survey of Graduate and Professional Institutions.* If an institution provided all of the information requested, the profile includes all of the items listed below. A number of graduate school administrators have submitted and paid for **Displays**, which appear near their profiles. In these, readers will find information an institution wants to emphasize. In addition, bolded reference lines at the end of a profile indicate the page number on which the reader will find a **Display** and/or **Close-Up**, if the institution has chosen to submit one or both. The absence of a **Display** or **Close-Up** does not reflect any type of editorial judgment on the part of Peterson's.

A ★ graphic next to the school's name indicates the institution has additional detailed information in a "Premium Profile" on Petersons.com. After reading their information here, you can learn more about the school by visiting www.petersons.com and searching for that particular institution's graduate program.

General Information

Type. An institution's control is indicated as independent (private nonprofit), independent with religious affiliation, proprietary (private profit-making), or state-supported or state-related (public). Whether an institution is coeducational or primarily for men or women is indicated. A few schools are designated as undergraduate: women (or men) only; graduate: coed. Institutional type is given as university, comprehensive, graduate only, or upper level.

CGS Membership. Membership in the Council of Graduate Schools in the United States and in Canada is indicated here.

Enrollment. Enrollment figures include total matriculated students (graduate, professional, and undergraduate), total full- and part-time matriculated graduate and professional students, and the number of women in each category.

Enrollment by Degree Level. Figures include the total number of students enrolled at each degree level--master's, doctoral, and other advanced degrees.

Graduate Faculty. The numbers of full-time and part-time/adjunct faculty members actively involved with graduate students through teaching or research are given, followed by numbers of women.

Graduate Expenses. Tuition and fees for the overall institution for 2016–17 are indicated on a full-time (per academic year, semester, quarter, etc.) and/or a part-time (per credit, semester hour, quarter hour, course, etc.) basis. In-state and out-of-state figures are supplied where applicable. For exact costs at any given time, contact the schools and programs directly. Keep in mind that the tuition of Canadian institutions is usually given in Canadian dollars.

Graduate Housing. Institutions were asked to indicate whether housing for single and married students is guaranteed or available on a first-come, first-served basis and whether that includes board and to indicate the typical cost per year.

Student Services. Each institution was asked which of the following services are available to graduate and professional students: campus employment opportunities, campus safety program, career counseling, child day-care facilities, disabled student services, exercise/wellness program, free psychological counseling, grant writing training, international student services, low-cost health insurance, multicultural affairs office, teacher training, and writing training.

Library Facilities. The main library name and the number of additional on-campus libraries, if any, are provided. Also provided are online resources, such as library catalog, Web page, and other libraries' catalogs, and numbers of titles, current serial subscriptions, and audiovisual materials.

Research Affiliations. Institutions were asked to name up to six independent research centers, laboratories, or institutes with which they maintain formal arrangements providing extra research or study opportunities for graduate students.

Computer Facilities

Institutions were asked to provide the total number of PCs and/or terminals available for student use, whether a campuswide network is available, and whether Internet access and/or online class registration is available. The institution's website also appears here if that information was supplied.

General Application Contact

The name, title, phone number, fax number, and e-mail address of the person to contact for further information about applying to graduate and professional programs appear here.

Graduate Units

Each major graduate and professional unit within the institution (school, college, institute, center, etc.) is listed below the general information. These units are arranged to show the hierarchical structure of the institution. Those units offering advanced degree programs through the graduate school are listed immediately beneath it. Professional schools not connected with the graduate school are listed separately.

Enrollment. The number of full- and part-time matriculated students and the number of women, minority-group members, and international students are given. Average age is indicated, followed by the number of applicants, percentage accepted, and the number enrolled.

Faculty. Full-time and part-time/adjunct figures are given, and the number of women is indicated.

Expenses. For individual program expenses, readers are advised to contact the institution.

Financial Support. Information is given on the number of fellowships and assistantships awarded in 2015–16 and the availability of other types of aid. The financial aid application deadline is also indicated.

Degree Program Information. The number of degrees awarded in calendar year 2016 is given, broken down by degree level, followed by the availability of part-time and evening/weekend programs. Degree programs offered through the subunits and the specific degrees awarded are listed. Special degree information is also included, such as that a degree is offered jointly with another university.

Applying. The application deadline (for domestic and international students) and application fee are given, followed by a person to contact and a phone number, fax number, and e-mail address (if provided).

Head. The head of the unit and his or her title are indicated, along with a phone number, fax number, and e-mail address (if provided).

Close-Ups of Institutions Offering Graduate and Professional Work

The **Close-Ups** in this section present an overview of accredited graduate and professional schools in the United States and U.S. territories and institutions in Canada, Mexico, Europe, and Africa that are accredited by U.S. accrediting bodies. Critical information sought by all prospective graduate students—regardless of their intended field of study—has been supplied by the schools themselves.

In addition to listing the degree programs available, each entry gives valuable information on research facilities, financial aid opportunities, tuition rates, living and housing costs, students, the faculty, location, the university, and application criteria—in short, facts that all prospective graduate students need to know about an institution when selecting a graduate program.

After using the **Close-Ups** and the other sections of this volume to identify those universities that are appropriate to your needs, refer to the specialized volumes for specific program information. Graduate and professional schools and colleges within the institutions represented in this book are considered in detail in the specialized volumes, which cover the humanities, arts, and social sciences; the biological/biomedical sciences and health-related medical professions; the physical sciences, mathematics, agricultural sciences, the environment, and natural resources; engineering and applied sciences; and business, education, information studies, law, and social work, respectively.

Appendixes

This section contains two appendixes. The first, *Institutional Changes Since the 2016 Edition,* lists institutions that have closed, moved, merged, or changed their name or status since the last edition of the guides. The second, *Abbreviations Used in the Guides,* gives abbreviations of degree names, along with what those abbreviations stand for. These appendixes are identical in all six volumes of *Peterson's Graduate and Professional Programs.*

Indexes

There are two indexes in this section. The first, **Profiles, Displays, and Close-Ups,** gives page references for all information on all graduate and professional schools in this volume. Location of the institution's **Profile** is indicated in normal type. An *italic* page number indicates that a **Display** follows the institution's **Profile**. A **boldface** page number indicates the location of an institution's **Close-Up**. The second, **Directories and Subject Areas in the Specialized Volumes**, gives references to the directories in other volumes of this set and also includes cross-references for subject area names not used in the directory structure, for example, City and Regional Planning (see Urban and Regional Planning).

Data Collection Procedures

The information published in the directories and **Profiles** of all the books is collected through *Peterson's Annual Survey of Graduate and Professional Institutions.* The survey is sent each spring to more than 2,200 institutions offering postbaccalaureate degree programs, including accredited institutions in the United States, U.S. territories, and Canada and those institutions outside the United States that are accredited by U.S. accrediting bodies. Deans and other administrators complete these surveys, providing information on programs in over 500 academic and professional fields covered in the guides as well as overall institutional information. While every effort has been made to ensure the accuracy and completeness of the data, information is sometimes unavailable or changes occur after publication deadlines. All usable information received in time for publication has been included. The omission of any particular item from a directory or **Profile** signifies either that the item is not applicable to the institution or program or that information was not available. **Profiles** of programs scheduled to begin during the 2015–16 academic year cannot, obviously, include statistics on enrollment or, in many cases, the number of faculty members. If no usable data were submitted by an institution, its name, address, and program name appear in order to indicate the availability of graduate work.

Criteria for Inclusion in This Guide

To be included in this guide, an institution must have full accreditation or be a candidate for accreditation (preaccreditation) status by an institutional or specialized accrediting body recognized by the U.S. Department of Education or the Council for Higher Education Accreditation (CHEA). Institutional accrediting bodies, which review each institution as a whole, include the six regional associations of schools and colleges (Middle States, New England, North Central, Northwest, Southern, and Western), each of which is responsible for a specified portion of the United States and its territories. Other institutional accrediting bodies are national in scope and accredit specific kinds of institutions (e.g., Bible colleges, independent colleges, and rabbinical and Talmudic schools). Program registration by the New York State Board of Regents is considered to be the equivalent of institutional accreditation, since the board requires that all programs offered by an institution meet its standards before recognition is granted. A Canadian institution must be chartered and authorized to grant degrees by the provincial government, affiliated with a chartered institution, or accredited by a recognized U.S. accrediting body. This guide also includes institutions outside the United States that are accredited by these U.S. accrediting bodies. There are recognized specialized or professional accrediting bodies in more than fifty different fields, each of which is authorized to accredit institutions or specific programs in its particular field. For specialized institutions that offer programs in one field only, we designate this to be the equivalent of institutional accreditation. A full explanation of the accrediting process and complete information on recognized institutional (regional and national) and specialized accrediting bodies can be found online at www.chea.org or at www.ed.gov/admins/finaid/accred/index.html.

NOTICE: Certain portions of or information contained in this book have been submitted and paid for by the educational institution identified, and such institutions take full responsibility for the accuracy, timeliness, completeness, and functionality of such contents. Such portions or information include (i) each display ad that comprises a half page of information covering a single educational institution or program and (ii) each two-page description of a graduate school or program that appears in the "Close-Ups of Institutions Offering Graduate and Professional Work" section on pages 863–916.

DIRECTORY OF GRADUATE AND PROFESSIONAL PROGRAMS BY FIELD

ACCOUNTING

Abilene Christian University	M
Adelphi University	M
Adrian College	M
Alabama State University	M
Albany State University	M
Albertus Magnus College	M
Alfred University	M
American Business & Technology University	M
American InterContinental University Online	M
American International College	M
American Public University System	M
American University	M,O
American University of Sharjah	M
Anderson University (IN)	M,D
Andrews University	M
Angelo State University	M
Appalachian State University	M
Argosy University, Atlanta	M,D
Argosy University, Chicago	M,D
Argosy University, Dallas	M,D,O
Argosy University, Denver	M,D
Argosy University, Hawai`i	M,D,O
Argosy University, Inland Empire	M,D
Argosy University, Los Angeles	M,D
Argosy University, Nashville	M,D
Argosy University, Orange County	M,D,O
Argosy University, Phoenix	M,D
Argosy University, Salt Lake City	M,D
Argosy University, San Diego	M,D
Argosy University, San Francisco Bay Area	M,D
Argosy University, Sarasota	M,D,O
Argosy University, Schaumburg	M,D,O
Argosy University, Seattle	M,D
Argosy University, Tampa	M,D
Argosy University, Twin Cities	M,D
Argosy University, Washington DC	M,D,O
Arizona State University at the Tempe campus	M,D
Arkansas State University	M
Assumption College	M,O
Auburn University	M
Auburn University at Montgomery	M
Aurora University	M
Averett University	M
Avila University	M
Babson College	M,O
Baker College Center for Graduate Studies–Online	M,D
Baldwin Wallace University	M
Ball State University	M
Barry University	M
Baruch College of the City University of New York	M,D
Bayamón Central University	M
Baylor University	M
Bay Path University	M
Belmont University	M
Benedictine University	M
Bentley University	M,D
Binghamton University, State University of New York	M*
Bloomfield College	M
Bloomsburg University of Pennsylvania	M
Bluffton University	M
Bob Jones University	M,D,O
Boise State University	M
Boston College	M
Bowling Green State University	M
Bradley University	M
Brenau University	M
Bridgewater State University	M
Brock University	M
Brooklyn College of the City University of New York	M
Bryant University	M
Butler University	M
Cabrini University	M
Cairn University	M,O
Caldwell University	M
California Baptist University	M
California State Polytechnic University, Pomona	M
California State University, Fresno	M
California State University, Fullerton	M
California State University, Los Angeles	M
California State University, Sacramento	M
California State University, San Bernardino	M
California Western School of Law	M,D
Canisius College	M
Capella University	M,D
Carnegie Mellon University	D
Case Western Reserve University	M,D*
The Catholic University of America	M
Centenary College	M
Central Michigan University	M,O
Central Washington University	M
Chaminade University of Honolulu	M
Chapman University	M
Charleston Southern University	M
Chatham University	M
Christian Brothers University	M,O
City University of Seattle	M,O
Clark Atlanta University	M
Clark University	M
Clayton State University	M
Cleary University	M,O
Clemson University	M
Cleveland State University	M
Coastal Carolina University	M,O
The College at Brockport, State University of New York	M
College of Charleston	M
The College of Saint Rose	M
College of Staten Island of the City University of New York	M
The College of William and Mary	M
Colorado Heights University	M
Colorado State University	M
Colorado State University–Global Campus	M
Colorado Technical University Colorado Springs	M,D
Colorado Technical University Denver South	M
Columbia University	M,D*
Cornell University	D
Daemen College	M
Dallas Baptist University	M
Davenport University	M
Delaware Valley University	M
Delta State University	M
DePaul University	M
DeSales University	M
DeVry University	M
Dominican College	M
Dominican University	M
Drexel University	M,D,O
Duke University	D*
Duquesne University	M
East Carolina University	M
Eastern Illinois University	M
Eastern Michigan University	M
East Tennessee State University	M
Edgewood College	M
Ellis University	M
Elmhurst College	M
Elms College	M
Emory University	M,D
Emporia State University	M
Everest University	M
Everest University	M
Everest University	M
Everglades University	M
Fairfield University	M,O
Fairleigh Dickinson University, College at Florham	M
Fairleigh Dickinson University, Metropolitan Campus	M,O
Fitchburg State University	M
Florida Agricultural and Mechanical University	M
Florida Atlantic University	M
Florida Gulf Coast University	M
Florida International University	M
Florida State University	M,D
Fontbonne University	M
Fordham University	M
Franklin University	M
Freed-Hardeman University	M
Friends University	M
George Fox University	M,D
George Mason University	M,O
The George Washington University	M*
Georgia College & State University	M
Georgia Southern University	M
Georgia State University	M
Golden Gate University	M,D,O
Gonzaga University	M
Governors State University	M
The Graduate Center, City University of New York	D
Grand Canyon University	M
Grand Valley State University	M
Harvard University	D*
Hawai`i Pacific University	M
HEC Montreal	M,O
Hendrix College	M
Herzing University Online	M
Hodges University	M
Hofstra University	M,O
Holy Family University	M
Hood College	M
Howard University	M
Hunter College of the City University of New York	M
Illinois State University	M
Indiana Tech	M
Indiana University–Purdue University Indianapolis	M
Indiana University South Bend	M
Indiana Wesleyan University	M,O
Instituto Tecnologico de Santo Domingo	M,O
Inter American University of Puerto Rico, Aguadilla Campus	M
Inter American University of Puerto Rico, Arecibo Campus	M
Inter American University of Puerto Rico, Barranquitas Campus	M
Inter American University of Puerto Rico, Metropolitan Campus	M
Inter American University of Puerto Rico, Ponce Campus	M
Inter American University of Puerto Rico, San Germán Campus	M,D
Iona College	M,O
Iowa State University of Science and Technology	M
Ithaca College	M
Jackson State University	M
Jacksonville University	M*
James Madison University	M
John Carroll University	M
Juniata College	M
Kansas State University	M
Kean University	M
Keiser University	M
Kennesaw State University	M
Kent State University	M,D
Keystone College	M
King University	M
Lakeland University	M
Lamar University	M
La Roche College	M
La Salle University	M,O
La Sierra University	M,O
Lehigh University	M
Lehman College of the City University of New York	M
Lenoir-Rhyne University	M
Lewis University	M
Liberty University	M,D,O
Lincoln University (MO)	M
Lindenwood University	M
Lipscomb University	M,O
Long Island University–LIU Brooklyn	M,O
Long Island University–LIU Post	M
Louisiana State University and Agricultural & Mechanical College	M,D
Louisiana Tech University	M,D
Loyola Marymount University	M
Loyola University Chicago	M
Loyola University Maryland	M,O
Maharishi University of Management	M,D
Manhattanville College	M*
Marquette University	M
Marshall University	M
Maryville University of Saint Louis	M,O
McGill University	M,D,O
Mercer University	M
Mercy College	M
Mercyhurst University	M,O
Merrimack College	M
Metropolitan State University of Denver	M
Miami University	M
Michigan State University	M,D
Michigan Technological University	M
Middle Tennessee State University	M
Millennia Atlantic University	M
Millsaps College	M
Minnesota State University Moorhead	M
Misericordia University	M
Mississippi College	M,O
Mississippi State University	M,D
Missouri State University	M
Molloy College	M
Monmouth University	M,O
Montana State University	M
Montclair State University	M,O
Moravian College	M
Mount Aloysius College	M
Murray State University	M
National University	M,O
New England College	M
New Jersey City University	M,O
New Mexico State University	M
New York Institute of Technology	M
New York University	M,D
Niagara University	M
North Carolina Agricultural and Technical State University	M
North Carolina State University	M
North Dakota State University	M
Northeastern Illinois University	M
Northeastern State University	M
Northeastern University	M
Northern Illinois University	M
Northern Kentucky University	M,O
Northwest Christian University	M
Northwestern University	M,D*
Nova Southeastern University	M*
Oakland University	M,O
Ohio Dominican University	M
The Ohio State University	M,D
Oklahoma Christian University	M
Oklahoma State University	M,D
Old Dominion University	M
Oral Roberts University	M
Oregon State University	M,D
Our Lady of the Lake University of San Antonio	M
Pace University	M,O
Pacific Lutheran University	M
Pacific States University	M,D
Penn State Erie, The Behrend College	M
Penn State Harrisburg	M
Penn State University Park	M,D
Pepperdine University	M
Pittsburg State University	M
Polytechnic University of Puerto Rico, Miami Campus	M
Polytechnic University of Puerto Rico, Orlando Campus	M
Pontifical Catholic University of Puerto Rico	M,O
Post University	M
Prairie View A&M University	M
Providence College	M
Purdue University Northwest	M
Queens College of the City University of New York	M
Regent University	M,D,O
Regis University	M,O
Rhode Island College	M,O
Rhodes College	M
Rider University	M
Robert Morris University Illinois	M
Rochester Institute of Technology	M
Rockhurst University	M,O
Rocky Mountain College	M
Roosevelt University	M
Rutgers University–Newark	M,D
Sacred Heart University	M,O
St. Ambrose University	M
St. Edward's University	M,O
St. Francis College	M
St. John's University (NY)	M
St. Joseph's College, Long Island Campus	M
St. Joseph's College, New York	M
Saint Joseph's College of Maine	M
Saint Joseph's University	M,O
Saint Leo University	M
Saint Louis University	M
St. Mary's University (United States)	M
Saint Mary's University of Minnesota	M
Saint Peter's University	M
St. Thomas University	M,O
Sam Houston State University	M
San Diego State University	M
San Francisco State University	M
San Jose State University	M
Seattle University	M
Seton Hall University	M,O
Seton Hill University	M,O
Shorter University	M
Slippery Rock University of Pennsylvania	M
Southeast Missouri State University	M
Southern Adventist University	M
Southern Illinois University Carbondale	M,D
Southern Illinois University Edwardsville	M
Southern Methodist University	M
Southern New Hampshire University	M,O
Southern Oregon University	M,O
Southern Utah University	M
Southwestern Adventist University	M
State University of New York at New Paltz	M
State University of New York College at Geneseo	M
State University of New York College at Old Westbury	M
State University of New York Polytechnic Institute	M
Stephen F. Austin State University	M
Stetson University	M
Stony Brook University, State University of New York	M,O
Strayer University	M
Suffolk University	M,O
Syracuse University	M,D
Tabor College	M
Temple University	M,D*
Tennessee Technological University	M
Texas A&M International University	M
Texas A&M University	M
Texas A&M University–Central Texas	M,O
Texas A&M University–Commerce	M
Texas A&M University–Corpus Christi	M
Texas A&M University–San Antonio	M
Texas A&M University–Texarkana	M
Texas Christian University	M
Texas Lutheran University	M
Texas State University	M
Texas Tech University	M,D
Texas Woman's University	M
Towson University	M
Trinity University	M
Troy University	M
Truman State University	M
Tulane University	M,D
Union University	M
Universidad del Este	M
Universidad del Turabo	M
Universidad Metropolitana	M
Université de Sherbrooke	M
Université du Québec à Montréal	M,O
Université du Québec à Trois-Rivières	M
Université du Québec en Outaouais	M,O
Université Laval	M,O
University at Albany, State University of New York	M
University at Buffalo, the State University of New York	M,D*
The University of Akron	M
The University of Alabama	M,D
The University of Alabama at Birmingham	M
The University of Alabama in Huntsville	M,O
University of Alberta	D
The University of Arizona	M
University of Arkansas	M
University of Baltimore	M,O
University of Bridgeport	M
The University of British Columbia	D
University of California, Berkeley	D,O
University of California, Davis	M
University of California, Irvine	M
University of California, Los Angeles	M,D
University of Central Arkansas	M
University of Central Florida	M
University of Central Missouri	M,D,O
University of Central Oklahoma	M
University of Charleston	M
University of Chicago	M,O
University of Cincinnati	M,D
University of Colorado Boulder	M,D
University of Colorado Denver	M
University of Connecticut	M*
University of Dallas	M,D
University of Dayton	M
University of Delaware	M*
University of Denver	M
University of Detroit Mercy	M,O
University of Florida	M,D
University of Georgia	M
University of Hartford	M,O
University of Hawaii at Manoa	M,D
University of Houston	M,D
University of Houston–Clear Lake	M

University of Houston–Victoria	M
University of Idaho	M
University of Illinois at Chicago	M
University of Illinois at Springfield	M
University of Illinois at Urbana–Champaign	M,D
The University of Iowa	M,D*
The University of Kansas	M*
University of Kentucky	M
University of La Verne	M
University of Lethbridge	M,D
University of Louisville	M
University of Maine	M,O
The University of Manchester	M
University of Mary Hardin-Baylor	M
University of Maryland University College	M,O
University of Massachusetts Amherst	M,D*
University of Massachusetts Boston	M
University of Massachusetts Dartmouth	M,O
University of Memphis	M,D
University of Michigan	M,D
University of Michigan–Dearborn	M
University of Michigan–Flint	M
University of Minnesota, Twin Cities Campus	M,D
University of Mississippi	M,D
University of Missouri	M,D,O
University of Missouri–Kansas City	M,D
University of Missouri–St. Louis	M,D,O
University of Montana	M
University of Nebraska at Kearney	M
University of Nebraska at Omaha	M
University of Nebraska–Lincoln	M,D
University of Nevada, Las Vegas	M,O
University of Nevada, Reno	M
University of New Hampshire	M
University of New Haven	M,O
University of New Mexico	M
University of New Orleans	M
University of North Alabama	M
The University of North Carolina at Chapel Hill	M,D
The University of North Carolina at Charlotte	M
The University of North Carolina at Greensboro	M,O
The University of North Carolina Wilmington	M
University of North Dakota	M
University of Northern Colorado	M
University of Northern Iowa	M
University of North Florida	M
University of North Texas	M,D,O
University of Notre Dame	M
University of Oklahoma	M,D*
University of Oregon	M,D
University of Pennsylvania	M,D*
University of Phoenix–Atlanta Campus	M
University of Phoenix–Augusta Campus	M
University of Phoenix–Bay Area Campus	M,D
University of Phoenix–Central Valley Campus	M
University of Phoenix–Charlotte Campus	M
University of Phoenix–Colorado Campus	M
University of Phoenix–Colorado Springs Downtown Campus	M
University of Phoenix–Columbus Georgia Campus	M
University of Phoenix–Dallas Campus	M
University of Phoenix–Hawaii Campus	M
University of Phoenix–Houston Campus	M
University of Phoenix–Jersey City Campus	M
University of Phoenix–Las Vegas Campus	M
University of Phoenix–New Mexico Campus	M
University of Phoenix–North Florida Campus	M
University of Phoenix–Online Campus	M,O
University of Phoenix–Phoenix Campus	M,O
University of Phoenix–Sacramento Valley Campus	M
University of Phoenix–San Antonio Campus	M
University of Phoenix–San Diego Campus	M
University of Phoenix–Southern Arizona Campus	M
University of Phoenix–Southern California Campus	M
University of Phoenix–South Florida Campus	M
University of Phoenix–Utah Campus	M
University of Phoenix–Washington D.C. Campus	M,D
University of Pittsburgh	M,D*
University of Puerto Rico, Río Piedras Campus	M,D
University of Rhode Island	M,D
University of Rochester	M*
University of St. Francis (IL)	M,O
University of St. Thomas (TX)	M
University of St. Thomas (MN)	M
University of San Diego	M
University of Saskatchewan	M
The University of Scranton	M
University of South Africa	M,D
University of South Alabama	M
University of South Carolina	M
The University of South Dakota	M
University of Southern California	M
University of Southern Maine	M
University of Southern Mississippi	M
University of South Florida	M,D
The University of Tampa	M
The University of Tennessee	M,D
The University of Tennessee at Chattanooga	M
The University of Texas at Arlington	M,D
The University of Texas at Austin	M,D
The University of Texas at Dallas	M,D*
The University of Texas at El Paso	M
The University of Texas at San Antonio	M,D
The University of Texas of the Permian Basin	M
The University of Texas Rio Grande Valley	M
University of the Cumberlands	M
University of the Incarnate Word	M
University of the Sacred Heart	M,O
The University of Toledo	M
The University of Tulsa	M
University of Utah	M,D*
University of Vermont	M
University of Virginia	M
University of Washington	M,D*
University of Washington, Tacoma	M
University of Waterloo	M,D
University of West Florida	M
University of West Georgia	M
University of Wisconsin–Madison	M,D
University of Wisconsin–Whitewater	M
University of Wyoming	M
Upper Iowa University	M
Utah State University	M
Utah Valley University	M
Utica College	M
Vanderbilt University	M*
Villanova University	M
Virginia Commonwealth University	M,D
Virginia International University	M,O
Virginia Polytechnic Institute and State University	M,D
Wagner College	M
Wake Forest University	M
Walden University	M,D,O
Walsh College of Accountancy and Business Administration	M
Washburn University	M
Washington State University	M
Washington University in St. Louis	M
Wayland Baptist University	M,D
Wayne State University	M,D,O
Webber International University	M
Weber State University	M
Webster University	M
Western Carolina University	M
Western Connecticut State University	M
Western Illinois University	M
Western Michigan University	M
Western New England University	M
Westminster College (UT)	M,O
West Texas A&M University	M
West Virginia University	M
Wheeling Jesuit University	M
Wichita State University	M
Wilfrid Laurier University	M,D
Wilkes University	M
Wilmington University	M,D
Wilson College	M
Worcester State University	M
Wright State University	M
Xavier University	M
Yale University	D*
Yeshiva University	M
York University	M,D
Youngstown State University	M

ACOUSTICS

Naval Postgraduate School	M,D
Penn State University Park	M,D
Rensselaer Polytechnic Institute	M,D
University of Massachusetts Dartmouth	M,D,O

ACTUARIAL SCIENCE

Ball State University	M
Boston University	M
California State University, East Bay	M
Central Connecticut State University	M,O
Columbia University	M*
Georgia State University	M
Lock Haven University of Pennsylvania	M
Maryville University of Saint Louis	M
Middle Tennessee State University	M
Oregon State University	M,D
Roosevelt University	M
St. John's University (NY)	M
Simon Fraser University	M,D
Temple University	M*
Université du Québec à Montréal	O
University of Illinois at Urbana–Champaign	M,D
The University of Iowa	M,D*
The University of Manchester	M,D
University of Nebraska–Lincoln	M
The University of Texas at Austin	M,D
The University of Texas at Dallas	M,D*
University of Waterloo	M,D

ACUPUNCTURE AND ORIENTAL MEDICINE

Academy for Five Element Acupuncture	M
Academy of Chinese Culture and Health Sciences	M
Acupuncture & Integrative Medicine College, Berkeley	M
Acupuncture and Massage College	M
American College of Acupuncture and Oriental Medicine	M
AOMA Graduate School of Integrative Medicine	M,D
Arizona School of Acupuncture and Oriental Medicine	M
Atlantic Institute of Oriental Medicine	M,D
Bastyr University	M,D,O
California Institute of Integral Studies	M,D
Canadian Memorial Chiropractic College	O
Colorado School of Traditional Chinese Medicine	M
Dongguk University Los Angeles	M
East West College of Natural Medicine	M
Emperor's College of Traditional Oriental Medicine	M,D
Five Branches University	M,D
Florida College of Integrative Medicine	M
Institute of Clinical Acupuncture and Oriental Medicine	M
Maryland University of Integrative Health	M,O
MCPHS University	M
Midwest College of Oriental Medicine	M,O
National College of Natural Medicine	M
New York Chiropractic College	M*
New York College of Health Professions	M
New York College of Traditional Chinese Medicine	M
Northwestern Health Sciences University	M
Oregon College of Oriental Medicine	M,D
Pacific College of Oriental Medicine	M,D
Pacific College of Oriental Medicine–Chicago	M
Pacific College of Oriental Medicine-New York	M
Seattle Institute of Oriental Medicine	M
South Baylo University	M
Southern California University of Health Sciences	M,D
Southwest Acupuncture College	M
Swedish Institute, College of Health Sciences	M
Tri-State College of Acupuncture	M,O
University of Bridgeport	M
WON Institute of Graduate Studies	M,O
World Medicine Institute	M
Yo San University of Traditional Chinese Medicine	M

ACUTE CARE/CRITICAL CARE NURSING

Allen College	M,D,O
Augusta University	D
Barry University	M,O
Case Western Reserve University	M*
The College of New Rochelle	M,O
Columbia University	M,O*
Drexel University	M
Duke University	M,D,O*
Georgetown University	M,D
Goldfarb School of Nursing at Barnes-Jewish College	M
Grand Canyon University	M,O
Inter American University of Puerto Rico, Arecibo Campus	M
Marquette University	M,D,O
Maryville University of Saint Louis	M,D
Mount Carmel College of Nursing	M,D
New York University	M,D,O
Northeastern University	M,D,O
Ohio University	M
Purdue University Northwest	M
San Francisco State University	M,O
Southern Adventist University	M
Texas Tech University Health Sciences Center	M,D,O
Texas Woman's University	M,D
Universidad de Iberoamerica	M,D
The University of Alabama in Huntsville	M,D,O
University of Cincinnati	M,D
University of Guelph	M,D,O
University of Illinois at Chicago	M,O
University of Miami	M,D
The University of North Carolina at Charlotte	M,D,O
University of Pennsylvania	M*
University of Pittsburgh	M,D*
University of Puerto Rico, Medical Sciences Campus	M
University of Rhode Island	M,D
University of Rochester	M,D*
University of South Africa	M,D
University of South Carolina	M,O
University of South Florida	M,D,O
The University of Texas Health Science Center at San Antonio	M,D,O
University of Virginia	M,D
Vanderbilt University	M,D,O*
Wayne State University	D,O
Wright State University	M

ADDICTIONS/SUBSTANCE ABUSE COUNSELING

Adler Graduate School	M
Adler University	M,D,O
Alliant International University–Los Angeles	M
Antioch University New England	M
Argosy University, Hawai`i	O
Arkansas State University	M,O
Cambridge College	M,O
Capella University	M,D
Carlow University	M,O
Cleveland State University	M,D,O
The College of New Jersey	M,O
College of St. Joseph	M
Coppin State University	M
East Carolina University	M,D,O
Fairfield University	M,O
The George Washington University	M*
Governors State University	M
Grand Canyon University	M
Hazelden Graduate School of Addiction Studies	M,O
Indiana University Northwest	M
Indiana University–Purdue University Indianapolis	M,D
Indiana Wesleyan University	M
Johns Hopkins University	M,D
Kean University	M
Lenoir-Rhyne University	M
Lewis & Clark College	M
Liberty University	M,D,O
Loma Linda University	M,D,O
Long Island University–Hudson at Westchester	M,O
Maryville University of Saint Louis	M
McNeese State University	M
Monmouth University	M,O
Montclair State University	O
Northeastern State University	M
Northwest Nazarene University	M
Pace University	M,D
Palm Beach Atlantic University	M
Post University	M
Regis University	M,D,O
Saint Mary's University of Minnesota	M,O
Salve Regina University	M,O
Slippery Rock University of Pennsylvania	M
Springfield College	M
Stony Brook University, State University of New York	M,O
Syracuse University	M,O
Troy University	M,O
United States International University–Africa	M
Universidad Central del Caribe	M
University of Arkansas at Pine Bluff	M
University of California, Berkeley	O
University of Central Oklahoma	M
University of Detroit Mercy	M,D,O
University of Illinois at Springfield	M,O
University of Lethbridge	M,D
University of Louisville	M,D,O
University of Nevada, Las Vegas	M,D,O
University of New Hampshire	M,O
The University of North Carolina at Charlotte	M,D,O
University of Oklahoma	M,O*
The University of South Dakota	M
University of Southern Maine	M,O
University of South Florida	M
The University of Tennessee at Martin	M
Viterbo University	M
Walden University	M,D
Washburn University	M
Waynesburg University	M,D

ADULT EDUCATION

Alverno College	M
Argosy University, Chicago	M,D,O
Argosy University, Hawai`i	M,D
Argosy University, Phoenix	M,D,O
Argosy University, Seattle	M,D
Armstrong State University	M,O
Athabasca University	M,O
Auburn University	M,D,O
Ball State University	M,D
Buffalo State College, State University of New York	M,O
California Baptist University	M
Capella University	M,D
Cleveland State University	M,D,O
Colorado State University	M,D
Concordia University (Canada)	M,O
Coppin State University	M
Cornell University	M,D
Dallas Theological Seminary	M,D,O
Defiance College	M
Delaware State University	M
DePaul University	M,D

*M—masters degree; D—doctorate; O—other advanced degree; *—Close-Up and/or Display*

East Carolina University	M
Eastern Washington University	M
Edgewood College	M,D,O
Florida Agricultural and Mechanical University	M,D
Florida Atlantic University	M,D,O
Florida International University	M,D,O
The George Washington University	O*
Grand Valley State University	M,O
Indiana University of Pennsylvania	M
Instituto Tecnologico de Santo Domingo	M,O
Kean University	M
Lesley University	M,D,O
Louisiana Tech University	M,D
Marshall University	M
Memorial University of Newfoundland	M,D,O
Merrimack College	M,O
Michigan State University	M,D,O
Millersville University of Pennsylvania	M,D
Montana State University	M,D,O
Morehead State University	M,O
Mount Saint Vincent University	M
National Louis University	M,D,O
North Carolina Agricultural and Technical State University	M
North Carolina State University	M,D
North Dakota State University	M,D,O
Northern Illinois University	M,D
Northwestern Oklahoma State University	M
Northwestern State University of Louisiana	M
Oregon State University	M
Penn State Harrisburg	M,D,O
Penn State University Park	M,D,O
Plymouth State University	D
Regent University	M,D,O
St. Francis Xavier University	M
Saint Joseph's College of Maine	M
Saint Joseph's University	M
San Francisco State University	M
Seattle University	M,O
Southern Arkansas University–Magnolia	M
State University of New York Empire State College	M
Teachers College, Columbia University	M,D
Texas A&M University–Kingsville	M,D
Texas A&M University–Texarkana	M
Texas State University	M,D
Trident University International	M
Troy University	M
Tusculum College	M
Universidad del Este	M
Universidad Metropolitana	M
University of Alberta	M,D,O
University of Arkansas	M,D
University of Arkansas at Little Rock	M
The University of British Columbia	M,D
University of Calgary	M,D
University of Central Arkansas	M,O
University of Central Oklahoma	M
University of Cincinnati	M,D,O
University of Colorado Denver	M
University of Connecticut	M,O*
University of Georgia	M,D,O
University of Houston–Victoria	M
University of Manitoba	M
University of Memphis	M,D
University of Minnesota, Twin Cities Campus	M,D,O
University of Missouri	M,D,O
University of Missouri–St. Louis	M,D,O
University of Nebraska–Lincoln	M,D,O
The University of North Carolina at Greensboro	M,D,O
University of North Florida	M
University of Oklahoma	M,D*
University of Phoenix–Bay Area Campus	M,D,O
University of Phoenix–Online Campus	M,O
University of Phoenix–Phoenix Campus	M
University of Phoenix–Sacramento Valley Campus	M,O
University of Phoenix–Southern Arizona Campus	M,O
University of Phoenix–Southern California Campus	M,O
University of Phoenix–Washington D.C. Campus	M,D,O
University of Regina	M
University of South Africa	M,D
The University of South Dakota	M,D,O
University of Southern Maine	M,O
University of South Florida	M,D,O
The University of Tennessee	M,D
University of the District of Columbia	O
University of the Incarnate Word	M,D
The University of West Alabama	M
University of Wisconsin–Milwaukee	D
University of Wisconsin–Platteville	M
Virginia Commonwealth University	M
Walden University	M,D,O
Western Kentucky University	M,D,O
Western Washington University	M
Widener University	M,D
Wright State University	O

ADULT NURSING

Adelphi University	M
Allen College	M,D,O
Armstrong State University	M,O
Bloomsburg University of Pennsylvania	M
Boston College	M,D
California Baptist University	M
Clarkson College	M,O
College of Mount Saint Vincent	M,O
College of Staten Island of the City University of New York	M,O
Columbia University	M,O*
Creighton University	M,D,O
Daemen College	M,D,O
Duke University	M,D,O*
Eastern Michigan University	M,O
Emory University	M
Felician University	M,O
Florida Southern College	M
The George Washington University	M,D,O*
Georgia State University	M,D,O
Goldfarb School of Nursing at Barnes-Jewish College	M
Gwynedd Mercy University	M,D
Hampton University	M,D
Hunter College of the City University of New York	M
Indiana University–Purdue University Fort Wayne	M,O
Kent State University	M,D,O
La Salle University	M,D,O
Lehman College of the City University of New York	M
Lewis University	M,D
Loma Linda University	M
Long Island University–LIU Brooklyn	M,O
Loyola University Chicago	M,D,O
Madonna University	M
Marian University (WI)	M
Marquette University	M,D,O
Maryville University of Saint Louis	M,D
Medical University of South Carolina	M,D
Molloy College	M,D,O
Monmouth University	M,D,O
Mount Carmel College of Nursing	M,D
Mount Saint Mary College	M,O
New York University	M,D,O
North Park University	M
Old Dominion University	M
Purdue University Northwest	M
Quinnipiac University	M,D
Research College of Nursing	M
Rush University	D
Rutgers University–Newark	M,D,O
Sage Graduate School	M,D,O
St. Catherine University	M,D
Saint Peter's University	M,D,O
Seattle Pacific University	M,O
Seattle University	M
Seton Hall University	M,D
Southern Adventist University	M
South University	M
Spalding University	M,D,O
Stony Brook University, State University of New York	M,D,O
Temple University	D*
Texas Christian University	M,O
Texas Woman's University	M,D
Troy University	M,D,O
Universidad del Turabo	M,O
University at Buffalo, the State University of New York	M,D,O*
University of Central Arkansas	M,O
University of Cincinnati	M,D
University of Colorado Colorado Springs	M,D
University of Colorado Denver	M,D
University of Delaware	M,O*
University of Hawaii at Manoa	M,D,O
University of Illinois at Chicago	M,O
The University of Kansas	M,D,O*
University of Massachusetts Amherst	M,D*
University of Massachusetts Dartmouth	M,D
University of Massachusetts Medical School	M,D,O
University of Miami	M,D
University of Minnesota, Twin Cities Campus	M
University of Missouri	M,D,O
University of Missouri–Kansas City	M,D
University of Missouri–St. Louis	M,D,O
The University of North Carolina at Chapel Hill	M,D,O
The University of North Carolina at Greensboro	M,D,O
University of North Florida	M,D,O
University of Pennsylvania	M*
University of Puerto Rico, Medical Sciences Campus	M
University of San Diego	M,D
University of South Carolina	M
University of Southern Maine	M,D,O
University of South Florida	M,D,O
The University of Tampa	M
The University of Texas at Austin	M,D
The University of Texas Rio Grande Valley	M
University of Wisconsin–Eau Claire	M,D
University of Wisconsin–Madison	D
University of Wisconsin–Oshkosh	M
Ursuline College	M,D
Vanderbilt University	M,D,O*
Villanova University	M,D,O
Virginia Commonwealth University	M,D,O
Walden University	M,D,O
Wayne State University	D
Western Connecticut State University	M,D
Wilmington University	M,D
Winona State University	M,D,O
Wright State University	M
York College of Pennsylvania	M,D

ADVERTISING AND PUBLIC RELATIONS

Academy of Art University	M
Arcadia University	M
Ball State University	M
Boston University	M
California Baptist University	M
California State University, Fullerton	M
Central Connecticut State University	M,O
Clarion University of Pennsylvania	O
Colorado State University	M,D
DePaul University	M
Emerson College	M
Georgetown University	M
Golden Gate University	M,D,O
Hofstra University	M
Iona College	M,O
Kansas State University	M
Kent State University	M
La Salle University	M,O
Lasell College	M,O
La Sierra University	M
Liberty University	M,D,O
Marquette University	M,O
Marshall University	M
Michigan State University	M,D
Mississippi College	M
Monmouth University	M,O
Montana State University Billings	M
New York University	M
Northern Kentucky University	M,O
Quinnipiac University	M
Rowan University	M
Royal Roads University	O
Sacred Heart University	M
San Diego State University	M
Savannah College of Art and Design	M
Southern Illinois University Edwardsville	M
Southern Methodist University	M
Suffolk University	M
Syracuse University	M
Universidad Autonoma de Guadalajara	M,D
Université Laval	O
The University of Alabama	M
University of Florida	M,D
University of Houston	M
University of Illinois at Urbana–Champaign	M
University of Maryland, College Park	M,D
University of Miami	M,D
University of Nebraska–Lincoln	M,D
University of North Texas	M,D,O
University of Saint Mary	M
University of Southern California	M
The University of Tennessee	M,D
The University of Texas at Austin	M,D
The University of Texas Rio Grande Valley	M,O
University of the Sacred Heart	M
University of Wisconsin–Stevens Point	M
Virginia Commonwealth University	M
Virginia International University	M,O
Wayne State University	M,D,O
Webster University	M
Western New England University	M
William Woods University	M,D,O

AEROSPACE/AERONAUTICAL ENGINEERING

Air Force Institute of Technology	M,D
American Public University System	M
Arizona State University at the Tempe campus	M,D
Auburn University	M,D
California Institute of Technology	M,D,O
California Polytechnic State University, San Luis Obispo	M
California State Polytechnic University, Pomona	M
California State University, Long Beach	M
Carleton University	M,D
Case Western Reserve University	M,D*
Concordia University (Canada)	M
Cornell University	M,D
École Polytechnique de Montréal	M,D,O
Embry-Riddle Aeronautical University–Daytona	M,D*
Embry-Riddle Aeronautical University–Worldwide	M
Florida Institute of Technology	M,D
The George Washington University	M,D,O*
Georgia Institute of Technology	M,D
Illinois Institute of Technology	M,D
Iowa State University of Science and Technology	M,D
Johns Hopkins University	M,O
Massachusetts Institute of Technology	M,D,O
McGill University	M,D
Middle Tennessee State University	M
Mississippi State University	M,D
Missouri University of Science and Technology	M,D
Naval Postgraduate School	M,D,O
New Mexico State University	M,D
North Carolina State University	M,D
The Ohio State University	M,D
Old Dominion University	M,D
Penn State University Park	M,D
Princeton University	M,D
Purdue University	M,D
Rensselaer Polytechnic Institute	M,D
Rutgers University–New Brunswick	M,D
San Diego State University	M,D
Stanford University	M,D,O
Stevens Institute of Technology	M,O
Syracuse University	M,D
Texas A&M University	M,D
Université Laval	M
University at Buffalo, the State University of New York	M,D*
The University of Alabama	M,D
The University of Alabama in Huntsville	M,D
The University of Arizona	M,D
University of California, Davis	M,D,O
University of California, Irvine	M,D
University of California, Los Angeles	M,D
University of California, San Diego	M,D
University of Central Florida	M
University of Central Missouri	M,D,O
University of Cincinnati	M,D
University of Colorado Boulder	M,D
University of Colorado Colorado Springs	M,D
University of Dayton	M,D
University of Florida	M,D
University of Illinois at Urbana–Champaign	M,D
The University of Kansas	M,D*
The University of Manchester	M,D
University of Maryland, College Park	M,D
University of Miami	M,D
University of Michigan	M,D
University of Minnesota, Twin Cities Campus	M,D
University of Missouri	M,D
University of Nevada, Las Vegas	M,D,O
University of Notre Dame	M,D
University of Oklahoma	M,D*
University of Ottawa	M,D
University of Southern California	M,D,O
The University of Tennessee	M,D
The University of Texas at Arlington	M,D
The University of Texas at Austin	M,D
University of Toronto	M,D
University of Virginia	M,D
University of Washington	M,D*
Utah State University	M,D
Virginia Polytechnic Institute and State University	M,D,O
Washington University in St. Louis	M,D
Webster University	M
Western Michigan University	M,D
West Virginia University	M,D
Wichita State University	M,D
Worcester Polytechnic Institute	M,D

AFRICAN-AMERICAN STUDIES

Boston University	M
Carnegie Mellon University	D
Clark Atlanta University	M,D
Columbia University	M,D*
Cornell University	M,D
Eastern Michigan University	O
Georgia State University	M
Harvard University	D*
Indiana University Bloomington	M
Michigan State University	M,D
Morgan State University	M,D
North Carolina Agricultural and Technical State University	M
Northwestern University	D*
Oblate School of Theology	M,D,O
The Ohio State University	M,D
Rutgers University–New Brunswick	D
Syracuse University	M
Temple University	M,D*
Trinity Lutheran Seminary	M
University at Albany, State University of New York	M
University of California, Berkeley	D
University of California, Los Angeles	M
University of California, Santa Barbara	D
The University of Kansas	M,O*
University of Louisville	M
University of Massachusetts Amherst	M,D*
University of Memphis	M,D,O
University of Wisconsin–Madison	M
West Virginia University	M,D
Yale University	D*

AFRICAN STUDIES

Arizona State University at the Tempe campus	M,D,O
California State University, Long Beach	M
Carnegie Mellon University	D
Claremont Graduate University	M,D,O
Columbia University	M,D*
Cornell University	M,D
Florida International University	M
Harvard University	D*
Howard University	M,D
Indiana University Bloomington	M
Michigan State University	M,D
New York University	M,D,O
Northwestern University	O*
The Ohio State University	M,D
Ohio University	M
Rice University	D

Rutgers University–New Brunswick	D
Stony Brook University, State University of New York	M,O
Syracuse University	M
University at Albany, State University of New York	M
The University of Arizona	M,D,O
University of California, Los Angeles	M
University of Illinois at Urbana–Champaign	M
The University of Kansas	M,O*
University of Louisville	M
The University of North Carolina at Charlotte	O
University of Pennsylvania	M,D*
University of Pittsburgh	O*
University of South Florida	M,O
The University of Texas at Austin	M,D
University of Wisconsin–Madison	M,D
University of Wisconsin–Milwaukee	D
Wayne State University	M,D,O
West Virginia University	M,D
Yale University	M*

AGRICULTURAL ECONOMICS AND AGRIBUSINESS

Alabama Agricultural and Mechanical University	M,D
Alcorn State University	M
American University of Beirut	M
Arizona State University at the Tempe campus	D
Auburn University	M
California Polytechnic State University, San Luis Obispo	M
Colorado State University	M,D
Cornell University	M,D
Delaware Valley University	M
Illinois State University	M
Instituto Centroamericano de Administración de Empresas	M
Iowa State University of Science and Technology	M,D
Kansas State University	M,D
Louisiana State University and Agricultural & Mechanical College	M,D
McGill University	M
Michigan State University	M,D
Mississippi State University	M
New Mexico State University	M,D
North Carolina Agricultural and Technical State University	M
North Carolina State University	M
North Dakota State University	M
Northwest Missouri State University	M
The Ohio State University	M,D
Oklahoma State University	M,D
Penn State University Park	M,D,O
Purdue University	M,D
Rutgers University–New Brunswick	M
South Carolina State University	M
Southern Illinois University Carbondale	M
Texas A&M University	M,D
Texas A&M University–Kingsville	M,D
Texas Tech University	M,D
Tropical Agriculture Research and Higher Education Center	M,D
Tuskegee University	M
Universidad del Este	M
Université Laval	M
University of Alberta	M,D
The University of Arizona	M
University of Arkansas	M
The University of British Columbia	M
University of California, Berkeley	D
University of California, Davis	M,D
University of California, Santa Barbara	M,D
University of Connecticut	M,D*
University of Delaware	M*
University of Florida	M,D
University of Georgia	M,D
University of Guelph	M,D
University of Idaho	M
University of Illinois at Urbana–Champaign	M,D
University of Kentucky	M,D
University of Maine	M
University of Manitoba	M,D
University of Maryland, College Park	M,D
University of Massachusetts Amherst	M,D*
University of Missouri	M,D,O
University of Nebraska–Lincoln	M,D
University of Nevada, Reno	M,D
University of Puerto Rico, Mayagüez Campus	M
University of Saskatchewan	M,D,O
The University of Tennessee at Martin	M
University of Vermont	M
University of Wisconsin–Madison	M,D
University of Wyoming	M
Virginia Polytechnic Institute and State University	M,D
Washington State University	M,D,O
West Texas A&M University	M
West Virginia University	M

AGRICULTURAL EDUCATION

Alcorn State University	M,O
Arkansas State University	M,O
California Polytechnic State University, San Luis Obispo	M
Clemson University	M
Cornell University	M,D
Eastern Kentucky University	M
Iowa State University of Science and Technology	M,D
Ithaca College	M
Kansas State University	M
Louisiana State University and Agricultural & Mechanical College	M,D
Mississippi State University	M,D
Montana State University	M
Murray State University	M
New Mexico State University	M
North Carolina Agricultural and Technical State University	M
North Carolina State University	M,O
North Dakota State University	M
Northwest Missouri State University	M
The Ohio State University	M
Oklahoma State University	M,D
Oregon State University	M
Penn State University Park	M,D,O
Purdue University	M,D,O
South Dakota State University	M
State University of New York at Oswego	M
Stephen F. Austin State University	M
Tarleton State University	M
Tennessee State University	M,D
Texas A&M University	M,D
Texas State University	M
Texas Tech University	M,D
The University of Arizona	M,O
University of Arkansas	M
University of Connecticut	M,D*
University of Delaware	M*
University of Florida	M,D
University of Georgia	M
University of Idaho	M
University of Illinois at Urbana–Champaign	M
University of Minnesota, Twin Cities Campus	M,D
University of Missouri	M,D,O
University of Nebraska–Lincoln	M
University of Puerto Rico, Mayagüez Campus	M
The University of Tennessee	M
University of Wisconsin–River Falls	M
Utah State University	M
West Virginia University	M,D

AGRICULTURAL ENGINEERING

Cornell University	M,D
Dalhousie University	M,D
Illinois Institute of Technology	M
Instituto Tecnológico y de Estudios Superiores de Monterrey, Campus Monterrey	M,D
Iowa State University of Science and Technology	M,D
Kansas State University	M,D
Louisiana State University and Agricultural & Mechanical College	M,D
McGill University	M,D
New York University	M,D
North Carolina State University	M,D,O
The Ohio State University	M,D
Oklahoma State University	M,D
Penn State University Park	M,D
Purdue University	M,D
South Dakota State University	M,D
Texas A&M University	M,D
Université Laval	M
The University of Arizona	M,D
University of Arkansas	M,D
University of Florida	M,D,O
University of Georgia	M,D
University of Illinois at Urbana–Champaign	M,D
University of Kentucky	M,D
University of Missouri	M,D
University of Nebraska–Lincoln	M,D
The University of Tennessee	M
University of Wisconsin–Madison	M,D
Utah State University	M,D
Virginia Polytechnic Institute and State University	M,D
Washington State University	M,D

AGRICULTURAL SCIENCES—GENERAL

Alabama Agricultural and Mechanical University	M,D
Alcorn State University	M
Angelo State University	M
Arkansas State University	M,O
Auburn University	M,D
Brigham Young University	M,D
California Polytechnic State University, San Luis Obispo	M
California State Polytechnic University, Pomona	M
Clemson University	M
Colorado State University	M,D
Dalhousie University	M
Illinois State University	M
Instituto Tecnológico y de Estudios Superiores de Monterrey, Campus Monterrey	M,D
Iowa State University of Science and Technology	M,D
Kansas State University	M,D,O
Louisiana State University and Agricultural & Mechanical College	M,D
McGill University	M,D,O
McNeese State University	M
Michigan State University	M,D
Mississippi State University	M,D
Missouri State University	M
Montana State University	M,D
Morehead State University	M
Murray State University	M
North Carolina Agricultural and Technical State University	M
North Carolina State University	M,D,O
North Dakota State University	M,D
Northwest Missouri State University	M
The Ohio State University	M,D
Oklahoma State University	M,D
Penn State University Park	M,D,O
Prairie View A&M University	M
Purdue University	M,D
Sam Houston State University	M
South Dakota State University	M,D
Southern Arkansas University–Magnolia	M
Southern Illinois University Carbondale	M
Southern University and Agricultural and Mechanical College	M
Tarleton State University	M
Tennessee State University	M,D
Texas A&M University	M,D
Texas A&M University–Commerce	M
Texas A&M University–Kingsville	M,D
Texas Tech University	M,D
Tropical Agriculture Research and Higher Education Center	M,D
Universidad Nacional Pedro Henriquez Urena	M
Université Laval	M,D,O
University of Alberta	M,D
The University of Arizona	M,D,O
University of Arkansas	M,D
The University of British Columbia	M,D
University of California, Davis	M
University of Connecticut	M,D*
University of Delaware	M,D*
University of Florida	M,D,O
University of Georgia	M,D
University of Guelph	M,D,O
University of Hawaii at Manoa	M,D
University of Illinois at Urbana–Champaign	M
The University of Iowa	M,D,O*
University of Kentucky	M,D
University of Lethbridge	M,D
University of Maine	M,D,O
University of Manitoba	M,D
University of Maryland, College Park	M,D
University of Maryland Eastern Shore	M,D
University of Minnesota, Twin Cities Campus	M,D
University of Missouri	M,D,O
University of Nebraska–Lincoln	M,D
University of Nevada, Reno	M,D
University of New Hampshire	M,D
University of Puerto Rico, Mayagüez Campus	M
University of Saskatchewan	M,D,O
University of South Africa	M,D
The University of Tennessee	M,D
The University of Tennessee at Martin	M
University of Vermont	M,D
University of Wisconsin–Madison	M,D
University of Wisconsin–River Falls	M
University of Wyoming	M,D
Utah State University	M,D
Virginia Polytechnic Institute and State University	M,D,O
Western Kentucky University	M
West Texas A&M University	M,D
West Virginia University	M,D

AGRONOMY AND SOIL SCIENCES

Alabama Agricultural and Mechanical University	M,D
Alcorn State University	M
Auburn University	M,D
Colorado State University	M,D
Cornell University	M,D
Dalhousie University	M
Iowa State University of Science and Technology	M,D
Kansas State University	M,D,O
McGill University	M,D
Michigan State University	M,D
Mississippi State University	M,D
North Carolina Agricultural and Technical State University	M
North Carolina State University	M,D
North Dakota State University	M,D
The Ohio State University	M,D
Oklahoma State University	M,D
Oregon State University	M,D
Penn State University Park	M,D
Purdue University	M,D
South Dakota State University	M,D
Southern Illinois University Carbondale	M
Tennessee State University	M,D
Texas A&M University	M,D
Texas A&M University–Kingsville	M
Texas Tech University	M,D
Tuskegee University	M
Université Laval	M,D
University of Alberta	M,D
The University of Arizona	M,D,O
University of Arkansas	M,D
The University of British Columbia	M,D
University of California, Davis	M,D
University of California, Riverside	M,D
University of Connecticut	M,D*
University of Delaware	M,D*
University of Florida	M,D
University of Georgia	M,D
University of Guelph	M,D
University of Idaho	M,D
University of Illinois at Urbana–Champaign	M,D
University of Kentucky	M,D
University of Manitoba	M,D
University of Minnesota, Twin Cities Campus	M,D
University of Missouri	M,D,O
University of Nebraska–Lincoln	M,D
University of Puerto Rico, Mayagüez Campus	M
University of Saskatchewan	M,D,O
University of Vermont	M,D
University of Wisconsin–Madison	M,D
University of Wyoming	M,D
Utah State University	M,D
Virginia Polytechnic Institute and State University	M,D
Washington State University	M,D,O
West Virginia University	D

ALLIED HEALTH—GENERAL

Alabama State University	M,D
American College of Healthcare Sciences	M,O
Andrews University	M
Athabasca University	M,O
A.T. Still University	M,D
Baylor University	M,D
Belmont University	M,D
Bennington College	O
Boston University	M,D
Brock University	M,D
Canisius College	M,O
Cleveland State University	M
The Commonwealth Medical College	D
Creighton University	M,D
Dominican College	M,D
Drexel University	M,D,O
Duquesne University	M,D,O
East Carolina University	M,D,O
Eastern Kentucky University	M
East Tennessee State University	M,D,O
Emory University	M,D
Ferris State University	M
Florida Agricultural and Mechanical University	M,D
Florida Gulf Coast University	M,D
Georgia Southern University	M,D,O
Georgia State University	M
Grand Valley State University	M,D
Hampton University	M
Harding University	M,D
Idaho State University	M,D,O
Ithaca College	M,D
Jacksonville University	M*
Loma Linda University	M,D
Long Island University–LIU Post	M,O
Marymount University	M,D,O
Maryville University of Saint Louis	M,D
Medical University of South Carolina	M,D
Mercy College	M,D
Midwestern University, Downers Grove Campus	D
Midwestern University, Glendale Campus	M,D
Minnesota State University Mankato	M,D,O
Misericordia University	M,D
Moravian College	M
New Jersey City University	M
Northeastern University	M,D,O
Northern Arizona University	M,D,O
Northern Kentucky University	M
Nova Southeastern University	M,D*
Oakland University	M,D,O
The Ohio State University	M
Old Dominion University	M,D
Oregon State University	M,D
Purdue University	M,D
Quinnipiac University	M
Regis University	M,D,O
Rosalind Franklin University of Medicine and Science	M,D,O
Rutgers University–Newark	M,D,O
Saint Louis University	M,D,O
Sam Houston State University	M
Seton Hall University	D
Shenandoah University	M,D,O
South Carolina State University	M
Southwestern Oklahoma State University	M
Temple University	M,D*
Tennessee State University	M,D,O
Texas A&M University	M,D
Texas Christian University	M,D,O
Texas State University	M,D
Texas Woman's University	M,D
Towson University	M

*M—masters degree; D—doctorate; O—other advanced degree; *—Close-Up and/or Display*

University at Buffalo, the State University of New York	M,D,O*
The University of Alabama at Birmingham	M,D,O
University of Detroit Mercy	M,D,O
University of Florida	M,D,O
University of Illinois at Chicago	M,D,O
The University of Kansas	M,D,O*
University of Kentucky	M,D
University of Massachusetts Lowell	M,D
University of Mississippi Medical Center	M
University of Nebraska Medical Center	M,D,O
University of Nevada, Las Vegas	M,D,O
University of New Mexico	M,D,O
The University of North Carolina at Chapel Hill	M,D
University of Northern Iowa	M,D
University of North Florida	M,D,O
University of Oklahoma Health Sciences Center	M,D,O
University of Phoenix–Las Vegas Campus	M
University of Puerto Rico, Medical Sciences Campus	M,D,O
University of South Alabama	M,D
The University of South Dakota	M,D,O
The University of Tennessee Health Science Center	M,D
The University of Texas at El Paso	D
The University of Texas Medical Branch	M,D
University of Vermont	M,D
University of Wisconsin–Milwaukee	M,D,O
Virginia Commonwealth University	D
Western University of Health Sciences	M,D
Wichita State University	M,D

ALLOPATHIC MEDICINE

Albany Medical College	D
Albert Einstein College of Medicine	D
American University of Beirut	M,D
Augusta University	D
Baylor College of Medicine	D
Boston University	D
Brown University	D
Case Western Reserve University	D*
Charles R. Drew University of Medicine and Science	D
Columbia University	M,D*
Creighton University	D
Dalhousie University	M,D
Dartmouth College	D*
Drexel University	D
Duke University	D*
East Carolina University	D
Eastern Virginia Medical School	D
East Tennessee State University	D
Emory University	D
Florida International University	M,D
Georgetown University	D
The George Washington University	D*
Harvard University	D*
Hofstra University	D
Howard University	D
Icahn School of Medicine at Mount Sinai	D
Indiana University–Purdue University Indianapolis	M,D
Instituto Tecnologico de Santo Domingo	M,D
Johns Hopkins University	D
Loma Linda University	M,D
Louisiana State University Health Sciences Center	M,D
Louisiana State University Health Sciences Center at Shreveport	D
Marshall University	D
Mayo Medical School	D
McGill University	M,D
Medical College of Wisconsin	D
Medical University of South Carolina	D
Meharry Medical College	D
Mercer University	M,D
Michigan State University	D
Morehouse School of Medicine	D
New York Medical College	D
New York University	M,D
Northeast Ohio Medical University	D
Northwestern University	*
The Ohio State University	D
Oregon Health & Science University	D
Penn State Hershey Medical Center	M,D
Ponce Health Sciences University	D
Pontificia Universidad Catolica Madre y Maestra	D
Queen's University at Kingston	D
Quinnipiac University	D
Rosalind Franklin University of Medicine and Science	D
Rush University	D
Rutgers University–Newark	D
Rutgers University–New Brunswick	D
Saint Louis University	D
Stanford University	D
State University of New York Downstate Medical Center	M,D
State University of New York Upstate Medical University	D
Stony Brook University, State University of New York	D
Temple University	D*
Texas Tech University Health Sciences Center	D
Thomas Jefferson University	D
Tufts University	D
Tulane University	D
Universidad Autonoma de Guadalajara	D
Universidad Central del Caribe	M,D
Universidad Central del Este	D
Universidad de Ciencias Medicas	M,D,O
Universidad de Iberoamerica	M,D
Universidad Iberoamericana	D
Universidad Nacional Pedro Henriquez Urena	D
Université de Montréal	D
Université de Sherbrooke	D
Université Laval	D,O
University at Buffalo, the State University of New York	D*
The University of Alabama at Birmingham	D
The University of Arizona	M,D
University of Arkansas for Medical Sciences	D
The University of British Columbia	M,D
University of Calgary	D
University of California, Berkeley	
University of California, Davis	D
University of California, Irvine	D
University of California, Los Angeles	D
University of California, San Diego	D
University of California, San Francisco	D
University of Central Florida	M,D
University of Chicago	D
University of Cincinnati	D
University of Colorado Denver	D
University of Connecticut Health Center	D*
University of Florida	D
University of Hawaii at Manoa	D
University of Illinois at Chicago	D
University of Illinois at Urbana–Champaign	
The University of Iowa	D*
The University of Kansas	D*
University of Kentucky	D
University of Louisville	D
University of Maryland, Baltimore	D
University of Massachusetts Medical School	D
University of Miami	D
University of Michigan	D
University of Minnesota, Duluth	D
University of Minnesota, Twin Cities Campus	M,D
University of Mississippi Medical Center	D
University of Missouri	D
University of Missouri–Kansas City	M,D
University of Nebraska Medical Center	D,O
University of New Mexico	D
The University of North Carolina at Chapel Hill	D
University of North Dakota	D
University of Oklahoma Health Sciences Center	D
University of Ottawa	M,D
University of Pennsylvania	D*
University of Pittsburgh	D*
University of Puerto Rico, Medical Sciences Campus	D
University of Rochester	D*
University of Saskatchewan	D
University of South Alabama	D
University of South Carolina	D
The University of South Dakota	D
University of Southern California	D
University of South Florida	M,D
The University of Tennessee Health Science Center	D
The University of Texas Health Science Center at Houston	D
The University of Texas Health Science Center at San Antonio	M,D
The University of Texas Medical Branch	D
The University of Texas Rio Grande Valley	D
The University of Texas Southwestern Medical Center	D
University of Toronto	M,D
University of Utah	D*
University of Virginia	M,D
University of Washington	D*
The University of Western Ontario	M,D
University of Wisconsin–Madison	D
Vanderbilt University	M,D*
Virginia Commonwealth University	D
Wake Forest University	D
Washington University in St. Louis	D
Wayne State University	D
West Virginia University	D
Wright State University	D
Yale University	D*

AMERICAN INDIAN/NATIVE AMERICAN STUDIES

Central Michigan University	M
Montana State University	M
Navajo Technical University	M
Northeastern State University	M
Trent University	M,D
The University of Arizona	M,D
University of California, Davis	M,D
University of California, Los Angeles	M
University of Idaho	D
The University of Kansas	M,O*
University of Lethbridge	M,D
University of Manitoba	M
University of New Mexico	M,D
University of Oklahoma	M*
The University of Tulsa	M,D,O
University of Wisconsin–Milwaukee	M
Washington University in St. Louis	M,D,O

AMERICAN STUDIES

American Public University System	M
American University	M,D,O
American University of Beirut	M,D
Appalachian State University	M
Armstrong State University	M
Baylor University	M
Boston University	D
Bowling Green State University	M,D
Brown University	M,D
California State University, Fullerton	M
California State University, Long Beach	M
The Catholic University of America	M,D
Central Michigan University	M,O
Claremont Graduate University	M,D,O
Clark University	M,D
The College at Brockport, State University of New York	M
The College of William and Mary	M,D
The Colorado College	M
Columbia University	M,D*
Cornell University	M,D
Drew University	M,D,O
East Carolina University	M
Emory & Henry College	M
Fairfield University	M
Florida State University	M
Georgetown University	M,D
The George Washington University	M,D*
Harvard University	D*
Inter American University of Puerto Rico, Metropolitan Campus	M,D
James Madison University	M
Kennesaw State University	M
Lake Forest College	M
La Salle University	M,O
Lehigh University	M,D,O
Michigan State University	M,D
Mississippi State University	M,D
Monmouth University	M
New Mexico Highlands University	M
New York University	M,D
Northwestern Oklahoma State University	M
Northwestern University	M*
Norwich University	M
Penn State Harrisburg	M,D,O
Pepperdine University	M
Providence College	M
Purdue University	M,D
Regent University	M
Rice University	D
Rutgers University–Newark	M,D
Saint Louis University	M,D
Stockton University	M,O
Texas Christian University	M,D
Trinity College (United States)	M
Universidad de las Américas Puebla	M
University at Buffalo, the State University of New York	M,D,O*
The University of Alabama	M
University of Colorado Denver	M
University of Dallas	M
University of Delaware	M*
University of Hawaii at Manoa	M,D,O
The University of Iowa	M,D*
The University of Kansas	M,D*
University of Louisiana at Lafayette	D
University of Maryland, College Park	M,D
University of Massachusetts Amherst	M,D*
University of Massachusetts Boston	M
University of Michigan	M,D
University of Michigan–Flint	M
University of Minnesota, Twin Cities Campus	D
University of Missouri–St. Louis	M,D
University of New Mexico	M,D
University of Rochester	M,D*
University of Southern California	D
University of Southern Maine	M,O
University of South Florida	M,D
The University of Texas at Austin	M,D
University of Utah	M,D*
University of Wisconsin–Madison	M,D
University of Wyoming	M
Utah State University	M
Washington State University	M,D
Wayne State University	M,D,O
West Virginia University	M,D
Wilfrid Laurier University	M,D
Yale University	D*

ANALYTICAL CHEMISTRY

Auburn University	M,D
Binghamton University, State University of New York	M,D*
Brigham Young University	M,D
California State University, Los Angeles	M
Cleveland State University	M,D
Cornell University	D
Eastern New Mexico University	M
Florida State University	M,D
Georgetown University	D
The George Washington University	M,D*
Georgia State University	M,D
Governors State University	M
Howard University	M,D
Illinois Institute of Technology	M,D
Indiana University Bloomington	M,D
Iowa State University of Science and Technology	D
Kansas State University	M,D
Laurentian University	M
Marquette University	M,D
McMaster University	M,D
Old Dominion University	M,D
Oregon State University	M,D
Purdue University	M,D
Rutgers University–Newark	M,D
Seton Hall University	M,D
Southern University and Agricultural and Mechanical College	M
Stevens Institute of Technology	M,D,O
Tufts University	M,D
University of Calgary	M,D
University of Cincinnati	M,D
University of Georgia	M,D
University of Louisville	M,D
The University of Manchester	M,D
University of Maryland, College Park	M,D
University of Massachusetts Lowell	M,D
University of Memphis	M,D
University of Michigan	D
University of Missouri	M,D
University of Missouri–Kansas City	M,D
University of Montana	M,D
University of Nebraska–Lincoln	M,D
University of Regina	M,D
The University of Tennessee	M,D
The University of Texas at Austin	D
The University of Toledo	M,D
Vanderbilt University	M,D*
Virginia Commonwealth University	M,D
Wake Forest University	M,D
Wayne State University	M,D
West Virginia University	M,D
Youngstown State University	M

ANATOMY

Albert Einstein College of Medicine	D
American University of Beirut	M,D
Auburn University	M,D
Augusta University	D
Barry University	M
Boston University	M,D
Case Western Reserve University	M*
Columbia University	M,D*
Cornell University	D
Creighton University	M
Dalhousie University	M,D
Des Moines University	M
Duke University	D*
East Carolina University	D
East Tennessee State University	D
Howard University	M,D
Indiana University–Purdue University Indianapolis	M,D
Johns Hopkins University	D
Loma Linda University	D
Louisiana State University Health Sciences Center	D
Louisiana State University Health Sciences Center at Shreveport	M,D
McGill University	M,D
New York Academy of Art	M
New York Chiropractic College	M*
New York Medical College	M,D
The Ohio State University	M,D
Palmer College of Chiropractic	M
Penn State Hershey Medical Center	M,D
Purdue University	M,D
Queen's University at Kingston	M,D
Rosalind Franklin University of Medicine and Science	D
Rush University	M,D
Saint Louis University	M,D
State University of New York Upstate Medical University	M,D
Stony Brook University, State University of New York	D
Universidad Central del Caribe	M,D
Universidad de Ciencias Medicas	M,D,O
Université Laval	O
University at Buffalo, the State University of New York	M,D*
University of California, Irvine	M,D
University of California, Los Angeles	M,D
University of Chicago	D
University of Colorado Denver	M,D
University of Georgia	M
University of Guelph	M,D
University of Illinois at Chicago	M
The University of Iowa	D*
The University of Kansas	M,D*
University of Kentucky	D
University of Louisville	M,D
University of Manitoba	M,D
University of Mississippi Medical Center	M,D
University of Missouri	M
University of Nebraska Medical Center	M,D
University of North Dakota	M,D
University of North Texas Health Science Center at Fort Worth	M,D
University of Prince Edward Island	M,D
University of Puerto Rico, Medical Sciences Campus	M,D
University of Rochester	D*
University of Saskatchewan	M,D
University of South Florida	M,D
The University of Tennessee	M,D
University of Utah	D*
The University of Western Ontario	M,D
Virginia Commonwealth University	D,O
Wake Forest University	D
Wayne State University	D
Wright State University	M
Youngstown State University	M

ANESTHESIOLOGIST ASSISTANT STUDIES

Case Western Reserve University	M*
Emory University	M
Nova Southeastern University	M,D*
Quinnipiac University	M
South University (GA)	M
Université Laval	O
University of Colorado Denver	M
University of Guelph	M,D,O
University of Missouri–Kansas City	M,D

ANIMAL BEHAVIOR

Arizona State University at the Tempe campus	M,D
Bucknell University	M
Cornell University	D
Emory University	D
Illinois State University	M,D
University of California, Davis	D
University of Colorado Boulder	M,D
University of Colorado Denver	M,D
University of Massachusetts Amherst	M,D*
University of Minnesota, Twin Cities Campus	M,D
University of Montana	M,D,O
The University of Tennessee	M,D
The University of Texas at Austin	D
University of Washington	D*

ANIMAL SCIENCES

Alcorn State University	M
American University of Beirut	M
Angelo State University	M
Auburn University	M,D
Bergin University of Canine Studies	M
Boise State University	M,D
Brigham Young University	M,D
California State University, Fresno	M
Clemson University	M,D
Colorado State University	M,D
Cornell University	M,D
Dalhousie University	M
Fort Valley State University	M
Iowa State University of Science and Technology	M,D
Kansas State University	M,D
Louisiana State University and Agricultural & Mechanical College	M,D
McGill University	M,D
Michigan State University	M,D
Mississippi State University	M,D
Montana State University	M,D
New Mexico State University	M,D
North Carolina Agricultural and Technical State University	M
North Carolina State University	M,D
North Dakota State University	M,D
The Ohio State University	M,D
Oklahoma State University	M,D
Oregon State University	M,D
Penn State University Park	M,D
Purdue University	M,D
Rutgers University–New Brunswick	M,D
South Dakota State University	M,D
Southern Illinois University Carbondale	M
Sul Ross State University	M
Texas A&M University	M,D
Texas A&M University–Kingsville	M
Texas Tech University	M,D
Tufts University	M
Tuskegee University	M
Universidad Nacional Pedro Henriquez Urena	M
Université Laval	M,D
The University of Arizona	M,D
University of Arkansas	M,D
The University of British Columbia	M,D
University of California, Davis	M,D
University of Connecticut	M,D*
University of Delaware	M,D*
University of Florida	M,D
University of Georgia	M,D
University of Guelph	M,D
University of Hawaii at Manoa	M
University of Idaho	M,D
University of Illinois at Urbana–Champaign	M,D
University of Kentucky	M,D
University of Maine	M,D,O
University of Manitoba	M,D
University of Maryland, College Park	M,D
University of Massachusetts Amherst	M,D*
University of Minnesota, Twin Cities Campus	M,D
University of Missouri	M,D
University of Nebraska–Lincoln	M,D
University of Nevada, Reno	M
University of New Hampshire	D
University of Puerto Rico, Mayagüez Campus	M
University of Rhode Island	M,D
University of Saint Joseph	M
University of Saskatchewan	M,D
The University of Tennessee	M,D
University of Vermont	M,D
University of Wisconsin–Madison	M,D
University of Wyoming	M,D
Utah State University	M,D
Virginia Polytechnic Institute and State University	M,D
Washington State University	M,D
West Texas A&M University	M
West Virginia University	M,D

ANTHROPOLOGY

American University	M,D,O
The American University in Cairo	M
American University of Beirut	M,D
Arizona State University at the Tempe campus	M,D,O
Ball State University	M,O
Binghamton University, State University of New York	M,D*
Biola University	M,D,O
Boise State University	M
Boston University	M,D
Brandeis University	M,D
Brigham Young University	M
Brown University	M,D
California State University, Bakersfield	M
California State University, Chico	M
California State University, East Bay	M
California State University, Fullerton	M
California State University, Long Beach	M
California State University, Los Angeles	M
California State University, Northridge	M
California State University, Sacramento	M
Canisius College	M
Carleton University	M
Case Western Reserve University	M,D*
The Catholic University of America	M
Central European University	M,D
The College of William and Mary	M,D
Colorado State University	M
Columbia University	M,D*
Concordia University (Canada)	M,D
Cornell University	D
Creighton University	M
Dalhousie University	M,D
East Carolina University	M
Eastern New Mexico University	M
Edinboro University of Pennsylvania	M
Emory University	D
Florida Atlantic University	M
George Mason University	M,D
The George Washington University	M,D*
Georgia State University	M
The Graduate Center, City University of New York	D
Harvard University	M,D*
Humboldt State University	M
Hunter College of the City University of New York	M
Idaho State University	M
Indiana University Bloomington	M,D
Iowa State University of Science and Technology	M
Johns Hopkins University	D
Kent State University	M
Louisiana State University and Agricultural & Mechanical College	M,D
McGill University	M,D
McMaster University	M,D
Memorial University of Newfoundland	M,D
Mercyhurst University	M
Michigan State University	M,D
Minnesota State University Mankato	M
Mississippi State University	M
Monmouth University	M
New Mexico Highlands University	M
New Mexico State University	M,O
The New School	M,D
New York University	M,D
North Carolina State University	M
North Dakota State University	M
Northern Arizona University	M
Northern Illinois University	M
Northwestern University	D*
The Ohio State University	M,D
Oregon State University	M,D
Penn State University Park	M,D
Portland State University	M,D,O
Princeton University	D
Purdue University	M,D
Rice University	M,D
Roosevelt University	M
Rutgers University–New Brunswick	M,D
San Diego State University	M
San Francisco State University	M
San Jose State University	M,O
Simon Fraser University	M,D
Sonoma State University	M
Southern Illinois University Carbondale	M,D
Southern Methodist University	M,D
Stanford University	M,D
Stony Brook University, State University of New York	M,D
Syracuse University	M,D
Teachers College, Columbia University	M,D
Temple University	D*
Texas A&M University	M,D
Texas State University	M
Texas Tech University	M
Trent University	M
Tulane University	D
Universidad de las Américas Puebla	M
Université de Montréal	M,D
Université Laval	M,D
University at Albany, State University of New York	M,D
University at Buffalo, the State University of New York	M,D*
The University of Alabama	M,D
The University of Alabama at Birmingham	M
University of Alaska Anchorage	M
University of Alaska Fairbanks	M,D
University of Alberta	M,D
The University of Arizona	M,D,O
University of Arkansas	M,D
The University of British Columbia	M,D
University of Calgary	M,D
University of California, Berkeley	D
University of California, Davis	M,D
University of California, Irvine	M,D
University of California, Los Angeles	M,D
University of California, Riverside	M,D
University of California, San Diego	D
University of California, San Francisco	D
University of California, Santa Barbara	M,D
University of California, Santa Cruz	D
University of Central Florida	M,O
University of Chicago	D
University of Cincinnati	M
University of Colorado Boulder	M,D
University of Colorado Denver	M
University of Connecticut	M,D*
University of Denver	M
University of Florida	M,D
University of Georgia	M,D
University of Guelph	M,D
University of Hawaii at Manoa	M,D
University of Houston	M
University of Idaho	M
University of Illinois at Chicago	M,D
University of Illinois at Urbana–Champaign	M,D
University of Indianapolis	M
The University of Iowa	M,D*
The University of Kansas	M,D*
University of Kentucky	M,D
University of Lethbridge	M,D
University of Louisville	M
University of Maine	D
The University of Manchester	M,D
University of Manitoba	M,D
University of Maryland, College Park	M
University of Massachusetts Amherst	M,D*
University of Memphis	M
University of Michigan	D
University of Minnesota, Duluth	M
University of Minnesota, Twin Cities Campus	M,D
University of Mississippi	M,D
University of Missouri	M,D
University of Montana	M,D
University of Nebraska–Lincoln	M
University of Nevada, Las Vegas	M,D
University of Nevada, Reno	M,D
University of New Brunswick Fredericton	M
University of New Mexico	M,D
The University of North Carolina at Chapel Hill	M,D
The University of North Carolina at Charlotte	M
University of North Georgia	M
University of North Texas	M,D,O
University of Oklahoma	M,D*
University of Oregon	M,D
University of Ottawa	M
University of Pennsylvania	M,D*
University of Pittsburgh	M,D*
University of Regina	M
University of Rhode Island	M
University of Saskatchewan	M
University of South Africa	M,D
University of South Carolina	M,D
University of Southern Mississippi	M
University of South Florida	M,D,O
The University of Tennessee	M,D
The University of Texas at Arlington	M
The University of Texas at Austin	M,D
The University of Texas at El Paso	M,O
The University of Texas at San Antonio	M,D
The University of Texas Rio Grande Valley	M
University of Toronto	M,D
The University of Tulsa	M,D
University of Utah	M,D*
University of Victoria	M
University of Virginia	M,D
University of Washington	M,D*
University of Waterloo	M
The University of Western Ontario	M,D
University of West Florida	M
University of Wisconsin–Madison	D
University of Wisconsin–Milwaukee	M,D,O
University of Wyoming	M,D
Vanderbilt University	M,D*
Washington State University	M,D
Washington University in St. Louis	D
Wayne State University	M,D,O
Western Kentucky University	M
Western Michigan University	M
Western Washington University	M
Wichita State University	M
Yale University	M,D*
York University	M,D

APPLIED ARTS AND DESIGN—GENERAL

Academy of Art University	M
Alfred University	M
Arizona State University at the Tempe campus	M,D
The Art Institute of Dallas, a campus of South University	M
Bowling Green State University	M
California College of the Arts	M
California Institute of the Arts	M,O
California State University, Fresno	M
California State University, Fullerton	M
California State University, Los Angeles	M
Carnegie Mellon University	M,D
College for Creative Studies	M
Concordia University (Canada)	M,O
Cranbrook Academy of Art	M
Drexel University	M
Emily Carr University of Art + Design	M
Fashion Institute of Technology	M*
Ferris State University	M
Florida Atlantic University	M
Howard University	M
Illinois Institute of Technology	M,D
Indiana University–Purdue University Indianapolis	M
Kansas State University	M
Louisiana State University and Agricultural & Mechanical College	M
Louisiana Tech University	M
Maryland Institute College of Art	M
Massachusetts College of Art and Design	M,O
Memphis College of Art	M
Miami International University of Art & Design	M
Millersville University of Pennsylvania	M
Minneapolis College of Art and Design	M
The New School	M
New York University	M
North Carolina State University	M,D
Northeastern University	M
NSCAD University	M
Oklahoma State University	M,D
Pacific Northwest College of Art	M
Pratt Institute	M,O*
Purdue University	M
Radford University	M
Rhode Island School of Design	M
Rutgers University–New Brunswick	M
San Diego State University	M
Savannah College of Art and Design	M,O
School of the Art Institute of Chicago	M
School of Visual Arts (NY)	M
Southern Illinois University Carbondale	M
Stanford University	M,D,O
Stephen F. Austin State University	M
Suffolk University	M
Syracuse University	M
University of Alberta	M
University of Baltimore	M
University of Bridgeport	M
University of California, Berkeley	M,O
University of California, Los Angeles	M
University of Central Oklahoma	M
University of Cincinnati	M
University of Connecticut	M*
University of Delaware	M*
University of Illinois at Chicago	M
University of Illinois at Urbana–Champaign	M,D
The University of Kansas	M*
University of Kentucky	M
University of Louisville	M,D
University of Massachusetts Dartmouth	M,O
University of Michigan	M,D
University of Minnesota, Twin Cities Campus	M,D,O
University of North Texas	M,D,O
University of Notre Dame	M
The University of Texas at Austin	M
University of Washington	M*
University of Wisconsin–Madison	M,D
Virginia Commonwealth University	M
Western Carolina University	M
Western Michigan University	M
Yale University	M*
York University	M

APPLIED BEHAVIOR ANALYSIS

Antioch University New England	M,O
Arizona State University at the Tempe campus	M,D
Assumption College	M,O
Auburn University	M,D
Aurora University	M
Ball State University	M
Baylor University	M,D,O
Caldwell University	M,D,O
California State University, Sacramento	M

*M—masters degree; D—doctorate; O—other advanced degree; *—Close-Up and/or Display*

California State University, Stanislaus	M
Capella University	M
The Chicago School of Professional Psychology	M,D
The Chicago School of Professional Psychology at Downtown Los Angeles	M,D
Drexel University	M,D
Eastern University	M,O
East Stroudsburg University of Pennsylvania	M
Endicott College	M,D
Fairfield University	M,O
Florida Institute of Technology	M,D
Florida International University	M,D
Florida State University	M
Georgian Court University	M,O
Hofstra University	M,D,O
James Madison University	M
Johns Hopkins University	O
Johnson State College	M
Lipscomb University	M,D,O
Long Island University–LIU Brooklyn	M,O
Long Island University–LIU Post	M,O
McNeese State University	M
Mercyhurst University	M
Missouri State University	M,O
Monmouth University	M,O
Mount Aloysius College	M
National University	M,O
Northeastern University	M,D,O
Northern Michigan University	M,O
Oakland University	M,O
Oklahoma City University	M
Oklahoma State University	M,D,O
Penn State Harrisburg	M,D,O
Philadelphia College of Osteopathic Medicine	M,D,O*
Queens College of the City University of New York	M,O
Regis College (MA)	M,D,O
Rollins College	M
Rowan University	M,O
Sage Graduate School	M,O
St. Cloud State University	M
Saint Peter's University	M,D,O
Shenandoah University	M
Simmons College	M,D,O
Spalding University	M
Teachers College, Columbia University	M,D,O
Tennessee Technological University	D
The University of Kansas	M,D*
University of Louisville	M,D,O
University of Massachusetts Dartmouth	M,O
University of Nebraska at Omaha	M,D,O
The University of North Carolina Wilmington	M
University of North Florida	M
University of North Texas	M,D,O
University of Pittsburgh	M,D*
University of Saint Joseph	M,O
University of Southern Maine	M,O
University of South Florida	M,D
The University of Texas at San Antonio	M,O
Wayne State University	M,D,O
Western New England University	M,D
Westfield State University	M
Wright State University	M
Youngstown State University	M

APPLIED ECONOMICS

Auburn University	D
Buffalo State College, State University of New York	M
Clemson University	M,D
Cornell University	M,D
DePaul University	M
East Carolina University	M
Florida State University	M,D
Georgia Southern University	M,O
HEC Montreal	M
Johns Hopkins University	M
Mills College	M
Mississippi State University	M,D
New York University	M,D,O
North Carolina Agricultural and Technical State University	M
Ohio University	M
Portland State University	M,D
Roosevelt University	M
St. Cloud State University	M
Southern Methodist University	M,D
Texas Tech University	M,D
Thomas Jefferson University	M,D,O
University of California, Santa Cruz	M
University of Cincinnati	M
University of Georgia	M,D
University of Houston	M,D
University of Idaho	M
University of Illinois at Urbana–Champaign	M,D
University of Massachusetts Boston	M
University of Michigan	M
University of Minnesota, Twin Cities Campus	M,D
University of Nevada, Reno	M,D
University of New Brunswick Fredericton	M
The University of North Carolina at Charlotte	M,O
The University of North Carolina at Greensboro	M
University of North Dakota	M
University of Oklahoma	M,D*
University of Pennsylvania	D*
University of Regina	M
University of Vermont	M
University of Wisconsin–Madison	M,D
University of Wyoming	M,D
Utah State University	M
Virginia Polytechnic Institute and State University	M,D
Western Kentucky University	M
Western Michigan University	M,D
Wright State University	M

APPLIED MATHEMATICS

Acadia University	M
Air Force Institute of Technology	M,D
Arizona State University at the Tempe campus	M,D,O
Auburn University	M,D
Bowie State University	M
Brown University	M,D
California Baptist University	M
California Institute of Technology	M,D
California State Polytechnic University, Pomona	M
California State University, East Bay	M
California State University, Fullerton	M
California State University, Long Beach	M,D
California State University, Los Angeles	M
California State University, Northridge	M
Case Western Reserve University	M,D*
Central European University	M,D
Claremont Graduate University	M,D
The College of William and Mary	M,D
Colorado School of Mines	M,D
Columbia University	M,D*
Cornell University	M,D
Dalhousie University	M,D
Delaware State University	M,D
DePaul University	M,D
École Polytechnique de Montréal	M,D,O
Elizabeth City State University	M
Florida Atlantic University	M,D
Florida Institute of Technology	M,D
Florida State University	M,D
The George Washington University	M,D,O*
Hampton University	M
Harvard University	M,D*
Howard University	M,D
Hunter College of the City University of New York	M
Illinois Institute of Technology	M,D
Indiana University Bloomington	M,D
Indiana University of Pennsylvania	M
Indiana University–Purdue University Fort Wayne	M,O
Indiana University–Purdue University Indianapolis	M,D
Indiana University South Bend	M
Inter American University of Puerto Rico, San Germán Campus	M
Iowa State University of Science and Technology	M,D
Johns Hopkins University	M,D,O
Kent State University	M,D
Lehigh University	M,D
Long Island University–LIU Post	M,O
Manhattan College	M
McGill University	M,D
Michigan State University	M,D
Missouri University of Science and Technology	M,D
Montclair State University	M
Naval Postgraduate School	M,D
New Jersey Institute of Technology	M,D,O
New Mexico Institute of Mining and Technology	M,D
North Carolina Agricultural and Technical State University	M
North Carolina Central University	M
North Carolina State University	M,D
North Dakota State University	M,D
Northeastern Illinois University	M
Northeastern University	M,D
Northwestern University	M,D*
Oakland University	M,D
Oklahoma State University	M,D
Oregon State University	M,D
Princeton University	D
Rensselaer Polytechnic Institute	M
Rice University	M,D
Rochester Institute of Technology	M
Rutgers University–Camden	M
Rutgers University–New Brunswick	M,D
San Diego State University	M
Santa Clara University	M,D,O
Simon Fraser University	M,D
Southern Illinois University Edwardsville	M
Southern Methodist University	M,D
Southern Oregon University	M
Stevens Institute of Technology	M
Stony Brook University, State University of New York	M,D,O
Temple University	M,D*
Texas Christian University	M,D
Texas State University	M
Towson University	M
The University of Akron	M
The University of Alabama	M,D
The University of Alabama at Birmingham	D
The University of Alabama in Huntsville	M,D
University of Alberta	M,D,O
The University of Arizona	M,D
University of Arkansas at Little Rock	M,O
The University of British Columbia	M,D
University of California, Berkeley	D
University of California, Davis	M,D
University of California, Irvine	M,D
University of California, Merced	M,D
University of California, San Diego	M,D
University of California, Santa Barbara	M,D
University of California, Santa Cruz	M,D
University of Central Arkansas	M
University of Central Missouri	M,D,O
University of Central Oklahoma	M
University of Chicago	D
University of Cincinnati	M,D
University of Colorado Boulder	M,D
University of Colorado Colorado Springs	M
University of Colorado Denver	M,D
University of Connecticut	M*
University of Dayton	M
University of Delaware	M,D*
University of Georgia	M,D
University of Guelph	M,D
University of Houston	M,D
University of Illinois at Urbana–Champaign	M,D
The University of Iowa	D*
University of Kentucky	M,D
University of Louisville	M,D
The University of Manchester	M,D
University of Maryland, Baltimore County	M,D
University of Maryland, College Park	M,D
University of Massachusetts Amherst	M,D*
University of Memphis	M,D
University of Michigan–Dearborn	M
University of Minnesota, Duluth	M
University of Missouri	M,D
University of New Hampshire	M,D
The University of North Carolina at Charlotte	M,D
University of Northern Iowa	M
University of Notre Dame	M,D
University of Pennsylvania	D*
University of Pittsburgh	M,D*
University of Puerto Rico, Mayagüez Campus	M
University of Rhode Island	M,D
University of Southern California	M,D
The University of Tennessee	M,D
The University of Tennessee at Chattanooga	M
The University of Texas at Arlington	M,D
The University of Texas at Austin	M,D
The University of Texas at Dallas	M,D*
The University of Texas at San Antonio	M
The University of Toledo	M,D
The University of Tulsa	M
University of Washington	M,D*
University of Waterloo	M,D
The University of Western Ontario	M,D
University of Wisconsin–Stout	M
Utah State University	M,D
Virginia Commonwealth University	M
Washington State University	M,D
Wayne State University	M,D
West Chester University of Pennsylvania	M,O
Western Illinois University	M,O
Western Michigan University	M,D
West Virginia University	M,D
Wichita State University	M,D
Worcester Polytechnic Institute	M,D,O
Wright State University	M
Yale University	M,D*
York University	M,D
Youngstown State University	M

APPLIED PHYSICS

Air Force Institute of Technology	M,D
Binghamton University, State University of New York	M,D*
California Institute of Technology	M,D
Carnegie Mellon University	M,D
Christopher Newport University	M
The College of William and Mary	M,D
Colorado School of Mines	M,D
Columbia University	M,D*
Cornell University	M,D
East Carolina University	M,D
George Mason University	M,D,O
Georgia Southern University	M
Harvard University	M,D*
Idaho State University	M,D
Illinois Institute of Technology	M,D
Iowa State University of Science and Technology	M,D
Johns Hopkins University	M,O
Laurentian University	M
Louisiana Tech University	M
Michigan Technological University	M,D
Mississippi State University	M,D
Naval Postgraduate School	M,D,O
New Jersey Institute of Technology	M,D,O
New York University	M,D
Northern Arizona University	M,D
Northwestern University	D*
Rice University	M,D
Rutgers University–Newark	M,D
Southern Illinois University Carbondale	M,D
Stanford University	M,D
Texas A&M University	M,D
Texas Tech University	M,D
Towson University	M
University of Arkansas	M,D
University of California, San Diego	M,D
University of Massachusetts Boston	M
University of Michigan	D
University of Missouri–St. Louis	M,D
The University of North Carolina at Charlotte	M,D
University of South Florida	M,D
The University of Texas at Austin	M,D
University of Washington	M,D*
Virginia Commonwealth University	M
West Virginia University	M,D
Yale University	M,D*

APPLIED PSYCHOLOGY

Angelo State University	M
Antioch University New England	M,D,O
Arizona State University at the Tempe campus	M
Athabasca University	M,O
Boston College	M,D
California State University, Chico	M
The Catholic University of America	M,D
Central Michigan University	M,D
The Chicago School of Professional Psychology: Online	M,O
Clayton State University	M
Clemson University	M
DEREE - The American College of Greece	M
Eastern Washington University	M
Fairfield University	M,O
Fordham University	M,D
Francis Marion University	M,O
George Mason University	M,D,O
The George Washington University	D*
Laurentian University	M
London Metropolitan University	M,D
Loras College	M
Lynn University	M
Mississippi State University	M,D
New York University	M,D,O
Oklahoma State University	M,D,O
Old Dominion University	D
Penn State Harrisburg	M,D,O
Rider University	M
Rutgers University–New Brunswick	M,D
Sacred Heart University	M
Saint Mary's University (Canada)	M,D
Tarleton State University	M
Teachers College, Columbia University	M,D
University of Arkansas at Little Rock	M
University of Baltimore	M
University of Calgary	M,D
University of Central Florida	M,D
University of Guelph	M,D
University of Maryland, Baltimore County	D
University of Pennsylvania	M,D*
University of Pittsburgh	M,D*
University of Regina	M,D
University of South Carolina Aiken	M
The University of Tennessee	M,D
The University of Texas at El Paso	M,O
The University of Texas of the Permian Basin	M
University of Windsor	M,D
University of Wisconsin–Stout	M
Walden University	M,D,O
William James College	M,D,O

APPLIED SCIENCE AND TECHNOLOGY

The College of William and Mary	M,D
Colorado State University–Pueblo	M
Harvard University	M,O*
James Madison University	M
Louisiana State University and Agricultural & Mechanical College	M
Missouri State University	M
Naval Postgraduate School	M,D
Saint Mary's University (Canada)	M
Southeastern Louisiana University	M
Southern Methodist University	M,D
Thomas Edison State University	O
University of Arkansas at Little Rock	M,D
University of California, Berkeley	D
University of California, Davis	M,D
University of Colorado Denver	M
University of Mississippi	M,D

APPLIED SOCIAL RESEARCH

American University	M,O
California State University, Dominguez Hills	M,O
Concordia University Irvine	M
Hunter College of the City University of New York	M
Laurentian University	M
Loma Linda University	M,D
The New School	M,D
New York University	M
Portland State University	M,D
Queens College of the City University of New York	M
University of California, Los Angeles	M,D
Virginia Commonwealth University	M,O
West Virginia University	M

APPLIED STATISTICS

American University	M,O
Binghamton University, State University of New York	M,D*
Bowling Green State University	M,D
Brigham Young University	M

California State University, East Bay	M
California State University, Long Beach	M
Cleveland State University	M
Colorado School of Mines	M,D
Cornell University	M,D
DePaul University	M,D
Florida State University	M,D
Indiana University Bloomington	M,D
Indiana University–Purdue University Fort Wayne	M,O
Indiana University–Purdue University Indianapolis	M,D
Instituto Tecnológico y de Estudios Superiores de Monterrey, Campus Monterrey	M,D
Kennesaw State University	M
Louisiana State University and Agricultural & Mechanical College	M
Loyola University Chicago	M
McMaster University	M
Michigan State University	M,D
New Jersey Institute of Technology	M,D,O
New Mexico State University	M,D,O
New York University	M
Northern Arizona University	M,O
Oakland University	M
Penn State University Park	M,D
Purdue University	M,D
Rochester Institute of Technology	M,O
Rutgers University–New Brunswick	M,D
St. Cloud State University	M
Stevens Institute of Technology	O
Syracuse University	M
Teachers College, Columbia University	M,D
The University of Alabama	M,D
University of Arkansas at Little Rock	M,O
University of California, Santa Barbara	M,D
University of Chicago	M
University of Colorado Denver	M,D
University of Guelph	M,D
University of Illinois at Urbana–Champaign	M,D
The University of Kansas	M,D,O*
University of Memphis	M,D
University of Michigan	M,D
University of Northern Colorado	M,D
University of Notre Dame	M,D
University of Pittsburgh	M,D*
University of South Carolina	M,D,O
The University of Tennessee at Chattanooga	M
The University of Texas at San Antonio	M,D
University of West Florida	M
Villanova University	M
West Chester University of Pennsylvania	M,O
Worcester Polytechnic Institute	M,D,O
Wright State University	M

AQUACULTURE

American University of Beirut	M
Auburn University	M,D
Clemson University	M,D
Dalhousie University	M
Kentucky State University	M
Memorial University of Newfoundland	M
Purdue University	M,D
Texas A&M University–Corpus Christi	M
University of Arkansas at Pine Bluff	M
University of Florida	M,D
University of Guelph	M
University of Rhode Island	M,D

ARCHAEOLOGY

American University of Beirut	M,D
Arizona State University at the Tempe campus	M,D,O
Boston University	M,D
Brown University	D
Bryn Mawr College	M,D
California State University, Northridge	M
California State University, San Bernardino	M
Columbia University	M,D*
Cornell University	M,D
Florida State University	M,D
Gordon-Conwell Theological Seminary	M,D
The Graduate Center, City University of New York	D
Harvard University	M,D*
Illinois State University	M
Indiana University of Pennsylvania	M
Johns Hopkins University	D
Massachusetts Institute of Technology	M,D,O
Memorial University of Newfoundland	M,D
Mercyhurst University	M
Michigan Technological University	M,D
New York University	M,D
Northern Arizona University	M
Princeton University	D
Rice University	M,D
St. Cloud State University	M
San Francisco State University	M
Simon Fraser University	M,D
Stanford University	M,D
Trinity International University	M,D,O
Tufts University	M
Universidad de las Américas Puebla	M
Université Laval	M,D
University of Alberta	M,D
The University of British Columbia	M,D
University of Calgary	M
University of California, Berkeley	M,D
University of California, Los Angeles	M,D
University of Colorado Denver	M
University of Denver	M
University of Georgia	M,D
University of Lethbridge	M,D
The University of Manchester	M,D
University of Massachusetts Boston	M
University of Memphis	M,D,O
University of Michigan	M,D
University of Minnesota, Twin Cities Campus	M,D
University of Missouri	M,D
University of Nebraska–Lincoln	M,D
University of New Mexico	M,D
The University of North Carolina at Chapel Hill	M,D
University of Pennsylvania	M,D*
University of Rhode Island	M
University of Saskatchewan	M,D
University of South Africa	M,D
University of South Florida	M,D,O
The University of Tennessee	M,D
The University of Texas at Austin	M,D
University of West Florida	M
University of Wisconsin–Madison	D
University of Wisconsin–Milwaukee	M,D,O
Washington State University	M,D
Washington University in St. Louis	M,D
Wheaton College	M,D
Yale University	M,D*

ARCHITECTURAL ENGINEERING

Carnegie Mellon University	M,D
Drexel University	M,D
Illinois Institute of Technology	M,D
Kansas State University	M
Lawrence Technological University	M,D
Milwaukee School of Engineering	M*
Penn State University Park	M,D
University of California, San Diego	M
University of Colorado Boulder	M,D
University of Detroit Mercy	M
The University of Kansas	M*
University of Louisiana at Lafayette	M
University of Massachusetts Amherst	M,D*
University of Miami	M,D
University of Nebraska–Lincoln	M,D
The University of Texas at Austin	M

ARCHITECTURAL HISTORY

Arizona State University at the Tempe campus	D
Cornell University	M,D
The Graduate Center, City University of New York	D
Harvard University	D*
Massachusetts Institute of Technology	M,D
New York University	M
Roger Williams University	M
Savannah College of Art and Design	M
University of California, Berkeley	M,D
University of Colorado Denver	D
University of Pittsburgh	M,D*
The University of Texas at Austin	M,D
University of Virginia	M,D
Virginia Commonwealth University	M,D

ARCHITECTURE

Academy of Art University	M
Andrews University	M
Arizona State University at the Tempe campus	M,D
Athabasca University	M,O
Auburn University	M
Ball State University	M
Boston Architectural College	M
California Baptist University	M
California College of the Arts	M
California Polytechnic State University, San Luis Obispo	M
California State Polytechnic University, Pomona	M
Carleton University	M
Carnegie Mellon University	M,D
The Catholic University of America	M
City College of the City University of New York	M
Clemson University	M,O
Columbia University	M,D*
Cooper Union for the Advancement of Science and Art	M
Cornell University	M,D
Cranbrook Academy of Art	M
Dalhousie University	M
Drury University	M
Ferris State University	M
Florida Agricultural and Mechanical University	M
Florida International University	M,O
Florida State University	M
Frank Lloyd Wright School of Architecture	M*
Georgia Institute of Technology	M,D
Hampton University	M
Harvard University	M,D*
Illinois Institute of Technology	M,D
Instituto Tecnológico y de Estudios Superiores de Monterrey, Campus Estado de México	M,D
Instituto Tecnológico y de Estudios Superiores de Monterrey, Campus Irapuato	M,D
Iowa State University of Science and Technology	M
Judson University	M
Kansas State University	M
Kennesaw State University	M
Kent State University	M
Lawrence Technological University	M,D,O
London Metropolitan University	M,D
Louisiana State University and Agricultural & Mechanical College	M
Louisiana Tech University	M,D
Marywood University	M
Massachusetts College of Art and Design	M
Massachusetts Institute of Technology	M,D
McGill University	M,D,O
Miami University	M
Montana State University	M
Morgan State University	M
New Jersey Institute of Technology	M,D
The New School	M
NewSchool of Architecture and Design	M
New York Institute of Technology	M
North Carolina State University	M
North Dakota State University	M
Northeastern University	M
The Ohio State University	M,D
Penn State University Park	M,D
Philadelphia University	M
Pontificia Universidad Catolica Madre y Maestra	M
Portland State University	M
Prairie View A&M University	M
Pratt Institute	M*
Princeton University	M,D
Rensselaer Polytechnic Institute	M,D
Rhode Island School of Design	M
Rice University	M,D
Rochester Institute of Technology	M
Roger Williams University	M
Savannah College of Art and Design	M
School of the Art Institute of Chicago	M
Southern California Institute of Architecture	M
Southern Illinois University Carbondale	M
Syracuse University	M
Temple University	M*
Texas A&M University	M,D,O
Texas Tech University	M,D
Tulane University	M
Universidad Autonoma de Guadalajara	M,D
Universidad Nacional Pedro Henriquez Urena	M
Université Laval	M
University at Buffalo, the State University of New York	M*
The University of Arizona	M,D,O
The University of British Columbia	M
University of Calgary	M,D
University of California, Berkeley	M,D
University of California, Los Angeles	M,D
University of Cincinnati	M
University of Colorado Denver	M
University of Florida	M,D
University of Hartford	M
University of Hawaii at Manoa	D
University of Houston	M
University of Idaho	M
University of Illinois at Chicago	M
University of Illinois at Urbana–Champaign	M,D
The University of Kansas	M,D,O*
University of Kentucky	M
The University of Manchester	M,D
University of Manitoba	M
University of Maryland, College Park	M
University of Massachusetts Amherst	M*
University of Memphis	M
University of Miami	M
University of Michigan	M
University of Minnesota, Twin Cities Campus	M
University of Nebraska–Lincoln	M,D
University of Nevada, Las Vegas	M,O
University of New Mexico	M,D
The University of North Carolina at Charlotte	M
The University of North Carolina at Greensboro	M,O
University of Notre Dame	M
University of Oklahoma	M*
University of Oregon	M
University of Pennsylvania	M,D,O*
University of Puerto Rico, Rí o Piedras Campus	M
University of Southern California	M,D
University of South Florida	M
The University of Tennessee	M
The University of Texas at Arlington	M
The University of Texas at Austin	M
The University of Texas at San Antonio	M
University of the District of Columbia	M
University of Toronto	M
University of Utah	M*
University of Washington	M,D,O*
University of Waterloo	M
University of Wisconsin–Milwaukee	M,D,O
Virginia Polytechnic Institute and State University	M,D,O
Washington State University	M
Washington University in St. Louis	M
Wentworth Institute of Technology	M
Woodbury University	M
Yale University	M,D*

ARCHIVES/ARCHIVAL ADMINISTRATION

Claremont Graduate University	M,D,O
Clayton State University	M
Columbia University	M*
Drexel University	M
Middle Tennessee State University	M,D,O
Montclair State University	M
New York University	M,D,O
Pratt Institute	M,O*
The University of British Columbia	M,D
University of California, Los Angeles	M,D,O
University of California, Riverside	M,D
University of Manitoba	M,D
University of Massachusetts Boston	M
University of Michigan	M,D
University of Rochester	M*
University of South Carolina	M,O
University of Wisconsin–Milwaukee	M,D,O
Wayne State University	M,D,O

ART/FINE ARTS

Academy of Art University	M
Adams State University	M
Adelphi University	M
Alfred University	M,D
Anna Maria College	M,O
Antioch University Midwest	M
Arizona State University at the Tempe campus	M,D
Art Center College of Design	M
Azusa Pacific University	M
Ball State University	M
Bard College	M
Barry University	M
Bob Jones University	M,D,O
Boise State University	M
Boston University	M
Bowling Green State University	M
Bradley University	M
Brigham Young University	M
Brooklyn College of the City University of New York	M
California College of the Arts	M
California Institute of the Arts	M,O
California State University, Chico	M
California State University, Fresno	M
California State University, Fullerton	M
California State University, Long Beach	M
California State University, Los Angeles	M
California State University, Northridge	M
California State University, Sacramento	M
California State University, San Bernardino	M
Carnegie Mellon University	M
Central Washington University	M
Christie's Education	O
City College of the City University of New York	M
Claremont Graduate University	M
Clemson University	M
The College at Brockport, State University of New York	M
College for Creative Studies	M
Colorado State University	M
Columbia University	M,D*
Columbus College of Art & Design	M
Concordia University (Canada)	M
Cornell University	M
Cranbrook Academy of Art	M
Drew University	M,D,O
Drury University	M
Duke University	M,D*
East Carolina University	M
Eastern Illinois University	M
Eastern Michigan University	M
East Tennessee State University	M
Edinboro University of Pennsylvania	M
Emily Carr University of Art + Design	M
Fairleigh Dickinson University, Metropolitan Campus	M
Ferris State University	M
Florida Atlantic University	M
Florida International University	M,O
Florida State University	M
Fontbonne University	M
Fort Hays State University	M
Framingham State University	M
Full Sail University	M
George Mason University	M
The George Washington University	M,O*
Georgia Southern University	M
Georgia State University	M
Governors State University	M
Hofstra University	M,D,O
Hollins University	M
Hood College	M,O
Houston Baptist University	M

*M—masters degree; D—doctorate; O—other advanced degree; *—Close-Up and/or Display*

Howard University	M
Hunter College of the City University of New York	M
Idaho State University	M
Illinois State University	M
Indiana State University	M
Indiana University Bloomington	M,D
Indiana University of Pennsylvania	M
Indiana University–Purdue University Indianapolis	M
Institute for Doctoral Studies in the Visual Arts	D
Inter American University of Puerto Rico, San Germán Campus	M
Iowa State University of Science and Technology	M
Jacksonville University	M*
James Madison University	M
John F. Kennedy University	M
Johnson State College	M
Kansas State University	M
Kean University	M
Kent State University	M
Laguna College of Art & Design	M
Lake Forest College	M
La Salle University	M,O
Lee University	M,O
Lehman College of the City University of New York	M
Lesley University	M,D,O
Liberty University	M
Lindenwood University	M
Long Island University–LIU Post	M
Louisiana State University and Agricultural & Mechanical College	M
Louisiana Tech University	M
Maine College of Art	M
Maryland Institute College of Art	M,O
Marywood University	M
Massachusetts College of Art and Design	M,O
Memphis College of Art	M
Miami University	M
Michigan State University	M
Millersville University of Pennsylvania	M
Mills College	M
Minneapolis College of Art and Design	M,O
Minnesota State University Mankato	M
Mississippi College	M
Missouri State University	M
Montana State University	M
Montclair State University	M
Moore College of Art & Design	M
Morehead State University	M
New Hampshire Institute of Art	M
New Jersey City University	M
New Mexico State University	M
The New School	M
New York Academy of Art	M
New York Institute of Technology	M
New York Studio School of Drawing, Painting and Sculpture	M,O*
New York University	M,D,O
Norfolk State University	M
Northeastern University	M
Northern Illinois University	M
Northwestern State University of Louisiana	M
Northwestern University	M*
Nova Southeastern University	M,D,O*
NSCAD University	M
The Ohio State University	M
Ohio University	M
Oregon College of Art & Craft	M
Otis College of Art and Design	M
Pace University	M,O
Pacific Northwest College of Art	M
Paris College of Art	M
Penn State University Park	M,D,O
Pennsylvania Academy of the Fine Arts	M,O
Philadelphia University	M
Pontifical Catholic University of Puerto Rico	M
Portland State University	M
Pratt Institute	M*
Purchase College, State University of New York	M
Purdue University	M
Queens College of the City University of New York	M
Radford University	M
Rensselaer Polytechnic Institute	M,D
Rhode Island College	M
Rhode Island School of Design	M
Rochester Institute of Technology	M,O
Rutgers University–New Brunswick	M
San Diego State University	M
San Francisco Art Institute	M,O
San Francisco State University	M
Savannah College of Art and Design	M
School of the Art Institute of Chicago	M
School of the Museum of Fine Arts, Boston	M,O
School of Visual Arts (NY)	M
Sotheby's Institute of Art–London	M
Sotheby's Institute of Art–New York	M
Southern Illinois University Carbondale	M
Southern Illinois University Edwardsville	M
Southern Methodist University	M
Southwest University of Visual Arts	M
Spring Hill College	M,O
Stanford University	M,D
State University of New York at New Paltz	M
State University of New York at Oswego	M
Stephen F. Austin State University	M
Stony Brook University, State University of New York	M
Sul Ross State University	M
Syracuse University	M
Temple University	M*
Texas A&M University	M
Texas A&M University–Corpus Christi	M
Texas Christian University	M
Texas Southern University	M
Texas Tech University	M,D
Texas Woman's University	M
Tiffin University	M
Towson University	M
Tufts University	M
Tulane University	M
United Theological Seminary of the Twin Cities	M,D,O
Universidad del Turabo	M
Université du Québec à Chicoutimi	M
Université du Québec à Montréal	M
Université Laval	M
University at Albany, State University of New York	M
University at Buffalo, the State University of New York	M,D*
The University of Alabama	M
University of Alaska Fairbanks	M
University of Alberta	M
The University of Arizona	M
University of Arkansas	M
University of Arkansas at Little Rock	M
The University of British Columbia	M,D,O
University of Calgary	M
University of California, Berkeley	M,O
University of California, Davis	M
University of California, Irvine	M,D
University of California, Los Angeles	M
University of California, Riverside	M
University of California, San Diego	M,D
University of California, Santa Barbara	M
University of California, Santa Cruz	M,D
University of Central Florida	M
University of Chicago	M
University of Cincinnati	M
University of Colorado Boulder	M
University of Colorado Denver	M
University of Dallas	M
University of Delaware	M*
University of Denver	M
University of Florida	M,D
University of Georgia	M,D
University of Guam	M
University of Guelph	M
University of Hartford	M
University of Hawaii at Manoa	M
University of Houston	M
University of Idaho	M
University of Illinois at Chicago	M,D
University of Illinois at Urbana–Champaign	M
University of Indianapolis	M
The University of Iowa	M*
The University of Kansas	M*
University of Kentucky	M
University of Lethbridge	M,D
University of Maine	M
The University of Manchester	M,D
University of Maryland, College Park	M
University of Massachusetts Amherst	M*
University of Massachusetts Dartmouth	M,O
University of Memphis	M,O
University of Miami	M
University of Michigan	M
University of Michigan–Flint	M
University of Minnesota, Duluth	M
University of Minnesota, Twin Cities Campus	M
University of Mississippi	M,D
University of Missouri	M
University of Missouri–Kansas City	M,D
University of Montana	M
University of Nebraska at Omaha	M
University of Nebraska–Lincoln	M
University of Nevada, Las Vegas	M
University of Nevada, Reno	M
University of New Hampshire	M
University of New Mexico	M
University of New Orleans	M
The University of North Carolina at Chapel Hill	M
The University of North Carolina at Greensboro	M
University of North Dakota	M
University of Northern Colorado	M
University of Northern Iowa	M
University of North Texas	M,D,O
University of Notre Dame	M
University of Oklahoma	M*
University of Oregon	M
University of Pennsylvania	M,O*
University of Regina	M
University of Rochester	M,D*
University of Saint Francis (IN)	M
University of Saskatchewan	M
The University of Scranton	M
University of South Carolina	M
The University of South Dakota	M
University of Southern California	M,D,O
University of South Florida	M
The University of Tennessee	M
The University of Texas at Arlington	M
The University of Texas at Austin	M
The University of Texas at El Paso	M
The University of Texas at San Antonio	M
The University of Texas at Tyler	M
The University of Texas Rio Grande Valley	M
The University of the Arts	M
The University of Tulsa	M
University of Utah	M*
University of Victoria	M
University of Washington	M*
University of Waterloo	M
University of Windsor	M
University of Wisconsin–Madison	M
University of Wisconsin–River Falls	M
University of Wisconsin–Stout	M
University of Wisconsin–Superior	M
Utah State University	M
Vermont College of Fine Arts	M
Virginia Commonwealth University	M,D
Washington State University	M
Washington University in St. Louis	M
Wayne State University	M
Webster University	M
Western Carolina University	M
Western Connecticut State University	M
West Texas A&M University	M
West Virginia University	M
Wichita State University	M
William Paterson University of New Jersey	M
Wilson College	M
Winthrop University	M
Yale University	M*
York University	M,D

ART EDUCATION

Academy of Art University	M
Adelphi University	M
Alabama Agricultural and Mechanical University	M
American University of Puerto Rico	M
Anna Maria College	M
Arcadia University	M,D,O
Arizona State University at the Tempe campus	M,D
Art Academy of Cincinnati	M
Boise State University	M
Boston University	M
Bowling Green State University	M
Bridgewater State University	M
Brigham Young University	M
Brooklyn College of the City University of New York	M
Buffalo State College, State University of New York	M
California State University, Long Beach	M
California State University, Los Angeles	M
California State University, Northridge	M
Carlow University	M
Carthage College	M,O
Case Western Reserve University	M*
Central Connecticut State University	M,O
Chatham University	M
Cleveland State University	M
The College of New Rochelle	M
The Colorado College	M
Colorado State University–Pueblo	M
Columbus State University	M
Concordia University (Canada)	M,D
Concordia University Wisconsin	M
Converse College	M
Delaware State University	M
East Carolina University	M
Eastern Illinois University	M
Eastern Kentucky University	M
Eastern Michigan University	M
Edinboro University of Pennsylvania	M
Ferris State University	M
Fitchburg State University	M,O
Florida Atlantic University	M
Florida International University	M,D,O
Florida State University	M,D
Fontbonne University	M
George Mason University	M
The George Washington University	M*
Georgia State University	M
Harding University	M,O
Harvard University	M*
Hofstra University	M,D,O
Indiana University Bloomington	M,D,O
Indiana University–Purdue University Indianapolis	M
Indiana University South Bend	M
James Madison University	M
Kean University	M
Kennesaw State University	M
Kent State University	M
Kutztown University of Pennsylvania	M
Lake Forest College	M
Lesley University	M,D,O
Long Island University–LIU Post	M,D,O
Manhattanville College	M*
Mansfield University of Pennsylvania	M
Maryland Institute College of Art	M
Maryville University of Saint Louis	M,D
Marywood University	M
Massachusetts College of Art and Design	M,O
Memphis College of Art	M
Miami University	M
Millersville University of Pennsylvania	M
Mills College	M,D,O
Minnesota State University Mankato	M
Mississippi College	M,D,O
Montclair State University	M
Moore College of Art & Design	M
Morehead State University	M
Nazareth College of Rochester	M
New Hampshire Institute of Art	M
New Jersey City University	M
New York University	M,O
The Ohio State University	M,D
Penn State University Park	M,D,O
Piedmont College	M,O
Plymouth State University	M
Pratt Institute	M,O*
Purdue University	M,D,O
Queens College of the City University of New York	M,O
Rhode Island College	M
Rhode Island School of Design	M
Rochester Institute of Technology	M
Rocky Mountain College of Art + Design	M
Saint Michael's College	M,O
Salem College	M
Salem State University	M
School of the Art Institute of Chicago	M
School of the Museum of Fine Arts, Boston	M,O
School of Visual Arts (NY)	M
School of Visual Arts (NY)	M
Simon Fraser University	M,D
Southern Connecticut State University	M
Southwestern Oklahoma State University	M
Spalding University	M
State University of New York at New Paltz	M
State University of New York at Oswego	M
Sul Ross State University	M
Syracuse University	M
Teachers College, Columbia University	M,D,O
Temple University	M*
Texas Tech University	M
Towson University	M,O
Troy University	M
Tufts University	M,D,O
The University of Alabama at Birmingham	M
The University of Arizona	M,D
University of Arkansas at Little Rock	M
The University of British Columbia	M,D
University of Central Florida	M
University of Cincinnati	M
University of Florida	M,D
University of Georgia	M,D,O
University of Idaho	M
University of Illinois at Urbana–Champaign	M,D
University of Indianapolis	M
The University of Iowa	M,D*
The University of Kansas	M*
University of Kentucky	M
University of Louisiana at Monroe	M,D
University of Louisville	M,D,O
University of Maryland, Baltimore County	M
University of Massachusetts Amherst	M*
University of Massachusetts Dartmouth	M
University of Minnesota, Twin Cities Campus	M,D,O
University of Missouri	M,D,O
University of Montana	M
University of Nebraska at Kearney	M
University of New Mexico	M
The University of North Carolina at Charlotte	M,D,O
The University of North Carolina at Pembroke	M
University of Northern Iowa	M
University of North Georgia	M,O
University of North Texas	M,D,O
University of Rio Grande	M
University of St. Francis (IL)	M,D,O
University of South Carolina	M,D
The University of South Dakota	M
The University of Tennessee	M,D,O
The University of Texas at Austin	M
The University of Texas at El Paso	M
The University of the Arts	M
The University of Toledo	M,D,O
University of Utah	M*
University of Victoria	M,D
University of Wisconsin–Madison	M,D
University of Wisconsin–Superior	M
Ursuline College	M
Vermont College of Fine Arts	M
Virginia Commonwealth University	M
Wayne State University	M,D,O
Western Kentucky University	M
Western Michigan University	M
West Virginia University	M
William Carey University	M,O

Winthrop University	M

ART HISTORY

Academy of Art University	M
American University	M
Arizona State University at the Tempe campus	M,D
Bard Graduate Center: Decorative Arts, Design History, Material Culture	M,D*
Binghamton University, State University of New York	M,D*
Boston University	M,D,O
Bowling Green State University	M
Brooklyn College of the City University of New York	M
Brown University	D
Bryn Mawr College	M,D
California State University, Chico	M
California State University, Fullerton	M
California State University, Long Beach	M
California State University, Los Angeles	M
California State University, Northridge	M
Caribbean University	M,D
Carleton University	M
Case Western Reserve University	M,D*
Christie's Education	M
City College of the City University of New York	M
Cleveland State University	M
Colorado State University	M
Columbia University	M,D*
Concordia University (Canada)	M,D
Cornell University	D
Dominican University of California	M
Duke University	M,D*
Emory University	D
Fashion Institute of Technology	M*
Florida State University	M,D,O
George Mason University	M
The George Washington University	M*
Georgia State University	M
The Graduate Center, City University of New York	D
Graduate Theological Union	M,D,O
Harvard University	D*
Howard University	M
Hunter College of the City University of New York	M
Illinois State University	M
Indiana University Bloomington	M,D
James Madison University	M
Johns Hopkins University	M,D
Kent State University	M
Lancaster Theological Seminary	M,D,O
Louisiana State University and Agricultural & Mechanical College	M
Massachusetts Institute of Technology	M,D
McGill University	M,D
Montana State University	M
New Mexico State University	M
New York University	M,D
Northwestern University	D*
The Ohio State University	M,D
Ohio University	M
Penn State University Park	M,D
Pratt Institute	M*
Purchase College, State University of New York	M
Queens College of the City University of New York	M
Rice University	D
Richmond, The American International University in London	M
Roger Williams University	M
Rutgers University–New Brunswick	M,D,O
San Diego State University	M
San Francisco Art Institute	M
San Francisco State University	M
San Jose State University	M,O
Savannah College of Art and Design	M
School of the Art Institute of Chicago	M
School of Visual Arts (NY)	M
Southern Methodist University	M,D
Stony Brook University, State University of New York	M,D
Sul Ross State University	M
Syracuse University	M
Temple University	M,D*
Texas Christian University	M
Texas Tech University	M
Towson University	M
Tufts University	M
Tulane University	M
Université de Montréal	M,D
Université du Québec à Montréal	M,D
Université Laval	M,D
University at Buffalo, the State University of New York	M*
The University of Alabama	M
The University of Alabama at Birmingham	M
University of Alberta	M
The University of Arizona	M,D
University of Arkansas at Little Rock	M
The University of British Columbia	M,D,O
University of California, Berkeley	D
University of California, Davis	M
University of California, Los Angeles	M,D
University of California, Riverside	M,D
University of California, San Diego	M,D
University of California, Santa Barbara	D
University of Chicago	M,D
University of Cincinnati	M
University of Colorado Boulder	M
University of Delaware	M,D*
University of Denver	M
University of Florida	M,D
University of Georgia	M,D
University of Hawaii at Manoa	M
University of Houston	M
University of Illinois at Chicago	M,D
University of Illinois at Urbana–Champaign	M,D
The University of Iowa	M,D*
The University of Kansas	M,D*
University of Kentucky	M
University of Louisville	M,D
The University of Manchester	D
University of Maryland, College Park	M,D
University of Massachusetts Amherst	M*
University of Memphis	M,O
University of Miami	M
University of Michigan	M,D
University of Minnesota, Twin Cities Campus	M,D
University of Missouri	M,D
University of Missouri–Kansas City	M,D
University of Montana	M
University of Nebraska–Lincoln	M
University of New Mexico	M,D
The University of North Carolina at Chapel Hill	M,D
University of North Texas	M,D,O
University of Notre Dame	M
University of Oklahoma	M,D*
University of Oregon	M,D
University of Pennsylvania	M,D*
University of Pittsburgh	M,D*
University of Rochester	M,D*
University of St. Thomas (MN)	M
University of South Africa	M,D
University of South Carolina	M
University of Southern California	M,D,O
University of South Florida	M
The University of Texas at Austin	M,D
The University of Texas at San Antonio	M
The University of Texas at Tyler	M
University of Toronto	M,D
University of Utah	M*
University of Victoria	M,D
University of Virginia	M,D
University of Washington	M,D*
University of Wisconsin–Madison	M,D
University of Wisconsin–Milwaukee	M,O
University of Wisconsin–Superior	M
Virginia Commonwealth University	M,D
Washington University in St. Louis	M,D
Wayne State University	M
Webster University	M
West Virginia University	M
Williams College	M
Yale University	D*
York University	M,D

ARTIFICIAL INTELLIGENCE/ROBOTICS

California State University, Northridge	M
Carnegie Mellon University	M,D
The College of William and Mary	M,D
Cornell University	M,D
Eastern Michigan University	M,O
Georgia Institute of Technology	D
Illinois Institute of Technology	M,D
Indiana University Bloomington	M,D
Instituto Tecnológico y de Estudios Superiores de Monterrey, Campus Monterrey	M,D
Johns Hopkins University	M
Northwestern University	M*
Oregon State University	M,D
Portland State University	M,D,O
South Dakota School of Mines and Technology	M
Stevens Institute of Technology	M,D,O
University of California, Riverside	M,D
University of California, San Diego	M,D
University of Georgia	M
University of Michigan	M,D
University of Nebraska at Omaha	M,O
University of Pennsylvania	M,D*
University of Pittsburgh	M,D*
University of Southern California	M,D
Villanova University	M,O
Worcester Polytechnic Institute	M,D

ARTS ADMINISTRATION

American University	M,O
Arizona State University at the Tempe campus	M,D
Baruch College of the City University of New York	M
Boston University	M,O
Brooklyn College of the City University of New York	M
Carnegie Mellon University	M
Christie's Education	M,O
Claremont Graduate University	M
The College at Brockport, State University of New York	M,O
College of Charleston	M,O
Colorado State University	M
Columbia College Chicago	M
Daemen College	M
Drexel University	M
Eastern Michigan University	M
Fashion Institute of Technology	M*
Florida State University	M,D
George Mason University	M,O
Goucher College	M
HEC Montreal	O
Indiana University Bloomington	M
Le Moyne College	M,O
Lindenwood University	M
London Metropolitan University	M,D
Montclair State University	M
Moore College of Art & Design	M
New York Institute of Technology	M,O
New York University	M
Northwestern University	M*
The Ohio State University	M
Pratt Institute	M*
Rhode Island College	M
Robert Morris University Illinois	M
Rocky Mountain College of Art + Design	M
Rowan University	M
Ryerson University	M
Saint Mary's University of Minnesota	M
St. Thomas University	M
Savannah College of Art and Design	M
School of the Art Institute of Chicago	M
Seattle University	M
Shenandoah University	M,D,O
Sotheby's Institute of Art–London	M
Sotheby's Institute of Art–New York	M
Southern Methodist University	M
Southern Utah University	M
Syracuse University	M,O
Teachers College, Columbia University	M,D,O
Temple University	M,D*
Universidad del Turabo	M
University at Buffalo, the State University of New York	M*
The University of Akron	M
University of Cincinnati	M,D
University of Kentucky	M
The University of Manchester	D
University of Michigan–Flint	M
University of New Orleans	M
The University of North Carolina at Charlotte	M,O
University of North Carolina School of the Arts	M
University of Oregon	M
University of Southern California	M
University of Wisconsin–Madison	M
Valparaiso University	M
Winthrop University	M

ARTS JOURNALISM

Academy of Art University	M
School of the Art Institute of Chicago	M
Syracuse University	M

ART THERAPY

Adler Graduate School	M
Adler University	M,D,O
Albertus Magnus College	M
Athabasca University	M,O
Caldwell University	M,O
California Institute of Integral Studies	M,D
California State University, Los Angeles	M
Cedar Crest College	M
The College of New Rochelle	M
Concordia University (Canada)	M
Drexel University	M,O
Eastern Virginia Medical School	M
Edinboro University of Pennsylvania	M,O
Emporia State University	M
The George Washington University	M,O*
Georgia College & State University	M
Goddard College	M
Hofstra University	M,O
Indiana University–Purdue University Indianapolis	M
Lesley University	M,D,O
Long Island University–LIU Post	M
Marylhurst University	M,O
Marywood University	M,O
Mount Mary University	M,D
Naropa University	M
New York University	M
Notre Dame de Namur University	M
Ottawa University	M
Phillips Graduate Institute	M
Pratt Institute	M*
Prescott College	M
Saint Mary-of-the-Woods College	M,O
School of the Art Institute of Chicago	M
School of Visual Arts (NY)	M
Seton Hill University	M
Southern Illinois University Edwardsville	M
Southwestern College (NM)	M
Springfield College	M,O
University of Louisville	M,D
University of Maryland, College Park	M,D,O
University of Wisconsin–Superior	M
Ursuline College	M

ASIAN-AMERICAN STUDIES

Binghamton University, State University of New York	M,O*
California State University, Long Beach	M
San Francisco State University	M
University of California, Los Angeles	M

ASIAN LANGUAGES

Cornell University	M,D
Harvard University	M,D*
Indiana University Bloomington	M,D
The Ohio State University	M,D
St. John's College (NM)	M
Stanford University	M,D
University of California, Berkeley	M,D
University of California, Irvine	M,D
University of California, Los Angeles	M,D
University of California, Santa Barbara	M,D
University of Chicago	D
University of Hawaii at Manoa	M,D
University of Illinois at Urbana–Champaign	M,D
The University of Iowa	M*
The University of Kansas	M*
University of Michigan	D
University of Minnesota, Twin Cities Campus	D
University of Oregon	M,D
University of Southern California	M,D
The University of Texas at Austin	M,D
University of Washington	M,D*
University of Wisconsin–Madison	M,D
Washington University in St. Louis	M,D
Yale University	D*

ASIAN STUDIES

Binghamton University, State University of New York	M,O*
Brown University	D
California Institute of Integral Studies	M,D
California State University, Long Beach	M
Columbia University	M,D,O*
Cornell University	M,D
Creighton University	M
Dallas Baptist University	M
Duke University	M,O*
Florida International University	M
Florida State University	M
Georgetown University	M
The George Washington University	M*
Harvard University	M,D*
Indiana University Bloomington	M,D
Johns Hopkins University	M,D,O
Maharishi University of Management	M,D
McGill University	M,D
New York University	M,D
The Ohio State University	M
Ohio University	M
Princeton University	D
Rutgers University–New Brunswick	M,D
St. John's College (NM)	M
St. John's University (NY)	M,O
San Diego State University	M
Seton Hall University	M
Stanford University	M
United Theological Seminary of the Twin Cities	M,D,O
University of Alberta	M
The University of Arizona	M,D
University of Bridgeport	M
The University of British Columbia	M,D
University of California, Berkeley	M,D
University of California, Los Angeles	M,D
University of California, Riverside	M
University of California, Santa Barbara	M,D
University of Chicago	M,D
University of Colorado Boulder	M,D
University of Hawaii at Manoa	O
University of Illinois at Urbana–Champaign	M,D
The University of Iowa	M*
The University of Kansas	M*
University of Maine	M,D
The University of Manchester	M,D
University of Michigan	M,D,O
University of Minnesota, Twin Cities Campus	D
University of Oregon	M
University of Pennsylvania	M,D*
University of Pittsburgh	M,O*
University of San Francisco	M
University of Southern California	M,D
The University of Texas at Austin	M,D
University of Toronto	M,D
University of Utah	M*
University of Victoria	M
University of Virginia	M
University of Washington	M,D*
University of Wisconsin–Madison	M,D
Valparaiso University	M
Washington University in St. Louis	M,D
Wayne State University	M,D,O
West Virginia University	M,D
Yale University	M*

*M—masters degree; D—doctorate; O—other advanced degree; *—Close-Up and/or Display*

ASTRONOMY

Boston University	M,D
Brigham Young University	M,D
California Institute of Technology	D
Case Western Reserve University	M,D*
Columbia University	M,D*
Cornell University	D
Dartmouth College	D*
George Mason University	M,D,O
Georgia State University	D
Harvard University	D*
Indiana University Bloomington	M,D
Johns Hopkins University	D
Louisiana State University and Agricultural & Mechanical College	M,D
Michigan State University	M,D
Minnesota State University Mankato	M
New Mexico State University	M,D
Northwestern University	D*
The Ohio State University	M,D
Ohio University	M,D
Penn State University Park	M,D
Princeton University	D
Rice University	M,D
Rutgers University–New Brunswick	M,D
Saint Mary's University (Canada)	M,D
San Diego State University	M
San Francisco State University	M
Stony Brook University, State University of New York	D
Université de Moncton	M
The University of Arizona	D
The University of British Columbia	M,D
University of Calgary	M,D
University of California, Los Angeles	M,D
University of California, Santa Cruz	D
University of Chicago	D
University of Delaware	M,D*
University of Florida	M,D
University of Hawaii at Manoa	M,D
University of Illinois at Urbana–Champaign	M,D
The University of Iowa	M*
The University of Kansas	M,D*
University of Kentucky	M,D
The University of Manchester	M,D
University of Maryland, College Park	M,D
University of Massachusetts Amherst	M,D*
University of Michigan	D
University of Missouri	M,D
University of Nebraska–Lincoln	M,D
University of Nevada, Las Vegas	M,D
The University of North Carolina at Chapel Hill	M,D
University of Pittsburgh	D*
University of Rochester	M,D*
University of South Carolina	M,D
The University of Texas at Austin	M,D
University of Toronto	M,D
University of Victoria	M,D
University of Virginia	M,D
University of Washington	M,D*
The University of Western Ontario	M,D
University of Wisconsin–Madison	D
Vanderbilt University	M,D*
Wesleyan University	M
West Chester University of Pennsylvania	M
Yale University	M,D*
York University	M,D

ASTROPHYSICS

Air Force Institute of Technology	M,D
Arizona State University at the Tempe campus	M,D
Cornell University	D
Harvard University	D*
Indiana University Bloomington	M,D
Iowa State University of Science and Technology	M,D
Louisiana State University and Agricultural & Mechanical College	M,D
McMaster University	D
Michigan State University	M,D
New Mexico Institute of Mining and Technology	M,D
New Mexico State University	M,D
Penn State University Park	M,D
Princeton University	D
Rochester Institute of Technology	M,D
Texas Christian University	M,D
Tufts University	M,D
University of Alaska Fairbanks	M,D
University of Alberta	M,D
University of California, Berkeley	D
University of California, Los Angeles	M,D
University of California, Santa Cruz	D
University of Chicago	D
University of Colorado Boulder	M,D
The University of Manchester	M,D
University of Michigan	D
University of Minnesota, Twin Cities Campus	M,D
University of Missouri–St. Louis	M,D
The University of North Carolina at Chapel Hill	M,D
The University of Toledo	M,D
University of Toronto	M,D
University of Victoria	M,D
Yale University	M,D*

ATHLETIC TRAINING AND SPORTS MEDICINE

Adrian College	M
Armstrong State University	M,O
A.T. Still University	M,D
Barry University	M
Bloomsburg University of Pennsylvania	M
Boston University	D
Brigham Young University	M,D
California Baptist University	M
California State University, Long Beach	M
California University of Pennsylvania	M
Chapman University	M
The College of St. Scholastica	M
Eastern Michigan University	M,O
East Stroudsburg University of Pennsylvania	M
Florida International University	M
Franklin College	M
Gannon University	M
Georgia State University	M
Indiana State University	M,D
Indiana University Bloomington	M,D
Inter American University of Puerto Rico, Metropolitan Campus	M
Kent State University	M,D
Lebanon Valley College	M
Lenoir-Rhyne University	M
Life University	M
Lock Haven University of Pennsylvania	M
London Metropolitan University	M,D
Long Island University–LIU Brooklyn	M,D
Manchester University	M
Marshall University	M
Missouri State University	M
Montana State University Billings	M
North Dakota State University	M,D
Ohio University	M
Old Dominion University	M,D
Oregon State University	M
Pacific University	M,D
Plymouth State University	M
Saint Louis University	M,D
Salisbury University	M
Samford University	M,D
San Jose State University	M,O
Seton Hall University	M
Shenandoah University	M,O
South Dakota State University	M,D
Spalding University	M
Springfield College	M,D
Stephen F. Austin State University	M
Temple University	M,D*
Texas A&M University	M,D
Texas State University	M
Texas Tech University Health Sciences Center	M
Truman State University	M
United States Sports Academy	M
Universidad del Turabo	M
University of Arkansas	M
University of Central Oklahoma	M
The University of Findlay	M,D
University of Florida	M,D
University of Idaho	M,D
The University of Iowa	M,D*
University of Kentucky	M
University of Miami	M,D
University of Nebraska at Omaha	M,D
The University of North Carolina at Chapel Hill	M
The University of North Carolina at Greensboro	M,D
University of Northern Iowa	M
University of Pittsburgh	M*
University of South Florida	M,D
The University of Tennessee	M,D
The University of Tennessee at Chattanooga	M
University of Wisconsin–La Crosse	M
Virginia Commonwealth University	M
Weber State University	M
West Chester University of Pennsylvania	M,O
Western Michigan University	M
West Virginia University	M,D
West Virginia Wesleyan College	M
Xavier University	M

ATMOSPHERIC SCIENCES

Bard College	M,O
Carnegie Mellon University	D
City College of the City University of New York	M
The College of William and Mary	M,D
Colorado State University	M,D
Columbia University	M,D*
Cornell University	M,D
Florida State University	M,D
George Mason University	D
Georgia Institute of Technology	M,D
Hampton University	M,D
Howard University	M,D
Massachusetts Institute of Technology	M,D
McGill University	M,D
Michigan Technological University	M,D,O
Millersville University of Pennsylvania	M
Mississippi State University	M,D
New Mexico Institute of Mining and Technology	M,D
North Carolina State University	M,D
Northern Arizona University	M,D
Nova Southeastern University	M,D,O*
The Ohio State University	M,D
Oregon State University	M,D
Princeton University	D
Purdue University	M,D
Rutgers University–New Brunswick	M,D
South Dakota School of Mines and Technology	M,D
Southern Methodist University	M,D
Stevens Institute of Technology	M,D,O
Stony Brook University, State University of New York	M,D
Texas Tech University	M,D
Université du Québec à Montréal	M,D,O
University at Albany, State University of New York	M,D
The University of Alabama in Huntsville	M,D
University of Alaska Fairbanks	M,D
The University of Arizona	M,D
The University of British Columbia	M,D
University of California, Davis	M,D
University of California, Los Angeles	M,D
University of Chicago	D
University of Colorado Boulder	M,D
University of Guelph	M,D
University of Houston	M,D
University of Illinois at Urbana–Champaign	M,D
The University of Kansas	M,D*
The University of Manchester	M,D
University of Maryland, Baltimore County	M,D
University of Michigan	M,D
University of Nevada, Reno	M,D
The University of North Carolina at Chapel Hill	M,D
University of North Dakota	M,D
University of South Florida	M,D
University of Utah	M,D*
University of Washington	M,D*
University of Wisconsin–Madison	M,D
University of Wyoming	M,D
Yale University	D*

AUTOMOTIVE ENGINEERING

Clemson University	M,D
College for Creative Studies	M
Lawrence Technological University	M,D
Michigan Technological University	M,D,O
Minnesota State University Mankato	M
University of Michigan	M,D
University of Michigan–Dearborn	M,D
The University of Tennessee at Chattanooga	M
Wayne State University	M,O

AVIATION

Embry-Riddle Aeronautical University–Prescott	M
Embry-Riddle Aeronautical University–Worldwide	D
Everglades University	M
Florida Institute of Technology	M,D
Lewis University	M
Southeastern Oklahoma State University	M
University of North Dakota	M
The University of Tennessee	M

AVIATION MANAGEMENT

Arizona State University at the Tempe campus	M
Delta State University	M
Embry-Riddle Aeronautical University–Daytona	M,D*
Embry-Riddle Aeronautical University–Worldwide	M
Florida Institute of Technology	M
Lewis University	M
Lynn University	M
Middle Tennessee State University	M
Purdue University	M
Southeastern Oklahoma State University	M
Vaughn College of Aeronautics and Technology	M

BACTERIOLOGY

Illinois State University	M,D
The University of Iowa	M,D*
University of Prince Edward Island	M,D
The University of Texas Medical Branch	D
University of Washington	D*
University of Wisconsin–Madison	M

BIOCHEMICAL ENGINEERING

Brown University	M,D
Cornell University	M,D
Dartmouth College	M,D*
Drexel University	M
Lehigh University	M,D
Rutgers University–New Brunswick	M,D
University of California, Irvine	M,D
University of Georgia	M
The University of Iowa	M,D*
The University of Manchester	M,D
University of Maryland, Baltimore County	M,D,O
The University of Western Ontario	M,D
Villanova University	M,O

BIOCHEMISTRY

Albert Einstein College of Medicine	D
American University of Beirut	M,D
Arizona State University at the Tempe campus	M,D
Auburn University	M,D
Augusta University	D
Baylor College of Medicine	D
Boston College	M,D
Boston University	M,D
Bradley University	M
Brandeis University	D
Brigham Young University	M,D
Brown University	M,D
California Institute of Technology	M,D
California Polytechnic State University, San Luis Obispo	M
California State University, East Bay	M
California State University, Long Beach	M
California State University, Los Angeles	M
California State University, Northridge	M
Carnegie Mellon University	M,D
Case Western Reserve University	M,D*
City College of the City University of New York	M,D
Clark University	M,D
Clemson University	D
Colorado State University	M,D
Colorado State University–Pueblo	M
Columbia University	M,D*
Cornell University	M,D
Dalhousie University	M,D
Dartmouth College	M,D*
Drexel University	M,D
Duke University	D*
East Carolina University	M,D
Eastern New Mexico University	M
East Tennessee State University	D
Emory University	D
Florida Institute of Technology	M
Florida State University	M,D
George Mason University	M,D
Georgetown University	M,D
The George Washington University	D*
Georgia State University	M,D
The Graduate Center, City University of New York	D
Harvard University	D*
Howard University	M,D
Hunter College of the City University of New York	M,D
Illinois Institute of Technology	M,D
Illinois State University	M,D
Indiana University Bloomington	M,D
Indiana University–Purdue University Indianapolis	M,D
Irell & Manella Graduate School of Biological Sciences	D*
Johns Hopkins University	M,D
Kansas State University	M,D
Kennesaw State University	M
Laurentian University	M
Lehigh University	M,D
Loma Linda University	M,D
Louisiana State University and Agricultural & Mechanical College	M,D
Louisiana State University Health Sciences Center at Shreveport	M,D
Loyola University Chicago	M,D
Massachusetts Institute of Technology	D
Mayo Graduate School	D
McGill University	M,D
McMaster University	M,D
Medical College of Wisconsin	D
Medical University of South Carolina	M,D
Memorial University of Newfoundland	M,D
Miami University	M,D
Michigan State University	M,D
Michigan Technological University	M,D,O
Mississippi College	M
Mississippi State University	M,D
Montana State University	M,D
Montclair State University	M
New York Medical College	M,D
North Carolina State University	D
North Dakota State University	M,D
Northern Michigan University	M
Northwestern University	D*
The Ohio State University	M,D
Ohio University	M,D
Oklahoma State University	M,D
Old Dominion University	M,D
Oregon Health & Science University	M,D
Oregon State University	M,D
Pace University	M
Penn State Hershey Medical Center	M,D
Penn State University Park	M,D
Purdue University	M,D
Queen's University at Kingston	M,D
Rensselaer Polytechnic Institute	M,D
Rice University	M,D
Rosalind Franklin University of Medicine and Science	D
Rush University	M,D
Rutgers University–Newark	M,D
Rutgers University–New Brunswick	M,D
Saint Louis University	D
San Diego State University	M,D
San Francisco State University	M
Seton Hall University	M,D
Simon Fraser University	M,D,O
Sonoma State University	M
Southern Illinois University Carbondale	M,D
Southern University and Agricultural and Mechanical College	M
Stanford University	D
State University of New York College of Environmental Science and Forestry	M,D
State University of New York Upstate Medical University	M,D
Stevens Institute of Technology	M,D,O

Stony Brook University, State University of New York	M,D
Syracuse University	D
Texas A&M University	M,D
Texas Christian University	M,D
Texas State University	M
Thomas Jefferson University	D
Tufts University	D
Tulane University	M
Universidad Central del Caribe	M,D
Université de Moncton	M
Université de Montréal	M,D,O
Université de Sherbrooke	M,D
Université Laval	M,D,O
University at Buffalo, the State University of New York	M,D*
The University of Alabama at Birmingham	D
University of Alaska Fairbanks	M,D
University of Alberta	M,D
The University of Arizona	M,D
University of Arkansas for Medical Sciences	M,D,O
The University of British Columbia	M,D
University of Calgary	M,D
University of California, Berkeley	D
University of California, Davis	M,D
University of California, Irvine	M,D
University of California, Los Angeles	M,D
University of California, Merced	M,D
University of California, Riverside	M,D
University of California, San Diego	M,D
University of California, San Francisco	D
University of California, Santa Barbara	D
University of California, Santa Cruz	M,D
University of Chicago	D
University of Cincinnati	M,D
University of Colorado Boulder	M,D
University of Colorado Denver	D
University of Connecticut Health Center	D*
University of Delaware	M,D*
University of Florida	D
University of Georgia	M,D
University of Guelph	M,D
University of Houston	M,D
University of Idaho	M,D
University of Illinois at Chicago	D
University of Illinois at Urbana–Champaign	M,D
The University of Iowa	M,D*
The University of Kansas	M,D*
University of Kentucky	D
University of Lethbridge	M,D
University of Louisville	M,D
The University of Manchester	M,D
University of Manitoba	M,D
University of Maryland, Baltimore	M,D
University of Maryland, Baltimore County	M,D,O
University of Maryland, College Park	M,D
University of Massachusetts Amherst	M,D*
University of Massachusetts Dartmouth	M,D
University of Massachusetts Lowell	M,D
University of Massachusetts Medical School	M,D
University of Miami	D
University of Michigan	M,D
University of Minnesota, Duluth	M,D
University of Minnesota, Twin Cities Campus	D
University of Mississippi Medical Center	D
University of Missouri	M,D
University of Missouri–Kansas City	D
University of Missouri–St. Louis	M,D
University of Montana	D
University of Nebraska–Lincoln	M,D
University of Nebraska Medical Center	M,D
University of Nevada, Las Vegas	M,D
University of Nevada, Reno	M,D
University of New Hampshire	M,D
University of New Mexico	M,D
The University of North Carolina at Chapel Hill	M,D
The University of North Carolina at Greensboro	M
University of North Dakota	M,D
University of North Texas	M,D,O
University of North Texas Health Science Center at Fort Worth	M,D
University of Notre Dame	M,D
University of Oklahoma	M,D*
University of Oklahoma Health Sciences Center	M,D
University of Oregon	M,D
University of Ottawa	M,D
University of Pennsylvania	D*
University of Puerto Rico, Medical Sciences Campus	M,D
University of Regina	M,D
University of Rhode Island	M,D
University of Rochester	D*
University of Saint Joseph	M
University of Saskatchewan	M,D
The University of Scranton	M
University of South Carolina	M,D
University of Southern California	M
University of Southern Mississippi	M,D
The University of Tennessee	M,D
The University of Texas at Austin	D
The University of Texas Health Science Center at Houston	M,D
The University of Texas Health Science Center at San Antonio	M,D
The University of Texas Medical Branch	D
The University of Texas Southwestern Medical Center	D
University of the Sciences	M,D
The University of Toledo	M,D
University of Toronto	M,D
The University of Tulsa	M
University of Utah	M,D*
University of Victoria	M,D
University of Virginia	D
University of Washington	D*
University of Waterloo	M,D
The University of Western Ontario	M,D
University of West Florida	M
University of Windsor	M,D
University of Wisconsin–Madison	M,D
Utah State University	M,D
Vanderbilt University	M,D*
Virginia Commonwealth University	M,D,O
Wake Forest University	D
Washington State University	M,D
Washington University in St. Louis	D
Wayne State University	M,D
Weill Cornell Medicine	M,D
Wesleyan University	D
West Virginia University	M,D
Worcester Polytechnic Institute	M,D
Wright State University	M
Yale University	D*
Youngstown State University	M

BIOENGINEERING

Alfred University	M,D
Baylor College of Medicine	D
California Institute of Technology	M,D
Carnegie Mellon University	M,D
Clemson University	M,D,O
Colorado School of Mines	M,D
Cornell University	M,D
Dalhousie University	M,D
Florida Atlantic University	M,D
George Mason University	D
Georgia Institute of Technology	M,D
Harvard University	M,D*
Illinois Institute of Technology	M,D
Johns Hopkins University	M,D
Kansas State University	M,D
Lehigh University	M,D
Louisiana State University and Agricultural & Mechanical College	M,D
Massachusetts Institute of Technology	M,D
McGill University	M,D
Mississippi State University	M,D
North Carolina Agricultural and Technical State University	M
North Carolina State University	M,D,O
Northeastern University	M,D,O
Northwestern University	D*
The Ohio State University	M,D
Oklahoma State University	M,D
Oregon State University	M,D
Penn State University Park	M,D
Rensselaer Polytechnic Institute	M,D
Rice University	M,D
Santa Clara University	M,D,O
South Dakota School of Mines and Technology	D
Stanford University	M,D
Syracuse University	M,D
Temple University	M,D*
Texas A&M University	M,D
Texas Tech University	M
Tufts University	M,D,O
University at Buffalo, the State University of New York	M,D*
University of Arkansas	M
University of California, Berkeley	D
University of California, Davis	M,D
University of California, Los Angeles	M,D
University of California, Merced	M,D
University of California, Riverside	M,D
University of California, San Diego	M,D
University of California, San Francisco	D
University of California, Santa Barbara	M,D
University of Chicago	D
University of Colorado Denver	M,D
University of Dayton	M
University of Denver	M,D
University of Florida	M,D,O
University of Georgia	M,D
University of Guelph	M,D
University of Hawaii at Manoa	M
University of Idaho	M,D
University of Illinois at Chicago	M,D
University of Illinois at Urbana–Champaign	M,D
The University of Kansas	M,D*
University of Louisville	M
University of Maryland, College Park	M,D
University of Missouri	M,D
University of Nebraska–Lincoln	M,D
University of Notre Dame	M,D
University of Ottawa	M,D
University of Pennsylvania	M,D*
University of Pittsburgh	M,D*
University of Saskatchewan	M,D
The University of Texas at Arlington	M,D
The University of Toledo	M,D
University of Utah	M,D*
University of Washington	M,D*
Virginia Commonwealth University	M,D
Virginia Polytechnic Institute and State University	M,D
Washington State University	M,D
Wilkes University	M

BIOETHICS

Albany Medical College	M,D,O
Case Western Reserve University	M*
Clarkson University	M,O
Cleveland State University	M,O
Columbia University	M*
Duke University	M*
Duquesne University	M,D,O
Emory University	M
Icahn School of Medicine at Mount Sinai	M
Indiana University–Purdue University Indianapolis	M,O
Instituto Tecnologico de Santo Domingo	M,O
Johns Hopkins University	M,D
Kansas City University of Medicine and Biosciences	M
Loma Linda University	M,O
Loyola Marymount University	M
Loyola University Chicago	D,O
McGill University	M,D,O
Medical College of Wisconsin	M,O
New York University	M
Northeast Ohio Medical University	M,D,O
Oregon State University	M
Saint Louis University	D,O
Stony Brook University, State University of New York	
Trinity International University	M
Université de Montréal	M,D,O
University of Mary	M
University of Pennsylvania	M*
University of Pittsburgh	M*
University of South Florida	O
The University of Tennessee	M,D
University of Toronto	M,D
University of Washington	M*
Washington State University	M,D,O
Washington University in St. Louis	M

BIOINFORMATICS

Arizona State University at the Tempe campus	M,D
Boston University	M,D
Brandeis University	M
California State University Channel Islands	M
California State University, Dominguez Hills	M
Dalhousie University	M,D
Duke University	D,O*
Emory University	M,D
Georgetown University	M,O
Georgia Institute of Technology	M,D
Georgia State University	M,D
Grand Valley State University	M
Hood College	M,O
Indiana University Bloomington	M,D
Indiana University–Purdue University Indianapolis	M,D
Iowa State University of Science and Technology	M,D
Johns Hopkins University	M,D,O
Marquette University	M,D
Massachusetts Institute of Technology	M,D
McGill University	M,D
Medical College of Wisconsin	M
Mississippi Valley State University	M
Morgan State University	M
New Jersey Institute of Technology	M,D,O
New Mexico State University	M,D
New York University	M,D
North Carolina State University	M,D
North Dakota State University	M,D
Northeastern University	M,D
Nova Southeastern University	M,D,O*
Oregon State University	D
Rice University	M,D
Rochester Institute of Technology	M
Rowan University	M
Rutgers University–Newark	M,D
Simon Fraser University	M,D,O
Stevens Institute of Technology	M,D,O
Stony Brook University, State University of New York	M,D
Tufts University	M,D
Université de Montréal	M,D
University at Buffalo, the State University of New York	M,D*
The University of Alabama at Birmingham	D
University of Arkansas at Little Rock	M,D
University of Arkansas for Medical Sciences	M,D,O
University of California, Los Angeles	M,D
University of California, Riverside	D
University of California, San Diego	D
University of California, San Francisco	D
University of California, Santa Cruz	M,D
University of Cincinnati	D,O
University of Colorado Denver	D
University of Georgia	M,D,O
University of Idaho	M,D
University of Illinois at Chicago	M,D
University of Illinois at Urbana–Champaign	M,D,O
The University of Iowa	M,D,O*
University of Maine	M,D
The University of Manchester	M,D
University of Maryland, College Park	D
University of Massachusetts Medical School	M,D
University of Michigan	M,D
University of Missouri	D
University of Missouri–Kansas City	M,D,O
University of Nebraska at Omaha	M,D,O
University of Nebraska–Lincoln	M,D
University of Nebraska Medical Center	M,D
The University of North Carolina at Chapel Hill	D
The University of North Carolina at Charlotte	M,D,O
University of Oklahoma	M,D*
University of Southern California	D
University of South Florida	M,D,O
The University of Texas at El Paso	M,D
The University of Texas Medical Branch	D
University of the Sciences	M
The University of Toledo	M,O
University of Utah	M,D,O*
University of Washington	M,D*
University of Wisconsin–Madison	M
Vanderbilt University	M,D*
Virginia Commonwealth University	M,D
Virginia Polytechnic Institute and State University	M,D
Wayne State University	M,D,O
Wesleyan University	D
Worcester Polytechnic Institute	M,D
Yale University	D*

BIOLOGICAL AND BIOMEDICAL SCIENCES—GENERAL

Acadia University	M
Adelphi University	M
Alabama Agricultural and Mechanical University	M,D
Alabama State University	M,D
Albert Einstein College of Medicine	D
Alcorn State University	M
American Museum of Natural History–Richard Gilder Graduate School	D
American University of Beirut	M,D
Andrews University	M
Angelo State University	M
Appalachian State University	M
Arizona State University at the Tempe campus	M,D
Arkansas State University	M,O
A.T. Still University	M,D
Auburn University	M,D
Austin Peay State University	M
Ball State University	M,D
Barry University	M
Baylor College of Medicine	M,D
Baylor University	M,D
Bemidji State University	M
Binghamton University, State University of New York	M,D*
Bloomsburg University of Pennsylvania	M
Boise State University	M,D
Boston College	D
Boston University	M,D
Bowling Green State University	M,D
Bradley University	M
Brandeis University	M,D,O
Brigham Young University	M,D
Brock University	M,D
Brooklyn College of the City University of New York	M
Brown University	M,D
Bucknell University	M
Buffalo State College, State University of New York	M
California Institute of Technology	D
California Polytechnic State University, San Luis Obispo	M
California State Polytechnic University, Pomona	M
California State University, Bakersfield	M
California State University, Chico	M
California State University, Dominguez Hills	M
California State University, East Bay	M
California State University, Fresno	M
California State University, Fullerton	M
California State University, Long Beach	M
California State University, Los Angeles	M
California State University, Northridge	M
California State University, Sacramento	M
California State University, San Bernardino	M

*M—masters degree; D—doctorate; O—other advanced degree; *—Close-Up and/or Display*

California State University, San Marcos	M
Carleton University	M,D
Carnegie Mellon University	M,D
Case Western Reserve University	M,D*
The Catholic University of America	M,D
Cedars-Sinai Medical Center	D
Central Connecticut State University	M,O
Central Michigan University	M
Central Washington University	M
Chatham University	M
Chicago State University	M
The Citadel, The Military College of South Carolina	M
City College of the City University of New York	M,D
Clark Atlanta University	M,D
Clark University	M,D
Clayton State University	M
Clemson University	M,D
Cleveland State University	M,D
Cold Spring Harbor Laboratory	D
The College at Brockport, State University of New York	M,O
College of Staten Island of the City University of New York	M
The College of William and Mary	M
Colorado State University	M,D
Colorado State University–Pueblo	M
Columbia University	M,D,O*
The Commonwealth Medical College	M
Concordia University (Canada)	M,D,O
Cornell University	M,D
Creighton University	M,D
Dalhousie University	M,D
Dartmouth College	D*
Delaware State University	M
Delta State University	M
DePaul University	M,D
Des Moines University	M
Dominican University of California	M
Drew University	M,D,O
Drexel University	M,D,O
Duke University	M,D*
Duquesne University	D
East Carolina University	M,D
Eastern Illinois University	M
Eastern Kentucky University	M
Eastern Mennonite University	M
Eastern Michigan University	M
Eastern New Mexico University	M
Eastern Virginia Medical School	M,D
Eastern Washington University	M
East Stroudsburg University of Pennsylvania	M
East Tennessee State University	M,D
Elizabeth City State University	M
Emory University	D
Emporia State University	M
Fairleigh Dickinson University, College at Florham	M
Fairleigh Dickinson University, Metropolitan Campus	M
Fayetteville State University	M
Fisk University	M
Fitchburg State University	M,O
Florida Atlantic University	M
Florida Institute of Technology	M,D
Florida International University	M,D
Florida State University	M,D
Fordham University	M,D,O
Fort Hays State University	M
Frostburg State University	M
George Mason University	M,D,O
Georgetown University	M,D
The George Washington University	M,D*
Georgia College & State University	M
Georgia Institute of Technology	M,D
Georgia Southern University	M
Georgia State University	M,D
Gerstner Sloan Kettering Graduate School of Biomedical Sciences	D*
Goucher College	O
The Graduate Center, City University of New York	D
Grand Valley State University	M
Hampton University	M
Harvard University	M,D,O*
Hofstra University	M,D,O
Hood College	M,O
Howard University	M,D
Humboldt State University	M
Hunter College of the City University of New York	M,D
Icahn School of Medicine at Mount Sinai	M,D
Idaho State University	M,D
Illinois Institute of Technology	M,D
Illinois State University	M,D
Indiana State University	M,D
Indiana University Bloomington	M,D
Indiana University of Pennsylvania	M
Indiana University–Purdue University Fort Wayne	M
Indiana University–Purdue University Indianapolis	M,D
Iowa State University of Science and Technology	M,D
Irell & Manella Graduate School of Biological Sciences	D*
Jackson State University	M,D
Jacksonville State University	M
James Madison University	M
John Carroll University	M
Johns Hopkins University	M,D
Kansas City University of Medicine and Biosciences	M
Kansas State University	M,D
Keck Graduate Institute	M,D,O
Kennesaw State University	M
Kent State University	M,D

Lake Erie College of Osteopathic Medicine	M,D,O
Lakehead University	M
Lamar University	M
Laurentian University	M,D
Lee University	M,O
Lehigh University	M,D
Lehman College of the City University of New York	M
Liberty University	M,O
London Metropolitan University	M,D
Long Island University–LIU Brooklyn	M,D,O
Long Island University–LIU Post	M,O
Louisiana State University and Agricultural & Mechanical College	M,D
Louisiana State University Health Sciences Center	D
Louisiana State University Health Sciences Center at Shreveport	M
Louisiana State University in Shreveport	M
Louisiana Tech University	M
Loyola University Chicago	M,D
Marquette University	M,D
Marshall University	M,D
Massachusetts Institute of Technology	M,D
Mayo Graduate School	D
McGill University	M,D
McMaster University	M,D
Medical College of Wisconsin	M,D,O
Medical University of South Carolina	M,D
Meharry Medical College	D
Memorial University of Newfoundland	M,D,O
Miami University	M,D
Michigan State University	M,D
Michigan Technological University	M,D
Middle Tennessee State University	M
Midwestern State University	M
Midwestern University, Downers Grove Campus	M
Midwestern University, Glendale Campus	M
Mills College	O
Minnesota State University Mankato	M
Mississippi College	M
Mississippi State University	M,D
Missouri State University	M
Missouri University of Science and Technology	M
Missouri Western State University	M
Molloy College	M,O
Montana State University	M,D
Montclair State University	M,D
Morehead State University	M
Morehouse School of Medicine	M,D
Morgan State University	M,D
Mount Allison University	M
Murray State University	M,D
National University	M,O
New Jersey Institute of Technology	M,D,O
New Mexico Institute of Mining and Technology	M,D
New Mexico State University	M,D
New York Medical College	M,D
New York University	M,D,O
North Carolina Agricultural and Technical State University	M
North Carolina Central University	M
North Carolina State University	M,D,O
North Dakota State University	M,D
Northeastern Illinois University	M
Northeastern University	M,D
Northern Arizona University	M,D
Northern Illinois University	M,D
Northern Michigan University	M
Northwestern University	D*
Northwest Missouri State University	M
Nova Southeastern University	M,D,O*
Oakland University	M,D,O
Occidental College	M
The Ohio State University	M,D
Ohio University	M,D
Oklahoma State University	M,D
Oklahoma State University Center for Health Sciences	M,D
Old Dominion University	M,D
Oregon Health & Science University	M,D,O
Oregon State University	M,D
Pace University	M,O
Penn State Hershey Medical Center	M,D
Penn State University Park	M,D
Philadelphia College of Osteopathic Medicine	M*
Pittsburg State University	M
Plymouth State University	M
Point Loma Nazarene University	M
Ponce Health Sciences University	D
Pontifical Catholic University of Puerto Rico	M
Portland State University	M,D
Purdue University	M,D
Purdue University Northwest	M
Queens College of the City University of New York	M,O
Queen's University at Kingston	M,D
Regis College (MA)	M,D,O
Regis University	M
Rensselaer Polytechnic Institute	M,D
Rhode Island College	M,O
Rochester Institute of Technology	M
The Rockefeller University	M,D*
Rosalind Franklin University of Medicine and Science	M,D
Rowan University	M
Rutgers University–Camden	M
Rutgers University–Newark	M,D,O

Rutgers University–New Brunswick	M,D
St. Cloud State University	M
Saint Francis University	M
St. Francis Xavier University	M
St. John's University (NY)	M,D
Saint Joseph's University	M
Saint Louis University	M,D
Salisbury University	M
Samford University	M,D,O
Sam Houston State University	M
San Diego State University	M,D
Sanford Burnham Prebys Medical Discovery Institute	D
San Francisco State University	M
San Jose State University	M,O
The Scripps Research Institute	D
Seton Hall University	M,D
Shippensburg University of Pennsylvania	M
Simon Fraser University	M,D,O
Smith College	M
Sonoma State University	M
South Carolina State University	M
South Dakota State University	M,D
Southeastern Louisiana University	M
Southeast Missouri State University	M
Southern Connecticut State University	M
Southern Illinois University Carbondale	M,D
Southern Illinois University Edwardsville	M
Southern Methodist University	M,D
Southern University and Agricultural and Mechanical College	M
Stanford University	M,D
State University of New York at Fredonia	M
State University of New York College at Oneonta	M
State University of New York Downstate Medical Center	M,D
State University of New York Upstate Medical University	M,D
Stephen F. Austin State University	M
Stevenson University	M
Stony Brook University, State University of New York	M,D,O
Sul Ross State University	M
Syracuse University	M,D,O
Tarleton State University	M
Teachers College, Columbia University	M,D
Temple University	M,D*
Tennessee State University	D
Tennessee Technological University	M,D
Texas A&M International University	M
Texas A&M University	M,D
Texas A&M University–Corpus Christi	M
Texas A&M University–Kingsville	M
Texas Christian University	M
Texas Southern University	M
Texas State University	M
Texas Tech University	M,D
Texas Tech University Health Sciences Center	M,D
Texas Woman's University	M,D
Thomas Jefferson University	M,D,O
Towson University	M
Trent University	M,D
Troy University	M,O
Truman State University	M
Tufts University	M,D,O
Tulane University	M,D
Tuskegee University	M,D
Uniformed Services University of the Health Sciences	M,D*
Universidad Central del Caribe	M,D
Universidad de Ciencias Medicas	M,D,O
Université de Moncton	M
Université de Montréal	M,D
Université de Sherbrooke	M,D,O
Université du Québec à Montréal	M,D
Université du Québec en Abitibi-Témiscamingue	M,D
Université du Québec, Institut National de la Recherche Scientifique	M,D
Université Laval	M,D,O
University at Albany, State University of New York	M,D
University at Buffalo, the State University of New York	M,D*
The University of Akron	M,D
The University of Alabama	M,D
The University of Alabama at Birmingham	M,D
The University of Alabama in Huntsville	M,D
University of Alaska Anchorage	M
University of Alberta	M,D
The University of Arizona	M,D
University of Arkansas	M,D
University of Arkansas at Little Rock	M
University of Arkansas for Medical Sciences	M,D,O
University of Calgary	M,D
University of California, Berkeley	D
University of California, Irvine	M,D
University of California, Los Angeles	M,D
University of California, Merced	M,D
University of California, Riverside	M,D
University of California, San Diego	M,D
University of California, San Francisco	D

University of Central Arkansas	M
University of Central Florida	M,D
University of Central Missouri	M,D,O
University of Central Oklahoma	M
University of Chicago	D
University of Cincinnati	M,D,O
University of Colorado Denver	M,D
University of Connecticut Health Center	D*
University of Dayton	M,D
University of Delaware	M,D*
University of Denver	M,D
University of Florida	M,D
University of Georgia	D
University of Guam	M
University of Guelph	M,D
University of Hartford	M
University of Hawaii at Manoa	M,D
University of Houston	M,D
University of Houston–Clear Lake	M
University of Houston–Victoria	M
University of Idaho	M,D
University of Illinois at Chicago	M,D
University of Illinois at Springfield	M
University of Illinois at Urbana–Champaign	M,D
University of Indianapolis	M
The University of Iowa	M,D*
The University of Kansas	D*
University of Kentucky	M,D
University of Lethbridge	M,D
University of Louisiana at Lafayette	M,D
University of Louisiana at Monroe	M
University of Louisville	M,D
University of Maine	M,D
The University of Manchester	M,D
University of Manitoba	M,D,O
University of Maryland, Baltimore	M,D
University of Maryland, Baltimore County	M,D,O
University of Maryland, College Park	M,D
University of Massachusetts Amherst	M,D*
University of Massachusetts Boston	M,D
University of Massachusetts Dartmouth	M
University of Massachusetts Lowell	M
University of Massachusetts Medical School	M,D
University of Memphis	M,D
University of Miami	M,D
University of Michigan	M,D
University of Michigan–Flint	M
University of Minnesota, Duluth	M,D
University of Minnesota, Twin Cities Campus	M
University of Mississippi	M,D
University of Mississippi Medical Center	M,D
University of Missouri	M,D
University of Missouri–Kansas City	M,D
University of Missouri–St. Louis	M,D,O
University of Montana	M,D
University of Nebraska at Kearney	M
University of Nebraska at Omaha	M,O
University of Nebraska–Lincoln	M,D
University of Nebraska Medical Center	M,D
University of Nevada, Las Vegas	M,D
University of Nevada, Reno	M
University of New Brunswick Fredericton	M,D
University of New Brunswick Saint John	M,D
University of New England	M
University of New Hampshire	M,D
University of New Mexico	M,D
University of New Orleans	M,D
The University of North Carolina at Chapel Hill	M,D
The University of North Carolina at Charlotte	M,D
The University of North Carolina at Greensboro	M
The University of North Carolina Wilmington	M,D
University of North Dakota	M,D
University of Northern Colorado	M
University of Northern Iowa	M
University of North Florida	M
University of North Texas	M,D,O
University of North Texas Health Science Center at Fort Worth	M,D
University of Notre Dame	M,D
University of Oklahoma	M,D*
University of Oklahoma Health Sciences Center	M,D
University of Oregon	M,D
University of Ottawa	M,D
University of Pennsylvania	M,D*
University of Pittsburgh	D*
University of Prince Edward Island	M
University of Puerto Rico, Mayagüez Campus	M
University of Puerto Rico, Medical Sciences Campus	M,D
University of Puerto Rico, Río Piedras Campus	M,D
University of Regina	M,D
University of Rhode Island	M,D
University of Rochester	M,D*
University of Saint Joseph	M
University of San Francisco	M
University of Saskatchewan	M,D
University of South Alabama	M,D
University of South Carolina	M,D,O

The University of South Dakota	M,D
University of Southern California	M,D,O
University of Southern Maine	M
University of Southern Mississippi	M,D
University of South Florida	M,D
The University of Tennessee	M,D
The University of Tennessee Health Science Center	M,D
The University of Tennessee–Oak Ridge National Laboratory	M,D
The University of Texas at Arlington	M,D
The University of Texas at Austin	M,D
The University of Texas at Dallas	M,D*
The University of Texas at El Paso	M,D
The University of Texas at San Antonio	M,D
The University of Texas at Tyler	M
The University of Texas Health Science Center at Houston	M,D
The University of Texas Health Science Center at San Antonio	D
The University of Texas Medical Branch	M,D
The University of Texas of the Permian Basin	M
The University of Texas Rio Grande Valley	M
The University of Texas Southwestern Medical Center	M,D
University of the Incarnate Word	M
University of the Pacific	M
The University of Toledo	M,D,O
The University of Tulsa	M,D
University of Utah	M,D,O*
University of Vermont	M,D,O
University of Victoria	M,D
University of Virginia	M,D
University of Washington	M,D*
University of Waterloo	M,D
The University of Western Ontario	M,D
University of West Florida	M
University of West Georgia	M,O
University of Windsor	M,D
University of Wisconsin–La Crosse	M
University of Wisconsin–Madison	
University of Wisconsin–Milwaukee	M,D
University of Wisconsin–Oshkosh	M
Utah State University	M,D
Vanderbilt University	M,D*
Villanova University	M
Virginia Commonwealth University	M,D,O
Virginia Polytechnic Institute and State University	M,D
Virginia State University	M
Wake Forest University	M,D
Walla Walla University	M
Washington State University	M,D
Washington University in St. Louis	D
Wayne State University	M,D
Weill Cornell Medicine	M,D
Wesleyan University	D
West Chester University of Pennsylvania	M,O
Western Carolina University	M
Western Connecticut State University	M
Western Illinois University	M,O
Western Kentucky University	M
Western Michigan University	M,D,O
Western University of Health Sciences	M
Western Washington University	M
West Texas A&M University	M
West Virginia University	M,D
Wichita State University	M
Wilfrid Laurier University	M
William Paterson University of New Jersey	M,D
Winthrop University	M
Worcester Polytechnic Institute	M,D
Wright State University	M,D
Yale University	D*
York University	M,D
Youngstown State University	M

BIOLOGICAL ANTHROPOLOGY

Duke University	D*
Kent State University	M,D
Mercyhurst University	M
University of Wisconsin–Milwaukee	M,D,O

BIOMATHEMATICS

The College of William and Mary	M,D
North Carolina State University	M,D
University of California, Los Angeles	M,D
The University of Texas Health Science Center at Houston	M,D

BIOMEDICAL ENGINEERING

Arizona State University at the Tempe campus	M,D
Baylor College of Medicine	D
Baylor University	M,D
Binghamton University, State University of New York	M,D*
Boston University	M,D
Brown University	M,D
Carleton University	M
Carnegie Mellon University	M,D
Case Western Reserve University	M,D*
The Catholic University of America	M,D
City College of the City University of New York	M,D
Clemson University	M,D,O
Cleveland State University	D
Colorado State University	M,D
Columbia University	M,D*
Cornell University	M,D
Dalhousie University	M,D
Dartmouth College	M,D*
Drexel University	M,D
Duke University	M,D*
East Carolina University	M
École Polytechnique de Montréal	M,D,O
Florida Agricultural and Mechanical University	M,D
Florida Institute of Technology	M,D
Florida International University	M,D
Florida State University	M,D
The George Washington University	M,D*
Georgia Institute of Technology	D
The Graduate Center, City University of New York	D
Harvard University	D*
Illinois Institute of Technology	M,D
Indiana University–Purdue University Indianapolis	M,D,O
Johns Hopkins University	M,D,O
Lawrence Technological University	M,D
Louisiana Tech University	M,D
Marquette University	M,D
Massachusetts Institute of Technology	M,D
Mayo Graduate School	D
McGill University	M,D
Mercer University	M
Michigan Technological University	M,D
Mississippi State University	M,D
New Jersey Institute of Technology	M,D
New York University	M,D
North Carolina State University	M,D
Northwestern University	M,D*
The Ohio State University	M,D
Ohio University	M
Old Dominion University	M,D
Oregon Health & Science University	D
Purdue University	M,D
Rensselaer Polytechnic Institute	M,D
Rice University	M,D
Rose-Hulman Institute of Technology	M
Rutgers University–Newark	O
Rutgers University–New Brunswick	M,D
St. Cloud State University	M
Saint Louis University	M,D
South Dakota School of Mines and Technology	M,D
Southern Illinois University Carbondale	M
Stanford University	M,D,O
State University of New York Downstate Medical Center	M,D
Stevens Institute of Technology	M,D,O
Stony Brook University, State University of New York	M,D,O
Tennessee State University	M,D
Texas A&M University	M,D
Tufts University	M,D
Tulane University	M,D
Université de Montréal	M,D,O
University at Buffalo, the State University of New York	M,D*
The University of Akron	M,D
The University of Alabama at Birmingham	M,D
University of Alberta	M,D
The University of Arizona	M,D
University of Arkansas	M
University of Bridgeport	M
University of Calgary	M,D
University of California, Davis	M,D
University of California, Irvine	M,D
University of California, Los Angeles	M,D
University of Central Oklahoma	M
University of Cincinnati	M,D
University of Connecticut	M,D*
University of Florida	M,D,O
University of Houston	D
The University of Iowa	M,D*
University of Kentucky	M,D
University of Maine	M,D
University of Massachusetts Boston	D
University of Massachusetts Dartmouth	M,D
University of Memphis	M,D
University of Miami	M,D
University of Michigan	M,D
University of Minnesota, Twin Cities Campus	M,D
University of Nebraska–Lincoln	M,D
University of Nevada, Las Vegas	M,D,O
University of Nevada, Reno	M,D
University of New Mexico	M,D
The University of North Carolina at Chapel Hill	M,D
University of North Texas	M,D,O
University of Oklahoma	M,D*
University of Ottawa	M
University of Portland	M
University of Rhode Island	M,D
University of Rochester	M,D*
University of Saskatchewan	M,D
University of Southern California	M,D
University of South Florida	M,D,O
The University of Tennessee	M,D
The University of Tennessee Health Science Center	M,D
The University of Texas at Austin	M,D
The University of Texas at Dallas	M,D*
The University of Texas at El Paso	M,D,O
The University of Texas at San Antonio	M,D
The University of Texas Health Science Center at San Antonio	M,D
The University of Texas Southwestern Medical Center	M,D
The University of Toledo	D
University of Toronto	M,D
University of Vermont	D
University of Virginia	M,D
University of Wisconsin–Madison	M,D
Vanderbilt University	M,D*
Virginia Commonwealth University	M,D
Virginia Polytechnic Institute and State University	M,D
Wake Forest University	M,D
Washington University in St. Louis	M,D
Wayne State University	M,D,O
Widener University	M
Worcester Polytechnic Institute	M,D,O
Wright State University	M
Yale University	M,D*

BIOMETRY

Cornell University	M,D
San Diego State University	M
University of Wisconsin–Madison	M

BIOPHYSICS

Albert Einstein College of Medicine	D
Baylor College of Medicine	D
Boston University	M,D
Brandeis University	D
California Institute of Technology	D
Carnegie Mellon University	M,D
Case Western Reserve University	M,D*
Columbia University	M,D*
Cornell University	D
Dalhousie University	M,D
East Carolina University	M,D
Emory University	D
Harvard University	D*
Howard University	D
Illinois State University	M,D
Iowa State University of Science and Technology	M,D
Johns Hopkins University	D
Medical College of Wisconsin	D
Northwestern University	D*
The Ohio State University	M,D
Oregon State University	M,D
Purdue University	M,D
Rensselaer Polytechnic Institute	M,D
Rosalind Franklin University of Medicine and Science	M,D
Stanford University	D
Stony Brook University, State University of New York	D
Syracuse University	D
Texas Christian University	M,D
Université de Sherbrooke	M,D
Université du Québec à Trois-Rivières	M,D
University at Buffalo, the State University of New York	M,D*
University of California, Berkeley	D
University of California, Davis	M,D
University of California, Irvine	D
University of California, San Diego	M,D
University of California, San Francisco	D
University of California, Santa Barbara	D
University of Chicago	D
University of Cincinnati	D
University of Colorado Denver	M,D
University of Guelph	M,D
University of Illinois at Chicago	M,D
University of Illinois at Urbana–Champaign	M,D
The University of Iowa	M,D*
The University of Kansas	M,D*
University of Louisville	M,D
The University of Manchester	M,D
University of Maryland, College Park	D
University of Miami	D
University of Michigan	D
University of Minnesota, Duluth	M,D
University of Minnesota, Twin Cities Campus	M,D
University of Mississippi Medical Center	D
University of Missouri–Kansas City	D
The University of North Carolina at Chapel Hill	M,D
University of Regina	M,D
University of Rochester	D*
University of Southern California	M
University of South Florida	M,D
The University of Texas Medical Branch	D
University of Toronto	M,D
University of Virginia	M,D
University of Washington	D*
The University of Western Ontario	M,D
University of Wisconsin–Madison	D
Vanderbilt University	M,D*
Washington State University	M,D
Weill Cornell Medicine	M,D
Wright State University	M
Yale University	D*

BIOPSYCHOLOGY

Adler University	M,D,O
American University	M,D,O
Argosy University, Atlanta	M,D,O
Argosy University, Twin Cities	M,D,O
Binghamton University, State University of New York	D*
Boston University	M
Carnegie Mellon University	D
Connecticut College	M
Cornell University	D
Drexel University	M,D
Duke University	D*
The Graduate Center, City University of New York	D
Harvard University	D*
Howard University	M,D
Indiana University–Purdue University Indianapolis	M,D
Louisiana State University and Agricultural & Mechanical College	M,D
Memorial University of Newfoundland	M,D
Northwestern University	D*
Oregon Health & Science University	D
Palo Alto University	D
Penn State University Park	M,D
Philadelphia College of Osteopathic Medicine	M,D,O*
Rutgers University–Newark	D
Rutgers University–New Brunswick	D
The University of British Columbia	M,D
University of Connecticut	M,D*
University of Michigan	D
University of Minnesota, Twin Cities Campus	D
University of Nebraska–Lincoln	M,D
The University of North Carolina at Chapel Hill	D
University of Oklahoma Health Sciences Center	M,D
University of Oregon	M,D
The University of Texas at Austin	D
University of Windsor	M,D
University of Wisconsin–Madison	D
Virginia Commonwealth University	D
Wayne State University	D

BIOSTATISTICS

American University of Beirut	M
Boston University	M,D
Brown University	M,D
California State University, East Bay	M
Case Western Reserve University	M,D*
Columbia University	M,D*
Dartmouth College	D*
Drexel University	M,D,O
Duke University	M*
Emory University	M,D
Florida International University	M,D
Florida State University	M,D
George Mason University	M,D,O
Georgetown University	M,O
The George Washington University	M,D*
Georgia Southern University	M,D
Georgia State University	M,D
Grand Valley State University	M
Harvard University	M,D*
Hunter College of the City University of New York	M
Indiana University Bloomington	M,D
Indiana University–Purdue University Indianapolis	M,D
Iowa State University of Science and Technology	M,D
Johns Hopkins University	M,D
Loma Linda University	M,D
Louisiana State University Health Sciences Center	M,D
McGill University	M,D,O
Medical College of Wisconsin	D
Medical University of South Carolina	M,D
Middle Tennessee State University	M
New Jersey Institute of Technology	M,D,O
New York Medical College	M
Northwestern University	D*
The Ohio State University	M,D
Old Dominion University	M,D
Oregon State University	M,D
Penn State Hershey Medical Center	D
Rice University	M,D
Rutgers University–New Brunswick	M,D,O
San Diego State University	M,D
Stanford University	M,D
Tufts University	M,D,O
Tulane University	M,D
University at Albany, State University of New York	M,D
University at Buffalo, the State University of New York	M,D*
The University of Alabama at Birmingham	M,D
University of Alberta	M,D,O
The University of Arizona	M,D
University of Arkansas for Medical Sciences	M,D,O
University of California, Berkeley	M,D
University of California, Davis	M,D
University of California, Los Angeles	M,D
University of California, San Diego	D
University of Cincinnati	M,D
University of Colorado Denver	M,D
University of Florida	M,D,O
University of Illinois at Chicago	M,D
The University of Iowa	M,D,O*
The University of Kansas	M,D,O*
University of Kentucky	D
University of Louisville	M,D

*M—masters degree; D—doctorate; O—other advanced degree; *—Close-Up and/or Display*

University of Maryland, Baltimore	M,D
University of Maryland, Baltimore County	M,D
University of Maryland, College Park	M,D
University of Massachusetts Amherst	M,D*
University of Memphis	M
University of Michigan	M,D
University of Minnesota, Twin Cities Campus	M,D
University of Nebraska Medical Center	D
The University of North Carolina at Chapel Hill	M,D
University of North Texas Health Science Center at Fort Worth	M,D
University of Oklahoma Health Sciences Center	M,D
University of Pennsylvania	M,D*
University of Pittsburgh	M,D*
University of Puerto Rico, Medical Sciences Campus	M
University of Rochester	M*
University of South Carolina	M,D
University of Southern California	M,D
University of Southern Mississippi	M
University of South Florida	M,D,O
The University of Texas Health Science Center at Houston	M,D
The University of Toledo	M,O
University of Toronto	M,D
University of Utah	M,D*
University of Vermont	M
University of Washington	M,D*
University of Waterloo	M,D
The University of Western Ontario	M,D
Virginia Commonwealth University	M,D
Washington University in St. Louis	M,D,O
West Virginia University	M,D
Yale University	M,D*

BIOSYSTEMS ENGINEERING

Auburn University	M,D
Clemson University	M,D
Michigan State University	M,D
South Dakota State University	M,D
The University of Arizona	M,D
University of Manitoba	M,D
University of Minnesota, Twin Cities Campus	M,D
The University of Tennessee	M,D

BIOTECHNOLOGY

American University	M
Arizona State University at the Tempe campus	M,D
Arkansas State University	M,O
Brandeis University	M
Brigham Young University	M,D
Brock University	M,D
Brown University	M,D
California State Polytechnic University, Pomona	M
California State University Channel Islands	M
California State University, Fullerton	M
Carnegie Mellon University	M
The Catholic University of America	M,D
Claflin University	M
Clarkson University	D
Columbia University	M,D*
Concordia University (Canada)	M,D,O
Cornell University	M,D
Dartmouth College	M,D*
Duquesne University	M
East Carolina University	M
Eastern Virginia Medical School	M
Florida Institute of Technology	M,D
The George Washington University	M,D,O*
Harvard University	M,O*
Hood College	M,O
Howard University	M,D
Husson University	M
Illinois State University	M
Indiana University Bloomington	M,D
Instituto Tecnológico y de Estudios Superiores de Monterrey, Campus Monterrey	M,D
Inter American University of Puerto Rico, Bayamón Campus	M
Johns Hopkins University	M
Kean University	M
Marywood University	M
McGill University	M,D,O
Middle Tennessee State University	M
Mount St. Mary's University (MD)	M
New Mexico State University	M,D
New York University	M
North Carolina State University	M
Northeastern University	M,D,O
Northwestern University	M,D*
Oregon State University	D
Penn State University Park	M,D
Purdue University	D
Purdue University Northwest	M
Regis College (MA)	M
Roosevelt University	M
St. John's University (NY)	M
San Francisco State University	M
San Jose State University	M,O
Simon Fraser University	M,D,O
Southeastern Oklahoma State University	M
Stephen F. Austin State University	M
Temple University	M,D*
Tennessee State University	M,D
Texas Tech University	M,D
Texas Tech University Health Sciences Center	M
Tufts University	M,D,O
Universidad de las Américas Puebla	M
University at Buffalo, the State University of New York	M*
The University of Alabama at Birmingham	M
The University of Alabama in Huntsville	M,D
University of Alberta	M,D
University of Calgary	M
University of California, Irvine	M
University of Central Florida	M,D
University of Delaware	M,D*
University of Guelph	M,D
University of Houston–Clear Lake	M
University of Illinois at Chicago	M,D
The University of Kansas	M*
The University of Manchester	M,D
University of Maryland, Baltimore County	M,O
University of Maryland University College	M,O
University of Massachusetts Amherst	M,D*
University of Massachusetts Boston	M,D
University of Massachusetts Dartmouth	M,D
University of Minnesota, Twin Cities Campus	M
University of Missouri–St. Louis	M,D
University of Nevada, Reno	M
University of North Texas Health Science Center at Fort Worth	M,D
University of Pennsylvania	M*
University of Rhode Island	M,D
University of San Francisco	M
University of Saskatchewan	M
University of South Florida	M,D,O
The University of Texas at Dallas	M,D*
The University of Texas at San Antonio	M,D
University of the Sciences	M
University of Toronto	M
University of Utah	M*
University of Washington	D*
University of West Florida	M
University of Wyoming	D
Virginia Polytechnic Institute and State University	M,D
Wayne State University	M,D
West Virginia State University	M
William Paterson University of New Jersey	M,D
Worcester Polytechnic Institute	M,D
Worcester State University	M

BOTANY

Auburn University	M,D
Claremont Graduate University	M,D
Colorado State University	M,D
Dalhousie University	M
Eastern New Mexico University	M
Emporia State University	M
Illinois State University	M,D
North Carolina State University	M,D
North Dakota State University	M,D
Oklahoma State University	M,D
Oregon State University	M,D
Purdue University	M,D
The University of British Columbia	M,D
University of California, Riverside	M,D
University of Connecticut	M,D*
University of Florida	M,D
University of Guelph	M,D
University of Hawaii at Manoa	M,D
The University of Kansas	M,D*
University of Maine	M,D
University of Manitoba	M,D
The University of North Carolina at Chapel Hill	M,D
University of North Dakota	M,D
University of Wisconsin–Madison	M,D
University of Wisconsin–Oshkosh	M
University of Wyoming	M,D

BROADCAST JOURNALISM

Emerson College	M
Northwestern University	M*
Quinnipiac University	M
Syracuse University	M
University of Maryland, College Park	M,D
University of Miami	M,D
University of the Sacred Heart	M,O

BUILDING SCIENCE

Arizona State University at the Tempe campus	M,D
Auburn University	M
Carnegie Mellon University	M,D
Georgia Institute of Technology	M,D
Pontificia Universidad Catolica Madre y Maestra	M
Rensselaer Polytechnic Institute	M,D
University of California, Berkeley	M,D
Virginia Polytechnic Institute and State University	M,D,O

BUSINESS ADMINISTRATION AND MANAGEMENT—GENERAL

Abilene Christian University	M
Adelphi University	M
Alabama Agricultural and Mechanical University	M,D
Alabama State University	M
Alaska Pacific University	M
Albany State University	M
Albertus Magnus College	M
Alcorn State University	M
Alfred University	M
Alliant International University–Los Angeles	D
Alliant International University–México City	M
Alliant International University–San Diego	M
Alvernia University	M
Alverno College	M
Amberton University	M
American Business & Technology University	M
The American College	M
American College of Thessaloniki	M,O
American Graduate University	M,O
American InterContinental University Houston	M
American InterContinental University Online	M
American International College	M
American Jewish University	M
American National University	M
American Public University System	M
American Sentinel University	M
The American University in Cairo	M,O
The American University in Dubai	M
American University of Armenia	M
American University of Beirut	M
The American University of Paris	M
American University of Sharjah	M
Anaheim University	M,D,O
Anderson University (IN)	M,D
Anderson University (SC)	M
Angelo State University	M
Anna Maria College	M,O
Antioch University Los Angeles	M
Antioch University Midwest	M
Antioch University New England	M
Antioch University Santa Barbara	M
Appalachian State University	M
Aquinas College (MI)	M
Arcadia University	M
Argosy University, Atlanta	M,D
Argosy University, Chicago	M,D
Argosy University, Dallas	M,D,O
Argosy University, Denver	M,D
Argosy University, Hawai`i	M,D,O
Argosy University, Inland Empire	M,D
Argosy University, Los Angeles	M,D
Argosy University, Nashville	M,D
Argosy University, Orange County	M,D,O
Argosy University, Phoenix	M,D
Argosy University, Salt Lake City	M,D
Argosy University, San Diego	M,D
Argosy University, San Francisco Bay Area	M,D
Argosy University, Sarasota	M,D,O
Argosy University, Schaumburg	M,D,O
Argosy University, Seattle	M,D
Argosy University, Tampa	M,D
Argosy University, Twin Cities	M,D
Argosy University, Washington DC	M,D,O
Arizona State University at the Tempe campus	M,D
Arkansas State University	M
Arkansas Tech University	M
Armstrong State University	M,O
Ashland University	M
Ashworth College	M
Aspen University	M,O
Assumption College	M,O
Athabasca University	M,D,O
Auburn University	M,D
Auburn University at Montgomery	M
Augsburg College	M
Augusta University	M
Aurora University	M
Austin Peay State University	M
Averett University	M
Avila University	M
Azusa Pacific University	M
Babson College	M,O
Baker College Center for Graduate Studies–Online	M,D
Baker University	M
Bakke Graduate University	M,D
Baldwin Wallace University	M
Ball State University	M,O
Barry University	M,O
Baruch College of the City University of New York	M,D,O
Bayamón Central University	M
Baylor University	M,D
Belhaven University (MS)	M
Bellarmine University	M
Bellevue University	M,D
Belmont University	M
Benedictine College	M
Benedictine University	M
Bentley University	M,D,O
Berkeley College–Woodland Park Campus	M
Berry College	M
Bethel College	M
Bethel University (MN)	M,D,O
Bethel University (TN)	M
Binghamton University, State University of New York	M,D*
Biola University	M
Black Hills State University	M
Bloomsburg University of Pennsylvania	M
Bluffton University	M
Bob Jones University	M,D,O
Boise State University	M
Boston College	M
Boston University	M,D
Bowie State University	M
Bowling Green State University	M
Bradley University	M
Brandeis University	M
Brandman University	M
Brenau University	M
Brescia University	M
Bridgewater State University	M
Briercrest Seminary	M
Brigham Young University	M
Bristol University	M
Broadview University–West Jordan	M
Brock University	M
Brooklyn College of the City University of New York	M
Bryan College	M
Bryant University	M
Bryan University	M
Butler University	M
Cairn University	M,O
Caldwell University	M
California Baptist University	M
California Coast University	M
California Intercontinental University	M,D
California International Business University	M,D
California Lutheran University	M,O
California Miramar University	M
California National University for Advanced Studies	M
California Polytechnic State University, San Luis Obispo	M
California State Polytechnic University, Pomona	M
California State University, Bakersfield	M
California State University Channel Islands	M
California State University, Chico	M
California State University, Dominguez Hills	M
California State University, East Bay	M
California State University, Fresno	M
California State University, Fullerton	M
California State University, Long Beach	M
California State University, Los Angeles	M,O
California State University, Monterey Bay	M
California State University, Northridge	M
California State University, Sacramento	M
California State University, San Bernardino	M
California State University, San Marcos	M
California State University, Stanislaus	M
California University of Management and Sciences	M,D
California University of Pennsylvania	M
Cambridge College	M
Cameron University	M
Campbellsville University	M
Campbell University	M
Canisius College	M
Cape Breton University	M
Capella University	M,D
Capital University	M
Capitol Technology University	M
Cardinal Stritch University	M
Carleton University	M,D
Carlos Albizu University, Miami Campus	M,D
Carlow University	M
Carnegie Mellon University	M,D
Carroll University	M
Carson-Newman University	M
Case Western Reserve University	M,D*
The Catholic University of America	M
Cedar Crest College	M
Cedarville University	M,D
Centenary College	M
Centenary College of Louisiana	M
Central Connecticut State University	M
Central European University	M,D
Central Michigan University	M,O
Chadron State College	M
Chaminade University of Honolulu	M
Champlain College	M
Chapman University	M
Charleston Southern University	M
Chatham University	M
Christian Brothers University	M,O
The Citadel, The Military College of South Carolina	M
City College of the City University of New York	M
City University of Seattle	M,O
Claflin University	M
Claremont Graduate University	M,D,O
Clarion University of Pennsylvania	M
Clark Atlanta University	M
Clarke University	M
Clarkson University	M
Clark University	M
Clayton State University	M
Cleary University	M,O
Clemson University	M
Cleveland State University	M,D
Coastal Carolina University	M,O
College of Charleston	M
College of Saint Elizabeth	M
College of St. Joseph	M
The College of Saint Rose	M
The College of St. Scholastica	M,O
College of Staten Island of the City University of New York	M
The College of William and Mary	M
Colorado Christian University	M
Colorado Mesa University	M
Colorado State University	M
Colorado State University–Global Campus	M

Colorado State University–Pueblo	M
Colorado Technical University Colorado Springs	M,D
Colorado Technical University Denver South	M
Columbia College (MO)	M
Columbia Southern University	M,D
Columbia University	M,D*
Columbus State University	M,O
Concordia University (United States)	M
Concordia University (Canada)	M,D,O
Concordia University Chicago	M
Concordia University Irvine	M
Concordia University, St. Paul	M
Concordia University Wisconsin	M
Copenhagen Business School	M,D
Corban University	M
Cornell University	M,D
Cornerstone University	M,O
Creighton University	M
Cumberland University	M
Curry College	M,O
Daemen College	M
Dakota State University	M,D,O
Dalhousie University	M,O
Dallas Baptist University	M
Daniel Webster College	M
Dartmouth College	M*
Davenport University	M
Defiance College	M
Delaware State University	M
Delaware Valley University	M
Delta State University	M
DePaul University	M
DeSales University	M
DeVry College of New York	M
DeVry University (Columbus, OH)	M,O
DeVry University (Chicago, IL)	M
DeVry University (Seven Hills, OH)	M
DeVry University (Orlando, FL)	M,O
DeVry University (Glendale, AZ)	M
DeVry University (Mesa, AZ)	M
DeVry University (Phoenix, AZ)	M
DeVry University (Alhambra, CA)	M,O
DeVry University (Anaheim, CA)	M,O
DeVry University (Fremont, CA)	M,O
DeVry University (Long Beach, CA)	M,O
DeVry University (Oakland, CA)	M,O
DeVry University (Oxnard, CA)	M,O
DeVry University (Palmdale, CA)	M,O
DeVry University (Pomona, CA)	M,O
DeVry University (San Diego, CA)	M,O
DeVry University (Kansas City, CA)	M,O
DeVry University (Colorado Springs, CO)	M
DeVry University (Jacksonville, FL)	M
DeVry University (Miramar, FL)	M
DeVry University (Alpharetta, GA)	M,O
DeVry University (Decatur, GA)	M,O
DeVry University (Duluth, GA)	M,O
DeVry University (Downers Grove, IL)	M,O
DeVry University (Elgin, IL)	M,O
DeVry University (Gurnee, IL)	M,O
DeVry University (Naperville, IL)	M,O
DeVry University (Tinley Park, IL)	M
DeVry University (Merrillville, IN)	M
DeVry University (Henderson, NV)	M
DeVry University (North Brunswick, NJ)	M
DeVry University (Paramus, NJ)	M
DeVry University (Charlotte, NC)	M
DeVry University (Fort Washington, PA)	M
DeVry University (King of Prussia, PA)	M
DeVry University (Nashville, TN)	M
DeVry University (Irving, TX)	M
DeVry University (Arlington, VA)	M
DeVry University (Chesapeake, VA)	M
DeVry University (Manassas,, VA)	M
Doane University	M
Dominican College	M
Dominican University	M
Dominican University of California	M
Drake University	M
Drexel University	M,D,O
Drury University	M
Duke University	M,D,O*
Duquesne University	M
D'Youville College	M
East Carolina University	M,D,O
Eastern Illinois University	M
Eastern Kentucky University	M
Eastern Mennonite University	M
Eastern Michigan University	M,O
Eastern Nazarene College	M
Eastern New Mexico University	M
Eastern Oregon University	M
Eastern University	M
Eastern Washington University	M
East Tennessee State University	M,O
East Texas Baptist University	M
Edgewood College	M
Ellis University	M
Elmhurst College	M
Elms College	M
Elon University	M
Embry-Riddle Aeronautical University–Daytona	M,D*
Embry-Riddle Aeronautical University–Worldwide	M
Emmanuel College (United States)	M,O
Emory University	M,D
Emporia State University	M
Endicott College	M
ESSEC Business School	M,D
Everest University	M
Everest University	M
Everest University	M
Everglades University	M
Excelsior College	M,O
Fairfield University	M,O
Fairleigh Dickinson University, College at Florham	M,O
Fairleigh Dickinson University, Metropolitan Campus	M,O
Fairmont State University	M
Fashion Institute of Technology	M*
Faulkner University	M
Fayetteville State University	M
Felician University	M
Ferris State University	M
Fisher College	M
Fitchburg State University	M
Florida Agricultural and Mechanical University	M
Florida Atlantic University	M
Florida Gulf Coast University	M
Florida Institute of Technology	M,D
Florida International University	M,D
Florida Memorial University	M
Florida National University	M
Florida Southern College	M
Florida State University	M,D
Fontbonne University	M
Fordham University	M
Fort Hays State University	M
Framingham State University	M
Franciscan University of Steubenville	M
Francis Marion University	M
Franklin Pierce University	M,D,O
Franklin University	M
Freed-Hardeman University	M
Fresno Pacific University	M
Frostburg State University	M
Full Sail University	M
Gannon University	M
Gardner-Webb University	M
Geneva College	M
George Fox University	M,D
George Mason University	M
Georgetown University	M
The George Washington University	M,D,O*
Georgia Christian University	M
Georgia College & State University	M
Georgia Institute of Technology	M,D
Georgian Court University	M,O
Georgia Southern University	M
Georgia Southwestern State University	M
Georgia State University	M,D
Globe University–Woodbury	M
Goddard College	M
Golden Gate University	M,D,O
Goldey-Beacom College	M
Gonzaga University	M
Goucher College	M
Governors State University	M
The Graduate Center, City University of New York	D
Grand Canyon University	M,D
Grand Valley State University	M
Grand View University	M
Granite State College	M
Grantham University	M,O
Green Mountain College	M
Gwynedd Mercy University	M
Hallmark University	M
Hamline University	M,D
Hampton University	M,D
Harding University	M
Hardin-Simmons University	M
Harvard University	M,D,O*
Hawai`i Pacific University	M
HEC Montreal	M,D,O
Heidelberg University	M
Henderson State University	M
Herzing University Online	M
High Point University	M
Hodges University	M
Hofstra University	M,O
Holy Family University	M
Holy Names University	M
Hood College	M
Houston Baptist University	M
Howard Payne University	M
Howard University	M
Hult International Business School (United States)	M
Hult International Business School (United States)	M
Humboldt State University	M
Husson University	M
Idaho State University	M,O
Illinois Institute of Technology	M,D
Illinois State University	M
IMCA–International Management Centres Association	M
Independence University	M
Indiana State University	M
Indiana Tech	M
Indiana University Bloomington	M,D
Indiana University Kokomo	M
Indiana University Northwest	M,O
Indiana University of Pennsylvania	M
Indiana University–Purdue University Fort Wayne	M
Indiana University–Purdue University Indianapolis	M
Indiana University South Bend	M
Indiana University Southeast	M
Indiana Wesleyan University	M,O
Instituto Centroamericano de Administración de Empresas	M
Instituto Tecnologico de Santo Domingo	M,O
Instituto Tecnológico y de Estudios Superiores de Monterrey, Campus Central de Veracruz	M
Instituto Tecnológico y de Estudios Superiores de Monterrey, Campus Ciudad de México	M,D
Instituto Tecnológico y de Estudios Superiores de Monterrey, Campus Ciudad Juárez	M
Instituto Tecnológico y de Estudios Superiores de Monterrey, Campus Ciudad Obregón	M
Instituto Tecnológico y de Estudios Superiores de Monterrey, Campus Cuernavaca	M
Instituto Tecnológico y de Estudios Superiores de Monterrey, Campus Estado de México	M,D
Instituto Tecnológico y de Estudios Superiores de Monterrey, Campus Guadalajara	M
Instituto Tecnológico y de Estudios Superiores de Monterrey, Campus Irapuato	M,D
Instituto Tecnológico y de Estudios Superiores de Monterrey, Campus Laguna	M
Instituto Tecnológico y de Estudios Superiores de Monterrey, Campus León	M
Instituto Tecnológico y de Estudios Superiores de Monterrey, Campus Monterrey	M,D
Instituto Tecnológico y de Estudios Superiores de Monterrey, Campus Querétaro	M
Instituto Tecnológico y de Estudios Superiores de Monterrey, Campus Sonora Norte	M
Instituto Tecnológico y de Estudios Superiores de Monterrey, Campus Toluca	M
Inter American University of Puerto Rico, Aguadilla Campus	M
Inter American University of Puerto Rico, Arecibo Campus	M
Inter American University of Puerto Rico, Barranquitas Campus	M
Inter American University of Puerto Rico, Fajardo Campus	M
Inter American University of Puerto Rico, Guayama Campus	M
Inter American University of Puerto Rico, Metropolitan Campus	M
Inter American University of Puerto Rico, San Germán Campus	M,D
International College of the Cayman Islands	M
International Technological University	M,D
International University in Geneva	M,D
The International University of Monaco	M
Iona College	M,O
Ithaca College	M
Jackson State University	M,D
Jacksonville State University	M
Jacksonville University	M*
James Madison University	M
John Brown University	M
John Carroll University	M
John F. Kennedy University	M,O
Johns Hopkins University	M
Johnson & Wales University	M
John Wesley University	M
Judson University	M
Kansas State University	M,O
Kansas Wesleyan University	M
Kaplan University, Davenport Campus	M
Kean University	M
Keiser University	M,D
Kennesaw State University	M,D
Kent State University	M
Kent State University at Stark	M
Kentucky State University	M
Kettering University	M
Keuka College	M
King University	M
Kutztown University of Pennsylvania	M
Lake Erie College	M
Lake Forest Graduate School of Management	M
Lakehead University–Orillia	M
Lakeland University	M
Lamar University	M
La Salle University	M,O
Lasell College	M,O
La Sierra University	M,O
Laurentian University	M
Lawrence Technological University	M,D
Lebanese American University	M
Lebanon Valley College	M
Lee University	M
Lehigh University	M
Le Moyne College	M
Lenoir-Rhyne University	M
LeTourneau University	M
Lewis University	M
Liberty University	M,D,O
LIM College	M
Limestone College	M
Lincoln Memorial University	M
Lincoln University (CA)	M,D
Lincoln University (MO)	M
Lincoln University (PA)	M
Lindenwood University	M,O
Lindenwood University–Belleville	M
Lipscomb University	M,O
Long Island University–Hudson at Rockland	M,O
Long Island University–Hudson at Westchester	M,O
Long Island University–LIU Brooklyn	M,O
Long Island University–LIU Post	M
Longwood University	M
Louisiana State University and Agricultural & Mechanical College	M,D
Louisiana State University in Shreveport	M
Louisiana Tech University	M,D
Lourdes University	M
Loyola Marymount University	M
Loyola University Chicago	M
Loyola University Maryland	M
Loyola University New Orleans	M
Lynchburg College	M
Lynn University	M
Maastricht School of Management	M,D
Madonna University	M
Maharishi University of Management	M,D
Malone University	M
Manhattan College	M
Marconi International University	M,D
Marian University (WI)	M
Marist College	M,O
Marlboro College	M
Marquette University	M,O
Marshall University	M
Maryland Institute College of Art	M
Marylhurst University	M
Marymount California University	M
Marymount University	M,O
Maryville University of Saint Louis	M,O
Marywood University	M
Massachusetts College of Liberal Arts	M,O
Massachusetts Institute of Technology	M,D
McGill University	M,D,O
McKendree University	M
McMaster University	M,D
McNeese State University	M
Medaille College	M
Melbourne Business School	M,D,O
Memorial University of Newfoundland	M
Mercer University	M
Mercer University	M
Mercy College	M
Meredith College	M
Merrimack College	M
Messiah College	M,O
Methodist University	M
Metropolitan College of New York	M
Metropolitan State University	M,D,O
Miami University	M
Michigan State University	M,D
Michigan Technological University	M
Mid-America Christian University	M
MidAmerica Nazarene University	M
Middlebury Institute of International Studies at Monterey	M
Middle Tennessee State University	M
Midway University	M
Midwestern State University	M
Millennia Atlantic University	M
Milligan College	M
Millikin University	M
Millsaps College	M
Mills College	M
Milwaukee School of Engineering	M*
Minnesota State University Mankato	M
Minnesota State University Moorhead	M
Minot State University	M
Misericordia University	M
Mississippi College	M,O
Mississippi State University	M,D
Missouri Baptist University	M,O
Missouri Southern State University	M
Missouri State University	M
Missouri Western State University	M
Molloy College	M
Monmouth University	M,O
Monroe College	M
Montclair State University	M,O
Moravian College	M
Morehead State University	M
Morgan State University	D
Mount Aloysius College	M
Mount Ida College	M
Mount Marty College	M
Mount Mary University	M
Mount Mercy University	M
Mount St. Joseph University	M
Mount Saint Mary College	M
Mount Saint Mary's University (CA)	M,D,O
Mount St. Mary's University (MD)	M
Mount Vernon Nazarene University	M
Murray State University	M
National American University	M
National Louis University	M
National University	M,O
National University College	M
Naval Postgraduate School	M
Nazareth College of Rochester	M
New Charter University	M
New England College	M
New Jersey City University	M,O
New Jersey Institute of Technology	M,D,O
Newman University	M
New Mexico Highlands University	M
New Mexico State University	M,D
New York Institute of Technology	M
New York University	M,D,O
Niagara University	M

*M—masters degree; D—doctorate; O—other advanced degree; *—Close-Up and/or Display*

Nicholls State University	M
Nichols College	M
North Carolina Agricultural and Technical State University	M
North Carolina Central University	M
North Carolina State University	M
North Central College	M
Northcentral University	M,D,O
North Dakota State University	M
Northeastern Illinois University	M
Northeastern State University	M
Northeastern University	M,D,O
Northern Arizona University	M
Northern Illinois University	M
Northern Kentucky University	M,O
Northern Michigan University	M
North Park University	M
Northwest Christian University	M
Northwestern Polytechnic University	M,D
Northwestern University	M,D*
Northwest Missouri State University	M
Northwest Nazarene University	M
Northwest University	M
Northwood University, Michigan Campus	M
Norwich University	M
Notre Dame de Namur University	M
Notre Dame of Maryland University	M
Nova Southeastern University	M*
Nyack College	M
Oakland City University	M
Oakland University	M,O
Oglala Lakota College	M
Ohio Dominican University	M
The Ohio State University	M,D
Ohio University	M
Oklahoma Baptist University	M
Oklahoma Christian University	M
Oklahoma City University	M
Oklahoma State University	M,D
Old Dominion University	M,D
Olivet Nazarene University	M
Open University	M
Oral Roberts University	M
Oregon State University	M,D
Ottawa University	M
Otterbein University	M
Our Lady of the Lake University of San Antonio	M
Pace University	M,D,O
Pacific Lutheran University	M
Pacific States University	M,D
Pacific University	M
Palm Beach Atlantic University	M
Park University	M,O
Penn State Erie, The Behrend College	M
Penn State Great Valley	M,O
Penn State University Park	M,D
Pepperdine University	M
Pfeiffer University	M
Philadelphia University	M
Phillips Theological Seminary	M,D
Piedmont College	M
Pinchot University	M
Pittsburg State University	M
Plymouth State University	M
Point Loma Nazarene University	M
Point Park University	M
Polytechnic University of Puerto Rico	M
Polytechnic University of Puerto Rico, Miami Campus	M
Polytechnic University of Puerto Rico, Orlando Campus	M
Pontifical Catholic University of Puerto Rico	M,D,O
Pontificia Universidad Catolica Madre y Maestra	M
Portland State University	M,D,O
Post University	M
Prairie View A&M University	M
Providence College	M
Purdue University	M,D
Purdue University Northwest	M
Queen's University at Kingston	M
Queens University of Charlotte	M
Quincy University	M
Quinnipiac University	M
Radford University	M
Ramapo College of New Jersey	M
Regent's University London	M
Regent University	M,D,O
Reinhardt University	M
Rensselaer at Hartford	M
Rensselaer Polytechnic Institute	M,D
Rice University	M
Rider University	M
Rivier University	M
Robert Morris University	M
Robert Morris University Illinois	M
Roberts Wesleyan College	M
Rochester Institute of Technology	M
Rockford University	M
Rockhurst University	M,O
Rollins College	M,D
Roosevelt University	M
Roseman University of Health Sciences	M,O
Rosemont College	M
Rowan University	M,O
Royal Military College of Canada	M
Royal Roads University	M,O
Rutgers University–Camden	M
Rutgers University–Newark	M,D
Sacred Heart University	M,D,O
Sage Graduate School	M
Saginaw Valley State University	M
St. Ambrose University	M,D
St. Bonaventure University	M
St. Catherine University	M
St. Cloud State University	M
St. Edward's University	M,O
Saint Francis University	M
St. John Fisher College	M
St. John's University (NY)	M
St. Joseph's College, Long Island Campus	M
St. Joseph's College, New York	M
Saint Joseph's College of Maine	M
Saint Joseph's University	M,O
Saint Leo University	M
Saint Louis University	M
Saint Martin's University	M
Saint Mary's College of California	M
Saint Mary's University (Canada)	M,D
St. Mary's University (United States)	M
Saint Mary's University of Minnesota	M,D
St. Norbert College	M
Saint Peter's University	M
St. Thomas Aquinas College	M
St. Thomas University	M,O
Saint Vincent College	M
Saint Xavier University	M,O
Salem International University	M
Salem State University	M
Salisbury University	M
Salve Regina University	M,O
Samford University	M
Sam Houston State University	M
San Diego State University	M
San Francisco State University	M
Santa Clara University	M
Savannah State University	M
Schiller International University (United States)	M
Schiller International University (Germany)	M
Schiller International University	M
Schiller International University (Spain)	M
Schreiner University	M
Seattle Pacific University	M
Seattle University	M,O
Seton Hall University	M,O
Seton Hill University	M,O
Shenandoah University	M,O
Shippensburg University of Pennsylvania	M,O
Shorter University	M
Silicon Valley University	M
Silver Lake College of the Holy Family	M
Simmons College	M
Simon Fraser University	M,D,O
SIT Graduate Institute	M
Slippery Rock University of Pennsylvania	M
Sonoma State University	M
Southeastern Louisiana University	M
Southeastern Oklahoma State University	M
Southeastern University (FL)	M
Southeast Missouri State University	M
Southern Adventist University	M
Southern Arkansas University–Magnolia	M
Southern Connecticut State University	M
Southern Illinois University Carbondale	M,D
Southern Illinois University Edwardsville	M
Southern Methodist University	M
Southern Nazarene University	M
Southern New Hampshire University	M,O
Southern Oregon University	M,O
Southern University and Agricultural and Mechanical College	M
Southern Utah University	M
Southern Wesleyan University	M
South University	M
South University	M
South University	M
South University (TX)	M
South University (MI)	M
South University (OH)	M
South University (NC)	M
South University (SC)	M
South University (GA)	M
South University (AL)	M
South University	M
Southwest Baptist University	M
Southwestern Adventist University	M
Southwestern College (KS)	M
Southwestern College (KS)	M
Southwestern Oklahoma State University	M
Southwest Minnesota State University	M
Southwest University	M
Spring Arbor University	M
Springfield College	M
Spring Hill College	M
Stanford University	M,D
State University of New York at New Paltz	M
State University of New York College at Geneseo	M
State University of New York College at Old Westbury	M
State University of New York Empire State College	M
State University of New York Polytechnic Institute	M
Stephen F. Austin State University	M
Stephens College	M
Stetson University	M
Stevens Institute of Technology	M,O
Stockton University	M
Stony Brook University, State University of New York	M,O
Stratford University (VA)	M,D
Strayer University	M
Suffolk University	M,O
Sullivan University	M,D
Sul Ross State University	M
Syracuse University	M,D
Tabor College	M
Tarleton State University	M
Taylor University	M
Temple University	M,D*
Tennessee State University	M
Tennessee Technological University	M
Texas A&M International University	M,D
Texas A&M University	M
Texas A&M University–Central Texas	M,O
Texas A&M University–Commerce	M
Texas A&M University–Corpus Christi	M
Texas A&M University–Kingsville	M
Texas A&M University–San Antonio	M
Texas A&M University–Texarkana	M
Texas Christian University	M
Texas Health and Science University	M,D
Texas Southern University	M
Texas State University	M
Texas Tech University	M,D
Texas Wesleyan University	M
Texas Woman's University	M
Thomas College	M
Thomas Edison State University	M
Thomas More College	M
Thomas University	M
Thompson Rivers University	M
Tiffin University	M
Trevecca Nazarene University	M
Trident University International	M,D
Trinity International University	M,D,O
Trinity University	M
Trinity Washington University	M
Trinity Western University	M
Troy University	M
Tulane University	M,D
Tusculum College	M
Union University	M
United States International University–Africa	M
Universidad Autonoma de Guadalajara	M,D
Universidad de las Americas, A.C.	M
Universidad de las Américas Puebla	M
Universidad del Este	M
Universidad del Turabo	M,D
Universidad Iberoamericana	M,D
Universidad Metropolitana	M
Université de Moncton	M
Université de Sherbrooke	M,D,O
Université du Québec à Chicoutimi	M
Université du Québec à Montréal	M,D,O
Université du Québec à Rimouski	M,O
Université du Québec à Trois-Rivières	M,D
Université du Québec en Abitibi-Témiscamingue	M
Université Laval	M,D,O
University at Albany, State University of New York	M
University at Buffalo, the State University of New York	M,D*
The University of Akron	M
The University of Alabama	M,D
The University of Alabama at Birmingham	M
The University of Alabama in Huntsville	M,O
University of Alaska Anchorage	M
University of Alaska Fairbanks	M
University of Alaska Southeast	M
University of Alberta	M,D
University of Antelope Valley	M
The University of Arizona	M,D,O
University of Arkansas	M,D
University of Arkansas at Little Rock	M,O
University of Baltimore	M,O
University of Bridgeport	M
The University of British Columbia	M,D
University of Calgary	M,D
University of California, Berkeley	M,D,O
University of California, Davis	M
University of California, Irvine	M,D
University of California, Los Angeles	M,D
University of California, Riverside	M,D
University of California, San Diego	M,D
University of Central Arkansas	M
University of Central Florida	M,D,O
University of Central Missouri	M,D,O
University of Charleston	M
University of Chicago	M,D,O
University of Cincinnati	M,D
University of Colorado Boulder	M
University of Colorado Colorado Springs	M
University of Colorado Denver	M
University of Connecticut	M,D*
University of Dallas	M,D
University of Dayton	M
University of Delaware	M,D*
University of Denver	M
University of Detroit Mercy	M,O
University of Dubuque	M
The University of Findlay	M,D
University of Florida	M,D
University of Georgia	M,D
University of Guam	M
University of Guelph	M,D
University of Hartford	M
University of Hawaii at Manoa	M
University of Houston	M,D
University of Houston–Clear Lake	M
University of Houston–Downtown	M
University of Houston–Victoria	M
University of Idaho	M,D
University of Illinois at Chicago	M,D
University of Illinois at Springfield	M
University of Illinois at Urbana–Champaign	M,D
University of Indianapolis	M,O
The University of Iowa	M,D*
The University of Kansas	M,D*
University of Kentucky	M,D
University of La Verne	M,D,O
University of Lethbridge	M,D
University of Louisiana at Lafayette	M
University of Louisville	M
University of Maine	M,O
University of Management and Technology	M,D,O
The University of Manchester	M
University of Manitoba	M,D
University of Mary	M
University of Mary Hardin-Baylor	M
University of Maryland, College Park	M,D
University of Maryland University College	M,D,O
University of Mary Washington	M
University of Massachusetts Amherst	M,D*
University of Massachusetts Boston	M
University of Massachusetts Dartmouth	M,O
University of Massachusetts Lowell	M,D
University of Memphis	M,D
University of Michigan	M,D
University of Michigan–Dearborn	M
University of Michigan–Flint	M,O
University of Minnesota, Duluth	M
University of Minnesota, Twin Cities Campus	M,D
University of Mississippi	M,D
University of Missouri	M,D
University of Missouri–Kansas City	M,D
University of Missouri–St. Louis	M,D,O
University of Mobile	M
University of Montana	M
University of Montevallo	M
University of Nebraska at Kearney	M
University of Nebraska at Omaha	M,O
University of Nebraska–Lincoln	M,D
University of Nevada, Las Vegas	M
University of Nevada, Reno	M
University of New Brunswick Fredericton	M
University of New Brunswick Saint John	M
University of New Hampshire	M,O
University of New Haven	M,O
University of New Mexico	M
University of New Orleans	M
University of North Alabama	M
The University of North Carolina at Chapel Hill	M,D
The University of North Carolina at Charlotte	M,D,O
The University of North Carolina at Greensboro	M,O
The University of North Carolina at Pembroke	M
The University of North Carolina Wilmington	M
University of North Dakota	M
University of Northern Iowa	M
University of North Florida	M
University of North Georgia	M
University of North Texas	M,D,O
University of Northwestern–St. Paul	M
University of Notre Dame	M
University of Oklahoma	M,D*
University of Oregon	M,D
University of Ottawa	M
University of Pennsylvania	M,D*
University of Phoenix–Atlanta Campus	M
University of Phoenix–Augusta Campus	M
University of Phoenix–Bay Area Campus	M,D
University of Phoenix–Central Valley Campus	M
University of Phoenix–Charlotte Campus	M
University of Phoenix–Colorado Campus	M
University of Phoenix–Colorado Springs Downtown Campus	M
University of Phoenix–Columbus Georgia Campus	M
University of Phoenix–Dallas Campus	M

University of Phoenix–Hawaii Campus M
University of Phoenix–Houston Campus M
University of Phoenix–Jersey City Campus M
University of Phoenix–Las Vegas Campus M
University of Phoenix–New Mexico Campus M
University of Phoenix–North Florida Campus M
University of Phoenix–Online Campus M,D,O
University of Phoenix–Phoenix Campus M,O
University of Phoenix–Sacramento Valley Campus M
University of Phoenix–San Antonio Campus M
University of Phoenix–San Diego Campus M
University of Phoenix–Southern Arizona Campus M
University of Phoenix–Southern California Campus M
University of Phoenix–South Florida Campus M
University of Phoenix–Utah Campus M
University of Phoenix–Washington D.C. Campus M,D
University of Phoenix–Western Washington Campus M
University of Pikeville M
University of Pittsburgh M,D*
University of Portland M
University of Puerto Rico, Mayagüez Campus M
University of Puerto Rico, Rí o Piedras Campus M,D
University of Redlands M
University of Regina M,O
University of Rhode Island M,D
University of Richmond M
University of Rochester M,D*
University of St. Francis (IL) M,O
University of Saint Francis (IN) M
University of Saint Joseph M
University of Saint Mary M
University of St. Thomas (TX) M
University of St. Thomas (MN) M
University of San Diego M
University of San Francisco M
University of Saskatchewan M
The University of Scranton M
University of Sioux Falls M
University of South Africa M,D
University of South Alabama M,D
University of South Carolina M,D
University of South Carolina Aiken M
The University of South Dakota M
University of Southern California M,D
University of Southern Indiana M
University of Southern Maine M,O
University of Southern Mississippi M
University of South Florida M,D
University of South Florida, St. Petersburg M
University of South Florida Sarasota-Manatee M
The University of Tampa M
The University of Tennessee M,D
The University of Tennessee at Chattanooga M
The University of Tennessee at Martin M
The University of Texas at Arlington M,D
The University of Texas at Austin M,D
The University of Texas at Dallas M,D*
The University of Texas at El Paso M,D,O
The University of Texas at San Antonio M,D,O
The University of Texas at Tyler M
The University of Texas of the Permian Basin M
The University of Texas Rio Grande Valley M,D
University of the Cumberlands M
University of the District of Columbia M
University of the Incarnate Word M,D
University of the Pacific M
University of the Potomac M
University of the Sacred Heart M,O
University of the Southwest M
University of the Virgin Islands M
University of the West M
The University of Toledo M
University of Toronto M,D
The University of Tulsa M
University of Utah M,D,O*
University of Vermont M
University of Victoria M
University of Virginia M,D,O
University of Washington M,D*
University of Washington, Bothell M
University of Washington, Tacoma M
University of Waterloo M
The University of West Alabama M
The University of Western Ontario M,D
University of West Florida M
University of West Georgia M
University of Windsor M
University of Wisconsin–Eau Claire M
University of Wisconsin–Green Bay M
University of Wisconsin–La Crosse M
University of Wisconsin–Madison M
University of Wisconsin–Milwaukee M,D,O
University of Wisconsin–Oshkosh M
University of Wisconsin–Parkside M
University of Wisconsin–River Falls M
University of Wisconsin–Stevens Point M
University of Wisconsin–Whitewater M
University of Wyoming M
Upper Iowa University M
Urbana University M
Ursuline College M
Utah State University M
Utah Valley University M
Valdosta State University M
Valparaiso University M,O
Vancouver Island University M
Vanderbilt University M*
Villanova University M
Virginia College in Birmingham M
Virginia Commonwealth University M,O
Virginia International University M,O
Virginia Polytechnic Institute and State University M,D
Viterbo University M
Wagner College M
Wake Forest University M
Walden University M,D,O
Walsh College of Accountancy and Business Administration M
Walsh University M
Warner University M
Washburn University M
Washington Adventist University M
Washington State University M,D
Washington University in St. Louis M,D
Wayland Baptist University M,D
Waynesburg University M,D
Wayne State College M
Wayne State University M,D,O
Webber International University M
Weber State University M
Webster University M
Wesleyan College M
Wesley College M
West Chester University of Pennsylvania M,O
Western Carolina University M
Western Connecticut State University M
Western Governors University M
Western Illinois University M,O
Western International University M
Western Kentucky University M
Western Michigan University M
Western New England University M
Western New Mexico University M
Western Washington University M
Westminster College (UT) M,O
West Texas A&M University M
West Virginia University M
West Virginia Wesleyan College M
Wheeling Jesuit University M
Whitworth University M
WHU - Otto Beisheim School of Management M
Wichita State University M
Widener University M
Wilfrid Laurier University M,D
Wilkes University M
Willamette University M
William Carey University M
William Paterson University of New Jersey M
William Woods University M,D,O
Wilmington University M,D
Wingate University M
Winston-Salem State University M
Winthrop University M
Woodbury University M
Worcester Polytechnic Institute M,D,O
Worcester State University M
Wright State University M
Xavier University M
Yale University M,D*
York College of Pennsylvania M
York University M,D
Youngstown State University M,O

BUSINESS EDUCATION

Alabama Agricultural and Mechanical University M,O
Arkansas State University O
Auburn University M,D,O
Ball State University M,O
Bloomsburg University of Pennsylvania M
Bowling Green State University M
Buffalo State College, State University of New York M
Canisius College M,O
Capella University D
Chadron State College M,O
Clemson University M,D
Colorado Christian University M
East Carolina University M
Eastern Kentucky University M
Emporia State University M
Florida Agricultural and Mechanical University M
Hofstra University M,D,O
Indiana University of Pennsylvania M
Inter American University of Puerto Rico, Metropolitan Campus M
Inter American University of Puerto Rico, San Germán Campus M
International College of the Cayman Islands M
Johnson & Wales University M
Lehman College of the City University of New York M
Lock Haven University of Pennsylvania M
Louisiana State University and Agricultural & Mechanical College M,D
Manhattanville College M*
Maryville University of Saint Louis M,O
Middle Tennessee State University M
Milwaukee School of Engineering M*
Mississippi College M,D,O
Mississippi State University M,D,O
Morehead State University M,O
New York University M,O
North Carolina Agricultural and Technical State University M
North Carolina State University M
Nova Southeastern University M*
Old Dominion University M,D
Pace University M,O
Pepperdine University M
Pontifical Catholic University of Puerto Rico M,D
Regis University M,O
Rider University O
Robert Morris University M,D,O
South Carolina State University M
Southern New Hampshire University M,D,O
Spalding University M
State University of New York at Oswego M
Temple University M*
Thomas College M
The University of British Columbia M,D
University of Delaware M,D*
University of Georgia M,D,O
University of Minnesota, Twin Cities Campus M,D
University of Missouri M,D,O
University of St. Francis (IL) M,O
University of South Carolina M,D
University of the Cumberlands M,D,O
The University of Toledo M,D,O
University of Washington M,D*
University of West Georgia M,D,O
University of Wisconsin–Whitewater M
Utah State University M,D
Washington State University M,D
Wayne State College M
West Chester University of Pennsylvania M,O
Wright State University M

CANADIAN STUDIES

Carleton University M,D
Queen's University at Kingston M,D
Saint Mary's University (Canada) M,O
Trent University M,D
Université de Saint-Boniface M
Université de Sherbrooke M,D
Université du Québec à Chicoutimi M
University at Buffalo, the State University of New York M,D,O*
University of Lethbridge M,D
University of Maine M,D
University of Manitoba M
University of Ottawa D
University of Regina M,D
University of Saskatchewan M,D
Wilfrid Laurier University M,D

CANCER BIOLOGY/ONCOLOGY

Augusta University D
Baylor College of Medicine D
Case Western Reserve University D*
Duke University D*
Emory University D
Gerstner Sloan Kettering Graduate School of Biomedical Sciences D*
Irell & Manella Graduate School of Biological Sciences D*
Long Island University–LIU Post M,O
Loyola University Chicago M,D,O
Mayo Graduate School D
McMaster University M,D
Medical University of South Carolina D
Meharry Medical College D
Memorial University of Newfoundland M,D
New York University M,D
Oregon Health & Science University D
Purdue University D
Queen's University at Kingston M,D
Rutgers University–Newark D,O
Rutgers University–New Brunswick M,D
Thomas Jefferson University D
Tufts University D
Université Laval O
University at Buffalo, the State University of New York M*
The University of Alabama at Birmingham D
University of Alberta M,D
The University of Arizona D
University of Calgary M,D
University of Chicago D
University of Cincinnati D
University of Colorado Denver D
University of Delaware M,D*
The University of Manchester M,D
University of Manitoba M
University of Maryland, Baltimore M,D
University of Massachusetts Medical School M,D
University of Miami D
University of Michigan M,D
University of Minnesota, Twin Cities Campus D
University of Nebraska Medical Center D
University of Pennsylvania D*
University of Regina M,D
University of Southern California D
University of South Florida M,D
The University of Texas Health Science Center at Houston M,D
The University of Texas Southwestern Medical Center D
University of the District of Columbia M
The University of Toledo M,D
University of Utah M,D*
University of Wisconsin–La Crosse M
University of Wisconsin–Madison D
University of Wisconsin–Milwaukee M
Vanderbilt University M,D*
Wake Forest University D
Wayne State University D
West Virginia University M,D
Yale University D*

CARDIOVASCULAR SCIENCES

Albany Medical College M,D
Augusta University D
Baylor College of Medicine D
Geneva College M
Johns Hopkins University M,D
Marquette University M
McMaster University M,D
Medical University of South Carolina D
Memorial University of Newfoundland M,D
Midwestern University, Glendale Campus M
Milwaukee School of Engineering M*
Queen's University at Kingston M,D
Quinnipiac University M
Université Laval O
University of Calgary M,D
University of Guelph M,D,O
University of Mary M
The University of South Dakota M,D
University of South Florida O
The University of Toledo M,D

CELL BIOLOGY

Albany College of Pharmacy and Health Sciences M
Albany Medical College M,D
Albert Einstein College of Medicine D
American University of Beirut M,D
Appalachian State University M
Arizona State University at the Tempe campus M,D
Auburn University M,D
Augusta University D
Baylor College of Medicine D
Boston University M,D
Brandeis University M,D
Brown University M,D
California Institute of Technology D
California State University, Sacramento M
Carnegie Mellon University M,D
Case Western Reserve University M,D*
The Catholic University of America M,D
Colorado State University M,D
Columbia University M,D*
Cornell University D
Dartmouth College D*
Drexel University M,D
Duke University D,O*
East Carolina University D
Eastern Michigan University M
Eastern New Mexico University M
Emory University D
Emporia State University M
Florida Institute of Technology M,D
Florida State University M,D
Georgia State University M,D
Grand Valley State University M
Harvard University D*
Illinois Institute of Technology M,D
Illinois State University M,D
Indiana State University M,D
Indiana University Bloomington M,D
Indiana University–Purdue University Indianapolis M,D
Iowa State University of Science and Technology M,D
Irell & Manella Graduate School of Biological Sciences D*
Johns Hopkins University D
Kent State University M,D
Lehigh University M,D
Louisiana State University Health Sciences Center D
Louisiana State University Health Sciences Center at Shreveport M,D
Loyola University Chicago M,D
Marquette University M,D

*M—masters degree; D—doctorate; O—other advanced degree; *—Close-Up and/or Display*

Massachusetts Institute of Technology	D
Mayo Graduate School	D
McGill University	M,D
McMaster University	M,D
Medical University of South Carolina	D
Michigan State University	M,D
Missouri State University	M
New York Medical College	M,D
New York University	D
North Carolina State University	M,D
North Dakota State University	M,D
Northwestern University	D*
The Ohio State University	M,D
Ohio University	M,D
Oregon Health & Science University	D
Oregon State University	M,D
Penn State Hershey Medical Center	D
Penn State University Park	M,D
Purdue University	M,D
Queen's University at Kingston	M,D
Quinnipiac University	M
Rice University	M,D
Rosalind Franklin University of Medicine and Science	D
Rush University	M,D
Rutgers University–Newark	D
Rutgers University–New Brunswick	M,D
San Diego State University	M,D
San Francisco State University	M
Sonoma State University	M
Southern Methodist University	M,D
State University of New York Downstate Medical Center	D
State University of New York Upstate Medical University	M,D
Stony Brook University, State University of New York	M,D
Texas Tech University Health Sciences Center	M,D
Thomas Jefferson University	M,D
Tufts University	D
Tulane University	M,D
Uniformed Services University of the Health Sciences	M,D*
Universidad Central del Caribe	M,D
Université de Montréal	M,D
Université de Sherbrooke	M,D
Université Laval	M,D
University at Albany, State University of New York	M,D
University at Buffalo, the State University of New York	D*
The University of Alabama at Birmingham	D
University of Alberta	M,D
The University of Arizona	M,D,O
University of Arkansas	M,D
The University of British Columbia	M,D
University of California, Berkeley	D
University of California, Davis	M,D
University of California, Irvine	M,D
University of California, Los Angeles	M,D
University of California, Riverside	M,D
University of California, San Francisco	D
University of California, Santa Barbara	M,D
University of California, Santa Cruz	M,D
University of Chicago	D
University of Cincinnati	D
University of Colorado Boulder	M,D
University of Colorado Denver	M,D
University of Connecticut Health Center	D*
University of Delaware	M,D*
University of Denver	M,D
University of Florida	M,D
University of Georgia	M,D
University of Guelph	M,D
University of Illinois at Chicago	M,D
University of Illinois at Urbana–Champaign	D
The University of Iowa	M,D*
The University of Kansas	M,D*
The University of Manchester	M,D
University of Maryland, Baltimore	M,D
University of Maryland, Baltimore County	D
University of Maryland, College Park	M,D
University of Massachusetts Amherst	M,D*
University of Massachusetts Medical School	M,D
University of Miami	D
University of Michigan	M,D
University of Minnesota, Twin Cities Campus	M,D
University of Missouri–Kansas City	D
University of Montana	D
University of Nebraska Medical Center	M,D
University of Nevada, Reno	M,D
University of New Haven	M,O
University of New Mexico	M,D
The University of North Carolina at Chapel Hill	M,D
University of North Dakota	M,D
University of Notre Dame	M,D
University of Oklahoma Health Sciences Center	M,D
University of Ottawa	M,D
University of Pennsylvania	D*
University of Pittsburgh	D*
University of Puerto Rico, Río Piedras Campus	M,D
University of Rhode Island	M,D
University of Saskatchewan	M,D
University of South Carolina	M,D
The University of South Dakota	M,D
University of Southern California	M,D
University of South Florida	M,D
The University of Texas at Austin	D
The University of Texas at Dallas	M,D*
The University of Texas at San Antonio	M,D
The University of Texas Health Science Center at Houston	M,D
The University of Texas Health Science Center at San Antonio	M,D
The University of Texas Medical Branch	D
The University of Texas Southwestern Medical Center	D
University of the Sciences	M
University of Toronto	M,D
University of Vermont	D
University of Virginia	D
University of Washington	D*
The University of Western Ontario	M,D
University of Wisconsin–La Crosse	M
University of Wisconsin–Madison	D
University of Wyoming	D
Vanderbilt University	M,D*
Washington State University	M,D
Washington University in St. Louis	D
Weill Cornell Medicine	M,D
Wesleyan University	D
West Virginia University	M,D
Yale University	D*

CELTIC LANGUAGES

Harvard University	D*

CERAMIC SCIENCES AND ENGINEERING

Alfred University	M,D
Missouri University of Science and Technology	M,D

CHEMICAL ENGINEERING

American University of Sharjah	M
Arizona State University at the Tempe campus	M,D
Auburn University	M,D
Brigham Young University	M,D
Brown University	M,D
Bucknell University	M
California Institute of Technology	M,D
California State University, Long Beach	M
Carnegie Mellon University	M,D
Case Western Reserve University	M,D*
City College of the City University of New York	M,D
Clarkson University	M,D
Clemson University	M,D
Cleveland State University	M,D
Colorado School of Mines	M,D
Colorado State University	M,D
Columbia University	M,D*
Cooper Union for the Advancement of Science and Art	M
Cornell University	M,D
Dalhousie University	M,D
Drexel University	M,D
École Polytechnique de Montréal	M,D,O
Fairleigh Dickinson University, College at Florham	M,O
Florida Agricultural and Mechanical University	M,D
Florida Institute of Technology	M,D
Florida State University	M,D
Georgia Institute of Technology	M,D
The Graduate Center, City University of New York	D
Howard University	M
Illinois Institute of Technology	M,D
Instituto Tecnológico y de Estudios Superiores de Monterrey, Campus Monterrey	M,D
Iowa State University of Science and Technology	M,D
Johns Hopkins University	M,D
Kansas State University	M,D,O
Lamar University	M,D
Lehigh University	M,D
Louisiana State University and Agricultural & Mechanical College	M,D
Louisiana Tech University	M,D
Manhattan College	M
Massachusetts Institute of Technology	M,D
McGill University	M,D
McMaster University	M,D
McNeese State University	M
Miami University	M
Michigan State University	M,D
Michigan Technological University	M,D
Mississippi State University	M,D
Missouri University of Science and Technology	M,D
Montana State University	M,D
New Jersey Institute of Technology	M,D
New Mexico State University	M,D
New York University	M,D
North Carolina Agricultural and Technical State University	M
North Carolina State University	M,D
Northeastern University	M,D,O
Northwestern University	M,D*
The Ohio State University	M,D
Ohio University	M,D
Oklahoma State University	M,D
Oregon State University	M,D
Penn State University Park	M,D
Princeton University	M,D
Purdue University	M,D
Queen's University at Kingston	M,D
Rensselaer Polytechnic Institute	M,D
Rice University	M,D
Rose-Hulman Institute of Technology	M
Rowan University	M
Royal Military College of Canada	M,D
Rutgers University–New Brunswick	M,D
South Dakota School of Mines and Technology	M,D
Stanford University	M,D
Stevens Institute of Technology	M,D,O
Syracuse University	M,D
Tennessee Technological University	M
Texas A&M University	M,D
Texas A&M University–Kingsville	M
Texas Tech University	M,D
Tufts University	M,D
Tulane University	M,D
Universidad de las Américas Puebla	M
Université de Sherbrooke	M,D
Université Laval	M,D
University at Buffalo, the State University of New York	M,D*
The University of Akron	M,D
The University of Alabama	M,D
The University of Alabama in Huntsville	M,D
University of Alberta	M,D
The University of Arizona	M,D
University of Arkansas	M,D
The University of British Columbia	M,D
University of Calgary	M,D
University of California, Berkeley	M,D
University of California, Davis	M,D
University of California, Irvine	M,D
University of California, Los Angeles	M,D
University of California, Riverside	M,D
University of California, San Diego	M,D
University of California, Santa Barbara	M,D
University of Cincinnati	M,D
University of Colorado Boulder	M,D
University of Connecticut	M,D*
University of Dayton	M
University of Delaware	M,D*
University of Florida	M,D,O
University of Houston	M,D
University of Idaho	M,D
University of Illinois at Chicago	M,D
University of Illinois at Urbana–Champaign	M,D
The University of Iowa	M,D*
The University of Kansas	M,D*
University of Kentucky	M,D
University of Louisiana at Lafayette	M
University of Louisville	M,D
University of Maine	M,D
The University of Manchester	M,D
University of Maryland, Baltimore County	M,D
University of Maryland, College Park	M,D
University of Massachusetts Amherst	M,D*
University of Massachusetts Lowell	M,D
University of Michigan	M,D,O
University of Minnesota, Twin Cities Campus	M,D
University of Missouri	M,D
University of Nebraska–Lincoln	M,D
University of Nevada, Reno	M,D
University of New Brunswick Fredericton	M,D
University of New Hampshire	M,D
University of New Mexico	M,D
University of North Dakota	M
University of Notre Dame	M,D
University of Oklahoma	M,D*
University of Ottawa	M,D
University of Pennsylvania	M,D*
University of Pittsburgh	M,D*
University of Puerto Rico, Mayagüez Campus	M,D
University of Rhode Island	M,D,O
University of Rochester	M,D*
University of Saskatchewan	M,D
University of South Africa	M
University of South Alabama	M
University of South Carolina	M,D
University of Southern California	M,D,O
University of South Florida	M,D,O
The University of Tennessee	M,D
The University of Tennessee at Chattanooga	M
The University of Texas at Austin	M,D
The University of Toledo	M,D
University of Toronto	M,D
The University of Tulsa	M,D
University of Utah	M,D*
University of Virginia	M,D
University of Washington	M,D*
University of Waterloo	M,D
The University of Western Ontario	M,D
University of Wisconsin–Madison	M,D
University of Wyoming	M,D
Vanderbilt University	M,D*
Villanova University	M,O
Virginia Commonwealth University	M,D
Virginia Polytechnic Institute and State University	M,D
Washington State University	M,D
Washington University in St. Louis	M,D
Wayne State University	M,D
Western Michigan University	M,D
West Virginia University	M,D
Widener University	M
Worcester Polytechnic Institute	M,D
Yale University	M,D*

CHEMICAL PHYSICS

Columbia University	M,D*
Cornell University	D
Harvard University	D*
Kent State University	M,D
Marquette University	M,D
McMaster University	M,D
Michigan State University	M,D
The Ohio State University	M,D
Tufts University	M,D
University of Colorado Boulder	M,D
University of Illinois at Urbana–Champaign	M,D
University of Louisville	M,D
University of Maryland, College Park	M,D
University of Minnesota, Twin Cities Campus	M,D
University of Nevada, Reno	D
The University of Tennessee	M,D
University of Utah	M,D*
Virginia Commonwealth University	M,D
Wesleyan University	D
West Virginia University	M,D

CHEMISTRY

Acadia University	M
American University	M
The American University in Cairo	M
American University of Beirut	M,D
Arizona State University at the Tempe campus	M,D
Arkansas State University	M,O
Auburn University	M,D
Ball State University	M,D
Baylor University	M,D
Binghamton University, State University of New York	M,D*
Boise State University	M
Boston College	M,D
Boston University	M,D
Bowling Green State University	M,D
Bradley University	M
Brandeis University	M,D
Brigham Young University	M,D
Brock University	M,D
Brooklyn College of the City University of New York	M,D
Brown University	D
Bryn Mawr College	M,D
Bucknell University	M
Buffalo State College, State University of New York	M
California Institute of Technology	M,D
California Polytechnic State University, San Luis Obispo	M
California State Polytechnic University, Pomona	M
California State University, East Bay	M
California State University, Fresno	M
California State University, Fullerton	M
California State University, Long Beach	M
California State University, Los Angeles	M
California State University, Northridge	M
California State University, Sacramento	M
Carleton University	M,D
Carnegie Mellon University	D
Case Western Reserve University	M,D*
Central Michigan University	M
Central Washington University	M
City College of the City University of New York	M,D
Clark Atlanta University	M,D
Clarkson University	M,D
Clark University	M,D
Clemson University	M,D
Cleveland State University	M,D
The College at Brockport, State University of New York	M,O
The College of William and Mary	M
Colorado School of Mines	M,D
Colorado State University	M,D
Colorado State University–Pueblo	M
Columbia University	M,D*
Columbus State University	M,O
Concordia University (Canada)	M,D
Cornell University	D
Dalhousie University	M,D
Dartmouth College	M,D*
Delaware State University	M,D
DePaul University	M,D
Drew University	M,D,O
Drexel University	M,D
Duke University	D*
Duquesne University	D
East Carolina University	M
Eastern Illinois University	M
Eastern Kentucky University	M
Eastern Michigan University	M
Eastern New Mexico University	M
East Tennessee State University	M
Emory University	D
Fairleigh Dickinson University, College at Florham	M
Fairleigh Dickinson University, Metropolitan Campus	M
Fisk University	M
Florida Agricultural and Mechanical University	M
Florida Atlantic University	M,D
Florida Institute of Technology	M,D

Florida International University	M,D
Florida State University	M,D
Furman University	M
George Mason University	M,D
Georgetown University	D
The George Washington University	M,D*
Georgia Institute of Technology	M,D
Georgia State University	M,D
The Graduate Center, City University of New York	D
Hampton University	M
Harvard University	D*
Howard University	M,D
Hunter College of the City University of New York	M,D
Idaho State University	M
Illinois Institute of Technology	M,D
Indiana University Bloomington	M,D
Indiana University of Pennsylvania	M
Indiana University–Purdue University Indianapolis	M,D
Instituto Tecnológico y de Estudios Superiores de Monterrey, Campus Monterrey	M,D
Iowa State University of Science and Technology	M,D
Jackson State University	M,D
Johns Hopkins University	M,D
Kansas State University	M,D
Kennesaw State University	M
Kent State University	M,D
Lakehead University	M
Lamar University	M
Laurentian University	M
Lehigh University	M,D
Long Island University–LIU Brooklyn	M,D,O
Louisiana State University and Agricultural & Mechanical College	M,D
Louisiana Tech University	M
Loyola University Chicago	M,D
Marquette University	M,D
Marshall University	M
Massachusetts Institute of Technology	D
McGill University	M,D
McMaster University	M,D
McNeese State University	M
MCPHS University	M,D
Memorial University of Newfoundland	M,D
Miami University	M,D
Michigan State University	M,D
Michigan Technological University	M,D
Middle Tennessee State University	M
Mississippi College	M
Mississippi State University	M,D
Missouri State University	M
Missouri University of Science and Technology	M,D
Missouri Western State University	M
Montana State University	M,D
Montclair State University	M
Morgan State University	M
Mount Allison University	M
Murray State University	M
New Jersey Institute of Technology	M,D,O
New Mexico Highlands University	M
New Mexico Institute of Mining and Technology	M,D
New Mexico State University	M,D
New York University	M,D,O
North Carolina Agricultural and Technical State University	M,D
North Carolina Central University	M
North Carolina State University	M,D
North Dakota State University	M,D
Northeastern Illinois University	M
Northeastern University	M,D
Northern Arizona University	M
Northern Illinois University	M,D
Northwestern University	D*
Oakland University	M,D
The Ohio State University	M,D
Oklahoma State University	M,D
Old Dominion University	M,D
Oregon State University	M,D
Pace University	M,O
Penn State University Park	M,D
Pittsburg State University	M
Pontifical Catholic University of Puerto Rico	M
Portland State University	M,D
Prairie View A&M University	M
Princeton University	M,D
Purdue University	M,D
Queens College of the City University of New York	M
Queen's University at Kingston	M,D
Rensselaer Polytechnic Institute	M,D
Rice University	M,D
Rochester Institute of Technology	M
Roosevelt University	M
Royal Military College of Canada	M,D
Rutgers University–Camden	M
Rutgers University–Newark	M,D
Rutgers University–New Brunswick	M,D
Sacred Heart University	M
St. Francis Xavier University	M
St. John's University (NY)	M
Saint Louis University	M,D
Sam Houston State University	M
San Diego State University	M,D
San Francisco State University	M
San Jose State University	M,O
The Scripps Research Institute	D
Seton Hall University	M,D
Simon Fraser University	M,D
Smith College	M
South Dakota State University	M,D
Southeast Missouri State University	M
Southern Connecticut State University	M
Southern Illinois University Carbondale	M,D
Southern Illinois University Edwardsville	M
Southern Methodist University	M,D
Southern University and Agricultural and Mechanical College	M
Stanford University	D
State University of New York at New Paltz	M,O
State University of New York at Oswego	M
State University of New York College of Environmental Science and Forestry	M,D
Stephen F. Austin State University	M
Stevens Institute of Technology	M,D,O
Stevenson University	M
Stony Brook University, State University of New York	M,D
Syracuse University	M,D
Teachers College, Columbia University	M,D
Temple University	M,D*
Tennessee State University	M
Tennessee Technological University	M,D
Texas A&M University	M,D
Texas A&M University–Kingsville	M
Texas Christian University	M,D
Texas Southern University	M
Texas State University	M
Texas Tech University	M,D
Texas Woman's University	M
Trent University	M
Tufts University	M,D
Tulane University	M,D
Tuskegee University	M
Universidad del Turabo	M,D
Université de Moncton	M
Université de Montréal	M,D
Université de Sherbrooke	M,D,O
Université du Québec à Montréal	M,D
Université du Québec à Trois-Rivières	M
Université Laval	M,D
University at Albany, State University of New York	M,D
University at Buffalo, the State University of New York	M,D*
The University of Akron	M,D
The University of Alabama	M,D
The University of Alabama at Birmingham	M,D
The University of Alabama in Huntsville	M,D
University of Alaska Fairbanks	M,D
University of Alberta	M,D
The University of Arizona	M,D
University of Arkansas	M,D
University of Arkansas at Little Rock	M
The University of British Columbia	M,D
University of Calgary	M,D
University of California, Berkeley	D
University of California, Davis	M,D
University of California, Irvine	M,D
University of California, Los Angeles	M,D
University of California, Merced	M,D
University of California, Riverside	M,D
University of California, San Diego	M,D
University of California, San Francisco	D
University of California, Santa Barbara	M,D
University of California, Santa Cruz	M,D
University of Central Florida	M,D,O
University of Chicago	D
University of Cincinnati	M,D
University of Colorado Boulder	M,D
University of Colorado Denver	M
University of Connecticut	M,D*
University of Dayton	M
University of Delaware	M,D*
University of Denver	M,D
University of Detroit Mercy	M,D
University of Florida	M,D
University of Georgia	M,D
University of Guelph	M,D
University of Hawaii at Manoa	M,D
University of Houston	M,D
University of Houston–Clear Lake	M
University of Idaho	M,D
University of Illinois at Chicago	M,D
University of Illinois at Urbana–Champaign	M,D
The University of Iowa	D*
The University of Kansas	M,D*
University of Kentucky	M,D
University of Lethbridge	M,D
University of Louisville	M,D
University of Maine	M,D
The University of Manchester	M,D
University of Manitoba	M,D
University of Maryland, Baltimore County	M,D,O
University of Maryland, College Park	M,D
University of Maryland Eastern Shore	M,D
University of Massachusetts Amherst	M,D*
University of Massachusetts Boston	M,D
University of Massachusetts Dartmouth	M,D
University of Massachusetts Lowell	M,D
University of Memphis	M,D
University of Miami	M,D
University of Michigan	D
University of Minnesota, Duluth	M
University of Minnesota, Twin Cities Campus	M,D
University of Mississippi	M,D
University of Missouri	M,D
University of Missouri–Kansas City	M,D
University of Missouri–St. Louis	M,D
University of Montana	M,D
University of Nebraska–Lincoln	M,D
University of Nevada, Las Vegas	M,D
University of Nevada, Reno	M,D
University of New Brunswick Fredericton	M,D
University of New Hampshire	M,D
University of New Mexico	M,D
University of New Orleans	M,D
The University of North Carolina at Chapel Hill	M,D
The University of North Carolina at Charlotte	M,D
The University of North Carolina at Greensboro	M
The University of North Carolina Wilmington	M
University of North Dakota	M,D
University of Northern Colorado	M,D
University of North Texas	M,D,O
University of Notre Dame	M,D
University of Oklahoma	M,D*
University of Oregon	M,D
University of Ottawa	M,D
University of Pennsylvania	M,D*
University of Pittsburgh	M,D*
University of Prince Edward Island	M
University of Puerto Rico, Mayagüez Campus	M,D
University of Puerto Rico, Río Piedras Campus	M,D
University of Regina	M,D
University of Rhode Island	M,D
University of Rochester	M,D*
University of Saint Joseph	M
University of San Francisco	M
University of Saskatchewan	M,D
The University of Scranton	M
University of South Carolina	M,D
The University of South Dakota	M,D
University of Southern California	D
University of Southern Mississippi	M,D
University of South Florida	M,D
The University of Tennessee	M,D
The University of Texas at Arlington	M,D
The University of Texas at Austin	D
The University of Texas at Dallas	M,D*
The University of Texas at El Paso	M,D
The University of Texas at San Antonio	M,D
The University of Texas Rio Grande Valley	M
University of the Sciences	M,D
The University of Toledo	M,D
University of Toronto	M,D
The University of Tulsa	M,D
University of Utah	M,D*
University of Vermont	M,D
University of Victoria	M,D
University of Virginia	M,D
University of Washington	M,D*
University of Waterloo	M,D
The University of Western Ontario	M,D
University of Windsor	M,D
University of Wisconsin–Madison	M,D
University of Wisconsin–Milwaukee	M,D
University of Wyoming	M,D
Utah State University	M,D
Vanderbilt University	M,D*
Villanova University	M
Virginia Commonwealth University	M,D
Virginia Polytechnic Institute and State University	M,D
Wake Forest University	M,D
Washington State University	M,D
Washington University in St. Louis	D
Wayne State University	M,D
Wesleyan University	D
West Chester University of Pennsylvania	O
Western Carolina University	M
Western Illinois University	M
Western Kentucky University	M
Western Michigan University	M,D,O
Western Washington University	M
West Texas A&M University	M
West Virginia University	M,D
Wichita State University	M,D
Wilfrid Laurier University	M
Worcester Polytechnic Institute	M,D
Wright State University	M
Yale University	D*
York University	M,D
Youngstown State University	M

CHILD AND FAMILY STUDIES

Alabama Agricultural and Mechanical University	M
Amberton University	M
Arizona State University at the Tempe campus	M,D
Asbury University	M
Assumption College	M,O
Auburn University	M,D
Bank Street College of Education	M
Bowling Green State University	M
Brandeis University	M,D
Brigham Young University	M,D
Brock University	M
California State University, East Bay	M
California State University, Los Angeles	M
California State University, San Marcos	M
Capella University	M
Carlow University	M,O
Central Michigan University	M,O
Central Washington University	M
Colorado State University	M,D
Concordia University (Canada)	M
Concordia University, St. Paul	M,D,O
Concordia University Wisconsin	M
Cornell University	M,D
Dallas Theological Seminary	M,D,O
East Carolina University	M,D
Fairfield University	M,O
Florida State University	M,D
Fontbonne University	M
Indiana University–Purdue University Indianapolis	M
Iowa State University of Science and Technology	M,D
Kansas State University	M,D,O
Kent State University	M
Liberty University	M,D,O
Loma Linda University	M,D,O
London Metropolitan University	M,D
Miami University	M
Michigan State University	M,D
Mississippi State University	M,D
Missouri State University	M
Montclair State University	M,D,O
Mount Saint Vincent University	M
North Carolina Agricultural and Technical State University	M
North Dakota State University	M,D,O
Northern Illinois University	M
The Ohio State University	M,D
Ohio University	M
Oklahoma State University	M,D
Oregon State University	M,D
Oxford Graduate School	M,D
Penn State University Park	M,D
Purdue University	M,D
Purdue University Northwest	M
Queens College of the City University of New York	M,O
Roberts Wesleyan College	M
St. Cloud State University	M
San Diego State University	M
South Carolina State University	M
Spring Arbor University	M
State University of New York at Oswego	M
Syracuse University	M,D
Texas State University	M
Texas Tech University	M,D
Texas Woman's University	M,D
Towson University	M,O
Tufts University	M,D
The University of Akron	M,D
The University of Alabama	M
The University of Arizona	M,D,O
University of Central Oklahoma	M
University of Connecticut	M,D*
University of Delaware	M,D*
University of Denver	M,D,O
University of Georgia	M,D,O
University of Guelph	M,D
University of Illinois at Springfield	M,O
University of Kentucky	M,D
University of La Verne	M
University of Manitoba	M
University of Maryland, College Park	M,D
University of Massachusetts Amherst	M,D,O*
University of Minnesota, Twin Cities Campus	M,D
University of Missouri	M,D
University of Montana	M,D,O
University of Nebraska–Lincoln	M,D
University of Nevada, Reno	M
University of New Hampshire	M,O
University of New Mexico	M,D
University of North Alabama	M
The University of North Carolina at Charlotte	M,D,O
The University of North Carolina at Greensboro	M,D
University of North Texas	M,D,O
University of Rhode Island	M
University of Southern California	M,D
University of Southern Mississippi	M
University of South Florida	M,D,O
The University of Tennessee	M,D
The University of Tennessee at Martin	M
The University of Texas at Austin	M,D
The University of Texas at Dallas	M,D*
University of Utah	M*
University of Victoria	M,D
University of Wisconsin–Madison	M,D
Utah State University	M,D
Vanderbilt University	M,D*
Walden University	M,D

*M—masters degree; D—doctorate; O—other advanced degree; *—Close-Up and/or Display*

Washington University in St. Louis	M,D,O
West Virginia University	M
Wheelock College	M

CHILD DEVELOPMENT

Appalachian State University	M
California State University, Los Angeles	M
California State University, San Bernardino	M
Chaminade University of Honolulu	M
East Carolina University	M,D
Erikson Institute	M
Fielding Graduate University	M,D,O
Kansas State University	M,O
Lee University	M
Michigan State University	M,D
Montclair State University	M,O
North Carolina Agricultural and Technical State University	M
North Dakota State University	M
Ohio University	M
Purdue University	M,D
Purdue University Northwest	M
Rutgers University–Camden	M,D
San Diego State University	M
San Jose State University	M,D,O
Sarah Lawrence College	M
Southern New Hampshire University	M,D,O
Texas Woman's University	M,D
Tufts University	M,D
The University of Akron	M
University of California, Davis	M
University of Florida	M
University of La Verne	M
University of Minnesota, Twin Cities Campus	M,D
University of Nebraska–Lincoln	M,D
The University of North Carolina at Charlotte	M,D,O
The University of Tennessee at Martin	M
The University of Texas at Austin	M,D
The University of West Alabama	M,O
University of Wyoming	M
Whittier College	M

CHINESE

Arizona State University at the Tempe campus	M,D
Clarkson University	M,O
DePaul University	M
Harvard University	D*
Hunter College of the City University of New York	M
Indiana University Bloomington	M,D
Middlebury College	M
New York University	M,D,O
The Ohio State University	M,D
Saginaw Valley State University	M
San Francisco State University	M
Stanford University	M,D
University of Alberta	M
University of California, Berkeley	D
University of California, Irvine	M,D
University of Colorado Boulder	M,D
University of Delaware	M*
University of Hawaii at Manoa	M,D,O
The University of Iowa	M*
The University of Manchester	M,D
University of Massachusetts Amherst	M*
University of Oregon	M,D
University of Pittsburgh	M*
University of Washington	M,D*
University of Wisconsin–Madison	M,D
Washington University in St. Louis	M,D

CHIROPRACTIC

Canadian Memorial Chiropractic College	D,O
Cleveland University–Kansas City	D
D'Youville College	D
Institut Franco-Europen de Chiropraxie	D
Life Chiropractic College West	D
Life University	D
Logan University	M,D
National University of Health Sciences	M,D
New York Chiropractic College	D*
Northwestern Health Sciences University	D
Palmer College of Chiropractic	D
Parker University	D
Sherman College of Chiropractic	D
Southern California University of Health Sciences	D
Texas Chiropractic College	D
Université du Québec à Trois-Rivières	D
University of Bridgeport	D
University of Western States	D

CIVIL ENGINEERING

American University of Beirut	M,D
American University of Sharjah	M
Arizona State University at the Tempe campus	M,D
Auburn University	M,D
Boise State University	M
Bradley University	M
Brigham Young University	M,D
Bucknell University	M
California Baptist University	M
California Institute of Technology	M,D,O
California Polytechnic State University, San Luis Obispo	M
California State Polytechnic University, Pomona	M
California State University, Fresno	M
California State University, Fullerton	M
California State University, Long Beach	M
California State University, Los Angeles	M
California State University, Northridge	M
California State University, Sacramento	M
Carleton University	M,D
Carnegie Mellon University	M,D
Case Western Reserve University	M,D*
The Catholic University of America	M,D,O
The Citadel, The Military College of South Carolina	M
City College of the City University of New York	M,D
Clarkson University	M,D
Clemson University	M,D
Cleveland State University	M,D
Colorado School of Mines	M,D
Colorado State University	M,D
Columbia University	M,D*
Concordia University (Canada)	M,D,O
Cooper Union for the Advancement of Science and Art	M
Cornell University	M,D
Dalhousie University	M,D
Drexel University	M,D
Duke University	M,D*
École Polytechnique de Montréal	M,D,O
Florida Agricultural and Mechanical University	M,D
Florida Atlantic University	M
Florida Institute of Technology	M,D
Florida International University	M,D
Florida State University	M,D
George Mason University	M,D
The George Washington University	M,D,O*
Georgia Institute of Technology	M,D
Georgia Southern University	M
The Graduate Center, City University of New York	D
Howard University	M
Idaho State University	M
Illinois Institute of Technology	M,D
Indiana University–Purdue University Fort Wayne	M
Instituto Tecnológico y de Estudios Superiores de Monterrey, Campus Monterrey	M,D
Iowa State University of Science and Technology	M,D
Johns Hopkins University	M,D
Kansas State University	M,D
Lawrence Technological University	M,D
Lehigh University	M,D
Louisiana State University and Agricultural & Mechanical College	M,D
Louisiana Tech University	M,D
Loyola Marymount University	M
Manhattan College	M
Marquette University	M,D,O
Massachusetts Institute of Technology	M,D,O
McGill University	M,D
McMaster University	M,D
McNeese State University	M
Memorial University of Newfoundland	M,D
Merrimack College	M
Michigan State University	M,D
Michigan Technological University	M,D
Milwaukee School of Engineering	M*
Mississippi State University	M,D
Missouri University of Science and Technology	M,D
Montana State University	M,D
Morgan State University	M,D
New Mexico State University	M,D
New York University	M,D
North Carolina Agricultural and Technical State University	M
North Carolina State University	M,D
North Dakota State University	M,D
Northeastern University	M,D,O
Northern Arizona University	M
Northwestern University	M,D*
Norwich University	M
The Ohio State University	M,D
Ohio University	M,D
Oklahoma State University	M,D
Old Dominion University	M,D
Oregon State University	M,D
Penn State University Park	M,D
Polytechnic University of Puerto Rico	M
Portland State University	M,D,O
Princeton University	M,D
Purdue University	M,D
Queen's University at Kingston	M,D
Rensselaer Polytechnic Institute	M,D
Rice University	M,D
Rose-Hulman Institute of Technology	M
Rowan University	M
Royal Military College of Canada	M,D
Rutgers University–New Brunswick	M,D
Saint Martin's University	M
San Diego State University	M
Santa Clara University	M,D,O
South Carolina State University	M
South Dakota School of Mines and Technology	M,D
South Dakota State University	M
Southern Illinois University Carbondale	M,D
Southern Illinois University Edwardsville	M
Southern Methodist University	M,D
Stanford University	M,D,O
Stevens Institute of Technology	M,D,O
Stony Brook University, State University of New York	M,D,O
Syracuse University	M,D
Temple University	M,O*
Tennessee State University	M,D
Tennessee Technological University	M
Texas A&M University	M,D
Texas A&M University–Kingsville	M
Texas Tech University	M,D
Trine University	M
Tufts University	M,D
United States Merchant Marine Academy	M
Université de Moncton	M
Université de Sherbrooke	M,D
Université Laval	M,D,O
University at Buffalo, the State University of New York	M,D*
The University of Akron	M,D
The University of Alabama	M,D
The University of Alabama at Birmingham	M,D
The University of Alabama in Huntsville	M,D
University of Alaska Anchorage	M,O
University of Alaska Fairbanks	M,D,O
University of Alberta	M,D
University of Arkansas	M,D
The University of British Columbia	M,D
University of Calgary	M,D
University of California, Berkeley	M,D
University of California, Davis	M,D,O
University of California, Irvine	M,D
University of California, Los Angeles	M,D
University of Central Florida	M,D,O
University of Cincinnati	M,D
University of Colorado Boulder	M,D
University of Colorado Denver	M,D
University of Connecticut	M,D*
University of Dayton	M
University of Delaware	M,D*
University of Detroit Mercy	M,D
University of Florida	M,D
University of Hawaii at Manoa	M,D
University of Houston	M,D
University of Idaho	M,D
University of Illinois at Chicago	M,D
University of Illinois at Urbana–Champaign	M,D
The University of Iowa	M,D*
The University of Kansas	M,D*
University of Kentucky	M,D
University of Louisiana at Lafayette	M
University of Louisville	M,D,O
University of Maine	M,D
The University of Manchester	M,D
University of Manitoba	M,D
University of Maryland, College Park	M,D
University of Massachusetts Amherst	M,D*
University of Massachusetts Dartmouth	M
University of Massachusetts Lowell	M,D
University of Memphis	M,D
University of Miami	M,D
University of Michigan	M,D,O
University of Minnesota, Twin Cities Campus	M,D,O
University of Missouri	M,D
University of Missouri–Kansas City	M,D,O
University of Nebraska–Lincoln	M,D
University of Nevada, Las Vegas	M,D
University of Nevada, Reno	M,D
University of New Brunswick Fredericton	M,D
University of New Hampshire	M,D
University of New Mexico	M,D
The University of North Carolina at Charlotte	M,D
University of North Dakota	M
University of North Florida	M
University of Notre Dame	M,D
University of Oklahoma	M,D*
University of Ottawa	M,D
University of Pittsburgh	M,D*
University of Portland	M
University of Puerto Rico, Mayagüez Campus	M,D
University of Rhode Island	M,D
University of Saskatchewan	M,D
University of South Alabama	M
University of South Carolina	M,D
University of Southern California	M,D,O
University of South Florida	M,D,O
The University of Tennessee	M,D
The University of Tennessee at Chattanooga	M
The University of Texas at Arlington	M,D
The University of Texas at Austin	M,D
The University of Texas at El Paso	M,D,O
The University of Texas at San Antonio	M,D
The University of Texas at Tyler	M
The University of Toledo	M,D
University of Toronto	M,D
University of Utah	M,D*
University of Vermont	M,D
University of Virginia	M,D
University of Washington	M,D*
University of Waterloo	M,D
The University of Western Ontario	M,D
University of Windsor	M,D
University of Wisconsin–Madison	M,D
University of Wisconsin–Milwaukee	M,D,O
University of Wyoming	M,D
Utah State University	M,D,O
Vanderbilt University	M,D*
Villanova University	M
Virginia Polytechnic Institute and State University	M,D,O
Washington State University	M,D
Wayne State University	M,D
Wentworth Institute of Technology	M
Western Michigan University	M
West Virginia University	M,D
Widener University	M
Worcester Polytechnic Institute	M,D,O
Youngstown State University	M

CLASSICS

American Public University System	M
Asbury University	M
Bethel Seminary	M,D,O
Boston College	M
Boston University	M,D
Brandeis University	M
Brigham Young University	M
Brock University	M
Brown University	M,D
Bryn Mawr College	M,D
The Catholic University of America	M,D,O
City College of the City University of New York	M
Columbia University	M,D*
Cornell University	D
Dalhousie University	M,D
Duke University	D*
Duquesne University	M
Florida State University	M,D
Fordham University	M,D
The Graduate Center, City University of New York	M,D
Harvard University	D*
Heritage Christian University	M
Hunter College of the City University of New York	M
Indiana University Bloomington	M,D
Johns Hopkins University	D
Knox Theological Seminary	M
Marshall University	M,O
McMaster University	M,D
Memorial University of Newfoundland	M
New York University	M,D,O
The Ohio State University	M,D
Princeton University	D
Queen's University at Kingston	M
Rutgers University–New Brunswick	M,D
San Francisco State University	M
Stanford University	M,D
Texas Tech University	M,D
Tufts University	M
Tulane University	M
Université de Montréal	M
University at Buffalo, the State University of New York	M,D,O*
University of Alberta	M,D
The University of Arizona	M
The University of British Columbia	M,D
University of Calgary	M,D
University of California, Berkeley	M,D
University of California, Irvine	M,D
University of California, Los Angeles	M,D
University of California, Riverside	D
University of California, Santa Barbara	M,D
University of Chicago	M,D
University of Cincinnati	M,D
University of Colorado Boulder	M,D
University of Dallas	M
University of Florida	M,D
University of Georgia	M
University of Illinois at Urbana–Champaign	M,D
The University of Iowa	M,D*
The University of Kansas	M*
University of Kentucky	M
The University of Manchester	D
University of Manitoba	M
University of Maryland, College Park	M
University of Massachusetts Amherst	M*
University of Massachusetts Boston	M
University of Michigan	M,D,O
University of Minnesota, Twin Cities Campus	M,D
University of Missouri	M,D
University of Nebraska–Lincoln	M
University of New Brunswick Fredericton	M
The University of North Carolina at Chapel Hill	M,D
The University of North Carolina at Greensboro	M
University of Oregon	M
University of Ottawa	M,D
University of Pennsylvania	M,D*
University of South Africa	M,D
University of Southern California	M,D
The University of Texas at Austin	M,D
University of Toronto	M,D
University of Victoria	M,D
University of Virginia	M,D
University of Washington	M,D*
The University of Western Ontario	M
University of Wisconsin–Madison	M,D
University of Wisconsin–Milwaukee	M,O
Vanderbilt University	M*

Villanova University	M
Washington University in St. Louis	M,D
Wayne State University	M
Yale University	M,D*

CLINICAL LABORATORY SCIENCES/ MEDICAL TECHNOLOGY

Albany College of Pharmacy and Health Sciences	M
Austin Peay State University	M
Baylor College of Medicine	M,D
The Catholic University of America	M,D
The College of William and Mary	M,D
Dominican University of California	M
Duke University	M*
Fairleigh Dickinson University, Metropolitan Campus	M
Inter American University of Puerto Rico, Metropolitan Campus	M
Medical College of Wisconsin	M,D
Michigan State University	M
Milwaukee School of Engineering	M*
Northern Michigan University	M
Northwestern University	M*
Pontifical Catholic University of Puerto Rico	O
Quinnipiac University	M
Rush University	M
Rutgers University–Newark	M
Rutgers University–New Brunswick	M
State University of New York Upstate Medical University	M
Tarleton State University	M
Thomas Jefferson University	M
Universidad de las Américas Puebla	M
Université de Sherbrooke	M,D
University at Buffalo, the State University of New York	M*
The University of Alabama at Birmingham	M,D
University of Alberta	M,D
University of California, San Diego	M,D
University of Colorado Denver	M,D
University of Florida	M,D
University of Maryland, Baltimore	M
University of Massachusetts Dartmouth	M,D
University of Massachusetts Lowell	M
University of Minnesota, Twin Cities Campus	M
University of Nebraska Medical Center	M,O
University of New Mexico	M,O
University of North Dakota	M
University of Pennsylvania	M*
University of Pittsburgh	D*
University of Puerto Rico, Medical Sciences Campus	M,O
University of Rhode Island	M,D
University of Southern Mississippi	M
The University of Tennessee Health Science Center	M,D
The University of Texas at Austin	M,D
The University of Texas Health Science Center at San Antonio	D
The University of Texas Medical Branch	M,D
University of Utah	M*
University of Vermont	M,D,O
University of Washington	M*
Virginia Commonwealth University	M,D

CLINICAL PSYCHOLOGY

Abilene Christian University	M
Acadia University	M
Adelphi University	D
Adler Graduate School	M
Adler University	M,D,O
Alabama Agricultural and Mechanical University	M,O
Alliant International University–Fresno	D
Alliant International University–Los Angeles	D
Alliant International University–Sacramento	D
Alliant International University–San Diego	M,D
Alliant International University–San Francisco	M,D,O
American International College	M
American University	M,D,O
American University of Beirut	M,D
Andrews University	M
Antioch University Los Angeles	M
Antioch University New England	M,D
Antioch University Santa Barbara	M,D
Appalachian State University	M
Argosy University, Atlanta	M,D,O
Argosy University, Chicago	M,D
Argosy University, Dallas	M,D
Argosy University, Denver	M,D
Argosy University, Hawai`i	M,D,O
Argosy University, Inland Empire	M,D
Argosy University, Los Angeles	M,D
Argosy University, Orange County	M,D
Argosy University, Phoenix	M,D
Argosy University, San Diego	M,D
Argosy University, San Francisco Bay Area	M,D
Argosy University, Schaumburg	M,D
Argosy University, Seattle	M,D,O
Argosy University, Tampa	M,D
Argosy University, Twin Cities	M,D,O
Argosy University, Washington DC	M,D
Arizona State University at the Tempe campus	M,D
Arkansas State University	M,O
Auburn University at Montgomery	M
Austin Peay State University	M
Azusa Pacific University	M,D
Ball State University	M,D
Barry University	M,O
Baylor University	D
Bay Path University	M
Benedictine University	M
Binghamton University, State University of New York	D*
Biola University	D
Bowling Green State University	M,D
Bradley University	M
Brigham Young University	D
California Institute of Integral Studies	M,D
California Lutheran University	M,D
California State University, Dominguez Hills	M
California State University, Fullerton	M
California State University, Northridge	M
California State University, San Bernardino	M
California University of Pennsylvania	M
Capella University	M,D
Cardinal Stritch University	M
Carlos Albizu University	M,D
Carlos Albizu University, Miami Campus	M,D
Case Western Reserve University	D*
The Catholic University of America	M,D
Central Michigan University	D
Chestnut Hill College	M,D,O
The Chicago School of Professional Psychology	D
The Chicago School of Professional Psychology at Downtown Los Angeles	M,D
The Chicago School of Professional Psychology at Irvine	D
City College of the City University of New York	M,D
Clark University	D
Clayton State University	M
College of St. Joseph	M
College of Staten Island of the City University of New York	M
Columbus State University	M,D,O
Concordia University (Canada)	D,O
Connecticut College	M
Dalhousie University	M,D
DePaul University	M,D
Drexel University	D
Duke University	D*
Duquesne University	M,D,O
East Carolina University	M,D
Eastern Illinois University	M,O
Eastern Kentucky University	M,O
Eastern Michigan University	M,D
Eastern Virginia Medical School	D
Eastern Washington University	M
Edinboro University of Pennsylvania	M,O
Emory University	D
Emporia State University	M
Evangel University	M
Fairfield University	M,O
Fairleigh Dickinson University, College at Florham	M
Fairleigh Dickinson University, Metropolitan Campus	M,D
Fielding Graduate University	M,D,O
Fisk University	M
Florida Institute of Technology	D
Florida International University	M,D,O
Florida State University	D
Fordham University	D
Franciscan University of Steubenville	M
Francis Marion University	M,O
Fuller Theological Seminary	M,D,O
Gallaudet University	M,D,O
Gannon University	M
Geneva College	M
George Fox University	M,D,O
The George Washington University	M,D*
Georgian Court University	M,O
Georgia Southern University	M,D
Georgia State University	D
Grace College	M
The Graduate Center, City University of New York	D
Hawai`i Pacific University	M
Hodges University	M
Hofstra University	M,D
Howard University	M,D
Husson University	M
Idaho State University	D
Illinois Institute of Technology	M,D
Illinois State University	M,D,O
Immaculata University	M,D,O
Indiana State University	M,D,O
Indiana University of Pennsylvania	M,D
Indiana University–Purdue University Indianapolis	M,D
The Institute for the Psychological Sciences	M,D
Jackson State University	D
James Madison University	M,D,O
John Brown University	M,O
Johns Hopkins University	M,O
Judson University	M
Kean University	M,D
Kent State University	M,D
LaGrange College	M
Lakehead University	M,D
Lamar University	M
La Salle University	M,D
Lenoir-Rhyne University	M
Lesley University	M,D,O
Lewis University	M
Liberty University	M,D,O
Lipscomb University	M,O
Lock Haven University of Pennsylvania	M
Loma Linda University	D
London Metropolitan University	M,D
Long Island University–Brentwood Campus	M,O
Long Island University–LIU Brooklyn	M,D,O
Long Island University–LIU Post	M,D,O
Louisiana State University and Agricultural & Mechanical College	M,D
Loyola University Chicago	M,D
Loyola University Maryland	M,D,O
Loyola University New Orleans	M
Lynchburg College	M
Madonna University	M
Marquette University	M,D
Marshall University	M,D,O
Marymount University	M,D
Marywood University	M,D
McGill University	M,D
McKendree University	M
Medaille College	M,D
Memorial University of Newfoundland	M,D
Mercer University	M,D
Merrimack College	M
Messiah College	M,O
Michigan School of Professional Psychology	M,D
Middle Tennessee State University	M,O
Midwestern State University	M
Midwestern University, Downers Grove Campus	M,D
Midwestern University, Glendale Campus	D
Millersville University of Pennsylvania	M
Minnesota State University Mankato	M,D
Mississippi State University	M,D,O
Missouri State University	M,O
Molloy College	M
Montclair State University	M
Morehead State University	M
Mount Mary University	M,O
Murray State University	M
National University	M,O
Neumann University	M,D,O
New Mexico Highlands University	M
The New School	M,D
Nicholls State University	M,O
Norfolk State University	M
North Dakota State University	M,D
Northern Arizona University	M
Northern Kentucky University	M
Northern State University	M
Northwestern State University of Louisiana	M
Northwestern University	D*
Northwest Nazarene University	M
Notre Dame de Namur University	M
Nova Southeastern University	M,D,O*
The Ohio State University	D
Ohio University	M,D
Oklahoma State University	M,D
Old Dominion University	D
Pace University	M,D
Pacifica Graduate Institute	M,D
Pacific University	M,D
Palo Alto University	D
Penn State Harrisburg	M,D,O
Pepperdine University	M,D
Philadelphia College of Osteopathic Medicine	M,D,O*
Pittsburg State University	M
Plymouth State University	M,O
Point Park University	M
Ponce Health Sciences University	D
Pontifical Catholic University of Puerto Rico	D
Pontificia Universidad Catolica Madre y Maestra	M
Prairie View A&M University	M,D
Purdue University	D
Queen's University at Kingston	M,D
Radford University	M
Regent University	M,D,O
Richmont Graduate University	M
Rivier University	M
Roger Williams University	M
Roosevelt University	M
Rosalind Franklin University of Medicine and Science	M,D
Rowan University	M,O
Rutgers University–New Brunswick	M,D
St. John's University (NY)	M,D,O
Saint Louis University	M,D
Saint Michael's College	M
Sam Houston State University	M,D,O
San Diego State University	M,D
San Francisco State University	M,O
San Jose State University	M,O
Saybrook University	M
Seattle Pacific University	D
Shippensburg University of Pennsylvania	M,O
Siena Heights University	M,O
Slippery Rock University of Pennsylvania	M
Sofia University	M,D
Sonoma State University	M
Southeastern Oklahoma State University	M
Southern Illinois University Carbondale	M,D
Southern Illinois University Edwardsville	M
Southern Methodist University	D
South University (OH)	M
Spalding University	M,D
Springfield College	M,D,O
State University of New York at Plattsburgh	M,O
Stony Brook University, State University of New York	D
Suffolk University	M,D,O
Syracuse University	M,D
Teachers College, Columbia University	M,D
Texas A&M University	M,D
Texas A&M University–Central Texas	M,O
Texas Tech University	M,D
Towson University	M
Trinity Washington University	M
Troy University	M,O
Uniformed Services University of the Health Sciences	D*
Union College (KY)	M
Union Institute & University	M
Universidad de Iberoamerica	M,D
Université Laval	D
University at Albany, State University of New York	M,D
The University of Akron	M
The University of Alabama	D
The University of Alabama at Birmingham	M,D
University of Alaska Anchorage	M,D
University of Alaska Fairbanks	D
University of Bridgeport	M
The University of British Columbia	M,D
University of Calgary	M,D
University of California, San Diego	D
University of California, Santa Barbara	M,D,O
University of Central Florida	M,D
University of Cincinnati	D
University of Colorado Denver	M,D
University of Connecticut	M,D*
University of Dayton	M,O
University of Delaware	D*
University of Denver	M,D
University of Detroit Mercy	M,D,O
University of Florida	M,D
University of Guelph	M,D
University of Hartford	M,D
University of Hawaii at Manoa	M,D,O
University of Houston	M,D
University of Houston–Clear Lake	M
University of Indianapolis	M,D
The University of Kansas	M,D*
University of La Verne	D
University of Louisiana at Monroe	M
University of Louisville	D
The University of Manchester	M,D
University of Manitoba	M,D
University of Mary Hardin-Baylor	M
University of Maryland, Baltimore County	M,D
University of Maryland, College Park	M,D
University of Massachusetts Amherst	M,D*
University of Massachusetts Boston	D
University of Massachusetts Dartmouth	M,O
University of Memphis	M,D,O
University of Miami	M,D
University of Michigan	D
University of Michigan–Dearborn	M
University of Minnesota, Twin Cities Campus	D
University of Mississippi	M,D
University of Missouri–Kansas City	M,D
University of Missouri–St. Louis	M,D,O
University of Montana	M,D,O
University of Montevallo	M
University of Nebraska–Lincoln	M,D
University of Nevada, Las Vegas	M,D,O
University of Nevada, Reno	D
University of New Brunswick Saint John	M,D
University of New Mexico	D
The University of North Carolina at Chapel Hill	D
The University of North Carolina at Greensboro	M,D
University of North Dakota	M,D
University of North Georgia	M
University of North Texas	M,D,O
University of Oregon	D
University of Phoenix–Phoenix Campus	M
University of Pittsburgh	D*
University of Puerto Rico, Rí o Piedras Campus	M,D
University of Regina	M,D
University of Rhode Island	M,D
University of Rochester	D*
University of Saint Francis (IN)	M,O
University of Saint Joseph	M,O
The University of Scranton	M
University of South Africa	M,D
University of South Alabama	M,D,O
University of South Carolina	M,D
University of South Carolina Aiken	M
The University of South Dakota	M,D

*M—masters degree; D—doctorate; O—other advanced degree; *—Close-Up and/or Display*

University of Southern California	M,D
University of Southern Mississippi	M,D
University of South Florida	D
The University of Tennessee	M,D
The University of Texas at Austin	D
The University of Texas at El Paso	M,D
The University of Texas at Tyler	M
The University of Texas of the Permian Basin	M
The University of Texas Rio Grande Valley	M
The University of Texas Southwestern Medical Center	D
University of the Cumberlands	D
The University of Toledo	M,D
The University of Tulsa	M,D
University of Utah	M,D*
University of Vermont	D
University of Victoria	M,D
University of Virginia	D
University of Washington	D*
University of Windsor	M,D
University of Wisconsin–Madison	D
University of Wisconsin–Milwaukee	M,D
University of Wisconsin–Stout	M
Utah State University	M,D
Valparaiso University	M
Vanguard University of Southern California	M
Virginia Commonwealth University	D
Virginia State University	M,D
Walden University	M,D,O
Washburn University	M
Washington State University	M,D
Waynesburg University	M,D
Wayne State University	M,D
West Chester University of Pennsylvania	M,O
Western Connecticut State University	M
Western Illinois University	M,O
Western Kentucky University	M,O
Western Michigan University	M,D
West Virginia University	M,D
Wheaton College	M,D
Wichita State University	D
Widener University	D
William James College	M,D,O
William Paterson University of New Jersey	M,D
Wilmington University	M
Wisconsin School of Professional Psychology	M,D
Wright Institute	D
Wright State University	D
Xavier University	M,D
Yale University	D*
Yeshiva University	D

CLINICAL RESEARCH

Albert Einstein College of Medicine	D
American University of Health Sciences	M
Augusta University	M
Boston University	M
Case Western Reserve University	M*
Clemson University	M,D,O
Duke University	M*
Eastern Michigan University	M,O
Emory University	M
Fordham University	M,D
Icahn School of Medicine at Mount Sinai	M,D
Johns Hopkins University	M,D
Loyola University Chicago	M
Medical College of Wisconsin	
Medical University of South Carolina	M
Memorial University of Newfoundland	M
Morehouse School of Medicine	M
New York University	M
Northwestern University	M,O*
Oregon Health & Science University	M,O
Palmer College of Chiropractic	M
Stanford University	M,D
Thomas Jefferson University	M,O
Trident University International	M,D,O
Tufts University	M,D,O
University of California, Berkeley	O
University of California, Davis	M
University of California, Los Angeles	M
University of California, San Diego	M
University of Colorado Denver	M,D
University of Connecticut Health Center	M*
University of Florida	M,D,O
The University of Iowa	M,D*
The University of Kansas	M*
University of Kentucky	M
University of Louisville	M,D
University of Maryland, Baltimore	M,D,O
University of Massachusetts Medical School	M,D
University of Michigan	M
University of Minnesota, Twin Cities Campus	M
The University of North Carolina Wilmington	M,O
University of Pittsburgh	M,O*
University of Puerto Rico, Medical Sciences Campus	M,O
University of Rochester	M*
University of Southern California	M,D,O
University of South Florida	M,D,O
The University of Texas Health Science Center at San Antonio	M
University of Virginia	M
University of Washington	M,D*
University of Wisconsin–Madison	M,D
Vanderbilt University	M*
Walden University	M,D,O
Washington University in St. Louis	M

CLOTHING AND TEXTILES

Academy of Art University	M
Alabama Agricultural and Mechanical University	M
Auburn University	M,D
Central Michigan University	M,O
Cornell University	M,D
Eastern Michigan University	M
Fashion Institute of Technology	M*
Georgia State University	M
Iowa State University of Science and Technology	M,D
Kansas State University	M,D
LIM College	M
The New School	M
North Carolina State University	D
North Dakota State University	M,O
Ohio University	M
Oklahoma State University	M,D
Oregon State University	M,D
Philadelphia University	M
Rutgers University–Newark	M
Savannah College of Art and Design	M
The University of Akron	M
The University of Alabama	M
University of Alberta	M,D
University of California, Davis	M
University of Delaware	M*
University of Georgia	M,D
The University of Manchester	M,D
University of Manitoba	M
University of Minnesota, Twin Cities Campus	M,D,O
University of Missouri	M,D
University of Nebraska–Lincoln	M,D
University of Rhode Island	M,O
The University of Tennessee	M,D
University of the Incarnate Word	M
Washington State University	M

COGNITIVE SCIENCES

American University	M,D,O
Arizona State University at the Tempe campus	M,D
Ball State University	M
Binghamton University, State University of New York	D*
Brandeis University	M,D
Brown University	M,D
Carleton University	D
Carnegie Mellon University	D
Case Western Reserve University	M*
Central European University	D
Claremont Graduate University	M,D,O
Cornell University	D
Dartmouth College	D*
Duke University	D*
Emory University	D
Florida International University	M,D
Florida State University	D
George Mason University	M,D,O
The George Washington University	D*
Georgia State University	D
The Graduate Center, City University of New York	D
Grand Canyon University	D
Harvard University	M,D*
Illinois State University	M,D,O
Indiana University Bloomington	D
Iowa State University of Science and Technology	D
Johns Hopkins University	D
Louisiana State University and Agricultural & Mechanical College	M,D
Massachusetts Institute of Technology	D
Michigan Technological University	M,D,O
Mississippi State University	M,D
The New School	M,D
New York University	M,D,O
North Dakota State University	M,D
Northwestern University	D*
The Ohio State University	D
Oregon State University	M,D
Purdue University	D
Queen's University at Kingston	M,D
Rensselaer Polytechnic Institute	D
Rice University	M,D
Rutgers University–Newark	D
Rutgers University–New Brunswick	D
Stony Brook University, State University of New York	D
Texas Christian University	M,D
Tufts University	M,D
University at Albany, State University of New York	M,D
The University of British Columbia	M,D
University of California, Merced	M,D
University of California, San Diego	D
University of California, Santa Barbara	M,D
University of Connecticut	M,D,O*
University of Delaware	M,D*
University of Denver	D
University of Guelph	M,D
The University of Kansas	M,D*
University of Louisiana at Lafayette	D
University of Louisville	D
University of Maryland, Baltimore County	D
University of Maryland, College Park	D
University of Massachusetts Amherst	M,D*
University of Massachusetts Boston	M
University of Michigan	D
University of Minnesota, Twin Cities Campus	D
University of Nebraska–Lincoln	M,D,O
University of Nevada, Reno	M,D
University of New Mexico	D
The University of North Carolina at Chapel Hill	D
The University of North Carolina at Charlotte	M,D,O
The University of North Carolina at Greensboro	M,D
University of Notre Dame	D
University of Oregon	M,D
University of Rochester	D*
University of Southern California	M,D
University of South Florida	D
The University of Texas at Dallas	M,D*
University of Washington	D*
University of Wisconsin–Madison	D
Wayne State University	M,D
Wilfrid Laurier University	M,D
Yale University	D*

COMMUNICATION—GENERAL

Abilene Christian University	M
American University	M,D
The American University in Cairo	M
The American University of Paris	M
Andrews University	M
Angelo State University	M
Arizona State University at the Tempe campus	M,D
Arkansas State University	M,O
Auburn University	M,O
Austin Peay State University	M
Ball State University	M,O
Barry University	M,O
Baylor University	M
Bay Path University	M
Bellarmine University	M
Bethel University (MN)	M,D,O
Boise State University	M
Boston University	M,D
Bowling Green State University	M,D
Brandeis University	M
Brigham Young University	M
Bryant University	M
California Baptist University	M
California State University, Chico	M
California State University, East Bay	M
California State University, Fresno	M
California State University, Fullerton	M
California State University, Long Beach	M
California State University, Los Angeles	M
California State University, Northridge	M
California State University, Sacramento	M
California State University, San Bernardino	M
Carleton University	M,D
Carnegie Mellon University	M,D
Central Connecticut State University	M,O
Central Michigan University	M
Chatham University	M
Clarion University of Pennsylvania	M
Clark University	M
Clemson University	M,D
Cleveland State University	M,D,O
The College at Brockport, State University of New York	M
College of Charleston	M
The College of New Rochelle	M,O
Columbia University	M,D*
Concordia University (Canada)	M,D,O
Cornell University	M,D
DePaul University	M
DEREE - The American College of Greece	M
DeVry University	M
Drake University	M
Drexel University	M
Drury University	M
Duquesne University	M,D
Eastern Michigan University	M
Eastern New Mexico University	M
Eastern University	M,O
Eastern Washington University	M
East Tennessee State University	M
Edinboro University of Pennsylvania	M
Emerson College	M
Fairfield University	M
Fairleigh Dickinson University, Metropolitan Campus	M
Fitchburg State University	M,O
Florida Institute of Technology	M
Florida International University	M
Florida State University	M,D
Fort Hays State University	M
George Mason University	M,D,O
Georgetown University	M
The George Washington University	M*
Georgia State University	M,D
Governors State University	M
Grand Valley State University	M
Harvard University	M,O*
Hawai`i Pacific University	M
Hofstra University	M
Howard University	M,D
Illinois Institute of Technology	M,D
Illinois State University	M
Indiana State University	M
Indiana University Bloomington	M,D
Indiana University of Pennsylvania	M,D
Indiana University–Purdue University Fort Wayne	M
Indiana University–Purdue University Indianapolis	M,D
Instituto Tecnologico de Santo Domingo	M,O
Instituto Tecnológico y de Estudios Superiores de Monterrey, Campus Ciudad Obregón	M
Instituto Tecnológico y de Estudios Superiores de Monterrey, Campus Monterrey	M,D
International University in Geneva	M,D
James Madison University	M
Johns Hopkins University	M
Kansas State University	M,D
Kean University	M
Kennesaw State University	M
Kent State University	M,D
La Salle University	M,O
Lasell College	M,O
La Sierra University	M
Liberty University	M
Lindenwood University	M,O
Lindenwood University–Belleville	M
Louisiana State University and Agricultural & Mechanical College	M,D
Loyola University Chicago	M
Lynn University	M,O
Marist College	M
Marquette University	M,O
Marshall University	M
Marywood University	M
McGill University	M,D
Michigan State University	M,D
Minnesota State University Mankato	M,O
Mississippi College	M
Missouri State University	M,O
Monmouth University	M,O
Montana State University Billings	M
Moore College of Art & Design	M
Morehead State University	M
New Mexico State University	M
New York Institute of Technology	M
New York University	M,D
Norfolk State University	M
North Carolina State University	M
North Dakota State University	M,D
Northeastern State University	M
Northern Arizona University	M
Northern Illinois University	M
Northern Kentucky University	M,O
Northwestern University	M,D*
Notre Dame of Maryland University	M
The Ohio State University	M,D
Ohio University	M,D
Penn State Harrisburg	M,D,O
Penn State University Park	M,D
Pepperdine University	M
Pittsburg State University	M
Point Park University	M
Purdue University	M,D
Purdue University Northwest	M
Queen's University at Kingston	M,D
Queens University of Charlotte	M
Quincy University	M
Quinnipiac University	M
Regent University	M,D
Rochester Institute of Technology	M,O
Roosevelt University	M
Rutgers University–New Brunswick	D
Sacred Heart University	M
Saginaw Valley State University	M
Saint Louis University	M
St. Mary's University (United States)	M,O
St. Thomas University	M,D,O
Sam Houston State University	M
San Diego State University	M
San Jose State University	M,O
Seton Hall University	M
Shippensburg University of Pennsylvania	M
Simmons College	M
Simon Fraser University	M,D
South Dakota State University	M
Southeastern Louisiana University	M
Southern Illinois University Carbondale	M,D
Southern Utah University	M
Spring Arbor University	M
Stanford University	M,D
State University of New York College at Potsdam	M
Stephen F. Austin State University	M
Stevens Institute of Technology	M,D,O
Stevenson University	M
Suffolk University	M
Summit University	M,D
Syracuse University	M,D
Tarleton State University	M
Teachers College, Columbia University	M,D
Temple University	M,D*
Texas A&M University	M,D
Texas A&M University–Corpus Christi	M
Texas Christian University	M
Texas Southern University	M
Texas State University	M
Texas Tech University	M
Tiffin University	M
Towson University	M
Trinity International University	M
Trinity Washington University	M
Troy University	M
Université de Montréal	M,D

Université du Québec à Montréal	M,D
Université du Québec à Trois-Rivières	M,O
University at Albany, State University of New York	M,D
University at Buffalo, the State University of New York	M,D*
The University of Akron	M
The University of Alabama	M,D
The University of Alabama at Birmingham	M
University of Alaska Fairbanks	M
University of Alberta	M
The University of Arizona	M,D
University of Arkansas	M
University of Bridgeport	M
University of Calgary	M,D
University of California, Davis	M
University of California, San Diego	D
University of California, Santa Barbara	D
University of California, Santa Cruz	O
University of Central Florida	M,O
University of Central Missouri	M,D,O
University of Cincinnati	M
University of Colorado Boulder	M,D
University of Colorado Colorado Springs	M
University of Colorado Denver	M
University of Connecticut	M*
University of Dayton	M
University of Delaware	M*
University of Denver	M,D,O
University of Dubuque	M
University of Florida	M,D
University of Georgia	M,D
University of Hartford	M
University of Hawaii at Manoa	M,O
University of Houston	M
University of Illinois at Chicago	M,D
University of Illinois at Springfield	M
University of Illinois at Urbana–Champaign	M,D
The University of Iowa	M,D*
The University of Kansas	M,D*
University of Kentucky	M,D
University of Louisiana at Lafayette	M
University of Louisiana at Monroe	M
University of Louisville	M
University of Maine	M,D
University of Maryland, Baltimore County	M
University of Maryland, College Park	M,D
University of Massachusetts Amherst	M,D*
University of Memphis	M,D
University of Miami	M,D
University of Michigan	D
University of Michigan–Flint	M
University of Minnesota, Twin Cities Campus	M,D,O
University of Missouri	M,D
University of Missouri–St. Louis	M
University of Montana	M
University of Nebraska at Omaha	M,O
University of Nebraska–Lincoln	M,D
University of Nevada, Las Vegas	M
University of New Mexico	M,D
The University of North Carolina at Chapel Hill	D
The University of North Carolina at Charlotte	M
The University of North Carolina at Greensboro	M
University of North Dakota	M,D
University of Northern Colorado	M
University of Northern Iowa	M
University of North Texas	M,D,O
University of Oklahoma	M,D*
University of Oregon	M,D
University of Ottawa	M
University of Pennsylvania	D*
University of Pittsburgh	M,D*
University of Portland	M
University of Puerto Rico, Río Piedras Campus	M
University of Rhode Island	M
University of San Francisco	M
University of South Africa	M,D
University of South Alabama	M
The University of South Dakota	M
University of Southern California	M,D
University of Southern Indiana	M
University of South Florida	M,D
The University of Tennessee	M,D
The University of Tennessee at Martin	M
The University of Texas at Arlington	M
The University of Texas at Austin	M,D
The University of Texas at Dallas	M,D*
The University of Texas at El Paso	M
The University of Texas at San Antonio	M
The University of Texas at Tyler	M
The University of Texas Rio Grande Valley	M,O
University of the Incarnate Word	M
University of the Pacific	M
University of the Sacred Heart	M,O
The University of Toledo	O
University of Utah	M,D*
University of Vermont	M
University of Washington	M,D*
University of West Florida	M
University of Windsor	M
University of Wisconsin–Madison	M,D
University of Wisconsin–Milwaukee	M,D,O
University of Wisconsin–Stevens Point	M
University of Wisconsin–Superior	M
University of Wisconsin–Whitewater	M
University of Wyoming	M
Utah State University	M
Valparaiso University	M,O
Villanova University	M
Virginia Commonwealth University	D
Virginia Polytechnic Institute and State University	M,D,O
Wake Forest University	M
Walden University	M,D,O
Washington State University	M,D
Wayne State College	M
Wayne State University	M,D,O
Weber State University	M
Webster University	M
West Chester University of Pennsylvania	M
Western Illinois University	M
Western Kentucky University	M,O
Western Michigan University	M
Western New England University	M
Westminster College (UT)	M
West Texas A&M University	M
West Virginia University	M,D
Wichita State University	M
Wilfrid Laurier University	M
William Paterson University of New Jersey	M
York University	M,D

COMMUNICATION DISORDERS

Abilene Christian University	M
Adelphi University	M,D
Alabama Agricultural and Mechanical University	M
Andrews University	M
Appalachian State University	M
Arizona State University at the Tempe campus	M,D
Arkansas State University	M,O
Armstrong State University	M
A.T. Still University	M,D
Auburn University	M,D
Baldwin Wallace University	M
Ball State University	M,D
Barry University	M
Baylor University	M
Biola University	M,O
Bloomsburg University of Pennsylvania	M,D
Boston University	M,D
Bowling Green State University	M,D
Brigham Young University	M
Brooklyn College of the City University of New York	M,D
Buffalo State College, State University of New York	M
California Baptist University	M
California State University, Chico	M
California State University, East Bay	M
California State University, Fresno	M
California State University, Fullerton	M
California State University, Long Beach	M
California State University, Los Angeles	M
California State University, Northridge	M
California State University, Sacramento	M
California State University, San Marcos	M
California University of Pennsylvania	M
Canisius College	M,O
Carlos Albizu University	M,D
Carlos Albizu University, Miami Campus	M,D
Case Western Reserve University	M,D*
Central Michigan University	M,D
Chapman University	M
Clarion University of Pennsylvania	M
Cleveland State University	M
The College of Saint Rose	M
Dalhousie University	M,D
Duquesne University	M,D
East Carolina University	M,D
Eastern Illinois University	M
Eastern Kentucky University	M
Eastern Michigan University	M
Eastern New Mexico University	M
Eastern Washington University	M
East Stroudsburg University of Pennsylvania	M
East Tennessee State University	M,D
Edinboro University of Pennsylvania	M
Elmhurst College	M
Elms College	M,O
Emerson College	M
Florida Atlantic University	M
Florida International University	M
Florida State University	M,D
Fontbonne University	M
Fort Hays State University	M
Gallaudet University	M,D,O
The George Washington University	M*
Georgia State University	M,D
Governors State University	M
The Graduate Center, City University of New York	D
Grand Valley State University	M
Hampton University	M
Harding University	M
Hofstra University	M,D
Howard University	M,D
Hunter College of the City University of New York	M
Idaho State University	M,D,O
Illinois State University	M
Indiana State University	M,D,O
Indiana University Bloomington	M,D
Indiana University of Pennsylvania	M
Iona College	M
Ithaca College	M
Jackson State University	M
Jacksonville University	M*
James Madison University	M,D
Kansas State University	M,O
Kean University	M
Kent State University	M,D,O
Lamar University	M,D
La Salle University	M
Lehman College of the City University of New York	M
Lewis & Clark College	M
Lindenwood University	M,D,O
Loma Linda University	M,D
Long Island University–LIU Brooklyn	M,D,O
Long Island University–LIU Post	M,D,O
Longwood University	M
Louisiana State University and Agricultural & Mechanical College	M,D
Louisiana State University Health Sciences Center	M,D
Louisiana Tech University	M,D
Loyola University Maryland	M
Marquette University	M,O
Marshall University	M
Marywood University	M
Massachusetts Institute of Technology	M,D
McGill University	M,D
Mercy College	M
MGH Institute of Health Professions	M,O
Miami University	M
Michigan State University	M,D
Minnesota State University Mankato	M
Minnesota State University Moorhead	M,O
Minot State University	M
Misericordia University	M
Mississippi University for Women	M,O
Molloy College	M
Monmouth University	M,O
Montclair State University	M,D
Murray State University	M
National University	M,O
Nazareth College of Rochester	M
New Mexico State University	M,D,O
New York Medical College	M
New York University	M,D
North Carolina Central University	M
Northeastern State University	M
Northeastern University	M,D,O
Northern Arizona University	M
Northern Illinois University	M,D
Northwestern University	M,D*
Nova Southeastern University	M,D*
The Ohio State University	M,D
Ohio University	M,D
Oklahoma State University	M
Old Dominion University	M
Our Lady of the Lake University of San Antonio	M
Pacific University	M,D
Penn State University Park	M,D,O
Portland State University	M
Purdue University	M,D
Queens College of the City University of New York	M
Radford University	M
Rockhurst University	M
Rocky Mountain University of Health Professions	D
Rush University	M,D
Sacred Heart University	M
St. Ambrose University	M
St. Cloud State University	M
St. John's University (NY)	M,D
Saint Louis University	M
Saint Mary's College	M
Saint Xavier University	M
Salus University	D
Samford University	M,D
San Diego State University	M,D
San Francisco State University	M
San Jose State University	M,D,O
Seton Hall University	M
South Carolina State University	M
Southeastern Louisiana University	M
Southeast Missouri State University	M
Southern Connecticut State University	M
Southern Illinois University Carbondale	M
Southern Illinois University Edwardsville	M
State University of New York at Fredonia	M
State University of New York at New Paltz	M
State University of New York at Plattsburgh	M
Stephen F. Austin State University	M
Stockton University	M
Syracuse University	M,D
Teachers College, Columbia University	M,D,O
Temple University	M,D*
Tennessee State University	M
Texas A&M University–Kingsville	M
Texas Christian University	M
Texas State University	M
Texas Tech University Health Sciences Center	M,D
Texas Woman's University	M
Touro College	M,D
Towson University	M,D
Truman State University	M
Universidad del Turabo	M
Université de Montréal	M,O
Université Laval	M
University at Buffalo, the State University of New York	M,D*
The University of Akron	M,D
The University of Alabama	M
University of Alberta	M,D
The University of Arizona	M,D,O
University of Arkansas	M
University of Arkansas for Medical Sciences	M,D
The University of British Columbia	M,D
University of California, San Diego	D
University of Central Arkansas	M,D
University of Central Florida	M,D,O
University of Central Missouri	M,D,O
University of Central Oklahoma	M
University of Cincinnati	M,D,O
University of Colorado Boulder	M,D
University of Connecticut	M,D*
University of Florida	M,D
University of Georgia	M,D,O
University of Hawaii at Manoa	M
University of Houston	M
University of Illinois at Urbana–Champaign	M,D
The University of Iowa	M,D*
The University of Kansas	M,D*
University of Kentucky	M
University of Louisiana at Lafayette	M,D
University of Louisiana at Monroe	M
University of Louisville	M,D
University of Maine	M
The University of Manchester	M,D
University of Maryland, College Park	M,D
University of Massachusetts Amherst	M,D*
University of Memphis	M,D
University of Minnesota, Duluth	M
University of Minnesota, Twin Cities Campus	M,D
University of Mississippi	M,D
University of Missouri	M,D
University of Montevallo	M
University of Nebraska at Kearney	M
University of Nebraska at Omaha	M
University of Nebraska–Lincoln	M,D
University of Nevada, Reno	M,D
University of New Hampshire	M
University of New Mexico	M
The University of North Carolina at Chapel Hill	M,D
The University of North Carolina at Greensboro	M,D
University of North Dakota	M,D
University of Northern Colorado	M,D
University of Northern Iowa	M
University of North Florida	M
University of North Texas	M,D,O
University of Oklahoma Health Sciences Center	M,D,O
University of Ottawa	M
University of Pittsburgh	M,D*
University of Puerto Rico, Medical Sciences Campus	M,D
University of Redlands	M
University of Rhode Island	M
University of San Diego	M
University of South Alabama	M,D
University of South Carolina	M,D
The University of South Dakota	M,D
University of Southern Mississippi	M,D
University of South Florida	M,D,O
The University of Tennessee	M,D,O
The University of Tennessee Health Science Center	M,D
The University of Texas at Austin	M,D
The University of Texas at Dallas	M,D*
The University of Texas at El Paso	M
The University of Texas Health Science Center at San Antonio	M,D
The University of Texas Rio Grande Valley	M
University of the District of Columbia	M
University of the Pacific	M
The University of Toledo	M,D
University of Toronto	M,D
The University of Tulsa	M
University of Utah	M,D*
University of Vermont	M
University of Virginia	M
University of Washington	M,D*
The University of Western Ontario	M
University of West Georgia	M,D,O
University of Wisconsin–Eau Claire	M

*M—masters degree; D—doctorate; O—other advanced degree; *—Close-Up and/or Display*

University of Wisconsin–Madison	M,D
University of Wisconsin–Milwaukee	M,O
University of Wisconsin–River Falls	M
University of Wisconsin–Stevens Point	M,D
University of Wisconsin–Whitewater	M
University of Wyoming	M
Utah State University	M,D,O
Vanderbilt University	M,D*
Washington State University	M
Washington University in St. Louis	M,D
Wayne State University	M,D
Webster University	M
West Chester University of Pennsylvania	M
Western Carolina University	M
Western Illinois University	M
Western Kentucky University	M
Western Michigan University	M,D
Western Washington University	M
West Texas A&M University	M
West Virginia University	M,D
Wichita State University	M,D
William Paterson University of New Jersey	M,D
Worcester State University	M
Yeshiva University	M,D

COMMUNITY COLLEGE EDUCATION

Argosy University, Chicago	M,D,O
Argosy University, Denver	M,D
Argosy University, Inland Empire	M,D
Argosy University, Los Angeles	M,D
Argosy University, Orange County	M,D
Argosy University, Phoenix	M,D,O
Argosy University, San Diego	M,D
Argosy University, San Francisco Bay Area	M,D
Argosy University, Seattle	M,D
Argosy University, Tampa	M,D,O
Argosy University, Washington DC	M,D,O
Arkansas State University	M,D,O
California State University, Fullerton	M,D
California State University, San Bernardino	M
California State University, Stanislaus	D
Central Michigan University	M,D,O
Drew University	M,D,O
East Carolina University	M,D,O
Eastern Illinois University	M
Eastern Michigan University	M,D,O
Elizabeth City State University	M
Ferris State University	D
Florida State University	M
George Mason University	M,D,O
Lenoir-Rhyne University	M
Marymount University	M,O
Mississippi State University	M,D,O
Morgan State University	D
North Carolina State University	M,D
Northern Arizona University	M,D,O
Old Dominion University	M,D
University of Arkansas at Little Rock	M,D
University of Central Florida	M,D,O
University of Missouri–St. Louis	M,D,O
University of Northern Iowa	M
University of South Florida	M,D,O
Wingate University	M,D

COMMUNITY HEALTH

Adelphi University	M,O
American University of Beirut	M
Arcadia University	M
Arizona State University at the Tempe campus	M,D,O
Baylor University	M,D
Bloomsburg University of Pennsylvania	M
Boston University	M,D
Brooklyn College of the City University of New York	M
Brown University	M,D
Canisius College	M,O
Columbia University	M,D*
Daemen College	M
Dalhousie University	M
East Carolina University	M,O
Eastern Kentucky University	M
George Mason University	M,O
The George Washington University	M,D*
Georgia Southern University	M,D
Hofstra University	M
Hunter College of the City University of New York	M
Icahn School of Medicine at Mount Sinai	M,D
Idaho State University	O
Independence University	M
Indiana University Bloomington	M,D
Indiana University–Purdue University Indianapolis	M,D
Johns Hopkins University	M,D
Louisiana State University Health Sciences Center	M,D
McGill University	M,D,O
Medical College of Wisconsin	M,D,O
Meharry Medical College	M
Memorial University of Newfoundland	M,D,O
Merrimack College	M
Midwestern State University	M,O
Minnesota State University Mankato	M,O
New Jersey City University	M
New York University	M,D
Northeastern University	M,D,O
Old Dominion University	M
Quinnipiac University	D
Saint Louis University	M
Southern Illinois University Carbondale	M
Southern New Hampshire University	M,O
State University of New York College at Cortland	M
State University of New York College at Potsdam	M
State University of New York Downstate Medical Center	M
Stony Brook University, State University of New York	M,D,O
Teachers College, Columbia University	M,D,O
Texas A&M University	M,D
Tulane University	M,D
Universidad de Ciencias Medicas	M,D,O
Université de Montréal	M,D,O
Université Laval	M,D,O
University at Buffalo, the State University of New York	M,D*
The University of Alabama	M
The University of Alabama at Birmingham	M
University of Alberta	M,D
University of Arkansas	M,D
University of Calgary	M,D
University of California, Los Angeles	M,D
University of Colorado Denver	M,D
University of Illinois at Chicago	M,D
University of Illinois at Springfield	M,O
University of Illinois at Urbana–Champaign	M,D
The University of Iowa	M,D*
University of Louisville	M
University of Manitoba	M,D,O
University of Massachusetts Amherst	M,D*
University of Massachusetts Medical School	M,D,O
University of Miami	D
University of Minnesota, Twin Cities Campus	M
University of Missouri	M,D
University of Montana	M
University of Nevada, Las Vegas	M,D
University of New Mexico	M
The University of North Carolina at Charlotte	M,D,O
The University of North Carolina at Greensboro	M,D
University of Northern British Columbia	M,D,O
University of Northern Iowa	M
University of North Florida	M,O
University of North Texas Health Science Center at Fort Worth	M,D
University of Ottawa	M,D,O
University of Phoenix–Central Valley Campus	M
University of Phoenix–Hawaii Campus	M
University of Pittsburgh	M,D,O*
University of Saskatchewan	M,D
University of South Florida	M,D,O
The University of Tennessee	M,D
The University of Texas Medical Branch	M,D
University of Toronto	M,D
University of Virginia	M,D
University of Washington	M,D*
University of West Florida	M
University of Wisconsin–La Crosse	M
University of Wisconsin–Madison	M,D
University of Wyoming	M,D
Virginia Commonwealth University	M,D
Virginia State University	M,D
Walden University	M,D,O
Washington State University	M,D,O
West Chester University of Pennsylvania	M,O
West Virginia University	M,D
William James College	M,D,O

COMMUNITY HEALTH NURSING

Allen College	M,D,O
Cleveland State University	M,D
Hampton University	M,D
Holy Names University	M,O
Hunter College of the City University of New York	M
Husson University	M,O
Independence University	M
Kean University	M
La Salle University	M,D,O
Louisiana State University Health Sciences Center	M,D,O
New Mexico State University	M,D
Oregon Health & Science University	M,O
Rush University	D
San Francisco State University	M,O
Seattle University	M
University of Cincinnati	M,D
University of Hartford	M
University of Hawaii at Manoa	M,D,O
University of Illinois at Chicago	M,O
The University of Kansas	M,D,O*
University of Maryland, Baltimore	M
University of Massachusetts Amherst	M,D*
University of Massachusetts Dartmouth	M,D
University of Minnesota, Twin Cities Campus	M
The University of North Carolina at Charlotte	M,D,O
University of North Dakota	M,D
University of Puerto Rico, Medical Sciences Campus	M
University of South Carolina	M
The University of Texas at Austin	M,D
The University of Texas Health Science Center at San Antonio	M,D,O
The University of Toledo	M,O
University of Washington, Tacoma	M
Worcester State University	M
Wright State University	M

COMPARATIVE AND INTERDISCIPLINARY ARTS

Bradley University	M
Brigham Young University	M
Columbia College Chicago	M
Florida Atlantic University	M
Goddard College	M
John F. Kennedy University	M
Ohio University	D
Simon Fraser University	M

COMPARATIVE LITERATURE

American University	M
The American University in Cairo	M,O
Antioch University Midwest	M
Arizona State University at the Tempe campus	M,D,O
Binghamton University, State University of New York	M,D*
Brigham Young University	M
Brock University	M
Brown University	D
California State University, Northridge	M
Carleton University	D
Carnegie Mellon University	M,D
Case Western Reserve University	M*
Claremont Graduate University	M,D
Columbia University	M,D*
Cornell University	D
Dartmouth College	M*
Duke University	D*
East Carolina University	M,D,O
Emory University	D,O
Fairleigh Dickinson University, Metropolitan Campus	M
Florida Atlantic University	M
Georgetown University	M,D
The Graduate Center, City University of New York	M,D
Harrison Middleton University	M,D
Harvard University	D*
Indiana University Bloomington	M,D
Johns Hopkins University	D
La Salle University	M,O
Louisiana State University and Agricultural & Mechanical College	M,D
New York University	M,D
Northwestern University	M,D*
Penn State University Park	M,D
Princeton University	D
Purdue University	M,D
Rutgers University–New Brunswick	M,D
San Francisco State University	M
Stanford University	D
Stony Brook University, State University of New York	M,D,O
Université de Montréal	M,D
Université de Sherbrooke	M,D
Université du Québec à Chicoutimi	M
Université du Québec à Montréal	M,D
Université du Québec à Rimouski	M,D
Université du Québec à Trois-Rivières	M
Université Laval	M,D
University at Buffalo, the State University of New York	M,D*
University of Arkansas	M,D
University of California, Berkeley	D
University of California, Davis	D
University of California, Irvine	M,D
University of California, Los Angeles	M,D
University of California, Riverside	M,D
University of California, Santa Barbara	D
University of California, Santa Cruz	M,D
University of Chicago	M,D
University of Colorado Boulder	M,D
University of Dallas	D
University of Georgia	M,D
University of Guelph	D
University of Houston	M
University of Illinois at Urbana–Champaign	M,D
University of Maryland, College Park	M,D
University of Massachusetts Amherst	M,D*
University of Memphis	M,D,O
University of Michigan	D
University of Minnesota, Twin Cities Campus	D
University of Missouri	M,D
University of Nebraska–Lincoln	M,D
University of New Hampshire	M,D
University of New Mexico	M,D
University of Notre Dame	D
University of Oregon	M,D
University of Pennsylvania	M,D*
University of Puerto Rico, Río Piedras Campus	M
University of South Carolina	M,D
University of Southern California	D
University of South Florida	O
The University of Texas at Austin	M,D
The University of Texas at Dallas	M,D*
University of Toronto	M,D
University of Utah	M,D*
University of Washington	M,D*
The University of Western Ontario	M,D
University of Wisconsin–Madison	M,D
University of Wisconsin–Milwaukee	M,D,O
Washington University in St. Louis	M,D
Western Kentucky University	M
Yale University	D*

COMPUTATIONAL BIOLOGY

Albert Einstein College of Medicine	D
Baylor College of Medicine	D
Carnegie Mellon University	M,D
Claremont Graduate University	M,D
The College of William and Mary	M,D
Cornell University	D
Duke University	D,O*
Florida State University	D
Harvard University	M*
Iowa State University of Science and Technology	M,D
Massachusetts Institute of Technology	D
New Jersey Institute of Technology	M,D,O
New York University	D
Princeton University	D
Rutgers University–Camden	M,D
Rutgers University–Newark	M
Rutgers University–New Brunswick	D
University of California, Irvine	D
University of Colorado Denver	M,D
University of Idaho	M,D
University of Illinois at Urbana–Champaign	M,D
The University of Iowa	M,D,O*
The University of Kansas	D*
University of Maryland, College Park	D
University of Massachusetts Medical School	M,D
The University of North Carolina at Chapel Hill	D
University of Pennsylvania	D*
University of Pittsburgh	D*
University of Rochester	D*
University of Southern California	D
University of South Florida	M,D
The University of Texas Medical Branch	D
University of Wyoming	D
Washington University in St. Louis	D
Wayne State University	M,D,O
Weill Cornell Medicine	D
Worcester Polytechnic Institute	M,D
Yale University	D*

COMPUTATIONAL SCIENCES

American University of Beirut	M,D
California Institute of Technology	M,D
Chapman University	M,D
Claremont Graduate University	M,D
The College of William and Mary	M
Cornell University	M,D
Emory University	D
Florida State University	M,D
Georgia Institute of Technology	M,D
Hampton University	M
Harvard University	M,D*
Lehigh University	M,D
Marquette University	M,D
Massachusetts Institute of Technology	M
McGill University	M,D
Memorial University of Newfoundland	M
Michigan Technological University	M,D,O
Middle Tennessee State University	D
North Carolina Agricultural and Technical State University	M
The Ohio State University	M,D
Oregon State University	M,D
Princeton University	D
Purdue University	M,D
Rice University	M,D
Sam Houston State University	M,D
San Diego State University	M,D
San Jose State University	M,O
Simon Fraser University	M,D
South Dakota State University	M,D
Southern Illinois University Edwardsville	M
Southern Methodist University	M,D
Stanford University	M,D
Stockton University	M
Temple University	M,D*
University at Buffalo, the State University of New York	O*
The University of Alabama at Birmingham	D
University of Alaska Fairbanks	M,D
University of California, San Diego	M,D
University of California, Santa Barbara	M,D
University of Chicago	M
University of Colorado Denver	M,D
The University of Iowa	D*
The University of Kansas	M,D*
University of Lethbridge	M,D
University of Manitoba	M
University of Massachusetts Dartmouth	D
University of Michigan–Dearborn	M
University of Minnesota, Duluth	M
University of Minnesota, Twin Cities Campus	M,D
University of Notre Dame	M,D
University of Pennsylvania	M,D*
University of Puerto Rico, Mayagüez Campus	M
University of Southern Mississippi	M,D

The University of Tennessee at Chattanooga	M,D
The University of Texas at Austin	M,D
The University of Texas at El Paso	M,D
University of Utah	M*
University of Washington	M,D*
Valparaiso University	M
Western Kentucky University	M
Western Michigan University	M,D

COMPUTER AND INFORMATION SYSTEMS SECURITY

American InterContinental University Online	M
American Public University System	M
Armstrong State University	M,O
Auburn University at Montgomery	M
Bay Path University	M
Benedictine University	M
Boston University	M,D,O
Brandeis University	M
California State University, San Bernardino	M
Capella University	M,D
Capitol Technology University	M
Carlow University	M
Carnegie Mellon University	M
Central Michigan University	O
Champlain College	M
City University of Seattle	M,O
Claremont Graduate University	M,D,O
Colorado Christian University	M
Colorado Technical University Colorado Springs	M,D
Colorado Technical University Denver South	M
Columbus State University	M,O
Concordia University (Canada)	M,D,O
Concordia University, Nebraska	M
Concordia University of Edmonton	M
Concordia University, St. Paul	M
Dakota State University	M,D,O
Davenport University	M
DePaul University	M,D
DeSales University	M,D,O
East Carolina University	M,D,O
Eastern Illinois University	M,O
Eastern Michigan University	O
East Stroudsburg University of Pennsylvania	M
EC-Council University	M
Embry-Riddle Aeronautical University–Daytona	M,D*
Fairfield University	M,O
Ferris State University	M
Florida Institute of Technology	M
Florida State University	M,D
Fordham University	M
George Mason University	M
The George Washington University	M,D,O*
Georgia Institute of Technology	M
Hampton University	M
Hofstra University	M
Hood College	M,O
Illinois Institute of Technology	M,D
Indiana University Bloomington	M,D
Inter American University of Puerto Rico, Guayama Campus	M
Iona College	M
James Madison University	M
John Marshall Law School	M,D
Johns Hopkins University	M,O
Kaplan University, Davenport Campus	M
Keiser University	M
Kennesaw State University	M,O
Kent State University	M,O
Lewis University	M
Liberty University	M,D,O
Lindenwood University	M,O
Lipscomb University	M,O
London Metropolitan University	M,D
Long Island University–Riverhead	M,O
Loyola University Maryland	O
Marymount University	M,O
Maryville University of Saint Louis	M,O
Marywood University	M
Mercy College	M
Mercyhurst University	M
Metropolitan State University	M,D,O
Middle Georgia State University	M
Missouri State University	M
Missouri Western State University	M
National University	M,O
Naval Postgraduate School	M,D
New Jersey Institute of Technology	M,D,O
New York Institute of Technology	M
New York University	O
Northeastern University	M,D,O
Northern Kentucky University	M,O
Northwestern University	M*
Norwich University	M
Nova Southeastern University	M,D*
Our Lady of the Lake University of San Antonio	M
Pace University	M,D,O
Penn State Great Valley	M,O
Purdue University	M
Regis University	M,O
Robert Morris University	M,D
Robert Morris University Illinois	M
Rochester Institute of Technology	M,O
Roger Williams University	M
Rowan University	O
Sacred Heart University	M,O
St. Cloud State University	M
Saint Leo University	M
St. Mary's University (United States)	M
Salem International University	M
Salve Regina University	M,O
Sam Houston State University	M,D
San Jose State University	M,O
Shippensburg University of Pennsylvania	M
State University of New York Polytechnic Institute	M
Stevens Institute of Technology	M,D,O
Stevenson University	M
Stratford University (VA)	M,D
Strayer University	M
Syracuse University	M,O
Texas A&M University–San Antonio	M
Towson University	M,D,O
Trident University International	M,D
Tuskegee University	M
Universidad del Este	M
Université de Sherbrooke	M
University at Albany, State University of New York	M
University of Advancing Technology	M
The University of Alabama at Birmingham	M
The University of Alabama in Huntsville	M,D,O
University of Colorado Colorado Springs	M,D
University of Dallas	M,D
University of Dayton	M
University of Detroit Mercy	M,D,O
University of Houston	M
University of Louisville	M,D,O
University of Maryland, Baltimore County	M,O
University of Maryland University College	M,O
University of Minnesota, Twin Cities Campus	M
University of Missouri–St. Louis	M,D,O
University of Nebraska at Omaha	M,D,O
University of New Haven	M,D,O
University of New Mexico	M
The University of North Carolina at Charlotte	M,D,O
University of Pittsburgh	M,D,O*
University of Rhode Island	M,D,O
University of St. Thomas (MN)	M,O
University of Southern California	M,D
University of South Florida	M
The University of Texas at Austin	M,D
The University of Texas at San Antonio	M,D,O
University of Utah	M,O*
University of Wisconsin–Madison	M
Utica College	M
Valparaiso University	M
Virginia International University	M,O
Virginia Polytechnic Institute and State University	M,O
Walden University	M,D,O
West Chester University of Pennsylvania	M,O
Western Governors University	M
Wilmington University	M

COMPUTER ART AND DESIGN

Academy of Art University	M
Alfred University	M
Art Center College of Design	M
The Art Institute of California–San Francisco, a campus of Argosy University	M
Bowling Green State University	M
California College of the Arts	M
Carnegie Mellon University	M
Chatham University	M
City College of the City University of New York	M
Claremont Graduate University	M
Clemson University	M
Concordia University (Canada)	M,O
Cornell University	M,D
DePaul University	M,D
DigiPen Institute of Technology	M
Digital Media Arts College	M
Drexel University	M
East Tennessee State University	M,O
Emily Carr University of Art + Design	M
Full Sail University	M
Georgia Institute of Technology	M,D
Georgian Court University	M,O
Goucher College	M
Indiana University Bloomington	M,D,O
International Technological University	M
Lindenwood University–Belleville	M
Lynn University	M,O
Michigan State University	M
Minneapolis College of Art and Design	O
New Mexico Highlands University	M
The New School	M
New York Institute of Technology	M
New York University	M
North Carolina Agricultural and Technical State University	M
North Carolina State University	D
The Ohio State University	M
Old Dominion University	M
Purdue University	M,D
Rensselaer Polytechnic Institute	M,D
Rhode Island School of Design	M
Rochester Institute of Technology	M
Savannah College of Art and Design	M,O
School of Visual Arts (NY)	M
Shepherd University (CA)	M
Stevens Institute of Technology	M,D,O
Syracuse University	M
Texas State University	M
Universidad Autonoma de Guadalajara	M,D
Universidad de las Américas Puebla	M
University of Alaska Fairbanks	M
University of California, Santa Cruz	M,D
University of Central Arkansas	M
University of Central Florida	M
University of Denver	M
University of Florida	M,D
The University of Kansas	M*
University of Maryland, Baltimore County	M
University of Massachusetts Dartmouth	M,O
University of Montana	M
University of Pennsylvania	M,D*
University of Rhode Island	M
University of Southern California	M
University of South Florida, St. Petersburg	M
University of Victoria	M
Virginia International University	M,O

COMPUTER EDUCATION

Arcadia University	M,D,O
Ball State University	M,D,O
Clarkson University	M,O
Eastern Washington University	M
Florida Institute of Technology	M
Illinois Institute of Technology	M,D
Indiana University–Purdue University Indianapolis	M,O
Kent State University	M,D
Lesley University	M,D,O
Marlboro College	M,O
Mississippi College	M,D,O
Ohio University	M,D
Stony Brook University, State University of New York	M
Teachers College, Columbia University	M,D
Thomas College	M
Troy University	M
University of Bridgeport	M,D,O
University of Illinois at Chicago	D
University of Mary Hardin-Baylor	M
University of Phoenix–Central Valley Campus	M
University of Phoenix–North Florida Campus	M
University of Phoenix–Online Campus	M,O
University of Phoenix–San Diego Campus	M
University of Phoenix–South Florida Campus	M
University of Phoenix–Washington D.C. Campus	M,D,O
Wright State University	M

COMPUTER ENGINEERING

Air Force Institute of Technology	M,D
American University of Beirut	M,D
American University of Sharjah	M
Arizona State University at the Tempe campus	M,D
Auburn University	M,D
Baylor University	M,D
Boise State University	M,D
Boston University	M,D,O
Brigham Young University	M,D
Brown University	M,D
California State University, Chico	M
California State University, Fullerton	M
California State University, Long Beach	M
Carnegie Mellon University	M,D
Case Western Reserve University	M,D*
Clarkson University	M,D
Clemson University	M,D
Colorado Technical University Colorado Springs	M
Colorado Technical University Denver South	M
Columbia University	M,D*
Concordia University (Canada)	M,D
Cornell University	M,D
Dalhousie University	M,D
Dartmouth College	M,D*
Drexel University	M
Duke University	M,D*
East Carolina University	M,D,O
École Polytechnique de Montréal	M,D,O
Embry-Riddle Aeronautical University–Daytona	M,D*
Fairfield University	M,O
Fairleigh Dickinson University, Metropolitan Campus	M
Florida Atlantic University	M,D
Florida Institute of Technology	M,D
Florida International University	M,D
George Mason University	M,D,O
The George Washington University	M,D,O*
Georgia Institute of Technology	M,D
Grand Valley State University	M
Illinois Institute of Technology	M,D
Indiana State University	M
Indiana University–Purdue University Fort Wayne	M
Indiana University–Purdue University Indianapolis	M,D
Instituto Tecnológico y de Estudios Superiores de Monterrey, Campus Chihuahua	M,O
International Technological University	M
Iowa State University of Science and Technology	M,D
Johns Hopkins University	M,D,O
Kansas State University	M,D
Kennesaw State University	M
Lakehead University	M
Lawrence Technological University	M,D
Lehigh University	M,D
Louisiana State University and Agricultural & Mechanical College	M,D
Manhattan College	M
Marquette University	M,D,O
Massachusetts Institute of Technology	M,D,O
McGill University	M,D
Memorial University of Newfoundland	M,D
Mercer University	M
Miami University	M
Michigan Technological University	M,D,O
Mississippi State University	M,D
Missouri University of Science and Technology	M,D
Montana State University	M,D
Naval Postgraduate School	M,D,O
New Jersey Institute of Technology	M,D
New Mexico State University	M,D,O
New York Institute of Technology	M
New York University	M,O
Norfolk State University	M
North Carolina Agricultural and Technical State University	M,D
North Carolina State University	M,D
North Dakota State University	M,D
Northeastern University	M,D,O
Northern Arizona University	M
Northwestern Polytechnic University	M,D
Northwestern University	M,D*
Oakland University	M,D
The Ohio State University	M,D
Oklahoma Christian University	M
Oklahoma State University	M,D
Old Dominion University	M,D
Oregon Health & Science University	M,D
Oregon State University	M,D
Polytechnic University of Puerto Rico	M
Portland State University	M,D
Purdue University	M,D
Purdue University Northwest	M
Queen's University at Kingston	M,D
Rensselaer at Hartford	M
Rensselaer Polytechnic Institute	M,D
Rice University	M,D
Rochester Institute of Technology	M
Rose-Hulman Institute of Technology	M
Royal Military College of Canada	M,D
Rutgers University–New Brunswick	M,D
St. Mary's University (United States)	M
Santa Clara University	M,D,O
Silicon Valley University	M
Southern Illinois University Carbondale	M,D
Southern Methodist University	M,D
Stevens Institute of Technology	M,D,O
Stony Brook University, State University of New York	M,D
Syracuse University	M,D
Tennessee State University	M,D
Texas A&M University	M,D
The University of Akron	M,D
The University of Alabama	M,D
The University of Alabama at Birmingham	D
The University of Alabama in Huntsville	M,D
University of Alberta	M,D
The University of Arizona	M,D
University of Arkansas	M,D
University of Bridgeport	M,D
The University of British Columbia	M,D
University of Calgary	M,D
University of California, Davis	M,D
University of California, Riverside	M
University of California, San Diego	M,D
University of California, Santa Barbara	M,D
University of California, Santa Cruz	M,D
University of Central Florida	M,D
University of Cincinnati	M,D
University of Colorado Boulder	M,D
University of Dayton	M,D
University of Delaware	M,D*
University of Denver	M,D
University of Detroit Mercy	M,D
University of Florida	M,D
University of Houston–Clear Lake	M
University of Idaho	M,D
University of Illinois at Chicago	M,D
University of Illinois at Urbana–Champaign	M,D
The University of Iowa	M,D*
The University of Kansas	M*
University of Louisiana at Lafayette	M,D
University of Louisville	M,D,O
University of Maine	M,D

*M—masters degree; D—doctorate; O—other advanced degree; *—Close-Up and/or Display*

University of Manitoba	M,D
University of Maryland, Baltimore County	M,D
University of Maryland, College Park	M,D
University of Massachusetts Amherst	M,D*
University of Massachusetts Dartmouth	M,D,O
University of Massachusetts Lowell	M,D
University of Memphis	M,D
University of Miami	M,D
University of Michigan	M,D
University of Michigan–Dearborn	M
University of Minnesota, Duluth	M
University of Minnesota, Twin Cities Campus	M,D
University of Missouri–Kansas City	M,D,O
University of Nebraska–Lincoln	M,D
University of Nevada, Las Vegas	M,D
University of Nevada, Reno	M,D
University of New Brunswick Fredericton	M,D
University of New Haven	M
University of New Mexico	M,D
The University of North Carolina at Charlotte	M,D
University of North Texas	M,D,O
University of Notre Dame	M,D
University of Oklahoma	M,D*
University of Ottawa	M,D
University of Pittsburgh	M,D*
University of Puerto Rico, Mayagüez Campus	M,D
University of Regina	M,D
University of Rhode Island	M,D
University of Rochester	M,D*
University of South Alabama	M
University of South Carolina	M,D
University of Southern California	M,D,O
University of South Florida	M,D
The University of Tennessee	M,D
The University of Texas at Arlington	M,D
The University of Texas at Austin	M,D
The University of Texas at Dallas	M,D*
The University of Texas at El Paso	M,D
The University of Texas at San Antonio	M,D
University of Toronto	M,D
The University of Tulsa	M,D
University of Victoria	M,D
University of Virginia	M,D
University of Washington, Bothell	M
University of Washington, Tacoma	M
University of Waterloo	M,D
The University of Western Ontario	M,D
University of Wisconsin–Milwaukee	M,D,O
Villanova University	M,O
Virginia Polytechnic Institute and State University	M,D,O
Washington State University	M,D
Washington University in St. Louis	M,D
Wayne State University	M,D
Western Michigan University	M,D
West Virginia University	D
Wichita State University	M,D
Worcester Polytechnic Institute	M,D,O
Wright State University	M,D
Youngstown State University	M

COMPUTER SCIENCE

Acadia University	M
Air Force Institute of Technology	M,D
Alabama Agricultural and Mechanical University	M
Alcorn State University	M
American Sentinel University	M
The American University in Cairo	M,O
American University of Armenia	M
American University of Beirut	M,D
Appalachian State University	M
Arizona State University at the Tempe campus	M,D
Arkansas State University	M
Armstrong State University	M
Auburn University	M,D
Ball State University	M
Baylor University	M,D
Binghamton University, State University of New York	M,D*
Boise State University	M,O
Boston University	M,D,O
Bowie State University	M,D
Bowling Green State University	M
Bradley University	M
Brandeis University	M
Bridgewater State University	M
Brigham Young University	M,D
Brock University	M
Brooklyn College of the City University of New York	M,O
Brown University	M,D
California Institute of Technology	M,D
California Polytechnic State University, San Luis Obispo	M
California State Polytechnic University, Pomona	M
California State University Channel Islands	M
California State University, Chico	M
California State University, Dominguez Hills	M
California State University, East Bay	M
California State University, Fresno	M
California State University, Fullerton	M
California State University, Long Beach	M
California State University, Los Angeles	M
California State University, Northridge	M
California State University, Sacramento	M
California State University, San Bernardino	M
California State University, San Marcos	M
Capitol Technology University	M
Carleton University	M,D
Carnegie Mellon University	M,D
Case Western Reserve University	M,D*
The Catholic University of America	M,D
Central Connecticut State University	M,O
Central Michigan University	M
Chicago State University	M
Christopher Newport University	M
The Citadel, The Military College of South Carolina	M
City College of the City University of New York	M,D
City University of Seattle	M,O
Clark Atlanta University	M
Clarkson University	M,D
Clemson University	M,D
Cleveland State University	M,D
Coastal Carolina University	M,D,O
College of Charleston	M
The College of Saint Rose	M,O
College of Staten Island of the City University of New York	M
The College of William and Mary	M,D
Colorado School of Mines	M,D
Colorado State University	M,D
Colorado Technical University Colorado Springs	M,D
Colorado Technical University Denver South	M
Columbia University	M,D*
Columbus State University	M,O
Concordia University (Canada)	M,D,O
Concordia University, Nebraska	M
Cornell University	M,D
Dakota State University	M,D,O
Dalhousie University	M,D
Dartmouth College	M,D*
DePaul University	M,D
DigiPen Institute of Technology	M
Drexel University	M,D
Duke University	M,D*
East Carolina University	M,D,O
Eastern Illinois University	M
Eastern Michigan University	M,O
Eastern Washington University	M
East Stroudsburg University of Pennsylvania	M
East Tennessee State University	M,O
École Polytechnique de Montréal	M,D,O
Emory University	M,D
Fairleigh Dickinson University, College at Florham	M
Fairleigh Dickinson University, Metropolitan Campus	M
Fitchburg State University	M
Florida Institute of Technology	M,D
Florida International University	M,D
Florida State University	M,D
Fontbonne University	M
Fordham University	M
Franklin University	M
Frostburg State University	M
Gannon University	M
George Mason University	M,D,O
Georgetown University	M,D
The George Washington University	M,D,O*
Georgia Institute of Technology	M,D
Georgia Southern University	M
Georgia Southwestern State University	M,O
Georgia State University	M,D
Governors State University	M
The Graduate Center, City University of New York	D
Grand Valley State University	M
Hampton University	M
Harvard University	M,D*
Hood College	M,O
Howard University	M
Illinois Institute of Technology	M,D
Indiana State University	M
Indiana University Bloomington	M,D
Indiana University–Purdue University Fort Wayne	M
Indiana University–Purdue University Indianapolis	M,D,O
Indiana University South Bend	M
Instituto Tecnológico y de Estudios Superiores de Monterrey, Campus Central de Veracruz	M
Instituto Tecnológico y de Estudios Superiores de Monterrey, Campus Ciudad de México	M,D
Instituto Tecnológico y de Estudios Superiores de Monterrey, Campus Cuernavaca	M,D
Instituto Tecnológico y de Estudios Superiores de Monterrey, Campus Estado de México	M,D
Instituto Tecnológico y de Estudios Superiores de Monterrey, Campus Irapuato	M,D
Instituto Tecnológico y de Estudios Superiores de Monterrey, Campus Monterrey	M,D
Inter American University of Puerto Rico, Fajardo Campus	M
Inter American University of Puerto Rico, Guayama Campus	M
Inter American University of Puerto Rico, Metropolitan Campus	M
Iona College	M
Iowa State University of Science and Technology	M,D
Jackson State University	M
Jacksonville State University	M
James Madison University	M
Johns Hopkins University	M,D,O
Kansas State University	M,D
Kennesaw State University	M
Kent State University	M,D
Kentucky State University	M
Knowledge Systems Institute	M
Kutztown University of Pennsylvania	M
Lakehead University	M
Lamar University	M
La Salle University	M,O
Lawrence Technological University	M
Lebanese American University	M
Lehigh University	M,D
Lehman College of the City University of New York	M
Long Island University–LIU Brooklyn	M,O
Louisiana State University and Agricultural & Mechanical College	M,D
Louisiana State University in Shreveport	M
Louisiana Tech University	M,D
Loyola University Chicago	M
Loyola University Maryland	M
Maharishi University of Management	M
Marist College	M,O
Marquette University	M,D
Marshall University	M
Massachusetts Institute of Technology	M,D,O
McGill University	M,D
McMaster University	M,D
McNeese State University	M
Memorial University of Newfoundland	M,D
Merrimack College	M
Metropolitan State University	M
Michigan State University	M,D
Michigan Technological University	M,D
Middle Tennessee State University	M
Midwestern State University	M
Mills College	M,O
Mississippi College	M
Mississippi State University	M,D
Missouri State University	M
Missouri University of Science and Technology	M,D
Monmouth University	M,O
Montana State University	M,D
Montclair State University	M,O
National University	M,O
Naval Postgraduate School	M,D,O
New Jersey Institute of Technology	M,D,O
New Mexico Highlands University	M
New Mexico Institute of Mining and Technology	M,D
New Mexico State University	M,D
New York Institute of Technology	M
New York University	M,D
Norfolk State University	M
North Carolina Agricultural and Technical State University	M
North Carolina State University	M,D
North Central College	M
Northeastern Illinois University	M
Northeastern University	M,D
Northern Arizona University	M
Northern Illinois University	M
Northern Kentucky University	M,O
Northwestern Polytechnic University	M,D
Northwestern University	M,D*
Northwest Missouri State University	M
Notre Dame College (OH)	M,O
Nova Southeastern University	M,D*
Oakland University	M,D
The Ohio State University	M,D
Ohio University	M,D
Oklahoma Christian University	M
Oklahoma City University	M
Oklahoma State University	M,D
Old Dominion University	M,D
Oregon Health & Science University	M,D
Oregon State University	M,D
Pace University	M,D,O
Pacific States University	M
Penn State Harrisburg	M,O
Penn State University Park	M,D
Polytechnic University of Puerto Rico	M
Portland State University	M,D
Prairie View A&M University	M,D
Princeton University	M,D
Purdue University	M,D
Purdue University Northwest	M
Queens College of the City University of New York	M
Queen's University at Kingston	M,D
Regis University	M,O
Rensselaer at Hartford	M
Rensselaer Polytechnic Institute	M,D
Rice University	M,D
Rivier University	M
Rochester Institute of Technology	M,D
Roosevelt University	M
Rowan University	M
Royal Military College of Canada	M
Rutgers University–Camden	M
Rutgers University–New Brunswick	M,D
Sacred Heart University	M,O
St. Cloud State University	M
St. Francis Xavier University	M
Saint Joseph's University	M,O
St. Mary's University (United States)	M
Saint Xavier University	M
Sam Houston State University	M,D
San Diego State University	M
San Francisco State University	M
San Jose State University	M,O
Santa Clara University	M,D,O
Seattle University	M
Shippensburg University of Pennsylvania	M
Silicon Valley University	M
Simon Fraser University	M,D
Sofia University	M,D
Southern Arkansas University–Magnolia	M
Southern Connecticut State University	M
Southern Illinois University Carbondale	M,D
Southern Illinois University Edwardsville	M
Southern Methodist University	M,D
Southern Oregon University	M
Southern University and Agricultural and Mechanical College	M
Stanford University	M,D
State University of New York at New Paltz	M
State University of New York Polytechnic Institute	M
Stephen F. Austin State University	M
Stevens Institute of Technology	M,D,O
Stony Brook University, State University of New York	M,D,O
Stratford University (VA)	M,D
Syracuse University	M
Télé-université	M,D
Temple University	M,D*
Tennessee Technological University	M
Texas A&M University	M,D
Texas A&M University–Corpus Christi	M
Texas A&M University–Kingsville	M
Texas Southern University	M
Texas Tech University	M,D
Towson University	M
Toyota Technological Institute at Chicago	D
Trent University	M
Troy University	M
Tufts University	M,D,O
Universidad Autonoma de Guadalajara	M,D
Universidad de las Américas Puebla	M,D
Université de Moncton	M,O
Université de Montréal	M,D
Université du Québec à Trois-Rivières	M
Université du Québec en Outaouais	M,D,O
Université Laval	M,D
University at Albany, State University of New York	M,D
University at Buffalo, the State University of New York	M,D,O*
University of Advancing Technology	M
The University of Akron	M
The University of Alabama	M,D
The University of Alabama at Birmingham	M,D
The University of Alabama in Huntsville	M,D,O
University of Alaska Fairbanks	M
University of Alberta	M,D
The University of Arizona	M,D
University of Arkansas	M,D
University of Arkansas at Little Rock	M,D
University of Bridgeport	M,D
The University of British Columbia	M,D
University of Calgary	M,D
University of California, Berkeley	M,D
University of California, Davis	M,D
University of California, Irvine	M,D
University of California, Los Angeles	M,D
University of California, Merced	M,D
University of California, Riverside	M,D
University of California, San Diego	M,D
University of California, Santa Barbara	M,D
University of California, Santa Cruz	M,D
University of Central Arkansas	M
University of Central Florida	M,D
University of Central Missouri	M,D,O
University of Central Oklahoma	M
University of Chicago	M,D
University of Cincinnati	M,D
University of Colorado Boulder	M,D
University of Colorado Colorado Springs	M
University of Colorado Denver	M,D
University of Connecticut	M,D*
University of Dayton	M
University of Delaware	M,D*
University of Denver	M,D
University of Detroit Mercy	M,D,O
University of Florida	M,D
University of Georgia	M,D
University of Guelph	M,D
University of Hawaii at Manoa	M,D,O
University of Houston	M,D
University of Houston–Clear Lake	M
University of Houston–Victoria	M
University of Idaho	M,D

University of Illinois at Chicago M,D
University of Illinois at Springfield M
University of Illinois at Urbana–Champaign M,D
The University of Iowa M,D*
The University of Kansas M,D*
University of Kentucky M,D
University of Lethbridge M,D
University of Louisiana at Lafayette M,D
University of Louisville M,D,O
University of Maine M,D,O
University of Management and Technology M,O
The University of Manchester M,D
University of Manitoba M,D
University of Maryland, Baltimore County M,D
University of Maryland, College Park M,D
University of Maryland Eastern Shore M
University of Massachusetts Amherst M,D*
University of Massachusetts Boston M,D
University of Massachusetts Dartmouth M,D,O
University of Massachusetts Lowell M,D
University of Memphis M,D
University of Miami M,D
University of Michigan M,D
University of Michigan–Flint M
University of Minnesota, Duluth M
University of Minnesota, Twin Cities Campus M,D
University of Missouri M,D
University of Missouri–Kansas City M,D,O
University of Missouri–St. Louis M,D
University of Montana M
University of Nebraska at Omaha M,O
University of Nebraska–Lincoln M,D
University of Nevada, Las Vegas M,D
University of Nevada, Reno M,D
University of New Brunswick Fredericton M,D
University of New Hampshire M,D,O
University of New Haven M,D,O
University of New Mexico M,D
University of New Orleans M
The University of North Carolina at Chapel Hill M,D
The University of North Carolina at Charlotte M,O
The University of North Carolina at Greensboro M
The University of North Carolina Wilmington M
University of North Dakota M,D
University of Northern British Columbia M,D,O
University of North Florida M
University of North Texas M,D,O
University of Notre Dame M,D
University of Oklahoma M,D*
University of Oregon M,D
University of Ottawa M,D
University of Pennsylvania M,D*
University of Pittsburgh M,D*
University of Portland M
University of Puerto Rico, Mayagüez Campus M,D
University of Regina M,D
University of Rhode Island M,D,O
University of Rochester M,D*
University of San Francisco M
University of Saskatchewan M,D
University of South Alabama M,D
University of South Carolina M,D
The University of South Dakota M
University of Southern California M,D
University of Southern Maine M,O
University of Southern Mississippi M,D
University of South Florida M,D
The University of Tennessee M,D
The University of Tennessee at Chattanooga M
The University of Texas at Arlington M,D
The University of Texas at Austin M,D
The University of Texas at Dallas M,D*
The University of Texas at El Paso M,D
The University of Texas at San Antonio M,D
The University of Texas at Tyler M
The University of Texas of the Permian Basin M
The University of Texas Rio Grande Valley M
The University of Toledo M,D
University of Toronto M,D
The University of Tulsa M,D
University of Utah M,D*
University of Vermont M,D
University of Victoria M,D
University of Virginia M,D
University of Washington M,D*
University of Waterloo M,D
The University of Western Ontario M,D
University of West Florida M
University of West Georgia M,O
University of Windsor M,D
University of Wisconsin–Madison M,D
University of Wisconsin–Milwaukee M
University of Wisconsin–Parkside M
University of Wisconsin–Platteville M
University of Wyoming M,D
Utah State University M,D
Vanderbilt University M,D*
Villanova University M,O
Virginia Commonwealth University M,D
Virginia International University M,O
Virginia Polytechnic Institute and State University M,D,O
Virginia State University M
Wake Forest University M
Washington State University M,D
Washington University in St. Louis M,D
Wayne State University M,D,O
Webster University M
Wesleyan University M,D
West Chester University of Pennsylvania M,O
Western Illinois University M
Western Kentucky University M
Western Michigan University M,D
Western Washington University M
West Virginia University M,D
Wichita State University M,D
Winston-Salem State University M
Worcester Polytechnic Institute M,D,O
Wright State University M,D
Yale University M,D*
York University M,D
Youngstown State University M

CONDENSED MATTER PHYSICS

Cleveland State University M
Iowa State University of Science and Technology M,D
Memorial University of Newfoundland M,D
Rutgers University–New Brunswick M,D
University of Alberta M,D
The University of Manchester M,D
University of Victoria M,D
West Virginia University M,D

CONFLICT RESOLUTION AND MEDIATION/PEACE STUDIES

Abilene Christian University M,O
American Public University System M
American University M,D,O
The American University of Paris M
Anabaptist Mennonite Biblical Seminary M,O
Antioch University Midwest M
Arcadia University M
Baptist Theological Seminary at Richmond M,D,O
Bethany Theological Seminary M,O
Bethel University (TN) M
Brandeis University M
California State University, Dominguez Hills M
Cambridge College M
Carleton University M,O
Champlain College M
Colgate Rochester Crozer Divinity School M,D,O
Colorado Technical University Colorado Springs M,D
Colorado Technical University Denver South M
Columbia College (SC) M
Columbia University M*
Cornell University M,D
Creighton University M,O
Dallas Baptist University M
Dominican University M
Drew University M,D,O
Duquesne University M,O
Eastern Mennonite University M,O
Excelsior College M,O
Fresno Pacific University M,O
George Mason University M,D,O
Georgetown University M
Henley-Putnam University M
Hult International Business School (United States) M
Kansas State University M,O
Kennesaw State University M,D
Lesley University M,D,O
Lipscomb University M,O
London Metropolitan University M,D
Middlebury Institute of International Studies at Monterey M
Montclair State University M,O
Naval Postgraduate School M,D
New York University M,O
Norwich University M
Nova Southeastern University M,D,O*
Old Dominion University M,D
Pepperdine University M
Portland State University M
Royal Roads University M,O
Saint Mary's College of California M
St. Mary's University (United States) M,O
Saint Paul University M
Salisbury University M
Salve Regina University M,D
Southern Methodist University M
Southern New Hampshire University M,O
Syracuse University O
Trident University International M,D
Tufts University M,D
United States International University–Africa M
United Theological Seminary of the Twin Cities M,D,O
Universidad del Turabo M
Université de Sherbrooke M,D,O
University of Arkansas at Little Rock O
University of Baltimore M
University of Bridgeport M
University of Denver M,O
University of Hawaii at Manoa M,O
University of Idaho D
The University of Manchester D
University of Massachusetts Amherst M,D*
University of Massachusetts Boston M,O
University of Massachusetts Lowell M
University of Missouri M,D,O
University of New Brunswick Fredericton M
University of New Haven M,O
The University of North Carolina at Greensboro M,O
The University of North Carolina Wilmington M,O
University of Notre Dame M,D
University of Phoenix–Online Campus M,O
University of San Diego M
University of the Sacred Heart M
University of Victoria M,D
University of Wisconsin–Milwaukee M,D,O
Walden University M,D,O
Wayne State University M,O
Wilfrid Laurier University D
Willamette University M,D
Yeshiva University M,D

CONSERVATION BIOLOGY

Antioch University New England M
Arizona State University at the Tempe campus M,D
California State University, Sacramento M
California State University, Stanislaus M
Central Michigan University M
Colorado State University M,D
Columbia University M,D*
Cornell University M,D
Florida Institute of Technology M
Fordham University M,D,O
Frostburg State University M
Illinois State University M,D
Oregon State University M,D
State University of New York College of Environmental Science and Forestry M,D
Texas State University M
Tropical Agriculture Research and Higher Education Center M,D
University at Albany, State University of New York M
University of Alberta M,D
University of Central Florida M,D,O
University of Hawaii at Hilo M
University of Illinois at Urbana–Champaign M,D
University of Maryland, College Park M
University of Minnesota, Twin Cities Campus M,D
University of Missouri M,D,O
University of Nevada, Reno D
University of New Hampshire M
University of Wisconsin–Madison M
University of Wisconsin–Stout M

CONSTRUCTION ENGINEERING

The American University in Cairo M
Arizona State University at the Tempe campus M,D
Auburn University M,D
Bradley University M
Colorado School of Mines M,D
Columbia University M,D*
Concordia University (Canada) M,D,O
George Mason University M,D
Illinois Institute of Technology M,D
Iowa State University of Science and Technology M,D
Lawrence Technological University M,D
Marquette University M,D,O
Massachusetts Institute of Technology M,D,O
Missouri University of Science and Technology M,D
Montana State University M,D
Ohio University M,D
Oregon State University M,D
Pittsburg State University M
Stanford University M,D,O
Stevens Institute of Technology M,O
The University of Alabama M,D
The University of Alabama at Birmingham M
University of Alberta M,D
University of Central Florida M,D,O
University of Colorado Boulder M,D
University of Michigan M,D,O
University of Missouri–Kansas City M,D,O
University of New Brunswick Fredericton M,D
University of Southern Mississippi M
University of Virginia D
University of Washington M,D*
Virginia Polytechnic Institute and State University M,D,O
Wentworth Institute of Technology M

CONSTRUCTION MANAGEMENT

Alabama Agricultural and Mechanical University M
The American University in Dubai M
Arizona State University at the Tempe campus M,D
Auburn University M
Bowling Green State University M
Brigham Young University M
California Baptist University M
California State University, Chico M
California State University, East Bay M
Carnegie Mellon University M,D
Central Connecticut State University M,O
Clemson University M
Colorado State University M
Columbia University M,D*
Drexel University M
East Carolina University M
Eastern Michigan University M
Florida International University M
Georgia Southern University M
Harrisburg University of Science and Technology M
Illinois Institute of Technology M,D
Indiana University–Purdue University Fort Wayne M
Instituto Tecnologico de Santo Domingo M,O
Kennesaw State University M
Louisiana State University and Agricultural & Mechanical College M,D
Marquette University M,D,O
Michigan State University M,D
Milwaukee School of Engineering M*
Missouri State University M
New England Institute of Technology M
NewSchool of Architecture and Design M
New York University M,D,O
North Carolina Agricultural and Technical State University M
Norwich University M
Philadelphia University M
Pittsburg State University M,O
Polytechnic University of Puerto Rico, Miami Campus M
Polytechnic University of Puerto Rico, Orlando Campus M
Purdue University M
South Dakota School of Mines and Technology M
State University of New York College of Environmental Science and Forestry M,D
Stevens Institute of Technology M,O
Texas A&M University M
Universidad de las Américas Puebla M
University of Alaska Fairbanks M,D,O
University of Arkansas at Little Rock M
University of California, Berkeley O
University of Denver M
University of Florida M,D
University of Houston M
The University of Kansas M*
University of Nevada, Las Vegas O
University of New Mexico M,D
The University of North Carolina at Charlotte M,O
University of North Florida M
University of Oklahoma M*
University of Southern California M,D,O
The University of Texas at Arlington M,D
The University of Texas at El Paso M,D,O
University of Washington M*
University of Wisconsin–Stout M
Virginia Polytechnic Institute and State University M,D,O
Wentworth Institute of Technology M
Western Carolina University M
Worcester Polytechnic Institute M,D,O

CONSUMER ECONOMICS

California State University, Long Beach M
Colorado State University M
Cornell University M,D
Iowa State University of Science and Technology M,D
Kansas State University M,D
North Carolina Agricultural and Technical State University M
North Dakota State University M,O
Ohio University M
Oklahoma State University M,D
Purdue University M,D
South Dakota State University M
State University of New York at Oswego M
Texas Tech University M,D
Université Laval O
The University of Alabama M
University of Georgia M,D
University of Guelph M
University of Idaho M
University of Illinois at Urbana–Champaign M,D
University of Missouri M,D,O
University of Nebraska–Lincoln M,D
University of South Carolina M
The University of Tennessee M,D
University of Utah M*
University of Wisconsin–Madison M,D
University of Wyoming M
Utah State University M

*M—masters degree; D—doctorate; O—other advanced degree; *—Close-Up and/or Display*

CORPORATE AND ORGANIZATIONAL COMMUNICATION

Argosy University, Schaumburg	M,D,O
Armstrong State University	M,O
Barry University	M,O
Baruch College of the City University of New York	M
Bellevue University	M
Boston University	M
Bowie State University	M,O
California State University, San Bernardino	M
Canisius College	M
Carnegie Mellon University	M
Central Connecticut State University	M,O
City College of the City University of New York	M
Columbia University	M*
Concordia University, St. Paul	M
Concordia University Wisconsin	M
Cornell University	M,D
Dallas Baptist University	M
DePaul University	M
Drexel University	M
Eastern Michigan University	M,O
East Tennessee State University	M
Emerson College	M
Fairleigh Dickinson University, College at Florham	M
Florida State University	M,D
Fordham University	M
Franklin University	M
Golden Gate University	M,D,O
HEC Montreal	O
High Point University	M
Howard University	M,D
Illinois Institute of Technology	M
Iowa State University of Science and Technology	M,D
John Carroll University	M
La Salle University	M,O
Lasell College	M,O
Loyola University Chicago	M
Manhattanville College	M*
Marist College	M
Minnesota State University Mankato	M,O
Mississippi College	M
Monmouth University	M,O
Murray State University	M
National University	M,O
New Mexico State University	M,D
New York University	M
Northeastern University	M
Northwestern University	M,D*
Ohio University	M,D
Radford University	M
Regent University	M,D,O
Regis College (MA)	M
Rider University	M
Roosevelt University	M
Rowan University	O
Sacred Heart University	M
St. Bonaventure University	M
Seton Hall University	M
Southern Illinois University Edwardsville	M
Spalding University	M
Stevens Institute of Technology	O
Suffolk University	M
Temple University	M*
Texas Christian University	M
Towson University	M
Troy University	M
Universidad Autonoma de Guadalajara	M,D
Universidad Iberoamericana	M,D
Université de Sherbrooke	M
University of Alaska Fairbanks	M
University of Central Florida	M,O
University of Colorado Denver	M
University of Denver	M,O
University of Nebraska–Lincoln	M,D
University of Oklahoma	M,D*
University of Portland	M
University of St. Thomas (MN)	M
University of Southern California	M
University of South Florida	M,O
University of Wisconsin–Stevens Point	M
University of Wisconsin–Whitewater	M
Washington State University	M,D
Webster University	M
Western Kentucky University	M,O
West Virginia University	M,D,O

COUNSELING PSYCHOLOGY

Abilene Christian University	M
Adelphi University	M
Adler Graduate School	M
Adler University	M,D,O
Alabama Agricultural and Mechanical University	M,O
Alaska Pacific University	M
Alfred University	M,D,O
Alliant International University–México City	M
Amberton University	M
American International College	M
Amridge University	M,D
Andrews University	M,D
Angelo State University	M
Anna Maria College	M
Antioch University Midwest	M
Antioch University New England	M
Appalachian State University	M
Argosy University, Chicago	D
Argosy University, Denver	M,D
Argosy University, Hawai`i	D
Argosy University, Inland Empire	M,D
Argosy University, Los Angeles	M,D
Argosy University, Nashville	M,D
Argosy University, Orange County	M,D
Argosy University, Phoenix	M
Argosy University, Salt Lake City	M,D
Argosy University, San Diego	M,D
Argosy University, San Francisco Bay Area	M,D
Argosy University, Sarasota	M,D
Argosy University, Schaumburg	M,O
Argosy University, Seattle	M,D
Argosy University, Tampa	M,D
Argosy University, Washington DC	M,D
Arizona State University at the Tempe campus	D
Ashland Theological Seminary	M,D,O
Assumption College	M,O
Athabasca University	M,O
Austin Peay State University	M
Avila University	M
Ball State University	M,D
Baruch College of the City University of New York	M
Bastyr University	M,O
Bay Path University	M
Becker College	M
Bethel University (MN)	M,D,O
Boston College	M,D
Boston Graduate School of Psychoanalysis	M
Boston University	M
Bowie State University	M
Bowling Green State University	M
Bradley University	M
Brandman University	M
Brigham Young University	M,D,O
Brooklyn College of the City University of New York	M,D,O
Caldwell University	M,O
California Baptist University	M
California Institute of Integral Studies	M,D
California State University, Bakersfield	M
California State University, Sacramento	M
California State University, San Bernardino	M
California State University, Stanislaus	M
California University of Pennsylvania	M
Cambridge College	M,O
Capella University	M
Carlos Albizu University, Miami Campus	M,D
Carlow University	M,D,O
Centenary College	M
Central Michigan University	M,D,O
Central Washington University	M
Chaminade University of Honolulu	M
Chatham University	M,D
Chestnut Hill College	M,O
City University of Seattle	M
Clemson University	M,D,O
Cleveland State University	M,D,O
The College at Brockport, State University of New York	M,O
The College of New Rochelle	M,O
College of Saint Elizabeth	M,D,O
College of St. Joseph	M
The College of Saint Rose	M,O
College of Staten Island of the City University of New York	M
Colorado Christian University	M
Concordia University Chicago	M
Concordia University Wisconsin	M
Dallas Baptist University	M
Delaware Valley University	M
DePaul University	M,D
Dominican University of California	M
Duquesne University	M,D,O
Eastern Nazarene College	M
Eastern University	M,O
Eastern Washington University	M
East Texas Baptist University	M
Edinboro University of Pennsylvania	M,O
Emporia State University	M
Evangel University	M
Fairfield University	M,O
Fairleigh Dickinson University, College at Florham	M
Felician University	M
Fitchburg State University	M
Florida International University	M,D,O
Florida State University	D
Fordham University	M,D
Fort Valley State University	M
Franciscan University of Steubenville	M
Francis Marion University	M,O
Frostburg State University	M
Gallaudet University	M,D,O
Gannon University	M
Gardner-Webb University	M
Geneva College	M
George Fox University	M,O
Georgian Court University	M,O
Georgia State University	M,O
Governors State University	M
Grace University	M
Grand Canyon University	M
Harding University	M
Hardin-Simmons University	M
Heidelberg University	M
Henderson State University	M,O
Hodges University	M
Hofstra University	M,O
Holy Family University	M
Holy Names University	M,O
Houston Baptist University	M
Howard University	D
Humboldt State University	M
Husson University	M
Idaho State University	M,D,O
Illinois State University	M,D,O
Immaculata University	M,D,O
Indiana University Northwest	M
Indiana Wesleyan University	M
Instituto Tecnologico de Santo Domingo	M,O
Inter American University of Puerto Rico, Aguadilla Campus	M
Inter American University of Puerto Rico, Metropolitan Campus	M,D
Inter American University of Puerto Rico, San Germán Campus	M,D
Iona College	M,O
Iowa State University of Science and Technology	D
Jacksonville University	M*
James Madison University	M,D,O
John Brown University	M,O
John Carroll University	M,O
John F. Kennedy University	M
Johns Hopkins University	M,O
Kean University	M
Kent State University	M
Kutztown University of Pennsylvania	M
Lamar University	M
Lancaster Bible College	M,D
La Salle University	M
Lee University	M
Lehigh University	M,D,O
Lenoir-Rhyne University	M
Lesley University	M,D,O
LeTourneau University	M
Lewis & Clark College	M
Lewis University	M
Liberty University	M,D,O
Lindenwood University	M,D,O
Lindsey Wilson College	M,D
Lipscomb University	M,O
Lock Haven University of Pennsylvania	M
London Metropolitan University	M,D
Long Island University–Brentwood Campus	M,O
Long Island University–Hudson at Rockland	M,O
Long Island University–Hudson at Westchester	M,O
Long Island University–LIU Brooklyn	M,O
Long Island University–LIU Post	M,D,O
Louisiana Tech University	M,D
Loyola Marymount University	M
Loyola University Chicago	D
Lynchburg College	M
Marist College	M,O
Marquette University	M,D
Marylhurst University	M,O
Marymount University	M,D
Marywood University	M
McGill University	M,D,O
McKendree University	M
McNeese State University	M
Medaille College	M,D
Mercy College	M,O
Messiah College	M,O
Mid-America Christian University	M
Middle Tennessee State University	M
Midwestern State University	M
Minnesota State University Mankato	M,D
Mississippi College	M,O
Missouri State University	M
Monmouth University	M,O
Montana State University Billings	M
Moody Theological SeminaryMichigan	M,O
Morehead State University	M
Mount Mary University	M,O
Mount Saint Mary's University (CA)	M,D,O
Naropa University	M
National University	M,O
New England College	M
New Mexico Highlands University	M
New Mexico State University	M,D,O
New York University	M,D,O
North Dakota State University	M,D
Northeastern State University	M
Northeastern University	M,D,O
Northern Arizona University	M,D,O
Northern Kentucky University	M
Northern State University	M
Northwest Christian University	M
Northwestern Oklahoma State University	M
Northwest University	M,D
Nova Southeastern University	M,D,O*
Nyack College	M
Oakland University	M,D,O
Old Dominion University	M,D,O
Ottawa University	M
Our Lady of the Lake University of San Antonio	D
Pace University	M,D
Pacifica Graduate Institute	M,D
Palm Beach Atlantic University	M
Palo Alto University	M
Philadelphia College of Osteopathic Medicine	M,D,O*
Phoenix Seminary	M,D,O
Prescott College	M
Providence University College & Theological Seminary	M,D,O
Purdue University Northwest	M
Radford University	M,D
Regent University	M,D,O
Regis College (MA)	M,D,O
Rhode Island College	M,O
Rivier University	M,D,O
Robert Morris University	M,D,O
Rosemont College	M
Rutgers University–New Brunswick	M
Sage Graduate School	M
St. Bonaventure University	M,O
St. Edward's University	M
St. John Fisher College	M
St. John's University (NY)	M,D,O
Saint Martin's University	M
St. Mary's University (United States)	M
Saint Mary's University of Minnesota	M,D,O
Saint Paul University	M
St. Thomas University	M
Salem State University	M,O
Salve Regina University	M,O
San Francisco State University	M,O
Santa Clara University	M,O
Saybrook University	M
The Seattle School of Theology and Psychology	M
Seton Hall University	M,D
Siena Heights University	M,O
Simpson University	M
Slippery Rock University of Pennsylvania	M
Sofia University	M,D
Sonoma State University	M
Southeastern Oklahoma State University	M
Southeastern University (FL)	M
Southeast Missouri State University	M,O
Southern Adventist University	M
Southern California Seminary	M,D
Southern Illinois University Carbondale	M,D
Southern Nazarene University	M
Southern Oregon University	M
South University	M
South University	M
South University (TX)	M
South University (MI)	M
South University (OH)	M
South University (NC)	M
South University (SC)	M
South University (GA)	M
South University (AL)	M
South University	M
Southwestern Assemblies of God University	M
Southwestern College (NM)	M,O
Spring Arbor University	M
Springfield College	M,D,O
State University of New York at New Paltz	M,O
State University of New York at Oswego	M
State University of New York at Plattsburgh	M,O
State University of New York College at Old Westbury	M
Stephens College	M,O
Suffolk University	M,D,O
Tarleton State University	M
Teachers College, Columbia University	M,D
Temple University	M,D,O*
Tennessee State University	M
Tennessee Technological University	M,O
Texas A&M International University	M
Texas A&M University	M,D
Texas A&M University–Texarkana	M
Texas Tech University	M,D
Texas Wesleyan University	M,D
Texas Woman's University	M,D,O
Touro College	M,D
Towson University	O
Trinity Christian College	M
Trinity International University	M,D,O
Trinity International University Florida	M
Trinity Washington University	M
Trinity Western University	M
Union College (KY)	M
United States International University–Africa	M
Universidad del Turabo	M,D,O
Universidad Metropolitana	M
University at Albany, State University of New York	M,D
University at Buffalo, the State University of New York	M,D,O*
The University of Akron	M,D
University of Alberta	M,D
The University of Arizona	M
University of Baltimore	M
University of Bridgeport	M
The University of British Columbia	M,D,O
University of Calgary	M,D
University of California, Berkeley	O
University of California, Santa Barbara	M,D,O
University of Central Arkansas	M
University of Central Missouri	M,D,O
University of Central Oklahoma	M
University of Colorado Denver	M
University of Dayton	M,O
University of Denver	M,D,O
University of Florida	M,D
University of Great Falls	M
University of Hawaii at Hilo	M
University of Houston	M,D
University of Houston–Victoria	M
University of Indianapolis	M,D
The University of Iowa	M,D,O*
The University of Kansas	M,D*
University of Kentucky	M,D,O
University of Lethbridge	M,D
University of Louisiana at Monroe	M
University of Louisville	M,D
The University of Manchester	M,D
University of Mary Hardin-Baylor	M

University of Maryland, College Park	M,D,O
University of Massachusetts Boston	M,D
University of Memphis	M,D
University of Miami	D
University of Minnesota, Twin Cities Campus	D
University of Missouri	M,D,O
University of Missouri–Kansas City	M,D,O
University of Missouri–St. Louis	M,D
University of Montana	M,D,O
University of Nebraska at Kearney	M,O
University of Nebraska–Lincoln	M,D,O
University of Nevada, Las Vegas	M,D,O
The University of North Carolina at Greensboro	M,D,O
The University of North Carolina at Pembroke	M
University of North Dakota	M
University of Northern Iowa	M
University of North Florida	M
University of North Georgia	M
University of North Texas	M,D,O
University of Notre Dame	D
University of Oklahoma	M,D*
University of Pennsylvania	M*
University of Phoenix–Las Vegas Campus	M
University of Phoenix–Phoenix Campus	M
University of Puget Sound	M
University of Rhode Island	M
University of Saint Francis (IN)	M,O
University of Saint Joseph	M,O
University of Saint Mary	M
University of St. Thomas (MN)	M,D,O
University of San Diego	M
University of San Francisco	M
The University of Scranton	M
University of South Africa	M,D
University of South Alabama	M,D,O
University of Southern Maine	M,O
University of Southern Mississippi	M,D
University of South Florida	O
The University of Tennessee	M,D
The University of Texas at Austin	M,D
The University of Texas at Tyler	M
University of the Cumberlands	M
University of the District of Columbia	M
University of the Southwest	M
University of Utah	M,D*
University of Vermont	M
University of Victoria	M,D
The University of Western Ontario	M
University of West Florida	M
University of Wisconsin–Madison	D
University of Wisconsin–Milwaukee	M,D
University of Wisconsin–Stout	M
Utah State University	M,D
Virginia Commonwealth University	M,D,O
Viterbo University	M
Walden University	M,D,O
Walla Walla University	M
Walsh University	M
Washington Adventist University	M
Washington State University	M,D
Washington University in St. Louis	M,D,O
Wayland Baptist University	M
Waynesburg University	M,D
Wayne State University	M,D,O
Webster University	M
Western Kentucky University	M
Western Michigan University	M,D
Western Washington University	M
Westfield State University	M
Westminster College (UT)	M
West Virginia University	D
Wheaton College	M,D
William Carey University	M
William James College	M,D,O
William Paterson University of New Jersey	M,D
Wilmington University	M
Winebrenner Theological Seminary	M,D
Wright Institute	M
Xavier University	M
Yeshiva University	M
Youngstown State University	M

COUNSELOR EDUCATION

Acadia University	M
Adams State University	M
Adler Graduate School	M
Adler University	M,D,O
Alabama Agricultural and Mechanical University	M,O
Alabama State University	M,D,O
Albany State University	M,O
Alcorn State University	M,O
Alfred University	M,D,O
Alliant International University–San Francisco	M
American International College	M,D,O
American Public University System	M
Amridge University	M,D
Angelo State University	M
Antioch University Seattle	M,D
Appalachian State University	M
Argosy University, Atlanta	M,D,O
Argosy University, Chicago	D
Argosy University, Dallas	D
Argosy University, Denver	M,D
Argosy University, Nashville	D
Argosy University, Salt Lake City	M,D
Argosy University, Sarasota	M,D,O
Argosy University, Tampa	M,D,O
Argosy University, Washington DC	M,D
Arizona State University at the Tempe campus	M
Arkansas State University	M,O
Arkansas Tech University	M,D,O
Ashland Theological Seminary	M,D,O
Athabasca University	M,O
Auburn University at Montgomery	M,O
Augusta University	M,O
Austin Peay State University	M,O
Azusa Pacific University	M
Ball State University	M,D
Barry University	M,D,O
Bayamón Central University	M,O
Becker College	M
Bellevue University	M
Bloomsburg University of Pennsylvania	M
Bob Jones University	M,D,O
Boise State University	M,O
Bowie State University	M
Bowling Green State University	M
Bradley University	M
Brandman University	M
Brandon University	M,O
Bridgewater State University	M,O
Brooklyn College of the City University of New York	M
Buena Vista University	M
Butler University	M
Caldwell University	M,O
California Baptist University	M
California Lutheran University	M,D
California State University, Bakersfield	M
California State University, Dominguez Hills	M
California State University, East Bay	M
California State University, Fresno	M
California State University, Fullerton	M
California State University, Long Beach	M
California State University, Los Angeles	M,D
California State University, Northridge	M
California State University, Sacramento	M
California State University, San Bernardino	M
California State University, Stanislaus	M
California University of Pennsylvania	M
Cambridge College	M,D,O
Campbell University	M
Canisius College	M
Capella University	M,D
Carlow University	M,O
Carson-Newman University	M
Carthage College	M,O
Central Connecticut State University	M,O
Central Methodist University	M
Central Michigan University	M
Central Washington University	M
Chadron State College	M,O
Chapman University	M,D,O
Chicago State University	M
The Citadel, The Military College of South Carolina	M,O
City University of Seattle	M,O
Clark Atlanta University	M
Clemson University	M,D,O
Cleveland State University	M,D,O
The College at Brockport, State University of New York	M,O
The College of New Jersey	M
College of St. Joseph	M
The College of Saint Rose	M,O
The College of William and Mary	M,D
Colorado State University	M,D
Columbia International University	M,D,O
Columbus State University	M,D,O
Concordia University Chicago	M,O
Concordia University Irvine	M
Concordia University Wisconsin	M
Creighton University	M
Dallas Baptist University	M,O
Delta State University	M,D,O
DePaul University	M,D
Doane University	M
Duquesne University	M,D,O
East Carolina University	M,D,O
East Central University	M
Eastern Illinois University	M
Eastern Kentucky University	M
Eastern Mennonite University	M
Eastern Michigan University	M,O
Eastern New Mexico University	M
Eastern University	M,O
Eastern Washington University	M
East Tennessee State University	M
Edinboro University of Pennsylvania	M,O
Emporia State University	M
Evangel University	M
Fairfield University	M,O
Faulkner University	M
Fitchburg State University	M,O
Florida Agricultural and Mechanical University	M,D
Florida Atlantic University	D
Florida International University	M,D,O
Fordham University	M,D
Fort Hays State University	M
Fort Valley State University	M,O
Freed-Hardeman University	M,O
Fresno Pacific University	M
Frostburg State University	M
Gallaudet University	M,D,O
Geneva College	M
George Fox University	M,O
George Mason University	M,D,O
The George Washington University	M,D,O*
Georgian Court University	M,O
Georgia Southern University	M,O
Georgia State University	M,O
Grambling State University	M,D,O
Gwynedd Mercy University	M
Hampton University	M,D,O
Harding University	M,O
Hardin-Simmons University	M
Henderson State University	M,O
Heritage University	M
Hofstra University	M,O
Houston Baptist University	M
Howard University	M
Hunter College of the City University of New York	M
Husson University	M
Idaho State University	M,D,O
Indiana State University	M,D,O
Indiana University Bloomington	M,D,O
Indiana University of Pennsylvania	M
Indiana University–Purdue University Fort Wayne	M,O
Indiana University–Purdue University Indianapolis	M,O
Indiana University South Bend	M
Indiana University Southeast	M
Indiana Wesleyan University	M
Inter American University of Puerto Rico, Arecibo Campus	M
Inter American University of Puerto Rico, Metropolitan Campus	M,D
Inter American University of Puerto Rico, San Germán Campus	M,D
Iowa State University of Science and Technology	M,D
Jackson State University	M
Jacksonville State University	M
John Brown University	M,O
John Carroll University	M,O
Johns Hopkins University	M,O
Johnson State College	M
Johnson University	M,D,O
Kansas State University	M,D
Kean University	M
Keene State College	M,O
Kent State University	M,D,O
Kutztown University of Pennsylvania	M
Lakeland University	M
Lamar University	M
Lancaster Bible College	M,D
La Sierra University	M,O
Lee University	M
Lehigh University	M,D,O
Lehman College of the City University of New York	M
Lenoir-Rhyne University	M
Lewis University	M
Liberty University	M,D,O
Lincoln Memorial University	M,D,O
Lincoln University (MO)	M
Lindenwood University–Belleville	M
Lindsey Wilson College	M,D
Loma Linda University	M,D,O
Long Island University–Brentwood Campus	M,O
Long Island University–Hudson at Rockland	M,O
Long Island University–Hudson at Westchester	M,O
Long Island University–LIU Brooklyn	M,O
Longwood University	M
Louisiana State University and Agricultural & Mechanical College	M,D,O
Louisiana State University in Shreveport	M
Louisiana Tech University	M,D
Loyola Marymount University	M
Loyola University Chicago	M,O
Loyola University Maryland	M,O
Lynchburg College	M
Lyndon State College	M
Malone University	M
Manhattan College	M,O
Marquette University	M,D
Marshall University	M,O
Marymount University	M,D
Marywood University	M
McDaniel College	M
McNeese State University	M,O
Mercer University	M,D
Mercy College	M,O
Messiah College	M,O
Michigan State University	M,D,O
Middle Tennessee State University	M
Midwestern State University	M
Minnesota State University Mankato	M,D
Minnesota State University Moorhead	M,O
Mississippi College	M,O
Mississippi State University	M,D,O
Missouri Baptist University	M,O
Missouri State University	M
Monmouth University	M,O
Montana State University Billings	M
Montana State University–Northern	M
Montclair State University	M,D
Morehead State University	M,O
Mount Mary University	M,O
Multnomah University	M
Murray State University	M,O
Naropa University	M
National Louis University	M,D,O
National University	M,O
New Jersey City University	M
New Mexico Highlands University	M
New Mexico State University	M,D,O
New York Institute of Technology	M
New York University	M,D,O
Niagara University	M,O
Nicholls State University	M,O
North Carolina Agricultural and Technical State University	M
North Carolina Central University	M
North Carolina State University	M,D
North Dakota State University	M,D
Northeastern Illinois University	M
Northeastern State University	M
Northern Arizona University	M,D,O
Northern Illinois University	M,D
Northern Kentucky University	M
Northern State University	M
Northwest Christian University	M
Northwestern Oklahoma State University	M
Northwestern State University of Louisiana	M,O
Northwest Missouri State University	M
Northwest Nazarene University	M
Nova Southeastern University	M,D,O*
Nyack College	M
Ohio University	M,D
Oklahoma City University	M
Old Dominion University	M,D,O
Oregon State University	M,D
Ottawa University	M
Our Lady of the Lake University of San Antonio	M
Palm Beach Atlantic University	M
Penn State University Park	M,D,O
Phillips Graduate Institute	M
Pittsburg State University	M
Plymouth State University	M
Point Loma Nazarene University	M
Pontifical Catholic University of Puerto Rico	M
Prairie View A&M University	M,D
Prescott College	M,D
Providence College	M
Purdue University	M,D,O
Purdue University Northwest	M
Queens College of the City University of New York	M,O
Quincy University	M
Radford University	M
Regent University	M,D,O
Regis University	M,D,O
Rhode Island College	M,O
Richmont Graduate University	M
Rider University	M,O
Rivier University	M,D,O
Rollins College	M
Roosevelt University	M
Rosemont College	M
Rowan University	M
Rutgers University–New Brunswick	M
Sage Graduate School	M,O
St. Bonaventure University	M,O
St. Cloud State University	M
St. John's University (NY)	M,D,O
St. Lawrence University	M,O
Saint Louis University	M,D,O
Saint Martin's University	M
Saint Mary's College of California	M,O
St. Mary's University (United States)	D
Saint Peter's University	M,O
St. Thomas University	M,O
Saint Xavier University	M
Salem College	M
Salem State University	M
Sam Houston State University	M,D
San Diego State University	M
San Francisco State University	M,O
San Jose State University	M,D,O
Santa Clara University	M,O
Seattle Pacific University	M,D,O
Seattle University	M,O
Seton Hall University	M,D
Shippensburg University of Pennsylvania	M,O
Simon Fraser University	M
Slippery Rock University of Pennsylvania	M
Sonoma State University	M
South Carolina State University	M
South Dakota State University	M
Southeastern Louisiana University	M
Southeastern Oklahoma State University	M
Southeastern University (FL)	M
Southeast Missouri State University	M,O
Southern Adventist University	M
Southern Arkansas University–Magnolia	M
Southern Connecticut State University	M,O
Southern Methodist University	M
Southern University and Agricultural and Mechanical College	M
Southwestern Oklahoma State University	M
Spalding University	M
Springfield College	M,D,O
State University of New York at New Paltz	M,O

*M—masters degree; D—doctorate; O—other advanced degree; *—Close-Up and/or Display*

State University of New York at Plattsburgh	M,O
State University of New York College at Oneonta	M,O
Stephen F. Austin State University	M
Stephens College	M,O
Stetson University	M
Suffolk University	M,D,O
Sul Ross State University	M
Summit University	M
Syracuse University	M,D
Texas A&M International University	M
Texas A&M University–Central Texas	M,O
Texas A&M University–Corpus Christi	M,D
Texas A&M University–Kingsville	M,D
Texas A&M University–San Antonio	M
Texas Christian University	M,O
Texas Southern University	M,D
Texas State University	M
Texas Tech University	M,D
Texas Wesleyan University	M,D
Texas Woman's University	M,D
Trevecca Nazarene University	M,D
Trinity Washington University	M
Troy University	M,O
Universidad del Turabo	M
Université de Moncton	M
Université Laval	M,D
University at Buffalo, the State University of New York	M,D,O*
The University of Akron	M,D
The University of Alabama	M,D,O
The University of Alabama at Birmingham	M
University of Alaska Anchorage	M
University of Alaska Fairbanks	M,O
University of Alberta	M,D
The University of Arizona	M
University of Arkansas	M,D,O
University of Arkansas at Little Rock	M
University of Central Arkansas	M
University of Central Florida	M,O
University of Central Missouri	M,D,O
University of Central Oklahoma	M
University of Cincinnati	M,D,O
University of Colorado Colorado Springs	M,D
University of Colorado Denver	M
University of Connecticut	M,D*
University of Dayton	M,O
University of Florida	M,D,O
University of Georgia	M,D,O
University of Guam	M
University of Hartford	M,O
University of Holy Cross	M
University of Houston–Clear Lake	M
University of Houston–Victoria	M
University of Idaho	M,O
University of Illinois at Urbana–Champaign	M,D,O
The University of Iowa	M,D*
University of La Verne	M,D,O
University of Lethbridge	M,D
University of Louisiana at Lafayette	M
University of Louisiana at Monroe	M
University of Louisville	M,D
University of Maine	M,D,O
University of Manitoba	M
University of Mary Hardin-Baylor	M
University of Maryland, College Park	M,D,O
University of Maryland Eastern Shore	M
University of Massachusetts Amherst	M,D,O*
University of Massachusetts Boston	M
University of Memphis	M,D
University of Miami	M,O
University of Minnesota, Twin Cities Campus	M,D,O
University of Missouri–Kansas City	M,D,O
University of Missouri–St. Louis	M,D
University of Montana	M,D,O
University of Montevallo	M
University of Nebraska at Kearney	M,O
University of Nebraska at Omaha	M
University of Nevada, Las Vegas	M,D,O
University of Nevada, Reno	M,D,O
University of New Mexico	M,D
University of New Orleans	M,D
University of North Alabama	M
The University of North Carolina at Chapel Hill	M
The University of North Carolina at Charlotte	M,D,O
The University of North Carolina at Greensboro	M,D,O
The University of North Carolina at Pembroke	M
University of Northern Colorado	M,D
University of Northern Iowa	M
University of North Florida	M,D
University of North Texas	M,D,O
University of Phoenix–Las Vegas Campus	M
University of Phoenix–New Mexico Campus	M
University of Phoenix–Phoenix Campus	M
University of Phoenix–Southern Arizona Campus	M,O
University of Phoenix–Southern California Campus	M
University of Puerto Rico, Río Piedras Campus	M,D
University of Puget Sound	M
University of Rochester	M,D*
University of Saint Francis (IN)	M,O
University of Saint Joseph	M,O
University of St. Thomas (TX)	M
University of San Diego	M
University of San Francisco	M
The University of Scranton	M
University of South Africa	M,D
University of South Alabama	M,D,O
University of South Carolina	D,O
The University of South Dakota	M,D,O
University of Southern California	M
University of Southern Maine	M,O
University of Southern Mississippi	M,D,O
University of South Florida	M,D,O
The University of Tennessee	M,D,O
The University of Tennessee at Chattanooga	M,D,O
The University of Tennessee at Martin	M
The University of Texas at Austin	M,D
The University of Texas at El Paso	M
The University of Texas at San Antonio	M,D
The University of Texas of the Permian Basin	M
The University of Texas Rio Grande Valley	M
University of the Cumberlands	M,D,O
University of the Southwest	M
The University of Toledo	M,D,O
University of Utah	M,D*
University of Vermont	M
University of Victoria	M,D
University of Virginia	M,D,O
The University of West Alabama	M,O
University of West Florida	M
University of West Georgia	M,D,O
University of Wisconsin–Madison	M
University of Wisconsin–Milwaukee	M,D
University of Wisconsin–Oshkosh	M
University of Wisconsin–Platteville	M
University of Wisconsin–River Falls	M,O
University of Wisconsin–Stevens Point	M
University of Wisconsin–Superior	M
University of Wyoming	M,D
Utah State University	M,D
Valdosta State University	M,O
Vanderbilt University	M,D*
Villanova University	M
Virginia Commonwealth University	M
Virginia Polytechnic Institute and State University	M,D,O
Virginia State University	M
Wake Forest University	M
Walden University	M,D
Walsh University	M
Waynesburg University	M,D
Wayne State College	M
Wayne State University	M,D,O
West Chester University of Pennsylvania	M,O
Western Connecticut State University	M
Western Illinois University	M
Western Kentucky University	M
Western Michigan University	M,D
Western Washington University	M
Westfield State University	M
Westminster College (PA)	M,O
West Texas A&M University	M
West Virginia University	M
Whitworth University	M
Wichita State University	M,D,O
Widener University	M,D
William Paterson University of New Jersey	M
Wilmington University	M,D
Winona State University	M
Winthrop University	M
Wright State University	M
Xavier University	M
Xavier University of Louisiana	M
Youngstown State University	M

CRIMINAL JUSTICE AND CRIMINOLOGY

Adler University	M,D,O
Adrian College	M
Albany State University	M
Albertus Magnus College	M
Alliant International University–San Francisco	M
American Public University System	M
American University	M,D,O
American University of Puerto Rico	M
Anderson University (SC)	M
Angelo State University	M
Anna Maria College	M
Appalachian State University	M
Arizona State University at the Tempe campus	M,D,O
Arkansas State University	M,O
Armstrong State University	M,O
Ashworth College	M
Auburn University at Montgomery	M,O
Ball State University	M,O
Baylor University	D
Bellevue University	M
Boise State University	M
Boston University	M
Bowling Green State University	M
Bridgewater State University	M
Buffalo State College, State University of New York	M
California Coast University	M
California State University, Chico	M
California State University, Fresno	M
California State University, Long Beach	M
California State University, Los Angeles	M
California State University, Sacramento	M
California State University, San Bernardino	M
California State University, Stanislaus	M
California University of Pennsylvania	M
Calumet College of Saint Joseph	M
Capella University	M,D
Caribbean University	M,D
Carnegie Mellon University	M
The Catholic University of America	M
Central Connecticut State University	M
Chaminade University of Honolulu	M,O
Charleston Southern University	M
Chicago State University	M
Clark Atlanta University	M
College of Saint Elizabeth	M
Colorado State University–Global Campus	M
Colorado Technical University Colorado Springs	M
Colorado Technical University Denver South	M
Columbia College (MO)	M
Columbia Southern University	M
Columbus State University	M
Concordia University, St. Paul	M,D,O
Coppin State University	M
Curry College	M
Dallas Baptist University	M
Defiance College	M
Delta State University	M
Drury University	M
East Carolina University	M,O
East Central University	M
Eastern Kentucky University	M
Eastern Michigan University	M
East Tennessee State University	M,O
Excelsior College	M,O
Fairleigh Dickinson University, Metropolitan Campus	M
Fairmont State University	M
Faulkner University	M
Fayetteville State University	M
Ferris State University	M
Florida Agricultural and Mechanical University	M
Florida Atlantic University	M
Florida Gulf Coast University	M
Florida International University	M
Florida State University	M,D
Gannon University	M
George Mason University	M,D,O
The George Washington University	M,O*
Georgia College & State University	M
Georgia State University	M,D,O
The Graduate Center, City University of New York	D
Grambling State University	M
Grand Valley State University	M
Hilbert College	M
Holy Family University	M
Husson University	M
Illinois State University	M
Indiana State University	M
Indiana University Bloomington	M,D
Indiana University Northwest	M,O
Indiana University of Pennsylvania	M,D
Indiana University–Purdue University Indianapolis	M,O
Inter American University of Puerto Rico, Aguadilla Campus	M
Inter American University of Puerto Rico, Metropolitan Campus	M
Inter American University of Puerto Rico, Ponce Campus	M
Iona College	M,O
Jackson State University	M
Jacksonville State University	M
John Jay College of Criminal Justice of the City University of New York	M,D
Johnson & Wales University	M
Kaplan University, Davenport Campus	M
Kean University	M
Keiser University	M
Kennesaw State University	M
Keuka College	M
Lamar University	M
Lasell College	M
Lewis University	M
Liberty University	M,D,O
Lincoln University (MO)	M
Lindenwood University	M,O
Lindenwood University–Belleville	M
Loma Linda University	M,D
London Metropolitan University	M,D
Long Island University–LIU Post	M,O
Loyola University Chicago	M
Loyola University New Orleans	M
Lynn University	M
Madonna University	M
Marian University (WI)	M
Marshall University	M
Marywood University	M
McNeese State University	M
Mercyhurst University	M,O
Merrimack College	M,O
Methodist University	M
Metropolitan State University	M
Michigan State University	M,D
Middle Tennessee State University	M
Midwestern State University	M,O
Mississippi College	M,O
Mississippi Valley State University	M
Missouri Southern State University	M
Missouri State University	M,O
Molloy College	M
Monmouth University	M,O
Monroe College	M
Morehead State University	M
Mount Mercy University	M
National University	M,O
New Charter University	M
New Jersey City University	M
New Mexico State University	M
Niagara University	M
Norfolk State University	M
North Carolina Central University	M
North Dakota State University	M,D
Northeastern State University	M
Northeastern University	M,D
Northern Arizona University	M
Northern Michigan University	M
Norwich University	M
Oklahoma City University	M
Old Dominion University	D
Penn State Harrisburg	M,D,O
Penn State University Park	M,D
Point Park University	M
Pontifical Catholic University of Puerto Rico	M
Pontificia Universidad Catolica Madre y Maestra	M
Portland State University	M,D
Radford University	M,O
Regent University	M,D
Regis University	M,O
Robert Morris University Illinois	M
Rochester Institute of Technology	M
Roger Williams University	M
Rowan University	M
Rutgers University–Camden	M
Rutgers University–Newark	M,D
Sacred Heart University	M
St. Ambrose University	M
St. Cloud State University	M
St. John's University (NY)	M
Saint Joseph's University	M,O
Saint Leo University	M
Saint Mary's University (Canada)	M
Saint Peter's University	M
St. Thomas University	M,O
Salem State University	M
Salve Regina University	M,O
Sam Houston State University	M,D
San Diego State University	M
San Francisco State University	M
Seattle University	M,O
Shippensburg University of Pennsylvania	M
Simon Fraser University	M,D
Simpson College	M
Slippery Rock University of Pennsylvania	M
Southeast Missouri State University	M
Southern Illinois University Carbondale	M,D
Southern University and Agricultural and Mechanical College	M
Southern University at New Orleans	M
South University	M
South University (SC)	M
South University (GA)	M
South University (AL)	M
South University	M
Southwestern College (KS)	M
Southwest University	M
Stockton University	M
Suffolk University	M
Sul Ross State University	M
Tarleton State University	M
Temple University	M,D*
Tennessee State University	M
Texas A&M International University	M
Texas A&M University–Central Texas	M,O
Texas A&M University–Kingsville	M
Texas Christian University	M
Texas Southern University	M,D
Texas State University	M,D
Tiffin University	M
Trident University International	M,D
Trine University	M
Troy University	M,O
Universidad del Este	M
Universidad del Turabo	M
Université de Montréal	M,D
University at Albany, State University of New York	M,D
The University of Alabama	M
The University of Alabama at Birmingham	M
University of Alaska Fairbanks	M
University of Alberta	M,D
University of Antelope Valley	M
University of Arkansas at Little Rock	M,D
University of Baltimore	M
University of California, Irvine	M,D
University of Central Florida	M,D,O
University of Central Missouri	M,D,O
University of Central Oklahoma	M
University of Cincinnati	M,D
University of Colorado Colorado Springs	M
University of Colorado Denver	M,D
University of Delaware	M,D*
University of Detroit Mercy	M,D,O
University of Florida	M,D

University of Great Falls	M
University of Guelph	M,D
University of Houston–Clear Lake	M
University of Houston–Downtown	M
University of Illinois at Chicago	M,D
University of Louisiana at Monroe	M
University of Louisville	M,D
University of Management and Technology	M,O
The University of Manchester	M,D
University of Maryland, College Park	M,D
University of Maryland Eastern Shore	M
University of Massachusetts Lowell	M
University of Memphis	M
University of Michigan–Flint	M
University of Minnesota, Duluth	M
University of Mississippi	M,D
University of Missouri–Kansas City	M
University of Missouri–St. Louis	M,D
University of Montana	M
University of Nebraska at Omaha	M,D,O
University of Nevada, Las Vegas	M,D
University of Nevada, Reno	M
University of New Haven	M,D,O
University of North Alabama	M
The University of North Carolina at Charlotte	M
The University of North Carolina at Greensboro	M
The University of North Carolina Wilmington	M
University of North Dakota	D
University of Northern Colorado	M
University of North Florida	M
University of North Georgia	M
University of North Texas	M,D,O
University of Oklahoma	M,O*
University of Ottawa	M,D
University of Pennsylvania	M,D*
University of Phoenix–Augusta Campus	M
University of Phoenix–Bay Area Campus	M
University of Phoenix–Dallas Campus	M
University of Phoenix–Jersey City Campus	M
University of Phoenix–Online Campus	M
University of Phoenix–Phoenix Campus	M
University of Phoenix–San Antonio Campus	M
University of Phoenix–Southern California Campus	M
University of Phoenix–Washington D.C. Campus	M
University of Phoenix–Western Washington Campus	M
University of Pittsburgh	M*
University of Regina	M
University of San Diego	M
University of South Africa	M,D
University of South Carolina	M,D
The University of South Dakota	M
The University of Southern Mississippi	M,D
University of South Florida	M,D,O
University of South Florida Sarasota-Manatee	M
The University of Tennessee	M,D
The University of Tennessee at Chattanooga	M
The University of Texas at Arlington	M
The University of Texas at Dallas	M,D*
The University of Texas at San Antonio	M
The University of Texas at Tyler	M
The University of Texas of the Permian Basin	M
The University of Texas Rio Grande Valley	M
University of the Fraser Valley	M
The University of Toledo	M,O
University of Toronto	M,D
University of West Florida	M
University of West Georgia	M,D,O
University of Windsor	M,D
University of Wisconsin–Milwaukee	M
University of Wisconsin–Platteville	M
Urbana University	M
Utica College	M
Virginia College in Birmingham	M
Virginia Commonwealth University	M,O
Virginia State University	M
Walden University	M,D,O
Waldorf College	M
Washburn University	M
Washington State University	M,D
Wayland Baptist University	M
Waynesburg University	M,D
Wayne State University	M
Webber International University	M
Webster University	M
West Chester University of Pennsylvania	M
Western Connecticut State University	M
Western Illinois University	M,O
Western Kentucky University	M
Western Oregon University	M
Westfield State University	M
West Liberty University	M
West Texas A&M University	M
West Virginia State University	M
Wichita State University	M
Widener University	M
Wilfrid Laurier University	M
Wilmington University	M
Wright State University	M
Xavier University	M
Youngstown State University	M

CULTURAL ANTHROPOLOGY

California Institute of Integral Studies	M,D
Concordia University (Canada)	M,D
Cornell University	D
Duke University	D*
Eastern University	M
The Graduate Center, City University of New York	D
Memorial University of Newfoundland	M,D
North Carolina State University	M
Northern Arizona University	M
Rice University	M,D
San Francisco State University	M
Southern Illinois University Edwardsville	M
University of California, Santa Barbara	M,D
University of California, Santa Cruz	D
University of Denver	M
University of Michigan	D
The University of Tennessee	M,D
University of Wisconsin–Madison	D
Washington State University	M,D

CULTURAL STUDIES

Ambrose University	M,O
American University	M,D,O
The American University of Paris	M
Appalachian State University	M
Arizona State University at the Tempe campus	M,D
Assemblies of God Theological Seminary	M,D
Athabasca University	M,O
Baptist Bible College	M
Baylor University	M,D
Binghamton University, State University of New York	M,D*
Biola University	M,D,O
Boston University	M
Brock University	M
Carnegie Mellon University	D
Central Michigan University	M
Chapman University	M,D,O
Charlotte Christian College and Theological Seminary	M
Claremont Graduate University	M,D,O
Columbia International University	M,D,O
Concordia University Irvine	M
Cornell University	M,D
Drew University	M,D,O
Eastern Michigan University	O
Florida State University	M,D,O
Gardner-Webb University	M,D
George Fox University	M,D,O
George Mason University	D
Goucher College	M
Grace Theological Seminary	M,D,O
Graduate Theological Union	M,D,O
Johnson University	M,D,O
La Salle University	M,O
Lewis & Clark College	M,O
Lincoln Christian University	M
Maranatha Baptist University	M
McMaster University	M,D
Michigan Technological University	M,D
New York University	M,D,O
North Central College	M
Northern Kentucky University	M,O
Northwest University	M
Old Dominion University	M,D
Pacific Northwest College of Art	M
Plymouth State University	M
Regent University	M,D
Regis College (MA)	M
St. Francis Xavier University	M
San Francisco State University	M
School of Visual Arts (NY)	M
Simon Fraser University	D
Southern Illinois University Carbondale	M
Stanford University	M,D
Stony Brook University, State University of New York	M,D,O
Summit University	M
Taylor College and Seminary	M,O
Texas A&M University	M
Texas A&M University–Kingsville	M
Texas Tech University	M,D
Trent University	D
Trinity College (United States)	M
Union Institute & University	M
Union University	M
University at Buffalo, the State University of New York	M*
University of Alaska Fairbanks	M
University of California, Davis	M,D
University of California, Irvine	D
University of California, Riverside	D
University of California, Santa Barbara	M,D
University of Denver	M,O
University of Hawaii at Hilo	M,D
University of Hawaii at Manoa	O
University of Houston	M
University of Houston–Clear Lake	M
University of Louisville	M,D
The University of Manchester	M,D
University of Minnesota, Twin Cities Campus	D
University of Montana	M,D,O
University of New Mexico	M,D
University of Pittsburgh	O*
University of Southern California	D
University of Southern Maine	M,O
The University of Texas at Austin	M,D
The University of Texas at San Antonio	M,D
University of the Sacred Heart	M
University of Washington, Bothell	M
Washington State University	M,D
West Chester University of Pennsylvania	M,O
Wheaton College	M,O
Wilfrid Laurier University	M
Wilson College	M

CURRICULUM AND INSTRUCTION

Acadia University	M
American College of Education	M
American InterContinental University Online	M
American Public University System	M
American University	M,O
Andrews University	M,D,O
Angelo State University	M
Appalachian State University	M
Arcadia University	M,D,O
Arizona State University at the Tempe campus	M
Arkansas Tech University	M,D,O
Arlington Baptist College	M
Armstrong State University	M,O
Ashland University	M
Auburn University	M,D,O
Augusta University	M,O
Aurora University	M,D
Austin Peay State University	M,O
Averett University	M
Azusa Pacific University	M
Ball State University	M,D
Barry University	D,O
Baylor University	M,D
Benedictine University	M
Berry College	M,O
Biola University	M,O
Black Hills State University	M
Bloomsburg University of Pennsylvania	M,O
Bluffton University	M
Bob Jones University	M,D,O
Boise State University	M,D
Boston College	M,D,O
Bowling Green State University	M
Bradley University	M,O
Brandon University	M,O
Brescia University	M
Buena Vista University	M
Caldwell University	M,D,O
California Baptist University	M
California Coast University	M,D
California State Polytechnic University, Pomona	M
California State University, Bakersfield	M
California State University, Chico	M
California State University, Dominguez Hills	M
California State University, Fresno	M
California State University, Los Angeles	M
California State University, Northridge	M
California State University, Sacramento	M
California State University, Stanislaus	M
Calvin College	M
Cambridge College	M,D,O
Capella University	M,D
Caribbean University	M,D
Carson-Newman University	M
Castleton University	M
Cedarville University	M,D
Central Michigan University	M,D,O
Central Washington University	M
Chapman University	M,D,O
City University of Seattle	M,O
Clarion University of Pennsylvania	M
Clark Atlanta University	M
Clemson University	M,D,O
The College at Brockport, State University of New York	M
The College of Idaho	M
The College of Saint Rose	M,O
The College of William and Mary	M,D
Colorado Christian University	M
Columbia International University	M,D,O
Columbus State University	M,D,O
Concordia University (United States)	M,D
Concordia University Ann Arbor	M
Concordia University Chicago	M
Concordia University Irvine	M
Concordia University, St. Paul	M,D,O
Concordia University Wisconsin	M
Coppin State University	M
Cornell University	M,D
Dakota Wesleyan University	M
Dallas Baptist University	M
Delaware State University	M
Delaware Valley University	M
DePaul University	M,D
Doane University	M
Dominican University	M
Drexel University	M,D
Duquesne University	M,O
East Carolina University	M,O
Eastern Kentucky University	M
Eastern Michigan University	M
Eastern New Mexico University	M
Eastern Washington University	M
East Tennessee State University	M,O
East Texas Baptist University	M
Emporia State University	M
Evangel University	M,D
Fairleigh Dickinson University, Metropolitan Campus	M
Ferris State University	M
Fitchburg State University	M
Florida Atlantic University	M,D,O
Florida Gulf Coast University	M
Florida International University	M,D,O
Florida State University	M,D,O
Fontbonne University	M
Fordham University	M,O
Framingham State University	M
Franciscan University of Steubenville	M
Franklin Pierce University	M,D,O
Freed-Hardeman University	M,O
Fresno Pacific University	M
Frostburg State University	M
Furman University	M,O
Gannon University	M,O
Gardner-Webb University	D
George Mason University	M
The George Washington University	M,D,O*
Georgia College & State University	O
Georgia Southern University	M,D
Georgia State University	M,D
Graceland University (IA)	M
Grambling State University	M,D,O
Grand Canyon University	M
Grand Valley State University	M
Harvard University	M*
Henderson State University	M,O
Hood College	M,O
Houston Baptist University	M
Idaho State University	M,O
Illinois State University	M,D
Indiana State University	M,D
Indiana University Bloomington	M,D,O
Indiana University of Pennsylvania	D
Indiana University–Purdue University Indianapolis	M,O
Inter American University of Puerto Rico, Arecibo Campus	M
Inter American University of Puerto Rico, Barranquitas Campus	M
Inter American University of Puerto Rico, Metropolitan Campus	M,D
Inter American University of Puerto Rico, San Germán Campus	D
Iowa State University of Science and Technology	M,D
John Brown University	M
Johnson State College	M
Kansas State University	M,D
Kean University	M
Keene State College	M,O
Kent State University	M,D,O
Kent State University at Stark	M
Kutztown University of Pennsylvania	M
LaGrange College	M,O
La Sierra University	M,D,O
Lee University	M,O
Lesley University	M,D,O
LeTourneau University	M
Lewis & Clark College	M
Liberty University	M,D,O
Lincoln Memorial University	M,D,O
Louisiana State University in Shreveport	M
Louisiana Tech University	M,D
Lourdes University	M
Loyola University Chicago	M,D
Loyola University Maryland	M
Lynchburg College	M
Lyndon State College	M
Malone University	M
Marian University (WI)	M,D
Marquette University	M,D,O
Martin Luther College	M
Massachusetts College of Liberal Arts	M,O
McDaniel College	M
McGill University	M,D,O
McKendree University	M,D,O
McNeese State University	M
Medaille College	M
Memorial University of Newfoundland	M,D,O
Mercer University	M,D,O
Merrimack College	M,O
Messiah College	M
Michigan State University	M,D,O
Middle Tennessee State University	M,O
Midwestern State University	M
Mills College	M,D,O
Minnesota State University Moorhead	M,O
Misericordia University	M
Mississippi College	M,D,O
Mississippi State University	M,D,O
Mississippi University for Women	M
Montana State University	M,D,O
Montana State University Billings	M
Montclair State University	M
Moravian College	M
Morehead State University	M,O
Mount Saint Vincent University	M
National Louis University	M,D,O
Newman University	M

*M—masters degree; D—doctorate; O—other advanced degree; *—Close-Up and/or Display*

New Mexico Highlands University	M
New Mexico State University	M,D,O
Nicholls State University	M
North Carolina State University	M,D
North Central College	M
North Dakota State University	M
Northeastern University	M,D
Northern Arizona University	M,D
Northern Illinois University	M,D
Northern Michigan University	M
Northern State University	M
Northwest Christian University	M
Northwestern Oklahoma State University	M
Northwestern State University of Louisiana	M
Northwest Nazarene University	M,D,O
Notre Dame de Namur University	M,D
Ohio Dominican University	M
Ohio University	M,D
Ohio Valley University	M
Oklahoma State University	M,D
Old Dominion University	M,D
Olivet Nazarene University	M
Oral Roberts University	M,D
Ottawa University	M
Our Lady of the Lake University of San Antonio	M
Pacific Lutheran University	M
Park University	M,O
Penn State Harrisburg	M,D,O
Penn State University Park	M,D,O
Peru State College	M
Piedmont College	M,O
Piedmont International University	M,D
Plymouth State University	M
Point Park University	M
Pontifical Catholic University of Puerto Rico	M,D
Prairie View A&M University	M
Purdue University	M,D,O
Quincy University	M
Radford University	M
Randolph College	M
Regent University	M,D,O
Regis University	M,O
Rider University	M,O
Rivier University	M,D,O
St. Catherine University	M
St. Cloud State University	M
St. Francis Xavier University	M
Saint Joseph's University	M,D,O
Saint Louis University	M,D
Saint Michael's College	M,O
Saint Vincent College	M
Saint Xavier University	M
Salem International University	M
Salisbury University	M
Sam Houston State University	M,D
San Diego State University	M
San Jose State University	M,D,O
Shawnee State University	M
Shaw University	M
Shepherd University (WV)	M
Shippensburg University of Pennsylvania	M
Simon Fraser University	M,D
Simpson University	M
Sonoma State University	M,D,O
South Dakota State University	M
Southeastern Louisiana University	M
Southern Arkansas University–Magnolia	M
Southern Illinois University Carbondale	M,D
Southern Illinois University Edwardsville	M
Southern New Hampshire University	M,D,O
Southwestern Adventist University	M
Southwestern Assemblies of God University	M
Southwestern College (KS)	M,D
Stanford University	M
State University of New York at Oswego	M
State University of New York at Plattsburgh	M
State University of New York College at Potsdam	M
Stephens College	M
Stetson University	M,O
Summit University	M
Syracuse University	M,D,O
Tarleton State University	M
Teachers College, Columbia University	M,D
Tennessee State University	M,D
Tennessee Technological University	M,O
Tennessee Wesleyan College	M
Texas A&M International University	M
Texas A&M University	M,D
Texas A&M University–Central Texas	M,O
Texas A&M University–Corpus Christi	M,D
Texas A&M University–Texarkana	M
Texas Christian University	M,O
Texas Southern University	M,D
Texas Tech University	M,D
Texas Woman's University	M,D
Trevecca Nazarene University	M,O
Trinity Washington University	M
Universidad Adventista de las Antillas	M
Universidad del Turabo	M,D
Universidad Metropolitana	M
Université de Montréal	M,D,O
Université Laval	M,D
University at Albany, State University of New York	M,D,O
University at Buffalo, the State University of New York	M,D,O*
The University of Akron	M
The University of Alabama at Birmingham	O
University of Arkansas	M,D,O
University of Arkansas at Little Rock	M
The University of British Columbia	M,D
University of Calgary	M,D
University of California, Davis	M,D
University of California, San Diego	M,D
University of Central Arkansas	M,O
University of Cincinnati	M,D
University of Colorado Boulder	M,D
University of Colorado Colorado Springs	M,D
University of Delaware	M,D,O*
University of Denver	M,D,O
University of Detroit Mercy	M,D,O
University of Florida	M,D,O
University of Hawaii at Manoa	M,D
University of Holy Cross	M
University of Houston	M,D
University of Houston–Clear Lake	M
University of Houston–Downtown	M
University of Houston–Victoria	M
University of Idaho	M,D,O
University of Illinois at Chicago	M,D
University of Illinois at Urbana–Champaign	M,D,O
University of Indianapolis	M
University of Jamestown	M
The University of Kansas	M,D*
University of Kentucky	M,D
University of Louisiana at Lafayette	M
University of Louisiana at Monroe	M,D
University of Louisville	M,D,O
University of Manitoba	M
University of Mary	M,D
University of Mary Hardin-Baylor	M,D
University of Maryland, College Park	M,D,O
University of Massachusetts Lowell	M
University of Memphis	M,D
University of Michigan–Dearborn	D,O
University of Michigan–Flint	M,D,O
University of Minnesota, Twin Cities Campus	M,D,O
University of Missouri	M,D,O
University of Missouri–Kansas City	M,D,O
University of Missouri–St. Louis	M,O
University of Montana	M,D
University of Nebraska at Kearney	M
University of Nebraska–Lincoln	M,D,O
University of Nevada, Las Vegas	M,D,O
University of Nevada, Reno	D
University of New England	M,O
University of New Hampshire	D
University of New Orleans	M,D
The University of North Carolina at Chapel Hill	M,D
The University of North Carolina at Charlotte	M,D,O
The University of North Carolina at Greensboro	M,D,O
The University of North Carolina Wilmington	M,D
University of Northern Iowa	D
University of North Texas	M,D,O
University of Oklahoma	M,D,O*
University of Phoenix–Central Valley Campus	M
University of Phoenix–Colorado Campus	M
University of Phoenix–Colorado Springs Downtown Campus	M,O
University of Phoenix–Dallas Campus	M
University of Phoenix–Hawaii Campus	M
University of Phoenix–Houston Campus	M
University of Phoenix–Las Vegas Campus	M
University of Phoenix–New Mexico Campus	M
University of Phoenix–North Florida Campus	M
University of Phoenix–Online Campus	M,D,O
University of Phoenix–Phoenix Campus	M
University of Phoenix–Sacramento Valley Campus	M,O
University of Phoenix–San Antonio Campus	M
University of Phoenix–San Diego Campus	M
University of Phoenix–Southern Arizona Campus	M,O
University of Phoenix–South Florida Campus	M
University of Phoenix–Utah Campus	M
University of Phoenix–Washington D.C. Campus	M,D,O
University of Puerto Rico, Río Piedras Campus	M,D
University of Regina	M
University of Rochester	M,D*
University of St. Francis (IL)	M,D,O
University of Saint Joseph	M
University of St. Thomas (MN)	M,O
University of St. Thomas (TX)	M
University of San Diego	M
University of San Francisco	M,D
University of Saskatchewan	M,D,O
The University of Scranton	M
University of South Africa	M,D
University of South Carolina	D
The University of South Dakota	M,D,O
University of Southern Mississippi	M,D,O
University of South Florida	M,D,O
University of South Florida Sarasota-Manatee	M
The University of Tampa	M
The University of Tennessee	M,D,O
The University of Tennessee at Martin	M
The University of Texas at Arlington	M
The University of Texas at Austin	M,D
The University of Texas at El Paso	M,D
The University of Texas at San Antonio	M,D
University of the Pacific	M,D
University of the Southwest	M
The University of Toledo	M,D,O
University of Vermont	M
University of Victoria	M,D
University of Virginia	M,D,O
University of Washington	M,D*
The University of West Alabama	M,O
The University of Western Ontario	M
University of West Florida	M,D,O
University of Wisconsin–Madison	M,D
University of Wisconsin–Milwaukee	M,D
University of Wisconsin–Oshkosh	M
University of Wisconsin–Superior	M
University of Wyoming	M,D
Utah State University	D
Virginia Polytechnic Institute and State University	M,D,O
Virginia Union University	M
Walden University	M,D,O
Walla Walla University	M
Washburn University	M
Washington State University	M,D
Waynesburg University	M,D
Wayne State College	M
Wayne State University	M,D,O
Weber State University	M
Western Connecticut State University	M
Western New England University	M
West Texas A&M University	M
West Virginia University	M,D
Wichita State University	M
Wilkes University	M,D
William Paterson University of New Jersey	M
William Woods University	M,D,O
Wisconsin Lutheran College	M
Wright State University	M,O
Xavier University of Louisiana	M
Youngstown State University	M

DANCE

Arizona State University at the Tempe campus	M
Bennington College	M
California Institute of the Arts	M,O
California State University, Fullerton	M
California State University, Long Beach	M
Case Western Reserve University	M*
The College at Brockport, State University of New York	M
Florida State University	M
The George Washington University	M,O*
Hollins University	M
Jacksonville University	M*
Mills College	M
New Mexico State University	M,D,O
New York University	M,D,O
Northern Illinois University	M
The Ohio State University	M,D
Saint Mary's College of California	M
Sam Houston State University	M
Sarah Lawrence College	M
Smith College	M
Temple University	M,D*
Texas Woman's University	M,D
Tulane University	M
Université du Québec à Montréal	M
The University of Arizona	M
University of California, Irvine	M
University of California, Los Angeles	M,D
University of California, Riverside	M
University of California, San Diego	M,D
University of Colorado Boulder	M,D
University of Hawaii at Manoa	M,D
University of Illinois at Urbana–Champaign	M
The University of Iowa	M*
University of Maryland, Baltimore County	M
University of Maryland, College Park	M
University of Michigan	M
University of New Mexico	M
The University of North Carolina at Greensboro	M
University of Oklahoma	M*
University of Oregon	M
The University of Texas at Austin	M,D
University of Utah	M*
University of Washington	M*
Washington University in St. Louis	M
Wayne State University	M,D,O
Wilson College	M
York University	M,D

DATABASE SYSTEMS

Austin Peay State University	M
Boston University	M,O
Case Western Reserve University	M*
Central European University	M,D
Claremont Graduate University	M,D,O
Clarion University of Pennsylvania	M
Colorado Technical University Colorado Springs	M,D
Colorado Technical University Denver South	M
Columbia University	M*
Elmhurst College	M
Fairfield University	M,O
Ferris State University	M
Fordham University	M
Illinois Institute of Technology	M,D
Indiana University Bloomington	M,D,O
Lewis University	M
Lipscomb University	M,O
London Metropolitan University	M,D
Manhattan College	M
Metropolitan State University	M,D,O
Michigan Technological University	M,D,O
Montclair State University	O
National University	M,O
New College of Florida	M
New York University	M,O
Northwestern University	M*
Penn State Great Valley	M,O
Pratt Institute	M,O*
Queens College of the City University of New York	M
Regis University	M,O
Robert Morris University	M,D
Rochester Institute of Technology	O
Rockhurst University	M,O
Sacred Heart University	M,O
St. John's University (NY)	M
Saint Mary's College	M
Saint Peter's University	M
Seattle University	M,O
Southern Methodist University	M
Stevens Institute of Technology	M,D,O
Syracuse University	M
Texas Tech University	M,D
Towson University	M,D,O
University of Houston–Downtown	M
The University of Iowa	M*
University of Maryland University College	M,O
University of Massachusetts Dartmouth	M
University of Michigan	M,D,O
University of Michigan–Dearborn	M
University of Minnesota, Twin Cities Campus	M
University of Nebraska at Omaha	M,D,O
University of New Haven	M
The University of North Carolina at Charlotte	M,O
University of Notre Dame	M
University of Oklahoma	M*
University of Rochester	M*
University of San Francisco	M
The University of South Dakota	M
University of South Florida	M,D
University of the Incarnate Word	M
University of Virginia	M
University of West Florida	M
University of Wisconsin–La Crosse	M
Villanova University	M
Virginia International University	M,O
Washington University in St. Louis	M
Worcester Polytechnic Institute	M,O

DECORATIVE ARTS

Bard Graduate Center: Decorative Arts, Design History, Material Culture	M,D*
Sotheby's Institute of Art–London	M
Sotheby's Institute of Art–New York	M

DEMOGRAPHY AND POPULATION STUDIES

The American University in Cairo	M,O
Bowling Green State University	M,D
Cornell University	M,D
Florida State University	M
Harvard University	M,D*
Johns Hopkins University	M,D
Miami University	M,D
New York University	M,D
Princeton University	D,O
Université de Montréal	M,D
Université du Québec, Institut National de la Recherche Scientifique	M,D,O
University at Albany, State University of New York	M,D,O
University of Alberta	M,D
University of California, Berkeley	M,D
University of California, Irvine	M
University of Guelph	M,D
University of Hawaii at Manoa	O
University of Pennsylvania	M,D*
University of Puerto Rico, Medical Sciences Campus	M
The University of Texas at San Antonio	D
University of Wisconsin–Madison	M,D

DENTAL HYGIENE

Boston University	M,D,O
Eastern Washington University	M
Idaho State University	M

Missouri Southern State University	M
The Ohio State University	M,D
Old Dominion University	M
Université de Montréal	O
University of Alberta	O
University of Bridgeport	M
University of Michigan	M
University of Missouri–Kansas City	M,D,O
University of New Mexico	M
The University of North Carolina at Chapel Hill	M,D

DENTISTRY

A.T. Still University	D
Augusta University	D
Case Western Reserve University	D*
Columbia University	D*
Creighton University	D
East Carolina University	D
Harvard University	M,D,O*
Howard University	D,O
Idaho State University	O
Indiana University–Purdue University Indianapolis	M,D,O
Loma Linda University	M,D,O
Louisiana State University Health Sciences Center	D
Marquette University	D
McGill University	M,D,O
Medical University of South Carolina	D
Meharry Medical College	D
Midwestern University, Downers Grove Campus	D
Midwestern University, Glendale Campus	D
New York University	D
Nova Southeastern University	M,D*
The Ohio State University	M,D
Oregon Health & Science University	D,O
Roseman University of Health Sciences	M,D,O
Rutgers University–Newark	M,D,O
Saint Louis University	M
Southern Illinois University Edwardsville	D
Stony Brook University, State University of New York	D,O
Temple University	D*
Texas A&M University	M,D,O
Tufts University	D
Universidad Central del Este	D
Universidad Iberoamericana	M,D
Universidad Nacional Pedro Henriquez Urena	D
Université Laval	D
University at Buffalo, the State University of New York	D*
The University of Alabama at Birmingham	D
University of Alberta	D
The University of British Columbia	D
University of California, Los Angeles	D,O
University of California, San Francisco	D
University of Colorado Denver	M,D
University of Connecticut Health Center	D,O*
University of Detroit Mercy	M,D,O
University of Florida	D,O
University of Illinois at Chicago	D
The University of Iowa	M,D,O*
University of Kentucky	D
University of Louisville	M,D
The University of Manchester	M,D
University of Manitoba	D
University of Maryland, Baltimore	D,O
University of Michigan	D
University of Minnesota, Twin Cities Campus	D
University of Mississippi Medical Center	M,D
University of Missouri–Kansas City	M,D,O
University of Nevada, Las Vegas	M,D
University of New England	D
The University of North Carolina at Chapel Hill	D
University of Oklahoma Health Sciences Center	D,O
University of Pennsylvania	D*
University of Pittsburgh	M,D,O*
University of Puerto Rico, Medical Sciences Campus	D
University of Saskatchewan	D
University of Southern California	D
The University of Tennessee Health Science Center	D
The University of Texas Health Science Center at Houston	M,D
The University of Texas Health Science Center at San Antonio	M,D,O
University of the Pacific	M,D,O
University of Toronto	D
University of Utah	D*
University of Washington	D*
The University of Western Ontario	D
Virginia Commonwealth University	M,D
Western University of Health Sciences	D
West Virginia University	D

DEVELOPMENTAL BIOLOGY

Albert Einstein College of Medicine	D
Baylor College of Medicine	D
Brigham Young University	M,D
California Institute of Technology	D
California State University, Sacramento	M
Carnegie Mellon University	M,D
Columbia University	M,D*
Cornell University	M,D
Duke University	O*
Emory University	D
Illinois State University	M,D
Iowa State University of Science and Technology	M,D
Irell & Manella Graduate School of Biological Sciences	D*
Johns Hopkins University	D
Louisiana State University Health Sciences Center	D
Marquette University	M,D
Massachusetts Institute of Technology	D
Medical University of South Carolina	D
New York University	M,D
Northwestern University	D*
The Ohio State University	M,D
Oregon Health & Science University	D
Oregon State University	M,D
Penn State Hershey Medical Center	D
Purdue University	M,D
Rutgers University–Newark	D,O
Rutgers University–New Brunswick	M,D
San Francisco State University	M
Stanford University	M,D
Stony Brook University, State University of New York	M,D
Thomas Jefferson University	M,D
Tufts University	D
University at Albany, State University of New York	D
The University of Alabama at Birmingham	D
The University of British Columbia	M,D
University of California, Davis	M,D
University of California, Irvine	M,D
University of California, Los Angeles	M,D
University of California, Riverside	M,D
University of California, San Francisco	D
University of California, Santa Barbara	M,D
University of California, Santa Cruz	M,D
University of Chicago	D
University of Cincinnati	D
University of Colorado Boulder	M,D
University of Colorado Denver	M,D
University of Connecticut Health Center	D*
University of Delaware	M,D*
University of Hawaii at Manoa	M,D
University of Illinois at Urbana–Champaign	D
The University of Kansas	M,D*
The University of Manchester	M,D
University of Massachusetts Amherst	D*
University of Miami	D
University of Michigan	M,D
University of Minnesota, Twin Cities Campus	M,D
University of Montana	D
The University of North Carolina at Chapel Hill	M,D
University of Pennsylvania	D*
University of Pittsburgh	D*
University of South Carolina	M,D
University of Southern California	D
The University of Texas Health Science Center at Houston	M,D
The University of Texas Southwestern Medical Center	D
Vanderbilt University	M,D*
Washington University in St. Louis	D
Wesleyan University	D
West Virginia University	M,D
Yale University	D*

DEVELOPMENTAL EDUCATION

Austin Peay State University	M
Eastern Michigan University	M,O
Ferris State University	M
Grambling State University	M,D,O
Instituto Tecnológico y de Estudios Superiores de Monterrey, Campus Ciudad Obregón	M
National Louis University	M,D,O
North Carolina State University	M,D,O
Penn State Harrisburg	M,D,O
Rutgers University–New Brunswick	M
Sam Houston State University	M,D
Texas State University	M,D
The University of Iowa	M,D*
Walden University	M,D,O

DEVELOPMENTAL PSYCHOLOGY

Andrews University	M,D
Arizona State University at the Tempe campus	M,D
Bay Path University	M
Bethel University (MN)	M,D,O
Boston College	M,D
Boston Graduate School of Psychoanalysis	O
Bowling Green State University	M,D
Brandeis University	M,D
Capella University	M
Carnegie Mellon University	D
Chatham University	M,D
Claremont Graduate University	M,D,O
Clark University	D
Clayton State University	M
Cornell University	M,D
Delaware Valley University	M
Duke University	D*
Emory University	D
Erikson Institute	M,O
Florida International University	M,D
Florida State University	D
Fordham University	D
George Mason University	M,D,O
Georgia State University	D
The Graduate Center, City University of New York	D
Harvard University	D*
Howard University	M,D
Humboldt State University	M
Illinois State University	M,D,O
Indiana University Bloomington	D
La Salle University	M,D
Louisiana State University and Agricultural & Mechanical College	M,D
Loyola University Chicago	M,D
McGill University	M,D,O
The New School	M,D
New York University	M,D
North Carolina State University	D
North Dakota State University	D
The Ohio State University	D
Pace University	M,D
Pontificia Universidad Catolica Madre y Maestra	M
Queen's University at Kingston	M,D
Regis University	M,D,O
San Francisco State University	M,O
Teachers College, Columbia University	M,D
Texas Christian University	M,D
Université de Montréal	M,D
The University of Alabama at Birmingham	M,D
The University of British Columbia	M,D
University of Connecticut	M,D*
University of Denver	D
University of Houston	M,D
University of Illinois at Chicago	M,D
The University of Kansas	M,D*
University of Louisville	D
The University of Manchester	M,D
University of Maryland, Baltimore County	D
University of Maryland, College Park	M,D
University of Massachusetts Amherst	M,D*
University of Miami	M,D
University of Michigan	D
University of Montana	M,D,O
University of Nebraska–Lincoln	M,D,O
University of New Mexico	D
The University of North Carolina at Chapel Hill	D
The University of North Carolina at Greensboro	M,D
University of Notre Dame	D
University of Oregon	M,D
University of Pittsburgh	M,D*
University of Rochester	D*
University of Southern California	M,D
The University of Texas at Austin	D
University of Victoria	M,D
University of Washington	D*
University of Wisconsin–Madison	D
University of Wisconsin–Milwaukee	M,D
Virginia Commonwealth University	D
Viterbo University	M
Washington University in St. Louis	D
Wayne State University	M,D
West Virginia University	M,D
Wilfrid Laurier University	M,D
Yale University	D*

DISABILITY STUDIES

Brandeis University	D
Brock University	M,O
California Baptist University	M
Chapman University	M,D,O
Montclair State University	M,O
Syracuse University	O
University of Hawaii at Manoa	O
University of Illinois at Chicago	M,D
University of Manitoba	M
University of Northern British Columbia	M,D,O
University of Pittsburgh	O*
Utah State University	M,D,O
York University	M,D

DISTANCE EDUCATION DEVELOPMENT

American Public University System	M
Athabasca University	M,D,O
Barry University	O
Boise State University	M,D,O
Brandeis University	M
California Baptist University	M
Capella University	M,D
Coastal Carolina University	M,O
Colorado Christian University	M
Colorado State University	M
Dallas Baptist University	M
Endicott College	M
Fairmont State University	M
The George Washington University	O*
Keiser University	M
Lenoir-Rhyne University	M
Lesley University	M,D,O
Liberty University	M,D,O
Millersville University of Pennsylvania	M
National University	M,O
New Mexico State University	O
New York Institute of Technology	M,O
Nova Southeastern University	M,D,O*
Post University	M
Regent University	M,D,O
Saginaw Valley State University	M
Télé-université	M,D
Texas Tech University	M,D
Thomas Edison State University	O
University of Colorado Denver	M
University of Maryland, Baltimore County	M,O
University of Maryland University College	M,O
University of South Florida	O
University of the Incarnate Word	M,D
Virginia Polytechnic Institute and State University	M,O
Walden University	M,D,O
Waynesburg University	M,D
Wayne State University	M,D,O
Western Illinois University	M,O
Wilkes University	M,D

EARLY CHILDHOOD EDUCATION

Alabama Agricultural and Mechanical University	M,D,O
Alabama State University	M,O
Albany State University	M,O
Albright College	M
American International College	M,D,O
Anna Maria College	M,O
Antioch University New England	M
Arcadia University	M,D,O
Arkansas State University	M,D,O
Armstrong State University	M,O
Auburn University	M,D,O
Auburn University at Montgomery	M,O
Augusta University	M,O
Bank Street College of Education	M
Barry University	M,D,O
Bayamón Central University	M,O
Berry College	M
Binghamton University, State University of New York	M*
Biola University	M,O
Bloomsburg University of Pennsylvania	M
Boise State University	M
Bowling Green State University	M
Brenau University	M,O
Bridgewater State University	M
Brooklyn College of the City University of New York	M,O
Buffalo State College, State University of New York	M
California State University, Dominguez Hills	M
California State University, East Bay	M
California State University, Fresno	M
California State University, Northridge	M
Cambridge College	M,D,O
Canisius College	M
Capella University	M
Caribbean University	M,D
Carlow University	M
Central Connecticut State University	M,O
Central Michigan University	M,O
Champlain College	M
Chatham University	M
Chestnut Hill College	M
Chicago State University	M
City College of the City University of New York	M
Clarion University of Pennsylvania	M
Cleveland State University	M
The College at Brockport, State University of New York	M
College of Charleston	M
The College of New Jersey	M
The College of New Rochelle	M
The College of Saint Rose	M,O
Colorado Christian University	M
Columbia International University	M,D,O
Columbus State University	M,O
Concordia University (United States)	M,D
Concordia University Chicago	M,D
Concordia University, Nebraska	M
Concordia University, St. Paul	M,D,O
Concordia University Wisconsin	M
Daemen College	M
Dallas Baptist University	M
DePaul University	M,D
Dominican University	M
Duquesne University	M
East Carolina University	M,D
Eastern Connecticut State University	M
Eastern Illinois University	M
Eastern Michigan University	M
Eastern Nazarene College	M,O
Eastern New Mexico University	M
Eastern University	M,O
Eastern Washington University	M
East Stroudsburg University of Pennsylvania	M
East Tennessee State University	M,D,O
Edinboro University of Pennsylvania	M,O
Ellis University	M
Elms College	M,O
Emporia State University	M
Endicott College	M

*M—masters degree; D—doctorate; O—other advanced degree; *—Close-Up and/or Display*

Erikson Institute	M,D
Fitchburg State University	M
Five Towns College	M,D
Florida Atlantic University	M,D,O
Florida International University	M,D,O
Florida State University	M,D,O
Fontbonne University	M
Fordham University	M,O
Framingham State University	M
Furman University	M,O
Gallaudet University	M,D,O
Gateway Seminary	M,D,O
George Mason University	M
The George Washington University	M*
Georgia College & State University	M
Georgia Southern University	M,O
Georgia Southwestern State University	M,O
Georgia State University	M,D,O
Gordon College	M,O
Governors State University	M
Grand Valley State University	M,O
Harding University	M,O
Hebrew College	M,O
Henderson State University	M,O
Hofstra University	M,D,O
Holy Family University	M
Hood College	M,O
Hunter College of the City University of New York	M,O
Indiana University–Purdue University Indianapolis	M,O
Inter American University of Puerto Rico, Guayama Campus	M
Iona College	M
Jackson State University	M,D,O
Jacksonville State University	M
James Madison University	M
John Carroll University	M
Johns Hopkins University	M
Jose Maria Vargas University	M
Kansas State University	M,O
Kean University	M
Kennesaw State University	M
Kent State University	M,D,O
Keuka College	M
Keystone College	M
Lander University	M
La Salle University	M,O
Lee University	M,O
Lehman College of the City University of New York	M
Le Moyne College	M,O
Lesley University	M,D,O
Lewis & Clark College	M
Lewis University	M,D,O
Liberty University	M,D,O
Lincoln University (PA)	M
London Metropolitan University	M,D
Long Island University–Brentwood Campus	M,O
Long Island University–Hudson at Rockland	M,O
Long Island University–Hudson at Westchester	M,O
Long Island University–LIU Brooklyn	M,O
Long Island University–LIU Post	M,D,O
Long Island University–Riverhead	M,O
Louisiana Tech University	M,D
Loyola University Maryland	M,O
Manhattan College	M,O
Manhattanville College	M*
Marshall University	M
Martin Luther College	M
Maryville University of Saint Louis	M,D
Marywood University	M
McNeese State University	M,O
Mercer University	M,D,O
Mercy College	M
Merrimack College	M,O
Middle Tennessee State University	M,O
Millersville University of Pennsylvania	M
Mills College	M,D,O
Mississippi State University	M,D,O
Missouri Southern State University	M
Missouri State University	M
Molloy College	M,O
Mount St. Joseph University	M,O
Mount Saint Mary College	M,O
Murray State University	M
National Louis University	M,D,O
National University	M,O
Nazareth College of Rochester	M
New Jersey City University	M
New Mexico State University	M,D,O
New York Institute of Technology	M
New York University	M
Niagara University	M,O
Norfolk State University	M
North Carolina Agricultural and Technical State University	M
Northeastern Illinois University	M
Northeastern State University	M
Northern Arizona University	M,D
Northern Illinois University	M,D
Northwestern College	M,O
Northwestern State University of Louisiana	M
Northwest Missouri State University	M
Oakland University	M,D,O
Oklahoma City University	M
Old Dominion University	M,D
Ottawa University	M
Pace University	M,O
Pacific Oaks College	M
Pacific University	M
Piedmont College	M,O
Pontificia Universidad Catolica Madre y Maestra	M
Prescott College	M,D
Radford University	M,O
Reinhardt University	M
Rhode Island College	M
Rivier University	M,D,O
Roberts Wesleyan College	M
Rockford University	M
Roosevelt University	M
Rutgers University–New Brunswick	M,D
Saginaw Valley State University	M
St. Bonaventure University	M
St. Catherine University	M
St. John's University (NY)	M
St. Joseph's College, Long Island Campus	M
Saint Mary's College of California	M
Saint Xavier University	M
Salem State University	M
Samford University	M,D,O
San Francisco State University	M,D,O
San Jose State University	M,D,O
Shaw University	M
Shippensburg University of Pennsylvania	M
Siena Heights University	M,O
Sonoma State University	M,D,O
South Carolina State University	M
Southern Oregon University	M
Southwestern College (KS)	M,D
Southwestern Oklahoma State University	M
Southwest Minnesota State University	M
Spring Hill College	M
State University of New York at Fredonia	M
State University of New York at New Paltz	M
State University of New York at Oswego	M
State University of New York at Plattsburgh	O
State University of New York College at Cortland	M
State University of New York College at Geneseo	M
State University of New York College at Potsdam	M
Stephen F. Austin State University	M
Syracuse University	M
Teachers College, Columbia University	M,D
Tennessee Technological University	M,O
Texas A&M University–Corpus Christi	M,D
Texas A&M University–Kingsville	M
Texas A&M University–San Antonio	M
Texas Woman's University	M,D
Theological University of the Caribbean	M,D
Towson University	M,O
Trident University International	M
Trinity Washington University	M
Troy University	M,O
Tufts University	M,D
Universidad del Turabo	M
University at Buffalo, the State University of New York	M,D,O*
The University of Alabama at Birmingham	M,D
University of Alaska Anchorage	M,O
University of Alaska Southeast	M
University of Arkansas	M
University of Arkansas at Pine Bluff	M
University of Bridgeport	M,D,O
The University of British Columbia	M,D
University of Central Florida	D
University of Central Missouri	M,D,O
University of Central Oklahoma	M
University of Cincinnati	M
University of Colorado Denver	M,D
University of Dayton	M
University of Denver	M,D,O
The University of Findlay	M,D
University of Florida	M,D,O
University of Georgia	M,D,O
University of Hartford	M
University of Hawaii at Manoa	M
University of Houston–Clear Lake	M
University of Illinois at Chicago	M,D
University of Kentucky	M,D
University of Louisiana at Monroe	M,D
University of Louisville	M,D,O
University of Maine	M,D,O
University of Maine at Farmington	M
University of Maryland, Baltimore County	M
University of Massachusetts Amherst	M,D,O*
University of Massachusetts Boston	M,D
University of Memphis	M,D
University of Miami	M,O
University of Michigan–Dearborn	M
University of Michigan–Flint	M,D,O
University of Minnesota, Twin Cities Campus	M,D,O
University of Missouri	M,D,O
University of Missouri–St. Louis	M,O
University of Nebraska at Kearney	M
University of Nebraska–Lincoln	M,D
University of Nevada, Las Vegas	M,D,O
University of New Hampshire	M
University of New Mexico	D
The University of North Carolina at Chapel Hill	M,D
The University of North Carolina at Charlotte	M,D,O
The University of North Carolina at Greensboro	M,D,O
The University of North Carolina Wilmington	M
University of North Dakota	M
University of Northern Colorado	M,D
University of Northern Iowa	M
University of North Georgia	M,O
University of North Texas	M,D,O
University of Phoenix–Bay Area Campus	M,D,O
University of Phoenix–North Florida Campus	M
University of Phoenix–Online Campus	M,O
University of Phoenix–Phoenix Campus	M
University of Phoenix–South Florida Campus	M
University of Phoenix–Washington D.C. Campus	M,D,O
University of Pittsburgh	M*
University of Puerto Rico, Río Piedras Campus	M
University of St. Thomas (MN)	M,O
University of South Alabama	M,D
University of South Carolina	M,D
University of South Carolina Upstate	M
The University of South Dakota	M,D,O
University of South Florida	M,D,O
The University of Tennessee	M,D,O
The University of Texas at Austin	M,D
The University of Texas at San Antonio	M,D
The University of Texas at Tyler	M
The University of Texas of the Permian Basin	M
The University of Texas Rio Grande Valley	M
University of the District of Columbia	M
University of the Sacred Heart	M,O
University of the Southwest	M
The University of Toledo	M,D,O
University of Utah	M,D*
University of Victoria	M,D
University of Virginia	M,D
The University of West Alabama	M,O
University of West Florida	M
University of West Georgia	M,D,O
University of Wisconsin–Milwaukee	M
University of Wisconsin–Oshkosh	M
Upper Iowa University	M
Ursuline College	M
Valdosta State University	M,O
Virginia Commonwealth University	M,O
Viterbo University	M,O
Wagner College	M
Walden University	M,D,O
Wayne State College	M
Wayne State University	M,D,O
Wesleyan College	M
West Chester University of Pennsylvania	M,O
Western Kentucky University	M,O
Western Oregon University	M
Westfield State University	M
West Virginia University	M,D
Wheelock College	M
Wichita State University	M
Widener University	M,D
Wilkes University	M,D
Worcester State University	M
Wright State University	M
Xavier University	M
Youngstown State University	M

EAST EUROPEAN AND RUSSIAN STUDIES

Boston College	M
Brown University	M,D
Carleton University	M,O
Columbia University	M,D*
Cornell University	M,D
Florida State University	M
Georgetown University	M
The George Washington University	M*
Harvard University	M*
Indiana University Bloomington	M,O
La Salle University	M,O
The Ohio State University	M,D
Stanford University	M
University of Alberta	M,D
The University of British Columbia	M,D
University of Illinois at Chicago	M,D
University of Illinois at Urbana–Champaign	M
The University of Kansas	M,O*
University of Michigan	M,O
The University of North Carolina at Chapel Hill	M
University of Pittsburgh	O*
University of Saskatchewan	M
The University of Texas at Austin	M
University of Toronto	M
University of Washington	M*
Yale University	M,D*

ECOLOGY

Baylor University	D
Brown University	D
California Institute of Integral Studies	M,D
California State University, Stanislaus	M
Clemson University	M,D
Colorado State University	M,D
Columbia University	M,D*
Cornell University	M,D
Dalhousie University	M
Dartmouth College	D*
Duke University	D,O*
Eastern Kentucky University	M
Eastern Michigan University	M
Eastern New Mexico University	M
Emory University	D
Florida Institute of Technology	M,D
Florida State University	M,D
Frostburg State University	M
George Mason University	M,D
Illinois State University	M,D
Indiana State University	M,D
Indiana University Bloomington	M,D,O
Inter American University of Puerto Rico, Bayamón Campus	M
Iowa State University of Science and Technology	M,D
Kent State University	M,D
Laurentian University	M,D
Lesley University	M,D,O
Marquette University	M,D
Michigan State University	D
Michigan Technological University	M,D
Montana State University	M,D
Montclair State University	M
North Dakota State University	M,D
Northeastern University	M,D
The Ohio State University	M,D
Ohio University	M,D
Oklahoma State University	M,D
Old Dominion University	D
Oregon State University	M,D
Penn State University Park	M,D
Princeton University	D
Purdue University	M,D
Rice University	M,D
Rutgers University–New Brunswick	M,D
San Diego State University	M,D
San Francisco State University	M
San Jose State University	M,O
Sonoma State University	M
Stanford University	M,D
State University of New York College of Environmental Science and Forestry	M,D
Stony Brook University, State University of New York	M,D
Tulane University	M,D
Universidad Nacional Pedro Henriquez Urena	M
University at Albany, State University of New York	D
University at Buffalo, the State University of New York	M,D,O*
University of Alberta	M,D
The University of Arizona	M,D
University of California, Davis	M,D
University of California, Irvine	M,D
University of California, Los Angeles	M,D
University of California, Santa Barbara	M,D
University of California, Santa Cruz	M,D
University of Chicago	D
University of Colorado Boulder	M,D
University of Colorado Denver	M,D
University of Connecticut	M,D*
University of Delaware	M,D*
University of Denver	M,D
University of Florida	M,D,O
University of Georgia	M,D
University of Guelph	M,D
University of Illinois at Urbana–Champaign	M,D
The University of Kansas	M,D*
University of Maine	M,D
The University of Manchester	M,D
University of Manitoba	M,D
University of Maryland, College Park	M,D
University of Michigan	M,D
University of Minnesota, Twin Cities Campus	M,D
University of Missouri	M,D
University of Montana	M,D
University of Nevada, Reno	D
University of New Haven	M,O
The University of North Carolina at Chapel Hill	M,D
University of North Dakota	M,D
University of Notre Dame	M,D
University of Oklahoma	D*
University of Oregon	M,D
University of Pittsburgh	D*
University of Puerto Rico, Río Piedras Campus	M,D
University of South Carolina	M,D
University of South Florida	M,D
The University of Tennessee	M,D
The University of Texas at Austin	D
The University of Toledo	M,D
University of Toronto	M,D
University of Washington	M,D*
University of Wisconsin–Madison	M
University of Wyoming	M,D
Utah State University	M,D
Washington University in St. Louis	D
Wesleyan University	D
Western Illinois University	D
Yale University	D*

ECONOMIC DEVELOPMENT

Albany State University	M
The American University in Cairo	M,O
Ball State University	M,O
The Catholic University of America	M
Claremont Graduate University	M,D,O
Cleveland State University	M,O
Concordia University (Canada)	O

Cornell University	M,D
East Carolina University	M,O
Eastern University	M
East Tennessee State University	M,O
Fordham University	M,O
Georgetown University	D
Georgia Institute of Technology	M,D
Georgia State University	M,D,O
Indiana University Bloomington	M,D,O
New Mexico State University	M,D,O
Northeastern University	M,D
State University of New York Empire State College	M
Troy University	M
Université de Sherbrooke	D
University of Central Arkansas	M,O
University of Colorado Denver	M
University of Houston–Victoria	M
The University of North Carolina at Greensboro	M,D,O
University of Pennsylvania	M,O*
University of Puerto Rico, Río Piedras Campus	M
University of Southern California	M,D
University of Southern Mississippi	M
University of Waterloo	M
Vanderbilt University	M,D*
Washington University in St. Louis	M,D,O
Wayne State University	M,D,O
Western Illinois University	M,O
West Virginia University	M,D
Williams College	M
Yale University	M*

ECONOMICS

Albany State University	M
American University	M,D,O
The American University in Cairo	M,O
American University of Armenia	M
American University of Beirut	M,D
Andrews University	M
Arizona State University at the Tempe campus	D
Assumption College	M,O
Auburn University	M
Bard College	M
Baruch College of the City University of New York	M
Baylor University	M
Binghamton University, State University of New York	M,D*
Boston College	D
Boston University	M,D
Bowling Green State University	M
Brandeis University	M,D
Brock University	M
Brooklyn College of the City University of New York	M
Brown University	D
Buffalo State College, State University of New York	M
California Lutheran University	M,O
California State Polytechnic University, Pomona	M
California State University, East Bay	M
California State University, Fullerton	M
California State University, Long Beach	M
California State University, Los Angeles	M
California University of Management and Sciences	M,D
Carleton University	M,D
Carnegie Mellon University	D
The Catholic University of America	M
Central European University	M,D
Central Michigan University	M
City College of the City University of New York	M
Claremont Graduate University	M,D,O
Clark Atlanta University	M
Clark University	D
Clemson University	M,D
Cleveland State University	M,O
Colorado State University	M,D
Columbia University	M,D*
Concordia University (Canada)	M,D,O
Copenhagen Business School	M,D
Cornell University	M,D
Dalhousie University	M,D
DePaul University	M
Drexel University	M,D,O
Duke University	M,D*
Eastern Illinois University	M
Eastern Michigan University	M,O
Emory University	D
Florida Atlantic University	M
Florida International University	M,D
Florida State University	M,D
Fordham University	M,D,O
George Mason University	M,D,O
Georgetown University	D
The George Washington University	M,D*
Georgia Institute of Technology	M,D
Georgia State University	M,D
The Graduate Center, City University of New York	D
Harvard University	D*
Hawai`i Pacific University	M
Howard University	M,D
Hunter College of the City University of New York	M,D
Illinois State University	M
Indiana University Bloomington	D
Indiana University–Purdue University Indianapolis	M
Instituto Tecnologico de Santo Domingo	M,O
Instituto Tecnológico y de Estudios Superiores de Monterrey, Campus Ciudad de México	M,D
Iowa State University of Science and Technology	M,D
Johns Hopkins University	D
Kansas State University	M,D
Kent State University	M
Lakehead University	M
Lee University	M,O
Lehigh University	M,D
Louisiana State University and Agricultural & Mechanical College	M,D
Louisiana Tech University	M,D
Loyola University Chicago	M
Marquette University	M,O
Massachusetts Institute of Technology	M,D
McGill University	M,D
McMaster University	M,D
Memorial University of Newfoundland	M
Miami University	M
Michigan State University	M,D
Middle Tennessee State University	M,D
Mississippi State University	M,D
Morgan State University	M
Murray State University	M
New Mexico State University	M,D,O
The New School	M,D
New York University	M,D,O
North Carolina State University	M,D
Northeastern University	M,D
Northern Illinois University	M,D
Northwestern University	D*
Oakland University	M,O
The Ohio State University	M,D
Ohio University	M
Oklahoma State University	M,D
Old Dominion University	M
Oregon State University	M,D
Pace University	O
Penn State University Park	M,D
Pepperdine University	M
Peru State College	M
Portland State University	M,D,O
Princeton University	D,O
Purdue University	D
Regis University	M,O
Rice University	M,D
Roosevelt University	M
Rutgers University–Newark	M,D
Rutgers University–New Brunswick	M,D
St. Cloud State University	M
San Diego State University	M
San Francisco State University	M
San Jose State University	M,O
Simon Fraser University	M,D
South Dakota State University	M
Southern Illinois University Carbondale	M,D
Southern Illinois University Edwardsville	M
Southern Methodist University	M,D
Stanford University	D
State University of New York College of Environmental Science and Forestry	M,D
Stony Brook University, State University of New York	M,D
Syracuse University	M,D
Teachers College, Columbia University	M,D
Temple University	M,D*
Texas A&M University	M,D
Texas Tech University	M,D
Troy University	M
Tufts University	M
Tulane University	M,D
Universidad de las Américas Puebla	M
Université de Moncton	M
Université de Montréal	M,D,O
Université de Sherbrooke	M
Université du Québec à Montréal	M,D
Université Laval	M,D
University at Albany, State University of New York	M,D,O
University at Buffalo, the State University of New York	M,D,O*
The University of Akron	M
The University of Alabama	M,D
University of Alaska Fairbanks	M
University of Alberta	M,D
The University of Arizona	M,D
University of Arkansas	M,D
The University of British Columbia	M,D
University of Calgary	M,D
University of California, Berkeley	D
University of California, Davis	M,D
University of California, Irvine	M,D
University of California, Los Angeles	M,D
University of California, Riverside	M,D
University of California, San Diego	D
University of California, Santa Barbara	M,D
University of California, Santa Cruz	D
University of Central Arkansas	M,O
University of Chicago	M,D,O
University of Cincinnati	D
University of Colorado Boulder	M,D
University of Colorado Denver	M
University of Connecticut	M,D*
University of Delaware	M,D*
University of Denver	M
University of Detroit Mercy	M,D,O
University of Florida	M,D
University of Georgia	M,D
University of Guelph	M,D
University of Hawaii at Manoa	M,D
University of Houston	M,D
University of Illinois at Chicago	M,D
University of Illinois at Urbana–Champaign	M,D
The University of Iowa	D*
The University of Kansas	M,D*
University of Kentucky	M,D
University of Lethbridge	M,D
University of Maine	M
The University of Manchester	D
University of Manitoba	M,D
University of Maryland, Baltimore County	M,D
University of Maryland, College Park	M,D
University of Massachusetts Amherst	M,D*
University of Memphis	M,D
University of Michigan	M,D
University of Minnesota, Twin Cities Campus	M,D
University of Mississippi	M,D
University of Missouri	M,D
University of Missouri–Kansas City	M,D
University of Missouri–St. Louis	M
University of Montana	M
University of Nebraska at Omaha	M
University of Nebraska–Lincoln	M,D
University of Nevada, Las Vegas	M
University of Nevada, Reno	M
University of New Brunswick Fredericton	M
University of New Hampshire	M,D
University of New Mexico	M,D
University of New Orleans	D
The University of North Carolina at Chapel Hill	M,D
The University of North Carolina at Charlotte	M,O
The University of North Carolina at Greensboro	D
University of North Florida	M
University of North Texas	M,D,O
University of Notre Dame	M,D
University of Oklahoma	M,D*
University of Oregon	M,D
University of Ottawa	M,D
University of Pennsylvania	M,D*
University of Pittsburgh	M,D*
University of Puerto Rico, Río Piedras Campus	M
University of Regina	M,D,O
University of Rhode Island	M,D
University of Rochester	M,D*
University of San Francisco	M
University of Saskatchewan	M,O
University of South Africa	M,D
University of South Carolina	M,D
University of Southern California	M,D
University of Southern Mississippi	M
University of South Florida	M,D
The University of Tennessee	M,D
The University of Texas at Arlington	M
The University of Texas at Austin	M,D
The University of Texas at Dallas	M,D*
The University of Texas at El Paso	M
The University of Texas at San Antonio	M
The University of Toledo	M,D,O
University of Toronto	M,D
University of Utah	M,D*
University of Victoria	M,D
University of Virginia	M,D
University of Washington	M,D*
University of Waterloo	M,D
The University of Western Ontario	M,D
University of Windsor	M
University of Wisconsin–Madison	D
University of Wisconsin–Milwaukee	M,D
University of Wyoming	M,D
Utah State University	M,D
Vanderbilt University	M,D*
Virginia Commonwealth University	M
Virginia Polytechnic Institute and State University	M,D
Virginia State University	M
Washington State University	M,D,O
Washington University in St. Louis	D
Wayne State University	M,D
Western Illinois University	M,O
Western Michigan University	M,D
West Texas A&M University	M
West Virginia University	M,D
Wichita State University	M
Wilfrid Laurier University	M,D
Wright State University	M
Yale University	M,D*
Yeshiva University	M,D
York University	M,D
Youngstown State University	M

EDUCATION—GENERAL

Abilene Christian University	M,D,O
Acacia University	M
Acadia University	M,D
Adams State University	M
Adelphi University	M,D,O
Alabama Agricultural and Mechanical University	M,O
Alabama State University	M,D,O
Alaska Pacific University	M
Albany State University	M,O
Albertus Magnus College	M
Albright College	M
Alcorn State University	M,O
Alfred University	M
Alliant International University–Los Angeles	M,O
Alliant International University–México City	M
Alliant International University–Sacramento	M,O
Alliant International University–San Diego	M,O
Alliant International University–San Francisco	M,O
Alvernia University	M
Alverno College	M
American College of Education	M
American InterContinental University Online	M
American International College	M,D,O
American Jewish University	M
American University	M,O
The American University in Cairo	M
The American University in Dubai	M
American University of Puerto Rico	M
Anderson University (IN)	M
Anderson University (SC)	M
Andrews University	M,D,O
Anna Maria College	M,O
Antioch University Los Angeles	M
Antioch University Midwest	M
Antioch University New England	M,O
Antioch University Santa Barbara	M
Antioch University Seattle	M
Aquinas College (MI)	M
Aquinas College (TN)	M
Arcadia University	M,D,O
Argosy University, Atlanta	M,D,O
Argosy University, Chicago	M,D,O
Argosy University, Dallas	M,D
Argosy University, Denver	M,D
Argosy University, Hawai`i	M,D
Argosy University, Inland Empire	M,D
Argosy University, Los Angeles	M,D
Argosy University, Nashville	M,D,O
Argosy University, Orange County	M,D
Argosy University, Phoenix	M,D,O
Argosy University, Salt Lake City	M,D
Argosy University, San Diego	M,D
Argosy University, San Francisco Bay Area	M,D
Argosy University, Sarasota	M,D,O
Argosy University, Seattle	M,D
Argosy University, Tampa	M,D,O
Argosy University, Twin Cities	M,D,O
Argosy University, Washington DC	M,D,O
Arizona State University at the Tempe campus	M,D,O
Arkansas State University	M,D,O
Arkansas Tech University	M,D,O
Arlington Baptist College	M
Armstrong State University	M,O
Ashland University	M,D
Athabasca University	M,D,O
Auburn University	M,D,O
Auburn University at Montgomery	M,O
Augsburg College	M
Augustana University	M
Augusta University	M,O
Aurora University	M,D
Austin College	M
Austin Peay State University	M,O
Averett University	M
Avila University	M,O
Azusa Pacific University	M,D,O
Baker University	M,D
Baldwin Wallace University	M
Ball State University	M,D,O
Bank Street College of Education	M
Bard College	M
Barry University	M,D,O
Bayamón Central University	M,O
Baylor University	M,D,O
Belhaven University (MS)	M
Bellarmine University	M,D,O
Bemidji State University	M
Benedictine College	M
Benedictine University	M
Berry College	M,O
Bethany College	M
Bethel College	M
Bethel University (MN)	M,D,O
Binghamton University, State University of New York	M,D,O*
Biola University	M,O
Bishop's University	M,O
Bloomsburg University of Pennsylvania	M,O
Bluefield College	M
Bluffton University	M
Boise State University	M,D,O
Boston College	M,D,O
Boston University	M,D,O
Bowie State University	M
Bradley University	M,D,O
Brandman University	M
Brandon University	M,O
Brenau University	M,O
Bridgewater State University	M,O
Brigham Young University	M,D,O
Brock University	M,D
Brooklyn College of the City University of New York	M,O
Brown University	M
Bucknell University	M
Buena Vista University	M
Butler University	M
Cabrini University	M
Cairn University	M

*M—masters degree; D—doctorate; O—other advanced degree; *—Close-Up and/or Display*

Caldwell University	M,D,O
California Baptist University	M
California Coast University	M,D
California Lutheran University	M,D
California Polytechnic State University, San Luis Obispo	M
California State University, Bakersfield	M
California State University, Dominguez Hills	M
California State University, East Bay	M
California State University, Fresno	M,D
California State University, Long Beach	M,D
California State University, Los Angeles	M,D,O
California State University, Monterey Bay	M
California State University, Northridge	M,D
California State University, Sacramento	M
California State University, San Bernardino	M
California State University, San Marcos	M,D
California State University, Stanislaus	M,D,O
California University of Pennsylvania	M
Calvin College	M
Cambridge College	M,D,O
Cameron University	M
Campbellsville University	M
Campbell University	M
Canisius College	M,O
Capella University	M,D
Cardinal Stritch University	M,D
Caribbean University	M,D
Carlow University	M
Carroll University	M
Carson-Newman University	M
Carthage College	M,O
Castleton University	M,O
The Catholic University of America	M,D,O
Cedar Crest College	M
Cedarville University	M,D
Centenary College	M
Centenary College of Louisiana	M
Central Connecticut State University	M,D,O
Central Methodist University	M
Central Michigan University	M,D,O
Central Washington University	M
Chadron State College	M,O
Chaminade University of Honolulu	M
Chapman University	M,D,O
Charleston Southern University	M
Chatham University	M
Chestnut Hill College	M
Cheyney University of Pennsylvania	M,O
Chicago State University	M,D
Chowan University	M
Christian Brothers University	M
Christopher Newport University	M
The Citadel, The Military College of South Carolina	M,O
City College of the City University of New York	M,O
City University of Seattle	M,O
Claremont Graduate University	M,D,O
Clarion University of Pennsylvania	M
Clark Atlanta University	M,D,O
Clarke University	M
Clarkson University	M,O
Clark University	M
Clayton State University	M
Clemson University	M,D,O
Cleveland State University	M,D,O
Coastal Carolina University	M,O
The College at Brockport, State University of New York	M,O
College of Charleston	M,O
The College of Idaho	M
College of Mount Saint Vincent	M,O
The College of New Jersey	M,O
The College of New Rochelle	M,O
College of Saint Elizabeth	M,D,O
College of St. Joseph	M
College of Saint Mary	M
The College of Saint Rose	M,O
The College of St. Scholastica	M,O
College of Staten Island of the City University of New York	M,O
The College of William and Mary	M,D,O
Colorado Christian University	M
The Colorado College	M
Colorado Mesa University	M
Colorado State University	M,D
Colorado State University–Global Campus	M
Colorado State University–Pueblo	M
Columbia College (MO)	M
Columbia College (SC)	M
Columbia International University	M,D,O
Columbus State University	M,D,O
Concordia College	M
Concordia University (United States)	M,D
Concordia University (Canada)	M,O
Concordia University Chicago	M
Concordia University Irvine	M
Concordia University, Nebraska	M
Concordia University, St. Paul	M,D,O
Concordia University Texas	M
Concordia University Wisconsin	M
Concord University	M
Converse College	M,O
Coppin State University	M
Corban University	M
Cornell University	M,D
Cornerstone University	M,O
Covenant College	M
Crandall University	M
Creighton University	M
Cumberland University	M
Curry College	M,O
Daemen College	M
Dakota State University	M
Dakota Wesleyan University	M
Dallas Baptist University	M
Defiance College	M
Delaware State University	M,D
Delta State University	M,D,O
DePaul University	M,D
DeSales University	M,O
DeVry University	M
DeVry University	M
DeVry University	M
DeVry University	M
DeVry University	M
Doane University	M
Dominican University	M
Dominican University of California	M
Dordt College	M
Drake University	M,D,O
Drexel University	M,D
Drury University	M
Duke University	M*
Duquesne University	M,D,O
D'Youville College	M,D
Earlham College	M
East Carolina University	M,D,O
East Central University	M
Eastern Connecticut State University	M
Eastern Illinois University	M,O
Eastern Kentucky University	M
Eastern Mennonite University	M
Eastern Michigan University	M,D,O
Eastern Nazarene College	M,O
Eastern New Mexico University	M
Eastern Oregon University	M
Eastern University	M,O
Eastern Washington University	M
East Stroudsburg University of Pennsylvania	M,D
East Tennessee State University	M,D,O
East Texas Baptist University	M
Edgewood College	M,D,O
Elizabeth City State University	M
Ellis University	M
Elms College	M,O
Elon University	M
Emmanuel College (United States)	M
Emory & Henry College	M
Emory University	M,D
Emporia State University	M
Evangel University	M
The Evergreen State College	M
Fairfield University	M,O
Fairleigh Dickinson University, College at Florham	M,O
Fairleigh Dickinson University, Metropolitan Campus	M,O
Fairmont State University	M
Faulkner University	M
Felician University	M,O
Ferris State University	M
Florida Agricultural and Mechanical University	M,D
Florida Atlantic University	M,D,O
Florida Gulf Coast University	M
Florida Institute of Technology	M
Florida International University	M,D,O
Florida Memorial University	M
Florida Southern College	M
Florida State University	M,D,O
Fontbonne University	M
Fordham University	M,D,O
Fort Hays State University	M,O
Franciscan University of Steubenville	M
Francis Marion University	M
Freed-Hardeman University	M,O
Fresno Pacific University	M,O
Frostburg State University	M
Furman University	M,O
Gallaudet University	M,D,O
Gannon University	M,O
Gardner-Webb University	M,D,O
Geneva College	M
George Fox University	M,D,O
George Mason University	M,D,O
Georgetown College	M
The George Washington University	M,D,O*
Georgia College & State University	M,O
Georgian Court University	M,O
Georgia Southern University	M,D,O
Georgia Southwestern State University	M,O
Georgia State University	M,D,O
Goddard College	M
Gonzaga University	M
Gordon College	M,O
Goucher College	M,O
Governors State University	M
Graceland University (IA)	M
Grambling State University	M,D,O
Grand Canyon University	M,D
Grand Valley State University	M,O
Grand View University	M
Gratz College	M
Greensboro College	M
Greenville College	M
Gwynedd Mercy University	M
Hamline University	M,D
Hampton University	M,D,O
Hannibal-LaGrange University	M
Harding University	M,O
Hardin-Simmons University	M,D
Harrison Middleton University	M,D
Harvard University	M,D*
Hastings College	M
Hebrew College	M,O
Hebrew Union College–Jewish Institute of Religion (NY)	M
Heidelberg University	M
Henderson State University	M,O
Heritage University	M
High Point University	M
Hofstra University	M,D,O
Hollins University	M
Holy Family University	M,D
Holy Names University	M,O
Hood College	M,O
Hope International University	M
Houston Baptist University	M
Howard University	M,D,O
Humboldt State University	M
Hunter College of the City University of New York	M,O
Huntington University	M,D
Idaho State University	M,D,O
Illinois College	M
Illinois State University	M,D,O
Indiana State University	M,D,O
Indiana University Bloomington	M,D,O
Indiana University East	M
Indiana University Northwest	M
Indiana University of Pennsylvania	M,D,O
Indiana University–Purdue University Fort Wayne	M,O
Indiana University–Purdue University Indianapolis	M,O
Indiana University South Bend	M
Indiana University Southeast	M
Institute for Christian Studies	M,D
Instituto Tecnologico de Santo Domingo	M,O
Instituto Tecnológico y de Estudios Superiores de Monterrey, Campus Central de Veracruz	M
Instituto Tecnológico y de Estudios Superiores de Monterrey, Campus Ciudad de México	M,D
Instituto Tecnológico y de Estudios Superiores de Monterrey, Campus Ciudad Juárez	M
Instituto Tecnológico y de Estudios Superiores de Monterrey, Campus Ciudad Obregón	M
Instituto Tecnológico y de Estudios Superiores de Monterrey, Campus Estado de México	M,D
Instituto Tecnológico y de Estudios Superiores de Monterrey, Campus Irapuato	M,D
Instituto Tecnológico y de Estudios Superiores de Monterrey, Campus Sonora Norte	M
Inter American University of Puerto Rico, Arecibo Campus	M
Inter American University of Puerto Rico, Barranquitas Campus	M
Inter American University of Puerto Rico, Metropolitan Campus	M,D
International Baptist College and Seminary	M
Iona College	M
Jackson State University	M,D,O
Jacksonville State University	M,O
John Brown University	M
John Carroll University	M
John F. Kennedy University	M
Johns Hopkins University	M,D,O
Johnson & Wales University	M
Johnson State College	M
Johnson University	M,D,O
Kansas State University	M,D
Kaplan University, Davenport Campus	M
Kean University	M
Keene State College	M,O
Keiser University	M
Kennesaw State University	M,D,O
Kent State University	M,D,O
Kent State University at Stark	M
King's College	M
Kutztown University of Pennsylvania	M
LaGrange College	M,O
Lake Erie College	M
Lake Forest College	M
Lakehead University	M,D
Lakeland University	M
Lamar University	M,D,O
Lander University	M
Langston University	M
La Salle University	M,O
Lasell College	M
La Sierra University	M,D,O
Lee University	M,O
Lehigh University	M,D,O
Lehman College of the City University of New York	M
Le Moyne College	M,O
Lenoir-Rhyne University	M
Lesley University	M,D,O
LeTourneau University	M
Lewis University	M,D,O
Liberty University	M,D,O
Lincoln Memorial University	M,D,O
Lindenwood University	M,D,O
Lindenwood University–Belleville	M
Lipscomb University	M,D,O
Lock Haven University of Pennsylvania	M
London Metropolitan University	M,D
Long Island University–Brentwood Campus	M,O
Long Island University–LIU Brooklyn	M,O
Long Island University–LIU Post	M,D,O
Long Island University–Riverhead	M,O
Longwood University	M
Louisiana College	M
Louisiana State University and Agricultural & Mechanical College	M,D,O
Louisiana State University in Shreveport	M
Louisiana Tech University	M,D
Loyola Marymount University	M,D
Loyola University Chicago	M,D,O
Loyola University Maryland	M,O
Lyndon State College	M
Lynn University	M,D
Madonna University	M
Malone University	M
Manhattan College	M,O
Manhattanville College	M,D,O*
Mansfield University of Pennsylvania	M
Maranatha Baptist University	M
Marian University (IN)	M
Marian University (WI)	M,D
Marist College	M,O
Marlboro College	M,O
Marquette University	M,D,O
Marshall University	M,D,O
Martin Luther College	M
Mary Baldwin College	M
Marygrove College	M
Marylhurst University	M
Marymount University	M
Maryville University of Saint Louis	M,D
Marywood University	M
Massachusetts College of Liberal Arts	M,O
McGill University	M,D,O
McKendree University	M,D,O
McNeese State University	O
McPherson College	M
Medaille College	M
Memorial University of Newfoundland	M,D,O
Mercer University	M,D,O
Mercy College	M,O
Meredith College	M
Merrimack College	M,O
Metropolitan State University of Denver	M
Miami University	M,D,O
Michigan State University	M,D,O
MidAmerica Nazarene University	M
Middle Tennessee State University	M,D,O
Midway University	M
Midwestern State University	M
Millersville University of Pennsylvania	M,D
Milligan College	M
Mills College	M,D,O
Minnesota State University Mankato	M,D,O
Minnesota State University Moorhead	M,O
Misericordia University	M
Mississippi College	M,D,O
Mississippi State University	M,D,O
Mississippi University for Women	M
Mississippi Valley State University	M
Missouri Baptist University	M,O
Missouri Southern State University	M
Molloy College	M,O
Monmouth University	M,O
Montana State University	M,D,O
Montana State University Billings	M,O
Montana State University–Northern	M
Montclair State University	M,D,O
Moravian College	M
Morehead State University	M,O
Morgan State University	M,D
Morningside College	M
Mount Mary University	M
Mount Mercy University	M
Mount St. Joseph University	M,O
Mount Saint Mary College	M,O
Mount Saint Mary's University (CA)	M,D,O
Mount St. Mary's University (MD)	M
Mount Saint Vincent University	M
Mount Vernon Nazarene University	M
Multnomah University	M
Murray State University	M,D,O
Muskingum University	M
Naropa University	M
National Louis University	M,D,O
National University	M,O
Nazareth College of Rochester	M
Neumann University	M
New England College	M,D
New Jersey City University	M,D
Newman University	M
New Mexico Highlands University	M
New Mexico State University	M,D,O
New York Institute of Technology	M,O
New York University	M,D,O
Niagara University	M,D,O
Nicholls State University	M
Nipissing University	M,O
Norfolk State University	M
North Carolina Agricultural and Technical State University	M
North Carolina Central University	M
North Carolina State University	M,D,O
North Central College	M
Northcentral University	M,D,O
North Dakota State University	M,D,O
Northeastern Illinois University	M
Northeastern State University	M
Northeastern University	M,D
Northern Arizona University	M,D,O
Northern Illinois University	M,D,O
Northern Kentucky University	M,D,O
Northern Michigan University	M
Northern State University	M
North Greenville University	M,D

North Park University	M
Northwest Christian University	M
Northwestern College	M,O
Northwestern Oklahoma State University	M
Northwestern State University of Louisiana	M,O
Northwestern University	M,D*
Northwest Missouri State University	M,O
Northwest Nazarene University	M,D,O
Northwest University	M
Notre Dame de Namur University	M,D
Notre Dame of Maryland University	M
Nova Southeastern University	M,D,O*
Oakland City University	M,D
Oakland University	M,D,O
Occidental College	M
Ohio Dominican University	M
The Ohio State University	M,D,O
The Ohio State University at Marion	M
The Ohio State University–Mansfield Campus	M
The Ohio State University–Newark Campus	M
Ohio University	M,D
Ohio Valley University	M
Oklahoma State University	M,D,O
Old Dominion University	M,D,O
Olivet Nazarene University	M
Open University	M
Oral Roberts University	M,D
Oregon State University	M,D
Oregon State University–Cascades	M
Ottawa University	M
Otterbein University	M
Our Lady of the Lake University of San Antonio	M,D
Pace University	M,O
Pacific Lutheran University	M
Pacific Oaks College	M
Pacific Union College	M
Pacific University	M
Palm Beach Atlantic University	M
Park University	M,O
Penn State Harrisburg	M,D,O
Penn State University Park	M,D,O
Peru State College	M
Piedmont College	M,O
Pittsburg State University	M,O
Plymouth State University	O
Point Loma Nazarene University	M
Point Park University	M
Pontifical Catholic University of Puerto Rico	M,D
Portland State University	M,D
Post University	M
Prairie View A&M University	M,D
Prescott College	M,D
Purdue University	M,D,O
Purdue University Northwest	M
Purdue University Northwest	M
Queens College of the City University of New York	M,O
Queen's University at Kingston	M,D
Queens University of Charlotte	M
Quincy University	M
Quinnipiac University	M,O
Radford University	M,O
Randolph College	M
Regent University	M,D,O
Regis College (MA)	M,D
Regis University	M
Reinhardt University	M
Relay Graduate School of Education	M
Rhode Island College	D
Rice University	M
Rider University	M,O
Rivier University	M,D,O
Robert Morris University	M,D,O
Roberts Wesleyan College	M
Rockford University	M
Rockhurst University	M
Roger Williams University	M
Rollins College	M
Roosevelt University	M,D
Rosemont College	M
Rowan University	M,D,O
Rutgers University–New Brunswick	M,D
Sacred Heart University	M,O
Sage Graduate School	M,D,O
Saginaw Valley State University	M,O
St. Ambrose University	M
St. Bonaventure University	M,O
St. Catherine University	M
St. Cloud State University	M,D
Saint Francis University	M
St. Francis Xavier University	M
St. John Fisher College	M,D,O
St. John's University (NY)	M,D,O
St. Joseph's College, New York	M
Saint Joseph's College of Maine	M
Saint Joseph's University	M,D,O
St. Lawrence University	M,O
Saint Leo University	M
Saint Louis University	M,D
Saint Martin's University	M
Saint Mary's College of California	M,D,O
St. Mary's College of Maryland	M
Saint Mary's University of Minnesota	M,O
Saint Michael's College	M,O
Saint Peter's University	M,D,O
St. Thomas Aquinas College	M,O
St. Thomas University	M,D,O
Saint Vincent College	M
Saint Xavier University	M
Salem College	M
Salem International University	M
Samford University	M,D,O
Sam Houston State University	M,D
San Diego State University	M,D
San Francisco State University	M,D,O
San Jose State University	M,D,O
Santa Clara University	M,O
Sarah Lawrence College	M
Schreiner University	M,O
Seattle Pacific University	D
Seattle University	M,D,O
Seton Hall University	M,D,O
Shawnee State University	M
Shenandoah University	M,D,O
Shippensburg University of Pennsylvania	M,D,O
Siena Heights University	M,O
Sierra Nevada College	M
Silver Lake College of the Holy Family	M
Simmons College	M,D,O
Simon Fraser University	M,D,O
Simpson College	M
Simpson University	M
Sinte Gleska University	M
Slippery Rock University of Pennsylvania	M,D
Smith College	M
Sonoma State University	M,D,O
South Carolina State University	M
South Dakota State University	M,D
Southeastern Louisiana University	M,D
Southeastern Oklahoma State University	M
Southeastern University (FL)	M
Southern Adventist University	M
Southern Arkansas University–Magnolia	M
Southern Connecticut State University	M,D,O
Southern Illinois University Carbondale	M,D
Southern Illinois University Edwardsville	M,D,O
Southern Methodist University	M,D
Southern New Hampshire University	M,D,O
Southern Oregon University	M
Southern University and Agricultural and Mechanical College	M,D
Southern Utah University	M,O
Southern Wesleyan University	M
Southwest Baptist University	M,O
Southwestern Adventist University	M
Southwestern Assemblies of God University	M
Southwestern College (KS)	M,D
Southwestern Oklahoma State University	M
Southwest Minnesota State University	M
Spalding University	M,D
Spring Arbor University	M
Springfield College	M
Spring Hill College	M
Stanford University	M,D
State University of New York at Fredonia	M
State University of New York at New Paltz	M,O
State University of New York at Oswego	M,O
State University of New York College at Cortland	M,O
State University of New York College at Geneseo	M
State University of New York College at Old Westbury	M
State University of New York College at Oneonta	M,O
State University of New York Empire State College	M
Stephen F. Austin State University	M,D
Stetson University	M,O
Stevenson University	M
Stockton University	M
Strayer University	M
Sul Ross State University	M,O
Sweet Briar College	M
Syracuse University	M,D,O
Taft University System	M
Tarleton State University	M,D,O
Teachers College, Columbia University	M,D
Temple University	M,D,O*
Tennessee State University	M,D,O
Tennessee Technological University	M,D,O
Tennessee Wesleyan College	M
Texas A&M International University	M
Texas A&M University	M,D
Texas A&M University–Commerce	M,D,O
Texas A&M University–Corpus Christi	M,D
Texas A&M University–Kingsville	M,D,O
Texas A&M University–Texarkana	M
Texas Christian University	M,D,O
Texas Southern University	M,D
Texas State University	M,D,O
Texas Tech University	M,D
Texas Wesleyan University	M,D
Texas Woman's University	M,D
Thomas More College	M
Thomas University	M
Thompson Rivers University	M
Tiffin University	M
Touro College	M
Touro University California	M,D
Towson University	M
Trevecca Nazarene University	M,O
Trident University International	M,D
Trinity International University	M
Trinity University	M
Trinity Washington University	M
Troy University	M,O
Truman State University	M
Tufts University	M,D,O
Tusculum College	M
Union College (KY)	M
Union Institute & University	D
Union University	M,D,O
Universidad Autonoma de Guadalajara	M,D
Universidad de las Americas, A.C.	M
Universidad de las Américas Puebla	M
Universidad del Turabo	M,D,O
Universidad Metropolitana	M
Université de Moncton	M
Université de Montréal	M,D,O
Université de Saint-Boniface	M
Université de Sherbrooke	M,O
Université du Québec à Chicoutimi	M,D
Université du Québec à Montréal	M,D,O
Université du Québec à Rimouski	M,D,O
Université du Québec à Trois-Rivières	M,D
Université du Québec en Abitibi-Témiscamingue	M,D,O
Université du Québec en Outaouais	M,D,O
Université Laval	M,D,O
Université Sainte-Anne	M
University at Albany, State University of New York	M,D,O
University at Buffalo, the State University of New York	M,D,O*
The University of Akron	M
The University of Alabama at Birmingham	M,D,O
University of Alaska Anchorage	M,O
University of Alaska Fairbanks	M,O
University of Alaska Southeast	M
The University of Arizona	M,D,O
University of Arkansas	M,D,O
University of Arkansas at Little Rock	M,D,O
University of Arkansas at Monticello	M
University of Arkansas at Pine Bluff	M
University of Bridgeport	M,D,O
The University of British Columbia	M,D,O
University of California, Berkeley	M,D,O
University of California, Davis	M,D
University of California, Irvine	M,D
University of California, Los Angeles	M,D
University of California, Riverside	M,D,O
University of California, San Diego	M,D
University of California, Santa Barbara	M,D,O
University of California, Santa Cruz	M,D
University of Central Arkansas	M,O
University of Central Missouri	M,D,O
University of Central Oklahoma	M
University of Cincinnati	M,D,O
University of Colorado Boulder	M,D
University of Colorado Colorado Springs	M,D
University of Colorado Denver	M,D,O
University of Connecticut	M,D*
University of Dayton	M
University of Delaware	M,D,O*
University of Denver	M,D,O
The University of Findlay	M,D
University of Florida	M,D,O
University of Georgia	M,D,O
University of Great Falls	M
University of Guam	M
University of Hartford	M,D,O
University of Hawaii at Hilo	M
University of Hawaii at Manoa	M,D,O
University of Holy Cross	M
University of Houston	M,D
University of Houston–Clear Lake	M,D
University of Houston–Victoria	M
University of Idaho	M,D,O
University of Illinois at Chicago	M,D
University of Illinois at Springfield	M,O
University of Illinois at Urbana–Champaign	M,D,O
University of Indianapolis	M
The University of Iowa	M,D,O*
University of Jamestown	M
The University of Kansas	M,D,O*
University of Kentucky	M,D,O
University of La Verne	M,O
University of Lethbridge	M,D
University of Louisiana at Lafayette	M,D
University of Louisiana at Monroe	M,D
University of Louisville	M,D,O
University of Maine	M,D,O
University of Maine at Farmington	M
The University of Manchester	M,D
University of Manitoba	M,D
University of Mary	M,D
University of Mary Hardin-Baylor	M,D
University of Maryland, Baltimore County	M,O
University of Maryland, College Park	M,D,O
University of Maryland Eastern Shore	M
University of Maryland University College	M,O
University of Mary Washington	M
University of Massachusetts Amherst	M,D,O*
University of Massachusetts Boston	M,D
University of Massachusetts Dartmouth	M,D,O
University of Massachusetts Lowell	M
University of Memphis	M,D,O
University of Miami	M,D,O
University of Michigan	M,D
University of Michigan–Dearborn	M
University of Michigan–Flint	M,D,O
University of Minnesota, Duluth	M,D
University of Minnesota, Twin Cities Campus	M,D,O
University of Mississippi	M,D,O
University of Missouri	M,D,O
University of Missouri–Kansas City	M,D,O
University of Missouri–St. Louis	M,D,O
University of Mobile	M
University of Montana	M,D,O
University of Montevallo	M,O
University of Nebraska at Kearney	M,O
University of Nebraska at Omaha	M,D,O
University of Nevada, Las Vegas	M,D,O
University of Nevada, Reno	M,D,O
University of New Brunswick Fredericton	M,D
University of New England	M,O
University of New Hampshire	M,D,O
University of New Mexico	M,D,O
University of New Orleans	M,D
University of North Alabama	M,O
The University of North Carolina at Chapel Hill	M,D
The University of North Carolina at Greensboro	M,D,O
The University of North Carolina at Pembroke	M
The University of North Carolina Wilmington	M,D
University of North Dakota	M,D,O
University of Northern British Columbia	M,D,O
University of Northern Colorado	M,D,O
University of Northern Iowa	M,D,O
University of North Florida	M,D
University of North Georgia	M,O
University of North Texas	M,D,O
University of Northwestern–St. Paul	M
University of Notre Dame	M
University of Oklahoma	M,D,O*
University of Oregon	M,D
University of Ottawa	M,D,O
University of Pennsylvania	M,D,O*
University of Phoenix–Bay Area Campus	M,D,O
University of Phoenix–Central Valley Campus	M
University of Phoenix–Colorado Campus	M
University of Phoenix–Colorado Springs Downtown Campus	M,O
University of Phoenix–Dallas Campus	M
University of Phoenix–Hawaii Campus	M
University of Phoenix–Houston Campus	M
University of Phoenix–Las Vegas Campus	M
University of Phoenix–New Mexico Campus	M
University of Phoenix–North Florida Campus	M
University of Phoenix–Online Campus	M,O
University of Phoenix–Phoenix Campus	M
University of Phoenix–Sacramento Valley Campus	M,O
University of Phoenix–San Diego Campus	M
University of Phoenix–Southern Arizona Campus	M,O
University of Phoenix–Southern California Campus	M,O
University of Phoenix–South Florida Campus	M
University of Phoenix–Utah Campus	M
University of Phoenix–Washington D.C. Campus	M,D,O
University of Pikeville	M
University of Pittsburgh	M,D*
University of Portland	M,D
University of Prince Edward Island	M
University of Puerto Rico, Río Piedras Campus	M,D
University of Puget Sound	M
University of Redlands	M,D,O
University of Regina	M,D,O
University of Rhode Island	M,D
University of Rio Grande	M
University of Rochester	M,D*
University of St. Francis (IL)	M,D,O

*M—masters degree; D—doctorate; O—other advanced degree; *—Close-Up and/or Display*

University of Saint Francis (IN)	M,O
University of Saint Joseph	M
University of Saint Mary	M
University of St. Thomas (MN)	M,D,O
University of St. Thomas (TX)	M
University of San Diego	M,D,O
University of San Francisco	M,D
University of Saskatchewan	M,D,O
The University of Scranton	M
University of Sioux Falls	M,O
University of South Africa	M,D
University of South Alabama	M,D,O
University of South Carolina	M,D,O
University of South Carolina Upstate	M
The University of South Dakota	M,D,O
University of Southern California	M,D
University of Southern Indiana	M
University of Southern Maine	M,D,O
University of Southern Mississippi	M,D,O
University of South Florida	M,D,O
University of South Florida, St. Petersburg	M
University of South Florida Sarasota-Manatee	M
The University of Tampa	M
The University of Tennessee	M,D,O
The University of Tennessee at Chattanooga	M,D,O
The University of Tennessee at Martin	M
The University of Texas at Arlington	M,D
The University of Texas at Austin	M,D
The University of Texas at El Paso	M,D
The University of Texas of the Permian Basin	M
The University of Texas Rio Grande Valley	M,D
University of the Cumberlands	M,D,O
University of the Incarnate Word	M,D
University of the Pacific	M,D,O
University of the Sacred Heart	M,O
University of the Southwest	M
University of the Virgin Islands	M
The University of Toledo	M,D,O
University of Toronto	M,D
The University of Tulsa	M
University of Utah	M,D*
University of Vermont	M,D
University of Victoria	M,D
University of Virginia	M,D,O
University of Washington	M,D*
University of Washington, Bothell	M
University of Washington, Tacoma	M
The University of West Alabama	M,O
The University of Western Ontario	M
University of West Florida	D
University of West Georgia	M,D,O
University of Windsor	M,D
University of Wisconsin–Eau Claire	M
University of Wisconsin–Green Bay	M
University of Wisconsin–La Crosse	M
University of Wisconsin–Madison	M,D,O
University of Wisconsin–Milwaukee	M,D,O
University of Wisconsin–Oshkosh	M
University of Wisconsin–Platteville	M
University of Wisconsin–River Falls	M
University of Wisconsin–Stevens Point	M
University of Wisconsin–Stout	M,D,O
University of Wisconsin–Superior	M
Upper Iowa University	M
Urbana University	M
Ursuline College	M
Utah State University	M,D,O
Utah Valley University	M
Utica College	M,O
Valley City State University	M
Valparaiso University	M
Vanderbilt University	M,D*
Vanguard University of Southern California	M
Villanova University	M
Virginia Commonwealth University	M,D,O
Virginia International University	M
Virginia Polytechnic Institute and State University	M,O
Virginia State University	M
Virginia Union University	M
Viterbo University	M,O
Wagner College	M,O
Wake Forest University	M
Walden University	M,D,O
Walla Walla University	M
Walsh University	M
Warner Pacific College	M
Warner University	M
Washburn University	M
Washington State University	M,D
Washington University in St. Louis	M,D
Wayland Baptist University	M
Wayne State College	M,O
Wayne State University	M,D,O
Weber State University	M
Webster University	M,O
Wesleyan College	M
Wesley College	M
West Chester University of Pennsylvania	M,O
Western Carolina University	M
Western Connecticut State University	M,D
Western Governors University	M,O
Western Illinois University	M,D,O
Western Michigan University	M,D,O
Western New Mexico University	M
Western Oregon University	M
Western State Colorado University	M
Western Washington University	M
Westfield State University	M,O
West Liberty University	M
Westminster College (PA)	M,O
Westminster College (UT)	M
West Texas A&M University	M
West Virginia University	M,D
West Virginia Wesleyan College	M
Wheaton College	M
Wheelock College	M
Whittier College	M
Whitworth University	M
Wichita State University	M,D,O
Widener University	M,D
Wilkes University	M,D
William Carey University	M,O
William Jessup University	M
William Jewell College	M
William Paterson University of New Jersey	M
Wilmington College	M
Wilmington University	M,D
Wilson College	M
Wingate University	M,D
Winona State University	M
Winston-Salem State University	M
Winthrop University	M
Wittenberg University	M
Worcester State University	M,O
Wright State University	M,O
Xavier University	M,D
Xavier University of Louisiana	M
York College of Pennsylvania	M
York University	M,D
Youngstown State University	M,D

EDUCATIONAL LEADERSHIP AND ADMINISTRATION

Abilene Christian University	M,D,O
Acacia University	M
Acadia University	M
Adelphi University	M,O
Alabama State University	M,D,O
Albany State University	M,O
Alliant International University–San Diego	M,D,O
Alliant International University–San Francisco	M,D,O
Alverno College	M
American College of Education	M
American InterContinental University Online	M
American International College	M,D,O
American Public University System	M
American University	M,O
The American University in Cairo	M
Andrews University	M,D,O
Angelo State University	M
Antioch University New England	M,O
Appalachian State University	M,D,O
Arcadia University	M,D,O
Argosy University, Atlanta	M,D,O
Argosy University, Chicago	M,D,O
Argosy University, Dallas	M,D
Argosy University, Denver	M,D
Argosy University, Hawai`i	M,D
Argosy University, Inland Empire	M,D
Argosy University, Los Angeles	M,D
Argosy University, Nashville	M,D,O
Argosy University, Orange County	M,D
Argosy University, Phoenix	M,D,O
Argosy University, Salt Lake City	M,D
Argosy University, San Diego	M,D
Argosy University, San Francisco Bay Area	M,D
Argosy University, Sarasota	M,D,O
Argosy University, Seattle	M,D
Argosy University, Tampa	M,D,O
Argosy University, Twin Cities	M,D,O
Argosy University, Washington DC	M,D,O
Arizona State University at the Tempe campus	M,D
Arkansas State University	M,D,O
Arkansas Tech University	M,D,O
Arlington Baptist College	M
Asbury University	M
Ashland University	M,D
Auburn University	M,D,O
Auburn University at Montgomery	M,O
Augusta University	M,O
Aurora University	M,D
Austin Peay State University	M,O
Averett University	M
Azusa Pacific University	M,D
Baldwin Wallace University	M
Ball State University	M,D,O
Bank Street College of Education	M
Barry University	M,D,O
Baruch College of the City University of New York	M,O
Bayamón Central University	M,O
Baylor University	M,O
Bay Path University	M
Bellarmine University	M,D,O
Benedictine College	M
Benedictine University	M,D
Berry College	O
Bethel University (MN)	M,D,O
Bethel University (TN)	M
Binghamton University, State University of New York	M,D,O*
Bob Jones University	M,D,O
Boise State University	M,D
Boston College	M,D,O
Bowie State University	M,D
Bowling Green State University	M,D,O
Bradley University	M
Brandeis University	M,O
Brandman University	M
Brandon University	M,O
Bridgewater State University	M,O
Brigham Young University	M,D
Brooklyn College of the City University of New York	M
Buffalo State College, State University of New York	O
Butler University	M
Cairn University	M
Caldwell University	M,D,O
California Baptist University	M
California Coast University	M,D
California Lutheran University	M,D
California State Polytechnic University, Pomona	M,D
California State University, Bakersfield	M
California State University, Dominguez Hills	M
California State University, East Bay	M,D
California State University, Fresno	M,D
California State University, Fullerton	M,D
California State University, Long Beach	M,D
California State University, Northridge	M,D
California State University, Sacramento	M
California State University, San Bernardino	M,D
California State University, San Marcos	M,D
California State University, Stanislaus	M,D
California University of Pennsylvania	M
Calumet College of Saint Joseph	M
Calvin College	M
Cambridge College	M,D,O
Cameron University	M
Campbell University	M
Canisius College	M,O
Capella University	M,D
Cardinal Stritch University	M,D
Caribbean University	M,D
Carlow University	M
Carson-Newman University	M
Carthage College	M,O
Castleton University	M,O
The Catholic University of America	M,D,O
Cedarville University	M,D
Centenary College	M
Central Connecticut State University	M,D,O
Central Michigan University	M,D,O
Central Washington University	M
Chadron State College	M,O
Chaminade University of Honolulu	M
Chapman University	M,D,O
Charleston Southern University	M
Chestnut Hill College	M
Cheyney University of Pennsylvania	M,O
Chicago State University	M,D
Christian Brothers University	M
The Citadel, The Military College of South Carolina	M,O
City College of the City University of New York	M,O
City University of Seattle	M,D,O
Claremont Graduate University	M,D,O
Clark Atlanta University	M,D,O
Clarke University	M
Clarkson University	M,O
Clemson University	M,D,O
Cleveland State University	M,D,O
Coastal Carolina University	M,O
The College at Brockport, State University of New York	M,O
The College of New Jersey	M,O
The College of New Rochelle	M,O
College of Saint Elizabeth	M,D,O
College of Saint Mary	M
The College of Saint Rose	M,O
College of Staten Island of the City University of New York	O
The College of William and Mary	M,D
Colorado Mesa University	M
Colorado State University	M,D
Colorado State University–Global Campus	M
Columbia College (MO)	M
Columbia College (SC)	M
Columbia International University	M,D,O
Columbus State University	M,D,O
Concordia University (United States)	M,D
Concordia University Ann Arbor	M
Concordia University Chicago	M,D,O
Concordia University Irvine	M
Concordia University, Nebraska	M
Concordia University, St. Paul	M,D,O
Concordia University Wisconsin	M
Concord University	M
Converse College	M,O
Creighton University	M,D
Dakota Wesleyan University	M
Dallas Baptist University	M
Dallas Theological Seminary	M,D,O
Delaware State University	M,D
Delaware Valley University	M
Delta State University	M,D,O
DePaul University	M,D
Doane University	M
Dominican University	M
Drexel University	M,D
Duquesne University	M,D,O
D'Youville College	M,D
East Carolina University	M,D,O
Eastern Illinois University	M,O
Eastern Kentucky University	M
Eastern Michigan University	M,D,O
Eastern Nazarene College	M,O
Eastern New Mexico University	M
Eastern University	M,O
East Stroudsburg University of Pennsylvania	M,D
East Tennessee State University	M,D,O
Edgewood College	M,D,O
Edinboro University of Pennsylvania	M
Elizabeth City State University	M
Ellis University	M
Elmhurst College	M
Emporia State University	M
Endicott College	M,D
Evangel University	M,D
Fairleigh Dickinson University, College at Florham	M
Fairleigh Dickinson University, Metropolitan Campus	M
Fayetteville State University	M,D
Felician University	M,O
Ferris State University	M,D
Fielding Graduate University	M,D,O
Fitchburg State University	M,O
Florida Agricultural and Mechanical University	M,D
Florida Atlantic University	M,D,O
Florida Gulf Coast University	M
Florida International University	M,D,O
Florida State University	M,D,O
Fordham University	M,D,O
Fort Hays State University	M,O
Fort Lewis College	M,O
Framingham State University	M
Franciscan University of Steubenville	M
Freed-Hardeman University	M,O
Fresno Pacific University	M
Frostburg State University	M
Furman University	M,O
Gannon University	D,O
Gardner-Webb University	M,D,O
Gateway Seminary	M,D,O
Geneva College	M
George Fox University	M,D,O
George Mason University	M,D,O
The George Washington University	M,D,O*
Georgia College & State University	O
Georgian Court University	M,O
Georgia Southern University	M,D,O
Georgia State University	M,D,O
Gordon College	M,O
Goucher College	M,O
Governors State University	M
Graceland University (IA)	M
Grambling State University	M,D,O
Grand Canyon University	M,D
Grand Valley State University	M,O
Granite State College	M
Gwynedd Mercy University	M
Hampton University	M,D
Harding University	M,O
Hardin-Simmons University	D
Harvard University	M,D*
Henderson State University	M,O
Heritage University	M
High Point University	M
Holy Family University	M,D
Hood College	M,O
Hope International University	M
Houston Baptist University	M
Howard Payne University	M
Howard University	M,D,O
Hunter College of the City University of New York	O
Huston-Tillotson University	M
Idaho State University	M,D,O
Illinois State University	M,D
Immaculata University	M,D,O
Indiana State University	M,D,O
Indiana University Bloomington	M,D,O
Indiana University Northwest	M
Indiana University of Pennsylvania	D,O
Indiana University–Purdue University Fort Wayne	M,O
Indiana University–Purdue University Indianapolis	M,O
Indiana Wesleyan University	M,O
Instituto Tecnologico de Santo Domingo	M,O
Instituto Tecnológico y de Estudios Superiores de Monterrey, Campus Central de Veracruz	M
Instituto Tecnológico y de Estudios Superiores de Monterrey, Campus Ciudad Juárez	M
Instituto Tecnológico y de Estudios Superiores de Monterrey, Campus Estado de México	M,D
Instituto Tecnológico y de Estudios Superiores de Monterrey, Campus Irapuato	M,D
Inter American University of Puerto Rico, Aguadilla Campus	M
Inter American University of Puerto Rico, Arecibo Campus	M
Inter American University of Puerto Rico, Barranquitas Campus	M
Inter American University of Puerto Rico, Fajardo Campus	M
Inter American University of Puerto Rico, Metropolitan Campus	M,D
Iona College	M
Iowa State University of Science and Technology	M,D
Jackson State University	M,D,O
Jacksonville State University	M,O
James Madison University	M
John Brown University	M
John Carroll University	M
Johns Hopkins University	M,D
Johnson & Wales University	D
Kansas State University	M,D

Kaplan University, Davenport Campus	M
Kean University	M,D
Keene State College	M,O
Keiser University	M,D,O
Kennesaw State University	M,D,O
Kent State University	M,D,O
Keystone College	M
Kutztown University of Pennsylvania	M
Lamar University	M,D
La Salle University	M,O
La Sierra University	M,D,O
Lee University	M,O
Lehigh University	M,D,O
Le Moyne College	M,O
Lenoir-Rhyne University	M
Lesley University	M,D,O
LeTourneau University	M
Lewis & Clark College	D,O
Lewis University	M,D
Liberty University	M,D,O
Lincoln Memorial University	M,D,O
Lincoln University (PA)	M
Lindenwood University	M,D,O
Lindenwood University–Belleville	M
Lindsey Wilson College	M
Lipscomb University	M,D,O
Lock Haven University of Pennsylvania	M
Long Island University–Hudson at Rockland	M,O
Long Island University–LIU Brooklyn	M,O
Long Island University–LIU Post	M,D,O
Loras College	M
Louisiana State University and Agricultural & Mechanical College	M,D,O
Louisiana State University in Shreveport	M
Louisiana Tech University	M,D
Lourdes University	M
Loyola Marymount University	M,D
Loyola University Chicago	M,D,O
Loyola University Maryland	M,O
Lynchburg College	M,D
Lynn University	M,D
Madonna University	M
Malone University	M
Manhattan College	M,O
Manhattanville College	M,D,O*
Marconi International University	M,D
Marian University (WI)	M,D
Marquette University	M,D,O
Marshall University	M,D,O
Martin Luther College	M
Marygrove College	M
Maryville University of Saint Louis	M,D
Marywood University	M,D
Massachusetts College of Liberal Arts	M,O
McDaniel College	M
McGill University	M,D,O
McKendree University	M,D,O
McNeese State University	M,O
Memorial University of Newfoundland	M,D,O
Mercer University	M,D,O
Mercy College	M,O
Mercyhurst University	M,O
Merrimack College	M,O
Michigan State University	M,D,O
Middle Tennessee State University	M,O
Midwestern State University	M
Millersville University of Pennsylvania	M,D
Mills College	M,D,O
Minnesota State University Mankato	M
Minnesota State University Moorhead	M,O
Mississippi College	M,D,O
Mississippi State University	M,D,O
Mississippi University for Women	M
Missouri Baptist University	M,O
Missouri State University	M,O
Monmouth University	M,O
Montana State University	M,D,O
Montclair State University	M,D
Morehead State University	M,O
Morgan State University	M,D
Mount Holyoke College	M
Mount Mercy University	M
Mount St. Joseph University	M,O
Murray State University	M,O
National Louis University	M,D,O
National University	M,O
Neumann University	D
New England College	M,D
New Jersey City University	M
Newman Theological College	M,O
Newman University	M
New Mexico Highlands University	M
New Mexico State University	M,D
New York University	M,D,O
Niagara University	M,D,O
Nicholls State University	M
Norfolk State University	M
North American University	M
North Carolina Agricultural and Technical State University	M
North Carolina Central University	M
North Carolina State University	M,D
North Central College	M
North Dakota State University	M,O
Northeastern Illinois University	M
Northeastern State University	M
Northeastern University	M,D
Northern Arizona University	M,D,O
Northern Illinois University	M,D,O
Northern Kentucky University	M,D,O
Northern Michigan University	M
Northern State University	M
Northwestern College	M,O
Northwestern Oklahoma State University	M
Northwestern State University of Louisiana	M,O
Northwestern University	M*
Northwest Missouri State University	M,O
Northwest Nazarene University	M,D,O
Notre Dame de Namur University	M
Notre Dame of Maryland University	M,D
Oakland City University	M,D
Oakland University	M,D,O
Oglala Lakota College	M
Ohio Dominican University	M
The Ohio State University	M,D,O
Ohio University	M,D
Oklahoma State University	M,D
Old Dominion University	M,D,O
Olivet Nazarene University	M
Oral Roberts University	M,D
Oregon State University	M
Ottawa University	M
Park University	M,O
Penn State University Park	M,D,O
Pepperdine University	M,D
Piedmont International University	M,D
Pittsburg State University	M,O
Plymouth State University	M,O
Point Loma Nazarene University	M
Point Park University	M
Pontifical Catholic University of Puerto Rico	D
Post University	M
Prairie View A&M University	M,D
Prescott College	M,D
Providence College	M
Purdue University	M,D,O
Purdue University Northwest	M
Queens College of the City University of New York	M,O
Queens University of Charlotte	M
Quincy University	M
Quinnipiac University	M,O
Radford University	M,O
Ramapo College of New Jersey	M
Regent University	M,D,O
Regis College (MA)	M,D
Regis University	M,O
Rhode Island College	M,O
Rider University	M,O
Rivier University	M,D,O
Robert Morris University	M,D,O
Robert Morris University Illinois	M
Rocky Mountain College	M
Roosevelt University	M
Rowan University	M,D,O
Rutgers University–Camden	M
Rutgers University–New Brunswick	M,D
Sacred Heart University	M,O
Sage Graduate School	D
Saginaw Valley State University	M,O
St. Ambrose University	M
St. Bonaventure University	M,O
St. Cloud State University	M,D
Saint Francis University	M
St. Francis Xavier University	M
St. John Fisher College	M,D
St. John's University (NY)	M,D,O
Saint Joseph's College of Maine	M
Saint Joseph's University	M,D,O
St. Lawrence University	M,O
Saint Leo University	M
Saint Louis University	M,D,O
Saint Martin's University	M
Saint Mary's College of California	M,D,O
St. Mary's University (United States)	M
Saint Mary's University of Minnesota	M,D,O
Saint Michael's College	M,O
Saint Peter's University	M,D
St. Thomas Aquinas College	M,O
St. Thomas University	M,D,O
Saint Vincent College	M
Saint Xavier University	M
Salem International University	M
Salem State University	M
Salisbury University	M
Samford University	M,D,O
Sam Houston State University	M,D
San Diego State University	M
San Francisco State University	M,D,O
San Jose State University	M,D,O
Santa Clara University	M,O
Schreiner University	M,O
Seattle Pacific University	M,D,O
Seattle University	M,D,O
Seton Hall University	D,O
Shasta Bible College	M
Shenandoah University	M,D,O
Shippensburg University of Pennsylvania	M,D
Siena Heights University	M,O
Sierra Nevada College	M
Silver Lake College of the Holy Family	M
Simon Fraser University	M,D
Simpson University	M
Slippery Rock University of Pennsylvania	M,D
Soka University of America	M
Sonoma State University	M,D,O
South Carolina State University	D,O
South Dakota State University	M
Southeastern Louisiana University	M,D
Southeastern Oklahoma State University	M
Southeastern University (FL)	M
Southeast Missouri State University	M,D,O
Southern Adventist University	M
Southern Arkansas University–Magnolia	M
Southern Connecticut State University	M,D,O
Southern Illinois University Carbondale	M,D
Southern Illinois University Edwardsville	M,D,O
Southern New Hampshire University	M,D,O
Southern Oregon University	M
Southern University and Agricultural and Mechanical College	M
Southwest Baptist University	M,O
Southwestern Adventist University	M
Southwestern Assemblies of God University	M
Southwestern College (KS)	M,D
Southwestern Oklahoma State University	M
Southwest Minnesota State University	M
Spalding University	M,D
Stanford University	M
State University of New York at New Paltz	M,O
State University of New York at Oswego	O
State University of New York at Plattsburgh	O
State University of New York College at Cortland	O
Stephen F. Austin State University	M,D
Stetson University	M
Stony Brook University, State University of New York	M,O
Suffolk University	M,O
Sul Ross State University	M
Summit University	M
Syracuse University	M,D,O
Tarleton State University	M,D,O
Teachers College, Columbia University	M,D
Temple University	M,D,O*
Tennessee Technological University	M,O
Tennessee Wesleyan College	M
Texas A&M International University	M
Texas A&M University	M,D
Texas A&M University–Central Texas	M,O
Texas A&M University–Corpus Christi	M,D
Texas A&M University–Kingsville	M
Texas A&M University–San Antonio	M
Texas A&M University–Texarkana	M
Texas Christian University	M,D,O
Texas Southern University	M,D
Texas State University	M,D
Texas Tech University	M,D
Texas Woman's University	M,D
Thomas Edison State University	M
Thomas More College	M
Tiffin University	M
Touro College	M
Towson University	O
Trevecca Nazarene University	M,D,O
Trident University International	M,D
Trinity Baptist College	M
Trinity International University	M
Trinity University	M
Trinity Washington University	M
Trinity Western University	M,O
Troy University	M,O
Union College (KY)	M
Union University	M,D,O
Universidad Adventista de las Antillas	M
Universidad del Turabo	M,D,O
Universidad Iberoamericana	M,D
Universidad Metropolitana	M
Université de Moncton	M
Université de Montréal	M,D,O
Université de Sherbrooke	M
Université du Québec à Trois-Rivières	O
Université Laval	M,D,O
University at Albany, State University of New York	M,D,O
University at Buffalo, the State University of New York	M,D,O*
The University of Akron	M
The University of Alabama	M,D,O
The University of Alabama at Birmingham	M,D,O
University of Alaska Anchorage	M,O
University of Alberta	M,D,O
The University of Arizona	M,D,O
University of Arkansas	M,D,O
University of Arkansas at Little Rock	M,D,O
University of Arkansas at Monticello	M
University of Bridgeport	M,D,O
The University of British Columbia	M,D
University of Calgary	M,D
University of California, Irvine	M,D
University of California, Los Angeles	D
University of California, Riverside	M,D,O
University of California, San Diego	M,D
University of Central Arkansas	M,O
University of Central Florida	M,D,O
University of Central Missouri	M,D,O
University of Central Oklahoma	M
University of Cincinnati	M,D,O
University of Colorado Colorado Springs	M,D
University of Colorado Denver	M,D,O
University of Dayton	M,D,O
University of Delaware	M,D,O*
University of Denver	M,D,O
University of Detroit Mercy	M,D,O
The University of Findlay	M,D
University of Florida	M,D,O
University of Georgia	M,D,O
University of Guam	M
University of Hartford	D,O
University of Hawaii at Manoa	M,D
University of Holy Cross	M
University of Houston	M,D
University of Houston–Clear Lake	M,D
University of Houston–Victoria	M
University of Idaho	M,O
University of Illinois at Chicago	M,D
University of Illinois at Springfield	M,O
University of Illinois at Urbana–Champaign	M,D,O
University of Indianapolis	M
The University of Iowa	M,D,O*
The University of Kansas	M,D*
University of Kentucky	M,D,O
University of La Verne	M,D,O
University of Lethbridge	M,D
University of Louisiana at Lafayette	M,D
University of Louisiana at Monroe	M,D
University of Louisville	M,D,O
University of Maine	M,D,O
University of Maine at Farmington	M
University of Manitoba	M
University of Mary	M,D
University of Mary Hardin-Baylor	M,D
University of Maryland, College Park	M,D,O
University of Maryland Eastern Shore	D
University of Massachusetts Amherst	M,D,O*
University of Massachusetts Dartmouth	D
University of Memphis	M,D
University of Michigan–Dearborn	M,D,O
University of Michigan–Flint	M,D,O
University of Minnesota, Twin Cities Campus	M,D
University of Missouri	M,D,O
University of Missouri–Kansas City	M,D,O
University of Missouri–St. Louis	M,D,O
University of Montana	M,D,O
University of Montevallo	M,O
University of Mount Union	M
University of Nebraska at Kearney	M,O
University of Nebraska at Omaha	M,D,O
University of Nebraska–Lincoln	M,D,O
University of Nevada, Las Vegas	M,D,O
University of Nevada, Reno	M,D,O
University of New England	M,D,O
University of New Hampshire	M,D,O
University of New Mexico	M,D,O
University of New Orleans	M,D
University of North Alabama	M,O
The University of North Carolina at Chapel Hill	M,D
The University of North Carolina at Charlotte	M,D,O
The University of North Carolina at Greensboro	M,D,O
The University of North Carolina at Pembroke	M
The University of North Carolina Wilmington	M,D
University of North Dakota	M,D,O
University of Northern Colorado	M,D,O
University of Northern Iowa	M,D
University of North Florida	M,D
University of North Georgia	M,O
University of North Texas	M,D,O
University of Oklahoma	M,D,O*
University of Pennsylvania	M,D*
University of Phoenix–Bay Area Campus	M,D,O
University of Phoenix–Colorado Campus	M
University of Phoenix–Colorado Springs Downtown Campus	M,O
University of Phoenix–Hawaii Campus	M
University of Phoenix–Las Vegas Campus	M
University of Phoenix–New Mexico Campus	M
University of Phoenix–North Florida Campus	M
University of Phoenix–Online Campus	M,D,O
University of Phoenix–Phoenix Campus	M
University of Phoenix–Southern Arizona Campus	M,O
University of Phoenix–Southern California Campus	M,O

*M—masters degree; D—doctorate; O—other advanced degree; *—Close-Up and/or Display*

University of Phoenix–South Florida Campus	M
University of Phoenix–Utah Campus	M
University of Phoenix–Washington D.C. Campus	M,D,O
University of Pikeville	M
University of Pittsburgh	M,D*
University of Portland	M,D
University of Prince Edward Island	M
University of Puerto Rico, Río Piedras Campus	M,D
University of Regina	M
University of Rio Grande	M
University of Rochester	M,D*
University of St. Francis (IL)	M,D,O
University of St. Thomas (MN)	M,D,O
University of St. Thomas (TX)	M
University of San Diego	M,D,O
University of San Francisco	M,D
University of Saskatchewan	M,D,O
The University of Scranton	M
University of Sioux Falls	M,O
University of South Africa	M,D
University of South Alabama	M,D,O
University of South Carolina	M,D,O
The University of South Dakota	M,D,O
University of Southern California	D
University of Southern Maine	M,O
University of Southern Mississippi	M,D,O
University of South Florida	M,D,O
University of South Florida, St. Petersburg	M
University of South Florida Sarasota-Manatee	M
The University of Tennessee	M,D,O
The University of Tennessee at Chattanooga	M,D,O
The University of Tennessee at Martin	M
The University of Texas at Arlington	M,D
The University of Texas at Austin	M,D
The University of Texas at El Paso	M,D
The University of Texas at San Antonio	M,D
The University of Texas at Tyler	M
The University of Texas of the Permian Basin	M
The University of Texas Rio Grande Valley	M,D
University of the Cumberlands	M,D,O
University of the Incarnate Word	M
University of the Pacific	M,D
University of the Southwest	M
The University of Toledo	M,D,O
University of Utah	M,D*
University of Vermont	M,D
University of Victoria	M,D
University of Virginia	M,D,O
University of Washington	M,D*
University of Washington, Bothell	M
University of Washington, Tacoma	M
The University of West Alabama	M,O
University of West Florida	M,D,O
University of West Georgia	M,D,O
University of Wisconsin–Madison	M,D,O
University of Wisconsin–Milwaukee	M,D,O
University of Wisconsin–Oshkosh	M
University of Wisconsin–Stevens Point	M
University of Wisconsin–Superior	M,O
University of Wisconsin–Whitewater	M
University of Wyoming	M,D,O
Upper Iowa University	M
Ursuline College	M
Utah Valley University	M
Valdosta State University	M
Valparaiso University	M
Vanderbilt University	D*
Villanova University	M
Virginia Commonwealth University	D
Virginia Polytechnic Institute and State University	M,D,O
Virginia State University	M,D
Virginia Theological Seminary	M,D
Viterbo University	M,O
Wagner College	M,O
Walden University	M,D,O
Waldorf College	M
Walla Walla University	M
Washburn University	M
Washington State University	M,D
Wayland Baptist University	M
Waynesburg University	M,D
Wayne State College	M,O
Wayne State University	M,D,O
Western Connecticut State University	D
Western Governors University	M,O
Western Illinois University	M,D,O
Western Kentucky University	M,D,O
Western Michigan University	M,D,O
Western New Mexico University	M
Western State Colorado University	M
Western Washington University	M
Westfield State University	M,O
Westminster College (PA)	M,O
West Texas A&M University	M
West Virginia University	M,D
Wheeling Jesuit University	M
Wheelock College	M
Whittier College	M
Whitworth University	M
Wichita State University	M,D,O
Widener University	M,D
Wilkes University	M,D
William Paterson University of New Jersey	M
William Woods University	M,D,O
Wilmington University	M,D
Wingate University	M,D
Winona State University	M,O
Winthrop University	M
Wisconsin Lutheran College	M
Worcester State University	M,O
Wright State University	M,O
Xavier University	M,D
Xavier University of Louisiana	M
Yeshiva University	M,D,O
York College of Pennsylvania	M
Youngstown State University	M,D

EDUCATIONAL MEASUREMENT AND EVALUATION

Abilene Christian University	O
American InterContinental University Online	M
Arizona State University at the Tempe campus	D
Ball State University	M,D,O
Baylor University	M,D,O
Boston College	M,D
Brandeis University	O
Cambridge College	M,D,O
Claremont Graduate University	M,D,O
Clemson University	D
College of Saint Mary	M
Duquesne University	M
Eastern Michigan University	M,O
Florida State University	M,D,O
Georgia State University	M,D
Houston Baptist University	M
Indiana University Bloomington	M,D,O
Iowa State University of Science and Technology	M,D
James Madison University	M,D
Kent State University	M,D
Louisiana State University and Agricultural & Mechanical College	M,D,O
Loyola University Chicago	M,D
McNeese State University	M,O
Michigan State University	M,D,O
Missouri State University	O
Missouri Western State University	M,O
Montclair State University	O
New Mexico State University	M,D,O
North Carolina State University	D
Ohio University	M,D
Old Dominion University	D
Rutgers University–New Brunswick	M
Seton Hall University	M,D,O
Southern Connecticut State University	M,D,O
Southwestern Oklahoma State University	M
Sul Ross State University	M,O
Syracuse University	M,D,O
Teachers College, Columbia University	M,D
Tennessee Technological University	D
Texas A&M University–San Antonio	M
Université Laval	M,D,O
University at Albany, State University of New York	M,D,O
The University of Akron	M,O
University of Arkansas	M,D
The University of British Columbia	M,D,O
University of Calgary	M,D
University of Colorado Boulder	D
University of Colorado Denver	M,D,O
University of Denver	M,D,O
University of Florida	M,D,O
University of Illinois at Chicago	M,D
The University of Iowa	M,D,O*
The University of Kansas	M,D*
University of Kentucky	M,D
University of Louisiana at Monroe	M,D
University of Louisville	M,D
University of Maryland, College Park	M,D
University of Massachusetts Amherst	M,D,O*
University of Memphis	M,D
University of Miami	M,D
University of Minnesota, Twin Cities Campus	M,D
University of Missouri–St. Louis	M,O
University of Nebraska–Lincoln	M,D,O
University of New England	M,O
The University of North Carolina at Chapel Hill	M,D
The University of North Carolina at Greensboro	D
University of North Dakota	D
University of Northern Colorado	M,D
University of Northern Iowa	M
University of North Texas	M,D,O
University of Oklahoma	M,D,O*
University of Pennsylvania	M,D*
University of Pittsburgh	M,D*
University of Puerto Rico, Río Piedras Campus	M
University of St. Thomas (TX)	M
University of South Carolina	M,D
University of Southern Mississippi	M,D
University of South Florida	M,D,O
The University of Tennessee	M,D,O
The University of Texas at El Paso	M
The University of Texas Rio Grande Valley	M
The University of Toledo	M,D,O
University of Victoria	M,D
University of Virginia	M,D,O
University of Washington	M,D*
University of Wisconsin–Milwaukee	M,D
Utah State University	M,D
Virginia Commonwealth University	D
Virginia Polytechnic Institute and State University	M,D,O
Walden University	M,D,O
Washington University in St. Louis	D
Wayland Baptist University	M
Wayne State University	M,D,O
Western Governors University	M,O
Western Michigan University	M,D,O
West Texas A&M University	M
Wilkes University	M,D

EDUCATIONAL MEDIA/INSTRUCTIONAL TECHNOLOGY

Abilene Christian University	M,O
Acadia University	M
Adelphi University	M,O
Alabama Agricultural and Mechanical University	M,O
Alabama State University	M,D,O
Alverno College	M
American College of Education	M
American InterContinental University Online	M
Antioch University New England	M,O
Appalachian State University	M,O
Arcadia University	M,D,O
Argosy University, Atlanta	M,D,O
Argosy University, Denver	M,D
Argosy University, Nashville	M,D,O
Argosy University, Orange County	M,D
Argosy University, Phoenix	M,D,O
Argosy University, San Francisco Bay Area	M,D
Argosy University, Sarasota	M,D,O
Argosy University, Seattle	M,D
Argosy University, Twin Cities	M,D,O
Arizona State University at the Tempe campus	M,O
Arkansas Tech University	M,D,O
Ashland University	M
Auburn University	M,D,O
Auburn University at Montgomery	M,O
Augustana University	M
Avila University	M
Azusa Pacific University	M
Baldwin Wallace University	M
Ball State University	M,D
Barry University	M,D,O
Bay Path University	M
Belhaven University (MS)	M
Bellevue University	M
Bloomsburg University of Pennsylvania	M,O
Boise State University	M,D,O
Bowling Green State University	M
Bridgewater State University	M
Brigham Young University	M,D
Buffalo State College, State University of New York	M
California Baptist University	M
California State Polytechnic University, Pomona	M
California State University, East Bay	M
California State University, Fullerton	M
California State University, Northridge	M
California State University, Sacramento	M
California State University, Stanislaus	M
Cambridge College	M,D,O
Canisius College	M,O
Capella University	M,D
Caribbean University	M,D
Central Connecticut State University	M,D,O
Central Michigan University	M,D,O
Chestnut Hill College	M,O
Chicago State University	M
Cleveland State University	D
Coastal Carolina University	M,O
College of Mount Saint Vincent	M,O
College of Saint Elizabeth	M,D,O
The College of William and Mary	M,D
Colorado Christian University	M
Colorado State University–Pueblo	M
Concordia University (United States)	M,D
Concordia University (Canada)	M,O
Concordia University Chicago	M
Concordia University Irvine	M
Concordia University, St. Paul	M,D,O
Dakota State University	M
Delaware Valley University	M
DeSales University	M,O
DeVry University	M
Drexel University	M,D
Drury University	M
Duquesne University	M,D,O
East Carolina University	M,O
Eastern Connecticut State University	M
Eastern Michigan University	M,O
Eastern New Mexico University	M
East Stroudsburg University of Pennsylvania	M
East Tennessee State University	M,O
Ellis University	M
Emporia State University	M
Fairfield University	M,O
Fairleigh Dickinson University, College at Florham	M,O
Fairleigh Dickinson University, Metropolitan Campus	M,O
Fairmont State University	M
Fielding Graduate University	M,D,O
Fitchburg State University	M,O
Florida Atlantic University	M
Florida Institute of Technology	M
Florida International University	M,D,O
Florida State University	M,D,O
Fontbonne University	M
Fort Hays State University	M
Framingham State University	M
Franklin University	M
Fresno Pacific University	M
Frostburg State University	M
Full Sail University	M
George Fox University	M,O
George Mason University	M
The George Washington University	M,O*
Georgia College & State University	M
Georgian Court University	M,O
Georgia Southern University	M,O
Georgia State University	M,D
Goucher College	M,O
Governors State University	M
Graceland University (IA)	M
Grambling State University	M,D,O
Grand Valley State University	M,O
Gratz College	O
Harrisburg University of Science and Technology	M
Harvard University	M,O*
Hofstra University	M,D,O
Idaho State University	M,D,O
Indiana State University	M,D
Indiana University Bloomington	M,D
Indiana University of Pennsylvania	M,D
Instituto Tecnológico y de Estudios Superiores de Monterrey, Campus Central de Veracruz	M
Instituto Tecnológico y de Estudios Superiores de Monterrey, Campus Ciudad de México	M,D
Instituto Tecnológico y de Estudios Superiores de Monterrey, Campus Ciudad Juárez	M,D
Instituto Tecnológico y de Estudios Superiores de Monterrey, Campus Estado de México	M,D
Instituto Tecnológico y de Estudios Superiores de Monterrey, Campus Irapuato	M,D
Inter American University of Puerto Rico, Metropolitan Campus	M
Iowa State University of Science and Technology	M,D
Jackson State University	M,D,O
Jacksonville State University	M
James Madison University	M
Johns Hopkins University	M
Johnson University	M,D,O
Kansas State University	M,D
Kaplan University, Davenport Campus	M
Keiser University	D,O
Kennesaw State University	M
Kent State University	M,D
Kutztown University of Pennsylvania	M
Lamar University	M,D
La Salle University	M,O
Lawrence Technological University	M
Lehigh University	M,D,O
Lenoir-Rhyne University	M
Lesley University	M,D,O
Lewis University	M
Liberty University	M,D,O
Lindenwood University	M,D,O
Lipscomb University	M,D,O
Long Island University–LIU Post	M,D,O
Longwood University	M
Louisiana State University and Agricultural & Mechanical College	M,D,O
Loyola University Maryland	M
Lynn University	M,O
Manhattan College	M
Marconi International University	M,D
Marian University (WI)	M,D
Marlboro College	M,O
Martin Luther College	M
Marygrove College	M
Massachusetts College of Liberal Arts	M,O
McDaniel College	M
McNeese State University	M,O
Memorial University of Newfoundland	M,D,O
Michigan State University	M,D,O
MidAmerica Nazarene University	M
Middle Tennessee State University	M,O
Midwestern State University	M
Misericordia University	M
Mississippi State University	M,D,O
Missouri Southern State University	M
Missouri State University	M
Montana State University Billings	M
Morehead State University	M,O
National Louis University	M,D,O
National University	M,O
Nazareth College of Rochester	M
New Jersey City University	M,D
New York Institute of Technology	M,O
New York University	M,D,O
North Carolina Agricultural and Technical State University	M
North Carolina Central University	M
North Carolina State University	M,D
Northeastern State University	M
Northern Arizona University	M,O
Northern Illinois University	M,D
Northern State University	M
Northwest Christian University	M
Northwestern State University of Louisiana	M,O
Northwestern University	M,D*
Northwest Missouri State University	M
Nova Southeastern University	M,D,O*
Ohio University	M,D
Old Dominion University	M,D
Ottawa University	M
Pace University	M,O

Penn State University Park M,D,O
Pepperdine University M,D
Piedmont College M,O
Pittsburg State University M
Plymouth State University M
Post University M
Purdue University M,D,O
Purdue University Northwest M
Quinnipiac University M
Radford University M
Ramapo College of New Jersey M
Regent University M,D,O
Robert Morris University Illinois M
Rochester Institute of Technology O
Rowan University M,O
Sacred Heart University M,O
Saginaw Valley State University M
St. Cloud State University M
Saint Joseph's University M,D,O
Saint Leo University M
Saint Mary's University of Minnesota M
St. Thomas University M,D,O
Saint Vincent College M
Saint Xavier University M
Salem State University M
Samford University M,D,O
San Diego State University M,D
San Francisco State University M
Seattle Pacific University M
Seton Hall University M
Simon Fraser University M,D
Slippery Rock University of Pennsylvania M,D
Southeast Missouri State University M
Southern Illinois University Edwardsville M,O
Southern New Hampshire University M,D,O
Southern University and Agricultural and Mechanical College M
Stanford University M
State University of New York College at Oneonta M,O
State University of New York College at Potsdam M
State University of New York Empire State College M
Stockton University M
Stony Brook University, State University of New York M,O
Strayer University M
Syracuse University M,O
Tarleton State University M
Teachers College, Columbia University M,D
Tennessee Technological University M,O
Texas A&M University M,D
Texas A&M University–Corpus Christi M,D
Texas A&M University–Kingsville M
Texas A&M University–Texarkana M
Texas State University M
Texas Tech University M,D
Thomas Edison State University O
Tiffin University M
Touro College M
Towson University M,D
Trident University International M,D
Université Laval M,D
University at Albany, State University of New York M,D,O
University at Buffalo, the State University of New York M,D,O*
The University of Akron M
University of Alaska Southeast M
University of Alberta M,D
University of Arkansas M
University of Arkansas at Little Rock M
University of California, Irvine M
University of Central Arkansas M
University of Central Florida M,D,O
University of Central Missouri M,D,O
University of Central Oklahoma M
University of Colorado Denver M
University of Dayton M
The University of Findlay M,D
University of Georgia M,D,O
University of Hartford M
University of Hawaii at Manoa M,D
University of Houston–Clear Lake M
University of Houston–Victoria M
The University of Kansas M,D*
University of Kentucky M,D
University of Maine M,D,O
University of Maryland, Baltimore County M,O
University of Maryland, College Park M,D,O
University of Massachusetts Amherst M,D,O*
University of Massachusetts Boston M,O
University of Memphis M,D
University of Michigan–Dearborn M
University of Michigan–Flint M,D,O
University of Minnesota, Twin Cities Campus M,D,O
University of Missouri M,D,O
University of Nebraska at Kearney M
University of Nevada, Las Vegas M,D,O
University of New Hampshire M,O
University of New Mexico M,D,O
The University of North Carolina at Charlotte M,D,O
The University of North Carolina at Greensboro M,D,O
The University of North Carolina Wilmington M
University of North Dakota M
University of Northern Colorado M,D
University of Northern Iowa M
University of North Florida M,D
University of Oklahoma M,D,O*
University of Pennsylvania M*
University of Phoenix–Online Campus D,O
University of Phoenix–Washington D.C. Campus M,D,O
University of St. Francis (IL) M,O
University of Saint Joseph M
University of San Francisco M,D
University of Sioux Falls M,O
University of South Africa M,D
University of South Alabama M,D,O
University of South Carolina M
University of South Carolina Aiken M
The University of South Dakota M
University of Southern Mississippi M,D,O
University of South Florida M,D,O
The University of Tampa M
The University of Tennessee M,D,O
The University of Tennessee at Chattanooga M,D,O
The University of Texas at Austin M,D
The University of Texas at San Antonio M,D,O
University of the Sacred Heart M
The University of Toledo M,D,O
University of Utah M,D*
University of Virginia M,D,O
University of Washington M,D*
The University of West Alabama M,O
University of West Florida M,D
University of West Georgia M,D,O
University of Wyoming M,D
Utah State University M,D,O
Utah Valley University M
Valley City State University M
Virginia Commonwealth University M
Virginia Polytechnic Institute and State University M,O
Walden University M,D,O
Wayland Baptist University M
Waynesburg University M,D
Wayne State University M,D,O
Webster University M,O
West Chester University of Pennsylvania M,O
Western Connecticut State University M
Western Governors University M,O
Western Illinois University M,O
Western Kentucky University M,O
Western Michigan University M,D,O
Western Oregon University M
Westfield State University M
West Texas A&M University M
West Virginia University M,D
Widener University M,D
Wilkes University M,D
William Woods University M,D,O
Wilmington University M,D
Wisconsin Lutheran College M
Worcester Polytechnic Institute M,D
York College of Pennsylvania M
Youngstown State University M

EDUCATIONAL POLICY

Alabama State University M,D,O
American University M,O
Arizona State University at the Tempe campus D
Ball State University D
The Catholic University of America M,D,O
Cleveland State University D
The College of William and Mary M,D
Cornell University M,D
Eastern Michigan University M
Florida State University M,D,O
The George Washington University M,D,O*
Georgia State University M,D,O
Harvard University M*
Howard University M,D,O
Illinois State University M,D
Indiana University Bloomington M,D,O
Johns Hopkins University D
Loyola University Chicago M,D
Marquette University M,D,O
Michigan State University D
New York University M,D
Niagara University M,D,O
The Ohio State University M,D,O
Penn State University Park M,D,O
Rutgers University–Camden M
Rutgers University–New Brunswick D
Stanford University M
Syracuse University O
Teachers College, Columbia University M,D
University of Alberta M,D,O
University of Arkansas D
The University of British Columbia M,D
University of Colorado Boulder M,D
University of Colorado Denver D
University of Denver M,D,O
University of Florida M,D,O
University of Georgia M,D,O
University of Hawaii at Manoa D
University of Illinois at Chicago M,D
University of Illinois at Urbana–Champaign M,D,O
The University of Iowa M,D,O*
The University of Kansas D*
University of Kentucky M,D
University of Maryland, Baltimore County M,D
University of Massachusetts Amherst M,D,O*
University of Massachusetts Dartmouth M,O
University of Minnesota, Twin Cities Campus M,D,O
University of Missouri–St. Louis D
The University of North Carolina Wilmington M
University of Pennsylvania M,D*
University of Pittsburgh D*
University of Rochester M,D*
University of St. Thomas (MN) M,D,O
University of Southern California D
The University of Texas at Arlington M,D
University of Washington M,D*
The University of Western Ontario M
University of Wisconsin–Madison M,D,O
Vanderbilt University M,D*
Virginia Commonwealth University D
Virginia Polytechnic Institute and State University M,D,O
Wayne State University M,D,O

EDUCATIONAL PSYCHOLOGY

Alliant International University–Irvine M,D,O
Alliant International University–Los Angeles M,D,O
Alliant International University–San Diego M,D,O
Alliant International University–San Francisco M,D,O
American International College M,D
Andrews University M,D
Auburn University M,D,O
Ball State University M,D
Baylor University M,D,O
Boston College M,D
Brigham Young University M,D
California Coast University M,D
California State University, Long Beach M
California State University, Northridge M
Capella University M,D
Chapman University M,D,O
Clark Atlanta University M
The College of Saint Rose M,O
Eastern Michigan University M,O
Edinboro University of Pennsylvania M,O
Florida Atlantic University M
Florida State University M,D
Fordham University M,D
George Mason University M,D,O
Georgia State University M,D
The Graduate Center, City University of New York D
Harvard University M*
Holy Names University M,O
Howard University D
Immaculata University M,D,O
Indiana University Bloomington M,D,O
Indiana University of Pennsylvania M,O
Instituto Tecnologico de Santo Domingo M,O
John Carroll University M
Kent State University M
La Sierra University M,O
McGill University M,D,O
Memorial University of Newfoundland M,D,O
Miami University M,O
Michigan School of Professional Psychology M,D
Michigan State University M,D,O
Mississippi State University M,D,O
Mount Saint Vincent University M
National Louis University M,D,O
New York University M,D
Northern Arizona University M,D,O
Northern Illinois University M,D,O
Oklahoma State University M,D,O
Old Dominion University D
Penn State University Park M,D,O
Pontifical Catholic University of Puerto Rico M
Purdue University M,D,O
Regent University M,D,O
Rutgers University–New Brunswick M,D
Simon Fraser University M,D
Southern Illinois University Carbondale M,D
State University of New York College at Oneonta M,O
Teachers College, Columbia University M,D,O
Temple University M,D,O*
Tennessee Technological University M,O
Texas A&M University M,D
Texas A&M University–Central Texas M,O
Texas Tech University M,D
Universidad de Iberoamerica M,D
Université de Moncton M
Université de Montréal M,D,O
Université du Québec à Trois-Rivières M,D
Université du Québec en Outaouais M
Université Laval M,D
University at Albany, State University of New York M,D,O
University at Buffalo, the State University of New York M,D,O*
University of Alberta M,D
The University of Arizona M,D,O
University of California, Davis M,D
University of California, Riverside M,D,O
University of Colorado Boulder M,D
University of Colorado Denver M,O
University of Georgia M,D,O
University of Hawaii at Manoa M,D
University of Houston M,D
University of Illinois at Chicago M,D
University of Illinois at Urbana–Champaign M,D,O
The University of Iowa M,D,O*
The University of Kansas M,D*
University of Kentucky M,D,O
University of Louisville M,D
The University of Manchester M,D
University of Manitoba M
University of Memphis M,D
University of Minnesota, Twin Cities Campus M,D,O
University of Missouri M,D,O
University of Missouri–St. Louis D
University of Nebraska–Lincoln M,D,O
University of Nevada, Reno M,D,O
University of New Mexico M,D
The University of North Carolina at Chapel Hill M,D
University of Northern Colorado M,D
University of Northern Iowa M
University of North Texas M,D,O
University of Oklahoma M,D,O*
University of Phoenix–Southern Arizona Campus M,O
University of Regina M
University of Saskatchewan M,D,O
University of South Africa M,D
University of South Carolina M,D
The University of South Dakota M,D,O
University of Southern California D
University of Southern Maine M,O
The University of Tennessee M,D,O
The University of Texas at Austin M,D
The University of Texas at El Paso M
The University of Texas Rio Grande Valley M
University of the Incarnate Word M
University of the Pacific M,D,O
The University of Toledo M,D,O
University of Utah M,D*
University of Victoria M,D
University of Virginia M,D,O
University of Washington M,D*
The University of Western Ontario M
University of Wisconsin–Madison M,D
University of Wisconsin–Milwaukee M,D
Virginia Commonwealth University D
Walden University M,D,O
Washington State University M,D
Wayne State University M,D,O
Webster University M,O
West Virginia University M
Wichita State University M,D,O
Widener University M,D

EDUCATION OF STUDENTS WITH SEVERE/MULTIPLE DISABILITIES

Cleveland State University M
Georgia State University M
Hunter College of the City University of New York M
Norfolk State University M
Syracuse University M
Teachers College, Columbia University M,D,O
University of Illinois at Urbana–Champaign M,D,O
West Virginia University M,D

EDUCATION OF THE GIFTED

Arkansas State University M,D,O
Ashland University M
Ball State University M,D,O
Barry University M,D,O
Bowling Green State University M
Canisius College M,O
Carlos Albizu University, Miami Campus M,D
Carthage College M,O
The College of New Rochelle O
Colorado Mesa University M
Converse College M
Drury University M
Elon University M
Emporia State University M
George Mason University M
Hardin-Simmons University M
Hofstra University M,D,O
James Madison University M
Johns Hopkins University M
Kent State University M,D,O
Liberty University M,D,O
Lindenwood University M,D,O
Lynn University M,D
Maryville University of Saint Louis M,D
Millersville University of Pennsylvania M
Mississippi University for Women M
Morehead State University M,O
Northeastern Illinois University M
Pacific University M
Purdue University M,D,O
St. Bonaventure University M,O

*M—masters degree; D—doctorate; O—other advanced degree; *—Close-Up and/or Display*

St. John's University (NY)	M,D,O
Saint Leo University	M
Saint Mary's University of Minnesota	M,O
St. Thomas University	M,D,O
Samford University	M,D,O
Southern Arkansas University–Magnolia	M
Southern Methodist University	M,D
Teachers College, Columbia University	M,D
Tennessee Technological University	D
Troy University	M
University at Buffalo, the State University of New York	M,D,O*
The University of Alabama	M,D,O
University of Arkansas at Little Rock	M,O
University of Central Arkansas	M,O
University of Louisiana at Lafayette	M
University of Louisiana at Monroe	M,D
University of Minnesota, Twin Cities Campus	M,D,O
University of Missouri	M,D
University of Nebraska at Kearney	M
The University of North Carolina at Charlotte	M,D,O
The University of North Carolina Wilmington	M
University of Northern Colorado	M,D
University of North Texas	M,D,O
University of Southern Maine	M,O
University of South Florida	M,D
The University of Texas Rio Grande Valley	M
The University of Toledo	M,D,O
University of Virginia	M,D,O
Viterbo University	M,O
Western Washington University	M
West Virginia University	M,D
Whitworth University	M
Wichita State University	M
William Carey University	M,O
Wilmington University	M,D
Wright State University	M
Youngstown State University	M

ELECTRICAL ENGINEERING

Air Force Institute of Technology	M,D
Alfred University	M,D
American University of Beirut	M,D
American University of Sharjah	M
Arizona State University at the Tempe campus	M,D,O
Auburn University	M,D
Baylor University	M,D
Binghamton University, State University of New York	M,D*
Boise State University	M,D
Boston University	M,D
Bradley University	M
Brigham Young University	M,D
Brown University	M,D
Bucknell University	M
California Institute of Technology	M,D,O
California Polytechnic State University, San Luis Obispo	M
California State Polytechnic University, Pomona	M
California State University, Chico	M
California State University, Fresno	M
California State University, Fullerton	M
California State University, Long Beach	M
California State University, Los Angeles	M
California State University, Northridge	M
California State University, Sacramento	M
Capitol Technology University	M
Carleton University	M,D
Carnegie Mellon University	M,D
Case Western Reserve University	M,D*
The Catholic University of America	M,D
City College of the City University of New York	M,D
Clarkson University	M,D
Clemson University	M,D
Cleveland State University	M,D
Colorado School of Mines	M,D
Colorado State University	M,D
Colorado Technical University Colorado Springs	M
Colorado Technical University Denver South	M
Columbia University	M,D*
Concordia University (Canada)	M,D
Cooper Union for the Advancement of Science and Art	M
Cornell University	M,D
Dalhousie University	M,D
DeVry University	M
Drexel University	M
Duke University	M,D*
École Polytechnique de Montréal	M,D,O
Embry-Riddle Aeronautical University–Daytona	M,D*
Fairfield University	M,O
Fairleigh Dickinson University, Metropolitan Campus	M
Florida Agricultural and Mechanical University	M,D
Florida Institute of Technology	M,D
Florida International University	M,D
Florida State University	M,D
Gannon University	M
George Mason University	M,D,O
The George Washington University	M,D,O*
Georgia Institute of Technology	M,D
Georgia Southern University	M
The Graduate Center, City University of New York	D
Grand Valley State University	M
Harvard University	M,D*
Howard University	M,D
Illinois Institute of Technology	M,D
Indiana University–Purdue University Fort Wayne	M
Indiana University–Purdue University Indianapolis	M,D
Instituto Tecnológico y de Estudios Superiores de Monterrey, Campus Chihuahua	M,O
Instituto Tecnológico y de Estudios Superiores de Monterrey, Campus Monterrey	M,D
International Technological University	M,D
Iowa State University of Science and Technology	M,D
Johns Hopkins University	M,D,O
Kansas State University	M,D
Kennesaw State University	M
Kettering University	M
Lakehead University	M
Lamar University	M,D
Lawrence Technological University	M,D
Lehigh University	M,D
Louisiana State University and Agricultural & Mechanical College	M,D
Louisiana Tech University	M,D
Manhattan College	M
Marquette University	M,D,O
Massachusetts Institute of Technology	M,D,O
McGill University	M,D
McMaster University	M,D
McNeese State University	M
Memorial University of Newfoundland	M,D
Mercer University	M
Miami University	M
Michigan State University	M,D
Michigan Technological University	M,D,O
Mississippi State University	M,D
Missouri University of Science and Technology	M,D
Montana State University	M,D
Montana Tech of The University of Montana	M
Morgan State University	M,D
Naval Postgraduate School	M,D,O
New Jersey Institute of Technology	M,D
New Mexico Institute of Mining and Technology	M
New Mexico State University	M,D,O
New York Institute of Technology	M
New York University	M,D
Norfolk State University	M
North Carolina Agricultural and Technical State University	M,D
North Carolina State University	M,D
North Dakota State University	M,D
Northeastern University	M,D,O
Northern Arizona University	M
Northern Illinois University	M
Northwestern Polytechnic University	M,D
Northwestern University	M,D*
Oakland University	M,D
The Ohio State University	M,D
Ohio University	M,D
Oklahoma Christian University	M
Oklahoma State University	M,D
Old Dominion University	M,D
Oregon Health & Science University	M,D
Oregon State University	M,D
Penn State Harrisburg	M,O
Penn State University Park	M,D
Pittsburg State University	M
Polytechnic University of Puerto Rico	M
Portland State University	M,D
Prairie View A&M University	M,D
Princeton University	M,D
Purdue University	M,D
Purdue University Northwest	M
Queen's University at Kingston	M,D
Rensselaer at Hartford	M
Rensselaer Polytechnic Institute	M,D
Rice University	M,D
Rochester Institute of Technology	M
Rose-Hulman Institute of Technology	M
Rowan University	M
Royal Military College of Canada	M,D
Rutgers University–New Brunswick	M,D
St. Cloud State University	M
St. Mary's University (United States)	M
San Diego State University	M
San Francisco State University	M
Santa Clara University	M,D,O
South Dakota School of Mines and Technology	M
South Dakota State University	M,D
Southern Illinois University Carbondale	M,D
Southern Illinois University Edwardsville	M
Southern Methodist University	M,D
Stanford University	M,D
State University of New York at New Paltz	M
Stevens Institute of Technology	M,D,O
Stony Brook University, State University of New York	M,D
Syracuse University	M,D,O
Temple University	M*
Tennessee State University	M,D
Tennessee Technological University	M
Texas A&M University	M,D
Texas A&M University–Kingsville	M
Texas State University	M
Texas Tech University	M,D
Tufts University	M,D,O
Tuskegee University	M
Universidad de las Américas Puebla	M
Université de Moncton	M
Université de Sherbrooke	M,D
Université du Québec à Trois-Rivières	M,D
Université Laval	M,D
University at Buffalo, the State University of New York	M,D*
The University of Akron	M,D
The University of Alabama	M,D
The University of Alabama at Birmingham	M
The University of Alabama in Huntsville	M,D
University of Alaska Fairbanks	M
University of Alberta	M,D
The University of Arizona	M,D
University of Arkansas	M,D
University of Bridgeport	M
The University of British Columbia	M,D
University of Calgary	M,D
University of California, Berkeley	M,D
University of California, Davis	M,D
University of California, Irvine	M,D
University of California, Los Angeles	M,D
University of California, Merced	M,D
University of California, Riverside	M,D
University of California, San Diego	M,D
University of California, Santa Barbara	M,D
University of California, Santa Cruz	M,D
University of Central Florida	M,D,O
University of Central Oklahoma	M
University of Cincinnati	M,D
University of Colorado Boulder	M,D
University of Colorado Colorado Springs	M
University of Colorado Denver	M,D
University of Connecticut	M,D*
University of Dayton	M,D
University of Delaware	M,D*
University of Denver	M,D
University of Detroit Mercy	M,D
University of Florida	M,D
University of Hawaii at Manoa	M,D
University of Houston	M,D
University of Idaho	M,D
University of Illinois at Chicago	M,D
University of Illinois at Urbana–Champaign	M,D
The University of Iowa	M,D*
The University of Kansas	M,D*
University of Kentucky	M,D
University of Louisville	M,D
University of Maine	M,D
The University of Manchester	M,D
University of Manitoba	M,D
University of Maryland, Baltimore County	M,D
University of Maryland, College Park	M,D
University of Massachusetts Amherst	M,D*
University of Massachusetts Dartmouth	M,D,O
University of Massachusetts Lowell	M,D
University of Memphis	M,D
University of Miami	M,D
University of Michigan	M,D
University of Michigan–Dearborn	M
University of Minnesota, Duluth	M
University of Minnesota, Twin Cities Campus	M,D
University of Missouri	M,D
University of Missouri–Kansas City	M,D,O
University of Nebraska–Lincoln	M,D
University of Nevada, Las Vegas	M,D
University of Nevada, Reno	M,D
University of New Brunswick Fredericton	M,D
University of New Hampshire	M,D
University of New Haven	M
University of New Mexico	M,D
The University of North Carolina at Charlotte	M,D
University of North Dakota	M
University of North Florida	M
University of North Texas	M,D,O
University of Notre Dame	M,D
University of Oklahoma	M,D*
University of Ottawa	M,D
University of Pennsylvania	M,D*
University of Pittsburgh	M,D*
University of Portland	M
University of Puerto Rico, Mayagüez Campus	M,D
University of Rhode Island	M,D
University of Rochester	M,D*
University of St. Thomas (MN)	M,O
University of Saskatchewan	M,D,O
University of South Alabama	M
University of South Carolina	M,D
University of Southern California	M,D,O
University of South Florida	M,D
The University of Tennessee	M,D
The University of Tennessee at Chattanooga	M
The University of Texas at Arlington	M,D
The University of Texas at Austin	M,D
The University of Texas at Dallas	M,D*
The University of Texas at El Paso	M,D
The University of Texas at San Antonio	M,D
The University of Texas at Tyler	M
The University of Texas Rio Grande Valley	M
University of the District of Columbia	M
The University of Toledo	M,D
University of Toronto	M,D
The University of Tulsa	M,D
University of Utah	M,D*
University of Vermont	M,D
University of Victoria	M,D
University of Virginia	M,D
University of Washington	M,D*
University of Waterloo	M,D
The University of Western Ontario	M,D
University of Windsor	M,D
University of Wisconsin–Madison	M,D
University of Wisconsin–Milwaukee	M,D,O
University of Wyoming	M,D
Utah State University	M,D
Vanderbilt University	M,D*
Villanova University	M,O
Virginia Commonwealth University	M,D
Virginia Polytechnic Institute and State University	M,D,O
Washington State University	M,D
Wayne State University	M,D
Western Michigan University	M,D
Western New England University	M
West Virginia University	M,D
Wichita State University	M,D
Widener University	M
Wilkes University	M
Worcester Polytechnic Institute	M,D,O
Wright State University	M
Yale University	M,D*
Youngstown State University	M

ELECTRONIC COMMERCE

California State University, Fullerton	M
Claremont Graduate University	M,D,O
Dalhousie University	M,D
DePaul University	M,D
Eastern Michigan University	M,O
Ellis University	M
Fairleigh Dickinson University, Metropolitan Campus	M
Florida Institute of Technology	M,D
HEC Montreal	M,O
Instituto Tecnológico y de Estudios Superiores de Monterrey, Campus Central de Veracruz	M
Instituto Tecnológico y de Estudios Superiores de Monterrey, Campus Ciudad Juárez	M
Instituto Tecnológico y de Estudios Superiores de Monterrey, Campus Estado de México	M,D
Instituto Tecnológico y de Estudios Superiores de Monterrey, Campus Irapuato	M,D
Lewis University	M
New York University	M,D,O
Northwestern University	M*
Pace University	O
Stevens Institute of Technology	M,O
Towson University	M,O
Universidad del Este	M
Université de Montréal	M,D
Université de Sherbrooke	M
Université Laval	M,O
University at Buffalo, the State University of New York	M,D,O*
The University of Akron	M
University of New Brunswick Saint John	M
University of North Florida	M
University of Ottawa	M,D,O
University of Phoenix–Colorado Campus	M
University of Phoenix–Columbus Georgia Campus	M
University of Phoenix–Dallas Campus	M
University of Phoenix–Houston Campus	M
University of Phoenix–New Mexico Campus	M
University of Phoenix–San Antonio Campus	M
University of Rochester	M*

ELECTRONIC MATERIALS

Colorado School of Mines	M,D
Princeton University	D
University of Arkansas	M,D

ELEMENTARY EDUCATION

Acacia University	M
Adelphi University	M
Alabama Agricultural and Mechanical University	M,D,O
Alabama State University	M,O
Alaska Pacific University	M
Albright College	M
Alcorn State University	M,O
American International College	M,D,O
American Public University System	M
American University of Puerto Rico	M
Andrews University	M,D,O
Anna Maria College	M,O
Antioch University New England	M,O
Appalachian State University	M
Arcadia University	M,D,O
Argosy University, Atlanta	M,D,O
Argosy University, Chicago	M,D,O
Argosy University, Denver	M,D

Argosy University, Hawai`i	M,D
Argosy University, Inland Empire	M,D
Argosy University, Los Angeles	M,D
Argosy University, Nashville	M,D,O
Argosy University, Orange County	M,D
Argosy University, Phoenix	M,D,O
Argosy University, San Diego	M,D
Argosy University, San Francisco Bay Area	M,D
Argosy University, Sarasota	M,D,O
Argosy University, Seattle	M,D
Argosy University, Tampa	M,D,O
Argosy University, Twin Cities	M,D,O
Argosy University, Washington DC	M,D,O
Arizona State University at the Tempe campus	M
Arkansas State University	M,D,O
Arkansas Tech University	M,D,O
Auburn University	M,D,O
Auburn University at Montgomery	M,O
Austin Peay State University	M,O
Ball State University	M,D,O
Bank Street College of Education	M
Barry University	M,D,O
Barton College	M
Bayamón Central University	M,O
Belhaven University (MS)	M
Bellarmine University	M,D,O
Benedictine University	M
Bethel University (MN)	M,D,O
Bloomsburg University of Pennsylvania	M
Blue Mountain College	M
Bob Jones University	M,D,O
Boston College	M
Bowie State University	M
Brandeis University	M,O
Bridgewater State University	M
Brooklyn College of the City University of New York	M,O
Brown University	M
Buffalo State College, State University of New York	M
California Lutheran University	M,D
California State University, Fullerton	M
California State University, Long Beach	M
California State University, Los Angeles	M
California State University, Northridge	M
California State University, Stanislaus	M
California University of Pennsylvania	M
Cambridge College	M,D,O
Campbell University	M
Canisius College	M,O
Capella University	M,D
Caribbean University	M,D
Carson-Newman University	M
Catawba College	M
Centenary College of Louisiana	M
Central Connecticut State University	M,O
Central Michigan University	M,D,O
Chadron State College	M,O
Chaminade University of Honolulu	M
Chapman University	M,D,O
Charleston Southern University	M
Chatham University	M
Chestnut Hill College	M
Cheyney University of Pennsylvania	M
Chicago State University	M
The Citadel, The Military College of South Carolina	M,O
City University of Seattle	M,O
College of Charleston	M
The College of New Jersey	M
The College of New Rochelle	M
College of St. Joseph	M
College of Staten Island of the City University of New York	M
Colorado Christian University	M
The Colorado College	M
Columbia College (SC)	M
Columbia International University	M,D,O
Concordia University (United States)	M,D
Concordia University Chicago	M
Concordia University, Nebraska	M
Converse College	M
Creighton University	M
Curry College	M,O
Dallas Baptist University	M
Delta State University	M,D,O
DePaul University	M,D
Dominican College	M
Dominican University	M
Drew University	M,D,O
Drury University	M
Duquesne University	M
D'Youville College	M,D
East Carolina University	M,O
Eastern Connecticut State University	M
Eastern Illinois University	M
Eastern Kentucky University	M
Eastern Michigan University	M
Eastern Nazarene College	M,O
Eastern New Mexico University	M
Eastern Oregon University	M
Eastern University	M,O
Eastern Washington University	M
East Stroudsburg University of Pennsylvania	M
East Tennessee State University	M,O
Elizabeth City State University	M
Elms College	M,O
Elon University	M
Emmanuel College (United States)	M
Emporia State University	M
Endicott College	M
Fairfield University	M,O
Fayetteville State University	M
Fitchburg State University	M
Florida Agricultural and Mechanical University	M
Florida Atlantic University	M
Florida Institute of Technology	M
Florida International University	M,D,O
Florida Memorial University	M
Florida State University	M,D,O
Fontbonne University	M
Fordham University	M,O
Framingham State University	M
Franklin Pierce University	M,D,O
Frostburg State University	M
Gallaudet University	M,D,O
Gardner-Webb University	M
George Mason University	M
The George Washington University	M*
Georgia Southern University	M
Georgia State University	M,D,O
Gonzaga University	M
Gordon College	M,O
Goucher College	M,O
Grand Canyon University	M
Grand Valley State University	M,O
Greensboro College	M
Greenville College	M
Hampton University	M
Harding University	M,O
Hawai`i Pacific University	M
High Point University	M
Hofstra University	M,D,O
Holy Family University	M
Hood College	M,O
Hope International University	M
Howard University	M
Hunter College of the City University of New York	M
Idaho State University	M,O
Indiana University Bloomington	M,D,O
Indiana University Northwest	M
Indiana University–Purdue University Fort Wayne	M
Indiana University South Bend	M
Indiana University Southeast	M
Inter American University of Puerto Rico, Aguadilla Campus	M
Inter American University of Puerto Rico, Arecibo Campus	M
Inter American University of Puerto Rico, Barranquitas Campus	M
Inter American University of Puerto Rico, Fajardo Campus	M
Inter American University of Puerto Rico, Guayama Campus	M
Inter American University of Puerto Rico, Metropolitan Campus	M
Inter American University of Puerto Rico, Ponce Campus	M
Inter American University of Puerto Rico, San Germán Campus	M
Iowa State University of Science and Technology	M,D
Ithaca College	M
Jackson State University	M,D,O
Jacksonville State University	M
James Madison University	M
Johns Hopkins University	M
Johnson & Wales University	M
Kansas State University	M,D
Kennesaw State University	M
Kutztown University of Pennsylvania	M
Lake Forest College	M
Lancaster Bible College	M,D
Langston University	M
Lasell College	M
Lee University	M,O
Lehman College of the City University of New York	M
Le Moyne College	M,O
Lesley University	M,D,O
Lewis & Clark College	M
Lewis University	M
Liberty University	M,D,O
Lincoln University (MO)	M
Lock Haven University of Pennsylvania	M
Long Island University–Brentwood Campus	M,O
Long Island University–Riverhead	M,O
Longwood University	M
Louisiana State University and Agricultural & Mechanical College	M,D,O
Loyola Marymount University	M
Loyola University Chicago	M,O
Loyola University Maryland	M,O
Manhattanville College	M*
Mansfield University of Pennsylvania	M
Marquette University	M,D,O
Marshall University	M,O
Mars Hill University	M
Mary Baldwin College	M
Marygrove College	M
Marylhurst University	M
Marymount University	M
Maryville University of Saint Louis	M,D
Marywood University	M
McDaniel College	M
McNeese State University	M,O
Medaille College	M
Mercy College	M
Merrimack College	M,O
Metropolitan College of New York	M
Metropolitan State University of Denver	M
Middle Tennessee State University	M,O
Mills College	M,D,O
Minot State University	M
Mississippi College	M,D,O
Mississippi State University	M,D,O
Missouri State University	M,O
Monmouth University	M,O
Morehead State University	M,O
Morgan State University	M
Mount Saint Mary College	M,O
Mount Saint Vincent University	M
Murray State University	M,O
National Louis University	M,D,O
Nazareth College of Rochester	M
New Jersey City University	M
New York University	M
Niagara University	M,O
Nicholls State University	M
North Carolina Agricultural and Technical State University	M
North Carolina State University	M
Northeastern Illinois University	M
Northeastern University	M,D
Northern Arizona University	M,D
Northern Illinois University	M,D
Northern Michigan University	M
Northwest Christian University	M
Northwestern Oklahoma State University	M
Northwestern State University of Louisiana	M,O
Northwestern University	M*
Northwest Missouri State University	M,O
Nyack College	M
Oakland University	M,O
Occidental College	M
Oklahoma City University	M
Old Dominion University	M
Olivet Nazarene University	M
Oregon State University	M
Ottawa University	M
Pace University	M,O
Pacific Union College	M
Pacific University	M
Pfeiffer University	M
Plymouth State University	M
Prescott College	M,D
Providence College	M
Purdue University	M,D,O
Purdue University Northwest	M
Queens College of the City University of New York	M,O
Queens University of Charlotte	M
Quinnipiac University	M
Regent University	M,D,O
Regis College (MA)	M,D
Regis University	M,O
Rhode Island College	M
Rider University	O
Rivier University	M,D,O
Rockford University	M
Rollins College	M
Roosevelt University	M
Rosemont College	M
Rowan University	M
Rutgers University–New Brunswick	M,D
Sage Graduate School	M
Saginaw Valley State University	M
St. John Fisher College	M,O
St. John's University (NY)	M
Saint Joseph's University	M,D,O
Saint Mary's University of Minnesota	M,O
Saint Peter's University	M,O
St. Thomas Aquinas College	M,O
St. Thomas University	M,D,O
Saint Xavier University	M
Salem College	M
Salem State University	M
Samford University	M,D,O
San Diego State University	M
San Francisco State University	M
San Jose State University	M,D,O
Seton Hill University	M,O
Shenandoah University	M,D,O
Shippensburg University of Pennsylvania	M
Siena Heights University	M,O
Sierra Nevada College	M
Simmons College	M,D,O
Sinte Gleska University	M
Slippery Rock University of Pennsylvania	M
Smith College	M
South Carolina State University	M
Southeastern Louisiana University	M
Southeastern University (FL)	M
Southeast Missouri State University	M,D,O
Southern Connecticut State University	M,O
Southern New Hampshire University	M,D,O
Southern Oregon University	M
Southern University and Agricultural and Mechanical College	M
Southwestern Oklahoma State University	M
Spalding University	M
Spring Hill College	M
Stanford University	M
State University of New York at New Paltz	M
State University of New York at Oswego	M
State University of New York at Plattsburgh	M,O
State University of New York College at Oneonta	M
State University of New York College at Potsdam	M
Stephen F. Austin State University	M
Stetson University	M
Sul Ross State University	M
Tarleton State University	M
Teachers College, Columbia University	M,D
Temple University	M,D,O*
Tennessee State University	M,D
Tennessee Technological University	M,O
Texas A&M University–Corpus Christi	M
Texas State University	M
Texas Tech University	M,D
Towson University	M
Trevecca Nazarene University	M,O
Trinity Washington University	M
Troy University	M,O
Tufts University	M,D
Union College (KY)	M
Universidad del Este	M
Universidad Metropolitana	M
Université de Sherbrooke	M,O
University at Buffalo, the State University of New York	M,D,O*
The University of Akron	M
The University of Alabama	M,D,O
The University of Alabama at Birmingham	M
University of Alaska Fairbanks	M
University of Alaska Southeast	M
University of Alberta	M,D
The University of Arizona	M,D
University of Bridgeport	M,D,O
University of California, Irvine	M,D
University of Central Florida	M,D
University of Central Missouri	M,D,O
University of Central Oklahoma	M
University of Cincinnati	M
University of Colorado Denver	M
University of Connecticut	M,D*
University of Florida	M,D,O
University of Georgia	M,D,O
University of Hartford	M
University of Illinois at Chicago	M,D
University of Indianapolis	M
The University of Iowa	M,D*
University of Kentucky	M,D
University of La Verne	M,D,O
University of Louisiana at Monroe	M,D
University of Louisville	M,D,O
University of Maine	M,D,O
University of Mary Hardin-Baylor	M,D
University of Maryland, Baltimore County	M
University of Mary Washington	M
University of Massachusetts Amherst	M,D,O*
University of Memphis	M,D
University of Minnesota, Twin Cities Campus	M,D,O
University of Missouri	M,D,O
University of Missouri–St. Louis	M,D,O
University of Montevallo	M
University of Nebraska at Kearney	M
University of Nebraska at Omaha	M
University of Nevada, Reno	M
University of New Hampshire	M,O
University of New Mexico	M
University of North Alabama	M
The University of North Carolina at Charlotte	M,O
The University of North Carolina at Greensboro	D
The University of North Carolina at Pembroke	M
The University of North Carolina Wilmington	M
University of North Dakota	M,D
University of Northern Iowa	M
University of North Florida	M
University of Pennsylvania	M*
University of Phoenix–Bay Area Campus	M,D,O
University of Phoenix–Central Valley Campus	M
University of Phoenix–Colorado Campus	M
University of Phoenix–Colorado Springs Downtown Campus	M,O
University of Phoenix–Hawaii Campus	M
University of Phoenix–Las Vegas Campus	M
University of Phoenix–New Mexico Campus	M
University of Phoenix–North Florida Campus	M
University of Phoenix–Online Campus	M,O
University of Phoenix–Phoenix Campus	M
University of Phoenix–Sacramento Valley Campus	M,O
University of Phoenix–San Diego Campus	M
University of Phoenix–Southern Arizona Campus	M,O
University of Phoenix–Southern California Campus	M,O
University of Phoenix–South Florida Campus	M
University of Phoenix–Utah Campus	M
University of Phoenix–Washington D.C. Campus	M,D,O

*M—masters degree; D—doctorate; O—other advanced degree; *—Close-Up and/or Display*

University of Pittsburgh M*
University of Puget Sound M
University of St. Francis (IL) M,D,O
University of Saint Mary M
University of St. Thomas (MN) M,O
University of St. Thomas (TX) M
University of South Alabama M,D
University of South Carolina M,D
University of South Carolina Upstate M
The University of South Dakota M
University of Southern Indiana M
University of Southern Mississippi M,D,O
University of South Florida M,D,O
University of South Florida, St. Petersburg M
University of South Florida Sarasota-Manatee M
The University of Tennessee M,D,O
The University of Tennessee at Chattanooga M,D,O
The University of Tennessee at Martin M
The University of Texas Rio Grande Valley M
University of the Cumberlands M,D,O
University of the District of Columbia M
University of the Incarnate Word M
The University of Toledo M,D,O
The University of Tulsa M
University of Utah M,D*
University of Virginia M,D,O
University of Washington, Tacoma M
The University of West Alabama M,O
University of West Florida M
University of Wisconsin–Milwaukee M
University of Wisconsin–Platteville M
University of Wisconsin–River Falls M
University of Wisconsin–Stevens Point M
Utah State University M
Utah Valley University M
Valley City State University M
Vanderbilt University M,D*
Virginia Commonwealth University M,O
Wagner College M
Walden University M,D,O
Washington State University M,D
Washington University in St. Louis M
Wayland Baptist University M
Wayne State College M
Wayne State University M,D,O
Western Governors University M,O
Western Illinois University M
Western Kentucky University M,O
Western New England University M
Western New Mexico University M
Western Washington University M
Westfield State University M
West Virginia University M
Wheaton College M
Wheelock College M
Whittier College M
Whitworth University M
Widener University M,D
William Carey University M,O
William Paterson University of New Jersey M
Wilmington University M,D
Wilson College M
Wingate University M,D
Worcester State University M
Wright State University M
Xavier University M

EMERGENCY MANAGEMENT

Adelphi University O
Adler University M,D,O
American Public University System M
Anna Maria College M,O
Arizona State University at the Tempe campus M,D
Arkansas State University M,O
Arkansas Tech University M
Auburn University at Montgomery M,O
Ball State University M,O
Benedictine University M
Boston University M
Brandman University M
California Maritime Academy M
California State University, Long Beach M
Capella University M,D
Columbia Southern University M
Drexel University M
Excelsior College M
Florida Institute of Technology M,D
Florida International University M
Fordham University M
Georgetown University M,D
The George Washington University M,D,O*
Georgia State University M,D,O
Grand Canyon University M
Indiana University of Pennsylvania M
Indiana University–Purdue University Indianapolis M,O
Jacksonville State University M,D
Lander University M
Lasell College M
Liberty University M,D,O
London Metropolitan University M,D
Lynn University M
Massachusetts Maritime Academy M
Metropolitan College of New York M
Millersville University of Pennsylvania M
National University M,O
New Jersey Institute of Technology M,D,O
New York Medical College O
Norwich University M
Nova Southeastern University M,D,O*
Oklahoma State University M,D
Pace University M
Park University M,O
Philadelphia University M
Regent University M
Royal Roads University M,O
Rutgers University–New Brunswick M,D,O
San Diego State University M,D
Sul Ross State University M
Syracuse University O
Trident University International M,D,O
Trine University M
Tulane University M,D
Université de Montréal O
University of Alaska Fairbanks M
University of Central Florida M,O
University of Chicago M
University of Colorado Denver M,D
University of Delaware M,D*
University of Denver M,O
University of Florida M
University of Hawaii at Manoa M,D,O
University of Illinois at Springfield M,O
University of Maryland, Baltimore County M,O
University of Nebraska Medical Center M
University of Nevada, Las Vegas M,D,O
University of New Haven M,O
The University of North Carolina at Charlotte M,O
University of North Texas M,D,O
University of South Florida O
The University of Toledo M,O
Upper Iowa University M
Virginia Commonwealth University M,O
Walden University M,D,O
Waldorf College M
West Chester University of Pennsylvania M,O
York University M

EMERGENCY MEDICAL SERVICES

Baylor University D
Creighton University M
Drexel University M
San Diego State University M,D
Université Laval O
University of Guelph M,D,O

ENERGY AND POWER ENGINEERING

Appalachian State University M
Arizona State University at the Tempe campus M,D
Carnegie Mellon University M,D
The Catholic University of America M,D
Cornell University M,D
Florida State University M,D
Georgia Southern University M
Instituto Tecnologico de Santo Domingo M,D,O
Kansas State University M,D
Lehigh University M
New Jersey Institute of Technology M,D
New York Institute of Technology M,O
North Carolina Agricultural and Technical State University M,D
Northeastern University M,D,O
Oregon State University M,D
Saginaw Valley State University M
San Francisco State University M
Santa Clara University M,D,O
Southern Illinois University Carbondale D
Stanford University M,D,O
Syracuse University M
Texas A&M University–Kingsville D
Texas Tech University M,D
Universidad Autonoma de Guadalajara M,D
University of Alberta M,D
University of Calgary M,D
University of Colorado Colorado Springs M,D
University of Illinois at Urbana–Champaign M,D
The University of Iowa M,D*
University of Massachusetts Lowell M,D
University of Memphis M,D
University of Michigan M,D
University of Michigan–Dearborn M
The University of North Carolina at Charlotte M,O
University of North Texas M,D,O
University of Rochester M*
The University of Tennessee D
The University of Tennessee at Chattanooga M,O
Washington State University M,D
Wayne State University M,O
Worcester Polytechnic Institute M,D

ENERGY MANAGEMENT AND POLICY

American University of Armenia M
Boston University M,D
Duke University M,O*
Eastern Illinois University M
Franklin Pierce University M,D,O
HEC Montreal O
Holy Names University M
Indiana University Bloomington M,D,O
Instituto Tecnologico de Santo Domingo M,D,O
Johns Hopkins University M,O
Kansas State University M,D
Michigan Technological University M,D
New York Institute of Technology M,O
New York University M,O
Oklahoma Baptist University M
Oklahoma City University M
Rice University M,D
Samford University M
Tulane University M,D
Université du Québec, Institut National de la Recherche Scientifique M,D
University of Calgary M,D
University of California, Berkeley M,D
University of Colorado Denver M
University of Delaware M,D*
University of Illinois at Urbana–Champaign M
University of Mary M
University of Phoenix–Bay Area Campus M,D
University of Phoenix–Online Campus M,O
University of Phoenix–Phoenix Campus M,O
University of Phoenix–Southern California Campus M
University of Pittsburgh M*
University of Rochester M*
University of San Francisco M
The University of Tulsa M
Vermont Law School M
Waynesburg University M,D

ENGINEERING AND APPLIED SCIENCES—GENERAL

Air Force Institute of Technology M,D
Alabama Agricultural and Mechanical University M,D
Alfred University M,D
The American University in Cairo M,D,O
American University of Beirut M,D
Arizona State University at the Tempe campus M,D
Arkansas State University M
Arkansas Tech University M
Auburn University M,D,O
Austin Peay State University M
Binghamton University, State University of New York M,D*
Boise State University M,D,O
Boston University M,D
Bradley University M
Brigham Young University M,D
Brown University M,D
Bucknell University M
California Institute of Technology M,D,O
California National University for Advanced Studies M
California Polytechnic State University, San Luis Obispo M
California State University, Chico M
California State University, East Bay M
California State University, Fresno M
California State University, Fullerton M
California State University, Los Angeles M
California State University, Northridge M
California State University, Sacramento M
Carleton University M,D
Case Western Reserve University M,D*
The Catholic University of America M,D,O
Central Connecticut State University M
Central Michigan University M
Central Washington University M
Christian Brothers University M
City College of the City University of New York M,D
Clarkson University M,D
Clemson University M,D,O
Cleveland State University M,D
Colorado School of Mines M,D,O
Colorado State University M,D
Colorado State University–Pueblo M
Columbia University M,D*
Concordia University (Canada) M,D,O
Cooper Union for the Advancement of Science and Art M
Cornell University M,D
Dalhousie University M,D
Dartmouth College M,D*
Drexel University M,D,O
Duke University M*
Eastern Illinois University M,O
Eastern Michigan University M
École Polytechnique de Montréal M,D,O
Fairfield University M,O
Fairleigh Dickinson University, Metropolitan Campus M
Florida Agricultural and Mechanical University M,D
Florida Atlantic University M,D
Florida Institute of Technology M,D
Florida International University M,D
Florida State University M,D
George Mason University M,D,O
The George Washington University M,D,O*
Georgia Institute of Technology M,D
Georgia Southern University M,O
The Graduate Center, City University of New York D
Grand Valley State University M
Grantham University M
Harvard University M,D*
Hofstra University M
Howard University M,D
Idaho State University M,D,O
Illinois Institute of Technology M,D
Indiana State University M
Indiana University–Purdue University Fort Wayne M,O
Instituto Tecnologico de Santo Domingo M,O
Instituto Tecnológico y de Estudios Superiores de Monterrey, Campus Ciudad Obregón M
Instituto Tecnológico y de Estudios Superiores de Monterrey, Campus Monterrey M,D
James Madison University M
Johns Hopkins University M,D,O
Kansas State University M,D,O
Kennesaw State University M,O
Kent State University M
Lakehead University M
Lamar University M,D
Laurentian University M,D
Lawrence Technological University M,D
Lehigh University M,D
LeTourneau University M
Liberty University M
Louisiana State University and Agricultural & Mechanical College M,D
Louisiana Tech University M,D
Manhattan College M
Marquette University M,D,O
Marshall University M
Massachusetts Institute of Technology M,D,O
McGill University M,D,O
McMaster University M,D
McNeese State University M,O
Memorial University of Newfoundland M,D
Mercer University M
Merrimack College M
Miami University M
Michigan State University M,D
Michigan Technological University M,D,O
Milwaukee School of Engineering M*
Mississippi State University M,D
Missouri Western State University M
Montana State University M,D
Montana Tech of The University of Montana M
Morgan State University M,D
New Jersey Institute of Technology M,D
New Mexico State University M,D,O
New York Institute of Technology M,O
New York University M,D,O
North Carolina Agricultural and Technical State University M,D
North Carolina State University M,D
Northeastern University M,D,O
Northern Arizona University M,D,O
Northern Illinois University M
Northwestern Polytechnic University M,D
Northwestern University M,D,O*
Oakland University M,D,O
The Ohio State University M,D
Ohio University M,D
Oklahoma Christian University M
Oklahoma State University M,D
Old Dominion University M,D
Open University M
Oregon State University M,D
Penn State Erie, The Behrend College M
Penn State Great Valley M,O
Penn State Harrisburg M,O
Penn State University Park M,D
Pontificia Universidad Catolica Madre y Maestra M
Portland State University M,D,O
Prairie View A&M University M,D
Princeton University M,D
Purdue University M,D,O
Purdue University Northwest M
Queen's University at Kingston M,D
Rensselaer at Hartford M
Rensselaer Polytechnic Institute M,D
Rice University M,D
Robert Morris University M
Rochester Institute of Technology M,D,O
Rose-Hulman Institute of Technology M
Rowan University M
Royal Military College of Canada M,D
Saginaw Valley State University M
St. Cloud State University M
San Diego State University M,D
San Francisco State University M
Santa Clara University M,D,O
Seattle University M
Simon Fraser University M,D
South Dakota School of Mines and Technology M,D
South Dakota State University M,D
Southern Illinois University Carbondale M,D
Southern Illinois University Edwardsville M
Southern Methodist University M,D
Southern University and Agricultural and Mechanical College M
Stanford University M,D,O
Stevens Institute of Technology M,D,O
Stony Brook University, State University of New York M,D,O
Syracuse University M,D,O
Temple University D*
Tennessee State University M,D
Tennessee Technological University M,D
Texas A&M University–Kingsville M,D
Texas State University M
Texas Tech University M,D
Trine University M
Tufts University M,D
Tuskegee University M,D
Universidad de las Américas Puebla M,D
Université de Moncton M

Université de Sherbrooke M,D,O
Université du Québec à Chicoutimi M,D
Université du Québec à Rimouski M
Université du Québec, École de technologie supérieure M,D,O
Université du Québec en Abitibi-Témiscamingue M,O
Université Laval M,D,O
University at Buffalo, the State University of New York M,D,O*
The University of Akron M,D
The University of Alabama M,D
The University of Alabama at Birmingham M,D
The University of Alabama in Huntsville M,D
University of Alaska Anchorage M,O
University of Alaska Fairbanks D
The University of Arizona M,D,O
University of Arkansas M,D
University of Bridgeport M,D
The University of British Columbia M,D
University of Calgary M,D
University of California, Berkeley M,D,O
University of California, Davis M,D,O
University of California, Irvine M,D
University of California, Los Angeles M,D
University of California, Merced M,D
University of California, Santa Barbara M,D
University of California, Santa Cruz M,D
University of Central Florida M,D,O
University of Central Oklahoma M
University of Cincinnati M,D
University of Colorado Boulder M,D
University of Colorado Colorado Springs M,D
University of Colorado Denver M,D
University of Connecticut M,D*
University of Delaware M,D*
University of Denver M,D
University of Detroit Mercy M,D
University of Florida M,D,O
University of Guelph M,D
University of Hartford M
University of Hawaii at Manoa M,D
University of Houston M,D
University of Idaho M,D
University of Illinois at Chicago M,D
University of Illinois at Urbana–Champaign M,D
The University of Iowa M,D*
The University of Kansas M,D*
University of Kentucky M,D
University of Louisville M,D,O
University of Maine M,D
University of Manitoba M,D
University of Maryland, Baltimore County M,D,O
University of Maryland, College Park M
University of Massachusetts Amherst M,D*
University of Massachusetts Dartmouth D
University of Massachusetts Lowell M,D
University of Memphis M,D
University of Miami M,D
University of Michigan M,D,O
University of Michigan–Dearborn M,D
University of Minnesota, Twin Cities Campus M,D,O
University of Mississippi M,D
University of Missouri–Kansas City M,D,O
University of Nebraska–Lincoln M,D
University of Nevada, Las Vegas M,D,O
University of Nevada, Reno M,D
University of New Brunswick Fredericton M,D,O
University of New Haven M,O
University of New Mexico M,D
University of New Orleans M,D
The University of North Carolina at Charlotte M,D,O
University of North Dakota D
University of North Texas M,D,O
University of Notre Dame M,D
University of Oklahoma M,D*
University of Ottawa M,D,O
University of Pennsylvania M,D,O*
University of Pittsburgh M,D*
University of Portland M
University of Puerto Rico, Mayagüez Campus M,D
University of Regina M,D
University of Rhode Island M,D,O
University of Rochester M,D*
University of St. Thomas (MN) M,O
University of Saskatchewan M,D,O
University of South Africa M
University of South Alabama M,D
University of South Carolina M,D
University of Southern California M,D,O
University of Southern Indiana M
University of South Florida M,D,O
The University of Tennessee M,D
The University of Texas at Arlington M,D
The University of Texas at Austin M,D
The University of Texas at Dallas M,D*
The University of Texas at El Paso M,D,O
The University of Texas at San Antonio M,D
University of the District of Columbia M
University of the Pacific M
The University of Toledo M
University of Toronto M,D
The University of Tulsa M,D
University of Utah M,D*
University of Vermont M,D
University of Victoria M,D
University of Virginia M,D
University of Washington M,D,O*
University of Waterloo M,D
The University of Western Ontario M,D
University of Windsor M,D
University of Wisconsin–Madison M,D
University of Wisconsin–Milwaukee M,D,O
University of Wisconsin–Platteville M
University of Wyoming M,D
Utah State University M,D,O
Vanderbilt University M,D*
Villanova University M,D,O
Virginia Commonwealth University M,D
Virginia Polytechnic Institute and State University M,D
Washington State University M,D,O
Washington University in St. Louis M,D
Wayne State University M,D,O
Western Michigan University M,D
Western New England University M,D
West Texas A&M University M
West Virginia University M,D,O
Wichita State University M,D
Widener University M
Wilkes University M
Worcester Polytechnic Institute M,D,O
Wright State University M,D
Yale University M,D*
Youngstown State University M

ENGINEERING DESIGN

Harvard University M,D*
Northwestern University M*
Oregon State University M,D
Penn State University Park M
Rochester Institute of Technology M
San Diego State University M,D
Stanford University M
Stevens Institute of Technology M
The University of Alabama at Birmingham M
University of Michigan M,D
Worcester Polytechnic Institute M,D,O

ENGINEERING MANAGEMENT

Air Force Institute of Technology M
American University of Beirut M,D
American University of Sharjah M
Arkansas State University M
California Maritime Academy M
California National University for Advanced Studies M
California State Polytechnic University, Pomona M
California State University, East Bay M
California State University, Long Beach M,D
California State University, Northridge M
Case Western Reserve University M*
The Catholic University of America M,O
Central Michigan University M,O
Clarkson University M
Colorado School of Mines M,D
Cornell University M,D
Dallas Baptist University M
Dartmouth College M*
Drexel University M,O
Duke University M*
Eastern Michigan University M
Embry-Riddle Aeronautical University–Worldwide M
Florida Institute of Technology M,D
Florida International University M
Gannon University M
The George Washington University M,D,O*
Georgia Southern University M
Indiana Tech M
Instituto Tecnológico y de Estudios Superiores de Monterrey, Campus Chihuahua M,O
International Technological University M
Johns Hopkins University M
Kansas State University M,D
Kettering University M
Lamar University M,D
Lawrence Technological University M,D
Lehigh University M,D
LeTourneau University M
Lipscomb University M
Long Island University–LIU Post M
Loyola Marymount University M
Marquette University M,D,O
Marshall University M
McNeese State University M
Mercer University M
Merrimack College M
Middle Tennessee State University M
Milwaukee School of Engineering M*
Missouri University of Science and Technology M,D
National University M,O
Naval Postgraduate School M,D,O
New Jersey Institute of Technology M,D
New Mexico Institute of Mining and Technology M
Northeastern University M,D,O
Northwestern University M*
Oakland University M,D,O
Oklahoma Christian University M
Old Dominion University M,D
Oregon State University M,D
Penn State Great Valley M,O
Penn State Harrisburg M,O
Point Park University M
Polytechnic University of Puerto Rico M
Polytechnic University of Puerto Rico, Orlando Campus M
Portland State University M,D,O
Rensselaer Polytechnic Institute M,D
Robert Morris University M
Rochester Institute of Technology M
Rose-Hulman Institute of Technology M
St. Cloud State University M
Saint Martin's University M
St. Mary's University (United States) M
Santa Clara University M,D,O
South Dakota School of Mines and Technology M
Southern Illinois University Carbondale M
Southern Methodist University M,D
Stanford University M,D
Stevens Institute of Technology M,D,O
Syracuse University M
Tarleton State University M
Temple University M,O*
Texas Tech University M,D
Trine University M
Tufts University M
Université de Sherbrooke M,O
The University of Alabama at Birmingham M,D
University of Alaska Anchorage M
University of Alaska Fairbanks M
University of Alberta M,D
The University of Arizona M,D,O
University of California, Berkeley M,D
University of California, Irvine M
University of Colorado Boulder M
University of Colorado Colorado Springs M,D
University of Dayton M
University of Denver M,D
University of Detroit Mercy M,D
University of Idaho M,D
The University of Kansas M*
University of Louisiana at Lafayette M
University of Louisville M,D,O
University of Management and Technology M
The University of Manchester M,D
University of Maryland, Baltimore County M,O
University of Michigan–Dearborn M
University of Minnesota, Duluth M
University of Missouri–Kansas City M,D,O
University of Nebraska–Lincoln M,D
University of New Brunswick Fredericton M
University of New Haven M,O
University of New Orleans M
The University of North Carolina at Charlotte M,O
University of Ottawa M,O
University of Regina M,O
University of St. Thomas (MN) M,O
University of Southern California M,D,O
University of South Florida M,D
The University of Tennessee M,D
The University of Tennessee at Chattanooga M,O
The University of Texas at Arlington M
The University of Texas Rio Grande Valley M
University of Waterloo M,D
University of Wisconsin–Milwaukee M,D,O
Valparaiso University M,O
Virginia Polytechnic Institute and State University M,O
Washington State University M,O
Wayne State University M,O
Webster University M
Western Michigan University M,D
Western New England University M,D
Wichita State University M,D
Widener University M
Wilkes University M

ENGINEERING PHYSICS

Air Force Institute of Technology M,D
Appalachian State University M
Cornell University M,D
École Polytechnique de Montréal M,D,O
Embry-Riddle Aeronautical University–Daytona M,D*
George Mason University M,D,O
McMaster University M,D
Michigan Technological University M,D
Rensselaer Polytechnic Institute M,D
Stanford University M,D
University of California, San Diego M,D
University of Central Oklahoma M
University of Maine M,D
University of Oklahoma M,D*
University of Saskatchewan M,D
The University of Tulsa M
University of Virginia M,D
University of Wisconsin–Madison M,D
Yale University M,D*

ENGLISH

Abilene Christian University M
Acadia University M
The American University in Cairo M,O
American University of Beirut M,D
Andrews University M
Angelo State University M
Appalachian State University M
Arcadia University M
Arizona State University at the Tempe campus M,D,O
Arkansas State University M,O
Arkansas Tech University M
Asbury University M
Auburn University M,D,O
Austin Peay State University M
Ball State University M,D
Baylor University M,D
Bemidji State University M
Binghamton University, State University of New York M,D*
Bob Jones University M,D,O
Boston College M,D
Boston University M,D
Bowie State University M
Bowling Green State University M,D
Bradley University M
Brandeis University M,D
Bridgewater State University M
Brigham Young University M
Brock University M
Brooklyn College of the City University of New York M
Brown University M,D
Bucknell University M
Buffalo State College, State University of New York M
Butler University M
California Baptist University M
California Polytechnic State University, San Luis Obispo M
California State Polytechnic University, Pomona M
California State University, Bakersfield M
California State University, Chico M
California State University, Dominguez Hills M,O
California State University, East Bay M
California State University, Fresno M
California State University, Fullerton M
California State University, Long Beach M
California State University, Los Angeles M,O
California State University, Northridge M
California State University, Sacramento M
California State University, San Bernardino M
California State University, San Marcos M
California State University, Stanislaus M,O
Carleton University M,D
Carnegie Mellon University M,D
Case Western Reserve University M,D*
The Catholic University of America M,D,O
Central Connecticut State University M,O
Central Michigan University M
Central Washington University M
Chapman University M
Chicago State University M
The Citadel, The Military College of South Carolina M
City College of the City University of New York M
Claremont Graduate University M,D
Clark Atlanta University M,D
Clark University M
Clemson University M
Cleveland State University M
The College at Brockport, State University of New York M,O
College of Charleston M
The College of New Jersey M
College of Staten Island of the City University of New York M
Colorado State University M
Columbia University M,D*
Concordia University (Canada) M,D
Converse College M
Cornell University M,D
Creighton University M
Dalhousie University M,D
DePaul University M
Dominican University of California M
Drew University M,D,O
Duke University D*
Duquesne University M,D
East Carolina University M,D,O
Eastern Illinois University M
Eastern Kentucky University M
Eastern Michigan University M,O
Eastern New Mexico University M
Eastern Washington University M
East Tennessee State University M,O
Emory University D,O
Emporia State University M

*M—masters degree; D—doctorate; O—other advanced degree; *—Close-Up and/or Display*

Fairleigh Dickinson University, Metropolitan Campus	M
Fayetteville State University	M
Fitchburg State University	M,O
Florida Atlantic University	M
Florida Gulf Coast University	M
Florida International University	M
Florida State University	M,D
Fordham University	M,D
Fort Hays State University	M
Gannon University	M
Gardner-Webb University	M
George Mason University	M,D,O
Georgetown University	M
The George Washington University	M,D*
Georgia College & State University	M
Georgia Southern University	M
Georgia State University	M,D
Governors State University	M
The Graduate Center, City University of New York	D
Grambling State University	M,D,O
Grand Valley State University	M
Hardin-Simmons University	M
Harvard University	M,D,O*
Heritage University	M
Hofstra University	M
Hollins University	M
Howard University	M,D
Humboldt State University	M
Hunter College of the City University of New York	M
Idaho State University	M,D,O
Illinois State University	M,D
Indiana State University	M
Indiana University Bloomington	M,D
Indiana University of Pennsylvania	M,D
Indiana University–Purdue University Fort Wayne	M,O
Indiana University–Purdue University Indianapolis	M,O
Indiana University South Bend	M
Inter American University of Puerto Rico, Metropolitan Campus	M
Iona College	M
Iowa State University of Science and Technology	M,D
Jackson State University	M
Jacksonville State University	M
James Madison University	M
John Carroll University	M
Johns Hopkins University	M,D
Kansas State University	M,O
Kent State University	M,D,O
Kutztown University of Pennsylvania	M
Lakehead University	M
Lamar University	M
La Salle University	M,O
La Sierra University	M
Lee University	M,O
Lehigh University	M,D
Lehman College of the City University of New York	M
Liberty University	M,D,O
Lipscomb University	M,D,O
Long Island University–LIU Brooklyn	M,D,O
Long Island University–LIU Post	M,O
Louisiana State University and Agricultural & Mechanical College	M,D
Louisiana Tech University	M,O
Loyola Marymount University	M
Loyola University Chicago	M,D
Marquette University	M,D
Marshall University	M,O
Mary Baldwin College	M
Marygrove College	M
Marymount University	M,O
McGill University	M,D
McMaster University	M,D
McNeese State University	M
Memorial University of Newfoundland	M,D
Mercy College	M
Miami University	M,D
Michigan State University	M,D
Middlebury College	M
Middle Tennessee State University	M,D
Midwestern State University	M,D
Millersville University of Pennsylvania	M
Mills College	M,O
Minnesota State University Mankato	M,O
Mississippi College	M
Mississippi State University	M
Missouri State University	M,O
Molloy College	M,O
Monmouth University	M
Montana State University	M
Montclair State University	M
Morehead State University	M
Morgan State University	M,D
Mount Mary University	M
Mount Saint Mary's University (CA)	M,D,O
Murray State University	M
National University	M,O
New Mexico Highlands University	M
New Mexico State University	M,D
New York University	M,D
North Carolina Agricultural and Technical State University	M
North Carolina Central University	M
North Carolina State University	M
North Dakota State University	M,D
Northeastern Illinois University	M
Northeastern State University	M
Northeastern University	M,D
Northern Arizona University	M,D,O
Northern Illinois University	M,D
Northern Kentucky University	M,O
Northern Michigan University	M,O
Northwestern State University of Louisiana	M
Northwestern University	M,D*
Northwest Missouri State University	M
Notre Dame de Namur University	M
Oakland University	M
Ohio Dominican University	M
The Ohio State University	M,D
Ohio University	M,D
Oklahoma State University	M,D
Old Dominion University	M,D
Oregon State University	M
Our Lady of the Lake University of San Antonio	M
Pace University	M,O
Penn State University Park	M,D
Pittsburg State University	M
Portland State University	M
Princeton University	D
Purdue University	M,D
Purdue University Northwest	M
Queens College of the City University of New York	M
Queen's University at Kingston	M,D
Radford University	M
Rhode Island College	M,O
Rice University	M,D
Rivier University	M
Roosevelt University	M
Rutgers University–Camden	M
Rutgers University–Newark	M
Rutgers University–New Brunswick	D
St. Bonaventure University	M
St. Cloud State University	M
St. John's University (NY)	M,D
Saint Louis University	M,D
Saint Louis University–Madrid Campus	M
St. Mary's University (United States)	M
Salem State University	M
Salisbury University	M
Sam Houston State University	M
San Diego State University	M
San Francisco State University	M,O
San Jose State University	M,O
Seton Hall University	M
Sewanee: The University of the South	M
Simon Fraser University	M,D
Sonoma State University	M
South Carolina State University	M
South Dakota State University	M
Southeastern Louisiana University	M
Southeast Missouri State University	M
Southern Connecticut State University	M
Southern Illinois University Carbondale	M,D
Southern Illinois University Edwardsville	M,O
Southern Methodist University	M,D
Spring Hill College	M,O
Stanford University	M,D
State University of New York at New Paltz	M
State University of New York at Oswego	M
State University of New York College at Cortland	M
State University of New York College at Potsdam	M
Stephen F. Austin State University	M
Stony Brook University, State University of New York	M,D,O
Sul Ross State University	M
Summit University	M
Syracuse University	M,D
Tarleton State University	M
Temple University	M,D*
Tennessee Technological University	M
Texas A&M International University	M,D
Texas A&M University	M,D
Texas A&M University–Corpus Christi	M
Texas A&M University–Kingsville	M
Texas A&M University–San Antonio	M
Texas A&M University–Texarkana	M
Texas Christian University	M,D
Texas Southern University	M
Texas State University	M
Texas Tech University	M,D
Texas Woman's University	M,D
Tiffin University	M
Trinity College (United States)	M
Trinity Western University	M
Truman State University	M
Tufts University	M,D
Tulane University	M
Universidad de las Américas Puebla	M
Université de Montréal	M,D
Université Laval	M,D
University at Albany, State University of New York	M,D
University at Buffalo, the State University of New York	M,D*
The University of Akron	M
The University of Alabama	M,D
The University of Alabama at Birmingham	M
The University of Alabama in Huntsville	M,O
University of Alaska Anchorage	M
University of Alaska Fairbanks	M
University of Alberta	M,D
The University of Arizona	M,D
University of Arkansas	M,D
The University of British Columbia	M,D
University of Calgary	M,D
University of California, Berkeley	D
University of California, Davis	M,D
University of California, Irvine	M,D
University of California, Los Angeles	M,D
University of California, Riverside	M,D
University of California, San Diego	M,D
University of California, Santa Barbara	D
University of California, Santa Cruz	M,D
University of Central Arkansas	M
University of Central Florida	M,D,O
University of Central Missouri	M,D,O
University of Central Oklahoma	M
University of Chicago	M,D
University of Cincinnati	M,D
University of Colorado Boulder	M,D
University of Colorado Denver	M
University of Connecticut	M,D*
University of Dallas	M
University of Dayton	M
University of Delaware	M,D*
University of Denver	M,D
University of Florida	M,D
University of Georgia	M,D
University of Guam	M
University of Guelph	M
University of Hawaii at Manoa	M,D
University of Houston–Clear Lake	M
University of Houston–Downtown	M
University of Idaho	M
University of Illinois at Chicago	M,D
University of Illinois at Springfield	M,O
University of Illinois at Urbana–Champaign	M,D
University of Indianapolis	M
The University of Iowa	M,D*
The University of Kansas	M,D*
University of Kentucky	M,D
University of La Verne	M,O
University of Lethbridge	M,D
University of Louisiana at Lafayette	M,D
University of Louisiana at Monroe	M
University of Louisville	M,D
University of Maine	M
The University of Manchester	D
University of Manitoba	M,D
University of Maryland, Baltimore County	M
University of Maryland, College Park	M,D
University of Massachusetts Amherst	M,D*
University of Massachusetts Boston	M
University of Memphis	M,D,O
University of Miami	M,D
University of Michigan	M,D,O
University of Michigan–Flint	M
University of Minnesota, Duluth	M
University of Minnesota, Twin Cities Campus	M,D
University of Mississippi	M,D
University of Missouri	M,D
University of Missouri–Kansas City	M,D
University of Missouri–St. Louis	M
University of Montana	M
University of Montevallo	M
University of Nebraska at Kearney	M
University of Nebraska at Omaha	M,O
University of Nebraska–Lincoln	M,D
University of Nevada, Las Vegas	M,D
University of Nevada, Reno	M,D
University of New Brunswick Fredericton	M,D
University of New Hampshire	M,D
University of New Mexico	M,D
University of New Orleans	M
University of North Alabama	M
The University of North Carolina at Chapel Hill	M,D
The University of North Carolina at Charlotte	M,O
The University of North Carolina at Greensboro	M,D
The University of North Carolina Wilmington	M
University of North Dakota	M,D
University of Northern Colorado	M
University of Northern Iowa	M
University of North Florida	M
University of North Texas	M,D,O
University of Notre Dame	M,D
University of Oklahoma	M,D*
University of Oregon	M,D
University of Ottawa	M,D
University of Pennsylvania	M,D*
University of Pittsburgh	M,D*
University of Puerto Rico, Mayagüez Campus	M
University of Puerto Rico, Rí o Piedras Campus	M,D
University of Regina	M
University of Rhode Island	M,D
University of Rochester	M,D*
University of St. Thomas (MN)	M
University of Saskatchewan	M,D
University of South Africa	M,D
University of South Alabama	M
University of South Carolina	M,D
The University of South Dakota	M,D
University of Southern California	M,D
University of Southern Indiana	M
University of Southern Mississippi	M,D
University of South Florida	M,D,O
The University of Tennessee	M,D
The University of Tennessee at Chattanooga	M,O
The University of Texas at Arlington	M,D
The University of Texas at Austin	M,D
The University of Texas at El Paso	M,D,O
The University of Texas at San Antonio	M,D
The University of Texas at Tyler	M
The University of Texas of the Permian Basin	M
The University of Texas Rio Grande Valley	M
The University of Toledo	M,O
University of Toronto	M,D
The University of Tulsa	M,D
University of Utah	M,D*
University of Vermont	M
University of Victoria	M,D
University of Virginia	M,D
University of Washington	M,D*
University of Waterloo	M,D
The University of Western Ontario	M,D
University of West Florida	M
University of West Georgia	M,O
University of Windsor	M
University of Wisconsin–Eau Claire	M
University of Wisconsin–Madison	M,D
University of Wisconsin–Milwaukee	M,D,O
University of Wisconsin–Oshkosh	M
University of Wisconsin–Stevens Point	M
University of Wyoming	M
Utah State University	M
Valdosta State University	M
Valparaiso University	M,O
Vanderbilt University	M,D*
Villanova University	M
Virginia Commonwealth University	M
Virginia Polytechnic Institute and State University	M,D,O
Wake Forest University	M
Washington State University	M,D
Washington University in St. Louis	M,D
Wayne State University	M,D
Weber State University	M
West Chester University of Pennsylvania	M,O
Western Carolina University	M
Western Connecticut State University	M
Western Illinois University	M,O
Western Kentucky University	M
Western Michigan University	M,D
Western Washington University	M
Westfield State University	M
West Texas A&M University	M
West Virginia University	M,D
Wichita State University	M
Wilfrid Laurier University	M,D
William Paterson University of New Jersey	M,D
Wilson College	M
Winona State University	M
Winthrop University	M
Wright State University	M
Xavier University	M
Yale University	M,D*
York University	M,D
Youngstown State University	M

ENGLISH AS A SECOND LANGUAGE

Acacia University	M
Adelphi University	M,O
Albright College	M
Alliant International University–San Diego	M,D,O
Alliant International University–San Francisco	M,O
American College of Education	M
American Public University System	M
American University	M,O
American University of Armenia	M
American University of Sharjah	M
Anaheim University	M,D,O
Andrews University	M,D,O
Arizona State University at the Tempe campus	M,D,O
Arkansas Tech University	M
Asbury University	M
Aurora University	M,D
Avila University	M,O
Azusa Pacific University	M
Ball State University	M
Barry University	M,D,O
Binghamton University, State University of New York	M*
Biola University	M,D,O
Bishop's University	M,O
Boise State University	M
Boricua College	M
Brigham Young University	M
Brock University	M
Brown University	M,D
Buena Vista University	M
California Baptist University	M
California State University, Chico	M
California State University, Dominguez Hills	M,O
California State University, East Bay	M
California State University, Fresno	M
California State University, Fullerton	M

California State University, Long Beach	M
California State University, Sacramento	M
California State University, Stanislaus	M,O
Cambridge College	M,D,O
Canisius College	M,O
Carlos Albizu University, Miami Campus	M,D
Carson-Newman University	M
Central Connecticut State University	M,O
Central Michigan University	M
Central Washington University	M
City College of the City University of New York	M
Cleveland State University	M
Coastal Carolina University	M,O
College of Charleston	O
The College of New Jersey	M,O
The College of New Rochelle	M,O
College of Saint Mary	M
College of Staten Island of the City University of New York	M,O
Colorado Mesa University	M
Columbia International University	M,D,O
Columbus State University	O
Concordia University (United States)	M,D
Concordia University (Canada)	M,O
Cornerstone University	M,O
Dallas Baptist University	M
DeSales University	M,O
Dominican University	M
Duquesne University	M
East Carolina University	M,D,O
Eastern Michigan University	M,O
Eastern Nazarene College	M,O
Eastern New Mexico University	M
Eastern University	M,O
Eastern Washington University	M
Edgewood College	M,D,O
Elms College	M,O
Emporia State University	M
Erikson Institute	M,O
Fairfield University	M,O
Florida Atlantic University	M,D,O
Florida International University	M,D,O
Fordham University	M,O
Framingham State University	M
Fresno Pacific University	M,O
Furman University	M,O
Gannon University	O
George Fox University	M,O
George Mason University	M
Gonzaga University	M
Gordon College	M,O
Grand Valley State University	M,O
Greensboro College	M
Hamline University	M,D
Harding University	M,O
Hawai`i Pacific University	M
Henderson State University	M,O
Heritage University	M
Hofstra University	M,D,O
Holy Family University	M
Holy Names University	M,O
Houston Baptist University	M
Humboldt State University	M
Hunter College of the City University of New York	M
Huntington University	M,D
Idaho State University	M,D,O
Immaculata University	M
Indiana State University	M,D,O
Indiana University Bloomington	M,D
Indiana University of Pennsylvania	M,D
Indiana University–Purdue University Fort Wayne	M,O
Indiana University–Purdue University Indianapolis	M,O
Inter American University of Puerto Rico, Arecibo Campus	M
Inter American University of Puerto Rico, Barranquitas Campus	M
Inter American University of Puerto Rico, Metropolitan Campus	M
Inter American University of Puerto Rico, Ponce Campus	M
Inter American University of Puerto Rico, San Germán Campus	M
Iowa State University of Science and Technology	M
James Madison University	M
Kean University	M
Kennesaw State University	M
Kent State University	M,D,O
Langston University	M
La Salle University	M,O
Lee University	M,O
Lehigh University	M,D,O
Lehman College of the City University of New York	M
Le Moyne College	M,O
Lesley University	M,D,O
Lewis University	M
Lindenwood University	M,D,O
Long Island University–Hudson at Westchester	M,O
Long Island University–LIU Brooklyn	M,O
Long Island University–LIU Post	M,D,O
Long Island University–Riverhead	M,O
Loyola University Chicago	M,O
Madonna University	M
Manhattanville College	M,O*
Marlboro College	M
Marymount University	M
McDaniel College	M
Mercy College	M,O
Merrimack College	M,O
Messiah College	M
Michigan State University	M,D
MidAmerica Nazarene University	M
Middlebury Institute of International Studies at Monterey	M
Middle Tennessee State University	M,O
Millersville University of Pennsylvania	M
Minnesota State University Mankato	M,O
Minnesota State University Moorhead	M
Mississippi College	M
Missouri State University	M,O
Missouri Western State University	M,O
Molloy College	M,O
Monmouth University	M,O
Montclair State University	M,O
Mount Saint Vincent University	M
Multnomah University	M
Murray State University	M
Nazareth College of Rochester	M
New Jersey City University	M
Newman University	M
New Mexico State University	M,D,O
The New School	M
New York University	M,D,O
Niagara University	M,O
Northeastern Illinois University	M
Northern Arizona University	M,D,O
Northern Michigan University	M,O
Northwest Christian University	M
Northwest Missouri State University	M,O
Notre Dame of Maryland University	M
Nyack College	M
Oakland University	M,O
Ohio Dominican University	M
Oklahoma City University	M
Pacific University	M
Penn State Harrisburg	M,D,O
Penn State University Park	M,D
Pontifical Catholic University of Puerto Rico	M
Portland State University	M
Post University	M
Providence University College & Theological Seminary	M,D,O
Queens College of the City University of New York	M
Quincy University	M
Regent University	M,D,O
Rhode Island College	M
Rider University	O
Rowan University	O
Rutgers University–New Brunswick	M,D
Sacred Heart University	M,O
St. Cloud State University	M
St. John's University (NY)	M,O
Saint Martin's University	M
Saint Michael's College	M,O
St. Thomas University	M,D,O
Saint Xavier University	M
Salem College	M
Salem State University	M
Salisbury University	M
San Diego State University	M,O
San Francisco State University	M
San Jose State University	M,O
Seattle Pacific University	M
Seattle University	M,O
Simmons College	M,D,O
Simon Fraser University	M
SIT Graduate Institute	M
Southeast Missouri State University	M
Southern Connecticut State University	M
Southern Illinois University Carbondale	M
Southern Illinois University Edwardsville	M,O
Southern New Hampshire University	M,D,O
Southwest Minnesota State University	M
State University of New York at Fredonia	M
State University of New York at New Paltz	M,O
State University of New York College at Cortland	M
Stony Brook University, State University of New York	M
Summit University	M
Syracuse University	M,O
Taylor College and Seminary	M,O
Teachers College, Columbia University	M,D,O
Temple University	M*
Texas A&M University–Kingsville	M,D
Touro College	M
Trevecca Nazarene University	M,O
Trinity Western University	M
Troy University	M
Universidad del Este	M
Universidad del Turabo	M
University at Buffalo, the State University of New York	M,D,O*
The University of Alabama	M,D
The University of Alabama at Birmingham	M,O
The University of Alabama in Huntsville	M,O
University of Alberta	M,D
The University of Arizona	M,D
University of Arkansas at Little Rock	M
The University of British Columbia	M,D
University of California, Berkeley	O
University of California, Los Angeles	M,D,O
University of California, Riverside	M,D,O
University of Central Florida	M,D,O
University of Central Missouri	M,D,O
University of Central Oklahoma	M
University of Cincinnati	M,D,O
University of Delaware	M,D,O*
The University of Findlay	M,D
University of Florida	M,D,O
University of Guam	M
University of Hawaii at Manoa	M,D,O
University of Idaho	M
University of Illinois at Chicago	M,D
University of Illinois at Springfield	M,O
University of Illinois at Urbana–Champaign	M,D
The University of Iowa	M,D*
University of Louisiana at Monroe	M,D
The University of Manchester	M,D
University of Manitoba	M
University of Maryland, Baltimore County	M,O
University of Maryland, College Park	M,D,O
University of Massachusetts Amherst	M,D,O*
University of Massachusetts Boston	M
University of Memphis	M,D,O
University of Minnesota, Twin Cities Campus	M
University of Missouri–St. Louis	M,O
University of Nebraska at Kearney	M
University of Nebraska at Omaha	M,O
University of Nevada, Las Vegas	M,D,O
University of Nevada, Reno	M
University of New Mexico	M,D
The University of North Carolina at Chapel Hill	M
The University of North Carolina at Charlotte	M,D,O
The University of North Carolina at Greensboro	M,D,O
The University of North Carolina Wilmington	M
University of Northern Iowa	M
University of North Florida	M
University of North Texas	M,D,O
University of Pennsylvania	M,D*
University of Phoenix–Online Campus	M,O
University of Phoenix–San Diego Campus	M
University of Phoenix–Southern California Campus	M,O
University of Phoenix–Washington D.C. Campus	M,D,O
University of Pittsburgh	M,D,O*
University of Portland	M,D
University of Puerto Rico, Río Piedras Campus	M
University of St. Francis (IL)	M,D,O
University of St. Thomas (MN)	M,O
University of St. Thomas (TX)	M
University of San Diego	M
University of San Francisco	M,D
University of South Africa	M,D
University of South Carolina	M,D,O
University of Southern California	M
University of Southern Maine	M,O
University of South Florida	M,D,O
The University of Tennessee	M,D,O
The University of Texas at Arlington	M
The University of Texas at El Paso	M,O
The University of Texas at San Antonio	M,D,O
The University of Texas of the Permian Basin	M
The University of Texas Rio Grande Valley	M
University of the Southwest	M
The University of Toledo	M,D,O
University of Washington	M,D*
University of Wisconsin–Milwaukee	M,D,O
University of Wisconsin–River Falls	M
Upper Iowa University	M
Utah Valley University	M
Valley City State University	M
Valparaiso University	M,O
Virginia International University	M
Walden University	M,D,O
Washington State University	M,D
Wayland Baptist University	M
Wayne State College	M
Wayne State University	M,D,O
West Chester University of Pennsylvania	M,O
Western Carolina University	M
Western Illinois University	M,O
Western Kentucky University	M
Western New Mexico University	M
West Virginia University	M
Wheaton College	M,O
Wilkes University	M,D
Wilmington University	M,D
Worcester State University	M,O
Wright State University	M

ENGLISH EDUCATION

Alabama Agricultural and Mechanical University	M,O
Alabama State University	M,O
Albany State University	M
Andrews University	M,D,O
Anna Maria College	M,O
Appalachian State University	M
Arcadia University	M,D,O
Arkansas State University	M,O
Arkansas Tech University	M
Auburn University	M,D,O
Binghamton University, State University of New York	M*
Bloomsburg University of Pennsylvania	M
Bob Jones University	M,D,O
Boise State University	M
Brooklyn College of the City University of New York	M
Brown University	M
Buffalo State College, State University of New York	M
California Baptist University	M
California State University, Northridge	M
Caribbean University	M,D
Carthage College	M,O
Chadron State College	M,O
Chaminade University of Honolulu	M
Chatham University	M
The Citadel, The Military College of South Carolina	M
City College of the City University of New York	M,O
Clarkson University	M,O
Clayton State University	M
The College at Brockport, State University of New York	M,O
College of St. Joseph	M
The Colorado College	M
Columbus State University	M,O
Converse College	M
Delta State University	M
Duquesne University	M
East Carolina University	M,D,O
Eastern Kentucky University	M
Eastern Michigan University	M
Eastern University	M,O
Elms College	M,O
Fitchburg State University	M,O
Florida Agricultural and Mechanical University	M
Florida Atlantic University	M
Florida Gulf Coast University	M
Florida International University	M,D,O
Florida State University	M,D,O
Framingham State University	M
Gardner-Webb University	M
George Mason University	M
Georgia Southern University	M
Georgia Southwestern State University	M,O
Georgia State University	M,D
Grand Valley State University	M
Harding University	M,O
Hofstra University	M,D,O
Hunter College of the City University of New York	M
Indiana University of Pennsylvania	M,D
Indiana University–Purdue University Fort Wayne	M,O
Iona College	M
Ithaca College	M
Jackson State University	M
Kansas State University	M,D
Kennesaw State University	M
Kent State University	M,D,O
Kutztown University of Pennsylvania	M
Lake Forest College	M
La Salle University	M,O
Lehman College of the City University of New York	M
Le Moyne College	M,O
Lincoln Memorial University	M,D,O
Lipscomb University	M,D,O
London Metropolitan University	M,D
Louisiana Tech University	M,D
Manhattanville College	M*
Marymount University	M,O
Mills College	M,D,O
Minnesota State University Mankato	M,O
Mississippi College	M,D,O
Missouri State University	M,O
Montclair State University	M,O
Morehead State University	M,O
National Louis University	M,D,O
New Mexico State University	M,D
New York University	M,D,O
North Carolina Agricultural and Technical State University	M
North Carolina State University	M
Northern Arizona University	M,D,O
Northwest Missouri State University	M
Occidental College	M
Plymouth State University	M
Purdue University	M,D,O
Queens College of the City University of New York	M,O
Quinnipiac University	M
Rhode Island College	M
Rider University	O
Rowan University	O
Rutgers University–New Brunswick	M
St. John Fisher College	M
San Francisco State University	M,O
Simon Fraser University	M,D
Slippery Rock University of Pennsylvania	M
Smith College	M
South Carolina State University	M
Southeastern Louisiana University	M

*M—masters degree; D—doctorate; O—other advanced degree; *—Close-Up and/or Display*

Southern Illinois University Edwardsville	M,O
Southern New Hampshire University	M,D,O
Southwestern Oklahoma State University	M
State University of New York at New Paltz	M,O
State University of New York at Plattsburgh	M
State University of New York College at Cortland	M
State University of New York College at Old Westbury	M
State University of New York College at Potsdam	M
Stony Brook University, State University of New York	M,D,O
Syracuse University	M
Teachers College, Columbia University	M,D,O
Temple University	M*
Trinity Washington University	M
University at Buffalo, the State University of New York	M,D,O*
The University of Alabama in Huntsville	M,O
The University of Arizona	M,D
University of Arkansas at Pine Bluff	M
University of Central Florida	M
University of Colorado Denver	M
University of Connecticut	M,D*
University of Florida	M,D,O
University of Georgia	M,D,O
University of Illinois at Springfield	M,O
University of Indianapolis	M
The University of Iowa	M,D*
University of Louisiana at Monroe	M,D
University of Maine	M
University of Manitoba	M
University of Maryland, Baltimore County	M
University of Michigan	D
University of Minnesota, Twin Cities Campus	M
University of Missouri	M,D,O
University of Montana	M
University of New Hampshire	M,D
University of New Mexico	M,D
The University of North Carolina at Chapel Hill	M
The University of North Carolina at Charlotte	M,O
The University of North Carolina at Greensboro	M,D
The University of North Carolina at Pembroke	M
The University of North Carolina Wilmington	M
University of Northern Iowa	M
University of North Georgia	M,O
University of Pennsylvania	M,D*
University of Phoenix–Online Campus	M,O
University of Phoenix–Washington D.C. Campus	M,D,O
University of Pittsburgh	M,D*
University of Puerto Rico, Mayagüez Campus	M
University of St. Francis (IL)	M,D,O
University of South Carolina	M,D
University of South Florida	M,D,O
University of South Florida, St. Petersburg	M
University of South Florida Sarasota-Manatee	M
The University of Tennessee	M,D,O
The University of Texas at El Paso	M,D,O
University of the District of Columbia	M
University of the Sacred Heart	M,O
The University of Toledo	M,D,O
The University of Tulsa	M
University of Victoria	M,D
University of Virginia	M,D,O
University of Washington	M,D*
The University of West Alabama	M
University of Wisconsin–Platteville	M
Valdosta State University	M
Valley City State University	M
Vanderbilt University	M,D*
Wagner College	M
Wayland Baptist University	M
Wayne State College	M
Wayne State University	M,D,O
Western Governors University	M,O
Western Kentucky University	M
Western Michigan University	M,D
Western New England University	M
Widener University	M,D
Wilkes University	M,D
William Carey University	M,O
William Jessup University	M
Worcester State University	M

ENTERTAINMENT MANAGEMENT

Berklee College of Music	M
California Intercontinental University	M
California State University, Fullerton	M
California State University, Northridge	M,O
Carnegie Mellon University	M
Columbia College Chicago	M
Full Sail University	M
Hofstra University	M,O
Neumann University	M
New York Institute of Technology	M,O
Syracuse University	M
Universidad Autonoma de Guadalajara	M,D
University of Colorado Denver	M
University of Dallas	M,D
University of Massachusetts Amherst	M
University of South Carolina	M
Valparaiso University	M

ENTOMOLOGY

Auburn University	M,D
Clemson University	M,D
Colorado State University	M,D
Cornell University	M,D
Illinois State University	M,D
Iowa State University of Science and Technology	M,D
Kansas State University	M,D
Louisiana State University and Agricultural & Mechanical College	M,D
McGill University	M,D
Michigan State University	M,D
Mississippi State University	M,D
New Mexico State University	M
North Carolina State University	M,D
North Dakota State University	M,D
The Ohio State University	M,D
Oklahoma State University	M,D
Penn State University Park	M,D
Purdue University	M,D
Rutgers University–New Brunswick	M,D
Simon Fraser University	M,D,O
State University of New York College of Environmental Science and Forestry	M,D
Texas A&M University	M,D
The University of Arizona	M,D
University of Arkansas	M,D
University of California, Davis	M,D
University of California, Riverside	M,D
University of Delaware	M,D*
University of Georgia	M,D
University of Guelph	M,D
University of Hawaii at Manoa	M,D
University of Idaho	M,D
University of Illinois at Urbana–Champaign	M,D
The University of Kansas	M,D*
University of Kentucky	M,D
University of Maine	M,D
University of Manitoba	M,D
University of Maryland, College Park	M,D
University of Minnesota, Twin Cities Campus	M,D
University of Missouri	M,D
University of Nebraska–Lincoln	M,D
University of North Dakota	M,D
The University of Tennessee	M,D
University of Wisconsin–Madison	M,D
University of Wyoming	M,D
Virginia Polytechnic Institute and State University	M,D
Washington State University	M,D
West Virginia University	M,D

ENTREPRENEURSHIP

American College of Thessaloniki	M,O
American Public University System	M
American University	M,D,O
Anaheim University	M,D,O
Arizona State University at the Tempe campus	M,D
Azusa Pacific University	M
Babson College	M,O
Bakke Graduate University	M,D
Baldwin Wallace University	M
Baruch College of the City University of New York	M,D
Bay Path University	M
Benedictine University	M
Brigham Young University	M
California Baptist University	M
California Intercontinental University	M,D
California Lutheran University	M,O
California State University, East Bay	M
California State University, Fullerton	M
California State University, San Bernardino	M
California University of Pennsylvania	M
Cambridge College	M
Cameron University	M
Capella University	M,D
Carlos Albizu University, Miami Campus	M,D
Carnegie Mellon University	D
City Vision University	M
Clemson University	M
Cogswell Polytechnical College	M
Columbia University	M*
Dallas Baptist University	M
Dartmouth College	D*
Delaware Valley University	M
DePaul University	M
Drexel University	M
Duke University	M,O*
Eastern Michigan University	M,O
East Tennessee State University	M,O
East Texas Baptist University	M
Everglades University	M
Fairfield University	M,O
Fairleigh Dickinson University, College at Florham	M,O
Fairleigh Dickinson University, Metropolitan Campus	M,O
Felician University	M
Florida Institute of Technology	M
Georgia State University	M,D
Grand Canyon University	M
Harrisburg University of Science and Technology	M
Hult International Business School (United States)	M
Illinois Institute of Technology	M
International University in Geneva	M,D
The International University of Monaco	M
James Madison University	M
Kaplan University, Davenport Campus	M
Lamar University	M
Lehigh University	M
Lenoir-Rhyne University	M
LIM College	M
Lincoln University (MO)	M
Lindenwood University	M
Loyola University Chicago	M
Loyola University New Orleans	M
Manhattanville College	M*
Marquette University	M,O
McGill University	M,D,O
Mercer University	M
Mercyhurst University	M,O
New York University	M,D,O
North Carolina State University	M
Northeastern University	M
Northwestern University	M,D*
Notre Dame de Namur University	M
Nova Southeastern University	M*
Oakland University	M,O
Oklahoma State University	M,D
Oral Roberts University	M
Pace University	M
Peru State College	M
Point Loma Nazarene University	M
Pontificia Universidad Catolica Madre y Maestra	M
Post University	M
Queen's University at Kingston	M
Regent University	M,D,O
Rensselaer Polytechnic Institute	M
Rochester Institute of Technology	M
Rockhurst University	M,O
Rollins College	M,D
Salve Regina University	M
Samford University	M
San Diego State University	M
San Francisco State University	M
Seton Hall University	M,O
Seton Hill University	M,O
South Carolina State University	M
Southeast Missouri State University	M
Southern Methodist University	M
Southern New Hampshire University	M,O
South University (GA)	M
Stevens Institute of Technology	M,O
Stratford University (VA)	M,D
Suffolk University	M,O
Syracuse University	M,D
Temple University	M,D*
Tufts University	M
Tulane University	M,D
United States International University–Africa	M
Université Laval	M,O
University at Albany, State University of New York	M
The University of Alabama in Huntsville	M,O
University of Arkansas at Little Rock	O
University of Baltimore	M
University of Bridgeport	M
University of Central Florida	M,O
University of Chicago	M,O
University of Colorado Boulder	M,D
University of Colorado Denver	M
University of Delaware	M,D*
University of Florida	M,D,O
University of Hawaii at Manoa	M,O
University of Houston–Victoria	M
University of Idaho	D
University of Louisville	M,D
The University of Manchester	M
University of Massachusetts Amherst	M,D*
University of Massachusetts Lowell	M,D
University of Minnesota, Twin Cities Campus	D
University of Missouri–Kansas City	M,D
University of Nevada, Las Vegas	M,O
University of New Brunswick Fredericton	M
University of New Mexico	M
University of Oklahoma	M,D,O*
University of Pennsylvania	M*
University of Portland	M
University of Rhode Island	M,D
University of Rio Grande	M
University of Rochester	M*
University of San Francisco	M
University of Sioux Falls	M
University of Southern California	M
University of South Florida	M,O
The University of Tampa	M
The University of Texas at Austin	M
The University of Texas at Dallas	M,D*
University of the Incarnate Word	M,D
University of Washington	M,D*
University of Waterloo	M
The University of Western Ontario	M,D
Valparaiso University	M,O
Virginia International University	M,O
Walden University	M,D,O
Washington University in St. Louis	M
West Chester University of Pennsylvania	M,O
Western Carolina University	M
Wichita State University	M
Wilkes University	M

ENVIRONMENTAL AND OCCUPATIONAL HEALTH

American University of Beirut	M
Anna Maria College	M
Augusta University	M
Boise State University	M,O
Boston University	M,D
California State University, Northridge	M
Capella University	M,D
Clemson University	M
Colorado State University	M,D
Columbia Southern University	M
Columbia University	M,D*
Duke University	O*
East Carolina University	M,D
Eastern Kentucky University	M
East Tennessee State University	M,D
Embry-Riddle Aeronautical University–Prescott	M
Embry-Riddle Aeronautical University–Worldwide	M
Emory University	M,D
Florida International University	M,D
Fort Valley State University	M
Gannon University	M
The George Washington University	D*
Georgia Southern University	M,D,O
Harvard University	M,D*
Hunter College of the City University of New York	M
Indiana State University	M
Indiana University Bloomington	M,D
Indiana University of Pennsylvania	M,D
Indiana University–Purdue University Indianapolis	M,D,O
Johns Hopkins University	M,D
Keene State College	M,O
Lewis University	M
Loma Linda University	M
Louisiana State University Health Sciences Center	M,D
McGill University	M,D,O
Meharry Medical College	M
Mercer University	M,D
Murray State University	M
New York Medical College	M,O
New York University	M,D
North Carolina Agricultural and Technical State University	M
Northeastern State University	M
Oakland University	M
Oregon State University	M,D
Purdue University	M,D
Rochester Institute of Technology	M
Rutgers University–New Brunswick	M,D,O
Saint Joseph's University	M
Saint Mary's University of Minnesota	M
San Diego State University	M,D
Southeastern Oklahoma State University	M
Syracuse University	O
Towson University	D
Trident University International	M,D,O
Tufts University	M,D
Tulane University	M,D
Uniformed Services University of the Health Sciences	M,D*
Universidad Autonoma de Guadalajara	M,D
Universidad de Ciencias Medicas	M,D,O
Université de Montréal	M
Université du Québec à Montréal	O
Université Laval	O
University at Albany, State University of New York	M,D
The University of Alabama at Birmingham	M,D
University of Alberta	M,D
University of Arkansas for Medical Sciences	M,D,O
The University of British Columbia	M,D
University of California, Berkeley	M,D
University of California, Irvine	M,D
University of California, Los Angeles	M,D
University of Central Missouri	M,D,O
University of Cincinnati	M,D
University of Colorado Denver	M,D
University of Connecticut	O*
University of Florida	M,D,O
University of Georgia	M,D
University of Illinois at Chicago	M,D
The University of Iowa	M,D,O*
The University of Kansas	M*
University of Louisville	M,D
University of Maryland, College Park	M
University of Massachusetts Amherst	M,D*
University of Memphis	M
University of Miami	M
University of Michigan	M,D
University of Minnesota, Twin Cities Campus	M,D,O
University of Nebraska Medical Center	D
University of Nevada, Reno	M,D
University of New Haven	M,O
University of North Alabama	M
The University of North Carolina at Chapel Hill	M,D
University of North Texas Health Science Center at Fort Worth	M,D
University of Oklahoma Health Sciences Center	M,D
University of Pennsylvania	M*
University of Pittsburgh	M,D*

University of Puerto Rico, Medical Sciences Campus	M,D
University of Saint Francis (IN)	M
University of South Alabama	M
University of South Carolina	M,D
University of Southern California	M
University of South Florida	M,D,O
The University of Texas at Tyler	M
University of the Sacred Heart	M
The University of Toledo	M,O
University of Toronto	M,D
University of Washington	M,D*
University of West Florida	M
University of Wisconsin–Milwaukee	D
University of Wisconsin–Whitewater	M
West Chester University of Pennsylvania	M,O
West Virginia University	D
Yale University	M,D*

ENVIRONMENTAL BIOLOGY

Baylor University	M,D
Chatham University	M
Dalhousie University	M
Emporia State University	M
Georgia State University	M,D
Governors State University	M
Hampton University	M
Hood College	M
Massachusetts Institute of Technology	M,D,O
Missouri University of Science and Technology	M
Morgan State University	D
Nicholls State University	M
Ohio University	M,D
Regis University	M
Rutgers University–New Brunswick	M,D
Sonoma State University	M
State University of New York College of Environmental Science and Forestry	M,D
Universidad del Turabo	M,D
University of Alberta	M,D
University of California, Santa Cruz	M,D
University of Guelph	M,D
University of Louisiana at Lafayette	M,D
University of Louisville	M,D
The University of Manchester	M,D
University of Massachusetts Amherst	M,D*
University of North Dakota	M,D
University of Southern California	M,D
University of Southern Mississippi	M,D
University of South Florida	M,D
University of West Florida	M
University of Wisconsin–Madison	M,D
Washington University in St. Louis	D
West Virginia University	M,D
Youngstown State University	M

ENVIRONMENTAL DESIGN

Arizona State University at the Tempe campus	D
Art Center College of Design	M
Bastyr University	M,O
Clemson University	D
Columbia University	M*
Cornell University	M
Kansas State University	D
Kent State University	M
Michigan State University	M,D
San Diego State University	M
Texas Tech University	M,D
Université de Montréal	M,D,O
University of Calgary	M,D
University of California, Berkeley	M,D
University of California, Irvine	D
University of Georgia	M
The University of Manchester	M,D
Virginia Polytechnic Institute and State University	M,D,O
Yale University	M,D*

ENVIRONMENTAL EDUCATION

Alaska Pacific University	M
Antioch University New England	M
Arcadia University	M,D,O
Ball State University	M,O
Brooklyn College of the City University of New York	M
Chatham University	M
Concordia University (United States)	M,D
Concordia University Wisconsin	M
Florida Atlantic University	M
Florida Institute of Technology	M
Goshen College	M
Hamline University	M,D
Instituto Tecnologico de Santo Domingo	M,D,O
Montclair State University	M
New York University	M
Oregon State University	M,D
Prescott College	M,D
Royal Roads University	M,O
Slippery Rock University of Pennsylvania	M
Southern Connecticut State University	M,O
Southern Oregon University	M
State University of New York College at Cortland	M
Université du Québec à Montréal	M,D,O
University of Colorado Denver	M
University of Florida	M,D,O
University of Minnesota, Twin Cities Campus	M,D,O
University of New Hampshire	M,D,O
The University of North Carolina Wilmington	M
University of South Africa	M,D
University of Victoria	M,D
Western Washington University	M
West Virginia University	M,D

ENVIRONMENTAL ENGINEERING

Air Force Institute of Technology	M
Arizona State University at the Tempe campus	M,D
Auburn University	M,D
California Institute of Technology	M,D
California Polytechnic State University, San Luis Obispo	M
California State University, Fullerton	M
Carleton University	M,D
Carnegie Mellon University	M,D
The Catholic University of America	M,D
Clarkson University	M,D
Clemson University	M,D
Cleveland State University	M,D
Colorado School of Mines	M,D
Columbia University	M,D*
Concordia University (Canada)	M,D,O
Cornell University	M,D
Dalhousie University	M,D
Dartmouth College	M,D*
Drexel University	M,D
Duke University	M,D*
École Polytechnique de Montréal	M,D,O
Florida Atlantic University	M
Florida International University	M
Florida State University	M,D
Gannon University	M
The George Washington University	M,D,O*
Georgia Institute of Technology	M,D
Harvard University	M,D*
Idaho State University	M
Illinois Institute of Technology	M,D
Instituto Tecnologico de Santo Domingo	M,O
Instituto Tecnológico y de Estudios Superiores de Monterrey, Campus Ciudad de México	M,D
Instituto Tecnológico y de Estudios Superiores de Monterrey, Campus Monterrey	M,D
Iowa State University of Science and Technology	M,D
Johns Hopkins University	M,D,O
Kansas State University	M,D
Lakehead University	M
Lamar University	M,D
Lehigh University	M,D
Louisiana State University and Agricultural & Mechanical College	M,D
Manhattan College	M
Marquette University	M,D,O
Marshall University	M
Massachusetts Institute of Technology	M,D,O
McGill University	M,D
Memorial University of Newfoundland	M
Mercer University	M
Michigan State University	M,D
Michigan Technological University	M,D,O
Missouri University of Science and Technology	M,D
Montana State University	M,D
Montana Tech of The University of Montana	M
National University	M,O
New Jersey Institute of Technology	M,D
New Mexico Institute of Mining and Technology	M
New Mexico State University	M,D
New York Institute of Technology	M
New York University	M
North Dakota State University	M,D
Northern Arizona University	M
Northwestern University	M,D*
Norwich University	M
Ohio University	M,D
Oklahoma State University	M,D
Old Dominion University	M,D
Oregon Health & Science University	M,D
Oregon State University	M,D
Penn State Harrisburg	M,O
Penn State University Park	M,D
Polytechnic University of Puerto Rico, Miami Campus	M
Polytechnic University of Puerto Rico, Orlando Campus	M
Portland State University	M,D
Princeton University	M,D
Purdue University	M,D
Rensselaer Polytechnic Institute	M,D
Rice University	M,D
Rose-Hulman Institute of Technology	M
Royal Military College of Canada	M,D
Rutgers University–New Brunswick	M,D
Southern Illinois University Carbondale	D
Southern Illinois University Edwardsville	M
Southern Methodist University	M,D
Stanford University	M,D,O
State University of New York College of Environmental Science and Forestry	M,D
Stevens Institute of Technology	M,D,O
Syracuse University	M
Temple University	M,O*
Tennessee State University	M,D
Texas A&M University–Kingsville	M,D
Texas Tech University	M,D
Tufts University	M,D
Universidad Central del Este	M
Universidad Nacional Pedro Henriquez Urena	M
Université de Sherbrooke	M
Université Laval	M,D
University at Buffalo, the State University of New York	M,D*
The University of Alabama	M,D
The University of Alabama at Birmingham	D
The University of Alabama in Huntsville	M,D
University of Alaska Anchorage	M
University of Alaska Fairbanks	M,D
University of Alberta	M,D
The University of Arizona	M,D
University of Arkansas	M
University of Calgary	M,D
University of California, Berkeley	M,D
University of California, Davis	M,D,O
University of California, Irvine	M,D
University of California, Los Angeles	M,D
University of California, Merced	M,D
University of California, Riverside	M,D
University of Central Florida	M,D
University of Cincinnati	M,D
University of Colorado Boulder	M,D
University of Colorado Denver	M,D
University of Connecticut	M,D*
University of Dayton	M
University of Delaware	M,D*
University of Detroit Mercy	M,D
University of Florida	M,D,O
University of Georgia	M
University of Guelph	M,D
University of Hawaii at Manoa	M,D
University of Illinois at Urbana–Champaign	M,D
The University of Iowa	M,D*
The University of Kansas	M,D*
University of Louisville	M,D,O
The University of Manchester	M,D
University of Maryland, Baltimore County	M,D
University of Maryland, College Park	M,D
University of Massachusetts Amherst	M,D*
University of Massachusetts Lowell	M,D
University of Memphis	M,D
University of Michigan	M,D,O
University of Missouri	M,D
University of Nebraska–Lincoln	M,D
University of Nevada, Las Vegas	M,D
University of New Brunswick Fredericton	M,D
University of New Hampshire	M,D
University of New Haven	M
The University of North Carolina at Chapel Hill	M,D
The University of North Carolina at Charlotte	M,D
University of North Dakota	M
University of Notre Dame	M,D
University of Oklahoma	M,D*
University of Pittsburgh	M,D*
University of Regina	M,D
University of Rhode Island	M,D
University of Southern California	M,D,O
University of South Florida	M,D
The University of Tennessee	M
The University of Texas at Austin	M,D
The University of Texas at El Paso	M,D,O
The University of Texas at San Antonio	M,D
The University of Texas at Tyler	M
University of Utah	M,D*
University of Vermont	M,D
University of Washington	M,D*
University of Waterloo	M,D
The University of Western Ontario	M,D
University of Windsor	M,D
University of Wisconsin–Madison	M,D
University of Wyoming	M
Utah State University	M,D,O
Vanderbilt University	M,D*
Villanova University	M,O
Virginia Polytechnic Institute and State University	M,D,O
Washington State University	M,D
Washington University in St. Louis	M,D
West Virginia University	M,D
Worcester Polytechnic Institute	M,D,O
Yale University	M,D*
Youngstown State University	M

ENVIRONMENTAL LAW

Baylor University	D
Chapman University	M,D
Florida State University	M,D
Georgetown University	M,D
Golden Gate University	M,D
Lehigh University	M,O
Lewis & Clark College	M,D
Montclair State University	O
Pace University	M,D
Stanford University	M,D
University of Calgary	M,O
University of Colorado Denver	M,D
University of Florida	M,D
University of Houston	M,D
University of Idaho	D
University of Pittsburgh	M*
The University of Tulsa	M,D,O
Vermont Law School	M
Western Michigan University Thomas M. Cooley Law School	M,D

ENVIRONMENTAL MANAGEMENT AND POLICY

Adelphi University	M
Air Force Institute of Technology	M
American Public University System	M
American University	M,D,O
American University of Beirut	M,D
Antioch University New England	M,D
Antioch University Seattle	M
Appalachian State University	M
Aquinas College (MI)	M
Arizona State University at the Tempe campus	M
Ball State University	M,O
Bard College	M,O
Baylor University	M
Bemidji State University	M
Boston University	M,D
California State University, Fullerton	M
Central European University	M,D
Clarkson University	M
Clark University	M
Clemson University	M,D
Cleveland State University	M,O
College of the Atlantic	M
Colorado Heights University	M
Columbia University	M*
Columbus State University	M
Concordia University (Canada)	M,D,O
Cornell University	M,D
Dalhousie University	M
Drexel University	M
Duke University	M,D*
Duquesne University	M,O
The Evergreen State College	M
Florida Gulf Coast University	M
Florida Institute of Technology	M
Florida International University	M
George Mason University	M,D
The George Washington University	M*
Georgia Institute of Technology	M,D
Georgia State University	M,D,O
Goucher College	M
Green Mountain College	M
Hardin-Simmons University	M
Harvard University	M,O*
Humboldt State University	M
Idaho State University	M
Illinois Institute of Technology	M
Indiana University Bloomington	M,D,O
Indiana University Northwest	M,O
Indiana University of Pennsylvania	M
Instituto Tecnologico de Santo Domingo	M,D,O
Instituto Tecnológico y de Estudios Superiores de Monterrey, Campus Estado de México	M,D
Instituto Tecnológico y de Estudios Superiores de Monterrey, Campus Irapuato	M,D
Inter American University of Puerto Rico, Metropolitan Campus	M
James Madison University	M
Johns Hopkins University	M,O
Kentucky State University	M
Lake Forest College	M
Lamar University	M,D
Lehigh University	M,O
Long Island University–LIU Post	M,O
Louisiana State University and Agricultural & Mechanical College	M,D
McGill University	M,D
Michigan Technological University	M,D
Middlebury Institute of International Studies at Monterey	M
Millersville University of Pennsylvania	M
Missouri State University	M,O
Montclair State University	M,D
Morehead State University	M
Naropa University	M
The New School	M,O
New York Institute of Technology	M,O
New York University	M,O
Northeastern Illinois University	M
Northeastern State University	M
Northern Arizona University	M,D
The Ohio State University	M,D
Ohio University	M
Oregon State University	M,D
Pace University	M
Penn State University Park	M
Plymouth State University	M
Point Park University	M
Polytechnic University of Puerto Rico	M
Polytechnic University of Puerto Rico, Miami Campus	M
Polytechnic University of Puerto Rico, Orlando Campus	M
Portland State University	M,D
Prescott College	M
Purdue University	M,D
Rice University	M
Royal Roads University	M,O
Sacred Heart University	M
St. Cloud State University	M
St. Edward's University	M
Samford University	M
San Francisco State University	M
San Jose State University	M,O

*M—masters degree; D—doctorate; O—other advanced degree; *—Close-Up and/or Display*

Shippensburg University of Pennsylvania	M
Simon Fraser University	M,D,O
Slippery Rock University of Pennsylvania	M
Southeast Missouri State University	M
Southern Illinois University Carbondale	M,D
Southern Illinois University Edwardsville	M
Southern New Hampshire University	M,O
State University of New York College of Environmental Science and Forestry	M,D
Stony Brook University, State University of New York	M,O
Tennessee Technological University	M
Texas Southern University	M,D
Texas State University	M
Texas Tech University	M,D
Towson University	M
Trent University	M,D
Tropical Agriculture Research and Higher Education Center	M,D
Troy University	M
Tufts University	M,D,O
Universidad Autonoma de Guadalajara	M,D
Universidad del Turabo	M,D
Universidad Metropolitana	M
Université de Montréal	O
Université du Québec à Chicoutimi	M
Université du Québec, Institut National de la Recherche Scientifique	M,D
Université Laval	M,D,O
University at Albany, State University of New York	M
University of Alaska Fairbanks	M
University of Alberta	M,D
The University of Arizona	M,D
University of Calgary	M,D,O
University of California, Berkeley	M,D,O
University of California, Santa Barbara	M,D
University of California, Santa Cruz	D
University of Central Missouri	M,D,O
University of Chicago	M
University of Colorado Boulder	M,D
University of Colorado Denver	M,D
University of Dayton	M,D
University of Delaware	M,D*
University of Denver	M,O
The University of Findlay	M,D
University of Guelph	M,D
University of Hawaii at Manoa	M,D,O
University of Houston–Clear Lake	M
University of Illinois at Springfield	M
University of Maine	D
The University of Manchester	M,D
University of Maryland, Baltimore County	M,D
University of Maryland Eastern Shore	M,D
University of Maryland University College	M,O
University of Massachusetts Amherst	M,D*
University of Massachusetts Dartmouth	M,O
University of Michigan	M,D
University of Minnesota, Twin Cities Campus	M,D
University of Montana	M
University of Nevada, Reno	M
University of New Brunswick Fredericton	M,D
University of New Hampshire	M
University of New Haven	M,O
University of New Mexico	M
The University of North Carolina at Chapel Hill	M,D
The University of North Carolina Wilmington	M
University of Northern British Columbia	M,D,O
University of Oregon	M,D
University of Pennsylvania	M*
University of Puerto Rico, Rí o Piedras Campus	M
University of Rhode Island	M,D
University of Rochester	M*
University of South Africa	M,D
University of South Carolina	M
University of South Florida	M,D,O
University of South Florida, St. Petersburg	M
The University of Tennessee	M,D
The University of Texas at Austin	M
University of Washington	M,D*
University of Waterloo	M,D
University of Wisconsin–Green Bay	M
Utah State University	M,D
Vanderbilt University	M,D*
Vermont Law School	M
Virginia Commonwealth University	M
Virginia Polytechnic Institute and State University	M,D,O
Webster University	M
Wesley College	M
Western State Colorado University	M
West Virginia University	M,D
Wilfrid Laurier University	M,D
Wilmington University	M,D
Yale University	M,D*
York University	M,D
Youngstown State University	M,O

ENVIRONMENTAL SCIENCES

Adelphi University	M
Alaska Pacific University	M
American University	M,O
American University of Beirut	M,D
Antioch University New England	M,D
Arizona State University at the Tempe campus	M,D,O
Arkansas State University	M,D
Ball State University	D
Baylor University	D
Binghamton University, State University of New York	M,D*
Boston University	M,D
Brigham Young University	M,D
Bryant University	M
California Institute of Technology	M,D
California State Polytechnic University, Pomona	M
California State University, Chico	M
California State University, East Bay	M
California State University, Northridge	M
California State University, San Bernardino	M
Carnegie Mellon University	D
Christopher Newport University	M
Clarkson University	M,D
Clemson University	M,D
Cleveland State University	M,D
The College at Brockport, State University of New York	M
College of Charleston	M
College of Staten Island of the City University of New York	M
The College of William and Mary	M,D
Columbia University	M,D*
Columbus State University	M,O
Cornell University	M,D
Dalhousie University	M
Drexel University	M,D
Duke University	M,D*
Duquesne University	M,O
East Stroudsburg University of Pennsylvania	M
Florida Agricultural and Mechanical University	M,D
Florida Gulf Coast University	M
Florida Institute of Technology	M,D
Florida International University	M
Florida State University	M,D
Gannon University	M
George Mason University	M,D
Georgia Southern University	O
The Graduate Center, City University of New York	D
Harvard University	M,D*
Howard University	M,D
Humboldt State University	M
Idaho State University	M,O
Indiana University Bloomington	M,D,O
Instituto Tecnologico de Santo Domingo	M,D,O
Instituto Tecnológico y de Estudios Superiores de Monterrey, Campus Ciudad de México	M,D
Inter American University of Puerto Rico, San Germán Campus	M
Iowa State University of Science and Technology	M,D
Jackson State University	M,D
Johns Hopkins University	M,O
Kansas State University	M,D,O
Laurentian University	M
Lehigh University	M,D
Louisiana State University and Agricultural & Mechanical College	M,D
Loyola Marymount University	M
Marshall University	M
Massachusetts Institute of Technology	M,D,O
McNeese State University	M
Memorial University of Newfoundland	M,D
Mercer University	M
Miami University	M
Michigan State University	M,D
Minnesota State University Mankato	M
Montana State University	M,D
Montclair State University	M
Murray State University	M
New Jersey Institute of Technology	M,D,O
New Mexico State University	M,D
New York University	M
North Carolina Agricultural and Technical State University	M
North Dakota State University	M,D
Northern Arizona University	M,D
Nova Southeastern University	M,D,O*
Oakland University	M,D
The Ohio State University	M,D
Oklahoma State University	M,D,O
Old Dominion University	M,D
Oregon Health & Science University	M,D
Oregon State University	M,D
Pace University	M
Penn State Harrisburg	M,O
Penn State University Park	M
Pontifical Catholic University of Puerto Rico	M
Portland State University	M,D
Queens College of the City University of New York	M
Rice University	M,D
Rochester Institute of Technology	M
Royal Military College of Canada	M,D
Rutgers University–Newark	M,D
Rutgers University–New Brunswick	M,D
Sitting Bull College	M
South Dakota School of Mines and Technology	D
Southeast Missouri State University	M
Southern Connecticut State University	M,O
Southern Illinois University Carbondale	D
Southern Illinois University Edwardsville	M
Southern Methodist University	M,D
Southern University and Agricultural and Mechanical College	M
Stanford University	M,D,O
State University of New York College of Environmental Science and Forestry	M,D
Stephen F. Austin State University	M
Stockton University	M
Tarleton State University	M
Tennessee Technological University	D
Texas A&M University–Corpus Christi	M
Texas Christian University	M
Texas Tech University	M,D
Thompson Rivers University	M
Towson University	M,O
Troy University	M
Tufts University	M,D
Tuskegee University	M
Universidad del Turabo	M,D
Universidad Nacional Pedro Henriquez Urena	M
Université de Sherbrooke	M,O
Université du Québec à Montréal	M,D,O
Université du Québec à Trois-Rivières	M,D
Université du Québec en Abitibi-Témiscamingue	M,D
Université Laval	M,D
University at Albany, State University of New York	M
University at Buffalo, the State University of New York	M,D,O*
The University of Alabama in Huntsville	M,D
University of Alaska Anchorage	M
University of Alaska Fairbanks	M
University of Alberta	M,D
The University of Arizona	M,D,O
University of California, Berkeley	M,D
University of California, Davis	M,D
University of California, Los Angeles	M,D
University of California, Riverside	M
University of California, Santa Barbara	M,D
University of Chicago	M
University of Cincinnati	M,D
University of Colorado Colorado Springs	M
University of Colorado Denver	M
University of Guam	M
University of Guelph	M,D
University of Hawaii at Hilo	M
University of Houston–Clear Lake	M
University of Idaho	M,D
University of Illinois at Springfield	M
University of Illinois at Urbana–Champaign	M,D
The University of Kansas	M,D*
University of Lethbridge	M,D
University of Maine	M,D
The University of Manchester	M,D
University of Manitoba	M,D
University of Maryland, Baltimore	M,D
University of Maryland, Baltimore County	M,D
University of Maryland, College Park	M,D
University of Maryland Eastern Shore	M,D
University of Massachusetts Boston	M,D
University of Massachusetts Lowell	M,D
University of Michigan	M,D
University of Michigan–Dearborn	M
University of Missouri	M,D,O
University of Montana	M
University of Nevada, Las Vegas	M,D,O
University of Nevada, Reno	M,D
University of New Hampshire	D,O
University of New Haven	M,O
University of New Orleans	M
The University of North Carolina at Chapel Hill	M,D
University of North Texas	M,D,O
University of Oklahoma	M,D*
University of Pennsylvania	M,D*
University of Pittsburgh	M,D*
University of Puerto Rico, Rí o Piedras Campus	M,D
University of Rhode Island	M,D
University of Saskatchewan	M
University of South Africa	M,D
University of South Florida	M,D
University of South Florida, St. Petersburg	M
The University of Tennessee at Chattanooga	M
The University of Texas at Arlington	M,D
The University of Texas at El Paso	M,D
The University of Texas at San Antonio	M,D
University of the Virgin Islands	M
The University of Toledo	M,D
University of Toronto	M,D
University of Utah	M*
University of Virginia	M,D
University of Waterloo	M,D
The University of Western Ontario	M,D
University of West Florida	M
University of Windsor	M,D
University of Wisconsin–Green Bay	M
Vanderbilt University	M*
Virginia Polytechnic Institute and State University	M,D,O
Washington State University	M,D
Wesleyan University	M
Western Connecticut State University	M
Western Illinois University	D
Western Washington University	M
West Texas A&M University	M
Wichita State University	M
Wilfrid Laurier University	M,D
Wright State University	M,D
Yale University	M,D*

EPIDEMIOLOGY

American University of Beirut	M
Boston University	M,D
Brown University	M,D
Capella University	D
Case Western Reserve University	M,D*
Columbia University	M,D*
Cornell University	M,D
Daemen College	M
Dalhousie University	M
Drexel University	M,D,O
Emory University	M,D
Florida International University	M,D
George Mason University	M,O
Georgetown University	M,O
The George Washington University	M*
Georgia Southern University	M,D
Harvard University	M,D*
Hunter College of the City University of New York	M
Indiana University Bloomington	M,D
Indiana University–Purdue University Indianapolis	M,D
Johns Hopkins University	M,D
Loma Linda University	M,D
Louisiana State University Health Sciences Center	M,D
McGill University	M,D,O
Medical College of Wisconsin	M,D,O
Medical University of South Carolina	M,D
Memorial University of Newfoundland	M,D,O
Michigan State University	M,D
New York Medical College	M
New York University	M,D
North Carolina State University	M,D
Northwestern University	D*
Oregon State University	M,D
Ponce Health Sciences University	M,D
Purdue University	M,D
Queen's University at Kingston	M,D
Rutgers University–Newark	M,O
Rutgers University–New Brunswick	M,D,O
San Diego State University	M,D
Stanford University	M,D
Thomas Edison State University	O
Tufts University	M,D,O
Tulane University	M,D
Université Laval	M,D
University at Albany, State University of New York	M,D
University at Buffalo, the State University of New York	M,D*
The University of Alabama at Birmingham	M,D
University of Alberta	M,D
The University of Arizona	M,D
University of Arkansas for Medical Sciences	M,D,O
The University of British Columbia	M,D
University of California, Berkeley	M,D
University of California, Davis	M,D
University of California, Irvine	M,D
University of California, Los Angeles	M,D
University of California, San Diego	D
University of Cincinnati	M,D
University of Colorado Denver	M,D
University of Florida	M,D,O
University of Guelph	M,D
University of Hawaii at Manoa	D
University of Illinois at Chicago	M,D
University of Illinois at Springfield	M,O
The University of Iowa	M,D*
The University of Kansas	M*
University of Kentucky	D
University of Louisville	M,D
University of Maryland, Baltimore	M,D
University of Maryland, Baltimore County	M,O
University of Maryland, College Park	M,D
University of Massachusetts Amherst	M,D*
University of Memphis	M
University of Miami	M,D
University of Michigan	M,D
University of Minnesota, Twin Cities Campus	M,D
University of Nebraska Medical Center	D
University of New Mexico	M
The University of North Carolina at Chapel Hill	M,D
University of North Texas Health Science Center at Fort Worth	M,D
University of Oklahoma Health Sciences Center	M,D
University of Ottawa	M
University of Pennsylvania	M*

University of Pittsburgh M,D*
University of Prince Edward Island M,D
University of Puerto Rico, Medical Sciences Campus M
University of Rochester D*
University of Saskatchewan M,D
University of South Carolina M,D
University of Southern California M,D
University of Southern Mississippi M
University of South Florida M,D,O
The University of Tennessee Health Science Center M,D
The University of Toledo M,O
University of Toronto M,D
University of Washington M,D*
The University of Western Ontario M,D
University of Wisconsin–Madison M,D
Virginia Commonwealth University M,D
Walden University M,D,O
Washington State University M,D
Washington University in St. Louis M,D,O
Weill Cornell Medicine M
Yale University M,D*

ERGONOMICS AND HUMAN FACTORS

Arizona State University at the Tempe campus M
Bentley University M
California State University, Long Beach M
The Catholic University of America M,D
Clemson University D
Cornell University M
Embry-Riddle Aeronautical University–Daytona M,D*
Florida Institute of Technology M,D
Georgia Institute of Technology M,D
Indiana University Bloomington M,D
Michigan Technological University M,D,O
Mississippi State University M,D
Missouri Western State University M
New York University M,D
North Carolina State University D
Old Dominion University D
Purdue University M,D
Tufts University M,D
Université de Montréal O
Université du Québec à Montréal O
The University of Alabama M
University of Cincinnati M,D
The University of Iowa M,D,O*
University of Miami M
University of Wisconsin–Milwaukee M,D,O
Wright State University M,D

ETHICS

American University M,D,O
Arizona State University at the Tempe campus M,D
Azusa Pacific University M
Chicago Theological Seminary M,D
Claremont Graduate University M,D
Claremont Lincoln University M
Claremont School of Theology M,D
Columbia University M*
Duke University M,O*
Emory University M,D
Fordham University M,O
Freed-Hardeman University M
George Mason University M
Georgetown University M,D
Graduate Theological Union M,D,O
John Brown University M
Kennesaw State University O
Lancaster Theological Seminary M,D,O
Lee University M
Loyola University Chicago M
Lutheran Theological Seminary Saskatoon M,D
Marquette University M,D
New England College of Business and Finance M
North Central College M
Northwestern University M*
Oregon State University M
Phillips Theological Seminary M,D
Santa Clara University M,D,O
Schreiner University M
Sonoma State University M
Southeastern Baptist Theological Seminary M,D
Southern Methodist University M,D
Southern New Hampshire University M,O
Spring Hill College M,O
Stevens Institute of Technology M,O
Suffolk University M,O
Texas State University M
Union Institute & University D
Université de Sherbrooke M,D,O
Université du Québec à Chicoutimi O
Université du Québec à Rimouski M,O
Université Laval O
University of Baltimore M
University of Chicago D
University of Detroit Mercy M,O
University of Maryland, Baltimore O
University of New England M,O
The University of North Carolina at Charlotte M,O
University of North Florida M,O
University of Pennsylvania M,D*
University of St. Thomas (MN) M,D
University of South Africa M,D
The University of Tennessee at Chattanooga M,O
Valparaiso University M,O
Viterbo University M,O
West Chester University of Pennsylvania M,O
Xavier University M

ETHNIC STUDIES

Colorado State University M
Cornell University M,D
Minnesota State University Mankato M
Northern Arizona University O
San Francisco State University M
United Theological Seminary of the Twin Cities M,D,O
Université Laval M,D
University of California, Berkeley D
University of California, Riverside D
University of California, San Diego D
University of Colorado Boulder D
University of New Mexico M,D

EVOLUTIONARY BIOLOGY

Arizona State University at the Tempe campus M,D
Brown University D
Clemson University M,D
Columbia University M,D*
Cornell University D
Dartmouth College D*
Emory University D
Florida State University M,D
Harvard University D*
Illinois State University M,D
Indiana State University M,D
Indiana University Bloomington M,D
Iowa State University of Science and Technology M,D
Johns Hopkins University D
Michigan State University D
Montclair State University M
Northeastern University M,D
The Ohio State University M,D
Ohio University M,D
Oklahoma State University M,D
Princeton University D
Purdue University M,D
Rice University M,D
Rutgers University–New Brunswick M,D
Sonoma State University M
Stony Brook University, State University of New York M,D
Tulane University M,D
University at Albany, State University of New York D
University at Buffalo, the State University of New York M,D,O*
University of Alberta M,D
The University of Arizona M,D
University of California, Davis D
University of California, Irvine M,D
University of California, Los Angeles M,D
University of California, Riverside M,D
University of California, Santa Barbara M,D
University of California, Santa Cruz M,D
University of Chicago D
University of Colorado Boulder M,D
University of Colorado Denver M,D
University of Delaware M,D*
University of Denver M,D
University of Guelph M,D
University of Illinois at Urbana–Champaign M,D
The University of Iowa M,D*
The University of Kansas M,D*
University of Louisiana at Lafayette M,D
The University of Manchester M,D
University of Maryland, College Park M,D
University of Massachusetts Amherst M,D*
University of Miami M,D
University of Michigan M,D
University of Minnesota, Twin Cities Campus M,D
University of Missouri M,D
University of Nevada, Reno D
University of New Hampshire D
The University of North Carolina at Chapel Hill M,D
University of Notre Dame M,D
University of Oklahoma D*
University of Oregon M,D
University of Pittsburgh D*
University of Puerto Rico, Río Piedras Campus M,D
University of South Carolina M,D
University of Southern California D
University of South Florida M,D
The University of Tennessee M,D
The University of Texas at Austin D
University of Toronto M,D
Washington University in St. Louis D
Wayne State University M,D
Wesleyan University D
West Virginia University M,D
Yale University D*

EXERCISE AND SPORTS SCIENCE

American Public University System M
American University M
Appalachian State University M
Arizona State University at the Tempe campus M,D
Arkansas State University M,O
Armstrong State University M,O
Ashland University M
Auburn University M,D,O
Auburn University at Montgomery M,O
Austin Peay State University M
Ball State University M,D
Barry University M
Baylor University M,D
Benedictine University M
Bloomsburg University of Pennsylvania M
Brigham Young University M,D
Brooklyn College of the City University of New York M
California Baptist University M
California State University, Fresno M
California State University, Long Beach M
California University of Pennsylvania M
Central Connecticut State University M,O
Central Michigan University M,D
Central Washington University M
Cleveland State University M
College of Saint Elizabeth M,O
The College of St. Scholastica M
Colorado State University M,D
Columbus State University M
Concordia University (Canada) M
Concordia University Chicago M
Concordia University, St. Paul M,D,O
Delaware State University M
Delta State University M
East Carolina University M,D,O
Eastern Illinois University M
Eastern Michigan University M
Eastern New Mexico University M
Eastern Washington University M
East Stroudsburg University of Pennsylvania M
East Tennessee State University M,D
Fairmont State University M
Florida Atlantic University M
Florida State University M,D
Gannon University M
Gardner-Webb University M
George Mason University M,D,O
The George Washington University M*
Georgia College & State University M
Georgia State University M
Howard University M
Indiana University Bloomington M,D
Indiana University of Pennsylvania M
Inter American University of Puerto Rico, Metropolitan Campus M
Iowa State University of Science and Technology M
Ithaca College M
James Madison University M
Kean University M
Kennesaw State University M
Kent State University M,D
Lakehead University M
Liberty University M,D,O
Life University M
Lipscomb University M
Logan University M,D
Long Island University–LIU Brooklyn M,D
Louisiana Tech University M
Manhattanville College M,O*
Marshall University M
Marywood University M
McDaniel College M
McNeese State University M
Memorial University of Newfoundland M
Merrimack College M
Miami University M
Middle Tennessee State University M,D
Midwestern State University M
Mississippi State University M,D
Montclair State University M,O
Morehead State University M
Murray State University M
New Mexico Highlands University M
North Dakota State University M,D
Northeastern Illinois University M
Northeastern University M,D,O
Northern Michigan University M
Northwest Missouri State University M
Oakland University M,D,O
Ohio University M,D
Old Dominion University M
Pittsburg State University M
Point Loma Nazarene University M
Purdue University M,D
Queens College of the City University of New York M,O
Queen's University at Kingston M,D
Rowan University M
Sacred Heart University M
St. Cloud State University M
Saint Mary's College of California M
San Diego State University M
San Jose State University M,O
Smith College M
South Dakota State University M,D
Southeast Missouri State University M
Southern Connecticut State University M
Southern Illinois University Edwardsville M
Southern Utah University M
Springfield College M,D
Syracuse University M
Tennessee State University M
Texas State University M
Texas Tech University M
Texas Woman's University M,D
United States Sports Academy M
University at Buffalo, the State University of New York M,D,O*
The University of Akron M
The University of Alabama M,D
University of Alberta M,D
University of Arkansas at Little Rock M
University of California, Davis M
University of Central Florida M,D
University of Central Oklahoma M
University of Connecticut M,D*
University of Dayton M
University of Florida M,D
University of Houston M,D
University of Houston–Clear Lake M
The University of Iowa M,D*
University of Kentucky M,D
University of Lethbridge M,D
University of Louisiana at Monroe M
University of Louisville M,D,O
University of Maine M,D,O
University of Mary M
University of Mary Hardin-Baylor M
University of Massachusetts Boston M,D
University of Memphis M
University of Miami M,D
University of Minnesota, Twin Cities Campus M,D,O
University of Mississippi M,D
University of Montana M
University of Nebraska at Kearney M
University of Nebraska at Omaha M,D
University of Nebraska–Lincoln M,D
University of Nevada, Las Vegas M,D
University of New Brunswick Fredericton M
University of New Hampshire M,O
University of New Mexico D
University of North Alabama M
The University of North Carolina at Chapel Hill M
The University of North Carolina at Pembroke M
University of Northern Colorado M,D
University of North Florida M,D
University of Oklahoma M,D*
University of Pittsburgh M,D*
University of Puerto Rico, Mayagüez Campus M
University of Puerto Rico, Río Piedras Campus M
University of Rhode Island M
University of South Alabama M
University of South Carolina M,D
The University of South Dakota M
University of South Florida M
The University of Tampa M
The University of Tennessee M,D,O
The University of Texas at Arlington M
The University of Texas at Austin M,D
The University of Texas Rio Grande Valley M
University of the Pacific M
The University of Toledo M,D
University of Utah M,D*
University of West Florida M
University of Wisconsin–La Crosse M
University of Wyoming M
Virginia Commonwealth University M
Virginia Polytechnic Institute and State University M,D
Wake Forest University M
Washington State University M
Wayne State College M
Wayne State University M,D
West Chester University of Pennsylvania M,O
Western Michigan University M
Western Washington University M
West Texas A&M University M
West Virginia University M,D
Wichita State University M
William Paterson University of New Jersey M,D

EXPERIMENTAL PSYCHOLOGY

Appalachian State University M
Auburn University M,D
Bowling Green State University M,D
Brooklyn College of the City University of New York M,D
California State University, Northridge M
California State University, San Bernardino M
Case Western Reserve University D*
The Catholic University of America M,D
Central Michigan University M,D
Central Washington University M
The College of William and Mary M
Cornell University D
Dallas Baptist University M
Duke University D*
Eastern Washington University M
Fairleigh Dickinson University, Metropolitan Campus M,O
The Graduate Center, City University of New York D
Harvard University D*
Howard University M,D
Idaho State University D
Iona College M,O

M—masters degree; D—doctorate; O—other advanced degree; *—Close-Up and/or Display

James Madison University	M
Kent State University	M,D
Lakehead University	M,D
Laurentian University	M
McGill University	M,D
McNeese State University	M
Memorial University of Newfoundland	M,D
Middle Tennessee State University	M,O
Missouri State University	M,O
Morehead State University	M
North Carolina State University	D
Ohio University	M,D
Old Dominion University	D
Radford University	M
Rivier University	M
Rochester Institute of Technology	M
St. John's University (NY)	M
Saint Louis University	M,D
San Jose State University	M,O
Seton Hall University	M
Southern Illinois University Carbondale	M,D
Southern Methodist University	M,D
Stony Brook University, State University of New York	D
Syracuse University	D
Texas A&M University–Central Texas	M,O
Texas Christian University	M,D
Texas Tech University	M,D
The University of Alabama	D
University of Central Florida	M,D
University of Central Oklahoma	M
University of Cincinnati	D
University of Connecticut	M,D*
University of Hartford	M
University of Maryland, College Park	M,D
University of Massachusetts Dartmouth	M,O
University of Memphis	M,D,O
University of Mississippi	M,D
University of Montana	M,D,O
University of New Brunswick Saint John	M,D
University of North Dakota	M,D
University of Regina	M,D
University of South Carolina	M,D
University of Southern Mississippi	M,D
The University of Tennessee	M,D
The University of Tennessee at Chattanooga	M
The University of Texas at Arlington	M,D
The University of Texas at El Paso	M,D
The University of Texas of the Permian Basin	M
The University of Texas Rio Grande Valley	M
The University of Toledo	M,D
University of Victoria	M,D
The University of West Alabama	M
University of Wisconsin–Oshkosh	M
Washington State University	M,D
Western Illinois University	M,O
Western Kentucky University	M,O
Western Washington University	M

FACILITIES MANAGEMENT

Cornell University	M
Indiana University–Purdue University Fort Wayne	M
Maastricht School of Management	M,D
Massachusetts Maritime Academy	M
Pratt Institute	M*
Université Laval	M,O
University of California, Berkeley	O
The University of Kansas	M,D,O*
University of New Haven	M,O
The University of North Carolina at Charlotte	M,O
Wentworth Institute of Technology	M

FAMILY AND CONSUMER SCIENCES-GENERAL

Alabama Agricultural and Mechanical University	M
Appalachian State University	M
Ball State University	M
Bowling Green State University	M
California State University, Fresno	M
California State University, Long Beach	M
California State University, Northridge	M
Central Michigan University	M,O
Central Washington University	M
Clemson University	D,O
East Carolina University	M
Eastern Illinois University	M
Florida State University	M,D
Fontbonne University	M
Illinois State University	M
Iowa State University of Science and Technology	M
Kansas State University	M,D,O
Lamar University	M
Louisiana State University and Agricultural & Mechanical College	M,D
Louisiana Tech University	M
New Mexico State University	M
North Dakota State University	M
The Ohio State University	M,D
Ohio University	M
Oklahoma State University	M,D
Prairie View A&M University	M
Purdue University	M,D
Queens College of the City University of New York	M,O
Sam Houston State University	M
San Francisco State University	M
South Carolina State University	M
South Dakota State University	M
Stephen F. Austin State University	M
Tennessee State University	M,D
Texas A&M University–Kingsville	M
Texas Southern University	M
Texas State University	M
Texas Tech University	M,D
Tufts University	M,D
The University of Alabama	M,D
University of Alberta	M,D
The University of Arizona	D
University of Arkansas	M
University of Central Arkansas	M
University of Central Oklahoma	M
University of Florida	M
University of Georgia	M,D
University of Houston	M
University of Louisiana at Monroe	M,D
University of Manitoba	M
University of Maryland, College Park	M,D
University of Memphis	M
University of Missouri	M,D,O
University of Nebraska–Lincoln	M,D
University of Northwestern–St. Paul	M
University of Puerto Rico, Rí o Piedras Campus	M
University of South Africa	M,D
The University of Tennessee	D
The University of Tennessee at Martin	M
The University of Texas at Austin	M,D
University of Wisconsin–Madison	M,D
University of Wisconsin–Stevens Point	M
Utah State University	M,D
Western Michigan University	M

FAMILY NURSE PRACTITIONER STUDIES

Albany State University	M
Allen College	M,D,O
Alverno College	M
American International College	M
Angelo State University	M
Arizona State University at the Tempe campus	M,D,O
Armstrong State University	M,O
Augsburg College	M,D
Augusta University	M,D,O
Austin Peay State University	M
Ball State University	M,D,O
Barry University	M,O
Baylor University	M,D
Bellarmine University	M,D
Bellin College	M
Bloomsburg University of Pennsylvania	M
Bowie State University	M
Brenau University	M
Brigham Young University	M
California Baptist University	M
California State University, Fresno	M
Carlow University	M,O
Carson-Newman University	M
Case Western Reserve University	M*
Cedarville University	M,D
Clarion University of Pennsylvania	M,D,O
Clarke University	D
Clarkson College	M,O
Clayton State University	M
College of Mount Saint Vincent	M,O
The College of New Rochelle	M,O
College of Staten Island of the City University of New York	D
Colorado Mesa University	M,D,O
Columbia University	M,O*
Columbus State University	M
Concordia University Wisconsin	M
Coppin State University	M,O
Cox College	M
Creighton University	M,D,O
Delta State University	M,D
DePaul University	M,D
DeSales University	M,D,O
Dominican College	M,D
Drexel University	M
Duke University	M,D,O*
Duquesne University	M,O
D'Youville College	M,D,O
Eastern Kentucky University	M
East Tennessee State University	M,D,O
Edinboro University of Pennsylvania	M,D
Emory University	M
Fairfield University	M,D
Felician University	M,O
Florida National University	M
Florida State University	M,D,O
Francis Marion University	M
Fresno Pacific University	M
Frontier Nursing University	M,D,O
Gannon University	M,O
Georgetown University	M,D
The George Washington University	M,D,O*
Georgia Southern University	M
Georgia State University	M,D,O
Goshen College	M
Graceland University (IA)	M,D,O
Grambling State University	M,O
Grand Canyon University	M,O
Gwynedd Mercy University	M,D
Hardin-Simmons University	M
Holy Names University	M,O
Howard University	M,O
Husson University	M,O
Illinois State University	M,D,O
Indiana State University	M,D
Indiana University–Purdue University Fort Wayne	M,O
Indiana University South Bend	M
James Madison University	M,D
Kent State University	M,D,O
La Salle University	M,D,O
Liberty University	M,D
Lincoln Memorial University	M
Long Island University–LIU Brooklyn	M,O
Long Island University–LIU Post	M,O
Louisiana State University Health Sciences Center	M,D,O
Loyola University Chicago	M,D,O
Malone University	M
Marquette University	M,D,O
Marymount University	M,D,O
Maryville University of Saint Louis	M,D
McGill University	M,D,O
McMurry University	M
McNeese State University	M,O
Medical University of South Carolina	M,D
Middle Tennessee State University	M,O
Midwestern State University	M
Millersville University of Pennsylvania	M
Missouri State University	M,D
Molloy College	M,D,O
Monmouth University	M,D,O
Montana State University	M,D,O
Mount Carmel College of Nursing	M,D
Mount Saint Mary College	M,O
Murray State University	M
New Mexico State University	M,D
New York University	M,D,O
Nicholls State University	M
Northeastern University	M,D,O
Northern Arizona University	M,D,O
Northern Michigan University	M,D
Oakland University	M,O
Ohio University	M
Old Dominion University	M,D
Oregon Health & Science University	M,D,O
Otterbein University	M,D,O
Pace University	M,D,O
Pacific Lutheran University	D
Palm Beach Atlantic University	M,D
Point Loma Nazarene University	M,O
Prairie View A&M University	M
Purdue University Northwest	M
Queen's University at Kingston	M,D,O
Quinnipiac University	M,D
Regis College (MA)	M,D,O
Regis University	M,D,O
Research College of Nursing	M
Rivier University	M
Rocky Mountain University of Health Professions	D
Rush University	D
Rutgers University–Newark	M,D,O
Sacred Heart University	M,D,O
Sage Graduate School	M,O
Saginaw Valley State University	M,D
Saint Francis Medical Center College of Nursing	M,D,O
St. John Fisher College	M,O
Saint Joseph's College of Maine	M,O
Salisbury University	D
Samford University	M,D
Samuel Merritt University	M,D,O
San Francisco State University	M,O
Seattle Pacific University	M,O
Seattle University	M
Shenandoah University	M,D,O
Simmons College	M,D,O
Sonoma State University	M
Southern Adventist University	M
Southern Connecticut State University	M
Southern Illinois University Edwardsville	M,D,O
Southern University and Agricultural and Mechanical College	M,D,O
South University	M
South University	M
South University	M
Spalding University	M,D,O
State University of New York Downstate Medical Center	M,O
State University of New York Polytechnic Institute	M,O
State University of New York Upstate Medical University	M,O
Stony Brook University, State University of New York	M,D,O
Temple University	D*
Tennessee State University	M,O
Tennessee Technological University	M
Texas A&M International University	M
Texas A&M University	M
Texas A&M University–Corpus Christi	M
Texas State University	M
Texas Tech University Health Sciences Center	M,D,O
Texas Woman's University	M,D
Troy University	M,D,O
Uniformed Services University of the Health Sciences	M,D*
Union University	M,D,O
United States University	M
Universidad del Turabo	M
University at Buffalo, the State University of New York	M,D,O*
The University of Alabama in Huntsville	M,D,O
The University of Arizona	M,D,O
University of Central Arkansas	M,O
University of Colorado Denver	M,D
University of Delaware	M,O*
University of Detroit Mercy	M,D,O
University of Hawaii at Manoa	M,D,O
University of Houston	M
University of Illinois at Chicago	M,O
University of Indianapolis	M,D
University of Louisville	M,D
University of Maine	M,O
University of Mary	M,D
University of Mary Hardin-Baylor	M,O
University of Massachusetts Amherst	M,D*
University of Massachusetts Lowell	M
University of Massachusetts Medical School	M,D,O
University of Memphis	M,O
University of Miami	M,D
University of Michigan–Flint	M,D,O
University of Minnesota, Twin Cities Campus	M
University of Missouri	M,D,O
University of Missouri–Kansas City	M,D
University of Missouri–St. Louis	M,D,O
University of Nevada, Las Vegas	M,D,O
University of New Hampshire	M,D,O
The University of North Carolina at Chapel Hill	M,D,O
The University of North Carolina at Charlotte	M,D,O
The University of North Carolina Wilmington	M,O
University of North Dakota	M,D
University of Northern Colorado	M,D
University of North Florida	M,D,O
University of North Georgia	M,O
University of Pennsylvania	M,O*
University of Phoenix–Hawaii Campus	M
University of Phoenix–Online Campus	M,O
University of Phoenix–Phoenix Campus	M,O
University of Phoenix–Sacramento Valley Campus	M
University of Phoenix–Southern California Campus	M,O
University of Pittsburgh	M,D*
University of Portland	M,D
University of Puerto Rico, Medical Sciences Campus	M
University of Rhode Island	M,D
University of Rochester	M,D*
University of St. Francis (IL)	M,D,O
University of Saint Francis (IN)	M,O
University of Saint Joseph	M,D
University of San Diego	M,D
University of San Francisco	D
The University of Scranton	M,D,O
University of South Carolina	M
University of Southern Maine	M,D,O
University of Southern Mississippi	M,D,O
University of South Florida	M,D,O
The University of Tampa	M
The University of Tennessee at Chattanooga	M,D,O
The University of Texas at Arlington	M,D
The University of Texas at Austin	M,D
The University of Texas at El Paso	M,D,O
The University of Texas at Tyler	M,D
The University of Texas Health Science Center at San Antonio	M,D,O
The University of Texas Rio Grande Valley	M
The University of Toledo	M,O
University of Victoria	M,D
University of Wisconsin–Eau Claire	M,D
University of Wisconsin–Milwaukee	M,D,O
University of Wisconsin–Oshkosh	M
Ursuline College	M,D
Vanderbilt University	M,D,O*
Villanova University	M,D,O
Virginia Commonwealth University	M,O
Walden University	M,D,O
Washington State University	M,D,O
Wayne State University	D
West Coast University	M,D
Western University of Health Sciences	M
Westminster College (UT)	M
West Texas A&M University	M
West Virginia Wesleyan College	M,O
Wilmington University	M,D
Winona State University	M,D,O
Winston-Salem State University	M,D
Wright State University	M

FILM, TELEVISION, AND VIDEO PRODUCTION

Academy of Art University	M
American Film Institute Conservatory	M
American University	M
Arizona State University at the Tempe campus	M
Art Center College of Design	M
The Art Institute of California–San Francisco, a campus of Argosy University	M
Bob Jones University	M,D,O
Boston University	M
Bowling Green State University	M,D
Brigham Young University	M
Brooklyn College of the City University of New York	M
California College of the Arts	M
California Institute of the Arts	M,O
California State University, Fullerton	M

California State University, Northridge	M
Carleton University	M
Carnegie Mellon University	M
Central Michigan University	M
Chapman University	M
Chatham University	M
Columbia College Chicago	M
Columbia University	M*
Concordia University (Canada)	M,D
DePaul University	M,D
Drexel University	M
Florida Atlantic University	M,O
Florida State University	M
Georgia State University	M,D
Hofstra University	M
Hollins University	M
Howard University	M
Johns Hopkins University	M
Lipscomb University	M
Loyola Marymount University	M
Maryland Institute College of Art	M
Massachusetts College of Art and Design	M,O
Miami International University of Art & Design	M
Minneapolis College of Art and Design	M
Missouri State University	M,O
Montana State University	M
Mount Saint Mary's University (CA)	M,D,O
National University	M
New York Film Academy	M
New York University	M
Northwestern University	M,D*
Ohio University	M
Quinnipiac University	M
Regent University	M,D
Rochester Institute of Technology	M
Sacred Heart University	M
St. Thomas University	M
San Diego State University	M
San Francisco State University	M
Savannah College of Art and Design	M
School of the Art Institute of Chicago	M
School of Visual Arts (NY)	M
Stanford University	M,D
Stevens Institute of Technology	M
Stony Brook University, State University of New York	M
Syracuse University	M
Temple University	M*
Universidad Autonoma de Guadalajara	M,D
The University of Alabama	M
The University of British Columbia	M,O
University of California, Los Angeles	M,D
University of California, Santa Barbara	D
University of Central Arkansas	M
University of Central Florida	M
University of Colorado Boulder	M
The University of Iowa	M*
University of Memphis	M,D
University of Miami	M,D
University of Montana	M
University of Nevada, Las Vegas	M,O
University of New Orleans	M
The University of North Carolina at Greensboro	M
University of North Carolina School of the Arts	M
University of North Texas	M,D,O
University of Oklahoma	M*
University of Regina	M
University of Southern California	M
The University of Texas at Arlington	M
The University of Texas at Austin	M,D
University of the Sacred Heart	M,O
University of Utah	M*
University of Victoria	M
Vermont College of Fine Arts	M
Western State Colorado University	M
York University	M,D

FILM, TELEVISION, AND VIDEO THEORY AND CRITICISM

California College of the Arts	M
Central Michigan University	M
Claremont Graduate University	M,D
College of Staten Island of the City University of New York	M
Concordia University (Canada)	M,D
DePaul University	M
Emory University	M,D,O
Hollins University	M
Indiana University Bloomington	M,D
National University	M,O
Ohio University	M
Salisbury University	M
San Francisco State University	M
Savannah College of Art and Design	M
Syracuse University	M
Tiffin University	M
Université de Montréal	M,D
Université Laval	M,D
University at Buffalo, the State University of New York	M,D,O*
The University of Arizona	M
The University of British Columbia	M,O
University of California, Santa Cruz	D
University of Chicago	D
University of Idaho	M
The University of Iowa	M,D*
The University of Kansas	M,D*
University of Miami	M,D
University of Michigan	D,O
University of Pittsburgh	M,D,O*
University of Southern California	M,D
University of South Florida	M
University of Toronto	M,D
University of Wisconsin–Madison	M,D
Wayne State University	M,D
Wilfrid Laurier University	M,D
Yale University	D*

FINANCE AND BANKING

Adelphi University	M
American Business & Technology University	M
The American College	M
American College of Thessaloniki	M,O
American InterContinental University Online	M
American Public University System	M
American University	M
The American University in Cairo	M,O
The American University in Dubai	M
American University of Beirut	M,D
Andrews University	M
Argosy University, Atlanta	M,D
Argosy University, Chicago	M,D
Argosy University, Dallas	M,D,O
Argosy University, Denver	M,D
Argosy University, Hawai`i	M,D,O
Argosy University, Inland Empire	M,D
Argosy University, Los Angeles	M,D
Argosy University, Nashville	M,D
Argosy University, Orange County	M,D,O
Argosy University, Phoenix	M,D
Argosy University, Salt Lake City	M,D
Argosy University, San Diego	M,D
Argosy University, San Francisco Bay Area	M,D
Argosy University, Sarasota	M,D,O
Argosy University, Schaumburg	M,D,O
Argosy University, Seattle	M,D
Argosy University, Tampa	M,D
Argosy University, Twin Cities	M,D
Argosy University, Washington DC	M,D,O
Arizona State University at the Tempe campus	M,D
Aspen University	M,O
Assumption College	M,O
Auburn University	M
Avila University	M
Azusa Pacific University	M
Baker College Center for Graduate Studies–Online	M,D
Barry University	O
Baruch College of the City University of New York	M,D
Bayamón Central University	M
Bellevue University	M,D
Benedictine University	M
Bentley University	M
Bluffton University	M
Boston College	M,D
Boston University	M
Brandeis University	M,D
Bridgewater State University	M
Brigham Young University	M
Brooklyn College of the City University of New York	M
Bryant University	M
Butler University	M
California College of the Arts	M
California Intercontinental University	M,D
California Lutheran University	M,O
California State University, East Bay	M
California State University, Fullerton	M
California State University, Los Angeles	M
California State University, San Bernardino	M
Capella University	M,D
Carnegie Mellon University	D
Case Western Reserve University	M*
Central European University	M,D
Central Michigan University	M
Charleston Southern University	M
City University of Seattle	M,O
Claremont McKenna College	M
Clark University	M
Cleary University	M,O
Cleveland State University	M,D,O
College for Financial Planning	M
The College of Saint Rose	O
Colorado Heights University	M
Colorado State University	M
Colorado State University–Global Campus	M
Colorado Technical University Colorado Springs	M,D
Colorado Technical University Denver South	M
Columbia Southern University	M
Columbia University	M,D*
Concordia University (Canada)	M,D,O
Concordia University Wisconsin	M
Cornell University	D
Curry College	M,O
Dalhousie University	M
Dallas Baptist University	M
Davenport University	M
Delaware Valley University	M
DePaul University	M
DeSales University	M
DeVry University	M
Drexel University	M,D,O
Duke University	M,D,O*
Duquesne University	M
Eastern Michigan University	M,O
East Tennessee State University	M,O
Edgewood College	M
Ellis University	M
Embry-Riddle Aeronautical University–Daytona	M,D*
Emory University	M,D
Fairfield University	M,O
Fairleigh Dickinson University, College at Florham	M,O
Fairleigh Dickinson University, Metropolitan Campus	M,O
Florida Agricultural and Mechanical University	M
Florida Atlantic University	M
Florida International University	M
Florida National University	M
Florida State University	M,D
Fordham University	M
Gannon University	M
Geneva College	M
George Fox University	M,D
Georgetown University	M,D
The George Washington University	M,D*
Georgia State University	M,D,O
Golden Gate University	M,D,O
Goldey-Beacom College	M
The Graduate Center, City University of New York	D
Grand Canyon University	M
Hawai`i Pacific University	M
HEC Montreal	M,O
Hofstra University	M,O
Holy Family University	M
Holy Names University	M
Hood College	M
Howard University	M
Hult International Business School (United States)	M
Hult International Business School (United States)	M
Hult International Business School (United States)	M
Illinois Institute of Technology	M,D
Indiana University Bloomington	M,D,O
Indiana University Southeast	M
Instituto Centroamericano de Administración de Empresas	M
Instituto Tecnologico de Santo Domingo	M,O
Instituto Tecnológico y de Estudios Superiores de Monterrey, Campus Central de Veracruz	M
Instituto Tecnológico y de Estudios Superiores de Monterrey, Campus Ciudad de México	M,D
Instituto Tecnológico y de Estudios Superiores de Monterrey, Campus Ciudad Obregón	M
Instituto Tecnológico y de Estudios Superiores de Monterrey, Campus Cuernavaca	M
Instituto Tecnológico y de Estudios Superiores de Monterrey, Campus Estado de México	M,D
Instituto Tecnológico y de Estudios Superiores de Monterrey, Campus Guadalajara	M
Instituto Tecnológico y de Estudios Superiores de Monterrey, Campus Irapuato	M,D
Instituto Tecnológico y de Estudios Superiores de Monterrey, Campus Monterrey	M
Inter American University of Puerto Rico, Aguadilla Campus	M
Inter American University of Puerto Rico, Arecibo Campus	M
Inter American University of Puerto Rico, Barranquitas Campus	M
Inter American University of Puerto Rico, Metropolitan Campus	M
Inter American University of Puerto Rico, Ponce Campus	M
Inter American University of Puerto Rico, San Germán Campus	M,D
The International University of Monaco	M
Iona College	M,O
Iowa State University of Science and Technology	M
Jacksonville University	M*
Johns Hopkins University	M,D,O
Kansas State University	M,O
Kaplan University, Davenport Campus	M
Kent State University	D
King University	M
Lake Forest Graduate School of Management	M
Lakeland University	M
La Salle University	M,O
La Sierra University	M,O
Lehigh University	M
Lewis University	M
Lincoln University (CA)	M,D
Lincoln University (PA)	M
Lindenwood University	M
Lipscomb University	M,O
Long Island University–Hudson at Westchester	M,O
Long Island University–LIU Post	M
Louisiana State University and Agricultural & Mechanical College	M,D
Louisiana Tech University	M,D
Loyola University Chicago	M
Loyola University Maryland	M
Manhattanville College	M*
Marquette University	M,O
Maryville University of Saint Louis	M,O
Marywood University	M
McGill University	M,D,O
Metropolitan College of New York	M
Michigan State University	M,D
Minnesota State University Moorhead	M
Mississippi College	M,O
Mississippi State University	M,D
Molloy College	M
Monmouth University	M,O
Mount Saint Mary College	M
National University	M,O
Naval Postgraduate School	M
New Charter University	M
New England College of Business and Finance	M
Newman University	M
New Mexico State University	M,O
The New School	M,D
New York Institute of Technology	M
New York University	M,D,O
Niagara University	M
North Central College	M
Northeastern Illinois University	M
Northeastern State University	M
Northeastern University	M
Northern State University	M
North Greenville University	M,D
Northwestern University	M,D*
Norwich University	M
Notre Dame de Namur University	M
Nova Southeastern University	M*
Oakland University	M,O
Ohio Dominican University	M
The Ohio State University	M
Ohio University	M
Oklahoma Christian University	M
Oklahoma State University	M,D
Old Dominion University	D
Oral Roberts University	M
Oregon State University	M,D
Ottawa University	M
Our Lady of the Lake University of San Antonio	M
Pace University	M,D,O
Pacific Lutheran University	M
Pacific States University	M,D
Pacific University	M
Park University	M,O
Penn State Great Valley	M,O
Penn State Harrisburg	M,D,O
Polytechnic University of Puerto Rico, Miami Campus	M
Polytechnic University of Puerto Rico, Orlando Campus	M
Pontifical Catholic University of Puerto Rico	M
Pontificia Universidad Catolica Madre y Maestra	M
Portland State University	M
Post University	M
Princeton University	M
Providence College	M
Purdue University	M
Queen's University at Kingston	M
Regent's University London	M
Regent University	M,D,O
Regis University	M,O
Rhode Island College	M,O
Robert Morris University Illinois	M
Rochester Institute of Technology	M
Rockhurst University	M,O
Rollins College	M,D
Rutgers University–Newark	M,D
Sacred Heart University	M,D,O
Sage Graduate School	M
St. Edward's University	M,O
St. John's University (NY)	M
Saint Joseph's University	M,O
Saint Louis University	M
Saint Mary's College of California	M
Saint Peter's University	M
St. Thomas Aquinas College	M
Saint Xavier University	M,O
Samford University	M
Sam Houston State University	M
San Diego State University	M
San Francisco State University	M
Santa Clara University	M
Schiller International University (United States)	M
Seattle University	M,O
Seton Hall University	M,O
Shippensburg University of Pennsylvania	M,O
Simon Fraser University	M,D,O
Slippery Rock University of Pennsylvania	M
Southeast Missouri State University	M
Southern Adventist University	M
Southern Illinois University Edwardsville	M
Southern Methodist University	M
Southern New Hampshire University	M,O
Southwestern Adventist University	M
State University of New York Polytechnic Institute	M
Stevens Institute of Technology	M,O
Stony Brook University, State University of New York	M,O
Stratford University (VA)	M,D
Strayer University	M
Suffolk University	M,O
Syracuse University	M,D
Télé-université	M,D
Temple University	M,D*
Tennessee Technological University	M
Texas A&M International University	M

*M—masters degree; D—doctorate; O—other advanced degree; *—Close-Up and/or Display*

Texas A&M University M
Texas A&M University–Commerce M
Texas A&M University–San Antonio M
Texas Christian University M
Texas State University M
Texas Tech University M,D
Tiffin University M
Trident University International M,D
Troy University M
Tulane University M,D
United States International University–Africa M
Universidad Central del Este M
Universidad de las Americas, A.C. M
Universidad de las Américas Puebla M
Universidad Metropolitana M
Université de Sherbrooke M
Université du Québec à Montréal O
Université du Québec à Trois-Rivières O
Université du Québec en Outaouais M,O
Université Laval M,O
University at Albany, State University of New York M,D,O
University at Buffalo, the State University of New York M,D*
The University of Akron M
The University of Alabama M,D
The University of Alabama at Birmingham M
The University of Alabama in Huntsville M,O
University of Alaska Fairbanks M
University of Alberta M,D
The University of Arizona M
University of Baltimore M
University of Bridgeport M
The University of British Columbia D
University of California, Berkeley D,O
University of California, Los Angeles M,D
University of California, San Diego M,D
University of California, Santa Barbara M,D
University of California, Santa Cruz M
University of Central Missouri M,D,O
University of Chicago M,O
University of Cincinnati M,D
University of Colorado Boulder M,D
University of Colorado Denver M
University of Connecticut M,D*
University of Dallas M,D
University of Dayton M
University of Delaware M*
University of Denver M
University of Detroit Mercy M,D,O
University of Florida M,D,O
University of Hawaii at Manoa M,D
University of Houston M
University of Houston–Clear Lake M
University of Houston–Downtown M
University of Houston–Victoria M
University of Illinois at Chicago M
University of Illinois at Urbana–Champaign M,D
The University of Iowa M,D*
University of La Verne M
University of Lethbridge M,D
University of Maine M,O
The University of Manchester M
University of Maryland University College M,O
University of Massachusetts Amherst M,D*
University of Massachusetts Boston M
University of Massachusetts Dartmouth M,O
University of Memphis M,D
University of Michigan–Dearborn M
University of Michigan–Flint M
University of Minnesota, Twin Cities Campus M,D
University of Missouri M,D
University of Missouri–Kansas City M,D
University of Missouri–St. Louis M,D,O
University of Nebraska–Lincoln M,D
University of Nevada, Reno M
University of New Haven M,O
University of New Mexico M
University of New Orleans M,D
University of North Alabama M
The University of North Carolina at Chapel Hill D
The University of North Carolina at Charlotte M,O
The University of North Carolina at Greensboro M,O
University of North Florida M
University of North Texas M,D,O
University of Notre Dame M
University of Oregon D
University of Ottawa D,O
University of Pennsylvania M,D*
University of Pittsburgh M,D*
University of Portland M
University of Puerto Rico, Mayagüez Campus M
University of Puerto Rico, Río Piedras Campus M,D
University of Rhode Island M,D
University of Rochester M*
University of St. Francis (IL) M,O
University of St. Thomas (TX) M
University of San Diego M
University of San Francisco M
University of Saskatchewan M
The University of Scranton M
University of Southern Maine M
University of South Florida M,D
The University of Tampa M
The University of Tennessee M,D
The University of Tennessee at Martin M
The University of Texas at Arlington M,D
The University of Texas at Austin M,D
The University of Texas at Dallas M,D*
The University of Texas at San Antonio M,D
The University of Texas Rio Grande Valley M,D
University of the Incarnate Word M
University of the West M
The University of Toledo M
University of Toronto M
The University of Tulsa M
University of Utah M,D*
University of Virginia M
University of Washington, Tacoma M
University of Waterloo M,D
The University of West Alabama M
The University of Western Ontario M,D
University of Wisconsin–Madison M,D
University of Wisconsin–Whitewater M
University of Wyoming M
Upper Iowa University M
Valparaiso University M,O
Vancouver Island University M
Vanderbilt University M*
Villanova University M
Virginia Commonwealth University M
Virginia International University M,O
Wagner College M
Walden University M,D,O
Walsh College of Accountancy and Business Administration M
Washington University in St. Louis M,D
Waynesburg University M,D
Wayne State University M,D
Webster University M
Western International University M
Western Michigan University Thomas M. Cooley Law School M,D
West Texas A&M University M
Wilfrid Laurier University M,D
Wilkes University M
Wilmington University M,D
Wright State University M
Xavier University M
Yale University D*
York College of Pennsylvania M
York University M,D
Youngstown State University M

FINANCIAL ENGINEERING

Baruch College of the City University of New York M
Claremont Graduate University M
Columbia University M,D*
HEC Montreal M
The International University of Monaco M
New York University M,O
North Carolina State University M
Princeton University M,D
Rensselaer Polytechnic Institute M
Stevens Institute of Technology M,D,O
Temple University M*
University of California, Berkeley M
University of California, Los Angeles M,D
University of Illinois at Urbana–Champaign M
The University of Tulsa M

FIRE PROTECTION ENGINEERING

Anna Maria College M
Oklahoma State University M,D
University of Maryland, College Park M
University of New Haven M,O
The University of North Carolina at Charlotte M,O
Worcester Polytechnic Institute M,D,O

FISH, GAME, AND WILDLIFE MANAGEMENT

American Public University System M
Arkansas Tech University M
Auburn University M,D
Brigham Young University M,D
Clemson University M,D
Colorado State University M,D
Cornell University M,D
Frostburg State University M
Humboldt State University M
Iowa State University of Science and Technology M,D
Louisiana State University and Agricultural & Mechanical College M,D
McGill University M,D
Memorial University of Newfoundland M,O
Michigan State University M,D
Mississippi State University M,D
Montana State University M,D
New Mexico State University M
North Carolina State University M,D
The Ohio State University M,D
Oregon State University M,D
Penn State University Park M,D
Purdue University M,D
Simon Fraser University M,D,O
South Dakota State University M,D
State University of New York College of Environmental Science and Forestry M,D
Sul Ross State University M
Tarleton State University M
Tennessee Technological University M
Texas A&M University M,D
Texas A&M University–Kingsville M,D
Texas State University M
Texas Tech University M,D
Université du Québec à Rimouski M,D,O
University of Arkansas at Pine Bluff M
University of Delaware M,D*
University of Florida M,D,O
University of Maine M,D
University of Maryland Eastern Shore M,D
University of Massachusetts Amherst M,D*
University of Miami M,D
University of Minnesota, Twin Cities Campus M,D
University of Missouri M,D,O
University of Montana M,D
University of New Hampshire M
University of North Dakota M,D
University of Rhode Island M,D
The University of Tennessee M
University of Washington M,D*
University of Wisconsin–Madison M,D
Utah State University M,D
Virginia Polytechnic Institute and State University M,D
West Virginia University M

FOLKLORE

The George Washington University M,D*
Indiana University Bloomington M,D
Memorial University of Newfoundland M,D
Penn State Harrisburg M,D,O
University of Alberta M,D
University of California, Berkeley M
University of Louisiana at Lafayette M,D
The University of North Carolina at Chapel Hill M
University of Oregon M
The University of Texas at Austin M,D
University of Wisconsin–Madison M,D
Utah State University M

FOOD SCIENCE AND TECHNOLOGY

Alabama Agricultural and Mechanical University M,D
American University of Beirut M
Auburn University M,D,O
Boston University M
Brigham Young University M
California State University, Fresno M
California State University, Long Beach M
Chapman University M
Clemson University M,D
Colorado State University M,D
Cornell University M,D
Dalhousie University M,D
Drexel University M
Florida State University M,D
Framingham State University M
Illinois Institute of Technology M
Iowa State University of Science and Technology M,D
Kansas State University M,D
London Metropolitan University M,D
Louisiana State University and Agricultural & Mechanical College M,D
Marlboro College M
McGill University M,D
Memorial University of Newfoundland M,D
Michigan State University M,D
Mississippi State University M,D
New Mexico State University M
New York University M,D
North Carolina State University M,D
North Dakota State University M,D,O
The Ohio State University M,D
Oklahoma State University M,D
Oregon State University M,D
Penn State University Park M,D
Purdue University M,D
Rutgers University–New Brunswick M,D
Texas A&M University M,D
Texas Tech University M,D
Texas Woman's University M,D
Tuskegee University M
Universidad de las Américas Puebla M
Université de Moncton M
Université Laval M,D
University of Arkansas M,D
The University of British Columbia M,D
University of California, Davis M,D
University of Delaware M,D*
University of Florida M,D
University of Georgia M,D
University of Guelph M,D
University of Hawaii at Manoa M
University of Idaho M,D
University of Illinois at Urbana–Champaign M,D
University of Kentucky M,D
University of Maine M,D,O
University of Manitoba M,D
University of Maryland, College Park M,D
University of Maryland Eastern Shore M,D
University of Massachusetts Amherst M,D*
University of Minnesota, Twin Cities Campus M,D
University of Mississippi M,D
University of Missouri M,D
University of Nebraska–Lincoln M,D
University of Puerto Rico, Mayagüez Campus M
University of Rhode Island M,D
University of Saskatchewan M,D
University of Southern California M,D,O
University of Southern Mississippi M,D
The University of Tennessee M,D
The University of Tennessee at Martin M
University of Vermont M,D
University of Wisconsin–Madison M,D
University of Wisconsin–Stout M
University of Wyoming M
Utah State University M,D
Washington State University M,D
Wayne State University M,D,O
West Virginia University M,D

FOREIGN LANGUAGES EDUCATION

Andrews University M,D,O
Appalachian State University M
Arizona State University at the Tempe campus M,D
Auburn University M,D,O
Augusta University M,O
Binghamton University, State University of New York M*
Bowling Green State University M
Brigham Young University M
Brooklyn College of the City University of New York M
California State University, Sacramento M
Caribbean University M,D
Central Connecticut State University M,O
City College of the City University of New York M
Clarkson University M,O
Cleveland State University M
College of Charleston M
The Colorado College M
Colorado State University–Pueblo M
Columbia University M,D*
Concordia College M
Cornell University M,D
Delaware State University M
DePaul University M,D
Duquesne University M
East Carolina University M
Eastern Michigan University M,O
Eastern University M,O
Elms College M,O
Florida International University M,D,O
Florida State University M,D,O
Framingham State University M
George Mason University M
The George Washington University M*
Georgia State University M
Harding University M,O
Hofstra University M,D,O
Hunter College of the City University of New York M
Indiana State University M,D,O
Indiana University Bloomington M,D
Indiana University of Pennsylvania M
Indiana University–Purdue University Indianapolis M,O
Inter American University of Puerto Rico, Arecibo Campus M
Inter American University of Puerto Rico, Barranquitas Campus M
Inter American University of Puerto Rico, Metropolitan Campus M
Iona College M
Ithaca College M
James Madison University M
Kean University M
Kennesaw State University M
Lamar University M
Le Moyne College M,O
London Metropolitan University M,D
Manhattanville College M*
Marquette University M
McGill University M,D,O
Michigan State University D
Middlebury Institute of International Studies at Monterey M
Middle Tennessee State University M
Mills College M,D,O
Mississippi State University M
Morehead State University M
New Mexico State University M,D,O
New York University M,D,O
Northern Arizona University M
Occidental College M
Pace University M,O
Plymouth State University M
Portland State University M
Purdue University M,D,O
Queens College of the City University of New York M,O
Quinnipiac University M
Rhode Island College M
Rider University O
Rivier University M
Rutgers University–New Brunswick M,D
Saginaw Valley State University M
St. John Fisher College M
Saint Xavier University M

Shippensburg University of Pennsylvania	M
SIT Graduate Institute	M
Smith College	M
Southern Connecticut State University	M
Southern Oregon University	M
Spalding University	M
State University of New York at Plattsburgh	M
State University of New York College at Old Westbury	M
Stony Brook University, State University of New York	M,O
Texas A&M International University	M,D
Texas A&M University–Kingsville	M
Universidad del Este	M
Université du Québec en Outaouais	O
University at Buffalo, the State University of New York	M,D,O*
University of Arkansas at Little Rock	M
University of California, Irvine	M,D
University of Central Arkansas	M
University of Connecticut	M,D*
University of Delaware	M*
University of Florida	M,D
University of Georgia	M,D,O
University of Hawaii at Hilo	M,D
University of Hawaii at Manoa	M,D,O
University of Illinois at Chicago	M,D
University of Illinois at Urbana–Champaign	M,D
University of Indianapolis	M
The University of Iowa	M,D*
University of Kentucky	M
University of Louisiana at Monroe	M,D
University of Maryland, Baltimore County	M
University of Maryland, College Park	D
University of Massachusetts Amherst	M*
University of Massachusetts Boston	M
University of Michigan	M,D
University of Minnesota, Twin Cities Campus	M
University of Mississippi	M,D
University of Missouri	M,D,O
University of Nebraska at Kearney	M
University of Nebraska at Omaha	M
University of Nevada, Reno	M
The University of North Carolina at Chapel Hill	M
The University of North Carolina at Charlotte	M,D,O
The University of North Carolina at Greensboro	M,D,O
University of Northern Colorado	M
University of Northern Iowa	M
University of Pittsburgh	M,D*
University of Puerto Rico, Rí o Piedras Campus	M,D
University of South Carolina	M,D
University of Southern Mississippi	M
University of South Florida	M,D,O
The University of Tennessee	M,D,O
University of the Sacred Heart	M,O
The University of Toledo	M,D,O
University of Utah	M,D*
University of Victoria	M
University of Virginia	M,D,O
University of Wisconsin–Madison	M,D
University of Wisconsin–Milwaukee	M,O
Vanderbilt University	M,D*
Virginia Polytechnic Institute and State University	M,D,O
Wagner College	M
Washington State University	M
Wayne State University	M,D,O
West Chester University of Pennsylvania	M,O
Western Kentucky University	M
Worcester State University	M

FORENSIC NURSING

Boston College	M,D
Cleveland State University	M,D
Duquesne University	M,O
Fitchburg State University	M,O
Monmouth University	M,D,O
National University	M,D,O

FORENSIC PSYCHOLOGY

Adler University	M,D,O
Alliant International University–Fresno	D
Alliant International University–Irvine	D
Alliant International University–Los Angeles	D
Alliant International University–Sacramento	D
Alliant International University–San Diego	D
Alliant International University–San Francisco	M,D
American International College	M
Argosy University, Atlanta	M,D,O
Argosy University, Chicago	D
Argosy University, Dallas	M
Argosy University, Denver	M,D
Argosy University, Hawai`i	M
Argosy University, Inland Empire	M,D
Argosy University, Los Angeles	M,D
Argosy University, Orange County	M
Argosy University, Phoenix	M
Argosy University, Salt Lake City	M,D
Argosy University, San Diego	M,D
Argosy University, San Francisco Bay Area	M
Argosy University, Sarasota	M,D
Argosy University, Schaumburg	M,O
Argosy University, Twin Cities	M,D,O
Argosy University, Washington DC	M,D
California Baptist University	M
Cambridge College	M,O
Castleton University	M
The Chicago School of Professional Psychology	M,D
The Chicago School of Professional Psychology at Downtown Los Angeles	D
The Chicago School of Professional Psychology at Irvine	D
The Chicago School of Professional Psychology: Online	M,O
College of Saint Elizabeth	M,D,O
Concordia University, St. Paul	M,D,O
Drexel University	D
Fairleigh Dickinson University, Metropolitan Campus	M
Fielding Graduate University	M,D,O
The George Washington University	O*
Holy Names University	M,O
Immaculata University	M,D,O
John Jay College of Criminal Justice of the City University of New York	M,D
London Metropolitan University	M,D
Marymount University	M
Montclair State University	O
Pontificia Universidad Catolica Madre y Maestra	M
Prairie View A&M University	M,D
Roger Williams University	M
Sage Graduate School	M,O
Saint Leo University	M
Tiffin University	M
Trine University	M
Universidad de Iberoamerica	M,D
University of Central Oklahoma	M
University of Denver	M,D
University of Houston–Victoria	M
University of Louisiana at Monroe	M
University of New Haven	M,D,O
University of North Dakota	M,D
Walden University	M,D,O
William James College	M,D,O

FORENSIC SCIENCES

Alabama State University	M
Albany State University	M
Alliant International University–Irvine	D
American Public University System	M
Arcadia University	M
Bay Path University	M
Boston University	M
Carlow University	M
Cedar Crest College	M
Chaminade University of Honolulu	M,O
Champlain College	M
The College at Brockport, State University of New York	M
DeSales University	M,O
Duquesne University	M
Emporia State University	M
Florida Gulf Coast University	M
Florida International University	M,D
George Mason University	M
The George Washington University	M,O*
Georgia State University	M,O
Golden Gate University	M,O
Indiana University–Purdue University Indianapolis	M
Iona College	M,O
James Madison University	M
John Jay College of Criminal Justice of the City University of New York	M,D
La Salle University	M,O
Marshall University	M,O
McGill University	M,D,O
Mercyhurst University	M
Michigan State University	M,D
Middle Georgia State University	M
Missouri Western State University	M,O
National University	M,O
Nebraska Wesleyan University	M
Norwich University	M
Oklahoma State University Center for Health Sciences	M
Pace University	M
Philadelphia College of Osteopathic Medicine	M*
Saint Leo University	M
Salve Regina University	M,O
Sam Houston State University	M,D
Seattle University	M,O
Stevenson University	M
Stratford University (VA)	M,D
Syracuse University	M,O
Texas Tech University	M
Towson University	M
Universidad del Turabo	M
University at Albany, State University of New York	M,D
The University of Alabama at Birmingham	M
University of California, Davis	M
University of Central Florida	M,D
University of Central Oklahoma	M
University of Charleston	M
University of Colorado Denver	M
University of Detroit Mercy	M,O
University of Florida	M,O
University of Houston–Victoria	M
University of Illinois at Chicago	M
University of New Haven	M,D,O
University of North Texas Health Science Center at Fort Worth	M,D
University of Rhode Island	M,D,O
University of St. Francis (IL)	M,O
University of Southern Mississippi	M,D
University of South Florida	M,D,O
Utica College	M
Virginia Commonwealth University	M
Webster University	M
West Virginia University	M,D

FORESTRY

Auburn University	M,D
California Polytechnic State University, San Luis Obispo	M
Clemson University	M,D
Colorado State University	M,D
Cornell University	M,D
Duke University	M,D*
Harvard University	M*
Humboldt State University	M
Iowa State University of Science and Technology	M,D
Lakehead University	M,D
Louisiana State University and Agricultural & Mechanical College	M,D
McGill University	M,D
Michigan State University	M,D
Michigan Technological University	M,D
Mississippi State University	M,D
North Carolina State University	M,D
Northern Arizona University	M,D
The Ohio State University	M,D
Oklahoma State University	M,D
Oregon State University	M,D
Penn State University Park	M,D
Purdue University	M,D
Southern Illinois University Carbondale	M
Southern University and Agricultural and Mechanical College	M
State University of New York College of Environmental Science and Forestry	M,D
Stephen F. Austin State University	M,D
Texas A&M University	M,D
Tropical Agriculture Research and Higher Education Center	M,D
Université du Québec en Abitibi-Témiscamingue	M,D
Université Laval	M,D
University of Alberta	M,D
The University of Arizona	M,D
University of Arkansas at Monticello	M
The University of British Columbia	M,D
University of California, Berkeley	M,D
University of Florida	M,D
University of Georgia	M,D
University of Kentucky	M
University of Maine	M,D
University of Massachusetts Amherst	M,D*
University of Minnesota, Twin Cities Campus	M,D
University of Missouri	M,D,O
University of Montana	M,D
University of New Brunswick Fredericton	M,D
University of New Hampshire	M
The University of Tennessee	M
University of Toronto	M,D
University of Vermont	M,D
University of Washington	M,D*
University of Wisconsin–Madison	M,D
Utah State University	M,D
Virginia Polytechnic Institute and State University	M,D
West Virginia University	M,D
Yale University	M,D*

FOUNDATIONS AND PHILOSOPHY OF EDUCATION

Antioch University New England	M,O
Arkansas State University	M,D,O
Ashland University	M
Azusa Pacific University	M
Ball State University	D
Bank Street College of Education	M
Binghamton University, State University of New York	M,D,O*
Brigham Young University	M,D
Central Washington University	M
Chicago State University	M
Columbia University	M,D*
Curry College	M,O
DePaul University	M,D
Duquesne University	M
Eastern Michigan University	M
Fairfield University	M,O
Fairleigh Dickinson University, Metropolitan Campus	M
Florida Atlantic University	M
Florida State University	M,D
Georgia State University	M,D
Harvard University	M,O*
Indiana University Bloomington	M,D,O
Iowa State University of Science and Technology	M,D
Johnson State College	M
Kent State University	M,D
Marquette University	M,D,O
McGill University	M,D,O
Millersville University of Pennsylvania	M,D
Mount Saint Vincent University	M
New York University	M,D
Niagara University	M
Northeastern State University	M
Northern Arizona University	M,D,O
Northern Illinois University	M,D,O
Purdue University	M,D,O
Rutgers University–New Brunswick	M,D
Saint Louis University	M,D
Simon Fraser University	M,D
Southeast Missouri State University	M
Southern Illinois University Edwardsville	M
Spring Hill College	M
Syracuse University	M,D,O
Teachers College, Columbia University	M,D,O
University at Buffalo, the State University of New York	M,D,O*
The University of British Columbia	M,D
University of California, Riverside	M,D,O
University of Cincinnati	M,D
University of Hawaii at Manoa	M,D
University of Houston	M,D
University of Houston–Clear Lake	M
The University of Iowa	M,D,O*
The University of Kansas	M,D*
University of Manitoba	M
University of Maryland, College Park	M,D,O
University of Minnesota, Twin Cities Campus	M,D,O
University of New Mexico	M,D
University of Pennsylvania	M,D*
University of Pittsburgh	M,D*
University of Rochester	D*
University of Saskatchewan	M,D,O
University of South Africa	M,D
University of South Carolina	D
The University of Tennessee	M,D,O
The University of Texas of the Permian Basin	M
The University of Toledo	M,D,O
University of Utah	M,D*
University of Victoria	M,D
University of Washington	M,D*
University of Wisconsin–Milwaukee	M,D
Wayne State University	M,D,O
Western Illinois University	M,O
Widener University	M,D

FRENCH

American University	M,O
Arizona State University at the Tempe campus	M
Asbury University	M
Binghamton University, State University of New York	M*
Boston College	M
Boston University	M,D
Bowling Green State University	M
Brigham Young University	M
Brooklyn College of the City University of New York	M
Brown University	D
California State University, Fullerton	M
California State University, Long Beach	M
California State University, Los Angeles	M
Carleton University	M
Case Western Reserve University	M*
Central Connecticut State University	M,O
Cleveland State University	M
Columbia University	M,D*
Concordia University (Canada)	M,O
Cornell University	D
Dalhousie University	M,D
DePaul University	M
Drew University	M,D,O
Duke University	D*
Eastern Michigan University	M,O
Eastern University	M,O
Emory University	D
Florida Atlantic University	M
Florida State University	M,D
George Mason University	M
Georgia State University	M,O
The Graduate Center, City University of New York	D
Harvard University	M,D*
Hofstra University	M,D,O
Howard University	M
Hunter College of the City University of New York	M
Illinois State University	M
Indiana University Bloomington	M,D
Johns Hopkins University	D
Lake Forest College	M
Louisiana State University and Agricultural & Mechanical College	M,D
McGill University	M,D
McMaster University	M
Memorial University of Newfoundland	M
Miami University	M
Michigan State University	M,D
Middlebury College	M,D
Middle Tennessee State University	M
Millersville University of Pennsylvania	M
Minnesota State University Mankato	M
Mississippi State University	M
Montclair State University	M
New York University	M,D,O

*M—masters degree; D—doctorate; O—other advanced degree; *—Close-Up and/or Display*

North Carolina State University	M
Northern Illinois University	M
Northwestern University	D,O*
The Ohio State University	M,D
Ohio University	M
Penn State University Park	M,D
Portland State University	M
Princeton University	D
Purdue University	M,D
Queens College of the City University of New York	M
Queen's University at Kingston	M,D
Rider University	O
Rutgers University–New Brunswick	M,D
Saint Louis University	M
San Francisco State University	M
San Jose State University	M,O
Simon Fraser University	M
Smith College	M
Southern Oregon University	M
Stanford University	M,D
State University of New York at New Paltz	M,O
Stony Brook University, State University of New York	M
Syracuse University	M
Tufts University	M
Tulane University	M,D
Université de Moncton	M,D
Université de Montréal	M,D
Université de Sherbrooke	M,D
Université du Québec à Chicoutimi	O
University at Buffalo, the State University of New York	M,D,O*
The University of Alabama	M,D
University of Alberta	M,D
The University of Arizona	M
University of Arkansas	M
The University of British Columbia	M,D
University of Calgary	M,D
University of California, Berkeley	D
University of California, Davis	D
University of California, Irvine	M,D
University of California, Los Angeles	M,D
University of California, Santa Barbara	D
University of Chicago	D
University of Cincinnati	M,D
University of Colorado Boulder	M,D
University of Delaware	M*
University of Florida	M,D
University of Georgia	M,D
University of Guelph	M
University of Hawaii at Manoa	M
University of Illinois at Chicago	M
University of Illinois at Urbana–Champaign	M,D
The University of Iowa	M,D*
The University of Kansas	M,D*
University of Lethbridge	M,D
University of Louisiana at Lafayette	M,D
University of Louisville	M
The University of Manchester	M,D
University of Manitoba	M,D
University of Maryland, College Park	M,D
University of Massachusetts Amherst	M*
University of Memphis	M
University of Miami	D
University of Michigan	D
University of Minnesota, Twin Cities Campus	M,D
University of Missouri	M,D
University of Missouri–Kansas City	M
University of Montana	M
University of Nebraska–Lincoln	M,D
University of Nevada, Reno	M
University of New Mexico	M,D
The University of North Carolina at Chapel Hill	M,D
The University of North Carolina at Greensboro	M
University of North Texas	M,D,O
University of Notre Dame	M
University of Oklahoma	M,D*
University of Oregon	M
University of Ottawa	M,D
University of Pennsylvania	M,D*
University of Pittsburgh	M,D*
University of Regina	M
University of Saskatchewan	M
University of South Africa	M,D
University of South Carolina	M,D
University of South Florida	M
The University of Tennessee	M,D
The University of Texas at Arlington	M
The University of Texas at Austin	M,D
The University of Toledo	M
University of Toronto	M,D
University of Utah	M,D*
University of Victoria	M
University of Virginia	M,D
University of Washington	M,D*
University of Waterloo	M,D
The University of Western Ontario	M,D
University of Wisconsin–Madison	M,D,O
University of Wisconsin–Milwaukee	M,O
University of Wyoming	M
Vanderbilt University	M,D*
Washington University in St. Louis	D
Wayne State University	M,D
West Chester University of Pennsylvania	M,O
Western Kentucky University	M
West Virginia University	M
Yale University	M,D*
York University	M,D

GAME DESIGN AND DEVELOPMENT

Academy of Art University	M
American University	M
Concordia University (Canada)	M,D,O
DePaul University	M,D
Full Sail University	M
Long Island University–LIU Post	M
Michigan State University	M
New York University	M
Rochester Institute of Technology	M
Sacred Heart University	M,O
Savannah College of Art and Design	M,O
Shepherd University (CA)	M
University of Advancing Technology	M
University of Central Florida	M
The University of North Carolina at Charlotte	M,O
University of Southern California	M,D
University of Utah	M*
Virginia International University	M,O
West Virginia University	O
Worcester Polytechnic Institute	M

GENDER STUDIES

American University	M,D,O
The American University in Cairo	M
Arizona State University at the Tempe campus	M,D,O
Brandeis University	M,D
California State University, Sacramento	M
Carnegie Mellon University	D
Central European University	M,D
Central Michigan University	M
The College of New Jersey	O
Cornell University	M,D
Delta State University	M
Dominican University of California	M
Eastern Michigan University	M,O
The George Washington University	O*
Indiana University Bloomington	D
Indiana University–Purdue University Indianapolis	M
Instituto Tecnologico de Santo Domingo	M,O
Memorial University of Newfoundland	M,D
Middle Tennessee State University	O
Minnesota State University Mankato	M
Northern Arizona University	O
Northwestern University	O*
The Ohio State University	M,D
Oregon State University	M,D
Queen's University at Kingston	M,D
Roosevelt University	M,O
Rutgers University–New Brunswick	M,D
Saint Mary's University (Canada)	M
San Diego State University	O
Simon Fraser University	M,D
Texas Woman's University	M,D
University at Buffalo, the State University of New York	M,D,O*
The University of Arizona	M,D,O
The University of British Columbia	M,D
University of California, Los Angeles	M,D
University of Central Florida	M,O
University of Colorado Denver	M
University of Florida	M,O
University of Lethbridge	M,D
University of Maine	M
University of Michigan–Flint	M
The University of North Carolina at Charlotte	M,D,O
The University of North Carolina at Greensboro	M,O
University of Northern British Columbia	M,D,O
University of Northern Iowa	M
University of Oklahoma	O*
University of Rhode Island	M,D
University of Saskatchewan	M,D
University of South Florida	M,O
The University of Toledo	O
University of Toronto	M,D
Wayne State University	M,D,O
Wilfrid Laurier University	M
York University	M,D

GENETIC COUNSELING

Arcadia University	M
Bay Path University	M
Boston University	M
Brandeis University	M
California State University, Stanislaus	M
Case Western Reserve University	M*
Emory University	M
Icahn School of Medicine at Mount Sinai	M,D
Johns Hopkins University	M,D
Long Island University–LIU Post	M,O
McGill University	M,D
Northwestern University	M*
Sarah Lawrence College	M
Université de Montréal	O
The University of Alabama at Birmingham	M
University of Arkansas for Medical Sciences	M,D
The University of British Columbia	M
University of California, Irvine	M
University of Cincinnati	M
University of Colorado Denver	M,D
University of Maryland, Baltimore	M
University of Michigan	M,D
University of Minnesota, Twin Cities Campus	M,D
The University of North Carolina at Greensboro	M
University of Oklahoma Health Sciences Center	M
University of Pittsburgh	M,D,O*
University of South Carolina	M
The University of Texas Health Science Center at Houston	M
University of Toronto	M,D
University of Wisconsin–Madison	M,D
Wayne State University	M

GENETICS

Albert Einstein College of Medicine	D
American University of Beirut	M,D
Baylor College of Medicine	D
Boston University	D
Brandeis University	M,D
California Institute of Technology	D
Carnegie Mellon University	M,D
Case Western Reserve University	D*
Clemson University	M,D
Columbia University	M,D*
Cornell University	D
Dartmouth College	D*
Drexel University	M,D
Duke University	D*
Emory University	D
Harvard University	D*
Illinois State University	M,D
Indiana University Bloomington	M,D
Iowa State University of Science and Technology	M,D
Irell & Manella Graduate School of Biological Sciences	D*
Johns Hopkins University	M,D
Kansas State University	M,D
Kent State University	M,D
Marquette University	M,D
Massachusetts Institute of Technology	D
Mayo Graduate School	D
McMaster University	M,D
Medical University of South Carolina	D
Michigan State University	M,D
Mississippi State University	M,D
New York University	M,D
North Carolina State University	M,D
The Ohio State University	M,D
Oregon Health & Science University	D
Purdue University	M,D
Rutgers University–New Brunswick	M,D
Stanford University	D
Stony Brook University, State University of New York	D
Thomas Jefferson University	D
Tufts University	D
Université de Montréal	O
Université du Québec à Chicoutimi	M
University at Buffalo, the State University of New York	M,D*
The University of Alabama at Birmingham	D
University of Alberta	M,D
The University of Arizona	M,D
The University of British Columbia	M,D
University of Calgary	M,D
University of California, Davis	M,D
University of California, Irvine	D
University of California, Riverside	D
University of California, San Francisco	D
University of Chicago	D
University of Colorado Boulder	M,D
University of Colorado Denver	M,D
University of Connecticut Health Center	D*
University of Delaware	M,D*
University of Florida	D
University of Georgia	M,D
University of Hawaii at Manoa	M,D
University of Illinois at Chicago	D
The University of Iowa	M,D*
The University of Manchester	M,D
University of Massachusetts Amherst	M,D*
University of Miami	M,D
University of Minnesota, Twin Cities Campus	M,D
University of Missouri	D
University of Nebraska Medical Center	M,D
University of New Hampshire	M,D
University of New Mexico	M,D
The University of North Carolina at Chapel Hill	M,D
University of North Dakota	M,D
University of North Texas Health Science Center at Fort Worth	M,D
University of Notre Dame	M,D
University of Oregon	M,D
University of Pennsylvania	D*
University of Puerto Rico, Rí o Piedras Campus	M,D
University of Rochester	D*
The University of Tennessee	M,D
The University of Texas Health Science Center at Houston	M,D
The University of Texas MD Anderson Cancer Center	M
The University of Texas Medical Branch	D
The University of Texas Southwestern Medical Center	D
University of Washington	M,D*
University of Wisconsin–Madison	M,D
University of Wyoming	D
Van Andel Institute Graduate School	D
Virginia Commonwealth University	M,D
Virginia Polytechnic Institute and State University	M,D
Washington State University	M,D
Washington University in St. Louis	M,D
Wesleyan University	D
West Virginia University	M,D
Yale University	D*

GENOMIC SCIENCES

Albert Einstein College of Medicine	D
Augusta University	M,D
Black Hills State University	M
Boston University	D
Case Western Reserve University	D*
Concordia University (Canada)	M,D,O
Cornell University	D
Duke University	D*
Harvard University	D*
Massachusetts Institute of Technology	M,D
New York University	D
North Carolina State University	M,D
North Dakota State University	M,D
Oregon State University	M,D
Purdue University	D
Thomas Jefferson University	D
University at Buffalo, the State University of New York	M,D*
The University of Alabama at Birmingham	D
University of California, Riverside	D
University of California, San Francisco	D
University of Chicago	D
University of Cincinnati	M,D
University of Connecticut	M*
University of Georgia	M,D
University of Maryland, Baltimore	M,D
University of Maryland, College Park	D
University of Pennsylvania	D*
University of Rochester	D*
University of Southern California	D
The University of Tennessee	M,D
The University of Tennessee–Oak Ridge National Laboratory	M,D
The University of Toledo	M,O
University of Washington	D*
Wake Forest University	D
Washington University in St. Louis	M
Wayne State University	M,D
Wesleyan University	D
West Virginia University	M,D
Yale University	D*

GEOCHEMISTRY

California Institute of Technology	M,D
California State University, Fullerton	M
Colorado School of Mines	M,D
Cornell University	M,D
Georgia State University	M,D
Indiana University Bloomington	M,D
Massachusetts Institute of Technology	M,D
McMaster University	M,D
Missouri University of Science and Technology	M,D
Montana Tech of The University of Montana	M
New Mexico Institute of Mining and Technology	M,D
Ohio University	M
Oregon State University	M,D
University of California, Los Angeles	M,D
University of Chicago	D
University of Hawaii at Manoa	M,D
The University of Manchester	M,D
University of Nevada, Reno	M,D
The University of Texas at Dallas	M,D*
Yale University	D*

GEODETIC SCIENCES

The Ohio State University	M,D
Université Laval	M,D
University of New Brunswick Fredericton	M,D

GEOGRAPHIC INFORMATION SYSTEMS

Acadia University	M
Appalachian State University	M
Arizona State University at the Tempe campus	M,D,O
Auburn University at Montgomery	M
Ball State University	M,O
Boston University	M,D
Central Michigan University	M
Chicago State University	M
Claremont Graduate University	M,D,O
Clark University	M
Cleveland State University	M,O
The College of William and Mary	M,D
East Carolina University	M,O
Eastern Illinois University	M
Eastern Michigan University	M,O
East Stroudsburg University of Pennsylvania	M
Elizabeth City State University	M
Elmhurst College	M
Florida State University	M,D
George Mason University	M,D,O
Georgia Institute of Technology	M,D
Georgia State University	O
Idaho State University	M,O
Indiana University of Pennsylvania	M,O

Indiana University–Purdue University Indianapolis	M,O
Johns Hopkins University	M,O
Long Island University–LIU Post	M,O
Michigan Technological University	M,D
Millersville University of Pennsylvania	M
Montclair State University	O
Naval Postgraduate School	M,D,O
North Carolina State University	M,D
Northeastern University	M
Northern Arizona University	M,O
Northern Kentucky University	M,O
Northwest Missouri State University	M,O
Oregon State University	M
Saint Louis University	M,D,O
Saint Mary's University of Minnesota	M,O
Salisbury University	M
Sam Houston State University	M,O
San Francisco State University	M
State University of New York College of Environmental Science and Forestry	M,D
Stony Brook University, State University of New York	O
Temple University	M,D,O*
Texas State University	D
Université du Québec à Montréal	O
Université Laval	M,O
University at Buffalo, the State University of New York	M,D,O*
The University of Alabama	M
University of Alaska Fairbanks	M,D
The University of Arizona	M,D,O
University of Central Arkansas	M,O
University of Colorado Denver	M,D
University of Denver	M,D,O
University of Florida	M,D
The University of Iowa	M,D,O*
University of Lethbridge	M,D
University of Maine	M,D,O
University of Maryland, Baltimore County	M,O
University of Memphis	M,D,O
University of Minnesota, Twin Cities Campus	M,D
University of Missouri	M,D,O
University of Nebraska at Omaha	M,O
University of New Hampshire	O
University of New Haven	M,O
University of North Alabama	M
The University of North Carolina at Charlotte	M,D
The University of North Carolina at Greensboro	M,D,O
University of Pennsylvania	M,D,O*
University of Pittsburgh	M,D*
University of Redlands	M
University of Southern California	M,O
University of South Florida	M,D,O
The University of Texas at Dallas	M,D*
The University of Toledo	M,D,O
University of Utah	M,D*
University of West Georgia	M,O
University of Wisconsin–Madison	M,D,O
University of Wisconsin–Milwaukee	M,O
Virginia Commonwealth University	O
Virginia Polytechnic Institute and State University	M,D
West Chester University of Pennsylvania	M,O
Western Illinois University	M,O
Western Michigan University	M,O
West Virginia University	M,D
Wilmington University	M

GEOGRAPHY

Appalachian State University	M
Arizona State University at the Tempe campus	M,D,O
Auburn University	M
Ball State University	M,O
Binghamton University, State University of New York	M*
Boston University	M,D
Brock University	M
California State University, East Bay	M
California State University, Fullerton	M
California State University, Long Beach	M
California State University, Los Angeles	M
California State University, Northridge	M
Carleton University	M,D
Central Connecticut State University	M
Chicago State University	M
Clark University	M,D
Concordia University (Canada)	M,D,O
Concord University	M
East Carolina University	M,O
Eastern Michigan University	M,O
Florida State University	M,D
Fort Hays State University	M
George Mason University	M,D,O
The George Washington University	M,O*
Georgia State University	M,D
Hunter College of the City University of New York	M,O
Indiana University Bloomington	M,D
Indiana University of Pennsylvania	M
Johns Hopkins University	M,D
Kansas State University	M,D,O
Kent State University	M,D
Louisiana State University and Agricultural & Mechanical College	M,D
Marshall University	M,O
McGill University	M,D
McMaster University	M,D
Memorial University of Newfoundland	M,D
Miami University	M
Michigan State University	M,D
Minnesota State University Mankato	M
Mississippi State University	M,D
Missouri State University	M
New Mexico State University	M
Northeastern Illinois University	M
Northern Arizona University	M,O
Northern Illinois University	M,D
The Ohio State University	M,D
Ohio University	M
Oklahoma State University	M,D
Oregon State University	M,D
Penn State University Park	M,D
Philadelphia University	M
Portland State University	M,D
Queen's University at Kingston	M,D
Rutgers University–New Brunswick	M,D
St. Cloud State University	M
Salem State University	M
San Diego State University	M,D
San Francisco State University	M
San Jose State University	M,O
Shippensburg University of Pennsylvania	M
Simon Fraser University	M,D
South Dakota State University	M
Southern Illinois University Carbondale	M,D
Southern Illinois University Edwardsville	M
Syracuse University	M,D
Temple University	M,D,O*
Texas A&M University	M,D
Texas State University	M,D
Texas Tech University	M,D
Towson University	M
Trent University	M,D
Université de Montréal	M,D,O
Université de Sherbrooke	M,D
Université du Québec à Montréal	M
Université Laval	M,D
University at Albany, State University of New York	M
University at Buffalo, the State University of New York	M,D,O*
The University of Alabama	M
The University of Arizona	M,D,O
University of Arkansas	M
The University of British Columbia	M,D
University of Calgary	M,D
University of California, Berkeley	D
University of California, Davis	M,D
University of California, Los Angeles	M,D
University of California, Santa Barbara	M,D
University of Central Arkansas	M,O
University of Cincinnati	M,D
University of Colorado Boulder	M,D
University of Colorado Colorado Springs	M
University of Connecticut	M,D*
University of Delaware	M,D*
University of Denver	M,D
University of Florida	M,D
University of Georgia	M,D
University of Guelph	M,D
University of Hawaii at Manoa	M,D,O
University of Idaho	M,D
University of Illinois at Chicago	M
University of Illinois at Urbana–Champaign	M,D
The University of Iowa	M,D,O*
The University of Kansas	M,D*
University of Kentucky	M,D
University of Lethbridge	M,D
University of Louisville	M
The University of Manchester	M,D
University of Manitoba	M,D
University of Maryland, Baltimore County	M,D
University of Maryland, College Park	M,D
University of Massachusetts Amherst	M*
University of Memphis	M,D,O
University of Miami	M
University of Minnesota, Twin Cities Campus	M,D
University of Missouri	M,O
University of Montana	M
University of Nebraska at Omaha	M,O
University of Nebraska–Lincoln	M,D
University of Nevada, Reno	M,D
University of New Mexico	M
University of New Orleans	M
The University of North Carolina at Chapel Hill	M,D
The University of North Carolina at Charlotte	M,D
The University of North Carolina at Greensboro	M,D,O
University of North Dakota	M
University of Northern Iowa	M
University of North Texas	M,D,O
University of Oklahoma	M,D*
University of Oregon	M,D
University of Ottawa	M,D
University of Prince Edward Island	M
University of Regina	M,D
University of Saskatchewan	M,D
University of South Africa	M,D
University of South Carolina	M,D
University of Southern California	M,O
University of Southern Mississippi	M,D
University of South Florida	M,D,O
The University of Tennessee	M,D
The University of Texas at Austin	M,D
The University of Texas at Dallas	M,D*
The University of Toledo	M,D,O
University of Toronto	M,D
University of Utah	M,D*
University of Victoria	M,D
University of Washington	M,D*
University of Waterloo	M,D
The University of Western Ontario	M,D
University of Wisconsin–Madison	M,D,O
University of Wisconsin–Milwaukee	M,D
University of Wyoming	M
Utah State University	M,D
Virginia Polytechnic Institute and State University	M,D
West Chester University of Pennsylvania	M,O
Western Illinois University	M,O
Western Michigan University	M,D,O
Western Washington University	M
West Virginia University	M,D
Wilfrid Laurier University	M,D
York University	M,D

GEOLOGICAL ENGINEERING

Arizona State University at the Tempe campus	M,D
Colorado School of Mines	M,D
Michigan Technological University	M,D
Missouri University of Science and Technology	M,D
Montana Tech of The University of Montana	M
New Mexico Institute of Mining and Technology	M
New Mexico State University	M,D
South Dakota School of Mines and Technology	M,D
The University of Akron	M
University of Alaska Anchorage	M
University of Alaska Fairbanks	M
The University of Arizona	M,D,O
The University of British Columbia	M,D
University of Hawaii at Manoa	M,D
University of Idaho	M,D
University of Minnesota, Twin Cities Campus	M,D,O
University of Nevada, Reno	M,D
University of North Dakota	M
University of Oklahoma	M,D*
University of Saskatchewan	M,D
University of Utah	M,D*
University of Wisconsin–Madison	M,D

GEOLOGY

Acadia University	M
American University of Beirut	M,D
Arizona State University at the Tempe campus	M,D
Auburn University	M
Ball State University	M,D
Binghamton University, State University of New York	M,D*
Boston College	M
Bowling Green State University	M
Brigham Young University	M
Brooklyn College of the City University of New York	M,D
California Institute of Technology	M,D
California State Polytechnic University, Pomona	M
California State University, Bakersfield	M
California State University, Chico	M
California State University, East Bay	M
California State University, Fresno	M
California State University, Fullerton	M
California State University, Long Beach	M
California State University, Los Angeles	M
California State University, Northridge	M
Case Western Reserve University	M,D*
Central Washington University	M
City College of the City University of New York	M
Colorado School of Mines	M,D
Cornell University	M,D
Duke University	M,D*
East Carolina University	M,O
Eastern Kentucky University	M,D
Florida Atlantic University	M,D
Florida State University	M,D
Fort Hays State University	M
Georgia State University	M
Hofstra University	M,D,O
Humboldt State University	M
Idaho State University	M,O
Indiana University Bloomington	M,D
Indiana University–Purdue University Indianapolis	M,D
Iowa State University of Science and Technology	M,D
Kansas State University	M
Kent State University	M,D
Lakehead University	M
Laurentian University	M,D
Lehigh University	M,D
Louisiana State University and Agricultural & Mechanical College	M,D
Massachusetts Institute of Technology	M,D
McMaster University	M,D
Memorial University of Newfoundland	M,D
Miami University	M,D
Michigan Technological University	M,D
Mississippi State University	M,D
Missouri State University	M
Missouri University of Science and Technology	M,D
Montana Tech of The University of Montana	M
New Mexico Institute of Mining and Technology	M,D
New Mexico State University	M
Northern Arizona University	M,D
Northern Illinois University	M,D
Northwestern University	D*
The Ohio State University	M,D
Ohio University	M
Oklahoma State University	M,D
Oregon State University	M,D
Portland State University	M,D
Queens College of the City University of New York	M
Queen's University at Kingston	M,D
Rensselaer Polytechnic Institute	M,D
Rutgers University–Newark	M
Rutgers University–New Brunswick	M,D
St. Francis Xavier University	M
San Diego State University	M
San Jose State University	M,O
South Dakota School of Mines and Technology	M,D
Southern Illinois University Carbondale	M,D
Southern Methodist University	M,D
Stephen F. Austin State University	M
Sul Ross State University	M
Syracuse University	M,D
Temple University	M,D*
Texas A&M University	M,D
Texas Christian University	M
Université du Québec à Montréal	M,D,O
Université Laval	M,D
University at Buffalo, the State University of New York	M,D*
The University of Akron	M
The University of Alabama	M,D
University of Alaska Fairbanks	M,D
University of Arkansas	M
The University of British Columbia	M,D
University of Calgary	M,D
University of California, Berkeley	M,D
University of California, Davis	M,D
University of California, Los Angeles	M,D
University of California, Riverside	M,D
University of Cincinnati	M,D
University of Colorado Boulder	M,D
University of Connecticut	M,D*
University of Delaware	M,D*
University of Florida	M,D
University of Georgia	M,D
University of Hawaii at Manoa	M,D
University of Houston	M,D
University of Idaho	M,D
University of Illinois at Chicago	M,D
University of Illinois at Urbana–Champaign	M,D
The University of Kansas	M,D*
University of Kentucky	M,D
University of Louisiana at Lafayette	M
University of Maine	M,O
University of Manitoba	M,D
University of Maryland, College Park	M,D
University of Memphis	M,D,O
University of Minnesota, Duluth	M,D
University of Minnesota, Twin Cities Campus	M,D
University of Missouri	M,D
University of Missouri–Kansas City	M,D
University of Montana	M,D
University of Nevada, Reno	M,D
University of New Brunswick Fredericton	M,D
University of New Hampshire	M
The University of North Carolina at Chapel Hill	M,D
University of North Dakota	M,D
University of Oklahoma	M,D*
University of Oregon	M,D
University of Pittsburgh	M,D*
University of Puerto Rico, Mayagüez Campus	M
University of Regina	M,D
University of Rochester	M,D*
University of Saskatchewan	M,D,O
University of South Carolina	M,D
University of Southern Mississippi	M,D
University of South Florida	M,D,O
The University of Tennessee	M,D
The University of Texas at Arlington	M,D
The University of Texas at Austin	M,D
The University of Texas at El Paso	M,D

*M—masters degree; D—doctorate; O—other advanced degree; *—Close-Up and/or Display*

The University of Texas at San Antonio	M
The University of Texas of the Permian Basin	M
The University of Toledo	M,D
University of Toronto	M,D
University of Utah	M,D*
University of Vermont	M
University of Washington	M,D*
The University of Western Ontario	M,D
University of Wisconsin–Madison	M,D
University of Wisconsin–Milwaukee	M,D
University of Wyoming	M,D
Utah State University	M
Vanderbilt University	M*
Washington State University	M,D
Wayne State University	M
West Chester University of Pennsylvania	M
Western Kentucky University	M
Western Washington University	M
West Virginia University	M,D
Wichita State University	M
Wright State University	M
Yale University	D*

GEOPHYSICS

Boise State University	M,D
Boston College	M
Bowling Green State University	M
California Institute of Technology	M,D
California State University, Long Beach	M
Colorado School of Mines	M,D
Cornell University	M,D
Florida State University	D
Idaho State University	M,O
Indiana University Bloomington	M,D
Louisiana State University and Agricultural & Mechanical College	M,D
Massachusetts Institute of Technology	M,D
Memorial University of Newfoundland	M,D
Michigan Technological University	M,D
Missouri University of Science and Technology	M,D
New Mexico Institute of Mining and Technology	M,D
Ohio University	M
Oregon State University	M,D
Rice University	M
Saint Louis University	M,D
Southern Methodist University	M,D
Stanford University	M,D
Texas A&M University	M,D
The University of Akron	M
University of Alaska Fairbanks	M,D
University of Alberta	M,D
The University of British Columbia	M,D
University of Calgary	M,D
University of California, Berkeley	M,D
University of California, Los Angeles	M,D
University of California, San Diego	M,D
University of Chicago	D
University of Colorado Boulder	M,D
University of Hawaii at Manoa	M,D
University of Houston	M,D
University of Manitoba	M,D
University of Memphis	M,D,O
University of Miami	M,D
University of Minnesota, Twin Cities Campus	M,D
University of Nevada, Reno	M,D
University of Oklahoma	M,D*
The University of Texas at Dallas	M,D*
The University of Texas at El Paso	M
The University of Tulsa	M,D
University of Utah	M,D*
University of Washington	M,D*
The University of Western Ontario	M,D
University of Wisconsin–Madison	M,D
University of Wyoming	M,D
West Virginia University	M,D
Wright State University	M
Yale University	D*

GEOSCIENCES

Arizona State University at the Tempe campus	M,D
Ball State University	M
Baylor University	M,D
Boston University	M,D
Brock University	M
Brooklyn College of the City University of New York	M
Brown University	D
California State University, Chico	M
California State University, San Bernardino	M
Carleton University	M,D
Case Western Reserve University	M,D*
City College of the City University of New York	M
Colorado State University	M,D
Columbia University	M,D*
Cornell University	M,D
Dalhousie University	M,D
Dartmouth College	M,D*
Eastern Michigan University	M
East Tennessee State University	M
Emporia State University	M,O
Florida Atlantic University	M,D
Florida Institute of Technology	M
Florida International University	M,D
Florida State University	M,D
Fort Hays State University	M
George Mason University	M,D,O
Georgia Institute of Technology	M,D
Georgia State University	M,D,O
The Graduate Center, City University of New York	D
Harvard University	M,D*
Hunter College of the City University of New York	M
Idaho State University	M,O
Indiana University Bloomington	M,D
Indiana University–Purdue University Indianapolis	M,D
Iowa State University of Science and Technology	M,D
Johns Hopkins University	M,D
Lehigh University	M,D
Long Island University–LIU Post	M,O
Massachusetts Institute of Technology	M,D
McGill University	M,D
McMaster University	M,D
Memorial University of Newfoundland	M,D
Michigan State University	M,D
Middle Tennessee State University	O
Mississippi State University	M,D
Missouri State University	M
Montana State University	M,D
Montana Tech of The University of Montana	M
Montclair State University	M
Murray State University	M
New Mexico Institute of Mining and Technology	M,D
North Carolina Central University	M
North Carolina State University	M,D
Northwestern University	D*
The Ohio State University	M,D
Pace University	M,O
Penn State University Park	M,D
Princeton University	D
Purdue University	M,D
Queens College of the City University of New York	M
Rice University	M,D
St. Francis Xavier University	M
Saint Louis University	M,D
St. Thomas University	M,D,O
San Francisco State University	M
Simon Fraser University	M,D
South Dakota State University	D
Southern Illinois University Carbondale	M,D
Stanford University	M,D,O
State University of New York at New Paltz	M,O
State University of New York College at Oneonta	M
Stony Brook University, State University of New York	M,D
Syracuse University	M,D
Teachers College, Columbia University	M,D
Texas Tech University	M,D
Université du Québec à Chicoutimi	M
Université du Québec à Montréal	M,D,O
Université du Québec, Institut National de la Recherche Scientifique	M,D
Université Laval	M,D
University at Buffalo, the State University of New York	M,D,O*
The University of Akron	M
The University of Alabama	M
University of Alberta	M,D
The University of Arizona	M,D
University of Arkansas at Little Rock	O
University of Calgary	M,D
University of California, Irvine	M,D
University of California, Los Angeles	M,D
University of California, San Diego	M,D
University of California, Santa Barbara	M,D
University of California, Santa Cruz	M,D
University of Chicago	D
University of Florida	M,D
University of Illinois at Chicago	M,D
University of Illinois at Urbana–Champaign	M,D
The University of Iowa	M,D*
University of Maine	M,D
The University of Manchester	M,D
University of Massachusetts Amherst	M,D*
University of Michigan	M,D
University of Missouri–Kansas City	M,D
University of Montana	M,D
University of Nebraska–Lincoln	M,D
University of Nevada, Las Vegas	M,D
University of New Hampshire	M,D,O
University of New Haven	M,O
University of New Mexico	M,D
University of New Orleans	M
The University of North Carolina at Charlotte	M,D
The University of North Carolina Wilmington	M
University of North Dakota	M,D
University of Northern Colorado	M
University of Northern Iowa	M
University of Notre Dame	M,D
University of Ottawa	M,D
University of Pennsylvania	M,D*
University of Rhode Island	M,D
University of Rochester	M,D*
University of South Carolina	M,D
University of Southern California	M,D
University of South Florida	M,D
The University of Texas at Austin	M,D
The University of Texas at Dallas	M,D*
The University of Tulsa	M,D
University of Victoria	M,D
University of Waterloo	M,D
The University of Western Ontario	M,D
University of West Florida	M
University of Windsor	M,D
Virginia Polytechnic Institute and State University	M,D
Washington University in St. Louis	D
Wesleyan University	M
West Chester University of Pennsylvania	M
Western Connecticut State University	M
Western Kentucky University	M
Western Michigan University	M,D,O
Yale University	D*
York University	M,D

GEOTECHNICAL ENGINEERING

Auburn University	M,D
Cornell University	M,D
Drexel University	M,D
École Polytechnique de Montréal	M,D,O
Illinois Institute of Technology	M,D
Iowa State University of Science and Technology	M,D
Kansas State University	M,D
Louisiana State University and Agricultural & Mechanical College	M,D
Massachusetts Institute of Technology	M,D,O
McGill University	M,D
Missouri University of Science and Technology	M,D
Northwestern University	M,D*
Norwich University	M
Ohio University	M,D
Old Dominion University	M
Oregon State University	M,D
Penn State University Park	M,D
Southern Illinois University Edwardsville	M
Stanford University	M,D,O
Tufts University	M,D
University of Alberta	M,D
University of Calgary	M,D
University of California, Berkeley	M,D
University of Colorado Boulder	M,D
University of Colorado Denver	M,D
University of Dayton	M
University of Delaware	M,D*
University of Massachusetts Amherst	M,D*
University of Missouri	M,D
University of New Brunswick Fredericton	M,D
University of Southern California	M,D,O
University of South Florida	M,D
The University of Texas at Austin	M,D
University of Washington	M,D*

GERMAN

Arizona State University at the Tempe campus	M
Bowling Green State University	M
Brown University	D
California State University, Fullerton	M
California State University, Long Beach	M
Central Connecticut State University	M,O
Columbia University	M,D*
Cornell University	M,D
Dalhousie University	M
DePaul University	M
Duke University	D*
Eastern Michigan University	M,O
Florida Atlantic University	M
Florida State University	M
Georgetown University	M,D
Georgia State University	O
The Graduate Center, City University of New York	M,D
Harvard University	D*
Illinois State University	M
Indiana University Bloomington	M,D
Johns Hopkins University	D
McGill University	M,D
Memorial University of Newfoundland	M
Michigan State University	M,D
Middlebury College	M,D
Middle Tennessee State University	M
Millersville University of Pennsylvania	M
Mississippi State University	M
New York University	M,D
Northwestern University	D*
The Ohio State University	M,D
Penn State University Park	M,D
Portland State University	M
Princeton University	D
Purdue University	M,D
Queen's University at Kingston	M,D
Rider University	O
Rutgers University–New Brunswick	M,D
San Francisco State University	M
Stanford University	M,D
Texas Tech University	M,D
Tufts University	M
Université de Montréal	M
University at Buffalo, the State University of New York	M,D,O*
The University of Alabama	M,D
University of Alberta	M,D
The University of Arizona	M,D
University of Arkansas	M
The University of British Columbia	M,D
University of Calgary	M,D
University of California, Berkeley	D
University of California, Davis	M,D
University of California, Irvine	M,D
University of California, Los Angeles	M,D
University of Chicago	M,D
University of Cincinnati	M,D
University of Colorado Boulder	M
University of Delaware	M*
University of Florida	M,D
University of Georgia	M
University of Illinois at Chicago	M,D
University of Illinois at Urbana–Champaign	M,D
The University of Kansas	M,D*
University of Kentucky	M
University of Lethbridge	M,D
The University of Manchester	M,D
University of Manitoba	M
University of Maryland, College Park	M,D
University of Massachusetts Amherst	M,D*
University of Michigan	M,D
University of Minnesota, Twin Cities Campus	M,D
University of Missouri	M
University of Montana	M
University of Nebraska–Lincoln	M,D
University of Nevada, Reno	M
University of New Mexico	M,D
The University of North Carolina at Chapel Hill	M,D
University of Oklahoma	M*
University of Oregon	M,D
University of Pennsylvania	M,D*
University of Saskatchewan	M
University of South Africa	M,D
University of South Carolina	M,D
The University of Tennessee	M,D
The University of Texas at Austin	M,D
The University of Toledo	M
University of Toronto	M,D
University of Vermont	M
University of Victoria	M
University of Virginia	M,D
University of Washington	M,D*
University of Waterloo	M,D
University of Wisconsin–Madison	M,D
University of Wisconsin–Milwaukee	M,O
University of Wyoming	M
Vanderbilt University	M,D*
Washington University in St. Louis	D
Wayne State University	M,D
West Chester University of Pennsylvania	M,O
Western Kentucky University	M
Yale University	D*

GERONTOLOGICAL NURSING

Allen College	M,D,O
Arizona State University at the Tempe campus	M,D,O
Armstrong State University	M,O
Augusta University	D
Ball State University	M,D,O
Boise State University	M,D,O
Boston College	M,D
California State University, Stanislaus	M
Capella University	M
Caribbean University	M,D
Case Western Reserve University	M*
College of Mount Saint Vincent	M,O
College of Staten Island of the City University of New York	M,O
Columbia University	M,O*
Concordia University Wisconsin	M
Creighton University	M,D,O
Duke University	M,D,O*
Felician University	M,O
Florida Southern College	M
Goldfarb School of Nursing at Barnes-Jewish College	M
Gwynedd Mercy University	M,D
Hampton University	M,D
Hunter College of the City University of New York	M
Independence University	M
Indiana University–Purdue University Fort Wayne	M,O
James Madison University	M,D
Kent State University	M,D,O
Keuka College	M
La Salle University	M,D,O
Lehman College of the City University of New York	M
Le Moyne College	M,O
Loma Linda University	M
Louisiana State University Health Sciences Center	M,D,O
Loyola University Chicago	M,D,O
Marquette University	M,D,O
Maryville University of Saint Louis	M,D
Medical University of South Carolina	M,D
Mercer University	M,D,O
MGH Institute of Health Professions	M,D,O
Middle Georgia State University	M
Molloy College	M,D,O
Monmouth University	M,D,O
Mount Carmel College of Nursing	M,D
Neumann University	M
New Mexico State University	M,D
New York University	M,O
Northeastern University	M,D,O
Oakland University	M,O
Old Dominion University	M

Oregon Health & Science University	M,D,O
Point Loma Nazarene University	M,O
Research College of Nursing	M
Rush University	D
Sage Graduate School	M,O
St. Catherine University	M,D
Saint Francis Medical Center College of Nursing	M,D,O
Salem State University	M
Seattle Pacific University	M,O
Seattle University	M
Seton Hall University	M,D
Southern University and Agricultural and Mechanical College	M,D,O
Stony Brook University, State University of New York	M,D,O
Texas Christian University	M,O
Texas Tech University Health Sciences Center	M,D,O
Uniformed Services University of the Health Sciences	M,D*
University at Buffalo, the State University of New York	M,D,O*
The University of Alabama in Huntsville	M,D,O
University of Colorado Colorado Springs	M,D
University of Delaware	M,O*
University of Illinois at Chicago	M,O
The University of Kansas	M,D,O*
University of Louisville	M,D
University of Maryland, Baltimore	M
University of Massachusetts Amherst	M,D*
University of Massachusetts Lowell	M
University of Massachusetts Medical School	M,D,O
University of Minnesota, Twin Cities Campus	M
University of Missouri	M,D,O
University of Missouri–Kansas City	M,D
University of Missouri–St. Louis	M,D,O
The University of North Carolina at Chapel Hill	M,D,O
The University of North Carolina at Charlotte	M,D,O
The University of North Carolina at Greensboro	M,D,O
University of North Dakota	M,D
University of Pennsylvania	M*
University of Phoenix–Bay Area Campus	M,D
University of Phoenix–Phoenix Campus	M,O
University of Pittsburgh	M,D*
University of Puerto Rico, Medical Sciences Campus	M
University of Rhode Island	M,D
University of Rochester	M,D*
University of San Diego	M,D
University of Southern Maine	M,D,O
University of South Florida	M,D,O
The University of Tennessee Health Science Center	M,D,O
The University of Texas at Austin	M,D
The University of Texas Health Science Center at San Antonio	M,D,O
University of Utah	M,O*
University of Wisconsin–Eau Claire	M,D
University of Wisconsin–Madison	D
Ursuline College	M,D
Vanderbilt University	M,D,O*
Walden University	M,D,O
Wayne State University	D
West Chester University of Pennsylvania	M,D,O
Western Connecticut State University	M,D
Wilmington University	M,D
York College of Pennsylvania	M,D

GERONTOLOGY

Adelphi University	M,O
Alliant International University–Los Angeles	M
Appalachian State University	M,O
Arizona State University at the Tempe campus	M,D,O
Arkansas State University	M,D,O
Bethel University (MN)	M,D,O
California State University, Fullerton	M
California State University, Long Beach	M
Capella University	M
Central Michigan University	M,O
The College at Brockport, State University of New York	M,O
Concordia University Chicago	M
DeSales University	M,D,O
East Carolina University	M,O
Eastern Illinois University	M
Eastern Michigan University	O
Fielding Graduate University	M,D,O
Georgia State University	M,O
Kansas State University	M,O
Lakehead University	M,D
La Salle University	M,D,O
Lindenwood University	M,O
Loma Linda University	M,D
Long Island University–LIU Brooklyn	M,O
Long Island University–LIU Post	M,O
Marywood University	M
McDaniel College	M,O
Mercer University	M,D
Miami University	M,D
Middle Tennessee State University	O
Minnesota State University Mankato	M
Morehead State University	M
Mount Saint Vincent University	M
North Dakota State University	M,O
Northeastern Illinois University	M
Oregon Health & Science University	M,O
Portland State University	O
Sage Graduate School	M
St. Cloud State University	M
Saint Joseph's University	M
San Diego State University	M
San Francisco State University	M
Simon Fraser University	M,D
Slippery Rock University of Pennsylvania	M
Temple University	D*
Texas State University	M
Texas Tech University	M,D
Towson University	M,O
Université de Sherbrooke	M
Université Laval	O
The University of Akron	D
University of Arkansas at Little Rock	O
University of Central Missouri	M,D,O
University of Central Oklahoma	M
University of Georgia	O
University of Illinois at Springfield	M,O
University of Indianapolis	M,D,O
The University of Kansas	M,D,O*
University of Kentucky	D,O
University of La Verne	M,O
University of Louisiana at Monroe	M,O
University of Louisville	M,D,O
University of Maryland, Baltimore	M,D
University of Maryland, Baltimore County	M,D
University of Massachusetts Boston	M,D,O
University of Michigan–Flint	M,D,O
University of Missouri	M,D,O
University of Missouri–St. Louis	M,O
University of Nebraska at Omaha	M,O
University of Nebraska–Lincoln	M,D
The University of North Carolina at Charlotte	M,D,O
The University of North Carolina at Greensboro	M,O
The University of North Carolina Wilmington	M,O
University of Northern Colorado	M
University of North Florida	M,O
University of North Texas	M,D,O
University of Phoenix–Central Valley Campus	M
University of Phoenix–Charlotte Campus	M
University of Phoenix–Colorado Springs Downtown Campus	M
University of Phoenix–Hawaii Campus	M
University of Phoenix–Washington D.C. Campus	M,D
University of Puerto Rico, Medical Sciences Campus	M,O
University of Regina	M
University of Saint Joseph	O
University of South Carolina	O
University of Southern California	M,D,O
University of South Florida	M,D,O
The University of Tennessee	M
The University of Toledo	M,O
University of Utah	M,O*
University of West Florida	M
University of Wisconsin–Milwaukee	M,D,O
Virginia Commonwealth University	M,D,O
Walden University	M,D
Washington University in St. Louis	M,D,O
Wayne State University	M,D,O
Webster University	M
West Chester University of Pennsylvania	M,O
Wichita State University	M
Youngstown State University	M

GRAPHIC DESIGN

Academy of Art University	M
Atlantic University College	M
Bob Jones University	M,D,O
Boston University	M
Bowling Green State University	M
California College of the Arts	M
California Institute of the Arts	M,O
California State University, Fullerton	M
California State University, Los Angeles	M
Central Connecticut State University	M
City College of the City University of New York	M
Digital Media Arts College	M
East Carolina University	M
Florida Atlantic University	M
Full Sail University	M
George Mason University	M
Georgia Southern University	M
Georgia State University	M
Illinois State University	M
Indiana State University	M
Inter American University of Puerto Rico, San Germán Campus	M
Iowa State University of Science and Technology	M
Kent State University	M
Louisiana State University and Agricultural & Mechanical College	M
Louisiana Tech University	M
Maryland Institute College of Art	M,O
Marywood University	M
Minneapolis College of Art and Design	M,O
Morehead State University	M
New York Institute of Technology	M
New York University	M
North Carolina Agricultural and Technical State University	M
North Carolina State University	M
Ohio University	M
Otis College of Art and Design	M
Pittsburg State University	M,O
Pratt Institute	M*
Rhode Island School of Design	M
Rochester Institute of Technology	M
San Diego State University	M
Savannah College of Art and Design	M
School of the Art Institute of Chicago	M
School of Visual Arts (NY)	M
State University of New York at Oswego	M
Suffolk University	M
Temple University	M*
Texas State University	M
Université Laval	M
University of Baltimore	M,D
University of Cincinnati	M
University of Guam	M
University of Illinois at Chicago	M
University of Illinois at Urbana–Champaign	M
University of Memphis	M,O
University of Miami	M
University of Minnesota, Duluth	M
University of Notre Dame	M
University of Pennsylvania	M,O*
The University of South Dakota	M
The University of Tennessee	M
University of Utah	M*
Vermont College of Fine Arts	M
Wayne State University	M
Western Illinois University	M,O
West Virginia University	M
Yale University	M*

HAZARDOUS MATERIALS MANAGEMENT

Humboldt State University	M
Idaho State University	M
Marquette University	M,D,O
New Mexico Institute of Mining and Technology	M
Rutgers University–New Brunswick	M,D
Tufts University	M,D
University of Alaska Fairbanks	M,D,O
The University of Manchester	M,D
University of New Haven	M
University of South Carolina	M,D
University of Southern California	M,D,O

HEALTH COMMUNICATION

Arkansas State University	M,O
Boston University	M
Brandman University	M
Chapman University	M
Chatham University	M
Cleveland State University	M,O
Cornell University	M,D
DePaul University	M
East Carolina University	M
Emerson College	M
Fitchburg State University	M,O
Fontbonne University	M
Gannon University	M
The George Washington University	M,D*
Indiana University–Purdue University Indianapolis	M,D
Johns Hopkins University	M,D
Kansas State University	M
Lasell College	M,O
Marquette University	M,O
Michigan State University	M
Ohio University	M,D
Southern Illinois University Edwardsville	M
Stony Brook University, State University of New York	M,O
Tufts University	M,D,O
University of Florida	M,D,O
University of Houston	M
University of Missouri	M,D
University of Southern California	M,D
Wayne State University	M,D,O

HEALTH EDUCATION

Adelphi University	M,O
Alabama State University	M
Albany State University	M,O
Alcorn State University	M,O
Allen College	M,D,O
American University	M,O
Arcadia University	M
Arizona State University at the Tempe campus	D
Arkansas State University	M,D,O
A.T. Still University	M,D
Auburn University	M,D,O
Augusta University	M,O
Austin Peay State University	M
Baylor University	M,D
Benedictine University	M
Brandeis University	D
Brigham Young University	M
California Baptist University	M
California Institute of Integral Studies	M,D
California State University, Long Beach	M
California State University, Northridge	M,O
California State University, San Marcos	M
Cambridge College	M,D,O
Central Washington University	M
The Citadel, The Military College of South Carolina	M
Cleveland State University	M
The College at Brockport, State University of New York	M
The College of New Jersey	M
College of Saint Mary	D
Colorado State University–Pueblo	M
Columbus State University	M
Daemen College	M
Dalhousie University	M
Delta State University	M
Drew University	M,D,O
East Carolina University	M
Eastern Kentucky University	M
Eastern Michigan University	M,O
Eastern University	M,O
East Stroudsburg University of Pennsylvania	M
Emory University	M,D
Excelsior College	M,O
Fairfield University	M,D
Florida State University	M,D
Fort Hays State University	M
Framingham State University	M
Georgia College & State University	M
Georgia Southern University	M,D
Georgia State University	M
Grand Canyon University	D
Harding University	M,O
Howard University	M
Idaho State University	M
Illinois State University	M
Indiana State University	M,D
Indiana University Bloomington	M,D
Indiana University of Pennsylvania	M
Indiana University–Purdue University Indianapolis	M,D
Inter American University of Puerto Rico, Metropolitan Campus	M
Inter American University of Puerto Rico, San Germán Campus	M
Ithaca College	M
Jackson State University	M
James Madison University	M
John F. Kennedy University	M
Johns Hopkins University	M,D
Keiser University	M
Kent State University	M,D
Lake Erie College of Osteopathic Medicine	M,D,O
Lehman College of the City University of New York	M
Lock Haven University of Pennsylvania	M
Logan University	M,D
Loma Linda University	M,D
Longwood University	M
Marshall University	M
Marymount University	M
Marywood University	D
Massachusetts College of Liberal Arts	M,O
Middle Tennessee State University	M
Mills College	M,D,O
Minnesota State University Mankato	M,O
Mississippi University for Women	M
Montana State University	M
Montclair State University	M
Morehead State University	M
Mount Mary University	M
New Jersey City University	M
New Mexico Highlands University	M
New York Medical College	O
Nicholls State University	M
North Carolina Agricultural and Technical State University	M
Northeastern State University	M
Northwestern State University of Louisiana	M
Northwest Missouri State University	M
Oklahoma State University	M,D,O
Penn State Harrisburg	M,D,O
Pennsylvania College of Health Sciences	M
Pittsburg State University	M
Plymouth State University	M
Portland State University	M,D,O
Prairie View A&M University	M
Purdue University	M,D
Rhode Island College	M,O
Rosalind Franklin University of Medicine and Science	M
Rutgers University–Newark	M,D
Rutgers University–New Brunswick	M,D,O
Sage Graduate School	M
Saint Francis University	M
Saint Joseph's College of Maine	M
Saint Joseph's University	M
San Francisco State University	M
Shenandoah University	M,D,O
Simmons College	M,D,O
Southeastern Louisiana University	M
Southern Connecticut State University	M
Southern Illinois University Carbondale	M,D
Southern Illinois University Edwardsville	M,D,O

*M—masters degree; D—doctorate; O—other advanced degree; *—Close-Up and/or Display*

State University of New York College at Cortland	M
Teachers College, Columbia University	M,D,O
Tennessee Technological University	M
Texas A&M University	M,D
Texas A&M University–Kingsville	M
Texas Southern University	M
Texas State University	M
Texas Woman's University	M,D
Thomas Jefferson University	M,D,O
Trident University International	M,D,O
Union College (KY)	M
The University of Alabama	M,D
The University of Alabama at Birmingham	D
University of Arkansas	M,D
University of Arkansas at Little Rock	M,D
University of Arkansas for Medical Sciences	M,D,O
University of Central Arkansas	M
University of Cincinnati	M,D
University of Colorado Denver	M,D
University of Florida	M,D,O
University of Georgia	M,D,O
University of Houston	M,D
University of Illinois at Chicago	M
University of Illinois at Springfield	M,O
The University of Kansas	M,D,O*
University of Louisville	M,D,O
University of Maryland, Baltimore County	M,O
University of Maryland, College Park	M,D
University of Massachusetts Amherst	M,D*
University of Michigan	M,D
University of Michigan–Flint	M
University of Missouri	M,D,O
University of Missouri–Kansas City	M,D
University of Montana	M
University of Nebraska at Omaha	M,D
University of New England	M,O
University of New Mexico	M
University of Northern Colorado	M
University of Northern Iowa	M
University of Oklahoma	M,D*
University of Oklahoma Health Sciences Center	D
University of Phoenix–Charlotte Campus	M
University of Phoenix–Colorado Springs Downtown Campus	M
University of Phoenix–Online Campus	M,O
University of Phoenix–Washington D.C. Campus	M,D
University of Pittsburgh	M,D*
University of Puerto Rico, Medical Sciences Campus	M
University of Rhode Island	M
University of St. Augustine for Health Sciences	D
University of San Francisco	M
University of South Africa	M,D
University of South Alabama	M
University of South Carolina	M,D,O
University of Southern California	M
University of Southern Mississippi	M
The University of Tennessee	M
The University of Texas at Austin	M,D
The University of Texas at San Antonio	M
The University of Texas at Tyler	M
The University of Toledo	M,D,O
University of Utah	M,D*
University of Waterloo	M,D
University of West Florida	M
University of Wisconsin–La Crosse	M
University of Wisconsin–Milwaukee	M,D,O
University of Wyoming	M
Utah State University	M
Virginia Commonwealth University	M,O
Virginia State University	M,D
Walden University	M,D,O
Washburn University	M
Washington University in St. Louis	M,O
Wayne State University	M,D
West Chester University of Pennsylvania	M,O
Western Illinois University	M,O
Western Michigan University	D,O
Western Oregon University	M
Western University of Health Sciences	M
Widener University	M,D
Wingate University	M,D
Worcester State University	M
Wright State University	M

HEALTH INFORMATICS

Adelphi University	M,O
American Sentinel University	M
Arkansas Tech University	M
Augusta University	M
Barry University	O
Benedictine University	M
Boston University	M,O
Brandeis University	M
Brooklyn College of the City University of New York	M,O
Canisius College	M,O
Capella University	M,D
Chatham University	M
Claremont Graduate University	M,D,O
Clarkson University	M,O
The College of St. Scholastica	M,O
Colorado Mesa University	M,D,O
Dakota State University	M,D,O
DePaul University	M,D
Drexel University	M
Duke University	M*
East Carolina University	M
Emory University	M,D
Excelsior College	M,O
Georgia State University	M,D,O
Golden Gate University	M,D,O
Grand Canyon University	M
Indiana University Bloomington	M,D
Indiana University–Purdue University Indianapolis	M,D
Jacksonville University	M*
Johns Hopkins University	M,D,O
Kennesaw State University	M,O
Lipscomb University	M,D,O
Logan University	M,D
Louisiana Tech University	M
Marshall University	M
Marymount University	M,O
Metropolitan State University	M,D,O
Middle Georgia State University	M
Midwestern State University	M,O
Millennia Atlantic University	M
Molloy College	M,D,O
Montana Tech of The University of Montana	O
National University	M,D,O
Northeastern University	M,D,O
Northern Kentucky University	M,O
Northwestern University	D*
Nova Southeastern University	M,D,O*
Oregon Health & Science University	M,D,O
Roberts Wesleyan College	M
Sacred Heart University	M
St. Joseph's College, Long Island Campus	M
St. Joseph's College, New York	M
Shenandoah University	M,D,O
Southern Illinois University Edwardsville	M
Southern New Hampshire University	M,O
Stephens College	M,O
Stevens Institute of Technology	M,D,O
Temple University	M*
Texas State University	M
Trident University International	M,D,O
The University of Alabama at Birmingham	M
University of Central Florida	M,O
The University of Findlay	M,D
University of Illinois at Chicago	M,O
University of Illinois at Urbana–Champaign	M,D,O
The University of Iowa	M,D,O*
The University of Kansas	M,O*
University of Maryland, Baltimore County	M
University of Maryland University College	M,O
University of Michigan	M,D
University of Michigan–Dearborn	M
University of Minnesota, Twin Cities Campus	M,D
University of Missouri	M,O
The University of North Carolina at Charlotte	M,O
University of Phoenix–Charlotte Campus	M
University of Phoenix–Online Campus	M,O
University of Phoenix–Washington D.C. Campus	M,D
University of Puerto Rico, Medical Sciences Campus	M
University of San Diego	M,D
University of South Carolina Upstate	M
University of South Florida	M,D,O
The University of Tennessee Health Science Center	M,D
The University of Texas Health Science Center at Houston	M,D,O
University of Toronto	M
University of Victoria	M
University of Virginia	M
University of Washington	M,D*
University of Waterloo	M,D
University of Wisconsin–Milwaukee	M
Virginia International University	M,O
Walden University	M,D,O
Weill Cornell Medicine	M

HEALTH LAW

Baylor University	D
Cleveland State University	M,D,O
DePaul University	M,D
Georgetown University	M,D
Hofstra University	M,D
Loyola University Chicago	M,D
Nova Southeastern University	M,D*
Seton Hall University	M,D
Southern Illinois University Carbondale	M
Suffolk University	M,D
Université de Sherbrooke	M,D,O
University of California, San Diego	M
University of Houston	M,D
The University of Manchester	M,D
University of Pittsburgh	M*
The University of Tulsa	M,D,O
Widener University	M,D

HEALTH PHYSICS/RADIOLOGICAL HEALTH

East Carolina University	M,D
Georgetown University	M
Georgia Institute of Technology	M,D
Idaho State University	M,D
Illinois Institute of Technology	M,D
McMaster University	M,D
Midwestern State University	M
Northwestern State University of Louisiana	M
Oregon State University	M,D
Purdue University	M,D
Quinnipiac University	M
Rutgers University–Newark	M
San Diego State University	M
Texas A&M University	M,D
Thomas Jefferson University	M
Université Laval	O
University of Alberta	M,D
University of Arkansas for Medical Sciences	M,D
University of Cincinnati	M
University of Kentucky	M
University of Massachusetts Lowell	M
University of Michigan	M,D,O
University of Missouri	M
University of Nevada, Las Vegas	M,D,O
University of Oklahoma Health Sciences Center	M,D
University of Toronto	M,D
Vanderbilt University	M,D*
Virginia Commonwealth University	D
Weber State University	M

HEALTH PROMOTION

American University	M
American University of Beirut	M
Arizona State University at the Tempe campus	M,D
Auburn University	M,D,O
Ball State University	M
Baylor University	M,D
Benedictine University	M
Boise State University	M,O
Bridgewater State University	M
Brigham Young University	M,D
California Baptist University	M
California State University, Fresno	M
Claremont Graduate University	M,D
Cleveland University–Kansas City	M
Concord University	M
East Carolina University	M
Eastern Kentucky University	M
Eastern Michigan University	M,O
Emory University	M
Fairmont State University	M
Florida Atlantic University	M
Florida International University	M,D
George Mason University	M,D,O
Georgetown University	M,D
Georgia College & State University	M
Goddard College	M
Harvard University	M,D*
Immaculata University	M
Independence University	M
Indiana University Bloomington	M,D
Instituto Tecnologico de Santo Domingo	M,O
Kent State University	M,D
Lehman College of the City University of New York	M
Liberty University	M,D,O
Lindenwood University	M
Lock Haven University of Pennsylvania	M
Manhattanville College	M,O*
Marymount University	M
McNeese State University	M
Merrimack College	M
Mississippi State University	M,D
Mount St. Joseph University	M,O
National University	M,D,O
Nebraska Methodist College	M
New York Medical College	M,O
New York University	M,D,O
North Dakota State University	M,D
Old Dominion University	M
Oregon State University	M,D
Plymouth State University	M
Portland State University	M,D,O
Rosalind Franklin University of Medicine and Science	M
Rowan University	M
San Diego State University	M,D
Simmons College	M,D,O
Sonoma State University	M
Springfield College	M,D
Tennessee Technological University	M
Texas A&M University	M,D
Union Institute & University	M
Universidad del Turabo	M
The University of Alabama	M,D
The University of Alabama at Birmingham	D
University of Alberta	M,O
University of Arkansas	M,D
University of Arkansas for Medical Sciences	M,D,O
University of Central Oklahoma	M
University of Chicago	M,D
University of Delaware	M*
University of Georgia	M,D
University of Kentucky	M,D
University of Louisville	M,D
University of Massachusetts Lowell	D
University of Michigan	M,D
University of Mississippi	M,D
University of Missouri	M,O
University of Nebraska–Lincoln	M,D
University of Nebraska Medical Center	D
University of North Alabama	M
The University of North Carolina at Chapel Hill	M
University of Northern Iowa	M
University of Oklahoma	M,D*
University of Oklahoma Health Sciences Center	M,D
University of Puerto Rico, Medical Sciences Campus	O
University of South Carolina	M,D,O
University of Southern California	M
The University of Tennessee	M
University of the Incarnate Word	M
The University of Toledo	M,D,O
University of Toronto	M,D
University of Utah	M,D*
University of Wisconsin–Milwaukee	M,D,O
University of Wisconsin–Stevens Point	M
University of Wyoming	M
Walden University	M,D,O
West Virginia University	M,D
Wilfrid Laurier University	M
Wright State University	M

HEALTH PSYCHOLOGY

Adler University	M,D,O
Alliant International University–Los Angeles	D
Appalachian State University	M
Argosy University, Atlanta	M,D,O
Argosy University, Chicago	D
Argosy University, Twin Cities	M,D,O
Argosy University, Washington DC	M,D
Bastyr University	M,O
California Institute of Integral Studies	M,D
California State University, Dominguez Hills	M
Central Connecticut State University	M
Central Michigan University	M,D
Chatham University	M,D
Claremont Graduate University	M,D,O
Connecticut College	M
Drexel University	D
Duke University	D*
East Carolina University	M,D
Fielding Graduate University	M,D,O
Georgian Court University	M,O
John F. Kennedy University	M
La Salle University	M,D
Lesley University	M,D,O
North Dakota State University	M,D
Northern Kentucky University	M,O
Oklahoma State University	M,D,O
Oregon State University	M,D
Penn State Harrisburg	M,D,O
Prescott College	M
Rhode Island College	M,O
Rutgers University–New Brunswick	D
San Diego State University	M,D
Saybrook University	M,D
Southwestern College (NM)	O
Stony Brook University, State University of New York	D
United States International University–Africa	M
The University of Alabama at Birmingham	M,D
The University of British Columbia	M,D
University of Colorado Denver	M,D
University of Florida	M,D
University of Michigan–Dearborn	M
University of Missouri–Kansas City	M,D
University of New Mexico	D
The University of North Carolina at Chapel Hill	M,D
The University of North Carolina at Charlotte	M,D,O
The University of Texas at Arlington	M,D
University of the Sciences	M
Virginia Commonwealth University	D
Virginia State University	M,D
Viterbo University	M
Walden University	M,D,O
Yeshiva University	D

HEALTH SERVICES MANAGEMENT AND HOSPITAL ADMINISTRATION

Adelphi University	M
Alaska Pacific University	M
Albany State University	M
American InterContinental University Online	M
American Public University System	M
American Sentinel University	M
American University of Beirut	M
Aquinas College (MI)	M
Aquinas Institute of Theology	M,D,O
Argosy University, Atlanta	M,D
Argosy University, Chicago	M,D
Argosy University, Dallas	M,D,O
Argosy University, Denver	M,D
Argosy University, Hawai`i	M,D,O
Argosy University, Inland Empire	M,D
Argosy University, Los Angeles	M,D
Argosy University, Nashville	M,D
Argosy University, Orange County	M,D,O
Argosy University, Phoenix	M,D
Argosy University, Salt Lake City	M,D
Argosy University, San Francisco Bay Area	M,D
Argosy University, Sarasota	M,D,O
Argosy University, Schaumburg	M,D,O
Argosy University, Seattle	M,D
Argosy University, Tampa	M,D
Argosy University, Twin Cities	M,D
Argosy University, Washington DC	M,D,O
Arizona State University at the Tempe campus	M,D
Arkansas State University	M,D,O
Armstrong State University	M
Ashworth College	M
Assumption College	M,O

A.T. Still University	M,D
Auburn University at Montgomery	M,D,O
Avila University	M
Baker College Center for Graduate Studies–Online	M,D
Baldwin Wallace University	M
Barry University	M,O
Baruch College of the City University of New York	M
Baylor University	M
Belhaven University (MS)	M
Bellevue University	M
Belmont University	M
Benedictine University	M
Binghamton University, State University of New York	M,D*
Bluffton University	M
Boston University	M,D
Brandeis University	M
Brandman University	M
Brenau University	M
Broadview University–West Jordan	M
Brooklyn College of the City University of New York	M
California Baptist University	M
California Coast University	M
California Intercontinental University	M,D
California State University, Bakersfield	M
California State University, Chico	M
California State University, East Bay	M
California State University, Fresno	M
California State University, Long Beach	M
California State University, Los Angeles	M,O
California State University, Northridge	M
California State University, San Bernardino	M
Cambridge College	M
Capella University	M,D
Carlow University	M
Carnegie Mellon University	M
Case Western Reserve University	M*
Central Michigan University	M,D,O
Champlain College	M
Clarkson University	M,O
Cleary University	M,O
Cleveland State University	M,O
The College at Brockport, State University of New York	M,O
College of Saint Elizabeth	M
Colorado Heights University	M
Colorado State University–Global Campus	M
Columbia Southern University	M
Columbia University	M*
Columbus State University	M
Concordia University, St. Paul	M
Concordia University Wisconsin	M
Copenhagen Business School	M,D
Cornell University	M,D
Daemen College	M
Dalhousie University	M,D
Dallas Baptist University	M
Dartmouth College	M,D*
Davenport University	M
Defiance College	M
Delta State University	M,D
DePaul University	M
DeSales University	M
Des Moines University	M
Dominican College	M
Drew University	M,D,O
Duke University	M,O*
Duquesne University	M,D
D'Youville College	M,D,O
Eastern Kentucky University	M
Eastern Mennonite University	M
Eastern Michigan University	M,O
Eastern University	M
East Tennessee State University	M,O
Ellis University	M
Elms College	M
Emory University	M,D
Excelsior College	M,O
Fairleigh Dickinson University, College at Florham	M
Fairleigh Dickinson University, Metropolitan Campus	M
Felician University	M
Florida Institute of Technology	M
Florida International University	M,D
Florida National University	M
Framingham State University	M
Francis Marion University	M
Franklin Pierce University	M,D,O
Friends University	M
George Mason University	M,D
The George Washington University	M,D,O*
Georgia Institute of Technology	M
Georgia Southern University	M,D
Georgia State University	M,D,O
Globe University–Woodbury	M
Goldey-Beacom College	M
Goldfarb School of Nursing at Barnes-Jewish College	M
Governors State University	M
Grambling State University	M
Grand Canyon University	M,O
Grand Valley State University	M,D
Grantham University	M
Gwynedd Mercy University	M
Harding University	M
Harrisburg University of Science and Technology	M
Harvard University	M,D*
Herzing University Online	M
Hilbert College	M
Hodges University	M
Hofstra University	M,O
Holy Family University	M
Hunter College of the City University of New York	M
Husson University	M
Independence University	M
Indiana Tech	M
Indiana University Bloomington	M,D
Indiana University Kokomo	M,O
Indiana University Northwest	M,O
Indiana University of Pennsylvania	M,D
Indiana University–Purdue University Indianapolis	M,D
Indiana Wesleyan University	M,O
Institute of Public Administration	M,O
Iona College	M,O
Johns Hopkins University	M,D,O
Kaplan University, Davenport Campus	M,O
Kean University	M
Keiser University	M
Kennesaw State University	M
King's College	M
King University	M
Lake Erie College	M
Lake Forest Graduate School of Management	M
Lakeland University	M
Lamar University	M
Lasell College	M,O
Lebanon Valley College	M
Lehigh University	M
Lenoir-Rhyne University	M
LeTourneau University	M
Lewis University	M
Liberty University	M,D,O
Lindenwood University	M,O
Lindenwood University–Belleville	M
Lipscomb University	M,O
Lock Haven University of Pennsylvania	M
Loma Linda University	M
London Metropolitan University	M,D
Long Island University–Hudson at Westchester	M,O
Long Island University–LIU Brooklyn	M,O
Louisiana State University Health Sciences Center	M,D
Louisiana State University in Shreveport	M
Loyola University Chicago	M,O
Loyola University New Orleans	M,D
Madonna University	M
Marshall University	M
Marylhurst University	M
Marymount University	M
Maryville University of Saint Louis	M,O
Marywood University	M
McGill University	M,D,O
MCPHS University	M
Medical University of South Carolina	M,D
Meharry Medical College	M
Mercy College	M
Metropolitan College of New York	M
Midwestern State University	M,O
Milwaukee School of Engineering	M*
Minnesota State University Moorhead	M,O
Misericordia University	M
Mississippi College	M
Missouri State University	M
Molloy College	M
Montana State University Billings	M
Moravian College	M
Mount Aloysius College	M
Mount Ida College	M
Mount St. Joseph University	D
Mount Saint Mary's University (CA)	M,D,O
Mount St. Mary's University (MD)	M
National University	M,D,O
Nebraska Methodist College	M
New Charter University	M
New England College	M
New Jersey City University	M
New Jersey Institute of Technology	M,D
New York Medical College	M,D,O
New York University	M,D,O
Niagara University	M
Northeast Ohio Medical University	M,D,O
Northwestern University	M,D*
Northwest Nazarene University	M
Ohio Dominican University	M
The Ohio State University	M,D
Ohio University	M
Oklahoma Christian University	M
Oklahoma State University Center for Health Sciences	M
Oregon Health & Science University	M,O
Oregon State University	M,D
Our Lady of the Lake College	M
Our Lady of the Lake University of San Antonio	M
Pace University	M
Pacific University	M
Park University	M,O
Penn State Great Valley	M,O
Penn State Harrisburg	M,D,O
Penn State University Park	M,D
Pennsylvania College of Health Sciences	M
Pfeiffer University	M
Point Loma Nazarene University	M
Portland State University	M,D
Post University	M
Queen's University at Kingston	M,D
Quinnipiac University	M
Regent University	M,D,O
Regis College (MA)	M,D,O
Regis University	M,D,O
Rice University	M
Robert Morris University Illinois	M
Roberts Wesleyan College	M
Rochester Institute of Technology	M,O
Rockhurst University	M,O
Roger Williams University	M
Rollins College	M
Rosalind Franklin University of Medicine and Science	M,O
Royal Roads University	O
Rush University	M,D
Rutgers University–Camden	M,O
Rutgers University–Newark	M,D,O
Rutgers University–New Brunswick	M,D,O
Sage Graduate School	M,D,O
Saginaw Valley State University	M
St. Ambrose University	M,D
St. Catherine University	M
St. Joseph's College, Long Island Campus	M
St. Joseph's College, New York	M
Saint Joseph's College of Maine	M
Saint Joseph's University	M,O
Saint Leo University	M
Saint Louis University	M,D
Saint Mary's University of Minnesota	M
St. Norbert College	M
Saint Peter's University	M
St. Thomas University	M,O
Saint Xavier University	M,O
Salve Regina University	M,O
Samford University	M,D
San Diego State University	M,D
San Francisco State University	M
Seton Hall University	M,D,O
Shenandoah University	M,O
Siena Heights University	M,O
Simmons College	M
Southeast Missouri State University	M
Southern Adventist University	M
Southern Illinois University Carbondale	M
Southern Nazarene University	M
Southern New Hampshire University	M,O
South University	M
South University (SC)	M
South University (GA)	M
South University (AL)	M
South University	M
Southwest Baptist University	M
Stevenson University	M
Stony Brook University, State University of New York	M,D,O
Stratford University (VA)	M,D
Strayer University	M
Suffolk University	M,O
Syracuse University	O
Temple University	M*
Texas A&M University	M,D
Texas A&M University–Corpus Christi	M
Texas A&M University–San Antonio	M
Texas Health and Science University	M,D
Texas Southern University	M
Texas State University	M
Texas Tech University	M,D
Texas Tech University Health Sciences Center	M
Texas Woman's University	M,D
Thomas Jefferson University	M,D,O
Tiffin University	M
Towson University	M,O
Trident University International	M,D,O
Trinity University	M
Trinity Western University	M,O
Troy University	M
Tufts University	M,D,O
Tulane University	M,D
Uniformed Services University of the Health Sciences	M,D*
Universidad de Ciencias Medicas	M,D,O
Universidad de Iberoamerica	M,D
Université de Montréal	M,O
University at Albany, State University of New York	M,D,O
University at Buffalo, the State University of New York	M,D,O*
The University of Akron	M
The University of Alabama at Birmingham	M,D
The University of Alabama in Huntsville	M,D,O
University of Alberta	M,D
University of Arkansas for Medical Sciences	M,D,O
University of Baltimore	M
The University of British Columbia	M,D
University of California, Berkeley	D
University of California, Irvine	M
University of California, Los Angeles	M,D
University of California, San Diego	M
University of Central Florida	M,O
University of Chicago	M,O
University of Colorado Denver	M,D
University of Connecticut	M,D*
University of Dallas	M,D
University of Detroit Mercy	M,D,O
University of Evansville	M
The University of Findlay	M,D
University of Florida	M,D
University of Georgia	M
University of Houston–Clear Lake	M
University of Illinois at Chicago	M,D
University of Illinois at Urbana–Champaign	M,D
The University of Iowa	M,D*
The University of Kansas	M,D*
University of Kentucky	M
University of La Verne	M,D,O
University of Louisville	M
University of Management and Technology	M
University of Mary	M
University of Maryland, Baltimore County	M,D,O
University of Maryland, College Park	M,D
University of Maryland University College	M,O
University of Massachusetts Amherst	M,D*
University of Massachusetts Dartmouth	M
University of Memphis	M
University of Michigan	M,D
University of Michigan–Flint	M
University of Minnesota, Twin Cities Campus	M,D
University of Missouri	M,D,O
University of Nevada, Las Vegas	M
University of New Haven	M,O
University of New Mexico	M
University of New Orleans	M
University of North Alabama	M
The University of North Carolina at Chapel Hill	M,D
The University of North Carolina at Charlotte	M,D,O
University of North Florida	M,O
University of North Texas	M,D,O
University of North Texas Health Science Center at Fort Worth	M,D
University of Oklahoma	M,O*
University of Oklahoma Health Sciences Center	M,D
University of Ottawa	M
University of Pennsylvania	M,D*
University of Phoenix–Atlanta Campus	M
University of Phoenix–Augusta Campus	M
University of Phoenix–Bay Area Campus	M,D
University of Phoenix–Central Valley Campus	M
University of Phoenix–Charlotte Campus	M
University of Phoenix–Colorado Campus	M
University of Phoenix–Colorado Springs Downtown Campus	M
University of Phoenix–Hawaii Campus	M
University of Phoenix–Houston Campus	M
University of Phoenix–New Mexico Campus	M
University of Phoenix–North Florida Campus	M
University of Phoenix–Online Campus	M,D,O
University of Phoenix–Phoenix Campus	M,O
University of Phoenix–Sacramento Valley Campus	M
University of Phoenix–San Antonio Campus	M
University of Phoenix–Southern California Campus	M
University of Phoenix–South Florida Campus	M
University of Phoenix–Washington D.C. Campus	M,D
University of Pittsburgh	M,D,O*
University of Portland	M
University of Puerto Rico, Medical Sciences Campus	M
University of Regina	M,D,O
University of Rhode Island	M,D
University of Rochester	M,D*
University of St. Francis (IL)	M
University of Saint Francis (IN)	M
University of Saint Mary	M
University of St. Thomas (MN)	M
University of San Francisco	M
University of Saskatchewan	M
The University of Scranton	M
University of Sioux Falls	M
University of South Africa	M,D
University of South Carolina	M,D
The University of South Dakota	M
University of Southern California	M,O
University of Southern Indiana	M
University of Southern Maine	M
University of Southern Mississippi	M
University of South Florida	M,D,O
The University of Tennessee	M
The University of Texas at Arlington	M
The University of Texas at Dallas	M,D*
The University of Texas at El Paso	M,D,O
The University of Texas at Tyler	M

*M—masters degree; D—doctorate; O—other advanced degree; *—Close-Up and/or Display*

University of the Incarnate Word	M
University of the Sciences	M,D
The University of Toledo	M,O
University of Toronto	M
University of Utah	M,D*
University of Virginia	M
University of Washington	M*
The University of Western Ontario	M,D
University of West Georgia	M,D,O
University of Wisconsin–Oshkosh	M
University of Wyoming	M,D
Utica College	M
Valdosta State University	M
Valparaiso University	M
Vanderbilt University	M*
Villanova University	M
Virginia College in Birmingham	M
Virginia Commonwealth University	M,D
Virginia International University	M,O
Viterbo University	M
Wagner College	M
Walden University	M,D,O
Walsh University	M,O
Washington Adventist University	M
Washington State University	M
Wayland Baptist University	M,D
Waynesburg University	M,D
Wayne State University	M,D
Weber State University	M
Webster University	M
West Chester University of Pennsylvania	M,O
West Coast University	M,D
Western Carolina University	M
Western Connecticut State University	M
Western Governors University	M
Western Illinois University	M,O
Western Kentucky University	M
Western Michigan University	M,D,O
Widener University	M
Wilkes University	M
William Woods University	M,D,O
Wilmington University	M,D
Wilson College	M
Winston-Salem State University	M
Worcester State University	M
Wright State University	M
Xavier University	M
Yale University	M,D*
York College of Pennsylvania	M
Youngstown State University	M

HEALTH SERVICES RESEARCH

Albany College of Pharmacy and Health Sciences	M,D
Brown University	D
Case Western Reserve University	M,D*
Clarkson University	M
Dartmouth College	M,D*
Emory University	M,D
Florida Agricultural and Mechanical University	M,D
The George Washington University	M,D,O*
Johns Hopkins University	M,D
Lakehead University	M
McMaster University	M,D
Northwestern University	D*
Old Dominion University	D
Penn State Hershey Medical Center	M
Stanford University	M,D
Texas A&M University	M,D
Thomas Jefferson University	M,D,O
The University of Alabama at Birmingham	M,D
University of Alberta	M,D
University of Arkansas for Medical Sciences	M,D,O
University of Cincinnati	M
University of Colorado Denver	M,D
University of Florida	M,D
University of Illinois at Chicago	M,D
University of La Verne	M
University of Maryland, Baltimore	M,D
University of Massachusetts Medical School	M,D
University of Minnesota, Twin Cities Campus	M,D
University of Nebraska Medical Center	D
University of New Brunswick Fredericton	M
The University of North Carolina at Charlotte	D
University of Ottawa	D,O
University of Pennsylvania	M*
University of Puerto Rico, Medical Sciences Campus	M
University of Rochester	M,D*
University of Southern California	D
The University of Tennessee Health Science Center	M,D
University of Utah	M,D*
University of Virginia	M
University of Washington	M,D*
Virginia Commonwealth University	D
Wake Forest University	M
Washington University in St. Louis	M,O
Weill Cornell Medicine	M

HIGHER EDUCATION

Abilene Christian University	M
Alliant International University–San Diego	M,D,O
Alliant International University–San Francisco	M,D,O
Andrews University	M,D,O
Angelo State University	M
Appalachian State University	M,O
Argosy University, Atlanta	M,D,O
Argosy University, Chicago	M,D,O
Argosy University, Dallas	M,D
Argosy University, Denver	M,D
Argosy University, Hawai`i	M,D
Argosy University, Inland Empire	M,D
Argosy University, Los Angeles	M,D
Argosy University, Nashville	M,D,O
Argosy University, Orange County	M,D
Argosy University, Phoenix	M,D,O
Argosy University, San Diego	M,D
Argosy University, San Francisco Bay Area	M,D
Argosy University, Sarasota	M,D,O
Argosy University, Seattle	M,D
Argosy University, Tampa	M,D,O
Argosy University, Twin Cities	M,D,O
Argosy University, Washington DC	M,D,O
Arizona State University at the Tempe campus	M
Auburn University	M,D,O
Aurora University	M,D
Azusa Pacific University	M,D
Ball State University	M,D
Barry University	M,D
Baruch College of the City University of New York	M
Bay Path University	M
Benedictine University	D
Boston College	M,D
Bowling Green State University	D
California Baptist University	M
California Lutheran University	M,D
California State University, Fullerton	M,D
California State University, Long Beach	M
California State University, Sacramento	M
Capella University	M,D
Central Michigan University	M,D,O
Chicago State University	M,D
Claremont Graduate University	M,D,O
Clemson University	M,D,O
Cleveland State University	D
College of Saint Elizabeth	M,D,O
The College of Saint Rose	M,O
Colorado State University	M,D
Columbia College (SC)	M
Columbus State University	M,D,O
Dallas Baptist University	M
Delta State University	D
Drexel University	M,D
Eastern Kentucky University	M
Eastern Michigan University	M,D,O
Florida Atlantic University	M,D,O
Florida International University	M,D,O
Florida State University	M,D
Geneva College	M
George Mason University	M,D,O
The George Washington University	M,D,O*
Georgia Southern University	M
Grambling State University	M,D,O
Grand Canyon University	D
Grand Valley State University	M,O
Illinois State University	M,D
Indiana State University	M,D,O
Indiana University Bloomington	M,D,O
Indiana University of Pennsylvania	M
Indiana University–Purdue University Indianapolis	M,O
Indiana Wesleyan University	M
Inter American University of Puerto Rico, Metropolitan Campus	M
Iowa State University of Science and Technology	M,D
James Madison University	M
John Brown University	M
Johnson University	M,D,O
Kaplan University, Davenport Campus	M
Kent State University	M,D,O
Lee University	M,O
Lewis University	M
Lincoln Memorial University	M,D,O
London Metropolitan University	M,D
Louisiana State University and Agricultural & Mechanical College	M,D,O
Louisiana Tech University	M,D
Loyola Marymount University	M
Loyola University Chicago	M,D
Lynchburg College	M
Maryville University of Saint Louis	M,D
Marywood University	M,D
McKendree University	M,D,O
Mercer University	M,D,O
Mercyhurst University	M,O
Merrimack College	M,O
Messiah College	M
Michigan State University	M,D,O
Minnesota State University Mankato	M
Mississippi College	M,D,O
Mississippi State University	M,D,O
Missouri State University	M
Montana State University	M,D,O
Morehead State University	M,O
Morgan State University	M,D
New England College	M,D
New York University	M,D
North Carolina State University	M,D
North Dakota State University	O
Northeastern University	M,D
Northern Arizona University	M,D,O
Northern Illinois University	M,D
Northern Michigan University	M
Oakland University	M,D,O
Ohio University	M,D
Oklahoma State University	M,D
Old Dominion University	M,D,O
Oral Roberts University	M,D
Oregon State University	M
Phillips Theological Seminary	M,D
Plymouth State University	D,O
Purdue University	M,D,O
Regent University	M,D,O
Regis College (MA)	M,D
Robert Morris University	M,D,O
Robert Morris University Illinois	M
Rowan University	M
St. Cloud State University	M,D
Saint Louis University	M,D,O
Saint Peter's University	D
Salem State University	M
Sam Houston State University	M,D
San Diego State University	M
San Jose State University	M,D,O
Seton Hall University	D
Shippensburg University of Pennsylvania	M
Siena Heights University	M,O
Slippery Rock University of Pennsylvania	M
Southeast Missouri State University	M,D,O
Southern Arkansas University–Magnolia	M
Southern Illinois University Carbondale	M
Southern Illinois University Edwardsville	M
Stony Brook University, State University of New York	M,O
Syracuse University	M,D
Taylor University	M
Teachers College, Columbia University	M,D
Texas Southern University	M,D
Texas State University	M
Texas Tech University	M,D
Tiffin University	M
Trident University International	M,D
Union University	M,D,O
Universidad Central del Este	M
Université de Sherbrooke	M,O
University at Buffalo, the State University of New York	M,D,O*
The University of Akron	M
The University of Alabama	M,D
The University of Arizona	M,D
University of Arkansas	M,D,O
University of Arkansas at Little Rock	M,D
The University of British Columbia	M,D
University of California, Riverside	M,D,O
University of Central Florida	M,D,O
University of Central Oklahoma	M
University of Dayton	D
University of Delaware	M,D,O*
University of Denver	M,D,O
University of Florida	M,D,O
University of Georgia	D
University of Houston	M,D
University of Houston–Victoria	M
The University of Iowa	M,D*
The University of Kansas	M,D*
University of Kentucky	M,D
University of Louisville	M,D,O
University of Maine	M,D,O
University of Manitoba	M
University of Mary Hardin-Baylor	M,D
University of Massachusetts Amherst	M,D,O*
University of Memphis	M,D
University of Miami	M,D,O
University of Minnesota, Twin Cities Campus	M,D
University of Missouri	M,D,O
University of Missouri–Kansas City	M,D,O
University of Missouri–St. Louis	M,D,O
University of Nevada, Las Vegas	M,D,O
University of New Hampshire	O
University of New Mexico	O
The University of North Carolina at Greensboro	D
The University of North Carolina Wilmington	M,D
University of Northern Colorado	D
University of Northern Iowa	M
University of North Texas	M,D,O
University of Oklahoma	M,D,O*
University of Pennsylvania	M,D*
University of Phoenix–Bay Area Campus	M,D,O
University of Phoenix–Online Campus	D,O
University of Phoenix–Washington D.C. Campus	M,D,O
University of Pittsburgh	M,D*
University of Rochester	M,D*
University of St. Francis (IL)	M,D,O
University of San Diego	M,D,O
University of South Carolina	M
The University of South Dakota	M,D,O
University of Southern California	D
University of Southern Maine	M,O
University of Southern Mississippi	M,D
University of South Florida	M,D,O
The University of Texas at Arlington	M,D
The University of Texas at San Antonio	M,D
University of the Incarnate Word	M,D
The University of Toledo	M,D,O
University of Utah	M,D*
University of Virginia	M,D,O
University of Washington	M,D*
The University of West Alabama	M
University of Wisconsin–La Crosse	M,D
University of Wisconsin–Madison	M,D,O
University of Wisconsin–Milwaukee	M,O
Upper Iowa University	M
Vanderbilt University	M,D*
Virginia Polytechnic Institute and State University	M,D,O
Walden University	M,D,O
Walsh University	M
Wayland Baptist University	M
Wayne State University	M,D,O
West Chester University of Pennsylvania	M,O
Western Governors University	M,O
Western Kentucky University	M
Western Michigan University	M,D
Western Washington University	M
West Virginia University	M,D
Wilkes University	M,D
Wilmington University	M,D
Wright State University	M,O

HISPANIC AND LATIN AMERICAN LANGUAGES

Boston University	M,D
Brigham Young University	M
California State University, San Marcos	M
Cornell University	D
Eastern Michigan University	M,O
The Graduate Center, City University of New York	D
Indiana University Bloomington	M,D
Indiana University of Pennsylvania	M
Michigan State University	M,D
Queens College of the City University of New York	M
Stony Brook University, State University of New York	M,D
Université de Montréal	M,D
University of California, Berkeley	D
University of California, Los Angeles	D
University of California, Santa Barbara	M,D
University of Colorado Boulder	M,D
University of Illinois at Chicago	M,D
University of Massachusetts Amherst	M,D*
University of Minnesota, Twin Cities Campus	M,D
The University of North Carolina at Greensboro	M,O
University of Pittsburgh	M,D*
The University of Texas at Austin	M,D
University of Washington	M*

HISPANIC STUDIES

Brown University	D
California State University, Los Angeles	M
California State University, Northridge	M
California State University, San Marcos	M
The Catholic University of America	M,D
Columbia University	M,D*
Eastern Michigan University	M,O
La Salle University	M,O
Louisiana State University and Agricultural & Mechanical College	M
McGill University	M,D
Michigan State University	M,D
Oregon State University	M
Pontifical Catholic University of Puerto Rico	M,O
Queen's University at Kingston	M
St. Thomas University	M,O
San Jose State University	M,O
Texas A&M International University	M,D
University of Alberta	M,D
The University of British Columbia	M,D
University of California, Riverside	M,D
University of California, Santa Barbara	M,D
University of Houston	M,D
University of Illinois at Chicago	M,D
University of Kentucky	M,D
The University of Manchester	M,D
University of Nevada, Las Vegas	M
The University of North Carolina at Greensboro	M,O
University of Puerto Rico, Mayagüez Campus	M
University of Puerto Rico, Rí o Piedras Campus	M,D
The University of Texas at Austin	M
University of Victoria	M
Villanova University	M

HISTORIC PRESERVATION

The American University of Rome	M
Arkansas State University	M,D
Ball State University	M
Boston Architectural College	M
Boston University	M
Buffalo State College, State University of New York	M,O
Clemson University	M
Cleveland State University	M,O
College of Charleston	M
Columbia University	M,O*
Cornell University	M,D
Delaware State University	M
Eastern Michigan University	M,O
The George Washington University	M,D*
Georgia State University	M,D
Goucher College	M
Michigan Technological University	M,D
Morgan State University	M,D
New York University	M
Penn State Harrisburg	M,D,O
Plymouth State University	M
Pratt Institute	M*
Roger Williams University	M
Rutgers University–New Brunswick	M,D,O
St. Cloud State University	M
Savannah College of Art and Design	M,O
School of the Art Institute of Chicago	M

Southeast Missouri State University	M,O
Syracuse University	O
Texas Tech University	M,D
Universidad Nacional Pedro Henriquez Urena	M
University at Buffalo, the State University of New York	M,D,O*
University of California, Los Angeles	M
University of Colorado Denver	M
University of Delaware	M,D*
University of Florida	M,D
University of Georgia	M
University of Hawaii at Manoa	O
University of Kentucky	M
University of Maryland, College Park	M,O
University of Massachusetts Amherst	M*
University of New Mexico	O
The University of North Carolina at Greensboro	M,O
University of Oregon	M
University of Pennsylvania	M,O*
University of Rochester	M*
University of South Carolina	M,O
The University of Texas at Austin	M
University of Vermont	M
University of Washington	O*
University of Wisconsin–Milwaukee	M,D,O
Ursuline College	M
Virginia Commonwealth University	O

HISTORY

Adams State University	M
American Public University System	M
American University	M,D
American University of Beirut	M,D
Appalachian State University	M
Arizona State University at the Tempe campus	M,D,O
Arkansas State University	M,O
Arkansas Tech University	M
Armstrong State University	M
Ashland University	M
Auburn University	M,D,O
Ball State University	M
Baylor University	M,D
Binghamton University, State University of New York	M,D*
Bob Jones University	M,D,O
Boise State University	M
Boston College	M,D
Boston University	M,D
Bowling Green State University	M,D
Brandeis University	M,D
Brock University	M
Brooklyn College of the City University of New York	M
Brown University	M,D
Buffalo State College, State University of New York	M
Butler University	M
California Polytechnic State University, San Luis Obispo	M
California State Polytechnic University, Pomona	M
California State University, Bakersfield	M
California State University, Chico	M
California State University, East Bay	M
California State University, Fresno	M
California State University, Fullerton	M
California State University, Long Beach	M
California State University, Los Angeles	M
California State University, Northridge	M
California State University, San Marcos	M
California State University, Stanislaus	M
Carleton University	M,D
Carnegie Mellon University	D
Case Western Reserve University	M,D*
The Catholic University of America	M,D
Central Connecticut State University	M,O
Central European University	M,D
Central Michigan University	M,O
Central Washington University	M
Centro de Estudios Avanzados de Puerto Rico y el Caribe	M,D
Chicago State University	M
The Citadel, The Military College of South Carolina	M
City College of the City University of New York	M
Claremont Graduate University	M,D,O
Clark Atlanta University	M,D
Clark University	M,D,O
Clayton State University	M
Clemson University	M
Cleveland State University	M
The College at Brockport, State University of New York	M
College of Charleston	M
College of Staten Island of the City University of New York	M
The College of William and Mary	M,D
Colorado State University	M
Columbia University	M,D*
Columbus State University	M,O
Concordia University (Canada)	M,D
Converse College	M
Cornell University	M,D
Dalhousie University	M,D
DePaul University	M
Dominican University of California	M
Drew University	M,D,O
Duke University	M,D*
Duquesne University	M
East Carolina University	M
Eastern Illinois University	M
Eastern Kentucky University	M
Eastern Michigan University	M
Eastern Washington University	M
East Stroudsburg University of Pennsylvania	M
East Tennessee State University	M,O
Edinboro University of Pennsylvania	M
Emory & Henry College	M
Emory University	D
Emporia State University	M
Fairleigh Dickinson University, Metropolitan Campus	M
Faulkner University	M
Fitchburg State University	M,O
Florida Agricultural and Mechanical University	M
Florida Atlantic University	M
Florida Gulf Coast University	M
Florida International University	M,D
Florida State University	M,D
Fordham University	M,D
Fort Hays State University	M
George Mason University	M,D
Georgetown University	M,D
The George Washington University	M,D*
Georgia College & State University	M
Georgia Southern University	M,O
Georgia State University	M,D
The Graduate Center, City University of New York	D
Hardin-Simmons University	M
Harvard University	D*
High Point University	M
Howard University	M,D
Hunter College of the City University of New York	M
Idaho State University	M
Illinois State University	M
Indiana State University	M
Indiana University Bloomington	M,D
Indiana University of Pennsylvania	M
Indiana University–Purdue University Indianapolis	M
Inter American University of Puerto Rico, Metropolitan Campus	M,D
Iona College	M
Iowa State University of Science and Technology	M,D
Jackson State University	M
Jacksonville State University	M
James Madison University	M
John Carroll University	M
Johns Hopkins University	D
Kansas State University	M,D
Kent State University	M,D
Lake Forest College	M
Lakehead University	M
Lamar University	M
La Salle University	M,O
Laurentian University	M
Lee University	M,O
Lehigh University	M,D
Lehman College of the City University of New York	M
Liberty University	M,D,O
Lincoln University (MO)	M
Long Island University–LIU Post	M,O
Louisiana State University and Agricultural & Mechanical College	M,D
Louisiana Tech University	M
Loyola University Chicago	M,D
Lynchburg College	M
Marquette University	M,D
Marshall University	M,O
McGill University	M,D
McMaster University	M,D
Memorial University of Newfoundland	M,D
Miami University	M
Michigan State University	M,D
Middle Tennessee State University	M,D
Midwestern State University	M
Millersville University of Pennsylvania	M
Minnesota State University Mankato	M
Mississippi College	M,O
Mississippi State University	M,D
Missouri State University	M,O
Monmouth University	M
Montana State University	M,D
Morgan State University	M,D
Murray State University	M
National University	M,O
Nebraska Wesleyan University	M
New Jersey Institute of Technology	M,D,O
New Mexico Highlands University	M
New Mexico State University	M
The New School	M,D
New York University	M,D,O
North Carolina Central University	M
North Carolina State University	M
North Dakota State University	M,D
Northeastern Illinois University	M
Northeastern University	M,D
Northern Arizona University	M
Northern Illinois University	M,D
Northwestern University	M,D*
Northwest Missouri State University	M,O
Norwich University	M
Oakland University	M
The Ohio State University	M,D
Ohio University	M,D
Oklahoma State University	M,D
Old Dominion University	M
Open University	M
Penn State University Park	M,D
Pittsburg State University	M
Pontifical Catholic University of Puerto Rico	M
Portland State University	M
Princeton University	D
Providence College	M
Purdue University	M,D
Purdue University Northwest	M
Queens College of the City University of New York	M
Regent University	M,D
Rhode Island College	M
Rice University	M,D
Roosevelt University	M
Rowan University	M,O
Rutgers University–Camden	M
Rutgers University–Newark	M
Rutgers University–New Brunswick	D
St. Cloud State University	M
St. John's University (NY)	M,D
Saint Louis University	M,D
Saint Mary's University (Canada)	M
Salem State University	M
Salisbury University	M
Samford University	M,D,O
Sam Houston State University	M
San Diego State University	M
San Francisco State University	M
San Jose State University	M,O
Sarah Lawrence College	M
Seton Hall University	M
Shippensburg University of Pennsylvania	M
Simon Fraser University	M,D
Slippery Rock University of Pennsylvania	M
Smith College	M
Sonoma State University	M
Southeastern Louisiana University	M
Southeast Missouri State University	M,O
Southern Connecticut State University	M
Southern Illinois University Carbondale	M,D
Southern Illinois University Edwardsville	M
Southern Methodist University	M,D
Southern University and Agricultural and Mechanical College	M
Southwestern Assemblies of God University	M
Spring Hill College	M,O
Stanford University	M,D
State University of New York at Oswego	M
State University of New York College at Cortland	M
Stephen F. Austin State University	M
Stony Brook University, State University of New York	M,D
Sul Ross State University	M
Syracuse University	M,D
Tarleton State University	M
Temple University	M,D*
Texas A&M International University	M,D
Texas A&M University	M,D
Texas A&M University–Central Texas	M,O
Texas A&M University–Corpus Christi	M
Texas Christian University	M,D
Texas Southern University	M
Texas State University	M
Texas Tech University	M,D
Texas Woman's University	M
Trinity Western University	M
Troy University	M
Tufts University	M,D
Tulane University	M,D
Union Institute & University	M
Université de Moncton	M
Université de Montréal	M,D
Université de Sherbrooke	M
Université du Québec à Montréal	M,D
Université Laval	M,D
University at Albany, State University of New York	M,D,O
University at Buffalo, the State University of New York	M,D*
The University of Akron	M,D
The University of Alabama	M,D
The University of Alabama at Birmingham	M
The University of Alabama in Huntsville	M
University of Alaska Fairbanks	M
University of Alberta	M,D
The University of Arizona	M,D,O
University of Arkansas	M,D
The University of British Columbia	M,D
University of Calgary	M,D
University of California, Berkeley	M,D
University of California, Davis	M,D
University of California, Irvine	M,D
University of California, Los Angeles	M,D
University of California, Riverside	M,D
University of California, San Diego	M,D
University of California, Santa Barbara	D
University of California, Santa Cruz	M,D
University of Central Arkansas	M
University of Central Florida	M
University of Central Missouri	M,D,O
University of Central Oklahoma	M
University of Chicago	D
University of Cincinnati	M,D
University of Colorado Boulder	M,D
University of Colorado Colorado Springs	M
University of Colorado Denver	M
University of Connecticut	M,D*
University of Delaware	M,D*
University of Denver	M,O
University of Florida	M,D
University of Georgia	M,D
University of Guelph	M,D
University of Hawaii at Manoa	M,D
University of Houston	M,D
University of Houston–Clear Lake	M
University of Idaho	M,D
University of Illinois at Chicago	M,D
University of Illinois at Springfield	M
University of Illinois at Urbana–Champaign	M,D
University of Indianapolis	M
The University of Iowa	M,D*
The University of Kansas	M,D*
University of Kentucky	M,D
University of Louisiana at Lafayette	M
University of Louisiana at Monroe	M
University of Louisville	M,O
University of Maine	M,D
The University of Manchester	D
University of Manitoba	M,D
University of Maryland, Baltimore County	M
University of Maryland, College Park	M,D
University of Massachusetts Amherst	M,D*
University of Massachusetts Boston	M
University of Memphis	M,D
University of Miami	M,D
University of Michigan	D,O
University of Minnesota, Twin Cities Campus	M,D
University of Mississippi	M,D
University of Missouri	M,D
University of Missouri–Kansas City	M,D
University of Montana	M,D
University of Nebraska at Kearney	M
University of Nebraska at Omaha	M
University of Nebraska–Lincoln	M,D
University of Nevada, Las Vegas	M,D
University of Nevada, Reno	M,D
University of New Brunswick Fredericton	M,D
University of New Hampshire	M,D
University of New Mexico	M,D
University of New Orleans	M
University of North Alabama	M
The University of North Carolina at Chapel Hill	M,D
The University of North Carolina at Charlotte	M
The University of North Carolina at Greensboro	M,D,O
The University of North Carolina Wilmington	M
University of North Dakota	M,D
University of Northern British Columbia	M,D,O
University of Northern Colorado	M
University of Northern Iowa	M
University of North Florida	M
University of North Georgia	M
University of North Texas	M,D,O
University of Notre Dame	M,D
University of Oklahoma	M,D*
University of Oregon	M,D
University of Ottawa	M,D
University of Pennsylvania	M,D*
University of Pittsburgh	M,D*
University of Puerto Rico, Río Piedras Campus	M,D
University of Regina	M
University of Rhode Island	M
University of Rochester	M,D*
University of Saskatchewan	M,D
University of South Africa	M,D
University of South Alabama	M
University of South Carolina	M,D,O
The University of South Dakota	M
University of Southern California	D
University of Southern Mississippi	M,D
University of South Florida	M,D
The University of Tennessee	M,D
The University of Texas at Arlington	M,D
The University of Texas at Austin	M,D
The University of Texas at Dallas	M,D*
The University of Texas at El Paso	M,D
The University of Texas at San Antonio	M
The University of Texas at Tyler	M
The University of Texas of the Permian Basin	M
The University of Texas Rio Grande Valley	M
The University of Toledo	M,D
University of Toronto	M,D
The University of Tulsa	M

*M—masters degree; D—doctorate; O—other advanced degree; *—Close-Up and/or Display*

- University of Utah M,D*
- University of Vermont M
- University of Victoria M,D
- University of Virginia M,D
- University of Washington M,D*
- University of Waterloo M,D
- The University of West Alabama M
- The University of Western Ontario M,D
- University of West Florida M
- University of West Georgia M,O
- University of Windsor M
- The University of Winnipeg M
- University of Wisconsin–Eau Claire M
- University of Wisconsin–Madison M,D
- University of Wisconsin–Milwaukee M,D
- University of Wisconsin–Stevens Point M
- University of Wyoming M
- Utah State University M
- Valparaiso University M,O
- Vanderbilt University M,D*
- Villanova University M
- Virginia Commonwealth University M,D
- Virginia Polytechnic Institute and State University M,D,O
- Washington State University M,D
- Washington University in St. Louis D
- Wayland Baptist University M
- Wayne State University M,D,O
- West Chester University of Pennsylvania M,O
- Western Carolina University M
- Western Connecticut State University M
- Western Illinois University M
- Western Kentucky University M
- Western Michigan University M,D
- Western Washington University M
- Westfield State University M
- West Texas A&M University M
- West Virginia University M,D
- Wichita State University M
- Wilfrid Laurier University M,D
- William Paterson University of New Jersey M,D
- Winthrop University M
- Worcester State University M
- Wright State University M
- Yale University M,D*
- York University M,D
- Youngstown State University M

HISTORY OF MEDICINE
- The College at Brockport, State University of New York M,O
- McGill University M,D
- Oregon State University M,D
- Rutgers University–New Brunswick D
- The University of Manchester M,D
- University of Minnesota, Twin Cities Campus M,D
- Yale University M,D*

HISTORY OF SCIENCE AND TECHNOLOGY
- Arizona State University at the Tempe campus M,D
- Brown University D
- Carnegie Mellon University D
- Cornell University M,D
- Drexel University M
- Georgia Institute of Technology M
- Harvard University M,D*
- Indiana University Bloomington M,D
- Iowa State University of Science and Technology M,D
- Johns Hopkins University M,D
- Massachusetts Institute of Technology D
- Oregon State University M,D
- Princeton University D
- Rensselaer Polytechnic Institute M,D
- Rutgers University–New Brunswick D
- University of California, Berkeley D
- University of California, San Diego D
- University of California, San Francisco M,D
- University of Delaware M,D*
- The University of Manchester M,D
- University of Minnesota, Twin Cities Campus M,D
- University of Notre Dame M,D
- University of Oklahoma M,D*
- University of Pennsylvania M,D*
- University of Pittsburgh M,D*
- University of Toronto M,D
- University of Wisconsin–Madison M,D
- Virginia Polytechnic Institute and State University M,D,O
- Wayne State University M,D,O
- West Virginia University M,D
- Yale University M,D*

HIV/AIDS NURSING
- University of Delaware M,O*

HOLOCAUST AND GENOCIDE STUDIES
- Chapman University M
- Clark University D
- Gratz College M,O
- Kean University M
- Seton Hill University O
- Stockton University M
- West Chester University of Pennsylvania M,O

HOME ECONOMICS EDUCATION
- Alabama Agricultural and Mechanical University M,O
- Cambridge College M,D,O
- Central Washington University M
- Eastern Kentucky University M
- Iowa State University of Science and Technology M,D
- Louisiana State University and Agricultural & Mechanical College M,D
- Montana State University M
- Purdue University M,D,O
- South Carolina State University M
- Texas Tech University M,D
- The University of British Columbia M,D
- University of Georgia M,D,O
- University of Nebraska–Lincoln M,D
- Utah State University M
- Wayne State College M

HOMELAND SECURITY
- American Public University System M
- American University M,D
- Angelo State University M
- Arizona State University at the Tempe campus M,D
- Auburn University at Montgomery M,O
- Ball State University M,O
- Capella University M
- Chaminade University of Honolulu M,O
- Columbus State University M
- Drexel University M
- Endicott College M
- Excelsior College M
- Fairleigh Dickinson University, Metropolitan Campus M
- George Mason University M,D,O
- Georgian Court University M,O
- Henley-Putnam University M
- Indiana University–Purdue University Indianapolis M,O
- Johns Hopkins University M,O
- Keiser University M
- Lasell College M
- London Metropolitan University M,D
- Long Island University–Riverhead M,O
- Missouri State University M,O
- Monmouth University M,O
- National Defense University M
- The National Graduate School of Quality Management M,D
- National University M,O
- Naval Postgraduate School M,D
- Northeastern University M,D
- Northwestern State University of Louisiana M
- Notre Dame College (OH) M,O
- Pace University M
- Penn State Harrisburg M,D,O
- Regent University M
- Saint Joseph's University M
- St. Mary's University (United States) M,O
- Salve Regina University M,O
- Sam Houston State University M
- Southern Illinois University Carbondale M
- Texas A&M University M,O
- Thomas Edison State University O
- Tiffin University M
- Towson University M,O
- University at Albany, State University of New York M,D,O
- University of Alaska Fairbanks M
- University of Central Florida M,O
- University of Colorado Denver M,D
- University of Denver M,D,O
- University of Illinois at Springfield M,O
- University of Management and Technology M
- University of Oklahoma Health Sciences Center M
- University of Phoenix–Online Campus M
- University of Phoenix–Phoenix Campus M
- University of Phoenix–Southern California Campus M
- University of Southern California M,O
- University of the District of Columbia M
- Upper Iowa University M
- Virginia Commonwealth University M,O
- Walden University M,D,O
- Wayland Baptist University M
- Western Kentucky University M
- Western Michigan University Thomas M. Cooley Law School M,D
- Wilmington University M,D

HORTICULTURE
- Auburn University M,D
- Colorado State University M,D
- Cornell University M,D
- Dalhousie University M
- Iowa State University of Science and Technology M,D
- Kansas State University M,D
- Michigan State University M,D
- Mississippi State University M,D
- New Mexico State University M,D
- North Carolina State University M,D,O
- The Ohio State University M,D
- Oklahoma State University M,D
- Oregon State University M,D
- Penn State University Park M,D
- Purdue University M,D
- Rutgers University–New Brunswick M,D
- Texas A&M University M,D
- Texas A&M University–Kingsville M,D
- Texas Tech University M,D
- Universidad Nacional Pedro Henriquez Urena M
- University of Arkansas M
- University of California, Davis M
- University of Delaware M*
- University of Florida M,D
- University of Georgia M,D
- University of Guelph M,D
- University of Hawaii at Manoa M,D
- University of Maine M,D,O
- University of Manitoba M,D
- University of Maryland, College Park M,D
- University of Missouri M,D
- University of Nebraska–Lincoln M,D
- University of Puerto Rico, Mayagüez Campus M
- University of South Africa M,D
- University of Vermont M,D
- University of Washington M,D*
- University of Wisconsin–Madison M,D
- Virginia Polytechnic Institute and State University M,D
- Washington State University M,D
- West Virginia University M,D

HOSPICE NURSING
- Madonna University M

HOSPITALITY MANAGEMENT
- Alabama Agricultural and Mechanical University M
- Auburn University M,D,O
- California State Polytechnic University, Pomona M
- California State University, Long Beach M
- California State University, Northridge M,O
- Cornell University M,D
- DePaul University M
- Drexel University M
- East Carolina University M
- Eastern Michigan University M,O
- Ecole Hôtelière de Lausanne M
- ESSEC Business School M,D
- Fairleigh Dickinson University, College at Florham M
- Fairleigh Dickinson University, Metropolitan Campus M
- Florida International University M
- Georgetown University M,D
- The George Washington University M,O*
- Glion Institute of Higher Education M
- Hawai`i Pacific University M
- Husson University M
- Iowa State University of Science and Technology M,D
- Johnson & Wales University M
- Kansas State University M,D
- Kent State University M
- Lasell College M,O
- Les Roches International School of Hotel Management M
- Lynn University M
- Marylhurst University M
- Michigan State University M
- Monroe College M
- New York University M,D,O
- Norwich University M
- Oklahoma State University M,D
- Penn State University Park M,D
- Pontificia Universidad Catolica Madre y Maestra M
- Purdue University M,D
- Rochester Institute of Technology M
- Roosevelt University M
- Royal Roads University M,O
- San Francisco State University M
- Schiller International University (United States) M
- South University (GA) M
- Stratford University (VA) M,D
- Stratford University (MD) M
- Strayer University M
- Syracuse University M
- Temple University M,D*
- Texas Tech University M,D
- Troy University M
- The University of Alabama M
- University of Central Florida M,D,O
- University of Delaware M*
- The University of Findlay M,D
- University of Guelph M
- University of Houston M
- University of Kentucky M
- University of Massachusetts Amherst M,D*
- University of Missouri M,D
- University of Nevada, Las Vegas M,D
- University of New Orleans M
- University of North Texas M,D,O
- University of South Carolina M
- University of South Florida Sarasota-Manatee M
- The University of Tennessee M
- Virginia International University M,O
- Virginia Polytechnic Institute and State University M,D
- Widener University M,D

HUMAN-COMPUTER INTERACTION
- Brandeis University M
- Carnegie Mellon University M,D
- Clemson University D
- Cornell University M,D
- Dalhousie University M
- DePaul University M,D
- Florida Institute of Technology M
- Georgia Institute of Technology M
- Indiana University Bloomington M,D
- Indiana University–Purdue University Indianapolis M,D
- Iowa State University of Science and Technology M,D
- Rensselaer Polytechnic Institute M
- Rochester Institute of Technology M
- State University of New York at Oswego M
- Tufts University O
- University of Baltimore M
- University of Illinois at Urbana–Champaign M,D,O

HUMAN DEVELOPMENT
- Alabama Agricultural and Mechanical University M
- Argosy University, Chicago D
- Arizona State University at the Tempe campus M,D
- Auburn University M,D
- Ball State University M,D,O
- Bowling Green State University M
- Bradley University M
- Brigham Young University M,D
- Brock University M,D
- Central Michigan University M,O
- Claremont Graduate University M,D,O
- Clemson University M,O
- Colorado State University M,D
- Cornell University M,D
- Duke University D*
- East Tennessee State University M
- Erikson Institute M,O
- Fielding Graduate University M,D,O
- Georgetown University M
- The George Washington University M*
- Harvard University M*
- Hofstra University M,D,O
- Hood College M
- Iowa State University of Science and Technology M,D
- Kansas State University M,D,O
- Kent State University M,D
- Laurentian University M
- Lindsey Wilson College M,D
- Marywood University D
- Mississippi State University M,D
- Montana State University M
- National Louis University M,D,O
- New York University M,D,O
- Northern Arizona University O
- Northwestern University D*
- The Ohio State University M,D
- Oklahoma State University M,D
- Oregon State University M,D
- Pacific Oaks College M
- Penn State University Park M,D
- Purdue University M,D
- St. Lawrence University M,O
- Saint Louis University M,D,O
- Saint Mary's University of Minnesota M
- Texas Tech University M,D
- Tufts University M,D
- The University of Alabama M
- The University of Arizona M,D,O
- The University of British Columbia M,D,O
- University of California, Berkeley M,D
- University of California, Davis D
- University of Central Oklahoma M
- University of Chicago D
- University of Colorado Denver M,O
- University of Connecticut M,D*
- University of Dayton M,O
- University of Delaware M,D*
- University of Guelph M,D
- University of Illinois at Chicago M,D
- University of Illinois at Springfield M
- University of Illinois at Urbana–Champaign M,D
- University of Maine M,D,O
- University of Maryland, College Park M,D
- University of Missouri M,D
- University of Nebraska–Lincoln M,D,O
- University of Nevada, Reno M
- University of New Mexico M,D
- The University of North Carolina at Greensboro M,D
- University of North Texas M,D,O
- University of Pennsylvania M,D*
- University of Rhode Island M
- University of Rochester M,D*
- University of St. Thomas (MN) M,D
- University of South Africa M,D
- The University of South Dakota M,D,O
- The University of Texas at Austin M,D
- University of Utah M*
- University of Victoria M,D
- University of Washington M,D*
- University of Wisconsin–Madison M,D
- University of Wisconsin–Stevens Point M
- Utah State University M,D
- Vanderbilt University M,D*
- Virginia Polytechnic Institute and State University M,D,O
- Washington State University D
- West Virginia University M,D
- Wheelock College M

HUMAN GENETICS
- Baylor College of Medicine D
- Case Western Reserve University D*
- Emory University M
- Johns Hopkins University D
- Louisiana State University Health Sciences Center D
- McGill University M,D
- Memorial University of Newfoundland M,D
- Sarah Lawrence College M
- Tulane University M

University of California, Los Angeles	M,D
University of Chicago	D
University of Manitoba	M,D
University of Maryland, Baltimore	M,D
University of Michigan	M,D
University of Pennsylvania	M*
University of Pittsburgh	M,D,O*
The University of Texas Health Science Center at Houston	M,D
University of Utah	M,D*
Vanderbilt University	D*
Virginia Commonwealth University	M,D,O
Wake Forest University	D
Washington University in St. Louis	D
West Virginia University	M,D

HUMANITIES

American Public University System	M
Antioch University New England	M
Arcadia University	M
Brandeis University	M
Brigham Young University	M
California Institute of Integral Studies	M,D
California State University, Dominguez Hills	M
Central Michigan University	M
Claremont Graduate University	M,D,O
The Colorado College	M
Concordia University (Canada)	D
Dominican University of California	M
Duke University	M*
Georgetown University	M,D
Harrison Middleton University	M,D
Hofstra University	M,D,O
Hollins University	M
Hood College	M
Illinois Institute of Technology	M,D
Instituto Tecnologico de Santo Domingo	M,O
Instituto Tecnológico y de Estudios Superiores de Monterrey, Campus Central de Veracruz	M
Instituto Tecnológico y de Estudios Superiores de Monterrey, Campus Ciudad de México	M,D
Instituto Tecnológico y de Estudios Superiores de Monterrey, Campus Ciudad Juárez	M
Instituto Tecnológico y de Estudios Superiores de Monterrey, Campus Estado de México	M,D
Instituto Tecnológico y de Estudios Superiores de Monterrey, Campus Irapuato	M,D
John Carroll University	M
Laurentian University	M
Loyola University Chicago	M
Marshall University	M,O
Memorial University of Newfoundland	M
Mount Saint Mary's University (CA)	M,D,O
New York University	M,O
Nova Southeastern University	M,D,O*
Old Dominion University	M
Penn State Harrisburg	M,D,O
Pepperdine University	M
Prescott College	M
St. Edward's University	M,O
Salve Regina University	M,D
Sam Houston State University	M,D,O
San Francisco State University	M
Simon Fraser University	M
Tiffin University	M
Towson University	M
Trinity Western University	M
Union Institute & University	D
United Theological Seminary of the Twin Cities	M,D,O
University of California, Santa Cruz	D
University of Chicago	M
University of Colorado Denver	M
University of Dallas	M
University of Houston–Clear Lake	M
University of Louisville	M,D
University of South Florida	M
The University of Texas at Dallas	M,D*
The University of Texas Medical Branch	M,D
University of Utah	M*
Virginia Commonwealth University	M,D,O
Virginia Polytechnic Institute and State University	M,D,O
Wayland Baptist University	M
Wilson College	M
Wright State University	M
York University	M,D

HUMAN RESOURCES DEVELOPMENT

Abilene Christian University	M
Amberton University	M
Antioch University Los Angeles	M
Azusa Pacific University	M
Barry University	M,D
Bowie State University	M
California State University, Sacramento	M
Claremont Graduate University	M,D,O
Clemson University	M,D,O
The College of New Rochelle	M,O
Drexel University	M,D
Florida International University	M,D,O
The George Washington University	M,D,O*
Grantham University	M,O
Illinois Institute of Technology	M,D
Indiana State University	M
Indiana Tech	M
Indiana University of Pennsylvania	M
Inter American University of Puerto Rico, Metropolitan Campus	M
Inter American University of Puerto Rico, San Germán Campus	M,D
Iowa State University of Science and Technology	M,D
John F. Kennedy University	M,O
Kentucky State University	M,D
La Salle University	M,O
Lincoln Memorial University	M,D,O
Louisiana State University and Agricultural & Mechanical College	M,D
Marquette University	M
McDaniel College	M
Midwestern State University	M
Mississippi State University	M,D,O
Moravian College	M
National Louis University	M
New York University	M,O
North Carolina State University	M
Northeastern Illinois University	M
Ottawa University	M
Penn State Great Valley	M,O
Penn State University Park	M,D,O
Pittsburg State University	M
Regent University	M,D,O
Rochester Institute of Technology	M
Rockhurst University	M,O
Rollins College	M
Roosevelt University	M
South Dakota State University	M
Texas A&M University	M,D
Towson University	M
Universidad Central del Este	M
Universidad Iberoamericana	M,D
University of Arkansas	M,D,O
University of Bridgeport	M
University of California, Los Angeles	M,D
University of Houston	M
University of Louisville	M,D,O
University of Minnesota, Twin Cities Campus	M,D,O
University of Missouri–St. Louis	M,O
University of Nebraska at Omaha	M,D,O
University of Nevada, Las Vegas	M,D,O
University of Regina	M
University of St. Thomas (MN)	M,D
The University of Scranton	M
University of South Africa	M,D
University of South Florida	O
The University of Tennessee	M
The University of Texas at Tyler	M,D
University of Wisconsin–Stout	M
Villanova University	M
Virginia Commonwealth University	M
Waldorf College	M
Webster University	M
Western Seminary	M
William Woods University	M,D,O
Xavier University	M,D

HUMAN RESOURCES MANAGEMENT

Adelphi University	M,O
Albany State University	M
Amberton University	M
American InterContinental University Online	M
American Public University System	M
American University of Beirut	M
Argosy University, Schaumburg	M,D,O
Ashworth College	M
Assumption College	M,O
Auburn University	M,D
Austin Peay State University	M
Averett University	M
Avila University	M
Azusa Pacific University	M
Baker College Center for Graduate Studies–Online	M,D
Baldwin Wallace University	M
Barry University	O
Baruch College of the City University of New York	M,D
Belhaven University (MS)	M
Bellevue University	M,D
Benedictine University	M
Brandman University	M
Briar Cliff University	M
Brigham Young University	M
Buffalo State College, State University of New York	M,O
California Coast University	M
California Intercontinental University	M,D
California State University, East Bay	M
California State University, Sacramento	M
Capella University	M,D
Caribbean University	M,D
Carlow University	M
The Catholic University of America	M
Central Michigan University	M,O
City University of Seattle	M,O
Claremont Graduate University	M
Clarkson University	M,O
Clayton State University	M
Clemson University	M,D,O
Cleveland State University	M
College of Saint Elizabeth	M
Colorado State University–Global Campus	M
Colorado Technical University Colorado Springs	M,D
Colorado Technical University Denver South	M
Columbia Southern University	M
Columbia University	M*
Concordia University, St. Paul	M
Concordia University Wisconsin	M
Cornell University	M,D
Dallas Baptist University	M
Davenport University	M
Delaware Valley University	M
DePaul University	M
DeSales University	M
DeVry University	M
East Central University	M
Eastern Michigan University	M,O
Emmanuel College (United States)	M,O
Everest University	M
Everest University	M
Everest University	M
Everglades University	M
Excelsior College	M,O
Fairfield University	M,O
Fairleigh Dickinson University, College at Florham	M
Fairleigh Dickinson University, Metropolitan Campus	M,O
Fitchburg State University	M
Florida Institute of Technology	M,D
Florida International University	M
Florida State University	M,D
Framingham State University	M
Franklin Pierce University	M,D,O
Gannon University	M
George Fox University	M,D
George Mason University	M
Georgetown University	M,D
The George Washington University	M,O*
Georgia State University	M,D
Golden Gate University	M,D,O
Goldey-Beacom College	M
Grambling State University	M
Grand Canyon University	M
Grantham University	M,O
Hawai`i Pacific University	M
HEC Montreal	M,O
Herzing University Online	M
Hofstra University	M,O
Holy Family University	M
Hood College	M
Houston Baptist University	M
Howard University	M
Indiana Tech	M
Indiana Wesleyan University	M,O
Instituto Tecnologico de Santo Domingo	M,O
Instituto Tecnológico y de Estudios Superiores de Monterrey, Campus Cuernavaca	M
Inter American University of Puerto Rico, Aguadilla Campus	M
Inter American University of Puerto Rico, Arecibo Campus	M
Inter American University of Puerto Rico, Bayamón Campus	M
Inter American University of Puerto Rico, Metropolitan Campus	M
Inter American University of Puerto Rico, Ponce Campus	M
Inter American University of Puerto Rico, San Germán Campus	M,D
International College of the Cayman Islands	M
Iona College	M,O
James Madison University	M
Kaplan University, Davenport Campus	M
King University	M
La Roche College	M,O
La Salle University	M,O
Lasell College	M,O
La Sierra University	M,O
Lewis University	M
Liberty University	M,D,O
Lincoln University (CA)	M,D
Lincoln University (PA)	M
Lindenwood University	M,O
Lindenwood University–Belleville	M
Lipscomb University	M,O
London Metropolitan University	M,D
Long Island University–LIU Brooklyn	M,O
Loyola University Chicago	M
Lynn University	M
Manhattanville College	M*
Marquette University	M,O
Marshall University	M
Marygrove College	M
Marymount University	M,O
Maryville University of Saint Louis	M,O
McKendree University	M
McMaster University	M,D
Mercy College	M
Mercyhurst University	M,O
Michigan State University	M,D
Middle Tennessee State University	M
Millennia Atlantic University	M
Misericordia University	M
Monmouth University	M,O
Moravian College	M
Mount Ida College	M
Mount Mercy University	M
National Louis University	M
National University	M,O
Nazareth College of Rochester	M
New Mexico Highlands University	M
New York Institute of Technology	M,O
New York University	M,D,O
Niagara University	M
North Carolina Agricultural and Technical State University	M
North Central College	M
Northern Michigan University	M
North Greenville University	M,D
Northwestern University	M,D*
Norwich University	M
Notre Dame de Namur University	M
Nova Southeastern University	M*
Oakland University	M,O
The Ohio State University	M,D
Oklahoma Christian University	M
Ottawa University	M
Pace University	M
Penn State Great Valley	M,O
Penn State Harrisburg	M,D,O
Penn State University Park	M
Pepperdine University	M
Polytechnic University of Puerto Rico, Miami Campus	M
Polytechnic University of Puerto Rico, Orlando Campus	M
Pontifical Catholic University of Puerto Rico	M,O
Pontificia Universidad Catolica Madre y Maestra	M
Purdue University	M,D
Regent's University London	M
Regent University	M,D,O
Regis University	M,O
Robert Morris University	M
Robert Morris University Illinois	M
Rollins College	M
Roosevelt University	M
Royal Roads University	M,O
Rutgers University–Newark	M,D
Rutgers University–New Brunswick	M,D
Sacred Heart University	M,O
Sage Graduate School	M
St. Ambrose University	M,D
Saint Francis University	M
St. Joseph's College, Long Island Campus	M
St. Joseph's College, New York	M
Saint Joseph's University	M,O
Saint Leo University	M
Saint Mary's University of Minnesota	M
Saint Peter's University	M
St. Thomas University	M,O
San Diego State University	M
Savannah State University	M
Seattle Pacific University	M
Southern New Hampshire University	M,O
State University of New York Polytechnic Institute	M
Stevens Institute of Technology	M
Stony Brook University, State University of New York	M,O
Strayer University	M
Tarleton State University	M
Temple University	M*
Tennessee State University	M,D
Tennessee Technological University	M
Texas A&M University–Central Texas	M,O
Texas A&M University–San Antonio	M
Texas State University	M
Thomas College	M
Thomas Edison State University	M,O
Tiffin University	M
Trident University International	M,D
Trinity Washington University	M
Troy University	M
United States International University–Africa	M
Universidad del Este	M
Universidad del Turabo	M
Universidad Metropolitana	M
University at Albany, State University of New York	M,D,O
University at Buffalo, the State University of New York	M,D,O*
The University of Alabama in Huntsville	M,O
University of Bridgeport	M
University of California, Berkeley	O
University of Colorado Denver	M
University of Connecticut	M*
University of Dallas	M,D
University of Denver	M,O
University of Florida	M,D
University of Georgia	M,D,O
University of Hawaii at Manoa	M
University of Houston–Clear Lake	M
University of Houston–Downtown	M
University of Illinois at Urbana–Champaign	M,D,O
University of La Verne	M,O
University of Lethbridge	M,D
University of Louisville	M,D,O
The University of Manchester	M
University of Mary	M
University of Minnesota, Twin Cities Campus	M
University of Missouri–St. Louis	M,D,O
University of Nebraska at Kearney	M
University of New Haven	M,O
University of New Mexico	M
University of North Florida	M
University of North Texas	M,D,O
University of Oklahoma	M,O*
University of Phoenix–Atlanta Campus	M
University of Phoenix–Augusta Campus	M
University of Phoenix–Bay Area Campus	M,D

*M—masters degree; D—doctorate; O—other advanced degree; *—Close-Up and/or Display*

University of Phoenix–Central Valley Campus	M
University of Phoenix–Colorado Campus	M
University of Phoenix–Colorado Springs Downtown Campus	M
University of Phoenix–Columbus Georgia Campus	M
University of Phoenix–Dallas Campus	M
University of Phoenix–Hawaii Campus	M
University of Phoenix–Houston Campus	M
University of Phoenix–Jersey City Campus	M
University of Phoenix–Las Vegas Campus	M
University of Phoenix–New Mexico Campus	M
University of Phoenix–North Florida Campus	M
University of Phoenix–Online Campus	M,O
University of Phoenix–Phoenix Campus	M,O
University of Phoenix–Sacramento Valley Campus	M
University of Phoenix–San Antonio Campus	M
University of Phoenix–San Diego Campus	M
University of Phoenix–Southern Arizona Campus	M
University of Phoenix–Southern California Campus	M
University of Phoenix–South Florida Campus	M
University of Phoenix–Utah Campus	M
University of Phoenix–Washington D.C. Campus	M,D
University of Pittsburgh	M,D*
University of Puerto Rico, Mayagüez Campus	M
University of Puerto Rico, Río Piedras Campus	M,D
University of Regina	M,O
University of Rhode Island	M,O
University of Saint Mary	M
University of South Carolina	M
The University of South Dakota	M
The University of Texas at Arlington	M
University of the Incarnate Word	M
University of the Sacred Heart	M
University of Toronto	M,D
University of Wisconsin–Madison	M,D
University of Wisconsin–Platteville	M
Upper Iowa University	M
Utah State University	M
Virginia International University	M,O
Walden University	M,D,O
Walsh College of Accountancy and Business Administration	M
Wayland Baptist University	M,D
Waynesburg University	M,D
Wayne State University	M,D
Webster University	M
West Chester University of Pennsylvania	M,O
Wilfrid Laurier University	M,D
Wilkes University	M
Wilmington University	M,D
York University	M,D

HUMAN SERVICES

Abilene Christian University	M,D,O
Albertus Magnus College	M
Amridge University	M,D
Bellevue University	M
Boricua College	M
Brandeis University	M
California State University, Sacramento	M
Capella University	M,D
Carlos Albizu University, Miami Campus	M,D
Chestnut Hill College	M,O
Concordia University Chicago	M,D
Concordia University Wisconsin	M,D
Coppin State University	M
Drury University	M
East Central University	M
Eastern Michigan University	O
Eastern New Mexico University	M
Ferris State University	M
Georgia State University	M,O
Judson University	M
Kansas State University	M,O
Kent State University	M,D,O
Lehigh University	M,D,O
Lenoir-Rhyne University	M
Liberty University	M,D,O
Lincoln University (PA)	M
Lindenwood University	M
Lock Haven University of Pennsylvania	M
McDaniel College	M
Mercer University	M,D
Minnesota State University Mankato	M
Minnesota State University Moorhead	M,O
Murray State University	M
National Louis University	M,D,O
National University	M,D,O
New England College	M
Northeastern University	M
Pontifical Catholic University of Puerto Rico	M,D
Post University	M
Purdue University Northwest	M
Roberts Wesleyan College	M
Rosemont College	M
St. Joseph's College, Long Island Campus	M
St. Joseph's College, New York	M
Saint Leo University	M
South Carolina State University	M
Southeastern University (FL)	M
Springfield College	M
Texas Southern University	M
Thomas University	M
Universidad del Turabo	M
Université de Montréal	D
University of Baltimore	M
University of Bridgeport	M
University of Central Missouri	M,D,O
University of Colorado Colorado Springs	M,D
University of Great Falls	M
University of Idaho	M,O
University of Illinois at Springfield	M,O
University of Illinois at Urbana–Champaign	M,D
University of Maryland, Baltimore County	M,D
University of Massachusetts Boston	M
University of Nebraska at Kearney	M
University of Northern Iowa	M
University of Northwestern–St. Paul	M
University of Oklahoma	M,O*
Upper Iowa University	M
Walden University	M,D
Warner Pacific College	M
Washburn University	M
Webster University	M
Western Michigan University	D,O
West Virginia University	M,D
Wichita State University	M
Wilmington University	M
Youngstown State University	M

HYDRAULICS

Auburn University	M,D
Drexel University	M,D
École Polytechnique de Montréal	M,D,O
McGill University	M,D
Missouri University of Science and Technology	M,D
Old Dominion University	M
University of Colorado Denver	M,D

HYDROGEOLOGY

California State University, Chico	M
Clemson University	M
East Carolina University	M,O
Indiana University Bloomington	M,D
Montana Tech of The University of Montana	M
Ohio University	M
University of Hawaii at Manoa	M,D
University of Nevada, Reno	M,D
University of South Florida	O
The University of Texas at Dallas	M,D*
West Virginia University	M,D

HYDROLOGY

Auburn University	M,D
Boise State University	M,D
California State University, Bakersfield	M
California State University, Chico	M
Colorado School of Mines	M,D
Cornell University	M,D
Drexel University	M,D
Idaho State University	M,O
Massachusetts Institute of Technology	M,D,O
Missouri University of Science and Technology	M,D
Murray State University	M
New Mexico Institute of Mining and Technology	M,D
New Mexico State University	M,D
Stanford University	M,D,O
Stevens Institute of Technology	M,D,O
Temple University	M,O*
Université du Québec, Institut National de la Recherche Scientifique	M,D
The University of Arizona	D,O
University of Calgary	M,D
University of California, Davis	M,D
University of Colorado Boulder	M,D
University of Colorado Denver	M,D
University of Florida	M,D
University of Idaho	M,D
University of Minnesota, Twin Cities Campus	M,D
University of Nevada, Reno	M,D
University of New Brunswick Fredericton	M,D
University of New Hampshire	M
University of Southern Mississippi	M,D
University of Washington	M,D*

ILLUSTRATION

Academy of Art University	M
Bob Jones University	M,D,O
California State University, Fullerton	M
East Carolina University	M
Fashion Institute of Technology	M*
Hollins University	M
Kent State University	M
Maryland Institute College of Art	M
Marywood University	M
Memphis College of Art	M
Mills College	M,O
Minneapolis College of Art and Design	M
Savannah College of Art and Design	M
School of Visual Arts (NY)	M
Syracuse University	M
University of Massachusetts Dartmouth	M,O
Western Connecticut State University	M

IMMUNOLOGY

Albany Medical College	M,D
Albert Einstein College of Medicine	D
American University of Beirut	M,D
Baylor College of Medicine	D
Boston University	D
California Institute of Technology	D
Case Western Reserve University	M,D*
Colorado State University	M,D
Cornell University	M,D
Creighton University	M,D
Dalhousie University	M,D
Dartmouth College	D*
Drexel University	M,D
Duke University	D*
East Carolina University	M,D
Emory University	D
Georgetown University	M,D
The George Washington University	D*
Hood College	M,O
Illinois State University	M,D
Indiana University–Purdue University Indianapolis	M,D
Iowa State University of Science and Technology	M,D
Irell & Manella Graduate School of Biological Sciences	D*
Johns Hopkins University	M,D
London Metropolitan University	M,D
Louisiana State University Health Sciences Center	D
Louisiana State University Health Sciences Center at Shreveport	M,D
Loyola University Chicago	M,D
Massachusetts Institute of Technology	D
Mayo Graduate School	D
McGill University	M,D
McMaster University	M,D
Medical University of South Carolina	M,D
Meharry Medical College	D
Memorial University of Newfoundland	M,D
Montana State University	M,D
New York Medical College	M,D
New York University	M,D
North Carolina State University	M,D
Oregon Health & Science University	D
Oregon State University	M,D
Penn State Hershey Medical Center	M,D
Purdue University	M,D
Queen's University at Kingston	M,D
Rosalind Franklin University of Medicine and Science	D
Rush University	M,D
Rutgers University–Newark	D
Rutgers University–New Brunswick	M,D
Saint Louis University	D
Stanford University	D
State University of New York Upstate Medical University	M,D
Stony Brook University, State University of New York	M,D
Thomas Jefferson University	D
Tufts University	D
Tulane University	M
Uniformed Services University of the Health Sciences	D*
Universidad Central del Caribe	M,D
Université de Montréal	M,D
Université de Sherbrooke	M,D
Université du Québec, Institut National de la Recherche Scientifique	M,D
Université Laval	M,D
University at Albany, State University of New York	M,D
University at Buffalo, the State University of New York	M,D*
University of Alberta	M,D
The University of Arizona	D
University of Arkansas for Medical Sciences	M,D,O
The University of British Columbia	M,D
University of Calgary	M,D
University of California, Berkeley	D
University of California, Davis	M,D
University of California, Los Angeles	M,D
University of Chicago	D
University of Cincinnati	M,D
University of Colorado Denver	D
University of Connecticut Health Center	D*
University of Florida	D
University of Guelph	M,D,O
University of Illinois at Chicago	D
The University of Iowa	M,D*
University of Kentucky	D
University of Louisville	M,D
The University of Manchester	M,D
University of Manitoba	M,D
University of Maryland, Baltimore	D
University of Massachusetts Medical School	M,D
University of Miami	D
University of Michigan	M,D
University of Minnesota, Duluth	M,D
University of Minnesota, Twin Cities Campus	D
University of Missouri	D
University of Montana	D
The University of North Carolina at Chapel Hill	M,D
University of North Dakota	M,D
University of North Texas Health Science Center at Fort Worth	M,D
University of Oklahoma Health Sciences Center	M,D
University of Ottawa	M,D
University of Pennsylvania	D*
University of Pittsburgh	D*
University of Prince Edward Island	M,D
University of Rochester	M,D*
University of Saskatchewan	M,D
The University of South Dakota	M,D
University of Southern California	M
University of Southern Maine	M
University of South Florida	M,D
The University of Texas Health Science Center at Houston	M,D
The University of Texas Health Science Center at San Antonio	M,D
The University of Texas Medical Branch	M,D
The University of Texas Southwestern Medical Center	D
The University of Toledo	M,D
University of Toronto	M,D
University of Washington	D*
The University of Western Ontario	M,D
University of Wisconsin–Milwaukee	M
Vanderbilt University	M,D*
Virginia Commonwealth University	M,D
Wake Forest University	D
Washington State University	M,D
Washington University in St. Louis	D
Wayne State University	M,D
Weill Cornell Medicine	M,D
West Virginia University	M,D
Wright State University	M
Yale University	D*

INDUSTRIAL/MANAGEMENT ENGINEERING

American University of Armenia	M
Arizona State University at the Tempe campus	M,D
Auburn University	M,D,O
Binghamton University, State University of New York	M,D*
Bradley University	M
Buffalo State College, State University of New York	M
California Polytechnic State University, San Luis Obispo	M
California State University, East Bay	M
California State University, Fresno	M
California State University, Northridge	M
Central Washington University	M
Clemson University	M,D
Cleveland State University	M,D
Colorado State University–Pueblo	M
Columbia University	M,D*
Concordia University (Canada)	M,D,O
Cornell University	M,D
Dalhousie University	M,D
Eastern Kentucky University	M
École Polytechnique de Montréal	M,D,O
Florida Agricultural and Mechanical University	M,D
Florida State University	M,D
Georgia Institute of Technology	M,D
Illinois State University	M
Indiana University–Purdue University Fort Wayne	M
Instituto Tecnologico de Santo Domingo	M,O
Instituto Tecnológico y de Estudios Superiores de Monterrey, Campus Chihuahua	M,O
Instituto Tecnológico y de Estudios Superiores de Monterrey, Campus Ciudad de México	M,D
Instituto Tecnológico y de Estudios Superiores de Monterrey, Campus Laguna	M
Instituto Tecnológico y de Estudios Superiores de Monterrey, Campus Monterrey	M,D
Iowa State University of Science and Technology	M,D
Kansas State University	M,D
Lamar University	M,D
Lawrence Technological University	M,D
Lehigh University	M,D
Louisiana Tech University	M
Mississippi State University	M,D
Montana State University	M,D
Montana Tech of The University of Montana	M
Morehead State University	M
Morgan State University	M,D
New Jersey Institute of Technology	M,D
New Mexico State University	M,D,O
New York University	M
North Carolina Agricultural and Technical State University	M,D
North Carolina State University	M,D
North Dakota State University	M,D
Northeastern University	M,D,O
Northern Illinois University	M
Northwestern University	M,D*
The Ohio State University	M,D
Ohio University	M,D
Oklahoma State University	M,D
Oregon State University	M,D
Penn State University Park	M,D
Purdue University	M,D
Rensselaer Polytechnic Institute	M,D

Rochester Institute of Technology M
Rutgers University–New Brunswick M,D
St. Mary's University (United States) M
South Dakota State University M
Southern Illinois University Edwardsville M
Stanford University M,D
Texas A&M University M,D
Texas A&M University–Kingsville M
Texas Southern University M
Texas State University M
Texas Tech University M,D
Universidad de las Américas Puebla M
Université de Moncton M
Université du Québec à Trois-Rivières M,O
Université Laval O
University at Buffalo, the State University of New York M,D*
The University of Alabama in Huntsville M,D
The University of Arizona M,D,O
University of Arkansas M,D
University of California, Berkeley M,D
University of Central Florida M,D,O
University of Cincinnati M,D
University of Florida M,D,O
University of Houston M,D
University of Illinois at Chicago M,D
University of Illinois at Urbana–Champaign M,D
The University of Iowa M,D*
University of Louisville M,D,O
University of Manitoba M,D
University of Massachusetts Amherst M,D*
University of Massachusetts Dartmouth M,D
University of Memphis M,D
University of Miami M,D
University of Michigan M,D
University of Michigan–Dearborn M
University of Minnesota, Twin Cities Campus M,D
University of Missouri M,D
University of Nebraska–Lincoln M,D
University of New Haven M,O
University of Oklahoma M,D*
University of Pittsburgh M,D*
University of Puerto Rico, Mayagüez Campus M
University of Regina M,D
University of Southern California M,D,O
University of South Florida M,D,O
The University of Tennessee M,D
The University of Tennessee at Chattanooga M
The University of Texas at Arlington M,D
The University of Texas at Austin M,D
The University of Texas at El Paso M,O
The University of Toledo M,D
University of Toronto M,D
University of Washington M,D*
University of Windsor M,D
University of Wisconsin–Madison M,D
University of Wisconsin–Milwaukee M,D,O
University of Wisconsin–Stout M
Virginia Polytechnic Institute and State University M,D,O
Wayne State University M,D
Western Michigan University M,D
West Virginia University M,D
Wichita State University M,D
Youngstown State University M

INDUSTRIAL AND LABOR RELATIONS

Baruch College of the City University of New York M
Carnegie Mellon University D
Cleveland State University M,D,O
Cornell University M,D
Georgetown University D
Georgia State University M,D
Indiana University of Pennsylvania M
Inter American University of Puerto Rico, Metropolitan Campus M,D
McMaster University M
Memorial University of Newfoundland M
Michigan State University M,D
New York Institute of Technology M,O
The Ohio State University M,D
Penn State University Park M
Queen's University at Kingston M
Rutgers University–New Brunswick M,D
Southern New Hampshire University M,O
State University of New York Empire State College M
Université de Montréal M,D,O
Université du Québec à Trois-Rivières O
Université du Québec en Outaouais M,D,O
Université Laval M,D
University of Alberta D
University of California, Berkeley D
University of Cincinnati M
University of Illinois at Urbana–Champaign M,D
The University of Manchester M
University of Massachusetts Amherst M*
University of Minnesota, Twin Cities Campus M
University of New Haven M,O
University of Rhode Island M,O
University of Toronto M,D
Wayne State University M,D
West Virginia University M

INDUSTRIAL AND MANUFACTURING MANAGEMENT

American InterContinental University Online M
The American University in Cairo M
Baruch College of the City University of New York M,D
Bluffton University M
California State University, East Bay M
Carnegie Mellon University M,D
Case Western Reserve University M,D*
Central Connecticut State University M,O
Central Michigan University M
Cleveland State University D
Colorado Technical University Colorado Springs M,D
Colorado Technical University Denver South M
DePaul University M
Duke University M,D,O*
East Carolina University M,D,O
Emory University M
Everglades University M
Georgetown University D
Harvard University D*
HEC Montreal M
Illinois Institute of Technology M
Instituto Tecnologico de Santo Domingo M,O
Instituto Tecnológico y de Estudios Superiores de Monterrey, Campus Estado de México M,D
Instituto Tecnológico y de Estudios Superiores de Monterrey, Campus Irapuato M,D
Inter American University of Puerto Rico, Metropolitan Campus M
Inter American University of Puerto Rico, San Germán Campus M,D
Kansas State University M
Marquette University M,O
McGill University M,D,O
Milwaukee School of Engineering M*
Mississippi State University M,D
Northern Illinois University M
Northwestern University M,D*
Notre Dame de Namur University M
Oakland University M,O
Penn State Erie, The Behrend College M
Polytechnic University of Puerto Rico M
Polytechnic University of Puerto Rico, Miami Campus M
Polytechnic University of Puerto Rico, Orlando Campus M
Portland State University M,D
Purdue University M
Regis University M,O
Rochester Institute of Technology M
San Francisco State University M
Southeast Missouri State University M
Southern New Hampshire University M,O
Stevens Institute of Technology M
Stony Brook University, State University of New York M,O
Texas A&M University–Kingsville M
Universidad de las Américas Puebla M
The University of Alabama M,D
University of Arkansas M
University of Bridgeport M
University of California, Los Angeles M,D
University of Central Missouri M,D,O
University of Chicago M,O
University of Cincinnati D
The University of Manchester M,D
University of Michigan–Flint M
University of Minnesota, Twin Cities Campus M,D
University of Missouri–St. Louis M,D,O
University of New Haven M,O
The University of North Carolina at Charlotte M,O
University of North Texas M,D,O
University of Pittsburgh M*
University of Portland M
University of Puerto Rico, Mayagüez Campus M
University of Puerto Rico, Río Piedras Campus M,D
University of Rochester M*
University of Southern Indiana M
The University of Tennessee M,D
The University of Texas at Arlington M,D
The University of Texas at Austin M,D
The University of Texas at Tyler M,D
University of Utah M,D,O*
University of Wisconsin–Milwaukee M,D
Virginia Commonwealth University M
Wayne State University M,D
Wilkes University M

INDUSTRIAL AND ORGANIZATIONAL PSYCHOLOGY

Adler University M,D,O
Alliant International University–Fresno M,D
Alliant International University–Los Angeles M,D
Alliant International University–San Diego M,D
Alliant International University–San Francisco M,D
American InterContinental University Online M
Angelo State University M
Anna Maria College M
Appalachian State University M
Argosy University, Atlanta M,D,O
Argosy University, Chicago M,D
Argosy University, Dallas M
Argosy University, Denver M,D
Argosy University, Inland Empire M,D
Argosy University, Phoenix M
Argosy University, Schaumburg M,O
Argosy University, Tampa M,D
Argosy University, Twin Cities M,D,O
Auburn University M,D
Austin Peay State University M
Baruch College of the City University of New York M,D
Bayamón Central University M
Bowling Green State University M,D
Brooklyn College of the City University of New York M,D
California State University, Long Beach M
California State University, Sacramento M
California State University, San Bernardino M
Capella University M,D
Carlos Albizu University M,D
Carlos Albizu University, Miami Campus M,D
Central Michigan University M,D
Chatham University M,D
The Chicago School of Professional Psychology M,D
The Chicago School of Professional Psychology at Downtown Los Angeles M
The Chicago School of Professional Psychology: Online M,D,O
Claremont Graduate University M,D,O
Clemson University D
Colorado State University M,D
East Carolina University M,D
Eastern Kentucky University M,O
Elmhurst College M
Emporia State University M
Fairleigh Dickinson University, College at Florham M
Florida Institute of Technology M,D
Florida International University M,D
George Mason University M,D,O
The Graduate Center, City University of New York D
Grand Canyon University D
Hofstra University M,D
Illinois Institute of Technology M,D
Illinois State University M,D,O
Indiana University–Purdue University Indianapolis M,D
Inter American University of Puerto Rico, Metropolitan Campus M,D
Iona College M,O
John F. Kennedy University M,O
Kean University M
Keiser University M,D
Lamar University M
London Metropolitan University M,D
Louisiana Tech University M,D
Middle Tennessee State University M,O
Minnesota State University Mankato M,D
Missouri State University M,O
Montclair State University M
New York University M,D,O
North Carolina State University D
Northern Kentucky University M,O
Ohio University M,D
Old Dominion University D
Philadelphia College of Osteopathic Medicine M,D,O*
Pontifical Catholic University of Puerto Rico D
Purdue University D
Radford University M
Rice University M,D
Roosevelt University M,D
St. Cloud State University M
Saint Joseph's University M
Saint Louis University M,D
Saint Mary's University (Canada) M,D
St. Mary's University (United States) M
San Diego State University M,D
San Francisco State University M,O
San Jose State University M,O
Seattle Pacific University M,D
Southern Illinois University Edwardsville M
Springfield College M,D,O
Teachers College, Columbia University M,D
Temple University M,D,O*
Texas A&M University M,D
Touro College M,D
University at Albany, State University of New York M,D
The University of Akron M,D
The University of Alabama in Huntsville M
University of Central Florida M,D
University of Connecticut M,D*
University of Detroit Mercy M,D,O
University of Guelph M,D
University of Houston M,D
The University of Manchester M
University of Maryland, Baltimore County M
University of Maryland, College Park M,D
University of Minnesota, Twin Cities Campus D
University of Missouri–St. Louis M,D,O
University of Nebraska at Omaha M,D,O
University of New Haven M,O
The University of North Carolina at Charlotte M,D,O
University of Oklahoma M,D*
University of Phoenix–Online Campus M,D,O
University of Phoenix–Washington D.C. Campus M,D
University of Puerto Rico, Río Piedras Campus M,D
University of South Africa M,D
University of South Florida D
The University of Tennessee D
The University of Tennessee at Chattanooga M
The University of Texas at Arlington M,D
University of the Incarnate Word M
The University of Tulsa M,D
University of West Florida M
University of Wisconsin–Oshkosh M
Walden University M,D,O
Wayne State University M,D
West Chester University of Pennsylvania M
Western Kentucky University M,O
Western Michigan University M,D
William James College M,D,O
Wright State University M,D
Xavier University M,D

INDUSTRIAL DESIGN

Academy of Art University M
Art Center College of Design M
Auburn University M
Brigham Young University M
California College of the Arts M
Carleton University M
Florida State University M
Georgia Institute of Technology M
Iowa State University of Science and Technology M
The New School M
North Carolina State University M
The Ohio State University M
Philadelphia University M
Pratt Institute M*
Rhode Island School of Design M
Rochester Institute of Technology M
San Francisco State University M
Savannah College of Art and Design M
University of Cincinnati M
University of Detroit Mercy M,D
University of Illinois at Urbana–Champaign M
University of Notre Dame M
The University of the Arts M
University of Washington M*
Wayne State University M

INDUSTRIAL HYGIENE

California State University, Northridge M
Montana Tech of The University of Montana M
Murray State University M
New York Medical College O
The University of Alabama at Birmingham M,D
University of Central Missouri M,D,O
University of Cincinnati M,D
The University of Iowa M,D,O*
University of Michigan M,D
University of Minnesota, Twin Cities Campus M,D
The University of North Carolina at Chapel Hill M,D
University of Puerto Rico, Medical Sciences Campus M
University of South Carolina M,D
The University of Toledo M,O
University of Wisconsin–Stout M
West Virginia University M

INFECTIOUS DISEASES

Cornell University M,D
Georgetown University M,D
The George Washington University M,D,O*
Johns Hopkins University M,D
Long Island University–LIU Post M,O
Loyola University Chicago M,D
Montana State University M,D
North Carolina State University M,D
Penn State Hershey Medical Center D
Rutgers University–Newark D,O
Thomas Jefferson University O
Tufts University M,D
Uniformed Services University of the Health Sciences D*
Université Laval O
University of Calgary M,D
University of California, Berkeley M,D

*M—masters degree; D—doctorate; O—other advanced degree; *—Close-Up and/or Display*

University of Georgia	M,D
University of Guelph	M,D,O
University of Minnesota, Twin Cities Campus	M,D
University of Pittsburgh	M,D*
The University of Texas Medical Branch	D
Yale University	D*

INFORMATION SCIENCE

Alcorn State University	M
American InterContinental University Atlanta	M
American InterContinental University Online	M
American University of Armenia	M
Arizona State University at the Tempe campus	M
Arkansas Tech University	M
Armstrong State University	M
Aspen University	M,O
Auburn University at Montgomery	M
Ball State University	M,O
Barry University	M
Bellevue University	M
Bentley University	M
Bradley University	M
Brigham Young University	M
Brooklyn College of the City University of New York	M,O
California State University, Fullerton	M
Capitol Technology University	M
Carleton University	M,D
Carnegie Mellon University	M,D
Case Western Reserve University	M,D*
Claremont Graduate University	M,D,O
Clark Atlanta University	M
Clarkson University	M
Clark University	M
Cleveland State University	M,D
Coleman University	M
The College of Saint Rose	M,O
Cornell University	D
Dakota State University	M,D,O
DePaul University	M,D
Drexel University	M,D
East Tennessee State University	M,O
Florida Institute of Technology	M
Florida International University	M,D
Gannon University	M
George Mason University	M,D,O
Georgia State University	M,D,O
Grand Valley State University	M
Harvard University	M,D,O*
Hood College	M,O
Indiana University Bloomington	M,D,O
Indiana University–Purdue University Fort Wayne	M
Indiana University–Purdue University Indianapolis	M
Instituto Tecnologico de Santo Domingo	M,O
Instituto Tecnológico y de Estudios Superiores de Monterrey, Campus Cuernavaca	M,D
Instituto Tecnológico y de Estudios Superiores de Monterrey, Campus Estado de México	M,D
Instituto Tecnológico y de Estudios Superiores de Monterrey, Campus Irapuato	M,D
Instituto Tecnológico y de Estudios Superiores de Monterrey, Campus Monterrey	M,D
Instituto Tecnológico y de Estudios Superiores de Monterrey, Campus Sonora Norte	M
Iowa State University of Science and Technology	M
Johns Hopkins University	M
Kansas State University	M,D
Kennesaw State University	M,O
Kent State University	M,O
Knowledge Systems Institute	M
Lawrence Technological University	M,D
Lehigh University	M
Long Island University–LIU Post	M,D,O
Loyola University Chicago	M,D,O
Marshall University	M
Maryville University of Saint Louis	M,O
Massachusetts Institute of Technology	M,D,O
Missouri University of Science and Technology	M
Naval Postgraduate School	M,D,O
New Jersey Institute of Technology	M,D,O
Northeastern University	M,D,O
Northern Kentucky University	M,O
Northwestern University	M*
Nova Southeastern University	M,D*
Oklahoma State University	M,D
Old Dominion University	D
Pace University	M,D,O
Penn State Great Valley	M,O
Penn State University Park	M,D
Regis University	M,O
Rensselaer at Hartford	M
Rensselaer Polytechnic Institute	M
Robert Morris University	M,D
Rochester Institute of Technology	M,D
Sacred Heart University	M,O
St. John's University (NY)	
St. Mary's University (United States)	M
Sam Houston State University	M,D
Simmons College	M,D,O
Southern Methodist University	M,D
State University of New York Polytechnic Institute	M
Stevens Institute of Technology	M,O
Stevenson University	M
Stratford University (VA)	M,D
Strayer University	M
Syracuse University	M,D
Temple University	M,D*
Texas Woman's University	M
Towson University	M,D,O
Trevecca Nazarene University	M,O
Université de Sherbrooke	M,D
University at Albany, State University of New York	M,D,O
The University of Alabama at Birmingham	M,D
University of Arkansas at Little Rock	M,D,O
University of California, Irvine	M,D
University of California, Merced	M,D
University of Central Missouri	M,D,O
University of Colorado Denver	M,D
University of Delaware	M,D*
University of Florida	M,D
University of Hawaii at Manoa	M,D
University of Houston	M,D
University of Houston–Clear Lake	M
University of Illinois at Urbana–Champaign	M,D,O
The University of Iowa	M,D,O*
University of Kentucky	M
University of Louisville	M,D
University of Maine	M,D,O
University of Maryland, Baltimore County	M,D
University of Maryland University College	M,O
University of Massachusetts Dartmouth	D
University of Michigan	M,D
University of Michigan–Dearborn	M
University of Michigan–Flint	M
University of Nebraska at Omaha	M,D,O
University of Nebraska–Lincoln	M,D
The University of North Carolina at Charlotte	M,D,O
University of North Texas	M,D,O
University of Oregon	M,D
University of Ottawa	M,O
University of Pennsylvania	M,D*
University of Pittsburgh	M,D,O*
University of Puerto Rico, Mayagüez Campus	M,D
University of Puerto Rico, Río Piedras Campus	M,O
University of South Africa	M,D
University of South Carolina Upstate	M
University of Southern Mississippi	M,O
University of South Florida	M
The University of Tennessee	M,D
The University of Texas at El Paso	M,D
The University of Texas at San Antonio	M,D,O
University of the Sacred Heart	O
University of Washington	M,D*
University of Waterloo	M,D
University of Wisconsin–Parkside	M
University of Wisconsin–Stout	M
Western Governors University	M
Youngstown State University	M

INFORMATION STUDIES

The Catholic University of America	M,O
Central Connecticut State University	M
Columbia University	M*
Cornell University	D
Dalhousie University	M
Dominican University	M,D,O
Emporia State University	M
Florida State University	M,D,O
Lock Haven University of Pennsylvania	M
Louisiana State University and Agricultural & Mechanical College	M
Mansfield University of Pennsylvania	M
McGill University	M,D,O
Metropolitan State University	M,D,O
Missouri Western State University	M
North Carolina Central University	M
Pratt Institute	M,O*
Queens College of the City University of New York	M,O
Queen's University at Kingston	M,D
Rutgers University–New Brunswick	M,D
St. Catherine University	M
St. John's University (NY)	M,O
Southern Connecticut State University	M,O
Syracuse University	M
Universidad del Turabo	M
Université de Montréal	M,D
University at Albany, State University of New York	M,O
University at Buffalo, the State University of New York	M,O*
The University of Alabama	M,D
University of Alberta	M
The University of Arizona	M,D
The University of British Columbia	M,D
University of California, Berkeley	M,D
University of California, Los Angeles	M,D,O
University of Hawaii at Manoa	M,O
University of Illinois at Urbana–Champaign	M,D,O
The University of Iowa	M,D*
University of Maryland, College Park	M,D
University of Michigan	M,D
University of Missouri	M,D,O
The University of North Carolina at Chapel Hill	M,D,O
The University of North Carolina at Greensboro	M
University of Pittsburgh	M,D*
University of Puerto Rico, Río Piedras Campus	M,O
University of Rhode Island	M
University of South Carolina	M,D,O
University of South Florida	M,O
The University of Texas at Austin	M,D
University of Toronto	M,D
The University of Western Ontario	M,D
University of Wisconsin–Madison	M,D
University of Wisconsin–Milwaukee	M,D,O
Valdosta State University	M
Wayne State University	M,O

INORGANIC CHEMISTRY

Auburn University	M,D
Binghamton University, State University of New York	M,D*
Boston College	M,D
Brandeis University	M,D
Cleveland State University	M,D
Cornell University	D
Eastern New Mexico University	M
Florida State University	M,D
Georgetown University	D
The George Washington University	M,D*
Harvard University	D*
Howard University	M,D
Illinois Institute of Technology	M,D
Indiana University Bloomington	M,D
Iowa State University of Science and Technology	M,D
Kansas State University	M,D
Marquette University	M,D
Massachusetts Institute of Technology	D
McMaster University	M,D
Old Dominion University	M,D
Oregon State University	M,D
Purdue University	M,D
Rice University	M,D
Rutgers University–Newark	M,D
Rutgers University–New Brunswick	M,D
Seton Hall University	M,D
Southern University and Agricultural and Mechanical College	M
Tufts University	M,D
University of Calgary	M,D
University of Cincinnati	M,D
University of Georgia	M,D
University of Louisville	M,D
The University of Manchester	M,D
University of Maryland, College Park	M,D
University of Massachusetts Lowell	M,D
University of Memphis	M,D
University of Miami	M,D
University of Michigan	D
University of Missouri–Kansas City	M,D
University of Montana	M,D
University of Nebraska–Lincoln	M,D
University of Notre Dame	M,D
University of Regina	M,D
University of Southern Mississippi	M,D
The University of Tennessee	M,D
The University of Texas at Austin	D
The University of Toledo	M,D
Vanderbilt University	M,D*
Virginia Commonwealth University	M,D
Wake Forest University	M,D
Wayne State University	M,D
Wesleyan University	D
West Virginia University	M,D
Yale University	D*
Youngstown State University	M

INSURANCE

California State University, Fullerton	M
Florida State University	M,D
Georgia State University	M,D,O
Olivet College	M
Pontificia Universidad Catolica Madre y Maestra	M
St. John's University (NY)	M
Temple University	D*
University of Colorado Denver	M
University of Florida	M,D,O
University of Pennsylvania	M,D*
University of Wisconsin–Madison	M,D
Virginia Commonwealth University	M
Western Michigan University Thomas M. Cooley Law School	M,D

INTELLECTUAL PROPERTY LAW

Baylor University	D
Boston University	M,D
Case Western Reserve University	M,D*
DePaul University	M,D
Fordham University	M,D
Golden Gate University	M,D
Michigan State University College of Law	M,D
Montclair State University	M,O
Santa Clara University	M,D,O
Suffolk University	M,D
University of Houston	M,D
University of Pittsburgh	M*
University of San Francisco	M
University of Washington	M,D*
Western Michigan University Thomas M. Cooley Law School	M,D
Yeshiva University	M,D

INTERDISCIPLINARY STUDIES

Alaska Pacific University	M
Amberton University	M
Antioch University New England	M
Arizona State University at the Tempe campus	M
Athabasca University	M,O
Baylor University	D
Boise State University	M
Bowling Green State University	M,D
Buffalo State College, State University of New York	M
California College of the Arts	M
California Institute of Integral Studies	M,D
California State University, Bakersfield	M
California State University, East Bay	M
California State University, Long Beach	M
California State University, San Bernardino	M
California State University, Stanislaus	M
Cambridge College	M,D,O
Campbell University	M
Central Washington University	M
Clarkson University	M,D
Concordia University (Canada)	M,D
Dalhousie University	D
Dallas Baptist University	M
DePaul University	M
Eastern Washington University	M
Emory University	D
Fitchburg State University	O
Florida Gulf Coast University	M
Florida Institute of Technology	M
Fresno Pacific University	M
Frostburg State University	M
George Mason University	M
Georgetown University	M,D
Goddard College	M
The Graduate Center, City University of New York	M,D
Harrison Middleton University	M,D
Hiram College	M
Hollins University	M
Idaho State University	M
Indiana University Southeast	M,O
Iowa State University of Science and Technology	M
Lehigh University	M,D
Lesley University	M,D,O
Long Island University–LIU Post	M,D,O
Marquette University	D
Marylhurst University	M
Marywood University	D
Massachusetts College of Art and Design	M,O
Michigan Technological University	M,D,O
Mills College	M,O
Minnesota State University Mankato	M
Montana State University Billings	M
Montana Tech of The University of Montana	M
New Mexico State University	M,D
New York University	M
Niagara University	M
Northeastern University	M,D,O
Nova Southeastern University	M,D,O*
The Ohio State University	M,D
Oregon State University	M
Regent University	M,D,O
Rensselaer Polytechnic Institute	M,D
Rochester Institute of Technology	M
Rosalind Franklin University of Medicine and Science	D
Rutgers University–New Brunswick	D
San Diego State University	M
Sonoma State University	M
Southern Illinois University Edwardsville	M
Southern Oregon University	M
State University of New York at Fredonia	M
Stephen F. Austin State University	M
Teachers College, Columbia University	M,D
Texas A&M University–Texarkana	M
Texas State University	M
Texas Tech University	M,D
Trinity Western University	M
Tufts University	D
Tulane University	D
Union Institute & University	M,D
The University of Alabama	D
The University of Alabama at Birmingham	D
University of Alaska Anchorage	M
University of Alaska Fairbanks	M,D
The University of Arizona	M,D
University of Arkansas	M,D
University of Arkansas at Little Rock	M
University of California, Santa Barbara	D
University of California, Santa Cruz	M,D
University of Central Florida	M,O
University of Central Oklahoma	M
University of Chicago	D
University of Cincinnati	D
University of Colorado Colorado Springs	M
University of Florida	M,D
University of Houston–Victoria	M
University of Idaho	M
University of Illinois at Chicago	D

University of Illinois at Springfield	M
University of Illinois at Urbana–Champaign	D
The University of Kansas	D*
University of Louisville	M,D
University of Maine	M,D
University of Manitoba	M,D
University of Massachusetts Medical School	M,D
University of Memphis	M,D,O
University of Minnesota, Twin Cities Campus	D
University of Missouri–Kansas City	D
University of Montana	M,D
University of New Brunswick Fredericton	M,D
University of North Alabama	M
The University of North Carolina at Charlotte	M,D,O
University of Northern British Columbia	M,D,O
University of North Texas	M,D,O
University of Oklahoma	M,D*
University of Oregon	M
University of Ottawa	D,O
University of Pittsburgh	D*
University of Regina	M
University of South Alabama	M,D
The University of South Dakota	M
University of South Florida	M,D
The University of Tennessee at Martin	M
The University of Texas at Arlington	M
The University of Texas at Dallas	M*
The University of Texas at El Paso	M
The University of Texas at San Antonio	M,D
The University of Texas at Tyler	M
The University of Texas Health Science Center at San Antonio	D
The University of Texas Rio Grande Valley	M
University of the Incarnate Word	M
University of Virginia	M,D
University of Washington, Tacoma	M
The University of Western Ontario	M,D
Virginia Commonwealth University	M
Virginia Polytechnic Institute and State University	M,D
Virginia State University	M
Walden University	M,D,O
Washington State University	D
Wayland Baptist University	M
Western Kentucky University	M,O
Western New Mexico University	M
West Texas A&M University	M
Worcester Polytechnic Institute	M,D,O
Wright State University	M
York University	M

INTERIOR DESIGN

Academy of Art University	M
Ball State University	M
Boston Architectural College	M
Brenau University	M
California State Polytechnic University, Pomona	M
Chatham University	M
Cornell University	M
Drexel University	M
Eastern Michigan University	M
Endicott College	M
Fashion Institute of Technology	M*
Florida International University	M,O
Florida State University	M
The George Washington University	M*
Georgia State University	M
Interior Designers Institute	M
Iowa State University of Science and Technology	M
Lawrence Technological University	M,O
Marymount University	M
Marywood University	M
Miami University	M
Michigan State University	M,D
Moore College of Art & Design	M
The New School	M
New York School of Interior Design	M
The Ohio State University	M
Oregon State University	M,D
Paris College of Art	M
Philadelphia University	M
Pontificia Universidad Catolica Madre y Maestra	M
Pratt Institute	M*
Queens University of Charlotte	M
Rhode Island School of Design	M
San Diego State University	M
Savannah College of Art and Design	M
School of the Art Institute of Chicago	M
Suffolk University	M
Texas Tech University	M,D
University of California, Berkeley	O
University of Cincinnati	M
University of Florida	M,D
University of Georgia	M,D
University of Kentucky	M
University of Manitoba	M
University of Massachusetts Amherst	M*
University of Memphis	M,O
University of Minnesota, Twin Cities Campus	M,D,O
University of Nebraska–Lincoln	M,D
The University of North Carolina at Greensboro	M,O
University of North Texas	M,D,O
University of Oklahoma	M,O*
University of Oregon	M
The University of Texas at Austin	M
Utah State University	M
Virginia Commonwealth University	M
Washington State University	M
Wayne State University	M

INTERNATIONAL AFFAIRS

Alliant International University–México City	M
American Graduate School in Paris	M,D
American Public University System	M
American University	M,D,O
The American University in Cairo	M,O
American University of Armenia	M
The American University of Paris	M
Appalachian State University	M
Arcadia University	M
Auburn University at Montgomery	M,D,O
Azusa Pacific University	M
Baylor University	M,D
Boston University	M
Brandeis University	M
Brigham Young University	M
Brock University	M
Brooklyn College of the City University of New York	M
California State University, Fresno	M
California State University, Stanislaus	M
Carleton University	M,D
The Catholic University of America	M,D
Central Connecticut State University	M
Central European University	M,D
Central Michigan University	M,O
Chapman University	M
City College of the City University of New York	M
Claremont Graduate University	M,D
Cleveland State University	M
Colorado School of Mines	O
Columbia University	M,D*
Concordia University Irvine	M
Cornell University	D
Creighton University	M
DePaul University	M
East Carolina University	M
Embry-Riddle Aeronautical University–Worldwide	M
Fairleigh Dickinson University, Metropolitan Campus	M
Florida International University	M,D
Florida State University	M
Fordham University	M,O
George Mason University	M
Georgetown University	M,D
The George Washington University	M,D*
Georgia Institute of Technology	M
Harvard University	D*
Hult International Business School (United States)	M
Hult International Business School (United States)	M
Instituto Tecnologico de Santo Domingo	M,O
Instituto Tecnológico y de Estudios Superiores de Monterrey, Campus Ciudad Obregón	M
International University in Geneva	M,D
Johns Hopkins University	M,D,O
Kansas State University	M
Kennesaw State University	M
Lebanese American University	M
Lesley University	M,D,O
Liberty University	M,D,O
London Metropolitan University	M,D
Loyola University Chicago	M,D
Marquette University	M,D
McMaster University	M,D
Middlebury Institute of International Studies at Monterey	M
Middle Tennessee State University	M
Missouri State University	M
Morgan State University	M
New England College	M
The New School	M
New York University	M,D,O
North Carolina State University	M
Northeastern University	M,D
Northwestern University	M,D,O*
Norwich University	M
Ohio University	M
Oklahoma State University	M,D,O
Old Dominion University	M,D
Penn State University Park	M
Pepperdine University	M
Pontificia Universidad Catolica Madre y Maestra	M
Princeton University	M,D
Queen's University at Kingston	M,D
Regent's University London	M
Regent University	M
Richmond, The American International University in London	M
Rutgers University–Camden	M
Rutgers University–Newark	M,D
Rutgers University–New Brunswick	M,D
St. John's University (NY)	M,O
St. Mary's University (United States)	M,O
Salve Regina University	M,O
San Francisco State University	M
Schiller International University	M
Seton Hall University	M,O
Simon Fraser University	M
SIT Graduate Institute	M
Stratford University (VA)	M,D
Syracuse University	M
Teachers College, Columbia University	M,D,O
Texas A&M University	M,O
Texas State University	M
Troy University	M
Tufts University	M,D
United States International University–Africa	M
Universidad de las Americas, A.C.	M
Universidad Nacional Pedro Henriquez Urena	M
Université de Montréal	M,O
Université Laval	M,D
University of Bridgeport	M
The University of British Columbia	M
University of California, Berkeley	M,D
University of California, San Diego	M,D
University of California, Santa Barbara	M,D
University of California, Santa Cruz	D
University of Central Oklahoma	M
University of Chicago	M
University of Colorado Boulder	M,D
University of Colorado Denver	M
University of Delaware	M,D*
University of Denver	M,D,O
University of Florida	M
University of Georgia	M,D
University of Hawaii at Manoa	O
University of Indianapolis	M
The University of Kansas	M*
University of Kentucky	M
University of Maine	M
The University of Manchester	D
University of Massachusetts Boston	M
University of Miami	M,D
University of Michigan–Flint	M
University of Northern British Columbia	M,D,O
University of North Georgia	M
University of North Texas	M,D,O
University of Oklahoma	M,O*
University of Oregon	M
University of Pennsylvania	M*
University of Pittsburgh	M,D,O*
University of Rhode Island	M
University of Rochester	M,D*
University of San Diego	M
University of San Francisco	M
University of South Carolina	M,D
University of Southern California	M,D
University of South Florida	M,D,O
University of the Pacific	M,D
University of Toronto	M
University of Utah	M,D*
University of Virginia	M,D
University of Washington	D*
University of Waterloo	M,D
University of Wyoming	M
Virginia International University	M
Virginia Polytechnic Institute and State University	M,D,O
Walden University	M,D,O
Webster University	M
Western Michigan University	M,D
West Virginia University	M,D
Wilfrid Laurier University	M,D
Yale University	M*
York University	M

INTERNATIONAL AND COMPARATIVE EDUCATION

American University	M
The American University in Cairo	M
Avila University	M,O
Bowling Green State University	M
California Baptist University	M
California State University, Dominguez Hills	M
The College of New Jersey	M,O
Drexel University	M,D
Florida International University	M,D,O
Florida State University	M,D
Gallaudet University	M,D,O
George Mason University	M
The George Washington University	M,D,O*
Harvard University	M*
Indiana University Bloomington	M,D,O
Lehigh University	M,D,O
Louisiana State University and Agricultural & Mechanical College	M,D
Middlebury Institute of International Studies at Monterey	M
Morehead State University	M,O
National University	M,O
New York University	M,D,O
SIT Graduate Institute	M
Stanford University	M,D
Teachers College, Columbia University	M,D
University of Bridgeport	M,D,O
University of Massachusetts Amherst	M,D,O*
University of Minnesota, Twin Cities Campus	M,D
University of Pennsylvania	M*
University of Pittsburgh	M,D*
University of San Francisco	M,D
University of South Africa	M,D
University of Wisconsin–Madison	M,D,O
Vanderbilt University	M,D*
Walden University	M,D,O
Wilkes University	M,D
Wright State University	M

INTERNATIONAL BUSINESS

Alliant International University–México City	M
American Business & Technology University	M
American InterContinental University Atlanta	M
American InterContinental University Online	M
American Public University System	M
The American University in Dubai	M
The American University of Paris	M
Anaheim University	M,D,O
Argosy University, Atlanta	M,D
Argosy University, Chicago	M,D
Argosy University, Dallas	M,D,O
Argosy University, Denver	M,D
Argosy University, Hawai`i	M,D,O
Argosy University, Inland Empire	M,D
Argosy University, Los Angeles	M,D
Argosy University, Nashville	M,D
Argosy University, Orange County	M,D,O
Argosy University, Phoenix	M,D
Argosy University, Salt Lake City	M,D
Argosy University, San Diego	M,D
Argosy University, San Francisco Bay Area	M,D
Argosy University, Sarasota	M,D,O
Argosy University, Schaumburg	M,D,O
Argosy University, Seattle	M,D
Argosy University, Tampa	M,D
Argosy University, Twin Cities	M,D
Argosy University, Washington DC	M,D,O
Arizona State University at the Tempe campus	M,D
Ashworth College	M
Assumption College	M,O
Avila University	M
Azusa Pacific University	M
Baldwin Wallace University	M
Barry University	O
Baruch College of the City University of New York	M,D
Benedictine University	M
Boston University	M,D
Brandeis University	M,D
Bristol University	M
Brooklyn College of the City University of New York	M
Bryant University	M
Butler University	M
California Intercontinental University	M,D
California Lutheran University	M,O
California State University, East Bay	M
California State University, Fullerton	M
California State University, Los Angeles	M
California State University, San Bernardino	M
California University of Management and Sciences	M,D
Canisius College	M
Central European University	M,D
Central Michigan University	M,O
Christian Brothers University	M,O
City University of Seattle	M,O
Clark University	M
Clayton State University	M
Cleveland State University	M,D,O
Colorado Heights University	M
Colorado State University–Global Campus	M
Columbia University	M*
Concordia University Wisconsin	M
Copenhagen Business School	M,D
Daemen College	M
Dallas Baptist University	M
Delaware Valley University	M
Dominican University of California	M
Duke University	M,O*
D'Youville College	M
Eastern Michigan University	M,O
Ellis University	M
Emerson College	M
ESSEC Business School	M,D
Everest University	M
Everest University	M
Everest University	M
Fairleigh Dickinson University, College at Florham	M,O
Fairleigh Dickinson University, Metropolitan Campus	M
Florida International University	M,D
Florida State University	M
Franklin University Switzerland	M
George Mason University	M
Georgetown University	M,D
The George Washington University	M,D*
Georgia Institute of Technology	M
Georgia State University	M
Golden Gate University	M,D,O
Goldey-Beacom College	M
Hallmark University	M
Harding University	M
Hawai`i Pacific University	M
HEC Montreal	M
Hofstra University	M,O
Hope International University	M
Houston Baptist University	M
Howard University	M
Hult International Business School (United States)	M
Hult International Business School (United States)	M
Hult International Business School (United States)	M
Hult International Business School (United States)	M

*M—masters degree; D—doctorate; O—other advanced degree; *—Close-Up and/or Display*

Indiana Tech	D
Instituto Tecnologico de Santo Domingo	M,O
Instituto Tecnológico y de Estudios Superiores de Monterrey, Campus Central de Veracruz	M
Instituto Tecnológico y de Estudios Superiores de Monterrey, Campus Chihuahua	M,O
Instituto Tecnológico y de Estudios Superiores de Monterrey, Campus Ciudad de México	M,D
Instituto Tecnológico y de Estudios Superiores de Monterrey, Campus Cuernavaca	M
Instituto Tecnológico y de Estudios Superiores de Monterrey, Campus Irapuato	M,D
Instituto Tecnológico y de Estudios Superiores de Monterrey, Campus Monterrey	M
Inter American University of Puerto Rico, Metropolitan Campus	M,D
Inter American University of Puerto Rico, San Germán Campus	M,D
International University in Geneva	M,D
The International University of Monaco	M
Iona College	M,O
John Brown University	M
John Marshall Law School	M,D
Kaplan University, Davenport Campus	M
Kean University	M
Keiser University	M,D
Lake Forest Graduate School of Management	M
La Salle University	M,O
Lenoir-Rhyne University	M
Lewis University	M
Liberty University	M,D,O
Lincoln University (CA)	M,D
Lindenwood University	M
Long Island University–LIU Post	M
Loyola University Chicago	M
Loyola University Maryland	M
Lynn University	M
Madonna University	M
Maine Maritime Academy	M
Manhattanville College	M*
Marconi International University	M,D
Marquette University	M,O
McGill University	M,D,O
McKendree University	M
Middlebury Institute of International Studies at Monterey	M
Milwaukee School of Engineering	M*
National University	M,O
New Jersey Institute of Technology	M,O
Newman University	M
New Mexico Highlands University	M
New York University	M,D
Niagara University	M
North Central College	M
Northeastern University	M,D
Northwestern University	M,D*
Northwest University	M
Norwich University	M
Nova Southeastern University	M*
Oakland University	M,O
Oklahoma Christian University	M
Oral Roberts University	M
Pace University	M,O
Pacific States University	M,D
Park University	M,O
Pepperdine University	M
Pittsburg State University	M
Polytechnic University of Puerto Rico	M
Polytechnic University of Puerto Rico, Miami Campus	M
Polytechnic University of Puerto Rico, Orlando Campus	M
Pontifical Catholic University of Puerto Rico	M
Pontificia Universidad Catolica Madre y Maestra	M
Portland State University	M
Providence College	M
Purdue University	M
Regent's University London	M
Rochester Institute of Technology	M
Rockhurst University	M,O
Rollins College	M,D
Roosevelt University	M
Rutgers University–Newark	D
St. John's University (NY)	M
Saint Joseph's University	M,O
Saint Louis University	M,D
Saint Mary's University of Minnesota	M
Saint Peter's University	M
St. Thomas University	M,O
Salem International University	M
San Francisco State University	M
Schiller International University (United States)	M
Schiller International University (Germany)	M
Schiller International University	M
Schiller International University (Spain)	M
Seton Hall University	M,O
SIT Graduate Institute	M
Sonoma State University	M
Southeast Missouri State University	M
Southern New Hampshire University	M,O
Southern Oregon University	M,O
State University of New York Empire State College	M
Stevens Institute of Technology	M
Stratford University (VA)	M,D
Suffolk University	M,O
Taylor University	M
Temple University	M,D*
Tennessee Technological University	M
Texas A&M International University	M,D
Texas A&M University–Corpus Christi	M
Texas A&M University–San Antonio	M
Tiffin University	M
Trident University International	M,D
Trinity Western University	M
Troy University	M
Tufts University	M,D
Tulane University	M,D
United States International University–Africa	M
Universidad Autonoma de Guadalajara	M,D
Universidad Metropolitana	M
Université de Sherbrooke	M
Université du Québec, École nationale d'administration publique	M,O
Université Laval	M,O
University at Buffalo, the State University of New York	M,D,O*
The University of Akron	M
University of Alberta	M
University of Baltimore	M
University of Bridgeport	M
University of California, Berkeley	O
University of California, Los Angeles	M,D
University of Chicago	M,O
University of Colorado Denver	M
University of Dallas	M,D
University of Florida	M,D
University of Hawaii at Manoa	M,D
University of Houston–Victoria	M
University of Kentucky	M
University of La Verne	M
University of Lethbridge	M,D
University of Louisville	M
University of Maine	M,O
The University of Manchester	M
University of Mary Hardin-Baylor	M
University of Maryland University College	M,O
University of Massachusetts Boston	M
University of Massachusetts Dartmouth	M,O
University of Michigan–Flint	M
University of Missouri–St. Louis	M,D,O
University of New Brunswick Saint John	M
University of New Haven	M,O
University of New Mexico	M
University of North Alabama	M
University of North Florida	M
University of Pennsylvania	M*
University of Phoenix–Atlanta Campus	M
University of Phoenix–Augusta Campus	M
University of Phoenix–Bay Area Campus	M,D
University of Phoenix–Central Valley Campus	M
University of Phoenix–Charlotte Campus	M
University of Phoenix–Colorado Campus	M
University of Phoenix–Colorado Springs Downtown Campus	M
University of Phoenix–Columbus Georgia Campus	M
University of Phoenix–Dallas Campus	M
University of Phoenix–Hawaii Campus	M
University of Phoenix–Houston Campus	M
University of Phoenix–Jersey City Campus	M
University of Phoenix–Las Vegas Campus	M
University of Phoenix–New Mexico Campus	M
University of Phoenix–North Florida Campus	M
University of Phoenix–Online Campus	M,O
University of Phoenix–Phoenix Campus	M,O
University of Phoenix–Sacramento Valley Campus	M
University of Phoenix–San Antonio Campus	M
University of Phoenix–San Diego Campus	M
University of Phoenix–Southern Arizona Campus	M
University of Phoenix–Southern California Campus	M
University of Phoenix–South Florida Campus	M
University of Phoenix–Utah Campus	M
University of Pittsburgh	O*
University of Puerto Rico, Rí o Piedras Campus	M,D
University of Regina	M,O
University of Rochester	M*
University of St. Thomas (TX)	M
University of San Diego	M
University of San Francisco	M
University of Saskatchewan	M,D
The University of Scranton	M
University of South Carolina	M
The University of Tampa	M
The University of Texas at Dallas	M,D*
The University of Texas at El Paso	M,D,O
University of the Incarnate Word	M
University of the West	M
The University of Toledo	M
University of Virginia	M,O
University of Washington	M,D,O*
The University of Western Ontario	M,D
University of Wisconsin–Oshkosh	M
Valparaiso University	M
Vancouver Island University	M
Villanova University	M
Virginia International University	M,O
Viterbo University	M
Wagner College	M
Walden University	M,D,O
Walsh College of Accountancy and Business Administration	M
Wayland Baptist University	M,D
Webster University	M
Western International University	M
Wilkes University	M
Wright State University	M
Xavier University	M
York University	M,D

INTERNATIONAL DEVELOPMENT

American University	M,D,O
Andrews University	M
Athabasca University	M,O
Boston University	M,D
Clark University	M
Dalhousie University	M
Duke University	M*
Eastern University	M
Fordham University	M,O
The George Washington University	M,D*
Harvard University	M*
Hope International University	M
Indiana University Bloomington	M,D,O
Johns Hopkins University	M,D,O
Lehigh University	M,D,O
Marymount California University	M
McGill University	M,D,O
Middlebury Institute of International Studies at Monterey	M
New York University	M,O
Norwich University	M
Ohio University	M
Old Dominion University	M,D
Rutgers University–Camden	M
Saint Mary's University (Canada)	M,O
St. Mary's University (United States)	M,O
Saint Mary's University of Minnesota	M
Tufts University	M,D
Tulane University	M,D
University of Denver	M,D,O
University of Florida	M,D,O
University of Guelph	M,D
University of Hawaii at Manoa	M,D,O
The University of Manchester	M,D
University of Massachusetts Boston	M,D
University of Minnesota, Twin Cities Campus	M
University of New Brunswick Fredericton	M
University of New Mexico	M,D
University of Ottawa	M
University of Pittsburgh	M,D*
University of San Francisco	M
University of Southern Mississippi	M,D
Walden University	M,D,O

INTERNATIONAL ECONOMICS

American University	M,D,O
Claremont Graduate University	M,D,O
Cleveland State University	M
Fordham University	M,O
Johns Hopkins University	M,D,O
The New School	M,D
Pace University	O
University of New Mexico	M,D
University of Wisconsin–Milwaukee	M,D
Valparaiso University	M
Wayne State University	M,D
West Virginia University	M,D
Wichita State University	M
Wilfrid Laurier University	M
Yale University	M*

INTERNATIONAL HEALTH

Arizona State University at the Tempe campus	M,D,O
Boston University	M,D
Brandeis University	M,D
Cedarville University	M,D
Central Michigan University	M,D,O
Duke University	M*
Emory University	M
George Mason University	M,O
Georgetown University	M,D
The George Washington University	M,D*
Harvard University	M,D*
Johns Hopkins University	M,D
Liberty University	M,O
Loma Linda University	M
Medical University of South Carolina	M
New York Medical College	O
New York University	M,D
Northwestern University	M*
Oregon State University	M,D
Park University	M,O
San Diego State University	M,D
Seton Hall University	M,O
Simon Fraser University	M,D,O
Syracuse University	M
Trident University International	M,D,O
Tufts University	M,D
Tulane University	M,D
Uniformed Services University of the Health Sciences	M,D*
University of Alberta	M,D
University of California, San Diego	D
University of Colorado Denver	M
University of Denver	M,D,O
University of Florida	M,D
University of Michigan	M,D
University of Minnesota, Twin Cities Campus	M,D
University of Missouri	M,O
University of Pennsylvania	M*
University of Southern California	M,O
University of South Florida	M,D,O
The University of Toledo	M,O
University of Washington	M,D*
Walden University	M,D,O
Washington University in St. Louis	M,D,O
William James College	M,D,O
Yale University	M,D*

INTERNATIONAL TRADE POLICY

The George Washington University	M*
Middlebury Institute of International Studies at Monterey	M

INTERNET AND INTERACTIVE MULTIMEDIA

Academy of Art University	M
Alfred University	M
Ball State University	M
Boston University	M,O
Brandeis University	M
Brooklyn College of the City University of New York	M
California State University, East Bay	M
Champlain College	M
Concordia University (Canada)	M,D,O
DePaul University	M,D
Duquesne University	M,O
Elon University	M
Excelsior College	M,O
Fairfield University	M,O
Full Sail University	M
Gannon University	M
Georgetown University	M
Georgia Institute of Technology	M,D
Indiana University–Purdue University Indianapolis	M,D
Ithaca College	M
Kutztown University of Pennsylvania	M
Lindenwood University	M
Lindenwood University–Belleville	M
Lindsey Wilson College	M
London Metropolitan University	M,D
Long Island University–LIU Post	M
Louisiana State University and Agricultural & Mechanical College	M
Lynn University	M,O
Marlboro College	M,O
Mississippi State University	M,D,O
Mount Mary University	M
National University	M,O
New Mexico Highlands University	M
New York University	M,O
North Central College	M
Northeastern University	M
Northwestern University	M*
The Ohio State University	M
Pace University	M,D,O
Philadelphia University	M
Pratt Institute	M*
Quinnipiac University	M
Robert Morris University	M,D
Rochester Institute of Technology	O
Rocky Mountain College of Art + Design	M
Sacred Heart University	M,O
Sam Houston State University	M
San Diego State University	M
Savannah College of Art and Design	M,O
School of Visual Arts (NY)	M
Southern New Hampshire University	M,O
State University of New York at Oswego	M
Stevens Institute of Technology	M,D,O
Tennessee Technological University	M
Touro College	M
Towson University	M,D,O
Universidad Autonoma de Guadalajara	M,D
University of Advancing Technology	M
University of Colorado Boulder	D
University of Georgia	M
University of Massachusetts Dartmouth	M,O
University of Miami	M
University of Montana	M
University of North Texas	M,D,O
University of Pennsylvania	M,O*
University of Southern California	M,D,O
University of South Florida	M,O
The University of Texas at Dallas	M,D*
University of the Sacred Heart	M,O
University of Utah	M*
Virginia Commonwealth University	M
Virginia Polytechnic Institute and State University	M,D,O
Webster University	M
Western Illinois University	M,O
Wilmington University	M
Worcester Polytechnic Institute	M

INTERNET ENGINEERING

Hofstra University	M
New Jersey Institute of Technology	M,D
University of Georgia	M
Wilmington University	M

INVESTMENT MANAGEMENT

Alaska Pacific University	M,O
DePaul University	M
Fordham University	M
The George Washington University	M,D*
Hofstra University	M,O
Johns Hopkins University	M,O
Lincoln University (CA)	M,D
Lynn University	M
Manhattanville College	M*
Marywood University	M
New York University	M,O
Oregon State University	M,D
Pace University	M,O
Regent University	M,D,O
Sacred Heart University	M,D,O
St. John's University (NY)	M
Saint Mary's College of California	M
Southern New Hampshire University	M,O
University of Colorado Denver	M
University of Houston–Downtown	M
The University of Iowa	M*
The University of Texas at Dallas	M*
The University of Tulsa	M
University of Wisconsin–Madison	D
University of Wisconsin–Milwaukee	M,D,O

ITALIAN

Binghamton University, State University of New York	M*
Boston College	M
Brown University	D
Central Connecticut State University	M,O
Columbia University	M,D*
Cornell University	D
DePaul University	M
Drew University	M,D,O
Duke University	D*
Florida State University	M
The Graduate Center, City University of New York	M,D
Harvard University	M,D*
Hunter College of the City University of New York	M
Indiana University Bloomington	M,D
Johns Hopkins University	D
McGill University	M,D
Middlebury College	M,D
New York University	M,D,O
Northwestern University	D,O*
The Ohio State University	M,D
Queens College of the City University of New York	M
Rutgers University–New Brunswick	M,D
San Francisco State University	M
Stanford University	M,D
Stony Brook University, State University of New York	M
University of Alberta	M,D
The University of Arizona	M
University of California, Berkeley	D
University of California, Los Angeles	M,D
University of Chicago	D
University of Illinois at Urbana–Champaign	M,D
The University of Manchester	M,D
University of Massachusetts Amherst	M*
University of Michigan	D
The University of North Carolina at Chapel Hill	M,D
University of Notre Dame	M
University of Oregon	M
University of Pennsylvania	M,D*
University of Pittsburgh	M*
University of South Africa	M,D
The University of Tennessee	D
The University of Texas at Austin	M,D
University of Toronto	M,D
University of Victoria	M
University of Virginia	M
University of Washington	M,D*
University of Wisconsin–Madison	M,D
Wayne State University	M
Yale University	D*

JAPANESE

Arizona State University at the Tempe campus	M
Columbia University	M,D*
DePaul University	M
Eastern Michigan University	M,O
Harvard University	D*
Indiana University Bloomington	M,D
Kent State University	M,D
New York University	M,D,O
The Ohio State University	M,D
Portland State University	M
Purdue University	M,D
San Francisco State University	M
Stanford University	M,D
University of Alberta	M
University of California, Berkeley	D
University of California, Irvine	M,D
University of Colorado Boulder	M,D
University of Hawaii at Manoa	M,D,O
The University of Manchester	M,D
University of Massachusetts Amherst	M*
University of Oregon	M,D
University of Pittsburgh	M*
University of Washington	M,D*
University of Wisconsin–Madison	M,D
Washington University in St. Louis	M,D

JEWISH STUDIES

American Jewish University	M
Biola University	M,D,O
Brandeis University	M,D
Brooklyn College of the City University of New York	M
Central Yeshiva Tomchei Tmimim-Lubavitch	M
Columbia University	M,D*
Concordia University (Canada)	M
Cornell University	M,D
Criswell College	M
Dallas Theological Seminary	M,D,O
Graduate Theological Union	M,D,O
Gratz College	M,O
Harvard University	M,D*
Hebrew College	M,O
Hebrew Union College–Jewish Institute of Religion (NY)	M
Indiana University Bloomington	M
The Jewish Theological Seminary	M,D
McGill University	M
New York University	M,D,O
Reconstructionist Rabbinical College	M,D,O
Rice University	D
Rutgers University–New Brunswick	M,O
Seton Hall University	M,O
Southern Evangelical Seminary	M,D,O
Spertus Institute for Jewish Learning and Leadership	M,D
Telshe Yeshiva–Chicago	O
Touro College	M
Towson University	M,O
University of California, Berkeley	D
University of California, San Diego	M,D
University of Connecticut	M*
University of Florida	M,D
University of Maryland, College Park	M
University of Michigan	M,D,O
University of St. Michael's College	M,D,O
University of Wisconsin–Madison	M,D
Washington University in St. Louis	M
Yeshiva University	M,D

JOURNALISM

American University	M
The American University in Cairo	M
Arizona State University at the Tempe campus	M,D
Arkansas State University	M
Arkansas Tech University	M
Ball State University	M
Baylor University	M
Bob Jones University	M,D,O
Boston University	M
California State University, Fresno	M
California State University, Northridge	M
Carleton University	M,D
Columbia College Chicago	M
Columbia University	M,D*
Concordia University (Canada)	M,O
CUNY Graduate School of Journalism	M,O
DePaul University	M
Drexel University	M
Emerson College	M
Florida Agricultural and Mechanical University	M
Florida International University	M
Full Sail University	M
Georgetown University	M,D
Harvard University	M,O*
Hofstra University	M
Indiana University Bloomington	M,D
Iowa State University of Science and Technology	M
Kansas State University	M
Kent State University	M
Lindenwood University	M
Marquette University	M,O
Marshall University	M
Michigan State University	M
National University	M
New York University	M,D,O
Northeastern University	M
Northwestern University	M*
Ohio University	M,D
Point Park University	M
Quinnipiac University	M
Regent University	M,D
Roosevelt University	M
Sacred Heart University	M
School of the Art Institute of Chicago	M
South Dakota State University	M
Stanford University	M,D
Stony Brook University, State University of New York	M,O
Syracuse University	M
Temple University	M*
Université Laval	O
The University of Alabama	M
The University of Arizona	M
University of Arkansas	M
The University of British Columbia	M
University of California, Berkeley	M
University of Colorado Boulder	M,D
University of Florida	M,D
University of Georgia	M,D
University of Illinois at Springfield	M
University of Illinois at Urbana–Champaign	M
The University of Iowa	M,D*
The University of Kansas	M*
University of King's College	M
University of Maryland, College Park	M,D
University of Memphis	M
University of Miami	M,D
University of Mississippi	M
University of Missouri	M,D
University of Montana	M
University of Nebraska–Lincoln	M
University of Nevada, Las Vegas	M
University of Nevada, Reno	M
University of North Texas	M,D,O
University of Oklahoma	M,D*
University of Oregon	M,D
University of Puerto Rico, Río Piedras Campus	M
University of Regina	M
University of South Carolina	M,D
University of Southern California	M
University of South Florida	M,O
University of South Florida, St. Petersburg	M
The University of Tennessee	M,D
The University of Texas at Austin	M,D
The University of Western Ontario	M
University of Wisconsin–Madison	M,D
Virginia Commonwealth University	M
Wayne State University	M,D,O
West Virginia University	M,O

KINESIOLOGY AND MOVEMENT STUDIES

A.T. Still University	M,D
Auburn University	M,D,O
Ball State University	M,D,O
Barry University	M
Baylor University	M,D
Boise State University	M
Bowling Green State University	M
Brooklyn College of the City University of New York	M
California Polytechnic State University, San Luis Obispo	M
California State Polytechnic University, Pomona	M
California State University, Chico	M
California State University, Fresno	M
California State University, Long Beach	M
California State University, Los Angeles	M,O
California State University, Northridge	M
Canisius College	M
Columbia University	M,D*
Dalhousie University	M
Dallas Baptist University	M
East Carolina University	M,D,O
Eastern Illinois University	M
Eastern Michigan University	M
East Tennessee State University	M,O
Fresno Pacific University	M
Georgia College & State University	M
Georgia Southern University	M
Georgia State University	D
Hardin-Simmons University	M
Humboldt State University	M
Indiana University Bloomington	M,D
Inter American University of Puerto Rico, San Germán Campus	M
Iowa State University of Science and Technology	M,D
Jacksonville University	M*
James Madison University	M
Kansas State University	M,D
Lakehead University	M
Lamar University	M
Louisiana State University and Agricultural & Mechanical College	M,D
McGill University	M,D,O
McMaster University	M,D
Memorial University of Newfoundland	M
Michigan State University	M,D
Michigan Technological University	M
Mississippi College	M
Mississippi State University	M,D
Missouri State University	M
New York University	M,D,O
Northeastern State University	M
Northwestern University	D*
The Ohio State University	M,D
Old Dominion University	D
Oregon State University	M,D
Penn State University Park	M,D,O
Point Loma Nazarene University	M
Purdue University	M,D
Saint Mary's College of California	M
Sam Houston State University	M
San Diego State University	M
San Francisco State University	M
San Jose State University	M,O
Sarah Lawrence College	M
Simon Fraser University	M,D
Sonoma State University	M
Southeastern Louisiana University	M
Southern Arkansas University–Magnolia	M
Southern Illinois University Carbondale	M
Southern Illinois University Edwardsville	M
Southwestern Oklahoma State University	M
Stephen F. Austin State University	M
Syracuse University	M,D,O
Tarleton State University	M
Teachers College, Columbia University	M,D
Temple University	M,D*
Tennessee Technological University	M
Texas A&M University	M,D
Texas A&M University–Corpus Christi	M,D
Texas A&M University–Kingsville	M
Texas A&M University–San Antonio	M
Texas Christian University	M
Texas Tech University	M
Texas Woman's University	M,D
Towson University	M
Université de Montréal	M,D,O
Université de Sherbrooke	M,O
Université du Québec à Montréal	M
Université Laval	M,D
The University of Alabama	M,D
University of Arkansas	M,D
The University of British Columbia	M,D
University of Calgary	M,D
University of Central Arkansas	M
University of Central Missouri	M,D,O
University of Colorado Boulder	M,D
University of Delaware	M,D*
University of Florida	M,D
University of Georgia	M,D
University of Hawaii at Manoa	M,D
University of Houston	M,D
University of Illinois at Chicago	M,D
University of Illinois at Urbana–Champaign	M,D
University of Kentucky	M,D
University of Lethbridge	M,D
University of Maine	M,D,O
University of Manitoba	M
University of Mary	M
University of Maryland, College Park	M,D
University of Massachusetts Amherst	M,D*
University of Michigan	M,D
University of Minnesota, Twin Cities Campus	M,D,O
University of Mississippi	M,D
University of Nevada, Las Vegas	M,D
University of New Hampshire	M,O
University of North Alabama	M
The University of North Carolina at Chapel Hill	M,D
The University of North Carolina at Charlotte	M
The University of North Carolina at Greensboro	M,D
University of North Dakota	M
University of Northern Iowa	M
University of North Texas	M,D,O
University of Ottawa	M
University of Puerto Rico, Mayagüez Campus	M
University of Regina	M,D
University of Saskatchewan	M,D,O
The University of South Dakota	M
University of Southern California	M,D
University of Southern Indiana	M
The University of Tennessee	M,D
The University of Texas at Austin	M,D
The University of Texas at El Paso	M
The University of Texas at San Antonio	M
The University of Texas at Tyler	M
The University of Texas of the Permian Basin	M
The University of Texas Rio Grande Valley	M
University of the Incarnate Word	M,D
University of Toronto	M,D
University of Victoria	M
University of Virginia	M,D
University of Waterloo	M,D
The University of Western Ontario	M,D
University of Windsor	M
University of Wisconsin–Madison	M,D
University of Wisconsin–Milwaukee	M,D
University of Wyoming	M
Washington University in St. Louis	D
Wayne State University	M,D,O
West Chester University of Pennsylvania	M,O
Western Illinois University	M
Wilfrid Laurier University	M
York University	M,D

LANDSCAPE ARCHITECTURE

Academy of Art University	M
Arizona State University at the Tempe campus	M,D
Auburn University	M
Ball State University	M
Bastyr University	M,O
Boston Architectural College	M
California State Polytechnic University, Pomona	M
Chatham University	M
City College of the City University of New York	M
Clemson University	M
Colorado State University	M,D
Columbia University	M*

*M—masters degree; D—doctorate; O—other advanced degree; *—Close-Up and/or Display*

Cornell University	M
Florida Agricultural and Mechanical University	M
Florida International University	M
Harvard University	M,D*
Illinois Institute of Technology	M,D
Iowa State University of Science and Technology	M
Kansas State University	M
Louisiana State University and Agricultural & Mechanical College	M
Mississippi State University	M
Morgan State University	M
North Carolina State University	M
The Ohio State University	M,D
Oklahoma State University	M,D
Penn State University Park	M,D
Polytechnic University of Puerto Rico	M
Pontificia Universidad Catolica Madre y Maestra	M
Rhode Island School of Design	M
State University of New York College of Environmental Science and Forestry	M
Temple University	M*
Texas A&M University	M,D
Texas Tech University	M,D
The University of Arizona	M,D,O
The University of British Columbia	M
University of California, Berkeley	M,D,O
University of Colorado Denver	M
University of Florida	M,D
University of Georgia	M
University of Guelph	M
University of Idaho	M
University of Illinois at Urbana–Champaign	M,D
The University of Manchester	M,D
University of Manitoba	M
University of Maryland, College Park	M
University of Massachusetts Amherst	M*
University of Michigan	M
University of Minnesota, Twin Cities Campus	M
University of New Mexico	M
University of Oklahoma	M*
University of Oregon	M
University of Pennsylvania	M,O*
The University of Tennessee	M
The University of Texas at Arlington	M
The University of Texas at Austin	M
University of Toronto	M
University of Virginia	M
University of Washington	M*
University of Wisconsin–Madison	M
Utah State University	M
Virginia Polytechnic Institute and State University	M,D,O
Washington State University	M

LATIN AMERICAN STUDIES

American University	M,O
Boricua College	M
Boston University	M
Brown University	M,D
California State University, Long Beach	M
California State University, Los Angeles	M
The Catholic University of America	M,D
Centro de Estudios Avanzados de Puerto Rico y el Caribe	M,D
Cleveland State University	M
Columbia University	M,D*
Cornell University	M,D
Duke University	M,D*
Florida International University	M
Georgetown University	M
The George Washington University	M*
Georgia State University	M,O
Indiana University Bloomington	M
La Salle University	M,O
Michigan State University	D
New York University	M,O
Northeastern Illinois University	M
The Ohio State University	M
Ohio University	M
San Diego State University	M
Simon Fraser University	M,O
Texas Christian University	M,D
Tulane University	M,D
University at Albany, State University of New York	M,D,O
University at Buffalo, the State University of New York	M*
The University of Arizona	M
University of California, Berkeley	M
University of California, Los Angeles	M
University of California, San Diego	M
University of California, Santa Barbara	M
University of Chicago	M
University of Connecticut	M*
University of Florida	M,O
University of Illinois at Chicago	M
University of Illinois at Urbana–Champaign	M
The University of Kansas	M,O*
The University of Manchester	M,D
University of Massachusetts Dartmouth	M,D
University of Miami	M
University of New Mexico	M,D
The University of North Carolina at Chapel Hill	M,D,O
The University of North Carolina at Charlotte	M,D,O
University of Notre Dame	M
University of Pittsburgh	O*
University of Southern California	D
University of South Florida	M,D,O
The University of Texas at Austin	M
The University of Texas at Dallas	M,D*
University of Utah	M*
University of Wisconsin–Madison	M,D
Vanderbilt University	M*
West Virginia University	M,D
Yale University	D*

LAW

Albany Law School	M,D
Alliant International University–San Francisco	D
American University	M,D
American University of Armenia	M
The American University of Paris	M
Appalachian School of Law	D
Arizona State University at the Tempe campus	M,D
Atlanta's John Marshall Law School	M,D
Ave Maria School of Law	D
Barry University	D
Baylor University	D
Belmont University	D
Boston College	D
Boston University	M,D
Brigham Young University	M,D
Brooklyn Law School	M,D
California Western School of Law	M,D
Campbell University	D
Capital University	M,D
Case Western Reserve University	M,D*
The Catholic University of America	M,D
Central European University	M,D
Champlain College	M
Chapman University	M,D
Charlotte School of Law	D
City University of New York School of Law	D
Cleveland State University	M,D,O
The College of William and Mary	M,D
Columbia University	M,D*
Concord Law School	D
Cornell University	M,D
Creighton University	M,D,O
Dalhousie University	M,D
DePaul University	M,D
Drake University	M,D
Duke University	M,D*
Dunlap-Stone University	M
Duquesne University	M,D
Elon University	D
Emory University	M,D,O
Empire College	M,D
Faulkner University	D
Florida Agricultural and Mechanical University	D
Florida Coastal School of Law	D
Florida International University	M,D
Florida State University	M,D
Fordham University	M,D
Friends University	M
George Mason University	M,D
Georgetown University	M,D
The George Washington University	M,D*
Georgia State University	D
Golden Gate University	M,D
Gonzaga University	D
Hamline University	M,D
Harvard University	M,D*
Hofstra University	M,D
Houston College of Law	D
Howard University	M,D
Humphreys College	D
Illinois Institute of Technology	M,D
Indiana University Bloomington	M,D,O
Indiana University–Purdue University Indianapolis	M,D
Instituto Tecnológico y de Estudios Superiores de Monterrey, Campus Ciudad de México	O
Inter American University of Puerto Rico School of Law	D
John F. Kennedy University	D
John Marshall Law School	M,D
The Judge Advocate General's School, U.S. Army	M
Kaplan University, Davenport Campus	M
Lewis & Clark College	M,D
Liberty University	D
Lincoln Memorial University	D
London Metropolitan University	M,D
Louisiana State University and Agricultural & Mechanical College	M,D
Loyola Marymount University	M,D
Loyola University Chicago	M,D
Loyola University New Orleans	M,D
Marquette University	D
Massachusetts School of Law at Andover	D
McGill University	M,D,O
Mercer University	D
Michigan State University College of Law	M,D
Mississippi College	D,O
Montclair State University	M,O
New England Law–Boston	M,D
New York Law School	M,D
New York University	M,D,O
North Carolina Central University	D
Northeastern University	M,D
Northern Illinois University	D
Northern Kentucky University	D
Northwestern University	M,D*
Nova Southeastern University	M,D*
Ohio Northern University	M,D
The Ohio State University	M,D
Oklahoma City University	M,D
Pace University	M,D
Penn State University - Dickinson Law	M,D
Penn State University Park	M,D
Pepperdine University	D
Pontifical Catholic University of Puerto Rico	D
Pontificia Universidad Catolica Madre y Maestra	M
Queen's University at Kingston	M,D
Quinnipiac University	M,D
Regent University	M,D
Roger Williams University	M,D
Rutgers University–Camden	D
Rutgers University–Newark	D
St. John's University (NY)	M,D
Saint Joseph's University	M,O
Saint Louis University	M,D
St. Mary's University (United States)	M,D
St. Thomas University	M,D
Samford University	M,D
San Joaquin College of Law	D
Santa Clara University	M,D,O
Seattle University	D
Seton Hall University	M,D
Southern Illinois University Carbondale	M,D
Southern Methodist University	M,D
Southern University and Agricultural and Mechanical College	D
Southwestern Law School	M,D
Stanford University	M,D
Stetson University	M,D
Suffolk University	M,D
Syracuse University	D
Taft University System	M,D
Temple University	M,D*
Texas A&M University	D
Texas Southern University	D
Texas Tech University	M,D
Thomas Jefferson School of Law	D
Touro College	M,D
Trine University	M
Trinity International University	D
Tufts University	M,D
Tulane University	M,D
Universidad Autonoma de Guadalajara	M,D
Universidad Central del Este	D
Universidad Iberoamericana	M,D
Université de Montréal	M,D,O
Université de Sherbrooke	M,D,O
Université du Québec à Montréal	O
Université Laval	M,D,O
University at Buffalo, the State University of New York	M,D*
The University of Akron	M,D
The University of Alabama	M,D
University of Alberta	M,D
The University of Arizona	M,D
University of Arkansas	M,D
University of Arkansas at Little Rock	D
University of Baltimore	M,D
The University of British Columbia	M,D
University of Calgary	M,D,O
University of California, Berkeley	M,D
University of California, Davis	M,D
University of California, Hastings College of the Law	M,D
University of California, Irvine	D
University of California, Los Angeles	M,D
University of California, San Diego	M
University of Chicago	M,D
University of Cincinnati	D
University of Colorado Boulder	D
University of Connecticut	D*
University of Dayton	M,D
University of Denver	M,D,O
University of Detroit Mercy	D
University of Florida	M,D
University of Georgia	M,D
University of Hawaii at Manoa	M,D,O
University of Houston	M,D
University of Idaho	D
University of Illinois at Urbana–Champaign	M,D
The University of Iowa	M,D*
The University of Kansas	D*
University of Kentucky	D
University of La Verne	D
University of Louisville	D
University of Maine	D
The University of Manchester	M,D
University of Manitoba	M
University of Maryland, Baltimore	M,D
University of Maryland, College Park	
University of Massachusetts Dartmouth	D
University of Memphis	D
University of Miami	M,D
University of Michigan	M,D
University of Minnesota, Twin Cities Campus	M,D
University of Mississippi	M,D
University of Missouri	M,D
University of Missouri–Kansas City	M,D
University of Montana	D
University of Nebraska–Lincoln	M,D
University of Nevada, Las Vegas	M,D
University of New Hampshire	M,D,O
University of New Mexico	D
University of North Alabama	M
The University of North Carolina at Chapel Hill	D
University of North Dakota	D
University of Notre Dame	M,D
University of Oklahoma	M,D*
University of Oregon	M,D
University of Ottawa	M,D
University of Pennsylvania	M,D*
University of Pittsburgh	M*
University of Puerto Rico, Río Piedras Campus	M,D
University of Richmond	D
University of St. Thomas (MN)	M,D
University of San Diego	M,D,O
University of San Francisco	M,D
University of Saskatchewan	M,D
University of South Africa	M,D
University of South Carolina	D
The University of South Dakota	D
University of Southern California	M,D
The University of Tennessee	D
The University of Texas at Austin	M,D
The University of Texas at Dallas	M,D*
University of the District of Columbia	M,D
University of the Pacific	M,D
The University of Toledo	M,D
University of Toronto	M,D
The University of Tulsa	M,D,O
University of Utah	M,D*
University of Victoria	M,D
University of Virginia	M,D
University of Washington	M,D*
The University of Western Ontario	M,D,O
University of Wisconsin–Madison	M,D
University of Wyoming	D
Valparaiso University	M,D
Vanderbilt University	M,D*
Vermont Law School	D
Villanova University	D
Wake Forest University	M,D
Walden University	M,D,O
Washburn University	M,D
Washington and Lee University	M,D
Washington University in St. Louis	M,D
Wayne State University	M,D
Western Michigan University Thomas M. Cooley Law School	M,D
Western New England University	M,D
Western State College of Law at Argosy University	D
West Virginia University	M,D
Whittier College	D
Widener University	M,D
Willamette University	M,D
Yale University	M,D*
Yeshiva University	M,D
York University	M,D

LEGAL AND JUSTICE STUDIES

American Public University System	M
American University	M,D
Arizona State University at the Tempe campus	M,D,O
Auburn University at Montgomery	M,O
Binghamton University, State University of New York	M,D*
Brock University	M
California University of Pennsylvania	M
Capital University	M
Carleton University	M,O
Case Western Reserve University	M,D*
The Catholic University of America	M,D,O
Central European University	M,D
Columbia University	M,D*
The George Washington University	M,D,O*
Golden Gate University	M,D
Governors State University	M
Harrison Middleton University	M,D
Harvard University	D*
Hodges University	M
Hofstra University	M,D
Illinois Institute of Technology	M,D
John Jay College of Criminal Justice of the City University of New York	M,D
John Marshall Law School	M,D
Kaplan University, Davenport Campus	M,O
Loyola University Chicago	M,O
Marlboro College	M
Marygrove College	M
Michigan State University College of Law	M,D
Mississippi College	M,O
Montclair State University	O
National Paralegal College	M
National University	M
New York University	M,D,O
Northeastern University	M,D
Nova Southeastern University	M,D*
Pace University	M,D
Prairie View A&M University	M,D
Prescott College	M
Queen's University at Kingston	M,D
Regent University	M,D
Rutgers University–New Brunswick	M,D
St. John's University (NY)	M
Saint Leo University	M
St. Mary's University (United States)	M
San Francisco State University	M
San Jose State University	M,O
Simon Fraser University	M,D
Southern Illinois University Carbondale	M
Southern New Hampshire University	M,O
Stanford University	M,D
Syracuse University	M,O
Taft University System	M,D
Temple University	M,D*
Texas State University	M
Touro College	M,D

Trident University International	M,D,O
Universidad Autonoma de Guadalajara	M,D
Université Laval	O
University of Baltimore	M
University of Calgary	M,O
University of California, Berkeley	D
University of California, San Diego	M
University of Charleston	M
University of Denver	M,O
University of Illinois at Springfield	M
University of Massachusetts Lowell	M
University of Montana	M
University of Nebraska–Lincoln	M
University of Nevada, Reno	M,D
University of New Hampshire	M
University of Pennsylvania	M,D*
University of Pittsburgh	M*
University of San Diego	M,D,O
University of South Florida	O
University of the District of Columbia	M,D
University of the Sacred Heart	M
University of Washington	M,D*
University of Windsor	M
Valparaiso University	O
Vermont Law School	M
Washburn University	M,D
Weber State University	M
Webster University	M
Western Michigan University Thomas M. Cooley Law School	M,D
West Virginia University	M
Wilfrid Laurier University	D

LEISURE STUDIES

Bowling Green State University	M
California State University, Long Beach	M
Dalhousie University	M
East Carolina University	M,O
Howard University	M
Indiana University Bloomington	M,D
Murray State University	M
Penn State University Park	M,D
Prescott College	M
San Francisco State University	M
Southeast Missouri State University	M
Southern Connecticut State University	M
Texas State University	M
Universidad Metropolitana	M
Université du Québec à Trois-Rivières	M,O
University of Georgia	M,D,O
University of Illinois at Urbana–Champaign	M,D
The University of Iowa	M,D*
University of Nebraska at Kearney	M
University of South Alabama	M
The University of Tennessee	M,D
The University of Toledo	M,D
University of Utah	M,D*
University of Victoria	M
University of Waterloo	M,D
University of West Florida	M

LIBERAL STUDIES

Abilene Christian University	M
Alaska Pacific University	M
Albertus Magnus College	M
Alvernia University	M
Antioch University Midwest	M
Arizona State University at the Tempe campus	M
Arkansas Tech University	M
Auburn University at Montgomery	M,D,O
Baker University	M
Barry University	M
Brooklyn College of the City University of New York	M
Cardinal Stritch University	M
Clayton State University	M
Coastal Carolina University	M
The College at Brockport, State University of New York	M
College of Staten Island of the City University of New York	M
The Colorado College	M
Concordia University Chicago	M
Converse College	M
Dallas Baptist University	M
Dartmouth College	M*
Delta State University	M
DePaul University	M
Drew University	M,D,O
Duke University	M*
East Tennessee State University	M,O
Excelsior College	M
Faulkner University	M
Florida Atlantic University	M
Florida International University	M
Fort Hays State University	M
Georgetown University	M,D
The Graduate Center, City University of New York	M
Hamline University	M
Harvard University	M,O*
Hawai`i Pacific University	M
Henderson State University	M
Hollins University	M
Houston Baptist University	M
Indiana University Northwest	M
Indiana University–Purdue University Indianapolis	M,D,O
Indiana University South Bend	M
Jacksonville State University	M
Johns Hopkins University	M,O
Kent State University	M
Lake Forest College	M
Louisiana State University and Agricultural & Mechanical College	M
Louisiana State University in Shreveport	M
Loyola University Maryland	M
Madonna University	M
McDaniel College	M
Metropolitan State University	M
Mississippi College	M
The New School	M
North Carolina State University	M
North Central College	M
Northern Arizona University	M
Northern Kentucky University	M
Northwestern University	M*
Notre Dame of Maryland University	M
Oakland University	M
Occidental College	M
Ohio Dominican University	M
Queens College of the City University of New York	M
Ramapo College of New Jersey	M
Reed College	M
Rice University	M
Rollins College	M
Rutgers University–Camden	M
St. Edward's University	M,O
St. John's College (MD)	M
St. John's College (NM)	M
St. John's University (NY)	M
St. Norbert College	M
San Diego State University	M
San Francisco State University	M
Simon Fraser University	M
Southern Methodist University	M
Spring Hill College	M,O
State University of New York College at Old Westbury	M
State University of New York Empire State College	M
Stony Brook University, State University of New York	M,O
Texas A&M University–Central Texas	M,O
Texas Christian University	M
Thomas Edison State University	M
Towson University	M
Tulane University	M
University at Albany, State University of New York	M
University of Chicago	M
University of Delaware	M*
University of Detroit Mercy	M,D,O
University of Memphis	M
University of Miami	M
University of Minnesota, Duluth	M
University of New Hampshire	M
University of North Carolina at Asheville	M,O
The University of North Carolina at Charlotte	M,D,O
The University of North Carolina at Greensboro	M
The University of North Carolina Wilmington	M
University of Oklahoma	M,O*
University of Pennsylvania	M*
University of St. Thomas (TX)	M
University of Southern Indiana	M
University of South Florida	M
University of South Florida, St. Petersburg	M
The University of Texas at El Paso	M
The University of Toledo	M
University of Wisconsin–Milwaukee	M
Ursuline College	M
Utica College	M
Valparaiso University	M,O
Vanderbilt University	M*
Virginia Polytechnic Institute and State University	M,O
Wake Forest University	M
Washburn University	M
Wesleyan University	M
Western Illinois University	M
West Virginia University	M
Wichita State University	M
Widener University	M
Winthrop University	M

LIBRARY SCIENCE

Appalachian State University	M,O
Azusa Pacific University	M,O
The Catholic University of America	M,O
Chicago State University	M
Clarion University of Pennsylvania	M,O
Dalhousie University	M
Dominican University	M,D,O
Drexel University	M,D,O
East Carolina University	M
Eastern Kentucky University	M
East Tennessee State University	M,O
Florida State University	M,D,O
Indiana University Bloomington	M,D,O
Indiana University–Purdue University Indianapolis	M,O
Instituto Tecnológico y de Estudios Superiores de Monterrey, Campus Irapuato	M,D
Inter American University of Puerto Rico, Barranquitas Campus	M
Inter American University of Puerto Rico, San Germán Campus	M
Kent State University	M,O
Kutztown University of Pennsylvania	M
Louisiana State University and Agricultural & Mechanical College	M
Mansfield University of Pennsylvania	M
McDaniel College	M
McGill University	M,D,O
McNeese State University	O
North Carolina Central University	M
Old Dominion University	M
Olivet Nazarene University	M
Pratt Institute	M,O*
Queens College of the City University of New York	M,O
Rowan University	M,D,O
Rutgers University–New Brunswick	M,D
St. Catherine University	M
St. John's University (NY)	M,O
Sam Houston State University	M
San Jose State University	M,O
Simmons College	M,D,O
Southern Arkansas University–Magnolia	M
Southern Connecticut State University	M,O
Syracuse University	M
Tennessee Technological University	M,O
Texas Woman's University	M
Trevecca Nazarene University	M,O
Universidad del Turabo	M,O
Université de Montréal	M,D
University at Albany, State University of New York	M,O
University at Buffalo, the State University of New York	M,O*
The University of Alabama	M,D
University of Alberta	M
The University of Arizona	M,D
The University of British Columbia	M,D
University of California, Los Angeles	M,D,O
University of Central Arkansas	M
University of Central Missouri	M,D,O
University of Central Oklahoma	M
University of Denver	M,D,O
University of Hawaii at Manoa	M,O
University of Houston–Clear Lake	M
University of Illinois at Urbana–Champaign	M,D,O
The University of Iowa	M,D*
University of Kentucky	M
University of Maryland, College Park	
University of Missouri	M,D,O
University of Nebraska at Kearney	M
The University of North Carolina at Chapel Hill	M,D,O
The University of North Carolina at Greensboro	M
University of Northern Colorado	M
University of Pittsburgh	M,D*
University of Puerto Rico, Río Piedras Campus	M,O
University of Rhode Island	M
University of South Carolina	M,D,O
University of Southern Mississippi	M,O
University of South Florida	M
University of Washington	M,D*
The University of Western Ontario	M,D
University of Wisconsin–Eau Claire	M
University of Wisconsin–Madison	M,D
University of Wisconsin–Milwaukee	M,D,O
Valdosta State University	M
Valley City State University	M
Wayne State University	M,O
Wright State University	M

LIGHTING DESIGN

The New School	M
New York School of Interior Design	M
Rensselaer Polytechnic Institute	M,D
University of Washington	M,D,O*

LIMNOLOGY

Baylor University	M,D
Cornell University	D
University of Alaska Fairbanks	M,D
University of Florida	M,D

LINGUISTICS

Arizona State University at the Tempe campus	M,D,O
Ball State University	M
Biola University	M,D,O
Boston College	M
Boston University	M
Brandeis University	M
Brigham Young University	M
Brown University	M,D
California State University, Fresno	M
California State University, Fullerton	M
California State University, Long Beach	M
California State University, Northridge	M
Carleton University	M
Carnegie Mellon University	M,D
Case Western Reserve University	M*
Cleveland State University	M
Concordia University (Canada)	M,O
Cornell University	M,D
East Carolina University	M,D,O
Eastern Michigan University	M,O
Florida Atlantic University	M
Florida International University	M
Gallaudet University	M,D,O
George Mason University	M,D,O
Georgetown University	M,D
Georgia State University	M,D
The Graduate Center, City University of New York	M,D
Graduate Institute of Applied Linguistics	M,O
Harvard University	D*
Hofstra University	M,D,O
Indiana State University	M,D,O
Indiana University Bloomington	M,D
Instituto Tecnologico de Santo Domingo	M,O
Iowa State University of Science and Technology	M,D
Massachusetts Institute of Technology	D
McGill University	M,D
Memorial University of Newfoundland	M,D
Michigan State University	M,D
Montclair State University	M,O
National University	M,O
New York University	M,D
Northeastern Illinois University	M
Northern Arizona University	M,D,O
Northwestern University	D*
Oakland University	M,O
The Ohio State University	M,D
Ohio University	M
Old Dominion University	M
Penn State University Park	M,D
Purdue University	M,D
Queens College of the City University of New York	M
Rice University	M,D
Rutgers University–New Brunswick	D
San Diego State University	M,O
San Francisco State University	M
San Jose State University	M,O
Simon Fraser University	M,D
Southern Illinois University Carbondale	M
Stanford University	M,D
Stony Brook University, State University of New York	M,D
Syracuse University	M,O
Teachers College, Columbia University	M,D,O
Texas Tech University	M,D
Trinity Western University	M
Universidad de las Américas Puebla	M
Université de Montréal	M,D,O
Université de Sherbrooke	M,D
Université du Québec à Chicoutimi	M
Université du Québec à Montréal	M,D
Université Laval	M,D
University at Buffalo, the State University of New York	M,D*
University of Alaska Fairbanks	M
University of Alberta	M,D
The University of Arizona	M,D
The University of British Columbia	M,D
University of Calgary	M,D
University of California, Berkeley	D
University of California, Davis	M,D
University of California, Los Angeles	M,D
University of California, San Diego	D
University of California, Santa Barbara	M,D
University of California, Santa Cruz	M,D
University of Chicago	M,D
University of Colorado Boulder	M,D
University of Colorado Denver	M
University of Connecticut	M,D*
University of Delaware	M,D*
University of Florida	M,D,O
University of Georgia	M,D
University of Hawaii at Manoa	M,D
University of Houston	M,D
University of Illinois at Chicago	M
University of Illinois at Urbana–Champaign	M,D
The University of Iowa	M,D*
The University of Kansas	M,D*
University of Louisville	M,D
The University of Manchester	M,D
University of Manitoba	M,D
University of Maryland, Baltimore County	M
University of Maryland, College Park	M,D
University of Massachusetts Amherst	M,D*
University of Massachusetts Boston	M
University of Memphis	M,D,O
University of Michigan	D
University of Minnesota, Twin Cities Campus	M,D
University of Montana	M,D
University of New Hampshire	M,D
University of New Mexico	M,D
The University of North Carolina at Chapel Hill	M,D
The University of North Carolina at Charlotte	M,O
University of North Dakota	M
University of North Texas	M,D,O
University of Oregon	M,D
University of Ottawa	M,D
University of Pennsylvania	M,D*
University of Pittsburgh	M,D*
University of Puerto Rico, Río Piedras Campus	M,D

*M—masters degree; D—doctorate; O—other advanced degree; *—Close-Up and/or Display*

University of Regina	M
University of Rochester	M*
University of South Africa	M,D
University of South Carolina	M,D,O
University of Southern California	M,D
The University of Tennessee	D
The University of Texas at Arlington	M,D
The University of Texas at Austin	M,D
The University of Texas at El Paso	M,O
University of Toronto	M,D
University of Utah	M,D*
University of Victoria	M,D
University of Virginia	M
University of Washington	M,D*
University of Wisconsin–Madison	M,D
University of Wisconsin–Milwaukee	M,D,O
Virginia International University	M
Wayne State University	M,D
Wesley Biblical Seminary	M
West Virginia University	M
Yale University	D*
York University	M,D

LOGISTICS

Air Force Institute of Technology	M,D
Alabama Agricultural and Mechanical University	M,D
American Public University System	M
Benedictine University	M
California State University, Long Beach	M
Case Western Reserve University	M,D*
Central Connecticut State University	M,O
Central Michigan University	M,O
Colorado Technical University Colorado Springs	M,D
Copenhagen Business School	M,D
East Carolina University	M,D,O
Embry-Riddle Aeronautical University–Worldwide	M
Florida Institute of Technology	M,D
Friends University	M
George Mason University	M,O
Georgia College & State University	M
Georgia Institute of Technology	M
Georgia Southern University	D
HEC Montreal	M
Kaplan University, Davenport Campus	M
Maryville University of Saint Louis	M,O
Michigan State University	M,D
Naval Postgraduate School	M
North Dakota State University	M,D
Norwich University	M
The Ohio State University	M
Polytechnic University of Puerto Rico, Miami Campus	M
Pontifical Catholic University of Puerto Rico	O
Pontificia Universidad Catolica Madre y Maestra	M
Rutgers University–Newark	M
Shippensburg University of Pennsylvania	M,O
Stevens Institute of Technology	O
Trident University International	M,D
Universidad del Turabo	M
University at Buffalo, the State University of New York	M,D*
The University of Alabama in Huntsville	M,O
University of Alaska Anchorage	M,O
University of Dallas	M,D
University of Houston	M
University of Louisville	M,D,O
University of Missouri–St. Louis	M,D,O
The University of North Carolina at Charlotte	M,O
University of North Florida	M
University of North Texas	M,D,O
University of St. Francis (IL)	M,O
University of South Africa	M,D
The University of Tennessee	M,D
The University of Tennessee at Chattanooga	M,O
The University of Texas at Arlington	M
University of Washington	O*
Virginia International University	M,O
Wright State University	M

MANAGEMENT INFORMATION SYSTEMS

Adelphi University	M
Air Force Institute of Technology	M
American Business & Technology University	M
American InterContinental University Atlanta	M
American Public University System	M
American Sentinel University	M
American University	M,D,O
The American University in Cairo	M
American University of Armenia	M
Argosy University, Atlanta	M,D
Argosy University, Chicago	M,D
Argosy University, Dallas	M,D,O
Argosy University, Denver	M,D
Argosy University, Hawai`i	M,D,O
Argosy University, Inland Empire	M,D
Argosy University, Los Angeles	M,D
Argosy University, Nashville	M,D
Argosy University, Orange County	M,D,O
Argosy University, Phoenix	M,D
Argosy University, Salt Lake City	M,D
Argosy University, San Diego	M,D
Argosy University, San Francisco Bay Area	M,D
Argosy University, Sarasota	M,D,O
Argosy University, Schaumburg	M,D,O
Argosy University, Seattle	M,D
Argosy University, Tampa	M,D
Argosy University, Twin Cities	M,D
Argosy University, Washington DC	M,D,O
Arizona State University at the Tempe campus	M,D
Arkansas State University	O
Aspen University	M,O
Auburn University	M,D
Auburn University at Montgomery	M
Avila University	M
Baker College Center for Graduate Studies–Online	M,D
Ball State University	M,O
Barry University	O
Baruch College of the City University of New York	M,D
Baylor University	M,D
Bay Path University	M
Bellevue University	M
Benedictine University	M
Boston University	M,O
Bowie State University	M,O
Brandeis University	M
Broadview University–West Jordan	M
California Intercontinental University	M,D
California Lutheran University	M,O
California State Polytechnic University, Pomona	M
California State University, East Bay	M
California State University, Fullerton	M
California State University, Los Angeles	M
California State University, Monterey Bay	M
California State University, San Bernardino	M
California University of Management and Sciences	M,D
Capella University	M,D
Capitol Technology University	M
Carnegie Mellon University	M,D
The Catholic University of America	M,O
Central European University	M,D
Central Michigan University	M,O
Central Penn College	M
Charleston Southern University	M
City College of the City University of New York	M,D
City University of Seattle	M,O
Claremont Graduate University	M,D,O
Clark University	M
Cleveland State University	M,D
Coastal Carolina University	M,D,O
College of Charleston	M
The College of Saint Rose	M,O
The College of St. Scholastica	M,O
Colorado State University	M
Colorado State University–Global Campus	M
Concordia University Wisconsin	M
Copenhagen Business School	M,D
Daemen College	M
Dakota State University	M,D,O
Dalhousie University	M
Dallas Baptist University	M
DePaul University	M,D
DeSales University	M
DeVry University	M
Duquesne University	M
East Carolina University	M,D,O
Eastern Michigan University	M,O
Ellis University	M
Elmhurst College	M
Embry-Riddle Aeronautical University–Worldwide	M
Emory University	M,D
Endicott College	M
Fairfield University	M,O
Fairleigh Dickinson University, Metropolitan Campus	M,O
Ferris State University	M
Florida Agricultural and Mechanical University	M
Florida Atlantic University	M
Florida Institute of Technology	M,D
Florida International University	M,D
Florida State University	M,D,O
Fordham University	M
Franklin Pierce University	M,D,O
Friends University	M
George Mason University	M
The George Washington University	M,D*
Georgia College & State University	M
Georgia Institute of Technology	M
Georgia Southern University	M,O
Georgia Southwestern State University	M,O
Georgia State University	M,D,O
Globe University–Woodbury	M
Golden Gate University	M,D,O
Goldey-Beacom College	M
Governors State University	M
The Graduate Center, City University of New York	D
Grand Canyon University	M
Grand Valley State University	M
Grantham University	M,O
Harrisburg University of Science and Technology	M
Hawai`i Pacific University	M
HEC Montreal	M
Hodges University	M
Hofstra University	M,O
Holy Family University	M
Hood College	M
Howard University	M
Idaho State University	M,O
Illinois Institute of Technology	M,D
Illinois State University	M
Indiana University Bloomington	M,D,O
Indiana University South Bend	M
Instituto Tecnológico y de Estudios Superiores de Monterrey, Campus Central de Veracruz	M
Instituto Tecnológico y de Estudios Superiores de Monterrey, Campus Ciudad de México	M,D
Instituto Tecnológico y de Estudios Superiores de Monterrey, Campus Ciudad Juárez	M
Instituto Tecnológico y de Estudios Superiores de Monterrey, Campus Ciudad Obregón	M
Instituto Tecnológico y de Estudios Superiores de Monterrey, Campus Estado de México	M,D
Instituto Tecnológico y de Estudios Superiores de Monterrey, Campus Irapuato	M,D
Instituto Tecnológico y de Estudios Superiores de Monterrey, Campus Laguna	M
Inter American University of Puerto Rico, Aguadilla Campus	M
Inter American University of Puerto Rico, Fajardo Campus	M
Inter American University of Puerto Rico, Metropolitan Campus	M
Inter American University of Puerto Rico, San Germán Campus	M,D
Iowa State University of Science and Technology	M,D
James Madison University	M
John Marshall Law School	M,D
Johns Hopkins University	M,O
Kaplan University, Davenport Campus	M
Kean University	M
Keiser University	M
Kent State University	D
Lake Erie College	M
Lenoir-Rhyne University	M
Lewis University	M
Liberty University	M,D,O
Lincoln University (CA)	M,D
Lindenwood University	M,O
Lipscomb University	M,O
London Metropolitan University	M,D
Long Island University–LIU Post	M
Louisiana State University and Agricultural & Mechanical College	M,D
Loyola University Chicago	M
Loyola University Maryland	M
Marist College	M,O
Marquette University	M,O
Marymount University	M,O
Marywood University	M
McGill University	M,D,O
McMaster University	D
Metropolitan State University	M,D,O
Michigan State University	M,D
Middle Georgia State University	M
Middle Tennessee State University	M
Minnesota State University Mankato	M,O
Minot State University	M
Misericordia University	M
Mississippi State University	M,D
Missouri State University	M
Missouri Western State University	M
Monmouth University	M,O
Morehead State University	M
National University	M,O
Naval Postgraduate School	M,D,O
New England Institute of Technology	M
New Jersey Institute of Technology	M,D,O
Newman University	M
New Mexico State University	M
New York University	M,D,O
North Carolina Agricultural and Technical State University	M
Northeastern University	M,D
Northwestern University	M*
Northwest Missouri State University	M
Norwich University	M
Nova Southeastern University	M,D*
Oakland University	M,D,O
The Ohio State University	M,D
Oklahoma State University	M,D
Our Lady of the Lake University of San Antonio	M
Pace University	M
Pacific States University	M,D
Park University	M,O
Penn State Harrisburg	M
Penn State University Park	M,D
Polytechnic University of Puerto Rico	M
Pontifical Catholic University of Puerto Rico	M,O
Prairie View A&M University	M,D
Purdue University	M
Regent's University London	M
Regis University	M,O
Rensselaer Polytechnic Institute	M
Rivier University	M
Robert Morris University	M,D
Robert Morris University Illinois	M
Rochester Institute of Technology	O
Roosevelt University	M
Rose-Hulman Institute of Technology	M
Rutgers University–Newark	M,D
Sacred Heart University	M,O
St. John's University (NY)	M
Saint Joseph's University	M
Saint Peter's University	M
San Diego State University	M
San Francisco State University	M
Santa Clara University	M
Schiller International University (United States)	M
Schiller International University (Germany)	M
Seattle Pacific University	M
Shepherd University (CA)	M
Shippensburg University of Pennsylvania	M,O
Southeastern Oklahoma State University	M
Southern Illinois University Edwardsville	M
Southern Methodist University	M
Southern New Hampshire University	M,O
Southern University at New Orleans	M
South University	M
South University	M
South University (TX)	M
South University (AL)	M
South University	M
Stevens Institute of Technology	M,D,O
Stony Brook University, State University of New York	M,D,O
Stratford University (VA)	M,D
Strayer University	M
Syracuse University	M,D,O
Tarleton State University	M
Temple University	M,D*
Tennessee Technological University	M
Texas A&M International University	M,D
Texas A&M University	M
Texas A&M University–Central Texas	M,O
Texas A&M University–San Antonio	M
Texas Southern University	M
Texas State University	M
Texas Tech University	M,D
Touro College	M
Towson University	M,D,O
Trident University International	M,D,O
Troy University	M
Tuskegee University	M
United States International University–Africa	M
Universidad del Este	M
Universidad del Turabo	D
Universidad Metropolitana	M
Université de Sherbrooke	M,O
Université du Québec à Montréal	M
Université Laval	M,O
University at Albany, State University of New York	M,D,O
University at Buffalo, the State University of New York	M,D,O*
The University of Akron	M
The University of Alabama at Birmingham	M
The University of Alabama in Huntsville	M,O
The University of Arizona	M,O
University of Arkansas	M
University of Arkansas at Little Rock	M,O
University of Baltimore	M,O
University of Bridgeport	M
The University of British Columbia	D
University of California, Berkeley	O
University of California, Los Angeles	M,D
University of California, Santa Cruz	M,D
University of Central Missouri	M,D,O
University of Cincinnati	M,D
University of Colorado Boulder	M,D
University of Colorado Denver	M,D
University of Dallas	M,D
University of Delaware	M,D*
University of Detroit Mercy	M,D,O
University of Florida	M,D,O
University of Georgia	D
University of Hawaii at Manoa	M,D,O
University of Houston–Clear Lake	M
University of Houston–Victoria	M
University of Illinois at Chicago	M,D
University of Illinois at Springfield	M
The University of Kansas	M*
University of La Verne	M,O
University of Lethbridge	M,D
University of Maine	M,D,O
University of Management and Technology	M,O
University of Mary Hardin-Baylor	M
University of Maryland University College	M,O
University of Massachusetts Boston	M
University of Michigan–Dearborn	M
University of Michigan–Flint	M
University of Minnesota, Twin Cities Campus	M,D
University of Mississippi	M,D
University of Missouri–St. Louis	M,D,O
University of Nebraska at Kearney	M
University of Nebraska at Omaha	M,D,O
University of Nebraska–Lincoln	M
University of Nevada, Las Vegas	M,O
University of Nevada, Reno	M
University of New Hampshire	M,O
University of New Mexico	M
University of North Alabama	M
The University of North Carolina at Chapel Hill	D
The University of North Carolina at Charlotte	M,D,O
The University of North Carolina at Greensboro	M,D,O

The University of North Carolina Wilmington	M
University of North Florida	M
University of North Texas	M,D,O
University of Oklahoma	M,O*
University of Oregon	M
University of Pennsylvania	M,D*
University of Phoenix–Atlanta Campus	M
University of Phoenix–Augusta Campus	M
University of Phoenix–Bay Area Campus	M,D
University of Phoenix–Central Valley Campus	M
University of Phoenix–Charlotte Campus	M
University of Phoenix–Colorado Campus	M
University of Phoenix–Colorado Springs Downtown Campus	M
University of Phoenix–Columbus Georgia Campus	M
University of Phoenix–Dallas Campus	M
University of Phoenix–Hawaii Campus	M
University of Phoenix–Houston Campus	M
University of Phoenix–Jersey City Campus	M
University of Phoenix–Las Vegas Campus	M
University of Phoenix–New Mexico Campus	M
University of Phoenix–North Florida Campus	M
University of Phoenix–Online Campus	M
University of Phoenix–Sacramento Valley Campus	M
University of Phoenix–San Antonio Campus	M
University of Phoenix–San Diego Campus	M
University of Phoenix–Southern Arizona Campus	M
University of Phoenix–South Florida Campus	M
University of Phoenix–Utah Campus	M
University of Phoenix–Washington D.C. Campus	M,D
University of Pittsburgh	M,D*
University of Redlands	M
University of Rochester	M*
University of St. Thomas (MN)	M,O
University of San Francisco	M
The University of Scranton	M
University of South Africa	M
University of South Alabama	M,D
University of South Florida	M,D,O
The University of Tampa	M
The University of Texas at Arlington	M,D
The University of Texas at Austin	M,D
The University of Texas at Dallas	M,D*
The University of Texas Rio Grande Valley	M
University of the Sacred Heart	M
University of the West	M
University of Utah	M,D,O*
University of Washington	M,D*
University of Wisconsin–Madison	D
Utah State University	M,D
Valparaiso University	M
Villanova University	M
Virginia Commonwealth University	M,D
Virginia International University	M,O
Virginia Polytechnic Institute and State University	M,D,O
Walden University	M,D,O
Walsh College of Accountancy and Business Administration	M
Wayland Baptist University	M,D
Wayne State University	M,D,O
Webster University	M
West Chester University of Pennsylvania	M,O
Western Governors University	M
Western International University	M
Wichita State University	M
Wilmington University	M,D
Winston-Salem State University	M
Worcester Polytechnic Institute	M,D,O
Wright State University	M

MANAGEMENT OF TECHNOLOGY

Air Force Institute of Technology	M,D
Arizona State University at the Tempe campus	M
Athabasca University	M,D,O
Boston University	M
California Lutheran University	M,O
California State University, Los Angeles	M
Cambridge College	M
Capella University	M,D
Carleton University	M
The Catholic University of America	M,O
Central Connecticut State University	M,O
Champlain College	M
City University of Seattle	M,O
Coleman University	M
Colorado School of Mines	M,D
Colorado Technical University Colorado Springs	M,D
Colorado Technical University Denver South	M
Columbia University	M*
Dallas Baptist University	M
DePaul University	M,D
East Carolina University	M,D,O
Eastern Michigan University	D
École Polytechnique de Montréal	M,D,O
Excelsior College	M,O
Fairfield University	M,O
Fairleigh Dickinson University, College at Florham	M,O
Florida Institute of Technology	M,D
George Mason University	M
Georgetown University	M,D
The George Washington University	M,D*
Golden Gate University	M,D,O
Harding University	M
Harrisburg University of Science and Technology	M
Harvard University	D*
Herzing University Online	M
Idaho State University	M
Illinois State University	M
Indiana State University	M,D
Instituto Centroamericano de Administración de Empresas	M
Instituto Tecnológico y de Estudios Superiores de Monterrey, Campus Cuernavaca	M,D
Instituto Tecnológico y de Estudios Superiores de Monterrey, Campus Irapuato	M,D
Iona College	M,O
Johns Hopkins University	M,O
Kansas State University	M
La Salle University	M,O
Lewis University	M
Liberty University	M,D,O
Lipscomb University	M,O
London Metropolitan University	M,D
Marist College	M,O
Marquette University	M,D
Marshall University	M
Mercer University	M
Murray State University	M
National University	M,O
New Jersey Institute of Technology	M,O
New York University	M,D,O
North Carolina Agricultural and Technical State University	M
North Carolina State University	D
Northern Kentucky University	M
Notre Dame de Namur University	M
Pacific States University	M,D
Pittsburg State University	M,O
Polytechnic University of Puerto Rico	M
Polytechnic University of Puerto Rico, Orlando Campus	M
Portland State University	M,D
Purdue University	M,D
Rensselaer Polytechnic Institute	M,D
Rollins College	M,D
Rutgers University–Newark	D
St. Ambrose University	M
Seton Hall University	M,O
Simon Fraser University	M,D,O
South Dakota School of Mines and Technology	M
Southeast Missouri State University	M
State University of New York Polytechnic Institute	M
Stevens Institute of Technology	M,D,O
Stevenson University	M
Stony Brook University, State University of New York	M
Texas State University	M
Towson University	M,O
Trevecca Nazarene University	M
University at Albany, State University of New York	M
University of Advancing Technology	M
The University of Akron	M
The University of Alabama in Huntsville	M,O
University of Bridgeport	M,D
University of California, Santa Barbara	M
University of California, Santa Cruz	M,D
University of Central Missouri	M,D,O
University of Colorado Denver	M
University of Dallas	M,D
University of Delaware	M*
University of Idaho	M,D
University of Illinois at Urbana–Champaign	M,D
University of Maryland University College	M,O
University of Massachusetts Dartmouth	M
University of Miami	M,D
University of Minnesota, Twin Cities Campus	M
University of New Mexico	M
University of North Dakota	M
University of Phoenix–Atlanta Campus	M
University of Phoenix–Augusta Campus	M
University of Phoenix–Bay Area Campus	M,D
University of Phoenix–Central Valley Campus	M
University of Phoenix–Charlotte Campus	M
University of Phoenix–Colorado Campus	M
University of Phoenix–Colorado Springs Downtown Campus	M
University of Phoenix–Columbus Georgia Campus	M
University of Phoenix–Dallas Campus	M
University of Phoenix–Hawaii Campus	M
University of Phoenix–Houston Campus	M
University of Phoenix–Jersey City Campus	M
University of Phoenix–Las Vegas Campus	M
University of Phoenix–New Mexico Campus	M
University of Phoenix–Online Campus	M,O
University of Phoenix–Phoenix Campus	M,O
University of Phoenix–Sacramento Valley Campus	M
University of Phoenix–San Antonio Campus	M
University of Phoenix–San Diego Campus	M
University of Phoenix–Southern Arizona Campus	M
University of Phoenix–Southern California Campus	M
University of Phoenix–Utah Campus	M
University of Portland	M
University of St. Thomas (MN)	M,O
University of South Florida	O
The University of Texas at Dallas	M*
The University of Texas at San Antonio	M,D,O
University of Toronto	M
University of Virginia	M
University of Washington	M,D*
University of Waterloo	M,D
University of Wisconsin–Madison	M
Walsh College of Accountancy and Business Administration	M
Washington State University	M,O
Wentworth Institute of Technology	M
Western Kentucky University	M
Wilfrid Laurier University	M,D

MANAGEMENT STRATEGY AND POLICY

Amberton University	M
American Public University System	M
American University	M,O
Antioch University Midwest	M
Antioch University Santa Barbara	M
Arizona State University at the Tempe campus	M,D
Austin Peay State University	M
Azusa Pacific University	M
Baldwin Wallace University	M
Bay Path University	M
Bellarmine University	M
Bentley University	O
Black Hills State University	M
Boston University	M,O
Brandeis University	M
California Miramar University	M
California State University, East Bay	M
California University of Pennsylvania	M
Capella University	M,D
Claremont Graduate University	M,D,O
Clemson University	M
The College of Saint Rose	M,O
Davenport University	M
Defiance College	M
DePaul University	M
Dominican University of California	M
Drexel University	M,D,O
Duke University	M,D,O*
Florida State University	M,D
Freed-Hardeman University	M
Friends University	M
The George Washington University	M,D,O*
Georgia State University	M,D
Grantham University	M,O
Gwynedd Mercy University	M
Harvard University	D*
HEC Montreal	M
Hofstra University	M,O
James Madison University	D
Lenoir-Rhyne University	M
LeTourneau University	M
Manhattanville College	M*
McGill University	M,D,O
Mercer University	M
Mercyhurst University	M,O
Messiah College	M,O
Michigan State University	M,D
Middlebury Institute of International Studies at Monterey	M
Middle Tennessee State University	M
Mount Mercy University	M
Neumann University	M
New England College	M
New York University	M,D,O
Niagara University	M
North Central College	M
Northwestern University	M,D*
Norwich University	M
Nova Southeastern University	M*
Oklahoma Wesleyan University	M
Oregon State University	M,D
Pace University	M
Philadelphia University	M
Pontificia Universidad Catolica Madre y Maestra	M
Regent University	M,D,O
Regis University	M,O
Robert Morris University Illinois	M
Roberts Wesleyan College	M
Rockhurst University	M,O
Sage Graduate School	M
St. John's University (NY)	M
Saint Joseph's University	M
Saint Mary-of-the-Woods College	M
Salve Regina University	M,O
San Jose State University	M,O
Southern Illinois University Edwardsville	M
Southern Methodist University	M
Stevens Institute of Technology	M
Suffolk University	M,O
Syracuse University	M
Taylor University	M
Temple University	D*
Tennessee State University	M,D
Tennessee Technological University	M
Tufts University	O
Tulane University	M,D
United States International University–Africa	M
Universidad del Este	M
The University of Arizona	M,D
The University of British Columbia	D
University of Calgary	M,D
University of California, Los Angeles	M,D
University of Charleston	M
University of Chicago	M,O
University of Colorado Denver	M
University of Dallas	M,D
University of Denver	M
University of Detroit Mercy	M,O
University of Illinois at Urbana–Champaign	M,D,O
University of Lethbridge	M,D
The University of Manchester	M
University of Massachusetts Amherst	M,D*
University of Michigan–Dearborn	M
University of Minnesota, Twin Cities Campus	M,D
University of Missouri–St. Louis	M,D,O
University of New Haven	M,O
University of New Mexico	M
The University of North Carolina at Chapel Hill	D
University of North Texas	M,D,O
University of Pittsburgh	M,D*
University of Rhode Island	M,D
University of Rochester	M*
University of St. Francis (IL)	M,O
University of South Florida	O
The University of Texas at Dallas	M,D*
University of Utah	M,D,O*
University of Virginia	M,O
The University of Western Ontario	M,D
University of West Florida	M
Valparaiso University	M,O
Vanderbilt University	M*
Villanova University	M
Virginia Commonwealth University	M
Walsh College of Accountancy and Business Administration	M
Western Governors University	M
Western International University	M
Xavier University	M

MANUFACTURING ENGINEERING

American University of Armenia	M
Arizona State University at the Tempe campus	M
Boston University	M,D
Bowling Green State University	M
Bradley University	M
California State University, Northridge	M
Clemson University	M
Cornell University	M,D
Eastern Kentucky University	M
East Tennessee State University	M,O
Fairfield University	M,O
Florida State University	M,D
Georgia Southern University	M,O
Grand Valley State University	M
Illinois Institute of Technology	M,D
Instituto Tecnológico y de Estudios Superiores de Monterrey, Campus Monterrey	M,D
Kansas State University	M,D
Kettering University	M
Lehigh University	M
Massachusetts Institute of Technology	M,D,O
Michigan State University	M,D
Minnesota State University Mankato	M
Missouri University of Science and Technology	M,D
New Jersey Institute of Technology	M,D
New York University	M
North Carolina State University	M
North Dakota State University	M,D
Oregon Institute of Technology	M
Oregon State University	M,D
Pittsburg State University	M
Polytechnic University of Puerto Rico	M
Portland State University	M,D
Rochester Institute of Technology	M
Southern Methodist University	M,D
Stevens Institute of Technology	M
Tennessee State University	M,D
Texas A&M University	M
Texas State University	M
Tufts University	O

*M—masters degree; D—doctorate; O—other advanced degree; *—Close-Up and/or Display*

Universidad Autonoma de Guadalajara M,D
Universidad de las Américas Puebla M
University of Calgary M,D
University of California, Irvine M,D
University of California, Los Angeles M
The University of Iowa M,D*
University of Kentucky M
University of Manitoba M,D
University of Maryland, College Park M,D
University of Michigan M,D
University of Michigan–Dearborn M
University of Missouri M,D
University of Nebraska–Lincoln M,D
University of New Mexico M
University of St. Thomas (MN) M,O
University of Southern California M,D,O
University of South Florida M,D
The University of Texas at El Paso M,O
The University of Texas at San Antonio M,D
The University of Texas Rio Grande Valley M
University of Toronto M
University of Windsor M,D
University of Wisconsin–Madison M
University of Wisconsin–Milwaukee M,D,O
University of Wisconsin–Stout M
Villanova University M,O
Wayne State University M
Western Illinois University M
Western Michigan University M
Western New England University M
Wichita State University M,D
Worcester Polytechnic Institute M,D

MARINE AFFAIRS
Dalhousie University M
Louisiana State University and Agricultural & Mechanical College M,D
Memorial University of Newfoundland M,D,O
Nova Southeastern University M,D,O*
Oregon State University M
Stevens Institute of Technology M
Stony Brook University, State University of New York M
Université du Québec à Rimouski M,O
University of Delaware M,D*
University of Maine M,D
University of Massachusetts Dartmouth M,D
University of Miami M
University of Rhode Island M,D
University of San Diego M
University of Washington M,O*
University of West Florida M

MARINE BIOLOGY
College of Charleston M
Florida Institute of Technology M,D
Montclair State University M
Nicholls State University M
Northeastern University M,D
Nova Southeastern University M,D,O*
Princeton University D
Rutgers University–New Brunswick M,D
San Francisco State University M
Texas A&M University at Galveston M,D
Texas State University M,D
University of Alaska Fairbanks M,D
University of California, San Diego M,D
University of California, Santa Barbara M,D
University of Colorado Boulder M,D
University of Guam M
University of Hawaii at Hilo M
University of Hawaii at Manoa M,D
University of Maine M,D
University of Massachusetts Dartmouth M
University of Miami M,D
University of New Hampshire M,D,O
The University of North Carolina Wilmington M,D
University of Oregon M,D
University of Southern California M,D
University of Southern Mississippi M,D
Western Illinois University M,O
Woods Hole Oceanographic Institution D

MARINE GEOLOGY
Cornell University M,D
Massachusetts Institute of Technology M,D
University of Delaware M,D*
University of Hawaii at Manoa M,D
University of Miami M,D
University of Washington M,D*
Woods Hole Oceanographic Institution D

MARINE SCIENCES
California State University, East Bay M
California State University, Fresno M
California State University, Monterey Bay M
Coastal Carolina University M,D,O
College of Charleston M
The College of William and Mary M,D
Cornell University M,D
Duke University D*
Florida Institute of Technology M,D
Florida State University M,D
Hawai`i Pacific University M
Instituto Tecnologico de Santo Domingo M,D,O
Jacksonville University M*
Medical University of South Carolina D
Memorial University of Newfoundland M,O
North Carolina State University M,D
Nova Southeastern University M,D,O*
Oregon State University M
San Francisco State University M
San Jose State University M,O
Savannah State University M
Southern Connecticut State University M,O
Stony Brook University, State University of New York M,D
Texas A&M University at Galveston M
Texas A&M University–Corpus Christi M,D
University of Alaska Fairbanks M,D
The University of British Columbia M,D
University of California, San Diego M
University of California, Santa Barbara M,D
University of California, Santa Cruz M,D
University of Delaware M,D*
University of Florida M,D
University of Georgia M,D
University of Hawaii at Manoa O
University of Maine M,D
University of Maryland, Baltimore M,D
University of Maryland, Baltimore County M,D
University of Maryland, College Park M,D
University of Maryland Eastern Shore M,D
University of Massachusetts Amherst M,D*
University of Massachusetts Boston M,D
University of Massachusetts Dartmouth M,D
University of Miami M,D
University of Michigan M,D,O
University of New England M
The University of North Carolina at Chapel Hill M,D
The University of North Carolina Wilmington M,D,O
University of Puerto Rico, Mayagüez Campus M,D
University of Rhode Island M,D
University of San Diego M
University of South Alabama M,D
University of South Carolina M,D
University of Southern California M,D
University of Southern Mississippi M,D
University of South Florida M,D
The University of Texas at Austin M,D
University of the Virgin Islands M
University of Wisconsin–La Crosse M
University of Wisconsin–Madison M,D
Western Washington University M

MARKETING
Adelphi University M
Alabama Agricultural and Mechanical University M,D
American Business & Technology University M
American College of Thessaloniki M,O
American InterContinental University Online M
American Public University System M
American University M
The American University in Dubai M
Aquinas College (MI) M
Argosy University, Atlanta M,D
Argosy University, Chicago M,D
Argosy University, Dallas M,D,O
Argosy University, Denver M,D
Argosy University, Hawai`i M,D,O
Argosy University, Inland Empire M,D
Argosy University, Los Angeles M,D
Argosy University, Nashville M,D
Argosy University, Orange County M,D,O
Argosy University, Phoenix M,D
Argosy University, Salt Lake City M,D
Argosy University, San Diego M,D
Argosy University, San Francisco Bay Area M,D
Argosy University, Sarasota M,D,O
Argosy University, Schaumburg M,D,O
Argosy University, Seattle M,D
Argosy University, Tampa M,D
Argosy University, Twin Cities M,D
Argosy University, Washington DC M,D,O
Arizona State University at the Tempe campus M,D
Ashworth College M
Assumption College M,O
Averett University M
Avila University M
Azusa Pacific University M
Baker College Center for Graduate Studies–Online M,D
Barry University O
Baruch College of the City University of New York M,D
Bayamón Central University M
Benedictine University M
Bentley University M
Boston University M
Brandeis University M
Brigham Young University M
Bristol University M
Butler University M
California Coast University M
California Intercontinental University M,D
California Lutheran University M,O
California State University, East Bay M
California State University, Fullerton M
California State University, Los Angeles M
California State University, San Bernardino M
Capella University M,D
Carnegie Mellon University D
Central Michigan University M,O
City College of the City University of New York M
City University of Seattle M,O
Clark University M
Cleveland State University M,D,O
Colorado Technical University Colorado Springs M,D
Colorado Technical University Denver South M
Columbia Southern University M
Columbia University M,D*
Concordia University (Canada) M,D,O
Concordia University Wisconsin M
Cornell University D
Daemen College M
Dallas Baptist University M
DePaul University M
DEREE - The American College of Greece M
DeSales University M
Drexel University M,D,O
Duke University M,D,O*
Duquesne University M
Eastern Michigan University M,O
East Tennessee State University M,O
Edgewood College M
Ellis University M
Emerson College M
Emory University M,D
Fairfield University M,O
Fairleigh Dickinson University, College at Florham M,O
Fairleigh Dickinson University, Metropolitan Campus M,O
Fashion Institute of Technology M*
Florida Agricultural and Mechanical University M
Florida Atlantic University M
Florida National University M
Florida State University M,D
Fordham University M
Franklin University M
Full Sail University M
Gannon University M
Geneva College M
George Fox University M,D
The George Washington University M,D*
Georgia State University M,D
Golden Gate University M,D,O
Goldey-Beacom College M
Grand Canyon University M
Harvard University D*
Hawai`i Pacific University M
HEC Montreal M
Herzing University Online M
Hofstra University M,O
Holy Names University M
Hood College M
Hope International University M
Howard University M
Hult International Business School (United States) M
Illinois Institute of Technology M
Indiana Tech M
Instituto Tecnologico de Santo Domingo M,O
Instituto Tecnológico y de Estudios Superiores de Monterrey, Campus Central de Veracruz M
Instituto Tecnológico y de Estudios Superiores de Monterrey, Campus Ciudad Obregón M
Instituto Tecnológico y de Estudios Superiores de Monterrey, Campus Cuernavaca M
Instituto Tecnológico y de Estudios Superiores de Monterrey, Campus Estado de México M,D
Instituto Tecnológico y de Estudios Superiores de Monterrey, Campus Monterrey M
Inter American University of Puerto Rico, Aguadilla Campus M
Inter American University of Puerto Rico, Fajardo Campus M
Inter American University of Puerto Rico, Guayama Campus M
Inter American University of Puerto Rico, Metropolitan Campus M
Inter American University of Puerto Rico, Ponce Campus M
Inter American University of Puerto Rico, San Germán Campus M,D
International University in Geneva M,D
The International University of Monaco M
Iona College M,O
Jacksonville University M*
Johns Hopkins University M
Kansas State University M
Kaplan University, Davenport Campus M
Keiser University M,D
Kent State University D
King University M
Lake Forest Graduate School of Management M
La Salle University M,O
Lasell College M,O
La Sierra University M,O
Lewis University M
Liberty University M,D,O
LIM College M
Lindenwood University M,O
Long Island University–LIU Post M
Loyola University Chicago M
Loyola University Maryland M
Loyola University New Orleans M
Lynn University M
Manhattanville College M*
Marist College M
Marquette University M,O
Maryville University of Saint Louis M,O
McGill University M,D,O
Melbourne Business School M,D,O
Michigan State University M,D
Milwaukee School of Engineering M*
Mississippi State University M,D
Molloy College M
Monmouth University M,O
National University M,O
National University College M
New England College M
New Mexico State University D
New York Institute of Technology M
New York University M,D,O
Niagara University M
North Central College M
Northeastern Illinois University M
Northwestern University M,D*
Notre Dame de Namur University M
Nova Southeastern University M*
Oakland University M,O
Oklahoma Christian University M
Oklahoma State University M,D
Old Dominion University D
Oral Roberts University M
Oregon State University M,D
Ottawa University M
Pace University M,D,O
Philadelphia University M
Polytechnic University of Puerto Rico, Miami Campus M
Pontifical Catholic University of Puerto Rico M
Pontificia Universidad Catolica Madre y Maestra M
Post University M
Providence College M
Queen's University at Kingston M
Regent's University London M
Regis University M,O
Roberts Wesleyan College M
Rollins College M,D
Roosevelt University M
Rowan University O
Rutgers University–Newark D
Sacred Heart University M,O
Sage Graduate School M
St. Bonaventure University M
St. Catherine University M
St. John's University (NY) M
Saint Joseph's University M,O
Saint Leo University M
Saint Peter's University M
St. Thomas Aquinas College M
Saint Xavier University M,O
Samford University M
San Diego State University M
San Francisco State University M
Seton Hall University M,O
Slippery Rock University of Pennsylvania M
Southern Adventist University M
Southern Methodist University M
Southern New Hampshire University M,O
Southwest Minnesota State University M
State University of New York Polytechnic Institute M
Stephen F. Austin State University M
Stevens Institute of Technology M,O
Stony Brook University, State University of New York M,O
Stratford University (VA) M,D
Strayer University M
Suffolk University M,O
Syracuse University M
Tarleton State University M
Temple University M,D*
Texas A&M University M
Texas A&M University–Commerce M
Texas Christian University M
Texas Tech University M,D
Tiffin University M
Trident University International M,D
United States International University–Africa M
Universidad del Turabo M
Universidad Iberoamericana M,D
Universidad Metropolitana M
Université de Sherbrooke M
Université Laval M,O
University at Albany, State University of New York M
The University of Akron M
The University of Alabama M,D
The University of Alabama at Birmingham M
The University of Alabama in Huntsville M,O
University of Alberta D
The University of Arizona M,D
University of Baltimore M
University of Bridgeport M
The University of British Columbia D
University of California, Berkeley D,O

University of California, Los Angeles	M,D
University of Central Missouri	M,D,O
University of Chicago	M,O
University of Cincinnati	M,D
University of Colorado Boulder	M,D
University of Colorado Denver	M
University of Connecticut	M,D*
University of Dallas	M,D
University of Dayton	M
University of Denver	M
University of Florida	M,D
University of Hawaii at Manoa	M,D
University of Houston	D
University of Houston–Victoria	M
The University of Iowa	M,D*
University of La Verne	M
University of Lethbridge	M,D
The University of Manchester	M
University of Massachusetts Amherst	M,D*
University of Massachusetts Dartmouth	M,O
University of Memphis	M,D
University of Michigan–Flint	M
University of Minnesota, Twin Cities Campus	M,D
University of Missouri	M,D
University of Missouri–St. Louis	M,D,O
University of Nebraska at Kearney	M
University of Nebraska–Lincoln	M,D
University of New Brunswick Fredericton	M,D
University of New Haven	M,O
University of New Mexico	M
The University of North Carolina at Chapel Hill	D
The University of North Carolina at Greensboro	M,D
University of North Texas	M,D,O
University of Oregon	D
University of Pennsylvania	M,D*
University of Phoenix–Atlanta Campus	M
University of Phoenix–Augusta Campus	M
University of Phoenix–Bay Area Campus	M,D
University of Phoenix–Central Valley Campus	M
University of Phoenix–Colorado Campus	M
University of Phoenix–Colorado Springs Downtown Campus	M
University of Phoenix–Columbus Georgia Campus	M
University of Phoenix–Dallas Campus	M
University of Phoenix–Hawaii Campus	M
University of Phoenix–Houston Campus	M
University of Phoenix–Jersey City Campus	M
University of Phoenix–Las Vegas Campus	M
University of Phoenix–New Mexico Campus	M
University of Phoenix–North Florida Campus	M
University of Phoenix–Online Campus	M,O
University of Phoenix–Phoenix Campus	M,O
University of Phoenix–Sacramento Valley Campus	M
University of Phoenix–San Antonio Campus	M
University of Phoenix–San Diego Campus	M
University of Phoenix–Southern Arizona Campus	M
University of Phoenix–Southern California Campus	M
University of Phoenix–South Florida Campus	M
University of Phoenix–Utah Campus	M
University of Pittsburgh	M,D*
University of Portland	M
University of Puerto Rico, Río Piedras Campus	M,D
University of Rhode Island	M,D
University of Rochester	M*
University of Saint Mary	M
University of San Francisco	M
University of Saskatchewan	M
The University of Scranton	M
University of Sioux Falls	M
University of South Africa	M,D
University of South Florida	M,D
The University of Tampa	M
The University of Tennessee	M,D
The University of Texas at Arlington	M,D
The University of Texas at Austin	M,D
The University of Texas at Dallas	M,D*
The University of Texas at San Antonio	M,D
The University of Texas Rio Grande Valley	M,D
University of the Cumberlands	M,D,O
University of the Incarnate Word	M
University of the Sacred Heart	M
The University of Toledo	M
University of Utah	M,D*
University of Virginia	M
The University of Western Ontario	M,D
University of Wisconsin–Madison	D
University of Wisconsin–Whitewater	M
Valparaiso University	M,O
Vancouver Island University	M
Vanderbilt University	M*
Villanova University	M
Virginia Commonwealth University	M
Virginia International University	M,O
Wagner College	M
Walden University	M,D,O
Walsh College of Accountancy and Business Administration	M
Walsh University	M
Webster University	M
Western International University	M
West Virginia University	M,O
Wilfrid Laurier University	M,D
Wilkes University	M
William Woods University	M,D,O
Wilmington University	M,D
Worcester Polytechnic Institute	M,D,O
Wright State University	M
Xavier University	M
Yale University	D*
York College of Pennsylvania	M
Youngstown State University	M

MARKETING RESEARCH

Baldwin Wallace University	M
Hofstra University	M,O
Instituto Tecnológico y de Estudios Superiores de Monterrey, Campus Irapuato	M,D
Marquette University	M
Michigan State University	M,D
Saint Leo University	M
Southern Illinois University Edwardsville	M
Towson University	M
Universidad Autonoma de Guadalajara	M,D
Universidad de las Americas, A.C.	M
University of Colorado Denver	M
The University of Texas at Arlington	M,D
University of Wisconsin–Madison	M

MARRIAGE AND FAMILY THERAPY

Abilene Christian University	M
Adler Graduate School	M
Adler University	M,D,O
Alliant International University–Irvine	M,D
Alliant International University–Los Angeles	M,D
Alliant International University–Sacramento	M,D
Alliant International University–San Diego	M,D
Amridge University	M,D
Antioch University New England	M,D,O
Appalachian State University	M
Argosy University, Atlanta	M,D,O
Argosy University, Chicago	D
Argosy University, Denver	M,D
Argosy University, Hawai`i	M
Argosy University, Inland Empire	M,D
Argosy University, Los Angeles	M,D
Argosy University, Orange County	M,D
Argosy University, Salt Lake City	M,D
Argosy University, San Diego	M,D
Argosy University, Sarasota	M,D
Argosy University, Tampa	M,D
Argosy University, Twin Cities	M,D,O
Argosy University, Washington DC	M,D
Arizona State University at the Tempe campus	M,D
Azusa Pacific University	M,D
Barry University	M,O
Bayamón Central University	M,O
Bethel Seminary	M,D,O
Brandman University	M
Briercrest Seminary	M
Brigham Young University	M,D
California Lutheran University	M,D
California State University, Chico	M
California State University, Dominguez Hills	M
California State University, East Bay	M
California State University, Fresno	M
California State University, Long Beach	M
California State University, Northridge	M
California State University, Sacramento	M
Cambridge College	M,O
Campbellsville University	M
Capella University	M
Carlos Albizu University, Miami Campus	M,D
Central Connecticut State University	M,O
Chaminade University of Honolulu	M
Chapman University	M
Chatham University	M,D
Chestnut Hill College	M,D,O
The Chicago School of Professional Psychology at Downtown Los Angeles	M,D
The Chicago School of Professional Psychology at Irvine	M,D
Christian Theological Seminary	M,D
The College of New Jersey	O
The College of New Rochelle	M
Colorado State University	M,D
Converse College	M
Denver Seminary	M,D,O
Dominican University of California	M
Drexel University	M,D
Duquesne University	M,D,O
East Carolina University	M,D
Eastern Nazarene College	M
Eastern University	D
Edgewood College	M
Evangelical Seminary	M
Fairfield University	M,O
Florida State University	M,D
Fresno Pacific University	M
Friends University	M
Fuller Theological Seminary	M,D,O
Geneva College	M
George Fox University	M,O
Gonzaga University	M
Grand Canyon University	M
Harding University	M
Hardin-Simmons University	M
Hofstra University	M,O
Hope International University	M
Idaho State University	M,D,O
Indiana University–Purdue University Fort Wayne	M,O
Indiana Wesleyan University	M
Instituto Tecnologico de Santo Domingo	M,O
Iona College	M
John Brown University	M,O
Johnson University	M,D,O
Kansas State University	M,D,O
Kean University	M,O
Kutztown University of Pennsylvania	M
Lancaster Bible College	M,D
La Salle University	M
Lee University	M
LeTourneau University	M
Lewis & Clark College	M
Liberty University	M,D,O
Lincoln Christian University	M
Lipscomb University	M,O
Loma Linda University	M,D,O
Long Island University–LIU Brooklyn	M,O
Loyola Marymount University	M
Maryville University of Saint Louis	M
Medaille College	M,D
Mercy College	M,O
Messiah College	M,O
Michigan State University	M,D
Mid-America Christian University	M
Mississippi College	M,O
Mount Mercy University	M
National University	M,O
New Mexico State University	M
Northcentral University	M,D,O
North Dakota State University	M,D,O
Northeastern Illinois University	M
Northern Kentucky University	M,O
Northwestern University	M*
Northwest Nazarene University	M
Notre Dame de Namur University	M
Nova Southeastern University	M,D,O*
Nyack College	M
Oklahoma Baptist University	M
Oklahoma State University	M,D
Oral Roberts University	M,D
Ottawa University	M
Pacific Lutheran University	M
Pacific Oaks College	M
Palm Beach Atlantic University	M
Pepperdine University	M,D
Phillips Graduate Institute	M
Purdue University	M,D
Purdue University Northwest	M
Reformed Theological Seminary–Jackson Campus	M,D,O
Regent University	M,D,O
Regis University	M,D,O
Richmont Graduate University	M
St. Cloud State University	M
Saint Louis University	M,D,O
Saint Mary's College of California	M,O
St. Mary's University (United States)	M,D
Saint Mary's University of Minnesota	M,O
Saint Paul University	M
St. Thomas University	M,O
San Francisco State University	M,O
Saybrook University	M,D
Seattle Pacific University	M,O
Seton Hall University	M,O
Seton Hill University	M
Shippensburg University of Pennsylvania	M,O
Sioux Falls Seminary	M,O
Sonoma State University	M
Southern California Seminary	M,D
Southern Nazarene University	M
Stephens College	M,O
Stetson University	M
Syracuse University	M,D
Texas A&M University–Central Texas	M,O
Texas State University	M
Texas Tech University	M,D
Texas Wesleyan University	M,D
Texas Woman's University	M,D
Thomas Jefferson University	M
Trevecca Nazarene University	M,D
Universidad de las Americas, A.C.	M
The University of Akron	M
The University of Alabama	M
University of Central Florida	M,O
University of Central Oklahoma	M
University of Colorado Denver	M
University of Denver	M,D,O
University of Florida	M,D,O
University of Guelph	M,D
University of Holy Cross	M
University of Houston–Clear Lake	M
The University of Iowa	M,D*
University of La Verne	M
University of Louisiana at Monroe	M,D
University of Louisville	M,D,O
University of Mary Hardin-Baylor	M
University of Maryland, College Park	M,D
University of Massachusetts Boston	M
University of Miami	M,O
University of Minnesota, Twin Cities Campus	M,D
University of Missouri–St. Louis	M,D
University of Mobile	M
University of Montevallo	M
University of Nebraska–Lincoln	M,D
University of Nevada, Las Vegas	M
University of New Hampshire	M,O
The University of North Carolina at Greensboro	M,D,O
University of Phoenix–Bay Area Campus	M
University of Phoenix–Central Valley Campus	M
University of Phoenix–Las Vegas Campus	M
University of Phoenix–Phoenix Campus	M
University of Phoenix–Southern California Campus	M
University of Rhode Island	M
University of Rochester	M*
University of Saint Joseph	M
University of St. Thomas (MN)	M,D,O
University of San Diego	M
University of San Francisco	M
University of Southern California	M
University of Southern Mississippi	M
University of South Florida	M,O
The University of Texas at Tyler	M
The University of West Alabama	M
The University of Winnipeg	M,O
University of Wisconsin–Milwaukee	M,D,O
University of Wisconsin–Stout	M
Utah State University	M,D
Valdosta State University	M,O
Walden University	M,D
Western Kentucky University	M
Western Seminary–Sacramento Campus	M
Western Seminary–San Jose Campus	M,O
Wheaton College	M,D

MASS COMMUNICATION

American University	M,D,O
Arizona State University at the Tempe campus	M,D
Arkansas State University	M
Auburn University	M,O
Boston University	M
Brigham Young University	M
California State University, Fresno	M
California State University, Fullerton	M
California State University, Northridge	M
Colorado State University	M,D
Drexel University	M
Florida International University	M
The George Washington University	M,O*
Georgia State University	M,D
Grambling State University	M
Howard University	M,D
Indiana University Bloomington	M,D
Iona College	M,O
Iowa State University of Science and Technology	M
Jackson State University	M
Kansas State University	M
Kent State University	M
Louisiana State University and Agricultural & Mechanical College	M,D
Lynn University	M,O
Marquette University	M,O
Middle Tennessee State University	M
Murray State University	M
North Dakota State University	M,D
Oklahoma State University	M
Penn State University Park	M,D
Point Park University	M
St. Cloud State University	M
San Jose State University	M,O
Southern Illinois University Carbondale	M,D
Southern Illinois University Edwardsville	M
Southern University and Agricultural and Mechanical College	M
Stephen F. Austin State University	M
Syracuse University	M,D
Texas Christian University	M
Texas State University	M
Texas Tech University	M,D
Université Laval	M,D
The University of Alabama	D
University of Arkansas at Little Rock	M
University of Colorado Boulder	M,D

*M—masters degree; D—doctorate; O—other advanced degree; *—Close-Up and/or Display*

University of Denver	M
University of Florida	M,D
University of Georgia	M,D
University of Houston	M
The University of Iowa	M,D*
University of Louisiana at Lafayette	M
University of Maine	M,D
University of Michigan	D
University of Minnesota, Twin Cities Campus	M,D
University of Nebraska–Lincoln	M
The University of North Carolina at Chapel Hill	M,D
University of Oklahoma	M,D*
University of Puerto Rico, Río Piedras Campus	M
University of Southern Mississippi	M,D
University of South Florida	M,O
University of Wisconsin–Madison	M,D
University of Wisconsin–Superior	M
University of Wisconsin–Whitewater	M
Virginia Commonwealth University	M

MATERIALS ENGINEERING

Alabama Agricultural and Mechanical University	M
Arizona State University at the Tempe campus	M,D
Auburn University	M,D
Binghamton University, State University of New York	M,D*
Boise State University	M,D
Boston University	M,D
California State University, Northridge	M
Carleton University	M,D
Carnegie Mellon University	M,D
Case Western Reserve University	M,D*
The Catholic University of America	M
Clarkson University	D
Clemson University	M,D
The College of William and Mary	M,D
Colorado School of Mines	M,D
Columbia University	M,D*
Cornell University	M,D
Dalhousie University	M,D
Dartmouth College	M,D*
Drexel University	M,D
Duke University	M*
Florida International University	M,D
Florida State University	M,D
Georgia Institute of Technology	M,D
Illinois Institute of Technology	M,D
Instituto Tecnológico y de Estudios Superiores de Monterrey, Campus Estado de México	M,D
Iowa State University of Science and Technology	M,D
Johns Hopkins University	M,D
Lehigh University	M,D
Massachusetts Institute of Technology	M,D,O
McGill University	M,D,O
McMaster University	M,D
Michigan State University	M,D
Michigan Technological University	M,D
New Jersey Institute of Technology	M,D,O
New Mexico Institute of Mining and Technology	M,D
North Carolina State University	M,D
Northwestern University	M,D,O*
The Ohio State University	M,D
Penn State University Park	M,D
Purdue University	M,D
Rensselaer Polytechnic Institute	M,D
Rochester Institute of Technology	M
Rutgers University–New Brunswick	M,D
Saginaw Valley State University	M
South Dakota School of Mines and Technology	M,D
Southern Methodist University	M,D
Stanford University	M,D,O
Stevens Institute of Technology	M,D
Stony Brook University, State University of New York	M,D
Texas A&M University	M,D
Texas State University	D
Tuskegee University	D
The University of Alabama	M,D
The University of Alabama at Birmingham	M,D
University of Alberta	M,D
The University of Arizona	M,D
The University of British Columbia	M,D
University of California, Berkeley	M,D
University of California, Davis	M,D
University of California, Irvine	M,D
University of California, Los Angeles	M,D
University of California, Riverside	M
University of California, Santa Barbara	M,D
University of Central Florida	M,D
University of Cincinnati	M,D
University of Connecticut	M*
University of Dayton	M,D
University of Delaware	M,D*
University of Denver	M,D
University of Florida	M,D
University of Illinois at Chicago	M,D
University of Illinois at Urbana–Champaign	M,D
The University of Iowa	M,D*
University of Kentucky	M,D
University of Maryland, College Park	M,D
University of Michigan	M,D
University of Minnesota, Twin Cities Campus	M,D
University of Nebraska–Lincoln	M,D
University of Nevada, Las Vegas	M,D,O
University of Nevada, Reno	M,D
University of Pennsylvania	M,D*
University of Southern California	M,D,O
University of South Florida	M,D,O
The University of Tennessee	M,D
The University of Texas at Arlington	M,D
The University of Texas at Austin	M,D
The University of Texas at Dallas	M,D*
The University of Texas at El Paso	M,D
The University of Texas at San Antonio	M,D
University of Toronto	M,D
University of Utah	M,D*
University of Washington	M,D*
The University of Western Ontario	M,D
University of Windsor	M,D
University of Wisconsin–Madison	M,D
University of Wisconsin–Milwaukee	M,D,O
Virginia Polytechnic Institute and State University	M,D
Washington State University	M,D
Worcester Polytechnic Institute	M,D
Wright State University	M

MATERIALS SCIENCES

Air Force Institute of Technology	M,D
Alabama Agricultural and Mechanical University	M,D
Alfred University	M,D
Arizona State University at the Tempe campus	M,D
Binghamton University, State University of New York	M,D*
Boston University	M,D
Brown University	M,D
California Institute of Technology	M,D
Carnegie Mellon University	M,D
Case Western Reserve University	M,D*
The Catholic University of America	M
Central Michigan University	D
Clarkson University	D
Clemson University	M,D
The College of William and Mary	M,D
Colorado School of Mines	M,D
Columbia University	M,D*
Cornell University	M,D
Dartmouth College	M,D*
Duke University	M,D*
Florida International University	M,D
Florida State University	M,D
Georgetown University	D
The George Washington University	M,D*
Harvard University	M,D*
Illinois Institute of Technology	M,D
Indiana University Bloomington	M,D
Instituto Tecnológico y de Estudios Superiores de Monterrey, Campus Estado de México	M,D
Iowa State University of Science and Technology	M,D
Jackson State University	M
Johns Hopkins University	M,D
Lehigh University	M,D
Massachusetts Institute of Technology	M,D,O
McMaster University	M,D
Michigan State University	M,D
Missouri State University	M
Montana Tech of The University of Montana	D
New Jersey Institute of Technology	M,D,O
Norfolk State University	M
North Carolina State University	M,D
North Dakota State University	M,D
Northwestern University	M,D,O*
The Ohio State University	M,D
Oregon State University	M,D
Penn State University Park	M,D
Princeton University	D
Rensselaer Polytechnic Institute	M,D
Rice University	M,D
Rochester Institute of Technology	M
Royal Military College of Canada	M,D
Rutgers University–New Brunswick	M,D
School of the Art Institute of Chicago	M
South Dakota School of Mines and Technology	M,D
Southern Methodist University	M,D
Stanford University	M,D,O
State University of New York College of Environmental Science and Forestry	M,D,O
Stevens Institute of Technology	M,D
Stony Brook University, State University of New York	M,D
Texas A&M University	M,D
Texas State University	M,D
Trent University	M
Université du Québec, Institut National de la Recherche Scientifique	M,D
The University of Alabama	D
The University of Alabama in Huntsville	M,D
The University of Arizona	M,D
The University of British Columbia	M,D
University of Calgary	M,D
University of California, Berkeley	M,D
University of California, Davis	M,D
University of California, Irvine	M,D
University of California, Los Angeles	M,D
University of California, Riverside	M
University of California, San Diego	M,D
University of California, Santa Barbara	M,D
University of Central Florida	M,D
University of Cincinnati	M,D
University of Connecticut	M,D*
University of Delaware	M,D*
University of Denver	M,D
University of Florida	M,D
University of Idaho	M,D
University of Illinois at Urbana–Champaign	M,D
University of Kentucky	M,D
The University of Manchester	M,D
University of Maryland, College Park	M,D
University of Michigan	M,D
University of Minnesota, Twin Cities Campus	M,D
University of Mississippi Medical Center	M,D
University of Nebraska–Lincoln	M,D
University of New Brunswick Fredericton	M,D
University of New Hampshire	M,D
The University of North Carolina at Chapel Hill	M,D
University of Pennsylvania	M,D*
University of Pittsburgh	M,D*
University of Rochester	M,D*
University of Southern California	M,D,O
University of South Florida	M,D,O
The University of Tennessee	M,D
The University of Texas at Arlington	M,D
The University of Texas at Austin	M,D
The University of Texas at Dallas	M,D*
The University of Texas at El Paso	M,D
The University of Toledo	M,D
University of Toronto	M,D
University of Utah	M,D*
University of Vermont	M,D
University of Virginia	M,D
University of Washington	M,D*
Vanderbilt University	M,D*
Virginia Polytechnic Institute and State University	M,D
Washington State University	M,D
Washington University in St. Louis	M,D
Wayne State University	M,D,O
Worcester Polytechnic Institute	M,D
Wright State University	M

MATERNAL AND CHILD/NEONATAL NURSING

Baylor University	M,D
Boston College	M,D
Case Western Reserve University	M*
Creighton University	M,D,O
Duke University	M,D,O*
Hardin-Simmons University	M
Lehman College of the City University of New York	M
Louisiana State University Health Sciences Center	M,D,O
Medical University of South Carolina	M,D
Northeastern University	M,D,O
Old Dominion University	M
Point Loma Nazarene University	M,O
Regis University	M,D,O
Rush University	D,O
St. Catherine University	M,D
Saint Francis Medical Center College of Nursing	M,D,O
Stony Brook University, State University of New York	M,D,O
University of Alberta	D
University of Cincinnati	M,D
University of Delaware	M,O*
University of Illinois at Chicago	M,O
University of Indianapolis	M,D
University of Louisville	M,D
University of Maryland, Baltimore	M
University of Missouri–Kansas City	M,D
University of Pennsylvania	M*
University of Pittsburgh	M,D*
University of Puerto Rico, Medical Sciences Campus	M
University of Rochester	M,D*
University of South Africa	M,D
University of Southern Mississippi	M,D,O
The University of Texas at Austin	M,D
Vanderbilt University	M,D,O*
Wayne State University	M,D

MATERNAL AND CHILD HEALTH

Bank Street College of Education	M
Columbia University	M,D*
East Carolina University	M,D
Instituto Tecnologico de Santo Domingo	M,O
Oakland University	D,O
Troy University	M,D,O
The University of Alabama at Birmingham	M,D
University of California, Davis	M
University of Maryland, College Park	M,D
University of Minnesota, Twin Cities Campus	M
The University of North Carolina at Chapel Hill	M,D
University of Puerto Rico, Medical Sciences Campus	M
University of South Florida	O
University of Washington	M,D*

MATHEMATICAL AND COMPUTATIONAL FINANCE

Boston University	M,D
Carnegie Mellon University	M,D
DePaul University	M,D
Florida State University	M,D
The George Washington University	M,D,O*
Georgia Institute of Technology	M
Illinois Institute of Technology	M,D
Johns Hopkins University	M,D
New Jersey Institute of Technology	M,D,O
New York University	M,D,O
North Carolina State University	M
Oregon State University	M,D
Purdue University	M,D
Rice University	M,D
Rochester Institute of Technology	M
Université de Montréal	M,D,O
University of Alberta	M,D,O
University of California, Santa Barbara	M,D
University of Chicago	M
University of Connecticut	M*
University of Dayton	M
The University of Manchester	M,D
University of Miami	M,D
The University of North Carolina at Charlotte	M,O
University of Notre Dame	M,D
University of Southern California	M,D
University of Toronto	M

MATHEMATICAL PHYSICS

Indiana University Bloomington	M,D
New Mexico Institute of Mining and Technology	M,D
University of Alberta	M,D,O
University of Colorado Boulder	M,D

MATHEMATICS

Alabama State University	M
American University	M,O
American University of Beirut	M,D
American University of Sharjah	M
Appalachian State University	M
Arizona State University at the Tempe campus	M,D,O
Arkansas State University	M
Auburn University	M,D
Aurora University	M
Ball State University	M
Baylor University	M,D
Bemidji State University	M
Binghamton University, State University of New York	M,D*
Boise State University	M
Boston College	D
Boston University	M,D
Bowling Green State University	M,D
Brandeis University	M,D,O
Brigham Young University	M,D
Brock University	M
Brooklyn College of the City University of New York	M
Brown University	D
Bryn Mawr College	M,D
Bucknell University	M
California Institute of Technology	D
California Polytechnic State University, San Luis Obispo	M
California State Polytechnic University, Pomona	M
California State University Channel Islands	M
California State University, East Bay	M
California State University, Fresno	M
California State University, Fullerton	M
California State University, Long Beach	M
California State University, Los Angeles	M
California State University, Northridge	M
California State University, Sacramento	M
California State University, San Bernardino	M
California State University, San Marcos	M
Carleton University	M,D
Carnegie Mellon University	M,D
Case Western Reserve University	M,D*
Central Connecticut State University	M,O
Central European University	M,D
Central Michigan University	M,D
Central Washington University	M
Chicago State University	M
City College of the City University of New York	M
Claremont Graduate University	M,D
Clark Atlanta University	M
Clarkson University	M,D
Clemson University	M,D
Cleveland State University	M
The College at Brockport, State University of New York	M,O
College of Charleston	M,O
Colorado State University	M,D
Columbia University	M,D*
Columbus State University	M,O
Concordia University (Canada)	M,D
Cornell University	D
Dalhousie University	M,D
Dartmouth College	M,D*
Delaware State University	M
DePaul University	M,D
Drew University	M,D,O
Drexel University	M,D
Duke University	D*
Duquesne University	M
East Carolina University	M,O
Eastern Illinois University	M
Eastern Kentucky University	M
Eastern Michigan University	M
Eastern Washington University	M

East Tennessee State University	M,O
Elizabeth City State University	M
Emory University	M,D
Emporia State University	M
Fairfield University	M
Fairleigh Dickinson University, Metropolitan Campus	M
Fayetteville State University	M
Florida Atlantic University	M,D
Florida Gulf Coast University	M
Florida International University	M
Florida State University	M,D
George Mason University	M,D,O
Georgetown University	M
The George Washington University	M,D,O*
Georgia Institute of Technology	M,D
Georgia Southern University	M
Georgia State University	M,D
The Graduate Center, City University of New York	D
Hardin-Simmons University	M
Harvard University	D*
Howard University	M,D
Hunter College of the City University of New York	M
Idaho State University	M,D
Illinois State University	M
Indiana State University	M
Indiana University Bloomington	M,D
Indiana University of Pennsylvania	M
Indiana University–Purdue University Fort Wayne	M,O
Indiana University–Purdue University Indianapolis	M,D
Instituto Tecnologico de Santo Domingo	M,D,O
Iowa State University of Science and Technology	M,D
Jackson State University	M
Jacksonville State University	M
John Carroll University	M
Johns Hopkins University	M,D
Kansas State University	M,D,O
Kent State University	M,D
Lakehead University	M
Lamar University	M
Lee University	M,O
Lehigh University	M,D
Lehman College of the City University of New York	M
Long Island University–LIU Post	M,O
Louisiana State University and Agricultural & Mechanical College	M,D
Louisiana Tech University	M,D
Loyola University Chicago	M
Manhattan College	M
Marquette University	M,D
Marshall University	M
Massachusetts Institute of Technology	D
McGill University	M,D
McMaster University	M,D
McNeese State University	M
Memorial University of Newfoundland	M,D
Miami University	M
Michigan State University	M,D
Michigan Technological University	M,D
Middle Tennessee State University	M
Minnesota State University Mankato	M
Mississippi College	M
Mississippi State University	M,D
Missouri State University	M
Missouri University of Science and Technology	M,D
Molloy College	M,O
Montana State University	M,D
Montclair State University	M
Morgan State University	M
Murray State University	M
New Jersey Institute of Technology	M,D,O
New Mexico Institute of Mining and Technology	M,D
New Mexico State University	M,D
New York University	M,D
North Carolina Agricultural and Technical State University	M
North Carolina Central University	M
North Carolina State University	M,D
North Dakota State University	M,D
Northeastern Illinois University	M
Northeastern University	M,D
Northern Arizona University	M,O
Northern Illinois University	M,D
Northwestern University	D*
Northwest Missouri State University	M
Oakland University	M
The Ohio State University	M,D
Ohio University	M,D
Oklahoma State University	M,D
Old Dominion University	M,D
Oregon State University	M,D
Pace University	M,O
Penn State University Park	M,D
Pepperdine University	M,D
Pittsburg State University	M
Portland State University	M,D,O
Princeton University	D
Purdue University	M,D
Purdue University Northwest	M
Queens College of the City University of New York	M
Queen's University at Kingston	M,D
Rensselaer Polytechnic Institute	M,D
Rhode Island College	M,O
Rice University	D
Rivier University	M
Rochester Institute of Technology	M,O
Roosevelt University	M
Rowan University	M
Royal Military College of Canada	M
Rutgers University–Camden	M
Rutgers University–Newark	D
Rutgers University–New Brunswick	M,D
St. Cloud State University	M
Saint Joseph's University	M,O
Saint Louis University	M,D
Salem State University	M
Samford University	M,D,O
Sam Houston State University	M
San Diego State University	M,D
San Francisco State University	M
San Jose State University	M,D,O
Simon Fraser University	M,D
Smith College	O
South Carolina State University	M
South Dakota State University	M,D
Southeast Missouri State University	M
Southern Connecticut State University	M
Southern Illinois University Carbondale	M,D
Southern Illinois University Edwardsville	M
Southern Methodist University	M,D
Southern University and Agricultural and Mechanical College	M
Stanford University	M,D
State University of New York College at Cortland	M
State University of New York College at Potsdam	M
Stephen F. Austin State University	M
Stevens Institute of Technology	M,D
Stony Brook University, State University of New York	M,D
Syracuse University	M,D
Tarleton State University	M
Temple University	M,D*
Tennessee State University	M,D
Tennessee Technological University	M
Texas A&M International University	M
Texas A&M University	M,D
Texas A&M University–Central Texas	M,O
Texas A&M University–Corpus Christi	M
Texas A&M University–Kingsville	M
Texas Christian University	M,D
Texas Southern University	M
Texas State University	M
Texas Tech University	M,D
Texas Woman's University	M
Tufts University	M,D
Tulane University	M,D
Université de Moncton	M
Université de Montréal	M,D,O
Université de Sherbrooke	M,D
Université du Québec à Montréal	M,D
Université du Québec à Trois-Rivières	M
Université Laval	M,D
University at Albany, State University of New York	M,D
University at Buffalo, the State University of New York	M,D*
The University of Akron	M
The University of Alabama	M,D
The University of Alabama at Birmingham	M
The University of Alabama in Huntsville	M,D
University of Alaska Fairbanks	M,D,O
University of Alberta	M,D,O
The University of Arizona	M,D
University of Arkansas	M,D
University of Arkansas at Little Rock	M,O
The University of British Columbia	M,D
University of Calgary	M,D
University of California, Berkeley	M,D
University of California, Davis	M,D
University of California, Irvine	M,D
University of California, Los Angeles	M,D
University of California, Riverside	M,D
University of California, San Diego	M,D
University of California, Santa Barbara	M,D
University of California, Santa Cruz	M,D
University of Central Arkansas	M
University of Central Florida	M,D,O
University of Central Missouri	M,D,O
University of Central Oklahoma	M
University of Chicago	D
University of Cincinnati	M,D
University of Colorado Boulder	M,D
University of Colorado Colorado Springs	D
University of Colorado Denver	M,D
University of Delaware	M,D*
University of Denver	M,D
University of Florida	M,D
University of Georgia	M,D
University of Guelph	M,D
University of Hawaii at Manoa	M,D
University of Houston	M,D
University of Houston–Clear Lake	M
University of Idaho	M,D
University of Illinois at Chicago	M,D
University of Illinois at Urbana–Champaign	M,D
The University of Iowa	M,D*
The University of Kansas	M,D*
University of Kentucky	M,D
University of Lethbridge	M,D
University of Louisiana at Lafayette	M,D
University of Louisville	M,D
The University of Manchester	M,D
University of Manitoba	M,D
University of Maryland, College Park	M,D
University of Massachusetts Amherst	M,D*
University of Massachusetts Lowell	D
University of Memphis	M,D
University of Miami	M,D
University of Michigan	M,D
University of Michigan–Flint	M
University of Minnesota, Twin Cities Campus	M,D,O
University of Mississippi	M,D
University of Missouri	M,D
University of Missouri–Kansas City	M,D
University of Missouri–St. Louis	M,D
University of Montana	M,D
University of Nebraska at Omaha	M
University of Nebraska–Lincoln	M,D
University of Nevada, Las Vegas	M,D
University of Nevada, Reno	M
University of New Brunswick Fredericton	M,D
University of New Hampshire	M,D
University of New Mexico	M,D
University of New Orleans	M
The University of North Carolina at Chapel Hill	M,D
The University of North Carolina at Charlotte	M,D,O
The University of North Carolina at Greensboro	M,D
The University of North Carolina Wilmington	M,O
University of North Dakota	M
University of Northern British Columbia	M,D,O
University of Northern Colorado	M,D
University of Northern Iowa	M
University of North Florida	M
University of North Texas	M,D,O
University of Notre Dame	M,D
University of Oklahoma	M,D*
University of Oregon	M,D
University of Ottawa	M,D
University of Pennsylvania	M,D*
University of Pittsburgh	M,D*
University of Puerto Rico, Mayagüez Campus	M
University of Puerto Rico, Rí o Piedras Campus	M,D
University of Regina	M,D
University of Rhode Island	M,D
University of Rochester	M,D*
University of Saskatchewan	M,D
University of South Alabama	M
University of South Carolina	M,D
The University of South Dakota	M
University of Southern California	M,D
University of Southern Mississippi	M,D
University of South Florida	M,D,O
The University of Tennessee	M,D
The University of Tennessee at Chattanooga	M
The University of Texas at Arlington	M,D
The University of Texas at Austin	M,D
The University of Texas at Dallas	M,D*
The University of Texas at El Paso	M
The University of Texas at San Antonio	M
The University of Texas at Tyler	M
The University of Texas Rio Grande Valley	M
University of the Incarnate Word	M
The University of Toledo	M,D
University of Toronto	M,D
The University of Tulsa	M,D
University of Utah	M,D*
University of Vermont	M,D
University of Victoria	M,D
University of Virginia	M,D
University of Washington	M,D*
University of Waterloo	M,D
The University of Western Ontario	M,D
University of West Florida	M
University of West Georgia	M,O
University of Windsor	M,D
University of Wisconsin–Madison	D
University of Wisconsin–Milwaukee	M,D
University of Wyoming	M,D
Utah State University	M,D
Vanderbilt University	M,D*
Villanova University	M
Virginia Commonwealth University	M
Virginia Polytechnic Institute and State University	M,D
Virginia State University	M
Wake Forest University	M
Washington State University	M,D
Washington University in St. Louis	M,D
Wayne State University	M,D
Wesleyan University	M,D
West Chester University of Pennsylvania	M,O
Western Connecticut State University	M
Western Illinois University	M,O
Western Kentucky University	M
Western Michigan University	M,D
Western Washington University	M
West Texas A&M University	M
West Virginia University	M,D
Wichita State University	M,D
Wilfrid Laurier University	M
Wilkes University	M
Worcester Polytechnic Institute	M,D,O
Wright State University	M
Yale University	M,D*
Yeshiva University	M,D
York University	M,D
Youngstown State University	M

MATHEMATICS EDUCATION

Acadia University	M
Alabama Agricultural and Mechanical University	M,O
Alabama State University	M,O
Albany State University	M
Appalachian State University	M
Arcadia University	M,D,O
Arizona State University at the Tempe campus	M,D,O
Arkansas State University	M
Asbury University	M
Auburn University	M,D,O
Ball State University	M
Bank Street College of Education	M
Bemidji State University	M
Bethel University (MN)	M,D,O
Binghamton University, State University of New York	M*
Bloomsburg University of Pennsylvania	M
Bob Jones University	M,D,O
Boise State University	M,O
Bowling Green State University	M,D
Bridgewater State University	M
Brigham Young University	M
Brooklyn College of the City University of New York	M
Buffalo State College, State University of New York	M
California State University, Bakersfield	M
California State University, Chico	M
California State University, Dominguez Hills	M
California State University, East Bay	M
California State University, Fresno	M
California State University, Fullerton	M
California State University, Long Beach	M
California State University, Northridge	M
California State University, San Bernardino	M
Cambridge College	M,D,O
Caribbean University	M,D
Central Michigan University	M,D
Chaminade University of Honolulu	M
Chatham University	M
The Citadel, The Military College of South Carolina	M
City College of the City University of New York	M,O
Clarion University of Pennsylvania	M
Clark Atlanta University	M
Clarkson University	M,O
Clayton State University	M
Clemson University	M,D,O
Cleveland State University	M
The College at Brockport, State University of New York	M,O
College of Charleston	M
The Colorado College	M
Columbus State University	M,O
Concordia University (United States)	M,D
Concordia University (Canada)	M,D
Converse College	M
Cornell University	M,D
Delaware State University	M
DePaul University	M,D
Drury University	M
Duquesne University	M
East Carolina University	M,O
Eastern Illinois University	M
Eastern Kentucky University	M
Eastern University	M,O
Eastern Washington University	M
Elizabeth City State University	M
Florida Agricultural and Mechanical University	M
Florida Atlantic University	M
Florida Institute of Technology	M,D,O
Florida International University	M,D,O
Florida State University	M,D,O
Framingham State University	M
Fresno Pacific University	M
George Mason University	M
The George Washington University	M*
Georgia Southwestern State University	M,O
Georgia State University	M,D,O
Gordon College	M,O
Grambling State University	M,D,O
Harding University	M,O
Harvard University	M,O*
High Point University	M
Hofstra University	M,D,O
Hood College	M,O

*M—masters degree; D—doctorate; O—other advanced degree; *—Close-Up and/or Display*

Hunter College of the City University of New York	M
Idaho State University	M,D
Illinois Institute of Technology	M,D
Illinois State University	M,D
Indiana University Bloomington	M,D,O
Indiana University of Pennsylvania	M
Indiana University–Purdue University Fort Wayne	M,O
Indiana University–Purdue University Indianapolis	M,D
Instituto Tecnológico y de Estudios Superiores de Monterrey, Campus Ciudad Obregón	M
Inter American University of Puerto Rico, Arecibo Campus	M
Inter American University of Puerto Rico, Barranquitas Campus	M
Inter American University of Puerto Rico, Metropolitan Campus	M
Inter American University of Puerto Rico, Ponce Campus	M
Inter American University of Puerto Rico, San Germán Campus	M
Iona College	M
Iowa State University of Science and Technology	M,D
Ithaca College	M
Jackson State University	M
James Madison University	M
Kaplan University, Davenport Campus	M
Kean University	M
Kennesaw State University	M
Kutztown University of Pennsylvania	M
Lake Forest College	M
Lee University	M,O
Lehman College of the City University of New York	M
Lesley University	M,D,O
Lewis University	M
Liberty University	M,D,O
Lipscomb University	M,D,O
Longwood University	M
Louisiana Tech University	M,D
Loyola Marymount University	M
Manhattanville College	M*
Marquette University	M,D
Miami University	M
Michigan State University	M,D
Middle Tennessee State University	M,D
Millersville University of Pennsylvania	M
Mills College	M,D,O
Minnesota State University Mankato	M
Minot State University	M
Mississippi College	M,D,O
Missouri State University	M
Missouri University of Science and Technology	M,D
Montana State University	M,D
Montclair State University	M,D,O
Morehead State University	M,D
Morgan State University	M,D
Mount Holyoke College	M
National Louis University	M,D,O
National University	M,O
New Jersey City University	M,D
New Mexico State University	M,D,O
New York Institute of Technology	M,O
New York University	M
Niagara University	M
North Carolina Central University	M
North Carolina State University	M,D
North Dakota State University	M,D,O
Northeastern Illinois University	M
Northeastern State University	M
Northern Arizona University	M,O
Northwest Missouri State University	M
Occidental College	M
The Ohio State University	M,D
Ohio University	M,D
Oklahoma State University	M,D
Oregon State University	M,D
Plymouth State University	M
Portland State University	M,D
Providence College	M
Purdue University	M,D,O
Purdue University Northwest	M
Queens College of the City University of New York	M,O
Quinnipiac University	M
Radford University	M
Regent University	M,D,O
Rhode Island College	M
Rider University	O
Rowan University	M,O
Rutgers University–Camden	M
Rutgers University–New Brunswick	M,D
St. Joseph's College, Long Island Campus	M
Saint Peter's University	M,D,O
Salem State University	M
Salisbury University	M
San Diego State University	M,D
San Francisco State University	M
San Jose State University	M,O
Seattle Pacific University	M
Shippensburg University of Pennsylvania	M
Simon Fraser University	M,D
Slippery Rock University of Pennsylvania	M
Smith College	M
South Carolina State University	M
Southeastern Oklahoma State University	M
Southern Illinois University Edwardsville	M
Southern University and Agricultural and Mechanical College	D
Southwestern Oklahoma State University	M
Southwest Minnesota State University	M
State University of New York at New Paltz	M
State University of New York at Plattsburgh	M
State University of New York College at Cortland	M
State University of New York College at Old Westbury	M
State University of New York College at Potsdam	M
Stephen F. Austin State University	M
Stevenson University	M
Stony Brook University, State University of New York	M,O
Syracuse University	M,D
Teachers College, Columbia University	M,D
Temple University	M*
Tennessee Technological University	M,O
Texas Christian University	M,O
Texas State University	M,D
Texas Woman's University	M
Touro College	M
Towson University	M
Troy University	M
Tufts University	M,D
Universidad Autonoma de Guadalajara	M,D
University at Buffalo, the State University of New York	M,D,O*
The University of Alabama in Huntsville	M,D
The University of Arizona	M
University of Arkansas	M
University of Arkansas at Pine Bluff	M
The University of British Columbia	M,D
University of California, Berkeley	M,D
University of California, San Diego	D
University of Central Arkansas	M
University of Central Florida	M,D,O
University of Cincinnati	M,D
University of Colorado Denver	M,D
University of Connecticut	M,D*
University of Dayton	M
University of Detroit Mercy	M,D
University of Florida	M,D,O
University of Georgia	M,D,O
University of Illinois at Chicago	M,D
University of Illinois at Urbana–Champaign	M,D
University of Indianapolis	M
The University of Iowa	M,D*
University of Louisiana at Monroe	M,D
University of Maine	M,D,O
University of Maryland, Baltimore County	M
University of Massachusetts Dartmouth	D
University of Miami	D
University of Minnesota, Twin Cities Campus	M
University of Missouri	M,D,O
University of Montana	M,D
University of Nebraska at Kearney	M
University of Nevada, Reno	M
University of New Hampshire	M,D
The University of North Carolina at Chapel Hill	M
The University of North Carolina at Charlotte	M,D
The University of North Carolina at Greensboro	M,D,O
The University of North Carolina at Pembroke	M
The University of North Carolina Wilmington	M
University of Northern Colorado	M,D
University of Northern Iowa	M
University of North Georgia	M,O
University of Phoenix–North Florida Campus	M
University of Phoenix–Online Campus	M,O
University of Phoenix–South Florida Campus	M
University of Phoenix–Washington D.C. Campus	M,D,O
University of Pittsburgh	M,D*
University of Puerto Rico, Rí o Piedras Campus	M,D
University of St. Francis (IL)	M,D,O
University of St. Thomas (MN)	M,O
University of South Africa	M,D
University of South Carolina	M,D
University of Southern Indiana	M
University of Southern Mississippi	M,D
University of South Florida	M,D,O
University of South Florida, St. Petersburg	M
The University of Tennessee	M,D,O
The University of Tennessee at Chattanooga	M
The University of Texas at Arlington	M,D
The University of Texas at Dallas	M*
The University of Texas at El Paso	M
The University of Texas at San Antonio	M
University of the District of Columbia	M
University of the Incarnate Word	M
University of the Sacred Heart	M,O
University of the Virgin Islands	M
The University of Toledo	M,D,O
The University of Tulsa	M
University of Utah	M,D*
University of Vermont	M
University of Victoria	M,D
University of Virginia	M,D,O
University of Washington	M,D*
University of Washington, Tacoma	M
The University of West Alabama	M
University of Wisconsin–Madison	M,D
University of Wisconsin–Oshkosh	M
University of Wisconsin–River Falls	M
University of Wyoming	M,D
Ursuline College	M
Utah Valley University	M
Virginia Polytechnic Institute and State University	M,D
Virginia State University	M
Wagner College	M
Walden University	M,D,O
Washington State University	M,D
Wayne State College	M
Wayne State University	M,D,O
Webster University	M,O
West Chester University of Pennsylvania	M,O
Western Governors University	M,O
Western Michigan University	M,D
Western New England University	M
Western Oregon University	M
West Virginia University	M,D
Widener University	M,D
Wilkes University	M,D
William Jessup University	M
Wright State University	M
Youngstown State University	M

MECHANICAL ENGINEERING

Alfred University	M,D
The American University in Cairo	M
American University of Beirut	M,D
American University of Sharjah	M
Arizona State University at the Tempe campus	M,D
Auburn University	M,D
Baylor University	M,D
Binghamton University, State University of New York	M,D*
Boise State University	M
Boston University	M,D
Bradley University	M
Brigham Young University	M,D
Brown University	M,D
Bucknell University	M
California Institute of Technology	M,D,O
California Polytechnic State University, San Luis Obispo	M
California State Polytechnic University, Pomona	M
California State University, Fresno	M
California State University, Fullerton	M
California State University, Long Beach	M,D
California State University, Los Angeles	M
California State University, Northridge	M
California State University, Sacramento	M
Carleton University	M,D
Carnegie Mellon University	M,D
Case Western Reserve University	M,D*
The Catholic University of America	M,D
City College of the City University of New York	M,D
Clarkson University	M,D
Clemson University	M,D
Cleveland State University	M,D
Colorado School of Mines	M,D
Colorado State University	M,D
Columbia University	M,D*
Concordia University (Canada)	M,D,O
Cooper Union for the Advancement of Science and Art	M
Cornell University	M,D
Dalhousie University	M,D
Dartmouth College	M,D*
Drexel University	M,D
Duke University	M,D*
École Polytechnique de Montréal	M,D,O
Embry-Riddle Aeronautical University–Daytona	M,D*
Fairfield University	M,O
Florida Agricultural and Mechanical University	M,D
Florida Atlantic University	M,D
Florida Institute of Technology	M,D
Florida International University	M,D
Florida State University	M,D
Gannon University	M
The George Washington University	M,D,O*
Georgia Institute of Technology	M,D
Georgia Southern University	M
The Graduate Center, City University of New York	D
Grand Valley State University	M
Harvard University	M,D*
Howard University	M,D
Idaho State University	M
Illinois Institute of Technology	M,D
Indiana University–Purdue University Fort Wayne	M
Indiana University–Purdue University Indianapolis	M,D,O
Instituto Tecnológico y de Estudios Superiores de Monterrey, Campus Chihuahua	M,O
Instituto Tecnológico y de Estudios Superiores de Monterrey, Campus Monterrey	M,D
Iowa State University of Science and Technology	M,D
Johns Hopkins University	M,D
Kansas State University	M,D
Kettering University	M
Lamar University	M,D
Lawrence Technological University	M,D
Lehigh University	M,D
Louisiana State University and Agricultural & Mechanical College	M,D
Louisiana Tech University	M,D
Loyola Marymount University	M
Manhattan College	M
Marquette University	M,D,O
Massachusetts Institute of Technology	M,D,O
McGill University	M,D
McMaster University	M,D
McNeese State University	M,O
Memorial University of Newfoundland	M,D
Mercer University	M
Merrimack College	M
Miami University	M
Michigan State University	M,D
Michigan Technological University	M,D,O
Mississippi State University	M,D
Missouri University of Science and Technology	M,D
Montana State University	M,D
Naval Postgraduate School	M,D,O
New Jersey Institute of Technology	M,D
New Mexico Institute of Mining and Technology	M
New Mexico State University	M,D
New York University	M,D
North Carolina Agricultural and Technical State University	M,D
North Carolina State University	M,D
North Dakota State University	M,D
Northeastern University	M,D,O
Northern Arizona University	M
Northern Illinois University	M
Northwestern University	M,D*
Oakland University	M,D
The Ohio State University	M,D
Ohio University	M,D
Oklahoma Christian University	M
Oklahoma State University	M,D
Old Dominion University	M,D
Oregon State University	M,D
Penn State University Park	M,D
Pittsburg State University	M
Polytechnic University of Puerto Rico	M
Portland State University	M,D,O
Princeton University	M,D
Purdue University	M,D,O
Purdue University Northwest	M
Queen's University at Kingston	M,D
Rensselaer at Hartford	M
Rensselaer Polytechnic Institute	M,D
Rice University	M,D
Rochester Institute of Technology	M
Rose-Hulman Institute of Technology	M
Rowan University	M
Royal Military College of Canada	M,D
Rutgers University–New Brunswick	M,D
St. Cloud State University	M
Saint Martin's University	M
San Diego State University	M,D
Santa Clara University	M,D,O
Simon Fraser University	M,D
South Carolina State University	M
South Dakota School of Mines and Technology	M,D
South Dakota State University	M,D
Southern Illinois University Carbondale	M,D
Southern Illinois University Edwardsville	M
Southern Methodist University	M,D
Stanford University	M,D,O
Stevens Institute of Technology	M,D,O
Stony Brook University, State University of New York	M,D
Syracuse University	M,D
Temple University	M*
Tennessee State University	M,D
Tennessee Technological University	M
Texas A&M University	M,D
Texas A&M University–Kingsville	M
Texas Tech University	M,D
Tufts University	M,D
Tuskegee University	M
Université de Moncton	M
Université de Sherbrooke	M,D
Université Laval	M,D
University at Buffalo, the State University of New York	M,D*
The University of Akron	M,D
The University of Alabama	M,D
The University of Alabama at Birmingham	M
The University of Alabama in Huntsville	M,D
University of Alaska Fairbanks	M
University of Alberta	M,D
The University of Arizona	M,D
University of Arkansas	M,D
University of Bridgeport	M
The University of British Columbia	M,D
University of Calgary	M,D
University of California, Berkeley	M,D
University of California, Davis	M,D,O
University of California, Irvine	M,D
University of California, Los Angeles	M,D
University of California, Merced	M,D
University of California, Riverside	M,D
University of California, San Diego	M,D

University of California, Santa Barbara	M,D
University of Central Florida	M,D
University of Central Oklahoma	M
University of Cincinnati	M,D
University of Colorado Boulder	M,D
University of Colorado Colorado Springs	M
University of Colorado Denver	M
University of Connecticut	M,D*
University of Dayton	M,D
University of Delaware	M,D*
University of Denver	M,D
University of Detroit Mercy	M,D
University of Florida	M,D
University of Hawaii at Manoa	M,D
University of Houston	M,D
University of Idaho	M,D
University of Illinois at Chicago	M,D
University of Illinois at Urbana–Champaign	M,D
The University of Iowa	M,D*
The University of Kansas	M,D*
University of Kentucky	M,D
University of Louisiana at Lafayette	M
University of Louisville	M,D
University of Maine	M,D
The University of Manchester	M,D
University of Manitoba	M,D
University of Maryland, Baltimore County	M,D,O
University of Maryland, College Park	M,D
University of Massachusetts Amherst	M,D*
University of Massachusetts Dartmouth	M
University of Massachusetts Lowell	M,D
University of Memphis	M,D
University of Miami	M,D
University of Michigan	M,D
University of Michigan–Dearborn	M
University of Minnesota, Twin Cities Campus	M,D
University of Missouri	M,D
University of Missouri–Kansas City	M,D,O
University of Nebraska–Lincoln	M,D
University of Nevada, Las Vegas	M,D,O
University of Nevada, Reno	M,D
University of New Brunswick Fredericton	M,D
University of New Hampshire	M,D
University of New Haven	M
University of New Mexico	M,D
University of New Orleans	M
The University of North Carolina at Charlotte	M,D
University of North Dakota	M
University of North Florida	M
University of North Texas	M,D,O
University of Notre Dame	M,D
University of Oklahoma	M,D*
University of Ottawa	M,D
University of Pennsylvania	M,D*
University of Pittsburgh	M,D*
University of Portland	M
University of Puerto Rico, Mayagüez Campus	M
University of Rochester	M,D*
University of St. Thomas (MN)	M,O
University of Saskatchewan	M,D
University of South Alabama	M
University of South Carolina	M,D
University of Southern California	M,D,O
University of South Florida	M,D
The University of Tennessee	M,D
The University of Tennessee at Chattanooga	M
The University of Texas at Arlington	M,D
The University of Texas at Austin	M,D
The University of Texas at Dallas	M,D*
The University of Texas at El Paso	M,D
The University of Texas at San Antonio	M,D
The University of Texas at Tyler	M
The University of Texas Rio Grande Valley	M
The University of Toledo	M,D
University of Toronto	M,D
The University of Tulsa	M,D
University of Utah	M,D*
University of Vermont	M,D
University of Victoria	M,D
University of Virginia	M,D
University of Washington	M,D*
University of Waterloo	M,D
The University of Western Ontario	M,D
University of Windsor	M,D
University of Wisconsin–Madison	M,D
University of Wisconsin–Milwaukee	M,D,O
University of Wyoming	M,D
Utah State University	M,D
Vanderbilt University	M,D*
Villanova University	M,O
Virginia Commonwealth University	M,D
Virginia Polytechnic Institute and State University	M,D
Washington State University	M,D
Washington University in St. Louis	M,D
Wayne State University	M,D
Western Michigan University	M,D
Western New England University	M
West Virginia University	M,D
Wichita State University	M,D
Widener University	M
Wilkes University	M
Worcester Polytechnic Institute	M,D,O
Wright State University	M
Yale University	M,D*
Youngstown State University	M

MECHANICS

Brown University	M,D
California Institute of Technology	M,D
Carnegie Mellon University	M,D
Columbia University	M,D*
Cornell University	M,D
Drexel University	M,D
École Polytechnique de Montréal	M,D,O
Georgia Institute of Technology	M
Iowa State University of Science and Technology	M,D
Johns Hopkins University	M
Lehigh University	M,D
Louisiana State University and Agricultural & Mechanical College	M,D
McGill University	M,D
Michigan State University	M,D
Michigan Technological University	M,D,O
Missouri University of Science and Technology	M,D
Montana State University	M,D
New Mexico Institute of Mining and Technology	M
Northwestern University	M,D*
Ohio University	M,D
Penn State University Park	M,D
Rutgers University–New Brunswick	M,D
San Diego State University	M,D
Southern Illinois University Carbondale	M
Stanford University	M,D,O
The University of Alabama	M,D
University of Calgary	M,D
University of California, Berkeley	M,D
University of California, Merced	M,D
University of California, San Diego	M,D
University of Cincinnati	M,D
University of Colorado Denver	M
University of Dayton	M
University of Illinois at Urbana–Champaign	M,D
University of Maryland, College Park	M,D
University of Massachusetts Amherst	M,D*
University of Massachusetts Dartmouth	D
University of Minnesota, Twin Cities Campus	M,D
University of Nebraska–Lincoln	M,D
University of New Brunswick Fredericton	M,D
University of Pennsylvania	M,D*
University of Southern California	M,D,O
The University of Texas at Austin	M,D
University of Washington	M,D*
University of Wisconsin–Madison	M,D
University of Wisconsin–Milwaukee	M,D,O
Virginia Polytechnic Institute and State University	M,D

MEDIA STUDIES

American University	M,D
American University of Beirut	M,D
Angelo State University	M
Arizona State University at the Tempe campus	M,D
Arkansas State University	M
Bob Jones University	M,D,O
Boston University	M,D
Brooklyn College of the City University of New York	M
California College of the Arts	M
Carnegie Mellon University	M
Central Michigan University	M
Champlain College	M
City College of the City University of New York	M
Claremont Graduate University	M,D,O
College of Staten Island of the City University of New York	M
Colorado State University	M,D
Concordia University (Canada)	M,D,O
Cornell University	M,D
Dallas Theological Seminary	M,D,O
DePaul University	M
Digital Media Arts College	M
Duke University	M*
Emerson College	M
Fairleigh Dickinson University, Metropolitan Campus	M
Fielding Graduate University	M,D,O
Florida Atlantic University	M,O
Florida State University	M,D
Fordham University	M
Full Sail University	M
Georgetown University	M,D
Georgia State University	M,D
Governors State University	M
Howard University	M,D
Hunter College of the City University of New York	M
Indiana State University	M
Indiana University Bloomington	M,D
Indiana University of Pennsylvania	D
International University in Geneva	M,D
Johns Hopkins University	M
La Salle University	M,O
Lindenwood University	M,O
Lindenwood University–Belleville	M
Long Island University–LIU Brooklyn	M,D,O
Louisiana State University and Agricultural & Mechanical College	M,D
Loyola University Maryland	M
Lynn University	M,O
Maryland Institute College of Art	M
Massachusetts College of Art and Design	M,O
Massachusetts Institute of Technology	M,D
Metropolitan College of New York	M
Michigan State University	M,D
Missouri Western State University	M
Monmouth University	M,O
New Mexico Highlands University	M
The New School	M,O
New York University	M,D,O
Norfolk State University	M
Northern Kentucky University	M,O
Northwestern University	M,D*
Ohio University	M,D
Pace University	M
Paris College of Art	M
Penn State University Park	M,D
Pepperdine University	M
Pratt Institute	M*
Robert Morris University Illinois	M
Rochester Institute of Technology	M
Rowan University	O
Rutgers University–New Brunswick	D
Sacred Heart University	M
Saginaw Valley State University	M
San Diego State University	M
San Francisco State University	M
San Jose State University	M,O
Savannah College of Art and Design	M
Southern Illinois University Carbondale	M,D
Southern Illinois University Edwardsville	O
Stanford University	M,D
Stevens Institute of Technology	M
Syracuse University	M
Temple University	M*
Trinity College (United States)	M
University at Buffalo, the State University of New York	M,D,O*
The University of Alabama	M
University of Bridgeport	M
University of California, Los Angeles	M,D
University of California, Santa Barbara	M,D
University of Chicago	D
University of Colorado Boulder	M,D
University of Denver	M
University of Illinois at Urbana–Champaign	M,D
The University of Iowa	M,D*
The University of Kansas	M,D*
University of Lethbridge	M,D
University of Maryland, College Park	M,D
University of Michigan	M
University of Missouri–Kansas City	M,D
University of Missouri–St. Louis	M
University of Nevada, Las Vegas	M
The University of North Carolina at Greensboro	M
University of Oregon	M,D
University of South Carolina	M,D
University of Southern California	M,D
University of South Florida	M
University of South Florida, St. Petersburg	M
The University of Tennessee	M,D
The University of Texas at Austin	M,D
The University of Western Ontario	M,D
University of Wisconsin–Madison	M,D
University of Wisconsin–Milwaukee	M,O
University of Wisconsin–Stevens Point	M
Valparaiso University	M,O
Virginia Commonwealth University	M,D
Virginia State University	M
Wayne State University	M,D,O
Webster University	M
West Virginia State University	M
Wilfrid Laurier University	M

MEDICAL/SURGICAL NURSING

Daemen College	M,D,O
Eastern Virginia Medical School	M
Inter American University of Puerto Rico, Arecibo Campus	M
Pontifical Catholic University of Puerto Rico	M
Saint Francis Medical Center College of Nursing	M,D,O
State University of New York Downstate Medical Center	M,O
Universidad Adventista de las Antillas	M
University of Maryland, Baltimore	M
University of South Africa	M,D
University of South Carolina	M
Ursuline College	M,D

MEDICAL ILLUSTRATION

Augusta University	M
Johns Hopkins University	M
Rochester Institute of Technology	M
University of Illinois at Chicago	M

MEDICAL IMAGING

Boston University	M
Cleveland State University	M
Illinois Institute of Technology	M,D
Medical College of Wisconsin	D
Medical University of South Carolina	D
New York University	D
Rutgers University–Newark	M
University of California, San Francisco	M
University of Cincinnati	M,D
University of Guelph	M,D,O
University of Southern California	M,D
Wayne State University	M,D,O

MEDICAL INFORMATICS

Arizona State University at the Tempe campus	M,D
Brandeis University	M
Cambridge College	M
Columbia University	M,D,O*
Dalhousie University	M,D
Excelsior College	M,O
Grand Valley State University	M
Johns Hopkins University	M,D,O
Medical College of Wisconsin	M
Michigan Technological University	M
Middle Tennessee State University	M
Milwaukee School of Engineering	M*
National University	M,D,O
Northwestern University	M,D*
Nova Southeastern University	M,D,O*
Oregon Health & Science University	M,D,O
Regis University	M,O
Rochester Institute of Technology	M
Rutgers University–Newark	M,D,O
Stanford University	M,D
The University of Arizona	M,D,O
University of California, Davis	M
University of Colorado Denver	M,D
University of Illinois at Urbana–Champaign	M,D,O
The University of Kansas	M,D,O*
University of Phoenix–Phoenix Campus	M,O
The University of Tennessee at Chattanooga	M,D,O
University of Washington	M,D*
University of Wisconsin–Milwaukee	D,O

MEDICAL MICROBIOLOGY

Creighton University	M,D
Idaho State University	M,D
Rutgers University–New Brunswick	M,D
Université du Québec, Institut National de la Recherche Scientifique	M,D
University of Alberta	M,D
University of Hawaii at Manoa	M,D
University of Manitoba	M,D
University of Minnesota, Duluth	M,D
University of Southern California	D
University of South Florida	M,D
University of Wisconsin–La Crosse	M
University of Wisconsin–Madison	D

MEDICAL PHYSICS

Cleveland State University	M
The College of William and Mary	M,D
Columbia University	M,D*
Duke University	M,D*
East Carolina University	M,D
Hampton University	M,D
Harvard University	D*
Hofstra University	M
Indiana University Bloomington	M,D
Louisiana State University and Agricultural & Mechanical College	M,D
Massachusetts Institute of Technology	M,D
McGill University	M,D
McMaster University	M,D
Oakland University	M,D
Oregon State University	M,D
Purdue University	M,D
Rush University	M,D
Southern Illinois University Carbondale	M
Stony Brook University, State University of New York	M,D
University at Buffalo, the State University of New York	M,D*
University of Alberta	M,D
The University of Arizona	M
University of California, Los Angeles	M,D
University of Chicago	D
University of Cincinnati	M
University of Colorado Boulder	M,D
University of Florida	M,D,O
University of Kentucky	M
University of Minnesota, Twin Cities Campus	M,D
University of Oklahoma Health Sciences Center	M,D
University of Pennsylvania	M,D*
University of South Florida	M,D
The University of Texas Health Science Center at Houston	M,D
The University of Texas Health Science Center at San Antonio	D
The University of Toledo	M,D
University of Utah	M,D*
University of Victoria	M,D

*M—masters degree; D—doctorate; O—other advanced degree; *—Close-Up and/or Display*

University of Wisconsin–Madison M,D
Virginia Commonwealth University M,D
Wayne State University M,D
Wright State University M

MEDICINAL AND PHARMACEUTICAL CHEMISTRY

Duquesne University M,D
Florida Agricultural and Mechanical University M,D
Idaho State University M,D
Medical University of South Carolina D
New Jersey Institute of Technology M,D,O
Northeastern University M,D,O
Oregon State University M,D
Purdue University D
Rutgers University–New Brunswick M,D
Temple University M,D*
University at Buffalo, the State University of New York M,D*
University of California, Irvine D
University of California, San Francisco D
University of Connecticut M,D*
University of Florida M,D
The University of Iowa M,D*
The University of Kansas M,D*
University of Michigan D
University of Minnesota, Twin Cities Campus M,D
University of Montana M,D
University of Rhode Island M,D
The University of Texas at Austin M,D
University of the Sciences M,D
The University of Toledo M,D
University of Utah M,D*
University of Washington D*
Virginia Commonwealth University M,D
Wayne State University M,D
West Virginia University M,D

MEDIEVAL AND RENAISSANCE STUDIES

Arizona State University at the Tempe campus M,D,O
California State University, Long Beach M
The Catholic University of America M,D,O
Central European University M,D
Columbia University M,D*
Cornell University M,D
Fordham University M,O
Georgetown University M,D
The Graduate Center, City University of New York M,D
Harvard University D*
Indiana University Bloomington M,D
Rutgers University–New Brunswick D
Southern Methodist University M
University of California, Santa Barbara M,D
University of Chicago D
University of Connecticut M,D*
University of Guelph D
University of Minnesota, Twin Cities Campus M,D
University of Notre Dame M,D
University of Pittsburgh O*
University of Toronto M,D
Yale University M,D*

METALLURGICAL ENGINEERING AND METALLURGY

Colorado School of Mines M,D
Michigan Technological University M,D
Missouri University of Science and Technology M,D
Montana Tech of The University of Montana M
The Ohio State University M,D
Université Laval M,D
The University of Alabama M,D
The University of British Columbia M,D
University of Connecticut M*
University of Idaho M,D
The University of Manchester M,D
University of Nebraska–Lincoln M,D
University of Nevada, Reno M,D
The University of Texas at El Paso M,D
University of Utah M,D*

METEOROLOGY

Ball State University M,O
Florida Institute of Technology M
Florida State University M,D
Iowa State University of Science and Technology M,D
McGill University M,D
Millersville University of Pennsylvania M
Mississippi State University M,D
Naval Postgraduate School M,D
North Carolina State University M,D
Northern Arizona University M,D
Penn State University Park M,D
Plymouth State University M
Saint Louis University M,D
San Jose State University M,O
Texas A&M University M,D
Université du Québec à Montréal M,D,O
University of California, San Diego M
University of Hawaii at Manoa M,D
University of Maryland, College Park M,D
University of Miami M,D
University of Oklahoma M,D*
Utah State University M,D
Yale University D*

MICROBIOLOGY

Albany Medical College M,D
Albert Einstein College of Medicine D
American University of Beirut M,D
Arizona State University at the Tempe campus M,D
Baylor College of Medicine D
Brandeis University M,D
Brigham Young University M,D
California State University, Long Beach M
Case Western Reserve University D*
The Catholic University of America M,D
Clemson University M,D
Colorado State University M,D
Columbia University M,D*
Cornell University D
Dalhousie University M,D
Dartmouth College D*
Drexel University M,D
Duke University D*
East Carolina University M,D
Eastern New Mexico University M
East Tennessee State University D
Emory University D
Emporia State University M
Georgetown University M,D
The George Washington University M,D,O*
Georgia State University M,D
Harvard University D*
Hood College M,O
Howard University D
Idaho State University M,D
Illinois Institute of Technology M,D
Illinois State University M,D
Indiana University Bloomington M,D
Indiana University–Purdue University Indianapolis M,D
Inter American University of Puerto Rico, Metropolitan Campus M
Iowa State University of Science and Technology M,D
Johns Hopkins University M,D
Loma Linda University M,D
Long Island University–LIU Post M,O
Louisiana State University Health Sciences Center D
Louisiana State University Health Sciences Center at Shreveport M,D
Loyola University Chicago M,D
Marquette University M,D
Massachusetts Institute of Technology D
McGill University M,D
Medical College of Wisconsin M,D
Medical University of South Carolina M,D
Meharry Medical College D
Miami University M,D
Michigan State University M,D
Montana State University M,D
New York Medical College M,D
New York University M,D
North Carolina State University M,D
North Dakota State University M,D
The Ohio State University M,D
Ohio University M,D
Oklahoma State University M,D
Oregon Health & Science University D
Oregon State University M,D
Penn State University Park M,D
Purdue University M,D
Queen's University at Kingston M,D
Rosalind Franklin University of Medicine and Science D
Rush University M,D
Rutgers University–Newark D
Rutgers University–New Brunswick M,D
Saint Louis University D
San Diego State University M
San Francisco State University M
Seton Hall University M,D
South Dakota State University M,D
Southern Illinois University Carbondale M,D
Southwestern Oklahoma State University M
Stanford University D
State University of New York Upstate Medical University M,D
Stony Brook University, State University of New York D
Texas A&M University M,D
Texas Tech University M,D
Thomas Jefferson University M,D
Tufts University D
Tulane University M
Universidad Central del Caribe M,D
Université de Montréal M,D
Université de Sherbrooke M,D
Université du Québec, Institut National de la Recherche Scientifique M,D
Université Laval M,D
University at Buffalo, the State University of New York M,D*
The University of Alabama at Birmingham D
University of Alberta M,D
The University of Arizona D
University of Arkansas for Medical Sciences M,D,O
The University of British Columbia M,D
University of Calgary M,D
University of California, Berkeley D
University of California, Davis M,D
University of California, Irvine M,D
University of California, Los Angeles M,D
University of California, Riverside M,D
University of Chicago D
University of Cincinnati M,D
University of Colorado Boulder M,D
University of Colorado Denver M,D
University of Delaware M,D*
University of Florida M,D
University of Georgia M,D
University of Guelph M,D
University of Hawaii at Manoa M,D
University of Idaho M,D
University of Illinois at Chicago D
University of Illinois at Urbana–Champaign M,D
The University of Iowa M,D*
The University of Kansas M,D*
University of Kentucky D
University of Louisville M,D
University of Maine M,D
The University of Manchester M,D
University of Manitoba M,D
University of Maryland, Baltimore D
University of Massachusetts Amherst M,D*
University of Massachusetts Medical School M,D
University of Miami D
University of Michigan M,D
University of Minnesota, Twin Cities Campus D
University of Mississippi Medical Center D
University of Missouri D
University of Montana D
University of Nebraska Medical Center M,D
University of New Hampshire M,D
University of New Mexico M,D
The University of North Carolina at Chapel Hill M,D
University of North Dakota M,D
University of North Texas Health Science Center at Fort Worth M,D
University of Oklahoma M,D*
University of Oklahoma Health Sciences Center M,D
University of Ottawa M,D
University of Pennsylvania D*
University of Pittsburgh M,D*
University of Puerto Rico, Medical Sciences Campus M,D
University of Rhode Island M,D
University of Rochester M,D*
University of Saskatchewan M,D
The University of South Dakota M,D
University of Southern California M
University of Southern Mississippi M,D
University of South Florida M,D
The University of Tennessee M,D
The University of Texas at Austin D
The University of Texas Health Science Center at Houston M,D
The University of Texas Health Science Center at San Antonio M,D
The University of Texas Medical Branch M,D
The University of Texas Southwestern Medical Center D
University of Victoria M,D
University of Virginia D
University of Washington D*
The University of Western Ontario M,D
University of Wisconsin–La Crosse M
University of Wisconsin–Madison D
University of Wisconsin–Milwaukee M
University of Wisconsin–Oshkosh M
University of Wyoming D
Vanderbilt University M,D*
Virginia Commonwealth University M,D,O
Wagner College M
Wake Forest University D
Washington State University M,D
Washington University in St. Louis D
Wayne State University M,D
West Virginia University M,D
Wright State University M
Yale University D*
Youngstown State University M

MIDDLE SCHOOL EDUCATION

Alaska Pacific University M
Albany State University M,O
American International College M,D,O
Appalachian State University M
Arkansas State University M,D,O
Augusta University M,O
Ball State University M,O
Bellarmine University M,D,O
Berry College M
Bloomsburg University of Pennsylvania M
Brenau University M,O
Brooklyn College of the City University of New York M,O
California Lutheran University M,D
California State University, Bakersfield M
Cambridge College M,D,O
Campbell University M
Canisius College M
Capella University M,D
Chestnut Hill College M
Chicago State University M
The Citadel, The Military College of South Carolina M
City College of the City University of New York M,O
Clarkson University M,O
Clemson University M,D,O
Cleveland State University M
The College at Brockport, State University of New York M
College of Mount Saint Vincent M,O
The College of Saint Rose M,O
Columbus State University M,O
Converse College M
Daemen College M
Drury University M
Duquesne University M
East Carolina University M
Eastern Illinois University M
Eastern Michigan University M
Eastern Nazarene College M,O
Eastern University M,O
East Tennessee State University M,O
Edinboro University of Pennsylvania M
Emory University M,D
Fayetteville State University M
Fitchburg State University M
Fontbonne University M
Gardner-Webb University M
Georgia Southern University M,O
Georgia Southwestern State University M,O
Georgia State University M,D
Gordon College M,O
Goucher College M,O
Grand Valley State University M,O
Hebrew College M,O
Henderson State University M,O
Huntington University M,D
James Madison University M
John Carroll University M
Kansas State University M,D
Kennesaw State University M
Kent State University M
LaGrange College M,O
La Salle University M,O
Lee University M,O
Le Moyne College M,O
Lesley University M,D,O
Lewis & Clark College M
Liberty University M,D,O
Long Island University–Hudson at Rockland M,O
Long Island University–LIU Post M,D,O
Longwood University M
Loyola University Maryland M,O
Manhattanville College M*
Mary Baldwin College M
Maryville University of Saint Louis M,D
McNeese State University O
Mercer University M,D,O
Merrimack College M,O
Middle Tennessee State University M,O
Minot State University M
Mississippi State University M,D,O
Morehead State University M,O
Morgan State University M
Mount St. Joseph University M,O
Mount Saint Mary College M,O
Mount Saint Vincent University M
Murray State University M,O
Nazareth College of Rochester M
New York Institute of Technology M
New York University M,D,O
Niagara University M,O
Nicholls State University M
North Carolina State University M
Northwestern State University of Louisiana M
Northwest Missouri State University M,O
Ohio University M,D
Old Dominion University M
Pacific University M
Piedmont College M,O
Quinnipiac University M
Roberts Wesleyan College M
Rowan University O
Saginaw Valley State University M
St. Bonaventure University M
St. John Fisher College M
St. John's University (NY) M,O
Saint Joseph's University M,D,O
Saint Peter's University M,O
St. Thomas Aquinas College M,O
Salem College M
Salem State University M
Salisbury University M
Seton Hill University M,O
Shenandoah University M,D,O
Shippensburg University of Pennsylvania M
Simmons College M,D,O
Smith College M
Southeast Missouri State University M
Spalding University M
State University of New York at Fredonia M
State University of New York at Oswego M
State University of New York College at Oneonta M
State University of New York College at Potsdam M
Temple University M*
Tennessee Technological University M
Theological University of the Caribbean M,D
Tufts University M,D
Union College (KY) M
University of Arkansas M,D,O
University of Arkansas at Little Rock M
University of Bridgeport M,D,O
University of Central Florida M
University of Dayton M
University of Georgia M,D,O

University of Kentucky M,D
University of Louisiana at Monroe M,D
University of Louisville M,D,O
University of Massachusetts Boston M,D
University of Massachusetts Dartmouth M,O
University of Memphis M,D
University of Missouri–St. Louis M,O
The University of North Carolina at Charlotte M,D,O
The University of North Carolina at Greensboro M,D,O
The University of North Carolina Wilmington M
University of Northern Iowa M
University of North Georgia M,O
University of Phoenix–Online Campus M,O
University of South Florida, St. Petersburg M
University of the Cumberlands M,D,O
University of the District of Columbia M
The University of Toledo M,D,O
University of Washington, Bothell M
University of West Florida M,O
University of Wisconsin–Milwaukee M
University of Wisconsin–Platteville M
Ursuline College M
Wagner College M
Western Kentucky University M,O
Wichita State University M
Widener University M,D
Wilkes University M,D
Winston-Salem State University M
Worcester State University M,O
Wright State University M
Youngstown State University M

MILITARY AND DEFENSE STUDIES

American Public University System M
Austin Peay State University M
Bellevue University M
East Carolina University M
Embry-Riddle Aeronautical University–Prescott M
The George Washington University M*
Hawai`i Pacific University M
Henley-Putnam University M
The Institute of World Politics M,O
Johns Hopkins University M
The Judge Advocate General's School, U.S. Army M
Liberty University M,D,O
London Metropolitan University M,D
Missouri State University M,O
National Defense University M
National Intelligence University M
Naval Postgraduate School M,D
Norwich University M
Royal Military College of Canada M,D
School of Advanced Air and Space Studies M
United States Army Command and General Staff College M
University of Calgary M,D
University of Colorado Denver M,D
University of Pittsburgh M*
University of West Florida M

MINERAL/MINING ENGINEERING

Colorado School of Mines M,D
Dalhousie University M,D
Laurentian University M,D
McGill University M,D,O
Michigan Technological University M,D
Missouri University of Science and Technology M,D
Montana Tech of The University of Montana M
New Mexico Institute of Mining and Technology M
Penn State University Park M,D
Queen's University at Kingston M,D
South Dakota School of Mines and Technology M
Southern Illinois University Carbondale M,D
Université du Québec en Abitibi-Témiscamingue M,O
Université Laval M,D
University of Alaska Fairbanks M
University of Alberta M,D
The University of Arizona M,D,O
The University of British Columbia M,D
University of Kentucky M,D
University of Nevada, Reno M
University of North Dakota M
The University of Texas at Austin M
University of Utah M,D*
Virginia Polytechnic Institute and State University M,D
West Virginia University M,D

MINERAL ECONOMICS

Colorado School of Mines M,D
Michigan Technological University M
The University of Texas at Austin M

MINERALOGY

Cornell University M,D
Indiana University Bloomington M,D
Université du Québec à Chicoutimi D
Université du Québec à Montréal M,D,O

MISSIONS AND MISSIOLOGY

Abilene Christian University M
Anabaptist Mennonite Biblical Seminary M,O
Anderson University (IN) M,D
Asbury Theological Seminary M,D,O
Ashland Theological Seminary M,D,O
Assemblies of God Theological Seminary M,D
Biblical Theological Seminary M,D,O
Biola University M,D,O
Briercrest Seminary M
Calvin Theological Seminary M,D
Catholic Theological Union M,D,O
Central Baptist Theological Seminary M,O
Charlotte Christian College and Theological Seminary M
Columbia International University M,D,O
Dallas Baptist University M
Dallas Theological Seminary M,D,O
Eastern University M,D
Evangelical Seminary M
Faulkner University M
Fresno Pacific University M
Fuller Theological Seminary M,D,O
Gardner-Webb University M,D
Georgia Christian University M,D
Global University M,D
Gordon-Conwell Theological Seminary M,D
Grace Mission University M,D
Grace Theological Seminary M,D,O
Grand Rapids Theological Seminary of Cornerstone University M
Hope International University M
Huntington University M,D
Liberty University M,D,O
Luther Seminary M,D
Milligan College M,D
Nazarene Theological Seminary M,D
Northwest Nazarene University M
Northwest University M
Nyack College M,D
Oral Roberts University M,D
Phillips Theological Seminary M,D
Providence University College & Theological Seminary M,D,O
Reformed Theological Seminary–Jackson Campus M,D,O
Regent University M,D
Rochester College M
Saint Paul University M
Simpson University M
Southeastern Baptist Theological Seminary M,D
Southern Adventist University M
The Southern Baptist Theological Seminary M,D
Southern Evangelical Seminary M,D,O
Southwestern Assemblies of God University M
Southwestern Baptist Theological Seminary M,D
Southwestern Christian University M
Summit University M,D
Taylor College and Seminary M,O
Theological University of the Caribbean M,D
Trinity International University M,D,O
Trinity Lutheran Seminary M
Trinity School for Ministry M,D,O
Tyndale University College & Seminary M,O
University of South Africa M,D
Villanova University M
Wesley Biblical Seminary M
Westminster Theological Seminary M,D,O
Wheaton College M,O

MODELING AND SIMULATION

Academy of Art University M
Arizona State University at the Tempe campus M,D
Carnegie Mellon University M,D
Columbus State University M,O
Naval Postgraduate School M,D
Old Dominion University M,D
Oregon State University M,D
Philadelphia University M
Portland State University M,D,O
Stevens Institute of Technology M,D,O
Trent University M,D
Université Laval M,O
University at Buffalo, the State University of New York M,D,O*
The University of Alabama in Huntsville M,D,O
University of California, San Diego M,D
University of Central Florida M,D,O
The University of Manchester M,D
University of Pittsburgh D*
University of Southern California M,D
Virginia Commonwealth University M,D
Worcester Polytechnic Institute M,D

MOLECULAR BIOLOGY

Albany College of Pharmacy and Health Sciences M
Albany Medical College M,D
Albert Einstein College of Medicine D
American University of Beirut M,D
Appalachian State University M
Arizona State University at the Tempe campus M,D
Arkansas State University M,D
Auburn University M,D
Baylor College of Medicine D
Boise State University M,D
Boston University M,D
Brandeis University M,D
Brigham Young University M,D
Brown University M,D
California Institute of Technology D
California State University, Sacramento M
Carnegie Mellon University M,D
Case Western Reserve University D*
Central Connecticut State University M,O
Clemson University D
Colorado State University M,D
Columbia University D*
Cornell University M,D
Dartmouth College D*
Drexel University M,D
Duke University D,O*
East Carolina University M,D
Eastern Michigan University M
Eastern New Mexico University M
Emory University D
Florida Institute of Technology M,D
Florida State University M,D
Georgetown University M,D
Georgia State University M,D
Grand Valley State University M
Harvard University D*
Hood College M,O
Howard University M,D
Illinois Institute of Technology M,D
Illinois State University M,D
Indiana State University M,D
Indiana University Bloomington M,D
Indiana University–Purdue University Indianapolis M,D
Inter American University of Puerto Rico, Metropolitan Campus M
Iowa State University of Science and Technology M,D
Irell & Manella Graduate School of Biological Sciences D*
Johns Hopkins University M,D
Kent State University M,D
Lehigh University M,D
Lipscomb University M
Louisiana State University Health Sciences Center at Shreveport M,D
Louisiana Tech University M
Loyola University Chicago M,D
Marquette University M,D
Massachusetts Institute of Technology D
Mayo Graduate School D
McMaster University M,D
Medical University of South Carolina M,D
Michigan State University M,D
Michigan Technological University M,D,O
Middle Tennessee State University D
Mississippi State University M,D
Missouri State University M
Montclair State University M,O
New Mexico State University M,D
New York Medical College M,D
New York University M,D
North Dakota State University M,D
Northwestern University D*
The Ohio State University M,D
Ohio University M,D
Oklahoma State University M,D
Oregon Health & Science University M,D
Oregon State University D
Pace University M
Penn State University Park M,D
Princeton University D
Purdue University M,D
Queen's University at Kingston M,D
Quinnipiac University M
Rosalind Franklin University of Medicine and Science D
Rutgers University–Newark M,D
Rutgers University–New Brunswick M,D
Saint Louis University D
San Diego State University M,D
San Francisco State University M
San Jose State University M,O
Seton Hall University M,D
Simon Fraser University M,D,O
Sonoma State University M
Southern Illinois University Carbondale M,D
Southern Methodist University M,D
State University of New York Downstate Medical Center D
State University of New York Upstate Medical University M,D
Stony Brook University, State University of New York M,D
Texas Woman's University M,D
Tufts University D
Tulane University M,D
Uniformed Services University of the Health Sciences M,D*
Universidad Central del Caribe M,D
Université de Montréal M,D
Université Laval M,D
University at Albany, State University of New York D
University at Buffalo, the State University of New York D*
The University of Alabama at Birmingham D
University of Alberta M,D
The University of Arizona M,D,O
University of Arkansas M,D
University of Arkansas for Medical Sciences M,D,O
The University of British Columbia M,D
University of Calgary M,D
University of California, Berkeley D
University of California, Davis M,D
University of California, Irvine M,D
University of California, Los Angeles M,D
University of California, Riverside M,D
University of California, San Francisco D
University of California, Santa Barbara M,D
University of California, Santa Cruz M,D
University of Chicago D
University of Cincinnati M,D
University of Colorado Boulder M,D
University of Colorado Denver M,D
University of Connecticut Health Center D*
University of Delaware M,D*
University of Denver M,D
University of Florida M,D
University of Georgia M,D
University of Guelph M,D
University of Hawaii at Manoa M,D
University of Illinois at Chicago D
The University of Iowa D*
The University of Kansas M,D*
University of Lethbridge M,D
University of Louisville M,D
University of Maine M,D
The University of Manchester M,D
University of Maryland, Baltimore M,D
University of Maryland, Baltimore County M,D
University of Maryland, College Park D
University of Miami D
University of Michigan M,D
University of Minnesota, Duluth M,D
University of Minnesota, Twin Cities Campus M,D
University of Missouri–Kansas City D
University of Montana D
University of Nebraska Medical Center M,D
University of Nevada, Reno M,D
University of New Haven M,O
University of New Mexico M,D
The University of North Carolina at Chapel Hill M,D
University of North Dakota M,D
University of North Texas M,D,O
University of North Texas Health Science Center at Fort Worth M,D
University of Notre Dame M,D
University of Oklahoma Health Sciences Center M,D
University of Oregon M,D
University of Ottawa M,D
University of Pennsylvania D*
University of Pittsburgh D*
University of Puerto Rico, Rí o Piedras Campus M,D
University of Rhode Island M,D
University of Rochester D*
University of South Carolina M,D
The University of South Dakota M,D
University of Southern California M,D
University of Southern Maine M
University of Southern Mississippi M,D
University of South Florida M,D
The University of Texas at Austin D
The University of Texas at Dallas M,D*
The University of Texas at San Antonio M,D
The University of Texas Health Science Center at Houston M,D
University of Utah D*
University of Vermont D
University of Washington D*
University of Wisconsin–La Crosse M
University of Wisconsin–Madison D
University of Wisconsin–Parkside M
University of Wyoming M,D
Vanderbilt University M,D*
Virginia Commonwealth University M,D
Wake Forest University D
Washington University in St. Louis D
Wayne State University M,D
Weill Cornell Medicine M,D
Wesleyan University D
West Virginia University M,D
Wright State University M
Yale University D*
Youngstown State University M

MOLECULAR BIOPHYSICS

Baylor College of Medicine D
California Institute of Technology M,D
Carnegie Mellon University D
Duke University O*
Florida State University D
Illinois Institute of Technology M,D
New York University D
Rutgers University–New Brunswick D
University at Buffalo, the State University of New York M,D*
University of Arkansas for Medical Sciences M,D,O
University of Chicago D
University of Massachusetts Amherst D*
University of Pennsylvania D*
University of Pittsburgh D*

*M—masters degree; D—doctorate; O—other advanced degree; *—Close-Up and/or Display*

The University of Texas Medical Branch	M,D
The University of Texas Southwestern Medical Center	D
Washington University in St. Louis	D
Wesleyan University	D
Yale University	D*

MOLECULAR GENETICS

Albert Einstein College of Medicine	D
Duke University	D*
Emory University	D
Georgia State University	M,D
Harvard University	D*
Illinois State University	M,D
Indiana University–Purdue University Indianapolis	M,D
Iowa State University of Science and Technology	M,D
Medical College of Wisconsin	M,D
Michigan State University	M,D
New York University	M,D
Northern Michigan University	M
The Ohio State University	M,D
Oklahoma State University	M,D
Penn State Hershey Medical Center	M,D
Rutgers University–Newark	D
Rutgers University–New Brunswick	M,D
Stony Brook University, State University of New York	D
University of Calgary	M,D
University of California, Irvine	M,D
University of California, Los Angeles	M,D
University of Cincinnati	M,D
University of Colorado Denver	D
University of Florida	M
University of Guelph	M,D
University of Illinois at Chicago	D
The University of Manchester	M,D
University of Maryland, College Park	M,D
University of Pittsburgh	D*
University of Rhode Island	M,D
The University of Texas Health Science Center at Houston	M,D
University of Toronto	M,D
University of Virginia	D
Van Andel Institute Graduate School	D
Wake Forest University	D
Washington University in St. Louis	D
Wayne State University	M,D,O
Wesleyan University	D

MOLECULAR MEDICINE

Augusta University	D
Baylor College of Medicine	D
Boston University	D
Case Western Reserve University	D*
Cleveland State University	M,D
Cornell University	M,D
Dartmouth College	D
Drexel University	M
Elmezzi Graduate School of Molecular Medicine	D
The George Washington University	D*
Hofstra University	D
Johns Hopkins University	D
Penn State Hershey Medical Center	D
Queen's University at Kingston	M,D
Rutgers University–Newark	D
Tufts University	D
The University of Alabama at Birmingham	D
The University of Arizona	M,D
University of Cincinnati	D
University of Maryland, Baltimore	M,D
University of South Florida	M,D
The University of Texas Health Science Center at San Antonio	M,D
University of Washington	D*
Wake Forest University	M,D
Wayne State University	M,D,O
Yale University	D*

MOLECULAR PATHOGENESIS

Dartmouth College	D*
Emory University	D
North Dakota State University	M,D
Oregon State University	D
Washington University in St. Louis	D

MOLECULAR PATHOLOGY

Rutgers University–Newark	D
Texas Tech University Health Sciences Center	M
University of Michigan	D
University of Pittsburgh	D*
The University of Texas Health Science Center at Houston	M,D
University of Wisconsin–Madison	D
Yale University	D*

MOLECULAR PHARMACOLOGY

Albert Einstein College of Medicine	D
Brown University	M,D
Harvard University	D*
Loyola University Chicago	M,D
Mayo Graduate School	D
Medical University of South Carolina	M,D
New York University	D
Purdue University	D
Rosalind Franklin University of Medicine and Science	M,D
Rutgers University–New Brunswick	M,D
Thomas Jefferson University	D
University at Buffalo, the State University of New York	D*
University of Massachusetts Medical School	M,D
University of Nevada, Reno	D
University of Pittsburgh	D*
University of Southern California	M,D
University of South Florida	M,D

MOLECULAR PHYSIOLOGY

Baylor College of Medicine	D
Case Western Reserve University	M,D*
Loyola University Chicago	M,D
Rutgers University–New Brunswick	M,D
Stony Brook University, State University of New York	D
University of California, Los Angeles	D
University of Illinois at Urbana–Champaign	M,D
The University of North Carolina at Chapel Hill	D
University of Pittsburgh	D*
University of Virginia	M,D
Vanderbilt University	M,D*
Yale University	D*

MOLECULAR TOXICOLOGY

Massachusetts Institute of Technology	D
New York University	M,D
North Carolina State University	M,D
Penn State Hershey Medical Center	D
University of California, Berkeley	D
University of California, Los Angeles	D
University of Cincinnati	M,D

MULTILINGUAL AND MULTICULTURAL EDUCATION

Alliant International University–San Francisco	M,O
American College of Education	M
American University	M,O
Azusa Pacific University	M
Bank Street College of Education	M
Belhaven University (MS)	M
Boise State University	M
Brooklyn College of the City University of New York	M
Brown University	M,D
Buffalo State College, State University of New York	M
California State University, Fullerton	M
California State University, Northridge	M
California State University, Sacramento	M
California State University, Stanislaus	M
Chicago State University	M
City College of the City University of New York	M
The College at Brockport, State University of New York	M,O
College of Mount Saint Vincent	M,O
The College of New Rochelle	M,O
Columbia International University	M,D,O
Dallas Baptist University	M
DePaul University	M,D
Eastern New Mexico University	M
Eastern University	M,O
Edgewood College	M,D,O
Fairfield University	M,O
Fairleigh Dickinson University, Metropolitan Campus	M
Florida Atlantic University	M,D,O
Florida International University	M,D,O
Gallaudet University	M,D,O
George Mason University	M
The George Washington University	M,D,O*
Georgia Southern University	D
Graduate Institute of Applied Linguistics	M,O
Heritage University	M
Hofstra University	M,D,O
Howard University	M,D
Hunter College of the City University of New York	M
Immaculata University	M
Indiana State University	M,D,O
Indiana University Bloomington	M,D
James Madison University	M
Kean University	M
Langston University	M
La Salle University	M,O
Lehman College of the City University of New York	M
Long Island University–LIU Brooklyn	M,O
Loyola Marymount University	M
Manhattan College	M,O
Minnesota State University Mankato	M
Molloy College	M,O
Mount St. Joseph University	M,O
New Jersey City University	M
New Mexico State University	M,D,O
New York University	M,D,O
Northeastern Illinois University	M
Northern Arizona University	M,O
Ohio University	M,D
Queens College of the City University of New York	M,O
Quincy University	M
Rowan University	M,O
Rutgers University–New Brunswick	M,D
St. John's University (NY)	M,O
Saint Mary's University of Minnesota	M,O
San Diego State University	M,D
Southern Connecticut State University	M
Southern Methodist University	M,D
State University of New York at New Paltz	M,O
State University of New York College at Geneseo	M
Sul Ross State University	M
Teachers College, Columbia University	M,D,O
Texas A&M University	M,D
Texas A&M University–Kingsville	M,D
Texas A&M University–San Antonio	M
Texas Southern University	M,D
Texas State University	M
Texas Tech University	M,D
University at Buffalo, the State University of New York	M,D,O*
University of Alaska Fairbanks	M
University of Alberta	M
University of Calgary	M,D
University of California, Riverside	M,D,O
University of California, San Diego	M,D
University of Colorado Boulder	M,D
University of Colorado Denver	M
University of Connecticut	M,D*
University of Delaware	M,D,O*
The University of Findlay	M,D
University of Houston–Clear Lake	M
University of Maryland, Baltimore County	M,D
University of Massachusetts Amherst	M,D,O*
University of Massachusetts Boston	M
University of Miami	D
University of Minnesota, Twin Cities Campus	M
University of New Mexico	M,D
The University of North Carolina at Greensboro	M,D,O
University of Pennsylvania	M*
University of St. Thomas (MN)	M,O
University of St. Thomas (TX)	M
University of San Francisco	M,D
University of Southern California	D
The University of Tennessee	M,D,O
The University of Texas at Arlington	M,D
The University of Texas at Austin	M,D
The University of Texas at El Paso	M,D,O
The University of Texas at San Antonio	M,D
The University of Texas Rio Grande Valley	M
University of the Southwest	M
University of Washington	M,D*
University of West Florida	D
University of Wisconsin–Milwaukee	D
Utah State University	M
Vanderbilt University	D*
Walden University	M,D,O
Wayne State University	M,D,O
Western New Mexico University	M
Western Oregon University	M
Xavier University	M

MUSEUM EDUCATION

Bank Street College of Education	M
Eastern Michigan University	O
The George Washington University	M*
Seton Hall University	M
Tufts University	M,D
The University of the Arts	M

MUSEUM STUDIES

American Museum of Natural History–Richard Gilder Graduate School	D
Arizona State University at the Tempe campus	M,D,O
Bard College	M
Baylor University	M
Boston University	M,D,O
California College of the Arts	M
California State University, Chico	M
California State University, Fullerton	M
Caribbean University	M,D
Case Western Reserve University	M*
Christie's Education	M
City College of the City University of New York	M
Claremont Graduate University	M,D,O
Cleveland State University	M
Columbia University	M,D*
Eastern Michigan University	M,O
Fashion Institute of Technology	M*
Florida International University	M,O
Florida State University	M,D,O
The George Washington University	M,D,O*
Harvard University	M,O*
Indiana University–Purdue University Indianapolis	M,O
John F. Kennedy University	M,O
Johns Hopkins University	M,O
Marist College	M
Maryland Institute College of Art	M
Morgan State University	M,D
New Mexico State University	M,O
The New School	M
New York University	M,O
Penn State Harrisburg	M,D,O
Pratt Institute	M,O*
St. John's University (NY)	M
San Francisco Art Institute	M
San Francisco State University	M
Seton Hall University	M
Southern Illinois University Edwardsville	O
Southern University at New Orleans	M
State University of New York College at Oneonta	M
Syracuse University	M
Texas Tech University	M,D
Trinity College (United States)	M
Tufts University	M,D,O
Université de Montréal	M
Université du Québec à Montréal	M
Université Laval	O
The University of British Columbia	M,D,O
University of Central Oklahoma	M
University of Colorado Boulder	M
University of Denver	M
University of Florida	M,D
University of Hawaii at Manoa	O
University of Illinois at Chicago	M,D
The University of Kansas	M,O*
University of Louisville	M,D
The University of Manchester	D
University of Michigan–Flint	M
University of Missouri–St. Louis	M,O
University of New Hampshire	M,D
The University of North Carolina at Greensboro	M,D,O
University of North Texas	M,D,O
University of Oklahoma	M,O*
University of San Francisco	M
University of South Carolina	M,O
University of South Florida	O
The University of the Arts	M
University of Toronto	M
The University of Tulsa	M
University of Washington	M*
University of West Georgia	M,O
University of Wisconsin–Milwaukee	M,D,O
Virginia Commonwealth University	M,D
Western Illinois University	M,O

MUSIC

Academy of Art University	M
American University	M,O
Andrews University	M
Appalachian State University	M
Aquinas Institute of Theology	M,D,O
Arizona State University at the Tempe campus	M,D
Arkansas State University	M,O
Austin Peay State University	M
Azusa Pacific University	M
Ball State University	M,D,O
The Baptist College of Florida	M
Bard College	M,O
Baylor University	M,D
Bennington College	M
Berklee College of Music	M,O
Bethesda University	M
Binghamton University, State University of New York	M*
Bob Jones University	M,D,O
Boise State University	M
Boston University	M,D,O
Bowling Green State University	M,D
Brandeis University	M,D
Brandon University	M
Brigham Young University	M
Brooklyn College of the City University of New York	M
Brown University	D
Butler University	M
California Baptist University	M
California Institute of Integral Studies	M,D
California Institute of the Arts	M,O
California State University, East Bay	M
California State University, Fresno	M
California State University, Fullerton	M
California State University, Long Beach	M
California State University, Los Angeles	M
California State University, Northridge	M
California State University, Sacramento	M
California State University, San Bernardino	M
Campbellsville University	M
Capital University	M
Carleton University	M
Carnegie Mellon University	M
Case Western Reserve University	M,D*
The Catholic University of America	M,D,O
Central Michigan University	M
Central Washington University	M
Charlotte Christian College and Theological Seminary	M
Claremont Graduate University	M,D
Cleveland Institute of Music	M,D,O
Cleveland State University	M
The Colburn School Conservatory of Music	M,O
Colorado State University	M
Columbia College Chicago	M
Columbia University	M,D*
Columbus State University	M,O
Concordia University (Canada)	O
Concordia University Chicago	M
Concordia University Wisconsin	M
Conservatorio de Musica de Puerto Rico	O
Converse College	M
Cornell University	M,D
Curtis Institute of Music	M
Dalhousie University	M
Dallas Baptist University	M
Dartmouth College	M*
DePaul University	M,O
Dominican University of California	M
Duke University	D*
Duquesne University	M,O
East Carolina University	M,D,O

Eastern Illinois University	M
Eastern Kentucky University	M
Eastern Michigan University	M
Eastern Washington University	M
Emory University	M
Emporia State University	M
Five Towns College	M,D
Florida Atlantic University	M
Florida International University	M
Florida State University	M,D
Fuller Theological Seminary	M,D,O
Garrett-Evangelical Theological Seminary	M,D
George Mason University	M,D
Georgia Christian University	M
Georgia Institute of Technology	M,D
Georgia Southern University	M
Georgia State University	M,D,O
The Graduate Center, City University of New York	D
Hardin-Simmons University	M
Harvard University	M,D*
Hebrew College	M,O
Hebrew Union College–Jewish Institute of Religion (NY)	M
Hollins University	M
Holy Names University	M,O
Hope International University	M
Houghton College	M
Howard University	M
Hunter College of the City University of New York	M
Illinois State University	M
Indiana State University	M
Indiana University Bloomington	M,D,O
Indiana University of Pennsylvania	M
Indiana University–Purdue University Indianapolis	M
Indiana University South Bend	M
Inter American University of Puerto Rico, San Germán Campus	M
Ithaca College	M
Jacksonville State University	M
Jacksonville University	M*
James Madison University	M,D
The Jewish Theological Seminary	M
Johns Hopkins University	M,D,O
The Juilliard School	M,D,O
Kansas State University	M
Kent State University	M,D,O
Lamar University	M
Lee University	M
Liberty University	M,D
Long Island University–LIU Post	M
Louisiana State University and Agricultural & Mechanical College	M,D
Loyola University New Orleans	M
Lynchburg College	M
Lynn University	M,O
Manhattan School of Music	M,D,O
Mansfield University of Pennsylvania	M
Marshall University	M
McGill University	M,D
McNally Smith College of Music	M
Memorial University of Newfoundland	M,D
Mercer University	M
Messiah College	M
Miami University	M
Michigan State University	M,D
Middle Tennessee State University	M
Midwestern Baptist Theological Seminary	M,D,O
Mills College	M
Minnesota State University Mankato	M
Mississippi College	M
Missouri State University	M
Montclair State University	M,O
Morehead State University	M
Morgan State University	M
Murray State University	M
New England Conservatory of Music	M,D,O
New Jersey City University	M
New Mexico State University	M
New Orleans Baptist Theological Seminary	M,D
The New School	M,O
New York University	M,D,O
Norfolk State University	M
North Carolina Central University	M
North Dakota State University	M,D
Northeastern Illinois University	M
Northern Arizona University	M,O
Northern Illinois University	M,O
Northern Kentucky University	M,O
North Park University	M
Northwestern State University of Louisiana	M
Northwestern University	M,D*
Notre Dame de Namur University	M,O
Oakland University	M,D
Oberlin College	M,O
The Ohio State University	M,D
Ohio University	M,O
Oklahoma City University	M
Oklahoma State University	M
Open University	M
Park University	M,O
Penn State University Park	M,D,O
Phillips Theological Seminary	M,D
Pittsburg State University	M
Point Park University	M
Portland State University	M
Pratt Institute	M*
Princeton University	D
Purchase College, State University of New York	M
Queens College of the City University of New York	M,O
Radford University	M
Reinhardt University	M
Rice University	M,D
Rider University	M
Roosevelt University	M,O
Rowan University	M
Rutgers University–Newark	M
Rutgers University–New Brunswick	M,D,O
St. Cloud State University	M
Saint John's University (MN)	M
Saint Joseph's College	M,O
St. Vladimir's Orthodox Theological Seminary	M,D
Samford University	M
Sam Houston State University	M
San Diego State University	M
San Francisco Conservatory of Music	M
San Francisco State University	M
San Jose State University	M,O
Savannah College of Art and Design	M
School of the Art Institute of Chicago	M
Seabury-Western Theological Seminary	M,D,O
Shenandoah University	M,D,O
Shepherd University (CA)	M
Southeastern Baptist Theological Seminary	M,D
Southeastern Louisiana University	M
Southern Illinois University Carbondale	M
Southern Illinois University Edwardsville	M
Southern Methodist University	M
Southern Oregon University	M
Southwestern Baptist Theological Seminary	M,D
Southwestern Oklahoma State University	M
Stanford University	M,D
State University of New York at New Paltz	M
State University of New York College at Potsdam	M
Stephen F. Austin State University	M
Stony Brook University, State University of New York	M,D
Syracuse University	M
Temple University	M,D*
Texas A&M University	M
Texas Christian University	M,D
Texas Southern University	M
Texas State University	M
Texas Tech University	M,D
Texas Woman's University	M
Towson University	M
Trinity College (Canada)	M,D,O
Trinity Lutheran Seminary	M
Truman State University	M
Tufts University	M
Tulane University	M
Université de Montréal	M,D,O
Université Laval	M,D
University at Buffalo, the State University of New York	M,D,O*
The University of Akron	M
The University of Alabama	M,D
The University of Alabama at Birmingham	M
University of Alaska Fairbanks	M
University of Alberta	M,D
The University of Arizona	M,D
University of Arkansas	M
The University of British Columbia	M,D
University of Calgary	M,D
University of California, Berkeley	D
University of California, Davis	M,D
University of California, Irvine	M
University of California, Los Angeles	M,D
University of California, Riverside	M,D
University of California, San Diego	M,D
University of California, Santa Barbara	M,D
University of California, Santa Cruz	M,D
University of Central Arkansas	M,O
University of Central Florida	M
University of Central Missouri	M,D,O
University of Central Oklahoma	M
University of Chicago	M,D
University of Cincinnati	M,D,O
University of Colorado Boulder	M,D
University of Colorado Denver	M
University of Connecticut	M,D*
University of Delaware	M*
University of Denver	M,O
University of Florida	M,D
University of Georgia	M,D
University of Hartford	M,D,O
University of Hawaii at Manoa	M,D
University of Houston	M,D
University of Idaho	M
University of Illinois at Urbana–Champaign	M,D
The University of Iowa	M,D*
The University of Kansas	M,D*
University of Kentucky	M,D
University of Lethbridge	M,D
University of Louisiana at Lafayette	M
University of Louisville	M
University of Maine	M
The University of Manchester	D
University of Manitoba	M
University of Maryland, Baltimore County	O
University of Maryland, College Park	M,D
University of Massachusetts Amherst	M,D*
University of Massachusetts Lowell	M
University of Memphis	M,D
University of Miami	M,D,O
University of Michigan	M,D,O
University of Michigan–Flint	M
University of Minnesota, Duluth	M
University of Minnesota, Twin Cities Campus	M,D
University of Mississippi	M,D
University of Missouri	M
University of Missouri–Kansas City	M,D
University of Montana	M
University of Nebraska at Omaha	M
University of Nebraska–Lincoln	M,D
University of Nevada, Las Vegas	M,D,O
University of Nevada, Reno	M
University of New Hampshire	M,D
University of New Mexico	M
University of New Orleans	M
The University of North Carolina at Chapel Hill	M,D
The University of North Carolina at Charlotte	O
The University of North Carolina at Greensboro	M,D
University of North Carolina School of the Arts	M,O
University of North Dakota	M,D
University of Northern Colorado	M,D
University of Northern Iowa	M
University of North Georgia	M
University of North Texas	M,D,O
University of Oklahoma	M,D,O*
University of Oregon	M,D
University of Ottawa	M,O
University of Pennsylvania	M,D*
University of Pittsburgh	M,D*
University of Redlands	M
University of Regina	M
University of Rhode Island	M
University of Rochester	M,D*
University of St. Thomas (MN)	M
University of St. Thomas (TX)	M
University of Saskatchewan	M
University of South Africa	M,D
University of South Alabama	M
University of South Carolina	M,D,O
The University of South Dakota	M
University of Southern California	M,D,O
University of Southern Maine	M
University of Southern Mississippi	M,D
University of South Florida	M,D
The University of Tennessee	M
The University of Tennessee at Chattanooga	M
The University of Texas at Arlington	M
The University of Texas at Austin	M,D
The University of Texas at El Paso	M
The University of Texas at San Antonio	M
The University of Texas Rio Grande Valley	M
The University of the Arts	M
University of the Pacific	M
The University of Toledo	M,O
University of Toronto	M,D
University of Utah	M,D*
University of Valley Forge	M
University of Victoria	M,D
University of Virginia	M,D
University of Washington	M,D*
The University of Western Ontario	M,D
University of West Georgia	M,O
University of Wisconsin–Madison	M,D
University of Wyoming	M
Valdosta State University	M
Vermont College of Fine Arts	M
Virginia Commonwealth University	M
Washington State University	M
Washington University in St. Louis	M,D
Wayne State University	M,D,O
Webster University	M
Wesleyan University	M,D
West Chester University of Pennsylvania	M,O
Western Illinois University	M
Western Michigan University	M,O
Western Oregon University	M
Western Washington University	M
West Texas A&M University	M
West Virginia University	M,D
Wichita State University	M
William Paterson University of New Jersey	M
Winthrop University	M
Wright State University	M
Yale University	M,D,O*
York University	M,D
Youngstown State University	M

MUSIC EDUCATION

Alabama Agricultural and Mechanical University	M
Alabama State University	M,O
Appalachian State University	M
Arcadia University	M,D,O
Arizona State University at the Tempe campus	M,D
Arkansas State University	M,O
Auburn University	M,D,O
Augusta University	M,O
Austin Peay State University	M
Azusa Pacific University	M
Ball State University	M,D,O
Bob Jones University	M,D,O
Boise State University	M
Boston University	M,D
Bowling Green State University	M,D
Brandon University	M
Brigham Young University	M
Brooklyn College of the City University of New York	M
Butler University	M
California Baptist University	M
California State University, Fresno	M
California State University, Fullerton	M
California State University, Los Angeles	M
California State University, Northridge	M
Campbellsville University	M
Capital University	M
Carnegie Mellon University	M
Case Western Reserve University	M,D*
The Catholic University of America	M,D,O
Central Connecticut State University	M,O
Central Methodist University	M
Central Michigan University	M
Cleveland State University	M
College of Charleston	M
The Colorado College	M
Colorado State University	M
Colorado State University–Pueblo	M
Columbus State University	M,O
Conservatorio de Musica de Puerto Rico	M
Converse College	M
DePaul University	M,O
Duquesne University	M,O
East Carolina University	M,O
Eastern Kentucky University	M
Eastern Washington University	M
Five Towns College	M,D
Florida Atlantic University	M
Florida International University	M
Florida State University	M,D
George Mason University	D,O
Georgia College & State University	M
Georgia Southern University	M
Georgia State University	M,D,O
Gordon College	M
Hampton University	M
Hardin-Simmons University	M
Hebrew College	M,O
Heidelberg University	M
Holy Names University	M,O
Howard University	M
Hunter College of the City University of New York	M
Indiana State University	M
Indiana University of Pennsylvania	M
Inter American University of Puerto Rico, Metropolitan Campus	M
Inter American University of Puerto Rico, San Germán Campus	M
Ithaca College	M
Jackson State University	M
James Madison University	M
Kent State University	M,D,O
Lake Forest College	M
Lebanon Valley College	M
Lee University	M
Lehman College of the City University of New York	M
Liberty University	M,D
Long Island University–LIU Post	M
Louisiana State University and Agricultural & Mechanical College	M,D
Loyola University Maryland	M
Manhattanville College	M*
Marywood University	M
McGill University	M,D
McKendree University	M,D,O
McNeese State University	O
Miami University	M
Michigan State University	M,D
Mississippi College	M
Montclair State University	M
Morehead State University	M
Murray State University	M
Nazareth College of Rochester	M
New Jersey City University	M
New Mexico State University	M
New York University	M,D,O
Norfolk State University	M
North Dakota State University	M,D,O
Northern State University	M
Northwestern University	M,D*
Northwest Missouri State University	M
Oakland University	M,D
Oberlin College	M,O
Ohio University	M,O
Oklahoma State University	M
Old Dominion University	M
Oregon State University	M
Penn State University Park	M,D,O
Piedmont College	M,O
Pittsburg State University	M
Plymouth State University	M
Portland State University	M
Queens College of the City University of New York	M,O
Radford University	M
Reinhardt University	M
Rhode Island College	M
Rider University	M
Roosevelt University	M,O

*M—masters degree; D—doctorate; O—other advanced degree; *—Close-Up and/or Display*

Rutgers University–New Brunswick	M,D,O
St. Cloud State University	M
Saint Xavier University	M
Samford University	M
San Diego State University	M
San Francisco State University	M
Shenandoah University	M,D,O
Silver Lake College of the Holy Family	M
Southern Illinois University Edwardsville	M,O
Southern Methodist University	M
Southwestern Oklahoma State University	M
State University of New York at Fredonia	M
State University of New York College at Potsdam	M
Syracuse University	M
Tarleton State University	M
Teachers College, Columbia University	M,D,O
Temple University	M,D*
Tennessee Technological University	M
Texas A&M University–Kingsville	M
Texas Christian University	M,D
Texas State University	M
Texas Tech University	M,D
Texas Woman's University	M
Towson University	M,O
Troy University	M
Union College (KY)	M
Université Laval	M,D
University at Buffalo, the State University of New York	M,D,O*
The University of Akron	M
The University of Alabama	M,D,O
The University of Arizona	M,D
University of Bridgeport	M,D,O
The University of British Columbia	M,D
University of Central Arkansas	M,O
University of Cincinnati	M
University of Colorado Boulder	M,D
University of Connecticut	M,D*
University of Dayton	M
University of Delaware	M*
University of Denver	M,O
University of Florida	M,D
University of Georgia	M,D,O
University of Hartford	M,D,O
University of Houston	M,D
University of Illinois at Urbana–Champaign	M,D
The University of Iowa	M,D*
The University of Kansas	M,D*
University of Kentucky	M,D
University of Louisiana at Lafayette	M
University of Louisiana at Monroe	M,D
University of Louisville	M,D,O
University of Maryland, Baltimore County	M
University of Maryland, College Park	M,D
University of Massachusetts Amherst	M,D*
University of Massachusetts Lowell	M
University of Memphis	M,D
University of Miami	M,D,O
University of Michigan	M,D,O
University of Minnesota, Duluth	M
University of Missouri	M,D,O
University of Missouri–Kansas City	M,D
University of Missouri–St. Louis	M
University of Nebraska at Kearney	M
University of Nebraska–Lincoln	M,D
University of New Mexico	M
The University of North Carolina at Chapel Hill	M
The University of North Carolina at Greensboro	M,D
University of North Dakota	M,D
University of Northern Colorado	M,D
University of Northern Iowa	M
University of North Texas	M,D,O
University of Oklahoma	M,D,O*
University of Oregon	M,D
University of Ottawa	M,O
University of Rhode Island	M,D
University of Rochester	M,D*
University of St. Thomas (MN)	M
University of South Alabama	M
University of South Carolina	M,D,O
The University of South Dakota	M
University of Southern California	M,D,O
University of Southern Maine	M
University of Southern Mississippi	M,D
University of South Florida	M,D
The University of Tennessee	M
The University of Tennessee at Chattanooga	M
The University of Texas at Arlington	M
The University of Texas at Austin	M,D
The University of Texas at El Paso	M
The University of Texas Rio Grande Valley	M
The University of the Arts	M
University of the Pacific	M
The University of Toledo	M,O
University of Toronto	M,D
University of Utah	M,D*
University of Victoria	M,D
University of Washington	M,D*
University of West Georgia	M,O
University of Wisconsin–Madison	M,D
University of Wisconsin–Stevens Point	M
University of Wyoming	M
VanderCook College of Music	M
Virginia Commonwealth University	M
Wayne State College	M
Wayne State University	M,O
Webster University	M
West Chester University of Pennsylvania	M,O
Western Connecticut State University	M
Western Kentucky University	M
Western Michigan University	M,O
West Virginia University	M,D
Wichita State University	M
Winthrop University	M
Wright State University	M
Youngstown State University	M

NANOTECHNOLOGY

Arizona State University at the Tempe campus	M,D
Carnegie Mellon University	D
The College of William and Mary	M,D
Cornell University	M,D
Indiana University of Pennsylvania	M
Johns Hopkins University	M
Michigan Technological University	M,D,O
North Dakota State University	M,D
South Dakota School of Mines and Technology	D
State University of New York Polytechnic Institute	M,D
Stevens Institute of Technology	D
University of Alberta	M,D
University of California, Riverside	M
University of California, San Diego	M,D
University of Central Florida	M
University of New Mexico	M,D
University of Pennsylvania	M*
University of South Florida	M,D
University of Washington	M,D*
Virginia Commonwealth University	M,D

NATIONAL SECURITY

American Public University System	M
Angelo State University	M
Bellevue University	M
California State University, San Bernardino	M
The Citadel, The Military College of South Carolina	M
Drexel University	M
George Mason University	M,D
The George Washington University	M,D*
Henley-Putnam University	D
Hult International Business School (United States)	M
The Institute of World Politics	M,O
Kansas State University	M,D
La Salle University	M,O
National Defense University	M
Naval Postgraduate School	M,D,O
Naval War College	M
New York University	M,O
Regent University	M,D
Texas A&M University	M,O
Trinity Washington University	M
Troy University	M
University of Central Florida	M,D,O
University of Nebraska at Omaha	M,O
University of New Haven	M,O
Virginia Polytechnic Institute and State University	M,O
Western Michigan University Thomas M. Cooley Law School	M,D

NATURAL RESOURCES

American University	M,D,O
Auburn University	M,D
Ball State University	M,O
Boise State University	M,D,O
California Polytechnic State University, San Luis Obispo	M
Central Washington University	M
Colorado State University	M,D
Cornell University	M,D
Dalhousie University	M
Delaware State University	M
Duke University	M,D*
Humboldt State University	M
Instituto Tecnologico de Santo Domingo	M,D,O
Iowa State University of Science and Technology	M,D
Laurentian University	M,D
Louisiana State University and Agricultural & Mechanical College	M,D
McGill University	M,D
Michigan State University	M,D
Montana State University	M
New Mexico Highlands University	M
North Carolina State University	M,D
North Dakota State University	M,D
Northeastern State University	M
The Ohio State University	M,D
Oklahoma State University	M,D
Oregon State University	M,D
Purdue University	M,D
State University of New York College of Environmental Science and Forestry	M,D
Sul Ross State University	M
Tarleton State University	M
Texas A&M University	M,D
Texas Tech University	M,D
Unity College	M
Universidad Metropolitana	M
Universidad Nacional Pedro Henriquez Urena	M
Université du Québec à Montréal	M,D,O
Université du Québec en Abitibi-Témiscamingue	M,D
University of Alaska Fairbanks	M,D
University of Alberta	M,D
University of Arkansas at Monticello	M
The University of British Columbia	M,D
University of California, Berkeley	M,D
University of Connecticut	M,D*
University of Delaware	M*
University of Florida	M,D
University of Georgia	M,D
University of Guelph	M,D
University of Hawaii at Manoa	M,D
University of Idaho	M,D
University of Illinois at Urbana–Champaign	M,D
University of Maine	M,D
The University of Manchester	M,D
University of Manitoba	M,D
University of Maryland, College Park	M,D
University of Michigan	M,D
University of Minnesota, Twin Cities Campus	M,D
University of Montana	M,D
University of Nebraska–Lincoln	M,D
University of New Brunswick Saint John	M
University of New Hampshire	M,D,O
University of New Mexico	M,D
University of Northern British Columbia	M,D,O
University of Rhode Island	M,D
University of San Francisco	M
University of South Africa	M,D
The University of Texas at Austin	M
University of Vermont	M,D
University of Washington	M,D*
University of Wisconsin–Madison	M,D
University of Wisconsin–Stevens Point	M
University of Wyoming	M,D
Utah State University	M
Virginia Polytechnic Institute and State University	M,D,O
Washington State University	M,D
West Virginia University	M,D

NATUROPATHIC MEDICINE

Bastyr University	D
Canadian College of Naturopathic Medicine	O
National College of Natural Medicine	M,D
Southwest College of Naturopathic Medicine and Health Sciences	D
Universidad del Turabo	D
University of Bridgeport	D

NEAR AND MIDDLE EASTERN LANGUAGES

The American University in Cairo	M
American University of Beirut	M,D
Bethel Seminary	M,D,O
Brandeis University	M,D
The Catholic University of America	M,D
DePaul University	M
Georgetown University	M,O
Harvard University	M,D*
Hebrew Union College–Jewish Institute of Religion (NY)	D
Indiana University Bloomington	M,D
Johns Hopkins University	D
London Metropolitan University	M,D
Middlebury College	M
The Ohio State University	M,D
Oral Roberts University	M,D
University of California, Los Angeles	M,D
University of Chicago	D
The University of Manchester	M,D
University of Michigan	M,D
University of South Africa	M,D
The University of Texas at Austin	M,D
University of Utah	M,D*
University of Wisconsin–Madison	M,D
Wayne State University	M
Yale University	M,D*

NEAR AND MIDDLE EASTERN STUDIES

The American University in Cairo	M,O
American University of Beirut	M,D
The American University of Paris	M
Brandeis University	M,D
Brown University	D
California State University, Long Beach	M
The Catholic University of America	M,D,O
Columbia University	M,D*
Cornell University	M,D
George Mason University	M,O
Georgetown University	M,O
The George Washington University	M*
Harvard University	M,D*
Johns Hopkins University	D
Liberty University	M
McGill University	M,D,O
New York University	M,D,O
Princeton University	M,D
Rice University	D
Southern Evangelical Seminary	M,D,O
Southwestern Baptist Theological Seminary	M,D
The University of Arizona	M,D,O
University of California, Berkeley	M,D
University of California, Los Angeles	M,D
University of Chicago	M,D
University of Illinois at Urbana–Champaign	M
The University of Kansas	M,O*
The University of Manchester	M,D
University of Memphis	M,D
University of Michigan	M,D
University of Pennsylvania	M,D*
University of South Africa	M,D
The University of Texas at Austin	M,D
University of Toronto	M,D
University of Utah	M,D*
University of Virginia	M
University of Washington	M,D*
University of Waterloo	M
University of Wisconsin–Madison	M,D
Washington University in St. Louis	M
Wayne State University	M
Yale University	M,D*

NEUROBIOLOGY

Albert Einstein College of Medicine	D
Boston University	M,D
Brandeis University	M,D
California Institute of Technology	D
Carnegie Mellon University	M,D
Columbia University	D*
Cornell University	D
Dalhousie University	M,D
Duke University	D*
Georgia State University	M,D
Harvard University	D*
Illinois State University	M,D
Indiana University–Purdue University Indianapolis	D
Louisiana State University Health Sciences Center	D
Massachusetts Institute of Technology	D
New York University	M,D
Northwestern University	M,D*
Penn State Hershey Medical Center	D
Purdue University	M,D
Queen's University at Kingston	M,D
Université Laval	M,D
University at Albany, State University of New York	D
The University of Alabama at Birmingham	D
University of Arkansas for Medical Sciences	M,D,O
University of California, Irvine	M,D
University of California, Los Angeles	M,D
University of Chicago	D
University of Colorado Boulder	M,D
University of Colorado Denver	M,D
University of Connecticut	M,D*
The University of Iowa	M,D*
University of Kentucky	D
University of Louisville	M,D
The University of Manchester	M,D
University of Maryland, Baltimore	D
University of Minnesota, Twin Cities Campus	M,D
The University of North Carolina at Chapel Hill	D
University of Oklahoma	D*
University of Pittsburgh	D*
University of Rochester	D*
University of Southern California	D
The University of Texas at Austin	D
The University of Texas at San Antonio	M,D
University of Utah	D*
University of Washington	D*
Virginia Commonwealth University	D
Wake Forest University	D
Wayne State University	M,D
Wesleyan University	D
West Virginia University	M,D
Yale University	D*

NEUROSCIENCE

Albany Medical College	M,D
Alliant International University–San Diego	M,D,O
American University	M,D,O
American University of Beirut	M,D
Argosy University, Chicago	D
Argosy University, Phoenix	M,D
Argosy University, Tampa	M,D
Arizona State University at the Tempe campus	M,D
Augusta University	D
Ball State University	M,D,O
Baylor College of Medicine	D
Boston University	D
Brandeis University	M,D
Brigham Young University	M,D
Brock University	M,D
Brown University	D
California Institute of Technology	M,D
Carleton University	M,D
Carnegie Mellon University	D
Case Western Reserve University	D*
Central Michigan University	M,D
College of Staten Island of the City University of New York	M
The College of William and Mary	M
Colorado State University	D
Connecticut College	M
Dalhousie University	M,D
Dartmouth College	D*
Delaware State University	M,D
Drexel University	M,D
Duke University	D,O*
Emory University	D
Fielding Graduate University	M,D,O
Florida Atlantic University	D
Florida International University	M,D
Florida State University	M,D
Gallaudet University	M,D,O
George Mason University	M,D,O
Georgetown University	D
Georgia State University	D
The Graduate Center, City University of New York	D

Harvard University	D*
Icahn School of Medicine at Mount Sinai	M,D
Illinois State University	M,D
Immaculata University	M,D,O
Indiana University Bloomington	D
Iowa State University of Science and Technology	M,D
Irell & Manella Graduate School of Biological Sciences	D*
Johns Hopkins University	D
Kent State University	M,D
Louisiana State University Health Sciences Center	D
Loyola University Chicago	M,D
Marquette University	M,D
Massachusetts Institute of Technology	D
Mayo Graduate School	D
McGill University	M,D
McMaster University	M,D
Medical College of Wisconsin	D
Medical University of South Carolina	M,D
Meharry Medical College	D
Memorial University of Newfoundland	M,D
Michigan State University	M,D
Montana State University	M,D
New York University	D
Northwestern University	D*
The Ohio State University	D
Ohio University	M,D
Oregon Health & Science University	D
Penn State Hershey Medical Center	M,D
Princeton University	D
Purdue University	D
Queens College of the City University of New York	M,O
Queen's University at Kingston	M,D
Rosalind Franklin University of Medicine and Science	D
Rush University	M,D
Rutgers University–Newark	D
Rutgers University–New Brunswick	M,D
Seton Hall University	M,D
State University of New York Downstate Medical Center	D
State University of New York Upstate Medical University	D
Stony Brook University, State University of New York	M,D
Syracuse University	M,D
Teachers College, Columbia University	M,D
Texas Christian University	M,D
Thomas Jefferson University	D
Tufts University	M,D
Tulane University	M,D
Uniformed Services University of the Health Sciences	D*
Universidad de Iberoamerica	M,D
Université de Montréal	M,D
University at Albany, State University of New York	M,D
University at Buffalo, the State University of New York	M,D*
The University of Alabama at Birmingham	M,D
University of Alaska Fairbanks	M,D
University of Alberta	M,D
The University of Arizona	D
The University of British Columbia	M,D
University of Calgary	M,D
University of California, Berkeley	D
University of California, Davis	D
University of California, Irvine	D
University of California, Los Angeles	D
University of California, Riverside	D
University of California, San Diego	D
University of California, San Francisco	D
University of California, Santa Barbara	D
University of Chicago	D
University of Cincinnati	D
University of Colorado Denver	D
University of Connecticut	M,D*
University of Connecticut Health Center	D*
University of Delaware	D*
University of Florida	D
University of Georgia	D
University of Guelph	M,D,O
University of Hartford	M
University of Idaho	M,D
University of Illinois at Chicago	M,D
University of Illinois at Urbana–Champaign	D
The University of Iowa	D*
The University of Kansas	M,D*
University of Lethbridge	M,D
The University of Manchester	M,D
University of Maryland, Baltimore	D
University of Maryland, Baltimore County	D
University of Maryland, College Park	M,D
University of Massachusetts Amherst	M,D*
University of Massachusetts Medical School	M,D
University of Miami	M,D
University of Michigan	D
University of Michigan–Flint	D,O
University of Minnesota, Twin Cities Campus	M,D
University of Mississippi Medical Center	D
University of Missouri	M,D,O
University of Missouri–St. Louis	M,D,O
University of Montana	M,D
University of Nebraska Medical Center	D
University of New Mexico	M,D
The University of North Carolina at Chapel Hill	D
University of Oklahoma Health Sciences Center	M,D
University of Oregon	M,D
University of Pennsylvania	D*
University of Pittsburgh	D*
University of Puerto Rico, Rí o Piedras Campus	M,D
University of Rochester	D*
The University of South Dakota	M,D
University of Southern California	M,D
University of South Florida	M,D,O
The University of Texas at Austin	D
The University of Texas at Dallas	M,D*
The University of Texas Health Science Center at Houston	M,D
The University of Texas Health Science Center at San Antonio	D
The University of Texas Medical Branch	D
The University of Texas Southwestern Medical Center	D
The University of Toledo	M,D
University of Utah	D*
University of Vermont	D
University of Virginia	D
The University of Western Ontario	M,D
University of Wisconsin–Madison	D
Virginia Commonwealth University	M,D,O
Wake Forest University	D
Washington State University	M,D
Washington University in St. Louis	D
Wayne State University	M,D
Weill Cornell Medicine	M,D
West Virginia University	D
Wilfrid Laurier University	M,D
Yale University	D*

NONPROFIT MANAGEMENT

Adler University	M,D,O
American Jewish University	M
American Public University System	M
American University	M,D,O
Antioch University Los Angeles	M
Antioch University Santa Barbara	M
Arizona State University at the Tempe campus	M,D,O
Assumption College	M,O
Auburn University at Montgomery	M,D,O
Azusa Pacific University	M
Baruch College of the City University of New York	M
Bay Path University	M
Bradley University	M
Brandeis University	M
Brigham Young University	M
California Baptist University	M
California Lutheran University	M,O
California State University, Northridge	O
Cambridge College	M
Capella University	D
Carlos Albizu University, Miami Campus	M,D
Case Western Reserve University	M,D,O*
Central Michigan University	M,O
Chaminade University of Honolulu	M
Cleary University	M,O
Cleveland State University	M,O
The College at Brockport, State University of New York	M,O
Columbia University	M*
Corban University	M
Daemen College	M
Dallas Baptist University	M
DePaul University	M
Eastern Mennonite University	M
Eastern Michigan University	M,O
Eastern University	M
East Tennessee State University	M,O
Fairleigh Dickinson University, Metropolitan Campus	M,O
Fielding Graduate University	M,D,O
Florida Atlantic University	M,D
Fontbonne University	M
Fordham University	M,D
The George Washington University	M,O*
Georgian Court University	M,O
Georgia Southern University	O
Georgia State University	M,D,O
Grand Valley State University	M
Gratz College	O
Hamline University	M,D
Hebrew Union College–Jewish Institute of Religion (NY)	M
High Point University	M
Hope International University	M
Indiana University Bloomington	M,D,O
Indiana University Northwest	M,O
Indiana University of Pennsylvania	D
Indiana University–Purdue University Indianapolis	M,O
Iona College	M,O
James Madison University	M
John Carroll University	M
Johns Hopkins University	M,O
Kean University	M
La Salle University	M
Lasell College	M,O
Lewis University	M
Lindenwood University	M
Lipscomb University	M,O
Long Island University–LIU Brooklyn	M,O
Long Island University–LIU Post	M,O
Louisiana State University in Shreveport	M
Marymount University	M,O
Metropolitan State University	M,D,O
Misericordia University	M
Mount Aloysius College	M
New England College	M
The New School	M
New York University	M,D,O
North Carolina State University	M,D,O
Northeastern University	M
Northern Kentucky University	M,O
North Park University	M
Norwich University	M
Notre Dame of Maryland University	M
Oakland University	M,O
Oklahoma State University	M,D,O
Oral Roberts University	M
Our Lady of the Lake University of San Antonio	M
Pace University	M
Park University	M,O
Penn State Harrisburg	M,D,O
Post University	M
Providence College	M
Regent University	M,D,O
Regis University	M,O
Rockhurst University	M,O
St. Cloud State University	M
Salve Regina University	M,O
San Francisco State University	M
Seton Hall University	M,O
Simmons College	M
Sonoma State University	M,O
Southern Adventist University	M
Southern New Hampshire University	M,O
Suffolk University	M,O
Texas A&M University	M,O
Tiffin University	M
Trinity Washington University	M
Trinity Western University	M,O
Troy University	M
Tufts University	O
Unification Theological Seminary	M,D
University at Albany, State University of New York	M,D,O
University of Arkansas at Little Rock	O
University of Central Florida	M,O
University of Colorado Denver	M,D
University of Florida	M
University of Georgia	M,D,O
University of Houston–Downtown	M
University of La Verne	M,O
University of Louisville	M,D
University of Maryland, Baltimore County	M,O
University of Michigan–Flint	M
University of Missouri	M,D,O
University of Missouri–St. Louis	M,O
University of Nevada, Las Vegas	M,D,O
The University of North Carolina at Charlotte	M,O
The University of North Carolina at Greensboro	M,O
University of Northern Iowa	M
University of North Florida	M,O
University of North Texas	M,D,O
University of Notre Dame	M
University of Oklahoma	M*
University of Pennsylvania	M,O*
University of Pittsburgh	M*
University of Portland	M
University of San Diego	M,D,O
University of San Francisco	M
University of Southern California	M,O
University of South Florida	O
The University of Tampa	M
The University of Tennessee at Chattanooga	M,O
The University of Texas at Dallas	M,D*
University of the Sacred Heart	M
University of the West	M
The University of Toledo	M,O
University of West Georgia	M,D,O
University of Wisconsin–Milwaukee	M,D,O
Upper Iowa University	M
Virginia Commonwealth University	M,O
Virginia Polytechnic Institute and State University	M,O
Walden University	M,D,O
Warner Pacific College	M
Wayne State University	M,D
Webster University	M
West Chester University of Pennsylvania	M,O
Western Michigan University	M,D,O
Worcester State University	M

NORTHERN STUDIES

University of Alaska Fairbanks	M
University of Manitoba	M

NUCLEAR ENGINEERING

Air Force Institute of Technology	M,D
Arizona State University at the Tempe campus	M,D,O
Colorado School of Mines	M,D
École Polytechnique de Montréal	M,D,O
Georgia Institute of Technology	M,D
Idaho State University	M,D
Kansas State University	M,D
Massachusetts Institute of Technology	M,D,O
McMaster University	M,D
Missouri University of Science and Technology	M,D
North Carolina State University	M,D
The Ohio State University	M,D
Oregon State University	M,D
Penn State University Park	M,D
Purdue University	M,D
Rensselaer Polytechnic Institute	M,D
Royal Military College of Canada	M,D
Stevens Institute of Technology	M,D,O
Texas A&M University	M,D
University of California, Berkeley	M,D
University of Cincinnati	M,D
University of Florida	M,D
University of Illinois at Urbana–Champaign	M,D
The University of Manchester	M,D
University of Maryland, College Park	M,D
University of Massachusetts Lowell	M,D
University of Michigan	M,D,O
University of Missouri	M,D,O
University of Nevada, Las Vegas	M,D,O
University of New Mexico	M,D
University of South Carolina	M,D
The University of Tennessee	M,D
The University of Tennessee at Chattanooga	M,O
University of Utah	M,D*
University of Wisconsin–Madison	M,D
Virginia Commonwealth University	M,D
Virginia Polytechnic Institute and State University	M,D

NURSE ANESTHESIA

Adventist University of Health Sciences	M
Albany Medical College	M
Arkansas State University	M,D,O
Augusta University	D
Barry University	M
Baylor College of Medicine	D
Bloomsburg University of Pennsylvania	M
Boston College	M,D
Bryan College of Health Sciences	M
California State University, Fullerton	M,D
Case Western Reserve University	M*
Central Connecticut State University	M,O
Columbia University	M,O*
DeSales University	M,D,O
Drexel University	M
Duke University	M,D,O*
Fairfield University	M,D
Florida Gulf Coast University	M
Gannon University	M,O
Georgetown University	M,D
Goldfarb School of Nursing at Barnes-Jewish College	M
Inter American University of Puerto Rico, Arecibo Campus	M
La Roche College	M
La Salle University	M,D,O
Lincoln Memorial University	M
Louisiana State University Health Sciences Center	M,D,O
Lourdes University	M
Marshall University	D
Mayo School of Health Sciences	D
Medical University of South Carolina	M
Middle Tennessee School of Anesthesia	M,D
Midwestern University, Glendale Campus	M
Millikin University	M,D
Missouri State University	D
Mount Marty College	M
Murray State University	M
National University	M,D,O
Newman University	M
Northeastern University	M,D,O
Oakland University	M,O
Old Dominion University	M
Oregon Health & Science University	M
Otterbein University	M,D,O
Our Lady of the Lake College	M
Quinnipiac University	D
Rosalind Franklin University of Medicine and Science	D
Rush University	D
Rutgers University–Newark	M,D,O
Saint Joseph's University	M
Saint Mary's University of Minnesota	M
Saint Vincent College	M,D
Samford University	M,D
Samuel Merritt University	M,D,O
Southern Illinois University Edwardsville	D
State University of New York Downstate Medical Center	M
Texas Christian University	D
Texas Wesleyan University	M,D
Uniformed Services University of the Health Sciences	M,D*
Union University	M,D,O
University at Buffalo, the State University of New York	M,D,O*
The University of Alabama at Birmingham	M,D
The University of British Columbia	M,D

*M—masters degree; D—doctorate; O—other advanced degree; *—Close-Up and/or Display*

University of Cincinnati	M,D
University of Detroit Mercy	M,D,O
The University of Kansas	D*
University of Miami	M,D
University of Michigan–Flint	M,D
University of Minnesota, Twin Cities Campus	M
University of New England	M
The University of North Carolina at Charlotte	M,D,O
The University of North Carolina at Greensboro	M,D,O
University of North Dakota	M,D
University of North Florida	M,D,O
University of Pennsylvania	M*
University of Pittsburgh	M,D*
The University of Scranton	M,D,O
University of South Carolina	M
University of South Florida	M,D,O
The University of Tennessee at Chattanooga	M,D,O
University of Wisconsin–La Crosse	M
Villanova University	M,D,O
Virginia Commonwealth University	M,D
Wayne State University	M,O
Webster University	M
Westminster College (UT)	M
York College of Pennsylvania	M,D

NURSE MIDWIFERY

Bastyr University	M,O
Baylor University	M,D
Bethel University (MN)	M,D,O
Case Western Reserve University	M*
Columbia University	M*
DeSales University	M,D,O
Emory University	M
Frontier Nursing University	M,D,O
Georgetown University	M,D
James Madison University	M,D
Marquette University	M,D,O
Midwives College of Utah	M
National College of Midwifery	M,D
New York University	M,D,O
Old Dominion University	M,D
Oregon Health & Science University	M,D,O
Philadelphia University	M,O
Seattle University	M
Shenandoah University	M,D,O
State University of New York Downstate Medical Center	M,O
Stony Brook University, State University of New York	M,D,O
University of Cincinnati	M,D
University of Colorado Denver	M,D
University of Illinois at Chicago	M,O
University of Indianapolis	M,D
The University of Kansas	M,D,O*
The University of Manchester	M,D
University of Maryland, Baltimore	M
University of Miami	M,D
University of Minnesota, Twin Cities Campus	M
University of Pennsylvania	M*
University of Puerto Rico, Medical Sciences Campus	M,O
University of South Africa	M,D
Vanderbilt University	M,D,O*
Wayne State University	M,D,O
West Virginia Wesleyan College	M,O

NURSING—GENERAL

Adelphi University	D
Albany State University	M
Alcorn State University	M
Allen College	M,D,O
Alverno College	M
American International College	M
American Sentinel University	M
American University of Beirut	M
Andrews University	M,D
Angelo State University	M
Aquinas College (TN)	M
Arizona State University at the Tempe campus	M,D,O
Arkansas State University	M,D,O
Arkansas Tech University	M
Armstrong State University	M,O
Athabasca University	M,O
Auburn University	M
Auburn University at Montgomery	M
Augsburg College	M,D
Augusta University	D
Aurora University	M
Austin Peay State University	M
Azusa Pacific University	M,D
Ball State University	M,D,O
Barry University	M,D,O
Baylor University	M,D
Bellarmine University	M,D
Bellin College	M
Belmont University	M,D
Benedictine University	M
Bethel College	M
Bethel University (MN)	M,D,O
Binghamton University, State University of New York	M,D,O*
Blessing-Rieman College of Nursing	M
Blessing–Rieman College of Nursing and Health Sciences	M
Bloomsburg University of Pennsylvania	M
Boise State University	M,D,O
Boston College	M,D
Bowie State University	M
Bradley University	M,D,O
Briar Cliff University	M
Brigham Young University	M
California Baptist University	M,D
California State University, Chico	M
California State University, Dominguez Hills	M
California State University, Fresno	M
California State University, Fullerton	M,D
California State University, Long Beach	M,D
California State University, Los Angeles	M,O
California State University, Sacramento	M
California State University, San Bernardino	M
California State University, Stanislaus	M
Capella University	M,D
Capital University	M
Cardinal Stritch University	M
Carlow University	D
Carson-Newman University	M
Case Western Reserve University	M,D*
The Catholic University of America	M,D,O
Cedar Crest College	M
Central Methodist University	M
Chatham University	M,D
Chicago State University	M
Clarion University of Pennsylvania	M,D
Clarke University	D
Clarkson College	M,O
Clayton State University	M
Clemson University	M,D
Cleveland State University	M,D
College of Mount Saint Vincent	M,O
The College of New Jersey	M,O
The College of New Rochelle	M,O
College of Saint Elizabeth	M
College of Saint Mary	M
The College of St. Scholastica	M,O
College of Staten Island of the City University of New York	M,D,O
Colorado Mesa University	M,D,O
Colorado State University–Pueblo	M
Columbia University	M,D,O*
Columbus State University	M
Concordia University Wisconsin	M
Coppin State University	M,O
Cox College	M
Creighton University	M,D,O
Curry College	M
Daemen College	M,D,O
Dalhousie University	M,D
Delaware State University	M
Delta State University	M,D
DePaul University	M,D
DeSales University	M,D,O
Drexel University	M,D
Duke University	D*
Duquesne University	M,D,O
D'Youville College	M,D,O
East Carolina University	M,D,O
Eastern Kentucky University	M
Eastern Mennonite University	M
Eastern New Mexico University	M
East Tennessee State University	M,D,O
Edgewood College	M,D
Edinboro University of Pennsylvania	M,D
EDP University of Puerto Rico–San Sebastian	M
Elmhurst College	M
Elms College	M,D
Emmanuel College (United States)	M,O
Emory University	M,D
Endicott College	M,D
Excelsior College	M
Fairfield University	M,D
Fairleigh Dickinson University, Metropolitan Campus	M,D,O
Felician University	M,D,O
Ferris State University	M
Florida Agricultural and Mechanical University	M,D
Florida Atlantic University	M,D,O
Florida International University	M,D
Florida National University	M
Florida Southern College	M
Florida State University	M,D,O
Fort Hays State University	M
Framingham State University	M
Franciscan University of Steubenville	M
Francis Marion University	M
Fresno Pacific University	M
Frontier Nursing University	M,D,O
Frostburg State University	M
Gannon University	M,D
Gardner-Webb University	M,D
George Mason University	M,D,O
Georgetown University	M,D
The George Washington University	M,D,O*
Georgia College & State University	M,D
Georgia Southern University	D
Georgia State University	M,D,O
Goldfarb School of Nursing at Barnes-Jewish College	M
Gonzaga University	M,D
Goshen College	M
Governors State University	M
Graceland University (IA)	M,D,O
The Graduate Center, City University of New York	D
Grambling State University	M,O
Grand Canyon University	M,O
Grand Valley State University	M,D
Grand View University	M
Gwynedd Mercy University	M,D
Hampton University	M,D
Hardin-Simmons University	M
Hawai`i Pacific University	M
Herzing University Online	M
Holy Family University	M
Holy Names University	M,O
Howard University	M,O
Hunter College of the City University of New York	M,O
Husson University	M,O
Idaho State University	M,O
Illinois State University	M,D,O
Immaculata University	M
Independence University	M
Indiana State University	M,D
Indiana University East	M
Indiana University Kokomo	M
Indiana University of Pennsylvania	D
Indiana University–Purdue University Fort Wayne	M,O
Indiana University–Purdue University Indianapolis	M,D,O
Indiana University South Bend	M
Indiana Wesleyan University	M
Inter American University of Puerto Rico, Arecibo Campus	M
Jacksonville State University	M
Jacksonville University	M,D*
James Madison University	M,D
Jefferson College of Health Sciences	M
Johns Hopkins University	M,D,O
Kaplan University, Davenport Campus	M
Kean University	M
Keiser University	M
Kennesaw State University	M,D
Kent State University	M,D,O
Kentucky State University	M,D
Keuka College	M
Lamar University	M
Lander University	M
La Roche College	M
La Salle University	M,D,O
Laurentian University	M
Lehman College of the City University of New York	M
Le Moyne College	M,O
Lenoir-Rhyne University	M
Lewis University	M,D
Liberty University	M,D
Lincoln Memorial University	M
Lindenwood University	M
Loma Linda University	D
Long Island University–LIU Brooklyn	M,O
Louisiana State University Health Sciences Center	M,D,O
Loyola University Chicago	M,D,O
Loyola University New Orleans	M,D
Lynchburg College	M
Madonna University	M
Malone University	M
Mansfield University of Pennsylvania	M
Marian University (WI)	M
Marquette University	M,D,O
Marshall University	M
Marymount University	M,D,O
Maryville University of Saint Louis	M,D
McGill University	M,D,O
McKendree University	M
McMaster University	M,D
McMurry University	M
McNeese State University	M,O
MCPHS University	M
Medical University of South Carolina	D
Memorial University of Newfoundland	M,D
Mercer University	M,D,O
Mercy College	M
Metropolitan State University	M,D
MGH Institute of Health Professions	M,D,O
Michigan State University	M,D
Middle Tennessee State University	M,O
Midwestern State University	M
Millersville University of Pennsylvania	M
Millikin University	M,D
Minnesota State University Moorhead	M,O
Misericordia University	M,D
Mississippi University for Women	M,O
Missouri Southern State University	M
Missouri State University	M,D
Missouri Western State University	M,O
Molloy College	M,D,O
Monmouth University	M,D,O
Moravian College	M
Morgan State University	M
Mount Carmel College of Nursing	M,D
Mount Marty College	M
Mount Mercy University	M
Mount St. Joseph University	M,D
Mount Saint Mary College	M,O
Mount Saint Mary's University (CA)	M,D,O
Murray State University	M
National University	M,D,O
Nebraska Methodist College	M
Nebraska Wesleyan University	M
Neumann University	M
New Mexico State University	M,D
New York University	M,D,O
Nicholls State University	M
North Dakota State University	M,D
Northeastern University	M,D,O
Northern Arizona University	M,D,O
Northern Illinois University	M
Northern Kentucky University	M,D,O
Northern Michigan University	M,D
North Park University	M
Northwestern State University of Louisiana	M
Norwich University	M
Nova Southeastern University	M,D*
Oakland University	M,D,O
The Ohio State University	M,D
Ohio University	M
Oklahoma Baptist University	M
Oklahoma City University	M,D
Old Dominion University	M,D
Oregon Health & Science University	M,D,O
Otterbein University	M,D,O
Our Lady of the Lake College	M
Pace University	M,D,O
Pacific Lutheran University	M,D
Palm Beach Atlantic University	M,D
Penn State University Park	M,D
Pittsburg State University	M
Point Loma Nazarene University	M,O
Pontifical Catholic University of Puerto Rico	M
Prairie View A&M University	M
Purdue University Northwest	M
Queen's University at Kingston	M,D,O
Queens University of Charlotte	M
Quinnipiac University	M,D
Radford University	D
Ramapo College of New Jersey	M
Regis College (MA)	M,D,O
Research College of Nursing	M
Resurrection University	M
Rhode Island College	M
Rivier University	M
Robert Morris University	M,D
Roberts Wesleyan College	M
Rowan University	M
Rush University	M,D,O
Rutgers University–Newark	M,D,O
Sacred Heart University	M,D,O
Sage Graduate School	M,D,O
Saginaw Valley State University	M
St. Ambrose University	M
Saint Anthony College of Nursing	M
St. Catherine University	M,D
Saint Francis Medical Center College of Nursing	M,D,O
St. John Fisher College	M,D,O
St. Joseph's College, Long Island Campus	M
St. Joseph's College, New York	M
Saint Joseph's College of Maine	M,O
Saint Louis University	M,D,O
Saint Mary's College	D
Saint Peter's University	M,D,O
Saint Xavier University	M,O
Salem State University	M
Salisbury University	M,D
Salve Regina University	D
Samford University	M,D
Samuel Merritt University	M,D,O
San Diego State University	M
San Francisco State University	M,O
Seattle Pacific University	M,O
Seattle University	M,D
Seton Hall University	M,D
Shenandoah University	M,D,O
Simmons College	M,D,O
Sonoma State University	M
South Dakota State University	M,D
Southeast Missouri State University	M
Southern Adventist University	M
Southern Connecticut State University	M
Southern Illinois University Edwardsville	M,D,O
Southern Nazarene University	M
Southern University and Agricultural and Mechanical College	M,D,O
South University	M
South University	M
South University	M
South University (MI)	M
South University (SC)	M
South University (GA)	M
South University (AL)	M
South University	M
Spalding University	M,D,O
Spring Arbor University	M
Spring Hill College	M,O
State University of New York Downstate Medical Center	M,O
State University of New York Upstate Medical University	M,O
Stevenson University	M
Stockton University	M
Stony Brook University, State University of New York	M,D,O
Tarleton State University	M
Temple University	D*
Tennessee State University	M,O
Tennessee Technological University	M
Texas A&M International University	M
Texas A&M University	M
Texas A&M University–Corpus Christi	M
Texas Christian University	M,D,O
Texas Tech University Health Sciences Center	M,D,O
Texas Woman's University	M,D
Thomas Edison State University	M,D
Thomas Jefferson University	M,D
Thomas University	M
Towson University	M,O
Trinity Western University	M
Troy University	M,D,O
Uniformed Services University of the Health Sciences	M,D*
Union University	M,D,O
Universidad Metropolitana	M,O
Université de Montréal	M,D,O
Université du Québec à Rimouski	M,O
Université du Québec à Trois-Rivières	M,O
Université du Québec en Outaouais	M,O
Université Laval	M,D,O

University at Buffalo, the State University of New York	M,D,O*
The University of Akron	M,D
The University of Alabama	M,D
The University of Alabama at Birmingham	M,D
The University of Alabama in Huntsville	M,D,O
University of Alaska Anchorage	M
University of Alberta	M,D
The University of Arizona	M,D,O
University of Arkansas	M
University of Arkansas for Medical Sciences	D
The University of British Columbia	M,D
University of Calgary	M,D,O
University of California, Irvine	M
University of California, Los Angeles	M,D
University of California, San Francisco	M,D
University of Central Arkansas	M,O
University of Central Florida	M,D,O
University of Central Missouri	M,D,O
University of Central Oklahoma	M
University of Cincinnati	M,D
University of Colorado Colorado Springs	M,D
University of Colorado Denver	M,D
University of Connecticut	M,D,O*
University of Delaware	M,O*
University of Detroit Mercy	M,D,O
University of Florida	M,D
University of Hartford	M
University of Hawaii at Hilo	D
University of Hawaii at Manoa	M,D,O
University of Houston	M
University of Illinois at Chicago	M,D,O
University of Indianapolis	M,D
The University of Iowa	M,D*
The University of Kansas	M,D,O*
University of Kentucky	D
University of Lethbridge	M,D
University of Louisiana at Lafayette	M
University of Louisville	M,D
University of Maine	M,O
The University of Manchester	M,D
University of Manitoba	M
University of Mary	M,D
University of Mary Hardin-Baylor	M,O
University of Maryland, Baltimore	M,D,O
University of Massachusetts Amherst	M,D*
University of Massachusetts Boston	M,D
University of Massachusetts Dartmouth	M,D
University of Massachusetts Lowell	M,D
University of Massachusetts Medical School	M,D,O
University of Memphis	M,O
University of Miami	M,D
University of Michigan	M,D,O
University of Michigan–Flint	M,D,O
University of Minnesota, Twin Cities Campus	M,D
University of Mississippi Medical Center	M,D
University of Missouri	M,D,O
University of Missouri–Kansas City	M,D
University of Missouri–St. Louis	M,D,O
University of Mobile	M
University of Nebraska Medical Center	D
University of Nevada, Las Vegas	M,D,O
University of Nevada, Reno	M,D
University of New Brunswick Fredericton	M
University of New Hampshire	M,D,O
University of New Mexico	M,D
University of North Alabama	M
The University of North Carolina at Chapel Hill	M,D,O
The University of North Carolina at Charlotte	M,D,O
The University of North Carolina at Greensboro	M,D,O
The University of North Carolina at Pembroke	M
The University of North Carolina Wilmington	M,O
University of North Dakota	M,D
University of Northern Colorado	M,D
University of North Florida	M,D,O
University of Oklahoma Health Sciences Center	M
University of Ottawa	M,D,O
University of Pennsylvania	M,D,O*
University of Phoenix–Atlanta Campus	M
University of Phoenix–Augusta Campus	M
University of Phoenix–Bay Area Campus	M,D
University of Phoenix–Central Valley Campus	M
University of Phoenix–Charlotte Campus	M
University of Phoenix–Colorado Campus	M
University of Phoenix–Colorado Springs Downtown Campus	M
University of Phoenix–Columbus Georgia Campus	M
University of Phoenix–Hawaii Campus	M
University of Phoenix–Houston Campus	M
University of Phoenix–New Mexico Campus	M
University of Phoenix–North Florida Campus	M
University of Phoenix–Online Campus	M,D,O
University of Phoenix–Phoenix Campus	M,O
University of Phoenix–Sacramento Valley Campus	M
University of Phoenix–San Antonio Campus	M
University of Phoenix–San Diego Campus	M
University of Phoenix–Southern California Campus	M,O
University of Phoenix–South Florida Campus	M
University of Phoenix–Utah Campus	M
University of Phoenix–Washington D.C. Campus	M,D
University of Pittsburgh	D*
University of Portland	M,D
University of Puerto Rico, Medical Sciences Campus	M
University of Regina	M
University of Rhode Island	M,D
University of Rochester	M,D*
University of St. Francis (IL)	M,D,O
University of Saint Francis (IN)	M,O
University of Saint Joseph	M,D
University of Saint Mary	M
University of San Diego	M,D
University of San Francisco	M,D
University of Saskatchewan	M
The University of Scranton	M,D,O
University of South Alabama	M,D,O
University of South Carolina	M,O
University of Southern Indiana	M,D
University of Southern Maine	M,D,O
University of Southern Mississippi	M,D,O
University of South Florida	M,D,O
The University of Tampa	M
The University of Tennessee	M,D
The University of Tennessee at Chattanooga	M,D,O
The University of Tennessee Health Science Center	M,D,O
The University of Texas at Arlington	M,D
The University of Texas at Austin	M,D
The University of Texas at El Paso	M,D,O
The University of Texas at Tyler	M,D
The University of Texas Health Science Center at Houston	M,D
The University of Texas Health Science Center at San Antonio	M,D,O
The University of Texas Medical Branch	M,D
The University of Texas Rio Grande Valley	M
University of the Incarnate Word	M,D
The University of Toledo	M,D,O
University of Toronto	M,D
University of Utah	M,D*
University of Vermont	M,D
University of Victoria	M,D
University of Virginia	M,D
University of Washington	M,D,O*
University of Washington, Bothell	M
University of Washington, Tacoma	M
The University of Western Ontario	M,D
University of West Florida	M
University of West Georgia	M,D,O
University of Windsor	M
University of Wisconsin–Eau Claire	M,D
University of Wisconsin–Madison	D
University of Wisconsin–Milwaukee	M,D,O
University of Wisconsin–Oshkosh	M
University of Wyoming	M
Urbana University	M
Ursuline College	M,D
Utah Valley University	M
Valparaiso University	M,D,O
Vanderbilt University	M,D,O*
Vanguard University of Southern California	M
Villanova University	M,D,O
Virginia Commonwealth University	M,D,O
Viterbo University	D
Walden University	M,D,O
Walsh University	M,D
Washburn University	M,D,O
Washington Adventist University	M
Washington State University	M,D,O
Waynesburg University	M,D
Wayne State University	D
Weber State University	M
Webster University	M
Wesley College	M
West Chester University of Pennsylvania	M,D,O
West Coast University	M,D
Western Carolina University	M,D,O
Western Connecticut State University	M,D
Western Kentucky University	M
Western Michigan University	M
Western University of Health Sciences	M,D
Westminster College (UT)	M
West Texas A&M University	M
West Virginia University	M,D,O
West Virginia Wesleyan College	M,O
Wheeling Jesuit University	M
Wichita State University	M,D
Widener University	M,D,O
Wilkes University	M,D
William Carey University	M
William Paterson University of New Jersey	M,D
Wilmington University	M,D
Wilson College	M
Winona State University	M,D,O
Winston-Salem State University	M,D
Wright State University	M
Xavier University	M,D,O
Yale University	M,D,O*
York College of Pennsylvania	M,D
York University	M
Youngstown State University	M

NURSING AND HEALTHCARE ADMINISTRATION

Adelphi University	M,O
Allen College	M,D,O
American International College	M
Arizona State University at the Tempe campus	M,D,O
Athabasca University	M,O
Augusta University	M
Austin Peay State University	M
Barry University	M,D,O
Bellarmine University	M,D
Blessing–Rieman College of Nursing and Health Sciences	M
Bloomsburg University of Pennsylvania	M
Bowie State University	M
Bradley University	M,D,O
Brenau University	M
California State University, Fullerton	M,D
California University of Pennsylvania	M
Capella University	M
Capital University	M
Carlow University	M
Cedar Crest College	M
Central Methodist University	M
Chatham University	M,D
Clarkson College	M,O
College of Mount Saint Vincent	M,O
The College of New Rochelle	M,O
Columbus State University	M
Cox College	M
Creighton University	M,D,O
Daemen College	M,D,O
DeSales University	M,D,O
Drexel University	M
Duke University	M,D,O*
Eastern Mennonite University	M
Eastern Michigan University	M,O
Edgewood College	M,D
Elms College	M,D
Emmanuel College (United States)	M,O
Emory University	M
Excelsior College	M
Fairfield University	M,D
Felician University	M,D,O
Ferris State University	M
Florida Agricultural and Mechanical University	M,D
Florida Atlantic University	M,D,O
Florida National University	M
Florida Southern College	M
Florida State University	M,D,O
Framingham State University	M
Franklin Pierce University	M,D,O
Frostburg State University	M
Gannon University	M,D
The George Washington University	M,D,O*
Georgia State University	M,D,O
Grand Valley State University	M,D
Grantham University	M
Herzing University Online	M
Holy Family University	M
Holy Names University	M,O
Immaculata University	M
Independence University	M
Indiana State University	M,D
Indiana University Kokomo	M
Indiana University of Pennsylvania	M
Indiana University–Purdue University Fort Wayne	M,O
Indiana University–Purdue University Indianapolis	M,O
Indiana Wesleyan University	M,O
James Madison University	M,D
Jefferson College of Health Sciences	M
Kaplan University, Davenport Campus	M
Kean University	M,D
Kent State University	M,D,O
Lamar University	M
La Roche College	M
La Salle University	M,D,O
Le Moyne College	M,O
Lenoir-Rhyne University	M
Lewis University	M,D
Liberty University	M,D
Loma Linda University	M
Long Island University–LIU Post	M,O
Louisiana State University Health Sciences Center	M,D,O
Lourdes University	M
Loyola University Chicago	M,D,O
Lynchburg College	M
Madonna University	M
Marquette University	M,D,O
McKendree University	M
McNeese State University	M,O
Medical University of South Carolina	M
Mercy College	M
Metropolitan State University	M,D
MidAmerica Nazarene University	M
Middle Tennessee State University	M
Milwaukee School of Engineering	M*
Missouri Western State University	M,O
Molloy College	M,D,O
Monmouth University	M,D,O
Montana State University	M,D,O
Moravian College	M
Mount Carmel College of Nursing	M,D
Mount Mary University	M
Mount Mercy University	M
Mount St. Joseph University	M
Mount Saint Mary College	M,O
National University	M,D,O
Nebraska Methodist College	M
New Mexico State University	M,D
Nicholls State University	M
Northeastern University	M,D,O
North Park University	M
Northwest Nazarene University	M
Norwich University	M
Ohio University	M
Oklahoma Wesleyan University	M
Old Dominion University	M,D
Otterbein University	M,D,O
Our Lady of the Lake College	M
Pace University	M,D,O
Palm Beach Atlantic University	M,D
Pennsylvania College of Health Sciences	M
Prairie View A&M University	M
Purdue University Northwest	M
Queens University of Charlotte	M
Quinnipiac University	D
Research College of Nursing	M
Roberts Wesleyan College	M
Rush University	M
Sacred Heart University	M,D,O
Saginaw Valley State University	M
Saint Francis Medical Center College of Nursing	M,D,O
Saint Joseph's College of Maine	M,O
Saint Joseph's University	M
Saint Peter's University	M,D,O
Salem State University	M
Salisbury University	M,D
Samford University	M,D
Samuel Merritt University	M,D,O
San Francisco State University	M,O
Seattle Pacific University	M,O
Seton Hall University	M,D
Shenandoah University	M,D,O
Southern Adventist University	M
Southern Illinois University Edwardsville	M,O
Southern Nazarene University	M
Southern University and Agricultural and Mechanical College	M,D,O
Spalding University	M,D,O
Spring Hill College	M,O
State University of New York Polytechnic Institute	M
Stony Brook University, State University of New York	M,O
Tarleton State University	M
Teachers College, Columbia University	M,D
Tennessee Technological University	M
Texas A&M University–Corpus Christi	M
Texas Christian University	M,D,O
Texas Tech University Health Sciences Center	M,D,O
Texas Woman's University	M,D
Trident University International	M,D,O
Union University	M,D,O
Universidad Metropolitana	M,O
University at Buffalo, the State University of New York	M,D,O*
University of Central Arkansas	M,O
University of Cincinnati	M,D
University of Colorado Denver	M,D
University of Delaware	M,O*
University of Hawaii at Manoa	M,D,O
University of Houston	M
University of Illinois at Chicago	M,O
University of Indianapolis	M,D
The University of Kansas	M,D,O*
University of Louisville	M,D
University of Mary	M,D
University of Mary Hardin-Baylor	M,O
University of Maryland, Baltimore	M
University of Massachusetts Amherst	M,D*
University of Massachusetts Medical School	M,D,O
University of Memphis	M,O
University of Minnesota, Twin Cities Campus	M
University of Missouri	M,D,O
University of Missouri–Kansas City	M,D
The University of North Carolina at Chapel Hill	M,D,O
The University of North Carolina at Charlotte	M,D,O
The University of North Carolina at Greensboro	M,D,O
The University of North Carolina at Pembroke	M
University of North Florida	M,D,O
University of Pennsylvania	M,D*
University of Phoenix–Bay Area Campus	M,D
University of Phoenix–Washington D.C. Campus	M,D
University of Pittsburgh	M,D*
University of Rochester	M,D*
University of St. Francis (IL)	M,D,O

*M—masters degree; D—doctorate; O—other advanced degree; *—Close-Up and/or Display*

University of Saint Mary	M
University of San Diego	M,D
University of San Francisco	M,D
The University of Scranton	M,D,O
University of South Alabama	M,D,O
University of South Carolina	M
University of Southern Maine	M,D,O
University of South Florida	M,D,O
The University of Tennessee at Chattanooga	M,D,O
The University of Tennessee Health Science Center	M,D,O
The University of Texas at Arlington	M,D
The University of Texas at Austin	M,D
The University of Texas at El Paso	M,D,O
The University of Texas at Tyler	M,D
The University of Texas Health Science Center at San Antonio	M,D,O
University of the Incarnate Word	M,D
The University of Toledo	M,O
University of Victoria	M,D
University of Virginia	M,D
University of Washington, Tacoma	M
University of West Florida	M
University of Wisconsin–Eau Claire	M,D
University of Wisconsin–Green Bay	M
Vanderbilt University	M,D,O*
Virginia Commonwealth University	M,D,O
Walden University	M,D,O
Walsh University	M,D
Washburn University	M,D,O
Washington Adventist University	M
Waynesburg University	M,D
Webster University	M
Western Governors University	M
Western University of Health Sciences	M
West Virginia Wesleyan College	M,O
Wilmington University	M,D
Wilson College	M
Winona State University	M,D,O
Wright State University	M
York College of Pennsylvania	M,D

NURSING EDUCATION

Albany State University	M
American International College	M
Angelo State University	M
Aquinas College (TN)	M
Arizona State University at the Tempe campus	M,D,O
Auburn University	M
Auburn University at Montgomery	M
Austin Peay State University	M
Azusa Pacific University	M,D
Ball State University	M,D,O
Barry University	M,O
Bellarmine University	M,D
Bellin College	M
Bethel University (MN)	M,D,O
Blessing–Rieman College of Nursing and Health Sciences	M
Bowie State University	M
Bradley University	M,D,O
Brenau University	M
California Baptist University	M
California State University, Fresno	M
California State University, Fullerton	M,D
California State University, Stanislaus	M
Capella University	M,D
Carlow University	M
Carson-Newman University	M
Case Western Reserve University	M*
Cedar Crest College	M
Central Methodist University	M
Chatham University	M,D
Clarion University of Pennsylvania	M,D,O
Clarkson College	M,O
Cleveland State University	M,D
College of Mount Saint Vincent	M,O
The College of New Rochelle	M,O
Colorado Mesa University	M,D,O
Columbus State University	M
Concordia University Wisconsin	M
Cox College	M
Daemen College	M,D,O
Delta State University	M,D
DeSales University	M,D,O
Drexel University	M
Duke University	M,D,O*
Duquesne University	M,O
Eastern Michigan University	M,O
Edgewood College	M,D
Edinboro University of Pennsylvania	M,D
Elms College	M,D
Emmanuel College (United States)	M,O
Excelsior College	M
Felician University	M,O
Ferris State University	M
Florida National University	M
Florida Southern College	M
Florida State University	M,D,O
Framingham State University	M
Francis Marion University	M
Franklin Pierce University	M,D,O
Frostburg State University	M
Georgetown University	M,D
The George Washington University	M,D,O*
Georgia Southern University	O
Goldfarb School of Nursing at Barnes-Jewish College	M
Graceland University (IA)	M,D,O
Grand Canyon University	M,O
Grand Valley State University	M,D
Grantham University	M
Gwynedd Mercy University	M,D
Herzing University Online	M
Holy Family University	M
Holy Names University	M,O
Husson University	M,O
Immaculata University	M
Indiana State University	M,D
Indiana University Kokomo	M
Indiana University of Pennsylvania	M
Indiana University–Purdue University Fort Wayne	M,O
Indiana University–Purdue University Indianapolis	M,O
Indiana Wesleyan University	M
Jefferson College of Health Sciences	M
Kaplan University, Davenport Campus	M
Kent State University	M,D,O
Lamar University	M
La Roche College	M
La Salle University	M,D,O
Le Moyne College	M,O
Lenoir-Rhyne University	M
Lewis University	M,D
Liberty University	M,D
Loma Linda University	M
Long Island University–LIU Brooklyn	M,O
Long Island University–LIU Post	M,O
Louisiana State University Health Sciences Center	M,D,O
Lourdes University	M
Marian University (WI)	M
McKendree University	M
McMurry University	M
McNeese State University	M
Medical University of South Carolina	M
Mercy College	M
Messiah College	M
Metropolitan State University	M,D
MGH Institute of Health Professions	M,D,O
MidAmerica Nazarene University	M
Middle Tennessee State University	M
Midwestern State University	M
Millersville University of Pennsylvania	M
Millikin University	M,D
Missouri State University	M,D
Missouri Western State University	M,O
Molloy College	M,D,O
Monmouth University	M,D,O
Montana State University	M,D,O
Moravian College	M
Mount Carmel College of Nursing	M,D
Mount Mercy University	M
Mount St. Joseph University	M
Mount Saint Mary College	M,O
Nebraska Methodist College	M
Neumann University	M
New York University	M,O
Nicholls State University	M
Northeastern State University	M
Norwich University	M
Ohio University	M
Oklahoma Baptist University	M
Oklahoma City University	M,D
Oklahoma Wesleyan University	M
Old Dominion University	M
Oregon Health & Science University	M,O
Otterbein University	M,D,O
Our Lady of the Lake College	M
Pace University	M,D,O
Pennsylvania College of Health Sciences	M
Prairie View A&M University	M
Queens University of Charlotte	M
Ramapo College of New Jersey	M
Regis College (MA)	M,D,O
Regis University	M,D,O
Rivier University	M
Roberts Wesleyan College	M
Sacred Heart University	M,D,O
Sage Graduate School	D
St. Catherine University	M,D
Saint Francis Medical Center College of Nursing	M,D,O
Saint Joseph's College of Maine	M,O
Salem State University	M
Salisbury University	M
Samford University	M,D
Seattle Pacific University	M,O
Seton Hall University	M,D
Shenandoah University	M,D,O
Southern Connecticut State University	M
Southern Illinois University Edwardsville	M,O
Southern Nazarene University	M
Southern University and Agricultural and Mechanical College	M,D,O
South University	M
South University (GA)	M
State University of New York College of Technology at Delhi	M
State University of New York Empire State College	M
State University of New York Polytechnic Institute	M,O
Stevenson University	M
Stony Brook University, State University of New York	M,O
Tarleton State University	M
Teachers College, Columbia University	M,D,O
Tennessee Technological University	M
Texas A&M University	M
Texas A&M University–Corpus Christi	M
Texas Christian University	M,O
Texas Tech University Health Sciences Center	M,D,O
Texas Woman's University	M,D
Thomas Edison State University	O
Towson University	M,O
Union University	M,D,O
The University of Alabama in Huntsville	M,D,O
University of Central Arkansas	M,O
University of Detroit Mercy	M,D,O
University of Hartford	M
University of Houston	M
University of Indianapolis	M,D
University of Louisville	M,D
University of Maine	M,O
University of Mary	M,D
University of Mary Hardin-Baylor	M,D,O
University of Maryland, Baltimore	M
University of Massachusetts Medical School	M,D,O
University of Memphis	M,O
University of Missouri–Kansas City	M,D
University of Missouri–St. Louis	M,D,O
University of New Brunswick Fredericton	M
The University of North Carolina at Chapel Hill	M,D,O
The University of North Carolina at Charlotte	M,D,O
The University of North Carolina at Greensboro	M,D,O
The University of North Carolina at Pembroke	M
University of North Dakota	M,D
University of Northern Colorado	M,D
University of Phoenix–Atlanta Campus	M
University of Phoenix–Augusta Campus	M
University of Phoenix–Bay Area Campus	M,D
University of Phoenix–Charlotte Campus	M
University of Phoenix–Hawaii Campus	M
University of Phoenix–New Mexico Campus	M
University of Phoenix–North Florida Campus	M
University of Phoenix–Online Campus	M,O
University of Phoenix–Phoenix Campus	M,O
University of Phoenix–Sacramento Valley Campus	M
University of Phoenix–San Diego Campus	M
University of Phoenix–Southern California Campus	M,O
University of Phoenix–South Florida Campus	M
University of Phoenix–Utah Campus	M
University of Phoenix–Washington D.C. Campus	M,D
University of Portland	M,D
University of Rhode Island	M,D
University of Rochester	M,D*
University of St. Francis (IL)	M,D,O
University of Saint Joseph	M,D
University of Saint Mary	M
University of South Alabama	M,D,O
University of Southern Maine	M,D,O
University of South Florida	M,D,O
The University of Tennessee at Chattanooga	M,D,O
The University of Texas at Arlington	M,D
The University of Texas at Austin	M,D
The University of Texas at El Paso	M,D,O
The University of Texas at Tyler	M,D
The University of Texas Health Science Center at San Antonio	M,D,O
The University of Toledo	M,O
University of Victoria	M,D
University of Washington, Tacoma	M
University of West Georgia	M,D,O
University of Wisconsin–Eau Claire	M,D
Ursuline College	M,D
Valparaiso University	M,D,O
Villanova University	M,D,O
Virginia Commonwealth University	M,D,O
Walden University	M,D,O
Walsh University	M,D
Washington Adventist University	M
Waynesburg University	M,D
Wayne State University	O
Webster University	M
West Chester University of Pennsylvania	M,D,O
Western Connecticut State University	D
Western Governors University	M
Westminster College (UT)	M
West Virginia Wesleyan College	M,O
Wilson College	M
Winona State University	M,D,O
Winston-Salem State University	M,D
Worcester State University	M
York College of Pennsylvania	M,D

NURSING INFORMATICS

Austin Peay State University	M
Columbus State University	M
Duke University	M,D,O*
Emporia State University	M
Excelsior College	M
Ferris State University	M
Georgia State University	M,D,O
Grantham University	M
Le Moyne College	M,O
National University	M,D,O
New York University	M,O
Rutgers University–Newark	M
Seattle Pacific University	M,O
Tennessee Technological University	M
Troy University	M,D,O
The University of North Carolina at Chapel Hill	M,D,O
University of Phoenix–Bay Area Campus	M,D
University of Phoenix–Charlotte Campus	M
University of Phoenix–Phoenix Campus	M,O
University of Phoenix–Southern California Campus	M,O
University of Phoenix–Washington D.C. Campus	M,D
University of Pittsburgh	M,D*
Vanderbilt University	M,D,O*
Walden University	M,D,O
Waynesburg University	M,D

NUTRITION

Abilene Christian University	O
Adelphi University	M,D,O
Alabama Agricultural and Mechanical University	M
American College of Healthcare Sciences	M,O
American University	M,O
American University of Beirut	M
Andrews University	M,O
Appalachian State University	M
Arizona State University at the Tempe campus	M,D
Auburn University	M,D,O
Ball State University	M
Bastyr University	M,O
Baylor University	M
Benedictine University	M
Boston University	M,D
Bowling Green State University	M
Brigham Young University	M
Brooklyn College of the City University of New York	M
California State Polytechnic University, Pomona	M
California State University, Chico	M
California State University, Long Beach	M
California State University, Los Angeles	M,O
Canisius College	M,O
Case Western Reserve University	M,D*
Cedar Crest College	O
Central Michigan University	M,D,O
Central Washington University	M
Chapman University	M
Clemson University	M
College of Saint Elizabeth	M,O
Colorado State University	M,D
Columbia University	M,D*
Cornell University	M,D
Drexel University	M
D'Youville College	M
East Carolina University	M
Eastern Illinois University	M
Eastern Kentucky University	M
Eastern Michigan University	M
East Tennessee State University	M
Emory University	M,D
Florida International University	M,D
Florida State University	M,D
Framingham State University	M
George Mason University	M
Georgia Southern University	O
Georgia State University	M
Harvard University	D*
Howard University	M,D
Hunter College of the City University of New York	M
Huntington College of Health Sciences	M,D
Idaho State University	M,O
Immaculata University	M
Indiana University Bloomington	M,D
Indiana University of Pennsylvania	M
Indiana University–Purdue University Indianapolis	M,D
Instituto Tecnologico de Santo Domingo	M,O
Iowa State University of Science and Technology	M,D
James Madison University	M
Johns Hopkins University	M,D
Kansas State University	M,D
Kent State University	M
Lehman College of the City University of New York	M
Liberty University	M,O
Life University	M
Lipscomb University	M
Logan University	M,D
Loma Linda University	M,D
London Metropolitan University	M,D
Long Island University–LIU Post	M,O
Louisiana Tech University	M
Loyola University Chicago	M,D,O
Marshall University	M
Marywood University	M,O
McGill University	M,D,O
McMaster University	M,D
McNeese State University	M
Meredith College	M,O
Michigan State University	M,D
Mississippi State University	M,D
Missouri State University	M,D,O
Montclair State University	M,O
Mount Mary University	M
Mount Saint Vincent University	M
New Mexico State University	M
New York Chiropractic College	M*
New York Institute of Technology	M
New York University	M,D

North Carolina Agricultural and Technical State University	M
North Carolina State University	M,D
North Dakota State University	M,D
Northeastern University	M
Northern Illinois University	M
The Ohio State University	M,D
Ohio University	M
Oklahoma State University	M,D
Oregon Health & Science University	M,O
Oregon State University	M,D
Penn State University Park	M,D
Purdue University	M,D
Queens College of the City University of New York	M,O
Rosalind Franklin University of Medicine and Science	M
Rush University	M
Rutgers University–Newark	M,D,O
Rutgers University–New Brunswick	M,D
Sacred Heart University	M
Sage Graduate School	M,O
Saint Louis University	M
Sam Houston State University	M
San Diego State University	M
San Jose State University	M,O
Saybrook University	M,D,O
Simmons College	M,D,O
South Carolina State University	M
South Dakota State University	M,D
Southeast Missouri State University	M
Southern Illinois University Carbondale	M
State University of New York College at Oneonta	M
Stony Brook University, State University of New York	M,O
Syracuse University	M
Teachers College, Columbia University	M,D,O
Texas A&M University	M,D
Texas State University	M
Texas Tech University	M,D
Texas Woman's University	M
Tufts University	M,D,O
Tuskegee University	M
Université de Moncton	M
Université de Montréal	M,D,O
Université Laval	M,D
University at Buffalo, the State University of New York	M,D,O*
The University of Alabama	M
The University of Alabama at Birmingham	M,D
The University of Arizona	M,D
University of Arkansas for Medical Sciences	M,D,O
University of Bridgeport	M
The University of British Columbia	M,D
University of California, Berkeley	D
University of California, Davis	M,D
University of Central Oklahoma	M
University of Chicago	D
University of Cincinnati	M
University of Connecticut	M,D*
University of Delaware	M*
University of Florida	M,D
University of Georgia	M,D
University of Guelph	M,D
University of Hawaii at Manoa	M,D
University of Houston	M,D
University of Illinois at Chicago	M,D
University of Illinois at Urbana–Champaign	M,D
The University of Kansas	M,D,O*
University of Kentucky	M,D
University of Maine	M,D,O
University of Manitoba	M,D
University of Maryland, College Park	M,D
University of Massachusetts Amherst	M,D*
University of Miami	M
University of Michigan	M,D
University of Minnesota, Twin Cities Campus	M,D
University of Mississippi	M,D
University of Missouri	M,D
University of Nebraska–Lincoln	M,D
University of Nebraska Medical Center	O
University of Nevada, Las Vegas	M,D
University of Nevada, Reno	M
University of New Hampshire	M,D
University of New Haven	M,O
University of New Mexico	M
The University of North Carolina at Chapel Hill	M,D
The University of North Carolina at Greensboro	M,D
University of North Florida	M
University of Oklahoma Health Sciences Center	M
University of Pittsburgh	M*
University of Puerto Rico, Medical Sciences Campus	M,D,O
University of Puerto Rico, Rí o Piedras Campus	M
University of Rhode Island	M,D
University of Saint Joseph	M
University of Southern Mississippi	M,D
University of South Florida	M,D,O
The University of Tampa	M
The University of Tennessee	M
The University of Tennessee at Martin	M
The University of Texas at Austin	M,D
The University of Texas Southwestern Medical Center	M
University of the District of Columbia	M
University of the Incarnate Word	M
The University of Toledo	M,O
University of Toronto	M,D
University of Utah	M,D*
University of Vermont	M,D
University of Washington	M,D*
University of Wisconsin–Madison	M,D
University of Wisconsin–Stevens Point	M
University of Wisconsin–Stout	M
University of Wyoming	M
Utah State University	M,D
Virginia Polytechnic Institute and State University	M,D
Washington State University	M
Wayne State University	M,D,O
West Virginia University	M
Winthrop University	M,O

OCCUPATIONAL HEALTH NURSING

Rutgers University–Newark	M,D,O
University of Cincinnati	M,D
University of Illinois at Chicago	M,O
University of Minnesota, Twin Cities Campus	M,D
The University of North Carolina at Chapel Hill	M
University of South Florida	M,D,O
University of the Sacred Heart	M

OCCUPATIONAL THERAPY

Abilene Christian University	M
Alabama State University	M
Allen College	M,D,O
Alvernia University	M
American International College	M
Arkansas State University	D
A.T. Still University	M,D
Augusta University	M
Barry University	M
Bay Path University	M
Belmont University	M,D
Boston University	D
Brenau University	M
Cabarrus College of Health Sciences	M
California State University, Dominguez Hills	M
Chatham University	M,D
Chicago State University	M
Clarkson University	M
Cleveland State University	M
College of Saint Mary	M
The College of St. Scholastica	M
Colorado State University	M,D
Columbia University	M,D*
Concordia University Wisconsin	M
Creighton University	D
Dalhousie University	M
Dominican College	M
Dominican University of California	M
Duquesne University	M,D
D'Youville College	M
East Carolina University	M,D,O
Eastern Kentucky University	M
Eastern Michigan University	M
Eastern Washington University	M
Elizabethtown College	M
Florida Agricultural and Mechanical University	M
Florida Gulf Coast University	M
Florida International University	M
Gannon University	M,D
Governors State University	M
Grand Valley State University	M
Husson University	M
Idaho State University	M
Indiana State University	M,D
Indiana University–Purdue University Indianapolis	M,D
Ithaca College	M
James Madison University	M
Jefferson College of Health Sciences	M
Kean University	M
Keuka College	M
Le Moyne College	M
Lenoir-Rhyne University	M
Loma Linda University	M,D
Long Island University–LIU Brooklyn	M,D
Louisiana State University Health Sciences Center	M
Maryville University of Saint Louis	M
McMaster University	M
Medical University of South Carolina	M
Mercy College	M
MGH Institute of Health Professions	D
Midwestern University, Downers Grove Campus	M
Midwestern University, Glendale Campus	M
Milligan College	M
Misericordia University	M,D
Missouri State University	M
Mount Mary University	M,D
New England Institute of Technology	M
New York Institute of Technology	M
New York University	M,D
Northeastern State University	M
Nova Southeastern University	M,D*
The Ohio State University	M
Pacific University	D
Philadelphia University	M,D
Queen's University at Kingston	M,D
Radford University	M
Regis College (MA)	M,D,O
Rochester Institute of Technology	M
Rockhurst University	M
Rocky Mountain University of Health Professions	D
Rush University	M
Sacred Heart University	M
Sage Graduate School	M
Saginaw Valley State University	M
St. Ambrose University	M
St. Catherine University	M,D
Saint Francis University	M
Saint Louis University	M
Salem State University	M
Samuel Merritt University	M
San Jose State University	M,O
Seton Hall University	M
Shawnee State University	M
Shenandoah University	M
Sonoma State University	M
South University	D
Spalding University	M
Springfield College	M
Stockton University	M
Stony Brook University, State University of New York	M,D,O
Temple University	M,D*
Tennessee State University	M
Texas Tech University Health Sciences Center	M
Texas Woman's University	M,D
Thomas Jefferson University	M,D
Touro College	M,D
Towson University	M
Tufts University	M,D,O
Tuskegee University	M
Université de Montréal	O
University at Buffalo, the State University of New York	M*
The University of Alabama at Birmingham	M,O
University of Alberta	M,D
The University of British Columbia	M
University of Central Arkansas	M
The University of Findlay	M,D
University of Florida	M
University of Illinois at Chicago	M,D
University of Indianapolis	M,D
The University of Kansas	M,D*
University of Louisiana at Monroe	M
University of Manitoba	M,D
University of Mary	M
University of Mississippi Medical Center	M
University of Missouri	M
University of New England	M
University of New Hampshire	M,O
University of New Mexico	M
The University of North Carolina at Chapel Hill	M,D
University of North Dakota	M
University of Oklahoma Health Sciences Center	M
University of Pittsburgh	M*
University of Puerto Rico, Medical Sciences Campus	M
University of Puget Sound	M,D
University of St. Augustine for Health Sciences	M,D
The University of Scranton	M
University of South Alabama	M
The University of South Dakota	M,D
University of Southern California	M,D
University of Southern Indiana	M
University of Southern Maine	M
The University of Tennessee Health Science Center	M,D
The University of Texas at El Paso	M
The University of Texas Health Science Center at San Antonio	M,D
The University of Texas Medical Branch	M
The University of Texas Rio Grande Valley	M
University of the Sciences	M,D
The University of Toledo	M,D
University of Toronto	M
University of Utah	M,D*
University of Washington	M,D*
The University of Western Ontario	M
University of Wisconsin–La Crosse	M
University of Wisconsin–Madison	M,D
University of Wisconsin–Milwaukee	M,D,O
Utica College	M
Virginia Commonwealth University	M,D
Washington University in St. Louis	M,D
Wayne State University	M
West Coast University	M,D
Western Michigan University	M
Western New Mexico University	M
West Virginia University	M
Winston-Salem State University	M
Worcester State University	M
Xavier University	M

OCEAN ENGINEERING

Florida Atlantic University	M,D
Florida Institute of Technology	M,D
Massachusetts Institute of Technology	M,D,O
Memorial University of Newfoundland	M,D
Oregon State University	M,D
Princeton University	D
Stevens Institute of Technology	M,D
Texas A&M University	M,D
University of Alaska Anchorage	M,O
University of California, San Diego	M,D
University of Delaware	M,D*
University of Florida	M,D
University of Hawaii at Manoa	M,D
University of Michigan	M,D,O
University of New Hampshire	M,D,O
University of Rhode Island	M,D
Virginia Polytechnic Institute and State University	M,D,O
Woods Hole Oceanographic Institution	D

OCEANOGRAPHY

Cornell University	D
Dalhousie University	M,D
Florida Institute of Technology	M,D
Florida State University	M,D
Louisiana State University and Agricultural & Mechanical College	M,D
Massachusetts Institute of Technology	M,D,O
McGill University	M,D
Memorial University of Newfoundland	M,D
Naval Postgraduate School	M,D
North Carolina State University	M,D
Nova Southeastern University	M,D,O*
Old Dominion University	M,D
Oregon State University	M,D
Princeton University	D
Rutgers University–New Brunswick	M,D
Texas A&M University	M,D
Université du Québec à Rimouski	M,D
Université Laval	D
University of Alaska Fairbanks	M,D
The University of British Columbia	M,D
University of California, Los Angeles	M,D
University of California, San Diego	M,D
University of Colorado Boulder	M,D
University of Delaware	M,D*
University of Hawaii at Manoa	M,D
University of Maine	M,D
University of Maryland, College Park	M,D
University of Miami	M,D
University of New Hampshire	M,D,O
University of Rhode Island	M,D
University of Southern California	M,D
University of South Florida	M,D
University of Victoria	M,D
University of Washington	M,D*
University of Wisconsin–Madison	M,D
Woods Hole Oceanographic Institution	D
Yale University	D*

ONCOLOGY NURSING

Case Western Reserve University	M*
Gwynedd Mercy University	M,D
Universidad Metropolitana	M,O
University of Delaware	M,O*
University of South Florida	M,D,O

OPERATIONS RESEARCH

Air Force Institute of Technology	M,D
Bowling Green State University	M
Capella University	M
Carnegie Mellon University	D
Case Western Reserve University	M,D*
Claremont Graduate University	M,D
The College of William and Mary	M
Colorado School of Mines	M,D
Columbia University	M,D*
Cornell University	M,D
École Polytechnique de Montréal	M,D,O
Florida Institute of Technology	M,D
George Mason University	M,D,O
Georgia Institute of Technology	M,D
Georgia State University	M,D
HEC Montreal	M
Idaho State University	M
Indiana University–Purdue University Fort Wayne	M,O
Iowa State University of Science and Technology	M,D
Johns Hopkins University	M,D
Kansas State University	M,D
Massachusetts Institute of Technology	M,D
Mississippi State University	M,D
Naval Postgraduate School	M,D
New Mexico Institute of Mining and Technology	M,D
North Carolina State University	M,D
Northeastern University	M,D,O
The Ohio State University	M
Princeton University	M,D
Rutgers University–New Brunswick	D
Simon Fraser University	M,D
Southern Illinois University Edwardsville	M
Southern Methodist University	M,D
The University of Alabama in Huntsville	M,D
University of Arkansas	M,D
The University of British Columbia	M
University of California, Berkeley	M,D
University of Colorado Boulder	M
University of Colorado Denver	M,D

*M—masters degree; D—doctorate; O—other advanced degree; *—Close-Up and/or Display*

University of Delaware	M*
University of Illinois at Chicago	M,D
The University of Iowa	M,D*
University of Massachusetts Amherst	M,D*
University of Michigan	M,D
The University of North Carolina at Chapel Hill	M,D
University of Southern California	M,D,O
The University of Texas at Austin	M,D
University of Waterloo	M,D
Virginia Commonwealth University	M,D

OPTICAL SCIENCES

Air Force Institute of Technology	M,D
Alabama Agricultural and Mechanical University	M,D
Cleveland State University	M
The College of William and Mary	M,D
Delaware State University	M,D
Duke University	M*
École Polytechnique de Montréal	M,D,O
Norfolk State University	M
North Carolina Agricultural and Technical State University	M,D
The Ohio State University	M,D
Rochester Institute of Technology	M,D
Rose-Hulman Institute of Technology	M
The University of Alabama in Huntsville	M,D
The University of Arizona	M,D,O
University of Central Florida	M,D
University of Colorado Boulder	M,D
University of Dayton	M,D
University of New Mexico	M,D
The University of North Carolina at Charlotte	M,D
University of Rochester	M,D*

OPTOMETRY

Ferris State University	D
Illinois College of Optometry	D
Indiana University Bloomington	M,D
Inter American University of Puerto Rico School of Optometry	D
Marshall B. Ketchum University	M,D
Midwestern University, Glendale Campus	D
New England College of Optometry	M,D
Northeastern State University	D
Nova Southeastern University	M,D*
The Ohio State University	M,D
Pacific University	M,D
Salus University	D
Southern College of Optometry	D
State University of New York College of Optometry	D
Université de Montréal	D
The University of Alabama at Birmingham	D
University of California, Berkeley	D,O
University of Houston	D
The University of Manchester	M,D
University of Missouri–St. Louis	D
University of the Incarnate Word	D
University of Waterloo	M,D
Western University of Health Sciences	D

ORAL AND DENTAL SCIENCES

A.T. Still University	M,D,O
Augusta University	M,D
Boston University	M,D,O
Case Western Reserve University	M,O*
Columbia University	M,D,O*
Dalhousie University	
Harvard University	M,D,O*
Howard University	D,O
Idaho State University	O
Jacksonville University	O*
Loma Linda University	M,O
Marquette University	M,O
McGill University	M,D,O
Metropolitan State University	M,D
New York University	M,D,O
The Ohio State University	M,D
Oregon Health & Science University	M,D,O
Rutgers University–Newark	M,D,O
Saint Louis University	M
Seton Hill University	M,O
Stony Brook University, State University of New York	M,D,O
Temple University	M,O*
Tufts University	M,O
Université de Montréal	M,O
Université Laval	M,O
University at Buffalo, the State University of New York	M,D,O*
The University of Alabama at Birmingham	M
University of Alberta	M,D
The University of British Columbia	M,D,O
University of California, Los Angeles	M,D
University of California, San Francisco	M,D
University of Colorado Denver	M,D
University of Connecticut Health Center	M,D*
University of Detroit Mercy	M,D,O
University of Florida	M,D,O
University of Illinois at Chicago	M,D
The University of Iowa	M,D,O*
University of Kentucky	M
University of Louisville	M,D
The University of Manchester	M,D
University of Manitoba	M,D
University of Maryland, Baltimore	M,D,O
University of Michigan	M,D
University of Minnesota, Twin Cities Campus	M,D,O
University of Mississippi Medical Center	M,D
University of Missouri–Kansas City	M,D,O
University of Nevada, Las Vegas	M,D
The University of North Carolina at Chapel Hill	M,D
University of Oklahoma Health Sciences Center	M
University of Pittsburgh	M,D,O*
University of Puerto Rico, Medical Sciences Campus	O
University of Rochester	M*
University of Southern California	M,D,O
The University of Tennessee Health Science Center	M,D
The University of Toledo	M
University of Toronto	M,D
University of Washington	M,D,O*
The University of Western Ontario	M
West Virginia University	M

ORGANIC CHEMISTRY

Auburn University	M,D
Binghamton University, State University of New York	M,D*
Boston College	M,D
Brandeis University	M,D
Cleveland State University	M,D
Cornell University	D
Eastern New Mexico University	M
Florida State University	M,D
Georgetown University	D
The George Washington University	M,D*
Georgia State University	M,D
Harvard University	D*
Howard University	M,D
Indiana University Bloomington	M,D
Instituto Tecnológico y de Estudios Superiores de Monterrey, Campus Monterrey	M,D
Iowa State University of Science and Technology	M,D
Kansas State University	M,D
Laurentian University	M
Marquette University	M,D
Massachusetts Institute of Technology	M,D,O
McMaster University	M,D
Old Dominion University	M,D
Oregon State University	M,D
Purdue University	M,D
Rice University	M,D
Rutgers University–Newark	M,D
Rutgers University–New Brunswick	M,D
Seton Hall University	M,D
Southern University and Agricultural and Mechanical College	M
State University of New York College of Environmental Science and Forestry	M,D
Tufts University	M,D
University of Calgary	M,D
University of Cincinnati	M,D
University of Georgia	M,D
University of Louisville	M,D
The University of Manchester	M,D
University of Maryland, College Park	M,D
University of Massachusetts Lowell	M,D
University of Miami	M,D
University of Michigan	D
University of Missouri–Kansas City	M,D
University of Montana	M,D
University of Nebraska–Lincoln	M,D
University of Notre Dame	M,D
University of Regina	M,D
University of Southern Mississippi	M,D
The University of Tennessee	M,D
The University of Texas at Austin	D
The University of Toledo	M,D
Vanderbilt University	M,D*
Virginia Commonwealth University	M,D
Wake Forest University	M,D
Wayne State University	M,D
Wesleyan University	D
West Virginia University	M,D
Yale University	D*
Youngstown State University	M

ORGANIZATIONAL BEHAVIOR

Argosy University, Chicago	D
Arizona State University at the Tempe campus	M,D
Baruch College of the City University of New York	M,D
Benedictine University	M
Boston College	D
Brigham Young University	M
Brooklyn College of the City University of New York	M,D
California Lutheran University	M,O
Carnegie Mellon University	D
Case Western Reserve University	M,D*
Concordia University, St. Paul	M
Cornell University	M,D
Drexel University	M,D,O
Fairleigh Dickinson University, College at Florham	M,O
Florida Institute of Technology	M
Florida State University	M,D
The Graduate Center, City University of New York	D
Harvard University	D*
International Institute for Restorative Practices	M,O
John Jay College of Criminal Justice of the City University of New York	M,D
Lake Forest Graduate School of Management	M
New York University	M,D,O
Northwestern University	M*
Phillips Graduate Institute	D
Purdue University	D
Saybrook University	M,D
Silver Lake College of the Holy Family	M
Suffolk University	M,O
Towson University	O
Universidad de las Americas, A.C.	M
Université de Sherbrooke	M
University at Albany, State University of New York	M,D,O
The University of British Columbia	D
University of California, Berkeley	D
University of California, Los Angeles	M,D
University of Chicago	M,O
University of Hartford	M
University of Hawaii at Manoa	M
The University of North Carolina at Chapel Hill	D
University of Oklahoma	M,O*
University of Pittsburgh	M,D*
The University of Texas at Austin	M
University of Utah	M,D*
Wayne State University	M,D
Western International University	M
Wilfrid Laurier University	M,D

ORGANIZATIONAL MANAGEMENT

Albertus Magnus College	M
Alvernia University	D
The American College	M
American Public University System	M
American University	M,O
Antioch University Los Angeles	M
Antioch University Seattle	M
Aquinas College (MI)	M
Argosy University, Chicago	D
Argosy University, Denver	M,D
Argosy University, Hawai`i	D
Argosy University, Inland Empire	M,D
Argosy University, Los Angeles	M,D
Argosy University, Orange County	D
Argosy University, San Diego	M,D
Argosy University, San Francisco Bay Area	M,D
Argosy University, Sarasota	M,D,O
Argosy University, Schaumburg	M,D,O
Argosy University, Seattle	M,D
Argosy University, Tampa	M,D
Argosy University, Twin Cities	M,D
Argosy University, Washington DC	M,D,O
Athabasca University	M,O
Atlantic University	M
Auburn University at Montgomery	M,O
Augsburg College	M
Avila University	M
Azusa Pacific University	M
Baker University	M
Bellevue University	M
Benedictine University	M,D
Bethel University (MN)	M,D,O
Bluffton University	M
Boise State University	M,O
Boston College	D
Boston University	M
Bowling Green State University	M
Brandman University	M
Brenau University	M
Briercrest Seminary	M
Cabrini University	M
Cairn University	M,O
California Baptist University	M
California Coast University	M,D
California College of the Arts	M
California Intercontinental University	M,D
California State University, East Bay	M
California State University, Fullerton	M
Cambridge College	M
Capella University	M,D
Carlos Albizu University, Miami Campus	M,D
Carlow University	M,D,O
Carson-Newman University	M
Central Penn College	M
The Chicago School of Professional Psychology	M,D
City University of Seattle	M,O
Cleary University	M,O
Clemson University	M,D,O
Cleveland State University	M,D,O
College of Saint Elizabeth	M
College of Saint Mary	M
The College of Saint Rose	O
Colorado State University–Global Campus	M
Columbia Southern University	M
Columbus State University	M,O
Concordia College–New York	M
Concordia University (Canada)	M,O
Concordia University Ann Arbor	M
Concordia University, St. Paul	M
Crandall University	M
Creighton University	M
Dallas Baptist University	M
DePaul University	M
Duke University	M,D,O*
Duquesne University	M
Eastern Connecticut State University	M
Eastern Mennonite University	M
Eastern Michigan University	M,O
Eastern University	M,D
Edgewood College	M
Emory & Henry College	M
Emory University	M,D
Endicott College	M
Evangel University	M
Fairleigh Dickinson University, College at Florham	M,O
Fielding Graduate University	M,D,O
Florida Institute of Technology	M
Gannon University	D
Gardner-Webb University	D
Geneva College	M
George Fox University	M,D
George Mason University	M
The George Washington University	M,O*
Georgia State University	M,D
Gonzaga University	M,D
Graceland University (IA)	M,D,O
Grand Canyon University	D
Grand View University	M
Granite State College	M
Grantham University	M
Harding University	M
Hawai`i Pacific University	M
HEC Montreal	M
Husson University	M
Immaculata University	M
Indiana Tech	M
Indiana University Bloomington	M,D,O
Indiana University–Purdue University Fort Wayne	M,O
Indiana University–Purdue University Indianapolis	M,O
Indiana Wesleyan University	M,D,O
Instituto Tecnologico de Santo Domingo	M,O
Jacksonville University	M*
James Madison University	D
John F. Kennedy University	M,O
Johns Hopkins University	M
Judson University	M
Kaplan University, Davenport Campus	M
Keiser University	D
LaGrange College	M
Lenoir-Rhyne University	M
Lewis University	M
Lincoln Christian University	M
Lipscomb University	M
Louisiana Tech University	M,D
Lourdes University	M
Loyola University New Orleans	M
Malone University	M
Manhattan College	M
Manhattanville College	M*
Mansfield University of Pennsylvania	M
Marian University (WI)	M
Marlboro College	M
Maryville University of Saint Louis	M
Medaille College	M
Mercer University	M,D
Mercy College	M
Mercyhurst University	M,O
Messiah College	M,O
Mid-America Christian University	M
Midway University	M
Misericordia University	M
Mount St. Joseph University	M
National University	M,O
Neumann University	M
Newman University	M
The New School	M,O
New York University	M,D,O
Nichols College	M
North Central College	M
Northeastern University	M,D
Northern Kentucky University	M
Northwestern University	M,D*
Northwest University	M
Norwich University	M
Nyack College	M
Oakland University	M,D,O
Oklahoma Christian University	M
Olivet Nazarene University	M
Our Lady of the Lake University of San Antonio	M,D
Oxford Graduate School	M,D
Palm Beach Atlantic University	M
Peirce College	M
Pepperdine University	M,D
Peru State College	M
Pfeiffer University	M
Pinchot University	M
Point Loma Nazarene University	M
Point Park University	M
Queens University of Charlotte	M
Quinnipiac University	M
Regent University	M,D,O
Regis University	M,O
Rider University	M
Robert Morris University	M,D
Rochester Institute of Technology	O
Roosevelt University	M,D
Rutgers University–Newark	D
Sage Graduate School	M
St. Ambrose University	M
St. Catherine University	M
St. Edward's University	M
St. Joseph's College, Long Island Campus	M
St. Joseph's College, New York	M
Saint Joseph's University	M
Saint Louis University	M,D,O
Saint Mary's College of California	M
Saint Mary's University of Minnesota	M
Saybrook University	M,D
Seattle University	M,O
Shenandoah University	M,D,O
Shippensburg University of Pennsylvania	M
Siena Heights University	M,O
Simpson University	M
Southeast Missouri State University	M
Southern New Hampshire University	M,O
South University	M

South University (MI)	M
South University (SC)	M
South University (GA)	M
Southwest University	M
State University of New York College at Potsdam	M
Stockton University	D
Summit University	M,D
Syracuse University	O
Thomas Edison State University	O
Trevecca Nazarene University	M,D
Trinity Washington University	M
Trinity Western University	M,O
Troy University	M
Union Institute & University	M
United States International University–Africa	M
Université Laval	M,O
University of Alberta	D
The University of Arizona	M,D
University of Central Arkansas	D
University of Charleston	D
University of Cincinnati	M
University of Colorado Boulder	M,D
University of Dallas	M,D
The University of Findlay	M,D
University of Guelph	M
University of Hawaii at Manoa	M,D
The University of Kansas	M,D,O*
University of La Verne	M,D,O
University of Maryland Eastern Shore	D
University of Massachusetts Amherst	M,D*
University of Massachusetts Dartmouth	M,O
University of Michigan–Flint	M
University of Missouri	M,D,O
University of Nebraska at Omaha	M
University of Nevada, Las Vegas	M,D,O
University of New Haven	M,O
University of New Mexico	M
University of Northwestern–St. Paul	M
University of Pennsylvania	M,O*
University of Phoenix–Bay Area Campus	M,D
University of Phoenix–Online Campus	D,O
University of Phoenix–Washington D.C. Campus	M,D
University of Portland	M,D
University of Regina	M,O
University of St. Thomas (MN)	M,D
University of San Francisco	M
The University of South Dakota	M
University of Southern California	M
The University of Texas at San Antonio	D
University of the Incarnate Word	M,D
Upper Iowa University	M
Vanderbilt University	M,D*
Viterbo University	M,O
Walden University	M,D,O
Waldorf College	M
Warner Pacific College	M
Washington University in St. Louis	M
Wayland Baptist University	M,D
Waynesburg University	M,D
Wayne State College	M
Wayne State University	M,D
Western International University	M
Western New England University	M
West Liberty University	M
Wheeling Jesuit University	M
Wilfrid Laurier University	M,D
Wilkes University	M
William Penn University	M
Williamson College	M
Wilmington University	M,D
Woodbury University	M
Worcester Polytechnic Institute	M,D,O
Worcester State University	M
Yale University	D*

OSTEOPATHIC MEDICINE

A.T. Still University	M,D
Des Moines University	D
Edward Via College of Osteopahtic Medicine–Virginia Campus	D
Edward Via College of Osteopathic Medicine–Carolinas Campus	D
Georgia Campus–Philadelphia College of Osteopathic Medicine	D*
Kansas City University of Medicine and Biosciences	D
Lake Erie College of Osteopathic Medicine	M,D,O
Liberty University	D
Lincoln Memorial University	D
Marian University (IN)	D
Michigan State University	D
Midwestern University, Downers Grove Campus	D
Midwestern University, Glendale Campus	D
New York Institute of Technology	M,D
Nova Southeastern University	M,D,O*
Ohio University	D
Oklahoma State University Center for Health Sciences	D
Philadelphia College of Osteopathic Medicine	D*
Rocky Vista University	D
Rowan University	D
Touro University California	M,D
University of North Texas Health Science Center at Fort Worth	M,D
University of Pikeville	D
Western University of Health Sciences	D
West Virginia School of Osteopathic Medicine	D

PACIFIC AREA/PACIFIC RIM STUDIES

University of Guam	M
University of Hawaii at Manoa	M,O
University of San Francisco	M
University of Victoria	M

PALEONTOLOGY

Cornell University	M,D
Duke University	D*
East Tennessee State University	M
South Dakota School of Mines and Technology	M,D
University of Chicago	D
The University of Manchester	M,D
The University of Texas at Dallas	M,D*
West Virginia University	M,D
Yale University	D*

PAPER AND PULP ENGINEERING

Georgia Institute of Technology	M,D
North Carolina State University	M,D
State University of New York College of Environmental Science and Forestry	M,D,O
The University of Manchester	M,D
University of Minnesota, Twin Cities Campus	M,D
Western Michigan University	M,D

PARASITOLOGY

Illinois State University	M,D
Louisiana State University Health Sciences Center	D
McGill University	M,D,O
Oregon State University	M,D
Tulane University	M,D,O
University of Notre Dame	M,D
University of Prince Edward Island	M,D
University of Washington	D*

PASTORAL MINISTRY AND COUNSELING

Abilene Christian University	M,D
Ambrose University	M,O
American Baptist Seminary of the West	M
Amridge University	M,D
Anderson University (SC)	M
Andover Newton Theological School	M,D
Andrews University	M,D,O
Anna Maria College	M
Appalachian Bible College	M
Aquinas Institute of Theology	M,D,O
Argosy University, Sarasota	M,D
Asbury Theological Seminary	M,D,O
Ashland Theological Seminary	M,D,O
Assemblies of God Theological Seminary	M,D
The Athenaeum of Ohio	M,O
Atlantic School of Theology	M,O
Atlantic University	O
Austin Presbyterian Theological Seminary	M,D
Ave Maria University	M,D
Azusa Pacific University	M
Bakke Graduate University	M,D
Baptist Bible College	M
The Baptist College of Florida	M
Baptist Theological Seminary at Richmond	M,D,O
Barry University	M,D
Bethany Theological Seminary	M,O
Bethel College	M
Bethel Seminary	M,D,O
Biblical Theological Seminary	M,D,O
Biola University	M,D,O
Bob Jones University	M,D,O
Boston College	M,D,O
Briercrest Seminary	M
Brite Divinity School	M,D,O
Cairn University	M
California Baptist University	M
Calvary Bible College and Theological Seminary	M
Calvin Theological Seminary	M,D
Campbell University	M,D
Canadian Southern Baptist Seminary	M
Cardinal Stritch University	M
Carolina Christian College	M
Carolina Graduate School of Divinity	D
Catholic Theological Union	M,D,O
The Catholic University of America	M,D,O
Cedarville University	M,D
Chaminade University of Honolulu	M
Charlotte Christian College and Theological Seminary	M
Chicago Theological Seminary	M,D
Christian Theological Seminary	M,D
Christ the King Seminary	M
Cincinnati Christian University	M
City Vision University	M
Claremont Lincoln University	M
Claremont School of Theology	M,D
Columbia International University	M,D,O
Concordia University, Nebraska	M
Corban University	M,D,O
Covenant Theological Seminary	M,D,O
Criswell College	M
Dallas Baptist University	M,D
Dallas Theological Seminary	M,D,O
Denver Seminary	M,D,O
Eastern Mennonite University	M,O
Eastern University	M,D
East Texas Baptist University	M
Ecumenical Theological Seminary	D
Emory University	M,D
Evangelical Seminary	M
Fairfield University	M,O
Faith Baptist Bible College and Theological Seminary	M
Faulkner University	M
Fordham University	M,D,O
Freed-Hardeman University	M
Fresno Pacific University	M
Fuller Theological Seminary	M,D,O
Gannon University	M,O
Gardner-Webb University	M,D
Garrett-Evangelical Theological Seminary	M,D
Gateway Seminary	M,D,O
General Theological Seminary	M,D,O
George Fox University	M,D,O
Georgia Christian University	M,D
Global University	M,D
Gordon-Conwell Theological Seminary	M,D
Grace Theological Seminary	M,D,O
Grace University	M
Grand Rapids Theological Seminary of Cornerstone University	M
Greenville College	M
Hampton University	M,D,O
Harding School of Theology	M,D
Harding University	M
Hardin-Simmons University	M,D
Hartford Seminary	M,D,O
Heritage Christian University	M
Hillsdale Free Will Baptist College	M
Holmes Institute	M
Holy Names University	M,O
Houston Baptist University	M
Houston Graduate School of Theology	M,D
Howard Payne University	M
Huntington University	M,D
Iliff School of Theology	M,D
Indiana Wesleyan University	M
Inter American University of Puerto Rico, Metropolitan Campus	D
International Baptist College and Seminary	M,D
Judson University	M
The King's University	M,D,O
Kingswood University	M
Knox Theological Seminary	D
Lancaster Bible College	M,D,O
La Salle University	M,D,O
La Sierra University	M
Lee University	M
Liberty University	M,D,O
Lincoln Christian Seminary	M,D
Lipscomb University	M,D,O
Loras College	M
Louisiana College	M
Loyola Marymount University	M
Loyola University Chicago	M,O
Loyola University Maryland	M,D,O
Lutheran School of Theology at Chicago	M,D
Lutheran Theological Seminary at Gettysburg	M,D
The Lutheran Theological Seminary at Philadelphia	M,D,O
Lutheran Theological Seminary Saskatoon	M,D
Luther Rice College & Seminary	M,D
Luther Seminary	M,D
Madonna University	M
Maple Springs Baptist Bible College and Seminary	M,D,O
Maranatha Baptist University	M
Martin University	M
Marymount University	M,D
The Master's College and Seminary	M,D
McCormick Theological Seminary	M,D,O
McMaster University	M,D,O
Meadville Lombard Theological School	M,D
Mercer University	M,D
Mid-America Christian University	M
Midwestern Baptist Theological Seminary	M,D,O
Milligan College	M,D
Missouri Baptist University	M,O
Moody Bible Institute	M,O
Mount Marty College	M
Mount St. Joseph University	M,O
Neumann University	M,D,O
New Brunswick Theological Seminary	M,D
New Orleans Baptist Theological Seminary	M,D
Northern Seminary	M,D
North Greenville University	M,D
North Park Theological Seminary	M,O
Northwest Nazarene University	M
Northwest University	M
Nyack College	M,D
Oakwood University	M
Oblate School of Theology	M,D,O
Oklahoma Christian University	M
Oral Roberts University	M,D
Ottawa University	M
Pacific Rim Christian University	M
Pentecostal Theological Seminary	M,D
Pepperdine University	M
Phillips Theological Seminary	D
Phoenix Seminary	M,D,O
Piedmont International University	M,D
Pittsburgh Theological Seminary	M,D
Point Loma Nazarene University	M
Providence University College & Theological Seminary	M,D,O
Reformed Theological Seminary–Charlotte Campus	M,D
Reformed Theological Seminary–Jackson Campus	M,D,O
Reformed Theological Seminary–Orlando Campus	M,D,O
Regent University	M,D
Regis College (Canada)	M,D,O
Richmont Graduate University	M,O
Sacred Heart Major Seminary	M
St. Ambrose University	M
St. Augustine's Seminary of Toronto	M,O
St. Bernard's School of Theology and Ministry	M,O
St. Catherine University	M,O
St. John's Seminary (CA)	M
Saint John's University (MN)	M
Saint Joseph's College of Maine	M
St. Joseph's Seminary	M
Saint Leo University	M
Saint Mary-of-the-Woods College	M,O
Saint Meinrad School of Theology	M
Saint Paul University	M,D,O
Saints Cyril and Methodius Seminary	M
St. Stephen's College	M,D
St. Thomas University	M,D,O
Saint Vincent Seminary	M
Santa Clara University	M,D,O
Seattle University	M
Selma University	M
Seminary of the Immaculate Conception	M,D,O
Seton Hall University	M,O
Shasta Bible College	M
Shepherds Theological Seminary	M
Shiloh University	M,D
Simpson University	M
Sioux Falls Seminary	M
Southeastern University (FL)	M
The Southern Baptist Theological Seminary	M,D
Southern Evangelical Seminary	M,D,O
Southern Wesleyan University	M
South University (MI)	D
South University (GA)	D
Southwestern Assemblies of God University	M
Southwestern Baptist Theological Seminary	M,D,O
Southwestern Christian University	M
Spring Arbor University	M
Spring Hill College	M,O
SUM Bible College & Theological Seminary	M
Summit University	M,D
Theological University of the Caribbean	M,D
Trevecca Nazarene University	M
Trinity College (Canada)	M,D,O
Trinity International University	M,D,O
Trinity Lutheran Seminary	M
Trinity School for Ministry	M,D,O
Trinity Western University	M,D
Tyndale University College & Seminary	M,O
Unification Theological Seminary	M,D
Union University	M,D
United Theological Seminary of the Twin Cities	M,D,O
University of Chicago	M
University of Dallas	M
University of Dayton	M,D
University of Fort Lauderdale	M
University of Northwestern–St. Paul	M
University of Portland	M
University of Saint Francis (IN)	M,O
University of Saint Mary of the Lake–Mundelein Seminary	M,D
University of St. Michael's College	M,D,O
University of St. Thomas (MN)	M
University of St. Thomas (TX)	M
University of South Africa	M,D
Valparaiso University	M
Viterbo University	M,O
Walsh University	M
Wayland Baptist University	M
Wesley Biblical Seminary	M
Western Seminary	M,D,O
Western Seminary–Sacramento Campus	M,O
Western Seminary–San Jose Campus	M,O
Western Theological Seminary	M,D,O
Westminster Theological Seminary	M,D,O
Wheaton College	M,D
Wilfrid Laurier University	M,D,O
Xavier University	M
Xavier University of Louisiana	M

PATHOBIOLOGY

Auburn University	M,D
Brown University	M,D
Columbia University	M,D*
Drexel University	M,D
Johns Hopkins University	D
Kansas State University	M,D
Medical University of South Carolina	D
Michigan State University	M,D
New York University	D
Penn State University Park	M,D
Purdue University	M,D
The University of Alabama at Birmingham	D
University of Cincinnati	D
University of Connecticut	M,D*
University of Illinois at Urbana–Champaign	M,D

*M—masters degree; D—doctorate; O—other advanced degree; *—Close-Up and/or Display*

University of Missouri	M,D
University of Toronto	M,D
University of Washington	D*
University of Wyoming	M
Wake Forest University	M,D
Yale University	D*

PATHOLOGY

Albert Einstein College of Medicine	D
Baylor College of Medicine	D
Boston University	D
Case Western Reserve University	M,D*
Colorado State University	M,D
Columbia University	M,D*
Dalhousie University	M,D
Duke University	M,D*
Harvard University	D*
Indiana University–Purdue University Indianapolis	M,D
Iowa State University of Science and Technology	M,D
Johns Hopkins University	D
Loma Linda University	D
McGill University	M,D
Medical University of South Carolina	M,D
Michigan State University	M,D
New York Medical College	M,D
North Carolina State University	M,D
North Dakota State University	M,D
Purdue University	M,D
Queen's University at Kingston	M,D
Quinnipiac University	M
Rosalind Franklin University of Medicine and Science	M
Rutgers University–Newark	D
Saint Louis University	D
Stony Brook University, State University of New York	M,D
Tufts University	M,D
Université de Montréal	M,D
Université Laval	O
University at Buffalo, the State University of New York	M,D*
University of Alberta	M,D
The University of British Columbia	M,D
University of Calgary	M,D
University of California, Davis	M,D
University of California, Irvine	D
University of California, Los Angeles	M,D
University of Cincinnati	D
University of Georgia	M,D
University of Guelph	M,D,O
The University of Iowa	M*
The University of Kansas	D*
University of Manitoba	M
University of Maryland, Baltimore	M
University of Michigan	D
University of Mississippi Medical Center	D
University of Missouri	M
University of Nebraska Medical Center	M,D
University of New Mexico	M,D
The University of North Carolina at Chapel Hill	D
University of Oklahoma Health Sciences Center	D
University of Pittsburgh	D*
University of Prince Edward Island	M,D
University of Rochester	D*
University of Saskatchewan	M,D
University of Southern California	M
University of South Florida	M,D
The University of Tennessee Health Science Center	M,D
The University of Texas Medical Branch	D
The University of Toledo	M,O
University of Utah	M,D*
University of Vermont	M
University of Virginia	D
University of Washington	D*
The University of Western Ontario	M,D
University of Wisconsin–Madison	D
Vanderbilt University	D*
Virginia Commonwealth University	D
Wayne State University	D
Yale University	M,D*

PEDIATRIC NURSING

Augusta University	M,D,O
Boston College	M,D
Caribbean University	M,D
Case Western Reserve University	M*
Columbia University	M,O*
Creighton University	M,D,O
Drexel University	M
Duke University	M,D,O*
Emory University	M
Georgia State University	M,D,O
Gwynedd Mercy University	M,D
Hampton University	M,D
Kent State University	M,D,O
Lehman College of the City University of New York	M
Loma Linda University	M
Marquette University	M,D,O
Maryville University of Saint Louis	M,D
MGH Institute of Health Professions	M,D,O
Molloy College	M,D,O
New York University	M,D,O
Northeastern University	M,D,O
Old Dominion University	M
Oregon Health & Science University	M,D,O
Queen's University at Kingston	M,D,O
Rush University	D,O
St. Catherine University	M,D
San Francisco State University	M,O
Seton Hall University	M,D
Spalding University	M,D,O
Stony Brook University, State University of New York	M,D,O
Texas Christian University	M,O
Texas Tech University Health Sciences Center	M,D,O
Texas Woman's University	M,D
University of Cincinnati	M,D
University of Colorado Denver	M,D
University of Delaware	M,O*
University of Illinois at Chicago	M,O
University of Maryland, Baltimore	M
University of Michigan	M,D,O
University of Minnesota, Twin Cities Campus	M
University of Missouri	M,D,O
University of Missouri–Kansas City	M,D
University of Missouri–St. Louis	M,D,O
The University of North Carolina at Chapel Hill	M,D,O
University of Pennsylvania	M*
University of Pittsburgh	M,D*
University of Puerto Rico, Medical Sciences Campus	M
University of Rochester	M,D*
University of South Carolina	M
University of South Florida	M,D,O
The University of Texas at Austin	M,D
The University of Texas Health Science Center at San Antonio	M,D,O
The University of Toledo	M,O
University of Wisconsin–Madison	D
Vanderbilt University	M,D,O*
Villanova University	M,D,O
Virginia Commonwealth University	M,D,O
Wayne State University	M,D,O
Wright State University	M

PERFUSION

Milwaukee School of Engineering	M*
Quinnipiac University	M
Rush University	M
The University of Arizona	M,D
University of Nebraska Medical Center	M

PETROLEUM ENGINEERING

Colorado School of Mines	M,D
Louisiana State University and Agricultural & Mechanical College	M,D
Missouri University of Science and Technology	M,D
Montana Tech of The University of Montana	M
New Mexico Institute of Mining and Technology	M,D
Texas A&M University	M,D
Texas A&M University–Kingsville	M
Texas Tech University	M,D
University of Alaska Fairbanks	M
University of Alberta	M,D
University of Calgary	M,D
University of Houston	M,D
The University of Kansas	M,D*
University of Louisiana at Lafayette	M
University of Oklahoma	M,D,O*
University of Pittsburgh	M,D*
University of Regina	M,D
University of Southern California	M,D,O
The University of Texas at Austin	M,D
The University of Tulsa	M,D
University of Utah	M,D*
University of Wyoming	M,D
West Virginia University	M,D

PHARMACEUTICAL ADMINISTRATION

Columbia University	M*
Duquesne University	M
Fairleigh Dickinson University, Metropolitan Campus	M,O
Florida Agricultural and Mechanical University	M,D
Idaho State University	M,D
New Jersey Institute of Technology	M,D
Northeast Ohio Medical University	M,D,O
Nova Southeastern University	D*
The Ohio State University	M,D
Purdue University	M,D,O
Rutgers University–Newark	M
St. John's University (NY)	M
San Diego State University	M
Temple University	M*
University of Florida	M,D
University of Georgia	D
University of Houston	M,D
University of Illinois at Chicago	M,D
University of Maryland, Baltimore	M,D
University of Michigan	D
University of Minnesota, Twin Cities Campus	M,D
The University of North Carolina at Chapel Hill	M,D
University of Southern California	M
University of the Sciences	M
The University of Toledo	M
University of Utah	M,D*
University of Wisconsin–Madison	M,D
Virginia Commonwealth University	M,D
West Virginia University	M,D

PHARMACEUTICAL ENGINEERING

New Jersey Institute of Technology	M,D
University of Michigan	M,D

PHARMACEUTICAL SCIENCES

Albany College of Pharmacy and Health Sciences	M,D
Auburn University	M,D
Boston University	M,D
Butler University	M,D
Campbell University	M,D
Chapman University	M,D
Creighton University	M,D
Drexel University	M
Duquesne University	M,D
East Tennessee State University	D
Florida Agricultural and Mechanical University	M,D
Idaho State University	M,D
Irell & Manella Graduate School of Biological Sciences	D*
Johns Hopkins University	M
Long Island University–Hudson at Rockland	M,O
Long Island University–LIU Brooklyn	M,D
MCPHS University	M,D
Memorial University of Newfoundland	M,D
Mercer University	D
Northeastern University	M,D,O
Northeast Ohio Medical University	M,D,O
Oregon State University	M,D
Purdue University	M,D
Queen's University at Kingston	M,D
Rowan University	M
Rush University	M,D
Rutgers University–New Brunswick	M,D
St. John's University (NY)	M,D
South Dakota State University	M,D
Stevens Institute of Technology	M,O
Temple University	M,D*
Texas Southern University	M,D
Texas Tech University Health Sciences Center	M,D
Université de Montréal	M,D,O
Université Laval	M,D,O
University at Buffalo, the State University of New York	M,D*
University of Alberta	M,D
The University of Arizona	M,D
The University of British Columbia	M,D
University of California, Irvine	D
University of California, San Francisco	D
University of Cincinnati	M,D
University of Colorado Denver	D
University of Connecticut	M,D*
University of Florida	M,D
University of Georgia	D
University of Hawaii at Hilo	D
University of Houston	M,D
University of Illinois at Chicago	M,D
The University of Iowa	M,D*
The University of Kansas	M*
University of Kentucky	M,D
The University of Manchester	M,D
University of Manitoba	M,D
University of Maryland, Baltimore	D
University of Michigan	D
University of Minnesota, Twin Cities Campus	M,D
University of Missouri–Kansas City	D
University of Montana	M,D
University of Nebraska Medical Center	M,D
University of New Mexico	M,D
The University of North Carolina at Chapel Hill	M,D
University of Oklahoma Health Sciences Center	M,D
University of Pittsburgh	M,D*
University of Puerto Rico, Medical Sciences Campus	M,D
University of Rhode Island	M,D
University of Saskatchewan	M,D
University of South Carolina	M,D
University of Southern California	M,D,O
University of South Florida	M,D
The University of Tennessee Health Science Center	M,D
The University of Texas at Austin	M,D
University of the Pacific	M,D
University of the Sciences	M,D
The University of Toledo	M
University of Toronto	M,D
University of Utah	M,D*
University of Washington	M,D*
University of Wisconsin–Madison	M,D
Virginia Commonwealth University	M,D
Wayne State University	M,D
Western University of Health Sciences	M
West Virginia University	M,D

PHARMACOLOGY

Albany College of Pharmacy and Health Sciences	M,D
Albany Medical College	M,D
Alliant International University–San Francisco	M
American University of Beirut	M,D
Argosy University, Hawai`i	M,O
Auburn University	M,D
Augusta University	D
Baylor College of Medicine	D
Boston University	M,D
Case Western Reserve University	D*
Columbia University	M,D*
Cornell University	M,D
Creighton University	M,D
Dalhousie University	M,D
Drexel University	M,D
Duke University	D*
Duquesne University	M,D
East Carolina University	D
East Tennessee State University	D
Emory University	D
Fairleigh Dickinson University, College at Florham	M,O
Florida Agricultural and Mechanical University	M,D
Georgetown University	M,D
Howard University	M,D
Idaho State University	M,D
Indiana University–Purdue University Indianapolis	M,D
Johns Hopkins University	D
Kent State University	M,D
Loma Linda University	D
London Metropolitan University	M,D
Long Island University–LIU Brooklyn	M,D
Louisiana State University Health Sciences Center	D
Louisiana State University Health Sciences Center at Shreveport	M,D
McGill University	M,D
McMaster University	M,D
MCPHS University	M,D
Medical College of Wisconsin	D
Meharry Medical College	D
Michigan State University	M,D
Montclair State University	M
New Jersey Institute of Technology	M,D
New York Medical College	M,D
North Carolina State University	M,D
Northeastern University	M,D,O
The Ohio State University	M,D
Oregon Health & Science University	D
Oregon State University	M,D
Purdue University	M,D
Queen's University at Kingston	M,D
Rush University	M,D
Rutgers University–Newark	D
Saint Louis University	D
Southern Illinois University Carbondale	M,D
State University of New York Upstate Medical University	D
Stony Brook University, State University of New York	D
Thomas Jefferson University	M
Tufts University	M,D
Tulane University	M
Universidad Central del Caribe	M,D
Université de Montréal	M,D
Université de Sherbrooke	M,D
University at Buffalo, the State University of New York	M,D*
The University of Alabama at Birmingham	D
University of Alberta	M,D
The University of Arizona	M,D
University of Arkansas for Medical Sciences	M,D,O
The University of British Columbia	M,D
University of California, Davis	M,D
University of California, Los Angeles	M,D
University of California, San Francisco	D
University of Cincinnati	D
University of Colorado Denver	D
University of Connecticut	M,D*
University of Florida	M,D
University of Georgia	M,D
University of Guelph	M,D
University of Hawaii at Hilo	M
University of Houston	M,D
University of Illinois at Chicago	D
The University of Iowa	M,D*
The University of Kansas	M,D*
University of Kentucky	D
University of Louisville	M,D
The University of Manchester	M,D
University of Manitoba	M,D
University of Maryland, Baltimore	M,D
University of Miami	D
University of Michigan	M,D
University of Minnesota, Duluth	M,D
University of Minnesota, Twin Cities Campus	M,D
University of Mississippi Medical Center	D
University of Missouri	M,D
University of Missouri–Kansas City	D
University of Nebraska Medical Center	D
The University of North Carolina at Chapel Hill	D
University of North Dakota	M,D
University of North Texas Health Science Center at Fort Worth	M,D
University of Pennsylvania	D*
University of Prince Edward Island	M,D
University of Puerto Rico, Medical Sciences Campus	M,D
University of Rhode Island	M,D
University of Rochester	M,D*
University of Saskatchewan	M,D
The University of South Dakota	M,D
University of South Florida	M,D
The University of Tennessee Health Science Center	M,D
The University of Texas at Austin	M,D
The University of Texas Health Science Center at San Antonio	D
The University of Texas Medical Branch	M,D
University of the Sciences	M,D
The University of Toledo	M,D
University of Toronto	M,D
University of Utah	D*
University of Vermont	M,D
University of Virginia	D
University of Washington	D*
University of Wisconsin–Madison	D

University of Wisconsin–Milwaukee	M
Vanderbilt University	D*
Virginia Commonwealth University	M,D,O
Wake Forest University	D
Wayne State University	M,D
Weill Cornell Medicine	M,D
West Virginia University	M,D
Wright State University	M
Yale University	D*

PHARMACY

Albany College of Pharmacy and Health Sciences	M,D
Appalachian College of Pharmacy	D
Auburn University	D
Belmont University	D
Butler University	M,D
Campbell University	M,D
Cedarville University	M,D
Chapman University	M,D
Chicago State University	D
Creighton University	D
Drake University	D
Duquesne University	D
D'Youville College	D
East Tennessee State University	D
Ferris State University	D
Florida Agricultural and Mechanical University	D
Georgia Campus–Philadelphia College of Osteopathic Medicine	D*
Hampton University	D
Harding University	D
Howard University	D
Husson University	D
Idaho State University	M,D
Keck Graduate Institute	D
Lake Erie College of Osteopathic Medicine	M,D,O
Lebanese American University	D
Lipscomb University	M,D
Loma Linda University	D
Long Island University–LIU Brooklyn	M,D
Manchester University	D
Marshall University	D
MCPHS University	D
Medical University of South Carolina	D
Mercer University	D
Midwestern University, Downers Grove Campus	D
Midwestern University, Glendale Campus	D
North Dakota State University	M,D
Northeastern University	M,D,O
Northeast Ohio Medical University	D
Nova Southeastern University	D*
Ohio Northern University	D
The Ohio State University	M,D
Oregon State University	D
Pacific University	D
Palm Beach Atlantic University	D
Purdue University	D
Regis University	M,D,O
Roosevelt University	D
Rosalind Franklin University of Medicine and Science	D
Roseman University of Health Sciences	D
Rutgers University–New Brunswick	M,D
St. John Fisher College	D
St. Louis College of Pharmacy	D
Samford University	D
Shenandoah University	D
South Dakota State University	D
Southern Illinois University Edwardsville	D
South University (SC)	D
South University (GA)	D
Southwestern Oklahoma State University	D
Texas A&M University	D
Texas Southern University	D
Thomas Jefferson University	D
Touro University California	M,D
Universidad de Ciencias Medicas	M,D,O
University at Buffalo, the State University of New York	D*
University of Alberta	M,D
The University of Arizona	D
University of Arkansas for Medical Sciences	M,D
The University of British Columbia	M,D
University of California, San Diego	D
University of California, San Francisco	D
University of Charleston	D
University of Cincinnati	D
University of Connecticut	D*
The University of Findlay	M,D
University of Florida	M,D
University of Georgia	M,D,O
University of Hawaii at Hilo	D
University of Houston	M,D
University of Illinois at Chicago	M,D
The University of Iowa	M,D*
University of Kentucky	D
University of Louisiana at Monroe	D
The University of Manchester	M,D
University of Maryland, Baltimore	M,D
University of Michigan	D
University of Minnesota, Duluth	M,D
University of Minnesota, Twin Cities Campus	D
University of Mississippi	M,D
University of Missouri–Kansas City	D
University of Montana	M,D
University of Nebraska Medical Center	D
University of New England	D
University of New Mexico	D
University of Oklahoma Health Sciences Center	D
University of Pittsburgh	D*
University of Puerto Rico, Medical Sciences Campus	M,D
University of Rhode Island	M,D
University of Saint Joseph	D
University of South Carolina	D
University of Southern California	D
University of South Florida	M,D,O
The University of Tennessee Health Science Center	M,D
The University of Texas at Austin	D
University of the Incarnate Word	D
University of the Pacific	D
University of the Sciences	D
University of Utah	D*
University of Washington	M,D*
University of Wisconsin–Madison	D
University of Wyoming	M,D
Virginia Commonwealth University	D
Washington State University	M,D
Wayne State University	M,D
West Coast University	M,D
Western New England University	D
Western University of Health Sciences	D
West Virginia University	M,D
Wilkes University	D
Wingate University	D
Xavier University of Louisiana	D

PHILANTHROPIC STUDIES

Indiana University–Purdue University Indianapolis	M,D
Saint Mary's University of Minnesota	M

PHILOSOPHY

Acadia University	M
American University	M
Arizona State University at the Tempe campus	M,D,O
Baylor University	M,D
Binghamton University, State University of New York	M,D*
Boston College	M,D
Boston University	M,D
Bowling Green State University	M,D
Brandeis University	M
Brock University	M
Brown University	D
California Institute of Integral Studies	M,D
California State University, Long Beach	M
California State University, Los Angeles	M,O
Carleton University	M
Carnegie Mellon University	M,D
The Catholic University of America	M,D,O
Central European University	M,D
Claremont Graduate University	M,D
Cleveland State University	M,O
Collège Dominicain de Philosophie et de Théologie	M,D
Colorado State University	M
Columbia University	M,D*
Concordia University (Canada)	M
Cornell University	D
Dalhousie University	M,D
Dallas Theological Seminary	M,D,O
Delta State University	M
Dominican School of Philosophy and Theology	M,O
Dominican University of California	M
Duke University	D*
Duquesne University	M,D
Eastern Michigan University	M
Emory University	D,O
Florida State University	M,D
Fordham University	M,D
Franciscan University of Steubenville	M
George Mason University	M
Georgetown University	M,D
The George Washington University	M*
Georgia State University	M
Gonzaga University	M
The Graduate Center, City University of New York	M,D
Harrison Middleton University	M,D
Harvard University	M,D*
Houston Baptist University	M
Howard University	M
Indiana University Bloomington	M,D
Indiana University–Purdue University Indianapolis	M,O
Institute for Christian Studies	M,D
Institute for Doctoral Studies in the Visual Arts	D
Johns Hopkins University	M,D
Kent State University	M
Lake Forest College	M
Liberty University	M
Louisiana State University and Agricultural & Mechanical College	M
Loyola Marymount University	M
Loyola University Chicago	M,D
Marquette University	M,D
Massachusetts Institute of Technology	D
McGill University	M,D
McMaster University	M,D
Memorial University of Newfoundland	M,D
Miami University	M
Michigan State University	M,D
Midwestern State University	M,D
Mount St. Mary's University (MD)	M
The New School	M,D
New York University	M,D
Northern Illinois University	M
Northwestern University	D*
The Ohio State University	M,D
Ohio University	M
Oklahoma State University	M
Open University	M
Penn State University Park	M,D
Princeton University	D
Purdue University	M,D
Queen's University at Kingston	M,D
Regis College (Canada)	M,D,O
Rice University	M,D
Rutgers University–New Brunswick	D
Saint Louis University	M,D
Saint Mary's University (Canada)	M
San Diego State University	M
San Francisco State University	M
San Jose State University	M,O
Simon Fraser University	M,D
Southeastern Baptist Theological Seminary	M,D
The Southern Baptist Theological Seminary	M,D
Southern Evangelical Seminary	M,D,O
Southern Illinois University Carbondale	M,D
Stanford University	M,D
Stony Brook University, State University of New York	M,D,O
Summit University	M
Syracuse University	M,D
Teachers College, Columbia University	M,D,O
Temple University	M,D*
Texas A&M University	M,D
Texas State University	M
Texas Tech University	M
Trinity Western University	M
Tufts University	M
Tulane University	M,D
Universidad Autonoma de Guadalajara	M,D
Université de Montréal	M,D
Université de Sherbrooke	M,D,O
Université du Québec à Montréal	M,D
Université du Québec à Trois-Rivières	M,D
Université Laval	M,D
University at Albany, State University of New York	M,D
University at Buffalo, the State University of New York	M,D*
University of Alberta	M,D
The University of Arizona	M,D
University of Arkansas	M,D
The University of British Columbia	M,D
University of Calgary	M,D
University of California, Berkeley	D
University of California, Davis	M,D
University of California, Irvine	M,D
University of California, Los Angeles	M,D
University of California, Riverside	M,D
University of California, San Diego	D
University of California, Santa Barbara	D
University of California, Santa Cruz	M,D
University of Chicago	M,D
University of Cincinnati	M,D
University of Colorado Boulder	M,D
University of Connecticut	M,D*
University of Dallas	M,D
University of Florida	M,D
University of Georgia	M,D
University of Guelph	M,D
University of Hawaii at Manoa	M,D
University of Houston	M
University of Idaho	M
University of Illinois at Chicago	M,D
University of Illinois at Urbana–Champaign	M,D
The University of Iowa	D*
The University of Kansas	M,D*
University of Kentucky	M,D
University of Lethbridge	M,D
University of Louisville	M
The University of Manchester	M,D
University of Manitoba	M
University of Maryland, College Park	M,D
University of Massachusetts Amherst	M,D*
University of Memphis	M,D
University of Miami	M,D
University of Michigan	M,D
University of Minnesota, Twin Cities Campus	M,D
University of Mississippi	M,D
University of Missouri	D
University of Missouri–St. Louis	M
University of Montana	M
University of Nebraska–Lincoln	M,D
University of Nevada, Reno	M
University of New Mexico	M,D
The University of North Carolina at Chapel Hill	M,D
The University of North Carolina at Charlotte	M,O
University of North Florida	M,O
University of North Georgia	M
University of North Texas	M,D,O
University of Notre Dame	D
University of Oklahoma	M,D*
University of Oregon	M,D
University of Ottawa	M,D
University of Pennsylvania	M,D*
University of Pittsburgh	M,D*
University of Puerto Rico, Rí o Piedras Campus	M
University of Regina	M
University of Rochester	M,D*
University of St. Thomas (TX)	M,D
University of Saskatchewan	M
University of South Africa	M,D
University of South Carolina	M,D
University of Southern California	M,D
University of South Florida	M,D
The University of Tennessee	M,D
The University of Texas at Austin	D
The University of Texas at El Paso	M
The University of Texas at San Antonio	M
The University of Toledo	M
University of Toronto	M,D
University of Utah	M,D*
University of Victoria	M
University of Virginia	M,D
University of Washington	M,D*
University of Waterloo	M,D
The University of Western Ontario	M,D
University of Windsor	M
University of Wisconsin–Madison	M,D
University of Wisconsin–Milwaukee	M
University of Wyoming	M
Vanderbilt University	M,D*
Villanova University	D
Virginia Polytechnic Institute and State University	M,D,O
Washington University in St. Louis	D
Wayne State University	M,D
West Chester University of Pennsylvania	M,O
Western Michigan University	M
Wilfrid Laurier University	M
Yale University	D*
York University	M,D

PHOTOGRAPHY

Academy of Art University	M
Ball State University	M
Bard College	M
Barry University	M
Bradley University	M
Brooklyn College of the City University of New York	M
California College of the Arts	M
California Institute of the Arts	M,O
California State University, Fullerton	M
California State University, Los Angeles	M
Claremont Graduate University	M
Columbia College Chicago	M
Columbia University	M*
Cornell University	M,D
Cranbrook Academy of Art	M
East Carolina University	M
Ferris State University	M
The George Washington University	M,O*
Georgia State University	M,D
Howard University	M
Illinois State University	M
Indiana State University	M
Inter American University of Puerto Rico, San Germán Campus	M
James Madison University	M
Lesley University	M
Louisiana State University and Agricultural & Mechanical College	M
Louisiana Tech University	M
Maryland Institute College of Art	M
Marywood University	M
Massachusetts College of Art and Design	M,O
Memphis College of Art	M
Mills College	M
Minneapolis College of Art and Design	M
New Hampshire Institute of Art	M
The New School	M
New York Film Academy	M
Ohio University	M
Oklahoma City University	M
Otis College of Art and Design	M
Paris College of Art	M
Pratt Institute	M*
Rhode Island School of Design	M
Rochester Institute of Technology	M
San Jose State University	M,O
Savannah College of Art and Design	M
School of the Art Institute of Chicago	M
School of Visual Arts (NY)	M
Southern Methodist University	M
Southwest University of Visual Arts	M
Syracuse University	M
Temple University	M*
Texas Christian University	M
The University of Alabama	M
University of Alaska Fairbanks	M
University of Colorado Boulder	M

*M—masters degree; D—doctorate; O—other advanced degree; *—Close-Up and/or Display*

University of Illinois at Urbana–Champaign	M
University of Massachusetts Dartmouth	M,O
University of Memphis	M,O
University of Miami	M
University of Montana	M
University of New Mexico	M,D
University of Notre Dame	M
University of Oklahoma	M*
University of Rochester	M*
The University of South Dakota	M
University of Southern California	M
The University of Tennessee	M
University of Utah	M*
University of Victoria	M
University of Washington	M*
Virginia Commonwealth University	M,D
Wayne State University	M
Wichita State University	M
Yale University	M*

PHOTONICS

Boston University	M,D
Duke University	M*
Lehigh University	M,D
Oklahoma State University	M,D
Princeton University	D
Stevens Institute of Technology	M,D,O
The University of Alabama in Huntsville	M,D
University of Arkansas	M,D
University of California, San Diego	M,D
University of California, Santa Barbara	M,D
University of Central Florida	M,D
University of New Mexico	M,D

PHYSICAL CHEMISTRY

Auburn University	M,D
Binghamton University, State University of New York	M,D*
Boston College	M,D
Brandeis University	M,D
Cleveland State University	M,D
Cornell University	D
Dartmouth College	M,D*
Eastern New Mexico University	M
Florida State University	M,D
The George Washington University	M,D*
Georgia State University	M,D
Harvard University	D*
Howard University	M,D
Indiana University Bloomington	M,D
Iowa State University of Science and Technology	M,D
Kansas State University	M,D
Laurentian University	M
Marquette University	M,D
Massachusetts Institute of Technology	D
McMaster University	M,D
Old Dominion University	M,D
Oregon State University	M,D
Purdue University	M,D
Rice University	M,D
Rutgers University–Newark	M,D
Rutgers University–New Brunswick	M,D
Seton Hall University	M,D
Southern University and Agricultural and Mechanical College	M
Tufts University	M,D
University of Calgary	M,D
University of Cincinnati	M,D
University of Georgia	M,D
University of Louisville	M,D
The University of Manchester	M,D
University of Maryland, College Park	M,D
University of Memphis	M,D
University of Miami	M,D
University of Michigan	D
University of Missouri–Kansas City	M,D
University of Montana	M,D
University of Nebraska–Lincoln	M,D
University of Notre Dame	M,D
University of Southern California	D
University of Southern Mississippi	M,D
The University of Tennessee	M,D
The University of Texas at Austin	D
The University of Toledo	M,D
Vanderbilt University	M,D*
Virginia Commonwealth University	M,D
Wake Forest University	M,D
Wayne State University	M,D
West Virginia University	M,D
Yale University	D*
Youngstown State University	M

PHYSICAL EDUCATION

Adams State University	M
Adelphi University	M,O
Alabama Agricultural and Mechanical University	M
Alabama State University	M
Albany State University	M,O
Alcorn State University	M,O
American University of Puerto Rico	M
Arizona State University at the Tempe campus	M
Arkansas State University	M,O
Armstrong State University	M,O
Ashland University	M
Auburn University	M,D,O
Auburn University at Montgomery	M,O
Augusta University	M,O
Azusa Pacific University	M
Ball State University	M
Baylor University	M,D
Bridgewater State University	M
Brigham Young University	M
Brooklyn College of the City University of New York	M
California Baptist University	M
California State University, Dominguez Hills	M
California State University, East Bay	M
California State University, Fullerton	M
California State University, Long Beach	M
California State University, Los Angeles	M,O
California State University, Sacramento	M
California State University, Stanislaus	M
Campbell University	M
Canisius College	M,O
Caribbean University	M,D
Central Connecticut State University	M,O
Central Washington University	M
Chicago State University	M
The Citadel, The Military College of South Carolina	M
Cleveland State University	M
The College at Brockport, State University of New York	M,O
The College of New Jersey	M
Colorado State University–Pueblo	M
Columbus State University	M
Concordia University Irvine	M
Delta State University	M
East Carolina University	M,D,O
Eastern Kentucky University	M
Eastern Michigan University	M
Eastern New Mexico University	M
Eastern University	M,O
Eastern Washington University	M
East Stroudsburg University of Pennsylvania	M
East Texas Baptist University	M
Emporia State University	M
Florida Agricultural and Mechanical University	M
Florida International University	M,D,O
Fort Hays State University	M
Gardner-Webb University	M
George Mason University	M
Georgia College & State University	M
Georgia State University	M
Goucher College	M,O
Henderson State University	M
Hofstra University	M,D,O
Howard University	M
Idaho State University	M
Illinois State University	M
Indiana State University	M,D
Indiana University Bloomington	M,D
Indiana University of Pennsylvania	M
Indiana University–Purdue University Indianapolis	M
Inter American University of Puerto Rico, Metropolitan Campus	M
Inter American University of Puerto Rico, San Germán Campus	M
Ithaca College	M
Jackson State University	M
Jacksonville State University	M,O
James Madison University	M
Longwood University	M
Louisiana Tech University	M
Massachusetts College of Liberal Arts	M,O
McDaniel College	M
McGill University	M,D,O
Memorial University of Newfoundland	M
Middle Tennessee State University	M
Millersville University of Pennsylvania	M
Minnesota State University Mankato	M
Mississippi State University	M,D
Missouri State University	M
Montclair State University	M
Morehead State University	M
Murray State University	M,O
North Carolina Agricultural and Technical State University	M
North Carolina Central University	M
Northern Illinois University	M
Northwest Missouri State University	M
The Ohio State University	M,D
Ohio University	M
Old Dominion University	M
Pittsburg State University	M
Plymouth State University	M
Prairie View A&M University	M
Purdue University	M,D
Queens College of the City University of New York	M,O
Rhode Island College	M,O
Salem State University	M
Samford University	M,D,O
Shenandoah University	M,D,O
Slippery Rock University of Pennsylvania	M
Sonoma State University	M
Southern Connecticut State University	M
Southern Illinois University Carbondale	M
Southern Illinois University Edwardsville	M
Springfield College	M,D,O
State University of New York College at Cortland	M
Stony Brook University, State University of New York	M,O
Sul Ross State University	M
Tarleton State University	M
Teachers College, Columbia University	M,D
Temple University	M,D*
Tennessee State University	M
Tennessee Technological University	M
Texas Southern University	M
Texas State University	M
Texas Woman's University	M,D
Troy University	M
Union College (KY)	M
United States Sports Academy	M
Universidad del Turabo	M
Universidad Metropolitana	M
Université de Montréal	M,D,O
Université de Sherbrooke	M,O
Université du Québec à Trois-Rivières	M
The University of Akron	M
The University of Alabama	M,D
University of Alberta	M,D
University of Arkansas	M
University of Arkansas at Pine Bluff	M
The University of British Columbia	M,D
University of Dayton	M
University of Florida	M,D
University of Georgia	M,D
University of Houston	M,D
University of Idaho	M,D
University of Indianapolis	M
The University of Kansas	M,D*
University of Kentucky	M,D
University of Louisville	M,D,O
University of Maine	M,D,O
University of Manitoba	M
University of Mary	M
University of Minnesota, Twin Cities Campus	M,D,O
University of Montana	M
University of Nebraska at Kearney	M
University of Nebraska at Omaha	M,D
University of New Brunswick Fredericton	M
University of New Hampshire	M,O
University of New Mexico	D
University of North Alabama	M
The University of North Carolina at Chapel Hill	M
The University of North Carolina at Pembroke	M
The University of North Carolina Wilmington	M
University of Northern Colorado	M,D
University of Northern Iowa	M
University of North Georgia	M,O
University of Puerto Rico, Mayagüez Campus	M
University of Rhode Island	M
University of Rio Grande	M
University of South Alabama	M
University of South Carolina	M,D
University of Southern Mississippi	M,D
University of South Florida	M
The University of Tennessee at Chattanooga	M
The University of Tennessee at Martin	M
The University of Texas at Austin	M,D
The University of Toledo	M
University of Toronto	M,D
University of Victoria	M
University of Virginia	M,D
University of Washington	M,D*
The University of West Alabama	M
University of West Florida	M,D
University of Wisconsin–La Crosse	M
University of Wyoming	M
Utah State University	M
Virginia Commonwealth University	M,D,O
Wayne State College	M
Wayne State University	M,D
West Chester University of Pennsylvania	M,O
Western Kentucky University	M
Western Michigan University	M
Western Washington University	M
Westfield State University	M
West Virginia University	M,D
Wilfrid Laurier University	M
William Woods University	M,D,O
Wingate University	M,D
Winthrop University	M
Wright State University	M

PHYSICAL THERAPY

Alabama State University	D
American International College	D
Andrews University	D
Angelo State University	D
Arcadia University	D
Arkansas State University	D
Armstrong State University	D
A.T. Still University	M,D
Augusta University	D
Azusa Pacific University	D
Baylor University	D
Bellarmine University	M,D
Belmont University	M,D
Boston University	D
Bradley University	D
California State University, Fresno	M,D
California State University, Long Beach	D
California State University, Northridge	M
Campbell University	M,D
Carroll University	M,D
Central Michigan University	M,D
Chapman University	D
Chatham University	D
Clarke University	D
Clarkson University	D
Cleveland State University	D
The College of St. Scholastica	D
College of Staten Island of the City University of New York	D
Columbia University	D*
Concordia University, St. Paul	M,D,O
Concordia University Wisconsin	M,D
Creighton University	D
Daemen College	D,O
Dalhousie University	M
Des Moines University	D
Dominican College	M,D
Drexel University	M,D,O
Duke University	D*
Duquesne University	M,D
D'Youville College	D,O
East Carolina University	D
Eastern Washington University	D
East Tennessee State University	D
Elon University	D
Emory University	D
Florida Agricultural and Mechanical University	D
Florida Gulf Coast University	D
Florida International University	D
Franklin Pierce University	M,D,O
Gannon University	D
George Fox University	D
The George Washington University	D*
Georgia State University	D
Governors State University	M,D
The Graduate Center, City University of New York	D
Grand Valley State University	D
Hampton University	D
Harding University	D
Hardin-Simmons University	D
Husson University	D
Idaho State University	D
Indiana State University	M,D
Indiana University–Purdue University Indianapolis	M,D
Ithaca College	D
Langston University	D
Lebanon Valley College	D
Loma Linda University	M,D
Long Island University–LIU Brooklyn	M,D
Louisiana State University Health Sciences Center	D
Lynchburg College	D
Marquette University	D
Marshall University	D
Marymount University	D
Maryville University of Saint Louis	D
Mayo School of Health Sciences	D
McMaster University	M
Medical University of South Carolina	D
Mercer University	M,D
Mercy College	D
MGH Institute of Health Professions	M,D,O
Midwestern University, Downers Grove Campus	D
Midwestern University, Glendale Campus	D
Misericordia University	D
Missouri State University	D
Mount St. Joseph University	D
Mount Saint Mary's University (CA)	M,D,O
Nazareth College of Rochester	D
Neumann University	D
New York Institute of Technology	D
New York Medical College	D
New York University	M,D,O
Northeastern University	M,D,O
Northern Arizona University	D
Northern Illinois University	M,D
Northwestern University	D*
Nova Southeastern University	M,D*
Oakland University	D,O
The Ohio State University	D
Ohio University	D
Old Dominion University	M,D
Pacific University	M,D
Queen's University at Kingston	M,D
Radford University	D
Regis University	M,D,O
Rockhurst University	D
Rocky Mountain University of Health Professions	D
Rosalind Franklin University of Medicine and Science	M,D
Rush University	M
Rutgers University–Camden	D
Rutgers University–Newark	D
Sacred Heart University	D,O
Sage Graduate School	D
St. Ambrose University	D
St. Catherine University	D
Saint Francis University	D
Saint Louis University	M,D
Samford University	M,D
Samuel Merritt University	D
San Diego State University	D
San Francisco State University	D
Seton Hall University	D
Shenandoah University	D
Simmons College	M,D,O
Slippery Rock University of Pennsylvania	D
Sonoma State University	M
Southwest Baptist University	D
Springfield College	D
State University of New York Upstate Medical University	D
Stockton University	D
Stony Brook University, State University of New York	M,D,O
Temple University	D*

Tennessee State University	D
Texas State University	D
Texas Tech University Health Sciences Center	D
Texas Woman's University	D
Thomas Jefferson University	D
Touro College	M,D
University at Buffalo, the State University of New York	D*
The University of Alabama at Birmingham	D
University of Alberta	M,D
University of California, San Francisco	D
University of Central Arkansas	D
University of Central Florida	D
University of Colorado Denver	D
University of Connecticut	D*
University of Dayton	D
University of Delaware	D*
University of Evansville	D
The University of Findlay	M,D
University of Florida	D
University of Hartford	M,D
University of Illinois at Chicago	M,D
University of Indianapolis	M,D
The University of Iowa	M,D*
University of Jamestown	D
The University of Kansas	D*
University of Kentucky	D
University of Manitoba	M,D
University of Mary	D
University of Mary Hardin-Baylor	D
University of Maryland, Baltimore	D
University of Maryland Eastern Shore	D
University of Massachusetts Lowell	D
University of Miami	D
University of Michigan–Flint	D,O
University of Minnesota, Twin Cities Campus	M,D
University of Mississippi Medical Center	M
University of Missouri	D
University of Montana	D
University of Nebraska Medical Center	D
University of Nevada, Las Vegas	D
University of New England	D
University of New Mexico	D
The University of North Carolina at Chapel Hill	M,D
University of North Dakota	M,D
University of North Florida	M,D
University of North Georgia	D
University of Oklahoma Health Sciences Center	M
University of Pittsburgh	M,D*
University of Puerto Rico, Medical Sciences Campus	M
University of Puget Sound	D
University of Rhode Island	D
University of St. Augustine for Health Sciences	D
University of Saint Mary	D
The University of Scranton	D
University of South Alabama	D
The University of South Dakota	D
University of Southern California	M,D
University of South Florida	D
The University of Tennessee at Chattanooga	D
The University of Tennessee Health Science Center	M,D
The University of Texas at El Paso	D
The University of Texas Health Science Center at San Antonio	M,D
The University of Texas Medical Branch	M,D
The University of Texas Southwestern Medical Center	D
University of the Pacific	M,D
University of the Sciences	D
The University of Toledo	M,D
University of Toronto	M
University of Utah	D*
University of Vermont	D
University of Washington	M,D*
The University of Western Ontario	M,O
University of Wisconsin–La Crosse	D
University of Wisconsin–Madison	D
University of Wisconsin–Milwaukee	D
Utica College	D
Virginia Commonwealth University	M,D
Walsh University	D
Washington University in St. Louis	D
Wayne State University	D
West Coast University	M,D
Western Carolina University	D
Western Kentucky University	D
Western University of Health Sciences	D
West Virginia University	D
Wheeling Jesuit University	D
Wichita State University	D
Widener University	M,D
Winston-Salem State University	D
Youngstown State University	D

PHYSICIAN ASSISTANT STUDIES

Albany Medical College	M
Alderson Broaddus University	M
Arcadia University	M
A.T. Still University	M,D
Augsburg College	M
Augusta University	M
Baldwin Wallace University	M
Barry University	M
Baylor College of Medicine	M
Bay Path University	M
Bethel University (MN)	M,D,O
Bethel University (TN)	M
Boston University	M
Butler University	M,D
California Baptist University	M
Campbell University	M,D
Carroll University	M
Case Western Reserve University	M*
Central Michigan University	M,D
Chatham University	M
Christian Brothers University	M
Clarkson University	M
Cleveland State University	M
Daemen College	M
Des Moines University	M
Drexel University	M
Duke University	M*
Duquesne University	M,D
D'Youville College	M
East Carolina University	M
Eastern Michigan University	M
Eastern Virginia Medical School	M
Elon University	M
Emory University	M
Florida International University	M
Francis Marion University	M
Franklin Pierce University	M,D,O
Gannon University	M
Gardner-Webb University	M
The George Washington University	M*
Grand Valley State University	M
Harding University	M
Hofstra University	M
Idaho State University	M
Indiana State University	M,D
James Madison University	M
Jefferson College of Health Sciences	M
Johnson & Wales University	M
Keiser University	M
Kettering College	M
King's College	M
Le Moyne College	M
Lenoir-Rhyne University	M
Lock Haven University of Pennsylvania	M
Loma Linda University	M
Long Island University–LIU Brooklyn	M,D
Louisiana State University Health Sciences Center	M
Marietta College	M
Marquette University	M
Marywood University	M
MCPHS University	M
Medical University of South Carolina	M
Mercer University	M,D
Mercy College	M
Mercyhurst University	M
Methodist University	M
MGH Institute of Health Professions	M
Midwestern University, Downers Grove Campus	M
Midwestern University, Glendale Campus	M
Missouri State University	M
Monmouth University	M,D,O
New York Institute of Technology	M
Northeastern University	M,D,O
Northern Arizona University	M
Nova Southeastern University	M,D*
Ohio Dominican University	M
Oregon Health & Science University	M
Our Lady of the Lake College	M
Pace University	M
Pacific University	M
Philadelphia College of Osteopathic Medicine	M*
Philadelphia University	M
Quinnipiac University	M
Rocky Mountain College	M
Rocky Mountain University of Health Professions	M
Rosalind Franklin University of Medicine and Science	M
Rush University	M
Rutgers University–Newark	M
St. Catherine University	M
Saint Francis University	M
Saint Louis University	M
Salus University	M
Samuel Merritt University	M
Seton Hall University	M
Seton Hill University	M
Shenandoah University	M
South College	M
Southern Illinois University Carbondale	M
South University	M
South University (GA)	M
Springfield College	M
Stony Brook University, State University of New York	M,D,O
Texas Tech University Health Sciences Center	M
Thomas Jefferson University	M
Touro College	M,D
Towson University	M
Trevecca Nazarene University	M
Tufts University	M,D,O
Union College (NE)	M
The University of Alabama at Birmingham	M
University of Arkansas for Medical Sciences	M,D
University of Bridgeport	M
University of Charleston	M
University of Colorado Denver	M
University of Dayton	M
University of Detroit Mercy	M,D,O
The University of Findlay	M,D
University of Florida	M
The University of Iowa	M*
University of Kentucky	M
University of Missouri–Kansas City	M,D
University of Mount Union	M
University of Nebraska Medical Center	M
University of New England	M
University of New Mexico	M
University of North Dakota	M
University of North Texas Health Science Center at Fort Worth	M
University of Oklahoma Health Sciences Center	M
University of Pittsburgh	M*
University of St. Francis (IL)	M,O
University of Saint Francis (IN)	M
University of South Alabama	M
The University of South Dakota	M
University of Southern California	M
The University of Tennessee Health Science Center	M,D
The University of Texas Health Science Center at San Antonio	M,D
The University of Texas Medical Branch	M
The University of Texas Southwestern Medical Center	M
University of the Cumberlands	M
University of the Sciences	M
The University of Toledo	M
University of Utah	M*
University of Wisconsin–La Crosse	M
University of Wisconsin–Madison	M
Wayne State University	M
Weill Cornell Medicine	M
Western Michigan University	M
Western University of Health Sciences	M
Wichita State University	M
Yale University	M*

PHYSICS

Alabama Agricultural and Mechanical University	M,D
American University of Beirut	M,D
Arizona State University at the Tempe campus	M,D
Auburn University	M,D
Ball State University	M
Baylor University	M,D
Binghamton University, State University of New York	M,D*
Boston College	M,D
Boston University	D
Bowling Green State University	M,D
Brandeis University	M,D
Brigham Young University	M,D
Brock University	M
Brooklyn College of the City University of New York	M
Brown University	M,D
Bryn Mawr College	M,D
California Institute of Technology	D
California State University, Fresno	M
California State University, Fullerton	M
California State University, Long Beach	M
California State University, Los Angeles	M
California State University, Northridge	M
Carleton University	M,D
Carnegie Mellon University	M,D
Case Western Reserve University	M,D*
The Catholic University of America	M,D
Central Michigan University	M,D
Christopher Newport University	M
City College of the City University of New York	M,D
Clark Atlanta University	M
Clarkson University	M,D
Clark University	D
Cleveland State University	M
The College of William and Mary	M,D
Colorado School of Mines	M,D
Colorado State University	M,D
Columbia University	M,D*
Concordia University (Canada)	M,D
Cornell University	M,D
Creighton University	M
Dalhousie University	M,D
Dartmouth College	D*
Delaware State University	M,D
DePaul University	M,D
Drexel University	M,D
Duke University	D*
East Carolina University	M,D
Eastern Michigan University	M
Emory University	D
Fisk University	M
Florida Agricultural and Mechanical University	M,D
Florida Atlantic University	M,D
Florida Institute of Technology	M,D
Florida International University	M,D
Florida State University	M,D
George Mason University	M,D,O
The George Washington University	M,D*
Georgia Institute of Technology	M,D
Georgia State University	M,D
The Graduate Center, City University of New York	D
Hampton University	M,D
Harvard University	D*
Howard University	M,D
Hunter College of the City University of New York	M,D
Idaho State University	M,D
Illinois Institute of Technology	M,D
Indiana University Bloomington	M,D
Indiana University of Pennsylvania	M
Indiana University–Purdue University Indianapolis	M,D
Iowa State University of Science and Technology	M,D
Johns Hopkins University	M,D
Kansas State University	M,D
Kennesaw State University	M
Kent State University	M,D
Lakehead University	M
Lehigh University	M,D
Louisiana State University and Agricultural & Mechanical College	M,D
Louisiana Tech University	M
Marshall University	M
Massachusetts Institute of Technology	M,D
McGill University	M,D
McMaster University	D
Memorial University of Newfoundland	M,D
Miami University	M
Michigan State University	M,D
Michigan Technological University	M,D
Minnesota State University Mankato	M
Mississippi State University	M,D
Missouri State University	M
Missouri University of Science and Technology	M,D
Montana State University	M,D
Naval Postgraduate School	M,D
New Mexico Institute of Mining and Technology	M,D
New Mexico State University	M,D
New York University	M,D,O
North Carolina Agricultural and Technical State University	M
North Carolina Central University	M
North Carolina State University	M,D
North Dakota State University	M,D
Northeastern University	M,D
Northern Arizona University	M,D
Northern Illinois University	M,D
Northwestern University	D*
Oakland University	M,D
The Ohio State University	M,D
Ohio University	M,D
Oklahoma State University	M,D
Old Dominion University	M,D
Oregon State University	M,D
Pace University	M,O
Penn State University Park	M,D
Pittsburg State University	M
Portland State University	M,D
Princeton University	D
Purdue University	M,D
Queens College of the City University of New York	M
Queen's University at Kingston	M,D
Rensselaer Polytechnic Institute	M,D
Rice University	M,D
Royal Military College of Canada	M
Rutgers University–New Brunswick	M,D
St. Francis Xavier University	M
San Diego State University	M
San Francisco State University	M
San Jose State University	M,O
Simon Fraser University	M,D
South Dakota School of Mines and Technology	M,D
South Dakota State University	M
Southern Illinois University Carbondale	M,D
Southern Methodist University	M,D
Southern University and Agricultural and Mechanical College	M
Stanford University	D
State University of New York College at Cortland	M
Stephen F. Austin State University	M
Stevens Institute of Technology	M,D,O
Stony Brook University, State University of New York	M,D
Syracuse University	M,D
Teachers College, Columbia University	M,D
Temple University	M,D*
Texas A&M University	M,D
Texas Christian University	M,D
Texas State University	M
Texas Tech University	M,D
Trent University	M
Tufts University	M,D
Tulane University	M,D
Université de Moncton	M
Université de Montréal	M,D
Université de Sherbrooke	M,D
Université du Québec à Trois-Rivières	M,D
Université Laval	M,D
University at Albany, State University of New York	M,D
University at Buffalo, the State University of New York	M,D*
The University of Akron	M
The University of Alabama	M,D
The University of Alabama at Birmingham	M,D

*M—masters degree; D—doctorate; O—other advanced degree; *—Close-Up and/or Display*

The University of Alabama in Huntsville	M,D
University of Alaska Fairbanks	M,D
University of Alberta	M,D
The University of Arizona	M,D
University of Arkansas	M,D
The University of British Columbia	M,D
University of Calgary	M,D
University of California, Berkeley	D
University of California, Davis	M,D
University of California, Irvine	M,D
University of California, Los Angeles	M,D
University of California, Merced	M,D
University of California, Riverside	M,D
University of California, San Diego	M,D
University of California, Santa Barbara	D
University of California, Santa Cruz	M,D
University of Central Florida	M,D
University of Chicago	M,D
University of Cincinnati	M,D
University of Colorado Boulder	M,D
University of Colorado Colorado Springs	D
University of Connecticut	M,D*
University of Delaware	M,D*
University of Denver	M,D
University of Florida	M,D
University of Georgia	M,D
University of Guelph	M,D
University of Hawaii at Manoa	M,D
University of Houston	M,D
University of Houston–Clear Lake	M
University of Idaho	M,D
University of Illinois at Chicago	M,D
University of Illinois at Urbana–Champaign	M,D
The University of Iowa	M,D*
The University of Kansas	M,D*
University of Kentucky	M,D
University of Lethbridge	M,D
University of Louisiana at Lafayette	M
University of Louisville	M,D
University of Maine	M,D
The University of Manchester	M,D
University of Manitoba	M,D
University of Maryland, Baltimore County	M,D
University of Maryland, College Park	M,D
University of Massachusetts Amherst	M,D*
University of Massachusetts Dartmouth	M
University of Massachusetts Lowell	M,D
University of Memphis	M
University of Miami	M,D
University of Michigan	D
University of Minnesota, Duluth	M
University of Minnesota, Twin Cities Campus	M,D
University of Mississippi	M,D
University of Missouri	M,D
University of Missouri–Kansas City	M,D
University of Missouri–St. Louis	M,D
University of Nebraska–Lincoln	M,D
University of Nevada, Las Vegas	M,D
University of Nevada, Reno	M,D
University of New Brunswick Fredericton	M,D
University of New Hampshire	M,D
University of New Mexico	M,D
University of New Orleans	M,D
The University of North Carolina at Chapel Hill	M,D
University of North Dakota	M,D
University of Northern Iowa	M
University of Notre Dame	M,D
University of Oklahoma	M,D*
University of Oregon	M,D
University of Ottawa	M,D
University of Pennsylvania	M,D*
University of Pittsburgh	M,D*
University of Puerto Rico, Mayagüez Campus	M
University of Puerto Rico, Rí o Piedras Campus	M,D
University of Regina	M,D
University of Rhode Island	M,D
University of Rochester	M,D*
University of Saskatchewan	M,D
University of South Carolina	M,D
The University of South Dakota	M,D
University of Southern California	M,D
University of Southern Mississippi	M,D
University of South Florida	M,D
The University of Tennessee	M,D
The University of Texas at Arlington	M,D
The University of Texas at Austin	M,D
The University of Texas at Dallas	M,D*
The University of Texas at El Paso	M
The University of Texas at San Antonio	M,D
The University of Texas Rio Grande Valley	M
The University of Toledo	M,D
University of Toronto	M,D
The University of Tulsa	M,D
University of Utah	M,D*
University of Vermont	M
University of Victoria	M,D
University of Virginia	M,D
University of Washington	M,D*
University of Waterloo	M,D
The University of Western Ontario	M,D
University of Windsor	M,D
University of Wisconsin–Madison	M,D
University of Wisconsin–Milwaukee	M,D
Utah State University	M,D
Vanderbilt University	M,D*
Virginia Commonwealth University	M
Virginia Polytechnic Institute and State University	M,D
Wake Forest University	M,D
Washington State University	M,D
Washington University in St. Louis	D
Wayne State University	M,D
Wesleyan University	D
Western Illinois University	M
Western Kentucky University	M
Western Michigan University	M,D,O
West Virginia University	M,D
Wichita State University	M,D
Worcester Polytechnic Institute	M,D
Wright State University	M
Yale University	D*
York University	M,D

PHYSIOLOGY

Albert Einstein College of Medicine	D
Augusta University	D
Ball State University	M
Boston University	M,D
Brigham Young University	M,D
Brown University	M,D
Case Western Reserve University	M,D*
Columbia University	M,D*
Cornell University	M,D
Dalhousie University	M,D
East Carolina University	D
Eastern Michigan University	M
East Stroudsburg University of Pennsylvania	M
East Tennessee State University	D
Georgetown University	M,D
Georgia Institute of Technology	M,D
Georgia State University	M,D
Gonzaga University	M
Harvard University	M,D*
Howard University	D
Illinois State University	M,D
Indiana State University	M,D
James Madison University	M
Johns Hopkins University	M,D
Kansas State University	D
Kent State University	M,D
Loma Linda University	D
Louisiana State University Health Sciences Center	D
Louisiana State University Health Sciences Center at Shreveport	M,D
Loyola University Chicago	M,D
Marquette University	M,D
McGill University	M,D
McMaster University	M,D
Medical College of Wisconsin	D
Michigan State University	M,D
Montclair State University	M
New York Medical College	M,D
New York University	D
North Carolina State University	M,D
Northwestern University	M*
Ohio University	M,D
Oregon Health & Science University	D
Penn State University Park	M,D
Purdue University	M,D
Queen's University at Kingston	M,D
Rocky Mountain University of Health Professions	D
Rosalind Franklin University of Medicine and Science	M,D
Rush University	D
Rutgers University–Newark	D
Rutgers University–New Brunswick	M,D
Saint Louis University	D
Salisbury University	M
San Francisco State University	M
San Jose State University	M,O
Southern Illinois University Carbondale	M,D
Southern Methodist University	M
Stanford University	D
State University of New York Upstate Medical University	M,D
Stony Brook University, State University of New York	D
Syracuse University	M
Teachers College, Columbia University	M,D
Tulane University	M
Universidad Central del Caribe	M,D
Université de Montréal	M,D
Université de Sherbrooke	M,D
Université Laval	M,D
University at Buffalo, the State University of New York	M,D*
University of Alberta	M,D
The University of Arizona	M,D
University of Arkansas for Medical Sciences	M,D,O
University of Calgary	M,D
University of California, Berkeley	M,D
University of California, Davis	M,D
University of California, Irvine	D
University of California, Los Angeles	M,D
University of Central Florida	M
University of Cincinnati	D
University of Colorado Boulder	M,D
University of Colorado Denver	D
University of Connecticut	M,D*
University of Delaware	M,D*
University of Florida	M,D
University of Georgia	M,D
University of Guelph	M,D
University of Hawaii at Manoa	M,D
University of Illinois at Chicago	M,D
University of Illinois at Urbana–Champaign	M,D
The University of Iowa	M,D*
The University of Kansas	D*
University of Kentucky	D
University of Louisville	M,D
The University of Manchester	M,D
University of Manitoba	M,D
University of Massachusetts Amherst	M,D*
University of Miami	D
University of Michigan	M,D
University of Minnesota, Duluth	M,D
University of Minnesota, Twin Cities Campus	D
University of Mississippi Medical Center	D
University of Missouri	M,D
University of Nebraska Medical Center	M,D
University of Nevada, Reno	D
University of New Mexico	M,D
University of North Dakota	M,D
University of North Texas Health Science Center at Fort Worth	M,D
University of Notre Dame	M,D
University of Oklahoma Health Sciences Center	M,D
University of Oregon	M,D
University of Pennsylvania	D*
University of Prince Edward Island	M,D
University of Puerto Rico, Medical Sciences Campus	M,D
University of Rochester	M,D*
University of Saskatchewan	M,D
The University of South Dakota	M,D
University of Southern California	M
University of South Florida	M,D
The University of Tennessee	M,D
The University of Texas Medical Branch	M,D
University of Toronto	M,D
University of Utah	M,D*
University of Virginia	D
University of Washington	D*
The University of Western Ontario	M,D
University of Wisconsin–La Crosse	M
University of Wisconsin–Madison	M,D
University of Wyoming	M,D
Virginia Commonwealth University	M,D,O
Wake Forest University	D
Wayne State University	M,D
Weill Cornell Medicine	M,D
Western Michigan University	M
West Virginia University	M,D
Wright State University	M
Yale University	D*
Youngstown State University	M

PLANETARY AND SPACE SCIENCES

Air Force Institute of Technology	M,D
Alabama Agricultural and Mechanical University	M,D
American Public University System	M
Arizona State University at the Tempe campus	M,D
California Institute of Technology	M,D
Cornell University	D
Florida Institute of Technology	M,D
Hampton University	M,D
Harvard University	M,D*
Massachusetts Institute of Technology	M,D
McGill University	M,D
St. Thomas University	M,D,O
The University of Arizona	M,D
University of Arkansas	M,D
University of California, Los Angeles	M,D
University of California, Santa Cruz	M,D
University of Chicago	D
University of Hawaii at Manoa	M,D
University of Houston	M,D
University of Maryland, Baltimore County	M
University of Michigan	M,D
University of New Mexico	M,D
University of North Dakota	M
Washington University in St. Louis	D
Western Connecticut State University	M
Yale University	M,D*
York University	M,D

PLANT BIOLOGY

Arizona State University at the Tempe campus	M,D
Clemson University	M,D
Cornell University	M,D
Florida State University	M,D
Illinois State University	M,D
Indiana University Bloomington	M,D
Iowa State University of Science and Technology	M,D
Michigan State University	M,D
New York University	M,D
North Carolina State University	M,D
Northwestern University	M,D*
Ohio University	M,D
Oklahoma State University	M,D
Penn State University Park	M,D
Rutgers University–New Brunswick	M,D
Southern Illinois University Carbondale	M,D
Université Laval	M,D
University of Alberta	M,D
University of California, Berkeley	D
University of California, Davis	M,D
University of California, Riverside	M,D
University of Florida	M,D
University of Georgia	M,D
University of Illinois at Urbana–Champaign	M,D
University of Maryland, College Park	M,D
University of Massachusetts Amherst	M,D*
University of Minnesota, Twin Cities Campus	M,D
University of Missouri	M,D
University of Oklahoma	M,D*
The University of Texas at Austin	M,D
University of Vermont	M,D
Washington University in St. Louis	D
Yale University	D*

PLANT MOLECULAR BIOLOGY

Cornell University	M,D
Illinois State University	M,D
Michigan Technological University	M,D
Oregon State University	D
Rutgers University–New Brunswick	M,D
University of California, Riverside	M,D
University of Florida	M,D
University of Massachusetts Amherst	M,D*

PLANT PATHOLOGY

Auburn University	M,D
Colorado State University	M,D
Cornell University	M,D
Dalhousie University	M
Iowa State University of Science and Technology	M,D
Kansas State University	M,D
Louisiana State University and Agricultural & Mechanical College	M,D
Michigan State University	M,D
Mississippi State University	M,D
Montana State University	M,D
New Mexico State University	M
North Carolina State University	M,D
North Dakota State University	M,D
The Ohio State University	M,D
Oklahoma State University	M,D
Oregon State University	M,D
Penn State University Park	M,D
Purdue University	M,D
Rutgers University–New Brunswick	M,D
State University of New York College of Environmental Science and Forestry	M,D
Texas A&M University	M,D
The University of Arizona	M,D
University of Arkansas	M
University of California, Davis	M,D
University of California, Riverside	M,D
University of Florida	M,D
University of Georgia	M,D
University of Guelph	M,D
University of Hawaii at Manoa	M,D
University of Kentucky	M,D
University of Maine	M,D
University of Minnesota, Twin Cities Campus	M,D
The University of Tennessee	M,D
University of Wisconsin–Madison	M,D
Virginia Polytechnic Institute and State University	M,D
Washington State University	M,D
West Virginia University	M,D

PLANT PHYSIOLOGY

Cornell University	M,D
Dalhousie University	M
Purdue University	M,D
University of Manitoba	M,D
University of Massachusetts Amherst	M,D*
The University of Tennessee	M,D
Virginia Polytechnic Institute and State University	M,D

PLANT SCIENCES

Alabama Agricultural and Mechanical University	M,D
American University of Beirut	M
Brigham Young University	M,D
California State University, Fresno	M
Clemson University	M,D
Colorado State University	M,D
Cornell University	M,D
Delaware State University	M
Illinois State University	M,D
Iowa State University of Science and Technology	M,D
Kansas State University	M,D,O
Lehman College of the City University of New York	D
McGill University	M,D,O
Michigan State University	M,D
Mississippi State University	M,D
Missouri State University	M
Montana State University	M,D
New Mexico State University	M
North Carolina Agricultural and Technical State University	M
North Dakota State University	M,D
The Ohio State University	D
Oklahoma State University	M,D
Penn State University Park	M,D
Purdue University	D
South Dakota State University	M,D
Southern Illinois University Carbondale	M

State University of New York College of Environmental Science and Forestry	M,D
Tennessee State University	M,D
Texas A&M University–Kingsville	M
Texas Tech University	M,D
Tuskegee University	M
University of Arkansas	D
The University of British Columbia	M,D
University of California, Riverside	M,D
University of Connecticut	M,D*
University of Delaware	M,D*
University of Florida	D
University of Georgia	M,D
University of Hawaii at Manoa	M,D
University of Idaho	M,D
University of Kentucky	M,D
University of Maine	M,D,O
The University of Manchester	M,D
University of Manitoba	M,D
University of Massachusetts Amherst	M,D*
University of Minnesota, Twin Cities Campus	M,D
University of Missouri	M,D
University of Saskatchewan	M,D
The University of Tennessee	M
University of Vermont	M,D
University of Wisconsin–Madison	M,D
Utah State University	M,D
West Texas A&M University	M
West Virginia University	D

PLASMA PHYSICS

Princeton University	D
University of Colorado Boulder	M,D
West Virginia University	M,D

PODIATRIC MEDICINE

Barry University	D
California School of Podiatric Medicine at Samuel Merritt University	D
Des Moines University	D
Kent State University	D
Midwestern University, Glendale Campus	D
New York College of Podiatric Medicine	D
Rosalind Franklin University of Medicine and Science	D
Temple University	D*

POLITICAL SCIENCE

Acadia University	M
American Public University System	M
American University	M,D,O
The American University in Cairo	M
American University of Armenia	M
American University of Beirut	M,D
Appalachian State University	M
Arizona State University at the Tempe campus	M,D
Arkansas State University	M,O
Ashland University	M
Auburn University	M,D,O
Auburn University at Montgomery	M,D,O
Ball State University	M
Baylor University	M,D
Binghamton University, State University of New York	M,D*
Boise State University	M
Boston College	M,D
Boston University	M,D
Bowling Green State University	
Brandeis University	M,D
Brigham Young University	M
Brock University	M
Brooklyn College of the City University of New York	M
Brown University	D
California Polytechnic State University, San Luis Obispo	M
California State University, Chico	M
California State University, Fullerton	M
California State University, Long Beach	M
California State University, Los Angeles	M
California State University, Northridge	M
California State University, Sacramento	M
Carleton University	M,D
Case Western Reserve University	M,D*
The Catholic University of America	M,D
Central European University	M,D
Central Michigan University	M,O
The Citadel, The Military College of South Carolina	M
Claremont Graduate University	M,D
Clark Atlanta University	M,D
Colorado State University	M,D
Columbia University	M,D*
Concordia University (Canada)	M,D
Converse College	M
Cornell University	D
Dalhousie University	M,D
Dominican University of California	M
Duke University	M,D*
East Carolina University	M,O
Eastern Illinois University	M
Eastern Kentucky University	M
East Stroudsburg University of Pennsylvania	M
East Tennessee State University	M,O
Edinboro University of Pennsylvania	M
Emory University	D
Fairleigh Dickinson University, Metropolitan Campus	M
Florida Agricultural and Mechanical University	M
Florida Atlantic University	M
Florida International University	M,D
Florida State University	M,D
Fordham University	M
George Mason University	M,D,O
Georgetown University	M,D
The George Washington University	M,D*
Georgia State University	M,D
Governors State University	M
The Graduate Center, City University of New York	M,D
Grambling State University	M
Harvard University	M,D*
Hillsdale College	M,D
Howard University	M,D
Hult International Business School (United States)	M
Idaho State University	M,D
Illinois State University	M
Indiana University Bloomington	M,D
Indiana University–Purdue University Indianapolis	M,O
Institute for Christian Studies	M,D
The Institute of World Politics	M,O
Iowa State University of Science and Technology	M
Jackson State University	M
Jacksonville State University	M
James Madison University	M
Johns Hopkins University	M,D,O
Kansas State University	M
Kaplan University, Davenport Campus	M,O
Kent State University	M,D
Lamar University	M
Lehigh University	M
Liberty University	M
Long Island University–LIU Brooklyn	M,D,O
Long Island University–LIU Post	M,O
Louisiana State University and Agricultural & Mechanical College	M,D
Loyola University Chicago	M,D
Marquette University	M
Marshall University	M
Massachusetts Institute of Technology	M,D
McGill University	M,D
McMaster University	M,D
Memorial University of Newfoundland	M
Miami University	M
Michigan State University	M,D
Middle Tennessee State University	M
Midwestern State University	M
Mississippi College	M,O
Mississippi State University	M,D
Missouri State University	M,O
Montclair State University	M,O
New Mexico Highlands University	M
New Mexico State University	M
The New School	M,D
New York University	M,D
Northeastern Illinois University	M
Northeastern University	M,D
Northern Arizona University	M,D,O
Northern Illinois University	M,D
Northwestern University	D*
The Ohio State University	D
Ohio University	M
Oklahoma State University	M,D
Penn State University Park	M,D
Pepperdine University	M
Portland State University	M,D
Princeton University	D
Purdue University	M,D
Queen's University at Kingston	M,D
Regent University	M
Rice University	D
Roosevelt University	M
Rutgers University–Newark	M
Rutgers University–New Brunswick	M,D
St. John's University (NY)	M,O
Saint Louis University	M
Sam Houston State University	M
San Diego State University	M
San Francisco State University	M
Simon Fraser University	M,D
Sonoma State University	M,O
Southern Connecticut State University	M
Southern Illinois University Carbondale	M,D
Southern University and Agricultural and Mechanical College	M
Stanford University	M,D
Stony Brook University, State University of New York	M,D
Suffolk University	M,O
Sul Ross State University	M
Syracuse University	M,D,O
Tarleton State University	M
Teachers College, Columbia University	M,D
Temple University	M,D*
Texas A&M International University	M,D
Texas A&M University	M,D
Texas A&M University–Central Texas	M,O
Texas State University	M
Texas Tech University	M,D
Texas Woman's University	M
Tulane University	D
Universidad Nacional Pedro Henriquez Urena	M
Université de Montréal	M,D
Université du Québec à Montréal	M,D
Université Laval	M,D
University at Albany, State University of New York	M,D
University at Buffalo, the State University of New York	M,D*
The University of Akron	M
The University of Alabama	M,D
University of Alberta	M,D
The University of Arizona	M,D
University of Arkansas	M
The University of British Columbia	M,D
University of Calgary	M,D
University of California, Berkeley	D
University of California, Davis	M,D
University of California, Irvine	D
University of California, Los Angeles	M,D
University of California, Riverside	M,D
University of California, San Diego	M,D
University of California, Santa Barbara	M,D
University of California, Santa Cruz	D
University of Central Florida	M,D,O
University of Central Oklahoma	M
University of Chicago	D
University of Cincinnati	M,D
University of Colorado Boulder	M,D
University of Colorado Denver	M,D
University of Connecticut	M,D*
University of Dallas	M,D
University of Delaware	M,D*
University of Florida	M,D,O
University of Georgia	M,D
University of Guelph	M
University of Hawaii at Manoa	M,D
University of Houston	M,D
University of Idaho	M,D
University of Illinois at Chicago	M,D
University of Illinois at Springfield	M
University of Illinois at Urbana–Champaign	M,D
The University of Iowa	D*
The University of Kansas	M,D*
University of Kentucky	M,D
University of Lethbridge	M,D
University of Louisville	M
The University of Manchester	M,D
University of Manitoba	M
University of Maryland, College Park	D
University of Massachusetts Amherst	M,D*
University of Memphis	M
University of Miami	M
University of Michigan	D
University of Michigan–Flint	M
University of Minnesota, Twin Cities Campus	D
University of Mississippi	M,D
University of Missouri	M,D
University of Missouri–Kansas City	M
University of Missouri–St. Louis	M,D
University of Montana	M
University of Nebraska at Omaha	M,O
University of Nebraska–Lincoln	M,D,O
University of Nevada, Las Vegas	M,D
University of Nevada, Reno	M,D
University of New Brunswick Fredericton	M
University of New Hampshire	M,O
University of New Mexico	M,D
University of New Orleans	M,D
University of North Alabama	M
The University of North Carolina at Chapel Hill	M,D,O
The University of North Carolina at Greensboro	M,O
University of Northern British Columbia	M,D,O
University of North Georgia	M
University of North Texas	M,D,O
University of Notre Dame	D
University of Oklahoma	M,D*
University of Oregon	M,D
University of Ottawa	M,D
University of Pennsylvania	M,D,O*
University of Pittsburgh	M,D*
University of Regina	M
University of Rhode Island	M
University of Rochester	D*
University of Saskatchewan	M
University of South Africa	M,D
University of South Carolina	M,D
The University of South Dakota	M,D
University of Southern California	M,D
University of Southern Mississippi	M,D
University of South Florida	M,D,O
The University of Tennessee	M,D
The University of Texas at Arlington	M
The University of Texas at Austin	M,D
The University of Texas at Dallas	M,D*
The University of Texas at El Paso	M
The University of Texas at San Antonio	M
The University of Texas at Tyler	M
The University of Texas of the Permian Basin	M
The University of Toledo	M,O
University of Toronto	M,D
University of Utah	M,D*
University of Victoria	M,D
University of Virginia	M,D
University of Washington	M,D*
University of Waterloo	M,D
The University of Western Ontario	M,D
University of West Florida	M
University of Windsor	M
University of Wisconsin–Madison	D
University of Wisconsin–Milwaukee	M,D
University of Wyoming	M
Utah State University	M
Vanderbilt University	M,D*
Villanova University	M
Virginia Commonwealth University	M,D,O
Virginia Polytechnic Institute and State University	M,D,O
Walden University	M,D,O
Washington State University	M,D,O
Washington University in St. Louis	D
Wayne State University	M,D
Western Illinois University	M
Western Kentucky University	M
Western Michigan University	M,D
Western Washington University	M
West Virginia University	M,D
Wilfrid Laurier University	M,D
Yale University	D*
York University	M,D

POLYMER SCIENCE AND ENGINEERING

Auburn University	M,D
California Polytechnic State University, San Luis Obispo	M
Carnegie Mellon University	M
Case Western Reserve University	M,D*
The College of William and Mary	M,D
Cornell University	M,D
Eastern Michigan University	M,O
Lehigh University	M,D
North Carolina State University	D
North Dakota State University	M,D
Pittsburg State University	M
Stevens Institute of Technology	M,D,O
The University of Akron	M,D
University of Connecticut	M,D*
The University of Manchester	M,D
University of Massachusetts Amherst	M,D*
University of Massachusetts Lowell	M,D
University of Missouri–Kansas City	M,D
University of Southern Mississippi	M,D
The University of Tennessee	M,D
University of Wisconsin–Madison	M,D
Wayne State University	M,D,O

PORTUGUESE

Brigham Young University	M
Emory University	D,O
Harvard University	M,D*
Indiana University Bloomington	M,D
Michigan State University	M,D
New York University	M,D
Northwestern University	D*
The Ohio State University	M,D
Princeton University	D
Tulane University	M,D
University of California, Los Angeles	M
University of California, Santa Barbara	M,D
University of Illinois at Urbana–Champaign	M,D
University of Maryland, College Park	M,D
University of Massachusetts Amherst	M,D*
University of Massachusetts Dartmouth	M,D
University of Minnesota, Twin Cities Campus	M,D
University of New Mexico	M,D
The University of North Carolina at Chapel Hill	M,D
University of South Africa	M,D
The University of Tennessee	D
The University of Texas at Austin	M,D
University of Toronto	M,D
University of Washington	M*
University of Wisconsin–Madison	M,D
Vanderbilt University	M,D*
Yale University	D*

PROJECT MANAGEMENT

Amberton University	M
American Business & Technology University	M
American Graduate University	M,O
American InterContinental University Online	M
American Public University System	M
American University	M,O
Aspen University	M,O
Athabasca University	M,D,O
Avila University	M
Bellevue University	M
Boston University	M,O
Brandeis University	M
Brenau University	M
California Intercontinental University	M,D
Capella University	M,D
Carlow University	M
The Catholic University of America	M,O
Christian Brothers University	M,O
City University of Seattle	M,O

*M—masters degree; D—doctorate; O—other advanced degree; *—Close-Up and/or Display*

Colorado Christian University	M
Colorado State University–Global Campus	M
Colorado Technical University Colorado Springs	M,D
Colorado Technical University Denver South	M
Dallas Baptist University	M
DeSales University	M,D,O
DeVry University	M
Drexel University	M
Ellis University	M
Embry-Riddle Aeronautical University–Worldwide	M
Everglades University	M
Ferris State University	M
Florida Institute of Technology	M,D
George Mason University	M,D
The George Washington University	M,D,O*
Granite State College	M
Grantham University	M,O
Harrisburg University of Science and Technology	M
Herzing University Online	M
Kaplan University, Davenport Campus	M
King University	M
Lakeland University	M
Lasell College	M,O
Lehigh University	M
Lewis University	M
Liberty University	M,D,O
Lindenwood University	M,O
Marlboro College	M
Marymount University	M,O
Maryville University of Saint Louis	M,O
Metropolitan State University	M,D,O
Mississippi State University	M,D
Missouri State University	M
Montana Tech of The University of Montana	M
Mount Aloysius College	M
National University	M,O
New England College	M
New York University	M,D,O
Northeastern University	M
Northwestern University	M*
Northwest University	M
Norwich University	M
Oklahoma Christian University	M
Penn State Erie, The Behrend College	M
Point Loma Nazarene University	M
Polytechnic University of Puerto Rico, Miami Campus	M
Post University	M
Queen's University at Kingston	M
Regis University	M,O
Robert Morris University	M,D
Rochester Institute of Technology	O
Royal Roads University	O
Saint Leo University	M
Saint Mary's University of Minnesota	M,O
Saint Xavier University	M,O
Sam Houston State University	M
Southern Illinois University Edwardsville	M
Southern New Hampshire University	M,O
Stevens Institute of Technology	M,O
Stevenson University	M
Texas A&M University–San Antonio	M
Trident University International	M,D
Universidad del Turabo	M
Universidad Nacional Pedro Henriquez Urena	M
Université du Québec à Chicoutimi	M
Université du Québec à Montréal	M,O
Université du Québec à Rimouski	M,O
Université du Québec en Abitibi-Témiscamingue	M,O
Université du Québec en Outaouais	M,O
The University of Alabama in Huntsville	M,O
University of Alaska Anchorage	M
University of Calgary	M,D
University of California, Berkeley	O
University of Dallas	M,D
University of Denver	M,O
University of Houston	M
The University of Kansas	M*
University of Management and Technology	M,D,O
The University of Manchester	M
University of Mary	M
University of Michigan–Dearborn	M
University of Nebraska at Omaha	M,D,O
University of North Alabama	M
University of Oklahoma	M,O*
University of Ottawa	M,O
University of Phoenix–Bay Area Campus	M,D
University of Phoenix–Online Campus	M,O
University of Phoenix–Phoenix Campus	M,O
University of Phoenix–Southern California Campus	M
University of Regina	M,O
The University of Tennessee at Chattanooga	M,O
The University of Texas at Dallas	M,D*
University of Wisconsin–Platteville	M
University of Wisconsin–Stout	M
Virginia International University	M,O
Viterbo University	M
Walden University	M,D,O
Wayland Baptist University	M,D
Western Carolina University	M,O
Wright State University	M

PSYCHIATRIC NURSING

Allen College	M,D,O
Alverno College	M
American University of Beirut	M
Arizona State University at the Tempe campus	M,D,O
Augusta University	D
Boston College	M,D
Case Western Reserve University	M*
Columbia University	M,O*
Creighton University	M,D,O
Drexel University	M
Fairfield University	M,D
Georgia Southern University	M
Georgia State University	M,D,O
Hampton University	M,D
Hunter College of the City University of New York	M,O
Husson University	M,O
Kent State University	M,D,O
Lincoln Memorial University	M
McNeese State University	M,O
MGH Institute of Health Professions	M,D,O
Midwestern State University	M
Molloy College	M,D,O
Monmouth University	M,D,O
Montana State University	M,D,O
New Mexico State University	M,D
New York University	M,D,O
Nicholls State University	M
Northeastern University	M,D,O
Oregon Health & Science University	M,O
Point Loma Nazarene University	M,O
Pontifical Catholic University of Puerto Rico	M
Rivier University	M
Rush University	D
Sage Graduate School	M,O
Saint Francis Medical Center College of Nursing	M,D,O
Seattle University	M
Shenandoah University	M,D,O
Southern Arkansas University–Magnolia	M
Stony Brook University, State University of New York	M,D,O
Uniformed Services University of the Health Sciences	M,D*
University at Buffalo, the State University of New York	M,D,O*
University of Cincinnati	M,D
University of Colorado Denver	M,D
University of Delaware	M,O*
The University of Kansas	M,D,O*
University of Louisville	M,D
University of Maryland, Baltimore	M
University of Michigan–Flint	M,D,O
University of Minnesota, Twin Cities Campus	M
University of Missouri	M,D,O
University of Missouri–St. Louis	M,D,O
The University of North Carolina at Chapel Hill	M,D,O
University of North Dakota	M,D
University of Pennsylvania	M*
University of Pittsburgh	M,D*
University of Puerto Rico, Medical Sciences Campus	M
University of Rochester	M,D*
University of St. Francis (IL)	M,D,O
University of Saint Joseph	M,D
University of San Diego	M,D
University of San Francisco	D
University of South Carolina	M,O
University of Southern Maine	M,D,O
University of Southern Mississippi	M,D,O
The University of Texas at Austin	M,D
The University of Texas Health Science Center at San Antonio	M,D,O
University of Virginia	M,D
University of Wisconsin–Madison	D
Vanderbilt University	M,D,O*
Virginia Commonwealth University	M,D,O
Washington State University	M,D,O
Wayne State University	M,O
West Virginia Wesleyan College	M,O

PSYCHOANALYSIS AND PSYCHOTHERAPY

Adler Graduate School	M
Adler University	M,D,O
Argosy University, Chicago	D
Atlantic University	O
Boston Graduate School of Psychoanalysis	M,D,O
Immaculata University	M,D,O
Naropa University	M
The New School	M,D
New York University	M,D,O
Prescott College	M
Regent University	M,D

PSYCHOLOGY—GENERAL

Abilene Christian University	M
Acadia University	M
Adelphi University	M,D
Adler University	M,D,O
Alabama Agricultural and Mechanical University	M,O
Alliant International University–Fresno	M,D
Alliant International University–Los Angeles	M,D
Alliant International University–Sacramento	M,D
Alliant International University–San Diego	M,D
Alliant International University–San Francisco	M,D,O
American International College	M
American Public University System	M
American University	M,D,O
American University of Beirut	M,D
Andrews University	M,D,O
Angelo State University	M
Antioch University Los Angeles	M
Antioch University Midwest	M
Antioch University Seattle	M,D
Appalachian State University	M
Arcadia University	M,D,O
Argosy University, Atlanta	M,D,O
Argosy University, Chicago	M,D
Argosy University, Dallas	M,D
Argosy University, Denver	M,D
Argosy University, Hawai`i	M,D,O
Argosy University, Inland Empire	M,D
Argosy University, Los Angeles	M,D
Argosy University, Nashville	M,D
Argosy University, Orange County	M,D
Argosy University, Phoenix	M,D
Argosy University, Salt Lake City	M,D
Argosy University, San Diego	M,D
Argosy University, San Francisco Bay Area	M,D
Argosy University, Sarasota	M,D
Argosy University, Schaumburg	M,O
Argosy University, Seattle	M,D,O
Argosy University, Tampa	M,D
Argosy University, Twin Cities	M,D,O
Argosy University, Washington DC	M,D
Arizona State University at the Tempe campus	M,D
Arkansas Tech University	M
Auburn University	M,D
Auburn University at Montgomery	M
Augusta University	M
Austin Peay State University	M
Avila University	M
Azusa Pacific University	M,D
Ball State University	M
Barry University	M,O
Baylor University	M,D
Binghamton University, State University of New York	D*
Biola University	D
Boston College	D
Boston Graduate School of Psychoanalysis	M
Boston University	M,D
Bowling Green State University	M,D
Brandeis University	M,D
Brandman University	M
Brenau University	M
Bridgewater State University	M
Brigham Young University	D
Brock University	M,D
Brooklyn College of the City University of New York	M,D
Brown University	M,D
Bucknell University	M
California Coast University	M
California Institute of Integral Studies	M,D
California Lutheran University	M,D
California Polytechnic State University, San Luis Obispo	M
California State Polytechnic University, Pomona	M
California State University, Chico	M
California State University, Dominguez Hills	M
California State University, Fresno	M
California State University, Fullerton	M
California State University, Long Beach	M
California State University, Los Angeles	M
California State University, Northridge	M
California State University, Sacramento	M
California State University, San Bernardino	M
California State University, San Marcos	M
California State University, Stanislaus	M
Cambridge College	M,O
Cameron University	M
Capella University	M,D
Cardinal Stritch University	M
Carleton University	M,D
Carlos Albizu University	M,D
Carlos Albizu University, Miami Campus	M,D
Carnegie Mellon University	D
Case Western Reserve University	M,D*
Castleton University	M
The Catholic University of America	M,D
Central Connecticut State University	M
Central Michigan University	M,D,O
Central Washington University	M
Chestnut Hill College	M,D,O
The Chicago School of Professional Psychology	M,D
The Chicago School of Professional Psychology at Irvine	D
The Chicago School of Professional Psychology: Online	M,D
The Citadel, The Military College of South Carolina	M,O
City College of the City University of New York	M,D
Claremont Graduate University	M,D,O
Clayton State University	M
Clemson University	D
Cleveland State University	M,D,O
The College at Brockport, State University of New York	M
College of Saint Elizabeth	M,D,O
College of St. Joseph	M
Colorado State University	M,D
Columbia University	M,D*
Concordia University (Canada)	M
Concordia University Chicago	M
Concordia University Wisconsin	M
Connecticut College	M
Cornell University	D
Dalhousie University	M,D
Dartmouth College	D*
DePaul University	M,D
Drexel University	M,D
Duke University	D*
Duquesne University	D
East Central University	M
Eastern Illinois University	M,O
Eastern Kentucky University	M,O
Eastern Michigan University	M,D
Eastern Washington University	M
East Tennessee State University	D
Emory University	D
Emporia State University	M
Evangel University	M
Fairleigh Dickinson University, College at Florham	M,O
Fairleigh Dickinson University, Metropolitan Campus	M,D,O
Fayetteville State University	M
Fielding Graduate University	M,D,O
Fisk University	M
Fitchburg State University	O
Florida Agricultural and Mechanical University	M
Florida Atlantic University	M
Florida Institute of Technology	M,D
Florida International University	M,D
Florida State University	M,D
Fordham University	M,D
Fort Hays State University	M,O
Framingham State University	M
Francis Marion University	M,O
Frostburg State University	M
Gardner-Webb University	M
Geneva College	M
George Mason University	M,D,O
Georgetown University	D
The George Washington University	M,D,O*
Georgia Institute of Technology	M,D
Georgia Southern University	M,D
Georgia State University	D
Goddard College	M
Golden Gate University	M,D,O
Governors State University	M
The Graduate Center, City University of New York	D
Grand Canyon University	D
Hampton University	M
Hardin-Simmons University	M
Harvard University	D*
Hofstra University	M,D
Hood College	M
Houston Baptist University	M
Howard University	M,D
Humboldt State University	M
Hunter College of the City University of New York	M
Idaho State University	D
Illinois Institute of Technology	M,D
Illinois State University	M,D,O
Immaculata University	M,D,O
Indiana State University	M,D
Indiana University Bloomington	D
Indiana University of Pennsylvania	M,D
Indiana University–Purdue University Indianapolis	M,D
Inter American University of Puerto Rico, Metropolitan Campus	M,D
Inter American University of Puerto Rico, San Germán Campus	M,D
Iona College	M,O
Iowa State University of Science and Technology	D
Jackson State University	D
Jacksonville State University	M
James Madison University	M
John F. Kennedy University	M,D,O
Johns Hopkins University	D
Kansas State University	M,D
Kean University	M
Keiser University	M,D
Kent State University	M,D
Lakehead University	M,D
Lamar University	M
La Salle University	M,D
Laurentian University	M
Lehigh University	M,D
Lesley University	M,D,O
LeTourneau University	M
Lewis & Clark College	M,O
Lipscomb University	M,O
Loma Linda University	D
Long Island University–LIU Brooklyn	M,D,O
Long Island University–LIU Post	M,O
Louisiana State University and Agricultural & Mechanical College	M,D
Louisiana Tech University	M,D
Loyola University Chicago	M,D
Loyola University Maryland	M,D,O
Madonna University	M
Mansfield University of Pennsylvania	M
Marietta College	M
Marist College	M,O
Marquette University	D
Marshall University	M,D,O
Martin University	M
Marywood University	M
McGill University	M,D

McMaster University	M,D
McNeese State University	M
Medaille College	M,D
Memorial University of Newfoundland	M,D
Mercy College	M
Metropolitan State University	M,D
Miami University	M,D
Michigan School of Professional Psychology	M,D
Michigan State University	M,D
Middle Tennessee State University	M,O
Millersville University of Pennsylvania	M
Minnesota State University Mankato	M,D
Mississippi State University	M,D
Missouri State University	M,O
Monmouth University	M,O
Montana State University	M
Montana State University Billings	M
Montclair State University	M
Morehead State University	M
Morgan State University	M,D
Mount Aloysius College	M
Murray State University	M
National Louis University	M,D,O
National University	M,O
New Mexico Highlands University	M
New Mexico State University	M,D
The New School	M,D
New York University	M,D,O
Norfolk State University	M,D
North Carolina Central University	M
North Carolina State University	D
Northcentral University	M,D,O
North Dakota State University	M,D
Northeastern State University	M
Northeastern University	M,D
Northern Arizona University	M
Northern Illinois University	M,D
Northern Michigan University	M,O
Northwestern State University of Louisiana	M
Northwestern University	D*
Northwest Missouri State University	M
Northwest University	M,D
Notre Dame de Namur University	M
Nova Southeastern University	M,D,O*
The Ohio State University	D
Ohio University	M,D
Oklahoma State University	M,D
Old Dominion University	M,D
Oregon State University	M,D
Our Lady of the Lake University of San Antonio	M
Pace University	M
Pacifica Graduate Institute	M,D
Pacific University	M,D
Palo Alto University	M,D
Penn State Harrisburg	M,D,O
Penn State University Park	M,D
Pepperdine University	M,D
Philadelphia College of Osteopathic Medicine	M,D,O*
Pittsburg State University	M
Pontifical Catholic University of Puerto Rico	M,D
Pontificia Universidad Catolica Madre y Maestra	M
Portland State University	M,D,O
Princeton University	D
Purdue University	D
Queens College of the City University of New York	M,O
Queen's University at Kingston	M,D
Radford University	M,D,O
Rhode Island College	M,O
Rice University	M,D
Rivier University	M
Rochester Institute of Technology	M,O
Roosevelt University	M,D
Rosalind Franklin University of Medicine and Science	M,D
Rowan University	M,O
Rutgers University–Camden	M
Rutgers University–Newark	D
Rutgers University–New Brunswick	D
Sage Graduate School	M,O
St. Cloud State University	M,D
St. John's University (NY)	M,D
Saint Joseph's University	M,O
Saint Louis University	M,D
Saint Mary's University (Canada)	M,D
Salem State University	M,O
Sam Houston State University	M,D,O
San Diego State University	M,D
San Francisco State University	M,O
San Jose State University	M,O
Saybrook University	M,D
The Seattle School of Theology and Psychology	M
Seattle University	M
Seton Hall University	M,D,O
Shippensburg University of Pennsylvania	M
Simon Fraser University	M,D
Sofia University	M,D
Southeastern Baptist Theological Seminary	M,D
Southeastern Louisiana University	M
Southern Adventist University	M
Southern California Seminary	M,D
Southern Connecticut State University	M
Southern Illinois University Carbondale	M,D
Southern Illinois University Edwardsville	M,O
Southern Methodist University	D
Southern Nazarene University	M
Southern New Hampshire University	M,O
Southern Oregon University	M
Southern University and Agricultural and Mechanical College	M
Southwestern College (NM)	O
Spalding University	M,D
Stanford University	D
State University of New York at New Paltz	M,O
State University of New York at Plattsburgh	M,O
Stephen F. Austin State University	M
Stony Brook University, State University of New York	M,D
Suffolk University	M,D,O
Sul Ross State University	M
Teachers College, Columbia University	M,D
Temple University	M,D*
Tennessee State University	M
Texas A&M International University	M
Texas A&M University	M,D
Texas A&M University–Corpus Christi	M
Texas A&M University–Kingsville	M
Texas A&M University–Texarkana	M
Texas Christian University	M,D
Texas Southern University	M
Texas State University	M
Texas Tech University	M,D
Texas Woman's University	M,D,O
Tiffin University	M
Tufts University	M,D
Tulane University	M,D
Uniformed Services University of the Health Sciences	D*
Union College (KY)	M
Universidad de las Americas, A.C.	M
Universidad de las Américas Puebla	M
Université de Montréal	M,D
Université de Sherbrooke	M
Université du Québec à Montréal	D
Université du Québec à Trois-Rivières	D,O
Université Laval	D
University at Albany, State University of New York	M,D
University at Buffalo, the State University of New York	M,D*
The University of Akron	M,D
The University of Alabama	D
The University of Alabama at Birmingham	M,D
The University of Alabama in Huntsville	M
University of Alaska Anchorage	M,D
University of Alaska Fairbanks	D
University of Alberta	M,D
University of Arkansas	M,D
University of Arkansas at Little Rock	M
The University of British Columbia	M,D
University of Calgary	M,D
University of California, Berkeley	D
University of California, Davis	D
University of California, Irvine	D
University of California, Los Angeles	M,D
University of California, Merced	M,D
University of California, Riverside	D
University of California, San Diego	D
University of California, Santa Barbara	D
University of California, Santa Cruz	D
University of Central Arkansas	M,D,O
University of Central Florida	M,D
University of Central Missouri	M,D,O
University of Central Oklahoma	M
University of Chicago	D
University of Cincinnati	D
University of Colorado Boulder	M,D
University of Colorado Colorado Springs	M,D
University of Connecticut	M,D*
University of Dallas	M
University of Dayton	M
University of Delaware	D*
University of Denver	M,D
University of Florida	M,D
University of Georgia	M,D
University of Guelph	M,D
University of Hartford	M,D
University of Hawaii at Manoa	M,D,O
University of Houston	M,D
University of Houston–Clear Lake	M
University of Houston–Victoria	M
University of Idaho	M
University of Illinois at Chicago	M,D
University of Illinois at Urbana–Champaign	M,D
University of Indianapolis	M,D
The University of Iowa	M,D,O*
The University of Kansas	M,D*
University of Kentucky	M,D
University of La Verne	M,D
University of Lethbridge	M,D
University of Louisiana at Lafayette	M
University of Louisiana at Monroe	M
University of Louisville	D
University of Maine	M,D
The University of Manchester	M,D
University of Manitoba	M,D
University of Maryland, Baltimore County	M,D
University of Maryland, College Park	M,D
University of Massachusetts Amherst	M,D*
University of Massachusetts Dartmouth	M,O
University of Massachusetts Lowell	M
University of Memphis	M,D,O
University of Miami	M,D
University of Michigan	D,O
University of Minnesota, Twin Cities Campus	D
University of Missouri	M,D
University of Missouri–Kansas City	M,D
University of Missouri–St. Louis	M,D,O
University of Montana	M,D,O
University of Nebraska at Omaha	M,D,O
University of Nebraska–Lincoln	M,D
University of Nevada, Las Vegas	M,D,O
University of Nevada, Reno	M,D
University of New Brunswick Fredericton	M,D
University of New Brunswick Saint John	M,D
University of New Hampshire	D
University of New Mexico	D
University of New Orleans	M,D
The University of North Carolina at Chapel Hill	D
The University of North Carolina at Charlotte	M,D,O
The University of North Carolina at Greensboro	M,D
The University of North Carolina Wilmington	M
University of North Dakota	M,D
University of Northern British Columbia	M,D,O
University of Northern Colorado	M,D
University of Northern Iowa	M
University of North Florida	M
University of North Texas	M,D,O
University of Notre Dame	D
University of Oklahoma	M,D,O*
University of Oregon	M,D
University of Ottawa	D
University of Pennsylvania	D*
University of Philosophical Research	M
University of Phoenix–Jersey City Campus	M
University of Phoenix–Online Campus	M,O
University of Phoenix–Phoenix Campus	M
University of Phoenix–Southern Arizona Campus	M
University of Phoenix–Southern California Campus	M
University of Phoenix–Washington D.C. Campus	M,D
University of Pittsburgh	D*
University of Puerto Rico, Rí o Piedras Campus	M,D
University of Regina	M,D
University of Rhode Island	M,D
University of Rochester	D*
University of Saint Francis (IN)	M,O
University of Saint Mary	M
University of St. Thomas (MN)	M,D,O
University of Saskatchewan	M,D
University of South Africa	M,D
University of South Alabama	M
University of South Carolina	M,D
The University of South Dakota	M,D
University of Southern California	M,D
University of Southern Mississippi	M,D
University of South Florida	D
University of South Florida, St. Petersburg	M
The University of Tennessee	M,D
The University of Tennessee at Chattanooga	M
The University of Texas at Arlington	M,D
The University of Texas at Austin	D
The University of Texas at Dallas	M,D*
The University of Texas at El Paso	M,D
The University of Texas at San Antonio	M,D
The University of Texas at Tyler	M
The University of Texas of the Permian Basin	M
The University of Texas Rio Grande Valley	M
University of the Incarnate Word	M
University of the Pacific	M
University of the Rockies	M,D
University of the West	M
The University of Toledo	M,D
University of Toronto	M,D
The University of Tulsa	M,D
University of Utah	D*
University of Vermont	D
University of Victoria	M,D
University of Virginia	M,D
University of Washington	D*
University of Waterloo	M,D
The University of Western Ontario	M,D
University of West Florida	M
University of West Georgia	M,D,O
University of Windsor	M,D
University of Wisconsin–Eau Claire	M,O
University of Wisconsin–La Crosse	M,O
University of Wisconsin–Madison	D
University of Wisconsin–Milwaukee	M,D
University of Wisconsin–Oshkosh	M
University of Wisconsin–Whitewater	M,O
University of Wyoming	M,D
Utah State University	M,D
Valdosta State University	M,O
Valparaiso University	M
Vanderbilt University	D*
Villanova University	M
Virginia Commonwealth University	D
Virginia Polytechnic Institute and State University	M,D
Virginia State University	M,D
Wake Forest University	M
Walden University	M,D,O
Washburn University	M
Washington State University	M,D
Washington University in St. Louis	D
Wayne State University	M,D
Webster University	M
West Chester University of Pennsylvania	M
Western Carolina University	M
Western Illinois University	M,O
Western Kentucky University	M,O
Western Michigan University	M,D
Western Washington University	M
Westfield State University	M
West Texas A&M University	M
West Virginia University	M,D
Wheaton College	M,D
Wichita State University	D
Widener University	
Wilfrid Laurier University	M,D
William Carey University	M
William James College	M,D,O
Winthrop University	M,O
Wisconsin School of Professional Psychology	M,D
Wright Institute	D
Wright State University	M,D
Xavier University	M,D
Yale University	D*
Yeshiva University	M,D
York University	M,D
Youngstown State University	M

PUBLIC ADMINISTRATION

Adelphi University	O
Adler University	M,D,O
Albany State University	M
American Public University System	M
American University	M,D,O
The American University in Cairo	M,O
American University of Beirut	M,D
Anna Maria College	M
Appalachian State University	M
Argosy University, Chicago	M,D
Argosy University, Dallas	M,D,O
Argosy University, Denver	M,D
Argosy University, Inland Empire	M,D
Argosy University, Los Angeles	M,D
Argosy University, Orange County	M,D,O
Argosy University, Phoenix	M,D
Argosy University, Salt Lake City	M,D
Argosy University, San Diego	M,D
Argosy University, San Francisco Bay Area	M,D
Argosy University, Sarasota	M,D,O
Argosy University, Schaumburg	M,D,O
Argosy University, Seattle	M,D
Argosy University, Tampa	M,D
Argosy University, Twin Cities	M,D
Argosy University, Washington DC	M,D,O
Arizona State University at the Tempe campus	M,D
Arkansas State University	M,O
Auburn University	M,D,O
Auburn University at Montgomery	M,D,O
Azusa Pacific University	M
Ball State University	M,O
Barry University	M
Baruch College of the City University of New York	M
Baylor University	M,D
Belhaven University (MS)	M
Bellevue University	M
Binghamton University, State University of New York	M*
Boise State University	M,D,O
Bowie State University	M
Bowling Green State University	M
Brandman University	M
Bridgewater State University	M
Brigham Young University	M
California Baptist University	M
California Lutheran University	M
California State Polytechnic University, Pomona	M
California State University, Bakersfield	M
California State University, Chico	M
California State University, Dominguez Hills	M
California State University, East Bay	M
California State University, Fresno	M
California State University, Fullerton	M

*M—masters degree; D—doctorate; O—other advanced degree; *—Close-Up and/or Display*

California State University, Long Beach	M
California State University, Los Angeles	M
California State University, Northridge	M,O
California State University, Sacramento	M
California State University, San Bernardino	M
California State University, Stanislaus	M
Capella University	M,D
Carleton University	M,D
Carnegie Mellon University	M
Central European University	M,D
Central Michigan University	M,O
Cheyney University of Pennsylvania	M
City College of the City University of New York	M,D
Clark Atlanta University	M
Clark University	M,O
Clemson University	M,O
Cleveland State University	M,D,O
The College at Brockport, State University of New York	M,O
College of Charleston	M
The College of New Rochelle	M
College of Saint Elizabeth	M
Columbia University	M*
Columbus State University	M
Concordia University (Canada)	M,D
Concordia University Wisconsin	M
Copenhagen Business School	M,D
Cumberland University	M
Dalhousie University	M,O
DePaul University	M
DeVry University	M
Drake University	M
Duquesne University	M,O
East Carolina University	M,O
Eastern Kentucky University	M
Eastern Michigan University	M,O
Eastern Washington University	M
East Stroudsburg University of Pennsylvania	M
East Tennessee State University	M,O
The Evergreen State College	M
Excelsior College	M
Fairfield University	M
Fairleigh Dickinson University, College at Florham	M
Fairleigh Dickinson University, Metropolitan Campus	M,O
Florida Agricultural and Mechanical University	M
Florida Atlantic University	M,D
Florida Gulf Coast University	M
Florida Institute of Technology	M,D
Florida International University	M,D
Florida National University	M
Florida State University	M,D,O
Framingham State University	M
Gallaudet University	M,D,O
Gannon University	M
George Mason University	M,D,O
The George Washington University	M,D*
Georgia College & State University	M
Georgia Southern University	M
Georgia State University	M,D
Golden Gate University	M,D,O
Governors State University	M
Grambling State University	M
Grand Canyon University	M
Grand Valley State University	M
Hamline University	M,D
Harrisburg University of Science and Technology	M
Harvard University	M*
Hilbert College	M
Hood College	M
Howard University	M
Idaho State University	M
Illinois Institute of Technology	M
Indiana State University	M
Indiana University Bloomington	M,D,O
Indiana University Kokomo	M,O
Indiana University Northwest	M,O
Indiana University–Purdue University Indianapolis	M,O
Institute of Public Administration	M,O
Instituto Tecnológico y de Estudios Superiores de Monterrey, Campus Ciudad Juárez	M
International University in Geneva	M,D
Iowa State University of Science and Technology	M
Jackson State University	M,D
James Madison University	M
John Jay College of Criminal Justice of the City University of New York	M
Johns Hopkins University	M,O
Kansas State University	M
Kean University	M
Kennesaw State University	M
Kent State University	M,D
Kentucky State University	M,D
Kutztown University of Pennsylvania	M
Lamar University	M
Liberty University	M,D,O
Lincoln University (MO)	M
Lindenwood University	M
London Metropolitan University	M,D
Long Island University–Hudson at Rockland	M,O
Long Island University–LIU Brooklyn	M,O
Long Island University–LIU Post	M,O
Louisiana State University and Agricultural & Mechanical College	M,D
Marist College	M
Marshall University	M
Marywood University	M
McMaster University	M,D
Metropolitan College of New York	M
Metropolitan State University	M,D,O
Mid-America Christian University	M
Middlebury Institute of International Studies at Monterey	M
Minnesota State University Mankato	M
Mississippi State University	M,D
Missouri State University	M,O
Montana State University	M
Montana State University Billings	M
Morehead State University	M
National University	M
New Charter University	M
New Mexico State University	M
New York University	M,D,O
North Carolina Central University	M
North Carolina State University	M,D
Northeastern University	M,D
Northern Arizona University	M,D,O
Northern Illinois University	M
Northern Kentucky University	M,O
Northern Michigan University	M
Northwestern University	M*
Norwich University	M
Notre Dame de Namur University	M
Nova Southeastern University	M*
Oakland University	M,O
Ohio Dominican University	M
The Ohio State University	M,D
Ohio University	M
Old Dominion University	M,D
Pace University	M
Park University	M,O
Penn State Harrisburg	M,D,O
Pontifical Catholic University of Puerto Rico	M
Portland State University	M,D
Post University	M
Regent University	M
Rhode Island College	M
Roger Williams University	M
Roosevelt University	M
Rutgers University–Camden	M
Rutgers University–Newark	M,D
Saginaw Valley State University	M
St. John's University (NY)	M,O
Saint Louis University	M,D,O
St. Mary's University (United States)	M,O
Saint Peter's University	M
St. Thomas University	M,O
Sam Houston State University	M
San Diego State University	M
San Francisco State University	M
San Jose State University	M,O
Savannah State University	M
Seattle University	M
Seton Hall University	M,O
Shippensburg University of Pennsylvania	M
Sonoma State University	M,O
Southeast Missouri State University	M
Southern Arkansas University–Magnolia	M
Southern Illinois University Carbondale	M
Southern Illinois University Edwardsville	M
Southern University and Agricultural and Mechanical College	M
Southern Utah University	M
South University (GA)	M
South University (AL)	M
South University	M
Stephen F. Austin State University	M
Strayer University	M
Suffolk University	M,O
Syracuse University	M,D
Tarleton State University	M
Tennessee State University	M,D
Texas A&M International University	M
Texas A&M University	M,O
Texas A&M University–Corpus Christi	M
Texas Southern University	M
Texas State University	M
Texas Tech University	M,D
Thomas Edison State University	M
Trident University International	M,D
Trine University	M
Troy University	M
Tufts University	O
Université de Moncton	M
Université de Sherbrooke	M
Université du Québec à Montréal	M
Université du Québec, École nationale d'administration publique	D,O
University at Albany, State University of New York	M,D,O
The University of Akron	M
The University of Alabama	M,D
The University of Alabama at Birmingham	M
University of Alaska Anchorage	M
University of Alaska Southeast	M
The University of Arizona	M,D,O
University of Arkansas	M
University of Arkansas at Little Rock	M
University of Baltimore	M,D
University of Central Florida	M,O
University of Central Oklahoma	M
University of Colorado Colorado Springs	M
University of Colorado Denver	M,D
University of Connecticut	M*
University of Dayton	M
University of Delaware	M*
University of Evansville	M
The University of Findlay	M,D
University of Georgia	M,D
University of Guam	M
University of Guelph	M
University of Hawaii at Manoa	M,O
University of Houston	M,D
University of Idaho	M,D
University of Illinois at Chicago	M,D
University of Illinois at Springfield	M,D,O
The University of Kansas	M,D*
University of Kentucky	M,D
University of La Verne	M,D
University of Louisville	M,D
University of Management and Technology	M,O
University of Manitoba	M
University of Maryland, College Park	M
University of Massachusetts Amherst	M*
University of Massachusetts Boston	M
University of Massachusetts Dartmouth	M,O
University of Memphis	M,O
University of Michigan–Dearborn	M
University of Michigan–Flint	M
University of Missouri	M,D,O
University of Missouri–Kansas City	M,D
University of Missouri–St. Louis	M,D,O
University of Montana	M
University of Nebraska at Omaha	M,D,O
University of Nevada, Las Vegas	M,D,O
University of Nevada, Reno	M
University of New Brunswick Fredericton	M
University of New Hampshire	M,O
University of New Haven	M,O
University of New Mexico	M
University of New Orleans	M
The University of North Carolina at Chapel Hill	M
The University of North Carolina at Charlotte	M,O
The University of North Carolina at Pembroke	M
The University of North Carolina Wilmington	M,O
University of North Dakota	M
University of North Florida	M,O
University of North Texas	M,D,O
University of Oklahoma	M*
University of Ottawa	D,O
University of Pennsylvania	M,O*
University of Phoenix–Atlanta Campus	M
University of Phoenix–Augusta Campus	M
University of Phoenix–Bay Area Campus	M,D
University of Phoenix–Central Valley Campus	M
University of Phoenix–Colorado Campus	M
University of Phoenix–Colorado Springs Downtown Campus	M
University of Phoenix–Columbus Georgia Campus	M
University of Phoenix–Dallas Campus	M
University of Phoenix–Hawaii Campus	M
University of Phoenix–Houston Campus	M
University of Phoenix–Jersey City Campus	M
University of Phoenix–Las Vegas Campus	M
University of Phoenix–North Florida Campus	M
University of Phoenix–Online Campus	M,O
University of Phoenix–Phoenix Campus	M
University of Phoenix–Sacramento Valley Campus	M
University of Phoenix–San Antonio Campus	M
University of Phoenix–San Diego Campus	M
University of Phoenix–Southern California Campus	M
University of Phoenix–South Florida Campus	M
University of Phoenix–Washington D.C. Campus	M,D
University of Pittsburgh	M,D*
University of Puerto Rico, Río Piedras Campus	M
University of Regina	M,D,O
University of Rhode Island	M
University of St. Thomas (TX)	M
University of San Francisco	M
University of South Africa	M,D
University of South Alabama	M
University of South Carolina	M
The University of South Dakota	M,D
University of Southern California	M,O
University of Southern Indiana	M
University of South Florida	O
The University of Tennessee	M
The University of Tennessee at Chattanooga	M,O
The University of Texas at Arlington	M
The University of Texas at Austin	M,D
The University of Texas at Dallas	M,D*
The University of Texas at San Antonio	M
The University of Texas at Tyler	M
The University of Texas Rio Grande Valley	M
University of the District of Columbia	M
University of the Virgin Islands	M
The University of Toledo	M,O
University of Utah	M,D*
University of Vermont	M
University of Victoria	M,D
University of Washington	M,D*
University of West Florida	M
University of West Georgia	M,D,O
The University of Winnipeg	M
University of Wisconsin–Oshkosh	M
University of Wyoming	M
Upper Iowa University	M
Villanova University	M
Virginia Commonwealth University	M,O
Virginia International University	M
Virginia Polytechnic Institute and State University	M,D,O
Walden University	M,D,O
Waldorf College	M
Washington Adventist University	M
Wayne State University	M
Webster University	M
West Chester University of Pennsylvania	M,O
Western International University	M
Western Kentucky University	M
Western Michigan University	M,D,O
West Virginia University	M
Wichita State University	M
Widener University	M
Wilmington University	M,D
Wright State University	M
York University	M

PUBLIC AFFAIRS

American University	M
Arizona State University at the Tempe campus	M,D
Cleveland State University	D
Concordia University (Canada)	O
Cornell University	M
Florida International University	M,D
George Mason University	M
The George Washington University	M,O*
Indiana University Bloomington	M,D,O
Indiana University Northwest	M,O
Indiana University of Pennsylvania	M
Indiana University–Purdue University Indianapolis	M,O
Indiana University South Bend	M
The Institute of World Politics	M,O
Jackson State University	M,D
McMaster University	M,D
Merrimack College	M
Metropolitan College of New York	M
Murray State University	M
New Mexico Highlands University	M
Notre Dame de Namur University	M
The Ohio State University	M,D
Park University	M,O
Penn State Harrisburg	M,D,O
Portland State University	M,D
Princeton University	M,D,O
Syracuse University	
Texas A&M University	M,O
The University of Alabama in Huntsville	M
University of Arkansas at Little Rock	M,O
University of Baltimore	M,D
University of Central Florida	M,D,O
University of Colorado Colorado Springs	M
University of Colorado Denver	M,D
University of Florida	M,D,O
University of Louisville	M,D
University of Massachusetts Boston	M,D,O
University of Minnesota, Twin Cities Campus	M,D
University of Missouri	M,D,O
University of Missouri–Kansas City	M,D
University of Nevada, Las Vegas	M,D,O
The University of North Carolina at Greensboro	M,O
University of San Francisco	M
University of Saskatchewan	M,D
University of South Florida	O
The University of Texas at Arlington	D
The University of Texas at Austin	M,D
The University of Texas Rio Grande Valley	M
University of Washington	M,D*
University of Waterloo	M
University of Wisconsin–Madison	M
Virginia Commonwealth University	M,D,O
Virginia Polytechnic Institute and State University	M,D,O
Washington State University	M,D,O
West Chester University of Pennsylvania	M,O
Western Carolina University	M
Western Michigan University	M,D,O
York University	M

PUBLIC HEALTH—GENERAL

Adelphi University	M,O
Allen College	M,D,O
American Public University System	M
American University of Armenia	M
Andrews University	M,O
Arcadia University	M
Argosy University, Atlanta	M
Argosy University, Chicago	M
Argosy University, Dallas	M
Argosy University, Denver	M
Argosy University, Hawai`i	M

Argosy University, Inland Empire	M
Argosy University, Los Angeles	M
Argosy University, Nashville	M
Argosy University, Orange County	M
Argosy University, Phoenix	M
Argosy University, Salt Lake City	M
Argosy University, San Diego	M
Argosy University, San Francisco Bay Area	M
Argosy University, Sarasota	M
Argosy University, Schaumburg	M
Argosy University, Seattle	M
Argosy University, Tampa	M
Argosy University, Twin Cities	M
Argosy University, Washington DC	M
Arizona State University at the Tempe campus	M,D,O
Armstrong State University	M
A.T. Still University	M,D
Auburn University at Montgomery	M,D,O
Augusta University	M
Austin Peay State University	M
Barry University	
Benedictine University	M
Boise State University	M,D,O
Boston University	M,D,O
Bowling Green State University	M
Brooklyn College of the City University of New York	M
Brown University	M
California Baptist University	M
California State University, Fresno	M
California State University, Fullerton	M
California State University, Northridge	M
California State University, San Bernardino	M
Case Western Reserve University	M*
Charles R. Drew University of Medicine and Science	M
Chicago State University	M
Claremont Graduate University	M,D
Clemson University	M,D,O
Cleveland State University	M
Columbia University	M,D*
Daemen College	M
Dartmouth College	M*
Davenport University	M
DePaul University	M
Des Moines University	M
Drexel University	M,D,O
East Carolina University	M
Eastern Virginia Medical School	M
East Stroudsburg University of Pennsylvania	M
East Tennessee State University	M,D,O
Elmhurst College	M
Emory University	M,D
Everglades University	M
Excelsior College	M,O
Florida Agricultural and Mechanical University	M,D
Florida International University	M,D
Florida State University	M
Fort Valley State University	M
George Mason University	M,O
Georgetown University	M,D
The George Washington University	M,D*
Georgia Southern University	M,D
Georgia State University	M,D,O
The Graduate Center, City University of New York	D
Grand Canyon University	M
Grand Valley State University	M
Harvard University	M,D*
Hofstra University	M
Howard University	M
Hunter College of the City University of New York	M
Idaho State University	M,O
Independence University	M
Indiana University Bloomington	M,D
Indiana University–Purdue University Indianapolis	M,D
Johns Hopkins University	M,D
Kansas State University	M,D,O
Kent State University	M,D
Lamar University	M
La Salle University	M
Laurentian University	D
Lenoir-Rhyne University	M
Loma Linda University	M,D
London Metropolitan University	M,D
Long Island University–LIU Brooklyn	M,D
Louisiana State University Health Sciences Center	M,D
Louisiana State University in Shreveport	M
Loyola University Chicago	M
Marshall University	M
Medical College of Wisconsin	M,D,O
Mercer University	M,D
Michigan State University	M
MidAmerica Nazarene University	M
Missouri State University	M
Monroe College	M
Montclair State University	M
Morehouse School of Medicine	M
Morgan State University	M,D
National University	M,D,O
New Mexico State University	M,O
New York Medical College	M,D,O
New York University	M,D
North Dakota State University	M,D
Northeast Ohio Medical University	M,D,O
Northern Illinois University	M
Northwestern University	M*
Nova Southeastern University	M,D,O*
The Ohio State University	M,D
Ohio University	M
Oregon State University	M,D
Penn State Hershey Medical Center	M,D
Ponce Health Sciences University	M,D
Portland State University	M,D,O
Purdue University	M,D
Queen's University at Kingston	M,D
Rutgers University–Camden	M,O
Rutgers University–Newark	M,O
Rutgers University–New Brunswick	M,D
St. Catherine University	M
St. John's University (NY)	M
Saint Louis University	M,D
Salus University	M
Samford University	M
San Diego State University	M,D
San Francisco State University	M
San Jose State University	M,O
Sarah Lawrence College	M
Simon Fraser University	M,D,O
Southern Connecticut State University	M
State University of New York Downstate Medical Center	M
Stony Brook University, State University of New York	M,O
Syracuse University	M
Tarleton State University	M
Temple University	M,D*
Tennessee State University	M
Texas A&M University	M,D
Thomas Jefferson University	M,O
Touro University California	M,D
Trident University International	M,D,O
Trinity Washington University	M
Tufts University	M,D,O
Tulane University	M,D
Uniformed Services University of the Health Sciences	M,D*
Université de Montréal	M,D,O
University at Albany, State University of New York	M,D
University at Buffalo, the State University of New York	M,D*
The University of Akron	M,D
The University of Alabama at Birmingham	M,D
University of Alaska Anchorage	M
University of Alberta	M,D
The University of Arizona	M,D
University of Arkansas for Medical Sciences	M,D,O
The University of British Columbia	M,D
University of California, Berkeley	M,D
University of California, Irvine	M,D
University of California, Los Angeles	M,D
University of California, San Diego	D
University of Colorado Denver	M,D
University of Connecticut Health Center	M*
University of Florida	M,D,O
University of Georgia	D
University of Hawaii at Manoa	M,D,O
University of Illinois at Chicago	M,D
University of Illinois at Springfield	M,O
University of Illinois at Urbana–Champaign	M,D
University of Indianapolis	M
The University of Iowa	M,D,O*
The University of Kansas	M*
University of Kentucky	M,D
University of Louisville	M,D
The University of Manchester	M,D
University of Maryland, College Park	M,D
University of Massachusetts Amherst	M,D*
University of Memphis	M
University of Miami	M,D
University of Michigan	M,D
University of Michigan–Flint	M
University of Minnesota, Twin Cities Campus	M,D,O
University of Missouri	M,O
University of Montana	M,O
University of Nebraska Medical Center	M
University of Nevada, Las Vegas	M,D
University of Nevada, Reno	M,D
University of New Hampshire	M,O
University of New Mexico	M
The University of North Carolina at Chapel Hill	M,D
The University of North Carolina at Charlotte	M,D,O
University of North Dakota	M,D
University of Northern Colorado	M
University of North Florida	M,O
University of North Texas Health Science Center at Fort Worth	M,D
University of Oklahoma Health Sciences Center	M,D
University of Ottawa	D
University of Pennsylvania	M*
University of Pittsburgh	M,D,O*
University of Rochester	M*
University of San Francisco	M
University of South Africa	M,D
University of South Carolina	M
University of Southern California	M,D
University of Southern Maine	M,O
University of Southern Mississippi	M
University of South Florida	M,D,O
The University of Tennessee	M
The University of Texas Health Science Center at Houston	M,D,O
The University of Texas Medical Branch	M
University of the Sciences	M
The University of Toledo	M,O
University of Toronto	M,D
University of Utah	M,D*
University of Virginia	M,D
University of Washington	M*
University of Waterloo	M,D
University of West Florida	M
University of Wisconsin–Madison	M
University of Wisconsin–Milwaukee	M,D,O
Valparaiso University	M,D,O
Vanderbilt University	M*
Virginia Commonwealth University	M,D
Virginia Polytechnic Institute and State University	M,D,O
Walden University	M,D,O
Washington University in St. Louis	M,D,O
Wayne State University	M,O
West Chester University of Pennsylvania	M,O
Western Kentucky University	M
Westminster College (UT)	M
West Virginia University	M,D
Wright State University	M
Yale University	M,D*

PUBLIC HISTORY

American Public University System	M
Arizona State University at the Tempe campus	M,D,O
Armstrong State University	M
California State University, East Bay	M
California State University, Sacramento	M,D
The College at Brockport, State University of New York	M
Drew University	M,D,O
Duquesne University	M
East Carolina University	M
Eastern Illinois University	M
Florida State University	M,D
Georgia College & State University	M
Georgia Southern University	M,O
Georgia State University	M,D
Indiana University of Pennsylvania	M
Indiana University–Purdue University Indianapolis	M
James Madison University	M
La Salle University	M,O
Lehigh University	M,D
Loyola University Chicago	M,D
Middle Tennessee State University	D
New York University	M,D,O
North Carolina State University	M
Northeastern University	M,D
Northern Kentucky University	M
Rutgers University–Camden	M
St. John's University (NY)	M,D
Shippensburg University of Pennsylvania	M
Sonoma State University	M
Southeast Missouri State University	M,O
University at Albany, State University of New York	M,D,O
University at Buffalo, the State University of New York	M,D*
University of Arkansas at Little Rock	M
University of California, Santa Barbara	D
University of Colorado Denver	M
University of Illinois at Springfield	M
University of Louisville	M,O
University of Maryland, Baltimore County	M,D
University of Missouri–St. Louis	M,O
University of North Alabama	M
University of Northern Iowa	M
University of South Carolina	M,O
The University of Texas at Austin	M,D
University of West Florida	M
University of West Georgia	M,O

PUBLIC POLICY

Adler University	M,D,O
Albany State University	M
American Public University System	M
American University	M,O
The American University in Cairo	M,O
The American University of Paris	M
Arizona State University at the Tempe campus	M,D
Auburn University at Montgomery	M,D,O
Baruch College of the City University of New York	M
Baylor University	M,D
Boise State University	M,D,O
Brandeis University	M
Brock University	M
Brooklyn College of the City University of New York	M
Brown University	M
California Lutheran University	M
California State University, East Bay	M
California State University, Long Beach	M
California State University, Sacramento	M
Carleton University	M,D
Carnegie Mellon University	M,D
The Catholic University of America	M
Central European University	M,D
Claremont Graduate University	M,D,O
Clemson University	D,O
The College of William and Mary	M
Columbia University	M*
Concordia University (Canada)	M,D
Cornell University	M,D
DePaul University	M
Duke University	M,D*
Duquesne University	M,O
Eastern Michigan University	M,O
Eastern University	M,D
Florida State University	M,D,O
Frederick S. Pardee RAND Graduate School	D
George Mason University	M,D
Georgetown University	M,D
The George Washington University	M,D*
Georgia Institute of Technology	M,D
Georgia State University	M,D,O
The Graduate Center, City University of New York	M,D
Harvard University	M,D*
Indiana University Bloomington	M,D,O
Indiana University–Purdue University Fort Wayne	M,O
The Institute of World Politics	M,O
Jackson State University	M,D
John Jay College of Criminal Justice of the City University of New York	M,D
Johns Hopkins University	M,D
Liberty University	M
Lincoln University (MO)	M
London Metropolitan University	M,D
Loyola University Chicago	M
McMaster University	M,D
Mills College	M
Mississippi State University	M,D
Monmouth University	M
Morehead State University	M
National Louis University	M,D,O
New England College	M
The New School	D
New York University	M
Northeastern University	M,D
Northwestern University	M,D*
Norwich University	M
The Ohio State University	M,D
Oregon State University	M,D
Pepperdine University	M
Portland State University	M,D
Princeton University	M,D
Queen's University at Kingston	M
Rochester Institute of Technology	M
Rutgers University–Camden	M
Rutgers University–Newark	M,D,O
Rutgers University–New Brunswick	M,D
Saint Louis University	M,D,O
St. Mary's University (United States)	M,O
San Francisco State University	M
Seton Hall University	M,O
Simmons College	M,D,O
Simon Fraser University	M
Southern University and Agricultural and Mechanical College	D
State University of New York Empire State College	M
Stony Brook University, State University of New York	M
Suffolk University	M,O
Trinity College (United States)	M
Tufts University	M
Union Institute & University	M,D
Universidad Autonoma de Guadalajara	M,D
Universidad del Este	M
Université de Montréal	O
University at Albany, State University of New York	M,D,O
The University of Arizona	M,D,O
University of Arkansas	D
University of California, Berkeley	M,D
University of California, Los Angeles	M
University of California, San Diego	M
University of Chicago	M,D
University of Colorado Boulder	M,D
University of Delaware	M,D*
University of Denver	M
University of Georgia	M,D
University of Guelph	M
University of Hawaii at Manoa	O
University of Kentucky	M,D
University of Louisville	M,D
University of Maryland, Baltimore County	M,D
University of Maryland, College Park	M,D
University of Massachusetts Amherst	M*
University of Massachusetts Boston	M,D
University of Massachusetts Dartmouth	M,O
University of Memphis	M,O
University of Michigan	M,D
University of Michigan–Dearborn	M
University of Minnesota, Twin Cities Campus	M,D
University of Missouri	M,D,O
University of Missouri–St. Louis	M,D,O
University of Nebraska–Lincoln	M,D,O

*M—masters degree; D—doctorate; O—other advanced degree; *—Close-Up and/or Display*

University of New Brunswick Fredericton	M
University of New Hampshire	M
The University of North Carolina at Chapel Hill	D
The University of North Carolina at Charlotte	M,D,O
University of Northern Iowa	M
University of Oklahoma	M,D*
University of Oregon	M
University of Pennsylvania	M,D*
University of Pittsburgh	M,D*
University of Puerto Rico, Rí o Piedras Campus	M
University of Regina	M,D,O
University of Rhode Island	M
University of Rochester	M*
University of St. Thomas (TX)	M
University of Saskatchewan	M,D
The University of South Dakota	M,D
University of Southern California	M,D,O
University of Southern Maine	M
The University of Texas at Austin	M,D
The University of Texas at Dallas	M,D*
The University of Texas Rio Grande Valley	M
University of the Pacific	M,D
University of Utah	M*
University of Virginia	M
University of Washington	M,D*
University of Washington, Bothell	M
Vanderbilt University	D*
Virginia Commonwealth University	D
Virginia Polytechnic Institute and State University	M,D
Walden University	M,D,O
Wayne State University	M,D
West Virginia University	M,D
Wilfrid Laurier University	M
William Paterson University of New Jersey	M,D
York University	M

PUBLISHING

Arizona State University at the Tempe campus	M,D,O
Brown University	M,D
Carnegie Mellon University	M
DePaul University	M
Drexel University	M
Emerson College	M
The George Washington University	M*
New York University	M
North Central College	M
Northwestern University	M*
Pace University	M,O
Rosemont College	M
Rowan University	O
Sam Houston State University	M
Simon Fraser University	M
University of Baltimore	M
University of Houston–Victoria	M
Vermont College of Fine Arts	M

QUALITY MANAGEMENT

California Intercontinental University	M,D
California State University, Dominguez Hills	M
Calumet College of Saint Joseph	M
East Carolina University	M,D,O
Eastern Michigan University	M,O
Florida Institute of Technology	M,D
Hofstra University	M,O
Instituto Tecnologico de Santo Domingo	M,O
Instituto Tecnológico y de Estudios Superiores de Monterrey, Campus Ciudad de México	M,D
Instituto Tecnológico y de Estudios Superiores de Monterrey, Campus Ciudad Juárez	M
Instituto Tecnológico y de Estudios Superiores de Monterrey, Campus Estado de México	M,D
Instituto Tecnológico y de Estudios Superiores de Monterrey, Campus Irapuato	M,D
Madonna University	M
Mount Mercy University	M
The National Graduate School of Quality Management	M,D
Northwestern University	M*
Penn State Erie, The Behrend College	M
Regis College (MA)	M
Rutgers University–New Brunswick	M,D
Southern New Hampshire University	M,O
Stevens Institute of Technology	M,O
Stevenson University	M
Trident University International	M,D,O
Universidad de las Americas, A.C.	M
Universidad del Turabo	M
The University of Alabama	M
University of Massachusetts Boston	M,O
The University of Tennessee at Chattanooga	M,O
University of Wisconsin–Stout	M

QUANTITATIVE ANALYSIS

Ball State University	M
Baruch College of the City University of New York	M
Columbia University	M,D*
Cornell University	M,D
Drexel University	M,D,O
Duke University	M,D,O*
Hofstra University	M,O
Instituto Tecnologico de Santo Domingo	M,O
La Salle University	M,O
Lehigh University	M
Northwestern University	M,D*
Purdue University	M,D
Rutgers University–Newark	M,O
St. John's University (NY)	M
San Francisco State University	M
University at Buffalo, the State University of New York	M,D*
The University of Alabama at Birmingham	M,D
The University of British Columbia	M,D
University of California, Santa Barbara	M,D
University of Cincinnati	M,D
University of Colorado Denver	M
University of Connecticut	M,O*
University of Florida	M,D,O
The University of Iowa	M,D,O*
University of Maryland, College Park	M,D
University of Minnesota, Twin Cities Campus	M,D,O
University of New Mexico	D
University of North Texas	M,D,O
University of Oregon	M
University of Pittsburgh	M,D*
University of Puerto Rico, Rí o Piedras Campus	M,D
University of South Africa	M,D
University of Southern California	M,D
The University of Texas at Arlington	M,D
The University of Texas at Austin	M,D
Vanderbilt University	M,D*
Virginia Commonwealth University	M
Virginia Polytechnic Institute and State University	M,O

RADIATION BIOLOGY

Auburn University	M,D
Colorado State University	M,D
Georgetown University	M
Université de Sherbrooke	M,D
The University of Iowa	M*
University of Oklahoma Health Sciences Center	M,D

RANGE SCIENCE

Colorado State University	M,D
Kansas State University	M,D,O
Montana State University	M,D
New Mexico State University	M,D
Oregon State University	M,D
Sul Ross State University	M
Texas A&M University	M,D
Texas A&M University–Kingsville	M
The University of Arizona	M,D
University of California, Berkeley	M
University of Wyoming	M,D
Utah State University	M,D

READING EDUCATION

Adelphi University	M
Alabama Agricultural and Mechanical University	M,D,O
Alabama State University	M,O
Alfred University	M
Alverno College	M
American International College	M,D,O
American Public University System	M
Appalachian State University	M
Arcadia University	M,D,O
Arkansas State University	M,D,O
Armstrong State University	M,O
Asbury University	M
Ashland University	M
Auburn University	M,D,O
Augustana University	M
Austin Peay State University	M,O
Baldwin Wallace University	M
Ball State University	M,D,O
Bank Street College of Education	M
Barry University	M,D,O
Belhaven University (MS)	M
Bellarmine University	M,D,O
Benedictine University	M
Berry College	M
Bethel University (MN)	M,D,O
Binghamton University, State University of New York	M*
Bloomsburg University of Pennsylvania	M
Blue Mountain College	M
Bluffton University	M
Boise State University	M
Boston College	M,O
Bowie State University	M
Bowling Green State University	M,O
Bridgewater State University	M,O
Brigham Young University	M
Buffalo State College, State University of New York	M
Caldwell University	M,D,O
California Baptist University	M
California State Polytechnic University, Pomona	M
California State University, East Bay	M
California State University, Fresno	M
California State University, Fullerton	M
California State University, Northridge	M
California State University, Sacramento	M
California State University, San Marcos	M,D
California State University, Stanislaus	M
California University of Pennsylvania	M
Calvin College	M
Cambridge College	M,D,O
Canisius College	M,O
Capella University	M,D
Cardinal Stritch University	M,D
Carthage College	M,O
Castleton University	M,O
Central Connecticut State University	M,O
Central Michigan University	M,D,O
Central Washington University	M
Chestnut Hill College	M
Chicago State University	M
The Citadel, The Military College of South Carolina	M,O
City College of the City University of New York	M
City University of Seattle	M,O
Clarion University of Pennsylvania	M
Clemson University	M,D,O
Coker College	M
The College at Brockport, State University of New York	M
The College of New Jersey	M,O
The College of New Rochelle	M
College of St. Joseph	M
The College of Saint Rose	M,O
Concordia University (United States)	M,D
Concordia University Chicago	M
Concordia University, Nebraska	M
Concordia University, St. Paul	M,D,O
Concordia University Wisconsin	M
Concord University	M
Converse College	O
Coppin State University	M
Crandall University	M
Curry College	M,O
Dallas Baptist University	M
Delaware State University	M
DePaul University	M,D
Dominican University	M
Drury University	M
Duquesne University	M
East Carolina University	M
Eastern Connecticut State University	M
Eastern Michigan University	M
Eastern Nazarene College	M,O
Eastern New Mexico University	M
Eastern University	M,O
Eastern Washington University	M
East Stroudsburg University of Pennsylvania	M
East Tennessee State University	M,O
Edgewood College	M,D,O
Edinboro University of Pennsylvania	M,O
Elms College	M,O
Emory & Henry College	M
Emporia State University	M
Endicott College	M
Evangel University	M
Fairleigh Dickinson University, College at Florham	M,O
Fairleigh Dickinson University, Metropolitan Campus	M,O
Fairmont State University	M
Ferris State University	M
Fitchburg State University	O
Florida Atlantic University	M
Florida International University	M,D,O
Florida Memorial University	M
Florida State University	M,D,O
Fontbonne University	M
Framingham State University	M
Fresno Pacific University	M,O
Frostburg State University	M
Furman University	M,O
Gannon University	M,O
Geneva College	M
George Fox University	M,O
George Mason University	M
Georgetown College	M
Georgia College & State University	M
Georgia Southern University	M,O
Georgia State University	M,D
Gordon College	M,O
Goucher College	M,O
Governors State University	M
Graceland University (IA)	M
Grambling State University	M,D,O
Grand Valley State University	M
Hamline University	M,D
Hannibal-LaGrange University	M
Harding University	M,O
Hardin-Simmons University	M
Harvard University	M*
Heritage University	M
Holy Family University	M
Hood College	M,O
Houston Baptist University	M
Idaho State University	M,O
Illinois State University	M
Indiana University Bloomington	M,D,O
Indiana University of Pennsylvania	M,O
Indiana University–Purdue University Indianapolis	M,O
Jacksonville State University	M
James Madison University	M
Johns Hopkins University	M
Johnson State College	M
Judson University	M,D
Kansas State University	M,D
Kaplan University, Davenport Campus	M
Kean University	M
Kennesaw State University	M
Kent State University	M
Kutztown University of Pennsylvania	M
La Salle University	M,O
Lehman College of the City University of New York	M
Le Moyne College	M,O
Lesley University	M,D,O
Lewis University	M
Liberty University	M,D,O
Lincoln University (PA)	M
Lipscomb University	M,D,O
Long Island University–Brentwood Campus	M,O
Long Island University–Hudson at Rockland	M,O
Long Island University–Hudson at Westchester	M,O
Long Island University–LIU Post	M,D,O
Longwood University	M
Lourdes University	M
Loyola Marymount University	M
Loyola University Chicago	M,O
Loyola University Maryland	M
Lynchburg College	M
Lyndon State College	M
Madonna University	M
Manhattanville College	M*
Marquette University	M,D,O
Marshall University	M,O
Marygrove College	M
Maryville University of Saint Louis	M,D
Marywood University	M
Massachusetts College of Liberal Arts	M,O
McDaniel College	M
McKendree University	M,D,O
McNeese State University	M,O
Medaille College	M
Mercer University	M,D,O
Mercy College	M,O
MGH Institute of Health Professions	M,O
Michigan State University	M
MidAmerica Nazarene University	M
Middle Tennessee State University	M,D
Midwestern State University	M
Millersville University of Pennsylvania	M
Misericordia University	M
Mississippi State University	M,D,O
Mississippi University for Women	M
Missouri State University	M
Montana State University Billings	M
Montclair State University	M
Morehead State University	M,O
Mount Mercy University	M
Mount St. Joseph University	M,O
Mount Saint Mary College	M,O
Mount Saint Vincent University	M
Murray State University	M,O
National Louis University	M,D,O
National University	M,O
Nazareth College of Rochester	M
Newman University	M
New York University	M
Niagara University	M
North Carolina Agricultural and Technical State University	M
Northeastern Illinois University	M
Northeastern State University	M
Northern Illinois University	M,D
Northern Michigan University	M
Northwestern Oklahoma State University	M
Northwestern State University of Louisiana	M,O
Northwest Missouri State University	M
Notre Dame College (OH)	M,O
Oakland University	M,D,O
Ohio University	M,D
Old Dominion University	M,D
Olivet Nazarene University	M
Oregon State University	M
Pace University	M,O
Park University	M,O
Penn State Harrisburg	M,D,O
Plymouth State University	M
Providence College	M
Purdue University	M,D,O
Queens College of the City University of New York	M,O
Queens University of Charlotte	M
Quincy University	M
Radford University	M
Regent University	M,D,O
Regis College (MA)	M,D
Regis University	M,O
Rhode Island College	M
Rider University	M,O
Rivier University	M,D,O
Roberts Wesleyan College	M
Rockford University	M
Roosevelt University	M
Rowan University	M,O
Rutgers University–New Brunswick	M,D
Sacred Heart University	O
Sage Graduate School	M
Saginaw Valley State University	M
St. Bonaventure University	M
Saint Francis University	M
St. John Fisher College	M
St. John's University (NY)	M,D,O
St. Joseph's College, Long Island Campus	M
St. Joseph's College, New York	M
Saint Joseph's University	M,D,O
Saint Martin's University	M
Saint Mary's College of California	M
Saint Mary's University of Minnesota	M,O
Saint Michael's College	M,O
Saint Peter's University	M,O
St. Thomas Aquinas College	M,O
St. Thomas University	M,D,O
Saint Xavier University	M
Salem College	M

Salem State University	M
Salisbury University	M,D
Sam Houston State University	M,D
San Diego State University	M
San Francisco State University	M,O
Seattle Pacific University	M
Seattle University	M,O
Shippensburg University of Pennsylvania	M
Siena Heights University	M,O
Simmons College	M,D,O
Simon Fraser University	D
Slippery Rock University of Pennsylvania	M
Sonoma State University	M,D,O
Southeastern Louisiana University	M
Southeastern Oklahoma State University	M
Southern Adventist University	M
Southern Connecticut State University	M,O
Southern Illinois University Edwardsville	M,O
Southern Methodist University	M,D
Southern New Hampshire University	M,D,O
Southern Oregon University	M
Southwestern Adventist University	M
Southwest Minnesota State University	M
Spring Arbor University	M
State University of New York at Fredonia	M
State University of New York at New Paltz	M
State University of New York at Oswego	M
State University of New York at Plattsburgh	M
State University of New York College at Cortland	M
State University of New York College at Geneseo	M
State University of New York College at Oneonta	M
State University of New York College at Potsdam	M
Sul Ross State University	M,O
Summit University	M
Syracuse University	M,D
Tarleton State University	M
Teachers College, Columbia University	M,D,O
Tennessee Technological University	M,D,O
Texas A&M University–Corpus Christi	M,D
Texas A&M University–Kingsville	M
Texas A&M University–San Antonio	M
Texas Christian University	M,O
Texas State University	M
Texas Tech University	M,D
Texas Woman's University	M,D
Touro College	M
Towson University	M,O
Trident University International	M
Trinity Washington University	M
Troy University	M
Union College (KY)	M
University at Albany, State University of New York	M,D,O
University at Buffalo, the State University of New York	M,D,O*
The University of Akron	M
The University of Alabama at Birmingham	M
The University of Arizona	M,D,O
University of Arkansas at Little Rock	M,D,O
University of Bridgeport	M,D,O
The University of British Columbia	M,D
University of California, Riverside	M,D,O
University of Central Arkansas	M
University of Central Florida	M,D,O
University of Central Missouri	M,D,O
University of Central Oklahoma	M
University of Cincinnati	M,D
University of Colorado Denver	M
University of Connecticut	M,D*
University of Dayton	M
The University of Findlay	M,D
University of Florida	M,D,O
University of Georgia	M,D,O
University of Guam	M
University of Houston–Clear Lake	M
University of Kentucky	M,D
University of La Verne	M,O
University of Louisiana at Monroe	M,D
University of Maine	M,D,O
University of Mary	M,D
University of Maryland, College Park	M,D,O
University of Massachusetts Amherst	M,D,O*
University of Memphis	M,D
University of Miami	D
University of Michigan–Flint	M,D,O
University of Minnesota, Twin Cities Campus	M,D,O
University of Missouri	M,D,O
University of Missouri–Kansas City	M,D,O
University of Missouri–St. Louis	M,O
University of Nebraska at Kearney	M
University of Nebraska at Omaha	M
University of Nevada, Reno	M,D
University of New England	M,O
University of New Mexico	M,D
The University of North Carolina at Chapel Hill	M,D
The University of North Carolina at Charlotte	M,O
The University of North Carolina at Greensboro	M,D,O
The University of North Carolina at Pembroke	M
The University of North Carolina Wilmington	M
University of North Dakota	M
University of Northern Colorado	M
University of Northern Iowa	M
University of North Florida	M
University of Oklahoma Health Sciences Center	M,D,O
University of Pennsylvania	M*
University of Phoenix–Online Campus	M,O
University of Phoenix–Phoenix Campus	M
University of Pittsburgh	M,D*
University of Portland	M,D
University of Rhode Island	M,D
University of St. Francis (IL)	M,D,O
University of Saint Joseph	M
University of St. Thomas (MN)	M,O
University of St. Thomas (TX)	M
University of San Diego	M
University of San Francisco	M,D
The University of Scranton	M
University of Sioux Falls	M,O
University of South Alabama	M,D
University of South Carolina	M,D
The University of South Dakota	M
University of Southern Maine	M,O
University of South Florida	M,D,O
University of South Florida, St. Petersburg	M
The University of Tennessee	M,D,O
The University of Texas at Austin	M,D
The University of Texas at El Paso	M,D
The University of Texas at San Antonio	M,D
The University of Texas at Tyler	M
The University of Texas of the Permian Basin	M
The University of Texas Rio Grande Valley	M
University of the Cumberlands	M,D,O
University of Utah	M,D*
University of Victoria	M,D
University of Virginia	M,D
University of Washington	M,D*
University of West Florida	M
University of West Georgia	M,D,O
University of Wisconsin–Eau Claire	M
University of Wisconsin–La Crosse	M
University of Wisconsin–Milwaukee	M
University of Wisconsin–Oshkosh	M
University of Wisconsin–River Falls	M
University of Wisconsin–Stevens Point	M
University of Wisconsin–Superior	M
Upper Iowa University	M
Ursuline College	M
Utah Valley University	M
Vanderbilt University	M,D*
Virginia Commonwealth University	M,O
Viterbo University	M,O
Wagner College	M
Walden University	M,D,O
Walla Walla University	M
Walsh University	M
Washburn University	M
Washington State University	M,D
Wayne State University	M,D,O
Webster University	M
West Chester University of Pennsylvania	M,O
Western Connecticut State University	M
Western Illinois University	M
Western Kentucky University	M,O
Western Michigan University	M,D
Western New Mexico University	M
Western State Colorado University	M
Westfield State University	M
Westminster College (PA)	M,O
West Texas A&M University	M
West Virginia University	M
Wheelock College	M
Widener University	M,D
Wilkes University	M,D
William Paterson University of New Jersey	M
Wilmington College	M
Wilmington University	M,D
Worcester State University	M,O
Xavier University	M
York College of Pennsylvania	M
Youngstown State University	M

REAL ESTATE

American University	M,O
Arizona State University at the Tempe campus	M,D
Auburn University	M
Baruch College of the City University of New York	M
Baylor University	D
Brandeis University	M
California State University, Sacramento	M
Clemson University	M
Cleveland State University	M,O
Columbia University	M*
Cornell University	M
DePaul University	M
Drexel University	M
Emory University	M
Florida International University	M
Georgetown University	M,D
The George Washington University	O*
Georgia State University	M,D,O
Instituto Centroamericano de Administración de Empresas	M
John Marshall Law School	M,D
Johns Hopkins University	M
Longwood University	M
Marquette University	M
Marylhurst University	M
Massachusetts Institute of Technology	M
Monmouth University	M,O
New York University	M,O
Northwestern University	M,D*
Pacific States University	M,D
Pontificia Universidad Catolica Madre y Maestra	M
Portland State University	M
Roosevelt University	M,O
Rutgers University–Newark	M
San Jose State University	M,O
Southern Methodist University	M
Syracuse University	M
Texas A&M University	M
Universidad Iberoamericana	M,D
University at Buffalo, the State University of New York	M*
University of California, Berkeley	D
University of Denver	M
University of Florida	M,D,O
University of Hawaii at Manoa	M
University of Illinois at Chicago	M
University of Maryland, College Park	M
University of Memphis	M,D
University of Miami	M,D
University of Missouri–Kansas City	M,D
The University of North Carolina at Charlotte	M,O
University of Pennsylvania	M,D*
University of St. Thomas (MN)	M
University of San Diego	M
University of South Africa	M,D
University of Southern California	M
University of South Florida	M,D
The University of Texas at Arlington	M,D
University of Utah	M*
University of Wisconsin–Madison	M,D
University of Wisconsin–Milwaukee	M,O
Villanova University	M
Virginia Commonwealth University	M,O

RECREATION AND PARK MANAGEMENT

Acadia University	M
Bowling Green State University	M
California State University, Chico	M
California State University, East Bay	M
California State University, Long Beach	M
California State University, Northridge	M,O
California State University, Sacramento	M
Central Michigan University	M,O
Clemson University	M,D,O
Colorado State University	M,D
Delta State University	M
East Carolina University	M,O
Eastern Kentucky University	M
Eastern Washington University	M
Florida International University	M,D,O
Frostburg State University	M
Hardin-Simmons University	M
Indiana State University	M,D
Indiana University Bloomington	M,D
Iona College	M,O
Kent State University	M
Lehman College of the City University of New York	M
Liberty University	M,D,O
Loyola Marymount University	M
Michigan State University	M,D
Middle Tennessee State University	M
Naropa University	M
New England College	M
North Carolina Central University	M
North Carolina State University	M,D
Northwest Missouri State University	M
Ohio University	M
Penn State University Park	M,D
Purdue University	M,D
San Francisco State University	M
San Jose State University	M,O
Slippery Rock University of Pennsylvania	M
South Dakota State University	M,D
Southern Adventist University	M
Southern Connecticut State University	M
Southern Illinois University Carbondale	M
Southern University and Agricultural and Mechanical College	M
Southwestern Oklahoma State University	M
Springfield College	M
State University of New York College at Cortland	M
Temple University	M,D*
Texas A&M University	M,D
Texas State University	M
Universidad Metropolitana	M
University of Alberta	M,D
University of Arkansas	M,D
University of Florida	M,D
University of Idaho	M,D
The University of Iowa	M,D*
University of Louisiana at Monroe	M
University of Manitoba	M
University of Mississippi	M,D
University of Montana	M,D
University of Nebraska at Kearney	M
University of Nebraska at Omaha	M,D
University of New Brunswick Fredericton	M
University of New Hampshire	M
The University of North Carolina at Greensboro	M
University of Rhode Island	M
The University of Tennessee	M,D
The University of Toledo	M,D
University of Utah	M,D*
University of Waterloo	M,D
University of Wisconsin–La Crosse	M
University of Wisconsin–Milwaukee	M,D,O
Utah State University	M,D
Virginia Commonwealth University	M
Western Illinois University	M
Western Kentucky University	M
West Virginia University	M
Winona State University	M,O
Wright State University	M

REHABILITATION COUNSELING

Adler University	M,D,O
Alabama Agricultural and Mechanical University	M,O
Alabama State University	M
Arkansas State University	M,O
Assumption College	M,O
Auburn University	M,D
Ball State University	M,D
Barry University	M,O
Bayamón Central University	M,O
Bowling Green State University	M
California State University, Fresno	M
California State University, Los Angeles	M,D
California State University, San Bernardino	M
Central Connecticut State University	M,O
Coppin State University	M
East Carolina University	M,D,O
East Central University	M
Edinboro University of Pennsylvania	M,O
Emporia State University	M
Florida International University	M,D,O
Fort Valley State University	M
The George Washington University	M*
Georgia State University	M
Hofstra University	M,O
Hunter College of the City University of New York	M
Illinois Institute of Technology	M,D
Jackson State University	M
Kent State University	M
Langston University	M
Louisiana State University Health Sciences Center	M
Maryville University of Saint Louis	M
Mercer University	M,D
Michigan State University	M,D,O
Minnesota State University Mankato	M
Mississippi State University	M,D,O
Montana State University Billings	M
Mount Mary University	M,O
Northeastern Illinois University	M
Ohio University	M,D
Pontifical Catholic University of Puerto Rico	M
Rutgers University–Newark	M,D
St. Bonaventure University	M,O
St. Cloud State University	M
Salve Regina University	M,O
San Diego State University	M
San Francisco State University	M,O
South Carolina State University	M
Southern University and Agricultural and Mechanical College	M
Springfield College	M
Texas Tech University Health Sciences Center	M
Thomas University	M
Troy University	M,O
University at Buffalo, the State University of New York	M,D,O*
The University of Arizona	M,D
University of Arkansas	M,D
University of Arkansas at Little Rock	M,O
University of Idaho	M,O
The University of Iowa	M,D*
The University of Kansas	M,D*
University of Kentucky	M,D
University of Louisiana at Lafayette	M
University of Maryland, College Park	M,D,O
University of Maryland Eastern Shore	M
University of Massachusetts Boston	M

*M—masters degree; D—doctorate; O—other advanced degree; *—Close-Up and/or Display*

University of Memphis	M,D
The University of North Carolina at Chapel Hill	M,D
University of Northern Colorado	M,D
University of North Florida	M,O
University of North Texas	M,D,O
University of Puerto Rico, Río Piedras Campus	M
University of Saint Francis (IN)	M,O
The University of Scranton	M
University of South Carolina	M,O
University of Southern Maine	M,O
University of South Florida	M,O
The University of Tennessee	M,D
The University of Texas at Austin	M,D
The University of Texas at El Paso	M
The University of Texas Rio Grande Valley	M,D
The University of Texas Southwestern Medical Center	M
University of the District of Columbia	M
University of Wisconsin–Madison	M,D
University of Wisconsin–Stout	M
Utah State University	M
Virginia Commonwealth University	M,O
Wayne State University	M,D,O
Western Michigan University	M
Western Oregon University	M
Western Washington University	M
West Virginia University	M
Wilberforce University	M
Winston-Salem State University	M
Wright State University	M

REHABILITATION SCIENCES

Alabama State University	M
Appalachian State University	M
Boston University	D
California University of Pennsylvania	M
Central Michigan University	M,D
Clarion University of Pennsylvania	M
Concordia University Wisconsin	M
Duquesne University	M,D
East Carolina University	M,D,O
East Stroudsburg University of Pennsylvania	M
George Mason University	D,O
Indiana University–Purdue University Indianapolis	M,D
Lasell College	M
Logan University	M,D
Loma Linda University	M,D
Marquette University	M,D
McGill University	M,D,O
McMaster University	M,D
Medical University of South Carolina	D
New York University	M,D
Northwestern University	D*
The Ohio State University	D
Queen's University at Kingston	M,D
Salus University	M,O
Temple University	M,D*
Texas Tech University Health Sciences Center	D
Université de Montréal	O
University at Buffalo, the State University of New York	M,D,O*
The University of Alabama at Birmingham	D
University of Alberta	D
The University of British Columbia	M,D
University of Cincinnati	D
University of Colorado Denver	D
University of Florida	D
University of Illinois at Urbana–Champaign	M,D
The University of Iowa	M,D*
The University of Kansas	M,D*
University of Kentucky	D
University of Manitoba	M,D
University of Maryland, Baltimore	D
University of Maryland Eastern Shore	M
University of Oklahoma Health Sciences Center	M
University of Ottawa	M
University of Pittsburgh	M,D*
University of South Carolina	M,O
University of South Florida	D
The University of Texas Medical Branch	M,D
University of Toronto	M,D
University of Utah	D*
University of Washington	M,D*
University of Wisconsin–La Crosse	M
Virginia Commonwealth University	D
Washington University in St. Louis	D
Western Michigan University	M

RELIABILITY ENGINEERING

Arizona State University at the Tempe campus	M
University of Maryland, College Park	M,D
The University of Tennessee	M,D

RELIGION

Abilene Christian University	M
Ambrose University	M,O
The American University of Rome	M
Amridge University	M,D
Arizona State University at the Tempe campus	M,D,O
The Baptist College of Florida	M
Baptist Theological Seminary at Richmond	M,D,O
Baylor University	M,D
Bellarmine University	M
Bethany Theological Seminary	M,O
Bethel Seminary	M,D,O
Bethesda University	M
Beulah Heights University	M
Biola University	M,D,O
Bob Jones University	M,D,O
Boston University	M,D
Briercrest Seminary	M
Brown University	D
Bryn Athyn College of the New Church	M
Cairn University	M
California Institute of Integral Studies	M,D
California State University, Long Beach	M
Calvin Theological Seminary	M,D
Canadian Southern Baptist Seminary	M
Cardinal Stritch University	M
The Catholic University of America	M,D,O
Charlotte Christian College and Theological Seminary	M
Chicago Theological Seminary	M,D
Christian Brothers University	M
Christian Theological Seminary	M,D
Cincinnati Christian University	M
Claremont Graduate University	M,D
Claremont Lincoln University	M
Claremont School of Theology	M,D
Columbia University	M,D*
Concordia University (Canada)	M,D
Concordia University Chicago	M
Concordia University Irvine	M
Concordia University of Edmonton	M
Cornell University	M,D
Dallas Baptist University	M
Dallas Theological Seminary	M,D,O
Delta State University	M
Denver Seminary	M,D,O
Dominican University of California	M
Drew University	M,D,O
Duke University	M,D*
Earlham School of Religion	M
Eastern Mennonite University	M,O
East Texas Baptist University	M
Elms College	M
Emory University	D
Faith Baptist Bible College and Theological Seminary	M
Florida International University	M
Florida State University	M,D
Fordham University	M,D,O
General Theological Seminary	M,D,O
Georgetown University	M,D
The George Washington University	M*
Georgia State University	M
Gordon-Conwell Theological Seminary	M,D
Graceland University (IA)	M
Graduate Theological Union	M,D,O
Grand Rapids Theological Seminary of Cornerstone University	M
Harding School of Theology	M,D
Hardin-Simmons University	M
Harrison Middleton University	M,D
Hartford Seminary	M,D,O
Harvard University	D*
Heritage Christian University	M
Holy Names University	M,O
Hope International University	M
Iliff School of Theology	M,D
Indiana University Bloomington	M,D
The Jewish Theological Seminary	M,D
John Carroll University	M
Kentucky Christian University	M
Knox Theological Seminary	M
Lancaster Theological Seminary	M,D,O
La Salle University	M,D,O
La Sierra University	M
Lee University	M
Liberty University	M,D,O
Loma Linda University	M
Louisville Presbyterian Theological Seminary	M,D
Lutheran Theological Seminary at Gettysburg	M,D
The Lutheran Theological Seminary at Philadelphia	M,D,O
Lutheran Theological Seminary Saskatoon	M,D
Luther Rice College & Seminary	M,D
Maranatha Baptist University	M
McGill University	M,D
McMaster University	M,D
Memorial University of Newfoundland	M
Milligan College	M,D
Missouri State University	M,O
Moody Theological SeminaryMichigan	M,O
Mount St. Joseph University	M,O
Mount Saint Mary's University (CA)	M,D,O
Naropa University	M
New Saint Andrews College	M,O
New York University	M,O
Northern Seminary	M,D
Northwestern University	M,D*
Northwest Nazarene University	M
Nyack College	M
Oblate School of Theology	M,D,O
Olivet Nazarene University	M
Oxford Graduate School	M,D
Pacific School of Religion	M,D,O
Pepperdine University	M
Point Loma Nazarene University	M
Princeton Theological Seminary	M,D
Princeton University	D
Providence College	M
Queen's University at Kingston	M
Reformed Theological Seminary–Charlotte Campus	M,D
Reformed Theological Seminary–Houston Campus	M
Reformed Theological Seminary–Jackson Campus	M,D,O
Reformed Theological Seminary–Washington D.C.	M
Regent University	M,D
Rice University	D
The Robert E. Webber Institute for Worship Studies	M,D
Rutgers University–New Brunswick	M,O
St. Bonaventure University	M
Saint Charles Borromeo Seminary, Overbrook	M
Saint John's Seminary (MA)	M
St. Joseph's Seminary	M
Saint Mary's University (Canada)	M
Salve Regina University	M,D
Santa Clara University	M,D,O
Seattle Pacific University	M,O
The Seattle School of Theology and Psychology	M
Selma University	M
Seton Hall University	M,O
Sioux Falls Seminary	M
Southern Adventist University	M
The Southern Baptist Theological Seminary	M,D
Southern California Seminary	M,D
Southern Evangelical Seminary	M,D,O
Southern Methodist University	M,D
Southwestern Assemblies of God University	M
Stanford University	D
SUM Bible College & Theological Seminary	M
Summit University	M,D
Syracuse University	M,D
Temple University	M,D*
Trevecca Nazarene University	M
Trinity International University Florida	M,O
Trinity School for Ministry	M,D,O
Unification Theological Seminary	M,D
Union University	M,D
United Theological Seminary of the Twin Cities	M,D,O
Université de Montréal	M,D,O
Université de Sherbrooke	M,D,O
Université du Québec à Montréal	M,D
Université Laval	M,D
The University of British Columbia	M,D
University of Calgary	M,D
University of California, Berkeley	D
University of California, Riverside	M,D
University of California, Santa Barbara	M,D
University of Chicago	M,D
University of Colorado Boulder	M
University of Denver	M,D,O
University of Florida	M,D
University of Georgia	M
University of Hawaii at Manoa	M
University of Illinois at Urbana–Champaign	M
The University of Iowa	M,D*
The University of Kansas	M*
University of Lethbridge	M,D
The University of Manchester	D
University of Manitoba	M,D
University of Michigan	M,D
University of Minnesota, Twin Cities Campus	M,D
University of Missouri	M
The University of North Carolina at Chapel Hill	M,D
The University of North Carolina at Charlotte	M
University of Notre Dame	M
University of Ottawa	M,D
University of Pennsylvania	D*
University of Regina	M
University of St. Thomas (MN)	M
University of St. Thomas (TX)	M
University of Saskatchewan	M
University of South Africa	M,D
University of South Carolina	M
University of South Florida	M,D
The University of Tennessee	M,D
University of the Cumberlands	M
University of the Incarnate Word	M
University of the West	M,D
University of Toronto	M,D
University of Valley Forge	M
University of Virginia	M,D
University of Washington	M,D*
University of Waterloo	D
The University of Winnipeg	M
Vancouver School of Theology	M,O
Vanderbilt University	M,D*
Vanguard University of Southern California	M
Virginia University of Lynchburg	M
Wake Forest University	M
Washington Adventist University	M
Washington University in St. Louis	M
Wayland Baptist University	M
Wesley Biblical Seminary	M
Western Michigan University	M,O
Western Seminary	M,O
Westminster Seminary California	M
Westminster Theological Seminary	M,D,O
Wilfrid Laurier University	M,D
WON Institute of Graduate Studies	M,O
Wycliffe College	M,D,O
Yale University	D*
Yeshiva Derech Chaim	D

RELIGIOUS EDUCATION

Andrews University	M,D,O
Asbury Theological Seminary	M,D,O
Azusa Pacific University	M
Baptist Theological Seminary at Richmond	M,D,O
Biola University	M,D,O
Boston College	M,D,O
Brandeis University	M,O
Brigham Young University	M
Calvin Theological Seminary	M,D
Carolina Christian College	M
Claremont School of Theology	M,D
Columbia International University	M,D,O
Concordia University Chicago	M
Concordia University, Nebraska	M
Dallas Baptist University	M
Dallas Theological Seminary	M,D,O
Felician University	M,O
Fordham University	M,D,O
Gardner-Webb University	M,D
Garrett-Evangelical Theological Seminary	M,D
Global University	M,D
Grand Rapids Theological Seminary of Cornerstone University	M
Gratz College	M,D,O
Hebrew College	M,O
Hebrew Union College–Jewish Institute of Religion (NY)	M
Inter American University of Puerto Rico, Metropolitan Campus	D
The Jewish Theological Seminary	M,D
Lancaster Theological Seminary	M,D,O
La Salle University	M,D,O
La Sierra University	M
Liberty University	M,D,O
Lincoln Christian Seminary	M,D
Loyola Marymount University	M
Maple Springs Baptist Bible College and Seminary	M,D,O
Midwestern Baptist Theological Seminary	M,D,O
Milligan College	M,D
Moody Theological SeminaryMichigan	M,O
Newman Theological College	M,O
New Orleans Baptist Theological Seminary	M,D
Oral Roberts University	M,D
Pfeiffer University	M
Phillips Theological Seminary	M,D
Pontifical Catholic University of Puerto Rico	M
Providence University College & Theological Seminary	M,D,O
Reformed Theological Seminary–Jackson Campus	M,D,O
Regent University	M,D,O
Rochester College	M
St. Augustine's Seminary of Toronto	M,O
Saint Mary's University of Minnesota	M
Saints Cyril and Methodius Seminary	M
St. Vladimir's Orthodox Theological Seminary	M,D
Selma University	M
Shasta Bible College	M
Southeastern Baptist Theological Seminary	M,D
Southern Adventist University	M
Southern Evangelical Seminary	M,D,O
Southwestern Assemblies of God University	M
Southwestern Baptist Theological Seminary	M,D
Summit University	M,D
Towson University	M,O
Trinity International University	M,D,O
Trinity Lutheran Seminary	M
Unification Theological Seminary	M,D
Union Presbyterian Seminary	M,D
University of Detroit Mercy	M,D,O
University of St. Michael's College	M,D,O
University of St. Thomas (TX)	M
University of St. Thomas (MN)	M
University of San Francisco	M,D
Walsh University	M
Wesley Biblical Seminary	M
Wheaton College	M
Xavier University	M
Yeshiva University	M,D,O

REPRODUCTIVE BIOLOGY

Cornell University	M,D
Eastern Virginia Medical School	M
Queen's University at Kingston	M,D
Rutgers University–New Brunswick	M,D
Tufts University	M,D
The University of British Columbia	M,D
University of Hawaii at Manoa	M,D
University of Saskatchewan	M,D
University of Wyoming	M,D
West Virginia University	M,D

RHETORIC

Abilene Christian University	M
Arizona State University at the Tempe campus	M,D,O
Ball State University	M,D
Bob Jones University	M,D,O
Boise State University	M
Bowling Green State University	M,D
Brigham Young University	M
California State University, Dominguez Hills	M,O
California State University, Northridge	M
California State University, Stanislaus	M,O
Carnegie Mellon University	M,D
The Catholic University of America	M,D,O

Clemson University	D
DePaul University	M
Duquesne University	M,D
East Carolina University	M,D,O
Eastern Washington University	M
Florida State University	M,D
Georgia State University	M,D
Hofstra University	M
Idaho State University	M
Indiana University Bloomington	M,D
Iowa State University of Science and Technology	M,D
James Madison University	M
Kent State University	M,D,O
Michigan State University	M,D
Michigan Technological University	M,D
Missouri Western State University	M,O
Monmouth University	M
National University	M,O
New Mexico Highlands University	M
New Mexico State University	M,D
North Carolina State University	D
North Dakota State University	M,D
Northern Arizona University	M,D,O
Northern Kentucky University	M,O
Northwestern University	M,D*
Ohio University	M,D
Rensselaer Polytechnic Institute	M,D
Rowan University	O
Salisbury University	M
San Diego State University	M
Southern Illinois University Carbondale	M,D
Syracuse University	M,D
Texas Christian University	M,D
Texas State University	M
Texas Tech University	M,D
Texas Woman's University	M,D
The University of Alabama	M,D
The University of Alabama at Birmingham	M
The University of Arizona	M,D
University of Arkansas at Little Rock	M
University of California, Berkeley	D
University of Colorado Denver	M
University of Denver	M,D
The University of Findlay	M,D
University of Houston–Downtown	M
The University of Iowa	M,D*
University of Louisiana at Lafayette	M,D
University of Louisville	M,D
University of Massachusetts Amherst	M,D*
University of Michigan–Flint	M
University of Nebraska–Lincoln	M,D
The University of North Carolina at Greensboro	M,D
University of Southern California	D
University of South Florida	M,D
The University of Tennessee at Chattanooga	M,O
The University of Texas at El Paso	M,D,O
The University of Texas Rio Grande Valley	M
University of Utah	M,D*
University of Wisconsin–Madison	M,D
University of Wisconsin–Milwaukee	M,D,O
Valdosta State University	M
Virginia Commonwealth University	M
Virginia Polytechnic Institute and State University	M,D,O
Wayne State University	M,D
Wright State University	M

ROMANCE LANGUAGES

Appalachian State University	M
Boston University	M,D
Clark Atlanta University	M,D
Columbia University	M,D*
Cornell University	M,D
Hunter College of the City University of New York	M
Johns Hopkins University	D
Michigan State University	M,D
New York University	M,D
Northern Illinois University	M
Queens College of the City University of New York	M
San Diego State University	M
Stony Brook University, State University of New York	M
Texas Tech University	M,D
University at Buffalo, the State University of New York	M,D*
The University of Alabama	M,D
University of California, Berkeley	D
University of Chicago	M,D
University of Cincinnati	M,D
University of Georgia	M,D
University of Illinois at Urbana–Champaign	D
University of Miami	D
University of Missouri	M,D
University of Missouri–Kansas City	M
University of New Orleans	M
The University of North Carolina at Chapel Hill	M,D
University of Notre Dame	M
University of Oregon	M,D
University of Pennsylvania	M,D*
University of South Africa	M,D
The University of Texas at Austin	M,D
University of Virginia	M,D
Washington University in St. Louis	D
Wayne State University	M

RURAL PLANNING AND STUDIES

Brandon University	M,O
Dalhousie University	M
East Carolina University	M,O
Iowa State University of Science and Technology	M,D
Université Laval	O
University of Alaska Fairbanks	M
University of Guelph	M,D
University of Montana	M
University of Wyoming	M

RURAL SOCIOLOGY

Auburn University	M
Cornell University	M,D
Iowa State University of Science and Technology	M,D
The Ohio State University	M,D
Penn State University Park	M,D,O
University of Alberta	M,D
University of Missouri	M,D
University of Montana	M
University of Wisconsin–Madison	M,D

RUSSIAN

American University	M,O
Boston College	M
Brown University	M,D
Columbia University	M,D*
Harvard University	D*
Kent State University	M,D
McGill University	M,D
Middlebury College	M,D
New York University	M
Penn State University Park	M,D
Princeton University	D
The University of Arizona	M
University of California, Berkeley	D
The University of Manchester	M,D
The University of North Carolina at Chapel Hill	M,D
University of Oregon	M
University of South Africa	M,D
The University of Tennessee	D
University of Washington	M,D*
University of Waterloo	M,D
Yale University	D*

SAFETY ENGINEERING

Embry-Riddle Aeronautical University–Prescott	M
Florida Institute of Technology	M
Indiana University Bloomington	M,D
Murray State University	M
New Jersey Institute of Technology	M,D
Rochester Institute of Technology	M
The University of Alabama at Birmingham	M
University of Minnesota, Duluth	M
University of Southern California	M,D,O
West Virginia University	M

SCANDINAVIAN LANGUAGES

Cornell University	M,D
Harvard University	D*
University of California, Berkeley	D
University of California, Los Angeles	M
University of Massachusetts Amherst	M,D*
University of Minnesota, Twin Cities Campus	M,D
University of Washington	M,D*
University of Wisconsin–Madison	M,D

SCHOOL NURSING

Cambridge College	M,D,O
Eastern Mennonite University	M
Eastern University	M,O
Felician University	M,O
Kean University	M
La Salle University	M,D,O
Monmouth University	M,D,O
Rowan University	M,D,O
Saint Joseph's University	M
Seton Hall University	M,D
University of Illinois at Chicago	M,O
West Chester University of Pennsylvania	M,D,O
Wright State University	M

SCHOOL PSYCHOLOGY

Abilene Christian University	O
Adelphi University	M
Alabama Agricultural and Mechanical University	M,O
Alfred University	M,D,O
Alliant International University–Irvine	M,D,O
Alliant International University–Los Angeles	M,D,O
Alliant International University–San Diego	M,D,O
Alliant International University–San Francisco	M,D,O
American Public University System	M
Andrews University	M,O
Appalachian State University	M
Arcadia University	M
Argosy University, Dallas	M,D
Argosy University, Hawai`i	M
Argosy University, Phoenix	M,D
Argosy University, Sarasota	M,D,O
Arkansas State University	M,O
Assumption College	M,O
Azusa Pacific University	M
Ball State University	M,D,O
Barry University	M,O
Baylor University	M,D,O
Bowling Green State University	M,O
Brigham Young University	M,D,O
Brooklyn College of the City University of New York	M,O
Caldwell University	M,O
California Baptist University	M
California State University, Chico	M
California State University, Dominguez Hills	M
California State University, East Bay	M
California State University, Los Angeles	M,D
California State University, Northridge	M
California State University, Sacramento	M
California University of Pennsylvania	M
Cambridge College	M,D,O
Canisius College	M
Capella University	M,D
Carlos Albizu University, Miami Campus	M,D
Central Connecticut State University	M,O
Central Michigan University	D,O
Central Washington University	M
Chaminade University of Honolulu	M
Chapman University	M,D,O
The Chicago School of Professional Psychology	D,O
The Citadel, The Military College of South Carolina	O
The College of New Rochelle	M
College of St. Joseph	M
The College of Saint Rose	M,O
The College of William and Mary	M,O
Creighton University	M
DePaul University	M,D
Duquesne University	M,D
Eastern Illinois University	M,O
Eastern Kentucky University	M,O
Eastern University	M,O
Eastern Washington University	M
Edinboro University of Pennsylvania	M,O
Emporia State University	M,O
Evangel University	M
Fairfield University	M,O
Fairleigh Dickinson University, Metropolitan Campus	M,D
Florida International University	M,D,O
Florida State University	D
Fordham University	M,D
Fort Hays State University	O
Francis Marion University	M,O
Fresno Pacific University	M
Gallaudet University	M,D,O
Gardner-Webb University	M
George Fox University	M,O
Georgian Court University	M,O
Georgia Southern University	M,O
Georgia State University	M,D,O
Grand Valley State University	M,O
Heidelberg University	M
Hofstra University	M,D
Houston Baptist University	M
Howard University	M,D
Humboldt State University	M
Husson University	M
Idaho State University	M,D,O
Illinois State University	D,O
Immaculata University	M,D,O
Indiana State University	M,D,O
Indiana University Bloomington	M,D,O
Indiana University of Pennsylvania	D,O
Inter American University of Puerto Rico, Metropolitan Campus	M,D
Inter American University of Puerto Rico, San Germán Campus	M,D
Iona College	M,O
James Madison University	M,D,O
Kean University	M,D,O
Keene State College	M,O
Kent State University	M,D,O
La Sierra University	M,O
Lehigh University	D,O
Lesley University	M,D,O
Lewis & Clark College	M,O
Lindenwood University	M,D,O
Long Island University–Hudson at Westchester	M,O
Louisiana State University and Agricultural & Mechanical College	M,D
Louisiana State University in Shreveport	O
Loyola Marymount University	M
Loyola University Chicago	D,O
Lynchburg College	M
Marist College	M,O
Marshall University	O
McGill University	M,D,O
McNeese State University	M
Mercer University	M,D
Mercy College	M
Merrimack College	M,O
Michigan State University	M,D,O
Middle Tennessee State University	M,O
Millersville University of Pennsylvania	M
Minnesota State University Mankato	M,D
Minnesota State University Moorhead	M,O
Minot State University	O
Mississippi State University	M,D,O
Monmouth University	M,O
Montana State University	M,D,O
Mount Saint Vincent University	M
National Louis University	M,D,O
National University	M,O
New Mexico State University	M,D,O
Niagara University	M
Nicholls State University	M,O
North Carolina State University	D
North Dakota State University	M,D
Northeastern University	M,D,O
Northern Arizona University	M,D,O
Northwest Nazarene University	M
Nova Southeastern University	M,D,O*
Old Dominion University	M,D,O
Oregon State University–Cascades	M
Ottawa University	M
Our Lady of the Lake University of San Antonio	M
Pace University	M,D
Penn State University Park	M,D,O
Philadelphia College of Osteopathic Medicine	M,D,O*
Pittsburg State University	O
Plymouth State University	M,O
Purdue University Northwest	M
Queens College of the City University of New York	M,O
Quincy University	M
Radford University	O
Rhode Island College	M,O
Rider University	O
Rochester Institute of Technology	M,O
Rowan University	M,O
Rutgers University–New Brunswick	M,D
St. John's University (NY)	M,D
Saint Mary's College of California	M,O
Sam Houston State University	M,D,O
San Diego State University	M
San Francisco State University	M,O
San Jose State University	M,D,O
Seattle University	M,O
Seton Hall University	M
Slippery Rock University of Pennsylvania	M
Southern Connecticut State University	M,O
Southern Illinois University Edwardsville	O
Southwestern Oklahoma State University	M
State University of New York at Plattsburgh	M,O
Stephen F. Austin State University	M
Suffolk University	M,D,O
Syracuse University	M,D,O
Teachers College, Columbia University	M,D,O
Temple University	M,D,O*
Tennessee Technological University	M,O
Texas A&M University	M,D
Texas A&M University–Central Texas	M,O
Texas State University	O
Texas Woman's University	M,D,O
Touro College	M,D
Towson University	O
Trinity University	M
Troy University	M,O
Tufts University	M,O
Union College (KY)	M
University at Albany, State University of New York	M,D,O
The University of Akron	M,D
University of Alberta	M,D
The University of Arizona	D,O
The University of British Columbia	M,D,O
University of Calgary	M,D
University of California, Riverside	M,D,O
University of California, Santa Barbara	M,D,O
University of Central Arkansas	M,D,O
University of Central Florida	O
University of Central Oklahoma	M
University of Cincinnati	D,O
University of Colorado Denver	M,O
University of Dayton	M,O
University of Delaware	M,D,O*
University of Denver	M,D,O
University of Detroit Mercy	M,D,O
University of Florida	M,D,O
University of Hartford	M
University of Houston–Clear Lake	M
University of Houston–Victoria	M
The University of Iowa	M,D,O*
The University of Kansas	D,O*
University of Kentucky	M,D,O
University of La Verne	M,O
University of Louisville	M,D
University of Manitoba	M,D
University of Maryland, College Park	M,D,O
University of Massachusetts Amherst	M,D,O*
University of Massachusetts Boston	M,D
University of Memphis	M,D,O
University of Minnesota, Twin Cities Campus	M,D,O
University of Missouri	M,D,O
University of Missouri–St. Louis	M,O
University of Montana	M,D,O
University of Nebraska at Kearney	M,O
University of Nebraska at Omaha	M,D,O
University of Nebraska–Lincoln	M,D,O
University of North Alabama	M
The University of North Carolina at Chapel Hill	M,D

*M—masters degree; D—doctorate; O—other advanced degree; *—Close-Up and/or Display*

The University of North Carolina at Greensboro	M,D,O
University of Northern Colorado	D,O
University of Northern Iowa	M,O
University of Phoenix–Colorado Campus	M
University of Phoenix–Colorado Springs Downtown Campus	M,O
University of Phoenix–Las Vegas Campus	M
University of Phoenix–Utah Campus	M
University of Rhode Island	M,D
University of South Carolina	D
The University of South Dakota	M,D,O
University of Southern Maine	M,D
University of Southern Mississippi	M,D
University of South Florida	M,D,O
The University of Tennessee	M,D,O
The University of Tennessee at Chattanooga	M,D,O
The University of Texas at Austin	M,D
The University of Texas at San Antonio	M,O
The University of Texas at Tyler	M
The University of Texas Rio Grande Valley	M
University of the Pacific	M,D,O
The University of Toledo	M,D,O
University of Utah	M,D*
University of Virginia	M,D
University of Washington	M,D*
The University of West Alabama	M,O
University of Wisconsin–Eau Claire	M,O
University of Wisconsin–La Crosse	M,O
University of Wisconsin–Milwaukee	D,O
University of Wisconsin–River Falls	M,O
University of Wisconsin–Stout	M,O
University of Wisconsin–Superior	M
University of Wisconsin–Whitewater	M,O
Utah State University	M,D
Valparaiso University	
Wayne State University	M,D,O
Western Illinois University	M,O
Western Kentucky University	M,O
Wichita State University	M,D,O
William James College	M,D,O
Worcester State University	O
Yeshiva University	D
Youngstown State University	M

SCIENCE EDUCATION

Acadia University	M
Alabama Agricultural and Mechanical University	M,O
Alabama State University	M,O
Albany State University	M
Alverno College	M
American University of Puerto Rico	M
Andrews University	M,D,O
Antioch University New England	M
Appalachian State University	M
Arcadia University	M,D,O
Arkansas State University	M,O
Asbury University	M
Athabasca University	M,O
Auburn University	M,D,O
Benedictine University	M
Bethel University (MN)	M,D,O
Binghamton University, State University of New York	M*
Biola University	M,O
Bloomsburg University of Pennsylvania	M
Boise State University	M,D,O
Boston College	M,D
Bowling Green State University	M
Bridgewater State University	M
Brigham Young University	M,D
Brooklyn College of the City University of New York	M
Brown University	M
Buffalo State College, State University of New York	M
California Baptist University	M
California State University, Bakersfield	M
California State University, Dominguez Hills	M
California State University, Fullerton	M
California State University, Long Beach	M
California State University, Northridge	M
Cambridge College	M,D,O
Caribbean University	M,D
Carthage College	M,O
Catawba College	M
Central Connecticut State University	M,O
Central Michigan University	M
Chaminade University of Honolulu	M
Chatham University	M
The Citadel, The Military College of South Carolina	M
City College of the City University of New York	M
Clarion University of Pennsylvania	M
Clark Atlanta University	M
Clarkson University	M,O
Clemson University	M,D,O
Cleveland State University	M
The College at Brockport, State University of New York	M,O
College of Charleston	M
The Colorado College	M
Colorado State University	M,D
Columbia University	M,D,O*
Columbus State University	M,O
Concordia University (United States)	M,D
Converse College	M
Delaware State University	M,D
DePaul University	M,D
Duquesne University	M
East Carolina University	M,O
Eastern Connecticut State University	M
Eastern Kentucky University	M
Eastern Michigan University	M
Eastern University	M,O
Elizabeth City State University	M
Elms College	M,O
Fairleigh Dickinson University, Metropolitan Campus	M
Fitchburg State University	M,O
Florida Agricultural and Mechanical University	M
Florida Atlantic University	M,D
Florida Institute of Technology	M,D,O
Florida International University	M,D,O
Florida State University	M,D,O
Fresno Pacific University	M
George Mason University	M
The George Washington University	M*
Georgia State University	M,D
Grambling State University	M,D,O
Hamline University	M,D
Hardin-Simmons University	M,D
Harrison Middleton University	M,D
Heritage University	M
Hofstra University	M,D,O
Hood College	M,O
Hunter College of the City University of New York	M
Illinois Institute of Technology	M,D
Indiana State University	M,D
Indiana University Bloomington	M,D,O
Instituto Tecnológico y de Estudios Superiores de Monterrey, Campus Monterrey	M,D
Inter American University of Puerto Rico, Arecibo Campus	M
Inter American University of Puerto Rico, Barranquitas Campus	M
Inter American University of Puerto Rico, Metropolitan Campus	M
Inter American University of Puerto Rico, Ponce Campus	M
Inter American University of Puerto Rico, San Germán Campus	M
Iona College	M
Iowa State University of Science and Technology	M
Ithaca College	M
Jackson State University	M
John Carroll University	M
Johns Hopkins University	M
Kaplan University, Davenport Campus	M
Kean University	M
Kutztown University of Pennsylvania	M
Lake Forest College	M
Laurentian University	O
Lawrence Technological University	M
Lebanon Valley College	M
Lehman College of the City University of New York	M
Lesley University	M,D,O
Lewis University	M
Louisiana Tech University	M,D
Lynchburg College	M
Lyndon State College	M
Manhattanville College	M*
McNeese State University	M
Michigan State University	M,D
Michigan Technological University	M,D,O
Middle Tennessee State University	M,D
Millersville University of Pennsylvania	M
Mills College	M,D,O
Minnesota State University Mankato	M
Minot State University	M
Mississippi College	M,D,O
Mississippi State University	M,D
Missouri State University	M
Montclair State University	M
Morehead State University	M
Morgan State University	M,D
National Louis University	M,D,O
New Mexico Institute of Mining and Technology	M
New Mexico State University	M,D,O
New York Institute of Technology	M,O
New York University	M,D,O
Niagara University	M
North Carolina Agricultural and Technical State University	M
North Carolina State University	M,D
North Dakota State University	M,D,O
Northeastern State University	M
Northern Arizona University	M,O
Northern Michigan University	M
Northwest Missouri State University	M
Occidental College	M
Ohio University	M
Oregon State University	M,D
Our Lady of the Lake University of San Antonio	M
Pacific University	M
Pepperdine University	M,D
Plymouth State University	M
Portland State University	M,D
Purdue University	M,D,O
Purdue University Northwest	M
Queens College of the City University of New York	M,O
Quinnipiac University	M
Rice University	M,D
Rider University	O
Rowan University	M
Rutgers University–New Brunswick	M,D
Saginaw Valley State University	M
Saint Xavier University	M
Salem State University	M
Samford University	M,D,O
San Diego State University	M,D
San Jose State University	M,O
Seattle Pacific University	M
Shippensburg University of Pennsylvania	M
Slippery Rock University of Pennsylvania	M
Smith College	M
South Carolina State University	M
Southern Connecticut State University	M,O
Southern University and Agricultural and Mechanical College	D
Southwestern Oklahoma State University	M
State University of New York at New Paltz	M,O
State University of New York at Plattsburgh	M
State University of New York College at Cortland	M
State University of New York College at Old Westbury	M
State University of New York College at Potsdam	M
Stevenson University	M
Stony Brook University, State University of New York	M,D,O
Syracuse University	M,D
Teachers College, Columbia University	M,D
Temple University	M*
Tennessee Technological University	M,O
Texas Christian University	M,O
Texas Tech University	M,D
Touro College	M
Troy University	M
Tufts University	M,D
Universidad Nacional Pedro Henriquez Urena	M
University at Buffalo, the State University of New York	M,D,O*
The University of Alabama in Huntsville	M,D
University of Arkansas at Pine Bluff	M
The University of British Columbia	M,D
University of California, Berkeley	M,D
University of California, San Diego	D
University of Central Florida	M,D,O
University of Chicago	D
University of Cincinnati	M,D,O
University of Colorado Denver	M,D
University of Connecticut	M,D*
The University of Findlay	M,D
University of Florida	M,D,O
University of Georgia	M,D,O
University of Illinois at Chicago	D
University of Illinois at Urbana–Champaign	M,D
University of Indianapolis	M
The University of Iowa	M,D*
University of Louisiana at Monroe	M,D
University of Maine	M,D,O
University of Maryland, Baltimore County	M
University of Massachusetts Amherst	M,D,O*
University of Miami	D
University of Michigan–Dearborn	M
University of Minnesota, Twin Cities Campus	M
University of Missouri	M,D,O
University of Nebraska at Kearney	M
University of Nebraska at Omaha	M,O
University of New Hampshire	M,D
University of New Haven	M,O
University of New Mexico	O
The University of North Carolina at Chapel Hill	M
The University of North Carolina at Greensboro	M,D,O
The University of North Carolina at Pembroke	M
The University of North Carolina Wilmington	M
University of Northern Colorado	M,D
University of Northern Iowa	M
University of North Texas Health Science Center at Fort Worth	M,D
University of Pennsylvania	M,O*
University of Phoenix–Online Campus	M,O
University of Pittsburgh	M,D*
University of Puerto Rico, Rí o Piedras Campus	M,D
University of St. Francis (IL)	M,D,O
University of South Africa	M,D
University of South Alabama	M,D
University of South Carolina	M,D
University of Southern Mississippi	M,D
University of South Florida	M,D,O
University of South Florida, St. Petersburg	M
The University of Tennessee	M,D,O
The University of Texas at Dallas	M*
The University of Texas at El Paso	M
The University of Toledo	M,D,O
The University of Tulsa	M
University of Utah	M,D*
University of Vermont	M,D
University of Victoria	M,D
University of Virginia	M,D,O
University of Washington	M,D*
University of Washington, Tacoma	M
The University of West Alabama	M
University of West Florida	M,D
University of Wisconsin–Madison	M,D
University of Wisconsin–River Falls	M
University of Wisconsin–Stevens Point	M
University of Wyoming	M
Ursuline College	M
Vanderbilt University	M,D*
Wagner College	M
Walden University	M,D,O
Wayland Baptist University	M
Wayne State College	M
Wayne State University	M,D,O
West Chester University of Pennsylvania	M,O
Western Governors University	M,O
Western Michigan University	M,D,O
Western Oregon University	M
Western Washington University	M
Widener University	M,D
Wilkes University	M,D
Wisconsin Lutheran College	M
Wright State University	M
Youngstown State University	M

SECONDARY EDUCATION

Acacia University	M
Adelphi University	M
Alabama Agricultural and Mechanical University	M,O
Alabama State University	M,O
Alcorn State University	M,O
American International College	M,D,O
American Public University System	M
Andrews University	M,D,O
Arcadia University	M,D,O
Argosy University, Atlanta	M,D,O
Argosy University, Chicago	M,D,O
Argosy University, Hawai'i	M,D
Argosy University, Inland Empire	M,D
Argosy University, Los Angeles	M,D
Argosy University, Nashville	M,D,O
Argosy University, Orange County	M,D
Argosy University, Phoenix	M,D,O
Argosy University, San Diego	M,D
Argosy University, San Francisco Bay Area	M,D
Argosy University, Sarasota	M,D,O
Argosy University, Seattle	M,D
Argosy University, Tampa	M,D,O
Argosy University, Twin Cities	M,D,O
Argosy University, Washington DC	M,D,O
Arizona State University at the Tempe campus	M
Armstrong State University	M,O
Auburn University	M,D,O
Auburn University at Montgomery	M,O
Augusta University	M,O
Austin Peay State University	M,O
Ball State University	M
Belhaven University (MS)	M
Bellarmine University	M,D,O
Benedictine University	M
Berry College	M
Bethel University (MN)	M,D,O
Binghamton University, State University of New York	M*
Bloomsburg University of Pennsylvania	M
Bob Jones University	M,D,O
Boston College	M
Bowie State University	M
Brandeis University	M,O
Brenau University	M,O
Bridgewater State University	M
Brooklyn College of the City University of New York	M
Brown University	M
California State University, Bakersfield	M
California State University, Fullerton	M
California State University, Long Beach	M
California State University, Northridge	M
California State University, Stanislaus	M
California University of Pennsylvania	M
Campbell University	M
Canisius College	M,O
Carson-Newman University	M
The Catholic University of America	M,D,O
Centenary College of Louisiana	M
Central Michigan University	M,D,O
Chadron State College	M,O
Chaminade University of Honolulu	M
Chapman University	M,D,O
Chatham University	M
Chestnut Hill College	M
Chicago State University	M
The Citadel, The Military College of South Carolina	M,O
City College of the City University of New York	M,O
Clemson University	M
Colgate University	M
The College of New Jersey	M
College of St. Joseph	M
The College of Saint Rose	M,O
College of Staten Island of the City University of New York	M
The Colorado College	M
Columbus State University	M,O
Concordia University (United States)	M,D
Concordia University Chicago	M

Concordia University, Nebraska	M
Converse College	M
Cornell University	M,D
Creighton University	M
Dakota Wesleyan University	M
Dallas Baptist University	M
Defiance College	M
Delta State University	M,D,O
DePaul University	M,D
DeSales University	M,O
Drew University	M,D,O
Drury University	M
Duquesne University	M
D'Youville College	M,D
Eastern Connecticut State University	M
Eastern Kentucky University	M
Eastern Michigan University	M
Eastern Nazarene College	M,O
Eastern New Mexico University	M
Eastern Oregon University	M
Eastern University	M,O
Eastern Washington University	M
East Stroudsburg University of Pennsylvania	M,D
East Tennessee State University	M,O
Edinboro University of Pennsylvania	M
Elms College	M,O
Emmanuel College (United States)	M,D
Emory University	M,D
Endicott College	M
Evangel University	M
Fairfield University	M,O
Fayetteville State University	M
Florida Agricultural and Mechanical University	M
Fontbonne University	M
Frostburg State University	M
Gallaudet University	M,D,O
George Mason University	M
The George Washington University	M*
Georgia College & State University	M
Georgia Southern University	M,O
Georgia State University	M,D
Gonzaga University	M
Gordon College	M,O
Goucher College	M,O
Grand Canyon University	M
Grand Valley State University	M,O
Greenville College	M
Hampton University	M
Harding University	M,O
Hawai`i Pacific University	M
High Point University	M
Hofstra University	M,D,O
Hood College	M,O
Hope International University	M
Howard University	M
Hunter College of the City University of New York	M
Idaho State University	M,O
Immaculata University	M,D,O
Indiana University Bloomington	M,D,O
Indiana University Northwest	M
Indiana University–Purdue University Fort Wayne	M
Indiana University South Bend	M
Indiana University Southeast	M
Instituto Tecnologico de Santo Domingo	M,O
Ithaca College	M
Jackson State University	M,D,O
Jacksonville State University	M
James Madison University	M
John Brown University	M
John Carroll University	M
Johns Hopkins University	M
Johnson & Wales University	M
Johnson State College	M
Kaplan University, Davenport Campus	M
Kennesaw State University	M
Kent State University	M
Kutztown University of Pennsylvania	M
LaGrange College	M,O
Lake Forest College	M
Lancaster Bible College	M,D
La Salle University	M,O
Lee University	M,O
Le Moyne College	M,O
Lenoir-Rhyne University	M
Lesley University	M,D,O
Lewis & Clark College	M
Lewis University	M
Liberty University	M,D,O
Lincoln University (MO)	M
Long Island University–LIU Post	M,D,O
Louisiana State University and Agricultural & Mechanical College	M,D,O
Loyola Marymount University	M
Loyola University Chicago	M,O
Loyola University Maryland	M,O
Manhattanville College	M*
Mansfield University of Pennsylvania	M
Marquette University	M,D,O
Marshall University	M
Marygrove College	M
Marymount University	M
Maryville University of Saint Louis	M,D
Marywood University	M
McDaniel College	M
McNeese State University	M,O
Medaille College	M
Mercer University	M,D,O
Mercy College	M
Mercyhurst University	M
Merrimack College	M,O
Middle Tennessee State University	M,O
Mills College	M,D,O
Mississippi College	M,D,O
Mississippi State University	M,D,O
Missouri State University	M,O
Monmouth University	M,O
Morehead State University	M,O
Morgan State University	M
Mount St. Joseph University	M,O
Mount Saint Mary College	M,O
Murray State University	M,O
National Louis University	M,D,O
New Jersey City University	M
New York Institute of Technology	M
New York University	M,D,O
Niagara University	M,O
Nicholls State University	M
Norfolk State University	M
North Carolina Agricultural and Technical State University	M
North Carolina State University	M
Northeastern Illinois University	M
Northeastern University	M,D
Northern Arizona University	M,D
Northern Illinois University	M,D
Northern Michigan University	M
Northwest Christian University	M
Northwestern Oklahoma State University	M
Northwestern State University of Louisiana	M,O
Northwestern University	M*
Northwest Missouri State University	M,O
Oakland University	M,O
Occidental College	M
Ohio University	M,D
Old Dominion University	M
Olivet Nazarene University	M
Pacific Union College	M
Pacific University	M
Piedmont College	M,O
Plymouth State University	M
Prescott College	M,D
Providence College	M
Queens College of the City University of New York	M,O
Quinnipiac University	M
Regis University	M,O
Rhode Island College	M
Roberts Wesleyan College	M
Rochester Institute of Technology	M
Rockford University	M
Roosevelt University	M
Rowan University	M
Saginaw Valley State University	M
St. Bonaventure University	M
St. John's University (NY)	M,O
Saint Joseph's University	M,D,O
Saint Mary's University of Minnesota	M,O
Saint Peter's University	M,O
St. Thomas Aquinas College	M,O
Saint Xavier University	M
Salem College	M
Salem State University	M
Salisbury University	M
Samford University	M,D,O
San Diego State University	M
San Francisco State University	M,O
Seattle Pacific University	M
Shenandoah University	M,D,O
Siena Heights University	M,O
Sierra Nevada College	M
Simmons College	M,D,O
Simpson College	M
Slippery Rock University of Pennsylvania	M
Smith College	M
South Carolina State University	M
Southeast Missouri State University	M,D,O
Southern New Hampshire University	M,D,O
Southern Oregon University	M
Southern University and Agricultural and Mechanical College	M
Southwestern Assemblies of God University	M
Southwestern Oklahoma State University	M
Spalding University	M
Springfield College	M
Spring Hill College	M
Stanford University	M
State University of New York at Fredonia	M
State University of New York at New Paltz	M,O
State University of New York at Oswego	M
State University of New York at Plattsburgh	M
State University of New York College at Cortland	M
State University of New York College at Geneseo	M
State University of New York College at Oneonta	M
State University of New York College at Potsdam	M
Stephen F. Austin State University	M,D
Sul Ross State University	M
Syracuse University	M,D
Tarleton State University	M
Teachers College, Columbia University	M,D
Temple University	M*
Tennessee Technological University	M,O
Texas A&M University–Corpus Christi	M
Texas Southern University	M,D
Texas State University	M
Texas Tech University	M,D
Towson University	M
Trevecca Nazarene University	M,O
Trinity Washington University	M
Troy University	M
Tufts University	M,D
Union College (KY)	M
Universidad Metropolitana	M
The University of Alabama	M,D,O
The University of Alabama at Birmingham	M
University of Alaska Fairbanks	M
University of Alaska Southeast	M
University of Alberta	M,D
The University of Arizona	M,D
University of Arkansas	M,O
University of Arkansas at Little Rock	M
University of Arkansas at Pine Bluff	M
University of Bridgeport	M,D,O
University of California, Irvine	M,D
University of Central Oklahoma	M
University of Cincinnati	M
University of Colorado Denver	M
University of Connecticut	M,D*
University of Dayton	M
University of Great Falls	M
University of Guam	M
University of Illinois at Chicago	M,D
University of Indianapolis	M
The University of Iowa	M,D*
University of Kentucky	M,D
University of La Verne	M,D,O
University of Louisiana at Monroe	M
University of Louisville	M,D,O
University of Maine	M,D,O
University of Mary Hardin-Baylor	M,D
University of Maryland, College Park	M,D,O
University of Massachusetts Amherst	M,D,O*
University of Massachusetts Dartmouth	M,O
University of Memphis	M,D
University of Michigan–Flint	M,D,O
University of Missouri–St. Louis	M,D,O
University of Montevallo	M
University of Nebraska at Kearney	M
University of Nebraska at Omaha	M,O
University of Nevada, Reno	M
University of New Hampshire	M,O
University of New Mexico	M
University of North Alabama	M
The University of North Carolina at Chapel Hill	M
The University of North Carolina at Charlotte	M,D,O
University of North Dakota	D
University of Northern Iowa	M
University of North Florida	M
University of North Georgia	M,O
University of Pennsylvania	M*
University of Phoenix–Bay Area Campus	M,D,O
University of Phoenix–Central Valley Campus	M
University of Phoenix–Colorado Campus	M
University of Phoenix–Colorado Springs Downtown Campus	M,O
University of Phoenix–Hawaii Campus	M
University of Phoenix–New Mexico Campus	M
University of Phoenix–North Florida Campus	M
University of Phoenix–Online Campus	M,O
University of Phoenix–Phoenix Campus	M
University of Phoenix–Sacramento Valley Campus	M,O
University of Phoenix–San Diego Campus	M
University of Phoenix–Southern Arizona Campus	M,O
University of Phoenix–Southern California Campus	M,O
University of Phoenix–South Florida Campus	M
University of Phoenix–Utah Campus	M
University of Phoenix–Washington D.C. Campus	M,D,O
University of Pittsburgh	M,D*
University of Puget Sound	M
University of St. Francis (IL)	M,D,O
University of St. Thomas (TX)	M
The University of Scranton	M
University of South Alabama	M,D
University of South Carolina	M,D
The University of South Dakota	M
University of Southern Indiana	M
University of South Florida	M,D,O
The University of Tennessee	M,D,O
The University of Tennessee at Chattanooga	M,D,O
The University of Tennessee at Martin	M
The University of Texas Rio Grande Valley	M
University of the Cumberlands	M,D,O
University of the District of Columbia	M
University of the Incarnate Word	M
The University of Toledo	M,D,O
The University of Tulsa	M
University of Utah	M,D*
University of Washington, Bothell	M
The University of West Alabama	M
University of West Florida	M,O
University of West Georgia	M,D,O
University of Wisconsin–Eau Claire	M
University of Wisconsin–Milwaukee	M
University of Wisconsin–Platteville	M
University of Wisconsin–Stevens Point	M
Utah State University	M
Vanderbilt University	M,D*
Villanova University	M
Virginia Commonwealth University	M,O
Wagner College	M
Wake Forest University	M
Washington State University	M,D
Washington University in St. Louis	M
Wayland Baptist University	M
Wayne State University	M,D,O
West Chester University of Pennsylvania	M,O
Western Kentucky University	M,O
Western New Mexico University	M
Western Oregon University	M
Western Washington University	M
Westfield State University	M
West Virginia University	M,D
Wheaton College	M
Whittier College	M
Whitworth University	M
Wichita State University	M
Wilkes University	M,D
William Carey University	M,O
William Paterson University of New Jersey	M
Wilmington University	M,D
Wilson College	M
Winthrop University	M
Worcester State University	M,O
Wright State University	M
Xavier University	M
Youngstown State University	M

SLAVIC LANGUAGES

Brigham Young University	D
Brown University	M,D
Columbia University	M,D*
Cornell University	M,D
Duke University	M,O*
Florida State University	M
Harvard University	D*
Indiana University Bloomington	M,D
New York University	M
Northwestern University	D*
The Ohio State University	M,D
Princeton University	D
Stanford University	D
University of Alberta	M,D
University of California, Berkeley	D
University of California, Los Angeles	M,D
University of Illinois at Chicago	M,D
University of Illinois at Urbana–Champaign	M,D
The University of Kansas	M,D*
The University of Manchester	M,D
University of Manitoba	M
University of Michigan	M,D
The University of North Carolina at Chapel Hill	M,D
University of Pittsburgh	M,D*
University of Southern California	M,D
The University of Texas at Austin	M,D
University of Toronto	M,D
University of Virginia	M,D
University of Washington	M,D*
University of Wisconsin–Madison	M,D
Yale University	D*

SOCIAL PSYCHOLOGY

Adler University	M,D,O
Alliant International University–Los Angeles	D
Alvernia University	M
Alverno College	M
The American University in Cairo	M
Andrews University	M
Arcadia University	M
Argosy University, Atlanta	M,D,O
Argosy University, Chicago	M,D
Argosy University, Dallas	M
Argosy University, Sarasota	M,D
Argosy University, Washington DC	M,D
Arizona State University at the Tempe campus	M,D
Ball State University	M
Becker College	M
Bowling Green State University	M,D
Brandeis University	M,D
Brock University	M,D
Brooklyn College of the City University of New York	M,D
California Institute of Integral Studies	M,D
California State University, East Bay	M
California State University, Fullerton	M
Canisius College	M
Carnegie Mellon University	D
Central Connecticut State University	M
Claremont Graduate University	M,D,O
Clark University	D
Cleveland State University	M,D,O

*M—masters degree; D—doctorate; O—other advanced degree; *—Close-Up and/or Display*

College of St. Joseph	M
Connecticut College	M
Cornell University	M,D
Delaware Valley University	M
Florida Agricultural and Mechanical University	M
Florida State University	D
Future Generations Graduate School	M
The George Washington University	D*
Georgia State University	D
The Graduate Center, City University of New York	D
Harvard University	D*
Heidelberg University	M
Hofstra University	M,D
Howard University	M,D
Humboldt State University	M
Husson University	M
Indiana University Bloomington	D
Indiana University of Pennsylvania	M
Indiana Wesleyan University	M
Iowa State University of Science and Technology	D
Lesley University	M,D,O
Loyola University Chicago	M,D,O
Marquette University	M,D
Martin University	M
Marymount California University	M
Missouri Valley College	M
Mount Aloysius College	M
The New School	M,O
New York University	M,D,O
Norfolk State University	M
North Carolina State University	M
North Dakota State University	M,D
Northeastern Illinois University	M
Northwestern University	D*
The Ohio State University	D
Oregon State University–Cascades	M
Penn State Harrisburg	M,D,O
Philadelphia University	M
Queen's University at Kingston	M,D
Rutgers University–Newark	D
Rutgers University–New Brunswick	D
Sage Graduate School	M
St. Bonaventure University	M,O
St. Cloud State University	M
Saint Martin's University	M
San Francisco State University	M,O
Southwestern College (NM)	O
Stony Brook University, State University of New York	D
Syracuse University	D
Teachers College, Columbia University	M,D
Temple University	M,D,O*
Texas Christian University	M,D
Texas State University	M
Thomas University	M
Troy University	M,O
Université du Québec à Rimouski	M
Université Laval	D
University at Albany, State University of New York	M,D
University of Alaska Anchorage	M,D
University of Alaska Fairbanks	M,D,O
University of Bridgeport	M
The University of British Columbia	M,D
University of Central Arkansas	M
University of Connecticut	M,D*
University of Delaware	D*
University of Denver	D
University of Guelph	M,D
University of Hawaii at Manoa	M,D,O
University of Houston	M,D
The University of Kansas	M,D*
University of Maryland, College Park	M,D
University of Massachusetts Amherst	M,D*
University of Massachusetts Lowell	M
University of Michigan	D
University of Minnesota, Twin Cities Campus	D
University of Missouri–Kansas City	M,D
University of Nebraska–Lincoln	M,D
University of Nevada, Reno	D
University of New Haven	M,O
The University of North Carolina at Chapel Hill	D
The University of North Carolina at Greensboro	M,D
University of Oregon	M,D
University of Phoenix–Phoenix Campus	M
University of Puerto Rico, Rí o Piedras Campus	M,D
University of Rochester	M,D*
University of South Carolina	M,D
University of Southern California	M,D
The University of Tennessee at Chattanooga	M,D,O
The University of Tennessee at Martin	M
University of Victoria	M,D
University of Washington	D*
University of Windsor	M,D
University of Wisconsin–Madison	D
University of Wisconsin–Milwaukee	M,D
University of Wisconsin–Superior	M
Virginia Commonwealth University	D
Walden University	M,D,O
Wayne State University	M,D
Western Illinois University	M,O
Wichita State University	D
Wilfrid Laurier University	M,D
Yale University	D*

SOCIAL SCIENCES

Augusta University	M
California Institute of Technology	M,D
California State University, Chico	M
California State University, San Bernardino	M
Campbellsville University	M
Carnegie Mellon University	D
The Citadel, The Military College of South Carolina	M
Columbia University	M,D*
Eastern Michigan University	M
Florida Agricultural and Mechanical University	M
Graduate Theological Union	M,D,O
Harrison Middleton University	M,D
Hollins University	M
Humboldt State University	M
Indiana University Bloomington	M,D,O
Indiana University–Purdue University Indianapolis	M,D
Johns Hopkins University	M,D
Massachusetts Institute of Technology	D
Mississippi College	M,O
Montclair State University	M
The New School	M,D
New York University	M,D
North Dakota State University	M
Nova Southeastern University	M,D,O*
The Ohio State University	M,D
Ohio University	M
St. Edward's University	M,O
Southern University and Agricultural and Mechanical College	M
Syracuse University	M,D
Texas A&M International University	M
Towson University	M
Troy University	M
University of California, Merced	M,D
University of California, Santa Barbara	D
University of California, Santa Cruz	D
University of Chicago	M,D
University of Florida	M,D,O
University of Illinois at Springfield	M,O
The University of Manchester	M,D
University of Maryland, Baltimore County	D
University of Memphis	M
University of Michigan	D
University of Michigan–Flint	M
University of Northern Iowa	M
University of Regina	M
The University of Texas at Tyler	M
University of Toronto	M,D
University of Washington	M,D*
Wilfrid Laurier University	M
Worcester Polytechnic Institute	M,D,O
Yale University	M,D*

SOCIAL SCIENCES EDUCATION

Acadia University	M
Alabama Agricultural and Mechanical University	M,O
Alabama State University	M,O
American Public University System	M
Andrews University	M,D,O
Appalachian State University	M
Arcadia University	M,D,O
Arkansas State University	M,D,O
Asbury University	M
Auburn University	M,D,O
Binghamton University, State University of New York	M*
Bloomsburg University of Pennsylvania	M
Bob Jones University	M,D,O
Bridgewater State University	M
Brooklyn College of the City University of New York	M
Brown University	M
Buffalo State College, State University of New York	M
California State University, East Bay	M
California State University, Fresno	M
Cambridge College	M,D,O
Caribbean University	M,D
Carthage College	M,O
Chadron State College	M,O
Chaminade University of Honolulu	M
Chatham University	M
The Citadel, The Military College of South Carolina	M
City College of the City University of New York	M,O
Clarkson University	M,O
The College at Brockport, State University of New York	M,O
College of St. Joseph	M
The Colorado College	M
Columbus State University	M,O
Concord University	M
Converse College	M
Delta State University	M
Duquesne University	M
East Carolina University	M
Eastern Kentucky University	M
Eastern University	M,O
East Stroudsburg University of Pennsylvania	M
Emporia State University	M
Fayetteville State University	M
Fitchburg State University	M,O
Florida Agricultural and Mechanical University	M
Florida Atlantic University	M
Florida International University	M,D,O
Florida State University	M,D,O
Framingham State University	M
George Mason University	M
Georgia State University	M,D
Grambling State University	M
Harding University	M,O
Hofstra University	M,D,O
Hunter College of the City University of New York	M
Indiana University Bloomington	M,D,O
Instituto Tecnologico de Santo Domingo	M,O
Inter American University of Puerto Rico, Arecibo Campus	M
Inter American University of Puerto Rico, Barranquitas Campus	M
Inter American University of Puerto Rico, Metropolitan Campus	M
Inter American University of Puerto Rico, Ponce Campus	M
Iona College	M
Ithaca College	M
Johns Hopkins University	M
Kutztown University of Pennsylvania	M
Lake Forest College	M
La Salle University	M,O
Lee University	M,O
Lehman College of the City University of New York	M
Le Moyne College	M,O
Lewis University	M
Long Island University–LIU Brooklyn	M,D,O
Louisiana Tech University	M,D
Manhattanville College	M*
Michigan State University	M,D
Mills College	M,D,O
Minnesota State University Mankato	M
Mississippi College	M,D,O
Missouri State University	M,O
Molloy College	M,O
Morehead State University	M,O
New York University	M,D,O
North Carolina State University	M
North Dakota State University	M,D,O
Northwest Missouri State University	M,O
Occidental College	M
Ohio University	M,D
Oregon State University	M,D
Pace University	M,O
Plymouth State University	M
Portland State University	M
Purdue University	M,D,O
Queens College of the City University of New York	M,O
Quinnipiac University	M
Rhode Island College	M
Rider University	O
Rivier University	M
Rutgers University–New Brunswick	M,D
St. John Fisher College	M
Samford University	M,D,O
Slippery Rock University of Pennsylvania	M
Smith College	M
South Carolina State University	M
Southwestern Oklahoma State University	M
Spring Hill College	M,O
State University of New York at New Paltz	M,O
State University of New York at Plattsburgh	M
State University of New York College at Old Westbury	M
State University of New York College at Potsdam	M
Stony Brook University, State University of New York	M,O
Syracuse University	M
Teachers College, Columbia University	M,D,O
Temple University	M*
Trinity Washington University	M
Troy University	M
University at Buffalo, the State University of New York	M,D,O*
University of Arkansas at Pine Bluff	M
The University of British Columbia	M,D
University of California, Santa Cruz	M
University of Central Florida	M,D
University of Cincinnati	M,D,O
University of Connecticut	M,D*
University of Florida	M,D,O
University of Georgia	M,D,O
University of Illinois at Chicago	D
University of Indianapolis	M
The University of Iowa	M,D*
University of Louisiana at Monroe	M,D
University of Maine	M,D,O
University of Maryland, Baltimore County	M
University of Minnesota, Twin Cities Campus	M
University of Missouri	M,D,O
The University of North Carolina at Chapel Hill	M
The University of North Carolina at Greensboro	M,D,O
The University of North Carolina at Pembroke	M
The University of North Carolina Wilmington	M
University of North Georgia	M,O
University of Pittsburgh	M,D*
University of Puerto Rico, Rí o Piedras Campus	M,D
University of St. Francis (IL)	M,D,O
University of South Carolina	M,D
University of Southern Mississippi	M,D,O
University of South Florida	M,D,O
The University of Tennessee	M,D,O
University of the District of Columbia	M
The University of Toledo	M,D,O
University of Victoria	M,D
University of Virginia	M,D,O
University of Washington	M,D*
The University of West Alabama	M
University of West Florida	D
University of Wisconsin–River Falls	M
Ursuline College	M
Virginia Polytechnic Institute and State University	M,D,O
Wagner College	M
Wayland Baptist University	M
Wayne State College	M
Wayne State University	M,D,O
Webster University	M,O
Western Governors University	M,O
Western Oregon University	M
Widener University	M,D
Wilkes University	M,D
William Carey University	M,O
Worcester State University	M

SOCIAL WORK

Abilene Christian University	M
Adelphi University	M,D
Alabama Agricultural and Mechanical University	M,O
Albany State University	M
American Jewish University	M
Andrews University	M
Appalachian State University	M
Arizona State University at the Tempe campus	M,D,O
Arkansas State University	M,O
Asbury University	M
Augsburg College	M
Aurora University	M,D
Austin Peay State University	M
Azusa Pacific University	M
Barry University	M,D
Baylor University	M,D
Binghamton University, State University of New York	M*
Boise State University	M
Boston College	M,D
Boston University	M,D
Bridgewater State University	M
Brigham Young University	M
Bryn Mawr College	M,D
California State University, Bakersfield	M
California State University, Chico	M
California State University, Dominguez Hills	M
California State University, East Bay	M
California State University, Fresno	M
California State University, Fullerton	M
California State University, Long Beach	M
California State University, Los Angeles	M
California State University, Monterey Bay	M
California State University, Northridge	M,O
California State University, Sacramento	M
California State University, San Bernardino	M
California State University, San Marcos	M
California State University, Stanislaus	M
California University of Pennsylvania	M
Campbellsville University	M
Capella University	D
Carleton University	M
Case Western Reserve University	M,D*
The Catholic University of America	M,D
Chicago State University	M
Clark Atlanta University	M,D
Clarke University	M
Cleveland State University	M
The College at Brockport, State University of New York	M,O
The College of St. Scholastica	M
College of Staten Island of the City University of New York	M
Colorado State University	M,D
Columbia University	M,D*
Concord University	M
Cornell University	M,D
Daemen College	M
Dalhousie University	M
Delaware State University	M
DePaul University	M
Dominican University	M
East Carolina University	M,O
Eastern Michigan University	M
Eastern Washington University	M
East Tennessee State University	M
Edinboro University of Pennsylvania	M
Fayetteville State University	M
Florida Agricultural and Mechanical University	M
Florida Atlantic University	M,D
Florida Gulf Coast University	M
Florida International University	M,D
Florida State University	M,D
Fordham University	M,D
Gallaudet University	M,D,O
George Fox University	M
George Mason University	M

Georgia State University	M,O
Governors State University	M
The Graduate Center, City University of New York	D
Grambling State University	M
Grand Valley State University	M
Gratz College	M,O
Hawai`i Pacific University	M
Howard University	M,D
Humboldt State University	M
Hunter College of the City University of New York	M,D
Illinois State University	M
Indiana State University	M
Indiana University East	M
Indiana University Northwest	M
Indiana University–Purdue University Indianapolis	M,D,O
Indiana University South Bend	M
Institute for Clinical Social Work	D
Inter American University of Puerto Rico, Metropolitan Campus	M
Jackson State University	M,D
Johnson C. Smith University	M
Kean University	M
Kennesaw State University	M
Kutztown University of Pennsylvania	M
Lakehead University	M
Laurentian University	M
Loma Linda University	M,D
London Metropolitan University	M,D
Long Island University–LIU Brooklyn	M,D
Long Island University–LIU Post	M,O
Louisiana State University and Agricultural & Mechanical College	M,D
Loyola University Chicago	M,D,O
Marshall University	M
Marywood University	M,D
McGill University	M,D,O
McMaster University	M
Memorial University of Newfoundland	M,D
Metropolitan State University of Denver	M
Michigan State University	M,D
Middle Tennessee State University	M
Millersville University of Pennsylvania	M,D
Minnesota State University Mankato	M
Missouri State University	M
Monmouth University	M,O
Morgan State University	M,D
Nazareth College of Rochester	M
Newman University	M
New Mexico Highlands University	M
New Mexico State University	M
New York University	M,D
Norfolk State University	M,D
North Carolina Agricultural and Technical State University	M
North Carolina State University	M
Northern Kentucky University	M
Northwest Nazarene University	M
Nyack College	M
The Ohio State University	M,D
The Ohio State University at Lima	M
The Ohio State University–Mansfield Campus	M
The Ohio State University–Newark Campus	M
Ohio University	M
Our Lady of the Lake University of San Antonio	M,D
Pacific University	M
Park University	M,O
Phillips Theological Seminary	M,D
Pontifical Catholic University of Puerto Rico	M
Portland State University	M,D
Quinnipiac University	M
Radford University	M
Ramapo College of New Jersey	M
Rhode Island College	M
Roberts Wesleyan College	M
Rutgers University–New Brunswick	M,D
Sacred Heart University	M
St. Ambrose University	M
St. Catherine University	M,D
St. Cloud State University	M
Saint Leo University	M
Saint Louis University	M
Salem State University	M
Salisbury University	M
Samford University	M
San Diego State University	M
San Francisco State University	M
San Jose State University	M,O
Savannah State University	M
Shippensburg University of Pennsylvania	M
Simmons College	M,D
Smith College	M,D
Southern Adventist University	M
Southern Connecticut State University	M
Southern Illinois University Carbondale	M
Southern Illinois University Edwardsville	M
Southern University at New Orleans	M
Spalding University	M
Springfield College	M,O
Stephen F. Austin State University	M
Stockton University	M
Stony Brook University, State University of New York	M,D
Syracuse University	M
Tarleton State University	M
Temple University	M*
Tennessee State University	M,D
Texas Christian University	M
Texas State University	M
Texas Tech University	M
Thompson Rivers University	M
Touro College	M
Troy University	M,O
Tulane University	M,D
Union University	M
Universidad del Este	M
Université de Moncton	M
Université de Montréal	O
Université de Sherbrooke	M
Université du Québec à Montréal	M
Université du Québec en Abitibi-Témiscamingue	M
Université du Québec en Outaouais	M
Université Laval	M,D
University at Albany, State University of New York	M,D
University at Buffalo, the State University of New York	M,D*
The University of Akron	M
The University of Alabama	M,D
University of Alaska Anchorage	M,O
University of Arkansas	M
University of Arkansas at Little Rock	M
The University of British Columbia	M,D
University of Calgary	M,D,O
University of California, Berkeley	M,D
University of California, Los Angeles	M,D
University of Central Florida	M,O
University of Chicago	M,D
University of Cincinnati	M
University of Denver	M,D,O
University of Georgia	M,D,O
University of Guam	M
University of Hawaii at Manoa	M,D
University of Houston	M,D
University of Illinois at Chicago	M,D,O
University of Illinois at Urbana–Champaign	M,D
The University of Iowa	M,D*
The University of Kansas	M,D*
University of Kentucky	M,D
University of Louisville	M,D,O
University of Maine	M,O
The University of Manchester	M,D
University of Manitoba	M,D
University of Maryland, Baltimore	M,D
University of Maryland, College Park	
University of Michigan	M,D
University of Minnesota, Duluth	M
University of Minnesota, Twin Cities Campus	M,D
University of Mississippi	M,D
University of Missouri	M,D,O
University of Missouri–Kansas City	M
University of Missouri–St. Louis	M
University of Montana	M
University of Nebraska at Omaha	M,O
University of Nevada, Las Vegas	M
University of Nevada, Reno	M
University of New England	M
University of New Hampshire	M,O
The University of North Carolina at Chapel Hill	M,D
The University of North Carolina at Charlotte	M
The University of North Carolina at Greensboro	M
The University of North Carolina at Pembroke	M
The University of North Carolina Wilmington	M
University of North Dakota	M
University of Northern British Columbia	M,D,O
University of Northern Iowa	M
University of Oklahoma	M*
University of Ottawa	M
University of Pennsylvania	M,D*
University of Pittsburgh	M,D,O*
University of Puerto Rico, Río Piedras Campus	M,D
University of Regina	M,D
University of St. Francis (IL)	M,O
University of St. Thomas (MN)	M
University of South Africa	M,D
University of South Carolina	M,D
University of Southern California	M,D
University of Southern Indiana	M
University of Southern Maine	M
University of Southern Mississippi	M
University of South Florida	M,D,O
The University of Tennessee	M,D
The University of Texas at Arlington	M,D
The University of Texas at Austin	M,D
The University of Texas at El Paso	M
The University of Texas at San Antonio	M
The University of Texas Rio Grande Valley	M
University of the Fraser Valley	M
The University of Toledo	M,O
University of Toronto	M,D
University of Utah	M,D*
University of Vermont	M
University of Victoria	M
University of Washington	M,D*
University of Washington, Tacoma	M
University of West Florida	M
University of Windsor	M
University of Wisconsin–Green Bay	M
University of Wisconsin–Madison	M,D
University of Wisconsin–Milwaukee	M,D,O
University of Wisconsin–Oshkosh	M
University of Wyoming	M
Valdosta State University	M
Virginia Commonwealth University	M,D
Walden University	M,D
Walla Walla University	M
Washburn University	M
Washington University in St. Louis	M,D,O
Wayne State University	M,D,O
West Chester University of Pennsylvania	M
Western Carolina University	M
Western Kentucky University	M
Western Michigan University	M
Western New Mexico University	M
West Texas A&M University	M
West Virginia University	M
Wheelock College	M
Wichita State University	M
Widener University	M,D
Wilfrid Laurier University	M,D
Winthrop University	M
Yeshiva University	M,D
York University	M,D

SOCIOLOGY

Acadia University	M
American University	M,O
The American University in Cairo	M
American University of Beirut	M,D
Appalachian State University	M,O
Arizona State University at the Tempe campus	M,D
Arkansas State University	M,O
Arkansas Tech University	M
Auburn University	M
Ball State University	M
Baylor University	M,D
Binghamton University, State University of New York	M,D*
Boston College	M,D
Boston University	M,D
Bowling Green State University	M,D
Brandeis University	M,D
Brigham Young University	M
Brock University	M
Brooklyn College of the City University of New York	M,D
Brown University	M,D
California State University, Bakersfield	M
California State University, Dominguez Hills	M,O
California State University, Fullerton	M
California State University, Los Angeles	M
California State University, Northridge	M
California State University, Sacramento	M
California State University, San Marcos	M
Carleton University	M,D
Case Western Reserve University	M,D*
The Catholic University of America	M
Central European University	M,D
City College of the City University of New York	M
Clark Atlanta University	M
Clemson University	M
Cleveland State University	M
Colorado State University	M,D
Columbia University	M,D*
Concordia University (Canada)	M,D
Cornell University	M,D
Dalhousie University	M,D
DePaul University	M
Duke University	M,D*
East Carolina University	M
Eastern Michigan University	M
East Tennessee State University	M
Emory University	D
Fayetteville State University	M
Florida Atlantic University	M
Florida International University	M,D
Florida State University	M,D
George Mason University	M,D
The George Washington University	M*
Georgia Southern University	M
Georgia State University	M,D
The Graduate Center, City University of New York	D
Harvard University	D*
Howard University	M,D
Humboldt State University	M
Hunter College of the City University of New York	M
Idaho State University	M
Illinois State University	M
Indiana University Bloomington	M,D
Indiana University of Pennsylvania	M
Indiana University–Purdue University Indianapolis	M
Iowa State University of Science and Technology	M,D
Jackson State University	M
Johns Hopkins University	M,D
Kansas State University	M,D
Kent State University	M,D
Lakehead University	M
Laurentian University	M
Lehigh University	M
Lincoln University (MO)	M
Louisiana State University and Agricultural & Mechanical College	M,D
Loyola University Chicago	M,D
Marshall University	M
McGill University	M,D,O
McMaster University	M,D
Memorial University of Newfoundland	M,D
Michigan State University	M,D
Middle Tennessee State University	M
Minnesota State University Mankato	M
Mississippi State University	M,D
Morehead State University	M
Morgan State University	M
New Mexico Highlands University	M
New Mexico State University	M
The New School	M,D
New York University	M,D
North Carolina State University	M,D
North Dakota State University	M
Northeastern University	M,D
Northern Arizona University	M
Northern Illinois University	M
Northwestern University	M,D*
The Ohio State University	D
Ohio University	M
Oklahoma City University	M
Oklahoma State University	M,D
Old Dominion University	M
Our Lady of the Lake University of San Antonio	M,D
Oxford Graduate School	M,D
Penn State University Park	M,D
Portland State University	M,D,O
Prairie View A&M University	M
Princeton University	D,O
Purdue University	M,D
Queens College of the City University of New York	M
Queen's University at Kingston	M,D
Rice University	D
Roosevelt University	M
Rutgers University–New Brunswick	M,D
St. John's University (NY)	M
Sam Houston State University	M
San Diego State University	M
San Jose State University	M,O
Shippensburg University of Pennsylvania	M
Simon Fraser University	M,D
South Dakota State University	M,D
Southeastern Louisiana University	M
Southern Connecticut State University	M
Southern Illinois University Carbondale	M,D
Southern Illinois University Edwardsville	M
Stanford University	D
Stony Brook University, State University of New York	M,D
Syracuse University	M,D
Teachers College, Columbia University	M,D
Temple University	M,D*
Texas A&M University	M,D
Texas A&M University–Kingsville	M
Texas Southern University	M
Texas State University	M
Texas Tech University	M
Texas Woman's University	M,D
Tulane University	M
Université de Montréal	M,D
Université du Québec à Montréal	M,D
Université Laval	M,D
University at Albany, State University of New York	M,D,O
University at Buffalo, the State University of New York	M,D*
The University of Akron	M,D
The University of Alabama at Birmingham	D
University of Alberta	M,D
The University of Arizona	M,D
University of Arkansas	M
The University of British Columbia	M,D
University of Calgary	M,D
University of California, Berkeley	D
University of California, Davis	M,D
University of California, Irvine	D
University of California, Los Angeles	M,D
University of California, Merced	M,D
University of California, Riverside	M,D
University of California, San Diego	D
University of California, San Francisco	D
University of California, Santa Barbara	D
University of California, Santa Cruz	D
University of Central Florida	M,D
University of Central Missouri	M,D,O
University of Central Oklahoma	M
University of Chicago	D
University of Cincinnati	M,D
University of Colorado Boulder	D
University of Colorado Colorado Springs	M
University of Colorado Denver	M
University of Connecticut	M,D*
University of Delaware	M,D*
University of Florida	M,D

*M—masters degree; D—doctorate; O—other advanced degree; *—Close-Up and/or Display*

University of Georgia	M,D
University of Guelph	M,D
University of Hawaii at Manoa	M,D
University of Houston	M
University of Houston–Clear Lake	M
University of Illinois at Chicago	M,D
University of Illinois at Urbana–Champaign	M,D
University of Indianapolis	M
The University of Iowa	M,D*
The University of Kansas	M,D*
University of Kentucky	M,D
University of Lethbridge	M,D
University of Louisville	M,D
The University of Manchester	M,D
University of Manitoba	M,D
University of Maryland, Baltimore County	M
University of Maryland, College Park	M,D
University of Massachusetts Amherst	M,D*
University of Massachusetts Boston	M,D
University of Memphis	M
University of Miami	M,D
University of Michigan	D
University of Minnesota, Duluth	M
University of Minnesota, Twin Cities Campus	M,D
University of Mississippi	M,D
University of Missouri	D
University of Missouri–Kansas City	M
University of Montana	M
University of Nebraska at Omaha	M
University of Nebraska–Lincoln	M,D
University of Nevada, Las Vegas	M,D
University of Nevada, Reno	M
University of New Brunswick Fredericton	M,D
University of New Hampshire	M,D
University of New Mexico	M,D
University of New Orleans	M
The University of North Carolina at Chapel Hill	M,D
The University of North Carolina at Charlotte	M
The University of North Carolina at Greensboro	M
The University of North Carolina Wilmington	M
University of North Dakota	M
University of Northern Colorado	M
University of North Texas	M,D,O
University of Notre Dame	D
University of Oklahoma	M,D*
University of Oregon	M,D
University of Ottawa	M
University of Pennsylvania	M,D*
University of Pittsburgh	M,D*
University of Puerto Rico, Rí o Piedras Campus	M
University of Regina	M
University of Saskatchewan	M,D
University of South Africa	M,D
University of South Alabama	M
University of South Carolina	M,D
University of Southern California	D
University of South Florida	M,D
The University of Tennessee	M,D
The University of Texas at Arlington	M
The University of Texas at Austin	M,D
The University of Texas at El Paso	M,O
The University of Texas at San Antonio	M
The University of Texas at Tyler	M
The University of Texas Rio Grande Valley	M
The University of Toledo	M
University of Toronto	M,D
University of Utah	M,D*
University of Victoria	M,D
University of Virginia	M,D
University of Washington	M,D*
University of Waterloo	M,D
The University of Western Ontario	M,D
University of West Florida	M
University of West Georgia	M,D,O
University of Windsor	M,D
University of Wisconsin–Madison	M,D
University of Wisconsin–Milwaukee	M,D
University of Wyoming	M
Utah State University	M,D
Vanderbilt University	M,D*
Virginia Commonwealth University	M,O
Virginia Polytechnic Institute and State University	M,D,O
Washington State University	M,D
Wayne State University	M,D
Western Illinois University	M
Western Kentucky University	M
Western Michigan University	M,D
West Virginia University	M
Wichita State University	M
Wilfrid Laurier University	M
William Paterson University of New Jersey	M,D
Yale University	D*
York University	M,D

SOFTWARE ENGINEERING

American Public University System	M
Arizona State University at the Tempe campus	M,D
Auburn University	M,D
Bowling Green State University	M
Brandeis University	M
California Baptist University	M
California State University, Fullerton	M
California State University, Northridge	M
California State University, Sacramento	M
Carnegie Mellon University	M,D
Carroll University	M
Cleveland State University	M,D
Colorado Technical University Colorado Springs	M,D
Colorado Technical University Denver South	M
Concordia University (Canada)	M,D,O
DePaul University	M,D
Drexel University	M
East Carolina University	M
Embry-Riddle Aeronautical University–Daytona	M,D*
Fairfield University	M,O
Florida Agricultural and Mechanical University	M
Florida Institute of Technology	M,D
Gannon University	M
Grand Valley State University	M
Illinois Institute of Technology	M,D
Instituto Tecnologico de Santo Domingo	M,O
International Technological University	M
Jacksonville State University	M
Kennesaw State University	M,O
Lipscomb University	M,O
Loyola University Chicago	M
Loyola University Maryland	M
Marist College	M,O
McMaster University	M,D
Mercer University	M
Monmouth University	M,O
National University	M,O
Naval Postgraduate School	M,D
New Jersey Institute of Technology	M,D,O
New York University	O
North Dakota State University	M,D,O
Northern Kentucky University	M,O
Northwestern University	M*
Nova Southeastern University	M,D*
Oakland University	M,D
Oklahoma Christian University	M
Pace University	M,D,O
Penn State Great Valley	M,O
Portland State University	M,D
Regis University	M,O
Rochester Institute of Technology	M
Rose-Hulman Institute of Technology	M
Royal Military College of Canada	M,D
St. Mary's University (United States)	M,O
Santa Clara University	M,D,O
Seattle University	M
Shippensburg University of Pennsylvania	M
Southern Methodist University	M,D
Stevens Institute of Technology	M,O
Stony Brook University, State University of New York	M,D,O
Stratford University (VA)	M,D
Strayer University	M
Syracuse University	M
Tennessee Technological University	M
Texas State University	M
Texas Tech University	M,D
Towson University	M,D,O
Université Laval	O
The University of Alabama in Huntsville	M,D,O
The University of British Columbia	M
University of Calgary	M,D
University of Colorado Colorado Springs	M,D
University of Connecticut	M,D*
University of Detroit Mercy	M,D
University of Houston–Clear Lake	M
University of Management and Technology	M,O
University of Massachusetts Dartmouth	M,O
University of Michigan–Dearborn	M
University of Minnesota, Twin Cities Campus	M
University of Missouri–Kansas City	M,D,O
University of Nebraska at Omaha	M,O
University of New Haven	M,O
University of North Florida	M
University of Regina	M
University of St. Thomas (MN)	M,O
University of St. Thomas (MN)	M,O
The University of Scranton	M
University of South Carolina	M,D
University of Southern California	M,D
University of Southern Maine	M,O
The University of Texas at Arlington	M,D
The University of Texas at Dallas	M,D*
The University of Texas at El Paso	M,D,O
University of Utah	M,O*
University of Washington, Bothell	M
University of Washington, Tacoma	M
University of Waterloo	M,D
University of West Florida	M
University of Wisconsin–La Crosse	M
Villanova University	M
Virginia International University	M,O
Virginia Polytechnic Institute and State University	M,O
West Virginia University	M

SPANISH

American University	M,O
Arizona State University at the Tempe campus	M,D
Asbury University	M
Auburn University	M
Baylor University	M
Binghamton University, State University of New York	M*
Boston College	M
Bowling Green State University	M
Brigham Young University	M
Brooklyn College of the City University of New York	M
California State University, Bakersfield	M
California State University, Fresno	M
California State University, Fullerton	M
California State University, Long Beach	M
California State University, Los Angeles	M
California State University, Northridge	M
California State University, San Bernardino	M
California State University, San Marcos	M
The Catholic University of America	M,D
Central Connecticut State University	M,O
Central Michigan University	M
City College of the City University of New York	M
Cleveland State University	M
Columbia University	M,D*
Cornell University	D
DePaul University	M
Duke University	D*
Eastern Michigan University	M,O
Eastern University	M,O
Emory University	D,O
Florida Atlantic University	M
Florida International University	M,D
Florida State University	M,D
Framingham State University	M
Georgetown University	M,D
Georgia Southern University	M
Georgia State University	M,O
Harvard University	M,D*
Howard University	M
Hunter College of the City University of New York	M
Illinois State University	M
Indiana State University	M,D,O
Indiana University Bloomington	M,D
Inter American University of Puerto Rico, Metropolitan Campus	M
Inter American University of Puerto Rico, Ponce Campus	M
Iona College	M
Ithaca College	M
Johns Hopkins University	D
Kean University	M
Lake Forest College	M
Lamar University	M
Lee University	M,O
Lehman College of the City University of New York	M
Loyola University Chicago	M
Marquette University	M
Michigan State University	M,D
Middlebury College	M,D
Middle Tennessee State University	M
Millersville University of Pennsylvania	M
Minnesota State University Mankato	M
Mississippi State University	M
Molloy College	M,O
Montclair State University	M
New Mexico State University	M,D,O
New York University	M,D,O
North Carolina State University	M
Northern Arizona University	M
Northern Illinois University	M
Northwestern University	D*
The Ohio State University	M,D
Ohio University	M
Penn State University Park	M,D
Pontifical Catholic University of Puerto Rico	M,O
Portland State University	M
Princeton University	D
Purdue University	M,D
Queens College of the City University of New York	M
Queen's University at Kingston	M
Rider University	O
Roosevelt University	M
Rutgers University–New Brunswick	M,D
St. John's University (NY)	M
Saint Louis University	M
Saint Louis University–Madrid Campus	M
Saint Xavier University	M
Salem State University	M
Samford University	M,D,O
Sam Houston State University	M
San Diego State University	M
San Francisco State University	M
San Jose State University	M,O
Smith College	M
Southern Oregon University	M
Stanford University	M,D
State University of New York at New Paltz	M,O
Syracuse University	M
Temple University	M,D*
Texas A&M University	M,D
Texas A&M University–Kingsville	M
Texas State University	M
Texas Tech University	M,D
Tulane University	M,D
Universidad Autonoma de Guadalajara	M,D
Université de Montréal	M
Université Laval	M,D
University at Albany, State University of New York	M,D
University at Buffalo, the State University of New York	M,D,O*
The University of Akron	M
The University of Alabama	M,D
The University of Arizona	M,D
University of Arkansas	M
University of Calgary	M,D
University of California, Berkeley	D
University of California, Davis	M,D
University of California, Irvine	M,D
University of California, Los Angeles	M
University of California, Riverside	M,D
University of California, Santa Barbara	M,D
University of Central Florida	M
University of Chicago	D
University of Cincinnati	M,D
University of Colorado Boulder	M,D
University of Colorado Denver	M
University of Delaware	M*
University of Florida	M,D
University of Georgia	M,D
University of Hawaii at Manoa	M
University of Houston	M,D
University of Illinois at Chicago	M,D
University of Illinois at Urbana–Champaign	M,D
The University of Iowa	M,D*
The University of Kansas	M,D*
University of Lethbridge	M,D
University of Louisville	M
The University of Manchester	M,D
University of Maryland, College Park	M,D
University of Massachusetts Amherst	M,D*
University of Miami	M,D
University of Michigan	D
University of Minnesota, Twin Cities Campus	M,D
University of Missouri	M,D
University of Missouri–Kansas City	M
University of Montana	M
University of Nebraska–Lincoln	M,D
University of Nevada, Reno	M
University of New Hampshire	M
University of New Mexico	M,D
The University of North Carolina at Chapel Hill	M,D
The University of North Carolina at Charlotte	M,O
The University of North Carolina at Greensboro	M,O
The University of North Carolina Wilmington	M,O
University of Northern Colorado	M
University of Northern Iowa	M
University of North Texas	M,D,O
University of Notre Dame	M
University of Oklahoma	M,D*
University of Oregon	M
University of Ottawa	M,D
University of Pennsylvania	M,D*
University of Pittsburgh	M,D*
University of Rhode Island	M
University of South Africa	M,D
University of South Carolina	M,D
University of Southern California	D
University of South Florida	M
The University of Tennessee	M,D
The University of Texas at Arlington	M
The University of Texas at Austin	M,D
The University of Texas at El Paso	M,O
The University of Texas at San Antonio	M
The University of Texas of the Permian Basin	M
The University of Texas Rio Grande Valley	M
The University of Toledo	M
University of Toronto	M,D
University of Utah	M,D*
University of Virginia	M,D
University of Washington	M*
The University of Western Ontario	M,D
University of Wisconsin–Madison	M,D
University of Wisconsin–Milwaukee	M,O
University of Wyoming	M
Vanderbilt University	M,D*
Washington University in St. Louis	D
Wayne State University	M,D
West Chester University of Pennsylvania	M,O
Western Kentucky University	M
Western Michigan University	M,D
West Virginia University	M
Wichita State University	M
Worcester State University	M
Yale University	D*

SPECIAL EDUCATION

Acacia University	M
Acadia University	M
Adams State University	M
Adelphi University	M,O
Alabama Agricultural and Mechanical University	M,D,O
Alabama State University	M,O
Albany State University	M,O

Albright College	M
Alcorn State University	M,O
Alliant International University–San Francisco	M,O
Alverno College	M
American International College	M,D,O
American Public University System	M
American University	M
American University of Puerto Rico	M
Andrews University	M
Antioch University New England	M,O
Appalachian State University	M
Arcadia University	M,D,O
Arizona State University at the Tempe campus	M,O
Arkansas State University	M,D,O
Armstrong State University	M,O
Asbury University	M
Ashland University	M
Assumption College	M,O
Auburn University	M,D
Auburn University at Montgomery	M,O
Augustana University	M
Augusta University	M,O
Austin Peay State University	M
Averett University	M
Azusa Pacific University	M
Baldwin Wallace University	M
Ball State University	M,D,O
Bank Street College of Education	M
Barry University	M,D,O
Bayamón Central University	M,O
Baylor University	M,D,O
Bay Path University	M
Bellarmine University	M,D,O
Bemidji State University	M
Benedictine University	M
Bethel University (MN)	M,D,O
Binghamton University, State University of New York	M*
Biola University	M,O
Bloomsburg University of Pennsylvania	M,O
Bluffton University	M
Bob Jones University	M,D,O
Boise State University	M
Boston College	M,O
Bowie State University	M
Bowling Green State University	M
Brandman University	M
Brandon University	M,O
Brenau University	M,O
Bridgewater State University	M
Brigham Young University	M,D,O
Brooklyn College of the City University of New York	M,O
Buffalo State College, State University of New York	M
Caldwell University	M,D,O
California Baptist University	M
California Lutheran University	M,D
California State Polytechnic University, Pomona	M
California State University, Bakersfield	M
California State University, Chico	M
California State University, Dominguez Hills	M
California State University, East Bay	M
California State University, Fresno	M
California State University, Fullerton	M
California State University, Long Beach	M
California State University, Los Angeles	M,D
California State University, Northridge	M
California State University, Sacramento	M
California State University, San Marcos	M,D
California State University, Stanislaus	M
California University of Pennsylvania	M
Cambridge College	M,D,O
Campbellsville University	M
Canisius College	M,O
Capella University	M,D
Cardinal Stritch University	M,D
Caribbean University	M,D
Carlos Albizu University, Miami Campus	M,D
Carlow University	M
Castleton University	M,O
The Catholic University of America	M,D,O
Centenary College	M
Central Connecticut State University	M,O
Central Michigan University	M,O
Central Washington University	M
Chaminade University of Honolulu	M
Chapman University	M,D,O
Chatham University	M
Chestnut Hill College	M,O
Cheyney University of Pennsylvania	M
Chicago State University	M
City College of the City University of New York	M,O
City University of Seattle	M,O
Claremont Graduate University	M,D,O
Clarion University of Pennsylvania	M
Clark Atlanta University	M
Clemson University	M,D,O
Cleveland State University	M
College of Charleston	M
The College of New Jersey	M,O
The College of New Rochelle	M
College of St. Joseph	M
The College of Saint Rose	M,O
College of Staten Island of the City University of New York	M,O
Colorado Christian University	M
Colorado Mesa University	M
Colorado State University–Pueblo	M
Columbus State University	M,O
Concordia College–New York	M
Concordia University (United States)	M,D
Concordia University, St. Paul	M,D,O
Concordia University Wisconsin	M
Concord University	M
Converse College	M
Coppin State University	M
Curry College	M,O
Daemen College	M
Dallas Baptist University	M
Defiance College	M
Delaware State University	M
Delta State University	M
DePaul University	M,D
DeSales University	M,O
Dominican College	M
Dominican University	M
Dominican University of California	M
Drew University	M,D,O
Drexel University	M,D
Drury University	M
Duquesne University	M,D
D'Youville College	M,D
East Carolina University	M,O
Eastern Illinois University	M
Eastern Kentucky University	M
Eastern Michigan University	M,O
Eastern Nazarene College	M,O
Eastern New Mexico University	M
Eastern University	M,O
Eastern Washington University	M
East Stroudsburg University of Pennsylvania	M
East Tennessee State University	M,D,O
Edgewood College	M,D,O
Edinboro University of Pennsylvania	M,O
Elmhurst College	M
Elms College	M,O
Elon University	M
Emporia State University	M
Endicott College	M,D
Fairfield University	M,O
Fairleigh Dickinson University, Metropolitan Campus	M
Fairmont State University	M
Ferris State University	M
Fitchburg State University	M
Florida Atlantic University	M,D
Florida Gulf Coast University	M
Florida International University	M,D,O
Florida Memorial University	M
Florida State University	M,D,O
Fontbonne University	M
Fordham University	M,O
Fort Hays State University	M
Framingham State University	M
Francis Marion University	M
Franklin Pierce University	M,D,O
Freed-Hardeman University	M,O
Fresno Pacific University	M
Frostburg State University	M
Furman University	M,O
Gallaudet University	M,D,O
Gannon University	O
Geneva College	M
George Fox University	M,O
George Mason University	M,D,O
Georgetown College	M
The George Washington University	M,D,O*
Georgia College & State University	M,O
Georgian Court University	M,O
Georgia Southern University	M,O
Georgia Southwestern State University	M,O
Georgia State University	M,D
Gonzaga University	M
Gordon College	M,O
Goucher College	M,O
Governors State University	M
Graceland University (IA)	M
Grambling State University	M
Grand Canyon University	M
Grand Valley State University	M
Greensboro College	M
Gwynedd Mercy University	M
Harding University	M,O
Hebrew College	M,O
Henderson State University	M,O
Heritage University	M
High Point University	M
Hofstra University	M,D,O
Holy Family University	M
Holy Names University	M,O
Hood College	M,O
Howard University	M
Hunter College of the City University of New York	M
Idaho State University	M,D,O
Illinois State University	M,D,O
Immaculata University	M,D,O
Indiana University Bloomington	M,D,O
Indiana University of Pennsylvania	M
Indiana University–Purdue University Fort Wayne	M,O
Indiana University–Purdue University Indianapolis	M,O
Indiana University South Bend	M
Inter American University of Puerto Rico, Barranquitas Campus	M
Inter American University of Puerto Rico, Fajardo Campus	M
Inter American University of Puerto Rico, Metropolitan Campus	M
Inter American University of Puerto Rico, San Germán Campus	M
Iona College	M
Iowa State University of Science and Technology	M,D
Jackson State University	M,O
Jacksonville State University	M
James Madison University	M
Johns Hopkins University	M,O
Johnson & Wales University	M
Johnson State College	M
Kansas State University	M,D
Kaplan University, Davenport Campus	M
Kean University	M
Keene State College	M,O
Kennesaw State University	M
Kent State University	M,D,O
Kentucky State University	M,D
Lamar University	M,D
Lancaster Bible College	M,D
La Salle University	M,O
Lasell College	M
Lee University	M,O
Lehigh University	M,D
Lehman College of the City University of New York	M
Le Moyne College	M,O
Lesley University	M,D,O
Lewis & Clark College	M
Lewis University	M
Liberty University	M,D,O
Lipscomb University	M,D,O
London Metropolitan University	M,D
Long Island University–Brentwood Campus	M,O
Long Island University–Hudson at Rockland	M,O
Long Island University–Hudson at Westchester	M,O
Long Island University–LIU Brooklyn	M,O
Long Island University–LIU Post	M,D,O
Long Island University–Riverhead	M,O
Longwood University	M
Loras College	M
Louisiana Tech University	M,D
Loyola Marymount University	M
Loyola University Chicago	M,O
Loyola University Maryland	M,O
Lynchburg College	M
Lyndon State College	M
Lynn University	M,D
Madonna University	M
Malone University	M
Manhattan College	M,O
Manhattanville College	M,O*
Mansfield University of Pennsylvania	M
Marian University (WI)	M,D
Marshall University	M
Martin Luther College	M
Marymount University	M
Marywood University	M
Massachusetts College of Liberal Arts	M,O
McDaniel College	M
McKendree University	M,D,O
McNeese State University	M,O
Medaille College	M
Mercyhurst University	M
Merrimack College	M,O
Messiah College	M
Metropolitan College of New York	M
Metropolitan State University of Denver	M
Michigan State University	M,D,O
MidAmerica Nazarene University	M
Middle Tennessee State University	M
Midwestern State University	M
Millersville University of Pennsylvania	M
Minnesota State University Mankato	M,O
Minnesota State University Moorhead	M,O
Minot State University	M
Misericordia University	M
Mississippi College	M,D,O
Mississippi State University	M,D,O
Mississippi Valley State University	M
Missouri State University	M
Missouri Western State University	M,O
Molloy College	M,O
Monmouth University	M,O
Montana State University Billings	M
Montclair State University	M
Morehead State University	M,O
Morningside College	M
Mount Mercy University	M
Mount St. Joseph University	M,O
Mount Saint Mary College	M,O
Mount Saint Vincent University	M
Murray State University	M
National Louis University	M,D,O
National University	M,O
National University College	M
Neumann University	M
New England College	M,D
New Jersey City University	M
New Mexico Highlands University	M
New Mexico State University	M,D,O
New York University	M
Niagara University	M,O
Norfolk State University	M
North Carolina Central University	M
North Carolina State University	M
Northeastern Illinois University	M
Northeastern University	M,D
Northern Arizona University	M,O
Northern Illinois University	M,D
Northern Kentucky University	M,O
Northern Michigan University	M
Northwestern State University of Louisiana	M,O
Northwest Missouri State University	M
Notre Dame College (OH)	M,O
Notre Dame de Namur University	M
Nyack College	M
Oakland University	M,O
The Ohio State University	D
Ohio University	M,D
Old Dominion University	M,D
Ottawa University	M
Pace University	M,O
Pacific Oaks College	M
Pacific University	M
Penn State University Park	M,D,O
Piedmont College	M,O
Pittsburg State University	M,O
Plymouth State University	M
Point Loma Nazarene University	M
Point Park University	M
Prairie View A&M University	M
Prescott College	M,D
Providence College	M
Purdue University	M,D,O
Purdue University Northwest	M
Queens College of the City University of New York	M,O
Quincy University	M
Radford University	M,O
Ramapo College of New Jersey	M
Randolph College	M
Regent University	M,D,O
Regis College (MA)	M,D
Regis University	M,O
Rhode Island College	M,O
Rider University	M,O
Rivier University	M,D,O
Robert Morris University	M,D,O
Roberts Wesleyan College	M
Rochester Institute of Technology	M
Rockford University	M
Roosevelt University	M
Rowan University	M,O
Rutgers University–New Brunswick	M,D
Sage Graduate School	M
Saginaw Valley State University	M
St. Ambrose University	M
St. Bonaventure University	M,O
St. Cloud State University	M
St. John Fisher College	M,O
St. John's University (NY)	M,D,O
St. Joseph's College, Long Island Campus	M
St. Joseph's College, New York	M
Saint Joseph's University	M,D,O
Saint Louis University	M,D
Saint Martin's University	M
Saint Mary's College of California	M
Saint Mary's University of Minnesota	M,O
Saint Michael's College	M,O
Saint Peter's University	M,O
St. Thomas Aquinas College	M,O
St. Thomas University	M,D,O
Saint Vincent College	M
Saint Xavier University	M
Salem College	M
Salem State University	M
Salus University	M,O
Samford University	M,D,O
Sam Houston State University	M,D
San Diego State University	M
San Francisco State University	M,O
Seattle University	M,O
Seton Hall University	M
Seton Hill University	M
Shenandoah University	M,D,O
Shippensburg University of Pennsylvania	M,D
Siena Heights University	M,O
Silver Lake College of the Holy Family	M
Simmons College	M,D,O
Slippery Rock University of Pennsylvania	M,D
Sonoma State University	M,D,O
South Carolina State University	M
Southeastern Louisiana University	M
Southeast Missouri State University	M
Southern Connecticut State University	M
Southern Illinois University Carbondale	M,D
Southern Illinois University Edwardsville	M,O
Southern Methodist University	M,D
Southern New Hampshire University	M,D,O
Southern Oregon University	M
Southern University and Agricultural and Mechanical College	M,D
Southwestern College (KS)	M,D
Southwestern Oklahoma State University	M
Southwest Minnesota State University	M
Spalding University	M
Spring Arbor University	M
Springfield College	M

*M—masters degree; D—doctorate; O—other advanced degree; *—Close-Up and/or Display*

State University of New York at New Paltz	M
State University of New York at Oswego	M
State University of New York at Plattsburgh	M
State University of New York College at Cortland	M
State University of New York College at Oneonta	M,O
State University of New York College at Potsdam	M
Stephen F. Austin State University	M
Syracuse University	M,D
Tarleton State University	M
Teachers College, Columbia University	M,D,O
Temple University	M,D,O*
Tennessee State University	M,D
Tennessee Technological University	M,O
Texas A&M International University	M
Texas A&M University	M,D
Texas A&M University–Corpus Christi	M
Texas A&M University–Kingsville	M
Texas A&M University–San Antonio	M
Texas A&M University–Texarkana	M
Texas Christian University	M,O
Texas State University	M
Texas Tech University	M,D
Texas Woman's University	M,D
Touro College	M
Towson University	M,O
Trevecca Nazarene University	M,O
Trinity Baptist College	M
Trinity Christian College	M
Trinity Washington University	M
Union College (KY)	M
Universidad del Este	M
Universidad del Turabo	M
Universidad Iberoamericana	M,D
Universidad Metropolitana	M
Université de Sherbrooke	M,O
University at Albany, State University of New York	M,D
University at Buffalo, the State University of New York	M,D,O*
The University of Akron	M
The University of Alabama	M,D,O
The University of Alabama at Birmingham	M
University of Alaska Anchorage	M,O
University of Alaska Fairbanks	M
University of Alberta	M,D
The University of Arizona	M,D
University of Arkansas	M
University of Arkansas at Little Rock	M,O
The University of British Columbia	M,D,O
University of California, Berkeley	M,D
University of California, Los Angeles	D
University of California, Riverside	M,D,O
University of Central Arkansas	M,O
University of Central Florida	M,D,O
University of Central Missouri	M,D,O
University of Central Oklahoma	M
University of Cincinnati	M,D
University of Colorado Colorado Springs	M,D
University of Colorado Denver	M,D
University of Denver	M,D,O
University of Detroit Mercy	M,D,O
University of Florida	M,D,O
University of Georgia	M,D,O
University of Guam	M
University of Hawaii at Manoa	M,D
University of Houston	M,D
University of Houston–Victoria	M
University of Idaho	M,D,O
University of Illinois at Chicago	M,D
University of Illinois at Urbana–Champaign	M,D,O
The University of Iowa	M,D*
The University of Kansas	M,D*
University of Kentucky	M,D
University of La Verne	M,D,O
University of Louisiana at Monroe	M,D
University of Louisville	M,D,O
University of Maine	M,D,O
University of Manitoba	M
University of Mary	M,D
University of Maryland Eastern Shore	M
University of Massachusetts Amherst	M,D,O*
University of Massachusetts Boston	M
University of Memphis	M,D
University of Miami	M,D,O
University of Michigan–Dearborn	M
University of Minnesota, Twin Cities Campus	M,D,O
University of Missouri	M,D
University of Missouri–Kansas City	M,D,O
University of Missouri–St. Louis	M,O
University of Nebraska at Kearney	M,O
University of Nebraska at Omaha	M
University of Nebraska–Lincoln	M,D,O
University of Nevada, Las Vegas	M,D,O
University of Nevada, Reno	M,D
University of New England	M,O
University of New Hampshire	M
University of New Mexico	M,D,O
University of New Orleans	M,D
University of North Alabama	M
The University of North Carolina at Charlotte	M,D,O
The University of North Carolina at Greensboro	M,D,O
The University of North Carolina Wilmington	M
University of North Dakota	M,D
University of Northern Colorado	M,D
University of Northern Iowa	M
University of North Florida	M
University of North Texas	M,D,O
University of Oklahoma	M,D*
University of Oklahoma Health Sciences Center	M,D,O
University of Phoenix–Bay Area Campus	M,D,O
University of Phoenix–Hawaii Campus	M
University of Phoenix–Online Campus	M,O
University of Phoenix–Phoenix Campus	M
University of Phoenix–Southern Arizona Campus	M,O
University of Phoenix–Utah Campus	M
University of Phoenix–Washington D.C. Campus	M,D,O
University of Pittsburgh	M,D*
University of Portland	M,D
University of Puerto Rico, Medical Sciences Campus	O
University of Puerto Rico, Río Piedras Campus	M
University of Rhode Island	M,D
University of Rio Grande	M
University of St. Francis (IL)	M,D,O
University of Saint Francis (IN)	M,O
University of Saint Joseph	M
University of Saint Mary	M
University of St. Thomas (MN)	M,O
University of St. Thomas (TX)	M
University of San Diego	M
University of San Francisco	M,D
University of Saskatchewan	M,D,O
University of South Alabama	M,D,O
University of South Carolina	M,D
University of South Carolina Upstate	M
The University of South Dakota	M,D,O
University of Southern Maine	M,O
University of Southern Mississippi	M,D,O
University of South Florida	M,D,O
The University of Tennessee	M,D,O
The University of Tennessee at Chattanooga	M,D,O
The University of Tennessee at Martin	M
The University of Texas at Austin	M,D
The University of Texas at El Paso	M
The University of Texas at San Antonio	M,D
The University of Texas at Tyler	M
The University of Texas Health Science Center at San Antonio	M,D
The University of Texas of the Permian Basin	M
The University of Texas Rio Grande Valley	M
University of the Cumberlands	M,D,O
University of the Pacific	M,D
University of the Southwest	M
The University of Toledo	M,D,O
University of Utah	M,D*
University of Vermont	M
University of Victoria	M,D
University of Virginia	M,D,O
University of Washington	M,D*
University of Washington, Tacoma	M
The University of West Alabama	M,O
The University of Western Ontario	M
University of West Florida	M
University of West Georgia	M,D,O
University of Wisconsin–Eau Claire	M
University of Wisconsin–La Crosse	M
University of Wisconsin–Madison	M,D
University of Wisconsin–Milwaukee	M,D,O
University of Wisconsin–Oshkosh	M
University of Wisconsin–Stevens Point	M
University of Wisconsin–Superior	M
University of Wisconsin–Whitewater	M,O
University of Wyoming	M,D,O
Ursuline College	M
Utah State University	M,D,O
Valdosta State University	M,O
Vanderbilt University	M,D*
Virginia Commonwealth University	M,D,O
Viterbo University	M,O
Wagner College	M
Walden University	M,D,O
Walla Walla University	M
Washburn University	M
Washington State University	M,D
Washington University in St. Louis	M,D
Wayland Baptist University	M
Waynesburg University	M,D
Wayne State College	M
Wayne State University	M,D,O
Webster University	M,O
West Chester University of Pennsylvania	M,O
Western Connecticut State University	M
Western Governors University	M,O
Western Illinois University	M
Western Kentucky University	M,O
Western Michigan University	M,D
Western New Mexico University	M
Western Oregon University	M
Westfield State University	M
West Texas A&M University	M
West Virginia University	M,D
Wheelock College	M
Whitworth University	M
Wichita State University	M
Widener University	M,D
Wilkes University	M,D
William Carey University	M,O
William Paterson University of New Jersey	M
Wilmington College	M
Wilmington University	M,D
Winona State University	M
Winston-Salem State University	M
Winthrop University	M
Worcester State University	M,O
Wright State University	M
Xavier University	M
Youngstown State University	M

SPEECH AND INTERPERSONAL COMMUNICATION

Ball State University	M
Bob Jones University	M,D,O
Bowling Green State University	M,D
Brooklyn College of the City University of New York	M,D
California State University, Fullerton	M
California State University, Northridge	M
Colorado State University	M
Eastern Illinois University	M
Georgia State University	M,D
Idaho State University	M
Indiana University Bloomington	M,D
Marquette University	M,O
New York University	M,D
North Dakota State University	M,D
Northeastern Illinois University	M
Northwestern University	M,D*
Ohio University	M,D
Old Dominion University	M
Portland State University	M,O
Rensselaer Polytechnic Institute	M,D
San Francisco State University	M
Seton Hall University	M
Southern Illinois University Carbondale	M,D
Southern Illinois University Edwardsville	M
Texas Christian University	M
The University of Alabama	M
University of Arkansas at Little Rock	M
University of California, Santa Barbara	D
University of Denver	M,D
University of Georgia	M,D
University of Hawaii at Manoa	M
University of Houston	M
The University of Iowa	M,D*
University of Louisiana at Monroe	M,D
University of Maryland, College Park	M,D
University of Nebraska–Lincoln	M,D
University of Nevada, Reno	M
University of South Carolina	M,D
University of Southern Mississippi	M,D
The University of Tennessee	M,D
University of Wisconsin–Madison	M,D
University of Wisconsin–Stevens Point	M
University of Wisconsin–Superior	M
Wake Forest University	M
Washington University in St. Louis	M,D

SPORT PSYCHOLOGY

Adler University	M,D,O
Argosy University, Atlanta	M,D,O
Argosy University, Inland Empire	M,D
Argosy University, Orange County	M
Argosy University, Phoenix	M,D
Argosy University, San Francisco Bay Area	M,D
Argosy University, Schaumburg	M,O
Ball State University	M
Barry University	M
California State University, Fresno	M
California State University, Long Beach	M
California University of Pennsylvania	M
Capella University	M
Chatham University	M,D
Cleveland State University	M
Florida State University	M,D
John F. Kennedy University	M
Lock Haven University of Pennsylvania	M
National University	M,O
Purdue University	M,D
Queen's University at Kingston	M,D
Seton Hall University	M
Southern Connecticut State University	M
Southern Illinois University Edwardsville	M
Springfield College	M,D,O
University of Denver	M,D
University of Rhode Island	M
The University of Texas at Austin	M,D
West Virginia University	M,D

SPORTS MANAGEMENT

Adelphi University	M
American Public University System	M
Angelo State University	M
Arkansas State University	M,O
Ashland University	M
Augustana University	M
Austin Peay State University	M
Ball State University	M
Barry University	M
Belhaven University (MS)	M
Bluffton University	M
Boise State University	M
Bowling Green State University	M
Bristol University	M
Brooklyn College of the City University of New York	M
California Baptist University	M
California State University, Long Beach	M
California University of Management and Sciences	M,D
California University of Pennsylvania	M
Canisius College	M
Cardinal Stritch University	M
Central Michigan University	M,O
Central Washington University	M
Clayton State University	M
Clemson University	M,D,O
Cleveland State University	M
Coastal Carolina University	M,D,O
Coker College	M
The College at Brockport, State University of New York	M,O
Columbia University	M*
Concordia University Irvine	M
Concordia University, St. Paul	M,D,O
Defiance College	M
DePaul University	M
Drexel University	M
East Carolina University	M,D,O
Eastern Kentucky University	M
Eastern Michigan University	M
Eastern New Mexico University	M
Eastern Washington University	M
East Stroudsburg University of Pennsylvania	M
East Tennessee State University	M,O
Endicott College	M
Fairleigh Dickinson University, College at Florham	M
Fairleigh Dickinson University, Metropolitan Campus	M
Florida Agricultural and Mechanical University	M
Florida International University	M,D,O
Florida State University	M,D,O
Franklin Pierce University	M,D,O
Georgetown University	M,D
The George Washington University	M,O*
Georgia Southern University	M
Georgia State University	M
Gonzaga University	M
Grambling State University	M
Hampton University	M
Hardin-Simmons University	M
Henderson State University	M
Hofstra University	M,O
Holy Names University	M
Howard Payne University	M
Howard University	M
Indiana State University	M,D
Indiana University Bloomington	M,D
Indiana University of Pennsylvania	M
Iona College	M,O
Kansas Wesleyan University	M
Kent State University	M
Keystone College	M
Lasell College	M,O
Lewis University	M
Liberty University	M,D,O
Lindenwood University	M
Lipscomb University	M,O
Lock Haven University of Pennsylvania	M
Lynn University	M
Manhattanville College	M*
Marquette University	M,O
Marshall University	M
Maryville University of Saint Louis	M,O
Mercyhurst University	M,O
Messiah College	M
Midwestern State University	M
Millersville University of Pennsylvania	M
Misericordia University	M
Mississippi State University	M,D
Missouri State University	M,O
Missouri Western State University	M
Montclair State University	M
Morehead State University	M
Mount Ida College	M
Mount St. Mary's University (MD)	M
National University	M,O
Neumann University	M
New England College	M
New Mexico Highlands University	M
New York University	M,O
North Carolina Central University	M
North Carolina State University	M,D
North Central College	M
Northeastern University	M
Northern Illinois University	M
Northern State University	M
Northwestern University	M*
Ohio Dominican University	M
Ohio University	M
Old Dominion University	M
Pittsburg State University	M
Point Loma Nazarene University	M
Purdue University	M,D
Robert Morris University	M,D,O
Robert Morris University Illinois	M

St. Cloud State University	M
St. John's University (NY)	M
Saint Leo University	M
Saint Mary's College of California	M
St. Thomas University	M,O
Sam Houston State University	M
San Diego State University	M
San Jose State University	M,O
Seattle University	M
Seton Hall University	M,O
Sonoma State University	M
Southeast Missouri State University	M
Southern Methodist University	M
Southern Nazarene University	M
Southern New Hampshire University	M,O
Springfield College	M,D,O
State University of New York College at Cortland	M
Syracuse University	M
Temple University	M,D*
Tennessee State University	M
Tennessee Technological University	M
Texas A&M University	M,D
Texas Tech University	M
Texas Woman's University	M,D
Tiffin University	M
Troy University	M
United States Sports Academy	M,D
The University of Alabama	M
University of Alberta	M
University of Arkansas	M,D
University of Arkansas at Little Rock	M
University of Central Florida	M
University of Colorado Denver	M
University of Dallas	M,D
University of Florida	M,D
University of Indianapolis	M
The University of Iowa	M,D*
University of Louisiana at Monroe	M
University of Louisville	M,D,O
University of Mary	M
University of Mary Hardin-Baylor	M
University of Massachusetts Amherst	M,D*
University of Miami	M
University of Michigan	M,D
University of Minnesota, Twin Cities Campus	M,D,O
University of Nebraska at Kearney	M
University of New Brunswick Fredericton	M
University of New Haven	M,O
University of New Mexico	D
The University of North Carolina at Chapel Hill	M
University of Northern Colorado	M,D
University of Northern Iowa	M
University of North Florida	M,D
University of Oregon	M
University of San Francisco	M
University of South Carolina	M
University of Southern Mississippi	M,D
University of South Florida	M
The University of Tennessee	M,D
University of the Incarnate Word	M
University of the Southwest	M
Upper Iowa University	M
Valparaiso University	M
Waldorf College	M
Washington State University	M,D
Wayland Baptist University	M
Wayne State College	M
Wayne State University	M,D
Webber International University	M
West Chester University of Pennsylvania	M,O
Western Illinois University	M
Western Kentucky University	M
Western Michigan University	M
Western New England University	M
West Texas A&M University	M
West Virginia University	M,D
Wichita State University	M
Wingate University	M,D
Winona State University	M,O
Xavier University	M

STATISTICS

Acadia University	M
American University	M,O
American University of Beirut	M,D
Arizona State University at the Tempe campus	M,D,O
Auburn University	M,D
Ball State University	M
Baruch College of the City University of New York	M
Baylor University	M,D
Bowling Green State University	M,D
Brigham Young University	M
Brock University	M
California State University, East Bay	M
Carnegie Mellon University	M,D
Central Connecticut State University	M,O
Claremont Graduate University	M,D
Clemson University	M,D
Colorado State University	M,D
Columbia University	M,D*
Concordia University (Canada)	M,D
Cornell University	M,D
Dalhousie University	M,D
Duke University	M,D*
East Carolina University	M,O
Florida Atlantic University	M,D
Florida International University	M
Florida State University	M,D
George Mason University	M,D,O
Georgetown University	M
The George Washington University	M,D,O*
Georgia Institute of Technology	M
Georgia State University	M,D
Hampton University	M
Harvard University	M,D*
Hunter College of the City University of New York	M
Indiana University Bloomington	M,D
Indiana University–Purdue University Indianapolis	M,D
Iowa State University of Science and Technology	M,D
Johns Hopkins University	M,D
Kansas State University	M,D,O
Lehigh University	M,D
Louisiana State University and Agricultural & Mechanical College	M
Louisiana Tech University	M,D
Loyola University Chicago	M
McGill University	M,D,O
McMaster University	M
McNeese State University	M
Memorial University of Newfoundland	M,D
Miami University	M
Michigan State University	M,D
Minnesota State University Mankato	M
Mississippi State University	M,D
Missouri University of Science and Technology	M,D
Montana State University	M,D
Montclair State University	M
Murray State University	M
New Jersey Institute of Technology	M,D,O
New Mexico Institute of Mining and Technology	M,D
New York University	M,D
North Carolina State University	M,D
North Dakota State University	M,D,O
Northern Arizona University	M,O
Northern Illinois University	M
Northwestern University	M,D*
Oakland University	O
The Ohio State University	M,D
Oklahoma State University	M,D
Old Dominion University	M,D
Oregon State University	M,D
Penn State University Park	M,D
Portland State University	M,D
Purdue University	M,D
Queen's University at Kingston	M,D
Rice University	M,D
Rochester Institute of Technology	O
Rutgers University–New Brunswick	M,D
Sam Houston State University	M
San Diego State University	M
San Jose State University	M,O
Simon Fraser University	M,D
South Dakota State University	M,D
Southern Illinois University Edwardsville	M
Southern Methodist University	M,D
Stanford University	M,D
Stephen F. Austin State University	M
Stevens Institute of Technology	M,O
Stony Brook University, State University of New York	M,D,O
Temple University	M,D*
Texas A&M University	M,D
Texas A&M University–Kingsville	M
Texas Tech University	M,D
Université de Montréal	M,D,O
Université Laval	M
University of Alaska Fairbanks	M,D,O
University of Alberta	M,D,O
The University of Arizona	M,D
University of Arkansas	M
The University of British Columbia	M,D
University of Calgary	M,D
University of California, Berkeley	M,D
University of California, Davis	M,D
University of California, Irvine	M,D
University of California, Los Angeles	M,D
University of California, Riverside	M
University of California, San Diego	M,D
University of California, Santa Barbara	M,D
University of California, Santa Cruz	M,D
University of Central Florida	M,O
University of Central Oklahoma	M
University of Chicago	M,D,O
University of Cincinnati	M,D
University of Colorado Denver	M,D
University of Connecticut	M,D*
University of Delaware	M*
University of Denver	M
University of Florida	M,D
University of Georgia	M,D
University of Guelph	M,D
University of Houston–Clear Lake	M
University of Idaho	M
University of Illinois at Chicago	M,D
University of Illinois at Urbana–Champaign	M,D
The University of Iowa	M,D,O*
The University of Kansas	M,D,O*
University of Kentucky	M,D
The University of Manchester	M,D
University of Manitoba	M,D
University of Maryland, Baltimore County	M,D
University of Maryland, College Park	M,D
University of Massachusetts Amherst	M,D*
University of Memphis	M,D
University of Michigan	M,D,O
University of Minnesota, Twin Cities Campus	M,D
University of Missouri	M,D
University of Missouri–Kansas City	M,D
University of Nebraska–Lincoln	M,D
University of New Brunswick Fredericton	M,D
University of New Mexico	M,D
The University of North Carolina at Chapel Hill	M,D
The University of North Carolina at Charlotte	M,O
The University of North Carolina Wilmington	M,O
University of North Florida	M
University of Notre Dame	M,D
University of Ottawa	M,D
University of Pennsylvania	M,D*
University of Pittsburgh	M,D*
University of Puerto Rico, Mayagüez Campus	M
University of Regina	M,D
University of Rhode Island	M,D,O
University of Rochester	M,D*
University of Saskatchewan	M,D
University of South Africa	M,D
University of South Carolina	M,D,O
University of Southern California	M,D
University of Southern Maine	M,O
University of South Florida	M,D
The University of Tennessee	M,D
The University of Texas at Austin	M,D
The University of Texas at Dallas	M,D*
The University of Texas at El Paso	M
The University of Texas at San Antonio	M,D
The University of Texas Rio Grande Valley	M
University of the Incarnate Word	M
The University of Toledo	M,D
University of Toronto	M,D
University of Utah	M,D*
University of Vermont	M
University of Victoria	M,D
University of Virginia	M,D
University of Washington	M,D*
University of Waterloo	M,D
The University of Western Ontario	M,D
University of Windsor	M,D
University of Wisconsin–Madison	M,D
University of Wyoming	M,D
Utah State University	M,D
Virginia Commonwealth University	M,D
Virginia Polytechnic Institute and State University	M,D
Washington University in St. Louis	M,D
Wayne State University	M,D
Western Michigan University	M,D,O
West Virginia University	M,D
Yale University	M,D*
York University	M,D
Youngstown State University	M

STRUCTURAL BIOLOGY

Baylor College of Medicine	D
Carnegie Mellon University	M,D
Columbia University	D*
Cornell University	M,D
Duke University	O*
Florida State University	M,D
Harvard University	D*
Illinois State University	M,D
Iowa State University of Science and Technology	M,D
Massachusetts Institute of Technology	D
Mayo Graduate School	D
Michigan State University	D
New York University	D
Northwestern University	D*
Oregon State University	D
Stanford University	D
Stony Brook University, State University of New York	D
Syracuse University	D
Tufts University	D
Tulane University	M,D
University at Albany, State University of New York	M,D
University at Buffalo, the State University of New York	M,D*
The University of Alabama at Birmingham	D
The University of Manchester	M,D
University of Minnesota, Twin Cities Campus	D
University of Pittsburgh	D*
University of Rochester	D*
The University of Texas Health Science Center at San Antonio	M,D
The University of Texas Medical Branch	D
University of Washington	D*
Weill Cornell Medicine	M,D

STRUCTURAL ENGINEERING

Auburn University	M,D
California State University, Northridge	M
Cornell University	M,D
Drexel University	M,D
École Polytechnique de Montréal	M,D,O
George Mason University	M,D
Illinois Institute of Technology	M,D
Instituto Tecnologico de Santo Domingo	M,O
Iowa State University of Science and Technology	M,D
Kansas State University	M,D
Louisiana State University and Agricultural & Mechanical College	M,D
Marquette University	M,D,O
Massachusetts Institute of Technology	M,D,O
McGill University	M,D
Northwestern University	M,D*
Norwich University	M
Ohio University	M,D
Old Dominion University	M
Oregon State University	M,D
Penn State Harrisburg	M,O
Pontificia Universidad Catolica Madre y Maestra	M
Southern Illinois University Edwardsville	M
Southern Methodist University	M,D
Stanford University	M,D,O
Stevens Institute of Technology	M,D,O
Tufts University	M,D
University at Buffalo, the State University of New York	M,D*
University of Alberta	M,D
University of Calgary	M,D
University of California, Berkeley	M,D
University of California, San Diego	M,D
University of Central Florida	M,D,O
University of Colorado Boulder	M,D
University of Colorado Denver	M,D
University of Dayton	M
University of Delaware	M,D*
The University of Manchester	M,D
University of Massachusetts Amherst	M,D*
University of Memphis	M,D
University of Michigan	M,D,O
University of Missouri	M,D
University of New Brunswick Fredericton	M,D
University of North Dakota	M
University of South Florida	M,D
The University of Texas at Tyler	M
University of Washington	M,D*

STUDENT AFFAIRS

Alfred University	M
Alliant International University–Los Angeles	M,D,O
Alliant International University–San Diego	M,D,O
Appalachian State University	M
Arkansas State University	M,O
Arkansas Tech University	M,D,O
Ashland University	M
Azusa Pacific University	M
Binghamton University, State University of New York	M*
Bloomsburg University of Pennsylvania	M
Bob Jones University	M,D,O
Bowling Green State University	M
Bucknell University	M
Buffalo State College, State University of New York	M
California State University, Long Beach	M
Canisius College	M,O
Central Michigan University	M,D,O
The Citadel, The Military College of South Carolina	M,O
Claremont Graduate University	M,D,O
Clemson University	M,D,O
College of Saint Elizabeth	M,D,O
The College of Saint Rose	M
Colorado State University	M,D
Concordia University Wisconsin	M
DePaul University	M,D
Eastern Illinois University	M
Eastern Michigan University	M,D,O
Fresno Pacific University	M,O
The George Washington University	M,D,O*
Grambling State University	M,D,O
Hampton University	M,D,O
Illinois State University	M
Indiana State University	M,D,O
Indiana University of Pennsylvania	M
Indiana University–Purdue University Indianapolis	M,O
Iowa State University of Science and Technology	M,D
Kansas State University	M,D
Kaplan University, Davenport Campus	M
Kent State University	M
Lewis University	M
Liberty University	M,D,O
Manhattan College	M,O
Marquette University	M,D,O
Merrimack College	M,O
Messiah College	M
Minnesota State University Mankato	M,D
Mississippi State University	M,D,O
Missouri State University	M
Monmouth University	M,O
New York University	M,D
Northern Arizona University	M,D,O
Northern Michigan University	M
Northwestern State University of Louisiana	M
Nova Southeastern University	M,D,O*
Ohio University	M,D

*M—masters degree; D—doctorate; O—other advanced degree; *—Close-Up and/or Display*

Oregon State University	M
Providence University College & Theological Seminary	M,D,O
Regent University	M,D,O
Rutgers University–New Brunswick	M
St. Cloud State University	M
St. Edward's University	M
Saint Louis University	M,D,O
Seton Hall University	M
Shippensburg University of Pennsylvania	M,O
Slippery Rock University of Pennsylvania	M
Southern Arkansas University–Magnolia	M
Southern Illinois University Edwardsville	M
Springfield College	M,D,O
State University of New York at Plattsburgh	M,O
Syracuse University	M
Texas State University	M
University of Arkansas at Little Rock	M,D
University of Bridgeport	M
University of Central Arkansas	M
University of Central Florida	M,D,O
University of Central Missouri	M,D,O
University of Central Oklahoma	M
University of Dayton	M,O
University of Florida	M,D,O
University of Georgia	M,D,O
The University of Iowa	M,D*
University of Louisville	M,D
University of Maryland, College Park	M,D,O
University of Minnesota, Twin Cities Campus	M,D,O
University of Nebraska at Kearney	M,O
University of Northern Colorado	D
University of Northern Iowa	M
University of Rhode Island	M
University of Rochester	M*
University of St. Thomas (MN)	M,D,O
University of South Carolina	M
University of Southern California	M
University of Southern Mississippi	M,D
University of South Florida	M,D,O
The University of Tennessee	M
The University of Tennessee at Martin	M
University of the Cumberlands	M,D,O
University of Utah	M,D*
University of Virginia	M,D,O
University of West Florida	M
University of Wisconsin–La Crosse	M,D
University of Wyoming	M,D
Virginia Commonwealth University	M
Virginia Polytechnic Institute and State University	M,D,O
Walsh University	M
West Chester University of Pennsylvania	M,O
Western Illinois University	M
Western Kentucky University	M
William James College	M,D,O

SUPPLY CHAIN MANAGEMENT

Alabama Agricultural and Mechanical University	M,D
American Graduate University	M,O
Arizona State University at the Tempe campus	M,D
Brigham Young University	M
Bryant University	M
California State University, East Bay	M
California State University, San Bernardino	M
Capella University	M,D
Case Western Reserve University	M,D*
Central Connecticut State University	M,O
Clayton State University	M
Concordia University (Canada)	M,D,O
Delaware Valley University	M
DeSales University	M
Eastern Michigan University	M,O
Elmhurst College	M
Embry-Riddle Aeronautical University–Worldwide	M
Ferris State University	M
Florida Institute of Technology	M,D
Fontbonne University	M
Friends University	M
Georgia Southern University	D
Golden Gate University	M,D,O
HEC Montreal	M,O
Howard University	M
Kansas State University	M,O
Kaplan University, Davenport Campus	M
Lindenwood University	M
Loyola University Chicago	M
Maine Maritime Academy	M
Marquette University	M,O
Maryville University of Saint Louis	M,O
Michigan State University	M,D
Moravian College	M
Naval Postgraduate School	M
North Carolina Agricultural and Technical State University	M
North Carolina State University	M
Norwich University	M
Nova Southeastern University	M*
Oregon State University	M,D
Penn State University Park	M,D
Polytechnic University of Puerto Rico, Miami Campus	M
Portland State University	M
Quinnipiac University	M
Rensselaer Polytechnic Institute	M
Rutgers University–Newark	D
St. Norbert College	M
Santa Clara University	M
Seton Hall University	M,O
Shippensburg University of Pennsylvania	M,O
Southern Arkansas University–Magnolia	M
Southern New Hampshire University	M,O
Strayer University	M
Suffolk University	M,O
Syracuse University	M,D
Texas A&M University–San Antonio	M
Texas Christian University	M
Towson University	M,O
The University of Akron	M
The University of Alabama in Huntsville	M,O
University of Dallas	M,D
University of Florida	M,D,O
University of Houston	M
University of Houston–Downtown	M
University of La Verne	M
University of Louisville	M,D,O
The University of Manchester	M
University of Massachusetts Dartmouth	M,O
University of Memphis	M,D
University of Michigan	M,D
University of Michigan–Dearborn	M
University of Minnesota, Twin Cities Campus	M
University of Missouri–St. Louis	M,D,O
The University of North Carolina at Charlotte	M,O
The University of North Carolina at Greensboro	M,D,O
University of North Texas	M,D,O
University of Rhode Island	M,D
University of San Diego	M,O
University of Southern California	M,D,O
The University of Tennessee at Chattanooga	M,O
The University of Texas at Austin	M,D
The University of Texas at Dallas	M*
University of Washington	M,D*
University of Wisconsin–Madison	M
University of Wisconsin–Platteville	M
University of Wisconsin–Stout	M
Walden University	M,D,O
Washington University in St. Louis	M
Western Illinois University	M,O
Wilfrid Laurier University	M,D
Wright State University	M

SURVEYING SCIENCE AND ENGINEERING

University of New Brunswick Fredericton	M,D

SURVEY METHODOLOGY

University of Maryland, College Park	M,D
University of Michigan	M,D,O
University of Nebraska–Lincoln	M,D

SUSTAINABILITY MANAGEMENT

American University	M
Anaheim University	M,D,O
Antioch University New England	M
Aquinas College (MI)	M
Argosy University, Chicago	M,D
Argosy University, Dallas	M,D,O
Argosy University, Denver	M,D
Argosy University, Hawai`i	M,D,O
Argosy University, Inland Empire	M,D
Argosy University, Los Angeles	M,D
Argosy University, Orange County	M,D,O
Argosy University, Phoenix	M,D
Argosy University, Salt Lake City	M,D
Argosy University, San Francisco Bay Area	M,D
Argosy University, Sarasota	M,D,O
Argosy University, Schaumburg	M,D,O
Argosy University, Seattle	M,D
Argosy University, Tampa	M,D
Argosy University, Twin Cities	M,D
Argosy University, Washington DC	M,D,O
Baldwin Wallace University	M
Bard College	M,O
Baruch College of the City University of New York	M,D
Brandeis University	M
Case Western Reserve University	D*
Chatham University	M
City University of Seattle	M,O
Clark University	M
Cleary University	M,O
Colorado State University	M
Columbia University	M*
DePaul University	M
Dominican University of California	M
Duquesne University	M
Edgewood College	M,D,O
Fairleigh Dickinson University, College at Florham	O
Franklin Pierce University	M,D,O
Goddard College	M
Illinois Institute of Technology	M
Indiana University Bloomington	M,D,O
Lipscomb University	M,O
Maastricht School of Management	M,D
Maharishi University of Management	M,D
Michigan Technological University	M,D,O
National University	M,O
The New School	M,O
Oklahoma State University	M,D,O
Oregon State University	M,D
Penn State Great Valley	M,O
Presidio Graduate School	M,O
Rochester Institute of Technology	M,D
San Francisco State University	M
Seattle Pacific University	M
Southern New Hampshire University	M,O
South University (GA)	M
State University of New York College of Environmental Science and Forestry	M,D,O
University of California, Berkeley	O
University of Colorado Denver	M
University of Maine	M,O
University of Michigan	M,D,O
University of New Hampshire	M,O
University of Portland	M
University of Saint Francis (IN)	M
University of Saskatchewan	M
University of Southern Maine	M
University of South Florida	M,O
University of Wisconsin–Green Bay	M
University of Wisconsin–Stout	M
University of Wisconsin–Superior	M
Valparaiso University	M,O

SUSTAINABLE DEVELOPMENT

Acadia University	M
American University	M,D,O
Antioch University Los Angeles	M
Antioch University New England	M,O
Appalachian State University	M
Arizona State University at the Tempe campus	M,D,O
Binghamton University, State University of New York	M*
Boston Architectural College	M
Brandeis University	M
California State University, Stanislaus	M
Carnegie Mellon University	M,D
City College of the City University of New York	M
Clarkson University	M,D
Clark University	M
Cleveland State University	M,O
Columbia University	M,D*
Cornell University	M,D
DePaul University	M
Eastern Illinois University	M
Emory University	M
Fashion Institute of Technology	M*
Future Generations Graduate School	M
Hawai`i Pacific University	M
HEC Montreal	O
Hofstra University	M
Instituto Centroamericano de Administración de Empresas	M
Instituto Tecnologico de Santo Domingo	M,O
Iowa State University of Science and Technology	M,D
Judson University	M
Lehigh University	M,O
Lenoir-Rhyne University	M
Lesley University	M,D,O
Lipscomb University	M,O
Long Island University–LIU Post	M,O
Minneapolis College of Art and Design	O
Mississippi State University	M,D
Montclair State University	M
New York School of Interior Design	M
New York University	M
Northern Arizona University	M
Pace University	M,D
Penn State University Park	M
Philadelphia University	M
Pratt Institute	M*
Ramapo College of New Jersey	M
Rochester Institute of Technology	M,D
St. Edward's University	M
San Jose State University	M,O
Savannah College of Art and Design	M
Saybrook University	M,D
SIT Graduate Institute	M
Southern Illinois University Edwardsville	M
Southern Methodist University	M,D
Stanford University	M,D,O
State University of New York College of Environmental Science and Forestry	M,D,O
Temple University	M,O*
Texas A&M University–Kingsville	D
Texas State University	M
Texas Tech University	M,D
Unity College	M
University of Alaska Fairbanks	M,D
University of Calgary	M,D
University of California, Berkeley	O
University of California, Santa Barbara	M,D
University of Colorado Denver	M,D
University of Florida	M,O
University of Georgia	M,D
University of Hawaii at Manoa	M,D,O
University of Maryland, College Park	M
University of Massachusetts Amherst	M*
University of Michigan	M,D
University of New Brunswick Fredericton	M
University of Oklahoma	M,D*
University of Southern California	M,D,O
University of South Florida	M,O
The University of Texas at Arlington	M
The University of Texas at Austin	M
University of Washington	M,D*
The University of Western Ontario	M,D
University of Wisconsin–Madison	M
Walden University	M,D,O
West Chester University of Pennsylvania	M,O
Western Illinois University	M,O
West Virginia University	D
Xavier University	M

SYSTEMS BIOLOGY

Albert Einstein College of Medicine	D
The George Washington University	D*
Harvard University	D*
Massachusetts Institute of Technology	D
Michigan State University	D
Northwestern University	D*
Purdue University	D
Rutgers University–New Brunswick	D
Stanford University	D
University of California, Irvine	D
University of California, Merced	M,D
University of California, San Diego	D
University of Chicago	D
University of Pittsburgh	D*
University of Toronto	M,D
Virginia Commonwealth University	D
Washington University in St. Louis	D
Weill Cornell Medicine	M,D

SYSTEMS ENGINEERING

Air Force Institute of Technology	M,D
Arizona State University at the Tempe campus	M
Auburn University	M,D,O
Boston University	M,D
California Institute of Technology	M,D
California State University, Fullerton	M
California State University, Northridge	M
Carleton University	M,D
Carnegie Mellon University	M
Case Western Reserve University	M,D*
The Catholic University of America	M,O
Colorado State University–Pueblo	M
Colorado Technical University Colorado Springs	M
Colorado Technical University Denver South	M
Concordia University (Canada)	M,D,O
Cornell University	M
Embry-Riddle Aeronautical University–Daytona	M,D*
Florida Institute of Technology	M,D
George Mason University	M,D,O
Georgetown University	M,D
The George Washington University	M,D,O*
Georgia Southern University	M
Harrisburg University of Science and Technology	M
Indiana University Bloomington	D
Indiana University–Purdue University Fort Wayne	M
Instituto Tecnológico y de Estudios Superiores de Monterrey, Campus Chihuahua	M,O
Instituto Tecnológico y de Estudios Superiores de Monterrey, Campus Monterrey	M,D
Iowa State University of Science and Technology	M
Johns Hopkins University	M,O
Kennesaw State University	M,O
Lehigh University	M,D
Loyola Marymount University	M
Massachusetts Institute of Technology	M
Mississippi State University	M,D
Missouri University of Science and Technology	M,D
National University	M,O
Naval Postgraduate School	M,D,O
New Mexico Institute of Mining and Technology	M
New Mexico State University	M,D,O
New York University	M
North Carolina Agricultural and Technical State University	M,D
Northeastern University	M,D,O
Oakland University	M,D,O
The Ohio State University	M,D
Ohio University	M
Old Dominion University	M,D
Penn State Great Valley	M,O
Regis University	M,O
Rensselaer Polytechnic Institute	M,D
Rochester Institute of Technology	M,D
Rose-Hulman Institute of Technology	M
Rutgers University–New Brunswick	M,D
Simon Fraser University	M,D
Southern Methodist University	M,D
Stevens Institute of Technology	M,D,O
Stony Brook University, State University of New York	M
Tennessee State University	M,D
Texas A&M University–Kingsville	D
Texas Tech University	M,D
The University of Alabama in Huntsville	M,D
University of Alberta	M,D
The University of Arizona	M,D,O

University of Arkansas at Little Rock M,D,O
University of California, Merced M,D
University of Colorado Colorado Springs M,D
University of Florida M,D,O
University of Houston–Clear Lake M
University of Illinois at Urbana–Champaign M,D
University of Maryland, Baltimore County M,O
University of Maryland, College Park M
University of Massachusetts Dartmouth M,D
University of Michigan M,D
University of Michigan–Dearborn M,D
University of Nebraska at Omaha M,O
University of New Hampshire M,D
University of New Mexico M,D
The University of North Carolina at Charlotte M,D,O
University of Pennsylvania M,D*
University of Regina M,D
University of St. Thomas (MN) M,O
University of South Alabama D
University of Southern California M,D,O
University of South Florida O
The University of Texas at Arlington M
The University of Texas at Dallas M,D*
The University of Texas at El Paso M,O
The University of Texas Rio Grande Valley M
University of Utah M,O*
University of Virginia M,D
University of Waterloo M,D
University of Wisconsin–Madison M,D
Virginia Polytechnic Institute and State University M,D,O
Wayne State University M,D,O
Western International University M
Worcester Polytechnic Institute M,O

SYSTEMS SCIENCE
Arizona State University at the Tempe campus M,D
Binghamton University, State University of New York M,D*
Carleton University M,D
Claremont Graduate University M,D,O
Eastern Illinois University M,O
Fairleigh Dickinson University, Metropolitan Campus M
Hood College M
Louisiana State University and Agricultural & Mechanical College M,D
Louisiana State University in Shreveport M
Miami University M
New Jersey Institute of Technology M,D,O
Oakland University M,D
Portland State University M,D,O
Rensselaer at Hartford M
Southern Methodist University M,D
Stevens Institute of Technology M,D,O
Strayer University M
Universidad Autonoma de Guadalajara M,D
University of Michigan M,D
University of Ottawa M,D,O
Worcester Polytechnic Institute M,D,O

TAXATION
American International College M
American University M,O
Appalachian State University M
Baruch College of the City University of New York M
Bentley University M
Boise State University M
Boston University M,D
Bryant University M
California Miramar University M
California Polytechnic State University, San Luis Obispo M
California State University, Fullerton M
California State University, Northridge M,O
Capital University M
Chapman University M,D
Cleveland State University M
DePaul University M,D
Fairfield University M,O
Fairleigh Dickinson University, College at Florham M,O
Fairleigh Dickinson University, Metropolitan Campus M
Florida Gulf Coast University M
Florida State University M,D
Fordham University M
Georgetown University M,D
Georgia State University M
Golden Gate University M,D,O
Goldey-Beacom College M
Gonzaga University M
Grand Valley State University M
HEC Montreal M,O
Hofstra University M,O
Illinois Institute of Technology M,D
Instituto Tecnologico de Santo Domingo M,O
James Madison University M
John Marshall Law School M,D
Long Island University–LIU Brooklyn M,O
Long Island University–LIU Post M
Loyola University Chicago M,D
Michigan State University M,D
Mississippi State University M
National Paralegal College M
New York Law School M,D
New York University M,D,O
Northeastern University M
Northern Illinois University M
Northern Kentucky University M,O
Northwestern University M,D*
Nova Southeastern University M*
Pace University M
Philadelphia University M
Robert Morris University M
St. John's University (NY) M
St. Thomas University M,D
San Jose State University M
Seton Hall University M,O
Southern Illinois University Edwardsville M
Southern Methodist University M,D
Southern New Hampshire University M,O
State University of New York College at Old Westbury M
Strayer University M
Suffolk University M,O
Taft University System M,D
Temple University M,D*
Texas Christian University M
Texas Tech University M,D
Troy University M,O
Université de Montréal M,D,O
Université de Sherbrooke M,O
University at Albany, State University of New York M
The University of Akron M
The University of Alabama M,D
The University of Alabama in Huntsville M
University of Baltimore M,D
University of Central Florida M
University of Cincinnati M
University of Colorado Denver M
University of Denver M
University of Florida M,D
University of Hartford M,O
University of Hawaii at Manoa M
University of Houston M,D
University of Illinois at Urbana–Champaign M,D
University of Miami M,D
University of Michigan M,D
University of Minnesota, Twin Cities Campus M
University of Mississippi M,D
University of Missouri M,D,O
University of Missouri–Kansas City M,D
University of New Haven M,O
University of New Mexico M
University of New Orleans M
The University of North Carolina Wilmington M
University of Notre Dame M
University of San Diego M,D,O
University of San Francisco M,D
University of Southern California M
University of South Florida M,D
The University of Texas at Arlington M,D
University of the Sacred Heart M
University of Washington M,D*
University of Waterloo M,D
University of Wisconsin–Madison M
University of Wisconsin–Milwaukee M,D,O
Villanova University M
Wake Forest University M
Walsh College of Accountancy and Business Administration M
Wayne State University M,D,O
Weber State University M
Western Michigan University Thomas M. Cooley Law School M,D
Wichita State University M
Widener University M

TECHNICAL COMMUNICATION
Auburn University M,D,O
Boise State University M
Bowling Green State University M,D
Drexel University M
East Carolina University M,D,O
Eastern Michigan University M,O
Eastern Washington University M
Harvard University M*
Lawrence Technological University M
Minnesota State University Mankato M,O
Missouri Western State University M,O
Montana Tech of The University of Montana M
New Jersey Institute of Technology M,D,O
North Carolina State University M,D
North Central College M
Northeastern University M
Texas State University M
University of Houston–Downtown M
University of Nebraska at Omaha M,O
University of South Florida O
University of Washington M,D,O*
University of Wisconsin–Milwaukee M,D,O
University of Wisconsin–Stout M

TECHNICAL WRITING
Carnegie Mellon University M
Drexel University M
Fitchburg State University M,O
Illinois Institute of Technology M,D
James Madison University M
Johns Hopkins University M,O
Laurentian University O
Louisiana Tech University M,O
Massachusetts Institute of Technology M
Metropolitan State University M
Texas Tech University M,D
The University of Alabama in Huntsville M,O
University of Arkansas at Little Rock M
The University of North Carolina at Charlotte M,O
The University of North Carolina at Greensboro M,D,O
University of the Sciences M,O
University of Waterloo M,D

TECHNOLOGY AND PUBLIC POLICY
Arizona State University at the Tempe campus M
Carnegie Mellon University M,D
Eastern Michigan University M
The George Washington University M,O*
Massachusetts Institute of Technology M,D
Rensselaer Polytechnic Institute M,D
Rochester Institute of Technology M
St. Cloud State University M
Stony Brook University, State University of New York D
University of Minnesota, Twin Cities Campus M
University of South Africa M,D
The University of Texas at Austin M

TELECOMMUNICATIONS
Ball State University M
Boston University M,O
California Miramar University M
Claremont Graduate University M,D,O
Drexel University M
Fairfield University M,O
Florida International University M
Franklin Pierce University M,D,O
The George Washington University M,D,O*
Illinois Institute of Technology M,D
Indiana University Bloomington M
Instituto Tecnologico de Santo Domingo M,O
Johns Hopkins University M,O
Michigan State University M
National University M,O
New Jersey Institute of Technology M,D
Northeastern University M,D,O
Ohio University M
Pace University M,D,O
Rochester Institute of Technology M
Roosevelt University M
Saint Mary's University of Minnesota M
Southern Methodist University M,D
State University of New York Polytechnic Institute M
Stevens Institute of Technology M,D,O
Stratford University (VA) M,D
Syracuse University M
Universidad del Turabo M
Université du Québec, Institut National de la Recherche Scientifique M,D
University of Alberta M,D
University of Arkansas M,D
University of California, San Diego M,D
University of California, Santa Cruz M,D
University of Colorado Boulder M
University of Florida M,D
University of Hawaii at Manoa O
University of Houston M
University of Louisiana at Lafayette M
University of Maryland, College Park M
University of Massachusetts Dartmouth M,D,O
University of Missouri–Kansas City M,D,O
The University of North Carolina at Chapel Hill M,D
University of Oklahoma M*
University of Pittsburgh M,D,O*
University of Southern California M,D,O
The University of Texas at Dallas M,D*

TELECOMMUNICATIONS MANAGEMENT
Alaska Pacific University M
Boston University M,O
California Miramar University M
Capitol Technology University M
Carnegie Mellon University M
Concordia University (Canada) M,D,O
East Carolina University M,D,O
Instituto Tecnológico y de Estudios Superiores de Monterrey, Campus Ciudad de México M
Instituto Tecnológico y de Estudios Superiores de Monterrey, Campus Ciudad Obregón M
Instituto Tecnológico y de Estudios Superiores de Monterrey, Campus Estado de México M,D
Instituto Tecnológico y de Estudios Superiores de Monterrey, Campus Irapuato M,D
Murray State University M
New York University M,D,O
Oklahoma State University M,D,O
San Diego State University M
Stevens Institute of Technology M,D,O
Strayer University M
Syracuse University M,O
University of Colorado Boulder M
University of South Africa M,D
University of Wisconsin–Stout M

TERATOLOGY
West Virginia University M,D

TEXTILE DESIGN
Academy of Art University M
Arizona State University at the Tempe campus M,D
California College of the Arts M
California State University, Los Angeles M
Concordia University (Canada) M
Cornell University M,D
Cranbrook Academy of Art M
Drexel University M
East Carolina University M
Illinois State University M
LIM College M
Massachusetts College of Art and Design M,O
The New School M
Oregon State University M,D
Paris College of Art M
Philadelphia University M
Rhode Island School of Design M
Savannah College of Art and Design M
School of the Art Institute of Chicago M,O
Temple University M*
University of California, Davis M
University of Cincinnati M
The University of Kansas M*
The University of Manchester M,D
University of Minnesota, Twin Cities Campus M,D,O
The University of North Carolina at Greensboro M,D
University of North Texas M,D,O
Wayne State University M

TEXTILE SCIENCES AND ENGINEERING
Cornell University M,D
North Carolina State University M,D
Philadelphia University M,D
University of Massachusetts Dartmouth M
The University of Texas at Austin M

THANATOLOGY
Brooklyn College of the City University of New York M
The College of New Rochelle M,O
Southwestern College (NM) M,O
University of Maryland, Baltimore O

THEATER
Academy of Art University M
American Conservatory Theater M,O
Arcadia University M,D,O
Arizona State University at the Tempe campus M,D
Baylor University M
Berklee College of Music M,O
Binghamton University, State University of New York M*
Bob Jones University M,D,O
Boston University M,O
Bowling Green State University M,D
Brandeis University M
Brigham Young University M
Brooklyn College of the City University of New York M
Brown University M,D
California Institute of Integral Studies M,D
California Institute of the Arts M,O
California State University, Fullerton M
California State University, Long Beach M
California State University, Los Angeles M
California State University, Northridge M
Carnegie Mellon University M
Case Western Reserve University M*
The Catholic University of America M
Central Washington University M
Columbia University M,D*
Columbus State University M
Cornell University D
Dell'Arte International School of Physical Theatre M
DePaul University M
Eastern Michigan University M
Emerson College M
Florida Atlantic University M
Florida State University M,D
Fontbonne University M
Fordham University M
The George Washington University M,O*
The Graduate Center, City University of New York D
Hollins University M,O
Hunter College of the City University of New York M
Idaho State University M
Illinois State University M
Indiana University Bloomington M,D
Kansas State University M
Kent State University M
Long Island University–LIU Post M

*M—masters degree; D—doctorate; O—other advanced degree; *—Close-Up and/or Display*

Louisiana State University and Agricultural & Mechanical College	M,D
Louisiana Tech University	M
Mary Baldwin College	M
Miami University	M
Michigan State University	M
Minnesota State University Mankato	M
Missouri State University	M
Montclair State University	M
Naropa University	M
The New School	M
New York University	M,D,O
Northern Illinois University	M
Northern Michigan University	M,O
Northwestern University	M,D*
The Ohio State University	M,D
Ohio University	M
Oklahoma State University	M
Pace University	M
Penn State University Park	M
Point Park University	M
Portland State University	M
Purchase College, State University of New York	M
Purdue University	M
Regent University	M,D
Roosevelt University	M
Rowan University	M
Rutgers University–New Brunswick	M
San Diego State University	M
San Francisco State University	M
San Jose State University	M,O
Sarah Lawrence College	M
Savannah College of Art and Design	M
Smith College	M
Southern Illinois University Carbondale	M,D
Southern Methodist University	M
Southern Oregon University	M
Stanford University	D
Stony Brook University, State University of New York	M
Temple University	M*
Texas State University	M
Texas Tech University	M
Texas Woman's University	M
Towson University	M
Tufts University	M,D
Tulane University	M
Université de Sherbrooke	M,D
Université Laval	M,D
University at Buffalo, the State University of New York	M,D*
The University of Akron	M
The University of Alabama	M
University of Alberta	M
The University of Arizona	M
University of Arkansas	M
The University of British Columbia	M,D
University of Calgary	M
University of California, Berkeley	D
University of California, Davis	M,D
University of California, Irvine	M,D
University of California, Los Angeles	M,D
University of California, San Diego	M,D
University of California, Santa Barbara	M,D
University of California, Santa Cruz	O
University of Central Florida	M
University of Central Missouri	M,D,O
University of Cincinnati	M,D
University of Colorado Boulder	M,D
University of Connecticut	M*
University of Delaware	M*
University of Florida	M
University of Georgia	M,D
University of Guelph	M
University of Hawaii at Manoa	M,D
University of Houston	M
University of Idaho	M
University of Illinois at Urbana–Champaign	M,D
The University of Iowa	M*
The University of Kansas	M,D*
University of Lethbridge	M,D
University of Louisville	M
The University of Manchester	D
University of Maryland, Baltimore County	M
University of Maryland, College Park	M,D
University of Massachusetts Amherst	M*
University of Memphis	M
University of Minnesota, Twin Cities Campus	M,D
University of Missouri	M,D
University of Missouri–Kansas City	M
University of Montana	M
University of Nebraska–Lincoln	M
University of Nevada, Las Vegas	M
University of New Mexico	M
University of New Orleans	M
The University of North Carolina at Chapel Hill	M
The University of North Carolina at Charlotte	M,D,O
The University of North Carolina at Greensboro	M
University of North Carolina School of the Arts	M
University of North Dakota	M
University of Oklahoma	M*
University of Oregon	M,D
University of Ottawa	M
University of Pittsburgh	M,D*
University of Portland	M
University of San Diego	M
University of Saskatchewan	M
University of South Carolina	M,D
The University of South Dakota	M
University of Southern California	M
University of Southern Mississippi	M
The University of Tennessee	M
The University of Texas at Austin	M,D
The University of Texas Rio Grande Valley	M,O
University of the Cumberlands	M,D,O
University of Toronto	M,D
University of Victoria	M
University of Virginia	M
University of Washington	M,D*
University of Wisconsin–Madison	M,D
University of Wisconsin–Superior	M
Utah State University	M
Villanova University	M
Virginia Commonwealth University	M
Virginia Polytechnic Institute and State University	M,D,O
Washington University in St. Louis	M
Wayne State University	M
Western Illinois University	M
West Virginia University	M
Yale University	M,D,O*
York University	M,D

THEOLOGY

Abilene Christian University	M
Acadia University	M,D
Ambrose University	M,O
American Baptist Seminary of the West	M
American Jewish University	M
Amridge University	M,D
Anabaptist Mennonite Biblical Seminary	M,O
Anderson University (IN)	M,D
Andover Newton Theological School	M,D
Andrews University	M,D,O
Apex School of Theology	M,D
Aquinas Institute of Theology	M,D,O
Arlington Baptist College	M
Asbury Theological Seminary	M,D,O
Ashland Theological Seminary	M,D,O
Assemblies of God Theological Seminary	M,D
The Athenaeum of Ohio	M,O
Atlantic School of Theology	M,O
Austin Graduate School of Theology	M
Austin Presbyterian Theological Seminary	M,D
Ave Maria University	M,D
Azusa Pacific University	M,D
Bakke Graduate University	M,D
Baptist Bible College	M
The Baptist College of Florida	M
Baptist Missionary Association Theological Seminary	M
Baptist Theological Seminary at Richmond	M,D,O
Barclay College	M
Barry University	M,D
Baylor University	M,D
Bethany Theological Seminary	M,O
Bethel College	M
Bethel Seminary	M,D,O
Bethesda University	M
Beth HaMedrash Shaarei Yosher Institute	
Beth Hatalmud Rabbinical College	
Beth Medrash Govoha	
Bethune-Cookman University	M
Bexley Hall Episcopal Seminary	M
Biblical Theological Seminary	M,D,O
Biola University	M,D,O
Bob Jones University	M,D,O
Boston College	M,D,O
Boston University	M,D
Briercrest Seminary	M
Brite Divinity School	M,D,O
Bryn Athyn College of the New Church	M
Cairn University	M
California Institute of Integral Studies	M,D
California Lutheran University	M,D,O
Calvary Bible College and Theological Seminary	M
Calvin Theological Seminary	M,D
Campbellsville University	M
Campbell University	M,D
Canadian Southern Baptist Seminary	M
Carey Theological College	M,D
Carolina Graduate School of Divinity	M
Carson-Newman University	M
Catholic Distance University	M
Catholic Theological Union	M,D,O
The Catholic University of America	M,D,O
Central Baptist Theological Seminary	M,O
Central Yeshiva Tomchei Tmimim-Lubavitch	M
Chaminade University of Honolulu	M
Charlotte Christian College and Theological Seminary	M
Chicago Theological Seminary	M,D
Christendom College	M
Christian Theological Seminary	M,D
Christ the King Seminary	M
Church Divinity School of the Pacific	M,D,O
Cincinnati Christian University	M
Claremont Graduate University	M,D
Claremont School of Theology	M,D
Colgate Rochester Crozer Divinity School	M,D,O
Collège Dominicain de Philosophie et de Théologie	M,D,O
College of Emmanuel and St. Chad	M,O
College of Saint Elizabeth	M
Columbia International University	M,D,O
Columbia Theological Seminary	M,D
Concordia Lutheran Seminary	M,O
Concordia Seminary	M,D,O
Concordia Theological Seminary	M,D
Concordia University (Canada)	M
Concordia University Irvine	M
Concordia University of Edmonton	M
Corban University	M,D,O
Covenant Theological Seminary	M,D,O
Creighton University	M
Criswell College	M
Crown College	M
Dallas Baptist University	M
Dallas Theological Seminary	M,D,O
Denver Seminary	M,D,O
Dominican House of Studies, Pontifical Faculty of the Immaculate Conception	M,D,O
Dominican School of Philosophy and Theology	M,O
Drew University	M,D,O
Duke University	M,D*
Duquesne University	M,D
Earlham School of Religion	M
Eastern Mennonite University	M,O
Eastern University	M,D
Ecumenical Theological Seminary	M
Eden Theological Seminary	M,D
Emory University	M,D
Episcopal Divinity School	M,D,O
Erskine Theological Seminary	M,D
Evangelical Seminary	M
Evangelical Seminary of Puerto Rico	M,D
Faith Baptist Bible College and Theological Seminary	M
Faith Evangelical College & Seminary	M,D
Faith Theological Seminary	M,D
Faulkner University	M
Fordham University	M,D
Franciscan School of Theology	M
Franciscan University of Steubenville	M
Freed-Hardeman University	M
Fresno Pacific University	M
Fuller Theological Seminary	M,D,O
Gannon University	M,O
Gardner-Webb University	M,D
Garrett-Evangelical Theological Seminary	M,D
Gateway Seminary	M,D,O
General Theological Seminary	M,D,O
George Fox University	M,D,O
Georgetown University	D
Georgia Christian University	M,D
Georgian Court University	M,O
Global University	M,D
Gonzaga University	M
Gordon-Conwell Theological Seminary	M,D
Graceland University (IA)	M
Grace Theological Seminary	M,D,O
Grace University	M
Graduate Theological Union	M,D,O
Grand Rapids Theological Seminary of Cornerstone University	M
Harding School of Theology	M,D
Hardin-Simmons University	M,D
Hartford Seminary	M,D,O
Harvard University	M*
Hebrew College	M
Hebrew Union College–Jewish Institute of Religion (NY)	M,D
Heritage College and Seminary	M,O
Holy Apostles College and Seminary	M,O
Holy Cross Greek Orthodox School of Theology	M
Hood Theological Seminary	M,D
Houston Baptist University	M
Houston Graduate School of Theology	M,D
Howard Payne University	M
Howard University	M,D
Iliff School of Theology	M,D
Indiana Wesleyan University	M
Institute for Christian Studies	M,D
Inter American University of Puerto Rico, Metropolitan Campus	D
Interdenominational Theological Center	M,D
International Baptist College and Seminary	M
The Jewish Theological Seminary	M,D,O
John Paul the Great Catholic University	M
Johnson University	M,D,O
Kehilath Yakov Rabbinical Seminary	
Kenrick-Glennon Seminary	M
Kentucky Christian University	M
The King's University	M,D,O
Kingswood University	M
Knox College	M,D
Knox Theological Seminary	M
Lakeland University	M
Lancaster Bible College	M,D,O
Lancaster Theological Seminary	M,D,O
La Salle University	M,D,O
Lee University	M
Lenoir-Rhyne University	M
Lexington Theological Seminary	M,D
Liberty University	M,D,O
Lincoln Christian Seminary	M,D
Lincoln Christian University	M
Lipscomb University	M,D,O
Logos Evangelical Seminary	M,D
Loras College	M
Louisiana College	M
Louisville Presbyterian Theological Seminary	M,D
Lourdes University	M
Loyola Marymount University	M
Loyola University Chicago	M,D,O
Loyola University Maryland	M,O
Loyola University New Orleans	M,O
Lubbock Christian University	M
Lutheran School of Theology at Chicago	M,D
Lutheran Theological Seminary at Gettysburg	M,D
The Lutheran Theological Seminary at Philadelphia	M,D,O
Lutheran Theological Seminary Saskatoon	M,D
Luther Rice College & Seminary	M,D
Luther Seminary	M,D
Machzikei Hadath Rabbinical College	O
Madonna University	M
Malone University	M
Maple Springs Baptist Bible College and Seminary	M,D,O
Maranatha Baptist University	M
Marquette University	M,D
Marylhurst University	M
The Master's College and Seminary	M,D
McCormick Theological Seminary	M,D,O
McGill University	M,D
McMaster University	M,D,O
Meadville Lombard Theological School	M,D
Memphis Theological Seminary	M,D
Mercer University	M,D
Mesivta of Eastern Parkway–Yeshiva Zichron Meilech	
Mesivta Torah Vodaath Rabbinical Seminary	
Mesivtha Tifereth Jerusalem of America	
Methodist Theological School in Ohio	M,D
Mid-America Baptist Theological Seminary	M,D
Mid-America Baptist Theological Seminary Northeast Branch	M
Mid-America Reformed Seminary	M
Midwestern Baptist Theological Seminary	M,D,O
Milligan College	M,D
Mirrer Yeshiva	
Moody Bible Institute	M,O
Moody Theological SeminaryMichigan	M,O
Moravian Theological Seminary	M,O
Mount Angel Seminary	M
Mount St. Joseph University	M,O
Mount St. Mary's University (MD)	M
Mount Vernon Nazarene University	M
Multnomah University	M,D
Naropa University	M
Nashotah House Theological Seminary	M,D,O
Nazarene Theological Seminary	M,D
Ner Israel Rabbinical College	M,D,O
Ner Israel Yeshiva College of Toronto	
New Brunswick Theological Seminary	M,D
Newman Theological College	M
Newman University	M
New Orleans Baptist Theological Seminary	M,D
New Saint Andrews College	M,O
New York Theological Seminary	M,D
Northeastern Seminary at Roberts Wesleyan College	M,D
Northern Seminary	M,D
North Park Theological Seminary	M,D
Northwest Nazarene University	M
Northwest University	M
Notre Dame Seminary	M
Nyack College	M,D
Oakland City University	M,D
Oblate School of Theology	M,D,O
Ohio Dominican University	M
Ohr Hameir Theological Seminary	
Oklahoma Christian University	M
Oklahoma Wesleyan University	M
Olivet Nazarene University	M
Oral Roberts University	M,D
Pacific School of Religion	M,D,O
Palm Beach Atlantic University	M
Payne Theological Seminary	M
Pentecostal Theological Seminary	M,D
Pfeiffer University	M
Phillips Theological Seminary	M,D
Phoenix Seminary	M,D,O
Piedmont International University	M,D
Pittsburgh Theological Seminary	M,D
Pontifical Catholic University of Puerto Rico	M
Pontifical College Josephinum	M
Pope St. John XXIII National Seminary	M
Princeton Theological Seminary	M,D
Providence College	M
Providence University College & Theological Seminary	M,D,O
Queen's University at Kingston	M,O
Rabbi Isaac Elchanan Theological Seminary	O
Rabbinical Academy Mesivta Rabbi Chaim Berlin	O
Rabbinical College Beth Shraga	
Rabbinical College Bobover Yeshiva B'nei Zion	
Rabbinical College Ch'san Sofer	
Rabbinical College of Long Island	
Rabbinical Seminary of America	
Reconstructionist Rabbinical College	M,D,O
Reformed Episcopal Seminary	M

Reformed Presbyterian Theological Seminary M,D
Reformed Theological Seminary–Atlanta Campus M,D,O
Reformed Theological Seminary–Charlotte Campus M,D
Reformed Theological Seminary–Jackson Campus M,D,O
Reformed Theological Seminary–Orlando Campus M,D,O
Reformed Theological Seminary–Washington D.C. M
Regent College M,O
Regent University M,D
Regis College (Canada) M,D,O
Sacred Heart Major Seminary M
Sacred Heart School of Theology M,O
St. Andrew's College M,D,O
St. Andrew's College in Winnipeg M
St. Augustine's Seminary of Toronto M,O
St. Bernard's School of Theology and Ministry M,O
St. Catherine University M,O
Saint Charles Borromeo Seminary, Overbrook M
St. John's Seminary (CA) M
Saint John's Seminary (MA) M
Saint John's University (MN) M
St. John's University (NY) M
St. Joseph's Seminary M
Saint Louis University M,D
Saint Mary-of-the-Woods College M,O
Saint Mary Seminary and Graduate School of Theology M,D
St. Mary's Seminary and University M,D,O
Saint Mary's University (Canada) M
St. Mary's University (United States) M
Saint Meinrad School of Theology M
St. Norbert College M
St. Patrick's Seminary & University M,O
Saint Paul School of Theology M,D
Saint Paul University M,D,O
St. Peter's Seminary M
Saints Cyril and Methodius Seminary M
St. Stephen's College M,D
St. Thomas University M,D,O
St. Tikhon's Orthodox Theological Seminary M
St. Vincent de Paul Regional Seminary M
Saint Vincent Seminary M
St. Vladimir's Orthodox Theological Seminary M,D
Samford University M,D
San Francisco Theological Seminary M,D
Santa Clara University M,D,O
Seabury-Western Theological Seminary M,D,O
Seattle Pacific University M,O
The Seattle School of Theology and Psychology M
Seattle University M,O
Seminary of the Immaculate Conception M,D,O
Seminary of the Southwest M,O
Seton Hall University M,O
Sewanee: The University of the South M,D
Shaw University M
Shepherds Theological Seminary M
Shepherd University (CA) M,D
Shiloh University M,D
Sh'or Yoshuv Rabbinical College
Sioux Falls Seminary M,D,O
Southeastern Baptist Theological Seminary M,D
Southern Adventist University M
The Southern Baptist Theological Seminary M,D
Southern California Seminary M,D
Southern Evangelical Seminary M,D,O
Southern Methodist University M,D
South Florida Bible College and Theological Seminary M
Southwestern Assemblies of God University M
Southwestern Baptist Theological Seminary M,D
Southwestern College (KS) M
Spring Arbor University M
Spring Hill College M,O
Starr King School for the Ministry M
SUM Bible College & Theological Seminary M
Summit University M,D
Talmudic University M
Taylor College and Seminary M,O
Toronto School of Theology M,D
Trinity College (Canada) M,D,O
Trinity International University M,D,O
Trinity Lutheran Seminary M
Trinity School for Ministry M,D,O
Trinity Western University M,D
Tri-State Bible College M
Tyndale University College & Seminary M,O
Unification Theological Seminary M,D
Union Theological Seminary in the City of New York M,D
United Talmudical Seminary
United Theological Seminary M,D
United Theological Seminary of the Twin Cities M,D,O
Université de Montréal M,D,O
Université de Sherbrooke M,D,O
Université du Québec à Chicoutimi M,D
Université Laval M,D
University of Chicago D
University of Dallas M
University of Dayton M,D
University of Denver D
University of Dubuque M,D
The University of Manchester D
University of Northwestern–St. Paul M
University of Notre Dame M,D
University of Philosophical Research M
University of Saint Francis (IN) M
University of Saint Mary of the Lake–Mundelein Seminary M,D
University of St. Michael's College M,D,O
University of St. Thomas (MN) M
University of St. Thomas (TX) M
The University of Scranton M
University of South Africa M,D
University of the West M
University of Valley Forge M
The University of Winnipeg M,O
Urshan Graduate School of Theology M
Ursuline College M
Valparaiso University M,O
Vancouver School of Theology M,O
Vanderbilt University M*
Vanguard University of Southern California M
Victoria University M,D,O
Villanova University M
Virginia Beach Theological Seminary M
Virginia Theological Seminary M,D
Virginia Union University M,D
Walsh University M
Wartburg Theological Seminary M
Wayland Baptist University M
Wesley Biblical Seminary M
Wesley Theological Seminary M,D
Western Seminary M,O
Western Seminary–Sacramento Campus M,O
Western Seminary–San Jose Campus M,O
Western Theological Seminary M,D,O
Westminster Seminary California M
Westminster Theological Seminary M,D,O
Wheaton College M,D
Whitworth University M
Wilfrid Laurier University M,D,O
Winebrenner Theological Seminary M,D
Wycliffe College M,D,O
Xavier University M
Xavier University of Louisiana M
Yale University M*
Yeshiva Beth Moshe O
Yeshiva Karlin Stolin Rabbinical Institute O
Yeshiva of Nitra Rabbinical College
Yeshiva Shaar Hatorah Talmudic Research Institute
Yeshivath Zichron Moshe O
Yeshiva Toras Chaim Talmudical Seminary

THEORETICAL CHEMISTRY

Carnegie Mellon University D
Cornell University D
Georgetown University D
Laurentian University M
University of Calgary M,D
The University of Manchester M,D
University of Regina M,D
The University of Tennessee M,D
Vanderbilt University M,D*
Wesleyan University D
West Virginia University M,D
Yale University D*

THEORETICAL PHYSICS

American University of Beirut M,D
Cornell University M,D
Delaware State University D
Emory University D
Harvard University D*
Rutgers University–New Brunswick M,D
The University of Manchester M,D
University of Victoria M,D
West Virginia University M,D

THERAPIES—DANCE, DRAMA, AND MUSIC

Antioch University New England M,O
Appalachian State University M
Arizona State University at the Tempe campus M,D
Berklee College of Music M
California Institute of Integral Studies M,D
Colorado State University M
Columbia College Chicago M,O
Concordia University (Canada) M
Drexel University M,O
East Carolina University M,O
Florida State University M,D
Georgia College & State University M
Immaculata University M
Indiana University–Purdue University Indianapolis M
Lesley University M,D,O
Loyola University New Orleans M
Maryville University of Saint Louis M
Michigan State University M,D
Molloy College M
Montclair State University M,O
Naropa University M
New York University M
Ohio University M,O
Pratt Institute M*
Radford University M
Saint Mary-of-the-Woods College M
Shenandoah University M,D,O
State University of New York at New Paltz M
Temple University M,D*
Texas Woman's University M
The University of Kansas M*
University of Kentucky M,D
University of Miami M,D,O
University of Missouri–Kansas City M,D
University of the Pacific M
Western Michigan University M,O
Wilfrid Laurier University M

TOXICOLOGY

American University of Beirut M,D
Colorado State University M,D
Columbia University M,D*
Cornell University M,D
Duke University O*
Florida Agricultural and Mechanical University M,D
The George Washington University M,O*
Indiana University Bloomington M,D,O
Indiana University–Purdue University Indianapolis M,D
Iowa State University of Science and Technology M,D
Johns Hopkins University M,D
Long Island University–LIU Brooklyn M,D
Louisiana State University and Agricultural & Mechanical College M,D
Massachusetts Institute of Technology M,D
Medical College of Wisconsin D
Medical University of South Carolina D
Michigan State University M,D
New York University M,D
North Carolina State University M,D
Oklahoma State University Center for Health Sciences M
Oregon State University M,D
Purdue University M,D
Queen's University at Kingston M,D
Rutgers University–New Brunswick M,D
St. John's University (NY) M
San Diego State University M,D
Simon Fraser University M,D,O
Syracuse University M,O
Texas Southern University M,D
Texas Tech University M,D
Thomas Jefferson University M
Université de Montréal O
University at Albany, State University of New York M,D
University at Buffalo, the State University of New York M,D*
The University of Alabama at Birmingham M,D
University of Arkansas for Medical Sciences M,D,O
University of California, Davis M,D
University of California, Irvine M,D
University of California, Los Angeles D
University of California, Riverside M,D
University of California, Santa Cruz M,D
University of Colorado Denver D
University of Connecticut M,D*
University of Florida M,D,O
University of Guelph M,D
University of Illinois at Chicago M
The University of Iowa M,D*
The University of Kansas M,D*
University of Kentucky M,D
University of Louisiana at Monroe D
University of Louisville M,D
The University of Manchester M,D
University of Maryland, Baltimore M,D
University of Maryland Eastern Shore M,D
University of Michigan M,D
University of Minnesota, Duluth M,D
University of Minnesota, Twin Cities Campus M,D
University of Mississippi Medical Center D
University of Missouri–Kansas City D
University of Montana M,D
University of Nebraska–Lincoln M,D
University of Nebraska Medical Center D
University of New Mexico M,D
The University of North Carolina at Chapel Hill M,D
University of Prince Edward Island M,D
University of Puerto Rico, Medical Sciences Campus M,D
University of Rhode Island M,D
University of Rochester D*
University of Saskatchewan M,D,O
University of South Alabama M
University of Southern California M,D
The University of Texas at Austin M,D
The University of Texas Health Science Center at San Antonio M
The University of Texas Medical Branch M,D
University of the Sciences M,D
University of Utah D*
University of Washington M,D*
University of Wisconsin–Madison M,D
University of Wisconsin–Milwaukee M
Utah State University M,D
Virginia Commonwealth University M,D,O
Wayne State University M,D
West Virginia University M,D
Wright State University M

TRANSCULTURAL NURSING

Augsburg College M,D
Rutgers University–Newark M,D,O

TRANSLATIONAL BIOLOGY

Baylor College of Medicine D
Cedars-Sinai Medical Center D
Rutgers University–New Brunswick M
University of California, Irvine M
The University of Iowa M,D*
University of Massachusetts Medical School M,D
The University of Texas at San Antonio D

TRANSLATION AND INTERPRETATION

American University of Sharjah M
Arizona State University at the Tempe campus M,D,O
Babel University Professional School of Translation M
Binghamton University, State University of New York D,O*
Columbia University M,D*
Concordia University (Canada) M,O
Drew University M,D,O
Gallaudet University M,D,O
Georgia State University O
Kent State University M,D
La Salle University M,O
London Metropolitan University M,D
Marygrove College O
Middlebury Institute of International Studies at Monterey M
Mills College M,O
Montclair State University O
New York University M
Rochester Institute of Technology M
Rutgers University–New Brunswick M,D
Texas A&M International University M,D
Universidad Autonoma de Guadalajara M,D
Université de Montréal M,D,O
Université Laval M,O
University of California, Santa Barbara M,D
University of Delaware M*
University of Denver M,O
University of Illinois at Urbana–Champaign M
The University of Manchester M,D
The University of North Carolina at Charlotte M,O
University of North Florida M
University of Ottawa M,D
University of Puerto Rico, Rí o Piedras Campus M,O
University of Rochester M,O*
University of Wisconsin–Milwaukee M,O
Wesley Biblical Seminary M
York University M

TRANSPERSONAL AND HUMANISTIC PSYCHOLOGY

Atlantic University M
California Institute of Integral Studies M,D
John F. Kennedy University M
Michigan School of Professional Psychology M,D
Saybrook University M,D
Seattle University M
Sofia University M,D

TRANSPORTATION AND HIGHWAY ENGINEERING

Arizona State University at the Tempe campus M,D,O
Art Center College of Design M
Auburn University M,D
The Catholic University of America M,D,O
College for Creative Studies M
Cornell University M,D
École Polytechnique de Montréal M,D,O
George Mason University M,D
Illinois Institute of Technology M,D
Iowa State University of Science and Technology M,D
Kansas State University M,D
Louisiana State University and Agricultural & Mechanical College M,D
Marquette University M,D,O
Marshall University M
Massachusetts Institute of Technology M,D,O
Morgan State University M
New Jersey Institute of Technology M,D
New York University M,D
North Dakota State University D
Northwestern University M,D*
Ohio University M,D

*M—masters degree; D—doctorate; O—other advanced degree; *—Close-Up and/or Display*

Old Dominion University M
Oregon State University M,D
Rensselaer Polytechnic Institute M,D
South Carolina State University M
Southern Illinois University Edwardsville M
Stevens Institute of Technology M,D,O
Texas Southern University M
University of Arkansas M,D
University of Calgary M,D
University of California, Berkeley M,D
University of California, Davis M,D
University of California, Irvine M,D
University of Central Florida M,D,O
University of Colorado Denver M,D
University of Dayton M
University of Delaware M,D*
University of Massachusetts Amherst M,D*
University of Memphis M,D
University of Missouri M,D
University of Nevada, Las Vegas M,D
University of New Brunswick Fredericton M,D
University of Southern California M,D,O
University of South Florida M,D,O
The University of Texas at Tyler M
University of Washington M,D*
Virginia Polytechnic Institute and State University M,O
Wentworth Institute of Technology M

TRANSPORTATION MANAGEMENT

American Public University System M
California Maritime Academy M
Florida Institute of Technology M,D
George Mason University M,O
Instituto Tecnologico de Santo Domingo M,O
Iowa State University of Science and Technology M
Maine Maritime Academy M
McGill University M,D
Morgan State University M
Naval Postgraduate School M
New Jersey Institute of Technology M,D
New York University M
North Dakota State University M,D
Pontifical Catholic University of Puerto Rico O
San Jose State University M
State University of New York Maritime College M
Temple University M,O*
Texas A&M University at Galveston M
Texas Southern University M
The University of British Columbia D
University of California, Davis M,D
University of California, Santa Barbara M,D
University of Hawaii at Manoa M,D,O
University of New Orleans M
The University of Tennessee M,D
University of Washington O*

TRAVEL AND TOURISM

Arizona State University at the Tempe campus M,D,O
California State University, Chico M
California State University, East Bay M
California State University, Fullerton M
California State University, Northridge M
Clemson University M,D,O
Colorado State University M,D
The George Washington University M,O*
Indiana University Bloomington M,D
Kent State University M
Lasell College M,O
Liberty University M,D,O
New York University M,O
North Carolina State University M,D
Penn State University Park M,D
Pontificia Universidad Catolica Madre y Maestra M
Purdue University M,D
Rochester Institute of Technology M
Royal Roads University M,O
San Francisco State University M
Savannah College of Art and Design M
Schiller International University (United States) M
Strayer University M
Syracuse University M
Temple University M,D*
Tropical Agriculture Research and Higher Education Center M,D
Université du Québec à Trois-Rivières M,O
University of Central Florida M,D,O
University of Florida M,D
University of Hawaii at Manoa M
University of Massachusetts Amherst M,D*
University of Minnesota, Twin Cities Campus M,D
University of New Orleans M
University of North Texas M,D,O
University of South Africa M,D
University of South Carolina M
University of South Florida M,O
The University of Tennessee M
Virginia Polytechnic Institute and State University M,D
Western Illinois University M

URBAN AND REGIONAL PLANNING

Alabama Agricultural and Mechanical University M
American University of Beirut M,D
American University of Sharjah M
Arizona State University at the Tempe campus M,D,O
Auburn University M
Ball State University M,O
Boston University M
California Polytechnic State University, San Luis Obispo M
California State Polytechnic University, Pomona M
The Catholic University of America M
Clark University M
Clemson University M
Cleveland State University M,O
College of Charleston O
Columbia University M,D*
Concordia University (Canada) O
Cornell University M,D
Dalhousie University M
Delta State University M
East Carolina University M,O
Eastern Kentucky University M
Eastern Michigan University M,O
Eastern University M
Eastern Washington University M
East Tennessee State University M,O
Florida Atlantic University M
Florida State University M,D
Future Generations Graduate School M
Georgetown University M,D
Georgia Institute of Technology M,D
Georgia State University M,D,O
Harvard University M,D*
Hunter College of the City University of New York M
Indiana University of Pennsylvania M
Iowa State University of Science and Technology M
Jackson State University M,D
Kansas State University M
Lesley University M,D,O
Massachusetts Institute of Technology M,D
McGill University M,D
Michigan State University M,D
Minnesota State University Mankato M,O
Missouri State University M
Morgan State University M
New York University M
North Dakota State University M
Northern Arizona University M,O
Northwest Nazarene University M
Northwest University M,D
The Ohio State University M,D
Philadelphia University M
Portland State University M
Pratt Institute M*
Queen's University at Kingston M
Rutgers University–New Brunswick M,D
San Diego State University M
Savannah State University M
State University of New York College of Environmental Science and Forestry M,D
Syracuse University O
Temple University M,O*
Texas A&M University M,D
Texas Southern University M,D
Texas State University M
Tufts University M
Université de Montréal M,D,O
Université du Québec à Rimouski M,D,O
Université du Québec en Outaouais M
Université Laval M,D
University at Albany, State University of New York M
University at Buffalo, the State University of New York M,D,O*
The University of Alabama M
The University of Arizona M
The University of British Columbia M,D
University of California, Berkeley M,D
University of California, Davis M
University of California, Irvine M,D
University of California, Los Angeles M,D
University of Central Arkansas M,O
University of Central Florida M,O
University of Cincinnati M
University of Colorado Denver M,D
University of Detroit Mercy M
University of Florida M,D
University of Hawaii at Manoa M,D,O
University of Idaho M
University of Illinois at Chicago M,D
University of Illinois at Urbana–Champaign M,D
The University of Iowa M*
The University of Kansas M*
University of Louisville M,D
University of Manitoba M
University of Maryland, College Park M,D
University of Massachusetts Amherst M,D*
University of Memphis M
University of Michigan M,D,O
University of Minnesota, Twin Cities Campus M,D
University of Nebraska–Lincoln M,D
University of New Brunswick Fredericton M
University of New Haven M,O
University of New Mexico M
University of New Orleans M
University of North Alabama M
The University of North Carolina at Chapel Hill M,D
The University of North Carolina at Charlotte M,O
University of Oklahoma M*
University of Oregon M
University of Pennsylvania M,D,O*
University of Pittsburgh M*
University of Puerto Rico, Río Piedras Campus M
University of Southern California M,D,O
University of Southern Maine M,O
University of South Florida M,D,O
The University of Texas at Arlington M,D
The University of Texas at Austin M,D
The University of Texas at San Antonio M
The University of Toledo M,D,O
University of Toronto M,D
University of Utah M,D*
University of Virginia M
University of Washington M,D*
University of Waterloo M,D
University of West Georgia M,D,O
University of Wisconsin–Madison M,D
University of Wisconsin–Milwaukee M,O
Utah State University M,D
Vanderbilt University M,D*
Virginia Commonwealth University M,O
Virginia Polytechnic Institute and State University M,D,O
Wayne State University M,O
West Chester University of Pennsylvania M,O
West Virginia University M,D

URBAN DESIGN

American University of Beirut M,D
Arizona State University at the Tempe campus M,D
Ball State University M
Carnegie Mellon University M,D
City College of the City University of New York M
Cornell University M,D
DePaul University M
Georgia Institute of Technology M,D
Harvard University M*
Hofstra University M
Judson University M
Kent State University M
Lawrence Technological University M,O
London Metropolitan University M,D
The New School M
New York Institute of Technology M
Prairie View A&M University M
Pratt Institute M*
Rice University M,D
Savannah College of Art and Design M
State University of New York College of Environmental Science and Forestry M
University at Buffalo, the State University of New York M,D,O*
University of California, Berkeley M,D
University of California, Los Angeles M,D
University of Colorado Denver M,D
University of Miami M
University of Michigan M
The University of North Carolina at Charlotte M
University of Pennsylvania M,D,O*
University of South Florida M
The University of Texas at Austin M
University of Toronto M
University of Utah M,D*
University of Washington M,D,O*
Washington University in St. Louis M

URBAN EDUCATION

Alvernia University M
Bakke Graduate University M,D
Brown University M
Cardinal Stritch University M,D
Cheyney University of Pennsylvania M
Claremont Graduate University M,D,O
Cleveland State University M,D
College of Mount Saint Vincent M,O
Eastern Michigan University M
Florida International University M,D,O
Georgia State University M,D,O
The Graduate Center, City University of New York D
Holy Names University M,O
Langston University M
Long Island University–LIU Brooklyn M,O
Loyola Marymount University M
Manhattanville College M,O*
Marygrove College M
Morgan State University D
New Jersey City University M
Norfolk State University M
Northeastern Illinois University M
Providence College M
Teachers College, Columbia University M,D
Temple University M*
University of Chicago M
University of Houston–Downtown M
University of Illinois at Chicago M,D
University of Michigan–Dearborn D
University of Nebraska at Omaha M,O
University of Pennsylvania M*
University of San Francisco M
University of Southern California D
University of Wisconsin–Milwaukee M,D
Vanderbilt University M,D*
Virginia Commonwealth University D

URBAN STUDIES

Arizona State University at the Tempe campus M,D,O
Azusa Pacific University M
Boston University M
Brooklyn College of the City University of New York M
Cleveland State University M,D,O
Columbus State University M
Concordia University (Canada) M,D,O
Eastern University M
Fordham University M
The Graduate Center, City University of New York M,D
Hunter College of the City University of New York M
Le Moyne College M,O
Long Island University–LIU Brooklyn M,D,O
Loyola University Chicago M
Massachusetts Institute of Technology M,D
Minnesota State University Mankato M,O
Moody Bible Institute M,O
New Jersey City University M
New Jersey Institute of Technology M,D
The New School M
New York University M
Norfolk State University M
North Dakota State University M,D
Northeastern University M,D,O
Old Dominion University D
Portland State University M,D
Queens College of the City University of New York M
Rutgers University–Newark M,D
Saint Louis University M,D,O
Savannah State University M
Simon Fraser University M,O
Temple University M,D,O*
Tufts University M
Université du Québec à Montréal M,D
Université du Québec, École nationale d'administrationbpublique M
Université du Québec, Institut National de la Recherche Scientifique M,D,O
University at Albany, State University of New York M,D,O
University of California, Irvine M,D
University of Delaware M,D*
University of Lethbridge M,D
University of Louisville M,D
University of Maryland, Baltimore County M,D
University of New Orleans M,D
University of Oklahoma M*
University of San Francisco M
The University of Texas at Arlington M
University of Wisconsin–Milwaukee M,D
Virginia Polytechnic Institute and State University M,D,O
Wayne State University M,D
Wright State University M

VETERINARY MEDICINE

Auburn University D
Colorado State University D
Cornell University D
Iowa State University of Science and Technology M
Kansas State University D
Louisiana State University and Agricultural & Mechanical College D
Michigan State University D
Mississippi State University D
North Carolina State University M,D
Oklahoma State University D
Oregon State University D
Purdue University D
Texas A&M University M,D
Tufts University M,D
Tuskegee University M,D
Université de Montréal D
University of California, Davis D
University of Florida D
University of Georgia M,D
University of Guelph M,D,O
University of Illinois at Urbana–Champaign D
University of Maryland, College Park D
University of Minnesota, Twin Cities Campus D
University of Missouri M,D
University of Pennsylvania D*
University of Prince Edward Island D
University of Saskatchewan M,D
The University of Tennessee D
University of Wisconsin–Madison M,D
Virginia Polytechnic Institute and State University M,D,O
Washington State University D
Western University of Health Sciences D

VETERINARY SCIENCES

Auburn University M,D
Clemson University M,D
Colorado State University M,D
Drexel University M
Iowa State University of Science and Technology M,D
Kansas State University M,O
Louisiana State University and Agricultural & Mechanical College M,D
Michigan State University M,D
Mississippi State University M,D
North Carolina State University M,D
The Ohio State University M,D
Oklahoma State University M,D
Penn State Hershey Medical Center M
Purdue University M,D
South Dakota State University M,D

Texas A&M University	M,D
Tuskegee University	M,D
Université de Montréal	M,D
University of California, Davis	M,O
University of Florida	M,D,O
University of Georgia	M
University of Guelph	M,D,O
University of Idaho	M,D
University of Illinois at Urbana–Champaign	M,D
University of Kentucky	M,D
University of Maryland, College Park	M,D
University of Minnesota, Twin Cities Campus	M,D
University of Missouri	M
University of Nebraska–Lincoln	M,D
University of Prince Edward Island	M,D
University of Saskatchewan	M,D
University of Washington	M*
University of Wisconsin–Madison	M,D
Utah State University	M,D
Virginia Polytechnic Institute and State University	M,D,O
Washington State University	M,D

VIROLOGY

Baylor College of Medicine	D
Case Western Reserve University	D*
Mayo Graduate School	D
McMaster University	M,D
Oregon State University	M,D
Penn State Hershey Medical Center	M,D
Purdue University	M,D
Rush University	M,D
Rutgers University–New Brunswick	M,D
Université de Montréal	D
Université du Québec, Institut National de la Recherche Scientifique	M,D
The University of Iowa	M,D*
University of Minnesota, Twin Cities Campus	D
University of Pennsylvania	D*
University of Pittsburgh	D*
University of Prince Edward Island	M,D
The University of Texas Health Science Center at Houston	M,D
The University of Texas Medical Branch	D
Yale University	D*

VISION SCIENCES

Eastern Virginia Medical School	O
Marshall B. Ketchum University	M,D
New England College of Optometry	M,D
Pacific University	M,D
Salus University	M,O
State University of New York College of Optometry	D
Université de Montréal	M,O
The University of Alabama at Birmingham	M,D
University of Alberta	M,D
University of California, Berkeley	M,D
University of Guelph	M,D,O
University of Houston	M,D
The University of Manchester	M,D
University of Massachusetts Boston	M
University of Pittsburgh	M,D*
University of Waterloo	M,D

VITICULTURE AND ENOLOGY

California State University, Fresno	M
University of California, Davis	M,D

VOCATIONAL AND TECHNICAL EDUCATION

Alabama Agricultural and Mechanical University	M
Alcorn State University	M,O
Appalachian State University	M
Bowling Green State University	M
Buffalo State College, State University of New York	M
California Baptist University	M
California State University, Sacramento	M
California University of Pennsylvania	M
Capella University	D
Central Connecticut State University	M
Central Washington University	M
Chicago State University	M
Clarion University of Pennsylvania	M
Concordia University (United States)	M,D
East Carolina University	M
Eastern Kentucky University	M
Eastern New Mexico University	M
Fitchburg State University	M
Florida Agricultural and Mechanical University	M
The George Washington University	O*
Idaho State University	M
Indiana State University	M
Indiana University of Pennsylvania	M
Inter American University of Puerto Rico, Metropolitan Campus	M
Iowa State University of Science and Technology	M,D
Jackson State University	M
James Madison University	M
Kent State University	M
Louisiana State University and Agricultural & Mechanical College	M,D
Marshall University	M
Middle Tennessee State University	M
Millersville University of Pennsylvania	M
Montana State University	M,D,O
Morehead State University	M
Murray State University	M
Niagara University	M
North Carolina Agricultural and Technical State University	M
North Dakota State University	M,D,O
Northern Arizona University	M,O
Old Dominion University	M,D
Penn State University Park	M,D,O
Pittsburg State University	M,O
Purdue University	M,D,O
South Carolina State University	M
Southern Illinois University Carbondale	M,D
State University of New York at Oswego	M
Temple University	M*
Texas State University	M
University of Arkansas	M,D,O
The University of British Columbia	M,D
University of Central Florida	M,D,O
University of Central Missouri	M,D,O
University of Georgia	M,D,O
University of Idaho	M,D,O
University of Maryland Eastern Shore	M
University of Minnesota, Twin Cities Campus	M,D,O
University of Missouri	M,D,O
University of Nebraska–Lincoln	M,D,O
University of New England	M,O
University of Northern Iowa	M,D
University of North Texas	M,D,O
University of Phoenix–Phoenix Campus	M
University of South Africa	M,D
University of South Florida	M,D,O
The University of Texas at Tyler	M,D
The University of Toledo	M,D,O
University of Victoria	M,D
University of West Florida	M,D,O
University of Wisconsin–Stout	M,D,O
Utah State University	M
Valley City State University	M
Virginia Polytechnic Institute and State University	M,D,O
Washington State University	M,D
Wayne State College	M
Wayne State University	M,D,O
Western Michigan University	M
Westfield State University	M,O
Wilmington University	M,D
Wright State University	M

WATER RESOURCES

Albany State University	M
California State University, Monterey Bay	M
Cornell University	M,D
Dalhousie University	M
Eastern Michigan University	M,O
Humboldt State University	M
Marquette University	M,D,O
Michigan Technological University	M,D,O
Missouri University of Science and Technology	M,D
Montclair State University	O
New Mexico State University	M,D
Old Dominion University	M
Oregon State University	M,D
Rutgers University–New Brunswick	M,D
State University of New York College of Environmental Science and Forestry	M,D
Tropical Agriculture Research and Higher Education Center	M,D
University of Alaska Fairbanks	M,D,O
The University of Arizona	M,D,O
The University of British Columbia	M,D
University of Calgary	M,D
University of California, Riverside	M,D
University of Colorado Denver	M
University of Florida	M,D
University of Idaho	M,D
University of Maine	M,D
University of Massachusetts Amherst	M,D*
University of Minnesota, Twin Cities Campus	M,D
University of Missouri	M,D,O
University of Nevada, Las Vegas	M
University of New Brunswick Fredericton	M,D
University of New Hampshire	M
University of New Mexico	M
University of Southern California	M,D,O
University of the District of Columbia	M
University of the Pacific	M,D
University of Wisconsin–Madison	M
University of Wisconsin–Milwaukee	M,D
University of Wyoming	M,D
Utah State University	M,D

WATER RESOURCES ENGINEERING

American University of Beirut	M,D
Carnegie Mellon University	M,D
Cornell University	M,D
Indiana University Bloomington	M,D,O
Kansas State University	M,D
Louisiana State University and Agricultural & Mechanical College	M,D
Marquette University	M,D,O
McGill University	M,D
New Mexico Institute of Mining and Technology	M
Norwich University	M
Ohio University	M,D
Oregon State University	M,D
Southern Methodist University	M,D
State University of New York College of Environmental Science and Forestry	M,D
Stevens Institute of Technology	M,D,O
Tufts University	M,D
University of Alberta	M,D
University of California, Berkeley	M,D
University of Colorado Boulder	M,D
University of Dayton	M
University of Delaware	M,D*
University of Guelph	M,D
University of Idaho	M,D
University of Massachusetts Amherst	M,D*
University of Memphis	M,D
University of Missouri	M,D
University of New Haven	M
University of South Florida	M,D,O
The University of Texas at Austin	M,D
The University of Texas at Tyler	M
Utah State University	M,D
Villanova University	M,O

WESTERN EUROPEAN STUDIES

American Public University System	M
American University	M,D,O
Armstrong State University	M
Baylor University	M,D
Boston College	M,D
Brown University	M,D
California State University, Long Beach	M
Carleton University	M,O
The Catholic University of America	M,D
Central Michigan University	M,O
Claremont Graduate University	M,D,O
Columbia University	M,D*
Cornell University	M,D
Creighton University	M
Drew University	M,D,O
East Carolina University	M
Georgetown University	M
The George Washington University	M*
Indiana University Bloomington	M
La Salle University	M,O
Mississippi State University	M,D
Monmouth University	M
New York University	M
San Diego State University	M
University of Colorado Denver	M
University of Connecticut	M*
University of Guelph	M
University of Illinois at Urbana–Champaign	M
University of Maine	M,D
University of Nevada, Reno	D
University of Pittsburgh	O*
University of Rochester	M,D*
University of South Florida	M,D
Wayne State University	M,D,O

WOMEN'S HEALTH NURSING

Boston College	M,D
California State University, Fullerton	M,D
Case Western Reserve University	M*
Drexel University	M
Duke University	M,D,O*
Emory University	M
Frontier Nursing University	M,D,O
Georgia State University	M,D,O
Hampton University	M,D
Kent State University	M,D,O
Loyola University Chicago	M,D,O
MGH Institute of Health Professions	M,D,O
Queen's University at Kingston	M,D,O
Rutgers University–Newark	M,D,O
San Francisco State University	M,O
Stony Brook University, State University of New York	M,D,O
Texas Woman's University	M,D
Uniformed Services University of the Health Sciences	M,D*
University of Cincinnati	M,D
University of Colorado Denver	M,D
University of Delaware	M,O*
University of Illinois at Chicago	M,O
University of Indianapolis	M,D
University of Louisville	M,D
University of Minnesota, Twin Cities Campus	M
University of Missouri–Kansas City	M,D
University of Missouri–St. Louis	M,D,O
University of Pennsylvania	M*
University of South Carolina	M
Vanderbilt University	M,D,O*
Virginia Commonwealth University	M,D,O

WOMEN'S STUDIES

American University	O
The American University in Cairo	M
Benedictine University	M
Brandeis University	M,D
California Institute of Integral Studies	M,D
Carnegie Mellon University	D
Chatham University	M
Claremont Graduate University	M,D
Clark Atlanta University	M,D
Cornell University	M,D
DePaul University	M
Eastern Michigan University	M,O
Emory University	D,O
Florida Atlantic University	M
The George Washington University	M,O*
Georgia State University	M,O
Grace Theological Seminary	M,D,O
The Graduate Center, City University of New York	M,D
Inter American University of Puerto Rico, Metropolitan Campus	M
The Jewish Theological Seminary	M,D
Kansas State University	O
Lakehead University	M,D
Lesley University	M,D,O
London Metropolitan University	M,D
Middle Tennessee State University	O
Minnesota State University Mankato	M
Mount Saint Vincent University	M
Northern Arizona University	O
The Ohio State University	M,D
Oregon State University	M,D
Queen's University at Kingston	M,D
Reconstructionist Rabbinical College	M,D,O
Roosevelt University	M,O
Rutgers University–New Brunswick	M,D
Saint Mary's University (Canada)	M
San Diego State University	M
San Francisco State University	M
Sarah Lawrence College	M
Simon Fraser University	M,D
Smith College	O
Southeastern Baptist Theological Seminary	M,D
Southern Connecticut State University	M
Stony Brook University, State University of New York	O
Texas Woman's University	M,D
Towson University	M,O
United Theological Seminary of the Twin Cities	M,D,O
Université Laval	O
University at Albany, State University of New York	M
The University of Alabama	M
The University of Arizona	M,D,O
University of California, Santa Barbara	M,D
University of Cincinnati	M,O
University of Colorado Denver	M
University of Florida	M,O
University of Georgia	O
University of Hawaii at Manoa	O
The University of Iowa	O*
University of Lethbridge	M,D
University of Louisville	M,O
University of Maryland, Baltimore County	O
University of Maryland, College Park	M,D
University of Michigan	D,O
University of Minnesota, Twin Cities Campus	D
The University of North Carolina at Charlotte	M,D,O
The University of North Carolina at Greensboro	M,D,O
University of Northern Iowa	M
University of Oklahoma	O*
University of Ottawa	M
University of Pittsburgh	O*
University of Regina	M
University of Saskatchewan	M,D
University of South Carolina	O
University of South Florida	M
The University of Toledo	O
University of Toronto	M,D
University of Washington	D*
University of Wisconsin–Madison	M,D
University of Wisconsin–Milwaukee	M,O
Western Seminary	M
Western Seminary–Sacramento Campus	O
Western Seminary–San Jose Campus	M,O
Wilson College	M
York University	M,D

WRITING

Abilene Christian University	M
Academy of Art University	M
Adelphi University	M
Albertus Magnus College	M
American University	M
Antioch University Los Angeles	M,O
Antioch University Midwest	M
Antioch University Santa Barbara	M
Arizona State University at the Tempe campus	M,D
Armstrong State University	M,O
Asbury University	M
Ashland University	M
Auburn University at Montgomery	M
Ball State University	M,D
Bay Path University	M
Bennington College	M
Binghamton University, State University of New York	M,D*
Boise State University	M
Boston University	M,D
Bowling Green State University	M,D
Brigham Young University	M

*M—masters degree; D—doctorate; O—other advanced degree; *—Close-Up and/or Display*

Brooklyn College of the City University of New York	M
Brown University	M,D
Butler University	M
California College of the Arts	M
California Institute of Integral Studies	M,D
California Institute of the Arts	M,O
California State University, East Bay	M
California State University, Fresno	M
California State University, Long Beach	M
California State University, Northridge	M
California State University, Sacramento	M
California State University, San Bernardino	M
California State University, San Marcos	M
California State University, Stanislaus	M,O
Carlow University	M
Carnegie Mellon University	M
Cedar Crest College	M
Central Michigan University	M
Chapman University	M
Chatham University	M
Chicago State University	M
City College of the City University of New York	M
Claremont Graduate University	M,D
Clemson University	M
Cleveland State University	M
Coastal Carolina University	M
The College at Brockport, State University of New York	M,O
Colorado State University	M
Columbia College Chicago	M
Columbia University	M*
Concordia University (Canada)	M
Cornell University	M,D
Creighton University	M
DePaul University	M
Dominican University of California	M
Drew University	M,D,O
East Carolina University	M,D,O
Eastern Kentucky University	M
Eastern Michigan University	M,O
Eastern Washington University	M
Emerson College	M
Fairfield University	M
Fairleigh Dickinson University, College at Florham	M
Florida International University	M
Florida State University	M,D
Full Sail University	M
George Mason University	M
Georgia College & State University	M
Georgia State University	M,D
Goddard College	M
Goucher College	M
Hamline University	M
Hofstra University	M
Hollins University	M,O
Holy Names University	M
Hunter College of the City University of New York	M
Illinois State University	M,D
Indiana State University	M
Indiana University Bloomington	M,D
Indiana University–Purdue University Indianapolis	M,O
Institute of American Indian Arts	M
Iowa State University of Science and Technology	M,D
James Madison University	M
Johns Hopkins University	M,O
Kean University	M
Kennesaw State University	M
Kent State University	M,D,O
Lake Forest College	M
La Sierra University	M
Lenoir-Rhyne University	M
Lesley University	M,D,O
Lindenwood University	M,O
London Metropolitan University	M,D
Long Island University–LIU Brooklyn	M,D,O
Louisiana State University and Agricultural & Mechanical College	M,D
Loyola Marymount University	M
Manhattanville College	M*
Massachusetts Institute of Technology	M
McNeese State University	M
Michigan State University	M,D
Mills College	M,O
Minnesota State University Mankato	M,O
Missouri State University	M,O
Missouri Western State University	M,O
Monmouth University	M
Montclair State University	O
Mount Mary University	M
Mount Saint Mary's University (CA)	M,D,O
Murray State University	M
Naropa University	M
National Louis University	M,D,O
National University	M,O
New England College	M
New Hampshire Institute of Art	M
New Mexico Highlands University	M
New Mexico State University	M,D
The New School	M
New York University	M
North Carolina State University	M
North Central College	M
North Dakota State University	M,D
Northeastern Illinois University	M
Northern Arizona University	M,D,O
Northern Kentucky University	M,O
Northern Michigan University	M,O
Northwestern University	M*
Oklahoma City University	M
Oklahoma State University	M,D
Old Dominion University	M
Oregon State University	M
Otis College of Art and Design	M
Our Lady of the Lake University of San Antonio	M
Pacific Lutheran University	M
Pacific University	M
Park University	M,O
Penn State Harrisburg	M,D,O
Pepperdine University	M
Pittsburg State University	M
Pratt Institute	M*
Purdue University	M,D
Queens College of the City University of New York	M
Queens University of Charlotte	M
Regent University	M,D
Regis College (MA)	O
Regis University	M,O
Rhode Island College	M,O
Rivier University	M
Roosevelt University	M
Rosemont College	M
Rowan University	M,O
Rutgers University–Camden	M
Rutgers University–Newark	M
Rutgers University–New Brunswick	M
St. Joseph's College, New York	M
Saint Joseph's University	M
Saint Mary's College of California	M
Salisbury University	M
Sam Houston State University	M
San Diego State University	M
San Francisco State University	M
San Jose State University	M,O
Sarah Lawrence College	M
Savannah College of Art and Design	M
School of the Art Institute of Chicago	M,O
School of Visual Arts (NY)	M
Seattle Pacific University	M
Seton Hill University	M,O
Sewanee: The University of the South	M
Simmons College	M,D,O
Sonoma State University	M
Southeastern Louisiana University	M
Southeast Missouri State University	M
Southern Illinois University Carbondale	M
Southern Illinois University Edwardsville	M
Southern New Hampshire University	M,O
Spalding University	M
Stony Brook University, State University of New York	M,O
Syracuse University	M,D
Temple University	M,D*
Texas State University	M
Tiffin University	M
Towson University	M
Trinity College (United States)	M
Union Institute & University	M
The University of Akron	M
The University of Alabama	M,D
The University of Alabama at Birmingham	M
University of Alaska Anchorage	M
University of Alaska Fairbanks	M
The University of Arizona	M
University of Arkansas	M
University of Arkansas at Little Rock	M
University of Baltimore	M
The University of British Columbia	M,O
University of California, Berkeley	O
University of California, Davis	M,D
University of California, Irvine	M
University of California, Riverside	M
University of California, San Diego	M,D
University of California, Santa Barbara	D
University of California, Santa Cruz	M
University of Central Arkansas	M
University of Central Florida	M,D,O
University of Central Oklahoma	M
University of Chicago	M
University of Colorado Boulder	M,D
University of Colorado Denver	M
University of Dayton	M
University of Denver	M,D
The University of Findlay	M,D
University of Florida	M,D
University of Georgia	M,D
University of Houston	M,D
University of Houston–Victoria	M
University of Idaho	M
University of Illinois at Urbana–Champaign	M,D
The University of Iowa	M,D*
The University of Kansas	M,D*
University of King's College	M
University of Louisiana at Lafayette	M,D
University of Louisville	M,D
The University of Manchester	D
University of Maryland, College Park	M,D
University of Massachusetts Amherst	M,D*
University of Massachusetts Boston	M
University of Massachusetts Dartmouth	M,O
University of Memphis	M,D,O
University of Miami	M,D
University of Michigan	M
University of Michigan–Flint	M
University of Missouri–Kansas City	M,D
University of Missouri–St. Louis	M
University of Montana	M
University of Nebraska at Kearney	M
University of Nebraska at Omaha	M,O
University of Nebraska–Lincoln	M,D
University of Nevada, Las Vegas	M,D,O
University of New Hampshire	M,D
University of New Mexico	M
The University of North Carolina at Charlotte	M,O
The University of North Carolina at Greensboro	M
The University of North Carolina Wilmington	M
University of Northern Iowa	M
University of North Florida	M
University of North Texas	M,D,O
University of Notre Dame	M
University of Oklahoma	M*
University of Oregon	M
University of Pennsylvania	M,D*
University of Pittsburgh	M,D*
University of Regina	M
University of San Francisco	M
University of South Carolina	M,D
University of Southern California	M,D
University of Southern Maine	M
University of South Florida	M,D,O
The University of Tampa	M
The University of Tennessee at Chattanooga	M,O
The University of Texas at Austin	M,D
The University of Texas at El Paso	M,D,O
The University of Texas Rio Grande Valley	M
University of the Sacred Heart	M,O
The University of Toledo	M,O
University of Toronto	M,D
University of Utah	M,D*
University of Victoria	M
University of Virginia	M
University of Washington	M*
University of Washington, Bothell	M
University of West Florida	M
University of Windsor	M
University of Wisconsin–Eau Claire	M
University of Wisconsin–Madison	M,D
University of Wisconsin–Milwaukee	M,D,O
University of Wyoming	M
Utah State University	M
Vanderbilt University	M*
Vermont College of Fine Arts	M
Virginia Commonwealth University	M
Virginia Polytechnic Institute and State University	M,D,O
Warren Wilson College	M
Washington University in St. Louis	M
Wayne State University	M,D
Western Connecticut State University	M
Western Illinois University	M,O
Western Kentucky University	M
Western Michigan University	M,D
Western New England University	M
Western State Colorado University	M
Westminster College (UT)	M
West Virginia University	M
West Virginia Wesleyan College	M
Wichita State University	M
Wilkes University	M
William Paterson University of New Jersey	M,D
Wright State University	M
Yale University	M,D,O*

ZOOLOGY

Auburn University	M,D
Canisius College	M
Colorado State University	M,D
Cornell University	D
Eastern New Mexico University	M
Emporia State University	M
Illinois State University	M,D
Indiana University Bloomington	M,D
Michigan State University	M,D
North Carolina State University	M,D
North Dakota State University	M,D
Oregon State University	M,D
Southern Illinois University Carbondale	M,D
Texas Tech University	M,D
Uniformed Services University of the Health Sciences	M,D*
The University of British Columbia	M,D
University of California, Davis	M
University of Chicago	D
University of Florida	M,D
University of Guelph	M,D
University of Hawaii at Manoa	M,D
University of Illinois at Urbana–Champaign	M,D
University of Maine	M,D
University of Manitoba	M,D
University of Montana	M,D
University of North Dakota	M,D
University of Wisconsin–Madison	M,D
University of Wisconsin–Oshkosh	M
University of Wyoming	M,D
Western Illinois University	M,O

DIRECTORY OF INSTITUTIONS AND THEIR OFFERINGS

ABILENE CHRISTIAN UNIVERSITY

Accounting	M
Business Administration and Management—General	M
Clinical Psychology	M
Communication Disorders	M
Communication—General	M
Conflict Resolution and Mediation/Peace Studies	M,O
Counseling Psychology	M
Education—General	M,D,O
Educational Leadership and Administration	M,D,O
Educational Measurement and Evaluation	O
Educational Media/Instructional Technology	M,O
English	M
Higher Education	M
Human Resources Development	M
Human Services	M,D,O
Liberal Studies	M
Marriage and Family Therapy	M
Missions and Missiology	M
Nutrition	O
Occupational Therapy	M
Pastoral Ministry and Counseling	M,D
Psychology—General	M
Religion	M
Rhetoric	M
School Psychology	O
Social Work	M
Theology	M
Writing	M

ACACIA UNIVERSITY

Education—General	M
Educational Leadership and Administration	M
Elementary Education	M
English as a Second Language	M
Secondary Education	M
Special Education	M

ACADEMY FOR FIVE ELEMENT ACUPUNCTURE

Acupuncture and Oriental Medicine	M

ACADEMY OF ART UNIVERSITY

Advertising and Public Relations	M
Applied Arts and Design—General	M
Architecture	M
Art Education	M
Art History	M
Art/Fine Arts	M
Arts Journalism	M
Clothing and Textiles	M
Computer Art and Design	M
Film, Television, and Video Production	M
Game Design and Development	M
Graphic Design	M
Illustration	M
Industrial Design	M
Interior Design	M
Internet and Interactive Multimedia	M
Landscape Architecture	M
Modeling and Simulation	M
Music	M
Photography	M
Textile Design	M
Theater	M
Writing	M

ACADEMY OF CHINESE CULTURE AND HEALTH SCIENCES

Acupuncture and Oriental Medicine	M

ACADIA UNIVERSITY

Applied Mathematics	M
Biological and Biomedical Sciences—General	M
Chemistry	M
Clinical Psychology	M
Computer Science	M
Counselor Education	M
Curriculum and Instruction	M
Education—General	M,D
Educational Leadership and Administration	M
Educational Media/Instructional Technology	M
English	M
Geographic Information Systems	M
Geology	M
Mathematics Education	M
Philosophy	M
Political Science	M
Psychology—General	M
Recreation and Park Management	M
Science Education	M
Social Sciences Education	M
Sociology	M
Special Education	M
Statistics	M
Sustainable Development	M
Theology	M,D

ACUPUNCTURE & INTEGRATIVE MEDICINE COLLEGE, BERKELEY

Acupuncture and Oriental Medicine	M

ACUPUNCTURE AND MASSAGE COLLEGE

Acupuncture and Oriental Medicine	M

ADAMS STATE UNIVERSITY

Art/Fine Arts	M
Counselor Education	M
Education—General	M
History	M
Physical Education	M
Special Education	M

ADELPHI UNIVERSITY

Accounting	M
Adult Nursing	M
Art Education	M
Art/Fine Arts	M
Biological and Biomedical Sciences—General	M
Business Administration and Management—General	M
Clinical Psychology	D
Communication Disorders	M,D
Community Health	M,O
Counseling Psychology	M
Education—General	M,D,O
Educational Leadership and Administration	M,O
Educational Media/Instructional Technology	M,O
Elementary Education	M
Emergency Management	O
English as a Second Language	M,O
Environmental Management and Policy	M
Environmental Sciences	M
Finance and Banking	M
Gerontology	M,O
Health Education	M,O
Health Informatics	M,O
Health Services Management and Hospital Administration	M
Human Resources Management	M,O
Management Information Systems	M
Marketing	M
Nursing and Healthcare Administration	M,O
Nursing—General	D
Nutrition	M,D,O
Physical Education	M,O
Psychology—General	M,D
Public Administration	O
Public Health—General	M,O
Reading Education	M
School Psychology	M
Secondary Education	M
Social Work	M,D
Special Education	M,O
Sports Management	M
Writing	M

ADLER GRADUATE SCHOOL

Addictions/Substance Abuse Counseling	M
Art Therapy	M
Clinical Psychology	M
Counseling Psychology	M
Counselor Education	M
Marriage and Family Therapy	M
Psychoanalysis and Psychotherapy	M

ADLER UNIVERSITY

Addictions/Substance Abuse Counseling	M,D,O
Art Therapy	M,D,O
Biopsychology	M,D,O
Clinical Psychology	M,D,O
Counseling Psychology	M,D,O
Counselor Education	M,D,O
Criminal Justice and Criminology	M,D,O
Emergency Management	M,D,O
Forensic Psychology	M,D,O
Health Psychology	M,D,O
Industrial and Organizational Psychology	M,D,O
Marriage and Family Therapy	M,D,O
Nonprofit Management	M,D,O
Psychoanalysis and Psychotherapy	M,D,O
Psychology—General	M,D,O
Public Administration	M,D,O
Public Policy	M,D,O
Rehabilitation Counseling	M,D,O
Social Psychology	M,D,O
Sport Psychology	M,D,O

ADRIAN COLLEGE

Accounting	M
Athletic Training and Sports Medicine	M
Criminal Justice and Criminology	M

ADVENTIST UNIVERSITY OF HEALTH SCIENCES

Nurse Anesthesia	M

AIR FORCE INSTITUTE OF TECHNOLOGY

Aerospace/Aeronautical Engineering	M,D
Applied Mathematics	M,D
Applied Physics	M,D
Astrophysics	M,D
Computer Engineering	M,D
Computer Science	M,D
Electrical Engineering	M,D
Engineering and Applied Sciences—General	M,D
Engineering Management	M
Engineering Physics	M,D
Environmental Engineering	M
Environmental Management and Policy	M
Logistics	M,D
Management Information Systems	M
Management of Technology	M,D
Materials Sciences	M,D
Nuclear Engineering	M,D
Operations Research	M,D
Optical Sciences	M,D
Planetary and Space Sciences	M,D
Systems Engineering	M,D

ALABAMA AGRICULTURAL AND MECHANICAL UNIVERSITY

Agricultural Economics and Agribusiness	M,D
Agricultural Sciences—General	M,D
Agronomy and Soil Sciences	M,D
Art Education	M
Biological and Biomedical Sciences—General	M,D
Business Administration and Management—General	M,D
Business Education	M,O
Child and Family Studies	M
Clinical Psychology	M,O
Clothing and Textiles	M
Communication Disorders	M
Computer Science	M
Construction Management	M
Counseling Psychology	M,O
Counselor Education	M,O
Early Childhood Education	M,D,O
Education—General	M,O
Educational Media/Instructional Technology	M,O
Elementary Education	M,D,O
Engineering and Applied Sciences—General	M,D
English Education	M,O
Family and Consumer Sciences-General	M
Food Science and Technology	M,D
Home Economics Education	M,O
Hospitality Management	M
Human Development	M
Logistics	M,D
Marketing	M,D
Materials Engineering	M
Materials Sciences	M,D
Mathematics Education	M,O
Music Education	M
Nutrition	M
Optical Sciences	M,D
Physical Education	M
Physics	M,D
Planetary and Space Sciences	M,D
Plant Sciences	M,D
Psychology—General	M,O
Reading Education	M,D,O
Rehabilitation Counseling	M,O
School Psychology	M,O
Science Education	M,O
Secondary Education	M,O
Social Sciences Education	M,O
Social Work	M,O
Special Education	M,D,O
Supply Chain Management	M,D
Urban and Regional Planning	M
Vocational and Technical Education	M

ALABAMA STATE UNIVERSITY

Accounting	M
Allied Health—General	M,D
Biological and Biomedical Sciences—General	M,D
Business Administration and Management—General	M
Counselor Education	M,D,O
Early Childhood Education	M,O
Education—General	M,D,O
Educational Leadership and Administration	M,D,O
Educational Media/Instructional Technology	M,D,O
Educational Policy	M,D,O
Elementary Education	M,O
English Education	M,O
Forensic Sciences	M
Health Education	M
Mathematics Education	M,O
Mathematics	M
Music Education	M,O
Occupational Therapy	M
Physical Education	M
Physical Therapy	D
Reading Education	M,O
Rehabilitation Counseling	M
Rehabilitation Sciences	M
Science Education	M,O
Secondary Education	M,O
Social Sciences Education	M,O
Special Education	M,O

ALASKA PACIFIC UNIVERSITY

Business Administration and Management—General	M
Counseling Psychology	M
Education—General	M
Elementary Education	M
Environmental Education	M
Environmental Sciences	M
Health Services Management and Hospital Administration	M
Interdisciplinary Studies	M
Investment Management	M,O
Liberal Studies	M
Middle School Education	M
Telecommunications Management	M

ALBANY COLLEGE OF PHARMACY AND HEALTH SCIENCES

Cell Biology	M
Clinical Laboratory Sciences/Medical Technology	M
Health Services Research	M,D
Molecular Biology	M
Pharmaceutical Sciences	M,D
Pharmacology	M,D
Pharmacy	M,D

ALBANY LAW SCHOOL

Law	M,D

ALBANY MEDICAL COLLEGE

Allopathic Medicine	D
Bioethics	M,D,O
Cardiovascular Sciences	M,D
Cell Biology	M,D
Immunology	M,D
Microbiology	M,D
Molecular Biology	M,D
Neuroscience	M,D
Nurse Anesthesia	M
Pharmacology	M,D
Physician Assistant Studies	M

ALBANY STATE UNIVERSITY

Accounting	M
Business Administration and Management—General	M
Counselor Education	M,O
Criminal Justice and Criminology	M
Early Childhood Education	M,O
Economic Development	M
Economics	M
Education—General	M,O
Educational Leadership and Administration	M,O
English Education	M
Family Nurse Practitioner Studies	M
Forensic Sciences	M
Health Education	M,O
Health Services Management and Hospital Administration	M
Human Resources Management	M
Mathematics Education	M
Middle School Education	M,O
Nursing Education	M
Nursing—General	M
Physical Education	M,O
Public Administration	M
Public Policy	M
Science Education	M
Social Work	M
Special Education	M,O
Water Resources	M

ALBERT EINSTEIN COLLEGE OF MEDICINE

Allopathic Medicine	D
Anatomy	D
Biochemistry	D
Biological and Biomedical Sciences—General	D
Biophysics	D
Cell Biology	D
Clinical Research	D
Computational Biology	D
Developmental Biology	D
Genetics	D
Genomic Sciences	D
Immunology	D
Microbiology	D
Molecular Biology	D
Molecular Genetics	D
Molecular Pharmacology	D
Neurobiology	D
Pathology	D
Physiology	D
Systems Biology	D

ALBERTUS MAGNUS COLLEGE

Accounting	M
Art Therapy	M
Business Administration and Management—General	M
Criminal Justice and Criminology	M
Education—General	M
Human Services	M
Liberal Studies	M
Organizational Management	M
Writing	M

ALBRIGHT COLLEGE

Early Childhood Education	M
Education—General	M
Elementary Education	M
English as a Second Language	M
Special Education	M

ALCORN STATE UNIVERSITY

Agricultural Economics and Agribusiness	M
Agricultural Education	M,O
Agricultural Sciences—General	M
Agronomy and Soil Sciences	M
Animal Sciences	M
Biological and Biomedical Sciences—General	M
Business Administration and Management—General	M
Computer Science	M
Counselor Education	M,O
Education—General	M,O
Elementary Education	M,O
Health Education	M,O
Information Science	M
Nursing—General	M
Physical Education	M,O
Secondary Education	M,O
Special Education	M,O
Vocational and Technical Education	M,O

ALDERSON BROADDUS UNIVERSITY

Physician Assistant Studies	M

ALFRED UNIVERSITY

Accounting	M
Applied Arts and Design—General	M
Art/Fine Arts	M,D
Bioengineering	M,D
Business Administration and Management—General	M
Ceramic Sciences and Engineering	M,D
Computer Art and Design	M
Counseling Psychology	M,D,O
Counselor Education	M,D,O
Education—General	M
Electrical Engineering	M,D

Engineering and Applied Sciences—General	M,D
Internet and Interactive Multimedia	M
Materials Sciences	M,D
Mechanical Engineering	M,D
Reading Education	M
School Psychology	M,D,O
Student Affairs	M

ALLEN COLLEGE

Acute Care/Critical Care Nursing	M,D,O
Adult Nursing	M,D,O
Community Health Nursing	M,D,O
Family Nurse Practitioner Studies	M,D,O
Gerontological Nursing	M,D,O
Health Education	M,D,O
Nursing and Healthcare Administration	M,D,O
Nursing—General	M,D,O
Occupational Therapy	M,D,O
Psychiatric Nursing	M,D,O
Public Health—General	M,D,O

ALLIANT INTERNATIONAL UNIVERSITY–FRESNO

Clinical Psychology	D
Forensic Psychology	D
Industrial and Organizational Psychology	M,D
Psychology—General	M,D

ALLIANT INTERNATIONAL UNIVERSITY–IRVINE

Educational Psychology	M,D,O
Forensic Psychology	D
Forensic Sciences	D
Marriage and Family Therapy	M,D
School Psychology	M,D,O

ALLIANT INTERNATIONAL UNIVERSITY–LOS ANGELES

Addictions/Substance Abuse Counseling	M
Business Administration and Management—General	D
Clinical Psychology	D
Education—General	M,O
Educational Psychology	M,D,O
Forensic Psychology	D
Gerontology	M
Health Psychology	D
Industrial and Organizational Psychology	M,D
Marriage and Family Therapy	M,D
Psychology—General	M,D
School Psychology	M,D,O
Social Psychology	D
Student Affairs	M,D,O

ALLIANT INTERNATIONAL UNIVERSITY–MÉXICO CITY

Business Administration and Management—General	M
Counseling Psychology	M
Education—General	M
International Affairs	M
International Business	M

ALLIANT INTERNATIONAL UNIVERSITY–SACRAMENTO

Clinical Psychology	D
Education—General	M,O
Forensic Psychology	D
Marriage and Family Therapy	M,D
Psychology—General	M,D

ALLIANT INTERNATIONAL UNIVERSITY–SAN DIEGO

Business Administration and Management—General	M
Clinical Psychology	M,D
Education—General	M,O
Educational Leadership and Administration	M,D,O
Educational Psychology	M,D,O
English as a Second Language	M,D,O
Forensic Psychology	D
Higher Education	M,D,O
Industrial and Organizational Psychology	M,D
Marriage and Family Therapy	M,D
Neuroscience	M,D,O
Psychology—General	M,D
School Psychology	M,D,O
Student Affairs	M,D,O

ALLIANT INTERNATIONAL UNIVERSITY–SAN FRANCISCO

Clinical Psychology	M,D,O
Counselor Education	M
Criminal Justice and Criminology	M
Education—General	M,O
Educational Leadership and Administration	M,D,O
Educational Psychology	M,D,O
English as a Second Language	M,O
Forensic Psychology	M,D
Higher Education	M,D,O
Industrial and Organizational Psychology	M,D
Law	D
Multilingual and Multicultural Education	M,O
Pharmacology	M
Psychology—General	M,D,O
School Psychology	M,D,O
Special Education	M,O

ALVERNIA UNIVERSITY

Business Administration and Management—General	M
Education—General	M
Liberal Studies	M
Occupational Therapy	M
Organizational Management	D
Social Psychology	M
Urban Education	M

ALVERNO COLLEGE

Adult Education	M
Business Administration and Management—General	M
Education—General	M
Educational Leadership and Administration	M
Educational Media/Instructional Technology	M
Family Nurse Practitioner Studies	M
Nursing—General	M
Psychiatric Nursing	M
Reading Education	M
Science Education	M
Social Psychology	M
Special Education	M

AMBERTON UNIVERSITY

Business Administration and Management—General	M
Child and Family Studies	M
Counseling Psychology	M
Human Resources Development	M
Human Resources Management	M
Interdisciplinary Studies	M
Management Strategy and Policy	M
Project Management	M

AMBROSE UNIVERSITY

Cultural Studies	M,O
Pastoral Ministry and Counseling	M,O
Religion	M,O
Theology	M,O

AMERICAN BAPTIST SEMINARY OF THE WEST

Pastoral Ministry and Counseling	M
Theology	M

AMERICAN BUSINESS & TECHNOLOGY UNIVERSITY

Accounting	M
Business Administration and Management—General	M
Finance and Banking	M
International Business	M
Management Information Systems	M
Marketing	M
Project Management	M

THE AMERICAN COLLEGE

Business Administration and Management—General	M
Finance and Banking	M
Organizational Management	M

AMERICAN COLLEGE OF ACUPUNCTURE AND ORIENTAL MEDICINE

Acupuncture and Oriental Medicine	M

AMERICAN COLLEGE OF EDUCATION

Curriculum and Instruction	M
Education—General	M
Educational Leadership and Administration	M
Educational Media/Instructional Technology	M
English as a Second Language	M
Multilingual and Multicultural Education	M

AMERICAN COLLEGE OF HEALTHCARE SCIENCES

Allied Health—General	M,O
Nutrition	M,O

AMERICAN COLLEGE OF THESSALONIKI

Business Administration and Management—General	M,O
Entrepreneurship	M,O
Finance and Banking	M,O
Marketing	M,O

AMERICAN CONSERVATORY THEATER

Theater	M,O

AMERICAN FILM INSTITUTE CONSERVATORY

Film, Television, and Video Production	M

AMERICAN GRADUATE SCHOOL IN PARIS

International Affairs	M,D

AMERICAN GRADUATE UNIVERSITY

Business Administration and Management—General	M,O
Project Management	M,O
Supply Chain Management	M,O

AMERICAN INTERCONTINENTAL UNIVERSITY ATLANTA

Information Science	M
International Business	M
Management Information Systems	M

AMERICAN INTERCONTINENTAL UNIVERSITY HOUSTON

Business Administration and Management—General	M

AMERICAN INTERCONTINENTAL UNIVERSITY ONLINE

Accounting	M
Business Administration and Management—General	M
Computer and Information Systems Security	M
Curriculum and Instruction	M
Education—General	M
Educational Leadership and Administration	M
Educational Measurement and Evaluation	M
Educational Media/Instructional Technology	M
Finance and Banking	M
Health Services Management and Hospital Administration	M
Human Resources Management	M
Industrial and Manufacturing Management	M
Industrial and Organizational Psychology	M
Information Science	M
International Business	M
Marketing	M
Project Management	M

AMERICAN INTERNATIONAL COLLEGE

Accounting	M
Business Administration and Management—General	M
Clinical Psychology	M
Counseling Psychology	M
Counselor Education	M,D,O
Early Childhood Education	M,D,O
Education—General	M,D,O
Educational Leadership and Administration	M,D,O
Educational Psychology	M,D
Elementary Education	M,D,O
Family Nurse Practitioner Studies	M
Forensic Psychology	M
Middle School Education	M,D,O
Nursing and Healthcare Administration	M
Nursing Education	M
Nursing—General	M
Occupational Therapy	M
Physical Therapy	D
Psychology—General	M
Reading Education	M,D,O
Secondary Education	M,D,O
Special Education	M,D,O
Taxation	M

AMERICAN JEWISH UNIVERSITY

Business Administration and Management—General	M
Education—General	M
Jewish Studies	M
Nonprofit Management	M
Social Work	M
Theology	M

AMERICAN MUSEUM OF NATURAL HISTORY–RICHARD GILDER GRADUATE SCHOOL

Biological and Biomedical Sciences—General	D
Museum Studies	D

AMERICAN NATIONAL UNIVERSITY

Business Administration and Management—General	M

AMERICAN PUBLIC UNIVERSITY SYSTEM

Accounting	M
Aerospace/Aeronautical Engineering	M
American Studies	M
Business Administration and Management—General	M
Classics	M
Computer and Information Systems Security	M
Conflict Resolution and Mediation/Peace Studies	M
Counselor Education	M
Criminal Justice and Criminology	M
Curriculum and Instruction	M
Distance Education Development	M
Educational Leadership and Administration	M
Elementary Education	M
Emergency Management	M
English as a Second Language	M
Entrepreneurship	M
Environmental Management and Policy	M
Exercise and Sports Science	M
Finance and Banking	M
Fish, Game, and Wildlife Management	M
Forensic Sciences	M
Health Services Management and Hospital Administration	M
History	M
Homeland Security	M
Human Resources Management	M
Humanities	M
International Affairs	M
International Business	M
Legal and Justice Studies	M
Logistics	M
Management Information Systems	M
Management Strategy and Policy	M
Marketing	M
Military and Defense Studies	M
National Security	M
Nonprofit Management	M
Organizational Management	M
Planetary and Space Sciences	M
Political Science	M
Project Management	M
Psychology—General	M
Public Administration	M
Public Health—General	M
Public History	M
Public Policy	M
Reading Education	M
School Psychology	M
Secondary Education	M
Social Sciences Education	M
Software Engineering	M
Special Education	M
Sports Management	M
Transportation Management	M
Western European Studies	M

AMERICAN SENTINEL UNIVERSITY

Business Administration and Management—General	M
Computer Science	M
Health Informatics	M
Health Services Management and Hospital Administration	M
Management Information Systems	M
Nursing—General	M

AMERICAN UNIVERSITY

Accounting	M,O
American Studies	M,D,O
Anthropology	M,D,O
Applied Social Research	M,O
Applied Statistics	M,O
Art History	M
Arts Administration	M,O
Biopsychology	M,D,O
Biotechnology	M
Chemistry	M
Clinical Psychology	M,D,O
Cognitive Sciences	M,D,O
Communication—General	M,D
Comparative Literature	M
Conflict Resolution and Mediation/Peace Studies	M,D,O
Criminal Justice and Criminology	M,D,O
Cultural Studies	M,D,O
Curriculum and Instruction	M,O
Economics	M,D,O
Education—General	M,O
Educational Leadership and Administration	M,O
Educational Policy	M,O
English as a Second Language	M,O
Entrepreneurship	M,D,O
Environmental Management and Policy	M,D,O
Environmental Sciences	M,O
Ethics	M,D,O
Exercise and Sports Science	M
Film, Television, and Video Production	M
Finance and Banking	M
French	M,O
Game Design and Development	M
Gender Studies	M,D,O
Health Education	M,O
Health Promotion	M
History	M,D
Homeland Security	M,D
International Affairs	M,D,O
International and Comparative Education	M
International Development	M,D,O
International Economics	M,D,O
Journalism	M
Latin American Studies	M,O
Law	M,D
Legal and Justice Studies	M,D
Management Information Systems	M,D,O
Management Strategy and Policy	M,O
Marketing	M
Mass Communication	M,D,O
Mathematics	M,O
Media Studies	M,D
Multilingual and Multicultural Education	M,O
Music	M,O
Natural Resources	M,D,O
Neuroscience	M,D,O
Nonprofit Management	M,D,O
Nutrition	M,O
Organizational Management	M,O
Philosophy	M
Political Science	M,D,O
Project Management	M,O
Psychology—General	M,D,O
Public Administration	M,D,O
Public Affairs	M
Public Policy	M,O
Real Estate	M,O
Russian	M,O
Sociology	M,O
Spanish	M,O
Special Education	M
Statistics	M,O
Sustainability Management	M
Sustainable Development	M,D,O
Taxation	M,O
Western European Studies	M,D,O
Women's Studies	O
Writing	M

THE AMERICAN UNIVERSITY IN CAIRO

Anthropology	M
Business Administration and Management—General	M,O
Chemistry	M
Communication—General	M
Comparative Literature	M,O
Computer Science	M,O
Construction Engineering	M
Demography and Population Studies	M,O
Economic Development	M,O

*M—masters degree; D—doctorate; O—other advanced degree; *—Close-Up and/or Display*

- Economics M,O
- Education—General M
- Educational Leadership and Administration M
- Engineering and Applied Sciences—General M,D,O
- English M,O
- Finance and Banking M,O
- Gender Studies M
- Industrial and Manufacturing Management M
- International Affairs M,O
- International and Comparative Education M
- Journalism M
- Management Information Systems M
- Mechanical Engineering M
- Near and Middle Eastern Languages M
- Near and Middle Eastern Studies M,O
- Political Science M
- Public Administration M,O
- Public Policy M,O
- Social Psychology M
- Sociology M
- Women's Studies M

THE AMERICAN UNIVERSITY IN DUBAI
- Business Administration and Management—General M
- Construction Management M
- Education—General M
- Finance and Banking M
- International Business M
- Marketing M

AMERICAN UNIVERSITY OF ARMENIA
- Business Administration and Management—General M
- Computer Science M
- Economics M
- Energy Management and Policy M
- English as a Second Language M
- Industrial/Management Engineering M
- Information Science M
- International Affairs M
- Law M
- Management Information Systems M
- Manufacturing Engineering M
- Political Science M
- Public Health—General M

AMERICAN UNIVERSITY OF BEIRUT
- Agricultural Economics and Agribusiness M
- Allopathic Medicine M,D
- American Studies M,D
- Anatomy M,D
- Animal Sciences M
- Anthropology M,D
- Aquaculture M
- Archaeology M,D
- Biochemistry M,D
- Biological and Biomedical Sciences—General M,D
- Biostatistics M
- Business Administration and Management—General M
- Cell Biology M,D
- Chemistry M,D
- Civil Engineering M,D
- Clinical Psychology M,D
- Community Health M
- Computational Sciences M,D
- Computer Engineering M,D
- Computer Science M,D
- Economics M,D
- Electrical Engineering M,D
- Engineering and Applied Sciences—General M,D
- Engineering Management M,D
- English M,D
- Environmental and Occupational Health M
- Environmental Management and Policy M,D
- Environmental Sciences M,D
- Epidemiology M
- Finance and Banking M,D
- Food Science and Technology M
- Genetics M,D
- Geology M,D
- Health Promotion M
- Health Services Management and Hospital Administration M
- History M,D
- Human Resources Management M
- Immunology M,D
- Mathematics M,D
- Mechanical Engineering M,D
- Media Studies M,D
- Microbiology M,D
- Molecular Biology M,D
- Near and Middle Eastern Languages M,D
- Near and Middle Eastern Studies M,D
- Neuroscience M,D
- Nursing—General M
- Nutrition M
- Pharmacology M,D
- Physics M,D
- Plant Sciences M
- Political Science M,D
- Psychiatric Nursing M
- Psychology—General M,D
- Public Administration M,D
- Sociology M,D
- Statistics M,D
- Theoretical Physics M,D
- Toxicology M,D
- Urban and Regional Planning M,D
- Urban Design M,D
- Water Resources Engineering M,D

AMERICAN UNIVERSITY OF HEALTH SCIENCES
- Clinical Research M

THE AMERICAN UNIVERSITY OF PARIS
- Business Administration and Management—General M
- Communication—General M
- Conflict Resolution and Mediation/Peace Studies M
- Cultural Studies M
- International Affairs M
- International Business M
- Law M
- Near and Middle Eastern Studies M
- Public Policy M

AMERICAN UNIVERSITY OF PUERTO RICO
- Art Education M
- Criminal Justice and Criminology M
- Education—General M
- Elementary Education M
- Physical Education M
- Science Education M
- Special Education M

THE AMERICAN UNIVERSITY OF ROME
- Historic Preservation M
- Religion M

AMERICAN UNIVERSITY OF SHARJAH
- Accounting M
- Business Administration and Management—General M
- Chemical Engineering M
- Civil Engineering M
- Computer Engineering M
- Electrical Engineering M
- Engineering Management M
- English as a Second Language M
- Mathematics M
- Mechanical Engineering M
- Translation and Interpretation M
- Urban and Regional Planning M

AMRIDGE UNIVERSITY
- Counseling Psychology M,D
- Counselor Education M,D
- Human Services M,D
- Marriage and Family Therapy M,D
- Pastoral Ministry and Counseling M,D
- Religion M,D
- Theology M,D

ANABAPTIST MENNONITE BIBLICAL SEMINARY
- Conflict Resolution and Mediation/Peace Studies M,O
- Missions and Missiology M,O
- Theology M,O

ANAHEIM UNIVERSITY
- Business Administration and Management—General M,D,O
- English as a Second Language M,D,O
- Entrepreneurship M,D,O
- International Business M,D,O
- Sustainability Management M,D,O

ANDERSON UNIVERSITY (IN)
- Accounting M,D
- Business Administration and Management—General M,D
- Education—General M
- Missions and Missiology M,D
- Theology M,D

ANDERSON UNIVERSITY (SC)
- Business Administration and Management—General M
- Criminal Justice and Criminology M
- Education—General M
- Pastoral Ministry and Counseling M

ANDOVER NEWTON THEOLOGICAL SCHOOL
- Pastoral Ministry and Counseling M,D
- Theology M,D

ANDREWS UNIVERSITY
- Accounting M
- Allied Health—General M
- Architecture M
- Biological and Biomedical Sciences—General M
- Clinical Psychology M
- Communication Disorders M
- Communication—General M
- Counseling Psychology M,D
- Curriculum and Instruction M,D,O
- Developmental Psychology M,D
- Economics M
- Education—General M,D,O
- Educational Leadership and Administration M,D,O
- Educational Psychology M,D
- Elementary Education M,D,O
- English as a Second Language M,D,O
- English Education M,D,O
- English M
- Finance and Banking M,D
- Foreign Languages Education M,D,O
- Higher Education M,D,O
- International Development M
- Music M
- Nursing—General M,D
- Nutrition M,O
- Pastoral Ministry and Counseling M,D,O
- Physical Therapy D
- Psychology—General M,D,O
- Public Health—General M,O
- Religious Education M,D,O
- School Psychology M,O
- Science Education M,D,O
- Secondary Education M,D,O
- Social Psychology M
- Social Sciences Education M,D,O
- Social Work M
- Special Education M
- Theology M,D,O

ANGELO STATE UNIVERSITY
- Accounting M
- Agricultural Sciences—General M
- Animal Sciences M
- Applied Psychology M
- Biological and Biomedical Sciences—General M
- Business Administration and Management—General M
- Communication—General M
- Counseling Psychology M
- Counselor Education M
- Criminal Justice and Criminology M
- Curriculum and Instruction M
- Educational Leadership and Administration M
- English M
- Family Nurse Practitioner Studies M
- Higher Education M
- Homeland Security M
- Industrial and Organizational Psychology M
- Media Studies M
- National Security M
- Nursing Education M
- Nursing—General M
- Physical Therapy D
- Psychology—General M
- Sports Management M

ANNA MARIA COLLEGE
- Art Education M
- Art/Fine Arts M,O
- Business Administration and Management—General M,O
- Counseling Psychology M
- Criminal Justice and Criminology M
- Early Childhood Education M,O
- Education—General M,O
- Elementary Education M,O
- Emergency Management M,O
- English Education M,O
- Environmental and Occupational Health M
- Fire Protection Engineering M
- Industrial and Organizational Psychology M
- Pastoral Ministry and Counseling M
- Public Administration M

ANTIOCH UNIVERSITY LOS ANGELES
- Business Administration and Management—General M
- Clinical Psychology M
- Education—General M
- Human Resources Development M
- Nonprofit Management M
- Organizational Management M
- Psychology—General M
- Sustainable Development M
- Writing M,O

ANTIOCH UNIVERSITY MIDWEST
- Art/Fine Arts M
- Business Administration and Management—General M
- Comparative Literature M
- Conflict Resolution and Mediation/Peace Studies M
- Counseling Psychology M
- Education—General M
- Liberal Studies M
- Management Strategy and Policy M
- Psychology—General M
- Writing M

ANTIOCH UNIVERSITY NEW ENGLAND
- Addictions/Substance Abuse Counseling M
- Applied Behavior Analysis M,O
- Applied Psychology M,D,O
- Business Administration and Management—General M
- Clinical Psychology M,D
- Conservation Biology M
- Counseling Psychology M
- Early Childhood Education M
- Education—General M,O
- Educational Leadership and Administration M,O
- Educational Media/Instructional Technology M,O
- Elementary Education M,O
- Environmental Education M
- Environmental Management and Policy M,D
- Environmental Sciences M,D
- Foundations and Philosophy of Education M,O
- Humanities M
- Interdisciplinary Studies M
- Marriage and Family Therapy M,D,O
- Science Education M
- Special Education M,O
- Sustainability Management M
- Sustainable Development M,O
- Therapies—Dance, Drama, and Music M,O

ANTIOCH UNIVERSITY SANTA BARBARA
- Business Administration and Management—General M
- Clinical Psychology M,D
- Education—General M
- Management Strategy and Policy M
- Nonprofit Management M
- Writing M

ANTIOCH UNIVERSITY SEATTLE
- Counselor Education M,D
- Education—General M
- Environmental Management and Policy M
- Organizational Management M
- Psychology—General M,D

AOMA GRADUATE SCHOOL OF INTEGRATIVE MEDICINE
- Acupuncture and Oriental Medicine M,D

APEX SCHOOL OF THEOLOGY
- Theology M,D

APPALACHIAN BIBLE COLLEGE
- Pastoral Ministry and Counseling M

APPALACHIAN COLLEGE OF PHARMACY
- Pharmacy D

APPALACHIAN SCHOOL OF LAW
- Law D

APPALACHIAN STATE UNIVERSITY
- Accounting M
- American Studies M
- Biological and Biomedical Sciences—General M
- Business Administration and Management—General M
- Cell Biology M
- Child Development M
- Clinical Psychology M
- Communication Disorders M
- Computer Science M
- Counseling Psychology M
- Counselor Education M
- Criminal Justice and Criminology M
- Cultural Studies M
- Curriculum and Instruction M
- Educational Leadership and Administration M,D,O
- Educational Media/Instructional Technology M,O
- Elementary Education M
- Energy and Power Engineering M
- Engineering Physics M
- English Education M
- English M
- Environmental Management and Policy M
- Exercise and Sports Science M
- Experimental Psychology M
- Family and Consumer Sciences-General M
- Foreign Languages Education M
- Geographic Information Systems M
- Geography M
- Gerontology M,O
- Health Psychology M
- Higher Education M,O
- History M
- Industrial and Organizational Psychology M
- International Affairs M
- Library Science M,O
- Marriage and Family Therapy M
- Mathematics Education M
- Mathematics M
- Middle School Education M
- Molecular Biology M
- Music Education M
- Music M
- Nutrition M
- Political Science M
- Psychology—General M
- Public Administration M
- Reading Education M
- Rehabilitation Sciences M
- Romance Languages M
- School Psychology M
- Science Education M
- Social Sciences Education M
- Social Work M
- Sociology M,O
- Special Education M
- Student Affairs M
- Sustainable Development M
- Taxation M
- Therapies—Dance, Drama, and Music M
- Vocational and Technical Education M

AQUINAS COLLEGE (MI)
- Business Administration and Management—General M
- Education—General M
- Environmental Management and Policy M
- Health Services Management and Hospital Administration M
- Marketing M
- Organizational Management M
- Sustainability Management M

AQUINAS COLLEGE (TN)
- Education—General M
- Nursing Education M
- Nursing—General M

AQUINAS INSTITUTE OF THEOLOGY
- Health Services Management and Hospital Administration M,D,O
- Music M,D,O
- Pastoral Ministry and Counseling M,D,O
- Theology M,D,O

ARCADIA UNIVERSITY
- Advertising and Public Relations M
- Art Education M,D,O
- Business Administration and Management—General M
- Community Health M
- Computer Education M,D,O

Conflict Resolution and Mediation/Peace Studies	M
Curriculum and Instruction	M,D,O
Early Childhood Education	M,D,O
Education—General	M,D,O
Educational Leadership and Administration	M,D,O
Educational Media/Instructional Technology	M,D,O
Elementary Education	M,D,O
English Education	M,D,O
English	M
Environmental Education	M,D,O
Forensic Sciences	M
Genetic Counseling	M
Health Education	M
Humanities	M
International Affairs	M
Mathematics Education	M,D,O
Music Education	M,D,O
Physical Therapy	D
Physician Assistant Studies	M
Psychology—General	M,D,O
Public Health—General	M
Reading Education	M,D,O
School Psychology	M
Science Education	M,D,O
Secondary Education	M,D,O
Social Psychology	M
Social Sciences Education	M,D,O
Special Education	M,D,O
Theater	M,D,O

ARGOSY UNIVERSITY, ATLANTA

Accounting	M,D
Biopsychology	M,D,O
Business Administration and Management—General	M,D
Clinical Psychology	M,D,O
Counselor Education	M,D,O
Education—General	M,D,O
Educational Leadership and Administration	M,D,O
Educational Media/Instructional Technology	M,D,O
Elementary Education	M,D,O
Finance and Banking	M,D
Forensic Psychology	M,D,O
Health Psychology	M,D,O
Health Services Management and Hospital Administration	M,D
Higher Education	M,D,O
Industrial and Organizational Psychology	M,D,O
International Business	M,D
Management Information Systems	M,D
Marketing	M,D
Marriage and Family Therapy	M,D,O
Psychology—General	M,D,O
Public Health—General	M
Secondary Education	M,D,O
Social Psychology	M,D,O
Sport Psychology	M,D,O

ARGOSY UNIVERSITY, CHICAGO

Accounting	M,D
Adult Education	M,D,O
Business Administration and Management—General	M,D
Clinical Psychology	M,D
Community College Education	M,D,O
Counseling Psychology	D
Counselor Education	D
Education—General	M,D,O
Educational Leadership and Administration	M,D,O
Elementary Education	M,D,O
Finance and Banking	M,D
Forensic Psychology	D
Health Psychology	D
Health Services Management and Hospital Administration	M,D
Higher Education	M,D,O
Human Development	D
Industrial and Organizational Psychology	M,D
International Business	M,D
Management Information Systems	M,D
Marketing	M,D
Marriage and Family Therapy	D
Neuroscience	D
Organizational Behavior	D
Organizational Management	D
Psychoanalysis and Psychotherapy	D
Psychology—General	M,D
Public Administration	M,D
Public Health—General	M
Secondary Education	M,D,O
Social Psychology	M,D
Sustainability Management	M,D

ARGOSY UNIVERSITY, DALLAS

Accounting	M,D,O
Business Administration and Management—General	M,D,O
Clinical Psychology	M,D
Counselor Education	D
Education—General	M,D
Educational Leadership and Administration	M,D
Finance and Banking	M,D,O
Forensic Psychology	M
Health Services Management and Hospital Administration	M,D,O
Higher Education	M,D
Industrial and Organizational Psychology	M
International Business	M,D,O
Management Information Systems	M,D,O
Marketing	M,D,O
Psychology—General	M,D
Public Administration	M,D,O
Public Health—General	M
School Psychology	M,D
Social Psychology	M
Sustainability Management	M,D,O

ARGOSY UNIVERSITY, DENVER

Accounting	M,D
Business Administration and Management—General	M,D
Clinical Psychology	M,D
Community College Education	M,D
Counseling Psychology	M,D
Counselor Education	M,D
Education—General	M,D
Educational Leadership and Administration	M,D
Educational Media/Instructional Technology	M,D
Elementary Education	M,D
Finance and Banking	M,D
Forensic Psychology	M,D
Health Services Management and Hospital Administration	M,D
Higher Education	M,D
Industrial and Organizational Psychology	M,D
International Business	M,D
Management Information Systems	M,D
Marketing	M,D
Marriage and Family Therapy	M,D
Organizational Management	M,D
Psychology—General	M,D
Public Administration	M,D
Public Health—General	M
Sustainability Management	M,D

ARGOSY UNIVERSITY, HAWAIʻI

Accounting	M,D,O
Addictions/Substance Abuse Counseling	O
Adult Education	M,D
Business Administration and Management—General	M,D,O
Clinical Psychology	M,D,O
Counseling Psychology	D
Education—General	M,D
Educational Leadership and Administration	M,D
Elementary Education	M,D
Finance and Banking	M,D,O
Forensic Psychology	M
Health Services Management and Hospital Administration	M,D,O
Higher Education	M,D
International Business	M,D,O
Management Information Systems	M,D,O
Marketing	M,D,O
Marriage and Family Therapy	M
Organizational Management	D
Pharmacology	M,O
Psychology—General	M,D,O
Public Health—General	M
School Psychology	M
Secondary Education	M,D
Sustainability Management	M,D,O

ARGOSY UNIVERSITY, INLAND EMPIRE

Accounting	M,D
Business Administration and Management—General	M,D
Clinical Psychology	M,D
Community College Education	M,D
Counseling Psychology	M,D
Education—General	M,D
Educational Leadership and Administration	M,D
Elementary Education	M,D
Finance and Banking	M,D
Forensic Psychology	M,D
Health Services Management and Hospital Administration	M,D
Higher Education	M,D
Industrial and Organizational Psychology	M,D
International Business	M,D
Management Information Systems	M,D
Marketing	M,D
Marriage and Family Therapy	M,D
Organizational Management	M,D
Psychology—General	M,D
Public Administration	M,D
Public Health—General	M
Secondary Education	M,D
Sport Psychology	M,D
Sustainability Management	M,D

ARGOSY UNIVERSITY, LOS ANGELES

Accounting	M,D
Business Administration and Management—General	M,D
Clinical Psychology	M,D
Community College Education	M,D
Counseling Psychology	M,D
Education—General	M,D
Educational Leadership and Administration	M,D
Elementary Education	M,D
Finance and Banking	M,D
Forensic Psychology	M,D
Health Services Management and Hospital Administration	M,D
Higher Education	M,D
International Business	M,D
Management Information Systems	M,D
Marketing	M,D
Marriage and Family Therapy	M,D
Organizational Management	M,D
Psychology—General	M,D
Public Administration	M,D
Public Health—General	M
Secondary Education	M,D
Sustainability Management	M,D

ARGOSY UNIVERSITY, NASHVILLE

Accounting	M,D
Business Administration and Management—General	M,D
Counseling Psychology	M,D
Counselor Education	D
Education—General	M,D,O
Educational Leadership and Administration	M,D,O
Educational Media/Instructional Technology	M,D,O
Elementary Education	M,D,O
Finance and Banking	M,D
Health Services Management and Hospital Administration	M,D
Higher Education	M,D,O
International Business	M,D
Management Information Systems	M,D
Marketing	M,D
Psychology—General	M,D
Public Health—General	M
Secondary Education	M,D,O

ARGOSY UNIVERSITY, ORANGE COUNTY

Accounting	M,D,O
Business Administration and Management—General	M,D,O
Clinical Psychology	M,D
Community College Education	M,D
Counseling Psychology	M,D
Education—General	M,D
Educational Leadership and Administration	M,D
Educational Media/Instructional Technology	M,D
Elementary Education	M,D
Finance and Banking	M,D,O
Forensic Psychology	M
Health Services Management and Hospital Administration	M,D,O
Higher Education	M,D
International Business	M,D,O
Management Information Systems	M,D,O
Marketing	M,D,O
Marriage and Family Therapy	M,D
Organizational Management	D
Psychology—General	M,D
Public Administration	M,D,O
Public Health—General	M
Secondary Education	M,D
Sport Psychology	M
Sustainability Management	M,D,O

ARGOSY UNIVERSITY, PHOENIX

Accounting	M,D
Adult Education	M,D,O
Business Administration and Management—General	M,D
Clinical Psychology	M,D
Community College Education	M,D,O
Counseling Psychology	M
Education—General	M,D,O
Educational Leadership and Administration	M,D,O
Educational Media/Instructional Technology	M,D,O
Elementary Education	M,D,O
Finance and Banking	M,D
Forensic Psychology	M
Health Services Management and Hospital Administration	M,D
Higher Education	M,D,O
Industrial and Organizational Psychology	M
International Business	M,D
Management Information Systems	M,D
Marketing	M,D
Neuroscience	M,D
Psychology—General	M,D
Public Administration	M,D
Public Health—General	M
School Psychology	M,D
Secondary Education	M,D,O
Sport Psychology	M,D
Sustainability Management	M,D

ARGOSY UNIVERSITY, SALT LAKE CITY

Accounting	M,D
Business Administration and Management—General	M,D
Counseling Psychology	M,D
Counselor Education	M,D
Education—General	M,D
Educational Leadership and Administration	M,D
Finance and Banking	M,D
Forensic Psychology	M,D
Health Services Management and Hospital Administration	M,D
International Business	M,D
Management Information Systems	M,D
Marketing	M,D
Marriage and Family Therapy	M,D
Psychology—General	M,D
Public Administration	M,D
Public Health—General	M
Sustainability Management	M,D

ARGOSY UNIVERSITY, SAN DIEGO

Accounting	M,D
Business Administration and Management—General	M,D
Clinical Psychology	M,D
Community College Education	M,D
Counseling Psychology	M,D
Education—General	M,D
Educational Leadership and Administration	M,D
Elementary Education	M,D
Finance and Banking	M,D
Forensic Psychology	M,D
Higher Education	M,D
International Business	M,D
Management Information Systems	M,D
Marketing	M,D
Marriage and Family Therapy	M,D
Organizational Management	M,D
Psychology—General	M,D
Public Administration	M,D
Public Health—General	M
Secondary Education	M,D

ARGOSY UNIVERSITY, SAN FRANCISCO BAY AREA

Accounting	M,D
Business Administration and Management—General	M,D
Clinical Psychology	M,D
Community College Education	M,D
Counseling Psychology	M,D
Education—General	M,D
Educational Leadership and Administration	M,D
Educational Media/Instructional Technology	M,D
Elementary Education	M,D
Finance and Banking	M,D
Forensic Psychology	M
Health Services Management and Hospital Administration	M,D
Higher Education	M,D
International Business	M,D
Management Information Systems	M,D
Marketing	M,D
Organizational Management	M,D
Psychology—General	M,D
Public Administration	M,D
Public Health—General	M
Secondary Education	M,D
Sport Psychology	M,D
Sustainability Management	M,D

ARGOSY UNIVERSITY, SARASOTA

Accounting	M,D,O
Business Administration and Management—General	M,D,O
Counseling Psychology	M,D
Counselor Education	M,D,O
Education—General	M,D,O
Educational Leadership and Administration	M,D,O
Educational Media/Instructional Technology	M,D,O
Elementary Education	M,D,O
Finance and Banking	M,D,O
Forensic Psychology	M,D
Health Services Management and Hospital Administration	M,D,O
Higher Education	M,D,O
International Business	M,D,O
Management Information Systems	M,D,O
Marketing	M,D,O
Marriage and Family Therapy	M,D
Organizational Management	M,D,O
Pastoral Ministry and Counseling	M,D
Psychology—General	M,D
Public Administration	M,D,O
Public Health—General	M
School Psychology	M,D,O
Secondary Education	M,D,O
Social Psychology	M,D
Sustainability Management	M,D,O

ARGOSY UNIVERSITY, SCHAUMBURG

Accounting	M,D,O
Business Administration and Management—General	M,D,O
Clinical Psychology	M,D
Corporate and Organizational Communication	M,D,O
Counseling Psychology	M,O
Finance and Banking	M,D,O
Forensic Psychology	M,O
Health Services Management and Hospital Administration	M,D,O
Human Resources Management	M,D,O
Industrial and Organizational Psychology	M,O
International Business	M,D,O
Management Information Systems	M,D,O
Marketing	M,D,O
Organizational Management	M,D,O
Psychology—General	M,O
Public Administration	M,D,O
Public Health—General	M
Sport Psychology	M,O
Sustainability Management	M,D,O

ARGOSY UNIVERSITY, SEATTLE

Accounting	M,D
Adult Education	M,D
Business Administration and Management—General	M,D
Clinical Psychology	M,D,O
Community College Education	M,D
Counseling Psychology	M,D
Education—General	M,D
Educational Leadership and Administration	M,D
Educational Media/Instructional Technology	M,D
Elementary Education	M,D
Finance and Banking	M,D
Health Services Management and Hospital Administration	M,D
Higher Education	M,D
International Business	M,D
Management Information Systems	M,D
Marketing	M,D
Organizational Management	M,D
Psychology—General	M,D,O
Public Administration	M,D
Public Health—General	M

*M—masters degree; D—doctorate; O—other advanced degree; *—Close-Up and/or Display*

Secondary Education	M,D
Sustainability Management	M,D

ARGOSY UNIVERSITY, TAMPA

Accounting	M,D
Business Administration and Management—General	M,D
Clinical Psychology	M,D
Community College Education	M,D,O
Counseling Psychology	M,D
Counselor Education	M,D,O
Education—General	M,D,O
Educational Leadership and Administration	M,D,O
Elementary Education	M,D,O
Finance and Banking	M,D
Health Services Management and Hospital Administration	M,D
Higher Education	M,D,O
Industrial and Organizational Psychology	M,D
International Business	M,D
Management Information Systems	M,D
Marketing	M,D
Marriage and Family Therapy	M,D
Neuroscience	M,D
Organizational Management	M,D
Psychology—General	M,D
Public Administration	M,D
Public Health—General	M
Secondary Education	M,D,O
Sustainability Management	M,D

ARGOSY UNIVERSITY, TWIN CITIES

Accounting	M,D
Biopsychology	M,D,O
Business Administration and Management—General	M,D
Clinical Psychology	M,D,O
Education—General	M,D,O
Educational Leadership and Administration	M,D,O
Educational Media/Instructional Technology	M,D,O
Elementary Education	M,D,O
Finance and Banking	M,D
Forensic Psychology	M,D,O
Health Psychology	M,D,O
Health Services Management and Hospital Administration	M,D
Higher Education	M,D,O
Industrial and Organizational Psychology	M,D,O
International Business	M,D
Management Information Systems	M,D
Marketing	M,D
Marriage and Family Therapy	M,D,O
Organizational Management	M,D
Psychology—General	M,D,O
Public Administration	M,D
Public Health—General	M
Secondary Education	M,D,O
Sustainability Management	M,D

ARGOSY UNIVERSITY, WASHINGTON DC

Accounting	M,D,O
Business Administration and Management—General	M,D,O
Clinical Psychology	M,D
Community College Education	M,D,O
Counseling Psychology	M,D
Counselor Education	M,D
Education—General	M,D,O
Educational Leadership and Administration	M,D,O
Elementary Education	M,D,O
Finance and Banking	M,D,O
Forensic Psychology	M,D
Health Psychology	M,D
Health Services Management and Hospital Administration	M,D,O
Higher Education	M,D,O
International Business	M,D,O
Management Information Systems	M,D,O
Marketing	M,D,O
Marriage and Family Therapy	M,D
Organizational Management	M,D,O
Psychology—General	M,D
Public Administration	M,D,O
Public Health—General	M
Secondary Education	M,D,O
Social Psychology	M,D
Sustainability Management	M,D,O

ARIZONA SCHOOL OF ACUPUNCTURE AND ORIENTAL MEDICINE

Acupuncture and Oriental Medicine	M

ARIZONA STATE UNIVERSITY AT THE TEMPE CAMPUS

Accounting	M,D
Aerospace/Aeronautical Engineering	M,D
African Studies	M,D,O
Agricultural Economics and Agribusiness	D
Animal Behavior	M,D
Anthropology	M,D,O
Applied Arts and Design—General	M,D
Applied Behavior Analysis	M,D
Applied Mathematics	M,D,O
Applied Psychology	M
Archaeology	M,D,O
Architectural History	D
Architecture	M,D
Art Education	M,D
Art History	M,D
Art/Fine Arts	M,D
Arts Administration	M,D
Astrophysics	M,D
Aviation Management	M
Biochemistry	M,D
Bioinformatics	M,D
Biological and Biomedical Sciences—General	M,D
Biomedical Engineering	M,D
Biotechnology	M,D
Building Science	M,D
Business Administration and Management—General	M,D
Cell Biology	M,D
Chemical Engineering	M,D
Chemistry	M,D
Child and Family Studies	M,D
Chinese	M,D
Civil Engineering	M,D
Clinical Psychology	M,D
Cognitive Sciences	M,D
Communication Disorders	M,D
Communication—General	M,D
Community Health	M,D,O
Comparative Literature	M,D,O
Computer Engineering	M,D
Computer Science	M,D
Conservation Biology	M,D
Construction Engineering	M,D
Construction Management	M,D
Counseling Psychology	D
Counselor Education	M
Criminal Justice and Criminology	M,D,O
Cultural Studies	M,D
Curriculum and Instruction	M
Dance	M
Developmental Psychology	M,D
Economics	D
Education—General	M,D,O
Educational Leadership and Administration	M,D
Educational Measurement and Evaluation	D
Educational Media/Instructional Technology	M,O
Educational Policy	D
Electrical Engineering	M,D,O
Elementary Education	M
Emergency Management	M,D
Energy and Power Engineering	M,D
Engineering and Applied Sciences—General	M,D
English as a Second Language	M,D,O
English	M,D,O
Entrepreneurship	M,D
Environmental Design	D
Environmental Engineering	M,D
Environmental Management and Policy	M
Environmental Sciences	M,D,O
Ergonomics and Human Factors	M
Ethics	M,D
Evolutionary Biology	M,D
Exercise and Sports Science	M,D
Family Nurse Practitioner Studies	M,D,O
Film, Television, and Video Production	M
Finance and Banking	M,D
Foreign Languages Education	M,D
French	M
Gender Studies	M,D,O
Geographic Information Systems	M,D,O
Geography	M,D,O
Geological Engineering	M,D
Geology	M,D
Geosciences	M,D
German	M
Gerontological Nursing	M,D,O
Gerontology	M,D,O
Health Education	D
Health Promotion	M,D
Health Services Management and Hospital Administration	M,D
Higher Education	M
History of Science and Technology	M,D
History	M,D,O
Homeland Security	M,D
Human Development	M,D
Industrial/Management Engineering	M,D
Information Science	M
Interdisciplinary Studies	M
International Business	M,D
International Health	M,D,O
Japanese	M
Journalism	M,D
Landscape Architecture	M,D
Law	M,D
Legal and Justice Studies	M,D,O
Liberal Studies	M
Linguistics	M,D,O
Management Information Systems	M,D
Management of Technology	M
Management Strategy and Policy	M,D
Manufacturing Engineering	M
Marketing	M,D
Marriage and Family Therapy	M,D
Mass Communication	M,D
Materials Engineering	M,D
Materials Sciences	M,D
Mathematics Education	M,D,O
Mathematics	M,D,O
Mechanical Engineering	M,D
Media Studies	M,D
Medical Informatics	M,D
Medieval and Renaissance Studies	M,D,O
Microbiology	M,D
Modeling and Simulation	M,D
Molecular Biology	M,D
Museum Studies	M,D,O
Music Education	M,D
Music	M,D
Nanotechnology	M,D
Neuroscience	M,D
Nonprofit Management	M,D,O
Nuclear Engineering	M,D,O
Nursing and Healthcare Administration	M,D,O
Nursing Education	M,D,O
Nursing—General	M,D,O
Nutrition	M,D
Organizational Behavior	M,D
Philosophy	M,D,O
Physical Education	M
Physics	M,D
Planetary and Space Sciences	M,D
Plant Biology	M,D
Political Science	M,D
Psychiatric Nursing	M,D,O
Psychology—General	M,D
Public Administration	M,D
Public Affairs	M,D
Public Health—General	M,D,O
Public History	M,D,O
Public Policy	M,D
Publishing	M,D,O
Real Estate	M,D
Reliability Engineering	M
Religion	M,D,O
Rhetoric	M,D,O
Secondary Education	M
Social Psychology	M,D
Social Work	M,D,O
Sociology	M,D
Software Engineering	M,D
Spanish	M,D
Special Education	M,O
Statistics	M,D,O
Supply Chain Management	M,D
Sustainable Development	M,D,O
Systems Engineering	M
Systems Science	M,D
Technology and Public Policy	M
Textile Design	M,D
Theater	M,D
Therapies—Dance, Drama, and Music	M,D
Translation and Interpretation	M,D,O
Transportation and Highway Engineering	M,D,O
Travel and Tourism	M,D,O
Urban and Regional Planning	M,D,O
Urban Design	M,D
Urban Studies	M,D,O
Writing	M,D

ARKANSAS STATE UNIVERSITY

Accounting	M
Addictions/Substance Abuse Counseling	M,O
Agricultural Education	M,O
Agricultural Sciences—General	M,O
Biological and Biomedical Sciences—General	M,O
Biotechnology	M,O
Business Administration and Management—General	M
Business Education	O
Chemistry	M,O
Clinical Psychology	M,O
Communication Disorders	M,O
Communication—General	M,O
Community College Education	M,D,O
Computer Science	M
Counselor Education	M,O
Criminal Justice and Criminology	M,O
Early Childhood Education	M,D,O
Education of the Gifted	M,D,O
Education—General	M,D,O
Educational Leadership and Administration	M,D,O
Elementary Education	M,D,O
Emergency Management	M,O
Engineering and Applied Sciences—General	M
Engineering Management	M
English Education	M,O
English	M,O
Environmental Sciences	M,D
Exercise and Sports Science	M,O
Foundations and Philosophy of Education	M,D,O
Gerontology	M,D,O
Health Communication	M,O
Health Education	M,D,O
Health Services Management and Hospital Administration	M,D,O
Historic Preservation	M,D
History	M,O
Journalism	M
Management Information Systems	O
Mass Communication	M
Mathematics Education	M
Mathematics	M
Media Studies	M
Middle School Education	M,D,O
Molecular Biology	M,D
Music Education	M,O
Music	M,O
Nurse Anesthesia	M,D,O
Nursing—General	M,D,O
Occupational Therapy	D
Physical Education	M,O
Physical Therapy	D
Political Science	M,O
Public Administration	M,O
Reading Education	M,D,O
Rehabilitation Counseling	M,O
School Psychology	M,O
Science Education	M,O
Social Sciences Education	M,D,O
Social Work	M,O
Sociology	M,O
Special Education	M,D,O
Sports Management	M,O
Student Affairs	M,O

ARKANSAS TECH UNIVERSITY

Business Administration and Management—General	M
Counselor Education	M,D,O
Curriculum and Instruction	M,D,O
Education—General	M,D,O
Educational Leadership and Administration	M,D,O
Educational Media/Instructional Technology	M,D,O
Elementary Education	M,D,O
Emergency Management	M
Engineering and Applied Sciences—General	M
English as a Second Language	M
English Education	M
English	M
Fish, Game, and Wildlife Management	M
Health Informatics	M
History	M
Information Science	M
Journalism	M
Liberal Studies	M
Nursing—General	M
Psychology—General	M
Sociology	M
Student Affairs	M,D,O

ARLINGTON BAPTIST COLLEGE

Curriculum and Instruction	M
Education—General	M
Educational Leadership and Administration	M
Theology	M

ARMSTRONG STATE UNIVERSITY

Adult Education	M,O
Adult Nursing	M,O
American Studies	M
Athletic Training and Sports Medicine	M,O
Business Administration and Management—General	M,O
Communication Disorders	M
Computer and Information Systems Security	M,O
Computer Science	M
Corporate and Organizational Communication	M,O
Criminal Justice and Criminology	M,O
Curriculum and Instruction	M,O
Early Childhood Education	M,O
Education—General	M,O
Exercise and Sports Science	M,O
Family Nurse Practitioner Studies	M,O
Gerontological Nursing	M,O
Health Services Management and Hospital Administration	M
History	M
Information Science	M
Nursing—General	M,O
Physical Education	M,O
Physical Therapy	D
Public Health—General	M
Public History	M
Reading Education	M,O
Secondary Education	M,O
Special Education	M,O
Western European Studies	M
Writing	M,O

ART ACADEMY OF CINCINNATI

Art Education	M

ART CENTER COLLEGE OF DESIGN

Art/Fine Arts	M
Computer Art and Design	M
Environmental Design	M
Film, Television, and Video Production	M
Industrial Design	M
Transportation and Highway Engineering	M

THE ART INSTITUTE OF CALIFORNIA–SAN FRANCISCO, A CAMPUS OF ARGOSY UNIVERSITY

Computer Art and Design	M
Film, Television, and Video Production	M

THE ART INSTITUTE OF DALLAS, A CAMPUS OF SOUTH UNIVERSITY

Applied Arts and Design—General	M

ASBURY THEOLOGICAL SEMINARY

Missions and Missiology	M,D,O
Pastoral Ministry and Counseling	M,D,O
Religious Education	M,D,O
Theology	M,D,O

ASBURY UNIVERSITY

Child and Family Studies	M
Classics	M
Educational Leadership and Administration	M
English as a Second Language	M
English	M
French	M
Mathematics Education	M
Reading Education	M
Science Education	M
Social Sciences Education	M
Social Work	M
Spanish	M
Special Education	M
Writing	M

ASHLAND THEOLOGICAL SEMINARY

Counseling Psychology	M,D,O
Counselor Education	M,D,O
Missions and Missiology	M,D,O
Pastoral Ministry and Counseling	M,D,O
Theology	M,D,O

ASHLAND UNIVERSITY

Business Administration and Management—General	M
Curriculum and Instruction	M

Education of the Gifted	M
Education—General	M,D
Educational Leadership and Administration	M,D
Educational Media/Instructional Technology	M
Exercise and Sports Science	M
Foundations and Philosophy of Education	M
History	M
Physical Education	M
Political Science	M
Reading Education	M
Special Education	M
Sports Management	M
Student Affairs	M
Writing	M

ASHWORTH COLLEGE

Business Administration and Management—General	M
Criminal Justice and Criminology	M
Health Services Management and Hospital Administration	M
Human Resources Management	M
International Business	M
Marketing	M

ASPEN UNIVERSITY

Business Administration and Management—General	M,O
Finance and Banking	M,O
Information Science	M,O
Management Information Systems	M,O
Project Management	M,O

ASSEMBLIES OF GOD THEOLOGICAL SEMINARY

Cultural Studies	M,D
Missions and Missiology	M,D
Pastoral Ministry and Counseling	M,D
Theology	M,D

ASSUMPTION COLLEGE

Accounting	M,O
Applied Behavior Analysis	M,O
Business Administration and Management—General	M,O
Child and Family Studies	M,O
Counseling Psychology	M,O
Economics	M,O
Finance and Banking	M,O
Health Services Management and Hospital Administration	M,O
Human Resources Management	M,O
International Business	M,O
Marketing	M,O
Nonprofit Management	M,O
Rehabilitation Counseling	M,O
School Psychology	M,O
Special Education	M,O

ATHABASCA UNIVERSITY

Adult Education	M,O
Allied Health—General	M,O
Applied Psychology	M,O
Architecture	M,O
Art Therapy	M,O
Business Administration and Management—General	M,D,O
Counseling Psychology	M,O
Counselor Education	M,O
Cultural Studies	M,O
Distance Education Development	M,D,O
Education—General	M,D,O
Interdisciplinary Studies	M,O
International Development	M,O
Management of Technology	M,D,O
Nursing and Healthcare Administration	M,O
Nursing—General	M,O
Organizational Management	M,O
Project Management	M,D,O
Science Education	M,O

THE ATHENAEUM OF OHIO

Pastoral Ministry and Counseling	M,O
Theology	M,O

ATLANTA'S JOHN MARSHALL LAW SCHOOL

Law	M,D

ATLANTIC INSTITUTE OF ORIENTAL MEDICINE

Acupuncture and Oriental Medicine	M,D

ATLANTIC SCHOOL OF THEOLOGY

Pastoral Ministry and Counseling	M,O
Theology	M,O

ATLANTIC UNIVERSITY

Organizational Management	M
Pastoral Ministry and Counseling	O
Psychoanalysis and Psychotherapy	O
Transpersonal and Humanistic Psychology	M

ATLANTIC UNIVERSITY COLLEGE

Graphic Design	M

A.T. STILL UNIVERSITY

Allied Health—General	M,D
Athletic Training and Sports Medicine	M,D
Biological and Biomedical Sciences—General	M,D
Communication Disorders	M,D
Dentistry	D
Health Education	M,D
Health Services Management and Hospital Administration	M,D
Kinesiology and Movement Studies	M,D
Occupational Therapy	M,D
Oral and Dental Sciences	M,D,O
Osteopathic Medicine	M,D
Physical Therapy	M,D
Physician Assistant Studies	M,D
Public Health—General	M,D

AUBURN UNIVERSITY

Accounting	M
Adult Education	M,D,O
Aerospace/Aeronautical Engineering	M,D
Agricultural Economics and Agribusiness	M
Agricultural Sciences—General	M,D
Agronomy and Soil Sciences	M,D
Analytical Chemistry	M,D
Anatomy	M,D
Animal Sciences	M,D
Applied Behavior Analysis	M,D
Applied Economics	D
Applied Mathematics	M,D
Aquaculture	M,D
Architecture	M
Biochemistry	M,D
Biological and Biomedical Sciences—General	M,D
Biosystems Engineering	M,D
Botany	M,D
Building Science	M
Business Administration and Management—General	M,D
Business Education	M,D,O
Cell Biology	M,D
Chemical Engineering	M,D
Chemistry	M,D
Child and Family Studies	M,D
Civil Engineering	M,D
Clothing and Textiles	M,D
Communication Disorders	M,D
Communication—General	M,O
Computer Engineering	M,D
Computer Science	M,D
Construction Engineering	M,D
Construction Management	M
Curriculum and Instruction	M,D,O
Early Childhood Education	M,D,O
Economics	M
Education—General	M,D,O
Educational Leadership and Administration	M,D,O
Educational Media/Instructional Technology	M,D,O
Educational Psychology	M,D,O
Electrical Engineering	M,D
Elementary Education	M,D,O
Engineering and Applied Sciences—General	M,D,O
English Education	M,D,O
English	M,D,O
Entomology	M,D
Environmental Engineering	M,D
Exercise and Sports Science	M,D,O
Experimental Psychology	M,D
Finance and Banking	M
Fish, Game, and Wildlife Management	M,D
Food Science and Technology	M,D,O
Foreign Languages Education	M,D,O
Forestry	M,D
Geography	M
Geology	M
Geotechnical Engineering	M,D
Health Education	M,D,O
Health Promotion	M,D,O
Higher Education	M,D,O
History	M,D,O
Horticulture	M,D
Hospitality Management	M,D,O
Human Development	M,D
Human Resources Management	M,D
Hydraulics	M,D
Hydrology	M,D
Industrial and Organizational Psychology	M,D
Industrial Design	M
Industrial/Management Engineering	M,D,O
Inorganic Chemistry	M,D
Kinesiology and Movement Studies	M,D,O
Landscape Architecture	M
Management Information Systems	M,D
Mass Communication	M,O
Materials Engineering	M,D
Mathematics Education	M,D,O
Mathematics	M,D
Mechanical Engineering	M,D
Molecular Biology	M,D
Music Education	M,D,O
Natural Resources	M,D
Nursing Education	M
Nursing—General	M
Nutrition	M,D,O
Organic Chemistry	M,D
Pathobiology	M,D
Pharmaceutical Sciences	M,D
Pharmacology	M,D
Pharmacy	D
Physical Chemistry	M,D
Physical Education	M,D,O
Physics	M,D
Plant Pathology	M,D
Political Science	M,D,O
Polymer Science and Engineering	M,D
Psychology—General	M,D
Public Administration	M,D,O
Radiation Biology	M,D
Reading Education	M,D,O
Real Estate	M
Rehabilitation Counseling	M,D
Rural Sociology	M
Science Education	M,D,O
Secondary Education	M,D,O
Social Sciences Education	M,D,O
Sociology	M
Software Engineering	M,D
Spanish	M
Special Education	M,D
Statistics	M,D
Structural Engineering	M,D
Systems Engineering	M,D,O
Technical Communication	M,D,O
Transportation and Highway Engineering	M,D
Urban and Regional Planning	M
Veterinary Medicine	D
Veterinary Sciences	M,D
Zoology	M,D

AUBURN UNIVERSITY AT MONTGOMERY

Accounting	M
Business Administration and Management—General	M
Clinical Psychology	M
Computer and Information Systems Security	M
Counselor Education	M,O
Criminal Justice and Criminology	M,O
Early Childhood Education	M,O
Education—General	M,O
Educational Leadership and Administration	M,O
Educational Media/Instructional Technology	M,O
Elementary Education	M,O
Emergency Management	M,O
Exercise and Sports Science	M,O
Geographic Information Systems	M
Health Services Management and Hospital Administration	M,D,O
Homeland Security	M,O
Information Science	M
International Affairs	M,D,O
Legal and Justice Studies	M,O
Liberal Studies	M,D,O
Management Information Systems	M
Nonprofit Management	M,D,O
Nursing Education	M
Nursing—General	M
Organizational Management	M,O
Physical Education	M,O
Political Science	M,D,O
Psychology—General	M
Public Administration	M,D,O
Public Health—General	M,D,O
Public Policy	M,D,O
Secondary Education	M,O
Special Education	M,O
Writing	M

AUGSBURG COLLEGE

Business Administration and Management—General	M
Education—General	M
Family Nurse Practitioner Studies	M,D
Nursing—General	M,D
Organizational Management	M
Physician Assistant Studies	M
Social Work	M
Transcultural Nursing	M,D

AUGUSTANA UNIVERSITY

Education—General	M
Educational Media/Instructional Technology	M
Reading Education	M
Special Education	M
Sports Management	M

AUGUSTA UNIVERSITY

Acute Care/Critical Care Nursing	D
Allopathic Medicine	D
Anatomy	D
Biochemistry	D
Business Administration and Management—General	M
Cancer Biology/Oncology	D
Cardiovascular Sciences	D
Cell Biology	D
Clinical Research	M
Counselor Education	M,O
Curriculum and Instruction	M,O
Dentistry	D
Early Childhood Education	M,O
Education—General	M,O
Educational Leadership and Administration	M,O
Environmental and Occupational Health	M
Family Nurse Practitioner Studies	M,D,O
Foreign Languages Education	M,O
Genomic Sciences	M,D
Gerontological Nursing	D
Health Education	M,O
Health Informatics	M
Medical Illustration	M
Middle School Education	M,O
Molecular Medicine	D
Music Education	M,O
Neuroscience	D
Nurse Anesthesia	D
Nursing and Healthcare Administration	M
Nursing—General	D
Occupational Therapy	M
Oral and Dental Sciences	M,D
Pediatric Nursing	M,D,O
Pharmacology	D
Physical Education	M,O
Physical Therapy	D
Physician Assistant Studies	M
Physiology	D
Psychiatric Nursing	D
Psychology—General	M
Public Health—General	M
Secondary Education	M,O
Social Sciences	M
Special Education	M,O

AURORA UNIVERSITY

Accounting	M
Applied Behavior Analysis	M
Business Administration and Management—General	M
Curriculum and Instruction	M,D
Education—General	M,D
Educational Leadership and Administration	M,D
English as a Second Language	M,D
Higher Education	M,D
Mathematics	M
Nursing—General	M
Social Work	M,D

AUSTIN COLLEGE

Education—General	M

AUSTIN GRADUATE SCHOOL OF THEOLOGY

Theology	M

AUSTIN PEAY STATE UNIVERSITY

Biological and Biomedical Sciences—General	M
Business Administration and Management—General	M
Clinical Laboratory Sciences/Medical Technology	M
Clinical Psychology	M
Communication—General	M
Counseling Psychology	M
Counselor Education	M,O
Curriculum and Instruction	M,O
Database Systems	M
Developmental Education	M
Education—General	M,O
Educational Leadership and Administration	M,O
Elementary Education	M,O
Engineering and Applied Sciences—General	M
English	M
Exercise and Sports Science	M
Family Nurse Practitioner Studies	M
Health Education	M
Human Resources Management	M
Industrial and Organizational Psychology	M
Management Strategy and Policy	M
Military and Defense Studies	M
Music Education	M
Music	M
Nursing and Healthcare Administration	M
Nursing Education	M
Nursing Informatics	M
Nursing—General	M
Psychology—General	M
Public Health—General	M
Reading Education	M,O
Secondary Education	M,O
Social Work	M
Special Education	M
Sports Management	M

AUSTIN PRESBYTERIAN THEOLOGICAL SEMINARY

Pastoral Ministry and Counseling	M,D
Theology	M,D

AVE MARIA SCHOOL OF LAW

Law	D

AVE MARIA UNIVERSITY

Pastoral Ministry and Counseling	M,D
Theology	M,D

AVERETT UNIVERSITY

Accounting	M
Business Administration and Management—General	M
Curriculum and Instruction	M
Education—General	M
Educational Leadership and Administration	M
Human Resources Management	M
Marketing	M
Special Education	M

AVILA UNIVERSITY

Accounting	M
Business Administration and Management—General	M
Counseling Psychology	M
Education—General	M,O
Educational Media/Instructional Technology	M
English as a Second Language	M,O
Finance and Banking	M
Health Services Management and Hospital Administration	M
Human Resources Management	M
International and Comparative Education	M,O
International Business	M
Management Information Systems	M
Marketing	M
Organizational Management	M
Project Management	M
Psychology—General	M

AZUSA PACIFIC UNIVERSITY

Art/Fine Arts	M
Business Administration and Management—General	M

*M—masters degree; D—doctorate; O—other advanced degree; *—Close-Up and/or Display*

Clinical Psychology	M,D
Counselor Education	M
Curriculum and Instruction	M
Education—General	M,D,O
Educational Leadership and Administration	M,D
Educational Media/Instructional Technology	M
English as a Second Language	M
Entrepreneurship	M
Ethics	M
Finance and Banking	M
Foundations and Philosophy of Education	M
Higher Education	M,D
Human Resources Development	M
Human Resources Management	M
International Affairs	M
International Business	M
Library Science	M,O
Management Strategy and Policy	M
Marketing	M
Marriage and Family Therapy	M,D
Multilingual and Multicultural Education	M
Music Education	M
Music	M
Nonprofit Management	M
Nursing Education	M,D
Nursing—General	M,D
Organizational Management	M
Pastoral Ministry and Counseling	M
Physical Education	M
Physical Therapy	D
Psychology—General	M,D
Public Administration	M
Religious Education	M
School Psychology	M
Social Work	M
Special Education	M
Student Affairs	M
Theology	M,D
Urban Studies	M

BABEL UNIVERSITY PROFESSIONAL SCHOOL OF TRANSLATION

Translation and Interpretation	M

BABSON COLLEGE

Accounting	M,O
Business Administration and Management—General	M,O
Entrepreneurship	M,O

BAKER COLLEGE CENTER FOR GRADUATE STUDIES–ONLINE

Accounting	M,D
Business Administration and Management—General	M,D
Finance and Banking	M,D
Health Services Management and Hospital Administration	M,D
Human Resources Management	M,D
Management Information Systems	M,D
Marketing	M,D

BAKER UNIVERSITY

Business Administration and Management—General	M
Education—General	M,D
Liberal Studies	M
Organizational Management	M

BAKKE GRADUATE UNIVERSITY

Business Administration and Management—General	M,D
Entrepreneurship	M,D
Pastoral Ministry and Counseling	M,D
Theology	M,D
Urban Education	M,D

BALDWIN WALLACE UNIVERSITY

Accounting	M
Business Administration and Management—General	M
Communication Disorders	M
Education—General	M
Educational Leadership and Administration	M
Educational Media/Instructional Technology	M
Entrepreneurship	M
Health Services Management and Hospital Administration	M
Human Resources Management	M
International Business	M
Management Strategy and Policy	M
Marketing Research	M
Physician Assistant Studies	M
Reading Education	M
Special Education	M
Sustainability Management	M

BALL STATE UNIVERSITY

Accounting	M
Actuarial Science	M
Adult Education	M,D
Advertising and Public Relations	M
Anthropology	M,O
Applied Behavior Analysis	M
Architecture	M
Art/Fine Arts	M
Biological and Biomedical Sciences—General	M,D
Business Administration and Management—General	M,O
Business Education	M,O
Chemistry	M,D
Clinical Psychology	M,D
Cognitive Sciences	M
Communication Disorders	M,D
Communication—General	M,O
Computer Education	M,D,O
Computer Science	M
Counseling Psychology	M,D
Counselor Education	M,D
Criminal Justice and Criminology	M,O
Curriculum and Instruction	M,D
Economic Development	M,O
Education of the Gifted	M,D,O
Education—General	M,D,O
Educational Leadership and Administration	M,D,O
Educational Measurement and Evaluation	M,D,O
Educational Media/Instructional Technology	M,D
Educational Policy	D
Educational Psychology	M,D
Elementary Education	M,D,O
Emergency Management	M,O
English as a Second Language	M
English	M,D
Environmental Education	M,O
Environmental Management and Policy	M,O
Environmental Sciences	D
Exercise and Sports Science	M,D
Family and Consumer Sciences-General	M
Family Nurse Practitioner Studies	M,D,O
Foundations and Philosophy of Education	D
Geographic Information Systems	M,O
Geography	M,O
Geology	M,D
Geosciences	M
Gerontological Nursing	M,D,O
Health Promotion	M
Higher Education	M,D
Historic Preservation	M
History	M
Homeland Security	M,O
Human Development	M,D,O
Information Science	M,O
Interior Design	M
Internet and Interactive Multimedia	M
Journalism	M
Kinesiology and Movement Studies	M,D,O
Landscape Architecture	M
Linguistics	M
Management Information Systems	M,O
Mathematics Education	M
Mathematics	M
Meteorology	M,O
Middle School Education	M,O
Music Education	M,D,O
Music	M,D,O
Natural Resources	M,O
Neuroscience	M,D,O
Nursing Education	M,D,O
Nursing—General	M,D,O
Nutrition	M
Photography	M
Physical Education	M
Physics	M
Physiology	M
Political Science	M
Psychology—General	M
Public Administration	M,O
Quantitative Analysis	M
Reading Education	M,D,O
Rehabilitation Counseling	M,D
Rhetoric	M,D
School Psychology	M,D,O
Secondary Education	M
Social Psychology	M
Sociology	M
Special Education	M,D,O
Speech and Interpersonal Communication	M
Sport Psychology	M
Sports Management	M
Statistics	M
Telecommunications	M
Urban and Regional Planning	M,O
Urban Design	M
Writing	M,D

BANK STREET COLLEGE OF EDUCATION

Child and Family Studies	M
Early Childhood Education	M
Education—General	M
Educational Leadership and Administration	M
Elementary Education	M
Foundations and Philosophy of Education	M
Maternal and Child Health	M
Mathematics Education	M
Multilingual and Multicultural Education	M
Museum Education	M
Reading Education	M
Special Education	M

BAPTIST BIBLE COLLEGE

Cultural Studies	M
Pastoral Ministry and Counseling	M
Theology	M

THE BAPTIST COLLEGE OF FLORIDA

Music	M
Pastoral Ministry and Counseling	M
Religion	M
Theology	M

BAPTIST MISSIONARY ASSOCIATION THEOLOGICAL SEMINARY

Theology	M

BAPTIST THEOLOGICAL SEMINARY AT RICHMOND

Conflict Resolution and Mediation/Peace Studies	M,D,O
Pastoral Ministry and Counseling	M,D,O
Religion	M,D,O
Religious Education	M,D,O
Theology	M,D,O

BARCLAY COLLEGE

Theology	M

BARD COLLEGE

Art/Fine Arts	M
Atmospheric Sciences	M,O
Economics	M
Education—General	M
Environmental Management and Policy	M,O
Museum Studies	M
Music	M,O
Photography	M
Sustainability Management	M,O

BARD GRADUATE CENTER: DECORATIVE ARTS, DESIGN HISTORY, MATERIAL CULTURE

Art History	M,D*
Decorative Arts	M,D

BARRY UNIVERSITY

Accounting	M
Acute Care/Critical Care Nursing	M,O
Anatomy	M
Art/Fine Arts	M
Athletic Training and Sports Medicine	M
Biological and Biomedical Sciences—General	M
Business Administration and Management—General	M,O
Clinical Psychology	M,O
Communication Disorders	M
Communication—General	M,O
Corporate and Organizational Communication	M,O
Counselor Education	M,D,O
Curriculum and Instruction	D,O
Distance Education Development	O
Early Childhood Education	M,D,O
Education of the Gifted	M,D,O
Education—General	M,D,O
Educational Leadership and Administration	M,D,O
Educational Media/Instructional Technology	M,D,O
Elementary Education	M,D,O
English as a Second Language	M,D,O
Exercise and Sports Science	M
Family Nurse Practitioner Studies	M,O
Finance and Banking	O
Health Informatics	O
Health Services Management and Hospital Administration	M,O
Higher Education	M,D
Human Resources Development	M,D
Human Resources Management	O
Information Science	M
International Business	O
Kinesiology and Movement Studies	M
Law	D
Liberal Studies	M
Management Information Systems	O
Marketing	O
Marriage and Family Therapy	M,O
Nurse Anesthesia	M
Nursing and Healthcare Administration	M,D,O
Nursing Education	M,O
Nursing—General	M,D,O
Occupational Therapy	M
Pastoral Ministry and Counseling	M,D
Photography	M
Physician Assistant Studies	M
Podiatric Medicine	D
Psychology—General	M,O
Public Administration	M
Public Health—General	
Reading Education	M,D,O
Rehabilitation Counseling	M,O
School Psychology	M,O
Social Work	M,D
Special Education	M,D,O
Sport Psychology	M
Sports Management	M
Theology	M,D

BARTON COLLEGE

Elementary Education	M

BARUCH COLLEGE OF THE CITY UNIVERSITY OF NEW YORK

Accounting	M,D
Arts Administration	M
Business Administration and Management—General	M,D,O
Corporate and Organizational Communication	M
Counseling Psychology	M
Economics	M
Educational Leadership and Administration	M,O
Entrepreneurship	M,D
Finance and Banking	M,D
Financial Engineering	M
Health Services Management and Hospital Administration	M
Higher Education	M
Human Resources Management	M,D
Industrial and Labor Relations	M
Industrial and Manufacturing Management	M,D
Industrial and Organizational Psychology	M,D
International Business	M,D
Management Information Systems	M,D
Marketing	M,D
Nonprofit Management	M
Organizational Behavior	M,D
Public Administration	M
Public Policy	M
Quantitative Analysis	M
Real Estate	M
Statistics	M
Sustainability Management	M,D
Taxation	M

BASTYR UNIVERSITY

Acupuncture and Oriental Medicine	M,D,O
Counseling Psychology	M,O
Environmental Design	M,O
Health Psychology	M,O
Landscape Architecture	M,O
Naturopathic Medicine	D
Nurse Midwifery	M,O
Nutrition	M,O

BAYAMÓN CENTRAL UNIVERSITY

Accounting	M
Business Administration and Management—General	M
Counselor Education	M,O
Early Childhood Education	M,O
Education—General	M,O
Educational Leadership and Administration	M,O
Elementary Education	M,O
Finance and Banking	M
Industrial and Organizational Psychology	M
Marketing	M
Marriage and Family Therapy	M,O
Rehabilitation Counseling	M,O
Special Education	M,O

BAYLOR COLLEGE OF MEDICINE

Allopathic Medicine	D
Biochemistry	D
Bioengineering	D
Biological and Biomedical Sciences—General	M,D
Biomedical Engineering	D
Biophysics	D
Cancer Biology/Oncology	D
Cardiovascular Sciences	D
Cell Biology	D
Clinical Laboratory Sciences/Medical Technology	M,D
Computational Biology	D
Developmental Biology	D
Genetics	D
Human Genetics	D
Immunology	D
Microbiology	D
Molecular Biology	D
Molecular Biophysics	D
Molecular Medicine	D
Molecular Physiology	D
Neuroscience	D
Nurse Anesthesia	D
Pathology	D
Pharmacology	D
Physician Assistant Studies	M
Structural Biology	D
Translational Biology	D
Virology	D

BAYLOR UNIVERSITY

Accounting	M
Allied Health—General	M,D
American Studies	M
Applied Behavior Analysis	M,D,O
Biological and Biomedical Sciences—General	M,D
Biomedical Engineering	M,D
Business Administration and Management—General	M,D
Chemistry	M,D
Clinical Psychology	D
Communication Disorders	M
Communication—General	M
Community Health	M,D
Computer Engineering	M,D
Computer Science	M,D
Criminal Justice and Criminology	D
Cultural Studies	M,D
Curriculum and Instruction	M,D
Ecology	D
Economics	M
Education—General	M,D,O
Educational Leadership and Administration	M,O
Educational Measurement and Evaluation	M,D,O
Educational Psychology	M,D,O
Electrical Engineering	M,D
Emergency Medical Services	D
English	M,D
Environmental Biology	M,D
Environmental Law	D
Environmental Management and Policy	M
Environmental Sciences	D
Exercise and Sports Science	M,D
Family Nurse Practitioner Studies	M,D
Geosciences	M,D
Health Education	M,D
Health Law	D
Health Promotion	M,D
Health Services Management and Hospital Administration	M
History	M,D
Intellectual Property Law	D
Interdisciplinary Studies	D
International Affairs	M,D
Journalism	M
Kinesiology and Movement Studies	M,D
Law	D
Limnology	M,D
Management Information Systems	M,D
Maternal and Child/Neonatal Nursing	M,D
Mathematics	M,D
Mechanical Engineering	M,D
Museum Studies	M
Music	M,D
Nurse Midwifery	M,D
Nursing—General	M,D
Nutrition	M

Philosophy	M,D
Physical Education	M,D
Physical Therapy	D
Physics	M,D
Political Science	M,D
Psychology—General	M,D
Public Administration	M,D
Public Policy	M,D
Real Estate	D
Religion	M,D
School Psychology	M,D,O
Social Work	M,D
Sociology	M,D
Spanish	M
Special Education	M,D,O
Statistics	M,D
Theater	M
Theology	M,D
Western European Studies	M,D

BAY PATH UNIVERSITY

Accounting	M
Clinical Psychology	M
Communication—General	M
Computer and Information Systems Security	M
Counseling Psychology	M
Developmental Psychology	M
Educational Leadership and Administration	M
Educational Media/Instructional Technology	M
Entrepreneurship	M
Forensic Sciences	M
Genetic Counseling	M
Higher Education	M
Management Information Systems	M
Management Strategy and Policy	M
Nonprofit Management	M
Occupational Therapy	M
Physician Assistant Studies	M
Special Education	
Writing	M

BECKER COLLEGE

Counseling Psychology	M
Counselor Education	M
Social Psychology	M

BELHAVEN UNIVERSITY (MS)

Business Administration and Management—General	M
Education—General	M
Educational Media/Instructional Technology	M
Elementary Education	M
Health Services Management and Hospital Administration	M
Human Resources Management	M
Multilingual and Multicultural Education	M
Public Administration	M
Reading Education	M
Secondary Education	M
Sports Management	M

BELLARMINE UNIVERSITY

Business Administration and Management—General	M
Communication—General	M
Education—General	M,D,O
Educational Leadership and Administration	M,D,O
Elementary Education	M,D,O
Family Nurse Practitioner Studies	M,D
Management Strategy and Policy	M
Middle School Education	M,D,O
Nursing and Healthcare Administration	M,D
Nursing Education	M,D
Nursing—General	M,D
Physical Therapy	M,D
Reading Education	M,D,O
Religion	M
Secondary Education	M,D,O
Special Education	M,D,O

BELLEVUE UNIVERSITY

Business Administration and Management—General	M,D
Corporate and Organizational Communication	M
Counselor Education	M
Criminal Justice and Criminology	M
Educational Media/Instructional Technology	M
Finance and Banking	M,D
Health Services Management and Hospital Administration	M
Human Resources Management	M,D
Human Services	M
Information Science	M
Management Information Systems	M
Military and Defense Studies	M
National Security	M
Organizational Management	M
Project Management	M
Public Administration	M

BELLIN COLLEGE

Family Nurse Practitioner Studies	M
Nursing Education	M
Nursing—General	M

BELMONT UNIVERSITY

Accounting	M
Allied Health—General	M,D
Business Administration and Management—General	M
Health Services Management and Hospital Administration	M
Law	D
Nursing—General	M,D
Occupational Therapy	M,D
Pharmacy	D
Physical Therapy	M,D

BEMIDJI STATE UNIVERSITY

Biological and Biomedical Sciences—General	M
Education—General	M
English	M
Environmental Management and Policy	M
Mathematics Education	M
Mathematics	M
Special Education	M

BENEDICTINE COLLEGE

Business Administration and Management—General	M
Education—General	M
Educational Leadership and Administration	M

BENEDICTINE UNIVERSITY

Accounting	M
Business Administration and Management—General	M
Clinical Psychology	M
Computer and Information Systems Security	M
Curriculum and Instruction	M
Education—General	M
Educational Leadership and Administration	M,D
Elementary Education	M
Emergency Management	M
Entrepreneurship	M
Exercise and Sports Science	M
Finance and Banking	M
Health Education	M
Health Informatics	M
Health Promotion	M
Health Services Management and Hospital Administration	M
Higher Education	D
Human Resources Management	M
International Business	M
Logistics	M
Management Information Systems	M
Marketing	M
Nursing—General	M
Nutrition	M
Organizational Behavior	M
Organizational Management	M,D
Public Health—General	M
Reading Education	M
Science Education	M
Secondary Education	M
Special Education	M
Women's Studies	M

BENNINGTON COLLEGE

Allied Health—General	O
Dance	M
Music	M
Writing	M

BENTLEY UNIVERSITY

Accounting	M,D
Business Administration and Management—General	M,D,O
Ergonomics and Human Factors	M
Finance and Banking	M
Information Science	M
Management Strategy and Policy	O
Marketing	M
Taxation	M

BERGIN UNIVERSITY OF CANINE STUDIES

Animal Sciences	M

BERKELEY COLLEGE–WOODLAND PARK CAMPUS

Business Administration and Management—General	M

BERKLEE COLLEGE OF MUSIC

Entertainment Management	M
Music	M,O
Theater	M,O
Therapies—Dance, Drama, and Music	M

BERRY COLLEGE

Business Administration and Management—General	M
Curriculum and Instruction	M,O
Early Childhood Education	M
Education—General	M,O
Educational Leadership and Administration	O
Middle School Education	M
Reading Education	M
Secondary Education	M

BETHANY COLLEGE

Education—General	M

BETHANY THEOLOGICAL SEMINARY

Conflict Resolution and Mediation/Peace Studies	M,O
Pastoral Ministry and Counseling	M,O
Religion	M,O
Theology	M,O

BETHEL COLLEGE

Business Administration and Management—General	M
Education—General	M
Nursing—General	M
Pastoral Ministry and Counseling	M
Theology	M

BETHEL SEMINARY

Classics	M,D,O
Marriage and Family Therapy	M,D,O
Near and Middle Eastern Languages	M,D,O
Pastoral Ministry and Counseling	M,D,O
Religion	M,D,O
Theology	M,D,O

BETHEL UNIVERSITY (MN)

Business Administration and Management—General	M,D,O
Communication—General	M,D,O
Counseling Psychology	M,D,O
Developmental Psychology	M,D,O
Education—General	M,D,O
Educational Leadership and Administration	M,D,O
Elementary Education	M,D,O
Gerontology	M,D,O
Mathematics Education	M,D,O
Nurse Midwifery	M,D,O
Nursing Education	M,D,O
Nursing—General	M,D,O
Organizational Management	M,D,O
Physician Assistant Studies	M,D,O
Reading Education	M,D,O
Science Education	M,D,O
Secondary Education	M,D,O
Special Education	M,D,O

BETHEL UNIVERSITY (TN)

Business Administration and Management—General	M
Conflict Resolution and Mediation/Peace Studies	M
Educational Leadership and Administration	M
Physician Assistant Studies	M

BETHESDA UNIVERSITY

Music	M
Religion	M
Theology	M

BETH HAMEDRASH SHAAREI YOSHER INSTITUTE

Theology	

BETH HATALMUD RABBINICAL COLLEGE

Theology	

BETH MEDRASH GOVOHA

Theology	

BETHUNE-COOKMAN UNIVERSITY

Theology	M

BEULAH HEIGHTS UNIVERSITY

Religion	M

BEXLEY HALL EPISCOPAL SEMINARY

Theology	M

BIBLICAL THEOLOGICAL SEMINARY

Missions and Missiology	M,D,O
Pastoral Ministry and Counseling	M,D,O
Theology	M,D,O

BINGHAMTON UNIVERSITY, STATE UNIVERSITY OF NEW YORK

Accounting	M
Analytical Chemistry	M,D
Anthropology	M,D
Applied Physics	M,D
Applied Statistics	M,D
Art History	M,D
Asian Studies	M,O
Asian-American Studies	M,O
Biological and Biomedical Sciences—General	M,D
Biomedical Engineering	M,D
Biopsychology	D
Business Administration and Management—General	M,D
Chemistry	M,D
Clinical Psychology	D
Cognitive Sciences	D
Comparative Literature	M,D
Computer Science	M,D
Cultural Studies	M,D
Early Childhood Education	M
Economics	M,D
Education—General	M,D,O
Educational Leadership and Administration	M,D,O
Electrical Engineering	M,D
Engineering and Applied Sciences—General	M,D*
English as a Second Language	M
English Education	M
English	M,D
Environmental Sciences	M,D
Foreign Languages Education	M
Foundations and Philosophy of Education	M,D,O
French	M
Geography	M
Geology	M,D
Health Services Management and Hospital Administration	M,D
History	M,D
Industrial/Management Engineering	M,D
Inorganic Chemistry	M,D
Italian	M
Legal and Justice Studies	M,D
Materials Engineering	M,D
Materials Sciences	M,D
Mathematics Education	M
Mathematics	M,D
Mechanical Engineering	M,D
Music	M
Nursing—General	M,D,O
Organic Chemistry	M,D
Philosophy	M,D
Physical Chemistry	M,D
Physics	M,D
Political Science	M,D
Psychology—General	D
Public Administration	M
Reading Education	M
Science Education	M
Secondary Education	M
Social Sciences Education	M
Social Work	M
Sociology	M,D
Spanish	M
Special Education	M
Student Affairs	M
Sustainable Development	M
Systems Science	M,D
Theater	M
Translation and Interpretation	D,O
Writing	M,D

BIOLA UNIVERSITY

Anthropology	M,D,O
Business Administration and Management—General	M
Clinical Psychology	D
Communication Disorders	M,O
Cultural Studies	M,D,O
Curriculum and Instruction	M,O
Early Childhood Education	M,O
Education—General	M,O
English as a Second Language	M,D,O
Jewish Studies	M,D,O
Linguistics	M,D,O
Missions and Missiology	M,D,O
Pastoral Ministry and Counseling	M,D,O
Psychology—General	D
Religion	M,D,O
Religious Education	M,D,O
Science Education	M,O
Special Education	M,O
Theology	M,D,O

BISHOP'S UNIVERSITY

Education—General	M,O
English as a Second Language	M,O

BLACK HILLS STATE UNIVERSITY

Business Administration and Management—General	M
Curriculum and Instruction	M
Genomic Sciences	M
Management Strategy and Policy	M

BLESSING-RIEMAN COLLEGE OF NURSING

Nursing—General	M

BLESSING–RIEMAN COLLEGE OF NURSING AND HEALTH SCIENCES

Nursing and Healthcare Administration	M
Nursing Education	M
Nursing—General	M

BLOOMFIELD COLLEGE

Accounting	M

BLOOMSBURG UNIVERSITY OF PENNSYLVANIA

Accounting	M
Adult Nursing	M
Athletic Training and Sports Medicine	M
Biological and Biomedical Sciences—General	M
Business Administration and Management—General	M
Business Education	M
Communication Disorders	M,D
Community Health	M
Counselor Education	M
Curriculum and Instruction	M,O
Early Childhood Education	M
Education—General	M,O
Educational Media/Instructional Technology	M,O
Elementary Education	M
English Education	M
Exercise and Sports Science	M
Family Nurse Practitioner Studies	M
Mathematics Education	M
Middle School Education	M
Nurse Anesthesia	M
Nursing and Healthcare Administration	M
Nursing—General	M
Reading Education	M
Science Education	M
Secondary Education	M
Social Sciences Education	M
Special Education	M,O
Student Affairs	M

BLUEFIELD COLLEGE

Education—General	M

BLUE MOUNTAIN COLLEGE

Elementary Education	M
Reading Education	M

BLUFFTON UNIVERSITY

Accounting	M
Business Administration and Management—General	M
Curriculum and Instruction	M
Education—General	M
Finance and Banking	M
Health Services Management and Hospital Administration	M
Industrial and Manufacturing Management	M
Organizational Management	M

*M—masters degree; D—doctorate; O—other advanced degree; *—Close-Up and/or Display*

Reading Education	M
Special Education	M
Sports Management	M

BOB JONES UNIVERSITY

Accounting	M,D,O
Art/Fine Arts	M,D,O
Business Administration and Management—General	M,D,O
Counselor Education	M,D,O
Curriculum and Instruction	M,D,O
Educational Leadership and Administration	M,D,O
Elementary Education	M,D,O
English Education	M,D,O
English	M,D,O
Film, Television, and Video Production	M,D,O
Graphic Design	M,D,O
History	M,D,O
Illustration	M,D,O
Journalism	M,D,O
Mathematics Education	M,D,O
Media Studies	M,D,O
Music Education	M,D,O
Music	M,D,O
Pastoral Ministry and Counseling	M,D,O
Religion	M,D,O
Rhetoric	M,D,O
Secondary Education	M,D,O
Social Sciences Education	M,D,O
Special Education	M,D,O
Speech and Interpersonal Communication	M,D,O
Student Affairs	M,D,O
Theater	M,D,O
Theology	M,D,O

BOISE STATE UNIVERSITY

Accounting	M
Animal Sciences	M,D
Anthropology	M
Art Education	M
Art/Fine Arts	M
Biological and Biomedical Sciences—General	M,D
Business Administration and Management—General	M
Chemistry	M
Civil Engineering	M
Communication—General	M
Computer Engineering	M,D
Computer Science	M,O
Counselor Education	M,O
Criminal Justice and Criminology	M
Curriculum and Instruction	M,D
Distance Education Development	M,D,O
Early Childhood Education	M
Education—General	M,D,O
Educational Leadership and Administration	M,D
Educational Media/Instructional Technology	M,D,O
Electrical Engineering	M,D
Engineering and Applied Sciences—General	M,D,O
English as a Second Language	M
English Education	M
Environmental and Occupational Health	M,O
Geophysics	M,D
Gerontological Nursing	M,D,O
Health Promotion	M,O
History	M
Hydrology	M,D
Interdisciplinary Studies	M
Kinesiology and Movement Studies	M
Materials Engineering	M,D
Mathematics Education	M,O
Mathematics	M
Mechanical Engineering	M
Molecular Biology	M,D
Multilingual and Multicultural Education	M
Music Education	M
Music	M
Natural Resources	M,D,O
Nursing—General	M,D,O
Organizational Management	M,O
Political Science	M
Public Administration	M,D,O
Public Health—General	M,D,O
Public Policy	M,D,O
Reading Education	M
Rhetoric	M
Science Education	M,D,O
Social Work	M
Special Education	M
Sports Management	M
Taxation	M
Technical Communication	M
Writing	M

BORICUA COLLEGE

English as a Second Language	M
Human Services	M
Latin American Studies	M

BOSTON ARCHITECTURAL COLLEGE

Architecture	M
Historic Preservation	M
Interior Design	M
Landscape Architecture	M
Sustainable Development	M

BOSTON COLLEGE

Accounting	M
Adult Nursing	M,D
Applied Psychology	M,D
Biochemistry	M,D
Biological and Biomedical Sciences—General	D
Business Administration and Management—General	M
Chemistry	M,D
Classics	M
Counseling Psychology	M,D
Curriculum and Instruction	M,D,O
Developmental Psychology	M,D
East European and Russian Studies	M
Economics	D
Education—General	M,D,O*
Educational Leadership and Administration	M,D,O
Educational Measurement and Evaluation	M,D
Educational Psychology	M,D
Elementary Education	M
English	M,D
Finance and Banking	M,D
Forensic Nursing	M,D
French	M
Geology	M
Geophysics	M
Gerontological Nursing	M,D
Higher Education	M,D
History	M,D
Inorganic Chemistry	M,D
Italian	M
Law	D
Linguistics	M
Maternal and Child/Neonatal Nursing	M,D
Mathematics	D
Nurse Anesthesia	M,D
Nursing—General	M,D
Organic Chemistry	M,D
Organizational Behavior	D
Organizational Management	D
Pastoral Ministry and Counseling	M,D,O
Pediatric Nursing	M,D
Philosophy	M,D
Physical Chemistry	M,D
Physics	M,D
Political Science	M,D
Psychiatric Nursing	M,D
Psychology—General	D
Reading Education	M,O
Religious Education	M,D,O
Russian	M
Science Education	M,D
Secondary Education	M
Social Work	M,D
Sociology	M,D
Spanish	M
Special Education	M,O
Theology	M,D,O
Western European Studies	M,D
Women's Health Nursing	M,D

BOSTON GRADUATE SCHOOL OF PSYCHOANALYSIS

Counseling Psychology	M
Developmental Psychology	O
Psychoanalysis and Psychotherapy	M,D,O
Psychology—General	M

BOSTON UNIVERSITY

Actuarial Science	M
Advertising and Public Relations	M
African-American Studies	M
Allied Health—General	M,D
Allopathic Medicine	D
American Studies	D
Anatomy	M,D
Anthropology	M,D
Archaeology	M,D
Art Education	M
Art History	M,D,O
Art/Fine Arts	M
Arts Administration	M,O
Astronomy	M,D
Athletic Training and Sports Medicine	D
Biochemistry	M,D
Bioinformatics	M,D
Biological and Biomedical Sciences—General	M,D
Biomedical Engineering	M,D
Biophysics	M,D
Biopsychology	M
Biostatistics	M,D
Business Administration and Management—General	M,D
Cell Biology	M,D
Chemistry	M,D
Classics	M,D
Clinical Research	M
Communication Disorders	M,D
Communication—General	M,D
Community Health	M,D
Computer and Information Systems Security	M,D,O
Computer Engineering	M,D,O
Computer Science	M,D,O
Corporate and Organizational Communication	M
Counseling Psychology	M
Criminal Justice and Criminology	M
Cultural Studies	M
Database Systems	M,O
Dental Hygiene	M,D,O
Economics	M,D
Education—General	M,D,O
Electrical Engineering	M,D
Emergency Management	M
Energy Management and Policy	M,D
Engineering and Applied Sciences—General	M,D
English	M,D
Environmental and Occupational Health	M,D
Environmental Management and Policy	M,D
Environmental Sciences	M,D
Epidemiology	M,D
Film, Television, and Video Production	M
Finance and Banking	M
Food Science and Technology	M
Forensic Sciences	M
French	M,D
Genetic Counseling	M
Genetics	D
Genomic Sciences	D
Geographic Information Systems	M,D
Geography	M,D
Geosciences	M,D
Graphic Design	M
Health Communication	M
Health Informatics	M,O
Health Services Management and Hospital Administration	M,D
Hispanic and Latin American Languages	M,D
Historic Preservation	M
History	M,D
Immunology	D
Intellectual Property Law	M,D
International Affairs	M*
International Business	M,D
International Development	M,D
International Health	M,D
Internet and Interactive Multimedia	M,O
Journalism	M
Latin American Studies	M
Law	M,D
Linguistics	M
Management Information Systems	M,O
Management of Technology	M
Management Strategy and Policy	M,O
Manufacturing Engineering	M,D
Marketing	M
Mass Communication	M
Materials Engineering	M,D
Materials Sciences	M,D
Mathematical and Computational Finance	M,D
Mathematics	M,D
Mechanical Engineering	M,D
Media Studies	M,D
Medical Imaging	M
Molecular Biology	M,D
Molecular Medicine	D
Museum Studies	M,D,O
Music Education	M,D
Music	M,D,O
Neurobiology	M,D
Neuroscience	D
Nutrition	M,D
Occupational Therapy	D
Oral and Dental Sciences	M,D,O
Organizational Management	M
Pathology	D
Pharmaceutical Sciences	M,D
Pharmacology	M,D
Philosophy	M,D
Photonics	M,D
Physical Therapy	D
Physician Assistant Studies	M
Physics	D
Physiology	M,D
Political Science	M,D
Project Management	M,O
Psychology—General	M,D
Public Health—General	M,D,O
Rehabilitation Sciences	D
Religion	M,D
Romance Languages	M,D
Social Work	M,D
Sociology	M,D
Systems Engineering	M,D
Taxation	M,D
Telecommunications Management	M,O
Telecommunications	M,O
Theater	M,O
Theology	M,D
Urban and Regional Planning	M
Urban Studies	M
Writing	M,D

BOWIE STATE UNIVERSITY

Applied Mathematics	M
Business Administration and Management—General	M
Computer Science	M,D
Corporate and Organizational Communication	M,O
Counseling Psychology	M
Counselor Education	M
Education—General	M
Educational Leadership and Administration	M,D
Elementary Education	M
English	M
Family Nurse Practitioner Studies	M
Human Resources Development	M
Management Information Systems	M,O
Nursing and Healthcare Administration	M
Nursing Education	M
Nursing—General	M
Public Administration	M
Reading Education	M
Secondary Education	M
Special Education	M

BOWLING GREEN STATE UNIVERSITY

Accounting	M
American Studies	M,D
Applied Arts and Design—General	M
Applied Statistics	M,D
Art Education	M
Art History	M
Art/Fine Arts	M
Biological and Biomedical Sciences—General	M,D
Business Administration and Management—General	M
Business Education	M
Chemistry	M,D
Child and Family Studies	M
Clinical Psychology	M,D
Communication Disorders	M,D
Communication—General	M,D
Computer Art and Design	M
Computer Science	M
Construction Management	M
Counseling Psychology	M
Counselor Education	M
Criminal Justice and Criminology	M
Curriculum and Instruction	M
Demography and Population Studies	M,D
Developmental Psychology	M,D
Early Childhood Education	M
Economics	M
Education of the Gifted	M
Educational Leadership and Administration	M,D,O
Educational Media/Instructional Technology	M
English	M,D
Experimental Psychology	M,D
Family and Consumer Sciences-General	M
Film, Television, and Video Production	M,D
Foreign Languages Education	M
French	M
Geology	M
Geophysics	M
German	M
Graphic Design	M
Higher Education	D
History	M,D
Human Development	M
Industrial and Organizational Psychology	M,D
Interdisciplinary Studies	M,D
International and Comparative Education	M
Kinesiology and Movement Studies	M
Leisure Studies	M
Manufacturing Engineering	M
Mathematics Education	M,D
Mathematics	M,D
Music Education	M,D
Music	M,D
Nutrition	M
Operations Research	M
Organizational Management	M
Philosophy	M,D
Physics	M
Political Science	
Psychology—General	M,D
Public Administration	M
Public Health—General	M
Reading Education	M,O
Recreation and Park Management	M
Rehabilitation Counseling	M
Rhetoric	M,D
School Psychology	M,O
Science Education	M
Social Psychology	M,D
Sociology	M,D
Software Engineering	M
Spanish	M
Special Education	M
Speech and Interpersonal Communication	M,D
Sports Management	M
Statistics	M,D
Student Affairs	M
Technical Communication	M,D
Theater	M,D
Vocational and Technical Education	M
Writing	M,D

BRADLEY UNIVERSITY

Accounting	M
Art/Fine Arts	M
Biochemistry	M
Biological and Biomedical Sciences—General	M
Business Administration and Management—General	M
Chemistry	M
Civil Engineering	M
Clinical Psychology	M
Comparative and Interdisciplinary Arts	M
Computer Science	M
Construction Engineering	M
Counseling Psychology	M
Counselor Education	M
Curriculum and Instruction	M,O
Education—General	M,D,O
Educational Leadership and Administration	M
Electrical Engineering	M
Engineering and Applied Sciences—General	M
English	M
Human Development	M
Industrial/Management Engineering	M
Information Science	M
Manufacturing Engineering	M
Mechanical Engineering	M
Nonprofit Management	M
Nursing and Healthcare Administration	M,D,O
Nursing Education	M,D,O
Nursing—General	M,D,O
Photography	M
Physical Therapy	D

BRANDEIS UNIVERSITY

Anthropology	M,D
Biochemistry	D
Bioinformatics	M
Biological and Biomedical Sciences—General	M,D,O
Biophysics	D
Biotechnology	M

Business Administration and Management—General	M
Cell Biology	M,D
Chemistry	M,D
Child and Family Studies	M,D
Classics	M
Cognitive Sciences	M,D
Communication—General	M
Computer and Information Systems Security	M
Computer Science	M
Conflict Resolution and Mediation/Peace Studies	M
Developmental Psychology	M,D
Disability Studies	D
Distance Education Development	M
Economics	M,D
Educational Leadership and Administration	M,O
Educational Measurement and Evaluation	O
Elementary Education	M,O
English	M,D
Finance and Banking	M,D
Gender Studies	M,D
Genetic Counseling	M
Genetics	M,D
Health Education	D
Health Informatics	M
Health Services Management and Hospital Administration	M
History	M,D
Human Services	M
Human-Computer Interaction	M
Humanities	M
Inorganic Chemistry	M,D
International Affairs	M
International Business	M,D
International Health	M,D
Internet and Interactive Multimedia	M
Jewish Studies	M,D
Linguistics	M
Management Information Systems	M
Management Strategy and Policy	M
Marketing	M
Mathematics	M,D,O
Medical Informatics	M
Microbiology	M,D
Molecular Biology	M,D
Music	M,D
Near and Middle Eastern Languages	M,D
Near and Middle Eastern Studies	M,D
Neurobiology	M,D
Neuroscience	M,D
Nonprofit Management	M
Organic Chemistry	M,D
Philosophy	M
Physical Chemistry	M,D
Physics	M,D
Political Science	M,D
Project Management	M
Psychology—General	M,D
Public Policy	M
Real Estate	M
Religious Education	M,O
Secondary Education	M,O
Social Psychology	M,D
Sociology	M,D
Software Engineering	M
Sustainability Management	M
Sustainable Development	M
Theater	M
Women's Studies	M,D

BRANDMAN UNIVERSITY

Business Administration and Management—General	M
Counseling Psychology	M
Counselor Education	M
Education—General	M
Educational Leadership and Administration	M
Emergency Management	M
Health Communication	M
Health Services Management and Hospital Administration	M
Human Resources Management	M
Marriage and Family Therapy	M
Organizational Management	M
Psychology—General	M
Public Administration	M
Special Education	M

BRANDON UNIVERSITY

Counselor Education	M,O
Curriculum and Instruction	M,O
Education—General	M,O
Educational Leadership and Administration	M,O
Music Education	M
Music	M
Rural Planning and Studies	M,O
Special Education	M,O

BRENAU UNIVERSITY

Accounting	M
Business Administration and Management—General	M
Early Childhood Education	M,O
Education—General	M,O
Family Nurse Practitioner Studies	M
Health Services Management and Hospital Administration	M
Interior Design	M
Middle School Education	M,O
Nursing and Healthcare Administration	M
Nursing Education	M
Occupational Therapy	M
Organizational Management	M
Project Management	M
Psychology—General	M
Secondary Education	M,O
Special Education	M,O

BRESCIA UNIVERSITY

Business Administration and Management—General	M
Curriculum and Instruction	M

BRIAR CLIFF UNIVERSITY

Human Resources Management	M
Nursing—General	M

BRIDGEWATER STATE UNIVERSITY

Accounting	M
Art Education	M
Business Administration and Management—General	M
Computer Science	M
Counselor Education	M,O
Criminal Justice and Criminology	M
Early Childhood Education	M
Education—General	M,O
Educational Leadership and Administration	M,O
Educational Media/Instructional Technology	M
Elementary Education	M
English	M
Finance and Banking	M
Health Promotion	M
Mathematics Education	M
Physical Education	M
Psychology—General	M
Public Administration	M
Reading Education	M,O
Science Education	M
Secondary Education	M
Social Sciences Education	M
Social Work	M
Special Education	M

BRIERCREST SEMINARY

Business Administration and Management—General	M
Marriage and Family Therapy	M
Missions and Missiology	M
Organizational Management	M
Pastoral Ministry and Counseling	M
Religion	M
Theology	M

BRIGHAM YOUNG UNIVERSITY

Agricultural Sciences—General	M,D
Analytical Chemistry	M,D
Animal Sciences	M,D
Anthropology	M
Applied Statistics	M
Art Education	M
Art/Fine Arts	M
Astronomy	M,D
Athletic Training and Sports Medicine	M,D
Biochemistry	M,D
Biological and Biomedical Sciences—General	M,D
Biotechnology	M,D
Business Administration and Management—General	M
Chemical Engineering	M,D
Chemistry	M,D
Child and Family Studies	M,D
Civil Engineering	M,D
Classics	M
Clinical Psychology	D
Communication Disorders	M
Communication—General	M
Comparative and Interdisciplinary Arts	M
Comparative Literature	M
Computer Engineering	M,D
Computer Science	M,D
Construction Management	M
Counseling Psychology	M,D,O
Developmental Biology	M,D
Education—General	M,D,O
Educational Leadership and Administration	M,D
Educational Media/Instructional Technology	M,D
Educational Psychology	M,D
Electrical Engineering	M,D
Engineering and Applied Sciences—General	M,D
English as a Second Language	M
English	M
Entrepreneurship	M
Environmental Sciences	M,D
Exercise and Sports Science	M,D
Family Nurse Practitioner Studies	M
Film, Television, and Video Production	M
Finance and Banking	M
Fish, Game, and Wildlife Management	M,D
Food Science and Technology	M
Foreign Languages Education	M
Foundations and Philosophy of Education	M,D
French	M
Geology	M
Health Education	M
Health Promotion	M,D
Hispanic and Latin American Languages	M
Human Development	M,D
Human Resources Management	M
Humanities	M
Industrial Design	M
Information Science	M
International Affairs	M
Law	M,D
Linguistics	M
Marketing	M
Marriage and Family Therapy	M,D
Mass Communication	M
Mathematics Education	M
Mathematics	M,D
Mechanical Engineering	M,D
Microbiology	M,D
Molecular Biology	M,D
Music Education	M
Music	M
Neuroscience	M,D
Nonprofit Management	M
Nursing—General	M
Nutrition	M
Organizational Behavior	M
Physical Education	M
Physics	M,D
Physiology	M,D
Plant Sciences	M,D
Political Science	M
Portuguese	M
Psychology—General	D
Public Administration	M
Reading Education	M
Religious Education	M
Rhetoric	M
School Psychology	M,D,O
Science Education	M,D
Slavic Languages	D
Social Work	M
Sociology	M
Spanish	M
Special Education	M,D,O
Statistics	M
Supply Chain Management	M
Theater	M
Writing	M

BRISTOL UNIVERSITY

Business Administration and Management—General	M
International Business	M
Marketing	M
Sports Management	M

BRITE DIVINITY SCHOOL

Pastoral Ministry and Counseling	M,D,O
Theology	M,D,O

BROADVIEW UNIVERSITY–WEST JORDAN

Business Administration and Management—General	M
Health Services Management and Hospital Administration	M
Management Information Systems	M

BROCK UNIVERSITY

Accounting	M
Allied Health—General	M,D
Biological and Biomedical Sciences—General	M,D
Biotechnology	M,D
Business Administration and Management—General	M
Chemistry	M,D
Child and Family Studies	M
Classics	M
Comparative Literature	M
Computer Science	M
Cultural Studies	M
Disability Studies	M,O
Economics	M
Education—General	M,D
English as a Second Language	M
English	M
Geography	M
Geosciences	M
History	M
Human Development	M,D
International Affairs	M
Legal and Justice Studies	M
Mathematics	M
Neuroscience	M,D
Philosophy	M
Physics	M
Political Science	M
Psychology—General	M,D
Public Policy	M
Social Psychology	M,D
Sociology	M
Statistics	M

BROOKLYN COLLEGE OF THE CITY UNIVERSITY OF NEW YORK

Accounting	M
Art Education	M
Art History	M
Art/Fine Arts	M
Arts Administration	M
Biological and Biomedical Sciences—General	M
Business Administration and Management—General	M
Chemistry	M,D
Communication Disorders	M,D
Community Health	M
Computer Science	M,O
Counseling Psychology	M,D,O
Counselor Education	M
Early Childhood Education	M,O
Economics	M
Education—General	M,O
Educational Leadership and Administration	M
Elementary Education	M,O
English Education	M
English	M
Environmental Education	M
Exercise and Sports Science	M
Experimental Psychology	M,D
Film, Television, and Video Production	M
Finance and Banking	M
Foreign Languages Education	M
French	M
Geology	M,D
Geosciences	M
Health Informatics	M,O
Health Services Management and Hospital Administration	M
History	M
Industrial and Organizational Psychology	M,D
Information Science	M,O
International Affairs	M
International Business	M
Internet and Interactive Multimedia	M
Jewish Studies	M
Kinesiology and Movement Studies	M
Liberal Studies	M
Mathematics Education	M
Mathematics	M
Media Studies	M
Middle School Education	M,O
Multilingual and Multicultural Education	M
Music Education	M
Music	M
Nutrition	M
Organizational Behavior	M,D
Photography	M
Physical Education	M
Physics	M
Political Science	M
Psychology—General	M,D
Public Health—General	M
Public Policy	M
School Psychology	M,O
Science Education	M
Secondary Education	M
Social Psychology	M,D
Social Sciences Education	M
Sociology	M,D
Spanish	M
Special Education	M,O
Speech and Interpersonal Communication	M,D
Sports Management	M
Thanatology	M
Theater	M
Urban Studies	M
Writing	M

BROOKLYN LAW SCHOOL

Law	M,D

BROWN UNIVERSITY

Allopathic Medicine	D
American Studies	M,D
Anthropology	M,D
Applied Mathematics	M,D
Archaeology	D
Art History	D
Asian Studies	D
Biochemical Engineering	M,D
Biochemistry	M,D
Biological and Biomedical Sciences—General	M,D
Biomedical Engineering	M,D
Biostatistics	M,D
Biotechnology	M,D
Cell Biology	M,D
Chemical Engineering	M,D
Chemistry	D
Classics	M,D
Cognitive Sciences	M,D
Community Health	M,D
Comparative Literature	D
Computer Engineering	M,D
Computer Science	M,D
East European and Russian Studies	M,D
Ecology	D
Economics	D
Education—General	M
Electrical Engineering	M,D
Elementary Education	M
Engineering and Applied Sciences—General	M,D
English as a Second Language	M,D
English Education	M
English	M,D
Epidemiology	M,D
Evolutionary Biology	D
French	D
Geosciences	D
German	D
Health Services Research	D
Hispanic Studies	D
History of Science and Technology	D
History	M,D
Italian	D
Latin American Studies	M,D
Linguistics	M,D
Materials Sciences	M,D
Mathematics	D
Mechanical Engineering	M,D
Mechanics	M,D
Molecular Biology	M,D
Molecular Pharmacology	M,D
Multilingual and Multicultural Education	M,D
Music	D
Near and Middle Eastern Studies	D
Neuroscience	D
Pathobiology	M,D
Philosophy	D
Physics	M,D
Physiology	M,D

*M—masters degree; D—doctorate; O—other advanced degree; *—Close-Up and/or Display*

Political Science D
Psychology—General M,D
Public Health—General M
Public Policy M
Publishing M,D
Religion D
Russian M,D
Science Education M
Secondary Education M
Slavic Languages M,D
Social Sciences Education M
Sociology M,D
Theater M,D
Urban Education M
Western European Studies M,D
Writing M,D

BRYAN COLLEGE
Business Administration and Management—General M

BRYAN COLLEGE OF HEALTH SCIENCES
Nurse Anesthesia M

BRYANT UNIVERSITY
Accounting M
Business Administration and Management—General M
Communication—General M
Environmental Sciences M
Finance and Banking M
International Business M
Supply Chain Management M
Taxation M

BRYAN UNIVERSITY
Business Administration and Management—General M

BRYN ATHYN COLLEGE OF THE NEW CHURCH
Religion M
Theology M

BRYN MAWR COLLEGE
Archaeology M,D
Art History M,D
Chemistry M,D
Classics M,D
Mathematics M,D
Physics M,D
Social Work M,D

BUCKNELL UNIVERSITY
Animal Behavior M
Biological and Biomedical Sciences—General M
Chemical Engineering M
Chemistry M
Civil Engineering M
Education—General M
Electrical Engineering M
Engineering and Applied Sciences—General M
English M
Mathematics M
Mechanical Engineering M
Psychology—General M
Student Affairs M

BUENA VISTA UNIVERSITY
Counselor Education M
Curriculum and Instruction M
Education—General M
English as a Second Language M

BUFFALO STATE COLLEGE, STATE UNIVERSITY OF NEW YORK
Adult Education M,O
Applied Economics M
Art Education M
Biological and Biomedical Sciences—General M
Business Education M
Chemistry M
Communication Disorders M
Criminal Justice and Criminology M
Early Childhood Education M
Economics M
Educational Leadership and Administration O
Educational Media/Instructional Technology M
Elementary Education M
English Education M
English M
Historic Preservation M,O
History M
Human Resources Management M,O
Industrial/Management Engineering M
Interdisciplinary Studies M
Mathematics Education M
Multilingual and Multicultural Education M
Reading Education M
Science Education M
Social Sciences Education M
Special Education M
Student Affairs M
Vocational and Technical Education M

BUTLER UNIVERSITY
Accounting M
Business Administration and Management—General M
Counselor Education M
Education—General M
Educational Leadership and Administration M
English M
Finance and Banking M
History M
International Business M
Marketing M
Music Education M
Music M
Pharmaceutical Sciences M,D
Pharmacy M,D
Physician Assistant Studies M,D
Writing M

CABARRUS COLLEGE OF HEALTH SCIENCES
Occupational Therapy M

CABRINI UNIVERSITY
Accounting M
Education—General M
Organizational Management M

CAIRN UNIVERSITY
Accounting M,O
Business Administration and Management—General M,O
Education—General M
Educational Leadership and Administration M
Organizational Management M,O
Pastoral Ministry and Counseling M
Religion M
Theology M

CALDWELL UNIVERSITY
Accounting M
Applied Behavior Analysis M,D,O
Art Therapy M,O
Business Administration and Management—General M
Counseling Psychology M,O
Counselor Education M,O
Curriculum and Instruction M,D,O
Education—General M,D,O
Educational Leadership and Administration M,D,O
Reading Education M,D,O
School Psychology M,O
Special Education M,D,O

CALIFORNIA BAPTIST UNIVERSITY
Accounting M
Adult Education M
Adult Nursing M
Advertising and Public Relations M
Applied Mathematics M
Architecture M
Athletic Training and Sports Medicine M
Business Administration and Management—General M
Civil Engineering M
Communication Disorders M
Communication—General M
Construction Management M
Counseling Psychology M
Counselor Education M
Curriculum and Instruction M
Disability Studies M
Distance Education Development M
Education—General M
Educational Leadership and Administration M
Educational Media/Instructional Technology M
English as a Second Language M
English Education M
English M
Entrepreneurship M
Exercise and Sports Science M
Family Nurse Practitioner Studies M
Forensic Psychology M
Health Education M
Health Promotion M
Health Services Management and Hospital Administration M
Higher Education M
International and Comparative Education M
Music Education M
Music M
Nonprofit Management M
Nursing Education M
Nursing—General M,D
Organizational Management M
Pastoral Ministry and Counseling M
Physical Education M
Physician Assistant Studies M
Public Administration M
Public Health—General M
Reading Education M
School Psychology M
Science Education M
Software Engineering M
Special Education M
Sports Management M
Vocational and Technical Education M

CALIFORNIA COAST UNIVERSITY
Business Administration and Management—General M
Criminal Justice and Criminology M
Curriculum and Instruction M,D
Education—General M,D
Educational Leadership and Administration M,D
Educational Psychology M,D
Health Services Management and Hospital Administration M
Human Resources Management M
Marketing M
Organizational Management M,D
Psychology—General M

CALIFORNIA COLLEGE OF THE ARTS
Applied Arts and Design—General M
Architecture M
Art/Fine Arts M
Computer Art and Design M
Film, Television, and Video Production M
Film, Television, and Video Theory and Criticism M
Finance and Banking M
Graphic Design M
Industrial Design M
Interdisciplinary Studies M
Media Studies M
Museum Studies M
Organizational Management M
Photography M
Textile Design M
Writing M

CALIFORNIA INSTITUTE OF INTEGRAL STUDIES
Acupuncture and Oriental Medicine M,D
Art Therapy M,D
Asian Studies M,D
Clinical Psychology M,D
Counseling Psychology M,D
Cultural Anthropology M,D
Ecology M,D
Health Education M,D
Health Psychology M,D
Humanities M,D
Interdisciplinary Studies M,D
Music M,D
Philosophy M,D
Psychology—General M,D
Religion M,D
Social Psychology M,D
Theater M,D
Theology M,D
Therapies—Dance, Drama, and Music M,D
Transpersonal and Humanistic Psychology M,D
Women's Studies M,D
Writing M,D

CALIFORNIA INSTITUTE OF TECHNOLOGY
Aerospace/Aeronautical Engineering M,D,O
Applied Mathematics M,D
Applied Physics M,D
Astronomy D
Biochemistry M,D
Bioengineering M,D
Biological and Biomedical Sciences—General D
Biophysics D
Cell Biology D
Chemical Engineering M,D
Chemistry M,D
Civil Engineering M,D,O
Computational Sciences M,D
Computer Science M,D
Developmental Biology D
Electrical Engineering M,D,O
Engineering and Applied Sciences—General M,D,O
Environmental Engineering M,D
Environmental Sciences M,D
Genetics D
Geochemistry M,D
Geology M,D
Geophysics M,D
Immunology D
Materials Sciences M,D
Mathematics D
Mechanical Engineering M,D,O
Mechanics M,D
Molecular Biology D
Molecular Biophysics M,D
Neurobiology D
Neuroscience M,D
Physics D
Planetary and Space Sciences M,D
Social Sciences M,D
Systems Engineering M,D

CALIFORNIA INSTITUTE OF THE ARTS
Applied Arts and Design—General M,O
Art/Fine Arts M,O
Dance M,O
Film, Television, and Video Production M,O
Graphic Design M,O
Music M,O
Photography M,O
Theater M,O
Writing M,O

CALIFORNIA INTERCONTINENTAL UNIVERSITY
Business Administration and Management—General M,D
Entertainment Management M
Entrepreneurship M,D
Finance and Banking M,D
Health Services Management and Hospital Administration M,D
Human Resources Management M,D
International Business M,D
Management Information Systems M,D
Marketing M,D
Organizational Management M,D
Project Management M,D
Quality Management M,D

CALIFORNIA INTERNATIONAL BUSINESS UNIVERSITY
Business Administration and Management—General M,D

CALIFORNIA LUTHERAN UNIVERSITY
Business Administration and Management—General M,O
Clinical Psychology M,D
Counselor Education M,D
Economics M,O
Education—General M,D
Educational Leadership and Administration M,D
Elementary Education M,D
Entrepreneurship M,O
Finance and Banking M,O
Higher Education M,D
International Business M,O
Management Information Systems M,O
Management of Technology M,O
Marketing M,O
Marriage and Family Therapy M,D
Middle School Education M,D
Nonprofit Management M,O
Organizational Behavior M,O
Psychology—General M,D
Public Administration M
Public Policy M
Special Education M,D
Theology M,D,O

CALIFORNIA MARITIME ACADEMY
Emergency Management M
Engineering Management M
Transportation Management M

CALIFORNIA MIRAMAR UNIVERSITY
Business Administration and Management—General M
Management Strategy and Policy M
Taxation M
Telecommunications Management M
Telecommunications M

CALIFORNIA NATIONAL UNIVERSITY FOR ADVANCED STUDIES
Business Administration and Management—General M
Engineering and Applied Sciences—General M
Engineering Management M

CALIFORNIA POLYTECHNIC STATE UNIVERSITY, SAN LUIS OBISPO
Aerospace/Aeronautical Engineering M
Agricultural Economics and Agribusiness M
Agricultural Education M
Agricultural Sciences—General M
Architecture M
Biochemistry M
Biological and Biomedical Sciences—General M
Business Administration and Management—General M
Chemistry M
Civil Engineering M
Computer Science M
Education—General M
Electrical Engineering M
Engineering and Applied Sciences—General M
English M
Environmental Engineering M
Forestry M
History M
Industrial/Management Engineering M
Kinesiology and Movement Studies M
Mathematics M
Mechanical Engineering M
Natural Resources M
Political Science M
Polymer Science and Engineering M
Psychology—General M
Taxation M
Urban and Regional Planning M

CALIFORNIA SCHOOL OF PODIATRIC MEDICINE AT SAMUEL MERRITT UNIVERSITY
Podiatric Medicine D

CALIFORNIA STATE POLYTECHNIC UNIVERSITY, POMONA
Accounting M
Aerospace/Aeronautical Engineering M
Agricultural Sciences—General M
Applied Mathematics M
Architecture M
Biological and Biomedical Sciences—General M
Biotechnology M
Business Administration and Management—General M
Chemistry M
Civil Engineering M
Computer Science M
Curriculum and Instruction M
Economics M
Educational Leadership and Administration M,D
Educational Media/Instructional Technology M
Electrical Engineering M
Engineering Management M
English M
Environmental Sciences M
Geology M
History M
Hospitality Management M
Interior Design M
Kinesiology and Movement Studies M
Landscape Architecture M
Management Information Systems M
Mathematics M
Mechanical Engineering M
Nutrition M
Psychology—General M
Public Administration M
Reading Education M

Special Education	M
Urban and Regional Planning	M

CALIFORNIA STATE UNIVERSITY, BAKERSFIELD

Anthropology	M
Biological and Biomedical Sciences—General	M
Business Administration and Management—General	M
Counseling Psychology	M
Counselor Education	M
Curriculum and Instruction	M
Education—General	M
Educational Leadership and Administration	M
English	M
Geology	M
Health Services Management and Hospital Administration	M
History	M
Hydrology	M
Interdisciplinary Studies	M
Mathematics Education	M
Middle School Education	M
Public Administration	M
Science Education	M
Secondary Education	M
Social Work	M
Sociology	M
Spanish	M
Special Education	M

CALIFORNIA STATE UNIVERSITY CHANNEL ISLANDS

Bioinformatics	M
Biotechnology	M
Business Administration and Management—General	M
Computer Science	M
Mathematics	M

CALIFORNIA STATE UNIVERSITY, CHICO

Anthropology	M
Applied Psychology	M
Art History	M
Art/Fine Arts	M
Biological and Biomedical Sciences—General	M
Business Administration and Management—General	M
Communication Disorders	M
Communication—General	M
Computer Engineering	M
Computer Science	M
Construction Management	M
Criminal Justice and Criminology	M
Curriculum and Instruction	M
Electrical Engineering	M
Engineering and Applied Sciences—General	M
English as a Second Language	M
English	M
Environmental Sciences	M
Geology	M
Geosciences	M
Health Services Management and Hospital Administration	M
History	M
Hydrogeology	M
Hydrology	M
Kinesiology and Movement Studies	M
Marriage and Family Therapy	M
Mathematics Education	M
Museum Studies	M
Nursing—General	M
Nutrition	M
Political Science	M
Psychology—General	M
Public Administration	M
Recreation and Park Management	M
School Psychology	M
Social Sciences	M
Social Work	M
Special Education	M
Travel and Tourism	M

CALIFORNIA STATE UNIVERSITY, DOMINGUEZ HILLS

Applied Social Research	M,O
Bioinformatics	M
Biological and Biomedical Sciences—General	M
Business Administration and Management—General	M
Clinical Psychology	M
Computer Science	M
Conflict Resolution and Mediation/Peace Studies	M
Counselor Education	M
Curriculum and Instruction	M
Early Childhood Education	M
Education—General	M
Educational Leadership and Administration	M
English as a Second Language	M,O
English	M,O
Health Psychology	M
Humanities	M
International and Comparative Education	M
Marriage and Family Therapy	M
Mathematics Education	M
Nursing—General	M
Occupational Therapy	M
Physical Education	M
Psychology—General	M
Public Administration	M
Quality Management	M
Rhetoric	M,O
School Psychology	M
Science Education	M
Social Work	M
Sociology	M,O
Special Education	M

CALIFORNIA STATE UNIVERSITY, EAST BAY

Actuarial Science	M
Anthropology	M
Applied Mathematics	M
Applied Statistics	M
Biochemistry	M
Biological and Biomedical Sciences—General	M
Biostatistics	M
Business Administration and Management—General	M
Chemistry	M
Child and Family Studies	M
Communication Disorders	M
Communication—General	M
Computer Science	M
Construction Management	M
Counselor Education	M
Early Childhood Education	M
Economics	M
Education—General	M
Educational Leadership and Administration	M,D
Educational Media/Instructional Technology	M
Engineering and Applied Sciences—General	M
Engineering Management	M
English as a Second Language	M
English	M
Entrepreneurship	M
Environmental Sciences	M
Finance and Banking	M
Geography	M
Geology	M
Health Services Management and Hospital Administration	M
History	M
Human Resources Management	M
Industrial and Manufacturing Management	M
Industrial/Management Engineering	M
Interdisciplinary Studies	M
International Business	M
Internet and Interactive Multimedia	M
Management Information Systems	M
Management Strategy and Policy	M
Marine Sciences	M
Marketing	M
Marriage and Family Therapy	M
Mathematics Education	M
Mathematics	M
Music	M
Organizational Management	M
Physical Education	M
Public Administration	M
Public History	M
Public Policy	M
Reading Education	M
Recreation and Park Management	M
School Psychology	M
Social Psychology	M
Social Sciences Education	M
Social Work	M
Special Education	M
Statistics	M
Supply Chain Management	M
Travel and Tourism	M
Writing	M

CALIFORNIA STATE UNIVERSITY, FRESNO

Accounting	M
Animal Sciences	M
Applied Arts and Design—General	M
Art/Fine Arts	M
Biological and Biomedical Sciences—General	M
Business Administration and Management—General	M
Chemistry	M
Civil Engineering	M
Communication Disorders	M
Communication—General	M
Computer Science	M
Counselor Education	M
Criminal Justice and Criminology	M
Curriculum and Instruction	M
Early Childhood Education	M
Education—General	M,D
Educational Leadership and Administration	M,D
Electrical Engineering	M
Engineering and Applied Sciences—General	M
English as a Second Language	M
English	M
Exercise and Sports Science	M
Family and Consumer Sciences-General	M
Family Nurse Practitioner Studies	M
Food Science and Technology	M
Geology	M
Health Promotion	M
Health Services Management and Hospital Administration	M
History	M
Industrial/Management Engineering	M
International Affairs	M
Journalism	M
Kinesiology and Movement Studies	M
Linguistics	M
Marine Sciences	M
Marriage and Family Therapy	M
Mass Communication	M
Mathematics Education	M
Mathematics	M
Mechanical Engineering	M
Music Education	M
Music	M
Nursing Education	M
Nursing—General	M
Physical Therapy	M,D
Physics	M
Plant Sciences	M
Psychology—General	M
Public Administration	M
Public Health—General	M
Reading Education	M
Rehabilitation Counseling	M
Social Sciences Education	M
Social Work	M
Spanish	M
Special Education	M
Sport Psychology	M
Viticulture and Enology	M
Writing	M

CALIFORNIA STATE UNIVERSITY, FULLERTON

Accounting	M
Advertising and Public Relations	M
American Studies	M
Anthropology	M
Applied Arts and Design—General	M
Applied Mathematics	M
Art History	M
Art/Fine Arts	M
Biological and Biomedical Sciences—General	M
Biotechnology	M
Business Administration and Management—General	M
Chemistry	M
Civil Engineering	M
Clinical Psychology	M
Communication Disorders	M
Communication—General	M
Community College Education	M,D
Computer Engineering	M
Computer Science	M
Counselor Education	M
Dance	M
Economics	M
Educational Leadership and Administration	M,D
Educational Media/Instructional Technology	M
Electrical Engineering	M
Electronic Commerce	M
Elementary Education	M
Engineering and Applied Sciences—General	M
English as a Second Language	M
English	M
Entertainment Management	M
Entrepreneurship	M
Environmental Engineering	M
Environmental Management and Policy	M
Film, Television, and Video Production	M
Finance and Banking	M
French	M
Geochemistry	M
Geography	M
Geology	M
German	M
Gerontology	M
Graphic Design	M
Higher Education	M,D
History	M
Illustration	M
Information Science	M
Insurance	M
International Business	M
Linguistics	M
Management Information Systems	M
Marketing	M
Mass Communication	M
Mathematics Education	M
Mathematics	M
Mechanical Engineering	M
Multilingual and Multicultural Education	M
Museum Studies	M
Music Education	M
Music	M
Nurse Anesthesia	M,D
Nursing and Healthcare Administration	M,D
Nursing Education	M,D
Nursing—General	M,D
Organizational Management	M
Photography	M
Physical Education	M
Physics	M
Political Science	M
Psychology—General	M
Public Administration	M
Public Health—General	M
Reading Education	M
Science Education	M
Secondary Education	M
Social Psychology	M
Social Work	M
Sociology	M
Software Engineering	M
Spanish	M
Special Education	M
Speech and Interpersonal Communication	M
Systems Engineering	M
Taxation	M
Theater	M
Travel and Tourism	M
Women's Health Nursing	M,D

CALIFORNIA STATE UNIVERSITY, LONG BEACH

Aerospace/Aeronautical Engineering	M
African Studies	M
American Studies	M
Anthropology	M
Applied Mathematics	M,D
Applied Statistics	M
Art Education	M
Art History	M
Art/Fine Arts	M
Asian Studies	M
Asian-American Studies	M
Athletic Training and Sports Medicine	M
Biochemistry	M
Biological and Biomedical Sciences—General	M
Business Administration and Management—General	M
Chemical Engineering	M
Chemistry	M
Civil Engineering	M
Communication Disorders	M
Communication—General	M
Computer Engineering	M
Computer Science	M
Consumer Economics	M
Counselor Education	M
Criminal Justice and Criminology	M
Dance	M
Economics	M
Education—General	M,D
Educational Leadership and Administration	M,D
Educational Psychology	M
Electrical Engineering	M
Elementary Education	M
Emergency Management	M
Engineering Management	M,D
English as a Second Language	M
English	M
Ergonomics and Human Factors	M
Exercise and Sports Science	M
Family and Consumer Sciences-General	M
Food Science and Technology	M
French	M
Geography	M
Geology	M
Geophysics	M
German	M
Gerontology	M
Health Education	M
Health Services Management and Hospital Administration	M
Higher Education	M
History	M
Hospitality Management	M
Industrial and Organizational Psychology	M
Interdisciplinary Studies	M
Kinesiology and Movement Studies	M
Latin American Studies	M
Leisure Studies	M
Linguistics	M
Logistics	M
Marriage and Family Therapy	M
Mathematics Education	M
Mathematics	M
Mechanical Engineering	M,D
Medieval and Renaissance Studies	M
Microbiology	M
Music	M
Near and Middle Eastern Studies	M
Nursing—General	M,D
Nutrition	M
Philosophy	M
Physical Education	M
Physical Therapy	D
Physics	M
Political Science	M
Psychology—General	M
Public Administration	M
Public Policy	M
Recreation and Park Management	M
Religion	M
Science Education	M
Secondary Education	M
Social Work	M
Spanish	M
Special Education	M
Sport Psychology	M
Sports Management	M
Student Affairs	M
Theater	M
Western European Studies	M
Writing	M

CALIFORNIA STATE UNIVERSITY, LOS ANGELES

Accounting	M
Analytical Chemistry	M
Anthropology	M
Applied Arts and Design—General	M
Applied Mathematics	M
Art Education	M
Art History	M
Art Therapy	M

*M—masters degree; D—doctorate; O—other advanced degree; *—Close-Up and/or Display*

Art/Fine Arts M
Biochemistry M
Biological and Biomedical Sciences—General M
Business Administration and Management—General M,O
Chemistry M
Child and Family Studies M
Child Development M
Civil Engineering M
Communication Disorders M
Communication—General M
Computer Science M
Counselor Education M,D
Criminal Justice and Criminology M
Curriculum and Instruction M
Economics M
Education—General M,D,O
Electrical Engineering M
Elementary Education M
Engineering and Applied Sciences—General M
English M,O
Finance and Banking M
French M
Geography M
Geology M
Graphic Design M
Health Services Management and Hospital Administration M,O
Hispanic Studies M
History M
International Business M
Kinesiology and Movement Studies M,O
Latin American Studies M
Management Information Systems M
Management of Technology M
Marketing M
Mathematics M
Mechanical Engineering M
Music Education M
Music M
Nursing—General M,O
Nutrition M,O
Philosophy M,O
Photography M
Physical Education M,O
Physics M
Political Science M
Psychology—General M
Public Administration M
Rehabilitation Counseling M,D
School Psychology M,D
Social Work M
Sociology M
Spanish M
Special Education M,D
Textile Design M
Theater M

CALIFORNIA STATE UNIVERSITY, MONTEREY BAY
Business Administration and Management—General M
Education—General M
Management Information Systems M
Marine Sciences M
Social Work M
Water Resources M

CALIFORNIA STATE UNIVERSITY, NORTHRIDGE
Anthropology M
Applied Mathematics M
Archaeology M
Art Education M
Art History M
Art/Fine Arts M
Artificial Intelligence/Robotics M
Biochemistry M
Biological and Biomedical Sciences—General M
Business Administration and Management—General M
Chemistry M
Civil Engineering M
Clinical Psychology M
Communication Disorders M
Communication—General M
Comparative Literature M
Computer Science M
Counselor Education M
Curriculum and Instruction M
Early Childhood Education M
Education—General M,D
Educational Leadership and Administration M,D
Educational Media/Instructional Technology M
Educational Psychology M
Electrical Engineering M
Elementary Education M
Engineering and Applied Sciences—General M
Engineering Management M
English Education M
English M
Entertainment Management M,O
Environmental and Occupational Health M
Environmental Sciences M
Experimental Psychology M
Family and Consumer Sciences-General M
Film, Television, and Video Production M
Geography M
Geology M
Health Education M,O
Health Services Management and Hospital Administration M
Hispanic Studies M
History M
Hospitality Management M,O
Industrial Hygiene M
Industrial/Management Engineering M
Journalism M
Kinesiology and Movement Studies M
Linguistics M
Manufacturing Engineering M
Marriage and Family Therapy M
Mass Communication M
Materials Engineering M
Mathematics Education M
Mathematics M
Mechanical Engineering M
Multilingual and Multicultural Education M
Music Education M
Music M
Nonprofit Management O
Physical Therapy M
Physics M
Political Science M
Psychology—General M
Public Administration M,O
Public Health—General M
Reading Education M
Recreation and Park Management M,O
Rhetoric M
School Psychology M
Science Education M
Secondary Education M
Social Work M,O
Sociology M
Software Engineering M
Spanish M
Special Education M
Speech and Interpersonal Communication M
Structural Engineering M
Systems Engineering M
Taxation M,O
Theater M
Travel and Tourism M
Writing M

CALIFORNIA STATE UNIVERSITY, SACRAMENTO
Accounting M
Anthropology M
Applied Behavior Analysis M
Art/Fine Arts M
Biological and Biomedical Sciences—General M
Business Administration and Management—General M
Cell Biology M
Chemistry M
Civil Engineering M
Communication Disorders M
Communication—General M
Computer Science M
Conservation Biology M
Counseling Psychology M
Counselor Education M
Criminal Justice and Criminology M
Curriculum and Instruction M
Developmental Biology M
Education—General M
Educational Leadership and Administration M
Educational Media/Instructional Technology M
Electrical Engineering M
Engineering and Applied Sciences—General M
English as a Second Language M
English M
Foreign Languages Education M
Gender Studies M
Higher Education M
Human Resources Development M
Human Resources Management M
Human Services M
Industrial and Organizational Psychology M
Marriage and Family Therapy M
Mathematics M
Mechanical Engineering M
Molecular Biology M
Multilingual and Multicultural Education M
Music M
Nursing—General M
Physical Education M
Political Science M
Psychology—General M
Public Administration M
Public History M,D
Public Policy M
Reading Education M
Real Estate M
Recreation and Park Management M
School Psychology M
Social Work M
Sociology M
Software Engineering M
Special Education M
Vocational and Technical Education M
Writing M

CALIFORNIA STATE UNIVERSITY, SAN BERNARDINO
Accounting M
Archaeology M
Art/Fine Arts M
Biological and Biomedical Sciences—General M
Business Administration and Management—General M
Child Development M
Clinical Psychology M
Communication—General M
Community College Education M
Computer and Information Systems Security M
Computer Science M
Corporate and Organizational Communication M
Counseling Psychology M
Counselor Education M
Criminal Justice and Criminology M
Education—General M
Educational Leadership and Administration M,D
English M
Entrepreneurship M
Environmental Sciences M
Experimental Psychology M
Finance and Banking M
Geosciences M
Health Services Management and Hospital Administration M
Industrial and Organizational Psychology M
Interdisciplinary Studies M
International Business M
Management Information Systems M
Marketing M
Mathematics Education M
Mathematics M
Music M
National Security M
Nursing—General M
Psychology—General M
Public Administration M
Public Health—General M
Rehabilitation Counseling M
Social Sciences M
Social Work M
Spanish M
Supply Chain Management M
Writing M

CALIFORNIA STATE UNIVERSITY, SAN MARCOS
Biological and Biomedical Sciences—General M
Business Administration and Management—General M
Child and Family Studies M
Communication Disorders M
Computer Science M
Education—General M,D
Educational Leadership and Administration M,D
English M
Health Education M
Hispanic and Latin American Languages M
Hispanic Studies M
History M
Mathematics M
Psychology—General M
Reading Education M,D
Social Work M
Sociology M
Spanish M
Special Education M,D
Writing M

CALIFORNIA STATE UNIVERSITY, STANISLAUS
Applied Behavior Analysis M
Business Administration and Management—General M
Community College Education D
Conservation Biology M
Counseling Psychology M
Counselor Education M
Criminal Justice and Criminology M
Curriculum and Instruction M
Ecology M
Education—General M,D,O
Educational Leadership and Administration M,D
Educational Media/Instructional Technology M
Elementary Education M
English as a Second Language M,O
English M,O
Genetic Counseling M
Gerontological Nursing M
History M
Interdisciplinary Studies M
International Affairs M
Multilingual and Multicultural Education M
Nursing Education M
Nursing—General M
Physical Education M
Psychology—General M
Public Administration M
Reading Education M
Rhetoric M,O
Secondary Education M
Social Work M
Special Education M
Sustainable Development M
Writing M,O

CALIFORNIA UNIVERSITY OF MANAGEMENT AND SCIENCES
Business Administration and Management—General M,D
Economics M,D
International Business M,D
Management Information Systems M,D
Sports Management M,D

CALIFORNIA UNIVERSITY OF PENNSYLVANIA
Athletic Training and Sports Medicine M
Business Administration and Management—General M
Clinical Psychology M
Communication Disorders M
Counseling Psychology M
Counselor Education M
Criminal Justice and Criminology M
Education—General M
Educational Leadership and Administration M
Elementary Education M
Entrepreneurship M
Exercise and Sports Science M
Legal and Justice Studies M
Management Strategy and Policy M
Nursing and Healthcare Administration M
Reading Education M
Rehabilitation Sciences M
School Psychology M
Secondary Education M
Social Work M
Special Education M
Sport Psychology M
Sports Management M
Vocational and Technical Education M

CALIFORNIA WESTERN SCHOOL OF LAW
Accounting M,D
Law M,D

CALUMET COLLEGE OF SAINT JOSEPH
Criminal Justice and Criminology M
Educational Leadership and Administration M
Quality Management M

CALVARY BIBLE COLLEGE AND THEOLOGICAL SEMINARY
Pastoral Ministry and Counseling M
Theology M

CALVIN COLLEGE
Curriculum and Instruction M
Education—General M
Educational Leadership and Administration M
Reading Education M

CALVIN THEOLOGICAL SEMINARY
Missions and Missiology M,D
Pastoral Ministry and Counseling M,D
Religion M,D
Religious Education M,D
Theology M,D

CAMBRIDGE COLLEGE
Addictions/Substance Abuse Counseling M,O
Business Administration and Management—General M
Conflict Resolution and Mediation/Peace Studies M
Counseling Psychology M,O
Counselor Education M,D,O
Curriculum and Instruction M,D,O
Early Childhood Education M,D,O
Education—General M,D,O
Educational Leadership and Administration M,D,O
Educational Measurement and Evaluation M,D,O
Educational Media/Instructional Technology M,D,O
Elementary Education M,D,O
English as a Second Language M,D,O
Entrepreneurship M
Forensic Psychology M,O
Health Education M,D,O
Health Services Management and Hospital Administration M
Home Economics Education M,D,O
Interdisciplinary Studies M,D,O
Management of Technology M
Marriage and Family Therapy M,O
Mathematics Education M,D,O
Medical Informatics M
Middle School Education M,D,O
Nonprofit Management M
Organizational Management M
Psychology—General M,O
Reading Education M,D,O
School Nursing M,D,O
School Psychology M,D,O
Science Education M,D,O
Social Sciences Education M,D,O
Special Education M,D,O

CAMERON UNIVERSITY
Business Administration and Management—General M
Education—General M
Educational Leadership and Administration M
Entrepreneurship M
Psychology—General M

CAMPBELLSVILLE UNIVERSITY
Business Administration and Management—General M
Education—General M
Marriage and Family Therapy M
Music Education M
Music M
Social Sciences M
Social Work M
Special Education M
Theology M

CAMPBELL UNIVERSITY
Business Administration and Management—General M
Counselor Education M
Education—General M
Educational Leadership and Administration M
Elementary Education M
Interdisciplinary Studies M
Law D
Middle School Education M
Pastoral Ministry and Counseling M,D
Pharmaceutical Sciences M,D
Pharmacy M,D

Physical Education	M
Physical Therapy	M,D
Physician Assistant Studies	M,D
Secondary Education	M
Theology	M,D

CANADIAN COLLEGE OF NATUROPATHIC MEDICINE

Naturopathic Medicine	O

CANADIAN MEMORIAL CHIROPRACTIC COLLEGE

Acupuncture and Oriental Medicine	O
Chiropractic	D,O

CANADIAN SOUTHERN BAPTIST SEMINARY

Pastoral Ministry and Counseling	M
Religion	M
Theology	M

CANISIUS COLLEGE

Accounting	M
Allied Health—General	M,O
Anthropology	M
Business Administration and Management—General	M
Business Education	M,O
Communication Disorders	M,O
Community Health	M,O
Corporate and Organizational Communication	M
Counselor Education	M
Early Childhood Education	M
Education of the Gifted	M,O
Education—General	M,O
Educational Leadership and Administration	M,O
Educational Media/Instructional Technology	M,O
Elementary Education	M,O
English as a Second Language	M,O
Health Informatics	M,O
International Business	M
Kinesiology and Movement Studies	M
Middle School Education	M
Nutrition	M,O
Physical Education	M,O
Reading Education	M,O
School Psychology	M
Secondary Education	M,O
Social Psychology	M
Special Education	M,O
Sports Management	M
Student Affairs	M,O
Zoology	M

CAPE BRETON UNIVERSITY

Business Administration and Management—General	M

CAPELLA UNIVERSITY

Accounting	M,D
Addictions/Substance Abuse Counseling	M,D
Adult Education	M,D
Applied Behavior Analysis	M
Business Administration and Management—General	M,D
Business Education	D
Child and Family Studies	M
Clinical Psychology	M,D
Computer and Information Systems Security	M,D
Counseling Psychology	M
Counselor Education	M,D
Criminal Justice and Criminology	M,D
Curriculum and Instruction	M,D
Developmental Psychology	M
Distance Education Development	M,D
Early Childhood Education	M
Education—General	M,D
Educational Leadership and Administration	M,D
Educational Media/Instructional Technology	M,D
Educational Psychology	M,D
Elementary Education	M,D
Emergency Management	M,D
Entrepreneurship	M,D
Environmental and Occupational Health	M,D
Epidemiology	D
Finance and Banking	M,D
Gerontological Nursing	M
Gerontology	M
Health Informatics	M
Health Services Management and Hospital Administration	M,D
Higher Education	M,D
Homeland Security	M
Human Resources Management	M,D
Human Services	M,D
Industrial and Organizational Psychology	M,D
Management Information Systems	M,D
Management of Technology	M,D
Management Strategy and Policy	M,D
Marketing	M,D
Marriage and Family Therapy	M
Middle School Education	M,D
Nonprofit Management	D
Nursing and Healthcare Administration	M
Nursing Education	M,D
Nursing—General	M,D
Operations Research	M
Organizational Management	M,D
Project Management	M,D
Psychology—General	M,D
Public Administration	M,D
Reading Education	M,D
School Psychology	M,D
Social Work	D
Special Education	M,D
Sport Psychology	M
Supply Chain Management	M,D
Vocational and Technical Education	D

CAPITAL UNIVERSITY

Business Administration and Management—General	M
Law	M,D
Legal and Justice Studies	M
Music Education	M
Music	M
Nursing and Healthcare Administration	M
Nursing—General	M
Taxation	M

CAPITOL TECHNOLOGY UNIVERSITY

Business Administration and Management—General	M
Computer and Information Systems Security	M
Computer Science	M
Electrical Engineering	M
Information Science	M
Management Information Systems	M
Telecommunications Management	M

CARDINAL STRITCH UNIVERSITY

Business Administration and Management—General	M
Clinical Psychology	M
Education—General	M,D
Educational Leadership and Administration	M,D
Liberal Studies	M
Nursing—General	M
Pastoral Ministry and Counseling	M
Psychology—General	M
Reading Education	M,D
Religion	M
Special Education	M,D
Sports Management	M
Urban Education	M,D

CAREY THEOLOGICAL COLLEGE

Theology	M,D

CARIBBEAN UNIVERSITY

Art History	M,D
Criminal Justice and Criminology	M,D
Curriculum and Instruction	M,D
Early Childhood Education	M,D
Education—General	M,D
Educational Leadership and Administration	M,D
Educational Media/Instructional Technology	M,D
Elementary Education	M,D
English Education	M,D
Foreign Languages Education	M,D
Gerontological Nursing	M,D
Human Resources Management	M,D
Mathematics Education	M,D
Museum Studies	M,D
Pediatric Nursing	M,D
Physical Education	M,D
Science Education	M,D
Social Sciences Education	M,D
Special Education	M,D

CARLETON UNIVERSITY

Aerospace/Aeronautical Engineering	M,D
Anthropology	M
Architecture	M
Art History	M
Biological and Biomedical Sciences—General	M,D
Biomedical Engineering	M
Business Administration and Management—General	M,D
Canadian Studies	M,D
Chemistry	M,D
Civil Engineering	M,D
Cognitive Sciences	D
Communication—General	M,D
Comparative Literature	D
Computer Science	M,D
Conflict Resolution and Mediation/Peace Studies	M,O
East European and Russian Studies	M,O
Economics	M,D
Electrical Engineering	M,D
Engineering and Applied Sciences—General	M,D
English	M,D
Environmental Engineering	M,D
Film, Television, and Video Production	M
French	M
Geography	M,D
Geosciences	M,D
History	M,D
Industrial Design	M
Information Science	M,D
International Affairs	M,D
Journalism	M,D
Legal and Justice Studies	M,O
Linguistics	M
Management of Technology	M
Materials Engineering	M,D
Mathematics	M,D
Mechanical Engineering	M,D
Music	M
Neuroscience	M,D
Philosophy	M
Physics	M,D
Political Science	M,D
Psychology—General	M,D
Public Administration	M,D
Public Policy	M,D
Social Work	M
Sociology	M,D
Systems Engineering	M,D
Systems Science	M,D
Western European Studies	M,O

CARLOS ALBIZU UNIVERSITY

Clinical Psychology	M,D
Communication Disorders	M,D
Industrial and Organizational Psychology	M,D
Psychology—General	M,D

CARLOS ALBIZU UNIVERSITY, MIAMI CAMPUS

Business Administration and Management—General	M,D
Clinical Psychology	M,D
Communication Disorders	M,D
Counseling Psychology	M,D
Education of the Gifted	M,D
English as a Second Language	M,D
Entrepreneurship	M,D
Human Services	M,D
Industrial and Organizational Psychology	M,D
Marriage and Family Therapy	M,D
Nonprofit Management	M,D
Organizational Management	M,D
Psychology—General	M,D
School Psychology	M,D
Special Education	M,D

CARLOW UNIVERSITY

Addictions/Substance Abuse Counseling	M,O
Art Education	M
Business Administration and Management—General	M
Child and Family Studies	M,O
Computer and Information Systems Security	M
Counseling Psychology	M,D,O
Counselor Education	M,O
Early Childhood Education	M
Education—General	M
Educational Leadership and Administration	M
Family Nurse Practitioner Studies	M,O
Forensic Sciences	M
Health Services Management and Hospital Administration	M
Human Resources Management	M
Nursing and Healthcare Administration	M
Nursing Education	M
Nursing—General	D
Organizational Management	M,D,O
Project Management	M
Special Education	M
Writing	M

CARNEGIE MELLON UNIVERSITY

Accounting	D
African Studies	D
African-American Studies	D
Applied Arts and Design—General	M,D
Applied Physics	M,D
Architectural Engineering	M,D
Architecture	M,D
Art/Fine Arts	M
Artificial Intelligence/Robotics	M,D
Arts Administration	M
Atmospheric Sciences	D
Biochemistry	M,D
Bioengineering	M,D
Biological and Biomedical Sciences—General	M,D
Biomedical Engineering	M,D
Biophysics	M,D
Biopsychology	D
Biotechnology	M
Building Science	M,D
Business Administration and Management—General	M,D
Cell Biology	M,D
Chemical Engineering	M,D
Chemistry	D
Civil Engineering	M,D
Cognitive Sciences	D
Communication—General	M,D
Comparative Literature	M,D
Computational Biology	M,D
Computer and Information Systems Security	M
Computer Art and Design	M
Computer Engineering	M,D
Computer Science	M,D
Construction Management	M,D
Corporate and Organizational Communication	M
Criminal Justice and Criminology	M
Cultural Studies	D
Developmental Biology	M,D
Developmental Psychology	D
Economics	D
Electrical Engineering	M,D
Energy and Power Engineering	M,D
English	M,D
Entertainment Management	M
Entrepreneurship	D
Environmental Engineering	M,D
Environmental Sciences	D
Film, Television, and Video Production	M
Finance and Banking	D
Gender Studies	D
Genetics	M,D
Health Services Management and Hospital Administration	M
History of Science and Technology	D
History	D
Human-Computer Interaction	M,D
Industrial and Labor Relations	D
Industrial and Manufacturing Management	M,D
Information Science	M,D
Linguistics	M,D
Management Information Systems	M,D
Marketing	D
Materials Engineering	M,D
Materials Sciences	M,D
Mathematical and Computational Finance	M,D
Mathematics	M,D
Mechanical Engineering	M,D
Mechanics	M,D
Media Studies	M
Modeling and Simulation	M,D
Molecular Biology	M,D
Molecular Biophysics	D
Music Education	M
Music	M
Nanotechnology	D
Neurobiology	M,D
Neuroscience	D
Operations Research	D
Organizational Behavior	D
Philosophy	M,D
Physics	M,D
Polymer Science and Engineering	M
Psychology—General	D
Public Administration	M
Public Policy	M,D
Publishing	M
Rhetoric	M,D
Social Psychology	D
Social Sciences	D
Software Engineering	M,D
Statistics	M,D
Structural Biology	M,D
Sustainable Development	M,D
Systems Engineering	M
Technical Writing	M
Technology and Public Policy	M,D
Telecommunications Management	M
Theater	M
Theoretical Chemistry	D
Urban Design	M,D
Water Resources Engineering	M,D
Women's Studies	D
Writing	M

CAROLINA CHRISTIAN COLLEGE

Pastoral Ministry and Counseling	M
Religious Education	M

CAROLINA GRADUATE SCHOOL OF DIVINITY

Pastoral Ministry and Counseling	D
Theology	M

CARROLL UNIVERSITY

Business Administration and Management—General	M
Education—General	M
Physical Therapy	M,D
Physician Assistant Studies	M
Software Engineering	M

CARSON-NEWMAN UNIVERSITY

Business Administration and Management—General	M
Counselor Education	M
Curriculum and Instruction	M
Education—General	M
Educational Leadership and Administration	M
Elementary Education	M
English as a Second Language	M
Family Nurse Practitioner Studies	M
Nursing Education	M
Nursing—General	M
Organizational Management	M
Secondary Education	M
Theology	M

CARTHAGE COLLEGE

Art Education	M,O
Counselor Education	M,O
Education of the Gifted	M,O
Education—General	M,O
Educational Leadership and Administration	M,O
English Education	M,O
Reading Education	M,O
Science Education	M,O
Social Sciences Education	M,O

CASE WESTERN RESERVE UNIVERSITY

Accounting	M,D
Acute Care/Critical Care Nursing	M
Aerospace/Aeronautical Engineering	M,D
Allopathic Medicine	D
Anatomy	M
Anesthesiologist Assistant Studies	M
Anthropology	M,D
Applied Mathematics	M,D
Art Education	M
Art History	M,D
Astronomy	M,D
Biochemistry	M,D
Bioethics	M
Biological and Biomedical Sciences—General	M,D
Biomedical Engineering	M,D*
Biophysics	M,D
Biostatistics	M,D

*M—masters degree; D—doctorate; O—other advanced degree; *—Close-Up and/or Display*

- Business Administration and Management—General M,D
- Cancer Biology/Oncology D
- Cell Biology M,D
- Chemical Engineering M,D
- Chemistry M,D
- Civil Engineering M,D
- Clinical Psychology D
- Clinical Research M
- Cognitive Sciences M
- Communication Disorders M,D
- Comparative Literature M
- Computer Engineering M,D
- Computer Science M,D
- Dance M
- Database Systems M
- Dentistry D
- Electrical Engineering M,D
- Engineering and Applied Sciences—General M,D
- Engineering Management M
- English M,D
- Epidemiology M,D
- Experimental Psychology D
- Family Nurse Practitioner Studies M
- Finance and Banking M
- French M
- Genetic Counseling M
- Genetics D
- Genomic Sciences D
- Geology M,D
- Geosciences M,D
- Gerontological Nursing M
- Health Services Management and Hospital Administration M
- Health Services Research M,D
- History M,D
- Human Genetics D
- Immunology M,D
- Industrial and Manufacturing Management M,D
- Information Science M,D
- Intellectual Property Law M,D
- Law M,D
- Legal and Justice Studies M,D
- Linguistics M
- Logistics M,D
- Materials Engineering M,D
- Materials Sciences M,D
- Maternal and Child/Neonatal Nursing M
- Mathematics M,D
- Mechanical Engineering M,D
- Microbiology D
- Molecular Biology D
- Molecular Medicine D
- Molecular Physiology M,D
- Museum Studies M
- Music Education M,D
- Music M,D
- Neuroscience D
- Nonprofit Management M,D,O
- Nurse Anesthesia M
- Nurse Midwifery M
- Nursing Education M
- Nursing—General M,D
- Nutrition M,D
- Oncology Nursing M
- Operations Research M,D
- Oral and Dental Sciences M,O
- Organizational Behavior M,D
- Pathology M,D
- Pediatric Nursing M
- Pharmacology D
- Physician Assistant Studies M
- Physics M,D
- Physiology M,D
- Political Science M,D
- Polymer Science and Engineering M,D
- Psychiatric Nursing M
- Psychology—General M,D
- Public Health—General M
- Social Work M,D
- Sociology M,D
- Supply Chain Management M,D
- Sustainability Management D
- Systems Engineering M,D
- Theater M
- Virology D
- Women's Health Nursing M

CASTLETON UNIVERSITY
- Curriculum and Instruction M
- Education—General M,O
- Educational Leadership and Administration M,O
- Forensic Psychology M
- Psychology—General M
- Reading Education M,O
- Special Education M,O

CATAWBA COLLEGE
- Elementary Education M
- Science Education M

CATHOLIC DISTANCE UNIVERSITY
- Theology M

CATHOLIC THEOLOGICAL UNION
- Missions and Missiology M,D,O
- Pastoral Ministry and Counseling M,D,O
- Theology M,D,O

THE CATHOLIC UNIVERSITY OF AMERICA
- Accounting M
- American Studies M,D
- Anthropology M
- Applied Psychology M,D
- Architecture M
- Biological and Biomedical Sciences—General M,D
- Biomedical Engineering M,D
- Biotechnology M,D
- Business Administration and Management—General M
- Cell Biology M,D
- Civil Engineering M,D,O
- Classics M,D,O
- Clinical Laboratory Sciences/Medical Technology M,D
- Clinical Psychology M,D
- Computer Science M,D
- Criminal Justice and Criminology M
- Economic Development M
- Economics M
- Education—General M,D,O
- Educational Leadership and Administration M,D,O
- Educational Policy M,D,O
- Electrical Engineering M,D
- Energy and Power Engineering M,D
- Engineering and Applied Sciences—General M,D,O
- Engineering Management M,O
- English M,D,O
- Environmental Engineering M,D
- Ergonomics and Human Factors M,D
- Experimental Psychology M,D
- Hispanic Studies M,D
- History M,D
- Human Resources Management M
- Information Studies M,O
- International Affairs M,D
- Latin American Studies M,D
- Law M,D
- Legal and Justice Studies M,D,O
- Library Science M,O
- Management Information Systems M,O
- Management of Technology M,O
- Materials Engineering M
- Materials Sciences M
- Mechanical Engineering M,D
- Medieval and Renaissance Studies M,D,O
- Microbiology M,D
- Music Education M,D,O
- Music M,D,O
- Near and Middle Eastern Languages M,D
- Near and Middle Eastern Studies M,D,O
- Nursing—General M,D,O
- Pastoral Ministry and Counseling M,D,O
- Philosophy M,D,O
- Physics M,D
- Political Science M,D
- Project Management M,O
- Psychology—General M,D
- Public Policy M
- Religion M,D,O
- Rhetoric M,D,O
- Secondary Education M,D,O
- Social Work M,D
- Sociology M
- Spanish M,D
- Special Education M,D,O
- Systems Engineering M,O
- Theater M
- Theology M,D,O
- Transportation and Highway Engineering M,D,O
- Urban and Regional Planning M
- Western European Studies M,D

CEDAR CREST COLLEGE
- Art Therapy M
- Business Administration and Management—General M
- Education—General M
- Forensic Sciences M
- Nursing and Healthcare Administration M
- Nursing Education M
- Nursing—General M
- Nutrition O
- Writing M

CEDARS-SINAI MEDICAL CENTER
- Biological and Biomedical Sciences—General D
- Translational Biology D

CEDARVILLE UNIVERSITY
- Business Administration and Management—General M,D
- Curriculum and Instruction M,D
- Education—General M,D
- Educational Leadership and Administration M,D
- Family Nurse Practitioner Studies M,D
- International Health M,D
- Pastoral Ministry and Counseling M,D
- Pharmacy M,D

CENTENARY COLLEGE
- Accounting M
- Business Administration and Management—General M
- Counseling Psychology M
- Education—General M
- Educational Leadership and Administration M
- Special Education M

CENTENARY COLLEGE OF LOUISIANA
- Business Administration and Management—General M
- Education—General M
- Elementary Education M
- Secondary Education M

CENTRAL BAPTIST THEOLOGICAL SEMINARY
- Missions and Missiology M,O
- Theology M,O

CENTRAL CONNECTICUT STATE UNIVERSITY
- Actuarial Science M,O
- Advertising and Public Relations M,O
- Art Education M,O
- Biological and Biomedical Sciences—General M,O
- Business Administration and Management—General M
- Communication—General M,O
- Computer Science M,O
- Construction Management M,O
- Corporate and Organizational Communication M,O
- Counselor Education M,O
- Criminal Justice and Criminology M
- Early Childhood Education M,O
- Education—General M,D,O
- Educational Leadership and Administration M,D,O
- Educational Media/Instructional Technology M,D,O
- Elementary Education M,O
- Engineering and Applied Sciences—General M
- English as a Second Language M,O
- English M,O
- Exercise and Sports Science M,O
- Foreign Languages Education M,O
- French M,O
- Geography M
- German M,O
- Graphic Design M
- Health Psychology M
- History M,O
- Industrial and Manufacturing Management M,O
- Information Studies M
- International Affairs M
- Italian M,O
- Logistics M,O
- Management of Technology M,O
- Marriage and Family Therapy M,O
- Mathematics M,O
- Molecular Biology M,O
- Music Education M,O
- Nurse Anesthesia M,O
- Physical Education M,O
- Psychology—General M
- Reading Education M,O
- Rehabilitation Counseling M,O
- School Psychology M,O
- Science Education M,O
- Social Psychology M
- Spanish M,O
- Special Education M,O
- Statistics M,O
- Supply Chain Management M,O
- Vocational and Technical Education M

CENTRAL EUROPEAN UNIVERSITY
- Anthropology M,D
- Applied Mathematics M,D
- Business Administration and Management—General M,D
- Cognitive Sciences D
- Database Systems M,D
- Economics M,D
- Environmental Management and Policy M,D
- Finance and Banking M,D
- Gender Studies M,D
- History M,D
- International Affairs M,D
- International Business M,D
- Law M,D
- Legal and Justice Studies M,D
- Management Information Systems M,D
- Mathematics M,D
- Medieval and Renaissance Studies M,D
- Philosophy M,D
- Political Science M,D
- Public Administration M,D
- Public Policy M,D
- Sociology M,D

CENTRAL METHODIST UNIVERSITY
- Counselor Education M
- Education—General M
- Music Education M
- Nursing and Healthcare Administration M
- Nursing Education M
- Nursing—General M

CENTRAL MICHIGAN UNIVERSITY
- Accounting M,O
- American Indian/Native American Studies M
- American Studies M,O
- Applied Psychology M,D
- Biological and Biomedical Sciences—General M
- Business Administration and Management—General M,O
- Chemistry M
- Child and Family Studies M,O
- Clinical Psychology D
- Clothing and Textiles M,O
- Communication Disorders M,D
- Communication—General M
- Community College Education M,D,O
- Computer and Information Systems Security O
- Computer Science M
- Conservation Biology M
- Counseling Psychology M,D,O
- Counselor Education M
- Cultural Studies M
- Curriculum and Instruction M,D,O
- Early Childhood Education M,O
- Economics M
- Education—General M,D,O
- Educational Leadership and Administration M,D,O
- Educational Media/Instructional Technology M,D,O
- Elementary Education M,D,O
- Engineering and Applied Sciences—General M
- Engineering Management M,O
- English as a Second Language M
- English M
- Exercise and Sports Science M,D
- Experimental Psychology M,D
- Family and Consumer Sciences-General M,O
- Film, Television, and Video Production M
- Film, Television, and Video Theory and Criticism M
- Finance and Banking M
- Gender Studies M
- Geographic Information Systems M
- Gerontology M,O
- Health Psychology M,D
- Health Services Management and Hospital Administration M,D,O
- Higher Education M,D,O
- History M,O
- Human Development M,O
- Human Resources Management M,O
- Humanities M
- Industrial and Manufacturing Management M
- Industrial and Organizational Psychology M,D
- International Affairs M,O
- International Business M,O
- International Health M,D,O
- Logistics M,O
- Management Information Systems M,O
- Marketing M,O
- Materials Sciences D
- Mathematics Education M,D
- Mathematics M,D
- Media Studies M
- Music Education M
- Music M
- Neuroscience M,D
- Nonprofit Management M,O
- Nutrition M,D,O
- Physical Therapy M,D
- Physician Assistant Studies M,D
- Physics M,D
- Political Science M,O
- Psychology—General M,D,O
- Public Administration M,O
- Reading Education M,D,O
- Recreation and Park Management M,O
- Rehabilitation Sciences M,D
- School Psychology D,O
- Science Education M
- Secondary Education M,D,O
- Spanish M
- Special Education M,O
- Sports Management M,O
- Student Affairs M,D,O
- Western European Studies M,O
- Writing M

CENTRAL PENN COLLEGE
- Management Information Systems M
- Organizational Management M

CENTRAL WASHINGTON UNIVERSITY
- Accounting M
- Art/Fine Arts M
- Biological and Biomedical Sciences—General M
- Chemistry M
- Child and Family Studies M
- Counseling Psychology M
- Counselor Education M
- Curriculum and Instruction M
- Education—General M
- Educational Leadership and Administration M
- Engineering and Applied Sciences—General M
- English as a Second Language M
- English M
- Exercise and Sports Science M
- Experimental Psychology M
- Family and Consumer Sciences-General M
- Foundations and Philosophy of Education M
- Geology M
- Health Education M
- History M
- Home Economics Education M
- Industrial/Management Engineering M
- Interdisciplinary Studies M
- Mathematics M
- Music M
- Natural Resources M
- Nutrition M
- Physical Education M
- Psychology—General M
- Reading Education M
- School Psychology M
- Special Education M
- Sports Management M
- Theater M
- Vocational and Technical Education M

CENTRAL YESHIVA TOMCHEI TMIMIM-LUBAVITCH
- Jewish Studies M
- Theology M

CENTRO DE ESTUDIOS AVANZADOS DE PUERTO RICO Y EL CARIBE
- History M,D
- Latin American Studies M,D

CHADRON STATE COLLEGE
- Business Administration and Management—General M
- Business Education M,O
- Counselor Education M,O
- Education—General M,O

Educational Leadership and Administration M,O
Elementary Education M,O
English Education M,O
Secondary Education M,O
Social Sciences Education M,O

CHAMINADE UNIVERSITY OF HONOLULU
Accounting M
Business Administration and Management—General M
Child Development M
Counseling Psychology M
Criminal Justice and Criminology M,O
Education—General M
Educational Leadership and Administration M
Elementary Education M
English Education M
Forensic Sciences M,O
Homeland Security M,O
Marriage and Family Therapy M
Mathematics Education M
Nonprofit Management M
Pastoral Ministry and Counseling M
School Psychology M
Science Education M
Secondary Education M
Social Sciences Education M
Special Education M
Theology M

CHAMPLAIN COLLEGE
Business Administration and Management—General M
Computer and Information Systems Security M
Conflict Resolution and Mediation/Peace Studies M
Early Childhood Education M
Forensic Sciences M
Health Services Management and Hospital Administration M
Internet and Interactive Multimedia M
Law M
Management of Technology M
Media Studies M*

CHAPMAN UNIVERSITY
Accounting M
Athletic Training and Sports Medicine M
Business Administration and Management—General M
Communication Disorders M
Computational Sciences M,D*
Counselor Education M,D,O
Cultural Studies M,D,O
Curriculum and Instruction M,D,O
Disability Studies M,D,O
Education—General M,D,O
Educational Leadership and Administration M,D,O
Educational Psychology M,D,O
Elementary Education M,D,O
English M
Environmental Law M,D
Film, Television, and Video Production M
Food Science and Technology M
Health Communication M
Holocaust and Genocide Studies M
International Affairs M
Law M,D
Marriage and Family Therapy M
Nutrition M
Pharmaceutical Sciences M,D
Pharmacy M,D
Physical Therapy D
School Psychology M,D,O
Secondary Education M,D,O
Special Education M,D,O
Taxation M,D
Writing M

CHARLES R. DREW UNIVERSITY OF MEDICINE AND SCIENCE
Allopathic Medicine D
Public Health—General M

CHARLESTON SOUTHERN UNIVERSITY
Accounting M
Business Administration and Management—General M
Criminal Justice and Criminology M
Education—General M
Educational Leadership and Administration M
Elementary Education M
Finance and Banking M
Management Information Systems M

CHARLOTTE CHRISTIAN COLLEGE AND THEOLOGICAL SEMINARY
Cultural Studies M
Missions and Missiology M
Music M
Pastoral Ministry and Counseling M
Religion M
Theology M

CHARLOTTE SCHOOL OF LAW
Law D

CHATHAM UNIVERSITY
Accounting M
Art Education M
Biological and Biomedical Sciences—General M
Business Administration and Management—General M
Communication—General M
Computer Art and Design M
Counseling Psychology M,D
Developmental Psychology M,D
Early Childhood Education M
Education—General M
Elementary Education M
English Education M
Environmental Biology M
Environmental Education M
Film, Television, and Video Production M
Health Communication M
Health Informatics M
Health Psychology M,D
Industrial and Organizational Psychology M,D
Interior Design M
Landscape Architecture M
Marriage and Family Therapy M,D
Mathematics Education M
Nursing and Healthcare Administration M,D
Nursing Education M,D
Nursing—General M,D
Occupational Therapy M,D
Physical Therapy D
Physician Assistant Studies M
Science Education M
Secondary Education M
Social Sciences Education M
Special Education M
Sport Psychology M,D
Sustainability Management M
Women's Studies M
Writing M

CHESTNUT HILL COLLEGE
Clinical Psychology M,D,O
Counseling Psychology M,O
Early Childhood Education M
Education—General M
Educational Leadership and Administration M
Educational Media/Instructional Technology M,O
Elementary Education M
Human Services M,O
Marriage and Family Therapy M,D,O
Middle School Education M
Psychology—General M,D,O
Reading Education M
Secondary Education M
Special Education M,O

CHEYNEY UNIVERSITY OF PENNSYLVANIA
Education—General M,O
Educational Leadership and Administration M,O
Elementary Education M
Public Administration M
Special Education M
Urban Education M

THE CHICAGO SCHOOL OF PROFESSIONAL PSYCHOLOGY
Applied Behavior Analysis M,D
Clinical Psychology D
Forensic Psychology M,D
Industrial and Organizational Psychology M,D
Organizational Management M,D
Psychology—General M,D
School Psychology D,O

THE CHICAGO SCHOOL OF PROFESSIONAL PSYCHOLOGY AT DOWNTOWN LOS ANGELES
Applied Behavior Analysis M,D
Clinical Psychology M,D
Forensic Psychology D
Industrial and Organizational Psychology M
Marriage and Family Therapy M,D

THE CHICAGO SCHOOL OF PROFESSIONAL PSYCHOLOGY AT IRVINE
Clinical Psychology D
Forensic Psychology D
Marriage and Family Therapy M,D
Psychology—General D

THE CHICAGO SCHOOL OF PROFESSIONAL PSYCHOLOGY: ONLINE
Applied Psychology M,O
Forensic Psychology M,O
Industrial and Organizational Psychology M,D,O
Psychology—General M,D

CHICAGO STATE UNIVERSITY
Biological and Biomedical Sciences—General M
Computer Science M
Counselor Education M
Criminal Justice and Criminology M
Early Childhood Education M
Education—General M,D
Educational Leadership and Administration M,D
Educational Media/Instructional Technology M
Elementary Education M
English M
Foundations and Philosophy of Education M
Geographic Information Systems M
Geography M
Higher Education M,D
History M
Library Science M
Mathematics M
Middle School Education M
Multilingual and Multicultural Education M
Nursing—General M
Occupational Therapy M
Pharmacy D
Physical Education M
Public Health—General M
Reading Education M
Secondary Education M
Social Work M
Special Education M
Vocational and Technical Education M
Writing M

CHICAGO THEOLOGICAL SEMINARY
Ethics M,D
Pastoral Ministry and Counseling M,D
Religion M,D
Theology M,D

CHOWAN UNIVERSITY
Education—General M

CHRISTENDOM COLLEGE
Theology M

CHRISTIAN BROTHERS UNIVERSITY
Accounting M,O
Business Administration and Management—General M,O
Education—General M
Educational Leadership and Administration M
Engineering and Applied Sciences—General M
International Business M,O
Physician Assistant Studies M
Project Management M,O
Religion M

CHRISTIAN THEOLOGICAL SEMINARY
Marriage and Family Therapy M,D
Pastoral Ministry and Counseling M,D
Religion M,D
Theology M,D

CHRISTIE'S EDUCATION
Art History M
Art/Fine Arts O
Arts Administration M,O
Museum Studies M

CHRISTOPHER NEWPORT UNIVERSITY
Applied Physics M
Computer Science M
Education—General M
Environmental Sciences M
Physics M

CHRIST THE KING SEMINARY
Pastoral Ministry and Counseling M
Theology M

CHURCH DIVINITY SCHOOL OF THE PACIFIC
Theology M,D,O

CINCINNATI CHRISTIAN UNIVERSITY
Pastoral Ministry and Counseling M
Religion M
Theology M

THE CITADEL, THE MILITARY COLLEGE OF SOUTH CAROLINA
Biological and Biomedical Sciences—General M
Business Administration and Management—General M
Civil Engineering M
Computer Science M
Counselor Education M,O
Education—General M,O
Educational Leadership and Administration M,O
Elementary Education M,O
English Education M
English M
Health Education M
History M
Mathematics Education M
Middle School Education M
National Security M
Physical Education M
Political Science M
Psychology—General M,O
Reading Education M,O
School Psychology O
Science Education M
Secondary Education M,O
Social Sciences Education M
Social Sciences M
Student Affairs M,O

CITY COLLEGE OF THE CITY UNIVERSITY OF NEW YORK
Architecture M
Art History M
Art/Fine Arts M
Atmospheric Sciences M
Biochemistry M,D
Biological and Biomedical Sciences—General M,D
Biomedical Engineering M,D
Business Administration and Management—General M
Chemical Engineering M,D
Chemistry M,D
Civil Engineering M,D
Classics M
Clinical Psychology M,D
Computer Art and Design M
Computer Science M,D
Corporate and Organizational Communication M
Early Childhood Education M
Economics M
Education—General M,O
Educational Leadership and Administration M,O
Electrical Engineering M,D
Engineering and Applied Sciences—General M,D
English as a Second Language M
English Education M,O
English M
Foreign Languages Education M
Geology M
Geosciences M
Graphic Design M
History M
International Affairs M
Landscape Architecture M
Management Information Systems M,D
Marketing M
Mathematics Education M,O
Mathematics M
Mechanical Engineering M,D
Media Studies M
Middle School Education M,O
Multilingual and Multicultural Education M
Museum Studies M
Physics M,D
Psychology—General M,D
Public Administration M,D
Reading Education M
Science Education M
Secondary Education M,O
Social Sciences Education M,O
Sociology M
Spanish M
Special Education M,O
Sustainable Development M
Urban Design M
Writing M

CITY UNIVERSITY OF NEW YORK SCHOOL OF LAW
Law D

CITY UNIVERSITY OF SEATTLE
Accounting M,O
Business Administration and Management—General M,O
Computer and Information Systems Security M,O
Computer Science M,O
Counseling Psychology M
Counselor Education M,O
Curriculum and Instruction M,O
Education—General M,O
Educational Leadership and Administration M,D,O
Elementary Education M,O
Finance and Banking M,O
Human Resources Management M,O
International Business M,O
Management Information Systems M,O
Management of Technology M,O
Marketing M,O
Organizational Management M,O
Project Management M,O
Reading Education M,O
Special Education M,O
Sustainability Management M,O

CITY VISION UNIVERSITY
Entrepreneurship M
Pastoral Ministry and Counseling M

CLAFLIN UNIVERSITY
Biotechnology M
Business Administration and Management—General M

CLAREMONT GRADUATE UNIVERSITY
African Studies M,D,O
American Studies M,D,O
Applied Mathematics M,D
Archives/Archival Administration M,D,O
Art/Fine Arts M
Arts Administration M
Botany M,D
Business Administration and Management—General M,D,O
Cognitive Sciences M,D,O
Comparative Literature M,D
Computational Biology M,D
Computational Sciences M,D
Computer and Information Systems Security M,D,O
Computer Art and Design M
Cultural Studies M,D,O
Database Systems M,D,O
Developmental Psychology M,D,O
Economic Development M,D,O
Economics M,D,O
Education—General M,D,O
Educational Leadership and Administration M,D,O
Educational Measurement and Evaluation M,D,O
Electronic Commerce M,D,O
English M,D
Ethics M,D
Film, Television, and Video Theory and Criticism M,D
Financial Engineering M
Geographic Information Systems M,D,O
Health Informatics M,D,O
Health Promotion M,D

*M—masters degree; D—doctorate; O—other advanced degree; *—Close-Up and/or Display*

Health Psychology	M,D,O
Higher Education	M,D,O
History	M,D,O
Human Development	M,D,O
Human Resources Development	M,D,O
Human Resources Management	M
Humanities	M,D,O
Industrial and Organizational Psychology	M,D,O
Information Science	M,D,O
International Affairs	M,D
International Economics	M,D,O
Management Information Systems	M,D,O
Management Strategy and Policy	M,D,O
Mathematics	M,D
Media Studies	M,D,O
Museum Studies	M,D,O
Music	M,D
Operations Research	M,D
Philosophy	M,D
Photography	M
Political Science	M,D
Psychology—General	M,D,O
Public Health—General	M,D
Public Policy	M,D,O
Religion	M,D
Social Psychology	M,D,O
Special Education	M,D,O
Statistics	M,D
Student Affairs	M,D,O
Systems Science	M,D,O
Telecommunications	M,D,O
Theology	M,D
Urban Education	M,D,O
Western European Studies	M,D,O
Women's Studies	M,D
Writing	M,D

CLAREMONT LINCOLN UNIVERSITY

Ethics	M
Pastoral Ministry and Counseling	M
Religion	M

CLAREMONT MCKENNA COLLEGE

Finance and Banking	M

CLAREMONT SCHOOL OF THEOLOGY

Ethics	M,D
Pastoral Ministry and Counseling	M,D
Religion	M,D
Religious Education	M,D
Theology	M,D

CLARION UNIVERSITY OF PENNSYLVANIA

Advertising and Public Relations	O
Business Administration and Management—General	M
Communication Disorders	M
Communication—General	M
Curriculum and Instruction	M
Database Systems	M
Early Childhood Education	M
Education—General	M
Family Nurse Practitioner Studies	M,D,O
Library Science	M,O
Mathematics Education	M
Nursing Education	M,D,O
Nursing—General	M,D
Reading Education	M
Rehabilitation Sciences	M
Science Education	M
Special Education	M
Vocational and Technical Education	M

CLARK ATLANTA UNIVERSITY

Accounting	M
African-American Studies	M,D
Biological and Biomedical Sciences—General	M,D
Business Administration and Management—General	M
Chemistry	M,D
Computer Science	M
Counselor Education	M
Criminal Justice and Criminology	M
Curriculum and Instruction	M
Economics	M
Education—General	M,D,O
Educational Leadership and Administration	M,D,O
Educational Psychology	M
English	M,D
History	M,D
Information Science	M
Mathematics Education	M
Mathematics	M
Physics	M
Political Science	M,D
Public Administration	M
Romance Languages	M,D
Science Education	M
Social Work	M,D
Sociology	M
Special Education	M
Women's Studies	M,D

CLARKE UNIVERSITY

Business Administration and Management—General	M
Education—General	M
Educational Leadership and Administration	M
Family Nurse Practitioner Studies	D
Nursing—General	D
Physical Therapy	D
Social Work	M

CLARKSON COLLEGE

Adult Nursing	M,O
Family Nurse Practitioner Studies	M,O
Nursing and Healthcare Administration	M,O
Nursing Education	M,O
Nursing—General	M,O

CLARKSON UNIVERSITY

Bioethics	M,O
Biotechnology	D
Business Administration and Management—General	M
Chemical Engineering	M,D
Chemistry	M,D
Chinese	M,O
Civil Engineering	M,D
Computer Education	M,O
Computer Engineering	M,D
Computer Science	M,D
Education—General	M,O
Educational Leadership and Administration	M,O
Electrical Engineering	M,D
Engineering and Applied Sciences—General	M,D
Engineering Management	M
English Education	M,O
Environmental Engineering	M,D
Environmental Management and Policy	M
Environmental Sciences	M,D
Foreign Languages Education	M,O
Health Informatics	M,O
Health Services Management and Hospital Administration	M,O
Health Services Research	M
Human Resources Management	M,O
Information Science	M
Interdisciplinary Studies	M,D
Materials Engineering	D
Materials Sciences	D
Mathematics Education	M,O
Mathematics	M,D
Mechanical Engineering	M,D
Middle School Education	M,O
Occupational Therapy	M
Physical Therapy	D
Physician Assistant Studies	M
Physics	M,D
Science Education	M,O
Social Sciences Education	M,O
Sustainable Development	M,D

CLARK UNIVERSITY

Accounting	M
American Studies	M,D
Biochemistry	M,D
Biological and Biomedical Sciences—General	M,D
Business Administration and Management—General	M
Chemistry	M,D
Clinical Psychology	D
Communication—General	M
Developmental Psychology	D
Economics	D
Education—General	M
English	M
Environmental Management and Policy	M
Finance and Banking	M
Geographic Information Systems	M
Geography	M,D
History	M,D,O
Holocaust and Genocide Studies	D
Information Science	M
International Business	M
International Development	M
Management Information Systems	M
Marketing	M
Physics	D
Public Administration	M,O
Social Psychology	D
Sustainability Management	M
Sustainable Development	M
Urban and Regional Planning	M

CLAYTON STATE UNIVERSITY

Accounting	M
Applied Psychology	M
Archives/Archival Administration	M
Biological and Biomedical Sciences—General	M
Business Administration and Management—General	M
Clinical Psychology	M
Developmental Psychology	M
Education—General	M
English Education	M
Family Nurse Practitioner Studies	M
History	M
Human Resources Management	M
International Business	M
Liberal Studies	M
Mathematics Education	M
Nursing—General	M
Psychology—General	M
Sports Management	M
Supply Chain Management	M

CLEARY UNIVERSITY

Accounting	M,O
Business Administration and Management—General	M,O
Finance and Banking	M,O
Health Services Management and Hospital Administration	M,O
Nonprofit Management	M,O
Organizational Management	M,O
Sustainability Management	M,O

CLEMSON UNIVERSITY

Accounting	M
Agricultural Education	M
Agricultural Sciences—General	M
Animal Sciences	M,D
Applied Economics	M,D
Applied Psychology	M
Aquaculture	M,D
Architecture	M,O
Art/Fine Arts	M
Automotive Engineering	M,D
Biochemistry	D
Bioengineering	M,D,O
Biological and Biomedical Sciences—General	M,D
Biomedical Engineering	M,D,O
Biosystems Engineering	M,D
Business Administration and Management—General	M
Business Education	M,D
Chemical Engineering	M,D
Chemistry	M,D
Civil Engineering	M,D
Clinical Research	M,D,O
Communication—General	M,D
Computer Art and Design	M
Computer Engineering	M,D
Computer Science	M,D
Construction Management	M
Counseling Psychology	M,D,O
Counselor Education	M,D,O
Curriculum and Instruction	M,D,O
Ecology	M,D
Economics	M,D
Education—General	M,D,O
Educational Leadership and Administration	M,D,O
Educational Measurement and Evaluation	D
Electrical Engineering	M,D
Engineering and Applied Sciences—General	M,D,O
English	M
Entomology	M,D
Entrepreneurship	M
Environmental and Occupational Health	M
Environmental Design	D
Environmental Engineering	M,D
Environmental Management and Policy	M,D
Environmental Sciences	M,D
Ergonomics and Human Factors	D
Evolutionary Biology	M,D
Family and Consumer Sciences-General	D,O
Fish, Game, and Wildlife Management	M,D
Food Science and Technology	M,D
Forestry	M,D
Genetics	M,D
Higher Education	M,D,O
Historic Preservation	M
History	M
Human Development	M,O
Human Resources Development	M,D,O
Human Resources Management	M,D,O
Human-Computer Interaction	D
Hydrogeology	M
Industrial and Organizational Psychology	D
Industrial/Management Engineering	M,D
Landscape Architecture	M
Management Strategy and Policy	M
Manufacturing Engineering	M
Materials Engineering	M,D
Materials Sciences	M,D
Mathematics Education	M,D,O
Mathematics	M,D
Mechanical Engineering	M,D
Microbiology	M,D
Middle School Education	M,D,O
Molecular Biology	D
Nursing—General	M,D
Nutrition	M
Organizational Management	M,D,O
Plant Biology	M,D
Plant Sciences	M,D
Psychology—General	D
Public Administration	M,O
Public Health—General	M,D,O
Public Policy	D,O
Reading Education	M,D,O
Real Estate	M
Recreation and Park Management	M,D,O
Rhetoric	D
Science Education	M,D,O
Secondary Education	M
Sociology	M
Special Education	M,D,O
Sports Management	M,D,O
Statistics	M,D
Student Affairs	M,D,O
Travel and Tourism	M,D,O
Urban and Regional Planning	M
Veterinary Sciences	M,D
Writing	M

CLEVELAND INSTITUTE OF MUSIC

Music	M,D,O

CLEVELAND STATE UNIVERSITY

Accounting	M
Addictions/Substance Abuse Counseling	M,D,O
Adult Education	M,D,O
Allied Health—General	M
Analytical Chemistry	M,D
Applied Statistics	M
Art Education	M
Art History	M
Bioethics	M,O
Biological and Biomedical Sciences—General	M,D
Biomedical Engineering	D
Business Administration and Management—General	M,D
Chemical Engineering	M,D
Chemistry	M,D
Civil Engineering	M,D
Communication Disorders	M
Communication—General	M,D,O
Community Health Nursing	M,D
Computer Science	M,D
Condensed Matter Physics	M
Counseling Psychology	M,D,O
Counselor Education	M,D,O
Early Childhood Education	M
Economic Development	M,O
Economics	M,O
Education of Students with Severe/Multiple Disabilities	M
Education—General	M,D,O
Educational Leadership and Administration	M,D,O
Educational Media/Instructional Technology	D
Educational Policy	D
Electrical Engineering	M,D
Engineering and Applied Sciences—General	M,D
English as a Second Language	M
English	M
Environmental Engineering	M,D
Environmental Management and Policy	M,O
Environmental Sciences	M,D
Exercise and Sports Science	M
Finance and Banking	M,D,O
Foreign Languages Education	M
Forensic Nursing	M,D
French	M
Geographic Information Systems	M,O
Health Communication	M,O
Health Education	M
Health Law	M,D,O
Health Services Management and Hospital Administration	M,O
Higher Education	D
Historic Preservation	M,O
History	M
Human Resources Management	M
Industrial and Labor Relations	M,D,O
Industrial and Manufacturing Management	D
Industrial/Management Engineering	M,D
Information Science	M,D
Inorganic Chemistry	M,D
International Affairs	M
International Business	M,D,O
International Economics	M
Latin American Studies	M
Law	M,D,O
Linguistics	M
Management Information Systems	M,D
Marketing	M,D,O
Mathematics Education	M
Mathematics	M
Mechanical Engineering	M,D
Medical Imaging	M
Medical Physics	M
Middle School Education	M
Molecular Medicine	M,D
Museum Studies	M
Music Education	M
Music	M
Nonprofit Management	M,O
Nursing Education	M,D
Nursing—General	M,D
Occupational Therapy	M
Optical Sciences	M
Organic Chemistry	M,D
Organizational Management	M,D,O
Philosophy	M,O
Physical Chemistry	M,D
Physical Education	M
Physical Therapy	D
Physician Assistant Studies	M
Physics	M
Psychology—General	M,D,O
Public Administration	M,D,O
Public Affairs	D
Public Health—General	M
Real Estate	M,O
Science Education	M
Social Psychology	M,D,O
Social Work	M
Sociology	M
Software Engineering	M,D
Spanish	M
Special Education	M
Sport Psychology	M
Sports Management	M
Sustainable Development	M,O
Taxation	M
Urban and Regional Planning	M,O
Urban Education	M,D
Urban Studies	M,D,O
Writing	M

CLEVELAND UNIVERSITY–KANSAS CITY

Chiropractic	D
Health Promotion	M

COASTAL CAROLINA UNIVERSITY

Accounting	M,O
Business Administration and Management—General	M,O
Computer Science	M,D,O
Distance Education Development	M,O
Education—General	M,O
Educational Leadership and Administration	M,O
Educational Media/Instructional Technology	M,O
English as a Second Language	M,O
Liberal Studies	M
Management Information Systems	M,D,O
Marine Sciences	M,D,O
Sports Management	M,D,O
Writing	M

COGSWELL POLYTECHNICAL COLLEGE

Entrepreneurship	M

COKER COLLEGE
Reading Education M
Sports Management M

THE COLBURN SCHOOL CONSERVATORY OF MUSIC
Music M,O

COLD SPRING HARBOR LABORATORY
Biological and Biomedical Sciences—General D

COLEMAN UNIVERSITY
Information Science M
Management of Technology M

COLGATE ROCHESTER CROZER DIVINITY SCHOOL
Conflict Resolution and Mediation/Peace Studies M,D,O
Theology M,D,O

COLGATE UNIVERSITY
Secondary Education M

THE COLLEGE AT BROCKPORT, STATE UNIVERSITY OF NEW YORK
Accounting M
American Studies M
Art/Fine Arts M
Arts Administration M,O
Biological and Biomedical Sciences—General M,O
Chemistry M,O
Communication—General M
Counseling Psychology M,O
Counselor Education M,O
Curriculum and Instruction M
Dance M
Early Childhood Education M
Education—General M,O
Educational Leadership and Administration M,O
English Education M,O
English M,O
Environmental Sciences M
Forensic Sciences M
Gerontology M,O
Health Education M
Health Services Management and Hospital Administration M,O
History of Medicine M,O
History M
Liberal Studies M
Mathematics Education M,O
Mathematics M,O
Middle School Education M
Multilingual and Multicultural Education M,O
Nonprofit Management M,O
Physical Education M,O
Psychology—General M
Public Administration M,O
Public History M
Reading Education M
Science Education M,O
Social Sciences Education M,O
Social Work M,O
Sports Management M,O
Writing M,O

COLLÈGE DOMINICAIN DE PHILOSOPHIE ET DE THÉOLOGIE
Philosophy M,D
Theology M,D,O

COLLEGE FOR CREATIVE STUDIES
Applied Arts and Design—General M
Art/Fine Arts M
Automotive Engineering M
Transportation and Highway Engineering M

COLLEGE FOR FINANCIAL PLANNING
Finance and Banking M

COLLEGE OF CHARLESTON
Accounting M
Arts Administration M,O
Business Administration and Management—General M
Communication—General M
Computer Science M
Early Childhood Education M
Education—General M,O
Elementary Education M
English as a Second Language O
English M
Environmental Sciences M
Foreign Languages Education M
Historic Preservation M
History M
Management Information Systems M
Marine Biology M
Marine Sciences M
Mathematics Education M
Mathematics M,O
Music Education M
Public Administration M
Science Education M
Special Education M
Urban and Regional Planning O

COLLEGE OF EMMANUEL AND ST. CHAD
Theology M,O

THE COLLEGE OF IDAHO
Curriculum and Instruction M
Education—General M

COLLEGE OF MOUNT SAINT VINCENT
Adult Nursing M,O
Education—General M,O
Educational Media/Instructional Technology M,O
Family Nurse Practitioner Studies M,O
Gerontological Nursing M,O
Middle School Education M,O
Multilingual and Multicultural Education M,O
Nursing and Healthcare Administration M,O
Nursing Education M,O
Nursing—General M,O
Urban Education M,O

THE COLLEGE OF NEW JERSEY
Addictions/Substance Abuse Counseling M,O
Counselor Education M
Early Childhood Education M
Education—General M,O
Educational Leadership and Administration M,O
Elementary Education M
English as a Second Language M,O
English M
Gender Studies O
Health Education M
International and Comparative Education M,O
Marriage and Family Therapy O
Nursing—General M,O
Physical Education M
Reading Education M,O
Secondary Education M
Special Education M,O

THE COLLEGE OF NEW ROCHELLE
Acute Care/Critical Care Nursing M,O
Art Education M
Art Therapy M
Communication—General M,O
Counseling Psychology M,O
Early Childhood Education M
Education of the Gifted O
Education—General M,O
Educational Leadership and Administration M,O
Elementary Education M
English as a Second Language M,O
Family Nurse Practitioner Studies M,O
Human Resources Development M,O
Marriage and Family Therapy M
Multilingual and Multicultural Education M,O
Nursing and Healthcare Administration M,O
Nursing Education M,O
Nursing—General M,O
Public Administration M
Reading Education M
School Psychology M
Special Education M
Thanatology M,O

COLLEGE OF SAINT ELIZABETH
Business Administration and Management—General M
Counseling Psychology M,D,O
Criminal Justice and Criminology M
Education—General M,D,O
Educational Leadership and Administration M,D,O
Educational Media/Instructional Technology M,D,O
Exercise and Sports Science M,O
Forensic Psychology M,D,O
Health Services Management and Hospital Administration M
Higher Education M,D,O
Human Resources Management M
Nursing—General M
Nutrition M,O
Organizational Management M
Psychology—General M,D,O
Public Administration M
Student Affairs M,D,O
Theology M

COLLEGE OF ST. JOSEPH
Addictions/Substance Abuse Counseling M
Business Administration and Management—General M
Clinical Psychology M
Counseling Psychology M
Counselor Education M
Education—General M
Elementary Education M
English Education M
Psychology—General M
Reading Education M
School Psychology M
Secondary Education M
Social Psychology M
Social Sciences Education M
Special Education M

COLLEGE OF SAINT MARY
Education—General M
Educational Leadership and Administration M
Educational Measurement and Evaluation M
English as a Second Language M
Health Education D
Nursing—General M
Occupational Therapy M
Organizational Management M

THE COLLEGE OF SAINT ROSE
Accounting M
Business Administration and Management—General M
Communication Disorders M
Computer Science M,O
Counseling Psychology M,O
Counselor Education M,O
Curriculum and Instruction M,O
Early Childhood Education M,O
Education—General M,O
Educational Leadership and Administration M,O
Educational Psychology M,O
Finance and Banking O
Higher Education M,O
Information Science M,O
Management Information Systems M,O
Management Strategy and Policy M,O
Middle School Education M,O
Organizational Management O
Reading Education M,O
School Psychology M,O
Secondary Education M,O
Special Education M,O
Student Affairs M

THE COLLEGE OF ST. SCHOLASTICA
Athletic Training and Sports Medicine M
Business Administration and Management—General M,O
Education—General M,O
Exercise and Sports Science M
Health Informatics M,O
Management Information Systems M,O
Nursing—General M,O
Occupational Therapy M
Physical Therapy D
Social Work M

COLLEGE OF STATEN ISLAND OF THE CITY UNIVERSITY OF NEW YORK
Accounting M
Adult Nursing M,O
Biological and Biomedical Sciences—General M
Business Administration and Management—General M
Clinical Psychology M
Computer Science M
Counseling Psychology M
Education—General M,O
Educational Leadership and Administration O
Elementary Education M
English as a Second Language M,O
English M
Environmental Sciences M
Family Nurse Practitioner Studies D
Film, Television, and Video Theory and Criticism M
Gerontological Nursing M,O
History M
Liberal Studies M
Media Studies M
Neuroscience M
Nursing—General M,D,O
Physical Therapy D
Secondary Education M
Social Work M
Special Education M,O

COLLEGE OF THE ATLANTIC
Environmental Management and Policy M

THE COLLEGE OF WILLIAM AND MARY
Accounting M
American Studies M,D
Anthropology M,D
Applied Mathematics M,D
Applied Physics M,D
Applied Science and Technology M,D
Artificial Intelligence/Robotics M,D
Atmospheric Sciences M,D
Biological and Biomedical Sciences—General M
Biomathematics M,D
Business Administration and Management—General M
Chemistry M
Clinical Laboratory Sciences/Medical Technology M,D
Computational Biology M,D
Computational Sciences M
Computer Science M,D
Counselor Education M,D
Curriculum and Instruction M,D
Education—General M,D,O*
Educational Leadership and Administration M,D
Educational Media/Instructional Technology M,D
Educational Policy M,D
Environmental Sciences M,D
Experimental Psychology M
Geographic Information Systems M,D
History M,D
Law M,D
Marine Sciences M,D
Materials Engineering M,D
Materials Sciences M,D
Medical Physics M,D
Nanotechnology M,D
Neuroscience M,D
Operations Research M
Optical Sciences M,D
Physics M,D
Polymer Science and Engineering M,D
Public Policy M
School Psychology M,O

COLORADO CHRISTIAN UNIVERSITY
Business Administration and Management—General M
Business Education M
Computer and Information Systems Security M
Counseling Psychology M
Curriculum and Instruction M
Distance Education Development M
Early Childhood Education M
Education—General M
Educational Media/Instructional Technology M
Elementary Education M
Project Management M
Special Education M

THE COLORADO COLLEGE
American Studies M
Art Education M
Education—General M
Elementary Education M
English Education M
Foreign Languages Education M
Humanities M
Liberal Studies M
Mathematics Education M
Music Education M
Science Education M
Secondary Education M
Social Sciences Education M

COLORADO HEIGHTS UNIVERSITY
Accounting M
Environmental Management and Policy M
Finance and Banking M
Health Services Management and Hospital Administration M
International Business M

COLORADO MESA UNIVERSITY
Business Administration and Management—General M
Education of the Gifted M
Education—General M
Educational Leadership and Administration M
English as a Second Language M
Family Nurse Practitioner Studies M,D,O
Health Informatics M,D,O
Nursing Education M,D,O
Nursing—General M,D,O
Special Education M

COLORADO SCHOOL OF MINES
Applied Mathematics M,D
Applied Physics M,D
Applied Statistics M,D
Bioengineering M,D
Chemical Engineering M,D
Chemistry M,D
Civil Engineering M,D
Computer Science M,D
Construction Engineering M,D
Electrical Engineering M,D
Electronic Materials M,D
Engineering and Applied Sciences—General M,D,O
Engineering Management M,D
Environmental Engineering M,D
Geochemistry M,D
Geological Engineering M,D
Geology M,D
Geophysics M,D
Hydrology M,D
International Affairs O
Management of Technology M,D
Materials Engineering M,D
Materials Sciences M,D
Mechanical Engineering M,D
Metallurgical Engineering and Metallurgy M,D
Mineral Economics M,D
Mineral/Mining Engineering M,D
Nuclear Engineering M,D
Operations Research M,D
Petroleum Engineering M,D
Physics M,D

COLORADO SCHOOL OF TRADITIONAL CHINESE MEDICINE
Acupuncture and Oriental Medicine M

COLORADO STATE UNIVERSITY
Accounting M
Adult Education M,D
Advertising and Public Relations M,D
Agricultural Economics and Agribusiness M,D
Agricultural Sciences—General M,D
Agronomy and Soil Sciences M,D
Animal Sciences M,D
Anthropology M
Art History M
Art/Fine Arts M
Arts Administration M
Atmospheric Sciences M,D
Biochemistry M,D
Biological and Biomedical Sciences—General M,D
Biomedical Engineering M,D
Botany M,D
Business Administration and Management—General M
Cell Biology M,D
Chemical Engineering M,D
Chemistry M,D
Child and Family Studies M,D
Civil Engineering M,D
Computer Science M,D
Conservation Biology M,D

*M—masters degree; D—doctorate; O—other advanced degree; *—Close-Up and/or Display*

Construction Management M
Consumer Economics M
Counselor Education M,D
Distance Education Development M
Ecology M,D
Economics M,D
Education—General M,D
Educational Leadership and Administration M,D
Electrical Engineering M,D
Engineering and Applied Sciences—General M,D
English M
Entomology M,D
Environmental and Occupational Health M,D
Ethnic Studies M
Exercise and Sports Science M,D
Finance and Banking M
Fish, Game, and Wildlife Management M,D
Food Science and Technology M,D
Forestry M,D
Geosciences M,D
Higher Education M,D
History M
Horticulture M,D
Human Development M,D
Immunology M,D
Industrial and Organizational Psychology M,D
Landscape Architecture M,D
Management Information Systems M
Marriage and Family Therapy M,D
Mass Communication M,D
Mathematics M,D
Mechanical Engineering M,D
Media Studies M,D
Microbiology M,D
Molecular Biology M,D
Music Education M
Music M
Natural Resources M,D
Neuroscience D
Nutrition M,D
Occupational Therapy M,D
Pathology M,D
Philosophy M
Physics M,D
Plant Pathology M,D
Plant Sciences M,D
Political Science M,D
Psychology—General M,D
Radiation Biology M,D
Range Science M,D
Recreation and Park Management M,D
Science Education M,D
Social Work M,D
Sociology M,D
Speech and Interpersonal Communication M
Statistics M,D
Student Affairs M,D
Sustainability Management M
Therapies—Dance, Drama, and Music M
Toxicology M,D
Travel and Tourism M,D
Veterinary Medicine D
Veterinary Sciences M,D
Writing M
Zoology M,D

COLORADO STATE UNIVERSITY–GLOBAL CAMPUS
Accounting M
Business Administration and Management—General M
Criminal Justice and Criminology M
Education—General M
Educational Leadership and Administration M
Finance and Banking M
Health Services Management and Hospital Administration M
Human Resources Management M
International Business M
Management Information Systems M
Organizational Management M
Project Management M

COLORADO STATE UNIVERSITY–PUEBLO
Applied Science and Technology M
Art Education M
Biochemistry M
Biological and Biomedical Sciences—General M
Business Administration and Management—General M
Chemistry M
Education—General M
Educational Media/Instructional Technology M
Engineering and Applied Sciences—General M
Foreign Languages Education M
Health Education M
Industrial/Management Engineering M
Music Education M
Nursing—General M
Physical Education M
Special Education M
Systems Engineering M

COLORADO TECHNICAL UNIVERSITY COLORADO SPRINGS
Accounting M,D
Business Administration and Management—General M,D
Computer and Information Systems Security M,D
Computer Engineering M
Computer Science M,D
Conflict Resolution and Mediation/Peace Studies M,D
Criminal Justice and Criminology M
Database Systems M,D
Electrical Engineering M
Finance and Banking M,D
Human Resources Management M,D
Industrial and Manufacturing Management M,D
Logistics M,D
Management of Technology M,D
Marketing M,D
Project Management M,D
Software Engineering M,D
Systems Engineering M

COLORADO TECHNICAL UNIVERSITY DENVER SOUTH
Accounting M
Business Administration and Management—General M
Computer and Information Systems Security M
Computer Engineering M
Computer Science M
Conflict Resolution and Mediation/Peace Studies M
Criminal Justice and Criminology M
Database Systems M
Electrical Engineering M
Finance and Banking M
Human Resources Management M
Industrial and Manufacturing Management M
Management of Technology M
Marketing M
Project Management M
Software Engineering M
Systems Engineering M

COLUMBIA COLLEGE (MO)
Business Administration and Management—General M
Criminal Justice and Criminology M
Education—General M
Educational Leadership and Administration M

COLUMBIA COLLEGE (SC)
Conflict Resolution and Mediation/Peace Studies M
Education—General M
Educational Leadership and Administration M
Elementary Education M
Higher Education M

COLUMBIA COLLEGE CHICAGO
Arts Administration M
Comparative and Interdisciplinary Arts M
Entertainment Management M
Film, Television, and Video Production M
Journalism M
Music M
Photography M
Therapies—Dance, Drama, and Music M,O
Writing M

COLUMBIA INTERNATIONAL UNIVERSITY
Counselor Education M,D,O
Cultural Studies M,D,O
Curriculum and Instruction M,D,O
Early Childhood Education M,D,O
Education—General M,D,O
Educational Leadership and Administration M,D,O
Elementary Education M,D,O
English as a Second Language M,D,O
Missions and Missiology M,D,O
Multilingual and Multicultural Education M,D,O
Pastoral Ministry and Counseling M,D,O
Religious Education M,D,O
Theology M,D,O

COLUMBIA SOUTHERN UNIVERSITY
Business Administration and Management—General M,D
Criminal Justice and Criminology M
Emergency Management M
Environmental and Occupational Health M
Finance and Banking M
Health Services Management and Hospital Administration M
Human Resources Management M
Marketing M
Organizational Management M

COLUMBIA THEOLOGICAL SEMINARY
Theology M,D

COLUMBIA UNIVERSITY
Accounting M,D
Actuarial Science M
Acute Care/Critical Care Nursing M,O
Adult Nursing M,O
African Studies M,D
African-American Studies M,D
Allopathic Medicine M,D
American Studies M,D
Anatomy M,D
Anthropology M,D
Applied Mathematics M,D
Applied Physics M,D
Archaeology M,D
Architecture M,D
Archives/Archival Administration M
Art History M,D
Art/Fine Arts M,D
Asian Studies M,D,O
Astronomy M,D
Atmospheric Sciences M,D
Biochemistry M,D
Bioethics M
Biological and Biomedical Sciences—General M,D,O*
Biomedical Engineering M,D
Biophysics M,D
Biostatistics M,D
Biotechnology M,D
Business Administration and Management—General M,D
Cell Biology M,D
Chemical Engineering M,D
Chemical Physics M,D
Chemistry M,D
Civil Engineering M,D
Classics M,D
Communication—General M,D
Community Health M,D
Comparative Literature M,D
Computer Engineering M,D
Computer Science M,D
Conflict Resolution and Mediation/Peace Studies M
Conservation Biology M,D
Construction Engineering M,D
Construction Management M,D
Corporate and Organizational Communication M
Database Systems M
Dentistry D
Developmental Biology M,D
East European and Russian Studies M,D
Ecology M,D
Economics M,D
Electrical Engineering M,D
Engineering and Applied Sciences—General M,D
English M,D
Entrepreneurship M
Environmental and Occupational Health M,D
Environmental Design M
Environmental Engineering M,D
Environmental Management and Policy M
Environmental Sciences M,D*
Epidemiology M,D
Ethics M
Evolutionary Biology M,D
Family Nurse Practitioner Studies M,O
Film, Television, and Video Production M
Finance and Banking M,D
Financial Engineering M,D
Foreign Languages Education M,D
Foundations and Philosophy of Education M,D
French M,D
Genetics M,D
Geosciences M,D
German M,D
Gerontological Nursing M,O
Health Services Management and Hospital Administration M
Hispanic Studies M,D
Historic Preservation M,O
History M,D
Human Resources Management M
Industrial/Management Engineering M,D
Information Studies M
International Affairs M,D
International Business M
Italian M,D
Japanese M,D
Jewish Studies M,D
Journalism M,D
Kinesiology and Movement Studies M,D
Landscape Architecture M
Latin American Studies M,D
Law M,D
Legal and Justice Studies M,D
Management of Technology M
Marketing M,D
Materials Engineering M,D
Materials Sciences M,D
Maternal and Child Health M,D
Mathematics M,D
Mechanical Engineering M,D*
Mechanics M,D
Medical Informatics M,D,O
Medical Physics M,D
Medieval and Renaissance Studies M,D
Microbiology M,D
Molecular Biology D
Museum Studies M,D
Music M,D
Near and Middle Eastern Studies M,D
Neurobiology D
Nonprofit Management M
Nurse Anesthesia M,O
Nurse Midwifery M
Nursing—General M,D,O
Nutrition M,D
Occupational Therapy M,D
Operations Research M,D
Oral and Dental Sciences M,D,O
Pathobiology M,D
Pathology M,D
Pediatric Nursing M,O
Pharmaceutical Administration M
Pharmacology M,D
Philosophy M,D
Photography M
Physical Therapy D
Physics M,D
Physiology M,D
Political Science M,D
Psychiatric Nursing M,O
Psychology—General M,D
Public Administration M
Public Health—General M,D
Public Policy M
Quantitative Analysis M,D
Real Estate M
Religion M,D
Romance Languages M,D
Russian M,D
Science Education M,D,O
Slavic Languages M,D
Social Sciences M,D
Social Work M,D
Sociology M,D
Spanish M,D
Sports Management M
Statistics M,D
Structural Biology D
Sustainability Management M
Sustainable Development M,D
Theater M,D*
Toxicology M,D
Translation and Interpretation M,D
Urban and Regional Planning M,D
Western European Studies M,D
Writing M

COLUMBUS COLLEGE OF ART & DESIGN
Art/Fine Arts M

COLUMBUS STATE UNIVERSITY
Art Education M
Business Administration and Management—General M,O
Chemistry M,O
Clinical Psychology M,D,O
Computer and Information Systems Security M,O
Computer Science M,O
Counselor Education M,D,O
Criminal Justice and Criminology M
Curriculum and Instruction M,D,O
Early Childhood Education M,O
Education—General M,D,O
Educational Leadership and Administration M,D,O
English as a Second Language O
English Education M,O
Environmental Management and Policy M
Environmental Sciences M,O
Exercise and Sports Science M
Family Nurse Practitioner Studies M
Health Education M
Health Services Management and Hospital Administration M
Higher Education M,D,O
History M,O
Homeland Security M
Mathematics Education M,O
Mathematics M,O
Middle School Education M,O
Modeling and Simulation M,O
Music Education M,O
Music M,O
Nursing and Healthcare Administration M
Nursing Education M
Nursing Informatics M
Nursing—General M
Organizational Management M,O
Physical Education M
Public Administration M
Science Education M,O
Secondary Education M,O
Social Sciences Education M,O
Special Education M,O
Theater M
Urban Studies M

THE COMMONWEALTH MEDICAL COLLEGE
Allied Health—General D
Biological and Biomedical Sciences—General M

CONCORDIA COLLEGE
Education—General M
Foreign Languages Education M

CONCORDIA COLLEGE–NEW YORK
Organizational Management M
Special Education M

CONCORDIA LUTHERAN SEMINARY
Theology M,O

CONCORDIA SEMINARY
Theology M,D,O

CONCORDIA THEOLOGICAL SEMINARY
Theology M,D

CONCORDIA UNIVERSITY (CANADA)
Adult Education M,O
Aerospace/Aeronautical Engineering M
Anthropology M,D
Applied Arts and Design—General M,O
Art Education M,D
Art History M,D
Art Therapy M
Art/Fine Arts M
Biological and Biomedical Sciences—General M,D,O
Biotechnology M,D,O
Business Administration and Management—General M,D,O
Chemistry M,D
Child and Family Studies M
Civil Engineering M,D,O
Clinical Psychology D,O
Communication—General M,D,O
Computer and Information Systems Security M,D,O
Computer Art and Design M,O
Computer Engineering M,D
Computer Science M,D,O

Construction Engineering	M,D,O
Cultural Anthropology	M,D
Economic Development	O
Economics	M,D,O
Education—General	M,O
Educational Media/Instructional Technology	M,O
Electrical Engineering	M,D
Engineering and Applied Sciences—General	M,D,O
English as a Second Language	M,O
English	M,D
Environmental Engineering	M,D,O
Environmental Management and Policy	M,D,O
Exercise and Sports Science	M
Film, Television, and Video Production	M,D
Film, Television, and Video Theory and Criticism	M,D
Finance and Banking	M,D,O
French	M,O
Game Design and Development	M,D,O
Genomic Sciences	M,D,O
Geography	M,D,O
History	M,D
Humanities	D
Industrial/Management Engineering	M,D,O
Interdisciplinary Studies	M,D
Internet and Interactive Multimedia	M,D,O
Jewish Studies	M
Journalism	M,O
Linguistics	M,O
Marketing	M,D,O
Mathematics Education	M,D
Mathematics	M,D
Mechanical Engineering	M,D,O
Media Studies	M,D,O
Music	O
Organizational Management	M,O
Philosophy	M
Physics	M,D
Political Science	M,D
Psychology—General	M
Public Administration	M,D
Public Affairs	O
Public Policy	M,D
Religion	M,D
Sociology	M,D
Software Engineering	M,D,O
Statistics	M,D
Supply Chain Management	M,D,O
Systems Engineering	M,D,O
Telecommunications Management	M,D,O
Textile Design	M
Theology	M
Therapies—Dance, Drama, and Music	M
Translation and Interpretation	M,O
Urban and Regional Planning	O
Urban Studies	M,D,O
Writing	M

CONCORDIA UNIVERSITY (UNITED STATES)

Business Administration and Management—General	M
Curriculum and Instruction	M,D
Early Childhood Education	M,D
Education—General	M,D
Educational Leadership and Administration	M,D
Educational Media/Instructional Technology	M,D
Elementary Education	M,D
English as a Second Language	M,D
Environmental Education	M,D
Mathematics Education	M,D
Reading Education	M,D
Science Education	M,D
Secondary Education	M,D
Special Education	M,D
Vocational and Technical Education	M,D

CONCORDIA UNIVERSITY ANN ARBOR

Curriculum and Instruction	M
Educational Leadership and Administration	M
Organizational Management	M

CONCORDIA UNIVERSITY CHICAGO

Business Administration and Management—General	M
Counseling Psychology	M
Counselor Education	M,O
Curriculum and Instruction	M
Early Childhood Education	M,D
Education—General	M
Educational Leadership and Administration	M,D,O
Educational Media/Instructional Technology	M
Elementary Education	M
Exercise and Sports Science	M
Gerontology	M
Human Services	M
Liberal Studies	M
Music	M
Psychology—General	M
Reading Education	M
Religion	M
Religious Education	M
Secondary Education	M

CONCORDIA UNIVERSITY IRVINE

Applied Social Research	M
Business Administration and Management—General	M
Counselor Education	M
Cultural Studies	M
Curriculum and Instruction	M
Education—General	M
Educational Leadership and Administration	M
Educational Media/Instructional Technology	M
International Affairs	M
Physical Education	M
Religion	M
Sports Management	M
Theology	M

CONCORDIA UNIVERSITY, NEBRASKA

Computer and Information Systems Security	M
Computer Science	M
Early Childhood Education	M
Education—General	M
Educational Leadership and Administration	M
Elementary Education	M
Pastoral Ministry and Counseling	M
Reading Education	M
Religious Education	M
Secondary Education	M

CONCORDIA UNIVERSITY OF EDMONTON

Computer and Information Systems Security	M
Religion	M
Theology	M

CONCORDIA UNIVERSITY, ST. PAUL

Business Administration and Management—General	M
Child and Family Studies	M,D,O
Computer and Information Systems Security	M
Corporate and Organizational Communication	M
Criminal Justice and Criminology	M,D,O
Curriculum and Instruction	M,D,O
Early Childhood Education	M,D,O
Education—General	M,D,O
Educational Leadership and Administration	M,D,O
Educational Media/Instructional Technology	M,D,O
Exercise and Sports Science	M,D,O
Forensic Psychology	M,D,O
Health Services Management and Hospital Administration	M
Human Resources Management	M
Organizational Behavior	M
Organizational Management	M
Physical Therapy	M,D,O
Reading Education	M,D,O
Special Education	M,D,O
Sports Management	M,D,O

CONCORDIA UNIVERSITY TEXAS

Education—General	M

CONCORDIA UNIVERSITY WISCONSIN

Art Education	M
Business Administration and Management—General	M
Child and Family Studies	M
Corporate and Organizational Communication	M
Counseling Psychology	M
Counselor Education	M
Curriculum and Instruction	M
Early Childhood Education	M
Education—General	M
Educational Leadership and Administration	M
Environmental Education	M
Family Nurse Practitioner Studies	M
Finance and Banking	M
Gerontological Nursing	M
Health Services Management and Hospital Administration	M
Human Resources Management	M
Human Services	M,D
International Business	M
Management Information Systems	M
Marketing	M
Music	M
Nursing Education	M
Nursing—General	M
Occupational Therapy	M
Physical Therapy	M,D
Psychology—General	M
Public Administration	M
Reading Education	M
Rehabilitation Sciences	M
Special Education	M
Student Affairs	M

CONCORD LAW SCHOOL

Law	D

CONCORD UNIVERSITY

Education—General	M
Educational Leadership and Administration	M
Geography	M
Health Promotion	M
Reading Education	M
Social Sciences Education	M
Social Work	M
Special Education	M

CONNECTICUT COLLEGE

Biopsychology	M
Clinical Psychology	M
Health Psychology	M
Neuroscience	M
Psychology—General	M
Social Psychology	M

CONSERVATORIO DE MUSICA DE PUERTO RICO

Music Education	M
Music	O

CONVERSE COLLEGE

Art Education	M
Education of the Gifted	M
Education—General	M,O
Educational Leadership and Administration	M,O
Elementary Education	M
English Education	M
English	M
History	M
Liberal Studies	M
Marriage and Family Therapy	M
Mathematics Education	M
Middle School Education	M
Music Education	M
Music	M
Political Science	M
Reading Education	O
Science Education	M
Secondary Education	M
Social Sciences Education	M
Special Education	M

COOPER UNION FOR THE ADVANCEMENT OF SCIENCE AND ART

Architecture	M
Chemical Engineering	M
Civil Engineering	M
Electrical Engineering	M
Engineering and Applied Sciences—General	M
Mechanical Engineering	M

COPENHAGEN BUSINESS SCHOOL

Business Administration and Management—General	M,D
Economics	M,D
Health Services Management and Hospital Administration	M,D
International Business	M,D
Logistics	M,D
Management Information Systems	M,D
Public Administration	M,D

COPPIN STATE UNIVERSITY

Addictions/Substance Abuse Counseling	M
Adult Education	M
Criminal Justice and Criminology	M
Curriculum and Instruction	M
Education—General	M
Family Nurse Practitioner Studies	M,O
Human Services	M
Nursing—General	M,O
Reading Education	M
Rehabilitation Counseling	M
Special Education	M

CORBAN UNIVERSITY

Business Administration and Management—General	M
Education—General	M
Nonprofit Management	M
Pastoral Ministry and Counseling	M,D,O
Theology	M,D,O

CORNELL UNIVERSITY

Accounting	D
Adult Education	M,D
Aerospace/Aeronautical Engineering	M,D
African Studies	M,D
African-American Studies	M,D
Agricultural Economics and Agribusiness	M,D
Agricultural Education	M,D
Agricultural Engineering	M,D
Agronomy and Soil Sciences	M,D
American Studies	M,D
Analytical Chemistry	D
Anatomy	D
Animal Behavior	D
Animal Sciences	M,D
Anthropology	D
Applied Economics	M,D
Applied Mathematics	M,D
Applied Physics	M,D
Applied Statistics	M,D
Archaeology	M,D
Architectural History	M,D
Architecture	M,D
Art History	D
Art/Fine Arts	M
Artificial Intelligence/Robotics	M,D
Asian Languages	M,D
Asian Studies	M,D
Astronomy	D
Astrophysics	D
Atmospheric Sciences	M,D
Biochemical Engineering	M,D
Biochemistry	M,D
Bioengineering	M,D
Biological and Biomedical Sciences—General	M,D
Biomedical Engineering	M,D
Biometry	M,D
Biophysics	D
Biopsychology	D
Biotechnology	M,D
Business Administration and Management—General	M,D
Cell Biology	D
Chemical Engineering	M,D
Chemical Physics	D
Chemistry	D
Child and Family Studies	M,D
Civil Engineering	M,D
Classics	D
Clothing and Textiles	M,D
Cognitive Sciences	D
Communication—General	M,D
Comparative Literature	D
Computational Biology	D
Computational Sciences	M,D
Computer Art and Design	M,D
Computer Engineering	M,D
Computer Science	M,D
Conflict Resolution and Mediation/Peace Studies	M,D
Conservation Biology	M,D
Consumer Economics	M,D
Corporate and Organizational Communication	M,D
Cultural Anthropology	D
Cultural Studies	M,D
Curriculum and Instruction	M,D
Demography and Population Studies	M,D
Developmental Biology	M,D
Developmental Psychology	M,D
East European and Russian Studies	M,D
Ecology	M,D
Economic Development	M,D
Economics	M,D
Education—General	M,D
Educational Policy	M,D
Electrical Engineering	M,D
Energy and Power Engineering	M,D
Engineering and Applied Sciences—General	M,D
Engineering Management	M,D
Engineering Physics	M,D
English	M,D
Entomology	M,D
Environmental Design	M
Environmental Engineering	M,D
Environmental Management and Policy	M,D
Environmental Sciences	M,D
Epidemiology	M,D
Ergonomics and Human Factors	M
Ethnic Studies	M,D
Evolutionary Biology	D
Experimental Psychology	D
Facilities Management	M
Finance and Banking	D
Fish, Game, and Wildlife Management	M,D
Food Science and Technology	M,D
Foreign Languages Education	M,D
Forestry	M,D
French	D
Gender Studies	M,D
Genetics	D
Genomic Sciences	D
Geochemistry	M,D
Geology	M,D
Geophysics	M,D
Geosciences	M,D
Geotechnical Engineering	M,D
German	M,D
Health Communication	M,D
Health Services Management and Hospital Administration	M,D
Hispanic and Latin American Languages	D
Historic Preservation	M,D
History of Science and Technology	M,D
History	M,D
Horticulture	M,D
Hospitality Management	M,D*
Human Development	M,D
Human Resources Management	M,D
Human-Computer Interaction	M,D
Hydrology	M,D
Immunology	M,D
Industrial and Labor Relations	M,D
Industrial/Management Engineering	M,D
Infectious Diseases	M,D
Information Science	D
Information Studies	D
Inorganic Chemistry	D
Interior Design	M
International Affairs	D
Italian	D
Jewish Studies	M,D
Landscape Architecture	M
Latin American Studies	M,D
Law	M,D
Limnology	D
Linguistics	M,D
Manufacturing Engineering	M,D
Marine Geology	M,D
Marine Sciences	M,D
Marketing	D
Materials Engineering	M,D
Materials Sciences	M,D
Mathematics Education	M,D
Mathematics	D
Mechanical Engineering	M,D
Mechanics	M,D
Media Studies	M,D
Medieval and Renaissance Studies	M,D
Microbiology	D
Mineralogy	M,D
Molecular Biology	M,D
Molecular Medicine	M,D
Music	M,D
Nanotechnology	M,D
Natural Resources	M,D
Near and Middle Eastern Studies	M,D
Neurobiology	D
Nutrition	M,D
Oceanography	D

*M—masters degree; D—doctorate; O—other advanced degree; *—Close-Up and/or Display*

Operations Research M,D
Organic Chemistry D
Organizational Behavior M,D
Paleontology M,D
Pharmacology M,D
Philosophy D
Photography M,D
Physical Chemistry D
Physics M,D
Physiology M,D
Planetary and Space Sciences D
Plant Biology M,D
Plant Molecular Biology M,D
Plant Pathology M,D
Plant Physiology M,D
Plant Sciences M,D
Political Science D
Polymer Science and Engineering M,D
Psychology—General D
Public Affairs M
Public Policy M,D
Quantitative Analysis M,D
Real Estate M
Religion M,D
Reproductive Biology M,D
Romance Languages M,D
Rural Sociology M,D
Scandinavian Languages M,D
Secondary Education M,D
Slavic Languages M,D
Social Psychology M,D
Social Work M,D
Sociology M,D
Spanish D
Statistics M,D
Structural Biology M,D
Structural Engineering M,D
Sustainable Development M,D
Systems Engineering M
Textile Design M,D
Textile Sciences and Engineering M,D
Theater D
Theoretical Chemistry D
Theoretical Physics M,D
Toxicology M,D
Transportation and Highway Engineering M,D
Urban and Regional Planning M,D
Urban Design M,D
Veterinary Medicine D
Water Resources Engineering M,D
Water Resources M,D
Western European Studies M,D
Women's Studies M,D
Writing M,D
Zoology D

CORNERSTONE UNIVERSITY
Business Administration and Management—General M,O
Education—General M,O
English as a Second Language M,O

COVENANT COLLEGE
Education—General M

COVENANT THEOLOGICAL SEMINARY
Pastoral Ministry and Counseling M,D,O
Theology M,D,O

COX COLLEGE
Family Nurse Practitioner Studies M
Nursing and Healthcare Administration M
Nursing Education M
Nursing—General M

CRANBROOK ACADEMY OF ART
Applied Arts and Design—General M
Architecture M
Art/Fine Arts M
Photography M
Textile Design M

CRANDALL UNIVERSITY
Education—General M
Organizational Management M
Reading Education M

CREIGHTON UNIVERSITY
Adult Nursing M,D,O
Allied Health—General M,D
Allopathic Medicine D
Anatomy M
Anthropology M
Asian Studies M
Biological and Biomedical Sciences—General M,D
Business Administration and Management—General M
Conflict Resolution and Mediation/Peace Studies M,O
Counselor Education M
Dentistry D
Education—General M
Educational Leadership and Administration M,D
Elementary Education M
Emergency Medical Services M
English M
Family Nurse Practitioner Studies M,D,O
Gerontological Nursing M,D,O
Immunology M,D
International Affairs M
Law M,D,O
Maternal and Child/Neonatal Nursing M,D,O
Medical Microbiology M,D
Nursing and Healthcare Administration M,D,O
Nursing—General M,D,O
Occupational Therapy D
Organizational Management M
Pediatric Nursing M,D,O
Pharmaceutical Sciences M,D
Pharmacology M,D
Pharmacy D
Physical Therapy D
Physics M
Psychiatric Nursing M,D,O
School Psychology M
Secondary Education M
Theology M
Western European Studies M
Writing M

CRISWELL COLLEGE
Jewish Studies M
Pastoral Ministry and Counseling M
Theology M

CROWN COLLEGE
Theology M

CUMBERLAND UNIVERSITY
Business Administration and Management—General M
Education—General M
Public Administration M

CUNY GRADUATE SCHOOL OF JOURNALISM
Journalism M,O*

CURRY COLLEGE
Business Administration and Management—General M,O
Criminal Justice and Criminology M
Education—General M,O
Elementary Education M,O
Finance and Banking M,O
Foundations and Philosophy of Education M,O
Nursing—General M
Reading Education M,O
Special Education M,O

CURTIS INSTITUTE OF MUSIC
Music M

DAEMEN COLLEGE
Accounting M
Adult Nursing M,D,O
Arts Administration M
Business Administration and Management—General M
Community Health M
Early Childhood Education M
Education—General M
Epidemiology M
Health Education M
Health Services Management and Hospital Administration M
International Business M
Management Information Systems M
Marketing M
Medical/Surgical Nursing M,D,O
Middle School Education M
Nonprofit Management M
Nursing and Healthcare Administration M,D,O
Nursing Education M,D,O
Nursing—General M,D,O
Physical Therapy D,O
Physician Assistant Studies M
Public Health—General M
Social Work M
Special Education M

DAKOTA STATE UNIVERSITY
Business Administration and Management—General M,D,O
Computer and Information Systems Security M,D,O
Computer Science M,D,O
Education—General M
Educational Media/Instructional Technology M
Health Informatics M,D,O
Information Science M,D,O
Management Information Systems M,D,O

DAKOTA WESLEYAN UNIVERSITY
Curriculum and Instruction M
Education—General M
Educational Leadership and Administration M
Secondary Education M

DALHOUSIE UNIVERSITY
Agricultural Engineering M,D
Agricultural Sciences—General M
Agronomy and Soil Sciences M
Allopathic Medicine M,D
Anatomy M,D
Animal Sciences M
Anthropology M,D
Applied Mathematics M,D
Aquaculture M
Architecture M
Biochemistry M,D
Bioengineering M,D
Bioinformatics M,D
Biological and Biomedical Sciences—General M,D
Biomedical Engineering M,D
Biophysics M,D
Botany M
Business Administration and Management—General M,O
Chemical Engineering M,D
Chemistry M,D
Civil Engineering M,D
Classics M,D
Clinical Psychology M,D
Communication Disorders M,D
Community Health M
Computer Engineering M,D
Computer Science M,D
Ecology M
Economics M,D
Electrical Engineering M,D
Electronic Commerce M,D
Engineering and Applied Sciences—General M,D
English M,D
Environmental Biology M
Environmental Engineering M,D
Environmental Management and Policy M
Environmental Sciences M
Epidemiology M
Finance and Banking M
Food Science and Technology M,D
French M,D
Geosciences M,D
German M
Health Education M
Health Services Management and Hospital Administration M,D
History M,D
Horticulture M
Human-Computer Interaction M
Immunology M,D
Industrial/Management Engineering M,D
Information Studies M
Interdisciplinary Studies D
International Development M
Kinesiology and Movement Studies M
Law M,D
Leisure Studies M
Library Science M
Management Information Systems M
Marine Affairs M
Materials Engineering M,D
Mathematics M,D
Mechanical Engineering M,D
Medical Informatics M,D
Microbiology M,D
Mineral/Mining Engineering M,D
Music M
Natural Resources M
Neurobiology M,D
Neuroscience M,D
Nursing—General M,D
Occupational Therapy M
Oceanography M,D
Oral and Dental Sciences
Pathology M,D
Pharmacology M,D
Philosophy M,D
Physical Therapy M
Physics M,D
Physiology M,D
Plant Pathology M
Plant Physiology M
Political Science M,D
Psychology—General M,D
Public Administration M,O
Rural Planning and Studies M
Social Work M
Sociology M,D
Statistics M,D
Urban and Regional Planning M
Water Resources M

DALLAS BAPTIST UNIVERSITY
Accounting M
Asian Studies M
Business Administration and Management—General M
Conflict Resolution and Mediation/Peace Studies M
Corporate and Organizational Communication M
Counseling Psychology M
Counselor Education M,O
Criminal Justice and Criminology M
Curriculum and Instruction M
Distance Education Development M
Early Childhood Education M
Education—General M
Educational Leadership and Administration M
Elementary Education M
Engineering Management M
English as a Second Language M
Entrepreneurship M
Experimental Psychology M
Finance and Banking M
Health Services Management and Hospital Administration M
Higher Education M
Human Resources Management M
Interdisciplinary Studies M
International Business M
Kinesiology and Movement Studies M
Liberal Studies M
Management Information Systems M
Management of Technology M
Marketing M
Missions and Missiology M
Multilingual and Multicultural Education M
Music M
Nonprofit Management M
Organizational Management M
Pastoral Ministry and Counseling M,D
Project Management M
Reading Education M
Religion M
Religious Education M
Secondary Education M
Special Education M
Theology M

DALLAS THEOLOGICAL SEMINARY
Adult Education M,D,O
Child and Family Studies M,D,O
Educational Leadership and Administration M,D,O
Jewish Studies M,D,O
Media Studies M,D,O
Missions and Missiology M,D,O
Pastoral Ministry and Counseling M,D,O
Philosophy M,D,O
Religion M,D,O
Religious Education M,D,O
Theology M,D,O

DANIEL WEBSTER COLLEGE
Business Administration and Management—General M

DARTMOUTH COLLEGE
Allopathic Medicine D
Astronomy D
Biochemical Engineering M,D
Biochemistry M,D
Biological and Biomedical Sciences—General D
Biomedical Engineering M,D
Biostatistics D
Biotechnology M,D
Business Administration and Management—General M
Cell Biology D
Chemistry M,D
Cognitive Sciences D
Comparative Literature M
Computer Engineering M,D
Computer Science M,D
Ecology D
Engineering and Applied Sciences—General M,D
Engineering Management M
Entrepreneurship D
Environmental Engineering M,D
Evolutionary Biology D
Genetics D
Geosciences M,D
Health Services Management and Hospital Administration M,D
Health Services Research M,D
Immunology D
Liberal Studies M*
Materials Engineering M,D
Materials Sciences M,D
Mathematics M,D
Mechanical Engineering M,D
Microbiology D
Molecular Biology D
Molecular Medicine
Molecular Pathogenesis D
Music M
Neuroscience D
Physical Chemistry M,D
Physics D
Psychology—General D
Public Health—General M

DAVENPORT UNIVERSITY
Accounting M
Business Administration and Management—General M
Computer and Information Systems Security M
Finance and Banking M
Health Services Management and Hospital Administration M
Human Resources Management M
Management Strategy and Policy M
Public Health—General M

DEFIANCE COLLEGE
Adult Education M
Business Administration and Management—General M
Criminal Justice and Criminology M
Education—General M
Health Services Management and Hospital Administration M
Management Strategy and Policy M
Secondary Education M
Special Education M
Sports Management M

DELAWARE STATE UNIVERSITY
Adult Education M
Applied Mathematics M,D
Art Education M
Biological and Biomedical Sciences—General M
Business Administration and Management—General M
Chemistry M,D
Curriculum and Instruction M
Education—General M,D
Educational Leadership and Administration M,D
Exercise and Sports Science M
Foreign Languages Education M
Historic Preservation M
Mathematics Education M
Mathematics M
Natural Resources M
Neuroscience M,D
Nursing—General M
Optical Sciences M,D
Physics M,D
Plant Sciences M
Reading Education M
Science Education M,D
Social Work M
Special Education M
Theoretical Physics D

DELAWARE VALLEY UNIVERSITY
Accounting M
Agricultural Economics and Agribusiness M
Business Administration and Management—General M
Counseling Psychology M
Curriculum and Instruction M
Developmental Psychology M

Educational Leadership and Administration M
Educational Media/Instructional Technology M
Entrepreneurship M
Finance and Banking M
Human Resources Management M
International Business M
Social Psychology M
Supply Chain Management M

DELL'ARTE INTERNATIONAL SCHOOL OF PHYSICAL THEATRE
Theater M

DELTA STATE UNIVERSITY
Accounting M
Aviation Management M
Biological and Biomedical Sciences—General M
Business Administration and Management—General M
Counselor Education M,D,O
Criminal Justice and Criminology M
Education—General M,D,O
Educational Leadership and Administration M,D,O
Elementary Education M,D,O
English Education M
Exercise and Sports Science M
Family Nurse Practitioner Studies M,D
Gender Studies M
Health Education M
Health Services Management and Hospital Administration M,D
Higher Education D
Liberal Studies M
Nursing Education M,D
Nursing—General M,D
Philosophy M
Physical Education M
Recreation and Park Management M
Religion M
Secondary Education M,D,O
Social Sciences Education M
Special Education M
Urban and Regional Planning M

DENVER SEMINARY
Marriage and Family Therapy M,D,O
Pastoral Ministry and Counseling M,D,O
Religion M,D,O
Theology M,D,O

DEPAUL UNIVERSITY
Accounting M
Adult Education M,D
Advertising and Public Relations M
Applied Economics M
Applied Mathematics M,D
Applied Statistics M,D
Biological and Biomedical Sciences—General M,D
Business Administration and Management—General M
Chemistry M,D
Chinese M
Clinical Psychology M,D
Communication—General M
Computer and Information Systems Security M,D
Computer Art and Design M,D
Computer Science M,D
Corporate and Organizational Communication M
Counseling Psychology M,D
Counselor Education M,D
Curriculum and Instruction M,D
Early Childhood Education M,D
Economics M
Education—General M,D
Educational Leadership and Administration M,D
Electronic Commerce M,D
Elementary Education M,D
English M
Entrepreneurship M
Family Nurse Practitioner Studies M,D
Film, Television, and Video Production M,D
Film, Television, and Video Theory and Criticism M
Finance and Banking M
Foreign Languages Education M,D
Foundations and Philosophy of Education M,D
French M
Game Design and Development M,D
German M
Health Communication M
Health Informatics M,D
Health Law M,D
Health Services Management and Hospital Administration M
History M
Hospitality Management M
Human Resources Management M
Human-Computer Interaction M,D
Industrial and Manufacturing Management M
Information Science M,D
Intellectual Property Law M,D
Interdisciplinary Studies M
International Affairs M
Internet and Interactive Multimedia M,D
Investment Management M
Italian M
Japanese M
Journalism M
Law M,D
Liberal Studies M
Management Information Systems M,D
Management of Technology M,D
Management Strategy and Policy M
Marketing M
Mathematical and Computational Finance M,D
Mathematics Education M,D
Mathematics M,D
Media Studies M
Multilingual and Multicultural Education M,D
Music Education M,O
Music M,O
Near and Middle Eastern Languages M
Nonprofit Management M
Nursing—General M,D
Organizational Management M
Physics M,D
Psychology—General M,D
Public Administration M
Public Health—General M
Public Policy M
Publishing M
Reading Education M,D
Real Estate M
Rhetoric M
School Psychology M,D
Science Education M,D
Secondary Education M,D
Social Work M
Sociology M
Software Engineering M,D
Spanish M
Special Education M,D
Sports Management M
Student Affairs M,D
Sustainability Management M
Sustainable Development M
Taxation M,D
Theater M
Urban Design M
Women's Studies M
Writing M

DEREE - THE AMERICAN COLLEGE OF GREECE
Applied Psychology M
Communication—General M
Marketing M

DESALES UNIVERSITY
Accounting M
Business Administration and Management—General M
Computer and Information Systems Security M,D,O
Education—General M,O
Educational Media/Instructional Technology M,O
English as a Second Language M,O
Family Nurse Practitioner Studies M,D,O
Finance and Banking M
Forensic Sciences M,O
Gerontology M,D,O
Health Services Management and Hospital Administration M
Human Resources Management M
Management Information Systems M
Marketing M
Nurse Anesthesia M,D,O
Nurse Midwifery M,D,O
Nursing and Healthcare Administration M,D,O
Nursing Education M,D,O
Nursing—General M,D,O
Project Management M,D,O
Secondary Education M,O
Special Education M,O
Supply Chain Management M

DES MOINES UNIVERSITY
Anatomy M
Biological and Biomedical Sciences—General M
Health Services Management and Hospital Administration M
Osteopathic Medicine D
Physical Therapy D
Physician Assistant Studies M
Podiatric Medicine D
Public Health—General M

DEVRY COLLEGE OF NEW YORK
Business Administration and Management—General M

DEVRY UNIVERSITY
Business Administration and Management—General M

DEVRY UNIVERSITY
Business Administration and Management—General M
Education—General M

DEVRY UNIVERSITY
Business Administration and Management—General M,O

DEVRY UNIVERSITY
Business Administration and Management—General M
Education—General M

DEVRY UNIVERSITY
Business Administration and Management—General M,O

DEVRY UNIVERSITY
Business Administration and Management—General M,O

DEVRY UNIVERSITY
Business Administration and Management—General M

DEVRY UNIVERSITY
Business Administration and Management—General M

DEVRY UNIVERSITY
Business Administration and Management—General M

DEVRY UNIVERSITY
Business Administration and Management—General M

DEVRY UNIVERSITY
Business Administration and Management—General M

DEVRY UNIVERSITY
Business Administration and Management—General M

DEVRY UNIVERSITY
Business Administration and Management—General M,O

DEVRY UNIVERSITY
Business Administration and Management—General M,O

DEVRY UNIVERSITY
Business Administration and Management—General M
Education—General M

DEVRY UNIVERSITY
Business Administration and Management—General M,O

DEVRY UNIVERSITY
Business Administration and Management—General M

DEVRY UNIVERSITY
Business Administration and Management—General M,O

DEVRY UNIVERSITY
Business Administration and Management—General M,O

DEVRY UNIVERSITY
Business Administration and Management—General M

DEVRY UNIVERSITY
Business Administration and Management—General M
Education—General M

DEVRY UNIVERSITY
Business Administration and Management—General M

DEVRY UNIVERSITY
Business Administration and Management—General M

DEVRY UNIVERSITY
Business Administration and Management—General M,O

DEVRY UNIVERSITY
Accounting M
Business Administration and Management—General M
Communication—General M
Education—General M
Educational Media/Instructional Technology M
Electrical Engineering M
Finance and Banking M
Human Resources Management M
Management Information Systems M
Project Management M
Public Administration M

DEVRY UNIVERSITY
Business Administration and Management—General M,O

DEVRY UNIVERSITY
Business Administration and Management—General M,O

DEVRY UNIVERSITY
Business Administration and Management—General M,O

DEVRY UNIVERSITY
Business Administration and Management—General M

DEVRY UNIVERSITY
Business Administration and Management—General M,O

DEVRY UNIVERSITY (NV)
Business Administration and Management—General M

DEVRY UNIVERSITY
Business Administration and Management—General M

DEVRY UNIVERSITY
Business Administration and Management—General M

DEVRY UNIVERSITY
Business Administration and Management—General M

DEVRY UNIVERSITY
Business Administration and Management—General M

DEVRY UNIVERSITY
Business Administration and Management—General M,O

DEVRY UNIVERSITY
Business Administration and Management—General M

DEVRY UNIVERSITY
Business Administration and Management—General M

DEVRY UNIVERSITY
Business Administration and Management—General M

DEVRY UNIVERSITY
Business Administration and Management—General M

DEVRY UNIVERSITY
Business Administration and Management—General M,O

DEVRY UNIVERSITY ONLINE
Business Administration and Management—General M

DIGIPEN INSTITUTE OF TECHNOLOGY
Computer Art and Design M
Computer Science M

DIGITAL MEDIA ARTS COLLEGE
Computer Art and Design M
Graphic Design M
Media Studies M

DOANE UNIVERSITY
Business Administration and Management—General M
Counselor Education M
Curriculum and Instruction M
Education—General M
Educational Leadership and Administration M

DOMINICAN COLLEGE
Accounting M
Allied Health—General M,D
Business Administration and Management—General M
Elementary Education M
Family Nurse Practitioner Studies M,D
Health Services Management and Hospital Administration M
Occupational Therapy M
Physical Therapy M,D
Special Education M

DOMINICAN HOUSE OF STUDIES, PONTIFICAL FACULTY OF THE IMMACULATE CONCEPTION
Theology M,D,O

DOMINICAN SCHOOL OF PHILOSOPHY AND THEOLOGY
Philosophy M,O
Theology M,O

DOMINICAN UNIVERSITY
Accounting M
Business Administration and Management—General M
Conflict Resolution and Mediation/Peace Studies M
Curriculum and Instruction M
Early Childhood Education M
Education—General M
Educational Leadership and Administration M
Elementary Education M
English as a Second Language M
Information Studies M,D,O
Library Science M,D,O
Reading Education M
Social Work M
Special Education M

DOMINICAN UNIVERSITY OF CALIFORNIA
Art History M
Biological and Biomedical Sciences—General M
Business Administration and Management—General M
Clinical Laboratory Sciences/Medical Technology M
Counseling Psychology M
Education—General M
English M
Gender Studies M
History M
Humanities M
International Business M
Management Strategy and Policy M
Marriage and Family Therapy M
Music M
Occupational Therapy M
Philosophy M
Political Science M
Religion M
Special Education M
Sustainability Management M
Writing M

DONGGUK UNIVERSITY LOS ANGELES
Acupuncture and Oriental Medicine M

DORDT COLLEGE
Education—General M

DRAKE UNIVERSITY
Business Administration and Management—General M
Communication—General M
Education—General M,D,O

*M—masters degree; D—doctorate; O—other advanced degree; *—Close-Up and/or Display*

Law	M,D
Pharmacy	D
Public Administration	M

DREW UNIVERSITY

American Studies	M,D,O
Art/Fine Arts	M,D,O
Biological and Biomedical Sciences—General	M,D,O
Chemistry	M,D,O
Community College Education	M,D,O
Conflict Resolution and Mediation/Peace Studies	M,D,O
Cultural Studies	M,D,O
Elementary Education	M,D,O
English	M,D,O
French	M,D,O
Health Education	M,D,O
Health Services Management and Hospital Administration	M,D,O
History	M,D,O
Italian	M,D,O
Liberal Studies	M,D,O
Mathematics	M,D,O
Public History	M,D,O
Religion	M,D,O
Secondary Education	M,D,O
Special Education	M,D,O
Theology	M,D,O
Translation and Interpretation	M,D,O
Western European Studies	M,D,O
Writing	M,D,O

DREXEL UNIVERSITY

Accounting	M,D,O
Acute Care/Critical Care Nursing	M
Allied Health—General	M,D,O
Allopathic Medicine	D
Applied Arts and Design—General	M*
Applied Behavior Analysis	M,D
Architectural Engineering	M,D
Archives/Archival Administration	M
Art Therapy	M,O
Arts Administration	M
Biochemical Engineering	M
Biochemistry	M,D
Biological and Biomedical Sciences—General	M,D,O
Biomedical Engineering	M,D
Biopsychology	M,D
Biostatistics	M,D,O
Business Administration and Management—General	M,D,O
Cell Biology	M,D
Chemical Engineering	M,D
Chemistry	M,D
Civil Engineering	M,D
Clinical Psychology	D
Communication—General	M
Computer Art and Design	M
Computer Engineering	M
Computer Science	M,D*
Construction Management	M
Corporate and Organizational Communication	M
Curriculum and Instruction	M,D
Economics	M,D,O
Education—General	M,D*
Educational Leadership and Administration	M,D
Educational Media/Instructional Technology	M,D
Electrical Engineering	M
Emergency Management	M
Emergency Medical Services	M
Engineering and Applied Sciences—General	M,D,O
Engineering Management	M,O
Entrepreneurship	M
Environmental Engineering	M,D
Environmental Management and Policy	M
Environmental Sciences	M,D
Epidemiology	M,D,O
Family Nurse Practitioner Studies	M
Film, Television, and Video Production	M
Finance and Banking	M,D,O
Food Science and Technology	M
Forensic Psychology	D
Genetics	M,D
Geotechnical Engineering	M,D
Health Informatics	M
Health Psychology	D
Higher Education	M,D
History of Science and Technology	M
Homeland Security	M
Hospitality Management	M
Human Resources Development	M,D
Hydraulics	M,D
Hydrology	M,D
Immunology	M,D
Information Science	M,D
Interior Design	M
International and Comparative Education	M,D
Journalism	M
Library Science	M,D,O
Management Strategy and Policy	M,D,O
Marketing	M,D,O
Marriage and Family Therapy	M,D
Mass Communication	M
Materials Engineering	M,D
Mathematics	M,D
Mechanical Engineering	M,D
Mechanics	M,D
Microbiology	M,D
Molecular Biology	M,D
Molecular Medicine	M
National Security	M
Neuroscience	M,D
Nurse Anesthesia	M
Nursing and Healthcare Administration	M
Nursing Education	M
Nursing—General	M,D
Nutrition	M
Organizational Behavior	M,D,O
Pathobiology	M,D
Pediatric Nursing	M
Pharmaceutical Sciences	M
Pharmacology	M,D
Physical Therapy	M,D,O
Physician Assistant Studies	M
Physics	M,D
Project Management	M
Psychiatric Nursing	M
Psychology—General	M,D
Public Health—General	M,D,O
Publishing	M
Quantitative Analysis	M,D,O
Real Estate	M
Software Engineering	M
Special Education	M,D
Sports Management	M
Structural Engineering	M,D
Technical Communication	M
Technical Writing	M
Telecommunications	M
Textile Design	M
Therapies—Dance, Drama, and Music	M,O
Veterinary Sciences	M
Women's Health Nursing	M

DRURY UNIVERSITY

Architecture	M
Art/Fine Arts	M
Business Administration and Management—General	M
Communication—General	M
Criminal Justice and Criminology	M
Education of the Gifted	M
Education—General	M
Educational Media/Instructional Technology	M
Elementary Education	M
Human Services	M
Mathematics Education	M
Middle School Education	M
Reading Education	M
Secondary Education	M
Special Education	M

DUKE UNIVERSITY

Accounting	D
Acute Care/Critical Care Nursing	M,D,O
Adult Nursing	M,D,O
Allopathic Medicine	D
Anatomy	D
Art History	M,D
Art/Fine Arts	M,D
Asian Studies	M,O
Biochemistry	D
Bioethics	M
Bioinformatics	D,O
Biological and Biomedical Sciences—General	M,D
Biological Anthropology	D
Biomedical Engineering	M,D
Biopsychology	D
Biostatistics	M
Business Administration and Management—General	M,D,O
Cancer Biology/Oncology	D
Cell Biology	D,O
Chemistry	D
Civil Engineering	M,D
Classics	D
Clinical Laboratory Sciences/Medical Technology	M
Clinical Psychology	D
Clinical Research	M
Cognitive Sciences	D
Comparative Literature	D
Computational Biology	D,O
Computer Engineering	M,D
Computer Science	M,D
Cultural Anthropology	D
Developmental Biology	O
Developmental Psychology	D
Ecology	D,O
Economics	M,D
Education—General	M
Electrical Engineering	M,D*
Energy Management and Policy	M,O
Engineering and Applied Sciences—General	M
Engineering Management	M
English	D
Entrepreneurship	M,O
Environmental and Occupational Health	O
Environmental Engineering	M,D
Environmental Management and Policy	M,D
Environmental Sciences	M,D
Ethics	M,O
Experimental Psychology	D
Family Nurse Practitioner Studies	M,D,O
Finance and Banking	M,D,O
Forestry	M,D
French	D
Genetics	D
Genomic Sciences	D
Geology	M,D
German	D
Gerontological Nursing	M,D,O
Health Informatics	M
Health Psychology	D
Health Services Management and Hospital Administration	M,O
History	M,D
Human Development	D
Humanities	M
Immunology	D
Industrial and Manufacturing Management	M,D,O
International Business	M,O
International Development	M
International Health	M
Italian	D
Latin American Studies	M,D
Law	M,D
Liberal Studies	M
Management Strategy and Policy	M,D,O
Marine Sciences	D
Marketing	M,D,O
Materials Engineering	M
Materials Sciences	M,D
Maternal and Child/Neonatal Nursing	M,D,O
Mathematics	D
Mechanical Engineering	M,D
Media Studies	M
Medical Physics	M,D
Microbiology	D
Molecular Biology	D,O
Molecular Biophysics	O
Molecular Genetics	D
Music	D
Natural Resources	M,D
Neurobiology	D
Neuroscience	D,O
Nurse Anesthesia	M,D,O
Nursing and Healthcare Administration	M,D,O
Nursing Education	M,D,O
Nursing Informatics	M,D,O
Nursing—General	D
Optical Sciences	M
Organizational Management	M,D,O
Paleontology	D
Pathology	M,D
Pediatric Nursing	M,D,O
Pharmacology	D
Philosophy	D
Photonics	M
Physical Therapy	D
Physician Assistant Studies	M
Physics	D
Political Science	M,D
Psychology—General	D
Public Policy	M,D
Quantitative Analysis	M,D,O
Religion	M,D
Slavic Languages	M,O
Sociology	M,D
Spanish	D
Statistics	M,D
Structural Biology	O
Theology	M,D
Toxicology	O
Women's Health Nursing	M,D,O

DUNLAP-STONE UNIVERSITY

Law	M

DUQUESNE UNIVERSITY

Accounting	M
Allied Health—General	M,D,O
Bioethics	M,D,O
Biological and Biomedical Sciences—General	D
Biotechnology	M
Business Administration and Management—General	M
Chemistry	D
Classics	M
Clinical Psychology	M,D,O
Communication Disorders	M,D
Communication—General	M,D
Conflict Resolution and Mediation/Peace Studies	M,O
Counseling Psychology	M,D,O
Counselor Education	M,D,O
Curriculum and Instruction	M,O
Early Childhood Education	M
Education—General	M,D,O
Educational Leadership and Administration	M,D,O
Educational Measurement and Evaluation	M
Educational Media/Instructional Technology	M,D,O
Elementary Education	M
English as a Second Language	M
English Education	M
English	M,D
Environmental Management and Policy	M,O
Environmental Sciences	M,O
Family Nurse Practitioner Studies	M,O
Finance and Banking	M
Foreign Languages Education	M
Forensic Nursing	M,O
Forensic Sciences	M
Foundations and Philosophy of Education	M
Health Services Management and Hospital Administration	M,D
History	M
Internet and Interactive Multimedia	M,O
Law	M,D
Management Information Systems	M
Marketing	M
Marriage and Family Therapy	M,D,O
Mathematics Education	M
Mathematics	M
Medicinal and Pharmaceutical Chemistry	M,D
Middle School Education	M
Music Education	M,O
Music	M,O
Nursing Education	M,O
Nursing—General	M,D,O
Occupational Therapy	M,D
Organizational Management	M
Pharmaceutical Administration	M
Pharmaceutical Sciences	M,D
Pharmacology	M,D
Pharmacy	D
Philosophy	M,D
Physical Therapy	M,D
Physician Assistant Studies	M,D
Psychology—General	D
Public Administration	M,O
Public History	M
Public Policy	M,O
Reading Education	M
Rehabilitation Sciences	M,D
Rhetoric	M,D
School Psychology	M,D
Science Education	M
Secondary Education	M
Social Sciences Education	M
Special Education	M,D
Sustainability Management	M
Theology	M,D

D'YOUVILLE COLLEGE

Business Administration and Management—General	M
Chiropractic	D
Education—General	M,D
Educational Leadership and Administration	M,D
Elementary Education	M,D
Family Nurse Practitioner Studies	M,D,O
Health Services Management and Hospital Administration	M,D,O
International Business	M
Nursing—General	M,D,O
Nutrition	M
Occupational Therapy	M
Pharmacy	D
Physical Therapy	D,O
Physician Assistant Studies	M
Secondary Education	M,D
Special Education	M,D

EARLHAM COLLEGE

Education—General	M

EARLHAM SCHOOL OF RELIGION

Religion	M
Theology	M

EAST CAROLINA UNIVERSITY

Accounting	M
Addictions/Substance Abuse Counseling	M,D,O
Adult Education	M
Allied Health—General	M,D,O
Allopathic Medicine	D
American Studies	M
Anatomy	D
Anthropology	M
Applied Economics	M
Applied Physics	M,D
Art Education	M
Art/Fine Arts	M
Biochemistry	M,D
Biological and Biomedical Sciences—General	M,D
Biomedical Engineering	M
Biophysics	M,D
Biotechnology	M
Business Administration and Management—General	M,D,O
Business Education	M
Cell Biology	D
Chemistry	M
Child and Family Studies	M,D
Child Development	M,D
Clinical Psychology	M,D
Communication Disorders	M,D
Community College Education	M,D,O
Community Health	M,O
Comparative Literature	M,D,O
Computer and Information Systems Security	M,D,O
Computer Engineering	M,D,O
Computer Science	M,D,O
Construction Management	M
Counselor Education	M,D,O
Criminal Justice and Criminology	M,O
Curriculum and Instruction	M,O
Dentistry	D
Early Childhood Education	M,D
Economic Development	M,O
Education—General	M,D,O
Educational Leadership and Administration	M,D,O
Educational Media/Instructional Technology	M,O
Elementary Education	M,O
English as a Second Language	M,D,O
English Education	M,D,O
English	M,D,O
Environmental and Occupational Health	M,D
Exercise and Sports Science	M,D,O
Family and Consumer Sciences-General	M
Foreign Languages Education	M
Geographic Information Systems	M,O
Geography	M,O
Geology	M,O
Gerontology	M,O
Graphic Design	M
Health Communication	M
Health Education	M
Health Informatics	M
Health Physics/Radiological Health	M,D
Health Promotion	M
Health Psychology	M,D
History	M
Hospitality Management	M
Hydrogeology	M,O
Illustration	M
Immunology	M,D
Industrial and Manufacturing Management	M,D,O

Industrial and Organizational Psychology	M,D
International Affairs	M
Kinesiology and Movement Studies	M,D,O
Leisure Studies	M,O
Library Science	M
Linguistics	M,D,O
Logistics	M,D,O
Management Information Systems	M,D,O
Management of Technology	M,D,O
Marriage and Family Therapy	M,D
Maternal and Child Health	M,D
Mathematics Education	M,O
Mathematics	M,O
Medical Physics	M,D
Microbiology	M,D
Middle School Education	M
Military and Defense Studies	M
Molecular Biology	M,D
Music Education	M,O
Music	M,D,O
Nursing—General	M,D,O
Nutrition	M
Occupational Therapy	M,D,O
Pharmacology	D
Photography	M
Physical Education	M,D,O
Physical Therapy	D
Physician Assistant Studies	M
Physics	M,D
Physiology	D
Political Science	M,O
Public Administration	M,O
Public Health—General	M
Public History	M
Quality Management	M,D,O
Reading Education	M
Recreation and Park Management	M,O
Rehabilitation Counseling	M,D,O
Rehabilitation Sciences	M,D,O
Rhetoric	M,D,O
Rural Planning and Studies	M,O
Science Education	M,O
Social Sciences Education	M
Social Work	M,O
Sociology	M
Software Engineering	M
Special Education	M,O
Sports Management	M,D,O
Statistics	M,O
Technical Communication	M,D,O
Telecommunications Management	M,D,O
Textile Design	M
Therapies—Dance, Drama, and Music	M,O
Urban and Regional Planning	M,O
Vocational and Technical Education	M
Western European Studies	M
Writing	M,D,O

EAST CENTRAL UNIVERSITY

Counselor Education	M
Criminal Justice and Criminology	M
Education—General	M
Human Resources Management	M
Human Services	M
Psychology—General	M
Rehabilitation Counseling	M

EASTERN CONNECTICUT STATE UNIVERSITY

Early Childhood Education	M
Education—General	M
Educational Media/Instructional Technology	M
Elementary Education	M
Organizational Management	M
Reading Education	M
Science Education	M
Secondary Education	M

EASTERN ILLINOIS UNIVERSITY

Accounting	M
Art Education	M
Art/Fine Arts	M
Biological and Biomedical Sciences—General	M
Business Administration and Management—General	M
Chemistry	M
Clinical Psychology	M,O
Communication Disorders	M
Community College Education	M
Computer and Information Systems Security	M,O
Computer Science	M
Counselor Education	M
Early Childhood Education	M
Economics	M
Education—General	M,O
Educational Leadership and Administration	M,O
Elementary Education	M
Energy Management and Policy	M
Engineering and Applied Sciences—General	M,O
English	M
Exercise and Sports Science	M
Family and Consumer Sciences-General	M
Geographic Information Systems	M
Gerontology	M
History	M
Kinesiology and Movement Studies	M
Mathematics Education	M
Mathematics	M
Middle School Education	M
Music	M
Nutrition	M
Political Science	M
Psychology—General	M,O
Public History	M
School Psychology	M,O
Special Education	M
Speech and Interpersonal Communication	M
Student Affairs	M
Sustainable Development	M
Systems Science	M,O

EASTERN KENTUCKY UNIVERSITY

Agricultural Education	M
Allied Health—General	M
Art Education	M
Biological and Biomedical Sciences—General	M
Business Administration and Management—General	M
Business Education	M
Chemistry	M
Clinical Psychology	M,O
Communication Disorders	M
Community Health	M
Counselor Education	M
Criminal Justice and Criminology	M
Curriculum and Instruction	M
Ecology	M
Education—General	M
Educational Leadership and Administration	M
Elementary Education	M
English Education	M
English	M
Environmental and Occupational Health	M
Family Nurse Practitioner Studies	M
Geology	M,D
Health Education	M
Health Promotion	M
Health Services Management and Hospital Administration	M
Higher Education	M
History	M
Home Economics Education	M
Industrial and Organizational Psychology	M,O
Industrial/Management Engineering	M
Library Science	M
Manufacturing Engineering	M
Mathematics Education	M
Mathematics	M
Music Education	M
Music	M
Nursing—General	M
Nutrition	M
Occupational Therapy	M
Physical Education	M
Political Science	M
Psychology—General	M,O
Public Administration	M
Recreation and Park Management	M
School Psychology	M,O
Science Education	M
Secondary Education	M
Social Sciences Education	M
Special Education	M
Sports Management	M
Urban and Regional Planning	M
Vocational and Technical Education	M
Writing	M

EASTERN MENNONITE UNIVERSITY

Biological and Biomedical Sciences—General	M
Business Administration and Management—General	M
Conflict Resolution and Mediation/Peace Studies	M,O
Counselor Education	M
Education—General	M
Health Services Management and Hospital Administration	M
Nonprofit Management	M
Nursing and Healthcare Administration	M
Nursing—General	M
Organizational Management	M
Pastoral Ministry and Counseling	M,O
Religion	M,O
School Nursing	M
Theology	M,O

EASTERN MICHIGAN UNIVERSITY

Accounting	M
Adult Nursing	M,O
African-American Studies	O
Art Education	M
Art/Fine Arts	M
Artificial Intelligence/Robotics	M,O
Arts Administration	M
Athletic Training and Sports Medicine	M,O
Biological and Biomedical Sciences—General	M
Business Administration and Management—General	M,O
Cell Biology	M
Chemistry	M
Clinical Psychology	M,D
Clinical Research	M,O
Clothing and Textiles	M
Communication Disorders	M
Communication—General	M
Community College Education	M,D,O
Computer and Information Systems Security	O
Computer Science	M,O
Construction Management	M
Corporate and Organizational Communication	M,O
Counselor Education	M,O
Criminal Justice and Criminology	M
Cultural Studies	O
Curriculum and Instruction	M
Developmental Education	M,O
Early Childhood Education	M
Ecology	M
Economics	M,O
Education—General	M,D,O
Educational Leadership and Administration	M,D,O
Educational Measurement and Evaluation	M,O
Educational Media/Instructional Technology	M,O
Educational Policy	M
Educational Psychology	M,O
Electronic Commerce	M,O
Elementary Education	M
Engineering and Applied Sciences—General	M
Engineering Management	M
English as a Second Language	M,O
English Education	M
English	M,O
Entrepreneurship	M,O
Exercise and Sports Science	M
Finance and Banking	M,O
Foreign Languages Education	M,O
Foundations and Philosophy of Education	M
French	M,O
Gender Studies	M,O
Geographic Information Systems	M,O
Geography	M,O
Geosciences	M
German	M,O
Gerontology	O
Health Education	M,O
Health Promotion	M,O
Health Services Management and Hospital Administration	M,O
Higher Education	M,D,O
Hispanic and Latin American Languages	M,O
Hispanic Studies	M,O
Historic Preservation	M,O
History	M
Hospitality Management	M,O
Human Resources Management	M,O
Human Services	O
Interior Design	M
International Business	M,O
Japanese	M,O
Kinesiology and Movement Studies	M
Linguistics	M,O
Management Information Systems	M,O
Management of Technology	D
Marketing	M,O
Mathematics	M
Middle School Education	M
Molecular Biology	M
Museum Education	O
Museum Studies	M,O
Music	M
Nonprofit Management	M,O
Nursing and Healthcare Administration	M,O
Nursing Education	M,O
Nutrition	M
Occupational Therapy	M
Organizational Management	M,O
Philosophy	M
Physical Education	M
Physician Assistant Studies	M
Physics	M
Physiology	M
Polymer Science and Engineering	M,O
Psychology—General	M,D
Public Administration	M,O
Public Policy	M,O
Quality Management	M,O
Reading Education	M
Science Education	M
Secondary Education	M
Social Sciences	M
Social Work	M
Sociology	M
Spanish	M,O
Special Education	M,O
Sports Management	M
Student Affairs	M,D,O
Supply Chain Management	M,O
Technical Communication	M,O
Technology and Public Policy	M
Theater	M
Urban and Regional Planning	M,O
Urban Education	M
Water Resources	M,O
Women's Studies	M,O
Writing	M,O

EASTERN NAZARENE COLLEGE

Business Administration and Management—General	M
Counseling Psychology	M
Early Childhood Education	M,O
Education—General	M,O
Educational Leadership and Administration	M,O
Elementary Education	M,O
English as a Second Language	M,O
Marriage and Family Therapy	M
Middle School Education	M,O
Reading Education	M,O
Secondary Education	M,O
Special Education	M,O

EASTERN NEW MEXICO UNIVERSITY

Analytical Chemistry	M
Anthropology	M
Biochemistry	M
Biological and Biomedical Sciences—General	M
Botany	M
Business Administration and Management—General	M
Cell Biology	M
Chemistry	M
Communication Disorders	M
Communication—General	M
Counselor Education	M
Curriculum and Instruction	M
Early Childhood Education	M
Ecology	M
Education—General	M
Educational Leadership and Administration	M
Educational Media/Instructional Technology	M
Elementary Education	M
English as a Second Language	M
English	M
Exercise and Sports Science	M
Human Services	M
Inorganic Chemistry	M
Microbiology	M
Molecular Biology	M
Multilingual and Multicultural Education	M
Nursing—General	M
Organic Chemistry	M
Physical Chemistry	M
Physical Education	M
Reading Education	M
Secondary Education	M
Special Education	M
Sports Management	M
Vocational and Technical Education	M
Zoology	M

EASTERN OREGON UNIVERSITY

Business Administration and Management—General	M
Education—General	M
Elementary Education	M
Secondary Education	M

EASTERN UNIVERSITY

Applied Behavior Analysis	M,O
Business Administration and Management—General	M
Communication—General	M,O
Counseling Psychology	M,O
Counselor Education	M,O
Cultural Anthropology	M
Early Childhood Education	M,O
Economic Development	M
Education—General	M,O
Educational Leadership and Administration	M,O
Elementary Education	M,O
English as a Second Language	M,O
English Education	M,O
Foreign Languages Education	M,O
French	M,O
Health Education	M,O
Health Services Management and Hospital Administration	M
International Development	M
Marriage and Family Therapy	D
Mathematics Education	M,O
Middle School Education	M,O
Missions and Missiology	M,D
Multilingual and Multicultural Education	M,O
Nonprofit Management	M
Organizational Management	M,D
Pastoral Ministry and Counseling	M,D
Physical Education	M,O
Public Policy	M,D
Reading Education	M,O
School Nursing	M,O
School Psychology	M,O
Science Education	M,O
Secondary Education	M,O
Social Sciences Education	M,O
Spanish	M,O
Special Education	M,O
Theology	M,D
Urban and Regional Planning	M
Urban Studies	M

EASTERN VIRGINIA MEDICAL SCHOOL

Allopathic Medicine	D
Art Therapy	M
Biological and Biomedical Sciences—General	M,D
Biotechnology	M
Clinical Psychology	D
Medical/Surgical Nursing	M
Physician Assistant Studies	M
Public Health—General	M
Reproductive Biology	M
Vision Sciences	O

EASTERN WASHINGTON UNIVERSITY

Adult Education	M
Applied Psychology	M
Biological and Biomedical Sciences—General	M
Business Administration and Management—General	M
Clinical Psychology	M
Communication Disorders	M
Communication—General	M
Computer Education	M
Computer Science	M
Counseling Psychology	M
Counselor Education	M
Curriculum and Instruction	M
Dental Hygiene	M
Early Childhood Education	M

*M—masters degree; D—doctorate; O—other advanced degree; *—Close-Up and/or Display*

Education—General M
Elementary Education M
English as a Second Language M
English M
Exercise and Sports Science M
Experimental Psychology M
History M
Interdisciplinary Studies M
Mathematics Education M
Mathematics M
Music Education M
Music M
Occupational Therapy M
Physical Education M
Physical Therapy D
Psychology—General M
Public Administration M
Reading Education M
Recreation and Park Management M
Rhetoric M
School Psychology M
Secondary Education M
Social Work M
Special Education M
Sports Management M
Technical Communication M
Urban and Regional Planning M
Writing M

EAST STROUDSBURG UNIVERSITY OF PENNSYLVANIA
Applied Behavior Analysis M
Athletic Training and Sports Medicine M
Biological and Biomedical Sciences—General M
Communication Disorders M
Computer and Information Systems Security M
Computer Science M
Early Childhood Education M
Education—General M,D
Educational Leadership and Administration M,D
Educational Media/Instructional Technology M
Elementary Education M
Environmental Sciences M
Exercise and Sports Science M
Geographic Information Systems M
Health Education M
History M
Physical Education M
Physiology M
Political Science M
Public Administration M
Public Health—General M
Reading Education M
Rehabilitation Sciences M
Secondary Education M,D
Social Sciences Education M
Special Education M
Sports Management M

EAST TENNESSEE STATE UNIVERSITY
Accounting M
Allied Health—General M,D,O
Allopathic Medicine D
Anatomy D
Art/Fine Arts M
Biochemistry D
Biological and Biomedical Sciences—General M,D
Business Administration and Management—General M,O
Chemistry M
Communication Disorders M,D
Communication—General M
Computer Art and Design M,O
Computer Science M,O
Corporate and Organizational Communication M
Counselor Education M
Criminal Justice and Criminology M,O
Curriculum and Instruction M,O
Early Childhood Education M,D,O
Economic Development M,O
Education—General M,D,O
Educational Leadership and Administration M,D,O
Educational Media/Instructional Technology M,O
Elementary Education M,O
English M,O
Entrepreneurship M,O
Environmental and Occupational Health M,D
Exercise and Sports Science M,D
Family Nurse Practitioner Studies M,D,O
Finance and Banking M,O
Geosciences M
Health Services Management and Hospital Administration M,O
History M,O
Human Development M
Information Science M,O
Kinesiology and Movement Studies M,O
Liberal Studies M,O
Library Science M,O
Manufacturing Engineering M,O
Marketing M,O
Mathematics M,O
Microbiology D
Middle School Education M,O
Nonprofit Management M,O
Nursing—General M,D,O
Nutrition M
Paleontology M
Pharmaceutical Sciences D
Pharmacology D
Pharmacy D
Physical Therapy D
Physiology D
Political Science M,O
Psychology—General D
Public Administration M,O
Public Health—General M,D,O
Reading Education M,O
Secondary Education M,O
Social Work M
Sociology M
Special Education M,D,O
Sports Management M,O
Urban and Regional Planning M,O

EAST TEXAS BAPTIST UNIVERSITY
Business Administration and Management—General M
Counseling Psychology M
Curriculum and Instruction M
Education—General M
Entrepreneurship M
Pastoral Ministry and Counseling M
Physical Education M
Religion M

EAST WEST COLLEGE OF NATURAL MEDICINE
Acupuncture and Oriental Medicine M

EC-COUNCIL UNIVERSITY
Computer and Information Systems Security M

ECOLE HÔTELIÈRE DE LAUSANNE
Hospitality Management M

ÉCOLE POLYTECHNIQUE DE MONTRÉAL
Aerospace/Aeronautical Engineering M,D,O
Applied Mathematics M,D,O
Biomedical Engineering M,D,O
Chemical Engineering M,D,O
Civil Engineering M,D,O
Computer Engineering M,D,O
Computer Science M,D,O
Electrical Engineering M,D,O
Engineering and Applied Sciences—General M,D,O
Engineering Physics M,D,O
Environmental Engineering M,D,O
Geotechnical Engineering M,D,O
Hydraulics M,D,O
Industrial/Management Engineering M,D,O
Management of Technology M,D,O
Mechanical Engineering M,D,O
Mechanics M,D,O
Nuclear Engineering M,D,O
Operations Research M,D,O
Optical Sciences M,D,O
Structural Engineering M,D,O
Transportation and Highway Engineering M,D,O

ECUMENICAL THEOLOGICAL SEMINARY
Pastoral Ministry and Counseling D
Theology M

EDEN THEOLOGICAL SEMINARY
Theology M,D

EDGEWOOD COLLEGE
Accounting M
Adult Education M,D,O
Business Administration and Management—General M
Education—General M,D,O
Educational Leadership and Administration M,D,O
English as a Second Language M,D,O
Finance and Banking M
Marketing M
Marriage and Family Therapy M
Multilingual and Multicultural Education M,D,O
Nursing and Healthcare Administration M,D
Nursing Education M,D
Nursing—General M,D
Organizational Management M
Reading Education M,D,O
Special Education M,D,O
Sustainability Management M,D,O

EDINBORO UNIVERSITY OF PENNSYLVANIA
Anthropology M
Art Education M
Art Therapy M,O
Art/Fine Arts M
Clinical Psychology M,O
Communication Disorders M
Communication—General M
Counseling Psychology M,O
Counselor Education M,O
Early Childhood Education M,O
Educational Leadership and Administration M
Educational Psychology M,O
Family Nurse Practitioner Studies M,D
History M
Middle School Education M
Nursing Education M,D
Nursing—General M,D
Political Science M
Reading Education M,O
Rehabilitation Counseling M,O
School Psychology M,O
Secondary Education M
Social Work M
Special Education M,O

EDP UNIVERSITY OF PUERTO RICO–SAN SEBASTIAN
Nursing—General M

EDWARD VIA COLLEGE OF OSTEOPATHIC MEDICINE–VIRGINIA CAMPUS
Osteopathic Medicine D

EDWARD VIA COLLEGE OF OSTEOPATHIC MEDICINE–CAROLINAS CAMPUS
Osteopathic Medicine D

ELIZABETH CITY STATE UNIVERSITY
Applied Mathematics M
Biological and Biomedical Sciences—General M
Community College Education M
Education—General M
Educational Leadership and Administration M
Elementary Education M
Geographic Information Systems M
Mathematics Education M
Mathematics M
Science Education M

ELIZABETHTOWN COLLEGE
Occupational Therapy M

ELLIS UNIVERSITY
Accounting M
Business Administration and Management—General M
Early Childhood Education M
Education—General M
Educational Leadership and Administration M
Educational Media/Instructional Technology M
Electronic Commerce M
Finance and Banking M
Health Services Management and Hospital Administration M
International Business M
Management Information Systems M
Marketing M
Project Management M

ELMEZZI GRADUATE SCHOOL OF MOLECULAR MEDICINE
Molecular Medicine D

ELMHURST COLLEGE
Accounting M
Business Administration and Management—General M
Communication Disorders M
Database Systems M
Educational Leadership and Administration M
Geographic Information Systems M
Industrial and Organizational Psychology M
Management Information Systems M
Nursing—General M
Public Health—General M
Special Education M
Supply Chain Management M

ELMS COLLEGE
Accounting M
Business Administration and Management—General M
Communication Disorders M,O
Early Childhood Education M,O
Education—General M,O
Elementary Education M,O
English as a Second Language M,O
English Education M,O
Foreign Languages Education M,O
Health Services Management and Hospital Administration M
Nursing and Healthcare Administration M,D
Nursing Education M,D
Nursing—General M,D
Reading Education M,O
Religion M
Science Education M,O
Secondary Education M,O
Special Education M,O

ELON UNIVERSITY
Business Administration and Management—General M
Education of the Gifted M
Education—General M
Elementary Education M
Internet and Interactive Multimedia M
Law D
Physical Therapy D
Physician Assistant Studies M
Special Education M

EMBRY-RIDDLE AERONAUTICAL UNIVERSITY–DAYTONA
Aerospace/Aeronautical Engineering M,D
Aviation Management M,D*
Business Administration and Management—General M,D
Computer and Information Systems Security M,D
Computer Engineering M,D
Electrical Engineering M,D
Engineering Physics M,D
Ergonomics and Human Factors M,D
Finance and Banking M,D
Mechanical Engineering M,D
Software Engineering M,D
Systems Engineering M,D

EMBRY-RIDDLE AERONAUTICAL UNIVERSITY–PRESCOTT
Aviation M
Environmental and Occupational Health M
Military and Defense Studies M
Safety Engineering M

EMBRY-RIDDLE AERONAUTICAL UNIVERSITY–WORLDWIDE
Aerospace/Aeronautical Engineering M
Aviation Management M
Aviation D
Business Administration and Management—General M
Engineering Management M
Environmental and Occupational Health M
International Affairs M
Logistics M
Management Information Systems M
Project Management M
Supply Chain Management M

EMERSON COLLEGE
Advertising and Public Relations M
Broadcast Journalism M
Communication Disorders M
Communication—General M
Corporate and Organizational Communication M
Health Communication M
International Business M
Journalism M
Marketing M
Media Studies M
Publishing M
Theater M
Writing M

EMILY CARR UNIVERSITY OF ART + DESIGN
Applied Arts and Design—General M
Art/Fine Arts M
Computer Art and Design M

EMMANUEL COLLEGE (UNITED STATES)
Business Administration and Management—General M,O
Education—General M
Elementary Education M
Human Resources Management M,O
Nursing and Healthcare Administration M,O
Nursing Education M,O
Nursing—General M,O
Secondary Education M

EMORY & HENRY COLLEGE
American Studies M
Education—General M
History M
Organizational Management M
Reading Education M

EMORY UNIVERSITY
Accounting M,D
Adult Nursing M
Allied Health—General M,D
Allopathic Medicine D
Anesthesiologist Assistant Studies M
Animal Behavior D
Anthropology D
Art History D
Biochemistry D
Bioethics M
Bioinformatics M,D
Biological and Biomedical Sciences—General D
Biophysics D
Biostatistics M,D
Business Administration and Management—General M,D
Cancer Biology/Oncology D
Cell Biology D
Chemistry D
Clinical Psychology D
Clinical Research M
Cognitive Sciences D
Comparative Literature D,O
Computational Sciences D
Computer Science M,D
Developmental Biology D
Developmental Psychology D
Ecology D
Economics D
Education—General M,D
English D,O
Environmental and Occupational Health M,D
Epidemiology M,D
Ethics M,D
Evolutionary Biology D
Family Nurse Practitioner Studies M
Film, Television, and Video Theory and Criticism M,D,O
Finance and Banking M,D
French D
Genetic Counseling M
Genetics D
Health Education M,D
Health Informatics M,D
Health Promotion M
Health Services Management and Hospital Administration M,D
Health Services Research M,D
History D
Human Genetics M
Immunology D
Industrial and Manufacturing Management M
Interdisciplinary Studies D
International Health M
Law M,D,O
Management Information Systems M,D
Marketing M,D
Mathematics M,D
Microbiology D

Middle School Education M,D
Molecular Biology D
Molecular Genetics D
Molecular Pathogenesis D
Music M
Neuroscience D
Nurse Midwifery M
Nursing and Healthcare Administration M
Nursing—General M,D
Nutrition M,D
Organizational Management M,D
Pastoral Ministry and Counseling M,D
Pediatric Nursing M
Pharmacology D
Philosophy D,O
Physical Therapy D
Physician Assistant Studies M
Physics D
Political Science D
Portuguese D,O
Psychology—General D
Public Health—General M,D
Real Estate M
Religion D
Secondary Education M,D
Sociology D
Spanish D,O
Sustainable Development M
Theology M,D
Theoretical Physics D
Women's Health Nursing M
Women's Studies D,O

EMPEROR'S COLLEGE OF TRADITIONAL ORIENTAL MEDICINE
Acupuncture and Oriental Medicine M,D

EMPIRE COLLEGE
Law M,D

EMPORIA STATE UNIVERSITY
Accounting M
Art Therapy M
Biological and Biomedical Sciences—General M
Botany M
Business Administration and Management—General M
Business Education M
Cell Biology M
Clinical Psychology M
Counseling Psychology M
Counselor Education M
Curriculum and Instruction M
Early Childhood Education M
Education of the Gifted M
Education—General M
Educational Leadership and Administration M
Educational Media/Instructional Technology M
Elementary Education M
English as a Second Language M
English M
Environmental Biology M
Forensic Sciences M
Geosciences M,O
History M
Industrial and Organizational Psychology M
Information Studies M
Mathematics M
Microbiology M
Music M
Nursing Informatics M
Physical Education M
Psychology—General M
Reading Education M
Rehabilitation Counseling M
School Psychology M,O
Social Sciences Education M
Special Education M
Zoology M

ENDICOTT COLLEGE
Applied Behavior Analysis M,D
Business Administration and Management—General M
Distance Education Development M
Early Childhood Education M
Educational Leadership and Administration M,D
Elementary Education M
Homeland Security M
Interior Design M
Management Information Systems M
Nursing—General M,D
Organizational Management M
Reading Education M
Secondary Education M
Special Education M,D
Sports Management M

EPISCOPAL DIVINITY SCHOOL
Theology M,D,O

ERIKSON INSTITUTE
Child Development M
Developmental Psychology M,O
Early Childhood Education M,D
English as a Second Language M,O
Human Development M,O

ERSKINE THEOLOGICAL SEMINARY
Theology M,D

ESSEC BUSINESS SCHOOL
Business Administration and Management—General M,D
Hospitality Management M,D
International Business M,D

EVANGELICAL SEMINARY
Marriage and Family Therapy M
Missions and Missiology M
Pastoral Ministry and Counseling M
Theology M

EVANGELICAL SEMINARY OF PUERTO RICO
Theology M,D

EVANGEL UNIVERSITY
Clinical Psychology M
Counseling Psychology M
Counselor Education M
Curriculum and Instruction M,D
Education—General M
Educational Leadership and Administration M,D
Organizational Management M
Psychology—General M
Reading Education M
School Psychology M
Secondary Education M

EVEREST UNIVERSITY
Accounting M
Business Administration and Management—General M
Human Resources Management M
International Business M

EVEREST UNIVERSITY
Accounting M
Business Administration and Management—General M
Human Resources Management M
International Business M

EVEREST UNIVERSITY
Accounting M
Business Administration and Management—General M
Human Resources Management M
International Business M

EVERGLADES UNIVERSITY
Accounting M
Aviation M
Business Administration and Management—General M
Entrepreneurship M
Human Resources Management M
Industrial and Manufacturing Management M
Project Management M
Public Health—General M

THE EVERGREEN STATE COLLEGE
Education—General M
Environmental Management and Policy M
Public Administration M

EXCELSIOR COLLEGE
Business Administration and Management—General M,O
Conflict Resolution and Mediation/Peace Studies M,O
Criminal Justice and Criminology M,O
Emergency Management M
Health Education M,O
Health Informatics M,O
Health Services Management and Hospital Administration M,O
Homeland Security M
Human Resources Management M,O
Internet and Interactive Multimedia M,O
Liberal Studies M
Management of Technology M,O
Medical Informatics M,O
Nursing and Healthcare Administration M
Nursing Education M
Nursing Informatics M
Nursing—General M
Public Administration M
Public Health—General M,O

FAIRFIELD UNIVERSITY
Accounting M,O
Addictions/Substance Abuse Counseling M,O
American Studies M
Applied Behavior Analysis M,O
Applied Psychology M,O
Business Administration and Management—General M,O
Child and Family Studies M,O
Clinical Psychology M,O
Communication—General M
Computer and Information Systems Security M,O
Computer Engineering M,O
Counseling Psychology M,O
Counselor Education M,O
Database Systems M,O
Education—General M,O
Educational Media/Instructional Technology M,O
Electrical Engineering M,O
Elementary Education M,O
Engineering and Applied Sciences—General M,O
English as a Second Language M,O
Entrepreneurship M,O
Family Nurse Practitioner Studies M,D
Finance and Banking M,O
Foundations and Philosophy of Education M,O
Health Education M,D
Human Resources Management M,O
Internet and Interactive Multimedia M,O
Management Information Systems M,O
Management of Technology M,O
Manufacturing Engineering M,O
Marketing M,O
Marriage and Family Therapy M,O
Mathematics M
Mechanical Engineering M,O
Multilingual and Multicultural Education M,O
Nurse Anesthesia M,D
Nursing and Healthcare Administration M,D
Nursing—General M,D
Pastoral Ministry and Counseling M,O
Psychiatric Nursing M,D
Public Administration M
School Psychology M,O
Secondary Education M,O
Software Engineering M,O
Special Education M,O
Taxation M,O
Telecommunications M,O
Writing M

FAIRLEIGH DICKINSON UNIVERSITY, COLLEGE AT FLORHAM
Accounting M
Biological and Biomedical Sciences—General M
Business Administration and Management—General M,O
Chemical Engineering M,O
Chemistry M
Clinical Psychology M
Computer Science M
Corporate and Organizational Communication M
Counseling Psychology M
Education—General M,O
Educational Leadership and Administration M
Educational Media/Instructional Technology M,O
Entrepreneurship M,O
Finance and Banking M,O
Health Services Management and Hospital Administration M
Hospitality Management M
Human Resources Management M
Industrial and Organizational Psychology M
International Business M,O
Management of Technology M,O
Marketing M,O
Organizational Behavior M,O
Organizational Management M,O
Pharmacology M,O
Psychology—General M,O
Public Administration M
Reading Education M,O
Sports Management M
Sustainability Management O
Taxation M,O
Writing M

FAIRLEIGH DICKINSON UNIVERSITY, METROPOLITAN CAMPUS
Accounting M,O
Art/Fine Arts M
Biological and Biomedical Sciences—General M
Business Administration and Management—General M,O
Chemistry M
Clinical Laboratory Sciences/Medical Technology M
Clinical Psychology M,D
Communication—General M
Comparative Literature M
Computer Engineering M
Computer Science M
Criminal Justice and Criminology M
Curriculum and Instruction M
Education—General M,O
Educational Leadership and Administration M
Educational Media/Instructional Technology M,O
Electrical Engineering M
Electronic Commerce M
Engineering and Applied Sciences—General M
English M
Entrepreneurship M,O
Experimental Psychology M,O
Finance and Banking M,O
Forensic Psychology M
Foundations and Philosophy of Education M
Health Services Management and Hospital Administration M
History M
Homeland Security M
Hospitality Management M
Human Resources Management M,O
International Affairs M
International Business M
Management Information Systems M,O
Marketing M,O
Mathematics M
Media Studies M
Multilingual and Multicultural Education M
Nonprofit Management M,O
Nursing—General M,D,O
Pharmaceutical Administration M,O
Political Science M
Psychology—General M,D,O
Public Administration M,O
Reading Education M,O
School Psychology M,D

Science Education M
Special Education M
Sports Management M
Systems Science M
Taxation M

FAIRMONT STATE UNIVERSITY
Business Administration and Management—General M
Criminal Justice and Criminology M
Distance Education Development M
Education—General M
Educational Media/Instructional Technology M
Exercise and Sports Science M
Health Promotion M
Reading Education M
Special Education M

FAITH BAPTIST BIBLE COLLEGE AND THEOLOGICAL SEMINARY
Pastoral Ministry and Counseling M
Religion M
Theology M

FAITH EVANGELICAL COLLEGE & SEMINARY
Theology M,D

FAITH THEOLOGICAL SEMINARY
Theology M,D

FASHION INSTITUTE OF TECHNOLOGY
Applied Arts and Design—General M*
Art History M
Arts Administration M*
Business Administration and Management—General M*
Clothing and Textiles M
Illustration M*
Interior Design M
Marketing M*
Museum Studies M*
Sustainable Development M

FAULKNER UNIVERSITY
Business Administration and Management—General M
Counselor Education M
Criminal Justice and Criminology M
Education—General M
History M
Law D
Liberal Studies M
Missions and Missiology M
Pastoral Ministry and Counseling M
Theology M

FAYETTEVILLE STATE UNIVERSITY
Biological and Biomedical Sciences—General M
Business Administration and Management—General M
Criminal Justice and Criminology M
Educational Leadership and Administration M,D
Elementary Education M
English M
Mathematics M
Middle School Education M
Psychology—General M
Secondary Education M
Social Sciences Education M
Social Work M
Sociology M

FELICIAN UNIVERSITY
Adult Nursing M,O
Business Administration and Management—General M
Counseling Psychology M
Education—General M,O
Educational Leadership and Administration M,O
Entrepreneurship M
Family Nurse Practitioner Studies M,O
Gerontological Nursing M,O
Health Services Management and Hospital Administration M
Nursing and Healthcare Administration M,D,O
Nursing Education M,O
Nursing—General M,D,O
Religious Education M,O
School Nursing M,O

FERRIS STATE UNIVERSITY
Allied Health—General M
Applied Arts and Design—General M
Architecture M
Art Education M
Art/Fine Arts M
Business Administration and Management—General M
Community College Education D
Computer and Information Systems Security M
Criminal Justice and Criminology M
Curriculum and Instruction M
Database Systems M
Developmental Education M
Education—General M
Educational Leadership and Administration M,D
Human Services M
Management Information Systems M
Nursing and Healthcare Administration M
Nursing Education M
Nursing Informatics M
Nursing—General M
Optometry D

*M—masters degree; D—doctorate; O—other advanced degree; *—Close-Up and/or Display*

Pharmacy	D
Photography	M
Project Management	M
Reading Education	M
Special Education	M
Supply Chain Management	M

FIELDING GRADUATE UNIVERSITY

Child Development	M,D,O
Clinical Psychology	M,D,O
Educational Leadership and Administration	M,D,O
Educational Media/Instructional Technology	M,D,O
Forensic Psychology	M,D,O
Gerontology	M,D,O
Health Psychology	M,D,O
Human Development	M,D,O
Media Studies	M,D,O
Neuroscience	M,D,O
Nonprofit Management	M,D,O
Organizational Management	M,D,O
Psychology—General	M,D,O

FISHER COLLEGE

Business Administration and Management—General	M

FISK UNIVERSITY

Biological and Biomedical Sciences—General	M
Chemistry	M
Clinical Psychology	M
Physics	M
Psychology—General	M

FITCHBURG STATE UNIVERSITY

Accounting	M
Art Education	M,O
Biological and Biomedical Sciences—General	M,O
Business Administration and Management—General	M
Communication—General	M,O
Computer Science	M
Counseling Psychology	M
Counselor Education	M,O
Curriculum and Instruction	M
Early Childhood Education	M
Educational Leadership and Administration	M,O
Educational Media/Instructional Technology	M,O
Elementary Education	M
English Education	M,O
English	M,O
Forensic Nursing	M,O
Health Communication	M,O
History	M,O
Human Resources Management	M
Interdisciplinary Studies	O
Middle School Education	M
Psychology—General	O
Reading Education	O
Science Education	M,O
Social Sciences Education	M,O
Special Education	M
Technical Writing	M,O
Vocational and Technical Education	M

FIVE BRANCHES UNIVERSITY

Acupuncture and Oriental Medicine	M,D

FIVE TOWNS COLLEGE

Early Childhood Education	M,D
Music Education	M,D
Music	M,D

FLORIDA AGRICULTURAL AND MECHANICAL UNIVERSITY

Accounting	M
Adult Education	M,D
Allied Health—General	M,D
Architecture	M
Biomedical Engineering	M,D
Business Administration and Management—General	M
Business Education	M
Chemical Engineering	M,D
Chemistry	M
Civil Engineering	M,D
Counselor Education	M,D
Criminal Justice and Criminology	M
Education—General	M,D
Educational Leadership and Administration	M,D
Electrical Engineering	M,D
Elementary Education	M
Engineering and Applied Sciences—General	M,D
English Education	M
Environmental Sciences	M,D
Finance and Banking	M
Health Services Research	M,D
History	M
Industrial/Management Engineering	M,D
Journalism	M
Landscape Architecture	M
Law	D
Management Information Systems	M
Marketing	M
Mathematics Education	M
Mechanical Engineering	M,D
Medicinal and Pharmaceutical Chemistry	M,D
Nursing and Healthcare Administration	M,D
Nursing—General	M,D
Occupational Therapy	M
Pharmaceutical Administration	M,D
Pharmaceutical Sciences	M,D
Pharmacology	M,D
Pharmacy	D
Physical Education	M
Physical Therapy	D
Physics	M,D
Political Science	M
Psychology—General	M
Public Administration	M
Public Health—General	M,D
Science Education	M
Secondary Education	M
Social Psychology	M
Social Sciences Education	M
Social Sciences	M
Social Work	M
Software Engineering	M
Sports Management	M
Toxicology	M,D
Vocational and Technical Education	M

FLORIDA ATLANTIC UNIVERSITY

Accounting	M
Adult Education	M,D,O
Anthropology	M
Applied Arts and Design—General	M
Applied Mathematics	M,D
Art Education	M
Art/Fine Arts	M
Bioengineering	M,D
Biological and Biomedical Sciences—General	M
Business Administration and Management—General	M
Chemistry	M,D
Civil Engineering	M
Communication Disorders	M
Comparative and Interdisciplinary Arts	M
Comparative Literature	M
Computer Engineering	M,D
Counselor Education	D
Criminal Justice and Criminology	M
Curriculum and Instruction	M,D,O
Early Childhood Education	M,D,O
Economics	M
Education—General	M,D,O
Educational Leadership and Administration	M,D,O
Educational Media/Instructional Technology	M
Educational Psychology	M
Elementary Education	M
Engineering and Applied Sciences—General	M,D
English as a Second Language	M,D,O
English Education	M
English	M
Environmental Education	M
Environmental Engineering	M
Exercise and Sports Science	M
Film, Television, and Video Production	M,O
Finance and Banking	M
Foundations and Philosophy of Education	M
French	M
Geology	M,D
Geosciences	M,D
German	M
Graphic Design	M
Health Promotion	M
Higher Education	M,D,O
History	M
Liberal Studies	M
Linguistics	M
Management Information Systems	M
Marketing	M
Mathematics Education	M
Mathematics	M,D
Mechanical Engineering	M,D
Media Studies	M,O
Multilingual and Multicultural Education	M,D,O
Music Education	M
Music	M
Neuroscience	D
Nonprofit Management	M,D
Nursing and Healthcare Administration	M,D,O
Nursing—General	M,D,O
Ocean Engineering	M,D
Physics	M,D
Political Science	M
Psychology—General	M,D
Public Administration	M,D
Reading Education	M
Science Education	M,D
Social Sciences Education	M
Social Work	M,D
Sociology	M
Spanish	M
Special Education	M,D
Statistics	M,D
Theater	M
Urban and Regional Planning	M
Women's Studies	M

FLORIDA COASTAL SCHOOL OF LAW

Law	D

FLORIDA COLLEGE OF INTEGRATIVE MEDICINE

Acupuncture and Oriental Medicine	M

FLORIDA GULF COAST UNIVERSITY

Accounting	M
Allied Health—General	M,D
Business Administration and Management—General	M
Criminal Justice and Criminology	M
Curriculum and Instruction	M
Education—General	M
Educational Leadership and Administration	M
English Education	M
English	M
Environmental Management and Policy	M
Environmental Sciences	M
Forensic Sciences	M
History	M
Interdisciplinary Studies	M
Mathematics	M
Nurse Anesthesia	M
Occupational Therapy	M
Physical Therapy	D
Public Administration	M
Social Work	M
Special Education	M
Taxation	M

FLORIDA INSTITUTE OF TECHNOLOGY

Aerospace/Aeronautical Engineering	M,D
Applied Behavior Analysis	M,D
Applied Mathematics	M,D
Aviation Management	M
Aviation	M,D
Biochemistry	M
Biological and Biomedical Sciences—General	M,D
Biomedical Engineering	M,D
Biotechnology	M,D
Business Administration and Management—General	M,D
Cell Biology	M,D
Chemical Engineering	M,D
Chemistry	M,D
Civil Engineering	M,D
Clinical Psychology	D
Communication—General	M
Computer and Information Systems Security	M
Computer Education	M
Computer Engineering	M,D
Computer Science	M,D
Conservation Biology	M
Ecology	M,D
Education—General	M
Educational Media/Instructional Technology	M
Electrical Engineering	M,D
Electronic Commerce	M,D
Elementary Education	M
Emergency Management	M,D
Engineering and Applied Sciences—General	M,D
Engineering Management	M,D
Entrepreneurship	M
Environmental Education	M
Environmental Management and Policy	M
Environmental Sciences	M,D
Ergonomics and Human Factors	M,D
Geosciences	M
Health Services Management and Hospital Administration	M
Human Resources Management	M,D
Human-Computer Interaction	M
Industrial and Organizational Psychology	M,D
Information Science	M
Interdisciplinary Studies	M
Logistics	M,D
Management Information Systems	M,D
Management of Technology	M,D
Marine Biology	M,D
Marine Sciences	M,D
Mathematics Education	M,D,O
Mechanical Engineering	M,D
Meteorology	M
Molecular Biology	M,D
Ocean Engineering	M,D
Oceanography	M,D
Operations Research	M,D
Organizational Behavior	M
Organizational Management	M
Physics	M,D
Planetary and Space Sciences	M,D
Project Management	M,D
Psychology—General	M,D
Public Administration	M,D
Quality Management	M,D
Safety Engineering	M
Science Education	M,D,O
Software Engineering	M,D
Supply Chain Management	M,D
Systems Engineering	M,D
Transportation Management	M,D

FLORIDA INTERNATIONAL UNIVERSITY

Accounting	M
Adult Education	M,D,O
African Studies	M
Allopathic Medicine	M,D
Applied Behavior Analysis	M,D
Architecture	M,O
Art Education	M,D,O
Art/Fine Arts	M,O
Asian Studies	M
Athletic Training and Sports Medicine	M
Biological and Biomedical Sciences—General	M,D
Biomedical Engineering	M,D
Biostatistics	M,D
Business Administration and Management—General	M,D
Chemistry	M,D
Civil Engineering	M,D
Clinical Psychology	M,D,O
Cognitive Sciences	M,D
Communication Disorders	M
Communication—General	M
Computer Engineering	M
Computer Science	M,D
Construction Management	M
Counseling Psychology	M,D,O
Counselor Education	M,D,O
Criminal Justice and Criminology	M
Curriculum and Instruction	M,D,O
Developmental Psychology	M,D
Early Childhood Education	M,D,O
Economics	M,D
Education—General	M,D,O
Educational Leadership and Administration	M,D,O
Educational Media/Instructional Technology	M,D,O
Electrical Engineering	M,D
Elementary Education	M,D,O
Emergency Management	M
Engineering and Applied Sciences—General	M,D
Engineering Management	M
English as a Second Language	M,D,O
English Education	M,D,O
English	M
Environmental and Occupational Health	M,D
Environmental Engineering	M
Environmental Management and Policy	M
Environmental Sciences	M
Epidemiology	M,D
Finance and Banking	M
Foreign Languages Education	M,D,O
Forensic Sciences	M,D
Geosciences	M,D
Health Promotion	M,D
Health Services Management and Hospital Administration	M,D
Higher Education	M,D,O
History	M,D
Hospitality Management	M
Human Resources Development	M,D,O
Human Resources Management	M
Industrial and Organizational Psychology	M,D
Information Science	M,D
Interior Design	M,O
International Affairs	M,D
International and Comparative Education	M,D,O
International Business	M,D
Journalism	M
Landscape Architecture	M
Latin American Studies	M
Law	M,D
Liberal Studies	M
Linguistics	M
Management Information Systems	M,D
Mass Communication	M
Materials Engineering	M,D
Materials Sciences	M,D
Mathematics Education	M,D,O
Mathematics	M
Mechanical Engineering	M,D
Multilingual and Multicultural Education	M,D,O
Museum Studies	M,O
Music Education	M
Music	M
Neuroscience	M,D
Nursing—General	M,D
Nutrition	M,D
Occupational Therapy	M
Physical Education	M,D,O
Physical Therapy	D
Physician Assistant Studies	M
Physics	M,D
Political Science	M,D
Psychology—General	M,D
Public Administration	M,D
Public Affairs	M,D
Public Health—General	M,D
Reading Education	M,D,O
Real Estate	M
Recreation and Park Management	M,D,O
Rehabilitation Counseling	M,D,O
Religion	M
School Psychology	M,D,O
Science Education	M,D,O
Social Sciences Education	M,D,O
Social Work	M,D
Sociology	M,D
Spanish	M,D
Special Education	M,D,O
Sports Management	M,D,O
Statistics	M
Telecommunications	M
Urban Education	M,D,O
Writing	M

FLORIDA MEMORIAL UNIVERSITY

Business Administration and Management—General	M
Education—General	M
Elementary Education	M
Reading Education	M
Special Education	M

FLORIDA NATIONAL UNIVERSITY

Business Administration and Management—General	M
Family Nurse Practitioner Studies	M
Finance and Banking	M
Health Services Management and Hospital Administration	M
Marketing	M
Nursing and Healthcare Administration	M
Nursing Education	M
Nursing—General	M
Public Administration	M

FLORIDA SOUTHERN COLLEGE

Adult Nursing	M
Business Administration and Management—General	M
Education—General	M
Gerontological Nursing	M
Nursing and Healthcare Administration	M
Nursing Education	M
Nursing—General	M

FLORIDA STATE UNIVERSITY

Accounting	M,D
American Studies	M
Analytical Chemistry	M,D
Applied Behavior Analysis	M
Applied Economics	M,D
Applied Mathematics	M,D
Applied Statistics	M,D
Archaeology	M,D
Architecture	M
Art Education	M,D
Art History	M,D,O
Art/Fine Arts	M
Arts Administration	M,D
Asian Studies	M
Atmospheric Sciences	M,D
Biochemistry	M,D
Biological and Biomedical Sciences—General	M,D
Biomedical Engineering	M,D
Biostatistics	M,D
Business Administration and Management—General	M,D
Cell Biology	M,D
Chemical Engineering	M,D
Chemistry	M,D
Child and Family Studies	M,D
Civil Engineering	M,D
Classics	M,D
Clinical Psychology	D
Cognitive Sciences	D
Communication Disorders	M,D
Communication—General	M,D
Community College Education	M
Computational Biology	D
Computational Sciences	M,D
Computer and Information Systems Security	M,D
Computer Science	M,D
Corporate and Organizational Communication	M,D
Counseling Psychology	D
Criminal Justice and Criminology	M,D
Cultural Studies	M,D,O
Curriculum and Instruction	M,D,O
Dance	M
Demography and Population Studies	M
Developmental Psychology	D
Early Childhood Education	M,D,O
East European and Russian Studies	M
Ecology	M,D
Economics	M,D
Education—General	M,D,O
Educational Leadership and Administration	M,D,O
Educational Measurement and Evaluation	M,D,O
Educational Media/Instructional Technology	M,D,O
Educational Policy	M,D,O
Educational Psychology	M,D
Electrical Engineering	M,D
Elementary Education	M,D,O
Energy and Power Engineering	M,D
Engineering and Applied Sciences—General	M,D
English Education	M,D,O
English	M,D
Environmental Engineering	M,D
Environmental Law	M,D
Environmental Sciences	M,D
Evolutionary Biology	M,D
Exercise and Sports Science	M,D
Family and Consumer Sciences-General	M,D
Family Nurse Practitioner Studies	M,D,O
Film, Television, and Video Production	M*
Finance and Banking	M,D
Food Science and Technology	M,D
Foreign Languages Education	M,D,O
Foundations and Philosophy of Education	M,D
French	M,D
Geographic Information Systems	M,D
Geography	M,D
Geology	M,D
Geophysics	D
Geosciences	M,D
German	M
Health Education	M,D
Higher Education	M,D
History	M,D
Human Resources Management	M,D
Industrial Design	M
Industrial/Management Engineering	M,D
Information Studies	M,D,O
Inorganic Chemistry	M,D
Insurance	M,D
Interior Design	M
International Affairs	M
International and Comparative Education	M,D
International Business	M
Italian	M
Law	M,D
Library Science	M,D,O
Management Information Systems	M,D,O
Management Strategy and Policy	M,D
Manufacturing Engineering	M,D
Marine Sciences	M,D
Marketing	M,D
Marriage and Family Therapy	M,D
Materials Engineering	M,D
Materials Sciences	M,D
Mathematical and Computational Finance	M,D
Mathematics Education	M,D,O
Mathematics	M,D
Mechanical Engineering	M,D
Media Studies	M,D
Meteorology	M,D
Molecular Biology	M,D
Molecular Biophysics	D
Museum Studies	M,D,O
Music Education	M,D
Music	M,D
Neuroscience	M,D
Nursing and Healthcare Administration	M,D,O
Nursing Education	M,D,O
Nursing—General	M,D,O
Nutrition	M,D
Oceanography	M,D
Organic Chemistry	M,D
Organizational Behavior	M,D
Philosophy	M,D
Physical Chemistry	M,D
Physics	M,D
Plant Biology	M,D
Political Science	M,D
Psychology—General	M,D
Public Administration	M,D,O
Public Health—General	M
Public History	M,D
Public Policy	M,D,O
Reading Education	M,D,O
Religion	M,D
Rhetoric	M,D
School Psychology	D
Science Education	M,D,O
Slavic Languages	M
Social Psychology	D
Social Sciences Education	M,D,O
Social Work	M,D
Sociology	M,D
Spanish	M,D
Special Education	M,D,O
Sport Psychology	M,D
Sports Management	M,D,O
Statistics	M,D
Structural Biology	M,D
Taxation	M,D
Theater	M,D
Therapies—Dance, Drama, and Music	M,D
Urban and Regional Planning	M,D
Writing	M,D

FONTBONNE UNIVERSITY

Accounting	M
Art Education	M
Art/Fine Arts	M
Business Administration and Management—General	M
Child and Family Studies	M
Communication Disorders	M
Computer Science	M
Curriculum and Instruction	M
Early Childhood Education	M
Education—General	M
Educational Media/Instructional Technology	M
Elementary Education	M
Family and Consumer Sciences-General	M
Health Communication	M
Middle School Education	M
Nonprofit Management	M
Reading Education	M
Secondary Education	M
Special Education	M
Supply Chain Management	M
Theater	M

FORDHAM UNIVERSITY

Accounting	M
Applied Psychology	M,D
Biological and Biomedical Sciences—General	M,D,O
Business Administration and Management—General	M
Classics	M,D
Clinical Psychology	D
Clinical Research	M,D
Computer and Information Systems Security	M
Computer Science	M
Conservation Biology	M,D,O
Corporate and Organizational Communication	M
Counseling Psychology	M,D
Counselor Education	M,D
Curriculum and Instruction	M,O
Database Systems	M
Developmental Psychology	D
Early Childhood Education	M,O
Economic Development	M,O
Economics	M,D,O
Education—General	M,D,O
Educational Leadership and Administration	M,D,O
Educational Psychology	M,D
Elementary Education	M,O
Emergency Management	M
English as a Second Language	M,O
English	M,D
Ethics	M,O
Finance and Banking	M
History	M,D
Intellectual Property Law	M,D
International Affairs	M,O
International Development	M,O
International Economics	M,O
Investment Management	M
Law	M,D
Management Information Systems	M
Marketing	M
Media Studies	M
Medieval and Renaissance Studies	M,O
Nonprofit Management	M,D
Pastoral Ministry and Counseling	M,D,O
Philosophy	M,D
Political Science	M
Psychology—General	M,D
Religion	M,D,O
Religious Education	M,D,O
School Psychology	M,D
Social Work	M,D
Special Education	M,O
Taxation	M
Theater	M
Theology	M,D
Urban Studies	M

FORT HAYS STATE UNIVERSITY

Art/Fine Arts	M
Biological and Biomedical Sciences—General	M
Business Administration and Management—General	M
Communication Disorders	M
Communication—General	M
Counselor Education	M
Education—General	M,O
Educational Leadership and Administration	M,O
Educational Media/Instructional Technology	M
English	M
Geography	M
Geology	M
Geosciences	M
Health Education	M
History	M
Liberal Studies	M
Nursing—General	M
Physical Education	M
Psychology—General	M,O
School Psychology	O
Special Education	M

FORT LEWIS COLLEGE

Educational Leadership and Administration	M,O

FORT VALLEY STATE UNIVERSITY

Animal Sciences	M
Counseling Psychology	M
Counselor Education	M,O
Environmental and Occupational Health	M
Public Health—General	M
Rehabilitation Counseling	M

FRAMINGHAM STATE UNIVERSITY

Art/Fine Arts	M
Business Administration and Management—General	M
Curriculum and Instruction	M
Early Childhood Education	M
Educational Leadership and Administration	M
Educational Media/Instructional Technology	M
Elementary Education	M
English as a Second Language	M
English Education	M
Food Science and Technology	M
Foreign Languages Education	M
Health Education	M
Health Services Management and Hospital Administration	M
Human Resources Management	M
Mathematics Education	M
Nursing and Healthcare Administration	M
Nursing Education	M
Nursing—General	M
Nutrition	M
Psychology—General	M
Public Administration	M
Reading Education	M
Social Sciences Education	M
Spanish	M
Special Education	M

FRANCISCAN SCHOOL OF THEOLOGY

Theology	M

FRANCISCAN UNIVERSITY OF STEUBENVILLE

Business Administration and Management—General	M
Clinical Psychology	M
Counseling Psychology	M
Curriculum and Instruction	M
Education—General	M
Educational Leadership and Administration	M
Nursing—General	M
Philosophy	M
Theology	M

FRANCIS MARION UNIVERSITY

Applied Psychology	M,O
Business Administration and Management—General	M
Clinical Psychology	M,O
Counseling Psychology	M,O
Education—General	M
Family Nurse Practitioner Studies	M
Health Services Management and Hospital Administration	M
Nursing Education	M
Nursing—General	M
Physician Assistant Studies	M
Psychology—General	M,O
School Psychology	M,O
Special Education	M

FRANKLIN COLLEGE

Athletic Training and Sports Medicine	M

FRANKLIN PIERCE UNIVERSITY

Business Administration and Management—General	M,D,O
Curriculum and Instruction	M,D,O
Elementary Education	M,D,O
Energy Management and Policy	M,D,O
Health Services Management and Hospital Administration	M,D,O
Human Resources Management	M,D,O
Management Information Systems	M,D,O
Nursing and Healthcare Administration	M,D,O
Nursing Education	M,D,O
Physical Therapy	M,D,O
Physician Assistant Studies	M,D,O
Special Education	M,D,O
Sports Management	M,D,O
Sustainability Management	M,D,O
Telecommunications	M,D,O

FRANKLIN UNIVERSITY

Accounting	M
Business Administration and Management—General	M
Computer Science	M
Corporate and Organizational Communication	M
Educational Media/Instructional Technology	M
Marketing	M

FRANKLIN UNIVERSITY SWITZERLAND

International Business	M

FRANK LLOYD WRIGHT SCHOOL OF ARCHITECTURE

Architecture	M*

FREDERICK S. PARDEE RAND GRADUATE SCHOOL

Public Policy	D

FREED-HARDEMAN UNIVERSITY

Accounting	M
Business Administration and Management—General	M
Counselor Education	M,O
Curriculum and Instruction	M,O
Education—General	M,O
Educational Leadership and Administration	M,O
Ethics	M
Management Strategy and Policy	M
Pastoral Ministry and Counseling	M
Special Education	M,O
Theology	M

FRESNO PACIFIC UNIVERSITY

Business Administration and Management—General	M
Conflict Resolution and Mediation/Peace Studies	M,O
Counselor Education	M
Curriculum and Instruction	M
Education—General	M,O
Educational Leadership and Administration	M
Educational Media/Instructional Technology	M
English as a Second Language	M,O
Family Nurse Practitioner Studies	M
Interdisciplinary Studies	M
Kinesiology and Movement Studies	M
Marriage and Family Therapy	M
Mathematics Education	M
Missions and Missiology	M
Nursing—General	M
Pastoral Ministry and Counseling	M
Reading Education	M,O
School Psychology	M
Science Education	M
Special Education	M
Student Affairs	M,O
Theology	M

FRIENDS UNIVERSITY

Accounting	M
Health Services Management and Hospital Administration	M
Law	M
Logistics	M
Management Information Systems	M
Management Strategy and Policy	M
Marriage and Family Therapy	M
Supply Chain Management	M

FRONTIER NURSING UNIVERSITY

Family Nurse Practitioner Studies	M,D,O
Nurse Midwifery	M,D,O
Nursing—General	M,D,O
Women's Health Nursing	M,D,O

FROSTBURG STATE UNIVERSITY

Biological and Biomedical Sciences—General	M
Business Administration and Management—General	M
Computer Science	M
Conservation Biology	M
Counseling Psychology	M
Counselor Education	M
Curriculum and Instruction	M
Ecology	M
Education—General	M
Educational Leadership and Administration	M
Educational Media/Instructional Technology	M
Elementary Education	M

*M—masters degree; D—doctorate; O—other advanced degree; *—Close-Up and/or Display*

Fish, Game, and Wildlife Management	M
Interdisciplinary Studies	M
Nursing and Healthcare Administration	M
Nursing Education	M
Nursing—General	M
Psychology—General	M
Reading Education	M
Recreation and Park Management	M
Secondary Education	M
Special Education	M

FULLER THEOLOGICAL SEMINARY

Clinical Psychology	M,D,O
Marriage and Family Therapy	M,D,O
Missions and Missiology	M,D,O
Music	M,D,O
Pastoral Ministry and Counseling	M,D,O
Theology	M,D,O

FULL SAIL UNIVERSITY

Art/Fine Arts	M
Business Administration and Management—General	M
Computer Art and Design	M
Educational Media/Instructional Technology	M
Entertainment Management	M
Game Design and Development	M
Graphic Design	M
Internet and Interactive Multimedia	M
Journalism	M
Marketing	M
Media Studies	M
Writing	M

FURMAN UNIVERSITY

Chemistry	M
Curriculum and Instruction	M,O
Early Childhood Education	M,O
Education—General	M,O
Educational Leadership and Administration	M,O
English as a Second Language	M,O
Reading Education	M,O
Special Education	M,O

FUTURE GENERATIONS GRADUATE SCHOOL

Social Psychology	M
Sustainable Development	M
Urban and Regional Planning	M

GALLAUDET UNIVERSITY

Clinical Psychology	M,D,O
Communication Disorders	M,D,O
Counseling Psychology	M,D,O
Counselor Education	M,D,O
Early Childhood Education	M,D,O
Education—General	M,D,O
Elementary Education	M,D,O
International and Comparative Education	M,D,O
Linguistics	M,D,O
Multilingual and Multicultural Education	M,D,O
Neuroscience	M,D,O
Public Administration	M,D,O
School Psychology	M,D,O
Secondary Education	M,D,O
Social Work	M,D,O
Special Education	M,D,O
Translation and Interpretation	M,D,O

GANNON UNIVERSITY

Athletic Training and Sports Medicine	M
Business Administration and Management—General	M
Clinical Psychology	M
Computer Science	M
Counseling Psychology	M
Criminal Justice and Criminology	M
Curriculum and Instruction	M,O
Education—General	M,O
Educational Leadership and Administration	D,O
Electrical Engineering	M
Engineering Management	M
English as a Second Language	O
English	M
Environmental and Occupational Health	M
Environmental Engineering	M
Environmental Sciences	M
Exercise and Sports Science	M
Family Nurse Practitioner Studies	M,O
Finance and Banking	M
Health Communication	M
Human Resources Management	M
Information Science	M
Internet and Interactive Multimedia	M
Marketing	M
Mechanical Engineering	M
Nurse Anesthesia	M,O
Nursing and Healthcare Administration	M,D
Nursing—General	M,D
Occupational Therapy	M,D
Organizational Management	D
Pastoral Ministry and Counseling	M,O
Physical Therapy	D
Physician Assistant Studies	M
Public Administration	M
Reading Education	M,O
Software Engineering	M
Special Education	O
Theology	M,O

GARDNER-WEBB UNIVERSITY

Business Administration and Management—General	M
Counseling Psychology	M
Cultural Studies	M,D
Curriculum and Instruction	D
Education—General	M,D,O
Educational Leadership and Administration	M,D,O
Elementary Education	M
English Education	M
English	M
Exercise and Sports Science	M
Middle School Education	M
Missions and Missiology	M,D
Nursing—General	M,D
Organizational Management	D
Pastoral Ministry and Counseling	M,D
Physical Education	M
Physician Assistant Studies	M
Psychology—General	M
Religious Education	M,D
School Psychology	M
Theology	M,D

GARRETT-EVANGELICAL THEOLOGICAL SEMINARY

Music	M,D
Pastoral Ministry and Counseling	M,D
Religious Education	M,D
Theology	M,D

GATEWAY SEMINARY

Early Childhood Education	M,D,O
Educational Leadership and Administration	M,D,O
Pastoral Ministry and Counseling	M,D,O
Theology	M,D,O

GENERAL THEOLOGICAL SEMINARY

Pastoral Ministry and Counseling	M,D,O
Religion	M,D,O
Theology	M,D,O

GENEVA COLLEGE

Business Administration and Management—General	M
Cardiovascular Sciences	M
Clinical Psychology	M
Counseling Psychology	M
Counselor Education	M
Education—General	M
Educational Leadership and Administration	M
Finance and Banking	M
Higher Education	M
Marketing	M
Marriage and Family Therapy	M
Organizational Management	M
Psychology—General	M
Reading Education	M
Special Education	M

GEORGE FOX UNIVERSITY

Accounting	M,D
Business Administration and Management—General	M,D
Clinical Psychology	M,D,O
Counseling Psychology	M,O
Counselor Education	M,O
Cultural Studies	M,D,O
Education—General	M,D,O
Educational Leadership and Administration	M,D,O
Educational Media/Instructional Technology	M,O
English as a Second Language	M,O
Finance and Banking	M,D
Human Resources Management	M,D
Marketing	M,D
Marriage and Family Therapy	M,O
Organizational Management	M,D
Pastoral Ministry and Counseling	M,D,O
Physical Therapy	D
Reading Education	M,O
School Psychology	M,O
Social Work	M
Special Education	M,O
Theology	M,D,O

GEORGE MASON UNIVERSITY

Accounting	M,O
Anthropology	M,D
Applied Physics	M,D,O
Applied Psychology	M,D,O
Art Education	M
Art History	M
Art/Fine Arts	M
Arts Administration	M,O
Astronomy	M,D,O
Atmospheric Sciences	D
Biochemistry	M,D
Bioengineering	D
Biological and Biomedical Sciences—General	M,D,O
Biostatistics	M,D,O
Business Administration and Management—General	M
Chemistry	M,D
Civil Engineering	M,D
Cognitive Sciences	M,D,O
Communication—General	M,D,O
Community College Education	M,D,O
Community Health	M,O
Computer and Information Systems Security	M
Computer Engineering	M,D,O
Computer Science	M,D,O
Conflict Resolution and Mediation/Peace Studies	M,D,O
Construction Engineering	M,D
Counselor Education	M,D,O
Criminal Justice and Criminology	M,D,O
Cultural Studies	D
Curriculum and Instruction	M
Developmental Psychology	M,D,O
Early Childhood Education	M
Ecology	M,D
Economics	M,D,O
Education of the Gifted	M
Education—General	M,D,O
Educational Leadership and Administration	M,D,O
Educational Media/Instructional Technology	M
Educational Psychology	M,D,O
Electrical Engineering	M,D,O
Elementary Education	M
Engineering and Applied Sciences—General	M,D,O
Engineering Physics	M,D,O
English as a Second Language	M
English Education	M
English	M,D,O
Environmental Management and Policy	M,D
Environmental Sciences	M,D
Epidemiology	M,O
Ethics	M
Exercise and Sports Science	M,D,O
Foreign Languages Education	M
Forensic Sciences	M
French	M
Geographic Information Systems	M,D,O
Geography	M,D,O
Geosciences	M,D,O
Graphic Design	M
Health Promotion	M,D,O
Health Services Management and Hospital Administration	M,D
Higher Education	M,D,O
History	M,D
Homeland Security	M,D,O
Human Resources Management	M
Industrial and Organizational Psychology	M,D,O
Information Science	M,D,O
Interdisciplinary Studies	M
International Affairs	M
International and Comparative Education	M
International Business	M
International Health	M,O
Law	M,D
Linguistics	M,D,O
Logistics	M,O
Management Information Systems	M
Management of Technology	M
Mathematics Education	M
Mathematics	M,D,O
Multilingual and Multicultural Education	M
Music Education	D,O
Music	M,D
National Security	M,D
Near and Middle Eastern Studies	M,O
Neuroscience	M,D,O
Nursing—General	M,D,O
Nutrition	M
Operations Research	M,D,O
Organizational Management	M
Philosophy	M
Physical Education	M
Physics	M,D,O
Political Science	M,D,O
Project Management	M,D
Psychology—General	M,D,O
Public Administration	M,D,O
Public Affairs	M
Public Health—General	M,O
Public Policy	M,D
Reading Education	M
Rehabilitation Sciences	D,O
Science Education	M
Secondary Education	M
Social Sciences Education	M
Social Work	M
Sociology	M,D
Special Education	M,D,O
Statistics	M,D,O
Structural Engineering	M,D
Systems Engineering	M,D,O
Transportation and Highway Engineering	M,D
Transportation Management	M,O
Writing	M

GEORGETOWN COLLEGE

Education—General	M
Reading Education	M
Special Education	M

GEORGETOWN UNIVERSITY

Acute Care/Critical Care Nursing	M,D
Advertising and Public Relations	M
Allopathic Medicine	D
American Studies	M,D
Analytical Chemistry	D
Asian Studies	M
Biochemistry	M,D
Bioinformatics	M,O
Biological and Biomedical Sciences—General	M,D
Biostatistics	M,O
Business Administration and Management—General	M
Chemistry	D
Communication—General	M
Comparative Literature	M,D
Computer Science	M,D
Conflict Resolution and Mediation/Peace Studies	M
East European and Russian Studies	M
Economic Development	D
Economics	D
Emergency Management	M,D
English	M
Environmental Law	M,D
Epidemiology	M,O
Ethics	M,D
Family Nurse Practitioner Studies	M,D
Finance and Banking	M,D
German	M,D
Health Law	M,D
Health Physics/Radiological Health	M
Health Promotion	M,D
History	M,D
Hospitality Management	M,D
Human Development	M
Human Resources Management	M,D
Humanities	M,D
Immunology	M,D
Industrial and Labor Relations	D
Industrial and Manufacturing Management	D
Infectious Diseases	M,D
Inorganic Chemistry	D
Interdisciplinary Studies	M,D
International Affairs	M,D
International Business	M,D
International Health	M,D
Internet and Interactive Multimedia	M
Journalism	M,D
Latin American Studies	M
Law	M,D
Liberal Studies	M,D
Linguistics	M,D
Management of Technology	M,D
Materials Sciences	D
Mathematics	M
Media Studies	M,D
Medieval and Renaissance Studies	M,D
Microbiology	M,D
Molecular Biology	M,D
Near and Middle Eastern Languages	M,O
Near and Middle Eastern Studies	M,O
Neuroscience	D
Nurse Anesthesia	M,D
Nurse Midwifery	M,D
Nursing Education	M,D
Nursing—General	M,D
Organic Chemistry	D
Pharmacology	M,D
Philosophy	M,D
Physiology	M,D
Political Science	M,D
Psychology—General	D
Public Health—General	M,D
Public Policy	M,D
Radiation Biology	M
Real Estate	M,D
Religion	M,D
Spanish	M,D
Sports Management	M,D
Statistics	M
Systems Engineering	M,D
Taxation	M,D
Theology	D
Theoretical Chemistry	D
Urban and Regional Planning	M,D
Western European Studies	M

THE GEORGE WASHINGTON UNIVERSITY

Accounting	M
Addictions/Substance Abuse Counseling	M
Adult Education	O
Adult Nursing	M,D,O
Aerospace/Aeronautical Engineering	M,D,O
Allopathic Medicine	D
American Studies	M,D
Analytical Chemistry	M,D
Anthropology	M,D
Applied Mathematics	M,D,O
Applied Psychology	D
Art Education	M
Art History	M
Art Therapy	M,O
Art/Fine Arts	M,O
Asian Studies	M
Biochemistry	D
Biological and Biomedical Sciences—General	M,D
Biomedical Engineering	M,D
Biostatistics	M,D
Biotechnology	M,D,O
Business Administration and Management—General	M,D,O
Chemistry	M,D
Civil Engineering	M,D,O
Clinical Psychology	M,D
Cognitive Sciences	D
Communication Disorders	M
Communication—General	M
Community Health	M,D
Computer and Information Systems Security	M,D,O
Computer Engineering	M,D,O
Computer Science	M,D,O
Counselor Education	M,D,O
Criminal Justice and Criminology	M,O
Curriculum and Instruction	M,D,O
Dance	M,O
Distance Education Development	O
Early Childhood Education	M
East European and Russian Studies	M
Economics	M,D
Education—General	M,D,O
Educational Leadership and Administration	M,D,O
Educational Media/Instructional Technology	M,O
Educational Policy	M,D,O
Electrical Engineering	M,D,O
Elementary Education	M
Emergency Management	M,D,O
Engineering and Applied Sciences—General	M,D,O*
Engineering Management	M,D,O
English	M,D
Environmental and Occupational Health	D
Environmental Engineering	M,D,O
Environmental Management and Policy	M

Epidemiology	M
Exercise and Sports Science	M
Family Nurse Practitioner Studies	M,D,O
Finance and Banking	M,D
Folklore	M,D
Foreign Languages Education	M
Forensic Psychology	O
Forensic Sciences	M,O
Gender Studies	O
Geography	M,O
Health Communication	M,D
Health Services Management and Hospital Administration	M,D,O
Health Services Research	M,D,O
Higher Education	M,D,O
Historic Preservation	M,D
History	M,D
Hospitality Management	M,O
Human Development	M
Human Resources Development	M,D,O
Human Resources Management	M,O
Immunology	D
Infectious Diseases	M,D,O
Inorganic Chemistry	M,D
Interior Design	M
International Affairs	M,D
International and Comparative Education	M,D,O
International Business	M,D
International Development	M,D
International Health	M,D
International Trade Policy	M
Investment Management	M,D
Latin American Studies	M
Law	M,D
Legal and Justice Studies	M,D,O
Management Information Systems	M,D
Management of Technology	M,D
Management Strategy and Policy	M,D,O
Marketing	M,D
Mass Communication	M,O
Materials Sciences	M,D
Mathematical and Computational Finance	M,D,O
Mathematics Education	M
Mathematics	M,D,O
Mechanical Engineering	M,D,O
Microbiology	M,D,O
Military and Defense Studies	M
Molecular Medicine	D
Multilingual and Multicultural Education	M,D,O
Museum Education	M
Museum Studies	M,D,O
National Security	M,D
Near and Middle Eastern Studies	M
Nonprofit Management	M,O
Nursing and Healthcare Administration	M,D,O
Nursing Education	M,D,O
Nursing—General	M,D,O
Organic Chemistry	M,D
Organizational Management	M,O
Philosophy	M
Photography	M,O
Physical Chemistry	M,D
Physical Therapy	D
Physician Assistant Studies	M
Physics	M,D
Political Science	M,D
Project Management	M,D,O
Psychology—General	M,D,O
Public Administration	M,D
Public Affairs	M,O
Public Health—General	M,D
Public Policy	M,D
Publishing	M
Real Estate	O
Rehabilitation Counseling	M
Religion	M
Science Education	M
Secondary Education	M
Social Psychology	D
Sociology	M
Special Education	M,D,O
Sports Management	M,O
Statistics	M,D,O
Student Affairs	M,D,O
Systems Biology	D
Systems Engineering	M,D,O
Technology and Public Policy	M,O
Telecommunications	M,D,O
Theater	M,O
Toxicology	M,O
Travel and Tourism	M,O
Vocational and Technical Education	O
Western European Studies	M
Women's Studies	M,O

GEORGIA CAMPUS–PHILADELPHIA COLLEGE OF OSTEOPATHIC MEDICINE

Osteopathic Medicine	D
Pharmacy	D*

GEORGIA CHRISTIAN UNIVERSITY

Business Administration and Management—General	M
Missions and Missiology	M,D
Music	M
Pastoral Ministry and Counseling	M,D
Theology	M,D

GEORGIA COLLEGE & STATE UNIVERSITY

Accounting	M
Art Therapy	M
Biological and Biomedical Sciences—General	M
Business Administration and Management—General	M
Criminal Justice and Criminology	M
Curriculum and Instruction	O
Early Childhood Education	M
Education—General	M,O
Educational Leadership and Administration	O
Educational Media/Instructional Technology	M
English	M
Exercise and Sports Science	M
Health Education	M
Health Promotion	M
History	M
Kinesiology and Movement Studies	M
Logistics	M
Management Information Systems	M
Music Education	M
Nursing—General	M,D
Physical Education	M
Public Administration	M
Public History	M
Reading Education	M
Secondary Education	M
Special Education	M,O
Therapies—Dance, Drama, and Music	M
Writing	M

GEORGIA INSTITUTE OF TECHNOLOGY

Aerospace/Aeronautical Engineering	M,D
Architecture	M,D
Artificial Intelligence/Robotics	D
Atmospheric Sciences	M,D
Bioengineering	M,D
Bioinformatics	M,D
Biological and Biomedical Sciences—General	M,D
Biomedical Engineering	D
Building Science	M,D
Business Administration and Management—General	M,D
Chemical Engineering	M,D
Chemistry	M,D
Civil Engineering	M,D
Computational Sciences	M,D
Computer and Information Systems Security	M
Computer Art and Design	M,D
Computer Engineering	M,D
Computer Science	M,D
Economic Development	M,D
Economics	M,D
Electrical Engineering	M,D
Engineering and Applied Sciences—General	M,D
Environmental Engineering	M
Environmental Management and Policy	M,D
Ergonomics and Human Factors	M,D
Geographic Information Systems	M,D
Geosciences	M,D
Health Physics/Radiological Health	M,D
Health Services Management and Hospital Administration	M
History of Science and Technology	M
Human-Computer Interaction	M
Industrial Design	M
Industrial/Management Engineering	M,D
International Affairs	M
International Business	M
Internet and Interactive Multimedia	M,D
Logistics	M
Management Information Systems	M
Materials Engineering	M,D
Mathematical and Computational Finance	M
Mathematics	M,D
Mechanical Engineering	M,D
Mechanics	M
Music	M,D
Nuclear Engineering	M,D
Operations Research	M,D
Paper and Pulp Engineering	M,D
Physics	M,D
Physiology	M,D
Psychology—General	M,D
Public Policy	M,D
Statistics	M
Urban and Regional Planning	M,D
Urban Design	M,D

GEORGIAN COURT UNIVERSITY

Applied Behavior Analysis	M,O
Business Administration and Management—General	M,O
Clinical Psychology	M,O
Computer Art and Design	M,O
Counseling Psychology	M,O
Counselor Education	M,O
Education—General	M,O
Educational Leadership and Administration	M,O
Educational Media/Instructional Technology	M,O
Health Psychology	M,O
Homeland Security	M,O
Nonprofit Management	M,O
School Psychology	M,O
Special Education	M,O
Theology	M,O

GEORGIA SOUTHERN UNIVERSITY

Accounting	M
Allied Health—General	M,D,O
Applied Economics	M,O
Applied Physics	M
Art/Fine Arts	M
Biological and Biomedical Sciences—General	M
Biostatistics	M,D
Business Administration and Management—General	M
Civil Engineering	M
Clinical Psychology	M,D
Community Health	M,D
Computer Science	M
Construction Management	M
Counselor Education	M,O
Curriculum and Instruction	M,D
Early Childhood Education	M,O
Education—General	M,D,O
Educational Leadership and Administration	M,D,O
Educational Media/Instructional Technology	M,O
Electrical Engineering	M
Elementary Education	M
Energy and Power Engineering	M
Engineering and Applied Sciences—General	M,O
Engineering Management	M
English Education	M
English	M
Environmental and Occupational Health	M,D,O
Environmental Sciences	O
Epidemiology	M,D
Family Nurse Practitioner Studies	M
Graphic Design	M
Health Education	M,D
Health Services Management and Hospital Administration	M,D
Higher Education	M
History	M,O
Kinesiology and Movement Studies	M
Logistics	D
Management Information Systems	M,O
Manufacturing Engineering	M,O
Mathematics	M
Mechanical Engineering	M
Middle School Education	M,O
Multilingual and Multicultural Education	D
Music Education	M
Music	M
Nonprofit Management	O
Nursing Education	O
Nursing—General	D
Nutrition	O
Psychiatric Nursing	M
Psychology—General	M,D
Public Administration	M
Public Health—General	M,D
Public History	M,O
Reading Education	M,O
School Psychology	M,O
Secondary Education	M,O
Sociology	M
Spanish	M
Special Education	M,O
Sports Management	M
Supply Chain Management	D
Systems Engineering	M

GEORGIA SOUTHWESTERN STATE UNIVERSITY

Business Administration and Management—General	M
Computer Science	M,O
Early Childhood Education	M,O
Education—General	M,O
English Education	M,O
Management Information Systems	M,O
Mathematics Education	M,O
Middle School Education	M,O
Special Education	M,O

GEORGIA STATE UNIVERSITY

Accounting	M
Actuarial Science	M
Adult Nursing	M,D,O
African-American Studies	M
Allied Health—General	M
Analytical Chemistry	M,D
Anthropology	M
Art Education	M
Art History	M
Art/Fine Arts	M
Astronomy	D
Athletic Training and Sports Medicine	M
Biochemistry	M,D
Bioinformatics	M,D
Biological and Biomedical Sciences—General	M,D*
Biostatistics	M,D
Business Administration and Management—General	M,D
Cell Biology	M,D
Chemistry	M,D
Clinical Psychology	D
Clothing and Textiles	M
Cognitive Sciences	D
Communication Disorders	M,D
Communication—General	M,D
Computer Science	M,D
Counseling Psychology	M,O
Counselor Education	M,O
Criminal Justice and Criminology	M,D,O
Curriculum and Instruction	M,D
Developmental Psychology	D
Early Childhood Education	M,D,O
Economic Development	M,D,O
Economics	M,D
Education of Students with Severe/Multiple Disabilities	M
Education—General	M,D,O
Educational Leadership and Administration	M,D,O
Educational Measurement and Evaluation	M,D
Educational Media/Instructional Technology	M,D
Educational Policy	M,D,O
Educational Psychology	M,D
Elementary Education	M,D,O
Emergency Management	M,D,O
English Education	M,D
English	M,D
Entrepreneurship	M,D
Environmental Biology	M,D
Environmental Management and Policy	M,D,O
Exercise and Sports Science	M
Family Nurse Practitioner Studies	M,D,O
Film, Television, and Video Production	M,D
Finance and Banking	M,D,O
Foreign Languages Education	M
Forensic Sciences	M,O
Foundations and Philosophy of Education	M,D
French	M,O
Geochemistry	M,D
Geographic Information Systems	O
Geography	M,D
Geology	M
Geosciences	M,D,O
German	O
Gerontology	M,O
Graphic Design	M
Health Education	M
Health Informatics	M,D,O
Health Services Management and Hospital Administration	M,D,O
Historic Preservation	M,D
History	M,D
Human Resources Management	M,D
Human Services	M,O
Industrial and Labor Relations	M,D
Information Science	M,D,O
Insurance	M,D,O
Interior Design	M
International Business	M
Kinesiology and Movement Studies	D
Latin American Studies	M,O
Law	D
Linguistics	M,D
Management Information Systems	M,D,O
Management Strategy and Policy	M,D
Marketing	M,D
Mass Communication	M,D
Mathematics Education	M,D,O
Mathematics	M,D
Media Studies	M,D
Microbiology	M,D
Middle School Education	M,D
Molecular Biology	M,D
Molecular Genetics	M,D
Music Education	M,D,O
Music	M,D,O
Neurobiology	M,D
Neuroscience	D
Nonprofit Management	M,D,O
Nursing and Healthcare Administration	M,D,O
Nursing Informatics	M,D,O
Nursing—General	M,D,O
Nutrition	M
Operations Research	M,D
Organic Chemistry	M,D
Organizational Management	M,D
Pediatric Nursing	M,D,O
Philosophy	M
Photography	M,D
Physical Chemistry	M,D
Physical Education	M
Physical Therapy	D
Physics	M,D
Physiology	M,D
Political Science	M,D
Psychiatric Nursing	M,D,O
Psychology—General	D
Public Administration	M,D
Public Health—General	M,D,O
Public History	M,D
Public Policy	M,D,O
Reading Education	M,D
Real Estate	M,D,O
Rehabilitation Counseling	M
Religion	M
Rhetoric	M,D
School Psychology	M,D,O
Science Education	M,D
Secondary Education	M,D
Social Psychology	D
Social Sciences Education	M,D
Social Work	M,O
Sociology	M,D
Spanish	M,O
Special Education	M,D
Speech and Interpersonal Communication	M,D
Sports Management	M
Statistics	M,D
Taxation	M
Translation and Interpretation	O
Urban and Regional Planning	M,D,O
Urban Education	M,D,O
Women's Health Nursing	M,D,O
Women's Studies	M,O
Writing	M,D

GERSTNER SLOAN KETTERING GRADUATE SCHOOL OF BIOMEDICAL SCIENCES

Biological and Biomedical Sciences—General	D
Cancer Biology/Oncology	D*

*M—masters degree; D—doctorate; O—other advanced degree; *—Close-Up and/or Display*

GLION INSTITUTE OF HIGHER EDUCATION
Hospitality Management M

GLOBAL UNIVERSITY
Missions and Missiology M,D
Pastoral Ministry and Counseling M,D
Religious Education M,D
Theology M,D

GLOBE UNIVERSITY–WOODBURY
Business Administration and Management—General M
Health Services Management and Hospital Administration M
Management Information Systems M

GODDARD COLLEGE
Art Therapy M
Business Administration and Management—General M
Comparative and Interdisciplinary Arts M
Education—General M
Health Promotion M
Interdisciplinary Studies M
Psychology—General M
Sustainability Management M
Writing M

GOLDEN GATE UNIVERSITY
Accounting M,D,O
Advertising and Public Relations M,D,O
Business Administration and Management—General M,D,O
Corporate and Organizational Communication M,D,O
Environmental Law M,D
Finance and Banking M,D,O
Forensic Sciences M,O
Health Informatics M,D,O
Human Resources Management M,D,O
Intellectual Property Law M,D
International Business M,D,O
Law M,D
Legal and Justice Studies M,D
Management Information Systems M,D,O
Management of Technology M,D,O
Marketing M,D,O
Psychology—General M,D,O
Public Administration M,D,O
Supply Chain Management M,D,O
Taxation M,D,O

GOLDEY-BEACOM COLLEGE
Business Administration and Management—General M
Finance and Banking M
Health Services Management and Hospital Administration M
Human Resources Management M
International Business M
Management Information Systems M
Marketing M
Taxation M

GOLDFARB SCHOOL OF NURSING AT BARNES-JEWISH COLLEGE
Acute Care/Critical Care Nursing M
Adult Nursing M
Gerontological Nursing M
Health Services Management and Hospital Administration M
Nurse Anesthesia M
Nursing Education M
Nursing—General M

GONZAGA UNIVERSITY
Accounting M
Business Administration and Management—General M
Education—General M
Elementary Education M
English as a Second Language M
Law D
Marriage and Family Therapy M
Nursing—General M,D
Organizational Management M,D
Philosophy M
Physiology M,D
Secondary Education M
Special Education M
Sports Management M
Taxation M
Theology M

GORDON COLLEGE
Early Childhood Education M,O
Education—General M,O
Educational Leadership and Administration M,O
Elementary Education M,O
English as a Second Language M,O
Mathematics Education M,O
Middle School Education M,O
Music Education M
Reading Education M,O
Secondary Education M,O
Special Education M,O

GORDON-CONWELL THEOLOGICAL SEMINARY
Archaeology M,D
Missions and Missiology M,D
Pastoral Ministry and Counseling M,D
Religion M,D
Theology M,D

GOSHEN COLLEGE
Environmental Education M
Family Nurse Practitioner Studies M
Nursing—General M

GOUCHER COLLEGE
Arts Administration M
Biological and Biomedical Sciences—General O
Business Administration and Management—General M
Computer Art and Design M
Cultural Studies M
Education—General M,O
Educational Leadership and Administration M,O
Educational Media/Instructional Technology M,O
Elementary Education M,O
Environmental Management and Policy M
Historic Preservation M
Middle School Education M,O
Physical Education M,O
Reading Education M,O
Secondary Education M,O
Special Education M,O
Writing M

GOVERNORS STATE UNIVERSITY
Accounting M
Addictions/Substance Abuse Counseling M
Analytical Chemistry M
Art/Fine Arts M
Business Administration and Management—General M
Communication Disorders M
Communication—General M
Computer Science M
Counseling Psychology M
Early Childhood Education M
Education—General M
Educational Leadership and Administration M
Educational Media/Instructional Technology M
English M
Environmental Biology M
Health Services Management and Hospital Administration M
Legal and Justice Studies M
Management Information Systems M
Media Studies M
Nursing—General M
Occupational Therapy M
Physical Therapy M,D
Political Science M
Psychology—General M
Public Administration M
Reading Education M
Social Work M
Special Education M

GRACE COLLEGE
Clinical Psychology M

GRACELAND UNIVERSITY (IA)
Curriculum and Instruction M
Education—General M
Educational Leadership and Administration M
Educational Media/Instructional Technology M
Family Nurse Practitioner Studies M,D,O
Nursing Education M,D,O
Nursing—General M,D,O
Organizational Management M,D,O
Reading Education M
Religion M
Special Education M
Theology M

GRACE MISSION UNIVERSITY
Missions and Missiology M,D

GRACE THEOLOGICAL SEMINARY
Cultural Studies M,D,O
Missions and Missiology M,D,O
Pastoral Ministry and Counseling M,D,O
Theology M,D,O
Women's Studies M,D,O

GRACE UNIVERSITY
Counseling Psychology M
Pastoral Ministry and Counseling M
Theology M

THE GRADUATE CENTER, CITY UNIVERSITY OF NEW YORK
Accounting D
Anthropology D
Archaeology D
Architectural History D
Art History D
Biochemistry D
Biological and Biomedical Sciences—General D
Biomedical Engineering D
Biopsychology D
Business Administration and Management—General D
Chemical Engineering D
Chemistry D
Civil Engineering D
Classics M,D
Clinical Psychology D
Cognitive Sciences D
Communication Disorders D
Comparative Literature M,D
Computer Science D
Criminal Justice and Criminology D
Cultural Anthropology D
Developmental Psychology D
Economics D
Educational Psychology D
Electrical Engineering D
Engineering and Applied Sciences—General D
English D
Environmental Sciences D
Experimental Psychology D
Finance and Banking D
French D
Geosciences D
German M,D
Hispanic and Latin American Languages D
History D
Industrial and Organizational Psychology D
Interdisciplinary Studies M,D
Italian M,D
Liberal Studies M
Linguistics M,D
Management Information Systems D
Mathematics D
Mechanical Engineering D
Medieval and Renaissance Studies M,D
Music D
Neuroscience D
Nursing—General D
Organizational Behavior D
Philosophy M,D
Physical Therapy D
Physics D
Political Science M,D
Psychology—General D
Public Health—General D
Public Policy M,D
Social Psychology D
Social Work D
Sociology D
Theater D
Urban Education D
Urban Studies M,D
Women's Studies M,D

GRADUATE INSTITUTE OF APPLIED LINGUISTICS
Linguistics M,O
Multilingual and Multicultural Education M,O

GRADUATE THEOLOGICAL UNION
Art History M,D,O
Cultural Studies M,D,O
Ethics M,D,O
Jewish Studies M,D,O
Religion M,D,O
Social Sciences M,D,O
Theology M,D,O

GRAMBLING STATE UNIVERSITY
Counselor Education M,D,O
Criminal Justice and Criminology M
Curriculum and Instruction M,D,O
Developmental Education M,D,O
Education—General M,D,O
Educational Leadership and Administration M,D,O
Educational Media/Instructional Technology M,D,O
English M,D,O
Family Nurse Practitioner Studies M,O
Health Services Management and Hospital Administration M
Higher Education M,D,O
Human Resources Management M
Mass Communication M
Mathematics Education M,D,O
Nursing—General M,O
Political Science M
Public Administration M
Reading Education M,D,O
Science Education M,D,O
Social Sciences Education M
Social Work M
Special Education M
Sports Management M
Student Affairs M,D,O

GRAND CANYON UNIVERSITY
Accounting M
Acute Care/Critical Care Nursing M,O
Addictions/Substance Abuse Counseling M
Business Administration and Management—General M,D
Cognitive Sciences D
Counseling Psychology M
Curriculum and Instruction M
Education—General M,D
Educational Leadership and Administration M,D
Elementary Education M
Emergency Management M
Entrepreneurship M
Family Nurse Practitioner Studies M,O
Finance and Banking M
Health Education D
Health Informatics M
Health Services Management and Hospital Administration M,O
Higher Education D
Human Resources Management M
Industrial and Organizational Psychology D
Management Information Systems M
Marketing M
Marriage and Family Therapy M
Nursing Education M,O
Nursing—General M,O
Organizational Management D
Psychology—General D
Public Administration M
Public Health—General M
Secondary Education M
Special Education M

GRAND RAPIDS THEOLOGICAL SEMINARY OF CORNERSTONE UNIVERSITY
Missions and Missiology M
Pastoral Ministry and Counseling M
Religion M
Religious Education M
Theology M

GRAND VALLEY STATE UNIVERSITY
Accounting M
Adult Education M,O
Allied Health—General M,D
Bioinformatics M
Biological and Biomedical Sciences—General M
Biostatistics M
Business Administration and Management—General M
Cell Biology M
Communication Disorders M
Communication—General M
Computer Engineering M
Computer Science M
Criminal Justice and Criminology M
Curriculum and Instruction M
Early Childhood Education M,O
Education—General M,O
Educational Leadership and Administration M,O
Educational Media/Instructional Technology M,O
Electrical Engineering M
Elementary Education M,O
Engineering and Applied Sciences—General M
English as a Second Language M,O
English Education M
English M
Health Services Management and Hospital Administration M,D
Higher Education M,O
Information Science M
Management Information Systems M
Manufacturing Engineering M
Mechanical Engineering M
Medical Informatics M
Middle School Education M,O
Molecular Biology M
Nonprofit Management M
Nursing and Healthcare Administration M,D
Nursing Education M,D
Nursing—General M,D
Occupational Therapy M
Physical Therapy D
Physician Assistant Studies M
Public Administration M
Public Health—General M
Reading Education M
School Psychology M,O
Secondary Education M,O
Social Work M
Software Engineering M
Special Education M
Taxation M

GRAND VIEW UNIVERSITY
Business Administration and Management—General M
Education—General M
Nursing—General M
Organizational Management M

GRANITE STATE COLLEGE
Business Administration and Management—General M
Educational Leadership and Administration M
Organizational Management M
Project Management M

GRANTHAM UNIVERSITY
Business Administration and Management—General M,O
Engineering and Applied Sciences—General M
Health Services Management and Hospital Administration M
Human Resources Development M,O
Human Resources Management M,O
Management Information Systems M,O
Management Strategy and Policy M,O
Nursing and Healthcare Administration M
Nursing Education M
Nursing Informatics M
Organizational Management M
Project Management M,O

GRATZ COLLEGE
Education—General M
Educational Media/Instructional Technology O
Holocaust and Genocide Studies M,O
Jewish Studies M,O
Nonprofit Management O
Religious Education M,D,O
Social Work M,O

GREEN MOUNTAIN COLLEGE
Business Administration and Management—General M
Environmental Management and Policy M

GREENSBORO COLLEGE
Education—General M
Elementary Education M
English as a Second Language M
Special Education M

GREENVILLE COLLEGE
Education—General M
Elementary Education M
Pastoral Ministry and Counseling M
Secondary Education M

GWYNEDD MERCY UNIVERSITY
Adult Nursing M,D
Business Administration and Management—General M
Counselor Education M
Education—General M
Educational Leadership and Administration M
Family Nurse Practitioner Studies M,D
Gerontological Nursing M,D

Health Services Management and Hospital Administration	M
Management Strategy and Policy	M
Nursing Education	M,D
Nursing—General	M,D
Oncology Nursing	M,D
Pediatric Nursing	M,D
Special Education	M

HALLMARK UNIVERSITY

Business Administration and Management—General	M
International Business	M

HAMLINE UNIVERSITY

Business Administration and Management—General	M,D
Education—General	M,D
English as a Second Language	M,D
Environmental Education	M,D
Law	M,D
Liberal Studies	M
Nonprofit Management	M,D
Public Administration	M,D
Reading Education	M,D
Science Education	M,D
Writing	M

HAMPTON UNIVERSITY

Adult Nursing	M,D
Allied Health—General	M
Applied Mathematics	M
Architecture	M
Atmospheric Sciences	M,D
Biological and Biomedical Sciences—General	M
Business Administration and Management—General	M,D
Chemistry	M
Communication Disorders	M
Community Health Nursing	M,D
Computational Sciences	M
Computer and Information Systems Security	M
Computer Science	M
Counselor Education	M,D,O
Education—General	M,D,O
Educational Leadership and Administration	M,D
Elementary Education	M
Environmental Biology	M
Gerontological Nursing	M,D
Medical Physics	M,D
Music Education	M
Nursing—General	M,D
Pastoral Ministry and Counseling	M,D,O
Pediatric Nursing	M,D
Pharmacy	D
Physical Therapy	D
Physics	M,D
Planetary and Space Sciences	M,D
Psychiatric Nursing	M,D
Psychology—General	M
Secondary Education	M
Sports Management	M
Statistics	M
Student Affairs	M,D,O
Women's Health Nursing	M,D

HANNIBAL-LAGRANGE UNIVERSITY

Education—General	M
Reading Education	M

HARDING SCHOOL OF THEOLOGY

Pastoral Ministry and Counseling	M,D
Religion	M,D
Theology	M,D

HARDING UNIVERSITY

Allied Health—General	M,D
Art Education	M,O
Business Administration and Management—General	M
Communication Disorders	M
Counseling Psychology	M
Counselor Education	M,O
Early Childhood Education	M,O
Education—General	M,O
Educational Leadership and Administration	M,O
Elementary Education	M,O
English as a Second Language	M,O
English Education	M,O
Foreign Languages Education	M,O
Health Education	M,O
Health Services Management and Hospital Administration	M
International Business	M
Management of Technology	M
Marriage and Family Therapy	M
Mathematics Education	M,O
Organizational Management	M
Pastoral Ministry and Counseling	M
Pharmacy	D
Physical Therapy	D
Physician Assistant Studies	M
Reading Education	M,O
Secondary Education	M,O
Social Sciences Education	M,O
Special Education	M,O

HARDIN-SIMMONS UNIVERSITY

Business Administration and Management—General	M
Counseling Psychology	M
Counselor Education	M
Education of the Gifted	M
Education—General	M,D
Educational Leadership and Administration	D
English	M
Environmental Management and Policy	M
Family Nurse Practitioner Studies	M
History	M
Kinesiology and Movement Studies	M
Marriage and Family Therapy	M
Maternal and Child/Neonatal Nursing	M
Mathematics	M
Music Education	M
Music	M
Nursing—General	M
Pastoral Ministry and Counseling	M,D
Physical Therapy	D
Psychology—General	M
Reading Education	M
Recreation and Park Management	M
Religion	M
Science Education	M,D
Sports Management	M
Theology	M,D

HARRISBURG UNIVERSITY OF SCIENCE AND TECHNOLOGY

Construction Management	M
Educational Media/Instructional Technology	M
Entrepreneurship	M
Health Services Management and Hospital Administration	M
Management Information Systems	M
Management of Technology	M
Project Management	M
Public Administration	M
Systems Engineering	M

HARRISON MIDDLETON UNIVERSITY

Comparative Literature	M,D
Education—General	M,D
Humanities	M,D
Interdisciplinary Studies	M,D
Legal and Justice Studies	M,D
Philosophy	M,D
Religion	M,D
Science Education	M,D
Social Sciences	M,D

HARTFORD SEMINARY

Pastoral Ministry and Counseling	M,D,O
Religion	M,D,O
Theology	M,D,O

HARVARD UNIVERSITY

Accounting	D
African Studies	D
African-American Studies	D
Allopathic Medicine	D
American Studies	D
Anthropology	M,D
Applied Mathematics	M,D
Applied Physics	M,D
Applied Science and Technology	M,O
Archaeology	M,D
Architectural History	D
Architecture	M,D
Art Education	M
Art History	D
Asian Languages	M,D
Asian Studies	M,D
Astronomy	D
Astrophysics	D
Biochemistry	D
Bioengineering	M,D
Biological and Biomedical Sciences—General	M,D,O
Biomedical Engineering	D
Biophysics	D*
Biopsychology	D
Biostatistics	M,D
Biotechnology	M,O
Business Administration and Management—General	M,D,O
Cell Biology	D
Celtic Languages	D
Chemical Physics	D
Chemistry	D
Chinese	D
Classics	D
Cognitive Sciences	M,D
Communication—General	M,O
Comparative Literature	D
Computational Biology	M
Computational Sciences	M,D
Computer Science	M,D
Curriculum and Instruction	M
Demography and Population Studies	M,D
Dentistry	M,D,O
Developmental Psychology	D
East European and Russian Studies	M
Economics	D
Education—General	M,D
Educational Leadership and Administration	M,D
Educational Media/Instructional Technology	M,O
Educational Policy	M
Educational Psychology	M
Electrical Engineering	M,D
Engineering and Applied Sciences—General	M,D
Engineering Design	M,D
English	M,D,O
Environmental and Occupational Health	M,D
Environmental Engineering	M,D
Environmental Management and Policy	M,O
Environmental Sciences	M,D
Epidemiology	M,D
Evolutionary Biology	D
Experimental Psychology	D
Forestry	M
Foundations and Philosophy of Education	M,O
French	M,D
Genetics	D
Genomic Sciences	D
Geosciences	M,D
German	D
Health Promotion	M,D
Health Services Management and Hospital Administration	M,D
History of Science and Technology	M,D
History	D
Human Development	M
Industrial and Manufacturing Management	D
Information Science	M,D,O
Inorganic Chemistry	D
International Affairs	D
International and Comparative Education	M
International Development	M
International Health	M,D
Italian	M,D
Japanese	D
Jewish Studies	M,D
Journalism	M,O
Landscape Architecture	M,D
Law	M,D
Legal and Justice Studies	D
Liberal Studies	M,O
Linguistics	D
Management of Technology	D
Management Strategy and Policy	D
Marketing	D
Materials Sciences	M,D
Mathematics Education	M,O
Mathematics	D
Mechanical Engineering	M,D
Medical Physics	D
Medieval and Renaissance Studies	D
Microbiology	D
Molecular Biology	D
Molecular Genetics	D
Molecular Pharmacology	D
Museum Studies	M,O
Music	M,D
Near and Middle Eastern Languages	M,D
Near and Middle Eastern Studies	M,D
Neurobiology	D
Neuroscience	D
Nutrition	D
Oral and Dental Sciences	M,D,O
Organic Chemistry	D
Organizational Behavior	D
Pathology	D
Philosophy	M,D
Physical Chemistry	D
Physics	D
Physiology	M,D
Planetary and Space Sciences	M,D
Political Science	M,D
Portuguese	M,D
Psychology—General	D
Public Administration	M
Public Health—General	M,D*
Public Policy	M,D
Reading Education	M
Religion	D
Russian	D
Scandinavian Languages	D
Slavic Languages	D
Social Psychology	D
Sociology	D
Spanish	M,D
Statistics	M,D
Structural Biology	D
Systems Biology	D
Technical Communication	M
Theology	M
Theoretical Physics	D
Urban and Regional Planning	M,D
Urban Design	M

HASTINGS COLLEGE

Education—General	M

HAWAI`I PACIFIC UNIVERSITY

Accounting	M
Business Administration and Management—General	M
Clinical Psychology	M
Communication—General	M
Economics	M
Elementary Education	M
English as a Second Language	M
Finance and Banking	M
Hospitality Management	M
Human Resources Management	M
International Business	M
Liberal Studies	M
Management Information Systems	M
Marine Sciences	M
Marketing	M
Military and Defense Studies	M
Nursing—General	M
Organizational Management	M
Secondary Education	M
Social Work	M
Sustainable Development	M

HAZELDEN GRADUATE SCHOOL OF ADDICTION STUDIES

Addictions/Substance Abuse Counseling	M,O

HEBREW COLLEGE

Early Childhood Education	M,O
Education—General	M,O
Jewish Studies	M,O
Middle School Education	M,O
Music Education	M,O
Music	M,O
Religious Education	M,O
Special Education	M,O
Theology	M

HEBREW UNION COLLEGE–JEWISH INSTITUTE OF RELIGION (NY)

Education—General	M
Jewish Studies	M
Music	M
Near and Middle Eastern Languages	D
Nonprofit Management	M
Religious Education	M
Theology	M,D

HEC MONTREAL

Accounting	M,O
Applied Economics	M
Arts Administration	O
Business Administration and Management—General	M,D,O
Corporate and Organizational Communication	O
Electronic Commerce	M,O
Energy Management and Policy	O
Finance and Banking	M,O
Financial Engineering	M
Human Resources Management	M,O
Industrial and Manufacturing Management	M
International Business	M
Logistics	M
Management Information Systems	M
Management Strategy and Policy	M
Marketing	M
Operations Research	M
Organizational Management	M
Supply Chain Management	M,O
Sustainable Development	O
Taxation	M,O

HEIDELBERG UNIVERSITY

Business Administration and Management—General	M
Counseling Psychology	M
Education—General	M
Music Education	M
School Psychology	M
Social Psychology	M

HENDERSON STATE UNIVERSITY

Business Administration and Management—General	M
Counseling Psychology	M,O
Counselor Education	M,O
Curriculum and Instruction	M,O
Early Childhood Education	M,O
Education—General	M,O
Educational Leadership and Administration	M,O
English as a Second Language	M,O
Liberal Studies	M
Middle School Education	M,O
Physical Education	M
Special Education	M,O
Sports Management	M

HENDRIX COLLEGE

Accounting	M

HENLEY-PUTNAM UNIVERSITY

Conflict Resolution and Mediation/Peace Studies	M
Homeland Security	M
Military and Defense Studies	M
National Security	D

HERITAGE CHRISTIAN UNIVERSITY

Classics	M
Pastoral Ministry and Counseling	M
Religion	M

HERITAGE COLLEGE AND SEMINARY

Theology	M,O

HERITAGE UNIVERSITY

Counselor Education	M
Education—General	M
Educational Leadership and Administration	M
English as a Second Language	M
English	M
Multilingual and Multicultural Education	M
Reading Education	M
Science Education	M
Special Education	M

HERZING UNIVERSITY ONLINE

Accounting	M
Business Administration and Management—General	M
Health Services Management and Hospital Administration	M
Human Resources Management	M
Management of Technology	M
Marketing	M
Nursing and Healthcare Administration	M
Nursing Education	M
Nursing—General	M
Project Management	M

HIGH POINT UNIVERSITY

Business Administration and Management—General	M
Corporate and Organizational Communication	M
Education—General	M
Educational Leadership and Administration	M
Elementary Education	M
History	M

*M—masters degree; D—doctorate; O—other advanced degree; *—Close-Up and/or Display*

Mathematics Education M
Nonprofit Management M
Secondary Education M
Special Education M

HILBERT COLLEGE
Criminal Justice and Criminology M
Health Services Management and Hospital Administration M
Public Administration M

HILLSDALE COLLEGE
Political Science M,D

HILLSDALE FREE WILL BAPTIST COLLEGE
Pastoral Ministry and Counseling M

HIRAM COLLEGE
Interdisciplinary Studies M

HODGES UNIVERSITY
Accounting M
Business Administration and Management—General M
Clinical Psychology M
Counseling Psychology M
Health Services Management and Hospital Administration M
Legal and Justice Studies M
Management Information Systems M

HOFSTRA UNIVERSITY
Accounting M,O
Advertising and Public Relations M
Allopathic Medicine D
Applied Behavior Analysis M,D,O
Art Education M,D,O
Art Therapy M,O
Art/Fine Arts M,D,O
Biological and Biomedical Sciences—General M,D,O
Business Administration and Management—General M,O
Business Education M,D,O
Clinical Psychology M,D
Communication Disorders M,D
Communication—General M
Community Health M
Computer and Information Systems Security M
Counseling Psychology M,O
Counselor Education M,O
Early Childhood Education M,D,O
Education of the Gifted M,D,O
Education—General M,D,O
Educational Media/Instructional Technology M,D,O
Elementary Education M,D,O
Engineering and Applied Sciences—General M
English as a Second Language M,D,O
English Education M,D,O
English M
Entertainment Management M,O
Film, Television, and Video Production M
Finance and Banking M,O
Foreign Languages Education M,D,O
French M,D,O
Geology M,D,O
Health Law M,D
Health Services Management and Hospital Administration M,O
Human Development M,D,O
Human Resources Management M,O
Humanities M,D,O
Industrial and Organizational Psychology M,D
International Business M,O
Internet Engineering M
Investment Management M,O
Journalism M
Law M,D
Legal and Justice Studies M,D
Linguistics M,D,O
Management Information Systems M,O
Management Strategy and Policy M,O
Marketing Research M,O
Marketing M,O
Marriage and Family Therapy M,O
Mathematics Education M,D,O
Medical Physics M
Molecular Medicine D
Multilingual and Multicultural Education M,D,O
Physical Education M,D,O
Physician Assistant Studies M
Psychology—General M,D
Public Health—General M
Quality Management M,O
Quantitative Analysis M,O
Rehabilitation Counseling M,O
Rhetoric M
School Psychology M,D
Science Education M,D,O
Secondary Education M,D,O
Social Psychology M,D
Social Sciences Education M,D,O
Special Education M,D,O
Sports Management M,O
Sustainable Development M
Taxation M,O
Urban Design M
Writing M

HOLLINS UNIVERSITY
Art/Fine Arts M
Dance M
Education—General M
English M
Film, Television, and Video Production M
Film, Television, and Video Theory and Criticism M
Humanities M
Illustration M
Interdisciplinary Studies M
Liberal Studies M
Music M
Social Sciences M
Theater M,O
Writing M,O

HOLMES INSTITUTE
Pastoral Ministry and Counseling M

HOLY APOSTLES COLLEGE AND SEMINARY
Theology M,O

HOLY CROSS GREEK ORTHODOX SCHOOL OF THEOLOGY
Theology M

HOLY FAMILY UNIVERSITY
Accounting M
Business Administration and Management—General M
Counseling Psychology M
Criminal Justice and Criminology M
Early Childhood Education M
Education—General M,D
Educational Leadership and Administration M,D
Elementary Education M
English as a Second Language M
Finance and Banking M
Health Services Management and Hospital Administration M
Human Resources Management M
Management Information Systems M
Nursing and Healthcare Administration M
Nursing Education M
Nursing—General M
Reading Education M
Special Education M

HOLY NAMES UNIVERSITY
Business Administration and Management—General M
Community Health Nursing M,O
Counseling Psychology M,O
Education—General M,O
Educational Psychology M,O
Energy Management and Policy M
English as a Second Language M,O
Family Nurse Practitioner Studies M,O
Finance and Banking M
Forensic Psychology M,O
Marketing M
Music Education M,O
Music M,O
Nursing and Healthcare Administration M,O
Nursing Education M,O
Nursing—General M,O
Pastoral Ministry and Counseling M,O
Religion M,O
Special Education M,O
Sports Management M
Urban Education M,O
Writing M

HOOD COLLEGE
Accounting M
Art/Fine Arts M,O
Bioinformatics M,O
Biological and Biomedical Sciences—General M,O*
Biotechnology M,O
Business Administration and Management—General M
Computer and Information Systems Security M,O
Computer Science M,O
Curriculum and Instruction M,O
Early Childhood Education M,O
Education—General M,O
Educational Leadership and Administration M,O
Elementary Education M,O
Environmental Biology M
Finance and Banking M
Human Development M
Human Resources Management M
Humanities M
Immunology M,O
Information Science M,O
Management Information Systems M
Marketing M
Mathematics Education M,O
Microbiology M,O
Molecular Biology M,O
Psychology—General M
Public Administration M
Reading Education M,O
Science Education M,O
Secondary Education M,O
Special Education M,O
Systems Science M

HOOD THEOLOGICAL SEMINARY
Theology M,D

HOPE INTERNATIONAL UNIVERSITY
Education—General M
Educational Leadership and Administration M
Elementary Education M
International Business M
International Development M
Marketing M
Marriage and Family Therapy M
Missions and Missiology M
Music M
Nonprofit Management M
Religion M
Secondary Education M

HOUGHTON COLLEGE
Music M

HOUSTON BAPTIST UNIVERSITY
Art/Fine Arts M
Business Administration and Management—General M
Counseling Psychology M
Counselor Education M
Curriculum and Instruction M
Education—General M
Educational Leadership and Administration M
Educational Measurement and Evaluation M
English as a Second Language M
Human Resources Management M
International Business M
Liberal Studies M
Pastoral Ministry and Counseling M
Philosophy M
Psychology—General M
Reading Education M
School Psychology M
Theology M

HOUSTON COLLEGE OF LAW
Law D

HOUSTON GRADUATE SCHOOL OF THEOLOGY
Pastoral Ministry and Counseling M,D
Theology M,D

HOWARD PAYNE UNIVERSITY
Business Administration and Management—General M
Educational Leadership and Administration M
Pastoral Ministry and Counseling M
Sports Management M
Theology M

HOWARD UNIVERSITY
Accounting M
African Studies M,D
Allopathic Medicine D
Analytical Chemistry M,D
Anatomy M,D
Applied Arts and Design—General M
Applied Mathematics M,D
Art History M
Art/Fine Arts M
Atmospheric Sciences M,D
Biochemistry M,D
Biological and Biomedical Sciences—General M,D
Biophysics D
Biopsychology M,D
Biotechnology M,D
Business Administration and Management—General M
Chemical Engineering M
Chemistry M,D
Civil Engineering M
Clinical Psychology M,D
Communication Disorders M,D
Communication—General M,D
Computer Science M
Corporate and Organizational Communication M,D
Counseling Psychology D
Counselor Education M
Dentistry D,O
Developmental Psychology M,D
Economics M,D
Education—General M,D,O
Educational Leadership and Administration M,D,O
Educational Policy M,D,O
Educational Psychology D
Electrical Engineering M,D
Elementary Education M
Engineering and Applied Sciences—General M,D
English M,D
Environmental Sciences M,D
Exercise and Sports Science M
Experimental Psychology M,D
Family Nurse Practitioner Studies M,O
Film, Television, and Video Production M
Finance and Banking M
French M
Health Education M
History M,D
Human Resources Management M
Inorganic Chemistry M,D
International Business M
Law M,D
Leisure Studies M
Management Information Systems M
Marketing M
Mass Communication M,D
Mathematics M,D
Mechanical Engineering M,D
Media Studies M,D
Microbiology D
Molecular Biology M,D
Multilingual and Multicultural Education M,D
Music Education M
Music M
Nursing—General M,O
Nutrition M,D
Oral and Dental Sciences D,O
Organic Chemistry M,D
Pharmacology M,D
Pharmacy D
Philosophy M
Photography M
Physical Chemistry M,D
Physical Education M
Physics M,D
Physiology D
Political Science M,D
Psychology—General M,D
Public Administration M
Public Health—General M
School Psychology M,D
Secondary Education M
Social Psychology M,D
Social Work M,D
Sociology M,D
Spanish M
Special Education M
Sports Management M
Supply Chain Management M
Theology M,D

HULT INTERNATIONAL BUSINESS SCHOOL (UNITED STATES)
Business Administration and Management—General M
Conflict Resolution and Mediation/Peace Studies M
Entrepreneurship M
Finance and Banking M
International Affairs M
International Business M
Marketing M
National Security M
Political Science M

HUMBOLDT STATE UNIVERSITY
Anthropology M
Biological and Biomedical Sciences—General M
Business Administration and Management—General M
Counseling Psychology M
Developmental Psychology M
Education—General M
English as a Second Language M
English M
Environmental Management and Policy M
Environmental Sciences M
Fish, Game, and Wildlife Management M
Forestry M
Geology M
Hazardous Materials Management M
Kinesiology and Movement Studies M
Natural Resources M
Psychology—General M
School Psychology M
Social Psychology M
Social Sciences M
Social Work M
Sociology M
Water Resources M

HUMPHREYS COLLEGE
Law D

HUNTER COLLEGE OF THE CITY UNIVERSITY OF NEW YORK
Accounting M
Adult Nursing M
Anthropology M
Applied Mathematics M
Applied Social Research M
Art History M
Art/Fine Arts M
Biochemistry M,D
Biological and Biomedical Sciences—General M,D
Biostatistics M
Chemistry M,D
Chinese M
Classics M
Communication Disorders M
Community Health Nursing M
Community Health M
Counselor Education M
Early Childhood Education M,O
Economics M,D
Education of Students with Severe/Multiple Disabilities M
Education—General M,O
Educational Leadership and Administration O
Elementary Education M
English as a Second Language M
English Education M
English M
Environmental and Occupational Health M
Epidemiology M
Foreign Languages Education M
French M
Geography M,O
Geosciences M
Gerontological Nursing M
Health Services Management and Hospital Administration M
History M
Italian M
Mathematics Education M
Mathematics M
Media Studies M
Multilingual and Multicultural Education M
Music Education M
Music M
Nursing—General M,O
Nutrition M
Physics M,D
Psychiatric Nursing M,O
Psychology—General M
Public Health—General M
Rehabilitation Counseling M
Romance Languages M
Science Education M
Secondary Education M
Social Sciences Education M
Social Work M,D
Sociology M

Spanish	M
Special Education	M
Statistics	M
Theater	M
Urban and Regional Planning	M
Urban Studies	M
Writing	M

HUNTINGTON COLLEGE OF HEALTH SCIENCES

Nutrition	M,D

HUNTINGTON UNIVERSITY

Education—General	M,D
English as a Second Language	M,D
Middle School Education	M,D
Missions and Missiology	M,D
Pastoral Ministry and Counseling	M,D

HUSSON UNIVERSITY

Biotechnology	M
Business Administration and Management—General	M
Clinical Psychology	M
Community Health Nursing	M,O
Counseling Psychology	M
Counselor Education	M
Criminal Justice and Criminology	M
Family Nurse Practitioner Studies	M,O
Health Services Management and Hospital Administration	M
Hospitality Management	M
Nursing Education	M,O
Nursing—General	M,O
Occupational Therapy	M
Organizational Management	M
Pharmacy	D
Physical Therapy	D
Psychiatric Nursing	M,O
School Psychology	M
Social Psychology	M

HUSTON-TILLOTSON UNIVERSITY

Educational Leadership and Administration	M

ICAHN SCHOOL OF MEDICINE AT MOUNT SINAI

Allopathic Medicine	D
Bioethics	M
Biological and Biomedical Sciences—General	M,D
Clinical Research	M,D
Community Health	M,D
Genetic Counseling	M,D
Neuroscience	M,D

IDAHO STATE UNIVERSITY

Allied Health—General	M,D,O
Anthropology	M
Applied Physics	M,D
Art/Fine Arts	M
Biological and Biomedical Sciences—General	M,D
Business Administration and Management—General	M,O
Chemistry	M
Civil Engineering	M
Clinical Psychology	D
Communication Disorders	M,D,O
Community Health	O
Counseling Psychology	M,D,O
Counselor Education	M,D,O
Curriculum and Instruction	M,O
Dental Hygiene	M
Dentistry	O
Education—General	M,D,O
Educational Leadership and Administration	M,D,O
Educational Media/Instructional Technology	M,D,O
Elementary Education	M,O
Engineering and Applied Sciences—General	M,D,O
English as a Second Language	M,D,O
English	M,D,O
Environmental Engineering	M
Environmental Management and Policy	M
Environmental Sciences	M,O
Experimental Psychology	D
Geographic Information Systems	M,O
Geology	M,O
Geophysics	M,O
Geosciences	M,O
Hazardous Materials Management	M
Health Education	M
Health Physics/Radiological Health	M,D
History	M
Hydrology	M,O
Interdisciplinary Studies	M
Management Information Systems	M,O
Management of Technology	M
Marriage and Family Therapy	M,D,O
Mathematics Education	M,D
Mathematics	M,D
Mechanical Engineering	M
Medical Microbiology	M,D
Medicinal and Pharmaceutical Chemistry	M,D
Microbiology	M,D
Nuclear Engineering	M,D
Nursing—General	M,O
Nutrition	M,O
Occupational Therapy	M
Operations Research	M
Oral and Dental Sciences	O
Pharmaceutical Administration	M,D
Pharmaceutical Sciences	M,D
Pharmacology	M,D
Pharmacy	M,D
Physical Education	M
Physical Therapy	D
Physician Assistant Studies	M
Physics	M,D
Political Science	M,D
Psychology—General	D
Public Administration	M
Public Health—General	M,O
Reading Education	M,O
Rhetoric	M
School Psychology	M,D,O
Secondary Education	M,O
Sociology	M
Special Education	M,D,O
Speech and Interpersonal Communication	M
Theater	M
Vocational and Technical Education	M

ILIFF SCHOOL OF THEOLOGY

Pastoral Ministry and Counseling	M,D
Religion	M,D
Theology	M,D

ILLINOIS COLLEGE

Education—General	M

ILLINOIS COLLEGE OF OPTOMETRY

Optometry	D

ILLINOIS INSTITUTE OF TECHNOLOGY

Aerospace/Aeronautical Engineering	M,D
Agricultural Engineering	M
Analytical Chemistry	M,D
Applied Arts and Design—General	M,D
Applied Mathematics	M,D
Applied Physics	M,D
Architectural Engineering	M,D
Architecture	M,D
Artificial Intelligence/Robotics	M,D
Biochemistry	M,D
Bioengineering	M,D
Biological and Biomedical Sciences—General	M,D
Biomedical Engineering	M,D
Business Administration and Management—General	M,D
Cell Biology	M,D
Chemical Engineering	M,D
Chemistry	M,D
Civil Engineering	M,D
Clinical Psychology	M,D
Communication—General	M,D
Computer and Information Systems Security	M,D
Computer Education	M,D
Computer Engineering	M,D
Computer Science	M,D
Construction Engineering	M,D
Construction Management	M,D
Corporate and Organizational Communication	M
Database Systems	M,D
Electrical Engineering	M,D
Engineering and Applied Sciences—General	M,D
Entrepreneurship	M
Environmental Engineering	M,D
Environmental Management and Policy	M
Finance and Banking	M,D
Food Science and Technology	M
Geotechnical Engineering	M,D
Health Physics/Radiological Health	M,D
Human Resources Development	M,D
Humanities	M,D
Industrial and Manufacturing Management	M
Industrial and Organizational Psychology	M,D
Inorganic Chemistry	M,D
Landscape Architecture	M,D
Law	M,D
Legal and Justice Studies	M,D
Management Information Systems	M,D
Manufacturing Engineering	M,D
Marketing	M
Materials Engineering	M,D
Materials Sciences	M,D
Mathematical and Computational Finance	M,D
Mathematics Education	M,D
Mechanical Engineering	M,D
Medical Imaging	M,D
Microbiology	M,D
Molecular Biology	M,D
Molecular Biophysics	M,D
Physics	M,D
Psychology—General	M,D
Public Administration	M
Rehabilitation Counseling	M,D
Science Education	M,D
Software Engineering	M,D
Structural Engineering	M,D
Sustainability Management	M
Taxation	M,D
Technical Writing	M,D
Telecommunications	M,D
Transportation and Highway Engineering	M,D

ILLINOIS STATE UNIVERSITY

Accounting	M
Agricultural Economics and Agribusiness	M
Agricultural Sciences—General	M
Animal Behavior	M,D
Archaeology	M
Art History	M
Art/Fine Arts	M
Bacteriology	M,D
Biochemistry	M,D
Biological and Biomedical Sciences—General	M,D
Biophysics	M,D
Biotechnology	M
Botany	M,D
Business Administration and Management—General	M
Cell Biology	M,D
Clinical Psychology	M,D,O
Cognitive Sciences	M,D,O
Communication Disorders	M
Communication—General	M
Conservation Biology	M,D
Counseling Psychology	M,D,O
Criminal Justice and Criminology	M
Curriculum and Instruction	M,D
Developmental Biology	M,D
Developmental Psychology	M,D,O
Ecology	M,D
Economics	M
Education—General	M,D,O
Educational Leadership and Administration	M,D
Educational Policy	M,D
English	M,D
Entomology	M,D
Evolutionary Biology	M,D
Family and Consumer Sciences-General	M
Family Nurse Practitioner Studies	M,D,O
French	M
Genetics	M,D
German	M
Graphic Design	M
Health Education	M
Higher Education	M,D
History	M
Immunology	M,D
Industrial and Organizational Psychology	M,D,O
Industrial/Management Engineering	M
Management Information Systems	M
Management of Technology	M
Mathematics Education	M,D
Mathematics	M
Microbiology	M,D
Molecular Biology	M,D
Molecular Genetics	M,D
Music	M
Neurobiology	M,D
Neuroscience	M,D
Nursing—General	M,D,O
Parasitology	M,D
Photography	M
Physical Education	M
Physiology	M,D
Plant Biology	M,D
Plant Molecular Biology	M,D
Plant Sciences	M,D
Political Science	M
Psychology—General	M,D,O
Reading Education	M
School Psychology	D,O
Social Work	M
Sociology	M
Spanish	M
Special Education	M,D,O
Structural Biology	M,D
Student Affairs	M
Textile Design	M
Theater	M
Writing	M,D
Zoology	M,D

IMCA–INTERNATIONAL MANAGEMENT CENTRES ASSOCIATION

Business Administration and Management—General	M

IMMACULATA UNIVERSITY

Clinical Psychology	M,D,O
Counseling Psychology	M,D,O
Educational Leadership and Administration	M,D,O
Educational Psychology	M,D,O
English as a Second Language	M
Forensic Psychology	M,D,O
Health Promotion	M
Multilingual and Multicultural Education	M
Neuroscience	M,D,O
Nursing and Healthcare Administration	M
Nursing Education	M
Nursing—General	M
Nutrition	M
Organizational Management	M
Psychoanalysis and Psychotherapy	M,D,O
Psychology—General	M,D,O
School Psychology	M,D,O
Secondary Education	M,D,O
Special Education	M,D,O
Therapies—Dance, Drama, and Music	M

INDEPENDENCE UNIVERSITY

Business Administration and Management—General	M
Community Health Nursing	M
Community Health	M
Gerontological Nursing	M
Health Promotion	M
Health Services Management and Hospital Administration	M
Nursing and Healthcare Administration	M
Nursing—General	M
Public Health—General	M

INDIANA STATE UNIVERSITY

Art/Fine Arts	M
Athletic Training and Sports Medicine	M,D
Biological and Biomedical Sciences—General	M,D
Business Administration and Management—General	M
Cell Biology	M,D
Clinical Psychology	M,D,O
Communication Disorders	M,D,O
Communication—General	M
Computer Engineering	M
Computer Science	M
Counselor Education	M,D,O
Criminal Justice and Criminology	M
Curriculum and Instruction	M,D
Ecology	M,D
Education—General	M,D,O
Educational Leadership and Administration	M,D,O
Educational Media/Instructional Technology	M,D
Engineering and Applied Sciences—General	M
English as a Second Language	M,D,O
English	M
Environmental and Occupational Health	M
Evolutionary Biology	M,D
Family Nurse Practitioner Studies	M,D
Foreign Languages Education	M,D,O
Graphic Design	M
Health Education	M,D
Higher Education	M,D,O
History	M
Human Resources Development	M
Linguistics	M,D,O
Management of Technology	M,D
Mathematics	M
Media Studies	M
Molecular Biology	M,D
Multilingual and Multicultural Education	M,D,O
Music Education	M
Music	M
Nursing and Healthcare Administration	M,D
Nursing Education	M,D
Nursing—General	M,D
Occupational Therapy	M,D
Photography	M
Physical Education	M,D
Physical Therapy	M,D
Physician Assistant Studies	M,D
Physiology	M,D
Psychology—General	M,D
Public Administration	M
Recreation and Park Management	M,D
School Psychology	M,D,O
Science Education	M,D
Social Work	M
Spanish	M,D,O
Sports Management	M,D
Student Affairs	M,D,O
Vocational and Technical Education	M
Writing	M

INDIANA TECH

Accounting	M
Business Administration and Management—General	M
Engineering Management	M
Health Services Management and Hospital Administration	M
Human Resources Development	M
Human Resources Management	M
International Business	D
Marketing	M
Organizational Management	M

INDIANA UNIVERSITY BLOOMINGTON

African Studies	M
African-American Studies	M
Analytical Chemistry	M,D
Anthropology	M,D
Applied Mathematics	M,D
Applied Statistics	M,D
Art Education	M,D,O
Art History	M,D
Art/Fine Arts	M,D
Artificial Intelligence/Robotics	M,D
Arts Administration	M
Asian Languages	M,D
Asian Studies	M,D
Astronomy	M,D
Astrophysics	M,D
Athletic Training and Sports Medicine	M,D
Biochemistry	M,D
Bioinformatics	M,D
Biological and Biomedical Sciences—General	M,D
Biostatistics	M,D
Biotechnology	M,D
Business Administration and Management—General	M,D
Cell Biology	M,D
Chemistry	M,D
Chinese	M,D
Classics	M,D
Cognitive Sciences	D
Communication Disorders	M,D
Communication—General	M,D
Community Health	M,D
Comparative Literature	M,D
Computer and Information Systems Security	M,D
Computer Art and Design	M,D,O
Computer Science	M,D
Counselor Education	M,D,O

*M—masters degree; D—doctorate; O—other advanced degree; *—Close-Up and/or Display*

Criminal Justice and Criminology M,D
Curriculum and Instruction M,D,O
Database Systems M,D,O
Developmental Psychology D
East European and Russian Studies M,O
Ecology M,D,O
Economic Development M,D,O
Economics D
Education—General M,D,O
Educational Leadership and Administration M,D,O
Educational Measurement and Evaluation M,D,O
Educational Media/Instructional Technology M,D
Educational Policy M,D,O
Educational Psychology M,D,O
Elementary Education M,D,O
Energy Management and Policy M,D,O
English as a Second Language M,D
English M,D
Environmental and Occupational Health M,D
Environmental Management and Policy M,D,O
Environmental Sciences M,D,O
Epidemiology M,D
Ergonomics and Human Factors M,D
Evolutionary Biology M,D
Exercise and Sports Science M,D
Film, Television, and Video Theory and Criticism M,D
Finance and Banking M,D,O
Folklore M,D
Foreign Languages Education M,D
Foundations and Philosophy of Education M,D,O
French M,D
Gender Studies D
Genetics M,D
Geochemistry M,D
Geography M,D
Geology M,D
Geophysics M,D
Geosciences M,D
German M,D
Health Education M,D
Health Informatics M,D
Health Promotion M,D
Health Services Management and Hospital Administration M,D
Higher Education M,D,O
Hispanic and Latin American Languages M,D
History of Science and Technology M,D
History M,D
Human-Computer Interaction M,D
Hydrogeology M,D
Information Science M,D,O
Inorganic Chemistry M,D
International and Comparative Education M,D,O
International Development M,D,O
Italian M,D
Japanese M,D
Jewish Studies M
Journalism M,D
Kinesiology and Movement Studies M,D
Latin American Studies M
Law M,D,O
Leisure Studies M,D
Library Science M,D,O
Linguistics M,D
Management Information Systems M,D,O
Mass Communication M,D
Materials Sciences M,D
Mathematical Physics M,D
Mathematics Education M,D,O
Mathematics M,D
Media Studies M,D
Medical Physics M,D
Medieval and Renaissance Studies M,D
Microbiology M,D
Mineralogy M,D
Molecular Biology M,D
Multilingual and Multicultural Education M,D
Music M,D,O
Near and Middle Eastern Languages M,D
Neuroscience D
Nonprofit Management M,D,O
Nutrition M,D
Optometry M,D
Organic Chemistry M,D
Organizational Management M,D,O
Philosophy M,D
Physical Chemistry M,D
Physical Education M,D
Physics M,D
Plant Biology M,D
Political Science M,D
Portuguese M,D
Psychology—General D
Public Administration M,D,O
Public Affairs M,D,O
Public Health—General M,D
Public Policy M,D,O
Reading Education M,D,O
Recreation and Park Management M,D
Religion M,D
Rhetoric M,D
Safety Engineering M,D
School Psychology M,D,O
Science Education M,D,O
Secondary Education M,D,O
Slavic Languages M,D
Social Psychology D
Social Sciences Education M,D,O
Social Sciences M,D,O
Sociology M,D
Spanish M,D
Special Education M,D,O
Speech and Interpersonal Communication M,D
Sports Management M,D
Statistics M,D
Sustainability Management M,D,O
Systems Engineering D
Telecommunications M
Theater M,D
Toxicology M,D,O
Travel and Tourism M,D
Water Resources Engineering M,D,O
Western European Studies M
Writing M,D
Zoology M,D

INDIANA UNIVERSITY EAST
Education—General M
Nursing—General M
Social Work M

INDIANA UNIVERSITY KOKOMO
Business Administration and Management—General M
Health Services Management and Hospital Administration M,O
Nursing and Healthcare Administration M
Nursing Education M
Nursing—General M
Public Administration M,O

INDIANA UNIVERSITY NORTHWEST
Addictions/Substance Abuse Counseling M
Business Administration and Management—General M,O
Counseling Psychology M
Criminal Justice and Criminology M,O
Education—General M
Educational Leadership and Administration M
Elementary Education M
Environmental Management and Policy M,O
Health Services Management and Hospital Administration M,O
Liberal Studies M
Nonprofit Management M,O
Public Administration M,O
Public Affairs M,O
Secondary Education M
Social Work M

INDIANA UNIVERSITY OF PENNSYLVANIA
Adult Education M
Applied Mathematics M
Archaeology M
Art/Fine Arts M
Biological and Biomedical Sciences—General M
Business Administration and Management—General M
Business Education M
Chemistry M
Clinical Psychology M,D
Communication Disorders M
Communication—General M,D
Counselor Education M
Criminal Justice and Criminology M,D
Curriculum and Instruction D
Education—General M,D,O
Educational Leadership and Administration D,O
Educational Media/Instructional Technology M,D
Educational Psychology M,O
Emergency Management M
English as a Second Language M,D
English Education M,D
English M,D
Environmental and Occupational Health M,D
Environmental Management and Policy M
Exercise and Sports Science M
Foreign Languages Education M
Geographic Information Systems M,O
Geography M
Health Education M
Health Services Management and Hospital Administration M,D
Higher Education M
Hispanic and Latin American Languages M
History M
Human Resources Development M
Industrial and Labor Relations M
Mathematics Education M
Mathematics M
Media Studies D
Music Education M
Music M
Nanotechnology M
Nonprofit Management D
Nursing and Healthcare Administration M
Nursing Education M
Nursing—General D
Nutrition M
Physical Education M
Physics M
Psychology—General M,D
Public Affairs M
Public History M
Reading Education M,O
School Psychology D,O
Social Psychology M
Sociology M
Special Education M
Sports Management M
Student Affairs M
Urban and Regional Planning M
Vocational and Technical Education M

INDIANA UNIVERSITY–PURDUE UNIVERSITY FORT WAYNE
Adult Nursing M,O
Applied Mathematics M,O
Applied Statistics M,O
Biological and Biomedical Sciences—General M
Business Administration and Management—General M
Civil Engineering M
Communication—General M
Computer Engineering M
Computer Science M
Construction Management M
Counselor Education M,O
Education—General M,O
Educational Leadership and Administration M,O
Electrical Engineering M
Elementary Education M
Engineering and Applied Sciences—General M,O
English as a Second Language M,O
English Education M,O
English M,O
Facilities Management M
Family Nurse Practitioner Studies M,O
Gerontological Nursing M,O
Industrial/Management Engineering M
Information Science M
Marriage and Family Therapy M,O
Mathematics Education M,O
Mathematics M,O
Mechanical Engineering M
Nursing and Healthcare Administration M,O
Nursing Education M,O
Nursing—General M,O
Operations Research M,O
Organizational Management M,O
Public Policy M,O
Secondary Education M
Special Education M,O
Systems Engineering M

INDIANA UNIVERSITY–PURDUE UNIVERSITY INDIANAPOLIS
Accounting M
Addictions/Substance Abuse Counseling M,D
Allopathic Medicine M,D
Anatomy M,D
Applied Arts and Design—General M
Applied Mathematics M,D
Applied Statistics M,D
Art Education M
Art Therapy M
Art/Fine Arts M
Biochemistry M,D
Bioethics M,O
Bioinformatics M,D
Biological and Biomedical Sciences—General M,D
Biomedical Engineering M,D,O
Biopsychology M,D
Biostatistics M,D
Business Administration and Management—General M
Cell Biology M,D
Chemistry M,D
Child and Family Studies M
Clinical Psychology M,D
Communication—General M,D
Community Health M,D
Computer Education M,O
Computer Engineering M,D
Computer Science M,D,O
Counselor Education M,O
Criminal Justice and Criminology M,O
Curriculum and Instruction M,O
Dentistry M,D,O
Early Childhood Education M,O
Economics M
Education—General M,O
Educational Leadership and Administration M,O
Electrical Engineering M,D
Emergency Management M,O
English as a Second Language M,O
English M,O
Environmental and Occupational Health M,D,O
Epidemiology M,D
Foreign Languages Education M,O
Forensic Sciences M
Gender Studies M
Geographic Information Systems M,O
Geology M,D
Geosciences M,D
Health Communication M,D
Health Education M,D
Health Informatics M,D
Health Services Management and Hospital Administration M,D
Higher Education M,O
History M
Homeland Security M,O
Human-Computer Interaction M,D
Immunology M,D
Industrial and Organizational Psychology M,D
Information Science M
Internet and Interactive Multimedia M,D
Law M,D
Liberal Studies M,D,O
Library Science M,O
Mathematics Education M,D
Mathematics M,D
Mechanical Engineering M,D,O
Microbiology M,D
Molecular Biology M,D
Molecular Genetics M,D
Museum Studies M,O
Music M
Neurobiology D
Nonprofit Management M,O
Nursing and Healthcare Administration M,O
Nursing Education M,O
Nursing—General M,D,O
Nutrition M,D
Occupational Therapy M,D
Organizational Management M,O
Pathology M,D
Pharmacology M,D
Philanthropic Studies M,D
Philosophy M,O
Physical Education M
Physical Therapy M,D
Physics M,D
Political Science M,O
Psychology—General M,D
Public Administration M,O
Public Affairs M,O
Public Health—General M,D
Public History M
Reading Education M,O
Rehabilitation Sciences M,D
Social Sciences M,D
Social Work M,D,O
Sociology M
Special Education M,O
Statistics M,D
Student Affairs M,O
Therapies—Dance, Drama, and Music M
Toxicology M,D
Writing M,O

INDIANA UNIVERSITY SOUTH BEND
Accounting M
Applied Mathematics M
Art Education M
Business Administration and Management—General M
Computer Science M
Counselor Education M
Education—General M
Elementary Education M
English M
Family Nurse Practitioner Studies M
Liberal Studies M
Management Information Systems M
Music M
Nursing—General M
Public Affairs M
Secondary Education M
Social Work M
Special Education M

INDIANA UNIVERSITY SOUTHEAST
Business Administration and Management—General M
Counselor Education M
Education—General M
Elementary Education M
Finance and Banking M
Interdisciplinary Studies M,O
Secondary Education M

INDIANA WESLEYAN UNIVERSITY
Accounting M,O
Addictions/Substance Abuse Counseling M
Business Administration and Management—General M,O
Counseling Psychology M
Counselor Education M
Educational Leadership and Administration M,O
Health Services Management and Hospital Administration M,O
Higher Education M
Human Resources Management M,O
Marriage and Family Therapy M
Nursing and Healthcare Administration M,O
Nursing Education M
Nursing—General M
Organizational Management M,D,O
Pastoral Ministry and Counseling M
Social Psychology M
Theology M

INSTITUTE FOR CHRISTIAN STUDIES
Education—General M,D
Philosophy M,D
Political Science M,D
Theology M,D

INSTITUTE FOR CLINICAL SOCIAL WORK
Social Work D

INSTITUTE FOR DOCTORAL STUDIES IN THE VISUAL ARTS
Art/Fine Arts D
Philosophy D

THE INSTITUTE FOR THE PSYCHOLOGICAL SCIENCES
Clinical Psychology M,D

INSTITUTE OF AMERICAN INDIAN ARTS
Writing M

INSTITUTE OF CLINICAL ACUPUNCTURE AND ORIENTAL MEDICINE
Acupuncture and Oriental Medicine M

INSTITUTE OF PUBLIC ADMINISTRATION
Health Services Management and Hospital Administration M,O
Public Administration M,O

THE INSTITUTE OF WORLD POLITICS
Military and Defense Studies M,O
National Security M,O
Political Science M,O
Public Affairs M,O
Public Policy M,O

INSTITUT FRANCO-EUROPEN DE CHIROPRAXIE
Chiropractic D

INSTITUTO CENTROAMERICANO DE ADMINISTRACIÓN DE EMPRESAS
Agricultural Economics and Agribusiness M
Business Administration and Management—General M
Finance and Banking M
Management of Technology M
Real Estate M
Sustainable Development M

INSTITUTO TECNOLOGICO DE SANTO DOMINGO
Accounting M,O
Adult Education M,O
Allopathic Medicine M,D
Bioethics M,O
Business Administration and Management—General M,O
Communication—General M,O
Construction Management M,O
Counseling Psychology M,O
Economics M,O
Education—General M,O
Educational Leadership and Administration M,O
Educational Psychology M,O
Energy and Power Engineering M,D,O
Energy Management and Policy M,D,O
Engineering and Applied Sciences—General M,O
Environmental Education M,D,O
Environmental Engineering M,O
Environmental Management and Policy M,D,O
Environmental Sciences M,D,O
Finance and Banking M,O
Gender Studies M,O
Health Promotion M,O
Human Resources Management M,O
Humanities M,O
Industrial and Manufacturing Management M,O
Industrial/Management Engineering M,O
Information Science M,O
International Affairs M,O
International Business M,O
Linguistics M,O
Marine Sciences M,D,O
Marketing M,O
Marriage and Family Therapy M,O
Maternal and Child Health M,O
Mathematics M,D,O
Natural Resources M,D,O
Nutrition M,O
Organizational Management M,O
Quality Management M,O
Quantitative Analysis M,O
Secondary Education M,O
Social Sciences Education M,O
Software Engineering M,O
Structural Engineering M,O
Sustainable Development M,O
Taxation M,O
Telecommunications M,O
Transportation Management M,O

INSTITUTO TECNOLÓGICO Y DE ESTUDIOS SUPERIORES DE MONTERREY, CAMPUS CENTRAL DE VERACRUZ
Business Administration and Management—General M
Computer Science M
Education—General M
Educational Leadership and Administration M
Educational Media/Instructional Technology M
Electronic Commerce M
Finance and Banking M
Humanities M
International Business M
Management Information Systems M
Marketing M

INSTITUTO TECNOLÓGICO Y DE ESTUDIOS SUPERIORES DE MONTERREY, CAMPUS CHIHUAHUA
Computer Engineering M,O
Electrical Engineering M,O
Engineering Management M,O
Industrial/Management Engineering M,O
International Business M,O
Mechanical Engineering M,O
Systems Engineering M,O

INSTITUTO TECNOLÓGICO Y DE ESTUDIOS SUPERIORES DE MONTERREY, CAMPUS CIUDAD DE MÉXICO
Business Administration and Management—General M,D
Computer Science M,D
Economics M,D
Education—General M,D
Educational Media/Instructional Technology M,D
Environmental Engineering M,D
Environmental Sciences M,D
Finance and Banking M,D
Humanities M,D
Industrial/Management Engineering M,D
International Business M,D
Law O
Management Information Systems M,D
Quality Management M,D
Telecommunications Management M

INSTITUTO TECNOLÓGICO Y DE ESTUDIOS SUPERIORES DE MONTERREY, CAMPUS CIUDAD JUÁREZ
Business Administration and Management—General M
Education—General M
Educational Leadership and Administration M
Educational Media/Instructional Technology M,D
Electronic Commerce M
Humanities M
Management Information Systems M
Public Administration M
Quality Management M

INSTITUTO TECNOLÓGICO Y DE ESTUDIOS SUPERIORES DE MONTERREY, CAMPUS CIUDAD OBREGÓN
Business Administration and Management—General M
Communication—General M
Developmental Education M
Education—General M
Engineering and Applied Sciences—General M
Finance and Banking M
International Affairs M
Management Information Systems M
Marketing M
Mathematics Education M
Telecommunications Management M

INSTITUTO TECNOLÓGICO Y DE ESTUDIOS SUPERIORES DE MONTERREY, CAMPUS CUERNAVACA
Business Administration and Management—General M
Computer Science M,D
Finance and Banking M
Human Resources Management M
Information Science M,D
International Business M
Management of Technology M,D
Marketing M

INSTITUTO TECNOLÓGICO Y DE ESTUDIOS SUPERIORES DE MONTERREY, CAMPUS ESTADO DE MÉXICO
Architecture M,D
Business Administration and Management—General M,D
Computer Science M,D
Education—General M,D
Educational Leadership and Administration M,D
Educational Media/Instructional Technology M,D
Electronic Commerce M,D
Environmental Management and Policy M,D
Finance and Banking M,D
Humanities M,D
Industrial and Manufacturing Management M,D
Information Science M,D
Management Information Systems M,D
Marketing M,D
Materials Engineering M,D
Materials Sciences M,D
Quality Management M,D
Telecommunications Management M,D

INSTITUTO TECNOLÓGICO Y DE ESTUDIOS SUPERIORES DE MONTERREY, CAMPUS GUADALAJARA
Business Administration and Management—General M
Finance and Banking M

INSTITUTO TECNOLÓGICO Y DE ESTUDIOS SUPERIORES DE MONTERREY, CAMPUS IRAPUATO
Architecture M,D
Business Administration and Management—General M,D
Computer Science M,D
Education—General M,D
Educational Leadership and Administration M,D
Educational Media/Instructional Technology M,D
Electronic Commerce M,D
Environmental Management and Policy M,D
Finance and Banking M,D
Humanities M,D
Industrial and Manufacturing Management M,D
Information Science M,D
International Business M,D
Library Science M,D
Management Information Systems M,D
Management of Technology M,D
Marketing Research M,D
Quality Management M,D
Telecommunications Management M,D

INSTITUTO TECNOLÓGICO Y DE ESTUDIOS SUPERIORES DE MONTERREY, CAMPUS LAGUNA
Business Administration and Management—General M
Industrial/Management Engineering M
Management Information Systems M

INSTITUTO TECNOLÓGICO Y DE ESTUDIOS SUPERIORES DE MONTERREY, CAMPUS LEÓN
Business Administration and Management—General M

INSTITUTO TECNOLÓGICO Y DE ESTUDIOS SUPERIORES DE MONTERREY, CAMPUS MONTERREY
Agricultural Engineering M,D
Agricultural Sciences—General M,D
Applied Statistics M,D
Artificial Intelligence/Robotics M,D
Biotechnology M,D
Business Administration and Management—General M,D
Chemical Engineering M,D
Chemistry M,D
Civil Engineering M,D
Communication—General M,D
Computer Science M,D
Electrical Engineering M,D
Engineering and Applied Sciences—General M,D
Environmental Engineering M,D
Finance and Banking M
Industrial/Management Engineering M,D
Information Science M,D
International Business M
Manufacturing Engineering M,D
Marketing M
Mechanical Engineering M,D
Organic Chemistry M,D
Science Education M,D
Systems Engineering M,D

INSTITUTO TECNOLÓGICO Y DE ESTUDIOS SUPERIORES DE MONTERREY, CAMPUS QUERÉTARO
Business Administration and Management—General M

INSTITUTO TECNOLÓGICO Y DE ESTUDIOS SUPERIORES DE MONTERREY, CAMPUS SONORA NORTE
Business Administration and Management—General M
Education—General M
Information Science M

INSTITUTO TECNOLÓGICO Y DE ESTUDIOS SUPERIORES DE MONTERREY, CAMPUS TOLUCA
Business Administration and Management—General M

INTER AMERICAN UNIVERSITY OF PUERTO RICO, AGUADILLA CAMPUS
Accounting M
Business Administration and Management—General M
Counseling Psychology M
Criminal Justice and Criminology M
Educational Leadership and Administration M
Elementary Education M
Finance and Banking M
Human Resources Management M
Management Information Systems M
Marketing M

INTER AMERICAN UNIVERSITY OF PUERTO RICO, ARECIBO CAMPUS
Accounting M
Acute Care/Critical Care Nursing M
Business Administration and Management—General M
Counselor Education M
Curriculum and Instruction M
Education—General M
Educational Leadership and Administration M
Elementary Education M
English as a Second Language M
Finance and Banking M
Foreign Languages Education M
Human Resources Management M
Mathematics Education M
Medical/Surgical Nursing M
Nurse Anesthesia M
Nursing—General M
Science Education M
Social Sciences Education M

INTER AMERICAN UNIVERSITY OF PUERTO RICO, BARRANQUITAS CAMPUS
Accounting M
Business Administration and Management—General M
Curriculum and Instruction M
Education—General M
Educational Leadership and Administration M
Elementary Education M
English as a Second Language M
Finance and Banking M
Foreign Languages Education M
Library Science M
Mathematics Education M
Science Education M
Social Sciences Education M
Special Education M

INTER AMERICAN UNIVERSITY OF PUERTO RICO, BAYAMÓN CAMPUS
Biotechnology M
Ecology M
Human Resources Management M

INTER AMERICAN UNIVERSITY OF PUERTO RICO, FAJARDO CAMPUS
Business Administration and Management—General M
Computer Science M
Educational Leadership and Administration M
Elementary Education M
Management Information Systems M
Marketing M
Special Education M

INTER AMERICAN UNIVERSITY OF PUERTO RICO, GUAYAMA CAMPUS
Business Administration and Management—General M
Computer and Information Systems Security M
Computer Science M
Early Childhood Education M
Elementary Education M
Marketing M

INTER AMERICAN UNIVERSITY OF PUERTO RICO, METROPOLITAN CAMPUS
Accounting M
American Studies M,D
Athletic Training and Sports Medicine M
Business Administration and Management—General M
Business Education M
Clinical Laboratory Sciences/Medical Technology M
Computer Science M
Counseling Psychology M,D
Counselor Education M,D
Criminal Justice and Criminology M
Curriculum and Instruction M,D
Education—General M,D
Educational Leadership and Administration M,D
Educational Media/Instructional Technology M
Elementary Education M
English as a Second Language M
English M
Environmental Management and Policy M
Exercise and Sports Science M
Finance and Banking M
Foreign Languages Education M
Health Education M
Higher Education M
History M,D
Human Resources Development M
Human Resources Management M
Industrial and Labor Relations M,D
Industrial and Manufacturing Management M
Industrial and Organizational Psychology M,D
International Business M,D
Management Information Systems M
Marketing M
Mathematics Education M
Microbiology M
Molecular Biology M
Music Education M
Pastoral Ministry and Counseling D
Physical Education M
Psychology—General M,D
Religious Education D
School Psychology M,D
Science Education M
Social Sciences Education M
Social Work M
Spanish M
Special Education M
Theology D
Vocational and Technical Education M
Women's Studies M

INTER AMERICAN UNIVERSITY OF PUERTO RICO, PONCE CAMPUS
Accounting M
Criminal Justice and Criminology M
Elementary Education M
English as a Second Language M
Finance and Banking M
Human Resources Management M
Marketing M
Mathematics Education M
Science Education M
Social Sciences Education M
Spanish M

INTER AMERICAN UNIVERSITY OF PUERTO RICO, SAN GERMÁN CAMPUS
Accounting M,D
Applied Mathematics M
Art/Fine Arts M

*M—masters degree; D—doctorate; O—other advanced degree; *—Close-Up and/or Display*

Business Administration and Management—General M,D
Business Education M
Counseling Psychology M,D
Counselor Education M,D
Curriculum and Instruction D
Elementary Education M
English as a Second Language M
Environmental Sciences M
Finance and Banking M,D
Graphic Design M
Health Education M
Human Resources Development M,D
Human Resources Management M,D
Industrial and Manufacturing Management M,D
International Business M,D
Kinesiology and Movement Studies M
Library Science M
Management Information Systems M,D
Marketing M,D
Mathematics Education M
Music Education M
Music M
Photography M
Physical Education M
Psychology—General M,D
School Psychology M,D
Science Education M
Special Education M

INTER AMERICAN UNIVERSITY OF PUERTO RICO SCHOOL OF LAW
Law D

INTER AMERICAN UNIVERSITY OF PUERTO RICO SCHOOL OF OPTOMETRY
Optometry D

INTERDENOMINATIONAL THEOLOGICAL CENTER
Theology M,D

INTERIOR DESIGNERS INSTITUTE
Interior Design M

INTERNATIONAL BAPTIST COLLEGE AND SEMINARY
Education—General M
Pastoral Ministry and Counseling M,D
Theology M

INTERNATIONAL COLLEGE OF THE CAYMAN ISLANDS
Business Administration and Management—General M
Business Education M
Human Resources Management M

INTERNATIONAL INSTITUTE FOR RESTORATIVE PRACTICES
Organizational Behavior M,O

INTERNATIONAL TECHNOLOGICAL UNIVERSITY
Business Administration and Management—General M,D
Computer Art and Design M
Computer Engineering M
Electrical Engineering M,D
Engineering Management M
Software Engineering M

INTERNATIONAL UNIVERSITY IN GENEVA
Business Administration and Management—General M,D
Communication—General M,D
Entrepreneurship M,D
International Affairs M,D
International Business M,D
Marketing M,D
Media Studies M,D
Public Administration M,D

THE INTERNATIONAL UNIVERSITY OF MONACO
Business Administration and Management—General M
Entrepreneurship M
Finance and Banking M
Financial Engineering M
International Business M
Marketing M

IONA COLLEGE
Accounting M,O
Advertising and Public Relations M,O
Business Administration and Management—General M,O
Communication Disorders M
Computer and Information Systems Security M
Computer Science M
Counseling Psychology M,O
Criminal Justice and Criminology M,O
Early Childhood Education M
Education—General M
Educational Leadership and Administration M
English Education M
English M
Experimental Psychology M,O
Finance and Banking M,O
Foreign Languages Education M
Forensic Sciences M,O
Health Services Management and Hospital Administration M,O
History M
Human Resources Management M,O
Industrial and Organizational Psychology M,O
International Business M,O
Management of Technology M,O
Marketing M,O
Marriage and Family Therapy M
Mass Communication M,O
Mathematics Education M
Nonprofit Management M,O
Psychology—General M,O
Recreation and Park Management M,O
School Psychology M,O
Science Education M
Social Sciences Education M
Spanish M
Special Education M
Sports Management M,O

IOWA STATE UNIVERSITY OF SCIENCE AND TECHNOLOGY
Accounting M
Aerospace/Aeronautical Engineering M,D
Agricultural Economics and Agribusiness M,D
Agricultural Education M,D
Agricultural Engineering M,D
Agricultural Sciences—General M,D
Agronomy and Soil Sciences M,D
Analytical Chemistry D
Animal Sciences M,D
Anthropology M
Applied Mathematics M,D
Applied Physics M,D
Architecture M
Art/Fine Arts M
Astrophysics M,D
Bioinformatics M,D
Biological and Biomedical Sciences—General M,D
Biophysics M,D
Biostatistics M,D
Cell Biology M,D
Chemical Engineering M,D
Chemistry M,D
Child and Family Studies M,D
Civil Engineering M,D
Clothing and Textiles M,D
Cognitive Sciences D
Computational Biology M,D
Computer Engineering M,D
Computer Science M,D
Condensed Matter Physics M,D
Construction Engineering M,D
Consumer Economics M,D
Corporate and Organizational Communication M,D
Counseling Psychology D
Counselor Education M,D
Curriculum and Instruction M,D
Developmental Biology M,D
Ecology M,D
Economics M,D
Educational Leadership and Administration M,D
Educational Measurement and Evaluation M,D
Educational Media/Instructional Technology M,D
Electrical Engineering M,D
Elementary Education M,D
English as a Second Language M
English M,D
Entomology M,D
Environmental Engineering M,D
Environmental Sciences M,D
Evolutionary Biology M,D
Exercise and Sports Science M
Family and Consumer Sciences-General M
Finance and Banking M
Fish, Game, and Wildlife Management M,D
Food Science and Technology M,D
Forestry M,D
Foundations and Philosophy of Education M,D
Genetics M,D
Geology M,D
Geosciences M,D
Geotechnical Engineering M,D
Graphic Design M
Higher Education M,D
History of Science and Technology M,D
History M,D
Home Economics Education M,D
Horticulture M,D
Hospitality Management M,D
Human Development M,D
Human Resources Development M,D
Human-Computer Interaction M,D
Immunology M,D
Industrial Design M
Industrial/Management Engineering M,D
Information Science M
Inorganic Chemistry M,D
Interdisciplinary Studies M
Interior Design M
Journalism M
Kinesiology and Movement Studies M,D
Landscape Architecture M
Linguistics M,D
Management Information Systems M,D
Mass Communication M
Materials Engineering M,D
Materials Sciences M,D
Mathematics Education M,D
Mathematics M,D
Mechanical Engineering M,D
Mechanics M,D
Meteorology M,D
Microbiology M,D
Molecular Biology M,D
Molecular Genetics M,D
Natural Resources M,D
Neuroscience M,D
Nutrition M,D
Operations Research M,D
Organic Chemistry M,D
Pathology M,D
Physical Chemistry M,D
Physics M,D
Plant Biology M,D
Plant Pathology M,D
Plant Sciences M,D
Political Science M
Psychology—General D
Public Administration M
Rhetoric M,D
Rural Planning and Studies M,D
Rural Sociology M,D
Science Education M
Social Psychology D
Sociology M,D
Special Education M,D
Statistics M,D
Structural Biology M,D
Structural Engineering M,D
Student Affairs M,D
Sustainable Development M,D
Systems Engineering M
Toxicology M,D
Transportation and Highway Engineering M,D
Transportation Management M
Urban and Regional Planning M
Veterinary Medicine M
Veterinary Sciences M,D
Vocational and Technical Education M,D
Writing M,D

IRELL & MANELLA GRADUATE SCHOOL OF BIOLOGICAL SCIENCES
Biochemistry D
Biological and Biomedical Sciences—General D*
Cancer Biology/Oncology D
Cell Biology D
Developmental Biology D
Genetics D
Immunology D
Molecular Biology D
Neuroscience D
Pharmaceutical Sciences D

ITHACA COLLEGE
Accounting M
Agricultural Education M
Allied Health—General M,D
Business Administration and Management—General M
Communication Disorders M
Elementary Education M
English Education M
Exercise and Sports Science M
Foreign Languages Education M
Health Education M
Internet and Interactive Multimedia M
Mathematics Education M
Music Education M
Music M
Occupational Therapy M
Physical Education M
Physical Therapy D
Science Education M
Secondary Education M
Social Sciences Education M
Spanish M

JACKSON STATE UNIVERSITY
Accounting M
Biological and Biomedical Sciences—General M,D
Business Administration and Management—General M,D
Chemistry M,D
Clinical Psychology D
Communication Disorders M
Computer Science M
Counselor Education M
Criminal Justice and Criminology M
Early Childhood Education M,D,O
Education—General M,D,O
Educational Leadership and Administration M,D,O
Educational Media/Instructional Technology M,D,O
Elementary Education M,D,O
English Education M
English M
Environmental Sciences M,D
Health Education M
History M
Mass Communication M
Materials Sciences M
Mathematics Education M
Mathematics M
Music Education M
Physical Education M
Political Science M
Psychology—General D
Public Administration M,D
Public Affairs M,D
Public Policy M,D
Rehabilitation Counseling M
Science Education M
Secondary Education M,D,O
Social Work M,D
Sociology M
Special Education M,O
Urban and Regional Planning M,D
Vocational and Technical Education M

JACKSONVILLE STATE UNIVERSITY
Biological and Biomedical Sciences—General M
Business Administration and Management—General M
Computer Science M
Counselor Education M
Criminal Justice and Criminology M
Early Childhood Education M
Education—General M,O
Educational Leadership and Administration M,O
Educational Media/Instructional Technology M
Elementary Education M
Emergency Management M,D
English M
History M
Liberal Studies M
Mathematics M
Music M
Nursing—General M
Physical Education M,O
Political Science M
Psychology—General M
Reading Education M
Secondary Education M
Software Engineering M
Special Education M

JACKSONVILLE UNIVERSITY
Accounting M
Allied Health—General M
Art/Fine Arts M
Business Administration and Management—General M*
Communication Disorders M
Counseling Psychology M
Dance M
Finance and Banking M
Health Informatics M
Kinesiology and Movement Studies M
Marine Sciences M
Marketing M
Music M
Nursing—General M,D
Oral and Dental Sciences O
Organizational Management M

JAMES MADISON UNIVERSITY
Accounting M
American Studies M
Applied Behavior Analysis M
Applied Science and Technology M
Art Education M
Art History M
Art/Fine Arts M
Biological and Biomedical Sciences—General M
Business Administration and Management—General M
Clinical Psychology M,D,O
Communication Disorders M,D
Communication—General M
Computer and Information Systems Security M
Computer Science M
Counseling Psychology M,D,O
Early Childhood Education M
Education of the Gifted M
Educational Leadership and Administration M
Educational Measurement and Evaluation M,D
Educational Media/Instructional Technology M
Elementary Education M
Engineering and Applied Sciences—General M
English as a Second Language M
English M
Entrepreneurship M
Environmental Management and Policy M
Exercise and Sports Science M
Experimental Psychology M
Family Nurse Practitioner Studies M,D
Foreign Languages Education M
Forensic Sciences M
Gerontological Nursing M,D
Health Education M
Higher Education M
History M
Human Resources Management M
Kinesiology and Movement Studies M
Management Information Systems M
Management Strategy and Policy D
Mathematics Education M
Middle School Education M
Multilingual and Multicultural Education M
Music Education M
Music M,D
Nonprofit Management M,D
Nurse Midwifery M,D
Nursing and Healthcare Administration M,D
Nursing—General M,D
Nutrition M
Occupational Therapy M
Organizational Management D
Photography M
Physical Education M
Physician Assistant Studies M
Physiology M
Political Science M
Psychology—General M
Public Administration M
Public History M
Reading Education M
Rhetoric M
School Psychology M,D,O
Secondary Education M
Special Education M
Taxation M
Technical Writing M
Vocational and Technical Education M
Writing M

JEFFERSON COLLEGE OF HEALTH SCIENCES

Nursing and Healthcare Administration	M
Nursing Education	M
Nursing—General	M
Occupational Therapy	M
Physician Assistant Studies	M

THE JEWISH THEOLOGICAL SEMINARY

Jewish Studies	M,D
Music	M
Religion	M,D
Religious Education	M,D
Theology	M,D,O
Women's Studies	M,D

JOHN BROWN UNIVERSITY

Business Administration and Management—General	M
Clinical Psychology	M,O
Counseling Psychology	M,O
Counselor Education	M,O
Curriculum and Instruction	M
Education—General	M
Educational Leadership and Administration	M
Ethics	M
Higher Education	M
International Business	M
Marriage and Family Therapy	M,O
Secondary Education	M

JOHN CARROLL UNIVERSITY

Accounting	M
Biological and Biomedical Sciences—General	M
Business Administration and Management—General	M
Corporate and Organizational Communication	M
Counseling Psychology	M,O
Counselor Education	M,O
Early Childhood Education	M
Education—General	M
Educational Leadership and Administration	M
Educational Psychology	M
English	M
History	M
Humanities	M
Mathematics	M
Middle School Education	M
Nonprofit Management	M
Religion	M
Science Education	M
Secondary Education	M

JOHN F. KENNEDY UNIVERSITY

Art/Fine Arts	M
Business Administration and Management—General	M,O
Comparative and Interdisciplinary Arts	M
Counseling Psychology	M
Education—General	M
Health Education	M
Health Psychology	M
Human Resources Development	M,O
Industrial and Organizational Psychology	M,O
Law	D
Museum Studies	M,O
Organizational Management	M,O
Psychology—General	M,D,O
Sport Psychology	M
Transpersonal and Humanistic Psychology	M

JOHN JAY COLLEGE OF CRIMINAL JUSTICE OF THE CITY UNIVERSITY OF NEW YORK

Criminal Justice and Criminology	M,D
Forensic Psychology	M,D
Forensic Sciences	M,D
Legal and Justice Studies	M,D
Organizational Behavior	M,D
Public Administration	M
Public Policy	M,D

JOHN MARSHALL LAW SCHOOL

Computer and Information Systems Security	M,D
International Business	M,D
Law	M,D
Legal and Justice Studies	M,D
Management Information Systems	M,D
Real Estate	M,D
Taxation	M,D

JOHN PAUL THE GREAT CATHOLIC UNIVERSITY

Theology	M

JOHNS HOPKINS UNIVERSITY

Addictions/Substance Abuse Counseling	M,D
Aerospace/Aeronautical Engineering	M,O
Allopathic Medicine	D
Anatomy	D
Anthropology	D
Applied Behavior Analysis	O
Applied Economics	M
Applied Mathematics	M,D,O
Applied Physics	M,O
Archaeology	D
Art History	M,D
Artificial Intelligence/Robotics	M
Asian Studies	M,D,O
Astronomy	D
Biochemistry	M,D
Bioengineering	M,D
Bioethics	M,D
Bioinformatics	M,D,O
Biological and Biomedical Sciences—General	M,D
Biomedical Engineering	M,D,O
Biophysics	D
Biostatistics	M,D
Biotechnology	M
Business Administration and Management—General	M
Cardiovascular Sciences	M,D
Cell Biology	D
Chemical Engineering	M,D
Chemistry	M,D
Civil Engineering	M,D
Classics	D
Clinical Psychology	M,D
Clinical Research	M,D
Cognitive Sciences	D
Communication—General	M
Community Health	M,D
Comparative Literature	D
Computer and Information Systems Security	M,O
Computer Engineering	M,D,O
Computer Science	M,D,O
Counseling Psychology	M,O
Counselor Education	M,O
Demography and Population Studies	M,D
Developmental Biology	D
Early Childhood Education	M
Economics	D
Education of the Gifted	M
Education—General	M,D,O
Educational Leadership and Administration	M,D
Educational Media/Instructional Technology	M
Educational Policy	D
Electrical Engineering	M,D,O
Elementary Education	M
Energy Management and Policy	M,O
Engineering and Applied Sciences—General	M,D,O
Engineering Management	M
English	M,D
Environmental and Occupational Health	M,D
Environmental Engineering	M,D,O
Environmental Management and Policy	M,O
Environmental Sciences	M,O
Epidemiology	M,D
Evolutionary Biology	D
Film, Television, and Video Production	M
Finance and Banking	M,D,O
French	D
Genetic Counseling	M,D
Genetics	M,D
Geographic Information Systems	M,O
Geography	M,D
Geosciences	M,D
German	D
Health Communication	M,D
Health Education	M,D
Health Informatics	M,D,O
Health Services Management and Hospital Administration	M,D,O
Health Services Research	M,D
History of Science and Technology	M,D
History	D
Homeland Security	M,O
Human Genetics	D
Immunology	M,D
Infectious Diseases	M,D
Information Science	M
International Affairs	M,D,O
International Development	M,D,O
International Economics	M,D,O
International Health	M,D
Investment Management	M,O
Italian	D
Liberal Studies	M,O
Management Information Systems	M,O
Management of Technology	M,O
Marketing	M
Materials Engineering	M,D
Materials Sciences	M,D
Mathematical and Computational Finance	M,D
Mathematics	M,D
Mechanical Engineering	M,D
Mechanics	M
Media Studies	M
Medical Illustration	M
Medical Informatics	M,D,O
Microbiology	M,D
Military and Defense Studies	M
Molecular Biology	M,D
Molecular Medicine	D
Museum Studies	M,O
Music	M,D,O
Nanotechnology	M
Near and Middle Eastern Languages	D
Near and Middle Eastern Studies	D
Neuroscience	D
Nonprofit Management	M,O
Nursing—General	M,D,O
Nutrition	M,D
Operations Research	M,D
Organizational Management	M
Pathobiology	D
Pathology	D
Pharmaceutical Sciences	M
Pharmacology	D
Philosophy	M,D
Physics	M,D
Physiology	M,D
Political Science	M,D,O
Psychology—General	D
Public Administration	M,O
Public Health—General	M,D
Public Policy	M,D
Reading Education	M
Real Estate	M
Romance Languages	D
Science Education	M
Secondary Education	M
Social Sciences Education	M
Social Sciences	M,D
Sociology	M,D
Spanish	D
Special Education	M,O
Statistics	M,O
Systems Engineering	M,O
Technical Writing	M,O
Telecommunications	M,O
Toxicology	M,D
Writing	M,O

JOHNSON & WALES UNIVERSITY

Business Administration and Management—General	M
Business Education	M
Criminal Justice and Criminology	M
Education—General	M
Educational Leadership and Administration	D
Elementary Education	M
Hospitality Management	M
Physician Assistant Studies	M
Secondary Education	M
Special Education	M

JOHNSON C. SMITH UNIVERSITY

Social Work	M

JOHNSON STATE COLLEGE

Applied Behavior Analysis	M
Art/Fine Arts	M
Counselor Education	M
Curriculum and Instruction	M
Education—General	M
Foundations and Philosophy of Education	M
Reading Education	M
Secondary Education	M
Special Education	M

JOHNSON UNIVERSITY

Counselor Education	M,D,O
Cultural Studies	M,D,O
Education—General	M,D,O
Educational Media/Instructional Technology	M,D,O
Higher Education	M,D,O
Marriage and Family Therapy	M,D,O
Theology	M,D,O

JOHN WESLEY UNIVERSITY

Business Administration and Management—General	M

JOSE MARIA VARGAS UNIVERSITY

Early Childhood Education	M

THE JUDGE ADVOCATE GENERAL'S SCHOOL, U.S. ARMY

Law	M
Military and Defense Studies	M

JUDSON UNIVERSITY

Architecture	M
Business Administration and Management—General	M
Clinical Psychology	M
Human Services	M
Organizational Management	M
Pastoral Ministry and Counseling	M
Reading Education	M,D
Sustainable Development	M
Urban Design	M

THE JUILLIARD SCHOOL

Music	M,D,O

JUNIATA COLLEGE

Accounting	M

KANSAS CITY UNIVERSITY OF MEDICINE AND BIOSCIENCES

Bioethics	M
Biological and Biomedical Sciences—General	M
Osteopathic Medicine	D

KANSAS STATE UNIVERSITY

Accounting	M
Advertising and Public Relations	M
Agricultural Economics and Agribusiness	M,D
Agricultural Education	M
Agricultural Engineering	M,D
Agricultural Sciences—General	M,D,O
Agronomy and Soil Sciences	M,D,O
Analytical Chemistry	M,D
Animal Sciences	M,D
Applied Arts and Design—General	M
Architectural Engineering	M
Architecture	M
Art/Fine Arts	M
Biochemistry	M,D
Bioengineering	M,D
Biological and Biomedical Sciences—General	M,D
Business Administration and Management—General	M,O
Chemical Engineering	M,D,O
Chemistry	M,D
Child and Family Studies	M,D,O
Child Development	M,O
Civil Engineering	M,D
Clothing and Textiles	M,D
Communication Disorders	M,O
Communication—General	M,D
Computer Engineering	M,D
Computer Science	M,D
Conflict Resolution and Mediation/Peace Studies	M,O
Consumer Economics	M,D
Counselor Education	M,D
Curriculum and Instruction	M,D
Early Childhood Education	M,O
Economics	M,D
Education—General	M,D
Educational Leadership and Administration	M,D
Educational Media/Instructional Technology	M,D
Electrical Engineering	M,D
Elementary Education	M,D
Energy and Power Engineering	M,D
Energy Management and Policy	M,D
Engineering and Applied Sciences—General	M,D,O
Engineering Management	M,D
English Education	M,D
English	M,O
Entomology	M,D
Environmental Design	D
Environmental Engineering	M,D
Environmental Sciences	M,D,O
Family and Consumer Sciences-General	M,D,O
Finance and Banking	M,O
Food Science and Technology	M,D
Genetics	M,D
Geography	M,D,O
Geology	M
Geotechnical Engineering	M,D
Gerontology	M,O
Health Communication	M
History	M,D
Horticulture	M,D
Hospitality Management	M,D
Human Development	M,D,O
Human Services	M,O
Industrial and Manufacturing Management	M
Industrial/Management Engineering	M,D
Information Science	M,D
Inorganic Chemistry	M,D
International Affairs	M
Journalism	M
Kinesiology and Movement Studies	M,D
Landscape Architecture	M
Management of Technology	M
Manufacturing Engineering	M,D
Marketing	M
Marriage and Family Therapy	M,D,O
Mass Communication	M
Mathematics	M,D,O
Mechanical Engineering	M,D
Middle School Education	M,D
Music	M
National Security	M,D
Nuclear Engineering	M,D
Nutrition	M,D
Operations Research	M,D
Organic Chemistry	M,D
Pathobiology	M,D
Physical Chemistry	M,D
Physics	M,D
Physiology	D
Plant Pathology	M,D
Plant Sciences	M,D,O
Political Science	M
Psychology—General	M,D
Public Administration	M
Public Health—General	M,D,O
Range Science	M,D,O
Reading Education	M,D
Sociology	M,D
Special Education	M,D
Statistics	M,D,O
Structural Engineering	M,D
Student Affairs	M,D
Supply Chain Management	M,O
Theater	M
Transportation and Highway Engineering	M,D
Urban and Regional Planning	M
Veterinary Medicine	D
Veterinary Sciences	M,O
Water Resources Engineering	M,D
Women's Studies	O

KANSAS WESLEYAN UNIVERSITY

Business Administration and Management—General	M
Sports Management	M

KAPLAN UNIVERSITY, DAVENPORT CAMPUS

Business Administration and Management—General	M
Computer and Information Systems Security	M
Criminal Justice and Criminology	M
Education—General	M
Educational Leadership and Administration	M
Educational Media/Instructional Technology	M
Entrepreneurship	M
Finance and Banking	M
Health Services Management and Hospital Administration	M,O
Higher Education	M

*M—masters degree; D—doctorate; O—other advanced degree; *—Close-Up and/or Display*

Human Resources Management M
International Business M
Law M
Legal and Justice Studies M,O
Logistics M
Management Information Systems M
Marketing M
Mathematics Education M
Nursing and Healthcare Administration M
Nursing Education M
Nursing—General M
Organizational Management M
Political Science M,O
Project Management M
Reading Education M
Science Education M
Secondary Education M
Special Education M
Student Affairs M
Supply Chain Management M

KEAN UNIVERSITY
Accounting M
Addictions/Substance Abuse Counseling M
Adult Education M
Art Education M
Art/Fine Arts M
Biotechnology M
Business Administration and Management—General M
Clinical Psychology M,D
Communication Disorders M
Communication—General M
Community Health Nursing M
Counseling Psychology M
Counselor Education M
Criminal Justice and Criminology M
Curriculum and Instruction M
Early Childhood Education M
Education—General M
Educational Leadership and Administration M,D
English as a Second Language M
Exercise and Sports Science M
Foreign Languages Education M
Health Services Management and Hospital Administration M
Holocaust and Genocide Studies M
Industrial and Organizational Psychology M
International Business M
Management Information Systems M
Marriage and Family Therapy M,O
Mathematics Education M
Multilingual and Multicultural Education M
Nonprofit Management M
Nursing and Healthcare Administration M,D
Nursing—General M
Occupational Therapy M
Psychology—General M
Public Administration M
Reading Education M
School Nursing M
School Psychology M,D,O
Science Education M
Social Work M
Spanish M
Special Education M
Writing M

KECK GRADUATE INSTITUTE
Biological and Biomedical Sciences—General M,D,O
Pharmacy D

KEENE STATE COLLEGE
Counselor Education M,O
Curriculum and Instruction M,O
Education—General M,O
Educational Leadership and Administration M,O
Environmental and Occupational Health M,O
School Psychology M,O
Special Education M,O

KEHILATH YAKOV RABBINICAL SEMINARY
Theology

KEISER UNIVERSITY
Accounting M
Business Administration and Management—General M,D
Computer and Information Systems Security M
Criminal Justice and Criminology M
Distance Education Development M
Education—General M
Educational Leadership and Administration M,D,O
Educational Media/Instructional Technology D,O
Health Education M
Health Services Management and Hospital Administration M
Homeland Security M
Industrial and Organizational Psychology M,D
International Business M,D
Management Information Systems M
Marketing M,D
Nursing—General M
Organizational Management D
Physician Assistant Studies M
Psychology—General M,D

KENNESAW STATE UNIVERSITY
Accounting M
American Studies M
Applied Statistics M
Architecture M
Art Education M
Biochemistry M
Biological and Biomedical Sciences—General M
Business Administration and Management—General M,D
Chemistry M
Communication—General M
Computer and Information Systems Security M,O
Computer Engineering M
Computer Science M
Conflict Resolution and Mediation/Peace Studies M,D
Construction Management M
Criminal Justice and Criminology M
Early Childhood Education M
Education—General M,D,O
Educational Leadership and Administration M,D,O
Educational Media/Instructional Technology M
Electrical Engineering M
Elementary Education M
Engineering and Applied Sciences—General M,O
English as a Second Language M
English Education M
Ethics O
Exercise and Sports Science M
Foreign Languages Education M
Health Informatics M,O
Health Services Management and Hospital Administration M
Information Science M,O
International Affairs M
Mathematics Education M
Middle School Education M
Nursing—General M,D
Physics M
Public Administration M
Reading Education M
Secondary Education M
Social Work M
Software Engineering M,O
Special Education M
Systems Engineering M,O
Writing M

KENRICK-GLENNON SEMINARY
Theology M

KENT STATE UNIVERSITY
Accounting M,D
Adult Nursing M,D,O
Advertising and Public Relations M
Anthropology M
Applied Mathematics M,D
Architecture M
Art Education M
Art History M
Art/Fine Arts M
Athletic Training and Sports Medicine M,D
Biological and Biomedical Sciences—General M,D
Biological Anthropology M,D
Business Administration and Management—General M
Cell Biology M,D
Chemical Physics M,D
Chemistry M,D
Child and Family Studies M
Clinical Psychology M,D
Communication Disorders M,D,O
Communication—General M,D
Computer and Information Systems Security M,O
Computer Education M,D
Computer Science M,D
Counseling Psychology M
Counselor Education M,D,O
Curriculum and Instruction M,D,O
Early Childhood Education M,D,O
Ecology M,D
Economics M
Education of the Gifted M,D,O
Education—General M,D,O
Educational Leadership and Administration M,D,O
Educational Measurement and Evaluation M,D
Educational Media/Instructional Technology M,D
Educational Psychology M
Engineering and Applied Sciences—General M
English as a Second Language M,D,O
English Education M,D,O
English M,D,O
Environmental Design M
Exercise and Sports Science M,D
Experimental Psychology M,D
Family Nurse Practitioner Studies M,D,O
Finance and Banking D
Foundations and Philosophy of Education M,D
Genetics M,D
Geography M,D
Geology M,D
Gerontological Nursing M,D,O
Graphic Design M
Health Education M,D
Health Promotion M,D
Higher Education M,D,O
History M,D
Hospitality Management M
Human Development M,D
Human Services M,D,O
Illustration M
Information Science M,O
Japanese M,D
Journalism M
Liberal Studies M
Library Science M,O
Management Information Systems D
Marketing D
Mass Communication M
Mathematics M,D
Middle School Education M
Molecular Biology M,D
Music Education M,D,O
Music M,D,O
Neuroscience M,D
Nursing and Healthcare Administration M,D,O
Nursing Education M,D,O
Nursing—General M,D,O
Nutrition M
Pediatric Nursing M,D,O
Pharmacology M,D
Philosophy M
Physics M,D
Physiology M,D
Podiatric Medicine D
Political Science M,D
Psychiatric Nursing M,D,O
Psychology—General M,D
Public Administration M,D
Public Health—General M,D
Reading Education M
Recreation and Park Management M
Rehabilitation Counseling M
Rhetoric M,D,O
Russian M,D
School Psychology M,D,O
Secondary Education M
Sociology M,D
Special Education M,D,O
Sports Management M
Student Affairs M
Theater M
Translation and Interpretation M,D
Travel and Tourism M
Urban Design M
Vocational and Technical Education M
Women's Health Nursing M,D,O
Writing M,D,O

KENT STATE UNIVERSITY AT STARK
Business Administration and Management—General M
Curriculum and Instruction M
Education—General M

KENTUCKY CHRISTIAN UNIVERSITY
Religion M
Theology M

KENTUCKY STATE UNIVERSITY
Aquaculture M
Business Administration and Management—General M
Computer Science M
Environmental Management and Policy M
Human Resources Development M,D
Nursing—General M,D
Public Administration M,D
Special Education M,D

KETTERING COLLEGE
Physician Assistant Studies M

KETTERING UNIVERSITY
Business Administration and Management—General M
Electrical Engineering M
Engineering Management M
Manufacturing Engineering M
Mechanical Engineering M

KEUKA COLLEGE
Business Administration and Management—General M
Criminal Justice and Criminology M
Early Childhood Education M
Gerontological Nursing M
Nursing—General M
Occupational Therapy M

KEYSTONE COLLEGE
Accounting M
Early Childhood Education M
Educational Leadership and Administration M
Sports Management M

KING'S COLLEGE
Education—General M
Health Services Management and Hospital Administration M
Physician Assistant Studies M

THE KING'S UNIVERSITY
Pastoral Ministry and Counseling M,D,O
Theology M,D,O

KINGSWOOD UNIVERSITY
Pastoral Ministry and Counseling M
Theology M

KING UNIVERSITY
Accounting M
Business Administration and Management—General M
Finance and Banking M
Health Services Management and Hospital Administration M
Human Resources Management M
Marketing M
Project Management M

KNOWLEDGE SYSTEMS INSTITUTE
Computer Science M
Information Science M

KNOX COLLEGE
Theology M,D

KNOX THEOLOGICAL SEMINARY
Classics M
Pastoral Ministry and Counseling D
Religion M
Theology M

KUTZTOWN UNIVERSITY OF PENNSYLVANIA
Art Education M
Business Administration and Management—General M
Computer Science M
Counseling Psychology M
Counselor Education M
Curriculum and Instruction M
Education—General M
Educational Leadership and Administration M
Educational Media/Instructional Technology M
Elementary Education M
English Education M
English M
Internet and Interactive Multimedia M
Library Science M
Marriage and Family Therapy M
Mathematics Education M
Public Administration M
Reading Education M
Science Education M
Secondary Education M
Social Sciences Education M
Social Work M

LAGRANGE COLLEGE
Clinical Psychology M
Curriculum and Instruction M,O
Education—General M,O
Middle School Education M,O
Organizational Management M
Secondary Education M,O

LAGUNA COLLEGE OF ART & DESIGN
Art/Fine Arts M

LAKE ERIE COLLEGE
Business Administration and Management—General M
Education—General M
Health Services Management and Hospital Administration M
Management Information Systems M

LAKE ERIE COLLEGE OF OSTEOPATHIC MEDICINE
Biological and Biomedical Sciences—General M,D,O
Health Education M,D,O
Osteopathic Medicine M,D,O
Pharmacy M,D,O

LAKE FOREST COLLEGE
American Studies M
Art Education M
Art/Fine Arts M
Education—General M
Elementary Education M
English Education M
Environmental Management and Policy M
French M
History M
Liberal Studies M
Mathematics Education M
Music Education M
Philosophy M
Science Education M
Secondary Education M
Social Sciences Education M
Spanish M
Writing M

LAKE FOREST GRADUATE SCHOOL OF MANAGEMENT
Business Administration and Management—General M
Finance and Banking M
Health Services Management and Hospital Administration M
International Business M
Marketing M
Organizational Behavior M

LAKEHEAD UNIVERSITY
Biological and Biomedical Sciences—General M
Chemistry M
Clinical Psychology M,D
Computer Engineering M
Computer Science M
Economics M
Education—General M,D
Electrical Engineering M
Engineering and Applied Sciences—General M
English M
Environmental Engineering M
Exercise and Sports Science M
Experimental Psychology M,D
Forestry M,D
Geology M
Gerontology M,D
Health Services Research M
History M
Kinesiology and Movement Studies M
Mathematics M
Physics M
Psychology—General M,D
Social Work M
Sociology M
Women's Studies M,D

LAKEHEAD UNIVERSITY–ORILLIA
Business Administration and Management—General M

LAKELAND UNIVERSITY
Accounting M
Business Administration and Management—General M

Counselor Education M
Education—General M
Finance and Banking M
Health Services Management and Hospital Administration M
Project Management M
Theology M

LAMAR UNIVERSITY
Accounting M
Biological and Biomedical Sciences—General M
Business Administration and Management—General M
Chemical Engineering M,D
Chemistry M
Clinical Psychology M
Communication Disorders M,D
Computer Science M
Counseling Psychology M
Counselor Education M
Criminal Justice and Criminology M
Education—General M,D,O
Educational Leadership and Administration M,D
Educational Media/Instructional Technology M,D
Electrical Engineering M,D
Engineering and Applied Sciences—General M,D
Engineering Management M,D
English M
Entrepreneurship M
Environmental Engineering M,D
Environmental Management and Policy M,D
Family and Consumer Sciences-General M
Foreign Languages Education M
Health Services Management and Hospital Administration M
History M
Industrial and Organizational Psychology M
Industrial/Management Engineering M,D
Kinesiology and Movement Studies M
Mathematics M
Mechanical Engineering M,D
Music M
Nursing and Healthcare Administration M
Nursing Education M
Nursing—General M
Political Science M
Psychology—General M
Public Administration M
Public Health—General M
Spanish M
Special Education M,D

LANCASTER BIBLE COLLEGE
Counseling Psychology M,D
Counselor Education M,D
Elementary Education M,D
Marriage and Family Therapy M,D
Pastoral Ministry and Counseling M,D,O
Secondary Education M,D
Special Education M,D
Theology M,D,O

LANCASTER THEOLOGICAL SEMINARY
Art History M,D,O
Ethics M,D,O
Religion M,D,O
Religious Education M,D,O
Theology M,D,O

LANDER UNIVERSITY
Early Childhood Education M
Education—General M
Emergency Management M
Nursing—General M

LANGSTON UNIVERSITY
Education—General M
Elementary Education M
English as a Second Language M
Multilingual and Multicultural Education M
Physical Therapy D
Rehabilitation Counseling M
Urban Education M

LA ROCHE COLLEGE
Accounting M
Human Resources Management M,O
Nurse Anesthesia M
Nursing and Healthcare Administration M
Nursing Education M
Nursing—General M

LA SALLE UNIVERSITY
Accounting M,O
Adult Nursing M,D,O
Advertising and Public Relations M,O
American Studies M,O
Art/Fine Arts M,O
Business Administration and Management—General M,O
Clinical Psychology M,D
Communication Disorders M
Communication—General M,O
Community Health Nursing M,D,O
Comparative Literature M,O
Computer Science M,O
Corporate and Organizational Communication M,O
Counseling Psychology M
Cultural Studies M,O
Developmental Psychology M,D
Early Childhood Education M,O
East European and Russian Studies M,O
Education—General M,O
Educational Leadership and Administration M,O
Educational Media/Instructional Technology M,O
English as a Second Language M,O
English Education M,O
English M,O
Family Nurse Practitioner Studies M,D,O
Finance and Banking M,O
Forensic Sciences M,O
Gerontological Nursing M,D,O
Gerontology M,D,O
Health Psychology M,D
Hispanic Studies M,O
History M,O
Human Resources Development M,O
Human Resources Management M,O
International Business M,O
Latin American Studies M,O
Management of Technology M,O
Marketing M,O
Marriage and Family Therapy M
Media Studies M,O
Middle School Education M,O
Multilingual and Multicultural Education M,O
National Security M,O
Nonprofit Management M
Nurse Anesthesia M,D,O
Nursing and Healthcare Administration M,D,O
Nursing Education M,D,O
Nursing—General M,D,O
Pastoral Ministry and Counseling M,D,O
Psychology—General M,D
Public Health—General M
Public History M,O
Quantitative Analysis M,O
Reading Education M,O
Religion M,D,O
Religious Education M,D,O
School Nursing M,D,O
Secondary Education M,O
Social Sciences Education M,O
Special Education M,O
Theology M,D,O
Translation and Interpretation M,O
Western European Studies M,O

LASELL COLLEGE
Advertising and Public Relations M,O
Business Administration and Management—General M,O
Communication—General M,O
Corporate and Organizational Communication M,O
Criminal Justice and Criminology M
Education—General M
Elementary Education M
Emergency Management M
Health Communication M,O
Health Services Management and Hospital Administration M,O
Homeland Security M
Hospitality Management M,O
Human Resources Management M,O
Marketing M,O
Nonprofit Management M,O
Project Management M,O
Rehabilitation Sciences M
Special Education M
Sports Management M,O
Travel and Tourism M,O

LA SIERRA UNIVERSITY
Accounting M,O
Advertising and Public Relations M
Business Administration and Management—General M,O
Communication—General M
Counselor Education M,O
Curriculum and Instruction M,D,O
Education—General M,D,O
Educational Leadership and Administration M,D,O
Educational Psychology M,O
English M
Finance and Banking M,O
Human Resources Management M,O
Marketing M,O
Pastoral Ministry and Counseling M
Religion M
Religious Education M
School Psychology M,O
Writing M

LAURENTIAN UNIVERSITY
Analytical Chemistry M
Applied Physics M
Applied Psychology M
Applied Social Research M
Biochemistry M
Biological and Biomedical Sciences—General M,D
Business Administration and Management—General M
Chemistry M
Ecology M,D
Engineering and Applied Sciences—General M,D
Environmental Sciences M
Experimental Psychology M
Geology M,D
History M
Human Development M
Humanities M
Mineral/Mining Engineering M,D
Natural Resources M,D
Nursing—General M
Organic Chemistry M
Physical Chemistry M
Psychology—General M
Public Health—General D
Science Education O
Social Work M
Sociology M
Technical Writing O
Theoretical Chemistry M

LAWRENCE TECHNOLOGICAL UNIVERSITY
Architectural Engineering M,D
Architecture M,D,O
Automotive Engineering M,D
Biomedical Engineering M,D
Business Administration and Management—General M,D
Civil Engineering M,D
Computer Engineering M,D
Computer Science M
Construction Engineering M,D
Educational Media/Instructional Technology M
Electrical Engineering M,D
Engineering and Applied Sciences—General M,D
Engineering Management M,D
Industrial/Management Engineering M,D
Information Science M,D
Interior Design M,O
Mechanical Engineering M,D
Science Education M
Technical Communication M
Urban Design M,O

LEBANESE AMERICAN UNIVERSITY
Business Administration and Management—General M
Computer Science M
International Affairs M
Pharmacy D

LEBANON VALLEY COLLEGE
Athletic Training and Sports Medicine M
Business Administration and Management—General M
Health Services Management and Hospital Administration M
Music Education M
Physical Therapy D
Science Education M

LEE UNIVERSITY
Art/Fine Arts M,O
Biological and Biomedical Sciences—General M,O
Business Administration and Management—General M
Child Development M
Counseling Psychology M
Counselor Education M
Curriculum and Instruction M,O
Early Childhood Education M,O
Economics M,O
Education—General M,O
Educational Leadership and Administration M,O
Elementary Education M,O
English as a Second Language M,O
English M,O
Ethics M
Higher Education M,O
History M,O
Marriage and Family Therapy M
Mathematics Education M,O
Mathematics M,O
Middle School Education M,O
Music Education M
Music M
Pastoral Ministry and Counseling M
Religion M
Secondary Education M,O
Social Sciences Education M,O
Spanish M,O
Special Education M,O
Theology M

LEHIGH UNIVERSITY
Accounting M
American Studies M,D,O
Applied Mathematics M,D
Biochemical Engineering M,D
Biochemistry M,D
Bioengineering M,D
Biological and Biomedical Sciences—General M,D
Business Administration and Management—General M
Cell Biology M,D
Chemical Engineering M,D
Chemistry M,D
Civil Engineering M,D
Computational Sciences M,D
Computer Engineering M,D
Computer Science M,D
Counseling Psychology M,D,O
Counselor Education M,D,O
Economics M,D
Education—General M,D,O
Educational Leadership and Administration M,D,O
Educational Media/Instructional Technology M,D,O
Electrical Engineering M,D
Energy and Power Engineering M
Engineering and Applied Sciences—General M,D
Engineering Management M,D
English as a Second Language M,D,O
English M,D
Entrepreneurship M
Environmental Engineering M,D
Environmental Law M,O
Environmental Management and Policy M,O
Environmental Sciences M,D
Finance and Banking M
Geology M,D
Geosciences M,D
Health Services Management and Hospital Administration M
History M,D
Human Services M,D,O
Industrial/Management Engineering M,D
Information Science M
Interdisciplinary Studies M,D
International and Comparative Education M,D,O
International Development M,D,O
Manufacturing Engineering M
Materials Engineering M,D
Materials Sciences M,D
Mathematics M,D
Mechanical Engineering M,D
Mechanics M,D
Molecular Biology M,D
Photonics M,D
Physics M,D
Political Science M
Polymer Science and Engineering M,D
Project Management M
Psychology—General M,D
Public History M,D
Quantitative Analysis M
School Psychology D,O
Sociology M
Special Education M,D
Statistics M,D
Sustainable Development M,O
Systems Engineering M,D

LEHMAN COLLEGE OF THE CITY UNIVERSITY OF NEW YORK
Accounting M
Adult Nursing M
Art/Fine Arts M
Biological and Biomedical Sciences—General M
Business Education M
Communication Disorders M
Computer Science M
Counselor Education M
Early Childhood Education M
Education—General M
Elementary Education M
English as a Second Language M
English Education M
English M
Gerontological Nursing M
Health Education M
Health Promotion M
History M
Maternal and Child/Neonatal Nursing M
Mathematics Education M
Mathematics M
Multilingual and Multicultural Education M
Music Education M
Nursing—General M
Nutrition M
Pediatric Nursing M
Plant Sciences D
Reading Education M
Recreation and Park Management M
Science Education M
Social Sciences Education M
Spanish M
Special Education M

LE MOYNE COLLEGE
Arts Administration M,O
Business Administration and Management—General M
Early Childhood Education M,O
Education—General M,O
Educational Leadership and Administration M,O
Elementary Education M,O
English as a Second Language M,O
English Education M,O
Foreign Languages Education M,O
Gerontological Nursing M,O
Middle School Education M,O
Nursing and Healthcare Administration M,O
Nursing Education M,O
Nursing Informatics M,O
Nursing—General M,O
Occupational Therapy M
Physician Assistant Studies M
Reading Education M,O
Secondary Education M,O
Social Sciences Education M,O
Special Education M,O
Urban Studies M,O

LENOIR-RHYNE UNIVERSITY
Accounting M
Addictions/Substance Abuse Counseling M
Athletic Training and Sports Medicine M
Business Administration and Management—General M
Clinical Psychology M
Community College Education M
Counseling Psychology M
Counselor Education M

*M—masters degree; D—doctorate; O—other advanced degree; *—Close-Up and/or Display*

- Distance Education Development M
- Education—General M
- Educational Leadership and Administration M
- Educational Media/Instructional Technology M
- Entrepreneurship M
- Health Services Management and Hospital Administration M
- Human Services M
- International Business M
- Management Information Systems M
- Management Strategy and Policy M
- Nursing and Healthcare Administration M
- Nursing Education M
- Nursing—General M
- Occupational Therapy M
- Organizational Management M
- Physician Assistant Studies M
- Public Health—General M
- Secondary Education M
- Sustainable Development M
- Theology M
- Writing M

LESLEY UNIVERSITY

- Adult Education M,D,O
- Art Education M,D,O
- Art Therapy M,D,O
- Art/Fine Arts M,D,O
- Clinical Psychology M,D,O
- Computer Education M,D,O
- Conflict Resolution and Mediation/Peace Studies M,D,O
- Counseling Psychology M,D,O
- Curriculum and Instruction M,D,O
- Distance Education Development M,D,O
- Early Childhood Education M,D,O
- Ecology M,D,O
- Education—General M,D,O
- Educational Leadership and Administration M,D,O
- Educational Media/Instructional Technology M,D,O
- Elementary Education M,D,O
- English as a Second Language M,D,O
- Health Psychology M,D,O
- Interdisciplinary Studies M,D,O
- International Affairs M,D,O
- Mathematics Education M,D,O
- Middle School Education M,D,O
- Photography M
- Psychology—General M,D,O
- Reading Education M,D,O
- School Psychology M,D,O
- Science Education M,D,O
- Secondary Education M,D,O
- Social Psychology M,D,O
- Special Education M,D,O
- Sustainable Development M,D,O
- Therapies—Dance, Drama, and Music M,D,O
- Urban and Regional Planning M,D,O
- Women's Studies M,D,O
- Writing M,D,O

LES ROCHES INTERNATIONAL SCHOOL OF HOTEL MANAGEMENT

- Hospitality Management M

LETOURNEAU UNIVERSITY

- Business Administration and Management—General M
- Counseling Psychology M
- Curriculum and Instruction M
- Education—General M
- Educational Leadership and Administration M
- Engineering and Applied Sciences—General M
- Engineering Management M
- Health Services Management and Hospital Administration M
- Management Strategy and Policy M
- Marriage and Family Therapy M
- Psychology—General M

LEWIS & CLARK COLLEGE

- Addictions/Substance Abuse Counseling M
- Communication Disorders M
- Counseling Psychology M
- Cultural Studies M,O
- Curriculum and Instruction M
- Early Childhood Education M
- Educational Leadership and Administration D,O
- Elementary Education M
- Environmental Law M,D
- Law M,D
- Marriage and Family Therapy M
- Middle School Education M
- Psychology—General M,O
- School Psychology M,O
- Secondary Education M
- Special Education M

LEWIS UNIVERSITY

- Accounting M
- Adult Nursing M,D
- Aviation Management M
- Aviation M
- Business Administration and Management—General M
- Clinical Psychology M
- Computer and Information Systems Security M
- Counseling Psychology M
- Counselor Education M
- Criminal Justice and Criminology M
- Database Systems M
- Early Childhood Education M,D,O
- Education—General M,D,O
- Educational Leadership and Administration M,D
- Educational Media/Instructional Technology M
- Electronic Commerce M
- Elementary Education M
- English as a Second Language M
- Environmental and Occupational Health M
- Finance and Banking M
- Health Services Management and Hospital Administration M
- Higher Education M
- Human Resources Management M
- International Business M
- Management Information Systems M
- Management of Technology M
- Marketing M
- Mathematics Education M
- Nonprofit Management M
- Nursing and Healthcare Administration M,D
- Nursing Education M,D
- Nursing—General M,D
- Organizational Management M
- Project Management M
- Reading Education M
- Science Education M
- Secondary Education M
- Social Sciences Education M
- Special Education M
- Sports Management M
- Student Affairs M

LEXINGTON THEOLOGICAL SEMINARY

- Theology M,D

LIBERTY UNIVERSITY

- Accounting M,D,O
- Addictions/Substance Abuse Counseling M,D,O
- Advertising and Public Relations M,D,O
- Art/Fine Arts M
- Biological and Biomedical Sciences—General M,O
- Business Administration and Management—General M,D,O
- Child and Family Studies M,D,O
- Clinical Psychology M,D,O
- Communication—General M
- Computer and Information Systems Security M,D,O
- Counseling Psychology M,D,O
- Counselor Education M,D,O
- Criminal Justice and Criminology M,D,O
- Curriculum and Instruction M,D,O
- Distance Education Development M,D,O
- Early Childhood Education M,D,O
- Education of the Gifted M,D,O
- Education—General M,D,O
- Educational Leadership and Administration M,D,O
- Educational Media/Instructional Technology M,D,O
- Elementary Education M,D,O
- Emergency Management M,D,O
- Engineering and Applied Sciences—General M
- English M,D,O
- Exercise and Sports Science M,D,O
- Family Nurse Practitioner Studies M,D
- Health Promotion M,D,O
- Health Services Management and Hospital Administration M,D,O
- History M,D,O
- Human Resources Management M,D,O
- Human Services M,D,O
- International Affairs M,D,O
- International Business M,D,O
- International Health M,O
- Law D
- Management Information Systems M,D,O
- Management of Technology M,D,O
- Marketing M,D,O
- Marriage and Family Therapy M,D,O
- Mathematics Education M,D,O
- Middle School Education M,D,O
- Military and Defense Studies M,D,O
- Missions and Missiology M,D,O
- Music Education M,D
- Music M,D
- Near and Middle Eastern Studies M
- Nursing and Healthcare Administration M,D
- Nursing Education M,D
- Nursing—General M,D
- Nutrition M,O
- Osteopathic Medicine D
- Pastoral Ministry and Counseling M,D,O
- Philosophy M
- Political Science M
- Project Management M,D,O
- Public Administration M,D,O
- Public Policy M
- Reading Education M,D,O
- Recreation and Park Management M,D,O
- Religion M,D,O
- Religious Education M,D,O
- Secondary Education M,D,O
- Special Education M,D,O
- Sports Management M,D,O
- Student Affairs M,D,O
- Theology M,D,O
- Travel and Tourism M,D,O

LIFE CHIROPRACTIC COLLEGE WEST

- Chiropractic D

LIFE UNIVERSITY

- Athletic Training and Sports Medicine M
- Chiropractic D
- Exercise and Sports Science M
- Nutrition M

LIM COLLEGE

- Business Administration and Management—General M
- Clothing and Textiles M
- Entrepreneurship M
- Marketing M
- Textile Design M

LIMESTONE COLLEGE

- Business Administration and Management—General M

LINCOLN CHRISTIAN SEMINARY

- Pastoral Ministry and Counseling M,D
- Religious Education M,D
- Theology M,D

LINCOLN CHRISTIAN UNIVERSITY

- Cultural Studies M
- Marriage and Family Therapy M
- Organizational Management M
- Theology M

LINCOLN MEMORIAL UNIVERSITY

- Business Administration and Management—General M
- Counselor Education M,D,O
- Curriculum and Instruction M,D,O
- Education—General M,D,O
- Educational Leadership and Administration M,D,O
- English Education M,D,O
- Family Nurse Practitioner Studies M
- Higher Education M,D,O
- Human Resources Development M,D,O
- Law D
- Nurse Anesthesia M
- Nursing—General M
- Osteopathic Medicine D
- Psychiatric Nursing M

LINCOLN UNIVERSITY (CA)

- Business Administration and Management—General M,D
- Finance and Banking M,D
- Human Resources Management M,D
- International Business M,D
- Investment Management M,D
- Management Information Systems M,D

LINCOLN UNIVERSITY (MO)

- Accounting M
- Business Administration and Management—General M
- Counselor Education M
- Criminal Justice and Criminology M
- Elementary Education M
- Entrepreneurship M
- History M
- Public Administration M
- Public Policy M
- Secondary Education M
- Sociology M

LINCOLN UNIVERSITY (PA)

- Business Administration and Management—General M
- Early Childhood Education M
- Educational Leadership and Administration M
- Finance and Banking M
- Human Resources Management M
- Human Services M
- Reading Education M

LINDENWOOD UNIVERSITY

- Accounting M
- Art/Fine Arts M
- Arts Administration M
- Business Administration and Management—General M,O
- Communication Disorders M,D,O
- Communication—General M,O
- Computer and Information Systems Security M,O
- Counseling Psychology M,D,O
- Criminal Justice and Criminology M,O
- Education of the Gifted M,D,O
- Education—General M,D,O
- Educational Leadership and Administration M,D,O
- Educational Media/Instructional Technology M,D,O
- English as a Second Language M,D,O
- Entrepreneurship M
- Finance and Banking M
- Gerontology M,O
- Health Promotion M
- Health Services Management and Hospital Administration M,O
- Human Resources Management M,O
- Human Services M
- International Business M
- Internet and Interactive Multimedia M
- Journalism M
- Management Information Systems M,O
- Marketing M,O
- Media Studies M,O
- Nonprofit Management M
- Nursing—General M
- Project Management M,O
- Public Administration M
- School Psychology M,D,O
- Sports Management M
- Supply Chain Management M
- Writing M,O

LINDENWOOD UNIVERSITY–BELLEVILLE

- Business Administration and Management—General M
- Communication—General M
- Computer Art and Design M
- Counselor Education M
- Criminal Justice and Criminology M
- Education—General M
- Educational Leadership and Administration M
- Health Services Management and Hospital Administration M
- Human Resources Management M
- Internet and Interactive Multimedia M
- Media Studies M

LINDSEY WILSON COLLEGE

- Counseling Psychology M,D
- Counselor Education M,D
- Educational Leadership and Administration M
- Human Development M,D
- Internet and Interactive Multimedia M

LIPSCOMB UNIVERSITY

- Accounting M,O
- Applied Behavior Analysis M,D,O
- Business Administration and Management—General M,O
- Clinical Psychology M,O
- Computer and Information Systems Security M,O
- Conflict Resolution and Mediation/Peace Studies M,O
- Counseling Psychology M,O
- Database Systems M,O
- Education—General M,D,O
- Educational Leadership and Administration M,D,O
- Educational Media/Instructional Technology M,D,O
- Engineering Management M
- English Education M,D,O
- English M,D,O
- Exercise and Sports Science M
- Film, Television, and Video Production M
- Finance and Banking M,O
- Health Informatics M,D,O
- Health Services Management and Hospital Administration M,O
- Human Resources Management M,O
- Management Information Systems M,O
- Management of Technology M,O
- Marriage and Family Therapy M,O
- Mathematics Education M,D,O
- Molecular Biology M
- Nonprofit Management M,O
- Nutrition M
- Organizational Management M
- Pastoral Ministry and Counseling M,D,O
- Pharmacy M,D
- Psychology—General M,O
- Reading Education M,D,O
- Software Engineering M,O
- Special Education M,D,O
- Sports Management M,O
- Sustainability Management M,O
- Sustainable Development M,O
- Theology M,D,O

LOCK HAVEN UNIVERSITY OF PENNSYLVANIA

- Actuarial Science M
- Athletic Training and Sports Medicine M
- Business Education M
- Clinical Psychology M
- Counseling Psychology M
- Education—General M
- Educational Leadership and Administration M
- Elementary Education M
- Health Education M
- Health Promotion M
- Health Services Management and Hospital Administration M
- Human Services M
- Information Studies M
- Physician Assistant Studies M
- Sport Psychology M
- Sports Management M

LOGAN UNIVERSITY

- Chiropractic M,D
- Exercise and Sports Science M,D
- Health Education M,D
- Health Informatics M,D
- Nutrition M,D
- Rehabilitation Sciences M,D

LOGOS EVANGELICAL SEMINARY

- Theology M,D

LOMA LINDA UNIVERSITY

- Addictions/Substance Abuse Counseling M,D,O
- Adult Nursing M
- Allied Health—General M,D
- Allopathic Medicine M,D
- Anatomy D
- Applied Social Research M,D
- Biochemistry M,D
- Bioethics M,O
- Biostatistics M,D
- Child and Family Studies M,D,O
- Clinical Psychology D
- Communication Disorders M,D
- Counselor Education M,D,O
- Criminal Justice and Criminology M,D
- Dentistry M,D,O
- Environmental and Occupational Health M
- Epidemiology M,D
- Gerontological Nursing M
- Gerontology M,D
- Health Education M,D
- Health Services Management and Hospital Administration M
- International Health M
- Marriage and Family Therapy M,D,O
- Microbiology M,D
- Nursing and Healthcare Administration M

Nursing Education M
Nursing—General D
Nutrition M,D
Occupational Therapy M,D
Oral and Dental Sciences M,O
Pathology D
Pediatric Nursing M
Pharmacology D
Pharmacy D
Physical Therapy M,D
Physician Assistant Studies M
Physiology D
Psychology—General D
Public Health—General M,D
Rehabilitation Sciences M,D
Religion M
Social Work M,D

LONDON METROPOLITAN UNIVERSITY
Applied Psychology M,D
Architecture M,D
Arts Administration M,D
Athletic Training and Sports Medicine M,D
Biological and Biomedical Sciences—General M,D
Child and Family Studies M,D
Clinical Psychology M,D
Computer and Information Systems Security M,D
Conflict Resolution and Mediation/Peace Studies M,D
Counseling Psychology M,D
Criminal Justice and Criminology M,D
Database Systems M,D
Early Childhood Education M,D
Education—General M,D
Emergency Management M,D
English Education M,D
Food Science and Technology M,D
Foreign Languages Education M,D
Forensic Psychology M,D
Health Services Management and Hospital Administration M,D
Higher Education M,D
Homeland Security M,D
Human Resources Management M,D
Immunology M,D
Industrial and Organizational Psychology M,D
International Affairs M,D
Internet and Interactive Multimedia M,D
Law M,D
Management Information Systems M,D
Management of Technology M,D
Military and Defense Studies M,D
Near and Middle Eastern Languages M,D
Nutrition M,D
Pharmacology M,D
Public Administration M,D
Public Health—General M,D
Public Policy M,D
Social Work M,D
Special Education M,D
Translation and Interpretation M,D
Urban Design M,D
Women's Studies M,D
Writing M,D

LONG ISLAND UNIVERSITY–BRENTWOOD CAMPUS
Clinical Psychology M,O
Counseling Psychology M,O
Counselor Education M,O
Early Childhood Education M,O
Education—General M,O
Elementary Education M,O
Reading Education M,O
Special Education M,O

LONG ISLAND UNIVERSITY–HUDSON AT ROCKLAND
Business Administration and Management—General M,O
Counseling Psychology M,O
Counselor Education M,O
Early Childhood Education M,O
Educational Leadership and Administration M,O
Middle School Education M,O
Pharmaceutical Sciences M,O
Public Administration M,O
Reading Education M,O
Special Education M,O

LONG ISLAND UNIVERSITY–HUDSON AT WESTCHESTER
Addictions/Substance Abuse Counseling M,O
Business Administration and Management—General M,O
Counseling Psychology M,O
Counselor Education M,O
Early Childhood Education M,O
English as a Second Language M,O
Finance and Banking M,O
Health Services Management and Hospital Administration M,O
Reading Education M,O
School Psychology M,O
Special Education M,O

LONG ISLAND UNIVERSITY–LIU BROOKLYN
Accounting M,O
Adult Nursing M,O
Applied Behavior Analysis M,O
Athletic Training and Sports Medicine M,D
Biological and Biomedical Sciences—General M,D,O
Business Administration and Management—General M,O
Chemistry M,D,O
Clinical Psychology M,D,O
Communication Disorders M,D,O
Computer Science M,O
Counseling Psychology M,O
Counselor Education M,O
Early Childhood Education M,O
Education—General M,O
Educational Leadership and Administration M,O
English as a Second Language M,O
English M,D,O
Exercise and Sports Science M,D
Family Nurse Practitioner Studies M,O
Gerontology M,O
Health Services Management and Hospital Administration M,O
Human Resources Management M,O
Marriage and Family Therapy M,O
Media Studies M,D,O
Multilingual and Multicultural Education M,O
Nonprofit Management M,O
Nursing Education M,O
Nursing—General M,O
Occupational Therapy M,D
Pharmaceutical Sciences M,D
Pharmacology M,D
Pharmacy M,D
Physical Therapy M,D
Physician Assistant Studies M,D
Political Science M,D,O
Psychology—General M,D,O
Public Administration M,O
Public Health—General M,D
Social Sciences Education M,D,O
Social Work M,D
Special Education M,O
Taxation M,O
Toxicology M,D
Urban Education M,O
Urban Studies M,D,O
Writing M,D,O

LONG ISLAND UNIVERSITY–LIU POST
Accounting M
Allied Health—General M,O
Applied Behavior Analysis M,O
Applied Mathematics M,O
Art Education M,D,O
Art Therapy M
Art/Fine Arts M
Biological and Biomedical Sciences—General M,O
Business Administration and Management—General M
Cancer Biology/Oncology M,O
Clinical Psychology M,D,O
Communication Disorders M,D,O
Counseling Psychology M,D,O
Criminal Justice and Criminology M,O
Early Childhood Education M,D,O
Education—General M,D,O
Educational Leadership and Administration M,D,O
Educational Media/Instructional Technology M,D,O
Engineering Management M
English as a Second Language M,D,O
English M,O
Environmental Management and Policy M,O
Family Nurse Practitioner Studies M,O
Finance and Banking M
Game Design and Development M
Genetic Counseling M,O
Geographic Information Systems M,O
Geosciences M,O
Gerontology M,O
History M,O
Infectious Diseases M,O
Information Science M,D,O
Interdisciplinary Studies M,D,O
International Business M
Internet and Interactive Multimedia M
Management Information Systems M
Marketing M
Mathematics M,O
Microbiology M,O
Middle School Education M,D,O
Music Education M
Music M
Nonprofit Management M,O
Nursing and Healthcare Administration M,O
Nursing Education M,O
Nutrition M,O
Political Science M,O
Psychology—General M,O
Public Administration M,O
Reading Education M,D,O
Secondary Education M,D,O
Social Work M,O
Special Education M,D,O
Sustainable Development M,O
Taxation M
Theater M

LONG ISLAND UNIVERSITY–RIVERHEAD
Computer and Information Systems Security M,O
Early Childhood Education M,O
Education—General M,O
Elementary Education M,O
English as a Second Language M,O
Homeland Security M,O
Special Education M,O

LONGWOOD UNIVERSITY
Business Administration and Management—General M
Communication Disorders M
Counselor Education M
Education—General M
Educational Media/Instructional Technology M
Elementary Education M
Health Education M
Mathematics Education M
Middle School Education M
Physical Education M
Reading Education M
Real Estate M
Special Education M

LORAS COLLEGE
Applied Psychology M
Educational Leadership and Administration M
Pastoral Ministry and Counseling M
Special Education M
Theology M

LOUISIANA COLLEGE
Education—General M
Pastoral Ministry and Counseling M
Theology M

LOUISIANA STATE UNIVERSITY AND AGRICULTURAL & MECHANICAL COLLEGE
Accounting M,D
Agricultural Economics and Agribusiness M,D
Agricultural Education M,D
Agricultural Engineering M,D
Agricultural Sciences—General M,D
Animal Sciences M,D
Anthropology M,D
Applied Arts and Design—General M
Applied Science and Technology M
Applied Statistics M
Architecture M
Art History M
Art/Fine Arts M
Astronomy M,D
Astrophysics M,D
Biochemistry M,D
Bioengineering M,D
Biological and Biomedical Sciences—General M,D
Biopsychology M,D
Business Administration and Management—General M,D
Business Education M,D
Chemical Engineering M,D
Chemistry M,D
Civil Engineering M,D
Clinical Psychology M,D
Cognitive Sciences M,D
Communication Disorders M,D
Communication—General M,D
Comparative Literature M,D
Computer Engineering M,D
Computer Science M,D
Construction Management M,D
Counselor Education M,D,O
Developmental Psychology M,D
Economics M,D
Education—General M,D,O
Educational Leadership and Administration M,D,O
Educational Measurement and Evaluation M,D,O
Educational Media/Instructional Technology M,D,O
Electrical Engineering M,D
Elementary Education M,D,O
Engineering and Applied Sciences—General M,D
English M,D
Entomology M,D
Environmental Engineering M,D
Environmental Management and Policy M,D
Environmental Sciences M,D
Family and Consumer Sciences-General M,D
Finance and Banking M,D
Fish, Game, and Wildlife Management M,D
Food Science and Technology M,D
Forestry M,D
French M,D
Geography M,D
Geology M,D
Geophysics M,D
Geotechnical Engineering M,D
Graphic Design M
Higher Education M,D,O
Hispanic Studies M
History M,D
Home Economics Education M,D
Human Resources Development M,D
Information Studies M
International and Comparative Education M,D
Internet and Interactive Multimedia M
Kinesiology and Movement Studies M,D
Landscape Architecture M
Law M,D
Liberal Studies M
Library Science M
Management Information Systems M,D
Marine Affairs M,D
Mass Communication M,D
Mathematics M,D
Mechanical Engineering M,D
Mechanics M,D
Media Studies M,D
Medical Physics M,D
Music Education M,D
Music M,D
Natural Resources M,D
Oceanography M,D
Petroleum Engineering M,D
Philosophy M
Photography M
Physics M,D
Plant Pathology M,D
Political Science M,D
Psychology—General M,D
Public Administration M,D
School Psychology M,D
Secondary Education M,D,O
Social Work M,D
Sociology M,D
Statistics M
Structural Engineering M,D
Systems Science M,D
Theater M,D
Toxicology M,D
Transportation and Highway Engineering M,D
Veterinary Medicine D
Veterinary Sciences M,D
Vocational and Technical Education M,D
Water Resources Engineering M,D
Writing M,D

LOUISIANA STATE UNIVERSITY HEALTH SCIENCES CENTER
Allopathic Medicine M,D
Anatomy D
Biological and Biomedical Sciences—General D
Biostatistics M,D
Cell Biology D
Communication Disorders M,D
Community Health Nursing M,D,O
Community Health M,D
Dentistry D
Developmental Biology D
Environmental and Occupational Health M,D
Epidemiology M,D
Family Nurse Practitioner Studies M,D,O
Gerontological Nursing M,D,O
Health Services Management and Hospital Administration M,D
Human Genetics D
Immunology D
Maternal and Child/Neonatal Nursing M,D,O
Microbiology D
Neurobiology D
Neuroscience D
Nurse Anesthesia M,D,O
Nursing and Healthcare Administration M,D,O
Nursing Education M,D,O
Nursing—General M,D,O
Occupational Therapy M
Parasitology D
Pharmacology D
Physical Therapy D
Physician Assistant Studies M
Physiology D
Public Health—General M,D
Rehabilitation Counseling M

LOUISIANA STATE UNIVERSITY HEALTH SCIENCES CENTER AT SHREVEPORT
Allopathic Medicine D
Anatomy M,D
Biochemistry M,D
Biological and Biomedical Sciences—General M
Cell Biology M,D
Immunology M,D
Microbiology M,D
Molecular Biology M,D
Pharmacology M,D
Physiology M,D

LOUISIANA STATE UNIVERSITY IN SHREVEPORT
Biological and Biomedical Sciences—General M
Business Administration and Management—General M
Computer Science M
Counselor Education M
Curriculum and Instruction M
Education—General M
Educational Leadership and Administration M
Health Services Management and Hospital Administration M
Liberal Studies M
Nonprofit Management M
Public Health—General M
School Psychology O
Systems Science M

LOUISIANA TECH UNIVERSITY
Accounting M,D
Adult Education M,D
Applied Arts and Design—General M
Applied Physics M
Architecture M,D

*M—masters degree; D—doctorate; O—other advanced degree; *—Close-Up and/or Display*

Art/Fine Arts M
Biological and Biomedical Sciences—General M
Biomedical Engineering M,D
Business Administration and Management—General M,D
Chemical Engineering M,D
Chemistry M
Civil Engineering M,D
Communication Disorders M,D
Computer Science M,D
Counseling Psychology M,D
Counselor Education M,D
Curriculum and Instruction M,D
Early Childhood Education M,D
Economics M,D
Education—General M,D
Educational Leadership and Administration M,D
Electrical Engineering M,D
Engineering and Applied Sciences—General M,D
English Education M,D
English M,O
Exercise and Sports Science M
Family and Consumer Sciences-General M
Finance and Banking M,D
Graphic Design M
Health Informatics M
Higher Education M,D
History M
Industrial and Organizational Psychology M,D
Industrial/Management Engineering M
Mathematics Education M,D
Mathematics M,D
Mechanical Engineering M,D
Molecular Biology M
Nutrition M
Organizational Management M,D
Photography M
Physical Education M
Physics M
Psychology—General M,D
Science Education M,D
Social Sciences Education M,D
Special Education M,D
Statistics M,D
Technical Writing M,O
Theater M

LOUISVILLE PRESBYTERIAN THEOLOGICAL SEMINARY
Religion M,D
Theology M,D

LOURDES UNIVERSITY
Business Administration and Management—General M
Curriculum and Instruction M
Educational Leadership and Administration M
Nurse Anesthesia M
Nursing and Healthcare Administration M
Nursing Education M
Organizational Management M
Reading Education M
Theology M

LOYOLA MARYMOUNT UNIVERSITY
Accounting M
Bioethics M
Business Administration and Management—General M
Civil Engineering M
Counseling Psychology M
Counselor Education M
Education—General M,D
Educational Leadership and Administration M,D
Elementary Education M
Engineering Management
English M
Environmental Sciences M
Film, Television, and Video Production M
Higher Education M
Law M,D
Marriage and Family Therapy M
Mathematics Education M
Mechanical Engineering M
Multilingual and Multicultural Education M
Pastoral Ministry and Counseling M
Philosophy M
Reading Education M
Recreation and Park Management M
Religious Education M
School Psychology M
Secondary Education M
Special Education M
Systems Engineering M
Theology M
Urban Education M
Writing M

LOYOLA UNIVERSITY CHICAGO
Accounting M
Adult Nursing M,D,O
Applied Statistics M
Biochemistry M,D
Bioethics D,O
Biological and Biomedical Sciences—General M,D
Business Administration and Management—General M
Cancer Biology/Oncology M,D,O
Cell Biology M,D
Chemistry M,D
Clinical Psychology M,D
Clinical Research M
Communication—General M
Computer Science M
Corporate and Organizational Communication M
Counseling Psychology D
Counselor Education M,O
Criminal Justice and Criminology M
Curriculum and Instruction M,D
Developmental Psychology M,D
Economics M
Education—General M,D,O
Educational Leadership and Administration M,D,O
Educational Measurement and Evaluation M,D
Educational Policy M,D
Elementary Education M,O
English as a Second Language M,O
English M,D
Entrepreneurship M
Ethics M
Family Nurse Practitioner Studies M,D,O
Finance and Banking M
Gerontological Nursing M,D,O
Health Law M,D
Health Services Management and Hospital Administration M,O
Higher Education M,D
History M,D
Human Resources Management M
Humanities M
Immunology M,D
Infectious Diseases M,D
Information Science M,D,O
International Affairs M,D
International Business M
Law M,D
Legal and Justice Studies M,O
Management Information Systems M
Marketing M
Mathematics M
Microbiology M,D
Molecular Biology M,D
Molecular Pharmacology M,D
Molecular Physiology M,D
Neuroscience M,D
Nursing and Healthcare Administration M,D,O
Nursing—General M,D,O
Nutrition M,D,O
Pastoral Ministry and Counseling M,O
Philosophy M,D
Physiology M,D
Political Science M,D
Psychology—General M,D
Public Health—General M
Public History M,D
Public Policy M
Reading Education M,O
School Psychology D,O
Secondary Education M,O
Social Psychology M,D,O
Social Work M,D,O
Sociology M,D
Software Engineering M
Spanish M
Special Education M,O
Statistics M
Supply Chain Management M
Taxation M,D
Theology M,D,O
Urban Studies M
Women's Health Nursing M,D,O

LOYOLA UNIVERSITY MARYLAND
Accounting M,O
Business Administration and Management—General M
Clinical Psychology M,D,O
Communication Disorders M
Computer and Information Systems Security O
Computer Science M
Counselor Education M,O
Curriculum and Instruction M
Early Childhood Education M,O
Education—General M,O
Educational Leadership and Administration M,O
Educational Media/Instructional Technology M
Elementary Education M,O
Finance and Banking M
International Business M
Liberal Studies M
Management Information Systems M
Marketing M
Media Studies M
Middle School Education M,O
Music Education M
Pastoral Ministry and Counseling M,D,O
Psychology—General M,D,O
Reading Education M
Secondary Education M,O
Software Engineering M
Special Education M,O
Theology M,O

LOYOLA UNIVERSITY NEW ORLEANS
Business Administration and Management—General M
Clinical Psychology M
Criminal Justice and Criminology M
Entrepreneurship M
Health Services Management and Hospital Administration M,D
Law M,D
Marketing M
Music M
Nursing—General M,D
Organizational Management M
Theology M,O
Therapies—Dance, Drama, and Music M

LUBBOCK CHRISTIAN UNIVERSITY
Theology M

LUTHERAN SCHOOL OF THEOLOGY AT CHICAGO
Pastoral Ministry and Counseling M,D
Theology M,D

LUTHERAN THEOLOGICAL SEMINARY AT GETTYSBURG
Pastoral Ministry and Counseling M,D
Religion M,D
Theology M,D

THE LUTHERAN THEOLOGICAL SEMINARY AT PHILADELPHIA
Pastoral Ministry and Counseling M,D,O
Religion M,D,O
Theology M,D,O

LUTHERAN THEOLOGICAL SEMINARY SASKATOON
Ethics M,D
Pastoral Ministry and Counseling M,D
Religion M,D
Theology M,D

LUTHER RICE COLLEGE & SEMINARY
Pastoral Ministry and Counseling M,D
Religion M,D
Theology M,D

LUTHER SEMINARY
Missions and Missiology M,D
Pastoral Ministry and Counseling M,D
Theology M,D

LYNCHBURG COLLEGE
Business Administration and Management—General M
Clinical Psychology M
Counseling Psychology M
Counselor Education M
Curriculum and Instruction M
Educational Leadership and Administration M,D
Higher Education M
History M
Music M
Nursing and Healthcare Administration M
Nursing—General M
Physical Therapy D
Reading Education M
School Psychology M
Science Education M
Special Education M

LYNDON STATE COLLEGE
Counselor Education M
Curriculum and Instruction M
Education—General M
Reading Education M
Science Education M
Special Education M

LYNN UNIVERSITY
Applied Psychology M
Aviation Management M
Business Administration and Management—General M
Communication—General M,O
Computer Art and Design M,O
Criminal Justice and Criminology M
Education of the Gifted M,D
Education—General M,D
Educational Leadership and Administration M,D
Educational Media/Instructional Technology M,O
Emergency Management M
Hospitality Management M
Human Resources Management M
International Business M
Internet and Interactive Multimedia M,O
Investment Management M
Marketing M
Mass Communication M,O
Media Studies M,O
Music M,O
Special Education M,D
Sports Management M

MAASTRICHT SCHOOL OF MANAGEMENT
Business Administration and Management—General M,D
Facilities Management M,D
Sustainability Management M,D

MACHZIKEI HADATH RABBINICAL COLLEGE
Theology O

MADONNA UNIVERSITY
Adult Nursing M
Business Administration and Management—General M
Clinical Psychology M
Criminal Justice and Criminology M
Education—General M
Educational Leadership and Administration M
English as a Second Language M
Health Services Management and Hospital Administration M
Hospice Nursing M
International Business M
Liberal Studies M
Nursing and Healthcare Administration M
Nursing—General M
Pastoral Ministry and Counseling M
Psychology—General M
Quality Management M
Reading Education M
Special Education M

Theology M

MAHARISHI UNIVERSITY OF MANAGEMENT
Accounting M,D
Asian Studies M,D
Business Administration and Management—General M,D
Computer Science M
Sustainability Management M,D

MAINE COLLEGE OF ART
Art/Fine Arts M

MAINE MARITIME ACADEMY
International Business M
Supply Chain Management M
Transportation Management M

MALONE UNIVERSITY
Business Administration and Management—General M
Counselor Education M
Curriculum and Instruction M
Education—General M
Educational Leadership and Administration M
Family Nurse Practitioner Studies M
Nursing—General M
Organizational Management M
Special Education M
Theology M

MANCHESTER UNIVERSITY
Athletic Training and Sports Medicine M
Pharmacy D

MANHATTAN COLLEGE
Applied Mathematics M
Business Administration and Management—General M
Chemical Engineering M
Civil Engineering M
Computer Engineering M
Counselor Education M,O
Database Systems M
Early Childhood Education M,O
Education—General M,O
Educational Leadership and Administration M,O
Educational Media/Instructional Technology M
Electrical Engineering M
Engineering and Applied Sciences—General M
Environmental Engineering M
Mathematics M
Mechanical Engineering M
Multilingual and Multicultural Education M,O
Organizational Management M
Special Education M,O
Student Affairs M,O

MANHATTAN SCHOOL OF MUSIC
Music M,D,O

MANHATTANVILLE COLLEGE
Accounting M
Art Education M
Business Education M
Corporate and Organizational Communication M
Early Childhood Education M
Education—General M,D,O*
Educational Leadership and Administration M,D,O
Elementary Education M
English as a Second Language M,O
English Education M
Entrepreneurship M
Exercise and Sports Science M,O
Finance and Banking M
Foreign Languages Education M
Health Promotion M,O
Human Resources Management M
International Business M
Investment Management M
Management Strategy and Policy M
Marketing M
Mathematics Education M
Middle School Education M
Music Education M
Organizational Management M
Reading Education M
Science Education M
Secondary Education M
Social Sciences Education M
Special Education M,O
Sports Management M
Urban Education M,O
Writing M

MANSFIELD UNIVERSITY OF PENNSYLVANIA
Art Education M
Education—General M
Elementary Education M
Information Studies M
Library Science M
Music M
Nursing—General M
Organizational Management M
Psychology—General M
Secondary Education M
Special Education M

MAPLE SPRINGS BAPTIST BIBLE COLLEGE AND SEMINARY
Pastoral Ministry and Counseling M,D,O
Religious Education M,D,O
Theology M,D,O

MARANATHA BAPTIST UNIVERSITY
Cultural Studies M
Education—General M
Pastoral Ministry and Counseling M

Religion M
Theology M

MARCONI INTERNATIONAL UNIVERSITY
Business Administration and Management—General M,D
Educational Leadership and Administration M,D
Educational Media/Instructional Technology M,D
International Business M,D

MARIAN UNIVERSITY (IN)
Education—General M
Osteopathic Medicine D

MARIAN UNIVERSITY (WI)
Adult Nursing M
Business Administration and Management—General M
Criminal Justice and Criminology M
Curriculum and Instruction M,D
Education—General M,D
Educational Leadership and Administration M,D
Educational Media/Instructional Technology M,D
Nursing Education M
Nursing—General M
Organizational Management M
Special Education M,D

MARIETTA COLLEGE
Physician Assistant Studies M
Psychology—General M

MARIST COLLEGE
Business Administration and Management—General M,O
Communication—General M
Computer Science M,O
Corporate and Organizational Communication M
Counseling Psychology M,O
Education—General M,O
Management Information Systems M,O
Management of Technology M,O
Marketing M
Museum Studies M
Psychology—General M,O
Public Administration M
School Psychology M,O
Software Engineering M,O

MARLBORO COLLEGE
Business Administration and Management—General M
Computer Education M,O
Education—General M,O
Educational Media/Instructional Technology M,O
English as a Second Language M
Food Science and Technology M
Internet and Interactive Multimedia M,O
Legal and Justice Studies M
Organizational Management M
Project Management M

MARQUETTE UNIVERSITY
Accounting M
Acute Care/Critical Care Nursing M,D,O
Adult Nursing M,D,O
Advertising and Public Relations M,O
Analytical Chemistry M,D
Bioinformatics M,D
Biological and Biomedical Sciences—General M,D
Biomedical Engineering M,D
Business Administration and Management—General M,O
Cardiovascular Sciences M
Cell Biology M,D
Chemical Physics M,D
Chemistry M,D
Civil Engineering M,D,O
Clinical Psychology M,D
Communication Disorders M,O
Communication—General M,O
Computational Sciences M,D
Computer Engineering M,D,O
Computer Science M,D
Construction Engineering M,D,O
Construction Management M,D,O
Counseling Psychology M,D
Counselor Education M,D
Curriculum and Instruction M,D,O
Dentistry D
Developmental Biology M,D
Ecology M,D
Economics M,O
Education—General M,D,O
Educational Leadership and Administration M,D,O
Educational Policy M,D,O
Electrical Engineering M,D,O
Elementary Education M,D,O
Engineering and Applied Sciences—General M,D,O
Engineering Management M,D,O
English M,D
Entrepreneurship M,O
Environmental Engineering M,D,O
Ethics M,D
Family Nurse Practitioner Studies M,D,O
Finance and Banking M,O
Foreign Languages Education M
Foundations and Philosophy of Education M,D,O
Genetics M,D
Gerontological Nursing M,D,O
Hazardous Materials Management M,D,O
Health Communication M,O
History M,D
Human Resources Development M
Human Resources Management M,O
Industrial and Manufacturing Management M,O
Inorganic Chemistry M,D
Interdisciplinary Studies D
International Affairs M,D
International Business M,O
Journalism M,O
Law D
Management Information Systems M,O
Management of Technology M,D
Marketing Research M
Marketing M,O
Mass Communication M,O
Mathematics Education M,D
Mathematics M,D
Mechanical Engineering M,D,O
Microbiology M,D
Molecular Biology M,D
Neuroscience M,D
Nurse Midwifery M,D,O
Nursing and Healthcare Administration M,D,O
Nursing—General M,D,O
Oral and Dental Sciences M,O
Organic Chemistry M,D
Pediatric Nursing M,D,O
Philosophy M,D
Physical Chemistry M,D
Physical Therapy D
Physician Assistant Studies M
Physiology M,D
Political Science M
Psychology—General D
Reading Education M,D,O
Real Estate M
Rehabilitation Sciences M,D
Secondary Education M,D,O
Social Psychology M,D
Spanish M
Speech and Interpersonal Communication M,O
Sports Management M,O
Structural Engineering M,D,O
Student Affairs M,D,O
Supply Chain Management M,O
Theology M,D
Transportation and Highway Engineering M,D,O
Water Resources Engineering M,D,O
Water Resources M,D,O

MARSHALL B. KETCHUM UNIVERSITY
Optometry M,D
Vision Sciences M,D

MARSHALL UNIVERSITY
Accounting M
Adult Education M
Advertising and Public Relations M
Allopathic Medicine D
Athletic Training and Sports Medicine M
Biological and Biomedical Sciences—General M,D
Business Administration and Management—General M
Chemistry M
Classics M,O
Clinical Psychology M,D,O
Communication Disorders M
Communication—General M
Computer Science M
Counselor Education M,O
Criminal Justice and Criminology M
Early Childhood Education M
Education—General M,D,O
Educational Leadership and Administration M,D,O
Elementary Education M,O
Engineering and Applied Sciences—General M
Engineering Management M
English M,O
Environmental Engineering M
Environmental Sciences M
Exercise and Sports Science M
Forensic Sciences M,O
Geography M,O
Health Education M
Health Informatics M
Health Services Management and Hospital Administration M
History M,O
Human Resources Management M
Humanities M,O
Information Science M
Journalism M
Management of Technology M
Mathematics M
Music M
Nurse Anesthesia D
Nursing—General M
Nutrition M
Pharmacy D
Physical Therapy D
Physics M
Political Science M
Psychology—General M,D,O
Public Administration M
Public Health—General M
Reading Education M,O
School Psychology O
Secondary Education M
Social Work M
Sociology M
Special Education M
Sports Management M
Transportation and Highway Engineering M
Vocational and Technical Education M

MARS HILL UNIVERSITY
Elementary Education M

MARTIN LUTHER COLLEGE
Curriculum and Instruction M
Early Childhood Education M
Education—General M
Educational Leadership and Administration M
Educational Media/Instructional Technology M
Special Education M

MARTIN UNIVERSITY
Pastoral Ministry and Counseling M
Psychology—General M
Social Psychology M

MARY BALDWIN COLLEGE
Education—General M
Elementary Education M
English M
Middle School Education M
Theater M

MARYGROVE COLLEGE
Education—General M
Educational Leadership and Administration M
Educational Media/Instructional Technology M
Elementary Education M
English M
Human Resources Management M
Legal and Justice Studies M
Reading Education M
Secondary Education M
Translation and Interpretation O
Urban Education M

MARYLAND INSTITUTE COLLEGE OF ART
Applied Arts and Design—General M
Art Education M
Art/Fine Arts M,O
Business Administration and Management—General M
Film, Television, and Video Production M
Graphic Design M,O
Illustration M
Media Studies M
Museum Studies M
Photography M

MARYLAND UNIVERSITY OF INTEGRATIVE HEALTH
Acupuncture and Oriental Medicine M,O

MARYLHURST UNIVERSITY
Art Therapy M,O
Business Administration and Management—General M
Counseling Psychology M,O
Education—General M
Elementary Education M
Health Services Management and Hospital Administration M
Hospitality Management M
Interdisciplinary Studies M
Real Estate M
Theology M

MARYMOUNT CALIFORNIA UNIVERSITY
Business Administration and Management—General M
International Development M
Social Psychology M

MARYMOUNT UNIVERSITY
Allied Health—General M,D,O
Business Administration and Management—General M,O
Clinical Psychology M,D
Community College Education M,O
Computer and Information Systems Security M,O
Counseling Psychology M,D
Counselor Education M,D
Education—General M
Elementary Education M
English as a Second Language M
English Education M,O
English M,O
Family Nurse Practitioner Studies M,D,O
Forensic Psychology M
Health Education M
Health Informatics M,O
Health Promotion M
Health Services Management and Hospital Administration M
Human Resources Management M,O
Interior Design M
Management Information Systems M,O
Nonprofit Management M,O
Nursing—General M,D,O
Pastoral Ministry and Counseling M,D
Physical Therapy D
Project Management M,O
Secondary Education M
Special Education M

MARYVILLE UNIVERSITY OF SAINT LOUIS
Accounting M,O
Actuarial Science M
Acute Care/Critical Care Nursing M,D
Addictions/Substance Abuse Counseling M
Adult Nursing M,D
Allied Health—General M,D
Art Education M,D
Business Administration and Management—General M,O
Business Education M,O
Computer and Information Systems Security M,O
Early Childhood Education M,D
Education of the Gifted M,D
Education—General M,D
Educational Leadership and Administration M,D
Elementary Education M,D
Family Nurse Practitioner Studies M,D
Finance and Banking M,O
Gerontological Nursing M,D
Health Services Management and Hospital Administration M,O
Higher Education M,D
Human Resources Management M,O
Information Science M,O
Logistics M,O
Marketing M,O
Marriage and Family Therapy M
Middle School Education M,D
Nursing—General M,D
Occupational Therapy M
Organizational Management M
Pediatric Nursing M,D
Physical Therapy D
Project Management M,O
Reading Education M,D
Rehabilitation Counseling M
Secondary Education M,D
Sports Management M,O
Supply Chain Management M,O
Therapies—Dance, Drama, and Music M

MARYWOOD UNIVERSITY
Architecture M
Art Education M
Art Therapy M,O
Art/Fine Arts M
Biotechnology M
Business Administration and Management—General M
Clinical Psychology M,D
Communication Disorders M
Communication—General M
Computer and Information Systems Security M
Counseling Psychology M
Counselor Education M
Criminal Justice and Criminology M
Early Childhood Education M
Education—General M
Educational Leadership and Administration M,D
Elementary Education M
Exercise and Sports Science M
Finance and Banking M
Gerontology M
Graphic Design M
Health Education D
Health Services Management and Hospital Administration M
Higher Education M,D
Human Development D
Illustration M
Interdisciplinary Studies D
Interior Design M
Investment Management M
Management Information Systems M
Music Education M
Nutrition M,O
Photography M
Physician Assistant Studies M
Psychology—General M
Public Administration M
Reading Education M
Secondary Education M
Social Work M,D
Special Education M

MASSACHUSETTS COLLEGE OF ART AND DESIGN
Applied Arts and Design—General M,O
Architecture M
Art Education M,O
Art/Fine Arts M,O
Film, Television, and Video Production M,O
Interdisciplinary Studies M,O
Media Studies M,O
Photography M,O
Textile Design M,O

MASSACHUSETTS COLLEGE OF LIBERAL ARTS
Business Administration and Management—General M,O
Curriculum and Instruction M,O
Education—General M,O
Educational Leadership and Administration M,O
Educational Media/Instructional Technology M,O
Health Education M,O
Physical Education M,O
Reading Education M,O
Special Education M,O

MASSACHUSETTS INSTITUTE OF TECHNOLOGY
Aerospace/Aeronautical Engineering M,D,O
Archaeology M,D,O

*M—masters degree; D—doctorate; O—other advanced degree; *—Close-Up and/or Display*

Architectural History	M,D
Architecture	M,D
Art History	M,D
Atmospheric Sciences	M,D
Biochemistry	D
Bioengineering	M,D
Bioinformatics	M,D
Biological and Biomedical Sciences—General	M,D
Biomedical Engineering	M,D
Business Administration and Management—General	M,D
Cell Biology	D
Chemical Engineering	M,D
Chemistry	D
Civil Engineering	M,D,O
Cognitive Sciences	D
Communication Disorders	M,D
Computational Biology	D
Computational Sciences	M
Computer Engineering	M,D,O
Computer Science	M,D,O
Construction Engineering	M,D,O
Developmental Biology	D
Economics	M,D
Electrical Engineering	M,D,O
Engineering and Applied Sciences—General	M,D,O
Environmental Biology	M,D,O
Environmental Engineering	M,D,O
Environmental Sciences	M,D,O
Genetics	D
Genomic Sciences	M,D
Geochemistry	M,D
Geology	M,D
Geophysics	M,D
Geosciences	M,D
Geotechnical Engineering	M,D,O
History of Science and Technology	D
Hydrology	M,D,O
Immunology	D
Information Science	M,D,O
Inorganic Chemistry	D
Linguistics	D
Manufacturing Engineering	M,D,O
Marine Geology	M,D
Materials Engineering	M,D,O
Materials Sciences	M,D,O
Mathematics	D
Mechanical Engineering	M,D,O
Media Studies	M,D
Medical Physics	M,D
Microbiology	D
Molecular Biology	D
Molecular Toxicology	D
Neurobiology	D
Neuroscience	D
Nuclear Engineering	M,D,O
Ocean Engineering	M,D,O
Oceanography	M,D,O
Operations Research	M,D
Organic Chemistry	M,D,O
Philosophy	D
Physical Chemistry	D
Physics	M,D
Planetary and Space Sciences	M,D
Political Science	M,D
Real Estate	M
Social Sciences	D
Structural Biology	D
Structural Engineering	M,D,O
Systems Biology	D
Systems Engineering	M
Technical Writing	M
Technology and Public Policy	M,D
Toxicology	M,D
Transportation and Highway Engineering	M,D,O
Urban and Regional Planning	M,D
Urban Studies	M,D
Writing	M

MASSACHUSETTS MARITIME ACADEMY

Emergency Management	M
Facilities Management	M

MASSACHUSETTS SCHOOL OF LAW AT ANDOVER

Law	D

THE MASTER'S COLLEGE AND SEMINARY

Pastoral Ministry and Counseling	M,D
Theology	M,D

MAYO GRADUATE SCHOOL

Biochemistry	D
Biological and Biomedical Sciences—General	D
Biomedical Engineering	D
Cancer Biology/Oncology	D
Cell Biology	D
Genetics	D
Immunology	D
Molecular Biology	D
Molecular Pharmacology	D
Neuroscience	D
Structural Biology	D
Virology	D

MAYO MEDICAL SCHOOL

Allopathic Medicine	D

MAYO SCHOOL OF HEALTH SCIENCES

Nurse Anesthesia	D
Physical Therapy	D

MCCORMICK THEOLOGICAL SEMINARY

Pastoral Ministry and Counseling	M,D,O
Theology	M,D,O

MCDANIEL COLLEGE

Counselor Education	M
Curriculum and Instruction	M
Educational Leadership and Administration	M
Educational Media/Instructional Technology	M
Elementary Education	M
English as a Second Language	M
Exercise and Sports Science	M
Gerontology	M,O*
Human Resources Development	M
Human Services	M
Liberal Studies	M
Library Science	M
Physical Education	M
Reading Education	M
Secondary Education	M
Special Education	M

MCGILL UNIVERSITY

Accounting	M,D,O
Aerospace/Aeronautical Engineering	M,D
Agricultural Economics and Agribusiness	M
Agricultural Engineering	M,D
Agricultural Sciences—General	M,D,O
Agronomy and Soil Sciences	M,D
Allopathic Medicine	M,D
Anatomy	M,D
Animal Sciences	M,D
Anthropology	M,D
Applied Mathematics	M,D
Architecture	M,D,O
Art History	M,D
Asian Studies	M,D
Atmospheric Sciences	M,D
Biochemistry	M,D
Bioengineering	M,D
Bioethics	M,D,O
Bioinformatics	M,D
Biological and Biomedical Sciences—General	M,D
Biomedical Engineering	M,D
Biostatistics	M,D,O
Biotechnology	M,D,O
Business Administration and Management—General	M,D,O
Cell Biology	M,D
Chemical Engineering	M,D
Chemistry	M,D
Civil Engineering	M,D
Clinical Psychology	M,D
Communication Disorders	M,D
Communication—General	M,D
Community Health	M,D,O
Computational Sciences	M,D
Computer Engineering	M,D
Computer Science	M,D
Counseling Psychology	M,D,O
Curriculum and Instruction	M,D,O
Dentistry	M,D,O
Developmental Psychology	M,D,O
Economics	M,D
Education—General	M,D,O
Educational Leadership and Administration	M,D,O
Educational Psychology	M,D,O
Electrical Engineering	M,D
Engineering and Applied Sciences—General	M,D,O
English	M,D
Entomology	M,D
Entrepreneurship	M,D,O
Environmental and Occupational Health	M,D,O
Environmental Engineering	M,D
Environmental Management and Policy	M,D
Epidemiology	M,D,O
Experimental Psychology	M,D
Family Nurse Practitioner Studies	M,D,O
Finance and Banking	M,D,O
Fish, Game, and Wildlife Management	M,D
Food Science and Technology	M,D
Foreign Languages Education	M,D,O
Forensic Sciences	M,D,O
Forestry	M,D
Foundations and Philosophy of Education	M,D,O
French	M,D
Genetic Counseling	M,D
Geography	M,D
Geosciences	M,D
Geotechnical Engineering	M,D
German	M,D
Health Services Management and Hospital Administration	M,D,O
Hispanic Studies	M,D
History of Medicine	M,D
History	M,D
Human Genetics	M,D
Hydraulics	M,D
Immunology	M,D
Industrial and Manufacturing Management	M,D,O
Information Studies	M,D,O
International Business	M,D,O
International Development	M,D,O
Italian	M,D
Jewish Studies	M
Kinesiology and Movement Studies	M,D,O
Law	M,D,O
Library Science	M,D,O
Linguistics	M,D
Management Information Systems	M,D,O
Management Strategy and Policy	M,D,O
Marketing	M,D,O
Materials Engineering	M,D,O
Mathematics	M,D
Mechanical Engineering	M,D
Mechanics	M,D
Medical Physics	M,D
Meteorology	M,D
Microbiology	M,D
Mineral/Mining Engineering	M,D,O
Music Education	M,D
Music	M,D
Natural Resources	M,D
Near and Middle Eastern Studies	M,D,O
Neuroscience	M,D
Nursing—General	M,D,O
Nutrition	M,D,O
Oceanography	M,D
Oral and Dental Sciences	M,D,O
Parasitology	M,D,O
Pathology	M,D
Pharmacology	M,D
Philosophy	M,D
Physical Education	M,D,O
Physics	M,D
Physiology	M,D
Planetary and Space Sciences	M,D
Plant Sciences	M,D,O
Political Science	M,D
Psychology—General	M,D
Rehabilitation Sciences	M,D,O
Religion	M,D
Russian	M,D
School Psychology	M,D,O
Social Work	M,D,O
Sociology	M,D,O
Statistics	M,D,O
Structural Engineering	M,D
Theology	M,D
Transportation Management	M,D
Urban and Regional Planning	M,D
Water Resources Engineering	M,D

MCKENDREE UNIVERSITY

Business Administration and Management—General	M
Clinical Psychology	M
Counseling Psychology	M
Curriculum and Instruction	M,D,O
Education—General	M,D,O
Educational Leadership and Administration	M,D,O
Higher Education	M,D,O
Human Resources Management	M
International Business	M
Music Education	M,D,O
Nursing and Healthcare Administration	M
Nursing Education	M
Nursing—General	M
Reading Education	M,D,O
Special Education	M,D,O

MCMASTER UNIVERSITY

Analytical Chemistry	M,D
Anthropology	M,D
Applied Statistics	M
Astrophysics	D
Biochemistry	M,D
Biological and Biomedical Sciences—General	M,D
Business Administration and Management—General	M,D
Cancer Biology/Oncology	M,D
Cardiovascular Sciences	M,D
Cell Biology	M,D
Chemical Engineering	M,D
Chemical Physics	M,D
Chemistry	M,D
Civil Engineering	M,D
Classics	M,D
Computer Science	M,D
Cultural Studies	M,D
Economics	M,D
Electrical Engineering	M,D
Engineering and Applied Sciences—General	M,D
Engineering Physics	M,D
English	M,D
French	M
Genetics	M,D
Geochemistry	M,D
Geography	M,D
Geology	M,D
Geosciences	M,D
Health Physics/Radiological Health	M,D
Health Services Research	M,D
History	M,D
Human Resources Management	M,D
Immunology	M,D
Industrial and Labor Relations	M
Inorganic Chemistry	M,D
International Affairs	M,D
Kinesiology and Movement Studies	M,D
Management Information Systems	D
Materials Engineering	M,D
Materials Sciences	M,D
Mathematics	M,D
Mechanical Engineering	M,D
Medical Physics	M,D
Molecular Biology	M,D
Neuroscience	M,D
Nuclear Engineering	M,D
Nursing—General	M,D
Nutrition	M,D
Occupational Therapy	M
Organic Chemistry	M,D
Pastoral Ministry and Counseling	M,D,O
Pharmacology	M,D
Philosophy	M,D
Physical Chemistry	M,D
Physical Therapy	M
Physics	D
Physiology	M,D
Political Science	M,D
Psychology—General	M,D
Public Administration	M,D
Public Affairs	M,D
Public Policy	M,D
Rehabilitation Sciences	M,D
Religion	M,D
Social Work	M
Sociology	M,D
Software Engineering	M,D
Statistics	M
Theology	M,D,O
Virology	M,D

MCMURRY UNIVERSITY

Family Nurse Practitioner Studies	M
Nursing Education	M
Nursing—General	M

MCNALLY SMITH COLLEGE OF MUSIC

Music	M

MCNEESE STATE UNIVERSITY

Addictions/Substance Abuse Counseling	M
Agricultural Sciences—General	M
Applied Behavior Analysis	M
Business Administration and Management—General	M
Chemical Engineering	M
Chemistry	M
Civil Engineering	M
Computer Science	M
Counseling Psychology	M
Counselor Education	M,O
Criminal Justice and Criminology	M
Curriculum and Instruction	M
Early Childhood Education	M,O
Education—General	O
Educational Leadership and Administration	M,O
Educational Measurement and Evaluation	M,O
Educational Media/Instructional Technology	M,O
Electrical Engineering	M
Elementary Education	M,O
Engineering and Applied Sciences—General	M,O
Engineering Management	M
English	M
Environmental Sciences	M
Exercise and Sports Science	M
Experimental Psychology	M
Family Nurse Practitioner Studies	M,O
Health Promotion	M
Library Science	O
Mathematics	M
Mechanical Engineering	M,O
Middle School Education	O
Music Education	O
Nursing and Healthcare Administration	M,O
Nursing Education	M
Nursing—General	M,O
Nutrition	M
Psychiatric Nursing	M,O
Psychology—General	M
Reading Education	M,O
School Psychology	M
Science Education	M
Secondary Education	M,O
Special Education	M,O
Statistics	M
Writing	M

MCPHERSON COLLEGE

Education—General	M

MCPHS UNIVERSITY

Acupuncture and Oriental Medicine	M
Chemistry	M,D
Health Services Management and Hospital Administration	M
Nursing—General	M
Pharmaceutical Sciences	M,D
Pharmacology	M,D
Pharmacy	D
Physician Assistant Studies	M

MEADVILLE LOMBARD THEOLOGICAL SCHOOL

Pastoral Ministry and Counseling	M,D
Theology	M,D

MEDAILLE COLLEGE

Business Administration and Management—General	M
Clinical Psychology	M,D
Counseling Psychology	M,D
Curriculum and Instruction	M
Education—General	M
Elementary Education	M
Marriage and Family Therapy	M,D
Organizational Management	M
Psychology—General	M,D
Reading Education	M
Secondary Education	M
Special Education	M

MEDICAL COLLEGE OF WISCONSIN

Allopathic Medicine	D
Biochemistry	D
Bioethics	M,O
Bioinformatics	M
Biological and Biomedical Sciences—General	M,D,O
Biophysics	D
Biostatistics	D*
Clinical Laboratory Sciences/Medical Technology	M,D
Clinical Research	M
Community Health	M,D,O
Epidemiology	M,D,O
Medical Imaging	D
Medical Informatics	M
Microbiology	M,D
Molecular Genetics	M,D
Neuroscience	D
Pharmacology	D
Physiology	D
Public Health—General	M,D,O
Toxicology	D

MEDICAL UNIVERSITY OF SOUTH CAROLINA

Adult Nursing	M,D
Allied Health—General	M,D
Allopathic Medicine	D
Biochemistry	M,D
Biological and Biomedical Sciences—General	M,D
Biostatistics	M,D
Cancer Biology/Oncology	D
Cardiovascular Sciences	D
Cell Biology	D
Clinical Research	M
Dentistry	D
Developmental Biology	D
Epidemiology	M,D
Family Nurse Practitioner Studies	M,D
Genetics	D
Gerontological Nursing	M,D
Health Services Management and Hospital Administration	M,D
Immunology	M,D
International Health	M
Marine Sciences	D
Maternal and Child/Neonatal Nursing	M,D
Medical Imaging	D
Medicinal and Pharmaceutical Chemistry	D
Microbiology	M,D
Molecular Biology	M,D
Molecular Pharmacology	M,D
Neuroscience	M,D
Nurse Anesthesia	M
Nursing and Healthcare Administration	M
Nursing Education	M
Nursing—General	D
Occupational Therapy	M
Pathobiology	D
Pathology	M,D
Pharmacy	D
Physical Therapy	D
Physician Assistant Studies	M
Rehabilitation Sciences	D
Toxicology	D

MEHARRY MEDICAL COLLEGE

Allopathic Medicine	D
Biological and Biomedical Sciences—General	D
Cancer Biology/Oncology	D
Community Health	M
Dentistry	D
Environmental and Occupational Health	M
Health Services Management and Hospital Administration	M
Immunology	D
Microbiology	D
Neuroscience	D
Pharmacology	D

MELBOURNE BUSINESS SCHOOL

Business Administration and Management—General	M,D,O
Marketing	M,D,O

MEMORIAL UNIVERSITY OF NEWFOUNDLAND

Adult Education	M,D,O
Anthropology	M,D
Aquaculture	M
Archaeology	M,D
Biochemistry	M,D
Biological and Biomedical Sciences—General	M,D,O
Biopsychology	M,D
Business Administration and Management—General	M
Cancer Biology/Oncology	M,D
Cardiovascular Sciences	M,D
Chemistry	M,D
Civil Engineering	M,D
Classics	M
Clinical Psychology	M,D
Clinical Research	M
Community Health	M,D,O
Computational Sciences	M
Computer Engineering	M,D
Computer Science	M,D
Condensed Matter Physics	M,D
Cultural Anthropology	M,D
Curriculum and Instruction	M,D,O
Economics	M
Education—General	M,D,O
Educational Leadership and Administration	M,D,O
Educational Media/Instructional Technology	M,D,O
Educational Psychology	M,D,O
Electrical Engineering	M,D
Engineering and Applied Sciences—General	M,D
English	M,D
Environmental Engineering	M
Environmental Sciences	M,D
Epidemiology	M,D,O
Exercise and Sports Science	M
Experimental Psychology	M,D
Fish, Game, and Wildlife Management	M,O
Folklore	M,D
Food Science and Technology	M,D
French	M
Gender Studies	M,D
Geography	M,D
Geology	M,D
Geophysics	M,D
Geosciences	M,D
German	M
History	M,D
Human Genetics	M,D
Humanities	M
Immunology	M,D
Industrial and Labor Relations	M
Kinesiology and Movement Studies	M
Linguistics	M,D
Marine Affairs	M,D,O
Marine Sciences	M,O
Mathematics	M,D
Mechanical Engineering	M,D
Music	M,D
Neuroscience	M,D
Nursing—General	M,D
Ocean Engineering	M,D
Oceanography	M,D
Pharmaceutical Sciences	M,D
Philosophy	M,D
Physical Education	M
Physics	M,D
Political Science	M
Psychology—General	M,D
Religion	M
Social Work	M,D
Sociology	M,D
Statistics	M,D

MEMPHIS COLLEGE OF ART

Applied Arts and Design—General	M
Art Education	M
Art/Fine Arts	M
Illustration	M
Photography	M

MEMPHIS THEOLOGICAL SEMINARY

Theology	M,D

MERCER UNIVERSITY

Accounting	M
Allopathic Medicine	M,D
Biomedical Engineering	M
Business Administration and Management—General	M
Clinical Psychology	M,D
Computer Engineering	M
Counselor Education	M,D
Curriculum and Instruction	M,D,O
Early Childhood Education	M,D,O
Education—General	M,D,O
Educational Leadership and Administration	M,D,O
Electrical Engineering	M
Engineering and Applied Sciences—General	M
Engineering Management	M
Entrepreneurship	M
Environmental and Occupational Health	M,D
Environmental Engineering	M
Environmental Sciences	M
Gerontological Nursing	M,D,O
Gerontology	M,D
Higher Education	M,D,O
Human Services	M,D
Law	D
Management of Technology	M
Management Strategy and Policy	M
Mechanical Engineering	M
Middle School Education	M,D,O
Music	M
Nursing—General	M,D,O
Organizational Management	M,D
Pastoral Ministry and Counseling	M,D
Pharmaceutical Sciences	D
Pharmacy	D
Physical Therapy	M,D
Physician Assistant Studies	M,D
Public Health—General	M,D
Reading Education	M,D,O
Rehabilitation Counseling	M,D
School Psychology	M,D
Secondary Education	M,D,O
Software Engineering	M
Theology	M,D

MERCY COLLEGE

Accounting	M
Allied Health—General	M,D
Business Administration and Management—General	M
Communication Disorders	M
Computer and Information Systems Security	M
Counseling Psychology	M,O
Counselor Education	M,O
Early Childhood Education	M
Education—General	M,O
Educational Leadership and Administration	M,O
Elementary Education	M
English as a Second Language	M,O
English	M
Health Services Management and Hospital Administration	M
Human Resources Management	M
Marriage and Family Therapy	M,O
Nursing and Healthcare Administration	M
Nursing Education	M
Nursing—General	M
Occupational Therapy	M
Organizational Management	M
Physical Therapy	D
Physician Assistant Studies	M
Psychology—General	M
Reading Education	M,O
School Psychology	M
Secondary Education	M

MERCYHURST UNIVERSITY

Accounting	M,O
Anthropology	M
Applied Behavior Analysis	M
Archaeology	M
Biological Anthropology	M
Computer and Information Systems Security	M
Criminal Justice and Criminology	M,O
Educational Leadership and Administration	M,O
Entrepreneurship	M,O
Forensic Sciences	M
Higher Education	M,O
Human Resources Management	M,O
Management Strategy and Policy	M,O
Organizational Management	M,O
Physician Assistant Studies	M
Secondary Education	M
Special Education	M
Sports Management	M,O

MEREDITH COLLEGE

Business Administration and Management—General	M
Education—General	M
Nutrition	M,O

MERRIMACK COLLEGE

Accounting	M
Adult Education	M,O
Business Administration and Management—General	M
Civil Engineering	M
Clinical Psychology	M
Community Health	M
Computer Science	M
Criminal Justice and Criminology	M,O
Curriculum and Instruction	M,O
Early Childhood Education	M,O
Education—General	M,O
Educational Leadership and Administration	M,O
Elementary Education	M,O
Engineering and Applied Sciences—General	M
Engineering Management	M
English as a Second Language	M,O
Exercise and Sports Science	M
Health Promotion	M
Higher Education	M,O
Mechanical Engineering	M
Middle School Education	M,O
Public Affairs	M
School Psychology	M,O
Secondary Education	M,O
Special Education	M,O
Student Affairs	M,O

MESIVTA OF EASTERN PARKWAY–YESHIVA ZICHRON MEILECH

Theology

MESIVTA TORAH VODAATH RABBINICAL SEMINARY

Theology

MESIVTHA TIFERETH JERUSALEM OF AMERICA

Theology

MESSIAH COLLEGE

Business Administration and Management—General	M,O
Clinical Psychology	M,O
Counseling Psychology	M,O
Counselor Education	M,O
Curriculum and Instruction	M
English as a Second Language	M
Higher Education	M
Management Strategy and Policy	M,O
Marriage and Family Therapy	M,O
Music	M
Nursing Education	M
Organizational Management	M,O
Special Education	M
Sports Management	M
Student Affairs	M

METHODIST THEOLOGICAL SCHOOL IN OHIO

Theology	M,D

METHODIST UNIVERSITY

Business Administration and Management—General	M
Criminal Justice and Criminology	M
Physician Assistant Studies	M

METROPOLITAN COLLEGE OF NEW YORK

Business Administration and Management—General	M
Elementary Education	M
Emergency Management	M
Finance and Banking	M
Health Services Management and Hospital Administration	M
Media Studies	M
Public Administration	M
Public Affairs	M
Special Education	M

METROPOLITAN STATE UNIVERSITY

Business Administration and Management—General	M,D,O
Computer and Information Systems Security	M,D,O
Computer Science	M
Criminal Justice and Criminology	M
Database Systems	M,D,O
Health Informatics	M,D,O
Information Studies	M,D,O
Liberal Studies	M
Management Information Systems	M,D,O
Nonprofit Management	M,D,O
Nursing and Healthcare Administration	M,D
Nursing Education	M,D
Nursing—General	M,D
Oral and Dental Sciences	M,D
Project Management	M,D,O
Psychology—General	M,D
Public Administration	M,D,O
Technical Writing	M

METROPOLITAN STATE UNIVERSITY OF DENVER

Accounting	M
Education—General	M
Elementary Education	M
Social Work	M
Special Education	M

MGH INSTITUTE OF HEALTH PROFESSIONS

Communication Disorders	M,O
Gerontological Nursing	M,D,O
Nursing Education	M,D,O
Nursing—General	M,D,O
Occupational Therapy	D
Pediatric Nursing	M,D,O
Physical Therapy	M,D,O
Physician Assistant Studies	M
Psychiatric Nursing	M,D,O
Reading Education	M,O
Women's Health Nursing	M,D,O

MIAMI INTERNATIONAL UNIVERSITY OF ART & DESIGN

Applied Arts and Design—General	M
Film, Television, and Video Production	M

MIAMI UNIVERSITY

Accounting	M
Architecture	M
Art Education	M
Art/Fine Arts	M
Biochemistry	M,D
Biological and Biomedical Sciences—General	M,D
Business Administration and Management—General	M
Chemical Engineering	M
Chemistry	M,D
Child and Family Studies	M
Communication Disorders	M
Computer Engineering	M
Demography and Population Studies	M,D
Economics	M
Education—General	M,D,O
Educational Psychology	M,O
Electrical Engineering	M
Engineering and Applied Sciences—General	M
English	M,D
Environmental Sciences	M
Exercise and Sports Science	M
French	M
Geography	M
Geology	M,D
Gerontology	M,D
History	M
Interior Design	M
Mathematics Education	M
Mathematics	M
Mechanical Engineering	M
Microbiology	M,D
Music Education	M
Music	M
Philosophy	M
Physics	M
Political Science	M
Psychology—General	M,D
Statistics	M
Systems Science	M
Theater	M

MICHIGAN SCHOOL OF PROFESSIONAL PSYCHOLOGY

Clinical Psychology	M,D
Educational Psychology	M,D
Psychology—General	M,D
Transpersonal and Humanistic Psychology	M,D

MICHIGAN STATE UNIVERSITY

Accounting	M,D
Adult Education	M,D,O
Advertising and Public Relations	M,D
African Studies	M,D
African-American Studies	M,D
Agricultural Economics and Agribusiness	M,D
Agricultural Sciences—General	M,D
Agronomy and Soil Sciences	M,D
Allopathic Medicine	D
American Studies	M,D
Animal Sciences	M,D
Anthropology	M,D
Applied Mathematics	M,D
Applied Statistics	M,D
Art/Fine Arts	M
Astronomy	M,D
Astrophysics	M,D
Biochemistry	M,D
Biological and Biomedical Sciences—General	M,D
Biosystems Engineering	M,D
Business Administration and Management—General	M,D
Cell Biology	M,D
Chemical Engineering	M,D

*M—masters degree; D—doctorate; O—other advanced degree; *—Close-Up and/or Display*

Chemical Physics M,D
Chemistry M,D
Child and Family Studies M,D
Child Development M,D
Civil Engineering M,D
Clinical Laboratory Sciences/Medical Technology M
Communication Disorders M,D
Communication—General M,D
Computer Art and Design M
Computer Science M,D
Construction Management M,D
Counselor Education M,D,O
Criminal Justice and Criminology M,D
Curriculum and Instruction M,D,O
Ecology D
Economics M,D
Education—General M,D,O
Educational Leadership and Administration M,D,O
Educational Measurement and Evaluation M,D,O
Educational Media/Instructional Technology M,D,O
Educational Policy D
Educational Psychology M,D,O
Electrical Engineering M,D
Engineering and Applied Sciences—General M,D
English as a Second Language M,D
English M,D
Entomology M,D
Environmental Design M,D
Environmental Engineering M,D
Environmental Sciences M,D
Epidemiology M,D
Evolutionary Biology D
Finance and Banking M,D
Fish, Game, and Wildlife Management M,D
Food Science and Technology M,D
Foreign Languages Education D
Forensic Sciences M,D
Forestry M,D
French M,D
Game Design and Development M
Genetics M,D
Geography M,D
Geosciences M,D
German M,D
Health Communication M
Higher Education M,D,O
Hispanic and Latin American Languages M,D
Hispanic Studies M,D
History M,D
Horticulture M,D
Hospitality Management M
Human Resources Management M,D
Industrial and Labor Relations M,D
Interior Design M,D
Journalism M
Kinesiology and Movement Studies M,D
Latin American Studies D
Linguistics M,D
Logistics M,D
Management Information Systems M,D
Management Strategy and Policy M,D
Manufacturing Engineering M,D
Marketing Research M,D
Marketing M,D
Marriage and Family Therapy M,D
Materials Engineering M,D
Materials Sciences M,D
Mathematics Education M,D
Mathematics M,D
Mechanical Engineering M,D
Mechanics M,D
Media Studies M,D
Microbiology M,D
Molecular Biology M,D
Molecular Genetics M,D
Music Education M,D
Music M,D
Natural Resources M,D
Neuroscience M,D
Nursing—General M,D
Nutrition M,D
Osteopathic Medicine D
Pathobiology M,D
Pathology M,D
Pharmacology M,D
Philosophy M,D
Physics M,D
Physiology M,D
Plant Biology M,D
Plant Pathology M,D
Plant Sciences M,D
Political Science M,D
Portuguese M,D
Psychology—General M,D
Public Health—General M
Reading Education M
Recreation and Park Management M,D
Rehabilitation Counseling M,D,O
Rhetoric M,D
Romance Languages M,D
School Psychology M,D,O
Science Education M,D
Social Sciences Education M,D
Social Work M,D
Sociology M,D
Spanish M,D
Special Education M,D,O
Statistics M,D
Structural Biology D
Supply Chain Management M,D
Systems Biology D
Taxation M,D
Telecommunications M
Theater M
Therapies—Dance, Drama, and Music M,D
Toxicology M,D
Urban and Regional Planning M,D
Veterinary Medicine D
Veterinary Sciences M,D
Writing M,D
Zoology M,D

MICHIGAN STATE UNIVERSITY COLLEGE OF LAW
Intellectual Property Law M,D
Law M,D
Legal and Justice Studies M,D

MICHIGAN TECHNOLOGICAL UNIVERSITY
Accounting M
Applied Physics M,D
Archaeology M,D
Atmospheric Sciences M,D,O
Automotive Engineering M,D,O
Biochemistry M,D,O
Biological and Biomedical Sciences—General M,D
Biomedical Engineering M,D
Business Administration and Management—General M
Chemical Engineering M,D
Chemistry M,D
Civil Engineering M,D
Cognitive Sciences M,D,O
Computational Sciences M,D,O
Computer Engineering M,D,O
Computer Science M,D
Cultural Studies M,D
Database Systems M,D,O
Ecology M,D
Electrical Engineering M,D,O
Energy Management and Policy M,D
Engineering and Applied Sciences—General M,D,O
Engineering Physics M,D
Environmental Engineering M,D,O
Environmental Management and Policy M,D
Ergonomics and Human Factors M,D,O
Forestry M,D
Geographic Information Systems M,D
Geological Engineering M,D
Geology M,D
Geophysics M,D
Historic Preservation M,D
Interdisciplinary Studies M,D,O
Kinesiology and Movement Studies M
Materials Engineering M,D
Mathematics M,D
Mechanical Engineering M,D,O
Mechanics M,D,O
Medical Informatics M
Metallurgical Engineering and Metallurgy M,D
Mineral Economics M
Mineral/Mining Engineering M,D
Molecular Biology M,D,O
Nanotechnology M,D,O
Physics M,D
Plant Molecular Biology M,D
Rhetoric M,D
Science Education M,D,O
Sustainability Management M,D,O
Water Resources M,D,O

MID-AMERICA BAPTIST THEOLOGICAL SEMINARY
Theology M,D

MID-AMERICA BAPTIST THEOLOGICAL SEMINARY NORTHEAST BRANCH
Theology M

MID-AMERICA CHRISTIAN UNIVERSITY
Business Administration and Management—General M
Counseling Psychology M
Marriage and Family Therapy M
Organizational Management M
Pastoral Ministry and Counseling M
Public Administration M

MIDAMERICA NAZARENE UNIVERSITY
Business Administration and Management—General M
Education—General M
Educational Media/Instructional Technology M
English as a Second Language M
Nursing and Healthcare Administration M
Nursing Education M
Public Health—General M
Reading Education M
Special Education M

MID-AMERICA REFORMED SEMINARY
Theology M

MIDDLEBURY COLLEGE
Chinese M
English M
French M,D
German M,D
Italian M,D
Near and Middle Eastern Languages M
Russian M,D
Spanish M,D

MIDDLEBURY INSTITUTE OF INTERNATIONAL STUDIES AT MONTEREY
Business Administration and Management—General M
Conflict Resolution and Mediation/Peace Studies M
English as a Second Language M
Environmental Management and Policy M
Foreign Languages Education M
International Affairs M
International and Comparative Education M
International Business M
International Development M
International Trade Policy M
Management Strategy and Policy M
Public Administration M
Translation and Interpretation M

MIDDLE GEORGIA STATE UNIVERSITY
Computer and Information Systems Security M
Forensic Sciences M
Gerontological Nursing M
Health Informatics M
Management Information Systems M

MIDDLE TENNESSEE SCHOOL OF ANESTHESIA
Nurse Anesthesia M,D

MIDDLE TENNESSEE STATE UNIVERSITY
Accounting M
Actuarial Science M
Aerospace/Aeronautical Engineering M
Archives/Archival Administration M,D,O
Aviation Management M
Biological and Biomedical Sciences—General M
Biostatistics M
Biotechnology M
Business Administration and Management—General M
Business Education M
Chemistry M
Clinical Psychology M,O
Computational Sciences D
Computer Science M
Counseling Psychology M
Counselor Education M
Criminal Justice and Criminology M
Curriculum and Instruction M,O
Early Childhood Education M,O
Economics M,D
Education—General M,D,O
Educational Leadership and Administration M,O
Educational Media/Instructional Technology M,O
Elementary Education M,O
Engineering Management M
English as a Second Language M,O
English M,D
Exercise and Sports Science M,D
Experimental Psychology M,O
Family Nurse Practitioner Studies M,O
Foreign Languages Education M
French M
Gender Studies O
Geosciences O
German M
Gerontology O
Health Education M
History M
Human Resources Management M
Industrial and Organizational Psychology M,O
International Affairs M
Management Information Systems M
Management Strategy and Policy M
Mass Communication M
Mathematics Education M,D
Mathematics M
Medical Informatics M
Middle School Education M,O
Molecular Biology D
Music M
Nursing and Healthcare Administration M
Nursing Education M
Nursing—General M,O
Physical Education M
Political Science M
Psychology—General M,O
Public History D
Reading Education M,D
Recreation and Park Management M
School Psychology M,O
Science Education M,D
Secondary Education M,O
Social Work M
Sociology M
Spanish M
Special Education M
Vocational and Technical Education M
Women's Studies O

MIDWAY UNIVERSITY
Business Administration and Management—General M
Education—General M
Organizational Management M

MIDWEST COLLEGE OF ORIENTAL MEDICINE
Acupuncture and Oriental Medicine M,O

MIDWESTERN BAPTIST THEOLOGICAL SEMINARY
Music M,D,O
Pastoral Ministry and Counseling M,D,O
Religious Education M,D,O
Theology M,D,O

MIDWESTERN STATE UNIVERSITY
Biological and Biomedical Sciences—General M
Business Administration and Management—General M
Clinical Psychology M
Community Health M,O
Computer Science M
Counseling Psychology M
Counselor Education M
Criminal Justice and Criminology M,O
Curriculum and Instruction M
Education—General M
Educational Leadership and Administration M
Educational Media/Instructional Technology M
English M,D
Exercise and Sports Science M
Family Nurse Practitioner Studies M
Health Informatics M,O
Health Physics/Radiological Health M
Health Services Management and Hospital Administration M,O
History M
Human Resources Development M
Nursing Education M
Nursing—General M
Philosophy M,D
Political Science M
Psychiatric Nursing M
Reading Education M
Special Education M
Sports Management M

MIDWESTERN UNIVERSITY, DOWNERS GROVE CAMPUS
Allied Health—General D
Biological and Biomedical Sciences—General M
Clinical Psychology M,D
Dentistry D
Occupational Therapy M
Osteopathic Medicine D
Pharmacy D
Physical Therapy D
Physician Assistant Studies M

MIDWESTERN UNIVERSITY, GLENDALE CAMPUS
Allied Health—General M,D
Biological and Biomedical Sciences—General M
Cardiovascular Sciences M
Clinical Psychology D
Dentistry D
Nurse Anesthesia M
Occupational Therapy M
Optometry D
Osteopathic Medicine D
Pharmacy D
Physical Therapy D
Physician Assistant Studies M
Podiatric Medicine D

MIDWIVES COLLEGE OF UTAH
Nurse Midwifery M

MILLENNIA ATLANTIC UNIVERSITY
Accounting M
Business Administration and Management—General M
Health Informatics M
Human Resources Management M

MILLERSVILLE UNIVERSITY OF PENNSYLVANIA
Adult Education M,D
Applied Arts and Design—General M
Art Education M
Art/Fine Arts M
Atmospheric Sciences M
Clinical Psychology M
Distance Education Development M
Early Childhood Education M
Education of the Gifted M
Education—General M,D
Educational Leadership and Administration M,D
Emergency Management M
English as a Second Language M
English M
Environmental Management and Policy M
Family Nurse Practitioner Studies M
Foundations and Philosophy of Education M,D
French M
Geographic Information Systems M
German M
History M
Mathematics Education M
Meteorology M
Nursing Education M
Nursing—General M
Physical Education M
Psychology—General M
Reading Education M
School Psychology M
Science Education M
Social Work M,D
Spanish M
Special Education M
Sports Management M
Vocational and Technical Education M

MILLIGAN COLLEGE
Business Administration and Management—General M
Education—General M
Missions and Missiology M,D
Occupational Therapy M
Pastoral Ministry and Counseling M,D
Religion M,D
Religious Education M,D
Theology M,D

MILLIKIN UNIVERSITY
Business Administration and Management—General M
Nurse Anesthesia M,D

Nursing Education	M,D
Nursing—General	M,D

MILLSAPS COLLEGE

Accounting	M
Business Administration and Management—General	M

MILLS COLLEGE

Applied Economics	M
Art Education	M,D,O
Art/Fine Arts	M
Biological and Biomedical Sciences—General	O
Business Administration and Management—General	M
Computer Science	M,O
Curriculum and Instruction	M,D,O
Dance	M
Early Childhood Education	M,D,O
Education—General	M,D,O
Educational Leadership and Administration	M,D,O
Elementary Education	M,D,O
English Education	M,D,O
English	M,O
Foreign Languages Education	M,D,O
Health Education	M,D,O
Illustration	M,O
Interdisciplinary Studies	M,O
Mathematics Education	M,D,O
Music	M
Photography	M
Public Policy	M
Science Education	M,D,O
Secondary Education	M,D,O
Social Sciences Education	M,D,O
Translation and Interpretation	M,O
Writing	M,O

MILWAUKEE SCHOOL OF ENGINEERING

Architectural Engineering	M
Business Administration and Management—General	M*
Business Education	M
Cardiovascular Sciences	M
Civil Engineering	M
Clinical Laboratory Sciences/Medical Technology	M
Construction Management	M
Engineering and Applied Sciences—General	M*
Engineering Management	M
Health Services Management and Hospital Administration	M
Industrial and Manufacturing Management	M
International Business	M
Marketing	M
Medical Informatics	M
Nursing and Healthcare Administration	M
Perfusion	M*

MINNEAPOLIS COLLEGE OF ART AND DESIGN

Applied Arts and Design—General	M
Art/Fine Arts	M,O
Computer Art and Design	O
Film, Television, and Video Production	M
Graphic Design	M,O
Illustration	M
Photography	M
Sustainable Development	O

MINNESOTA STATE UNIVERSITY MANKATO

Allied Health—General	M,D,O
Anthropology	M
Art Education	M
Art/Fine Arts	M
Astronomy	M
Automotive Engineering	M
Biological and Biomedical Sciences—General	M
Business Administration and Management—General	M
Clinical Psychology	M,D
Communication Disorders	M
Communication—General	M,O
Community Health	M,O
Corporate and Organizational Communication	M,O
Counseling Psychology	M,D
Counselor Education	M,D
Education—General	M,D,O
Educational Leadership and Administration	M
English as a Second Language	M,O
English Education	M,O
English	M,O
Environmental Sciences	M
Ethnic Studies	M
French	M
Gender Studies	M
Geography	M
Gerontology	M
Health Education	M,O
Higher Education	M
History	M
Human Services	M
Industrial and Organizational Psychology	M,D
Interdisciplinary Studies	M
Management Information Systems	M,O
Manufacturing Engineering	M
Mathematics Education	M
Mathematics	M
Multilingual and Multicultural Education	M
Music	M
Physical Education	M
Physics	M
Psychology—General	M,D
Public Administration	M
Rehabilitation Counseling	M
School Psychology	M,D
Science Education	M
Social Sciences Education	M
Social Work	M
Sociology	M
Spanish	M
Special Education	M,O
Statistics	M
Student Affairs	M,D
Technical Communication	M,O
Theater	M
Urban and Regional Planning	M,O
Urban Studies	M,O
Women's Studies	M
Writing	M,O

MINNESOTA STATE UNIVERSITY MOORHEAD

Accounting	M
Business Administration and Management—General	M
Communication Disorders	M,O
Counselor Education	M,O
Curriculum and Instruction	M,O
Education—General	M,O
Educational Leadership and Administration	M,O
English as a Second Language	M
Finance and Banking	M
Health Services Management and Hospital Administration	M,O
Human Services	M,O
Nursing—General	M,O
School Psychology	M,O
Special Education	M,O

MINOT STATE UNIVERSITY

Business Administration and Management—General	M
Communication Disorders	M
Elementary Education	M
Management Information Systems	M
Mathematics Education	M
Middle School Education	M
School Psychology	O
Science Education	M
Special Education	M

MIRRER YESHIVA

Theology	

MISERICORDIA UNIVERSITY

Accounting	M
Allied Health—General	M,D
Business Administration and Management—General	M
Communication Disorders	M
Curriculum and Instruction	M
Education—General	M
Educational Media/Instructional Technology	M
Health Services Management and Hospital Administration	M
Human Resources Management	M
Management Information Systems	M
Nonprofit Management	M
Nursing—General	M,D
Occupational Therapy	M,D
Organizational Management	M
Physical Therapy	D
Reading Education	M
Special Education	M
Sports Management	M

MISSISSIPPI COLLEGE

Accounting	M,O
Advertising and Public Relations	M
Art Education	M,D,O
Art/Fine Arts	M
Biochemistry	M
Biological and Biomedical Sciences—General	M
Business Administration and Management—General	M,O
Business Education	M,D,O
Chemistry	M
Communication—General	M
Computer Education	M,D,O
Computer Science	M
Corporate and Organizational Communication	M
Counseling Psychology	M,O
Counselor Education	M,O
Criminal Justice and Criminology	M,O
Curriculum and Instruction	M,D,O
Education—General	M,D,O
Educational Leadership and Administration	M,D,O
Elementary Education	M,D,O
English as a Second Language	M
English Education	M,D,O
English	M
Finance and Banking	M,O
Health Services Management and Hospital Administration	M
Higher Education	M,D,O
History	M,O
Kinesiology and Movement Studies	M
Law	D,O
Legal and Justice Studies	M,O
Liberal Studies	M
Marriage and Family Therapy	M,O
Mathematics Education	M,D,O
Mathematics	M
Music Education	M
Music	M
Political Science	M,O
Science Education	M,D,O
Secondary Education	M,D,O
Social Sciences Education	M,D,O
Social Sciences	M,O
Special Education	M,D,O

MISSISSIPPI STATE UNIVERSITY

Accounting	M,D
Aerospace/Aeronautical Engineering	M,D
Agricultural Economics and Agribusiness	M
Agricultural Education	M,D
Agricultural Sciences—General	M,D
Agronomy and Soil Sciences	M,D
American Studies	M,D
Animal Sciences	M,D
Anthropology	M
Applied Economics	M,D
Applied Physics	M,D
Applied Psychology	M,D
Atmospheric Sciences	M,D
Biochemistry	M,D
Bioengineering	M,D
Biological and Biomedical Sciences—General	M,D
Biomedical Engineering	M,D
Business Administration and Management—General	M,D
Business Education	M,D,O
Chemical Engineering	M,D
Chemistry	M,D
Child and Family Studies	M,D
Civil Engineering	M,D
Clinical Psychology	M,D,O
Cognitive Sciences	M,D
Community College Education	M,D,O
Computer Engineering	M,D
Computer Science	M,D
Counselor Education	M,D,O
Curriculum and Instruction	M,D,O
Early Childhood Education	M,D,O
Economics	M,D
Education—General	M,D,O
Educational Leadership and Administration	M,D,O
Educational Media/Instructional Technology	M,D,O
Educational Psychology	M,D,O
Electrical Engineering	M,D
Elementary Education	M,D,O
Engineering and Applied Sciences—General	M,D
English	M
Entomology	M,D
Ergonomics and Human Factors	M,D
Exercise and Sports Science	M,D
Finance and Banking	M,D
Fish, Game, and Wildlife Management	M,D
Food Science and Technology	M,D
Foreign Languages Education	M
Forestry	M,D
French	M
Genetics	M,D
Geography	M,D
Geology	M,D
Geosciences	M,D
German	M
Health Promotion	M,D
Higher Education	M,D,O
History	M,D
Horticulture	M,D
Human Development	M,D
Human Resources Development	M,D,O
Industrial and Manufacturing Management	M,D
Industrial/Management Engineering	M,D
Internet and Interactive Multimedia	M,D,O
Kinesiology and Movement Studies	M,D
Landscape Architecture	M
Management Information Systems	M,D
Marketing	M,D
Mathematics	M,D
Mechanical Engineering	M,D
Meteorology	M,D
Middle School Education	M,D,O
Molecular Biology	M,D
Nutrition	M,D
Operations Research	M,D
Physical Education	M,D
Physics	M,D
Plant Pathology	M,D
Plant Sciences	M,D
Political Science	M,D
Project Management	M,D
Psychology—General	M,D
Public Administration	M,D
Public Policy	M,D
Reading Education	M,D,O
Rehabilitation Counseling	M,D,O
School Psychology	M,D,O
Science Education	M,D
Secondary Education	M,D,O
Sociology	M,D
Spanish	M
Special Education	M,D,O
Sports Management	M,D
Statistics	M,D
Student Affairs	M,D,O
Sustainable Development	M,D
Systems Engineering	M,D
Taxation	M
Veterinary Medicine	D
Veterinary Sciences	M,D
Western European Studies	M,D

MISSISSIPPI UNIVERSITY FOR WOMEN

Communication Disorders	M,O
Curriculum and Instruction	M
Education of the Gifted	M
Education—General	M
Educational Leadership and Administration	M
Health Education	M
Nursing—General	M,O
Reading Education	M

MISSISSIPPI VALLEY STATE UNIVERSITY

Bioinformatics	M
Criminal Justice and Criminology	M
Education—General	M
Special Education	M

MISSOURI BAPTIST UNIVERSITY

Business Administration and Management—General	M,O
Counselor Education	M,O
Education—General	M,O
Educational Leadership and Administration	M,O
Pastoral Ministry and Counseling	M,O

MISSOURI SOUTHERN STATE UNIVERSITY

Business Administration and Management—General	M
Criminal Justice and Criminology	M
Dental Hygiene	M
Early Childhood Education	M
Education—General	M
Educational Media/Instructional Technology	M
Nursing—General	M

MISSOURI STATE UNIVERSITY

Accounting	M
Agricultural Sciences—General	M
Applied Behavior Analysis	M,O
Applied Science and Technology	M
Art/Fine Arts	M
Athletic Training and Sports Medicine	M
Biological and Biomedical Sciences—General	M
Business Administration and Management—General	M
Cell Biology	M
Chemistry	M
Child and Family Studies	M
Clinical Psychology	M,O
Communication—General	M,O
Computer and Information Systems Security	M
Computer Science	M
Construction Management	M
Counseling Psychology	M
Counselor Education	M
Criminal Justice and Criminology	M,O
Early Childhood Education	M
Educational Leadership and Administration	M,O
Educational Measurement and Evaluation	O
Educational Media/Instructional Technology	M
Elementary Education	M,O
English as a Second Language	M,O
English Education	M,O
English	M,O
Environmental Management and Policy	M,O
Experimental Psychology	M,O
Family Nurse Practitioner Studies	M,D
Film, Television, and Video Production	M,O
Geography	M
Geology	M
Geosciences	M
Health Services Management and Hospital Administration	M
Higher Education	M
History	M,O
Homeland Security	M,O
Industrial and Organizational Psychology	M,O
International Affairs	M
Kinesiology and Movement Studies	M
Management Information Systems	M
Materials Sciences	M
Mathematics Education	M
Mathematics	M
Military and Defense Studies	M,O
Molecular Biology	M
Music	M
Nurse Anesthesia	D
Nursing Education	M,D
Nursing—General	M,D
Nutrition	M,D,O
Occupational Therapy	M
Physical Education	M
Physical Therapy	D
Physician Assistant Studies	M
Physics	M
Plant Sciences	M
Political Science	M,O
Project Management	M
Psychology—General	M,O
Public Administration	M,O
Public Health—General	M
Reading Education	M
Religion	M,O

*M—masters degree; D—doctorate; O—other advanced degree; *—Close-Up and/or Display*

Science Education M
Secondary Education M,O
Social Sciences Education M,O
Social Work M
Special Education M
Sports Management M,O
Student Affairs M
Theater M
Urban and Regional Planning M
Writing M,O

MISSOURI UNIVERSITY OF SCIENCE AND TECHNOLOGY
Aerospace/Aeronautical Engineering M,D
Applied Mathematics M,D
Biological and Biomedical Sciences—General M
Ceramic Sciences and Engineering M,D
Chemical Engineering M,D
Chemistry M,D
Civil Engineering M,D
Computer Engineering M,D
Computer Science M,D
Construction Engineering M,D
Electrical Engineering M,D
Engineering Management M,D
Environmental Biology M
Environmental Engineering M,D
Geochemistry M,D
Geological Engineering M,D
Geology M,D
Geophysics M,D
Geotechnical Engineering M,D
Hydraulics M,D
Hydrology M,D
Information Science M
Manufacturing Engineering M,D
Mathematics Education M,D
Mathematics M,D
Mechanical Engineering M,D
Mechanics M,D
Metallurgical Engineering and Metallurgy M,D
Mineral/Mining Engineering M,D
Nuclear Engineering M,D
Petroleum Engineering M,D
Physics M,D
Statistics M,D
Systems Engineering M,D
Water Resources M,D

MISSOURI VALLEY COLLEGE
Social Psychology M

MISSOURI WESTERN STATE UNIVERSITY
Biological and Biomedical Sciences—General M
Business Administration and Management—General M
Chemistry M
Computer and Information Systems Security M
Educational Measurement and Evaluation M,O
Engineering and Applied Sciences—General M
English as a Second Language M,O
Ergonomics and Human Factors M
Forensic Sciences M,O
Information Studies M
Management Information Systems M
Media Studies M
Nursing and Healthcare Administration M,O
Nursing Education M,O
Nursing—General M,O
Rhetoric M,O
Special Education M,O
Sports Management M
Technical Communication M,O
Writing M,O

MOLLOY COLLEGE
Accounting M
Adult Nursing M,D,O
Biological and Biomedical Sciences—General M,O
Business Administration and Management—General M
Clinical Psychology M
Communication Disorders M
Criminal Justice and Criminology M
Early Childhood Education M,O
Education—General M,O
English as a Second Language M,O
English M,O
Family Nurse Practitioner Studies M,D,O
Finance and Banking M
Gerontological Nursing M,D,O
Health Informatics M,D,O
Health Services Management and Hospital Administration M
Marketing M
Mathematics M,O
Multilingual and Multicultural Education M,O
Nursing and Healthcare Administration M,D,O
Nursing Education M,D,O
Nursing—General M,D,O
Pediatric Nursing M,D,O
Psychiatric Nursing M,D,O
Social Sciences Education M,O
Spanish M,O
Special Education M,O
Therapies—Dance, Drama, and Music M

MONMOUTH UNIVERSITY
Accounting M,O
Addictions/Substance Abuse Counseling M,O
Adult Nursing M,D,O
Advertising and Public Relations M,O
American Studies M
Anthropology M
Applied Behavior Analysis M,O
Business Administration and Management—General M,O*
Communication Disorders M,O
Communication—General M,O
Computer Science M,O
Corporate and Organizational Communication M,O
Counseling Psychology M,O
Counselor Education M,O
Criminal Justice and Criminology M,O
Education—General M,O
Educational Leadership and Administration M,O
Elementary Education M,O
English as a Second Language M,O
English M
Family Nurse Practitioner Studies M,D,O
Finance and Banking M,O
Forensic Nursing M,D,O
Gerontological Nursing M,D,O
History M
Homeland Security M,O
Human Resources Management M,O
Management Information Systems M,O
Marketing M,O
Media Studies M,O
Nursing and Healthcare Administration M,D,O
Nursing Education M,D,O
Nursing—General M,D,O
Physician Assistant Studies M,D,O
Psychiatric Nursing M,D,O
Psychology—General M,O
Public Policy M
Real Estate M,O
Rhetoric M
School Nursing M,D,O
School Psychology M,O
Secondary Education M,O
Social Work M,O
Software Engineering M,O
Special Education M,O
Student Affairs M,O
Western European Studies M
Writing M

MONROE COLLEGE
Business Administration and Management—General M
Criminal Justice and Criminology M
Hospitality Management M
Public Health—General M

MONTANA STATE UNIVERSITY
Accounting M
Adult Education M,D,O
Agricultural Education M
Agricultural Sciences—General M,D
American Indian/Native American Studies M
Animal Sciences M,D
Architecture M
Art History M
Art/Fine Arts M
Biochemistry M,D
Biological and Biomedical Sciences—General M,D
Chemical Engineering M,D
Chemistry M,D
Civil Engineering M,D
Computer Engineering M,D
Computer Science M,D
Construction Engineering M,D
Curriculum and Instruction M,D,O
Ecology M,D
Education—General M,D,O
Educational Leadership and Administration M,D,O
Electrical Engineering M,D
Engineering and Applied Sciences—General M,D
English M
Environmental Engineering M,D
Environmental Sciences M,D
Family Nurse Practitioner Studies M,D,O
Film, Television, and Video Production M
Fish, Game, and Wildlife Management M,D
Geosciences M,D
Health Education M
Higher Education M,D,O
History M,D
Home Economics Education M
Human Development M
Immunology M,D
Industrial/Management Engineering M,D
Infectious Diseases M,D
Mathematics Education M,D
Mathematics M,D
Mechanical Engineering M,D
Mechanics M,D
Microbiology M,D
Natural Resources M
Neuroscience M,D
Nursing and Healthcare Administration M,D,O
Nursing Education M,D,O
Physics M,D
Plant Pathology M,D
Plant Sciences M,D
Psychiatric Nursing M,D,O
Psychology—General M
Public Administration M
Range Science M,D
School Psychology M,D,O
Statistics M,D
Vocational and Technical Education M,D,O

MONTANA STATE UNIVERSITY BILLINGS
Advertising and Public Relations M
Athletic Training and Sports Medicine M
Communication—General M
Counseling Psychology M
Counselor Education M
Curriculum and Instruction M
Education—General M,O
Educational Media/Instructional Technology M
Health Services Management and Hospital Administration M
Interdisciplinary Studies M
Psychology—General M
Public Administration M
Reading Education M
Rehabilitation Counseling M
Special Education M

MONTANA STATE UNIVERSITY–NORTHERN
Counselor Education M
Education—General M

MONTANA TECH OF THE UNIVERSITY OF MONTANA
Electrical Engineering M
Engineering and Applied Sciences—General M
Environmental Engineering M
Geochemistry M
Geological Engineering M
Geology M
Geosciences M
Health Informatics O
Hydrogeology M
Industrial Hygiene M
Industrial/Management Engineering M
Interdisciplinary Studies M
Materials Sciences D
Metallurgical Engineering and Metallurgy M
Mineral/Mining Engineering M
Petroleum Engineering M
Project Management M
Technical Communication M

MONTCLAIR STATE UNIVERSITY
Accounting M,O
Addictions/Substance Abuse Counseling O
Applied Mathematics M
Archives/Archival Administration M
Art Education M
Art/Fine Arts M
Arts Administration M
Biochemistry M
Biological and Biomedical Sciences—General M
Business Administration and Management—General M,O
Chemistry M
Child and Family Studies M,D,O
Child Development M,O
Clinical Psychology M
Communication Disorders M,D
Computer Science M,O
Conflict Resolution and Mediation/Peace Studies M,O
Counselor Education M,D
Curriculum and Instruction M
Database Systems O
Disability Studies M,O
Ecology M
Education—General M,D,O
Educational Leadership and Administration M,D
Educational Measurement and Evaluation O
English as a Second Language M,O
English Education M,O
English M
Environmental Education M
Environmental Law O
Environmental Management and Policy M,D
Environmental Sciences M
Evolutionary Biology M
Exercise and Sports Science M,O
Forensic Psychology O
French M
Geographic Information Systems O
Geosciences M
Health Education M
Industrial and Organizational Psychology M
Intellectual Property Law M,O
Law M,O
Legal and Justice Studies O
Linguistics M,O
Marine Biology M
Mathematics Education M,D,O
Mathematics M
Molecular Biology M,O
Music Education M
Music M,O
Nutrition M,O
Pharmacology M
Physical Education M
Physiology M
Political Science M,O
Psychology—General M
Public Health—General M
Reading Education M
Science Education M
Social Sciences M
Spanish M
Special Education M
Sports Management M
Statistics M
Sustainable Development M
Theater M
Therapies—Dance, Drama, and Music M,O
Translation and Interpretation O
Water Resources O
Writing O

MOODY BIBLE INSTITUTE
Pastoral Ministry and Counseling M,O
Theology M,O
Urban Studies M,O

MOODY THEOLOGICAL SEMINARYMICHIGAN
Counseling Psychology M,O
Religion M,O
Religious Education M,O
Theology M,O

MOORE COLLEGE OF ART & DESIGN
Art Education M
Art/Fine Arts M
Arts Administration M
Communication—General M
Interior Design M

MORAVIAN COLLEGE
Accounting M
Allied Health—General M
Business Administration and Management—General M
Curriculum and Instruction M
Education—General M
Health Services Management and Hospital Administration M
Human Resources Development M
Human Resources Management M
Nursing and Healthcare Administration M
Nursing Education M
Nursing—General M
Supply Chain Management M

MORAVIAN THEOLOGICAL SEMINARY
Theology M,O

MOREHEAD STATE UNIVERSITY
Adult Education M,O
Agricultural Sciences—General M
Art Education M
Art/Fine Arts M
Biological and Biomedical Sciences—General M
Business Administration and Management—General M
Business Education M,O
Clinical Psychology M
Communication—General M
Counseling Psychology M
Counselor Education M,O
Criminal Justice and Criminology M
Curriculum and Instruction M,O
Education of the Gifted M,O
Education—General M,O
Educational Leadership and Administration M,O
Educational Media/Instructional Technology M,O
Elementary Education M,O
English Education M,O
English M
Environmental Management and Policy M
Exercise and Sports Science M
Experimental Psychology M
Foreign Languages Education M
Gerontology M
Graphic Design M
Health Education M
Higher Education M,O
Industrial/Management Engineering M
International and Comparative Education M,O
Management Information Systems M
Mathematics Education M
Middle School Education M,O
Music Education M
Music M
Physical Education M
Psychology—General M
Public Administration M
Public Policy M
Reading Education M,O
Science Education M
Secondary Education M,O
Social Sciences Education M,O
Sociology M
Special Education M,O
Sports Management M
Vocational and Technical Education M

MOREHOUSE SCHOOL OF MEDICINE
Allopathic Medicine D
Biological and Biomedical Sciences—General M,D
Clinical Research M
Public Health—General M

MORGAN STATE UNIVERSITY
African-American Studies M,D
Architecture M
Bioinformatics M
Biological and Biomedical Sciences—General M,D
Business Administration and Management—General D
Chemistry M
Civil Engineering M,D
Community College Education D
Economics M
Education—General M,D
Educational Leadership and Administration M,D
Electrical Engineering M,D
Elementary Education M

Engineering and Applied Sciences—General M,D
English M,D
Environmental Biology D
Higher Education M,D
Historic Preservation M,D
History M,D
Industrial/Management Engineering M,D
International Affairs M
Landscape Architecture M
Mathematics Education M,D
Mathematics M
Middle School Education M
Museum Studies M,D
Music M
Nursing—General M
Psychology—General M,D
Public Health—General M,D
Science Education M,D
Secondary Education M
Social Work M,D
Sociology M
Transportation and Highway Engineering M
Transportation Management M
Urban and Regional Planning M
Urban Education D

MORNINGSIDE COLLEGE
Education—General M
Special Education M

MOUNT ALLISON UNIVERSITY
Biological and Biomedical Sciences—General M
Chemistry M

MOUNT ALOYSIUS COLLEGE
Accounting M
Applied Behavior Analysis M
Business Administration and Management—General M
Health Services Management and Hospital Administration M
Nonprofit Management M
Project Management M
Psychology—General M
Social Psychology M

MOUNT ANGEL SEMINARY
Theology M

MOUNT CARMEL COLLEGE OF NURSING
Acute Care/Critical Care Nursing M,D
Adult Nursing M,D
Family Nurse Practitioner Studies M,D
Gerontological Nursing M,D
Nursing and Healthcare Administration M,D
Nursing Education M,D
Nursing—General M,D

MOUNT HOLYOKE COLLEGE
Educational Leadership and Administration M
Mathematics Education M

MOUNT IDA COLLEGE
Business Administration and Management—General M
Health Services Management and Hospital Administration M
Human Resources Management M
Sports Management M

MOUNT MARTY COLLEGE
Business Administration and Management—General M
Nurse Anesthesia M
Nursing—General M
Pastoral Ministry and Counseling M

MOUNT MARY UNIVERSITY
Art Therapy M,D
Business Administration and Management—General M
Clinical Psychology M,O
Counseling Psychology M,O
Counselor Education M,O
Education—General M
English M
Health Education M
Internet and Interactive Multimedia M
Nursing and Healthcare Administration M
Nutrition M
Occupational Therapy M,D
Rehabilitation Counseling M,O
Writing M

MOUNT MERCY UNIVERSITY
Business Administration and Management—General M
Criminal Justice and Criminology M
Education—General M
Educational Leadership and Administration M
Human Resources Management M
Management Strategy and Policy M
Marriage and Family Therapy M
Nursing and Healthcare Administration M
Nursing Education M
Nursing—General M
Quality Management M
Reading Education M
Special Education M

MOUNT ST. JOSEPH UNIVERSITY
Business Administration and Management—General M
Early Childhood Education M,O
Education—General M,O
Educational Leadership and Administration M,O
Health Promotion M,O
Health Services Management and Hospital Administration D
Middle School Education M,O
Multilingual and Multicultural Education M,O
Nursing and Healthcare Administration M
Nursing Education M
Nursing—General M,D
Organizational Management M
Pastoral Ministry and Counseling M,O
Physical Therapy D
Reading Education M,O
Religion M,O
Secondary Education M,O
Special Education M,O
Theology M,O

MOUNT SAINT MARY COLLEGE
Adult Nursing M,O
Business Administration and Management—General M
Early Childhood Education M,O
Education—General M,O
Elementary Education M,O
Family Nurse Practitioner Studies M,O
Finance and Banking M
Middle School Education M,O
Nursing and Healthcare Administration M,O
Nursing Education M,O
Nursing—General M,O
Reading Education M,O
Secondary Education M,O
Special Education M,O

MOUNT SAINT MARY'S UNIVERSITY (CA)
Business Administration and Management—General M,D,O
Counseling Psychology M,D,O
Education—General M,D,O
English M,D,O
Film, Television, and Video Production M,D,O
Health Services Management and Hospital Administration M,D,O
Humanities M,D,O
Nursing—General M,D,O
Physical Therapy M,D,O
Religion M,D,O
Writing M,D,O

MOUNT ST. MARY'S UNIVERSITY (MD)
Biotechnology M
Business Administration and Management—General M
Education—General M
Health Services Management and Hospital Administration M
Philosophy M
Sports Management M
Theology M

MOUNT SAINT VINCENT UNIVERSITY
Adult Education M
Child and Family Studies M
Curriculum and Instruction M
Education—General M
Educational Psychology M
Elementary Education M
English as a Second Language M
Foundations and Philosophy of Education M
Gerontology M
Middle School Education M
Nutrition M
Reading Education M
School Psychology M
Special Education M
Women's Studies M

MOUNT VERNON NAZARENE UNIVERSITY
Business Administration and Management—General M
Education—General M
Theology M

MULTNOMAH UNIVERSITY
Counselor Education M
Education—General M
English as a Second Language M
Theology M,D

MURRAY STATE UNIVERSITY
Accounting M
Agricultural Education M
Agricultural Sciences—General M
Biological and Biomedical Sciences—General M,D
Business Administration and Management—General M
Chemistry M
Clinical Psychology M
Communication Disorders M
Corporate and Organizational Communication M
Counselor Education M,O
Early Childhood Education M
Economics M
Education—General M,D,O
Educational Leadership and Administration M,O
Elementary Education M,O
English as a Second Language M
English M
Environmental and Occupational Health M
Environmental Sciences M
Exercise and Sports Science M
Family Nurse Practitioner Studies M
Geosciences M
History M
Human Services M
Hydrology M
Industrial Hygiene M
Leisure Studies M
Management of Technology M
Mass Communication M
Mathematics M
Middle School Education M,O
Music Education M
Music M
Nurse Anesthesia M
Nursing—General M
Physical Education M,O
Psychology—General M
Public Affairs M
Reading Education M,O
Safety Engineering M
Secondary Education M,O
Special Education M
Statistics M
Telecommunications Management M
Vocational and Technical Education M
Writing M

MUSKINGUM UNIVERSITY
Education—General M

NAROPA UNIVERSITY
Art Therapy M
Counseling Psychology M
Counselor Education M
Education—General M
Environmental Management and Policy M
Psychoanalysis and Psychotherapy M
Recreation and Park Management M
Religion M
Theater M
Theology M
Therapies—Dance, Drama, and Music M
Writing M

NASHOTAH HOUSE THEOLOGICAL SEMINARY
Theology M,D,O

NATIONAL AMERICAN UNIVERSITY
Business Administration and Management—General M

NATIONAL COLLEGE OF MIDWIFERY
Nurse Midwifery M,D

NATIONAL COLLEGE OF NATURAL MEDICINE
Acupuncture and Oriental Medicine M
Naturopathic Medicine M,D

NATIONAL DEFENSE UNIVERSITY
Homeland Security M
Military and Defense Studies M
National Security M

THE NATIONAL GRADUATE SCHOOL OF QUALITY MANAGEMENT
Homeland Security M,D
Quality Management M,D

NATIONAL INTELLIGENCE UNIVERSITY
Military and Defense Studies M

NATIONAL LOUIS UNIVERSITY
Adult Education M,D,O
Business Administration and Management—General M
Counselor Education M,D,O
Curriculum and Instruction M,D,O
Developmental Education M,D,O
Early Childhood Education M,D,O
Education—General M,D,O
Educational Leadership and Administration M,D,O
Educational Media/Instructional Technology M,D,O
Educational Psychology M,D,O
Elementary Education M,D,O
English Education M,D,O
Human Development M,D,O
Human Resources Development M
Human Resources Management M
Human Services M,D,O
Mathematics Education M,D,O
Psychology—General M,D,O
Public Policy M,D,O
Reading Education M,D,O
School Psychology M,D,O
Science Education M,D,O
Secondary Education M,D,O
Special Education M,D,O
Writing M,D,O

NATIONAL PARALEGAL COLLEGE
Legal and Justice Studies M
Taxation M

NATIONAL UNIVERSITY
Accounting M,O
Applied Behavior Analysis M,O
Biological and Biomedical Sciences—General M,O
Business Administration and Management—General M,O
Clinical Psychology M,O
Communication Disorders M,O
Computer and Information Systems Security M,O
Computer Science M,O
Corporate and Organizational Communication M,O
Counseling Psychology M,O
Counselor Education M,O
Criminal Justice and Criminology M,O
Database Systems M,O
Distance Education Development M,O
Early Childhood Education M,O
Education—General M,O
Educational Leadership and Administration M,O
Educational Media/Instructional Technology M,O
Emergency Management M,O
Engineering Management M,O
English M,O
Environmental Engineering M,O
Film, Television, and Video Production M
Film, Television, and Video Theory and Criticism M,O
Finance and Banking M,O
Forensic Nursing M,D,O
Forensic Sciences M,O
Health Informatics M,D,O
Health Promotion M,D,O
Health Services Management and Hospital Administration M,D,O
History M,O
Homeland Security M,O
Human Resources Management M,O
Human Services M,D,O
International and Comparative Education M,O
International Business M,O
Internet and Interactive Multimedia M,O
Journalism M
Legal and Justice Studies M
Linguistics M,O
Management Information Systems M,O
Management of Technology M,O
Marketing M,O
Marriage and Family Therapy M,O
Mathematics Education M,O
Medical Informatics M,D,O
Nurse Anesthesia M,D,O
Nursing and Healthcare Administration M,D,O
Nursing Informatics M,D,O
Nursing—General M,D,O
Organizational Management M,O
Project Management M,O
Psychology—General M,O
Public Administration M
Public Health—General M,D,O
Reading Education M,O
Rhetoric M,O
School Psychology M,O
Software Engineering M,O
Special Education M,O
Sport Psychology M,O
Sports Management M,O
Sustainability Management M,O
Systems Engineering M,O
Telecommunications M,O
Writing M,O

NATIONAL UNIVERSITY COLLEGE
Business Administration and Management—General M
Marketing M
Special Education M

NATIONAL UNIVERSITY OF HEALTH SCIENCES
Chiropractic M,D

NAVAJO TECHNICAL UNIVERSITY
American Indian/Native American Studies M

NAVAL POSTGRADUATE SCHOOL
Acoustics M,D
Aerospace/Aeronautical Engineering M,D,O
Applied Mathematics M,D
Applied Physics M,D,O
Applied Science and Technology M,D
Business Administration and Management—General M
Computer and Information Systems Security M,D
Computer Engineering M,D,O
Computer Science M,D,O
Conflict Resolution and Mediation/Peace Studies M,D
Electrical Engineering M,D,O
Engineering Management M,D,O
Finance and Banking M
Geographic Information Systems M,D,O
Homeland Security M,D
Information Science M,D,O
Logistics M
Management Information Systems M,D,O
Mechanical Engineering M,D,O
Meteorology M,D
Military and Defense Studies M,D
Modeling and Simulation M,D
National Security M,D,O
Oceanography M,D
Operations Research M,D
Physics M,D
Software Engineering M,D
Supply Chain Management M
Systems Engineering M,D,O
Transportation Management M

NAVAL WAR COLLEGE
National Security M

*M—masters degree; D—doctorate; O—other advanced degree; *—Close-Up and/or Display*

NAZARENE THEOLOGICAL SEMINARY

Missions and Missiology	M,D
Theology	M,D

NAZARETH COLLEGE OF ROCHESTER

Art Education	M
Business Administration and Management—General	M
Communication Disorders	M
Early Childhood Education	M
Education—General	M
Educational Media/Instructional Technology	M
Elementary Education	M
English as a Second Language	M
Human Resources Management	M
Middle School Education	M
Music Education	M
Physical Therapy	D
Reading Education	M
Social Work	M

NEBRASKA METHODIST COLLEGE

Health Promotion	M
Health Services Management and Hospital Administration	M
Nursing and Healthcare Administration	M
Nursing Education	M
Nursing—General	M

NEBRASKA WESLEYAN UNIVERSITY

Forensic Sciences	M
History	M
Nursing—General	M

NER ISRAEL RABBINICAL COLLEGE

Theology	M,D,O

NER ISRAEL YESHIVA COLLEGE OF TORONTO

Theology	

NEUMANN UNIVERSITY

Clinical Psychology	M,D,O
Education—General	M
Educational Leadership and Administration	D
Entertainment Management	M
Gerontological Nursing	M
Management Strategy and Policy	M
Nursing Education	M
Nursing—General	M
Organizational Management	M
Pastoral Ministry and Counseling	M,D,O
Physical Therapy	D
Special Education	M
Sports Management	M

NEW BRUNSWICK THEOLOGICAL SEMINARY

Pastoral Ministry and Counseling	M,D
Theology	M,D

NEW CHARTER UNIVERSITY

Business Administration and Management—General	M
Criminal Justice and Criminology	M
Finance and Banking	M
Health Services Management and Hospital Administration	M
Public Administration	M

NEW COLLEGE OF FLORIDA

Database Systems	M

NEW ENGLAND COLLEGE

Accounting	M
Business Administration and Management—General	M
Counseling Psychology	M
Education—General	M,D
Educational Leadership and Administration	M,D
Health Services Management and Hospital Administration	M
Higher Education	M,D
Human Services	M
International Affairs	M
Management Strategy and Policy	M
Marketing	M
Nonprofit Management	M
Project Management	M
Public Policy	M
Recreation and Park Management	M
Special Education	M,D
Sports Management	M
Writing	M

NEW ENGLAND COLLEGE OF BUSINESS AND FINANCE

Ethics	M
Finance and Banking	M

NEW ENGLAND COLLEGE OF OPTOMETRY

Optometry	M,D
Vision Sciences	M,D

NEW ENGLAND CONSERVATORY OF MUSIC

Music	M,D,O

NEW ENGLAND INSTITUTE OF TECHNOLOGY

Construction Management	M
Management Information Systems	M
Occupational Therapy	M

NEW ENGLAND LAW–BOSTON

Law	M,D

NEW HAMPSHIRE INSTITUTE OF ART

Art Education	M
Art/Fine Arts	M
Photography	M
Writing	M

NEW JERSEY CITY UNIVERSITY

Accounting	M,O
Allied Health—General	M
Art Education	M
Art/Fine Arts	M
Business Administration and Management—General	M,O
Community Health	M
Counselor Education	M
Criminal Justice and Criminology	M
Early Childhood Education	M
Education—General	M,D
Educational Leadership and Administration	M
Educational Media/Instructional Technology	M,D
Elementary Education	M
English as a Second Language	M
Health Education	M
Health Services Management and Hospital Administration	M
Mathematics Education	M
Multilingual and Multicultural Education	M
Music Education	M
Music	M
Secondary Education	M
Special Education	M
Urban Education	M
Urban Studies	M

NEW JERSEY INSTITUTE OF TECHNOLOGY

Applied Mathematics	M,D,O
Applied Physics	M,D,O
Applied Statistics	M,D,O
Architecture	M,D
Bioinformatics	M,D,O
Biological and Biomedical Sciences—General	M,D,O
Biomedical Engineering	M,D
Biostatistics	M,D,O
Business Administration and Management—General	M,D,O
Chemical Engineering	M,D
Chemistry	M,D,O
Computational Biology	M,D,O
Computer and Information Systems Security	M,D,O
Computer Engineering	M,D
Computer Science	M,D,O
Electrical Engineering	M,D
Emergency Management	M,D,O
Energy and Power Engineering	M,D
Engineering and Applied Sciences—General	M,D
Engineering Management	M,D
Environmental Engineering	M,D
Environmental Sciences	M,D,O
Health Services Management and Hospital Administration	M,D
History	M,D,O
Industrial/Management Engineering	M,D
Information Science	M,D,O
International Business	M,O
Internet Engineering	M,D
Management Information Systems	M,D,O
Management of Technology	M,O
Manufacturing Engineering	M,D
Materials Engineering	M,D,O
Materials Sciences	M,D,O
Mathematical and Computational Finance	M,D,O
Mathematics	M,D,O
Mechanical Engineering	M,D
Medicinal and Pharmaceutical Chemistry	M,D,O
Pharmaceutical Administration	M,D
Pharmaceutical Engineering	M,D
Pharmacology	M,D
Safety Engineering	M,D
Software Engineering	M,D,O
Statistics	M,D,O
Systems Science	M,D,O
Technical Communication	M,D,O
Telecommunications	M,D
Transportation and Highway Engineering	M,D
Transportation Management	M,D
Urban Studies	M,D

NEWMAN THEOLOGICAL COLLEGE

Educational Leadership and Administration	M,O
Religious Education	M,O
Theology	M

NEWMAN UNIVERSITY

Business Administration and Management—General	M
Curriculum and Instruction	M
Education—General	M
Educational Leadership and Administration	M
English as a Second Language	M
Finance and Banking	M
International Business	M
Management Information Systems	M
Nurse Anesthesia	M
Organizational Management	M
Reading Education	M
Social Work	M
Theology	M

NEW MEXICO HIGHLANDS UNIVERSITY

American Studies	M
Anthropology	M
Business Administration and Management—General	M
Chemistry	M
Clinical Psychology	M
Computer Art and Design	M
Computer Science	M
Counseling Psychology	M
Counselor Education	M
Curriculum and Instruction	M
Education—General	M
Educational Leadership and Administration	M
English	M
Exercise and Sports Science	M
Health Education	M
History	M
Human Resources Management	M
International Business	M
Internet and Interactive Multimedia	M
Media Studies	M
Natural Resources	M
Political Science	M
Psychology—General	M
Public Affairs	M
Rhetoric	M
Social Work	M
Sociology	M
Special Education	M
Sports Management	M
Writing	M

NEW MEXICO INSTITUTE OF MINING AND TECHNOLOGY

Applied Mathematics	M,D
Astrophysics	M,D
Atmospheric Sciences	M,D
Biological and Biomedical Sciences—General	M,D
Chemistry	M,D
Computer Science	M,D
Electrical Engineering	M
Engineering Management	M
Environmental Engineering	M
Geochemistry	M,D
Geological Engineering	M
Geology	M,D
Geophysics	M,D
Geosciences	M,D
Hazardous Materials Management	M
Hydrology	M,D
Materials Engineering	M,D
Mathematical Physics	M,D
Mathematics	M,D
Mechanical Engineering	M
Mechanics	M
Mineral/Mining Engineering	M
Operations Research	M,D
Petroleum Engineering	M,D
Physics	M,D
Science Education	M
Statistics	M,D
Systems Engineering	M
Water Resources Engineering	M

NEW MEXICO STATE UNIVERSITY

Accounting	M
Aerospace/Aeronautical Engineering	M,D
Agricultural Economics and Agribusiness	M,D
Agricultural Education	M
Animal Sciences	M,D
Anthropology	M,O
Applied Statistics	M,D,O
Art History	M
Art/Fine Arts	M
Astronomy	M,D
Astrophysics	M,D
Bioinformatics	M,D
Biological and Biomedical Sciences—General	M,D
Biotechnology	M,D
Business Administration and Management—General	M,D
Chemical Engineering	M,D
Chemistry	M,D
Civil Engineering	M,D
Communication Disorders	M,D,O
Communication—General	M
Community Health Nursing	M,D
Computer Engineering	M,D,O
Computer Science	M,D
Corporate and Organizational Communication	M,D
Counseling Psychology	M,D,O
Counselor Education	M,D,O
Criminal Justice and Criminology	M
Curriculum and Instruction	M,D,O
Dance	M,D,O
Distance Education Development	O
Early Childhood Education	M,D,O
Economic Development	M,D,O
Economics	M,D,O
Education—General	M,D,O
Educational Leadership and Administration	M,D
Educational Measurement and Evaluation	M,D,O
Electrical Engineering	M,D,O
Engineering and Applied Sciences—General	M,D,O
English as a Second Language	M,D,O
English Education	M,D
English	M,D
Entomology	M
Environmental Engineering	M,D
Environmental Sciences	M,D
Family and Consumer Sciences-General	M
Family Nurse Practitioner Studies	M,D
Finance and Banking	M,O
Fish, Game, and Wildlife Management	M
Food Science and Technology	M
Foreign Languages Education	M,D,O
Geography	M
Geological Engineering	M,D
Geology	M
Gerontological Nursing	M,D
History	M
Horticulture	M,D
Hydrology	M,D
Industrial/Management Engineering	M,D,O
Interdisciplinary Studies	M,D
Management Information Systems	M
Marketing	D
Marriage and Family Therapy	M
Mathematics Education	M,D,O
Mathematics	M,D
Mechanical Engineering	M,D
Molecular Biology	M,D
Multilingual and Multicultural Education	M,D,O
Museum Studies	M,O
Music Education	M
Music	M
Nursing and Healthcare Administration	M,D
Nursing—General	M,D
Nutrition	M
Physics	M,D
Plant Pathology	M
Plant Sciences	M
Political Science	M
Psychiatric Nursing	M,D
Psychology—General	M,D
Public Administration	M
Public Health—General	M,O
Range Science	M,D
Rhetoric	M,D
School Psychology	M,D,O
Science Education	M,D,O
Social Work	M
Sociology	M
Spanish	M,D,O
Special Education	M,D,O
Systems Engineering	M,D,O
Water Resources	M,D
Writing	M,D

NEW ORLEANS BAPTIST THEOLOGICAL SEMINARY

Music	M,D
Pastoral Ministry and Counseling	M,D
Religious Education	M,D
Theology	M,D

NEW SAINT ANDREWS COLLEGE

Religion	M,O
Theology	M,O

THE NEW SCHOOL

Anthropology	M,D
Applied Arts and Design—General	M
Applied Social Research	M,D
Architecture	M
Art/Fine Arts	M
Clinical Psychology	M,D
Clothing and Textiles	M
Cognitive Sciences	M,D
Computer Art and Design	M
Developmental Psychology	M,D
Economics	M,D
English as a Second Language	M
Environmental Management and Policy	M,O
Finance and Banking	M,D
History	M,D
Industrial Design	M
Interior Design	M
International Affairs	M
International Economics	M,D
Liberal Studies	M
Lighting Design	M
Media Studies	M,O
Museum Studies	M
Music	M,O
Nonprofit Management	M
Organizational Management	M,O
Philosophy	M,D
Photography	M
Political Science	M,D
Psychoanalysis and Psychotherapy	M,D
Psychology—General	M,D
Public Policy	D
Social Psychology	M,O
Social Sciences	M,D
Sociology	M,D
Sustainability Management	M,O
Textile Design	M
Theater	M
Urban Design	M
Urban Studies	M
Writing	M

NEWSCHOOL OF ARCHITECTURE AND DESIGN

Architecture	M
Construction Management	M

NEW YORK ACADEMY OF ART

Anatomy	M
Art/Fine Arts	M

NEW YORK CHIROPRACTIC COLLEGE

Acupuncture and Oriental Medicine	M
Anatomy	M
Chiropractic	D*
Nutrition	M

NEW YORK COLLEGE OF HEALTH PROFESSIONS

Acupuncture and Oriental Medicine	M

NEW YORK COLLEGE OF PODIATRIC MEDICINE

Podiatric Medicine	D

NEW YORK COLLEGE OF TRADITIONAL CHINESE MEDICINE

Acupuncture and Oriental Medicine	M

NEW YORK FILM ACADEMY

Film, Television, and Video Production	M
Photography	M

NEW YORK INSTITUTE OF TECHNOLOGY

Accounting	M
Architecture	M
Art/Fine Arts	M
Arts Administration	M,O
Business Administration and Management—General	M
Communication—General	M
Computer and Information Systems Security	M
Computer Art and Design	M
Computer Engineering	M
Computer Science	M
Counselor Education	M
Distance Education Development	M,O
Early Childhood Education	M
Education—General	M,O
Educational Media/Instructional Technology	M,O
Electrical Engineering	M
Energy and Power Engineering	M,O
Energy Management and Policy	M,O
Engineering and Applied Sciences—General	M,O
Entertainment Management	M,O
Environmental Engineering	M
Environmental Management and Policy	M,O
Finance and Banking	M
Graphic Design	M
Human Resources Management	M,O
Industrial and Labor Relations	M,O
Marketing	M
Mathematics Education	M,O
Middle School Education	M
Nutrition	M
Occupational Therapy	M
Osteopathic Medicine	M,D
Physical Therapy	D
Physician Assistant Studies	M
Science Education	M,O
Secondary Education	M
Urban Design	M

NEW YORK LAW SCHOOL

Law	M,D
Taxation	M,D

NEW YORK MEDICAL COLLEGE

Allopathic Medicine	D
Anatomy	M,D
Biochemistry	M,D
Biological and Biomedical Sciences—General	M,D
Biostatistics	M
Cell Biology	M,D
Communication Disorders	M
Emergency Management	O
Environmental and Occupational Health	M,O
Epidemiology	M
Health Education	O
Health Promotion	M,O
Health Services Management and Hospital Administration	M,D,O
Immunology	M,D
Industrial Hygiene	O
International Health	O
Microbiology	M,D
Molecular Biology	M,D
Pathology	M,D
Pharmacology	M,D
Physical Therapy	D
Physiology	M,D
Public Health—General	M,D,O

NEW YORK SCHOOL OF INTERIOR DESIGN

Interior Design	M
Lighting Design	M
Sustainable Development	M

NEW YORK STUDIO SCHOOL OF DRAWING, PAINTING AND SCULPTURE

Art/Fine Arts	M,O*

NEW YORK THEOLOGICAL SEMINARY

Theology	M,D

NEW YORK UNIVERSITY

Accounting	M,D
Acute Care/Critical Care Nursing	M,D,O
Adult Nursing	M,D,O
Advertising and Public Relations	M
African Studies	M,D,O
Agricultural Engineering	M,D
Allopathic Medicine	M,D
American Studies	M,D
Anthropology	M,D
Applied Arts and Design—General	M
Applied Economics	M,D,O
Applied Physics	M,D
Applied Psychology	M,D,O
Applied Social Research	M
Applied Statistics	M
Archaeology	M,D
Architectural History	M
Archives/Archival Administration	M,D,O
Art Education	M,O
Art History	M,D
Art Therapy	M
Art/Fine Arts	M,D,O
Arts Administration	M
Asian Studies	M,D
Bioethics	M
Bioinformatics	M,D
Biological and Biomedical Sciences—General	M,D,O
Biomedical Engineering	M,D
Biotechnology	M
Business Administration and Management—General	M,D,O
Business Education	M,O
Cancer Biology/Oncology	M,D
Cell Biology	D
Chemical Engineering	M,D
Chemistry	M,D,O
Chinese	M,D,O
Civil Engineering	M,D
Classics	M,D,O
Clinical Research	M
Cognitive Sciences	M,D,O
Communication Disorders	M,D
Communication—General	M,D
Community Health	M,D
Comparative Literature	M,D
Computational Biology	D
Computer and Information Systems Security	O
Computer Art and Design	M
Computer Engineering	M,O
Computer Science	M,D
Conflict Resolution and Mediation/Peace Studies	M,O
Construction Management	M,D,O
Corporate and Organizational Communication	M
Counseling Psychology	M,D,O
Counselor Education	M,D,O
Cultural Studies	M,D,O
Dance	M,D,O
Database Systems	M,O
Demography and Population Studies	M,D
Dentistry	D
Developmental Biology	M,D
Developmental Psychology	M,D
Early Childhood Education	M
Economics	M,D,O
Education—General	M,D,O
Educational Leadership and Administration	M,D,O
Educational Media/Instructional Technology	M,D,O
Educational Policy	M,D
Educational Psychology	M,D
Electrical Engineering	M,D
Electronic Commerce	M,D,O
Elementary Education	M
Energy Management and Policy	M,O
Engineering and Applied Sciences—General	M,D,O
English as a Second Language	M,D,O
English Education	M,D,O
English	M,D
Entrepreneurship	M,D,O
Environmental and Occupational Health	M,D*
Environmental Education	M
Environmental Engineering	M
Environmental Management and Policy	M,O
Environmental Sciences	M
Epidemiology	M,D
Ergonomics and Human Factors	M,D
Family Nurse Practitioner Studies	M,D,O
Film, Television, and Video Production	M
Finance and Banking	M,D,O
Financial Engineering	M,O
Food Science and Technology	M,D
Foreign Languages Education	M,D,O
Foundations and Philosophy of Education	M,D
French	M,D,O
Game Design and Development	M
Genetics	M,D
Genomic Sciences	D
German	M,D
Gerontological Nursing	M,O
Graphic Design	M
Health Promotion	M,D,O
Health Services Management and Hospital Administration	M,D,O
Higher Education	M,D
Historic Preservation	
History	M,D,O
Hospitality Management	M,D,O
Human Development	M,D,O
Human Resources Development	M,O
Human Resources Management	M,D,O
Humanities	M,O
Immunology	M,D
Industrial and Organizational Psychology	M,D,O
Industrial/Management Engineering	M
Interdisciplinary Studies	M
International Affairs	M,D,O
International and Comparative Education	M,D,O
International Business	M,D
International Development	M,O
International Health	M,D
Internet and Interactive Multimedia	M,O
Investment Management	M,O
Italian	M,D,O
Japanese	M,D,O
Jewish Studies	M,D,O
Journalism	M,D,O
Kinesiology and Movement Studies	M,D,O
Latin American Studies	M,O
Law	M,D,O
Legal and Justice Studies	M,D,O
Linguistics	M,D
Management Information Systems	M,D,O
Management of Technology	M,D,O
Management Strategy and Policy	M,D,O
Manufacturing Engineering	M
Marketing	M,D,O
Mathematical and Computational Finance	M,D,O
Mathematics Education	M
Mathematics	M,D*
Mechanical Engineering	M,D
Media Studies	M,D,O
Medical Imaging	D
Microbiology	M,D
Middle School Education	M,D,O
Molecular Biology	M,D
Molecular Biophysics	D
Molecular Genetics	M,D
Molecular Pharmacology	D
Molecular Toxicology	M,D
Multilingual and Multicultural Education	M,D,O
Museum Studies	M,O
Music Education	M,D,O
Music	M,D,O
National Security	M,O
Near and Middle Eastern Studies	M,D,O
Neurobiology	M,D
Neuroscience	D
Nonprofit Management	M,D,O
Nurse Midwifery	M,D,O
Nursing Education	M,O
Nursing Informatics	M,O
Nursing—General	M,D,O
Nutrition	M,D
Occupational Therapy	M,D
Oral and Dental Sciences	M,D,O
Organizational Behavior	M,D,O
Organizational Management	M,D,O
Pathobiology	D
Pediatric Nursing	M,D,O
Philosophy	M,D
Physical Therapy	M,D,O
Physics	M,D,O
Physiology	D
Plant Biology	M,D
Political Science	M,D
Portuguese	M,D
Project Management	M,D,O
Psychiatric Nursing	M,D,O
Psychoanalysis and Psychotherapy	M,D,O
Psychology—General	M,D,O
Public Administration	M,D,O
Public Health—General	M,D
Public History	M,D,O
Public Policy	M
Publishing	M
Reading Education	M
Real Estate	M,O
Rehabilitation Sciences	M,D
Religion	M,O
Romance Languages	M,D
Russian	M
Science Education	M,D,O
Secondary Education	M,D,O
Slavic Languages	M
Social Psychology	M,D,O
Social Sciences Education	M,D,O
Social Sciences	M,D
Social Work	M,D
Sociology	M,D
Software Engineering	O
Spanish	M,D,O
Special Education	M
Speech and Interpersonal Communication	M,D
Sports Management	M,O
Statistics	M,D
Structural Biology	D
Student Affairs	M,D
Sustainable Development	M
Systems Engineering	M
Taxation	M,D,O
Telecommunications Management	M,D,O
Theater	M,D,O
Therapies—Dance, Drama, and Music	M
Toxicology	M,D
Translation and Interpretation	M
Transportation and Highway Engineering	M,D
Transportation Management	M
Travel and Tourism	M,O
Urban and Regional Planning	M
Urban Studies	M
Western European Studies	M
Writing	M

NIAGARA UNIVERSITY

Accounting	M
Business Administration and Management—General	M
Counselor Education	M,O
Criminal Justice and Criminology	M
Early Childhood Education	M,O
Education—General	M,D,O
Educational Leadership and Administration	M,D,O
Educational Policy	M,D,O
Elementary Education	M,O
English as a Second Language	M,O
Finance and Banking	M
Foundations and Philosophy of Education	M
Health Services Management and Hospital Administration	M
Human Resources Management	M
Interdisciplinary Studies	M
International Business	M
Management Strategy and Policy	M
Marketing	M
Mathematics Education	M
Middle School Education	M,O
Reading Education	M
School Psychology	M
Science Education	M
Secondary Education	M,O
Special Education	M,O
Vocational and Technical Education	M

NICHOLLS STATE UNIVERSITY

Business Administration and Management—General	M
Clinical Psychology	M,O
Counselor Education	M,O
Curriculum and Instruction	M
Education—General	M
Educational Leadership and Administration	M
Elementary Education	M
Environmental Biology	M
Family Nurse Practitioner Studies	M
Health Education	M
Marine Biology	M
Middle School Education	M
Nursing and Healthcare Administration	M
Nursing Education	M
Nursing—General	M
Psychiatric Nursing	M
School Psychology	M,O
Secondary Education	M

NICHOLS COLLEGE

Business Administration and Management—General	M
Organizational Management	M

NIPISSING UNIVERSITY

Education—General	M,O

NORFOLK STATE UNIVERSITY

Art/Fine Arts	M
Clinical Psychology	M
Communication—General	M
Computer Engineering	M
Computer Science	M
Criminal Justice and Criminology	M
Early Childhood Education	M
Education of Students with Severe/Multiple Disabilities	M
Education—General	M
Educational Leadership and Administration	M
Electrical Engineering	M
Materials Sciences	M
Media Studies	M
Music Education	M
Music	M
Optical Sciences	M
Psychology—General	M,D
Secondary Education	M
Social Psychology	M
Social Work	M,D
Special Education	M
Urban Education	M
Urban Studies	M

NORTH AMERICAN UNIVERSITY

Educational Leadership and Administration	M

NORTH CAROLINA AGRICULTURAL AND TECHNICAL STATE UNIVERSITY

Accounting	M
Adult Education	M
African-American Studies	M
Agricultural Economics and Agribusiness	M
Agricultural Education	M
Agricultural Sciences—General	M
Agronomy and Soil Sciences	M
Animal Sciences	M
Applied Economics	M
Applied Mathematics	M
Bioengineering	M
Biological and Biomedical Sciences—General	M
Business Administration and Management—General	M
Business Education	M
Chemical Engineering	M
Chemistry	M,D
Child and Family Studies	M
Child Development	M
Civil Engineering	M
Computational Sciences	M
Computer Art and Design	M
Computer Engineering	M,D
Computer Science	M
Construction Management	M
Consumer Economics	M
Counselor Education	M
Early Childhood Education	M
Education—General	M
Educational Leadership and Administration	M
Educational Media/Instructional Technology	M
Electrical Engineering	M,D
Elementary Education	M
Energy and Power Engineering	M,D
Engineering and Applied Sciences—General	M,D
English Education	M
English	M
Environmental and Occupational Health	M

*M—masters degree; D—doctorate; O—other advanced degree; *—Close-Up and/or Display*

Environmental Sciences M
Graphic Design M
Health Education M
Human Resources Management M
Industrial/Management Engineering M,D
Management Information Systems M
Management of Technology M
Mathematics M
Mechanical Engineering M,D
Nutrition M
Optical Sciences M,D
Physical Education M
Physics M
Plant Sciences M
Reading Education M
Science Education M
Secondary Education M
Social Work M
Supply Chain Management M
Systems Engineering M,D
Vocational and Technical Education M

NORTH CAROLINA CENTRAL UNIVERSITY

Applied Mathematics M
Biological and Biomedical Sciences—General M
Business Administration and Management—General M
Chemistry M
Communication Disorders M
Counselor Education M
Criminal Justice and Criminology M
Education—General M
Educational Leadership and Administration M
Educational Media/Instructional Technology M
English M
Geosciences M
History M
Information Studies M
Law D
Library Science M
Mathematics Education M
Mathematics M
Music M
Physical Education M
Physics M
Psychology—General M
Public Administration M
Recreation and Park Management M
Special Education M
Sports Management M

NORTH CAROLINA STATE UNIVERSITY

Accounting M
Adult Education M,D
Aerospace/Aeronautical Engineering M,D
Agricultural Economics and Agribusiness M
Agricultural Education M,O
Agricultural Engineering M,D,O
Agricultural Sciences—General M,D,O
Agronomy and Soil Sciences M,D
Animal Sciences M,D
Anthropology M
Applied Arts and Design—General M,D
Applied Mathematics M,D
Architecture M
Atmospheric Sciences M,D
Biochemistry D
Bioengineering M,D,O
Bioinformatics M,D
Biological and Biomedical Sciences—General M,D,O
Biomathematics M,D
Biomedical Engineering M,D
Biotechnology M
Botany M,D
Business Administration and Management—General M
Business Education M
Cell Biology M,D
Chemical Engineering M,D
Chemistry M,D
Civil Engineering M,D
Clothing and Textiles D
Communication—General M
Community College Education M,D
Computer Art and Design D
Computer Engineering M,D
Computer Science M,D
Counselor Education M,D
Cultural Anthropology M
Curriculum and Instruction M,D
Developmental Education M,D,O
Developmental Psychology D
Economics M,D
Education—General M,D,O
Educational Leadership and Administration M,D
Educational Measurement and Evaluation D
Educational Media/Instructional Technology M,D
Electrical Engineering M,D
Elementary Education M
Engineering and Applied Sciences—General M,D
English Education M
English M
Entomology M,D
Entrepreneurship M
Epidemiology M,D
Ergonomics and Human Factors D
Experimental Psychology D
Financial Engineering M
Fish, Game, and Wildlife Management M,D
Food Science and Technology M,D
Forestry M,D
French M
Genetics M,D
Genomic Sciences M,D
Geographic Information Systems M,D
Geosciences M,D
Graphic Design M
Higher Education M,D
History M
Horticulture M,D,O
Human Resources Development M
Immunology M,D
Industrial and Organizational Psychology D
Industrial Design M
Industrial/Management Engineering M,D
Infectious Diseases M,D
International Affairs M
Landscape Architecture M
Liberal Studies M
Management of Technology D
Manufacturing Engineering M
Marine Sciences M,D
Materials Engineering M,D
Materials Sciences M,D
Mathematical and Computational Finance M
Mathematics Education M,D
Mathematics M,D
Mechanical Engineering M,D
Meteorology M,D
Microbiology M,D
Middle School Education M
Molecular Toxicology M,D
Natural Resources M,D
Nonprofit Management M,D,O
Nuclear Engineering M,D
Nutrition M,D
Oceanography M,D
Operations Research M,D
Paper and Pulp Engineering M,D
Pathology M,D
Pharmacology M,D
Physics M,D
Physiology M,D
Plant Biology M,D
Plant Pathology M,D
Polymer Science and Engineering D
Psychology—General D
Public Administration M,D
Public History M
Recreation and Park Management M,D
Rhetoric D
School Psychology D
Science Education M,D
Secondary Education M
Social Psychology M
Social Sciences Education M
Social Work M
Sociology M,D
Spanish M
Special Education M
Sports Management M,D
Statistics M,D
Supply Chain Management M
Technical Communication M
Textile Sciences and Engineering M,D
Toxicology M,D
Travel and Tourism M,D
Veterinary Medicine M,D
Veterinary Sciences M,D
Writing M
Zoology M,D

NORTH CENTRAL COLLEGE

Business Administration and Management—General M
Computer Science M
Cultural Studies M
Curriculum and Instruction M
Education—General M
Educational Leadership and Administration M
Ethics M
Finance and Banking M
Human Resources Management M
International Business M
Internet and Interactive Multimedia M
Liberal Studies M
Management Strategy and Policy M
Marketing M
Organizational Management M
Publishing M
Sports Management M
Technical Communication M
Writing M

NORTHCENTRAL UNIVERSITY

Business Administration and Management—General M,D,O
Education—General M,D,O
Marriage and Family Therapy M,D,O
Psychology—General M,D,O

NORTH DAKOTA STATE UNIVERSITY

Accounting M
Adult Education M,D,O
Agricultural Economics and Agribusiness M
Agricultural Education M
Agricultural Sciences—General M,D
Agronomy and Soil Sciences M,D
Animal Sciences M,D
Anthropology M
Applied Mathematics M,D
Architecture M
Athletic Training and Sports Medicine M,D
Biochemistry M,D
Bioinformatics M,D
Biological and Biomedical Sciences—General M,D
Botany M,D
Business Administration and Management—General M
Cell Biology M,D
Chemistry M,D
Child and Family Studies M,D,O
Child Development M
Civil Engineering M,D
Clinical Psychology M,D
Clothing and Textiles M,O
Cognitive Sciences M,D
Communication—General M,D
Computer Engineering M,D
Consumer Economics M,O
Counseling Psychology M,D
Counselor Education M,D
Criminal Justice and Criminology M,D
Curriculum and Instruction M
Developmental Psychology D
Ecology M,D
Education—General M,D,O
Educational Leadership and Administration M,O
Electrical Engineering M,D
English M,D
Entomology M,D
Environmental Engineering M,D
Environmental Sciences M,D
Exercise and Sports Science M,D
Family and Consumer Sciences-General M
Food Science and Technology M,D,O
Genomic Sciences M,D
Gerontology M,O
Health Promotion M,D
Health Psychology M,D
Higher Education O
History M,D
Industrial/Management Engineering M,D
Logistics M,D
Manufacturing Engineering M,D
Marriage and Family Therapy M,D,O
Mass Communication M,D
Materials Sciences M,D
Mathematics Education M,D,O
Mathematics M,D
Mechanical Engineering M,D
Microbiology M,D
Molecular Biology M,D
Molecular Pathogenesis M,D
Music Education M,D,O
Music M,D
Nanotechnology M,D
Natural Resources M,D
Nursing—General M,D
Nutrition M,D
Pathology M,D
Pharmacy M,D
Physics M,D
Plant Pathology M,D
Plant Sciences M,D
Polymer Science and Engineering M,D
Psychology—General M,D
Public Health—General M,D
Rhetoric M,D
School Psychology M,D
Science Education M,D,O
Social Psychology M,D
Social Sciences Education M,D,O
Social Sciences M
Sociology M
Software Engineering M,D,O
Speech and Interpersonal Communication M,D
Statistics M,D,O
Transportation and Highway Engineering D
Transportation Management M,D
Urban and Regional Planning M
Urban Studies M,D
Vocational and Technical Education M,D,O
Writing M,D
Zoology M,D

NORTHEASTERN ILLINOIS UNIVERSITY

Accounting M
Applied Mathematics M
Biological and Biomedical Sciences—General M
Business Administration and Management—General M
Chemistry M
Computer Science M
Counselor Education M
Early Childhood Education M
Education of the Gifted M
Education—General M
Educational Leadership and Administration M
Elementary Education M
English as a Second Language M
English M
Environmental Management and Policy M
Exercise and Sports Science M
Finance and Banking M
Geography M
Gerontology M
History M
Human Resources Development M
Latin American Studies M
Linguistics M
Marketing M
Marriage and Family Therapy M
Mathematics Education M
Mathematics M
Multilingual and Multicultural Education M
Music M
Political Science M
Reading Education M
Rehabilitation Counseling M
Secondary Education M
Social Psychology M
Special Education M
Speech and Interpersonal Communication M
Urban Education M
Writing M

NORTHEASTERN SEMINARY AT ROBERTS WESLEYAN COLLEGE

Theology M,D

NORTHEASTERN STATE UNIVERSITY

Accounting M
Addictions/Substance Abuse Counseling M
American Indian/Native American Studies M
Business Administration and Management—General M
Communication Disorders M
Communication—General M
Counseling Psychology M
Counselor Education M
Criminal Justice and Criminology M
Early Childhood Education M
Education—General M
Educational Leadership and Administration M
Educational Media/Instructional Technology M
English M
Environmental and Occupational Health M
Environmental Management and Policy M
Finance and Banking M
Foundations and Philosophy of Education M
Health Education M
Kinesiology and Movement Studies M
Mathematics Education M
Natural Resources M
Nursing Education M
Occupational Therapy M
Optometry D
Psychology—General M
Reading Education M
Science Education M

NORTHEASTERN UNIVERSITY

Accounting M
Acute Care/Critical Care Nursing M,D,O
Allied Health—General M,D,O
Applied Arts and Design—General M
Applied Behavior Analysis M,D,O
Applied Mathematics M,D
Architecture M
Art/Fine Arts M
Bioengineering M,D,O
Bioinformatics M,D
Biological and Biomedical Sciences—General M,D
Biotechnology M,D,O
Business Administration and Management—General M,D,O
Chemical Engineering M,D,O
Chemistry M,D
Civil Engineering M,D,O
Communication Disorders M,D,O
Community Health M,D,O
Computer and Information Systems Security M,D,O
Computer Engineering M,D,O
Computer Science M,D
Corporate and Organizational Communication M
Counseling Psychology M,D,O
Criminal Justice and Criminology M,D
Curriculum and Instruction M,D
Ecology M,D
Economic Development M,D
Economics M,D
Education—General M,D
Educational Leadership and Administration M,D
Electrical Engineering M,D,O
Elementary Education M,D
Energy and Power Engineering M,D,O
Engineering and Applied Sciences—General M,D,O
Engineering Management M,D,O
English M,D
Entrepreneurship M
Evolutionary Biology M,D
Exercise and Sports Science M,D,O
Family Nurse Practitioner Studies M,D,O
Finance and Banking M
Geographic Information Systems M
Gerontological Nursing M,D,O
Health Informatics M,D,O
Higher Education M,D
History M,D
Homeland Security M,D
Human Services M
Industrial/Management Engineering M,D,O
Information Science M,D,O
Interdisciplinary Studies M,D,O
International Affairs M,D
International Business M,D
Internet and Interactive Multimedia M
Journalism M
Law M,D
Legal and Justice Studies M,D
Management Information Systems M,D

Marine Biology M,D
Maternal and Child/Neonatal Nursing M,D,O
Mathematics M,D
Mechanical Engineering M,D,O
Medicinal and Pharmaceutical Chemistry M,D,O
Nonprofit Management M
Nurse Anesthesia M,D,O
Nursing and Healthcare Administration M,D,O
Nursing—General M,D,O
Nutrition M
Operations Research M,D,O
Organizational Management M,D
Pediatric Nursing M,D,O
Pharmaceutical Sciences M,D,O
Pharmacology M,D,O
Pharmacy M,D,O
Physical Therapy M,D,O
Physician Assistant Studies M,D,O
Physics M,D
Political Science M,D
Project Management M
Psychiatric Nursing M,D,O
Psychology—General M,D
Public Administration M,D
Public History M,D
Public Policy M,D
School Psychology M,D,O
Secondary Education M,D
Sociology M,D
Special Education M,D
Sports Management M
Systems Engineering M,D,O
Taxation M
Technical Communication M
Telecommunications M,D,O
Urban Studies M,D,O

NORTHEAST OHIO MEDICAL UNIVERSITY
Allopathic Medicine D
Bioethics M,D,O
Health Services Management and Hospital Administration M,D,O
Pharmaceutical Administration M,D,O
Pharmaceutical Sciences M,D,O
Pharmacy D
Public Health—General M,D,O

NORTHERN ARIZONA UNIVERSITY
Allied Health—General M,D,O
Anthropology M
Applied Physics M,D
Applied Statistics M,O
Archaeology M
Atmospheric Sciences M,D
Biological and Biomedical Sciences—General M,D
Business Administration and Management—General M
Chemistry M
Civil Engineering M
Clinical Psychology M
Communication Disorders M
Communication—General M
Community College Education M,D,O
Computer Engineering M
Computer Science M
Counseling Psychology M,D,O
Counselor Education M,D,O
Criminal Justice and Criminology M
Cultural Anthropology M
Curriculum and Instruction M,D
Early Childhood Education M,D
Education—General M,D,O
Educational Leadership and Administration M,D,O
Educational Media/Instructional Technology M,O
Educational Psychology M,D,O
Electrical Engineering M
Elementary Education M,D
Engineering and Applied Sciences—General M,D,O
English as a Second Language M,D,O
English Education M,D,O
English M,D,O
Environmental Engineering M
Environmental Management and Policy M,D
Environmental Sciences M,D
Ethnic Studies O
Family Nurse Practitioner Studies M,D,O
Foreign Languages Education M
Forestry M,D
Foundations and Philosophy of Education M,D,O
Gender Studies O
Geographic Information Systems M,O
Geography M,O
Geology M,D
Higher Education M,D,O
History M
Human Development O
Liberal Studies M
Linguistics M,D,O
Mathematics Education M,O
Mathematics M,O
Mechanical Engineering M
Meteorology M,D
Multilingual and Multicultural Education M,O
Music M,O
Nursing—General M,D,O
Physical Therapy D
Physician Assistant Studies M
Physics M,D
Political Science M,D,O
Psychology—General M
Public Administration M,D,O
Rhetoric M,D,O
School Psychology M,D,O
Science Education M,O
Secondary Education M,D
Sociology M
Spanish M
Special Education M,O
Statistics M,O
Student Affairs M,D,O
Sustainable Development M
Urban and Regional Planning M,O
Vocational and Technical Education M,O
Women's Studies O
Writing M,D,O

NORTHERN ILLINOIS UNIVERSITY
Accounting M
Adult Education M,D
Anthropology M
Art/Fine Arts M
Biological and Biomedical Sciences—General M,D
Business Administration and Management—General M
Chemistry M,D
Child and Family Studies M
Communication Disorders M,D
Communication—General M
Computer Science M
Counselor Education M,D
Curriculum and Instruction M,D
Dance M
Early Childhood Education M,D
Economics M,D
Education—General M,D,O
Educational Leadership and Administration M,D,O
Educational Media/Instructional Technology M,D
Educational Psychology M,D,O
Electrical Engineering M
Elementary Education M,D
Engineering and Applied Sciences—General M
English M,D
Foundations and Philosophy of Education M,D,O
French M
Geography M,D
Geology M,D
Higher Education M,D
History M,D
Industrial and Manufacturing Management M
Industrial/Management Engineering M
Law D
Mathematics M,D
Mechanical Engineering M
Music M,O
Nursing—General M
Nutrition M
Philosophy M
Physical Education M
Physical Therapy M,D
Physics M,D
Political Science M,D
Psychology—General M,D
Public Administration M
Public Health—General M
Reading Education M,D
Romance Languages M
Secondary Education M,D
Sociology M
Spanish M
Special Education M,D
Sports Management M
Statistics M
Taxation M
Theater M

NORTHERN KENTUCKY UNIVERSITY
Accounting M,O
Advertising and Public Relations M,O
Allied Health—General M
Business Administration and Management—General M,O
Clinical Psychology M
Communication—General M,O
Computer and Information Systems Security M,O
Computer Science M,O
Counseling Psychology M
Counselor Education M
Cultural Studies M,O
Education—General M,D,O
Educational Leadership and Administration M,D,O
English M,O
Geographic Information Systems M,O
Health Informatics M,O
Health Psychology M,O
Industrial and Organizational Psychology M,O
Information Science M,O
Law D
Liberal Studies M
Management of Technology M
Marriage and Family Therapy M,O
Media Studies M,O
Music M,O
Nonprofit Management M,O
Nursing—General M,D,O
Organizational Management M
Public Administration M,O
Public History M
Rhetoric M,O
Social Work M
Software Engineering M,O
Special Education M,O
Taxation M,O
Writing M,O

NORTHERN MICHIGAN UNIVERSITY
Applied Behavior Analysis M,O
Biochemistry M
Biological and Biomedical Sciences—General M
Business Administration and Management—General M
Clinical Laboratory Sciences/Medical Technology M
Criminal Justice and Criminology M
Curriculum and Instruction M
Education—General M
Educational Leadership and Administration M
Elementary Education M
English as a Second Language M,O
English M,O
Exercise and Sports Science M
Family Nurse Practitioner Studies M,D
Higher Education M
Human Resources Management M
Molecular Genetics M
Nursing—General M,D
Psychology—General M,O
Public Administration M
Reading Education M
Science Education M
Secondary Education M
Special Education M
Student Affairs M
Theater M,O
Writing M,O

NORTHERN SEMINARY
Pastoral Ministry and Counseling M,D
Religion M,D
Theology M,D

NORTHERN STATE UNIVERSITY
Clinical Psychology M
Counseling Psychology M
Counselor Education M
Curriculum and Instruction M
Education—General M
Educational Leadership and Administration M
Educational Media/Instructional Technology M
Finance and Banking M
Music Education M
Sports Management M

NORTH GREENVILLE UNIVERSITY
Education—General M,D
Finance and Banking M,D
Human Resources Management M,D
Pastoral Ministry and Counseling M,D

NORTH PARK THEOLOGICAL SEMINARY
Pastoral Ministry and Counseling M,O
Theology M,D

NORTH PARK UNIVERSITY
Adult Nursing M
Business Administration and Management—General M
Education—General M
Music M
Nonprofit Management M
Nursing and Healthcare Administration M
Nursing—General M

NORTHWEST CHRISTIAN UNIVERSITY
Accounting M
Business Administration and Management—General M
Counseling Psychology M
Counselor Education M
Curriculum and Instruction M
Education—General M
Educational Media/Instructional Technology M
Elementary Education M
English as a Second Language M
Secondary Education M

NORTHWESTERN COLLEGE
Early Childhood Education M,O
Education—General M,O
Educational Leadership and Administration M,O

NORTHWESTERN HEALTH SCIENCES UNIVERSITY
Acupuncture and Oriental Medicine M
Chiropractic D

NORTHWESTERN OKLAHOMA STATE UNIVERSITY
Adult Education M
American Studies M
Counseling Psychology M
Counselor Education M
Curriculum and Instruction M
Education—General M
Educational Leadership and Administration M
Elementary Education M
Reading Education M
Secondary Education M

NORTHWESTERN POLYTECHNIC UNIVERSITY
Business Administration and Management—General M,D
Computer Engineering M,D
Computer Science M,D
Electrical Engineering M,D
Engineering and Applied Sciences—General M,D

NORTHWESTERN STATE UNIVERSITY OF LOUISIANA
Adult Education M
Art/Fine Arts M
Clinical Psychology M
Counselor Education M,O
Curriculum and Instruction M
Early Childhood Education M
Education—General M,O
Educational Leadership and Administration M,O
Educational Media/Instructional Technology M,O
Elementary Education M,O
English M
Health Education M
Health Physics/Radiological Health M
Homeland Security M
Middle School Education M
Music M
Nursing—General M
Psychology—General M
Reading Education M,O
Secondary Education M,O
Special Education M,O
Student Affairs M

NORTHWESTERN UNIVERSITY
Accounting M,D
African Studies O
African-American Studies D
Allopathic Medicine
American Studies M
Anthropology D
Applied Mathematics M,D
Applied Physics D
Art History D
Art/Fine Arts M
Artificial Intelligence/Robotics M
Arts Administration M
Astronomy D
Biochemistry D
Bioengineering D
Biological and Biomedical Sciences—General D
Biomedical Engineering M,D
Biophysics D
Biopsychology D
Biostatistics D
Biotechnology M,D
Broadcast Journalism M
Business Administration and Management—General M,D
Cell Biology D
Chemical Engineering M,D
Chemistry D
Civil Engineering M,D
Clinical Laboratory Sciences/Medical Technology M
Clinical Psychology D
Clinical Research M,O
Cognitive Sciences D
Communication Disorders M,D
Communication—General M,D
Comparative Literature M,D
Computer and Information Systems Security M
Computer Engineering M,D
Computer Science M,D
Corporate and Organizational Communication M,D
Database Systems M
Developmental Biology D
Economics D
Education—General M,D*
Educational Leadership and Administration M
Educational Media/Instructional Technology M,D
Electrical Engineering M,D
Electronic Commerce M
Elementary Education M
Engineering and Applied Sciences—General M,D,O
Engineering Design M
Engineering Management M
English M,D
Entrepreneurship M,D
Environmental Engineering M,D
Epidemiology D
Ethics M
Film, Television, and Video Production M,D
Finance and Banking M,D
French D,O
Gender Studies O
Genetic Counseling M
Geology D
Geosciences D
Geotechnical Engineering M,D
German D
Health Informatics D
Health Services Management and Hospital Administration M,D
Health Services Research D
History M,D
Human Development D
Human Resources Management M,D
Industrial and Manufacturing Management M,D
Industrial/Management Engineering M,D
Information Science M
International Affairs M,D,O
International Business M,D
International Health M
Internet and Interactive Multimedia M

*M—masters degree; D—doctorate; O—other advanced degree; *—Close-Up and/or Display*

Italian D,O
Journalism M
Kinesiology and Movement Studies D
Law M,D*
Liberal Studies M
Linguistics D
Management Information Systems M
Management Strategy and Policy M,D
Marketing M,D
Marriage and Family Therapy M
Materials Engineering M,D,O
Materials Sciences M,D,O
Mathematics D
Mechanical Engineering M,D
Mechanics M,D
Media Studies M,D
Medical Informatics M,D
Molecular Biology D
Music Education M,D
Music M,D
Neurobiology M,D
Neuroscience D
Organizational Behavior M
Organizational Management M,D
Philosophy D
Physical Therapy D
Physics D
Physiology M
Plant Biology M,D
Political Science D
Portuguese D
Project Management M
Psychology—General D
Public Administration M
Public Health—General M
Public Policy M,D
Publishing M
Quality Management M
Quantitative Analysis M,D
Real Estate M,D
Rehabilitation Sciences D
Religion M,D
Rhetoric M,D
Secondary Education M
Slavic Languages D
Social Psychology D
Sociology M,D
Software Engineering M
Spanish D
Speech and Interpersonal Communication M,D
Sports Management M
Statistics M,D
Structural Biology D
Structural Engineering M,D
Systems Biology D
Taxation M,D
Theater M,D
Transportation and Highway Engineering M,D
Writing M

NORTHWEST MISSOURI STATE UNIVERSITY

Agricultural Economics and Agribusiness M
Agricultural Education M
Agricultural Sciences—General M
Biological and Biomedical Sciences—General M
Business Administration and Management—General M
Computer Science M
Counselor Education M
Early Childhood Education M
Education—General M,O
Educational Leadership and Administration M,O
Educational Media/Instructional Technology M
Elementary Education M,O
English as a Second Language M,O
English Education M
English M
Exercise and Sports Science M
Geographic Information Systems M,O
Health Education M
History M,O
Management Information Systems M
Mathematics Education M
Mathematics M
Middle School Education M,O
Music Education M
Physical Education M
Psychology—General M
Reading Education M
Recreation and Park Management M
Science Education M
Secondary Education M,O
Social Sciences Education M,O
Special Education M

NORTHWEST NAZARENE UNIVERSITY

Addictions/Substance Abuse Counseling M
Business Administration and Management—General M
Clinical Psychology M
Counselor Education M
Curriculum and Instruction M,D,O
Education—General M,D,O
Educational Leadership and Administration M,D,O
Health Services Management and Hospital Administration M
Marriage and Family Therapy M
Missions and Missiology M
Nursing and Healthcare Administration M
Pastoral Ministry and Counseling M
Religion M
School Psychology M
Social Work M
Theology M

Urban and Regional Planning M

NORTHWEST UNIVERSITY

Business Administration and Management—General M
Counseling Psychology M,D
Cultural Studies M
Education—General M
International Business M
Missions and Missiology M
Organizational Management M
Pastoral Ministry and Counseling M
Project Management M
Psychology—General M,D
Theology M
Urban and Regional Planning M,D

NORTHWOOD UNIVERSITY, MICHIGAN CAMPUS

Business Administration and Management—General M

NORWICH UNIVERSITY

American Studies M
Business Administration and Management—General M
Civil Engineering M
Computer and Information Systems Security M
Conflict Resolution and Mediation/Peace Studies M
Construction Management M
Criminal Justice and Criminology M
Emergency Management M
Environmental Engineering M
Finance and Banking M
Forensic Sciences M
Geotechnical Engineering M
History M
Hospitality Management M
Human Resources Management M
International Affairs M
International Business M
International Development M
Logistics M
Management Information Systems M
Management Strategy and Policy M
Military and Defense Studies M
Nonprofit Management M
Nursing and Healthcare Administration M
Nursing Education M
Nursing—General M
Organizational Management M
Project Management M
Public Administration M
Public Policy M
Structural Engineering M
Supply Chain Management M
Water Resources Engineering M

NOTRE DAME COLLEGE (OH)

Computer Science M,O
Homeland Security M,O
Reading Education M,O
Special Education M,O

NOTRE DAME DE NAMUR UNIVERSITY

Art Therapy M
Business Administration and Management—General M
Clinical Psychology M
Curriculum and Instruction M,D
Education—General M,D
Educational Leadership and Administration M
English M
Entrepreneurship M
Finance and Banking M
Human Resources Management M
Industrial and Manufacturing Management M
Management of Technology M
Marketing M
Marriage and Family Therapy M
Music M,O
Psychology—General M
Public Administration M
Public Affairs M
Special Education M

NOTRE DAME OF MARYLAND UNIVERSITY

Business Administration and Management—General M
Communication—General M
Education—General M
Educational Leadership and Administration M,D
English as a Second Language M
Liberal Studies M
Nonprofit Management M

NOTRE DAME SEMINARY

Theology M

NOVA SOUTHEASTERN UNIVERSITY

Accounting M
Allied Health—General M,D
Anesthesiologist Assistant Studies M,D
Art/Fine Arts M,D,O
Atmospheric Sciences M,D,O
Bioinformatics M,D,O
Biological and Biomedical Sciences—General M,D,O
Business Administration and Management—General M
Business Education M
Clinical Psychology M,D,O
Communication Disorders M,D
Computer and Information Systems Security M,D
Computer Science M,D
Conflict Resolution and Mediation/Peace Studies M,D,O
Counseling Psychology M,D,O
Counselor Education M,D,O

Dentistry M,D
Distance Education Development M,D,O
Education—General M,D,O
Educational Media/Instructional Technology M,D,O
Emergency Management M,D,O
Entrepreneurship M
Environmental Sciences M,D,O
Finance and Banking M
Health Informatics M,D,O
Health Law M,D
Human Resources Management M
Humanities M,D,O
Information Science M,D
Interdisciplinary Studies M,D,O
International Business M
Law M,D
Legal and Justice Studies M,D
Management Information Systems M,D
Management Strategy and Policy M
Marine Affairs M,D,O
Marine Biology M,D,O
Marine Sciences M,D,O
Marketing M
Marriage and Family Therapy M,D,O
Medical Informatics M,D,O
Nursing—General M,D
Occupational Therapy M,D
Oceanography M,D,O
Optometry M,D
Osteopathic Medicine M,D,O
Pharmaceutical Administration D
Pharmacy D*
Physical Therapy M,D
Physician Assistant Studies M,D
Psychology—General M,D,O
Public Administration M
Public Health—General M,D,O
School Psychology M,D,O
Social Sciences M,D,O
Software Engineering M,D
Student Affairs M,D,O
Supply Chain Management M
Taxation M

NSCAD UNIVERSITY

Applied Arts and Design—General M
Art/Fine Arts M

NYACK COLLEGE

Business Administration and Management—General M
Counseling Psychology M
Counselor Education M
Elementary Education M
English as a Second Language M
Marriage and Family Therapy M
Missions and Missiology M,D
Organizational Management M
Pastoral Ministry and Counseling M,D
Religion M
Social Work M
Special Education M
Theology M,D

OAKLAND CITY UNIVERSITY

Business Administration and Management—General M
Education—General M,D
Educational Leadership and Administration M,D
Theology M,D

OAKLAND UNIVERSITY

Accounting M,O
Allied Health—General M,D,O
Applied Behavior Analysis M,O
Applied Mathematics M,D
Applied Statistics M
Biological and Biomedical Sciences—General M,D,O
Business Administration and Management—General M,O
Chemistry M,D
Computer Engineering M,D
Computer Science M,D
Counseling Psychology M,D,O
Early Childhood Education M,D,O
Economics M,O
Education—General M,D,O
Educational Leadership and Administration M,D,O
Electrical Engineering M,D
Elementary Education M,O
Engineering and Applied Sciences—General M,D,O
Engineering Management M,D,O
English as a Second Language M,O
English M
Entrepreneurship M,O
Environmental and Occupational Health M
Environmental Sciences M,D
Exercise and Sports Science M,D,O
Family Nurse Practitioner Studies M,O
Finance and Banking M,O
Gerontological Nursing M,O
Higher Education M,D,O
History M
Human Resources Management M,O
Industrial and Manufacturing Management M,O
International Business M,O
Liberal Studies M
Linguistics M,O
Management Information Systems M,D,O
Marketing M,O
Maternal and Child Health D,O
Mathematics M
Mechanical Engineering M,D
Medical Physics M,D
Music Education M,D
Music M,D
Nonprofit Management M,O

Nurse Anesthesia M,O
Nursing—General M,D,O
Organizational Management M,D,O
Physical Therapy D,O
Physics M,D
Public Administration M,O
Reading Education M,D,O
Secondary Education M,O
Software Engineering M,D
Special Education M,O
Statistics O
Systems Engineering M,D,O
Systems Science M,D

OAKWOOD UNIVERSITY

Pastoral Ministry and Counseling M

OBERLIN COLLEGE

Music Education M,O
Music M,O

OBLATE SCHOOL OF THEOLOGY

African-American Studies M,D,O
Pastoral Ministry and Counseling M,D,O
Religion M,D,O
Theology M,D,O

OCCIDENTAL COLLEGE

Biological and Biomedical Sciences—General M
Education—General M
Elementary Education M
English Education M
Foreign Languages Education M
Liberal Studies M
Mathematics Education M
Science Education M
Secondary Education M
Social Sciences Education M

OGLALA LAKOTA COLLEGE

Business Administration and Management—General M
Educational Leadership and Administration M

OHIO DOMINICAN UNIVERSITY

Accounting M
Business Administration and Management—General M
Curriculum and Instruction M
Education—General M
Educational Leadership and Administration M
English as a Second Language M
English M
Finance and Banking M
Health Services Management and Hospital Administration M
Liberal Studies M
Physician Assistant Studies M
Public Administration M
Sports Management M
Theology M

OHIO NORTHERN UNIVERSITY

Law M,D
Pharmacy D

THE OHIO STATE UNIVERSITY

Accounting M,D
Aerospace/Aeronautical Engineering M,D
African Studies M,D
African-American Studies M,D
Agricultural Economics and Agribusiness M,D
Agricultural Education M
Agricultural Engineering M,D
Agricultural Sciences—General M,D
Agronomy and Soil Sciences M,D
Allied Health—General M
Allopathic Medicine D
Anatomy M,D
Animal Sciences M,D
Anthropology M,D
Architecture M,D
Art Education M,D
Art History M,D
Art/Fine Arts M
Arts Administration M
Asian Languages M,D
Asian Studies M
Astronomy M,D
Atmospheric Sciences M,D
Biochemistry M,D
Bioengineering M,D
Biological and Biomedical Sciences—General M,D
Biomedical Engineering M,D
Biophysics M,D
Biostatistics M,D
Business Administration and Management—General M,D
Cell Biology M,D
Chemical Engineering M,D
Chemical Physics M,D
Chemistry M,D
Child and Family Studies M,D
Chinese M,D
Civil Engineering M,D
Classics M,D
Clinical Psychology D
Cognitive Sciences D
Communication Disorders M,D
Communication—General M,D
Computational Sciences M,D
Computer Art and Design M
Computer Engineering M,D
Computer Science M,D
Dance M,D
Dental Hygiene M,D
Dentistry M,D
Developmental Biology M,D
Developmental Psychology D
East European and Russian Studies M,D

Ecology	M,D
Economics	M,D
Education—General	M,D,O
Educational Leadership and Administration	M,D,O
Educational Policy	M,D,O
Electrical Engineering	M,D
Engineering and Applied Sciences—General	M,D
English	M,D
Entomology	M,D
Environmental Management and Policy	M,D
Environmental Sciences	M,D
Evolutionary Biology	M,D
Family and Consumer Sciences-General	M,D
Finance and Banking	M
Fish, Game, and Wildlife Management	M,D
Food Science and Technology	M,D
Forestry	M,D
French	M,D
Gender Studies	M,D
Genetics	M,D
Geodetic Sciences	M,D
Geography	M,D
Geology	M,D
Geosciences	M,D
German	M,D
Health Services Management and Hospital Administration	M,D
History	M,D
Horticulture	M,D
Human Development	M,D
Human Resources Management	M,D
Industrial and Labor Relations	M,D
Industrial Design	M
Industrial/Management Engineering	M,D
Interdisciplinary Studies	M,D
Interior Design	M
Internet and Interactive Multimedia	M
Italian	M,D
Japanese	M,D
Kinesiology and Movement Studies	M,D
Landscape Architecture	M,D
Latin American Studies	M
Law	M,D
Linguistics	M,D
Logistics	M
Management Information Systems	M,D
Materials Engineering	M,D
Materials Sciences	M,D
Mathematics Education	M,D
Mathematics	M,D
Mechanical Engineering	M,D
Metallurgical Engineering and Metallurgy	M,D
Microbiology	M,D
Molecular Biology	M,D
Molecular Genetics	M,D
Music	M,D
Natural Resources	M,D
Near and Middle Eastern Languages	M,D
Neuroscience	D
Nuclear Engineering	M,D
Nursing—General	M,D
Nutrition	M,D
Occupational Therapy	M
Operations Research	M
Optical Sciences	M,D
Optometry	M,D
Oral and Dental Sciences	M,D
Pharmaceutical Administration	M,D
Pharmacology	M,D
Pharmacy	M,D
Philosophy	M,D
Physical Education	M,D
Physical Therapy	D
Physics	M,D
Plant Pathology	M,D
Plant Sciences	D
Political Science	D
Portuguese	M,D
Psychology—General	D
Public Administration	M,D
Public Affairs	M,D
Public Health—General	M,D
Public Policy	M,D
Rehabilitation Sciences	D
Rural Sociology	M,D
Slavic Languages	M,D
Social Psychology	D
Social Sciences	M,D
Social Work	M,D
Sociology	D
Spanish	M,D
Special Education	D
Statistics	M,D
Systems Engineering	M,D
Theater	M,D
Urban and Regional Planning	M,D
Veterinary Sciences	M,D
Women's Studies	M,D

THE OHIO STATE UNIVERSITY AT LIMA

Social Work	M

THE OHIO STATE UNIVERSITY AT MARION

Education—General	M

THE OHIO STATE UNIVERSITY–MANSFIELD CAMPUS

Education—General	M
Social Work	M

THE OHIO STATE UNIVERSITY–NEWARK CAMPUS

Education—General	M
Social Work	M

OHIO UNIVERSITY

Acute Care/Critical Care Nursing	M
African Studies	M
Applied Economics	M
Art History	M
Art/Fine Arts	M
Asian Studies	M
Astronomy	M,D
Athletic Training and Sports Medicine	M
Biochemistry	M,D
Biological and Biomedical Sciences—General	M,D
Biomedical Engineering	M
Business Administration and Management—General	M
Cell Biology	M,D
Chemical Engineering	M,D
Child and Family Studies	M
Child Development	M
Civil Engineering	M,D
Clinical Psychology	M,D
Clothing and Textiles	M
Communication Disorders	M,D
Communication—General	M,D
Comparative and Interdisciplinary Arts	D
Computer Education	M,D
Computer Science	M,D
Construction Engineering	M,D
Consumer Economics	M
Corporate and Organizational Communication	M,D
Counselor Education	M,D
Curriculum and Instruction	M,D
Ecology	M,D
Economics	M
Education—General	M,D
Educational Leadership and Administration	M,D
Educational Measurement and Evaluation	M,D
Educational Media/Instructional Technology	M,D
Electrical Engineering	M,D
Engineering and Applied Sciences—General	M,D
English	M,D
Environmental Biology	M,D
Environmental Engineering	M,D
Environmental Management and Policy	M
Evolutionary Biology	M,D
Exercise and Sports Science	M,D
Experimental Psychology	M,D
Family and Consumer Sciences-General	M
Family Nurse Practitioner Studies	M
Film, Television, and Video Production	M
Film, Television, and Video Theory and Criticism	M
Finance and Banking	M
French	M
Geochemistry	M
Geography	M
Geology	M
Geophysics	M
Geotechnical Engineering	M,D
Graphic Design	M
Health Communication	M,D
Health Services Management and Hospital Administration	M
Higher Education	M,D
History	M,D
Hydrogeology	M
Industrial and Organizational Psychology	M,D
Industrial/Management Engineering	M,D
International Affairs	M
International Development	M
Journalism	M,D
Latin American Studies	M
Linguistics	M
Mathematics Education	M,D
Mathematics	M,D
Mechanical Engineering	M,D
Mechanics	M,D
Media Studies	M,D
Microbiology	M,D
Middle School Education	M,D
Molecular Biology	M,D
Multilingual and Multicultural Education	M,D
Music Education	M,O
Music	M,O
Neuroscience	M,D
Nursing and Healthcare Administration	M
Nursing Education	M
Nursing—General	M
Nutrition	M
Osteopathic Medicine	D
Philosophy	M
Photography	M
Physical Education	M
Physical Therapy	D
Physics	M,D
Physiology	M,D
Plant Biology	M,D
Political Science	M
Psychology—General	M,D
Public Administration	M
Public Health—General	M
Reading Education	M,D
Recreation and Park Management	M
Rehabilitation Counseling	M,D
Rhetoric	M,D
Science Education	M
Secondary Education	M,D
Social Sciences Education	M,D
Social Sciences	M
Social Work	M
Sociology	M
Spanish	M
Special Education	M,D
Speech and Interpersonal Communication	M,D
Sports Management	M
Structural Engineering	M,D
Student Affairs	M,D
Systems Engineering	M
Telecommunications	M
Theater	M
Therapies—Dance, Drama, and Music	M,O
Transportation and Highway Engineering	M,D
Water Resources Engineering	M,D

OHIO VALLEY UNIVERSITY

Curriculum and Instruction	M
Education—General	M

OHR HAMEIR THEOLOGICAL SEMINARY

Theology	

OKLAHOMA BAPTIST UNIVERSITY

Business Administration and Management—General	M
Energy Management and Policy	M
Marriage and Family Therapy	M
Nursing Education	M
Nursing—General	M

OKLAHOMA CHRISTIAN UNIVERSITY

Accounting	M
Business Administration and Management—General	M
Computer Engineering	M
Computer Science	M
Electrical Engineering	M
Engineering and Applied Sciences—General	M
Engineering Management	M
Finance and Banking	M
Health Services Management and Hospital Administration	M
Human Resources Management	M
International Business	M
Marketing	M
Mechanical Engineering	M
Organizational Management	M
Pastoral Ministry and Counseling	M
Project Management	M
Software Engineering	M
Theology	M

OKLAHOMA CITY UNIVERSITY

Applied Behavior Analysis	M
Business Administration and Management—General	M
Computer Science	M
Counselor Education	M
Criminal Justice and Criminology	M
Early Childhood Education	M
Elementary Education	M
Energy Management and Policy	M
English as a Second Language	M
Law	M,D
Music	M
Nursing Education	M,D
Nursing—General	M,D
Photography	M
Sociology	M
Writing	M

OKLAHOMA STATE UNIVERSITY

Accounting	M,D
Agricultural Economics and Agribusiness	M,D
Agricultural Education	M,D
Agricultural Engineering	M,D
Agricultural Sciences—General	M,D
Agronomy and Soil Sciences	M,D
Animal Sciences	M,D
Applied Arts and Design—General	M,D
Applied Behavior Analysis	M,D,O
Applied Mathematics	M,D
Applied Psychology	M,D,O
Biochemistry	M,D
Bioengineering	M,D
Biological and Biomedical Sciences—General	M,D
Botany	M,D
Business Administration and Management—General	M,D
Chemical Engineering	M,D
Chemistry	M,D
Child and Family Studies	M,D
Civil Engineering	M,D
Clinical Psychology	M,D
Clothing and Textiles	M,D
Communication Disorders	M
Computer Engineering	M,D
Computer Science	M,D
Consumer Economics	M,D
Curriculum and Instruction	M,D
Ecology	M,D
Economics	M,D
Education—General	M,D,O
Educational Leadership and Administration	M,D
Educational Psychology	M,D,O
Electrical Engineering	M,D
Emergency Management	M,D
Engineering and Applied Sciences—General	M,D
English	M,D
Entomology	M,D
Entrepreneurship	M,D
Environmental Engineering	M,D
Environmental Sciences	M,D,O
Evolutionary Biology	M,D
Family and Consumer Sciences-General	M,D
Finance and Banking	M,D
Fire Protection Engineering	M,D
Food Science and Technology	M,D
Forestry	M,D
Geography	M,D
Geology	M,D
Health Education	M,D,O
Health Psychology	M,D,O
Higher Education	M,D
History	M,D
Horticulture	M,D
Hospitality Management	M,D
Human Development	M,D
Industrial/Management Engineering	M,D
Information Science	M,D
International Affairs	M,D,O
Landscape Architecture	M,D
Management Information Systems	M,D
Marketing	M,D
Marriage and Family Therapy	M,D
Mass Communication	M
Mathematics Education	M,D
Mathematics	M,D
Mechanical Engineering	M,D
Microbiology	M,D
Molecular Biology	M,D
Molecular Genetics	M,D
Music Education	M
Music	M
Natural Resources	M,D
Nonprofit Management	M,D,O
Nutrition	M,D
Philosophy	M
Photonics	M,D
Physics	M,D
Plant Biology	M,D
Plant Pathology	M,D
Plant Sciences	M,D
Political Science	M,D
Psychology—General	M,D
Sociology	M,D
Statistics	M,D
Sustainability Management	M,D,O
Telecommunications Management	M,D,O
Theater	M
Veterinary Medicine	D
Veterinary Sciences	M,D
Writing	M,D

OKLAHOMA STATE UNIVERSITY CENTER FOR HEALTH SCIENCES

Biological and Biomedical Sciences—General	M,D
Forensic Sciences	M
Health Services Management and Hospital Administration	M
Osteopathic Medicine	D
Toxicology	M

OKLAHOMA WESLEYAN UNIVERSITY

Management Strategy and Policy	M
Nursing and Healthcare Administration	M
Nursing Education	M
Theology	M

OLD DOMINION UNIVERSITY

Accounting	M
Adult Nursing	M
Aerospace/Aeronautical Engineering	M,D
Allied Health—General	M,D
Analytical Chemistry	M,D
Applied Psychology	D
Athletic Training and Sports Medicine	M,D
Biochemistry	M,D
Biological and Biomedical Sciences—General	M,D
Biomedical Engineering	M,D
Biostatistics	M,D
Business Administration and Management—General	M,D
Business Education	M,D
Chemistry	M,D
Civil Engineering	M,D
Clinical Psychology	D
Communication Disorders	M
Community College Education	M,D
Community Health	M
Computer Art and Design	M
Computer Engineering	M,D
Computer Science	M,D
Conflict Resolution and Mediation/Peace Studies	M,D
Counseling Psychology	M,D,O
Counselor Education	M,D,O
Criminal Justice and Criminology	D
Cultural Studies	M,D
Curriculum and Instruction	M,D
Dental Hygiene	M
Early Childhood Education	M,D
Ecology	D
Economics	M
Education—General	M,D,O
Educational Leadership and Administration	M,D,O

*M—masters degree; D—doctorate; O—other advanced degree; *—Close-Up and/or Display*

Educational Measurement and Evaluation D
Educational Media/Instructional Technology M,D
Educational Psychology D
Electrical Engineering M,D
Elementary Education M
Engineering and Applied Sciences—General M,D
Engineering Management M,D
English M,D
Environmental Engineering M,D
Environmental Sciences M,D
Ergonomics and Human Factors D
Exercise and Sports Science M
Experimental Psychology D
Family Nurse Practitioner Studies M,D
Finance and Banking D
Geotechnical Engineering M
Gerontological Nursing M
Health Promotion M
Health Services Research D
Higher Education M,D,O
History M
Humanities M
Hydraulics M
Industrial and Organizational Psychology D
Information Science D
Inorganic Chemistry M,D
International Affairs M,D
International Development M,D
Kinesiology and Movement Studies D
Library Science M
Linguistics M
Marketing D
Maternal and Child/Neonatal Nursing M
Mathematics M,D
Mechanical Engineering M,D
Middle School Education M
Modeling and Simulation M,D
Music Education M
Nurse Anesthesia M
Nurse Midwifery M,D
Nursing and Healthcare Administration M,D
Nursing Education M
Nursing—General M,D
Oceanography M,D
Organic Chemistry M,D
Pediatric Nursing M
Physical Chemistry M,D
Physical Education M
Physical Therapy M,D
Physics M,D
Psychology—General M,D
Public Administration M,D
Reading Education M,D
School Psychology M,D,O
Secondary Education M
Sociology M
Special Education M,D
Speech and Interpersonal Communication M
Sports Management M
Statistics M,D
Structural Engineering M
Systems Engineering M,D
Transportation and Highway Engineering M
Urban Studies D
Vocational and Technical Education M,D
Water Resources M
Writing M

OLIVET COLLEGE
Insurance M

OLIVET NAZARENE UNIVERSITY
Business Administration and Management—General M
Curriculum and Instruction M
Education—General M
Educational Leadership and Administration M
Elementary Education M
Library Science M
Organizational Management M
Reading Education M
Religion M
Secondary Education M
Theology M

OPEN UNIVERSITY
Business Administration and Management—General M
Education—General M
Engineering and Applied Sciences—General M
History M
Music M
Philosophy M

ORAL ROBERTS UNIVERSITY
Accounting M
Business Administration and Management—General M
Curriculum and Instruction M,D
Education—General M,D
Educational Leadership and Administration M,D
Entrepreneurship M
Finance and Banking M
Higher Education M,D
International Business M
Marketing M
Marriage and Family Therapy M,D
Missions and Missiology M,D
Near and Middle Eastern Languages M,D
Nonprofit Management M
Pastoral Ministry and Counseling M,D
Religious Education M,D
Theology M,D

OREGON COLLEGE OF ART & CRAFT
Art/Fine Arts M

OREGON COLLEGE OF ORIENTAL MEDICINE
Acupuncture and Oriental Medicine M,D

OREGON HEALTH & SCIENCE UNIVERSITY
Allopathic Medicine D
Biochemistry M,D
Biological and Biomedical Sciences—General M,D,O
Biomedical Engineering D
Biopsychology D
Cancer Biology/Oncology D
Cell Biology D
Clinical Research M,O
Community Health Nursing M,O
Computer Engineering M,D
Computer Science M,D
Dentistry D,O
Developmental Biology D
Electrical Engineering M,D
Environmental Engineering M,D
Environmental Sciences M,D
Family Nurse Practitioner Studies M,D,O
Genetics D
Gerontological Nursing M,D,O
Gerontology M,O
Health Informatics M,D,O
Health Services Management and Hospital Administration M,O
Immunology D
Medical Informatics M,D,O
Microbiology D
Molecular Biology M,D
Neuroscience D
Nurse Anesthesia M
Nurse Midwifery M,D,O
Nursing Education M,O
Nursing—General M,D,O
Nutrition M,O
Oral and Dental Sciences M,D,O
Pediatric Nursing M,D,O
Pharmacology D
Physician Assistant Studies M
Physiology D
Psychiatric Nursing M,O

OREGON INSTITUTE OF TECHNOLOGY
Manufacturing Engineering M

OREGON STATE UNIVERSITY
Accounting M,D
Actuarial Science M,D
Adult Education M
Agricultural Education M
Agronomy and Soil Sciences M,D
Allied Health—General M,D
Analytical Chemistry M,D
Animal Sciences M,D
Anthropology M,D
Applied Mathematics M,D
Artificial Intelligence/Robotics M,D
Athletic Training and Sports Medicine M
Atmospheric Sciences M,D
Biochemistry M,D
Bioengineering M,D
Bioethics M
Bioinformatics D
Biological and Biomedical Sciences—General M,D
Biophysics M,D
Biostatistics M,D
Biotechnology D
Botany M,D
Business Administration and Management—General M,D
Cell Biology M,D
Chemical Engineering M,D
Chemistry M,D
Child and Family Studies M,D
Civil Engineering M,D
Clothing and Textiles M,D
Cognitive Sciences M,D
Computational Sciences M,D
Computer Engineering M,D
Computer Science M,D
Conservation Biology M,D
Construction Engineering M,D
Counselor Education M,D
Developmental Biology M,D
Ecology M,D
Economics M,D
Education—General M,D
Educational Leadership and Administration M
Electrical Engineering M,D
Elementary Education M
Energy and Power Engineering M,D
Engineering and Applied Sciences—General M,D
Engineering Design M,D
Engineering Management M,D
English M
Environmental and Occupational Health M,D
Environmental Education M,D
Environmental Engineering M,D
Environmental Management and Policy M,D
Environmental Sciences M,D
Epidemiology M,D
Ethics M
Finance and Banking M,D
Fish, Game, and Wildlife Management M,D
Food Science and Technology M,D
Forestry M,D
Gender Studies M,D
Genomic Sciences M,D
Geochemistry M,D
Geographic Information Systems M
Geography M,D
Geology M,D
Geophysics M,D
Geotechnical Engineering M,D
Health Physics/Radiological Health M,D
Health Promotion M,D
Health Psychology M,D
Health Services Management and Hospital Administration M,D
Higher Education M
Hispanic Studies M
History of Medicine M,D
History of Science and Technology M,D
Horticulture M,D
Human Development M,D
Immunology M,D
Industrial/Management Engineering M,D
Inorganic Chemistry M,D
Interdisciplinary Studies M
Interior Design M,D
International Health M,D
Investment Management M,D
Kinesiology and Movement Studies M,D
Management Strategy and Policy M,D
Manufacturing Engineering M,D
Marine Affairs M
Marine Sciences M
Marketing M,D
Materials Sciences M,D
Mathematical and Computational Finance M,D
Mathematics Education M,D
Mathematics M,D
Mechanical Engineering M,D
Medical Physics M,D
Medicinal and Pharmaceutical Chemistry M,D
Microbiology M,D
Modeling and Simulation M,D
Molecular Biology D
Molecular Pathogenesis D
Music Education M
Natural Resources M,D
Nuclear Engineering M,D
Nutrition M,D
Ocean Engineering M,D
Oceanography M,D
Organic Chemistry M,D
Parasitology M,D
Pharmaceutical Sciences M,D
Pharmacology M,D
Pharmacy D
Physical Chemistry M,D
Physics M,D
Plant Molecular Biology D
Plant Pathology M,D
Psychology—General M,D
Public Health—General M,D
Public Policy M,D
Range Science M,D
Reading Education M
Science Education M,D
Social Sciences Education M,D
Statistics M,D
Structural Biology D
Structural Engineering M,D
Student Affairs M
Supply Chain Management M,D
Sustainability Management M,D
Textile Design M,D
Toxicology M,D
Transportation and Highway Engineering M,D
Veterinary Medicine D
Virology M,D
Water Resources Engineering M,D
Water Resources M,D
Women's Studies M,D
Writing M
Zoology M,D

OREGON STATE UNIVERSITY–CASCADES
Education—General M
School Psychology M
Social Psychology M

OTIS COLLEGE OF ART AND DESIGN
Art/Fine Arts M
Graphic Design M
Photography M
Writing M

OTTAWA UNIVERSITY
Art Therapy M
Business Administration and Management—General M
Counseling Psychology M
Counselor Education M
Curriculum and Instruction M
Early Childhood Education M
Education—General M
Educational Leadership and Administration M
Educational Media/Instructional Technology M
Elementary Education M
Finance and Banking M
Human Resources Development M
Human Resources Management M
Marketing M
Marriage and Family Therapy M
Pastoral Ministry and Counseling M
School Psychology M
Special Education M

OTTERBEIN UNIVERSITY
Business Administration and Management—General M
Education—General M
Family Nurse Practitioner Studies M,D,O
Nurse Anesthesia M,D,O
Nursing and Healthcare Administration M,D,O
Nursing Education M,D,O
Nursing—General M,D,O

OUR LADY OF THE LAKE COLLEGE
Health Services Management and Hospital Administration M
Nurse Anesthesia M
Nursing and Healthcare Administration M
Nursing Education M
Nursing—General M
Physician Assistant Studies M

OUR LADY OF THE LAKE UNIVERSITY OF SAN ANTONIO
Accounting M
Business Administration and Management—General M
Communication Disorders M
Computer and Information Systems Security M
Counseling Psychology D
Counselor Education M
Curriculum and Instruction M
Education—General M,D
English M
Finance and Banking M
Health Services Management and Hospital Administration M
Management Information Systems M
Nonprofit Management M
Organizational Management M,D
Psychology—General M
School Psychology M
Science Education M
Social Work M,D
Sociology M,D
Writing M

OXFORD GRADUATE SCHOOL
Child and Family Studies M,D
Organizational Management M,D
Religion M,D
Sociology M,D

PACE UNIVERSITY
Accounting M,O
Addictions/Substance Abuse Counseling M,D
Art/Fine Arts M,O
Biochemistry M
Biological and Biomedical Sciences—General M,O
Business Administration and Management—General M,D,O
Business Education M,O
Chemistry M,O
Clinical Psychology M,D
Computer and Information Systems Security M,D,O
Computer Science M,D,O
Counseling Psychology M,D
Developmental Psychology M,D
Early Childhood Education M,O
Economics O
Education—General M,O
Educational Media/Instructional Technology M,O
Electronic Commerce O
Elementary Education M,O
Emergency Management M
English M,O
Entrepreneurship M
Environmental Law M,D
Environmental Management and Policy M
Environmental Sciences M
Family Nurse Practitioner Studies M,D,O
Finance and Banking M,D,O
Foreign Languages Education M,O
Forensic Sciences M
Geosciences M,O
Health Services Management and Hospital Administration M
Homeland Security M
Human Resources Management M
Information Science M,D,O
International Business M,O
International Economics O
Internet and Interactive Multimedia M,D,O
Investment Management M,O
Law M,D
Legal and Justice Studies M,D
Management Information Systems M
Management Strategy and Policy M
Marketing M,D,O
Mathematics M,O
Media Studies M
Molecular Biology M
Nonprofit Management M
Nursing and Healthcare Administration M,D,O
Nursing Education M,D,O
Nursing—General M,D,O
Physician Assistant Studies M
Physics M,O
Psychology—General M
Public Administration M
Publishing M,O
Reading Education M,O
School Psychology M,D
Social Sciences Education M,O
Software Engineering M,D,O
Special Education M,O
Sustainable Development M,D
Taxation M
Telecommunications M,D,O
Theater M

PACIFICA GRADUATE INSTITUTE
Clinical Psychology M,D
Counseling Psychology M,D
Psychology—General M,D

PACIFIC COLLEGE OF ORIENTAL MEDICINE
Acupuncture and Oriental Medicine M,D

PACIFIC COLLEGE OF ORIENTAL MEDICINE–CHICAGO
Acupuncture and Oriental Medicine M

PACIFIC COLLEGE OF ORIENTAL MEDICINE-NEW YORK
Acupuncture and Oriental Medicine M

PACIFIC LUTHERAN UNIVERSITY
Accounting M
Business Administration and Management—General M
Curriculum and Instruction M
Education—General M
Family Nurse Practitioner Studies D
Finance and Banking M
Marriage and Family Therapy M
Nursing—General M,D
Writing M

PACIFIC NORTHWEST COLLEGE OF ART
Applied Arts and Design—General M
Art/Fine Arts M
Cultural Studies M

PACIFIC OAKS COLLEGE
Early Childhood Education M
Education—General M
Human Development M
Marriage and Family Therapy M
Special Education M

PACIFIC RIM CHRISTIAN UNIVERSITY
Pastoral Ministry and Counseling M

PACIFIC SCHOOL OF RELIGION
Religion M,D,O
Theology M,D,O

PACIFIC STATES UNIVERSITY
Accounting M,D
Business Administration and Management—General M,D
Computer Science M
Finance and Banking M,D
International Business M,D
Management Information Systems M,D
Management of Technology M,D
Real Estate M,D

PACIFIC UNION COLLEGE
Education—General M
Elementary Education M
Secondary Education M

PACIFIC UNIVERSITY
Athletic Training and Sports Medicine M,D
Business Administration and Management—General M
Clinical Psychology M,D
Communication Disorders M,D
Early Childhood Education M
Education of the Gifted M
Education—General M
Elementary Education M
English as a Second Language M
Finance and Banking M
Health Services Management and Hospital Administration M
Middle School Education M
Occupational Therapy D
Optometry M,D
Pharmacy D
Physical Therapy M,D
Physician Assistant Studies M
Psychology—General M,D
Science Education M
Secondary Education M
Social Work M
Special Education M
Vision Sciences M,D
Writing M

PALM BEACH ATLANTIC UNIVERSITY
Addictions/Substance Abuse Counseling M
Business Administration and Management—General M
Counseling Psychology M
Counselor Education M
Education—General M
Family Nurse Practitioner Studies M,D
Marriage and Family Therapy M
Nursing and Healthcare Administration M,D
Nursing—General M,D
Organizational Management M
Pharmacy D
Theology M

PALMER COLLEGE OF CHIROPRACTIC
Anatomy M
Chiropractic D
Clinical Research M

PALO ALTO UNIVERSITY
Biopsychology D
Clinical Psychology D
Counseling Psychology M
Psychology—General M,D

PARIS COLLEGE OF ART
Art/Fine Arts M
Interior Design M
Media Studies M
Photography M
Textile Design M

PARKER UNIVERSITY
Chiropractic D

PARK UNIVERSITY
Business Administration and Management—General M,O
Curriculum and Instruction M,O
Education—General M,O
Educational Leadership and Administration M,O
Emergency Management M,O
Finance and Banking M,O
Health Services Management and Hospital Administration M,O
International Business M,O
International Health M,O
Management Information Systems M,O
Music M,O
Nonprofit Management M,O
Public Administration M,O
Public Affairs M,O
Reading Education M,O
Social Work M,O
Writing M,O

PAYNE THEOLOGICAL SEMINARY
Theology M

PEIRCE COLLEGE
Organizational Management M

PENN STATE ERIE, THE BEHREND COLLEGE
Accounting M
Business Administration and Management—General M
Engineering and Applied Sciences—General M
Industrial and Manufacturing Management M
Project Management M
Quality Management M

PENN STATE GREAT VALLEY
Business Administration and Management—General M,O
Computer and Information Systems Security M,O
Database Systems M,O
Engineering and Applied Sciences—General M,O
Engineering Management M,O
Finance and Banking M,O
Health Services Management and Hospital Administration M,O
Human Resources Development M,O
Human Resources Management M,O
Information Science M,O
Software Engineering M,O
Sustainability Management M,O
Systems Engineering M,O

PENN STATE HARRISBURG
Accounting M
Adult Education M,D,O
American Studies M,D,O
Applied Behavior Analysis M,D,O
Applied Psychology M,D,O
Clinical Psychology M,D,O
Communication—General M,D,O
Computer Science M,O
Criminal Justice and Criminology M,D,O
Curriculum and Instruction M,D,O
Developmental Education M,D,O
Education—General M,D,O
Electrical Engineering M,O
Engineering and Applied Sciences—General M,O
Engineering Management M,O
English as a Second Language M,D,O
Environmental Engineering M,O
Environmental Sciences M,O
Finance and Banking M,D,O
Folklore M,D,O
Health Education M,D,O
Health Psychology M,D,O
Health Services Management and Hospital Administration M,D,O
Historic Preservation M,D,O
Homeland Security M,D,O
Human Resources Management M,D,O
Humanities M,D,O
Management Information Systems M
Museum Studies M,D,O
Nonprofit Management M,D,O
Psychology—General M,D,O
Public Administration M,D,O
Public Affairs M,D,O
Reading Education M,D,O
Social Psychology M,D,O
Structural Engineering M,O
Writing M,D,O

PENN STATE HERSHEY MEDICAL CENTER
Allopathic Medicine M,D
Anatomy M,D
Biochemistry M,D
Biological and Biomedical Sciences—General M,D
Biostatistics D
Cell Biology D
Developmental Biology D
Health Services Research M
Immunology M,D
Infectious Diseases D
Molecular Genetics M,D
Molecular Medicine D
Molecular Toxicology D
Neurobiology D
Neuroscience M,D
Public Health—General M,D
Veterinary Sciences M

Virology M,D

PENN STATE UNIVERSITY - DICKINSON LAW
Law M,D

PENN STATE UNIVERSITY PARK
Accounting M,D
Acoustics M,D
Adult Education M,D,O
Aerospace/Aeronautical Engineering M,D
Agricultural Economics and Agribusiness M,D,O
Agricultural Education M,D,O
Agricultural Engineering M,D
Agricultural Sciences—General M,D,O
Agronomy and Soil Sciences M,D
Animal Sciences M,D
Anthropology M,D
Applied Statistics M,D
Architectural Engineering M,D
Architecture M,D
Art Education M,D,O
Art History M,D
Art/Fine Arts M,D,O
Astronomy M,D
Astrophysics M,D
Biochemistry M,D
Bioengineering M,D
Biological and Biomedical Sciences—General M,D
Biopsychology M,D
Biotechnology M,D
Business Administration and Management—General M,D
Cell Biology M,D
Chemical Engineering M,D
Chemistry M,D
Child and Family Studies M,D
Civil Engineering M,D
Communication Disorders M,D,O
Communication—General M,D
Comparative Literature M,D
Computer Science M,D
Counselor Education M,D,O
Criminal Justice and Criminology M,D
Curriculum and Instruction M,D,O
Ecology M,D
Economics M,D
Education—General M,D,O
Educational Leadership and Administration M,D,O
Educational Media/Instructional Technology M,D,O
Educational Policy M,D,O
Educational Psychology M,D,O
Electrical Engineering M,D
Engineering and Applied Sciences—General M,D
Engineering Design M
English as a Second Language M,D
English M,D
Entomology M,D
Environmental Engineering M,D
Environmental Management and Policy M
Environmental Sciences M
Fish, Game, and Wildlife Management M,D
Food Science and Technology M,D
Forestry M,D
French M,D
Geography M,D
Geosciences M,D
Geotechnical Engineering M,D
German M,D
Health Services Management and Hospital Administration M,D
History M,D
Horticulture M,D
Hospitality Management M,D
Human Development M,D
Human Resources Development M,D,O
Human Resources Management M
Industrial and Labor Relations M
Industrial/Management Engineering M,D
Information Science M,D
International Affairs M
Kinesiology and Movement Studies M,D,O
Landscape Architecture M,D
Law M,D
Leisure Studies M,D
Linguistics M,D
Management Information Systems M,D
Mass Communication M,D
Materials Engineering M,D
Materials Sciences M,D
Mathematics M,D
Mechanical Engineering M,D
Mechanics M,D
Media Studies M,D
Meteorology M,D
Microbiology M,D
Mineral/Mining Engineering M,D
Molecular Biology M,D
Music Education M,D,O
Music M,D,O
Nuclear Engineering M,D
Nursing—General M,D
Nutrition M,D
Pathobiology M,D
Philosophy M,D
Physics M,D
Physiology M,D
Plant Biology M,D
Plant Pathology M,D
Plant Sciences M,D
Political Science M,D
Psychology—General M,D
Recreation and Park Management M,D
Rural Sociology M,D,O
Russian M,D
School Psychology M,D,O
Sociology M,D
Spanish M,D
Special Education M,D,O
Statistics M,D
Supply Chain Management M,D
Sustainable Development M
Theater M
Travel and Tourism M,D
Vocational and Technical Education M,D,O

PENNSYLVANIA ACADEMY OF THE FINE ARTS
Art/Fine Arts M,O

PENNSYLVANIA COLLEGE OF HEALTH SCIENCES
Health Education M
Health Services Management and Hospital Administration M
Nursing and Healthcare Administration M
Nursing Education M

PENTECOSTAL THEOLOGICAL SEMINARY
Pastoral Ministry and Counseling M,D
Theology M,D

PEPPERDINE UNIVERSITY
Accounting M
American Studies M
Business Administration and Management—General M
Business Education M
Clinical Psychology M,D
Communication—General M
Conflict Resolution and Mediation/Peace Studies M
Economics M
Educational Leadership and Administration M,D
Educational Media/Instructional Technology M,D
Human Resources Management M
Humanities M
International Affairs M
International Business M
Law D
Marriage and Family Therapy M,D
Mathematics M,D
Media Studies M
Organizational Management M,D
Pastoral Ministry and Counseling M
Political Science M
Psychology—General M,D
Public Policy M
Religion M
Science Education M,D
Writing M

PERU STATE COLLEGE
Curriculum and Instruction M
Economics M
Education—General M
Entrepreneurship M
Organizational Management M

PFEIFFER UNIVERSITY
Business Administration and Management—General M
Elementary Education M
Health Services Management and Hospital Administration M
Organizational Management M
Religious Education M
Theology M

PHILADELPHIA COLLEGE OF OSTEOPATHIC MEDICINE
Applied Behavior Analysis M,D,O
Biological and Biomedical Sciences—General M
Biopsychology M,D,O
Clinical Psychology M,D,O
Counseling Psychology M,D,O
Forensic Sciences M
Industrial and Organizational Psychology M,D,O
Osteopathic Medicine D
Physician Assistant Studies M*
Psychology—General M,D,O*
School Psychology M,D,O

PHILADELPHIA UNIVERSITY
Architecture M
Art/Fine Arts M
Business Administration and Management—General M
Clothing and Textiles M
Construction Management M
Emergency Management M
Geography M
Industrial Design M
Interior Design M
Internet and Interactive Multimedia M
Management Strategy and Policy M
Marketing M
Modeling and Simulation M
Nurse Midwifery M,O
Occupational Therapy M,D
Physician Assistant Studies M
Social Psychology M
Sustainable Development M
Taxation M
Textile Design M

*M—masters degree; D—doctorate; O—other advanced degree; *—Close-Up and/or Display*

- Textile Sciences and Engineering M,D
- Urban and Regional Planning M

PHILLIPS GRADUATE INSTITUTE
- Art Therapy M
- Counselor Education M
- Marriage and Family Therapy M
- Organizational Behavior D

PHILLIPS THEOLOGICAL SEMINARY
- Business Administration and Management—General M,D
- Ethics M,D
- Higher Education M,D
- Missions and Missiology M,D
- Music M,D
- Pastoral Ministry and Counseling D
- Religious Education M,D
- Social Work M,D
- Theology M,D

PHOENIX SEMINARY
- Counseling Psychology M,D,O
- Pastoral Ministry and Counseling M,D,O
- Theology M,D,O

PIEDMONT COLLEGE
- Art Education M,O
- Business Administration and Management—General M
- Curriculum and Instruction M,O
- Early Childhood Education M,O
- Education—General M,O
- Educational Media/Instructional Technology M,O
- Middle School Education M,O
- Music Education M,O
- Secondary Education M,O
- Special Education M,O

PIEDMONT INTERNATIONAL UNIVERSITY
- Curriculum and Instruction M,D
- Educational Leadership and Administration M,D
- Pastoral Ministry and Counseling M,D
- Theology M,D

PINCHOT UNIVERSITY
- Business Administration and Management—General M
- Organizational Management M

PITTSBURGH THEOLOGICAL SEMINARY
- Pastoral Ministry and Counseling M,D
- Theology M,D

PITTSBURG STATE UNIVERSITY
- Accounting M
- Biological and Biomedical Sciences—General M
- Business Administration and Management—General M
- Chemistry M
- Clinical Psychology M
- Communication—General M
- Construction Engineering M
- Construction Management M,O
- Counselor Education M
- Education—General M,O
- Educational Leadership and Administration M,O
- Educational Media/Instructional Technology M
- Electrical Engineering M
- English M
- Exercise and Sports Science M
- Graphic Design M,O
- Health Education M
- History M
- Human Resources Development M
- International Business M
- Management of Technology M,O
- Manufacturing Engineering M,O
- Mathematics M
- Mechanical Engineering M
- Music Education M
- Music M
- Nursing—General M
- Physical Education M
- Physics M
- Polymer Science and Engineering M
- Psychology—General M
- School Psychology O
- Special Education M,O
- Sports Management M
- Vocational and Technical Education M,O
- Writing M

PLYMOUTH STATE UNIVERSITY
- Adult Education D
- Art Education M
- Athletic Training and Sports Medicine M
- Biological and Biomedical Sciences—General M
- Business Administration and Management—General M
- Clinical Psychology M,O
- Counselor Education M
- Cultural Studies M
- Curriculum and Instruction M
- Education—General O
- Educational Leadership and Administration M,O
- Educational Media/Instructional Technology M
- Elementary Education M
- English Education M
- Environmental Management and Policy M
- Foreign Languages Education M
- Health Education M
- Health Promotion M
- Higher Education D,O
- Historic Preservation M
- Mathematics Education M
- Meteorology M
- Music Education M
- Physical Education M
- Reading Education M
- School Psychology M,O
- Science Education M
- Secondary Education M
- Social Sciences Education M
- Special Education M

POINT LOMA NAZARENE UNIVERSITY
- Biological and Biomedical Sciences—General M
- Business Administration and Management—General M
- Counselor Education M
- Education—General M
- Educational Leadership and Administration M
- Entrepreneurship M
- Exercise and Sports Science M
- Family Nurse Practitioner Studies M,O
- Gerontological Nursing M,O
- Health Services Management and Hospital Administration M
- Kinesiology and Movement Studies M
- Maternal and Child/Neonatal Nursing M,O
- Nursing—General M,O
- Organizational Management M
- Pastoral Ministry and Counseling M
- Project Management M
- Psychiatric Nursing M,O
- Religion M
- Special Education M
- Sports Management M

POINT PARK UNIVERSITY
- Business Administration and Management—General M
- Clinical Psychology M
- Communication—General M
- Criminal Justice and Criminology M
- Curriculum and Instruction M
- Education—General M
- Educational Leadership and Administration M
- Engineering Management M
- Environmental Management and Policy M
- Journalism M
- Mass Communication M
- Music M
- Organizational Management M
- Special Education M
- Theater M

POLYTECHNIC UNIVERSITY OF PUERTO RICO
- Business Administration and Management—General M
- Civil Engineering M
- Computer Engineering M
- Computer Science M
- Electrical Engineering M
- Engineering Management M
- Environmental Management and Policy M
- Industrial and Manufacturing Management M
- International Business M
- Landscape Architecture M
- Management Information Systems M
- Management of Technology M
- Manufacturing Engineering M
- Mechanical Engineering M

POLYTECHNIC UNIVERSITY OF PUERTO RICO, MIAMI CAMPUS
- Accounting M
- Business Administration and Management—General M
- Construction Management M
- Environmental Engineering M
- Environmental Management and Policy M
- Finance and Banking M
- Human Resources Management M
- Industrial and Manufacturing Management M
- International Business M
- Logistics M
- Marketing M
- Project Management M
- Supply Chain Management M

POLYTECHNIC UNIVERSITY OF PUERTO RICO, ORLANDO CAMPUS
- Accounting M
- Business Administration and Management—General M
- Construction Management M
- Engineering Management M
- Environmental Engineering M
- Environmental Management and Policy M
- Finance and Banking M
- Human Resources Management M
- Industrial and Manufacturing Management M
- International Business M
- Management of Technology M

PONCE HEALTH SCIENCES UNIVERSITY
- Allopathic Medicine D
- Biological and Biomedical Sciences—General D
- Clinical Psychology D
- Epidemiology M,D
- Public Health—General M,D

PONTIFICAL CATHOLIC UNIVERSITY OF PUERTO RICO
- Accounting M,O
- Art/Fine Arts M
- Biological and Biomedical Sciences—General M
- Business Administration and Management—General M,D,O
- Business Education M,D
- Chemistry M
- Clinical Laboratory Sciences/Medical Technology O
- Clinical Psychology D
- Counselor Education M
- Criminal Justice and Criminology M
- Curriculum and Instruction M,D
- Education—General M,D
- Educational Leadership and Administration D
- Educational Psychology M
- English as a Second Language M
- Environmental Sciences M
- Finance and Banking M
- Hispanic Studies M,O
- History M
- Human Resources Management M,O
- Human Services M,D
- Industrial and Organizational Psychology D
- International Business M
- Law D
- Logistics O
- Management Information Systems M,O
- Marketing M
- Medical/Surgical Nursing M
- Nursing—General M
- Psychiatric Nursing M
- Psychology—General M,D
- Public Administration M
- Rehabilitation Counseling M
- Religious Education M
- Social Work M
- Spanish M,O
- Theology M
- Transportation Management O

PONTIFICAL COLLEGE JOSEPHINUM
- Theology M

PONTIFICIA UNIVERSIDAD CATOLICA MADRE Y MAESTRA
- Allopathic Medicine D
- Architecture M
- Building Science M
- Business Administration and Management—General M
- Clinical Psychology M
- Criminal Justice and Criminology M
- Developmental Psychology M
- Early Childhood Education M
- Engineering and Applied Sciences—General M
- Entrepreneurship M
- Finance and Banking M
- Forensic Psychology M
- Hospitality Management M
- Human Resources Management M
- Insurance M
- Interior Design M
- International Affairs M
- International Business M
- Landscape Architecture M
- Law M
- Logistics M
- Management Strategy and Policy M
- Marketing M
- Psychology—General M
- Real Estate M
- Structural Engineering M
- Travel and Tourism M

POPE ST. JOHN XXIII NATIONAL SEMINARY
- Theology M

PORTLAND STATE UNIVERSITY
- Anthropology M,D,O
- Applied Economics M,D
- Applied Social Research M,D
- Architecture M
- Art/Fine Arts M
- Artificial Intelligence/Robotics M,D,O
- Biological and Biomedical Sciences—General M,D
- Business Administration and Management—General M,D,O
- Chemistry M,D
- Civil Engineering M,D,O
- Communication Disorders M
- Computer Engineering M,D
- Computer Science M,D
- Conflict Resolution and Mediation/Peace Studies M
- Criminal Justice and Criminology M,D
- Economics M,D,O
- Education—General M,D
- Electrical Engineering M,D
- Engineering and Applied Sciences—General M,D,O
- Engineering Management M,D,O
- English as a Second Language M
- English M
- Environmental Engineering M,D
- Environmental Management and Policy M,D
- Environmental Sciences M,D
- Finance and Banking M
- Foreign Languages Education M
- French M
- Geography M,D
- Geology M,D
- German M
- Gerontology O
- Health Education M,D,O
- Health Promotion M,D,O
- Health Services Management and Hospital Administration M,D
- History M
- Industrial and Manufacturing Management M,D
- International Business M
- Japanese M
- Management of Technology M,D
- Manufacturing Engineering M,D
- Mathematics Education M,D
- Mathematics M,D,O
- Mechanical Engineering M,D,O
- Modeling and Simulation M,D,O
- Music Education M
- Music M
- Physics M,D
- Political Science M,D
- Psychology—General M,D,O
- Public Administration M,D
- Public Affairs M,D
- Public Health—General M,D,O
- Public Policy M,D
- Real Estate M
- Science Education M,D
- Social Sciences Education M
- Social Work M,D
- Sociology M,D,O
- Software Engineering M,D
- Spanish M
- Speech and Interpersonal Communication M,O
- Statistics M,D
- Supply Chain Management M
- Systems Science M,D,O
- Theater M
- Urban and Regional Planning M
- Urban Studies M,D

POST UNIVERSITY
- Accounting M
- Addictions/Substance Abuse Counseling M
- Business Administration and Management—General M
- Distance Education Development M
- Education—General M
- Educational Leadership and Administration M
- Educational Media/Instructional Technology M
- English as a Second Language M
- Entrepreneurship M
- Finance and Banking M
- Health Services Management and Hospital Administration M
- Human Services M
- Marketing M
- Nonprofit Management M
- Project Management M
- Public Administration M

PRAIRIE VIEW A&M UNIVERSITY
- Accounting M
- Agricultural Sciences—General M
- Architecture M
- Business Administration and Management—General M
- Chemistry M
- Clinical Psychology M,D
- Computer Science M,D
- Counselor Education M,D
- Curriculum and Instruction M
- Education—General M,D
- Educational Leadership and Administration M,D
- Electrical Engineering M,D
- Engineering and Applied Sciences—General M,D
- Family and Consumer Sciences-General M
- Family Nurse Practitioner Studies M
- Forensic Psychology M,D
- Health Education M
- Legal and Justice Studies M,D
- Management Information Systems M,D
- Nursing and Healthcare Administration M
- Nursing Education M
- Nursing—General M
- Physical Education M
- Sociology M
- Special Education M
- Urban Design M

PRATT INSTITUTE
- Applied Arts and Design—General M,O*
- Architecture M*
- Archives/Archival Administration M,O
- Art Education M,O
- Art History M
- Art Therapy M
- Art/Fine Arts M*
- Arts Administration M
- Database Systems M,O
- Facilities Management M
- Graphic Design M
- Historic Preservation M
- Industrial Design M
- Information Studies M,O*
- Interior Design M
- Internet and Interactive Multimedia M
- Library Science M,O
- Media Studies M*
- Museum Studies M,O
- Music M
- Photography M
- Sustainable Development M
- Therapies—Dance, Drama, and Music M
- Urban and Regional Planning M
- Urban Design M
- Writing M

PRESCOTT COLLEGE

Art Therapy	M
Counseling Psychology	M
Counselor Education	M,D
Early Childhood Education	M,D
Education—General	M,D
Educational Leadership and Administration	M,D
Elementary Education	M,D
Environmental Education	M,D
Environmental Management and Policy	M
Health Psychology	M
Humanities	M
Legal and Justice Studies	M
Leisure Studies	M
Psychoanalysis and Psychotherapy	M
Secondary Education	M,D
Special Education	M,D

PRESIDIO GRADUATE SCHOOL

Sustainability Management	M,O

PRINCETON THEOLOGICAL SEMINARY

Religion	M,D
Theology	M,D

PRINCETON UNIVERSITY

Aerospace/Aeronautical Engineering	M,D
Anthropology	D
Applied Mathematics	D
Archaeology	D
Architecture	M,D
Asian Studies	D
Astronomy	D
Astrophysics	D
Atmospheric Sciences	D
Chemical Engineering	M,D
Chemistry	M,D
Civil Engineering	M,D
Classics	D
Comparative Literature	D
Computational Biology	D
Computational Sciences	D
Computer Science	M,D
Demography and Population Studies	D,O
Ecology	D
Economics	D,O
Electrical Engineering	M,D
Electronic Materials	D
Engineering and Applied Sciences—General	M,D
English	D
Environmental Engineering	M,D
Evolutionary Biology	D
Finance and Banking	M
Financial Engineering	M,D
French	D
Geosciences	D
German	D
History of Science and Technology	D
History	D
International Affairs	M,D
Marine Biology	D
Materials Sciences	D
Mathematics	D
Mechanical Engineering	M,D
Molecular Biology	D
Music	D
Near and Middle Eastern Studies	M,D
Neuroscience	D
Ocean Engineering	D
Oceanography	D
Operations Research	M,D
Philosophy	D
Photonics	D
Physics	D
Plasma Physics	D
Political Science	D
Portuguese	D
Psychology—General	D
Public Affairs	M,D,O
Public Policy	M,D
Religion	D
Russian	D
Slavic Languages	D
Sociology	D,O
Spanish	D

PROVIDENCE COLLEGE

Accounting	M
American Studies	M
Business Administration and Management—General	M
Counselor Education	M
Educational Leadership and Administration	M
Elementary Education	M
Finance and Banking	M
History	M
International Business	M
Marketing	M
Mathematics Education	M
Nonprofit Management	M
Reading Education	M
Religion	M
Secondary Education	M
Special Education	M
Theology	M
Urban Education	M

PROVIDENCE UNIVERSITY COLLEGE & THEOLOGICAL SEMINARY

Counseling Psychology	M,D,O
English as a Second Language	M,D,O
Missions and Missiology	M,D,O
Pastoral Ministry and Counseling	M,D,O
Religious Education	M,D,O
Student Affairs	M,D,O
Theology	M,D,O

PURCHASE COLLEGE, STATE UNIVERSITY OF NEW YORK

Art History	M
Art/Fine Arts	M
Music	M
Theater	M

PURDUE UNIVERSITY

Aerospace/Aeronautical Engineering	M,D
Agricultural Economics and Agribusiness	M,D
Agricultural Education	M,D,O
Agricultural Engineering	M,D
Agricultural Sciences—General	M,D
Agronomy and Soil Sciences	M,D
Allied Health—General	M,D
American Studies	M,D
Analytical Chemistry	M,D
Anatomy	M,D
Animal Sciences	M,D
Anthropology	M,D
Applied Arts and Design—General	M
Applied Statistics	M,D
Aquaculture	M,D
Art Education	M,D,O
Art/Fine Arts	M
Atmospheric Sciences	M,D
Aviation Management	M
Biochemistry	M,D
Biological and Biomedical Sciences—General	M,D
Biomedical Engineering	M,D
Biophysics	M,D
Biotechnology	D
Botany	M,D
Business Administration and Management—General	M,D
Cancer Biology/Oncology	D
Cell Biology	M,D
Chemical Engineering	M,D
Chemistry	M,D
Child and Family Studies	M,D
Child Development	M,D
Civil Engineering	M,D
Clinical Psychology	D
Cognitive Sciences	D
Communication Disorders	M,D
Communication—General	M,D
Comparative Literature	M,D
Computational Sciences	M,D
Computer and Information Systems Security	M
Computer Art and Design	M,D
Computer Engineering	M,D
Computer Science	M,D
Construction Management	M
Consumer Economics	M,D
Counselor Education	M,D,O
Curriculum and Instruction	M,D,O
Developmental Biology	M,D
Ecology	M,D
Economics	D
Education of the Gifted	M,D,O
Education—General	M,D,O
Educational Leadership and Administration	M,D,O
Educational Media/Instructional Technology	M,D,O
Educational Psychology	M,D,O
Electrical Engineering	M,D
Elementary Education	M,D,O
Engineering and Applied Sciences—General	M,D,O
English Education	M,D,O
English	M,D
Entomology	M,D
Environmental and Occupational Health	M,D
Environmental Engineering	M,D
Environmental Management and Policy	M,D
Epidemiology	M,D
Ergonomics and Human Factors	M,D
Evolutionary Biology	M,D
Exercise and Sports Science	M,D
Family and Consumer Sciences-General	M,D
Finance and Banking	M
Fish, Game, and Wildlife Management	M,D
Food Science and Technology	M,D
Foreign Languages Education	M,D,O
Forestry	M,D
Foundations and Philosophy of Education	M,D,O
French	M,D
Genetics	M,D
Genomic Sciences	D
Geosciences	M,D
German	M,D
Health Education	M,D
Health Physics/Radiological Health	M,D
Higher Education	M,D,O
History	M,D
Home Economics Education	M,D,O
Horticulture	M,D
Hospitality Management	M,D
Human Development	M,D
Human Resources Management	M,D
Immunology	M,D
Industrial and Manufacturing Management	M
Industrial and Organizational Psychology	D
Industrial/Management Engineering	M,D
Inorganic Chemistry	M,D
International Business	M
Japanese	M,D
Kinesiology and Movement Studies	M,D
Linguistics	M,D
Management Information Systems	M
Management of Technology	M,D
Marriage and Family Therapy	M,D
Materials Engineering	M,D
Mathematical and Computational Finance	M,D
Mathematics Education	M,D,O
Mathematics	M,D
Mechanical Engineering	M,D,O
Medical Physics	M,D
Medicinal and Pharmaceutical Chemistry	D
Microbiology	M,D
Molecular Biology	M,D
Molecular Pharmacology	D
Natural Resources	M,D
Neurobiology	M,D
Neuroscience	D
Nuclear Engineering	M,D
Nutrition	M,D
Organic Chemistry	M,D
Organizational Behavior	D
Pathobiology	M,D
Pathology	M,D
Pharmaceutical Administration	M,D,O
Pharmaceutical Sciences	M,D
Pharmacology	M,D
Pharmacy	D
Philosophy	M,D
Physical Chemistry	M,D
Physical Education	M,D
Physics	M,D
Physiology	M,D
Plant Pathology	M,D
Plant Physiology	M,D
Plant Sciences	D
Political Science	M,D
Psychology—General	D
Public Health—General	M,D
Quantitative Analysis	M,D
Reading Education	M,D,O
Recreation and Park Management	M,D
Science Education	M,D,O
Social Sciences Education	M,D,O
Sociology	M,D
Spanish	M,D
Special Education	M,D,O
Sport Psychology	M,D
Sports Management	M,D
Statistics	M,D
Systems Biology	D
Theater	M
Toxicology	M,D
Travel and Tourism	M,D
Veterinary Medicine	D
Veterinary Sciences	M,D
Virology	M,D
Vocational and Technical Education	M,D,O
Writing	M,D

PURDUE UNIVERSITY NORTHWEST

Accounting	M
Acute Care/Critical Care Nursing	M
Adult Nursing	M
Biological and Biomedical Sciences—General	M
Biotechnology	M
Business Administration and Management—General	M
Child and Family Studies	M
Child Development	M
Communication—General	M
Computer Engineering	M
Computer Science	M
Counseling Psychology	M
Counselor Education	M
Education—General	M
Educational Leadership and Administration	M
Educational Media/Instructional Technology	M
Electrical Engineering	M
Engineering and Applied Sciences—General	M
English	M
Family Nurse Practitioner Studies	M
History	M
Human Services	M
Marriage and Family Therapy	M
Mathematics Education	M
Mathematics	M
Mechanical Engineering	M
Nursing and Healthcare Administration	M
Nursing—General	M
School Psychology	M
Science Education	M
Special Education	M

PURDUE UNIVERSITY NORTHWEST

Education—General	M
Elementary Education	M

QUEENS COLLEGE OF THE CITY UNIVERSITY OF NEW YORK

Accounting	M
Applied Behavior Analysis	M,O
Applied Social Research	M
Art Education	M,O
Art History	M
Art/Fine Arts	M
Biological and Biomedical Sciences—General	M,O
Chemistry	M
Child and Family Studies	M,O
Communication Disorders	M
Computer Science	M
Counselor Education	M,O
Database Systems	M
Education—General	M,O
Educational Leadership and Administration	M,O
Elementary Education	M,O
English as a Second Language	M
English Education	M,O
English	M
Environmental Sciences	M
Exercise and Sports Science	M,O
Family and Consumer Sciences-General	M,O
Foreign Languages Education	M,O
French	M
Geology	M
Geosciences	M
Hispanic and Latin American Languages	M
History	M
Information Studies	M,O
Italian	M
Liberal Studies	M
Library Science	M,O
Linguistics	M
Mathematics Education	M,O
Mathematics	M
Multilingual and Multicultural Education	M,O
Music Education	M,O
Music	M,O
Neuroscience	M,O
Nutrition	M,O
Physical Education	M,O
Physics	M
Psychology—General	M,O
Reading Education	M,O
Romance Languages	M
School Psychology	M,O
Science Education	M,O
Secondary Education	M,O
Social Sciences Education	M,O
Sociology	M
Spanish	M
Special Education	M,O
Urban Studies	M
Writing	M

QUEEN'S UNIVERSITY AT KINGSTON

Allopathic Medicine	D
Anatomy	M,D
Biochemistry	M,D
Biological and Biomedical Sciences—General	M,D
Business Administration and Management—General	M
Canadian Studies	M,D
Cancer Biology/Oncology	M,D
Cardiovascular Sciences	M,D
Cell Biology	M,D
Chemical Engineering	M,D
Chemistry	M,D
Civil Engineering	M,D
Classics	M
Clinical Psychology	M,D
Cognitive Sciences	M,D
Communication—General	M,D
Computer Engineering	M,D
Computer Science	M,D
Developmental Psychology	M,D
Education—General	M,D
Electrical Engineering	M,D
Engineering and Applied Sciences—General	M,D
English	M,D
Entrepreneurship	M
Epidemiology	M,D
Exercise and Sports Science	M,D
Family Nurse Practitioner Studies	M,D,O
Finance and Banking	M
French	M,D
Gender Studies	M,D
Geography	M,D
Geology	M,D
German	M,D
Health Services Management and Hospital Administration	M,D
Hispanic Studies	M
Immunology	M,D
Industrial and Labor Relations	M
Information Studies	M,D
International Affairs	M,D
Law	M,D
Legal and Justice Studies	M,D
Marketing	M
Mathematics	M,D
Mechanical Engineering	M,D
Microbiology	M,D
Mineral/Mining Engineering	M,D
Molecular Biology	M,D
Molecular Medicine	M,D
Neurobiology	M,D
Neuroscience	M,D
Nursing—General	M,D,O
Occupational Therapy	M,D
Pathology	M,D
Pediatric Nursing	M,D,O
Pharmaceutical Sciences	M,D
Pharmacology	M,D
Philosophy	M,D
Physical Therapy	M,D
Physics	M,D
Physiology	M,D
Political Science	M,D
Project Management	M
Psychology—General	M,D
Public Health—General	M,D
Public Policy	M
Rehabilitation Sciences	M,D
Religion	M
Reproductive Biology	M,D

*M—masters degree; D—doctorate; O—other advanced degree; *—Close-Up and/or Display*

Social Psychology M,D
Sociology M,D
Spanish M
Sport Psychology M,D
Statistics M,D
Theology M,O
Toxicology M,D
Urban and Regional Planning M
Women's Health Nursing M,D,O
Women's Studies M,D

QUEENS UNIVERSITY OF CHARLOTTE
Business Administration and Management—General M
Communication—General M
Education—General M
Educational Leadership and Administration M
Elementary Education M
Interior Design M
Nursing and Healthcare Administration M
Nursing Education M
Nursing—General M
Organizational Management M
Reading Education M
Writing M

QUINCY UNIVERSITY
Business Administration and Management—General M
Communication—General M
Counselor Education M
Curriculum and Instruction M
Education—General M
Educational Leadership and Administration M
English as a Second Language M
Multilingual and Multicultural Education M
Reading Education M
School Psychology M
Special Education M

QUINNIPIAC UNIVERSITY
Adult Nursing M,D
Advertising and Public Relations M
Allied Health—General M
Allopathic Medicine D
Anesthesiologist Assistant Studies M
Broadcast Journalism M
Business Administration and Management—General M
Cardiovascular Sciences M
Cell Biology M
Clinical Laboratory Sciences/Medical Technology M
Communication—General M
Community Health D
Education—General M,O
Educational Leadership and Administration M,O
Educational Media/Instructional Technology M
Elementary Education M
English Education M
Family Nurse Practitioner Studies M,D
Film, Television, and Video Production M
Foreign Languages Education M
Health Physics/Radiological Health M
Health Services Management and Hospital Administration M
Internet and Interactive Multimedia M
Journalism M
Law M,D
Mathematics Education M
Middle School Education M
Molecular Biology M
Nurse Anesthesia D
Nursing and Healthcare Administration D
Nursing—General M,D
Organizational Management M
Pathology M
Perfusion M
Physician Assistant Studies M
Science Education M
Secondary Education M
Social Sciences Education M
Social Work M
Supply Chain Management M

RABBI ISAAC ELCHANAN THEOLOGICAL SEMINARY
Theology O

RABBINICAL ACADEMY MESIVTA RABBI CHAIM BERLIN
Theology O

RABBINICAL COLLEGE BETH SHRAGA
Theology

RABBINICAL COLLEGE BOBOVER YESHIVA B'NEI ZION
Theology

RABBINICAL COLLEGE CH'SAN SOFER
Theology

RABBINICAL COLLEGE OF LONG ISLAND
Theology

RABBINICAL SEMINARY OF AMERICA
Theology

RADFORD UNIVERSITY
Applied Arts and Design—General M
Art/Fine Arts M
Business Administration and Management—General M
Clinical Psychology M
Communication Disorders M
Corporate and Organizational Communication M
Counseling Psychology M,D
Counselor Education M
Criminal Justice and Criminology M,O
Curriculum and Instruction M
Early Childhood Education M,O
Education—General M,O
Educational Leadership and Administration M,O
Educational Media/Instructional Technology M
English M
Experimental Psychology M
Industrial and Organizational Psychology M
Mathematics Education M
Music Education M
Music M
Nursing—General D
Occupational Therapy M
Physical Therapy D
Psychology—General M,D,O
Reading Education M
School Psychology O
Social Work M
Special Education M,O
Therapies—Dance, Drama, and Music M

RAMAPO COLLEGE OF NEW JERSEY
Business Administration and Management—General M
Educational Leadership and Administration M
Educational Media/Instructional Technology M
Liberal Studies M
Nursing Education M
Nursing—General M
Social Work M
Special Education M
Sustainable Development M

RANDOLPH COLLEGE
Curriculum and Instruction M
Education—General M
Special Education M

RECONSTRUCTIONIST RABBINICAL COLLEGE
Jewish Studies M,D,O
Theology M,D,O
Women's Studies M,D,O

REED COLLEGE
Liberal Studies M

REFORMED EPISCOPAL SEMINARY
Theology M

REFORMED PRESBYTERIAN THEOLOGICAL SEMINARY
Theology M,D

REFORMED THEOLOGICAL SEMINARY–ATLANTA CAMPUS
Theology M,D,O

REFORMED THEOLOGICAL SEMINARY–CHARLOTTE CAMPUS
Pastoral Ministry and Counseling M,D
Religion M,D
Theology M,D

REFORMED THEOLOGICAL SEMINARY–HOUSTON CAMPUS
Religion M

REFORMED THEOLOGICAL SEMINARY–JACKSON CAMPUS
Marriage and Family Therapy M,D,O
Missions and Missiology M,D,O
Pastoral Ministry and Counseling M,D,O
Religion M,D,O
Religious Education M,D,O
Theology M,D,O

REFORMED THEOLOGICAL SEMINARY–ORLANDO CAMPUS
Pastoral Ministry and Counseling M,D,O
Theology M,D,O

REFORMED THEOLOGICAL SEMINARY–WASHINGTON D.C.
Religion M
Theology M

REGENT COLLEGE
Theology M,O

REGENT'S UNIVERSITY LONDON
Business Administration and Management—General M
Finance and Banking M
Human Resources Management M
International Affairs M
International Business M
Management Information Systems M
Marketing M

REGENT UNIVERSITY
Accounting M,D,O
Adult Education M,D,O
American Studies M
Business Administration and Management—General M,D,O
Clinical Psychology M,D,O
Communication—General M,D
Corporate and Organizational Communication M,D,O
Counseling Psychology M,D,O
Counselor Education M,D,O
Criminal Justice and Criminology M,D
Cultural Studies M,D
Curriculum and Instruction M,D,O
Distance Education Development M,D,O
Education—General M,D,O
Educational Leadership and Administration M,D,O
Educational Media/Instructional Technology M,D,O
Educational Psychology M,D,O
Elementary Education M,D,O
Emergency Management M
English as a Second Language M,D,O
Entrepreneurship M,D,O
Film, Television, and Video Production M,D
Finance and Banking M,D,O
Health Services Management and Hospital Administration M,D,O
Higher Education M,D,O
History M,D
Homeland Security M
Human Resources Development M,D,O
Human Resources Management M,D,O
Interdisciplinary Studies M,D,O
International Affairs M
Investment Management M,D,O
Journalism M,D
Law M,D
Legal and Justice Studies M,D
Management Strategy and Policy M,D,O
Marriage and Family Therapy M,D,O
Mathematics Education M,D,O
Missions and Missiology M,D
National Security M,D
Nonprofit Management M,D,O
Organizational Management M,D,O
Pastoral Ministry and Counseling M,D
Political Science M
Psychoanalysis and Psychotherapy M,D
Public Administration M
Reading Education M,D,O
Religion M,D
Religious Education M,D,O
Special Education M,D,O
Student Affairs M,D,O
Theater M,D
Theology M,D
Writing M,D

REGIS COLLEGE (CANADA)
Pastoral Ministry and Counseling M,D,O
Philosophy M,D,O
Theology M,D,O

REGIS COLLEGE (MA)
Applied Behavior Analysis M,D,O
Biological and Biomedical Sciences—General M,D,O
Biotechnology M
Corporate and Organizational Communication M
Counseling Psychology M,D,O
Cultural Studies M
Education—General M,D
Educational Leadership and Administration M,D
Elementary Education M,D
Family Nurse Practitioner Studies M,D,O
Health Services Management and Hospital Administration M,D,O
Higher Education M,D
Nursing Education M,D,O
Nursing—General M,D,O
Occupational Therapy M,D,O
Quality Management M
Reading Education M,D
Special Education M,D
Writing O

REGIS UNIVERSITY
Accounting M,O
Addictions/Substance Abuse Counseling M,D,O
Allied Health—General M,D,O
Biological and Biomedical Sciences—General M
Business Education M,O
Computer and Information Systems Security M,O
Computer Science M,O
Counselor Education M,D,O
Criminal Justice and Criminology M,O
Curriculum and Instruction M,O
Database Systems M,O
Developmental Psychology M,D,O
Economics M,O
Education—General M
Educational Leadership and Administration M,O
Elementary Education M,O
Environmental Biology M
Family Nurse Practitioner Studies M,D,O
Finance and Banking M,O
Health Services Management and Hospital Administration M,D,O
Human Resources Management M,O
Industrial and Manufacturing Management M,O
Information Science M,O
Management Information Systems M,O
Management Strategy and Policy M,O
Marketing M,O
Marriage and Family Therapy M,D,O
Maternal and Child/Neonatal Nursing M,D,O
Medical Informatics M,O
Nonprofit Management M,O
Nursing Education M,D,O
Organizational Management M,O
Pharmacy M,D,O
Physical Therapy M,D,O
Project Management M,O
Reading Education M,O
Secondary Education M,O
Software Engineering M,O
Special Education M,O
Systems Engineering M,O
Writing M,O

REINHARDT UNIVERSITY
Business Administration and Management—General M
Early Childhood Education M
Education—General M
Music Education M
Music M

RELAY GRADUATE SCHOOL OF EDUCATION
Education—General M

RENSSELAER AT HARTFORD
Business Administration and Management—General M
Computer Engineering M
Computer Science M
Electrical Engineering M
Engineering and Applied Sciences—General M
Information Science M
Mechanical Engineering M
Systems Science M

RENSSELAER POLYTECHNIC INSTITUTE
Acoustics M,D
Aerospace/Aeronautical Engineering M,D
Applied Mathematics M
Architecture M,D
Art/Fine Arts M,D
Biochemistry M,D
Bioengineering M,D
Biological and Biomedical Sciences—General M,D
Biomedical Engineering M,D
Biophysics M,D
Building Science M,D
Business Administration and Management—General M,D
Chemical Engineering M,D
Chemistry M,D
Civil Engineering M,D
Cognitive Sciences D
Computer Art and Design M,D
Computer Engineering M,D
Computer Science M,D
Electrical Engineering M,D
Engineering and Applied Sciences—General M,D
Engineering Management M,D
Engineering Physics M,D
Entrepreneurship M
Environmental Engineering M,D
Financial Engineering M
Geology M,D
History of Science and Technology M,D
Human-Computer Interaction M
Industrial/Management Engineering M,D
Information Science M
Interdisciplinary Studies M,D
Lighting Design M,D
Management Information Systems M
Management of Technology M,D
Materials Engineering M,D
Materials Sciences M,D
Mathematics M,D
Mechanical Engineering M,D
Nuclear Engineering M,D
Physics M,D
Rhetoric M,D
Speech and Interpersonal Communication M,D
Supply Chain Management M
Systems Engineering M,D
Technology and Public Policy M,D
Transportation and Highway Engineering M,D

RESEARCH COLLEGE OF NURSING
Adult Nursing M
Family Nurse Practitioner Studies M
Gerontological Nursing M
Nursing and Healthcare Administration M
Nursing—General M

RESURRECTION UNIVERSITY
Nursing—General M

RHODE ISLAND COLLEGE
Accounting M,O
Art Education M
Art/Fine Arts M
Arts Administration M
Biological and Biomedical Sciences—General M,O
Counseling Psychology M,O
Counselor Education M,O
Early Childhood Education M
Education—General D
Educational Leadership and Administration M,O
Elementary Education M
English as a Second Language M
English Education M
English M,O
Finance and Banking M,O
Foreign Languages Education M
Health Education M
Health Psychology M,O
History M
Mathematics Education M
Mathematics M,O
Music Education M
Nursing—General M
Physical Education M,O
Psychology—General M,O
Public Administration M
Reading Education M
School Psychology M,O
Secondary Education M
Social Sciences Education M
Social Work M

Special Education	M,O
Writing	M,O

RHODE ISLAND SCHOOL OF DESIGN

Applied Arts and Design—General	M
Architecture	M
Art Education	M
Art/Fine Arts	M
Computer Art and Design	M
Graphic Design	M
Industrial Design	M
Interior Design	M
Landscape Architecture	M
Photography	M
Textile Design	M

RHODES COLLEGE

Accounting	M

RICE UNIVERSITY

African Studies	D
American Studies	D
Anthropology	M,D
Applied Mathematics	M,D
Applied Physics	M,D
Archaeology	M,D
Architecture	M,D
Art History	D
Astronomy	M,D
Biochemistry	M,D
Bioengineering	M,D
Bioinformatics	M,D
Biomedical Engineering	M,D
Biostatistics	M,D
Business Administration and Management—General	M
Cell Biology	M,D
Chemical Engineering	M,D
Chemistry	M,D
Civil Engineering	M,D
Cognitive Sciences	M,D
Computational Sciences	M,D
Computer Engineering	M,D
Computer Science	M,D
Cultural Anthropology	M,D
Ecology	M,D
Economics	M,D
Education—General	M
Electrical Engineering	M,D
Energy Management and Policy	M,D
Engineering and Applied Sciences—General	M,D
English	M,D
Environmental Engineering	M,D
Environmental Management and Policy	M
Environmental Sciences	M,D
Evolutionary Biology	M,D
Geophysics	M
Geosciences	M,D
Health Services Management and Hospital Administration	M
History	M,D
Industrial and Organizational Psychology	M,D
Inorganic Chemistry	M,D
Jewish Studies	D
Liberal Studies	M
Linguistics	M,D
Materials Sciences	M,D
Mathematical and Computational Finance	M,D
Mathematics	D
Mechanical Engineering	M,D
Music	M,D
Near and Middle Eastern Studies	D
Organic Chemistry	M,D
Philosophy	M,D
Physical Chemistry	M,D
Physics	M,D
Political Science	D
Psychology—General	M,D
Religion	D
Science Education	M,D
Sociology	D
Statistics	M,D
Urban Design	M,D

RICHMOND, THE AMERICAN INTERNATIONAL UNIVERSITY IN LONDON

Art History	M
International Affairs	M

RICHMONT GRADUATE UNIVERSITY

Clinical Psychology	M
Counselor Education	M
Marriage and Family Therapy	M
Pastoral Ministry and Counseling	M,O

RIDER UNIVERSITY

Accounting	M
Applied Psychology	M
Business Administration and Management—General	M
Business Education	O
Corporate and Organizational Communication	M
Counselor Education	M,O
Curriculum and Instruction	M,O
Education—General	M,O
Educational Leadership and Administration	M,O
Elementary Education	O
English as a Second Language	O
English Education	O
Foreign Languages Education	O
French	O
German	O
Mathematics Education	O
Music Education	M
Music	M
Organizational Management	M
Reading Education	M,O
School Psychology	O
Science Education	O
Social Sciences Education	O
Spanish	O
Special Education	M,O

RIVIER UNIVERSITY

Business Administration and Management—General	M
Clinical Psychology	M
Computer Science	M
Counseling Psychology	M,D,O
Counselor Education	M,D,O
Curriculum and Instruction	M,D,O
Early Childhood Education	M,D,O
Education—General	M,D,O
Educational Leadership and Administration	M,D,O
Elementary Education	M,D,O
English	M
Experimental Psychology	M
Family Nurse Practitioner Studies	M
Foreign Languages Education	M
Management Information Systems	M
Mathematics	M
Nursing Education	M
Nursing—General	M
Psychiatric Nursing	M
Psychology—General	M
Reading Education	M,D,O
Social Sciences Education	M
Special Education	M,D,O
Writing	M

THE ROBERT E. WEBBER INSTITUTE FOR WORSHIP STUDIES

Religion	M,D

ROBERT MORRIS UNIVERSITY

Business Administration and Management—General	M
Business Education	M,D,O
Computer and Information Systems Security	M,D
Counseling Psychology	M,D,O
Database Systems	M,D
Education—General	M,D,O
Educational Leadership and Administration	M,D,O
Engineering and Applied Sciences—General	M
Engineering Management	M
Higher Education	M,D,O
Human Resources Management	M
Information Science	M,D
Internet and Interactive Multimedia	M,D
Management Information Systems	M,D
Nursing—General	M,D
Organizational Management	M,D
Project Management	M,D
Special Education	M,D,O
Sports Management	M,D,O
Taxation	M

ROBERT MORRIS UNIVERSITY ILLINOIS

Accounting	M
Arts Administration	M
Business Administration and Management—General	M
Computer and Information Systems Security	M
Criminal Justice and Criminology	M
Educational Leadership and Administration	M
Educational Media/Instructional Technology	M
Finance and Banking	M
Health Services Management and Hospital Administration	M
Higher Education	M
Human Resources Management	M
Management Information Systems	M
Management Strategy and Policy	M
Media Studies	M
Sports Management	M

ROBERTS WESLEYAN COLLEGE

Business Administration and Management—General	M
Child and Family Studies	M
Early Childhood Education	M
Education—General	M
Health Informatics	M
Health Services Management and Hospital Administration	M
Human Services	M
Management Strategy and Policy	M
Marketing	M
Middle School Education	M
Nursing and Healthcare Administration	M
Nursing Education	M
Nursing—General	M
Reading Education	M
Secondary Education	M
Social Work	M
Special Education	M

ROCHESTER COLLEGE

Missions and Missiology	M
Religious Education	M

ROCHESTER INSTITUTE OF TECHNOLOGY

Accounting	M
Applied Mathematics	M
Applied Statistics	M,O
Architecture	M
Art Education	M
Art/Fine Arts	M,O
Astrophysics	M,D
Bioinformatics	M
Biological and Biomedical Sciences—General	M
Business Administration and Management—General	M
Chemistry	M
Communication—General	M,O
Computer and Information Systems Security	M,O
Computer Art and Design	M
Computer Engineering	M
Computer Science	M,D
Criminal Justice and Criminology	M
Database Systems	O
Educational Media/Instructional Technology	O
Electrical Engineering	M
Engineering and Applied Sciences—General	M,D,O
Engineering Design	M
Engineering Management	M
Entrepreneurship	M
Environmental and Occupational Health	M
Environmental Sciences	M
Experimental Psychology	M
Film, Television, and Video Production	M
Finance and Banking	M
Game Design and Development	M
Graphic Design	M
Health Services Management and Hospital Administration	M,O
Hospitality Management	M
Human Resources Development	M
Human-Computer Interaction	M
Industrial and Manufacturing Management	M
Industrial Design	M
Industrial/Management Engineering	M
Information Science	M,D
Interdisciplinary Studies	M
International Business	M
Internet and Interactive Multimedia	O
Management Information Systems	O
Manufacturing Engineering	M
Materials Engineering	M
Materials Sciences	M
Mathematical and Computational Finance	M
Mathematics	M,O
Mechanical Engineering	M
Media Studies	M
Medical Illustration	M
Medical Informatics	M
Occupational Therapy	M
Optical Sciences	M,D
Organizational Management	O
Photography	M
Project Management	O
Psychology—General	M,O
Public Policy	M
Safety Engineering	M
School Psychology	M,O
Secondary Education	M
Software Engineering	M
Special Education	M
Statistics	O
Sustainability Management	M,D
Sustainable Development	M,D
Systems Engineering	M,D
Technology and Public Policy	M
Telecommunications	M
Translation and Interpretation	M
Travel and Tourism	M

THE ROCKEFELLER UNIVERSITY

Biological and Biomedical Sciences—General	M,D*

ROCKFORD UNIVERSITY

Business Administration and Management—General	M
Early Childhood Education	M
Education—General	M
Elementary Education	M
Reading Education	M
Secondary Education	M
Special Education	M

ROCKHURST UNIVERSITY

Accounting	M,O
Business Administration and Management—General	M,O
Communication Disorders	M
Database Systems	M,O
Education—General	M
Entrepreneurship	M,O
Finance and Banking	M,O
Health Services Management and Hospital Administration	M,O
Human Resources Development	M,O
International Business	M,O
Management Strategy and Policy	M,O
Nonprofit Management	M,O
Occupational Therapy	M
Physical Therapy	D

ROCKY MOUNTAIN COLLEGE

Accounting	M
Educational Leadership and Administration	M
Physician Assistant Studies	M

ROCKY MOUNTAIN COLLEGE OF ART + DESIGN

Art Education	M
Arts Administration	M
Internet and Interactive Multimedia	M

ROCKY MOUNTAIN UNIVERSITY OF HEALTH PROFESSIONS

Communication Disorders	D
Family Nurse Practitioner Studies	D
Occupational Therapy	D
Physical Therapy	D
Physician Assistant Studies	M
Physiology	D

ROCKY VISTA UNIVERSITY

Osteopathic Medicine	D

ROGER WILLIAMS UNIVERSITY

Architectural History	M
Architecture	M
Art History	M
Clinical Psychology	M
Computer and Information Systems Security	M
Criminal Justice and Criminology	M
Education—General	M
Forensic Psychology	M
Health Services Management and Hospital Administration	M
Historic Preservation	M
Law	M,D
Public Administration	M

ROLLINS COLLEGE

Applied Behavior Analysis	M
Business Administration and Management—General	M,D
Counselor Education	M
Education—General	M
Elementary Education	M
Entrepreneurship	M,D
Finance and Banking	M,D
Health Services Management and Hospital Administration	M
Human Resources Development	M
Human Resources Management	M
International Business	M,D
Liberal Studies	M
Management of Technology	M,D
Marketing	M,D

ROOSEVELT UNIVERSITY

Accounting	M
Actuarial Science	M
Anthropology	M
Applied Economics	M
Biotechnology	M
Business Administration and Management—General	M
Chemistry	M
Clinical Psychology	M
Communication—General	M
Computer Science	M
Corporate and Organizational Communication	M
Counselor Education	M
Early Childhood Education	M
Economics	M
Education—General	M,D
Educational Leadership and Administration	M
Elementary Education	M
English	M
Gender Studies	M,O
History	M
Hospitality Management	M
Human Resources Development	M
Human Resources Management	M
Industrial and Organizational Psychology	M,D
International Business	M
Journalism	M
Management Information Systems	M
Marketing	M
Mathematics	M
Music Education	M,O
Music	M,O
Organizational Management	M,D
Pharmacy	D
Political Science	M
Psychology—General	M,D
Public Administration	M
Reading Education	M
Real Estate	M,O
Secondary Education	M
Sociology	M
Spanish	M
Special Education	M
Telecommunications	M
Theater	M
Women's Studies	M,O
Writing	M

ROSALIND FRANKLIN UNIVERSITY OF MEDICINE AND SCIENCE

Allied Health—General	M,D,O
Allopathic Medicine	D
Anatomy	D
Biochemistry	D
Biological and Biomedical Sciences—General	M,D
Biophysics	M,D
Cell Biology	D
Clinical Psychology	M,D
Health Education	M
Health Promotion	M
Health Services Management and Hospital Administration	M,O
Immunology	D
Interdisciplinary Studies	D
Microbiology	D
Molecular Biology	D
Molecular Pharmacology	M,D
Neuroscience	D

*M—masters degree; D—doctorate; O—other advanced degree; *—Close-Up and/or Display*

Nurse Anesthesia	D
Nutrition	M
Pathology	M
Pharmacy	D
Physical Therapy	M,D
Physician Assistant Studies	M
Physiology	M,D
Podiatric Medicine	D
Psychology—General	M,D

ROSE-HULMAN INSTITUTE OF TECHNOLOGY

Biomedical Engineering	M
Chemical Engineering	M
Civil Engineering	M
Computer Engineering	M
Electrical Engineering	M
Engineering and Applied Sciences—General	M
Engineering Management	M
Environmental Engineering	M
Management Information Systems	M
Mechanical Engineering	M
Optical Sciences	M
Software Engineering	M
Systems Engineering	M

ROSEMAN UNIVERSITY OF HEALTH SCIENCES

Business Administration and Management—General	M,O
Dentistry	M,D,O
Pharmacy	D

ROSEMONT COLLEGE

Business Administration and Management—General	M
Counseling Psychology	M
Counselor Education	M
Education—General	M
Elementary Education	M
Human Services	M
Publishing	M
Writing	M

ROWAN UNIVERSITY

Advertising and Public Relations	M
Applied Behavior Analysis	M,O
Arts Administration	M
Bioinformatics	M
Biological and Biomedical Sciences—General	M
Business Administration and Management—General	M,O
Chemical Engineering	M
Civil Engineering	M
Clinical Psychology	M,O
Computer and Information Systems Security	O
Computer Science	M
Corporate and Organizational Communication	O
Counselor Education	M
Criminal Justice and Criminology	M
Education—General	M,D,O
Educational Leadership and Administration	M,D,O
Educational Media/Instructional Technology	M,O
Electrical Engineering	M
Elementary Education	M
Engineering and Applied Sciences—General	M
English as a Second Language	O
English Education	O
Exercise and Sports Science	M
Health Promotion	M
Higher Education	M
History	M,O
Library Science	M,D,O
Marketing	O
Mathematics Education	M,O
Mathematics	M
Mechanical Engineering	M
Media Studies	O
Middle School Education	O
Multilingual and Multicultural Education	M,O
Music	M
Nursing—General	M
Osteopathic Medicine	D
Pharmaceutical Sciences	M
Psychology—General	M,O
Publishing	O
Reading Education	M,O
Rhetoric	O
School Nursing	M,D,O
School Psychology	M,O
Science Education	M
Secondary Education	M
Special Education	M,O
Theater	M
Writing	M,O

ROYAL MILITARY COLLEGE OF CANADA

Business Administration and Management—General	M
Chemical Engineering	M,D
Chemistry	M,D
Civil Engineering	M,D
Computer Engineering	M,D
Computer Science	M
Electrical Engineering	M,D
Engineering and Applied Sciences—General	M,D
Environmental Engineering	M,D
Environmental Sciences	M,D
Materials Sciences	M,D
Mathematics	M
Mechanical Engineering	M,D
Military and Defense Studies	M,D
Nuclear Engineering	M,D
Physics	M
Software Engineering	M,D

ROYAL ROADS UNIVERSITY

Advertising and Public Relations	O
Business Administration and Management—General	M,O
Conflict Resolution and Mediation/Peace Studies	M,O
Emergency Management	M,O
Environmental Education	M,O
Environmental Management and Policy	M,O
Health Services Management and Hospital Administration	O
Hospitality Management	M,O
Human Resources Management	M,O
Project Management	O
Travel and Tourism	M,O

RUSH UNIVERSITY

Adult Nursing	D
Allopathic Medicine	D
Anatomy	M,D
Biochemistry	M,D
Cell Biology	M,D
Clinical Laboratory Sciences/Medical Technology	M
Communication Disorders	M,D
Community Health Nursing	D
Family Nurse Practitioner Studies	D
Gerontological Nursing	D
Health Services Management and Hospital Administration	M,D
Immunology	M,D
Maternal and Child/Neonatal Nursing	D,O
Medical Physics	M,D
Microbiology	M,D
Neuroscience	M,D
Nurse Anesthesia	D
Nursing and Healthcare Administration	M
Nursing—General	M,D,O
Nutrition	M
Occupational Therapy	M
Pediatric Nursing	D,O
Perfusion	M
Pharmaceutical Sciences	M,D
Pharmacology	M,D
Physical Therapy	M
Physician Assistant Studies	M
Physiology	D
Psychiatric Nursing	D
Virology	M,D

RUTGERS UNIVERSITY–CAMDEN

Applied Mathematics	M
Biological and Biomedical Sciences—General	M
Business Administration and Management—General	M
Chemistry	M
Child Development	M,D
Computational Biology	M,D
Computer Science	M
Criminal Justice and Criminology	M
Educational Leadership and Administration	M
Educational Policy	M
English	M
Health Services Management and Hospital Administration	M,O
History	M
International Affairs	M
International Development	M
Law	D
Liberal Studies	M
Mathematics Education	M
Mathematics	M
Physical Therapy	D
Psychology—General	M
Public Administration	M
Public Health—General	M,O
Public History	M
Public Policy	M
Writing	M

RUTGERS UNIVERSITY–NEWARK

Accounting	M,D
Adult Nursing	M,D,O
Allied Health—General	M,D,O
Allopathic Medicine	D
American Studies	M,D
Analytical Chemistry	M,D
Applied Physics	M,D
Biochemistry	M,D
Bioinformatics	M,D
Biological and Biomedical Sciences—General	M,D,O
Biomedical Engineering	O
Biopsychology	D
Business Administration and Management—General	M,D
Cancer Biology/Oncology	D,O
Cell Biology	D
Chemistry	M,D
Clinical Laboratory Sciences/Medical Technology	M
Clothing and Textiles	M
Cognitive Sciences	D
Computational Biology	M
Criminal Justice and Criminology	M,D
Dentistry	M,D,O
Developmental Biology	D,O
Economics	M,D
English	M
Environmental Sciences	M,D
Epidemiology	M,O
Family Nurse Practitioner Studies	M,D,O
Finance and Banking	M,D
Geology	M
Health Education	M,D
Health Physics/Radiological Health	M
Health Services Management and Hospital Administration	M,D,O
History	M
Human Resources Management	M,D
Immunology	D
Infectious Diseases	D,O
Inorganic Chemistry	M,D
International Affairs	M,D
International Business	D
Law	D
Logistics	M
Management Information Systems	M,D
Management of Technology	D
Marketing	D
Mathematics	D
Medical Imaging	M
Medical Informatics	M,D,O
Microbiology	D
Molecular Biology	M,D
Molecular Genetics	D
Molecular Medicine	D
Molecular Pathology	D
Music	M
Neuroscience	D
Nurse Anesthesia	M,D,O
Nursing Informatics	M
Nursing—General	M,D,O
Nutrition	M,D,O
Occupational Health Nursing	M,D,O
Oral and Dental Sciences	M,D,O
Organic Chemistry	M,D
Organizational Management	D
Pathology	D
Pharmaceutical Administration	M
Pharmacology	D
Physical Chemistry	M,D
Physical Therapy	D
Physician Assistant Studies	M
Physiology	D
Political Science	M
Psychology—General	D
Public Administration	M,D
Public Health—General	M,O
Public Policy	M,D,O
Quantitative Analysis	M,O
Real Estate	M
Rehabilitation Counseling	M,D
Social Psychology	D
Supply Chain Management	D
Transcultural Nursing	M,D,O
Urban Studies	M,D
Women's Health Nursing	M,D,O
Writing	M

RUTGERS UNIVERSITY–NEW BRUNSWICK

Aerospace/Aeronautical Engineering	M,D
African Studies	D
African-American Studies	D
Agricultural Economics and Agribusiness	M
Allopathic Medicine	D
Animal Sciences	M,D
Anthropology	M,D
Applied Arts and Design—General	M
Applied Mathematics	M,D
Applied Psychology	M,D
Applied Statistics	M,D
Art History	M,D,O
Art/Fine Arts	M
Asian Studies	M,D
Astronomy	M,D
Atmospheric Sciences	M,D
Biochemical Engineering	M,D
Biochemistry	M,D
Biological and Biomedical Sciences—General	M,D
Biomedical Engineering	M,D
Biopsychology	D
Biostatistics	M,D,O
Cancer Biology/Oncology	M,D
Cell Biology	M,D
Chemical Engineering	M,D
Chemistry	M,D
Civil Engineering	M,D
Classics	M,D
Clinical Laboratory Sciences/Medical Technology	M
Clinical Psychology	M,D
Cognitive Sciences	D
Communication—General	D
Comparative Literature	M,D
Computational Biology	D
Computer Engineering	M,D
Computer Science	M,D
Condensed Matter Physics	M,D
Counseling Psychology	M
Counselor Education	M
Developmental Biology	M,D
Developmental Education	M
Early Childhood Education	M,D
Ecology	M,D
Economics	M,D
Education—General	M,D
Educational Leadership and Administration	M,D
Educational Measurement and Evaluation	M
Educational Policy	D
Educational Psychology	M,D
Electrical Engineering	M,D
Elementary Education	M,D
Emergency Management	M,D,O
English as a Second Language	M,D
English Education	M
English	D
Entomology	M,D
Environmental and Occupational Health	M,D,O
Environmental Biology	M,D
Environmental Engineering	M,D
Environmental Sciences	M,D
Epidemiology	M,D,O
Evolutionary Biology	M,D
Food Science and Technology	M,D
Foreign Languages Education	M,D
Foundations and Philosophy of Education	M,D
French	M,D
Gender Studies	M,D
Genetics	M,D
Geography	M,D
Geology	M,D
German	M,D
Hazardous Materials Management	M,D
Health Education	M,D,O
Health Psychology	D
Health Services Management and Hospital Administration	M,D,O
Historic Preservation	M,D,O
History of Medicine	D
History of Science and Technology	D
History	D
Horticulture	M,D
Human Resources Management	M,D
Immunology	M,D
Industrial and Labor Relations	M,D
Industrial/Management Engineering	M,D
Information Studies	M,D
Inorganic Chemistry	M,D
Interdisciplinary Studies	D
International Affairs	M,D
Italian	M,D
Jewish Studies	M,O
Legal and Justice Studies	M,D
Library Science	M,D
Linguistics	D
Marine Biology	M,D
Materials Engineering	M,D
Materials Sciences	M,D
Mathematics Education	M,D
Mathematics	M,D
Mechanical Engineering	M,D
Mechanics	M,D
Media Studies	D
Medical Microbiology	M,D
Medicinal and Pharmaceutical Chemistry	M,D
Medieval and Renaissance Studies	D
Microbiology	M,D
Molecular Biology	M,D
Molecular Biophysics	D
Molecular Genetics	M,D
Molecular Pharmacology	M,D
Molecular Physiology	M,D
Multilingual and Multicultural Education	M,D
Music Education	M,D,O
Music	M,D,O
Neuroscience	M,D
Nutrition	M,D
Oceanography	M,D
Operations Research	D
Organic Chemistry	M,D
Pharmaceutical Sciences	M,D
Pharmacy	M,D
Philosophy	D
Physical Chemistry	M,D
Physics	M,D
Physiology	M,D
Plant Biology	M,D
Plant Molecular Biology	M,D
Plant Pathology	M,D
Political Science	M,D
Psychology—General	D
Public Health—General	M,D
Public Policy	M,D
Quality Management	M,D
Reading Education	M,D
Religion	M,O
Reproductive Biology	M,D
School Psychology	M,D
Science Education	M,D
Social Psychology	D
Social Sciences Education	M,D
Social Work	M,D*
Sociology	M,D
Spanish	M,D
Special Education	M,D
Statistics	M,D
Student Affairs	M
Systems Biology	D
Systems Engineering	M,D
Theater	M
Theoretical Physics	M,D
Toxicology	M,D
Translation and Interpretation	M,D
Translational Biology	M
Urban and Regional Planning	M,D
Virology	M,D
Water Resources	M,D
Women's Studies	M,D
Writing	M

RYERSON UNIVERSITY

Arts Administration	M

SACRED HEART MAJOR SEMINARY

Pastoral Ministry and Counseling	M
Theology	M

SACRED HEART SCHOOL OF THEOLOGY

Theology	M,O

SACRED HEART UNIVERSITY

Accounting	M,O
Advertising and Public Relations	M
Applied Psychology	M
Business Administration and Management—General	M,D,O
Chemistry	M
Communication Disorders	M
Communication—General	M
Computer and Information Systems Security	M,O
Computer Science	M,O

Corporate and Organizational Communication	M
Criminal Justice and Criminology	M
Database Systems	M,O
Education—General	M,O
Educational Leadership and Administration	M,O
Educational Media/Instructional Technology	M,O
English as a Second Language	M,O
Environmental Management and Policy	M
Exercise and Sports Science	M
Family Nurse Practitioner Studies	M,D,O
Film, Television, and Video Production	M
Finance and Banking	M,D,O
Game Design and Development	M,O
Health Informatics	M
Human Resources Management	M,O
Information Science	M,O
Internet and Interactive Multimedia	M,O
Investment Management	M,D,O
Journalism	M
Management Information Systems	M,O
Marketing	M,O
Media Studies	M
Nursing and Healthcare Administration	M,D,O
Nursing Education	M,D,O
Nursing—General	M,D,O
Nutrition	M
Occupational Therapy	M
Physical Therapy	D,O
Reading Education	O
Social Work	M

SAGE GRADUATE SCHOOL

Adult Nursing	M,D,O
Applied Behavior Analysis	M,O
Business Administration and Management—General	M
Counseling Psychology	M
Counselor Education	M,O
Education—General	M,D,O
Educational Leadership and Administration	D
Elementary Education	M
Family Nurse Practitioner Studies	M,O
Finance and Banking	M
Forensic Psychology	M,O
Gerontological Nursing	M,O
Gerontology	M
Health Education	M
Health Services Management and Hospital Administration	M,D,O
Human Resources Management	M
Management Strategy and Policy	M
Marketing	M
Nursing Education	D
Nursing—General	M,D,O
Nutrition	M,O
Occupational Therapy	M
Organizational Management	M
Physical Therapy	D
Psychiatric Nursing	M,O
Psychology—General	M,O
Reading Education	M
Social Psychology	M
Special Education	M

SAGINAW VALLEY STATE UNIVERSITY

Business Administration and Management—General	M
Chinese	M
Communication—General	M
Distance Education Development	M
Early Childhood Education	M
Education—General	M,O
Educational Leadership and Administration	M,O
Educational Media/Instructional Technology	M
Elementary Education	M
Energy and Power Engineering	M
Engineering and Applied Sciences—General	M
Family Nurse Practitioner Studies	M,D
Foreign Languages Education	M
Health Services Management and Hospital Administration	M
Materials Engineering	M
Media Studies	M
Middle School Education	M
Nursing and Healthcare Administration	M
Nursing—General	M
Occupational Therapy	M
Public Administration	M
Reading Education	M
Science Education	M
Secondary Education	M
Special Education	M

ST. AMBROSE UNIVERSITY

Accounting	M
Business Administration and Management—General	M,D
Communication Disorders	M
Criminal Justice and Criminology	M
Education—General	M
Educational Leadership and Administration	M
Health Services Management and Hospital Administration	M,D
Human Resources Management	M,D
Management of Technology	M
Nursing—General	M
Occupational Therapy	M
Organizational Management	M
Pastoral Ministry and Counseling	M
Physical Therapy	D
Social Work	M
Special Education	M

ST. ANDREW'S COLLEGE

Theology	M,D,O

ST. ANDREW'S COLLEGE IN WINNIPEG

Theology	M

SAINT ANTHONY COLLEGE OF NURSING

Nursing—General	M

ST. AUGUSTINE'S SEMINARY OF TORONTO

Pastoral Ministry and Counseling	M,O
Religious Education	M,O
Theology	M,O

ST. BERNARD'S SCHOOL OF THEOLOGY AND MINISTRY

Pastoral Ministry and Counseling	M,O
Theology	M,O

ST. BONAVENTURE UNIVERSITY

Business Administration and Management—General	M
Corporate and Organizational Communication	M
Counseling Psychology	M,O
Counselor Education	M,O
Early Childhood Education	M
Education of the Gifted	M,O
Education—General	M,O
Educational Leadership and Administration	M,O
English	M
Marketing	M
Middle School Education	M
Reading Education	M
Rehabilitation Counseling	M,O
Religion	M
Secondary Education	M
Social Psychology	M,O
Special Education	M,O

ST. CATHERINE UNIVERSITY

Adult Nursing	M,D
Business Administration and Management—General	M
Curriculum and Instruction	M
Early Childhood Education	M
Education—General	M
Gerontological Nursing	M,D
Health Services Management and Hospital Administration	M
Information Studies	M
Library Science	M
Marketing	M
Maternal and Child/Neonatal Nursing	M,D
Nursing Education	M,D
Nursing—General	M,D
Occupational Therapy	M,D
Organizational Management	M
Pastoral Ministry and Counseling	M,O
Pediatric Nursing	M,D
Physical Therapy	D
Physician Assistant Studies	M
Public Health—General	M
Social Work	M,D
Theology	M,O

SAINT CHARLES BORROMEO SEMINARY, OVERBROOK

Religion	M
Theology	M

ST. CLOUD STATE UNIVERSITY

Applied Behavior Analysis	M
Applied Economics	M
Applied Statistics	M
Archaeology	M
Biological and Biomedical Sciences—General	M
Biomedical Engineering	M
Business Administration and Management—General	M
Child and Family Studies	M
Communication Disorders	M
Computer and Information Systems Security	M
Computer Science	M
Counselor Education	M
Criminal Justice and Criminology	M
Curriculum and Instruction	M
Economics	M
Education—General	M,D
Educational Leadership and Administration	M,D
Educational Media/Instructional Technology	M
Electrical Engineering	M
Engineering and Applied Sciences—General	M
Engineering Management	M
English as a Second Language	M
English	M
Environmental Management and Policy	M
Exercise and Sports Science	M
Geography	M
Gerontology	M
Higher Education	M,D
Historic Preservation	M
History	M
Industrial and Organizational Psychology	M
Marriage and Family Therapy	M
Mass Communication	M
Mathematics	M
Mechanical Engineering	M
Music Education	M
Music	M
Nonprofit Management	M
Psychology—General	M,D
Rehabilitation Counseling	M
Social Psychology	M
Social Work	M
Special Education	M
Sports Management	M
Student Affairs	M
Technology and Public Policy	M

ST. EDWARD'S UNIVERSITY

Accounting	M,O
Business Administration and Management—General	M,O
Counseling Psychology	M
Environmental Management and Policy	M
Finance and Banking	M,O
Humanities	M,O
Liberal Studies	M,O
Organizational Management	M
Social Sciences	M,O
Student Affairs	M
Sustainable Development	M

ST. FRANCIS COLLEGE

Accounting	M

SAINT FRANCIS MEDICAL CENTER COLLEGE OF NURSING

Family Nurse Practitioner Studies	M,D,O
Gerontological Nursing	M,D,O
Maternal and Child/Neonatal Nursing	M,D,O
Medical/Surgical Nursing	M,D,O
Nursing and Healthcare Administration	M,D,O
Nursing Education	M,D,O
Nursing—General	M,D,O
Psychiatric Nursing	M,D,O

SAINT FRANCIS UNIVERSITY

Biological and Biomedical Sciences—General	M
Business Administration and Management—General	M
Education—General	M
Educational Leadership and Administration	M
Health Education	M
Human Resources Management	M
Occupational Therapy	M
Physical Therapy	D
Physician Assistant Studies	M
Reading Education	M

ST. FRANCIS XAVIER UNIVERSITY

Adult Education	M
Biological and Biomedical Sciences—General	M
Chemistry	M
Computer Science	M
Cultural Studies	M
Curriculum and Instruction	M
Education—General	M
Educational Leadership and Administration	M
Geology	M
Geosciences	M
Physics	M

ST. JOHN FISHER COLLEGE

Business Administration and Management—General	M
Counseling Psychology	M
Education—General	M,D,O
Educational Leadership and Administration	M,D
Elementary Education	M,O
English Education	M
Family Nurse Practitioner Studies	M,O
Foreign Languages Education	M
Middle School Education	M
Nursing—General	M,D,O
Pharmacy	D
Reading Education	M
Social Sciences Education	M
Special Education	M,O

ST. JOHN'S COLLEGE (MD)

Liberal Studies	M

ST. JOHN'S COLLEGE (NM)

Asian Languages	M
Asian Studies	M
Liberal Studies	M

ST. JOHN'S SEMINARY (CA)

Pastoral Ministry and Counseling	M
Theology	M

SAINT JOHN'S SEMINARY (MA)

Religion	M
Theology	M

SAINT JOHN'S UNIVERSITY (MN)

Music	M
Pastoral Ministry and Counseling	M
Theology	M

ST. JOHN'S UNIVERSITY (NY)

Accounting	M
Actuarial Science	M
Asian Studies	M,O
Biological and Biomedical Sciences—General	M,D
Biotechnology	M
Business Administration and Management—General	M
Chemistry	M
Clinical Psychology	M,D,O
Communication Disorders	M,D
Counseling Psychology	M,D,O
Counselor Education	M,D,O
Criminal Justice and Criminology	M
Database Systems	M
Early Childhood Education	M
Education of the Gifted	M,D,O
Education—General	M,D,O
Educational Leadership and Administration	M,D,O
Elementary Education	M
English as a Second Language	M,O
English	M,D
Experimental Psychology	M
Finance and Banking	M
History	M,D
Information Science	
Information Studies	M,O
Insurance	M
International Affairs	M,O
International Business	M
Investment Management	M
Law	M,D
Legal and Justice Studies	M
Liberal Studies	M
Library Science	M,O
Management Information Systems	M
Management Strategy and Policy	M
Marketing	M
Middle School Education	M,O
Multilingual and Multicultural Education	M,O
Museum Studies	M
Pharmaceutical Administration	M
Pharmaceutical Sciences	M,D
Political Science	M,D
Psychology—General	M,D
Public Administration	M,O
Public Health—General	M
Public History	M,D
Quantitative Analysis	M
Reading Education	M,D,O
School Psychology	M,D
Secondary Education	M,O
Sociology	M
Spanish	M
Special Education	M,D,O
Sports Management	M
Taxation	M
Theology	M
Toxicology	M

SAINT JOSEPH'S COLLEGE

Music	M,O

ST. JOSEPH'S COLLEGE, LONG ISLAND CAMPUS

Accounting	M
Business Administration and Management—General	M
Early Childhood Education	M
Health Informatics	M
Health Services Management and Hospital Administration	M
Human Resources Management	M
Human Services	M
Mathematics Education	M
Nursing—General	M
Organizational Management	M
Reading Education	M
Special Education	M

ST. JOSEPH'S COLLEGE, NEW YORK

Accounting	M
Business Administration and Management—General	M
Education—General	M
Health Informatics	M
Health Services Management and Hospital Administration	M
Human Resources Management	M
Human Services	M
Nursing—General	M
Organizational Management	M
Reading Education	M
Special Education	M
Writing	M

SAINT JOSEPH'S COLLEGE OF MAINE

Accounting	M
Adult Education	M
Business Administration and Management—General	M
Education—General	M
Educational Leadership and Administration	M
Family Nurse Practitioner Studies	M,O
Health Education	M
Health Services Management and Hospital Administration	M
Nursing and Healthcare Administration	M,O
Nursing Education	M,O
Nursing—General	M,O
Pastoral Ministry and Counseling	M

ST. JOSEPH'S SEMINARY

Pastoral Ministry and Counseling	M
Religion	M
Theology	M

SAINT JOSEPH'S UNIVERSITY

Accounting	M,O
Adult Education	M
Biological and Biomedical Sciences—General	M
Business Administration and Management—General	M,O
Computer Science	M,O
Criminal Justice and Criminology	M,O
Curriculum and Instruction	M,D,O
Education—General	M,D,O
Educational Leadership and Administration	M,D,O

*M—masters degree; D—doctorate; O—other advanced degree; *—Close-Up and/or Display*

Educational Media/Instructional Technology	M,D,O
Elementary Education	M,D,O
Environmental and Occupational Health	M
Finance and Banking	M,O
Gerontology	M
Health Education	M
Health Services Management and Hospital Administration	M,O
Homeland Security	M
Human Resources Management	M,O
Industrial and Organizational Psychology	M
International Business	M,O
Law	M,O
Management Information Systems	M
Management Strategy and Policy	M
Marketing	M,O
Mathematics	M,O
Middle School Education	M,D,O
Nurse Anesthesia	M
Nursing and Healthcare Administration	M
Organizational Management	M
Psychology—General	M,O
Reading Education	M,D,O
School Nursing	M
Secondary Education	M,D,O
Special Education	M,D,O
Writing	M

ST. LAWRENCE UNIVERSITY

Counselor Education	M,O
Education—General	M,O
Educational Leadership and Administration	M,O
Human Development	M,O

SAINT LEO UNIVERSITY

Accounting	M
Business Administration and Management—General	M
Computer and Information Systems Security	M
Criminal Justice and Criminology	M
Education of the Gifted	M
Education—General	M
Educational Leadership and Administration	M
Educational Media/Instructional Technology	M
Forensic Psychology	M
Forensic Sciences	M
Health Services Management and Hospital Administration	M
Human Resources Management	M
Human Services	M
Legal and Justice Studies	M
Marketing Research	M
Marketing	M
Pastoral Ministry and Counseling	M
Project Management	M
Social Work	M
Sports Management	M

ST. LOUIS COLLEGE OF PHARMACY

Pharmacy	D*

SAINT LOUIS UNIVERSITY

Accounting	M
Allied Health—General	M,D,O
Allopathic Medicine	D
American Studies	M,D
Anatomy	M,D
Athletic Training and Sports Medicine	M,D
Biochemistry	D
Bioethics	D,O
Biological and Biomedical Sciences—General	M,D
Biomedical Engineering	M,D
Business Administration and Management—General	M
Chemistry	M,D
Clinical Psychology	M,D
Communication Disorders	M
Communication—General	M
Community Health	M
Counselor Education	M,D,O
Curriculum and Instruction	M,D
Dentistry	M
Education—General	M,D
Educational Leadership and Administration	M,D,O
English	M,D
Experimental Psychology	M,D
Finance and Banking	M
Foundations and Philosophy of Education	M,D
French	M
Geographic Information Systems	M,D,O
Geophysics	M,D
Geosciences	M,D
Health Services Management and Hospital Administration	M,D
Higher Education	M,D,O
History	M,D
Human Development	M,D,O
Immunology	D
Industrial and Organizational Psychology	M,D
International Business	M,D
Law	M,D
Marriage and Family Therapy	M,D,O
Mathematics	M,D
Meteorology	M,D
Microbiology	D
Molecular Biology	D
Nursing—General	M,D,O
Nutrition	M*
Occupational Therapy	M
Oral and Dental Sciences	M
Organizational Management	M,D,O
Pathology	D
Pharmacology	D
Philosophy	M,D
Physical Therapy	M,D
Physician Assistant Studies	M
Physiology	D
Political Science	M
Psychology—General	M,D
Public Administration	M,D,O
Public Health—General	M,D
Public Policy	M,D,O
Social Work	M
Spanish	M
Special Education	M,D
Student Affairs	M,D,O
Theology	M,D
Urban Studies	M,D,O

SAINT LOUIS UNIVERSITY–MADRID CAMPUS

English	M
Spanish	M

SAINT MARTIN'S UNIVERSITY

Business Administration and Management—General	M
Civil Engineering	M
Counseling Psychology	M
Counselor Education	M
Education—General	M
Educational Leadership and Administration	M
Engineering Management	M
English as a Second Language	M
Mechanical Engineering	M
Reading Education	M
Social Psychology	M
Special Education	M

SAINT MARY-OF-THE-WOODS COLLEGE

Art Therapy	M,O
Management Strategy and Policy	M
Pastoral Ministry and Counseling	M,O
Theology	M,O
Therapies—Dance, Drama, and Music	M

SAINT MARY'S COLLEGE

Communication Disorders	M
Database Systems	M
Nursing—General	D

SAINT MARY'S COLLEGE OF CALIFORNIA

Business Administration and Management—General	M
Conflict Resolution and Mediation/Peace Studies	M
Counselor Education	M,O
Dance	M
Early Childhood Education	M
Education—General	M,D,O
Educational Leadership and Administration	M,D,O
Exercise and Sports Science	M
Finance and Banking	M
Investment Management	M
Kinesiology and Movement Studies	M
Marriage and Family Therapy	M,O
Organizational Management	M
Reading Education	M
School Psychology	M,O
Special Education	M
Sports Management	M
Writing	M

ST. MARY'S COLLEGE OF MARYLAND

Education—General	M

SAINT MARY SEMINARY AND GRADUATE SCHOOL OF THEOLOGY

Theology	M,D

ST. MARY'S SEMINARY AND UNIVERSITY

Theology	M,D,O

SAINT MARY'S UNIVERSITY (CANADA)

Applied Psychology	M,D
Applied Science and Technology	M
Astronomy	M,D
Business Administration and Management—General	M,D
Canadian Studies	M,O
Criminal Justice and Criminology	M
Gender Studies	M
History	M
Industrial and Organizational Psychology	M,D
International Development	M,O
Philosophy	M
Psychology—General	M,D
Religion	M
Theology	M
Women's Studies	M

ST. MARY'S UNIVERSITY (UNITED STATES)

Accounting	M
Business Administration and Management—General	M
Communication—General	M,O
Computer and Information Systems Security	M
Computer Engineering	M
Computer Science	M
Conflict Resolution and Mediation/Peace Studies	M,O
Counseling Psychology	M
Counselor Education	D
Educational Leadership and Administration	M
Electrical Engineering	M
Engineering Management	M
English	M
Homeland Security	M,O
Industrial and Organizational Psychology	M
Industrial/Management Engineering	M
Information Science	M
International Affairs	M,O
International Development	M,O
Law	M,D
Legal and Justice Studies	M
Marriage and Family Therapy	M,D
Public Administration	M,O
Public Policy	M,O
Software Engineering	M,O
Theology	M

SAINT MARY'S UNIVERSITY OF MINNESOTA

Accounting	M
Addictions/Substance Abuse Counseling	M,O
Arts Administration	M
Business Administration and Management—General	M,D
Counseling Psychology	M,D,O
Education of the Gifted	M,O
Education—General	M,O
Educational Leadership and Administration	M,D,O
Educational Media/Instructional Technology	M
Elementary Education	M,O
Environmental and Occupational Health	M
Geographic Information Systems	M,O
Health Services Management and Hospital Administration	M
Human Development	M
Human Resources Management	M
International Business	M
International Development	M
Marriage and Family Therapy	M,O
Multilingual and Multicultural Education	M,O
Nurse Anesthesia	M
Organizational Management	M
Philanthropic Studies	M
Project Management	M,O
Reading Education	M,O
Religious Education	M
Secondary Education	M,O
Special Education	M,O
Telecommunications	M

SAINT MEINRAD SCHOOL OF THEOLOGY

Pastoral Ministry and Counseling	M
Theology	M

SAINT MICHAEL'S COLLEGE

Art Education	M,O
Clinical Psychology	M
Curriculum and Instruction	M,O
Education—General	M,O
Educational Leadership and Administration	M,O
English as a Second Language	M,O
Reading Education	M,O
Special Education	M,O

ST. NORBERT COLLEGE

Business Administration and Management—General	M
Health Services Management and Hospital Administration	M
Liberal Studies	M
Supply Chain Management	M
Theology	M

ST. PATRICK'S SEMINARY & UNIVERSITY

Theology	M,O

SAINT PAUL SCHOOL OF THEOLOGY

Theology	M,D

SAINT PAUL UNIVERSITY

Conflict Resolution and Mediation/Peace Studies	M
Counseling Psychology	M
Marriage and Family Therapy	M
Missions and Missiology	M
Pastoral Ministry and Counseling	M,D,O
Theology	M,D,O

ST. PETER'S SEMINARY

Theology	M

SAINT PETER'S UNIVERSITY

Accounting	M
Adult Nursing	M,D,O
Applied Behavior Analysis	M,D,O
Business Administration and Management—General	M
Counselor Education	M,O
Criminal Justice and Criminology	M
Database Systems	M
Education—General	M,D,O
Educational Leadership and Administration	M,D
Elementary Education	M,O
Finance and Banking	M
Health Services Management and Hospital Administration	M
Higher Education	D
Human Resources Management	M
International Business	M
Management Information Systems	M
Marketing	M
Mathematics Education	M,D,O
Middle School Education	M,O
Nursing and Healthcare Administration	M,D,O
Nursing—General	M,D,O
Public Administration	M
Reading Education	M,O
Secondary Education	M,O
Special Education	M,O

SAINTS CYRIL AND METHODIUS SEMINARY

Pastoral Ministry and Counseling	M
Religious Education	M
Theology	M

ST. STEPHEN'S COLLEGE

Pastoral Ministry and Counseling	M,D
Theology	M,D

ST. THOMAS AQUINAS COLLEGE

Business Administration and Management—General	M
Education—General	M,O
Educational Leadership and Administration	M,O
Elementary Education	M,O
Finance and Banking	M
Marketing	M
Middle School Education	M,O
Reading Education	M,O
Secondary Education	M,O
Special Education	M,O

ST. THOMAS UNIVERSITY

Accounting	M,O
Arts Administration	M
Business Administration and Management—General	M,O
Communication—General	M,D,O
Counseling Psychology	M
Counselor Education	M,O
Criminal Justice and Criminology	M,O
Education of the Gifted	M,D,O
Education—General	M,D,O
Educational Leadership and Administration	M,D,O
Educational Media/Instructional Technology	M,D,O
Elementary Education	M,D,O
English as a Second Language	M,D,O
Film, Television, and Video Production	M
Geosciences	M,D,O
Health Services Management and Hospital Administration	M,O
Hispanic Studies	M,O
Human Resources Management	M,O
International Business	M,O
Law	M,D
Marriage and Family Therapy	M,O
Pastoral Ministry and Counseling	M,D,O
Planetary and Space Sciences	M,D,O
Public Administration	M,O
Reading Education	M,D,O
Special Education	M,D,O
Sports Management	M,O
Taxation	M,D
Theology	M,D,O

ST. TIKHON'S ORTHODOX THEOLOGICAL SEMINARY

Theology	M

SAINT VINCENT COLLEGE

Business Administration and Management—General	M
Curriculum and Instruction	M
Education—General	M
Educational Leadership and Administration	M
Educational Media/Instructional Technology	M
Nurse Anesthesia	M,D
Special Education	M

ST. VINCENT DE PAUL REGIONAL SEMINARY

Theology	M

SAINT VINCENT SEMINARY

Pastoral Ministry and Counseling	M
Theology	M

ST. VLADIMIR'S ORTHODOX THEOLOGICAL SEMINARY

Music	M,D
Religious Education	M,D
Theology	M,D

SAINT XAVIER UNIVERSITY

Business Administration and Management—General	M,O
Communication Disorders	M
Computer Science	M
Counselor Education	M
Curriculum and Instruction	M
Early Childhood Education	M
Education—General	M
Educational Leadership and Administration	M
Educational Media/Instructional Technology	M
Elementary Education	M
English as a Second Language	M
Finance and Banking	M,O
Foreign Languages Education	M
Health Services Management and Hospital Administration	M,O
Marketing	M,O
Music Education	M
Nursing—General	M,O
Project Management	M,O
Reading Education	M
Science Education	M
Secondary Education	M
Spanish	M
Special Education	M

SALEM COLLEGE

Art Education	M
Counselor Education	M
Education—General	M
Elementary Education	M
English as a Second Language	M
Middle School Education	M

Reading Education M
Secondary Education M
Special Education M

SALEM INTERNATIONAL UNIVERSITY
Business Administration and Management—General M
Computer and Information Systems Security M
Curriculum and Instruction M
Education—General M
Educational Leadership and Administration M
International Business M

SALEM STATE UNIVERSITY
Art Education M
Business Administration and Management—General M
Counseling Psychology M,O
Counselor Education M
Criminal Justice and Criminology M
Early Childhood Education M
Educational Leadership and Administration M
Educational Media/Instructional Technology M
Elementary Education M
English as a Second Language M
English M
Geography M
Gerontological Nursing M
Higher Education M
History M
Mathematics Education M
Mathematics M
Middle School Education M
Nursing and Healthcare Administration M
Nursing Education M
Nursing—General M
Occupational Therapy M
Physical Education M
Psychology—General M,O
Reading Education M
Science Education M
Secondary Education M
Social Work M
Spanish M
Special Education M

SALISBURY UNIVERSITY
Athletic Training and Sports Medicine M
Biological and Biomedical Sciences—General M
Business Administration and Management—General M
Conflict Resolution and Mediation/Peace Studies M
Curriculum and Instruction M
Educational Leadership and Administration M
English as a Second Language M
English M
Family Nurse Practitioner Studies D
Film, Television, and Video Theory and Criticism M
Geographic Information Systems M
History M
Mathematics Education M
Middle School Education M
Nursing and Healthcare Administration M,D
Nursing Education M
Nursing—General M,D
Physiology M
Reading Education M,D
Rhetoric M
Secondary Education M
Social Work M
Writing M

SALUS UNIVERSITY
Communication Disorders D
Optometry D
Physician Assistant Studies M
Public Health—General M
Rehabilitation Sciences M,O
Special Education M,O
Vision Sciences M,O

SALVE REGINA UNIVERSITY
Addictions/Substance Abuse Counseling M,O
Business Administration and Management—General M,O
Computer and Information Systems Security M,O
Conflict Resolution and Mediation/Peace Studies M,D
Counseling Psychology M,O
Criminal Justice and Criminology M,O
Entrepreneurship M
Forensic Sciences M,O
Health Services Management and Hospital Administration M,O
Homeland Security M,O
Humanities M,D
International Affairs M,O
Management Strategy and Policy M,O
Nonprofit Management M,O
Nursing—General D
Rehabilitation Counseling M,O
Religion M,D

SAMFORD UNIVERSITY
Athletic Training and Sports Medicine M,D
Biological and Biomedical Sciences—General M,D,O
Business Administration and Management—General M
Communication Disorders M,D
Early Childhood Education M,D,O
Education of the Gifted M,D,O
Education—General M,D,O
Educational Leadership and Administration M,D,O
Educational Media/Instructional Technology M,D,O
Elementary Education M,D,O
Energy Management and Policy M
Entrepreneurship M
Environmental Management and Policy M
Family Nurse Practitioner Studies M,D
Finance and Banking M
Health Services Management and Hospital Administration M,D
History M,D,O
Law M,D
Marketing M
Mathematics M,D,O
Music Education M
Music M
Nurse Anesthesia M,D
Nursing and Healthcare Administration M,D
Nursing Education M,D
Nursing—General M,D
Pharmacy D
Physical Education M,D,O
Physical Therapy M,D
Public Health—General M
Science Education M,D,O
Secondary Education M,D,O
Social Sciences Education M,D,O
Social Work M
Spanish M,D,O
Special Education M,D,O
Theology M,D

SAM HOUSTON STATE UNIVERSITY
Accounting M
Agricultural Sciences—General M
Allied Health—General M
Biological and Biomedical Sciences—General M
Business Administration and Management—General M
Chemistry M
Clinical Psychology M,D,O
Communication—General M
Computational Sciences M,D
Computer and Information Systems Security M,D
Computer Science M,D
Counselor Education M,D
Criminal Justice and Criminology M,D
Curriculum and Instruction M,D
Dance M
Developmental Education M,D
Education—General M,D
Educational Leadership and Administration M,D
English M
Family and Consumer Sciences-General M
Finance and Banking M
Forensic Sciences M,D
Geographic Information Systems M,O
Higher Education M,D
History M
Homeland Security M
Humanities M,D,O
Information Science M,D
Internet and Interactive Multimedia M
Kinesiology and Movement Studies M
Library Science M
Mathematics M
Music M
Nutrition M
Political Science M
Project Management M
Psychology—General M,D,O
Public Administration M
Publishing M
Reading Education M,D
School Psychology M,D,O
Sociology M
Spanish M
Special Education M,D
Sports Management M
Statistics M
Writing M

SAMUEL MERRITT UNIVERSITY
Family Nurse Practitioner Studies M,D,O
Nurse Anesthesia M,D,O
Nursing and Healthcare Administration M,D,O
Nursing—General M,D,O
Occupational Therapy M
Physical Therapy D
Physician Assistant Studies M

SAN DIEGO STATE UNIVERSITY
Accounting M
Advertising and Public Relations M
Aerospace/Aeronautical Engineering M,D
Anthropology M
Applied Arts and Design—General M
Applied Mathematics M
Art History M
Art/Fine Arts M
Asian Studies M
Astronomy M
Biochemistry M,D
Biological and Biomedical Sciences—General M,D
Biometry M
Biostatistics M,D
Business Administration and Management—General M
Cell Biology M,D
Chemistry M,D
Child and Family Studies M
Child Development M
Civil Engineering M
Clinical Psychology M,D
Communication Disorders M,D
Communication—General M
Computational Sciences M,D
Computer Science M
Counselor Education M
Criminal Justice and Criminology M
Curriculum and Instruction M
Ecology M,D
Economics M
Education—General M,D
Educational Leadership and Administration M
Educational Media/Instructional Technology M,D
Electrical Engineering M
Elementary Education M
Emergency Management M,D
Emergency Medical Services M,D
Engineering and Applied Sciences—General M,D
Engineering Design M,D
English as a Second Language M,O
English M
Entrepreneurship M
Environmental and Occupational Health M,D
Environmental Design M
Epidemiology M,D
Exercise and Sports Science M
Film, Television, and Video Production M
Finance and Banking M
Gender Studies O
Geography M,D
Geology M
Gerontology M
Graphic Design M
Health Physics/Radiological Health M
Health Promotion M,D
Health Psychology M,D
Health Services Management and Hospital Administration M,D
Higher Education M
History M
Human Resources Management M
Industrial and Organizational Psychology M,D
Interdisciplinary Studies M
Interior Design M
International Health M,D
Internet and Interactive Multimedia M
Kinesiology and Movement Studies M
Latin American Studies M
Liberal Studies M
Linguistics M,O
Management Information Systems M
Marketing M
Mathematics Education M,D
Mathematics M,D
Mechanical Engineering M,D
Mechanics M,D
Media Studies M
Microbiology M
Molecular Biology M,D
Multilingual and Multicultural Education M,D
Music Education M
Music M
Nursing—General M
Nutrition M
Pharmaceutical Administration M
Philosophy M
Physical Therapy D
Physics M
Political Science M
Psychology—General M,D
Public Administration M
Public Health—General M,D
Reading Education M
Rehabilitation Counseling M
Rhetoric M
Romance Languages M
School Psychology M
Science Education M,D
Secondary Education M
Social Work M
Sociology M
Spanish M
Special Education M
Sports Management M
Statistics M
Telecommunications Management M
Theater M
Toxicology M,D
Urban and Regional Planning M
Western European Studies M
Women's Studies M
Writing M

SANFORD BURNHAM PREBYS MEDICAL DISCOVERY INSTITUTE
Biological and Biomedical Sciences—General D

SAN FRANCISCO ART INSTITUTE
Art History M
Art/Fine Arts M,O
Museum Studies M

SAN FRANCISCO CONSERVATORY OF MUSIC
Music M

SAN FRANCISCO STATE UNIVERSITY
Accounting M
Acute Care/Critical Care Nursing M,O
Adult Education M
Anthropology M
Archaeology M
Art History M
Art/Fine Arts M
Asian-American Studies M
Astronomy M
Biochemistry M
Biological and Biomedical Sciences—General M
Biotechnology M
Business Administration and Management—General M
Cell Biology M
Chemistry M
Chinese M
Classics M
Clinical Psychology M,O
Communication Disorders M
Community Health Nursing M,O
Comparative Literature M
Computer Science M
Counseling Psychology M,O
Counselor Education M,O
Criminal Justice and Criminology M
Cultural Anthropology M
Cultural Studies M
Developmental Biology M
Developmental Psychology M,O
Early Childhood Education M,D,O
Ecology M
Economics M
Education—General M,D,O
Educational Leadership and Administration M,D,O
Educational Media/Instructional Technology M
Electrical Engineering M
Elementary Education M
Energy and Power Engineering M
Engineering and Applied Sciences—General M
English as a Second Language M
English Education M,O
English M,O
Entrepreneurship M
Environmental Management and Policy M
Ethnic Studies M
Family and Consumer Sciences-General M
Family Nurse Practitioner Studies M,O
Film, Television, and Video Production M
Film, Television, and Video Theory and Criticism M
Finance and Banking M
French M
Geographic Information Systems M
Geography M
Geosciences M
German M
Gerontology M
Health Education M
Health Services Management and Hospital Administration M
History M
Hospitality Management M
Humanities M
Industrial and Manufacturing Management M
Industrial and Organizational Psychology M,O
Industrial Design M
International Affairs M
International Business M
Italian M
Japanese M
Kinesiology and Movement Studies M
Legal and Justice Studies M
Leisure Studies M
Liberal Studies M
Linguistics M
Management Information Systems M
Marine Biology M
Marine Sciences M
Marketing M
Marriage and Family Therapy M,O
Mathematics Education M
Mathematics M
Media Studies M
Microbiology M
Molecular Biology M
Museum Studies M
Music Education M
Music M
Nonprofit Management M
Nursing and Healthcare Administration M,O
Nursing—General M,O
Pediatric Nursing M,O
Philosophy M
Physical Therapy D
Physics M
Physiology M
Political Science M
Psychology—General M,O
Public Administration M
Public Health—General M
Public Policy M
Quantitative Analysis M

*M—masters degree; D—doctorate; O—other advanced degree; *—Close-Up and/or Display*

Reading Education M,O
Recreation and Park Management M
Rehabilitation Counseling M,O
School Psychology M,O
Secondary Education M,O
Social Psychology M,O
Social Work M
Spanish M
Special Education M,O
Speech and Interpersonal Communication M
Sustainability Management M
Theater M
Travel and Tourism M
Women's Health Nursing M,O
Women's Studies M
Writing M

SAN FRANCISCO THEOLOGICAL SEMINARY
Theology M,D

SAN JOAQUIN COLLEGE OF LAW
Law D

SAN JOSE STATE UNIVERSITY
Accounting M
Anthropology M,O
Art History M,O
Athletic Training and Sports Medicine M,O
Biological and Biomedical Sciences—General M,O
Biotechnology M,O
Chemistry M,O
Child Development M,D,O
Clinical Psychology M,O
Communication Disorders M,D,O
Communication—General M,O
Computational Sciences M,O
Computer and Information Systems Security M,O
Computer Science M,O
Counselor Education M,D,O
Curriculum and Instruction M,D,O
Early Childhood Education M,D,O
Ecology M,O
Economics M,O
Education—General M,D,O
Educational Leadership and Administration M,D,O
Elementary Education M,D,O
English as a Second Language M,O
English M,O
Environmental Management and Policy M,O
Exercise and Sports Science M,O
Experimental Psychology M,O
French M,O
Geography M,O
Geology M,O
Higher Education M,D,O
Hispanic Studies M,O
History M,O
Industrial and Organizational Psychology M,O
Kinesiology and Movement Studies M,O
Legal and Justice Studies M,O
Library Science M,O
Linguistics M,O
Management Strategy and Policy M,O
Marine Sciences M,O
Mass Communication M,O
Mathematics Education M,O
Mathematics M,D,O
Media Studies M,O
Meteorology M,O
Molecular Biology M,O
Music M,O
Nutrition M,O
Occupational Therapy M,O
Philosophy M,O
Photography M,O
Physics M,O
Physiology M,O
Psychology—General M,O
Public Administration M,O
Public Health—General M,O
Real Estate M,O
Recreation and Park Management M,O
School Psychology M,D,O
Science Education M,O
Social Work M,O
Sociology M,O
Spanish M,O
Sports Management M,O
Statistics M,O
Sustainable Development M,O
Taxation M
Theater M,O
Transportation Management M
Writing M,O

SANTA CLARA UNIVERSITY
Applied Mathematics M,D,O
Bioengineering M,D,O
Business Administration and Management—General M
Civil Engineering M,D,O
Computer Engineering M,D,O
Computer Science M,D,O
Counseling Psychology M,O
Counselor Education M,O
Education—General M,O
Educational Leadership and Administration M,O
Electrical Engineering M,D,O
Energy and Power Engineering M,D,O
Engineering and Applied Sciences—General M,D,O
Engineering Management M,D,O
Ethics M,D,O
Finance and Banking M
Intellectual Property Law M,D,O
Law M,D,O
Management Information Systems M
Mechanical Engineering M,D,O
Pastoral Ministry and Counseling M,D,O
Religion M,D,O
Software Engineering M,D,O
Supply Chain Management M
Theology M,D,O

SARAH LAWRENCE COLLEGE
Child Development M
Dance M
Education—General M
Genetic Counseling M
History M
Human Genetics M
Kinesiology and Movement Studies M
Public Health—General M
Theater M
Women's Studies M
Writing M

SAVANNAH COLLEGE OF ART AND DESIGN
Advertising and Public Relations M
Applied Arts and Design—General M,O
Architectural History M
Architecture M
Art History M
Art/Fine Arts M
Arts Administration M
Clothing and Textiles M
Computer Art and Design M,O
Film, Television, and Video Production M
Film, Television, and Video Theory and Criticism M
Game Design and Development M,O
Graphic Design M
Historic Preservation M,O
Illustration M
Industrial Design M
Interior Design M
Internet and Interactive Multimedia M,O
Media Studies M
Music M
Photography M
Sustainable Development M
Textile Design M
Theater M
Travel and Tourism M
Urban Design M
Writing M

SAVANNAH STATE UNIVERSITY
Business Administration and Management—General M
Human Resources Management M
Marine Sciences M
Public Administration M
Social Work M
Urban and Regional Planning M
Urban Studies M

SAYBROOK UNIVERSITY
Clinical Psychology M
Counseling Psychology M
Health Psychology M,D
Marriage and Family Therapy M,D
Nutrition M,D,O
Organizational Behavior M,D
Organizational Management M,D
Psychology—General M,D
Sustainable Development M,D
Transpersonal and Humanistic Psychology M,D

SCHILLER INTERNATIONAL UNIVERSITY (GERMANY)
Business Administration and Management—General M
International Business M
Management Information Systems M

SCHILLER INTERNATIONAL UNIVERSITY
Business Administration and Management—General M
International Affairs M
International Business M

SCHILLER INTERNATIONAL UNIVERSITY (SPAIN)
Business Administration and Management—General M
International Business M

SCHILLER INTERNATIONAL UNIVERSITY (UNITED STATES)
Business Administration and Management—General M
Finance and Banking M
Hospitality Management M
International Business M
Management Information Systems M
Travel and Tourism M

SCHOOL OF ADVANCED AIR AND SPACE STUDIES
Military and Defense Studies M

SCHOOL OF THE ART INSTITUTE OF CHICAGO
Applied Arts and Design—General M
Architecture M
Art Education M
Art History M
Art Therapy M
Art/Fine Arts M
Arts Administration M
Arts Journalism M
Film, Television, and Video Production M
Graphic Design M
Historic Preservation M
Interior Design M
Journalism M
Materials Sciences M
Music M
Photography M
Textile Design M,O
Writing M,O

SCHOOL OF THE MUSEUM OF FINE ARTS, BOSTON
Art Education M,O
Art/Fine Arts M,O

SCHOOL OF VISUAL ARTS (NY)
Applied Arts and Design—General M
Art Education M
Art History M
Art Therapy M
Art/Fine Arts M
Computer Art and Design M
Cultural Studies M
Film, Television, and Video Production M
Graphic Design M
Illustration M
Internet and Interactive Multimedia M
Photography M
Writing M

SCHREINER UNIVERSITY
Business Administration and Management—General M
Education—General M,O
Educational Leadership and Administration M,O
Ethics M

THE SCRIPPS RESEARCH INSTITUTE
Biological and Biomedical Sciences—General D
Chemistry D

SEABURY-WESTERN THEOLOGICAL SEMINARY
Music M,D,O
Theology M,D,O

SEATTLE INSTITUTE OF ORIENTAL MEDICINE
Acupuncture and Oriental Medicine M

SEATTLE PACIFIC UNIVERSITY
Adult Nursing M,O
Business Administration and Management—General M
Clinical Psychology D
Counselor Education M,D,O
Education—General D
Educational Leadership and Administration M,D,O
Educational Media/Instructional Technology M
English as a Second Language M
Family Nurse Practitioner Studies M,O
Gerontological Nursing M,O
Human Resources Management M
Industrial and Organizational Psychology M,D
Management Information Systems M
Marriage and Family Therapy M,O
Mathematics Education M
Nursing and Healthcare Administration M,O
Nursing Education M,O
Nursing Informatics M,O
Nursing—General M,O
Reading Education M
Religion M,O
Science Education M
Secondary Education M
Sustainability Management M
Theology M,O
Writing M

THE SEATTLE SCHOOL OF THEOLOGY AND PSYCHOLOGY
Counseling Psychology M
Psychology—General M
Religion M
Theology M

SEATTLE UNIVERSITY
Accounting M
Adult Education M,O
Adult Nursing M
Arts Administration M
Business Administration and Management—General M,O
Community Health Nursing M
Computer Science M
Counselor Education M,O
Criminal Justice and Criminology M,O
Database Systems M,O
Education—General M,D,O
Educational Leadership and Administration M,D,O
Engineering and Applied Sciences—General M
English as a Second Language M,O
Family Nurse Practitioner Studies M
Finance and Banking M,O
Forensic Sciences M,O
Gerontological Nursing M
Law D
Nurse Midwifery M
Nursing—General M,D
Organizational Management M,O
Pastoral Ministry and Counseling M
Psychiatric Nursing M
Psychology—General M
Public Administration M
Reading Education M,O
School Psychology M,O
Software Engineering M
Special Education M,O
Sports Management M
Theology M,O
Transpersonal and Humanistic Psychology M

SELMA UNIVERSITY
Pastoral Ministry and Counseling M
Religion M
Religious Education M

SEMINARY OF THE IMMACULATE CONCEPTION
Pastoral Ministry and Counseling M,D,O
Theology M,D,O

SEMINARY OF THE SOUTHWEST
Theology M,O

SETON HALL UNIVERSITY
Accounting M,O
Adult Nursing M,D
Allied Health—General D
Analytical Chemistry M,D
Asian Studies M
Athletic Training and Sports Medicine M
Biochemistry M,D
Biological and Biomedical Sciences—General M,D
Business Administration and Management—General M,O
Chemistry M,D
Communication Disorders M
Communication—General M
Corporate and Organizational Communication M
Counseling Psychology M,D
Counselor Education M,D
Education—General M,D,O
Educational Leadership and Administration D,O
Educational Measurement and Evaluation M,D,O
Educational Media/Instructional Technology M
English M
Entrepreneurship M,O
Experimental Psychology M
Finance and Banking M,O
Gerontological Nursing M,D
Health Law M,D
Health Services Management and Hospital Administration M,D,O
Higher Education D
History M
Inorganic Chemistry M,D
International Affairs M,O
International Business M,O
International Health M,O
Jewish Studies M,O
Law M,D
Management of Technology M,O
Marketing M,O
Marriage and Family Therapy M,O
Microbiology M,D
Molecular Biology M,D
Museum Education M
Museum Studies M
Neuroscience M,D
Nonprofit Management M,O
Nursing and Healthcare Administration M,D
Nursing Education M,D
Nursing—General M,D
Occupational Therapy M
Organic Chemistry M,D
Pastoral Ministry and Counseling M,O
Pediatric Nursing M,D
Physical Chemistry M,D
Physical Therapy D
Physician Assistant Studies M
Psychology—General M,D,O
Public Administration M,O
Public Policy M,O
Religion M,O
School Nursing M,D
School Psychology M
Special Education M
Speech and Interpersonal Communication M
Sport Psychology M
Sports Management M,O
Student Affairs M
Supply Chain Management M,O
Taxation M,O
Theology M,O

SETON HILL UNIVERSITY
Accounting M,O
Art Therapy M
Business Administration and Management—General M,O
Elementary Education M,O
Entrepreneurship M,O
Holocaust and Genocide Studies O
Marriage and Family Therapy M
Middle School Education M,O
Oral and Dental Sciences M,O
Physician Assistant Studies M
Special Education M
Writing M,O

SEWANEE: THE UNIVERSITY OF THE SOUTH
English M
Theology M,D
Writing M

SHASTA BIBLE COLLEGE
Educational Leadership and Administration M
Pastoral Ministry and Counseling M
Religious Education M

SHAWNEE STATE UNIVERSITY
Curriculum and Instruction M
Education—General M
Occupational Therapy M

SHAW UNIVERSITY
Curriculum and Instruction M
Early Childhood Education M
Theology M

SHENANDOAH UNIVERSITY
Allied Health—General M,D,O
Applied Behavior Analysis M
Arts Administration M,D,O
Athletic Training and Sports Medicine M,O
Business Administration and Management—General M,O
Education—General M,D,O
Educational Leadership and Administration M,D,O
Elementary Education M,D,O
Family Nurse Practitioner Studies M,D,O
Health Education M,D,O
Health Informatics M,D,O
Health Services Management and Hospital Administration M,O
Middle School Education M,D,O
Music Education M,D,O
Music M,D,O
Nurse Midwifery M,D,O
Nursing and Healthcare Administration M,D,O
Nursing Education M,D,O
Nursing—General M,D,O
Occupational Therapy M
Organizational Management M,D,O
Pharmacy D
Physical Education M,D,O
Physical Therapy D
Physician Assistant Studies M
Psychiatric Nursing M,D,O
Secondary Education M,D,O
Special Education M,D,O
Therapies—Dance, Drama, and Music M,D,O

SHEPHERDS THEOLOGICAL SEMINARY
Pastoral Ministry and Counseling M
Theology M

SHEPHERD UNIVERSITY (CA)
Computer Art and Design M
Game Design and Development M
Management Information Systems M
Music M
Theology M,D

SHEPHERD UNIVERSITY (WV)
Curriculum and Instruction M

SHERMAN COLLEGE OF CHIROPRACTIC
Chiropractic D*

SHILOH UNIVERSITY
Pastoral Ministry and Counseling M,D
Theology M,D

SHIPPENSBURG UNIVERSITY OF PENNSYLVANIA
Biological and Biomedical Sciences—General M
Business Administration and Management—General M,O
Clinical Psychology M,O
Communication—General M
Computer and Information Systems Security M
Computer Science M
Counselor Education M,O
Criminal Justice and Criminology M
Curriculum and Instruction M
Early Childhood Education M
Education—General M,D,O
Educational Leadership and Administration M,D
Elementary Education M
Environmental Management and Policy M
Finance and Banking M,O
Foreign Languages Education M
Geography M
Higher Education M
History M
Logistics M,O
Management Information Systems M,O
Marriage and Family Therapy M,O
Mathematics Education M
Middle School Education M
Organizational Management M
Psychology—General M
Public Administration M
Public History M
Reading Education M
Science Education M
Social Work M
Sociology M
Software Engineering M
Special Education M,D
Student Affairs M,O
Supply Chain Management M,O

SHORTER UNIVERSITY
Accounting M
Business Administration and Management—General M

SH'OR YOSHUV RABBINICAL COLLEGE
Theology

SIENA HEIGHTS UNIVERSITY
Clinical Psychology M,O
Counseling Psychology M,O
Early Childhood Education M,O
Education—General M,O
Educational Leadership and Administration M,O
Elementary Education M,O
Health Services Management and Hospital Administration M,O
Higher Education M,O
Organizational Management M,O
Reading Education M,O
Secondary Education M,O
Special Education M,O

SIERRA NEVADA COLLEGE
Education—General M
Educational Leadership and Administration M
Elementary Education M
Secondary Education M

SILICON VALLEY UNIVERSITY
Business Administration and Management—General M
Computer Engineering M
Computer Science M

SILVER LAKE COLLEGE OF THE HOLY FAMILY
Business Administration and Management—General M
Education—General M
Educational Leadership and Administration M
Music Education M
Organizational Behavior M
Special Education M

SIMMONS COLLEGE
Applied Behavior Analysis M,D,O
Business Administration and Management—General M
Communication—General M
Education—General M,D,O
Elementary Education M,D,O
English as a Second Language M,D,O
Family Nurse Practitioner Studies M,D,O
Health Education M,D,O
Health Promotion M,D,O
Health Services Management and Hospital Administration M
Information Science M,D,O
Library Science M,D,O
Middle School Education M,D,O
Nonprofit Management M
Nursing—General M,D,O
Nutrition M,D,O
Physical Therapy M,D,O
Public Policy M,D,O
Reading Education M,D,O
Secondary Education M,D,O
Social Work M,D
Special Education M,D,O
Writing M,D,O

SIMON FRASER UNIVERSITY
Actuarial Science M,D
Anthropology M,D
Applied Mathematics M,D
Archaeology M,D
Art Education M,D
Biochemistry M,D,O
Bioinformatics M,D,O
Biological and Biomedical Sciences—General M,D,O
Biotechnology M,D,O
Business Administration and Management—General M,D,O
Chemistry M,D
Communication—General M,D
Comparative and Interdisciplinary Arts M
Computational Sciences M,D
Computer Science M,D
Counselor Education M
Criminal Justice and Criminology M,D
Cultural Studies D
Curriculum and Instruction M,D
Economics M,D
Education—General M,D,O
Educational Leadership and Administration M,D
Educational Media/Instructional Technology M,D
Educational Psychology M,D
Engineering and Applied Sciences—General M,D
English as a Second Language M
English Education M,D
English M,D
Entomology M,D,O
Environmental Management and Policy M,D,O
Finance and Banking M,D,O
Fish, Game, and Wildlife Management M,D,O
Foundations and Philosophy of Education M,D
French M
Gender Studies M,D
Geography M,D
Geosciences M,D
Gerontology M,D
History M,D
Humanities M
International Affairs M
International Health M,D,O
Kinesiology and Movement Studies M,D
Latin American Studies M,O
Legal and Justice Studies M,D
Liberal Studies M
Linguistics M,D
Management of Technology M,D,O
Mathematics Education M,D
Mathematics M,D
Mechanical Engineering M,D
Molecular Biology M,D,O
Operations Research M,D
Philosophy M,D
Physics M,D
Political Science M,D
Psychology—General M,D
Public Health—General M,D,O
Public Policy M
Publishing M
Reading Education D
Sociology M,D
Statistics M,D
Systems Engineering M,D
Toxicology M,D,O
Urban Studies M,O
Women's Studies M,D

SIMPSON COLLEGE
Criminal Justice and Criminology M
Education—General M
Secondary Education M

SIMPSON UNIVERSITY
Counseling Psychology M
Curriculum and Instruction M
Education—General M
Educational Leadership and Administration M
Missions and Missiology M
Organizational Management M
Pastoral Ministry and Counseling M

SINTE GLESKA UNIVERSITY
Education—General M
Elementary Education M

SIOUX FALLS SEMINARY
Marriage and Family Therapy M,O
Pastoral Ministry and Counseling M
Religion M
Theology M,D,O

SIT GRADUATE INSTITUTE
Business Administration and Management—General M
English as a Second Language M
Foreign Languages Education M
International Affairs M
International and Comparative Education M
International Business M
Sustainable Development M

SITTING BULL COLLEGE
Environmental Sciences M

SLIPPERY ROCK UNIVERSITY OF PENNSYLVANIA
Accounting M
Addictions/Substance Abuse Counseling M
Business Administration and Management—General M
Clinical Psychology M
Counseling Psychology M
Counselor Education M
Criminal Justice and Criminology M
Education—General M,D
Educational Leadership and Administration M,D
Educational Media/Instructional Technology M,D
Elementary Education M
English Education M
Environmental Education M
Environmental Management and Policy M
Finance and Banking M
Gerontology M
Higher Education M
History M
Marketing M
Mathematics Education M
Physical Education M
Physical Therapy D
Reading Education M
Recreation and Park Management M
School Psychology M
Science Education M
Secondary Education M
Social Sciences Education M
Special Education M,D
Student Affairs M

SMITH COLLEGE
Biological and Biomedical Sciences—General M
Chemistry M
Dance M
Education—General M
Elementary Education M
English Education M
Exercise and Sports Science M
Foreign Languages Education M
French M
History M
Mathematics Education M
Mathematics O
Middle School Education M
Science Education M
Secondary Education M
Social Sciences Education M
Social Work M,D
Spanish M
Theater M
Women's Studies O

SOFIA UNIVERSITY
Clinical Psychology M,D
Computer Science M,D
Counseling Psychology M,D
Psychology—General M,D
Transpersonal and Humanistic Psychology M,D

SOKA UNIVERSITY OF AMERICA
Educational Leadership and Administration M

SONOMA STATE UNIVERSITY
Anthropology M
Biochemistry M
Biological and Biomedical Sciences—General M
Business Administration and Management—General M
Cell Biology M
Clinical Psychology M
Counseling Psychology M
Counselor Education M
Curriculum and Instruction M,D,O
Early Childhood Education M,D,O
Ecology M
Education—General M,D,O
Educational Leadership and Administration M,D,O
English M
Environmental Biology M
Ethics M
Evolutionary Biology M
Family Nurse Practitioner Studies M
Health Promotion M
History M
Interdisciplinary Studies M
International Business M
Kinesiology and Movement Studies M
Marriage and Family Therapy M
Molecular Biology M
Nonprofit Management M,O
Nursing—General M
Occupational Therapy M
Physical Education M
Physical Therapy M
Political Science M,O
Public Administration M,O
Public History M
Reading Education M,D,O
Special Education M,D,O
Sports Management M
Writing M

SOTHEBY'S INSTITUTE OF ART–LONDON
Art/Fine Arts M
Arts Administration M
Decorative Arts M

SOTHEBY'S INSTITUTE OF ART–NEW YORK
Art/Fine Arts M
Arts Administration M
Decorative Arts M

SOUTH BAYLO UNIVERSITY
Acupuncture and Oriental Medicine M

SOUTH CAROLINA STATE UNIVERSITY
Agricultural Economics and Agribusiness M
Allied Health—General M
Biological and Biomedical Sciences—General M
Business Education M
Child and Family Studies M
Civil Engineering M
Communication Disorders M
Counselor Education M
Early Childhood Education M
Education—General M
Educational Leadership and Administration D,O
Elementary Education M
English Education M
English M
Entrepreneurship M
Family and Consumer Sciences-General M
Home Economics Education M
Human Services M
Mathematics Education M
Mathematics M
Mechanical Engineering M
Nutrition M
Rehabilitation Counseling M
Science Education M
Secondary Education M
Social Sciences Education M
Special Education M
Transportation and Highway Engineering M
Vocational and Technical Education M

SOUTH COLLEGE
Physician Assistant Studies M

SOUTH DAKOTA SCHOOL OF MINES AND TECHNOLOGY
Artificial Intelligence/Robotics M
Atmospheric Sciences M,D
Bioengineering D
Biomedical Engineering M,D
Chemical Engineering M,D
Civil Engineering M,D
Construction Management M
Electrical Engineering M
Engineering and Applied Sciences—General M,D
Engineering Management M
Environmental Sciences D
Geological Engineering M,D
Geology M,D
Management of Technology M
Materials Engineering M,D

*M—masters degree; D—doctorate; O—other advanced degree; *—Close-Up and/or Display*

Materials Sciences	M,D
Mechanical Engineering	M,D
Mineral/Mining Engineering	M
Nanotechnology	D
Paleontology	M,D
Physics	M,D

SOUTH DAKOTA STATE UNIVERSITY

Agricultural Education	M
Agricultural Engineering	M,D
Agricultural Sciences—General	M,D
Agronomy and Soil Sciences	M,D
Animal Sciences	M,D
Athletic Training and Sports Medicine	M,D
Biological and Biomedical Sciences—General	M,D
Biosystems Engineering	M,D
Chemistry	M,D
Civil Engineering	M
Communication—General	M
Computational Sciences	M,D
Consumer Economics	M
Counselor Education	M
Curriculum and Instruction	M
Economics	M
Education—General	M,D
Educational Leadership and Administration	M
Electrical Engineering	M,D
Engineering and Applied Sciences—General	M,D
English	M
Exercise and Sports Science	M,D
Family and Consumer Sciences-General	M
Fish, Game, and Wildlife Management	M,D
Geography	M
Geosciences	D
Human Resources Development	M
Industrial/Management Engineering	M
Journalism	M
Mathematics	M,D
Mechanical Engineering	M,D
Microbiology	M,D
Nursing—General	M,D
Nutrition	M,D
Pharmaceutical Sciences	M,D
Pharmacy	D
Physics	M
Plant Sciences	M,D
Recreation and Park Management	M,D
Sociology	M,D
Statistics	M,D
Veterinary Sciences	M,D

SOUTHEASTERN BAPTIST THEOLOGICAL SEMINARY

Ethics	M,D
Missions and Missiology	M,D
Music	M,D
Philosophy	M,D
Psychology—General	M,D
Religious Education	M,D
Theology	M,D
Women's Studies	M,D

SOUTHEASTERN LOUISIANA UNIVERSITY

Applied Science and Technology	M
Biological and Biomedical Sciences—General	M
Business Administration and Management—General	M
Communication Disorders	M
Communication—General	M
Counselor Education	M
Curriculum and Instruction	M
Education—General	M,D
Educational Leadership and Administration	M,D
Elementary Education	M
English Education	M
English	M
Health Education	M
History	M
Kinesiology and Movement Studies	M
Music	M
Psychology—General	M
Reading Education	M
Sociology	M
Special Education	M
Writing	M

SOUTHEASTERN OKLAHOMA STATE UNIVERSITY

Aviation Management	M
Aviation	M
Biotechnology	M
Business Administration and Management—General	M
Clinical Psychology	M
Counseling Psychology	M
Counselor Education	M
Education—General	M
Educational Leadership and Administration	M
Environmental and Occupational Health	M
Management Information Systems	M
Mathematics Education	M
Reading Education	M

SOUTHEASTERN UNIVERSITY (FL)

Business Administration and Management—General	M
Counseling Psychology	M
Counselor Education	M
Education—General	M
Educational Leadership and Administration	M
Elementary Education	M
Human Services	M
Pastoral Ministry and Counseling	M

SOUTHEAST MISSOURI STATE UNIVERSITY

Accounting	M
Biological and Biomedical Sciences—General	M
Business Administration and Management—General	M
Chemistry	M
Communication Disorders	M
Counseling Psychology	M,O
Counselor Education	M,O
Criminal Justice and Criminology	M
Educational Leadership and Administration	M,D,O
Educational Media/Instructional Technology	M
Elementary Education	M,D,O
English as a Second Language	M
English	M
Entrepreneurship	M
Environmental Management and Policy	M
Environmental Sciences	M
Exercise and Sports Science	M
Finance and Banking	M
Foundations and Philosophy of Education	M
Health Services Management and Hospital Administration	M
Higher Education	M,D,O
Historic Preservation	M,O
History	M,O
Industrial and Manufacturing Management	M
International Business	M
Leisure Studies	M
Management of Technology	M
Mathematics	M
Middle School Education	M
Nursing—General	M
Nutrition	M
Organizational Management	M
Public Administration	M
Public History	M,O
Secondary Education	M,D,O
Special Education	M
Sports Management	M
Writing	M

SOUTHERN ADVENTIST UNIVERSITY

Accounting	M
Acute Care/Critical Care Nursing	M
Adult Nursing	M
Business Administration and Management—General	M
Counseling Psychology	M
Counselor Education	M
Education—General	M
Educational Leadership and Administration	M
Family Nurse Practitioner Studies	M
Finance and Banking	M
Health Services Management and Hospital Administration	M
Marketing	M
Missions and Missiology	M
Nonprofit Management	M
Nursing and Healthcare Administration	M
Nursing—General	M
Psychology—General	M
Reading Education	M
Recreation and Park Management	M
Religion	M
Religious Education	M
Social Work	M
Theology	M

SOUTHERN ARKANSAS UNIVERSITY–MAGNOLIA

Adult Education	M
Agricultural Sciences—General	M
Business Administration and Management—General	M
Computer Science	M
Counselor Education	M
Curriculum and Instruction	M
Education of the Gifted	M
Education—General	M
Educational Leadership and Administration	M
Higher Education	M
Kinesiology and Movement Studies	M
Library Science	M
Psychiatric Nursing	M
Public Administration	M
Student Affairs	M
Supply Chain Management	M

THE SOUTHERN BAPTIST THEOLOGICAL SEMINARY

Missions and Missiology	M,D
Pastoral Ministry and Counseling	M,D
Philosophy	M,D
Religion	M,D
Theology	M,D

SOUTHERN CALIFORNIA INSTITUTE OF ARCHITECTURE

Architecture	M

SOUTHERN CALIFORNIA SEMINARY

Counseling Psychology	M,D
Marriage and Family Therapy	M,D
Psychology—General	M,D
Religion	M,D
Theology	M,D

SOUTHERN CALIFORNIA UNIVERSITY OF HEALTH SCIENCES

Acupuncture and Oriental Medicine	M,D
Chiropractic	D

SOUTHERN COLLEGE OF OPTOMETRY

Optometry	D

SOUTHERN CONNECTICUT STATE UNIVERSITY

Art Education	M
Biological and Biomedical Sciences—General	M
Business Administration and Management—General	M
Chemistry	M
Communication Disorders	M
Computer Science	M
Counselor Education	M,O
Education—General	M,D,O
Educational Leadership and Administration	M,D,O
Educational Measurement and Evaluation	M,D,O
Elementary Education	M,O
English as a Second Language	M
English	M
Environmental Education	M,O
Environmental Sciences	M,O
Exercise and Sports Science	M
Family Nurse Practitioner Studies	M
Foreign Languages Education	M
Health Education	M
History	M
Information Studies	M,O
Leisure Studies	M
Library Science	M,O
Marine Sciences	M,O
Mathematics	M
Multilingual and Multicultural Education	M
Nursing Education	M
Nursing—General	M
Physical Education	M
Political Science	M
Psychology—General	M
Public Health—General	M
Reading Education	M,O
Recreation and Park Management	M
School Psychology	M,O
Science Education	M,O
Social Work	M
Sociology	M
Special Education	M
Sport Psychology	M
Women's Studies	M

SOUTHERN EVANGELICAL SEMINARY

Jewish Studies	M,D,O
Missions and Missiology	M,D,O
Near and Middle Eastern Studies	M,D,O
Pastoral Ministry and Counseling	M,D,O
Philosophy	M,D,O
Religion	M,D,O
Religious Education	M,D,O
Theology	M,D,O

SOUTHERN ILLINOIS UNIVERSITY CARBONDALE

Accounting	M,D
Agricultural Economics and Agribusiness	M
Agricultural Sciences—General	M
Agronomy and Soil Sciences	M
Animal Sciences	M
Anthropology	M,D
Applied Arts and Design—General	M
Applied Physics	M,D
Architecture	M
Art/Fine Arts	M
Biochemistry	M,D
Biological and Biomedical Sciences—General	M,D
Biomedical Engineering	M
Business Administration and Management—General	M,D
Chemistry	M,D
Civil Engineering	M,D
Clinical Psychology	M,D
Communication Disorders	M
Communication—General	M,D
Community Health	M
Computer Engineering	M,D
Computer Science	M,D
Counseling Psychology	M,D
Criminal Justice and Criminology	M,D
Cultural Studies	M
Curriculum and Instruction	M,D
Economics	M,D
Education—General	M,D
Educational Leadership and Administration	M,D
Educational Psychology	M,D
Electrical Engineering	M,D
Energy and Power Engineering	D
Engineering and Applied Sciences—General	M,D
Engineering Management	M
English as a Second Language	M
English	M,D
Environmental Engineering	D
Environmental Management and Policy	M,D
Environmental Sciences	D
Experimental Psychology	M,D
Forestry	M
Geography	M,D
Geology	M,D
Geosciences	M,D
Health Education	M,D
Health Law	M
Health Services Management and Hospital Administration	M
Higher Education	M
History	M,D
Homeland Security	M
Kinesiology and Movement Studies	M
Law	M,D
Legal and Justice Studies	M
Linguistics	M
Mass Communication	M,D
Mathematics	M,D
Mechanical Engineering	M,D
Mechanics	M
Media Studies	M,D
Medical Physics	M
Microbiology	M,D
Mineral/Mining Engineering	M,D
Molecular Biology	M,D
Music	M
Nutrition	M
Pharmacology	M,D
Philosophy	M,D
Physical Education	M
Physician Assistant Studies	M
Physics	M,D
Physiology	M,D
Plant Biology	M,D
Plant Sciences	M
Political Science	M,D
Psychology—General	M,D
Public Administration	M
Recreation and Park Management	M
Rhetoric	M,D
Social Work	M
Sociology	M,D
Special Education	M,D
Speech and Interpersonal Communication	M,D
Theater	M,D
Vocational and Technical Education	M,D
Writing	M
Zoology	M,D

SOUTHERN ILLINOIS UNIVERSITY EDWARDSVILLE

Accounting	M
Advertising and Public Relations	M
Applied Mathematics	M
Art Therapy	M
Art/Fine Arts	M
Biological and Biomedical Sciences—General	M
Business Administration and Management—General	M
Chemistry	M
Civil Engineering	M
Clinical Psychology	M
Communication Disorders	M
Computational Sciences	M
Computer Science	M
Corporate and Organizational Communication	M
Cultural Anthropology	M
Curriculum and Instruction	M
Dentistry	D
Economics	M
Education—General	M,D,O
Educational Leadership and Administration	M,D,O
Educational Media/Instructional Technology	M,O
Electrical Engineering	M
Engineering and Applied Sciences—General	M
English as a Second Language	M,O
English Education	M,O
English	M,O
Environmental Engineering	M
Environmental Management and Policy	M
Environmental Sciences	M
Exercise and Sports Science	M
Family Nurse Practitioner Studies	M,D,O
Finance and Banking	M
Foundations and Philosophy of Education	M
Geography	M
Geotechnical Engineering	M
Health Communication	M
Health Education	M,D,O
Health Informatics	M
Higher Education	M
History	M
Industrial and Organizational Psychology	M
Industrial/Management Engineering	M
Interdisciplinary Studies	M
Kinesiology and Movement Studies	M
Management Information Systems	M
Management Strategy and Policy	M
Marketing Research	M
Mass Communication	M
Mathematics Education	M
Mathematics	M
Mechanical Engineering	M
Media Studies	O
Museum Studies	O
Music Education	M,O
Music	M
Nurse Anesthesia	D
Nursing and Healthcare Administration	M,O
Nursing Education	M,O
Nursing—General	M,D,O
Operations Research	M
Pharmacy	D
Physical Education	M
Project Management	M
Psychology—General	M,O
Public Administration	M
Reading Education	M,O
School Psychology	O
Social Work	M
Sociology	M
Special Education	M,O
Speech and Interpersonal Communication	M

Sport Psychology M
Statistics M
Structural Engineering M
Student Affairs M
Sustainable Development M
Taxation M
Transportation and Highway Engineering M
Writing M

SOUTHERN METHODIST UNIVERSITY
Accounting M
Advertising and Public Relations M
Anthropology M,D
Applied Economics M,D
Applied Mathematics M,D
Applied Science and Technology M,D
Art History M,D
Art/Fine Arts M
Arts Administration M
Atmospheric Sciences M,D
Biological and Biomedical Sciences—General M,D
Business Administration and Management—General M
Cell Biology M,D
Chemistry M,D
Civil Engineering M,D
Clinical Psychology D
Computational Sciences M,D
Computer Engineering M,D
Computer Science M,D
Conflict Resolution and Mediation/Peace Studies M
Counselor Education M
Database Systems M
Economics M,D
Education of the Gifted M,D
Education—General M,D
Electrical Engineering M,D
Engineering and Applied Sciences—General M,D
Engineering Management M,D
English M,D
Entrepreneurship M
Environmental Engineering M,D
Environmental Sciences M,D
Ethics M,D
Experimental Psychology M,D
Finance and Banking M
Geology M,D
Geophysics M,D
History M,D
Information Science M,D
Law M,D
Liberal Studies M
Management Information Systems M
Management Strategy and Policy M
Manufacturing Engineering M,D
Marketing M
Materials Engineering M,D
Materials Sciences M,D
Mathematics M,D
Mechanical Engineering M,D
Medieval and Renaissance Studies M
Molecular Biology M,D
Multilingual and Multicultural Education M,D
Music Education M
Music M
Operations Research M,D
Photography M
Physics M,D
Physiology M
Psychology—General D
Reading Education M,D
Real Estate M
Religion M,D
Software Engineering M,D
Special Education M,D
Sports Management M
Statistics M,D
Structural Engineering M,D
Sustainable Development M,D
Systems Engineering M,D
Systems Science M,D
Taxation M,D
Telecommunications M,D
Theater M
Theology M,D
Water Resources Engineering M,D

SOUTHERN NAZARENE UNIVERSITY
Business Administration and Management—General M
Counseling Psychology M
Health Services Management and Hospital Administration M
Marriage and Family Therapy M
Nursing and Healthcare Administration M
Nursing Education M
Nursing—General M
Psychology—General M
Sports Management M

SOUTHERN NEW HAMPSHIRE UNIVERSITY
Accounting M,O
Business Administration and Management—General M,O
Business Education M,D,O
Child Development M,D,O
Community Health M,O
Conflict Resolution and Mediation/Peace Studies M,O
Curriculum and Instruction M,D,O
Education—General M,D,O
Educational Leadership and Administration M,D,O
Educational Media/Instructional Technology M,D,O
Elementary Education M,D,O
English as a Second Language M,D,O
English Education M,D,O
Entrepreneurship M,O
Environmental Management and Policy M,O
Ethics M,O
Finance and Banking M,O
Health Informatics M,O
Health Services Management and Hospital Administration M,O
Human Resources Management M,O
Industrial and Labor Relations M,O
Industrial and Manufacturing Management M,O
International Business M,O
Internet and Interactive Multimedia M,O
Investment Management M,O
Legal and Justice Studies M,O
Management Information Systems M,O
Marketing M,O
Nonprofit Management M,O
Organizational Management M,O
Project Management M,O
Psychology—General M,O
Quality Management M,O
Reading Education M,D,O
Secondary Education M,D,O
Special Education M,D,O
Sports Management M,O
Supply Chain Management M,O
Sustainability Management M,O
Taxation M,O
Writing M,O

SOUTHERN OREGON UNIVERSITY
Accounting M,O
Applied Mathematics M
Business Administration and Management—General M,O
Computer Science M
Counseling Psychology M
Early Childhood Education M
Education—General M
Educational Leadership and Administration M
Elementary Education M
Environmental Education M
Foreign Languages Education M
French M
Interdisciplinary Studies M
International Business M,O
Music M
Psychology—General M
Reading Education M
Secondary Education M
Spanish M
Special Education M
Theater M

SOUTHERN UNIVERSITY AND AGRICULTURAL AND MECHANICAL COLLEGE
Agricultural Sciences—General M
Analytical Chemistry M
Biochemistry M
Biological and Biomedical Sciences—General M
Business Administration and Management—General M
Chemistry M
Computer Science M
Counselor Education M
Criminal Justice and Criminology M
Education—General M,D
Educational Leadership and Administration M
Educational Media/Instructional Technology M
Elementary Education M
Engineering and Applied Sciences—General M
Environmental Sciences M
Family Nurse Practitioner Studies M,D,O
Forestry M
Gerontological Nursing M,D,O
History M
Inorganic Chemistry M
Law D
Mass Communication M
Mathematics Education D
Mathematics M
Nursing and Healthcare Administration M,D,O
Nursing Education M,D,O
Nursing—General M,D,O
Organic Chemistry M
Physical Chemistry M
Physics M
Political Science M
Psychology—General M
Public Administration M
Public Policy D
Recreation and Park Management M
Rehabilitation Counseling M
Science Education D
Secondary Education M
Social Sciences M
Special Education M,D

SOUTHERN UNIVERSITY AT NEW ORLEANS
Criminal Justice and Criminology M
Management Information Systems M
Museum Studies M
Social Work M

SOUTHERN UTAH UNIVERSITY
Accounting M
Arts Administration M
Business Administration and Management—General M
Communication—General M
Education—General M,O
Exercise and Sports Science M
Public Administration M

SOUTHERN WESLEYAN UNIVERSITY
Business Administration and Management—General M
Education—General M
Pastoral Ministry and Counseling M

SOUTH FLORIDA BIBLE COLLEGE AND THEOLOGICAL SEMINARY
Theology M

SOUTH UNIVERSITY (AL)
Business Administration and Management—General M
Counseling Psychology M
Criminal Justice and Criminology M
Health Services Management and Hospital Administration M
Management Information Systems M
Nursing—General M
Public Administration M

SOUTH UNIVERSITY
Business Administration and Management—General M
Counseling Psychology M
Criminal Justice and Criminology M
Family Nurse Practitioner Studies M
Health Services Management and Hospital Administration M
Management Information Systems M
Nursing—General M
Occupational Therapy D
Public Administration M

SOUTH UNIVERSITY
Adult Nursing M
Business Administration and Management—General M
Criminal Justice and Criminology M
Family Nurse Practitioner Studies M
Health Services Management and Hospital Administration M
Management Information Systems M
Nursing Education M
Nursing—General M
Physician Assistant Studies M

SOUTH UNIVERSITY (GA)
Anesthesiologist Assistant Studies M
Business Administration and Management—General M
Counseling Psychology M
Criminal Justice and Criminology M
Entrepreneurship M
Health Services Management and Hospital Administration M
Hospitality Management M
Nursing Education M
Nursing—General M
Organizational Management M
Pastoral Ministry and Counseling D
Pharmacy
Physician Assistant Studies M
Public Administration M
Sustainability Management M

SOUTH UNIVERSITY (MI)
Business Administration and Management—General M
Counseling Psychology M
Nursing—General M
Organizational Management M
Pastoral Ministry and Counseling D

SOUTH UNIVERSITY (NC)
Business Administration and Management—General M
Counseling Psychology M

SOUTH UNIVERSITY (OH)
Business Administration and Management—General M
Clinical Psychology M
Counseling Psychology M

SOUTH UNIVERSITY (SC)
Business Administration and Management—General M
Counseling Psychology M
Criminal Justice and Criminology M
Health Services Management and Hospital Administration M
Nursing—General M
Organizational Management M
Pharmacy D

SOUTH UNIVERSITY (TX)
Business Administration and Management—General M
Counseling Psychology M
Management Information Systems M

SOUTH UNIVERSITY
Business Administration and Management—General M
Counseling Psychology M
Nursing—General M

SOUTH UNIVERSITY
Business Administration and Management—General M
Counseling Psychology M
Family Nurse Practitioner Studies M
Management Information Systems M
Nursing—General M

Organizational Management M

SOUTHWEST ACUPUNCTURE COLLEGE
Acupuncture and Oriental Medicine M

SOUTHWEST BAPTIST UNIVERSITY
Business Administration and Management—General M
Education—General M,O
Educational Leadership and Administration M,O
Health Services Management and Hospital Administration M
Physical Therapy D

SOUTHWEST COLLEGE OF NATUROPATHIC MEDICINE AND HEALTH SCIENCES
Naturopathic Medicine D

SOUTHWESTERN ADVENTIST UNIVERSITY
Accounting M
Business Administration and Management—General M
Curriculum and Instruction M
Education—General M
Educational Leadership and Administration M
Finance and Banking M
Reading Education M

SOUTHWESTERN ASSEMBLIES OF GOD UNIVERSITY
Counseling Psychology M
Curriculum and Instruction M
Education—General M
Educational Leadership and Administration M
History M
Missions and Missiology M
Pastoral Ministry and Counseling M
Religion M
Religious Education M
Secondary Education M
Theology M

SOUTHWESTERN BAPTIST THEOLOGICAL SEMINARY
Missions and Missiology M,D
Music M,D
Near and Middle Eastern Studies M,D
Pastoral Ministry and Counseling M,D,O
Religious Education M,D
Theology M,D

SOUTHWESTERN CHRISTIAN UNIVERSITY
Missions and Missiology M
Pastoral Ministry and Counseling M

SOUTHWESTERN COLLEGE (KS)
Business Administration and Management—General M
Criminal Justice and Criminology M
Curriculum and Instruction M,D
Early Childhood Education M,D
Education—General M,D
Educational Leadership and Administration M,D
Special Education M,D
Theology M

SOUTHWESTERN COLLEGE (NM)
Art Therapy M
Counseling Psychology M,O
Health Psychology O
Psychology—General O
Social Psychology O
Thanatology M,O

SOUTHWESTERN LAW SCHOOL
Law M,D

SOUTHWESTERN OKLAHOMA STATE UNIVERSITY
Allied Health—General M
Art Education M
Business Administration and Management—General M
Counselor Education M
Early Childhood Education M
Education—General M
Educational Leadership and Administration M
Educational Measurement and Evaluation M
Elementary Education M
English Education M
Kinesiology and Movement Studies M
Mathematics Education M
Microbiology M
Music Education M
Music M
Pharmacy D
Recreation and Park Management M
School Psychology M
Science Education M
Secondary Education M
Social Sciences Education M
Special Education M

SOUTHWEST MINNESOTA STATE UNIVERSITY
Business Administration and Management—General M
Early Childhood Education M
Education—General M
Educational Leadership and Administration M
English as a Second Language M
Marketing M
Mathematics Education M
Reading Education M

*M—masters degree; D—doctorate; O—other advanced degree; *—Close-Up and/or Display*

Special Education M

SOUTHWEST UNIVERSITY
Business Administration and Management—General M
Criminal Justice and Criminology M
Organizational Management M

SOUTHWEST UNIVERSITY OF VISUAL ARTS
Art/Fine Arts M
Photography M

SPALDING UNIVERSITY
Adult Nursing M,D,O
Applied Behavior Analysis M
Art Education M
Athletic Training and Sports Medicine M
Business Education M
Clinical Psychology M,D
Corporate and Organizational Communication M
Counselor Education M
Education—General M,D
Educational Leadership and Administration M,D
Elementary Education M
Family Nurse Practitioner Studies M,D,O
Foreign Languages Education M
Middle School Education M
Nursing and Healthcare Administration M,D,O
Nursing—General M,D,O
Occupational Therapy M
Pediatric Nursing M,D,O
Psychology—General M,D
Secondary Education M
Social Work M
Special Education M
Writing M

SPERTUS INSTITUTE FOR JEWISH LEARNING AND LEADERSHIP
Jewish Studies M,D

SPRING ARBOR UNIVERSITY
Business Administration and Management—General M
Child and Family Studies M
Communication—General M
Counseling Psychology M
Education—General M
Nursing—General M
Pastoral Ministry and Counseling M
Reading Education M
Special Education M
Theology M

SPRINGFIELD COLLEGE
Addictions/Substance Abuse Counseling M
Art Therapy M,O
Athletic Training and Sports Medicine M,D
Business Administration and Management—General M
Clinical Psychology M,D,O
Counseling Psychology M,D,O
Counselor Education M,D,O
Education—General M
Exercise and Sports Science M,D
Health Promotion M,D
Human Services M
Industrial and Organizational Psychology M,D,O
Occupational Therapy M
Physical Education M,D,O
Physical Therapy D
Physician Assistant Studies M
Recreation and Park Management M
Rehabilitation Counseling M
Secondary Education M
Social Work M,O
Special Education M
Sport Psychology M,D,O
Sports Management M,D,O
Student Affairs M,D,O

SPRING HILL COLLEGE
Art/Fine Arts M,O
Business Administration and Management—General M
Early Childhood Education M
Education—General M
Elementary Education M
English M,O
Ethics M,O
Foundations and Philosophy of Education M
History M,O
Liberal Studies M,O
Nursing and Healthcare Administration M,O
Nursing—General M,O
Pastoral Ministry and Counseling M,O
Secondary Education M
Social Sciences Education M,O
Theology M,O

STANFORD UNIVERSITY
Aerospace/Aeronautical Engineering M,D,O
Allopathic Medicine D
Anthropology M,D
Applied Arts and Design—General M,D,O
Applied Physics M,D
Archaeology M,D
Art/Fine Arts M,D
Asian Languages M,D
Asian Studies M
Biochemistry D
Bioengineering M,D
Biological and Biomedical Sciences—General M,D
Biomedical Engineering M,D,O
Biophysics D
Biostatistics M,D
Business Administration and Management—General M,D
Chemical Engineering M,D
Chemistry D
Chinese M,D
Civil Engineering M,D,O
Classics M,D
Clinical Research M,D
Communication—General M,D
Comparative Literature D
Computational Sciences M,D
Computer Science M,D
Construction Engineering M,D,O
Cultural Studies M,D
Curriculum and Instruction M
Developmental Biology M,D
East European and Russian Studies M
Ecology M,D
Economics D
Education—General M,D
Educational Leadership and Administration M
Educational Media/Instructional Technology M
Educational Policy M
Electrical Engineering M,D
Elementary Education M
Energy and Power Engineering M,D,O
Engineering and Applied Sciences—General M,D,O
Engineering Design M
Engineering Management M,D
Engineering Physics M,D
English M,D
Environmental Engineering M,D,O
Environmental Law M,D
Environmental Sciences M,D,O
Epidemiology M,D
Film, Television, and Video Production M,D
French M,D
Genetics D
Geophysics M,D
Geosciences M,D,O
Geotechnical Engineering M,D,O
German M,D
Health Services Research M,D
History M,D
Hydrology M,D,O
Immunology D*
Industrial/Management Engineering M,D
International and Comparative Education M,D
Italian M,D
Japanese M,D
Journalism M,D
Law M,D
Legal and Justice Studies M,D
Linguistics M,D
Materials Engineering M,D,O
Materials Sciences M,D,O
Mathematics M,D
Mechanical Engineering M,D,O
Mechanics M,D,O
Media Studies M,D
Medical Informatics M,D
Microbiology D
Music M,D
Philosophy M,D
Physics D
Physiology D
Political Science M,D
Psychology—General D
Religion D
Secondary Education M
Slavic Languages D
Sociology D
Spanish M,D
Statistics M,D
Structural Biology D
Structural Engineering M,D,O
Sustainable Development M,D,O
Systems Biology D
Theater D

STARR KING SCHOOL FOR THE MINISTRY
Theology M

STATE UNIVERSITY OF NEW YORK AT FREDONIA
Biological and Biomedical Sciences—General M
Communication Disorders M
Early Childhood Education M
Education—General M
English as a Second Language M
Interdisciplinary Studies M
Middle School Education M
Music Education M
Reading Education M
Secondary Education M

STATE UNIVERSITY OF NEW YORK AT NEW PALTZ
Accounting M
Art Education M
Art/Fine Arts M
Business Administration and Management—General M
Chemistry M,O
Communication Disorders M
Computer Science M
Counseling Psychology M,O
Counselor Education M,O
Early Childhood Education M
Education—General M,O
Educational Leadership and Administration M,O
Electrical Engineering M
Elementary Education M
English as a Second Language M,O
English Education M,O
English M
French M,O
Geosciences M,O
Mathematics Education M
Multilingual and Multicultural Education M,O
Music M
Psychology—General M,O
Reading Education M
Science Education M,O
Secondary Education M,O
Social Sciences Education M,O
Spanish M,O
Special Education M
Therapies—Dance, Drama, and Music M

STATE UNIVERSITY OF NEW YORK AT OSWEGO
Agricultural Education M
Art Education M
Art/Fine Arts M
Business Education M
Chemistry M
Child and Family Studies M
Consumer Economics M
Counseling Psychology M
Curriculum and Instruction M
Early Childhood Education M
Education—General M,O
Educational Leadership and Administration O
Elementary Education M
English M
Graphic Design M
History M
Human-Computer Interaction M
Internet and Interactive Multimedia M
Middle School Education M
Reading Education M
Secondary Education M
Special Education M
Vocational and Technical Education M

STATE UNIVERSITY OF NEW YORK AT PLATTSBURGH
Clinical Psychology M,O
Communication Disorders M
Counseling Psychology M,O
Counselor Education M,O
Curriculum and Instruction M
Early Childhood Education O
Educational Leadership and Administration O
Elementary Education M,O
English Education M
Foreign Languages Education M
Mathematics Education M
Psychology—General M,O
Reading Education M
School Psychology M,O
Science Education M
Secondary Education M
Social Sciences Education M
Special Education M
Student Affairs M,O

STATE UNIVERSITY OF NEW YORK COLLEGE AT CORTLAND
Community Health M
Early Childhood Education M
Education—General M,O
Educational Leadership and Administration O
English as a Second Language M
English Education M
English M
Environmental Education M
Health Education M
History M
Mathematics Education M
Mathematics M
Physical Education M
Physics M
Reading Education M
Recreation and Park Management M
Science Education M
Secondary Education M
Special Education M
Sports Management M

STATE UNIVERSITY OF NEW YORK COLLEGE AT GENESEO
Accounting M
Business Administration and Management—General M
Early Childhood Education M
Education—General M
Multilingual and Multicultural Education M
Reading Education M
Secondary Education M

STATE UNIVERSITY OF NEW YORK COLLEGE AT OLD WESTBURY
Accounting M
Business Administration and Management—General M
Counseling Psychology M
Education—General M
English Education M
Foreign Languages Education M
Liberal Studies M
Mathematics Education M
Science Education M
Social Sciences Education M
Taxation M

STATE UNIVERSITY OF NEW YORK COLLEGE AT ONEONTA
Biological and Biomedical Sciences—General M
Counselor Education M,O
Education—General M,O
Educational Media/Instructional Technology M,O
Educational Psychology M,O
Elementary Education M
Geosciences M
Middle School Education M
Museum Studies M
Nutrition M
Reading Education M
Secondary Education M
Special Education M,O

STATE UNIVERSITY OF NEW YORK COLLEGE AT POTSDAM
Communication—General M
Community Health M
Curriculum and Instruction M
Early Childhood Education M
Educational Media/Instructional Technology M
Elementary Education M
English Education M
English M
Mathematics Education M
Mathematics M
Middle School Education M
Music Education M
Music M
Organizational Management M
Reading Education M
Science Education M
Secondary Education M
Social Sciences Education M
Special Education M

STATE UNIVERSITY OF NEW YORK COLLEGE OF ENVIRONMENTAL SCIENCE AND FORESTRY
Biochemistry M,D
Chemistry M,D
Conservation Biology M,D
Construction Management M,D
Ecology M,D
Economics M,D
Entomology M,D
Environmental Biology M,D
Environmental Engineering M,D
Environmental Management and Policy M,D
Environmental Sciences M,D
Fish, Game, and Wildlife Management M,D
Forestry M,D
Geographic Information Systems M,D
Landscape Architecture M
Materials Sciences M,D,O
Natural Resources M,D
Organic Chemistry M,D
Paper and Pulp Engineering M,D,O
Plant Pathology M,D
Plant Sciences M,D
Sustainability Management M,D,O
Sustainable Development M,D,O
Urban and Regional Planning M,D
Urban Design M
Water Resources Engineering M,D
Water Resources M,D

STATE UNIVERSITY OF NEW YORK COLLEGE OF OPTOMETRY
Optometry D
Vision Sciences D

STATE UNIVERSITY OF NEW YORK COLLEGE OF TECHNOLOGY AT DELHI
Nursing Education M

STATE UNIVERSITY OF NEW YORK DOWNSTATE MEDICAL CENTER
Allopathic Medicine M,D
Biological and Biomedical Sciences—General M,D
Biomedical Engineering M,D
Cell Biology D
Community Health M
Family Nurse Practitioner Studies M,O
Medical/Surgical Nursing M,O
Molecular Biology D
Neuroscience D
Nurse Anesthesia M
Nurse Midwifery M,O
Nursing—General M,O
Public Health—General M

STATE UNIVERSITY OF NEW YORK EMPIRE STATE COLLEGE
Adult Education M
Business Administration and Management—General M
Economic Development M
Education—General M
Educational Media/Instructional Technology M
Industrial and Labor Relations M
International Business M
Liberal Studies M
Nursing Education M
Public Policy M

STATE UNIVERSITY OF NEW YORK MARITIME COLLEGE
Transportation Management M

STATE UNIVERSITY OF NEW YORK POLYTECHNIC INSTITUTE
Accounting M
Business Administration and Management—General M
Computer and Information Systems Security M
Computer Science M
Family Nurse Practitioner Studies M,O
Finance and Banking M
Human Resources Management M
Information Science M

Management of Technology	M
Marketing	M
Nanotechnology	M,D
Nursing and Healthcare Administration	M
Nursing Education	M,O
Telecommunications	M

STATE UNIVERSITY OF NEW YORK UPSTATE MEDICAL UNIVERSITY

Allopathic Medicine	D
Anatomy	M,D
Biochemistry	M,D
Biological and Biomedical Sciences—General	M,D
Cell Biology	M,D
Clinical Laboratory Sciences/Medical Technology	M
Family Nurse Practitioner Studies	M,O
Immunology	M,D
Microbiology	M,D
Molecular Biology	M,D
Neuroscience	D
Nursing—General	M,O
Pharmacology	D
Physical Therapy	D
Physiology	M,D

STEPHEN F. AUSTIN STATE UNIVERSITY

Accounting	M
Agricultural Education	M
Applied Arts and Design—General	M
Art/Fine Arts	M
Athletic Training and Sports Medicine	M
Biological and Biomedical Sciences—General	M
Biotechnology	M
Business Administration and Management—General	M
Chemistry	M
Communication Disorders	M
Communication—General	M
Computer Science	M
Counselor Education	M
Early Childhood Education	M
Education—General	M,D
Educational Leadership and Administration	M,D
Elementary Education	M
English	M
Environmental Sciences	M
Family and Consumer Sciences-General	M
Forestry	M,D
Geology	M
History	M
Interdisciplinary Studies	M
Kinesiology and Movement Studies	M
Marketing	M
Mass Communication	M
Mathematics Education	M
Mathematics	M
Music	M
Physics	M
Psychology—General	M
Public Administration	M
School Psychology	M
Secondary Education	M,D
Social Work	M
Special Education	M
Statistics	M

STEPHENS COLLEGE

Business Administration and Management—General	M
Counseling Psychology	M,O
Counselor Education	M,O
Curriculum and Instruction	M
Health Informatics	M,O
Marriage and Family Therapy	M,O

STETSON UNIVERSITY

Accounting	M
Business Administration and Management—General	M
Counselor Education	M
Curriculum and Instruction	M,O
Education—General	M,O
Educational Leadership and Administration	M
Elementary Education	M
Law	M,D
Marriage and Family Therapy	M

STEVENS INSTITUTE OF TECHNOLOGY

Aerospace/Aeronautical Engineering	M,O
Analytical Chemistry	M,D,O
Applied Mathematics	M
Applied Statistics	O
Artificial Intelligence/Robotics	M,D,O
Atmospheric Sciences	M,D,O
Biochemistry	M,D,O
Bioinformatics	M,D,O
Biomedical Engineering	M,D,O
Business Administration and Management—General	M,O
Chemical Engineering	M,D,O
Chemistry	M,D,O
Civil Engineering	M,D,O
Communication—General	M,D,O
Computer and Information Systems Security	M,D,O
Computer Art and Design	M,D,O
Computer Engineering	M,D,O
Computer Science	M,D,O
Construction Engineering	M,O
Construction Management	M,O
Corporate and Organizational Communication	O
Database Systems	M,D,O
Electrical Engineering	M,D,O
Electronic Commerce	M,O
Engineering and Applied Sciences—General	M,D,O
Engineering Design	M
Engineering Management	M,D,O
Entrepreneurship	M,O
Environmental Engineering	M,D,O
Ethics	M,O
Film, Television, and Video Production	M
Finance and Banking	M,O
Financial Engineering	M,D,O
Health Informatics	M,D,O
Human Resources Management	M
Hydrology	M,D,O
Industrial and Manufacturing Management	M
Information Science	M,O
International Business	M
Internet and Interactive Multimedia	M,D,O
Logistics	O
Management Information Systems	M,D,O
Management of Technology	M,D,O
Management Strategy and Policy	M
Manufacturing Engineering	M
Marine Affairs	M
Marketing	M,O
Materials Engineering	M,D
Materials Sciences	M,D
Mathematics	M,D
Mechanical Engineering	M,D,O
Media Studies	M
Modeling and Simulation	M,D,O
Nanotechnology	D
Nuclear Engineering	M,D,O
Ocean Engineering	M,D
Pharmaceutical Sciences	M,O
Photonics	M,D,O
Physics	M,D,O
Polymer Science and Engineering	M,D,O
Project Management	M,O
Quality Management	M,O
Software Engineering	M,O
Statistics	M,O
Structural Engineering	M,D,O
Systems Engineering	M,D,O
Systems Science	M,D,O
Telecommunications Management	M,D,O
Telecommunications	M,D,O
Transportation and Highway Engineering	M,D,O
Water Resources Engineering	M,D,O

STEVENSON UNIVERSITY

Biological and Biomedical Sciences—General	M
Chemistry	M
Communication—General	M
Computer and Information Systems Security	M
Education—General	M
Forensic Sciences	M
Health Services Management and Hospital Administration	M
Information Science	M
Management of Technology	M
Mathematics Education	M
Nursing Education	M
Nursing—General	M
Project Management	M
Quality Management	M
Science Education	M

STOCKTON UNIVERSITY

American Studies	M,O
Business Administration and Management—General	M
Communication Disorders	M
Computational Sciences	M
Criminal Justice and Criminology	M
Education—General	M
Educational Media/Instructional Technology	M
Environmental Sciences	M
Holocaust and Genocide Studies	M
Nursing—General	M
Occupational Therapy	M
Organizational Management	D
Physical Therapy	D
Social Work	M

STONY BROOK UNIVERSITY, STATE UNIVERSITY OF NEW YORK

Accounting	M,O
Addictions/Substance Abuse Counseling	M,O
Adult Nursing	M,D,O
African Studies	M,O
Allopathic Medicine	D
Anatomy	D
Anthropology	M,D
Applied Mathematics	M,D,O
Art History	M,D
Art/Fine Arts	M
Astronomy	D
Atmospheric Sciences	M,D
Biochemistry	M,D
Bioethics	
Bioinformatics	M,D
Biological and Biomedical Sciences—General	M,D,O
Biomedical Engineering	M,D,O
Biophysics	D
Business Administration and Management—General	M,O
Cell Biology	M,D
Chemistry	M,D
Civil Engineering	M,D,O
Clinical Psychology	D
Cognitive Sciences	D
Community Health	M,D,O
Comparative Literature	M,D,O
Computer Education	M
Computer Engineering	M,D
Computer Science	M,D,O
Cultural Studies	M,D,O
Dentistry	D,O
Developmental Biology	M,D
Ecology	M,D
Economics	M,D
Educational Leadership and Administration	M,O
Educational Media/Instructional Technology	M,O
Electrical Engineering	M,D
Engineering and Applied Sciences—General	M,D,O
English as a Second Language	M
English Education	M,D,O
English	M,D,O
Environmental Management and Policy	M,O
Evolutionary Biology	M,D
Experimental Psychology	D
Family Nurse Practitioner Studies	M,D,O
Film, Television, and Video Production	M
Finance and Banking	M,O
Foreign Languages Education	M,O
French	M
Genetics	D
Geographic Information Systems	O
Geosciences	M,D
Gerontological Nursing	M,D,O
Health Communication	M,O
Health Psychology	D
Health Services Management and Hospital Administration	M,D,O
Higher Education	M,O
Hispanic and Latin American Languages	M,D
History	M,D
Human Resources Management	M,O
Immunology	M,D
Industrial and Manufacturing Management	M,O
Italian	M
Journalism	M,O
Liberal Studies	M,O
Linguistics	M,D
Management Information Systems	M,D,O
Management of Technology	M
Marine Affairs	M
Marine Sciences	M,D
Marketing	M,O
Materials Engineering	M,D
Materials Sciences	M,D
Maternal and Child/Neonatal Nursing	M,D,O
Mathematics Education	M,O
Mathematics	M,D
Mechanical Engineering	M,D
Medical Physics	M,D
Microbiology	D
Molecular Biology	M,D
Molecular Genetics	D
Molecular Physiology	D
Music	M,D
Neuroscience	M,D
Nurse Midwifery	M,D,O
Nursing and Healthcare Administration	M,O
Nursing Education	M,O
Nursing—General	M,D,O
Nutrition	M,O
Occupational Therapy	M,D,O
Oral and Dental Sciences	M,D,O
Pathology	M,D
Pediatric Nursing	M,D,O
Pharmacology	D
Philosophy	M,D,O
Physical Education	M,O
Physical Therapy	M,D,O
Physician Assistant Studies	M,D,O
Physics	M,D
Physiology	D
Political Science	M,D
Psychiatric Nursing	M,D,O
Psychology—General	M,D
Public Health—General	M,O
Public Policy	M
Romance Languages	M
Science Education	M,D,O
Social Psychology	D
Social Sciences Education	M,O
Social Work	M,D
Sociology	M,D
Software Engineering	M,D,O
Statistics	M,D,O
Structural Biology	D
Systems Engineering	M
Technology and Public Policy	D
Theater	M
Women's Health Nursing	M,D,O
Women's Studies	O
Writing	M,O

STRATFORD UNIVERSITY (MD)

Hospitality Management	M

STRATFORD UNIVERSITY (VA)

Business Administration and Management—General	M,D
Computer and Information Systems Security	M,D
Computer Science	M,D
Entrepreneurship	M,D
Finance and Banking	M,D
Forensic Sciences	M,D
Health Services Management and Hospital Administration	M,D
Hospitality Management	M,D
Information Science	M,D
International Affairs	M,D
International Business	M,D
Management Information Systems	M,D
Marketing	M,D
Software Engineering	M,D
Telecommunications	M,D

STRAYER UNIVERSITY

Accounting	M
Business Administration and Management—General	M
Computer and Information Systems Security	M
Education—General	M
Educational Media/Instructional Technology	M
Finance and Banking	M
Health Services Management and Hospital Administration	M
Hospitality Management	M
Human Resources Management	M
Information Science	M
Management Information Systems	M
Marketing	M
Public Administration	M
Software Engineering	M
Supply Chain Management	M
Systems Science	M
Taxation	M
Telecommunications Management	M
Travel and Tourism	M

SUFFOLK UNIVERSITY

Accounting	M,O
Advertising and Public Relations	M
Applied Arts and Design—General	M
Business Administration and Management—General	M,O
Clinical Psychology	M,D,O
Communication—General	M
Corporate and Organizational Communication	M
Counseling Psychology	M,D,O
Counselor Education	M,D,O
Criminal Justice and Criminology	M
Educational Leadership and Administration	M,O
Entrepreneurship	M,O
Ethics	M,O
Finance and Banking	M,O
Graphic Design	M
Health Law	M,D
Health Services Management and Hospital Administration	M,O
Intellectual Property Law	M,D
Interior Design	M
International Business	M,O
Law	M,D
Management Strategy and Policy	M,O
Marketing	M,O
Nonprofit Management	M,O
Organizational Behavior	M,O
Political Science	M,O
Psychology—General	M,D,O
Public Administration	M,O
Public Policy	M,O
School Psychology	M,D,O
Supply Chain Management	M,O
Taxation	M,O

SULLIVAN UNIVERSITY

Business Administration and Management—General	M,D

SUL ROSS STATE UNIVERSITY

Animal Sciences	M
Art Education	M
Art History	M
Art/Fine Arts	M
Biological and Biomedical Sciences—General	M
Business Administration and Management—General	M
Counselor Education	M
Criminal Justice and Criminology	M
Education—General	M,O
Educational Leadership and Administration	M
Educational Measurement and Evaluation	M,O
Elementary Education	M
Emergency Management	M
English	M
Fish, Game, and Wildlife Management	M
Geology	M
History	M
Multilingual and Multicultural Education	M
Natural Resources	M
Physical Education	M
Political Science	M
Psychology—General	M
Range Science	M
Reading Education	M,O
Secondary Education	M

SUM BIBLE COLLEGE & THEOLOGICAL SEMINARY

Pastoral Ministry and Counseling	M
Religion	M
Theology	M

SUMMIT UNIVERSITY

Communication—General	M,D
Counselor Education	M

*M—masters degree; D—doctorate; O—other advanced degree; *—Close-Up and/or Display*

Cultural Studies	M
Curriculum and Instruction	M
Educational Leadership and Administration	M
English as a Second Language	M
English	M
Missions and Missiology	M,D
Organizational Management	M,D
Pastoral Ministry and Counseling	M,D
Philosophy	M
Reading Education	M
Religion	M,D
Religious Education	M,D
Theology	M,D

SWEDISH INSTITUTE, COLLEGE OF HEALTH SCIENCES

Acupuncture and Oriental Medicine	M

SWEET BRIAR COLLEGE

Education—General	M

SYRACUSE UNIVERSITY

Accounting	M,D
Addictions/Substance Abuse Counseling	M,O
Advertising and Public Relations	M
Aerospace/Aeronautical Engineering	M,D
African Studies	M
African-American Studies	M
Anthropology	M,D
Applied Arts and Design—General	M
Applied Statistics	M
Architecture	M
Art Education	M
Art History	M
Art/Fine Arts	M
Arts Administration	M,O
Arts Journalism	M
Biochemistry	D
Bioengineering	M,D
Biological and Biomedical Sciences—General	M,D,O
Biophysics	D
Broadcast Journalism	M
Business Administration and Management—General	M,D*
Chemical Engineering	M,D
Chemistry	M,D
Child and Family Studies	M,D
Civil Engineering	M,D
Clinical Psychology	M,D
Communication Disorders	M,D
Communication—General	M,D
Computer and Information Systems Security	M,O
Computer Art and Design	M
Computer Engineering	M,D
Computer Science	M
Conflict Resolution and Mediation/Peace Studies	O
Counselor Education	M,D
Curriculum and Instruction	M,D,O
Database Systems	M
Disability Studies	O
Early Childhood Education	M
Economics	M,D
Education of Students with Severe/Multiple Disabilities	M
Education—General	M,D,O
Educational Leadership and Administration	M,D,O
Educational Measurement and Evaluation	M,D,O
Educational Media/Instructional Technology	M,O
Educational Policy	O
Electrical Engineering	M,D,O
Emergency Management	O
Energy and Power Engineering	M
Engineering and Applied Sciences—General	M,D,O
Engineering Management	M
English as a Second Language	M,O
English Education	M
English	M,D
Entertainment Management	M
Entrepreneurship	M,D
Environmental and Occupational Health	O
Environmental Engineering	M
Exercise and Sports Science	M
Experimental Psychology	D
Film, Television, and Video Production	M
Film, Television, and Video Theory and Criticism	M
Finance and Banking	M,D
Forensic Sciences	M,O
Foundations and Philosophy of Education	M,D,O
French	M
Geography	M,D
Geology	M,D
Geosciences	M,D
Health Services Management and Hospital Administration	O
Higher Education	M,D
Historic Preservation	O
History	M,D
Hospitality Management	M
Illustration	M
Information Science	M,D
Information Studies	M
International Affairs	M
International Health	M
Journalism	M
Kinesiology and Movement Studies	M,D,O
Law	D
Legal and Justice Studies	M,O
Library Science	M
Linguistics	M,O
Management Information Systems	M,D,O
Management Strategy and Policy	M
Marketing	M
Marriage and Family Therapy	M,D
Mass Communication	M,D
Mathematics Education	M,D
Mathematics	M,D
Mechanical Engineering	M,D
Media Studies	M
Museum Studies	M
Music Education	M
Music	M
Neuroscience	M,D
Nutrition	M
Organizational Management	O
Philosophy	M,D
Photography	M
Physics	M,D
Physiology	M
Political Science	M,D,O
Public Administration	M,D
Public Affairs	
Public Health—General	M
Reading Education	M,D
Real Estate	M
Religion	M,D
Rhetoric	M,D
School Psychology	M,D,O
Science Education	M,D
Secondary Education	M,D
Social Psychology	D
Social Sciences Education	M
Social Sciences	M,D
Social Work	M
Sociology	M,D
Software Engineering	M
Spanish	M
Special Education	M,D
Sports Management	M
Structural Biology	D
Student Affairs	M
Supply Chain Management	M,D
Telecommunications Management	M,O
Telecommunications	M
Toxicology	M,O
Travel and Tourism	M
Urban and Regional Planning	O
Writing	M,D

TABOR COLLEGE

Accounting	M
Business Administration and Management—General	M

TAFT UNIVERSITY SYSTEM

Education—General	M
Law	M,D
Legal and Justice Studies	M,D
Taxation	M,D

TALMUDIC UNIVERSITY

Theology	M

TARLETON STATE UNIVERSITY

Agricultural Education	M
Agricultural Sciences—General	M
Applied Psychology	M
Biological and Biomedical Sciences—General	M
Business Administration and Management—General	M
Clinical Laboratory Sciences/Medical Technology	M
Communication—General	M
Counseling Psychology	M
Criminal Justice and Criminology	M
Curriculum and Instruction	M
Education—General	M,D,O
Educational Leadership and Administration	M,D,O
Educational Media/Instructional Technology	M
Elementary Education	M
Engineering Management	M
English	M
Environmental Sciences	M
Fish, Game, and Wildlife Management	M
History	M
Human Resources Management	M
Kinesiology and Movement Studies	M
Management Information Systems	M
Marketing	M
Mathematics	M
Music Education	M
Natural Resources	M
Nursing and Healthcare Administration	M
Nursing Education	M
Nursing—General	M
Physical Education	M
Political Science	M
Public Administration	M
Public Health—General	M
Reading Education	M
Secondary Education	M
Social Work	M
Special Education	M

TAYLOR COLLEGE AND SEMINARY

Cultural Studies	M,O
English as a Second Language	M,O
Missions and Missiology	M,O
Theology	M,O

TAYLOR UNIVERSITY

Business Administration and Management—General	M
Higher Education	M
International Business	M
Management Strategy and Policy	M

TEACHERS COLLEGE, COLUMBIA UNIVERSITY

Adult Education	M,D
Anthropology	M,D
Applied Behavior Analysis	M,D,O
Applied Psychology	M,D
Applied Statistics	M,D
Art Education	M,D,O
Arts Administration	M,D,O
Biological and Biomedical Sciences—General	M,D
Chemistry	M,D
Clinical Psychology	M,D
Communication Disorders	M,D,O
Communication—General	M,D
Community Health	M,D,O
Computer Education	M,D
Counseling Psychology	M,D
Curriculum and Instruction	M,D
Developmental Psychology	M,D
Early Childhood Education	M,D
Economics	M,D
Education of Students with Severe/Multiple Disabilities	M,D,O
Education of the Gifted	M,D
Education—General	M,D
Educational Leadership and Administration	M,D
Educational Measurement and Evaluation	M,D
Educational Media/Instructional Technology	M,D
Educational Policy	M,D
Educational Psychology	M,D,O
Elementary Education	M,D
English as a Second Language	M,D,O
English Education	M,D,O
Foundations and Philosophy of Education	M,D,O
Geosciences	M,D
Health Education	M,D,O
Higher Education	M,D
Industrial and Organizational Psychology	M,D
Interdisciplinary Studies	M,D
International Affairs	M,D,O
International and Comparative Education	M,D
Kinesiology and Movement Studies	M,D
Linguistics	M,D,O
Mathematics Education	M,D
Multilingual and Multicultural Education	M,D,O
Music Education	M,D,O
Neuroscience	M,D
Nursing and Healthcare Administration	M,D
Nursing Education	M,D,O
Nutrition	M,D,O
Philosophy	M,D,O
Physical Education	M,D
Physics	M,D
Physiology	M,D
Political Science	M,D
Psychology—General	M,D
Reading Education	M,D,O
School Psychology	M,D,O
Science Education	M,D
Secondary Education	M,D
Social Psychology	M,D
Social Sciences Education	M,D,O
Sociology	M,D
Special Education	M,D,O
Urban Education	M,D

TÉLÉ-UNIVERSITÉ

Computer Science	M,D
Distance Education Development	M,D
Finance and Banking	M,D

TELSHE YESHIVA–CHICAGO

Jewish Studies	O

TEMPLE UNIVERSITY

Accounting	M,D
Actuarial Science	M
Adult Nursing	D
African-American Studies	M,D
Allied Health—General	M,D
Allopathic Medicine	D
Anthropology	D
Applied Mathematics	M,D
Architecture	M
Art Education	M
Art History	M,D
Art/Fine Arts	M
Arts Administration	M,D
Athletic Training and Sports Medicine	M,D
Bioengineering	M,D
Biological and Biomedical Sciences—General	M,D
Biotechnology	M,D
Business Administration and Management—General	M,D
Business Education	M
Chemistry	M,D
Civil Engineering	M,O
Communication Disorders	M,D
Communication—General	M,D
Computational Sciences	M,D
Computer Science	M,D
Corporate and Organizational Communication	M
Counseling Psychology	M,D,O
Criminal Justice and Criminology	M,D
Dance	M,D
Dentistry	D
Economics	M,D
Education—General	M,D,O
Educational Leadership and Administration	M,D,O
Educational Psychology	M,D,O
Electrical Engineering	M
Elementary Education	M,D,O
Engineering and Applied Sciences—General	D
Engineering Management	M,O
English as a Second Language	M
English Education	M
English	M,D
Entrepreneurship	M,D
Environmental Engineering	M,O
Family Nurse Practitioner Studies	D
Film, Television, and Video Production	M
Finance and Banking	M,D
Financial Engineering	M
Geographic Information Systems	M,D,O
Geography	M,D,O
Geology	M,D
Gerontology	D
Graphic Design	M
Health Informatics	M
Health Services Management and Hospital Administration	M
History	M,D
Hospitality Management	M,D*
Human Resources Management	M
Hydrology	M,O
Industrial and Organizational Psychology	M,D,O
Information Science	M,D
Insurance	D
International Business	M,D
Journalism	M
Kinesiology and Movement Studies	M,D
Landscape Architecture	M
Law	M,D
Legal and Justice Studies	M,D
Management Information Systems	M,D
Management Strategy and Policy	D
Marketing	M,D
Mathematics Education	M
Mathematics	M,D
Mechanical Engineering	M
Media Studies	M
Medicinal and Pharmaceutical Chemistry	M,D
Middle School Education	M
Music Education	M,D
Music	M,D
Nursing—General	D
Occupational Therapy	M,D
Oral and Dental Sciences	M,O
Pharmaceutical Administration	M
Pharmaceutical Sciences	M,D
Philosophy	M,D
Photography	M
Physical Education	M,D
Physical Therapy	D
Physics	M,D
Podiatric Medicine	D
Political Science	M,D
Psychology—General	M,D
Public Health—General	M,D
Recreation and Park Management	M,D
Rehabilitation Sciences	M,D
Religion	M,D
School Psychology	M,D,O
Science Education	M
Secondary Education	M
Social Psychology	M,D,O
Social Sciences Education	M
Social Work	M
Sociology	M,D
Spanish	M,D
Special Education	M,D,O
Sports Management	M,D*
Statistics	M,D
Sustainable Development	M,O
Taxation	M,D
Textile Design	M
Theater	M
Therapies—Dance, Drama, and Music	M,D
Transportation Management	M,O
Travel and Tourism	M,D
Urban and Regional Planning	M,O
Urban Education	M
Urban Studies	M,D,O
Vocational and Technical Education	M
Writing	M,D

TENNESSEE STATE UNIVERSITY

Agricultural Education	M,D
Agricultural Sciences—General	M,D
Agronomy and Soil Sciences	M,D
Allied Health—General	M,D,O
Biological and Biomedical Sciences—General	D
Biomedical Engineering	M,D
Biotechnology	M,D
Business Administration and Management—General	M
Chemistry	M
Civil Engineering	M,D
Communication Disorders	M
Computer Engineering	M,D
Counseling Psychology	M
Criminal Justice and Criminology	M
Curriculum and Instruction	M,D
Education—General	M,D,O
Electrical Engineering	M,D
Elementary Education	M,D
Engineering and Applied Sciences—General	M,D
Environmental Engineering	M,D
Exercise and Sports Science	M
Family and Consumer Sciences-General	M,D
Family Nurse Practitioner Studies	M,O
Human Resources Management	M,D
Management Strategy and Policy	M,D
Manufacturing Engineering	M,D
Mathematics	M,D
Mechanical Engineering	M,D
Nursing—General	M,O

Occupational Therapy	M
Physical Education	M
Physical Therapy	D
Plant Sciences	M,D
Psychology—General	M
Public Administration	M,D
Public Health—General	M
Social Work	M,D
Special Education	M,D
Sports Management	M
Systems Engineering	M,D

TENNESSEE TECHNOLOGICAL UNIVERSITY

Accounting	M
Applied Behavior Analysis	D
Biological and Biomedical Sciences—General	M,D
Business Administration and Management—General	M
Chemical Engineering	M
Chemistry	M,D
Civil Engineering	M
Computer Science	M
Counseling Psychology	M,O
Curriculum and Instruction	M,O
Early Childhood Education	M,O
Education of the Gifted	D
Education—General	M,D,O
Educational Leadership and Administration	M,O
Educational Measurement and Evaluation	D
Educational Media/Instructional Technology	M,O
Educational Psychology	M,O
Electrical Engineering	M
Elementary Education	M,O
Engineering and Applied Sciences—General	M,D
English	M
Environmental Management and Policy	M
Environmental Sciences	D
Family Nurse Practitioner Studies	M
Finance and Banking	M
Fish, Game, and Wildlife Management	M
Health Education	M
Health Promotion	M
Human Resources Management	M
International Business	M
Internet and Interactive Multimedia	M
Kinesiology and Movement Studies	M
Library Science	M,O
Management Information Systems	M
Management Strategy and Policy	M
Mathematics Education	M,O
Mathematics	M
Mechanical Engineering	M
Middle School Education	M
Music Education	M
Nursing and Healthcare Administration	M
Nursing Education	M
Nursing Informatics	M
Nursing—General	M
Physical Education	M
Reading Education	M,D,O
School Psychology	M,O
Science Education	M,O
Secondary Education	M,O
Software Engineering	M
Special Education	M,O
Sports Management	M

TENNESSEE WESLEYAN COLLEGE

Curriculum and Instruction	M
Education—General	M
Educational Leadership and Administration	M

TEXAS A&M INTERNATIONAL UNIVERSITY

Accounting	M
Biological and Biomedical Sciences—General	M
Business Administration and Management—General	M,D
Counseling Psychology	M
Counselor Education	M
Criminal Justice and Criminology	M
Curriculum and Instruction	M
Education—General	M
Educational Leadership and Administration	M
English	M,D
Family Nurse Practitioner Studies	M
Finance and Banking	M
Foreign Languages Education	M,D
Hispanic Studies	M,D
History	M,D
International Business	M,D
Management Information Systems	M,D
Mathematics	M
Nursing—General	M
Political Science	M,D
Psychology—General	M
Public Administration	M
Social Sciences	M
Special Education	M
Translation and Interpretation	M,D

TEXAS A&M UNIVERSITY

Accounting	M
Aerospace/Aeronautical Engineering	M,D
Agricultural Economics and Agribusiness	M,D
Agricultural Education	M,D
Agricultural Engineering	M,D
Agricultural Sciences—General	M,D
Agronomy and Soil Sciences	M,D
Allied Health—General	M,D
Animal Sciences	M,D
Anthropology	M,D
Applied Physics	M,D
Architecture	M,D,O
Art/Fine Arts	M
Athletic Training and Sports Medicine	M,D
Biochemistry	M,D
Bioengineering	M,D
Biological and Biomedical Sciences—General	M,D
Biomedical Engineering	M,D
Business Administration and Management—General	M
Chemical Engineering	M,D
Chemistry	M,D
Civil Engineering	M,D
Clinical Psychology	M,D
Communication—General	M,D
Community Health	M,D
Computer Engineering	M,D
Computer Science	M,D
Construction Management	M
Counseling Psychology	M,D
Cultural Studies	M
Curriculum and Instruction	M,D
Dentistry	M,D,O
Economics	M,D
Education—General	M,D
Educational Leadership and Administration	M,D
Educational Media/Instructional Technology	M,D
Educational Psychology	M,D
Electrical Engineering	M,D
English	M,D
Entomology	M,D
Family Nurse Practitioner Studies	M
Finance and Banking	M
Fish, Game, and Wildlife Management	M,D
Food Science and Technology	M,D
Forestry	M,D
Geography	M,D
Geology	M,D
Geophysics	M,D
Health Education	M,D
Health Physics/Radiological Health	M,D
Health Promotion	M,D
Health Services Management and Hospital Administration	M,D
Health Services Research	M,D
History	M,D
Homeland Security	M,O
Horticulture	M,D
Human Resources Development	M,D
Industrial and Organizational Psychology	M,D
Industrial/Management Engineering	M,D
International Affairs	M,O
Kinesiology and Movement Studies	M,D
Landscape Architecture	M,D
Law	D
Management Information Systems	M
Manufacturing Engineering	M
Marketing	M
Materials Engineering	M,D
Materials Sciences	M,D
Mathematics	M,D
Mechanical Engineering	M,D
Meteorology	M,D
Microbiology	M,D
Multilingual and Multicultural Education	M,D
Music	M
National Security	M,O
Natural Resources	M,D
Nonprofit Management	M,O
Nuclear Engineering	M,D
Nursing Education	M
Nursing—General	M
Nutrition	M,D
Ocean Engineering	M,D
Oceanography	M,D
Petroleum Engineering	M,D
Pharmacy	D
Philosophy	M,D
Physics	M,D
Plant Pathology	M,D
Political Science	M,D
Psychology—General	M,D
Public Administration	M,O
Public Affairs	M,O
Public Health—General	M,D
Range Science	M,D
Real Estate	M
Recreation and Park Management	M,D
School Psychology	M,D
Sociology	M,D
Spanish	M,D
Special Education	M,D
Sports Management	M,D
Statistics	M,D
Urban and Regional Planning	M,D
Veterinary Medicine	M,D
Veterinary Sciences	M,D

TEXAS A&M UNIVERSITY AT GALVESTON

Marine Biology	M,D
Marine Sciences	M
Transportation Management	M

TEXAS A&M UNIVERSITY–CENTRAL TEXAS

Accounting	M,O
Business Administration and Management—General	M,O
Clinical Psychology	M,O
Counselor Education	M,O
Criminal Justice and Criminology	M,O
Curriculum and Instruction	M,O
Educational Leadership and Administration	M,O
Educational Psychology	M,O
Experimental Psychology	M,O
History	M,O
Human Resources Management	M,O
Liberal Studies	M,O
Management Information Systems	M,O
Marriage and Family Therapy	M,O
Mathematics	M,O
Political Science	M,O
School Psychology	M,O

TEXAS A&M UNIVERSITY–COMMERCE

Accounting	M
Agricultural Sciences—General	M
Business Administration and Management—General	M
Education—General	M,D,O
Finance and Banking	M
Marketing	M

TEXAS A&M UNIVERSITY–CORPUS CHRISTI

Accounting	M
Aquaculture	M
Art/Fine Arts	M
Biological and Biomedical Sciences—General	M
Business Administration and Management—General	M
Communication—General	M
Computer Science	M
Counselor Education	M,D
Curriculum and Instruction	M,D
Early Childhood Education	M,D
Education—General	M,D
Educational Leadership and Administration	M,D
Educational Media/Instructional Technology	M,D
Elementary Education	M
English	M
Environmental Sciences	M
Family Nurse Practitioner Studies	M
Health Services Management and Hospital Administration	M
History	M
International Business	M
Kinesiology and Movement Studies	M,D
Marine Sciences	M,D
Mathematics	M
Nursing and Healthcare Administration	M
Nursing Education	M
Nursing—General	M
Psychology—General	M
Public Administration	M
Reading Education	M,D
Secondary Education	M
Special Education	M

TEXAS A&M UNIVERSITY–KINGSVILLE

Adult Education	M,D
Agricultural Economics and Agribusiness	M,D
Agricultural Sciences—General	M,D
Agronomy and Soil Sciences	M
Animal Sciences	M
Biological and Biomedical Sciences—General	M
Business Administration and Management—General	M
Chemical Engineering	M
Chemistry	M
Civil Engineering	M
Communication Disorders	M
Computer Science	M
Counselor Education	M,D
Criminal Justice and Criminology	M
Cultural Studies	M
Early Childhood Education	M
Education—General	M,D,O
Educational Leadership and Administration	M
Educational Media/Instructional Technology	M
Electrical Engineering	M
Energy and Power Engineering	D
Engineering and Applied Sciences—General	M,D
English as a Second Language	M,D
English	M
Environmental Engineering	M,D
Family and Consumer Sciences-General	M
Fish, Game, and Wildlife Management	M,D
Foreign Languages Education	M
Health Education	M
Horticulture	M,D
Industrial and Manufacturing Management	M
Industrial/Management Engineering	M
Kinesiology and Movement Studies	M
Mathematics	M
Mechanical Engineering	M
Multilingual and Multicultural Education	M,D
Music Education	M
Petroleum Engineering	M
Plant Sciences	M
Psychology—General	M
Range Science	M
Reading Education	M
Sociology	M
Spanish	M
Special Education	M
Statistics	M
Sustainable Development	D
Systems Engineering	D

TEXAS A&M UNIVERSITY–SAN ANTONIO

Accounting	M
Business Administration and Management—General	M
Computer and Information Systems Security	M
Counselor Education	M
Early Childhood Education	M
Educational Leadership and Administration	M
Educational Measurement and Evaluation	M
English	M
Finance and Banking	M
Health Services Management and Hospital Administration	M
Human Resources Management	M
International Business	M
Kinesiology and Movement Studies	M
Management Information Systems	M
Multilingual and Multicultural Education	M
Project Management	M
Reading Education	M
Special Education	M
Supply Chain Management	M

TEXAS A&M UNIVERSITY–TEXARKANA

Accounting	M
Adult Education	M
Business Administration and Management—General	M
Counseling Psychology	M
Curriculum and Instruction	M
Education—General	M
Educational Leadership and Administration	M
Educational Media/Instructional Technology	M
English	M
Interdisciplinary Studies	M
Psychology—General	M
Special Education	M

TEXAS CHIROPRACTIC COLLEGE

Chiropractic	D

TEXAS CHRISTIAN UNIVERSITY

Accounting	M
Adult Nursing	M,O
Allied Health—General	M,D,O
American Studies	M,D
Applied Mathematics	M,D
Art History	M
Art/Fine Arts	M
Astrophysics	M,D
Biochemistry	M,D
Biological and Biomedical Sciences—General	M
Biophysics	M,D
Business Administration and Management—General	M
Chemistry	M,D
Cognitive Sciences	M,D
Communication Disorders	M
Communication—General	M
Corporate and Organizational Communication	M
Counselor Education	M,O
Criminal Justice and Criminology	M
Curriculum and Instruction	M,O
Developmental Psychology	M,D
Education—General	M,D,O
Educational Leadership and Administration	M,D,O
English	M,D
Environmental Sciences	M
Experimental Psychology	M,D
Finance and Banking	M
Geology	M
Gerontological Nursing	M,O
History	M,D
Kinesiology and Movement Studies	M
Latin American Studies	M,D
Liberal Studies	M
Marketing	M
Mass Communication	M
Mathematics Education	M,O
Mathematics	M,D
Music Education	M,D
Music	M,D
Neuroscience	M,D
Nurse Anesthesia	D
Nursing and Healthcare Administration	M,D,O
Nursing Education	M,O
Nursing—General	M,D,O
Pediatric Nursing	M,O
Photography	M
Physics	M,D
Psychology—General	M,D
Reading Education	M,O
Rhetoric	M,D
Science Education	M,O
Social Psychology	M,D
Social Work	M

*M—masters degree; D—doctorate; O—other advanced degree; *—Close-Up and/or Display*

Special Education M,O
Speech and Interpersonal Communication M
Supply Chain Management M
Taxation M

TEXAS HEALTH AND SCIENCE UNIVERSITY
Business Administration and Management—General M,D
Health Services Management and Hospital Administration M,D

TEXAS LUTHERAN UNIVERSITY
Accounting M

TEXAS SOUTHERN UNIVERSITY
Art/Fine Arts M
Biological and Biomedical Sciences—General M
Business Administration and Management—General M
Chemistry M
Communication—General M
Computer Science M
Counselor Education M,D
Criminal Justice and Criminology M,D
Curriculum and Instruction M,D
Education—General M,D
Educational Leadership and Administration M,D
English M
Environmental Management and Policy M,D
Family and Consumer Sciences-General M
Health Education M
Health Services Management and Hospital Administration M
Higher Education M,D
History M
Human Services M
Industrial/Management Engineering M
Law D
Management Information Systems M
Mathematics M
Multilingual and Multicultural Education M,D
Music M
Pharmaceutical Sciences M,D
Pharmacy D
Physical Education M
Psychology—General M
Public Administration M
Secondary Education M,D
Sociology M
Toxicology M,D
Transportation and Highway Engineering M
Transportation Management M
Urban and Regional Planning M,D

TEXAS STATE UNIVERSITY
Accounting M
Adult Education M,D
Agricultural Education M
Allied Health—General M,D
Anthropology M
Applied Mathematics M
Athletic Training and Sports Medicine M
Biochemistry M
Biological and Biomedical Sciences—General M
Business Administration and Management—General M
Chemistry M
Child and Family Studies M
Communication Disorders M
Communication—General M
Computer Art and Design M
Conservation Biology M
Counselor Education M
Criminal Justice and Criminology M,D
Developmental Education M,D
Education—General M,D,O
Educational Leadership and Administration M,D
Educational Media/Instructional Technology M
Electrical Engineering M
Elementary Education M
Engineering and Applied Sciences—General M
English M
Environmental Management and Policy M
Ethics M
Exercise and Sports Science M
Family and Consumer Sciences-General M
Family Nurse Practitioner Studies M
Finance and Banking M
Fish, Game, and Wildlife Management M
Geographic Information Systems D
Geography M,D
Gerontology M
Graphic Design M
Health Education M
Health Informatics M
Health Services Management and Hospital Administration M
Higher Education M
History M
Human Resources Management M
Industrial/Management Engineering M
Interdisciplinary Studies M
International Affairs M
Legal and Justice Studies M
Leisure Studies M
Management Information Systems M
Management of Technology M
Manufacturing Engineering M
Marine Biology M,D
Marriage and Family Therapy M
Mass Communication M
Materials Engineering D
Materials Sciences M,D
Mathematics Education M,D
Mathematics M
Multilingual and Multicultural Education M
Music Education M
Music M
Nutrition M
Philosophy M
Physical Education M
Physical Therapy D
Physics M
Political Science M
Psychology—General M
Public Administration M
Reading Education M
Recreation and Park Management M
Rhetoric M
School Psychology O
Secondary Education M
Social Psychology M
Social Work M
Sociology M
Software Engineering M
Spanish M
Special Education M
Student Affairs M
Sustainable Development M
Technical Communication M
Theater M
Urban and Regional Planning M
Vocational and Technical Education M
Writing M

TEXAS TECH UNIVERSITY
Accounting M,D
Agricultural Economics and Agribusiness M,D
Agricultural Education M,D
Agricultural Sciences—General M,D
Agronomy and Soil Sciences M,D
Animal Sciences M,D
Anthropology M
Applied Economics M,D
Applied Physics M,D
Architecture M,D
Art Education M
Art History M
Art/Fine Arts M,D
Atmospheric Sciences M,D
Bioengineering M
Biological and Biomedical Sciences—General M,D
Biotechnology M,D
Business Administration and Management—General M,D
Chemical Engineering M,D
Chemistry M,D
Child and Family Studies M,D
Civil Engineering M,D
Classics M,D
Clinical Psychology M,D
Communication—General M
Computer Science M,D
Consumer Economics M,D
Counseling Psychology M,D
Counselor Education M,D
Cultural Studies M,D
Curriculum and Instruction M,D
Database Systems M,D
Distance Education Development M,D
Economics M,D
Education—General M,D
Educational Leadership and Administration M,D
Educational Media/Instructional Technology M,D
Educational Psychology M,D
Electrical Engineering M,D
Elementary Education M,D
Energy and Power Engineering M,D
Engineering and Applied Sciences—General M,D
Engineering Management M,D
English M,D
Environmental Design M,D
Environmental Engineering M,D
Environmental Management and Policy M,D
Environmental Sciences M,D
Exercise and Sports Science M
Experimental Psychology M,D
Family and Consumer Sciences-General M,D
Finance and Banking M,D
Fish, Game, and Wildlife Management M,D
Food Science and Technology M,D
Forensic Sciences M
Geography M,D
Geosciences M,D
German M,D
Gerontology M,D
Health Services Management and Hospital Administration M,D
Higher Education M,D
Historic Preservation M,D
History M,D
Home Economics Education M,D
Horticulture M,D
Hospitality Management M,D
Human Development M,D
Industrial/Management Engineering M,D
Interdisciplinary Studies M,D
Interior Design M,D
Kinesiology and Movement Studies M
Landscape Architecture M
Law M,D
Linguistics M,D
Management Information Systems M,D
Marketing M,D
Marriage and Family Therapy M,D
Mass Communication M,D
Mathematics M,D
Mechanical Engineering M,D
Microbiology M,D
Multilingual and Multicultural Education M,D
Museum Studies M,D
Music Education M,D
Music M,D
Natural Resources M,D
Nutrition M,D
Petroleum Engineering M,D
Philosophy M
Physics M,D
Plant Sciences M,D
Political Science M,D
Psychology—General M,D
Public Administration M,D
Reading Education M,D
Rhetoric M,D
Romance Languages M,D
Science Education M,D
Secondary Education M,D
Social Work M
Sociology M
Software Engineering M,D
Spanish M,D
Special Education M,D
Sports Management M
Statistics M,D
Sustainable Development M,D
Systems Engineering M,D
Taxation M,D
Technical Writing M,D
Theater M
Toxicology M,D
Zoology M,D

TEXAS TECH UNIVERSITY HEALTH SCIENCES CENTER
Acute Care/Critical Care Nursing M,D,O
Allopathic Medicine D
Athletic Training and Sports Medicine M
Biological and Biomedical Sciences—General M,D
Biotechnology M
Cell Biology M,D
Communication Disorders M,D
Family Nurse Practitioner Studies M,D,O
Gerontological Nursing M,D,O
Health Services Management and Hospital Administration M
Molecular Pathology M
Nursing and Healthcare Administration M,D,O
Nursing Education M,D,O
Nursing—General M,D,O
Occupational Therapy M
Pediatric Nursing M,D,O
Pharmaceutical Sciences M,D
Physical Therapy D
Physician Assistant Studies M
Rehabilitation Counseling M
Rehabilitation Sciences D

TEXAS WESLEYAN UNIVERSITY
Business Administration and Management—General M
Counseling Psychology M,D
Counselor Education M,D
Education—General M,D
Marriage and Family Therapy M,D
Nurse Anesthesia M,D

TEXAS WOMAN'S UNIVERSITY
Accounting M
Acute Care/Critical Care Nursing M,D
Adult Nursing M,D
Allied Health—General M,D
Art/Fine Arts M
Biological and Biomedical Sciences—General M,D
Business Administration and Management—General M
Chemistry M
Child and Family Studies M,D
Child Development M,D
Communication Disorders M
Counseling Psychology M,D,O
Counselor Education M,D
Curriculum and Instruction M,D
Dance M,D
Early Childhood Education M,D
Education—General M,D
Educational Leadership and Administration M,D
English M,D
Exercise and Sports Science M,D
Family Nurse Practitioner Studies M,D
Food Science and Technology M,D
Gender Studies M,D
Health Education M,D
Health Services Management and Hospital Administration M,D
History M
Information Science M
Kinesiology and Movement Studies M,D
Library Science M
Marriage and Family Therapy M,D
Mathematics Education M
Mathematics M
Molecular Biology M,D
Music Education M
Music M
Nursing and Healthcare Administration M,D
Nursing Education M,D
Nursing—General M,D
Nutrition M
Occupational Therapy M,D
Pediatric Nursing M,D
Physical Education M,D
Physical Therapy D
Political Science M
Psychology—General M,D,O
Reading Education M,D
Rhetoric M,D
School Psychology M,D,O
Sociology M,D
Special Education M,D
Sports Management M,D
Theater M
Therapies—Dance, Drama, and Music M
Women's Health Nursing M,D
Women's Studies M,D

THEOLOGICAL UNIVERSITY OF THE CARIBBEAN
Early Childhood Education M,D
Middle School Education M,D
Missions and Missiology M,D
Pastoral Ministry and Counseling M,D

THOMAS COLLEGE
Business Administration and Management—General M
Business Education M
Computer Education M
Human Resources Management M

THOMAS EDISON STATE UNIVERSITY
Applied Science and Technology O
Business Administration and Management—General M
Distance Education Development O
Educational Leadership and Administration M
Educational Media/Instructional Technology O
Epidemiology O
Homeland Security O
Human Resources Management M,O
Liberal Studies M
Nursing Education O
Nursing—General M,D
Organizational Management O
Public Administration M

THOMAS JEFFERSON SCHOOL OF LAW
Law D

THOMAS JEFFERSON UNIVERSITY
Allopathic Medicine D
Applied Economics M,D,O
Biochemistry D
Biological and Biomedical Sciences—General M,D,O
Cancer Biology/Oncology D
Cell Biology M,D
Clinical Laboratory Sciences/Medical Technology M
Clinical Research M,O
Developmental Biology M,D
Genetics D
Genomic Sciences D
Health Education M,D,O
Health Physics/Radiological Health M
Health Services Management and Hospital Administration M,D,O
Health Services Research M,D,O
Immunology D
Infectious Diseases O
Marriage and Family Therapy M
Microbiology M,D
Molecular Pharmacology D
Neuroscience D
Nursing—General M,D
Occupational Therapy M,D
Pharmacology M
Pharmacy D
Physical Therapy D
Physician Assistant Studies M
Public Health—General M,O
Toxicology M

THOMAS MORE COLLEGE
Business Administration and Management—General M
Education—General M
Educational Leadership and Administration M

THOMAS UNIVERSITY
Business Administration and Management—General M
Education—General M
Human Services M
Nursing—General M
Rehabilitation Counseling M
Social Psychology M

THOMPSON RIVERS UNIVERSITY
Business Administration and Management—General M
Education—General M
Environmental Sciences M
Social Work M

TIFFIN UNIVERSITY
Art/Fine Arts M
Business Administration and Management—General M
Communication—General M
Criminal Justice and Criminology M
Education—General M
Educational Leadership and Administration M
Educational Media/Instructional Technology M
English M

Film, Television, and Video Theory and Criticism M
Finance and Banking M
Forensic Psychology M
Health Services Management and Hospital Administration M
Higher Education M
Homeland Security M
Human Resources Management M
Humanities M
International Business M
Marketing M
Nonprofit Management M
Psychology—General M
Sports Management M
Writing M

TORONTO SCHOOL OF THEOLOGY
Theology M,D

TOURO COLLEGE
Communication Disorders M,D
Counseling Psychology M,D
Education—General M
Educational Leadership and Administration M
Educational Media/Instructional Technology M
English as a Second Language M
Industrial and Organizational Psychology M,D
Internet and Interactive Multimedia M
Jewish Studies M
Law M,D
Legal and Justice Studies M,D
Management Information Systems M
Mathematics Education M
Occupational Therapy M,D
Physical Therapy M,D
Physician Assistant Studies M,D
Reading Education M
School Psychology M,D
Science Education M
Social Work M
Special Education M

TOURO UNIVERSITY CALIFORNIA
Education—General M,D
Osteopathic Medicine M,D
Pharmacy M,D
Public Health—General M,D

TOWSON UNIVERSITY
Accounting M
Allied Health—General M
Applied Mathematics M
Applied Physics M
Art Education M,O
Art History M
Art/Fine Arts M
Biological and Biomedical Sciences—General M
Child and Family Studies M,O
Clinical Psychology M
Communication Disorders M,D
Communication—General M
Computer and Information Systems Security M,D,O
Computer Science M
Corporate and Organizational Communication M
Counseling Psychology O
Database Systems M,D,O
Early Childhood Education M,O
Education—General M
Educational Leadership and Administration O
Educational Media/Instructional Technology M,D
Electronic Commerce M,O
Elementary Education M
Environmental and Occupational Health D
Environmental Management and Policy M
Environmental Sciences M,O
Forensic Sciences M
Geography M
Gerontology M,O
Health Services Management and Hospital Administration M,O
Homeland Security M,O
Human Resources Development M
Humanities M
Information Science M,D,O
Internet and Interactive Multimedia M,D,O
Jewish Studies M,O
Kinesiology and Movement Studies M
Liberal Studies M
Management Information Systems M,D,O
Management of Technology M,O
Marketing Research M
Mathematics Education M
Music Education M,O
Music M
Nursing Education M,O
Nursing—General M,O
Occupational Therapy M
Organizational Behavior O
Physician Assistant Studies M
Reading Education M,O
Religious Education M,O
School Psychology O
Secondary Education M
Social Sciences M
Software Engineering M,D,O
Special Education M,O
Supply Chain Management M,O
Theater M
Women's Studies M,O

Writing M

TOYOTA TECHNOLOGICAL INSTITUTE AT CHICAGO
Computer Science D

TRENT UNIVERSITY
American Indian/Native American Studies M,D
Anthropology M
Biological and Biomedical Sciences—General M,D
Canadian Studies M,D
Chemistry M
Computer Science M
Cultural Studies D
Environmental Management and Policy M,D
Geography M,D
Materials Sciences M
Modeling and Simulation M,D
Physics M

TREVECCA NAZARENE UNIVERSITY
Business Administration and Management—General M
Counselor Education M,D
Curriculum and Instruction M,O
Education—General M,O
Educational Leadership and Administration M,D,O
Elementary Education M,O
English as a Second Language M,O
Information Science M,O
Library Science M,O
Management of Technology M
Marriage and Family Therapy M,D
Organizational Management M,D
Pastoral Ministry and Counseling M
Physician Assistant Studies M
Religion M
Secondary Education M,O
Special Education M,O

TRIDENT UNIVERSITY INTERNATIONAL
Adult Education M
Business Administration and Management—General M,D
Clinical Research M,D,O
Computer and Information Systems Security M,D
Conflict Resolution and Mediation/Peace Studies M,D
Criminal Justice and Criminology M,D
Early Childhood Education M
Education—General M,D
Educational Leadership and Administration M,D
Educational Media/Instructional Technology M,D
Emergency Management M,D,O
Environmental and Occupational Health M,D,O
Finance and Banking M,D
Health Education M,D,O
Health Informatics M,D,O
Health Services Management and Hospital Administration M,D,O
Higher Education M,D
Human Resources Management M,D
International Business M,D
International Health M,D,O
Legal and Justice Studies M,D,O
Logistics M,D
Management Information Systems M,D,O
Marketing M,D
Nursing and Healthcare Administration M,D,O
Project Management M,D
Public Administration M,D
Public Health—General M,D,O
Quality Management M,D,O
Reading Education M

TRINE UNIVERSITY
Civil Engineering M
Criminal Justice and Criminology M
Emergency Management M
Engineering and Applied Sciences—General M
Engineering Management M
Forensic Psychology M
Law M
Public Administration M

TRINITY BAPTIST COLLEGE
Educational Leadership and Administration M
Special Education M

TRINITY CHRISTIAN COLLEGE
Counseling Psychology M
Special Education M

TRINITY COLLEGE (CANADA)
Music M,D,O
Pastoral Ministry and Counseling M,D,O
Theology M,D,O

TRINITY COLLEGE (UNITED STATES)
American Studies M
Cultural Studies M
English M
Media Studies M
Museum Studies M
Public Policy M
Writing M

TRINITY INTERNATIONAL UNIVERSITY
Archaeology M,D,O
Bioethics M
Business Administration and Management—General M,D,O
Communication—General M

Counseling Psychology M,D,O
Education—General M
Educational Leadership and Administration M
Law D
Missions and Missiology M,D,O
Pastoral Ministry and Counseling M,D,O
Religious Education M,D,O
Theology M,D,O

TRINITY INTERNATIONAL UNIVERSITY FLORIDA
Counseling Psychology M
Religion M,O

TRINITY LUTHERAN SEMINARY
African-American Studies M
Missions and Missiology M
Music M
Pastoral Ministry and Counseling M
Religious Education M
Theology M

TRINITY SCHOOL FOR MINISTRY
Missions and Missiology M,D,O
Pastoral Ministry and Counseling M,D,O
Religion M,D,O
Theology M,D,O

TRINITY UNIVERSITY
Accounting M
Business Administration and Management—General M
Education—General M
Educational Leadership and Administration M
Health Services Management and Hospital Administration M
School Psychology M

TRINITY WASHINGTON UNIVERSITY
Business Administration and Management—General M
Clinical Psychology M
Communication—General M
Counseling Psychology M
Counselor Education M
Curriculum and Instruction M
Early Childhood Education M
Education—General M
Educational Leadership and Administration M
Elementary Education M
English Education M
Human Resources Management M
National Security M
Nonprofit Management M
Organizational Management M
Public Health—General M
Reading Education M
Secondary Education M
Social Sciences Education M
Special Education M

TRINITY WESTERN UNIVERSITY
Business Administration and Management—General M
Counseling Psychology M
Educational Leadership and Administration M,O
English as a Second Language M
English M
Health Services Management and Hospital Administration M,O
History M
Humanities M
Interdisciplinary Studies M
International Business M
Linguistics M
Nonprofit Management M,O
Nursing—General M
Organizational Management M,O
Pastoral Ministry and Counseling M,D
Philosophy M
Theology M,D

TRI-STATE BIBLE COLLEGE
Theology M

TRI-STATE COLLEGE OF ACUPUNCTURE
Acupuncture and Oriental Medicine M,O

TROPICAL AGRICULTURE RESEARCH AND HIGHER EDUCATION CENTER
Agricultural Economics and Agribusiness M,D
Agricultural Sciences—General M,D
Conservation Biology M,D
Environmental Management and Policy M,D
Forestry M,D
Travel and Tourism M,D
Water Resources M,D

TROY UNIVERSITY
Accounting M
Addictions/Substance Abuse Counseling M,O
Adult Education M
Adult Nursing M,D,O
Art Education M
Biological and Biomedical Sciences—General M,O
Business Administration and Management—General M
Clinical Psychology M,O
Communication—General M
Computer Education M
Computer Science M
Corporate and Organizational Communication M
Counselor Education M,O

Criminal Justice and Criminology M,O
Early Childhood Education M,O
Economic Development M
Economics M
Education of the Gifted M
Education—General M,O
Educational Leadership and Administration M,O
Elementary Education M,O
English as a Second Language M
Environmental Management and Policy M
Environmental Sciences M
Family Nurse Practitioner Studies M,D,O
Finance and Banking M
Health Services Management and Hospital Administration M
History M
Hospitality Management M
Human Resources Management M
International Affairs M
International Business M
Management Information Systems M
Maternal and Child Health M,D,O
Mathematics Education M
Music Education M
National Security M
Nonprofit Management M
Nursing Informatics M,D,O
Nursing—General M,D,O
Organizational Management M
Physical Education M
Public Administration M
Reading Education M
Rehabilitation Counseling M,O
School Psychology M,O
Science Education M
Secondary Education M
Social Psychology M,O
Social Sciences Education M
Social Sciences M
Social Work M,O
Sports Management M
Taxation M,O

TRUMAN STATE UNIVERSITY
Accounting M
Athletic Training and Sports Medicine M
Biological and Biomedical Sciences—General M
Communication Disorders M
Education—General M
English M
Music M

TUFTS UNIVERSITY
Allopathic Medicine D
Analytical Chemistry M,D
Animal Sciences M
Archaeology M
Art Education M,D,O
Art History M
Art/Fine Arts M
Astrophysics M,D
Biochemistry D
Bioengineering M,D,O
Bioinformatics M,D
Biological and Biomedical Sciences—General M,D,O
Biomedical Engineering M,D
Biostatistics M,D,O
Biotechnology M,D,O
Cancer Biology/Oncology D
Cell Biology D
Chemical Engineering M,D
Chemical Physics M,D
Chemistry M,D
Child and Family Studies M,D
Child Development M,D
Civil Engineering M,D
Classics M
Clinical Research M,D,O
Cognitive Sciences M,D
Computer Science M,D,O
Conflict Resolution and Mediation/Peace Studies M,D
Dentistry D
Developmental Biology D
Early Childhood Education M,D
Economics M
Education—General M,D,O
Electrical Engineering M,D,O
Elementary Education M,D
Engineering and Applied Sciences—General M,D*
Engineering Management M
English M,D
Entrepreneurship M
Environmental and Occupational Health M,D
Environmental Engineering M,D
Environmental Management and Policy M,D,O
Environmental Sciences M,D
Epidemiology M,D,O
Ergonomics and Human Factors M,D
Family and Consumer Sciences-General M,D
French M
Genetics D
Geotechnical Engineering M,D
German M
Hazardous Materials Management M,D
Health Communication M,D,O
Health Services Management and Hospital Administration M,D,O
History M,D
Human Development M,D

*M—masters degree; D—doctorate; O—other advanced degree; *—Close-Up and/or Display*

Human-Computer Interaction	O
Immunology	D
Infectious Diseases	M,D
Inorganic Chemistry	M,D
Interdisciplinary Studies	D
International Affairs	M,D
International Business	M,D
International Development	M,D
International Health	M,D
Law	M,D
Management Strategy and Policy	O
Manufacturing Engineering	O
Mathematics Education	M,D
Mathematics	M,D
Mechanical Engineering	M,D
Microbiology	D
Middle School Education	M,D
Molecular Biology	D
Molecular Medicine	D
Museum Education	M,D
Museum Studies	M,D,O
Music	M
Neuroscience	M,D
Nonprofit Management	O
Nutrition	M,D,O
Occupational Therapy	M,D,O
Oral and Dental Sciences	M,O
Organic Chemistry	M,D
Pathology	M,D
Pharmacology	M,D
Philosophy	M
Physical Chemistry	M,D
Physician Assistant Studies	M,D,O
Physics	M,D
Psychology—General	M,D
Public Administration	O
Public Health—General	M,D,O
Public Policy	M
Reproductive Biology	M,D
School Psychology	M,O
Science Education	M,D
Secondary Education	M,D
Structural Biology	D
Structural Engineering	M,D
Theater	M,D
Urban and Regional Planning	M
Urban Studies	M
Veterinary Medicine	M,D
Water Resources Engineering	M,D

TULANE UNIVERSITY

Accounting	M,D
Allopathic Medicine	D
Anthropology	D
Architecture	M
Art History	M
Art/Fine Arts	M
Biochemistry	M
Biological and Biomedical Sciences—General	M,D
Biomedical Engineering	M,D
Biostatistics	M,D
Business Administration and Management—General	M,D
Cell Biology	M,D
Chemical Engineering	M,D
Chemistry	M,D
Classics	M
Community Health	M,D
Dance	M
Ecology	M,D
Economics	M,D
Emergency Management	M,D
Energy Management and Policy	M,D
English	M
Entrepreneurship	M,D
Environmental and Occupational Health	M,D
Epidemiology	M,D
Evolutionary Biology	M,D
Finance and Banking	M,D
French	M,D
Health Services Management and Hospital Administration	M,D
History	M,D
Human Genetics	M
Immunology	M
Interdisciplinary Studies	D
International Business	M,D
International Development	M,D
International Health	M,D
Latin American Studies	M,D
Law	M,D
Liberal Studies	M
Management Strategy and Policy	M,D
Mathematics	M,D
Microbiology	M
Molecular Biology	M,D
Music	M
Neuroscience	M,D
Parasitology	M,D,O
Pharmacology	M
Philosophy	M,D
Physics	M,D
Physiology	M
Political Science	D
Portuguese	M,D
Psychology—General	M,D
Public Health—General	M,D
Social Work	M,D
Sociology	M
Spanish	M,D
Structural Biology	M,D
Theater	M

TUSCULUM COLLEGE

Adult Education	M
Business Administration and Management—General	M
Education—General	M

TUSKEGEE UNIVERSITY

Agricultural Economics and Agribusiness	M
Agronomy and Soil Sciences	M
Animal Sciences	M
Biological and Biomedical Sciences—General	M,D
Chemistry	M
Computer and Information Systems Security	M
Electrical Engineering	M
Engineering and Applied Sciences—General	M,D
Environmental Sciences	M
Food Science and Technology	M
Management Information Systems	M
Materials Engineering	D
Mechanical Engineering	M
Nutrition	M
Occupational Therapy	M
Plant Sciences	M
Veterinary Medicine	M,D
Veterinary Sciences	M,D

TYNDALE UNIVERSITY COLLEGE & SEMINARY

Missions and Missiology	M,O
Pastoral Ministry and Counseling	M,O
Theology	M,O

UNIFICATION THEOLOGICAL SEMINARY

Nonprofit Management	M,D
Pastoral Ministry and Counseling	M,D
Religion	M,D
Religious Education	M,D
Theology	M,D

UNIFORMED SERVICES UNIVERSITY OF THE HEALTH SCIENCES

Biological and Biomedical Sciences—General	M,D
Cell Biology	M,D
Clinical Psychology	D
Environmental and Occupational Health	M,D
Family Nurse Practitioner Studies	M,D
Gerontological Nursing	M,D
Health Services Management and Hospital Administration	M,D
Immunology	D
Infectious Diseases	D*
International Health	M,D
Molecular Biology	M,D*
Neuroscience	D*
Nurse Anesthesia	M,D
Nursing—General	M,D
Psychiatric Nursing	M,D
Psychology—General	D
Public Health—General	M,D
Women's Health Nursing	M,D
Zoology	M,D

UNION COLLEGE (KY)

Clinical Psychology	M
Counseling Psychology	M
Education—General	M
Educational Leadership and Administration	M
Elementary Education	M
Health Education	M
Middle School Education	M
Music Education	M
Physical Education	M
Psychology—General	M
Reading Education	M
School Psychology	M
Secondary Education	M
Special Education	M

UNION COLLEGE (NE)

Physician Assistant Studies	M

UNION INSTITUTE & UNIVERSITY

Clinical Psychology	M
Cultural Studies	M
Education—General	D
Ethics	D
Health Promotion	M
History	M
Humanities	D
Interdisciplinary Studies	M,D
Organizational Management	M
Public Policy	M,D
Writing	M

UNION PRESBYTERIAN SEMINARY

Religious Education	M,D

UNION THEOLOGICAL SEMINARY IN THE CITY OF NEW YORK

Theology	M,D

UNION UNIVERSITY

Accounting	M
Business Administration and Management—General	M
Cultural Studies	M
Education—General	M,D,O
Educational Leadership and Administration	M,D,O
Family Nurse Practitioner Studies	M,D,O
Higher Education	M,D,O
Nurse Anesthesia	M,D,O
Nursing and Healthcare Administration	M,D,O
Nursing Education	M,D,O
Nursing—General	M,D,O
Pastoral Ministry and Counseling	M,D
Religion	M,D
Social Work	M

UNITED STATES ARMY COMMAND AND GENERAL STAFF COLLEGE

Military and Defense Studies	M

UNITED STATES INTERNATIONAL UNIVERSITY–AFRICA

Addictions/Substance Abuse Counseling	M
Business Administration and Management—General	M
Conflict Resolution and Mediation/Peace Studies	M
Counseling Psychology	M
Entrepreneurship	M
Finance and Banking	M
Health Psychology	M
Human Resources Management	M
International Affairs	M
International Business	M
Management Information Systems	M
Management Strategy and Policy	M
Marketing	M
Organizational Management	M

UNITED STATES MERCHANT MARINE ACADEMY

Civil Engineering	M

UNITED STATES SPORTS ACADEMY

Athletic Training and Sports Medicine	M
Exercise and Sports Science	M
Physical Education	M
Sports Management	M,D

UNITED STATES UNIVERSITY

Family Nurse Practitioner Studies	M

UNITED TALMUDICAL SEMINARY

Theology	

UNITED THEOLOGICAL SEMINARY

Theology	M,D

UNITED THEOLOGICAL SEMINARY OF THE TWIN CITIES

Art/Fine Arts	M,D,O
Asian Studies	M,D,O
Conflict Resolution and Mediation/Peace Studies	M,D,O
Ethnic Studies	M,D,O
Humanities	M,D,O
Pastoral Ministry and Counseling	M,D,O
Religion	M,D,O
Theology	M,D,O
Women's Studies	M,D,O

UNITY COLLEGE

Natural Resources	M
Sustainable Development	M

UNIVERSIDAD ADVENTISTA DE LAS ANTILLAS

Curriculum and Instruction	M
Educational Leadership and Administration	M
Medical/Surgical Nursing	M

UNIVERSIDAD AUTONOMA DE GUADALAJARA

Advertising and Public Relations	M,D
Allopathic Medicine	D
Architecture	M,D
Business Administration and Management—General	M,D
Computer Art and Design	M,D
Computer Science	M,D
Corporate and Organizational Communication	M,D
Education—General	M,D
Energy and Power Engineering	M,D
Entertainment Management	M,D
Environmental and Occupational Health	M,D
Environmental Management and Policy	M,D
Film, Television, and Video Production	M,D
International Business	M,D
Internet and Interactive Multimedia	M,D
Law	M,D
Legal and Justice Studies	M,D
Manufacturing Engineering	M,D
Marketing Research	M,D
Mathematics Education	M,D
Philosophy	M,D
Public Policy	M,D
Spanish	M,D
Systems Science	M,D
Translation and Interpretation	M,D

UNIVERSIDAD CENTRAL DEL CARIBE

Addictions/Substance Abuse Counseling	M
Allopathic Medicine	M,D
Anatomy	M,D
Biochemistry	M,D
Biological and Biomedical Sciences—General	M,D
Cell Biology	M,D
Immunology	M,D
Microbiology	M,D
Molecular Biology	M,D
Pharmacology	M,D
Physiology	M,D

UNIVERSIDAD CENTRAL DEL ESTE

Allopathic Medicine	D
Dentistry	D
Environmental Engineering	M
Finance and Banking	M
Higher Education	M
Human Resources Development	M
Law	D

UNIVERSIDAD DE CIENCIAS MEDICAS

Allopathic Medicine	M,D,O
Anatomy	M,D,O
Biological and Biomedical Sciences—General	M,D,O
Community Health	M,D,O
Environmental and Occupational Health	M,D,O
Health Services Management and Hospital Administration	M,D,O
Pharmacy	M,D,O

UNIVERSIDAD DE IBEROAMERICA

Acute Care/Critical Care Nursing	M,D
Allopathic Medicine	M,D
Clinical Psychology	M,D
Educational Psychology	M,D
Forensic Psychology	M,D
Health Services Management and Hospital Administration	M,D
Neuroscience	M,D

UNIVERSIDAD DE LAS AMERICAS, A.C.

Business Administration and Management—General	M
Education—General	M
Finance and Banking	M
International Affairs	M
Marketing Research	M
Marriage and Family Therapy	M
Organizational Behavior	M
Psychology—General	M
Quality Management	M

UNIVERSIDAD DE LAS AMÉRICAS PUEBLA

American Studies	M
Anthropology	M
Archaeology	M
Biotechnology	M
Business Administration and Management—General	M
Chemical Engineering	M
Clinical Laboratory Sciences/Medical Technology	M
Computer Art and Design	M
Computer Science	M,D
Construction Management	M
Economics	M
Education—General	M
Electrical Engineering	M
Engineering and Applied Sciences—General	M,D
English	M
Finance and Banking	M
Food Science and Technology	M
Industrial and Manufacturing Management	M
Industrial/Management Engineering	M
Linguistics	M
Manufacturing Engineering	M
Psychology—General	M

UNIVERSIDAD DEL ESTE

Accounting	M
Adult Education	M
Agricultural Economics and Agribusiness	M
Business Administration and Management—General	M
Computer and Information Systems Security	M
Criminal Justice and Criminology	M
Electronic Commerce	M
Elementary Education	M
English as a Second Language	M
Foreign Languages Education	M
Human Resources Management	M
Management Information Systems	M
Management Strategy and Policy	M
Public Policy	M
Social Work	M
Special Education	M

UNIVERSIDAD DEL TURABO

Accounting	M
Adult Nursing	M,O
Art/Fine Arts	M
Arts Administration	M
Athletic Training and Sports Medicine	M
Business Administration and Management—General	M,D
Chemistry	M,D
Communication Disorders	M
Conflict Resolution and Mediation/Peace Studies	M
Counseling Psychology	M,D,O
Counselor Education	M
Criminal Justice and Criminology	M
Curriculum and Instruction	M,D
Early Childhood Education	M
Education—General	M,D,O
Educational Leadership and Administration	M,D,O
English as a Second Language	M
Environmental Biology	M,D
Environmental Management and Policy	M,D
Environmental Sciences	M,D
Family Nurse Practitioner Studies	M
Forensic Sciences	M
Health Promotion	M
Human Resources Management	M
Human Services	M
Information Studies	M
Library Science	M,O
Logistics	M
Management Information Systems	D
Marketing	M
Naturopathic Medicine	D
Physical Education	M
Project Management	M
Quality Management	M
Special Education	M
Telecommunications	M

UNIVERSIDAD IBEROAMERICANA

Allopathic Medicine	D

Business Administration and Management—General	M,D
Corporate and Organizational Communication	M,D
Dentistry	M,D
Educational Leadership and Administration	M,D
Human Resources Development	M,D
Law	M,D
Marketing	M,D
Real Estate	M,D
Special Education	M,D

UNIVERSIDAD METROPOLITANA

Accounting	M
Adult Education	M
Business Administration and Management—General	M
Counseling Psychology	M
Curriculum and Instruction	M
Education—General	M
Educational Leadership and Administration	M
Elementary Education	M
Environmental Management and Policy	M
Finance and Banking	M
Human Resources Management	M
International Business	M
Leisure Studies	M
Management Information Systems	M
Marketing	M
Natural Resources	M
Nursing and Healthcare Administration	M,O
Nursing—General	M,O
Oncology Nursing	M,O
Physical Education	M
Recreation and Park Management	M
Secondary Education	M
Special Education	M

UNIVERSIDAD NACIONAL PEDRO HENRIQUEZ URENA

Agricultural Sciences—General	M
Allopathic Medicine	D
Animal Sciences	M
Architecture	M
Dentistry	D
Ecology	M
Environmental Engineering	M
Environmental Sciences	M
Historic Preservation	M
Horticulture	M
International Affairs	M
Natural Resources	M
Political Science	M
Project Management	M
Science Education	M

UNIVERSITÉ DE MONCTON

Astronomy	M
Biochemistry	M
Biological and Biomedical Sciences—General	M
Business Administration and Management—General	M
Chemistry	M
Civil Engineering	M
Computer Science	M,O
Counselor Education	M
Economics	M
Education—General	M
Educational Leadership and Administration	M
Educational Psychology	M
Electrical Engineering	M
Engineering and Applied Sciences—General	M
Food Science and Technology	M
French	M,D
History	M
Industrial/Management Engineering	M
Mathematics	M
Mechanical Engineering	M
Nutrition	M
Physics	M
Public Administration	M
Social Work	M

UNIVERSITÉ DE MONTRÉAL

Allopathic Medicine	D
Anthropology	M,D
Art History	M,D
Biochemistry	M,D,O
Bioethics	M,D,O
Bioinformatics	M,D
Biological and Biomedical Sciences—General	M,D
Biomedical Engineering	M,D,O
Cell Biology	M,D
Chemistry	M,D
Classics	M
Communication Disorders	M,O
Communication—General	M,D
Community Health	M,D,O
Comparative Literature	M,D
Computer Science	M,D
Criminal Justice and Criminology	M,D
Curriculum and Instruction	M,D,O
Demography and Population Studies	M,D
Dental Hygiene	O
Developmental Psychology	M,D
Economics	M,D,O
Education—General	M,D,O
Educational Leadership and Administration	M,D,O
Educational Psychology	M,D,O
Electronic Commerce	M,D
Emergency Management	O
English	M,D
Environmental and Occupational Health	M
Environmental Design	M,D,O
Environmental Management and Policy	O
Ergonomics and Human Factors	O
Film, Television, and Video Theory and Criticism	M,D
French	M,D
Genetic Counseling	O
Genetics	O
Geography	M,D,O
German	M
Health Services Management and Hospital Administration	M,O
Hispanic and Latin American Languages	M,D
History	M,D
Human Services	D
Immunology	M,D
Industrial and Labor Relations	M,D,O
Information Studies	M,D
International Affairs	M,O
Kinesiology and Movement Studies	M,D,O
Law	M,D,O
Library Science	M,D
Linguistics	M,D,O
Mathematical and Computational Finance	M,D,O
Mathematics	M,D,O
Microbiology	M,D
Molecular Biology	M,D
Museum Studies	M
Music	M,D,O
Neuroscience	M,D
Nursing—General	M,D,O
Nutrition	M,D,O
Occupational Therapy	O
Optometry	D
Oral and Dental Sciences	M,O
Pathology	M,D
Pharmaceutical Sciences	M,D,O
Pharmacology	M,D
Philosophy	M,D
Physical Education	M,D,O
Physics	M,D
Physiology	M,D
Political Science	M,D
Psychology—General	M,D
Public Health—General	M,D,O
Public Policy	O
Rehabilitation Sciences	O
Religion	M,D,O
Social Work	O
Sociology	M,D
Spanish	M
Statistics	M,D,O
Taxation	M,D,O
Theology	M,D,O
Toxicology	O
Translation and Interpretation	M,D,O
Urban and Regional Planning	M,D,O
Veterinary Medicine	D
Veterinary Sciences	M,D
Virology	D
Vision Sciences	M,O

UNIVERSITÉ DE SAINT-BONIFACE

Canadian Studies	M
Education—General	M

UNIVERSITÉ DE SHERBROOKE

Accounting	M
Allopathic Medicine	D
Biochemistry	M,D
Biological and Biomedical Sciences—General	M,D,O
Biophysics	M,D
Business Administration and Management—General	M,D,O
Canadian Studies	M,D
Cell Biology	M,D
Chemical Engineering	M,D
Chemistry	M,D,O
Civil Engineering	M,D
Clinical Laboratory Sciences/Medical Technology	M,D
Comparative Literature	M,D
Computer and Information Systems Security	M
Conflict Resolution and Mediation/Peace Studies	M,D,O
Corporate and Organizational Communication	M
Economic Development	D
Economics	M
Education—General	M,O
Educational Leadership and Administration	M
Electrical Engineering	M,D
Electronic Commerce	M
Elementary Education	M,O
Engineering and Applied Sciences—General	M,D,O
Engineering Management	M,O
Environmental Engineering	M
Environmental Sciences	M,O
Ethics	M,D,O
Finance and Banking	M
French	M,D
Geography	M,D
Gerontology	M
Health Law	M,D,O
Higher Education	M,O
History	M
Immunology	M,D
Information Science	M,D
International Business	M
Kinesiology and Movement Studies	M,O
Law	M,D,O
Linguistics	M,D
Management Information Systems	M,O
Marketing	M
Mathematics	M,D
Mechanical Engineering	M,D
Microbiology	M,D
Organizational Behavior	M
Pharmacology	M,D
Philosophy	M,D,O
Physical Education	M,O
Physics	M,D
Physiology	M,D
Psychology—General	M
Public Administration	M
Radiation Biology	M,D
Religion	M,D,O
Social Work	M
Special Education	M,O
Taxation	M,O
Theater	M,D
Theology	M,D,O

UNIVERSITÉ DU QUÉBEC À CHICOUTIMI

Art/Fine Arts	M
Business Administration and Management—General	M
Canadian Studies	M
Comparative Literature	M
Education—General	M,D
Engineering and Applied Sciences—General	M,D
Environmental Management and Policy	M
Ethics	O
French	O
Genetics	M
Geosciences	M
Linguistics	M
Mineralogy	D
Project Management	M
Theology	M,D

UNIVERSITÉ DU QUÉBEC À MONTRÉAL

Accounting	M,O
Actuarial Science	O
Art History	M,D
Art/Fine Arts	M
Atmospheric Sciences	M,D,O
Biological and Biomedical Sciences—General	M,D
Business Administration and Management—General	M,D,O
Chemistry	M,D
Communication—General	M,D
Comparative Literature	M,D
Dance	M
Economics	M,D
Education—General	M,D,O
Environmental and Occupational Health	O
Environmental Education	M,D,O
Environmental Sciences	M,D,O
Ergonomics and Human Factors	O
Finance and Banking	O
Geographic Information Systems	O
Geography	M
Geology	M,D,O
Geosciences	M,D,O
History	M,D
Kinesiology and Movement Studies	M
Law	O
Linguistics	M,D
Management Information Systems	M
Mathematics	M,D
Meteorology	M,D,O
Mineralogy	M,D,O
Museum Studies	M
Natural Resources	M,D,O
Philosophy	M,D
Political Science	M,D
Project Management	M,O
Psychology—General	D
Public Administration	M
Religion	M,D
Social Work	M
Sociology	M,D
Urban Studies	M,D

UNIVERSITÉ DU QUÉBEC À RIMOUSKI

Business Administration and Management—General	M,O
Comparative Literature	M,D
Education—General	M,D,O
Engineering and Applied Sciences—General	M
Ethics	M,O
Fish, Game, and Wildlife Management	M,D,O
Marine Affairs	M,O
Nursing—General	M,O
Oceanography	M,D
Project Management	M,O
Social Psychology	M
Urban and Regional Planning	M,D,O

UNIVERSITÉ DU QUÉBEC À TROIS-RIVIÈRES

Accounting	M
Biophysics	M,D
Business Administration and Management—General	M,D
Chemistry	M
Chiropractic	D
Communication—General	M,O
Comparative Literature	M
Computer Science	M
Education—General	M,D
Educational Leadership and Administration	O
Educational Psychology	M,D
Electrical Engineering	M,D
Environmental Sciences	M,D
Finance and Banking	O
Industrial and Labor Relations	O
Industrial/Management Engineering	M,O
Leisure Studies	M,O
Mathematics	M
Nursing—General	M,O
Philosophy	M,D
Physical Education	M
Physics	M,D
Psychology—General	D,O
Travel and Tourism	M,O

UNIVERSITÉ DU QUÉBEC, ÉCOLE DE TECHNOLOGIE SUPÉRIEURE

Engineering and Applied Sciences—General	M,D,O

UNIVERSITÉ DU QUÉBEC, ÉCOLE NATIONALE D'ADMINISTRATION PUBLIQUE

International Business	M,O
Public Administration	D,O
Urban Studies	M

UNIVERSITÉ DU QUÉBEC EN ABITIBI-TÉMISCAMINGUE

Biological and Biomedical Sciences—General	M,D
Business Administration and Management—General	M
Education—General	M,D,O
Engineering and Applied Sciences—General	M,O
Environmental Sciences	M,D
Forestry	M,D
Mineral/Mining Engineering	M,O
Natural Resources	M,D
Project Management	M,O
Social Work	M

UNIVERSITÉ DU QUÉBEC EN OUTAOUAIS

Accounting	M,O
Computer Science	M,D,O
Education—General	M,D,O
Educational Psychology	M
Finance and Banking	M,O
Foreign Languages Education	O
Industrial and Labor Relations	M,D,O
Nursing—General	M,O
Project Management	M,O
Social Work	M
Urban and Regional Planning	M

UNIVERSITÉ DU QUÉBEC, INSTITUT NATIONAL DE LA RECHERCHE SCIENTIFIQUE

Biological and Biomedical Sciences—General	M,D
Demography and Population Studies	M,D,O
Energy Management and Policy	M,D
Environmental Management and Policy	M,D
Geosciences	M,D
Hydrology	M,D
Immunology	M,D
Materials Sciences	M,D
Medical Microbiology	M,D
Microbiology	M,D
Telecommunications	M,D
Urban Studies	M,D,O
Virology	M,D

UNIVERSITÉ LAVAL

Accounting	M,O
Advertising and Public Relations	O
Aerospace/Aeronautical Engineering	M
Agricultural Economics and Agribusiness	M
Agricultural Engineering	M
Agricultural Sciences—General	M,D,O
Agronomy and Soil Sciences	M,D
Allopathic Medicine	D,O
Anatomy	O
Anesthesiologist Assistant Studies	O
Animal Sciences	M,D
Anthropology	M,D
Archaeology	M,D
Architecture	M
Art History	M,D
Art/Fine Arts	M
Biochemistry	M,D,O
Biological and Biomedical Sciences—General	M,D,O
Business Administration and Management—General	M,D,O
Cancer Biology/Oncology	O
Cardiovascular Sciences	O
Cell Biology	M,D
Chemical Engineering	M,D
Chemistry	M,D
Civil Engineering	M,D,O
Clinical Psychology	D
Communication Disorders	M
Community Health	M,D,O
Comparative Literature	M,D
Computer Science	M,D
Consumer Economics	O
Counselor Education	M,D
Curriculum and Instruction	M,D
Dentistry	D
Economics	M,D
Education—General	M,D,O
Educational Leadership and Administration	M,D,O

*M—masters degree; D—doctorate; O—other advanced degree; *—Close-Up and/or Display*

Educational Measurement and Evaluation	M,D,O
Educational Media/Instructional Technology	M,D
Educational Psychology	M,D
Electrical Engineering	M,D
Electronic Commerce	M,O
Emergency Medical Services	O
Engineering and Applied Sciences—General	M,D,O
English	M,D
Entrepreneurship	M,O
Environmental and Occupational Health	O
Environmental Engineering	M,D
Environmental Management and Policy	M,D,O
Environmental Sciences	M,D
Epidemiology	M,D
Ethics	O
Ethnic Studies	M,D
Facilities Management	M,O
Film, Television, and Video Theory and Criticism	M,D
Finance and Banking	M,O
Food Science and Technology	M,D
Forestry	M,D
Geodetic Sciences	M,D
Geographic Information Systems	M,O
Geography	M,D
Geology	M,D
Geosciences	M,D
Gerontology	O
Graphic Design	M
Health Physics/Radiological Health	O
History	M,D
Immunology	M,D
Industrial and Labor Relations	M,D
Industrial/Management Engineering	O
Infectious Diseases	O
International Affairs	M,D
International Business	M,O
Journalism	O
Kinesiology and Movement Studies	M,D
Law	M,D,O
Legal and Justice Studies	O
Linguistics	M,D
Management Information Systems	M,O
Marketing	M,O
Mass Communication	M,D
Mathematics	M,D
Mechanical Engineering	M,D
Metallurgical Engineering and Metallurgy	M,D
Microbiology	M,D
Mineral/Mining Engineering	M,D
Modeling and Simulation	M,O
Molecular Biology	M,D
Museum Studies	O
Music Education	M,D
Music	M,D
Neurobiology	M,D
Nursing—General	M,D,O
Nutrition	M,D
Oceanography	D
Oral and Dental Sciences	M,O
Organizational Management	M,O
Pathology	O
Pharmaceutical Sciences	M,D,O
Philosophy	M,D
Physics	M,D
Physiology	M,D
Plant Biology	M,D
Political Science	M,D
Psychology—General	D
Religion	M,D
Rural Planning and Studies	O
Social Psychology	D
Social Work	M,D
Sociology	M,D
Software Engineering	O
Spanish	M,D
Statistics	M
Theater	M,D
Theology	M,D
Translation and Interpretation	M,O
Urban and Regional Planning	M,D
Women's Studies	O

UNIVERSITÉ SAINTE-ANNE

Education—General	M

UNIVERSITY AT ALBANY, STATE UNIVERSITY OF NEW YORK

Accounting	M
African Studies	M
African-American Studies	M
Anthropology	M,D
Art/Fine Arts	M
Atmospheric Sciences	M,D
Biological and Biomedical Sciences—General	M,D
Biostatistics	M,D
Business Administration and Management—General	M
Cell Biology	M,D
Chemistry	M,D
Clinical Psychology	M,D
Cognitive Sciences	M,D
Communication—General	M,D
Computer and Information Systems Security	M
Computer Science	M,D
Conservation Biology	M
Counseling Psychology	M,D
Criminal Justice and Criminology	M,D
Curriculum and Instruction	M,D,O
Demography and Population Studies	M,D,O
Developmental Biology	D
Ecology	D
Economics	M,D,O
Education—General	M,D,O
Educational Leadership and Administration	M,D,O
Educational Measurement and Evaluation	M,D,O
Educational Media/Instructional Technology	M,D,O
Educational Psychology	M,D,O
English	M,D
Entrepreneurship	M
Environmental and Occupational Health	M,D
Environmental Management and Policy	M
Environmental Sciences	M
Epidemiology	M,D
Evolutionary Biology	D
Finance and Banking	M,D,O
Forensic Sciences	M,D
Geography	M
Health Services Management and Hospital Administration	M,D,O
History	M,D,O
Homeland Security	M,D,O
Human Resources Management	M,D,O
Immunology	M,D
Industrial and Organizational Psychology	M,D
Information Science	M,D,O
Information Studies	M,O
Latin American Studies	M,D,O
Liberal Studies	M
Library Science	M,O
Management Information Systems	M,D,O
Management of Technology	M
Marketing	M
Mathematics	M,D
Molecular Biology	D
Neurobiology	D
Neuroscience	M,D
Nonprofit Management	M,D,O
Organizational Behavior	M,D,O
Philosophy	M,D
Physics	M,D
Political Science	M,D
Psychology—General	M,D
Public Administration	M,D,O
Public Health—General	M,D
Public History	M,D,O
Public Policy	M,D,O
Reading Education	M,D,O
School Psychology	M,D,O
Social Psychology	M,D
Social Work	M,D
Sociology	M,D,O
Spanish	M,D
Special Education	M,D
Structural Biology	M,D
Taxation	M
Toxicology	M,D
Urban and Regional Planning	M
Urban Studies	M,D,O
Women's Studies	M

UNIVERSITY AT BUFFALO, THE STATE UNIVERSITY OF NEW YORK

Accounting	M,D
Adult Nursing	M,D,O
Aerospace/Aeronautical Engineering	M,D
Allied Health—General	M,D,O
Allopathic Medicine	D
American Studies	M,D,O
Anatomy	M,D
Anthropology	M,D
Architecture	M
Art History	M
Art/Fine Arts	M,D
Arts Administration	M
Biochemistry	M,D
Bioengineering	M,D
Bioinformatics	M,D
Biological and Biomedical Sciences—General	M,D
Biomedical Engineering	M,D
Biophysics	M,D
Biostatistics	M,D
Biotechnology	M
Business Administration and Management—General	M,D
Canadian Studies	M,D,O
Cancer Biology/Oncology	M
Cell Biology	D
Chemical Engineering	M,D
Chemistry	M,D
Civil Engineering	M,D
Classics	M,D,O
Clinical Laboratory Sciences/Medical Technology	M
Communication Disorders	M,D
Communication—General	M,D
Community Health	M,D
Comparative Literature	M,D
Computational Sciences	O
Computer Science	M,D,O
Counseling Psychology	M,D,O
Counselor Education	M,D,O
Cultural Studies	M
Curriculum and Instruction	M,D,O
Dentistry	D
Early Childhood Education	M,D,O
Ecology	M,D,O
Economics	M,D,O
Education of the Gifted	M,D,O
Education—General	M,D,O
Educational Leadership and Administration	M,D,O
Educational Media/Instructional Technology	M,D,O
Educational Psychology	M,D,O
Electrical Engineering	M,D*
Electronic Commerce	M,D,O
Elementary Education	M,D,O
Engineering and Applied Sciences—General	M,D,O*
English as a Second Language	M,D,O
English Education	M,D,O
English	M,D
Environmental Engineering	M,D
Environmental Sciences	M,D,O
Epidemiology	M,D
Evolutionary Biology	M,D,O
Exercise and Sports Science	M,D,O
Family Nurse Practitioner Studies	M,D,O
Film, Television, and Video Theory and Criticism	M,D,O
Finance and Banking	M,D
Foreign Languages Education	M,D,O
Foundations and Philosophy of Education	M,D,O
French	M,D,O
Gender Studies	M,D,O
Genetics	M,D
Genomic Sciences	M,D
Geographic Information Systems	M,D,O
Geography	M,D,O
Geology	M,D
Geosciences	M,D,O
German	M,D,O
Gerontological Nursing	M,D,O
Health Services Management and Hospital Administration	M,D,O
Higher Education	M,D,O
Historic Preservation	M,D,O
History	M,D
Human Resources Management	M,D,O
Immunology	M,D
Industrial/Management Engineering	M,D
Information Studies	M,O
International Business	M,D,O
Latin American Studies	M
Law	M,D
Library Science	M,O
Linguistics	M,D
Logistics	M,D
Management Information Systems	M,D,O
Mathematics Education	M,D,O
Mathematics	M,D
Mechanical Engineering	M,D
Media Studies	M,D,O
Medical Physics	M,D
Medicinal and Pharmaceutical Chemistry	M,D
Microbiology	M,D
Modeling and Simulation	M,D,O
Molecular Biology	D
Molecular Biophysics	M,D
Molecular Pharmacology	D
Multilingual and Multicultural Education	M,D,O
Music Education	M,D,O
Music	M,D,O
Neuroscience	M,D
Nurse Anesthesia	M,D,O
Nursing and Healthcare Administration	M,D,O
Nursing—General	M,D,O
Nutrition	M,D,O
Occupational Therapy	M
Oral and Dental Sciences	M,D,O
Pathology	M,D
Pharmaceutical Sciences	M,D
Pharmacology	M,D
Pharmacy	D
Philosophy	M,D
Physical Therapy	D
Physics	M,D
Physiology	M,D
Political Science	M,D
Psychiatric Nursing	M,D,O
Psychology—General	M,D
Public Health—General	M,D
Public History	M,D
Quantitative Analysis	M,D
Reading Education	M,D,O
Real Estate	M
Rehabilitation Counseling	M,D,O
Rehabilitation Sciences	M,D,O
Romance Languages	M,D
Science Education	M,D,O
Social Sciences Education	M,D,O
Social Work	M,D
Sociology	M,D
Spanish	M,D,O
Special Education	M,D,O
Structural Biology	M,D
Structural Engineering	M,D
Theater	M,D
Toxicology	M,D
Urban and Regional Planning	M,D,O
Urban Design	M,D,O

UNIVERSITY OF ADVANCING TECHNOLOGY

Computer and Information Systems Security	M
Computer Science	M
Game Design and Development	M
Internet and Interactive Multimedia	M
Management of Technology	M

THE UNIVERSITY OF AKRON

Accounting	M
Applied Mathematics	M
Arts Administration	M
Biological and Biomedical Sciences—General	M,D
Biomedical Engineering	M,D
Business Administration and Management—General	M
Chemical Engineering	M,D
Chemistry	M,D
Child and Family Studies	M,D
Child Development	M
Civil Engineering	M,D
Clinical Psychology	M
Clothing and Textiles	M
Communication Disorders	M,D
Communication—General	M
Computer Engineering	M,D
Computer Science	M
Counseling Psychology	M,D
Counselor Education	M,D
Curriculum and Instruction	M
Economics	M
Education—General	M
Educational Leadership and Administration	M
Educational Measurement and Evaluation	M,O
Educational Media/Instructional Technology	M
Electrical Engineering	M,D
Electronic Commerce	M
Elementary Education	M
Engineering and Applied Sciences—General	M,D
English	M
Exercise and Sports Science	M
Finance and Banking	M
Geological Engineering	M
Geology	M
Geophysics	M
Geosciences	M
Gerontology	D
Health Services Management and Hospital Administration	M
Higher Education	M
History	M,D
Industrial and Organizational Psychology	M,D
International Business	M
Law	M,D
Management Information Systems	M
Management of Technology	M
Marketing	M
Marriage and Family Therapy	M
Mathematics	M
Mechanical Engineering	M,D
Music Education	M
Music	M
Nursing—General	M,D
Physical Education	M
Physics	M
Political Science	M
Polymer Science and Engineering	M,D
Psychology—General	M,D
Public Administration	M
Public Health—General	M,D
Reading Education	M
School Psychology	M,D
Social Work	M
Sociology	M,D
Spanish	M
Special Education	M
Supply Chain Management	M
Taxation	M
Theater	M
Writing	M

THE UNIVERSITY OF ALABAMA

Accounting	M,D
Advertising and Public Relations	M
Aerospace/Aeronautical Engineering	M,D
American Studies	M
Anthropology	M,D
Applied Mathematics	M,D
Applied Statistics	M,D
Art History	M
Art/Fine Arts	M
Biological and Biomedical Sciences—General	M,D
Business Administration and Management—General	M,D
Chemical Engineering	M,D
Chemistry	M,D
Child and Family Studies	M
Civil Engineering	M,D
Clinical Psychology	D
Clothing and Textiles	M
Communication Disorders	M
Communication—General	M,D
Community Health	M
Computer Engineering	M,D
Computer Science	M,D
Construction Engineering	M,D
Consumer Economics	M
Counselor Education	M,D,O
Criminal Justice and Criminology	M
Economics	M,D
Education of the Gifted	M,D,O
Educational Leadership and Administration	M,D,O
Electrical Engineering	M,D
Elementary Education	M,D,O
Engineering and Applied Sciences—General	M,D
English as a Second Language	M,D
English	M,D
Environmental Engineering	M,D
Ergonomics and Human Factors	M
Exercise and Sports Science	M,D
Experimental Psychology	D
Family and Consumer Sciences-General	M,D
Film, Television, and Video Production	M
Finance and Banking	M,D
French	M,D
Geographic Information Systems	M
Geography	M
Geology	M,D
Geosciences	M
German	M,D
Health Education	M,D
Health Promotion	M,D
Higher Education	M,D
History	M,D

Hospitality Management	M
Human Development	M
Industrial and Manufacturing Management	M,D
Information Studies	M,D
Interdisciplinary Studies	D
Journalism	M
Kinesiology and Movement Studies	M,D
Law	M,D
Library Science	M,D
Marketing	M,D
Marriage and Family Therapy	M
Mass Communication	D
Materials Engineering	M,D
Materials Sciences	D
Mathematics	M,D
Mechanical Engineering	M,D
Mechanics	M,D
Media Studies	M
Metallurgical Engineering and Metallurgy	M,D
Music Education	M,D,O
Music	M,D
Nursing—General	M,D
Nutrition	M
Photography	M
Physical Education	M,D
Physics	M,D
Political Science	M,D
Psychology—General	D
Public Administration	M,D
Quality Management	M
Rhetoric	M,D
Romance Languages	M,D
Secondary Education	M,D,O
Social Work	M,D
Spanish	M,D
Special Education	M,D,O
Speech and Interpersonal Communication	M
Sports Management	M
Taxation	M,D
Theater	M
Urban and Regional Planning	M
Women's Studies	M
Writing	M,D

THE UNIVERSITY OF ALABAMA AT BIRMINGHAM

Accounting	M
Allied Health—General	M,D,O
Allopathic Medicine	D
Anthropology	M
Applied Mathematics	D
Art Education	M
Art History	M
Biochemistry	D
Bioinformatics	D
Biological and Biomedical Sciences—General	M,D
Biomedical Engineering	M,D
Biostatistics	M,D
Biotechnology	M
Business Administration and Management—General	M
Cancer Biology/Oncology	D
Cell Biology	D
Chemistry	M,D
Civil Engineering	M,D
Clinical Laboratory Sciences/Medical Technology	M,D
Clinical Psychology	M,D
Communication—General	M
Community Health	M
Computational Sciences	D
Computer and Information Systems Security	M
Computer Engineering	D
Computer Science	M,D
Construction Engineering	M
Counselor Education	M
Criminal Justice and Criminology	M
Curriculum and Instruction	O
Dentistry	D
Developmental Biology	D
Developmental Psychology	M,D
Early Childhood Education	M,D
Education—General	M,D,O
Educational Leadership and Administration	M,D,O
Electrical Engineering	M
Elementary Education	M
Engineering and Applied Sciences—General	M,D
Engineering Design	M
Engineering Management	M,D
English as a Second Language	M,O
English	M
Environmental and Occupational Health	M,D
Environmental Engineering	D
Epidemiology	M,D
Finance and Banking	M
Forensic Sciences	M
Genetic Counseling	M
Genetics	D
Genomic Sciences	D
Health Education	D
Health Informatics	M
Health Promotion	D
Health Psychology	M,D
Health Services Management and Hospital Administration	M,D
Health Services Research	M,D
History	M
Industrial Hygiene	M,D
Information Science	M,D
Interdisciplinary Studies	D
Management Information Systems	M
Marketing	M
Materials Engineering	M,D
Maternal and Child Health	M,D
Mathematics	M
Mechanical Engineering	M
Microbiology	D
Molecular Biology	D
Molecular Medicine	D
Music	M
Neurobiology	D
Neuroscience	M,D
Nurse Anesthesia	M,D
Nursing—General	M,D
Nutrition	M,D
Occupational Therapy	M,O
Optometry	D
Oral and Dental Sciences	M
Pathobiology	D
Pharmacology	D
Physical Therapy	D
Physician Assistant Studies	M
Physics	M,D
Psychology—General	M,D
Public Administration	M
Public Health—General	M,D
Quantitative Analysis	M,D
Reading Education	M
Rehabilitation Sciences	D
Rhetoric	M
Safety Engineering	M
Secondary Education	M
Sociology	D
Special Education	M
Structural Biology	D
Toxicology	M,D
Vision Sciences	M,D
Writing	M

THE UNIVERSITY OF ALABAMA IN HUNTSVILLE

Accounting	M,O
Acute Care/Critical Care Nursing	M,D,O
Aerospace/Aeronautical Engineering	M,D
Applied Mathematics	M,D
Atmospheric Sciences	M,D
Biological and Biomedical Sciences—General	M,D
Biotechnology	M,D
Business Administration and Management—General	M,O
Chemical Engineering	M,D
Chemistry	M,D
Civil Engineering	M,D
Computer and Information Systems Security	M,D,O
Computer Engineering	M,D
Computer Science	M,D,O
Electrical Engineering	M,D
Engineering and Applied Sciences—General	M,D
English as a Second Language	M,O
English Education	M,O
English	M,O
Entrepreneurship	M,O
Environmental Engineering	M,D
Environmental Sciences	M,D
Family Nurse Practitioner Studies	M,D,O
Finance and Banking	M,O
Gerontological Nursing	M,D,O
Health Services Management and Hospital Administration	M,D,O
History	M
Human Resources Management	M,O
Industrial and Organizational Psychology	M
Industrial/Management Engineering	M,D
Logistics	M,O
Management Information Systems	M,O
Management of Technology	M,O
Marketing	M,O
Materials Sciences	M,D
Mathematics Education	M,D
Mathematics	M,D
Mechanical Engineering	M,D
Modeling and Simulation	M,D,O
Nursing Education	M,D,O
Nursing—General	M,D,O
Operations Research	M,D
Optical Sciences	M,D
Photonics	M,D
Physics	M,D
Project Management	M,O
Psychology—General	M
Public Affairs	M
Science Education	M,D
Software Engineering	M,D,O
Supply Chain Management	M,O
Systems Engineering	M,D
Taxation	M
Technical Writing	M,O

UNIVERSITY OF ALASKA ANCHORAGE

Anthropology	M
Biological and Biomedical Sciences—General	M
Business Administration and Management—General	M
Civil Engineering	M,O
Clinical Psychology	M,D
Counselor Education	M
Early Childhood Education	M,O
Education—General	M,O
Educational Leadership and Administration	M,O
Engineering and Applied Sciences—General	M,O
Engineering Management	M
English	M
Environmental Engineering	M
Environmental Sciences	M
Geological Engineering	M
Interdisciplinary Studies	M
Logistics	M,O
Nursing—General	M
Ocean Engineering	M,O
Project Management	M
Psychology—General	M,D
Public Administration	M
Public Health—General	M
Social Psychology	M,D
Social Work	M,O
Special Education	M,O
Writing	M

UNIVERSITY OF ALASKA FAIRBANKS

Anthropology	M,D
Art/Fine Arts	M
Astrophysics	M,D
Atmospheric Sciences	M,D
Biochemistry	M,D
Business Administration and Management—General	M
Chemistry	M,D
Civil Engineering	M,D,O
Clinical Psychology	D
Communication—General	M
Computational Sciences	M,D
Computer Art and Design	M
Computer Science	M
Construction Management	M,D,O
Corporate and Organizational Communication	M
Counselor Education	M,O
Criminal Justice and Criminology	M
Cultural Studies	M
Economics	M
Education—General	M,O
Electrical Engineering	M
Elementary Education	M
Emergency Management	M
Engineering and Applied Sciences—General	D
Engineering Management	M
English	M
Environmental Engineering	M,D
Environmental Management and Policy	M
Environmental Sciences	M
Finance and Banking	M
Geographic Information Systems	M,D
Geological Engineering	M
Geology	M,D
Geophysics	M,D
Hazardous Materials Management	M,D,O
History	M
Homeland Security	M
Interdisciplinary Studies	M,D
Limnology	M,D
Linguistics	M
Marine Biology	M,D
Marine Sciences	M,D
Mathematics	M,D,O
Mechanical Engineering	M
Mineral/Mining Engineering	M
Multilingual and Multicultural Education	M
Music	M
Natural Resources	M,D
Neuroscience	M,D
Northern Studies	M
Oceanography	M,D
Petroleum Engineering	M
Photography	M
Physics	M,D
Psychology—General	D
Rural Planning and Studies	M
Secondary Education	M
Social Psychology	M,D,O
Special Education	M
Statistics	M,D,O
Sustainable Development	M,D
Water Resources	M,D,O
Writing	M

UNIVERSITY OF ALASKA SOUTHEAST

Business Administration and Management—General	M
Early Childhood Education	M
Education—General	M
Educational Media/Instructional Technology	M
Elementary Education	M
Public Administration	M
Secondary Education	M

UNIVERSITY OF ALBERTA

Accounting	D
Adult Education	M,D,O
Agricultural Economics and Agribusiness	M,D
Agricultural Sciences—General	M,D
Agronomy and Soil Sciences	M,D
Anthropology	M,D
Applied Arts and Design—General	M
Applied Mathematics	M,D,O
Archaeology	M,D
Art History	M
Art/Fine Arts	M
Asian Studies	M
Astrophysics	M,D
Biochemistry	M,D
Biological and Biomedical Sciences—General	M,D
Biomedical Engineering	M,D
Biostatistics	M,D,O
Biotechnology	M,D
Business Administration and Management—General	M,D
Cancer Biology/Oncology	M,D
Cell Biology	M,D
Chemical Engineering	M,D
Chemistry	M,D
Chinese	M
Civil Engineering	M,D
Classics	M,D
Clinical Laboratory Sciences/Medical Technology	M,D
Clothing and Textiles	M,D
Communication Disorders	M,D
Communication—General	M
Community Health	M,D
Computer Engineering	M,D
Computer Science	M,D
Condensed Matter Physics	M,D
Conservation Biology	M,D
Construction Engineering	M,D
Counseling Psychology	M,D
Counselor Education	M,D
Criminal Justice and Criminology	M,D
Demography and Population Studies	M,D
Dental Hygiene	O
Dentistry	D
East European and Russian Studies	M,D
Ecology	M,D
Economics	M,D
Educational Leadership and Administration	M,D,O
Educational Media/Instructional Technology	M,D
Educational Policy	M,D,O
Educational Psychology	M,D
Electrical Engineering	M,D
Elementary Education	M,D
Energy and Power Engineering	M,D
Engineering Management	M,D
English as a Second Language	M,D
English	M,D
Environmental and Occupational Health	M,D
Environmental Biology	M,D
Environmental Engineering	M,D
Environmental Management and Policy	M,D
Environmental Sciences	M,D
Epidemiology	M,D
Evolutionary Biology	M,D
Exercise and Sports Science	M,D
Family and Consumer Sciences-General	M,D
Finance and Banking	M,D
Folklore	M,D
Forestry	M,D
French	M,D
Genetics	M,D
Geophysics	M,D
Geosciences	M,D
Geotechnical Engineering	M,D
German	M,D
Health Physics/Radiological Health	M,D
Health Promotion	M,O
Health Services Management and Hospital Administration	M,D
Health Services Research	M,D
Hispanic Studies	M,D
History	M,D
Immunology	M,D
Industrial and Labor Relations	D
Information Studies	M
International Business	M
International Health	M,D
Italian	M,D
Japanese	M
Law	M,D
Library Science	M
Linguistics	M,D
Marketing	D
Materials Engineering	M,D
Maternal and Child/Neonatal Nursing	D
Mathematical and Computational Finance	M,D,O
Mathematical Physics	M,D,O
Mathematics	M,D,O
Mechanical Engineering	M,D
Medical Microbiology	M,D
Medical Physics	M,D
Microbiology	M,D
Mineral/Mining Engineering	M,D
Molecular Biology	M,D
Multilingual and Multicultural Education	M
Music	M,D
Nanotechnology	M,D
Natural Resources	M,D
Neuroscience	M,D
Nursing—General	M,D
Occupational Therapy	M,D
Oral and Dental Sciences	M,D
Organizational Management	D
Pathology	M,D
Petroleum Engineering	M,D
Pharmaceutical Sciences	M,D
Pharmacology	M,D
Pharmacy	M,D
Philosophy	M,D
Physical Education	M,D
Physical Therapy	M,D
Physics	M,D
Physiology	M,D
Plant Biology	M,D
Political Science	M,D
Psychology—General	M,D
Public Health—General	M,D
Recreation and Park Management	M,D
Rehabilitation Sciences	D
Rural Sociology	M,D
School Psychology	M,D
Secondary Education	M,D
Slavic Languages	M,D
Sociology	M,D

*M—masters degree; D—doctorate; O—other advanced degree; *—Close-Up and/or Display*

Special Education	M,D
Sports Management	M
Statistics	M,D,O
Structural Engineering	M,D
Systems Engineering	M,D
Telecommunications	M,D
Theater	M
Vision Sciences	M,D
Water Resources Engineering	M,D

UNIVERSITY OF ANTELOPE VALLEY

Business Administration and Management—General	M
Criminal Justice and Criminology	M

THE UNIVERSITY OF ARIZONA

Accounting	M
Aerospace/Aeronautical Engineering	M,D
African Studies	M,D,O
Agricultural Economics and Agribusiness	M
Agricultural Education	M,O
Agricultural Engineering	M,D
Agricultural Sciences—General	M,D,O
Agronomy and Soil Sciences	M,D,O
Allopathic Medicine	M,D
American Indian/Native American Studies	M,D
Animal Sciences	M,D
Anthropology	M,D,O
Applied Mathematics	M,D
Architecture	M,D,O
Art Education	M,D
Art History	M,D
Art/Fine Arts	M
Asian Studies	M,D
Astronomy	D
Atmospheric Sciences	M,D
Biochemistry	M,D
Biological and Biomedical Sciences—General	M,D
Biomedical Engineering	M,D
Biostatistics	M,D
Biosystems Engineering	M,D
Business Administration and Management—General	M,D,O
Cancer Biology/Oncology	D
Cell Biology	M,D,O
Chemical Engineering	M,D
Chemistry	M,D
Child and Family Studies	M,D,O
Classics	M
Communication Disorders	M,D,O
Communication—General	M,D
Computer Engineering	M,D
Computer Science	M,D
Counseling Psychology	M
Counselor Education	M
Dance	M
Ecology	M,D
Economics	M,D
Education—General	M,D,O
Educational Leadership and Administration	M,D,O
Educational Psychology	M,D,O
Electrical Engineering	M,D
Elementary Education	M,D
Engineering and Applied Sciences—General	M,D,O
Engineering Management	M,D,O
English as a Second Language	M,D
English Education	M,D
English	M,D
Entomology	M,D
Environmental Engineering	M,D
Environmental Management and Policy	M,D
Environmental Sciences	M,D,O
Epidemiology	M,D
Evolutionary Biology	M,D
Family and Consumer Sciences-General	D
Family Nurse Practitioner Studies	M,D,O
Film, Television, and Video Theory and Criticism	M
Finance and Banking	M
Forestry	M,D
French	M
Gender Studies	M,D,O
Genetics	M,D
Geographic Information Systems	M,D,O
Geography	M,D,O
Geological Engineering	M,D,O
Geosciences	M,D
German	M,D
Higher Education	M,D
History	M,D,O
Human Development	M,D,O
Hydrology	D,O
Immunology	D
Industrial/Management Engineering	M,D,O
Information Studies	M,D
Interdisciplinary Studies	M,D
Italian	M
Journalism	M
Landscape Architecture	M,D,O
Latin American Studies	M
Law	M,D
Library Science	M,D
Linguistics	M,D
Management Information Systems	M,O
Management Strategy and Policy	M,D
Marketing	M,D
Materials Engineering	M,D
Materials Sciences	M,D
Mathematics Education	M
Mathematics	M,D
Mechanical Engineering	M,D
Medical Informatics	M,D,O
Medical Physics	M
Microbiology	D
Mineral/Mining Engineering	M,D,O
Molecular Biology	M,D,O
Molecular Medicine	M,D
Music Education	M,D
Music	M,D
Near and Middle Eastern Studies	M,D,O
Neuroscience	D
Nursing—General	M,D,O
Nutrition	M,D
Optical Sciences	M,D,O
Organizational Management	M,D
Perfusion	M,D
Pharmaceutical Sciences	M,D
Pharmacology	M,D
Pharmacy	D
Philosophy	M,D
Physics	M,D
Physiology	M,D
Planetary and Space Sciences	M,D
Plant Pathology	M,D
Political Science	M,D
Public Administration	M,D,O
Public Health—General	M,D
Public Policy	M,D,O
Range Science	M,D
Reading Education	M,D,O
Rehabilitation Counseling	M,D
Rhetoric	M,D
Russian	M
School Psychology	D,O
Secondary Education	M,D
Sociology	M,D
Spanish	M,D
Special Education	M,D
Statistics	M,D
Systems Engineering	M,D,O
Theater	M
Urban and Regional Planning	M
Water Resources	M,D,O
Women's Studies	M,D,O
Writing	M

UNIVERSITY OF ARKANSAS

Accounting	M
Adult Education	M,D
Agricultural Economics and Agribusiness	M
Agricultural Education	M
Agricultural Engineering	M,D
Agricultural Sciences—General	M,D
Agronomy and Soil Sciences	M,D
Animal Sciences	M,D
Anthropology	M,D
Applied Physics	M,D
Art/Fine Arts	M
Athletic Training and Sports Medicine	M
Bioengineering	M
Biological and Biomedical Sciences—General	M,D
Biomedical Engineering	M
Business Administration and Management—General	M,D
Cell Biology	M,D
Chemical Engineering	M,D
Chemistry	M,D
Civil Engineering	M,D
Communication Disorders	M
Communication—General	M,D
Community Health	M,D
Comparative Literature	M,D
Computer Engineering	M,D
Computer Science	M,D
Counselor Education	M,D,O
Curriculum and Instruction	M,D,O
Early Childhood Education	M
Economics	M,D
Education—General	M,D,O
Educational Leadership and Administration	M,D,O
Educational Measurement and Evaluation	M,D
Educational Media/Instructional Technology	M
Educational Policy	D
Electrical Engineering	M,D
Electronic Materials	M,D
Engineering and Applied Sciences—General	M,D
English	M,D
Entomology	M,D
Environmental Engineering	M
Family and Consumer Sciences-General	M
Food Science and Technology	M,D
French	M
Geography	M
Geology	M
German	M
Health Education	M,D
Health Promotion	M,D
Higher Education	M,D,O
History	M,D
Horticulture	M
Human Resources Development	M,D,O
Industrial and Manufacturing Management	M
Industrial/Management Engineering	M,D
Interdisciplinary Studies	M,D
Journalism	M
Kinesiology and Movement Studies	M,D
Law	M,D
Management Information Systems	M
Mathematics Education	M
Mathematics	M,D
Mechanical Engineering	M,D
Middle School Education	M,D,O
Molecular Biology	M,D
Music	M
Nursing—General	M
Operations Research	M,D
Philosophy	M,D
Photonics	M,D
Physical Education	M
Physics	M,D
Planetary and Space Sciences	M,D
Plant Pathology	M
Plant Sciences	D
Political Science	M
Psychology—General	M,D
Public Administration	M
Public Policy	D
Recreation and Park Management	M,D
Rehabilitation Counseling	M,D
Secondary Education	M,O
Social Work	M
Sociology	M
Spanish	M
Special Education	M
Sports Management	M,D
Statistics	M
Telecommunications	M,D
Theater	M
Transportation and Highway Engineering	M,D
Vocational and Technical Education	M,D,O
Writing	M

UNIVERSITY OF ARKANSAS AT LITTLE ROCK

Adult Education	M
Applied Mathematics	M,O
Applied Psychology	M
Applied Science and Technology	M,D
Applied Statistics	M,O
Art Education	M
Art History	M
Art/Fine Arts	M
Bioinformatics	M,D
Biological and Biomedical Sciences—General	M
Business Administration and Management—General	M,O
Chemistry	M
Community College Education	M,D
Computer Science	M,D
Conflict Resolution and Mediation/Peace Studies	O
Construction Management	M
Counselor Education	M
Criminal Justice and Criminology	M,D
Curriculum and Instruction	M
Education of the Gifted	M,O
Education—General	M,D,O
Educational Leadership and Administration	M,D,O
Educational Media/Instructional Technology	M
English as a Second Language	M
Entrepreneurship	O
Exercise and Sports Science	M
Foreign Languages Education	M
Geosciences	O
Gerontology	O
Health Education	M,D
Higher Education	M,D
Information Science	M,D,O
Interdisciplinary Studies	M
Law	D
Management Information Systems	M,O
Mass Communication	M
Mathematics	M,O
Middle School Education	M
Nonprofit Management	O
Psychology—General	M
Public Administration	M
Public Affairs	M,O
Public History	M
Reading Education	M,D,O
Rehabilitation Counseling	M,O
Rhetoric	M
Secondary Education	M
Social Work	M
Special Education	M,O
Speech and Interpersonal Communication	M
Sports Management	M
Student Affairs	M,D
Systems Engineering	M,D,O
Technical Writing	M
Writing	M

UNIVERSITY OF ARKANSAS AT MONTICELLO

Education—General	M
Educational Leadership and Administration	M
Forestry	M
Natural Resources	M

UNIVERSITY OF ARKANSAS AT PINE BLUFF

Addictions/Substance Abuse Counseling	M
Aquaculture	M
Early Childhood Education	M
Education—General	M
English Education	M
Fish, Game, and Wildlife Management	M
Mathematics Education	M
Physical Education	M
Science Education	M
Secondary Education	M
Social Sciences Education	M

UNIVERSITY OF ARKANSAS FOR MEDICAL SCIENCES

Allopathic Medicine	D
Biochemistry	M,D,O
Bioinformatics	M,D,O
Biological and Biomedical Sciences—General	M,D,O
Biostatistics	M,D,O
Communication Disorders	M,D
Environmental and Occupational Health	M,D,O
Epidemiology	M,D,O
Genetic Counseling	M,D
Health Education	M,D,O
Health Physics/Radiological Health	M,D
Health Promotion	M,D,O
Health Services Management and Hospital Administration	M,D,O
Health Services Research	M,D,O
Immunology	M,D,O
Microbiology	M,D,O
Molecular Biology	M,D,O
Molecular Biophysics	M,D,O
Neurobiology	M,D,O
Nursing—General	D
Nutrition	M,D,O
Pharmacology	M,D,O
Pharmacy	M,D
Physician Assistant Studies	M,D
Physiology	M,D,O
Public Health—General	M,D,O
Toxicology	M,D,O

UNIVERSITY OF BALTIMORE

Accounting	M,O
Applied Arts and Design—General	M
Applied Psychology	M
Business Administration and Management—General	M,O
Conflict Resolution and Mediation/Peace Studies	M
Counseling Psychology	M
Criminal Justice and Criminology	M
Entrepreneurship	M
Ethics	M
Finance and Banking	M
Graphic Design	M,D
Health Services Management and Hospital Administration	M
Human Services	M
Human-Computer Interaction	M
International Business	M
Law	M,D
Legal and Justice Studies	M
Management Information Systems	M,O
Marketing	M
Public Administration	M,D
Public Affairs	M,D
Publishing	M
Taxation	M,D
Writing	M

UNIVERSITY OF BRIDGEPORT

Accounting	M
Acupuncture and Oriental Medicine	M
Applied Arts and Design—General	M
Asian Studies	M
Biomedical Engineering	M
Business Administration and Management—General	M
Chiropractic	D
Clinical Psychology	M
Communication—General	M
Computer Education	M,D,O
Computer Engineering	M,D
Computer Science	M,D
Conflict Resolution and Mediation/Peace Studies	M
Counseling Psychology	M
Dental Hygiene	M
Early Childhood Education	M,D,O
Education—General	M,D,O
Educational Leadership and Administration	M,D,O
Electrical Engineering	M
Elementary Education	M,D,O
Engineering and Applied Sciences—General	M,D
Entrepreneurship	M
Finance and Banking	M
Human Resources Development	M
Human Resources Management	M
Human Services	M
Industrial and Manufacturing Management	M
International Affairs	M
International and Comparative Education	M,D,O
International Business	M
Management Information Systems	M
Management of Technology	M,D
Marketing	M
Mechanical Engineering	M
Media Studies	M
Middle School Education	M,D,O
Music Education	M,D,O
Naturopathic Medicine	D
Nutrition	M
Physician Assistant Studies	M
Reading Education	M,D,O
Secondary Education	M,D,O
Social Psychology	M
Student Affairs	M

THE UNIVERSITY OF BRITISH COLUMBIA

Accounting	D
Adult Education	M,D
Agricultural Economics and Agribusiness	M
Agricultural Sciences—General	M,D
Agronomy and Soil Sciences	M,D
Allopathic Medicine	M,D
Animal Sciences	M,D
Anthropology	M,D
Applied Mathematics	M,D
Archaeology	M,D
Architecture	M
Archives/Archival Administration	M,D
Art Education	M,D

Art History	M,D,O
Art/Fine Arts	M,D,O
Asian Studies	M,D
Astronomy	M,D
Atmospheric Sciences	M,D
Biochemistry	M,D
Biopsychology	M,D
Botany	M,D
Business Administration and Management—General	M,D
Business Education	M,D
Cell Biology	M,D
Chemical Engineering	M,D
Chemistry	M,D
Civil Engineering	M,D
Classics	M,D
Clinical Psychology	M,D
Cognitive Sciences	M,D
Communication Disorders	M,D
Computer Engineering	M,D
Computer Science	M,D
Counseling Psychology	M,D,O
Curriculum and Instruction	M,D
Dentistry	D
Developmental Biology	M,D
Developmental Psychology	M,D
Early Childhood Education	M,D
East European and Russian Studies	M,D
Economics	M,D
Education—General	M,D,O
Educational Leadership and Administration	M,D
Educational Measurement and Evaluation	M,D,O
Educational Policy	M,D
Electrical Engineering	M,D
Engineering and Applied Sciences—General	M,D
English as a Second Language	M,D
English	M,D
Environmental and Occupational Health	M,D
Epidemiology	M,D
Film, Television, and Video Production	M,O
Film, Television, and Video Theory and Criticism	M,O
Finance and Banking	D
Food Science and Technology	M,D
Forestry	M,D
Foundations and Philosophy of Education	M,D
French	M,D
Gender Studies	M,D
Genetic Counseling	M
Genetics	M,D
Geography	M,D
Geological Engineering	M,D
Geology	M,D
Geophysics	M,D
German	M,D
Health Psychology	M,D
Health Services Management and Hospital Administration	M,D
Higher Education	M,D
Hispanic Studies	M,D
History	M,D
Home Economics Education	M,D
Human Development	M,D,O
Immunology	M,D
Information Studies	M,D
International Affairs	M
Journalism	M
Kinesiology and Movement Studies	M,D
Landscape Architecture	M
Law	M,D
Library Science	M,D
Linguistics	M,D
Management Information Systems	D
Management Strategy and Policy	D
Marine Sciences	M,D
Marketing	D
Materials Engineering	M,D
Materials Sciences	M,D
Mathematics Education	M,D
Mathematics	M,D
Mechanical Engineering	M,D
Metallurgical Engineering and Metallurgy	M,D
Microbiology	M,D
Mineral/Mining Engineering	M,D
Molecular Biology	M,D
Museum Studies	M,D,O
Music Education	M,D
Music	M,D
Natural Resources	M,D
Neuroscience	M,D
Nurse Anesthesia	M,D
Nursing—General	M,D
Nutrition	M,D
Occupational Therapy	M
Oceanography	M,D
Operations Research	M
Oral and Dental Sciences	M,D,O
Organizational Behavior	D
Pathology	M,D
Pharmaceutical Sciences	M,D
Pharmacology	M,D
Pharmacy	M,D
Philosophy	M,D
Physical Education	M,D
Physics	M,D
Plant Sciences	M,D
Political Science	M,D
Psychology—General	M,D
Public Health—General	M,D
Quantitative Analysis	M,D
Reading Education	M,D
Rehabilitation Sciences	M,D
Religion	M,D
Reproductive Biology	M,D
School Psychology	M,D,O
Science Education	M,D
Social Psychology	M,D
Social Sciences Education	M,D
Social Work	M,D
Sociology	M,D
Software Engineering	M
Special Education	M,D,O
Statistics	M,D
Theater	M,D
Transportation Management	D
Urban and Regional Planning	M,D
Vocational and Technical Education	M,D
Water Resources	M,D
Writing	M,O
Zoology	M,D

UNIVERSITY OF CALGARY

Adult Education	M,D
Allopathic Medicine	D
Analytical Chemistry	M,D
Anthropology	M,D
Applied Psychology	M,D
Archaeology	M
Architecture	M,D
Art/Fine Arts	M
Astronomy	M,D
Biochemistry	M,D
Biological and Biomedical Sciences—General	M,D
Biomedical Engineering	M,D
Biotechnology	M
Business Administration and Management—General	M,D
Cancer Biology/Oncology	M,D
Cardiovascular Sciences	M,D
Chemical Engineering	M,D
Chemistry	M,D
Civil Engineering	M,D
Classics	M,D
Clinical Psychology	M,D
Communication—General	M,D
Community Health	M,D
Computer Engineering	M,D
Computer Science	M,D
Counseling Psychology	M,D
Curriculum and Instruction	M,D
Economics	M,D
Educational Leadership and Administration	M,D
Educational Measurement and Evaluation	M,D
Electrical Engineering	M,D
Energy and Power Engineering	M,D
Energy Management and Policy	M,D
Engineering and Applied Sciences—General	M,D
English	M,D
Environmental Design	M,D
Environmental Engineering	M,D
Environmental Law	M,O
Environmental Management and Policy	M,D,O
French	M,D
Genetics	M,D
Geography	M,D
Geology	M,D
Geophysics	M,D
Geosciences	M,D
Geotechnical Engineering	M,D
German	M,D
History	M,D
Hydrology	M,D
Immunology	M,D
Infectious Diseases	M,D
Inorganic Chemistry	M,D
Kinesiology and Movement Studies	M,D
Law	M,D,O
Legal and Justice Studies	M,O
Linguistics	M,D
Management Strategy and Policy	M,D
Manufacturing Engineering	M,D
Materials Sciences	M,D
Mathematics	M,D
Mechanical Engineering	M,D
Mechanics	M,D
Microbiology	M,D
Military and Defense Studies	M,D
Molecular Biology	M,D
Molecular Genetics	M,D
Multilingual and Multicultural Education	M,D
Music	M,D
Neuroscience	M,D
Nursing—General	M,D,O
Organic Chemistry	M,D
Pathology	M,D
Petroleum Engineering	M,D
Philosophy	M,D
Physical Chemistry	M,D
Physics	M,D
Physiology	M,D
Political Science	M,D
Project Management	M,D
Psychology—General	M,D
Religion	M,D
School Psychology	M,D
Social Work	M,D,O
Sociology	M,D
Software Engineering	M,D
Spanish	M,D
Statistics	M,D
Structural Engineering	M,D
Sustainable Development	M,D
Theater	M
Theoretical Chemistry	M,D
Transportation and Highway Engineering	M,D
Water Resources	M,D

UNIVERSITY OF CALIFORNIA, BERKELEY

Accounting	D,O
Addictions/Substance Abuse Counseling	O
African-American Studies	D
Agricultural Economics and Agribusiness	D
Allopathic Medicine	
Anthropology	D
Applied Arts and Design—General	M,O
Applied Mathematics	D
Applied Science and Technology	D
Archaeology	M,D
Architectural History	M,D
Architecture	M,D
Art History	D
Art/Fine Arts	M,O
Asian Languages	M,D
Asian Studies	M,D
Astrophysics	D
Biochemistry	D
Bioengineering	D
Biological and Biomedical Sciences—General	D
Biophysics	D
Biostatistics	M,D
Building Science	M,D
Business Administration and Management—General	M,D,O
Cell Biology	D
Chemical Engineering	M,D
Chemistry	D
Chinese	D
Civil Engineering	M,D
Classics	M,D
Clinical Research	O
Comparative Literature	D
Computer Science	M,D
Construction Management	O
Counseling Psychology	O
Demography and Population Studies	M,D
Economics	D
Education—General	M,D,O
Electrical Engineering	M,D
Energy Management and Policy	M,D
Engineering and Applied Sciences—General	M,D,O
Engineering Management	M,D
English as a Second Language	O
English	D
Environmental and Occupational Health	M,D
Environmental Design	M,D
Environmental Engineering	M,D
Environmental Management and Policy	M,D,O
Environmental Sciences	M,D
Epidemiology	M,D
Ethnic Studies	D
Facilities Management	O
Finance and Banking	D,O
Financial Engineering	M
Folklore	M
Forestry	M,D
French	D
Geography	D
Geology	M,D
Geophysics	M,D
Geotechnical Engineering	M,D
German	D
Health Services Management and Hospital Administration	D
Hispanic and Latin American Languages	D
History of Science and Technology	D
History	M,D
Human Development	M,D
Human Resources Management	O
Immunology	D
Industrial and Labor Relations	D
Industrial/Management Engineering	M,D
Infectious Diseases	M,D
Information Studies	M,D
Interior Design	O
International Affairs	M,D
International Business	O
Italian	D
Japanese	D
Jewish Studies	D
Journalism	M
Landscape Architecture	M,D,O
Latin American Studies	M
Law	M,D
Legal and Justice Studies	D
Linguistics	D
Management Information Systems	O
Marketing	D,O
Materials Engineering	M,D
Materials Sciences	M,D
Mathematics Education	M,D
Mathematics	M,D
Mechanical Engineering	M,D
Mechanics	M,D
Microbiology	D
Molecular Biology	D
Molecular Toxicology	D
Music	D
Natural Resources	M,D
Near and Middle Eastern Studies	M,D
Neuroscience	D
Nuclear Engineering	M,D
Nutrition	D
Operations Research	M,D
Optometry	D,O
Organizational Behavior	D
Philosophy	D
Physics	D
Physiology	M,D
Plant Biology	D
Political Science	D
Project Management	O
Psychology—General	D
Public Health—General	M,D
Public Policy	M,D
Range Science	M
Real Estate	D
Religion	D
Rhetoric	D
Romance Languages	D
Russian	D
Scandinavian Languages	D
Science Education	M,D
Slavic Languages	D
Social Work	M,D
Sociology	D
Spanish	D
Special Education	M,D
Statistics	M,D
Structural Engineering	M,D
Sustainability Management	O
Sustainable Development	O
Theater	D
Transportation and Highway Engineering	M,D
Urban and Regional Planning	M,D
Urban Design	M,D
Vision Sciences	M,D
Water Resources Engineering	M,D
Writing	O

UNIVERSITY OF CALIFORNIA, DAVIS

Accounting	M
Aerospace/Aeronautical Engineering	M,D,O
Agricultural Economics and Agribusiness	M,D
Agricultural Sciences—General	M
Agronomy and Soil Sciences	M,D
Allopathic Medicine	D
American Indian/Native American Studies	M,D
Animal Behavior	D
Animal Sciences	M,D
Anthropology	M,D
Applied Mathematics	M,D
Applied Science and Technology	M,D
Art History	M
Art/Fine Arts	M
Atmospheric Sciences	M,D
Biochemistry	M,D
Bioengineering	M,D
Biomedical Engineering	M,D
Biophysics	M,D
Biostatistics	M,D
Business Administration and Management—General	M
Cell Biology	M,D
Chemical Engineering	M,D
Chemistry	M,D
Child Development	M
Civil Engineering	M,D,O
Clinical Research	M
Clothing and Textiles	M
Communication—General	M
Comparative Literature	D
Computer Engineering	M,D
Computer Science	M,D
Cultural Studies	M,D
Curriculum and Instruction	M,D
Developmental Biology	M,D
Ecology	M,D
Economics	M,D
Education—General	M,D
Educational Psychology	M,D
Electrical Engineering	M,D
Engineering and Applied Sciences—General	M,D,O
English	M,D
Entomology	M,D
Environmental Engineering	M,D,O
Environmental Sciences	M,D
Epidemiology	M,D
Evolutionary Biology	D
Exercise and Sports Science	M
Food Science and Technology	M,D
Forensic Sciences	M
French	D
Genetics	M,D
Geography	M,D
Geology	M,D
German	M,D
History	M,D
Horticulture	M
Human Development	D
Hydrology	M,D
Immunology	M,D
Law	M,D
Linguistics	M,D
Materials Engineering	M,D
Materials Sciences	M,D
Maternal and Child Health	M
Mathematics	M,D
Mechanical Engineering	M,D,O
Medical Informatics	M
Microbiology	M,D
Molecular Biology	M,D
Music	M,D
Neuroscience	D
Nutrition	M,D
Pathology	M,D
Pharmacology	M,D
Philosophy	M,D

*M—masters degree; D—doctorate; O—other advanced degree; *—Close-Up and/or Display*

Physics	M,D
Physiology	M,D
Plant Biology	M,D
Plant Pathology	M,D
Political Science	M,D
Psychology—General	D
Sociology	M,D
Spanish	M,D
Statistics	M,D
Textile Design	M
Theater	M,D
Toxicology	M,D
Transportation and Highway Engineering	M,D
Transportation Management	M,D
Urban and Regional Planning	M
Veterinary Medicine	D
Veterinary Sciences	M,O
Viticulture and Enology	M,D
Writing	M,D
Zoology	M

UNIVERSITY OF CALIFORNIA, HASTINGS COLLEGE OF THE LAW

Law	M,D

UNIVERSITY OF CALIFORNIA, IRVINE

Accounting	M
Aerospace/Aeronautical Engineering	M,D
Allopathic Medicine	D
Anatomy	M,D
Anthropology	M,D
Applied Mathematics	M,D
Art/Fine Arts	M,D
Asian Languages	M,D
Biochemical Engineering	M,D
Biochemistry	M,D
Biological and Biomedical Sciences—General	M,D
Biomedical Engineering	M,D
Biophysics	D
Biotechnology	M
Business Administration and Management—General	M,D
Cell Biology	M,D
Chemical Engineering	M,D
Chemistry	M,D
Chinese	M,D
Civil Engineering	M,D
Classics	M,D
Comparative Literature	M,D
Computational Biology	D
Computer Science	M,D
Criminal Justice and Criminology	M,D
Cultural Studies	D
Dance	M
Demography and Population Studies	M
Developmental Biology	M,D
Ecology	M,D
Economics	M,D
Education—General	M,D
Educational Leadership and Administration	M,D
Educational Media/Instructional Technology	M
Electrical Engineering	M,D
Elementary Education	M,D
Engineering and Applied Sciences—General	M,D
Engineering Management	M
English	M,D
Environmental and Occupational Health	M,D
Environmental Design	D
Environmental Engineering	M,D
Epidemiology	M,D
Evolutionary Biology	M,D
Foreign Languages Education	M,D
French	M,D
Genetic Counseling	M
Genetics	D
Geosciences	M,D
German	M,D
Health Services Management and Hospital Administration	M
History	M,D
Information Science	M,D
Japanese	M,D
Law	D
Manufacturing Engineering	M,D
Materials Engineering	M,D
Materials Sciences	M,D
Mathematics	M,D
Mechanical Engineering	M,D
Medicinal and Pharmaceutical Chemistry	D
Microbiology	M,D
Molecular Biology	M,D
Molecular Genetics	M,D
Music	M
Neurobiology	M,D
Neuroscience	D
Nursing—General	M
Pathology	D
Pharmaceutical Sciences	D
Philosophy	M,D
Physics	M,D
Physiology	D
Political Science	D
Psychology—General	D
Public Health—General	M,D
Secondary Education	M,D
Sociology	D
Spanish	M,D
Statistics	M,D
Systems Biology	D
Theater	M,D
Toxicology	M,D
Translational Biology	M
Transportation and Highway Engineering	M,D
Urban and Regional Planning	M,D
Urban Studies	M,D
Writing	M

UNIVERSITY OF CALIFORNIA, LOS ANGELES

Accounting	M,D
Aerospace/Aeronautical Engineering	M,D
African Studies	M
African-American Studies	M
Allopathic Medicine	D
American Indian/Native American Studies	M
Anatomy	M,D
Anthropology	M,D
Applied Arts and Design—General	M
Applied Social Research	M,D
Archaeology	M,D
Architecture	M,D
Archives/Archival Administration	M,D,O
Art History	M,D
Art/Fine Arts	M
Asian Languages	M,D
Asian Studies	M,D
Asian-American Studies	M
Astronomy	M,D
Astrophysics	M,D
Atmospheric Sciences	M,D
Biochemistry	M,D
Bioengineering	M,D
Bioinformatics	M,D
Biological and Biomedical Sciences—General	M,D
Biomathematics	M,D
Biomedical Engineering	M,D
Biostatistics	M,D
Business Administration and Management—General	M,D
Cell Biology	M,D
Chemical Engineering	M,D
Chemistry	M,D
Civil Engineering	M,D
Classics	M,D
Clinical Research	M
Community Health	M,D
Comparative Literature	M,D
Computer Science	M,D
Dance	M,D
Dentistry	D,O
Developmental Biology	M,D
Ecology	M,D
Economics	M,D
Education—General	M,D
Educational Leadership and Administration	D
Electrical Engineering	M,D
Engineering and Applied Sciences—General	M,D
English as a Second Language	M,D,O
English	M,D
Environmental and Occupational Health	M,D
Environmental Engineering	M,D
Environmental Sciences	M,D
Epidemiology	M,D
Evolutionary Biology	M,D
Film, Television, and Video Production	M,D
Finance and Banking	M,D
Financial Engineering	M,D
French	M,D
Gender Studies	M,D
Geochemistry	M,D
Geography	M,D
Geology	M,D
Geophysics	M,D
Geosciences	M,D
German	M,D
Health Services Management and Hospital Administration	M,D
Hispanic and Latin American Languages	D
Historic Preservation	M
History	M,D
Human Genetics	M,D
Human Resources Development	M,D
Immunology	M,D
Industrial and Manufacturing Management	M,D
Information Studies	M,D,O
International Business	M,D
Italian	M,D
Latin American Studies	M
Law	M,D
Library Science	M,D,O
Linguistics	M,D
Management Information Systems	M,D
Management Strategy and Policy	M,D
Manufacturing Engineering	M
Marketing	M,D
Materials Engineering	M,D
Materials Sciences	M,D
Mathematics	M,D
Mechanical Engineering	M,D
Media Studies	M,D
Medical Physics	M,D
Microbiology	M,D
Molecular Biology	M,D
Molecular Genetics	M,D
Molecular Physiology	D
Molecular Toxicology	D
Music	M,D
Near and Middle Eastern Languages	M,D
Near and Middle Eastern Studies	M,D
Neurobiology	M,D
Neuroscience	D
Nursing—General	M,D
Oceanography	M,D
Oral and Dental Sciences	M,D
Organizational Behavior	M,D
Pathology	M,D
Pharmacology	M,D
Philosophy	M,D
Physics	M,D
Physiology	M,D
Planetary and Space Sciences	M,D
Political Science	M,D
Portuguese	M
Psychology—General	M,D
Public Health—General	M,D
Public Policy	M
Scandinavian Languages	M
Slavic Languages	M,D
Social Work	M,D
Sociology	M,D
Spanish	M
Special Education	D
Statistics	M,D
Theater	M,D
Toxicology	D
Urban and Regional Planning	M,D
Urban Design	M,D

UNIVERSITY OF CALIFORNIA, MERCED

Applied Mathematics	M,D
Biochemistry	M,D
Bioengineering	M,D
Biological and Biomedical Sciences—General	M,D
Chemistry	M,D
Cognitive Sciences	M,D
Computer Science	M,D
Electrical Engineering	M,D
Engineering and Applied Sciences—General	M,D
Environmental Engineering	M,D
Information Science	M,D
Mechanical Engineering	M,D
Mechanics	M,D
Physics	M,D
Psychology—General	M,D
Social Sciences	M,D
Sociology	M,D
Systems Biology	M,D
Systems Engineering	M,D

UNIVERSITY OF CALIFORNIA, RIVERSIDE

Agronomy and Soil Sciences	M,D
Anthropology	M,D
Archives/Archival Administration	M,D
Art History	M,D
Art/Fine Arts	M
Artificial Intelligence/Robotics	M,D
Asian Studies	M
Biochemistry	M,D
Bioengineering	M,D
Bioinformatics	D
Biological and Biomedical Sciences—General	M,D
Botany	M,D
Business Administration and Management—General	M,D
Cell Biology	M,D
Chemical Engineering	M,D
Chemistry	M,D
Classics	D
Comparative Literature	M,D
Computer Engineering	M
Computer Science	M,D*
Cultural Studies	D
Dance	M
Developmental Biology	M,D
Economics	M,D
Education—General	M,D,O
Educational Leadership and Administration	M,D,O
Educational Psychology	M,D,O
Electrical Engineering	M,D
English as a Second Language	M,D,O
English	M,D
Entomology	M,D
Environmental Engineering	M,D
Environmental Sciences	M
Ethnic Studies	D
Evolutionary Biology	M,D
Foundations and Philosophy of Education	M,D,O
Genetics	D
Genomic Sciences	D
Geology	M,D
Higher Education	M,D,O
Hispanic Studies	M,D
History	M,D
Materials Engineering	M
Materials Sciences	M
Mathematics	M,D
Mechanical Engineering	M,D
Microbiology	M,D
Molecular Biology	M,D
Multilingual and Multicultural Education	M,D,O
Music	M,D
Nanotechnology	M
Neuroscience	D
Philosophy	M,D
Physics	M,D
Plant Biology	M,D
Plant Molecular Biology	M,D
Plant Pathology	M,D
Plant Sciences	M,D
Political Science	M,D
Psychology—General	D
Reading Education	M,D,O
Religion	M,D
School Psychology	M,D,O
Sociology	M,D
Spanish	M,D
Special Education	M,D,O
Statistics	M
Toxicology	M,D
Water Resources	M,D
Writing	M

UNIVERSITY OF CALIFORNIA, SAN DIEGO

Aerospace/Aeronautical Engineering	M,D
Allopathic Medicine	D
Anthropology	D
Applied Mathematics	M,D
Applied Physics	M,D
Architectural Engineering	M
Art History	M,D
Art/Fine Arts	M,D
Artificial Intelligence/Robotics	M,D
Biochemistry	M,D
Bioengineering	M,D*
Bioinformatics	D
Biological and Biomedical Sciences—General	M,D*
Biophysics	M,D
Biostatistics	D
Business Administration and Management—General	M,D
Chemical Engineering	M,D
Chemistry	M,D
Clinical Laboratory Sciences/Medical Technology	M,D
Clinical Psychology	D
Clinical Research	M
Cognitive Sciences	D
Communication Disorders	D
Communication—General	D
Computational Sciences	M,D
Computer Engineering	M,D
Computer Science	M,D
Curriculum and Instruction	M,D
Dance	M,D
Economics	D
Education—General	M,D
Educational Leadership and Administration	M,D
Electrical Engineering	M,D
Engineering Physics	M,D
English	M,D
Epidemiology	D
Ethnic Studies	D
Finance and Banking	M,D
Geophysics	M,D
Geosciences	M,D
Health Law	M
Health Services Management and Hospital Administration	M
History of Science and Technology	D
History	M,D
International Affairs	M,D
International Health	D
Jewish Studies	M,D
Latin American Studies	M
Law	M
Legal and Justice Studies	M
Linguistics	D
Marine Biology	M,D
Marine Sciences	M
Materials Sciences	M,D
Mathematics Education	D
Mathematics	M,D
Mechanical Engineering	M,D
Mechanics	M,D
Meteorology	M
Modeling and Simulation	M,D
Multilingual and Multicultural Education	M,D
Music	M,D
Nanotechnology	M,D
Neuroscience	D
Ocean Engineering	M,D
Oceanography	M,D
Pharmacy	D
Philosophy	D
Photonics	M,D
Physics	M,D
Political Science	M,D
Psychology—General	D
Public Health—General	D
Public Policy	M
Science Education	D
Sociology	D
Statistics	M,D
Structural Engineering	M,D
Systems Biology	D*
Telecommunications	M,D
Theater	M,D
Writing	M,D

UNIVERSITY OF CALIFORNIA, SAN FRANCISCO

Allopathic Medicine	D
Anthropology	D
Biochemistry	D
Bioengineering	D
Bioinformatics	D
Biological and Biomedical Sciences—General	D
Biophysics	D
Cell Biology	D
Chemistry	D
Dentistry	D
Developmental Biology	D
Genetics	D
Genomic Sciences	D
History of Science and Technology	M,D
Medical Imaging	M
Medicinal and Pharmaceutical Chemistry	D
Molecular Biology	D
Neuroscience	D
Nursing—General	M,D
Oral and Dental Sciences	M,D
Pharmaceutical Sciences	D
Pharmacology	D
Pharmacy	D*
Physical Therapy	D
Sociology	D

UNIVERSITY OF CALIFORNIA, SANTA BARBARA

African-American Studies	D
Agricultural Economics and Agribusiness	M,D
Anthropology	M,D

Applied Mathematics	M,D
Applied Statistics	M,D
Art History	D
Art/Fine Arts	M
Asian Languages	M,D
Asian Studies	M,D
Biochemistry	D
Bioengineering	M,D
Biophysics	D
Cell Biology	M,D
Chemical Engineering	M,D
Chemistry	M,D
Classics	M,D
Clinical Psychology	M,D,O
Cognitive Sciences	M,D
Communication—General	D
Comparative Literature	D
Computational Sciences	M,D
Computer Engineering	M,D
Computer Science	M,D
Counseling Psychology	M,D,O
Cultural Anthropology	M,D
Cultural Studies	M,D
Developmental Biology	M,D
Ecology	M,D
Economics	M,D
Education—General	M,D,O
Electrical Engineering	M,D
Engineering and Applied Sciences—General	M,D
English	D
Environmental Management and Policy	M,D
Environmental Sciences	M,D
Evolutionary Biology	M,D
Film, Television, and Video Production	D
Finance and Banking	M,D
French	D
Geography	M,D
Geosciences	M,D
Hispanic and Latin American Languages	M,D
Hispanic Studies	M,D
History	D
Interdisciplinary Studies	D
International Affairs	M,D
Latin American Studies	M
Linguistics	M,D
Management of Technology	M
Marine Biology	M,D
Marine Sciences	M,D
Materials Engineering	M,D
Materials Sciences	M,D
Mathematical and Computational Finance	M,D
Mathematics	M,D
Mechanical Engineering	M,D
Media Studies	M,D
Medieval and Renaissance Studies	M,D
Molecular Biology	M,D
Music	M,D
Neuroscience	D
Philosophy	D
Photonics	M,D
Physics	D
Political Science	M,D
Portuguese	M,D
Psychology—General	D
Public History	D
Quantitative Analysis	M,D
Religion	M,D
School Psychology	M,D,O
Social Sciences	D
Sociology	D
Spanish	M,D
Speech and Interpersonal Communication	D
Statistics	M,D
Sustainable Development	M,D
Theater	M,D
Translation and Interpretation	M,D
Transportation Management	M,D
Women's Studies	M,D
Writing	D

UNIVERSITY OF CALIFORNIA, SANTA CRUZ

Anthropology	D
Applied Economics	M
Applied Mathematics	M,D
Art/Fine Arts	M,D
Astronomy	D
Astrophysics	D
Biochemistry	M,D
Bioinformatics	M,D
Cell Biology	M,D
Chemistry	M,D
Communication—General	O
Comparative Literature	M,D
Computer Art and Design	M,D
Computer Engineering	M,D
Computer Science	M,D
Cultural Anthropology	D
Developmental Biology	M,D
Ecology	M,D
Economics	D
Education—General	M,D
Electrical Engineering	M,D
Engineering and Applied Sciences—General	M,D
English	M,D
Environmental Biology	M,D
Environmental Management and Policy	D
Evolutionary Biology	M,D
Film, Television, and Video Theory and Criticism	D
Finance and Banking	M*
Geosciences	M,D
History	M,D
Humanities	D
Interdisciplinary Studies	M,D
International Affairs	D
Linguistics	M,D
Management Information Systems	M,D
Management of Technology	M,D
Marine Sciences	M,D
Mathematics	M,D
Molecular Biology	M,D
Music	M,D
Philosophy	M,D
Physics	M,D
Planetary and Space Sciences	M,D
Political Science	D
Psychology—General	D
Social Sciences Education	M
Social Sciences	D
Sociology	D
Statistics	M,D
Telecommunications	M,D
Theater	O
Toxicology	M,D
Writing	M

UNIVERSITY OF CENTRAL ARKANSAS

Accounting	M
Adult Education	M,O
Adult Nursing	M,O
Applied Mathematics	M
Biological and Biomedical Sciences—General	M
Business Administration and Management—General	M
Communication Disorders	M,D
Computer Art and Design	M
Computer Science	M
Counseling Psychology	M
Counselor Education	M
Curriculum and Instruction	M,O
Economic Development	M,O
Economics	M,O
Education of the Gifted	M,O
Education—General	M,O
Educational Leadership and Administration	M,O
Educational Media/Instructional Technology	M
English	M
Family and Consumer Sciences-General	M
Family Nurse Practitioner Studies	M,O
Film, Television, and Video Production	M
Foreign Languages Education	M
Geographic Information Systems	M,O
Geography	M,O
Health Education	M
History	M
Kinesiology and Movement Studies	M
Library Science	M
Mathematics Education	M
Mathematics	M
Music Education	M,O
Music	M,O
Nursing and Healthcare Administration	M,O
Nursing Education	M,O
Nursing—General	M,O
Occupational Therapy	M
Organizational Management	D
Physical Therapy	D
Psychology—General	M,D,O
Reading Education	M
School Psychology	M,D,O
Social Psychology	M
Special Education	M,O
Student Affairs	M
Urban and Regional Planning	M,O
Writing	M

UNIVERSITY OF CENTRAL FLORIDA

Accounting	M
Aerospace/Aeronautical Engineering	M
Allopathic Medicine	M,D
Anthropology	M,O
Applied Psychology	M,D
Art Education	M
Art/Fine Arts	M
Biological and Biomedical Sciences—General	M,D
Biotechnology	M,D
Business Administration and Management—General	M,D,O
Chemistry	M,D,O
Civil Engineering	M,D,O
Clinical Psychology	M,D
Communication Disorders	M,D,O
Communication—General	M,O
Community College Education	M,D,O
Computer Art and Design	M
Computer Engineering	M,D
Computer Science	M,D
Conservation Biology	M,D,O
Construction Engineering	M,D,O
Corporate and Organizational Communication	M,O
Counselor Education	M,O
Criminal Justice and Criminology	M,D,O
Early Childhood Education	D
Educational Leadership and Administration	M,D,O
Educational Media/Instructional Technology	M,D,O
Electrical Engineering	M,D,O
Elementary Education	M,D
Emergency Management	M,O
Engineering and Applied Sciences—General	M,D,O
English as a Second Language	M,D,O
English Education	M
English	M,D,O
Entrepreneurship	M,O
Environmental Engineering	M,D
Exercise and Sports Science	M,D
Experimental Psychology	M,D
Film, Television, and Video Production	M
Forensic Sciences	M,D
Game Design and Development	M
Gender Studies	M,O
Health Informatics	M,O
Health Services Management and Hospital Administration	M,O
Higher Education	M,D,O
History	M
Homeland Security	M,O
Hospitality Management	M,D,O
Industrial and Organizational Psychology	M,D
Industrial/Management Engineering	M,D,O
Interdisciplinary Studies	M,O
Marriage and Family Therapy	M,O
Materials Engineering	M,D
Materials Sciences	M,D
Mathematics Education	M,D,O
Mathematics	M,D,O
Mechanical Engineering	M,D
Middle School Education	M
Modeling and Simulation	M,D,O
Music	M
Nanotechnology	M
National Security	M,D,O
Nonprofit Management	M,O
Nursing—General	M,D,O
Optical Sciences	M,D
Photonics	M,D
Physical Therapy	D
Physics	M,D
Physiology	M
Political Science	M,D,O
Psychology—General	M,D
Public Administration	M,O
Public Affairs	M,D,O
Reading Education	M,D,O
School Psychology	O
Science Education	M,D,O
Social Sciences Education	M,D
Social Work	M,O
Sociology	M,D
Spanish	M
Special Education	M,D,O
Sports Management	M
Statistics	M,O
Structural Engineering	M,D,O
Student Affairs	M,D,O
Taxation	M
Theater	M
Transportation and Highway Engineering	M,D,O
Travel and Tourism	M,D,O
Urban and Regional Planning	M,O
Vocational and Technical Education	M,D,O
Writing	M,D,O

UNIVERSITY OF CENTRAL MISSOURI

Accounting	M,D,O
Aerospace/Aeronautical Engineering	M,D,O
Applied Mathematics	M,D,O
Biological and Biomedical Sciences—General	M,D,O
Business Administration and Management—General	M,D,O
Communication Disorders	M,D,O
Communication—General	M,D,O
Computer Science	M,D,O
Counseling Psychology	M,D,O
Counselor Education	M,D,O
Criminal Justice and Criminology	M,D,O
Early Childhood Education	M,D,O
Education—General	M,D,O
Educational Leadership and Administration	M,D,O
Educational Media/Instructional Technology	M,D,O
Elementary Education	M,D,O
English as a Second Language	M,D,O
English	M,D,O
Environmental and Occupational Health	M,D,O
Environmental Management and Policy	M,D,O
Finance and Banking	M,D,O
Gerontology	M,D,O
History	M,D,O
Human Services	M,D,O
Industrial and Manufacturing Management	M,D,O
Industrial Hygiene	M,D,O
Information Science	M,D,O
Kinesiology and Movement Studies	M,D,O
Library Science	M,D,O
Management Information Systems	M,D,O
Management of Technology	M,D,O
Marketing	M,D,O
Mathematics	M,D,O
Music	M,D,O
Nursing—General	M,D,O
Psychology—General	M,D,O
Reading Education	M,D,O
Sociology	M,D,O
Special Education	M,D,O
Student Affairs	M,D,O
Theater	M,D,O
Vocational and Technical Education	M,D,O

UNIVERSITY OF CENTRAL OKLAHOMA

Accounting	M
Addictions/Substance Abuse Counseling	M
Adult Education	M
Applied Arts and Design—General	M
Applied Mathematics	M
Athletic Training and Sports Medicine	M
Biological and Biomedical Sciences—General	M
Biomedical Engineering	M
Child and Family Studies	M
Communication Disorders	M
Computer Science	M
Counseling Psychology	M
Counselor Education	M
Criminal Justice and Criminology	M
Early Childhood Education	M
Education—General	M
Educational Leadership and Administration	M
Educational Media/Instructional Technology	M
Electrical Engineering	M
Elementary Education	M
Engineering and Applied Sciences—General	M
Engineering Physics	M
English as a Second Language	M
English	M
Exercise and Sports Science	M
Experimental Psychology	M
Family and Consumer Sciences-General	M
Forensic Psychology	M
Forensic Sciences	M
Gerontology	M
Health Promotion	M
Higher Education	M
History	M
Human Development	M
Interdisciplinary Studies	M
International Affairs	M
Library Science	M
Marriage and Family Therapy	M
Mathematics	M
Mechanical Engineering	M
Museum Studies	M
Music	M
Nursing—General	M
Nutrition	M
Political Science	M
Psychology—General	M
Public Administration	M
Reading Education	M
School Psychology	M
Secondary Education	M
Sociology	M
Special Education	M
Statistics	M
Student Affairs	M
Writing	M

UNIVERSITY OF CHARLESTON

Accounting	M
Business Administration and Management—General	M
Forensic Sciences	M
Legal and Justice Studies	M
Management Strategy and Policy	M
Organizational Management	D
Pharmacy	D
Physician Assistant Studies	M

UNIVERSITY OF CHICAGO

Accounting	M,O
Allopathic Medicine	D
Anatomy	D
Anthropology	D
Applied Mathematics	D
Applied Statistics	M
Art History	M,D
Art/Fine Arts	M
Asian Languages	D
Asian Studies	M,D
Astronomy	D
Astrophysics	D
Atmospheric Sciences	D
Biochemistry	D
Bioengineering	D
Biological and Biomedical Sciences—General	D
Biophysics	D
Business Administration and Management—General	M,D,O
Cancer Biology/Oncology	D
Cell Biology	D
Chemistry	D
Classics	M,D
Comparative Literature	M,D
Computational Sciences	M
Computer Science	M,D
Developmental Biology	D
Ecology	D
Economics	M,D,O
Emergency Management	M
English	M,D
Entrepreneurship	M,O
Environmental Management and Policy	M
Environmental Sciences	M
Ethics	D
Evolutionary Biology	D
Film, Television, and Video Theory and Criticism	D
Finance and Banking	M,O
French	D
Genetics	D
Genomic Sciences	D
Geochemistry	D
Geophysics	D

*M—masters degree; D—doctorate; O—other advanced degree; *—Close-Up and/or Display*

Geosciences D
German M,D
Health Promotion M,D
Health Services Management and Hospital Administration M,O
History D
Human Development D
Human Genetics D
Humanities M
Immunology D
Industrial and Manufacturing Management M,O
Interdisciplinary Studies D
International Affairs M
International Business M,O
Italian D
Latin American Studies M
Law M,D
Liberal Studies M
Linguistics M,D
Management Strategy and Policy M,O
Marketing M,O
Mathematical and Computational Finance M
Mathematics D
Media Studies D
Medical Physics D
Medieval and Renaissance Studies D
Microbiology D
Molecular Biology D
Molecular Biophysics D
Music M,D
Near and Middle Eastern Languages D
Near and Middle Eastern Studies M,D
Neurobiology D
Neuroscience D
Nutrition D
Organizational Behavior M,O
Paleontology D
Pastoral Ministry and Counseling M
Philosophy M,D
Physics M,D
Planetary and Space Sciences D
Political Science D
Psychology—General D
Public Policy M,D
Religion M,D
Romance Languages M,D
Science Education D
Social Sciences M,D
Social Work M,D
Sociology D
Spanish D
Statistics M,D,O
Systems Biology D
Theology D
Urban Education M
Writing M
Zoology D

UNIVERSITY OF CINCINNATI

Accounting M,D
Acute Care/Critical Care Nursing M,D
Adult Education M,D,O
Adult Nursing M,D
Aerospace/Aeronautical Engineering M,D
Allopathic Medicine D
Analytical Chemistry M,D
Anthropology M
Applied Arts and Design—General M
Applied Economics M
Applied Mathematics M,D
Architecture M
Art Education M
Art History M
Art/Fine Arts M
Arts Administration M,D
Biochemistry M,D
Bioinformatics D,O
Biological and Biomedical Sciences—General M,D,O
Biomedical Engineering M,D
Biophysics D
Biostatistics M,D
Business Administration and Management—General M,D
Cancer Biology/Oncology D
Cell Biology D
Chemical Engineering M,D
Chemistry M,D
Civil Engineering M,D
Classics M,D
Clinical Psychology D
Communication Disorders M,D,O
Communication—General M
Community Health Nursing M,D
Computer Engineering M,D
Computer Science M,D
Counselor Education M,D,O
Criminal Justice and Criminology M,D
Curriculum and Instruction M,D
Developmental Biology D
Early Childhood Education M
Economics D
Education—General M,D,O
Educational Leadership and Administration M,D,O
Electrical Engineering M,D
Elementary Education M
Engineering and Applied Sciences—General M,D
English as a Second Language M,D,O
English M,D
Environmental and Occupational Health M,D
Environmental Engineering M,D
Environmental Sciences M,D
Epidemiology M,D
Ergonomics and Human Factors M,D
Experimental Psychology D
Finance and Banking M,D
Foundations and Philosophy of Education M,D
French M,D
Genetic Counseling M
Genomic Sciences M,D
Geography M,D
Geology M,D
German M,D
Graphic Design M
Health Education M,D
Health Physics/Radiological Health M
Health Services Research M
History M,D
Immunology M,D
Industrial and Labor Relations M
Industrial and Manufacturing Management D
Industrial Design M
Industrial Hygiene M,D
Industrial/Management Engineering M,D
Inorganic Chemistry M,D
Interdisciplinary Studies D
Interior Design M
Law D
Management Information Systems M,D
Marketing M,D
Materials Engineering M,D
Materials Sciences M,D
Maternal and Child/Neonatal Nursing M,D
Mathematics Education M,D
Mathematics M,D
Mechanical Engineering M,D
Mechanics M,D
Medical Imaging M,D
Medical Physics M
Microbiology M,D
Molecular Biology M,D
Molecular Genetics M,D
Molecular Medicine D
Molecular Toxicology M,D
Music Education M
Music M,D,O
Neuroscience D
Nuclear Engineering M,D
Nurse Anesthesia M,D
Nurse Midwifery M,D
Nursing and Healthcare Administration M,D
Nursing—General M,D
Nutrition M
Occupational Health Nursing M,D
Organic Chemistry M,D
Organizational Management M
Pathobiology D
Pathology D
Pediatric Nursing M,D
Pharmaceutical Sciences M,D
Pharmacology D
Pharmacy D
Philosophy M,D
Physical Chemistry M,D
Physics M,D
Physiology D
Political Science M,D
Psychiatric Nursing M,D
Psychology—General D
Quantitative Analysis M,D
Reading Education M,D
Rehabilitation Sciences D
Romance Languages M,D
School Psychology D,O
Science Education M,D,O
Secondary Education M
Social Sciences Education M,D,O
Social Work M
Sociology M,D
Spanish M,D
Special Education M,D
Statistics M,D
Taxation M
Textile Design M
Theater M,D
Urban and Regional Planning M
Women's Health Nursing M,D
Women's Studies M,O

UNIVERSITY OF COLORADO BOULDER

Accounting M,D
Aerospace/Aeronautical Engineering M,D
Animal Behavior M,D
Anthropology M,D
Applied Mathematics M,D
Architectural Engineering M,D
Art History M
Art/Fine Arts M
Asian Studies M,D
Astrophysics M,D
Atmospheric Sciences M,D
Biochemistry M,D
Business Administration and Management—General M
Cell Biology M,D
Chemical Engineering M,D
Chemical Physics M,D
Chemistry M,D
Chinese M,D
Civil Engineering M,D
Classics M,D
Communication Disorders M,D
Communication—General M,D
Comparative Literature M,D
Computer Engineering M,D
Computer Science M,D
Construction Engineering M,D
Curriculum and Instruction M,D
Dance M,D
Developmental Biology M,D
Ecology M,D
Economics M,D
Education—General M,D
Educational Measurement and Evaluation D
Educational Policy M,D
Educational Psychology M,D
Electrical Engineering M,D
Engineering and Applied Sciences—General M,D
Engineering Management M
English M,D
Entrepreneurship M,D
Environmental Engineering M,D
Environmental Management and Policy M,D
Ethnic Studies D
Evolutionary Biology M,D
Film, Television, and Video Production M
Finance and Banking M,D
French M,D
Genetics M,D
Geography M,D
Geology M,D
Geophysics M,D
Geotechnical Engineering M,D
German M
Hispanic and Latin American Languages M,D
History M,D
Hydrology M,D
International Affairs M,D
Internet and Interactive Multimedia D
Japanese M,D
Journalism M,D
Kinesiology and Movement Studies M,D
Law D
Linguistics M,D
Management Information Systems M,D
Marine Biology M,D
Marketing M,D
Mass Communication M,D
Mathematical Physics M,D
Mathematics M,D
Mechanical Engineering M,D
Media Studies M,D
Medical Physics M,D
Microbiology M,D
Molecular Biology M,D
Multilingual and Multicultural Education M,D
Museum Studies M
Music Education M,D
Music M,D
Neurobiology M,D
Oceanography M,D
Operations Research M
Optical Sciences M,D
Organizational Management M,D
Philosophy M,D
Photography M
Physics M,D
Physiology M,D
Plasma Physics M,D
Political Science M,D
Psychology—General M,D
Public Policy M,D
Religion M
Sociology D
Spanish M,D
Structural Engineering M,D
Telecommunications Management M
Telecommunications M
Theater M,D
Water Resources Engineering M,D
Writing M,D

UNIVERSITY OF COLORADO COLORADO SPRINGS

Adult Nursing M,D
Aerospace/Aeronautical Engineering M,D
Applied Mathematics M
Business Administration and Management—General M
Communication—General M
Computer and Information Systems Security M,D
Computer Science M
Counselor Education M,D
Criminal Justice and Criminology M
Curriculum and Instruction M,D
Education—General M,D
Educational Leadership and Administration M,D
Electrical Engineering M
Energy and Power Engineering M,D
Engineering and Applied Sciences—General M,D
Engineering Management M,D
Environmental Sciences M
Geography M
Gerontological Nursing M,D
History M
Human Services M,D
Interdisciplinary Studies M
Mathematics D
Mechanical Engineering M
Nursing—General M,D
Physics D
Psychology—General M,D
Public Administration M
Public Affairs M
Sociology M
Software Engineering M,D
Special Education M,D
Systems Engineering M,D

UNIVERSITY OF COLORADO DENVER

Accounting M
Adult Education M
Adult Nursing M,D
Allopathic Medicine D
American Studies M
Anatomy M,D
Anesthesiologist Assistant Studies M
Animal Behavior M,D
Anthropology M
Applied Mathematics M,D
Applied Science and Technology M
Applied Statistics M,D
Archaeology M
Architectural History D
Architecture M
Art/Fine Arts M
Biochemistry D
Bioengineering M,D
Bioinformatics D
Biological and Biomedical Sciences—General M,D
Biophysics M,D
Biostatistics M,D
Business Administration and Management—General M
Cancer Biology/Oncology D
Cell Biology M,D
Chemistry M
Civil Engineering M,D
Clinical Laboratory Sciences/Medical Technology M,D
Clinical Psychology M,D
Clinical Research M,D
Communication—General M
Community Health M,D
Computational Biology M,D
Computational Sciences M,D
Computer Science M,D
Corporate and Organizational Communication M
Counseling Psychology M
Counselor Education M
Criminal Justice and Criminology M,D
Dentistry M,D
Developmental Biology M,D
Distance Education Development M
Early Childhood Education M,D
Ecology M,D
Economic Development M
Economics M
Education—General M,D,O
Educational Leadership and Administration M,D,O
Educational Measurement and Evaluation M,D,O
Educational Media/Instructional Technology M
Educational Policy D
Educational Psychology M,O
Electrical Engineering M,D
Elementary Education M
Emergency Management M,D
Energy Management and Policy M
Engineering and Applied Sciences—General M,D
English Education M
English M
Entertainment Management M
Entrepreneurship M
Environmental and Occupational Health M,D
Environmental Education M
Environmental Engineering M,D
Environmental Law M,D
Environmental Management and Policy M,D
Environmental Sciences M
Epidemiology M,D
Evolutionary Biology M,D
Family Nurse Practitioner Studies M,D
Finance and Banking M
Forensic Sciences M
Gender Studies M
Genetic Counseling M,D
Genetics M,D
Geographic Information Systems M,D
Geotechnical Engineering M,D
Health Education M,D
Health Psychology M,D
Health Services Management and Hospital Administration M,D
Health Services Research M,D
Historic Preservation M
History M
Homeland Security M,D
Human Development M,O
Human Resources Management M
Humanities M
Hydraulics M,D
Hydrology M,D
Immunology D
Information Science M,D
Insurance M
International Affairs M
International Business M
International Health M
Investment Management M
Landscape Architecture M
Linguistics M
Management Information Systems M,D
Management of Technology M
Management Strategy and Policy M
Marketing Research M
Marketing M
Marriage and Family Therapy M
Mathematics Education M,D
Mathematics M,D
Mechanical Engineering M
Mechanics M
Medical Informatics M,D
Microbiology M,D
Military and Defense Studies M,D
Molecular Biology M,D
Molecular Genetics D
Multilingual and Multicultural Education M
Music M

Neurobiology	M,D
Neuroscience	D
Nonprofit Management	M,D
Nurse Midwifery	M,D
Nursing and Healthcare Administration	M,D
Nursing—General	M,D
Operations Research	M,D
Oral and Dental Sciences	M,D
Pediatric Nursing	M,D
Pharmaceutical Sciences	D
Pharmacology	D
Physical Therapy	D
Physician Assistant Studies	M
Physiology	D
Political Science	M,D
Psychiatric Nursing	M,D
Public Administration	M,D
Public Affairs	M,D
Public Health—General	M,D
Public History	M
Quantitative Analysis	M
Reading Education	M
Rehabilitation Sciences	D
Rhetoric	M
School Psychology	M,O
Science Education	M,D
Secondary Education	M
Sociology	M
Spanish	M
Special Education	M,D
Sports Management	M
Statistics	M,D
Structural Engineering	M,D
Sustainability Management	M
Sustainable Development	M,D
Taxation	M
Toxicology	D
Transportation and Highway Engineering	M,D
Urban and Regional Planning	M,D
Urban Design	M,D
Water Resources	M
Western European Studies	M
Women's Health Nursing	M,D
Women's Studies	M
Writing	M

UNIVERSITY OF CONNECTICUT

Accounting	M
Adult Education	M,O
Agricultural Economics and Agribusiness	M,D
Agricultural Education	M,D
Agricultural Sciences—General	M,D
Agronomy and Soil Sciences	M,D
Animal Sciences	M,D
Anthropology	M,D
Applied Arts and Design—General	M
Applied Mathematics	M
Biomedical Engineering	M,D
Biopsychology	M,D
Botany	M,D
Business Administration and Management—General	M,D
Chemical Engineering	M,D
Chemistry	M,D
Child and Family Studies	M,D
Civil Engineering	M,D
Clinical Psychology	M,D
Cognitive Sciences	M,D,O
Communication Disorders	M,D
Communication—General	M
Computer Science	M,D
Counselor Education	M,D
Developmental Psychology	M,D
Ecology	M,D
Economics	M,D
Education—General	M,D
Electrical Engineering	M,D
Elementary Education	M,D
Engineering and Applied Sciences—General	M,D
English Education	M,D
English	M,D
Environmental and Occupational Health	O
Environmental Engineering	M,D
Exercise and Sports Science	M,D
Experimental Psychology	M,D
Finance and Banking	M,D
Foreign Languages Education	M,D
Genomic Sciences	M
Geography	M,D
Geology	M,D
Health Services Management and Hospital Administration	M,D
History	M,D
Human Development	M,D
Human Resources Management	M
Industrial and Organizational Psychology	M,D
Jewish Studies	M
Latin American Studies	M
Law	D
Linguistics	M,D
Marketing	M,D
Materials Engineering	M
Materials Sciences	M,D
Mathematical and Computational Finance	M
Mathematics Education	M,D
Mechanical Engineering	M,D
Medicinal and Pharmaceutical Chemistry	M,D
Medieval and Renaissance Studies	M,D
Metallurgical Engineering and Metallurgy	M
Multilingual and Multicultural Education	M,D
Music Education	M,D
Music	M,D
Natural Resources	M,D
Neurobiology	M,D
Neuroscience	M,D
Nursing—General	M,D,O
Nutrition	M,D
Pathobiology	M,D
Pharmaceutical Sciences	M,D
Pharmacology	M,D
Pharmacy	D
Philosophy	M,D
Physical Therapy	D
Physics	M,D
Physiology	M,D*
Plant Sciences	M,D
Political Science	M,D
Polymer Science and Engineering	M,D
Psychology—General	M,D
Public Administration	M
Quantitative Analysis	M,O
Reading Education	M,D
Science Education	M,D
Secondary Education	M,D
Social Psychology	M,D
Social Sciences Education	M,D
Sociology	M,D
Software Engineering	M,D
Statistics	M,D
Theater	M
Toxicology	M,D
Western European Studies	M

UNIVERSITY OF CONNECTICUT HEALTH CENTER

Allopathic Medicine	D
Biochemistry	D
Biological and Biomedical Sciences—General	D*
Cell Biology	D*
Clinical Research	M
Dentistry	D,O
Developmental Biology	D
Genetics	D*
Immunology	D*
Molecular Biology	D*
Neuroscience	D*
Oral and Dental Sciences	M,D*
Public Health—General	M

UNIVERSITY OF DALLAS

Accounting	M,D
American Studies	M
Art/Fine Arts	M
Business Administration and Management—General	M,D
Classics	M
Comparative Literature	D
Computer and Information Systems Security	M,D
English	M
Entertainment Management	M,D
Finance and Banking	M,D
Health Services Management and Hospital Administration	M,D
Human Resources Management	M,D
Humanities	M
International Business	M,D
Logistics	M,D
Management Information Systems	M,D
Management of Technology	M,D
Management Strategy and Policy	M,D
Marketing	M,D
Organizational Management	M,D
Pastoral Ministry and Counseling	M
Philosophy	M,D
Political Science	M,D
Project Management	M,D
Psychology—General	M
Sports Management	M,D
Supply Chain Management	M,D
Theology	M

UNIVERSITY OF DAYTON

Accounting	M
Aerospace/Aeronautical Engineering	M,D
Applied Mathematics	M
Bioengineering	M
Biological and Biomedical Sciences—General	M,D
Business Administration and Management—General	M
Chemical Engineering	M
Chemistry	M
Civil Engineering	M
Clinical Psychology	M,O
Communication—General	M
Computer and Information Systems Security	M
Computer Engineering	M,D
Computer Science	M
Counseling Psychology	M,O
Counselor Education	M,O
Early Childhood Education	M
Education—General	M
Educational Leadership and Administration	M,D,O
Educational Media/Instructional Technology	M
Electrical Engineering	M,D
Engineering Management	M
English	M
Environmental Engineering	M
Environmental Management and Policy	M,D
Exercise and Sports Science	M
Finance and Banking	M
Geotechnical Engineering	M
Higher Education	D
Human Development	M,O
Law	M,D
Marketing	M
Materials Engineering	M,D
Mathematical and Computational Finance	M
Mathematics Education	M
Mechanical Engineering	M,D
Mechanics	M
Middle School Education	M
Music Education	M
Optical Sciences	M,D
Pastoral Ministry and Counseling	M,D
Physical Education	M
Physical Therapy	D
Physician Assistant Studies	M
Psychology—General	M
Public Administration	M
Reading Education	M
School Psychology	M,O
Secondary Education	M
Structural Engineering	M
Student Affairs	M,O
Theology	M,D
Transportation and Highway Engineering	M
Water Resources Engineering	M
Writing	M

UNIVERSITY OF DELAWARE

Accounting	M
Adult Nursing	M,O
Agricultural Economics and Agribusiness	M
Agricultural Education	M
Agricultural Sciences—General	M,D
Agronomy and Soil Sciences	M,D
American Studies	M
Animal Sciences	M,D
Applied Arts and Design—General	M
Applied Mathematics	M,D
Art History	M,D
Art/Fine Arts	M
Astronomy	M,D
Biochemistry	M,D
Biological and Biomedical Sciences—General	M,D
Biotechnology	M,D
Business Administration and Management—General	M,D
Business Education	M,D
Cancer Biology/Oncology	M,D
Cell Biology	M,D
Chemical Engineering	M,D
Chemistry	M,D
Child and Family Studies	M,D
Chinese	M
Civil Engineering	M,D
Clinical Psychology	D
Clothing and Textiles	M
Cognitive Sciences	M,D
Communication—General	M
Computer Engineering	M,D
Computer Science	M,D
Criminal Justice and Criminology	M,D
Curriculum and Instruction	M,D,O
Developmental Biology	M,D
Ecology	M,D
Economics	M,D
Education—General	M,D,O
Educational Leadership and Administration	M,D,O
Electrical Engineering	M,D
Emergency Management	M,D
Energy Management and Policy	M,D
Engineering and Applied Sciences—General	M,D
English as a Second Language	M,D,O
English	M,D
Entomology	M,D
Entrepreneurship	M,D
Environmental Engineering	M,D
Environmental Management and Policy	M,D
Evolutionary Biology	M,D
Family Nurse Practitioner Studies	M,O
Finance and Banking	M
Fish, Game, and Wildlife Management	M,D
Food Science and Technology	M,D
Foreign Languages Education	M
French	M
Genetics	M,D
Geography	M,D
Geology	M,D
Geotechnical Engineering	M,D
German	M
Gerontological Nursing	M,O
Health Promotion	M
Higher Education	M,D,O
Historic Preservation	M,D
History of Science and Technology	M,D
History	M,D
HIV/AIDS Nursing	M,O
Horticulture	M
Hospitality Management	M
Human Development	M,D
Information Science	M,D
International Affairs	M,D
Kinesiology and Movement Studies	M,D
Liberal Studies	M
Linguistics	M,D
Management Information Systems	M,D
Management of Technology	M
Marine Affairs	M,D
Marine Geology	M,D
Marine Sciences	M,D
Materials Engineering	M,D
Materials Sciences	M,D
Maternal and Child/Neonatal Nursing	M,O
Mathematics	M,D
Mechanical Engineering	M,D
Microbiology	M,D
Molecular Biology	M,D
Multilingual and Multicultural Education	M,D,O
Music Education	M
Music	M
Natural Resources	M
Neuroscience	D
Nursing and Healthcare Administration	M,O
Nursing—General	M,O
Nutrition	M
Ocean Engineering	M,D
Oceanography	M,D
Oncology Nursing	M,O
Operations Research	M
Pediatric Nursing	M,O
Physical Therapy	D
Physics	M,D
Physiology	M,D
Plant Sciences	M,D
Political Science	M,D
Psychiatric Nursing	M,O
Psychology—General	D
Public Administration	M*
Public Policy	M,D
School Psychology	M,D,O
Social Psychology	D
Sociology	M,D
Spanish	M
Statistics	M
Structural Engineering	M,D
Theater	M
Translation and Interpretation	M
Transportation and Highway Engineering	M,D
Urban Studies	M,D
Water Resources Engineering	M,D
Women's Health Nursing	M,O

UNIVERSITY OF DENVER

Accounting	M
Anthropology	M
Archaeology	M
Art History	M
Art/Fine Arts	M
Bioengineering	M,D
Biological and Biomedical Sciences—General	M,D
Business Administration and Management—General	M
Cell Biology	M,D
Chemistry	M,D
Child and Family Studies	M,D,O
Clinical Psychology	M,D
Cognitive Sciences	D
Communication—General	M,D,O
Computer Art and Design	M
Computer Engineering	M,D
Computer Science	M,D
Conflict Resolution and Mediation/Peace Studies	M,O
Construction Management	M
Corporate and Organizational Communication	M,O
Counseling Psychology	M,D,O
Cultural Anthropology	M
Cultural Studies	M,O
Curriculum and Instruction	M,D,O
Developmental Psychology	D
Early Childhood Education	M,D,O
Ecology	M,D
Economics	M
Education—General	M,D,O
Educational Leadership and Administration	M,D,O
Educational Measurement and Evaluation	M,D,O
Educational Policy	M,D,O
Electrical Engineering	M,D
Emergency Management	M,O
Engineering and Applied Sciences—General	M,D
Engineering Management	M,D
English	M,D
Environmental Management and Policy	M,O
Evolutionary Biology	M,D
Finance and Banking	M
Forensic Psychology	M,D
Geographic Information Systems	M,D,O
Geography	M,D
Higher Education	M,D,O
History	M,O
Homeland Security	M,D,O
Human Resources Management	M,O
International Affairs	M,D,O
International Development	M,D,O
International Health	M,D,O
Law	M,D,O
Legal and Justice Studies	M,O
Library Science	M,D,O
Management Strategy and Policy	M
Marketing	M
Marriage and Family Therapy	M,D,O
Mass Communication	M
Materials Engineering	M,D
Materials Sciences	M,D
Mathematics	M,D
Mechanical Engineering	M,D
Media Studies	M
Molecular Biology	M,D
Museum Studies	M
Music Education	M,O

*M—masters degree; D—doctorate; O—other advanced degree; *—Close-Up and/or Display*

Music	M,O
Physics	M,D
Project Management	M,O
Psychology—General	M,D
Public Policy	M
Real Estate	M
Religion	M,D,O
Rhetoric	M,D
School Psychology	M,D,O
Social Psychology	D
Social Work	M,D,O
Special Education	M,D,O
Speech and Interpersonal Communication	M,D
Sport Psychology	M,D
Statistics	M
Taxation	M
Theology	D
Translation and Interpretation	M,O
Writing	M,D

UNIVERSITY OF DETROIT MERCY

Accounting	M,O
Addictions/Substance Abuse Counseling	M,D,O
Allied Health—General	M,D,O
Architectural Engineering	M
Business Administration and Management—General	M,O
Chemistry	M,D
Civil Engineering	M,D
Clinical Psychology	M,D,O
Computer and Information Systems Security	M,D,O
Computer Engineering	M,D
Computer Science	M,D,O
Criminal Justice and Criminology	M,D,O
Curriculum and Instruction	M,D,O
Dentistry	M,D,O
Economics	M,D,O
Educational Leadership and Administration	M,D,O
Electrical Engineering	M,D
Engineering and Applied Sciences—General	M,D
Engineering Management	M,D
Environmental Engineering	M,D
Ethics	M,O
Family Nurse Practitioner Studies	M,D,O
Finance and Banking	M,D,O
Forensic Sciences	M,O
Health Services Management and Hospital Administration	M,D,O
Industrial and Organizational Psychology	M,D,O
Industrial Design	M,D
Law	D
Liberal Studies	M,D,O
Management Information Systems	M,D,O
Management Strategy and Policy	M,O
Mathematics Education	M,D
Mechanical Engineering	M,D
Nurse Anesthesia	M,D,O
Nursing Education	M,D,O
Nursing—General	M,D,O
Oral and Dental Sciences	M,D,O
Physician Assistant Studies	M,D,O
Religious Education	M,D,O
School Psychology	M,D,O
Software Engineering	M,D
Special Education	M,D,O
Urban and Regional Planning	M

UNIVERSITY OF DUBUQUE

Business Administration and Management—General	M
Communication—General	M
Theology	M,D

UNIVERSITY OF EVANSVILLE

Health Services Management and Hospital Administration	M
Physical Therapy	D
Public Administration	M

THE UNIVERSITY OF FINDLAY

Athletic Training and Sports Medicine	M,D
Business Administration and Management—General	M,D
Early Childhood Education	M,D
Education—General	M,D
Educational Leadership and Administration	M,D
Educational Media/Instructional Technology	M,D
English as a Second Language	M,D
Environmental Management and Policy	M,D
Health Informatics	M,D
Health Services Management and Hospital Administration	M,D
Hospitality Management	M,D
Multilingual and Multicultural Education	M,D
Occupational Therapy	M,D
Organizational Management	M,D
Pharmacy	M,D
Physical Therapy	M,D
Physician Assistant Studies	M,D
Public Administration	M,D
Reading Education	M,D
Rhetoric	M,D
Science Education	M,D
Writing	M,D

UNIVERSITY OF FLORIDA

Accounting	M,D
Advertising and Public Relations	M,D
Aerospace/Aeronautical Engineering	M,D
Agricultural Economics and Agribusiness	M,D
Agricultural Education	M,D
Agricultural Engineering	M,D,O
Agricultural Sciences—General	M,D,O
Agronomy and Soil Sciences	M,D
Allied Health—General	M,D,O
Allopathic Medicine	D
Animal Sciences	M,D
Anthropology	M,D
Aquaculture	M,D
Architecture	M,D
Art Education	M,D
Art History	M,D
Art/Fine Arts	M,D
Astronomy	M,D
Athletic Training and Sports Medicine	M,D
Biochemistry	D
Bioengineering	M,D,O
Biological and Biomedical Sciences—General	M,D
Biomedical Engineering	M,D,O
Biostatistics	M,D,O
Botany	M,D
Business Administration and Management—General	M,D
Cell Biology	M,D
Chemical Engineering	M,D,O
Chemistry	M,D
Child Development	M
Civil Engineering	M,D
Classics	M,D
Clinical Laboratory Sciences/Medical Technology	M,D
Clinical Psychology	M,D
Clinical Research	M,D,O
Communication Disorders	M,D
Communication—General	M,D
Computer Art and Design	M,D
Computer Engineering	M,D
Computer Science	M,D
Construction Management	M,D
Counseling Psychology	M,D
Counselor Education	M,D,O
Criminal Justice and Criminology	M,D
Curriculum and Instruction	M,D,O
Dentistry	D,O
Early Childhood Education	M,D,O
Ecology	M,D,O
Economics	M,D
Education—General	M,D,O
Educational Leadership and Administration	M,D,O
Educational Measurement and Evaluation	M,D,O
Educational Policy	M,D,O
Electrical Engineering	M,D
Elementary Education	M,D,O
Emergency Management	M
Engineering and Applied Sciences—General	M,D,O
English as a Second Language	M,D,O
English Education	M,D,O
English	M,D
Entrepreneurship	M,D,O
Environmental and Occupational Health	M,D,O
Environmental Education	M,D,O
Environmental Engineering	M,D,O
Environmental Law	M,D
Epidemiology	M,D,O
Exercise and Sports Science	M,D
Family and Consumer Sciences-General	M
Finance and Banking	M,D,O
Fish, Game, and Wildlife Management	M,D,O
Food Science and Technology	M,D
Foreign Languages Education	M,D
Forensic Sciences	M,O
Forestry	M,D
French	M,D
Gender Studies	M,O
Genetics	D
Geographic Information Systems	M,D
Geography	M,D
Geology	M,D
Geosciences	M,D
German	M,D
Health Communication	M,D,O
Health Education	M,D,O
Health Psychology	M,D
Health Services Management and Hospital Administration	M,D
Health Services Research	M,D
Higher Education	M,D,O
Historic Preservation	M,D
History	M,D
Horticulture	M,D
Human Resources Management	M,D
Hydrology	M,D
Immunology	D
Industrial/Management Engineering	M,D,O
Information Science	M,D
Insurance	M,D,O
Interdisciplinary Studies	M,D
Interior Design	M,D
International Affairs	M
International Business	M,D
International Development	M,D,O
International Health	M,D
Jewish Studies	M,D
Journalism	M,D
Kinesiology and Movement Studies	M,D
Landscape Architecture	M,D
Latin American Studies	M,O
Law	M,D
Limnology	M,D
Linguistics	M,D,O
Management Information Systems	M,D,O
Marine Sciences	M,D
Marketing	M,D
Marriage and Family Therapy	M,D,O
Mass Communication	M,D
Materials Engineering	M,D
Materials Sciences	M,D
Mathematics Education	M,D,O
Mathematics	M,D
Mechanical Engineering	M,D
Medical Physics	M,D,O
Medicinal and Pharmaceutical Chemistry	M,D
Microbiology	M,D
Molecular Biology	M,D
Molecular Genetics	M
Museum Studies	M,D
Music Education	M,D
Music	M,D
Natural Resources	M,D
Neuroscience	D
Nonprofit Management	M
Nuclear Engineering	M,D
Nursing—General	M,D
Nutrition	M,D
Occupational Therapy	M
Ocean Engineering	M,D
Oral and Dental Sciences	M,D,O
Pharmaceutical Administration	M,D
Pharmaceutical Sciences	M,D
Pharmacology	M,D
Pharmacy	M,D
Philosophy	M,D
Physical Education	M,D
Physical Therapy	D
Physician Assistant Studies	M
Physics	M,D
Physiology	M,D
Plant Biology	M,D
Plant Molecular Biology	M,D
Plant Pathology	M,D
Plant Sciences	D
Political Science	M,D,O
Psychology—General	M,D
Public Affairs	M,D,O
Public Health—General	M,D,O
Quantitative Analysis	M,D,O
Reading Education	M,D,O
Real Estate	M,D,O
Recreation and Park Management	M,D
Rehabilitation Sciences	D
Religion	M,D
School Psychology	M,D,O
Science Education	M,D,O
Social Sciences Education	M,D,O
Social Sciences	M,D,O
Sociology	M,D
Spanish	M,D
Special Education	M,D,O
Sports Management	M,D
Statistics	M,D
Student Affairs	M,D,O
Supply Chain Management	M,D,O
Sustainable Development	M,O
Systems Engineering	M,D,O
Taxation	M,D
Telecommunications	M,D
Theater	M
Toxicology	M,D,O
Travel and Tourism	M,D
Urban and Regional Planning	M,D
Veterinary Medicine	D
Veterinary Sciences	M,D,O
Water Resources	M,D
Women's Studies	M,O
Writing	M,D
Zoology	M,D

UNIVERSITY OF FORT LAUDERDALE

Pastoral Ministry and Counseling	M

UNIVERSITY OF GEORGIA

Accounting	M
Adult Education	M,D,O
Agricultural Economics and Agribusiness	M,D
Agricultural Education	M
Agricultural Engineering	M,D
Agricultural Sciences—General	M,D
Agronomy and Soil Sciences	M,D
Analytical Chemistry	M,D
Anatomy	M
Animal Sciences	M,D
Anthropology	M,D
Applied Economics	M,D
Applied Mathematics	M,D
Archaeology	M,D
Art Education	M,D,O
Art History	M,D
Art/Fine Arts	M,D
Artificial Intelligence/Robotics	M
Biochemical Engineering	M
Biochemistry	M,D
Bioengineering	M,D
Bioinformatics	M,D,O
Biological and Biomedical Sciences—General	D
Business Administration and Management—General	M,D
Business Education	M,D,O
Cell Biology	M,D
Chemistry	M,D
Child and Family Studies	M,D,O
Classics	M
Clothing and Textiles	M,D
Communication Disorders	M,D,O
Communication—General	M,D
Comparative Literature	M,D
Computer Science	M,D
Consumer Economics	M,D
Counselor Education	M,D,O
Early Childhood Education	M,D,O
Ecology	M,D
Economics	M,D
Education—General	M,D,O
Educational Leadership and Administration	M,D,O
Educational Media/Instructional Technology	M,D,O
Educational Policy	M,D,O
Educational Psychology	M,D,O
Elementary Education	M,D,O
English Education	M,D,O
English	M,D
Entomology	M,D
Environmental and Occupational Health	M
Environmental Design	M
Environmental Engineering	M
Family and Consumer Sciences-General	M,D
Food Science and Technology	M,D
Foreign Languages Education	M,D,O
Forestry	M,D
French	M,D
Genetics	M,D
Genomic Sciences	M,D
Geography	M,D
Geology	M,D
German	M
Gerontology	O
Health Education	M,D,O
Health Promotion	M,D
Health Services Management and Hospital Administration	M
Higher Education	D
Historic Preservation	M
History	M,D
Home Economics Education	M,D,O
Horticulture	M,D
Human Resources Management	M,D,O
Infectious Diseases	M,D
Inorganic Chemistry	M,D
Interior Design	M,D
International Affairs	M,D
Internet and Interactive Multimedia	M
Internet Engineering	M
Journalism	M,D
Kinesiology and Movement Studies	M,D
Landscape Architecture	M
Law	M,D
Leisure Studies	M,D,O
Linguistics	M,D
Management Information Systems	D
Marine Sciences	M,D
Mass Communication	M,D
Mathematics Education	M,D,O
Mathematics	M,D
Microbiology	M,D
Middle School Education	M,D,O
Molecular Biology	M,D
Music Education	M,D,O
Music	M,D
Natural Resources	M,D
Neuroscience	D
Nonprofit Management	M,D,O
Nutrition	M,D
Organic Chemistry	M,D
Pathology	M,D
Pharmaceutical Administration	D
Pharmaceutical Sciences	D
Pharmacology	M,D
Pharmacy	M,D,O
Philosophy	M,D
Physical Chemistry	M,D
Physical Education	M,D
Physics	M,D
Physiology	M,D
Plant Biology	M,D
Plant Pathology	M,D
Plant Sciences	M,D
Political Science	M,D
Psychology—General	M,D
Public Administration	M,D
Public Health—General	D
Public Policy	M,D
Reading Education	M,D,O
Religion	M
Romance Languages	M,D
Science Education	M,D,O
Social Sciences Education	M,D,O
Social Work	M,D,O
Sociology	M,D
Spanish	M,D
Special Education	M,D,O
Speech and Interpersonal Communication	M,D
Statistics	M,D
Student Affairs	M,D,O
Sustainable Development	M,D
Theater	M,D
Veterinary Medicine	M,D
Veterinary Sciences	M
Vocational and Technical Education	M,D,O
Women's Studies	O
Writing	M,D

UNIVERSITY OF GREAT FALLS

Counseling Psychology	M
Criminal Justice and Criminology	M
Education—General	M
Human Services	M
Secondary Education	M

UNIVERSITY OF GUAM

Art/Fine Arts	M
Biological and Biomedical Sciences—General	M
Business Administration and Management—General	M
Counselor Education	M
Education—General	M
Educational Leadership and Administration	M
English as a Second Language	M
English	M
Environmental Sciences	M
Graphic Design	M
Marine Biology	M
Pacific Area/Pacific Rim Studies	M
Public Administration	M
Reading Education	M

Secondary Education	M
Social Work	M
Special Education	M

UNIVERSITY OF GUELPH

Acute Care/Critical Care Nursing	M,D,O
Agricultural Economics and Agribusiness	M,D
Agricultural Sciences—General	M,D,O
Agronomy and Soil Sciences	M,D
Anatomy	M,D
Anesthesiologist Assistant Studies	M,D,O
Animal Sciences	M,D
Anthropology	M,D
Applied Mathematics	M,D
Applied Psychology	M,D
Applied Statistics	M,D
Aquaculture	M
Art/Fine Arts	M
Atmospheric Sciences	M,D
Biochemistry	M,D
Bioengineering	M,D
Biological and Biomedical Sciences—General	M,D
Biophysics	M,D
Biotechnology	M,D
Botany	M,D
Business Administration and Management—General	M,D
Cardiovascular Sciences	M,D,O
Cell Biology	M,D
Chemistry	M,D
Child and Family Studies	M,D
Clinical Psychology	M,D
Cognitive Sciences	M,D
Comparative Literature	D
Computer Science	M,D
Consumer Economics	M
Criminal Justice and Criminology	M,D
Demography and Population Studies	M,D
Ecology	M,D
Economics	M,D
Emergency Medical Services	M,D,O
Engineering and Applied Sciences—General	M,D
English	M
Entomology	M,D
Environmental Biology	M,D
Environmental Engineering	M,D
Environmental Management and Policy	M,D
Environmental Sciences	M,D
Epidemiology	M,D
Evolutionary Biology	M,D
Food Science and Technology	M,D
French	M
Geography	M,D
History	M,D
Horticulture	M,D
Hospitality Management	M
Human Development	M,D
Immunology	M,D,O
Industrial and Organizational Psychology	M,D
Infectious Diseases	M,D,O
International Development	M,D
Landscape Architecture	M
Marriage and Family Therapy	M,D
Mathematics	M,D
Medical Imaging	M,D,O
Medieval and Renaissance Studies	D
Microbiology	M,D
Molecular Biology	M,D
Molecular Genetics	M,D
Natural Resources	M,D
Neuroscience	M,D,O
Nutrition	M,D
Organizational Management	M
Pathology	M,D,O
Pharmacology	M,D
Philosophy	M,D
Physics	M,D
Physiology	M,D
Plant Pathology	M,D
Political Science	M
Psychology—General	M,D
Public Administration	M
Public Policy	M
Rural Planning and Studies	M,D
Social Psychology	M,D
Sociology	M,D
Statistics	M,D
Theater	M
Toxicology	M,D
Veterinary Medicine	M,D,O
Veterinary Sciences	M,D,O
Vision Sciences	M,D,O
Water Resources Engineering	M,D
Western European Studies	M
Zoology	M,D

UNIVERSITY OF HARTFORD

Accounting	M,O
Architecture	M
Art/Fine Arts	M*
Biological and Biomedical Sciences—General	M
Business Administration and Management—General	M*
Clinical Psychology	M,D
Communication—General	M
Community Health Nursing	M
Counselor Education	M,O
Early Childhood Education	M
Education—General	M,D,O*
Educational Leadership and Administration	D,O
Educational Media/Instructional Technology	M
Elementary Education	M
Engineering and Applied Sciences—General	M*
Experimental Psychology	M
Music Education	M,D,O
Music	M,D,O*
Neuroscience	M
Nursing Education	M
Nursing—General	M
Organizational Behavior	M
Physical Therapy	M,D
Psychology—General	M,D*
School Psychology	M
Taxation	M,O

UNIVERSITY OF HAWAII AT HILO

Conservation Biology	M
Counseling Psychology	M
Cultural Studies	M,D
Education—General	M
Environmental Sciences	M
Foreign Languages Education	M,D
Marine Biology	M
Nursing—General	D
Pharmaceutical Sciences	D*
Pharmacology	M
Pharmacy	D

UNIVERSITY OF HAWAII AT MANOA

Accounting	M,D
Adult Nursing	M,D,O
Agricultural Sciences—General	M,D
Allopathic Medicine	D
American Studies	M,D,O
Animal Sciences	M
Anthropology	M,D
Architecture	D
Art History	M
Art/Fine Arts	M
Asian Languages	M,D
Asian Studies	O
Astronomy	M,D
Bioengineering	M
Biological and Biomedical Sciences—General	M,D
Botany	M,D
Business Administration and Management—General	M
Chemistry	M,D
Chinese	M,D,O
Civil Engineering	M,D
Clinical Psychology	M,D,O
Communication Disorders	M
Communication—General	M,O
Community Health Nursing	M,D,O
Computer Science	M,D,O
Conflict Resolution and Mediation/Peace Studies	M,O
Cultural Studies	O
Curriculum and Instruction	M,D
Dance	M,D
Demography and Population Studies	O
Developmental Biology	M,D
Disability Studies	O
Early Childhood Education	M
Economics	M,D
Education—General	M,D,O
Educational Leadership and Administration	M,D
Educational Media/Instructional Technology	M,D
Educational Policy	D
Educational Psychology	M,D
Electrical Engineering	M,D
Emergency Management	M,D,O
Engineering and Applied Sciences—General	M,D
English as a Second Language	M,D,O
English	M,D
Entomology	M,D
Entrepreneurship	M,O
Environmental Engineering	M,D
Environmental Management and Policy	M,D,O
Epidemiology	D
Family Nurse Practitioner Studies	M,D,O
Finance and Banking	M,D
Food Science and Technology	M
Foreign Languages Education	M,D,O
Foundations and Philosophy of Education	M,D
French	M
Genetics	M,D
Geochemistry	M,D
Geography	M,D,O
Geological Engineering	M,D
Geology	M,D
Geophysics	M,D
Historic Preservation	O
History	M,D
Horticulture	M,D
Human Resources Management	M
Hydrogeology	M,D
Information Science	M,D
Information Studies	M,O
International Affairs	O
International Business	M,D
International Development	M,D,O
Japanese	M,D,O
Kinesiology and Movement Studies	M,D
Law	M,D,O
Library Science	M,O
Linguistics	M,D
Management Information Systems	M,D,O
Marine Biology	M,D
Marine Geology	M,D
Marine Sciences	O
Marketing	M,D
Mathematics	M,D
Mechanical Engineering	M,D
Medical Microbiology	M,D
Meteorology	M,D
Microbiology	M,D
Molecular Biology	M,D
Museum Studies	O
Music	M,D
Natural Resources	M,D
Nursing and Healthcare Administration	M,D,O
Nursing—General	M,D,O
Nutrition	M,D
Ocean Engineering	M,D
Oceanography	M,D
Organizational Behavior	M
Organizational Management	M,D
Pacific Area/Pacific Rim Studies	M,O
Philosophy	M,D
Physics	M,D
Physiology	M,D
Planetary and Space Sciences	M,D
Plant Pathology	M,D
Plant Sciences	M,D
Political Science	M,D
Psychology—General	M,D,O
Public Administration	M,O
Public Health—General	M,D,O
Public Policy	O
Real Estate	M
Religion	M
Reproductive Biology	M,D
Social Psychology	M,D,O
Social Work	M,D
Sociology	M,D
Spanish	M
Special Education	M,D
Speech and Interpersonal Communication	M
Sustainable Development	M,D,O
Taxation	M
Telecommunications	O
Theater	M,D
Transportation Management	M,D,O
Travel and Tourism	M
Urban and Regional Planning	M,D,O
Women's Studies	O
Zoology	M,D

UNIVERSITY OF HOLY CROSS

Counselor Education	M
Curriculum and Instruction	M
Education—General	M
Educational Leadership and Administration	M
Marriage and Family Therapy	M

UNIVERSITY OF HOUSTON

Accounting	M,D
Advertising and Public Relations	M
Anthropology	M
Applied Economics	M,D
Applied Mathematics	M,D
Architecture	M
Art History	M
Art/Fine Arts	M
Atmospheric Sciences	M,D
Biochemistry	M,D
Biological and Biomedical Sciences—General	M,D
Biomedical Engineering	D
Business Administration and Management—General	M,D
Chemical Engineering	M,D
Chemistry	M,D
Civil Engineering	M,D
Clinical Psychology	M,D
Communication Disorders	M
Communication—General	M
Comparative Literature	M
Computer and Information Systems Security	M
Computer Science	M,D
Construction Management	M
Counseling Psychology	M,D
Cultural Studies	M
Curriculum and Instruction	M,D
Developmental Psychology	M,D
Economics	M,D
Education—General	M,D
Educational Leadership and Administration	M,D
Educational Psychology	M,D
Electrical Engineering	M,D
Engineering and Applied Sciences—General	M,D
Environmental Law	M,D
Exercise and Sports Science	M,D
Family and Consumer Sciences-General	M
Family Nurse Practitioner Studies	M
Finance and Banking	M
Foundations and Philosophy of Education	M,D
Geology	M,D
Geophysics	M,D
Health Communication	M
Health Education	M,D
Health Law	M,D
Higher Education	M,D
Hispanic Studies	M,D
History	M,D
Hospitality Management	M
Human Resources Development	M
Industrial and Organizational Psychology	M,D
Industrial/Management Engineering	M,D
Information Science	M,D
Intellectual Property Law	M,D
Kinesiology and Movement Studies	M,D
Law	M,D
Linguistics	M,D
Logistics	M
Marketing	D
Mass Communication	M
Mathematics	M,D
Mechanical Engineering	M,D
Music Education	M,D
Music	M,D
Nursing and Healthcare Administration	M
Nursing Education	M
Nursing—General	M
Nutrition	M,D
Optometry	D
Petroleum Engineering	M,D
Pharmaceutical Administration	M,D
Pharmaceutical Sciences	M,D
Pharmacology	M,D
Pharmacy	M,D
Philosophy	M
Physical Education	M,D
Physics	M,D
Planetary and Space Sciences	M,D
Political Science	M,D
Project Management	M
Psychology—General	M,D
Public Administration	M,D
Social Psychology	M,D
Social Work	M,D
Sociology	M
Spanish	M,D
Special Education	M,D
Speech and Interpersonal Communication	M
Supply Chain Management	M
Taxation	M,D
Telecommunications	M
Theater	M
Vision Sciences	M,D
Writing	M,D

UNIVERSITY OF HOUSTON–CLEAR LAKE

Accounting	M
Biological and Biomedical Sciences—General	M
Biotechnology	M
Business Administration and Management—General	M
Chemistry	M
Clinical Psychology	M
Computer Engineering	M
Computer Science	M
Counselor Education	M
Criminal Justice and Criminology	M
Cultural Studies	M
Curriculum and Instruction	M
Early Childhood Education	M
Education—General	M,D
Educational Leadership and Administration	M,D
Educational Media/Instructional Technology	M
English	M
Environmental Management and Policy	M
Environmental Sciences	M
Exercise and Sports Science	M
Finance and Banking	M
Foundations and Philosophy of Education	M
Health Services Management and Hospital Administration	M
History	M
Human Resources Management	M
Humanities	M
Information Science	M
Library Science	M
Management Information Systems	M
Marriage and Family Therapy	M
Mathematics	M
Multilingual and Multicultural Education	M
Physics	M
Psychology—General	M
Reading Education	M
School Psychology	M
Sociology	M
Software Engineering	M
Statistics	M
Systems Engineering	M

UNIVERSITY OF HOUSTON–DOWNTOWN

Business Administration and Management—General	M
Criminal Justice and Criminology	M
Curriculum and Instruction	M
Database Systems	M
English	M
Finance and Banking	M
Human Resources Management	M
Investment Management	M
Nonprofit Management	M
Rhetoric	M
Supply Chain Management	M
Technical Communication	M
Urban Education	M

UNIVERSITY OF HOUSTON–VICTORIA

Accounting	M
Adult Education	M
Biological and Biomedical Sciences—General	M
Business Administration and Management—General	M
Computer Science	M
Counseling Psychology	M
Counselor Education	M
Curriculum and Instruction	M

*M—masters degree; D—doctorate; O—other advanced degree; *—Close-Up and/or Display*

Economic Development	M
Education—General	M
Educational Leadership and Administration	M
Educational Media/Instructional Technology	M
Entrepreneurship	M
Finance and Banking	M
Forensic Psychology	M
Forensic Sciences	M
Higher Education	M
Interdisciplinary Studies	M
International Business	M
Management Information Systems	M
Marketing	M
Psychology—General	M
Publishing	M
School Psychology	M
Special Education	M
Writing	M

UNIVERSITY OF IDAHO

Accounting	M
Agricultural Economics and Agribusiness	M
Agricultural Education	M
Agronomy and Soil Sciences	M,D
American Indian/Native American Studies	D
Animal Sciences	M,D
Anthropology	M
Applied Economics	M
Architecture	M
Art Education	M
Art/Fine Arts	M
Athletic Training and Sports Medicine	M,D
Biochemistry	M,D
Bioengineering	M,D
Bioinformatics	M,D
Biological and Biomedical Sciences—General	M,D
Business Administration and Management—General	M,D
Chemical Engineering	M,D
Chemistry	M,D
Civil Engineering	M,D
Computational Biology	M,D
Computer Engineering	M,D
Computer Science	M,D
Conflict Resolution and Mediation/Peace Studies	D
Consumer Economics	M
Counselor Education	M,O
Curriculum and Instruction	M,D,O
Education—General	M,D,O
Educational Leadership and Administration	M,O
Electrical Engineering	M,D
Engineering and Applied Sciences—General	M,D
Engineering Management	M,D
English as a Second Language	M
English	M
Entomology	M,D
Entrepreneurship	D
Environmental Law	D
Environmental Sciences	M,D
Film, Television, and Video Theory and Criticism	M
Food Science and Technology	M,D
Geography	M,D
Geological Engineering	M,D
Geology	M,D
History	M,D
Human Services	M,O
Hydrology	M,D
Interdisciplinary Studies	M
Landscape Architecture	M
Law	D
Management of Technology	M,D
Materials Sciences	M,D
Mathematics	M,D
Mechanical Engineering	M,D
Metallurgical Engineering and Metallurgy	M,D
Microbiology	M,D
Music	M
Natural Resources	M,D
Neuroscience	M,D
Philosophy	M
Physical Education	M,D
Physics	M,D
Plant Sciences	M,D
Political Science	M,D
Psychology—General	M
Public Administration	M,D
Recreation and Park Management	M,D
Rehabilitation Counseling	M,O
Special Education	M,D,O
Statistics	M
Theater	M
Urban and Regional Planning	M
Veterinary Sciences	M,D
Vocational and Technical Education	M,D,O
Water Resources Engineering	M,D
Water Resources	M,D
Writing	M

UNIVERSITY OF ILLINOIS AT CHICAGO

Accounting	M
Acute Care/Critical Care Nursing	M,O
Adult Nursing	M,O
Allied Health—General	M,D,O
Allopathic Medicine	D
Anatomy	M
Anthropology	M,D
Applied Arts and Design—General	M
Architecture	M
Art History	M,D
Art/Fine Arts	M,D
Biochemistry	D
Bioengineering	M,D
Bioinformatics	M,D
Biological and Biomedical Sciences—General	M,D
Biophysics	M,D
Biostatistics	M,D
Biotechnology	M,D
Business Administration and Management—General	M,D
Cell Biology	M,D
Chemical Engineering	M,D
Chemistry	M,D
Civil Engineering	M,D
Communication—General	M,D
Community Health Nursing	M,O
Community Health	M,D
Computer Education	D
Computer Engineering	M,D
Computer Science	M,D
Criminal Justice and Criminology	M,D
Curriculum and Instruction	M,D
Dentistry	D
Developmental Psychology	M,D
Disability Studies	M,D
Early Childhood Education	M,D
East European and Russian Studies	M,D
Economics	M,D
Education—General	M,D
Educational Leadership and Administration	M,D
Educational Measurement and Evaluation	M,D
Educational Policy	M,D
Educational Psychology	M,D
Electrical Engineering	M,D*
Elementary Education	M,D
Engineering and Applied Sciences—General	M,D
English as a Second Language	M,D
English	M,D
Environmental and Occupational Health	M,D
Epidemiology	M,D
Family Nurse Practitioner Studies	M,O
Finance and Banking	M
Foreign Languages Education	M,D
Forensic Sciences	M
French	M
Genetics	D
Geography	M
Geology	M,D
Geosciences	M,D
German	M,D
Gerontological Nursing	M,O
Graphic Design	M
Health Education	M
Health Informatics	M,O
Health Services Management and Hospital Administration	M,D
Health Services Research	M,D
Hispanic and Latin American Languages	M,D
Hispanic Studies	M,D
History	M,D
Human Development	M,D
Immunology	D
Industrial/Management Engineering	M,D
Interdisciplinary Studies	D
Kinesiology and Movement Studies	M,D
Latin American Studies	M
Linguistics	M
Management Information Systems	M,D
Materials Engineering	M,D
Maternal and Child/Neonatal Nursing	M,O
Mathematics Education	M,D
Mathematics	M,D
Mechanical Engineering	M,D
Medical Illustration	M
Microbiology	D
Molecular Biology	D
Molecular Genetics	D
Museum Studies	M,D
Neuroscience	M,D
Nurse Midwifery	M,O
Nursing and Healthcare Administration	M,O
Nursing—General	M,D,O
Nutrition	M,D
Occupational Health Nursing	M,O
Occupational Therapy	M,D
Operations Research	M,D
Oral and Dental Sciences	M,D
Pediatric Nursing	M,O
Pharmaceutical Administration	M,D
Pharmaceutical Sciences	M,D
Pharmacology	D
Pharmacy	M,D
Philosophy	M,D
Physical Therapy	M,D
Physics	M,D
Physiology	M,D
Political Science	M,D
Psychology—General	M,D
Public Administration	M,D
Public Health—General	M,D
Real Estate	M
School Nursing	M,O
Science Education	D
Secondary Education	M,D
Slavic Languages	M,D
Social Sciences Education	D
Social Work	M,D,O
Sociology	M,D
Spanish	M,D
Special Education	M,D
Statistics	M,D
Toxicology	M
Urban and Regional Planning	M,D
Urban Education	M,D
Women's Health Nursing	M,O

UNIVERSITY OF ILLINOIS AT SPRINGFIELD

Accounting	M
Addictions/Substance Abuse Counseling	M,O
Biological and Biomedical Sciences—General	M
Business Administration and Management—General	M
Child and Family Studies	M,O
Communication—General	M
Community Health	M,O
Computer Science	M
Education—General	M,O
Educational Leadership and Administration	M,O
Emergency Management	M,O
English as a Second Language	M,O
English Education	M,O
English	M,O
Environmental Management and Policy	M
Environmental Sciences	M
Epidemiology	M,O
Gerontology	M,O
Health Education	M,O
History	M
Homeland Security	M,O
Human Development	M
Human Services	M,O
Interdisciplinary Studies	M
Journalism	M
Legal and Justice Studies	M
Management Information Systems	M
Political Science	M
Public Administration	M,D,O
Public Health—General	M,O
Public History	M
Social Sciences	M,O

UNIVERSITY OF ILLINOIS AT URBANA–CHAMPAIGN

Accounting	M,D
Actuarial Science	M,D
Advertising and Public Relations	M
Aerospace/Aeronautical Engineering	M,D
African Studies	M
Agricultural Economics and Agribusiness	M,D
Agricultural Education	M
Agricultural Engineering	M,D
Agricultural Sciences—General	M
Agronomy and Soil Sciences	M,D
Allopathic Medicine	
Animal Sciences	M,D
Anthropology	M,D
Applied Arts and Design—General	M,D
Applied Economics	M,D
Applied Mathematics	M,D
Applied Statistics	M,D
Architecture	M,D
Art Education	M,D
Art History	M,D
Art/Fine Arts	M
Asian Languages	M,D
Asian Studies	M,D
Astronomy	M,D
Atmospheric Sciences	M,D
Biochemistry	M,D
Bioengineering	M,D
Bioinformatics	M,D,O
Biological and Biomedical Sciences—General	M,D
Biophysics	M,D
Business Administration and Management—General	M,D
Cell Biology	D
Chemical Engineering	M,D
Chemical Physics	M,D
Chemistry	M,D
Civil Engineering	M,D
Classics	M,D
Communication Disorders	M,D
Communication—General	M,D
Community Health	M,D
Comparative Literature	M,D
Computational Biology	M,D
Computer Engineering	M,D
Computer Science	M,D
Conservation Biology	M,D
Consumer Economics	M,D
Counselor Education	M,D,O
Curriculum and Instruction	M,D,O
Dance	M
Developmental Biology	D
East European and Russian Studies	M
Ecology	M,D
Economics	M,D
Education of Students with Severe/Multiple Disabilities	M,D,O
Education—General	M,D,O
Educational Leadership and Administration	M,D,O
Educational Policy	M,D,O
Educational Psychology	M,D,O
Electrical Engineering	M,D
Energy and Power Engineering	M,D
Energy Management and Policy	M
Engineering and Applied Sciences—General	M,D
English as a Second Language	M,D
English	M,D
Entomology	M,D
Environmental Engineering	M,D
Environmental Sciences	M,D
Evolutionary Biology	M,D
Finance and Banking	M,D
Financial Engineering	M
Food Science and Technology	M,D
Foreign Languages Education	M,D
French	M,D
Geography	M,D
Geology	M,D
Geosciences	M,D
German	M,D
Graphic Design	M
Health Informatics	M,D,O
Health Services Management and Hospital Administration	M,D
History	M,D
Human Development	M,D
Human Resources Management	M,D,O
Human Services	M,D
Human-Computer Interaction	M,D,O
Industrial and Labor Relations	M,D
Industrial Design	M
Industrial/Management Engineering	M,D
Information Science	M,D,O
Information Studies	M,D,O
Interdisciplinary Studies	D
Italian	M,D
Journalism	M
Kinesiology and Movement Studies	M,D
Landscape Architecture	M,D
Latin American Studies	M
Law	M,D
Leisure Studies	M,D
Library Science	M,D,O
Linguistics	M,D
Management of Technology	M,D
Management Strategy and Policy	M,D,O
Materials Engineering	M,D
Materials Sciences	M,D
Mathematics Education	M,D
Mathematics	M,D
Mechanical Engineering	M,D
Mechanics	M,D
Media Studies	M,D
Medical Informatics	M,D,O
Microbiology	M,D
Molecular Physiology	M,D
Music Education	M,D
Music	M,D
Natural Resources	M,D
Near and Middle Eastern Studies	M
Neuroscience	D
Nuclear Engineering	M,D
Nutrition	M,D
Pathobiology	M,D
Philosophy	M,D
Photography	M
Physics	M,D
Physiology	M,D
Plant Biology	M,D
Political Science	M,D
Portuguese	M,D
Psychology—General	M,D
Public Health—General	M,D
Rehabilitation Sciences	M,D
Religion	M
Romance Languages	D
Science Education	M,D
Slavic Languages	M,D
Social Work	M,D
Sociology	M,D
Spanish	M,D
Special Education	M,D,O
Statistics	M,D
Systems Engineering	M,D
Taxation	M,D
Theater	M,D
Translation and Interpretation	M
Urban and Regional Planning	M,D
Veterinary Medicine	D
Veterinary Sciences	M,D
Western European Studies	M
Writing	M,D
Zoology	M,D

UNIVERSITY OF INDIANAPOLIS

Anthropology	M
Art Education	M
Art/Fine Arts	M
Biological and Biomedical Sciences—General	M
Business Administration and Management—General	M,O
Clinical Psychology	M,D
Counseling Psychology	M,D
Curriculum and Instruction	M
Education—General	M
Educational Leadership and Administration	M
Elementary Education	M
English Education	M
English	M
Family Nurse Practitioner Studies	M,D
Foreign Languages Education	M
Gerontology	M,D,O
History	M
International Affairs	M
Maternal and Child/Neonatal Nursing	M,D
Mathematics Education	M
Nurse Midwifery	M,D
Nursing and Healthcare Administration	M,D
Nursing Education	M,D
Nursing—General	M,D
Occupational Therapy	M,D
Physical Education	M
Physical Therapy	M,D
Psychology—General	M,D
Public Health—General	M
Science Education	M
Secondary Education	M
Social Sciences Education	M
Sociology	M
Sports Management	M
Women's Health Nursing	M,D

THE UNIVERSITY OF IOWA

Accounting	M,D
Actuarial Science	M,D
Agricultural Sciences—General	M,D,O
Allopathic Medicine	D
American Studies	M,D
Anatomy	D
Anthropology	M,D
Applied Mathematics	D
Art Education	M,D
Art History	M,D
Art/Fine Arts	M
Asian Languages	M
Asian Studies	M
Astronomy	M
Athletic Training and Sports Medicine	M,D
Bacteriology	M,D
Biochemical Engineering	M,D
Biochemistry	M,D
Bioinformatics	M,D,O
Biological and Biomedical Sciences—General	M,D
Biomedical Engineering	M,D
Biophysics	M,D
Biostatistics	M,D,O
Business Administration and Management—General	M,D
Cell Biology	M,D
Chemical Engineering	M,D
Chemistry	D
Chinese	M
Civil Engineering	M,D
Classics	M,D
Clinical Research	M,D
Communication Disorders	M,D
Communication—General	M,D
Community Health	M,D
Computational Biology	M,D,O
Computational Sciences	D
Computer Engineering	M,D
Computer Science	M,D
Counseling Psychology	M,D,O
Counselor Education	M,D
Dance	M
Database Systems	M
Dentistry	M,D,O
Developmental Education	M,D
Economics	D
Education—General	M,D,O
Educational Leadership and Administration	M,D,O
Educational Measurement and Evaluation	M,D,O
Educational Policy	M,D,O
Educational Psychology	M,D,O
Electrical Engineering	M,D
Elementary Education	M,D
Energy and Power Engineering	M,D
Engineering and Applied Sciences—General	M,D*
English as a Second Language	M,D
English Education	M,D
English	M,D
Environmental and Occupational Health	M,D,O
Environmental Engineering	M,D
Epidemiology	M,D
Ergonomics and Human Factors	M,D,O
Evolutionary Biology	M,D
Exercise and Sports Science	M,D
Film, Television, and Video Production	M
Film, Television, and Video Theory and Criticism	M,D
Finance and Banking	M,D
Foreign Languages Education	M,D
Foundations and Philosophy of Education	M,D,O
French	M,D
Genetics	M,D
Geographic Information Systems	M,D,O
Geography	M,D,O
Geosciences	M,D
Health Informatics	M,D,O
Health Services Management and Hospital Administration	M,D
Higher Education	M,D
History	M,D
Immunology	M,D
Industrial Hygiene	M,D,O
Industrial/Management Engineering	M,D
Information Science	M,D,O
Information Studies	M,D
Investment Management	M
Journalism	M,D
Law	M,D
Leisure Studies	M,D
Library Science	M,D
Linguistics	M,D
Manufacturing Engineering	M,D
Marketing	M,D
Marriage and Family Therapy	M,D
Mass Communication	M,D
Materials Engineering	M,D
Mathematics Education	M,D
Mathematics	M,D
Mechanical Engineering	M,D
Media Studies	M,D
Medicinal and Pharmaceutical Chemistry	M,D
Microbiology	M,D
Molecular Biology	D
Music Education	M,D
Music	M,D
Neurobiology	M,D
Neuroscience	D
Nursing—General	M,D
Operations Research	M,D
Oral and Dental Sciences	M,D,O
Pathology	M
Pharmaceutical Sciences	M,D
Pharmacology	M,D
Pharmacy	M,D
Philosophy	D
Physical Therapy	M,D
Physician Assistant Studies	M
Physics	M,D
Physiology	M,D
Political Science	D
Psychology—General	M,D,O
Public Health—General	M,D,O
Quantitative Analysis	M,D,O
Radiation Biology	M
Recreation and Park Management	M,D
Rehabilitation Counseling	M,D
Rehabilitation Sciences	M,D
Religion	M,D
Rhetoric	M,D
School Psychology	M,D,O
Science Education	M,D
Secondary Education	M,D
Social Sciences Education	M,D
Social Work	M,D
Sociology	M,D
Spanish	M,D
Special Education	M,D
Speech and Interpersonal Communication	M,D
Sports Management	M,D
Statistics	M,D,O
Student Affairs	M,D
Theater	M
Toxicology	M,D
Translational Biology	M,D
Urban and Regional Planning	M
Virology	M,D
Women's Studies	O
Writing	M,D

UNIVERSITY OF JAMESTOWN

Curriculum and Instruction	M
Education—General	M
Physical Therapy	D

THE UNIVERSITY OF KANSAS

Accounting	M
Adult Nursing	M,D,O
Aerospace/Aeronautical Engineering	M,D
African Studies	M,O
African-American Studies	M,O
Allied Health—General	M,D,O
Allopathic Medicine	D
American Indian/Native American Studies	M,O
American Studies	M,D
Anatomy	M,D
Anthropology	M,D
Applied Arts and Design—General	M
Applied Behavior Analysis	M,D
Applied Statistics	M,D,O
Architectural Engineering	M
Architecture	M,D,O
Art Education	M
Art History	M,D
Art/Fine Arts	M
Asian Languages	M
Asian Studies	M
Astronomy	M,D
Atmospheric Sciences	M,D
Biochemistry	M,D
Bioengineering	M,D
Biological and Biomedical Sciences—General	D*
Biophysics	M,D
Biostatistics	M,D,O
Biotechnology	M
Botany	M,D
Business Administration and Management—General	M,D
Cell Biology	M,D
Chemical Engineering	M,D
Chemistry	M,D
Civil Engineering	M,D
Classics	M
Clinical Psychology	M,D
Clinical Research	M
Cognitive Sciences	M,D
Communication Disorders	M,D
Communication—General	M,D
Community Health Nursing	M,D,O
Computational Biology	D
Computational Sciences	M,D
Computer Art and Design	M
Computer Engineering	M
Computer Science	M,D
Construction Management	M
Counseling Psychology	M,D
Curriculum and Instruction	M,D
Developmental Biology	M,D
Developmental Psychology	M,D
East European and Russian Studies	M,O
Ecology	M,D
Economics	M,D
Education—General	M,D,O
Educational Leadership and Administration	M,D
Educational Measurement and Evaluation	M,D
Educational Media/Instructional Technology	M,D
Educational Policy	D
Educational Psychology	M,D
Electrical Engineering	M,D
Engineering and Applied Sciences—General	M,D
Engineering Management	M
English	M,D
Entomology	M,D
Environmental and Occupational Health	M
Environmental Engineering	M,D
Environmental Sciences	M,D
Epidemiology	M
Evolutionary Biology	M,D
Facilities Management	M,D,O
Film, Television, and Video Theory and Criticism	M,D
Foundations and Philosophy of Education	M,D
French	M,D
Geography	M,D
Geology	M,D
German	M,D
Gerontological Nursing	M,D,O
Gerontology	M,D,O
Health Education	M,D,O
Health Informatics	M,O
Health Services Management and Hospital Administration	M,D
Higher Education	M,D
History	M,D
Interdisciplinary Studies	D
International Affairs	M
Journalism	M
Latin American Studies	M,O
Law	D
Linguistics	M,D
Management Information Systems	M
Mathematics	M,D
Mechanical Engineering	M,D
Media Studies	M,D
Medical Informatics	M,D,O
Medicinal and Pharmaceutical Chemistry	M,D
Microbiology	M,D
Molecular Biology	M,D
Museum Studies	M,O
Music Education	M,D
Music	M,D
Near and Middle Eastern Studies	M,O
Neuroscience	M,D
Nurse Anesthesia	D
Nurse Midwifery	M,D,O
Nursing and Healthcare Administration	M,D,O
Nursing—General	M,D,O
Nutrition	M,D,O
Occupational Therapy	M,D
Organizational Management	M,D,O
Pathology	D
Petroleum Engineering	M,D
Pharmaceutical Sciences	M
Pharmacology	M,D
Philosophy	M,D
Physical Education	M,D
Physical Therapy	D
Physics	M,D
Physiology	D
Political Science	M,D
Project Management	M
Psychiatric Nursing	M,D,O
Psychology—General	M,D
Public Administration	M,D
Public Health—General	M
Rehabilitation Counseling	M,D
Rehabilitation Sciences	M,D
Religion	M
School Psychology	D,O
Slavic Languages	M,D
Social Psychology	M,D
Social Work	M,D
Sociology	M,D
Spanish	M,D
Special Education	M,D
Statistics	M,D,O
Textile Design	M
Theater	M,D
Therapies—Dance, Drama, and Music	M
Toxicology	M,D
Urban and Regional Planning	M
Writing	M,D

UNIVERSITY OF KENTUCKY

Accounting	M
Agricultural Economics and Agribusiness	M,D
Agricultural Engineering	M,D
Agricultural Sciences—General	M,D
Agronomy and Soil Sciences	M,D
Allied Health—General	M,D
Allopathic Medicine	D
Anatomy	D
Animal Sciences	M,D
Anthropology	M,D
Applied Arts and Design—General	M
Applied Mathematics	M,D
Architecture	M
Art Education	M
Art History	M
Art/Fine Arts	M
Arts Administration	M
Astronomy	M,D
Athletic Training and Sports Medicine	M
Biochemistry	D
Biological and Biomedical Sciences—General	M,D
Biomedical Engineering	M,D
Biostatistics	D
Business Administration and Management—General	M,D
Chemical Engineering	M,D
Chemistry	M,D
Child and Family Studies	M,D
Civil Engineering	M,D
Classics	M
Clinical Research	M
Communication Disorders	M
Communication—General	M,D
Computer Science	M,D
Counseling Psychology	M,D,O
Curriculum and Instruction	M,D
Dentistry	D
Early Childhood Education	M,D
Economics	M,D
Education—General	M,D,O
Educational Leadership and Administration	M,D,O
Educational Measurement and Evaluation	M,D
Educational Media/Instructional Technology	M,D
Educational Policy	M,D
Educational Psychology	M,D,O
Electrical Engineering	M,D
Elementary Education	M,D
Engineering and Applied Sciences—General	M,D
English	M,D
Entomology	M,D
Epidemiology	D
Exercise and Sports Science	M,D
Food Science and Technology	M,D
Foreign Languages Education	M
Forestry	M
Geography	M,D
Geology	M,D
German	M
Gerontology	D,O
Health Physics/Radiological Health	M
Health Promotion	M,D
Health Services Management and Hospital Administration	M
Higher Education	M,D
Hispanic Studies	M,D
Historic Preservation	M
History	M,D
Hospitality Management	M
Immunology	D
Information Science	M
Interior Design	M
International Affairs	M
International Business	M
Kinesiology and Movement Studies	M,D
Law	D
Library Science	M
Manufacturing Engineering	M
Materials Engineering	M,D
Materials Sciences	M,D
Mathematics	M,D
Mechanical Engineering	M,D
Medical Physics	M
Microbiology	D
Middle School Education	M,D
Mineral/Mining Engineering	M,D
Music Education	M,D
Music	M,D
Neurobiology	D
Nursing—General	D
Nutrition	M,D
Oral and Dental Sciences	M
Pharmaceutical Sciences	M,D
Pharmacology	D
Pharmacy	D
Philosophy	M,D
Physical Education	M,D
Physical Therapy	D
Physician Assistant Studies	M
Physics	M,D
Physiology	D
Plant Pathology	M,D
Plant Sciences	M,D
Political Science	M,D
Psychology—General	M,D
Public Administration	M,D
Public Health—General	M,D
Public Policy	M,D
Reading Education	M,D
Rehabilitation Counseling	M,D
Rehabilitation Sciences	D
School Psychology	M,D,O
Secondary Education	M,D
Social Work	M,D
Sociology	M,D
Special Education	M,D
Statistics	M,D
Therapies—Dance, Drama, and Music	M,D
Toxicology	M,D
Veterinary Sciences	M,D

UNIVERSITY OF KING'S COLLEGE

Journalism	M
Writing	M

UNIVERSITY OF LA VERNE

Accounting	M
Business Administration and Management—General	M,D,O
Child and Family Studies	M
Child Development	M
Clinical Psychology	D
Counselor Education	M,D,O
Education—General	M,O
Educational Leadership and Administration	M,D,O
Elementary Education	M,D,O
English	M,O
Finance and Banking	M
Gerontology	M,O
Health Services Management and Hospital Administration	M,D,O
Health Services Research	M

*M—masters degree; D—doctorate; O—other advanced degree; *—Close-Up and/or Display*

Human Resources Management	M,O
International Business	M
Law	D
Management Information Systems	M,O
Marketing	M
Marriage and Family Therapy	M
Nonprofit Management	M,O
Organizational Management	M,D,O
Psychology—General	M,D
Public Administration	M,D
Reading Education	M,O
School Psychology	M,O
Secondary Education	M,D,O
Special Education	M,D,O
Supply Chain Management	M

UNIVERSITY OF LETHBRIDGE

Accounting	M,D
Addictions/Substance Abuse Counseling	M,D
Agricultural Sciences—General	M,D
American Indian/Native American Studies	M,D
Anthropology	M,D
Archaeology	M,D
Art/Fine Arts	M,D
Biochemistry	M,D
Biological and Biomedical Sciences—General	M,D
Business Administration and Management—General	M,D
Canadian Studies	M,D
Chemistry	M,D
Computational Sciences	M,D
Computer Science	M,D
Counseling Psychology	M,D
Counselor Education	M,D
Economics	M,D
Education—General	M,D
Educational Leadership and Administration	M,D
English	M,D
Environmental Sciences	M,D
Exercise and Sports Science	M,D
Finance and Banking	M,D
French	M,D
Gender Studies	M,D
Geographic Information Systems	M,D
Geography	M,D
German	M,D
Human Resources Management	M,D
International Business	M,D
Kinesiology and Movement Studies	M,D
Management Information Systems	M,D
Management Strategy and Policy	M,D
Marketing	M,D
Mathematics	M,D
Media Studies	M,D
Molecular Biology	M,D
Music	M,D
Neuroscience	M,D
Nursing—General	M,D
Philosophy	M,D
Physics	M,D
Political Science	M,D
Psychology—General	M,D
Religion	M,D
Sociology	M,D
Spanish	M,D
Theater	M,D
Urban Studies	M,D
Women's Studies	M,D

UNIVERSITY OF LOUISIANA AT LAFAYETTE

American Studies	D
Architectural Engineering	M
Biological and Biomedical Sciences—General	M,D
Business Administration and Management—General	M
Chemical Engineering	M
Civil Engineering	M
Cognitive Sciences	D
Communication Disorders	M,D
Communication—General	M
Computer Engineering	M,D
Computer Science	M,D
Counselor Education	M
Curriculum and Instruction	M
Education of the Gifted	M
Education—General	M,D
Educational Leadership and Administration	M,D
Engineering Management	M
English	M,D
Environmental Biology	M,D
Evolutionary Biology	M,D
Folklore	M,D
French	M,D
Geology	M
History	M
Mass Communication	M
Mathematics	M,D
Mechanical Engineering	M
Music Education	M
Music	M
Nursing—General	M
Petroleum Engineering	M
Physics	M
Psychology—General	M
Rehabilitation Counseling	M
Rhetoric	M,D
Telecommunications	M
Writing	M,D

UNIVERSITY OF LOUISIANA AT MONROE

Art Education	M,D
Biological and Biomedical Sciences—General	M
Clinical Psychology	M
Communication Disorders	M
Communication—General	M
Counseling Psychology	M
Counselor Education	M
Criminal Justice and Criminology	M
Curriculum and Instruction	M,D
Early Childhood Education	M,D
Education of the Gifted	M,D
Education—General	M,D
Educational Leadership and Administration	M,D
Educational Measurement and Evaluation	M,D
Elementary Education	M,D
English as a Second Language	M,D
English Education	M,D
English	M
Exercise and Sports Science	M
Family and Consumer Sciences-General	M,D
Foreign Languages Education	M,D
Forensic Psychology	M
Gerontology	M,O
History	M
Marriage and Family Therapy	M,D
Mathematics Education	M,D
Middle School Education	M,D
Music Education	M,D
Occupational Therapy	M
Pharmacy	D
Psychology—General	M
Reading Education	M,D
Recreation and Park Management	M
Science Education	M,D
Secondary Education	M
Social Sciences Education	M,D
Special Education	M,D
Speech and Interpersonal Communication	M,D
Sports Management	M
Toxicology	D

UNIVERSITY OF LOUISVILLE

Accounting	M
Addictions/Substance Abuse Counseling	M,D,O
African Studies	M
African-American Studies	M
Allopathic Medicine	D
Analytical Chemistry	M,D
Anatomy	M,D
Anthropology	M
Applied Arts and Design—General	M,D
Applied Behavior Analysis	M,D,O
Applied Mathematics	M,D
Art Education	M,D,O
Art History	M,D
Art Therapy	M,D
Biochemistry	M,D
Bioengineering	M
Biological and Biomedical Sciences—General	M,D
Biophysics	M,D
Biostatistics	M,D
Business Administration and Management—General	M
Chemical Engineering	M,D
Chemical Physics	M,D
Chemistry	M,D
Civil Engineering	M,D,O
Clinical Psychology	D
Clinical Research	M,D
Cognitive Sciences	D
Communication Disorders	M,D
Communication—General	M
Community Health	M
Computer and Information Systems Security	M,D,O
Computer Engineering	M,D,O
Computer Science	M,D,O
Counseling Psychology	M,D
Counselor Education	M,D
Criminal Justice and Criminology	M,D
Cultural Studies	M,D
Curriculum and Instruction	M,D,O
Dentistry	M,D
Developmental Psychology	D
Early Childhood Education	M,D,O
Education—General	M,D,O
Educational Leadership and Administration	M,D,O
Educational Measurement and Evaluation	M,D
Educational Psychology	M,D
Electrical Engineering	M,D
Elementary Education	M,D,O
Engineering and Applied Sciences—General	M,D,O
Engineering Management	M,D,O
English	M,D
Entrepreneurship	M,D
Environmental and Occupational Health	M,D
Environmental Biology	M,D
Environmental Engineering	M,D,O
Epidemiology	M,D
Exercise and Sports Science	M,D,O
Family Nurse Practitioner Studies	M,D
French	M
Geography	M
Gerontological Nursing	M,D
Gerontology	M,D,O
Health Education	M,D,O
Health Promotion	M,D
Health Services Management and Hospital Administration	M
Higher Education	M,D,O
History	M,O
Human Resources Development	M,D,O
Human Resources Management	M,D,O
Humanities	M,D
Immunology	M,D
Industrial/Management Engineering	M,D,O
Information Science	M,D
Inorganic Chemistry	M,D
Interdisciplinary Studies	M,D
International Business	M
Law	D
Linguistics	M,D
Logistics	M,D,O
Marriage and Family Therapy	M,D,O
Maternal and Child/Neonatal Nursing	M,D
Mathematics	M,D
Mechanical Engineering	M,D
Microbiology	M,D
Middle School Education	M,D,O
Molecular Biology	M,D
Museum Studies	M,D
Music Education	M,D,O
Music	M
Neurobiology	M,D
Nonprofit Management	M,D
Nursing and Healthcare Administration	M,D
Nursing Education	M,D
Nursing—General	M,D
Oral and Dental Sciences	M,D
Organic Chemistry	M,D
Pharmacology	M,D
Philosophy	M
Physical Chemistry	M,D
Physical Education	M,D,O
Physics	M,D
Physiology	M,D
Political Science	M,D
Psychiatric Nursing	M,D
Psychology—General	D
Public Administration	M,D
Public Affairs	M,D
Public Health—General	M,D
Public History	M,O
Public Policy	M,D
Rhetoric	M,D
School Psychology	M,D
Secondary Education	M,D,O
Social Work	M,D,O
Sociology	M,D
Spanish	M
Special Education	M,D,O
Sports Management	M,D,O
Student Affairs	M,D
Supply Chain Management	M,D,O
Theater	M
Toxicology	M,D
Urban and Regional Planning	M,D
Urban Studies	M,D
Women's Health Nursing	M,D
Women's Studies	M,O
Writing	M,D

UNIVERSITY OF MAINE

Accounting	M,O
Agricultural Economics and Agribusiness	M
Agricultural Sciences—General	M,D,O
Animal Sciences	M,D,O
Anthropology	D
Art/Fine Arts	M
Asian Studies	M,D
Bioinformatics	M,D
Biological and Biomedical Sciences—General	M,D
Biomedical Engineering	M,D
Botany	M,D
Business Administration and Management—General	M,O
Canadian Studies	M,D
Chemical Engineering	M,D
Chemistry	M,D
Civil Engineering	M,D
Communication Disorders	M
Communication—General	M,D
Computer Engineering	M,D
Computer Science	M,D,O
Counselor Education	M,D,O
Early Childhood Education	M,D,O
Ecology	M,D
Economics	M
Education—General	M,D,O
Educational Leadership and Administration	M,D,O
Educational Media/Instructional Technology	M,D,O
Electrical Engineering	M,D
Elementary Education	M,D,O
Engineering and Applied Sciences—General	M,D
Engineering Physics	M,D
English Education	M
English	M
Entomology	M,D
Environmental Management and Policy	D
Environmental Sciences	M,D
Exercise and Sports Science	M,D,O
Family Nurse Practitioner Studies	M,O
Finance and Banking	M,O
Fish, Game, and Wildlife Management	M,D
Food Science and Technology	M,D,O
Forestry	M,D
Gender Studies	M
Geographic Information Systems	M,D,O
Geology	M,O
Geosciences	M,D
Higher Education	M,D,O
History	M,D
Horticulture	M,D,O
Human Development	M,D,O
Information Science	M,D,O
Interdisciplinary Studies	M,D
International Affairs	M
International Business	M,O
Kinesiology and Movement Studies	M,D,O
Law	D
Management Information Systems	M,D,O
Marine Affairs	M,D
Marine Biology	M,D
Marine Sciences	M,D
Mass Communication	M,D
Mathematics Education	M,D,O
Mechanical Engineering	M,D
Microbiology	M,D
Molecular Biology	M,D
Music	M
Natural Resources	M,D
Nursing Education	M,O
Nursing—General	M,O
Nutrition	M,D,O
Oceanography	M,D
Physical Education	M,D,O
Physics	M,D
Plant Pathology	M,D
Plant Sciences	M,D,O
Psychology—General	M,D
Reading Education	M,D,O
Science Education	M,D,O
Secondary Education	M,D,O
Social Sciences Education	M,D,O
Social Work	M,O
Special Education	M,D,O
Sustainability Management	M,O
Water Resources	M,D
Western European Studies	M,D
Zoology	M,D

UNIVERSITY OF MAINE AT FARMINGTON

Early Childhood Education	M
Education—General	M
Educational Leadership and Administration	M

UNIVERSITY OF MANAGEMENT AND TECHNOLOGY

Business Administration and Management—General	M,D,O
Computer Science	M,O
Criminal Justice and Criminology	M,O
Engineering Management	M
Health Services Management and Hospital Administration	M
Homeland Security	M
Management Information Systems	M,O
Project Management	M,D,O
Public Administration	M,O
Software Engineering	M,O

THE UNIVERSITY OF MANCHESTER

Accounting	M
Actuarial Science	M,D
Aerospace/Aeronautical Engineering	M,D
Analytical Chemistry	M,D
Anthropology	M,D
Applied Mathematics	M,D
Archaeology	M,D
Architecture	M,D
Art History	D
Art/Fine Arts	M,D
Arts Administration	D
Asian Studies	M,D
Astronomy	M,D
Astrophysics	M,D
Atmospheric Sciences	M,D
Biochemical Engineering	M,D
Biochemistry	M,D
Bioinformatics	M,D
Biological and Biomedical Sciences—General	M,D
Biophysics	M,D
Biotechnology	M,D
Business Administration and Management—General	M
Cancer Biology/Oncology	M,D
Cell Biology	M,D
Chemical Engineering	M,D
Chemistry	M,D
Chinese	M,D
Civil Engineering	M,D
Classics	D
Clinical Psychology	M,D
Clothing and Textiles	M,D
Communication Disorders	M,D
Computer Science	M,D
Condensed Matter Physics	M,D
Conflict Resolution and Mediation/Peace Studies	D
Counseling Psychology	M,D
Criminal Justice and Criminology	M,D
Cultural Studies	M,D
Dentistry	M,D
Developmental Biology	M,D
Developmental Psychology	M,D
Ecology	M,D
Economics	D
Education—General	M,D
Educational Psychology	M,D
Electrical Engineering	M,D
Engineering Management	M,D
English as a Second Language	M,D
English	D
Entrepreneurship	M
Environmental Biology	M,D
Environmental Design	M,D
Environmental Engineering	M,D
Environmental Management and Policy	M,D
Environmental Sciences	M,D
Evolutionary Biology	M,D
Finance and Banking	M
French	M,D
Genetics	M,D
Geochemistry	M,D
Geography	M,D
Geosciences	M,D
German	M,D
Hazardous Materials Management	M,D
Health Law	M,D

Hispanic Studies	M,D
History of Medicine	M,D
History of Science and Technology	M,D
History	D
Human Resources Management	M
Immunology	M,D
Industrial and Labor Relations	M
Industrial and Manufacturing Management	M,D
Industrial and Organizational Psychology	M
Inorganic Chemistry	M,D
International Affairs	D
International Business	M
International Development	M,D
Italian	M,D
Japanese	M,D
Landscape Architecture	M,D
Latin American Studies	M,D
Law	M,D
Linguistics	M,D
Management Strategy and Policy	M
Marketing	M
Materials Sciences	M,D
Mathematical and Computational Finance	M,D
Mathematics	M,D
Mechanical Engineering	M,D
Metallurgical Engineering and Metallurgy	M,D
Microbiology	M,D
Modeling and Simulation	M,D
Molecular Biology	M,D
Molecular Genetics	M,D
Museum Studies	D
Music	D
Natural Resources	M,D
Near and Middle Eastern Languages	M,D
Near and Middle Eastern Studies	M,D
Neurobiology	M,D
Neuroscience	M,D
Nuclear Engineering	M,D
Nurse Midwifery	M,D
Nursing—General	M,D
Optometry	M,D
Oral and Dental Sciences	M,D
Organic Chemistry	M,D
Paleontology	M,D
Paper and Pulp Engineering	M,D
Pharmaceutical Sciences	M,D
Pharmacology	M,D
Pharmacy	M,D
Philosophy	M,D
Physical Chemistry	M,D
Physics	M,D
Physiology	M,D
Plant Sciences	M,D
Political Science	M,D
Polymer Science and Engineering	M,D
Project Management	M
Psychology—General	M,D
Public Health—General	M,D
Religion	D
Russian	M,D
Slavic Languages	M,D
Social Sciences	M,D
Social Work	M,D
Sociology	M,D
Spanish	M,D
Statistics	M,D
Structural Biology	M,D
Structural Engineering	M,D
Supply Chain Management	M
Textile Design	M,D
Theater	D
Theology	D
Theoretical Chemistry	M,D
Theoretical Physics	M,D
Toxicology	M,D
Translation and Interpretation	M,D
Vision Sciences	M,D
Writing	D

UNIVERSITY OF MANITOBA

Adult Education	M
Agricultural Economics and Agribusiness	M,D
Agricultural Sciences—General	M,D
Agronomy and Soil Sciences	M,D
American Indian/Native American Studies	M
Anatomy	M,D
Animal Sciences	M,D
Anthropology	M,D
Architecture	M
Archives/Archival Administration	M,D
Biochemistry	M,D
Biological and Biomedical Sciences—General	M,D,O
Biosystems Engineering	M,D
Botany	M,D
Business Administration and Management—General	M,D
Canadian Studies	M
Cancer Biology/Oncology	M
Chemistry	M,D
Child and Family Studies	M
Civil Engineering	M,D
Classics	M
Clinical Psychology	M,D
Clothing and Textiles	M
Community Health	M,D,O
Computational Sciences	M
Computer Engineering	M,D
Computer Science	M,D
Counselor Education	M
Curriculum and Instruction	M
Dentistry	D
Disability Studies	M
Ecology	M,D
Economics	M,D
Education—General	M,D
Educational Leadership and Administration	M
Educational Psychology	M
Electrical Engineering	M,D
Engineering and Applied Sciences—General	M,D
English as a Second Language	M
English Education	M
English	M,D
Entomology	M,D
Environmental Sciences	M,D
Family and Consumer Sciences-General	M
Food Science and Technology	M,D
Foundations and Philosophy of Education	M
French	M,D
Geography	M,D
Geology	M,D
Geophysics	M,D
German	M
Higher Education	M
History	M,D
Horticulture	M,D
Human Genetics	M,D
Immunology	M,D
Industrial/Management Engineering	M,D
Interdisciplinary Studies	M,D
Interior Design	M
Kinesiology and Movement Studies	M
Landscape Architecture	M
Law	M
Linguistics	M,D
Manufacturing Engineering	M,D
Mathematics	M,D
Mechanical Engineering	M,D
Medical Microbiology	M,D
Microbiology	M,D
Music	M
Natural Resources	M,D
Northern Studies	M
Nursing—General	M
Nutrition	M,D
Occupational Therapy	M,D
Oral and Dental Sciences	M,D
Pathology	M
Pharmaceutical Sciences	M,D
Pharmacology	M,D
Philosophy	M
Physical Education	M
Physical Therapy	M,D
Physics	M,D
Physiology	M,D
Plant Physiology	M,D
Plant Sciences	M,D
Political Science	M
Psychology—General	M,D
Public Administration	M
Recreation and Park Management	M
Rehabilitation Sciences	M,D
Religion	M,D
School Psychology	M,D
Slavic Languages	M
Social Work	M,D
Sociology	M,D
Special Education	M
Statistics	M,D
Urban and Regional Planning	M
Zoology	M,D

UNIVERSITY OF MARY

Bioethics	M
Business Administration and Management—General	M
Cardiovascular Sciences	M
Curriculum and Instruction	M,D
Education—General	M,D
Educational Leadership and Administration	M,D
Energy Management and Policy	M
Exercise and Sports Science	M
Family Nurse Practitioner Studies	M,D
Health Services Management and Hospital Administration	M
Human Resources Management	M
Kinesiology and Movement Studies	M
Nursing and Healthcare Administration	M,D
Nursing Education	M,D
Nursing—General	M,D
Occupational Therapy	M
Physical Education	M
Physical Therapy	D
Project Management	M
Reading Education	M,D
Special Education	M,D
Sports Management	M

UNIVERSITY OF MARY HARDIN-BAYLOR

Accounting	M
Business Administration and Management—General	M
Clinical Psychology	M
Computer Education	M
Counseling Psychology	M
Counselor Education	M
Curriculum and Instruction	M,D
Education—General	M,D
Educational Leadership and Administration	M,D
Elementary Education	M,D
Exercise and Sports Science	M
Family Nurse Practitioner Studies	M,O
Higher Education	M,D
International Business	M
Management Information Systems	M
Marriage and Family Therapy	M
Nursing and Healthcare Administration	M,O
Nursing Education	M,D,O
Nursing—General	M,O
Physical Therapy	D
Secondary Education	M,D
Sports Management	M

UNIVERSITY OF MARYLAND, BALTIMORE

Allopathic Medicine	D
Biochemistry	M,D
Biological and Biomedical Sciences—General	M,D
Biostatistics	M,D
Cancer Biology/Oncology	M,D
Cell Biology	M,D
Clinical Laboratory Sciences/Medical Technology	M
Clinical Research	M,D,O
Community Health Nursing	M
Dentistry	D,O
Environmental Sciences	M,D
Epidemiology	M,D
Ethics	O
Genetic Counseling	M
Genomic Sciences	M,D
Gerontological Nursing	M
Gerontology	M,D
Health Services Research	M,D
Human Genetics	M,D
Immunology	D
Law	M,D
Marine Sciences	M,D
Maternal and Child/Neonatal Nursing	M
Medical/Surgical Nursing	M
Microbiology	D
Molecular Biology	M,D
Molecular Medicine	M,D
Neurobiology	D
Neuroscience	D
Nurse Midwifery	M
Nursing and Healthcare Administration	M
Nursing Education	M
Nursing—General	M,D,O
Oral and Dental Sciences	M,D,O
Pathology	M
Pediatric Nursing	M
Pharmaceutical Administration	M,D
Pharmaceutical Sciences	D
Pharmacology	M,D
Pharmacy	M,D
Physical Therapy	D
Psychiatric Nursing	M
Rehabilitation Sciences	D
Social Work	M,D
Thanatology	O
Toxicology	M,D

UNIVERSITY OF MARYLAND, BALTIMORE COUNTY

Applied Mathematics	M,D
Applied Psychology	D
Art Education	M
Atmospheric Sciences	M,D
Biochemical Engineering	M,D,O
Biochemistry	M,D,O
Biological and Biomedical Sciences—General	M,D,O
Biostatistics	M,D
Biotechnology	M,O
Cell Biology	D
Chemical Engineering	M,D
Chemistry	M,D,O
Clinical Psychology	M,D
Cognitive Sciences	D
Communication—General	M
Computer and Information Systems Security	M,O
Computer Art and Design	M
Computer Engineering	M,D
Computer Science	M,D
Dance	M
Developmental Psychology	D
Distance Education Development	M,O
Early Childhood Education	M
Economics	M,D
Education—General	M,O
Educational Media/Instructional Technology	M,O
Educational Policy	M,D
Electrical Engineering	M,D
Elementary Education	M
Emergency Management	M,O
Engineering and Applied Sciences—General	M,D,O
Engineering Management	M,O
English as a Second Language	M,O
English Education	M
English	M
Environmental Engineering	M,D
Environmental Management and Policy	M,D
Environmental Sciences	M,D
Epidemiology	M,O
Foreign Languages Education	M
Geographic Information Systems	M,O
Geography	M,D
Gerontology	M,D
Health Education	M,O
Health Informatics	M
Health Services Management and Hospital Administration	M,D,O
History	M
Human Services	M,D
Industrial and Organizational Psychology	M
Information Science	M,D
Linguistics	M
Marine Sciences	M,D
Mathematics Education	M
Mechanical Engineering	M,D,O
Molecular Biology	M,D
Multilingual and Multicultural Education	M,D
Music Education	M
Music	O
Neuroscience	D
Nonprofit Management	M,O
Physics	M,D
Planetary and Space Sciences	M
Psychology—General	M,D
Public History	M,D
Public Policy	M,D
Science Education	M
Social Sciences Education	M
Social Sciences	D
Sociology	M
Statistics	M,D
Systems Engineering	M,O
Theater	M
Urban Studies	M,D
Women's Studies	O

UNIVERSITY OF MARYLAND, COLLEGE PARK

Advertising and Public Relations	M,D
Aerospace/Aeronautical Engineering	M,D
Agricultural Economics and Agribusiness	M,D
Agricultural Sciences—General	M,D
American Studies	M,D
Analytical Chemistry	M,D
Animal Sciences	M,D
Anthropology	M
Applied Mathematics	M,D
Architecture	M
Art History	M,D
Art Therapy	M,D,O
Art/Fine Arts	M
Astronomy	M,D
Biochemistry	M,D
Bioengineering	M,D
Bioinformatics	D
Biological and Biomedical Sciences—General	M,D
Biophysics	D
Biostatistics	M,D
Broadcast Journalism	M,D
Business Administration and Management—General	M,D
Cell Biology	M,D
Chemical Engineering	M,D
Chemical Physics	M,D
Chemistry	M,D
Child and Family Studies	M,D
Civil Engineering	M,D
Classics	M
Clinical Psychology	M,D
Cognitive Sciences	D
Communication Disorders	M,D
Communication—General	M,D
Comparative Literature	M,D
Computational Biology	D
Computer Engineering	M,D
Computer Science	M,D
Conservation Biology	M
Counseling Psychology	M,D,O
Counselor Education	M,D,O
Criminal Justice and Criminology	M,D
Curriculum and Instruction	M,D,O
Dance	M
Developmental Psychology	M,D
Ecology	M,D
Economics	M,D
Education—General	M,D,O
Educational Leadership and Administration	M,D,O
Educational Measurement and Evaluation	M,D
Educational Media/Instructional Technology	M,D,O
Electrical Engineering	M,D*
Engineering and Applied Sciences—General	M
English as a Second Language	M,D,O
English	M,D
Entomology	M,D
Environmental and Occupational Health	M
Environmental Engineering	M,D
Environmental Sciences	M,D
Epidemiology	M,D
Evolutionary Biology	M,D
Experimental Psychology	M,D
Family and Consumer Sciences-General	M,D
Fire Protection Engineering	M
Food Science and Technology	M,D
Foreign Languages Education	D
Foundations and Philosophy of Education	M,D,O
French	M,D
Genomic Sciences	D
Geography	M,D
Geology	M,D
German	M,D
Health Education	M,D
Health Services Management and Hospital Administration	M,D
Historic Preservation	M,O
History	M,D
Horticulture	M,D
Human Development	M,D

*M—masters degree; D—doctorate; O—other advanced degree; *—Close-Up and/or Display*

Industrial and Organizational Psychology	M,D
Information Studies	M,D
Inorganic Chemistry	M,D
Jewish Studies	M
Journalism	M,D
Kinesiology and Movement Studies	M,D
Landscape Architecture	M
Law	
Library Science	
Linguistics	M,D
Manufacturing Engineering	M,D
Marine Sciences	M,D
Marriage and Family Therapy	M,D
Materials Engineering	M,D
Materials Sciences	M,D
Maternal and Child Health	M,D
Mathematics	M,D
Mechanical Engineering	M,D
Mechanics	M,D
Media Studies	M,D
Meteorology	M,D
Molecular Biology	D
Molecular Genetics	M,D
Music Education	M,D
Music	M,D
Natural Resources	M,D
Neuroscience	M,D
Nuclear Engineering	M,D
Nutrition	M,D
Oceanography	M,D
Organic Chemistry	M,D
Philosophy	M,D
Physical Chemistry	M,D
Physics	M,D
Plant Biology	M,D
Political Science	D
Portuguese	M,D
Psychology—General	M,D
Public Administration	M
Public Health—General	M,D
Public Policy	M,D
Quantitative Analysis	M,D
Reading Education	M,D,O
Real Estate	M
Rehabilitation Counseling	M,D,O
Reliability Engineering	M,D
School Psychology	M,D,O
Secondary Education	M,D,O
Social Psychology	M,D
Social Work	
Sociology	M,D
Spanish	M,D
Speech and Interpersonal Communication	M,D
Statistics	M,D
Student Affairs	M,D,O
Survey Methodology	M,D
Sustainable Development	M
Systems Engineering	M
Telecommunications	M
Theater	M,D
Urban and Regional Planning	M,D
Veterinary Medicine	D
Veterinary Sciences	M,D
Women's Studies	M,D
Writing	M,D

UNIVERSITY OF MARYLAND EASTERN SHORE

Agricultural Sciences—General	M,D
Chemistry	M,D
Computer Science	M
Counselor Education	M
Criminal Justice and Criminology	M
Education—General	M
Educational Leadership and Administration	D
Environmental Management and Policy	M,D
Environmental Sciences	M,D
Fish, Game, and Wildlife Management	M,D
Food Science and Technology	M,D
Marine Sciences	M,D
Organizational Management	D
Physical Therapy	D
Rehabilitation Counseling	M
Rehabilitation Sciences	M
Special Education	M
Toxicology	M,D
Vocational and Technical Education	M

UNIVERSITY OF MARYLAND UNIVERSITY COLLEGE

Accounting	M,O
Biotechnology	M,O
Business Administration and Management—General	M,D,O
Computer and Information Systems Security	M,O
Database Systems	M,O
Distance Education Development	M,O
Education—General	M,O
Environmental Management and Policy	M,O
Finance and Banking	M,O
Health Informatics	M,O
Health Services Management and Hospital Administration	M,O
Information Science	M,O
International Business	M,O
Management Information Systems	M,O
Management of Technology	M,O

UNIVERSITY OF MARY WASHINGTON

Business Administration and Management—General	M
Education—General	M
Elementary Education	M

UNIVERSITY OF MASSACHUSETTS AMHERST

Accounting	M,D
Adult Nursing	M,D
African-American Studies	M,D
Agricultural Economics and Agribusiness	M,D
American Studies	M,D
Animal Behavior	M,D
Animal Sciences	M,D
Anthropology	M,D
Applied Mathematics	M,D
Architectural Engineering	M,D
Architecture	M
Art Education	M
Art History	M
Art/Fine Arts	M
Astronomy	M,D
Biochemistry	M,D
Biological and Biomedical Sciences—General	M,D
Biostatistics	M,D
Biotechnology	M,D
Business Administration and Management—General	M,D
Cell Biology	M,D
Chemical Engineering	M,D
Chemistry	M,D
Child and Family Studies	M,D,O
Chinese	M
Civil Engineering	M,D
Classics	M
Clinical Psychology	M,D
Cognitive Sciences	M,D
Communication Disorders	M,D
Communication—General	M,D
Community Health Nursing	M,D
Community Health	M,D
Comparative Literature	M,D
Computer Engineering	M,D
Computer Science	M,D
Conflict Resolution and Mediation/Peace Studies	M,D
Counselor Education	M,D,O
Developmental Biology	D
Developmental Psychology	M,D
Early Childhood Education	M,D,O
Economics	M,D
Education—General	M,D,O
Educational Leadership and Administration	M,D,O
Educational Measurement and Evaluation	M,D,O
Educational Media/Instructional Technology	M,D,O
Educational Policy	M,D,O
Electrical Engineering	M,D
Elementary Education	M,D,O
Engineering and Applied Sciences—General	M,D
English as a Second Language	M,D,O
English	M,D
Entertainment Management	
Entrepreneurship	M,D
Environmental and Occupational Health	M,D
Environmental Biology	M,D
Environmental Engineering	M,D
Environmental Management and Policy	M,D
Epidemiology	M,D
Evolutionary Biology	M,D
Family Nurse Practitioner Studies	M,D
Finance and Banking	M,D
Fish, Game, and Wildlife Management	M,D
Food Science and Technology	M,D
Foreign Languages Education	M
Forestry	M,D
French	M
Genetics	M,D
Geography	M
Geosciences	M,D
Geotechnical Engineering	M,D
German	M,D
Gerontological Nursing	M,D
Health Education	M,D
Health Services Management and Hospital Administration	M,D
Higher Education	M,D,O
Hispanic and Latin American Languages	M,D
Historic Preservation	M
History	M,D
Hospitality Management	M,D
Industrial and Labor Relations	M
Industrial/Management Engineering	M,D
Interior Design	M
International and Comparative Education	M,D,O
Italian	M
Japanese	M
Kinesiology and Movement Studies	M,D
Landscape Architecture	M
Linguistics	M,D
Management Strategy and Policy	M,D
Marine Sciences	M,D
Marketing	M,D
Mathematics	M,D
Mechanical Engineering	M,D
Mechanics	M,D
Microbiology	M,D*
Molecular Biophysics	D
Multilingual and Multicultural Education	M,D,O
Music Education	M,D
Music	M,D
Neuroscience	M,D
Nursing and Healthcare Administration	M,D
Nursing—General	M,D
Nutrition	M,D
Operations Research	M,D
Organizational Management	M,D
Philosophy	M,D
Physics	M,D
Physiology	M,D
Plant Biology	M,D
Plant Molecular Biology	M,D
Plant Physiology	M,D
Plant Sciences	M,D
Political Science	M,D
Polymer Science and Engineering	M,D
Portuguese	M,D
Psychology—General	M,D
Public Administration	M
Public Health—General	M,D
Public Policy	M
Reading Education	M,D,O
Rhetoric	M,D
Scandinavian Languages	M,D
School Psychology	M,D,O
Science Education	M,D,O
Secondary Education	M,D,O
Social Psychology	M,D
Sociology	M,D
Spanish	M,D
Special Education	M,D,O
Sports Management	M,D
Statistics	M,D
Structural Engineering	M,D
Sustainable Development	M
Theater	M
Transportation and Highway Engineering	M,D
Travel and Tourism	M,D
Urban and Regional Planning	M,D
Water Resources Engineering	M,D
Water Resources	M,D
Writing	M,D

UNIVERSITY OF MASSACHUSETTS BOSTON

Accounting	M
American Studies	M
Applied Economics	M
Applied Physics	M
Archaeology	M
Archives/Archival Administration	M
Biological and Biomedical Sciences—General	M,D
Biomedical Engineering	D
Biotechnology	M,D
Business Administration and Management—General	M
Chemistry	M,D
Classics	M
Clinical Psychology	D
Cognitive Sciences	M
Computer Science	M,D
Conflict Resolution and Mediation/Peace Studies	M,O
Counseling Psychology	M,D
Counselor Education	M
Early Childhood Education	M,D
Education—General	M,D
Educational Media/Instructional Technology	M,O
English as a Second Language	M
English	M
Environmental Sciences	M,D
Exercise and Sports Science	M,D
Finance and Banking	M
Foreign Languages Education	M
Gerontology	M,D,O
History	M
Human Services	M
International Affairs	M
International Business	M
International Development	M,D
Linguistics	M
Management Information Systems	M
Marine Sciences	M,D
Marriage and Family Therapy	M
Middle School Education	M,D
Multilingual and Multicultural Education	M
Nursing—General	M,D
Public Administration	M
Public Affairs	M,D,O
Public Policy	M,D
Quality Management	M,O
Rehabilitation Counseling	M
School Psychology	M,D
Sociology	M,D
Special Education	M
Vision Sciences	M
Writing	M

UNIVERSITY OF MASSACHUSETTS DARTMOUTH

Accounting	M,O
Acoustics	M,D,O
Adult Nursing	M,D
Applied Arts and Design—General	M,O
Applied Behavior Analysis	M,O
Art Education	M
Art/Fine Arts	M,O
Biochemistry	M,D
Biological and Biomedical Sciences—General	M
Biomedical Engineering	M,D
Biotechnology	M,D
Business Administration and Management—General	M,O
Chemistry	M,D
Civil Engineering	M
Clinical Laboratory Sciences/Medical Technology	M,D
Clinical Psychology	M,O
Community Health Nursing	M,D
Computational Sciences	D
Computer Art and Design	M,O
Computer Engineering	M,D,O
Computer Science	M,D,O
Database Systems	M
Education—General	M,D,O
Educational Leadership and Administration	D
Educational Policy	M,O
Electrical Engineering	M,D,O
Engineering and Applied Sciences—General	D
Environmental Management and Policy	M,O
Experimental Psychology	M,O
Finance and Banking	M,O
Health Services Management and Hospital Administration	M
Illustration	M,O
Industrial/Management Engineering	M,D
Information Science	D
International Business	M,O
Internet and Interactive Multimedia	M,O
Latin American Studies	M,D
Law	D
Management of Technology	M
Marine Affairs	M,D
Marine Biology	M
Marine Sciences	M,D
Marketing	M,O
Mathematics Education	D
Mechanical Engineering	M
Mechanics	D
Middle School Education	M,O
Nursing—General	M,D
Organizational Management	M,O
Photography	M,O
Physics	M
Portuguese	M,D
Psychology—General	M,O
Public Administration	M,O
Public Policy	M,O
Secondary Education	M,O
Software Engineering	M,O
Supply Chain Management	M,O
Systems Engineering	M,D
Telecommunications	M,D,O
Textile Sciences and Engineering	M
Writing	M,O

UNIVERSITY OF MASSACHUSETTS LOWELL

Allied Health—General	M,D
Analytical Chemistry	M,D
Biochemistry	M,D
Biological and Biomedical Sciences—General	M
Business Administration and Management—General	M,D
Chemical Engineering	M,D
Chemistry	M,D
Civil Engineering	M,D
Clinical Laboratory Sciences/Medical Technology	M
Computer Engineering	M,D
Computer Science	M,D
Conflict Resolution and Mediation/Peace Studies	M
Criminal Justice and Criminology	M
Curriculum and Instruction	M
Education—General	M
Electrical Engineering	M,D
Energy and Power Engineering	M,D
Engineering and Applied Sciences—General	M,D
Entrepreneurship	M,D
Environmental Engineering	M,D
Environmental Sciences	M,D
Family Nurse Practitioner Studies	M
Gerontological Nursing	M
Health Physics/Radiological Health	M
Health Promotion	D
Inorganic Chemistry	M,D
Legal and Justice Studies	M
Mathematics	D
Mechanical Engineering	M,D
Music Education	M
Music	M
Nuclear Engineering	M,D
Nursing—General	M,D
Organic Chemistry	M,D
Physical Therapy	D
Physics	M,D*
Polymer Science and Engineering	M,D
Psychology—General	M
Social Psychology	M

UNIVERSITY OF MASSACHUSETTS MEDICAL SCHOOL

Adult Nursing	M,D,O
Allopathic Medicine	D
Biochemistry	M,D
Bioinformatics	M,D
Biological and Biomedical Sciences—General	M,D
Cancer Biology/Oncology	M,D
Cell Biology	M,D
Clinical Research	M,D
Community Health	M,D,O
Computational Biology	M,D
Family Nurse Practitioner Studies	M,D,O
Gerontological Nursing	M,D,O
Health Services Research	M,D
Immunology	M,D
Interdisciplinary Studies	M,D
Microbiology	M,D
Molecular Pharmacology	M,D
Neuroscience	M,D
Nursing and Healthcare Administration	M,D,O
Nursing Education	M,D,O
Nursing—General	M,D,O

Translational Biology	M,D

UNIVERSITY OF MEMPHIS

Accounting	M,D
Adult Education	M,D
African-American Studies	M,D,O
Analytical Chemistry	M,D
Anthropology	M
Applied Mathematics	M,D
Applied Statistics	M,D
Archaeology	M,D,O
Architecture	M
Art History	M,O
Art/Fine Arts	M,O
Biological and Biomedical Sciences—General	M,D
Biomedical Engineering	M,D
Biostatistics	M
Business Administration and Management—General	M,D
Chemistry	M,D
Civil Engineering	M,D
Clinical Psychology	M,D,O
Communication Disorders	M,D
Communication—General	M,D
Comparative Literature	M,D,O
Computer Engineering	M,D
Computer Science	M,D
Counseling Psychology	M,D
Counselor Education	M,D
Criminal Justice and Criminology	M
Curriculum and Instruction	M,D
Early Childhood Education	M,D
Economics	M,D
Education—General	M,D,O
Educational Leadership and Administration	M,D
Educational Measurement and Evaluation	M,D
Educational Media/Instructional Technology	M,D
Educational Psychology	M,D
Electrical Engineering	M,D
Elementary Education	M,D
Energy and Power Engineering	M,D
Engineering and Applied Sciences—General	M,D
English as a Second Language	M,D,O
English	M,D,O
Environmental and Occupational Health	M
Environmental Engineering	M,D
Epidemiology	M
Exercise and Sports Science	M
Experimental Psychology	M,D,O
Family and Consumer Sciences-General	M
Family Nurse Practitioner Studies	M,O
Film, Television, and Video Production	M,D
Finance and Banking	M,D
French	M
Geographic Information Systems	M,D,O
Geography	M,D,O
Geology	M,D,O
Geophysics	M,D,O
Graphic Design	M,O
Health Services Management and Hospital Administration	M
Higher Education	M,D
History	M,D
Industrial/Management Engineering	M,D
Inorganic Chemistry	M,D
Interdisciplinary Studies	M,D,O
Interior Design	M,O
Journalism	M
Law	D
Liberal Studies	M
Linguistics	M,D,O
Marketing	M,D
Mathematics	M,D
Mechanical Engineering	M,D
Middle School Education	M,D
Music Education	M,D
Music	M,D
Near and Middle Eastern Studies	M,D
Nursing and Healthcare Administration	M,O
Nursing Education	M,O
Nursing—General	M,O
Philosophy	M,D
Photography	M,O
Physical Chemistry	M,D
Physics	M
Political Science	M
Psychology—General	M,D,O
Public Administration	M,O
Public Health—General	M
Public Policy	M,O
Reading Education	M,D
Real Estate	M,D
Rehabilitation Counseling	M,D
School Psychology	M,D,O
Secondary Education	M,D
Social Sciences	M
Sociology	M
Special Education	M,D
Statistics	M,D
Structural Engineering	M,D
Supply Chain Management	M,D
Theater	M
Transportation and Highway Engineering	M,D
Urban and Regional Planning	M,D
Water Resources Engineering	M,D
Writing	M,D,O

UNIVERSITY OF MIAMI

Acute Care/Critical Care Nursing	M,D
Adult Nursing	M,D
Advertising and Public Relations	M,D
Aerospace/Aeronautical Engineering	M,D
Allopathic Medicine	D
Architectural Engineering	M,D
Architecture	M
Art History	M
Art/Fine Arts	M
Athletic Training and Sports Medicine	M,D
Biochemistry	D
Biological and Biomedical Sciences—General	M,D
Biomedical Engineering	M,D
Biophysics	D
Broadcast Journalism	M,D
Cancer Biology/Oncology	D
Cell Biology	D
Chemistry	M,D
Civil Engineering	M,D
Clinical Psychology	M,D
Communication—General	M,D
Community Health	D
Computer Engineering	M,D
Computer Science	M,D
Counseling Psychology	D
Counselor Education	M,O
Developmental Biology	D
Developmental Psychology	M,D
Early Childhood Education	M,O
Education—General	M,D,O
Educational Measurement and Evaluation	M,D
Electrical Engineering	M,D
Engineering and Applied Sciences—General	M,D
English	M,D
Environmental and Occupational Health	M
Epidemiology	M,D
Ergonomics and Human Factors	M
Evolutionary Biology	M,D
Exercise and Sports Science	M,D
Family Nurse Practitioner Studies	M,D
Film, Television, and Video Production	M,D
Film, Television, and Video Theory and Criticism	M,D
Fish, Game, and Wildlife Management	M,D
French	D
Genetics	M,D
Geography	M
Geophysics	M,D
Graphic Design	M
Higher Education	M,D,O
History	M,D
Immunology	D
Industrial/Management Engineering	M,D
Inorganic Chemistry	M,D
International Affairs	M,D
Internet and Interactive Multimedia	M
Journalism	M,D
Latin American Studies	M
Law	M,D
Liberal Studies	M
Management of Technology	M,D
Marine Affairs	M
Marine Biology	M,D
Marine Geology	M,D
Marine Sciences	M,D
Marriage and Family Therapy	M,O
Mathematical and Computational Finance	M,D
Mathematics Education	D
Mathematics	M,D
Mechanical Engineering	M,D
Meteorology	M,D
Microbiology	D
Molecular Biology	D
Multilingual and Multicultural Education	D
Music Education	M,D,O
Music	M,D,O
Neuroscience	M,D
Nurse Anesthesia	M,D
Nurse Midwifery	M,D
Nursing—General	M,D
Nutrition	M
Oceanography	M,D
Organic Chemistry	M,D
Pharmacology	D
Philosophy	M,D
Photography	M
Physical Chemistry	M,D
Physical Therapy	D
Physics	M,D
Physiology	D
Political Science	M
Psychology—General	M,D
Public Health—General	M,D
Reading Education	D
Real Estate	M,D
Romance Languages	D
Science Education	D
Sociology	M,D
Spanish	M,D
Special Education	M,D,O
Sports Management	M
Taxation	M,D
Therapies—Dance, Drama, and Music	M,D,O
Urban Design	M
Writing	M,D

UNIVERSITY OF MICHIGAN

Accounting	M,D
Aerospace/Aeronautical Engineering	M,D
Allopathic Medicine	D
American Studies	M,D
Analytical Chemistry	D
Anthropology	D
Applied Arts and Design—General	M,D
Applied Economics	M
Applied Physics	D
Applied Statistics	M,D
Archaeology	M,D
Architecture	M
Archives/Archival Administration	M,D
Art History	M,D
Art/Fine Arts	M
Artificial Intelligence/Robotics	M,D
Asian Languages	D
Asian Studies	M,D,O
Astronomy	D
Astrophysics	D
Atmospheric Sciences	M,D
Automotive Engineering	M,D
Biochemistry	M,D
Bioinformatics	M,D
Biological and Biomedical Sciences—General	M,D
Biomedical Engineering	M,D
Biophysics	D
Biopsychology	D
Biostatistics	M,D
Business Administration and Management—General	M,D
Cancer Biology/Oncology	M,D
Cell Biology	M,D
Chemical Engineering	M,D,O
Chemistry	D
Civil Engineering	M,D,O
Classics	M,D,O
Clinical Psychology	D
Clinical Research	M
Cognitive Sciences	D
Communication—General	D
Comparative Literature	D
Computer Engineering	M,D
Computer Science	M,D
Construction Engineering	M,D,O
Cultural Anthropology	D
Dance	M
Database Systems	M,D,O
Dental Hygiene	M
Dentistry	D
Developmental Biology	M,D
Developmental Psychology	D
East European and Russian Studies	M,O
Ecology	M,D
Economics	M,D
Education—General	M,D
Electrical Engineering	M,D
Energy and Power Engineering	M,D
Engineering and Applied Sciences—General	M,D,O
Engineering Design	M,D
English Education	D
English	M,D,O
Environmental and Occupational Health	M,D
Environmental Engineering	M,D,O
Environmental Management and Policy	M,D
Environmental Sciences	M,D
Epidemiology	M,D
Evolutionary Biology	M,D
Film, Television, and Video Theory and Criticism	D,O
Foreign Languages Education	M,D
French	D
Genetic Counseling	M,D
Geosciences	M,D
German	M,D
Health Education	M,D
Health Informatics	M,D
Health Physics/Radiological Health	M,D,O
Health Promotion	M,D
Health Services Management and Hospital Administration	M,D
History	D,O
Human Genetics	M,D
Immunology	M,D
Industrial Hygiene	M,D
Industrial/Management Engineering	M,D
Information Science	M,D*
Information Studies	M,D
Inorganic Chemistry	D
International Health	M,D
Italian	D
Jewish Studies	M,D,O
Kinesiology and Movement Studies	M,D
Landscape Architecture	M
Law	M,D
Linguistics	D
Manufacturing Engineering	M,D
Marine Sciences	M,D,O
Mass Communication	D
Materials Engineering	M,D
Materials Sciences	M,D
Mathematics	M,D
Mechanical Engineering	M,D
Media Studies	M
Medicinal and Pharmaceutical Chemistry	D
Microbiology	M,D
Molecular Biology	M,D
Molecular Pathology	D
Music Education	M,D,O
Music	M,D,O
Natural Resources	M,D
Near and Middle Eastern Languages	M,D
Near and Middle Eastern Studies	M,D
Neuroscience	D
Nuclear Engineering	M,D,O
Nursing—General	M,D,O
Nutrition	M,D
Ocean Engineering	M,D,O
Operations Research	M,D
Oral and Dental Sciences	M,D
Organic Chemistry	D
Pathology	D
Pediatric Nursing	M,D,O
Pharmaceutical Administration	D
Pharmaceutical Engineering	M,D
Pharmaceutical Sciences	D
Pharmacology	M,D
Pharmacy	D
Philosophy	M,D
Physical Chemistry	D
Physics	D
Physiology	M,D
Planetary and Space Sciences	M,D
Political Science	D
Psychology—General	D,O
Public Health—General	M,D
Public Policy	M,D
Religion	M,D
Slavic Languages	M,D
Social Psychology	D
Social Sciences	D
Social Work	M,D
Sociology	D
Spanish	D
Sports Management	M,D
Statistics	M,D,O
Structural Engineering	M,D,O
Supply Chain Management	M,D
Survey Methodology	M,D,O
Sustainability Management	M,D,O
Sustainable Development	M,D
Systems Engineering	M,D
Systems Science	M,D
Taxation	M,D
Toxicology	M,D
Urban and Regional Planning	M,D,O
Urban Design	M
Women's Studies	D,O
Writing	M

UNIVERSITY OF MICHIGAN–DEARBORN

Accounting	M
Applied Mathematics	M
Automotive Engineering	M,D
Business Administration and Management—General	M
Clinical Psychology	M
Computational Sciences	M
Computer Engineering	M
Curriculum and Instruction	D,O
Database Systems	M
Early Childhood Education	M
Education—General	M
Educational Leadership and Administration	M,D,O
Educational Media/Instructional Technology	M
Electrical Engineering	M
Energy and Power Engineering	M
Engineering and Applied Sciences—General	M,D
Engineering Management	M
Environmental Sciences	M
Finance and Banking	M
Health Informatics	M
Health Psychology	M
Industrial/Management Engineering	M
Information Science	M
Management Information Systems	M
Management Strategy and Policy	M
Manufacturing Engineering	M
Mechanical Engineering	M
Project Management	M
Public Administration	M
Public Policy	M
Science Education	M
Software Engineering	M
Special Education	M
Supply Chain Management	M
Systems Engineering	M,D
Urban Education	D

UNIVERSITY OF MICHIGAN–FLINT

Accounting	M
American Studies	M
Art/Fine Arts	M
Arts Administration	M
Biological and Biomedical Sciences—General	M
Business Administration and Management—General	M,O
Communication—General	M
Computer Science	M
Criminal Justice and Criminology	M
Curriculum and Instruction	M,D,O
Early Childhood Education	M,D,O
Education—General	M,D,O
Educational Leadership and Administration	M,D,O
Educational Media/Instructional Technology	M,D,O
English	M
Family Nurse Practitioner Studies	M,D,O
Finance and Banking	M
Gender Studies	M
Gerontology	M,D,O
Health Education	M
Health Services Management and Hospital Administration	M
Industrial and Manufacturing Management	M

*M—masters degree; D—doctorate; O—other advanced degree; *—Close-Up and/or Display*

Information Science	M
International Affairs	M
International Business	M
Management Information Systems	M
Marketing	M
Mathematics	M
Museum Studies	M
Music	M
Neuroscience	D,O
Nonprofit Management	M
Nurse Anesthesia	M,D
Nursing—General	M,D,O
Organizational Management	M
Physical Therapy	D,O
Political Science	M
Psychiatric Nursing	M,D,O
Public Administration	M
Public Health—General	M
Reading Education	M,D,O
Rhetoric	M
Secondary Education	M,D,O
Social Sciences	M
Writing	M

UNIVERSITY OF MINNESOTA, DULUTH

Allopathic Medicine	D
Anthropology	M
Applied Mathematics	M
Art/Fine Arts	M
Biochemistry	M,D
Biological and Biomedical Sciences—General	M,D
Biophysics	M,D
Business Administration and Management—General	M
Chemistry	M
Communication Disorders	M
Computational Sciences	M
Computer Engineering	M
Computer Science	M
Criminal Justice and Criminology	M
Education—General	M,D
Electrical Engineering	M
Engineering Management	M
English	M
Geology	M,D
Graphic Design	M
Immunology	M,D
Liberal Studies	M
Medical Microbiology	M,D
Molecular Biology	M,D
Music Education	M
Music	M
Pharmacology	M,D
Pharmacy	M,D
Physics	M
Physiology	M,D
Safety Engineering	M
Social Work	M
Sociology	M
Toxicology	M,D

UNIVERSITY OF MINNESOTA, TWIN CITIES CAMPUS

Accounting	M,D
Adult Education	M,D,O
Adult Nursing	M
Aerospace/Aeronautical Engineering	M,D
Agricultural Education	M,D
Agricultural Sciences—General	M,D
Agronomy and Soil Sciences	M,D
Allopathic Medicine	M,D
American Studies	D
Animal Behavior	M,D
Animal Sciences	M,D
Anthropology	M,D
Applied Arts and Design—General	M,D,O
Applied Economics	M,D
Archaeology	M,D
Architecture	M
Art Education	M,D,O
Art History	M,D
Art/Fine Arts	M
Asian Languages	D
Asian Studies	D
Astrophysics	M,D
Biochemistry	D
Biological and Biomedical Sciences—General	M
Biomedical Engineering	M,D
Biophysics	M,D
Biopsychology	D
Biostatistics	M,D
Biosystems Engineering	M,D
Biotechnology	M
Business Administration and Management—General	M,D
Business Education	M,D
Cancer Biology/Oncology	D
Cell Biology	M,D
Chemical Engineering	M,D
Chemical Physics	M,D
Chemistry	M,D
Child and Family Studies	M,D
Child Development	M,D
Civil Engineering	M,D,O
Classics	M,D
Clinical Laboratory Sciences/Medical Technology	M
Clinical Psychology	D
Clinical Research	M
Clothing and Textiles	M,D,O
Cognitive Sciences	D
Communication Disorders	M,D
Communication—General	M,D,O
Community Health Nursing	M
Community Health	M
Comparative Literature	D
Computational Sciences	M,D
Computer and Information Systems Security	M
Computer Engineering	M,D
Computer Science	M,D
Conservation Biology	M,D
Counseling Psychology	D
Counselor Education	M,D,O
Cultural Studies	D
Curriculum and Instruction	M,D,O
Database Systems	M
Dentistry	D
Developmental Biology	M,D
Early Childhood Education	M,D,O
Ecology	M,D
Economics	M,D
Education of the Gifted	M,D,O
Education—General	M,D,O
Educational Leadership and Administration	M,D
Educational Measurement and Evaluation	M,D
Educational Media/Instructional Technology	M,D,O
Educational Policy	M,D,O
Educational Psychology	M,D,O
Electrical Engineering	M,D
Elementary Education	M,D,O
Engineering and Applied Sciences—General	M,D,O
English as a Second Language	M
English Education	M
English	M,D
Entomology	M,D
Entrepreneurship	D
Environmental and Occupational Health	M,D,O
Environmental Education	M,D,O
Environmental Management and Policy	M,D
Epidemiology	M,D
Evolutionary Biology	M,D
Exercise and Sports Science	M,D,O
Family Nurse Practitioner Studies	M
Finance and Banking	M,D
Fish, Game, and Wildlife Management	M,D
Food Science and Technology	M,D
Foreign Languages Education	M
Forestry	M,D
Foundations and Philosophy of Education	M,D,O
French	M,D
Genetic Counseling	M,D
Genetics	M,D
Geographic Information Systems	M,D
Geography	M,D
Geological Engineering	M,D,O
Geology	M,D
Geophysics	M,D
German	M,D
Gerontological Nursing	M
Health Informatics	M,D
Health Services Management and Hospital Administration	M,D
Health Services Research	M,D
Higher Education	M,D
Hispanic and Latin American Languages	M,D
History of Medicine	M,D
History of Science and Technology	M,D
History	M,D
Human Resources Development	M,D,O
Human Resources Management	M
Hydrology	M,D
Immunology	D
Industrial and Labor Relations	M
Industrial and Manufacturing Management	M,D
Industrial and Organizational Psychology	D
Industrial Hygiene	M,D
Industrial/Management Engineering	M,D
Infectious Diseases	M,D
Interdisciplinary Studies	D
Interior Design	M,D,O
International and Comparative Education	M,D
International Development	M
International Health	M,D
Kinesiology and Movement Studies	M,D,O
Landscape Architecture	M
Law	M,D
Linguistics	M,D
Management Information Systems	M,D
Management of Technology	M
Management Strategy and Policy	M,D
Marketing	M,D
Marriage and Family Therapy	M,D
Mass Communication	M,D
Materials Engineering	M,D
Materials Sciences	M,D
Maternal and Child Health	M
Mathematics Education	M
Mathematics	M,D,O
Mechanical Engineering	M,D
Mechanics	M,D
Medical Physics	M,D
Medicinal and Pharmaceutical Chemistry	M,D
Medieval and Renaissance Studies	M,D
Microbiology	D
Molecular Biology	M,D
Multilingual and Multicultural Education	M
Music	M,D
Natural Resources	M,D
Neurobiology	M,D
Neuroscience	M,D
Nurse Anesthesia	M
Nurse Midwifery	M
Nursing and Healthcare Administration	M
Nursing—General	M,D
Nutrition	M,D
Occupational Health Nursing	M,D
Oral and Dental Sciences	M,D,O
Paper and Pulp Engineering	M,D
Pediatric Nursing	M
Pharmaceutical Administration	M,D
Pharmaceutical Sciences	M,D
Pharmacology	M,D
Pharmacy	D
Philosophy	M,D
Physical Education	M,D,O
Physical Therapy	M,D
Physics	M,D
Physiology	D
Plant Biology	M,D
Plant Pathology	M,D
Plant Sciences	M,D
Political Science	D
Portuguese	M,D
Psychiatric Nursing	M
Psychology—General	D
Public Affairs	M,D
Public Health—General	M,D,O
Public Policy	M,D
Quantitative Analysis	M,D,O
Reading Education	M,D,O
Religion	M,D
Scandinavian Languages	M,D
School Psychology	M,D,O
Science Education	M
Social Psychology	D
Social Sciences Education	M
Social Work	M,D
Sociology	M,D
Software Engineering	M
Spanish	M,D
Special Education	M,D,O
Sports Management	M,D,O
Statistics	M,D
Structural Biology	D
Student Affairs	M,D,O
Supply Chain Management	M
Taxation	M
Technology and Public Policy	M
Textile Design	M,D,O
Theater	M,D
Toxicology	M,D
Travel and Tourism	M,D
Urban and Regional Planning	M,D
Veterinary Medicine	D
Veterinary Sciences	M,D
Virology	D
Vocational and Technical Education	M,D,O
Water Resources	M,D
Women's Health Nursing	M
Women's Studies	D

UNIVERSITY OF MISSISSIPPI

Accounting	M,D
Anthropology	M,D
Applied Science and Technology	M,D
Art/Fine Arts	M,D
Biological and Biomedical Sciences—General	M,D
Business Administration and Management—General	M,D
Chemistry	M,D
Clinical Psychology	M,D
Communication Disorders	M,D
Criminal Justice and Criminology	M,D
Economics	M,D
Education—General	M,D,O
Engineering and Applied Sciences—General	M,D
English	M,D
Exercise and Sports Science	M,D
Experimental Psychology	M,D
Food Science and Technology	M,D
Foreign Languages Education	M,D
Health Promotion	M,D
History	M,D
Journalism	M
Kinesiology and Movement Studies	M,D
Law	M,D
Management Information Systems	M,D
Mathematics	M,D
Music	M,D
Nutrition	M,D
Pharmacy	M,D
Philosophy	M,D
Physics	M,D
Political Science	M,D
Recreation and Park Management	M,D
Social Work	M,D
Sociology	M,D
Taxation	M,D

UNIVERSITY OF MISSISSIPPI MEDICAL CENTER

Allied Health—General	M
Allopathic Medicine	D
Anatomy	M,D
Biochemistry	D
Biological and Biomedical Sciences—General	M,D
Biophysics	D
Dentistry	M,D
Materials Sciences	M,D
Microbiology	D
Neuroscience	D
Nursing—General	M,D
Occupational Therapy	M
Oral and Dental Sciences	M,D
Pathology	D
Pharmacology	D
Physical Therapy	M
Physiology	D
Toxicology	D

UNIVERSITY OF MISSOURI

Accounting	M,D,O
Adult Education	M,D,O
Adult Nursing	M,D,O
Aerospace/Aeronautical Engineering	M,D
Agricultural Economics and Agribusiness	M,D,O
Agricultural Education	M,D,O
Agricultural Engineering	M,D
Agricultural Sciences—General	M,D,O
Agronomy and Soil Sciences	M,D,O
Allopathic Medicine	D
Analytical Chemistry	M,D
Anatomy	M
Animal Sciences	M,D
Anthropology	M,D
Applied Mathematics	M,D
Archaeology	M,D
Art Education	M,D,O
Art History	M,D
Art/Fine Arts	M
Astronomy	M,D
Biochemistry	M,D
Bioengineering	M,D
Bioinformatics	D
Biological and Biomedical Sciences—General	M,D
Business Administration and Management—General	M,D
Business Education	M,D,O
Chemical Engineering	M,D
Chemistry	M,D
Child and Family Studies	M,D
Civil Engineering	M,D
Classics	M,D
Clothing and Textiles	M,D
Communication Disorders	M,D
Communication—General	M,D
Community Health	M,D
Comparative Literature	M,D
Computer Science	M,D
Conflict Resolution and Mediation/Peace Studies	M,D,O
Conservation Biology	M,D,O
Consumer Economics	M,D,O
Counseling Psychology	M,D,O
Curriculum and Instruction	M,D,O
Early Childhood Education	M,D,O
Ecology	M,D
Economics	M,D
Education of the Gifted	M,D
Education—General	M,D,O
Educational Leadership and Administration	M,D,O
Educational Media/Instructional Technology	M,D,O
Educational Psychology	M,D,O
Electrical Engineering	M,D
Elementary Education	M,D,O
English Education	M,D,O
English	M,D
Entomology	M,D
Environmental Engineering	M,D
Environmental Sciences	M,D,O
Evolutionary Biology	M,D
Family and Consumer Sciences-General	M,D,O
Family Nurse Practitioner Studies	M,D,O
Finance and Banking	M,D
Fish, Game, and Wildlife Management	M,D,O
Food Science and Technology	M,D
Foreign Languages Education	M,D,O
Forestry	M,D,O
French	M,D
Genetics	D
Geographic Information Systems	M,D,O
Geography	M,O
Geology	M,D
Geotechnical Engineering	M,D
German	M
Gerontological Nursing	M,D,O
Gerontology	M,D,O
Health Communication	M,D
Health Education	M,D,O
Health Informatics	M,O
Health Physics/Radiological Health	M
Health Promotion	M,O
Health Services Management and Hospital Administration	M,D,O
Higher Education	M,D,O
History	M,D
Horticulture	M,D
Hospitality Management	M,D
Human Development	M,D
Immunology	D
Industrial/Management Engineering	M,D
Information Studies	M,D,O
International Health	M,O
Journalism	M,D
Law	M,D
Library Science	M,D,O
Manufacturing Engineering	M,D
Marketing	M,D
Mathematics Education	M,D,O
Mathematics	M,D
Mechanical Engineering	M,D
Microbiology	D
Music Education	M,D,O
Music	M
Neuroscience	M,D,O
Nonprofit Management	M,D,O
Nuclear Engineering	M,D,O
Nursing and Healthcare Administration	M,D,O
Nursing—General	M,D,O
Nutrition	M,D
Occupational Therapy	M
Organizational Management	M,D,O
Pathobiology	M,D
Pathology	M
Pediatric Nursing	M,D,O
Pharmacology	M,D
Philosophy	D
Physical Therapy	D
Physics	M,D

Physiology M,D
Plant Biology M,D
Plant Sciences M,D
Political Science M,D
Psychiatric Nursing M,D,O
Psychology—General M,D
Public Administration M,D,O
Public Affairs M,D,O
Public Health—General M,O
Public Policy M,D,O
Reading Education M,D,O
Religion M
Romance Languages M,D
Rural Sociology M,D
School Psychology M,D,O
Science Education M,D,O
Social Sciences Education M,D,O
Social Work M,D,O
Sociology D
Spanish M,D
Special Education M,D
Statistics M,D
Structural Engineering M,D
Taxation M,D,O
Theater M,D
Transportation and Highway Engineering M,D
Veterinary Medicine M,D
Veterinary Sciences M
Vocational and Technical Education M,D,O
Water Resources Engineering M,D
Water Resources M,D,O

UNIVERSITY OF MISSOURI–KANSAS CITY

Accounting M,D
Adult Nursing M,D
Allopathic Medicine M,D
Analytical Chemistry M,D
Anesthesiologist Assistant Studies M,D
Art History M,D
Art/Fine Arts M,D
Biochemistry D
Bioinformatics M,D,O
Biological and Biomedical Sciences—General M,D
Biophysics D
Business Administration and Management—General M,D
Cell Biology D
Chemistry M,D
Civil Engineering M,D,O
Clinical Psychology M,D
Computer Engineering M,D,O
Computer Science M,D,O
Construction Engineering M,D,O
Counseling Psychology M,D,O
Counselor Education M,D,O
Criminal Justice and Criminology M
Curriculum and Instruction M,D,O
Dental Hygiene M,D,O
Dentistry M,D,O
Economics M,D
Education—General M,D,O
Educational Leadership and Administration M,D,O
Electrical Engineering M,D,O
Engineering and Applied Sciences—General M,D,O
Engineering Management M,D,O
English M,D
Entrepreneurship M,D
Family Nurse Practitioner Studies M,D
Finance and Banking M,D
French M
Geology M,D
Geosciences M,D
Gerontological Nursing M,D
Health Education M,D
Health Psychology M,D
Higher Education M,D,O
History M,D
Inorganic Chemistry M,D
Interdisciplinary Studies D
Law M,D
Maternal and Child/Neonatal Nursing M,D
Mathematics M,D
Mechanical Engineering M,D,O
Media Studies M,D
Molecular Biology D
Music Education M,D
Music M,D
Nursing and Healthcare Administration M,D
Nursing Education M,D
Nursing—General M,D
Oral and Dental Sciences M,D,O
Organic Chemistry M,D
Pediatric Nursing M,D
Pharmaceutical Sciences D
Pharmacology D
Pharmacy D
Physical Chemistry M,D
Physician Assistant Studies M,D
Physics M,D
Political Science M
Polymer Science and Engineering M,D
Psychology—General M,D
Public Administration M,D
Public Affairs M,D
Reading Education M,D,O
Real Estate M,D
Romance Languages M
Social Psychology M,D
Social Work M
Sociology M
Software Engineering M,D,O
Spanish M
Special Education M,D,O
Statistics M,D
Taxation M,D
Telecommunications M,D,O
Theater M
Therapies—Dance, Drama, and Music M,D
Toxicology D
Women's Health Nursing M,D
Writing M,D

UNIVERSITY OF MISSOURI–ST. LOUIS

Accounting M,D,O
Adult Education M,D,O
Adult Nursing M,D,O
American Studies M,D
Applied Physics M,D
Astrophysics M,D
Biochemistry M,D
Biological and Biomedical Sciences—General M,D,O
Biotechnology M,D
Business Administration and Management—General M,D,O
Chemistry M,D
Clinical Psychology M,D,O
Communication—General M
Community College Education M,D,O
Computer and Information Systems Security M,D,O
Computer Science M,D
Counseling Psychology M,D
Counselor Education M,D
Criminal Justice and Criminology M,D
Curriculum and Instruction M,O
Early Childhood Education M,O
Economics M
Education—General M,D,O
Educational Leadership and Administration M,D,O
Educational Measurement and Evaluation M,O
Educational Policy D
Educational Psychology D
Elementary Education M,D,O
English as a Second Language M,O
English M
Family Nurse Practitioner Studies M,D,O
Finance and Banking M,D,O
Gerontological Nursing M,D,O
Gerontology M,O
Higher Education M,D,O
Human Resources Development M,O
Human Resources Management M,D,O
Industrial and Manufacturing Management M,D,O
Industrial and Organizational Psychology M,D,O
International Business M,D,O
Logistics M,D,O
Management Information Systems M,D,O
Management Strategy and Policy M,D,O
Marketing M,D,O
Marriage and Family Therapy M,D
Mathematics M,D
Media Studies M
Middle School Education M,O
Museum Studies M,O
Music Education M
Neuroscience M,D,O
Nonprofit Management M,O
Nursing Education M,D,O
Nursing—General M,D,O
Optometry D
Pediatric Nursing M,D,O
Philosophy M
Physics M,D
Political Science M,D
Psychiatric Nursing M,D,O
Psychology—General M,D,O
Public Administration M,D,O
Public History M,O
Public Policy M,D,O
Reading Education M,O
School Psychology M,O
Secondary Education M,D,O
Social Work M
Special Education M,O
Supply Chain Management M,D,O
Women's Health Nursing M,D,O
Writing M

UNIVERSITY OF MOBILE

Business Administration and Management—General M
Education—General M
Marriage and Family Therapy M
Nursing—General M

UNIVERSITY OF MONTANA

Accounting M
Analytical Chemistry M,D
Animal Behavior M,D,O
Anthropology M,D
Art Education M
Art History M
Art/Fine Arts M
Biochemistry D
Biological and Biomedical Sciences—General M,D
Business Administration and Management—General M
Cell Biology D
Chemistry M,D
Child and Family Studies M,D,O
Clinical Psychology M,D,O
Communication—General M
Community Health M
Computer Art and Design M
Computer Science M
Counseling Psychology M,D,O
Counselor Education M,D,O
Criminal Justice and Criminology M
Cultural Studies M,D,O
Curriculum and Instruction M,D
Developmental Biology D
Developmental Psychology M,D,O
Ecology M,D
Economics M
Education—General M,D,O
Educational Leadership and Administration M,D,O
English Education M
English M
Environmental Management and Policy M
Environmental Sciences M
Exercise and Sports Science M
Experimental Psychology M,D,O
Film, Television, and Video Production M
Fish, Game, and Wildlife Management M,D
Forestry M,D
French M
Geography M
Geology M,D
Geosciences M,D
German M
Health Education M
History M,D
Immunology D
Inorganic Chemistry M,D
Interdisciplinary Studies M,D
Internet and Interactive Multimedia M
Journalism M
Law D
Legal and Justice Studies M
Linguistics M,D
Mathematics Education M,D
Mathematics M,D
Medicinal and Pharmaceutical Chemistry M,D
Microbiology D
Molecular Biology D
Music M
Natural Resources M,D
Neuroscience M,D
Organic Chemistry M,D
Pharmaceutical Sciences M,D
Pharmacy M,D
Philosophy M
Photography M
Physical Chemistry M,D
Physical Education M
Physical Therapy D
Political Science M
Psychology—General M,D,O
Public Administration M
Public Health—General M,O
Recreation and Park Management M,D
Rural Planning and Studies M
Rural Sociology M
School Psychology M,D,O
Social Work M
Sociology M
Spanish M
Theater M
Toxicology M,D
Writing M
Zoology M,D

UNIVERSITY OF MONTEVALLO

Business Administration and Management—General M
Clinical Psychology M
Communication Disorders M
Counselor Education M
Education—General M,O
Educational Leadership and Administration M,O
Elementary Education M
English M
Marriage and Family Therapy M
Secondary Education M

UNIVERSITY OF MOUNT UNION

Educational Leadership and Administration M
Physician Assistant Studies M

UNIVERSITY OF NEBRASKA AT KEARNEY

Accounting M
Art Education M
Biological and Biomedical Sciences—General M
Business Administration and Management—General M
Communication Disorders M
Counseling Psychology M,O
Counselor Education M,O
Curriculum and Instruction M
Early Childhood Education M
Education of the Gifted M
Education—General M,O
Educational Leadership and Administration M,O
Educational Media/Instructional Technology M
Elementary Education M
English as a Second Language M
English M
Exercise and Sports Science M
Foreign Languages Education M
History M
Human Resources Management M
Human Services M
Leisure Studies M
Library Science M
Management Information Systems M
Marketing M
Mathematics Education M
Music Education M
Physical Education M
Reading Education M
Recreation and Park Management M
School Psychology M,O
Science Education M
Secondary Education M
Special Education M,O
Sports Management M
Student Affairs M,O
Writing M

UNIVERSITY OF NEBRASKA AT OMAHA

Accounting M
Applied Behavior Analysis M,D,O
Art/Fine Arts M
Artificial Intelligence/Robotics M,O
Athletic Training and Sports Medicine M,D
Bioinformatics M,D,O
Biological and Biomedical Sciences—General M,O
Business Administration and Management—General M,O
Communication Disorders M
Communication—General M,O
Computer and Information Systems Security M,D,O
Computer Science M,O
Counselor Education M
Criminal Justice and Criminology M,D,O
Database Systems M,D,O
Economics M
Education—General M,D,O
Educational Leadership and Administration M,D,O
Elementary Education M
English as a Second Language M,O
English M,O
Exercise and Sports Science M,D
Foreign Languages Education M
Geographic Information Systems M,O
Geography M,O
Gerontology M,O
Health Education M,D
History M
Human Resources Development M,D,O
Industrial and Organizational Psychology M,D,O
Information Science M,D,O
Management Information Systems M,D,O
Mathematics M
Music M
National Security M,O
Organizational Management M
Physical Education M,D
Political Science M,O
Project Management M,D,O
Psychology—General M,D,O
Public Administration M,D,O
Reading Education M
Recreation and Park Management M,D
School Psychology M,D,O
Science Education M,O
Secondary Education M,O
Social Work M,O
Sociology M
Software Engineering M,O
Special Education M
Systems Engineering M,O
Technical Communication M,O
Urban Education M,O
Writing M,O

UNIVERSITY OF NEBRASKA–LINCOLN

Accounting M,D
Actuarial Science M
Adult Education M,D,O
Advertising and Public Relations M,D
Agricultural Economics and Agribusiness M,D
Agricultural Education M
Agricultural Engineering M,D
Agricultural Sciences—General M,D
Agronomy and Soil Sciences M,D
Analytical Chemistry M,D
Animal Sciences M,D
Anthropology M
Archaeology M,D
Architectural Engineering M,D
Architecture M,D
Art History M
Art/Fine Arts M
Astronomy M,D
Biochemistry M,D
Bioengineering M,D
Bioinformatics M,D
Biological and Biomedical Sciences—General M,D
Biomedical Engineering M,D
Biopsychology M,D
Business Administration and Management—General M,D
Chemical Engineering M,D
Chemistry M,D
Child and Family Studies M,D
Child Development M,D
Civil Engineering M,D
Classics M
Clinical Psychology M,D
Clothing and Textiles M,D
Cognitive Sciences M,D,O
Communication Disorders M,D
Communication—General M,D
Comparative Literature M,D
Computer Engineering M,D
Computer Science M,D
Consumer Economics M,D
Corporate and Organizational Communication M,D
Counseling Psychology M,D,O

*M—masters degree; D—doctorate; O—other advanced degree; *—Close-Up and/or Display*

Curriculum and Instruction	M,D,O
Developmental Psychology	M,D,O
Early Childhood Education	M,D
Economics	M,D
Educational Leadership and Administration	M,D,O
Educational Measurement and Evaluation	M,D,O
Educational Psychology	M,D,O
Electrical Engineering	M,D
Engineering and Applied Sciences—General	M,D
Engineering Management	M,D
English	M,D
Entomology	M,D
Environmental Engineering	M,D
Exercise and Sports Science	M,D
Family and Consumer Sciences-General	M,D
Finance and Banking	M,D
Food Science and Technology	M,D
French	M,D
Geography	M,D
Geosciences	M,D
German	M,D
Gerontology	M,D
Health Promotion	M,D
History	M,D
Home Economics Education	M,D
Horticulture	M,D
Human Development	M,D,O
Industrial/Management Engineering	M,D
Information Science	M,D
Inorganic Chemistry	M,D
Interior Design	M,D
Journalism	M
Law	M,D
Legal and Justice Studies	M
Management Information Systems	M
Manufacturing Engineering	M,D
Marketing	M,D
Marriage and Family Therapy	M,D
Mass Communication	M
Materials Engineering	M,D
Materials Sciences	M,D
Mathematics	M,D
Mechanical Engineering	M,D
Mechanics	M,D
Metallurgical Engineering and Metallurgy	M,D
Music Education	M,D
Music	M,D
Natural Resources	M,D
Nutrition	M,D
Organic Chemistry	M,D
Philosophy	M,D
Physical Chemistry	M,D
Physics	M,D
Political Science	M,D,O
Psychology—General	M,D
Public Policy	M,D,O
Rhetoric	M,D
School Psychology	M,D,O
Social Psychology	M,D
Sociology	M,D
Spanish	M,D
Special Education	M,D,O
Speech and Interpersonal Communication	M,D
Statistics	M,D
Survey Methodology	M,D
Theater	M
Toxicology	M,D
Urban and Regional Planning	M,D
Veterinary Sciences	M,D
Vocational and Technical Education	M,D,O
Writing	M,D

UNIVERSITY OF NEBRASKA MEDICAL CENTER

Allied Health—General	M,D,O
Allopathic Medicine	D,O
Anatomy	M,D
Biochemistry	M,D
Bioinformatics	M,D
Biological and Biomedical Sciences—General	M,D
Biostatistics	D
Cancer Biology/Oncology	D
Cell Biology	M,D
Clinical Laboratory Sciences/Medical Technology	M,O
Emergency Management	M
Environmental and Occupational Health	D
Epidemiology	D
Genetics	M,D
Health Promotion	D
Health Services Research	D
Microbiology	M,D
Molecular Biology	M,D
Neuroscience	D
Nursing—General	D
Nutrition	O
Pathology	M,D
Perfusion	M
Pharmaceutical Sciences	M,D
Pharmacology	D
Pharmacy	D
Physical Therapy	D
Physician Assistant Studies	M
Physiology	M,D
Public Health—General	M
Toxicology	D

UNIVERSITY OF NEVADA, LAS VEGAS

Accounting	M,O
Addictions/Substance Abuse Counseling	M,D,O
Aerospace/Aeronautical Engineering	M,D,O
Allied Health—General	M,D,O
Anthropology	M,D
Architecture	M,O
Art/Fine Arts	M
Astronomy	M,D
Biochemistry	M,D
Biological and Biomedical Sciences—General	M,D
Biomedical Engineering	M,D,O
Business Administration and Management—General	M
Chemistry	M,D
Civil Engineering	M,D
Clinical Psychology	M,D,O
Communication—General	M
Community Health	M,D
Computer Engineering	M,D
Computer Science	M,D
Construction Management	O
Counseling Psychology	M,D,O
Counselor Education	M,D,O
Criminal Justice and Criminology	M,D
Curriculum and Instruction	M,D,O
Dentistry	M,D
Early Childhood Education	M,D,O
Economics	M
Education—General	M,D,O
Educational Leadership and Administration	M,D,O
Educational Media/Instructional Technology	M,D,O
Electrical Engineering	M,D
Emergency Management	M,D,O
Engineering and Applied Sciences—General	M,D,O
English as a Second Language	M,D,O
English	M,D
Entrepreneurship	M,O
Environmental Engineering	M,D
Environmental Sciences	M,D,O
Exercise and Sports Science	M,D
Family Nurse Practitioner Studies	M,D,O
Film, Television, and Video Production	M,O
Geosciences	M,D
Health Physics/Radiological Health	M,D,O
Health Services Management and Hospital Administration	M
Higher Education	M,D,O
Hispanic Studies	M
History	M,D
Hospitality Management	M,D
Human Resources Development	M,D,O
Journalism	M
Kinesiology and Movement Studies	M,D
Law	M,D
Management Information Systems	M,O
Marriage and Family Therapy	M
Materials Engineering	M,D,O
Mathematics	M,D
Mechanical Engineering	M,D,O
Media Studies	M
Music	M,D,O
Nonprofit Management	M,D,O
Nuclear Engineering	M,D,O
Nursing—General	M,D,O
Nutrition	M,D
Oral and Dental Sciences	M,D
Organizational Management	M,D,O
Physical Therapy	D
Physics	M,D
Political Science	M,D
Psychology—General	M,D,O
Public Administration	M,D,O
Public Affairs	M,D,O
Public Health—General	M,D
Social Work	M
Sociology	M,D
Special Education	M,D,O
Theater	M
Transportation and Highway Engineering	M,D
Water Resources	M
Writing	M,D,O

UNIVERSITY OF NEVADA, RENO

Accounting	M
Agricultural Economics and Agribusiness	M,D
Agricultural Sciences—General	M,D
Animal Sciences	M
Anthropology	M,D
Applied Economics	M,D
Art/Fine Arts	M
Atmospheric Sciences	M,D
Biochemistry	M,D
Biological and Biomedical Sciences—General	M
Biomedical Engineering	M,D
Biotechnology	M
Business Administration and Management—General	M
Cell Biology	M,D
Chemical Engineering	M,D
Chemical Physics	D
Chemistry	M,D
Child and Family Studies	M
Civil Engineering	M,D
Clinical Psychology	D
Cognitive Sciences	M,D
Communication Disorders	M,D
Computer Engineering	M,D
Computer Science	M,D
Conservation Biology	D
Counselor Education	M,D,O
Criminal Justice and Criminology	M
Curriculum and Instruction	D
Ecology	D
Economics	M
Education—General	M,D,O
Educational Leadership and Administration	M,D,O
Educational Psychology	M,D,O
Electrical Engineering	M,D
Elementary Education	M
Engineering and Applied Sciences—General	M,D
English as a Second Language	M
English	M,D
Environmental and Occupational Health	M,D
Environmental Management and Policy	M
Environmental Sciences	M,D
Evolutionary Biology	D
Finance and Banking	M
Foreign Languages Education	M
French	M
Geochemistry	M,D
Geography	M,D
Geological Engineering	M,D
Geology	M,D
Geophysics	M,D
German	M
History	M,D
Human Development	M
Hydrogeology	M,D
Hydrology	M,D
Journalism	M
Legal and Justice Studies	M,D
Management Information Systems	M
Materials Engineering	M,D
Mathematics Education	M
Mathematics	M
Mechanical Engineering	M,D
Metallurgical Engineering and Metallurgy	M,D
Mineral/Mining Engineering	M
Molecular Biology	M,D
Molecular Pharmacology	D
Music	M
Nursing—General	M,D
Nutrition	M
Philosophy	M
Physics	M,D
Physiology	D
Political Science	M,D
Psychology—General	M,D
Public Administration	M
Public Health—General	M,D
Reading Education	M,D
Secondary Education	M
Social Psychology	D
Social Work	M
Sociology	M
Spanish	M
Special Education	M,D
Speech and Interpersonal Communication	M
Western European Studies	D

UNIVERSITY OF NEW BRUNSWICK FREDERICTON

Anthropology	M
Applied Economics	M
Biological and Biomedical Sciences—General	M,D
Business Administration and Management—General	M
Chemical Engineering	M,D
Chemistry	M,D
Civil Engineering	M,D
Classics	M
Computer Engineering	M,D
Computer Science	M,D
Conflict Resolution and Mediation/Peace Studies	M
Construction Engineering	M,D
Economics	M
Education—General	M,D
Electrical Engineering	M,D
Engineering and Applied Sciences—General	M,D,O
Engineering Management	M
English	M,D
Entrepreneurship	M
Environmental Engineering	M,D
Environmental Management and Policy	M,D
Exercise and Sports Science	M
Forestry	M,D
Geodetic Sciences	M,D
Geology	M,D
Geotechnical Engineering	M,D
Health Services Research	M
History	M,D
Hydrology	M,D
Interdisciplinary Studies	M,D
International Development	M
Marketing	M,D
Materials Sciences	M,D
Mathematics	M,D
Mechanical Engineering	M,D
Mechanics	M,D
Nursing Education	M
Nursing—General	M
Physical Education	M
Physics	M,D
Political Science	M
Psychology—General	M,D
Public Administration	M
Public Policy	M
Recreation and Park Management	M
Sociology	M,D
Sports Management	M
Statistics	M,D
Structural Engineering	M,D
Surveying Science and Engineering	M,D
Sustainable Development	M
Transportation and Highway Engineering	M,D
Urban and Regional Planning	M
Water Resources	M,D

UNIVERSITY OF NEW BRUNSWICK SAINT JOHN

Biological and Biomedical Sciences—General	M,D
Business Administration and Management—General	M
Clinical Psychology	M,D
Electronic Commerce	M
Experimental Psychology	M,D
International Business	M
Natural Resources	M
Psychology—General	M,D

UNIVERSITY OF NEW ENGLAND

Biological and Biomedical Sciences—General	M
Curriculum and Instruction	M,O
Dentistry	D
Education—General	M,O
Educational Leadership and Administration	M,D,O
Educational Measurement and Evaluation	M,O
Ethics	M,O
Health Education	M,O
Marine Sciences	M
Nurse Anesthesia	M
Occupational Therapy	M
Pharmacy	D
Physical Therapy	D
Physician Assistant Studies	M
Reading Education	M,O
Social Work	M
Special Education	M,O
Vocational and Technical Education	M,O

UNIVERSITY OF NEW HAMPSHIRE

Accounting	M
Addictions/Substance Abuse Counseling	M,O
Agricultural Sciences—General	M,D
Animal Sciences	D
Applied Mathematics	M,D
Art/Fine Arts	M
Biochemistry	M,D
Biological and Biomedical Sciences—General	M,D
Business Administration and Management—General	M,O*
Chemical Engineering	M,D
Chemistry	M,D
Child and Family Studies	M,O
Civil Engineering	M,D
Communication Disorders	M
Comparative Literature	M,D
Computer Science	M,D,O
Conservation Biology	M
Curriculum and Instruction	D
Early Childhood Education	M
Economics	M,D
Education—General	M,D,O
Educational Leadership and Administration	M,D,O
Educational Media/Instructional Technology	M,O
Electrical Engineering	M,D
Elementary Education	M,O
English Education	M,D
English	M,D
Environmental Education	M,D,O
Environmental Engineering	M,D
Environmental Management and Policy	M
Environmental Sciences	D,O
Evolutionary Biology	D
Exercise and Sports Science	M,O
Family Nurse Practitioner Studies	M,D,O
Fish, Game, and Wildlife Management	M
Forestry	M
Genetics	M,D
Geographic Information Systems	O
Geology	M
Geosciences	M,D,O
Higher Education	O
History	M,D
Hydrology	M
Kinesiology and Movement Studies	M,O
Law	M,D,O
Legal and Justice Studies	M
Liberal Studies	M
Linguistics	M,D
Management Information Systems	M,O
Marine Biology	M,D,O
Marriage and Family Therapy	M,O
Materials Sciences	M,D
Mathematics Education	M,D
Mathematics	M,D
Mechanical Engineering	M,D
Microbiology	M,D
Museum Studies	M,D
Music	M,D
Natural Resources	M,D,O
Nursing—General	M,D,O
Nutrition	M,D
Occupational Therapy	M,O
Ocean Engineering	M,D,O
Oceanography	M,D,O
Physical Education	M,O
Physics	M,D
Political Science	M,O
Psychology—General	D
Public Administration	M,O
Public Health—General	M,O
Public Policy	M
Recreation and Park Management	M
Science Education	M,D
Secondary Education	M,O
Social Work	M,O
Sociology	M,D
Spanish	M
Special Education	M
Sustainability Management	M,O
Systems Engineering	M,D
Water Resources	M
Writing	M,D

UNIVERSITY OF NEW HAVEN

Accounting	M,O
Business Administration and Management—General	M,O
Cell Biology	M,O
Computer and Information Systems Security	M,D,O
Computer Engineering	M
Computer Science	M,D,O
Conflict Resolution and Mediation/Peace Studies	M,O
Criminal Justice and Criminology	M,D,O
Database Systems	M
Ecology	M,O
Electrical Engineering	M
Emergency Management	M,O
Engineering and Applied Sciences—General	M,O
Engineering Management	M,O
Environmental and Occupational Health	M,O
Environmental Engineering	M
Environmental Management and Policy	M,O
Environmental Sciences	M,O
Facilities Management	M,O
Finance and Banking	M,O
Fire Protection Engineering	M,O
Forensic Psychology	M,D,O
Forensic Sciences	M,D,O
Geographic Information Systems	M,O
Geosciences	M,O
Hazardous Materials Management	M
Health Services Management and Hospital Administration	M,O
Human Resources Management	M,O
Industrial and Labor Relations	M,O
Industrial and Manufacturing Management	M,O
Industrial and Organizational Psychology	M,O
Industrial/Management Engineering	M,O
International Business	M,O
Management Strategy and Policy	M,O
Marketing	M,O
Mechanical Engineering	M
Molecular Biology	M,O
National Security	M,O
Nutrition	M,O
Organizational Management	M,O
Public Administration	M,O
Science Education	M,O
Social Psychology	M,O
Software Engineering	M,O
Sports Management	M,O
Taxation	M,O
Urban and Regional Planning	M,O
Water Resources Engineering	M

UNIVERSITY OF NEW MEXICO

Accounting	M
Allied Health—General	M,D,O
Allopathic Medicine	D
American Indian/Native American Studies	M,D
American Studies	M,D
Anthropology	M,D
Archaeology	M,D
Architecture	M,D
Art Education	M
Art History	M,D
Art/Fine Arts	M
Biochemistry	M,D
Biological and Biomedical Sciences—General	M,D
Biomedical Engineering	M,D
Business Administration and Management—General	M
Cell Biology	M,D
Chemical Engineering	M,D
Chemistry	M,D
Child and Family Studies	M,D
Civil Engineering	M,D
Clinical Laboratory Sciences/Medical Technology	M,O
Clinical Psychology	D
Cognitive Sciences	D
Communication Disorders	M
Communication—General	M,D
Community Health	M
Comparative Literature	M,D
Computer and Information Systems Security	M
Computer Engineering	M,D
Computer Science	M,D
Construction Management	M,D
Counselor Education	M,D
Cultural Studies	M,D
Dance	M
Dental Hygiene	M
Developmental Psychology	D
Early Childhood Education	D
Economics	M,D
Education—General	M,D,O
Educational Leadership and Administration	M,D,O
Educational Media/Instructional Technology	M,D,O
Educational Psychology	M,D
Electrical Engineering	M,D
Elementary Education	M
Engineering and Applied Sciences—General	M,D
English as a Second Language	M,D
English Education	M,D
English	M,D
Entrepreneurship	M
Environmental Management and Policy	M
Epidemiology	M
Ethnic Studies	M,D
Exercise and Sports Science	D
Finance and Banking	M
Foundations and Philosophy of Education	M,D
French	M,D
Genetics	M,D
Geography	M
Geosciences	M,D
German	M,D
Health Education	M
Health Psychology	D
Health Services Management and Hospital Administration	M
Higher Education	O
Historic Preservation	O
History	M,D
Human Development	M,D
Human Resources Management	M
International Business	M
International Development	M,D
International Economics	M,D
Landscape Architecture	M
Latin American Studies	M,D
Law	D
Linguistics	M,D
Management Information Systems	M
Management of Technology	M
Management Strategy and Policy	M
Manufacturing Engineering	M
Marketing	M
Mathematics	M,D
Mechanical Engineering	M,D
Microbiology	M,D
Molecular Biology	M,D
Multilingual and Multicultural Education	M,D
Music Education	M
Music	M
Nanotechnology	M,D
Natural Resources	M,D
Neuroscience	M,D
Nuclear Engineering	M,D
Nursing—General	M,D
Nutrition	M
Occupational Therapy	M
Optical Sciences	M,D
Organizational Management	M
Pathology	M,D
Pharmaceutical Sciences	M,D
Pharmacy	D
Philosophy	M,D
Photography	M,D
Photonics	M,D
Physical Education	D
Physical Therapy	D
Physician Assistant Studies	M
Physics	M,D
Physiology	M,D
Planetary and Space Sciences	M,D
Political Science	M,D
Portuguese	M,D
Psychology—General	D
Public Administration	M
Public Health—General	M
Quantitative Analysis	D
Reading Education	M,D
Science Education	O
Secondary Education	M
Sociology	M,D
Spanish	M,D
Special Education	M,D,O
Sports Management	D
Statistics	M,D
Systems Engineering	M,D
Taxation	M
Theater	M
Toxicology	M,D
Urban and Regional Planning	M
Water Resources	M
Writing	M

UNIVERSITY OF NEW ORLEANS

Accounting	M
Art/Fine Arts	M
Arts Administration	M
Biological and Biomedical Sciences—General	M,D
Business Administration and Management—General	M
Chemistry	M,D
Computer Science	M
Counselor Education	M,D
Curriculum and Instruction	M,D
Economics	D
Education—General	M,D
Educational Leadership and Administration	M,D
Engineering and Applied Sciences—General	M,D
Engineering Management	M
English	M
Environmental Sciences	M
Film, Television, and Video Production	M
Finance and Banking	M,D
Geography	M
Geosciences	M
Health Services Management and Hospital Administration	M
History	M
Hospitality Management	M
Mathematics	M
Mechanical Engineering	M
Music	M
Physics	M,D
Political Science	M,D
Psychology—General	M,D
Public Administration	M
Romance Languages	M
Sociology	M
Special Education	M,D
Taxation	M
Theater	M
Transportation Management	M
Travel and Tourism	M
Urban and Regional Planning	M
Urban Studies	M,D

UNIVERSITY OF NORTH ALABAMA

Accounting	M
Business Administration and Management—General	M
Child and Family Studies	M
Counselor Education	M
Criminal Justice and Criminology	M
Education—General	M,O
Educational Leadership and Administration	M,O
Elementary Education	M
English	M
Environmental and Occupational Health	M
Exercise and Sports Science	M
Finance and Banking	M
Geographic Information Systems	M
Health Promotion	M
Health Services Management and Hospital Administration	M
History	M
Interdisciplinary Studies	M
International Business	M
Kinesiology and Movement Studies	M
Law	M
Management Information Systems	M
Nursing—General	M
Physical Education	M
Political Science	M
Project Management	M
Public History	M
School Psychology	M
Secondary Education	M
Special Education	M
Urban and Regional Planning	M

UNIVERSITY OF NORTH CAROLINA AT ASHEVILLE

Liberal Studies	M,O

THE UNIVERSITY OF NORTH CAROLINA AT CHAPEL HILL

Accounting	M,D
Adult Nursing	M,D,O
Allied Health—General	M,D
Allopathic Medicine	D
Anthropology	M,D
Archaeology	M,D
Art History	M,D
Art/Fine Arts	M
Astronomy	M,D
Astrophysics	M,D
Athletic Training and Sports Medicine	M
Atmospheric Sciences	M,D
Biochemistry	M,D
Bioinformatics	D
Biological and Biomedical Sciences—General	M,D
Biomedical Engineering	M,D
Biophysics	M,D
Biopsychology	D
Biostatistics	M,D
Botany	M,D
Business Administration and Management—General	M,D
Cell Biology	M,D
Chemistry	M,D
Classics	M,D
Clinical Psychology	D
Cognitive Sciences	D
Communication Disorders	M,D
Communication—General	D
Computational Biology	D
Computer Science	M,D
Counselor Education	M
Curriculum and Instruction	M,D
Dental Hygiene	M,D
Dentistry	D
Developmental Biology	M,D
Developmental Psychology	D
Early Childhood Education	M,D
East European and Russian Studies	M
Ecology	M,D
Economics	M,D
Education—General	M,D
Educational Leadership and Administration	M,D
Educational Measurement and Evaluation	M,D
Educational Psychology	M,D
English as a Second Language	M
English Education	M
English	M,D
Environmental and Occupational Health	M,D
Environmental Engineering	M,D
Environmental Management and Policy	M,D
Environmental Sciences	M,D
Epidemiology	M,D
Evolutionary Biology	M,D
Exercise and Sports Science	M
Family Nurse Practitioner Studies	M,D,O
Finance and Banking	D
Folklore	M
Foreign Languages Education	M
French	M,D
Genetics	M,D
Geography	M,D
Geology	M,D
German	M,D
Gerontological Nursing	M,D,O
Health Promotion	M
Health Psychology	M,D
Health Services Management and Hospital Administration	M,D
History	M,D
Immunology	M,D
Industrial Hygiene	M,D
Information Studies	M,D,O
Italian	M,D
Kinesiology and Movement Studies	M,D
Latin American Studies	M,D,O
Law	D
Library Science	M,D,O
Linguistics	M,D
Management Information Systems	D
Management Strategy and Policy	D
Marine Sciences	M,D
Marketing	D
Mass Communication	M,D
Materials Sciences	M,D
Maternal and Child Health	M,D
Mathematics Education	M
Mathematics	M,D
Microbiology	M,D
Molecular Biology	M,D
Molecular Physiology	D
Music Education	M
Music	M,D
Neurobiology	D
Neuroscience	D
Nursing and Healthcare Administration	M,D,O
Nursing Education	M,D,O
Nursing Informatics	M,D,O
Nursing—General	M,D,O
Nutrition	M,D
Occupational Health Nursing	M
Occupational Therapy	M,D
Operations Research	M,D
Oral and Dental Sciences	M,D
Organizational Behavior	D
Pathology	D
Pediatric Nursing	M,D,O
Pharmaceutical Administration	M,D
Pharmaceutical Sciences	M,D
Pharmacology	D
Philosophy	M,D
Physical Education	M
Physical Therapy	M,D
Physics	M,D
Political Science	M,D,O
Portuguese	M,D
Psychiatric Nursing	M,D,O
Psychology—General	D
Public Administration	M
Public Health—General	M,D
Public Policy	D
Reading Education	M,D
Rehabilitation Counseling	M,D
Religion	M,D
Romance Languages	M,D
Russian	M,D
School Psychology	M,D
Science Education	M
Secondary Education	M
Slavic Languages	M,D
Social Psychology	D
Social Sciences Education	M
Social Work	M,D
Sociology	M,D
Spanish	M,D
Sports Management	M
Statistics	M,D
Telecommunications	M,D
Theater	M
Toxicology	M,D
Urban and Regional Planning	M,D

THE UNIVERSITY OF NORTH CAROLINA AT CHARLOTTE

Accounting	M
Acute Care/Critical Care Nursing	M,D,O
Addictions/Substance Abuse Counseling	M,D,O
African Studies	O
Anthropology	M
Applied Economics	M,O
Applied Mathematics	M,D
Applied Physics	M,D
Architecture	M
Art Education	M,D,O
Arts Administration	M,O
Bioinformatics	M,D,O
Biological and Biomedical Sciences—General	M,D
Business Administration and Management—General	M,D,O
Chemistry	M,D
Child and Family Studies	M,D,O
Child Development	M,D,O
Civil Engineering	M,D
Cognitive Sciences	M,D,O
Communication—General	M
Community Health Nursing	M,D,O
Community Health	M,D,O
Computer and Information Systems Security	M,D,O
Computer Engineering	M,D
Computer Science	M,O
Construction Management	M,O
Counselor Education	M,D,O
Criminal Justice and Criminology	M
Curriculum and Instruction	M,D,O
Database Systems	M,O
Early Childhood Education	M,D,O
Economics	M,O
Education of the Gifted	M,D,O
Educational Leadership and Administration	M,D,O

*M—masters degree; D—doctorate; O—other advanced degree; *—Close-Up and/or Display*

Educational Media/Instructional Technology	M,D,O
Electrical Engineering	M,D
Elementary Education	M,O
Emergency Management	M,O
Energy and Power Engineering	M,O
Engineering and Applied Sciences—General	M,D,O
Engineering Management	M,O
English as a Second Language	M,D,O
English Education	M,O
English	M,O
Environmental Engineering	M,D
Ethics	M,O
Facilities Management	M,O
Family Nurse Practitioner Studies	M,D,O
Finance and Banking	M,O
Fire Protection Engineering	M,O
Foreign Languages Education	M,D,O
Game Design and Development	M,O
Gender Studies	M,D,O
Geographic Information Systems	M,D
Geography	M,D
Geosciences	M,D
Gerontological Nursing	M,D,O
Gerontology	M,D,O
Health Informatics	M,O
Health Psychology	M,D,O
Health Services Management and Hospital Administration	M,D,O
Health Services Research	D
History	M
Industrial and Manufacturing Management	M,O
Industrial and Organizational Psychology	M,D,O
Information Science	M,D,O
Interdisciplinary Studies	M,D,O
Kinesiology and Movement Studies	M
Latin American Studies	M,D,O
Liberal Studies	M,D,O
Linguistics	M,O
Logistics	M,O
Management Information Systems	M,D,O
Mathematical and Computational Finance	M,O
Mathematics Education	M,D
Mathematics	M,D,O
Mechanical Engineering	M,D
Middle School Education	M,D,O
Music	O
Nonprofit Management	M,O
Nurse Anesthesia	M,D,O
Nursing and Healthcare Administration	M,D,O
Nursing Education	M,D,O
Nursing—General	M,D,O
Optical Sciences	M,D
Philosophy	M,O
Psychology—General	M,D,O
Public Administration	M,O
Public Health—General	M,D,O
Public Policy	M,D,O
Reading Education	M,O
Real Estate	M,O
Religion	M
Secondary Education	M,D,O
Social Work	M
Sociology	M
Spanish	M,O
Special Education	M,D,O
Statistics	M,O
Supply Chain Management	M,O
Systems Engineering	M,D,O
Technical Writing	M,O
Theater	M,D,O
Translation and Interpretation	M,O
Urban and Regional Planning	M,O
Urban Design	M
Women's Studies	M,D,O
Writing	M,O

THE UNIVERSITY OF NORTH CAROLINA AT GREENSBORO

Accounting	M,O
Adult Education	M,D,O
Adult Nursing	M,D,O
Applied Economics	M
Architecture	M,O
Art/Fine Arts	M
Athletic Training and Sports Medicine	M,D
Biochemistry	M
Biological and Biomedical Sciences—General	M
Business Administration and Management—General	M,O
Chemistry	M
Child and Family Studies	M,D
Classics	M
Clinical Psychology	M,D
Cognitive Sciences	M,D
Communication Disorders	M,D
Communication—General	M
Community Health	M,D
Computer Science	M
Conflict Resolution and Mediation/Peace Studies	M,O
Counseling Psychology	M,D,O
Counselor Education	M,D,O
Criminal Justice and Criminology	M
Curriculum and Instruction	M,D,O
Dance	M
Developmental Psychology	M,D
Early Childhood Education	M,D,O
Economic Development	M,D,O
Economics	D
Education—General	M,D,O
Educational Leadership and Administration	M,D,O
Educational Measurement and Evaluation	D
Educational Media/Instructional Technology	M,D,O
Elementary Education	D
English as a Second Language	M,D,O
English Education	M,D
English	M,D
Film, Television, and Video Production	M
Finance and Banking	M,O
Foreign Languages Education	M,D,O
French	M
Gender Studies	M,O
Genetic Counseling	M
Geographic Information Systems	M,D,O
Geography	M,D,O
Gerontological Nursing	M,D,O
Gerontology	M,O
Higher Education	D
Hispanic and Latin American Languages	M,O
Hispanic Studies	M,O
Historic Preservation	M,O
History	M,D,O
Human Development	M,D
Information Studies	M
Interior Design	M,O
Kinesiology and Movement Studies	M,D
Liberal Studies	M
Library Science	M
Management Information Systems	M,D,O
Marketing	M,D
Marriage and Family Therapy	M,D,O
Mathematics Education	M,D,O
Mathematics	M,D
Media Studies	M
Middle School Education	M,D,O
Multilingual and Multicultural Education	M,D,O
Museum Studies	M,D,O
Music Education	M,D
Music	M,D
Nonprofit Management	M,O
Nurse Anesthesia	M,D,O
Nursing and Healthcare Administration	M,D,O
Nursing Education	M,D,O
Nursing—General	M,D,O
Nutrition	M,D
Political Science	M,O
Psychology—General	M,D
Public Affairs	M,O
Reading Education	M,D,O
Recreation and Park Management	M
Rhetoric	M,D
School Psychology	M,D,O
Science Education	M,D,O
Social Psychology	M,D
Social Sciences Education	M,D,O
Social Work	M
Sociology	M
Spanish	M,O
Special Education	M,D,O
Supply Chain Management	M,D,O
Technical Writing	M,D,O
Textile Design	M,D
Theater	M
Women's Studies	M,D,O
Writing	M

THE UNIVERSITY OF NORTH CAROLINA AT PEMBROKE

Art Education	M
Business Administration and Management—General	M
Counseling Psychology	M
Counselor Education	M
Education—General	M
Educational Leadership and Administration	M
Elementary Education	M
English Education	M
Exercise and Sports Science	M
Mathematics Education	M
Nursing and Healthcare Administration	M
Nursing Education	M
Nursing—General	M
Physical Education	M
Public Administration	M
Reading Education	M
Science Education	M
Social Sciences Education	M
Social Work	M

UNIVERSITY OF NORTH CAROLINA SCHOOL OF THE ARTS

Arts Administration	M
Film, Television, and Video Production	M
Music	M,O
Theater	M

THE UNIVERSITY OF NORTH CAROLINA WILMINGTON

Accounting	M
Applied Behavior Analysis	M
Biological and Biomedical Sciences—General	M,D
Business Administration and Management—General	M
Chemistry	M
Clinical Research	M,O
Computer Science	M
Conflict Resolution and Mediation/Peace Studies	M,O
Criminal Justice and Criminology	M
Curriculum and Instruction	M,D
Early Childhood Education	M
Education of the Gifted	M
Education—General	M,D
Educational Leadership and Administration	M,D
Educational Media/Instructional Technology	M
Educational Policy	M
Elementary Education	M
English as a Second Language	M
English Education	M
English	M
Environmental Education	M
Environmental Management and Policy	M
Family Nurse Practitioner Studies	M,O
Geosciences	M
Gerontology	M,O
Higher Education	M,D
History	M
Liberal Studies	M
Management Information Systems	M
Marine Biology	M,D
Marine Sciences	M,D,O
Mathematics Education	M
Mathematics	M,O
Middle School Education	M
Nursing—General	M,O
Physical Education	M
Psychology—General	M
Public Administration	M,O
Reading Education	M
Science Education	M
Social Sciences Education	M
Social Work	M
Sociology	M
Spanish	M,O
Special Education	M
Statistics	M,O
Taxation	M
Writing	M

UNIVERSITY OF NORTH DAKOTA

Accounting	M
Allopathic Medicine	D
Anatomy	M,D
Applied Economics	M
Art/Fine Arts	M
Atmospheric Sciences	M,D
Aviation	M
Biochemistry	M,D
Biological and Biomedical Sciences—General	M,D
Botany	M,D
Business Administration and Management—General	M
Cell Biology	M,D
Chemical Engineering	M
Chemistry	M,D
Civil Engineering	M
Clinical Laboratory Sciences/Medical Technology	M
Clinical Psychology	M,D
Communication Disorders	M,D
Communication—General	M,D
Community Health Nursing	M,D
Computer Science	M
Counseling Psychology	M
Criminal Justice and Criminology	D
Early Childhood Education	M
Ecology	M,D
Education—General	M,D,O
Educational Leadership and Administration	M,D,O
Educational Measurement and Evaluation	D
Educational Media/Instructional Technology	M
Electrical Engineering	M
Elementary Education	M,D
Engineering and Applied Sciences—General	D
English	M,D
Entomology	M,D
Environmental Biology	M,D
Environmental Engineering	M
Experimental Psychology	M,D
Family Nurse Practitioner Studies	M,D
Fish, Game, and Wildlife Management	M,D
Forensic Psychology	M,D
Genetics	M,D
Geography	M
Geological Engineering	M
Geology	M,D
Geosciences	M,D
Gerontological Nursing	M,D
History	M,D
Immunology	M,D
Kinesiology and Movement Studies	M
Law	D
Linguistics	M
Management of Technology	M
Mathematics	M
Mechanical Engineering	M
Microbiology	M,D
Mineral/Mining Engineering	M
Molecular Biology	M,D
Music Education	M,D
Music	M,D
Nurse Anesthesia	M,D
Nursing Education	M,D
Nursing—General	M,D
Occupational Therapy	M
Pharmacology	M,D
Physical Therapy	M,D
Physician Assistant Studies	M
Physics	M,D
Physiology	M,D
Planetary and Space Sciences	M
Psychiatric Nursing	M,D
Psychology—General	M,D
Public Administration	M
Public Health—General	M,D
Reading Education	M
Secondary Education	D
Social Work	M
Sociology	M
Special Education	M,D
Structural Engineering	M
Theater	M
Zoology	M,D

UNIVERSITY OF NORTHERN BRITISH COLUMBIA

Community Health	M,D,O
Computer Science	M,D,O
Disability Studies	M,D,O
Education—General	M,D,O
Environmental Management and Policy	M,D,O
Gender Studies	M,D,O
History	M,D,O
Interdisciplinary Studies	M,D,O
International Affairs	M,D,O
Mathematics	M,D,O
Natural Resources	M,D,O
Political Science	M,D,O
Psychology—General	M,D,O
Social Work	M,D,O

UNIVERSITY OF NORTHERN COLORADO

Accounting	M
Applied Statistics	M,D
Art/Fine Arts	M
Biological and Biomedical Sciences—General	M
Chemistry	M,D
Communication Disorders	M,D
Communication—General	M
Counselor Education	M,D
Criminal Justice and Criminology	M
Early Childhood Education	M,D
Education of the Gifted	M,D
Education—General	M,D,O
Educational Leadership and Administration	M,D,O
Educational Measurement and Evaluation	M,D
Educational Media/Instructional Technology	M,D
Educational Psychology	M,D
English	M
Exercise and Sports Science	M,D
Family Nurse Practitioner Studies	M,D
Foreign Languages Education	M
Geosciences	M
Gerontology	M
Health Education	M
Higher Education	D
History	M
Library Science	M
Mathematics Education	M,D
Mathematics	M,D
Music Education	M,D
Music	M,D
Nursing Education	M,D
Nursing—General	M,D
Physical Education	M,D
Psychology—General	M,D
Public Health—General	M
Reading Education	M
Rehabilitation Counseling	M,D
School Psychology	D,O
Science Education	M,D
Sociology	M
Spanish	M
Special Education	M,D
Sports Management	M,D
Student Affairs	D

UNIVERSITY OF NORTHERN IOWA

Accounting	M
Allied Health—General	M,D
Applied Mathematics	M
Art Education	M
Art/Fine Arts	M
Athletic Training and Sports Medicine	M
Biological and Biomedical Sciences—General	M
Business Administration and Management—General	M
Communication Disorders	M
Communication—General	M
Community College Education	M
Community Health	M
Counseling Psychology	M
Counselor Education	M
Curriculum and Instruction	D
Early Childhood Education	M
Education—General	M,D,O
Educational Leadership and Administration	M,D
Educational Measurement and Evaluation	M
Educational Media/Instructional Technology	M
Educational Psychology	M
Elementary Education	M
English as a Second Language	M
English Education	M
English	M
Foreign Languages Education	M
Gender Studies	M
Geography	M
Geosciences	M
Health Education	M
Health Promotion	M
Higher Education	M
History	M
Human Services	M
Kinesiology and Movement Studies	M
Mathematics Education	M
Mathematics	M
Middle School Education	M
Music Education	M
Music	M
Nonprofit Management	M
Physical Education	M
Physics	M
Psychology—General	M
Public History	M
Public Policy	M
Reading Education	M

School Psychology	M,O
Science Education	M
Secondary Education	M
Social Sciences	M
Social Work	M
Spanish	M
Special Education	M
Sports Management	M
Student Affairs	M
Vocational and Technical Education	M,D
Women's Studies	M
Writing	M

UNIVERSITY OF NORTH FLORIDA

Accounting	M
Adult Education	M
Adult Nursing	M,D,O
Allied Health—General	M,D,O
Applied Behavior Analysis	M
Biological and Biomedical Sciences—General	M
Business Administration and Management—General	M
Civil Engineering	M
Communication Disorders	M
Community Health	M,O
Computer Science	M
Construction Management	M
Counseling Psychology	M
Counselor Education	M,D
Criminal Justice and Criminology	M
Economics	M
Education—General	M,D
Educational Leadership and Administration	M,D
Educational Media/Instructional Technology	M,D
Electrical Engineering	M
Electronic Commerce	M
Elementary Education	M
English as a Second Language	M
English	M
Ethics	M,O
Exercise and Sports Science	M,D
Family Nurse Practitioner Studies	M,D,O
Finance and Banking	M
Gerontology	M,O
Health Services Management and Hospital Administration	M,O
History	M
Human Resources Management	M
International Business	M
Logistics	M
Management Information Systems	M
Mathematics	M
Mechanical Engineering	M
Nonprofit Management	M,O
Nurse Anesthesia	M,D,O
Nursing and Healthcare Administration	M,D,O
Nursing—General	M,D,O
Nutrition	M
Philosophy	M,O
Physical Therapy	M,D
Psychology—General	M
Public Administration	M,O
Public Health—General	M,O
Reading Education	M
Rehabilitation Counseling	M,O
Secondary Education	M
Software Engineering	M
Special Education	M
Sports Management	M,D
Statistics	M
Translation and Interpretation	M
Writing	M

UNIVERSITY OF NORTH GEORGIA

Anthropology	M
Art Education	M,O
Business Administration and Management—General	M
Clinical Psychology	M
Counseling Psychology	M
Criminal Justice and Criminology	M
Early Childhood Education	M,O
Education—General	M,O
Educational Leadership and Administration	M,O
English Education	M,O
Family Nurse Practitioner Studies	M,O
History	M
International Affairs	M
Mathematics Education	M,O
Middle School Education	M,O
Music	M
Philosophy	M
Physical Education	M,O
Physical Therapy	D
Political Science	M
Secondary Education	M,O
Social Sciences Education	M,O

UNIVERSITY OF NORTH TEXAS

Accounting	M,D,O
Advertising and Public Relations	M,D,O
Anthropology	M,D,O
Applied Arts and Design—General	M,D,O
Applied Behavior Analysis	M,D,O
Art Education	M,D,O
Art History	M,D,O
Art/Fine Arts	M,D,O
Biochemistry	M,D,O
Biological and Biomedical Sciences—General	M,D,O
Biomedical Engineering	M,D,O
Business Administration and Management—General	M,D,O
Chemistry	M,D,O
Child and Family Studies	M,D,O
Clinical Psychology	M,D,O
Communication Disorders	M,D,O
Communication—General	M,D,O
Computer Engineering	M,D,O
Computer Science	M,D,O
Counseling Psychology	M,D,O
Counselor Education	M,D,O
Criminal Justice and Criminology	M,D,O
Curriculum and Instruction	M,D,O
Early Childhood Education	M,D,O
Economics	M,D,O
Education of the Gifted	M,D,O
Education—General	M,D,O
Educational Leadership and Administration	M,D,O
Educational Measurement and Evaluation	M,D,O
Educational Psychology	M,D,O
Electrical Engineering	M,D,O
Emergency Management	M,D,O
Energy and Power Engineering	M,D,O
Engineering and Applied Sciences—General	M,D,O
English as a Second Language	M,D,O
English	M,D,O
Environmental Sciences	M,D,O
Film, Television, and Video Production	M,D,O
Finance and Banking	M,D,O
French	M,D,O
Geography	M,D,O
Gerontology	M,D,O
Health Services Management and Hospital Administration	M,D,O
Higher Education	M,D,O
History	M,D,O
Hospitality Management	M,D,O
Human Development	M,D,O
Human Resources Management	M,D,O
Industrial and Manufacturing Management	M,D,O
Information Science	M,D,O
Interdisciplinary Studies	M,D,O
Interior Design	M,D,O
International Affairs	M,D,O
Internet and Interactive Multimedia	M,D,O
Journalism	M,D,O
Kinesiology and Movement Studies	M,D,O
Linguistics	M,D,O
Logistics	M,D,O
Management Information Systems	M,D,O
Management Strategy and Policy	M,D,O
Marketing	M,D,O
Mathematics	M,D,O
Mechanical Engineering	M,D,O
Molecular Biology	M,D,O
Museum Studies	M,D,O
Music Education	M,D,O
Music	M,D,O
Nonprofit Management	M,D,O
Philosophy	M,D,O
Political Science	M,D,O
Psychology—General	M,D,O
Public Administration	M,D,O
Quantitative Analysis	M,D,O
Rehabilitation Counseling	M,D,O
Sociology	M,D,O
Spanish	M,D,O
Special Education	M,D,O
Supply Chain Management	M,D,O
Textile Design	M,D,O
Travel and Tourism	M,D,O
Vocational and Technical Education	M,D,O
Writing	M,D,O

UNIVERSITY OF NORTH TEXAS HEALTH SCIENCE CENTER AT FORT WORTH

Anatomy	M,D
Biochemistry	M,D
Biological and Biomedical Sciences—General	M,D
Biostatistics	M,D
Biotechnology	M,D
Community Health	M,D
Environmental and Occupational Health	M,D
Epidemiology	M,D
Forensic Sciences	M,D
Genetics	M,D
Health Services Management and Hospital Administration	M,D
Immunology	M,D
Microbiology	M,D
Molecular Biology	M,D
Osteopathic Medicine	M,D
Pharmacology	M,D
Physician Assistant Studies	M
Physiology	M,D
Public Health—General	M,D
Science Education	M,D

UNIVERSITY OF NORTHWESTERN–ST. PAUL

Business Administration and Management—General	M
Education—General	M
Family and Consumer Sciences-General	M
Human Services	M
Organizational Management	M
Pastoral Ministry and Counseling	M
Theology	M

UNIVERSITY OF NOTRE DAME

Accounting	M
Aerospace/Aeronautical Engineering	M,D
Applied Arts and Design—General	M
Applied Mathematics	M,D
Applied Statistics	M,D
Architecture	M
Art History	M
Art/Fine Arts	M
Biochemistry	M,D
Bioengineering	M,D
Biological and Biomedical Sciences—General	M,D
Business Administration and Management—General	M
Cell Biology	M,D
Chemical Engineering	M,D
Chemistry	M,D
Civil Engineering	M,D
Cognitive Sciences	D
Comparative Literature	D
Computational Sciences	M,D
Computer Engineering	M,D
Computer Science	M,D
Conflict Resolution and Mediation/Peace Studies	M,D
Counseling Psychology	D
Database Systems	M
Developmental Psychology	D
Ecology	M,D
Economics	M,D
Education—General	M
Electrical Engineering	M,D
Engineering and Applied Sciences—General	M,D
English	M,D
Environmental Engineering	M,D
Evolutionary Biology	M,D
Finance and Banking	M
French	M
Genetics	M,D
Geosciences	M,D
Graphic Design	M
History of Science and Technology	M,D
History	M,D
Industrial Design	M
Inorganic Chemistry	M,D
Italian	M
Latin American Studies	M
Law	M,D
Mathematical and Computational Finance	M,D
Mathematics	M,D
Mechanical Engineering	M,D
Medieval and Renaissance Studies	M,D
Molecular Biology	M,D
Nonprofit Management	M
Organic Chemistry	M,D
Parasitology	M,D
Philosophy	D
Photography	M
Physical Chemistry	M,D
Physics	M,D
Physiology	M,D
Political Science	D
Psychology—General	D
Religion	M
Romance Languages	M
Sociology	D
Spanish	M
Statistics	M,D
Taxation	M
Theology	M,D
Writing	M

UNIVERSITY OF OKLAHOMA

Accounting	M,D
Addictions/Substance Abuse Counseling	M,O
Adult Education	M,D
Aerospace/Aeronautical Engineering	M,D
American Indian/Native American Studies	M
Anthropology	M,D
Applied Economics	M,D
Architecture	M
Art History	M,D
Art/Fine Arts	M
Biochemistry	M,D
Bioinformatics	M,D
Biological and Biomedical Sciences—General	M,D
Biomedical Engineering	M,D
Business Administration and Management—General	M,D*
Chemical Engineering	M,D
Chemistry	M,D
Civil Engineering	M,D
Communication—General	M,D
Computer Engineering	M,D
Computer Science	M,D
Construction Management	M
Corporate and Organizational Communication	M,D
Counseling Psychology	M,D
Criminal Justice and Criminology	M,O
Curriculum and Instruction	M,D,O
Dance	M
Database Systems	M
Ecology	D
Economics	M,D
Education—General	M,D,O
Educational Leadership and Administration	M,D,O
Educational Measurement and Evaluation	M,D,O
Educational Media/Instructional Technology	M,D,O
Educational Psychology	M,D,O
Electrical Engineering	M,D
Engineering and Applied Sciences—General	M,D
Engineering Physics	M,D
English	M,D
Entrepreneurship	M,D,O
Environmental Engineering	M,D
Environmental Sciences	M,D
Evolutionary Biology	D
Exercise and Sports Science	M,D
Film, Television, and Video Production	M
French	M,D
Gender Studies	O
Geography	M,D
Geological Engineering	M,D
Geology	M,D
Geophysics	M,D
German	M
Health Education	M,D
Health Promotion	M,D
Health Services Management and Hospital Administration	M,O
Higher Education	M,D,O
History of Science and Technology	M,D
History	M,D
Human Resources Management	M,O
Human Services	M,O
Industrial and Organizational Psychology	M,D
Industrial/Management Engineering	M,D
Interdisciplinary Studies	M,D
Interior Design	M,O
International Affairs	M,O
Journalism	M,D
Landscape Architecture	M
Law	M,D
Liberal Studies	M,O
Management Information Systems	M,O
Mass Communication	M,D
Mathematics	M,D*
Mechanical Engineering	M,D
Meteorology	M,D
Microbiology	M,D
Museum Studies	M,O
Music Education	M,D,O
Music	M,D,O
Neurobiology	D
Nonprofit Management	M
Organizational Behavior	M,O
Petroleum Engineering	M,D,O
Philosophy	M,D
Photography	M
Physics	M,D
Plant Biology	M,D
Political Science	M,D
Project Management	M,O
Psychology—General	M,D,O
Public Administration	M
Public Policy	M,D
Social Work	M
Sociology	M,D
Spanish	M,D
Special Education	M,D
Sustainable Development	M,D
Telecommunications	M
Theater	M
Urban and Regional Planning	M
Urban Studies	M
Women's Studies	O
Writing	M

UNIVERSITY OF OKLAHOMA HEALTH SCIENCES CENTER

Allied Health—General	M,D,O
Allopathic Medicine	D
Biochemistry	M,D
Biological and Biomedical Sciences—General	M,D
Biopsychology	M,D
Biostatistics	M,D
Cell Biology	M,D
Communication Disorders	M,D,O
Dentistry	D,O
Environmental and Occupational Health	M,D
Epidemiology	M,D
Genetic Counseling	M
Health Education	D
Health Physics/Radiological Health	M,D
Health Promotion	M,D
Health Services Management and Hospital Administration	M,D
Homeland Security	M
Immunology	M,D
Medical Physics	M,D
Microbiology	M,D
Molecular Biology	M,D
Neuroscience	M,D
Nursing—General	M
Nutrition	M
Occupational Therapy	M
Oral and Dental Sciences	M
Pathology	D
Pharmaceutical Sciences	M,D
Pharmacy	D
Physical Therapy	M
Physician Assistant Studies	M
Physiology	M,D
Public Health—General	M,D
Radiation Biology	M,D
Reading Education	M,D,O
Rehabilitation Sciences	M
Special Education	M,D,O

UNIVERSITY OF OREGON

Accounting	M,D
Anthropology	M,D
Architecture	M
Art History	M,D
Art/Fine Arts	M
Arts Administration	M
Asian Languages	M,D
Asian Studies	M
Biochemistry	M,D
Biological and Biomedical Sciences—General	M,D

*M—masters degree; D—doctorate; O—other advanced degree; *—Close-Up and/or Display*

Biopsychology	M,D
Business Administration and Management—General	M,D
Chemistry	M,D
Chinese	M,D
Classics	M
Clinical Psychology	D
Cognitive Sciences	M,D
Communication—General	M,D
Comparative Literature	M,D
Computer Science	M,D
Dance	M
Developmental Psychology	M,D
Ecology	M,D
Economics	M,D
Education—General	M,D
English	M,D
Environmental Management and Policy	M,D
Evolutionary Biology	M,D
Finance and Banking	D
Folklore	M
French	M
Genetics	M,D
Geography	M,D
Geology	M,D
German	M,D
Historic Preservation	M
History	M,D
Information Science	M,D
Interdisciplinary Studies	M
Interior Design	M
International Affairs	M
Italian	M
Japanese	M,D
Journalism	M,D
Landscape Architecture	M
Law	M,D
Linguistics	M,D
Management Information Systems	M
Marine Biology	M,D
Marketing	D
Mathematics	M,D
Media Studies	M,D
Molecular Biology	M,D
Music Education	M,D
Music	M,D
Neuroscience	M,D
Philosophy	M,D
Physics	M,D
Physiology	M,D
Political Science	M,D
Psychology—General	M,D
Public Policy	M
Quantitative Analysis	M
Romance Languages	M,D
Russian	M
Social Psychology	M,D
Sociology	M,D
Spanish	M
Sports Management	M
Theater	M,D
Urban and Regional Planning	M
Writing	M

UNIVERSITY OF OTTAWA

Aerospace/Aeronautical Engineering	M,D
Allopathic Medicine	M,D
Anthropology	M
Biochemistry	M,D
Bioengineering	M,D
Biological and Biomedical Sciences—General	M,D
Biomedical Engineering	M
Business Administration and Management—General	M
Canadian Studies	D
Cell Biology	M,D
Chemical Engineering	M,D
Chemistry	M,D
Civil Engineering	M,D
Classics	M,D
Communication Disorders	M
Communication—General	M
Community Health	M,D,O
Computer Engineering	M,D
Computer Science	M,D
Criminal Justice and Criminology	M,D
Economics	M,D
Education—General	M,D,O
Electrical Engineering	M,D
Electronic Commerce	M,D,O
Engineering and Applied Sciences—General	M,D,O
Engineering Management	M,O
English	M,D
Epidemiology	M
Finance and Banking	D,O
French	M,D
Geography	M,D
Geosciences	M,D
Health Services Management and Hospital Administration	M
Health Services Research	D,O
History	M,D
Immunology	M,D
Information Science	M,O
Interdisciplinary Studies	D,O
International Development	M
Kinesiology and Movement Studies	M
Law	M,D
Linguistics	M,D
Mathematics	M,D
Mechanical Engineering	M,D
Microbiology	M,D
Molecular Biology	M,D
Music Education	M,O
Music	M,O
Nursing—General	M,D,O
Philosophy	M,D
Physics	M,D
Political Science	M,D
Project Management	M,O
Psychology—General	D
Public Administration	D,O
Public Health—General	D
Rehabilitation Sciences	M
Religion	M,D
Social Work	M
Sociology	M
Spanish	M,D
Statistics	M,D
Systems Science	M,D,O
Theater	M
Translation and Interpretation	M,D
Women's Studies	M

UNIVERSITY OF PENNSYLVANIA

Accounting	M,D
Acute Care/Critical Care Nursing	M
Adult Nursing	M
African Studies	M,D
Allopathic Medicine	D
Anthropology	M,D
Applied Economics	D
Applied Mathematics	D
Applied Psychology	M,D
Archaeology	M,D
Architecture	M,D,O
Art History	M,D
Art/Fine Arts	M,O
Artificial Intelligence/Robotics	M,D
Asian Studies	M,D
Biochemistry	D
Bioengineering	M,D
Bioethics	M
Biological and Biomedical Sciences—General	M,D
Biostatistics	M,D
Biotechnology	M
Business Administration and Management—General	M,D
Cancer Biology/Oncology	D
Cell Biology	D
Chemical Engineering	M,D
Chemistry	M,D
Classics	M,D
Clinical Laboratory Sciences/Medical Technology	M
Communication—General	D
Comparative Literature	M,D
Computational Biology	D
Computational Sciences	M,D
Computer Art and Design	M,D
Computer Science	M,D
Counseling Psychology	M
Criminal Justice and Criminology	M,D
Demography and Population Studies	M,D
Dentistry	D
Developmental Biology	D
Economic Development	M,O
Economics	M,D
Education—General	M,D,O*
Educational Leadership and Administration	M,D
Educational Measurement and Evaluation	M,D
Educational Media/Instructional Technology	M
Educational Policy	M,D
Electrical Engineering	M,D
Elementary Education	M
Engineering and Applied Sciences—General	M,D,O*
English as a Second Language	M,D
English Education	M,D
English	M,D
Entrepreneurship	M
Environmental and Occupational Health	M
Environmental Management and Policy	M
Environmental Sciences	M,D
Epidemiology	M
Ethics	M,D
Family Nurse Practitioner Studies	M,O
Finance and Banking	M,D
Foundations and Philosophy of Education	M,D
French	M,D
Genetics	D
Genomic Sciences	D
Geographic Information Systems	M,D,O
Geosciences	M,D
German	M,D
Gerontological Nursing	M
Graphic Design	M,O
Health Services Management and Hospital Administration	M,D
Health Services Research	M
Higher Education	M,D
Historic Preservation	M,O
History of Science and Technology	M,D
History	M,D
Human Development	M,D
Human Genetics	M
Immunology	D
Information Science	M,D
Insurance	M,D
International Affairs	M
International and Comparative Education	M
International Business	M
International Health	M
Internet and Interactive Multimedia	M,O
Italian	M,D
Landscape Architecture	M,O
Law	M,D
Legal and Justice Studies	M,D
Liberal Studies	M
Linguistics	M,D
Management Information Systems	M,D
Marketing	M,D
Materials Engineering	M,D
Materials Sciences	M,D
Maternal and Child/Neonatal Nursing	M
Mathematics	M,D
Mechanical Engineering	M,D
Mechanics	M,D
Medical Physics	M,D
Microbiology	D
Molecular Biology	D
Molecular Biophysics	D
Multilingual and Multicultural Education	M
Music	M,D
Nanotechnology	M
Near and Middle Eastern Studies	M,D
Neuroscience	D
Nonprofit Management	M,O
Nurse Anesthesia	M
Nurse Midwifery	M
Nursing and Healthcare Administration	M,D
Nursing—General	M,D,O
Organizational Management	M,O
Pediatric Nursing	M
Pharmacology	D
Philosophy	M,D
Physics	M,D
Physiology	D
Political Science	M,D,O
Psychiatric Nursing	M
Psychology—General	D
Public Administration	M,O
Public Health—General	M
Public Policy	M,D
Reading Education	M
Real Estate	M,D
Religion	D
Romance Languages	M,D
Science Education	M,O
Secondary Education	M
Social Work	M,D
Sociology	M,D
Spanish	M,D
Statistics	M,D
Systems Engineering	M,D
Urban and Regional Planning	M,D,O
Urban Design	M,D,O
Urban Education	M
Veterinary Medicine	D
Virology	D
Women's Health Nursing	M
Writing	M,D

UNIVERSITY OF PHILOSOPHICAL RESEARCH

Psychology—General	M
Theology	M

UNIVERSITY OF PHOENIX–ATLANTA CAMPUS

Accounting	M
Business Administration and Management—General	M
Health Services Management and Hospital Administration	M
Human Resources Management	M
International Business	M
Management Information Systems	M
Management of Technology	M
Marketing	M
Nursing Education	M
Nursing—General	M
Public Administration	M

UNIVERSITY OF PHOENIX–AUGUSTA CAMPUS

Accounting	M
Business Administration and Management—General	M
Criminal Justice and Criminology	M
Health Services Management and Hospital Administration	M
Human Resources Management	M
International Business	M
Management Information Systems	M
Management of Technology	M
Marketing	M
Nursing Education	M
Nursing—General	M
Public Administration	M

UNIVERSITY OF PHOENIX–BAY AREA CAMPUS

Accounting	M,D
Adult Education	M,D,O
Business Administration and Management—General	M,D
Criminal Justice and Criminology	M
Early Childhood Education	M,D,O
Education—General	M,D,O
Educational Leadership and Administration	M,D,O
Elementary Education	M,D,O
Energy Management and Policy	M,D
Gerontological Nursing	M,D
Health Services Management and Hospital Administration	M,D
Higher Education	M,D,O
Human Resources Management	M,D
International Business	M,D
Management Information Systems	M,D
Management of Technology	M,D
Marketing	M,D
Marriage and Family Therapy	M
Nursing and Healthcare Administration	M,D
Nursing Education	M,D
Nursing Informatics	M,D
Nursing—General	M,D
Organizational Management	M,D
Project Management	M,D
Public Administration	M,D
Secondary Education	M,D,O
Special Education	M,D,O

UNIVERSITY OF PHOENIX–CENTRAL VALLEY CAMPUS

Accounting	M
Business Administration and Management—General	M
Community Health	M
Computer Education	M
Curriculum and Instruction	M
Education—General	M
Elementary Education	M
Gerontology	M
Health Services Management and Hospital Administration	M
Human Resources Management	M
International Business	M
Management Information Systems	M
Management of Technology	M
Marketing	M
Marriage and Family Therapy	M
Nursing—General	M
Public Administration	M
Secondary Education	M

UNIVERSITY OF PHOENIX–CHARLOTTE CAMPUS

Accounting	M
Business Administration and Management—General	M
Gerontology	M
Health Education	M
Health Informatics	M
Health Services Management and Hospital Administration	M
International Business	M
Management Information Systems	M
Management of Technology	M
Nursing Education	M
Nursing Informatics	M
Nursing—General	M

UNIVERSITY OF PHOENIX–COLORADO CAMPUS

Accounting	M
Business Administration and Management—General	M
Curriculum and Instruction	M
Education—General	M
Educational Leadership and Administration	M
Electronic Commerce	M
Elementary Education	M
Health Services Management and Hospital Administration	M
Human Resources Management	M
International Business	M
Management Information Systems	M
Management of Technology	M
Marketing	M
Nursing—General	M
Public Administration	M
School Psychology	M
Secondary Education	M

UNIVERSITY OF PHOENIX–COLORADO SPRINGS DOWNTOWN CAMPUS

Accounting	M
Business Administration and Management—General	M
Curriculum and Instruction	M,O
Education—General	M,O
Educational Leadership and Administration	M,O
Elementary Education	M,O
Gerontology	M
Health Education	M
Health Services Management and Hospital Administration	M
Human Resources Management	M
International Business	M
Management Information Systems	M
Management of Technology	M
Marketing	M
Nursing—General	M
Public Administration	M
School Psychology	M,O
Secondary Education	M,O

UNIVERSITY OF PHOENIX–COLUMBUS GEORGIA CAMPUS

Accounting	M
Business Administration and Management—General	M
Electronic Commerce	M
Human Resources Management	M
International Business	M
Management Information Systems	M
Management of Technology	M
Marketing	M
Nursing—General	M
Public Administration	M

UNIVERSITY OF PHOENIX–DALLAS CAMPUS

Accounting	M
Business Administration and Management—General	M
Criminal Justice and Criminology	M
Curriculum and Instruction	M
Education—General	M
Electronic Commerce	M
Human Resources Management	M
International Business	M
Management Information Systems	M
Management of Technology	M
Marketing	M
Public Administration	M

UNIVERSITY OF PHOENIX–HAWAII CAMPUS

Accounting	M
Business Administration and Management—General	M
Community Health	M
Curriculum and Instruction	M
Education—General	M

Educational Leadership and Administration	M
Elementary Education	M
Family Nurse Practitioner Studies	M
Gerontology	M
Health Services Management and Hospital Administration	M
Human Resources Management	M
International Business	M
Management Information Systems	M
Management of Technology	M
Marketing	M
Nursing Education	M
Nursing—General	M
Public Administration	M
Secondary Education	M
Special Education	M

UNIVERSITY OF PHOENIX–HOUSTON CAMPUS

Accounting	M
Business Administration and Management—General	M
Curriculum and Instruction	M
Education—General	M
Electronic Commerce	M
Health Services Management and Hospital Administration	M
Human Resources Management	M
International Business	M
Management Information Systems	M
Management of Technology	M
Marketing	M
Nursing—General	M
Public Administration	M

UNIVERSITY OF PHOENIX–JERSEY CITY CAMPUS

Accounting	M
Business Administration and Management—General	M
Criminal Justice and Criminology	M
Human Resources Management	M
International Business	M
Management Information Systems	M
Management of Technology	M
Marketing	M
Psychology—General	M
Public Administration	M

UNIVERSITY OF PHOENIX–LAS VEGAS CAMPUS

Accounting	M
Allied Health—General	M
Business Administration and Management—General	M
Counseling Psychology	M
Counselor Education	M
Curriculum and Instruction	M
Education—General	M
Educational Leadership and Administration	M
Elementary Education	M
Human Resources Management	M
International Business	M
Management Information Systems	M
Management of Technology	M
Marketing	M
Marriage and Family Therapy	M
Public Administration	M
School Psychology	M

UNIVERSITY OF PHOENIX–NEW MEXICO CAMPUS

Accounting	M
Business Administration and Management—General	M
Counselor Education	M
Curriculum and Instruction	M
Education—General	M
Educational Leadership and Administration	M
Electronic Commerce	M
Elementary Education	M
Health Services Management and Hospital Administration	M
Human Resources Management	M
International Business	M
Management Information Systems	M
Management of Technology	M
Marketing	M
Nursing Education	M
Nursing—General	M
Secondary Education	M

UNIVERSITY OF PHOENIX–NORTH FLORIDA CAMPUS

Accounting	M
Business Administration and Management—General	M
Computer Education	M
Curriculum and Instruction	M
Early Childhood Education	M
Education—General	M
Educational Leadership and Administration	M
Elementary Education	M
Health Services Management and Hospital Administration	M
Human Resources Management	M
International Business	M
Management Information Systems	M
Marketing	M
Mathematics Education	M
Nursing Education	M
Nursing—General	M
Public Administration	M
Secondary Education	M

UNIVERSITY OF PHOENIX–ONLINE CAMPUS

Accounting	M,O
Adult Education	M,O
Business Administration and Management—General	M,D,O
Computer Education	M,O
Conflict Resolution and Mediation/Peace Studies	M,O
Criminal Justice and Criminology	M
Curriculum and Instruction	M,D,O
Early Childhood Education	M,O
Education—General	M,O
Educational Leadership and Administration	M,D,O
Educational Media/Instructional Technology	D,O
Elementary Education	M,O
Energy Management and Policy	M,O
English as a Second Language	M,O
English Education	M,O
Family Nurse Practitioner Studies	M,O
Health Education	M,O
Health Informatics	M,O
Health Services Management and Hospital Administration	M,D,O
Higher Education	D,O
Homeland Security	M
Human Resources Management	M,O
Industrial and Organizational Psychology	M,D,O
International Business	M,O
Management Information Systems	M
Management of Technology	M,O
Marketing	M,O
Mathematics Education	M,O
Middle School Education	M,O
Nursing Education	M,O
Nursing—General	M,D,O
Organizational Management	D,O
Project Management	M,O
Psychology—General	M,O
Public Administration	M,O
Reading Education	M,O
Science Education	M,O
Secondary Education	M,O
Special Education	M,O

UNIVERSITY OF PHOENIX–PHOENIX CAMPUS

Accounting	M,O
Adult Education	M
Business Administration and Management—General	M,O
Clinical Psychology	M
Counseling Psychology	M
Counselor Education	M
Criminal Justice and Criminology	M
Curriculum and Instruction	M
Early Childhood Education	M
Education—General	M
Educational Leadership and Administration	M
Elementary Education	M
Energy Management and Policy	M,O
Family Nurse Practitioner Studies	M,O
Gerontological Nursing	M,O
Health Services Management and Hospital Administration	M,O
Homeland Security	M
Human Resources Management	M,O
International Business	M,O
Management of Technology	M,O
Marketing	M,O
Marriage and Family Therapy	M
Medical Informatics	M,O
Nursing Education	M,O
Nursing Informatics	M,O
Nursing—General	M,O
Project Management	M,O
Psychology—General	M
Public Administration	M
Reading Education	M
Secondary Education	M
Social Psychology	M
Special Education	M
Vocational and Technical Education	M

UNIVERSITY OF PHOENIX–SACRAMENTO VALLEY CAMPUS

Accounting	M
Adult Education	M,O
Business Administration and Management—General	M
Curriculum and Instruction	M,O
Education—General	M,O
Elementary Education	M,O
Family Nurse Practitioner Studies	M
Health Services Management and Hospital Administration	M
Human Resources Management	M
International Business	M
Management Information Systems	M
Management of Technology	M
Marketing	M
Nursing Education	M
Nursing—General	M
Public Administration	M
Secondary Education	M,O

UNIVERSITY OF PHOENIX–SAN ANTONIO CAMPUS

Accounting	M
Business Administration and Management—General	M
Criminal Justice and Criminology	M
Curriculum and Instruction	M
Electronic Commerce	M
Health Services Management and Hospital Administration	M
Human Resources Management	M
International Business	M
Management Information Systems	M
Management of Technology	M
Marketing	M
Nursing—General	M
Public Administration	M

UNIVERSITY OF PHOENIX–SAN DIEGO CAMPUS

Accounting	M
Business Administration and Management—General	M
Computer Education	M
Curriculum and Instruction	M
Education—General	M
Elementary Education	M
English as a Second Language	M
Human Resources Management	M
International Business	M
Management Information Systems	M
Management of Technology	M
Marketing	M
Nursing Education	M
Nursing—General	M
Public Administration	M
Secondary Education	M

UNIVERSITY OF PHOENIX–SOUTHERN ARIZONA CAMPUS

Accounting	M
Adult Education	M,O
Business Administration and Management—General	M
Counselor Education	M,O
Curriculum and Instruction	M,O
Education—General	M,O
Educational Leadership and Administration	M,O
Educational Psychology	M,O
Elementary Education	M,O
Human Resources Management	M
International Business	M
Management Information Systems	M
Management of Technology	M
Marketing	M
Psychology—General	M
Secondary Education	M,O
Special Education	M,O

UNIVERSITY OF PHOENIX–SOUTHERN CALIFORNIA CAMPUS

Accounting	M
Adult Education	M,O
Business Administration and Management—General	M
Counselor Education	M
Criminal Justice and Criminology	M
Education—General	M,O
Educational Leadership and Administration	M,O
Elementary Education	M,O
Energy Management and Policy	M
English as a Second Language	M,O
Family Nurse Practitioner Studies	M,O
Health Services Management and Hospital Administration	M
Homeland Security	M
Human Resources Management	M
International Business	M
Management of Technology	M
Marketing	M
Marriage and Family Therapy	M
Nursing Education	M,O
Nursing Informatics	M,O
Nursing—General	M,O
Project Management	M
Psychology—General	M
Public Administration	M
Secondary Education	M,O

UNIVERSITY OF PHOENIX–SOUTH FLORIDA CAMPUS

Accounting	M
Business Administration and Management—General	M
Computer Education	M
Curriculum and Instruction	M
Early Childhood Education	M
Education—General	M
Educational Leadership and Administration	M
Elementary Education	M
Health Services Management and Hospital Administration	M
Human Resources Management	M
International Business	M
Management Information Systems	M
Marketing	M
Mathematics Education	M
Nursing Education	M
Nursing—General	M
Public Administration	M
Secondary Education	M

UNIVERSITY OF PHOENIX–UTAH CAMPUS

Accounting	M
Business Administration and Management—General	M
Curriculum and Instruction	M
Education—General	M
Educational Leadership and Administration	M
Elementary Education	M
Human Resources Management	M
International Business	M
Management Information Systems	M
Management of Technology	M
Marketing	M
Nursing Education	M
Nursing—General	M
School Psychology	M
Secondary Education	M
Special Education	M

UNIVERSITY OF PHOENIX–WASHINGTON D.C. CAMPUS

Accounting	M,D
Adult Education	M,D,O
Business Administration and Management—General	M,D
Computer Education	M,D,O
Criminal Justice and Criminology	M
Curriculum and Instruction	M,D,O
Early Childhood Education	M,D,O
Education—General	M,D,O
Educational Leadership and Administration	M,D,O
Educational Media/Instructional Technology	M,D,O
Elementary Education	M,D,O
English as a Second Language	M,D,O
English Education	M,D,O
Gerontology	M,D
Health Education	M,D
Health Informatics	M,D
Health Services Management and Hospital Administration	M,D
Higher Education	M,D,O
Human Resources Management	M,D
Industrial and Organizational Psychology	M,D
Management Information Systems	M,D
Mathematics Education	M,D,O
Nursing and Healthcare Administration	M,D
Nursing Education	M,D
Nursing Informatics	M,D
Nursing—General	M,D
Organizational Management	M,D
Psychology—General	M,D
Public Administration	M,D
Secondary Education	M,D,O
Special Education	M,D,O

UNIVERSITY OF PHOENIX–WESTERN WASHINGTON CAMPUS

Business Administration and Management—General	M
Criminal Justice and Criminology	M

UNIVERSITY OF PIKEVILLE

Business Administration and Management—General	M
Education—General	M
Educational Leadership and Administration	M
Osteopathic Medicine	D

UNIVERSITY OF PITTSBURGH

Accounting	M,D
Acute Care/Critical Care Nursing	M,D
African Studies	O
Allopathic Medicine	D
Anthropology	M,D
Applied Behavior Analysis	M,D
Applied Mathematics	M,D
Applied Psychology	M,D
Applied Statistics	M,D
Architectural History	M,D
Art History	M,D
Artificial Intelligence/Robotics	M,D
Asian Studies	M,O
Astronomy	D
Athletic Training and Sports Medicine	M
Bioengineering	M,D
Bioethics	M
Biological and Biomedical Sciences—General	D
Biostatistics	M,D
Business Administration and Management—General	M,D
Cell Biology	D
Chemical Engineering	M,D
Chemistry	M,D
Chinese	M
Civil Engineering	M,D
Clinical Laboratory Sciences/Medical Technology	D
Clinical Psychology	D
Clinical Research	M,O
Communication Disorders	M,D
Communication—General	M,D
Community Health	M,D,O
Computational Biology	D
Computer and Information Systems Security	M,D,O
Computer Engineering	M,D
Computer Science	M,D
Criminal Justice and Criminology	M
Cultural Studies	O
Dentistry	M,D,O
Developmental Biology	D
Developmental Psychology	M,D
Disability Studies	O
Early Childhood Education	M
East European and Russian Studies	O
Ecology	D
Economics	M,D
Education—General	M,D*
Educational Leadership and Administration	M,D
Educational Measurement and Evaluation	M,D
Educational Policy	D
Electrical Engineering	M,D
Elementary Education	M
Energy Management and Policy	M
Engineering and Applied Sciences—General	M,D
English as a Second Language	M,D,O

*M—masters degree; D—doctorate; O—other advanced degree; *—Close-Up and/or Display*

English Education	M,D
English	M,D
Environmental and Occupational Health	M,D
Environmental Engineering	M,D
Environmental Law	M
Environmental Sciences	M,D
Epidemiology	M,D
Evolutionary Biology	D
Exercise and Sports Science	M,D
Family Nurse Practitioner Studies	M,D
Film, Television, and Video Theory and Criticism	M,D,O
Finance and Banking	M,D
Foreign Languages Education	M,D
Foundations and Philosophy of Education	M,D
French	M,D
Genetic Counseling	M,D,O
Geographic Information Systems	M,D
Geology	M,D
Gerontological Nursing	M,D
Health Education	M,D
Health Law	M
Health Services Management and Hospital Administration	M,D,O
Higher Education	M,D
Hispanic and Latin American Languages	M,D
History of Science and Technology	M,D
History	M,D
Human Genetics	M,D,O
Human Resources Management	M,D
Immunology	D
Industrial and Manufacturing Management	M
Industrial/Management Engineering	M,D
Infectious Diseases	M,D
Information Science	M,D,O
Information Studies	M,D
Intellectual Property Law	M
Interdisciplinary Studies	D
International Affairs	M,D,O
International and Comparative Education	M,D
International Business	O
International Development	M,D
Italian	M
Japanese	M
Latin American Studies	O
Law	M
Legal and Justice Studies	M
Library Science	M,D
Linguistics	M,D
Management Information Systems	M,D
Management Strategy and Policy	M,D
Marketing	M,D
Materials Sciences	M,D
Maternal and Child/Neonatal Nursing	M,D
Mathematics Education	M,D
Mathematics	M,D
Mechanical Engineering	M,D
Medieval and Renaissance Studies	O
Microbiology	M,D
Military and Defense Studies	M
Modeling and Simulation	D
Molecular Biology	D
Molecular Biophysics	D
Molecular Genetics	D
Molecular Pathology	D
Molecular Pharmacology	D
Molecular Physiology	D
Music	M,D
Neurobiology	D
Neuroscience	D
Nonprofit Management	M
Nurse Anesthesia	M,D
Nursing and Healthcare Administration	M,D
Nursing Informatics	M,D
Nursing—General	D
Nutrition	M
Occupational Therapy	M
Oral and Dental Sciences	M,D,O
Organizational Behavior	M,D
Pathology	D
Pediatric Nursing	M,D
Petroleum Engineering	M,D
Pharmaceutical Sciences	M,D
Pharmacy	D
Philosophy	M,D
Physical Therapy	M,D
Physician Assistant Studies	M
Physics	M,D*
Political Science	M,D
Psychiatric Nursing	M,D
Psychology—General	D
Public Administration	M,D
Public Health—General	M,D,O
Public Policy	M,D
Quantitative Analysis	M,D
Reading Education	M,D
Rehabilitation Sciences	M,D
Science Education	M,D
Secondary Education	M,D
Slavic Languages	M,D
Social Sciences Education	M,D
Social Work	M,D,O
Sociology	M,D
Spanish	M,D
Special Education	M,D
Statistics	M,D
Structural Biology	D
Systems Biology	D
Telecommunications	M,D,O
Theater	M,D
Urban and Regional Planning	M
Virology	D
Vision Sciences	M,D
Western European Studies	O
Women's Studies	O
Writing	M,D

UNIVERSITY OF PORTLAND

Biomedical Engineering	M
Business Administration and Management—General	M
Civil Engineering	M
Communication—General	M
Computer Science	M
Corporate and Organizational Communication	M
Education—General	M,D
Educational Leadership and Administration	M,D
Electrical Engineering	M
Engineering and Applied Sciences—General	M
English as a Second Language	M,D
Entrepreneurship	M
Family Nurse Practitioner Studies	M,D
Finance and Banking	M
Health Services Management and Hospital Administration	M
Industrial and Manufacturing Management	M
Management of Technology	M
Marketing	M
Mechanical Engineering	M
Nonprofit Management	M
Nursing Education	M,D
Nursing—General	M,D
Organizational Management	M,D
Pastoral Ministry and Counseling	M
Reading Education	M,D
Special Education	M,D
Sustainability Management	M
Theater	M

UNIVERSITY OF PRINCE EDWARD ISLAND

Anatomy	M,D
Bacteriology	M,D
Biological and Biomedical Sciences—General	M
Chemistry	M
Education—General	M
Educational Leadership and Administration	M
Epidemiology	M,D
Geography	M
Immunology	M,D
Parasitology	M,D
Pathology	M,D
Pharmacology	M,D
Physiology	M,D
Toxicology	M,D
Veterinary Medicine	D
Veterinary Sciences	M,D
Virology	M,D

UNIVERSITY OF PUERTO RICO, MAYAGÜEZ CAMPUS

Agricultural Economics and Agribusiness	M
Agricultural Education	M
Agricultural Sciences—General	M
Agronomy and Soil Sciences	M
Animal Sciences	M
Applied Mathematics	M
Biological and Biomedical Sciences—General	M
Business Administration and Management—General	M
Chemical Engineering	M,D
Chemistry	M,D
Civil Engineering	M,D
Computational Sciences	M
Computer Engineering	M,D
Computer Science	M,D
Electrical Engineering	M,D
Engineering and Applied Sciences—General	M,D
English Education	M
English	M
Exercise and Sports Science	M
Finance and Banking	M
Food Science and Technology	M
Geology	M
Hispanic Studies	M
Horticulture	M
Human Resources Management	M
Industrial and Manufacturing Management	M
Industrial/Management Engineering	M
Information Science	M,D
Kinesiology and Movement Studies	M
Marine Sciences	M,D
Mathematics	M
Mechanical Engineering	M
Physical Education	M
Physics	M
Statistics	M

UNIVERSITY OF PUERTO RICO, MEDICAL SCIENCES CAMPUS

Acute Care/Critical Care Nursing	M
Adult Nursing	M
Allied Health—General	M,D,O
Allopathic Medicine	D
Anatomy	M,D
Biochemistry	M,D
Biological and Biomedical Sciences—General	M,D
Biostatistics	M
Clinical Laboratory Sciences/Medical Technology	M,O
Clinical Research	M,O
Communication Disorders	M,D
Community Health Nursing	M
Demography and Population Studies	M
Dentistry	D
Environmental and Occupational Health	M,D
Epidemiology	M
Family Nurse Practitioner Studies	M
Gerontological Nursing	M
Gerontology	M,O
Health Education	M
Health Informatics	M
Health Promotion	O
Health Services Management and Hospital Administration	M
Health Services Research	M
Industrial Hygiene	M
Maternal and Child Health	M
Maternal and Child/Neonatal Nursing	M
Microbiology	M,D
Nurse Midwifery	M,O
Nursing—General	M
Nutrition	M,D,O
Occupational Therapy	M
Oral and Dental Sciences	O
Pediatric Nursing	M
Pharmaceutical Sciences	M,D
Pharmacology	M,D
Pharmacy	M,D
Physical Therapy	M
Physiology	M,D
Psychiatric Nursing	M
Special Education	O
Toxicology	M,D

UNIVERSITY OF PUERTO RICO, RÍO PIEDRAS CAMPUS

Accounting	M,D
Architecture	M
Biological and Biomedical Sciences—General	M,D
Business Administration and Management—General	M,D
Cell Biology	M,D
Chemistry	M,D
Clinical Psychology	M,D
Communication—General	M
Comparative Literature	M
Counselor Education	M,D
Curriculum and Instruction	M,D
Early Childhood Education	M
Ecology	M,D
Economic Development	M
Economics	M
Education—General	M,D
Educational Leadership and Administration	M,D
Educational Measurement and Evaluation	M
English as a Second Language	M
English	M,D
Environmental Management and Policy	M
Environmental Sciences	M,D
Evolutionary Biology	M,D
Exercise and Sports Science	M
Family and Consumer Sciences-General	M
Finance and Banking	M,D
Foreign Languages Education	M,D
Genetics	M,D
Hispanic Studies	M,D
History	M,D
Human Resources Management	M,D
Industrial and Manufacturing Management	M,D
Industrial and Organizational Psychology	M,D
Information Science	M,O
Information Studies	M,O
International Business	M,D
Journalism	M
Law	M,D
Library Science	M,O
Linguistics	M,D
Marketing	M,D
Mass Communication	M
Mathematics Education	M,D
Mathematics	M,D
Molecular Biology	M,D
Neuroscience	M,D
Nutrition	M
Philosophy	M
Physics	M,D
Psychology—General	M,D
Public Administration	M
Public Policy	M
Quantitative Analysis	M,D
Rehabilitation Counseling	M
Science Education	M,D
Social Psychology	M,D
Social Sciences Education	M,D
Social Work	M,D
Sociology	M
Special Education	M
Translation and Interpretation	M,O
Urban and Regional Planning	M

UNIVERSITY OF PUGET SOUND

Counseling Psychology	M
Counselor Education	M
Education—General	M
Elementary Education	M
Occupational Therapy	M,D
Physical Therapy	D
Secondary Education	M

UNIVERSITY OF REDLANDS

Business Administration and Management—General	M
Communication Disorders	M
Education—General	M,D,O
Geographic Information Systems	M
Management Information Systems	M
Music	M

UNIVERSITY OF REGINA

Adult Education	M
Analytical Chemistry	M,D
Anthropology	M
Applied Economics	M
Applied Psychology	M,D
Art/Fine Arts	M
Biochemistry	M,D
Biological and Biomedical Sciences—General	M,D
Biophysics	M,D
Business Administration and Management—General	M,O
Canadian Studies	M,D
Cancer Biology/Oncology	M,D
Chemistry	M,D
Clinical Psychology	M,D
Computer Engineering	M,D
Computer Science	M,D
Criminal Justice and Criminology	M
Curriculum and Instruction	M
Economics	M,D,O
Education—General	M,D,O
Educational Leadership and Administration	M
Educational Psychology	M
Engineering and Applied Sciences—General	M,D
Engineering Management	M,O
English	M
Environmental Engineering	M,D
Experimental Psychology	M,D
Film, Television, and Video Production	M
French	M
Geography	M,D
Geology	M,D
Gerontology	M
Health Services Management and Hospital Administration	M,D,O
History	M
Human Resources Development	M
Human Resources Management	M,O
Industrial/Management Engineering	M,D
Inorganic Chemistry	M,D
Interdisciplinary Studies	M
International Business	M,O
Journalism	M
Kinesiology and Movement Studies	M,D
Linguistics	M
Mathematics	M,D
Music	M
Nursing—General	M
Organic Chemistry	M,D
Organizational Management	M,O
Petroleum Engineering	M,D
Philosophy	M
Physics	M,D
Political Science	M
Project Management	M,O
Psychology—General	M,D
Public Administration	M,D,O
Public Policy	M,D,O
Religion	M
Social Sciences	M
Social Work	M,D
Sociology	M
Software Engineering	M
Statistics	M,D
Systems Engineering	M,D
Theoretical Chemistry	M,D
Women's Studies	M
Writing	M

UNIVERSITY OF RHODE ISLAND

Accounting	M,D
Acute Care/Critical Care Nursing	M,D
Animal Sciences	M,D
Anthropology	M
Applied Mathematics	M,D
Aquaculture	M,D
Archaeology	M
Biochemistry	M,D
Biological and Biomedical Sciences—General	M,D
Biomedical Engineering	M,D
Biotechnology	M,D
Business Administration and Management—General	M,D*
Cell Biology	M,D
Chemical Engineering	M,D,O
Chemistry	M,D
Child and Family Studies	M
Civil Engineering	M,D
Clinical Laboratory Sciences/Medical Technology	M,D
Clinical Psychology	M,D
Clothing and Textiles	M,O
Communication Disorders	M
Communication—General	M
Computer and Information Systems Security	M,D,O
Computer Art and Design	M
Computer Engineering	M,D
Computer Science	M,D,O
Counseling Psychology	M
Economics	M,D
Education—General	M,D
Electrical Engineering	M,D
Engineering and Applied Sciences—General	M,D,O
English	M,D
Entrepreneurship	M,D
Environmental Engineering	M,D
Environmental Management and Policy	M,D
Environmental Sciences	M,D
Exercise and Sports Science	M
Family Nurse Practitioner Studies	M,D
Finance and Banking	M,D
Fish, Game, and Wildlife Management	M,D
Food Science and Technology	M,D
Forensic Sciences	M,D,O
Gender Studies	M,D
Geosciences	M,D
Gerontological Nursing	M,D

Health Education M
Health Services Management and Hospital Administration M,D
History M
Human Development M
Human Resources Management M,O
Industrial and Labor Relations M,O
Information Studies M
International Affairs M
Library Science M
Management Strategy and Policy M,D
Marine Affairs M,D
Marine Sciences M,D
Marketing M,D
Marriage and Family Therapy M
Mathematics M,D
Medicinal and Pharmaceutical Chemistry M,D
Microbiology M,D
Molecular Biology M,D
Molecular Genetics M,D
Music Education M,D
Music M
Natural Resources M,D
Nursing Education M,D
Nursing—General M,D
Nutrition M,D
Ocean Engineering M,D
Oceanography M,D
Pharmaceutical Sciences M,D
Pharmacology M,D
Pharmacy M,D
Physical Education M
Physical Therapy D
Physics M,D
Political Science M
Psychology—General M,D
Public Administration M
Public Policy M
Reading Education M,D
Recreation and Park Management M
School Psychology M,D
Spanish M
Special Education M,D
Sport Psychology M
Statistics M,D,O
Student Affairs M
Supply Chain Management M,D
Toxicology M,D

UNIVERSITY OF RICHMOND
Business Administration and Management—General M
Law D

UNIVERSITY OF RIO GRANDE
Art Education M
Education—General M
Educational Leadership and Administration M
Entrepreneurship M
Physical Education M
Special Education M

UNIVERSITY OF ROCHESTER
Accounting M
Acute Care/Critical Care Nursing M,D
Allopathic Medicine D
American Studies M,D
Anatomy D
Archives/Archival Administration M
Art History M,D
Art/Fine Arts M,D
Astronomy M,D
Biochemistry D
Biological and Biomedical Sciences—General M,D
Biomedical Engineering M,D
Biophysics D
Biostatistics M
Business Administration and Management—General M,D
Chemical Engineering M,D*
Chemistry M,D
Clinical Psychology D
Clinical Research M
Cognitive Sciences D
Computational Biology D
Computer Engineering M,D
Computer Science M,D
Counselor Education M,D
Curriculum and Instruction M,D
Database Systems M
Developmental Psychology D
Economics M,D
Education—General M,D
Educational Leadership and Administration M,D
Educational Policy M,D
Electrical Engineering M,D
Electronic Commerce M
Energy and Power Engineering M
Energy Management and Policy M
Engineering and Applied Sciences—General M,D
English M,D
Entrepreneurship M
Environmental Management and Policy M
Epidemiology D
Family Nurse Practitioner Studies M,D
Finance and Banking M
Foundations and Philosophy of Education D
Genetics D
Genomic Sciences D
Geology M,D
Geosciences M,D
Gerontological Nursing M,D
Health Services Management and Hospital Administration M,D
Health Services Research M,D
Higher Education M,D
Historic Preservation M
History M,D
Human Development M,D
Immunology M,D
Industrial and Manufacturing Management M
International Affairs M,D
International Business M
Linguistics M
Management Information Systems M
Management Strategy and Policy M
Marketing M
Marriage and Family Therapy M
Materials Sciences M,D
Maternal and Child/Neonatal Nursing M,D
Mathematics M,D
Mechanical Engineering M,D
Microbiology M,D
Molecular Biology D
Music Education M,D
Music M,D
Neurobiology D
Neuroscience D
Nursing and Healthcare Administration M,D
Nursing Education M,D
Nursing—General M,D
Optical Sciences M,D
Oral and Dental Sciences M
Pathology D
Pediatric Nursing M,D
Pharmacology M,D
Philosophy M,D
Photography M
Physics M,D
Physiology M,D
Political Science D
Psychiatric Nursing M,D
Psychology—General D
Public Health—General M
Public Policy M
Social Psychology M,D
Statistics M,D
Structural Biology D
Student Affairs M
Toxicology D
Translation and Interpretation M,O
Western European Studies M,D

UNIVERSITY OF ST. AUGUSTINE FOR HEALTH SCIENCES
Health Education D
Occupational Therapy M,D
Physical Therapy D

UNIVERSITY OF ST. FRANCIS (IL)
Accounting M,O
Art Education M,D,O
Business Administration and Management—General M,O
Business Education M,O
Curriculum and Instruction M,D,O
Education—General M,D,O
Educational Leadership and Administration M,D,O
Educational Media/Instructional Technology M,O
Elementary Education M,D,O
English as a Second Language M,D,O
English Education M,D,O
Family Nurse Practitioner Studies M,D,O
Finance and Banking M,O
Forensic Sciences M,O
Health Services Management and Hospital Administration M
Higher Education M,D,O
Logistics M,O
Management Strategy and Policy M,O
Mathematics Education M,D,O
Nursing and Healthcare Administration M,D,O
Nursing Education M,D,O
Nursing—General M,D,O
Physician Assistant Studies M,O
Psychiatric Nursing M,D,O
Reading Education M,D,O
Science Education M,D,O
Secondary Education M,D,O
Social Sciences Education M,D,O
Social Work M,O
Special Education M,D,O

UNIVERSITY OF SAINT FRANCIS (IN)
Art/Fine Arts M
Business Administration and Management—General M
Clinical Psychology M,O
Counseling Psychology M,O
Counselor Education M,O
Education—General M,O
Environmental and Occupational Health M
Family Nurse Practitioner Studies M,O
Health Services Management and Hospital Administration M
Nursing—General M,O
Pastoral Ministry and Counseling M,O
Physician Assistant Studies M
Psychology—General M,O
Rehabilitation Counseling M,O
Special Education M,O
Sustainability Management M
Theology M

UNIVERSITY OF SAINT JOSEPH
Animal Sciences M
Applied Behavior Analysis M,O
Biochemistry M
Biological and Biomedical Sciences—General M
Business Administration and Management—General M
Chemistry M
Clinical Psychology M,O
Counseling Psychology M,O
Counselor Education M,O
Curriculum and Instruction M
Education—General M
Educational Media/Instructional Technology M
Family Nurse Practitioner Studies M,D
Gerontology O
Marriage and Family Therapy M
Nursing Education M,D
Nursing—General M,D
Nutrition M
Pharmacy D
Psychiatric Nursing M,D
Reading Education M
Special Education M

UNIVERSITY OF SAINT MARY
Advertising and Public Relations M
Business Administration and Management—General M
Counseling Psychology M
Education—General M
Elementary Education M
Health Services Management and Hospital Administration M
Human Resources Management M
Marketing M
Nursing and Healthcare Administration M
Nursing Education M
Nursing—General M
Physical Therapy D
Psychology—General M
Special Education M

UNIVERSITY OF SAINT MARY OF THE LAKE–MUNDELEIN SEMINARY
Pastoral Ministry and Counseling M,D
Theology M,D

UNIVERSITY OF ST. MICHAEL'S COLLEGE
Jewish Studies M,D,O
Pastoral Ministry and Counseling M,D,O
Religious Education M,D,O
Theology M,D,O

UNIVERSITY OF ST. THOMAS (MN)
Accounting M
Art History M
Business Administration and Management—General M
Computer and Information Systems Security M,O
Corporate and Organizational Communication M
Counseling Psychology M,D,O
Curriculum and Instruction M,O
Early Childhood Education M,O
Education—General M,D,O
Educational Leadership and Administration M,D,O
Educational Policy M,D,O
Electrical Engineering M,O
Elementary Education M,O
Engineering and Applied Sciences—General M,O
Engineering Management M,O
English as a Second Language M,O
English M
Ethics M,D
Health Services Management and Hospital Administration M
Human Development M,D
Human Resources Development M,D
Law M,D
Management Information Systems M,O
Management of Technology M,O
Manufacturing Engineering M,O
Marriage and Family Therapy M,D,O
Mathematics Education M,O
Mechanical Engineering M,O
Multilingual and Multicultural Education M,O
Music Education M
Music M
Organizational Management M,D
Pastoral Ministry and Counseling M
Psychology—General M,D,O
Reading Education M,O
Real Estate M
Religion M
Religious Education M
Social Work M
Software Engineering M,O
Special Education M,O
Student Affairs M,D,O
Systems Engineering M,O
Theology M

UNIVERSITY OF ST. THOMAS (TX)
Accounting M
Business Administration and Management—General M
Counselor Education M
Curriculum and Instruction M
Education—General M
Educational Leadership and Administration M
Educational Measurement and Evaluation M
Elementary Education M
English as a Second Language M
Finance and Banking M
International Business M
Liberal Studies M
Multilingual and Multicultural Education M
Music M
Pastoral Ministry and Counseling M
Philosophy M,D
Public Administration M
Public Policy M
Reading Education M
Religion M
Religious Education M
Secondary Education M
Special Education M
Theology M

UNIVERSITY OF SAN DIEGO
Accounting M
Adult Nursing M,D
Business Administration and Management—General M
Communication Disorders M
Conflict Resolution and Mediation/Peace Studies M
Counseling Psychology M
Counselor Education M
Criminal Justice and Criminology M
Curriculum and Instruction M
Education—General M,D,O
Educational Leadership and Administration M,D,O
English as a Second Language M
Family Nurse Practitioner Studies M,D
Finance and Banking M
Gerontological Nursing M,D
Health Informatics M,D
Higher Education M,D,O
International Affairs M
International Business M
Law M,D,O
Legal and Justice Studies M,D,O
Marine Affairs M
Marine Sciences M
Marriage and Family Therapy M
Nonprofit Management M,D,O
Nursing and Healthcare Administration M,D
Nursing—General M,D
Psychiatric Nursing M,D
Reading Education M
Real Estate M
Special Education M
Supply Chain Management M,O
Taxation M,D,O
Theater M

UNIVERSITY OF SAN FRANCISCO
Asian Studies M
Biological and Biomedical Sciences—General M
Biotechnology M
Business Administration and Management—General M
Chemistry M
Communication—General M
Computer Science M
Counseling Psychology M
Counselor Education M
Curriculum and Instruction M,D
Database Systems M
Economics M
Education—General M,D
Educational Leadership and Administration M,D
Educational Media/Instructional Technology M,D
Energy Management and Policy M
English as a Second Language M,D
Entrepreneurship M
Family Nurse Practitioner Studies D
Finance and Banking M
Health Education M
Health Services Management and Hospital Administration M
Intellectual Property Law M
International Affairs M
International and Comparative Education M,D
International Business M
International Development M
Law M,D
Management Information Systems M
Marketing M
Marriage and Family Therapy M
Multilingual and Multicultural Education M,D
Museum Studies M
Natural Resources M
Nonprofit Management M
Nursing and Healthcare Administration M,D
Nursing—General M,D
Organizational Management M
Pacific Area/Pacific Rim Studies M
Psychiatric Nursing D
Public Administration M
Public Affairs M
Public Health—General M
Reading Education M,D
Religious Education M,D
Special Education M,D
Sports Management M
Taxation M,D
Urban Education M
Urban Studies M
Writing M

UNIVERSITY OF SASKATCHEWAN
Accounting M
Agricultural Economics and Agribusiness M,D,O

*M—masters degree; D—doctorate; O—other advanced degree; *—Close-Up and/or Display*

Agricultural Sciences—General	M,D,O
Agronomy and Soil Sciences	M,D,O
Allopathic Medicine	D
Anatomy	M,D
Animal Sciences	M,D
Anthropology	M
Archaeology	M,D
Art/Fine Arts	M
Biochemistry	M,D
Bioengineering	M,D
Biological and Biomedical Sciences—General	M,D
Biomedical Engineering	M,D
Biotechnology	M
Business Administration and Management—General	M
Canadian Studies	M,D
Cell Biology	M,D
Chemical Engineering	M,D
Chemistry	M,D
Civil Engineering	M,D
Community Health	M,D
Computer Science	M,D
Curriculum and Instruction	M,D,O
Dentistry	D
East European and Russian Studies	M
Economics	M,O
Education—General	M,D,O
Educational Leadership and Administration	M,D,O
Educational Psychology	M,D,O
Electrical Engineering	M,D,O
Engineering and Applied Sciences—General	M,D,O
Engineering Physics	M,D
English	M,D
Environmental Sciences	M
Epidemiology	M,D
Finance and Banking	M
Food Science and Technology	M,D
Foundations and Philosophy of Education	M,D,O
French	M
Gender Studies	M,D
Geography	M,D
Geological Engineering	M,D
Geology	M,D,O
German	M
Health Services Management and Hospital Administration	M
History	M,D
Immunology	M,D
International Business	M,D
Kinesiology and Movement Studies	M,D,O
Law	M,D
Marketing	M
Mathematics	M,D
Mechanical Engineering	M,D
Microbiology	M,D
Music	M
Nursing—General	M
Pathology	M,D
Pharmaceutical Sciences	M,D
Pharmacology	M,D
Philosophy	M
Physics	M,D
Physiology	M,D
Plant Sciences	M,D
Political Science	M
Psychology—General	M,D
Public Affairs	M,D
Public Policy	M,D
Religion	M
Reproductive Biology	M,D
Sociology	M,D
Special Education	M,D,O
Statistics	M,D
Sustainability Management	M
Theater	M
Toxicology	M,D,O
Veterinary Medicine	M,D
Veterinary Sciences	M,D
Women's Studies	M,D

THE UNIVERSITY OF SCRANTON

Accounting	M
Art/Fine Arts	M
Biochemistry	M
Business Administration and Management—General	M
Chemistry	M
Clinical Psychology	M
Counseling Psychology	M
Counselor Education	M
Curriculum and Instruction	M
Education—General	M
Educational Leadership and Administration	M
Family Nurse Practitioner Studies	M,D,O
Finance and Banking	M
Health Services Management and Hospital Administration	M
Human Resources Development	M
International Business	M
Management Information Systems	M
Marketing	M
Nurse Anesthesia	M,D,O
Nursing and Healthcare Administration	M,D,O
Nursing—General	M,D,O
Occupational Therapy	M
Physical Therapy	D
Reading Education	M
Rehabilitation Counseling	M
Secondary Education	M
Software Engineering	M
Theology	M

UNIVERSITY OF SIOUX FALLS

Business Administration and Management—General	M
Education—General	M,O
Educational Leadership and Administration	M,O
Educational Media/Instructional Technology	M,O
Entrepreneurship	M
Health Services Management and Hospital Administration	M
Marketing	M
Reading Education	M,O

UNIVERSITY OF SOUTH AFRICA

Accounting	M,D
Acute Care/Critical Care Nursing	M,D
Adult Education	M,D
Agricultural Sciences—General	M,D
Anthropology	M,D
Archaeology	M,D
Art History	M,D
Business Administration and Management—General	M,D
Chemical Engineering	M
Classics	M,D
Clinical Psychology	M,D
Communication—General	M,D
Counseling Psychology	M,D
Counselor Education	M,D
Criminal Justice and Criminology	M,D
Curriculum and Instruction	M,D
Economics	M,D
Education—General	M,D
Educational Leadership and Administration	M,D
Educational Media/Instructional Technology	M,D
Educational Psychology	M,D
Engineering and Applied Sciences—General	M
English as a Second Language	M,D
English	M,D
Environmental Education	M,D
Environmental Management and Policy	M,D
Environmental Sciences	M,D
Ethics	M,D
Family and Consumer Sciences-General	M,D
Foundations and Philosophy of Education	M,D
French	M,D
Geography	M,D
German	M,D
Health Education	M,D
Health Services Management and Hospital Administration	M,D
History	M,D
Horticulture	M,D
Human Development	M,D
Human Resources Development	M,D
Industrial and Organizational Psychology	M,D
Information Science	M,D
International and Comparative Education	M,D
Italian	M,D
Law	M,D
Linguistics	M,D
Logistics	M,D
Management Information Systems	M
Marketing	M,D
Maternal and Child/Neonatal Nursing	M,D
Mathematics Education	M,D
Medical/Surgical Nursing	M,D
Missions and Missiology	M,D
Music	M,D
Natural Resources	M,D
Near and Middle Eastern Languages	M,D
Near and Middle Eastern Studies	M,D
Nurse Midwifery	M,D
Pastoral Ministry and Counseling	M,D
Philosophy	M,D
Political Science	M,D
Portuguese	M,D
Psychology—General	M,D
Public Administration	M,D
Public Health—General	M,D
Quantitative Analysis	M,D
Real Estate	M,D
Religion	M,D
Romance Languages	M,D
Russian	M,D
Science Education	M,D
Social Work	M,D
Sociology	M,D
Spanish	M,D
Statistics	M,D
Technology and Public Policy	M,D
Telecommunications Management	M,D
Theology	M,D
Travel and Tourism	M,D
Vocational and Technical Education	M,D

UNIVERSITY OF SOUTH ALABAMA

Accounting	M
Allied Health—General	M,D
Allopathic Medicine	D
Biological and Biomedical Sciences—General	M,D
Business Administration and Management—General	M,D
Chemical Engineering	M
Civil Engineering	M
Clinical Psychology	M,D,O
Communication Disorders	M,D
Communication—General	M
Computer Engineering	M
Computer Science	M,D
Counseling Psychology	M,D,O
Counselor Education	M,D,O
Early Childhood Education	M,D
Education—General	M,D,O
Educational Leadership and Administration	M,D,O
Educational Media/Instructional Technology	M,D,O
Electrical Engineering	M
Elementary Education	M,D
Engineering and Applied Sciences—General	M,D
English	M
Environmental and Occupational Health	M
Exercise and Sports Science	M
Health Education	M
History	M
Interdisciplinary Studies	M,D
Leisure Studies	M
Management Information Systems	M,D
Marine Sciences	M,D
Mathematics	M
Mechanical Engineering	M
Music Education	M
Music	M
Nursing and Healthcare Administration	M,D,O
Nursing Education	M,D,O
Nursing—General	M,D,O
Occupational Therapy	M
Physical Education	M
Physical Therapy	D
Physician Assistant Studies	M
Psychology—General	M
Public Administration	M
Reading Education	M,D
Science Education	M,D
Secondary Education	M,D
Sociology	M
Special Education	M,D,O
Systems Engineering	D
Toxicology	M

UNIVERSITY OF SOUTH CAROLINA

Accounting	M
Acute Care/Critical Care Nursing	M,O
Adult Nursing	M
Allopathic Medicine	D
Anthropology	M,D
Applied Statistics	M,D,O
Archives/Archival Administration	M,O
Art Education	M,D
Art History	M
Art/Fine Arts	M
Astronomy	M,D
Biochemistry	M,D
Biological and Biomedical Sciences—General	M,D,O
Biostatistics	M,D
Business Administration and Management—General	M,D
Business Education	M,D
Cell Biology	M,D
Chemical Engineering	M,D
Chemistry	M,D
Civil Engineering	M,D
Clinical Psychology	M,D
Communication Disorders	M,D
Community Health Nursing	M
Comparative Literature	M,D
Computer Engineering	M,D
Computer Science	M,D
Consumer Economics	M
Counselor Education	D,O
Criminal Justice and Criminology	M,D
Curriculum and Instruction	D
Developmental Biology	M,D
Early Childhood Education	M,D
Ecology	M,D
Economics	M,D
Education—General	M,D,O
Educational Leadership and Administration	M,D,O
Educational Measurement and Evaluation	M,D
Educational Media/Instructional Technology	M
Educational Psychology	M,D
Electrical Engineering	M,D
Elementary Education	M,D
Engineering and Applied Sciences—General	M,D
English as a Second Language	M,D,O
English Education	M,D
English	M,D
Entertainment Management	M
Environmental and Occupational Health	M,D
Environmental Management and Policy	M
Epidemiology	M,D
Evolutionary Biology	M,D
Exercise and Sports Science	M,D
Experimental Psychology	M,D
Family Nurse Practitioner Studies	M
Foreign Languages Education	M,D
Foundations and Philosophy of Education	D
French	M,D
Genetic Counseling	M
Geography	M,D
Geology	M,D
Geosciences	M,D
German	M,D
Gerontology	O
Hazardous Materials Management	M,D
Health Education	M,D,O
Health Promotion	M,D,O
Health Services Management and Hospital Administration	M,D
Higher Education	M
Historic Preservation	M,O
History	M,D,O
Hospitality Management	M
Human Resources Management	M
Industrial Hygiene	M,D
Information Studies	M,D,O
International Affairs	M,D
International Business	M
Journalism	M,D
Law	D
Library Science	M,D,O
Linguistics	M,D,O
Marine Sciences	M,D
Mathematics Education	M,D
Mathematics	M,D
Mechanical Engineering	M,D
Media Studies	M
Medical/Surgical Nursing	M
Molecular Biology	M,D
Museum Studies	M,O
Music Education	M,D,O
Music	M,D,O
Nuclear Engineering	M,D
Nurse Anesthesia	M
Nursing and Healthcare Administration	M
Nursing—General	M,O
Pediatric Nursing	M
Pharmaceutical Sciences	M,D
Pharmacy	D
Philosophy	M,D
Physical Education	M,D
Physics	M,D
Political Science	M,D
Psychiatric Nursing	M,O
Psychology—General	M,D
Public Administration	M
Public Health—General	M
Public History	M,O
Reading Education	M,D
Rehabilitation Counseling	M,O
Rehabilitation Sciences	M,O
Religion	M
School Psychology	D
Science Education	M,D
Secondary Education	M,D
Social Psychology	M,D
Social Sciences Education	M,D
Social Work	M,D
Sociology	M,D
Software Engineering	M,D
Spanish	M,D
Special Education	M,D
Speech and Interpersonal Communication	M,D
Sports Management	M
Statistics	M,D,O
Student Affairs	M
Theater	M,D
Travel and Tourism	M
Women's Health Nursing	M
Women's Studies	O
Writing	M,D

UNIVERSITY OF SOUTH CAROLINA AIKEN

Applied Psychology	M
Business Administration and Management—General	M
Clinical Psychology	M
Educational Media/Instructional Technology	M

UNIVERSITY OF SOUTH CAROLINA UPSTATE

Early Childhood Education	M
Education—General	M
Elementary Education	M
Health Informatics	M
Information Science	M
Special Education	M

THE UNIVERSITY OF SOUTH DAKOTA

Accounting	M
Addictions/Substance Abuse Counseling	M
Adult Education	M,D,O
Allied Health—General	M,D,O
Allopathic Medicine	D
Art Education	M
Art/Fine Arts	M
Biological and Biomedical Sciences—General	M,D
Business Administration and Management—General	M
Cardiovascular Sciences	M,D
Cell Biology	M,D
Chemistry	M,D
Clinical Psychology	M,D
Communication Disorders	M,D
Communication—General	M
Computer Science	M
Counselor Education	M,D,O
Criminal Justice and Criminology	M
Curriculum and Instruction	M,D,O
Database Systems	M
Early Childhood Education	M,D,O
Education—General	M,D,O
Educational Leadership and Administration	M,D,O
Educational Media/Instructional Technology	M
Educational Psychology	M,D,O
Elementary Education	M
English	M,D
Exercise and Sports Science	M
Graphic Design	M
Health Services Management and Hospital Administration	M
Higher Education	M,D,O
History	M
Human Development	M,D,O
Human Resources Management	M
Immunology	M,D
Interdisciplinary Studies	M
Kinesiology and Movement Studies	M
Law	D
Mathematics	M
Microbiology	M,D
Molecular Biology	M,D
Music Education	M
Music	M

Neuroscience	M,D
Occupational Therapy	M,D
Organizational Management	M
Pharmacology	M,D
Photography	M
Physical Therapy	D
Physician Assistant Studies	M
Physics	M,D
Physiology	M,D
Political Science	M,D
Psychology—General	M,D
Public Administration	M,D
Public Policy	M,D
Reading Education	M
School Psychology	M,D,O
Secondary Education	M
Special Education	M,D,O
Theater	M

UNIVERSITY OF SOUTHERN CALIFORNIA

Accounting	M
Advertising and Public Relations	M
Aerospace/Aeronautical Engineering	M,D,O
Allopathic Medicine	D
American Studies	D
Applied Mathematics	M,D
Architecture	M,D
Art History	M,D,O
Art/Fine Arts	M,D,O
Artificial Intelligence/Robotics	M,D
Arts Administration	M
Asian Languages	M,D
Asian Studies	M,D
Biochemistry	M
Bioinformatics	D
Biological and Biomedical Sciences—General	M,D,O
Biomedical Engineering	M,D
Biophysics	M
Biostatistics	M,D
Business Administration and Management—General	M,D
Cancer Biology/Oncology	D
Cell Biology	M,D
Chemical Engineering	M,D,O
Chemistry	D
Child and Family Studies	M,D
Civil Engineering	M,D,O
Classics	M,D
Clinical Psychology	M,D
Clinical Research	M,D,O
Cognitive Sciences	M,D
Communication—General	M,D
Comparative Literature	D
Computational Biology	D
Computer and Information Systems Security	M,D
Computer Art and Design	M
Computer Engineering	M,D,O
Computer Science	M,D
Construction Management	M,D,O
Corporate and Organizational Communication	M
Counselor Education	M
Cultural Studies	D
Dentistry	D
Developmental Biology	D
Developmental Psychology	M,D
Economic Development	M,D
Economics	M,D
Education—General	M,D
Educational Leadership and Administration	D
Educational Policy	D
Educational Psychology	D
Electrical Engineering	M,D,O
Engineering and Applied Sciences—General	M,D,O
Engineering Management	M,D,O
English as a Second Language	M
English	M,D
Entrepreneurship	M
Environmental and Occupational Health	M
Environmental Biology	M,D
Environmental Engineering	M,D,O
Epidemiology	M,D
Evolutionary Biology	D
Film, Television, and Video Production	M
Film, Television, and Video Theory and Criticism	M,D
Food Science and Technology	M,D,O
Game Design and Development	M,D
Genomic Sciences	D
Geographic Information Systems	M,O
Geography	M,D
Geosciences	M,D
Geotechnical Engineering	M,D,O
Gerontology	M,D,O
Hazardous Materials Management	M,D,O
Health Communication	M,D
Health Education	M
Health Promotion	M
Health Services Management and Hospital Administration	M,O
Health Services Research	D
Higher Education	D
History	D
Homeland Security	M,O
Immunology	M
Industrial/Management Engineering	M,D,O
International Affairs	M,D
International Health	M,O
Internet and Interactive Multimedia	M,D,O
Journalism	M
Kinesiology and Movement Studies	M,D
Latin American Studies	D
Law	M,D
Linguistics	M,D
Manufacturing Engineering	M,D,O
Marine Biology	M,D
Marine Sciences	M,D
Marriage and Family Therapy	M
Materials Engineering	M,D,O
Materials Sciences	M,D,O
Mathematical and Computational Finance	M,D
Mathematics	M,D
Mechanical Engineering	M,D,O
Mechanics	M,D,O
Media Studies	M,D
Medical Imaging	M,D
Medical Microbiology	D
Microbiology	M
Modeling and Simulation	M,D
Molecular Biology	M,D
Molecular Pharmacology	M,D
Multilingual and Multicultural Education	D
Music Education	M,D,O
Music	M,D,O
Neurobiology	D
Neuroscience	M,D
Nonprofit Management	M,O
Occupational Therapy	M,D
Oceanography	M,D
Operations Research	M,D,O
Oral and Dental Sciences	M,D,O
Organizational Management	M
Pathology	M
Petroleum Engineering	M,D,O
Pharmaceutical Administration	M
Pharmaceutical Sciences	M,D,O
Pharmacy	D
Philosophy	M,D
Photography	M
Physical Chemistry	D
Physical Therapy	M,D
Physician Assistant Studies	M
Physics	M,D
Physiology	M
Political Science	M,D
Psychology—General	M,D
Public Administration	M,O
Public Health—General	M,D
Public Policy	M,D,O
Quantitative Analysis	M,D
Real Estate	M
Rhetoric	D
Safety Engineering	M,D,O
Slavic Languages	M,D
Social Psychology	M,D
Social Work	M,D
Sociology	D
Software Engineering	M,D
Spanish	D
Statistics	M,D
Student Affairs	M
Supply Chain Management	M,D,O
Sustainable Development	M,D,O
Systems Engineering	M,D,O
Taxation	M
Telecommunications	M,D,O
Theater	M
Toxicology	M,D
Transportation and Highway Engineering	M,D,O
Urban and Regional Planning	M,D,O
Urban Education	D
Water Resources	M,D,O
Writing	M,D

UNIVERSITY OF SOUTHERN INDIANA

Business Administration and Management—General	M
Communication—General	M
Education—General	M
Elementary Education	M
Engineering and Applied Sciences—General	M
English	M
Health Services Management and Hospital Administration	M
Industrial and Manufacturing Management	M
Kinesiology and Movement Studies	M
Liberal Studies	M
Mathematics Education	M
Nursing—General	M,D
Occupational Therapy	M
Public Administration	M
Secondary Education	M
Social Work	M

UNIVERSITY OF SOUTHERN MAINE

Accounting	M
Addictions/Substance Abuse Counseling	M,O
Adult Education	M,O
Adult Nursing	M,D,O
American Studies	M,O
Applied Behavior Analysis	M,O
Biological and Biomedical Sciences—General	M
Business Administration and Management—General	M,O
Computer Science	M,O
Counseling Psychology	M,O
Counselor Education	M,O
Cultural Studies	M,O
Education of the Gifted	M,O
Education—General	M,D,O
Educational Leadership and Administration	M,O
Educational Psychology	M,O
English as a Second Language	M,O
Family Nurse Practitioner Studies	M,D,O
Finance and Banking	M
Gerontological Nursing	M,D,O
Health Services Management and Hospital Administration	M
Higher Education	M,O
Immunology	M
Molecular Biology	M
Music Education	M
Music	M
Nursing and Healthcare Administration	M,D,O
Nursing Education	M,D,O
Nursing—General	M,D,O
Occupational Therapy	M
Psychiatric Nursing	M,D,O
Public Health—General	M,O
Public Policy	M
Reading Education	M,O
Rehabilitation Counseling	M,O
School Psychology	M,D
Social Work	M
Software Engineering	M,O
Special Education	M,O
Statistics	M,O
Sustainability Management	M
Urban and Regional Planning	M,O
Writing	M

UNIVERSITY OF SOUTHERN MISSISSIPPI

Accounting	M
Anthropology	M
Biochemistry	M,D
Biological and Biomedical Sciences—General	M,D
Biostatistics	M
Business Administration and Management—General	M
Chemistry	M,D
Child and Family Studies	M
Clinical Laboratory Sciences/Medical Technology	M
Clinical Psychology	M,D
Communication Disorders	M,D
Computational Sciences	M,D
Computer Science	M,D
Construction Engineering	M
Counseling Psychology	M,D
Counselor Education	M,D,O
Criminal Justice and Criminology	M,D
Curriculum and Instruction	M,D,O
Economic Development	M
Economics	M
Education—General	M,D,O
Educational Leadership and Administration	M,D,O
Educational Measurement and Evaluation	M,D
Educational Media/Instructional Technology	M,D,O
Elementary Education	M,D,O
English	M,D
Environmental Biology	M,D
Epidemiology	M
Experimental Psychology	M,D
Family Nurse Practitioner Studies	M,D,O
Food Science and Technology	M,D
Foreign Languages Education	M
Forensic Sciences	M,D
Geography	M,D
Geology	M,D
Health Education	M
Health Services Management and Hospital Administration	M
Higher Education	M,D
History	M,D
Hydrology	M,D
Information Science	M,O
Inorganic Chemistry	M,D
International Development	M,D
Library Science	M,O
Marine Biology	M,D
Marine Sciences	M,D
Marriage and Family Therapy	M
Mass Communication	M,D
Maternal and Child/Neonatal Nursing	M,D,O
Mathematics Education	M,D
Mathematics	M,D
Microbiology	M,D
Molecular Biology	M,D
Music Education	M,D
Music	M,D
Nursing—General	M,D,O
Nutrition	M,D
Organic Chemistry	M,D
Physical Chemistry	M,D
Physical Education	M,D
Physics	M,D
Political Science	M,D
Polymer Science and Engineering	M,D
Psychiatric Nursing	M,D,O
Psychology—General	M,D
Public Health—General	M
School Psychology	M,D
Science Education	M,D
Social Sciences Education	M,D,O
Social Work	M
Special Education	M,D,O
Speech and Interpersonal Communication	M,D
Sports Management	M,D
Student Affairs	M,D
Theater	M

UNIVERSITY OF SOUTH FLORIDA

Accounting	M,D
Acute Care/Critical Care Nursing	M,D,O
Addictions/Substance Abuse Counseling	M
Adult Education	M,D,O
Adult Nursing	M,D,O
African Studies	M,O
Allopathic Medicine	M,D
American Studies	M,D
Anatomy	M,D
Anthropology	M,D,O
Applied Behavior Analysis	M,D
Applied Physics	M,D
Archaeology	M,D,O
Architecture	M
Art History	M
Art/Fine Arts	M
Athletic Training and Sports Medicine	M,D
Atmospheric Sciences	M,D
Bioethics	O
Bioinformatics	M,D,O
Biological and Biomedical Sciences—General	M,D
Biomedical Engineering	M,D,O
Biophysics	M,D
Biostatistics	M,D,O
Biotechnology	M,D,O
Business Administration and Management—General	M,D
Cancer Biology/Oncology	M,D
Cardiovascular Sciences	O
Cell Biology	M,D
Chemical Engineering	M,D,O
Chemistry	M,D
Child and Family Studies	M,D,O
Civil Engineering	M,D,O
Clinical Psychology	D
Clinical Research	M,D,O
Cognitive Sciences	D
Communication Disorders	M,D,O
Communication—General	M,D
Community College Education	M,D,O
Community Health	M,D,O
Comparative Literature	O
Computational Biology	M,D
Computer and Information Systems Security	M
Computer Engineering	M,D
Computer Science	M,D
Corporate and Organizational Communication	M,O
Counseling Psychology	O
Counselor Education	M,D,O
Criminal Justice and Criminology	M,D,O
Curriculum and Instruction	M,D,O
Database Systems	M,D
Distance Education Development	O
Early Childhood Education	M,D,O
Ecology	M,D
Economics	M,D
Education of the Gifted	M,D
Education—General	M,D,O
Educational Leadership and Administration	M,D,O
Educational Measurement and Evaluation	M,D,O
Educational Media/Instructional Technology	M,D,O
Electrical Engineering	M,D
Elementary Education	M,D,O
Emergency Management	O
Engineering and Applied Sciences—General	M,D,O
Engineering Management	M,D
English as a Second Language	M,D,O
English Education	M,D,O
English	M,D,O
Entrepreneurship	M,O
Environmental and Occupational Health	M,D,O
Environmental Biology	M,D
Environmental Engineering	M,D
Environmental Management and Policy	M,D,O
Environmental Sciences	M,D
Epidemiology	M,D,O
Evolutionary Biology	M,D
Exercise and Sports Science	M
Family Nurse Practitioner Studies	M,D,O
Film, Television, and Video Theory and Criticism	M
Finance and Banking	M,D
Foreign Languages Education	M,D,O
Forensic Sciences	M,D,O
French	M
Gender Studies	M,O
Geographic Information Systems	M,D,O
Geography	M,D,O
Geology	M,D,O
Geosciences	M,D
Geotechnical Engineering	M,D
Gerontological Nursing	M,D,O
Gerontology	M,D,O
Health Informatics	M,D,O
Health Services Management and Hospital Administration	M,D,O
Higher Education	M,D,O
History	M,D
Human Resources Development	O
Humanities	M
Hydrogeology	O
Immunology	M,D
Industrial and Organizational Psychology	D
Industrial/Management Engineering	M,D,O
Information Science	M
Information Studies	M,O
Interdisciplinary Studies	M,D

*M—masters degree; D—doctorate; O—other advanced degree; *—Close-Up and/or Display*

International Affairs	M,D,O
International Health	M,D,O
Internet and Interactive Multimedia	M,O
Journalism	M,O
Latin American Studies	M,D,O
Legal and Justice Studies	O
Liberal Studies	M
Library Science	M
Management Information Systems	M,D,O
Management of Technology	O
Management Strategy and Policy	O
Manufacturing Engineering	M,D
Marine Sciences	M,D
Marketing	M,D
Marriage and Family Therapy	M,O
Mass Communication	M,O
Materials Engineering	M,D,O
Materials Sciences	M,D,O
Maternal and Child Health	O
Mathematics Education	M,D,O
Mathematics	M,D,O
Mechanical Engineering	M,D
Media Studies	M
Medical Microbiology	M,D
Medical Physics	M,D
Microbiology	M,D
Molecular Biology	M,D
Molecular Medicine	M,D
Molecular Pharmacology	M,D
Museum Studies	O
Music Education	M,D
Music	M,D
Nanotechnology	M,D
Neuroscience	M,D,O
Nonprofit Management	O
Nurse Anesthesia	M,D,O
Nursing and Healthcare Administration	M,D,O
Nursing Education	M,D,O
Nursing—General	M,D,O
Nutrition	M,D,O
Occupational Health Nursing	M,D,O
Oceanography	M,D
Oncology Nursing	M,D,O
Pathology	M,D
Pediatric Nursing	M,D,O
Pharmaceutical Sciences	M,D
Pharmacology	M,D
Pharmacy	M,D,O
Philosophy	M,D
Physical Education	M
Physical Therapy	D
Physics	M,D
Physiology	M,D
Political Science	M,D,O
Psychology—General	D
Public Administration	O
Public Affairs	O
Public Health—General	M,D,O*
Reading Education	M,D,O
Real Estate	M,D
Rehabilitation Counseling	M,O
Rehabilitation Sciences	D
Religion	M,D
Rhetoric	M,D
School Psychology	M,D,O
Science Education	M,D,O
Secondary Education	M,D,O
Social Sciences Education	M,D,O
Social Work	M,D,O
Sociology	M,D
Spanish	M
Special Education	M,D,O
Sports Management	M
Statistics	M,D
Structural Engineering	M,D
Student Affairs	M,D,O
Sustainability Management	M,O
Sustainable Development	M,O
Systems Engineering	O
Taxation	M,D
Technical Communication	O
Transportation and Highway Engineering	M,D,O
Travel and Tourism	M,O
Urban and Regional Planning	M,D,O
Urban Design	M
Vocational and Technical Education	M,D,O
Water Resources Engineering	M,D,O
Western European Studies	M,D
Women's Studies	M
Writing	M,D,O

UNIVERSITY OF SOUTH FLORIDA, ST. PETERSBURG

Business Administration and Management—General	M
Computer Art and Design	M
Education—General	M
Educational Leadership and Administration	M
Elementary Education	M
English Education	M
Environmental Management and Policy	M
Environmental Sciences	M
Journalism	M
Liberal Studies	M
Mathematics Education	M
Media Studies	M
Middle School Education	M
Psychology—General	M
Reading Education	M
Science Education	M

UNIVERSITY OF SOUTH FLORIDA SARASOTA-MANATEE

Business Administration and Management—General	M
Criminal Justice and Criminology	M
Curriculum and Instruction	M
Education—General	M
Educational Leadership and Administration	M
Elementary Education	M
English Education	M
Hospitality Management	M

THE UNIVERSITY OF TAMPA

Accounting	M
Adult Nursing	M
Business Administration and Management—General	M
Curriculum and Instruction	M
Education—General	M
Educational Media/Instructional Technology	M
Entrepreneurship	M
Exercise and Sports Science	M
Family Nurse Practitioner Studies	M
Finance and Banking	M
International Business	M
Management Information Systems	M
Marketing	M
Nonprofit Management	M
Nursing—General	M
Nutrition	M
Writing	M

THE UNIVERSITY OF TENNESSEE

Accounting	M,D
Adult Education	M,D
Advertising and Public Relations	M,D
Aerospace/Aeronautical Engineering	M,D
Agricultural Education	M
Agricultural Engineering	M
Agricultural Sciences—General	M,D
Analytical Chemistry	M,D
Anatomy	M,D
Animal Behavior	M,D
Animal Sciences	M,D
Anthropology	M,D
Applied Mathematics	M,D
Applied Psychology	M,D
Archaeology	M,D
Architecture	M
Art Education	M,D,O
Art/Fine Arts	M
Athletic Training and Sports Medicine	M,D
Aviation	M
Biochemistry	M,D
Bioethics	M,D
Biological and Biomedical Sciences—General	M,D
Biomedical Engineering	M,D
Biosystems Engineering	M,D
Business Administration and Management—General	M,D
Chemical Engineering	M,D
Chemical Physics	M,D
Chemistry	M,D
Child and Family Studies	M,D
Civil Engineering	M,D
Clinical Psychology	M,D
Clothing and Textiles	M,D
Communication Disorders	M,D,O
Communication—General	M,D
Community Health	M,D
Computer Engineering	M,D
Computer Science	M,D
Consumer Economics	M,D
Counseling Psychology	M,D
Counselor Education	M,D,O
Criminal Justice and Criminology	M,D
Cultural Anthropology	M,D
Curriculum and Instruction	M,D,O
Early Childhood Education	M,D,O
Ecology	M,D
Economics	M,D
Education—General	M,D,O
Educational Leadership and Administration	M,D,O
Educational Measurement and Evaluation	M,D,O
Educational Media/Instructional Technology	M,D,O
Educational Psychology	M,D,O
Electrical Engineering	M,D
Elementary Education	M,D,O
Energy and Power Engineering	D
Engineering and Applied Sciences—General	M,D
Engineering Management	M,D
English as a Second Language	M,D,O
English Education	M,D,O
English	M,D
Entomology	M,D
Environmental Engineering	M
Environmental Management and Policy	M,D
Evolutionary Biology	M,D
Exercise and Sports Science	M,D,O
Experimental Psychology	M,D
Family and Consumer Sciences-General	D
Finance and Banking	M,D
Fish, Game, and Wildlife Management	M
Food Science and Technology	M,D
Foreign Languages Education	M,D,O
Forestry	M
Foundations and Philosophy of Education	M,D,O
French	M,D
Genetics	M,D
Genomic Sciences	M,D
Geography	M,D
Geology	M,D
German	M,D
Gerontology	M
Graphic Design	M
Health Education	M
Health Promotion	M
Health Services Management and Hospital Administration	M
History	M,D
Hospitality Management	M
Human Resources Development	M
Industrial and Manufacturing Management	M,D
Industrial and Organizational Psychology	D
Industrial/Management Engineering	M,D
Information Science	M,D
Inorganic Chemistry	M,D
Italian	D
Journalism	M,D
Kinesiology and Movement Studies	M,D
Landscape Architecture	M
Law	D
Leisure Studies	M,D
Linguistics	D
Logistics	M,D
Marketing	M,D
Materials Engineering	M,D
Materials Sciences	M,D
Mathematics Education	M,D,O
Mathematics	M,D
Mechanical Engineering	M,D
Media Studies	M,D
Microbiology	M,D
Multilingual and Multicultural Education	M,D,O
Music Education	M
Music	M
Nuclear Engineering	M,D
Nursing—General	M,D
Nutrition	M
Organic Chemistry	M,D
Philosophy	M,D
Photography	M
Physical Chemistry	M,D
Physics	M,D
Physiology	M,D
Plant Pathology	M,D
Plant Physiology	M,D
Plant Sciences	M
Political Science	M,D
Polymer Science and Engineering	M,D
Portuguese	D
Psychology—General	M,D
Public Administration	M
Public Health—General	M
Reading Education	M,D,O
Recreation and Park Management	M,D
Rehabilitation Counseling	M,D
Reliability Engineering	M,D
Religion	M,D
Russian	D
School Psychology	M,D,O
Science Education	M,D,O
Secondary Education	M,D,O
Social Sciences Education	M,D,O
Social Work	M,D
Sociology	M,D
Spanish	M,D
Special Education	M,D,O
Speech and Interpersonal Communication	M,D
Sports Management	M,D
Statistics	M,D
Student Affairs	M
Theater	M
Theoretical Chemistry	M,D
Transportation Management	M,D
Travel and Tourism	M
Veterinary Medicine	D

THE UNIVERSITY OF TENNESSEE AT CHATTANOOGA

Accounting	M
Applied Mathematics	M
Applied Statistics	M
Athletic Training and Sports Medicine	M
Automotive Engineering	M
Business Administration and Management—General	M
Chemical Engineering	M
Civil Engineering	M
Computational Sciences	M,D
Computer Science	M
Counselor Education	M,D,O
Criminal Justice and Criminology	M
Education—General	M,D,O
Educational Leadership and Administration	M,D,O
Educational Media/Instructional Technology	M,D,O
Electrical Engineering	M
Elementary Education	M,D,O
Energy and Power Engineering	M,O
Engineering Management	M,O
English	M,O
Environmental Sciences	M
Ethics	M,O
Experimental Psychology	M
Family Nurse Practitioner Studies	M,D,O
Industrial and Organizational Psychology	M
Industrial/Management Engineering	M
Logistics	M,O
Mathematics Education	M
Mathematics	M
Mechanical Engineering	M
Medical Informatics	M,D,O
Music Education	M
Music	M
Nonprofit Management	M,O
Nuclear Engineering	M,O
Nurse Anesthesia	M,D,O
Nursing and Healthcare Administration	M,D,O
Nursing Education	M,D,O
Nursing—General	M,D,O
Physical Education	M
Physical Therapy	D
Project Management	M,O
Psychology—General	M
Public Administration	M,O
Quality Management	M,O
Rhetoric	M,O
School Psychology	M,D,O
Secondary Education	M,D,O
Social Psychology	M,D,O
Special Education	M,D,O
Supply Chain Management	M,O
Writing	M,O

THE UNIVERSITY OF TENNESSEE AT MARTIN

Addictions/Substance Abuse Counseling	M
Agricultural Economics and Agribusiness	M
Agricultural Sciences—General	M
Business Administration and Management—General	M
Child and Family Studies	M
Child Development	M
Communication—General	M
Counselor Education	M
Curriculum and Instruction	M
Education—General	M
Educational Leadership and Administration	M
Elementary Education	M
Family and Consumer Sciences-General	M
Finance and Banking	M
Food Science and Technology	M
Interdisciplinary Studies	M
Nutrition	M
Physical Education	M
Secondary Education	M
Social Psychology	M
Special Education	M
Student Affairs	M

THE UNIVERSITY OF TENNESSEE HEALTH SCIENCE CENTER

Allied Health—General	M,D
Allopathic Medicine	D
Biological and Biomedical Sciences—General	M,D
Biomedical Engineering	M,D
Clinical Laboratory Sciences/Medical Technology	M,D
Communication Disorders	M,D
Dentistry	D
Epidemiology	M,D
Gerontological Nursing	M,D,O
Health Informatics	M,D
Health Services Research	M,D
Nursing and Healthcare Administration	M,D,O
Nursing—General	M,D,O
Occupational Therapy	M,D
Oral and Dental Sciences	M,D
Pathology	M,D
Pharmaceutical Sciences	M,D
Pharmacology	M,D
Pharmacy	M,D
Physical Therapy	M,D
Physician Assistant Studies	M,D

THE UNIVERSITY OF TENNESSEE–OAK RIDGE NATIONAL LABORATORY

Biological and Biomedical Sciences—General	M,D
Genomic Sciences	M,D

THE UNIVERSITY OF TEXAS AT ARLINGTON

Accounting	M,D
Aerospace/Aeronautical Engineering	M,D
Anthropology	M
Applied Mathematics	M,D
Architecture	M
Art/Fine Arts	M
Bioengineering	M,D
Biological and Biomedical Sciences—General	M,D
Business Administration and Management—General	M,D
Chemistry	M,D
Civil Engineering	M,D
Communication—General	M
Computer Engineering	M,D
Computer Science	M,D
Construction Management	M,D
Criminal Justice and Criminology	M
Curriculum and Instruction	M
Economics	M
Education—General	M,D
Educational Leadership and Administration	M,D
Educational Policy	M,D
Electrical Engineering	M,D
Engineering and Applied Sciences—General	M,D
Engineering Management	M
English as a Second Language	M
English	M,D
Environmental Sciences	M,D
Exercise and Sports Science	M
Experimental Psychology	M,D
Family Nurse Practitioner Studies	M,D
Film, Television, and Video Production	M
Finance and Banking	M,D
French	M
Geology	M,D

Health Psychology	M,D
Health Services Management and Hospital Administration	M
Higher Education	M,D
History	M,D
Human Resources Management	M
Industrial and Manufacturing Management	M,D
Industrial and Organizational Psychology	M,D
Industrial/Management Engineering	M,D
Interdisciplinary Studies	M
Landscape Architecture	M
Linguistics	M,D
Logistics	M
Management Information Systems	M,D
Marketing Research	M,D
Marketing	M,D
Materials Engineering	M,D
Materials Sciences	M,D
Mathematics Education	M,D
Mathematics	M,D
Mechanical Engineering	M,D
Multilingual and Multicultural Education	M,D
Music Education	M
Music	M
Nursing and Healthcare Administration	M,D
Nursing Education	M,D
Nursing—General	M,D
Physics	M,D
Political Science	M
Psychology—General	M,D
Public Administration	M
Public Affairs	D
Quantitative Analysis	M,D
Real Estate	M,D
Social Work	M,D
Sociology	M
Software Engineering	M,D
Spanish	M
Sustainable Development	M
Systems Engineering	M
Taxation	M,D
Urban and Regional Planning	M,D
Urban Studies	M

THE UNIVERSITY OF TEXAS AT AUSTIN

Accounting	M,D
Actuarial Science	M,D
Adult Nursing	M,D
Advertising and Public Relations	M,D
Aerospace/Aeronautical Engineering	M,D
African Studies	M,D
American Studies	M,D
Analytical Chemistry	D
Animal Behavior	D
Anthropology	M,D
Applied Arts and Design—General	M
Applied Mathematics	M,D
Applied Physics	M,D
Archaeology	M,D
Architectural Engineering	M
Architectural History	M,D
Architecture	M
Art Education	M
Art History	M,D
Art/Fine Arts	M
Asian Languages	M,D
Asian Studies	M,D
Astronomy	M,D
Biochemistry	D
Biological and Biomedical Sciences—General	M,D
Biomedical Engineering	M,D
Biopsychology	D
Business Administration and Management—General	M,D
Cell Biology	D
Chemical Engineering	M,D
Chemistry	D
Child and Family Studies	M,D
Child Development	M,D
Civil Engineering	M,D
Classics	M,D
Clinical Laboratory Sciences/Medical Technology	M,D
Clinical Psychology	D
Communication Disorders	M,D
Communication—General	M,D
Community Health Nursing	M,D
Comparative Literature	M,D
Computational Sciences	M,D
Computer and Information Systems Security	M,D
Computer Engineering	M,D
Computer Science	M,D
Counseling Psychology	M,D
Counselor Education	M,D
Cultural Studies	M,D
Curriculum and Instruction	M,D
Dance	M,D
Developmental Psychology	D
Early Childhood Education	M,D
East European and Russian Studies	M
Ecology	D
Economics	M,D
Education—General	M,D
Educational Leadership and Administration	M,D
Educational Media/Instructional Technology	M,D
Educational Psychology	M,D
Electrical Engineering	M,D
Engineering and Applied Sciences—General	M,D
English	M,D
Entrepreneurship	M
Environmental Engineering	M,D
Environmental Management and Policy	M
Evolutionary Biology	D
Exercise and Sports Science	M,D
Family and Consumer Sciences-General	M,D
Family Nurse Practitioner Studies	M,D
Film, Television, and Video Production	M,D
Finance and Banking	M,D
Folklore	M,D
French	M,D
Geography	M,D
Geology	M,D
Geosciences	M,D
Geotechnical Engineering	M,D
German	M,D
Gerontological Nursing	M,D
Health Education	M,D
Hispanic and Latin American Languages	M,D
Hispanic Studies	M
Historic Preservation	M
History	M,D
Human Development	M,D
Industrial and Manufacturing Management	M,D
Industrial/Management Engineering	M,D
Information Studies	M,D
Inorganic Chemistry	D
Interior Design	M
Italian	M,D
Journalism	M,D
Kinesiology and Movement Studies	M,D
Landscape Architecture	M
Latin American Studies	M
Law	M,D
Linguistics	M,D
Management Information Systems	M,D
Marine Sciences	M,D
Marketing	M,D
Materials Engineering	M,D
Materials Sciences	M,D
Maternal and Child/Neonatal Nursing	M,D
Mathematics	M,D
Mechanical Engineering	M,D
Mechanics	M,D
Media Studies	M,D
Medicinal and Pharmaceutical Chemistry	M,D
Microbiology	D
Mineral Economics	M
Mineral/Mining Engineering	M
Molecular Biology	D
Multilingual and Multicultural Education	M,D
Music Education	M,D
Music	M,D
Natural Resources	M
Near and Middle Eastern Languages	M,D
Near and Middle Eastern Studies	M,D
Neurobiology	D
Neuroscience	D
Nursing and Healthcare Administration	M,D
Nursing Education	M,D
Nursing—General	M,D
Nutrition	M,D
Operations Research	M,D
Organic Chemistry	D
Organizational Behavior	M
Pediatric Nursing	M,D
Petroleum Engineering	M,D
Pharmaceutical Sciences	M,D
Pharmacology	M,D
Pharmacy	D
Philosophy	D
Physical Chemistry	D
Physical Education	M,D
Physics	M,D
Plant Biology	M,D
Political Science	M,D
Portuguese	M,D
Psychiatric Nursing	M,D
Psychology—General	D
Public Administration	M,D
Public Affairs	M,D
Public History	M,D
Public Policy	M,D
Quantitative Analysis	M,D
Reading Education	M,D
Rehabilitation Counseling	M,D
Romance Languages	M,D
School Psychology	M,D
Slavic Languages	M,D
Social Work	M,D
Sociology	M,D
Spanish	M,D
Special Education	M,D
Sport Psychology	M,D
Statistics	M,D
Supply Chain Management	M,D
Sustainable Development	M
Technology and Public Policy	M
Textile Sciences and Engineering	M
Theater	M,D
Toxicology	M,D
Urban and Regional Planning	M,D
Urban Design	M
Water Resources Engineering	M,D
Writing	M,D

THE UNIVERSITY OF TEXAS AT DALLAS

Accounting	M,D
Actuarial Science	M,D
Applied Mathematics	M,D
Biological and Biomedical Sciences—General	M,D
Biomedical Engineering	M,D
Biotechnology	M,D
Business Administration and Management—General	M,D*
Cell Biology	M,D
Chemistry	M,D
Child and Family Studies	M,D
Cognitive Sciences	M,D
Communication Disorders	M,D
Communication—General	M,D
Comparative Literature	M,D
Computer Engineering	M,D
Computer Science	M,D
Criminal Justice and Criminology	M,D
Economics	M,D
Electrical Engineering	M,D
Engineering and Applied Sciences—General	M,D
Entrepreneurship	M,D
Finance and Banking	M,D
Geochemistry	M,D
Geographic Information Systems	M,D
Geography	M,D
Geophysics	M,D
Geosciences	M,D
Health Services Management and Hospital Administration	M,D
History	M,D
Humanities	M,D
Hydrogeology	M,D
Interdisciplinary Studies	M
International Business	M,D
Internet and Interactive Multimedia	M,D
Investment Management	M
Latin American Studies	M,D
Law	M,D
Management Information Systems	M,D
Management of Technology	M
Management Strategy and Policy	M,D
Marketing	M,D
Materials Engineering	M,D
Materials Sciences	M,D
Mathematics Education	M
Mathematics	M,D
Mechanical Engineering	M,D
Molecular Biology	M,D
Neuroscience	M,D
Nonprofit Management	M,D
Paleontology	M,D
Physics	M,D
Political Science	M,D
Project Management	M,D
Psychology—General	M,D
Public Administration	M,D
Public Policy	M,D
Science Education	M
Software Engineering	M,D
Statistics	M,D
Supply Chain Management	M
Systems Engineering	M,D
Telecommunications	M,D

THE UNIVERSITY OF TEXAS AT EL PASO

Accounting	M
Allied Health—General	D
Anthropology	M,O
Applied Psychology	M,O
Art Education	M
Art/Fine Arts	M
Bioinformatics	M,D
Biological and Biomedical Sciences—General	M,D
Biomedical Engineering	M,D,O
Business Administration and Management—General	M,D,O
Chemistry	M,D
Civil Engineering	M,D,O
Clinical Psychology	M,D
Communication Disorders	M
Communication—General	M
Computational Sciences	M,D
Computer Engineering	M,D
Computer Science	M,D
Construction Management	M,D,O
Counselor Education	M
Curriculum and Instruction	M,D
Economics	M
Education—General	M,D
Educational Leadership and Administration	M,D
Educational Measurement and Evaluation	M
Educational Psychology	M
Electrical Engineering	M,D
Engineering and Applied Sciences—General	M,D,O
English as a Second Language	M,O
English Education	M,D,O
English	M,D,O
Environmental Engineering	M,D,O
Environmental Sciences	M,D
Experimental Psychology	M,D
Family Nurse Practitioner Studies	M,D,O
Geology	M,D
Geophysics	M
Health Services Management and Hospital Administration	M,D,O
History	M,D
Industrial/Management Engineering	M,O
Information Science	M,D
Interdisciplinary Studies	M
International Business	M,D,O
Kinesiology and Movement Studies	M
Liberal Studies	M
Linguistics	M,O
Manufacturing Engineering	M,O
Materials Engineering	M,D
Materials Sciences	M,D
Mathematics Education	M
Mathematics	M
Mechanical Engineering	M,D
Metallurgical Engineering and Metallurgy	M,D
Multilingual and Multicultural Education	M,D,O
Music Education	M
Music	M
Nursing and Healthcare Administration	M,D,O
Nursing Education	M,D,O
Nursing—General	M,D,O
Occupational Therapy	M
Philosophy	M
Physical Therapy	D
Physics	M
Political Science	M
Psychology—General	M,D
Reading Education	M,D
Rehabilitation Counseling	M
Rhetoric	M,D,O
Science Education	M
Social Work	M
Sociology	M,O
Software Engineering	M,D,O
Spanish	M,O
Special Education	M
Statistics	M
Systems Engineering	M,O
Writing	M,D,O

THE UNIVERSITY OF TEXAS AT SAN ANTONIO

Accounting	M,D
Anthropology	M,D
Applied Behavior Analysis	M,O
Applied Mathematics	M
Applied Statistics	M,D
Architecture	M
Art History	M
Art/Fine Arts	M
Biological and Biomedical Sciences—General	M,D
Biomedical Engineering	M,D
Biotechnology	M,D
Business Administration and Management—General	M,D,O
Cell Biology	M,D
Chemistry	M,D
Civil Engineering	M,D
Communication—General	M
Computer and Information Systems Security	M,D,O
Computer Engineering	M,D
Computer Science	M,D
Counselor Education	M,D
Criminal Justice and Criminology	M
Cultural Studies	M,D
Curriculum and Instruction	M,D
Demography and Population Studies	D
Early Childhood Education	M,D
Economics	M
Educational Leadership and Administration	M,D
Educational Media/Instructional Technology	M,D,O
Electrical Engineering	M,D
Engineering and Applied Sciences—General	M,D
English as a Second Language	M,D,O
English	M,D
Environmental Engineering	M,D
Environmental Sciences	M,D
Finance and Banking	M,D
Geology	M
Health Education	M
Higher Education	M,D
History	M
Information Science	M,D,O
Interdisciplinary Studies	M,D
Kinesiology and Movement Studies	M
Management of Technology	M,D,O
Manufacturing Engineering	M,D
Marketing	M,D
Materials Engineering	M,D
Mathematics Education	M
Mathematics	M
Mechanical Engineering	M,D
Molecular Biology	M,D
Multilingual and Multicultural Education	M,D
Music	M
Neurobiology	M,D
Organizational Management	D
Philosophy	M
Physics	M,D
Political Science	M
Psychology—General	M,D
Public Administration	M
Reading Education	M,D
School Psychology	M,O
Social Work	M
Sociology	M
Spanish	M
Special Education	M,D
Statistics	M,D
Translational Biology	D
Urban and Regional Planning	M

THE UNIVERSITY OF TEXAS AT TYLER

Art History	M
Art/Fine Arts	M
Biological and Biomedical Sciences—General	M
Business Administration and Management—General	M
Civil Engineering	M

*M—masters degree; D—doctorate; O—other advanced degree; *—Close-Up and/or Display*

- Clinical Psychology M
- Communication—General M
- Computer Science M
- Counseling Psychology M
- Criminal Justice and Criminology M
- Early Childhood Education M
- Educational Leadership and Administration M
- Electrical Engineering M
- English M
- Environmental and Occupational Health M
- Environmental Engineering M
- Family Nurse Practitioner Studies M,D
- Health Education M
- Health Services Management and Hospital Administration M
- History M
- Human Resources Development M,D
- Industrial and Manufacturing Management M,D
- Interdisciplinary Studies M
- Kinesiology and Movement Studies M
- Marriage and Family Therapy M
- Mathematics M
- Mechanical Engineering M
- Nursing and Healthcare Administration M,D
- Nursing Education M,D
- Nursing—General M,D
- Political Science M
- Psychology—General M
- Public Administration M
- Reading Education M
- School Psychology M
- Social Sciences M
- Sociology M
- Special Education M
- Structural Engineering M
- Transportation and Highway Engineering M
- Vocational and Technical Education M,D
- Water Resources Engineering M

THE UNIVERSITY OF TEXAS HEALTH SCIENCE CENTER AT HOUSTON

- Allopathic Medicine D
- Biochemistry M,D
- Biological and Biomedical Sciences—General M,D
- Biomathematics M,D
- Biostatistics M,D
- Cancer Biology/Oncology M,D
- Cell Biology M,D
- Dentistry M,D
- Developmental Biology M,D
- Genetic Counseling M
- Genetics M,D
- Health Informatics M,D,O
- Human Genetics M,D
- Immunology M,D
- Medical Physics M,D
- Microbiology M,D
- Molecular Biology M,D
- Molecular Genetics M,D
- Molecular Pathology M,D
- Neuroscience M,D
- Nursing—General M,D
- Public Health—General M,D,O
- Virology M,D

THE UNIVERSITY OF TEXAS HEALTH SCIENCE CENTER AT SAN ANTONIO

- Acute Care/Critical Care Nursing M,D,O
- Allopathic Medicine M,D
- Biochemistry M,D
- Biological and Biomedical Sciences—General D
- Biomedical Engineering M,D
- Cell Biology M,D
- Clinical Laboratory Sciences/Medical Technology D
- Clinical Research M
- Communication Disorders M,D
- Community Health Nursing M,D,O
- Dentistry M,D,O
- Family Nurse Practitioner Studies M,D,O
- Gerontological Nursing M,D,O
- Immunology M,D
- Interdisciplinary Studies D
- Medical Physics D
- Microbiology M,D
- Molecular Medicine M,D
- Neuroscience D
- Nursing and Healthcare Administration M,D,O
- Nursing Education M,D,O
- Nursing—General M,D,O
- Occupational Therapy M,D
- Pediatric Nursing M,D,O
- Pharmacology D
- Physical Therapy M,D
- Physician Assistant Studies M,D
- Psychiatric Nursing M,D,O
- Special Education M,D
- Structural Biology M,D
- Toxicology M

THE UNIVERSITY OF TEXAS MD ANDERSON CANCER CENTER

- Genetics M

THE UNIVERSITY OF TEXAS MEDICAL BRANCH

- Allied Health—General M,D
- Allopathic Medicine D
- Bacteriology D
- Biochemistry D
- Bioinformatics D
- Biological and Biomedical Sciences—General M,D
- Biophysics D
- Cell Biology D
- Clinical Laboratory Sciences/Medical Technology M,D
- Community Health M,D
- Computational Biology D
- Genetics D
- Humanities M,D
- Immunology M,D
- Infectious Diseases D
- Microbiology M,D
- Molecular Biophysics M,D
- Neuroscience D
- Nursing—General M,D
- Occupational Therapy M
- Pathology D
- Pharmacology M,D
- Physical Therapy M,D
- Physician Assistant Studies M
- Physiology M,D
- Public Health—General M
- Rehabilitation Sciences M,D
- Structural Biology D
- Toxicology M,D
- Virology D

THE UNIVERSITY OF TEXAS OF THE PERMIAN BASIN

- Accounting M
- Applied Psychology M
- Biological and Biomedical Sciences—General M
- Business Administration and Management—General M
- Clinical Psychology M
- Computer Science M
- Counselor Education M
- Criminal Justice and Criminology M
- Early Childhood Education M
- Education—General M
- Educational Leadership and Administration M
- English as a Second Language M
- English M
- Experimental Psychology M
- Foundations and Philosophy of Education M
- Geology M
- History M
- Kinesiology and Movement Studies M
- Political Science M
- Psychology—General M
- Reading Education M
- Spanish M
- Special Education M

THE UNIVERSITY OF TEXAS RIO GRANDE VALLEY

- Accounting M
- Adult Nursing M
- Advertising and Public Relations M,O
- Allopathic Medicine D
- Anthropology M
- Art/Fine Arts M
- Biological and Biomedical Sciences—General M
- Business Administration and Management—General M,D
- Chemistry M
- Clinical Psychology M
- Communication Disorders M
- Communication—General M,O
- Computer Science M
- Counselor Education M
- Criminal Justice and Criminology M
- Early Childhood Education M
- Education of the Gifted M
- Education—General M,D
- Educational Leadership and Administration M,D
- Educational Measurement and Evaluation M
- Educational Psychology M
- Electrical Engineering M
- Elementary Education M
- Engineering Management M
- English as a Second Language M
- English M
- Exercise and Sports Science M
- Experimental Psychology M
- Family Nurse Practitioner Studies M
- Finance and Banking M,D
- History M
- Interdisciplinary Studies M
- Kinesiology and Movement Studies M
- Management Information Systems M
- Manufacturing Engineering M
- Marketing M,D
- Mathematics M
- Mechanical Engineering M
- Multilingual and Multicultural Education M
- Music Education M
- Music M
- Nursing—General M
- Occupational Therapy M
- Physics M
- Psychology—General M
- Public Administration M
- Public Affairs M
- Public Policy M
- Reading Education M
- Rehabilitation Counseling M,D
- Rhetoric M
- School Psychology M
- Secondary Education M
- Social Work M
- Sociology M
- Spanish M
- Special Education M
- Statistics M
- Systems Engineering M
- Theater M,O
- Writing M

THE UNIVERSITY OF TEXAS SOUTHWESTERN MEDICAL CENTER

- Allopathic Medicine D
- Biochemistry D
- Biological and Biomedical Sciences—General M,D
- Biomedical Engineering M,D
- Cancer Biology/Oncology D
- Cell Biology D
- Clinical Psychology D
- Developmental Biology D
- Genetics D
- Immunology D
- Microbiology D
- Molecular Biophysics D
- Neuroscience D
- Nutrition M
- Physical Therapy D
- Physician Assistant Studies M
- Rehabilitation Counseling M

THE UNIVERSITY OF THE ARTS

- Art Education M
- Art/Fine Arts M
- Industrial Design M
- Museum Education M
- Museum Studies M
- Music Education M
- Music M

UNIVERSITY OF THE CUMBERLANDS

- Accounting M
- Business Administration and Management—General M
- Business Education M,D,O
- Clinical Psychology D
- Counseling Psychology M
- Counselor Education M,D,O
- Education—General M,D,O
- Educational Leadership and Administration M,D,O
- Elementary Education M,D,O
- Marketing M,D,O
- Middle School Education M,D,O
- Physician Assistant Studies M
- Reading Education M,D,O
- Religion M
- Secondary Education M,D,O
- Special Education M,D,O
- Student Affairs M,D,O
- Theater M,D,O

UNIVERSITY OF THE DISTRICT OF COLUMBIA

- Adult Education O
- Architecture M
- Business Administration and Management—General M
- Cancer Biology/Oncology M
- Communication Disorders M
- Counseling Psychology M
- Early Childhood Education M
- Electrical Engineering M
- Elementary Education M
- Engineering and Applied Sciences—General M
- English Education M
- Homeland Security M
- Law M,D
- Legal and Justice Studies M,D
- Mathematics Education M
- Middle School Education M
- Nutrition M
- Public Administration M
- Rehabilitation Counseling M
- Secondary Education M
- Social Sciences Education M
- Water Resources M

UNIVERSITY OF THE FRASER VALLEY

- Criminal Justice and Criminology M
- Social Work M

UNIVERSITY OF THE INCARNATE WORD

- Accounting M
- Adult Education M,D
- Biological and Biomedical Sciences—General M
- Business Administration and Management—General M,D
- Clothing and Textiles M
- Communication—General M
- Database Systems M
- Distance Education Development M,D
- Education—General M,D
- Educational Leadership and Administration M
- Educational Psychology M
- Elementary Education M
- Entrepreneurship M,D
- Finance and Banking M
- Health Promotion M
- Health Services Management and Hospital Administration M
- Higher Education M,D
- Human Resources Management M
- Industrial and Organizational Psychology M
- Interdisciplinary Studies M
- International Business M
- Kinesiology and Movement Studies M,D
- Marketing M
- Mathematics Education M
- Mathematics M
- Nursing and Healthcare Administration M,D
- Nursing—General M,D
- Nutrition M
- Optometry D
- Organizational Management M,D
- Pharmacy D
- Psychology—General M
- Religion M
- Secondary Education M
- Sports Management M
- Statistics M

UNIVERSITY OF THE PACIFIC

- Biological and Biomedical Sciences—General M
- Business Administration and Management—General M
- Communication Disorders M
- Communication—General M
- Curriculum and Instruction M,D
- Dentistry M,D,O
- Education—General M,D,O
- Educational Leadership and Administration M,D
- Educational Psychology M,D,O
- Engineering and Applied Sciences—General M
- Exercise and Sports Science M
- International Affairs M,D
- Law M,D
- Music Education M
- Music M
- Pharmaceutical Sciences M,D
- Pharmacy D
- Physical Therapy M,D
- Psychology—General M
- Public Policy M,D
- School Psychology M,D,O
- Special Education M,D
- Therapies—Dance, Drama, and Music M
- Water Resources M,D

UNIVERSITY OF THE POTOMAC

- Business Administration and Management—General M

UNIVERSITY OF THE ROCKIES

- Psychology—General M,D

UNIVERSITY OF THE SACRED HEART

- Accounting M,O
- Advertising and Public Relations M
- Broadcast Journalism M,O
- Business Administration and Management—General M,O
- Communication—General M,O
- Conflict Resolution and Mediation/Peace Studies M
- Cultural Studies M
- Early Childhood Education M,O
- Education—General M,O
- Educational Media/Instructional Technology M
- English Education M,O
- Environmental and Occupational Health M
- Film, Television, and Video Production M,O
- Foreign Languages Education M,O
- Human Resources Management M
- Information Science O
- Internet and Interactive Multimedia M,O
- Legal and Justice Studies M
- Management Information Systems M
- Marketing M
- Mathematics Education M,O
- Nonprofit Management M
- Occupational Health Nursing M
- Taxation M
- Writing M,O

UNIVERSITY OF THE SCIENCES

- Biochemistry M,D
- Bioinformatics M
- Biotechnology M
- Cell Biology M
- Chemistry M,D
- Health Psychology M
- Health Services Management and Hospital Administration M,D
- Medicinal and Pharmaceutical Chemistry M,D
- Occupational Therapy M,D
- Pharmaceutical Administration M
- Pharmaceutical Sciences M,D
- Pharmacology M,D
- Pharmacy D
- Physical Therapy D
- Physician Assistant Studies M
- Public Health—General M
- Technical Writing M,O
- Toxicology M,D

UNIVERSITY OF THE SOUTHWEST

- Business Administration and Management—General M
- Counseling Psychology M
- Counselor Education M
- Curriculum and Instruction M
- Early Childhood Education M
- Education—General M
- Educational Leadership and Administration M
- English as a Second Language M
- Multilingual and Multicultural Education M
- Special Education M
- Sports Management M

UNIVERSITY OF THE VIRGIN ISLANDS

- Business Administration and Management—General M
- Education—General M
- Environmental Sciences M
- Marine Sciences M
- Mathematics Education M
- Public Administration M

UNIVERSITY OF THE WEST

- Business Administration and Management—General M
- Finance and Banking M
- International Business M
- Management Information Systems M
- Nonprofit Management M
- Psychology—General M
- Religion M,D
- Theology M

THE UNIVERSITY OF TOLEDO

Accounting	M
Analytical Chemistry	M,D
Applied Mathematics	M,D
Art Education	M,D,O
Astrophysics	M,D
Biochemistry	M,D
Bioengineering	M,D
Bioinformatics	M,O
Biological and Biomedical Sciences—General	M,D,O
Biomedical Engineering	D
Biostatistics	M,O
Business Administration and Management—General	M
Business Education	M,D,O
Cancer Biology/Oncology	M,D
Cardiovascular Sciences	M,D
Chemical Engineering	M,D
Chemistry	M,D
Civil Engineering	M,D
Clinical Psychology	M,D
Communication Disorders	M,D
Communication—General	O
Community Health Nursing	M,O
Computer Science	M,D
Counselor Education	M,D,O
Criminal Justice and Criminology	M,O
Curriculum and Instruction	M,D,O
Early Childhood Education	M,D,O
Ecology	M,D
Economics	M,D,O
Education of the Gifted	M,D,O
Education—General	M,D,O
Educational Leadership and Administration	M,D,O
Educational Measurement and Evaluation	M,D,O
Educational Media/Instructional Technology	M,D,O
Educational Psychology	M,D,O
Electrical Engineering	M,D
Elementary Education	M,D,O
Emergency Management	M,O
Engineering and Applied Sciences—General	M
English as a Second Language	M,D,O
English Education	M,D,O
English	M,O
Environmental and Occupational Health	M,O
Environmental Sciences	M,D
Epidemiology	M,O
Exercise and Sports Science	M,D
Experimental Psychology	M,D
Family Nurse Practitioner Studies	M,O
Finance and Banking	M
Foreign Languages Education	M,D,O
Foundations and Philosophy of Education	M,D,O
French	M
Gender Studies	O
Genomic Sciences	M,O
Geographic Information Systems	M,D,O
Geography	M,D,O
Geology	M,D
German	M
Gerontology	M,O
Health Education	M,D,O
Health Promotion	M,D,O
Health Services Management and Hospital Administration	M,O
Higher Education	M,D,O
History	M,D
Immunology	M,D
Industrial Hygiene	M,O
Industrial/Management Engineering	M,D
Inorganic Chemistry	M,D
International Business	M
International Health	M,O
Law	M,D
Leisure Studies	M,D
Liberal Studies	M
Marketing	M
Materials Sciences	M,D
Mathematics Education	M,D,O
Mathematics	M,D
Mechanical Engineering	M,D
Medical Physics	M,D
Medicinal and Pharmaceutical Chemistry	M,D
Middle School Education	M,D,O
Music Education	M,O
Music	M,O
Neuroscience	M,D
Nonprofit Management	M,O
Nursing and Healthcare Administration	M,O
Nursing Education	M,O
Nursing—General	M,D,O
Nutrition	M,O
Occupational Therapy	M,D
Oral and Dental Sciences	M
Organic Chemistry	M,D
Pathology	M,O
Pediatric Nursing	M,O
Pharmaceutical Administration	M
Pharmaceutical Sciences	M
Pharmacology	M,D
Philosophy	M
Physical Chemistry	M,D
Physical Education	M
Physical Therapy	M,D
Physician Assistant Studies	M
Physics	M,D
Political Science	M,O
Psychology—General	M,D
Public Administration	M,O
Public Health—General	M,O
Recreation and Park Management	M,D
School Psychology	M,D,O
Science Education	M,D,O
Secondary Education	M,D,O
Social Sciences Education	M,D,O
Social Work	M,O
Sociology	M
Spanish	M
Special Education	M,D,O
Statistics	M,D
Urban and Regional Planning	M,D,O
Vocational and Technical Education	M,D,O
Women's Studies	O
Writing	M,O

UNIVERSITY OF TORONTO

Aerospace/Aeronautical Engineering	M,D
Allopathic Medicine	M,D
Anthropology	M,D
Architecture	M
Art History	M,D
Asian Studies	M,D
Astronomy	M,D
Astrophysics	M,D
Biochemistry	M,D
Bioethics	M,D
Biomedical Engineering	M,D
Biophysics	M,D
Biostatistics	M,D
Biotechnology	M
Business Administration and Management—General	M,D
Cell Biology	M,D
Chemical Engineering	M,D
Chemistry	M,D
Civil Engineering	M,D
Classics	M,D
Communication Disorders	M,D
Community Health	M,D
Comparative Literature	M,D
Computer Engineering	M,D
Computer Science	M,D
Criminal Justice and Criminology	M,D
Dentistry	D
East European and Russian Studies	M
Ecology	M,D
Economics	M,D
Education—General	M,D
Electrical Engineering	M,D
Engineering and Applied Sciences—General	M,D
English	M,D
Environmental and Occupational Health	M,D
Environmental Sciences	M,D
Epidemiology	M,D
Evolutionary Biology	M,D
Film, Television, and Video Theory and Criticism	M,D
Finance and Banking	M
Forestry	M,D
French	M,D
Gender Studies	M,D
Genetic Counseling	M,D
Geography	M,D
Geology	M,D
German	M,D
Health Informatics	M
Health Physics/Radiological Health	M,D
Health Promotion	M,D
Health Services Management and Hospital Administration	M
History of Science and Technology	M,D
History	M,D
Human Resources Management	M,D
Immunology	M,D
Industrial and Labor Relations	M,D
Industrial/Management Engineering	M,D
Information Studies	M,D
International Affairs	M
Italian	M,D
Kinesiology and Movement Studies	M,D
Landscape Architecture	M
Law	M,D
Linguistics	M,D
Management of Technology	M
Manufacturing Engineering	M
Materials Engineering	M,D
Materials Sciences	M,D
Mathematical and Computational Finance	M
Mathematics	M,D
Mechanical Engineering	M,D
Medieval and Renaissance Studies	M,D
Molecular Genetics	M,D
Museum Studies	M
Music Education	M,D
Music	M,D
Near and Middle Eastern Studies	M,D
Nursing—General	M,D
Nutrition	M,D
Occupational Therapy	M
Oral and Dental Sciences	M,D
Pathobiology	M,D
Pharmaceutical Sciences	M,D
Pharmacology	M,D
Philosophy	M,D
Physical Education	M,D
Physical Therapy	M
Physics	M,D
Physiology	M,D
Political Science	M,D
Portuguese	M,D
Psychology—General	M,D
Public Health—General	M,D
Rehabilitation Sciences	M,D
Religion	M,D
Slavic Languages	M,D
Social Sciences	M,D
Social Work	M,D
Sociology	M,D
Spanish	M,D
Statistics	M,D
Systems Biology	M,D
Theater	M,D
Urban and Regional Planning	M,D
Urban Design	M,D
Women's Studies	M,D
Writing	M,D

THE UNIVERSITY OF TULSA

Accounting	M
American Indian/Native American Studies	M,D,O
Anthropology	M,D
Applied Mathematics	
Art/Fine Arts	M
Biochemistry	M
Biological and Biomedical Sciences—General	M,D
Business Administration and Management—General	M
Chemical Engineering	M,D
Chemistry	M,D
Clinical Psychology	M,D
Communication Disorders	M
Computer Engineering	M,D
Computer Science	M,D
Education—General	M
Electrical Engineering	M,D
Elementary Education	M
Energy Management and Policy	M
Engineering and Applied Sciences—General	M,D
Engineering Physics	M
English Education	M
English	M,D
Environmental Law	M,D,O
Finance and Banking	M
Financial Engineering	M
Geophysics	M,D
Geosciences	M,D
Health Law	M,D,O
History	M
Industrial and Organizational Psychology	M,D
Investment Management	M
Law	M,D,O
Mathematics Education	M
Mathematics	M,D
Mechanical Engineering	M,D
Museum Studies	M
Petroleum Engineering	M,D
Physics	M,D
Psychology—General	M,D
Science Education	M
Secondary Education	M

UNIVERSITY OF UTAH

Accounting	M,D
Allopathic Medicine	D
American Studies	M,D
Anatomy	D
Anthropology	M,D
Architecture	M
Art Education	M
Art History	M
Art/Fine Arts	M
Asian Studies	M
Atmospheric Sciences	M,D
Biochemistry	M,D
Bioengineering	M,D*
Bioinformatics	M,D,O
Biological and Biomedical Sciences—General	M,D,O
Biostatistics	M,D
Biotechnology	M
Business Administration and Management—General	M,D,O
Cancer Biology/Oncology	M,D
Chemical Engineering	M,D
Chemical Physics	M,D
Chemistry	M,D
Child and Family Studies	M
Civil Engineering	M,D
Clinical Laboratory Sciences/Medical Technology	M
Clinical Psychology	M,D
Communication Disorders	M,D
Communication—General	M,D
Comparative Literature	M,D
Computational Sciences	M
Computer and Information Systems Security	M,O
Computer Science	M,D
Consumer Economics	M
Counseling Psychology	M,D
Counselor Education	M,D
Dance	M
Dentistry	D
Early Childhood Education	M,D
Economics	M,D
Education—General	M,D
Educational Leadership and Administration	M,D
Educational Media/Instructional Technology	M,D
Educational Psychology	M,D
Electrical Engineering	M,D
Elementary Education	M,D
Engineering and Applied Sciences—General	M,D
English	M,D
Environmental Engineering	M,D
Environmental Sciences	M
Exercise and Sports Science	M,D
Film, Television, and Video Production	M
Finance and Banking	M,D
Foreign Languages Education	M,D
Foundations and Philosophy of Education	M,D
French	M,D
Game Design and Development	M
Geographic Information Systems	M,D
Geography	M,D
Geological Engineering	M,D
Geology	M,D
Geophysics	M,D
Gerontological Nursing	M,O
Gerontology	M,O
Graphic Design	M
Health Education	M,D
Health Promotion	M,D
Health Services Management and Hospital Administration	M,D
Health Services Research	M,D
Higher Education	M,D
History	M,D
Human Development	M
Human Genetics	M,D
Humanities	M
Industrial and Manufacturing Management	M,D,O
International Affairs	M,D
Internet and Interactive Multimedia	M
Latin American Studies	M
Law	M,D
Leisure Studies	M,D
Linguistics	M,D
Management Information Systems	M,D,O
Management Strategy and Policy	M,D,O
Marketing	M,D
Materials Engineering	M,D
Materials Sciences	M,D
Mathematics Education	M,D
Mathematics	M,D
Mechanical Engineering	M,D
Medical Physics	M,D
Medicinal and Pharmaceutical Chemistry	M,D
Metallurgical Engineering and Metallurgy	M,D
Mineral/Mining Engineering	M,D
Molecular Biology	D
Music Education	M,D
Music	M,D
Near and Middle Eastern Languages	M,D
Near and Middle Eastern Studies	M,D
Neurobiology	D
Neuroscience	D
Nuclear Engineering	M,D
Nursing—General	M,D
Nutrition	M,D
Occupational Therapy	M,D
Organizational Behavior	M,D
Pathology	M,D
Petroleum Engineering	M,D
Pharmaceutical Administration	M,D
Pharmaceutical Sciences	M,D
Pharmacology	D
Pharmacy	D
Philosophy	M,D
Photography	M
Physical Therapy	D
Physician Assistant Studies	M
Physics	M,D
Physiology	M,D
Political Science	M,D
Psychology—General	D
Public Administration	M,D
Public Health—General	M,D
Public Policy	M
Reading Education	M,D
Real Estate	M
Recreation and Park Management	M,D
Rehabilitation Sciences	D
Rhetoric	M,D
School Psychology	M,D
Science Education	M,D
Secondary Education	M,D
Social Work	M,D
Sociology	M,D
Software Engineering	M,O
Spanish	M,D
Special Education	M,D
Statistics	M,D
Student Affairs	M,D
Systems Engineering	M,O
Toxicology	D
Urban and Regional Planning	M,D
Urban Design	M,D
Writing	M,D

UNIVERSITY OF VALLEY FORGE

Music	M
Religion	M
Theology	M

UNIVERSITY OF VERMONT

Accounting	M
Agricultural Economics and Agribusiness	M
Agricultural Sciences—General	M,D
Agronomy and Soil Sciences	M,D
Allied Health—General	M,D
Animal Sciences	M,D
Applied Economics	M
Biological and Biomedical Sciences—General	M,D,O
Biomedical Engineering	D
Biostatistics	M
Business Administration and Management—General	M
Cell Biology	D
Chemistry	M,D
Civil Engineering	M,D

*M—masters degree; D—doctorate; O—other advanced degree; *—Close-Up and/or Display*

Clinical Laboratory Sciences/Medical Technology	M,D,O
Clinical Psychology	D
Communication Disorders	M
Communication—General	M
Computer Science	M,D
Counseling Psychology	M
Counselor Education	M
Curriculum and Instruction	M
Education—General	M,D
Educational Leadership and Administration	M,D
Electrical Engineering	M,D
Engineering and Applied Sciences—General	M,D
English	M
Environmental Engineering	M,D
Food Science and Technology	M,D
Forestry	M,D
Geology	M
German	M
Historic Preservation	M
History	M
Horticulture	M,D
Materials Sciences	M,D
Mathematics Education	M
Mathematics	M
Mechanical Engineering	M,D
Molecular Biology	D
Natural Resources	M,D
Neuroscience	D
Nursing—General	M,D
Nutrition	M,D
Pathology	M
Pharmacology	M,D
Physical Therapy	D
Physics	M
Plant Biology	M,D
Plant Sciences	M,D
Psychology—General	D
Public Administration	M
Science Education	M,D
Social Work	M
Special Education	M
Statistics	M

UNIVERSITY OF VICTORIA

Anthropology	M
Art Education	M,D
Art History	M,D
Art/Fine Arts	M
Asian Studies	M
Astronomy	M,D
Astrophysics	M,D
Biochemistry	M,D
Biological and Biomedical Sciences—General	M,D
Business Administration and Management—General	M
Chemistry	M,D
Child and Family Studies	M,D
Classics	M,D
Clinical Psychology	M,D
Computer Art and Design	M
Computer Engineering	M,D
Computer Science	M,D
Condensed Matter Physics	M,D
Conflict Resolution and Mediation/Peace Studies	M,D
Counseling Psychology	M,D
Counselor Education	M,D
Curriculum and Instruction	M,D
Developmental Psychology	M,D
Early Childhood Education	M,D
Economics	M,D
Education—General	M,D
Educational Leadership and Administration	M,D
Educational Measurement and Evaluation	M,D
Educational Psychology	M,D
Electrical Engineering	M,D
Engineering and Applied Sciences—General	M,D
English Education	M,D
English	M,D
Environmental Education	M,D
Experimental Psychology	M,D
Family Nurse Practitioner Studies	M,D
Film, Television, and Video Production	M
Foreign Languages Education	M
Foundations and Philosophy of Education	M,D
French	M
Geography	M,D
Geosciences	M,D
German	M
Health Informatics	M
Hispanic Studies	M
History	M,D
Human Development	M,D
Italian	M
Kinesiology and Movement Studies	M
Law	M,D
Leisure Studies	M
Linguistics	M,D
Mathematics Education	M,D
Mathematics	M,D
Mechanical Engineering	M,D
Medical Physics	M,D
Microbiology	M,D
Music Education	M,D
Music	M,D
Nursing and Healthcare Administration	M,D
Nursing Education	M,D
Nursing—General	M,D
Oceanography	M,D
Pacific Area/Pacific Rim Studies	M
Philosophy	M
Photography	M
Physical Education	M
Physics	M,D
Political Science	M,D
Psychology—General	M,D
Public Administration	M,D
Reading Education	M,D
Science Education	M,D
Social Psychology	M,D
Social Sciences Education	M,D
Social Work	M
Sociology	M,D
Special Education	M,D
Statistics	M,D
Theater	M
Theoretical Physics	M,D
Vocational and Technical Education	M,D
Writing	M

UNIVERSITY OF VIRGINIA

Accounting	M
Acute Care/Critical Care Nursing	M,D
Aerospace/Aeronautical Engineering	M,D
Allopathic Medicine	M,D
Anthropology	M,D
Architectural History	M,D
Art History	M,D
Asian Studies	M
Astronomy	M,D
Biochemistry	D
Biological and Biomedical Sciences—General	M,D
Biomedical Engineering	M,D
Biophysics	M,D
Business Administration and Management—General	M,D,O
Cell Biology	D
Chemical Engineering	M,D
Chemistry	M,D
Civil Engineering	M,D
Classics	M,D
Clinical Psychology	D
Clinical Research	M
Communication Disorders	M
Community Health	M,D
Computer Engineering	M,D
Computer Science	M,D
Construction Engineering	D
Counselor Education	M,D,O
Curriculum and Instruction	M,D,O
Database Systems	M
Early Childhood Education	M,D
Economics	M,D
Education of the Gifted	M,D,O
Education—General	M,D,O
Educational Leadership and Administration	M,D,O
Educational Measurement and Evaluation	M,D,O
Educational Media/Instructional Technology	M,D,O
Educational Psychology	M,D,O
Electrical Engineering	M,D
Elementary Education	M,D,O
Engineering and Applied Sciences—General	M,D
Engineering Physics	M,D
English Education	M,D,O
English	M,D
Environmental Sciences	M,D
Finance and Banking	M
Foreign Languages Education	M,D,O
French	M,D
German	M,D
Health Informatics	M
Health Services Management and Hospital Administration	M
Health Services Research	M
Higher Education	M,D,O
History	M,D
Interdisciplinary Studies	M,D
International Affairs	M,D
International Business	M,O
Italian	M
Kinesiology and Movement Studies	M,D
Landscape Architecture	M
Law	M,D
Linguistics	M
Management of Technology	M
Management Strategy and Policy	M,O
Marketing	M
Materials Sciences	M,D
Mathematics Education	M,D,O
Mathematics	M,D
Mechanical Engineering	M,D
Microbiology	D
Molecular Genetics	D
Molecular Physiology	M,D
Music	M,D
Near and Middle Eastern Studies	M
Neuroscience	D
Nursing and Healthcare Administration	M,D
Nursing—General	M,D
Pathology	D
Pharmacology	D
Philosophy	M,D
Physical Education	M,D
Physics	M,D
Physiology	D
Political Science	M,D
Psychiatric Nursing	M,D
Psychology—General	M,D
Public Health—General	M,D
Public Policy	M
Reading Education	M,D
Religion	M,D
Romance Languages	M,D
School Psychology	M,D
Science Education	M,D,O
Slavic Languages	M,D
Social Sciences Education	M,D,O
Sociology	M,D
Spanish	M,D
Special Education	M,D,O
Statistics	M,D
Student Affairs	M,D,O
Systems Engineering	M,D
Theater	M
Urban and Regional Planning	M
Writing	M

UNIVERSITY OF WASHINGTON

Accounting	M,D
Aerospace/Aeronautical Engineering	M,D
Allopathic Medicine	D
Animal Behavior	D
Anthropology	M,D
Applied Arts and Design—General	M
Applied Mathematics	M,D
Applied Physics	M,D
Architecture	M,D,O
Art History	M,D
Art/Fine Arts	M
Asian Languages	M,D
Asian Studies	M,D
Astronomy	M,D
Atmospheric Sciences	M,D
Bacteriology	D
Biochemistry	D
Bioengineering	M,D
Bioethics	M
Bioinformatics	M,D
Biological and Biomedical Sciences—General	M,D
Biophysics	D
Biostatistics	M,D
Biotechnology	D
Business Administration and Management—General	M,D
Business Education	M,D
Cell Biology	D*
Chemical Engineering	M,D
Chemistry	M,D
Chinese	M,D
Civil Engineering	M,D
Classics	M,D
Clinical Laboratory Sciences/Medical Technology	M
Clinical Psychology	D
Clinical Research	M,D
Cognitive Sciences	D
Communication Disorders	M,D
Communication—General	M,D
Community Health	M,D
Comparative Literature	M,D
Computational Sciences	M,D
Computer Science	M,D
Construction Engineering	M,D
Construction Management	M
Curriculum and Instruction	M,D
Dance	M
Dentistry	D
Developmental Psychology	D
East European and Russian Studies	M
Ecology	M,D
Economics	M,D
Education—General	M,D
Educational Leadership and Administration	M,D
Educational Measurement and Evaluation	M,D
Educational Media/Instructional Technology	M,D
Educational Policy	M,D
Educational Psychology	M,D
Electrical Engineering	M,D
Engineering and Applied Sciences—General	M,D,O
English as a Second Language	M,D
English Education	M,D
English	M,D
Entrepreneurship	M,D
Environmental and Occupational Health	M,D
Environmental Engineering	M,D
Environmental Management and Policy	M,D
Epidemiology	M,D
Fish, Game, and Wildlife Management	M,D
Forestry	M,D
Foundations and Philosophy of Education	M,D
French	M,D
Genetics	M,D
Genomic Sciences	D
Geography	M,D
Geology	M,D
Geophysics	M,D
Geotechnical Engineering	M,D
German	M,D
Health Informatics	M,D
Health Services Management and Hospital Administration	M
Health Services Research	M,D
Higher Education	M,D
Hispanic and Latin American Languages	M
Historic Preservation	O
History	M,D
Horticulture	M,D
Human Development	M,D
Hydrology	M,D
Immunology	D
Industrial Design	M
Industrial/Management Engineering	M,D
Information Science	M,D
Intellectual Property Law	M,D
International Affairs	D
International Business	M,D,O
International Health	M,D
Italian	M,D
Japanese	M,D
Landscape Architecture	M
Law	M,D
Legal and Justice Studies	M,D
Library Science	M,D
Lighting Design	M,D,O
Linguistics	M,D
Logistics	O
Management Information Systems	M,D
Management of Technology	M,D
Marine Affairs	M,O
Marine Geology	M,D
Materials Engineering	M,D
Materials Sciences	M,D
Maternal and Child Health	M,D
Mathematics Education	M,D
Mathematics	M,D
Mechanical Engineering	M,D
Mechanics	M,D
Medical Informatics	M,D
Medicinal and Pharmaceutical Chemistry	D
Microbiology	D
Molecular Biology	D
Molecular Medicine	D
Multilingual and Multicultural Education	M,D
Museum Studies	M
Music Education	M,D
Music	M,D
Nanotechnology	M,D
Natural Resources	M,D
Near and Middle Eastern Studies	M,D
Neurobiology	D
Nursing—General	M,D,O
Nutrition	M,D
Occupational Therapy	M,D
Oceanography	M,D
Oral and Dental Sciences	M,D,O
Parasitology	D
Pathobiology	D
Pathology	D
Pharmaceutical Sciences	M,D
Pharmacology	D
Pharmacy	M,D
Philosophy	M,D
Photography	M
Physical Education	M,D
Physical Therapy	M,D
Physics	M,D
Physiology	D
Political Science	M,D
Portuguese	M
Psychology—General	D
Public Administration	M,D
Public Affairs	M,D
Public Health—General	M
Public Policy	M,D
Reading Education	M,D
Rehabilitation Sciences	M,D
Religion	M,D
Russian	M,D
Scandinavian Languages	M,D
School Psychology	M,D
Science Education	M,D
Slavic Languages	M,D
Social Psychology	D
Social Sciences Education	M,D
Social Sciences	M,D
Social Work	M,D
Sociology	M,D
Spanish	M
Special Education	M,D
Statistics	M,D
Structural Biology	D
Structural Engineering	M,D
Supply Chain Management	M,D
Sustainable Development	M,D
Taxation	M,D
Technical Communication	M,D,O
Theater	M,D
Toxicology	M,D
Transportation and Highway Engineering	M,D
Transportation Management	O
Urban and Regional Planning	M,D
Urban Design	M,D,O
Veterinary Sciences	M
Women's Studies	D
Writing	M

UNIVERSITY OF WASHINGTON, BOTHELL

Business Administration and Management—General	M
Computer Engineering	M
Cultural Studies	M
Education—General	M
Educational Leadership and Administration	M
Middle School Education	M
Nursing—General	M
Public Policy	M
Secondary Education	M
Software Engineering	M
Writing	M

UNIVERSITY OF WASHINGTON, TACOMA

Accounting	M
Business Administration and Management—General	M
Community Health Nursing	M
Computer Engineering	M
Education—General	M
Educational Leadership and Administration	M
Elementary Education	M
Finance and Banking	M
Interdisciplinary Studies	M
Mathematics Education	M
Nursing and Healthcare Administration	M
Nursing Education	M
Nursing—General	M
Science Education	M
Social Work	M

Software Engineering	M
Special Education	M

UNIVERSITY OF WATERLOO

Accounting	M,D
Actuarial Science	M,D
Anthropology	M
Applied Mathematics	M,D
Architecture	M
Art/Fine Arts	M
Biochemistry	M,D
Biological and Biomedical Sciences—General	M,D
Biostatistics	M,D
Business Administration and Management—General	M
Chemical Engineering	M,D
Chemistry	M,D
Civil Engineering	M,D
Computer Engineering	M,D
Computer Science	M,D
Economic Development	M
Economics	M,D
Electrical Engineering	M,D
Engineering and Applied Sciences—General	M,D
Engineering Management	M,D
English	M,D
Entrepreneurship	M
Environmental Engineering	M,D
Environmental Management and Policy	M,D
Environmental Sciences	M,D
Finance and Banking	M,D
French	M,D
Geography	M,D
Geosciences	M,D
German	M,D
Health Education	M,D
Health Informatics	M,D
History	M,D
Information Science	M,D
International Affairs	M,D
Kinesiology and Movement Studies	M,D
Leisure Studies	M,D
Management of Technology	M,D
Mathematics	M,D
Mechanical Engineering	M,D
Near and Middle Eastern Studies	M
Operations Research	M,D
Optometry	M,D
Philosophy	M,D
Physics	M,D
Political Science	M,D
Psychology—General	M,D
Public Affairs	M
Public Health—General	M,D
Recreation and Park Management	M,D
Religion	D
Russian	M,D
Sociology	M,D
Software Engineering	M,D
Statistics	M,D
Systems Engineering	M,D
Taxation	M,D
Technical Writing	M,D
Urban and Regional Planning	M,D
Vision Sciences	M,D

THE UNIVERSITY OF WEST ALABAMA

Adult Education	M
Business Administration and Management—General	M
Child Development	M,O
Counselor Education	M,O
Curriculum and Instruction	M,O
Early Childhood Education	M,O
Education—General	M,O
Educational Leadership and Administration	M,O
Educational Media/Instructional Technology	M,O
Elementary Education	M,O
English Education	M
Experimental Psychology	M
Finance and Banking	M
Higher Education	M
History	M
Marriage and Family Therapy	M
Mathematics Education	M
Physical Education	M
School Psychology	M,O
Science Education	M
Secondary Education	M
Social Sciences Education	M
Special Education	M,O

THE UNIVERSITY OF WESTERN ONTARIO

Allopathic Medicine	M,D
Anatomy	M,D
Anthropology	M,D
Applied Mathematics	M,D
Astronomy	M,D
Biochemical Engineering	M,D
Biochemistry	M,D
Biological and Biomedical Sciences—General	M,D
Biophysics	M,D
Biostatistics	M,D
Business Administration and Management—General	M,D
Cell Biology	M,D
Chemical Engineering	M,D
Chemistry	M,D
Civil Engineering	M,D
Classics	M
Communication Disorders	M
Comparative Literature	M,D
Computer Engineering	M,D
Computer Science	M,D
Counseling Psychology	M
Curriculum and Instruction	M
Dentistry	D
Economics	M,D
Education—General	M
Educational Policy	M
Educational Psychology	M
Electrical Engineering	M,D
Engineering and Applied Sciences—General	M,D
English	M,D
Entrepreneurship	M,D
Environmental Engineering	M,D
Environmental Sciences	M,D
Epidemiology	M,D
Finance and Banking	M,D
French	M,D
Geography	M,D
Geology	M,D
Geophysics	M,D
Geosciences	M,D
Health Services Management and Hospital Administration	M,D
History	M,D
Immunology	M,D
Information Studies	M,D
Interdisciplinary Studies	M,D
International Business	M,D
Journalism	M
Kinesiology and Movement Studies	M,D
Law	M,D,O
Library Science	M,D
Management Strategy and Policy	M,D
Marketing	M,D
Materials Engineering	M,D
Mathematics	M,D
Mechanical Engineering	M,D
Media Studies	M,D
Microbiology	M,D
Music	M,D
Neuroscience	M,D
Nursing—General	M,D
Occupational Therapy	M
Oral and Dental Sciences	M
Pathology	M,D
Philosophy	M,D
Physical Therapy	M,O
Physics	M,D
Physiology	M,D
Political Science	M,D
Psychology—General	M,D
Sociology	M,D
Spanish	M,D
Special Education	M
Statistics	M,D
Sustainable Development	M,D

UNIVERSITY OF WESTERN STATES

Chiropractic	D*

UNIVERSITY OF WEST FLORIDA

Accounting	M
Anthropology	M
Applied Statistics	M
Archaeology	M
Biochemistry	M
Biological and Biomedical Sciences—General	M
Biotechnology	M
Business Administration and Management—General	M
Communication—General	M
Community Health	M
Computer Science	M
Counseling Psychology	M
Counselor Education	M
Criminal Justice and Criminology	M
Curriculum and Instruction	M,D,O
Database Systems	M
Early Childhood Education	M
Education—General	D
Educational Leadership and Administration	M,D,O
Educational Media/Instructional Technology	M,D
Elementary Education	M
English	M
Environmental and Occupational Health	M
Environmental Biology	M
Environmental Sciences	M
Exercise and Sports Science	M
Geosciences	M
Gerontology	M
Health Education	M
History	M
Industrial and Organizational Psychology	M
Leisure Studies	M
Management Strategy and Policy	M
Marine Affairs	M
Mathematics	M
Middle School Education	M,O
Military and Defense Studies	M
Multilingual and Multicultural Education	D
Nursing and Healthcare Administration	M
Nursing—General	M
Physical Education	M,D
Political Science	M
Psychology—General	M
Public Administration	M
Public Health—General	M
Public History	M
Reading Education	M
Science Education	M,D
Secondary Education	M,O
Social Sciences Education	D
Social Work	M
Sociology	M
Software Engineering	M
Special Education	M
Student Affairs	M
Vocational and Technical Education	M,D,O
Writing	M

UNIVERSITY OF WEST GEORGIA

Accounting	M
Biological and Biomedical Sciences—General	M,O
Business Administration and Management—General	M
Business Education	M,D,O
Communication Disorders	M,D,O
Computer Science	M,O
Counselor Education	M,D,O
Criminal Justice and Criminology	M,D,O
Early Childhood Education	M,D,O
Education—General	M,D,O
Educational Leadership and Administration	M,D,O
Educational Media/Instructional Technology	M,D,O
English	M,O
Geographic Information Systems	M,O
Health Services Management and Hospital Administration	M,D,O
History	M,O
Mathematics	M,O
Museum Studies	M,O
Music Education	M,O
Music	M,O
Nonprofit Management	M,D,O
Nursing Education	M,D,O
Nursing—General	M,D,O
Psychology—General	M,D,O
Public Administration	M,D,O
Public History	M,O
Reading Education	M,D,O
Secondary Education	M,D,O
Sociology	M,D,O
Special Education	M,D,O
Urban and Regional Planning	M,D,O

UNIVERSITY OF WINDSOR

Applied Psychology	M,D
Art/Fine Arts	M
Biochemistry	M,D
Biological and Biomedical Sciences—General	M,D
Biopsychology	M,D
Business Administration and Management—General	M
Chemistry	M,D
Civil Engineering	M,D
Clinical Psychology	M,D
Communication—General	M
Computer Science	M,D
Criminal Justice and Criminology	M,D
Economics	M
Education—General	M,D
Electrical Engineering	M,D
Engineering and Applied Sciences—General	M,D
English	M
Environmental Engineering	M,D
Environmental Sciences	M,D
Geosciences	M,D
History	M
Industrial/Management Engineering	M,D
Kinesiology and Movement Studies	M
Legal and Justice Studies	M
Manufacturing Engineering	M,D
Materials Engineering	M,D
Mathematics	M,D
Mechanical Engineering	M,D
Nursing—General	M
Philosophy	M
Physics	M,D
Political Science	M
Psychology—General	M,D
Social Psychology	M,D
Social Work	M
Sociology	M,D
Statistics	M,D
Writing	M

THE UNIVERSITY OF WINNIPEG

History	M
Marriage and Family Therapy	M,O
Public Administration	M
Religion	M
Theology	M,O

UNIVERSITY OF WISCONSIN–EAU CLAIRE

Adult Nursing	M,D
Business Administration and Management—General	M
Communication Disorders	M
Education—General	M
English	M
Family Nurse Practitioner Studies	M,D
Gerontological Nursing	M,D
History	M
Library Science	M
Nursing and Healthcare Administration	M,D
Nursing Education	M,D
Nursing—General	M,D
Psychology—General	M,O
Reading Education	M
School Psychology	M,O
Secondary Education	M
Special Education	M
Writing	M

UNIVERSITY OF WISCONSIN–GREEN BAY

Business Administration and Management—General	M
Education—General	M
Environmental Management and Policy	M
Environmental Sciences	M
Nursing and Healthcare Administration	M
Social Work	M
Sustainability Management	M

UNIVERSITY OF WISCONSIN–LA CROSSE

Athletic Training and Sports Medicine	M
Biological and Biomedical Sciences—General	M
Business Administration and Management—General	M
Cancer Biology/Oncology	M
Cell Biology	M
Community Health	M
Database Systems	M
Education—General	M
Exercise and Sports Science	M
Health Education	M
Higher Education	M,D
Marine Sciences	M
Medical Microbiology	M
Microbiology	M
Molecular Biology	M
Nurse Anesthesia	M
Occupational Therapy	M
Physical Education	M
Physical Therapy	D
Physician Assistant Studies	M
Physiology	M
Psychology—General	M,O
Reading Education	M
Recreation and Park Management	M
Rehabilitation Sciences	M
School Psychology	M,O
Software Engineering	M
Special Education	M
Student Affairs	M,D

UNIVERSITY OF WISCONSIN–MADISON

Accounting	M,D
Adult Nursing	D
African Studies	M,D
African-American Studies	M
Agricultural Economics and Agribusiness	M,D
Agricultural Engineering	M,D
Agricultural Sciences—General	M,D
Agronomy and Soil Sciences	M,D
Allopathic Medicine	D
American Studies	M,D
Animal Sciences	M,D
Anthropology	D
Applied Arts and Design—General	M,D
Applied Economics	M,D
Archaeology	D
Art Education	M,D
Art History	M,D
Art/Fine Arts	M
Arts Administration	M
Asian Languages	M,D
Asian Studies	M,D
Astronomy	D
Atmospheric Sciences	M,D
Bacteriology	M
Biochemistry	M,D
Bioinformatics	M
Biological and Biomedical Sciences—General	
Biomedical Engineering	M,D
Biometry	M
Biophysics	D
Biopsychology	D
Botany	M,D
Business Administration and Management—General	M
Cancer Biology/Oncology	D
Cell Biology	D
Chemical Engineering	M,D
Chemistry	M,D
Child and Family Studies	M,D
Chinese	M,D
Civil Engineering	M,D
Classics	M,D
Clinical Psychology	D
Clinical Research	M,D
Cognitive Sciences	D
Communication Disorders	M,D
Communication—General	M,D
Community Health	M,D*
Comparative Literature	M,D
Computer and Information Systems Security	M
Computer Science	M,D
Conservation Biology	M
Consumer Economics	M,D
Counseling Psychology	D
Counselor Education	M
Cultural Anthropology	D
Curriculum and Instruction	M,D
Demography and Population Studies	M,D
Developmental Psychology	D
Ecology	M
Economics	D
Education—General	M,D,O
Educational Leadership and Administration	M,D,O
Educational Policy	M,D,O
Educational Psychology	M,D
Electrical Engineering	M,D
Engineering and Applied Sciences—General	M,D
Engineering Physics	M,D
English	M,D
Entomology	M,D

*M—masters degree; D—doctorate; O—other advanced degree; *—Close-Up and/or Display*

Environmental Biology M,D
Environmental Engineering M,D
Epidemiology M,D
Family and Consumer Sciences-General M,D
Film, Television, and Video Theory and Criticism M,D
Finance and Banking M,D
Fish, Game, and Wildlife Management M,D
Folklore M,D
Food Science and Technology M,D
Foreign Languages Education M,D
Forestry M,D
French M,D,O
Genetic Counseling M,D
Genetics M,D
Geographic Information Systems M,D,O
Geography M,D,O
Geological Engineering M,D
Geology M,D
Geophysics M,D
German M,D
Gerontological Nursing D
Higher Education M,D,O
History of Science and Technology M,D
History M,D
Horticulture M,D
Human Development M,D
Human Resources Management M,D
Industrial/Management Engineering M,D
Information Studies M,D
Insurance M,D
International and Comparative Education M,D,O
Investment Management D
Italian M,D
Japanese M,D
Jewish Studies M,D
Journalism M,D
Kinesiology and Movement Studies M,D
Landscape Architecture M
Latin American Studies M,D
Law M,D
Library Science M,D
Linguistics M,D
Management Information Systems D
Management of Technology M
Manufacturing Engineering M
Marine Sciences M,D
Marketing Research M
Marketing D
Mass Communication M,D
Materials Engineering M,D
Mathematics Education M,D
Mathematics D
Mechanical Engineering M,D
Mechanics M,D
Media Studies M,D
Medical Microbiology D
Medical Physics M,D
Microbiology D
Molecular Biology D
Molecular Pathology D
Music Education M,D
Music M,D
Natural Resources M,D
Near and Middle Eastern Languages M,D
Near and Middle Eastern Studies M,D
Neuroscience D
Nuclear Engineering M,D
Nursing—General D
Nutrition M,D
Occupational Therapy M,D
Oceanography M,D
Pathology D
Pediatric Nursing D
Pharmaceutical Administration M,D
Pharmaceutical Sciences M,D
Pharmacology D
Pharmacy D
Philosophy M,D
Physical Therapy D
Physician Assistant Studies M
Physics M,D
Physiology M,D
Plant Pathology M,D
Plant Sciences M,D
Political Science D
Polymer Science and Engineering M,D
Portuguese M,D
Psychiatric Nursing D
Psychology—General D
Public Affairs M
Public Health—General M
Real Estate M,D
Rehabilitation Counseling M,D
Rhetoric M,D
Rural Sociology M,D
Scandinavian Languages M,D
Science Education M,D
Slavic Languages M,D
Social Psychology D
Social Work M,D
Sociology M,D
Spanish M,D
Special Education M,D
Speech and Interpersonal Communication M,D
Statistics M,D
Supply Chain Management M
Sustainable Development M
Systems Engineering M,D
Taxation M
Theater M,D
Toxicology M,D
Urban and Regional Planning M,D
Veterinary Medicine M,D
Veterinary Sciences M,D
Water Resources M
Women's Studies M,D
Writing M,D
Zoology M,D

UNIVERSITY OF WISCONSIN–MILWAUKEE

Adult Education D
African Studies D
Allied Health—General M,D,O
American Indian/Native American Studies M
Anthropology M,D,O
Archaeology M,D,O
Architecture M,D,O
Archives/Archival Administration M,D,O
Art History M,O
Biological and Biomedical Sciences—General M,D
Biological Anthropology M,D,O
Business Administration and Management—General M,D,O
Cancer Biology/Oncology M
Chemistry M,D
Civil Engineering M,D,O
Classics M,O
Clinical Psychology M,D
Communication Disorders M,O
Communication—General M,D,O
Comparative Literature M,D,O
Computer Engineering M,D,O
Computer Science M
Conflict Resolution and Mediation/Peace Studies M,D,O
Counseling Psychology M,D
Counselor Education M,D
Criminal Justice and Criminology M
Curriculum and Instruction M,D
Developmental Psychology M,D
Early Childhood Education M
Economics M,D
Education—General M,D,O
Educational Leadership and Administration M,D,O
Educational Measurement and Evaluation M,D
Educational Psychology M,D
Electrical Engineering M,D,O
Elementary Education M
Engineering and Applied Sciences—General M,D,O
Engineering Management M,D,O
English as a Second Language M,D,O
English M,D,O
Environmental and Occupational Health D
Ergonomics and Human Factors M,D,O
Family Nurse Practitioner Studies M,D,O
Foreign Languages Education M,O
Foundations and Philosophy of Education M,D
French M,O
Geographic Information Systems M,O
Geography M,D
Geology M,D
German M,O
Gerontology M,D,O
Health Education M,D,O
Health Informatics M
Health Promotion M,D,O
Higher Education M,O
Historic Preservation M,D,O
History M,D
Immunology M
Industrial and Manufacturing Management M,D
Industrial/Management Engineering M,D,O
Information Studies M,D,O
International Economics M,D
Investment Management M,D,O
Kinesiology and Movement Studies M,D
Liberal Studies M
Library Science M,D,O
Linguistics M,D,O
Manufacturing Engineering M,D,O
Marriage and Family Therapy M,D,O
Materials Engineering M,D,O
Mathematics M,D
Mechanical Engineering M,D,O
Mechanics M,D,O
Media Studies M,O
Medical Informatics D,O
Microbiology M
Middle School Education M
Multilingual and Multicultural Education D
Museum Studies M,D,O
Nonprofit Management M,D,O
Nursing—General M,D,O
Occupational Therapy M,D,O
Pharmacology M
Philosophy M
Physical Therapy D
Physics M,D
Political Science M,D
Psychology—General M,D
Public Health—General M,D,O
Reading Education M
Real Estate M,O
Recreation and Park Management M,D,O
Rhetoric M,D,O
School Psychology D,O
Secondary Education M
Social Psychology M,D
Social Work M,D,O
Sociology M,D
Spanish M,O
Special Education M,D,O
Taxation M,D,O
Technical Communication M,D,O
Toxicology M
Translation and Interpretation M,O
Urban and Regional Planning M,O
Urban Education M,D
Urban Studies M,D
Water Resources M,D
Women's Studies M,O
Writing M,D,O

UNIVERSITY OF WISCONSIN–OSHKOSH

Adult Nursing M
Biological and Biomedical Sciences—General M
Botany M
Business Administration and Management—General M
Counselor Education M
Curriculum and Instruction M
Early Childhood Education M
Education—General M
Educational Leadership and Administration M
English M
Experimental Psychology M
Family Nurse Practitioner Studies M
Health Services Management and Hospital Administration M
Industrial and Organizational Psychology M
International Business M
Mathematics Education M
Microbiology M
Nursing—General M
Psychology—General M
Public Administration M
Reading Education M
Social Work M
Special Education M
Zoology M

UNIVERSITY OF WISCONSIN–PARKSIDE

Business Administration and Management—General M
Computer Science M
Information Science M
Molecular Biology M

UNIVERSITY OF WISCONSIN–PLATTEVILLE

Adult Education M
Computer Science M
Counselor Education M
Criminal Justice and Criminology M
Education—General M
Elementary Education M
Engineering and Applied Sciences—General M
English Education M
Human Resources Management M
Middle School Education M
Project Management M
Secondary Education M
Supply Chain Management M

UNIVERSITY OF WISCONSIN–RIVER FALLS

Agricultural Education M
Agricultural Sciences—General M
Art/Fine Arts M
Business Administration and Management—General M
Communication Disorders M
Counselor Education M,O
Education—General M
Elementary Education M
English as a Second Language M
Mathematics Education M
Reading Education M
School Psychology M,O
Science Education M
Social Sciences Education M

UNIVERSITY OF WISCONSIN–STEVENS POINT

Advertising and Public Relations M
Business Administration and Management—General M
Communication Disorders M,D
Communication—General M
Corporate and Organizational Communication M
Counselor Education M
Education—General M
Educational Leadership and Administration M
Elementary Education M
English M
Family and Consumer Sciences-General M
Health Promotion M
History M
Human Development M
Media Studies M
Music Education M
Natural Resources M
Nutrition M
Reading Education M
Science Education M
Secondary Education M
Special Education M
Speech and Interpersonal Communication M

UNIVERSITY OF WISCONSIN–STOUT

Applied Mathematics M
Applied Psychology M
Art/Fine Arts M
Clinical Psychology M
Conservation Biology M
Construction Management M
Counseling Psychology M
Education—General M,D,O
Food Science and Technology M
Human Resources Development M
Industrial Hygiene M
Industrial/Management Engineering M
Information Science M
Manufacturing Engineering M
Marriage and Family Therapy M
Nutrition M
Project Management M
Quality Management M
Rehabilitation Counseling M
School Psychology M,O
Supply Chain Management M
Sustainability Management M
Technical Communication M
Telecommunications Management M
Vocational and Technical Education M,D,O

UNIVERSITY OF WISCONSIN–SUPERIOR

Art Education M
Art History M
Art Therapy M
Art/Fine Arts M
Communication—General M
Counselor Education M
Curriculum and Instruction M
Education—General M
Educational Leadership and Administration M,O
Mass Communication M
Reading Education M
School Psychology M
Social Psychology M
Special Education M
Speech and Interpersonal Communication M
Sustainability Management M
Theater M

UNIVERSITY OF WISCONSIN–WHITEWATER

Accounting M
Business Administration and Management—General M
Business Education M
Communication Disorders M
Communication—General M
Corporate and Organizational Communication M
Educational Leadership and Administration M
Environmental and Occupational Health M
Finance and Banking M
Marketing M
Mass Communication M
Psychology—General M,O
School Psychology M,O
Special Education M,O

UNIVERSITY OF WYOMING

Accounting M
Agricultural Economics and Agribusiness M
Agricultural Sciences—General M,D
Agronomy and Soil Sciences M,D
American Studies M
Animal Sciences M,D
Anthropology M,D
Applied Economics M
Atmospheric Sciences M,D
Biotechnology D
Botany M,D
Business Administration and Management—General M
Cell Biology D
Chemical Engineering M,D
Chemistry M,D
Child Development M
Civil Engineering M,D
Communication Disorders M
Communication—General M
Community Health M,D
Computational Biology D
Computer Science M,D
Consumer Economics M
Counselor Education M,D
Curriculum and Instruction M,D
Ecology M,D
Economics M,D
Educational Leadership and Administration M,D,O
Educational Media/Instructional Technology M,D
Electrical Engineering M,D
Engineering and Applied Sciences—General M,D
English M
Entomology M,D
Environmental Engineering M
Exercise and Sports Science M
Finance and Banking M
Food Science and Technology M
French M
Genetics D
Geography M
Geology M,D
Geophysics M,D
German M
Health Education M
Health Promotion M
Health Services Management and Hospital Administration M,D
History M
International Affairs M
Kinesiology and Movement Studies M
Law D
Mathematics Education M,D
Mathematics M,D
Mechanical Engineering M,D
Microbiology D
Molecular Biology M,D
Music Education M
Music M
Natural Resources M,D
Nursing—General M
Nutrition M

Pathobiology	M
Petroleum Engineering	M,D
Pharmacy	M,D
Philosophy	M
Physical Education	M
Physiology	M,D
Political Science	M
Psychology—General	M,D
Public Administration	M
Range Science	M,D
Reproductive Biology	M,D
Rural Planning and Studies	M
Science Education	M
Social Work	M
Sociology	M
Spanish	M
Special Education	M,D,O
Statistics	M,D
Student Affairs	M,D
Water Resources	M,D
Writing	M
Zoology	M,D

UPPER IOWA UNIVERSITY

Accounting	M
Business Administration and Management—General	M
Early Childhood Education	M
Education—General	M
Educational Leadership and Administration	M
Emergency Management	M
English as a Second Language	M
Finance and Banking	M
Higher Education	M
Homeland Security	M
Human Resources Management	M
Human Services	M
Nonprofit Management	M
Organizational Management	M
Public Administration	M
Reading Education	M
Sports Management	M

URBANA UNIVERSITY

Business Administration and Management—General	M
Criminal Justice and Criminology	M
Education—General	M
Nursing—General	M

URSHAN GRADUATE SCHOOL OF THEOLOGY

Theology	M

URSULINE COLLEGE

Adult Nursing	M,D
Art Education	M
Art Therapy	M
Business Administration and Management—General	M
Early Childhood Education	M
Education—General	M
Educational Leadership and Administration	M
Family Nurse Practitioner Studies	M,D
Gerontological Nursing	M,D
Historic Preservation	M
Liberal Studies	M
Mathematics Education	M
Medical/Surgical Nursing	M,D
Middle School Education	M
Nursing Education	M,D
Nursing—General	M,D
Reading Education	M
Science Education	M
Social Sciences Education	M
Special Education	M
Theology	M

UTAH STATE UNIVERSITY

Accounting	M
Aerospace/Aeronautical Engineering	M,D
Agricultural Education	M
Agricultural Engineering	M,D
Agricultural Sciences—General	M,D
Agronomy and Soil Sciences	M,D
American Studies	M
Animal Sciences	M,D
Applied Economics	M
Applied Mathematics	M,D
Art/Fine Arts	M
Biochemistry	M,D
Biological and Biomedical Sciences—General	M,D
Business Administration and Management—General	M
Business Education	M,D
Chemistry	M,D
Child and Family Studies	M,D
Civil Engineering	M,D,O
Clinical Psychology	M,D
Communication Disorders	M,D,O
Communication—General	M
Computer Science	M,D
Consumer Economics	M
Counseling Psychology	M,D
Counselor Education	M,D
Curriculum and Instruction	D
Disability Studies	M,D,O
Ecology	M,D
Economics	M,D
Education—General	M,D,O
Educational Measurement and Evaluation	M,D
Educational Media/Instructional Technology	M,D,O
Electrical Engineering	M,D
Elementary Education	M
Engineering and Applied Sciences—General	M,D,O
English	M
Environmental Engineering	M,D,O
Environmental Management and Policy	M,D
Family and Consumer Sciences-General	M,D
Fish, Game, and Wildlife Management	M,D
Folklore	M
Food Science and Technology	M,D
Forestry	M,D
Geography	M,D
Geology	M
Health Education	M
History	M
Home Economics Education	M
Human Development	M,D
Human Resources Management	M
Interior Design	M
Landscape Architecture	M
Management Information Systems	M,D
Marriage and Family Therapy	M,D
Mathematics	M,D
Mechanical Engineering	M,D
Meteorology	M,D
Multilingual and Multicultural Education	M
Natural Resources	M
Nutrition	M,D
Physical Education	M
Physics	M,D
Plant Sciences	M,D
Political Science	M
Psychology—General	M,D
Range Science	M,D
Recreation and Park Management	M,D
Rehabilitation Counseling	M
School Psychology	M,D
Secondary Education	M
Sociology	M,D
Special Education	M,D,O
Statistics	M,D
Theater	M
Toxicology	M,D
Urban and Regional Planning	M,D
Veterinary Sciences	M,D
Vocational and Technical Education	M
Water Resources Engineering	M,D
Water Resources	M,D
Writing	M

UTAH VALLEY UNIVERSITY

Accounting	M
Business Administration and Management—General	M
Education—General	M
Educational Leadership and Administration	M
Educational Media/Instructional Technology	M
Elementary Education	M
English as a Second Language	M
Mathematics Education	M
Nursing—General	M
Reading Education	M

UTICA COLLEGE

Accounting	M
Computer and Information Systems Security	M
Criminal Justice and Criminology	M
Education—General	M,O
Forensic Sciences	M
Health Services Management and Hospital Administration	M
Liberal Studies	M
Occupational Therapy	M
Physical Therapy	D

VALDOSTA STATE UNIVERSITY

Business Administration and Management—General	M
Counselor Education	M,O
Early Childhood Education	M,O
Educational Leadership and Administration	M
English Education	M
English	M
Health Services Management and Hospital Administration	M
Information Studies	M
Library Science	M
Marriage and Family Therapy	M,O
Music	M
Psychology—General	M,O
Rhetoric	M
Social Work	M
Special Education	M,O

VALLEY CITY STATE UNIVERSITY

Education—General	M
Educational Media/Instructional Technology	M
Elementary Education	M
English as a Second Language	M
English Education	M
Library Science	M
Vocational and Technical Education	M

VALPARAISO UNIVERSITY

Arts Administration	M
Asian Studies	M
Business Administration and Management—General	M,O
Clinical Psychology	M
Communication—General	M,O
Computational Sciences	M
Computer and Information Systems Security	M
Education—General	M
Educational Leadership and Administration	M
Engineering Management	M,O
English as a Second Language	M,O
English	M,O
Entertainment Management	M
Entrepreneurship	M,O
Ethics	M,O
Finance and Banking	M,O
Health Services Management and Hospital Administration	M
History	M,O
International Business	M
International Economics	M
Law	M,D
Legal and Justice Studies	O
Liberal Studies	M,O
Management Information Systems	M
Management Strategy and Policy	M,O
Marketing	M,O
Media Studies	M,O
Nursing Education	M,D,O
Nursing—General	M,D,O
Pastoral Ministry and Counseling	M
Psychology—General	M
Public Health—General	M,D,O
School Psychology	
Sports Management	M
Sustainability Management	M,O
Theology	M,O

VAN ANDEL INSTITUTE GRADUATE SCHOOL

Genetics	D
Molecular Genetics	D

VANCOUVER ISLAND UNIVERSITY

Business Administration and Management—General	M
Finance and Banking	M
International Business	M
Marketing	M

VANCOUVER SCHOOL OF THEOLOGY

Religion	M,O
Theology	M,O

VANDERBILT UNIVERSITY

Accounting	M
Acute Care/Critical Care Nursing	M,D,O
Adult Nursing	M,D,O
Allopathic Medicine	M,D
Analytical Chemistry	M,D
Anthropology	M,D
Astronomy	M,D
Biochemistry	M,D
Bioinformatics	M,D
Biological and Biomedical Sciences—General	M,D
Biomedical Engineering	M,D
Biophysics	M,D
Business Administration and Management—General	M
Cancer Biology/Oncology	M,D
Cell Biology	M,D
Chemical Engineering	M,D
Chemistry	M,D
Child and Family Studies	M,D
Civil Engineering	M,D
Classics	M
Clinical Research	M
Communication Disorders	M,D
Computer Science	M,D
Counselor Education	M,D
Developmental Biology	M,D
Economic Development	M,D
Economics	M,D
Education—General	M,D*
Educational Leadership and Administration	D
Educational Policy	M,D
Electrical Engineering	M,D
Elementary Education	M,D
Engineering and Applied Sciences—General	M,D
English Education	M,D
English	M,D
Environmental Engineering	M,D
Environmental Management and Policy	M,D
Environmental Sciences	M
Family Nurse Practitioner Studies	M,D,O
Finance and Banking	M
Foreign Languages Education	M,D
French	M,D
Geology	M
German	M,D
Gerontological Nursing	M,D,O
Health Physics/Radiological Health	M,D
Health Services Management and Hospital Administration	M
Higher Education	M,D
History	M,D
Human Development	M,D
Human Genetics	D
Immunology	M,D
Inorganic Chemistry	M,D
International and Comparative Education	M,D
Latin American Studies	M
Law	M,D
Liberal Studies	M
Management Strategy and Policy	M
Marketing	M
Materials Sciences	M,D
Maternal and Child/Neonatal Nursing	M,D,O
Mathematics	M,D
Mechanical Engineering	M,D
Microbiology	M,D
Molecular Biology	M,D
Molecular Physiology	M,D
Multilingual and Multicultural Education	D
Nurse Midwifery	M,D,O
Nursing and Healthcare Administration	M,D,O
Nursing Informatics	M,D,O
Nursing—General	M,D,O
Organic Chemistry	M,D
Organizational Management	M,D
Pathology	D
Pediatric Nursing	M,D,O
Pharmacology	D
Philosophy	M,D
Physical Chemistry	M,D
Physics	M,D
Political Science	M,D
Portuguese	M,D
Psychiatric Nursing	M,D,O
Psychology—General	D
Public Health—General	M
Public Policy	D
Quantitative Analysis	M,D
Reading Education	M,D
Religion	M,D
Science Education	M,D
Secondary Education	M,D
Sociology	M,D
Spanish	M,D
Special Education	M,D
Theology	M
Theoretical Chemistry	M,D
Urban and Regional Planning	M,D
Urban Education	M,D
Women's Health Nursing	M,D,O
Writing	M

VANDERCOOK COLLEGE OF MUSIC

Music Education	M

VANGUARD UNIVERSITY OF SOUTHERN CALIFORNIA

Clinical Psychology	M
Education—General	M
Nursing—General	M
Religion	M
Theology	M

VAUGHN COLLEGE OF AERONAUTICS AND TECHNOLOGY

Aviation Management	M

VERMONT COLLEGE OF FINE ARTS

Art Education	M
Art/Fine Arts	M
Film, Television, and Video Production	M
Graphic Design	M
Music	M
Publishing	M
Writing	M

VERMONT LAW SCHOOL

Energy Management and Policy	M
Environmental Law	M
Environmental Management and Policy	M
Law	D
Legal and Justice Studies	M

VICTORIA UNIVERSITY

Theology	M,D,O

VILLANOVA UNIVERSITY

Accounting	M
Adult Nursing	M,D,O
Applied Statistics	M
Artificial Intelligence/Robotics	M,O
Biochemical Engineering	M,O
Biological and Biomedical Sciences—General	M
Business Administration and Management—General	M
Chemical Engineering	M,O
Chemistry	M
Civil Engineering	M
Classics	M
Communication—General	M
Computer Engineering	M,O
Computer Science	M,O
Counselor Education	M
Database Systems	M
Education—General	M
Educational Leadership and Administration	M
Electrical Engineering	M,O
Engineering and Applied Sciences—General	M,D,O
English	M
Environmental Engineering	M,O
Family Nurse Practitioner Studies	M,D,O
Finance and Banking	M
Health Services Management and Hospital Administration	M
Hispanic Studies	M
History	M
Human Resources Development	M
International Business	M
Law	D
Management Information Systems	M
Management Strategy and Policy	M
Manufacturing Engineering	M,O
Marketing	M
Mathematics	M
Mechanical Engineering	M,O
Missions and Missiology	M
Nurse Anesthesia	M,D,O
Nursing Education	M,D,O
Nursing—General	M,D,O
Pediatric Nursing	M,D,O
Philosophy	D
Political Science	M

*M—masters degree; D—doctorate; O—other advanced degree; *—Close-Up and/or Display*

Psychology—General	M
Public Administration	M
Real Estate	M
Secondary Education	M
Software Engineering	M
Taxation	M
Theater	M
Theology	M
Water Resources Engineering	M,O

VIRGINIA BEACH THEOLOGICAL SEMINARY

Theology	M

VIRGINIA COLLEGE IN BIRMINGHAM

Business Administration and Management—General	M
Criminal Justice and Criminology	M
Health Services Management and Hospital Administration	M

VIRGINIA COMMONWEALTH UNIVERSITY

Accounting	M,D
Adult Education	M
Adult Nursing	M,D,O
Advertising and Public Relations	M
Allied Health—General	D
Allopathic Medicine	D
Analytical Chemistry	M,D
Anatomy	D,O
Applied Arts and Design—General	M
Applied Mathematics	M
Applied Physics	M
Applied Social Research	M,O
Architectural History	M,D
Art Education	M
Art History	M,D
Art/Fine Arts	M,D
Athletic Training and Sports Medicine	M
Biochemistry	M,D,O
Bioengineering	M,D
Bioinformatics	M,D
Biological and Biomedical Sciences—General	M,D,O
Biomedical Engineering	M,D
Biopsychology	D
Biostatistics	M,D
Business Administration and Management—General	M,O
Chemical Engineering	M,D
Chemical Physics	M,D
Chemistry	M,D
Clinical Laboratory Sciences/Medical Technology	M,D
Clinical Psychology	D
Communication—General	D
Community Health	M,D
Computer Science	M,D
Counseling Psychology	M,D,O
Counselor Education	M
Criminal Justice and Criminology	M,O
Dentistry	M,D
Developmental Psychology	D
Early Childhood Education	M,O
Economics	M
Education—General	M,D,O
Educational Leadership and Administration	D
Educational Measurement and Evaluation	D
Educational Media/Instructional Technology	M
Educational Policy	D
Educational Psychology	D
Electrical Engineering	M,D
Elementary Education	M,O
Emergency Management	M,O
Engineering and Applied Sciences—General	M,D
English	M
Environmental Management and Policy	M
Epidemiology	M,D
Exercise and Sports Science	M
Family Nurse Practitioner Studies	M,O
Finance and Banking	M
Forensic Sciences	M
Genetics	M,D
Geographic Information Systems	O
Gerontology	M,D,O
Health Education	M,O
Health Physics/Radiological Health	D
Health Psychology	D
Health Services Management and Hospital Administration	M,D
Health Services Research	D
Historic Preservation	O
History	M,D
Homeland Security	M,O
Human Genetics	M,D,O
Human Resources Development	M
Humanities	M,D,O
Immunology	M,D
Industrial and Manufacturing Management	M
Inorganic Chemistry	M,D
Insurance	M
Interdisciplinary Studies	M
Interior Design	M
Internet and Interactive Multimedia	M
Journalism	M
Management Information Systems	M,D
Management Strategy and Policy	M
Marketing	M
Mass Communication	M
Mathematics	M
Mechanical Engineering	M,D
Media Studies	M,D
Medical Physics	M,D
Medicinal and Pharmaceutical Chemistry	M,D
Microbiology	M,D,O
Modeling and Simulation	M,D
Molecular Biology	M,D
Museum Studies	M,D
Music Education	M
Music	M
Nanotechnology	M,D
Neurobiology	D
Neuroscience	M,D,O
Nonprofit Management	M,O
Nuclear Engineering	M,D
Nurse Anesthesia	M,D
Nursing and Healthcare Administration	M,D,O
Nursing Education	M,D,O
Nursing—General	M,D,O
Occupational Therapy	M,D
Operations Research	M,D
Organic Chemistry	M,D
Pathology	D
Pediatric Nursing	M,D,O
Pharmaceutical Administration	M,D
Pharmaceutical Sciences	M,D
Pharmacology	M,D,O
Pharmacy	D
Photography	M,D
Physical Chemistry	M,D
Physical Education	M,D,O
Physical Therapy	M,D
Physics	M
Physiology	M,D,O
Political Science	M,D,O
Psychiatric Nursing	M,D,O
Psychology—General	D
Public Administration	M,O
Public Affairs	M,D,O
Public Health—General	M,D
Public Policy	D
Quantitative Analysis	M
Reading Education	M,O
Real Estate	M,O
Recreation and Park Management	M
Rehabilitation Counseling	M,O
Rehabilitation Sciences	D
Rhetoric	M
Secondary Education	M,O
Social Psychology	D
Social Work	M,D
Sociology	M,O
Special Education	M,D,O
Statistics	M,D
Student Affairs	M
Systems Biology	D
Theater	M
Toxicology	M,D,O
Urban and Regional Planning	M,O
Urban Education	D
Women's Health Nursing	M,D,O
Writing	M

VIRGINIA INTERNATIONAL UNIVERSITY

Accounting	M,O
Advertising and Public Relations	M,O
Business Administration and Management—General	M,O
Computer and Information Systems Security	M,O
Computer Art and Design	M,O
Computer Science	M,O
Database Systems	M,O
Education—General	M
English as a Second Language	M
Entrepreneurship	M,O
Finance and Banking	M,O
Game Design and Development	M,O
Health Informatics	M,O
Health Services Management and Hospital Administration	M,O
Hospitality Management	M,O
Human Resources Management	M,O
International Affairs	M
International Business	M,O
Linguistics	M
Logistics	M,O
Management Information Systems	M,O
Marketing	M,O
Project Management	M,O
Public Administration	M
Software Engineering	M,O

VIRGINIA POLYTECHNIC INSTITUTE AND STATE UNIVERSITY

Accounting	M,D
Aerospace/Aeronautical Engineering	M,D,O
Agricultural Economics and Agribusiness	M,D
Agricultural Engineering	M,D
Agricultural Sciences—General	M,D,O
Agronomy and Soil Sciences	M,D
Animal Sciences	M,D
Applied Economics	M,D
Architecture	M,D,O
Bioengineering	M,D
Bioinformatics	M,D
Biological and Biomedical Sciences—General	M,D
Biomedical Engineering	M,D
Biotechnology	M,D
Building Science	M,D,O
Business Administration and Management—General	M,D
Chemical Engineering	M,D
Chemistry	M,D
Civil Engineering	M,D,O
Communication—General	M,D,O
Computer and Information Systems Security	M,O
Computer Engineering	M,D,O
Computer Science	M,D,O
Construction Engineering	M,D,O
Construction Management	M,D,O
Counselor Education	M,D,O
Curriculum and Instruction	M,D,O
Distance Education Development	M,O
Economics	M,D
Education—General	M,O
Educational Leadership and Administration	M,D,O
Educational Measurement and Evaluation	M,D,O
Educational Media/Instructional Technology	M,O
Educational Policy	M,D,O
Electrical Engineering	M,D,O
Engineering and Applied Sciences—General	M,D
Engineering Management	M,O
English	M,D,O
Entomology	M,D
Environmental Design	M,D,O
Environmental Engineering	M,D,O
Environmental Management and Policy	M,D,O
Environmental Sciences	M,D,O
Exercise and Sports Science	M,D
Fish, Game, and Wildlife Management	M,D
Foreign Languages Education	M,D,O
Forestry	M,D
Genetics	M,D
Geographic Information Systems	M,D
Geography	M,D
Geosciences	M,D
Higher Education	M,D,O
History of Science and Technology	M,D,O
History	M,D,O
Horticulture	M,D
Hospitality Management	M,D
Human Development	M,D,O
Humanities	M,D,O
Industrial/Management Engineering	M,D,O
Interdisciplinary Studies	M,D
International Affairs	M,D,O
Internet and Interactive Multimedia	M,D,O
Landscape Architecture	M,D,O
Liberal Studies	M,O
Management Information Systems	M,D,O
Materials Engineering	M,D
Materials Sciences	M,D
Mathematics Education	M,D
Mathematics	M,D
Mechanical Engineering	M,D
Mechanics	M,D
Mineral/Mining Engineering	M,D
National Security	M,O
Natural Resources	M,D,O
Nonprofit Management	M,O
Nuclear Engineering	M,D
Nutrition	M,D
Ocean Engineering	M,D,O
Philosophy	M,D,O
Physics	M,D
Plant Pathology	M,D
Plant Physiology	M,D
Political Science	M,D,O
Psychology—General	M,D
Public Administration	M,D,O
Public Affairs	M,D,O
Public Health—General	M,D,O
Public Policy	M,D
Quantitative Analysis	M,O
Rhetoric	M,D,O
Social Sciences Education	M,D,O
Sociology	M,D,O
Software Engineering	M,O
Statistics	M,D
Student Affairs	M,D,O
Systems Engineering	M,D,O
Theater	M,D,O
Transportation and Highway Engineering	M,O
Travel and Tourism	M,D
Urban and Regional Planning	M,D,O
Urban Studies	M,D,O
Veterinary Medicine	M,D,O
Veterinary Sciences	M,D,O
Vocational and Technical Education	M,D,O
Writing	M,D,O

VIRGINIA STATE UNIVERSITY

Biological and Biomedical Sciences—General	M
Clinical Psychology	M,D
Community Health	M,D
Computer Science	M
Counselor Education	M
Criminal Justice and Criminology	M
Economics	M
Education—General	M
Educational Leadership and Administration	M,D
Health Education	M,D
Health Psychology	M,D
Interdisciplinary Studies	M
Mathematics Education	M
Mathematics	M
Media Studies	M
Psychology—General	M,D

VIRGINIA THEOLOGICAL SEMINARY

Educational Leadership and Administration	M,D
Theology	M,D

VIRGINIA UNION UNIVERSITY

Curriculum and Instruction	M
Education—General	M
Theology	M,D

VIRGINIA UNIVERSITY OF LYNCHBURG

Religion	M

VITERBO UNIVERSITY

Addictions/Substance Abuse Counseling	M
Business Administration and Management—General	M
Counseling Psychology	M
Developmental Psychology	M
Early Childhood Education	M,O
Education of the Gifted	M,O
Education—General	M,O
Educational Leadership and Administration	M,O
Ethics	M,O
Health Psychology	M
Health Services Management and Hospital Administration	M
International Business	M
Nursing—General	D
Organizational Management	M,O
Pastoral Ministry and Counseling	M,O
Project Management	M
Reading Education	M,O
Special Education	M,O

WAGNER COLLEGE

Accounting	M
Business Administration and Management—General	M
Early Childhood Education	M
Education—General	M,O
Educational Leadership and Administration	M,O
Elementary Education	M
English Education	M
Finance and Banking	M
Foreign Languages Education	M
Health Services Management and Hospital Administration	M
International Business	M
Marketing	M
Mathematics Education	M
Microbiology	M
Middle School Education	M
Reading Education	M
Science Education	M
Secondary Education	M
Social Sciences Education	M
Special Education	M

WAKE FOREST UNIVERSITY

Accounting	M
Allopathic Medicine	D
Analytical Chemistry	M,D
Anatomy	D
Biochemistry	D
Biological and Biomedical Sciences—General	M,D
Biomedical Engineering	M,D
Business Administration and Management—General	M
Cancer Biology/Oncology	D
Chemistry	M,D
Communication—General	M
Computer Science	M
Counselor Education	M
Education—General	M
English	M
Exercise and Sports Science	M
Genomic Sciences	D
Health Services Research	M
Human Genetics	D
Immunology	D
Inorganic Chemistry	M,D
Law	M,D
Liberal Studies	M
Mathematics	M
Microbiology	D
Molecular Biology	D
Molecular Genetics	D
Molecular Medicine	M,D
Neurobiology	D
Neuroscience	D
Organic Chemistry	M,D
Pathobiology	M,D
Pharmacology	D
Physical Chemistry	M,D
Physics	M,D
Physiology	D
Psychology—General	M
Religion	M
Secondary Education	M
Speech and Interpersonal Communication	M
Taxation	M

WALDEN UNIVERSITY

Accounting	M,D,O
Addictions/Substance Abuse Counseling	M,D
Adult Education	M,D,O
Adult Nursing	M,D,O
Applied Psychology	M,D,O
Business Administration and Management—General	M,D,O
Child and Family Studies	M,D
Clinical Psychology	M,D,O
Clinical Research	M,D,O
Communication—General	M,D,O
Community Health	M,D,O
Computer and Information Systems Security	M,D,O
Conflict Resolution and Mediation/Peace Studies	M,D,O
Counseling Psychology	M,D,O
Counselor Education	M,D
Criminal Justice and Criminology	M,D,O
Curriculum and Instruction	M,D,O
Developmental Psychology	M,D,O
Distance Education Development	M,D,O
Early Childhood Education	M,D,O
Education—General	M,D,O
Educational Leadership and Administration	M,D,O
Educational Measurement and Evaluation	M,D,O
Educational Media/Instructional Technology	M,D,O
Educational Psychology	M,D,O

Elementary Education	M,D,O
Emergency Management	M,D,O
English as a Second Language	M,D,O
Entrepreneurship	M,D,O
Epidemiology	M,D,O
Family Nurse Practitioner Studies	M,D,O
Finance and Banking	M,D,O
Forensic Psychology	M,D,O
Gerontological Nursing	M,D,O
Gerontology	M,D
Health Education	M,D,O
Health Informatics	M,D,O
Health Promotion	M,D,O
Health Psychology	M,D,O
Health Services Management and Hospital Administration	M,D,O
Higher Education	M,D,O
Homeland Security	M,D,O
Human Resources Management	M,D,O
Human Services	M,D
Industrial and Organizational Psychology	M,D,O
Interdisciplinary Studies	M,D,O
International Affairs	M,D,O
International and Comparative Education	M,D,O
International Business	M,D,O
International Development	M,D,O
International Health	M,D,O
Law	M,D,O
Management Information Systems	M,D,O
Marketing	M,D,O
Marriage and Family Therapy	M,D
Mathematics Education	M,D,O
Multilingual and Multicultural Education	M,D,O
Nonprofit Management	M,D,O
Nursing and Healthcare Administration	M,D,O
Nursing Education	M,D,O
Nursing Informatics	M,D,O
Nursing—General	M,D,O
Organizational Management	M,D,O
Political Science	M,D,O
Project Management	M,D,O
Psychology—General	M,D,O
Public Administration	M,D,O
Public Health—General	M,D,O
Public Policy	M,D,O
Reading Education	M,D,O
Science Education	M,D,O
Social Psychology	M,D,O
Social Work	M,D
Special Education	M,D,O
Supply Chain Management	M,D,O
Sustainable Development	M,D,O

WALDORF COLLEGE

Criminal Justice and Criminology	M
Educational Leadership and Administration	M
Emergency Management	M
Human Resources Development	M
Organizational Management	M
Public Administration	M
Sports Management	M

WALLA WALLA UNIVERSITY

Biological and Biomedical Sciences—General	M
Counseling Psychology	M
Curriculum and Instruction	M
Education—General	M
Educational Leadership and Administration	M
Reading Education	M
Social Work	M
Special Education	M

WALSH COLLEGE OF ACCOUNTANCY AND BUSINESS ADMINISTRATION

Accounting	M
Business Administration and Management—General	M
Finance and Banking	M
Human Resources Management	M
International Business	M
Management Information Systems	M
Management of Technology	M
Management Strategy and Policy	M
Marketing	M
Taxation	M

WALSH UNIVERSITY

Business Administration and Management—General	M
Counseling Psychology	M
Counselor Education	M
Education—General	M
Health Services Management and Hospital Administration	M,O
Higher Education	M
Marketing	M
Nursing and Healthcare Administration	M,D
Nursing Education	M,D
Nursing—General	M,D
Pastoral Ministry and Counseling	M
Physical Therapy	D
Reading Education	M
Religious Education	M
Student Affairs	M
Theology	M

WARNER PACIFIC COLLEGE

Education—General	M
Human Services	M
Nonprofit Management	M
Organizational Management	M

WARNER UNIVERSITY

Business Administration and Management—General	M
Education—General	M

WARREN WILSON COLLEGE

Writing	M

WARTBURG THEOLOGICAL SEMINARY

Theology	M

WASHBURN UNIVERSITY

Accounting	M
Addictions/Substance Abuse Counseling	M
Business Administration and Management—General	M
Clinical Psychology	M
Criminal Justice and Criminology	M
Curriculum and Instruction	M
Education—General	M
Educational Leadership and Administration	M
Health Education	M
Human Services	M
Law	M,D
Legal and Justice Studies	M,D
Liberal Studies	M
Nursing and Healthcare Administration	M,D,O
Nursing—General	M,D,O
Psychology—General	M
Reading Education	M
Social Work	M
Special Education	M

WASHINGTON ADVENTIST UNIVERSITY

Business Administration and Management—General	M
Counseling Psychology	M
Health Services Management and Hospital Administration	M
Nursing and Healthcare Administration	M
Nursing Education	M
Nursing—General	M
Public Administration	M
Religion	M

WASHINGTON AND LEE UNIVERSITY

Law	M,D

WASHINGTON STATE UNIVERSITY

Accounting	M
Agricultural Economics and Agribusiness	M,D,O
Agricultural Engineering	M,D
Agronomy and Soil Sciences	M,D,O
American Studies	M,D
Animal Sciences	M,D
Anthropology	M,D
Applied Mathematics	M,D
Archaeology	M,D
Architecture	M
Art/Fine Arts	M
Biochemistry	M,D
Bioengineering	M,D
Bioethics	M,D,O
Biological and Biomedical Sciences—General	M,D
Biophysics	M,D
Business Administration and Management—General	M,D
Business Education	M,D
Cell Biology	M,D
Chemical Engineering	M,D
Chemistry	M,D
Civil Engineering	M,D
Clinical Psychology	M,D
Clothing and Textiles	M
Communication Disorders	M
Communication—General	M,D
Community Health	M,D,O
Computer Engineering	M,D
Computer Science	M,D
Corporate and Organizational Communication	M,D
Counseling Psychology	M,D
Criminal Justice and Criminology	M,D
Cultural Anthropology	M,D
Cultural Studies	M,D
Curriculum and Instruction	M,D
Economics	M,D,O
Education—General	M,D
Educational Leadership and Administration	M,D
Educational Psychology	M,D
Electrical Engineering	M,D
Elementary Education	M,D
Energy and Power Engineering	M,D
Engineering and Applied Sciences—General	M,D,O
Engineering Management	M,O
English as a Second Language	M,D
English	M,D
Entomology	M,D
Environmental Engineering	M,D
Environmental Sciences	M,D
Epidemiology	M,D
Exercise and Sports Science	M
Experimental Psychology	M,D
Family Nurse Practitioner Studies	M,D,O
Food Science and Technology	M,D
Foreign Languages Education	M
Genetics	M,D
Geology	M,D
Health Services Management and Hospital Administration	M
History	M,D
Horticulture	M,D
Human Development	D
Immunology	M,D
Interdisciplinary Studies	D
Interior Design	M
Landscape Architecture	M
Management of Technology	M,O
Materials Engineering	M,D
Materials Sciences	M,D
Mathematics Education	M,D
Mathematics	M,D
Mechanical Engineering	M,D
Microbiology	M,D
Music	M
Natural Resources	M,D
Neuroscience	M,D
Nursing—General	M,D,O
Nutrition	M
Pharmacy	M,D
Physics	M,D
Plant Pathology	M,D
Political Science	M,D,O
Psychiatric Nursing	M,D,O
Psychology—General	M,D
Public Affairs	M,D,O
Reading Education	M,D
Secondary Education	M,D
Sociology	M,D
Special Education	M,D
Sports Management	M,D
Veterinary Medicine	D
Veterinary Sciences	M,D
Vocational and Technical Education	M,D

WASHINGTON UNIVERSITY IN ST. LOUIS

Accounting	M
Aerospace/Aeronautical Engineering	M,D
Allopathic Medicine	D
American Indian/Native American Studies	M,D,O
Anthropology	D
Archaeology	M,D
Architecture	M
Art History	M,D
Art/Fine Arts	M
Asian Languages	M,D
Asian Studies	M,D
Biochemistry	D
Bioethics	M
Biological and Biomedical Sciences—General	D
Biomedical Engineering	M,D
Biostatistics	M,D,O
Business Administration and Management—General	M,D
Cell Biology	D
Chemical Engineering	M,D
Chemistry	D
Child and Family Studies	M,D,O
Chinese	M,D
Classics	M,D
Clinical Research	M
Communication Disorders	M,D
Comparative Literature	M,D
Computational Biology	D
Computer Engineering	M,D
Computer Science	M,D
Counseling Psychology	M,D,O
Dance	M
Database Systems	M
Developmental Biology	D
Developmental Psychology	D
Ecology	D
Economic Development	M,D,O
Economics	D
Education—General	M,D
Educational Measurement and Evaluation	D
Elementary Education	M
Engineering and Applied Sciences—General	M,D
English	M,D
Entrepreneurship	M
Environmental Biology	D
Environmental Engineering	M,D
Epidemiology	M,D,O
Evolutionary Biology	D
Finance and Banking	M,D
French	D
Genetics	M,D
Genomic Sciences	M
Geosciences	D
German	D
Gerontology	M,D,O
Health Education	M,O
Health Services Research	M,O
History	D
Human Genetics	D
Immunology	D
International Health	M,D,O
Japanese	M,D
Jewish Studies	M
Kinesiology and Movement Studies	D
Law	M,D
Materials Sciences	M,D
Mathematics	M,D
Mechanical Engineering	M,D
Microbiology	D
Molecular Biology	D
Molecular Biophysics	D
Molecular Genetics	D
Molecular Pathogenesis	D
Music	M,D
Near and Middle Eastern Studies	M
Neuroscience	D
Occupational Therapy	M,D
Organizational Management	M
Philosophy	D
Physical Therapy	D
Physics	D
Planetary and Space Sciences	D
Plant Biology	D
Political Science	D
Psychology—General	D
Public Health—General	M,D,O
Rehabilitation Sciences	D
Religion	M
Romance Languages	D
Secondary Education	M
Social Work	M,D,O
Spanish	D
Special Education	M,D
Speech and Interpersonal Communication	M,D
Statistics	M,D
Supply Chain Management	M
Systems Biology	D
Theater	M
Urban Design	M
Writing	M

WAYLAND BAPTIST UNIVERSITY

Accounting	M,D
Business Administration and Management—General	M,D
Counseling Psychology	M
Criminal Justice and Criminology	M
Education—General	M
Educational Leadership and Administration	M
Educational Measurement and Evaluation	M
Educational Media/Instructional Technology	M
Elementary Education	M
English as a Second Language	M
English Education	M
Health Services Management and Hospital Administration	M,D
Higher Education	M
History	M
Homeland Security	M
Human Resources Management	M,D
Humanities	M
Interdisciplinary Studies	M
International Business	M,D
Management Information Systems	M,D
Organizational Management	M,D
Pastoral Ministry and Counseling	M
Project Management	M,D
Religion	M
Science Education	M
Secondary Education	M
Social Sciences Education	M
Special Education	M
Sports Management	M
Theology	M

WAYNESBURG UNIVERSITY

Addictions/Substance Abuse Counseling	M,D
Business Administration and Management—General	M,D
Clinical Psychology	M,D
Counseling Psychology	M,D
Counselor Education	M,D
Criminal Justice and Criminology	M,D
Curriculum and Instruction	M,D
Distance Education Development	M,D
Educational Leadership and Administration	M,D
Educational Media/Instructional Technology	M,D
Energy Management and Policy	M,D
Finance and Banking	M,D
Health Services Management and Hospital Administration	M,D
Human Resources Management	M,D
Nursing and Healthcare Administration	M,D
Nursing Education	M,D
Nursing Informatics	M,D
Nursing—General	M,D
Organizational Management	M,D
Special Education	M,D

WAYNE STATE COLLEGE

Business Administration and Management—General	M
Business Education	M
Communication—General	M
Counselor Education	M
Curriculum and Instruction	M
Early Childhood Education	M
Education—General	M,O
Educational Leadership and Administration	M,O
Elementary Education	M
English as a Second Language	M
English Education	M
Exercise and Sports Science	M
Home Economics Education	M
Mathematics Education	M
Music Education	M
Organizational Management	M
Physical Education	M
Science Education	M
Social Sciences Education	M
Special Education	M
Sports Management	M
Vocational and Technical Education	M

WAYNE STATE UNIVERSITY

Accounting	M,D,O
Acute Care/Critical Care Nursing	D,O
Adult Nursing	D
Advertising and Public Relations	M,D,O
African Studies	M,D,O
Allopathic Medicine	D
American Studies	M,D,O
Analytical Chemistry	M,D
Anatomy	D
Anthropology	M,D,O
Applied Behavior Analysis	M,D,O

*M—masters degree; D—doctorate; O—other advanced degree; *—Close-Up and/or Display*

Applied Mathematics	M,D
Archives/Archival Administration	M,D,O
Art Education	M,D,O
Art History	M
Art/Fine Arts	M
Asian Studies	M,D,O
Automotive Engineering	M,O
Biochemistry	M,D
Bioinformatics	M,D,O
Biological and Biomedical Sciences—General	M,D
Biomedical Engineering	M,D,O
Biopsychology	D
Biotechnology	M,D
Business Administration and Management—General	M,D,O
Cancer Biology/Oncology	D
Chemical Engineering	M,D
Chemistry	M,D
Civil Engineering	M,D
Classics	M
Clinical Psychology	M,D
Cognitive Sciences	M,D
Communication Disorders	M,D
Communication—General	M,D,O
Computational Biology	M,D,O
Computer Engineering	M,D
Computer Science	M,D,O
Conflict Resolution and Mediation/Peace Studies	M,O
Counseling Psychology	M,D,O
Counselor Education	M,D,O
Criminal Justice and Criminology	M
Curriculum and Instruction	M,D,O
Dance	M,D,O
Developmental Psychology	M,D
Distance Education Development	M,D,O
Early Childhood Education	M,D,O
Economic Development	M,D,O
Economics	M,D
Education—General	M,D,O
Educational Leadership and Administration	M,D,O
Educational Measurement and Evaluation	M,D,O
Educational Media/Instructional Technology	M,D,O
Educational Policy	M,D,O
Educational Psychology	M,D,O
Electrical Engineering	M,D
Elementary Education	M,D,O
Energy and Power Engineering	M,O
Engineering and Applied Sciences—General	M,D,O
Engineering Management	M,O
English as a Second Language	M,D,O
English Education	M,D,O
English	M,D
Evolutionary Biology	M,D
Exercise and Sports Science	M,D
Family Nurse Practitioner Studies	D
Film, Television, and Video Theory and Criticism	M,D
Finance and Banking	M,D
Food Science and Technology	M,D,O
Foreign Languages Education	M,D,O
Foundations and Philosophy of Education	M,D,O
French	M,D
Gender Studies	M,D,O
Genetic Counseling	M
Genomic Sciences	M,D
Geology	M
German	M,D
Gerontological Nursing	D
Gerontology	M,D,O
Graphic Design	M
Health Communication	M,D,O
Health Education	M,D
Health Services Management and Hospital Administration	M,D
Higher Education	M,D,O
History of Science and Technology	M,D,O
History	M,D,O
Human Resources Management	M,D
Immunology	M,D
Industrial and Labor Relations	M,D
Industrial and Manufacturing Management	M,D
Industrial and Organizational Psychology	M,D
Industrial Design	M
Industrial/Management Engineering	M,D
Information Studies	M,O
Inorganic Chemistry	M,D
Interior Design	M
International Economics	M,D
Italian	M
Journalism	M,D,O
Kinesiology and Movement Studies	M,D,O
Law	M,D
Library Science	M,O
Linguistics	M,D
Management Information Systems	M,D,O
Manufacturing Engineering	M
Materials Sciences	M,D,O
Maternal and Child/Neonatal Nursing	M,D
Mathematics Education	M,D,O
Mathematics	M,D
Mechanical Engineering	M,D
Media Studies	M,D,O
Medical Imaging	M,D,O
Medical Physics	M,D
Medicinal and Pharmaceutical Chemistry	M,D
Microbiology	M,D
Molecular Biology	M,D
Molecular Genetics	M,D,O
Molecular Medicine	M,D,O
Multilingual and Multicultural Education	M,D,O
Music Education	M,O
Music	M,D,O
Near and Middle Eastern Languages	M
Near and Middle Eastern Studies	M
Neurobiology	M,D
Neuroscience	M,D
Nonprofit Management	M,D
Nurse Anesthesia	M,O
Nurse Midwifery	M,D,O
Nursing Education	O
Nursing—General	D
Nutrition	M,D,O
Occupational Therapy	M
Organic Chemistry	M,D
Organizational Behavior	M,D
Organizational Management	M,D
Pathology	D
Pediatric Nursing	M,D,O
Pharmaceutical Sciences	M,D
Pharmacology	M,D
Pharmacy	M,D
Philosophy	M,D
Photography	M
Physical Chemistry	M,D
Physical Education	M,D
Physical Therapy	D
Physician Assistant Studies	M
Physics	M,D
Physiology	M,D
Political Science	M,D
Polymer Science and Engineering	M,D,O
Psychiatric Nursing	M,O
Psychology—General	M,D
Public Administration	M
Public Health—General	M,O
Public Policy	M,D
Reading Education	M,D,O
Rehabilitation Counseling	M,D,O
Rhetoric	M,D
Romance Languages	M
School Psychology	M,D,O
Science Education	M,D,O
Secondary Education	M,D,O
Social Psychology	M,D
Social Sciences Education	M,D,O
Social Work	M,D,O
Sociology	M,D
Spanish	M,D
Special Education	M,D,O
Sports Management	M,D
Statistics	M,D
Systems Engineering	M,D,O
Taxation	M,D,O
Textile Design	M
Theater	M
Toxicology	M,D
Urban and Regional Planning	M,O
Urban Studies	M,D
Vocational and Technical Education	M,D,O
Western European Studies	M,D,O
Writing	M,D

WEBBER INTERNATIONAL UNIVERSITY

Accounting	M
Business Administration and Management—General	M
Criminal Justice and Criminology	M
Sports Management	M

WEBER STATE UNIVERSITY

Accounting	M
Athletic Training and Sports Medicine	M
Business Administration and Management—General	M
Communication—General	M
Curriculum and Instruction	M
Education—General	M
English	M
Health Physics/Radiological Health	M
Health Services Management and Hospital Administration	M
Legal and Justice Studies	M
Nursing—General	M
Taxation	M

WEBSTER UNIVERSITY

Accounting	M
Advertising and Public Relations	M
Aerospace/Aeronautical Engineering	M
Art History	M
Art/Fine Arts	M
Business Administration and Management—General	M
Communication Disorders	M
Communication—General	M
Computer Science	M
Corporate and Organizational Communication	M
Counseling Psychology	M
Criminal Justice and Criminology	M
Education—General	M,O
Educational Media/Instructional Technology	M,O
Educational Psychology	M,O
Engineering Management	M
Environmental Management and Policy	M
Finance and Banking	M
Forensic Sciences	M
Gerontology	M
Health Services Management and Hospital Administration	M
Human Resources Development	M
Human Resources Management	M
Human Services	M
International Affairs	M
International Business	M
Internet and Interactive Multimedia	M
Legal and Justice Studies	M
Management Information Systems	M
Marketing	M
Mathematics Education	M,O
Media Studies	M
Music Education	M
Music	M
Nonprofit Management	M
Nurse Anesthesia	M
Nursing and Healthcare Administration	M
Nursing Education	M
Nursing—General	M
Psychology—General	M
Public Administration	M
Reading Education	M
Social Sciences Education	M,O
Special Education	M,O

WEILL CORNELL MEDICINE

Biochemistry	M,D
Biological and Biomedical Sciences—General	M,D
Biophysics	M,D
Cell Biology	M,D
Computational Biology	D
Epidemiology	M
Health Informatics	M
Health Services Research	M
Immunology	M,D
Molecular Biology	M,D
Neuroscience	M,D
Pharmacology	M,D
Physician Assistant Studies	M
Physiology	M,D
Structural Biology	M,D
Systems Biology	M,D

WENTWORTH INSTITUTE OF TECHNOLOGY

Architecture	M
Civil Engineering	M
Construction Engineering	M
Construction Management	M
Facilities Management	M
Management of Technology	M
Transportation and Highway Engineering	M

WESLEYAN COLLEGE

Business Administration and Management—General	M
Early Childhood Education	M
Education—General	M

WESLEYAN UNIVERSITY

Astronomy	M
Biochemistry	D
Bioinformatics	D
Biological and Biomedical Sciences—General	D
Cell Biology	D
Chemical Physics	D
Chemistry	D
Computer Science	M,D
Developmental Biology	D
Ecology	D
Environmental Sciences	M
Evolutionary Biology	D
Genetics	D
Genomic Sciences	D
Geosciences	M
Inorganic Chemistry	D
Liberal Studies	M
Mathematics	M,D
Molecular Biology	D
Molecular Biophysics	D
Molecular Genetics	D
Music	M,D
Neurobiology	D
Organic Chemistry	D
Physics	D
Theoretical Chemistry	D

WESLEY BIBLICAL SEMINARY

Linguistics	M
Missions and Missiology	M
Pastoral Ministry and Counseling	M
Religion	M
Religious Education	M
Theology	M
Translation and Interpretation	M

WESLEY COLLEGE

Business Administration and Management—General	M
Education—General	M
Environmental Management and Policy	M
Nursing—General	M

WESLEY THEOLOGICAL SEMINARY

Theology	M,D

WEST CHESTER UNIVERSITY OF PENNSYLVANIA

Applied Mathematics	M,O
Applied Statistics	M,O
Astronomy	M
Athletic Training and Sports Medicine	M,O
Biological and Biomedical Sciences—General	M,O
Business Administration and Management—General	M,O
Business Education	M,O
Chemistry	O
Clinical Psychology	M,O
Communication Disorders	M
Communication—General	M
Community Health	M,O
Computer and Information Systems Security	M,O
Computer Science	M,O
Counselor Education	M,O
Criminal Justice and Criminology	M
Cultural Studies	M,O
Early Childhood Education	M,O
Education—General	M,O
Educational Media/Instructional Technology	M,O
Emergency Management	M,O
English as a Second Language	M,O
English	M,O
Entrepreneurship	M,O
Environmental and Occupational Health	M,O
Ethics	M,O
Exercise and Sports Science	M,O
Foreign Languages Education	M,O
French	M,O
Geographic Information Systems	M,O
Geography	M,O
Geology	M
Geosciences	M
German	M,O
Gerontological Nursing	M,D,O
Gerontology	M,O
Health Education	M,O
Health Services Management and Hospital Administration	M,O
Higher Education	M,O
History	M,O
Holocaust and Genocide Studies	M,O
Human Resources Management	M,O
Industrial and Organizational Psychology	M
Kinesiology and Movement Studies	M,O
Management Information Systems	M,O
Mathematics Education	M,O
Mathematics	M,O
Music Education	M,O
Music	M,O
Nonprofit Management	M,O
Nursing Education	M,D,O
Nursing—General	M,D,O
Philosophy	M,O
Physical Education	M,O
Psychology—General	M
Public Administration	M,O
Public Affairs	M,O
Public Health—General	M,O
Reading Education	M,O
School Nursing	M,D,O
Science Education	M,O
Secondary Education	M,O
Social Work	M
Spanish	M,O
Special Education	M,O
Sports Management	M,O
Student Affairs	M,O
Sustainable Development	M,O
Urban and Regional Planning	M,O

WEST COAST UNIVERSITY

Family Nurse Practitioner Studies	M,D
Health Services Management and Hospital Administration	M,D
Nursing—General	M,D
Occupational Therapy	M,D
Pharmacy	M,D
Physical Therapy	M,D

WESTERN CAROLINA UNIVERSITY

Accounting	M
Applied Arts and Design—General	M
Art/Fine Arts	M
Biological and Biomedical Sciences—General	M
Business Administration and Management—General	M
Chemistry	M
Communication Disorders	M
Construction Management	M
Education—General	M
English as a Second Language	M
English	M
Entrepreneurship	M
Health Services Management and Hospital Administration	M
History	M
Nursing—General	M,D,O
Physical Therapy	D
Project Management	M,O
Psychology—General	M
Public Affairs	M
Social Work	M

WESTERN CONNECTICUT STATE UNIVERSITY

Accounting	M
Adult Nursing	M,D
Art/Fine Arts	M
Biological and Biomedical Sciences—General	M
Business Administration and Management—General	M
Clinical Psychology	M
Counselor Education	M
Criminal Justice and Criminology	M
Curriculum and Instruction	M
Education—General	M,D
Educational Leadership and Administration	D
Educational Media/Instructional Technology	M
English	M
Environmental Sciences	M
Geosciences	M
Gerontological Nursing	M,D
Health Services Management and Hospital Administration	M
History	M
Illustration	M
Mathematics	M
Music Education	M
Nursing Education	D
Nursing—General	M,D
Planetary and Space Sciences	M
Reading Education	M
Special Education	M

Writing	M

WESTERN GOVERNORS UNIVERSITY

Business Administration and Management—General	M
Computer and Information Systems Security	M
Education—General	M,O
Educational Leadership and Administration	M,O
Educational Measurement and Evaluation	M,O
Educational Media/Instructional Technology	M,O
Elementary Education	M,O
English Education	M,O
Health Services Management and Hospital Administration	M
Higher Education	M,O
Information Science	M
Management Information Systems	M
Management Strategy and Policy	M
Mathematics Education	M,O
Nursing and Healthcare Administration	M
Nursing Education	M
Science Education	M,O
Social Sciences Education	M,O
Special Education	M,O

WESTERN ILLINOIS UNIVERSITY

Accounting	M
Applied Mathematics	M,O
Biological and Biomedical Sciences—General	M,O
Business Administration and Management—General	M,O
Chemistry	M
Clinical Psychology	M,O
Communication Disorders	M
Communication—General	M
Computer Science	M
Counselor Education	M
Criminal Justice and Criminology	M,O
Distance Education Development	M,O
Ecology	D
Economic Development	M,O
Economics	M,O
Education—General	M,D,O
Educational Leadership and Administration	M,D,O
Educational Media/Instructional Technology	M,O
Elementary Education	M
English as a Second Language	M,O
English	M,O
Environmental Sciences	D
Experimental Psychology	M,O
Foundations and Philosophy of Education	M,O
Geographic Information Systems	M,O
Geography	M,O
Graphic Design	M,O
Health Education	M,O
Health Services Management and Hospital Administration	M,O
History	M
Internet and Interactive Multimedia	M,O
Kinesiology and Movement Studies	M
Liberal Studies	M
Manufacturing Engineering	M
Marine Biology	M,O
Mathematics	M,O
Museum Studies	M,O
Music	M
Physics	M
Political Science	M
Psychology—General	M,O
Reading Education	M
Recreation and Park Management	M
School Psychology	M,O
Social Psychology	M,O
Sociology	M
Special Education	M
Sports Management	M
Student Affairs	M
Supply Chain Management	M,O
Sustainable Development	M,O
Theater	M
Travel and Tourism	M
Writing	M,O
Zoology	M,O

WESTERN INTERNATIONAL UNIVERSITY

Business Administration and Management—General	M
Finance and Banking	M
International Business	M
Management Information Systems	M
Management Strategy and Policy	M
Marketing	M
Organizational Behavior	M
Organizational Management	M
Public Administration	M
Systems Engineering	M

WESTERN KENTUCKY UNIVERSITY

Adult Education	M,D,O
Agricultural Sciences—General	M
Anthropology	M
Applied Economics	M
Art Education	M
Biological and Biomedical Sciences—General	M
Business Administration and Management—General	M
Chemistry	M
Clinical Psychology	M,O
Communication Disorders	M
Communication—General	M,O
Comparative Literature	M
Computational Sciences	M
Computer Science	M
Corporate and Organizational Communication	M,O
Counseling Psychology	M
Counselor Education	M
Criminal Justice and Criminology	M
Early Childhood Education	M,O
Educational Leadership and Administration	M,D,O
Educational Media/Instructional Technology	M,O
Elementary Education	M,O
English as a Second Language	M
English Education	M
English	M
Experimental Psychology	M,O
Foreign Languages Education	M
French	M
Geology	M
Geosciences	M
German	M
Health Services Management and Hospital Administration	M
Higher Education	M
History	M
Homeland Security	M
Industrial and Organizational Psychology	M,O
Interdisciplinary Studies	M,O
Management of Technology	M
Marriage and Family Therapy	M
Mathematics	M
Middle School Education	M,O
Music Education	M
Nursing—General	M
Physical Education	M
Physical Therapy	D
Physics	M
Political Science	M
Psychology—General	M,O
Public Administration	M
Public Health—General	M
Reading Education	M,O
Recreation and Park Management	M
School Psychology	M,O
Secondary Education	M,O
Social Work	M
Sociology	M
Spanish	M
Special Education	M,O
Sports Management	M
Student Affairs	M
Writing	M

WESTERN MICHIGAN UNIVERSITY

Accounting	M
Aerospace/Aeronautical Engineering	M,D
Anthropology	M
Applied Arts and Design—General	M
Applied Economics	M,D
Applied Mathematics	M,D
Art Education	M
Athletic Training and Sports Medicine	M
Biological and Biomedical Sciences—General	M,D,O
Business Administration and Management—General	M
Chemical Engineering	M,D
Chemistry	M,D,O
Civil Engineering	M
Clinical Psychology	M,D
Communication Disorders	M,D
Communication—General	M
Computational Sciences	M,D
Computer Engineering	M,D
Computer Science	M,D
Counseling Psychology	M,D
Counselor Education	M,D
Economics	M,D
Education—General	M,D,O
Educational Leadership and Administration	M,D,O
Educational Measurement and Evaluation	M,D,O
Educational Media/Instructional Technology	M,D,O
Electrical Engineering	M,D
Engineering and Applied Sciences—General	M,D
Engineering Management	M,D
English Education	M,D
English	M,D
Exercise and Sports Science	M
Family and Consumer Sciences-General	M
Geographic Information Systems	M,O
Geography	M,D,O
Geosciences	M,D,O
Health Education	D,O
Health Services Management and Hospital Administration	M,D,O
Higher Education	M,D
History	M,D
Human Services	D,O
Industrial and Organizational Psychology	M,D
Industrial/Management Engineering	M,D
International Affairs	M,D
Manufacturing Engineering	M
Mathematics Education	M,D
Mathematics	M,D
Mechanical Engineering	M,D
Music Education	M,O
Music	M,O
Nonprofit Management	M,D,O
Nursing—General	M
Occupational Therapy	M
Paper and Pulp Engineering	M,D
Philosophy	M
Physical Education	M
Physician Assistant Studies	M
Physics	M,D,O
Physiology	M
Political Science	M,D
Psychology—General	M,D
Public Administration	M,D,O
Public Affairs	M,D,O
Reading Education	M,D
Rehabilitation Counseling	M
Rehabilitation Sciences	M
Religion	M,O
Science Education	M,D,O
Social Work	M
Sociology	M,D
Spanish	M,D
Special Education	M,D
Sports Management	M
Statistics	M,D,O
Therapies—Dance, Drama, and Music	M,O
Vocational and Technical Education	M
Writing	M,D

WESTERN MICHIGAN UNIVERSITY THOMAS M. COOLEY LAW SCHOOL

Environmental Law	M,D
Finance and Banking	M,D
Homeland Security	M,D
Insurance	M,D
Intellectual Property Law	M,D
Law	M,D
Legal and Justice Studies	M,D
National Security	M,D
Taxation	M,D

WESTERN NEW ENGLAND UNIVERSITY

Accounting	M
Advertising and Public Relations	M
Applied Behavior Analysis	M,D
Business Administration and Management—General	M
Communication—General	M
Curriculum and Instruction	M
Electrical Engineering	M
Elementary Education	M
Engineering and Applied Sciences—General	M,D
Engineering Management	M,D
English Education	M
Law	M,D
Manufacturing Engineering	M
Mathematics Education	M
Mechanical Engineering	M
Organizational Management	M
Pharmacy	D
Sports Management	M
Writing	M

WESTERN NEW MEXICO UNIVERSITY

Business Administration and Management—General	M
Education—General	M
Educational Leadership and Administration	M
Elementary Education	M
English as a Second Language	M
Interdisciplinary Studies	M
Multilingual and Multicultural Education	M
Occupational Therapy	M
Reading Education	M
Secondary Education	M
Social Work	M
Special Education	M

WESTERN OREGON UNIVERSITY

Criminal Justice and Criminology	M
Early Childhood Education	M
Education—General	M
Educational Media/Instructional Technology	M
Health Education	M
Mathematics Education	M
Multilingual and Multicultural Education	M
Music	M
Rehabilitation Counseling	M
Science Education	M
Secondary Education	M
Social Sciences Education	M
Special Education	M

WESTERN SEMINARY

Human Resources Development	M
Pastoral Ministry and Counseling	M,D,O
Religion	M,O
Theology	M,O
Women's Studies	M

WESTERN SEMINARY–SACRAMENTO CAMPUS

Marriage and Family Therapy	M
Pastoral Ministry and Counseling	M,O
Theology	M,O
Women's Studies	O

WESTERN SEMINARY–SAN JOSE CAMPUS

Marriage and Family Therapy	M,O
Pastoral Ministry and Counseling	M,O
Theology	M,O
Women's Studies	M,O

WESTERN STATE COLLEGE OF LAW AT ARGOSY UNIVERSITY

Law	D

WESTERN STATE COLORADO UNIVERSITY

Education—General	M
Educational Leadership and Administration	M
Environmental Management and Policy	M
Film, Television, and Video Production	M
Reading Education	M
Writing	M

WESTERN THEOLOGICAL SEMINARY

Pastoral Ministry and Counseling	M,D,O
Theology	M,D,O

WESTERN UNIVERSITY OF HEALTH SCIENCES

Allied Health—General	M,D
Biological and Biomedical Sciences—General	M
Dentistry	D
Family Nurse Practitioner Studies	M
Health Education	M
Nursing and Healthcare Administration	M
Nursing—General	M,D
Optometry	D
Osteopathic Medicine	D
Pharmaceutical Sciences	M
Pharmacy	D
Physical Therapy	D
Physician Assistant Studies	M
Veterinary Medicine	D

WESTERN WASHINGTON UNIVERSITY

Adult Education	M
Anthropology	M
Biological and Biomedical Sciences—General	M
Business Administration and Management—General	M
Chemistry	M
Communication Disorders	M
Computer Science	M
Counseling Psychology	M
Counselor Education	M
Education of the Gifted	M
Education—General	M
Educational Leadership and Administration	M
Elementary Education	M
English	M
Environmental Education	M
Environmental Sciences	M
Exercise and Sports Science	M
Experimental Psychology	M
Geography	M
Geology	M
Higher Education	M
History	M
Marine Sciences	M
Mathematics	M
Music	M
Physical Education	M
Political Science	M
Psychology—General	M
Rehabilitation Counseling	M
Science Education	M
Secondary Education	M

WESTFIELD STATE UNIVERSITY

Applied Behavior Analysis	M
Counseling Psychology	M
Counselor Education	M
Criminal Justice and Criminology	M
Early Childhood Education	M
Education—General	M,O
Educational Leadership and Administration	M,O
Educational Media/Instructional Technology	M
Elementary Education	M
English	M
History	M
Physical Education	M
Psychology—General	M
Reading Education	M
Secondary Education	M
Special Education	M
Vocational and Technical Education	M,O

WEST LIBERTY UNIVERSITY

Criminal Justice and Criminology	M
Education—General	M
Organizational Management	M

WESTMINSTER COLLEGE (PA)

Counselor Education	M,O
Education—General	M,O
Educational Leadership and Administration	M,O
Reading Education	M,O

WESTMINSTER COLLEGE (UT)

Accounting	M,O
Business Administration and Management—General	M,O
Communication—General	M
Counseling Psychology	M
Education—General	M
Family Nurse Practitioner Studies	M
Nurse Anesthesia	M
Nursing Education	M
Nursing—General	M
Public Health—General	M
Writing	M

WESTMINSTER SEMINARY CALIFORNIA

Religion	M
Theology	M

*M—masters degree; D—doctorate; O—other advanced degree; *—Close-Up and/or Display*

WESTMINSTER THEOLOGICAL SEMINARY
Missions and Missiology M,D,O
Pastoral Ministry and Counseling M,D,O
Religion M,D,O
Theology M,D,O

WEST TEXAS A&M UNIVERSITY
Accounting M
Agricultural Economics and Agribusiness M
Agricultural Sciences—General M,D
Animal Sciences M
Art/Fine Arts M
Biological and Biomedical Sciences—General M
Business Administration and Management—General M
Chemistry M
Communication Disorders M
Communication—General M
Counselor Education M
Criminal Justice and Criminology M
Curriculum and Instruction M
Economics M
Education—General M
Educational Leadership and Administration M
Educational Measurement and Evaluation M
Educational Media/Instructional Technology M
Engineering and Applied Sciences—General M
English M
Environmental Sciences M
Exercise and Sports Science M
Family Nurse Practitioner Studies M
Finance and Banking M
History M
Interdisciplinary Studies M
Mathematics M
Music M
Nursing—General M
Plant Sciences M
Psychology—General M
Reading Education M
Social Work M
Special Education M
Sports Management M

WEST VIRGINIA SCHOOL OF OSTEOPATHIC MEDICINE
Osteopathic Medicine D

WEST VIRGINIA STATE UNIVERSITY
Biotechnology M
Criminal Justice and Criminology M
Media Studies M

WEST VIRGINIA UNIVERSITY
Accounting M
Aerospace/Aeronautical Engineering M,D
African Studies M,D
African-American Studies M,D
Agricultural Economics and Agribusiness M
Agricultural Education M,D
Agricultural Sciences—General M,D
Agronomy and Soil Sciences D
Allopathic Medicine D
American Studies M,D
Analytical Chemistry M,D
Animal Sciences M,D
Applied Mathematics M,D
Applied Physics M,D
Applied Social Research M
Art Education M
Art History M
Art/Fine Arts M
Asian Studies M,D
Athletic Training and Sports Medicine M,D
Biochemistry M,D
Biological and Biomedical Sciences—General M,D
Biostatistics M,D
Business Administration and Management—General M
Cancer Biology/Oncology M,D
Cell Biology M,D
Chemical Engineering M,D
Chemical Physics M,D
Chemistry M,D
Child and Family Studies M
Civil Engineering M,D
Clinical Psychology M,D
Communication Disorders M,D
Communication—General M,D
Community Health M,D
Computer Engineering D
Computer Science M,D
Condensed Matter Physics M,D
Corporate and Organizational Communication M,D,O
Counseling Psychology D
Counselor Education M
Curriculum and Instruction M,D
Dentistry D
Developmental Biology M,D
Developmental Psychology M,D
Early Childhood Education M,D
Economic Development M,D
Economics M,D
Education of Students with Severe/Multiple Disabilities M,D
Education of the Gifted M,D
Education—General M,D
Educational Leadership and Administration M,D
Educational Media/Instructional Technology M,D
Educational Psychology M
Electrical Engineering M,D
Elementary Education M
Engineering and Applied Sciences—General M,D,O
English as a Second Language M
English M,D
Entomology M,D
Environmental and Occupational Health D
Environmental Biology M,D
Environmental Education M,D
Environmental Engineering M,D
Environmental Management and Policy M,D
Evolutionary Biology M,D
Exercise and Sports Science M,D
Fish, Game, and Wildlife Management M
Food Science and Technology M,D
Forensic Sciences M,D
Forestry M,D
French M
Game Design and Development O
Genetics M,D
Genomic Sciences M,D
Geographic Information Systems M,D
Geography M,D
Geology M,D
Geophysics M,D
Graphic Design M
Health Promotion M,D
Higher Education M,D
History of Science and Technology M,D
History M,D
Horticulture M,D
Human Development M,D
Human Genetics M,D
Human Services M,D
Hydrogeology M,D
Immunology M,D
Industrial and Labor Relations M
Industrial Hygiene M
Industrial/Management Engineering M,D
Inorganic Chemistry M,D
International Affairs M,D
International Economics M,D
Journalism M,O
Latin American Studies M,D
Law M,D
Legal and Justice Studies M
Liberal Studies M
Linguistics M
Marketing M,O
Mathematics Education M,D
Mathematics M,D
Mechanical Engineering M,D
Medicinal and Pharmaceutical Chemistry M,D
Microbiology M,D
Mineral/Mining Engineering M,D
Molecular Biology M,D
Music Education M,D
Music M,D
Natural Resources M,D
Neurobiology M,D
Neuroscience D
Nursing—General M,D,O
Nutrition M
Occupational Therapy M
Oral and Dental Sciences M
Organic Chemistry M,D
Paleontology M,D
Petroleum Engineering M,D
Pharmaceutical Administration M,D
Pharmaceutical Sciences M,D
Pharmacology M,D
Pharmacy M,D
Physical Chemistry M,D
Physical Education M,D
Physical Therapy D
Physics M,D
Physiology M,D
Plant Pathology M,D
Plant Sciences D
Plasma Physics M,D
Political Science M,D
Psychology—General M,D
Public Administration M
Public Health—General M,D
Public Policy M,D
Reading Education M
Recreation and Park Management M
Rehabilitation Counseling M
Reproductive Biology M,D
Safety Engineering M
Secondary Education M,D
Social Work M
Sociology M
Software Engineering M
Spanish M
Special Education M,D
Sport Psychology M,D
Sports Management M,D
Statistics M,D
Sustainable Development D
Teratology M,D
Theater M
Theoretical Chemistry M,D
Theoretical Physics M,D
Toxicology M,D
Urban and Regional Planning M,D
Writing M

WEST VIRGINIA WESLEYAN COLLEGE
Athletic Training and Sports Medicine M
Business Administration and Management—General M
Education—General M
Family Nurse Practitioner Studies M,O
Nurse Midwifery M,O
Nursing and Healthcare Administration M,O
Nursing Education M,O
Nursing—General M,O
Psychiatric Nursing M,O
Writing M

WHEATON COLLEGE
Archaeology M,D
Clinical Psychology M,D
Counseling Psychology M,D
Cultural Studies M,O
Education—General M
Elementary Education M
English as a Second Language M,O
Marriage and Family Therapy M,D
Missions and Missiology M,O
Pastoral Ministry and Counseling M,D
Psychology—General M,D
Religious Education M
Secondary Education M
Theology M,D

WHEELING JESUIT UNIVERSITY
Accounting M
Business Administration and Management—General M
Educational Leadership and Administration M
Nursing—General M
Organizational Management M
Physical Therapy D

WHEELOCK COLLEGE
Child and Family Studies M
Early Childhood Education M
Education—General M
Educational Leadership and Administration M
Elementary Education M
Human Development M
Reading Education M
Social Work M
Special Education M

WHITTIER COLLEGE
Child Development M
Education—General M
Educational Leadership and Administration M
Elementary Education M
Law D
Secondary Education M

WHITWORTH UNIVERSITY
Business Administration and Management—General M
Counselor Education M
Education of the Gifted M
Education—General M
Educational Leadership and Administration M
Elementary Education M
Secondary Education M
Special Education M
Theology M

WHU - OTTO BEISHEIM SCHOOL OF MANAGEMENT
Business Administration and Management—General M

WICHITA STATE UNIVERSITY
Accounting M
Aerospace/Aeronautical Engineering M,D
Allied Health—General M,D
Anthropology M
Applied Mathematics M,D
Art/Fine Arts M
Biological and Biomedical Sciences—General M
Business Administration and Management—General M
Chemistry M,D
Clinical Psychology D
Communication Disorders M,D
Communication—General M
Computer Engineering M,D
Computer Science M,D
Counselor Education M,D,O
Criminal Justice and Criminology M
Curriculum and Instruction M
Early Childhood Education M
Economics M
Education of the Gifted M
Education—General M,D,O
Educational Leadership and Administration M,D,O
Educational Psychology M,D,O
Electrical Engineering M,D
Engineering and Applied Sciences—General M,D
Engineering Management M,D
English M
Entrepreneurship M
Environmental Sciences M
Exercise and Sports Science M
Geology M
Gerontology M
History M
Human Services M
Industrial/Management Engineering M,D
International Economics M
Liberal Studies M
Management Information Systems M
Manufacturing Engineering M,D
Mathematics M,D
Mechanical Engineering M,D
Middle School Education M
Music Education M
Music M
Nursing—General M,D
Photography M
Physical Therapy D
Physician Assistant Studies M
Physics M,D
Psychology—General D
Public Administration M
School Psychology M,D,O
Secondary Education M
Social Psychology D
Social Work M
Sociology M
Spanish M
Special Education M
Sports Management M
Taxation M
Writing M

WIDENER UNIVERSITY
Adult Education M,D
Biomedical Engineering M
Business Administration and Management—General M
Chemical Engineering M
Civil Engineering M
Clinical Psychology D
Counselor Education M,D
Criminal Justice and Criminology M
Early Childhood Education M,D
Education—General M,D
Educational Leadership and Administration M,D
Educational Media/Instructional Technology M,D
Educational Psychology M,D
Electrical Engineering M
Elementary Education M,D
Engineering and Applied Sciences—General M
Engineering Management M
English Education M,D
Foundations and Philosophy of Education M,D
Health Education M,D
Health Law M,D
Health Services Management and Hospital Administration M
Hospitality Management M,D
Law M,D
Liberal Studies M
Mathematics Education M,D
Mechanical Engineering M
Middle School Education M,D
Nursing—General M,D,O
Physical Therapy M,D
Psychology—General
Public Administration M
Reading Education M,D
Science Education M,D
Social Sciences Education M,D
Social Work M,D
Special Education M,D
Taxation M

WILBERFORCE UNIVERSITY
Rehabilitation Counseling M

WILFRID LAURIER UNIVERSITY
Accounting M,D
American Studies M,D
Biological and Biomedical Sciences—General M
Business Administration and Management—General M,D
Canadian Studies M,D
Chemistry M
Cognitive Sciences M,D
Communication—General M
Conflict Resolution and Mediation/Peace Studies D
Criminal Justice and Criminology M
Cultural Studies M
Developmental Psychology M,D
Economics M,D
English M,D
Environmental Management and Policy M,D
Environmental Sciences M,D
Film, Television, and Video Theory and Criticism M,D
Finance and Banking M,D
Gender Studies M
Geography M,D
Health Promotion M
History M,D
Human Resources Management M,D
International Affairs M,D
International Economics M
Kinesiology and Movement Studies M
Legal and Justice Studies D
Management of Technology M,D
Marketing M,D
Mathematics M
Media Studies M
Neuroscience M,D
Organizational Behavior M,D
Organizational Management M,D
Pastoral Ministry and Counseling M,D,O
Philosophy M
Physical Education M
Political Science M,D
Psychology—General M,D
Public Policy M
Religion M,D
Social Psychology M,D
Social Sciences M
Social Work M,D
Sociology M
Supply Chain Management M,D
Theology M,D,O
Therapies—Dance, Drama, and Music M

WILKES UNIVERSITY
Accounting M
Bioengineering M

Business Administration and Management—General	M
Curriculum and Instruction	M,D
Distance Education Development	M,D
Early Childhood Education	M,D
Education—General	M,D
Educational Leadership and Administration	M,D
Educational Measurement and Evaluation	M,D
Educational Media/Instructional Technology	M,D
Electrical Engineering	M
Engineering and Applied Sciences—General	M
Engineering Management	M
English as a Second Language	M,D
English Education	M,D
Entrepreneurship	M
Finance and Banking	M
Health Services Management and Hospital Administration	M
Higher Education	M,D
Human Resources Management	M
Industrial and Manufacturing Management	M
International and Comparative Education	M,D
International Business	M
Marketing	M
Mathematics Education	M,D
Mathematics	M
Mechanical Engineering	M
Middle School Education	M,D
Nursing—General	M,D
Organizational Management	M
Pharmacy	D
Reading Education	M,D
Science Education	M,D
Secondary Education	M,D
Social Sciences Education	M,D
Special Education	M,D
Writing	M

WILLAMETTE UNIVERSITY

Business Administration and Management—General	M
Conflict Resolution and Mediation/Peace Studies	M,D
Law	M,D

WILLIAM CAREY UNIVERSITY

Art Education	M,O
Business Administration and Management—General	M
Counseling Psychology	M
Education of the Gifted	M,O
Education—General	M,O
Elementary Education	M,O
English Education	M,O
Nursing—General	M
Psychology—General	M
Secondary Education	M,O
Social Sciences Education	M,O
Special Education	M,O

WILLIAM JAMES COLLEGE

Applied Psychology	M,D,O
Clinical Psychology	M,D,O
Community Health	M,D,O
Counseling Psychology	M,D,O
Forensic Psychology	M,D,O
Industrial and Organizational Psychology	M,D,O
International Health	M,D,O
Psychology—General	M,D,O
School Psychology	M,D,O
Student Affairs	M,D,O

WILLIAM JESSUP UNIVERSITY

Education—General	M
English Education	M
Mathematics Education	M

WILLIAM JEWELL COLLEGE

Education—General	M

WILLIAM PATERSON UNIVERSITY OF NEW JERSEY

Art/Fine Arts	M
Biological and Biomedical Sciences—General	M,D
Biotechnology	M,D
Business Administration and Management—General	M
Clinical Psychology	M,D
Communication Disorders	M,D
Communication—General	M
Counseling Psychology	M,D
Counselor Education	M
Curriculum and Instruction	M
Education—General	M
Educational Leadership and Administration	M
Elementary Education	M
English	M,D
Exercise and Sports Science	M,D
History	M,D
Music	M
Nursing—General	M,D
Public Policy	M,D
Reading Education	M
Secondary Education	M
Sociology	M,D
Special Education	M
Writing	M,D

WILLIAM PENN UNIVERSITY

Organizational Management	M

WILLIAMS COLLEGE

Art History	M
Economic Development	M

WILLIAMSON COLLEGE

Organizational Management	M

WILLIAM WOODS UNIVERSITY

Advertising and Public Relations	M,D,O
Business Administration and Management—General	M,D,O
Curriculum and Instruction	M,D,O
Educational Leadership and Administration	M,D,O
Educational Media/Instructional Technology	M,D,O
Health Services Management and Hospital Administration	M,D,O
Human Resources Development	M,D,O
Marketing	M,D,O
Physical Education	M,D,O

WILMINGTON COLLEGE

Education—General	M
Reading Education	M
Special Education	M

WILMINGTON UNIVERSITY

Accounting	M,D
Adult Nursing	M,D
Business Administration and Management—General	M,D
Clinical Psychology	M
Computer and Information Systems Security	M
Counseling Psychology	M
Counselor Education	M,D
Criminal Justice and Criminology	M
Education of the Gifted	M,D
Education—General	M,D
Educational Leadership and Administration	M,D
Educational Media/Instructional Technology	M,D
Elementary Education	M,D
English as a Second Language	M,D
Environmental Management and Policy	M,D
Family Nurse Practitioner Studies	M,D
Finance and Banking	M,D
Geographic Information Systems	M
Gerontological Nursing	M,D
Health Services Management and Hospital Administration	M,D
Higher Education	M,D
Homeland Security	M,D
Human Resources Management	M,D
Human Services	M
Internet and Interactive Multimedia	M
Internet Engineering	M
Management Information Systems	M,D
Marketing	M,D
Nursing and Healthcare Administration	M,D
Nursing—General	M,D
Organizational Management	M,D
Public Administration	M,D
Reading Education	M,D
Secondary Education	M,D
Special Education	M,D
Vocational and Technical Education	M,D

WILSON COLLEGE

Accounting	M
Art/Fine Arts	M
Cultural Studies	M
Dance	M
Education—General	M
Elementary Education	M
English	M
Health Services Management and Hospital Administration	M
Humanities	M
Nursing and Healthcare Administration	M
Nursing Education	M
Nursing—General	M
Secondary Education	M
Women's Studies	M

WINEBRENNER THEOLOGICAL SEMINARY

Counseling Psychology	M,D
Theology	M,D

WINGATE UNIVERSITY

Business Administration and Management—General	M
Community College Education	M,D
Education—General	M,D
Educational Leadership and Administration	M,D
Elementary Education	M,D
Health Education	M,D
Pharmacy	D
Physical Education	M,D
Sports Management	M,D

WINONA STATE UNIVERSITY

Adult Nursing	M,D,O
Counselor Education	M
Education—General	M
Educational Leadership and Administration	M,O
English	M
Family Nurse Practitioner Studies	M,D,O
Nursing and Healthcare Administration	M,D,O
Nursing Education	M,D,O
Nursing—General	M,D,O
Recreation and Park Management	M,O
Special Education	M
Sports Management	M,O

WINSTON-SALEM STATE UNIVERSITY

Business Administration and Management—General	M
Computer Science	M
Education—General	M
Family Nurse Practitioner Studies	M,D
Health Services Management and Hospital Administration	M
Management Information Systems	M
Middle School Education	M
Nursing Education	M,D
Nursing—General	M,D
Occupational Therapy	M
Physical Therapy	D
Rehabilitation Counseling	M
Special Education	M

WINTHROP UNIVERSITY

Art Education	M
Art/Fine Arts	M
Arts Administration	M
Biological and Biomedical Sciences—General	M
Business Administration and Management—General	M
Counselor Education	M
Education—General	M
Educational Leadership and Administration	M
English	M
History	M
Liberal Studies	M
Music Education	M
Music	M
Nutrition	M,O
Physical Education	M
Psychology—General	M,O
Secondary Education	M
Social Work	M
Special Education	M

WISCONSIN LUTHERAN COLLEGE

Curriculum and Instruction	M
Educational Leadership and Administration	M
Educational Media/Instructional Technology	M
Science Education	M

WISCONSIN SCHOOL OF PROFESSIONAL PSYCHOLOGY

Clinical Psychology	M,D
Psychology—General	M,D

WITTENBERG UNIVERSITY

Education—General	M

WON INSTITUTE OF GRADUATE STUDIES

Acupuncture and Oriental Medicine	M,O
Religion	M,O

WOODBURY UNIVERSITY

Architecture	M
Business Administration and Management—General	M
Organizational Management	M

WOODS HOLE OCEANOGRAPHIC INSTITUTION

Marine Biology	D
Marine Geology	D
Ocean Engineering	D
Oceanography	D

WORCESTER POLYTECHNIC INSTITUTE

Aerospace/Aeronautical Engineering	M,D
Applied Mathematics	M,D,O
Applied Statistics	M,D,O
Artificial Intelligence/Robotics	M,D
Biochemistry	M,D
Bioinformatics	M,D
Biological and Biomedical Sciences—General	M,D
Biomedical Engineering	M,D,O
Biotechnology	M,D
Business Administration and Management—General	M,D,O
Chemical Engineering	M,D
Chemistry	M,D
Civil Engineering	M,D,O
Computational Biology	M,D
Computer Engineering	M,D,O
Computer Science	M,D,O
Construction Management	M,D,O
Database Systems	M,O
Educational Media/Instructional Technology	M,D
Electrical Engineering	M,D,O
Energy and Power Engineering	M,D
Engineering and Applied Sciences—General	M,D,O
Engineering Design	M,D,O
Environmental Engineering	M,D,O
Fire Protection Engineering	M,D,O
Game Design and Development	M
Interdisciplinary Studies	M,D,O
Internet and Interactive Multimedia	M
Management Information Systems	M,D,O
Manufacturing Engineering	M,D
Marketing	M,D,O
Materials Engineering	M,D
Materials Sciences	M,D
Mathematics	M,D,O
Mechanical Engineering	M,D,O
Modeling and Simulation	M,D
Organizational Management	M,D,O
Physics	M,D
Social Sciences	M,D,O
Systems Engineering	M,O
Systems Science	M,D,O

WORCESTER STATE UNIVERSITY

Accounting	M
Biotechnology	M
Business Administration and Management—General	M
Communication Disorders	M
Community Health Nursing	M
Early Childhood Education	M
Education—General	M,O
Educational Leadership and Administration	M,O
Elementary Education	M
English as a Second Language	M,O
English Education	M
Foreign Languages Education	M
Health Education	M
Health Services Management and Hospital Administration	M
History	M
Middle School Education	M,O
Nonprofit Management	M
Nursing Education	M
Occupational Therapy	M
Organizational Management	M
Reading Education	M,O
School Psychology	O
Secondary Education	M,O
Social Sciences Education	M
Spanish	M
Special Education	M,O

WORLD MEDICINE INSTITUTE

Acupuncture and Oriental Medicine	M

WRIGHT INSTITUTE

Clinical Psychology	D
Counseling Psychology	M
Psychology—General	D

WRIGHT STATE UNIVERSITY

Accounting	M
Acute Care/Critical Care Nursing	M
Adult Education	O
Adult Nursing	M
Allopathic Medicine	D
Anatomy	M
Applied Behavior Analysis	M
Applied Economics	M
Applied Mathematics	M
Applied Statistics	M
Biochemistry	M
Biological and Biomedical Sciences—General	M,D
Biomedical Engineering	M
Biophysics	M
Business Administration and Management—General	M
Business Education	M
Chemistry	M
Clinical Psychology	D
Community Health Nursing	M
Computer Education	M
Computer Engineering	M,D
Computer Science	M,D
Counselor Education	M
Criminal Justice and Criminology	M
Curriculum and Instruction	M,O
Early Childhood Education	M
Economics	M
Education of the Gifted	M
Education—General	M,O
Educational Leadership and Administration	M,O
Electrical Engineering	M
Elementary Education	M
Engineering and Applied Sciences—General	M,D
English as a Second Language	M
English	M
Environmental Sciences	M,D
Ergonomics and Human Factors	M,D
Family Nurse Practitioner Studies	M
Finance and Banking	M
Geology	M
Geophysics	M
Health Education	M
Health Promotion	M
Health Services Management and Hospital Administration	M
Higher Education	M,O
History	M
Humanities	M
Immunology	M
Industrial and Organizational Psychology	M,D
Interdisciplinary Studies	M
International and Comparative Education	M
International Business	M
Library Science	M
Logistics	M
Management Information Systems	M
Marketing	M
Materials Engineering	M
Materials Sciences	M
Mathematics Education	M
Mathematics	M
Mechanical Engineering	M
Medical Physics	M
Microbiology	M
Middle School Education	M
Molecular Biology	M
Music Education	M
Music	M
Nursing and Healthcare Administration	M
Nursing—General	M
Pediatric Nursing	M

*M—masters degree; D—doctorate; O—other advanced degree; *—Close-Up and/or Display*

Pharmacology	M
Physical Education	M
Physics	M
Physiology	M
Project Management	M
Psychology—General	M,D
Public Administration	M
Public Health—General	M
Recreation and Park Management	M
Rehabilitation Counseling	M
Rhetoric	M
School Nursing	M
Science Education	M
Secondary Education	M
Special Education	M
Supply Chain Management	M
Toxicology	M
Urban Studies	M
Vocational and Technical Education	M
Writing	M

WYCLIFFE COLLEGE

Religion	M,D,O
Theology	M,D,O

XAVIER UNIVERSITY

Accounting	M
Athletic Training and Sports Medicine	M
Business Administration and Management—General	M
Clinical Psychology	M,D
Counseling Psychology	M
Counselor Education	M
Criminal Justice and Criminology	M
Early Childhood Education	M
Education—General	M,D
Educational Leadership and Administration	M,D
Elementary Education	M
English	M
Ethics	M
Finance and Banking	M
Health Services Management and Hospital Administration	M*
Human Resources Development	M,D
Industrial and Organizational Psychology	M,D
International Business	M
Management Strategy and Policy	M
Marketing	M
Multilingual and Multicultural Education	M
Nursing—General	M,D,O
Occupational Therapy	M
Pastoral Ministry and Counseling	M
Psychology—General	M,D
Reading Education	M
Religious Education	M
Secondary Education	M
Special Education	M
Sports Management	M
Sustainable Development	M
Theology	M

XAVIER UNIVERSITY OF LOUISIANA

Counselor Education	M
Curriculum and Instruction	M
Education—General	M
Educational Leadership and Administration	M
Pastoral Ministry and Counseling	M
Pharmacy	D
Theology	M

YALE UNIVERSITY

Accounting	D
African Studies	M
African-American Studies	D
Allopathic Medicine	D
American Studies	D
Anthropology	M,D
Applied Arts and Design—General	M
Applied Mathematics	M,D
Applied Physics	M,D
Archaeology	M,D
Architecture	M,D
Art History	D
Art/Fine Arts	M
Asian Languages	D
Asian Studies	M
Astronomy	M,D
Astrophysics	M,D
Atmospheric Sciences	D
Biochemistry	D
Bioinformatics	D
Biological and Biomedical Sciences—General	D
Biomedical Engineering	M,D
Biophysics	D
Biostatistics	M,D
Business Administration and Management—General	M,D
Cancer Biology/Oncology	D
Cell Biology	D
Chemical Engineering	M,D
Chemistry	D
Classics	M,D
Clinical Psychology	D
Cognitive Sciences	D
Comparative Literature	D
Computational Biology	D
Computer Science	M,D
Developmental Biology	D
Developmental Psychology	D
East European and Russian Studies	M,D
Ecology	D
Economic Development	M
Economics	M,D
Electrical Engineering	M,D
Engineering and Applied Sciences—General	M,D*
Engineering Physics	M,D
English	M,D
Environmental and Occupational Health	M,D
Environmental Design	M,D
Environmental Engineering	M,D
Environmental Management and Policy	M,D
Environmental Sciences	M,D
Epidemiology	M,D
Evolutionary Biology	D
Film, Television, and Video Theory and Criticism	D
Finance and Banking	D
Forestry	M,D
French	M,D
Genetics	D
Genomic Sciences	D
Geochemistry	D
Geology	D
Geophysics	D
Geosciences	D
German	D
Graphic Design	M
Health Services Management and Hospital Administration	M,D
History of Medicine	M,D
History of Science and Technology	M,D
History	M,D
Immunology	D
Infectious Diseases	D
Inorganic Chemistry	D
International Affairs	M
International Economics	M
International Health	M,D
Italian	D
Latin American Studies	D
Law	M,D
Linguistics	D
Marketing	D
Mathematics	M,D
Mechanical Engineering	M,D
Medieval and Renaissance Studies	M,D
Meteorology	D
Microbiology	D
Molecular Biology	D
Molecular Biophysics	D
Molecular Medicine	D
Molecular Pathology	D
Molecular Physiology	D
Music	M,D,O
Near and Middle Eastern Languages	M,D
Near and Middle Eastern Studies	M,D
Neurobiology	D
Neuroscience	D
Nursing—General	M,D,O
Oceanography	D
Organic Chemistry	D
Organizational Management	D
Paleontology	D
Pathobiology	D
Pathology	M,D
Pharmacology	D
Philosophy	D
Photography	M
Physical Chemistry	D
Physician Assistant Studies	M
Physics	D
Physiology	D
Planetary and Space Sciences	M,D
Plant Biology	D
Political Science	D
Portuguese	D
Psychology—General	D
Public Health—General	M,D
Religion	D
Russian	D
Slavic Languages	D
Social Psychology	D
Social Sciences	M,D
Sociology	D
Spanish	D
Statistics	M,D
Theater	M,D,O
Theology	M
Theoretical Chemistry	D
Virology	D
Writing	M,D,O

YESHIVA BETH MOSHE

Theology	O

YESHIVA DERECH CHAIM

Religion	D

YESHIVA KARLIN STOLIN RABBINICAL INSTITUTE

Theology	O

YESHIVA OF NITRA RABBINICAL COLLEGE

Theology	

YESHIVA SHAAR HATORAH TALMUDIC RESEARCH INSTITUTE

Theology	

YESHIVATH ZICHRON MOSHE

Theology	O

YESHIVA TORAS CHAIM TALMUDICAL SEMINARY

Theology	

YESHIVA UNIVERSITY

Accounting	M
Clinical Psychology	D
Communication Disorders	M,D
Conflict Resolution and Mediation/Peace Studies	M,D
Counseling Psychology	M
Economics	M,D
Educational Leadership and Administration	M,D,O
Health Psychology	D
Intellectual Property Law	M,D
Jewish Studies	M,D
Law	M,D
Mathematics	M,D
Psychology—General	M,D
Religious Education	M,D,O
School Psychology	D
Social Work	M,D

YORK COLLEGE OF PENNSYLVANIA

Adult Nursing	M,D
Business Administration and Management—General	M
Education—General	M
Educational Leadership and Administration	M
Educational Media/Instructional Technology	M
Finance and Banking	M
Gerontological Nursing	M,D
Health Services Management and Hospital Administration	M
Marketing	M
Nurse Anesthesia	M,D
Nursing and Healthcare Administration	M,D
Nursing Education	M,D
Nursing—General	M,D
Reading Education	M

YORK UNIVERSITY

Accounting	M,D
Anthropology	M,D
Applied Arts and Design—General	M
Applied Mathematics	M,D
Art History	M,D
Art/Fine Arts	M,D
Astronomy	M,D
Biological and Biomedical Sciences—General	M,D
Business Administration and Management—General	M,D
Chemistry	M,D
Communication—General	M,D
Computer Science	M,D
Dance	M,D
Disability Studies	M,D
Economics	M,D
Education—General	M,D
Emergency Management	M
English	M,D
Environmental Management and Policy	M,D
Film, Television, and Video Production	M,D
Finance and Banking	M,D
French	M,D
Gender Studies	M,D
Geography	M,D
Geosciences	M,D
History	M,D
Human Resources Management	M,D
Humanities	M,D
Interdisciplinary Studies	M
International Affairs	M
International Business	M,D
Kinesiology and Movement Studies	M,D
Law	M,D
Linguistics	M,D
Mathematics	M,D
Music	M,D
Nursing—General	M
Philosophy	M,D
Physics	M,D
Planetary and Space Sciences	M,D
Political Science	M,D
Psychology—General	M,D
Public Administration	M
Public Affairs	M
Public Policy	M
Social Work	M,D
Sociology	M,D
Statistics	M,D
Theater	M,D
Translation and Interpretation	M
Women's Studies	M,D

YO SAN UNIVERSITY OF TRADITIONAL CHINESE MEDICINE

Acupuncture and Oriental Medicine	M

YOUNGSTOWN STATE UNIVERSITY

Accounting	M
Analytical Chemistry	M
Anatomy	M
Applied Behavior Analysis	M
Applied Mathematics	M
Biochemistry	M
Biological and Biomedical Sciences—General	M
Business Administration and Management—General	M,O
Chemistry	M
Civil Engineering	M
Computer Engineering	M
Computer Science	M
Counseling Psychology	M
Counselor Education	M
Criminal Justice and Criminology	M
Curriculum and Instruction	M
Early Childhood Education	M
Economics	M
Education of the Gifted	M
Education—General	M,D
Educational Leadership and Administration	M,D
Educational Media/Instructional Technology	M
Electrical Engineering	M
Engineering and Applied Sciences—General	M
English	M
Environmental Biology	M
Environmental Engineering	M
Environmental Management and Policy	M,O
Finance and Banking	M
Gerontology	M
Health Services Management and Hospital Administration	M
History	M
Human Services	M
Industrial/Management Engineering	M
Information Science	M
Inorganic Chemistry	M
Marketing	M
Mathematics Education	M
Mathematics	M
Mechanical Engineering	M
Microbiology	M
Middle School Education	M
Molecular Biology	M
Music Education	M
Music	M
Nursing—General	M
Organic Chemistry	M
Physical Chemistry	M
Physical Therapy	D
Physiology	M
Psychology—General	M
Reading Education	M
School Psychology	M
Science Education	M
Secondary Education	M
Special Education	M
Statistics	M

PROFILES OF INSTITUTIONS OFFERING GRADUATE AND PROFESSIONAL WORK

ABILENE CHRISTIAN UNIVERSITY, Abilene, TX 79699-9100

General Information Independent-religious, coed, university. CGS member. *Enrollment:* 4,544 graduate, professional, and undergraduate students; 527 full-time matriculated graduate/professional students (369 women), 256 part-time matriculated graduate/professional students (138 women). *Enrollment by degree level:* 761 master's, 17 doctoral, 22 other advanced degrees. *Graduate faculty:* 23 full-time (7 women), 86 part-time/adjunct (33 women). *Graduate housing:* On-campus housing not available. *Student services:* Campus employment opportunities, campus safety program, career counseling, exercise/wellness program, grant writing training, international student services, low-cost health insurance, multicultural affairs office, services for students with disabilities, teacher training, writing training. *Library:* Brown Library. *Collection:* Books: 554,015 (physical), 230,490 (digital/electronic); Serial titles: 5,381 (physical), 47,873 (digital/electronic); Databases: 112. Weekly public service hours: 97; students can reserve study rooms. *Research affiliation:* Los Alamos National Laboratory (particle physics), Fermilab (peanut toxins).

Computer facilities: Computer purchase and lease plans are available. 466 computers available on campus for general student use. A campuswide network can be accessed from student residence rooms and from off campus. Online class registration is available.
Website: http://www.acu.edu/

General Application Contact: Corey Patterson, Director of Graduate Admission and Recruiting, 325-674-6566, Fax: 325-674-6717, E-mail: gradinfo@acu.edu.

GRADUATE UNITS

Graduate School Students: 527 full-time (369 women), 256 part-time (138 women); includes 239 minority (129 Black or African American, non-Hispanic/Latino; 2 American Indian or Alaska Native, non-Hispanic/Latino; 7 Asian, non-Hispanic/Latino; 85 Hispanic/Latino; 16 Two or more races, non-Hispanic/Latino), 22 international. Average age 32. 1,098 applicants, 45% accepted, 404 enrolled. *Faculty:* 23 full-time (7 women), 86 part-time/adjunct (33 women). *Financial support:* In 2015–16, 177 students received support, including 39 research assistantships with partial tuition reimbursements available (averaging $5,800 per year), 12 teaching assistantships with partial tuition reimbursements available (averaging $5,800 per year); career-related internships or fieldwork, Federal Work-Study, institutionally sponsored loans, scholarships/grants, and tuition waivers (partial) also available. Support available to part-time students. Financial award application deadline: 4/1; financial award applicants required to submit FAFSA. In 2015, 324 master's, 4 doctorates, 48 other advanced degrees awarded. *Degree program information:* Part-time and evening/weekend programs available. Part-time, evening/weekend, online learning. *Application deadline:* For fall admission, 4/1 priority date for domestic students; for spring admission, 11/1 priority date for domestic students. Applications are processed on a rolling basis. *Application fee:* $50. Electronic applications accepted. *Application Contact:* Corey Patterson, Director of Graduate Admission and Recruiting, 325-674-6566, Fax: 325-674-3717, E-mail: gradinfo@acu.edu. *Interim Dean of Graduate School,* Dr. Donnie Snider, 325-674-2223, Fax: 325-674-6717, E-mail: gradinfo@acu.edu.

College of Arts and Sciences Students: 189 full-time (135 women), 54 part-time (44 women); includes 82 minority (53 Black or African American, non-Hispanic/Latino; 4 Asian, non-Hispanic/Latino; 23 Hispanic/Latino; 2 Two or more races, non-Hispanic/Latino), 3 international. 208 applicants, 59% accepted, 90 enrolled. *Faculty:* 3 full-time (0 women), 39 part-time/adjunct (15 women). *Financial support:* In 2015–16, 58 students received support, including 21 research assistantships (averaging $5,800 per year), 12 teaching assistantships (averaging $5,800 per year); career-related internships or fieldwork, Federal Work-Study, and tuition waivers (partial) also available. Support available to part-time students. Financial award application deadline: 4/1; financial award applicants required to submit FAFSA. In 2015, 112 master's, 44 other advanced degrees awarded. *Degree program information:* Part-time programs available. Part-time, online learning. Offers arts and sciences (MA, MLA, MS, Certificate, Specialist); clinical psychology (MS); communication (MA); composition/rhetoric (MA); conflict resolution (Certificate); conflict resolution and reconciliation (MA); counseling psychology (MS); liberal arts (MLA); literature (MA); organizational development (MS); psychology (MS, Specialist); school psychology (Specialist); writing (MA). *Application deadline:* For fall admission, 4/1 priority date for domestic students; for spring admission, 11/1 for domestic students. Applications are processed on a rolling basis. *Application fee:* $50. Electronic applications accepted. *Application Contact:* Corey Patterson, Director of Graduate Admission and Recruiting, 325-674-6566, Fax: 325-674-6717, E-mail: gradinfo@acu.edu. *Dean,* Dr. Greg Straughn, 325-674-2209, Fax: 325-674-6800, E-mail: gregory.straughn@acu.edu.

College of Biblical Studies Students: 99 full-time (46 women), 112 part-time (35 women); includes 46 minority (28 Black or African American, non-Hispanic/Latino; 1 Asian, non-Hispanic/Latino; 15 Hispanic/Latino; 2 Two or more races, non-Hispanic/Latino), 16 international. 218 applicants, 52% accepted, 98 enrolled. *Faculty:* 14 full-time (3 women), 10 part-time/adjunct (2 women). *Financial support:* In 2015–16, 37 students received support. Research assistantships, teaching assistantships, career-related internships or fieldwork, and Federal Work-Study available. Support available to part-time students. Financial award application deadline: 4/1; financial award applicants required to submit FAFSA. In 2015, 53 master's, 4 doctorates awarded. *Degree program information:* Part-time and evening/weekend programs available. Part-time, evening/weekend. Offers ancient and Oriental Christianity (MA); Biblical studies (M Div, MA, MACM, MAGS, MMFT, D Min); Christian ministry (MACM); divinity (M Div); global service (MAGS); marriage and family therapy (MMFT); ministry (D Min); modern and American Christianity (MA); New Testament (MA); Old Testament (MA); theology (MA). *Application deadline:* For fall admission, 4/1 priority date for domestic students; for spring admission, 11/1 for domestic students. Applications are processed on a rolling basis. *Application fee:* $50. Electronic applications accepted. *Application Contact:* Corey Patterson, Director of Graduate Admission and Recruiting, 325-674-6566, Fax: 325-674-6717, E-mail: gradinfo@acu.edu. *Dean,* Dr. Ken Cukrowski, 325-674-3700, Fax: 325-674-6180, E-mail: cukrowski@bible.acu.edu.

College of Business Administration Students: 13 full-time (3 women), 15 part-time (4 women); includes 3 minority (1 Black or African American, non-Hispanic/Latino; 1 Asian, non-Hispanic/Latino; 1 Hispanic/Latino), 2 international. 56 applicants, 52% accepted, 26 enrolled. *Faculty:* 20 part-time/adjunct (2 women). *Financial support:* In 2015–16, 9 students received support. Federal Work-Study and scholarships/grants available. Support available to part-time students. Financial award application deadline: 4/1; financial award applicants required to submit FAFSA. In 2015, 49 master's awarded. *Degree program information:* Part-time programs available. Part-time, online learning. Offers accountancy (M Acc); business administration (M Acc, MBA). *Application deadline:* For fall admission, 4/1 priority date for domestic students; for spring admission, 11/1 for domestic students. Applications are processed on a rolling basis. *Application fee:* $50. Electronic applications accepted. *Application Contact:* Corey Patterson, Director of Graduate Admission and Recruiting, 325-674-6566, Fax: 325-674-6717, E-mail: gradinfo@acu.edu. *Interim Dean,* Dr. Brad Crisp, 325-674-2053, Fax: 325-674-2564, E-mail: cbc06d@acu.edu.

College of Education and Human Services Students: 225 full-time (185 women), 75 part-time (55 women); includes 108 minority (47 Black or African American, non-Hispanic/Latino; 2 American Indian or Alaska Native, non-Hispanic/Latino; 1 Asian, non-Hispanic/Latino; 46 Hispanic/Latino; 12 Two or more races, non-Hispanic/Latino), 1 international. 560 applicants, 39% accepted, 190 enrolled. *Faculty:* 6 full-time (4 women), 37 part-time/adjunct (16 women). *Financial support:* In 2015–16, 82 students received support. Career-related internships or fieldwork and scholarships/grants available. Financial award application deadline: 4/1; financial award applicants required to submit FAFSA. In 2015, 113 master's, 4 other advanced degrees awarded. Offers communication sciences and disorders (MS); dietetic internship (Certificate); education and human services (M Ed, MS, MSSW, Ed D, Certificate, Post-Master's Certificate); enrollment management (Certificate); higher education (M Ed); leadership of digital learning (M Ed, Certificate); leadership of learning (M Ed, Certificate); occupational therapy (MS); organizational leadership (Ed D); social work (MSSW); superintendency (Post-Master's Certificate); teaching and learning (M Ed). *Application deadline:* For fall admission, 8/15 priority date for domestic students; for winter admission, 10/1 priority date for domestic students; for spring admission, 12/15 priority date for domestic students; for summer admission, 4/15 for domestic students. Applications are processed on a rolling basis. *Application fee:* $50. Electronic applications accepted. *Application Contact:* Corey Patterson, Director of Graduate Admission and Recruiting, 325-674-6566, Fax: 325-674-6717, E-mail: gradinfo@acu.edu. *Dean,* Dr. Donnie Snider, 325-674-2700, E-mail: dcs03b@acu.edu.

ACACIA UNIVERSITY, Tempe, AZ 85284

General Information Private, coed, graduate-only institution.

GRADUATE UNITS

American Graduate School of Education Offers educational administration (M Ed); elementary education (MA); English as a second language (M Ed); secondary education (MA); special education (M Ed).

ACADEMY FOR FIVE ELEMENT ACUPUNCTURE, Gainesville, FL 32601

General Information Independent, coed, graduate-only institution.

GRADUATE UNITS

Graduate Program Offers acupuncture (M Ac).

ACADEMY OF ART UNIVERSITY, San Francisco, CA 94105-3410

General Information Proprietary, coed, comprehensive institution. *Enrollment:* 13,800 graduate, professional, and undergraduate students; 2,961 full-time matriculated graduate/professional students (1,798 women), 1,713 part-time matriculated graduate/professional students (1,070 women). *Enrollment by degree level:* 4,674 master's. *Graduate faculty:* 208 full-time (71 women), 652 part-time/adjunct (275 women). *Tuition, area resident:* Part-time $935 per unit. *Graduate housing:* Room and/or apartments guaranteed to single students; on-campus housing not available to married students. *Student services:* Campus employment opportunities, campus safety program, career counseling, international student services, low-cost health insurance, services for students with disabilities, teacher training, writing training. *Library:* Academy of Art University Library. *Collection:* Books: 36,000 (physical), 8,000 (digital/electronic); Serial titles: 197 (physical), 400,000 (digital/electronic); Databases: 21. Weekly public service hours: 83; students can reserve study rooms.

Computer facilities: 900 computers available on campus for general student use. A campuswide network can be accessed. Online class registration, support for students taking online courses are available.
Website: http://www.academyart.edu/

General Application Contact: 800-544-ARTS, E-mail: info@academyart.edu.

GRADUATE UNITS

Graduate Program Students: 2,961 full-time (1,798 women), 1,713 part-time (1,070 women); includes 844 minority (282 Black or African American, non-Hispanic/Latino; 22 American Indian or Alaska Native, non-Hispanic/Latino; 251 Asian, non-Hispanic/Latino; 222 Hispanic/Latino; 14 Native Hawaiian or other Pacific Islander, non-Hispanic/Latino; 53 Two or more races, non-Hispanic/Latino), 2,524 international. Average age 30. 1,661 applicants, 100% accepted, 952 enrolled. *Faculty:* 208 full-time (71 women), 652 part-time/adjunct (275 women). *Financial support:* Career-related internships or fieldwork, Federal Work-Study, and scholarships/grants available. Financial award application deadline: 8/10; financial award applicants required to submit FAFSA. In 2015, 1,255 master's awarded. *Degree program information:* Part-time and evening/weekend programs available. Part-time, evening/weekend, 100% online. Offers costume design (MFA); fashion journalism (MA). *Application deadline:* Applications are processed on a rolling basis. *Application fee:* $100. Electronic applications accepted. *Application Contact:* 800-544-ARTS, E-mail: info@academyart.edu.

School of Acting Students: 25 full-time (14 women), 2 part-time (1 woman); includes 9 minority (1 Black or African American, non-Hispanic/Latino; 1 Asian, non-Hispanic/Latino; 5 Hispanic/Latino; 2 Two or more races, non-Hispanic/Latino), 12 international. Average age 27. 27 applicants, 100% accepted, 8 enrolled. *Faculty:* 1 (woman) full-time, 15 part-time/adjunct (9 women). *Financial support:* Career-related internships or fieldwork, Federal Work-Study, and scholarships/grants available. Financial award application deadline: 8/10; financial award applicants required to submit FAFSA. In 2015, 6 master's awarded. *Degree program information:* Part-time and evening/weekend programs available. Part-time, evening/weekend. Offers acting (MFA). *Application deadline:* Applications are processed on a rolling basis. *Application fee:* $100. Electronic applications accepted. *Application Contact:* 800-544-ARTS, E-mail: info@academyart.edu.

School of Advertising Students: 103 full-time (61 women), 49 part-time (31 women); includes 23 minority (7 Black or African American, non-Hispanic/Latino; 8 Asian, non-Hispanic/Latino; 7 Hispanic/Latino; 1 Two or more races, non-Hispanic/Latino), 100 international. Average age 28. 36 applicants, 100% accepted, 17 enrolled. *Faculty:* 9 full-time (2 women), 24 part-time/adjunct (5 women). *Financial support:* Career-related internships or fieldwork, Federal Work-Study, and scholarships/grants available. Financial award application deadline: 8/10; financial award applicants required to submit FAFSA. In 2015, 92 master's awarded. *Degree program information:* Part-time programs available. Part-time, 100% online. Offers advertising (MFA). *Application deadline:* Applications are processed on a rolling basis. *Application fee:* $100. Electronic applications accepted. *Application Contact:* 800-544-ARTS, E-mail: info@academyart.edu.

School of Animation and Visual Effects Students: 332 full-time (153 women), 176 part-time (69 women); includes 91 minority (24 Black or African American, non-Hispanic/Latino; 3 American Indian or Alaska Native, non-Hispanic/Latino; 29 Asian, non-Hispanic/Latino; 29 Hispanic/Latino; 3 Native Hawaiian or other Pacific Islander, non-Hispanic/Latino; 3 Two or more races, non-Hispanic/Latino), 301 international. Average age 29. 130 applicants, 100% accepted, 93 enrolled. *Faculty:* 21 full-time (6 women), 67 part-time/adjunct (14 women). *Financial support:* Career-related internships or fieldwork, Federal Work-Study, and scholarships/grants available. Financial award application deadline: 8/10; financial award applicants required to submit FAFSA. In 2015, 180 master's awarded. *Degree program information:* Part-time and evening/weekend programs available. Part-time, evening/weekend, 100% online. Offers 3D animation (MFA); 3D modeling (MFA); storyboarding (MFA); traditional animation (MFA); visual effects (MFA). *Application deadline:* Applications are processed on a rolling basis. *Application fee:* $100. Electronic applications accepted. *Application Contact:* 800-544-ARTS, E-mail: info@academyart.edu.

School of Architecture Students: 123 full-time (42 women), 88 part-time (34 women); includes 36 minority (7 Black or African American, non-Hispanic/Latino; 12 Asian, non-Hispanic/Latino; 17 Hispanic/Latino), 74 international. Average age 34. 107 applicants, 100% accepted, 31 enrolled. *Faculty:* 8 full-time (2 women), 29 part-time/adjunct (9 women). *Financial support:* Career-related internships or fieldwork, Federal Work-Study, and scholarships/grants available. Financial award application deadline: 8/10; financial award applicants required to submit FAFSA. In 2015, 54 master's awarded. *Degree program information:* Part-time and evening/weekend programs available. Part-time, evening/weekend, 100% online. Offers architecture (M Arch). *Application deadline:* Applications are processed on a rolling basis. *Application fee:* $100. Electronic applications accepted. *Application Contact:* 800-544-ARTS, E-mail: info@academyart.edu.

School of Art Education Students: 36 full-time (33 women), 15 part-time (14 women); includes 8 minority (3 Black or African American, non-Hispanic/Latino; 2 American Indian or Alaska Native, non-Hispanic/Latino; 1 Asian, non-Hispanic/Latino; 1 Hispanic/Latino; 1 Two or more races, non-Hispanic/Latino), 25 international. Average age 31. 30 applicants, 100% accepted, 17 enrolled. *Faculty:* 2 full-time (both women), 10 part-time/adjunct (all women). *Financial support:* Career-related internships or fieldwork, Federal Work-Study, and scholarships/grants available. Financial award application deadline: 8/10; financial award applicants required to submit FAFSA. In 2015, 13 master's awarded. *Degree program information:* Part-time and evening/weekend programs available. Part-time, evening/weekend, 100% online. Offers art education (MA, MAT). *Application deadline:* Applications are processed on a rolling basis. *Application fee:* $100. Electronic applications accepted. *Application Contact:* 800-544-ARTS, E-mail: info@academyart.edu.

School of Art History Students: 16 full-time (15 women), 31 part-time (27 women); includes 9 minority (1 Black or African American, non-Hispanic/Latino; 1 American Indian or Alaska Native, non-Hispanic/Latino; 1 Asian, non-Hispanic/Latino; 5 Hispanic/Latino; 1 Two or more races, non-Hispanic/Latino), 3 international. Average age 34. 35 applicants, 100% accepted, 16 enrolled. *Faculty:* 3 part-time/adjunct (all women). *Financial support:* Career-related internships or fieldwork, Federal Work-Study, and scholarships/grants available. Financial award application deadline: 8/10; financial award applicants required to submit FAFSA. *Degree program information:* Part-time and evening/weekend programs available. Part-time, evening/weekend, 100% online. Offers art history (MA). *Application deadline:* Applications are processed on a rolling basis. *Application fee:* $100. Electronic applications accepted. *Application Contact:* 800-544-ARTS, E-mail: info@academyart.edu.

School of Fashion Students: 419 full-time (374 women), 199 part-time (175 women); includes 169 minority (80 Black or African American, non-Hispanic/Latino; 3 American Indian or Alaska Native, non-Hispanic/Latino; 44 Asian, non-Hispanic/Latino; 32 Hispanic/Latino; 10 Two or more races, non-Hispanic/Latino), 348 international. Average age 29. 205 applicants, 100% accepted, 130 enrolled. *Faculty:* 23 full-time (14 women), 70 part-time/adjunct (54 women). *Financial support:* Career-related internships or fieldwork, Federal Work-Study, and scholarships/grants available. Financial award application deadline: 8/10; financial award applicants required to submit FAFSA. In 2015, 181 master's awarded. *Degree program information:* Part-time and evening/weekend programs available. Part-time, evening/weekend, 100% online. Offers fashion design (MFA); fashion merchandising (MFA); fashion textiles (MFA); knitwear (MFA). *Application deadline:* Applications are processed on a rolling basis. *Application fee:* $100. Electronic applications accepted. *Application Contact:* 800-544-ARTS, E-mail: info@academyart.edu.

School of Fine Art Students: 90 full-time (55 women), 176 part-time (127 women); includes 50 minority (13 Black or African American, non-Hispanic/Latino; 3 American Indian or Alaska Native, non-Hispanic/Latino; 13 Asian, non-Hispanic/Latino; 14 Hispanic/Latino; 2 Native Hawaiian or other Pacific Islander, non-Hispanic/Latino; 5 Two or more races, non-Hispanic/Latino), 69 international. Average age 41. 69 applicants, 100% accepted, 39 enrolled. *Faculty:* 19 full-time (7 women), 36 part-time/adjunct (16 women). *Financial support:* Career-related internships or fieldwork, Federal Work-Study, and scholarships/grants available. Financial award application deadline: 8/10; financial award applicants required to submit FAFSA. In 2015, 63 master's awarded. *Degree program information:* Part-time and evening/weekend programs available. Part-time, evening/weekend, 100% online. Offers figurative painting (MFA); non-figurative painting (MFA); printmaking (MFA); sculpture (MFA). *Application deadline:* Applications are processed on a rolling basis. *Application fee:* $100. Electronic applications accepted. *Application Contact:* 800-544-ARTS, E-mail: info@academyart.edu.

School of Game Development Students: 99 full-time (21 women), 38 part-time (12 women); includes 26 minority (3 Black or African American, non-Hispanic/Latino; 9 Asian, non-Hispanic/Latino; 8 Hispanic/Latino; 1 Native Hawaiian or other Pacific Islander, non-Hispanic/Latino; 5 Two or more races, non-Hispanic/Latino), 71 international. Average age 28. 45 applicants, 100% accepted, 34 enrolled. *Faculty:* 12 full-time (0 women), 21 part-time/adjunct (0 women). *Financial support:* Career-related internships or fieldwork, Federal Work-Study, and scholarships/grants available. Financial award application deadline: 8/10; financial award applicants required to submit FAFSA. In 2015, 35 master's awarded. *Degree program information:* Part-time and evening/weekend programs available. Part-time, evening/weekend, 100% online. Offers game development (MFA). *Application deadline:* Applications are processed on a rolling basis. *Application fee:* $100. Electronic applications accepted. *Application Contact:* 800-544-ARTS, E-mail: info@academyart.edu.

School of Graphic Design Students: 222 full-time (164 women), 139 part-time (96 women); includes 51 minority (14 Black or African American, non-Hispanic/Latino; 1 American Indian or Alaska Native, non-Hispanic/Latino; 18 Asian, non-Hispanic/Latino; 16 Hispanic/Latino; 1 Native Hawaiian or other Pacific Islander, non-Hispanic/Latino; 1 Two or more races, non-Hispanic/Latino), 247 international. Average age 28. 184 applicants, 100% accepted, 105 enrolled. *Faculty:* 9 full-time (1 woman), 32 part-time/adjunct (13 women). *Financial support:* Career-related internships or fieldwork, Federal Work-Study, and scholarships/grants available. Financial award application deadline: 8/10; financial award applicants required to submit FAFSA. In 2015, 32 master's awarded. *Degree program information:* Part-time and evening/weekend programs available. Part-time, evening/weekend, 100% online. Offers graphic design (MFA). *Application deadline:* Applications are processed on a rolling basis. *Application fee:* $100. Electronic applications accepted. *Application Contact:* 800-544-ARTS, E-mail: info@academyart.edu.

School of Illustration Students: 172 full-time (111 women), 116 part-time (78 women); includes 35 minority (9 Black or African American, non-Hispanic/Latino; 10 Asian, non-Hispanic/Latino; 13 Hispanic/Latino; 3 Two or more races, non-Hispanic/Latino), 144 international. Average age 31. 88 applicants, 100% accepted, 59 enrolled. *Faculty:* 11 full-time (2 women), 37 part-time/adjunct (16 women). *Financial support:* Career-related internships or fieldwork, Federal Work-Study, and scholarships/grants available. Financial award application deadline: 8/10; financial award applicants required to submit FAFSA. In 2015, 64 master's awarded. *Degree program information:* Part-time and evening/weekend programs available. Part-time, evening/weekend, 100% online. Offers illustration (MFA). *Application deadline:* Applications are processed on a rolling basis. *Application fee:* $100. Electronic applications accepted. *Application Contact:* 800-544-ARTS, E-mail: info@academyart.edu.

School of Industrial Design Students: 116 full-time (42 women), 50 part-time (21 women); includes 17 minority (3 Black or African American, non-Hispanic/Latino; 6 Asian, non-Hispanic/Latino; 6 Hispanic/Latino; 2 Native Hawaiian or other Pacific Islander, non-Hispanic/Latino), 123 international. Average age 28. 89 applicants, 100% accepted, 36 enrolled. *Faculty:* 5 full-time (0 women), 24 part-time/adjunct (6 women). *Financial support:* Career-related internships or fieldwork, Federal Work-Study, and scholarships/grants available. Financial award application deadline: 8/10; financial award applicants required to submit FAFSA. In 2015, 21 master's awarded. *Degree program information:* Part-time and evening/weekend programs available. Part-time, evening/weekend, 100% online. Offers industrial design (MFA). *Application deadline:* Applications are processed on a rolling basis. *Application fee:* $100. Electronic applications accepted. *Application Contact:* 800-544-ARTS, E-mail: info@academyart.edu.

School of Interior Architecture and Design Students: 132 full-time (104 women), 98 part-time (83 women); includes 32 minority (14 Black or African American, non-Hispanic/Latino; 7 Asian, non-Hispanic/Latino; 9 Hispanic/Latino; 2 Two or more races, non-Hispanic/Latino), 108 international. Average age 32. 120 applicants, 100% accepted, 67 enrolled. *Faculty:* 3 full-time (2 women), 24 part-time/adjunct (11 women). *Financial support:* Career-related internships or fieldwork, Federal Work-Study, and scholarships/grants available. Financial award application deadline: 8/10; financial award applicants required to submit FAFSA. In 2015, 129 master's awarded. *Degree program information:* Part-time and evening/weekend programs available. Part-time, evening/weekend, 100% online. Offers interior architecture and design (MFA). *Application deadline:* Applications are processed on a rolling basis. *Application fee:* $100. Electronic applications accepted. *Application Contact:* 800-544-ARTS, E-mail: info@academyart.edu.

School of Jewelry and Metal Arts Students: 37 full-time (32 women), 7 part-time (6 women); includes 4 minority (3 Asian, non-Hispanic/Latino; 1 Hispanic/Latino), 32 international. Average age 29. 23 applicants, 100% accepted, 12 enrolled. *Faculty:* 2 full-time (both women), 8 part-time/adjunct (6 women). *Financial support:* Career-related internships or fieldwork, Federal Work-Study, and scholarships/grants available. Financial award application deadline: 8/10; financial award applicants required to submit FAFSA. In 2015, 7 master's awarded. *Degree program information:* Part-time and evening/weekend programs available. Part-time, evening/weekend, 100% online. Offers jewelry and metal arts (MFA). *Application deadline:* Applications are processed on a rolling basis. *Application fee:* $100. Electronic applications accepted. *Application Contact:* 800-544-ARTS, E-mail: info@academyart.edu.

School of Landscape Architecture Students: 36 full-time (22 women), 5 part-time (1 woman); includes 2 minority (1 Black or African American, non-Hispanic/Latino; 1 Asian, non-Hispanic/Latino), 34 international. Average age 27. 31 applicants, 100% accepted, 9 enrolled. *Faculty:* 1 (woman) full-time, 15 part-time/adjunct (6 women). *Financial support:* Career-related internships or fieldwork, Federal Work-Study, and scholarships/grants available. Financial award application deadline: 8/10; financial award applicants required to submit FAFSA. In 2015, 2 master's awarded. *Degree program information:* Part-time and evening/weekend programs available. Part-time, evening/weekend, 100% online. Offers landscape architecture (MFA). *Application deadline:* Applications are processed on a rolling basis. *Application fee:* $100. Electronic applications accepted. *Application Contact:* 800-544-ARTS, E-mail: info@academyart.edu.

School of Motion Pictures and Television Students: 232 full-time (114 women), 83 part-time (37 women); includes 50 minority (23 Black or African American, non-Hispanic/Latino; 3 American Indian or Alaska Native, non-Hispanic/Latino; 7 Asian, non-Hispanic/Latino; 12 Hispanic/Latino; 1 Native Hawaiian or other Pacific Islander, non-Hispanic/Latino; 4 Two or more races, non-Hispanic/Latino), 200 international. Average age 29. 113 applicants, 100% accepted, 56 enrolled. *Faculty:* 9 full-time (1 woman), 47 part-time/adjunct (10 women). *Financial support:* Career-related internships or fieldwork, Federal Work-Study, and scholarships/grants available. Financial award application deadline: 8/10; financial award applicants required to submit FAFSA. In 2015, 90 master's awarded. *Degree program information:* Part-time and evening/weekend programs available. Part-time, evening/weekend, 100% online. Offers motion pictures and television (MFA). *Application deadline:* Applications are processed on a rolling basis. *Application fee:* $100. Electronic applications accepted. *Application Contact:* 800-544-ARTS, E-mail: info@academyart.edu.

School of Multimedia Communications Students: 68 full-time (47 women), 34 part-time (23 women); includes 13 minority (8 Black or African American, non-Hispanic/Latino; 2 Asian, non-Hispanic/Latino; 2 Hispanic/Latino; 1 Two or more races, non-Hispanic/Latino), 74 international. Average age 27. 34 applicants, 100% accepted, 20 enrolled. *Faculty:* 5 full-time (1 woman), 13 part-time/adjunct (4 women). *Financial support:* Career-related internships or fieldwork, Federal Work-Study, and scholarships/grants available. Financial award application deadline: 8/10; financial award applicants required to submit FAFSA. In 2015, 65 master's awarded. *Degree program information:* Part-time and evening/weekend programs available. Part-time, evening/weekend, 100% online. Offers multimedia communications (MA). *Application deadline:* Applications are processed on a rolling basis. *Application fee:* $100. Electronic applications accepted. *Application Contact:* 800-544-ARTS, E-mail: info@academyart.edu.

School of Music Production and Sound Design for Visual Media Students: 109 full-time (50 women), 26 part-time (11 women); includes 20 minority (10 Black or African

American, non-Hispanic/Latino; 1 American Indian or Alaska Native, non-Hispanic/Latino; 5 Asian, non-Hispanic/Latino; 4 Hispanic/Latino), 86 international. Average age 29. 31 applicants, 100% accepted, 20 enrolled. *Faculty:* 4 full-time (0 women), 24 part-time/adjunct (3 women). *Financial support:* Career-related internships or fieldwork, Federal Work-Study, and scholarships/grants available. Financial award application deadline: 8/10; financial award applicants required to submit FAFSA. In 2015, 31 master's awarded. *Degree program information:* Part-time and evening/weekend programs available. Part-time, evening/weekend, 100% online. Offers music production and sound design for visual media (MFA). *Application deadline:* Applications are processed on a rolling basis. *Application fee:* $100. Electronic applications accepted. *Application Contact:* 800-544-ARTS, E-mail: info@academyart.edu.

School of Photography Students: 122 full-time (56 women), 142 part-time (84 women); includes 54 minority (16 Black or African American, non-Hispanic/Latino; 2 American Indian or Alaska Native, non-Hispanic/Latino; 12 Asian, non-Hispanic/Latino; 15 Hispanic/Latino; 4 Native Hawaiian or other Pacific Islander, non-Hispanic/Latino; 5 Two or more races, non-Hispanic/Latino), 78 international. Average age 36. 83 applicants, 100% accepted, 53 enrolled. *Faculty:* 6 full-time (3 women), 29 part-time/adjunct (11 women). *Financial support:* Career-related internships or fieldwork, Federal Work-Study, and scholarships/grants available. Financial award application deadline: 8/10; financial award applicants required to submit FAFSA. In 2015, 69 master's awarded. *Degree program information:* Part-time and evening/weekend programs available. Part-time, evening/weekend, 100% online. Offers photography (MFA). *Application deadline:* Applications are processed on a rolling basis. *Application fee:* $100. Electronic applications accepted. *Application Contact:* 800-544-ARTS, E-mail: info@academyart.edu.

School of Visual Development Students: 158 full-time (85 women), 58 part-time (32 women); includes 43 minority (9 Black or African American, non-Hispanic/Latino; 1 American Indian or Alaska Native, non-Hispanic/Latino; 20 Asian, non-Hispanic/Latino; 10 Hispanic/Latino; 3 Two or more races, non-Hispanic/Latino), 113 international. Average age 28. 41 applicants, 100% accepted, 31 enrolled. *Faculty:* 5 full-time (0 women), 7 part-time/adjunct (1 woman). *Financial support:* Career-related internships or fieldwork, Federal Work-Study, and scholarships/grants available. Financial award application deadline: 8/10; financial award applicants required to submit FAFSA. In 2015, 20 master's awarded. *Degree program information:* Part-time and evening/weekend programs available. Part-time, evening/weekend, 100% online. Offers visual development (MFA). *Application deadline:* Applications are processed on a rolling basis. *Application fee:* $100. Electronic applications accepted. *Application Contact:* 800-544-ARTS, E-mail: info@academyart.edu.

School of Web Design and New Media Students: 275 full-time (172 women), 151 part-time (87 women); includes 76 minority (21 Black or African American, non-Hispanic/Latino; 39 Asian, non-Hispanic/Latino; 12 Hispanic/Latino; 4 Two or more races, non-Hispanic/Latino), 262 international. Average age 30. 90 applicants, 100% accepted, 72 enrolled. *Faculty:* 9 full-time (2 women), 39 part-time/adjunct (14 women). *Financial support:* Career-related internships or fieldwork, Federal Work-Study, and scholarships/grants available. Financial award application deadline: 8/10; financial award applicants required to submit FAFSA. In 2015, 89 master's awarded. *Degree program information:* Part-time and evening/weekend programs available. Part-time, evening/weekend, 100% online. Offers Web design and new media (MFA). *Application deadline:* Applications are processed on a rolling basis. *Application fee:* $100. Electronic applications accepted. *Application Contact:* 800-544-ARTS, E-mail: info@academyart.edu.

School of Writing for Film, Television and Digital Media Students: 11 full-time (6 women), 11 part-time (5 women); includes 9 minority (5 Black or African American, non-Hispanic/Latino; 1 American Indian or Alaska Native, non-Hispanic/Latino; 2 Hispanic/Latino; 1 Two or more races, non-Hispanic/Latino), 2 international. Average age 36. 23 applicants, 100% accepted, 9 enrolled. *Faculty:* 1 full-time (0 women), 8 part-time/adjunct (2 women). *Financial support:* Career-related internships or fieldwork, Federal Work-Study, and scholarships/grants available. Financial award application deadline: 8/10; financial award applicants required to submit FAFSA. *Degree program information:* Part-time and evening/weekend programs available. Part-time, evening/weekend, 100% online. Offers writing for film, television and digital media (MFA). *Application deadline:* Applications are processed on a rolling basis. *Application fee:* $100. Electronic applications accepted. *Application Contact:* 800-544-ARTS, E-mail: info@academyart.edu.

See Display below and Close-Up on page 863.

ACADEMY OF CHINESE CULTURE AND HEALTH SCIENCES, Oakland, CA 94612

General Information Private, coed, graduate-only institution. *Graduate housing:* On-campus housing not available.

GRADUATE UNITS

Program in Traditional Chinese Medicine ***Degree program information:*** Part-time and evening/weekend programs available. Part-time, evening/weekend. Offers traditional Chinese medicine (MS).

ACADIA UNIVERSITY, Wolfville, NS B4P 2R6, Canada

General Information Province-supported, coed, comprehensive institution. *Graduate housing:* Room and/or apartments available on a first-come, first-served basis to single students; on-campus housing not available to married students. Housing application deadline: 5/31. *Research affiliation:* Atlantic Research Laboratory.

GRADUATE UNITS

Divinity College ***Degree program information:*** Part-time programs available. Part-time. Offers divinity (M Div); theology (MA, D Min).

Faculty of Arts Offers arts (MA); English (MA); political science (MA); social and political thought (MA); sociology (MA).

Faculty of Professional Studies Offers educational studies (PhD).

School of Education Offers counseling (M Ed); cultural and media studies (M Ed); curriculum studies (M Ed); inclusive education (M Ed); leadership (M Ed); learning and technology (M Ed); science, math and technology (M Ed).

School of Recreation Management and Community Development Offers recreation management and community development (MR).

Faculty of Pure and Applied Science Offers applied geomatics (M Sc); applied mathematics and statistics (M Sc); biology (M Sc); chemistry (M Sc); clinical psychology (M Sc); earth and environmental science (M Sc); pure and applied science (M Sc).

Jodrey School of Computer Science Offers computer science (M Sc).

ACUPUNCTURE & INTEGRATIVE MEDICINE COLLEGE, BERKELEY, Berkeley, CA 94704

General Information Independent, coed, graduate-only institution. *Enrollment by degree level:* 104 master's. *Graduate faculty:* 29 part-time/adjunct (17 women). *Tuition, area resident:* Full-time $11,000. *Required fees:* $60. *Graduate housing:* On-campus housing not available. *Student services:* Campus employment opportunities. *Library:* AIMC Berkeley Library plus 1 other. *Collection:* Books: 2,500 (physical). Weekly public service hours: 40.

Computer facilities: 2 computers available on campus for general student use. Website: http://aimc.edu/

General Application Contact: Julie Scheff, Admissions Manager, 510-666-8248 Ext. 121, Fax: 510-666-0111, E-mail: rmcneilly@aimc.edu.

GRADUATE UNITS

Program in Oriental Medicine Students: 61 full-time (48 women), 43 part-time (36 women); includes 30 minority (4 Black or African American, non-Hispanic/Latino; 9 Asian, non-Hispanic/Latino; 8 Hispanic/Latino; 1 Native Hawaiian or other Pacific Islander, non-Hispanic/Latino; 8 Two or more races, non-Hispanic/Latino), 5 international. Average age 37. 40 applicants, 85% accepted, 29 enrolled. *Faculty:* 29 part-time/adjunct (17 women). *Financial support:* Federal Work-Study available. Support available to part-time students. Financial award application deadline: 7/31; financial award applicants required to submit FAFSA. In 2015, 33 master's awarded. *Degree program information:* Part-time programs available. Part-time. Offers Oriental medicine (MS). *Application deadline:* For fall admission, 3/15 priority date for domestic and international students; for winter admission, 7/15 priority date for domestic and international students; for spring admission, 11/15 priority date for domestic and international students. *Application fee:* $100 ($200 for international students). Electronic applications accepted. *Application Contact:* Julie Scheff. *President*, Yasou Tanaka, 510-666-8248, Fax: 510-666-0111, E-mail: ytanaka@aimc.edu.

ACUPUNCTURE AND MASSAGE COLLEGE, Miami, FL 33176

General Information Proprietary, coed, graduate-only institution.

GRADUATE UNITS

Program in Oriental Medicine Offers Oriental medicine (MOM).

ADAMS STATE UNIVERSITY, Alamosa, CO 81101

General Information State-supported, coed, comprehensive institution. *Graduate housing:* Rooms and/or apartments available to single and married students. Housing application deadline: 5/15. *Research affiliation:* Sandia National Laboratories (science education).

GRADUATE UNITS

The Graduate School *Degree program information:* Part-time programs available. Part-time, online learning. Offers art (MA); counseling (MA); education (MA); history (MA); human performance and physical education (MA); special education (MA).

ADELPHI UNIVERSITY, Garden City, NY 11530-0701

General Information Independent, coed, university. *Graduate housing:* Room and/or apartments available on a first-come, first-served basis to single students; on-campus housing not available to married students. Housing application deadline: 5/1. *Research affiliation:* The Hagedorn Foundation, North Shore Long Island Jewish Health System (medicine), National Science Foundation, The Research Corporation, Mount Sinai Medical Center, Albert Einstein College of Medicine.

GRADUATE UNITS

College of Arts and Sciences *Degree program information:* Part-time programs available. Part-time. Offers arts and sciences (MA, MFA, MS); biology (MS); creative writing (MFA); environmental studies (MS); studio art (MA). Electronic applications accepted.

College of Nursing and Public Health *Degree program information:* Part-time and evening/weekend programs available. Part-time, evening/weekend. Offers adult health nurse (MS); health information technology (Advanced Certificate); nurse practitioner in adult health nursing (Certificate); nursing (PhD); nursing administration (MS, Certificate); nutrition (MS); public health (MPH). Electronic applications accepted.

Derner Institute of Advanced Psychological Studies *Degree program information:* Part-time programs available. Part-time. Offers clinical psychology (PhD); general psychology (MA); mental health counseling (MA); school psychology (MA). Electronic applications accepted.

Robert B. Willumstad School of Business *Degree program information:* Part-time and evening/weekend programs available. Part-time, evening/weekend. Offers accounting (MBA); business (MBA, Certificate); finance (MBA); health services administration (MBA); human resource management (Certificate); management (MBA); management information systems (MBA); marketing (MBA); sport management (MBA). Electronic applications accepted.

Ruth S. Ammon School of Education *Degree program information:* Part-time and evening/weekend programs available. Part-time, evening/weekend. Offers adolescent education (MA); aging (Certificate); art education (MA); audiology (MS, DA); birth-grade 12 (MS); birth-grade 6 (MS); childhood education (MA); community health education (MA, Certificate); education (MA, MS, DA, Certificate); educational leadership and technology (MA, Certificate); grades 5-12 (MS); physical/educational human performance science (MA); school health education (MA); special education (MS, Certificate); speech-language pathology (MS, DA); teaching English to speakers of other languages (MA, Certificate). Electronic applications accepted.

School of Social Work *Degree program information:* Part-time and evening/weekend programs available. Part-time, evening/weekend. Offers social welfare (DSW); social work (MSW, PhD). Electronic applications accepted.

University College Offers emergency management (Certificate).

ADLER GRADUATE SCHOOL, Richfield, MN 55423

General Information Independent, coed, graduate-only institution. *Enrollment by degree level:* 311 master's. *Graduate faculty:* 9 full-time (all women), 61 part-time/adjunct (46 women). *Required fees:* $530 per credit. *Graduate housing:* On-campus housing not available. *Student services:* Career counseling, international student services, multicultural affairs office, services for students with disabilities, writing training. *Library:* Adler Graduate School Library.

Computer facilities: 12 computers available on campus for general student use. A campuswide network can be accessed. Online class registration is available. Website: http://www.alfredadler.edu/

General Application Contact: Evelyn B. Haas, Director of Admissions, 612-767-7044, Fax: 612-861-7559, E-mail: ev@alfredadler.edu.

GRADUATE UNITS

Program in Adlerian Counseling and Psychotherapy Students: 311 part-time (243 women); includes 51 minority (40 Black or African American, non-Hispanic/Latino; 6 American Indian or Alaska Native, non-Hispanic/Latino; 5 Hispanic/Latino). Average age 40. *Faculty:* 61 part-time/adjunct (46 women). *Financial support:* Career-related internships or fieldwork and tuition waivers available. Support available to part-time students. Financial award applicants required to submit FAFSA. *Degree program information:* Part-time and evening/weekend programs available. Part-time, evening/weekend. Offers Adlerian studies (MA); art therapy (MA); clinical mental health counseling (MA); co-occurring substance abuse and mental health disorders (MA); marriage and family therapy (MA); school counseling (MA). *Application deadline:* Applications are processed on a rolling basis. *Application fee:* $50. Electronic applications accepted. *Application Contact:* Evelyn B. Haas, Director of Admissions, 612-767-7044, Fax: 612-861-7559, E-mail: ev@alfredadler.edu. *President*, Dr. Dan Haugen, 612-767-7048, Fax: 612-861-7559, E-mail: haugen@alfredadler.edu.

ADLER UNIVERSITY, Chicago, IL 60602

General Information Independent, coed, graduate-only institution. *Graduate housing:* On-campus housing not available. *Research affiliation:* LGBTQ Mental Health and Inclusion Center, Adler Child Guidance Center, Adler Institute on Social Exclusion, Adler Institute on Public Safety and Social Justice.

GRADUATE UNITS

Programs in Psychology *Degree program information:* Part-time and evening/weekend programs available. Part-time, evening/weekend, online learning. Offers advanced Adlerian psychotherapy (Certificate); art therapy (MA); clinical mental health counseling (MA); clinical neuropsychology (Certificate); clinical psychology (Psy D); community psychology (MA); counseling and organizational psychology (MA); counseling psychology (MA); counselor education and supervision (PhD); couple and family therapy (DCFT); criminology (MA); emergency management leadership (MA); forensic psychology (MA); marriage and family counseling (MA); marriage and family therapy (Certificate); military psychology (MA); nonprofit management (MA); organizational psychology (MA); police psychology (MA); public policy and administration (MA); rehabilitation counseling (MA); sport and health psychology (MA); substance abuse counseling (Certificate). Electronic applications accepted.

ADRIAN COLLEGE, Adrian, MI 49221-2575

General Information Independent-religious, coed, comprehensive institution. *Graduate housing:* On-campus housing not available.

GRADUATE UNITS

Graduate Programs Offers accounting (MS); athletic training (MS); criminal justice (MA).

ADVENTIST UNIVERSITY OF HEALTH SCIENCES, Orlando, FL 32803

General Information Independent, coed, comprehensive institution.

GRADUATE UNITS

Program in Nurse Anesthesia Offers nurse anesthesia (MS).

AIR FORCE INSTITUTE OF TECHNOLOGY, Dayton, OH 45433-7765

General Information Federally supported, coed, primarily men, graduate-only institution. *Graduate housing:* On-campus housing not available. *Research affiliation:* U.S. Air Force Office of Scientific Research, U.S. Air Force Research Laboratory, Dayton Area Graduate Studies Institute (aerospace), Department of Energy, National Security Agency.

GRADUATE UNITS

Graduate School of Engineering and Management *Degree program information:* Part-time programs available. Part-time. Offers aeronautical engineering (MS, PhD); applied mathematics (MS, PhD); applied physics (MS, PhD); astronautical engineering (MS, PhD); computer engineering (MS, PhD); computer systems/science (MS); cost analysis (MS); electrical engineering (MS, PhD); electro-optics (MS, PhD); engineering and management (MS, PhD); environmental and engineering management (MS); environmental engineering science (MS); information resource/systems management (MS); logistics management (MS); materials science (MS, PhD); nuclear engineering (MS, PhD); operations research (MS, PhD); space operations (MS); space physics (MS); systems engineering (MS, PhD).

ALABAMA AGRICULTURAL AND MECHANICAL UNIVERSITY, Huntsville, AL 35811

General Information State-supported, coed, university. CGS member. *Graduate housing:* Rooms and/or apartments available on a first-come, first-served basis to single students and available to married students. Housing application deadline: 5/1. *Research affiliation:* NASA (utilization of space resources), Boeing Defense and Space Group (plant science), Lawrence Livermore National Laboratory (chemistry, physics), Alabama Supercomputer Network, Nichols Research Corporation (computer science), Hughes Aircraft Corporation (physics).

GRADUATE UNITS

School of Graduate Studies Electronic applications accepted.

College of Agricultural, Life and Natural Sciences *Degree program information:* Part-time and evening/weekend programs available. Part-time, evening/weekend. Offers agricultural, life and natural sciences (MS, MURP, PhD); apparel, merchandising and design (MS); biology (MS, PhD); family and consumer sciences (MS); food science (MS, PhD); human development and family studies (MS); nutrition and hospitality management (MS); plant and soil science (MS, PhD); urban and regional planning (MURP). Electronic applications accepted.

College of Business and Public Affairs *Degree program information:* Part-time and evening/weekend programs available. Part-time, evening/weekend. Offers agribusiness (PhD); business and public affairs (MBA, MS); logistics and supply chain management (MBA). Electronic applications accepted.

College of Education, Humanities, and Behavioral Sciences *Degree program information:* Part-time and evening/weekend programs available. Part-time, evening/weekend. Offers art education (MS); biology (M Ed); business/marketing education (M Ed, Ed S); chemistry (M Ed); collaborative teacher secondary education (M Ed, Ed S); early childhood education (MS Ed, Ed S); education (M Ed, Ed S); education, humanities, and behavioral sciences (M Ed, MS, MS Ed, Ed S); elementary education (MS Ed, Ed S); English language arts (M Ed); family/consumer science education (M Ed, Ed S); general science (M Ed); general social science (M Ed); mathematics (M Ed, Ed S); music education (M Ed); physical education (MS); physics (M Ed, Ed S); psychology and counseling (MS, Ed S); reading/literacy (PhD);

social work (MSW); special education collaborative teacher training (MS Ed, Ed S); speech-language pathology (MS); technology education (M Ed). Electronic applications accepted.

College of Engineering, Technology, and Physical Sciences Degree program information: Part-time and evening/weekend programs available. Part-time, evening/weekend. Offers computer science (MS); construction management (MS); engineering, technology, and physical sciences (M Eng, MS, PhD); industrial technology (MS); material engineering (M Eng); physics (MS, PhD). Electronic applications accepted.

ALABAMA STATE UNIVERSITY, Montgomery, AL 36101-0271

General Information State-supported, coed, comprehensive institution. CGS member. *Enrollment:* 5,383 graduate, professional, and undergraduate students; 291 full-time matriculated graduate/professional students (200 women), 328 part-time matriculated graduate/professional students (229 women). *Enrollment by degree level:* 429 master's, 153 doctoral, 37 other advanced degrees. *Graduate faculty:* 54 full-time (28 women), 23 part-time/adjunct (14 women). *Tuition, area resident:* Full-time $3087; part-time $2744 per credit. Tuition, nonresident: full-time $6174; part-time $5488 per credit. *Required fees:* $2284; $1142 per credit. $571 per semester. Tuition and fees vary according to class time, course level, course load, degree level, program and student level. *Graduate housing:* On-campus housing not available. *Student services:* Campus employment opportunities, campus safety program, career counseling, child daycare facilities, exercise/wellness program, free psychological counseling, international student services, low-cost health insurance, services for students with disabilities, teacher training, writing training. *Library:* Levi Watkins Learning Center plus 1 other. *Collection:* Books: 434,772 (physical), 69,699 (digital/electronic); Serial titles: 1,607 (physical), 4,986 (digital/electronic); Databases: 171. Study areas open 24 hours, 5–7 days a week.

Computer facilities: 541 computers available on campus for general student use. A campuswide network can be accessed from student residence rooms and from off campus. Online class registration is available.
Website: http://www.alasu.edu/

General Application Contact: Dr. William Person, Dean of Graduate Studies, 334-229-4274, Fax: 334-229-4928, E-mail: wperson@alasu.edu.

GRADUATE UNITS

College of Business Administration Students: 8 full-time (4 women), 6 part-time (3 women); includes 11 minority (10 Black or African American, non-Hispanic/Latino; 1 Hispanic/Latino), 1 international. Average age 32. 24 applicants, 33% accepted, 5 enrolled. *Faculty:* 4 full-time (1 woman), 1 part-time/adjunct (0 women). *Financial support:* Fellowships and unspecified assistantships available. Financial award application deadline: 6/30; financial award applicants required to submit FAFSA. In 2015, 21 master's awarded. *Degree program information:* Part-time programs available. Part-time. Offers accountancy (M Acc); business administration (M Acc). *Application deadline:* For fall admission, 7/15 for domestic students; for spring admission, 12/15 for domestic students. *Application fee:* $25. Electronic applications accepted. *Application Contact:* Dr. William Person, Dean of Graduate Studies, 334-229-4274, Fax: 334-229-4928, E-mail: wperson@alasu.edu. *Dean*, Dr. Le-Quita Booth, 334-229-4124, E-mail: lbooth@alasu.edu.

College of Education Students: 84 full-time (56 women), 263 part-time (193 women); includes 332 minority (324 Black or African American, non-Hispanic/Latino; 1 Asian, non-Hispanic/Latino; 2 Hispanic/Latino; 5 Two or more races, non-Hispanic/Latino), 2 international. Average age 35. 206 applicants, 46% accepted, 52 enrolled. *Faculty:* 7 full-time (4 women), 7 part-time/adjunct (4 women). *Financial support:* In 2015–16, 4 students received support. Research assistantships and unspecified assistantships available. Financial award application deadline: 6/30. In 2015, 70 master's, 9 doctorates, 27 other advanced degrees awarded. *Degree program information:* Part-time programs available. Part-time. Offers counselor education (M Ed, MS, Ed S); early childhood education (M Ed, Ed S); education (M Ed, MS, Ed D, Ed S); educational administration (M Ed, Ed D, Ed S); elementary education (M Ed, Ed S); health education (M Ed); library education media (M Ed, Ed S); physical education (M Ed); secondary education (M Ed, Ed S); special education (M Ed). *Application deadline:* For fall admission, 7/15 for domestic students; for spring admission, 12/15 for domestic students. Applications are processed on a rolling basis. *Application fee:* $25. *Application Contact:* Dr. William Person, Dean of Graduate Studies, 334-229-4274, Fax: 334-229-4928, E-mail: wperson@alasu.edu. *Interim Dean*, Dr. Doris Screws, 334-229-4250, E-mail: dscrews@alasu.edu.

College of Health Sciences Students: 182 full-time (128 women), 24 part-time (16 women); includes 97 minority (80 Black or African American, non-Hispanic/Latino; 1 American Indian or Alaska Native, non-Hispanic/Latino; 11 Asian, non-Hispanic/Latino; 3 Hispanic/Latino; 2 Two or more races, non-Hispanic/Latino), 4 international. Average age 26. 222 applicants, 32% accepted, 66 enrolled. *Financial support:* In 2015–16, 3 students received support. Research assistantships and unspecified assistantships available. Financial award application deadline: 6/30. In 2015, 36 master's, 29 doctorates awarded. Offers health sciences (MRC, MS, DPT); occupational therapy (MS); physical therapy (DPT); prosthetics and orthotics (MS); rehabilitation counseling (MRC). *Application deadline:* For fall admission, 7/15 for domestic students; for spring admission, 12/15 for domestic students. Applications are processed on a rolling basis. *Application fee:* $25. *Application Contact:* Dr. William Person, Dean of Graduate Studies, 334-229-4274, Fax: 334-229-4928, E-mail: wperson@alasu.edu. *Acting Dean*, Dr. Leon Wilson, 334-229-4232, E-mail: lwilson@alasu.edu.

College of Science, Mathematics and Technology Students: 16 full-time (12 women), 25 part-time (11 women); includes 33 minority (30 Black or African American, non-Hispanic/Latino; 1 American Indian or Alaska Native, non-Hispanic/Latino; 1 Asian, non-Hispanic/Latino; 1 Two or more races, non-Hispanic/Latino), 5 international. Average age 30. 39 applicants, 26% accepted, 3 enrolled. *Faculty:* 11 full-time (4 women). *Financial support:* In 2015–16, 22 students received support. Research assistantships and scholarships/grants available. Financial award application deadline: 6/30; financial award applicants required to submit CSS PROFILE or FAFSA. In 2015, 4 master's, 3 doctorates awarded. Offers biological sciences (MS, PhD); forensic science (MS); mathematics (MS); science, mathematics and technology (MS, PhD). *Application deadline:* For fall admission, 7/15 for domestic students; for spring admission, 12/15 for domestic students. Applications are processed on a rolling basis. *Application fee:* $25. *Application Contact:* Dr. William Person, Dean of Graduate Studies, 334-229-4274, Fax: 334-229-4928, E-mail: wperson@alasu.edu. *Dean*, Dr. Kennedy Weskesa, 334-229-4316, Fax: 334-229-4916, E-mail: weskesa@alasu.edu.

ALASKA PACIFIC UNIVERSITY, Anchorage, AK 99508-4672

General Information Independent, coed, comprehensive institution. *Graduate housing:* Room and/or apartments available on a first-come, first-served basis to single students; on-campus housing not available to married students. Housing application deadline: 8/15.

GRADUATE UNITS

Graduate Programs ***Degree program information:*** Part-time and evening/weekend programs available. Part-time, evening/weekend. Offers business administration (MBA); counseling psychology (MSCP); environmental science (MSES, MSOEE); health services administration (MBA); information and communication technology (MBAICT); investment (CGS); outdoor and environmental education (MSOEE); self-designed study (MA); teaching (MAT); teaching (K-8) (MAT). Electronic applications accepted.

ALBANY COLLEGE OF PHARMACY AND HEALTH SCIENCES, Albany, NY 12208

General Information Independent, coed, comprehensive institution. *Graduate housing:* Room and/or apartments available on a first-come, first-served basis to single students; on-campus housing not available to married students. Housing application deadline: 7/1.

GRADUATE UNITS

School of Arts and Sciences Offers clinical laboratory sciences (MS); cytotechnology and molecular cytology (MS); molecular biosciences (MS). Electronic applications accepted.

School of Pharmacy and Pharmaceutical Sciences Offers health outcomes research (MS); pharmaceutical sciences (MS); pharmacy (Pharm D). Electronic applications accepted.

ALBANY LAW SCHOOL, Albany, NY 12208-3494

General Information Independent, coed, graduate-only institution. *Graduate housing:* On-campus housing not available.

GRADUATE UNITS

Professional Program ***Degree program information:*** Part-time programs available. Part-time. Offers law (LL M, JD). JD/MBA offered jointly with The College of Saint Rose, The Sage Colleges, Union Graduate College, and University at Albany, State University of New York; JD/MPA, JD/MRP, and JD/MSW offered jointly with University at Albany, State University of New York.

ALBANY MEDICAL COLLEGE, Albany, NY 12208-3479

General Information Independent, coed, graduate-only institution. *Graduate housing:* On-campus housing not available. *Research affiliation:* X-Ray Optical Systems (diagnostic equipment), Integrated Tissue Dynamics INTIGYN (integrated tissue dynamics), Regenerative Research Foundation (biomedical research), Wadsworth Center for Laboratories and Research (biomedical research), ORDWAY Research Institute (biomedical research), General Electric Company (GE) (imaging).

GRADUATE UNITS

Alden March Bioethics Institute ***Degree program information:*** Part-time and evening/weekend programs available. Part-time, evening/weekend, online learning. Offers bioethics (MS, DPS); clinical ethics (Certificate); clinical ethics consultation (Certificate). Electronic applications accepted.

Center for Cardiovascular Sciences ***Degree program information:*** Part-time programs available. Part-time. Offers cardiovascular sciences (MS, PhD).

Center for Cell Biology and Cancer Research ***Degree program information:*** Part-time programs available. Part-time. Offers cell biology and cancer research (MS, PhD).

Center for Immunology and Microbial Disease ***Degree program information:*** Part-time programs available. Part-time. Offers immunology and microbial disease (MS, PhD).

Center for Neuropharmacology and Neuroscience Offers neuropharmacology and neuroscience (MS, PhD).

Center for Nurse Anesthesiology Offers anesthesia (MS). Electronic applications accepted.

Center for Physician Assistant Studies Offers physician assistant studies (MS). Electronic applications accepted.

Professional Program Offers medicine (MD). Electronic applications accepted.

ALBANY STATE UNIVERSITY, Albany, GA 31705-2717

General Information State-supported, coed, comprehensive institution. *Graduate housing:* Room and/or apartments available on a first-come, first-served basis to single students; on-campus housing not available to married students. Housing application deadline: 6/30.

GRADUATE UNITS

College of Arts and Humanities ***Degree program information:*** Part-time programs available. Part-time. Offers English education (M Ed); public administration (MPA); social work (MSW). Electronic applications accepted.

College of Business ***Degree program information:*** Part-time and evening/weekend programs available. Part-time, evening/weekend. Offers accounting (MBA); general (MBA); healthcare (MBA). Electronic applications accepted.

College of Education ***Degree program information:*** Part-time and evening/weekend programs available. Part-time, evening/weekend, online learning. Offers early childhood education (M Ed); education specialist (Ed S); educational leadership and administration (M Ed); health, physical education and recreation (M Ed); middle grades education (M Ed); school counseling (M Ed); special education (M Ed). Electronic applications accepted.

College of Sciences and Health Professions ***Degree program information:*** Part-time and evening/weekend programs available. Part-time, evening/weekend, online learning. Offers criminal justice (MS); mathematics education (M Ed); nursing (MSN); science education (M Ed). Electronic applications accepted.

ALBERT EINSTEIN COLLEGE OF MEDICINE, Bronx, NY 10461

General Information Independent, coed, graduate-only institution.

GRADUATE UNITS

Graduate Division of Biomedical Sciences Students: 393 full-time; includes 45 minority (13 Black or African American, non-Hispanic/Latino; 24 Asian, non-Hispanic/Latino; 8 Hispanic/Latino), 101 international. Average age 25. *Faculty:* 172 full-time, 17 part-time/adjunct. *Financial support:* In 2015–16, 229 fellowships were awarded. In 2015, 37 doctorates awarded. Offers anatomy (PhD); biochemistry (PhD); biomedical sciences (PhD); cell and developmental biology (PhD); cell biology (PhD); clinical investigation (PhD); computational genetics (PhD); developmental and molecular biology (PhD); microbiology and immunology (PhD); molecular genetics (PhD); molecular pharmacology (PhD); neuroscience (PhD); pathology (PhD); physiology and biophysics (PhD); systems and computational biology (PhD); translational genetics (PhD). *Application deadline:* For fall admission, 12/15 for domestic students. Applications are processed on a rolling basis. *Application fee:* $75. Electronic applications accepted. *Application Contact:* Salvatore Calabro, Assistant Director of

Admissions, 718-430-2345, Fax: 718-430-8655, E-mail: phd@einstein.yu.edu. *Assistant Dean for Graduate Studies*, Dr. Victoria H. Freedman, 718-430-2345, Fax: 718-430-8655.

Medical Scientist Training Program

Professional Program in Medicine Offers medicine (MD).

ALBERTUS MAGNUS COLLEGE, New Haven, CT 06511-1189

General Information Independent-religious, coed, comprehensive institution. *Enrollment:* 227 full-time matriculated graduate/professional students (171 women), 91 part-time matriculated graduate/professional students (67 women). *Enrollment by degree level:* 318 master's. *Graduate faculty:* 29 full-time (11 women), 59 part-time/adjunct (27 women). *Tuition, area resident:* Full-time $15,736; part-time $1944 per course. Tuition and fees vary according to course load and program. *Graduate housing:* On-campus housing not available. *Student services:* Campus employment opportunities, career counseling, free psychological counseling, international student services, services for students with disabilities, teacher training, writing training. *Library:* Rosary Hall.

Computer facilities: 117 computers available on campus for general student use. A campuswide network can be accessed from student residence rooms and from off campus. Online class registration, online class sessions - Moodle are available.
Website: http://www.albertus.edu/

General Application Contact: Anthony Reich, Director of Admission, Division of Professional and Graduate Studies, 203-773-5032, E-mail: arreich@albertus.edu.

GRADUATE UNITS

Master of Arts in Art Therapy Program Students: 22 full-time (all women), 16 part-time (15 women); includes 1 minority (Hispanic/Latino). Average age 28. 25 applicants, 72% accepted, 13 enrolled. *Faculty:* 3 full-time (all women), 13 part-time/adjunct (10 women). *Financial support:* Federal Work-Study and unspecified assistantships available. Support available to part-time students. Financial award application deadline: 8/15; financial award applicants required to submit FAFSA. In 2015, 21 master's awarded. *Degree program information:* Part-time programs available. Part-time. Offers art therapy (MAAT). *Application deadline:* For fall admission, 5/1 for domestic students; for spring admission, 11/1 for domestic students. Applications are processed on a rolling basis. *Application fee:* $50. Electronic applications accepted. *Application Contact:* Dr. Sean O'Connell, Vice President for Academic Affairs, 203-777-8539, Fax: 203-777-3701, E-mail: soconnell@albertus.edu. *Director*, Abbe Miller, 203-773-8543, Fax: 203-773-3117, E-mail: amiller@albertus.edu.

Master of Arts in Leadership Program Students: 4 full-time (3 women), 8 part-time (5 women); includes 8 minority (5 Black or African American, non-Hispanic/Latino; 3 Hispanic/Latino). Average age 44. *Faculty:* 2 full-time (0 women), 4 part-time/adjunct (2 women). *Financial support:* Federal Work-Study and unspecified assistantships available. Support available to part-time students. Financial award applicants required to submit FAFSA. In 2015, 7 master's awarded. *Degree program information:* Part-time and evening/weekend programs available. Part-time, evening/weekend, blended/hybrid learning. Offers leadership (MA). *Application deadline:* Applications are processed on a rolling basis. *Application fee:* $50. Electronic applications accepted. *Application Contact:* Anthony Reich, Director of Admission, Division of Professional and Graduate Studies, 203-773-5032, Fax: 203-773-5257, E-mail: leadership@albertus.edu. *Director*, Dr. Howard Fero, 203-773-4424, E-mail: hfero@albertus.edu.

Master of Arts in Liberal Studies Program Students: 2 full-time (both women), 1 (woman) part-time; includes 2 minority (both Black or African American, non-Hispanic/Latino). Average age 38. *Faculty:* 10 full-time (3 women). *Financial support:* Federal Work-Study and unspecified assistantships available. Support available to part-time students. Financial award application deadline: 8/15; financial award applicants required to submit FAFSA. *Degree program information:* Part-time and evening/weekend programs available. Part-time, evening/weekend, blended/hybrid learning. Offers liberal studies (MALS). *Application deadline:* For fall admission, 8/31 for domestic students; for spring admission, 1/10 for domestic students. Applications are processed on a rolling basis. *Application fee:* $50. Electronic applications accepted. *Application Contact:* Anthony Reich, Director of Admission, Division of Professional and Graduate Studies, 203-773-5032, Fax: 203-773-5257, E-mail: arreich@albertus.edu. *Director, Liberal Studies Program*, Prof. Julia A. Coash, 203-773-8993, Fax: 203-773-5257, E-mail: jcoash@albertus.edu.

Master of Business Administration Program Students: 79 full-time (51 women), 20 part-time (12 women); includes 57 minority (39 Black or African American, non-Hispanic/Latino; 2 Asian, non-Hispanic/Latino; 15 Hispanic/Latino; 1 Two or more races, non-Hispanic/Latino), 1 international. Average age 35. *Faculty:* 7 full-time (2 women), 24 part-time/adjunct (6 women). *Financial support:* Federal Work-Study and unspecified assistantships available. Support available to part-time students. Financial award applicants required to submit FAFSA. In 2015, 63 master's awarded. *Degree program information:* Part-time and evening/weekend programs available. Part-time, evening/weekend, 100% online, blended/hybrid learning. Offers business administration (MBA). Program also offered in East Hartford, CT. *Application deadline:* Applications are processed on a rolling basis. *Application fee:* $50. Electronic applications accepted. *Application Contact:* Anthony Reich, Director of Admission, Division of Professional and Graduate Studies, 203-773-5302, E-mail: arreich@albertus.edu. *Director, MBA Programs*, Dr. Wayne Gineo, 203-672-6670, E-mail: wgineo@albertus.edu.

Master of Fine Arts in Creative Writing Program Students: 6 full-time (4 women), 1 (woman) part-time; includes 2 minority (both Black or African American, non-Hispanic/Latino). Average age 40. *Faculty:* 5 full-time (1 woman), 1 part-time/adjunct (0 women). *Financial support:* Federal Work-Study and unspecified assistantships available. Support available to part-time students. Financial award applicants required to submit FAFSA. In 2015, 5 master's awarded. *Degree program information:* Part-time and evening/weekend programs available. Part-time, evening/weekend, blended/hybrid learning. Offers creative writing (MFA). *Application deadline:* For fall admission, 8/15 for domestic students; for spring admission, 1/15 for domestic students. Applications are processed on a rolling basis. *Application fee:* $50. Electronic applications accepted. *Application Contact:* Prof. Sarah Harris Wallman, Co-Director, 203-777-4473, Fax: 203-777-3701, E-mail: swallman@albertus.edu. *Co-Director*, Charles Rafferty, 203-773-6901, Fax: 203-777-3701, E-mail: crafferty@albertus.edu.

Master of Science in Accounting Program Students: 9 full-time (5 women), 7 part-time (5 women); includes 5 minority (1 Black or African American, non-Hispanic/Latino; 4 Hispanic/Latino), 1 international. *Financial support:* Federal Work-Study and unspecified assistantships available. Support available to part-time students. Financial award applicants required to submit FAFSA. *Degree program information:* Part-time and evening/weekend programs available. Part-time, evening/weekend, 100% online, blended/hybrid learning. Offers accounting (MSA). *Application deadline:* Applications are processed on a rolling basis. *Application fee:* $50. Electronic applications accepted. *Application Contact:* Dr. Sean O'Connell, Vice President for Academic Affairs, 203-777-8539, Fax: 203-777-3701, E-mail: soconnell@albertus.edu. *Director of the Business Programs*, Dr. Nancy Fallon, 203-773-8567, E-mail: nfallon@albertus.edu.

Master of Science in Criminal Justice Program Students: 7 full-time (5 women), 7 part-time (5 women); includes 9 minority (7 Black or African American, non-Hispanic/Latino; 2 Hispanic/Latino). Average age 32. *Financial support:* Federal Work-Study and unspecified assistantships available. Support available to part-time students. Financial award applicants required to submit FAFSA. *Degree program information:* Part-time and evening/weekend programs available. Part-time, evening/weekend, 100% online, blended/hybrid learning. Offers corrections administration (MS); juvenile justice (MS). *Application fee:* $50. *Application Contact:* Dr. Sean O'Connell, Vice President for Academic Affairs, 203-777-8539, Fax: 203-777-3701, E-mail: soconnell@albertus.edu. *Coordinator*, Michael Geary, 203-773-8088, E-mail: mgeary@albertus.edu.

Master of Science in Education Program Students: 3 full-time (2 women), 4 part-time (all women); includes 3 minority (2 Black or African American, non-Hispanic/Latino; 1 Hispanic/Latino). Average age 33. *Faculty:* 3 full-time (1 woman), 9 part-time/adjunct (4 women). *Financial support:* Federal Work-Study and unspecified assistantships available. Support available to part-time students. Financial award applicants required to submit FAFSA. In 2015, 1 master's awarded. *Degree program information:* Part-time and evening/weekend programs available. Part-time, evening/weekend, blended/hybrid learning. Offers education (MS Ed). *Application deadline:* For fall admission, 8/15 for domestic students; for spring admission, 1/15 for domestic students. *Application fee:* $50. *Application Contact:* Anthony Reich, Director of Admission, Division of Professional and Graduate Studies, 203-773-5032, E-mail: arreich@albertus.edu. *Director, Education Programs*, Dr. Joan Venditto, 203-773-8087, Fax: 203-773-4422, E-mail: jvenditto@albertus.edu.

Master of Science in Human Services Program Students: 51 full-time (44 women), 2 part-time (both women); includes 33 minority (28 Black or African American, non-Hispanic/Latino; 3 Hispanic/Latino; 2 Two or more races, non-Hispanic/Latino). Average age 38. *Faculty:* 3 full-time (1 woman), 6 part-time/adjunct (4 women). *Financial support:* Federal Work-Study and unspecified assistantships available. Support available to part-time students. Financial award applicants required to submit FAFSA. In 2015, 18 master's awarded. *Degree program information:* Part-time and evening/weekend programs available. Part-time, evening/weekend, blended/hybrid learning. Offers human services (MS). *Application deadline:* For fall admission, 8/15 for domestic students; for spring admission, 1/15 for domestic students. Applications are processed on a rolling basis. *Application fee:* $50. Electronic applications accepted. *Application Contact:* Dr. Ragaa Mazen, Director of the Master of Human Services Program, 203-773-8574, Fax: 203-777-3701, E-mail: rmazen@albertus.edu. *Director of the Master of Human Services Program*, Ragaa Mazen, 203-773-8574, E-mail: rmazen@albertus.edu.

Program in Management and Organizational Leadership Students: 44 full-time (33 women), 13 part-time (6 women); includes 34 minority (25 Black or African American, non-Hispanic/Latino; 1 American Indian or Alaska Native, non-Hispanic/Latino; 7 Hispanic/Latino; 1 Native Hawaiian or other Pacific Islander, non-Hispanic/Latino). Average age 40. *Faculty:* 8 full-time (2 women), 5 part-time/adjunct (1 woman). *Financial support:* Federal Work-Study and unspecified assistantships available. Support available to part-time students. Financial award applicants required to submit FAFSA. In 2015, 37 master's awarded. *Degree program information:* Part-time and evening/weekend programs available. Part-time, evening/weekend, blended/hybrid learning. Offers management and organizational leadership (MS). *Application deadline:* For fall admission, 8/14 for domestic students; for spring admission, 1/15 for domestic students. Applications are processed on a rolling basis. *Application fee:* $50. Electronic applications accepted. *Application Contact:* Anthony Reich, Director of Admission, Division of Professional and Graduate Studies, 203-773-5032, E-mail: arreich@albertus.edu. *Director of Leadership Programs*, Dr. Howard Fero, 203-773-4424, E-mail: hfero@albertus.edu.

ALBRIGHT COLLEGE, Reading, PA 19612-5234

General Information Independent-religious, coed, comprehensive institution. *Graduate housing:* On-campus housing not available.

GRADUATE UNITS

Graduate Division ***Degree program information:*** Part-time and evening/weekend programs available. Part-time, evening/weekend. Offers early childhood education (MS); elementary education (MS); English as a second language (MA); general education (MA); special education (MS). Electronic applications accepted.

ALCORN STATE UNIVERSITY, Lorman, MS 39096-7500

General Information State-supported, coed, comprehensive institution. CGS member. *Graduate housing:* Room and/or apartments available on a first-come, first-served basis to single students; on-campus housing not available to married students.

GRADUATE UNITS

School of Graduate Studies ***Degree program information:*** Part-time programs available. Part-time. Offers workforce education leadership (MS). Electronic applications accepted.

School of Agriculture and Applied Science Offers agricultural economics (MS Ag); agronomy (MS Ag); animal science (MS Ag).

School of Arts and Sciences Offers arts and sciences (MS); biology (MS); computer and information sciences (MS).

School of Business Offers business (MBA).

School of Nursing Offers rural nursing (MSN).

School of Psychology and Education Offers agricultural education (MS Ed); elementary education (MS Ed, Ed S); guidance and counseling (MS Ed); industrial education (MS Ed); secondary education (MS Ed); special education (MS Ed).

ALDERSON BROADDUS UNIVERSITY, Philippi, WV 26416

General Information Independent-religious, coed, comprehensive institution. *Graduate housing:* Rooms and/or apartments available on a first-come, first-served basis to single and married students. Housing application deadline: 8/21.

GRADUATE UNITS

Program in Physician Assistant Studies Offers physician assistant studies (MPAS). Electronic applications accepted.

ALFRED UNIVERSITY, Alfred, NY 14802-1205

General Information Independent, coed, university. *Enrollment:* 2,286 graduate, professional, and undergraduate students; 195 full-time matriculated graduate/professional students (108 women), 286 part-time matriculated graduate/professional students (208 women). *Enrollment by degree level:* 360 master's, 67 doctoral, 42 other advanced degrees. *Graduate faculty:* 81 full-time (30 women). *Tuition, area resident:* Full-time $38,020; part-time $810 per credit. *Required fees:* $970; $82 per semester. *Graduate housing:* Room and/or apartments available on a first-come, first-served basis to single students; on-campus housing not available to married students. Typical cost: $12,196 (including board). Room and board charges vary according to board plan, campus/location and housing facility selected. Housing application deadline: 5/1. *Student services:* Campus employment opportunities, campus safety program, career counseling, free psychological counseling, international student services, low-cost health insurance, multicultural affairs office, services for students with disabilities, teacher training, writing training. *Library:* Herrick Memorial Library plus 1 other. *Collection:* Books: 265,169 (physical), 571,609 (digital/electronic); Databases: 176. Study areas open 24 hours, 5–7 days a week; students can reserve study rooms. *Research affiliation:* Center for High Temperature Characterization (materials science), New York State Center for Advanced Ceramic Technology (ceramic engineering and materials science), Center for Glass Research (glass engineering and science), National Science Foundation Industry-University Center for Glass Research, Whitewares Research Center Industry University Center (whitewares processing, traditional ceramics), National Science Foundation Industry-University Center for Biosurfaces (bioceramics).

Computer facilities: Computer purchase and lease plans are available. A campuswide network can be accessed from student residence rooms and from off campus. Online class registration, online bill pay are available.
Website: http://www.alfred.edu/

General Application Contact: Sara Love, Coordinator of Graduate Admissions, 607-871-2115, Fax: 607-871-2198, E-mail: gradinquiry@alfred.edu.

GRADUATE UNITS

Graduate School Students: 193 full-time (107 women), 276 part-time (202 women); includes 152 minority (82 Black or African American, non-Hispanic/Latino; 1 American Indian or Alaska Native, non-Hispanic/Latino; 10 Asian, non-Hispanic/Latino; 58 Hispanic/Latino; 1 Two or more races, non-Hispanic/Latino), 23 international. Average age 25. 561 applicants, 50% accepted, 234 enrolled. *Faculty:* 87 full-time (24 women), 7 part-time/adjunct (2 women). *Financial support:* In 2015–16, 150 students received support, including 6 fellowships with full tuition reimbursements available (averaging $22,520 per year), 45 research assistantships with partial tuition reimbursements available (averaging $19,010 per year), 36 teaching assistantships with full tuition reimbursements available (averaging $27,270 per year); career-related internships or fieldwork and unspecified assistantships also available. Financial award application deadline: 8/1; financial award applicants required to submit FAFSA. In 2015, 161 master's, 6 doctorates, 68 other advanced degrees awarded. *Degree program information:* Part-time programs available. Part-time. Offers mental health counseling (MS Ed); school counseling (MS Ed, CAS); school psychology (MA, Psy D, CAS). *Application deadline:* For fall admission, 8/1 for domestic students, 2/15 for international students; for spring admission, 12/1 for domestic students, 10/1 for international students. Applications are processed on a rolling basis. *Application fee:* $60. Electronic applications accepted. *Application Contact:* Sara Love, Graduate Admissions Coordinator, 607-871-2115, Fax: 607-871-2198, E-mail: gradinquiry@alfred.edu. *Provost and Vice President of Academic Affairs,* Dr. Rick Stephens, 607-871-2967, Fax: 607-871-2198, E-mail: stephens@alfred.edu.

College of Ceramics Financial support: Fellowships with full tuition reimbursements, research assistantships with full tuition reimbursements, teaching assistantships with full tuition reimbursements, and tuition waivers (full and partial) available. Financial award applicants required to submit FAFSA. Offers biomaterials engineering (MS); ceramic art (MFA); ceramic engineering (MS, PhD); ceramics (MFA, MS, PhD); electrical engineering (MS); electronic integrated arts (MFA); glass science (MS, PhD); materials science and engineering (MS, PhD); mechanical engineering (MS); sculpture/dimensional studies (MFA). *Application deadline:* For fall admission, 3/1 priority date for domestic students, 3/15 for international students; for spring admission, 12/1 for domestic students, 10/1 for international students. Applications are processed on a rolling basis. *Application fee:* $60. Electronic applications accepted. *Application Contact:* Sara Love, Coordinator of Graduate Admissions, 607-871-2115, Fax: 607-871-2198, E-mail: gradinquiry@alfred.edu. *Vice President,* Dr. Doreen Edwards, 607-871-2422, E-mail: dedwards@alfred.edu.

Division of Education Financial support: Research assistantships with partial tuition reimbursements, tuition waivers (partial), and unspecified assistantships available. Financial award applicants required to submit FAFSA. *Degree program information:* Part-time programs available. Part-time. Offers college student development (MS Ed); literacy (MS Ed). *Application deadline:* For fall admission, 8/1 for domestic students, 3/15 for international students; for spring admission, 12/1 for domestic students, 10/1 for international students. Applications are processed on a rolling basis. *Application fee:* $60. Electronic applications accepted. *Application Contact:* Sara Love, Coordinator of Graduate Admissions, 607-871-2115, Fax: 607-871-2198, E-mail: gradinquiry@alfred.edu. *Program Director,* Kevin Curtin, 607-871-2699.

School of Business Financial support: Research assistantships with partial tuition reimbursements, tuition waivers (partial), and unspecified assistantships available. Financial award applicants required to submit FAFSA. *Degree program information:* Part-time programs available. Part-time. Offers accounting (MBA); business administration (MBA). *Application deadline:* For fall admission, 8/1 for domestic students, 3/15 for international students; for winter admission, 12/1 for domestic students; for spring admission, 10/1 for international students. Applications are processed on a rolling basis. *Application fee:* $60. Electronic applications accepted. *Application Contact:* Sara Love, Coordinator of Graduate Admissions, 607-871-2115, Fax: 607-871-2198, E-mail: gradinquiry@alfred.edu. *Dean of the College of Professional Studies,* Dr. Nancy Evangelista, 607-871-2124, Fax: 607-871-2114, E-mail: fevangel@alfred.edu.

ALLEN COLLEGE, Waterloo, IA 50703

General Information Independent, coed, primarily women, comprehensive institution. *Enrollment:* 611 graduate, professional, and undergraduate students; 61 full-time matriculated graduate/professional students (54 women), 163 part-time matriculated graduate/professional students (144 women). *Enrollment by degree level:* 210 master's, 14 doctoral, 17 other advanced degrees. *Graduate faculty:* 3 full-time (all women), 28 part-time/adjunct (27 women). *Tuition, area resident:* Full-time $15,940; part-time $4623 per credit hour. *Required fees:* $1240; $360 per unit. $360. Tuition and fees vary according to degree level and program. *Graduate housing:* On-campus housing not available. *Student services:* Campus safety program, career counseling, free psychological counseling. *Library:* Barrett Library. *Collection:* Books: 12,926 (physical), 200 (digital/electronic); Serial titles: 218 (physical), 279 (digital/electronic); Databases: 38. Weekly public service hours: 50; study areas open 24 hours, 5–7 days a week; students can reserve study rooms.

Computer facilities: 32 computers available on campus for general student use. A campuswide network can be accessed from student residence rooms and from off campus.
Website: http://www.allencollege.edu/

General Application Contact: Adriane McKernan, Administrative Assistant to Student Services, 319-226-2014, Fax: 319-226-2010, E-mail: admissions@allencollege.edu.

GRADUATE UNITS

Graduate Programs Students: 61 full-time (54 women), 163 part-time (144 women); includes 9 minority (5 Black or African American, non-Hispanic/Latino; 2 Hispanic/Latino; 2 Two or more races, non-Hispanic/Latino), 2 international. Average age 34. 212 applicants, 60% accepted, 94 enrolled. *Faculty:* 3 full-time (all women), 21 part-time/adjunct (20 women). *Financial support:* Institutionally sponsored loans, scholarships/grants, and traineeships available. Support available to part-time students. Financial award application deadline: 8/15; financial award applicants required to submit FAFSA. In 2015, 51 master's, 1 doctorate awarded. *Degree program information:* Part-time programs available. Part-time, blended/hybrid learning. Offers acute care nurse practitioner (Post-Master's Certificate); adult nurse practitioner (Post-Master's Certificate); adult psychiatric-mental health nurse practitioner (Post-Master's Certificate); adult-gerontology acute care nurse practitioner (MSN); community public health (Post-Master's Certificate); community/public health nursing (MSN); family nurse practitioner (MSN, Post-Master's Certificate); gerontological nurse practitioner (Post-Master's Certificate); health sciences (Ed D); leadership in health care delivery (MSN, Post-Master's Certificate); nursing (DNP); occupational therapy (MS). *Application deadline:* For fall admission, 2/1 priority date for domestic students; for spring admission, 9/1 priority date for domestic students. Applications are processed on a rolling basis. *Application fee:* $50. Electronic applications accepted. *Application Contact:* Molly Quinn, Administrative Assistant for Student Services, 319-226-2014, Fax: 319-226-2010, E-mail: admissions@allencollege.edu. *Vice Chancellor for Academic Affairs,* Nancy Kramer, 319-226-2040, Fax: 319-226-2070, E-mail: nancy.kramer@allencollege.edu.

ALLIANT INTERNATIONAL UNIVERSITY–FRESNO, Fresno, CA 93727

General Information Independent, coed, graduate-only institution. *Graduate housing:* On-campus housing not available.

GRADUATE UNITS

California School of Forensic Studies Offers clinical forensic psychology (PhD, Psy D); forensic studies (PhD, Psy D); victimology (Psy D). Electronic applications accepted.

California School of Professional Psychology Offers clinical psychology (PhD, Psy D); organizational behavior (MA); organizational development (Psy D); professional psychology (MA, PhD, Psy D). Electronic applications accepted.

ALLIANT INTERNATIONAL UNIVERSITY–IRVINE, Irvine, CA 92606

General Information Independent, coed, graduate-only institution. *Graduate housing:* On-campus housing not available.

GRADUATE UNITS

California School of Forensic Studies Offers forensic studies (Psy D). Electronic applications accepted.

California School of Professional Psychology ***Degree program information:*** Part-time programs available. Part-time. Offers couple and family therapy (MA, Psy D); professional psychology (MA, Psy D). Electronic applications accepted.

Shirley M. Hufstedler School of Education ***Degree program information:*** Part-time and evening/weekend programs available. Part-time, evening/weekend, online learning. Offers education (MA, Psy D, Certificate, Credential); educational psychology (Psy D); pupil personnel services (Credential); school psychology (MA). Electronic applications accepted.

ALLIANT INTERNATIONAL UNIVERSITY–LOS ANGELES, Alhambra, CA 91803-1360

General Information Independent, coed, graduate-only institution. *Graduate housing:* Room and/or apartments available to single students; on-campus housing not available to married students.

GRADUATE UNITS

California School of Forensic Studies Offers forensic psychology (Psy D).

California School of Professional Psychology Offers chemical dependency (MA); clinical health psychology (Psy D); clinical psychology (PhD, Psy D); family/child and couple clinical psychology (Psy D); gerontology (MA); Latin American family therapy (MA); multi-interest option (Psy D); multicultural community-clinical psychology (Psy D); professional psychology (MA, PhD, Psy D). Electronic applications accepted.

Organizational Psychology Division Degree program information: Part-time programs available. Part-time. Offers organizational psychology (MA, PhD). Electronic applications accepted.

Marshall Goldsmith School of Management Offers management (DBA).

Business Division Offers business (DBA).

Shirley M. Hufstedler School of Education ***Degree program information:*** Part-time and evening/weekend programs available. Part-time, evening/weekend, online learning. Offers education (MA, Psy D, Credential); educational psychology (Psy D); pupil personnel services (Credential); school psychology (MA); teaching (MA, Credential). Electronic applications accepted.

ALLIANT INTERNATIONAL UNIVERSITY–MÉXICO CITY, CP06700 Mexico City, Mexico

General Information Independent, coed, comprehensive institution. *Graduate housing:* On-campus housing not available.

GRADUATE UNITS

California School of Professional Psychology Offers counseling psychology (MA).

School of Management ***Degree program information:*** Part-time and evening/weekend programs available. Part-time, evening/weekend. Offers business administration (MBA); international business administration (MIBA); international studies (MA). Electronic applications accepted.

International Studies Division Degree program information: Part-time and evening/weekend programs available. Part-time, evening/weekend. Offers international relations (MA). Electronic applications accepted.

Shirley M. Hufstedler School of Education ***Degree program information:*** Part-time and evening/weekend programs available. Part-time, evening/weekend, online learning. Offers teaching (MA).

ALLIANT INTERNATIONAL UNIVERSITY–SACRAMENTO, Sacramento, CA 95833

General Information Independent, coed, graduate-only institution. *Graduate housing:* On-campus housing not available.

GRADUATE UNITS

California School of Forensic Studies Offers clinical forensic psychology (Psy D); forensic studies (Psy D). Electronic applications accepted.

California School of Professional Psychology ***Degree program information:*** Part-time programs available. Part-time. Offers clinical psychology (Psy D); couple and family therapy (MA, Psy D); professional psychology (MA, Psy D). Electronic applications accepted.

Shirley M. Hufstedler School of Education Offers education (MA, Credential); teaching (MA, Credential). Electronic applications accepted.

ALLIANT INTERNATIONAL UNIVERSITY–SAN DIEGO, San Diego, CA 92131-1799

General Information Independent, coed, graduate-only institution. *Graduate housing:* Rooms and/or apartments available on a first-come, first-served basis to single and married students.

GRADUATE UNITS

Alliant School of Management ***Degree program information:*** Part-time and evening/weekend programs available. Part-time, evening/weekend. Offers management (MA, MBA). Electronic applications accepted.

Business and Management Division Degree program information: Part-time and evening/weekend programs available. Part-time, evening/weekend. Offers business administration (MBA). Electronic applications accepted.

California School of Forensic Studies Offers clinical forensic psychology (Psy D); forensic studies (Psy D).

California School of Professional Psychology ***Degree program information:*** Part-time programs available. Part-time. Offers clinical psychology (PhD, Psy D); marital and family therapy (MA, Psy D); professional psychology (MA, MS, PhD, Psy D).

Organizational Psychology Division Degree program information: Part-time and evening/weekend programs available. Part-time, evening/weekend. Offers clinical/industrial organizational psychology (PhD); consulting psychology (PhD); industrial/organizational psychology (MA, MS, PhD); leadership (PhD). Electronic applications accepted.

Shirley M. Hufstedler School of Education ***Degree program information:*** Part-time and evening/weekend programs available. Part-time, evening/weekend, online learning. Offers education (MA, Ed D, Psy D, Certificate, Credential); educational administration (MA); educational leadership and management (K-12) (Ed D); educational psychology (Psy D); higher education (Ed D, Certificate); preliminary administrative services (Credential); preliminary single subject (Credential); professional clear multiple subject (Credential); professional clear single subject (Credential); pupil personnel services (Credential); school neuropsychology (Certificate); school psychology (MA); school-based mental health (Certificate); teacher education (MA); teaching English to speakers of other languages (MA, Ed D, Certificate). Electronic applications accepted.

ALLIANT INTERNATIONAL UNIVERSITY–SAN FRANCISCO, San Francisco, CA 94133-1221

General Information Independent, coed, graduate-only institution. *Graduate housing:* On-campus housing not available.

GRADUATE UNITS

California School of Forensic Studies Offers applied criminology (MS); clinical forensic psychology (PhD, Psy D); victimology (MS).

California School of Professional Psychology Offers clinical counseling (MA); clinical psychology (PhD, Psy D, Certificate); professional psychology (MA, Post-Doctoral MS, PhD, Psy D, Certificate); psychopharmacology (Post-Doctoral MS). Electronic applications accepted.

Organizational Psychology Division Degree program information: Part-time and evening/weekend programs available. Part-time, evening/weekend. Offers organizational psychology (MA, PhD). Electronic applications accepted.

San Francisco Law School ***Degree program information:*** Part-time and evening/weekend programs available. Part-time, evening/weekend. Offers law (JD). Electronic applications accepted.

Shirley M. Hufstedler School of Education ***Degree program information:*** Part-time and evening/weekend programs available. Part-time, evening/weekend, online learning. Offers auditory oral education (Certificate); CLAD (Certificate); community college administration (Ed D); education (MA, Ed D, Psy D, Certificate, Credential); education specialist: mild/moderate disabilities (Credential); educational administration (MA); educational leadership and management (K-12) (Ed D); educational psychology (Psy D); higher education (Ed D); preliminary administrative services (Credential); preliminary multiple subject (Credential); preliminary single subject (Credential); professional clear multiple subject (Credential); professional clear single subject (Credential); pupil personnel services (Credential); school psychology (MA); special education (MA); teaching (MA); TESOL (Certificate). Electronic applications accepted.

ALVERNIA UNIVERSITY, Reading, PA 19607-1799

General Information Independent-religious, coed, comprehensive institution. *Graduate housing:* On-campus housing not available.

GRADUATE UNITS

Graduate Studies ***Degree program information:*** Part-time and evening/weekend programs available. Part-time, evening/weekend. Offers business (MBA); community counseling (MA); leadership (PhD); liberal studies (MALS); occupational therapy (MSOT); urban education (M Ed). Electronic applications accepted.

ALVERNO COLLEGE, Milwaukee, WI 53234-3922

General Information Independent-religious, Undergraduate: women only; graduate: coed, comprehensive institution. *Enrollment:* 2,209 graduate, professional, and undergraduate students; 405 full-time matriculated graduate/professional students (367 women), 243 part-time matriculated graduate/professional students (220 women). *Enrollment by degree level:* 648 master's. *Graduate faculty:* 26 full-time (24 women), 39 part-time/adjunct (29 women). Tuition and fees vary according to program. *Graduate housing:* On-campus housing not available. *Student services:* Campus employment opportunities, campus safety program, career counseling, child daycare facilities, exercise/wellness program, free psychological counseling, low-cost health insurance, multicultural affairs office, services for students with disabilities. *Library:* Alverno College Library. *Collection:* Books: 67,349 (physical), 205,487 (digital/electronic); Serial titles: 2,575 (physical), 67,667 (digital/electronic); Databases: 42.

Computer facilities: 737 computers available on campus for general student use. A campuswide network can be accessed from student residence rooms and from off campus. Online class registration is available.

Website: http://www.alverno.edu/

General Application Contact: Janet Stikel, Associate Director of Adult and Graduate Admissions, 414-382-6112, Fax: 414-382-6354, E-mail: janet.stikel@alverno.edu.

GRADUATE UNITS

JoAnn McGrath School of Nursing Students: 97 full-time (90 women), 87 part-time (82 women); includes 43 minority (18 Black or African American, non-Hispanic/Latino; 11 Asian, non-Hispanic/Latino; 9 Hispanic/Latino; 5 Two or more races, non-Hispanic/Latino), 1 international. Average age 36. 73 applicants, 95% accepted, 45 enrolled. *Faculty:* 8 full-time (all women), 8 part-time/adjunct (4 women). *Financial support:* In 2015–16, 1 student received support. Federal Work-Study and scholarships/grants available. Support available to part-time students. Financial award applicants required to submit FAFSA. In 2015, 33 master's awarded. *Degree program information:* Part-time and evening/weekend programs available. Part-time, evening/weekend. Offers clinical nurse specialist (MSN); family nurse practitioner (MSN); mental health nurse practitioner (MSN). *Application deadline:* For fall admission, 7/15 priority date for domestic and international students; for spring admission, 12/15 priority date for domestic and international students. Applications are processed on a rolling basis. *Application fee:* $0. Electronic applications accepted. *Application Contact:* Dr. Carol Sabel, RN, Graduate Program Director, 414-382-6309, Fax: 414-382-6354, E-mail: carol.sabel@alverno.edu. *Interim Dean,* Margaret Rauschenberger, 414-382-6276, Fax: 414-382-6354, E-mail: margaret.rauschenberger@alverno.edu.

School of Arts and Sciences Students: 91 full-time (86 women), 13 part-time (all women); includes 42 minority (26 Black or African American, non-Hispanic/Latino; 1 American Indian or Alaska Native, non-Hispanic/Latino; 3 Asian, non-Hispanic/Latino; 10 Hispanic/Latino; 1 Native Hawaiian or other Pacific Islander, non-Hispanic/Latino; 1 Two or more races, non-Hispanic/Latino), 1 international. Average age 34. 39 applicants, 92% accepted, 25 enrolled. *Faculty:* 6 full-time (all women), 7 part-time/adjunct (6 women). *Financial support:* In 2015–16, 2 students received support. Federal Work-Study and scholarships/grants available. Support available to part-time students. Financial award applicants required to submit FAFSA. In 2015, 34 master's awarded. *Degree program information:* Part-time and evening/weekend programs available. Part-time, evening/weekend. Offers community-based research and consultation (MSCP); professional counselor (MSCP). *Application deadline:* For fall admission, 7/15 priority date for domestic and international students; for spring admission, 12/15 priority date for domestic and international students. Applications are processed on a rolling basis. *Application fee:* $0. Electronic applications accepted. *Application Contact:* Mariana Sanabria, Graduate Admissions Counselor, 414-382-6113, Fax: 414-382-6354, E-mail: mariana.sanabria@alverno.edu. *Program Director, Master of Science in Community Psychology,* Dr. Sandra Graham, 414-382-6366, Fax: 414-382-6354, E-mail: sandra.graham@alverno.edu.

School of Business Students: 59 full-time (50 women); includes 17 minority (5 Black or African American, non-Hispanic/Latino; 1 American Indian or Alaska Native, non-Hispanic/Latino; 2 Asian, non-Hispanic/Latino; 9 Hispanic/Latino), 1 international. Average age 34. 35 applicants, 97% accepted, 23 enrolled. *Faculty:* 7 full-time (5 women). *Financial support:* Federal Work-Study and scholarships/grants available. Support available to part-time students. Financial award applicants required to submit FAFSA. In 2015, 35 master's awarded. *Degree program information:* Evening/weekend programs available. Evening/weekend. Offers business (MBA). *Application deadline:* For fall admission, 7/15 priority date for domestic and international students; for spring admission, 12/15 priority date for domestic and international students. Applications are processed on a rolling basis. *Application fee:* $0. Electronic applications accepted. *Application Contact:* Janet Stikel, Associate Director of Adult and Graduate Admissions, 414-382-6112, Fax: 414-382-6354, E-mail: janet.stikel@alverno.edu. *MBA Program Director,* Patricia Jensen, 414-382-6321, E-mail: patricia.jensen@alverno.edu.

School of Education Students: 78 full-time (72 women), 80 part-time (73 women); includes 50 minority (26 Black or African American, non-Hispanic/Latino; 1 American Indian or Alaska Native, non-Hispanic/Latino; 5 Asian, non-Hispanic/Latino; 15 Hispanic/Latino; 3 Two or more races, non-Hispanic/Latino), 3 international. Average age 36. 81 applicants, 95% accepted, 62 enrolled. *Faculty:* 5 full-time (all women), 24 part-time/adjunct (19 women). *Financial support:* In 2015–16, 2 students received support. Federal Work-Study and scholarships/grants available. Support available to part-time students. Financial award applicants required to submit FAFSA. In 2015, 75 master's awarded. *Degree program information:* Part-time and evening/weekend programs available. Part-time, evening/weekend. Offers adaptive education (MA); administrative leadership (MA); adult education and organizational development (MA); adult educational and instructional design (MA); adult educational and instructional technology (MA); global connections in the humanities (MA); instructional leadership (MA); instructional technology for K-12 settings (MA); professional development (MA); reading education (MA); reading education with adaptive education (MA); science education (MA); special education (MA); teaching in alternative schools (MA). *Application deadline:* For fall admission, 7/15 priority date for domestic and international students; for spring admission, 12/15 priority date for domestic and international students. Applications are processed on a rolling basis. *Application fee:* $0. Electronic applications accepted. *Application Contact:* Katie Kipp, Graduate Admissions Counselor, 414-382-6045, Fax: 414-382-6354, E-mail: katie.kipp@alverno.edu. *Associate Dean, Graduate Program,* Dr. Desiree Pointer-Mace, 414-382-6345, Fax: 414-382-6332, E-mail: desiree.pointer-mace@alverno.edu.

AMBERTON UNIVERSITY, Garland, TX 75041-5595

General Information Independent-religious, coed, upper-level institution. *Graduate housing:* On-campus housing not available.

GRADUATE UNITS

Graduate School ***Degree program information:*** Part-time and evening/weekend programs available. Part-time, evening/weekend. Offers counseling (MA); family studies (MS); general business (MBA); human relations and business (MS); human resources training and development (MS); management (MBA); managerial science (MS); professional development (MA); project management (MBA); strategic leadership (MBA).

AMBROSE UNIVERSITY, Calgary, AB T3H 0L5, Canada

General Information Independent-religious, coed, comprehensive institution. *Enrollment:* 920 graduate, professional, and undergraduate students; 55 full-time matriculated graduate/professional students (18 women), 128 part-time matriculated graduate/professional students (64 women). *Enrollment by degree level:* 135 master's, 48 other advanced degrees. *Graduate faculty:* 7 full-time (0 women), 24 part-time/adjunct (2 women). *Graduate housing:* Room and/or apartments available on a first-come, first-served basis to single students; on-campus housing not available to married students. Housing application deadline: 8/20. *Student services:* Campus employment opportunities, career counseling, international student services, services for students with disabilities, writing training. *Library:* Archibald Foundation Library. *Collection:* Books: 125,000 (physical), 150,000 (digital/electronic); Serial titles: 185,000 (physical), 65,704 (digital/electronic); Databases: 42. Weekly public service hours: 81; students can reserve study rooms.

Computer facilities: 20 computers available on campus for general student use. A campuswide network can be accessed from student residence rooms. Online class registration is available.
Website: http://www.ambrose.edu/

General Application Contact: Kalie Eeles, Enrollment Advisor, 403-410-2954, Fax: 403-571-2556, E-mail: enrolment@ambrose.edu.

GRADUATE UNITS

Ambrose Seminary Students: 62 full-time (23 women), 145 part-time (67 women); includes 96 minority (8 Black or African American, non-Hispanic/Latino; 1 American Indian or Alaska Native, non-Hispanic/Latino; 84 Asian, non-Hispanic/Latino; 3 Hispanic/Latino). Average age 42. *Faculty:* 11 full-time (1 woman), 20 part-time/adjunct (4 women). *Financial support:* Career-related internships or fieldwork and scholarships/grants available. Support available to part-time students. Financial award application deadline: 3/30. In 2015, 21 master's, 1 other advanced degree awarded. *Degree program information:* Part-time programs available. Part-time, blended/hybrid learning. Offers biblical/theological studies (MA); Chinese ministries (Certificate); Christian studies (MCS, Certificate, Diploma); intercultural ministries (M Div, MA, Certificate, Diploma); leadership and ministry (MA, Certificate, Diploma); pastoral ministries (M Div). *Application deadline:* For fall admission, 7/15 for domestic students, 3/1 for international students; for winter admission, 11/15 for domestic students, 7/1 for international students. Applications are processed on a rolling basis. *Application fee:* $70 ($100 for international students). Electronic applications accepted. *Application Contact:* Kalie Eeles, Enrollment Advisor, 403-410-2954, Fax: 403-571-2556, E-mail: enrolment@ambrose.edu. *Dean of Theology,* Jo-Ann Badley, 403-410-2000 Ext. 3994, Fax: 403-571-2556, E-mail: jbadley@ambrose.edu.

AMERICAN BAPTIST SEMINARY OF THE WEST, Berkeley, CA 94704-3029

General Information Independent-religious, coed, graduate-only institution. *Graduate housing:* Rooms and/or apartments available on a first-come, first-served basis to single and married students. Housing application deadline: 5/1.

GRADUATE UNITS

Graduate and Professional Programs ***Degree program information:*** Part-time and evening/weekend programs available. Part-time, evening/weekend, online learning. Offers community leadership (MA); theology (M Div, MA). MA program in theology offered jointly with Graduate Theological Union. Electronic applications accepted.

AMERICAN BUSINESS & TECHNOLOGY UNIVERSITY, Saint Joseph, MO 64506

General Information Proprietary, coed, comprehensive institution.

GRADUATE UNITS

Programs in Business Administration Online learning. Offers business administration (MBA); financial management (MBA); global business management (MBA); information systems management (MBA); marketing and social media (MBA); project and operations management (MBA); public accounting (MBA).

THE AMERICAN COLLEGE, Bryn Mawr, PA 19010-2105

General Information Independent, coed, graduate-only institution. *Graduate housing:* On-campus housing not available.

GRADUATE UNITS

Graduate Programs ***Degree program information:*** Part-time and evening/weekend programs available. Part-time, evening/weekend, online learning. Offers financial services (MSFS); leadership (MSM). Electronic applications accepted.

AMERICAN COLLEGE OF ACUPUNCTURE AND ORIENTAL MEDICINE, Houston, TX 77063

General Information Proprietary, coed, graduate-only institution. *Research affiliation:* Montrose Clinic (HIV/AIDS research and treatment), Rice University Wellness Center (student and staff care), Baylor College of Medicine (acupuncture for osteoarthritis of the knee), Memorial Herman Healthcare System, Tianjing Hospital, China (traditional Chinese medicine).

GRADUATE UNITS

Graduate Studies ***Degree program information:*** Part-time programs available. Part-time.

AMERICAN COLLEGE OF EDUCATION, Chicago, IL 60606

General Information Private, coed, graduate-only institution.

GRADUATE UNITS

Graduate Programs Offers curriculum and instruction (M Ed); educational leadership (M Ed); educational technology (M Ed).

AMERICAN COLLEGE OF HEALTHCARE SCIENCES, Portland, OR 97239-3719

General Information Independent, coed. *Graduate housing:* On-campus housing not available.

GRADUATE UNITS

Graduate Programs ***Degree program information:*** Part-time and evening/weekend programs available. Part-time, evening/weekend, online learning. Offers aromatherapy (Graduate Certificate); complementary alternative medicine (MS, Graduate Certificate); herbal medicine (Graduate Certificate); nutrition (Graduate Certificate).

AMERICAN COLLEGE OF THESSALONIKI, GR-555-10 Pylea, Thessaloniki, Greece

General Information Independent, coed, comprehensive institution.

GRADUATE UNITS

Department of Business Administration ***Degree program information:*** Part-time and evening/weekend programs available. Part-time, evening/weekend. Offers banking and finance (MBA); entrepreneurship (MBA, Certificate); finance (Certificate); management (MBA, Certificate); marketing (MBA, Certificate). Electronic applications accepted.

AMERICAN CONSERVATORY THEATER, San Francisco, CA 94108-5800

General Information Independent, coed, graduate-only institution. *Graduate housing:* On-campus housing not available.

GRADUATE UNITS

Program in Acting Offers acting (MFA, Certificate).

AMERICAN FILM INSTITUTE CONSERVATORY, Los Angeles, CA 90027-1657

General Information Independent, coed, graduate-only institution. *Enrollment by degree level:* 328 master's. *Graduate faculty:* 11 full-time (2 women), 64 part-time/adjunct (22 women). *Tuition, area resident:* Full-time $44,082. *Required fees:* $2948. Full-time tuition and fees vary according to student level. *Graduate housing:* On-campus housing not available. *Student services:* Campus safety program, career counseling, free psychological counseling, international student services. *Library:* Louis B. Mayer Library. *Collection:* Books: 39,694 (physical), 519 (digital/electronic); Serial titles: 17 (physical), 4 (digital/electronic); Databases: 2. Weekly public service hours: 74.

Computer facilities: 31 computers available on campus for general student use.
Website: http://www.afi.com/Conservatory/

General Application Contact: Stacy Gaspard, Enrollment Counselor, 323-856-7740, Fax: 323-856-7683, E-mail: admissions@afi.com.

GRADUATE UNITS

Graduate Program Students: 324 full-time (142 women), 4 part-time (3 women); includes 65 minority (13 Black or African American, non-Hispanic/Latino; 2 American Indian or Alaska Native, non-Hispanic/Latino; 15 Asian, non-Hispanic/Latino; 27 Hispanic/Latino; 8 Two or more races, non-Hispanic/Latino), 117 international. Average age 26. 629 applicants, 32% accepted, 136 enrolled. *Faculty:* 11 full-time (2 women), 64 part-time/adjunct (22 women). *Financial support:* In 2015–16, 101 students received support, including 14 teaching assistantships (averaging $3,000 per year); career-related internships or fieldwork, scholarships/grants, and unspecified assistantships also available. Financial award applicants required to submit FAFSA. In 2015, 121 master's awarded. Offers cinematography (MFA); directing (MFA); editing (MFA); producing (MFA); production design (MFA); screenwriting (MFA). *Application deadline:* For fall admission, 12/1 for domestic and international students. *Application fee:* $75. Electronic applications accepted. *Application Contact:* Stacy Gaspard, Enrollment Counselor, 323-856-7740, Fax: 323-856-7683, E-mail: admissions@afi.com.

AMERICAN GRADUATE SCHOOL IN PARIS, F-75006 Paris, France

General Information Independent, coed, graduate-only institution.

GRADUATE UNITS

Program in International Relations and Diplomacy Offers international relations and diplomacy (MA, PhD).

AMERICAN GRADUATE UNIVERSITY, Covina, CA 91724

General Information Proprietary, coed, graduate-only institution.

GRADUATE UNITS

Program in Acquisition Management ***Degree program information:*** Part-time programs available. Part-time, online learning. Offers acquisition management (MAM, Certificate). Electronic applications accepted.

Program in Business Administration ***Degree program information:*** Part-time programs available. Part-time, online learning. Offers acquisition and contracting (MBA); general management (MBA); project management (MBA); supply chain management (MBA). Electronic applications accepted.

Program in Contract Management ***Degree program information:*** Part-time programs available. Part-time, online learning. Offers contract management (MCM, Certificate). Electronic applications accepted.

Program in Leadership and Management Online learning. Offers leadership and management (MLM).

Program in Project Management ***Degree program information:*** Part-time programs available. Part-time, online learning. Offers project management (MPM, Certificate). Electronic applications accepted.

Program in Supply Chain Management ***Degree program information:*** Part-time programs available. Part-time, online learning. Offers supply chain management (MSCM, Certificate).

AMERICAN INTERCONTINENTAL UNIVERSITY ATLANTA, Atlanta, GA 30328

General Information Proprietary, coed, comprehensive institution. CGS member. *Graduate housing:* On-campus housing not available.

GRADUATE UNITS

Program in Global Technology Management ***Degree program information:*** Part-time and evening/weekend programs available. Part-time, evening/weekend, online learning. Offers global technology management (MBA). Electronic applications accepted.

Program in Information Technology ***Degree program information:*** Part-time and evening/weekend programs available. Part-time, evening/weekend. Offers information technology (MIT). Electronic applications accepted.

AMERICAN INTERCONTINENTAL UNIVERSITY HOUSTON, Houston, TX 77042

General Information Proprietary, coed, comprehensive institution.

GRADUATE UNITS

School of Business Offers management (MBA).

AMERICAN INTERCONTINENTAL UNIVERSITY ONLINE, Schaumburg, IL 60173

General Information Proprietary, coed, comprehensive institution. CGS member.

GRADUATE UNITS

Program in Business Administration ***Degree program information:*** Evening/weekend programs available. Evening/weekend, online learning. Offers accounting and finance (MBA); finance (MBA); healthcare management (MBA); human resource management (MBA); international business (MBA); management (MBA); marketing (MBA); operations management (MBA); organizational psychology and development (MBA); project management (MBA). Electronic applications accepted.

Program in Education ***Degree program information:*** Evening/weekend programs available. Evening/weekend, online learning. Offers curriculum and instruction (M Ed); educational assessment and evaluation (M Ed); instructional technology (M Ed); leadership of educational organizations (M Ed). Electronic applications accepted.

Program in Information Technology ***Degree program information:*** Evening/weekend programs available. Evening/weekend, online learning. Offers Internet security (MIT); IT project management (MIT). Electronic applications accepted.

AMERICAN INTERNATIONAL COLLEGE, Springfield, MA 01109-3189

General Information Independent, coed, comprehensive institution. *Enrollment:* 3,542 graduate, professional, and undergraduate students; 1,861 full-time matriculated graduate/professional students (1,454 women), 158 part-time matriculated graduate/professional students (98 women). *Enrollment by degree level:* 1,642 master's, 201 doctoral, 290 other advanced degrees. *Graduate faculty:* 21 full-time (19 women), 229 part-time/adjunct (163 women). *Tuition, area resident:* Full-time $10,500; part-time $700 per semester hour. *Required fees:* $60; $60 per unit. $30 per semester. One-time fee: $50. Tuition and fees vary according to course load, campus/location and program. *Graduate housing:* Room and/or apartments available on a first-come, first-served basis to single students; on-campus housing not available to married students. Typical cost: $10,330 per year ($16,570 including board). Room and board charges vary according to board plan and housing facility selected. Housing application deadline: 7/30. *Student services:* Campus employment opportunities, campus safety program, career counseling, exercise/wellness program, free psychological counseling, international student services, low-cost health insurance, multicultural affairs office, services for students with disabilities, writing training. *Library:* James J. Shea Sr. Library. *Collection:* Books: 54,178 (physical), 132,997 (digital/electronic); Serial titles: 278 (physical), 84 (digital/electronic); Databases: 55. Weekly public service hours: 80; students can reserve study rooms.

Computer facilities: Computer purchase and lease plans are available. 208 computers available on campus for general student use. A campuswide network can be accessed from student residence rooms and from off campus. Online class registration is available.
Website: http://www.aic.edu/

General Application Contact: Kerry Barnes, Director of Graduate Admissions, 413-205-3703, Fax: 413-205-3051, E-mail: kerry.barnes@aic.edu.

GRADUATE UNITS

School of Graduate and Adult Education Students: 1,645 full-time (1,290 women), 152 part-time (94 women); includes 233 minority (91 Black or African American, non-Hispanic/Latino; 4 American Indian or Alaska Native, non-Hispanic/Latino; 17 Asian, non-Hispanic/Latino; 93 Hispanic/Latino; 2 Native Hawaiian or other Pacific Islander, non-Hispanic/Latino; 26 Two or more races, non-Hispanic/Latino), 12 international. Average age 34. 843 applicants, 72% accepted, 415 enrolled. *Faculty:* 8 full-time (5 women), 218 part-time/adjunct (142 women). *Financial support:* In 2015–16, 4 fellowships with full tuition reimbursements (averaging $1,500 per year) were awarded; career-related internships or fieldwork also available. Financial award applicants required to submit FAFSA. In 2015, 580 master's, 17 doctorates, 64 other advanced degrees awarded. *Degree program information:* Part-time and evening/weekend programs available. Part-time, evening/weekend. Offers clinical psychology (MA); counseling psychology (MA); early childhood education (M Ed, CAGS); educational leadership and supervision (Ed D); educational psychology (MA, Ed D); elementary education (M Ed, CAGS); forensic psychology (MS); general psychology (MA); middle education/secondary education (M Ed, CAGS); moderate disabilities (M Ed, CAGS); reading specialist (M Ed, CAGS); school adjustment counseling (MAEP, CAGS); school guidance counseling (MAEP, CAGS); school leadership (M Ed, CAGS); teaching and learning (Ed D). *Application deadline:* Applications are processed on a rolling basis. *Application fee:* $50. Electronic applications accepted. *Application Contact:* Kerry Barnes, Director of Graduate Admissions, 413-205-3703, Fax: 413-205-3051, E-mail: kerry.barnes@aic.edu. *Dean of the School of Business, Arts and Sciences*, Susanne Swanker, 413-205-3216, Fax: 413-205-3943, E-mail: susanne.swanker@aic.edu.

Graduate Business Programs Students: 53 full-time (19 women), 6 part-time (2 women); includes 27 minority (17 Black or African American, non-Hispanic/Latino; 1 Asian, non-Hispanic/Latino; 5 Hispanic/Latino; 4 Two or more races, non-Hispanic/Latino), 5 international. Average age 28. 43 applicants, 72% accepted, 25 enrolled. *Faculty:* 10 part-time/adjunct (2 women). *Financial support:* Application deadline: 4/1; applicants required to submit FAFSA. In 2015, 33 master's awarded. *Degree program information:* Part-time and evening/weekend programs available. Part-time, evening/weekend. Offers accounting and taxation (MSAT); business (MBA, MSAT); resort and casino management (MBA). *Application deadline:* For fall admission, 4/1 for domestic students, 6/1 priority date for international students; for spring admission, 12/1 for domestic students, 10/1 priority date for international students. Applications are processed on a rolling basis. *Application fee:* $50. Electronic applications accepted. *Application Contact:* Kerry Barnes, Director of Graduate Admissions, 413-205-3703, Fax: 413-205-3943, E-mail: kerry.barnes@aic.edu. *Director of Business Programs*, Dr. Rob Poole, 413-205-3547, E-mail: rob.poole@aic.edu.

School of Health Sciences Students: 216 full-time (164 women), 5 part-time (4 women); includes 57 minority (27 Black or African American, non-Hispanic/Latino; 1 American Indian or Alaska Native, non-Hispanic/Latino; 12 Asian, non-Hispanic/Latino; 9 Hispanic/Latino; 2 Native Hawaiian or other Pacific Islander, non-Hispanic/Latino; 6 Two or more races, non-Hispanic/Latino), 3 international. Average age 28. 361 applicants, 40% accepted, 80 enrolled. *Faculty:* 14 full-time (13 women), 11 part-time/adjunct (all women). *Financial support:* Career-related internships or fieldwork and traineeships available. Financial award application deadline: 4/1; financial award applicants required to submit FAFSA. In 2015, 29 master's, 33 doctorates awarded. *Degree program information:* Part-time programs available. Part-time, 100% online. Offers family nurse practitioner (MSN); health sciences (MSN, MSOT, DPT); nursing administration (MSN); nursing education (MSN); occupational therapy (MSOT); physical therapy (DPT). *Application deadline:* For fall and spring admission, 12/1 priority date for domestic and international students. *Application fee:* $50. Electronic applications accepted. *Application Contact:* Kerry Barnes, Director of Graduate Admissions, 413-205-3703, Fax: 413-205-3051, E-mail: kerry.barnes@aic.edu. *Dean*, Dr. Cesarina Thompson, 413-205-3056, Fax: 413-654-1430, E-mail: cesarina.thompson@aic.edu.

AMERICAN JEWISH UNIVERSITY, Bel Air, CA 90077-1599

General Information Independent-religious, coed, comprehensive institution. *Graduate housing:* Rooms and/or apartments available on a first-come, first-served basis to single and married students. Housing application deadline: 6/1.

GRADUATE UNITS

Graduate School of Education Offers education (MA Ed); education for working professionals (MA Ed).

Graduate School of Nonprofit Management ***Degree program information:*** Part-time and evening/weekend programs available. Part-time, evening/weekend. Offers general nonprofit administration (MBA); Jewish communal studies (MAJCS); Jewish nonprofit administration (MBA); nonprofit management (MAJCS, MBA).

Ziegler School of Rabbinic Studies Offers rabbinic studies (MARS).

AMERICAN MUSEUM OF NATURAL HISTORY–RICHARD GILDER GRADUATE SCHOOL, New York, NY 10024

General Information Independent, coed, graduate-only institution.

GRADUATE UNITS

Program in Comparative Biology Offers comparative biology (PhD).

AMERICAN NATIONAL UNIVERSITY, Salem, VA 24153

General Information Proprietary, coed, comprehensive institution.

GRADUATE UNITS

Program in Business Administration Offers business administration (MBA).

AMERICAN PUBLIC UNIVERSITY SYSTEM, Charles Town, WV 25414

General Information Proprietary, coed, comprehensive institution. CGS member. *Enrollment:* 52,513 graduate, professional, and undergraduate students; 531 full-time matriculated graduate/professional students (233 women), 9,094 part-time matriculated graduate/professional students (3,735 women). *Enrollment by degree level:* 9,625 master's. *Graduate faculty:* 431 full-time (241 women), 1,839 part-time/adjunct (865 women). *Tuition, area resident:* Part-time $350 per credit hour. *Graduate housing:* On-campus housing not available. *Student services:* Career counseling, international student services, teacher training. *Library:* APUS Online Library.

Computer facilities: Online class registration is available.
Website: http://www.apus.edu/

General Application Contact: Terry Grant, Vice President of Enrollment Management, 877-468-6268, Fax: 304-724-3780, E-mail: info@apus.edu.

GRADUATE UNITS

AMU/APU Graduate Programs Students: 531 full-time (233 women), 9,094 part-time (3,735 women); includes 3,140 minority (1,679 Black or African American, non-Hispanic/Latino; 55 American Indian or Alaska Native, non-Hispanic/Latino; 252 Asian, non-Hispanic/Latino; 773 Hispanic/Latino; 75 Native Hawaiian or other Pacific Islander, non-Hispanic/Latino; 306 Two or more races, non-Hispanic/Latino), 111 international. Average age 37. *Faculty:* 431 full-time (241 women), 1,839 part-time/adjunct (865 women). *Financial support:* Applicants required to submit FAFSA. In 2015, 3,391 master's awarded. *Degree program information:* Part-time and evening/weekend programs available. Part-time, evening/weekend, online only. Offers accounting (MBA, MS); analytics (MBA); criminal justice (MA); educational leadership (M Ed); emergency and disaster management (MA); entrepreneurship (MBA); environmental policy and management (MS); finance (MBA); general (MBA); global business management (MBA); government contracting and acquisition (MBA); health care administration (MBA); history (MA); homeland security (MA); homeland security resource allocation (MBA); humanities (MA); information technology (MS); information technology management (MBA); intelligence studies (MA); international relations and conflict resolution (MA); legal studies (MA); management (MA); marketing (MBA); military history (MA); military studies (MA); national security studies (MA); nonprofit management (MBA); political science (MA); psychology (MA); public administration (MPA); public health (MPH); reverse logistics management (MA); school counseling (M Ed); security management (MA); space studies (MS); sports and health sciences (MS); sports management (MBA); teaching (M Ed); transportation and logistics management (MA). *Application deadline:* Applications are processed on a rolling basis. *Application fee:* $0. Electronic applications accepted. *Application Contact:* Terry Grant, Vice President of Enrollment Management, 877-468-6268, Fax: 304-724-3780, E-mail: info@apus.edu. *Executive Vice President and Provost*, Dr. Karan Powell, 877-468-6268, Fax: 304-724-3780.

AMERICAN SENTINEL UNIVERSITY, Aurora, CO 80014

General Information Proprietary, coed, comprehensive institution.

GRADUATE UNITS

Graduate Programs ***Degree program information:*** Part-time and evening/weekend programs available. Part-time, evening/weekend, online learning. Electronic applications accepted.

AMERICAN UNIVERSITY, Washington, DC 20016-8001

General Information Independent-religious, coed, university. CGS member. *Enrollment:* 13,200 graduate, professional, and undergraduate students; 2,911 full-time matriculated graduate/professional students (1,789 women), 2,281 part-time matriculated graduate/professional students (1,421 women). *Enrollment by degree level:* 3,394 master's, 1,695 doctoral, 103 other advanced degrees. *Graduate faculty:* 793 full-time (389 women), 635 part-time/adjunct (266 women). *Tuition, area resident:* Full-time $27,468; part-time $1526 per credit hour. *Required fees:* $430. Tuition and fees vary according to course level and program. *Graduate housing:* On-campus housing not available. *Student services:* Campus employment opportunities, campus safety program, career counseling, child daycare facilities, exercise/wellness program, free psychological counseling, grant writing training, international student services, multicultural affairs office, services for students with disabilities, teacher training, writing training. *Library:* Bender Library plus 1 other. *Collection:* Books: 700,000 (physical), 300,000 (digital/electronic); Serial titles: 650 (physical), 125,000 (digital/electronic); Databases: 300. Study areas open 24 hours, 5–7 days a week; students can reserve study rooms.

Computer facilities: 700 computers available on campus for general student use. A campuswide network can be accessed from student residence rooms and from off campus. Online class registration, online e-support through Blackboard platform are available.
Website: http://www.american.edu/

General Application Contact: 202-885-1000.

GRADUATE UNITS

College of Arts and Sciences Students: 570 full-time (388 women), 504 part-time (354 women); includes 238 minority (113 Black or African American, non-Hispanic/Latino; 6 American Indian or Alaska Native, non-Hispanic/Latino; 32 Asian, non-Hispanic/Latino; 61 Hispanic/Latino; 1 Native Hawaiian or other Pacific Islander, non-Hispanic/Latino; 25 Two or more races, non-Hispanic/Latino), 138 international. Average age 30. 1,871 applicants, 57% accepted, 360 enrolled. *Faculty:* 362 full-time (197 women), 247 part-time/adjunct (125 women). *Financial support:* Institutionally sponsored loans, scholarships/grants, and unspecified assistantships available. In 2015, 325 master's, 40 doctorates, 37 other advanced degrees awarded. *Degree program information:* Part-time and evening/weekend programs available. Part-time, evening/weekend, 100% online. Offers addiction and addictive behavior (Certificate); anthropology (PhD); applied microeconomics (Certificate); applied statistics (Certificate); art history (MA); art management (MA); arts and sciences (M Ed, MA, MAT, MFA, MS, PhD, Certificate,

Graduate Certificate); audio production (Certificate); audio technology (MA); behavior, cognition, and neuroscience (PhD); biology (MA, MS); chemistry (MS); clinical psychology (PhD); creative writing (MFA); economics (MA, PhD); environmental assessment (Graduate Certificate); environmental science (MS); ethics, peace, and global affairs (MA); gender analysis in economics (Certificate); health promotion management (MS); history (MA, PhD); international arts management (Certificate); international economic relations (Certificate); international economics (MA); literature (MA); mathematics (MA); nutrition education (MS, Certificate); philosophy (MA); professional science: biotechnology (MS); professional science: environmental assessment (MS); professional science: quantitative analysis (MS); psychobiology of healing (Certificate); psychology (MA); public anthropology (MA, Certificate); public sociology (Certificate); social research (Certificate); sociology (MA); Spanish: Latin American studies (MA); statistics (MS); studio art (MFA); teaching English as a foreign language (MA); teaching English to speakers of other languages (MA, Certificate); technology in arts management (Certificate); translation: French (Certificate); translation: Russian (Certificate); translation: Spanish (Certificate); women's, gender, and sexuality studies (Graduate Certificate). *Application deadline:* For fall admission, 2/1 for domestic students; for spring admission, 11/1 for domestic students. Applications are processed on a rolling basis. *Application fee:* $55. Electronic applications accepted. *Application Contact:* Kathleen Clowery, Associate Director, Graduate Enrollment Management, 202-885-3621, Fax: 202-885-2429, E-mail: clowery@american.edu. *Dean*, Dr. Peter Starr, 202-885-2446, Fax: 202-885-2429, E-mail: pstarr@american.edu.

School of Education Students: 52 full-time (47 women), 128 part-time (104 women); includes 57 minority (30 Black or African American, non-Hispanic/Latino; 1 American Indian or Alaska Native, non-Hispanic/Latino; 9 Asian, non-Hispanic/Latino; 13 Hispanic/Latino; 4 Two or more races, non-Hispanic/Latino), 8 international. Average age 28. 190 applicants, 93% accepted, 77 enrolled. *Faculty:* 16 full-time (12 women), 29 part-time/adjunct (21 women). *Financial support:* Institutionally sponsored loans available. Financial award application deadline: 2/1. In 2015, 109 master's, 10 other advanced degrees awarded. *Degree program information:* Part-time and evening/weekend programs available. Part-time, evening/weekend. Offers bilingual education (MA, Certificate); curriculum and instruction (M Ed, Certificate); education policy and leadership (M Ed); international training and education (MA); special education: learning disabilities (MA); teacher education (MAT, Certificate). *Application deadline:* For fall admission, 2/1 priority date for domestic students; for spring admission, 11/1 for domestic students. Applications are processed on a rolling basis. *Application fee:* $55. *Application Contact:* Kathleen Clowery, Director, Graduate Admissions, 202-885-3620, Fax: 202-885-1344, E-mail: clowery@american.edu. *Dean*, Cheryl Holcomb-McCoy, 202-885-3720, E-mail: educate@american.edu.

Kogod School of Business Students: 187 full-time (94 women), 267 part-time (138 women); includes 140 minority (60 Black or African American, non-Hispanic/Latino; 34 Asian, non-Hispanic/Latino; 37 Hispanic/Latino; 1 Native Hawaiian or other Pacific Islander, non-Hispanic/Latino; 8 Two or more races, non-Hispanic/Latino), 90 international. Average age 29. 853 applicants, 57% accepted, 220 enrolled. *Faculty:* 75 full-time (25 women), 43 part-time/adjunct (12 women). *Financial support:* Application deadline: 2/1. In 2015, 289 master's, 8 other advanced degrees awarded. *Degree program information:* Part-time and evening/weekend programs available. Part-time, evening/weekend, 100% online. Offers accounting (MS, Certificate); analytics (MS); business (MBA, MS, Certificate); entrepreneurship (Certificate); finance (MS, Certificate); forensic accounting (Certificate); marketing (MS); real estate (MS, Certificate); sustainability management (MS); tax (Certificate); taxation (MS, Certificate). *Application deadline:* Applications are processed on a rolling basis. *Application fee:* $100. Electronic applications accepted. *Application Contact:* Jason Kennedy, Associate Director of Graduate Admissions, 202-885-1968, E-mail: jkennedy@american.edu. *Dean*, John T. Delaney, 202-885-1908, Fax: 202-885-8044.

Multidisciplinary Program in Game Design Students: 17 full-time (11 women), 3 part-time (0 women); includes 10 minority (2 Black or African American, non-Hispanic/Latino; 1 American Indian or Alaska Native, non-Hispanic/Latino; 1 Asian, non-Hispanic/Latino; 5 Hispanic/Latino; 1 Two or more races, non-Hispanic/Latino), 3 international. Average age 29. 15 applicants, 87% accepted, 11 enrolled. Offers game design (MA). Program is a partnership between the School of Communication and the College of Arts and Sciences. *Application deadline:* For fall admission, 2/1 for domestic students. Applications are processed on a rolling basis. *Application fee:* $55. Electronic applications accepted. *Application Contact:* Kathleen Clowery, Associate Director, Graduate Enrollment Management, 202-885-3621, Fax: 202-885-2429, E-mail: clowery@american.edu. *Director, American University Game Lab and Studio*, Grace Lindsay, 202-885-6933, E-mail: grace@american.edu.

School of Communication Students: 211 full-time (132 women), 291 part-time (202 women); includes 167 minority (100 Black or African American, non-Hispanic/Latino; 5 American Indian or Alaska Native, non-Hispanic/Latino; 15 Asian, non-Hispanic/Latino; 34 Hispanic/Latino; 13 Two or more races, non-Hispanic/Latino), 52 international. 567 applicants, 67% accepted, 198 enrolled. *Faculty:* 39 full-time (20 women). *Financial support:* In 2015–16, 210 students received support, including 3 fellowships with partial tuition reimbursements available (averaging $20,000 per year), 30 research assistantships with partial tuition reimbursements available (averaging $15,000 per year), 30 teaching assistantships with partial tuition reimbursements available (averaging $15,000 per year); career-related internships or fieldwork, Federal Work-Study, institutionally sponsored loans, scholarships/grants, tuition waivers (partial), and unspecified assistantships also available. Support available to part-time students. Financial award application deadline: 2/1; financial award applicants required to submit FAFSA. In 2015, 185 master's, 5 doctorates awarded. *Degree program information:* Part-time and evening/weekend programs available. Part-time, evening/weekend, 100% online. Offers broadcast journalism (MA); communication (MA, MFA, PhD); film and electronic media (MFA); film and media arts (MA); interactive journalism (MA); international journalism (MA); international media (MA); investigative journalism (MA); media industries and institutions (PhD); media, public issues, and engagement (PhD); media, technology, and culture (PhD); political communication (MA); producing for film and video (MA); strategic communication (MA). *Application deadline:* For fall admission, 2/1 priority date for domestic and international students; for spring admission, 11/1 for domestic and international students. Applications are processed on a rolling basis. *Application fee:* $55. Electronic applications accepted. *Application Contact:* Marc Tomik, Director of Graduate Programs, 202-885-2040, Fax: 202-885-2019, E-mail: mtomik@american.edu. *Dean*, Jeffrey Rutenbeck, 202-885-2058, Fax: 202-885-2099, E-mail: jeff@american.edu.

School of International Service Students: 578 full-time (351 women), 502 part-time (295 women); includes 268 minority (96 Black or African American, non-Hispanic/Latino; 9 American Indian or Alaska Native, non-Hispanic/Latino; 59 Asian, non-Hispanic/Latino; 89 Hispanic/Latino; 1 Native Hawaiian or other Pacific Islander, non-Hispanic/Latino; 14 Two or more races, non-Hispanic/Latino), 140 international. Average age 28. 1,810 applicants, 80% accepted, 415 enrolled. *Faculty:* 118 full-time (53 women), 60 part-time/adjunct (24 women). *Financial support:* Application deadline: 1/15. In 2015, 399 master's, 7 doctorates, 7 other advanced degrees awarded. *Degree program information:* Part-time and evening/weekend programs available. Part-time, evening/weekend, 100% online. Offers comparative and regional studies (Certificate); cross-cultural communication (Certificate); development management (MS); ethics, peace, and global affairs (MA); European studies (Certificate); global environmental policy (MA, Certificate); global information technology (Certificate); international affairs (MA); international arts management (Certificate); international communication (MA, Certificate); international development (MA); international economic policy (Certificate); international economic relations (Certificate); international economics (MA); international media (MA); international peace and conflict resolution (MA, Certificate); international politics (Certificate); international relations (MA, PhD); international service (MIS); peacebuilding (Certificate); social enterprise (MA); the Americas (Certificate); United States foreign policy (Certificate). *Application deadline:* For fall admission, 1/15 for domestic students; for spring admission, 10/1 for domestic students, 9/15 for international students. *Application fee:* $55. Electronic applications accepted. *Application Contact:* Jia Jiang, Associate Director, Graduate Education Enrollment, 202-885-1689, Fax: 202-885-1109, E-mail: jiang@american.edu. *Dean*, Dr. James Goldgeier, 202-885-1603, Fax: 202-885-2494, E-mail: goldgeier@american.edu.

School of Professional and Extended Studies Students: 25 part-time (21 women); includes 2 minority (1 American Indian or Alaska Native, non-Hispanic/Latino; 1 Hispanic/Latino). Average age 40. *Faculty:* 24 full-time (9 women), 9 part-time/adjunct (5 women). 100% online. Offers customizable modular studies (MS); project monitoring and evaluation (Graduate Certificate); strategic management and executive leadership for law enforcement (Graduate Certificate). *Application Contact:* Alycia Johnson, Director, Recruitment and Admission, 202-895-4919, Fax: 202-895-4960, E-mail: janjigia@american.edu. *Dean*, Carola Weil, 202-885-5990, Fax: 202-895-4960, E-mail: weil@american.edu.

School of Public Affairs Students: 289 full-time (167 women), 302 part-time (194 women); includes 172 minority (84 Black or African American, non-Hispanic/Latino; 7 American Indian or Alaska Native, non-Hispanic/Latino; 37 Asian, non-Hispanic/Latino; 40 Hispanic/Latino; 2 Native Hawaiian or other Pacific Islander, non-Hispanic/Latino; 2 Two or more races, non-Hispanic/Latino), 34 international. Average age 30. 891 applicants, 70% accepted, 234 enrolled. *Faculty:* 77 full-time (34 women), 68 part-time/adjunct (22 women). *Financial support:* Institutionally sponsored loans and scholarships/grants available. Financial award application deadline: 2/1. In 2015, 265 master's, 9 doctorates, 5 other advanced degrees awarded. *Degree program information:* Part-time and evening/weekend programs available. Part-time, evening/weekend, 100% online. Offers justice, law and criminology (MS, PhD); key executive leadership (MPA); leadership for organizational change (Certificate); nonprofit management (Certificate); organization development (MSOD, Certificate); organizational development (MSOD); political communication (MA); political science (MA, PhD); public administration (MPA, PhD, Certificate); public administration and policy (MPA, MPAP, MPP, MSOD, PhD, Certificate); public affairs (MA, MPA, MPAP, MPP, MS, MSOD, PhD, Certificate); public financial management (Certificate); public management (Certificate); public policy (MPP); public policy (Certificate); public policy analysis (Certificate); terrorism and homeland security policy (MS); women, policy and political leadership (Certificate). *Application deadline:* For fall admission, 2/1 for domestic and international students. *Application fee:* $55. Electronic applications accepted. *Dean*, Dr. Barbara Romzek, 202-885-2940, Fax: 202-885-2353, E-mail: bromzek@american.edu.

Washington College of Law Students: 1,075 full-time (657 women), 393 part-time (220 women); includes 392 minority (78 Black or African American, non-Hispanic/Latino; 2 American Indian or Alaska Native, non-Hispanic/Latino; 83 Asian, non-Hispanic/Latino; 210 Hispanic/Latino; 3 Native Hawaiian or other Pacific Islander, non-Hispanic/Latino; 16 Two or more races, non-Hispanic/Latino), 169 international. Average age 27. 5,124 applicants, 26% accepted, 256 enrolled. *Faculty:* 78 full-time (40 women), 138 part-time/adjunct (43 women). *Financial support:* Institutionally sponsored loans available. Financial award application deadline: 3/1; financial award applicants required to submit FAFSA. In 2015, 148 master's, 468 doctorates awarded. *Degree program information:* Part-time and evening/weekend programs available. Part-time, evening/weekend. Offers advocacy (LL M); information justice and intellectual property (LL M); international human rights and humanitarian law (LL M); international legal studies (LL M); juridical science (SJD); law (JD); law and government (LL M). *Application deadline:* For fall admission, 7/1 for domestic students, 5/1 for international students; for spring admission, 11/1 for domestic students, 10/1 for international students. *Application Contact:* Hilary Lappin, Associate Director, Graduate Admissions, 202-274-4114, Fax: 202-274-4107, E-mail: hlappin@wcl.american.edu. *Dean*, Camille A. Nelson, 202-274-4004, Fax: 202-274-4005.

THE AMERICAN UNIVERSITY IN CAIRO, 11835 New Cairo, Egypt

General Information Independent, coed, comprehensive institution. CGS member. *Enrollment:* 6,835 graduate, professional, and undergraduate students; 276 full-time matriculated graduate/professional students (154 women), 902 part-time matriculated graduate/professional students (586 women). *Enrollment by degree level:* 1,134 master's, 43 doctoral, 1 other advanced degree. *Graduate faculty:* 168 full-time (68 women), 30 part-time/adjunct (0 women). *Tuition, area resident:* Full-time $20,412; part-time $13,608. *Required fees:* $598; $598. Tuition and fees vary according to course load and program. *Graduate housing:* Room and/or apartments available on a first-come, first-served basis to single students; on-campus housing not available to married students. Typical cost: $5840 per year. Room charges vary according to housing facility selected. *Student services:* Campus employment opportunities, campus safety program, career counseling, child daycare facilities, free psychological counseling, grant writing training, international student services, low-cost health insurance, multicultural affairs office, services for students with disabilities, writing training. *Library:* American University in Cairo Library plus 1 other. *Collection:* Books: 512,980 (physical), 2,663 (digital/electronic); Databases: 133. Weekly public service hours: 80.

Computer facilities: 120 computers available on campus for general student use. A campuswide network can be accessed from student residence rooms and from off campus. Online class registration, Blackboard, on-line unofficial transcripts, ID creation are available.
Website: http://www.aucegypt.edu/

General Application Contact: Maha Hegazi, Assistant Director for Graduate Admissions, 20-22615-1462, E-mail: mahahegazi@aucegypt.edu.

GRADUATE UNITS

Graduate School of Education Students: 3 full-time (2 women), 68 part-time (59 women). Average age 32. 55 applicants, 62% accepted, 15 enrolled. *Faculty:* 8 full-time (7 women). *Financial support:* Fellowships with partial tuition reimbursements, scholarships/grants, tuition waivers (partial), and unspecified assistantships available. Financial award application deadline: 3/10. In 2015, 20 master's awarded. *Degree* *program information:* Part-time and evening/weekend programs available. Part-time, evening/weekend. Offers educational leadership (MA); international and comparative education (MA). *Application deadline:* For fall admission, 2/1 priority date for domestic and international students; for spring admission, 10/15 priority date for domestic and international students. Applications are processed on a rolling basis. *Application fee:* $75. Electronic applications accepted. *Application Contact:* Maha Hegazi, Director for Graduate Admissions, 20-22615-1462, E-mail: mahahegazi@aucegypt.edu. *Dean,* Dr. Ted Purinton, 20-2615-1490, E-mail: tedpurinton@aucegypt.edu.

School of Business Students: 58 full-time (20 women), 76 part-time (42 women), 3 international. Average age 29. 221 applicants, 38% accepted, 34 enrolled. *Faculty:* 24 full-time (5 women), 6 part-time/adjunct (0 women). *Financial support:* Fellowships with partial tuition reimbursements, scholarships/grants, tuition waivers (partial), and unspecified assistantships available. Financial award application deadline: 3/10. In 2015, 68 master's awarded. *Degree program information:* Part-time and evening/weekend programs available. Part-time, evening/weekend. Offers business administration (MBA, Diploma); economics (MA); economics in international development (MA); finance (MS). *Application deadline:* For fall admission, 2/1 priority date for domestic and international students; for spring admission, 10/15 priority date for domestic and international students. Applications are processed on a rolling basis. *Application fee:* $75. Electronic applications accepted. *Application Contact:* Maha Hegazi, Director of Graduate Admissions, 20-22615-1462, E-mail: mahahegazi@aucegypt.edu. *Dean,* Dr. AbdelKrim Seghir, 20-22615-3290, E-mail: kseghir@aucegypt.edu.

School of Global Affairs and Public Policy Students: 84 full-time (57 women), 246 part-time (166 women), 46 international. Average age 29. 447 applicants, 49% accepted, 83 enrolled. *Faculty:* 25 full-time (13 women), 6 part-time/adjunct (0 women). *Financial support:* Fellowships with partial tuition reimbursements, scholarships/grants, and unspecified assistantships available. Financial award application deadline: 3/10. In 2015, 88 master's awarded. *Degree program information:* Part-time and evening/weekend programs available. Part-time, evening/weekend. Offers gender and women's studies in the Middle East and North Africa (MA); gendered political economies (MA); geographies of gender and justice (MA); global affairs (MGA); global affairs and public policy (LL M, MA, MGA, MPA, MPP, Diploma); journalism and mass communication (MA); public administration (MPA, Diploma); public policy (MPP, Diploma). *Application deadline:* For fall admission, 2/1 for domestic and international students; for spring admission, 10/15 for domestic and international students. Applications are processed on a rolling basis. *Application fee:* $75. Electronic applications accepted. *Application Contact:* Maha Hegazi, Director for Graduate Admissions, 20-22615-1462, E-mail: mahahegazi@aucegypt.edu. *Dean,* Dr. Nabil Fahmy, 20-2615-2671, E-mail: nfahmy@aucegypt.edu.

Center for Migration and Refugee Studies Offers forced migration and refugee studies (Diploma); migration and refugee studies (MA). *Application Contact:* Wesley Clark, Director of North American Admissions and Financial Aid, 646-810-9433 Ext. 4547, E-mail: wclark@aucnyo.edu. *Director,* Dr. Ibrahim Awad, 20-2-2615-1398, E-mail: iawad@aucegypt.edu.

Middle East Studies Center Offers Middle East studies (MA, Diploma). *Application deadline:* For fall admission, 3/31 for domestic students; for spring admission, 1/10 for domestic students. *Application fee:* $45. *Application Contact:* Mary Davidson, Coordinator of Student Affairs, 212-730-8800, Fax: 212-730-1600, E-mail: mdavidson@aucnyo.edu. *Director,* Sandrine Gamblin, 20-2-2615-1750.

School of Humanities and Social Sciences Students: 61 full-time (41 women), 219 part-time (167 women), 39 international. Average age 31. 324 applicants, 57% accepted, 79 enrolled. *Faculty:* 57 full-time (36 women), 3 part-time/adjunct (0 women). *Financial support:* Fellowships with partial tuition reimbursements, scholarships/grants, tuition waivers (partial), and unspecified assistantships available. Financial award application deadline: 3/10. In 2015, 67 master's awarded. *Degree program information:* Part-time and evening/weekend programs available. Part-time, evening/weekend. Offers Arabic language and literature (MA); community psychology (MA); comparative literary studies (Graduate Diploma); counseling psychology (MA); Egyptology and Coptology (MA); English and comparative literature (MA); humanities and social sciences (MA, Graduate Diploma); Islamic art and architecture (MA); Islamic studies (MA); Middle Eastern history (MA); political science (MA); sociology and anthropology (MA). *Application deadline:* For fall admission, 2/1 priority date for domestic and international students; for spring admission, 10/15 priority date for domestic and international students. Applications are processed on a rolling basis. *Application fee:* $75. Electronic applications accepted. *Application Contact:* Maha Hegazi, Director for Graduate Admissions, 20-22615-1462, E-mail: mahahegazi@aucegypt.edu. *Dean,* Dr. Nathaniel Bowditch, 20-2-2615-1788, E-mail: nbowditch@aucegypt.edu.

School of Sciences and Engineering Students: 61 full-time (29 women), 268 part-time (132 women), 11 international. Average age 28. 310 applicants, 43% accepted, 56 enrolled. *Faculty:* 54 full-time (7 women), 15 part-time/adjunct (0 women). *Financial support:* Fellowships with partial tuition reimbursements, scholarships/grants, and unspecified assistantships available. Financial award application deadline: 3/10. In 2015, 63 master's, 3 doctorates awarded. *Degree program information:* Part-time and evening/weekend programs available. Part-time, evening/weekend. Offers computer science (MS, Graduate Diploma); computing (M Comp); construction engineering (M Eng, MS); food chemistry (M Chem); mechanical engineering (MS); product development and systems management (M Eng); sciences and engineering (M Chem, M Comp, M Eng, MS, PhD, Graduate Diploma). *Application deadline:* For fall admission, 2/1 priority date for domestic and international students; for spring admission, 10/15 priority date for domestic and international students. Applications are processed on a rolling basis. *Application fee:* $75. Electronic applications accepted. *Application Contact:* Maha Hegazi, Director for Graduate Admissions, 20-22615-1462, E-mail: mahahegazi@aucegypt.edu. *Interim Dean,* Dr. Mohamed Naguib Abou Zeid, 20-2615-2926, E-mail: nagiba@aucegypt.edu.

THE AMERICAN UNIVERSITY IN DUBAI, Dubai, United Arab Emirates

General Information Proprietary, coed, comprehensive institution. *Graduate housing:* Room and/or apartments available on a first-come, first-served basis to single students; on-campus housing not available to married students. Housing application deadline: 7/31.

GRADUATE UNITS

Graduate Programs ***Degree program information:*** Part-time and evening/weekend programs available. Part-time, evening/weekend. Offers construction management (MS); education (M Ed); finance (MBA); generalist (MBA); marketing (MBA). Electronic applications accepted.

AMERICAN UNIVERSITY OF ARMENIA, Yerevan 3750198, Armenia

General Information Independent, coed, graduate-only institution. *Research affiliation:* Samsung (cryptography), Volkswagen Foundation (cryptography), Mentor Graphics (data compression algorithms), IBM (big data and data analytics), Johns Hopkins University Bloomberg School of Public Health (public health), Institut de Medecine Sociale et Preventive, Universite de Geneve (Geneva, Switzerland) (tobacco control/health education).

GRADUATE UNITS

Graduate Programs ***Degree program information:*** Part-time and evening/weekend programs available. Part-time, evening/weekend. Offers business administration (MBA); computer and information science (MS); economics (MS); industrial engineering and systems management (ME); law (LL M); political science and international affairs (MPSIA); public health (MPH); teaching English as a foreign language (MA).

AMERICAN UNIVERSITY OF BEIRUT, 107 2020 Beirut, Lebanon

General Information Independent, coed, university. CGS member. *Enrollment:* 8,643 graduate, professional, and undergraduate students; 1,075 full-time matriculated graduate/professional students (600 women), 548 part-time matriculated graduate/professional students (360 women). *Enrollment by degree level:* 1,108 master's, 515 doctoral. *Graduate faculty:* 516 full-time (152 women), 23 part-time/adjunct (8 women). *Tuition, area resident:* Full-time $16,254; part-time $903 per credit. *Required fees:* $699. Tuition and fees vary according to course load and program. *Graduate housing:* Room and/or apartments available on a first-come, first-served basis to single students; on-campus housing not available to married students. Typical cost: $2732 per year. Housing application deadline: 6/30. *Student services:* Campus employment opportunities, campus safety program, career counseling, exercise/wellness program, free psychological counseling, grant writing training, international student services, low-cost health insurance, services for students with disabilities, teacher training, writing training. *Library:* Jafet Library plus 3 others. *Collection:* Books: 450,000 (physical), 350,000 (digital/electronic); Serial titles: 5,000 (physical), 80,000 (digital/electronic); Databases: 250. Weekly public service hours: 109; students can reserve study rooms. *Research affiliation:* LORE Foundation (education), MasterCard Foundation (public health), St. Jude's Children Research Hospital Inc. (pediatric oncology), Ford Foundation (sexual health), Computers & Communication Technology SAL (CCT) (engineering and technology), Elanco Animal Health (agriculture).

Computer facilities: 1,863 computers available on campus for general student use. A campuswide network can be accessed from student residence rooms and from off campus. Online class registration is available.
Website: http://www.aub.edu.lb/

General Application Contact: Dr. Salim Kanaan, Director, Admissions Office, 961-1350000 Ext. 2594, Fax: 961-1750775, E-mail: sk00@aub.edu.lb.

GRADUATE UNITS

Graduate Programs Students: 1,075 full-time (600 women), 548 part-time (360 women). Average age 26. 1,924 applicants, 45% accepted, 492 enrolled. *Faculty:* 516 full-time (152 women), 23 part-time/adjunct (8 women). *Financial support:* In 2015–16, 350 students received support, including 1,066 research assistantships (averaging $5,458 per year); career-related internships or fieldwork, institutionally sponsored loans, scholarships/grants, health care benefits, and unspecified assistantships also available. Financial award application deadline: 12/18; financial award applicants required to submit CSS PROFILE. In 2015, 439 master's, 96 doctorates awarded. *Degree program information:* Part-time and evening/weekend programs available. Part-time, evening/weekend. *Application deadline:* For fall admission, 2/10 priority date for domestic and international students; for spring admission, 11/1 for domestic and international students. *Application fee:* $50. Electronic applications accepted. *Application Contact:* Dr. Salim Kanaan, Director, Admissions Office, 961-1350000 Ext. 2594, Fax: 961-1750775, E-mail: sk00@aub.edu.lb. *Graduate Council Chairperson,* Dr. Rabih Talhouk, 961-1374374 Ext. 4193, E-mail: rtalhouk@aub.edu.lb.

Faculty of Agricultural and Food Sciences Students: 13 full-time (5 women), 55 part-time (41 women). Average age 26. 93 applicants, 52% accepted, 25 enrolled. *Faculty:* 19 full-time (4 women). *Financial support:* In 2015–16, 1 research assistantship with partial tuition reimbursement (averaging $1,800 per year), 48 teaching assistantships with tuition reimbursements (averaging $1,400 per year) were awarded; scholarships/grants, health care benefits, and unspecified assistantships also available. Financial award application deadline: 2/2. In 2015, 27 master's awarded. *Degree program information:* Part-time programs available. Part-time. Offers agricultural economics (MS); animal sciences (MS); ecosystem management (MSES); food technology (MS); irrigation (MS); nutrition (MS); plant protection (MS); plant science (MS); poultry science (MS); rural community development (MS). *Application deadline:* For fall admission, 2/10 for domestic and international students; for spring admission, 11/2 for domestic and international students. *Application fee:* $50. Electronic applications accepted. *Application Contact:* Dr. Rabih Talhouk, Director, Graduate Council, 961-1350000 Ext. 4386, Fax: 961-1374374, E-mail: graduate.council@aub.edu.lb. *Dean,* Prof. Nahla Hwalla, 961-1343002 Ext. 4400, Fax: 961-1744460, E-mail: nahla@aub.edu.lb.

Faculty of Arts and Sciences Students: 258 full-time (190 women), 207 part-time (142 women). Average age 27. 241 applicants, 71% accepted, 98 enrolled. *Faculty:* 114 full-time (36 women), 4 part-time/adjunct (2 women). *Financial support:* Research assistantships, career-related internships or fieldwork, institutionally sponsored loans, scholarships/grants, health care benefits, and unspecified assistantships available. Financial award application deadline: 2/4; financial award applicants required to submit FAFSA. In 2015, 47 master's, 3 doctorates awarded. *Degree program information:* Part-time programs available. Part-time. Offers anthropology (MA); Arab and Middle Eastern history (PhD); Arabic language and literature (MA, PhD); archaeology (MA); biology (MS); cell and molecular biology (PhD); chemistry (MS); clinical psychology (MA); computational sciences (MS); computer science (MS); economics (MA); English language (MA); English literature (MA); environmental policy planning (MS); financial economics (MAFE); geology (MS); history (MA); mathematics (MA, MS); media studies (MA); Middle Eastern studies (MA); physics (MS); political studies (MA); psychology (MA); public administration (MA); sociology (MA); statistics (MA, MS); theoretical physics (PhD); transnational American studies (MA). *Application deadline:* For fall admission, 4/1 for domestic and international students; for spring admission, 11/1 for domestic and international students. *Application fee:* $50. Electronic applications accepted. *Application Contact:* Dr. Salim Kanaan, Director, Admissions Office, 961-1350000 Ext. 2590, Fax: 961-1750775, E-mail: sk00@aub.edu.lb. *Dean,* Dr. Patrick McGreevy, 961-1374374 Ext. 3800, Fax: 961-1744461, E-mail: pm07@aub.edu.lb.

Faculty of Engineering and Architecture Students: 276 full-time (133 women), 58 part-time (26 women). Average age 27. 265 applicants, 66% accepted, 85 enrolled. *Faculty:* 100 full-time (22 women), 1 part-time/adjunct (0 women). *Financial support:* In 2015–16, 190 students received support, including 4 fellowships with full tuition reimbursements available (averaging $24,800 per year), 82 research assistantships with full tuition reimbursements available (averaging $24,800 per year), 131 teaching assistantships with full tuition reimbursements available (averaging $9,800 per year); career-related internships or fieldwork, institutionally sponsored loans, scholarships/grants, health care benefits, and unspecified assistantships also available. In 2015, 120 master's, 10 doctorates awarded. *Degree program information:* Part-time programs available. Part-time. Offers applied energy (ME); civil engineering (PhD); electrical and computer engineering (PhD); energy studies (MS); engineering management (MEM); environmental and water resources (ME); environmental technology (MSES); mechanical engineering (ME, PhD); urban design (MUD); urban planning and policy (MUPP). *Application deadline:* For fall admission, 2/5 priority date for domestic and international students; for spring admission, 11/1 priority date for domestic students, 11/1 for international students. *Application fee:* $50. Electronic applications accepted. *Application Contact:* Dr. Salim Kanaan, Director, Admissions Office, 961-1350000 Ext. 2594, Fax: 961-1750775, E-mail: sk00@aub.edu.lb. *Dean*, Prof. Makram T. Suidan, 961-1350000 Ext. 3400, Fax: 961-1744462, E-mail: msuidan@aub.edu.lb.

Faculty of Health Sciences Students: 49 full-time (38 women), 99 part-time (81 women). Average age 27. 115 applicants, 71% accepted, 40 enrolled. *Faculty:* 30 full-time (21 women), 3 part-time/adjunct (1 woman). *Financial support:* In 2015–16, 70 students received support. Scholarships/grants, health care benefits, and unspecified assistantships available. Financial award application deadline: 4/1. In 2015, 51 master's awarded. *Degree program information:* Part-time programs available. Part-time. Offers environmental sciences (MS); epidemiology (MS); epidemiology and biostatistics (MPH); health management and policy (MPH); health promotion and community health (MPH). *Application deadline:* For fall admission, 1/4 priority date for domestic and international students; for spring admission, 11/1 for domestic and international students. *Application fee:* $50. Electronic applications accepted. *Application Contact:* Mitra Tauk, Administrative Coordinator, 961-1350000 Ext. 4687, Fax: 961-1744470, E-mail: mt12@aub.edu.lb. *Dean*, Iman Adel Nuwayhid, 961-1759683, Fax: 961-1744470, E-mail: nuwayhid@aub.edu.lb.

Faculty of Medicine Students: 381 full-time (173 women), 61 part-time (51 women). Average age 23. *Faculty:* 302 full-time (95 women), 64 part-time/adjunct (11 women). *Financial support:* In 2015–16, 273 students received support, including 45 teaching assistantships (averaging $9,000 per year); career-related internships or fieldwork, institutionally sponsored loans, scholarships/grants, health care benefits, and unspecified assistantships also available. Financial award application deadline: 2/2. In 2015, 14 master's awarded. *Degree program information:* Part-time programs available. Part-time. Offers anatomy, cell biology and human morphology (MS); biochemistry and medical genetics (MS); biomedical sciences (PhD); experimental pathology, immunology and microbiology (MS); medicine (MD); neuroscience (MS); pharmacology and toxicology (MS). *Application deadline:* For fall admission, 4/30 for domestic and international students; for spring admission, 11/1 for domestic and international students. *Application fee:* $50. Electronic applications accepted. *Application Contact:* Dr. Salim Kanaan, Director, Admissions Office, 961-1350000 Ext. 2594, Fax: 961-1750775, E-mail: sk00@aub.edu.lb. *Dean*, Dr. Mohamed Sayegh, 961-1350000 Ext. 4700, Fax: 961-1744464, E-mail: msayegh@aub.edu.lb.

Rafic Hariri School of Nursing Students: 2 full-time (both women), 56 part-time (49 women). Average age 29. 22 applicants, 100% accepted, 10 enrolled. *Faculty:* 9 full-time (8 women), 13 part-time/adjunct (11 women). *Financial support:* In 2015–16, 17 teaching assistantships with partial tuition reimbursements were awarded; unspecified assistantships also available. Financial award application deadline: 12/20. In 2015, 11 master's awarded. *Degree program information:* Part-time programs available. Part-time. Offers psychiatric mental health nursing (MSN). *Application deadline:* For fall admission, 4/1 for domestic and international students; for spring admission, 11/1 for domestic and international students. Applications are processed on a rolling basis. *Application fee:* $50. Electronic applications accepted. *Application Contact:* Dr. Salim Kanaan, Director, Admissions Office, 961-1350000 Ext. 2594, Fax: 961-1750775, E-mail: sk00@aub.edu.lb. *Director*, Dr. Huda Huijer Abu-Saad, 961-1374374 Ext. 5952, Fax: 961-1744476, E-mail: hh35@aub.edu.lb.

Suliman S. Olayan School of Business Students: 113 full-time (56 women), 31 part-time (16 women). Average age 29. 226 applicants, 61% accepted, 79 enrolled. *Faculty:* 30 full-time (9 women), 9 part-time/adjunct (2 women). *Financial support:* In 2015–16, 20 students received support, including 24 teaching assistantships with partial tuition reimbursements available (averaging $14,800 per year); scholarships/grants and unspecified assistantships also available. Support available to part-time students. Financial award application deadline: 2/20. In 2015, 89 master's awarded. *Degree program information:* Part-time and evening/weekend programs available. Part-time, evening/weekend. Offers business (EMBA, M Fin, MBA, MHRM); business administration (MBA); executive business administration (EMBA); finance (M Fin); human resource management (MHRM). *Application fee:* $50. Electronic applications accepted. *Application Contact:* Dr. Rabih Talhouk, Graduate Council Chair, 961-1350000 Ext. 3895, E-mail: rtalhouk@aub.edu.lb. *Dean*, Prof. Salim Chahine, 961-1374374 Ext. 3787, E-mail: sc09@aub.edu.lb.

AMERICAN UNIVERSITY OF HEALTH SCIENCES, Signal Hill, CA 90755

General Information Proprietary, coed, comprehensive institution.

GRADUATE UNITS

School of Clinical Research Offers clinical research (MSCR).

THE AMERICAN UNIVERSITY OF PARIS, 75007 Paris, France

General Information Independent, coed, comprehensive institution. *Graduate housing:* Room and/or apartments available on a first-come, first-served basis to single students; on-campus housing not available to married students.

GRADUATE UNITS

Graduate Programs Offers cross-cultural and sustainable business management (MA); cultural translation (MA); global communications (MA); global communications and civil society (MA); international affairs (MA); international affairs, conflict resolution and civil society development (MA); Middle East and Islamic studies (MA); Middle East and Islamic studies and international affairs (MA); public policy and international affairs (MA); public policy and international law (MA). Electronic applications accepted.

AMERICAN UNIVERSITY OF PUERTO RICO, Bayamon, PR 00960-2037

General Information Independent, coed, comprehensive institution.

GRADUATE UNITS

Program in Criminal Justice ***Degree program information:*** Evening/weekend programs available. Evening/weekend. Offers criminal justice (MA).

Program in Education Offers art education (M Ed); elementary education 4-6 (M Ed); elementary education K-3 (M Ed); general science education (M Ed); physical education (M Ed); special education (M Ed).

THE AMERICAN UNIVERSITY OF ROME, 00153 Rome, Italy

General Information Independent, coed, comprehensive institution. *Research affiliation:* ARCA - Association for Research into Crimes against Art (art crime prevention), ENFSI - European Network of Forensic Science Institutes (forensic archaeology), Conservation Science in Cultural Heritage.

GRADUATE UNITS

Graduate School Offers religious studies (MA); sustainable cultural heritage (MA). Electronic applications accepted.

AMERICAN UNIVERSITY OF SHARJAH, Sharjah, United Arab Emirates

General Information Independent, coed, comprehensive institution. *Graduate housing:* Room and/or apartments available on a first-come, first-served basis to single students; on-campus housing not available to married students. Housing application deadline: 7/1. *Research affiliation:* Emirates Foundation (philanthropy), International Atomic Energy Agency (energy), National Research Foundation, Advanced Technology Investment Company (technology and investment), Qatar National Research Foundation.

GRADUATE UNITS

Graduate Programs ***Degree program information:*** Part-time and evening/weekend programs available. Part-time, evening/weekend. Offers accounting (MS); business (EMBA, MBA); chemical engineering (MS Ch E); civil engineering (MSCE); computer engineering (MS); electrical engineering (MSEE); engineering systems management (MS); mathematics (MS); mechanical engineering (MSME); mechatronics engineering (MS); teaching English to speakers of other languages (MA); translation and interpreting (MA); urban planning (MUP). Electronic applications accepted.

AMRIDGE UNIVERSITY, Montgomery, AL 36117

General Information Independent-religious, coed, university. *Enrollment:* 636 graduate, professional, and undergraduate students; 94 full-time matriculated graduate/professional students (49 women), 227 part-time matriculated graduate/professional students (146 women). *Enrollment by degree level:* 228 master's, 93 doctoral. *Graduate faculty:* 22 full-time (3 women), 10 part-time/adjunct (6 women). *Tuition, area resident:* Full-time $12,870; part-time $715 per credit hour. *Required fees:* $1300; $650 per semester. *Graduate housing:* On-campus housing not available. *Student services:* Campus safety program, career counseling, services for students with disabilities. *Library:* Southern Christian University Library.

Computer facilities: 5 computers available on campus for general student use. A campuswide network can be accessed from off campus. Online class registration, access to over 20 million monographs and journals online are available.
Website: http://www.amridgeuniversity.edu/

General Application Contact: Kristen Holcomb, Admissions Officer, 888-790-8080 Ext. 1, Fax: 334-387-3878, E-mail: admissions@amridgeuniversity.edu.

GRADUATE UNITS

Graduate and Professional Programs Students: 94 full-time (49 women), 227 part-time (146 women); includes 126 minority (120 Black or African American, non-Hispanic/Latino; 3 Asian, non-Hispanic/Latino; 3 Hispanic/Latino). *Faculty:* 22 full-time (3 women), 10 part-time/adjunct (6 women). *Financial support:* Federal Work-Study and scholarships/grants available. Support available to part-time students. Financial award applicants required to submit FAFSA. *Degree program information:* Part-time and evening/weekend programs available. Part-time, evening/weekend, online learning. Offers Biblical studies (MA, PhD); Christian ministry (MS); family therapy (D Min); human services (MS); leadership and management (MS); marriage and family therapy (M Div, MA, PhD); ministerial leadership (M Div, MS); New Testament studies (MA); Old Testament studies (MA); professional counseling (M Div, MA, PhD); theology (M Div, D Min). *Application deadline:* For fall admission, 9/1 priority date for domestic students; for spring admission, 1/1 priority date for domestic students. Applications are processed on a rolling basis. *Application fee:* $50. Electronic applications accepted. *Application Contact:* Kristen Holcomb, Admissions Officer, 888-790-8080 Ext. 1, Fax: 334-387-3878, E-mail: admissions@amridgeuniversity.edu. *Enrollment Management Coordinator*, Brooks Housley, 800-351-4040 Ext. 7520, Fax: 334-387-3878, E-mail: brookshousley@amridgeuniversity.edu.

ANABAPTIST MENNONITE BIBLICAL SEMINARY, Elkhart, IN 46517-1999

General Information Independent-religious, coed, graduate-only institution. *Graduate housing:* Rooms and/or apartments available on a first-come, first-served basis to single and married students. Housing application deadline: 5/1.

GRADUATE UNITS

Graduate and Professional Programs ***Degree program information:*** Part-time programs available. Part-time. Offers Christian formation (MA); divinity (M Div); mission and evangelism (MA); peace studies (MA); theological studies (MA, Certificate). Electronic applications accepted.

ANAHEIM UNIVERSITY, Anaheim, CA 92806-5150

General Information Proprietary, coed, graduate-only institution.

GRADUATE UNITS

Program in Teaching English to Speakers of Other Languages Online learning. Offers teaching English to speakers of other languages (MA, Ed D, Certificate, Diploma).

Programs in Business Administration Online learning. Offers entrepreneurship (ME, DBA); global sustainable management (MBA); international business (MBA, DBA, Certificate, Diploma); management (DBA); sustainable management (DBA, Certificate, Diploma).

ANDERSON UNIVERSITY, Anderson, IN 46012-3495

General Information Independent-religious, coed, comprehensive institution. *Graduate housing:* Room and/or apartments available to single students; on-campus housing not available to married students. Housing application deadline: 6/1.

GRADUATE UNITS

Falls School of Business Offers accountancy (MA); business administration (MBA, DBA).

School of Education Offers education (M Ed).

School of Theology ***Degree program information:*** Part-time programs available. Part-time. Offers missions (MA); theology (M Div, MTS, D Min).

ANDERSON UNIVERSITY, Anderson, SC 29621-4035

General Information Independent-religious, coed, comprehensive institution.

GRADUATE UNITS

College of Business Offers business (MBA).

College of Education Offers education (M Ed).

Command College Online learning. Offers executive leadership (MA).

School of Christian Ministry Online learning. Offers Christian ministry (M Min).

ANDOVER NEWTON THEOLOGICAL SCHOOL, Newton Centre, MA 02459-2243

General Information Independent-religious, coed, graduate-only institution. *Enrollment by degree level:* 211 master's, 38 doctoral. *Graduate faculty:* 11 full-time (6 women), 29 part-time/adjunct (16 women). *Graduate housing:* Rooms and/or apartments available on a first-come, first-served basis to single and married students. Housing application deadline: 7/1. *Student services:* Campus employment opportunities, international student services, low-cost health insurance, services for students with disabilities, writing training. *Library:* Franklin Trask Library.

Computer facilities: 16 computers available on campus for general student use. A campuswide network can be accessed from student residence rooms. Online class registration is available.
Website: http://www.ants.edu/

General Application Contact: Robert Ochoa, Director of Admissions, 617-831-2430, Fax: 617-831-1630, E-mail: admissions@ants.edu.

GRADUATE UNITS

Graduate and Professional Programs Students: 65 full-time (35 women), 170 part-time (101 women). *Faculty:* 11 full-time (6 women), 29 part-time/adjunct (16 women). *Financial support:* Career-related internships or fieldwork and scholarships/grants available. Support available to part-time students. Financial award application deadline: 4/15; financial award applicants required to submit FAFSA. *Degree program information:* Part-time programs available. Part-time. Offers divinity (M Div); global interreligious leadership (MA); pastoral studies (MA); theological research (MA); theological studies (MA); theology (D Min). *Application deadline:* For fall admission, 4/1 priority date for domestic students, 4/1 for international students; for winter admission, 9/1 for domestic students; for spring admission, 10/1 priority date for domestic students. Applications are processed on a rolling basis. *Application fee:* $50. Electronic applications accepted. *Application Contact:* Robert Ochoa, Director of Admissions, 617-831-2430, Fax: 617-831-1630, E-mail: admissions@ants.edu. *President,* Martin Copenhaver, 617-964-1100 Ext. 2410, Fax: 617-965-9756, E-mail: mcopenhaver@ants.edu.

ANDREWS UNIVERSITY, Berrien Springs, MI 49104

General Information Independent-religious, coed, university. CGS member. *Enrollment:* 3,366 graduate, professional, and undergraduate students; 874 full-time matriculated graduate/professional students (351 women), 711 part-time matriculated graduate/professional students (195 women). *Enrollment by degree level:* 964 master's, 587 doctoral, 34 other advanced degrees. *Graduate faculty:* 168 full-time (62 women), 32 part-time/adjunct (11 women). *Graduate housing:* Rooms and/or apartments available on a first-come, first-served basis to single and married students. *Student services:* Campus employment opportunities, campus safety program, career counseling, child daycare facilities, free psychological counseling, international student services, low-cost health insurance. *Library:* James White Library plus 2 others. *Collection:* Books: 883,990 (physical), 420,000 (digital/electronic); Serial titles: 890,766 (physical), 472,945 (digital/electronic); Databases: 150. *Research affiliation:* Argonne National Laboratory (physics), Deutches Electronen Synchroton (physics), RAND Corporation (drug abuse).

Computer facilities: Computer purchase and lease plans are available. 151 computers available on campus for general student use. A campuswide network can be accessed from student residence rooms and from off campus. Online class registration, degree audit are available.
Website: http://www.andrews.edu/

General Application Contact: Monica Wringer, Supervisor of Graduate Admission, 800-253-2874, Fax: 269-471-3228, E-mail: graduate@andrews.edu.

GRADUATE UNITS

School of Graduate Studies Students: 874 full-time (351 women), 711 part-time (195 women); includes 706 minority (371 Black or African American, non-Hispanic/Latino; 3 American Indian or Alaska Native, non-Hispanic/Latino; 86 Asian, non-Hispanic/Latino; 224 Hispanic/Latino; 4 Native Hawaiian or other Pacific Islander, non-Hispanic/Latino; 18 Two or more races, non-Hispanic/Latino), 349 international. Average age 38. 1,189 applicants, 48% accepted, 327 enrolled. *Faculty:* 168 full-time (62 women), 32 part-time/adjunct (11 women). *Financial support:* Fellowships, research assistantships, teaching assistantships, career-related internships or fieldwork, Federal Work-Study, institutionally sponsored loans, scholarships/grants, tuition waivers (partial), and unspecified assistantships available. Support available to part-time students. Financial award applicants required to submit FAFSA. In 2015, 261 master's, 106 doctorates, 11 other advanced degrees awarded. *Degree program information:* Part-time and evening/weekend programs available. Part-time, evening/weekend, online learning. *Application deadline:* Applications are processed on a rolling basis. *Application fee:* $40. *Application Contact:* Monica Wringer, Supervisor of Graduate Admission, 800-253-2874, Fax: 269-471-6321, E-mail: graduate@andrews.edu. *Dean,* Dr. Christon Arthur, 269-471-3405.

College of Arts and Sciences Students: 78 full-time (59 women), 38 part-time (25 women); includes 55 minority (30 Black or African American, non-Hispanic/Latino; 5 Asian, non-Hispanic/Latino; 16 Hispanic/Latino; 1 Native Hawaiian or other Pacific Islander, non-Hispanic/Latino; 3 Two or more races, non-Hispanic/Latino), 30 international. Average age 31. 121 applicants, 55% accepted, 39 enrolled. *Faculty:* 76 full-time (31 women), 3 part-time/adjunct (1 woman). *Financial support:* Fellowships, research assistantships, teaching assistantships, career-related internships or fieldwork, Federal Work-Study, and institutionally sponsored loans available. Financial award applicants required to submit FAFSA. In 2015, 55 master's awarded. *Degree program information:* Part-time and evening/weekend programs available. Part-time, evening/weekend. Offers arts and sciences (M Mus, MA, MAT, MIDA, MS, MSA, MSW); biology (MAT, MS); communication (MA); community and international development (MS); English (MA, MAT); international development (MIDA, MS); international development administration (MIDA); music (M Mus, MA); social work (MSW). *Application deadline:* Applications are processed on a rolling basis. *Application fee:* $40. *Application Contact:* Monica Wringer, Supervisor of Graduate Admission, 800-253-2874, Fax: 269-471-6321, E-mail: graduate@andrews.edu. *Dean,* Dr. Keith Mattingly, 269-471-3411.

School of Architecture, Art and Design Students: 14 full-time (6 women), 1 (woman) part-time; includes 8 minority (3 Black or African American, non-Hispanic/Latino; 1 Asian, non-Hispanic/Latino; 4 Hispanic/Latino), 5 international. Average age 24. 19 applicants, 84% accepted, 4 enrolled. *Faculty:* 9 full-time (3 women), 1 (woman) part-time/adjunct. In 2015, 12 master's awarded. Offers architecture, art and design (M Arch). *Application deadline:* Applications are processed on a rolling basis. *Application fee:* $40. Electronic applications accepted. *Application Contact:* Monica Wringer, Supervisor of Graduate Admission, 800-253-2874, Fax: 269-471-6321, E-mail: graduate@andrews.edu. *Dean,* Carey Carscallen, 269-471-6003.

School of Business Students: 15 full-time (4 women), 37 part-time (17 women); includes 18 minority (7 Black or African American, non-Hispanic/Latino; 4 Asian, non-Hispanic/Latino; 6 Hispanic/Latino; 1 Native Hawaiian or other Pacific Islander, non-Hispanic/Latino), 15 international. Average age 33. 72 applicants, 47% accepted, 17 enrolled. *Faculty:* 8 full-time (3 women). *Financial support:* Fellowships, research assistantships, teaching assistantships, and Federal Work-Study available. In 2015, 18 master's awarded. *Degree program information:* Part-time programs available. Part-time. Offers business (MBA, MSA). *Application deadline:* For fall admission, 8/15 for domestic students. Applications are processed on a rolling basis. *Application fee:* $40. *Application Contact:* Monica Wringer, Supervisor of Graduate Admission, 800-253-2874, Fax: 269-471-6321, E-mail: graduate@andrews.edu. *Dean,* Dr. Allen Stembridge, 269-471-3632.

School of Education Students: 143 full-time (93 women), 76 part-time (46 women); includes 77 minority (47 Black or African American, non-Hispanic/Latino; 7 Asian, non-Hispanic/Latino; 20 Hispanic/Latino; 3 Two or more races, non-Hispanic/Latino), 46 international. Average age 41. 128 applicants, 37% accepted, 29 enrolled. *Faculty:* 21 full-time (9 women), 5 part-time/adjunct (2 women). *Financial support:* Fellowships, research assistantships, teaching assistantships, career-related internships or fieldwork, Federal Work-Study, institutionally sponsored loans, and tuition waivers (partial) available. Support available to part-time students. In 2015, 23 master's, 25 doctorates, 5 other advanced degrees awarded. *Degree program information:* Part-time programs available. Part-time. Offers clinical mental health counseling (MA); community counseling (MA); counseling psychology (PhD); curriculum and instruction (MA, Ed D, PhD, Ed S); education (MA, MAT, MS, Ed D, PhD, Ed S); educational administration and leadership (MA, Ed D, PhD, Ed S); educational and developmental psychology (MA, Ed D, PhD); educational psychology (Ed D, PhD); elementary education (MAT); higher education administration (MA, Ed D, PhD, Ed S); leadership (MA, Ed D, PhD, Ed S); school counseling (MA); school psychology (Ed S); secondary education (MAT); special education (MS); teacher education (MAT). *Application deadline:* Applications are processed on a rolling basis. *Application fee:* $40. *Application Contact:* Monica Wringer, Supervisor of Graduate Admission, 800-253-2874, Fax: 269-471-6321, E-mail: graduate@andrews.edu. *Dean,* Dr. Robson Marinho, 269-471-3464.

Seventh-day Adventist Theological Seminary Students: 454 full-time (77 women), 500 part-time (71 women); includes 469 minority (252 Black or African American, non-Hispanic/Latino; 1 American Indian or Alaska Native, non-Hispanic/Latino; 51 Asian, non-Hispanic/Latino; 157 Hispanic/Latino; 1 Native Hawaiian or other Pacific Islander, non-Hispanic/Latino; 7 Two or more races, non-Hispanic/Latino), 222 international. Average age 40. 587 applicants, 46% accepted, 149 enrolled. *Faculty:* 40 full-time (5 women), 12 part-time/adjunct (2 women). *Financial support:* Fellowships, research assistantships, teaching assistantships, career-related internships or fieldwork, Federal Work-Study, and institutionally sponsored loans available. In 2015, 178 master's, 51 doctorates awarded. Offers ministry (M Div, D Min); pastoral ministry (MA); religious education (MA, Ed D, PhD, Ed S); theology (M Th, Th D); youth ministry (MA). *Application deadline:* Applications are processed on a rolling basis. *Application fee:* $40. *Application Contact:* Monica Wringer, Director, 800-253-2874, Fax: 269-471-6321. *Dean,* Dr. Jiri Moskala, 269-471-3537.

School of Health Professions Students: 170 full-time (112 women), 59 part-time (35 women); includes 79 minority (32 Black or African American, non-Hispanic/Latino; 2 American Indian or Alaska Native, non-Hispanic/Latino; 18 Asian, non-Hispanic/Latino; 21 Hispanic/Latino; 1 Native Hawaiian or other Pacific Islander, non-Hispanic/Latino; 5 Two or more races, non-Hispanic/Latino), 31 international. Average age 30. 262 applicants, 50% accepted, 89 enrolled. *Faculty:* 13 full-time (10 women), 11 part-time/adjunct (5 women). In 2015, 4 master's, 44 doctorates, 11 other advanced degrees awarded. Offers health professions (MPH, MS, MSMLS, DNP, DPT, Dr Sc PT, TDPT, Certificate); medical laboratory sciences (MSMLS); nursing (MS, DNP); nutrition (MS); nutrition and dietetics (Certificate); physical therapy (DPT, Dr Sc PT, TDPT); public health (MPH); speech-language pathology (MS). *Application fee:* $40. *Application Contact:* Monica Wringer, Supervisor of Graduate Admission, 800-253-2874, Fax: 269-471-3228, E-mail: graduate@andrews.edu. *Dean,* Dr. Emmanuel Rudatsikira, 269-471-6649, E-mail: rudatsikira@andrews.edu.

ANGELO STATE UNIVERSITY, San Angelo, TX 76909

General Information State-supported, coed, comprehensive institution. *Enrollment:* 8,483 graduate, professional, and undergraduate students; 585 full-time matriculated graduate/professional students (401 women), 499 part-time matriculated graduate/professional students (332 women). *Enrollment by degree level:* 1,009 master's, 75 doctoral. *Graduate faculty:* 126 full-time (52 women). *International tuition:* $10,746 full-time. *Tuition, area resident:* Full-time $3726; part-time $2484 per year. Tuition, state resident: full-time $3726; part-time $2484 per year. Tuition, nonresident: full-time $10,746; part-time $7164 per year. *Required fees:* $2538; $1702 per unit. *Graduate housing:* Room and/or apartments available on a first-come, first-served basis to single students; on-campus housing not available to married students. Typical cost: $7702 (including board). Room and board charges vary according to board plan, campus/location and housing facility selected. Housing application deadline: 7/15. *Student services:* Campus employment opportunities, campus safety program, career counseling, free psychological counseling, grant writing training, international student services, low-cost health insurance, multicultural affairs office, services for students with disabilities, writing training. *Library:* Porter Henderson Library plus 1 other. Study areas open 24 hours, 5–7 days a week. *Research affiliation:* Zinpro Corporation (animal nutrition), Purina (animal nutrition), Texas Space Consortium (space research and technology), TASCO (animal nutrition), Mannatech, Inc. (nutrition).

Computer facilities: Computer purchase and lease plans are available. 640 computers available on campus for general student use. A campuswide network can be accessed from student residence rooms and from off campus. Online class registration, online courses, tuition payments, book purchase, parking permits, university calendar, library card catalog and library resources, discounted hardware and software are available.
Website: http://www.angelo.edu/

General Application Contact: Jennifer McAndrews, Graduate Admissions Assistant, 325-942-2169, Fax: 325-942-2194, E-mail: jmcandrews@angelo.edu.

GRADUATE UNITS

College of Graduate Studies *Financial support:* Research assistantships, teaching assistantships, career-related internships or fieldwork, Federal Work-Study, scholarships/grants, and unspecified assistantships available. Support available to part-time students. Financial award application deadline: 3/1. *Degree program information:* Part-time and evening/weekend programs available. Part-time, evening/weekend, online learning. *Application deadline:* For fall admission, 7/15 priority date for domestic students, 6/10 for international students; for spring admission, 12/1 priority date for domestic students, 11/1 for international students. Applications are processed on a rolling basis. *Application fee:* $40 ($50 for international students). Electronic applications accepted. *Application Contact:* Jennifer Page McAndrews, Graduate Admissions Coordinator, 325-486-6481, Fax: 325-942-2194, E-mail: jennifer.mcandrews@angelo.edu. *Dean,* Dr. Susan E. Keith, 325-942-2169, Fax: 325-942-2194, E-mail: susan.keith@angelo.edu.

Archer College of Health and Human Services Faculty: 21 full-time. *Financial support:* Research assistantships available. Offers family nurse practitioner (MSN); health and human services (MSN, DPT); nurse educator (MSN); physical therapy (DPT). *Application deadline:* For fall admission, 7/15 priority date for domestic students, 6/10 for international students; for spring admission, 12/1 priority date for domestic students, 11/1 for international students. *Application fee:* $40 ($50 for international students). *Application Contact:* Dr. Leslie M. Mayrand, Dean, 325-486-6258, Fax: 325-942-2631, E-mail: leslie.mayrand@angelo.edu. *Dean,* Dr. Leslie M. Mayrand, 325-486-6258, Fax: 325-942-2631, E-mail: leslie.mayrand@angelo.edu.

College of Arts and Sciences Financial support: Research assistantships, teaching assistantships, career-related internships or fieldwork, Federal Work-Study, scholarships/grants, and unspecified assistantships available. Support available to part-time students. Financial award application deadline: 3/1; financial award applicants required to submit FAFSA. *Degree program information:* Part-time and evening/weekend programs available. Part-time, evening/weekend. Offers agriculture (M Ag); animal science (MS); arts and sciences (M Ag, MA, MS); biology (MS); communication (MA); English (MA); psychology (MS). *Application deadline:* For fall admission, 7/15 priority date for domestic students, 6/10 for international students; for spring admission, 12/1 priority date for domestic students, 11/1 for international students. Applications are processed on a rolling basis. *Application fee:* $40 ($50 for international students). Electronic applications accepted. *Application Contact:* Dr. Paul Swets, Dean, 325-942-2470, Fax: 325-942-2340, E-mail: paul.swets@angelo.edu. *Dean,* Dr. Paul Swets, 325-942-2470, Fax: 325-942-2340, E-mail: paul.swets@angelo.edu.

College of Business Financial support: Career-related internships or fieldwork, Federal Work-Study, and scholarships/grants available. Support available to part-time students. Financial award application deadline: 3/1; financial award applicants required to submit FAFSA. *Degree program information:* Part-time and evening/weekend programs available. Part-time, evening/weekend. Offers business (MBA, MPAC); business administration (MBA); professional accountancy (MPAC). *Application deadline:* For fall admission, 7/15 priority date for domestic students, 6/10 for international students; for spring admission, 12/1 priority date for domestic students, 11/1 for international students. Applications are processed on a rolling basis. *Application fee:* $40 ($50 for international students). Electronic applications accepted. *Application Contact:* Dr. Clifton T. Jones, Dean, 325-942-2337, Fax: 325-942-2718, E-mail: clifton.jones@angelo.edu. *Dean,* Dr. Clifton T. Jones, 325-942-2337, Fax: 325-942-2718, E-mail: clifton.jones@angelo.edu.

College of Education Financial support: Career-related internships or fieldwork, Federal Work-Study, scholarships/grants, and unspecified assistantships available. Support available to part-time students. Financial award application deadline: 3/1; financial award applicants required to submit FAFSA. *Degree program information:* Part-time and evening/weekend programs available. Part-time, evening/weekend. Offers coaching, sport, recreation and fitness administration (M Ed); curriculum and instruction (M Ed, MA); education (M Ed, MA); educational administration (M Ed); guidance and counseling (M Ed); school administration (M Ed); student development and leadership in higher education (M Ed). *Application deadline:* For fall admission, 7/15 priority date for domestic students, 6/10 for international students; for spring admission, 12/1 priority date for domestic students, 11/1 for international students. Applications are processed on a rolling basis. *Application fee:* $40 ($50 for international students). Electronic applications accepted. *Application Contact:* Dr. John J. Miazga, Jr., Dean, 325-942-2212, E-mail: john.miazga@angelo.edu. *Dean,* Dr. John J. Miazga, Jr., 325-942-2212, E-mail: john.miazga@angelo.edu.

Kay Bailey Hutchison Center for Security Studies Financial support: Federal Work-Study and scholarships/grants available. Support available to part-time students. Financial award application deadline: 3/1; financial award applicants required to submit FAFSA. *Degree program information:* Part-time and evening/weekend programs available. Part-time, evening/weekend, online learning. Offers criminal justice (MS); homeland security (MS); intelligence, security studies, and analysis (MSS); security studies (MSS). *Application deadline:* For fall admission, 7/15 priority date for domestic students, 6/10 for international students; for spring admission, 12/1 priority date for domestic students, 11/1 for international students. Applications are processed on a rolling basis. *Application fee:* $40 ($50 for international students). Electronic applications accepted. *Application Contact:* Dr. William A. Taylor, Chair, 325-486-6689, Fax: 325-942-2544, E-mail: william.taylor@angelo.edu. *Chair,* Dr. William A. Taylor, 325-486-6689, Fax: 325-942-2544, E-mail: william.taylor@angelo.edu.

ANNA MARIA COLLEGE, Paxton, MA 01612

General Information Independent-religious, coed, comprehensive institution. *Graduate housing:* On-campus housing not available.

GRADUATE UNITS

Graduate Division ***Degree program information:*** Part-time and evening/weekend programs available. Part-time, evening/weekend. Offers art and visual art (MA); business administration (MBA, AC); counseling psychology (MA); criminal justice (MS); early childhood education (M Ed); education (CAGS); elementary education (M Ed); emergency management (MS, Graduate Certificate); English language arts (M Ed); fire science (MA); industrial/organizational psychology (MS); justice administration (MS); occupational and environmental health and safety (MS); pastoral ministry (MA); public administration (MPA); security management (MA); teacher of visual art (M Ed); visual arts (M Ed). Electronic applications accepted.

ANTIOCH UNIVERSITY LOS ANGELES, Culver City, CA 90230

General Information Independent, coed, upper-level institution. *Graduate housing:* On-campus housing not available.

GRADUATE UNITS

Graduate Programs ***Degree program information:*** Part-time and evening/weekend programs available. Part-time, evening/weekend, online learning. Offers clinical psychology (MA); creative writing (MFA); education (MA); human resource development (MA); leadership (MA); nonprofit management (MA); organizational development (MA); pedagogy of creative writing (Certificate); psychology (MA); urban sustainability (MA).

ANTIOCH UNIVERSITY MIDWEST, Yellow Springs, OH 45387-1609

General Information Independent, coed, upper-level institution. *Graduate housing:* On-campus housing not available.

GRADUATE UNITS

Graduate Programs ***Degree program information:*** Part-time and evening/weekend programs available. Part-time, evening/weekend, online learning. Offers conflict analysis and management (MA); liberal and professional studies (MA); management and leading change (MA). Electronic applications accepted.

School of Education Degree program information: Part-time and evening/weekend programs available. Part-time, evening/weekend. Offers education (M Ed). Electronic applications accepted.

ANTIOCH UNIVERSITY NEW ENGLAND, Keene, NH 03431-3552

General Information Independent, coed, graduate-only institution. *Graduate housing:* On-campus housing not available. *Research affiliation:* Cheshire Medical Center Cardiac Rehabilitation Program (clinical psychology), Northeast Foundation for Children (education), Pine Hill Waldorf School (education), Harris Center for Conservation Education (environmental studies).

GRADUATE UNITS

Graduate School ***Degree program information:*** Evening/weekend programs available. Evening/weekend. Offers advocacy for social justice and sustainability (MS); applied behavior analysis (Certificate); applied behavior analysis internship (Certificate); autism spectrum disorders (Certificate); clinical mental health counseling (MA); clinical psychology (Psy D); conservation biology (MS); dance/movement therapy and counseling (M Ed, MA, PMC); early childhood education (M Ed); elementary education (M Ed, Certificate); environmental education (MS); environmental studies (PhD); foundations of education (M Ed); integrated learning (M Ed); marriage and family therapy (MA, PhD, Certificate); principal certification (PMC); resource management and conservation (MS); science teacher certification (MS); self-designed studies (MS); special education (M Ed); substance abuse counseling (MA); sustainability (MBA); sustainable development and climate change (MS); teaching (M Ed, PMC); Waldorf teacher training (M Ed, Certificate). Electronic applications accepted.

ANTIOCH UNIVERSITY SANTA BARBARA, Santa Barbara, CA 93101-1581

General Information Independent, coed, upper-level institution. *Enrollment:* 252 graduate, professional, and undergraduate students; 206 full-time matriculated graduate/professional students (152 women), 45 part-time matriculated graduate/professional students (31 women). *Enrollment by degree level:* 175 master's, 69 doctoral, 7 other advanced degrees. *Graduate housing:* On-campus housing not available. *Student services:* Campus employment opportunities, international student services, services for students with disabilities, writing training. *Library:* Sage Library.

Computer facilities: 16 computers available on campus for general student use. A campuswide network can be accessed. Online class registration is available. Website: http://www.antiochsb.edu/

GRADUATE UNITS

Program in Business Administration Students: 31 full-time (24 women); includes 11 minority (1 Black or African American, non-Hispanic/Latino; 2 Asian, non-Hispanic/Latino; 7 Hispanic/Latino; 1 Two or more races, non-Hispanic/Latino). Average age 34. Offers non-profit management (MBA); social business (MBA); strategic leadership (MBA).

Program in Clinical Psychology Students: 143 full-time (102 women), 37 part-time (24 women); includes 66 minority (7 Black or African American, non-Hispanic/Latino; 1 Asian, non-Hispanic/Latino; 56 Hispanic/Latino; 1 Native Hawaiian or other Pacific Islander, non-Hispanic/Latino; 1 Two or more races, non-Hispanic/Latino), 2 international. Average age 36. Offers clinical psychology (MA, Psy D). *Application deadline:* Applications are processed on a rolling basis. *Application fee:* $60. Electronic applications accepted. *Director of Clinical Training,* Dr. Sharleen O'Brien, 805-962-8179 Ext. 320, Fax: 805-962-4786, E-mail: sdolan@antioch.edu.

Program in Education/Teacher Credentialing Students: 32 full-time (26 women), 8 part-time (7 women); includes 23 minority (2 Black or African American, non-Hispanic/Latino; 3 Asian, non-Hispanic/Latino; 17 Hispanic/Latino; 1 Two or more races, non-Hispanic/Latino). Average age 34. *Degree program information:* Part-time programs available. Part-time. Offers education/teacher credentialing (M Ed, MA). *Application deadline:* Applications are processed on a rolling basis. *Application fee:* $60. Electronic applications accepted. *Interim Chair,* Dr. Marianne D'Emidio-Caston, 805-962-8179 Ext. 114, Fax: 805-962-4786, E-mail: mcaston@antioch.edu.

Program in Writing and Contemporary Media ***Degree program information:*** Part-time programs available. Part-time. Offers writing and contemporary media (MFA).

ANTIOCH UNIVERSITY SEATTLE, Seattle, WA 98121-1814

General Information Independent, coed, university. *Enrollment:* 386 full-time matriculated graduate/professional students (313 women), 154 part-time matriculated graduate/professional students (132 women). *Enrollment by degree level:* 439 master's, 100 doctoral, 1 other advanced degree. *Required fees:* $100; $100. *Graduate housing:* On-campus housing not available. *Student services:* Campus employment opportunities, career counseling, free psychological counseling, international student services, services for students with disabilities, teacher training, writing training. *Library:* Antioch Seattle Library.
Website: http://www.antiochsea.edu/

General Application Contact: Eileen Knight, Recruitment and Admissions Director, 206-268-4200, Fax: 206-268-4242, E-mail: eknight@antioch.edu.

GRADUATE UNITS

Graduate Programs Students: 386 full-time (313 women), 154 part-time (132 women); includes 95 minority (17 Black or African American, non-Hispanic/Latino; 3 American Indian or Alaska Native, non-Hispanic/Latino; 13 Asian, non-Hispanic/Latino; 32 Hispanic/Latino; 1 Native Hawaiian or other Pacific Islander, non-Hispanic/Latino; 29 Two or more races, non-Hispanic/Latino), 1 international. Average age 37. *Financial support:* In 2015–16, 4 fellowships (averaging $14,400 per year), 19 research assistantships (averaging $8,280 per year) were awarded; Federal Work-Study, institutionally sponsored loans, and unspecified assistantships also available. Financial award application deadline: 6/15. *Degree program information:* Part-time and evening/weekend programs available. Part-time, evening/weekend. Offers counseling (MA); education (MA); psychology (MA, Psy D). *Application deadline:* Applications are processed on a rolling basis. Electronic applications accepted. *Application Contact:* Eileen Knight, Recruitment and Admissions Director, 206-268-4200, E-mail: psmithmentz@antiochsea.edu. *Vice President of Academic Affairs*, Peter Rojcewicz, 206-268-4108, E-mail: projcewicz@antioch.edu.

Center for Creative Change Students: 26 full-time (17 women), 4 part-time (all women); includes 2 minority (both Black or African American, non-Hispanic/Latino). Average age 40. *Faculty:* 3 full-time (all women), 6 part-time/adjunct (all women). *Financial support:* Research assistantships, Federal Work-Study, institutionally sponsored loans, and unspecified assistantships available. Financial award application deadline: 6/15. *Degree program information:* Evening/weekend programs available. Evening/weekend. Offers environment and community (MA); organizational development (MA); whole systems design (MA). *Application deadline:* For fall admission, 8/15 priority date for domestic students; for spring admission, 2/3 priority date for domestic students. Applications are processed on a rolling basis. Electronic applications accepted. *Application Contact:* Eileen Knight, Recruitment and Admissions Director, 206-268-4200, E-mail: eknight@antioch.edu. *Director*, Betsy Geist, 206-268-4904, E-mail: bgeist@antioch.edu.

AOMA GRADUATE SCHOOL OF INTEGRATIVE MEDICINE, Austin, TX 78757

General Information Proprietary, coed, graduate-only institution.

GRADUATE UNITS

Doctor of Acupuncture and Oriental Medicine Program Offers acupuncture and Oriental medicine (DAOM). Electronic applications accepted.

Master of Acupuncture and Oriental Medicine Program Offers acupuncture and Oriental medicine (MAcOM). Electronic applications accepted.

APEX SCHOOL OF THEOLOGY, Durham, NC 27703

General Information Independent-religious, coed, comprehensive institution. *Graduate housing:* On-campus housing not available.

GRADUATE UNITS

Graduate Programs

APPALACHIAN BIBLE COLLEGE, Bradley, WV 25818

General Information Independent-religious, coed, comprehensive institution.

GRADUATE UNITS

Graduate School Online learning.

APPALACHIAN COLLEGE OF PHARMACY, Oakwood, VA 24631

General Information Independent, coed, graduate-only institution.

GRADUATE UNITS

Doctor of Pharmacy Program Offers pharmacy (Pharm D).

APPALACHIAN SCHOOL OF LAW, Grundy, VA 24614

General Information Independent, coed, graduate-only institution. *Graduate housing:* On-campus housing not available.

GRADUATE UNITS

Professional Program in Law Offers law (JD). Electronic applications accepted.

APPALACHIAN STATE UNIVERSITY, Boone, NC 28608

General Information State-supported, coed, comprehensive institution. CGS member. *Graduate housing:* On-campus housing not available.

GRADUATE UNITS

Cratis D. Williams Graduate School ***Degree program information:*** Part-time and evening/weekend programs available. Part-time, evening/weekend, online learning. Offers appropriate technology (MS); cell and molecular biology (MS); child development: birth through kindergarten (MA); clinical health psychology (MA); clinical mental health counseling (MA); college student development (MA); computer science (MS); criminal justice (MS); curriculum specialist (MA); educational administration (Ed S); educational media (MA); elementary education (MA); engineering physics (MS); English (MA); English education (MA); exercise science (MS); general biology (MS); general experimental psychology (MA); general history (MA); general management (MBA); geography (MA); gerontology (MA, Graduate Certificate); higher education (MA, Ed S); industrial and organizational psychology (MA); library science (MLS); licensure (superintendent) (Ed D); marriage and family therapy (MA); mathematics (MA); mathematics education (MA); middle grades education (MA); nutrition (MS); political science (MA); public administration (MPA); reading education (MA); renewable energy engineering (MS); romance languages (MA); school administration (MSA); school counseling (MA); social work (MSW); sociology (Graduate Certificate); special education (MA); speech-language pathology (MS); taxation (MS). Electronic applications accepted.

Center for Appalachian Studies Degree program information: Part-time programs available. Part-time. Offers culture (MA); roots and music (MA); sustainable development (MA). Electronic applications accepted.

School of Music Degree program information: Part-time programs available. Part-time. Offers music education (MM); music performance (MM); music therapy (MMT). Electronic applications accepted.

AQUINAS COLLEGE, Grand Rapids, MI 49506-1799

General Information Independent-religious, coed, comprehensive institution. *Graduate housing:* On-campus housing not available.

GRADUATE UNITS

School of Education ***Degree program information:*** Part-time and evening/weekend programs available. Part-time, evening/weekend. Offers education (M Ed, MAT, MSE).

School of Management ***Degree program information:*** Part-time and evening/weekend programs available. Part-time, evening/weekend. Offers health care administration (MM); marketing management (MM); organizational leadership (MM); sustainable business (MM, MSB).

AQUINAS COLLEGE, Nashville, TN 37205-2005

General Information Independent-religious, coed, comprehensive institution.

GRADUATE UNITS

School of Education Offers 7-12 (MAT); K-6 (MAT); teaching and learning (M Ed).

School of Nursing Offers nursing education (MSN).

AQUINAS INSTITUTE OF THEOLOGY, St. Louis, MO 63108

General Information Independent-religious, coed, graduate-only institution. *Graduate housing:* On-campus housing not available.

GRADUATE UNITS

Graduate and Professional Programs ***Degree program information:*** Part-time and evening/weekend programs available. Part-time, evening/weekend, online learning. Offers biblical studies (Certificate); church music (MM); health care mission (MAHCM); ministry (M Div); pastoral care (Certificate); pastoral ministry (MAPM); pastoral studies (MAPS); preaching (D Min); spiritual direction (Certificate); theology (M Div, MA); Thomistic studies (Certificate).

ARCADIA UNIVERSITY, Glenside, PA 19038-3295

General Information Independent-religious, coed, comprehensive institution. CGS member. *Enrollment:* 3,984 graduate, professional, and undergraduate students; 505 full-time matriculated graduate/professional students (126 women), 734 part-time matriculated graduate/professional students (177 women). *Enrollment by degree level:* 790 master's, 354 doctoral, 95 other advanced degrees. *Graduate faculty:* 71 full-time, 135 part-time/adjunct. *Tuition, area resident:* Full-time $28,364; part-time $720 per credit hour. Tuition and fees vary according to course load and program. *Graduate housing:* On-campus housing not available. *Student services:* Campus safety program, career counseling, international student services, low-cost health insurance, multicultural affairs office, writing training. *Library:* Bette E. Landman Library. *Collection:* Books: 106,873 (physical), 97,476 (digital/electronic); Databases: 25.

Computer facilities: 120 computers available on campus for general student use. A campuswide network can be accessed from student residence rooms and from off campus. Online class registration is available.
Website: http://www.arcadia.edu/

General Application Contact: Information Contact, 215-572-2910, Fax: 215-572-4049, E-mail: admiss@arcadia.edu.

GRADUATE UNITS

Graduate Studies Students: 506 full-time (381 women), 749 part-time (567 women); includes 238 minority (116 Black or African American, non-Hispanic/Latino; 2 American Indian or Alaska Native, non-Hispanic/Latino; 73 Asian, non-Hispanic/Latino; 27 Hispanic/Latino; 1 Native Hawaiian or other Pacific Islander, non-Hispanic/Latino; 19 Two or more races, non-Hispanic/Latino), 29 international. Average age 32. 3,969 applicants, 24% accepted, 338 enrolled. *Financial support:* Research assistantships, teaching assistantships, career-related internships or fieldwork, scholarships/grants, tuition waivers (partial), and unspecified assistantships available. Support available to part-time students. In 2015, 438 master's, 140 doctorates, 78 other advanced degrees awarded. *Degree program information:* Part-time and evening/weekend programs available. Part-time, evening/weekend, online learning. Offers business administration (IMBA, MBA); community counseling (MACP); English (MAE); fine arts, theater, and music (MAH); forensic science (MSFS); genetic counseling (MSGC); health communications (MA); health education (MA, MSHE); history, philosophy, and religion (MAH); international peace and conflict resolution (MAIPCR); literature and language (MAH); new media marketing (MA); physical therapy (DPT); physician assistant (MM Sc); public health (MPH); school counseling (MACP). *Application fee:* $50. Electronic applications accepted. *Application Contact:* 215-572-2910, Fax: 215-572-4049, E-mail: admiss@arcadia.edu. *Dean of Graduate and Undergraduate Studies*, Dr. Nancy Rosoff, 215-572-2921, E-mail: rosoffn@arcadia.edu.

School of Education Students: 29 full-time (22 women), 400 part-time (309 women); includes 92 minority (70 Black or African American, non-Hispanic/Latino; 1 American Indian or Alaska Native, non-Hispanic/Latino; 10 Asian, non-Hispanic/Latino; 6 Hispanic/Latino; 5 Two or more races, non-Hispanic/Latino), 7 international. Average age 35. 287 applicants, 68% accepted, 63 enrolled. *Faculty:* 14 full-time (10 women), 54 part-time/adjunct (39 women). *Financial support:* Career-related internships or fieldwork, tuition waivers (partial), and unspecified assistantships available. In 2015, 152 master's, 9 doctorates, 64 CASs awarded. *Degree program information:* Part-time and evening/weekend programs available. Part-time, evening/weekend, online learning. Offers art education (M Ed); computer education (CAS); curriculum (CAS); curriculum studies (M Ed); early childhood education (M Ed, CAS); educational leadership (M Ed, Ed D, CAS); elementary education (M Ed, CAS); English education (MA Ed); environmental education (MA Ed, CAS); history education (MA Ed); instructional technology (M Ed); language arts (M Ed, CAS); library science (M Ed); mathematics education (M Ed, MA Ed, CAS); music education (MA Ed); psychology (MA Ed); reading (M Ed, CAS); science education (M Ed, CAS); secondary education (M Ed, CAS); special education (M Ed, Ed D, CAS); theater arts (MA Ed); written communication (MA Ed). *Application deadline:* Applications are processed on a rolling basis. *Application fee:* $50. Electronic applications accepted. *Application Contact:* 215-572-2925, Fax: 215-572-2126, E-mail: grad@arcadia.edu. *Dean of the School of Education*, Dr. Graciela Slesaransky-Poe, 215-572-2938.

ARGOSY UNIVERSITY, ATLANTA, Atlanta, GA 30328

General Information Proprietary, coed, university.

GRADUATE UNITS

College of Business Offers accounting (DBA); corporate compliance (MBA); customized professional concentration (MBA, DBA); finance (MBA); healthcare administration (MBA); information systems (DBA); information systems management (MBA); international business (MBA, DBA); management (MBA, MSM, DBA); marketing (MBA, DBA).

College of Education Offers educational leadership (MAEd, Ed D, Ed S); teaching and learning (MAEd, Ed D, Ed S).

College of Health Sciences Offers public health (MPH).

Georgia School of Professional Psychology Offers clinical psychology (MA, Psy D, Postdoctoral Respecialization Certificate); community counseling (MA); counselor education and supervision (Ed D); forensic psychology (MA); industrial organizational psychology (MA); marriage and family therapy (Certificate); sport-exercise psychology (MA).

ARGOSY UNIVERSITY, CHICAGO, Chicago, IL 60601

General Information Proprietary, coed, university.

GRADUATE UNITS

College of Business Online learning. Offers accounting (DBA); customized professional concentration (MBA, DBA); finance (MBA); fraud examination (MBA); global business sustainability (DBA); healthcare administration (MBA); information systems (DBA); information systems management (MBA); international business (MBA, DBA); management (MBA, MSM, DBA); marketing (MBA, DBA); organizational leadership (Ed D); public administration (MBA); sustainable management (MBA).

College of Education Online learning. Offers adult education and training (MA Ed); community college executive leadership (Ed D); educational leadership (MA Ed, Ed D, Ed S); instructional leadership (Ed D, Ed S).

College of Health Sciences Offers public health (MPH).

Illinois School of Professional Psychology Online learning. Offers child and adolescent psychology (Psy D); client-centered and experiential psychotherapies (Psy D); clinical psychology (MA, Psy D); community counseling (MA); counseling psychology (Ed D); counselor education and supervision (Ed D); diversity and multicultural psychology (Psy D); family psychology (Psy D); forensic psychology (Psy D); health psychology (Psy D); industrial organizational psychology (MA); neuropsychology (Psy D); organizational consulting (Psy D); psychoanalytic psychology (Psy D); psychology and spirituality (Psy D).

ARGOSY UNIVERSITY, DALLAS, Farmers Branch, TX 75244

General Information Proprietary, coed, university.

GRADUATE UNITS

College of Business Offers accounting (DBA, AGC); corporate compliance (MBA, Graduate Certificate); customized professional concentration (MBA); finance (MBA, Graduate Certificate); fraud examination (MBA, Graduate Certificate); global business sustainability (DBA, AGC); healthcare administration (Graduate Certificate); healthcare management (MBA); information systems (MBA, DBA, AGC); information systems management (Graduate Certificate); international business (MBA, DBA, AGC, Graduate Certificate); management (MBA, DBA, AGC, Graduate Certificate); marketing (MBA, DBA, AGC, Graduate Certificate); public administration (MBA, Graduate Certificate); sustainable management (MBA, Graduate Certificate).

College of Education Offers educational administration (MA Ed); educational leadership (Ed D); higher and postsecondary education (MA Ed); instructional leadership (MA Ed); school psychology (MA).

College of Health Sciences Offers public health (MPH).

College of Psychology and Behavioral Sciences Offers clinical psychology (MA, Psy D); community counseling (MA); counselor education and supervision (Ed D); forensic psychology (MA); industrial organizational psychology (MA); psychology and behavioral sciences (MA, Ed D, Psy D).

ARGOSY UNIVERSITY, DENVER, Denver, CO 80231

General Information Proprietary, coed, university.

GRADUATE UNITS

College of Business Offers accounting (DBA); corporate compliance (MBA); customized professional concentration (MBA, DBA); finance (MBA); fraud examination (MBA); global business sustainability (DBA); healthcare administration (MBA); information systems (DBA); information systems management (MBA); international business (MBA, DBA); management (MBA, MSM, DBA); marketing (MBA, DBA); organizational leadership (Ed D); public administration (MBA); sustainable management (MBA).

College of Education Offers community college executive leadership (Ed D); educational leadership (MA Ed, Ed D); instructional leadership (MA Ed, Ed D).

College of Health Sciences Offers public health (MPH).

College of Psychology and Behavioral Sciences Offers clinical mental health counseling (MA); clinical psychology (MA, Psy D); counseling psychology (Ed D); counselor education and supervision (Ed D); forensic psychology (MA); industrial organizational psychology (MA); marriage and family therapy (MA, DMFT).

ARGOSY UNIVERSITY, HAWAI`I, Honolulu, HI 96813

General Information Proprietary, coed, university.

GRADUATE UNITS

College of Business Offers accounting (DBA); corporate compliance (MBA); customized professional concentration (MBA, DBA); finance (MBA, Certificate); fraud examination (MBA); global business sustainability (DBA); healthcare administration (MBA, Certificate); information systems (DBA); information systems management (MBA, Certificate); international business (MBA, DBA, Certificate); management (MBA, MSM, DBA); marketing (MBA, DBA, Certificate); organizational leadership (Ed D); public administration (MBA); sustainable management (MBA).

College of Education Offers adult education and training (MAEd); educational leadership (Ed D); instructional leadership (Ed D); school psychology (MA).

College of Health Sciences Offers public health (MPH).

Hawai'i School of Professional Psychology Offers clinical psychology (MA, Psy D, Postdoctoral Respecialization Certificate); counseling psychology (Ed D); forensic psychology (MA); marriage and family therapy (MA); professional psychology (MA, MS, Ed D, Psy D, Certificate, Postdoctoral Respecialization Certificate); psychopharmacology (MS, Certificate); substance abuse counseling (Certificate).

ARGOSY UNIVERSITY, INLAND EMPIRE, Ontario, CA 91761

General Information Proprietary, coed, university.

GRADUATE UNITS

College of Business Offers accounting (DBA); corporate compliance (MBA); customized professional concentration (MBA, DBA); finance (MBA); fraud examination (MBA); global business sustainability (DBA); healthcare administration (MBA); information systems (DBA); information systems management (MBA); international business (MBA, DBA); management (MBA, MSM, DBA); marketing (MBA, DBA); organizational leadership (Ed D); public administration (MBA); sustainable management (MBA).

College of Education Offers community college executive leadership (Ed D); educational leadership (MA Ed, Ed D); instructional leadership (MA Ed, Ed D).

College of Health Sciences Offers public health (MPH).

College of Psychology and Behavioral Sciences Offers clinical psychology/marriage and family therapy (MA); counseling psychology (Ed D); counseling psychology/marriage and family therapy (MA); forensic psychology (MA); industrial organizational psychology (MA); sport-exercise psychology (MA).

ARGOSY UNIVERSITY, LOS ANGELES, Santa Monica, CA 90045

General Information Proprietary, coed, university.

GRADUATE UNITS

College of Business Offers accounting (DBA); corporate compliance (MBA); customized professional concentration (MBA, DBA); finance (MBA); fraud examination (MBA); global business sustainability (DBA); healthcare administration (MBA); information systems (DBA); information systems management (MBA); international business (MBA, DBA); management (MBA, MSM, DBA); marketing (MBA, DBA); organizational leadership (Ed D); public administration (MBA); sustainable management (MBA).

College of Education Offers community college executive leadership (Ed D); educational leadership (MA Ed, Ed D); instructional leadership (MA Ed, Ed D).

College of Health Sciences Offers public health (MPH).

College of Psychology and Behavioral Sciences Offers clinical psychology/marriage and family therapy (MA); counseling psychology (Ed D); counseling psychology/marriage and family therapy (MA); forensic psychology (MA).

ARGOSY UNIVERSITY, NASHVILLE, Nashville, TN 37214

General Information Proprietary, coed, university.

GRADUATE UNITS

College of Business Offers accounting (DBA); customized professional concentration (MBA, DBA); finance (MBA); healthcare administration (MBA); information systems (MBA, DBA); international business (MBA, DBA); management (MBA, MSM, DBA); marketing (MBA, DBA).

College of Education Offers education (MA Ed, Ed D, Ed S); education technology (Ed D); educational leadership (MA Ed, Ed S); higher education administration (Ed D); instructional leadership (MA Ed, Ed S); K-12 education (Ed D).

College of Health Sciences Offers public health (MPH).

College of Psychology and Behavioral Sciences Offers counselor education and supervision (Ed D); mental health counseling (MA).

ARGOSY UNIVERSITY, ORANGE COUNTY, Orange, CA 92868

General Information Proprietary, coed, university.

GRADUATE UNITS

American School of Professional Psychology ***Degree program information:*** Part-time and evening/weekend programs available. Part-time, evening/weekend. Offers child and adolescent psychology (Psy D); counseling psychology (Ed D); forensic psychology (MA); marriage and family therapy (MA); professional psychology (MA, Ed D, Psy D); sport-exercise psychology (MA). Electronic applications accepted.

College of Business Offers accounting (DBA, Adv C); corporate compliance (MBA); customized professional concentration (MBA, DBA); finance (MBA, Certificate); fraud examination (MBA); global business sustainability (DBA); healthcare administration (MBA, Certificate); information systems (DBA, Adv C, Certificate); information systems management (MBA); international business (MBA, DBA, Adv C, Certificate); management (MBA, MSM, DBA, Adv C); marketing (MBA, DBA, Adv C, Certificate); organizational leadership (Ed D); public administration (MBA, Certificate); sustainable management (MBA).

College of Education Offers community college executive leadership (Ed D); educational leadership (MA Ed, Ed D); instructional leadership (MA Ed, Ed D).

College of Health Sciences Offers public health (MPH).

ARGOSY UNIVERSITY, PHOENIX, Phoenix, AZ 85021

General Information Proprietary, coed, university.

GRADUATE UNITS

Arizona School of Professional Psychology Offers clinical psychology (MA); forensic psychology (MA); industrial organizational psychology (MA); mental health counseling (MA); neuropsychology (Psy D); professional psychology (MA, Psy D); sport–exercise psychology (MA); sports-exercise psychology (Psy D).

College of Business Offers accounting (DBA); corporate compliance (MBA); customized professional concentration (MBA, DBA); finance (MBA); fraud examination (MBA); global business sustainability (DBA); healthcare administration (MBA); information systems (DBA); information systems management (MBA); international business (MBA, DBA); management (MBA, DBA); marketing (MBA, DBA); public administration (MBA); sustainable management (MBA).

College of Education Offers adult education and training (MA Ed); advanced educational administration (Ed D, Ed S); community college executive leadership (Ed D); educational administration (MA Ed); educational leadership (MA Ed, Ed D, Ed S); higher and postsecondary education (MA Ed); initial educational administration (Ed D, Ed S); school psychology (MA, Psy D); teaching and learning (MA Ed, Ed D, Ed S).

College of Health Sciences Offers public health (MPH).

ARGOSY UNIVERSITY, SALT LAKE CITY, Draper, UT 84020

General Information Proprietary, coed, university.

GRADUATE UNITS

College of Business Offers accounting (DBA); corporate compliance (MBA); customized professional concentration (MBA, DBA); finance (MBA); fraud examination (MBA); global business sustainability (DBA); healthcare administration (MBA); information systems (DBA); information systems management (MBA); international business (MBA, DBA); management (MBA, DBA); marketing (MBA, DBA); public administration (MBA); sustainable management (MBA).

College of Education Offers educational leadership (MA Ed, Ed D).

College of Health Sciences Offers public health (MPH).

College of Psychology and Behavioral Sciences Offers counseling psychology (Ed D); counselor education and supervision (Ed D); forensic psychology (MA); marriage and family therapy (MA, DMFT); mental health counseling (MA).

ARGOSY UNIVERSITY, SAN DIEGO, San Diego, CA 92108

General Information Proprietary, coed, university.

GRADUATE UNITS

College of Business Offers accounting (DBA); corporate compliance (MBA); customized professional concentration (MBA, DBA); finance (MBA); fraud examination (MBA); global business sustainability (DBA); information systems (DBA); information systems management (MBA); international business (MBA, DBA); management (MBA, MSM, DBA); marketing (MBA, DBA); organizational leadership (Ed D); public administration (MBA).

College of Education Offers community college executive leadership (Ed D); educational leadership (MA Ed, Ed D); instructional leadership (MA Ed, Ed D).

College of Health Sciences Offers public health (MPH).

College of Psychology and Behavioral Sciences Offers clinical psychology/marriage and family therapy (MA); counseling psychology (Ed D); counseling psychology/marriage and family therapy (MA); forensic psychology (MA).

ARGOSY UNIVERSITY, SAN FRANCISCO BAY AREA, Alameda, CA 94501

General Information Proprietary, coed, university.

GRADUATE UNITS
American School of Professional Psychology Offers clinical psychology (MA, Psy D); counseling psychology (MA, Ed D); forensic psychology (MA); sport-exercise psychology (MA).
College of Business Offers accounting (DBA); corporate compliance (MBA); customized professional concentration (MBA, DBA); finance (MBA); fraud examination (MBA); global business sustainability (DBA); healthcare administration (MBA); information systems (DBA); information systems management (MBA); international business (MBA, DBA); management (MBA, MSM, DBA); marketing (MBA, DBA); organizational leadership (Ed D); public administration (MBA); sustainable management (MBA).
College of Education Offers community college executive leadership (Ed D); educational leadership (MA Ed, Ed D); instructional leadership (MA Ed, Ed D).
College of Health Sciences Offers public health (MPH).

ARGOSY UNIVERSITY, SARASOTA, Sarasota, FL 34235

General Information Proprietary, coed, university.
GRADUATE UNITS
College of Business Offers accounting (DBA, Adv C); corporate compliance (MBA, DBA, Certificate); customized professional concentration (MBA, DBA); finance (MBA, Certificate); fraud examination (MBA, Certificate); global business sustainability (DBA, Adv C); healthcare administration (MBA, Certificate); information systems (DBA, Adv C, Certificate); information systems management (MBA); international business (MBA, DBA, Adv C, Certificate); management (MBA, MSM, DBA, Adv C, Certificate); marketing (MBA, DBA, Adv C, Certificate); organizational leadership (Ed D); public administration (MBA, Certificate); sustainable management (MBA, Certificate).
College of Education Offers community college executive leadership (Ed D); educational leadership (MA Ed, Ed D, Ed S); school counseling (MA, Ed S); school psychology (MA); teaching and learning (MA Ed, Ed D, Ed S).
College of Health Sciences Offers public health (MPH).
College of Psychology and Behavioral Sciences Offers community counseling (MA); counseling psychology (Ed D); counselor education and supervision (Ed D); forensic psychology (MA); marriage and family therapy (MA); mental health counseling (MA); pastoral community counseling (Ed D).

ARGOSY UNIVERSITY, SCHAUMBURG, Schaumburg, IL 60173-5403

General Information Proprietary, coed, university.
GRADUATE UNITS
College of Behavioral Sciences Offers clinical mental health counseling (MA); forensic psychology (MA, Post-Graduate Certificate); industrial organizational psychology (MA); sport-exercise psychology (MA).
College of Health Sciences Offers public health (MPH).
Graduate School of Business and Management Offers accounting (DBA, Adv C); customized professional concentration (MBA, DBA); finance (MBA, Certificate); fraud examination (MBA); healthcare administration (MBA, Certificate); human resource management (MS); information systems (Adv C, Certificate); information systems management (MBA); international business (MBA, DBA, Adv C, Certificate); management (MBA, MSM, DBA, Adv C, Certificate); marketing (MBA, DBA, Adv C, Certificate); organizational leadership (MS, Ed D); public administration (MBA); sustainable management (MBA).
Illinois School of Professional Psychology Offers clinical psychology (MA, Psy D).

ARGOSY UNIVERSITY, SEATTLE, Seattle, WA 98121

General Information Proprietary, coed, university.
GRADUATE UNITS
College of Business Offers accounting (DBA); corporate compliance (MBA); customized professional concentration (MBA, DBA); finance (MBA); fraud examination (MBA); global business sustainability (DBA); healthcare administration (MBA); information systems (DBA); information systems management (MBA); international business (MBA, DBA); management (MBA, MSM, DBA); marketing (MBA, DBA); organizational leadership (Ed D); public administration (MBA); sustainable management (MBA).
College of Education Offers adult education and training (MA Ed); community college executive leadership (Ed D); educational leadership (MA Ed, Ed D); higher and postsecondary education (MA Ed); instructional leadership (MA Ed, Ed D).
College of Health Sciences Offers public health (MPH).
College of Psychology and Behavioral Sciences Offers clinical psychology (MA, Psy D, Postdoctoral Respecialization Certificate); counseling psychology (MA, Ed D); psychology and behavioral sciences (MA, Ed D, Psy D, Postdoctoral Respecialization Certificate).

ARGOSY UNIVERSITY, TAMPA, Tampa, FL 33607

General Information Proprietary, coed, university.
GRADUATE UNITS
College of Business Offers accounting (DBA); corporate compliance (MBA); customized professional concentration (MBA, DBA); finance (MBA); fraud examination (MBA); global business sustainability (DBA); healthcare administration (MBA); information systems (DBA); information systems management (MBA); international business (MBA, DBA); management (MBA, MSM, DBA); marketing (MBA, DBA); organizational leadership (Ed D); public administration (MBA); sustainable management (MBA).
College of Education Offers community college executive leadership (Ed D); educational leadership (MA Ed, Ed D, Ed S); school counseling (MA); teaching and learning (MA Ed, Ed D, Ed S).
College of Health Sciences Offers public health (MPH).
Florida School of Professional Psychology Offers clinical psychology (MA, Psy D); counselor education and supervision (Ed D); industrial organizational psychology (MA); marriage and family therapy (MA); mental health counseling (MA).

ARGOSY UNIVERSITY, TWIN CITIES, Eagan, MN 55121

General Information Proprietary, coed, university.
GRADUATE UNITS
College of Business Offers accounting (DBA); customized professional concentration (MBA, DBA); finance (MBA); fraud examination (MBA); global business sustainability (DBA); healthcare administration (MBA); information systems (DBA); information systems management (MBA); international business (MBA, DBA); management (MBA, MSM, DBA); marketing (MBA, DBA); organizational leadership (Ed D); public administration (MBA); sustainable management (MBA).
College of Education Offers advanced educational administration (Ed D, Ed S); educational leadership (MA Ed, Ed D, Ed S); higher and postsecondary education (MA Ed); initial educational administration (Ed D, Ed S); instructional leadership (MA Ed, Ed D, Ed S).
College of Health Sciences Offers health services management (MS); public health (MPH).
Minnesota School of Professional Psychology Offers clinical psychology (MA, Psy D); forensic counseling (Post-Graduate Certificate); forensic psychology (MA); industrial organizational psychology (MA); marriage and family therapy (MA, DMFT).

ARGOSY UNIVERSITY, WASHINGTON DC, Arlington, VA 22209

General Information Proprietary, coed, university.
GRADUATE UNITS
American School of Professional Psychology Offers clinical psychology (MA, Psy D); community counseling (MA); counseling psychology (Ed D); counselor education and supervision (Ed D); forensic psychology (MA).
College of Business Offers accounting (DBA); customized professional concentration (MBA, DBA); finance (MBA); fraud examination (MBA); global business sustainability (DBA); healthcare administration (MBA); information systems (DBA); information systems management (MBA); international business (MBA, DBA, Certificate); management (MBA, MSM, DBA); marketing (MBA, DBA, Certificate); organizational leadership (Ed D); public administration (MBA); sustainable management (MBA).
College of Education Offers community college executive leadership (Ed D); educational leadership (MA Ed, Ed D, Ed S); instructional leadership (MA Ed, Ed D, Ed S).
College of Health Sciences Offers public health (MPH).

ARIZONA SCHOOL OF ACUPUNCTURE AND ORIENTAL MEDICINE, Tucson, AZ 85712

General Information Proprietary, coed, graduate-only institution.
Website: http://www.asaom.edu/
General Application Contact: Tim Dunn, Admissions Director, 520-795-0787 Ext. 104, Fax: 877-222-4606, E-mail: admissions@asaom.edu.
GRADUATE UNITS
Graduate Programs Offers acupuncture (M Ac, M Ac OM). *Admissions Director*, Tim Dunn, 520-795-0787 Ext. 104, Fax: 877-222-4606, E-mail: admissions@asaom.edu.

ARIZONA STATE UNIVERSITY AT THE TEMPE CAMPUS, Tempe, AZ 85287

General Information State-supported, coed, university. CGS member. *Graduate housing:* Room and/or apartments available to single students; on-campus housing not available to married students. *Research affiliation:* Arizona Public Service (electrical, computer and energy engineering), Banner Health (health, biomedical, and life sciences), Honeywell (mechanical and aerospace engineering), Mayo Clinic (healthcare, biomedical informatics), Raytheon Corporation (computer science and engineering), Translational Genomics Research Institute (TGEN) (biomedicine).
GRADUATE UNITS
College of Health Solutions Offers audiology (Au D); behavioral health (DBH); biomedical informatics (MS, PhD); communication disorders (MS); health solutions (MS, Au D, DBH, PhD); speech and hearing science (PhD).
School of Nutrition and Health Promotion Offers clinical exercise physiology (MS); exercise and wellness (MS); nutrition (MS); obesity prevention and management (MS); physical activity, nutrition and wellness (PhD).
College of Liberal Arts and Sciences ***Degree program information:*** Part-time programs available. Part-time, online learning. Offers American media and popular culture (MAS); applied behavior analysis (MS); applied linguistics (PhD); behavioral neuroscience (PhD); biochemistry (MS, PhD); chemistry (MS, PhD); clinical psychology (PhD); cognitive science (PhD); creative writing (MFA); developmental psychology (PhD); English (MA, PhD); film and media studies (MAS); liberal arts and sciences (MA, MAS, MFA, MLS, MNS, MS, MTESOL, MUEP, PSM, PSM, PhD, Graduate Certificate); liberal studies (MLS); linguistics (Graduate Certificate); nanoscience (PSM, PSM); physics (MNS, PhD); quantitative psychology (PhD); science and technology policy (MS); social psychology (PhD); teaching English to speakers of other languages (MTESOL); translation studies (Graduate Certificate). Electronic applications accepted.
Hugh Downs School of Human Communication Degree program information: Evening/weekend programs available. Evening/weekend. Offers communication (PhD). Electronic applications accepted.
School of Earth and Space Exploration Offers astrophysics (MS, PhD); exploration systems design (PhD); geological sciences (MS, PhD). PhD in exploration systems design is offered in collaboration with the Ira A. Fulton School of Engineering. Electronic applications accepted.
School of Geographical Sciences and Urban Planning Offers geographic information systems (MAS); geographical information science (Graduate Certificate); geography (MA, PhD); transportation systems (Graduate Certificate); urban and environmental planning (MUEP); urban planning (PhD). Electronic applications accepted.
School of Historical, Philosophical and Religious Studies Degree program information: Part-time programs available. Part-time. Offers European history (MA, PhD); medieval studies (Graduate Certificate); North American history (MA, PhD); philosophy (MA, PhD); public history (MA); religious studies (MA, PhD); Renaissance studies (Graduate Certificate); scholarly publishing (Graduate Certificate). Electronic applications accepted.
School of Human Evolution and Social Change Offers anthropology (MA, PhD); applied mathematics for the life and social sciences (PhD); environmental social science (PhD); global health (MA, PhD); immigration studies (Graduate Certificate). Electronic applications accepted.
School of International Letters and Cultures Offers Asian languages and civilizations: Chinese (MA); Asian languages and civilizations: Japanese (MA); Chinese (MA, PhD); comparative literature (MA); cultural studies (PhD); French (MA); German (MA); Japanese (MA); language and culture (MA); linguistics (MA); literature (MA, PhD); literature and culture (MA); Spanish (MA, PhD). Electronic applications accepted.
School of Life Sciences Offers animal behavior (PhD); applied ethics (biomedical and health ethics) (MA); biology (MS, PhD); environmental life sciences (PhD); evolutionary biology (PhD); history and philosophy of science (PhD); human and social dimensions of science and technology (PhD); microbiology (PhD); molecular and cellular biology (PhD); neuroscience (PhD). Electronic applications accepted.

School of Mathematical and Statistical Sciences Degree program information: Part-time programs available. Part-time. Offers applied mathematics (PhD); mathematics (MA, PhD); mathematics education (PhD); statistics (MS, PhD, Graduate Certificate). Electronic applications accepted.

School of Politics and Global Studies Degree program information: Part-time programs available. Part-time. Offers political science (MA, PhD). Electronic applications accepted.

School of Social and Family Dynamics Offers family and human development (MS, PhD); infant-family practice (MAS); marriage and family therapy (MAS); sociology (MA, PhD). Electronic applications accepted.

School of Social Transformation Degree program information: Part-time programs available. Part-time. Offers African studies (Graduate Certificate); gender studies (PhD, Graduate Certificate); justice studies (MS, PhD); social and cultural pedagogy (MA); socio-economic justice (Graduate Certificate). Electronic applications accepted.

College of Nursing and Health Innovation Online learning. Offers advanced nursing practice (DNP); clinical research management (MS); community and public health practice (Graduate Certificate); family mental health nurse practitioner (Graduate Certificate); family nurse practitioner (Graduate Certificate); geriatric nursing (Graduate Certificate); healthcare innovation (MHI); nurse education in academic and practice settings (Graduate Certificate); nurse educator (MS); nursing and healthcare innovation (PhD). Electronic applications accepted.

College of Public Programs ***Degree program information:*** Part-time and evening/weekend programs available. Part-time, evening/weekend, online learning. Electronic applications accepted.

School of Community Resources and Development Degree program information: Part-time and evening/weekend programs available. Part-time, evening/weekend. Offers community resources and development (MS, PhD); nonprofit leadership and management (Graduate Certificate); nonprofit studies (MNpS); sustainable tourism (MAS). Electronic applications accepted.

School of Criminology and Criminal Justice Degree program information: Part-time and evening/weekend programs available. Part-time, evening/weekend, online learning. Offers corrections management (Graduate Certificate); criminal justice (MA); criminology and criminal justice (MS, PhD); law enforcement administration (Graduate Certificate). Electronic applications accepted.

School of Public Affairs Degree program information: Part-time and evening/weekend programs available. Part-time, evening/weekend. Offers emergency management and homeland security (MA); program evaluation (MS); public administration (MPA, PhD); public policy (MPP). Electronic applications accepted.

School of Social Work Degree program information: Part-time programs available. Part-time. Offers advanced direct practice (MSW); assessment of integrative health modalities (Graduate Certificate); gerontology (Graduate Certificate); Latino cultural competency (Graduate Certificate); planning, administration and community practice (MSW); social work (PhD); trauma and bereavement (Graduate Certificate). Electronic applications accepted.

Graduate College ***Degree program information:*** Part-time and evening/weekend programs available. Part-time, evening/weekend, online learning. Offers human and social dimensions of science and technology (PhD); neuroscience (PhD). Electronic applications accepted.

Herberger Institute for Design and the Arts Offers design and the arts (M Arch, MA, MFA, MLA, MM, MS, MSD, MUD, DMA, PhD). Electronic applications accepted.

The Design School Offers architecture (M Arch); building design/built environment (MS); design (MSD, PhD); design, environment and the arts (PhD); digital culture (PhD); healthcare and healing environments (PhD); history, theory, and criticism (PhD); landscape architecture (MLA); urban design (MUD). Electronic applications accepted.

School of Art Offers art education (MA); art history (MA); ceramics (MFA); design, environment and the arts (PhD); drawing (MFA); fibers (MFA); intermedia (MFA); metals (MFA); museum studies (MFA); painting (MFA); printmaking (MFA); sculpture (MFA); wood (MFA). Electronic applications accepted.

School of Arts, Media and Engineering Offers media arts and sciences (PhD). Electronic applications accepted.

School of Film, Dance and Theatre Offers dance (MFA); interdisciplinary digital media and performance (MFA); theatre (MA, MFA, PhD). Electronic applications accepted.

School of Music Offers composition (MM, DMA); conducting (DMA); ethnomusicology (MA); interdisciplinary digital media/performance (DMA); music education (MM, PhD); music history and literature (MA); music therapy (MM); performance (MM, DMA). Electronic applications accepted.

Ira A. Fulton Schools of Engineering ***Degree program information:*** Part-time and evening/weekend programs available. Part-time, evening/weekend, online learning. Offers aerospace engineering (MS, PhD); chemical engineering (MS, PhD); construction (MS); embedded systems (M Eng); engineering (M Eng, MA, MCS, MS, MSE, PSM, PhD, Graduate Certificate); enterprise systems innovation and management (MSE); materials science and engineering (MS, PhD); mechanical engineering (MS, PhD); modeling and simulation (M Eng); quality and reliability engineering (M Eng); software engineering (MSE); solar energy engineering and commercialization (PSM); systems engineering (M Eng). Electronic applications accepted.

The Polytechnic School Degree program information: Part-time and evening/weekend programs available. Part-time, evening/weekend. Offers applied psychology (MS); aviation management and human factors (MS); environmental technology management (MS); global technology and development (MS); graphic information technology (MS); management of technology (MS); manufacturing engineering technology (MS); simulation, modeling, and applied cognitive science (PhD); technology and innovation (MS, PhD). Electronic applications accepted.

School of Biological and Health Systems Engineering Degree program information: Part-time and evening/weekend programs available. Part-time, evening/weekend. Offers biological design (PhD); biomedical engineering (MS, PhD). Electronic applications accepted.

School of Computing, Informatics, and Decision Systems Engineering Degree program information: Part-time and evening/weekend programs available. Part-time, evening/weekend, online learning. Offers computer engineering (MS, PhD); computer science (MCS, MS, PhD); industrial engineering (MS, PhD); software engineering (MS). Electronic applications accepted.

School of Electrical, Computer and Energy Engineering Degree program information: Part-time and evening/weekend programs available. Part-time, evening/weekend, online learning. Offers electrical engineering (MS, MSE, PhD); nuclear power generation (Graduate Certificate). Electronic applications accepted.

School of Sustainable Engineering and the Built Environment Degree program information: Part-time and evening/weekend programs available. Part-time, evening/weekend, online learning. Offers civil, environmental and sustainable engineering (MS, MSE, PhD); construction engineering (MSE); construction management (MS, PhD). Electronic applications accepted.

Mary Lou Fulton Teachers College ***Degree program information:*** Part-time and evening/weekend programs available. Part-time, evening/weekend, online learning. Offers autism spectrum disorder (Graduate Certificate); curriculum and instruction (M Ed, MA); education (M Ed, MA, MC, MPE, Ed D, PhD, Graduate Certificate); educational leadership (M Ed); educational policy and evaluation (PhD); educational technology (M Ed); elementary education (M Ed); higher and post-secondary education (M Ed); instructional design and performance improvement (Graduate Certificate); leadership and innovation (Ed D); online teaching for grades K-12 (Graduate Certificate); physical education (MPE); secondary education (M Ed); special education (M Ed). Electronic applications accepted.

New College of Interdisciplinary Arts and Sciences ***Degree program information:*** Part-time and evening/weekend programs available. Part-time, evening/weekend. Offers applied ethics and the professions (MA); communication studies (MA); interdisciplinary studies (MA); psychology (MS); social justice and human rights (MA). Electronic applications accepted.

Sandra Day O'Connor College of Law Students: 623 full-time (232 women); includes 146 minority (10 Black or African American, non-Hispanic/Latino; 20 American Indian or Alaska Native, non-Hispanic/Latino; 21 Asian, non-Hispanic/Latino; 69 Hispanic/Latino; 4 Native Hawaiian or other Pacific Islander, non-Hispanic/Latino; 22 Two or more races, non-Hispanic/Latino), 31 international. Average age 28. 1,423 applicants, 43% accepted, 215 enrolled. *Faculty:* 68 full-time (29 women), 77 part-time/adjunct (20 women). *Financial support:* Research assistantships, teaching assistantships, career-related internships or fieldwork, Federal Work-Study, institutionally sponsored loans, scholarships/grants, tuition waivers (full and partial), and unspecified assistantships available. Financial award application deadline: 3/15; financial award applicants required to submit FAFSA. In 2015, 36 master's, 229 doctorates awarded. Online learning. Offers biotechnology and genomics (LL M); global legal studies (LL M); law (MLS, JD); law (customized) (LL M); sports law and business (MSLB); tribal policy, law and government (LL M). JD/MD offered jointly with Mayo Medical School. *Application deadline:* For fall admission, 2/1 priority date for domestic and international students. Applications are processed on a rolling basis. *Application fee:* $65. Electronic applications accepted. *Application Contact:* Chitra Damania, Director of Operations, 480-965-1474, Fax: 480-727-7930, E-mail: law.admissions@asu.edu. *Dean/Professor,* Douglas Sylvester, 480-965-6188, Fax: 480-965-6521, E-mail: douglas.sylvester@asu.edu.

School of Letters and Sciences ***Degree program information:*** Part-time and evening/weekend programs available. Part-time, evening/weekend, online learning. Offers biomedical and health ethics (MA); counseling (MC); counseling psychology (PhD); ethics and emerging technologies (MA); letters and sciences (MA, MC, PhD); public administration, policy and ethics (MA); science, technology and ethics (MA). Electronic applications accepted.

School of Sustainability ***Degree program information:*** Part-time and evening/weekend programs available. Part-time, evening/weekend. Offers sustainability (MA, MS, PhD); sustainable technology and management (Graduate Certificate). Electronic applications accepted.

Thunderbird School of Global Management Students: 241 full-time (85 women), 191 part-time (55 women). *Faculty:* 22 full-time (6 women), 33 part-time/adjunct (15 women). *Financial support:* Career-related internships or fieldwork, Federal Work-Study, scholarships/grants, and unspecified assistantships available. Online learning. Offers global affairs and management (MA); global management (MGM). *Application deadline:* For fall admission, 6/10 for domestic students, 4/30 for international students. *Application fee:* $125. *Application Contact:* Keaton Allen, Director of Admissions, 602-978-7964, Fax: 602-439-5432, E-mail: keaton.allen@asu.edu.

Walter Cronkite School of Journalism and Mass Communication Offers journalism and mass communication (PhD); mass communication (MMC). Electronic applications accepted.

W. P. Carey School of Business ***Degree program information:*** Part-time and evening/weekend programs available. Part-time, evening/weekend, online learning. Offers business (M Acc, M Tax, MBA, MRED, MS, PhD, Graduate Certificate); business administration (PhD); economics (PhD); entrepreneurship (MBA); finance (MBA); health sector management (MBA); information management (MS); international business (MBA); leadership (MBA); marketing (MBA); organizational behavior (PhD); real estate development (MRED); strategic management (PhD); supply chain management (MBA, PhD). Electronic applications accepted.

Morrison School of Agribusiness Degree program information: Part-time and evening/weekend programs available. Part-time, evening/weekend. Offers agribusiness (PhD). Electronic applications accepted.

School of Accountancy Degree program information: Part-time and evening/weekend programs available. Part-time, evening/weekend. Offers accountancy (M Acc, M Tax); business administration (PhD). Electronic applications accepted.

ARKANSAS STATE UNIVERSITY, State University, AR 72467

General Information State-supported, coed, comprehensive institution. CGS member. *Enrollment:* 13,410 graduate, professional, and undergraduate students; 736 full-time matriculated graduate/professional students (398 women), 3,082 part-time matriculated graduate/professional students (2,086 women). *Enrollment by degree level:* 2,911 master's, 269 doctoral, 638 other advanced degrees. *Graduate faculty:* 276 full-time (111 women). *International tuition:* $9844 full-time. Tuition, state resident: full-time $4572; part-time $254 per credit hour. Tuition, nonresident: full-time $9144; part-time $508 per credit hour. *Required fees:* $1188; $66 per credit hour. $25 per term. Tuition and fees vary according to course load and program. *Graduate housing:* Rooms and/or apartments available on a first-come, first-served basis to single and married students. Typical cost: $5600 per year ($8940 including board) for single students. Room and board charges vary according to board plan and housing facility selected. *Student services:* Campus employment opportunities, campus safety program, career counseling, child daycare facilities, exercise/wellness program, free psychological counseling, international student services, multicultural affairs office, services for students with disabilities. *Library:* Dean B. Ellis Library. *Collection:* Books: 386,049 (physical), 452,194 (digital/electronic); Serial titles: 353 (physical), 40,469 (digital/electronic); Databases: 163. Weekly public service hours: 103; students can reserve study rooms. *Research affiliation:* Oak Ridge Associated Universities (scientific research and education development), Applied Biotechnologies Institute (recombinant proteins), Biostrategies, LLC (biotechnology), Infinite Enzymes (plant biotechnology), Nature West (physical, engineering, and life sciences), GeneCoMe (biotechnology).

Computer facilities: Computer purchase and lease plans are available. 800 computers available on campus for general student use. A campuswide network can be accessed

from student residence rooms and from off campus. Online class registration is available.
Website: http://www.astate.edu/

General Application Contact: Vickey Ring, Graduate Admissions Coordinator, 870-972-2737, Fax: 870-972-3917, E-mail: vickeyring@astate.edu.

GRADUATE UNITS

Graduate School Students: 736 full-time (398 women), 3,082 part-time (2,086 women); includes 705 minority (516 Black or African American, non-Hispanic/Latino; 20 American Indian or Alaska Native, non-Hispanic/Latino; 34 Asian, non-Hispanic/Latino; 78 Hispanic/Latino; 4 Native Hawaiian or other Pacific Islander, non-Hispanic/Latino; 53 Two or more races, non-Hispanic/Latino), 257 international. Average age 34. 4,009 applicants, 56% accepted, 1510 enrolled. *Faculty:* 276 full-time (111 women). *Financial support:* In 2015–16, 288 students received support. Fellowships, research assistantships, teaching assistantships, career-related internships or fieldwork, scholarships/grants, and unspecified assistantships available. Financial award application deadline: 7/1; financial award applicants required to submit FAFSA. In 2015, 1,266 master's, 43 doctorates, 321 other advanced degrees awarded. *Degree program information:* Part-time programs available. Part-time, online learning. *Application deadline:* Applications are processed on a rolling basis. Electronic applications accepted. *Application Contact:* Vickey Ring, Graduate Admissions Coordinator, 870-972-3029, Fax: 870-972-3857, E-mail: vickeyring@astate.edu. *Dean of the Graduate School*, Dr. Andrew Sustich, 870-972-3029, Fax: 870-972-3857, E-mail: sustich@astate.edu.

College of Agriculture and Technology Students: 14 full-time (7 women), 27 part-time (8 women); includes 11 minority (8 Black or African American, non-Hispanic/Latino; 3 Asian, non-Hispanic/Latino), 3 international. Average age 32. 34 applicants, 59% accepted, 13 enrolled. *Faculty:* 15 full-time (3 women). *Financial support:* In 2015–16, 8 students received support. Teaching assistantships, career-related internships or fieldwork, scholarships/grants, and unspecified assistantships available. Financial award application deadline: 7/1; financial award applicants required to submit FAFSA. In 2015, 12 master's awarded. *Degree program information:* Part-time programs available. Part-time. Offers agricultural education (SCCT); agriculture (MSA); vocational-technical administration (SCCT). *Application deadline:* For fall admission, 7/1 for domestic and international students; for spring admission, 11/15 for domestic students, 11/14 for international students. Applications are processed on a rolling basis. *Application fee:* $30 ($40 for international students). Electronic applications accepted. *Application Contact:* Vickey Ring, Graduate Admissions Coordinator, 870-972-2737, Fax: 870-972-3917, E-mail: vickeyring@astate.edu. *Dean*, Dr. Timothy Burcham, 870-972-2085, Fax: 870-972-3885, E-mail: tburcham@astate.edu.

College of Business Students: 73 full-time (36 women), 114 part-time (52 women); includes 33 minority (18 Black or African American, non-Hispanic/Latino; 6 Asian, non-Hispanic/Latino; 6 Hispanic/Latino; 3 Two or more races, non-Hispanic/Latino), 55 international. Average age 29. 231 applicants, 60% accepted, 85 enrolled. *Faculty:* 25 full-time (4 women). *Financial support:* In 2015–16, 28 students received support. Teaching assistantships, career-related internships or fieldwork, scholarships/grants, and unspecified assistantships available. Financial award application deadline: 7/1; financial award applicants required to submit FAFSA. In 2015, 94 master's awarded. *Degree program information:* Part-time and evening/weekend programs available. Part-time, evening/weekend. Offers accountancy (M Acc); business (M Acc, MBA, SCCT); business administration (MBA); business administration education (SCCT); business technology education (SCCT). *Application deadline:* For fall admission, 7/1 for domestic and international students; for spring admission, 11/15 for domestic students, 11/14 for international students. Applications are processed on a rolling basis. *Application fee:* $30 ($40 for international students). Electronic applications accepted. *Application Contact:* Vickey Ring, Graduate Admissions Coordinator, 870-972-2737, Fax: 870-972-3917, E-mail: vickeyring@astate.edu. *Dean*, Dr. Shane Hunt, 870-972-3035, Fax: 870-972-3744, E-mail: shunt@astate.edu.

College of Education and Behavioral Science Students: 135 full-time (89 women), 2,322 part-time (1,658 women); includes 422 minority (322 Black or African American, non-Hispanic/Latino; 12 American Indian or Alaska Native, non-Hispanic/Latino; 10 Asian, non-Hispanic/Latino; 39 Hispanic/Latino; 2 Native Hawaiian or other Pacific Islander, non-Hispanic/Latino; 37 Two or more races, non-Hispanic/Latino), 6 international. Average age 35. 1,875 applicants, 73% accepted, 1006 enrolled. *Faculty:* 52 full-time (28 women). *Financial support:* In 2015–16, 58 students received support. Fellowships, teaching assistantships, career-related internships or fieldwork, scholarships/grants, and unspecified assistantships available. Financial award application deadline: 7/1; financial award applicants required to submit FAFSA. In 2015, 848 master's, 6 doctorates, 321 other advanced degrees awarded. *Degree program information:* Part-time programs available. Part-time, online learning. Offers clinical mental health counseling (Graduate Certificate); college student personnel services (MS); community college administration (SCCT); curriculum and instruction (MSE); dyslexia therapy (Graduate Certificate); early childhood education (MSE); early childhood services (MS); education and behavioral science (MAT, MRC, MS, MSE, Ed D, Ed S, Graduate Certificate, SCCT); educational leadership (MSE, Ed D, Ed S); educational theory and practice (MSE); exercise science (MS); middle level education (MAT, MSE); physical education (MSE, SCCT); psychological science (MS); psychology and counseling (Ed S); reading (MSE, Ed S); rehabilitation counseling (MRC); school counseling (MSE); special education - gifted, talented, and creative (MSE); special education - instructional specialist grades 4-12 (MSE); special education - instructional specialist grades P-4 (MSE); special education, K-12 (MSE); sports administration (MS); student affairs (Graduate Certificate). *Application deadline:* Applications are processed on a rolling basis. Electronic applications accepted. *Application Contact:* Vickey Ring, Graduate Admissions Coordinator, 870-972-2737, Fax: 870-972-3917, E-mail: vickeyring@astate.edu. *Dean*, Dr. Mary Jane Bradley, 870-972-3057, Fax: 870-972-3828, E-mail: mbradley@astate.edu.

College of Engineering Students: 27 full-time (7 women), 27 part-time (4 women); includes 1 minority (Black or African American, non-Hispanic/Latino), 52 international. Average age 24. 169 applicants, 36% accepted, 30 enrolled. *Faculty:* 7 full-time (0 women). *Financial support:* In 2015–16, 20 students received support. Career-related internships or fieldwork, scholarships/grants, and unspecified assistantships available. Financial award application deadline: 7/1; financial award applicants required to submit FAFSA. In 2015, 4 master's awarded. *Degree program information:* Part-time programs available. Part-time. Offers engineering (MS Eng); engineering management (MEM). *Application deadline:* For fall admission, 6/1 for domestic and international students; for spring admission, 10/15 for domestic and international students. Applications are processed on a rolling basis. *Application fee:* $30 ($40 for international students). Electronic applications accepted. *Application Contact:* Vickey Ring, Graduate Admissions Coordinator, 870-972-2737, Fax: 870-972-3917, E-mail: vickeyring@astate.edu. *Interim Dean*, Dr. Paul Mixon, 870-972-2088, Fax: 870-972-3539, E-mail: pmixon@astate.edu.

College of Fine Arts Students: 3 full-time (2 women), 6 part-time (2 women); includes 3 minority (all Black or African American, non-Hispanic/Latino), 1 international. Average age 25. 7 applicants, 57% accepted, 3 enrolled. *Faculty:* 21 full-time (6 women). *Financial support:* In 2015–16, 7 students received support. Teaching assistantships, career-related internships or fieldwork, scholarships/grants, and unspecified assistantships available. Financial award application deadline: 7/1; financial award applicants required to submit FAFSA. In 2015, 7 master's awarded. *Degree program information:* Part-time programs available. Part-time. Offers fine arts (MM, MME, SCCT); music education (MME, SCCT); music performance (MM). *Application deadline:* For fall admission, 7/1 for domestic and international students; for spring admission, 11/15 for domestic students, 11/14 for international students. Applications are processed on a rolling basis. *Application fee:* $30 ($40 for international students). Electronic applications accepted. *Application Contact:* Vickey Ring, Graduate Admissions Coordinator, 870-972-2737, Fax: 870-972-3917, E-mail: vickeyring@astate.edu. *Dean*, Dr. Don Bowyer, 870-972-3053, Fax: 870-972-3932, E-mail: dbowyer@astate.edu.

College of Humanities and Social Sciences Students: 55 full-time (27 women), 260 part-time (135 women); includes 103 minority (77 Black or African American, non-Hispanic/Latino; 3 American Indian or Alaska Native, non-Hispanic/Latino; 2 Asian, non-Hispanic/Latino; 18 Hispanic/Latino; 3 Two or more races, non-Hispanic/Latino), 20 international. Average age 35. 249 applicants, 63% accepted, 93 enrolled. *Faculty:* 50 full-time (21 women). *Financial support:* In 2015–16, 47 students received support. Fellowships, teaching assistantships, career-related internships or fieldwork, scholarships/grants, and unspecified assistantships available. Financial award application deadline: 7/1; financial award applicants required to submit FAFSA. In 2015, 85 master's, 2 doctorates awarded. *Degree program information:* Part-time programs available. Part-time. Offers criminal justice (MA); English (MA); English education (MSE, SCCT); heritage studies (MA, PhD); history (MA); history education (SCCT); humanities and social sciences (MA, MPA, MSE, PhD, SCCT); political science (MA); political science education (SCCT); public administration (MPA); social science education (MSE); sociology (MA); sociology education (SCCT). *Application deadline:* Applications are processed on a rolling basis. Electronic applications accepted. *Application Contact:* Vickey Ring, Graduate Admissions Coordinator, 870-972-2737, Fax: 870-972-3917, E-mail: vickeyring@astate.edu. *Interim Dean*, Dr. Brad Rawlins, 870-972-3973, Fax: 870-972-3976, E-mail: brawlins@astate.edu.

College of Media and Communication Students: 15 full-time (6 women), 27 part-time (17 women); includes 20 minority (17 Black or African American, non-Hispanic/Latino; 1 Asian, non-Hispanic/Latino; 1 Hispanic/Latino; 1 Two or more races, non-Hispanic/Latino), 14 international. Average age 28. 49 applicants, 47% accepted, 15 enrolled. *Faculty:* 13 full-time (6 women). *Financial support:* In 2015–16, 20 students received support. Career-related internships or fieldwork, scholarships/grants, and unspecified assistantships available. Financial award application deadline: 7/1; financial award applicants required to submit FAFSA. In 2015, 30 master's awarded. *Degree program information:* Part-time programs available. Part-time. Offers communication studies (MA, SCCT); health communications (Graduate Certificate); mass communications (MSMC); media and communication (MA, MSMC, Graduate Certificate, SCCT). *Application deadline:* For fall admission, 7/1 for domestic and international students; for spring admission, 11/15 for domestic students, 11/14 for international students. Applications are processed on a rolling basis. *Application fee:* $30 ($40 for international students). Electronic applications accepted. *Application Contact:* Vickey Ring, Graduate Admissions Coordinator, 870-972-2737, Fax: 870-972-3917, E-mail: vickeyring@astate.edu. *Dean*, Dr. Brad Rawlins, 870-972-2468, Fax: 870-972-3856, E-mail: brawlins@astate.edu.

College of Nursing and Health Professions Students: 288 full-time (176 women), 200 part-time (165 women); includes 89 minority (58 Black or African American, non-Hispanic/Latino; 5 American Indian or Alaska Native, non-Hispanic/Latino; 9 Asian, non-Hispanic/Latino; 11 Hispanic/Latino; 2 Native Hawaiian or other Pacific Islander, non-Hispanic/Latino; 4 Two or more races, non-Hispanic/Latino), 5 international. Average age 30. 769 applicants, 25% accepted, 172 enrolled. *Faculty:* 41 full-time (28 women). *Financial support:* In 2015–16, 32 students received support. Fellowships, career-related internships or fieldwork, scholarships/grants, and unspecified assistantships available. Financial award application deadline: 7/1; financial award applicants required to submit FAFSA. In 2015, 150 master's, 31 doctorates awarded. *Degree program information:* Part-time programs available. Part-time. Offers addiction studies (Graduate Certificate); aging studies (Graduate Certificate); communication disorders (MCD); disaster preparedness and emergency management (MS); dyslexia therapy (Graduate Certificate); health care management (Graduate Certificate); health sciences (MS); health sciences education (Graduate Certificate); healthcare emergency management (Graduate Certificate); nurse anesthesia (MSN); nursing (MSN); nursing and health professions (MCD, MS, MSN, MSW, DNP, DOT, DPT, Graduate Certificate); nursing practice (DNP); occupational therapy (DOT); physical therapy (DPT); social work (MSW). *Application deadline:* Applications are processed on a rolling basis. Electronic applications accepted. *Application Contact:* Vickey Ring, Graduate Admissions Coordinator, 870-972-2737, Fax: 870-972-3917, E-mail: vickeyring@astate.edu. *Dean*, Dr. Susan Hanrahan, 870-972-3112, Fax: 870-972-2040, E-mail: hanrahan@astate.edu.

College of Sciences and Mathematics Students: 126 full-time (48 women), 63 part-time (31 women); includes 15 minority (6 Black or African American, non-Hispanic/Latino; 3 Asian, non-Hispanic/Latino; 3 Hispanic/Latino; 3 Two or more races, non-Hispanic/Latino), 101 international. Average age 27. 571 applicants, 37% accepted, 61 enrolled. *Faculty:* 52 full-time (15 women). *Financial support:* In 2015–16, 68 students received support. Fellowships, teaching assistantships, career-related internships or fieldwork, scholarships/grants, and unspecified assistantships available. Financial award application deadline: 7/1; financial award applicants required to submit FAFSA. In 2015, 36 master's, 4 doctorates awarded. *Degree program information:* Part-time programs available. Part-time. Offers biological sciences (MA); biology (MS); biology education (MSE, SCCT); biotechnology (PSM); chemistry (MS); chemistry education (MSE, SCCT); computer science (MS); environmental sciences (MS, PhD); mathematics (MS); mathematics education (MSE); molecular biosciences (MS, PhD); sciences and mathematics (MA, MS, MSE, PSM, PhD, SCCT). *Application deadline:* Applications are processed on a rolling basis. Electronic applications accepted. *Application Contact:* Vickey Ring, Graduate Admissions Coordinator, 870-972-2737, Fax: 870-972-3917, E-mail: vickeyring@astate.edu. *Dean*, Dr. John Pratte, 870-972-3079, Fax: 870-972-3827, E-mail: jpratte@astate.edu.

ARKANSAS TECH UNIVERSITY, Russellville, AR 72801

General Information State-supported, coed, comprehensive institution. *Enrollment:* 12,054 graduate, professional, and undergraduate students; 259 full-time matriculated graduate/professional students (139 women), 622 part-time matriculated graduate/professional students (433 women). *Enrollment by degree level:* 870 master's,

11 other advanced degrees. *Graduate faculty:* 86 full-time (38 women), 14 part-time/adjunct (10 women). *Graduate housing:* Room and/or apartments available on a first-come, first-served basis to single students; on-campus housing not available to married students. Housing application deadline: 8/1. *Student services:* Campus employment opportunities, campus safety program, career counseling, exercise/wellness program, free psychological counseling, international student services, low-cost health insurance, multicultural affairs office, services for students with disabilities, teacher training. *Library:* Ross Pendergraft Library and Technology Center. *Collection:* Books: 289,198 (physical), 47,410 (digital/electronic); Databases: 198. Students can reserve study rooms.

Computer facilities: Computer purchase and lease plans are available. 1,124 computers available on campus for general student use. A campuswide network can be accessed from student residence rooms and from off campus. Online class registration is available.
Website: http://www.atu.edu/

General Application Contact: Dr. Mary B. Gunter, Dean of Graduate College, 479-968-0398, Fax: 479-964-0542, E-mail: gradcollege@atu.edu.

GRADUATE UNITS

College of Arts and Humanities Students: 67 full-time (38 women), 114 part-time (86 women); includes 20 minority (7 Black or African American, non-Hispanic/Latino; 3 Asian, non-Hispanic/Latino; 7 Hispanic/Latino; 3 Two or more races, non-Hispanic/Latino), 50 international. Average age 31. *Financial support:* In 2015–16, research assistantships with full tuition reimbursements (averaging $4,800 per year), teaching assistantships with full tuition reimbursements (averaging $4,800 per year) were awarded; career-related internships or fieldwork, Federal Work-Study, scholarships/grants, health care benefits, and unspecified assistantships also available. Support available to part-time students. Financial award application deadline: 4/15; financial award applicants required to submit FAFSA. In 2015, 60 master's awarded. *Degree program information:* Part-time programs available. Part-time. Offers applied sociology (MS); English (M Ed, MA); history (MA); liberal arts (MLA); multi-media journalism (MA); psychology (MS); teaching English as a second language (MA). *Application deadline:* For fall admission, 3/1 priority date for domestic students, 5/1 priority date for international students; for spring admission, 10/1 priority date for domestic and international students. Applications are processed on a rolling basis. *Application fee:* $25 ($75 for international students). Electronic applications accepted. *Application Contact:* Dr. Mary B. Gunter, Dean of Graduate College, 479-968-0398, Fax: 479-964-0542, E-mail: gradcollege@atu.edu. *Dean*, Dr. Jeffrey Woods, 479-968-0274, Fax: 479-964-0812, E-mail: jwoods@atu.edu.

College of Business Students: 15 full-time (8 women), 51 part-time (30 women); includes 14 minority (12 Black or African American, non-Hispanic/Latino; 2 Hispanic/Latino), 2 international. Average age 35. *Financial support:* Application deadline: 4/15; applicants required to submit FAFSA. *Degree program information:* Part-time and evening/weekend programs available. Part-time, evening/weekend, online only. Offers business (MSBA). *Application deadline:* For fall admission, 3/1 priority date for domestic students, 5/1 priority date for international students; for spring admission, 10/1 priority date for domestic and international students. Applications are processed on a rolling basis. *Application fee:* $25 ($75 for international students). Electronic applications accepted. *Application Contact:* Dr. Mary B. Gunter, Dean of Graduate College, 479-968-0398, Fax: 479-964-0542, E-mail: gradcollege@atu.edu. *Dean*, Dr. Ed Bashaw, 479-968-0490, E-mail: ebashaw@atu.edu.

College of Education Students: 73 full-time (52 women), 359 part-time (267 women); includes 100 minority (70 Black or African American, non-Hispanic/Latino; 1 American Indian or Alaska Native, non-Hispanic/Latino; 6 Asian, non-Hispanic/Latino; 13 Hispanic/Latino; 10 Two or more races, non-Hispanic/Latino), 5 international. Average age 32. *Financial support:* In 2015–16, research assistantships with full tuition reimbursements (averaging $4,800 per year), teaching assistantships with full tuition reimbursements (averaging $4,800 per year) were awarded; career-related internships or fieldwork, Federal Work-Study, scholarships/grants, health care benefits, and unspecified assistantships also available. Support available to part-time students. Financial award application deadline: 4/15; financial award applicants required to submit FAFSA. In 2015, 166 master's, 7 other advanced degrees awarded. *Degree program information:* Part-time and evening/weekend programs available. Part-time, evening/weekend, online learning. Offers college student personnel (MS); educational leadership (M Ed, Ed S); elementary education (M Ed); instructional improvement (M Ed); instructional technology (M Ed); school counseling and leadership (M Ed); school leadership (Ed D); strength and conditioning studies (MS); teaching (MAT); teaching, learning, and leadership (M Ed). *Application deadline:* For fall admission, 3/1 priority date for domestic students, 5/1 priority date for international students; for spring admission, 10/1 priority date for domestic and international students. Applications are processed on a rolling basis. *Application fee:* $25 ($75 for international students). Electronic applications accepted. *Application Contact:* Dr. Mary B. Gunter, Dean of Graduate College, 479-968-0398, Fax: 479-964-0542, E-mail: gradcollege@atu.edu. *Dean*, Dr. Mary Gunter, 479-964-3217, E-mail: mgunter@atu.edu.

College of Engineering and Applied Sciences Students: 63 full-time (22 women), 44 part-time (12 women); includes 8 minority (3 Black or African American, non-Hispanic/Latino; 1 Asian, non-Hispanic/Latino; 1 Hispanic/Latino; 3 Two or more races, non-Hispanic/Latino), 44 international. Average age 30. *Financial support:* In 2015–16, research assistantships with full tuition reimbursements (averaging $4,800 per year), teaching assistantships with full tuition reimbursements (averaging $4,800 per year) were awarded; career-related internships or fieldwork, Federal Work-Study, scholarships/grants, health care benefits, and unspecified assistantships also available. Support available to part-time students. Financial award application deadline: 4/15; financial award applicants required to submit FAFSA. In 2015, 50 degrees awarded. *Degree program information:* Part-time programs available. Part-time, online learning. Offers emergency management (MS); engineering (M Engr); information technology (MS). *Application deadline:* For fall admission, 3/1 priority date for domestic students, 5/1 priority date for international students; for spring admission, 10/1 priority date for domestic and international students. Applications are processed on a rolling basis. *Application fee:* $25 ($75 for international students). Electronic applications accepted. *Application Contact:* Dr. Mary B. Gunter, Dean of Graduate College, 479-968-0398, Fax: 479-964-0542, E-mail: gradcollege@atu.edu. *Dean*, Dr. Douglas Barlow, 479-968-0353, E-mail: dbarlow@atu.edu.

College of Natural and Health Sciences Students: 7 full-time (4 women), 49 part-time (29 women); includes 9 minority (6 Black or African American, non-Hispanic/Latino; 1 Asian, non-Hispanic/Latino; 2 Two or more races, non-Hispanic/Latino), 1 international. Average age 36. *Financial support:* In 2015–16, research assistantships with full tuition reimbursements (averaging $4,800 per year), teaching assistantships with full tuition reimbursements (averaging $4,800 per year) were awarded; career-related internships or fieldwork, Federal Work-Study, scholarships/grants, health care benefits, and unspecified assistantships also available. Support available to part-time students. Financial award application deadline: 4/15; financial award applicants required to submit FAFSA. In 2015, 15 master's awarded. *Degree program information:* Part-time programs available. Part-time. Offers fisheries and wildlife biology (MS); health informatics (MS); nursing (MSN). *Application deadline:* For fall admission, 3/1 priority date for domestic students, 5/1 priority date for international students; for spring admission, 10/1 priority date for domestic and international students. Applications are processed on a rolling basis. *Application fee:* $25 ($75 for international students). Electronic applications accepted. *Application Contact:* Dr. Mary B. Gunter, Dean of Graduate College, 479-968-0398, Fax: 479-964-0542, E-mail: gradcollege@atu.edu. *Dean*, Dr. Jeff Robertson, 479-968-0498, E-mail: jrobertson@atu.edu.

ARLINGTON BAPTIST COLLEGE, Arlington, TX 76012-3425

General Information Independent-religious, coed, comprehensive institution.

GRADUATE UNITS

Program in Biblical and Theological Studies Offers Biblical and theological studies (MA). Electronic applications accepted.

Program in Education Offers curriculum and instruction (M Ed); educational leadership (M Ed).

ARMSTRONG STATE UNIVERSITY, Savannah, GA 31419-1997

General Information State-supported, coed, comprehensive institution. *Enrollment:* 7,103 graduate, professional, and undergraduate students; 328 full-time matriculated graduate/professional students (244 women), 428 part-time matriculated graduate/professional students (330 women). *Enrollment by degree level:* 636 master's, 95 doctoral, 25 other advanced degrees. *Graduate faculty:* 74 full-time (52 women), 12 part-time/adjunct (8 women). Tuition, state resident: part-time $211 per credit hour. Tuition, nonresident: part-time $782 per credit hour. *Required fees:* $1224 per unit. $612 per semester. Tuition and fees vary according to course load, campus/location and program. *Graduate housing:* Room and/or apartments available on a first-come, first-served basis to single students; on-campus housing not available to married students. Typical cost: $6400 per year. Room charges vary according to board plan and housing facility selected. Housing application deadline: 7/1. *Student services:* Campus employment opportunities, campus safety program, career counseling, exercise/wellness program, free psychological counseling, international student services, low-cost health insurance, multicultural affairs office, services for students with disabilities, teacher training, writing training. *Library:* Lane Library plus 1 other. *Collection:* Books: 218,237 (physical), 140,000 (digital/electronic); Serial titles: 500 (physical), 2,000 (digital/electronic); Databases: 300. Weekly public service hours: 104; students can reserve study rooms.

Computer facilities: 300 computers available on campus for general student use. A campuswide network can be accessed from student residence rooms. Online class registration is available.
Website: http://www.armstrong.edu/

General Application Contact: McKenzie Peterman, Assistant Director of Graduate Admissions, 912-344-2503, Fax: 912-344-3417, E-mail: graduate@armstrong.edu.

GRADUATE UNITS

School of Graduate Studies Students: 328 full-time (244 women), 428 part-time (330 women); includes 228 minority (178 Black or African American, non-Hispanic/Latino; 11 Asian, non-Hispanic/Latino; 28 Hispanic/Latino; 11 Two or more races, non-Hispanic/Latino), 13 international. Average age 31. 495 applicants, 53% accepted, 208 enrolled. *Faculty:* 74 full-time (52 women), 12 part-time/adjunct (8 women). *Financial support:* In 2015–16, 65 research assistantships with full tuition reimbursements (averaging $5,000 per year) were awarded; Federal Work-Study, scholarships/grants, and unspecified assistantships also available. Financial award application deadline: 3/15; financial award applicants required to submit FAFSA. In 2015, 293 master's, 20 doctorates, 37 other advanced degrees awarded. *Degree program information:* Part-time and evening/weekend programs available. Part-time, evening/weekend, 100% online. Offers adolescent and adult education (Certificate); adult education and community leadership (M Ed); adult-gerontological acute care nurse practitioner (Certificate); adult-gerontological clinical nurse specialist (Certificate); adult-gerontological primary care nurse practitioner (Certificate); American and European history (MA); communication sciences (MS); computer science (MSCIS); criminal justice (MS); curriculum and instruction (M Ed); cyber crime (Certificate); early childhood education (M Ed, MAT); family nurse practitioner (MSN); health services administration (MHSA); physical therapy (DPT); professional communication and leadership (MA, Certificate); public health (MPH); public history (MA); reading (Certificate); reading specialist education (M Ed); secondary education (MAT); special education (M Ed, MAT); special education transition specialist (Certificate); sports health sciences (MSSM); strength and conditioning (Certificate). *Application deadline:* For fall admission, 7/1 priority date for domestic students, 5/1 priority date for international students; for spring admission, 11/15 priority date for domestic students, 9/15 priority date for international students; for summer admission, 4/15 priority date for domestic students, 9/15 priority date for international students. Applications are processed on a rolling basis. *Application fee:* $30. Electronic applications accepted. *Application Contact:* McKenzie Peterman, Assistant Director of Graduate Admissions, 912-344-2503, Fax: 912-344-3417, E-mail: graduate@armstrong.edu. *Associate Provost for Academic Affairs and Graduate Studies*, Donna Brooks, 912-344-2589, Fax: 912-344-3417, E-mail: graduate@armstrong.edu.

ART ACADEMY OF CINCINNATI, Cincinnati, OH 45202

General Information Independent, coed, comprehensive institution. *Graduate housing:* Rooms and/or apartments available on a first-come, first-served basis to single and married students. Housing application deadline: 5/1.

GRADUATE UNITS

Program in Art Education ***Degree program information:*** Part-time programs available. Part-time. Offers art education (MAAE). Offered during summer only. Electronic applications accepted.

ART CENTER COLLEGE OF DESIGN, Pasadena, CA 91103

General Information Independent, coed, comprehensive institution. *Enrollment:* 2,133 graduate, professional, and undergraduate students; 161 full-time matriculated graduate/professional students (80 women), 57 part-time matriculated graduate/professional students (19 women). *Enrollment by degree level:* 218 master's. *Graduate housing:* On-campus housing not available. *Student services:* Campus employment opportunities, career counseling, exercise/wellness program, free psychological counseling, international student services, low-cost health insurance, services for students with disabilities. *Library:* James Lemont Fogg Memorial Library. *Collection:* Books: 93,839 (physical), 4,117 (digital/electronic); Serial titles: 420 (physical), 25,266 (digital/electronic); Databases: 38. Weekly public service hours: 75.

Computer facilities: Computer purchase and lease plans are available. 557 computers available on campus for general student use. A campuswide network can be accessed from off campus. Online class registration is available.
Website: http://www.artcenter.edu/

General Application Contact: Brooke Randolph, Director, Graduate Admissions, 626-396-2372, Fax: 626-795-0578, E-mail: gradadmissions@artcenter.edu.

GRADUATE UNITS

Graduate Art Program Students: 24 full-time (12 women), 8 part-time (3 women); includes 10 minority (2 Asian, non-Hispanic/Latino; 4 Hispanic/Latino; 2 Native Hawaiian or other Pacific Islander, non-Hispanic/Latino; 2 Two or more races, non-Hispanic/Latino), 8 international. Average age 32. 112 applicants, 32% accepted, 12 enrolled. *Financial support:* Application deadline: 2/1; applicants required to submit FAFSA. In 2015, 13 degrees awarded. Offers art (MFA). *Application deadline:* For fall admission, 2/1 priority date for domestic and international students; for spring admission, 10/1 priority date for domestic and international students. *Application fee:* $50 ($70 for international students). Electronic applications accepted. *Application Contact:* Brooke Randolph, Director, Graduate Admissions, 626-396-2372, E-mail: gradadmissions@artcenter.edu. *Chair,* Jason Smith, E-mail: jasonesmith0@gmail.com.

Graduate Environmental Design Program Students: 20 full-time (14 women); includes 3 minority (all Asian, non-Hispanic/Latino), 16 international. Average age 26. 40 applicants, 80% accepted, 12 enrolled. *Financial support:* Application deadline: 2/1; applicants required to submit FAFSA. In 2015, 11 master's awarded. Offers furniture and fixtures (MS); spatial experience (MS). *Application deadline:* For fall admission, 2/1 priority date for domestic and international students. *Application fee:* $50 ($70 for international students). Electronic applications accepted. *Application Contact:* Brooke Randolph, Director, Graduate Admissions, 626-396-2372, E-mail: gradadmissions@artcenter.edu. *Chair,* David Mocarski, 626-396-2220, E-mail: david.mocarski@artcenter.edu.

Graduate Film Program Students: 27 full-time (6 women), 23 part-time (10 women); includes 12 minority (3 Black or African American, non-Hispanic/Latino; 5 Asian, non-Hispanic/Latino; 2 Hispanic/Latino; 2 Two or more races, non-Hispanic/Latino), 32 international. Average age 27. 53 applicants, 55% accepted, 11 enrolled. *Financial support:* Application deadline: 2/1; applicants required to submit FAFSA. In 2015, 14 master's awarded. Offers film (MFA). *Application deadline:* For fall admission, 2/1 priority date for domestic and international students; for spring admission, 10/1 priority date for domestic and international students. Applications are processed on a rolling basis. *Application fee:* $50 ($70 for international students). Electronic applications accepted. *Application Contact:* Brooke Randolph, Director, Graduate Admissions, 626-396-2372, E-mail: gradadmissions@artcenter.edu. *Chair,* Ross La Manna, 626-396-2354, E-mail: ross.lamanna@artcenter.edu.

Graduate Industrial Design Program Students: 29 full-time (12 women), 14 part-time (4 women); includes 5 minority (3 Asian, non-Hispanic/Latino; 2 Hispanic/Latino), 20 international. Average age 30. 106 applicants, 19% accepted, 14 enrolled. *Financial support:* Application deadline: 2/1; applicants required to submit FAFSA. In 2015, 14 master's awarded. Offers industrial design (MS). *Application deadline:* For fall admission, 2/1 priority date for domestic and international students. *Application fee:* $50 ($70 for international students). Electronic applications accepted. *Application Contact:* Brooke Randolph, Director, Graduate Admissions, 626-396-2372, E-mail: gradadmissions@artcenter.edu. *Chair,* Andy Ogden, 626-396-2465, E-mail: andy.ogden@artcenter.edu.

Graduate Media Design Practices Program Students: 41 full-time (33 women), 2 part-time (1 woman); includes 15 minority (9 Asian, non-Hispanic/Latino; 3 Hispanic/Latino; 1 Native Hawaiian or other Pacific Islander, non-Hispanic/Latino; 2 Two or more races, non-Hispanic/Latino), 17 international. Average age 26. 99 applicants, 46% accepted, 25 enrolled. *Financial support:* Application deadline: 2/1; applicants required to submit FAFSA. In 2015, 13 master's awarded. Offers media design practices (MFA). *Application deadline:* For fall admission, 2/1 priority date for domestic and international students. *Application fee:* $50 ($70 for international students). Electronic applications accepted. *Application Contact:* Brooke Randolph, Director, Graduate Admissions, 626-396-2372, E-mail: gradadmissions@artcenter.edu. *Chair,* Anne Burdick, 626-396-2359, E-mail: anne.burdick@artcenter.edu.

Graduate Transportation Design Program Students: 19 full-time (3 women), 10 part-time (1 woman); includes 5 minority (3 Asian, non-Hispanic/Latino; 2 Hispanic/Latino), 19 international. Average age 30. 26 applicants, 54% accepted, 11 enrolled. *Financial support:* Application deadline: 2/1; applicants required to submit FAFSA. Offers transportation systems (MS). *Application deadline:* For fall admission, 2/1 priority date for domestic and international students. *Application fee:* $50 ($70 for international students). Electronic applications accepted. *Application Contact:* Brooke Randolph, Director, Graduate Admissions, 626-396-2372, E-mail: gradadmissions@artcenter.edu. *Executive Director,* Geoff Wardle, 626-396-2421, E-mail: gwardle@artcenter.edu.

THE ART INSTITUTE OF CALIFORNIA–SAN FRANCISCO, A CAMPUS OF ARGOSY UNIVERSITY, San Francisco, CA 94102

General Information Proprietary, coed, comprehensive institution.

GRADUATE UNITS

Program in Computer Animation Offers computer animation (MFA).

THE ART INSTITUTE OF DALLAS, A CAMPUS OF SOUTH UNIVERSITY, Dallas, TX 75231-5993

General Information Proprietary, coed, comprehensive institution.

GRADUATE UNITS

Program in Design and Media Management Offers design and media management (MA).

ASBURY THEOLOGICAL SEMINARY, Wilmore, KY 40390-1199

General Information Independent-religious, coed, primarily men, graduate-only institution. *Enrollment by degree level:* 1,143 master's, 247 doctoral, 38 other advanced degrees. *Graduate faculty:* 64 full-time (10 women), 163 part-time/adjunct (30 women). *Tuition, area resident:* Part-time $599 per credit hour. *Required fees:* $200 per semester. One-time fee: $100 part-time. Part-time tuition and fees vary according to course load and program. *Graduate housing:* Rooms and/or apartments available on a first-come, first-served basis to single and married students. Housing application deadline: 8/15. *Student services:* Campus employment opportunities, campus safety program, career counseling, exercise/wellness program, free psychological counseling, international student services, low-cost health insurance, multicultural affairs office, services for students with disabilities, writing training. *Library:* B.L. Fisher Library plus 1 other.

Computer facilities: 38 computers available on campus for general student use. Online class registration is available.
Website: http://www.asburyseminary.edu/

General Application Contact: Kevin Bish, Vice President of Enrollment Management, 859-858-2211, Fax: 859-858-2287, E-mail: admissions.office@asburyseminary.edu.

GRADUATE UNITS

Graduate and Professional Programs ***Financial support:*** Career-related internships or fieldwork, Federal Work-Study, institutionally sponsored loans, and scholarships/grants available. Support available to part-time students. Financial award applicants required to submit FAFSA. *Degree program information:* Part-time programs available. Part-time, online learning. Offers theology (M Div, MA, MAAS, MACE, MACL, MACM, MACP, MAMFC, MAMHC, MAPC, MASF, MAYM, Th M, D Min, PhD, Certificate). *Application deadline:* For fall admission, 8/15 for domestic students; for spring admission, 1/15 for domestic students; for summer admission, 5/15 for domestic students. Applications are processed on a rolling basis. *Application fee:* $50. Electronic applications accepted. *Application Contact:* Kevin Bish, Vice President of Enrollment Management, 859-858-2211, Fax: 859-858-2287, E-mail: admissions.office@asburyseminary.edu. *Provost,* Dr. Douglas K. Matthews, 859-858-2206, Fax: 859-858-2025, E-mail: doug.matthews@asburyseminary.edu.

ASBURY UNIVERSITY, Wilmore, KY 40390-1198

General Information Independent-religious, coed, comprehensive institution. *Graduate housing:* On-campus housing not available.

GRADUATE UNITS

School of Graduate and Professional Studies ***Degree program information:*** Part-time programs available. Part-time. Offers biology: alternative certificate (MA Ed); chemistry: alternative certificate (MA Ed); child and family services (MSW); English (MA Ed); English as a second language (MA Ed); ESL (MA Ed); French (MA Ed); Latin: alternative certificate (MA Ed); mathematics: alternative certificate (MA Ed); reading/writing endorsement (MA Ed); social studies (MA Ed); social work (MSW); Spanish (MA Ed); special education (MA Ed); special education: alternative certificate (MA Ed); teacher as leader endorsement (MA Ed). Electronic applications accepted.

ASHLAND THEOLOGICAL SEMINARY, Ashland, OH 44805

General Information Independent-religious, coed, graduate-only institution. *Graduate housing:* Rooms and/or apartments available on a first-come, first-served basis to single and married students. Housing application deadline: 8/30. *Research affiliation:* Tel Gezer Excavation and Publication Program (archaeological studies), Tyndale House, Cambridge England (faculty study and research).

GRADUATE UNITS

Graduate Programs ***Degree program information:*** Part-time programs available. Part-time. Offers biblical and theological studies (MAR); Biblical, historical and theological studies (MA); Christian ministry (MAPT); Christian studies (Diploma); clinical counseling (MACC); counseling (MAC); ministry (D Min); pastoral ministry (M Div). MAC program offered in Detroit, MI. Electronic applications accepted.

ASHLAND UNIVERSITY, Ashland, OH 44805-3702

General Information Independent-religious, coed, comprehensive institution. *Graduate housing:* On-campus housing not available. *Research affiliation:* Teacher Quality Project (TQP) (education).

GRADUATE UNITS

College of Arts and Sciences Offers American history and government (MAHG); arts and sciences (MAHG, MFA); creative writing (MFA). Electronic applications accepted.

Dauch College of Business and Economics ***Degree program information:*** Part-time and evening/weekend programs available. Part-time, evening/weekend. Offers business and economics (MBA). Electronic applications accepted.

Dwight Schar College of Education ***Degree program information:*** Part-time and evening/weekend programs available. Part-time, evening/weekend. Offers adapted physical education (M Ed); applied exercise science (M Ed); classroom instruction (M Ed); curriculum specialist (M Ed); education (M Ed, Ed D); educational leadership studies (Ed D); intervention specialist, mild/moderate (M Ed); intervention specialist, moderate/intensive (M Ed); literacy (M Ed); principalship (M Ed); pupil services (M Ed); sport education (M Ed); sport management (M Ed); talented and gifted (M Ed); teacher leader (M Ed); technology facilitator (M Ed).

ASHWORTH COLLEGE, Norcross, GA 30092

General Information Proprietary, coed, comprehensive institution.

GRADUATE UNITS

Graduate Programs Offers business administration (MBA); criminal justice (MS); health care administration (MBA, MS); human resource management (MBA, MS); international business (MBA); management (MS); marketing (MBA, MS).

ASPEN UNIVERSITY, Denver, CO 80246-1930

General Information Independent, coed, comprehensive institution. *Graduate housing:* On-campus housing not available.

GRADUATE UNITS

Program in Business Administration ***Degree program information:*** Part-time and evening/weekend programs available. Part-time, evening/weekend, online learning. Offers business administration (MBA); finance (MBA); information management (MBA); project management (MBA, Certificate). Electronic applications accepted.

Program in Information Technology ***Degree program information:*** Part-time and evening/weekend programs available. Part-time, evening/weekend, online learning. Offers information technology (MS, Certificate). Electronic applications accepted.

Programs in Information Management ***Degree program information:*** Part-time and evening/weekend programs available. Part-time, evening/weekend, online learning. Offers information management (MS); information systems (Certificate). Electronic applications accepted.

ASSEMBLIES OF GOD THEOLOGICAL SEMINARY, Springfield, MO 65802

General Information Independent-religious, coed, graduate-only institution. *Enrollment by degree level:* 109 master's, 214 doctoral. *Graduate faculty:* 6 full-time (1 woman), 22 part-time/adjunct (4 women). *Graduate housing:* On-campus housing not available. *Student services:* Campus safety program, career counseling, free psychological counseling, international student services, services for students with disabilities, writing training. *Library:* Cordas C. Burnett Library plus 2 others.

Computer facilities: 18 computers available on campus for general student use. A campuswide network can be accessed. Online class registration is available.
Website: http://www.agts.edu/

General Application Contact: Keena Morris, Admissions Coordinator, 417-268-1000, Fax: 417-268-1001, E-mail: morriske@evangel.edu.

GRADUATE UNITS

Graduate and Professional Programs Students: 63 full-time (21 women), 260 part-time (75 women); includes 54 minority (19 Black or African American, non-Hispanic/Latino; 5 American Indian or Alaska Native, non-Hispanic/Latino; 3 Asian, non-Hispanic/Latino; 17 Hispanic/Latino; 4 Native Hawaiian or other Pacific Islander, non-Hispanic/Latino; 6 Two or more races, non-Hispanic/Latino), 19 international. Average age 40. 95 applicants, 74% accepted, 47 enrolled. *Faculty:* 6 full-time (1 woman), 22 part-time/adjunct (4 women). *Financial support:* Career-related internships or fieldwork, Federal Work-Study, and scholarships/grants available. Support available to part-time students. Financial award application deadline: 7/15; financial award applicants required to submit FAFSA. In 2015, 56 master's, 21 doctorates awarded. *Degree program information:* Part-time and evening/weekend programs available. Part-time, evening/weekend, 100% online. Offers Biblical interpretation and theology (PhD); Christian ministries (MA); divinity (M Div); intercultural studies (MA, PhD); ministry (D Min); missiology (DAIS); pastoral studies (MPL); theological studies (MA, Th M). *Application deadline:* For fall admission, 7/1 priority date for domestic students, 6/1 priority date for international students; for spring admission, 12/1 priority date for domestic students, 11/1 priority date for international students. Applications are processed on a rolling basis. *Application fee:* $75. Electronic applications accepted. *Application Contact:* Keena Morris, Admissions Coordinator, 417-268-1000, Fax: 417-268-1001. *Dean*, James H. Railey, 417-268-1000, Fax: 417-268-1001.

ASSUMPTION COLLEGE, Worcester, MA 01609-1296

General Information Independent-religious, coed, comprehensive institution. *Enrollment:* 2,433 graduate, professional, and undergraduate students; 161 full-time matriculated graduate/professional students (112 women), 247 part-time matriculated graduate/professional students (161 women). *Enrollment by degree level:* 389 master's, 19 other advanced degrees. *Graduate faculty:* 17 full-time (7 women), 54 part-time/adjunct (18 women). *Tuition, area resident:* Full-time $11,250; part-time $625 per credit. *Required fees:* $70 per term. Full-time tuition and fees vary according to course load and program. *Graduate housing:* On-campus housing not available. *Student services:* Campus employment opportunities, campus safety program, career counseling, exercise/wellness program, international student services, low-cost health insurance, multicultural affairs office, services for students with disabilities. *Library:* Emmanuel d'Alzon Library. *Collection:* Books: 219,895 (physical), 8,579 (digital/electronic); Serial titles: 396 (physical), 318 (digital/electronic); Databases: 98. Weekly public service hours: 106; students can reserve study rooms.

Computer facilities: Computer purchase and lease plans are available. 361 computers available on campus for general student use. A campuswide network can be accessed from student residence rooms and from off campus. Online class registration is available.
Website: http://www.assumption.edu/

General Application Contact: Karen Stoyanoff, Director of Recruitment for Graduate Enrollment, 508-767-7442, Fax: 508-799-4412, E-mail: graduate@assumption.edu.

GRADUATE UNITS

Applied Behavior Analysis Program ***Financial support:*** Tuition waivers and institutional discounts available. Financial award application deadline: 6/1; financial award applicants required to submit FAFSA. *Degree program information:* Part-time and evening/weekend programs available. Part-time, evening/weekend. Offers applied behavior analysis (MA, CAGS). *Application deadline:* For fall admission, 6/1 for domestic and international students. *Application fee:* $30. Electronic applications accepted. *Application Contact:* Karen Stoyanoff, Director of Recruitment for Graduate Enrollment, 508-767-7442, Fax: 508-799-4412, E-mail: graduate@assumption.edu. *Director*, Dr. Karen Lionello-DeNolf, 508-767-7498, E-mail: k.lionellodenolf@assumption.edu.

Business Studies Program Students: 42 full-time (18 women), 119 part-time (55 women); includes 28 minority (10 Black or African American, non-Hispanic/Latino; 8 Asian, non-Hispanic/Latino; 8 Hispanic/Latino; 2 Two or more races, non-Hispanic/Latino), 2 international. Average age 30. 34 applicants, 50% accepted, 16 enrolled. *Faculty:* 5 full-time (2 women), 18 part-time/adjunct (5 women). *Financial support:* In 2015–16, 21 students received support. Tuition waivers (full and partial), unspecified assistantships, and institutional discounts available. Financial award application deadline: 5/1; financial award applicants required to submit FAFSA. In 2015, 80 master's, 1 other advanced degree awarded. *Degree program information:* Part-time and evening/weekend programs available. Part-time, evening/weekend. Offers accounting (MBA); business studies (CAGS); finance/economics (MBA); human resources (MBA); international business (MBA); management (MBA); marketing (MBA); nonprofit leadership (MBA). *Application deadline:* For fall admission, 5/1 for domestic and international students; for winter admission, 1/1 for domestic students, 2/1 for international students; for spring admission, 10/15 for domestic and international students; for summer admission, 3/1 for domestic and international students. Applications are processed on a rolling basis. *Application fee:* $30. Electronic applications accepted. *Application Contact:* Karen Stoyanoff, Director of Recruitment for Graduate Enrollment, 508-767-7442, Fax: 508-799-4412, E-mail: graduate@assumption.edu. *Director*, Eric Drouart, 508-767-7457, E-mail: edrouart@assumption.edu.

Clinical Counseling Program Students: 36 full-time (27 women), 23 part-time (22 women); includes 10 minority (2 Black or African American, non-Hispanic/Latino; 2 Asian, non-Hispanic/Latino; 4 Hispanic/Latino; 2 Two or more races, non-Hispanic/Latino), 1 international. Average age 27. 70 applicants, 59% accepted, 16 enrolled. *Faculty:* 5 full-time (2 women), 7 part-time/adjunct (3 women). *Financial support:* In 2015–16, 13 students received support, including 12 fellowships with full tuition reimbursements available; tuition waivers (full and partial), unspecified assistantships, and institutional discounts also available. Financial award application deadline: 3/7; financial award applicants required to submit FAFSA. In 2015, 34 master's, 1 other advanced degree awarded. *Degree program information:* Part-time and evening/weekend programs available. Part-time, evening/weekend. Offers child and family interventions (MA); cognitive-behavioral therapies (MA); counseling psychology (CAGS). *Application deadline:* For fall admission, 3/7 for domestic and international students; for winter admission, 2/1 for domestic and international students; for spring admission, 10/5 for domestic and international students; for summer admission, 2/8 for domestic and international students. *Application fee:* $30. Electronic applications accepted. *Application Contact:* Karen Stoyanoff, Director of Recruitment for Graduate Enrollment, 508-767-7442, Fax: 508-799-4412, E-mail: graduate@assumption.edu. *Director*, Dr. Leonard A. Doerfler, 508-767-7549, Fax: 508-767-7263, E-mail: doerfler@assumption.edu.

Health Advocacy Program Students: 7 part-time (all women). Average age 51. 9 applicants, 67% accepted, 4 enrolled. *Faculty:* 1 (woman) full-time, 4 part-time/adjunct (0 women). *Financial support:* In 2015–16, 1 student received support. Tuition waivers (full and partial) and institutional discounts available. Financial award applicants required to submit FAFSA. In 2015, 3 other advanced degrees awarded. *Degree program information:* Part-time and evening/weekend programs available. Part-time, evening/weekend, 100% online. Offers health advocacy (MA, Professional Certificate). *Application deadline:* For fall admission, 5/1 for domestic and international students; for spring admission, 10/15 for domestic and international students. Applications are processed on a rolling basis. *Application fee:* $30. Electronic applications accepted. *Application Contact:* Karen Stoyanoff, Director of Recruitment for Graduate Enrollment, 508-767-7442, Fax: 508-799-4412, E-mail: graduate@assumption.edu. *Director*, Lea Christo, 508-767-7503, E-mail: l.christo@assumption.edu.

Rehabilitation Counseling Program Students: 32 full-time (22 women), 38 part-time (27 women); includes 13 minority (9 Black or African American, non-Hispanic/Latino; 1 Asian, non-Hispanic/Latino; 2 Hispanic/Latino; 1 Two or more races, non-Hispanic/Latino). Average age 32. 38 applicants, 66% accepted, 19 enrolled. *Faculty:* 3 full-time (1 woman), 14 part-time/adjunct (3 women). *Financial support:* In 2015–16, 5 students received support. Scholarships/grants, tuition waivers (full and partial), unspecified assistantships, and institutional discounts available. Financial award application deadline: 3/29; financial award applicants required to submit FAFSA. In 2015, 32 master's, 2 other advanced degrees awarded. *Degree program information:* Part-time and evening/weekend programs available. Part-time, evening/weekend, blended/hybrid learning. Offers rehabilitation counseling (MA, CAGS). *Application deadline:* For fall admission, 5/1 for domestic and international students; for spring admission, 10/15 for domestic and international students; for summer admission, 3/1 for domestic and international students. Applications are processed on a rolling basis. *Application fee:* $30. Electronic applications accepted. *Application Contact:* Karen Stoyanoff, Director of Recruitment for Graduate Enrollment, 508-767-7442, Fax: 508-799-4915, E-mail: graduate@assumption.edu. *Director*, Dr. Nicholas Cioe, 508-767-7370, Fax: 508-798-2872, E-mail: nj.cioe@assumption.edu.

School Counseling Program Students: 39 full-time (35 women), 16 part-time (15 women); includes 6 minority (all Hispanic/Latino). Average age 26. 40 applicants, 75% accepted, 12 enrolled. *Faculty:* 2 full-time, 6 part-time/adjunct (3 women). *Financial support:* In 2015–16, 4 students received support. Tuition waivers (full and partial), unspecified assistantships, and institutional discounts available. Financial award application deadline: 5/1; financial award applicants required to submit FAFSA. In 2015, 26 master's, 8 other advanced degrees awarded. *Degree program information:* Part-time and evening/weekend programs available. Part-time, evening/weekend. Offers resiliency (CAGS); school counseling (MA, CAGS). *Application deadline:* For fall admission, 5/1 for domestic and international students; for spring admission, 10/15 for domestic and international students; for summer admission, 3/1 for domestic and international students. Applications are processed on a rolling basis. *Application fee:* $30. Electronic applications accepted. *Application Contact:* Karen Stoyanoff, Director of Recruitment for Graduate Enrollment, 508-767-7442, Fax: 508-799-4915, E-mail: graduate@assumption.edu. *Interim Director*, Dr. Evans Tsoules, 508-767-7089, Fax: 508-767-7263, E-mail: etsoules@assumption.edu.

Special Education Program Students: 6 full-time (5 women), 32 part-time (28 women); includes 1 minority (Hispanic/Latino). Average age 27. 20 applicants, 90% accepted, 11 enrolled. *Faculty:* 1 (woman) full-time, 5 part-time/adjunct (4 women). *Financial support:* In 2015–16, 2 students received support. Tuition waivers (full and partial), unspecified assistantships, and institutional discounts available. Financial award application deadline: 5/1; financial award applicants required to submit FAFSA. In 2015, 18 master's, 9 other advanced degrees awarded. *Degree program information:* Part-time and evening/weekend programs available. Part-time, evening/weekend. Offers positive behavior support (CAGS); special education (MA). *Application deadline:* For fall admission, 5/1 for domestic and international students; for spring admission, 10/15 for domestic and international students; for summer admission, 3/1 for domestic and international students. Applications are processed on a rolling basis. *Application fee:* $30. Electronic applications accepted. *Application Contact:* Karen Stoyanoff, Director of Recruitment for Graduate Enrollment, 508-767-7442, Fax: 508-799-4915, E-mail: graduate@assumption.edu. *Director*, Dr. Nanho Vander Hart, 508-767-7380, Fax: 508-767-7263, E-mail: nvanderh@assumption.edu.

ATHABASCA UNIVERSITY, Athabasca, AB T9S 3A3, Canada

General Information Province-supported, coed, comprehensive institution. *Enrollment:* 4,118 part-time matriculated graduate/professional students (2,948 women). *Enrollment by degree level:* 3,637 master's, 63 doctoral, 1,418 other advanced degrees. *Graduate faculty:* 184 full-time (83 women), 66 part-time/adjunct (40 women). *Required fees:* $5000 Canadian dollars. *Graduate housing:* On-campus housing not available. *Student services:* International student services, services for students with disabilities, writing training. *Library:* Athabasca University Library. *Research affiliation:* SAP (software), IBM (software).

Computer facilities: Computer purchase and lease plans are available. 28 computers available on campus for general student use. A campuswide network can be accessed from off campus. Online class registration is available.
Website: http://www.athabascau.ca/

General Application Contact: Information Contact, 800-788-9041, Fax: 780-675-6437.

GRADUATE UNITS

Centre for Distance Education Students: 394 part-time. Average age 36. *Faculty:* 11 full-time (4 women), 1 (woman) part-time/adjunct. In 2015, 56 master's, 4 doctorates, 13 other advanced degrees awarded. *Degree program information:* Part-time programs available. Part-time, online learning. Offers distance education (MDE, Ed D); distance education technology (Advanced Diploma). *Application deadline:* For fall admission, 3/1 for domestic and international students. *Application fee:* $80. Electronic applications accepted. *Application Contact:* Centre for Distance Education, 800-788-9041 Ext. 6179, Fax: 780-675-6170, E-mail: mde@athabascau.ca. *Chair*, Dr. Martha Clevelan-Innis, 800-788-9041 Ext. 6426, E-mail: martic@athabascau.ca.

Centre for Interdisciplinary Studies Students: 607 part-time. Average age 35. *Faculty:* 10 full-time (4 women), 12 part-time/adjunct (9 women). In 2015, 92 master's, 7 other advanced degrees awarded. *Degree program information:* Part-time and evening/weekend programs available. Part-time, evening/weekend, online learning. Offers adult education (MA); community studies (MA); cultural studies (MA); educational studies (MA); global change (MA); heritage resource management (Postbaccalaureate Certificate); legislative drafting (Postbaccalaureate Certificate); work, organization, and leadership (MA). *Application deadline:* For fall admission, 3/1 for domestic and international students; for winter admission, 9/1 for domestic and international students. *Application fee:* $80. Electronic applications accepted. *Program Director*, Dr. Wendell Kisner, 780-675-6792, Fax: 780-675-6921, E-mail: wendell@athabascau.ca.

Faculty of Business Students: 819 part-time. Average age 36. *Faculty:* 9 full-time (6 women), 2 part-time/adjunct (0 women). *Financial support:* Scholarships/grants available. In 2015, 177 master's, 4 doctorates, 175 other advanced degrees awarded. *Degree program information:* Part-time and evening/weekend programs available. Part-time, evening/weekend, online learning. Offers business administration (MBA);

information technology management (MBA); innovative management (DBA); management (GDM); project management (MBA, GDM). *Application deadline:* For fall admission, 6/15 for domestic and international students; for winter admission, 10/15 for domestic and international students; for spring admission, 2/15 for domestic and international students. Applications are processed on a rolling basis. *Application fee:* $200. Electronic applications accepted. *Application Contact:* Shannon Oscroft, Receptionist and Customer Service Representative, 780-459-1144, E-mail: shannono@athabascau.ca. *Dean,* Dr. Deborah Hurst, 780-509-7566, E-mail: fbdean@fb.athabascau.ca.

Faculty of Health Disciplines Students: 1,687 part-time. Average age 38. *Faculty:* 11 full-time (all women), 1 (woman) part-time/adjunct. In 2015, 243 master's, 5 other advanced degrees awarded. *Degree program information:* Part-time programs available. Part-time, online learning. Offers advanced nursing practice (MN, Advanced Diploma); generalist (MN); health studies (MHS). *Application deadline:* For fall admission, 3/1 for domestic and international students. *Application fee:* $80. Electronic applications accepted. *Application Contact:* Donna Dunn Hart, Academic Student Advisor, Graduate Programs, 800-788-9041 Ext. 6300, Fax: 780-675-6468, E-mail: donnad@athabascau.ca. *Dean,* Dr. Margaret Edwards, 800-788-9041 Ext. 6381, Fax: 780-675-6468, E-mail: marge@athabascau.ca.

Faculty of Science and Technology Students: 233 part-time. Average age 36. *Faculty:* 11 full-time (1 woman), 2 part-time/adjunct (0 women). In 2015, 23 master's, 1 other advanced degree awarded. *Degree program information:* Part-time programs available. Part-time, online learning. Offers architecture (Postgraduate Diploma); information systems (M Sc). *Application deadline:* For fall admission, 3/1 for domestic students, 2/1 for international students. *Application fee:* $80. Electronic applications accepted. *Application Contact:* Karie Chambers, Student Support and Program Advisor, 780-675-6789, Fax: 780-675-6148, E-mail: karie-lynnc@athabascau.ca. *Dean,* Dr. Lisa Carter, 780-675-6281, E-mail: lisac@athabascau.ca.

Program in Counseling Students: 352 part-time. Average age 35. *Faculty:* 5 full-time (2 women). In 2015, 70 master's, 1 Advanced Certificate awarded. Offers applied psychology (Post Master's Certificate); art therapy (MC); career counseling (MC); counseling (Advanced Certificate); counseling psychology (MC); school counseling (MC). *Application deadline:* For fall admission, 3/1 for domestic and international students. *Application fee:* $80. *Application Contact:* Information Contact, 800-788-9041, Fax: 780-675-6437. *Chair,* Dr. Paul Jerry, 866-313-4373, E-mail: paulj@athabascau.ca.

THE ATHENAEUM OF OHIO, Cincinnati, OH 45230-5900

General Information Independent-religious, coed, graduate-only institution. *Graduate housing:* On-campus housing not available. *Library:* Eugene H. Maly Memorial Library.

Computer facilities: 3 computers available on campus for general student use. Website: http://www.mtsm.org/

General Application Contact: Nicholas Jobe, Registrar, 513-231-2223, Fax: 513-231-3254, E-mail: njobe@athenaeum.edu.

GRADUATE UNITS

Graduate Programs ***Financial support:*** Scholarships/grants available. Support available to part-time students. Financial award application deadline: 8/1. *Degree program information:* Part-time and evening/weekend programs available. Part-time, evening/weekend. Offers biblical studies (MABS); divinity (M Div); lay ministry (Certificate); pastoral ministry (MA); theology (MA Th). *Application deadline:* For fall admission, 4/15 priority date for domestic students; for winter admission, 11/1 priority date for domestic students. *Application fee:* $30. *Application Contact:* Nicholas Jobe, Registrar, 513-231-2223, Fax: 513-231-3254, E-mail: njobe@athenaeum.edu. *Dean,* Fr. David J. Endres, 513-231-2223, Fax: 513-231-3254, E-mail: dendres@athenaeum.edu.

ATLANTA'S JOHN MARSHALL LAW SCHOOL, Atlanta, GA 30309

General Information Private, coed, graduate-only institution.

GRADUATE UNITS

JD and LL M Programs ***Degree program information:*** Part-time and evening/weekend programs available. Part-time, evening/weekend, online learning. Offers American legal studies (LL M); employment law (LL M); law (JD). Electronic applications accepted.

ATLANTIC INSTITUTE OF ORIENTAL MEDICINE, Fort Lauderdale, FL 33301

General Information Independent, coed, graduate-only institution. *Enrollment by degree level:* 123 master's, 19 doctoral. *Graduate faculty:* 7 full-time (1 woman), 15 part-time/adjunct (6 women). *Tuition, area resident:* Full-time $17,000. *Required fees:* $250. One-time fee: $450 full-time. *Student services:* Campus employment opportunities, campus safety program, career counseling, exercise/wellness program, international student services. *Collection:* Books: 3,100 (physical). Weekly public service hours: 50.

Computer facilities: 4 computers available on campus for general student use. A campuswide network can be accessed. Online class registration is available. Website: http://www.atom.edu/

General Application Contact: Karen Gemignani, Admissions Counselor, 954-763-9840 Ext. 213, Fax: 954-763-9844, E-mail: admissions@atom.edu.

GRADUATE UNITS

Graduate Program Students: 142 full-time (109 women); includes 23 minority (3 Black or African American, non-Hispanic/Latino; 7 Asian, non-Hispanic/Latino; 13 Hispanic/Latino), 7 international. *Faculty:* 7 full-time (1 woman), 15 part-time/adjunct (6 women). *Degree program information:* Evening/weekend programs available. Evening/weekend. Offers Oriental medicine (MS, DAOM). *Application deadline:* For fall admission, 7/1 for domestic students, 5/1 for international students; for spring admission, 11/30 for domestic students, 2/28 for international students. Applications are processed on a rolling basis. *Application fee:* $20 ($30 for international students). *Application Contact:* Milagros Ferreira, Registrar, 954-763-9840 Ext. 207, Fax: 954-763-9844, E-mail: registrar@atom.edu. *President,* Dr. Johanna C. Yen, 954-763-9840 Ext. 202, Fax: 954-763-9844, E-mail: president@atom.edu.

ATLANTIC SCHOOL OF THEOLOGY, Halifax, NS B3H 3B5, Canada

General Information Independent, coed, graduate-only institution. *Graduate housing:* Rooms and/or apartments available on a first-come, first-served basis to single and married students. Housing application deadline: 6/1.

GRADUATE UNITS

Graduate and Professional Programs ***Degree program information:*** Part-time programs available. Part-time, online learning. Offers ministry (M Div); theological studies (Graduate Certificate).

ATLANTIC UNIVERSITY, Virginia Beach, VA 23451-2061

General Information Independent, coed, primarily women, graduate-only institution. *Graduate housing:* On-campus housing not available.

GRADUATE UNITS

Program in Integrated Imagery - Regression Hypnosis Offers integrated imagery - regression hypnosis (Graduate Certificate).

Program in Leadership Studies Online learning. Offers global leadership (MA); mindful leadership (MA); organizational leadership (MA).

Program in Transpersonal Studies ***Degree program information:*** Part-time and evening/weekend programs available. Part-time, evening/weekend, online learning. Offers transpersonal studies (MA). Electronic applications accepted.

Spiritual Guidance Mentor Program Offers spiritual guidance mentor (Certificate).

ATLANTIC UNIVERSITY COLLEGE, Guaynabo, PR 00970

General Information Independent, coed, comprehensive institution.

GRADUATE UNITS

Program in Graphic Arts ***Degree program information:*** Part-time programs available. Part-time. Offers digital graphic design (MGD).

A.T. STILL UNIVERSITY, Kirksville, MO 63501

General Information Independent, coed, graduate-only institution. *Enrollment by degree level:* 619 master's, 2,505 doctoral, 102 other advanced degrees. *Graduate faculty:* 231 full-time (107 women), 509 part-time/adjunct (244 women). *Graduate housing:* Rooms and/or apartments available on a first-come, first-served basis to single and married students. Typical cost: $425 per year for single students; $425 per year for married students. Room charges vary according to campus/location and housing facility selected. Housing application deadline: 3/1. *Student services:* Campus employment opportunities, campus safety program, career counseling, exercise/wellness program, free psychological counseling, multicultural affairs office, services for students with disabilities. *Library:* A.T. Still Memorial Library plus 1 other. *Research affiliation:* Truman State University (osteopathic clinical research), The University of Arizona-College of Medicine-Phoenix (osteopathic and biomedical clinical research), Pennsylvania State University (exercise pressor reflex), Banner Heart Hospital (education and readmissions), Zimmer DeNovo (orthopedic clinical trials), Nordic Academy of Osteopathy (osteopathic clinical research).

Computer facilities: 45 computers available on campus for general student use. A campuswide network can be accessed from student residence rooms. Website: http://www.atsu.edu/

General Application Contact: Donna Sparks, Associate Director for Admissions, 660-626-2237, Fax: 660-626-2969, E-mail: admissions@atsu.edu.

GRADUATE UNITS

Arizona School of Dentistry and Oral Health Students: 316 full-time (152 women), 2 part-time (both women); includes 117 minority (8 Black or African American, non-Hispanic/Latino; 3 American Indian or Alaska Native, non-Hispanic/Latino; 73 Asian, non-Hispanic/Latino; 23 Hispanic/Latino; 2 Native Hawaiian or other Pacific Islander, non-Hispanic/Latino; 8 Two or more races, non-Hispanic/Latino), 3 international. Average age 28. 2,696 applicants, 5% accepted, 76 enrolled. *Faculty:* 58 full-time (29 women), 132 part-time/adjunct (88 women). *Financial support:* In 2015–16, 30 students received support. Federal Work-Study and scholarships/grants available. Financial award application deadline: 5/1; financial award applicants required to submit FAFSA. In 2015, 69 doctorates, 5 Certificates awarded. Offers dental medicine (DMD); orthodontics (Certificate). *Application deadline:* For fall admission, 11/15 for domestic and international students; for summer admission, 11/15 for domestic and international students. Applications are processed on a rolling basis. *Application fee:* $70. Electronic applications accepted. *Application Contact:* Donna Sparks, Associate Director, Admissions Processing, 660-626-2117, Fax: 660-626-2969, E-mail: admissions@atsu.edu. *Dean,* Dr. Jack Dillenberg, 480-219-6000, Fax: 480-219-6110, E-mail: jdillenberg@atsu.edu.

Arizona School of Health Sciences Students: 509 full-time (339 women), 397 part-time (310 women); includes 203 minority (41 Black or African American, non-Hispanic/Latino; 5 American Indian or Alaska Native, non-Hispanic/Latino; 83 Asian, non-Hispanic/Latino; 57 Hispanic/Latino; 2 Native Hawaiian or other Pacific Islander, non-Hispanic/Latino; 15 Two or more races, non-Hispanic/Latino), 60 international. Average age 33. 3,902 applicants, 10% accepted, 245 enrolled. *Faculty:* 54 full-time (31 women), 188 part-time/adjunct (132 women). *Financial support:* In 2015–16, 158 students received support. Federal Work-Study and scholarships/grants available. Financial award application deadline: 5/1; financial award applicants required to submit FAFSA. In 2015, 178 master's, 271 doctorates awarded. *Degree program information:* Part-time and evening/weekend programs available. Part-time, evening/weekend, 100% online. Offers advanced occupational therapy (MS); advanced physician assistant studies (MS); athletic training (MS, DAT); audiology (Au D); occupational therapy (OTD); physical therapy (DPT); physician assistant studies (MS); transitional audiology (Au D); transitional physical therapy (DPT). *Application deadline:* Applications are processed on a rolling basis. *Application fee:* $70. Electronic applications accepted. *Application Contact:* Donna Sparks, Associate Director, Admissions Processing, 660-626-2117, Fax: 660-626-2969, E-mail: admissions@atsu.edu. *Dean,* Dr. Randy Danielsen, 480-219-6000, Fax: 480-219-6110, E-mail: rdanielsen@atsu.edu.

College of Graduate Health Studies Students: 456 full-time (271 women), 391 part-time (232 women); includes 291 minority (126 Black or African American, non-Hispanic/Latino; 7 American Indian or Alaska Native, non-Hispanic/Latino; 71 Asian, non-Hispanic/Latino; 80 Hispanic/Latino; 4 Native Hawaiian or other Pacific Islander, non-Hispanic/Latino; 3 Two or more races, non-Hispanic/Latino), 21 international. Average age 37. 286 applicants, 99% accepted, 221 enrolled. *Faculty:* 29 full-time (18 women), 89 part-time/adjunct (46 women). *Financial support:* In 2015–16, 30 students received support. Scholarships/grants available. Financial award application deadline: 5/1; financial award applicants required to submit FAFSA. In 2015, 130 master's, 74 doctorates awarded. *Degree program information:* Part-time and evening/weekend programs available. Part-time, evening/weekend, 100% online, blended/hybrid learning. Offers dental public health (MPH); health administration (MHA, DHA); health education (DH Ed); health sciences (DH Sc); kinesiology (MS); public health (MPH); school health education (MS). *Application deadline:* For fall admission, 5/16 for domestic and international students; for winter admission, 8/1 for domestic and international students; for spring admission, 11/7 for domestic and international students; for summer admission, 1/23 for domestic and international students. Applications are processed on a rolling basis. *Application fee:* $70. Electronic applications accepted. *Application Contact:* Amie Waldemer, Associate Director, Online Admissions, 480-219-6146, E-mail: awaldemer@atsu.edu. *Interim Dean,* Dr. Donald Altman, 660-626-2820, Fax: 660-626-2826, E-mail: daltman@atsu.edu.

Kirksville College of Osteopathic Medicine Students: 724 full-time (302 women), 7 part-time (1 woman); includes 129 minority (18 Black or African American, non-Hispanic/Latino; 2 American Indian or Alaska Native, non-Hispanic/Latino; 49 Asian, non-Hispanic/Latino; 31 Hispanic/Latino; 29 Two or more races, non-Hispanic/Latino), 3 international. Average age 26. 5,061 applicants, 8% accepted, 188 enrolled. *Faculty:* 40 full-time (7 women), 32 part-time/adjunct (4 women). *Financial support:* In 2015–16, 243 students received support, including 25 fellowships with full tuition reimbursements available (averaging $52,320 per year); Federal Work-Study and scholarships/grants also available. Financial award application deadline: 5/1; financial award applicants required to submit FAFSA. In 2015, 12 master's, 156 doctorates awarded. Offers biomedical sciences (MS); osteopathic medicine (DO). *Application deadline:* For fall admission, 2/1 for domestic students; for summer admission, 2/1 for domestic students. Applications are processed on a rolling basis. *Application fee:* $70. Electronic applications accepted. *Application Contact:* Donna Sparks, Associate Director, Admissions Processing, 660-626-2117, Fax: 660-626-2969, E-mail: admissions@atsu.edu. *Dean*, Dr. Margaret Wilson, 660-626-2354, Fax: 660-626-2080, E-mail: mwilson@atsu.edu.

Missouri School of Dentistry and Oral Health Students: 126 full-time (75 women); includes 32 minority (1 Black or African American, non-Hispanic/Latino; 1 American Indian or Alaska Native, non-Hispanic/Latino; 21 Asian, non-Hispanic/Latino; 7 Hispanic/Latino; 2 Two or more races, non-Hispanic/Latino). Average age 26. 1,269 applicants, 8% accepted, 42 enrolled. *Faculty:* 11 full-time (4 women), 34 part-time/adjunct (8 women). *Financial support:* In 2015–16, 19 students received support. Federal Work-Study and scholarships/grants available. Financial award application deadline: 5/1; financial award applicants required to submit FAFSA. Offers dental medicine (DMD). *Application deadline:* For fall admission, 12/1 for domestic students; for summer admission, 12/1 for domestic students. Applications are processed on a rolling basis. *Application fee:* $70. Electronic applications accepted. *Application Contact:* Donna Sparks, Associate Director for Admissions, 660-626-2237, Fax: 660-626-2969, E-mail: admissions@atsu.edu. *Dean*, Dr. Christopher G. Halliday, 660-626-2800.

School of Osteopathic Medicine in Arizona Students: 428 full-time (211 women), 1 (woman) part-time; includes 204 minority (6 Black or African American, non-Hispanic/Latino; 1 American Indian or Alaska Native, non-Hispanic/Latino; 138 Asian, non-Hispanic/Latino; 34 Hispanic/Latino; 25 Two or more races, non-Hispanic/Latino). Average age 27. 5,978 applicants, 4% accepted, 108 enrolled. *Faculty:* 39 full-time (18 women), 34 part-time/adjunct (10 women). *Financial support:* In 2015–16, 30 students received support, including 2 fellowships (averaging $48,600 per year); Federal Work-Study and scholarships/grants also available. Financial award application deadline: 5/1; financial award applicants required to submit FAFSA. In 2015, 104 doctorates awarded. Offers osteopathic medicine (DO). *Application deadline:* For fall admission, 3/1 for domestic students; for summer admission, 3/1 for domestic students. Applications are processed on a rolling basis. *Application fee:* $70. Electronic applications accepted. *Application Contact:* Donna Sparks, Associate Director for Admissions, 660-626-2117, Fax: 660-626-2969, E-mail: admissions@atsu.edu. *Dean*, Dr. Kay Kalousek, 480-219-6000, Fax: 480-219-6110, E-mail: kkalousek@atsu.edu.

AUBURN UNIVERSITY, Auburn University, AL 36849

General Information State-supported, coed, university. CGS member. *Enrollment:* 27,287 graduate, professional, and undergraduate students; 3,175 full-time matriculated graduate/professional students (1,814 women), 2,216 part-time matriculated graduate/professional students (1,012 women). *Enrollment by degree level:* 2,516 master's, 2,730 doctoral, 140 other advanced degrees. *Graduate faculty:* 1,145 full-time (431 women), 144 part-time/adjunct (64 women). Tuition, state resident: full-time $8802; part-time $489 per credit hour. Tuition, nonresident: full-time $26,406; part-time $1467 per credit hour. *Required fees:* $808 per semester. Tuition and fees vary according to degree level and program. *Graduate housing:* Rooms and/or apartments available on a first-come, first-served basis to single and married students. Typical cost: $12,584 (including board) for married students. *Student services:* Campus employment opportunities, campus safety program, career counseling, exercise/wellness program, free psychological counseling, international student services, low-cost health insurance, multicultural affairs office, services for students with disabilities, teacher training, writing training. *Library:* R. B. Draughon Library plus 3 others. *Collection:* Books: 4.7 million (physical), 964,981 (digital/electronic); Serial titles: 60,607 (physical), 81,832 (digital/electronic); Databases: 239. Study areas open 24 hours, 5–7 days a week. *Research affiliation:* National Center of Excellence for Airliner Cabin Environmental Research (aerospace, polymer and fibers engineering), National Textile Center Consortium (polymer and fibers engineering), National Asphalt Pavement Association (asphalt technology, civil engineering), Consortium for Vehicle Electronics (mechanical and automotive engineering, electrical engineering), Tay-Sachs Gene Therapy Consortium (veterinary medicine, clinical sciences), Higher Education Consortium for Special Education (special and rehabilitative education).

Computer facilities: Computer purchase and lease plans are available. 1,722 computers available on campus for general student use. A campuswide network can be accessed from student residence rooms and from off campus. Online class registration, Bursar payments online, course materials are available.
Website: http://www.auburn.edu/

General Application Contact: Dr. George Flowers, Dean of the Graduate School, 334-844-2125, E-mail: flowegt@auburn.edu.

GRADUATE UNITS

College of Veterinary Medicine Students: 501 full-time (390 women), 87 part-time (60 women); includes 49 minority (9 Black or African American, non-Hispanic/Latino; 3 American Indian or Alaska Native, non-Hispanic/Latino; 9 Asian, non-Hispanic/Latino; 19 Hispanic/Latino; 9 Two or more races, non-Hispanic/Latino), 23 international. Average age 26. 1,197 applicants, 19% accepted, 134 enrolled. *Faculty:* 97 full-time (40 women), 4 part-time/adjunct (2 women). *Financial support:* Fellowships, research assistantships, teaching assistantships, and Federal Work-Study available. Support available to part-time students. Financial award application deadline: 3/15; financial award applicants required to submit FAFSA. In 2015, 12 master's, 119 doctorates awarded. *Degree program information:* Part-time programs available. Part-time. Offers biomedical sciences (MS, PhD); veterinary medicine (MS, DVM, PhD). *Application deadline:* Applications are processed on a rolling basis. *Application fee:* $50 ($60 for international students). *Application Contact:* Dr. George Flowers, Interim Dean of the Graduate School, 334-844-4700. *Acting Dean*, Dr. Calvin Johnson, 334-844-2650.

Graduate School Students: 3,175 full-time (1,814 women), 2,216 part-time (1,012 women); includes 798 minority (441 Black or African American, non-Hispanic/Latino; 26 American Indian or Alaska Native, non-Hispanic/Latino; 129 Asian, non-Hispanic/Latino; 131 Hispanic/Latino; 4 Native Hawaiian or other Pacific Islander, non-Hispanic/Latino; 67 Two or more races, non-Hispanic/Latino), 1,055 international. Average age 29. 6,372 applicants, 47% accepted, 1841 enrolled. *Faculty:* 1,145 full-time (431 women), 144 part-time/adjunct (64 women). *Financial support:* Fellowships, research assistantships, teaching assistantships, career-related internships or fieldwork, and Federal Work-Study available. Support available to part-time students. Financial award applicants required to submit FAFSA. In 2015, 1,107 master's, 519 doctorates, 155 other advanced degrees awarded. *Degree program information:* Part-time and evening/weekend programs available. Part-time, evening/weekend. Offers applied economics (PhD); cell and molecular biology (PhD); real estate development (MRED); rural sociology (MS); sociology (MA, MS); sociology and rural sociology (MA, MS). *Application fee:* $50 ($60 for international students). *Dean*, Dr. George Flowers, 334-844-4700, E-mail: gradadm@auburn.edu.

College of Agriculture Students: 142 full-time (68 women), 132 part-time (50 women); includes 17 minority (6 Black or African American, non-Hispanic/Latino; 2 American Indian or Alaska Native, non-Hispanic/Latino; 2 Asian, non-Hispanic/Latino; 5 Hispanic/Latino; 2 Two or more races, non-Hispanic/Latino), 114 international. Average age 28. 175 applicants, 52% accepted, 78 enrolled. *Faculty:* 120 full-time (34 women), 13 part-time/adjunct (1 woman). *Financial support:* Fellowships, research assistantships, teaching assistantships, and Federal Work-Study available. Support available to part-time students. Financial award application deadline: 3/15; financial award applicants required to submit FAFSA. In 2015, 51 master's, 19 doctorates awarded. *Degree program information:* Part-time programs available. Part-time. Offers agricultural economics (M Ag, MS); agriculture (M Ag, M Aq, MS, PhD); agronomy and soils (M Ag, MS, PhD); animal sciences (M Ag, MS, PhD); entomology (M Ag, MS, PhD); fisheries and allied aquacultures (M Aq, MS, PhD); horticulture (M Ag, MS, PhD); plant pathology (M Ag, MS, PhD); poultry science (M Ag, MS, PhD). *Application deadline:* Applications are processed on a rolling basis. *Application fee:* $50 ($60 for international students). Electronic applications accepted. *Application Contact:* Dr. George Flowers, Dean of the Graduate School, 334-844-2125. *Dean*, William Batchelor, 334-844-2345.

College of Architecture, Design, and Construction Students: 82 full-time (39 women), 71 part-time (26 women); includes 31 minority (16 Black or African American, non-Hispanic/Latino; 4 Asian, non-Hispanic/Latino; 9 Hispanic/Latino; 1 Native Hawaiian or other Pacific Islander, non-Hispanic/Latino; 1 Two or more races, non-Hispanic/Latino), 40 international. Average age 30. 222 applicants, 72% accepted, 64 enrolled. *Faculty:* 56 full-time (13 women), 13 part-time/adjunct (5 women). *Financial support:* Fellowships and Federal Work-Study available. Support available to part-time students. Financial award application deadline: 3/15; financial award applicants required to submit FAFSA. In 2015, 56 master's awarded. *Degree program information:* Part-time programs available. Part-time. Offers architecture, design, and construction (MBC, MCP, MID, MIDC, ML Arch); building construction (MBC); community planning (MCP); construction management (MBC); industrial design (MID); integrated design and construction (MIDC); landscape architecture (ML Arch). *Application deadline:* Applications are processed on a rolling basis. *Application fee:* $50 ($60 for international students). Electronic applications accepted. *Application Contact:* Dr. George Flowers, Dean of the Graduate School, 334-844-2125. *Dean*, Dr. Vini Nathan, 334-844-4285.

College of Business Students: 174 full-time (84 women), 537 part-time (152 women); includes 113 minority (57 Black or African American, non-Hispanic/Latino; 3 American Indian or Alaska Native, non-Hispanic/Latino; 27 Asian, non-Hispanic/Latino; 18 Hispanic/Latino; 8 Two or more races, non-Hispanic/Latino), 48 international. Average age 33. 782 applicants, 58% accepted, 326 enrolled. *Faculty:* 77 full-time (22 women), 22 part-time/adjunct (8 women). *Financial support:* Fellowships, research assistantships, teaching assistantships, career-related internships or fieldwork, and Federal Work-Study available. Support available to part-time students. Financial award application deadline: 3/15; financial award applicants required to submit FAFSA. In 2015, 265 master's, 9 doctorates awarded. *Degree program information:* Part-time programs available. Part-time. Offers accountancy (M Acc); business (M Acc, MBA, MRED, MS, PhD); business administration (MBA); finance (MS); human resource management (PhD); management (MS, PhD); management information systems (MS, PhD). *Application deadline:* Applications are processed on a rolling basis. *Application fee:* $50 ($60 for international students). Electronic applications accepted. *Application Contact:* Dr. George Flowers, Dean of the Graduate School, 334-844-2125. *Dean*, Dr. Bill Hardgrave, 334-844-4832, E-mail: bch0014@auburn.edu.

College of Education Students: 465 full-time (310 women), 531 part-time (356 women); includes 252 minority (194 Black or African American, non-Hispanic/Latino; 3 American Indian or Alaska Native, non-Hispanic/Latino; 6 Asian, non-Hispanic/Latino; 32 Hispanic/Latino; 1 Native Hawaiian or other Pacific Islander, non-Hispanic/Latino; 16 Two or more races, non-Hispanic/Latino), 32 international. Average age 33. 765 applicants, 58% accepted, 292 enrolled. *Faculty:* 97 full-time (64 women), 16 part-time/adjunct (14 women). *Financial support:* Fellowships, research assistantships, teaching assistantships, career-related internships or fieldwork, and Federal Work-Study available. Support available to part-time students. Financial award application deadline: 3/15; financial award applicants required to submit FAFSA. In 2015, 241 master's, 61 doctorates, 66 other advanced degrees awarded. *Degree program information:* Part-time programs available. Part-time. Offers adult education (M Ed, MS, PhD, Ed S); business education (M Ed, MS, PhD); collaborative teacher special education (M Ed, MS); curriculum supervision (M Ed, PhD); early childhood education (M Ed, MS, PhD, Ed S); early childhood special education (M Ed, MS); education (M Ed, MS, Ed D, PhD, Ed S, Graduate Certificate); educational psychology (PhD); elementary education (M Ed, MS, PhD, Ed S); exercise science (M Ed, MS, PhD); foreign languages (M Ed, MS); health promotion (M Ed, MS); higher education administration (M Ed, PhD); kinesiology (PhD); library media (M Ed, Ed S); music education (M Ed, MS, PhD, Ed S); physical education/teacher education (M Ed, MS, Ed D, Ed S); postsecondary education (PhD); reading education (PhD, Ed S); rehabilitation counseling (M Ed, MS, PhD); school administration (M Ed, PhD, Ed S); secondary education (M Ed, MS, PhD, Ed S). *Application fee:* $50 ($60 for international students). Electronic applications accepted. *Application Contact:* Dr. George Flowers, Dean of the Graduate School, 334-844-2125. *Dean*, Dr. Betty Lou Whitford, 334-844-4446.

College of Human Sciences Students: 81 full-time (66 women), 55 part-time (40 women); includes 25 minority (12 Black or African American, non-Hispanic/Latino; 1 American Indian or Alaska Native, non-Hispanic/Latino; 4 Asian, non-Hispanic/Latino; 5 Hispanic/Latino; 3 Two or more races, non-Hispanic/Latino), 34 international. Average age 29. 138 applicants, 54% accepted, 51 enrolled. *Faculty:* 49 full-time (32 women), 1 (woman) part-time/adjunct. *Financial support:* Fellowships, research assistantships, teaching assistantships, career-related internships or fieldwork, and Federal Work-Study available. Support available to part-time students. Financial award application deadline: 3/15; financial award applicants required to submit FAFSA. In 2015, 19 master's, 11 doctorates awarded. *Degree program information:* Part-time programs available. Part-time. Offers apparel and textiles (MS); global hospitality and retailing (Graduate Certificate); human development and family studies

(MS, PhD); human sciences (MS, PhD, Graduate Certificate); integrated textile and apparel science (PhD); nutrition (MS, PhD). *Application deadline:* Applications are processed on a rolling basis. *Application fee:* $50 ($60 for international students). Electronic applications accepted. *Application Contact:* Dr. George Flowers, Dean of the Graduate School, 334-844-2125. *Dean*, Dr. June Henton, 334-844-3790, E-mail: jhenton@humsci.auburn.edu.

College of Liberal Arts Students: 256 full-time (187 women), 162 part-time (86 women); includes 55 minority (32 Black or African American, non-Hispanic/Latino; 3 American Indian or Alaska Native, non-Hispanic/Latino; 4 Asian, non-Hispanic/Latino; 10 Hispanic/Latino; 6 Two or more races, non-Hispanic/Latino), 36 international. Average age 29. 872 applicants, 25% accepted, 127 enrolled. *Faculty:* 294 full-time (143 women), 70 part-time/adjunct (33 women). *Financial support:* Fellowships, research assistantships, teaching assistantships, career-related internships or fieldwork, and Federal Work-Study available. Support available to part-time students. Financial award application deadline: 3/15; financial award applicants required to submit FAFSA. In 2015, 108 master's, 50 doctorates, 6 other advanced degrees awarded. *Degree program information:* Part-time programs available. Part-time. Offers applied behavior analysis in developmental disabilities (MS); audiology (MCD, MS, Au D); clinical psychology (PhD); communication (MA); communication studies (Graduate Certificate); economics (MS); English (MA, PhD); experimental psychology (PhD); history (MA, PhD, Graduate Certificate); industrial/organizational psychology (PhD); liberal arts (MA, MCD, MHS, MPA, MS, MTPC, Au D, PhD, Graduate Certificate); mass communications (MA); public administration (MPA, PhD, Graduate Certificate); Spanish (MHS); speech pathology (MCD, MS); technical communication (MTPC). *Application deadline:* Applications are processed on a rolling basis. *Application fee:* $50 ($60 for international students). Electronic applications accepted. *Application Contact:* Dr. George Flowers, Dean of the Graduate School, 334-844-2125. *Dean*, Dr. Joe Aistrup, 334-844-2183.

College of Sciences and Mathematics Students: 215 full-time (84 women), 150 part-time (58 women); includes 38 minority (12 Black or African American, non-Hispanic/Latino; 1 American Indian or Alaska Native, non-Hispanic/Latino; 14 Asian, non-Hispanic/Latino; 6 Hispanic/Latino; 5 Two or more races, non-Hispanic/Latino), 140 international. Average age 28. 303 applicants, 47% accepted, 80 enrolled. *Faculty:* 163 full-time (34 women), 18 part-time/adjunct (3 women). *Financial support:* Fellowships, research assistantships, teaching assistantships, career-related internships or fieldwork, and Federal Work-Study available. Support available to part-time students. Financial award applicants required to submit FAFSA. In 2015, 63 master's, 25 doctorates awarded. *Degree program information:* Part-time programs available. Part-time. Offers analytical chemistry (MS, PhD); applied mathematics (MAM, MS); biochemistry (MS, PhD); botany (MS); geography (MS); geology (MS); inorganic chemistry (MS, PhD); mathematics (MS, PhD); organic chemistry (MS, PhD); physical chemistry (MS, PhD); physics (MS, PhD); probability and statistics (M Prob S); sciences and mathematics (M Prob S, MAM, MS, PhD); statistics (MS); zoology (MS). *Application deadline:* Applications are processed on a rolling basis. *Application fee:* $50 ($60 for international students). *Application Contact:* Dr. George Flowers, Dean of the Graduate School, 334-844-2125. *Interim Dean*, Nicholas Giordano, 334-844-5737.

Ginn College of Engineering Students: 552 full-time (128 women), 299 part-time (54 women); includes 58 minority (22 Black or African American, non-Hispanic/Latino; 2 American Indian or Alaska Native, non-Hispanic/Latino; 15 Asian, non-Hispanic/Latino; 16 Hispanic/Latino; 3 Two or more races, non-Hispanic/Latino), 500 international. Average age 27. 1,323 applicants, 44% accepted, 167 enrolled. *Faculty:* 149 full-time (12 women), 12 part-time/adjunct (2 women). *Financial support:* Fellowships, research assistantships, teaching assistantships, and Federal Work-Study available. Support available to part-time students. Financial award application deadline: 3/15; financial award applicants required to submit FAFSA. In 2015, 228 master's, 73 doctorates, 24 other advanced degrees awarded. *Degree program information:* Part-time programs available. Part-time. Offers aerospace engineering (MAE, MS, PhD); biosystems engineering (MS, PhD); chemical engineering (M Ch E, MS, PhD); computer science and software engineering (MS, MSWE, PhD); construction engineering and management (MCE, MS, PhD); electrical and computer engineering (MEE, MS, PhD); engineering (M Ch E, M Mtl E, MAE, MCE, MEE, MISE, MME, MS, MSWE, PhD, Graduate Certificate); environmental engineering (MCE, MS, PhD); geotechnical/materials engineering (MCE, MS, PhD); hydraulics/hydrology (MCE, MS, PhD); industrial and systems engineering (MISE, MS, PhD, Graduate Certificate); materials engineering (M Mtl E, MS, PhD); mechanical engineering (MME, MS, PhD); polymer and fiber engineering (MS, PhD); structural engineering (MCE, MS, PhD); transportation engineering (MCE, MS, PhD). *Application deadline:* Applications are processed on a rolling basis. *Application fee:* $50 ($60 for international students). Electronic applications accepted. *Application Contact:* Dr. George Flowers, Dean of the Graduate School, 334-844-2125. *Dean*, Dr. Chris Roberts, 334-844-2308.

School of Forestry and Wildlife Sciences Students: 36 full-time (15 women), 30 part-time (11 women); includes 2 minority (both Black or African American, non-Hispanic/Latino), 26 international. Average age 28. 27 applicants, 52% accepted, 11 enrolled. *Faculty:* 30 full-time (7 women), 2 part-time/adjunct (1 woman). *Financial support:* Fellowships, research assistantships, teaching assistantships, and Federal Work-Study available. Support available to part-time students. Financial award application deadline: 3/15; financial award applicants required to submit FAFSA. In 2015, 13 master's, 4 doctorates awarded. *Degree program information:* Part-time programs available. Part-time. Offers forest economics (PhD); forestry (MS, PhD); natural resource conservation (MNR); wildlife sciences (MS, PhD). *Application deadline:* Applications are processed on a rolling basis. *Application fee:* $50 ($60 for international students). Electronic applications accepted. *Application Contact:* Dr. George Flowers, Dean of the Graduate School, 334-844-2125. *Dean*, Dr. Graeme Lockaby, 334-844-4000, Fax: 334-844-1084, E-mail: brinker@forestry.auburn.edu.

School of Nursing Students: 13 full-time (all women), 107 part-time (101 women); includes 21 minority (14 Black or African American, non-Hispanic/Latino; 1 American Indian or Alaska Native, non-Hispanic/Latino; 2 Asian, non-Hispanic/Latino; 1 Hispanic/Latino; 3 Two or more races, non-Hispanic/Latino), 1 international. Average age 34. 78 applicants, 53% accepted, 35 enrolled. *Faculty:* 21 full-time (18 women). In 2015, 32 master's awarded. Offers nursing educator (MSN); primary care practitioner (MSN). *Application Contact:* Dr. George Flowers, Dean of the Graduate School, 334-844-4700, E-mail: gradadm@auburn.edu. *Dean*, Dr. Gregg Newschwander, 334-844-3658, E-mail: gen0002@auburn.edu.

Harrison School of Pharmacy Students: 623 full-time (412 women), 11 part-time (7 women); includes 122 minority (52 Black or African American, non-Hispanic/Latino; 7 American Indian or Alaska Native, non-Hispanic/Latino; 41 Asian, non-Hispanic/Latino; 9 Hispanic/Latino; 2 Native Hawaiian or other Pacific Islander, non-Hispanic/Latino; 11 Two or more races, non-Hispanic/Latino), 31 international. Average age 25. 577 applicants, 52% accepted, 160 enrolled. *Faculty:* 54 full-time (32 women), 1 (woman) part-time/adjunct. *Financial support:* Fellowships, research assistantships, teaching assistantships, and Federal Work-Study available. Support available to part-time students. Financial award applicants required to submit FAFSA. In 2015, 1 master's, 144 doctorates awarded. *Degree program information:* Part-time programs available. Part-time. Offers pharmacal sciences (MS, PhD); pharmaceutical sciences (PhD); pharmacy (MS, PhD, Pharm D); pharmacy care systems (MS, PhD). *Application deadline:* Applications are processed on a rolling basis. *Application fee:* $50 ($60 for international students). Electronic applications accepted. *Application Contact:* Dr. George Flowers, Dean of the Graduate School, 334-844-2125. *Dean*, Dr. R. Lee Evans, 334-844-8348.

AUBURN UNIVERSITY AT MONTGOMERY, Montgomery, AL 36124-4023

General Information State-supported, coed, comprehensive institution. *Enrollment:* 4,919 graduate, professional, and undergraduate students; 217 full-time matriculated graduate/professional students (131 women), 445 part-time matriculated graduate/professional students (312 women). *Enrollment by degree level:* 583 master's, 15 doctoral, 64 other advanced degrees. *Graduate faculty:* 91 full-time (39 women), 23 part-time/adjunct (8 women). Tuition, state resident: full-time $6462; part-time $359 per credit hour. Tuition, nonresident: full-time $14,526; part-time $807 per credit hour. *Required fees:* $554. *Graduate housing:* Rooms and/or apartments available on a first-come, first-served basis to single and married students. Typical cost: $4450 per year ($5650 including board) for single students. Room and board charges vary according to housing facility selected. Housing application deadline: 5/1. *Student services:* Campus employment opportunities, campus safety program, career counseling, exercise/wellness program, free psychological counseling, international student services, low-cost health insurance, multicultural affairs office, services for students with disabilities. *Library:* Auburn University at Montgomery Library. *Collection:* Books: 341,449 (physical), 74,467 (digital/electronic); Serial titles: 108 (physical), 83 (digital/electronic); Databases: 155. Weekly public service hours: 86; students can reserve study rooms.

Computer facilities: 600 computers available on campus for general student use. A campuswide network can be accessed. Online class registration is available.
Website: http://www.aum.edu/

General Application Contact: Ashley Warren, Administrative Coordinator, Provost's Office, 334-244-3623, Fax: 334-244-3947, E-mail: awarren3@aum.edu.

GRADUATE UNITS

College of Arts and Sciences Students: 44 full-time (22 women), 76 part-time (54 women); includes 21 minority (16 Black or African American, non-Hispanic/Latino; 1 American Indian or Alaska Native, non-Hispanic/Latino; 1 Asian, non-Hispanic/Latino; 1 Hispanic/Latino; 2 Two or more races, non-Hispanic/Latino), 20 international. Average age 32. 75 applicants, 80% accepted, 38 enrolled. *Faculty:* 33 full-time (12 women), 1 part-time/adjunct. *Financial support:* In 2015–16, 9 teaching assistantships were awarded; career-related internships or fieldwork and scholarships/grants also available. Support available to part-time students. Financial award application deadline: 3/1; financial award applicants required to submit FAFSA. In 2015, 10 master's awarded. *Degree program information:* Part-time and evening/weekend programs available. Part-time, evening/weekend. Offers arts and sciences (MA, MIR, MPA, MPS, MS, MSJPS, PhD, Certificate); clinical psychology (MS); teaching of writing (MA). *Application deadline:* Applications are processed on a rolling basis. Electronic applications accepted. *Application Contact:* Dr. Pamela Tidwell, Associate Dean, 334-244-3362, Fax: 334-244-3826, E-mail: ptidwell@aum.edu. *Dean*, Dr. Michael Burger, 334-244-3678, Fax: 334-244-3826, E-mail: mburger1@aum.edu.

Department of Mathematics and Computer Science Students: 12 full-time (2 women), 6 part-time (2 women); includes 2 minority (1 Black or African American, non-Hispanic/Latino; 1 Asian, non-Hispanic/Latino), 16 international. Average age 27. 14 applicants, 93% accepted, 8 enrolled. *Faculty:* 7 full-time (3 women). *Financial support:* In 2015–16, 1 teaching assistantship was awarded. In 2015, 2 master's awarded. Offers cybersystems and information security (MS). *Application Contact:* Dr. Pamela Tidwell, Associate Dean, 334-244-3362, Fax: 334-244-3826, E-mail: ptidwell@aum.edu. *Dean*, Dr. Karen Stine, 334-244-3689, Fax: 334-244-3826, E-mail: kstine@aum.edu.

College of Business Students: 77 full-time (37 women), 45 part-time (21 women); includes 16 minority (12 Black or African American, non-Hispanic/Latino; 1 American Indian or Alaska Native, non-Hispanic/Latino; 2 Hispanic/Latino; 1 Two or more races, non-Hispanic/Latino), 31 international. Average age 29. 95 applicants, 89% accepted, 59 enrolled. *Faculty:* 16 full-time (5 women), 6 part-time/adjunct (1 woman). *Financial support:* Research assistantships, career-related internships or fieldwork, and scholarships/grants available. Support available to part-time students. Financial award application deadline: 3/1; financial award applicants required to submit FAFSA. In 2015, 79 master's awarded. *Degree program information:* Part-time and evening/weekend programs available. Part-time, evening/weekend. Offers business (EMBA, M Acc, MBA, MSISM); business administration (MBA); information systems (MSISM). *Application deadline:* Applications are processed on a rolling basis. Electronic applications accepted. *Application Contact:* Jennifer Taylor, Assistant Director of Graduate Programs, 334-244-3587, Fax: 334-244-3137, E-mail: jtaylor5@aum.edu. *Dean*, Dr. Rhea Ingram, 334-244-3476, Fax: 334-244-3792, E-mail: wingram4@aum.edu.

School of Accountancy Students: 11 full-time (8 women), 11 part-time (6 women); includes 4 minority (3 Black or African American, non-Hispanic/Latino; 1 Hispanic/Latino), 1 international. 28 applicants, 93% accepted, 20 enrolled. *Faculty:* 3 full-time (1 woman), 2 part-time/adjunct (1 woman). *Financial support:* Scholarships/grants available. *Degree program information:* Part-time programs available. Part-time. Offers accountancy (M Acc). *Application fee:* $25. Electronic applications accepted. *Graduate Advisor*, Rhonda Seay, 334-244-3115, E-mail: rseay@aum.edu.

College of Education Students: 77 full-time (60 women), 227 part-time (173 women); includes 88 minority (84 Black or African American, non-Hispanic/Latino; 4 Asian, non-Hispanic/Latino), 7 international. Average age 34. 249 applicants, 77% accepted, 102 enrolled. *Faculty:* 25 full-time (15 women), 12 part-time/adjunct (7 women). *Financial support:* In 2015–16, 5 teaching assistantships were awarded; career-related internships or fieldwork and scholarships/grants also available. Support available to part-time students. Financial award application deadline: 3/1; financial award applicants required to submit FAFSA. In 2015, 108 master's awarded. *Degree program information:* Part-time and evening/weekend programs available. Part-time, evening/weekend. Offers counseling education (M Ed, Ed S); early childhood special education (M Ed); education (M Ed, Ed S); elementary education (M Ed, Ed S); exercise science (M Ed); instructional leadership (Ed S); instructional technology (Ed S); physical education (Ed S); secondary education (M Ed); special education (Ed S); special education/collaborative teacher (M Ed). *Application deadline:* Applications are processed on a rolling basis. Electronic applications accepted. *Application Contact:* Dr. Rhonda Morton, Associate Dean/Graduate Coordinator, 334-224-3287, Fax: 334-244-3978, E-mail: rmorton@aum.edu. *Dean*, Dr. Sheila Austin, 334-244-3425, Fax: 334-244-3102, E-mail: saustin1@aum.edu.

College of Nursing and Health Sciences Offers nurse educator (MSN); nurse practitioner (MSN). *Application Contact:* Dr. Barbara Wilder, Graduate Program Director, 334-844-6766, E-mail: wildebf@auburn.edu. *Dean*, Dr. Jean Leuner, 334-244-3658, E-mail: jleuner@aum.edu.

College of Public Policy and Justice Students: 19 full-time (12 women), 93 part-time (61 women); includes 35 minority (30 Black or African American, non-Hispanic/Latino; 2 American Indian or Alaska Native, non-Hispanic/Latino; 1 Hispanic/Latino; 2 Two or more races, non-Hispanic/Latino), 4 international. Average age 34. 42 applicants, 90% accepted, 15 enrolled. *Financial support:* In 2015–16, 6 teaching assistantships were awarded; career-related internships or fieldwork and scholarships/grants also available. Support available to part-time students. Financial award application deadline: 3/1; financial award applicants required to submit FAFSA. In 2015, 34 master's awarded. *Degree program information:* Part-time and evening/weekend programs available. Part-time, evening/weekend. Offers criminal studies (MSJPS); geographic information systems (MS); homeland security (MSJPS); homeland security and emergency management (MS); international relations (MIR); legal studies (MSJPS); nonprofit management and leadership (Certificate); organizational leadership (MSJPS); paralegal (Certificate); political science (MPS); public administration (MPA); public administration and public policy (PhD); public health care administration and policy (Certificate); public policy and justice (MA, MIR, MPA, MPS, MS, MSJPS, PhD, Certificate). *Application deadline:* Applications are processed on a rolling basis. Electronic applications accepted. *Dean*, Dr. Keivan Deravi, 334-244-3422, Fax: 334-244-3920, E-mail: mderavi@aum.edu.

AUGSBURG COLLEGE, Minneapolis, MN 55454-1351

General Information Independent-religious, coed, comprehensive institution. *Graduate housing:* On-campus housing not available.

GRADUATE UNITS

Program in Business Administration ***Degree program information:*** Evening/weekend programs available. Evening/weekend. Offers business administration (MBA). Electronic applications accepted.

Program in Education ***Degree program information:*** Part-time and evening/weekend programs available. Part-time, evening/weekend. Offers education (MAE). Electronic applications accepted.

Program in Leadership ***Degree program information:*** Part-time and evening/weekend programs available. Part-time, evening/weekend. Offers leadership (MA).

Program in Physician Assistant Studies Offers physician assistant studies (MS).

Program in Social Work ***Degree program information:*** Part-time and evening/weekend programs available. Part-time, evening/weekend. Offers social work (MSW).

Programs in Nursing Offers nursing (MA, DNP).

AUGUSTANA UNIVERSITY, Sioux Falls, SD 57197

General Information Independent-religious, coed, comprehensive institution. *Enrollment:* 1,837 graduate, professional, and undergraduate students; 224 part-time matriculated graduate/professional students (173 women). *Enrollment by degree level:* 224 master's. *Graduate faculty:* 10 full-time (4 women), 3 part-time/adjunct (2 women). *Graduate housing:* Rooms and/or apartments available on a first-come, first-served basis to single and married students. Housing application deadline: 9/1. *Student services:* Campus employment opportunities, campus safety program, career counseling, child daycare facilities, exercise/wellness program, free psychological counseling, international student services, low-cost health insurance, multicultural affairs office, services for students with disabilities, teacher training, writing training. *Library:* Mikkelsen Library. Students can reserve study rooms. *Research affiliation:* Binghamton University, State University of New York (chemistry), Sanford Underground Science and Engineering Lab (physics), JR Macdonald Laboratory (physics), NASA (computer science), Labratori Nazionalidd Gran Sasso, Italy (physics), Sanford Research (biology and biochemistry).

Computer facilities: Computer purchase and lease plans are available. 250 computers available on campus for general student use. A campuswide network can be accessed from student residence rooms and from off campus. Online class registration is available.
Website: http://www.augie.edu/

General Application Contact: Jody Nitz, Administrative Assistant, Graduate Education, 605-274-4043, Fax: 605-274-4450, E-mail: nancy.wright@augie.edu.

GRADUATE UNITS

MA in Education Program Students: 203 part-time (167 women); includes 4 minority (2 Black or African American, non-Hispanic/Latino; 1 Hispanic/Latino; 1 Two or more races, non-Hispanic/Latino), 3 international. Average age 33. 39 applicants, 95% accepted, 33 enrolled. *Faculty:* 5 full-time (2 women), 5 part-time/adjunct (3 women). *Financial support:* Application deadline: 3/1; applicants required to submit FAFSA. In 2015, 47 master's awarded. *Degree program information:* Part-time and evening/weekend programs available. Part-time, evening/weekend, online only, 100% online. Offers instructional strategies (MA); reading (MA); special populations (MA); technology (MA). *Application deadline:* For fall admission, 8/1 for domestic and international students; for spring admission, 11/1 for domestic and international students; for summer admission, 4/1 for domestic and international students. Applications are processed on a rolling basis. *Application fee:* $50. Electronic applications accepted. *Application Contact:* Jody Nitz, Graduate Coordinator, 605-274-4043, Fax: 605-274-4450, E-mail: graduate@augie.edu. *Associate Vice President for Graduate and Continuing Education*, Dr. Jerry Jorgensen, 605-274-4045, E-mail: jerry.jorgensen@augie.edu.

Sports Administration and Leadership Program Students: 20 part-time (5 women); includes 1 minority (Black or African American, non-Hispanic/Latino). Average age 24. 10 applicants, 90% accepted, 9 enrolled. *Faculty:* 4 full-time (1 woman). *Financial support:* In 2015–16, 15 students received support. Unspecified assistantships available. Financial award application deadline: 3/1; financial award applicants required to submit FAFSA. In 2015, 2 master's awarded. *Degree program information:* Part-time programs available. Part-time. Offers sports administration and leadership (MA). *Application deadline:* For fall admission, 6/1 priority date for domestic and international students. Applications are processed on a rolling basis. *Application fee:* $50. Electronic applications accepted. *Application Contact:* Jody Nitz, Graduate Education Assistant, 605-274-4043, Fax: 605-274-4450, E-mail: graduate@augie.edu. *Sports Administration and Leadership Master's Program Director*, Dr. Sherry Barkley, 605-274-4312, E-mail: sherry.barkley@augie.edu.

AUGUSTA UNIVERSITY, Augusta, GA 30912

General Information State-supported, coed, comprehensive institution. CGS member. *Enrollment:* 2,296 full-time matriculated graduate/professional students (1,289 women), 430 part-time matriculated graduate/professional students (324 women). *Enrollment by degree level:* 984 master's, 1,669 doctoral, 73 other advanced degrees. *Graduate faculty:* 643 full-time (238 women), 114 part-time/adjunct (57 women). *Graduate housing:* Rooms and/or apartments available on a first-come, first-served basis to single and married students. *Student services:* Campus employment opportunities, campus safety program, career counseling, child daycare facilities, exercise/wellness program, free psychological counseling, international student services, low-cost health insurance, multicultural affairs office. *Library:* Main library plus 2 others. *Research affiliation:* Georgia Center of Innovation for Life Sciences (research commercialization and economic development), Georgia Research Alliance (science and technology development), Georgia Cancer Coalition (cancer research programs), Advanced Technology Development Center (biotechnology transfer), Medical College of Georgia Research Institute, Inc. (biomedical research).

Computer facilities: A campuswide network can be accessed from student residence rooms. Online class registration is available.
Website: http://www.gru.edu/

General Application Contact: Scott Argos, Interim Director of Academic Admissions, 706-721-2725, Fax: 706-721-7279, E-mail: admissions@georgiahealth.edu.

GRADUATE UNITS

College of Allied Health Sciences ***Financial support:*** Federal Work-Study available. Support available to part-time students. Financial award application deadline: 5/31; financial award applicants required to submit FAFSA. Online learning. Offers allied health sciences (MHS, MPA, MPH, MS, DPT); clinical laboratory sciences (MHS); environmental health (MPH); health informatics (MPH); health management (MPH); medical illustration (MS); occupational therapy (MHS); physical therapy (DPT); physician assistant (MPA); social and behavioral sciences (MPH). *Application deadline:* For fall admission, 6/15 for domestic students, 1/15 for international students. Applications are processed on a rolling basis. *Application Contact:* Tonya Ryans, Administrative Assistant, 706-721-2623, Fax: 706-721-7279, E-mail: toryans@augusta.edu. *Dean and Professor*, Dr. Andrew Balas, 706-721-2621, Fax: 706-721-7312, E-mail: andrew.balas@augusta.edu.

The Dental College of Georgia Students: 320 full-time (140 women), 2 part-time (1 woman); includes 103 minority (39 Black or African American, non-Hispanic/Latino; 1 American Indian or Alaska Native, non-Hispanic/Latino; 35 Asian, non-Hispanic/Latino; 17 Hispanic/Latino; 11 Two or more races, non-Hispanic/Latino). Average age 26. 309 applicants, 26% accepted, 70 enrolled. *Faculty:* 53 full-time (10 women), 14 part-time/adjunct (4 women). *Financial support:* Federal Work-Study and scholarships/grants available. Financial award application deadline: 5/1; financial award applicants required to submit FAFSA. Offers dentistry (DMD). *Application deadline:* For fall admission, 10/15 for domestic students. *Application fee:* $30. Electronic applications accepted. *Application Contact:* Dr. Carole M. Hanes, Associate Dean for Students, Admissions, and Alumni, 706-721-2813, Fax: 706-723-0237, E-mail: chanes@augusta.edu. *Dean*, Dr. Carol Lefebrve, 706-721-2117, Fax: 706-723-0237, E-mail: clefebvr@augusta.edu.

The Graduate School ***Financial support:*** Fellowships with partial tuition reimbursements, research assistantships with partial tuition reimbursements, teaching assistantships, career-related internships or fieldwork, Federal Work-Study, institutionally sponsored loans, scholarships/grants, traineeships, and unspecified assistantships available. Support available to part-time students. Financial award application deadline: 5/31; financial award applicants required to submit FAFSA. *Degree program information:* Part-time programs available. Part-time, online learning. Offers adult gerontology acute care nurse practitioner (DNP); biochemistry and cancer biology (PhD); cellular biology and anatomy (PhD); clinical nurse leader (MSN); family nurse practitioner (MSN, Post-Master's Certificate); genomic medicine (MS, PhD); molecular medicine (PhD); neuroscience (PhD); nursing (DNP); nursing anesthesia (DNP); oral biology and maxillofacial pathology (MS, PhD); pediatric nurse practitioner (DNP); pharmacology (PhD); physiology (PhD); psychiatric mental health nurse practitioner (DNP); vascular biology (PhD). *Application fee:* $50. Electronic applications accepted. *Dean*, Dr. Mitchell Watsky, 706-721-3278, Fax: 706-721-6829, E-mail: mwatsky@augusta.edu.

College of Education ***Financial support:*** Career-related internships or fieldwork, Federal Work-Study, institutionally sponsored loans, and unspecified assistantships available. Support available to part-time students. Financial award application deadline: 4/15; financial award applicants required to submit FAFSA. *Degree program information:* Part-time and evening/weekend programs available. Part-time, evening/weekend. Offers counseling (M Ed, Ed S); curriculum and instruction (M Ed, Ed S); early childhood education (MAT); education (M Ed, MAT, Ed S); foreign language education (MAT); health and physical education (MAT); leadership (Ed S); middle grades education (MAT); music education (MAT); secondary education (MAT); special education (MAT); teacher leadership (M Ed). *Application deadline:* For fall admission, 7/16 priority date for domestic students. Applications are processed on a rolling basis. *Application fee:* $20. *Application Contact:* Liz Graves, Graduate Admissions and MAT Advisor, 706-729-2980, E-mail: margraves@augusta.edu. *Dean*, Dr. Zach Kelehear, 706-737-1499, Fax: 706-667-4706, E-mail: zkelehear@augusta.edu.

College of Science and Mathematics Offers psychological sciences (MS); science and mathematics (MS). *Application Contact:* Dr. John C. Sutherland, Associate Dean of Research and Graduate Studies, 706-667-4095, E-mail: jsutherland@augusta.edu. *Dean*, Dr. Rickey P. Hicks, 706-721-3278, Fax: 706-721-6829, E-mail: rhicks@augusta.edu.

Hull College of Business ***Financial support:*** Research assistantships with partial tuition reimbursements, Federal Work-Study, and institutionally sponsored loans available. Support available to part-time students. Financial award application deadline: 4/15; financial award applicants required to submit FAFSA. *Degree program information:* Part-time and evening/weekend programs available. Part-time, evening/weekend. Offers business (MBA). *Application deadline:* For fall admission, 7/2 for domestic and international students; for spring admission, 12/2 priority date for domestic students, 12/2 for international students; for summer admission, 4/2 for domestic and international students. Applications are processed on a rolling basis. *Application fee:* $20. *Application Contact:* Melissa Furman, Assistant Dean, 706-737-1560, Fax: 706-667-4064, E-mail: mfurman@augusta.edu. *Interim Dean*, Dr. Mark Thompson, 706-737-1418, Fax: 706-667-4064, E-mail: mark.thompson@augusta.edu.

Medical College of Georgia ***Financial support:*** Fellowships with tuition reimbursements, career-related internships or fieldwork, Federal Work-Study, institutionally sponsored loans, and scholarships/grants available. Support available to part-time students. Financial award application deadline: 5/1; financial award applicants required to submit FAFSA. Offers medicine (MD). *Application deadline:* For fall admission, 8/14 for domestic students. Applications are processed on a rolling basis. *Application fee:* $0. *Application Contact:* Esther Holland, Director of Admissions, 706-721-3186, Fax: 706-721-0959, E-mail: eholland@augusta.edu. *Dean*, Dr. Peter Buckley, 706-721-2231, Fax: 706-721-7035, E-mail: pbuckley@gru.edu.

AURORA UNIVERSITY, Aurora, IL 60506-4892

General Information Independent, coed, comprehensive institution. *Enrollment:* 5,423 graduate, professional, and undergraduate students; 569 full-time matriculated graduate/professional students (494 women), 1,274 part-time matriculated graduate/professional students (918 women). *Enrollment by degree level:* 1,476 master's, 219 doctoral, 148 other advanced degrees. *Graduate faculty:* 50 full-time (29 women), 123 part-time/adjunct (84 women). *Tuition, area resident:* Full-time $10,800; part-time $600 per credit hour. Tuition and fees vary according to degree level, campus/location and program. *Graduate housing:* On-campus housing not available. *Student services:* Campus employment opportunities, campus safety program, career counseling, exercise/wellness program, free psychological counseling, international student services, low-cost health insurance, multicultural affairs office, services for students with disabilities, teacher training, writing training. *Library:* Charles B. Phillips Library. *Collection:* Books: 51,754 (physical), 148,030 (digital/electronic); Serial titles: 52 (physical), 43,714 (digital/electronic); Databases: 79. Weekly public service hours: 102; students can reserve study rooms.

Computer facilities: 167 computers available on campus for general student use. A campuswide network can be accessed from student residence rooms and from off campus. Online class registration, Moodle Learning Management System are available. Website: http://www.aurora.edu/

General Application Contact: Jason Harmon, Director of Orchard Center and Graduate Enrollment, 630-947-8905, E-mail: jharmon@aurora.edu.

GRADUATE UNITS

College of Arts and Sciences Students: 27 part-time (18 women); includes 1 minority (Black or African American, non-Hispanic/Latino). Average age 32. 9 applicants, 100% accepted, 7 enrolled. *Faculty:* 3 full-time (1 woman), 5 part-time/adjunct (0 women). *Financial support:* Federal Work-Study, scholarships/grants, and unspecified assistantships available. Support available to part-time students. Financial award application deadline: 4/1; financial award applicants required to submit FAFSA. In 2015, 7 master's awarded. *Degree program information:* Part-time and evening/weekend programs available. Part-time, evening/weekend. Offers mathematics (MS). *Application deadline:* For fall admission, 6/1 for international students; for spring admission, 10/1 for international students. Applications are processed on a rolling basis. *Application fee:* $0. Electronic applications accepted. *Application Contact:* Jason Harmon, Director of Orchard Center and Graduate Enrollment, 630-947-8905, E-mail: jharmon@aurora.edu. *Chair*, Dr. Regina Rahn, 630-844-5651, E-mail: rrahn@aurora.edu.

Dunham School of Business Students: 58 full-time (40 women), 190 part-time (103 women); includes 76 minority (33 Black or African American, non-Hispanic/Latino; 1 Asian, non-Hispanic/Latino; 37 Hispanic/Latino; 5 Two or more races, non-Hispanic/Latino). Average age 33. 119 applicants, 97% accepted, 65 enrolled. *Faculty:* 7 full-time (1 woman), 16 part-time/adjunct (6 women). *Financial support:* In 2015–16, 55 students received support. Federal Work-Study, scholarships/grants, and unspecified assistantships available. Support available to part-time students. Financial award applicants required to submit FAFSA. In 2015, 99 master's awarded. *Degree program information:* Part-time and evening/weekend programs available. Part-time, evening/weekend. Offers accountancy (MS); business (MBA); digital marketing and analytics (MS). *Application deadline:* For fall admission, 6/1 for international students; for spring admission, 10/1 for international students. Applications are processed on a rolling basis. *Application fee:* $0. Electronic applications accepted. *Application Contact:* Liz Burton, Recruiting Specialist, 630-947-8903, E-mail: lburton@aurora.edu. *Provost*, Dr. Joan Poor, 630-844-5430, E-mail: jpoor@aurora.edu.

School of Education Students: 17 full-time (14 women), 553 part-time (357 women); includes 65 minority (26 Black or African American, non-Hispanic/Latino; 2 American Indian or Alaska Native, non-Hispanic/Latino; 4 Asian, non-Hispanic/Latino; 31 Hispanic/Latino; 1 Native Hawaiian or other Pacific Islander, non-Hispanic/Latino; 1 Two or more races, non-Hispanic/Latino). Average age 36. 109 applicants, 99% accepted, 86 enrolled. *Faculty:* 25 full-time (16 women), 41 part-time/adjunct (23 women). *Financial support:* In 2015–16, 1 student received support. Federal Work-Study, scholarships/grants, and unspecified assistantships available. Support available to part-time students. Financial award applicants required to submit FAFSA. In 2015, 152 master's, 23 doctorates awarded. *Degree program information:* Part-time and evening/weekend programs available. Part-time, evening/weekend. Offers curriculum and instruction (MA); curriculum and instruction with bilingual/ESL education (MA); educational leadership (MA); leadership in adult and higher education (Ed D); leadership in curriculum and instruction (Ed D); leadership in educational administration (Ed D). *Application deadline:* For fall admission, 6/1 for international students; for spring admission, 10/1 for international students. Applications are processed on a rolling basis. *Application fee:* $0. Electronic applications accepted. *Application Contact:* Marcia Gaspari, Graduate Education Recruiter, 630-844-4643, E-mail: mgaspari@aurora.edu. *Executive Director*, Dr. Jocelyn Booth, 630-844-1542, Fax: 630-844-4647, E-mail: jbooth@aurora.edu.

School of Nursing and Allied Health Students: 16 full-time (all women), 86 part-time (83 women); includes 20 minority (5 Black or African American, non-Hispanic/Latino; 3 Asian, non-Hispanic/Latino; 11 Hispanic/Latino; 1 Two or more races, non-Hispanic/Latino). Average age 37. 64 applicants, 89% accepted, 38 enrolled. *Faculty:* 4 full-time (3 women), 6 part-time/adjunct (5 women). *Financial support:* In 2015–16, 28 students received support. Federal Work-Study, scholarships/grants, and unspecified assistantships available. Support available to part-time students. Financial award applicants required to submit FAFSA. In 2015, 15 master's awarded. *Degree program information:* Part-time and evening/weekend programs available. Part-time, evening/weekend. Offers applied behavior analysis (MS); nursing (MSN). *Application deadline:* For fall admission, 6/1 for international students; for spring admission, 10/1 for international students. Applications are processed on a rolling basis. *Application fee:* $0. Electronic applications accepted. *Application Contact:* Jason Harmon, Director of Orchard Center and Graduate Enrollment, 630-947-8905, E-mail: jharmon@aurora.edu. *Executive Director*, Dr. Brenda Shostrom, 630-844-5135, E-mail: bshostrom@aurora.edu.

School of Social Work Students: 471 full-time (418 women), 267 part-time (224 women); includes 195 minority (83 Black or African American, non-Hispanic/Latino; 1 American Indian or Alaska Native, non-Hispanic/Latino; 14 Asian, non-Hispanic/Latino; 88 Hispanic/Latino; 9 Two or more races, non-Hispanic/Latino). Average age 30. 393 applicants, 99% accepted, 299 enrolled. *Faculty:* 9 full-time (6 women), 52 part-time/adjunct (47 women). *Financial support:* In 2015–16, 723 students received support. Federal Work-Study, scholarships/grants, and unspecified assistantships available. Support available to part-time students. Financial award applicants required to submit FAFSA. In 2015, 252 master's, 3 doctorates awarded. *Degree program information:* Part-time and evening/weekend programs available. Part-time, evening/weekend. Offers social work (MSW, DSW). *Application deadline:* For fall admission, 6/1 for international students; for spring admission, 10/1 for international students. Applications are processed on a rolling basis. *Application fee:* $0. Electronic applications accepted. *Application Contact:* Debbie Enlow, Senior Recruiter/Advisor for Adult and Graduate Studies, 630-947-8904, E-mail: denlow@aurora.edu. *Executive Director*, Dr. Fred McKenzie, 630-947-8930, E-mail: mckenzie@aurora.edu.

AUSTIN COLLEGE, Sherman, TX 75090-4400

General Information Independent-religious, coed, comprehensive institution. *Enrollment:* 1,272 graduate, professional, and undergraduate students; 16 full-time matriculated graduate/professional students (8 women). *Enrollment by degree level:* 16 master's. *Graduate faculty:* 5 full-time (4 women), 1 (woman) part-time/adjunct. *Graduate housing:* Room and/or apartments available on a first-come, first-served basis to single students; on-campus housing not available to married students. Housing application deadline: 5/1. *Student services:* Campus employment opportunities, campus safety program, career counseling, free psychological counseling, teacher training. *Library:* Abell Library. *Collection:* Books: 227,390 (physical). Study areas open 24 hours, 5–7 days a week; students can reserve study rooms.

Computer facilities: 160 computers available on campus for general student use. A campuswide network can be accessed from student residence rooms and from off campus. Online class registration is available.
Website: http://www.austincollege.edu/

General Application Contact: Nikki Christensen, Administrative Assistant, Academic Affairs, 903-813-2327, E-mail: nchristensen@austincollege.edu.

GRADUATE UNITS

Austin Teacher Program Students: 16 full-time (8 women); includes 5 minority (1 Black or African American, non-Hispanic/Latino; 1 Asian, non-Hispanic/Latino; 2 Hispanic/Latino; 1 Two or more races, non-Hispanic/Latino). *Faculty:* 5 full-time (4 women), 1 (woman) part-time/adjunct. *Financial support:* Career-related internships or fieldwork, Federal Work-Study, scholarships/grants, and unspecified assistantships available. Support available to part-time students. Financial award application deadline: 4/1; financial award applicants required to submit FAFSA. *Degree program information:* Part-time programs available. Part-time. Offers teaching (MAT). *Application deadline:* For fall admission, 5/1 priority date for domestic students; for spring admission, 1/15 priority date for domestic students. Applications are processed on a rolling basis. *Application fee:* $35. Electronic applications accepted. *Application Contact:* Nikki Christensen, 903-813-2327, E-mail: nchristensen@austincollege.edu. *Department Chair*, Julia Shahid, 903-813-2457, E-mail: jshahid@austincollege.edu.

AUSTIN GRADUATE SCHOOL OF THEOLOGY, Austin, TX 78752

General Information Independent-religious, coed, upper-level institution. *Enrollment:* 60 graduate, professional, and undergraduate students; 4 full-time matriculated graduate/professional students (2 women), 18 part-time matriculated graduate/professional students (5 women). *Enrollment by degree level:* 22 master's. *Graduate faculty:* 4 full-time (0 women), 4 part-time/adjunct (0 women). *Tuition, area resident:* Full-time $6300; part-time $4200 per credit. *Required fees:* $350; $350 per semester. $175 per semester. *Graduate housing:* On-campus housing not available. *Student services:* Campus employment opportunities, international student services, services for students with disabilities. *Library:* David Worley Library.

Computer facilities: 8 computers available on campus for general student use. A campuswide network can be accessed from off campus.
Website: http://www.austingrad.edu/

General Application Contact: Lauren Day, Director of Public Relations and Recruitment, 512-476-2772 Ext. 119, Fax: 512-476-3919, E-mail: lday@austingrad.edu.

GRADUATE UNITS

Program in Theological Studies Students: 4 full-time (2 women), 18 part-time (5 women). *Faculty:* 4 full-time (0 women), 4 part-time/adjunct (0 women). *Financial support:* Federal Work-Study and scholarships/grants available. Support available to part-time students. Financial award application deadline: 7/1. *Degree program information:* Part-time programs available. Part-time. Offers theological studies (MATS). *Application deadline:* For fall admission, 7/1 priority date for domestic and international students; for spring admission, 10/1 priority date for domestic and international students. Applications are processed on a rolling basis. *Application fee:* $25. Electronic applications accepted. *Application Contact:* Lauren Day, Director of Communications and Recruitment, 512-476-2772 Ext. 107, Fax: 512-476-3919, E-mail: lday@austingrad.edu. *Coordinator/Student Advisor*, Dr. Jeffery Peterson, 512-476-2772, Fax: 512-476-3919, E-mail: stanglin@austingrad.edu.

AUSTIN PEAY STATE UNIVERSITY, Clarksville, TN 37044

General Information State-supported, coed, comprehensive institution. CGS member. *Enrollment:* 10,099 graduate, professional, and undergraduate students; 252 full-time matriculated graduate/professional students (182 women), 641 part-time matriculated graduate/professional students (472 women). *Enrollment by degree level:* 858 master's, 35 other advanced degrees. *Graduate faculty:* 127 full-time (63 women), 19 part-time/adjunct (all women). Tuition, state resident: full-time $8080; part-time $404 per credit hour. Tuition, nonresident: full-time $21,680; part-time $1084 per credit hour. *Required fees:* $1453; $72.65 per credit hour. *Graduate housing:* Rooms and/or apartments available on a first-come, first-served basis to single and married students. Typical cost: $6500 per year ($9750 including board) for single students; $6500 per year ($9750 including board) for married students. Room and board charges vary according to board plan, campus/location and housing facility selected. *Student services:* Campus employment opportunities, career counseling, child daycare facilities, exercise/wellness program, free psychological counseling, international student services, low-cost health insurance, multicultural affairs office, services for students with disabilities, teacher training, writing training. *Library:* Felix G. Woodward Library. *Collection:* Books: 218,354 (physical), 317,822 (digital/electronic); Serial titles: 2,800 (physical), 53,798 (digital/electronic); Databases: 266. Weekly public service hours: 109.

Computer facilities: Computer purchase and lease plans are available. 1,062 computers available on campus for general student use. A campuswide network can be accessed from student residence rooms and from off campus. Online class registration is available.
Website: http://www.apsu.edu/

General Application Contact: June D. Lee, Graduate Coordinator, 800-859-4723, Fax: 931-221-7641, E-mail: gradadmissions@apsu.edu.

GRADUATE UNITS

College of Graduate Studies Students: 250 full-time (181 women), 608 part-time (448 women); includes 178 minority (103 Black or African American, non-Hispanic/Latino; 2 Asian, non-Hispanic/Latino; 36 Hispanic/Latino; 37 Two or more races, non-Hispanic/Latino), 4 international. Average age 33. 430 applicants, 78% accepted, 266 enrolled. *Faculty:* 127 full-time (63 women), 19 part-time/adjunct (all women). *Financial support:* In 2015–16, 136 students received support, including 136 research assistantships with full tuition reimbursements available (averaging $5,184 per year); career-related internships or fieldwork, Federal Work-Study, institutionally sponsored loans, scholarships/grants, and unspecified assistantships also available. Support available to part-time students. Financial award application deadline: 3/1; financial award applicants required to submit FAFSA. In 2015, 308 master's, 13 other advanced degrees awarded. *Degree program information:* Part-time and evening/weekend programs available. Part-time, evening/weekend, online learning. *Application deadline:* For fall admission, 8/3 priority date for domestic students. Applications are processed on a rolling basis. *Application fee:* $25. Electronic applications accepted. *Application Contact:* June D. Lee, Graduate Coordinator, 931-221-6189, Fax: 931-221-7641, E-mail: gradadmissions@apsu.edu. *Associate Provost for Research/Dean of the College of Graduate Studies*, Dr. Raj Dakshinamurthy, 931-221-7414, Fax: 931-221-7641, E-mail: dakshinamurthyr@apsu.edu.

The Austin Peay Center at Ft. Campbell Students: 6 full-time (3 women), 27 part-time (19 women); includes 15 minority (14 Black or African American, non-Hispanic/Latino; 1 Two or more races, non-Hispanic/Latino), 1 international. Average age 40. 14 applicants, 86% accepted, 8 enrolled. *Faculty:* 7 full-time (3 women). *Financial support:* Career-related internships or fieldwork, Federal Work-Study, institutionally sponsored loans, scholarships/grants, and unspecified assistantships available. Support available to part-time students. Financial award application deadline: 3/1; financial award applicants required to submit FAFSA. In 2015, 7 master's awarded. *Degree program information:* Part-time programs available. Part-time, online learning. Offers engineering technology (MS); human resources leadership (MPS); strategic leadership (MPS); training and development (MPS). *Application deadline:* For fall admission, 8/3 priority date for domestic students. Applications are processed on a rolling basis. *Application fee:* $25. Electronic applications accepted. *Application Contact:* June D. Lee, Graduate Coordinator, 800-859-4723, Fax: 931-221-7641, E-mail: gradadmissions@apsu.edu. *Executive Director*, Dr. William Cox, 931-221-1412, Fax: 931-221-1450, E-mail: coxw@apsu.edu.

College of Arts and Letters Students: 46 full-time (28 women), 87 part-time (45 women); includes 31 minority (16 Black or African American, non-Hispanic/Latino; 6 Hispanic/Latino; 9 Two or more races, non-Hispanic/Latino). Average age 33. 64 applicants, 91% accepted, 44 enrolled. *Faculty:* 35 full-time (11 women), 5 part-time/adjunct (all women). *Financial support:* In 2015–16, research assistantships with full tuition reimbursements (averaging $5,184 per year) were awarded; career-related internships or fieldwork, Federal Work-Study, institutionally sponsored loans, scholarships/grants, and unspecified assistantships also available. Support available to part-time students. Financial award application deadline: 3/1; financial award applicants required to submit FAFSA. In 2015, 37 master's awarded. *Degree program information:* Part-time programs available. Part-time, online learning. Offers arts and letters (M Mu, MA); communication arts (MA); English (MA); military history (MA); music education (M Mu); music performance (M Mu). *Application deadline:* For fall admission, 8/3 priority date for domestic students. Applications are processed on a rolling basis. *Application fee:* $25. Electronic applications accepted. *Application Contact:* June D. Lee, Graduate Coordinator, 800-859-4723, Fax: 931-221-7641, E-mail: gradadmissions@apsu.edu. *Dean*, Dr. Dixie Webb, 931-221-6445, Fax: 931-221-1024, E-mail: webbd@apsu.edu.

College of Behavioral and Health Sciences Students: 117 full-time (94 women), 223 part-time (186 women); includes 80 minority (56 Black or African American, non-Hispanic/Latino; 1 Asian, non-Hispanic/Latino; 10 Hispanic/Latino; 13 Two or more races, non-Hispanic/Latino), 1 international. Average age 33. 129 applicants, 98% accepted, 99 enrolled. *Faculty:* 32 full-time (21 women), 7 part-time/adjunct (all women). *Financial support:* In 2015–16, research assistantships with full tuition reimbursements (averaging $5,184 per year) were awarded; career-related internships or fieldwork, Federal Work-Study, institutionally sponsored loans, scholarships/grants, and unspecified assistantships also available. Support available to part-time students. Financial award application deadline: 3/1; financial award applicants required to submit FAFSA. In 2015, 145 master's awarded. *Degree program information:* Part-time and evening/weekend programs available. Part-time, evening/weekend, online learning. Offers behavioral and health sciences (MA, MS, MSN, MSW); family nurse practitioner (MSN); industrial-organizational psychology (MS); mental health counseling (MS); nursing administration (MSN); nursing education (MSN); nursing informatics (MSN); public health education (MS); school counseling (MS); social work (MSW); sports and wellness leadership (MS). *Application deadline:* For fall admission, 8/3 priority date for domestic students. Applications are processed on a rolling basis. *Application fee:* $25. Electronic applications accepted. *Application Contact:* June D. Lee, Graduate Coordinator, 800-859-4723, Fax: 931-221-7641, E-mail: gradadmissions@apsu.edu. *Dean*, Dr. David Denton, 931-221-7423, Fax: 931-221-6382, E-mail: dentond@apsu.edu.

College of Business Students: 1 full-time (0 women), 68 part-time (41 women); includes 13 minority (6 Black or African American, non-Hispanic/Latino; 6 Hispanic/Latino; 1 Two or more races, non-Hispanic/Latino). Average age 34. 35 applicants, 83% accepted, 26 enrolled. *Faculty:* 9 full-time (4 women). *Financial support:* In 2015–16, research assistantships with full tuition reimbursements (averaging $5,184 per year) were awarded; career-related internships or fieldwork, Federal Work-Study, institutionally sponsored loans, scholarships/grants, and unspecified assistantships also available. Support available to part-time students. Financial award application deadline: 3/1; financial award applicants required to submit FAFSA. In 2015, 26 master's awarded. *Degree program information:* Part-time and evening/weekend programs available. Part-time, evening/weekend, online learning. Offers management (MS). *Application deadline:* For fall admission, 8/3 priority date for domestic students. Applications are processed on a rolling basis. *Application fee:* $25. Electronic applications accepted. *Application Contact:* June D. Lee, Graduate Coordinator, 800-859-4723, Fax: 931-221-7641, E-mail: gradadmissions@apsu.edu. *Interim Dean*, Dr. Rex Gandy, 931-221-7674, Fax: 931-221-7355, E-mail: gandyr@apsu.edu.

College of Education Students: 76 full-time (55 women), 177 part-time (148 women); includes 46 minority (22 Black or African American, non-Hispanic/Latino; 1 Asian, non-Hispanic/Latino; 13 Hispanic/Latino; 10 Two or more races, non-Hispanic/Latino), 2 international. Average age 33. 86 applicants, 90% accepted, 60 enrolled. *Faculty:* 20 full-time (14 women), 6 part-time/adjunct (all women). *Financial support:* In 2015–16, research assistantships with full tuition reimbursements (averaging $5,184 per year) were awarded; career-related internships or fieldwork, Federal Work-Study, institutionally sponsored loans, scholarships/grants, and unspecified assistantships also available. Support available to part-time students. Financial award application deadline: 3/1; financial award applicants required to submit FAFSA. In 2015, 81 master's, 13 other advanced degrees awarded. *Degree program information:* Part-time and evening/weekend programs available. Part-time, evening/weekend, online learning. Offers administration and supervision (Ed S); counseling and guidance (Ed S); curriculum and instruction (MA Ed); education (MA Ed, MAT, Ed S); education leadership (MA Ed); elementary education (Ed S); elementary education K-6 (MAT); reading (MA Ed); secondary education (Ed S); secondary education 7-12 (MAT); special education K-12 (MAT). *Application deadline:* For fall admission, 8/3 priority date for domestic students. Applications are processed on a rolling basis. *Application fee:* $25. Electronic applications accepted. *Application Contact:* June D. Lee, Graduate Coordinator, 800-859-4723, Fax: 931-221-7641, E-mail: gradadmissions@apsu.edu. *Director*, Dr. Carlette Hardin, 931-221-7696, Fax: 931-221-1292, E-mail: hardinc@apsu.edu.

College of Science and Mathematics Students: 6 full-time (2 women), 53 part-time (28 women); includes 7 minority (3 Black or African American, non-Hispanic/Latino; 1 Hispanic/Latino; 3 Two or more races, non-Hispanic/Latino). Average age 32. 73 applicants, 44% accepted, 29 enrolled. *Faculty:* 24 full-time (10 women), 1 (woman) part-time/adjunct. *Financial support:* In 2015–16, research assistantships with full tuition reimbursements (averaging $5,184 per year) were awarded; career-related internships or fieldwork, Federal Work-Study, institutionally sponsored loans, scholarships/grants, and unspecified assistantships also available. Support available to part-time students. Financial award application deadline: 3/1; financial award applicants required to submit FAFSA. In 2015, 9 master's awarded. *Degree program information:* Part-time programs available. Part-time, online learning. Offers clinical laboratory science (MS); data management and analysis (PSM); predictive analytics (PSM); science and mathematics (MS, PSM). *Application deadline:* For fall admission, 8/3 priority date for domestic students. Applications are processed on a rolling basis. *Application fee:* $25. Electronic applications accepted. *Application Contact:* June D. Lee, Graduate Coordinator, 800-859-4723, Fax: 931-221-7641, E-mail: gradadmissions@apsu.edu. *Dean*, Dr. Jaime Taylor, 931-221-7971, Fax: 931-221-7984, E-mail: taylorj@apsu.edu.

AUSTIN PRESBYTERIAN THEOLOGICAL SEMINARY, Austin, TX 78705-5797

General Information Independent-religious, coed, graduate-only institution. *Enrollment by degree level:* 127 master's, 35 doctoral. *Graduate faculty:* 20 full-time (6 women), 5 part-time/adjunct (1 woman). *Tuition, area resident:* Full-time $12,900; part-time $215 per credit. *Required fees:* $120; $120 per unit. $25 per semester. One-time fee: $175 full-time; $120 part-time. Tuition and fees vary according to degree level and program. *Graduate housing:* Rooms and/or apartments available on a first-come, first-served basis to single and married students. Typical cost: $1980 per year ($2030 including board) for single students; $7200 per year ($7250 including board) for married students. Room and board charges vary according to housing facility selected. Housing application deadline: 5/31. *Student services:* Campus employment opportunities, campus safety program, career counseling, free psychological counseling, international student services, services for students with disabilities, writing training. *Library:* Stitt Library. *Collection:* Books: 142,236 (physical), 174,522 (digital/electronic); Serial titles: 1,250 (physical), 51,810 (digital/electronic); Databases: 80. Weekly public service hours: 37; students can reserve study rooms.

Computer facilities: 20 computers available on campus for general student use. A campuswide network can be accessed from student residence rooms and from off campus.
Website: http://www.austinseminary.edu/

General Application Contact: Dr. Jack Barden, Vice President for Admissions, 512-404-4827, Fax: 512-472-7089, E-mail: admissions@austinseminary.edu.

GRADUATE UNITS

Graduate and Professional Programs Students: 88 full-time (50 women), 74 part-time (41 women). *Faculty:* 20 full-time (6 women), 5 part-time/adjunct (1 woman). *Financial support:* Fellowships, career-related internships or fieldwork, institutionally sponsored loans, scholarships/grants, and tutorships available. Support available to part-time students. Financial award application deadline: 3/1; financial award applicants required to submit FAFSA. *Degree program information:* Part-time programs available. Part-time. Offers divinity (M Div); ministry (D Min); ministry practice (MA); theological studies (MA); youth ministry (MA). M Div/MSSW offered in collaboration with The University of Texas at Austin School of Social Work. *Application deadline:* For fall admission, 5/1 for domestic students, 1/1 for international students; for summer admission, 2/2 for domestic students. Applications are processed on a rolling basis. *Application fee:* $65. *Application Contact:* Dr. Jack Barden, Vice President for Admissions, 512-404-4827, Fax: 512-472-7089, E-mail: admissions@austinseminary.edu. *Academic Dean*, Dr. David Jensen, 512-404-4821, Fax: 512-479-0738, E-mail: dean@austinseminary.edu.

AVE MARIA SCHOOL OF LAW, Naples, FL 34119

General Information Independent-religious, coed, graduate-only institution. *Enrollment by degree level:* 268 doctoral. *Graduate faculty:* 27 full-time (7 women), 12 part-time/adjunct (3 women). *Tuition, area resident:* Full-time $39,450. *Required fees:* $2256. *Graduate housing:* Rooms and/or apartments available on a first-come, first-served basis to single and married students. Typical cost: $8919 per year ($13,131 including board) for single students; $8919 per year ($13,131 including board) for married students. Housing application deadline: 5/1. *Student services:* Campus employment opportunities, campus safety program, career counseling, international student services, services for students with disabilities, writing training. *Library:* Ave Maria School of Law Library. *Collection:* Books: 51,666 (physical), 48,101 (digital/electronic); Serial titles: 2,182 (physical), 29,717 (digital/electronic); Databases: 216. Weekly public service hours: 40; study areas open 24 hours, 5–7 days a week; students can reserve study rooms.

Computer facilities: 20 computers available on campus for general student use. A campuswide network can be accessed from off campus. Online class registration is available.
Website: http://www.avemarialaw.edu/

General Application Contact: Claire T. O'Keefe, Director of Admissions, 239-687-5423, Fax: 239-352-2890, E-mail: info@avemarialaw.edu.

GRADUATE UNITS

Professional Program Students: 268 full-time (135 women); includes 95 minority (25 Black or African American, non-Hispanic/Latino; 5 American Indian or Alaska Native, non-Hispanic/Latino; 2 Asian, non-Hispanic/Latino; 62 Hispanic/Latino; 1 Native Hawaiian or other Pacific Islander, non-Hispanic/Latino), 5 international. Average age 26. 766 applicants, 57% accepted, 118 enrolled. *Faculty:* 27 full-time (7 women), 12 part-time/adjunct (3 women). *Financial support:* In 2015–16, 218 students received support. Research assistantships, career-related internships or fieldwork, Federal Work-Study, and scholarships/grants available. Financial award application deadline: 6/1; financial award applicants required to submit FAFSA. In 2015, 88 doctorates awarded. Offers law (JD). *Application deadline:* For fall admission, 7/15 priority date for domestic and international students. Applications are processed on a rolling basis. *Application fee:* $0. Electronic applications accepted. *Application Contact:* Claire T. O'Keefe, Director of Admissions, 239-687-5423, Fax: 239-352-2890, E-mail: info@avemarialaw.edu. *President/Dean*, Kevin Cieply, 239-687-5300, E-mail: kcieply@avemarialaw.edu.

AVE MARIA UNIVERSITY, Ave Maria, FL 34142

General Information Independent-religious, coed, comprehensive institution. *Graduate housing:* Room and/or apartments available on a first-come, first-served basis to single students; on-campus housing not available to married students. Housing application deadline: 7/15.

GRADUATE UNITS

Graduate Programs

AVERETT UNIVERSITY, Danville, VA 24541-3692

General Information Independent-religious, coed, comprehensive institution. *Enrollment:* 894 graduate, professional, and undergraduate students; 45 full-time matriculated graduate/professional students (34 women), 347 part-time matriculated graduate/professional students (191 women). *Enrollment by degree level:* 392 master's. *Graduate faculty:* 12 full-time (3 women), 32 part-time/adjunct (14 women). Tuition and fees vary according to campus/location and program. *Graduate housing:* On-campus housing not available. *Student services:* Campus employment opportunities, campus safety program, career counseling, free psychological counseling, services for students with disabilities, teacher training, writing training. *Library:* Mary B. Blount Library. *Collection:* Books: 96,376 (physical), 192,345 (digital/electronic); Serial titles: 567 (physical), 32,185 (digital/electronic); Databases: 124. Weekly public service hours: 81; students can reserve study rooms.

Computer facilities: 150 computers available on campus for general student use. A campuswide network can be accessed from student residence rooms. Online class registration is available.
Website: http://www.averett.edu/

General Application Contact: Melissa Anderson, Director of Admissions, Graduate and Professional Studies, 804-729-8285, E-mail: manderson@averett.edu.

GRADUATE UNITS

Master in Education Program Students: 16 full-time (14 women), 73 part-time (61 women); includes 24 minority (22 Black or African American, non-Hispanic/Latino; 1 American Indian or Alaska Native, non-Hispanic/Latino; 1 Hispanic/Latino). Average age 38. 129 applicants, 56% accepted, 65 enrolled. *Faculty:* 4 full-time (2 women), 8 part-time/adjunct (6 women). *Financial support:* Tuition waivers (full) available. Financial award application deadline: 3/1; financial award applicants required to submit FAFSA. In 2015, 34 master's awarded. *Degree program information:* Part-time programs available. Part-time, online only, 100% online. Offers administration and supervision (M Ed); curriculum and instruction (M Ed); special education with endorsement (M Ed); special education with licensure (M Ed). Program offered on Danville Campus only. *Application deadline:* Applications are processed on a rolling basis. Electronic applications accepted. *Education Chair*, Dr. Sue Davis, 434-791-5741, Fax: 434-791-5020, E-mail: suedavis@averett.edu.

Master of Accountancy Program Students: 2 part-time (0 women), 1 international. Average age 23. 6 applicants, 67% accepted, 1 enrolled. *Faculty:* 2 full-time (1 woman). *Financial support:* Tuition waivers (full) available. Financial award application deadline: 3/1; financial award applicants required to submit FAFSA. In 2015, 2 master's awarded. *Degree program information:* Part-time programs available. Part-time, online only, 100% online. Offers accountancy (M Acc). *Application deadline:* Applications are processed on a rolling basis. Electronic applications accepted. *Application Contact:* Melissa Anderson, Director of Admissions, Graduate and Professional Studies, 804-729-8285, E-mail: manderson@averett.edu. *Director of the Master in Accountancy Program*, Dr. Peggy C. Wright, 434-791-7118, E-mail: pwright@averett.edu.

Master of Business Administration Program Students: 29 full-time (20 women), 272 part-time (130 women); includes 142 minority (117 Black or African American, non-Hispanic/Latino; 6 American Indian or Alaska Native, non-Hispanic/Latino; 9 Asian, non-Hispanic/Latino; 10 Hispanic/Latino), 8 international. Average age 38. 363 applicants, 89% accepted, 294 enrolled. *Faculty:* 7 full-time (1 woman), 24 part-time/adjunct (8 women). *Financial support:* Tuition waivers (full) available. Financial award application deadline: 3/1; financial award applicants required to submit FAFSA. In 2015, 151 master's awarded. *Degree program information:* Part-time and evening/weekend programs available. Part-time, evening/weekend, 100% online, blended/hybrid learning. Offers business administration (MBA); human resources management (MBA); leadership (MBA); marketing (MBA). *Application deadline:* Applications are processed on a rolling basis. Electronic applications accepted. *Application Contact:* Melissa Anderson, Director of Admissions, Graduate and Professional Studies, 804-729-8285, E-mail: manderson@averett.edu. *Chair, Business Department*, Dr. Peggy C. Wright, 434-791-7118, E-mail: pwright@averett.edu.

AVILA UNIVERSITY, Kansas City, MO 64145-1698

General Information Independent-religious, coed, comprehensive institution. *Enrollment:* 1,866 graduate, professional, and undergraduate students; 331 full-time matriculated graduate/professional students (227 women), 120 part-time matriculated graduate/professional students (90 women). *Enrollment by degree level:* 370 master's, 81 other advanced degrees. *Graduate faculty:* 24 full-time (15 women), 43 part-time/adjunct (23 women). *Tuition, area resident:* Full-time $6600; part-time $550 per credit hour. Full-time tuition and fees vary according to program. *Graduate housing:* Room and/or apartments available on a first-come, first-served basis to single students; on-campus housing not available to married students. Typical cost: $3300 per year ($6600 including board). *Student services:* Campus employment opportunities, campus safety program, career counseling, child daycare facilities, exercise/wellness program, free psychological counseling, international student services, low-cost health insurance, multicultural affairs office, services for students with disabilities, teacher training, writing training. *Library:* Hooley-Bundshu Library plus 1 other. *Collection:* Books: 39,963 (physical), 309,288 (digital/electronic); Serial titles: 205 (physical), 389,497 (digital/electronic); Databases: 72. Weekly public service hours: 91; students can reserve study rooms.

Computer facilities: 141 computers available on campus for general student use. A campuswide network can be accessed from student residence rooms and from off campus. Online class registration, laptop checkout through library checkout are available.
Website: http://www.avila.edu/

General Application Contact: Office of Admissions, 816-501-2400, E-mail: admissionsoffice@avila.edu.

GRADUATE UNITS

Department of Psychology Students: 93 full-time (76 women), 24 part-time (20 women); includes 47 minority (35 Black or African American, non-Hispanic/Latino; 2 American Indian or Alaska Native, non-Hispanic/Latino; 2 Asian, non-Hispanic/Latino; 5 Hispanic/Latino; 3 Two or more races, non-Hispanic/Latino), 1 international. Average age 34. 57 applicants, 72% accepted, 26 enrolled. *Faculty:* 7 full-time (6 women), 12 part-time/adjunct (6 women). *Financial support:* In 2015–16, 16 students received support, including 6 research assistantships with partial tuition reimbursements available; career-related internships or fieldwork, scholarships/grants, and unspecified assistantships also available. Support available to part-time students. Financial award applicants required to submit FAFSA. In 2015, 37 master's awarded. *Degree program information:* Part-time programs available. Part-time. Offers counseling psychology (MS); general psychology (MS). *Application deadline:* Applications are processed on a rolling basis. *Application fee:* $0. Electronic applications accepted. *Application Contact:* Tamika Doolin, Graduate Admissions Advisor, 816-501-3661, Fax: 816-501-2455, E-mail: gradpsych@avila.edu. *Director of Graduate Psychology Enrollment Management*, Aaron R. Coffey, 816-501-0419, Fax: 816-501-2455, E-mail: aaron.coffey@avila.edu.

School of Business Students: 70 full-time (29 women), 31 part-time (21 women); includes 25 minority (19 Black or African American, non-Hispanic/Latino; 2 Asian, non-Hispanic/Latino; 2 Hispanic/Latino; 2 Two or more races, non-Hispanic/Latino), 33 international. Average age 30. 35 applicants, 86% accepted, 28 enrolled. *Faculty:* 9 full-time (4 women), 14 part-time/adjunct (4 women). *Financial support:* In 2015–16, 12 students received support. Career-related internships or fieldwork and scholarships/grants available. Support available to part-time students. Financial award applicants required to submit FAFSA. In 2015, 44 master's awarded. *Degree program information:* Part-time and evening/weekend programs available. Part-time, evening/weekend. Offers accounting (MBA); finance (MBA); health care administration (MBA); international business (MBA); management (MBA); management information systems (MBA); marketing (MBA). *Application deadline:* For fall admission, 7/30 priority date for domestic and international students; for winter admission, 11/30 priority date for domestic and international students; for spring admission, 2/28 priority date for domestic and international students; for summer admission, 6/1 priority date for domestic and international students. Applications are processed on a rolling basis. *Application fee:* $0. Electronic applications accepted. *Application Contact:* Sarah Belanus, MBA Admissions Director, 816-501-3601, Fax: 816-501-2463, E-mail: sarah.belanus@avila.edu. *Dean*, Dr. Richard Woodall, 816-501-3720, Fax: 816-501-2463, E-mail: richard.woodall@avila.edu.

School of Education Students: 85 full-time (63 women), 9 part-time (6 women); includes 13 minority (10 Black or African American, non-Hispanic/Latino; 1 Asian, non-Hispanic/Latino; 1 Hispanic/Latino; 1 Two or more races, non-Hispanic/Latino), 4 international. Average age 33. 61 applicants, 67% accepted, 37 enrolled. *Faculty:* 7 full-time (6 women), 11 part-time/adjunct (10 women). *Financial support:* In 2015–16, 4 students received support. Unspecified assistantships available. Financial award applicants required to submit FAFSA. In 2015, 37 master's awarded. *Degree program information:* Part-time and evening/weekend programs available. Part-time, evening/weekend, online learning. Offers English for speakers of other languages (Advanced Certificate); international advocacy and leadership (MA, Certificate); teaching and learning (MA); TESL (MA). *Application deadline:* Applications are processed on a rolling basis. Electronic applications accepted. *Application Contact:* Cory Roup, Graduate Education Enrollment and Academic Advisor, 816-501-2464, E-mail: cory.roup@avila.edu. *Director of Graduate Education*, Dr. Stacy Keith, 816-501-2446, Fax: 816-501-2915, E-mail: stacy.keith@avila.edu.

School of Professional Studies Students: 83 full-time (59 women), 56 part-time (43 women); includes 49 minority (36 Black or African American, non-Hispanic/Latino; 11 Hispanic/Latino; 2 Two or more races, non-Hispanic/Latino), 8 international. Average age 38. 47 applicants, 64% accepted, 27 enrolled. *Faculty:* 2 full-time (1 woman), 10 part-time/adjunct (7 women). *Financial support:* In 2015–16, 19 students received support. Unspecified assistantships available. Support available to part-time students. Financial award applicants required to submit FAFSA. In 2015, 25 degrees awarded. *Degree program information:* Part-time and evening/weekend programs available. Part-time-only, evening/weekend, 100% online, blended/hybrid learning. Offers executive leadership development (MS); fundraising (MA); instructional design and technology (MA, MS); leadership coaching (MS); organizational development (MS); project management (MA); strategic human resources (MS). *Application deadline:* Applications are processed on a rolling basis. *Application fee:* $0. Electronic applications accepted. *Application Contact:* Linda Dubar, School of Professional Studies, 816-501-3737, Fax: 816-941-4650, E-mail: advantage@avila.edu. *Dean*, Dr. Steve Iliff, 816-501-3737, Fax: 816-941-4650, E-mail: advantage@avila.edu.

AZUSA PACIFIC UNIVERSITY, Azusa, CA 91702-7000

General Information Independent-religious, coed, university. CGS member. *Graduate housing:* On-campus housing not available.

GRADUATE UNITS

Center for Adult and Professional Studies Online learning. Offers leadership and organizational studies (MA).

College of Liberal Arts and Sciences ***Degree program information:*** Part-time and evening/weekend programs available. Part-time, evening/weekend, online learning. Offers fine arts in visual art (MFA); liberal arts and sciences (MA, MFA); teaching English to speakers of other languages (MA); transformational urban leadership (MA).

Haggard Graduate School of Theology ***Degree program information:*** Part-time and evening/weekend programs available. Part-time, evening/weekend. Offers biblical studies (MA); Christian education in youth ministry (MA); church leadership and development (MAPS); divinity (M Div); ministry (D Min); religion: Biblical studies (MAR); religion: theology and ethics (MA); theology (M Div, MA, MAPS, MAR, D Min); urban studies (MAPS); worship leadership (MAPS); youth and family ministry (MAPS).

School of Behavioral and Applied Sciences Offers behavioral and applied sciences (M Ed, MA, MSW, DPT, Ed D, PhD, Psy D); clinical psychology (MA, Psy D); college student affairs (M Ed); educational leadership (Ed D); global leadership (MA); higher education leadership (Ed D); organizational leadership (MA); physical therapy (DPT); social work (MSW).

School of Business and Management ***Degree program information:*** Part-time and evening/weekend programs available. Part-time, evening/weekend. Offers business administration (MBA); diversity for strategic advantage (MA); entrepreneurship (MBA); finance (MBA); human and organizational development (MA); human resources and organizational development (MBA); human resources management (MA); international business (MBA); marketing (MBA); non-profit management (MA); organizational development and change (MA); performance improvement (MA); public administration (MA); strategic management (MBA).

School of Education ***Degree program information:*** Part-time and evening/weekend programs available. Part-time, evening/weekend. Offers curriculum and instruction in multicultural contexts (MA Ed); digital teaching and learning (MA Ed); education (M Ed, MA, MA Ed, Ed D, Credential); educational counseling (MA); educational psychology (MA); educational technology (M Ed); educational technology and learning (MA); physical education (M Ed); school administration (MA); school librarianship (MA); special education (MA Ed); special education and educational technology (M Ed); teacher librarian services (Credential); teaching (MA Ed).

School of Music ***Degree program information:*** Part-time and evening/weekend programs available. Part-time, evening/weekend. Offers education (M Mus); performance (M Mus).

School of Nursing ***Degree program information:*** Part-time and evening/weekend programs available. Part-time, evening/weekend. Offers nursing (MSN); nursing education (PhD).

BABEL UNIVERSITY PROFESSIONAL SCHOOL OF TRANSLATION, Honolulu, HI 96815

General Information Proprietary, coed, primarily women, graduate-only institution. *Graduate housing:* On-campus housing not available.

GRADUATE UNITS

Program in Translation ***Degree program information:*** Part-time and evening/weekend programs available. Part-time, evening/weekend, online learning. Offers translation (MS).

BABSON COLLEGE, Babson Park, MA 02457-0310

General Information Independent, coed, comprehensive institution. *Graduate housing:* Rooms and/or apartments available on a first-come, first-served basis to single and married students. Housing application deadline: 5/1.

GRADUATE UNITS

F. W. Olin Graduate School of Business ***Degree program information:*** Part-time and evening/weekend programs available. Part-time, evening/weekend, online learning. Offers accounting (MSA); advanced management (Certificate); business administration (MBA); global entrepreneurship (MS); technological entrepreneurship (MS). Electronic applications accepted.

BAKER COLLEGE CENTER FOR GRADUATE STUDIES–ONLINE, Flint, MI 48507-9843

General Information Independent, coed, graduate-only institution. *Graduate housing:* On-campus housing not available.

GRADUATE UNITS

Graduate Programs ***Degree program information:*** Part-time and evening/weekend programs available. Part-time, evening/weekend, online learning. Offers accounting (MBA); business administration (DBA); finance (MBA); general business (MBA); health care management (MBA); human resources management (MBA); information management (MBA); leadership studies (MBA); management information systems (MSIS); marketing (MBA). Electronic applications accepted.

BAKER UNIVERSITY, Baldwin City, KS 66006-0065

General Information Independent-religious, coed, comprehensive institution. *Enrollment:* 309 full-time matriculated graduate/professional students (194 women), 800 part-time matriculated graduate/professional students (509 women). *Enrollment by degree level:* 965 master's, 144 doctoral. *Graduate housing:* On-campus housing not available. *Student services:* Campus safety program, international student services, services for students with disabilities. *Library:* Baker University Library.

Computer facilities: 140 computers available on campus for general student use. A campuswide network can be accessed from student residence rooms. Online class registration is available.
Website: http://www.bakeru.edu/

General Application Contact: Kelly Belk, Vice President of Enrollment Management, 913-491-4432, E-mail: kbelk@bakeru.edu.

GRADUATE UNITS

School of Education Students: 23 full-time (18 women), 409 part-time (307 women); includes 50 minority (24 Black or African American, non-Hispanic/Latino; 6 American Indian or Alaska Native, non-Hispanic/Latino; 3 Asian, non-Hispanic/Latino; 10 Hispanic/Latino; 1 Native Hawaiian or other Pacific Islander, non-Hispanic/Latino; 6 Two or more races, non-Hispanic/Latino). Average age 36. *Financial support:* Applicants required to submit FAFSA. In 2015, 147 master's, 20 doctorates awarded. *Degree program information:* Part-time and evening/weekend programs available. Part-time, evening/weekend, 100% online. Offers education (MA Ed, MSSE, MSSL, MST, Ed D). Master-level programs also offered in Wichita, KS. *Application deadline:* Applications are processed on a rolling basis. Electronic applications accepted. *Application Contact:* Linda Reynolds, Director of Graduate Education Enrollment, 913-344-6037, E-mail: linda.reynolds@bakeru.edu. *Dean of the School of Education*, Dr. Marc Childress, 913-344-1235, E-mail: marcus.childress@bakeru.edu.

School of Professional and Graduate Studies Students: 220 full-time (119 women), 318 part-time (181 women); includes 125 minority (65 Black or African American, non-Hispanic/Latino; 11 American Indian or Alaska Native, non-Hispanic/Latino; 18 Asian, non-Hispanic/Latino; 25 Hispanic/Latino; 1 Native Hawaiian or other Pacific Islander, non-Hispanic/Latino; 5 Two or more races, non-Hispanic/Latino), 3 international. Average age 34. *Financial support:* Applicants required to submit FAFSA. In 2015, 237 master's awarded. *Degree program information:* Part-time and evening/weekend programs available. Part-time, evening/weekend, online learning. Offers business (MAOL, MBA, MSM, MSSM); liberal arts (MLA). *Application deadline:* Applications are processed on a rolling basis. *Application fee:* $45. *Application Contact:* Kelly Belk, Vice President of Enrollment Management, 913-491-4432, E-mail: kelly.belk@learn.bakeru.edu. *Dean of the School of Professional and Graduate Studies*, Dr. Jacob Bucher, 785-594-8475, E-mail: jacob.bucher@bakeru.edu.

BAKKE GRADUATE UNIVERSITY, Dallas, TX 75243-7039

General Information Independent-religious, coed, primarily men, graduate-only institution. *Enrollment by degree level:* 45 master's, 129 doctoral. *Graduate faculty:* 5 full-time (3 women), 27 part-time/adjunct (12 women). *International tuition:* $3000 full-time. *Tuition, area resident:* Full-time $6000; part-time $2000 per semester. *Required fees:* $300; $200 per semester. $50 per semester. One-time fee: $300 full-time. *Graduate housing:* On-campus housing not available. *Student services:* Career counseling, writing training. *Library:* Bakke Graduate University Library. *Collection:* Books: 43,788 (physical), 4,625 (digital/electronic); Serial titles: 5,000 (digital/electronic); Databases: 3,000. Weekly public service hours: 40.

Computer facilities: 4 computers available on campus for general student use. Online class registration is available.
Website: https://www.bgu.edu/

General Application Contact: Diana Bakke, Admissions Coordinator, 214-329-4447 Ext. 122, Fax: 214-347-9367, E-mail: diana.bakke@bgu.edu.

GRADUATE UNITS

Programs in Pastoral Ministry and Business Students: 120 full-time (48 women), 54 part-time (24 women). *Faculty:* 5 full-time (3 women), 27 part-time/adjunct (12 women). *Financial support:* Scholarships/grants and tuition waivers (partial) available. Financial award applicants required to submit FAFSA. *Degree program information:* Part-time programs available. Part-time, online learning. Offers business administration (MBA); church and ministry multiplication (D Min); global urban leadership (MA); leadership (D Min); ministry in complex contexts (D Min); social and civic entrepreneurship (MA); theology of work (D Min); theology reflection (D Min); transformational leadership (DTL); urban youth ministry (D Min). *Application deadline:* For fall admission, 7/1 priority date for domestic students; for winter admission, 12/1 for domestic students; for spring admission, 3/15 for domestic students. Applications are processed on a rolling basis. *Application fee:* $50. Electronic applications accepted. *Application Contact:* Diana Bakke, Admissions Coordinator, 214-329-4447 Ext. 122, Fax: 214-347-9367, E-mail: diana.bakke@bgu.edu. *Director of Graduate Programs*, Dr. Gwen Dewey, 214-329-4447 Ext. 119, E-mail: gwend@bgu.edu.

BALDWIN WALLACE UNIVERSITY, Berea, OH 44017-2088

General Information Independent-religious, coed, comprehensive institution. *Enrollment:* 4,009 graduate, professional, and undergraduate students; 372 full-time matriculated graduate/professional students (214 women), 212 part-time matriculated graduate/professional students (120 women). *Enrollment by degree level:* 584 master's. *Graduate faculty:* 36 full-time (16 women), 33 part-time/adjunct (8 women). *Graduate housing:* Room and/or apartments available to single students; on-campus housing not available to married students. *Student services:* Campus employment opportunities, campus safety program, career counseling, exercise/wellness program, free psychological counseling, international student services, low-cost health insurance, multicultural affairs office, services for students with disabilities, teacher training, writing training. *Library:* Ritter Library plus 2 others. *Collection:* Books: 100,135 (physical), 393,409 (digital/electronic); Serial titles: 96 (physical), 60,604 (digital/electronic); Databases: 250. Weekly public service hours: 90; study areas open 24 hours, 5–7 days a week; students can reserve study rooms. *Research affiliation:* Cuyahoga Community College (early childhood education), Berea City Schools (co-teaching models), Head Start Programs (early childhood education).

Computer facilities: 520 computers available on campus for general student use. A campuswide network can be accessed from student residence rooms. Online class registration is available.
Website: http://www.bw.edu/

General Application Contact: Winifred W. Gerhardt, Director of Transfer, Adult and Graduate Admission, 440-826-2222, Fax: 440-826-3830, E-mail: admission@bw.edu.

GRADUATE UNITS

Graduate Programs Students: 372 full-time (214 women), 212 part-time (120 women); includes 82 minority (29 Black or African American, non-Hispanic/Latino; 1 American Indian or Alaska Native, non-Hispanic/Latino; 18 Asian, non-Hispanic/Latino; 23 Hispanic/Latino; 11 Two or more races, non-Hispanic/Latino), 4 international. Average age 33. 335 applicants, 61% accepted, 140 enrolled. *Faculty:* 36 full-time (16 women), 33 part-time/adjunct (8 women). In 2015, 221 master's awarded. *Degree program information:* Part-time and evening/weekend programs available. Part-time, evening/weekend, 100% online, blended/hybrid learning. Offers physician assistant (MMS); speech-language pathology (MS). *Application deadline:* Applications are processed on a rolling basis. *Application fee:* $25. Electronic applications accepted. *Application Contact:* Winifred W. Gerhardt, Director of Transfer, Adult and Graduate Admission, 440-826-2222, Fax: 440-826-3830, E-mail: admission@bw.edu. *Provost, Academic Affairs*, Stephen D. Stahl, 440-826-2251, Fax: 440-826-2329, E-mail: sstahl@bw.edu.

School of Business Students: 212 full-time (93 women), 135 part-time (62 women); includes 63 minority (23 Black or African American, non-Hispanic/Latino; 1 American Indian or Alaska Native, non-Hispanic/Latino; 17 Asian, non-Hispanic/Latino; 17 Hispanic/Latino; 5 Two or more races, non-Hispanic/Latino), 4 international. Average age 35. 136 applicants, 77% accepted, 59 enrolled. *Faculty:* 19 full-time (7 women), 26 part-time/adjunct (6 women). *Financial support:* Applicants required to submit FAFSA. In 2015, 152 master's awarded. *Degree program information:* Part-time and evening/weekend programs available. Part-time, evening/weekend, blended/hybrid learning. Offers accounting (MBA); analytics (MBA); entrepreneurship (MBA); executive management (MBA); health care (MBA); human resources (MBA); international management (MBA); management (MBA); sustainability (MBA). *Application deadline:* For fall admission, 7/25 priority date for domestic students, 4/30 priority date for international students; for spring admission, 12/15 priority date for domestic students, 9/30 priority date for international students; for summer admission, 4/15 for domestic students. Applications are processed on a rolling basis. Electronic applications accepted. *Application Contact:* Laura Spencer, Graduate Application Specialist, 440-826-2191, Fax: 440-826-3868, E-mail: lspencer@bw.edu. *MBA Program Director*, Dale Kramer, 440-826-3331, Fax: 440-826-3868, E-mail: dkramer@bw.edu.

School of Education Students: 89 full-time (61 women), 77 part-time (58 women); includes 14 minority (6 Black or African American, non-Hispanic/Latino; 1 Asian, non-Hispanic/Latino; 3 Hispanic/Latino; 4 Two or more races, non-Hispanic/Latino). Average age 30. 106 applicants, 58% accepted, 46 enrolled. *Faculty:* 8 full-time (3 women), 18 part-time/adjunct (7 women). *Financial support:* Career-related internships or fieldwork available. Financial award applicants required to submit FAFSA. In 2015, 52 master's awarded. *Degree program information:* Part-time and evening/weekend programs available. Part-time, evening/weekend, 100% online, blended/hybrid learning. Offers leadership in higher education (MA Ed); literacy (MA Ed); mild/moderate educational needs (MA Ed); school leadership (MA Ed); technology leadership (MA Ed). *Application deadline:* For fall admission, 8/15 priority date for domestic students; for spring admission, 12/15 priority date for domestic students. Applications are processed on a rolling basis. *Application fee:* $25. Electronic applications accepted. *Application Contact:* Winifred W. Gerhardt, Director of Transfer, Adult and Graduate Admission, 440-826-2222, Fax: 440-826-3830, E-mail: admission@bw.edu. *Dean*, Dr. Karen Kaye, 440-826-2168, Fax: 440-826-3779, E-mail: kkaye@bw.edu.

BALL STATE UNIVERSITY, Muncie, IN 47306

General Information State-supported, coed, university. CGS member. *Enrollment:* 21,196 graduate, professional, and undergraduate students; 1,361 full-time matriculated graduate/professional students (869 women), 3,048 part-time matriculated graduate/professional students (2,282 women). *Enrollment by degree level:* 3,882 master's, 389 doctoral, 138 other advanced degrees. *Graduate faculty:* 441 full-time (201 women), 83 part-time/adjunct (58 women). *Tuition, area resident:* Full-time $6948; part-time $2316 per semester. Tuition, state resident: full-time $10,422; part-time $3474 per semester. Tuition, nonresident: full-time $19,062; part-time $6354 per semester. *Required fees:* $651 per semester. Tuition and fees vary according to campus/location, program and reciprocity agreements. *Graduate housing:* Rooms and/or apartments available on a first-come, first-served basis to single and married students. Housing application deadline: 6/1. *Student services:* Campus employment opportunities, campus safety program, career counseling, child daycare facilities, exercise/wellness program, free psychological counseling, grant writing training, international student services, low-cost health insurance, multicultural affairs office, services for students with disabilities, teacher training, writing training. *Library:* Bracken Library plus 2 others. *Collection:* Books: 810,080 (physical), 10,367 (digital/electronic); Serial titles: 13,487 (physical), 61,564 (digital/electronic); Databases: 257. Weekly public service hours: 123; students can reserve study rooms. *Research affiliation:* DowAgro (biochemistry), Lilly Company (biochemistry), Cisco (networking, information management), Element (biochemistry), ConforMis (biomechanics), Monell (chemistry).

Computer facilities: Computer purchase and lease plans are available. 602 computers available on campus for general student use. A campuswide network can be accessed from student residence rooms and from off campus. Online class registration, room reservations, testing and test results, manage and pay tuition, order/buy textbooks, request room repairs, order transcripts, manage meal plan, manage and prepay long distance service, undergraduate degree progress report are available.
Website: http://www.bsu.edu/

General Application Contact: Dr. Carolyn Kapinus, Acting Associate Vice President for Research/Dean of the Graduate School, 765-285-1300, Fax: 765-285-1994, E-mail: ckapinus@bsu.edu.

GRADUATE UNITS

Graduate School Students: 1,361 full-time (869 women), 3,048 part-time (2,282 women); includes 487 minority (208 Black or African American, non-Hispanic/Latino; 10 American Indian or Alaska Native, non-Hispanic/Latino; 84 Asian, non-Hispanic/Latino; 139 Hispanic/Latino; 7 Native Hawaiian or other Pacific Islander, non-Hispanic/Latino; 39 Two or more races, non-Hispanic/Latino), 315 international. Average age 29. 2,738 applicants, 65% accepted, 1314 enrolled. *Faculty:* 457 full-time (214 women), 85 part-time/adjunct (60 women). *Financial support:* In 2015–16, 914 students received support, including 278 research assistantships with partial tuition reimbursements available (averaging $10,189 per year), 391 teaching assistantships with partial tuition reimbursements available (averaging $10,108 per year); unspecified assistantships also available. Financial award application deadline: 3/1; financial award applicants required to submit FAFSA. In 2015, 1,464 master's, 82 doctorates, 426 other advanced degrees awarded. *Degree program information:* Part-time and evening/weekend programs available. Part-time, evening/weekend, 100% online, blended/hybrid learning. *Application deadline:* For fall admission, 3/1 priority date for domestic students, 1/1 priority date for international students; for spring admission, 12/1 priority date for domestic students, 7/1 priority date for international students. Applications are processed on a rolling basis. *Application fee:* $60. Electronic applications accepted. *Acting Associate Vice President for Research and Dean of the Graduate School*, Dr. Carolyn Capinus, 765-285-1300, Fax: 765-285-1994, E-mail: ckapinus@bsu.edu.

College of Applied Sciences and Technology Students: 107 full-time (74 women), 493 part-time (391 women); includes 40 minority (17 Black or African American, non-Hispanic/Latino; 9 Asian, non-Hispanic/Latino; 10 Hispanic/Latino; 4 Two or more races, non-Hispanic/Latino), 16 international. Average age 31. 353 applicants, 46% accepted, 136 enrolled. *Faculty:* 44 full-time (25 women), 16 part-time/adjunct (12 women). *Financial support:* In 2015–16, 94 students received support, including 61 research assistantships with partial tuition reimbursements available (averaging $12,405 per year), 2 teaching assistantships with partial tuition reimbursements available (averaging $12,151 per year); unspecified assistantships also available. Financial award application deadline: 3/1; financial award applicants required to submit FAFSA. In 2015, 215 master's, 12 doctorates, 1 other advanced degree awarded. *Degree program information:* Part-time and evening/weekend programs available. Part-time, evening/weekend, 100% online. Offers adult/gerontology nurse practitioner (Post Master's Certificate); applied sciences and technology (MA, MS, DNP, PhD, Certificate, Post Master's Certificate, Postbaccalaureate Certificate); athletic coaching education (Certificate); career and technical education (MA); evidence-based clinical practice (Postbaccalaureate Certificate); exercise science (MA, MS); family and consumer science (MS); family and consumer sciences (MA); family nurse practitioner (Post Master's Certificate); family nurse practitioner for the adult nurse practitioner or adult/gerontology nurse practitioner (Post Master's Certificate); human bioenergetics (PhD); nurse educator (Post Master's Certificate); nursing (MS); nursing education (Postbaccalaureate Certificate); nursing practice (DNP); nutrition and dietetics (MA, MS); physical education (MS); physical education and sport (MA, MS); technology education (MA); wellness management (MA, MS). *Application deadline:* For fall admission, 3/1 priority date for domestic students, 1/1 priority date for international students; for spring admission, 1/1 priority date for domestic students, 7/1 priority date for international students. Applications are processed on a rolling basis. *Application fee:* $60. Electronic applications accepted. *Dean*, Dr. Mitchell Whaley, 765-285-5818, Fax: 765-285-1071, E-mail: mwhaley@bsu.edu.

College of Architecture and Planning Students: 119 full-time (52 women), 42 part-time (22 women); includes 15 minority (7 Black or African American, non-Hispanic/Latino; 2 Asian, non-Hispanic/Latino; 6 Hispanic/Latino), 47 international. Average age 25. 154 applicants, 81% accepted, 70 enrolled. *Faculty:* 36 full-time (14 women), 2 part-time/adjunct (0 women). *Financial support:* In 2015–16, 89 students received support, including 19 research assistantships with partial tuition reimbursements available (averaging $5,089 per year), 43 teaching assistantships with partial tuition reimbursements available (averaging $3,729 per year); unspecified assistantships also available. Financial award application deadline: 3/1; financial award applicants required to submit FAFSA. In 2015, 81 master's, 5 other advanced degrees awarded. *Degree program information:* Part-time programs available. Part-time. Offers architecture (M Arch, M Arch II); architecture and planning (M Arch, M Arch II, MLA, MS, MUD, MURP, Certificate); digital fabrication (Certificate); historic preservation (MS); landscape architecture (MLA); urban and regional planning (MURP); urban design (MUD). *Application deadline:* For fall admission, 1/15 for domestic students. Applications are processed on a rolling basis. *Application fee:* $60. Electronic applications accepted. *Application Contact:* Stephanie D. Wilson, Graduate Recruiter, 765-285-6130, Fax: 765-285-1328, E-mail: shuffman@bsu.edu. *Interim Dean*, Dr. Phil Repp, 765-285-5859, Fax: 765-285-3726, E-mail: prepp@bsu.edu.

College of Communication, Information, and Media Students: 117 full-time (58 women), 82 part-time (45 women); includes 23 minority (13 Black or African American, non-Hispanic/Latino; 1 American Indian or Alaska Native, non-Hispanic/Latino; 2 Asian, non-Hispanic/Latino; 5 Hispanic/Latino; 2 Two or more races, non-Hispanic/Latino), 28 international. Average age 27. 194 applicants, 78% accepted, 104 enrolled. *Faculty:* 29 full-time (14 women), 3 part-time/adjunct (1 woman). *Financial support:* In 2015–16, 103 students received support, including 39 research assistantships with partial tuition reimbursements available (averaging $9,108 per year), 31 teaching assistantships with partial tuition reimbursements available (averaging $11,238 per year); unspecified assistantships also available. Financial award application deadline: 3/1; financial award applicants required to submit FAFSA. In 2015, 99 master's, 3 other advanced degrees awarded. *Degree program information:* Part-time programs available. Part-time, 100% online, blended/hybrid learning. Offers communication studies (MA); communication, information, and media (MA, MS, Certificate); emerging media and visual reporting (Certificate); emerging media design and development (MA); information and communication sciences (MS); information and communication technologies (Certificate); journalism (MA); literary journalism (Certificate); public relations (MA); telecommunications (MA). *Application deadline:* For fall admission, 1/1 priority date for international students; for spring admission, 7/1 priority date for international students. Applications are processed on a rolling basis. *Application fee:* $60. Electronic applications accepted. *Dean*, Roger Lavery, 765-285-6000, Fax: 765-285-6002, E-mail: rlavery@bsu.edu.

College of Fine Arts Students: 60 full-time (24 women), 49 part-time (31 women); includes 10 minority (4 Black or African American, non-Hispanic/Latino; 4 Asian, non-Hispanic/Latino; 1 Hispanic/Latino; 1 Two or more races, non-Hispanic/Latino), 23 international. Average age 28. 104 applicants, 64% accepted, 38 enrolled. *Faculty:* 68 full-time (27 women), 2 part-time/adjunct (both women). *Financial support:* In 2015–16, 80 students received support, including 1 research assistantship with partial tuition reimbursement available (averaging $9,584 per year), 67 teaching assistantships with partial tuition reimbursements available (averaging $9,261 per year); unspecified assistantships also available. Financial award application deadline: 3/1; financial award applicants required to submit FAFSA. In 2015, 13 master's, 18 other advanced degrees awarded. *Degree program information:* Part-time programs available. Part-time. Offers fine arts (MFA); music (MA, MM, DA, Artist Diploma); visual arts studio (MA). *Application deadline:* For fall admission, 1/1 priority date for international students; for spring admission, 6/1 priority date for international students. Applications are processed on a rolling basis. *Application fee:* $60. Electronic applications accepted. *Application Contact:* Stephanie D. Wilson, Graduate Recruiter, 765-285-6130, Fax: 765-285-1328, E-mail: shuffman@bsu.edu. *Dean*, Dr. Robert Kvam, 765-285-5495, Fax: 765-285-3790, E-mail: rkvam@bsu.edu.

College of Sciences and Humanities Students: 378 full-time (216 women), 258 part-time (147 women); includes 47 minority (17 Black or African American, non-Hispanic/Latino; 1 American Indian or Alaska Native, non-Hispanic/Latino; 10 Asian, non-Hispanic/Latino; 15 Hispanic/Latino; 4 Two or more races, non-Hispanic/Latino), 122 international. Average age 26. 636 applicants, 59% accepted, 222 enrolled. *Faculty:* 158 full-time (67 women), 5 part-time/adjunct (4 women). *Financial support:* In 2015–16, 317 students received support, including 74 research assistantships with partial tuition reimbursements available (averaging $9,833 per year), 200 teaching assistantships with partial tuition reimbursements available (averaging $11,500 per year); unspecified assistantships also available. Financial award application deadline: 3/1; financial award applicants required to submit FAFSA. In 2015, 214 master's, 14 doctorates, 5 other advanced degrees awarded. *Degree program information:* Part-time programs available. Part-time, 100% online, blended/hybrid learning. Offers actuarial science (MA); anthropology (MA); audiology (Au D); biology (MA, MS); chemistry (MA, MS); clinical psychology (MA); cognitive and social processes (MA); computer science (MA, MS); elementary mathematics teacher leadership (Certificate); emergency management and homeland security (Certificate); English (MA, PhD); environmental science (PhD); geographic information systems (Certificate); geography (MS); geology (MA, MS); history (MA); interpretive ethnography (Certificate); linguistics (MA); mathematics (MA, MS); mathematics education (MA); middle school mathematics education (Certificate); natural resources and environmental management (MA, MS); physics (MA, MAE, MS); physiology (MA, MS); political science (MA); post-secondary foundational mathematics teaching (MA, Certificate); professional meteorology and climatology (Certificate); public administration (MPA, Certificate); sciences and humanities (MA, MAE, MPA, MS, Au D, PhD, Certificate); sociology (MA); speech-language pathology (MA); statistical modeling (Certificate); statistics (MA, MS); teaching English to speakers of other languages (TESOL) and linguistics (MA). *Application deadline:* For fall admission, 1/1 priority date for international students; for spring admission, 7/1 priority date for international students. Applications are processed on a rolling basis. *Application fee:* $60. Electronic applications accepted. *Dean*, Dr. Michael Maggioto, 765-285-1042, Fax: 765-285-8980, E-mail: mmaggiatto@bsu.edu.

Miller College of Business Students: 81 full-time (42 women), 227 part-time (87 women); includes 24 minority (10 Black or African American, non-Hispanic/Latino; 7 Asian, non-Hispanic/Latino; 5 Hispanic/Latino; 1 Native Hawaiian or other Pacific Islander, non-Hispanic/Latino; 1 Two or more races, non-Hispanic/Latino), 16 international. Average age 29. 168 applicants, 77% accepted, 92 enrolled. *Faculty:* 21 full-time (2 women). *Financial support:* In 2015–16, 40 students received support, including 13 research assistantships with partial tuition reimbursements available (averaging $10,162 per year), 18 teaching assistantships with partial tuition reimbursements available (averaging $9,883 per year); unspecified assistantships also available. Financial award application deadline: 3/1; financial award applicants required to submit FAFSA. In 2015, 117 master's, 16 other advanced degrees awarded. *Degree program information:* Part-time and evening/weekend programs available. Part-time, evening/weekend, 100% online, blended/hybrid learning. Offers accounting (MS); business administration (MBA, Certificate, Graduate Certificate); business education (MA); business essentials (Graduate Certificate); community and economic development (Certificate); health economics, policy and administration (Certificate); information systems and operations management (MA, Certificate); information systems security management (Certificate); selling and sales management (Certificate). *Application deadline:* For fall admission, 7/1 for domestic students; for spring admission, 12/1 for domestic students; for summer admission, 4/1 for domestic students. Applications are processed on a rolling basis. *Application fee:* $60. Electronic applications accepted. *Application Contact:* Stephanie D. Wilson, Graduate Recruiter, 765-285-6130, Fax: 765-285-1328, E-mail: shuffman@bsu.edu. *Dean*, Dr. Jennifer Bott, 765-285-5323, Fax: 765-285-5323, E-mail: jpbott@bsu.edu.

Teachers College Students: 523 full-time (414 women), 1,937 part-time (1,582 women); includes 338 minority (145 Black or African American, non-Hispanic/Latino; 8 American Indian or Alaska Native, non-Hispanic/Latino; 52 Asian, non-Hispanic/Latino; 100 Hispanic/Latino; 6 Native Hawaiian or other Pacific Islander, non-Hispanic/Latino; 27 Two or more races, non-Hispanic/Latino), 66 international. Average age 30. 1,259 applicants, 67% accepted, 698 enrolled. *Faculty:* 87 full-time (59 women), 56 part-time/adjunct (41 women). *Financial support:* In 2015–16, 210 students received support, including 80 research assistantships with partial tuition reimbursements available (averaging $10,509 per year), 35 teaching assistantships with partial tuition reimbursements available (averaging $10,098 per year); unspecified assistantships also available. Financial award application deadline: 3/1; financial award applicants required to submit FAFSA. In 2015, 725 master's, 44 doctorates, 378 other advanced degrees awarded. *Degree program information:* Part-time and evening/weekend programs available. Part-time, evening/weekend, 100% online, blended/hybrid learning. Offers adult and community education (MA); adult education (MA, Ed D, Certificate); adult, higher and community education (Ed D); applied behavior analysis (MA, Certificate); autism (Certificate); charter school leadership (Certificate); college and university teaching (Certificate); community college leadership (Certificate); community education (Certificate); computer education (Certificate); counseling (MA); counseling psychology (MA, PhD); curriculum and educational technology (MA); diversity studies (Certificate); early childhood administration (Certificate); education (MA, MAE, MS, Ed D, PhD, Certificate, Ed S); educational administration and supervision (MA, Ed D); educational psychology (MA, MS); educational psychology (PhD); educational studies (PhD); elementary education (MAE, Ed D, PhD); enhanced teaching practice for elementary teachers (Certificate); executive development for public service (MA); gifted and talented education (Certificate); human development and learning (Certificate); identity and leadership development for counselors (Certificate); instructional design and assessment (Certificate); literacy instruction (Certificate); middle-level education (Certificate); neuropsychology (Certificate); qualitative research in education (Certificate); quantitative psychology (MS); response to intervention (Certificate); school psychology (MA, PhD, Ed S); school psychology (Ed S); school superintendency (Ed S); secondary education (MA); social psychology (MA); social psychology and clinical mental health counseling (MA); special education (MA, MAE, Ed D); student affairs administration in higher education (MA). *Application deadline:* For fall admission, 1/1 priority date for international students. Applications are processed on a rolling basis. *Application fee:* $60. Electronic applications accepted. *Application Contact:* Stephanie D. Wilson, Graduate Recruiter, 765-285-6130, Fax: 765-285-1328, E-mail: shuffman@bsu.edu. *Dean*, Dr. John E. Jacobson, 765-285-5251, Fax: 765-285-5455, E-mail: jejacobson@bsu.edu.

BANK STREET COLLEGE OF EDUCATION, New York, NY 10025

General Information Independent, coed, graduate-only institution. *Research affiliation:* Annenberg Institute (education), Stanford University (education), Educational Development Center (education), Mathematica Policy Research, Inc. (education), Center for Teaching Quality (education).

GRADUATE UNITS

Graduate School Offers advanced literacy specialization (Ed M); bilingual childhood special education (Ed M); bilingual early childhood general education (MS Ed); bilingual early childhood special and general education (MS Ed); bilingual early childhood special education (Ed M, MS Ed); bilingual elementary/childhood general education (MS Ed); bilingual elementary/childhood special and general education (MS Ed); bilingual elementary/childhood special education (MS Ed); child life (MS); early childhood and elementary/childhood education (MS Ed); early childhood education (MS Ed); early childhood leadership (MS Ed); early childhood special and general education (MS Ed); early childhood special education (Ed M, MS Ed); education (Ed M, MS, MS Ed); educational leadership (MS Ed); elementary/childhood education (MS Ed); elementary/childhood special and general education (MS Ed); elementary/childhood special education (MS Ed); elementary/childhood special education certification (Ed M); infant and family development (MS Ed); infant and family early childhood special and general education (MS Ed); infant and family/early childhood special education (Ed M); leadership for educational change (Ed M, MS Ed); leadership in community-based learning (MS Ed); leadership in mathematics education (MS Ed); leadership in museum education (MS Ed); leadership in the arts: creative writing (MS Ed); leadership in the arts: visual arts (MS Ed); museum education (MS Ed); museum education: elementary education certification (MS Ed); reading and literacy (MS Ed); teaching literacy (MS Ed); teaching literacy and childhood general education (MS Ed). Electronic applications accepted.

BAPTIST BIBLE COLLEGE, Springfield, MO 65803-3498

General Information Independent-religious, coed, comprehensive institution. *Enrollment:* 8 full-time matriculated graduate/professional students (1 woman), 45 part-time matriculated graduate/professional students (9 women). *Enrollment by degree level:* 53 master's. *Graduate faculty:* 3 full-time (0 women), 3 part-time/adjunct (0 women). *Tuition, area resident:* Part-time $325 per credit hour. *Required fees:* $100. *Graduate housing:* Rooms and/or apartments available on a first-come, first-served basis to single and married students. Typical cost: $5600 (including board) for single students. *Student services:* Campus employment opportunities, campus safety program, free psychological counseling, international student services. *Library:* G. B. Vick Memorial Library plus 1 other.

Computer facilities: 50 computers available on campus for general student use.
Website: http://www.gobbc.edu/

General Application Contact: Emily Milioni, Graduate School Secretary, 417-268-6025, Fax: 800-819-8330, E-mail: emilioni@gobbc.edu.

GRADUATE UNITS

Graduate School of Theology Students: 8 full-time (1 woman), 45 part-time (9 women); includes 5 minority (2 Black or African American, non-Hispanic/Latino; 1 Asian, non-Hispanic/Latino; 2 Hispanic/Latino), 3 international. Average age 28. *Faculty:* 3 full-time (0 women), 3 part-time/adjunct (0 women). *Financial support:* Application deadline: 3/6; applicants required to submit FAFSA. In 2015, 12 master's awarded. *Degree program information:* Part-time programs available. Part-time. Offers biblical counseling (MA); biblical studies (MA); church ministry (MA); intercultural studies (MA); theology (M Div). *Application deadline:* For fall admission, 8/1 priority date for domestic students; for spring admission, 1/14 for domestic students. Applications are processed on a rolling basis. *Application fee:* $40. Electronic applications accepted. *Application Contact:* Emily Milioni, Administrative Assistant, 417-268-6025, Fax: 800-819-8330, E-mail: emilioni@gobbc.edu. *Vice President*, Dr. Gregory T. Christopher, 417-268-6008, Fax: 800-819-8330, E-mail: gchristopher@gobbc.edu.

THE BAPTIST COLLEGE OF FLORIDA, Graceville, FL 32440-1898

General Information Independent-religious, coed, comprehensive institution. *Enrollment:* 481 graduate, professional, and undergraduate students; 33 full-time matriculated graduate/professional students (6 women). *Enrollment by degree level:* 33 master's. *Graduate faculty:* 12 full-time (0 women). *Tuition, area resident:* Part-time $320 per credit hour. *Required fees:* $600. *Graduate housing:* Rooms and/or apartments available on a first-come, first-served basis to single and married students. Typical cost: $4200 (including board) for single students; $3000 per year for married students. *Student services:* Campus employment opportunities, campus safety program, exercise/wellness program, free psychological counseling, services for students with disabilities, writing training. *Library:* Ida J. MacMillan Library plus 1 other. *Collection:* Books: 88,931 (digital/electronic); Serial titles: 5,602 (digital/electronic); Databases: 16. Weekly public service hours: 66.

Computer facilities: 25 computers available on campus for general student use. A campuswide network can be accessed from student residence rooms. Online class registration is available.
Website: http://www.baptistcollege.edu/

General Application Contact: Sandra Richards, Director of Admissions, 850-261-3261 Ext. 415.

GRADUATE UNITS

Graduate Programs Students: 33 full-time (6 women); includes 2 minority (1 Black or African American, non-Hispanic/Latino; 1 Hispanic/Latino). Average age 28. 10 applicants, 100% accepted, 10 enrolled. *Faculty:* 12 full-time (0 women). *Financial support:* In 2015–16, 2 students received support. In 2015, 3 master's awarded. *Degree program information:* Part-time programs available. Part-time, 100% online, blended/hybrid learning. Offers Christian ministry (MA); Christian studies (MA); music and worship leadership (MA). *Application deadline:* For fall admission, 8/15 for domestic students; for spring admission, 1/15 for domestic students. Applications are processed on a rolling basis. *Application fee:* $25. Electronic applications accepted. *Application Contact:* Sandra Richards, Director of Admissions, 850-263-3261 Ext. 415. *Chair of the Graduate Division*, Dr. Ed Scott, 850-263-3261 Ext. 488, E-mail: eescott@baptistcollege.edu.

BAPTIST MISSIONARY ASSOCIATION THEOLOGICAL SEMINARY, Jacksonville, TX 75766-5407

General Information Independent-religious, coed, primarily men, comprehensive institution. *Graduate housing:* Rooms and/or apartments available on a first-come, first-served basis to single and married students. Housing application deadline: 6/1.

GRADUATE UNITS

Graduate and Professional Programs *Degree program information:* Part-time programs available. Part-time. Offers theology (M Div, MAR). Electronic applications accepted.

BAPTIST THEOLOGICAL SEMINARY AT RICHMOND, Richmond, VA 23227

General Information Independent-religious, coed, graduate-only institution. *Enrollment by degree level:* 55 master's, 9 doctoral, 3 other advanced degrees. *Graduate faculty:* 4 full-time (1 woman), 12 part-time/adjunct (4 women). *Tuition, area resident:* Full-time $29,700; part-time $19,800 per year. *Required fees:* $620; $620 per year. *Graduate housing:* Rooms and/or apartments available on a first-come, first-served basis to single and married students. Typical cost: $9000 (including board) for single students; $9360 (including board) for married students. Room and board charges vary according to housing facility selected. Housing application deadline: 2/15. *Student services:* Campus employment opportunities, campus safety program, exercise/wellness program, free psychological counseling, international student services, services for students with disabilities. *Library:* Morton Library. Students can reserve study rooms.

Computer facilities: 2 computers available on campus for general student use. A campuswide network can be accessed. Online class registration is available.
Website: http://www.btsr.edu/

General Application Contact: Melissa Fallen, Director of Admissions and Recruitment, 804-204-1208, E-mail: admissions@btsr.edu.

GRADUATE UNITS

Graduate and Professional Programs Students: 37 full-time (20 women), 30 part-time (18 women); includes 10 minority (9 Black or African American, non-Hispanic/Latino; 1 Hispanic/Latino), 3 international. *Faculty:* 4 full-time (1 woman), 12 part-time/adjunct (4 women). *Financial support:* Teaching assistantships, scholarships/grants, and tuition waivers (partial) available. Financial award application deadline: 2/1. *Degree program information:* Part-time programs available. Part-time, online learning. Offers Biblical interpretation (M Div); Christian education formation (M Div); Christian ministry (MCM); justice and peacebuilding (M Div, D Min); theological studies (MTS, Graduate Certificate); youth and student ministries (M Div). *Application deadline:* For fall admission, 7/1 for domestic students, 5/1 for international students; for winter admission, 12/15 for domestic students, 9/1 for international students; for spring admission, 1/15 for domestic students, 10/1 for international students. Applications are processed on a rolling basis. *Application fee:* $35. *Application Contact:* Melissa Fallen, Director of Admissions and Recruitment, 804-204-1208, E-mail: admissions@btsr.edu. *President*, Dr. Ronald W. Crawford, 804-204-1201, Fax: 804-355-8182, E-mail: rcrawford@btsr.edu.

BARCLAY COLLEGE, Haviland, KS 67059-0288

General Information Independent-religious, coed, comprehensive institution.

GRADUATE UNITS

Master of Arts Program Online learning. Offers transformational leadership (MA). Electronic applications accepted.

BARD COLLEGE, Annandale-on-Hudson, NY 12504

General Information Independent, coed, comprehensive institution. *Graduate housing:* Room and/or apartments available on a first-come, first-served basis to single students; on-campus housing not available to married students.

GRADUATE UNITS

Bard Center for Environmental Policy *Degree program information:* Part-time programs available. Part-time. Offers climate science and policy (MS, Professional Certificate); environmental policy (MS, Professional Certificate); sustainability (MBA). Electronic applications accepted.

Center for Curatorial Studies Offers curatorial studies (MA). Electronic applications accepted.

Conservatory of Music Offers music (MFA, MM); vocal arts (MM).

The Conductors Institute Offers conducting (MFA).

International Center of Photography Offers advanced photographic studies (MFA).

Levy Economics Institute Offers economic theory and policy (MS).

Longy School of Music ***Degree program information:*** Part-time programs available. Part-time. Offers chamber ensemble (Artist Diploma); collaborative piano (MM, Artist Diploma, GPD); composition (MM); Dalcroze eurhythmics (MM); early music (MM, Artist Diploma, GPD); instrumental performance (MM, Artist Diploma, GPD); modern American music (MM, GPD); opera performance (MM, GPD); organ performance (MM, Artist Diploma, GPD); piano performance (MM, Artist Diploma, GPD); vocal performance (MM, Artist Diploma, GPD). Electronic applications accepted.

Master of Arts in Teaching Program ***Degree program information:*** Part-time and evening/weekend programs available. Part-time, evening/weekend. Offers teaching (MAT). Electronic applications accepted.

Milton Avery Graduate School of the Arts Offers arts (MFA). Electronic applications accepted.

BARD GRADUATE CENTER: DECORATIVE ARTS, DESIGN HISTORY, MATERIAL CULTURE, New York, NY 10024-3602

General Information Independent, coed, primarily women, graduate-only institution. *Enrollment by degree level:* 44 master's, 38 doctoral. *Graduate faculty:* 18 full-time (8 women), 5 part-time/adjunct (4 women). *Graduate housing:* Rooms and/or apartments available on a first-come, first-served basis to single and married students. Housing application deadline: 4/1. *Student services:* Campus employment opportunities, campus safety program, career counseling, free psychological counseling, grant writing training, low-cost health insurance, writing training. *Research affiliation:* Association of Research Institutes in Art History, Metropolitan Museum of Art, New York Historical Society, American Museum of Natural History, Museum of Arts and Design, The Frick Collection.

Computer facilities: 15 computers available on campus for general student use. Website: http://www.bgc.bard.edu/

General Application Contact: Elena Pinto Simon, Dean, Academic Administration and Student Affairs, 212-501-3057, Fax: 212-501-3065, E-mail: simon@bgc.bard.edu.

GRADUATE UNITS

Graduate Studies Students: 70 full-time (58 women), 12 part-time (all women). *Faculty:* 18 full-time (8 women), 5 part-time/adjunct (4 women). *Financial support:* Fellowships with tuition reimbursements, research assistantships, teaching assistantships, career-related internships or fieldwork, institutionally sponsored loans, scholarships/grants, traineeships, health care benefits, and unspecified assistantships available. Financial award application deadline: 1/8; financial award applicants required to submit FAFSA. In 2015, 22 master's, 4 doctorates awarded. *Degree program information:* Part-time programs available. Part-time. Offers decorative arts, design history, and material culture (M Phil, MA, PhD). *Application deadline:* For fall admission, 1/6 for domestic and international students. *Application fee:* $70. *Application Contact:* Elena Pinto Simon, Dean, Academic Administration and Student Affairs, 212-501-3057, Fax: 212-501-3065, E-mail: simon@bgc.bard.edu. *Founder and Director,* Susan Weber, 212-501-3000, Fax: 212-501-3079.

BARRY UNIVERSITY, Miami Shores, FL 33161-6695

General Information Independent-religious, coed, university. *Graduate housing:* On-campus housing not available. *Research affiliation:* Baxter Corporation (immunology, diagnostics), Coulter Corporation (immunology, cytology), Cordis Corporation (cardiac product development), Diamedix (immunological diagnostics), Noven Pharmaceutical, Sano Pharmaceuticals.

GRADUATE UNITS

Andreas School of Business ***Degree program information:*** Part-time and evening/weekend programs available. Part-time, evening/weekend. Offers accounting (MSA); business (MBA, MSA, MSM, Certificate); business administration (MBA); finance (Certificate); health services administration (Certificate); international business (Certificate); management (MSM); management information systems (Certificate); marketing (Certificate). Electronic applications accepted.

College of Arts and Sciences ***Degree program information:*** Part-time and evening/weekend programs available. Part-time, evening/weekend. Offers arts and sciences (MA, MFA, MS, D Min, Certificate, SSP); broadcasting (Certificate); clinical psychology (MS); communication (MA); liberal studies (MA); ministry (D Min); organizational communication (MS); pastoral ministry for Hispanics (MA); pastoral theology (MA); photography (MA, MFA); practical theology (MA); school psychology (MS, SSP). Electronic applications accepted.

College of Health Sciences ***Degree program information:*** Part-time and evening/weekend programs available. Part-time, evening/weekend. Offers anesthesiology (MS); biology (MS); biomedical sciences (MS); health care leadership (Certificate); health care planning and informatics (Certificate); health sciences (MS, Certificate); health services administration (MS); histotechnology (Certificate); long term care management (Certificate); medical group practice management (Certificate); occupational therapy (MS); quality improvement and outcomes management (Certificate). Electronic applications accepted.

Dwayne O. Andreas School of Law Offers law (JD).

Physician Assistant Program Offers physician assistant (MCMS). Electronic applications accepted.

School of Adult and Continuing Education ***Degree program information:*** Part-time and evening/weekend programs available. Part-time, evening/weekend. Offers administrative studies (MA); adult and continuing education (MA, MPA, MS, MSN, PhD, Certificate); information technology (MS); public administration (MPA). Electronic applications accepted.

Division of Nursing ***Degree program information:*** Part-time and evening/weekend programs available. Part-time, evening/weekend. Offers acute care nurse practitioner (MSN); family nurse practitioner (MSN); nurse practitioner (Certificate); nursing (MSN, PhD, Certificate); nursing administration (MSN, PhD, Certificate); nursing education (MSN, Certificate). Electronic applications accepted.

School of Education ***Degree program information:*** Part-time and evening/weekend programs available. Part-time, evening/weekend, online learning. Offers accomplished teacher (Ed S); advanced teaching and learning with technology (Certificate); counseling (MS, PhD, Ed S); culture, language and literacy (TESOL) (PhD); curriculum evaluation and research (PhD); distance education (Certificate); early childhood (Ed S); early childhood education (PhD); education (MS, Ed D, PhD, Certificate, Ed S); education for teachers of students with hearing impairments (MS); educational computing and technology (MS, Ed S); educational leadership (MS, Ed D, Certificate, Ed S); educational technology (PhD); elementary (Ed S); elementary education (MS, PhD); elementary education/ESOL (MS); ESOL (Ed S); exceptional student education (MS, Ed S); gifted (Ed S); higher education administration (PhD); higher education technology integration (Certificate); human resource development (PhD); human resource development and administration (MS); human resources: not for profit and religious organizations (Certificate); K-12 technology integration (Certificate); leadership (PhD); marital, couple and family counseling/therapy (MS, Ed S); mental health counseling (MS, Ed S); Montessori (Ed S); Montessori education (MS, Ed S); PKP/elementary (Ed S); pre-k/primary (MS); pre-k/primary/ESOL (MS); reading (MS, Ed S); reading, language and cognition (PhD); rehabilitation counseling (MS, Ed S); school counseling (MS, Ed S); technology and TESOL (MS, Ed S); TESOL (MS); TESOL international (MS). Electronic applications accepted.

School of Human Performance and Leisure Sciences ***Degree program information:*** Part-time and evening/weekend programs available. Part-time, evening/weekend. Offers athletic training (MS); biomechanics (MS); exercise science (MS); general movement science (MS); human performance and leisure sciences (MS); sport and exercise psychology (MS); sport management (MS). Electronic applications accepted.

School of Podiatric Medicine Offers anatomy (MS); podiatric medicine (MS, DPM); podiatric medicine and surgery (DPM). Electronic applications accepted.

School of Social Work ***Degree program information:*** Part-time and evening/weekend programs available. Part-time, evening/weekend. Offers social work (MSW, PhD). Electronic applications accepted.

BARTON COLLEGE, Wilson, NC 27893-7000

General Information Independent-religious, coed, comprehensive institution.

GRADUATE UNITS

Program in Elementary Education Offers elementary education (M Ed). Electronic applications accepted.

BARUCH COLLEGE OF THE CITY UNIVERSITY OF NEW YORK, New York, NY 10010-5585

General Information State and locally supported, coed, comprehensive institution. *Graduate housing:* On-campus housing not available.

GRADUATE UNITS

School of Public Affairs ***Degree program information:*** Part-time and evening/weekend programs available. Part-time, evening/weekend. Offers educational leadership (MS Ed); general public administration (MPA); health care policy (MPA); higher education administration (MS Ed); nonprofit administration (MPA); policy analysis and evaluation (MPA); public affairs (MPA, MS Ed, Advanced Certificate); public management (MPA); school building leadership (Advanced Certificate); school district leadership (Advanced Certificate). Electronic applications accepted.

Weissman School of Arts and Sciences Students: 164 full-time (107 women), 99 part-time (59 women); includes 67 minority (24 Black or African American, non-Hispanic/Latino; 2 American Indian or Alaska Native, non-Hispanic/Latino; 14 Asian, non-Hispanic/Latino; 23 Hispanic/Latino; 4 Two or more races, non-Hispanic/Latino), 73 international. 918 applicants, 26% accepted, 136 enrolled. *Faculty:* 34 full-time (12 women), 19 part-time/adjunct (6 women). *Financial support:* In 2015–16, 20 students received support. Career-related internships or fieldwork, Federal Work-Study, scholarships/grants, traineeships, tuition waivers (partial), and unspecified assistantships available. Financial award applicants required to submit FAFSA. In 2015, 113 master's awarded. *Degree program information:* Part-time and evening/weekend programs available. Part-time, evening/weekend. Offers arts administration (MA); arts and sciences (MA, MS); corporate communication (MA); financial engineering (MS); industrial/organizational psychology (MS); mental health counseling (MA). *Application fee:* $125. Electronic applications accepted. *Application Contact:* Michael J. Lovaglio, Director of Graduate Programs, 646-312-3897, Fax: 646-312-3871, E-mail: wsas.graduate.studies@baruch.cuny.edu. *Director of Graduate Programs,* Michael J. Lovaglio, 646-312-3897, E-mail: michael.lovaglio@baruch.cuny.edu.

Zicklin School of Business ***Degree program information:*** Part-time and evening/weekend programs available. Part-time, evening/weekend. Offers accounting (MBA, MS, PhD); business (MBA, MS, PhD, Certificate); business administration (MBA); decision sciences (MBA); economics (MBA); entrepreneurship (MBA, MS); finance (MBA, MS, PhD); general business administration (MBA); health care administration (MBA); industrial and labor relations (MS); industrial and organizational psychology (MBA, MS, PhD); information systems (MBA, MS, PhD); international business (MBA); management (PhD); marketing (MBA, MS, PhD); operations management (MBA); organizational behavior/human resources management (MBA); quantitative methods and modeling (MBA, MS); real estate (MBA, MS); statistics (MBA, MS); sustainable business (MBA); taxation (MBA, MS). JD/MBA offered jointly with Brooklyn Law School and New York Law School. Electronic applications accepted.

BASTYR UNIVERSITY, Kenmore, WA 98028-4966

General Information Independent, coed, upper-level institution. *Graduate housing:* Room and/or apartments available on a first-come, first-served basis to single students; on-campus housing not available to married students. Housing application deadline: 5/1. *Research affiliation:* University of Washington (health), Fred Hutchinson Cancer Research Center (oncology), Seattle Cancer Care Alliance (oncology), Benaroya Research Institute at Virginia Mason (health).

GRADUATE UNITS

School of Acupuncture and Oriental Medicine ***Degree program information:*** Evening/weekend programs available. Evening/weekend. Offers acupuncture and Oriental medicine (MS, DAOM, Certificate). Electronic applications accepted.

School of Natural Health Arts and Sciences ***Degree program information:*** Part-time programs available. Part-time. Offers counseling psychology (MA); holistic landscape design (Certificate); midwifery (MS); nutrition (MS); nutrition and clinical health psychology (MS).

School of Naturopathic Medicine ***Degree program information:*** Part-time programs available. Part-time. Offers naturopathic medicine (ND). Electronic applications accepted.

BAYAMÓN CENTRAL UNIVERSITY, Bayamón, PR 00960-1725

General Information Independent-religious, coed, comprehensive institution. *Graduate housing:* On-campus housing not available.

GRADUATE UNITS

Graduate Programs ***Degree program information:*** Part-time and evening/weekend programs available. Part-time, evening/weekend. Offers accounting (MBA); administration and supervision (MA Ed); commercial education (MA Ed); elementary education (K–3) (MA Ed); family counseling (Graduate Certificate); finance (MBA); general business (MBA); guidance and counseling (MA Ed); management (MBA); marketing (MBA); organizational psychology (MA); pre-elementary teacher (MA Ed); rehabilitation counseling (MA Ed); special education (MA Ed).

BAYLOR COLLEGE OF MEDICINE, Houston, TX 77030-3498

General Information Independent, coed, graduate-only institution. CGS member. *Graduate housing:* On-campus housing not available. *Research affiliation:* Veterans Affairs Medical Center (biomedical research), Texas Children's Hospital (pediatric biomedical research), St. Luke's Episcopal Hospital (biomedical research), National Space Biomedical Research Institute (biomedical research), Harris Health System (biomedical research), Children's Nutrition Research Center (pediatric nutrition).

GRADUATE UNITS

Graduate School of Biomedical Sciences Offers biochemistry (PhD); biochemistry and molecular biology (PhD); biomedical sciences (MS, PhD); cardiovascular sciences (PhD); cell and molecular biology (PhD); clinical scientist training (MS, PhD); developmental biology (PhD); genetics (PhD); human genetics (PhD); immunology (PhD); microbiology (PhD); molecular and cellular biology (PhD); molecular and human genetics (PhD); molecular physiology and biophysics (PhD); molecular virology and microbiology (PhD); neuroscience (PhD); pharmacology (PhD); structural and computational biology and molecular biophysics (PhD); translational biology and molecular medicine (PhD); virology (PhD). Electronic applications accepted.

Medical School Offers medicine (MD). Electronic applications accepted.

School of Allied Health Sciences Offers allied health sciences (MS, DNP); nurse anesthesia (DNP); physician assistant (MS). Electronic applications accepted.

BAYLOR UNIVERSITY, Waco, TX 76798

General Information Independent-religious, coed, university. CGS member. *Enrollment:* 16,787 graduate, professional, and undergraduate students; 2,175 full-time matriculated graduate/professional students (998 women), 378 part-time matriculated graduate/professional students (195 women). *Enrollment by degree level:* 1,348 master's, 1,182 doctoral, 23 other advanced degrees. *Graduate faculty:* 789. *Graduate housing:* Rooms and/or apartments available to single and married students. *Student services:* Campus employment opportunities, campus safety program, career counseling, exercise/wellness program, free psychological counseling, international student services, low-cost health insurance, multicultural affairs office, services for students with disabilities. *Library:* Moody Memorial Library plus 8 others. *Research affiliation:* National Center for Supercomputing Applications (physics), Sandia National Laboratories (physics), Zyvex Corporation (physics), OXiGENE, Inc. (pharmaceuticals), Brookhaven National Laboratory (physics), Fermi National Accelerator Laboratory (physics).

Computer facilities: Computer purchase and lease plans are available. A campuswide network can be accessed from student residence rooms and from off campus. Online class registration is available.
Website: http://www.baylor.edu/

General Application Contact: Lori McNamara, Admissions Coordinator, 254-710-3588, Fax: 254-710-3870.

GRADUATE UNITS

Diana R. Garland School of Social Work Students: 90 full-time (72 women), 25 part-time (22 women); includes 30 minority (12 Black or African American, non-Hispanic/Latino; 2 Asian, non-Hispanic/Latino; 11 Hispanic/Latino; 5 Two or more races, non-Hispanic/Latino), 2 international. Average age 27. 190 applicants, 72% accepted, 71 enrolled. *Faculty:* 11 full-time (5 women), 13 part-time/adjunct (7 women). *Financial support:* In 2015–16, 138 students received support, including 12 research assistantships with tuition reimbursements available (averaging $6,800 per year); career-related internships or fieldwork, Federal Work-Study, institutionally sponsored loans, scholarships/grants, traineeships, tuition waivers (full and partial), and unspecified assistantships also available. Support available to part-time students. Financial award application deadline: 6/1; financial award applicants required to submit FAFSA. In 2015, 69 master's awarded. *Degree program information:* Part-time programs available. Part-time, blended/hybrid learning. Offers social work (MSW, PhD). *Application deadline:* For spring admission, 3/15 for domestic and international students. Applications are processed on a rolling basis. *Application fee:* $45. Electronic applications accepted. *Application Contact:* Dr. Crystal Diaz-Espinoza, Director of Recruitment and Career Services, 254-710-4479, Fax: 254-710-6455, E-mail: crystal_diaz-espinoza@baylor.edu. *Associate Dean for Academic Affairs,* Dr. David Pooler, 254-710-3884, Fax: 254-710-7412, E-mail: david_pooler@baylor.edu.

George W. Truett Theological Seminary Students: 283 full-time (95 women), 79 part-time (28 women); includes 87 minority (51 Black or African American, non-Hispanic/Latino; 6 Asian, non-Hispanic/Latino; 21 Hispanic/Latino; 9 Two or more races, non-Hispanic/Latino), 20 international. Average age 30. 167 applicants, 90% accepted, 107 enrolled. *Faculty:* 21 full-time (2 women), 16 part-time/adjunct (4 women). *Financial support:* In 2015–16, 348 students received support, including 28 teaching assistantships (averaging $5,140 per year); research assistantships, career-related internships or fieldwork, Federal Work-Study, institutionally sponsored loans, scholarships/grants, tuition waivers (partial), and unspecified assistantships also available. Support available to part-time students. Financial award application deadline: 3/1; financial award applicants required to submit FAFSA. In 2015, 73 master's, 7 doctorates awarded. *Degree program information:* Part-time programs available. Part-time. Offers theology (M Div, MACM, MTS, D Min). M Div/MBA offered jointly with Hankamer School of Business. *Application deadline:* For fall admission, 5/1 for domestic and international students; for spring admission, 11/15 for domestic and international students; for summer admission, 4/1 for domestic and international students. Applications are processed on a rolling basis. *Application fee:* $35. Electronic applications accepted. *Application Contact:* Carley Joy Lund, Administrative Associate, Admissions Services, 254-710-7334, Fax: 254-710-7233, E-mail: carley_collier@baylor.edu. *Dean,* Dr. Todd D. Still, 254-710-3755, Fax: 254-710-3753, E-mail: todd_still@baylor.edu.

Graduate School Students: 1,409 full-time (650 women), 284 part-time (155 women); includes 314 minority (62 Black or African American, non-Hispanic/Latino; 3 American Indian or Alaska Native, non-Hispanic/Latino; 62 Asian, non-Hispanic/Latino; 125 Hispanic/Latino; 1 Native Hawaiian or other Pacific Islander, non-Hispanic/Latino; 61 Two or more races, non-Hispanic/Latino), 201 international. 1,692 applicants. *Faculty:* 789. *Financial support:* Fellowships, research assistantships with tuition reimbursements, teaching assistantships with tuition reimbursements, career-related internships or fieldwork, Federal Work-Study, institutionally sponsored loans, scholarships/grants, health care benefits, tuition waivers (full and partial), and unspecified assistantships available. Support available to part-time students. Financial award applicants required to submit FAFSA. In 2015, 511 master's, 128 doctorates, 7 other advanced degrees awarded. *Degree program information:* Part-time and evening/weekend programs available. Part-time, evening/weekend, 100% online, blended/hybrid learning. Offers emergency medicine (D Sc PA); health care administration (MHA); health sciences (MHA, MS, D Sc, D Sc PA, DPT, DScPT); nutrition (MS); orthopedics (D Sc); physical therapy (DPT, DScPT). *Application deadline:* For fall admission, 2/15 for domestic students; for spring admission, 12/1 for domestic students; for summer admission, 5/1 for domestic students. Applications are processed on a rolling basis. *Application fee:* $50. Electronic applications accepted. *Application Contact:* Lori McNamara, Graduate Admissions Coordinator, 254-710-3588, Fax: 254-710-3870, E-mail: lori_mcnamara@baylor.edu. *Dean,* Dr. Larry Lyon, 254-710-3588, Fax: 254-710-3870, E-mail: larry_lyon@baylor.edu.

College of Arts and Sciences Degree program information: Part-time and evening/weekend programs available. Part-time, evening/weekend. Offers American religion and culture (PhD); American studies (MA); arts and sciences (IMES, MA, MES, MFA, MIJ, MPPA, MS, MSCSD, MSW, PhD, Psy D); biology (MA, MS, PhD); British religion and culture (PhD); chemistry (MS, PhD); clinical psychology (Psy D); communication (MA); directing (MFA); ecological, earth and environmental sciences (PhD); English (MA, PhD); environmental biology (MS); environmental science (MES, MS); geology (MS, PhD); history (MA); international journalism (MIJ); international studies (MA); journalism (MA); limnology (MS); mathematics (MS, PhD); museum studies (MA); philosophy (MA, PhD); physics (MA, MS, PhD); political science (MA, PhD); psychology (MA, PhD); public policy and administration (MPPA); religion (MA, PhD); sociology (MA, PhD); Spanish (MA); statistical science (MA, PhD); theatre studies (MA). Electronic applications accepted.

Hankamer School of Business Degree program information: Part-time programs available. Part-time. Offers accounting and business law (M Acc, MT); business (M Acc, MBA, MS Eco, MSIS, MT, PhD); business administration (MBA); economics (MS Eco); information systems (MSIS, PhD); information systems management (MBA).

Institute of Biomedical Studies Students: 28 full-time (9 women), 1 part-time (0 women); includes 5 minority (1 Black or African American, non-Hispanic/Latino; 2 Asian, non-Hispanic/Latino; 2 Hispanic/Latino), 14 international. Average age 24. 69 applicants, 10% accepted, 5 enrolled. *Faculty:* 17 part-time/adjunct (3 women). *Financial support:* In 2015–16, 22 students received support, including 11 research assistantships (averaging $20,000 per year), 11 teaching assistantships (averaging $20,000 per year); tuition waivers also available. In 2015, 5 doctorates awarded. Offers biomedical studies (MS, PhD). *Application deadline:* Applications are processed on a rolling basis. *Application fee:* $25. *Application Contact:* Rhonda Bellert, Administrative Assistant, 254-710-2514, Fax: 254-710-2199, E-mail: rhonda_bellert@baylor.edu. *Graduate Program Director,* Dr. Chris Kearney, 254-710-2131, Fax: 254-710-3878, E-mail: chris_kearney@baylor.edu.

Louise Herrington School of Nursing Degree program information: Part-time programs available. Part-time, online learning. Offers family nurse practitioner (MSN); neonatal nurse practitioner (MSN); nurse-midwifery (DNP). Electronic applications accepted.

Robbins College of Health and Human Sciences Offers communication sciences and disorders (MA, MSCSD); community health (MPH); exercise physiology (MS); health and human sciences (MA, MPH, MS, MS Ed, PhD); kinesiology, exercise nutrition and health promotion (PhD); nutrition sciences (MS); sport pedagogy (MS).

School of Education Degree program information: Part-time programs available. Part-time, online learning. Offers applied behavior analysis (MS Ed); curriculum and instruction (MA, MS Ed, Ed D, PhD); education (MA, MPH, MS Ed, Ed D, PhD, Ed S); educational administration (MS Ed, Ed S); educational psychology (MA, PhD); exceptionalities (PhD); learning and development (PhD); measurement (PhD); school psychology (Ed S). Electronic applications accepted.

School of Engineering and Computer Science Degree program information: Part-time programs available. Part-time. Offers biomedical engineering (MSBME); computer science (MS, PhD); electrical and computer engineering (MS, PhD); engineering (ME); engineering and computer science (ME, MS, MSBME, PhD); mechanical engineering (MS, PhD).

School of Music Offers church music (MM, DMA); collaborative piano (MM); composition (MM); conducting (MM); music history and literature (MM); music theory (MM); performance (MM); piano pedagogy and performance (MM).

School of Law Students: 394 full-time (181 women), 4 part-time (2 women); includes 92 minority (11 Black or African American, non-Hispanic/Latino; 7 American Indian or Alaska Native, non-Hispanic/Latino; 18 Asian, non-Hispanic/Latino; 52 Hispanic/Latino; 1 Native Hawaiian or other Pacific Islander, non-Hispanic/Latino; 3 Two or more races, non-Hispanic/Latino). Average age 24. 1,693 applicants, 36% accepted, 75 enrolled. *Faculty:* 30 full-time (7 women), 45 part-time/adjunct (5 women). *Financial support:* In 2015–16, 259 students received support. Career-related internships or fieldwork, Federal Work-Study, and scholarships/grants available. Financial award application deadline: 3/1; financial award applicants required to submit FAFSA. In 2015, 116 doctorates awarded. Offers administrative practice (JD); business litigation (JD); business transactions (JD); criminal practice (JD); estate planning (JD); general civil litigation (JD); healthcare (JD); intellectual property (JD); law (JD); real estate and natural resources (JD). *Application deadline:* For fall admission, 3/1 for domestic and international students; for spring admission, 11/1 for domestic and international students; for summer admission, 2/1 for domestic and international students. Applications are processed on a rolling basis. *Application fee:* $0. Electronic applications accepted. *Application Contact:* Nicole Neeley, Assistant Dean of Admissions, 254-710-1911, Fax: 254-710-2316, E-mail: nicole_neeley@baylor.edu. *Dean,* Bradley J. B. Toben, 254-710-1911, Fax: 254-710-2316.

BAY PATH UNIVERSITY, Longmeadow, MA 01106-2292

General Information Independent, Undergraduate: women only; graduate: coed, comprehensive institution. *Enrollment:* 3,107 graduate, professional, and undergraduate students; 569 full-time matriculated graduate/professional students (466 women), 682 part-time matriculated graduate/professional students (589 women). *Enrollment by degree level:* 1,244 master's, 7 other advanced degrees. *Graduate faculty:* 15 full-time (10 women), 79 part-time/adjunct (55 women). *Graduate housing:* Room and/or apartments available on a first-come, first-served basis to single students; on-campus housing not available to married students. Housing application deadline: 7/2. *Student services:* Campus employment opportunities, campus safety program, career counseling, exercise/wellness program, free psychological counseling, international student services, low-cost health insurance, multicultural affairs office, services for students with disabilities. *Library:* Hatch Library. *Collection:* Books: 52,343 (physical), 315,000 (digital/electronic); Serial titles: 120 (physical), 49,000 (digital/electronic); Databases: 102. Weekly public service hours: 86; students can reserve study rooms.

Computer facilities: 235 computers available on campus for general student use. A campuswide network can be accessed from student residence rooms and from off campus. Online class registration is available.
Website: http://www.baypath.edu/

General Application Contact: Diane Ranaldi, Dean of Graduate Admissions, 413-565-1332, Fax: 413-565-1250, E-mail: dranaldi@baypath.edu.

GRADUATE UNITS

Program in Accounting Students: 1 (woman) full-time, 26 part-time (20 women); includes 11 minority (5 Black or African American, non-Hispanic/Latino; 1 American Indian or Alaska Native, non-Hispanic/Latino; 1 Asian, non-Hispanic/Latino; 3 Hispanic/Latino; 1 Two or more races, non-Hispanic/Latino). Average age 33. 17 applicants, 76% accepted, 7 enrolled. *Financial support:* In 2015–16, 3 students received support. Scholarships/grants available. Financial award applicants required to submit FAFSA. In 2015, 3 master's awarded. *Degree program information:* Part-time and evening/weekend programs available. Part-time, evening/weekend, online only, 100% online. Offers accounting (MS). *Application deadline:* Applications are processed on a rolling basis. *Application fee:* $45. Electronic applications accepted. *Application Contact:* Diane Ranaldi, Dean of Graduate Admissions, 413-565-1332, Fax: 413-565-1250, E-mail: dranaldi@baypath.edu. *Director,* Kara Stevens, 413-565-1344, E-mail: kastevens@baypath.edu.

Program in Clinical Mental Health Counseling Students: 66 full-time (63 women), 70 part-time (63 women); includes 36 minority (16 Black or African American, non-Hispanic/Latino; 14 Hispanic/Latino; 6 Two or more races, non-Hispanic/Latino), 7 international. Average age 32. 97 applicants, 79% accepted, 54 enrolled. *Financial support:* In 2015–16, 7 students received support. Scholarships/grants available. Financial award applicants required to submit FAFSA. In 2015, 21 master's awarded. *Degree program information:* Part-time programs available. Part-time. Offers clinical mental health counseling (MS). Program also offered in Sturbridge and Burlington, MA. *Application deadline:* Applications are processed on a rolling basis. *Application fee:* $45. Electronic applications accepted. *Application Contact:* Diane Ranaldi, Dean of Graduate Admissions, 413-565-1332, Fax: 413-565-1250, E-mail: dranaldi@baypath.edu. *Director,* Dr. Mark Benander, 413-565-1332, E-mail: mbenander@baypath.edu.

Program in Communications ***Financial support:*** Scholarships/grants available. Financial award applicants required to submit FAFSA. *Degree program information:* Part-time and evening/weekend programs available. Part-time, evening/weekend, 100% online, blended/hybrid learning. Offers communications (MS). *Application deadline:* Applications are processed on a rolling basis. *Application fee:* $45. Electronic applications accepted. *Application Contact:* Diane Ranaldi, Dean of Graduate Admissions, 413-565-1332, Fax: 413-565-1250, E-mail: dranaldi@baypath.edu. *Director,* Robin Saunders, 413-565-1009, E-mail: rsaunders@baypath.edu.

Program in Communications and Information Management Students: 48 full-time (19 women), 27 part-time (23 women); includes 15 minority (8 Black or African American, non-Hispanic/Latino; 2 Asian, non-Hispanic/Latino; 3 Hispanic/Latino; 2 Two or more races, non-Hispanic/Latino), 33 international. Average age 32. 24 applicants, 88% accepted, 17 enrolled. *Financial support:* In 2015–16, 3 students received support. Scholarships/grants available. Financial award applicants required to submit FAFSA. In 2015, 28 master's awarded. *Degree program information:* Part-time and evening/weekend programs available. Part-time, evening/weekend, online learning. Offers communications and information management (MS). *Application deadline:* Applications are processed on a rolling basis. *Application fee:* $45. Electronic applications accepted. *Application Contact:* Diane Ranaldi, Dean of Graduate Admissions, 413-565-1332, Fax: 413-565-1250, E-mail: dranaldi@baypath.edu. *Program Director,* Robin Saunders, 413-565-1009.

Program in Creative Nonfiction Students: 18 full-time (all women), 16 part-time (15 women); includes 5 minority (3 Black or African American, non-Hispanic/Latino; 1 Hispanic/Latino; 1 Two or more races, non-Hispanic/Latino). Average age 49. 25 applicants, 92% accepted, 18 enrolled. *Financial support:* In 2015–16, 2 students received support. Scholarships/grants available. Financial award applicants required to submit FAFSA. *Degree program information:* Part-time and evening/weekend programs available. Part-time, evening/weekend, online only, 100% online. Offers creative nonfiction (MFA). *Application deadline:* Applications are processed on a rolling basis. *Application fee:* $45. Electronic applications accepted. *Application Contact:* Diane Ranaldi, Dean of Graduate Admissions, 413-565-1332, Fax: 413-565-1250, E-mail: dranaldi@baypath.edu. *Director,* Leanne James Blackwell, 413-565-1232, E-mail: ljblackwell@baypath.edu.

Program in Cybersecurity Management Students: 12 full-time (9 women), 26 part-time (15 women); includes 14 minority (9 Black or African American, non-Hispanic/Latino; 4 Hispanic/Latino; 1 Native Hawaiian or other Pacific Islander, non-Hispanic/Latino). Average age 41. 38 applicants, 87% accepted, 22 enrolled. *Financial support:* Scholarships/grants available. Financial award applicants required to submit FAFSA. In 2015, 4 master's awarded. *Degree program information:* Part-time and evening/weekend programs available. Part-time, evening/weekend, 100% online. Offers cybersecurity management (MS). *Application deadline:* Applications are processed on a rolling basis. *Application fee:* $45. Electronic applications accepted. *Application Contact:* Diane Ranaldi, Dean of Graduate Admissions, 413-565-1332, Fax: 413-565-1250, E-mail: dranaldi@baypath.edu. *Director,* Dr. Larry Snyder, 413-565-1294, E-mail: lsnyder@baypath.edu.

Program in Developmental Psychology Students: 2 full-time (both women), 13 part-time (all women); includes 6 minority (5 Black or African American, non-Hispanic/Latino; 1 Hispanic/Latino). Average age 31. 18 applicants, 67% accepted, 8 enrolled. *Financial support:* In 2015–16, 1 student received support. Scholarships/grants available. Financial award applicants required to submit FAFSA. In 2015, 8 master's awarded. *Degree program information:* Part-time and evening/weekend programs available. Part-time, evening/weekend. Offers developmental psychology (MS); mental health counseling (MS). *Application deadline:* Applications are processed on a rolling basis. *Application fee:* $45. Electronic applications accepted. *Application Contact:* Diane Ranaldi, Dean of Graduate Admissions, 413-565-1332, Fax: 413-565-1250, E-mail: dranaldi@baypath.edu. *Program Director,* Dr. Mark Benander, 413-565-1332, E-mail: mbenander@baypath.edu.

Program in Education Students: 56 full-time (52 women), 298 part-time (261 women); includes 52 minority (30 Black or African American, non-Hispanic/Latino; 4 Asian, non-Hispanic/Latino; 11 Hispanic/Latino; 7 Two or more races, non-Hispanic/Latino). Average age 32. 180 applicants, 73% accepted, 119 enrolled. *Financial support:* In 2015–16, 1 student received support. Scholarships/grants available. Financial award applicants required to submit FAFSA. *Degree program information:* Part-time and evening/weekend programs available. Part-time, evening/weekend, blended/hybrid learning. Offers education. *Application deadline:* Applications are processed on a rolling basis. *Application fee:* $45. Electronic applications accepted. *Application Contact:* Diane Ranaldi, Dean of Graduate Admissions, 413-565-1332, Fax: 413-565-1250, E-mail: dranaldi@baypath.edu. *Associate Provost and Dean,* Dr. Liz Fleming, 413-565-1332, E-mail: lfleming@baypath.edu.

Program in Entrepreneurial Thinking and Innovative Practices Students: 33 full-time (29 women), 47 part-time (42 women); includes 26 minority (10 Black or African American, non-Hispanic/Latino; 1 Asian, non-Hispanic/Latino; 12 Hispanic/Latino; 3 Two or more races, non-Hispanic/Latino). Average age 35. 79 applicants, 90% accepted, 55 enrolled. *Financial support:* In 2015–16, 4 students received support. Scholarships/grants available. Financial award applicants required to submit FAFSA. In 2015, 34 master's awarded. *Degree program information:* Part-time and evening/weekend programs available. Part-time, evening/weekend, 100% online, blended/hybrid learning. Offers entrepreneurial thinking and innovative practices (MBA). *Application deadline:* Applications are processed on a rolling basis. *Application fee:* $45. Electronic applications accepted. *Application Contact:* Diane Ranaldi, Dean of Graduate Admissions, 413-565-1332, Fax: 413-565-1250, E-mail: dranaldi@baypath.edu. *Program Director,* Mo Sattar, 413-565-1228, E-mail: msattar@baypath.edu.

Program in Forensics Students: 4 full-time (all women), 8 part-time (6 women); includes 2 minority (both Hispanic/Latino). Average age 27. 20 applicants, 35% accepted, 7 enrolled. *Financial support:* In 2015–16, 5 students received support. Scholarships/grants available. Financial award applicants required to submit FAFSA. In 2015, 3 master's awarded. *Degree program information:* Part-time and evening/weekend programs available. Part-time, evening/weekend. Offers forensics (MS). *Application deadline:* Applications are processed on a rolling basis. *Application fee:* $45. Electronic applications accepted. *Application Contact:* Diane Ranaldi, Dean of Graduate Admissions, 413-565-1332, Fax: 413-565-1250, E-mail: dranaldi@baypath.edu. *Program Director,* Dr. Sandra Haddad, 413-565-1355, E-mail: shaddad@baypath.edu.

Program in Genetic Counseling ***Financial support:*** Scholarships/grants available. Financial award applicants required to submit FAFSA. *Degree program information:* Evening/weekend programs available. Evening/weekend, blended/hybrid learning. Offers genetic counseling (MS). *Application deadline:* Applications are processed on a rolling basis. *Application fee:* $45. Electronic applications accepted. *Application Contact:* Diane Ranaldi, Dean of Graduate Admissions, 413-565-1332, Fax: 413-565-1250, E-mail: dranaldi@baypath.edu. *Associate Provost/Dean,* Dr. Liz Fleming, 413-565-1332, E-mail: lfleming@baypath.edu.

Program in Higher Education Administration Students: 10 full-time (7 women), 44 part-time (37 women); includes 12 minority (7 Black or African American, non-Hispanic/Latino; 1 American Indian or Alaska Native, non-Hispanic/Latino; 3 Hispanic/Latino; 1 Two or more races, non-Hispanic/Latino). Average age 38. 46 applicants, 87% accepted, 33 enrolled. *Financial support:* In 2015–16, 1 student received support. Scholarships/grants available. Financial award applicants required to submit FAFSA. In 2015, 15 master's awarded. *Degree program information:* Part-time and evening/weekend programs available. Part-time, evening/weekend, 100% online. Offers enrollment management (MS); general administration (MS); institutional advancement (MS); online teaching and program administration (MS). *Application deadline:* Applications are processed on a rolling basis. *Application fee:* $45. Electronic applications accepted. *Application Contact:* Diane Ranaldi, Dean of Graduate Admissions, 413-565-1332, Fax: 413-565-1250, E-mail: dranaldi@baypath.edu. *Program Director,* Dr. Lauren Way, 413-565-1193, E-mail: lway@baypath.edu.

Program in Information Management Students: 4 full-time (0 women), all international. Average age 31. *Financial support:* Scholarships/grants available. Financial award applicants required to submit FAFSA. *Degree program information:* Part-time and evening/weekend programs available. Part-time, evening/weekend, 100% online, blended/hybrid learning. Offers information management (MS). *Application deadline:* Applications are processed on a rolling basis. *Application fee:* $45. Electronic applications accepted. *Application Contact:* Diane Ranaldi, Dean of Graduate Admissions, 413-565-1332, Fax: 413-565-1250, E-mail: dranaldi@baypath.edu. *Director,* Robin Saunders, 413-565-1009, E-mail: rsaunders@baypath.edu.

Program in Leadership and Negotiation Students: 3 full-time (all women), 31 part-time (27 women); includes 5 minority (3 Black or African American, non-Hispanic/Latino; 2 Hispanic/Latino), 1 international. Average age 39. 23 applicants, 100% accepted, 19 enrolled. *Financial support:* In 2015–16, 1 student received support. Scholarships/grants available. Financial award applicants required to submit FAFSA. *Degree program information:* Part-time and evening/weekend programs available. Part-time, evening/weekend, 100% online, blended/hybrid learning. Offers leadership and negotiation (MS). *Application deadline:* Applications are processed on a rolling basis. *Application fee:* $45. Electronic applications accepted. *Application Contact:* Diane Ranaldi, Dean of Graduate Admissions, 413-565-1332, Fax: 413-565-1250, E-mail: dranaldi@baypath.edu. *Director,* Dr. Joshua Weiss, E-mail: joweiss@baypath.edu.

Program in Nonprofit Management and Philanthropy Students: 11 full-time (10 women), 37 part-time (33 women); includes 13 minority (10 Black or African American, non-Hispanic/Latino; 1 Asian, non-Hispanic/Latino; 2 Hispanic/Latino). Average age 36. 32 applicants, 100% accepted, 29 enrolled. *Financial support:* In 2015–16, 24 students received support. Scholarships/grants available. Financial award applicants required to submit FAFSA. In 2015, 13 master's awarded. *Degree program information:* Part-time and evening/weekend programs available. Part-time, evening/weekend, 100% online, blended/hybrid learning. Offers nonprofit management and philanthropy (MS). *Application deadline:* Applications are processed on a rolling basis. *Application fee:* $45. Electronic applications accepted. *Application Contact:* Diane Ranaldi, Dean of Graduate Admissions, 413-565-1332, Fax: 413-565-1250, E-mail: dranaldi@baypath.edu. *Program Director,* Jeffrey Greim, 413-565-1010, Fax: 413-565-1116, E-mail: jgriem@baypath.edu.

Program in Occupational Therapy Students: 241 full-time (219 women), 13 part-time (all women); includes 39 minority (6 Black or African American, non-Hispanic/Latino; 8 Asian, non-Hispanic/Latino; 16 Hispanic/Latino; 9 Two or more races, non-Hispanic/Latino), 1 international. Average age 26. 357 applicants, 66% accepted, 130 enrolled. *Financial support:* In 2015–16, 83 students received support. Scholarships/grants available. Financial award applicants required to submit FAFSA. In 2015, 119 master's awarded. *Degree program information:* Part-time programs available. Part-time. Offers occupational therapy (MOT). *Application deadline:* For fall admission, 3/1 priority date for domestic students. Applications are processed on a rolling basis. *Application fee:* $45. Electronic applications accepted. *Application Contact:* Diane Ranaldi, Dean of Graduate Admissions, 413-565-1332, Fax: 413-565-1250, E-mail: dranaldi@baypath.edu. *Assistant Dean/Program Director,* Dr. Lori Vaughn, 413-565-1012, E-mail: lvaughn@baypath.edu.

Program in Physician Assistant Studies Students: 59 full-time (29 women); includes 6 minority (1 Asian, non-Hispanic/Latino; 1 Hispanic/Latino; 4 Two or more races, non-Hispanic/Latino). Average age 28. 872 applicants, 4% accepted, 30 enrolled. *Financial support:* Unspecified assistantships available. Financial award applicants required to submit FAFSA. In 2015, 23 master's awarded. Offers physician assistant studies (MS). *Application deadline:* For fall admission, 10/1 for domestic students. *Application fee:* $60. *Application Contact:* Diane Ranaldi, Dean of Graduate Admissions, 413-565-1332, Fax: 413-565-1250, E-mail: dranaldi@baypath.edu. *Director,* Theresa Riethle, 413-565-1206, E-mail: triethle@baypath.edu.

Program in Strategic Fundraising and Philanthropy Students: 1 (woman) full-time, 14 part-time (13 women); includes 3 minority (all Black or African American, non-Hispanic/Latino). Average age 35. 9 applicants, 78% accepted, 7 enrolled. *Financial support:* Scholarships/grants available. Financial award applicants required to submit FAFSA. In 2015, 3 master's awarded. *Degree program information:* Part-time and evening/weekend programs available. Part-time, evening/weekend, 100% online, blended/hybrid learning. Offers higher education (MS). *Application deadline:* Applications are processed on a rolling basis. *Application fee:* $45. Electronic applications accepted. *Application Contact:* Diane Ranaldi, Dean of Graduate Admissions, 413-565-1332, Fax: 413-565-1250, E-mail: dranaldi@baypath.edu. *Program Director,* Jeffrey Greim, 413-565-1045, E-mail: jgreim@baypath.edu.

BECKER COLLEGE, Worcester, MA 01609

General Information Independent, coed, comprehensive institution.

GRADUATE UNITS

Program in Mental Health Counseling Offers community mental health (MA); school consultation (MA). Electronic applications accepted.

BELHAVEN UNIVERSITY, Jackson, MS 39202-1789

General Information Independent-religious, coed, comprehensive institution. *Enrollment:* 4,452 graduate, professional, and undergraduate students; 23 full-time matriculated graduate/professional students (20 women), 1,678 part-time matriculated graduate/professional students (1,258 women). *Enrollment by degree level:* 1,631 master's, 70 other advanced degrees. *Graduate faculty:* 37 full-time (17 women), 86 part-time/adjunct (44 women). *Tuition, area resident:* Full-time $9990; part-time $6600 per credit hour. *Graduate housing:* On-campus housing not available. *Student services:* Career counseling, free psychological counseling. *Library:* Warren A. Hood Library plus 1 other. *Collection:* Books: 95,316 (physical); Serial titles: 527 (physical); Databases: 42. Weekly public service hours: 104.

Computer facilities: 36 computers available on campus for general student use. A campuswide network can be accessed from student residence rooms and from off campus. Online class registration is available.
Website: http://www.belhaven.edu/

General Application Contact: Dr. Audrey Kelleher, Vice President for Adult and Graduate Marketing and Development, 407-804-1424, Fax: 407-620-5210, E-mail: akelleher@belhaven.edu.

GRADUATE UNITS

School of Business Students: 22 full-time (19 women), 1,120 part-time (793 women); includes 946 minority (899 Black or African American, non-Hispanic/Latino; 6 American Indian or Alaska Native, non-Hispanic/Latino; 3 Asian, non-Hispanic/Latino; 17 Hispanic/Latino; 3 Native Hawaiian or other Pacific Islander, non-Hispanic/Latino; 18 Two or more races, non-Hispanic/Latino). Average age 36. *Faculty:* 26 full-time (8 women), 61 part-time/adjunct (29 women). *Financial support:* Applicants required to submit FAFSA. In 2015, 274 master's awarded. *Degree program information:* Part-time and evening/weekend programs available. Part-time, evening/weekend, online learning. Offers business administration (MBA); health administration (MBA, MHA); human resources (MBA, MSL); leadership (MBA); public administration (MPA); sports administration (MBA, MSA). MBA program also offered in Houston, TX, Memphis, TN and Orlando, FL. *Application deadline:* Applications are processed on a rolling basis. *Application fee:* $25. Electronic applications accepted. *Application Contact:* Dr. Audrey Kelleher, Vice President of Adult and Graduate Marketing and Development, 407-804-1424, Fax: 407-620-5210, E-mail: akelleher@belhaven.edu. *Dean,* Dr. Ralph Mason, 601-968-8949, Fax: 601-968-8951, E-mail: cmason@belhaven.edu.

School of Education Students: 2 full-time (both women), 483 part-time (395 women); includes 314 minority (309 Black or African American, non-Hispanic/Latino; 1 American Indian or Alaska Native, non-Hispanic/Latino; 1 Asian, non-Hispanic/Latino; 1 Hispanic/Latino; 2 Two or more races, non-Hispanic/Latino). Average age 35. *Faculty:* 7 full-time (5 women), 24 part-time/adjunct (17 women). *Financial support:* Federal Work-Study, scholarships/grants, tuition waivers (full), and unspecified assistantships available. Support available to part-time students. Financial award applicants required to submit FAFSA. In 2015, 69 master's awarded. *Degree program information:* Part-time and evening/weekend programs available. Part-time, evening/weekend, online learning. Offers educational technology (M Ed); elementary education (M Ed, MAT); reading literacy (M Ed); secondary education (M Ed, MAT). *Application deadline:* Applications are processed on a rolling basis. *Application fee:* $25. Electronic applications accepted. *Application Contact:* Sean Kirnan, Assistant Vice President for Adult and Graduate Enrollment and Student Services, 601-968-8727, Fax: 601-968-5953, E-mail: gradadmission@belhaven.edu. *Dean,* Dr. David Hand, 601-965-7020, E-mail: dhand@belhaven.edu.

BELLARMINE UNIVERSITY, Louisville, KY 40205-0671

General Information Independent-religious, coed, comprehensive institution. *Enrollment:* 3,846 graduate, professional, and undergraduate students; 317 full-time matriculated graduate/professional students (205 women), 408 part-time matriculated graduate/professional students (290 women). *Enrollment by degree level:* 405 master's, 278 doctoral, 42 other advanced degrees. *Graduate faculty:* 60 full-time (39 women), 59 part-time/adjunct (41 women). Tuition and fees vary according to program. *Graduate housing:* Room and/or apartments available on a first-come, first-served basis to single students; on-campus housing not available to married students. *Student services:* Campus employment opportunities, campus safety program, career counseling, exercise/wellness program, free psychological counseling, grant writing training, international student services, multicultural affairs office, services for students with disabilities, teacher training, writing training. *Library:* W. L. Lyons Brown Library.

Computer facilities: 437 computers available on campus for general student use. A campuswide network can be accessed from student residence rooms and from off campus. Online class registration is available.
Website: http://www.bellarmine.edu/

General Application Contact: Dr. Sara Pettingill, Dean of Graduate Admission, 502-272-8401, Fax: 502-272-8002, E-mail: spettingill@bellarmine.edu.

GRADUATE UNITS

Annsley Frazier Thornton School of Education Students: 36 full-time (28 women), 201 part-time (148 women); includes 39 minority (27 Black or African American, non-Hispanic/Latino; 2 Asian, non-Hispanic/Latino; 8 Hispanic/Latino; 2 Two or more races, non-Hispanic/Latino). Average age 35. *Faculty:* 12 full-time (7 women), 46 part-time/adjunct (34 women). *Financial support:* Scholarships/grants available. Financial award applicants required to submit FAFSA. In 2015, 85 master's, 3 doctorates awarded. *Degree program information:* Part-time and evening/weekend programs available. Part-time, evening/weekend. Offers education and social change (PhD); elementary education (MA Ed, MAT); learning and behavior disorders (MA Ed, MAT); middle grades education (MA Ed, MAT); principalship (Ed S); reading and writing (MA Ed); secondary education (MAT); teacher leadership (MA Ed). *Application deadline:* Applications are processed on a rolling basis. *Application fee:* $40. Electronic applications accepted. *Application Contact:* Theresa Klapheke, Administrative Director of Graduate Programs, 502-272-8271, Fax: 502-272-8002, E-mail: tklapheke@bellarmine.edu. *Dean,* Dr. Robert Cooter, 502-272-8191, Fax: 502-272-8189, E-mail: rcooter@bellarmine.edu.

Bellarmine College (Arts and Sciences) Students: 7 part-time (all women). Average age 50. *Faculty:* 2 full-time (1 woman), 1 part-time/adjunct (0 women). *Degree program information:* Part-time programs available. Part-time. Offers spirituality (MA). *Application deadline:* For spring admission, 3/15 for domestic students. *Application fee:* $25. *Application Contact:* Dr. Sara Pettingill, Dean of Graduate Admission, 502-272-8401, E-mail: spettingill@bellarmine.edu. *Interim Program Director,* Dr. Justin Klassen, 502-272-8178, E-mail: jklassen@bellarmine.edu.

Donna and Allan Lansing School of Nursing and Health Sciences Students: 210 full-time (144 women), 91 part-time (83 women); includes 22 minority (6 Black or African American, non-Hispanic/Latino; 1 American Indian or Alaska Native, non-Hispanic/Latino; 7 Asian, non-Hispanic/Latino; 4 Hispanic/Latino; 4 Two or more races, non-Hispanic/Latino), 2 international. Average age 28. *Faculty:* 27 full-time (24 women), 8 part-time/adjunct (7 women). *Financial support:* Career-related internships or fieldwork and scholarships/grants available. In 2015, 33 master's, 64 doctorates awarded. *Degree program information:* Part-time and evening/weekend programs available. Part-time, evening/weekend. Offers family nurse practitioner (MSN); health science (MHS); nursing administration (MSN); nursing education (MSN); nursing practice (DNP); physical therapy (DPT). *Application fee:* $40. Electronic applications accepted. *Application Contact:* Julie Armstrong-Binnix, Health Science Recruiter, 800-274-4723 Ext. 8364, E-mail: julieab@bellarmine.edu. *Dean,* Dr. Mark Wiegand, 800-274-4723 Ext. 8368, E-mail: mwiegand@bellarmine.edu.

School of Communication Students: 5 full-time (all women), 27 part-time (17 women); includes 11 minority (10 Black or African American, non-Hispanic/Latino; 1 Two or more races, non-Hispanic/Latino), 1 international. Average age 29. *Faculty:* 5 full-time (3 women). In 2015, 18 master's awarded. *Degree program information:* Part-time and evening/weekend programs available. Part-time, evening/weekend. Offers communication (MA). *Application deadline:* Applications are processed on a rolling basis. *Application fee:* $40. Electronic applications accepted. *Application Contact:* Dr. Sara Pettingill, Dean of Graduate Admission, 502-272-8401, Fax: 502-272-8002, E-mail: spettingill@bellarmine.edu. *Dean,* Dr. Lara Needham, 502-272-7965, E-mail: lneedham@bellarmine.edu.

School of Continuing and Professional Studies Students: 27 part-time (5 women); includes 4 minority (1 Black or African American, non-Hispanic/Latino; 1 Asian, non-Hispanic/Latino; 2 Hispanic/Latino). Average age 31. *Faculty:* 1 part-time/adjunct (0 women). In 2015, 1 master's awarded. *Degree program information:* Part-time and evening/weekend programs available. Part-time, evening/weekend. Offers analytics (MSA). *Application fee:* $40. Electronic applications accepted. *Application Contact:* Dr. Sara Pettingill, Dean of Graduate Admission, 502-272-8401, E-mail: spettingill@bellarmine.edu. *Vice President of Enrollment Management/Dean of the School of Professional and Continuing Studies,* Dr. Sean Ryan, 502-272-8376, E-mail: sryan@bellarmine.edu.

W. Fielding Rubel School of Business Students: 66 full-time (28 women), 55 part-time (30 women); includes 19 minority (12 Black or African American, non-Hispanic/Latino; 1 Asian, non-Hispanic/Latino; 6 Hispanic/Latino). Average age 30. *Faculty:* 14 full-time (4 women), 3 part-time/adjunct (0 women). *Financial support:* Career-related internships or fieldwork, scholarships/grants, and unspecified assistantships available. Support available to part-time students. Financial award application deadline: 7/1. In 2015, 94 master's awarded. *Degree program information:* Part-time and evening/weekend programs available. Part-time, evening/weekend. Offers business (EMBA, MBA, MST). *Application deadline:* Applications are processed on a rolling basis. *Application fee:* $40. Electronic applications accepted. *Application Contact:* Dr. Sara Pettingill, Dean of Graduate Admission, 800-274-4723 Ext. 8258, Fax: 502-272-8002, E-mail: spettingill@bellarmine.edu. *Dean,* Dr. Robert L. Brown, 800-272-8249, Fax: 502-272-8013, E-mail: dbauer@bellarmine.edu.

BELLEVUE UNIVERSITY, Bellevue, NE 68005-3098

General Information Independent, coed, comprehensive institution. *Graduate housing:* Room and/or apartments available on a first-come, first-served basis to single students; on-campus housing not available to married students.

GRADUATE UNITS

Graduate School ***Degree program information:*** Part-time and evening/weekend programs available. Part-time, evening/weekend, online learning.

College of Arts and Sciences Online learning. Offers clinical counseling (MS); healthcare administration (MHA); human services (MA); international security and intelligence studies (MS); managerial communication (MA).

College of Business Offers acquisition and contract management (MS); business administration (MBA); finance (MS); human capital management (PhD); management (MSM).

College of Information Technology Offers computer information systems (MS); cybersecurity (MS); management of information systems (MS); project management (MPM).

College of Professional Studies

BELLIN COLLEGE, Green Bay, WI 54305

General Information Independent, coed, primarily women, comprehensive institution. *Graduate housing:* On-campus housing not available.

GRADUATE UNITS

School of Nursing Offers family nurse practitioner (MSN); nurse educator (MSN).

BELMONT UNIVERSITY, Nashville, TN 37212-3757

General Information Independent-religious, coed, university. *Enrollment:* 7,350 graduate, professional, and undergraduate students; 1,244 full-time matriculated graduate/professional students (808 women), 123 part-time matriculated graduate/professional students (74 women). *Enrollment by degree level:* 566 master's, 801 doctoral. *Graduate faculty:* 143 full-time (73 women), 77 part-time/adjunct (42 women). *Graduate housing:* On-campus housing not available. *Student services:* Campus employment opportunities, campus safety program, career counseling, exercise/wellness program, free psychological counseling, international student services, low-cost health insurance, multicultural affairs office, services for students with disabilities. *Library:* Lila D. Bunch Library plus 1 other.

Computer facilities: Computer purchase and lease plans are available. 500 computers available on campus for general student use. A campuswide network can be accessed from student residence rooms and from off campus. Online class registration, individual student information via BANNER Web are available.
Website: http://www.belmont.edu/

General Application Contact: David Mee, Dean of Enrollment Services, 615-460-6785, Fax: 615-460-5434, E-mail: david.mee@belmont.edu.

GRADUATE UNITS

College of Health Sciences Students: 371 full-time (324 women), 10 part-time (all women); includes 30 minority (10 Black or African American, non-Hispanic/Latino; 9 Asian, non-Hispanic/Latino; 6 Hispanic/Latino; 5 Two or more races, non-Hispanic/Latino), 2 international. Average age 26. *Faculty:* 54 full-time (50 women), 92 part-time/adjunct (81 women). *Financial support:* Teaching assistantships with full tuition reimbursements, career-related internships or fieldwork, scholarships/grants, and traineeships available. Financial award application deadline: 3/1; financial award applicants required to submit FAFSA. *Degree program information:* Part-time programs available. Part-time, online learning. Offers nursing (MSN, DNP); occupational therapy (MSOT, OTD); physical therapy (DPT). *Application deadline:* Applications are processed on a rolling basis. *Application fee:* $50. Electronic applications accepted. *Application Contact:* David Mee, Dean of Enrollment Services, 615-460-6785, Fax: 615-460-5434, E-mail: david.mee@belmont.edu. *Dean*, Dr. Cathy Taylor, 615-460-6916, Fax: 615-460-6750.

College of Law Students: 239 full-time (130 women); includes 32 minority (9 Black or African American, non-Hispanic/Latino; 9 Asian, non-Hispanic/Latino; 8 Hispanic/Latino; 1 Native Hawaiian or other Pacific Islander, non-Hispanic/Latino; 5 Two or more races, non-Hispanic/Latino). Average age 26. *Faculty:* 15 full-time (7 women), 14 part-time/adjunct (6 women). *Financial support:* Applicants required to submit FAFSA. Offers law (JD). *Application deadline:* For fall admission, 7/31 priority date for domestic students, 7/30 priority date for international students. Applications are processed on a rolling basis. Electronic applications accepted. *Application Contact:* David Mee, Dean of Enrollment Services, 615-460-6785, Fax: 615-460-5434, E-mail: david.mee@belmont.edu. *Dean*, Alberto R. Gonzales, 615-460-8259, E-mail: alberto.gonzales@belmont.edu.

College of Pharmacy Students: 290 full-time (165 women); includes 56 minority (18 Black or African American, non-Hispanic/Latino; 31 Asian, non-Hispanic/Latino; 4 Hispanic/Latino; 3 Two or more races, non-Hispanic/Latino), 2 international. Average age 25. *Faculty:* 25 full-time (16 women), 4 part-time/adjunct (3 women). *Financial support:* Applicants required to submit FAFSA. Offers pharmacy (Pharm D). *Application deadline:* For fall admission, 8/31 priority date for domestic students; for spring admission, 3/1 for domestic students. Applications are processed on a rolling basis. *Application fee:* $50. Electronic applications accepted. *Application Contact:* Dr. Elinor Gray, Dean of Enrollment Services, 615-460-6747, Fax: 615-460-6741, E-mail: elinor.gray@belmont.edu. *Dean*, Dr. Phil Johnston, 615-460-6746, Fax: 615-460-6741, E-mail: phil.johnston@belmont.edu.

Jack C. Massey Graduate School of Business Students: 161 full-time (71 women), 66 part-time (28 women); includes 37 minority (12 Black or African American, non-Hispanic/Latino; 12 Asian, non-Hispanic/Latino; 7 Hispanic/Latino; 6 Two or more races, non-Hispanic/Latino), 15 international. Average age 28. 148 applicants, 64% accepted, 77 enrolled. *Faculty:* 46 full-time (16 women), 27 part-time/adjunct (11 women). *Financial support:* Scholarships/grants, tuition waivers (partial), and unspecified assistantships available. Financial award application deadline: 7/1; financial award applicants required to submit FAFSA. In 2015, 136 master's awarded. *Degree program information:* Part-time and evening/weekend programs available. Part-time, evening/weekend. Offers accounting (M Acc); business (AMBA, PMBA); healthcare (MBA). *Application deadline:* For fall admission, 7/1 for domestic and international students; for spring admission, 11/1 for domestic and international students. Applications are processed on a rolling basis. *Application fee:* $50. Electronic applications accepted. *Application Contact:* Tonya Hollin, Admissions Assistant, 615-460-6480, Fax: 615-460-6353, E-mail: masseyadmissions@belmont.edu. *Dean*, Dr. Patrick Raines, 615-460-6480, Fax: 615-460-6455, E-mail: pat.raines@belmont.edu.

BEMIDJI STATE UNIVERSITY, Bemidji, MN 56601-2699

General Information State-supported, coed, comprehensive institution. *Graduate housing:* Room and/or apartments available on a first-come, first-served basis to single students; on-campus housing not available to married students. Housing application deadline: 8/1. *Research affiliation:* National Interscholastic Athletic Administrators Association, Sanford Research, Mossy Oak, Bass Pro Shops.

GRADUATE UNITS

School of Graduate Studies ***Degree program information:*** Part-time programs available. Part-time, online learning. Offers biology (MS); education (MS); English (MA, MS); environmental studies (MS); mathematics (MS); mathematics (elementary and middle level education) (MS); special education (M Sp Ed). Electronic applications accepted.

BENEDICTINE COLLEGE, Atchison, KS 66002-1499

General Information Independent-religious, coed, comprehensive institution. *Enrollment:* 2,189 graduate, professional, and undergraduate students; 37 full-time matriculated graduate/professional students (13 women), 19 part-time matriculated graduate/professional students (14 women). *Enrollment by degree level:* 46 master's, 10 other advanced degrees. *Graduate faculty:* 10 part-time/adjunct (1 woman). *Tuition, area resident:* Part-time $695 per credit hour. *Required fees:* $50 per course. Tuition and fees vary according to program. *Graduate housing:* Room and/or apartments available on a first-come, first-served basis to single students; on-campus housing not available to married students. Typical cost: $9165 (including board). Room and board charges vary according to board plan and housing facility selected. *Student services:* Campus employment opportunities, campus safety program, career counseling, exercise/wellness program, free psychological counseling, international student services, services for students with disabilities, teacher training. *Library:* Benedictine College Library. *Collection:* Books: 198,277 (physical), 113,412 (digital/electronic); Databases: 88.

Computer facilities: Computer purchase and lease plans are available. 100 computers available on campus for general student use. A campuswide network can be accessed from student residence rooms and from off campus. Online class registration is available.
Website: http://www.benedictine.edu/

General Application Contact: Dr. Cheryl Reding, Director, Graduate Programs in Education, 913-360-7384, E-mail: creding@benedictine.edu.

GRADUATE UNITS

Master of Arts in Education Program Students: 1 (woman) full-time, 2 part-time (both women). Average age 28. *Faculty:* 3 part-time/adjunct (1 woman). *Financial support:* Unspecified assistantships available. Financial award applicants required to submit FAFSA. In 2015, 3 master's awarded. *Degree program information:* Part-time and evening/weekend programs available. Part-time, evening/weekend. Offers education (MA). *Application deadline:* Applications are processed on a rolling basis. *Application fee:* $50. Electronic applications accepted. *Application Contact:* Dr. Cheryl Reding, Director, Graduate Programs in Education, 913-360-7384, E-mail: creding@benedictine.edu. *Director, Graduate Programs in Education*, Dr. Cheryl Reding, 913-360-7384, E-mail: creding@benedictine.edu.

Master of Arts in School Leadership Program Students: 7 full-time (4 women), 7 part-time (2 women); includes 1 minority (Hispanic/Latino), 1 international. Average age 34. 4 applicants, 100% accepted, 3 enrolled. *Faculty:* 3 part-time/adjunct (1 woman). *Financial support:* Scholarships/grants and unspecified assistantships available. Financial award applicants required to submit FAFSA. In 2015, 8 master's awarded. *Degree program information:* Part-time and evening/weekend programs available. Part-time, evening/weekend. Offers school leadership (MA). *Application deadline:* Applications are processed on a rolling basis. *Application fee:* $50. Electronic applications accepted. *Application Contact:* Dr. Cheryl Reding, Director, Graduate Programs in Education, 913-360-7384, E-mail: creding@benedictine.edu. *Director, Graduate Programs in Education*, Dr. Cheryl Reding, 913-360-7384, E-mail: creding@benedictine.edu.

Master of Business Administration Program Students: 20 full-time (7 women), 1 international. Average age 25. 18 applicants, 83% accepted, 14 enrolled. *Faculty:* 6 part-time/adjunct (0 women). *Financial support:* In 2015–16, 7 students received support. Unspecified assistantships available. Financial award application deadline: 3/15; financial award applicants required to submit FAFSA. In 2015, 12 master's awarded. *Degree program information:* Part-time and evening/weekend programs available. Part-time, evening/weekend. Offers business administration (MBA). *Application deadline:* Applications are processed on a rolling basis. *Application fee:* $50. Electronic applications accepted. *Application Contact:* Michael King, Chair, School of Business, 913-360-7160, E-mail: mking@benedictine.edu. *Chair, School of Business*, Michael King, 913-360-7160, E-mail: mking@benedictine.edu.

BENEDICTINE UNIVERSITY, Lisle, IL 60532

General Information Independent-religious, coed, comprehensive institution. *Graduate housing:* Rooms and/or apartments available on a first-come, first-served basis to single and married students.

GRADUATE UNITS

Graduate Programs ***Degree program information:*** Part-time and evening/weekend programs available. Part-time, evening/weekend, online learning. Offers accountancy (MS); accounting (MBA); administration of health care institutions (MPH); clinical exercise physiology (MS); clinical psychology (MS); curriculum and instruction and collaborative teaching (M Ed); dietetics (MPH); disaster management (MPH); elementary education (MA Ed); entrepreneurship and managing innovation (MBA); financial management (MBA); health administration (MBA); health education (MPH); health information systems (MPH); higher education and organizational change (Ed D); human resource management (MBA); information systems security (MBA); international business (MBA); leadership (MS); leadership and administration (M Ed); management and organizational behavior (MS); management consulting (MBA); management information systems (MS); marketing management (MBA); nursing (MSN); nutrition and wellness (MS); operations management and logistics (MBA); organization development (PhD); organizational leadership (MBA); reading and literacy (M Ed); science content and process (MS); secondary education (MA Ed); special education (MA Ed); values-driven leadership (DBA, PhD). Electronic applications accepted.

BENNINGTON COLLEGE, Bennington, VT 05201

General Information Independent, coed, comprehensive institution. *Enrollment:* 801 graduate, professional, and undergraduate students; 118 full-time matriculated graduate/professional students (92 women), 13 part-time matriculated graduate/professional students (12 women). *Enrollment by degree level:* 118 master's, 13 other advanced degrees. *Graduate faculty:* 35 full-time (16 women), 19 part-time/adjunct (10 women). *Graduate housing:* Room and/or apartments available on a first-come, first-served basis to single students; on-campus housing not available to married students. *Student services:* Campus employment opportunities, campus safety program, career counseling, exercise/wellness program, free psychological counseling, international student services, low-cost health insurance, teacher training, writing training. *Library:* Crossett Library plus 1 other. *Collection:* Books: 89,063 (physical), 114,788 (digital/electronic); Serial titles: 238 (physical), 48,077 (digital/electronic); Databases: 56. Weekly public service hours: 103; students can reserve study rooms.

Computer facilities: 40 computers available on campus for general student use. A campuswide network can be accessed from student residence rooms and from off campus. Online class registration is available.
Website: http://www.bennington.edu/

General Application Contact: Janet Marsden, Vice President for Admissions and Communications, 802-440-4312, Fax: 802-440-4320, E-mail: admissions@bennington.edu.

GRADUATE UNITS

Graduate Programs Students: 119 full-time (94 women), 13 part-time (12 women); includes 20 minority (6 Black or African American, non-Hispanic/Latino; 3 American Indian or Alaska Native, non-Hispanic/Latino; 8 Asian, non-Hispanic/Latino; 3 Hispanic/Latino), 1 international. Average age 39. 188 applicants, 52% accepted, 45 enrolled. *Faculty:* 41 full-time (19 women), 21 part-time/adjunct (12 women). *Financial support:* In 2015–16, 20 students received support, including 2 teaching assistantships (averaging $21,580 per year); scholarships/grants and unspecified assistantships also available. Financial award application deadline: 4/1; financial award applicants required to submit FAFSA. In 2015, 54 master's, 11 other advanced degrees awarded. *Degree program information:* Part-time programs available. Part-time, online learning. Offers allied and health sciences (Certificate); dance (MFA); music (MFA); writing (MFA). *Application deadline:* Applications are processed on a rolling basis. *Application fee:* $60. *Application Contact:* Janet Marsden, Vice President for Admissions and Communications, 802-440-4312, Fax: 802-440-4320, E-mail: admissions@bennington.edu. *Associate Dean of the College*, Duncan Dobbelmann, 802-440-4400, Fax: 802-440-4876, E-mail: duncand@bennington.edu.

BENTLEY UNIVERSITY, Waltham, MA 02452-4705

General Information Independent, coed, comprehensive institution. *Enrollment:* 5,552 graduate, professional, and undergraduate students; 765 full-time matriculated graduate/professional students (421 women), 584 part-time matriculated graduate/professional students (287 women). *Enrollment by degree level:* 1,298 master's, 34 doctoral, 15 other advanced degrees. *Graduate faculty:* 83 full-time (35 women), 24 part-time/adjunct (6 women). *Tuition, area resident:* Full-time $32,520; part-time $1365 per credit. *Required fees:* $455. *Graduate housing:* Room and/or apartments available on a first-come, first-served basis to single students; on-campus housing not available to married students. Typical cost: $11,130 per year ($16,730 including board). *Student services:* Campus employment opportunities, campus safety program, career counseling, exercise/wellness program, free psychological counseling, international student services, low-cost health insurance, multicultural affairs office, services for students with disabilities. *Library:* Bentley Library plus 1 other. *Collection:* Books:

182,399 (physical), 195,405 (digital/electronic); Serial titles: 1,500 (physical), 80,726 (digital/electronic); Databases: 98. Students can reserve study rooms.

Computer facilities: Computer purchase and lease plans are available. 4,472 computers available on campus for general student use. A campuswide network can be accessed from student residence rooms and from off campus. Online class registration, grade checking, online admission, Blackboard, resume review, student employment, interlibrary loan, free software are available.
Website: http://www.bentley.edu/

General Application Contact: Sharon Hill, Assistant Dean/Director of Graduate Admissions, 781-891-2108, Fax: 781-891-2464, E-mail: bentleygraduateadmissions@bentley.edu.

GRADUATE UNITS

Graduate School of Business Students: 765 full-time (421 women), 584 part-time (287 women); includes 137 minority (27 Black or African American, non-Hispanic/Latino; 3 American Indian or Alaska Native, non-Hispanic/Latino; 65 Asian, non-Hispanic/Latino; 30 Hispanic/Latino; 12 Two or more races, non-Hispanic/Latino), 593 international. Average age 28. 1,797 applicants, 74% accepted, 586 enrolled. *Faculty:* 83 full-time (35 women), 24 part-time/adjunct (6 women). *Financial support:* In 2015–16, 296 students received support. Scholarships/grants, tuition waivers (partial), and unspecified assistantships available. Financial award application deadline: 6/1; financial award applicants required to submit CSS PROFILE or FAFSA. In 2015, 628 master's, 7 doctorates, 101 other advanced degrees awarded. *Degree program information:* Part-time and evening/weekend programs available. Part-time, evening/weekend, online learning. Offers accountancy (PhD); accounting (GBC); business (MBA, MSA, MSF, MSFP, MSHFID, MSIT, MSMA, MST, PhD, Certificate, GBC, GSS); business administration (MBA); business analytics (GBC); business ethics (GBC); finance (MSF); financial planning (MSFP); fraud and forensic accounting (GBC); human factors in information design (MSHFID); information technology (MSIT); marketing analytics (MSMA); taxation (MST). *Application deadline:* For fall admission, 12/1 priority date for domestic and international students; for spring admission, 10/1 priority date for domestic and international students. Applications are processed on a rolling basis. *Application fee:* $50. Electronic applications accepted. *Application Contact:* Sharon Hill, Assistant Graduate Dean/Director of Graduate Admissions, 781-891-2108, Fax: 781-891-2464, E-mail: bentleygraduateadmissions@bentley.edu. *Dean*, Dr. Roy A. Wiggins, III, 781-891-3166.

BERGIN UNIVERSITY OF CANINE STUDIES, Rohnert Park, CA 94928

General Information Independent, coed, comprehensive institution. *Enrollment by degree level:* 26 master's. *Graduate faculty:* 1 (woman) full-time, 5 part-time/adjunct (4 women). *Tuition, area resident:* Full-time $18,375. *Required fees:* $600. One-time fee: $300 full-time. *Graduate housing:* On-campus housing not available. *Student services:* Career counseling, free psychological counseling, international student services, services for students with disabilities.
Website: http://www.berginu.edu/

General Application Contact: Connie Van Guilder, Director, Student Services, 707-545-3647 Ext. 21, Fax: 707-545-0800, E-mail: connie@berginu.edu.

GRADUATE UNITS

Program in Canine Life Sciences Online learning. Offers canine life sciences (MS).

BERKELEY COLLEGE–WOODLAND PARK CAMPUS, Woodland Park, NJ 07424-3353

General Information Proprietary, coed, comprehensive institution.

GRADUATE UNITS

MBA Program Offers management (MBA).

BERKLEE COLLEGE OF MUSIC, Boston, MA 02215-3693

General Information Independent, coed, comprehensive institution. *Enrollment:* 5,272 graduate, professional, and undergraduate students; 147 full-time matriculated graduate/professional students (47 women), 13 part-time matriculated graduate/professional students (9 women). *Enrollment by degree level:* 160 master's. *Graduate faculty:* 37 full-time (9 women), 33 part-time/adjunct (6 women). *Tuition, area resident:* Full-time $46,000. Tuition and fees vary according to campus/location and program. *Graduate housing:* On-campus housing not available. *Student services:* Campus employment opportunities, campus safety program, career counseling, exercise/wellness program, free psychological counseling, grant writing training, international student services, low-cost health insurance, multicultural affairs office, services for students with disabilities, teacher training, writing training. *Library:* The Stan Getz Media Center and Library.

Computer facilities: Computer purchase and lease plans are available. A campuswide network can be accessed from student residence rooms. Online class registration is available.
Website: http://www.berklee.edu/

General Application Contact: 617-747-2221, Fax: 617-747-2047, E-mail: admissions@berklee.edu.

GRADUATE UNITS

Berklee Graduate Programs Students: 147 full-time (47 women), 13 part-time (9 women); includes 21 minority (7 Black or African American, non-Hispanic/Latino; 1 American Indian or Alaska Native, non-Hispanic/Latino; 2 Asian, non-Hispanic/Latino; 9 Hispanic/Latino; 2 Two or more races, non-Hispanic/Latino), 85 international. Average age 26. 619 applicants, 37% accepted, 160 enrolled. *Faculty:* 37 full-time (9 women), 33 part-time/adjunct (6 women). *Financial support:* In 2015–16, 141 students received support, including 141 fellowships with partial tuition reimbursements available (averaging $17,189 per year), 49 research assistantships (averaging $3,710 per year); career-related internships or fieldwork, scholarships/grants, and tuition waivers (full and partial) also available. Support available to part-time students. Financial award application deadline: 2/1; financial award applicants required to submit CSS PROFILE or FAFSA. In 2015, 108 master's awarded. *Degree program information:* Part-time programs available. Part-time, blended/hybrid learning. Offers contemporary performance (MM); global entertainment and music business (MA); music production, technology, and innovation (MM); music therapy (MA); scoring for film, television, and video games (MM). Production; global entertainment and music business; music production, technology, and innovation; and scoring for film, television, and video games programs offered at Valencia, Spain campus. *Application deadline:* For fall admission, 2/1 for domestic and international students. *Application fee:* $150. Electronic applications accepted. *Application Contact:* Kellee Webb, Senior Assistant Director of Admissions, 617-747-2221, E-mail: admissions@berklee.edu. *Dean, Institutional Assessment and Graduate Studies*, Camille Colatosti, PhD, E-mail: ccolatosti@berklee.edu.

The Boston Conservatory at Berklee Students: 164 full-time (101 women), 25 part-time (16 women); includes 30 minority (27 Asian, non-Hispanic/Latino; 3 Hispanic/Latino). *Faculty:* 34 full-time (18 women), 55 part-time/adjunct (25 women). *Financial support:* Federal Work-Study, institutionally sponsored loans, scholarships/grants, and work assistantships available. Financial award application deadline: 12/1; financial award applicants required to submit FAFSA. In 2015, 81 master's, 8 other advanced degrees awarded. *Degree program information:* Part-time programs available. Part-time. Offers bassoon performance (MM); cello performance (MM); choral conducting (MM); clarinet performance (MM); collaborative piano (MM); composition (MM); contemporary music performance (MM); double bass performance (MM); flute performance (MM); harp performance (MM); horn performance (MM); marimba performance (MM); music and autism (Certificate); music education (MM); music education and autism (MM); music performance (ADP); musical theater (MFA); oboe performance (MM); opera performance (MM); orchestral conducting (MM); percussion performance (MM); piano performance (MM); saxophone performance (MM); trombone performance (MM); trumpet performance (MM). *Application deadline:* For fall admission, 12/1 for domestic and international students; for spring admission, 11/1 for domestic and international students. *Application fee:* $100. Electronic applications accepted. *Application Contact:* Director of Admissions, 617-912-9153, Fax: 617-912-9101, E-mail: admissions@bostonconservatory.edu. *Dean of the Conservatory*, Dr. Michael Nash, 617-912-9166, Fax: 617-536-3176, E-mail: mnash@bostonconservatory.edu.

BERRY COLLEGE, Mount Berry, GA 30149-0159

General Information Independent-religious, coed, comprehensive institution. *Enrollment:* 2,245 graduate, professional, and undergraduate students; 50 full-time matriculated graduate/professional students (36 women), 72 part-time matriculated graduate/professional students (45 women). *Enrollment by degree level:* 44 master's, 78 other advanced degrees. *Graduate faculty:* 1 full-time (0 women), 19 part-time/adjunct (11 women). *Tuition, area resident:* Full-time $10,368; part-time $576 per credit hour. *Required fees:* $150. *Graduate housing:* On-campus housing not available. *Student services:* Campus employment opportunities, campus safety program, career counseling, child daycare facilities, exercise/wellness program, free psychological counseling, grant writing training, international student services, multicultural affairs office, services for students with disabilities, teacher training, writing training. *Library:* Memorial Library plus 2 others. *Collection:* Books: 214,409 (physical), 374,448 (digital/electronic); Serial titles: 7,978 (physical), 44,764 (digital/electronic); Databases: 224. Weekly public service hours: 106; students can reserve study rooms. *Research affiliation:* Rome/Floyd County Commission on Children and Youth (education and psychology), Georgia Professional Standards Commission (education), Koch Foundation (business and economics), South Rome Early Learning Center (education), Marcus Autism Center (psychology and education), South Rome Development Corporation (education).

Computer facilities: 200 computers available on campus for general student use. A campuswide network can be accessed from student residence rooms and from off campus. Online class registration is available.
Website: http://www.berry.edu/

General Application Contact: Brett Kennedy, Assistant Vice President of Enrollment Management, 706-236-2215, Fax: 706-290-2178, E-mail: admissions@berry.edu.

GRADUATE UNITS

Graduate Programs Students: 50 full-time (36 women), 72 part-time (45 women); includes 20 minority (15 Black or African American, non-Hispanic/Latino; 4 Hispanic/Latino; 1 Two or more races, non-Hispanic/Latino). Average age 36. *Faculty:* 1 full-time (0 women), 19 part-time/adjunct (11 women). *Financial support:* In 2015–16, 28 students received support, including 11 research assistantships with full tuition reimbursements available (averaging $6,117 per year); scholarships/grants, tuition waivers (partial), and unspecified assistantships also available. Support available to part-time students. Financial award application deadline: 3/1; financial award applicants required to submit FAFSA. In 2015, 23 master's, 12 other advanced degrees awarded. *Degree program information:* Part-time and evening/weekend programs available. Part-time, evening/weekend. Offers curriculum and instruction (M Ed, Ed S); early childhood education (M Ed, MAT); educational leadership (Ed S); middle grades education (MAT); middle-grades education (M Ed); middle-grades education and reading (M Ed, MAT); reading (M Ed); secondary education (MAT). *Application deadline:* For fall admission, 7/22 for domestic students, 5/1 for international students; for spring admission, 12/1 for domestic students, 2/1 for international students. Applications are processed on a rolling basis. *Application fee:* $25 ($30 for international students). Electronic applications accepted. *Application Contact:* Brett Kennedy, Assistant Vice President of Enrollment Management, 706-236-2215, Fax: 706-290-2178, E-mail: admissions@berry.edu. *Provost and Vice President for Academic Affairs*, Dr. Kathy Brittain Richardson, 706-236-2216, Fax: 706-290-2179, E-mail: provostoffice@berry.edu.

Campbell School of Business Students: 1 full-time (0 women), 22 part-time (16 women); includes 1 minority (Hispanic/Latino). Average age 32. *Faculty:* 3 part-time/adjunct (1 woman). *Financial support:* In 2015–16, 16 students received support, including 5 research assistantships with full tuition reimbursements available (averaging $6,912 per year); scholarships/grants, tuition waivers (partial), and unspecified assistantships also available. Support available to part-time students. Financial award application deadline: 3/1; financial award applicants required to submit FAFSA. In 2015, 7 master's awarded. *Degree program information:* Part-time and evening/weekend programs available. Part-time, evening/weekend. Offers business (MBA). *Application deadline:* For fall admission, 7/22 for domestic students; for spring admission, 12/1 for domestic students. Applications are processed on a rolling basis. *Application fee:* $25 ($30 for international students). Electronic applications accepted. *Application Contact:* Brett Kennedy, Assistant Vice President of Enrollment Management, 706-236-2215, Fax: 706-290-2178, E-mail: admissions@berry.edu. *Dean*, Dr. John Grout, 706-236-2233, Fax: 706-802-6728, E-mail: jgrout@berry.edu.

BETHANY COLLEGE, Bethany, WV 26032

General Information Independent-religious, coed, comprehensive institution. *Graduate housing:* Room and/or apartments available on a first-come, first-served basis to single students; on-campus housing not available to married students.

GRADUATE UNITS

Master of Arts in Teaching Program ***Degree program information:*** Part-time programs available. Part-time. Offers teaching (MAT). Electronic applications accepted.

BETHANY THEOLOGICAL SEMINARY, Richmond, IN 47374-4019

General Information Independent-religious, coed, graduate-only institution. *Graduate housing:* On-campus housing not available.

GRADUATE UNITS

Graduate and Professional Programs ***Degree program information:*** Part-time programs available. Part-time, online learning. Offers biblical studies (MA Th); ministry studies (M Div); peace studies (M Div, MA Th); theological studies (MA Th, CATS); youth ministry (M Div).

BETHEL COLLEGE, Mishawaka, IN 46545-5591

General Information Independent-religious, coed, comprehensive institution. *Enrollment:* 1,719 graduate, professional, and undergraduate students; 45 full-time matriculated graduate/professional students (25 women), 185 part-time matriculated graduate/professional students (95 women). *Enrollment by degree level:* 230 master's. *Graduate faculty:* 37 part-time/adjunct (14 women). *Tuition, area resident:* Full-time $6480; part-time $3240 per credit hour. *Required fees:* $75 per semester. Tuition and fees vary according to course load and program. *Graduate housing:* On-campus housing not available. *Student services:* Campus employment opportunities, campus safety program, career counseling, free psychological counseling, international student services, services for students with disabilities, writing training. *Library:* Otis and Elizabeth Bowen Library. *Collection:* Books: 130,699 (physical), 8,189 (digital/electronic); Serial titles: 450 (physical), 47,876 (digital/electronic); Databases: 50. Weekly public service hours: 83.

Computer facilities: 132 computers available on campus for general student use. A campuswide network can be accessed from student residence rooms. Online class registration is available.
Website: http://www.bethelcollege.edu/

General Application Contact: Dr. Toni Steffensen Pauls, Vice President of Adult and Graduate Studies, 574-807-7550, Fax: 574-807-7551.

GRADUATE UNITS

Adult and Graduate Programs Students: 45 full-time (25 women), 185 part-time (95 women); includes 43 minority (27 Black or African American, non-Hispanic/Latino; 1 American Indian or Alaska Native, non-Hispanic/Latino; 1 Asian, non-Hispanic/Latino; 9 Hispanic/Latino; 5 Two or more races, non-Hispanic/Latino), 5 international. Average age 37. 225 applicants, 95% accepted, 203 enrolled. *Faculty:* 37 part-time/adjunct (14 women). *Financial support:* Career-related internships or fieldwork available. Financial award applicants required to submit FAFSA. In 2015, 47 master's awarded. *Degree program information:* Part-time and evening/weekend programs available. Part-time, evening/weekend. Offers business administration (MBA); education (M Ed, MAT); ministries (M Min); nursing (MSN); theological studies (MATS). *Application deadline:* For fall admission, 5/1 for international students; for spring admission, 10/1 for international students. Applications are processed on a rolling basis. *Application fee:* $0. Electronic applications accepted. *Vice President for Adult and Graduate Studies,* Dr. Toni Pauls, 574-807-7400, Fax: 574-807-7551, E-mail: toni.pauls@bethelcollege.edu.

BETHEL SEMINARY, St. Paul, MN 55112-6998

General Information Independent-religious, coed, graduate-only institution. *Enrollment by degree level:* 500 master's, 64 doctoral, 11 other advanced degrees. *Graduate faculty:* 15 full-time (3 women), 76 part-time/adjunct (31 women). *Student services:* Campus employment opportunities, campus safety program, career counseling, child daycare facilities, free psychological counseling, international student services, multicultural affairs office, writing training. *Library:* Carl H. Lundquist Library plus 2 others.

Computer facilities: 19 computers available on campus for general student use. Online class registration is available.
Website: http://seminary.bethel.edu/

General Application Contact: Jen Niska, Director of Admissions, 651-638-6288, Fax: 651-638-6002, E-mail: seminary-admissions@bethel.edu.

GRADUATE UNITS

Graduate and Professional Programs Students: 418 full-time (184 women), 157 part-time (36 women); includes 138 minority (48 Black or African American, non-Hispanic/Latino; 45 Asian, non-Hispanic/Latino; 28 Hispanic/Latino; 2 Native Hawaiian or other Pacific Islander, non-Hispanic/Latino; 15 Two or more races, non-Hispanic/Latino), 15 international. Average age 37. 322 applicants, 75% accepted, 174 enrolled. *Faculty:* 15 full-time (3 women), 76 part-time/adjunct (31 women). *Financial support:* In 2015–16, 404 students received support. Teaching assistantships, career-related internships or fieldwork, Federal Work-Study, and scholarships/grants available. Financial award applicants required to submit FAFSA. In 2015, 168 master's, 24 doctorates, 6 other advanced degrees awarded. *Degree program information:* Part-time and evening/weekend programs available. Part-time, evening/weekend, blended/hybrid learning. Offers Anglican studies (Certificate); children's and family ministry (MA); Christian studies (Certificate); Christian thought (MA); Greek and Hebrew language (M Div); Greek language (M Div); Hebrew language (M Div); marriage and family therapy (MA, Certificate); ministry (D Min); ministry practice (MA, Certificate); theological studies (MA, Certificate); transformational leadership (MA); young life youth ministry (Certificate). *Application deadline:* For fall admission, 8/1 priority date for domestic students, 8/1 for international students; for winter admission, 12/1 priority date for domestic students; for spring admission, 1/1 priority date for domestic students. Applications are processed on a rolling basis. *Application fee:* $0. Electronic applications accepted. *Application Contact:* Jen Niska, Director of Admissions, 651-638-6288, Fax: 651-638-6002, E-mail: seminary-admissions@bethel.edu. *Vice-President and Dean, Bethel Seminary,* Dr. David Clark, 651-638-6659.

BETHEL UNIVERSITY, St. Paul, MN 55112-6999

General Information Independent-religious, coed, comprehensive institution. *Enrollment:* 4,791 graduate, professional, and undergraduate students; 772 full-time matriculated graduate/professional students (537 women), 372 part-time matriculated graduate/professional students (232 women). *Enrollment by degree level:* 915 master's, 196 doctoral, 33 other advanced degrees. *Graduate faculty:* 21 full-time (15 women), 74 part-time/adjunct (38 women). *Graduate housing:* Rooms and/or apartments available on a first-come, first-served basis to single and married students. *Student services:* Campus employment opportunities, campus safety program, career counseling, international student services, low-cost health insurance, multicultural affairs office, services for students with disabilities, teacher training, writing training. *Library:* Bethel University Library plus 1 other. *Collection:* Books: 141,904 (physical), 153,597 (digital/electronic); Serial titles: 890 (physical), 31,538 (digital/electronic); Databases: 93. Weekly public service hours: 96; students can reserve study rooms.

Computer facilities: Computer purchase and lease plans are available. 420 computers available on campus for general student use. A campuswide network can be accessed from student residence rooms and from off campus. Online class registration is available.
Website: http://www.bethel.edu/

General Application Contact: Director of Admissions, 651-635-8000, Fax: 651-635-8004, E-mail: gs@bethel.edu.

GRADUATE UNITS

Graduate School Students: 772 full-time (537 women), 372 part-time (232 women); includes 188 minority (94 Black or African American, non-Hispanic/Latino; 3 American Indian or Alaska Native, non-Hispanic/Latino; 43 Asian, non-Hispanic/Latino; 31 Hispanic/Latino; 1 Native Hawaiian or other Pacific Islander, non-Hispanic/Latino; 16 Two or more races, non-Hispanic/Latino), 33 international. Average age 37. 663 applicants, 49% accepted, 232 enrolled. *Faculty:* 21 full-time (15 women), 74 part-time/adjunct (38 women). *Financial support:* In 2015–16, 132 students received support. Teaching assistantships, career-related internships or fieldwork, and scholarships/grants available. Support available to part-time students. Financial award applicants required to submit FAFSA. In 2015, 272 master's, 16 doctorates, 65 other advanced degrees awarded. *Degree program information:* Part-time and evening/weekend programs available. Part-time, evening/weekend, 100% online, blended/hybrid learning. Offers business administration (MBA); child and adolescent mental health (Certificate); classroom management (Certificate); communication (MA); counseling psychology (MA); educational leadership (Ed D); gerontology (MA, Certificate); international baccalaureate teaching and learning (Certificate); K-12 education (MA); leadership foundations (Certificate); literacy education (MA); nurse educator (Certificate); nurse-midwifery (MS); nursing (MS); physician assistant (MS); special education (MA); STEM education (Certificate); strategic leadership (MA); teaching (MA). *Application deadline:* Applications are processed on a rolling basis. *Application fee:* $0. Electronic applications accepted. *Application Contact:* Director of Admissions, 651-635-8000, Fax: 651-635-8004, E-mail: gs@bethel.edu. *Vice-President/Dean,* Dick Crombie, 651-635-8000, Fax: 651-635-8004, E-mail: gs@bethel.edu.

BETHEL UNIVERSITY, McKenzie, TN 38201

General Information Independent-religious, coed, comprehensive institution. *Graduate housing:* Room and/or apartments available on a first-come, first-served basis to single students; on-campus housing not available to married students. Housing application deadline: 7/31.

GRADUATE UNITS

Graduate Programs ***Degree program information:*** Part-time and evening/weekend programs available. Part-time, evening/weekend. Offers administration and supervision (MA Ed); business administration (MBA); conflict resolution (MA); physician assistant studies (MS).

BETHESDA UNIVERSITY, Anaheim, CA 92801

General Information Independent-religious, coed, comprehensive institution.

GRADUATE UNITS

Graduate and Professional Programs Offers biblical studies (MA); music (MA); theology (M Div).

BETH HAMEDRASH SHAAREI YOSHER INSTITUTE, Brooklyn, NY 11204

General Information Independent-religious, men only, comprehensive institution.

GRADUATE UNITS

Graduate Programs

BETH HATALMUD RABBINICAL COLLEGE, Brooklyn, NY 11214

General Information Independent-religious, men only, comprehensive institution.

GRADUATE UNITS

Graduate Programs

BETH MEDRASH GOVOHA, Lakewood, NJ 08701-2797

General Information Independent-religious, men only.

GRADUATE UNITS

Graduate Programs

BETHUNE-COOKMAN UNIVERSITY, Daytona Beach, FL 32114-3099

General Information Independent-religious, coed, comprehensive institution.

GRADUATE UNITS

School of Graduate Studies Online learning. Offers transformative leadership (MS). Electronic applications accepted.

BEULAH HEIGHTS UNIVERSITY, Atlanta, GA 30316

General Information Independent-religious, coed, comprehensive institution.

GRADUATE UNITS

Graduate School Offers biblical studies (MA); leadership studies (MA). Electronic applications accepted.

BEXLEY HALL EPISCOPAL SEMINARY, Columbus, OH 43209-2325

General Information Independent-religious, coed, graduate-only institution.

GRADUATE UNITS

Graduate Programs Offers ministry (M Div, MA).

BIBLICAL THEOLOGICAL SEMINARY, Hatfield, PA 19440-2499

General Information Independent-religious, coed, graduate-only institution. *Enrollment by degree level:* 194 master's, 33 doctoral, 33 other advanced degrees. *Graduate faculty:* 9 full-time (0 women), 21 part-time/adjunct (4 women). *Tuition, area resident:* Full-time $11,880; part-time $5940 per credit. *Required fees:* $75; $75 per credit. $25 per trimester. *Graduate housing:* Rooms and/or apartments available on a first-come, first-served basis to single and married students. Typical cost: $7210 per year for single students; $14,420 per year for married students. Housing application deadline: 8/30. *Student services:* Campus employment opportunities, career counseling, international student services. *Library:* BTS Library plus 1 other. *Collection:* Books: 43,390 (physical), 140,000 (digital/electronic); Serial titles: 13,572 (physical), 220 (digital/electronic); Databases: 10. Weekly public service hours: 50. *Research affiliation:* Christian Counseling and Education Foundation (psychology).

Computer facilities: 20 computers available on campus for general student use. A campuswide network can be accessed from off campus.
Website: http://www.biblical.edu/

General Application Contact: Dr. Malcolm Walls, Director of Student Advancement, 215-368-5000 Ext. 109, Fax: 215-368-7002, E-mail: mwalls@biblical.edu.

GRADUATE UNITS

Graduate and Professional Programs Students: 138 full-time (46 women), 122 part-time (46 women); includes 109 minority (64 Black or African American, non-Hispanic/Latino; 1 American Indian or Alaska Native, non-Hispanic/Latino; 37 Asian, non-Hispanic/Latino; 6 Hispanic/Latino; 1 Two or more races, non-Hispanic/Latino), 70 international. Average age 38. 245 applicants, 53% accepted, 109 enrolled. *Faculty:* 9 full-time (0 women), 21 part-time/adjunct (4 women). *Financial support:* In 2015–16, 173 students received support. Career-related internships or fieldwork, institutionally sponsored loans, and scholarships/grants available. Support available to part-time students. Financial award application deadline: 8/30; financial award applicants required to submit FAFSA. In 2015, 63 master's, 2 doctorates awarded. *Degree program information:* Part-time and evening/weekend programs available. Part-time, evening/weekend. Offers advanced missional leadership (D Min); advanced pastoral studies (Certificate); biblical counseling (Certificate); biblical studies (MA, Certificate); counseling (MA); ministry (M Div, MA); missional theology (MA). *Application deadline:* Applications are processed on a rolling basis. *Application fee:* $30. Electronic applications accepted. *Application Contact:* Dr. Malcolm Walls, Director of Student Advancement, 215-368-5000 Ext. 109, Fax: 215-368-7002, E-mail: mwalls@biblical.edu. *Director of Student Advancement*, Dr. Malcolm Walls, 215-368-5000 Ext. 109, Fax: 215-368-7002, E-mail: mwalls@biblical.edu.

BINGHAMTON UNIVERSITY, STATE UNIVERSITY OF NEW YORK, Binghamton, NY 13902-6000

General Information State-supported, coed, university. CGS member. *Enrollment:* 16,913 graduate, professional, and undergraduate students; 2,116 full-time matriculated graduate/professional students (950 women), 1,212 part-time matriculated graduate/professional students (645 women). *Enrollment by degree level:* 1,921 master's, 1,365 doctoral, 42 other advanced degrees. *Graduate faculty:* 605 full-time (233 women), 280 part-time/adjunct (106 women). *Graduate housing:* Room and/or apartments available on a first-come, first-served basis to single students; on-campus housing not available to married students. *Student services:* Campus employment opportunities, campus safety program, career counseling, child daycare facilities, exercise/wellness program, free psychological counseling, grant writing training, international student services, low-cost health insurance, multicultural affairs office, services for students with disabilities, teacher training, writing training. *Library:* Glenn G. Bartle Library plus 2 others. *Collection:* Books: 2.3 million (physical), 1.2 million (digital/electronic); Serial titles: 729 (physical), 93,414 (digital/electronic); Databases: 234. Weekly public service hours: 148; study areas open 24 hours, 5–7 days a week; students can reserve study rooms. *Research affiliation:* United Health Services Hospitals (health care, engineering), Mount Sinai Hospital (health care, engineering), Lockheed Martin Corporation (engineering, management, mathematics), Matco Company (engineering), IBM (engineering), Universal Instruments (engineering).

Computer facilities: 1,190 computers available on campus for general student use. A campuswide network can be accessed from student residence rooms and from off campus. Online class registration, course management system, personal Web space, wiki, virtual desktop are available.
Website: http://www.binghamton.edu/

General Application Contact: Dr. Susan Strehle, Vice Provost and Dean of the Graduate School, 607-777-2070, Fax: 607-777-2501, E-mail: sstrehle@binghamton.edu.

GRADUATE UNITS

Graduate School Students: 2,116 full-time (950 women), 1,212 part-time (645 women); includes 423 minority (120 Black or African American, non-Hispanic/Latino; 17 American Indian or Alaska Native, non-Hispanic/Latino; 135 Asian, non-Hispanic/Latino; 130 Hispanic/Latino; 21 Native Hawaiian or other Pacific Islander, non-Hispanic/Latino), 1,446 international. Average age 29. 4,649 applicants, 56% accepted, 1197 enrolled. *Faculty:* 605 full-time (233 women), 280 part-time/adjunct (106 women). *Financial support:* In 2015–16, 995 students received support, including 7 fellowships with full tuition reimbursements available (averaging $11,000 per year), 180 research assistantships with full tuition reimbursements available (averaging $15,000 per year), 543 teaching assistantships with full tuition reimbursements available (averaging $15,000 per year); career-related internships or fieldwork, Federal Work-Study, institutionally sponsored loans, scholarships/grants, traineeships, health care benefits, tuition waivers (full and partial), and unspecified assistantships also available. Support available to part-time students. Financial award applicants required to submit FAFSA. In 2015, 1,027 master's, 138 doctorates, 38 other advanced degrees awarded. *Degree program information:* Part-time and evening/weekend programs available. Part-time, evening/weekend, online learning. Offers sustainable communities (MA, MS). *Application deadline:* Applications are processed on a rolling basis. *Application fee:* $75. Electronic applications accepted. *Application Contact:* Kishan Zuber, Recruiting and Admissions Coordinator, 607-777-2151, Fax: 607-777-2501, E-mail: kzuber@binghamton.edu. *Vice Provost and Dean of the Graduate School*, Dr. Susan Strehle, 607-777-2070, Fax: 607-777-2501, E-mail: sstrehle@binghamton.edu.

College of Community and Public Affairs Students: 195 full-time (152 women), 113 part-time (94 women); includes 52 minority (23 Black or African American, non-Hispanic/Latino; 1 American Indian or Alaska Native, non-Hispanic/Latino; 6 Asian, non-Hispanic/Latino; 22 Hispanic/Latino), 16 international. Average age 30. 333 applicants, 78% accepted, 133 enrolled. *Faculty:* 26 full-time (19 women), 12 part-time/adjunct (7 women). *Financial support:* In 2015–16, 77 students received support. Career-related internships or fieldwork, Federal Work-Study, institutionally sponsored loans, scholarships/grants, health care benefits, and unspecified assistantships available. Financial award applicants required to submit FAFSA. In 2015, 106 master's awarded. *Degree program information:* Part-time and evening/weekend programs available. Part-time, evening/weekend. Offers community and public affairs (MPA, MS, MSW); public administration (MPA); social work (MSW); student affairs administration (MS). *Application deadline:* Applications are processed on a rolling basis. *Application fee:* $75. Electronic applications accepted. *Application Contact:* Kishan Zuber, Recruiting and Admissions Coordinator, 607-777-2151, Fax: 607-777-2501, E-mail: kzuber@binghamton.edu. *Dean*, Dr. Laura Bronstein, 607-777-5572, Fax: 607-777-2406, E-mail: lbronst@binghamton.edu.

Decker School of Nursing Students: 75 full-time (64 women), 111 part-time (93 women); includes 28 minority (13 Black or African American, non-Hispanic/Latino; 1 American Indian or Alaska Native, non-Hispanic/Latino; 7 Asian, non-Hispanic/Latino; 7 Hispanic/Latino), 10 international. Average age 37. 96 applicants, 79% accepted, 45 enrolled. *Faculty:* 43 full-time (40 women), 21 part-time/adjunct (14 women). *Financial support:* In 2015–16, 35 students received support, including 1 fellowship with partial tuition reimbursement available (averaging $16,500 per year), research assistantships with full tuition reimbursements available (averaging $12,500 per year), 1 teaching assistantship with full tuition reimbursement available (averaging $16,500 per year); career-related internships or fieldwork, Federal Work-Study, institutionally sponsored loans, traineeships, health care benefits, tuition waivers (full and partial), and unspecified assistantships also available. Financial award applicants required to submit FAFSA. In 2015, 61 master's, 13 doctorates, 9 other advanced degrees awarded. *Degree program information:* Part-time and evening/weekend programs available. Part-time, evening/weekend. Offers nursing (MS, DNP, PhD, Certificate). *Application fee:* $75. Electronic applications accepted. *Application Contact:* Kishan Zuber, Director of Graduate Studies, 607-777-2151, Fax: 607-777-2501, E-mail: kzuber@binghamton.edu. *Dean*, Dr. Pamela Stewart-Fahs, 607-777-2311, Fax: 607-777-4440, E-mail: psfahs@binghamton.edu.

School of Arts and Sciences Students: 589 full-time (288 women), 523 part-time (278 women); includes 146 minority (29 Black or African American, non-Hispanic/Latino; 11 American Indian or Alaska Native, non-Hispanic/Latino; 33 Asian, non-Hispanic/Latino; 58 Hispanic/Latino; 15 Native Hawaiian or other Pacific Islander, non-Hispanic/Latino), 396 international. Average age 30. 1,233 applicants, 52% accepted, 254 enrolled. *Faculty:* 376 full-time (138 women), 172 part-time/adjunct (63 women). *Financial support:* In 2015–16, 590 students received support, including 2 fellowships with full tuition reimbursements available (averaging $8,000 per year), 42 research assistantships with full tuition reimbursements available (averaging $16,500 per year), 429 teaching assistantships with full tuition reimbursements available (averaging $15,000 per year); career-related internships or fieldwork, Federal Work-Study, institutionally sponsored loans, scholarships/grants, health care benefits, tuition waivers (full and partial), and unspecified assistantships also available. Financial award applicants required to submit FAFSA. In 2015, 170 master's, 76 doctorates, 12 other advanced degrees awarded. *Degree program information:* Part-time and evening/weekend programs available. Part-time, evening/weekend. Offers analytical chemistry (PhD); anthropology (MA, PhD); applied statistics (MA); art history (MA, PhD); arts and sciences (MA, MM, MS, PhD, Certificate); Asian and Asian American studies (MA, Certificate); behavioral neuroscience (PhD); biological sciences (MA, MS, PhD); biomedical anthropology (MS); chemistry (MA, MS); clinical psychology (PhD); cognitive and behavioral science (PhD); comparative literature (MA, PhD); creative writing (MA); economics (MA, PhD); English (PhD); English/American literature (MA); environmental chemistry (PhD); French (MA); geography (MA); geological sciences (MA, PhD); history (MA, PhD); inorganic chemistry (PhD); Italian (MA); mathematical sciences (MA, PhD); music (MM); organic chemistry (PhD); philosophy (MA, PhD); philosophy, interpretation and culture (MA, PhD); physical chemistry (PhD); physics, applied physics, and astronomy (MS, PhD); political science (MA, PhD); social, political, ethical and legal philosophy (MA, PhD); sociology (MA, PhD); Spanish (MA); theater (MA); translation research and instruction (PhD, Certificate). *Application deadline:* Applications are processed on a rolling basis. *Application fee:* $75. Electronic applications accepted. *Application Contact:* Kishan Zuber, Recruiting and Admissions Coordinator, 607-777-2151, Fax: 607-777-2501, E-mail: kzuber@binghamton.edu. *Dean*, Dr. Anne E. McCall, 607-777-2145, E-mail: amccall@binghamton.edu.

School of Education Students: 84 full-time (62 women), 124 part-time (98 women); includes 24 minority (10 Black or African American, non-Hispanic/Latino; 3 American Indian or Alaska Native, non-Hispanic/Latino; 4 Asian, non-Hispanic/Latino; 5 Hispanic/Latino; 2 Native Hawaiian or other Pacific Islander, non-Hispanic/Latino), 6 international. Average age 31. 141 applicants, 84% accepted, 83 enrolled. *Faculty:* 19 full-time (13 women), 18 part-time/adjunct (12 women). *Financial support:* In 2015–16, 41 students received support, including 2 fellowships with full tuition reimbursements available (averaging $10,000 per year), 3 teaching assistantships with full tuition reimbursements available (averaging $15,500 per year); career-related internships or fieldwork, Federal Work-Study, institutionally sponsored loans, scholarships/grants, health care benefits, tuition waivers (full and partial), and unspecified assistantships also available. Financial award applicants required to submit FAFSA. In 2015, 78 master's, 5 doctorates, 5 other advanced degrees awarded. *Degree program information:* Part-time and evening/weekend programs available. Part-time, evening/weekend. Offers biology education (MAT, MS Ed); chemistry education (MAT, MS Ed); childhood education (MS Ed); earth science education (MAT, MS Ed); education (MAT, MS, MS Ed, Ed D, Certificate); educational leadership (Certificate); educational studies (MS); educational theory and practice (Ed D); English education (MAT, MS Ed); French education (MAT, MS Ed); literacy education (MS Ed); mathematical sciences education (MAT, MS Ed); physics (MAT, MS Ed); social studies (MAT, MS Ed); Spanish education (MAT, MS Ed); special education (MS Ed); TESOL education (MA, MS Ed). *Application fee:* $75. Electronic applications accepted. *Application Contact:* Kishan Zuber, Recruiting and Admissions Coordinator, 607-777-2151, Fax: 607-777-2501, E-mail: kzuber@binghamton.edu. *Dean*, Dr. Susan Strehle, 607-777-7329, E-mail: sstrehle@binghamton.edu.

School of Management Students: 357 full-time (185 women), 31 part-time (19 women); includes 70 minority (12 Black or African American, non-Hispanic/Latino; 43 Asian, non-Hispanic/Latino; 14 Hispanic/Latino; 1 Native Hawaiian or other Pacific Islander, non-Hispanic/Latino), 183 international. Average age 25. 805 applicants, 59% accepted, 252 enrolled. *Faculty:* 42 full-time (9 women), 32 part-time/adjunct (5 women). *Financial support:* In 2015–16, 46 students received support, including 16 teaching assistantships with full tuition reimbursements available (averaging $17,000 per year); career-related internships or fieldwork, Federal Work-Study, institutionally sponsored loans, scholarships/grants, health care benefits, tuition waivers (full and partial), and unspecified assistantships also available. Financial award applicants required to submit FAFSA. In 2015, 278 master's, 7 doctorates awarded. *Degree program information:* Part-time and evening/weekend programs available. Part-time, evening/weekend. Offers accounting (MS); business administration (MBA); corporate executive (MBA); executive business administration (MBA); health care professional executive (MBA); management (MBA, MS, PhD); professional business administration (MBA). *Application deadline:* Applications are processed on a rolling basis. *Application fee:* $75. Electronic applications accepted. *Application Contact:* Kishan Zuber, Recruiting and Admissions Coordinator, 607-777-2151, Fax: 607-777-2501, E-mail: kzuber@binghamton.edu. *Dean*, Dr. Upinder Dhillon, 607-777-4381, E-mail: dhillon@binghamton.edu.

Thomas J. Watson School of Engineering and Applied Science Students: 816 full-time (199 women), 310 part-time (63 women); includes 103 minority (33 Black or African American, non-Hispanic/Latino; 1 American Indian or Alaska Native, non-Hispanic/Latino; 42 Asian, non-Hispanic/Latino; 24 Hispanic/Latino; 3 Native Hawaiian or other Pacific Islander, non-Hispanic/Latino), 835 international. Average age 27. 2,041 applicants, 51% accepted, 430 enrolled. *Faculty:* 99 full-time (14 women), 25 part-time/adjunct (5 women). *Financial support:* In 2015–16, 268 students received support, including 2 fellowships with full tuition reimbursements available (averaging $10,000 per year), 138 research assistantships with full tuition reimbursements available (averaging $16,500 per year), 94 teaching assistantships with full tuition reimbursements available (averaging $16,500 per year); career-related internships or fieldwork, Federal Work-Study, institutionally sponsored loans, scholarships/grants, health care benefits, tuition waivers (full and partial), and unspecified assistantships also available. Financial award application deadline: 2/15; financial award applicants required to submit FAFSA. In 2015, 334 master's, 37 doctorates awarded. *Degree program information:* Part-time and evening/weekend programs available. Part-time, evening/weekend, online learning. Offers biomedical engineering (MS, PhD); computer science (MS, PhD); electrical and computer engineering (M Eng, MS, PhD); engineering and applied science (M Eng, MS, PhD); executive health systems (MS); industrial and systems engineering (M Eng); materials science and engineering (MS, PhD); mechanical engineering (M Eng, MS, PhD); systems science and industrial engineering (MS, PhD). *Application deadline:* Applications are processed on a rolling basis. *Application fee:* $75. Electronic applications accepted. *Application Contact:* Kishan Zuber, Recruiting and Admissions Coordinator, 607-777-2151, Fax: 607-777-2501, E-mail: kzuber@binghamton.edu. *Coordinator of Graduate Programs, The Watson School*, Ellen Tilden, 607-777-2873, E-mail: etilden@binghamton.edu.

See Display below and Close-Up on page 865.

BIOLA UNIVERSITY, La Mirada, CA 90639-0001

General Information Independent-religious, coed, university. *Enrollment:* 6,222 graduate, professional, and undergraduate students; 877 full-time matriculated graduate/professional students (330 women), 1,108 part-time matriculated graduate/professional students (389 women). *Graduate faculty:* 167. *Graduate housing:* Rooms and/or apartments available on a first-come, first-served basis to single and married students. *Student services:* Campus employment opportunities, campus safety program, career counseling, exercise/wellness program, international student services, low-cost health insurance, multicultural affairs office, services for students with disabilities, teacher training, writing training. *Library:* Biola University Library plus 1 other. *Collection:* Books: 550,000 (physical); Databases: 259. Weekly public service hours: 100; students can reserve study rooms.

Computer facilities: A campuswide network can be accessed from student residence rooms and from off campus. Online class registration is available.
Website: http://www.biola.edu/

General Application Contact: Graduate Admissions, 562-903-4752, E-mail: graduate.admissions@biola.edu.

GRADUATE UNITS

Cook School of Intercultural Studies Students: 89 full-time (41 women), 124 part-time (67 women); includes 72 minority (9 Black or African American, non-Hispanic/Latino; 2 American Indian or Alaska Native, non-Hispanic/Latino; 41 Asian, non-Hispanic/Latino; 17 Hispanic/Latino; 3 Two or more races, non-Hispanic/Latino), 26 international. *Faculty:* 19. *Financial support:* Scholarships/grants available. Support available to part-time students. Financial award applicants required to submit FAFSA. In 2015, 28 master's, 16 doctorates awarded. *Degree program information:* Part-time programs available. Part-time, 100% online. Offers anthropology (MA); applied linguistics (MA); intercultural education (PhD); intercultural studies (MA, PhD); linguistics (Certificate); linguistics and Biblical languages (MA); missiology (D Miss); missions (MA); teaching English to speakers of other languages (MA, Certificate); teaching English to speakers of other languages (online) (MA). *Application deadline:* For fall admission, 7/1 for domestic students, 6/1 for international students; for spring admission, 12/1 for domestic students; for summer admission, 5/1 for domestic students. Applications are processed on a rolling basis. *Application fee:* $65. Electronic applications accepted. *Application Contact:* Graduate Admissions Office, 562-903-4752, E-mail: graduate.admissions@biola.edu. *Dean*, Dr. Bulus Y. Galadima, 562-903-4844.

Crowell School of Business Students: 11 full-time (3 women), 49 part-time (15 women); includes 27 minority (5 Black or African American, non-Hispanic/Latino; 13 Asian, non-Hispanic/Latino; 9 Hispanic/Latino), 1 international. *Faculty:* 11. *Financial support:* Scholarships/grants available. Support available to part-time students. Financial award applicants required to submit FAFSA. In 2015, 10 master's awarded. *Degree program information:* Part-time and evening/weekend programs available. Part-time, evening/weekend. Offers business (MBA, MP Acc). *Application deadline:* For fall admission, 4/15 priority date for domestic and international students; for spring admission, 12/1 for domestic students. Applications are processed on a rolling basis. *Application fee:* $65. Electronic applications accepted. *Application Contact:* Christina Gramenz, MBA Coordinator, 562-777-4015, E-mail: mba@biola.edu. *Dean*, Dr. Gary Lindblad, 562-777-4015, Fax: 562-906-4545, E-mail: mba@biola.edu.

Rosemead School of Psychology Students: 115 full-time (85 women), 13 part-time (9 women); includes 69 minority (7 Black or African American, non-Hispanic/Latino; 1 American Indian or Alaska Native, non-Hispanic/Latino; 31 Asian, non-Hispanic/Latino; 23 Hispanic/Latino; 7 Two or more races, non-Hispanic/Latino), 3 international. 96 applicants, 41% accepted, 21 enrolled. *Faculty:* 24. *Financial support:* Scholarships/grants and unspecified assistantships available. Financial award applicants required to submit FAFSA. In 2015, 19 doctorates awarded. Offers clinical psychology (PhD, Psy D). *Application deadline:* For fall admission, 12/1 priority date for domestic students, 12/1 for international students. *Application fee:* $65. Electronic applications accepted. *Application Contact:* Jon Garcia, Graduate Admissions Counselor, 562-903-4752, E-mail: graduate.admissions@biola.edu. *Dean*, Dr. Clark Campbell, 562-903-4867, Fax: 562-903-4864.

School of Arts and Sciences Students: 31 full-time (8 women), 262 part-time (45 women); includes 80 minority (21 Black or African American, non-Hispanic/Latino; 1 American Indian or Alaska Native, non-Hispanic/Latino; 31 Asian, non-Hispanic/Latino; 19 Hispanic/Latino; 8 Two or more races, non-Hispanic/Latino), 15 international. 168 applicants, 70% accepted, 77 enrolled. *Faculty:* 20. *Financial support:* Scholarships/grants and unspecified assistantships available. Support available to part-time students. Financial award applicants required to submit FAFSA. In 2015, 64 master's awarded. *Degree program information:* Part-time and evening/weekend programs available. Part-time, evening/weekend, online learning. Offers Christian apologetics (MA, Certificate); science and religion (MA); speech language pathology (MA). *Application deadline:* For fall admission, 7/1 for domestic students, 6/1 for international students; for spring admission, 12/1 for domestic students. Applications are processed on a rolling basis. *Application fee:* $65. Electronic applications accepted. *Application Contact:* Graduate Admissions Office, 562-903-4752, E-mail: graduate.admissions@biola.edu.

School of Education Students: 65 full-time (58 women), 128 part-time (107 women); includes 97 minority (8 Black or African American, non-Hispanic/Latino; 1 American Indian or Alaska Native, non-Hispanic/Latino; 51 Asian, non-Hispanic/Latino; 30

Hispanic/Latino; 7 Two or more races, non-Hispanic/Latino), 4 international. 164 applicants, 87% accepted, 116 enrolled. *Faculty:* 16. *Financial support:* Scholarships/grants available. Support available to part-time students. Financial award applicants required to submit FAFSA. In 2015, 25 master's awarded. *Degree program information:* Part-time and evening/weekend programs available. Part-time, evening/weekend, online learning. Offers curriculum and instruction (Certificate); early childhood (MA Ed, MAT); multiple subject (MAT); single subject (MAT); special education (MA Ed, MAT, Certificate). *Application deadline:* For fall admission, 7/1 for domestic students, 6/1 for international students; for spring admission, 12/1 for domestic students; for summer admission, 5/1 for domestic students. Applications are processed on a rolling basis. *Application fee:* $65. Electronic applications accepted. *Application Contact:* Graduate Admissions Office, 562-903-4752, E-mail: graduate.admissions@biola.edu. *Dean*, Dr. June Hetzel, 562-903-4715.

Talbot School of Theology Students: 562 full-time (110 women), 548 part-time (164 women); includes 542 minority (40 Black or African American, non-Hispanic/Latino; 2 American Indian or Alaska Native, non-Hispanic/Latino; 378 Asian, non-Hispanic/Latino; 84 Hispanic/Latino; 1 Native Hawaiian or other Pacific Islander, non-Hispanic/Latino; 37 Two or more races, non-Hispanic/Latino), 105 international. 437 applicants, 78% accepted, 241 enrolled. *Faculty:* 77. *Financial support:* Scholarships/grants and unspecified assistantships available. Support available to part-time students. Financial award applicants required to submit FAFSA. In 2015, 177 master's, 24 doctorates awarded. *Degree program information:* Part-time and evening/weekend programs available. Part-time, evening/weekend. Offers adult/family ministry (MACE); Bible exposition (MA, Th M); Biblical and theological studies (Certificate); biblical and theological studies/diversified (MA); children's ministry (MACE); Christian education (M Div); cross-cultural education ministry (MACE); educational studies (Ed D, PhD); evangelism and discipleship (M Div); general Christian education (MACE); Messianic Jewish studies (M Div, Certificate); missions and intercultural studies (M Div); New Testament (MA, Th M); Old Testament (MA); Old Testament and Semitics (Th M); pastoral and general ministry (M Div); pastoral care and counseling (M Div, MACML); philosophy (MA); preaching and pastoral ministry (MACML); spiritual formation (M Div, Certificate); spiritual formation and soul care (MA); sports ministry (MACML); theology (MA, Th M, D Min, Certificate); youth ministry (MACE). *Application deadline:* For fall admission, 7/1 for domestic students, 6/1 for international students; for spring admission, 12/1 priority date for domestic students. Applications are processed on a rolling basis. *Application fee:* $65. Electronic applications accepted. *Application Contact:* Graduate Admissions Office, 562-903-4752, E-mail: graduate.admissions@biola.edu. *Dean*, Dr. Clint Arnold, 562-903-4816, Fax: 562-903-4748.

BISHOP'S UNIVERSITY, Sherbrooke, QC J1M 0C8, Canada

General Information Province-supported, coed, comprehensive institution. *Graduate housing:* Room and/or apartments available on a first-come, first-served basis to single students; on-campus housing not available to married students. Housing application deadline: 7/1.

GRADUATE UNITS

School of Education ***Degree program information:*** Part-time programs available. Part-time, online learning. Offers advanced studies in education (Diploma); education (M Ed, MA); teaching English as a second language (Certificate).

BLACK HILLS STATE UNIVERSITY, Spearfish, SD 57799

General Information State-supported, coed, comprehensive institution. *Graduate housing:* Room and/or apartments available on a first-come, first-served basis to single students; on-campus housing not available to married students. Housing application deadline: 4/1.

GRADUATE UNITS

Graduate Studies ***Degree program information:*** Part-time and evening/weekend programs available. Part-time, evening/weekend, online learning. Offers business administration (MBA); curriculum and instruction (MS); integrative genomics (MS); strategic leadership (MS). Electronic applications accepted.

BLESSING-RIEMAN COLLEGE OF NURSING, Quincy, IL 62305-7005

General Information Independent, coed, primarily women, comprehensive institution. *Graduate housing:* Rooms and/or apartments available on a first-come, first-served basis to single and married students.

GRADUATE UNITS

Program in Nursing ***Degree program information:*** Part-time programs available. Part-time. Offers nursing (MSN). Electronic applications accepted.

BLESSING–RIEMAN COLLEGE OF NURSING AND HEALTH SCIENCES, Quincy, IL 62305-7005

General Information Independent, coed, comprehensive institution. *Graduate housing:* On-campus housing not available. *Student services:* Campus safety program, services for students with disabilities.
Website: http://www.brcn.edu/

GRADUATE UNITS

Master of Science in Nursing Program ***Financial support:*** In 2015–16, 20,350 students received support. Scholarships/grants available. Financial award application deadline: 4/30; financial award applicants required to submit FAFSA. In 2015, 8 master's awarded. *Degree program information:* Part-time programs available. Part-time-only, online only, 100% online. Offers nursing administration (MSN); nursing education (MSN). *Application deadline:* Applications are processed on a rolling basis. Electronic applications accepted. *Application Contact:* Heather Mutter, Admissions Counselor, 217-228-5520 Ext. 6964, Fax: 217-223-1781, E-mail: hmutter@brcn.edu. *Administrative Coordinator, Accreditation*, Dr. Karen Mayville, 217-228-5520 Ext. 6968, Fax: 217-223-4661, E-mail: kmayville@brcn.edu.

BLOOMFIELD COLLEGE, Bloomfield, NJ 07003-9981

General Information Independent-religious, coed, comprehensive institution.

GRADUATE UNITS

Program in Accounting Offers accounting (MS).

BLOOMSBURG UNIVERSITY OF PENNSYLVANIA, Bloomsburg, PA 17815-1301

General Information State-supported, coed, comprehensive institution. CGS member. *Research affiliation:* Marine Science Consortium (biology), American Chemical Society Petroleum Research Fund (chemistry), Consortium of Big Ten Universities Research and Training Reactors (physics), Melanoma Research Fund (biology), Merck & Company, Inc. (biology).

GRADUATE UNITS

School of Graduate Studies ***Degree program information:*** Part-time and evening/weekend programs available. Part-time, evening/weekend. Electronic applications accepted.

College of Business Offers accounting (M Acc); business (M Acc, M Ed, MBA); business administration (MBA); business education (M Ed). Electronic applications accepted.

College of Education Offers college student affairs (M Ed); curriculum and instruction (M Ed, Certificate); early childhood education (M Ed); education (M Ed, MS, Certificate); education of the deaf/hard of hearing (MS); elementary school counseling (M Ed); language arts (M Ed); math (M Ed); middle level education grades 4-8 (M Ed); reading (M Ed); school counseling and student affairs (M Ed); school principal (Certificate); science (M Ed); secondary school counseling (M Ed); social studies (M Ed); special education (M Ed, MS, Certificate). Electronic applications accepted.

College of Science and Technology Offers adult and family nurse practitioner (MSN); audiology (Au D); biology (MS); clinical athletic training (MS); community health (MSN); corporate instructional technology (MS); elearning developer (Certificate); exercise science (MS); nurse anesthesia (MSN); nursing (MSN); nursing administration (MSN); school-based speech-language pathology (M Ed); science and technology (M Ed, MS, MSN, Au D, Certificate); speech pathology (M Ed, MS); speech-language pathology (MS). Electronic applications accepted.

BLUEFIELD COLLEGE, Bluefield, VA 24605-1799

General Information Independent-religious, coed, comprehensive institution. *Enrollment:* 972 graduate, professional, and undergraduate students; 13 full-time matriculated graduate/professional students (9 women), 4 part-time matriculated graduate/professional students (all women). *Enrollment by degree level:* 17 master's. *Graduate faculty:* 1 (woman) full-time, 2 part-time/adjunct (1 woman). *Tuition, area resident:* Full-time $5520; part-time $460 per credit. *Library:* Easley Library. *Collection:* Books: 44,352 (physical), 165,829 (digital/electronic); Serial titles: 7,976 (physical), 334 (digital/electronic); Databases: 72. Students can reserve study rooms.

Computer facilities: 110 computers available on campus for general student use. A campuswide network can be accessed from student residence rooms. Online class registration is available. Website: http://www.bluefield.edu/

General Application Contact: Trent Argo, Vice President for Enrollment Management, 276-326-4231, Fax: 276-326-4395, E-mail: targo@bluefield.edu.

GRADUATE UNITS

School of Education Students: 13 full-time (9 women), 4 part-time (all women). Average age 32. 9 applicants, 33% accepted, 3 enrolled. *Faculty:* 2 full-time (both women), 2 part-time/adjunct (1 woman). *Financial support:* Applicants required to submit FAFSA. In 2015, 4 master's awarded. *Degree program information:* Part-time programs available. Part-time, online only, 100% online. Offers education (MA Ed). *Application deadline:* Applications are processed on a rolling basis. *Application fee:* $0. Electronic applications accepted. *Dean*, Dr. Donna Hardy Watson, 276-326-4475, E-mail: dwatson@bluefield.edu.

BLUE MOUNTAIN COLLEGE, Blue Mountain, MS 38610

General Information Independent-religious, coed, comprehensive institution. *Graduate housing:* Room and/or apartments available on a first-come, first-served basis to single students; on-campus housing not available to married students.

GRADUATE UNITS

Program in Elementary Education ***Degree program information:*** Part-time and evening/weekend programs available. Part-time, evening/weekend. Offers elementary education (M Ed). Electronic applications accepted.

Program in Literacy/Reading (K-12) ***Degree program information:*** Part-time and evening/weekend programs available. Part-time, evening/weekend. Offers literacy/reading (K-12) (M Ed). Electronic applications accepted.

BLUFFTON UNIVERSITY, Bluffton, OH 45817

General Information Independent-religious, coed, comprehensive institution. *Enrollment:* 1,011 graduate, professional, and undergraduate students; 92 full-time matriculated graduate/professional students (54 women), 1 (woman) part-time matriculated graduate/professional student. *Enrollment by degree level:* 93 master's. *Graduate faculty:* 11 full-time (4 women), 5 part-time/adjunct (0 women). *Tuition, area resident:* Full-time $6420. Tuition and fees vary according to program. *Graduate housing:* Room and/or apartments available on a first-come, first-served basis to single students; on-campus housing not available to married students. Typical cost: $3780 per year. *Student services:* Campus employment opportunities, career counseling, low-cost health insurance, multicultural affairs office, services for students with disabilities, writing training. *Library:* Musselman Library plus 1 other. *Collection:* Books: 91,624 (physical), 241,791 (digital/electronic); Serial titles: 1,094 (physical), 232,693 (digital/electronic); Databases: 323. Weekly public service hours: 81; students can reserve study rooms.

Computer facilities: 170 computers available on campus for general student use. A campuswide network can be accessed from student residence rooms and from off campus. Online class registration is available.
Website: http://www.bluffton.edu/

General Application Contact: Rebecca Cox, 419-488-3257, Fax: 419-358-3399.

GRADUATE UNITS

Programs in Business ***Financial support:*** Scholarships/grants, tuition waivers, and unspecified assistantships available. Financial award application deadline: 5/1. *Degree program information:* Evening/weekend programs available. Evening/weekend, online learning. Offers accounting and financial management (MBA); business administration (MBA); health care management (MBA); leadership (MBA); organizational management (MA); production and operations management (MBA); sport management (MBA). *Application deadline:* For fall admission, 7/31 priority date for domestic and international students. Applications are processed on a rolling basis. *Application fee:* $25. Electronic applications accepted. *Administrative Assistant for Graduate Programs in Business*, Dr. George Lehman, 419-358-3065.

Programs in Education ***Financial support:*** Health care benefits available. Support available to part-time students. Financial award application deadline: 9/15; financial award applicants required to submit FAFSA. *Degree program information:* Part-time programs available. Part-time. Offers intervention specialist (MA Ed); leadership (MA Ed); reading (MA Ed); sport management (MA Ed). *Application deadline:* For fall admission, 8/15 priority date for domestic students, 6/15 priority date for international students; for spring admission, 12/15 priority date for domestic students, 9/15 priority date for international students. Applications are processed on a rolling basis. *Application fee:* $25. Electronic applications accepted. *Application Contact:* Nancey Schortgen, Program Representative, 419-358-3202, Fax: 419-358-3399, E-mail: schortgenn@bluffton.edu.

BOB JONES UNIVERSITY, Greenville, SC 29614

General Information Independent-religious, coed, university.

GRADUATE UNITS

Graduate Programs

BOISE STATE UNIVERSITY, Boise, ID 83725-0399

General Information State-supported, coed, university. CGS member. *Enrollment:* 22,113 graduate, professional, and undergraduate students; 903 full-time matriculated graduate/professional students (505 women), 2,088 part-time matriculated graduate/professional students (1,309 women). *Enrollment by degree level:* 1,971 master's, 209 doctoral, 107 other advanced degrees. *Graduate faculty:* 457. Tuition, state resident: full-time $6058; part-time $358 per credit hour. Tuition, nonresident: full-time $20,108; part-time $608 per credit hour. *Required fees:* $2108. Tuition and fees vary according to program. *Graduate housing:* Rooms and/or apartments available on a first-come, first-served basis to single and married students. Housing application deadline: 6/1. *Student services:* Campus employment opportunities, campus safety program, career counseling, child daycare facilities, exercise/wellness program, free psychological counseling, grant writing training, international student services, low-cost health insurance, multicultural affairs office, services for students with disabilities, teacher training, writing training. *Library:* Albertsons Library. *Research affiliation:* American Chemical Society (petroleum research), Federal Aviation Administration (airliner cabin environment research), Lee Pesky Learning Center (elementary mathematics education), Prewitt & Associates, Inc. (C-130 drop zones), Bechtel BWXT Idaho, LLC (energy policy analysis), Argonne National Laboratory (energy policy analysis).

Computer facilities: 900 computers available on campus for general student use. A campuswide network can be accessed from student residence rooms and from off campus. Online class registration is available.
Website: http://www.boisestate.edu/

General Application Contact: Dr. John R. Pelton, Dean, 208-426-3647, Fax: 208-426-2789, E-mail: jpelton@boisestate.edu.

GRADUATE UNITS

College of Arts and Sciences Students: 233 full-time (115 women), 122 part-time (75 women); includes 37 minority (2 Black or African American, non-Hispanic/Latino; 3 American Indian or Alaska Native, non-Hispanic/Latino; 10 Asian, non-Hispanic/Latino; 18 Hispanic/Latino; 1 Native Hawaiian or other Pacific Islander, non-Hispanic/Latino; 3 Two or more races, non-Hispanic/Latino), 24 international. Average age 32. 495 applicants, 26% accepted, 93 enrolled. *Faculty:* 140. *Financial support:* In 2015–16, 61 students received support, including 39 research assistantships (averaging $8,157 per year), 108 teaching assistantships (averaging $8,021 per year); scholarships/grants and unspecified assistantships also available. Financial award applicants required to submit FAFSA. In 2015, 81 master's, 1 doctorate awarded. *Degree program information:* Part-time programs available. Part-time. Offers anthropology (MA); applied anthropology (MAA); applied historical research (MAHR); art education (MA); arts and sciences (M E Sci, MA, MAA, MAHR, MFA, MM, MS, PhD); biology (MA, MS); biomolecular sciences (PhD); chemistry (MS); communication (MA); creative writing (MFA); earth science (M E Sci); English (MA); geophysics (MS, PhD); geosciences (MS, PhD); history (MA); hydrology (MS); interdisciplinary studies (MA, MS); mathematics (MS); mathematics education (MS); music education (MM); performance (MM); raptor biology (MS); rhetoric and composition (MA); teaching English language (MA); technical communication (MA); visual arts (MFA). *Application deadline:* For fall admission, 5/1 for domestic and international students. *Application fee:* $65 ($95 for international students). Electronic applications accepted. *Dean,* Dr. Tony Roark, 208-426-1414, Fax: 208-426-3006.

College of Business and Economics Students: 146 full-time (52 women), 187 part-time (59 women); includes 33 minority (3 Black or African American, non-Hispanic/Latino; 1 American Indian or Alaska Native, non-Hispanic/Latino; 8 Asian, non-Hispanic/Latino; 16 Hispanic/Latino; 5 Two or more races, non-Hispanic/Latino), 12 international. Average age 33. 234 applicants, 63% accepted, 116 enrolled. *Faculty:* 22. *Financial support:* In 2015–16, 29 students received support, including 2 research assistantships (averaging $7,596 per year); scholarships/grants and unspecified assistantships also available. Financial award applicants required to submit FAFSA. In 2015, 125 master's awarded. *Degree program information:* Part-time programs available. Part-time, 100% online. Offers accountancy (MSA); accountancy taxation (MSAT); business administration (MBA); business and economics (MBA, MSA, MSAT). *Application deadline:* For fall admission, 5/1 for domestic and international students. Applications are processed on a rolling basis. *Application fee:* $65 ($95 for international students). Electronic applications accepted. *Application Contact:* Trisha Stevens-Lamb, Director, Career Start MBA, 208-426-1120, E-mail: trishastevenslamb@boisestate.edu. *Dean,* Dr. Kenneth J. Petersen, 208-426-1125.

College of Education Students: 131 full-time (106 women), 762 part-time (486 women); includes 88 minority (13 Black or African American, non-Hispanic/Latino; 4 American Indian or Alaska Native, non-Hispanic/Latino; 19 Asian, non-Hispanic/Latino; 46 Hispanic/Latino; 4 Native Hawaiian or other Pacific Islander, non-Hispanic/Latino; 2 Two or more races, non-Hispanic/Latino), 32 international. Average age 37. 399 applicants, 61% accepted, 146 enrolled. *Faculty:* 106. *Financial support:* In 2015–16, 36 students received support, including 1 teaching assistantship (averaging $2,148 per year); scholarships/grants and unspecified assistantships also available. Financial award applicants required to submit FAFSA. In 2015, 234 master's, 12 doctorates awarded. *Degree program information:* Part-time programs available. Part-time, 100% online, blended/hybrid learning. Offers bilingual education (M Ed); counselor education (MA, Graduate Certificate); curriculum and instruction (Ed D); early and special education (M Ed); early childhood intervention (MIT); education (M Ed, MA, MET, MIT, MPE, MS, MS Ed, Ed D, Graduate Certificate); education, curriculum and instruction (MA); educational leadership (M Ed); educational technology (MET, MS, Ed D); English as a new language (M Ed); literacy (MA); online teaching (Graduate Certificate); school technology coordination (Graduate Certificate); special education (MIT); technology integration (Graduate Certificate). *Application fee:* $65 ($95 for international students). Electronic applications accepted. *Dean,* Dr. Rich Osguthorpe, 208-426-1611, E-mail: richardosguthorpe@boisestate.edu.

College of Engineering Students: 136 full-time (42 women), 231 part-time (117 women); includes 52 minority (15 Black or African American, non-Hispanic/Latino; 17 Asian, non-Hispanic/Latino; 15 Hispanic/Latino; 5 Two or more races, non-Hispanic/Latino), 78 international. Average age 34. 309 applicants, 51% accepted, 81 enrolled. *Faculty:* 78. *Financial support:* In 2015–16, 50 students received support, including 63 research assistantships (averaging $9,326 per year), 7 teaching assistantships with partial tuition reimbursements available (averaging $10,656 per year); scholarships/grants and unspecified assistantships also available. Financial award applicants required to submit FAFSA. In 2015, 72 master's, 1 doctorate awarded. *Degree program information:* Part-time programs available. Part-time, online learning. Offers civil engineering (M Engr, MS); computer science (MS); computer science teacher endorsement (Graduate Certificate); electrical and computer engineering (M Engr, MS, PhD); engineering (M Engr, MS, PhD, Graduate Certificate); mechanical engineering (M Engr, MS); organizational performance and workplace learning (MS); STEM education (Graduate Certificate); workplace e-learning and performance support (Graduate Certificate); workplace instructional design (Graduate Certificate); workplace performance improvement (Graduate Certificate). *Application fee:* $65 ($95 for international students). Electronic applications accepted. *Dean,* Dr. Amy Moll, 208-426-5719.

Micron School of Materials Science and Engineering Students: 37 full-time (13 women), 6 part-time (3 women); includes 6 minority (5 Asian, non-Hispanic/Latino; 1 Hispanic/Latino), 8 international. Average age 29. 61 applicants, 36% accepted, 7 enrolled. *Faculty:* 16. *Financial support:* In 2015–16, 6 students received support, including 32 research assistantships (averaging $8,599 per year); scholarships/grants and unspecified assistantships also available. Financial award application deadline: 1/15; financial award applicants required to submit FAFSA. In 2015, 10 master's, 1 doctorate awarded. Offers materials science and engineering (M Engr, MS, PhD). *Application deadline:* For fall admission, 1/15 priority date for domestic and international students. *Application fee:* $65 ($95 for international students). Electronic applications accepted. *Application Contact:* Dr. David Estrada, Graduate Program Coordinator, 208-426-5693, E-mail: daveestrada@boisestate.edu. *Department Chair,* Dr. Janet Callahan, 208-426-5983, E-mail: janetcallahan@boisestate.edu.

College of Health Sciences Students: 221 full-time (174 women), 183 part-time (138 women); includes 42 minority (11 Black or African American, non-Hispanic/Latino; 3 Asian, non-Hispanic/Latino; 24 Hispanic/Latino; 1 Native Hawaiian or other Pacific Islander, non-Hispanic/Latino; 3 Two or more races, non-Hispanic/Latino). Average age 35. 246 applicants, 49% accepted, 85 enrolled. *Faculty:* 72. *Financial support:* In 2015–16, 79 students received support, including 4 research assistantships (averaging $3,510 per year); scholarships/grants and unspecified assistantships also available. Financial award applicants required to submit FAFSA. In 2015, 151 master's, 13 other advanced degrees awarded. *Degree program information:* Part-time programs available. Part-time, 100% online. Offers athletic leadership (MAL); community and environmental health (MHS); health science (MHS); health sciences (MAL, MHS, MK, MSN, MSW, DNP, Graduate Certificate); health services leadership (Graduate Certificate); kinesiology (MK). *Application deadline:* Applications are processed on a rolling basis. *Application fee:* $65 ($95 for international students). Electronic applications accepted. *Application Contact:* Dr. Tedd McDonald, Program Director, 208-426-2425, E-mail: tmcdonal@boisestate.edu. *Dean,* Dr. Tim Dunnagan, 208-426-4150, Fax: 208-426-3469.

School of Nursing Students: 1 (woman) full-time, 91 part-time (73 women); includes 11 minority (5 Black or African American, non-Hispanic/Latino; 2 Asian, non-Hispanic/Latino; 3 Hispanic/Latino; 1 Native Hawaiian or other Pacific Islander, non-Hispanic/Latino). Average age 43. 32 applicants, 44% accepted, 12 enrolled. *Financial support:* In 2015–16, 1 student received support. Scholarships/grants and unspecified assistantships available. Financial award application deadline: 10/15; financial award applicants required to submit FAFSA. In 2015, 3 master's awarded. Offers acute care adult gerontology (Graduate Certificate); adult gerontology acute care (MSN); adult gerontology primary care (MSN); healthcare simulation (Graduate Certificate); nursing practice (DNP); primary care adult gerontology (Graduate Certificate). *Application deadline:* For spring admission, 10/15 priority date for domestic and international students. Applications are processed on a rolling basis. *Application fee:* $65 ($95 for international students). Electronic applications accepted. *Application Contact:* Dr. Dawn Weiler, Program Coordinator, 208-426-1239, E-mail: dweiler@boisestate.edu. *Director,* Dr. Ann Hubbert, 208-426-3404, E-mail: annhubbert@boisestate.edu.

School of Social Work Students: 177 full-time (146 women), 23 part-time (22 women); includes 13 minority (2 Black or African American, non-Hispanic/Latino; 10 Hispanic/Latino; 1 Two or more races, non-Hispanic/Latino). Average age 34. 139 applicants, 46% accepted, 47 enrolled. *Financial support:* In 2015–16, 37 students received support, including 2 research assistantships (averaging $4,083 per year); scholarships/grants and unspecified assistantships also available. Financial award applicants required to submit FAFSA. In 2015, 104 master's awarded. *Degree program information:* Part-time programs available. Part-time, 100% online. Offers social work (MSW). *Application deadline:* For fall admission, 1/10 for domestic and international students. *Application fee:* $65 ($95 for international students). Electronic applications accepted. *Application Contact:* Dr. Jo Powers, MSW Coordinator, 208-426-3184, Fax: 208-426-2789, E-mail: lplatt@boisestate.edu. *Director,* Dr. Randy Magen, 208-426-1789, E-mail: randymagen@boisestate.edu.

School of Public Service Students: 63 full-time (32 women), 111 part-time (68 women); includes 21 minority (1 American Indian or Alaska Native, non-Hispanic/Latino; 2 Asian, non-Hispanic/Latino; 16 Hispanic/Latino; 1 Native Hawaiian or other Pacific Islander, non-Hispanic/Latino; 1 Two or more races, non-Hispanic/Latino), 2 international. Average age 36. 114 applicants, 48% accepted, 44 enrolled. *Faculty:* 28. *Financial support:* In 2015–16, 51 students received support, including 4 research assistantships (averaging $5,064 per year); scholarships/grants and unspecified assistantships also available. Financial award applicants required to submit FAFSA. In 2015, 44 master's awarded. *Degree program information:* Part-time programs available. Part-time. Offers criminal justice (MA); political science (MA); public policy and administration (MPA, PhD, Graduate Certificate); public service (MA, MPA, PhD, Graduate Certificate). *Application fee:* $65 ($95 for international students). Electronic applications accepted. *Dean,* Dr. Corey Cook, 208-426-3349.

BORICUA COLLEGE, New York, NY 10032-1560

General Information Independent, coed, comprehensive institution. *Enrollment:* 70 full-time matriculated graduate/professional students (60 women). *Enrollment by degree level:* 70 master's. *Graduate faculty:* 2 full-time (1 woman), 6 part-time/adjunct (4 women). *Tuition, area resident:* Full-time $13,000. *Required fees:* $100. One-time fee: $100 full-time. *Student services:* Career counseling. *Library:* Boricua College Library plus 1 other.

Computer facilities: 120 computers available on campus for general student use.
Website: http://www.boricuacollege.edu/

General Application Contact: Brenda Rodriguez, Director of Admissions, 347-964-8680, E-mail: brodriguez@boricuacollege.edu.

GRADUATE UNITS

Program in Human Services ***Financial support:*** Career-related internships or fieldwork and Federal Work-Study available. Financial award applicants required to submit FAFSA. *Degree program information:* Evening/weekend programs available. Evening/weekend. Offers human services (MS). Program offered in Brooklyn and Manhattan. *Application deadline:* Applications are processed on a rolling basis.

Application fee: $100. *Application Contact:* Miriam Pfeffer, Director of Admissions, 718-782-2200 Ext. 210, E-mail: mpfeffer@boricuacollege.edu. *Co-Chairperson*, Victor Garcia, 718-782-2200 Ext. 271.

Program in Latin American and Caribbean Studies ***Financial support:*** Career-related internships or fieldwork and Federal Work-Study available. Financial award applicants required to submit FAFSA. *Degree program information:* Evening/weekend programs available. Evening/weekend. Offers Latin American and Caribbean studies (MA). Program offered in Brooklyn and Manhattan. *Application deadline:* Applications are processed on a rolling basis. *Application fee:* $100. *Application Contact:* Miriam Pfeffer, Director of Admissions, 718-782-2200 Ext. 210, E-mail: mpfeffer@boricuacollege.edu. *Senior Vice President*, Dr. Maria Montes, 718-782-2200 Ext. 222.

Program in TESOL Education (K-12) ***Financial support:*** Career-related internships or fieldwork and Federal Work-Study available. Financial award applicants required to submit FAFSA. *Degree program information:* Evening/weekend programs available. Evening/weekend. Offers TESOL education (MS). *Application deadline:* Applications are processed on a rolling basis. *Application fee:* $100. *Application Contact:* Dr. Shivaji Sengupta, Vice President, 212-694-1000 Ext. 650, Fax: 212-694-1015, E-mail: ssengupta@boricuacollege.edu. *Co-Chairperson*, Dr. Joseph H. Gaines, 212-694-1000.

BOSTON ARCHITECTURAL COLLEGE, Boston, MA 02115-2795

General Information Independent, coed, comprehensive institution.

GRADUATE UNITS

Graduate Programs Offers architecture (M Arch); historic preservation (MDS); interior design (MID); landscape architecture (MLA); sustainable design (MDS). Electronic applications accepted.

BOSTON COLLEGE, Chestnut Hill, MA 02467-3800

General Information Independent-religious, coed, university. CGS member. *Enrollment:* 13,705 graduate, professional, and undergraduate students; 3,491 full-time matriculated graduate/professional students (2,011 women), 1,022 part-time matriculated graduate/professional students (555 women). *Graduate faculty:* 786. Tuition and fees vary according to program. *Graduate housing:* On-campus housing not available. *Student services:* Campus employment opportunities, campus safety program, career counseling, child daycare facilities, exercise/wellness program, free psychological counseling, grant writing training, international student services, low-cost health insurance, multicultural affairs office, services for students with disabilities, teacher training, writing training. *Library:* O'Neill Library plus 8 others. *Collection:* Books: 3 million (physical); Serial titles: 3,546 (physical), 44,891 (digital/electronic). Study areas open 24 hours, 5–7 days a week; students can reserve study rooms.

Computer facilities: Computer purchase and lease plans are available. 1,000 computers available on campus for general student use. A campuswide network can be accessed from student residence rooms and from off campus. Online class registration is available.
Website: http://www.bc.edu/

General Application Contact: Robert V. Howe, Associate Dean, 617-552-3265, Fax: 617-552-3700, E-mail: hower@bc.edu.

GRADUATE UNITS

Carroll School of Management ***Degree program information:*** Part-time and evening/weekend programs available. Part-time, evening/weekend. Offers accounting (MSA); business administration (MBA); finance (MSF, PhD); management (MBA, MSA, MSF, PhD); management and organization (PhD). Electronic applications accepted.

Graduate School of Arts and Sciences Students: 805 full-time (353 women), 30 part-time (12 women). 2,202 applicants, 28% accepted, 191 enrolled. *Faculty:* 461 full-time (146 women). *Financial support:* In 2015–16, fellowships with tuition reimbursements (averaging $21,000 per year), research assistantships with tuition reimbursements (averaging $21,000 per year) were awarded; teaching assistantships with tuition reimbursements, career-related internships or fieldwork, Federal Work-Study, scholarships/grants, tuition waivers (full and partial), and unspecified assistantships also available. Support available to part-time students. Financial award application deadline: 3/1; financial award applicants required to submit FAFSA. *Degree program information:* Part-time programs available. Part-time. Offers arts and sciences (MA, MS, MST, PhD); biochemistry (PhD); biology (PhD); classics (MA); earth and environmental sciences (MS); economics (PhD); English (MA, PhD); European national studies (MA); French (MA); Greek (MA); history (MA, PhD); inorganic chemistry (PhD); Irish studies (MA, PhD); Italian (MA); Latin (MA); linguistics (MA); mathematics (PhD); medieval studies (MA); organic chemistry (PhD); philosophy (MA, PhD); philosophy and theology (MA); physical chemistry (PhD); physics (MS, PhD); political science (MA, PhD); psychology (PhD); Russian (MA); science education (MST); Slavic studies (MA); sociology (MA, PhD); Spanish (MA); theology (PhD). *Application deadline:* For fall admission, 1/2 priority date for domestic and international students. *Application fee:* $75. Electronic applications accepted. *Application Contact:* Robert V. Howe, Associate Dean, 617-552-3265, Fax: 617-552-3700, E-mail: hower@bc.edu. *Dean*, Dr. Gregory Kalscheur, 617-552-6850, E-mail: gregory.kalscheur@bc.edu.

Graduate School of Social Work ***Degree program information:*** Part-time programs available. Part-time. Offers social work (MSW, PhD). Electronic applications accepted.

Law School Offers law (JD). Electronic applications accepted.

Lynch School of Education Students: 512 full-time (406 women), 287 part-time (205 women); includes 162 minority (49 Black or African American, non-Hispanic/Latino; 36 Asian, non-Hispanic/Latino; 56 Hispanic/Latino; 21 Two or more races, non-Hispanic/Latino), 95 international. Average age 26. 1,385 applicants, 58% accepted, 322 enrolled. *Faculty:* 62 full-time (37 women). *Financial support:* Fellowships with tuition reimbursements, research assistantships with tuition reimbursements, teaching assistantships with tuition reimbursements, career-related internships or fieldwork, Federal Work-Study, scholarships/grants, traineeships, health care benefits, tuition waivers (partial), and unspecified assistantships available. Support available to part-time students. Financial award applicants required to submit FAFSA. In 2015, 249 master's, 38 doctorates, 5 other advanced degrees awarded. *Degree program information:* Part-time and evening/weekend programs available. Part-time, evening/weekend. Offers applied developmental and educational psychology (MA, PhD); counseling psychology (PhD); curriculum and instruction (M Ed, PhD, CAES); education (M Ed, MA, MAT, MS, MST, Ed D, PhD, CAES); educational leadership (M Ed, Ed D, CAES); educational research, measurement, and evaluation (M Ed, MS, PhD); elementary education (M Ed, MAT); higher education (MA, PhD); mental health counseling (MA); reading and literacy (M Ed, MAT, CAES); secondary education (M Ed, MAT, MST); special needs: moderate disabilities (M Ed, CAES); special needs: severe disabilities (M Ed, CAES). *Application deadline:* For fall admission, 12/1 priority date for domestic and international students; for spring admission, 11/1 for domestic and international students. *Application fee:* $65. Electronic applications accepted. *Application Contact:* Kimberly Rose, Graduate Admission Assistant, 617-552-4214, Fax: 617-552-0398, E-mail: roseki@bc.edu. *Dean*, Dr. Maureen Kenny, 617-552-4200, Fax: 617-552-0812.

School of Theology and Ministry ***Degree program information:*** Part-time programs available. Part-time. Offers church leadership (MA); divinity (M Div); pastoral ministry (MA); religious education (MA, PhD); sacred theology (STD, STL); social justice/social ministry (MA); spiritual direction (MA); theological studies (MTS); theology (Th M, PhD); youth ministry (MA). Electronic applications accepted.

William F. Connell School of Nursing Students: 185 full-time (167 women), 66 part-time (56 women); includes 31 minority (10 Black or African American, non-Hispanic/Latino; 12 Asian, non-Hispanic/Latino; 7 Hispanic/Latino; 2 Two or more races, non-Hispanic/Latino), 7 international. Average age 32. 313 applicants, 66% accepted, 91 enrolled. *Faculty:* 53 full-time (48 women), 47 part-time/adjunct (44 women). *Financial support:* In 2015–16, 1 fellowship with full tuition reimbursement (averaging $23,700 per year), 25 teaching assistantships (averaging $4,370 per year) were awarded; research assistantships, scholarships/grants, health care benefits, tuition waivers (partial), and unspecified assistantships also available. Support available to part-time students. Financial award application deadline: 3/1; financial award applicants required to submit FAFSA. In 2015, 98 master's, 5 doctorates awarded. *Degree program information:* Part-time programs available. Part-time. Offers adult-gerontology nursing (MS); family health nursing (MS); forensic nursing (MS); nurse anesthesia (MS); nursing (PhD); pediatric nursing (MS); psychiatric-mental health nursing (MS); women's health nursing (MS). *Application deadline:* For fall admission, 9/30 for domestic and international students; for winter admission, 1/15 for domestic and international students; for spring admission, 3/15 for domestic and international students. Applications are processed on a rolling basis. *Application fee:* $40. Electronic applications accepted. *Application Contact:* MaryBeth Crowley, Graduate Programs Assistant, 617-552-4928, Fax: 617-552-2121, E-mail: csongrad@bc.edu. *Dean*, Dr. Susan Gennaro, 617-552-4251, Fax: 617-552-0931, E-mail: susan.gennaro@bc.edu.

BOSTON GRADUATE SCHOOL OF PSYCHOANALYSIS, Brookline, MA 02446-4602

General Information Independent, coed, graduate-only institution. *Graduate housing:* On-campus housing not available. *Research affiliation:* Boston Institute for Psychotherapy (psychotherapy).

GRADUATE UNITS

BGSP-New Jersey Offers psychoanalysis (MA); psychoanalytic counseling (MA). Programs offered in conjunction with Academic of Clinical and Applied Psychoanalysis in Livingston, NJ.

CAGS and Certificate Programs ***Degree program information:*** Part-time programs available. Part-time. Offers child and adolescent intervention (CAGS); psychoanalysis (Certificate); psychoanalytic psychotherapy (CAGS).

Doctoral Programs ***Degree program information:*** Part-time programs available. Part-time. Offers psychoanalysis (Psya D); psychoanalysis, society and culture (Psya D).

Master's Programs ***Degree program information:*** Part-time programs available. Part-time. Offers mental health counseling (MA); psychoanalysis (MA); psychoanalysis, society and culture (MA).

New York Graduate School of Psychoanalysis ***Degree program information:*** Part-time programs available. Part-time. Offers psychoanalysis (MA).

BOSTON UNIVERSITY, Boston, MA 02215

General Information Independent, coed, university. CGS member. *Enrollment:* 32,158 graduate, professional, and undergraduate students; 9,314 full-time matriculated graduate/professional students (5,223 women), 4,640 part-time matriculated graduate/professional students (2,543 women). *Enrollment by degree level:* 8,672 master's, 5,079 doctoral, 203 other advanced degrees. *Graduate housing:* On-campus housing not available. *Student services:* Campus employment opportunities, campus safety program, career counseling, child daycare facilities, exercise/wellness program, free psychological counseling, international student services, low-cost health insurance, services for students with disabilities, writing training. *Library:* Mugar Memorial Library plus 21 others. *Collection:* Books: 2.4 million (physical), 1.2 million (digital/electronic); Databases: 496. Weekly public service hours: 123; students can reserve study rooms. *Research affiliation:* Society for the Preservation of New England Antiquities, NASA-Ames Research Center, Massachusetts Historical Society, Woods Hole Oceanographic Institution-Marine Biological Laboratory.

Computer facilities: Computer purchase and lease plans are available. 250 computers available on campus for general student use. A campuswide network can be accessed from student residence rooms and from off campus. Online class registration, research and educational networks are available.
Website: http://www.bu.edu/

GRADUATE UNITS

College of Communication Students: 333 full-time (256 women), 16 part-time (12 women); includes 47 minority (7 Black or African American, non-Hispanic/Latino; 1 American Indian or Alaska Native, non-Hispanic/Latino; 8 Asian, non-Hispanic/Latino; 24 Hispanic/Latino; 7 Two or more races, non-Hispanic/Latino), 149 international. Average age 24. 975 applicants, 61% accepted, 222 enrolled. *Faculty:* 67 full-time, 73 part-time/adjunct. *Financial support:* In 2015–16, 125 students received support, including 5 research assistantships (averaging $10,000 per year), 50 teaching assistantships (averaging $8,000 per year); career-related internships or fieldwork, Federal Work-Study, institutionally sponsored loans, scholarships/grants, health care benefits, and unspecified assistantships also available. Support available to part-time students. Financial award application deadline: 5/1; financial award applicants required to submit FAFSA. In 2015, 169 master's awarded. *Degree program information:* Part-time programs available. Part-time. Offers advertising (MS); communication (MA, MFA, MS, PhD); film and television (MFA, MS); journalism (MS). *Application deadline:* For fall admission, 5/1 for domestic and international students. Applications are processed on a rolling basis. *Application fee:* $95. Electronic applications accepted. *Application Contact:* Manny Dotel, Assistant Director, Graduate Affairs, 617-353-3481, E-mail: comgrad@bu.edu. *Dean*, Thomas Fiedler, 617-353-3450, Fax: 617-358-0399, E-mail: comdean@bu.edu.

Division of Emerging Media Studies Students: 23 full-time (18 women), 2 part-time (1 woman); includes 3 minority (1 Asian, non-Hispanic/Latino; 2 Hispanic/Latino), 11 international. Average age 25. 72 applicants, 44% accepted, 15 enrolled. *Faculty:* 4 full-time (1 woman). *Financial support:* Fellowships, research assistantships, teaching assistantships, career-related internships or fieldwork, Federal Work-Study, institutionally sponsored loans, scholarships/grants, health care benefits, and unspecified assistantships available. Financial award application deadline: 5/1; financial award applicants required to submit FAFSA. In 2015, 7 master's awarded. *Degree program information:* Part-time programs available. Part-time. Offers emerging media studies (MA, PhD). *Application deadline:* For fall admission, 5/1 for domestic and international students. Applications are processed on a rolling basis. *Application fee:* $95. Electronic applications accepted. *Application Contact:* Haley Nielsen, Administrator of Admission and Financial Aid, 617-353-3481, E-mail: comgrad@bu.edu. *Professor of Emerging Media/Chair of the Division of Emerging Media Studies*, Dr. James Katz, 617-353-7733, E-mail: katz2020@bu.edu.

College of Engineering Students: 696 full-time (203 women), 131 part-time (32 women); includes 114 minority (8 Black or African American, non-Hispanic/Latino; 1 American Indian or Alaska Native, non-Hispanic/Latino; 69 Asian, non-Hispanic/Latino; 21 Hispanic/Latino; 1 Native Hawaiian or other Pacific Islander, non-Hispanic/Latino; 14 Two or more races, non-Hispanic/Latino), 447 international. Average age 25. 1,931 applicants, 25% accepted, 245 enrolled. *Faculty:* 112 full-time (12 women), 9 part-time/adjunct (1 woman). *Financial support:* In 2015–16, 458 students received support, including 70 fellowships with full tuition reimbursements available (averaging $28,950 per year), 241 research assistantships with full tuition reimbursements available (averaging $19,300 per year), 62 teaching assistantships with full tuition reimbursements available (averaging $19,300 per year); career-related internships or fieldwork, Federal Work-Study, institutionally sponsored loans, scholarships/grants, traineeships, health care benefits, and tuition waivers (full and partial) also available. Financial award application deadline: 1/15; financial award applicants required to submit FAFSA. In 2015, 232 master's, 47 doctorates awarded. *Degree program information:* Part-time programs available. Part-time, online learning. Offers biomedical engineering (M Eng, MS, PhD); computer engineering (M Eng, MS, PhD); electrical engineering (M Eng, MS, PhD); engineering (M Eng, MS, PhD); manufacturing engineering (M Eng, MS); materials science and engineering (M Eng, MS, PhD); mechanical engineering (M Eng, MS, PhD); photonics (MS); systems engineering (M Eng, MS, PhD). *Application fee:* $70. Electronic applications accepted. *Application Contact:* Director of Graduate Programs, 617-353-9760, Fax: 617-353-0259, E-mail: enggrad@bu.edu. *Dean*, Dr. Kenneth R. Lutchen, 617-353-2800, Fax: 617-358-3468, E-mail: klutch@bu.edu.

College of Fine Arts Students: 966 full-time (598 women), 48 part-time (25 women); includes 133 minority (42 Black or African American, non-Hispanic/Latino; 2 American Indian or Alaska Native, non-Hispanic/Latino; 33 Asian, non-Hispanic/Latino; 39 Hispanic/Latino; 2 Native Hawaiian or other Pacific Islander, non-Hispanic/Latino; 15 Two or more races, non-Hispanic/Latino), 249 international. Average age 32. 1,472 applicants, 32% accepted, 169 enrolled. *Faculty:* 70 full-time, 38 part-time/adjunct. *Financial support:* Fellowships, teaching assistantships, Federal Work-Study, and scholarships/grants available. Support available to part-time students. Financial award application deadline: 1/1. In 2015, 307 master's, 65 doctorates, 15 other advanced degrees awarded. *Degree program information:* Part-time programs available. Part-time. Offers fine arts (MA, MFA, MM, DMA, Artist Diploma, CAS, Certificate, Performance Diploma). *Application deadline:* For fall admission, 1/15 for domestic and international students. *Application fee:* $80. Electronic applications accepted. *Application Contact:* Mark Krone, Manager, Graduate Admissions and Online Marketing, 617-353-3350, E-mail: arts@bu.edu. *Dean*, Lynne Allen, 617-353-3350.

School of Music Students: 356 full-time (216 women), 4 part-time (3 women); includes 40 minority (10 Black or African American, non-Hispanic/Latino; 15 Asian, non-Hispanic/Latino; 9 Hispanic/Latino; 6 Two or more races, non-Hispanic/Latino), 180 international. Average age 27. 1,027 applicants, 35% accepted, 111 enrolled. *Faculty:* 36 full-time, 21 part-time/adjunct. *Financial support:* Fellowships, teaching assistantships, scholarships/grants, and unspecified assistantships available. Financial award application deadline: 12/1. In 2015, 149 master's, 64 doctorates awarded. *Degree program information:* Part-time programs available. Part-time. Offers choral conducting (MM); collaborative piano (DMA); composition and theory (DMA); conducting (Performance Diploma); historical performance (MM, Artist Diploma); music education (MM, DMA, CAS); music theory (MM); opera performance (Certificate); performance (MM). CAS offered online only. *Application deadline:* For fall admission, 12/1 priority date for domestic and international students. *Application fee:* $95. Electronic applications accepted. *Application Contact:* Shaun Ramsay, Assistant Director, Admissions and Student Affairs, 617-353-3341, E-mail: arts@bu.edu. *Director*, Shiela Kibbe, 617-353-3341, Fax: 617-353-7455, E-mail: cfamusic@bu.edu.

School of Theatre Students: 42 full-time (27 women), 4 part-time (1 woman); includes 4 minority (1 Black or African American, non-Hispanic/Latino; 2 Asian, non-Hispanic/Latino; 1 Hispanic/Latino), 5 international. 142 applicants, 15% accepted, 16 enrolled. *Faculty:* 16 full-time, 9 part-time/adjunct. *Financial support:* Fellowships, teaching assistantships, scholarships/grants, and unspecified assistantships available. Financial award application deadline: 2/1. In 2015, 17 master's awarded. Offers design (MFA); lighting crafts (Certificate); management (MFA); production (MFA); scenic painting (Certificate). *Application deadline:* For fall admission, 2/1 priority date for domestic and international students. *Application fee:* $95. Electronic applications accepted. *Application Contact:* Mark Krone, Manager, Graduate Admissions and Online Marketing, 617-353-3350, E-mail: arts@bu.edu. *Director*, Jim Petosa, 617-353-3390.

School of Visual Arts Students: 198 full-time (166 women), 3 part-time (all women); includes 23 minority (4 Black or African American, non-Hispanic/Latino; 5 Asian, non-Hispanic/Latino; 9 Hispanic/Latino; 5 Two or more races, non-Hispanic/Latino), 45 international. Average age 31. 257 applicants, 27% accepted, 21 enrolled. *Faculty:* 17 full-time, 4 part-time/adjunct. *Financial support:* Fellowships, teaching assistantships, scholarships/grants, and unspecified assistantships available. Financial award application deadline: 2/1. In 2015, 50 master's awarded. Offers art education (MA); graphic design (MFA); painting (MFA); sculpture (MFA); studio teaching (MA). *Application deadline:* For fall admission, 2/1 for domestic and international students. Applications are processed on a rolling basis. *Application fee:* $80. *Application Contact:* Jessica Caccamo, Assistant Director, 617-353-3371, E-mail: visuarts@bu.edu. *Interim Director*, Jeannette Guillemin, 617-353-3371.

College of Health and Rehabilitation Sciences: Sargent College Students: 459 full-time (385 women), 36 part-time (33 women); includes 91 minority (5 Black or African American, non-Hispanic/Latino; 43 Asian, non-Hispanic/Latino; 26 Hispanic/Latino; 17 Two or more races, non-Hispanic/Latino), 21 international. Average age 25. 2,072 applicants, 16% accepted, 126 enrolled. *Faculty:* 54 full-time (42 women), 44 part-time/adjunct (28 women). *Financial support:* In 2015–16, 302 students received support, including 24 research assistantships with full tuition reimbursements available (averaging $21,000 per year), 18 teaching assistantships (averaging $2,500 per year); career-related internships or fieldwork, Federal Work-Study, institutionally sponsored loans, scholarships/grants, and health care benefits also available. Support available to part-time students. Financial award application deadline: 1/1; financial award applicants required to submit FAFSA. In 2015, 106 master's, 63 doctorates awarded. Blended/hybrid learning. Offers health and rehabilitation sciences (MS, DPT, OTD, PhD); human physiology (MS, PhD); nutrition (MS); occupational therapy (OTD); physical therapy (DPT); rehabilitation sciences (PhD); speech, language and hearing sciences (PhD); speech-language pathology (MS). *Application deadline:* For fall admission, 1/1 priority date for domestic and international students. Applications are processed on a rolling basis. *Application fee:* $80. Electronic applications accepted. *Application Contact:* Sharon Sankey, Assistant Dean, Student Services, 617-353-2713, Fax: 617-353-7500, E-mail: ssankey@bu.edu. *Dean*, Dr. Christopher Moore, 617-353-2705, Fax: 617-353-7500, E-mail: mooreca@bu.edu.

Graduate School of Arts and Sciences Students: 1,591 full-time (799 women), 168 part-time (87 women); includes 197 minority (29 Black or African American, non-Hispanic/Latino; 79 Asian, non-Hispanic/Latino; 61 Hispanic/Latino; 28 Two or more races, non-Hispanic/Latino), 663 international. Average age 28. 7,667 applicants, 25% accepted, 461 enrolled. *Financial support:* In 2015–16, 1,375 students received support, including 210 fellowships with full tuition reimbursements available (averaging $21,000 per year), 400 research assistantships with full tuition reimbursements available (averaging $21,000 per year), 575 teaching assistantships with full tuition reimbursements available (averaging $21,000 per year); career-related internships or fieldwork, Federal Work-Study, scholarships/grants, traineeships, health care benefits, and unspecified assistantships also available. Financial award application deadline: 1/15. In 2015, 399 master's, 187 doctorates awarded. Offers African American studies (MA); American and New England studies (PhD); anthropology (PhD); applied anthropology (MA); archaeology (MA, PhD); art history (MA, PhD); arts and sciences (MA, MAEP, MFA, MS, PhD, Certificate); astronomy (MA, PhD); bioinformatics (MS, PhD); biology (MA, PhD); biostatistics (MA, PhD); chemistry (MA, PhD); classical studies (MA, PhD); composition (MA); computer science (MS, PhD); creative writing (MFA); cyber security (MS); data-centric computing (MS); earth sciences (MA, PhD); economic policy (MAEP); economics (MA, PhD); energy and environment (MA); English (MA, PhD); ethnomusicology (MA, PhD); French language and literature (MA, PhD); geography (MA, PhD); global development economics (MA); global development policy (MA); Hispanic language and literatures (MA, PhD); historical musicology (MA, PhD); history (MA, PhD); international relations and environmental policy (MA); linguistics (MA); mathematics (MA, PhD); molecular biology, cell biology, and biochemistry (MA, PhD); museum studies (Certificate); music education (MA); music theory (MA); philosophy (MA, PhD); physics (PhD); playwriting (MFA); political science (MA, PhD); preservation studies (MA); psychological and brain sciences (MA, PhD); remote sensing and geospatial sciences (MA); sociology (MA, PhD); statistical practice (MS). *Application deadline:* For fall admission, 1/15 priority date for domestic and international students; for spring admission, 10/15 priority date for domestic and international students. *Application fee:* $95. Electronic applications accepted. *Application Contact:* Martin Gastmann, Assistant Director of Admissions and Financial Aid, 617-353-2696, Fax: 617-358-5492, E-mail: grs@bu.edu. *Associate Dean*, Dr. W. Jeffrey Hughes, 617-353-2696, Fax: 617-358-5492.

Editorial Institute Students: 16 full-time (9 women), 6 part-time (5 women); includes 5 minority (4 Hispanic/Latino; 1 Two or more races, non-Hispanic/Latino), 1 international. Average age 34. 7 applicants, 43% accepted, 3 enrolled. *Financial support:* In 2015–16, 18 students received support, including 3 fellowships with full tuition reimbursements available (averaging $21,000 per year), 4 research assistantships with full tuition reimbursements available (averaging $21,000 per year), 3 teaching assistantships with full tuition reimbursements available (averaging $21,000 per year); Federal Work-Study, scholarships/grants, and health care benefits also available. Financial award application deadline: 1/15. Offers editorial studies (MA, PhD). *Application deadline:* For fall admission, 4/15 for domestic and international students. *Application fee:* $95. Electronic applications accepted. *Application Contact:* Allison Vanouse, Administrative Assistant, 617-358-1937, Fax: 617-353-6917, E-mail: avanouse@bu.edu. *Co-Director*, Archie Burnett, 617-353-6631, E-mail: burnetta@bu.edu.

Frederick S. Pardee School of Global Studies Students: 74 full-time (43 women), 12 part-time (9 women); includes 10 minority (3 Black or African American, non-Hispanic/Latino; 2 Asian, non-Hispanic/Latino; 4 Hispanic/Latino; 1 Two or more races, non-Hispanic/Latino), 29 international. Average age 26. 295 applicants, 72% accepted, 26 enrolled. *Faculty:* 33 full-time (8 women), 10 part-time/adjunct (4 women). *Financial support:* In 2015–16, 29 students received support. Federal Work-Study, scholarships/grants, and unspecified assistantships available. Financial award application deadline: 1/15. In 2015, 41 master's awarded. Offers global development policy (MA); international affairs (MA); international relations and environmental policy (MA); international relations and international communication (MA); international relations and religion (MA); international relations, mid-career (MA); Latin American studies (MA). *Application deadline:* For fall admission, 4/15 for domestic and international students; for spring admission, 10/15 for domestic and international students. Applications are processed on a rolling basis. *Application fee:* $95. Electronic applications accepted. *Application Contact:* Michael Williams, Graduate Program Administrator, 617-353-9349, Fax: 617-353-9290, E-mail: psgsgrad@bu.edu. *Dean*, Adil Najam, Fax: 617-353-9290, E-mail: anajam@bu.edu.

Graduate Division of Religious Studies Students: 51 full-time (21 women), 6 part-time (1 woman); includes 10 minority (3 Black or African American, non-Hispanic/Latino; 3 Asian, non-Hispanic/Latino; 2 Hispanic/Latino; 2 Two or more races, non-Hispanic/Latino), 6 international. Average age 32. 102 applicants, 14% accepted, 4 enrolled. *Financial support:* In 2015–16, 52 students received support, including 18 fellowships with full tuition reimbursements available (averaging $21,000 per year), 2 research assistantships with full tuition reimbursements available (averaging $21,000 per year), 17 teaching assistantships with full tuition reimbursements available (averaging $21,000 per year); career-related internships or fieldwork, Federal Work-Study, scholarships/grants, health care benefits, and unspecified assistantships also available. Financial award application deadline: 1/15. In 2015, 13 master's, 13 doctorates awarded. Offers religious studies (MA, PhD). *Application deadline:* For fall admission, 1/15 for domestic and international students. *Application fee:* $95. Electronic applications accepted. *Application Contact:* Karen Nardella, Department Administrator, 617-353-2636, Fax: 617-358-3087, E-mail: kcn@bu.edu. *Director*, Jonathan Klawans, 617-353-4432, Fax: 617-358-3087, E-mail: jklawans@bu.edu.

Henry M. Goldman School of Dental Medicine Students: 812 full-time (428 women), 2 part-time (1 woman); includes 195 minority (12 Black or African American, non-Hispanic/Latino; 127 Asian, non-Hispanic/Latino; 42 Hispanic/Latino; 14 Two or more races, non-Hispanic/Latino), 316 international. Average age 28. 6,681 applicants, 8% accepted, 263 enrolled. *Faculty:* 136 full-time (60 women), 90 part-time/adjunct (31 women). *Financial support:* In 2015–16, 125 students received support. Career-related internships or fieldwork, institutionally sponsored loans, scholarships/grants, and stipends available. Financial award application deadline: 4/18; financial award applicants required to submit FAFSA. In 2015, 23 master's, 204 doctorates, 59 other advanced degrees awarded. Offers dental public health (MS, MSD, D Sc D); dentistry (DMD); endodontics (MSD, D Sc D, CAGS); operative dentistry (MSD, D Sc D, CAGS); oral and maxillofacial surgery (MSD, D Sc D, CAGS); oral biology (MSD, D Sc D); orthodontics (MSD, D Sc D); pediatric dentistry (MSD, D Sc D, CAGS); periodontology (MSD, D Sc D, CAGS); prosthodontics (D Sc D). *Application deadline:* For fall admission, 12/1 for domestic and international students. Applications are processed on a rolling basis.

Application fee: $75 ($105 for international students). Electronic applications accepted. *Application Contact:* Admissions Representative, 617-638-4787, Fax: 617-638-4798, E-mail: sdmadmis@bu.edu. *Dean*, Dr. Jeffrey W. Hutter, 617-638-4780.

Metropolitan College Students: 329 full-time (167 women), 2,097 part-time (998 women); includes 611 minority (195 Black or African American, non-Hispanic/Latino; 4 American Indian or Alaska Native, non-Hispanic/Latino; 198 Asian, non-Hispanic/Latino; 171 Hispanic/Latino; 4 Native Hawaiian or other Pacific Islander, non-Hispanic/Latino; 39 Two or more races, non-Hispanic/Latino), 512 international. Average age 32. 1,745 applicants, 70% accepted, 748 enrolled. *Faculty:* 36 full-time (12 women), 199 part-time/adjunct (57 women). *Financial support:* In 2015–16, 948 students received support, including 60 research assistantships (averaging $8,200 per year), 8 teaching assistantships (averaging $2,500 per year); career-related internships or fieldwork, scholarships/grants, and unspecified assistantships also available. Support available to part-time students. Financial award applicants required to submit FAFSA. In 2015, 1,034 master's awarded. *Degree program information:* Part-time and evening/weekend programs available. Part-time, evening/weekend, 100% online, blended/hybrid learning. Offers actuarial science (MS); advertising (MS); arts administration (MS, Graduate Certificate); banking and financial services management (MSM); business (MLA); business continuity in emergency management (MSM); city planning (MCP); communications (MLA); computer information systems (MS); computer networks (Certificate); computer science (MS); criminal justice (MCJ); data analytics (Certificate); digital forensics (Certificate); financial economics (MSAS); food policy (MLA); fundraising management (Graduate Certificate); health communication (MS); health informatics (Certificate); history and culture (MLA); information technology project management (Certificate); innovation and technology (MSAS); insurance management (MSM); international marketing management (MSM); leadership (MS); project management (MS); software engineering in health care systems (Certificate); telecommunications (MS); urban affairs (MUA). *Application deadline:* Applications are processed on a rolling basis. *Application fee:* $85. Electronic applications accepted. *Application Contact:* Kristin McAullife, Director, Enrollment Services, 617-353-6000, E-mail: met@bu.edu. *Dean*, Dr. Tanya Zlateva, 617-353-3010, Fax: 617-353-6066.

Questrom School of Business Students: 561 full-time (234 women), 676 part-time (278 women); includes 191 minority (24 Black or African American, non-Hispanic/Latino; 1 American Indian or Alaska Native, non-Hispanic/Latino; 96 Asian, non-Hispanic/Latino; 50 Hispanic/Latino; 1 Native Hawaiian or other Pacific Islander, non-Hispanic/Latino; 19 Two or more races, non-Hispanic/Latino), 321 international. Average age 29. 1,094 applicants, 35% accepted, 146 enrolled. *Faculty:* 95 full-time (27 women), 49 part-time/adjunct (13 women). *Financial support:* Career-related internships or fieldwork, Federal Work-Study, institutionally sponsored loans, scholarships/grants, and tuition waivers (partial) available. Support available to part-time students. Financial award applicants required to submit FAFSA. In 2015, 489 master's, 9 doctorates awarded. *Degree program information:* Part-time and evening/weekend programs available. Part-time, evening/weekend. Offers business (EMBA); business administration (MBA); management (PhD); management studies (MSMS); mathematical finance (MS, PhD). *Application deadline:* For fall admission, 3/22 for domestic and international students; for spring admission, 11/9 for domestic students. *Application fee:* $125. Electronic applications accepted. *Application Contact:* Meredith C. Siegel, Assistant Dean, Graduate Admission, 617-353-2670, Fax: 617-353-7368, E-mail: mba@bu.edu. *Professor/Dean*, Kenneth W. Freeman, 617-353-9720, Fax: 617-353-5581, E-mail: kfreeman@bu.edu.

School of Education Students: 204 full-time (154 women), 303 part-time (216 women); includes 113 minority (34 Black or African American, non-Hispanic/Latino; 27 Asian, non-Hispanic/Latino; 37 Hispanic/Latino; 15 Two or more races, non-Hispanic/Latino), 54 international. Average age 28. 1,061 applicants, 62% accepted, 227 enrolled. *Faculty:* 57 full-time, 39 part-time/adjunct. *Financial support:* In 2015–16, 314 students received support, including 38 fellowships with full tuition reimbursements available, 16 research assistantships, 32 teaching assistantships with partial tuition reimbursements available; career-related internships or fieldwork, Federal Work-Study, and scholarships/grants also available. Support available to part-time students. Financial award applicants required to submit FAFSA. In 2015, 270 master's, 16 doctorates, 5 other advanced degrees awarded. *Degree program information:* Part-time and evening/weekend programs available. Part-time, evening/weekend. Offers education (Ed M, MAT, Ed D, PhD, CAGS). *Application deadline:* For fall admission, 1/15 priority date for domestic and international students; for spring admission, 9/15 priority date for domestic and international students. Applications are processed on a rolling basis. *Application fee:* $80. Electronic applications accepted. *Application Contact:* Katharine Nelson, Director of Graduate Student Services, 617-353-4237, E-mail: sedgrad@bu.edu. *Dean*, Dr. Hardin Coleman, 617-353-3213.

School of Law Students: 869 full-time (482 women), 148 part-time (59 women); includes 183 minority (31 Black or African American, non-Hispanic/Latino; 1 American Indian or Alaska Native, non-Hispanic/Latino; 65 Asian, non-Hispanic/Latino; 70 Hispanic/Latino; 16 Two or more races, non-Hispanic/Latino), 173 international. Average age 27. 4,218 applicants, 39% accepted, 208 enrolled. *Faculty:* 48 full-time (21 women), 87 part-time/adjunct (27 women). *Financial support:* In 2015–16, 600 students received support. Career-related internships or fieldwork, Federal Work-Study, institutionally sponsored loans, and scholarships/grants available. Financial award application deadline: 3/1; financial award applicants required to submit FAFSA. In 2015, 208 master's, 246 doctorates awarded. Offers intellectual property law (LL M); international business law (LL M); taxation (LL M). MD/JD offered jointly with the School of Medicine. *Application deadline:* For fall admission, 4/1 for domestic and international students. Applications are processed on a rolling basis. *Application fee:* $85. Electronic applications accepted. *Application Contact:* Alissa Leonard, Director of Admissions and Financial Aid, 617-353-3100, Fax: 617-353-0578, E-mail: bulawadm@bu.edu. *Dean*, Maureen A. O'Rourke, 617-353-3112, Fax: 617-353-7400, E-mail: lawdean@bu.edu.

School of Medicine Students: 1,573 full-time (872 women), 112 part-time (60 women); includes 494 minority (54 Black or African American, non-Hispanic/Latino; 2 American Indian or Alaska Native, non-Hispanic/Latino; 287 Asian, non-Hispanic/Latino; 111 Hispanic/Latino; 3 Native Hawaiian or other Pacific Islander, non-Hispanic/Latino; 37 Two or more races, non-Hispanic/Latino), 151 international. Average age 26. *Financial support:* In 2015–16, 363 students received support. Fellowships, research assistantships, teaching assistantships, career-related internships or fieldwork, Federal Work-Study, and institutionally sponsored loans available. Support available to part-time students. Financial award application deadline: 4/17; financial award applicants required to submit FAFSA. In 2015, 344 master's, 197 doctorates awarded. *Degree program information:* Part-time and evening/weekend programs available. Part-time, evening/weekend. Offers medicine (MA, MS, MD, PhD). *Application Contact:* Dr. Robert Witzburg, Associate Dean for Admissions, 617-638-4630. *Dean*, Dr. Karen H. Antman, 617-638-5300.

Division of Graduate Medical Sciences Students: 832 full-time (508 women), 92 part-time (47 women); includes 264 minority (29 Black or African American, non-Hispanic/Latino; 2 American Indian or Alaska Native, non-Hispanic/Latino; 142 Asian, non-Hispanic/Latino; 62 Hispanic/Latino; 1 Native Hawaiian or other Pacific Islander, non-Hispanic/Latino; 28 Two or more races, non-Hispanic/Latino), 103 international. Average age 26. 2,525 applicants, 32% accepted, 386 enrolled. *Faculty:* 1,020 full-time (460 women), 517 part-time/adjunct (212 women). *Financial support:* In 2015–16, fellowships (averaging $32,250 per year), research assistantships (averaging $32,250 per year), teaching assistantships (averaging $32,250 per year) were awarded; Federal Work-Study, scholarships/grants, and traineeships also available. Financial award applicants required to submit FAFSA. In 2015, 211 master's, 63 doctorates awarded. *Degree program information:* Part-time programs available. Part-time. Offers anatomy and neurobiology (MA, PhD); behavioral neuroscience (PhD); biochemistry (MA, PhD); bioimaging (MA); biomedical forensic sciences (MS); biomedical sciences (PhD); cell and molecular biology (PhD); clinical investigation (MA); forensic anthropology (MS); genetic counseling (MS); genetics and genomics (PhD); healthcare emergency management (MS); immunology (PhD); medical anthropology and cross cultural practice (MA); medical sciences (MA, MS, PhD); mental health counseling and behavioral medicine (MA); microbiology (PhD); molecular medicine (PhD); neuroscience (PhD); nutrition and metabolism (MA, PhD); oral biology (PhD); oral health sciences (MS); pathology and laboratory medicine (PhD); pharmacology and experimental therapeutics (MA, PhD); physician assistant (MS); physiology and biophysics (MA, PhD). *Application deadline:* For fall admission, 1/31 for domestic and international students; for spring admission, 10/15 for domestic and international students. *Application fee:* $95. Electronic applications accepted. *Application Contact:* GMS Admissions Office, 617-638-5255, Fax: 617-638-5740, E-mail: askgms@bu.edu. *Associate Provost*, Dr. Linda Hyman, 617-638-5255, Fax: 617-638-5740.

School of Public Health Students: 607 full-time (488 women), 353 part-time (295 women); includes 263 minority (72 Black or African American, non-Hispanic/Latino; 2 American Indian or Alaska Native, non-Hispanic/Latino; 103 Asian, non-Hispanic/Latino; 57 Hispanic/Latino; 1 Native Hawaiian or other Pacific Islander, non-Hispanic/Latino; 28 Two or more races, non-Hispanic/Latino), 110 international. Average age 27. 2,594 applicants, 43% accepted, 396 enrolled. *Faculty:* 153 full-time, 271 part-time/adjunct. *Financial support:* In 2015–16, 494 students received support. Fellowships, career-related internships or fieldwork, Federal Work-Study, institutionally sponsored loans, scholarships/grants, traineeships, and tuition waivers (partial) available. Support available to part-time students. Financial award application deadline: 5/29; financial award applicants required to submit FAFSA. In 2015, 442 master's, 18 doctorates awarded. *Degree program information:* Part-time and evening/weekend programs available. Part-time, evening/weekend. Offers biostatistics (MA, MPH, PhD); community health sciences (MPH, Dr PH); environmental health (MPH, MS, PhD); epidemiology (MPH, MS, PhD); global health (MPH, Dr PH); health services research (MS); public health (MA, MPH, MS, Dr PH, PhD). *Application deadline:* For fall admission, 1/1 priority date for domestic and international students; for spring admission, 10/1 priority date for domestic and international students. Applications are processed on a rolling basis. *Application fee:* $120. Electronic applications accepted. *Application Contact:* LePhan Quan, Associate Director of Admissions, 617-638-4640, Fax: 617-638-5299, E-mail: asksph@bu.edu. *Dean*, Dr. Sandro Galea, 617-638-4640, Fax: 617-638-5299, E-mail: asksph@bu.edu.

School of Social Work Students: 170 full-time (152 women), 510 part-time (459 women); includes 175 minority (63 Black or African American, non-Hispanic/Latino; 2 American Indian or Alaska Native, non-Hispanic/Latino; 24 Asian, non-Hispanic/Latino; 76 Hispanic/Latino; 10 Two or more races, non-Hispanic/Latino), 3 international. Average age 32. 937 applicants, 64% accepted, 179 enrolled. *Faculty:* 27 full-time (18 women), 29 part-time/adjunct (21 women). *Financial support:* In 2015–16, 158 students received support. Career-related internships or fieldwork, Federal Work-Study, institutionally sponsored loans, and scholarships/grants available. Support available to part-time students. Financial award application deadline: 3/1; financial award applicants required to submit FAFSA. In 2015, 226 master's awarded. *Degree program information:* Part-time and evening/weekend programs available. Part-time, evening/weekend, 100% online. Offers clinical practice with individuals, families, and groups (MSW); social work (PhD). *Application deadline:* For fall admission, 1/13 priority date for domestic students, 1/13 for international students. *Application fee:* $95. Electronic applications accepted. *Application Contact:* Julie Billings, Admissions and Financial Aid Coordinator, 617-353-3750, Fax: 617-353-5612, E-mail: busswad@bu.edu. *Dean*, Gail Steketee, 617-353-3760, Fax: 617-353-5612.

School of Theology Students: 263 full-time (126 women), 46 part-time (20 women); includes 61 minority (36 Black or African American, non-Hispanic/Latino; 1 American Indian or Alaska Native, non-Hispanic/Latino; 6 Asian, non-Hispanic/Latino; 13 Hispanic/Latino; 5 Two or more races, non-Hispanic/Latino), 45 international. Average age 34. 287 applicants, 69% accepted, 89 enrolled. *Financial support:* In 2015–16, 261 students received support, including 73 fellowships (averaging $12,000 per year), 66 research assistantships (averaging $3,000 per year), 49 teaching assistantships (averaging $4,000 per year); Federal Work-Study, institutionally sponsored loans, scholarships/grants, health care benefits, and unspecified assistantships also available. Support available to part-time students. Financial award application deadline: 7/15; financial award applicants required to submit FAFSA. In 2015, 78 master's, 13 doctorates awarded. *Degree program information:* Part-time programs available. Part-time, blended/hybrid learning. Offers theology (M Div, MSM, MTS, STM, D Min, PhD). *Application deadline:* For fall admission, 1/15 priority date for domestic and international students; for spring admission, 10/15 priority date for domestic and international students. Applications are processed on a rolling basis. *Application fee:* $95. Electronic applications accepted. *Application Contact:* Rev. Anastasia Kidd, Director of Admissions and College Relations, 617-353-3036, Fax: 617-358-0140, E-mail: sthadmis@bu.edu. *Dean*, Rev. Dr. Mary Elizabeth Moore, 617-353-3050, Fax: 617-353-3061, E-mail: memoore@bu.edu.

BOWIE STATE UNIVERSITY, Bowie, MD 20715-9465

General Information State-supported, coed, comprehensive institution. CGS member. *Enrollment:* 5,430 graduate, professional, and undergraduate students; 484 full-time matriculated graduate/professional students (296 women), 701 part-time matriculated graduate/professional students (511 women). *Enrollment by degree level:* 1,130 master's, 55 doctoral. *Graduate faculty:* 62 full-time (32 women), 62 part-time/adjunct (23 women). Tuition, state resident: full-time $9384; part-time $2346 per year. Tuition, nonresident: full-time $16,344; part-time $4086 per year. *Required fees:* $2552; $325 per semester. *Graduate housing:* Room and/or apartments available on a first-come, first-served basis to single students; on-campus housing not available to married students. Housing application deadline: 8/1. *Student services:* Campus employment opportunities, campus safety program, career counseling, exercise/wellness program, free psychological counseling, international student services, low-cost health insurance, services for students with disabilities, teacher training, writing training. *Library:* Thurgood Marshall Library.

Computer facilities: 3,800 computers available on campus for general student use. A campuswide network can be accessed from student residence rooms and from off campus. Online class registration is available.
Website: http://www.bowiestate.edu/

General Application Contact: Dr. Cosmas Nwkeafor, Interim Dean, 301-860-3406, Fax: 301-860-3414, E-mail: graduatestudiesandresearch@bowiestate.edu.

GRADUATE UNITS

Graduate Programs *Degree program information:* Part-time and evening/weekend programs available. Part-time, evening/weekend. Offers administration of nursing services (MS); applied and computational mathematics (MS); business administration (MBA); computer science (MS, App Sc D); counseling psychology (MA); educational leadership (Ed D); elementary and secondary school administration (M Ed); elementary education (M Ed); English (MA); family nurse practitioner (MS); guidance and counseling (M Ed); human resource development (MA); information systems analyst (Certificate); management information systems (MS); mental health counseling (MA); nursing education (MS); organizational communication (MA, Certificate); public administration (MPA); reading education (M Ed); school administration and supervision (M Ed); secondary education (M Ed); special education (M Ed); teaching (MAT). Electronic applications accepted.

BOWLING GREEN STATE UNIVERSITY, Bowling Green, OH 43403

General Information State-supported, coed, university. CGS member. *Graduate housing:* On-campus housing not available. *Research affiliation:* Spectra Group, Inc. (photoscience).

GRADUATE UNITS

Graduate College *Degree program information:* Part-time and evening/weekend programs available. Part-time, evening/weekend. Electronic applications accepted.

College of Arts and Sciences Degree program information: Part-time programs available. Part-time. Offers 2-D studio art (MA, MFA); 3-D studio art (MA, MFA); American culture studies (MA, PhD); applied philosophy (PhD); applied statistics (MS); art education (MA); art history (MA); arts and sciences (MA, MAT, MFA, MPA, MS, PhD); biological sciences (MAT, MS, PhD); chemistry (MAT, MS); clinical psychology (MA, PhD); communication studies (MA, PhD); computer art (MA); computer science (MS); creative writing (MFA); demography and population studies (MA); design (MFA); developmental psychology (MA, PhD); digital arts (MFA); English (MA, PhD); experimental psychology (MA, PhD); fiction (MFA); French (MA, MAT); French education (MAT); geology (MS); geophysics (MS); German (MA, MAT); graphics (MFA); history (MA, MAT, PhD); industrial/organizational psychology (MA, PhD); institutional theory and history (PhD); literature (MA); mathematics (MA, MAT, PhD); philosophy (MA); photochemical sciences (PhD); physics (MAT, MS); poetry (MFA); popular culture (MA); public administration (MPA); public history (MA); quantitative psychology (MA, PhD); rhetoric and writing (PhD); scientific and technical communication (MA); social psychology (MA); sociology (PhD); Spanish (MA, MAT); Spanish education (MAT); statistics (PhD); theatre and film (MA, PhD). Electronic applications accepted.

College of Business Administration Degree program information: Part-time and evening/weekend programs available. Part-time, evening/weekend. Offers accountancy (M Acc); applied statistics (MS); business (MBA); business administration (M Acc, MA, MBA, MOD, MS); economics (MA); organization development (MOD). Electronic applications accepted.

College of Education and Human Development Degree program information: Part-time and evening/weekend programs available. Part-time, evening/weekend. Offers assistive technology (M Ed); business education (M Ed); classroom technology (M Ed); college student personnel (MA); counseling (M Ed, MA); cross-cultural and international education (MA); curriculum (M Ed); curriculum and teaching (M Ed); developmental kinesiology (M Ed); early childhood intervention (M Ed); education and human development (M Ed, MA, MFCS, MRC, Ed D, PhD, Ed S, Sp Ed); education and intervention services (M Ed, MA, MRC, Ed S, Sp Ed); educational administration and supervision (M Ed, Ed S); food and nutrition (MFCS); gifted education (M Ed); hearing impaired intervention (M Ed); higher education administration (PhD); human development and family studies (MFCS); leadership and policy studies (M Ed, MA, Ed D, PhD, Ed S); leadership studies (Ed D); master teaching (M Ed); mental health counseling (MA); mild/moderate intervention (M Ed); moderate/intensive intervention (M Ed); reading (M Ed, Ed S); recreation and leisure (M Ed); rehabilitation counseling (MRC); school counseling (M Ed); school psychology (M Ed, Sp Ed); special education (M Ed); sport administration (M Ed). Electronic applications accepted.

College of Health and Human Services Degree program information: Part-time and evening/weekend programs available. Part-time, evening/weekend. Offers communication disorders (PhD); criminal justice (MSCJ); health and human services (MPH, MS, MSCJ, PhD); public health (MPH); speech-language pathology (MS). Electronic applications accepted.

College of Musical Arts Degree program information: Part-time programs available. Part-time. Offers composition (MM); contemporary music (DMA); ethnomusicology (MM); music education (MM); music history (MM); music theory (MM); performance (MM). Electronic applications accepted.

College of Technology Degree program information: Part-time programs available. Part-time. Offers career and technology education (M Ed); construction management (MIT); manufacturing technology (MIT); technology (M Ed, MIT). Electronic applications accepted.

Interdisciplinary Studies Degree program information: Part-time programs available. Part-time. Offers interdisciplinary studies (M Ed, MA, MS, PhD). Electronic applications accepted.

BRADLEY UNIVERSITY, Peoria, IL 61625-0002

General Information Independent, coed, comprehensive institution. CGS member. *Graduate housing:* On-campus housing not available. *Research affiliation:* Illinois Manufacturing Extension Center, Northern Research Laboratory, Peoria School of Medicine, Caterpillar, Inc., Ford Motor Credit/Visteon.

GRADUATE UNITS

Graduate School Students: 444 full-time (250 women), 437 part-time (168 women); includes 50 minority (21 Black or African American, non-Hispanic/Latino; 2 American Indian or Alaska Native, non-Hispanic/Latino; 19 Asian, non-Hispanic/Latino; 8 Hispanic/Latino), 472 international. Average age 23. 1,062 applicants, 57% accepted, 274 enrolled. *Faculty:* 194 full-time (78 women), 24 part-time/adjunct (15 women). *Financial support:* In 2015–16, 3 fellowships with full tuition reimbursements (averaging $25,000 per year), 68 research assistantships with full tuition reimbursements (averaging $19,640 per year) were awarded; career-related internships or fieldwork, institutionally sponsored loans, scholarships/grants, tuition waivers (partial), and unspecified assistantships also available. Support available to part-time students. Financial award application deadline: 4/1. In 2015, 261 master's, 24 doctorates awarded. *Degree program information:* Part-time and evening/weekend programs available. Part-time, evening/weekend. *Application deadline:* For fall admission, 5/15 priority date for domestic and international students; for spring admission, 10/15 priority date for domestic and international students. Applications are processed on a rolling basis. *Application fee:* $40 ($50 for international students). Electronic applications accepted. *Application Contact:* Kayla Carroll, Director of International Admissions and Student Services, 309-677-2375, E-mail: klcarroll@fsmail.bradley.edu. *Dean of the Graduate School*, Jeffrey Bakken, 309-677-2375, E-mail: jbakken@bradley.edu.

College of Education and Health Sciences Degree program information: Part-time and evening/weekend programs available. Part-time, evening/weekend. Offers education and health sciences (MA, MSN, DPT, Certificate); human development counseling (MA); leadership in educational administration (MA); non-profit leadership (MA); nursing (DNP, Certificate); nursing administration (MSN); nursing education (MSN); physical therapy (DPT); teacher education (MA, Certificate). Electronic applications accepted.

College of Engineering and Technology Degree program information: Part-time and evening/weekend programs available. Part-time, evening/weekend. Offers civil engineering and construction (MSCE); electrical and computer engineering (MSEE); engineering and technology (MS, MSCE, MSEE, MSME); industrial engineering (MS); manufacturing engineering (MS); mechanical engineering (MSME). Electronic applications accepted.

College of Liberal Arts and Sciences Degree program information: Part-time and evening/weekend programs available. Part-time, evening/weekend. Offers biology (MS); chemistry (MS); computer information systems (MS); computer science (MS); English (MA); liberal arts and sciences (MA, MS). Electronic applications accepted.

Foster College of Business Degree program information: Part-time and evening/weekend programs available. Part-time, evening/weekend. Offers accounting (MSA); business (MBA, MSA); business administration (MBA). Electronic applications accepted.

Slane College of Communications and Fine Arts Degree program information: Part-time and evening/weekend programs available. Part-time, evening/weekend. Offers ceramics (MA, MFA); communications and fine arts (MA, MFA); drawing (MA, MFA); interdisciplinary art (MA, MFA); painting (MA, MFA); photography (MA, MFA); printmaking (MA, MFA); sculpture (MA, MFA); visual communications (MA, MFA). Electronic applications accepted.

BRANDEIS UNIVERSITY, Waltham, MA 02454-9110

General Information Independent, coed, university. *Enrollment:* 5,752 graduate, professional, and undergraduate students; 1,675 full-time matriculated graduate/professional students (935 women), 387 part-time matriculated graduate/professional students (131 women). *Enrollment by degree level:* 1,348 master's, 668 doctoral, 46 other advanced degrees. *Graduate faculty:* 358 full-time (140 women), 160 part-time/adjunct (82 women). *Graduate housing:* Room and/or apartments available on a first-come, first-served basis to single students; on-campus housing not available to married students. Housing application deadline: 6/1. *Student services:* Campus employment opportunities, campus safety program, career counseling, child daycare facilities, exercise/wellness program, free psychological counseling, grant writing training, international student services, low-cost health insurance, multicultural affairs office, services for students with disabilities, teacher training, writing training. *Library:* Goldfarb Library plus 1 other. *Collection:* Books: 982,634 (physical), 721,705 (digital/electronic).

Computer facilities: Computer purchase and lease plans are available. 130 computers available on campus for general student use. A campuswide network can be accessed from student residence rooms and from off campus. Online class registration, educational software are available.
Website: http://www.brandeis.edu/

General Application Contact: 781-736-2000.

GRADUATE UNITS

Graduate School of Arts and Sciences Students: 819 full-time (385 women), 26 part-time (18 women); includes 90 minority (17 Black or African American, non-Hispanic/Latino; 1 American Indian or Alaska Native, non-Hispanic/Latino; 28 Asian, non-Hispanic/Latino; 32 Hispanic/Latino; 1 Native Hawaiian or other Pacific Islander, non-Hispanic/Latino; 11 Two or more races, non-Hispanic/Latino), 231 international. 3,033 applicants, 27% accepted, 329 enrolled. *Faculty:* 297 full-time (121 women), 126 part-time/adjunct (63 women). *Financial support:* In 2015–16, 298 fellowships with tuition reimbursements, 108 research assistantships with tuition reimbursements, 162 teaching assistantships with partial tuition reimbursements were awarded; Federal Work-Study, scholarships/grants, health care benefits, tuition waivers (full and partial), and unspecified assistantships also available. Support available to part-time students. Financial award application deadline: 4/15; financial award applicants required to submit FAFSA. In 2015, 244 master's, 70 doctorates awarded. *Degree program information:* Part-time programs available. Part-time, blended/hybrid learning. Offers acting (MFA); anthropology (MA, PhD); anthropology and women's, gender, and sexuality studies (MA); anthropology/women's, gender, and sexuality studies (MA); arts and sciences (Ed M, MA, MAT, MFA, MS, PhD, CAGS, Postbaccalaureate Certificate); biochemistry and biophysics (PhD); biotechnology (MS); brain, body and behavior (PhD); classical studies (MA); cognitive neuroscience (PhD); comparative humanities (MA); composition and theory (MA, MFA, PhD); computational linguistics (MA); computer science (MA, PhD); English (MA, PhD); English and women's and gender studies (MA); English and women's, gender, and sexuality studies (MA); general psychology (MA); genetic counseling (MS); genetics (PhD); global studies (MA); history (MA, PhD); inorganic chemistry (MA, MS, PhD); Jewish day school (MAT); mathematics (MA, PhD, Postbaccalaureate Certificate); microbiology (PhD); molecular and cell biology (MS, PhD); molecular biology (PhD); musicology (MA, MFA, PhD); Near Eastern and Judaic studies (MA, PhD); Near Eastern and Judaic studies and women's, gender, and sexuality studies (MA); near Eastern and Judaic studies and women's, gender, and sexuality studies (MA); neurobiology (PhD); neuroscience (MS, PhD); organic chemistry (MA, MS, PhD); philosophy (MA); physical chemistry (MS, PhD); physics (MS, PhD); politics (MA, PhD); premedical studies (Postbaccalaureate Certificate); public elementary education (MAT); public policy and women's, gender, and sexuality studies (MA); quantitative biology (PhD); secondary education (MAT); social policy and sociology (PhD); social/developmental psychology (PhD); sociology (MA, PhD); sociology and women's and gender studies (MA); sociology and women's, gender, and sexuality studies (MA); studio art (Postbaccalaureate Certificate); sustainable international development and women's, gender, and sexuality studies (MA); teacher leadership (Ed M, CAGS); teaching of Hebrew (MAT); women's and gender studies (MA). *Application deadline:* For fall admission, 1/15 priority date for domestic and international students; for spring admission, 11/1 for domestic and international students. *Application fee:* $75. Electronic applications accepted. *Application Contact:* Laurie F. Nichols, Director of Admission and Recruitment, Graduate School of Arts and Sciences, 781-736-3410, Fax: 781-736-3412, E-mail: gradschool@brandeis.edu. *Dean*, Eric Chasalow, 781-736-3410, Fax: 781-736-3412, E-mail: gradschool@brandeis.edu.

The Heller School for Social Policy and Management ***Degree program information:*** Part-time programs available. Part-time. Offers aging (MPP); assets and inequalities (PhD); behavioral health (MPP); child, youth, and family management (MBA); children, youth and families (MPP, PhD); coexistence and conflict (MA); general social policy (MPP); global health and development (PhD); health (MPP); health and behavioral health (PhD); health care management (MBA); international development (MA); international health policy and management (MS); poverty alleviation and development (MPP); social impact management (MBA); social policy and management (MBA); sustainable development (MBA). Electronic applications accepted.

International Business School (IBS) Students: 387 full-time (174 women), 26 part-time (11 women); includes 270 minority (21 Black or African American, non-Hispanic/Latino; 226 Asian, non-Hispanic/Latino; 23 Hispanic/Latino). Average age 26. 1,383 applicants, 26% accepted, 139 enrolled. *Faculty:* 32 full-time (13 women), 27 part-time/adjunct (4 women). *Financial support:* In 2015–16, 176 students received support, including 11 fellowships (averaging $9,545 per year); research assistantships, teaching assistantships, career-related internships or fieldwork, institutionally sponsored loans, scholarships/grants, and health care benefits also available. Financial award application deadline: 1/15. In 2015, 171 master's, 3 doctorates awarded. Offers asset management (MBA); business economics (MA, MBA); corporate finance (MBA); data analytics (MBA); finance (MSF); global trade (PhD); international business (MA, MBA, MSF, PhD); international economic policy analysis (MBA); macroeconomics (PhD); marketing (MBA); real estate (MBA); risk management (MBA); sustainability (MBA). *Application deadline:* For fall admission, 11/1 for domestic and international students; for winter admission, 1/15 for domestic and international students; for spring admission, 3/15 for domestic students, 3/15 priority date for international students; for summer admission, 5/1 for domestic and international students. *Application fee:* $100. Electronic applications accepted. *Application Contact:* Kelly Sugrue, Director of Admissions, 781-736-2252, Fax: 781-736-2263, E-mail: globaladmissions@brandeis.edu. *Dean*, Bruce Magid, 781-736-4663.

Rabb School of Continuing Studies, Division of Graduate Professional Studies Students: 5 full-time (2 women), 331 part-time (130 women); includes 79 minority (32 Black or African American, non-Hispanic/Latino; 1 American Indian or Alaska Native, non-Hispanic/Latino; 32 Asian, non-Hispanic/Latino; 6 Hispanic/Latino; 1 Native Hawaiian or other Pacific Islander, non-Hispanic/Latino; 7 Two or more races, non-Hispanic/Latino). Average age 35. 117 applicants, 97% accepted, 88 enrolled. *Faculty:* 45 part-time/adjunct (12 women). In 2015, 105 master's, 5 other advanced degrees awarded. *Degree program information:* Part-time programs available. Part-time-only. Offers bioinformatics (MS); digital marketing and design (MS); health and medical informatics (MS); information security (MS); information technology management (MS); instructional design and technology (MS); learning analytics (Graduate Certificate); project and program management (MS); software engineering (MSE); strategic analytics (MS); user-centered design (MS); virtual management (MS). *Application deadline:* For fall admission, 8/16 priority date for domestic and international students; for spring admission, 12/13 priority date for domestic and international students; for summer admission, 4/25 priority date for domestic and international students. Applications are processed on a rolling basis. *Application fee:* $50. Electronic applications accepted. *Application Contact:* Frances Stearns, Director of Admissions and Recruitment, 781-736-8785, Fax: 781-736-3420, E-mail: fstearns@brandeis.edu. *Executive Director*, Anne M. Marando, 781-736-8782, Fax: 781-736-3420, E-mail: marando@brandeis.edu.

BRANDMAN UNIVERSITY, Irvine, CA 92618

General Information Independent, coed, comprehensive institution.

GRADUATE UNITS

School of Arts and Sciences Offers psychology (MA).

School of Business and Professional Studies Offers business administration (MBA); human resources (MS); organizational leadership (MA); public administration (MPA).

School of Education Offers education (MA); educational leadership (MA); school counseling (MA); special education (MA); teaching (MA).

School of Nursing and Health Professions Offers health administration (MHA); health risk and crisis communication (MS).

BRANDON UNIVERSITY, Brandon, MB R7A 6A9, Canada

General Information Province-supported, coed, comprehensive institution. *Graduate housing:* Room and/or apartments available on a first-come, first-served basis to single students; on-campus housing not available to married students.

GRADUATE UNITS

Department of Rural Development Offers rural development (MRD, Diploma). Electronic applications accepted.

Faculty of Education Offers curriculum and instruction (M Ed, Diploma); educational administration (M Ed, Diploma); guidance and counseling (M Ed, Diploma); special education (M Ed, Diploma).

School of Music Students: 13 full-time (7 women), 1 (woman) part-time, 9 international. Average age 25. 8 applicants, 38% accepted. *Faculty:* 9 full-time (5 women), 1 (woman) part-time/adjunct. *Financial support:* In 2015–16, 11 students received support, including 12 teaching assistantships (averaging $3,000 per year); research assistantships also available. Financial award application deadline: 5/1. In 2015, 2 master's awarded. *Degree program information:* Part-time programs available. Part-time. Offers composition (M Mus); music education (M Mus); performance and literature (M Mus). *Application deadline:* For spring admission, 5/1 priority date for domestic and international students. Applications are processed on a rolling basis. *Application fee:* $60 ($125 for international students). Electronic applications accepted. *Application Contact:* Kerry DuWors, Graduate Music Department, 204-727-9566, Fax: 204-728-6839, E-mail: duworsk@brandonu.ca. *Acting Dean*, Greg Gatien, 204-727-9633, Fax: 204-728-6839, E-mail: gatieng@brandonu.ca.

BRENAU UNIVERSITY, Gainesville, GA 30501

General Information Independent, women only, comprehensive institution. *Graduate housing:* Room and/or apartments available on a first-come, first-served basis to single students; on-campus housing not available to married students.

GRADUATE UNITS

Sydney O. Smith Graduate School ***Degree program information:*** Part-time and evening/weekend programs available. Part-time, evening/weekend, online learning. Electronic applications accepted.

College of Health and Science Degree program information: Part-time and evening/weekend programs available. Part-time, evening/weekend. Offers family nurse practitioner (MSN); nurse educator (MSN); nursing management (MSN); occupational therapy (MS); psychology (MS). Electronic applications accepted.

School of Business and Mass Communication Degree program information: Part-time and evening/weekend programs available. Part-time, evening/weekend, online learning. Offers accounting (MBA); business administration (MBA); healthcare management (MBA); organizational leadership (MS); project management (MBA). Electronic applications accepted.

School of Education Degree program information: Part-time and evening/weekend programs available. Part-time, evening/weekend, online learning. Offers early childhood (Ed S); early childhood education (M Ed, MAT); middle grades (Ed S); middle grades education (M Ed, MAT); secondary education (MAT); special education (M Ed, MAT). Electronic applications accepted.

School of Fine Arts and Humanities Degree program information: Part-time programs available. Part-time. Offers interior design (MID). Electronic applications accepted.

BRESCIA UNIVERSITY, Owensboro, KY 42301-3023

General Information Independent-religious, coed, comprehensive institution. *Enrollment:* 1,061 graduate, professional, and undergraduate students; 8 full-time matriculated graduate/professional students (5 women), 10 part-time matriculated graduate/professional students (3 women). *Enrollment by degree level:* 18 master's. *Graduate faculty:* 8 full-time (5 women). *Tuition, area resident:* Part-time $500 per credit hour. *Required fees:* $125. *Graduate housing:* Room and/or apartments available on a first-come, first-served basis to single students; on-campus housing not available to married students. *Student services:* Campus employment opportunities, campus safety program, career counseling, exercise/wellness program, free psychological counseling, international student services, low-cost health insurance, services for students with disabilities, teacher training. *Library:* Fr. Leonard Alvey Library. *Collection:* Books: 72,970 (physical), 1,245 (digital/electronic); Databases: 75. Students can reserve study rooms.

Computer facilities: Computer purchase and lease plans are available. 90 computers available on campus for general student use. A campuswide network can be accessed from student residence rooms and from off campus.
Website: http://www.brescia.edu/

General Application Contact: Christy Rohner, Director of Admissions, 270-686-4243, Fax: 270-686-4201, E-mail: admissions@brescia.edu.

GRADUATE UNITS

Program in Business Administration Students: 3 full-time (1 woman), 5 part-time (1 woman); includes 3 minority (1 Asian, non-Hispanic/Latino; 2 Hispanic/Latino). *Faculty:* 3 full-time (1 woman). *Financial support:* Institutionally sponsored loans available. Support available to part-time students. Financial award application deadline: 3/1; financial award applicants required to submit FAFSA. *Degree program information:* Part-time and evening/weekend programs available. Part-time, evening/weekend. Offers business administration (MBA). *Application deadline:* Applications are processed on a rolling basis. *Application fee:* $50. Electronic applications accepted. *Application Contact:* Christy Rohner, Director of Admissions, 270-686-4243, Fax: 270-686-4201, E-mail: admissions@brescia.edu.

Program in Management ***Financial support:*** Institutionally sponsored loans available. Support available to part-time students. Financial award application deadline: 3/1; financial award applicants required to submit FAFSA. *Degree program information:* Part-time and evening/weekend programs available. Part-time, evening/weekend. Offers management (MSM). *Application deadline:* Applications are processed on a rolling basis. *Application fee:* $50. *Application Contact:* Christy Rohner, Director of Admissions, 270-686-4243, Fax: 270-686-4201, E-mail: admissions@brescia.edu.

Program in Teacher Leadership Students: 2 part-time. *Financial support:* Institutionally sponsored loans available. Support available to part-time students. Financial award application deadline: 3/1; financial award applicants required to submit FAFSA. *Degree program information:* Part-time and evening/weekend programs available. Part-time, evening/weekend. Offers teacher leadership (MSTL). *Application deadline:* Applications are processed on a rolling basis. *Application fee:* $50. Electronic applications accepted. *Application Contact:* Christy Rohner, Director of Admissions, 270-686-4243, Fax: 270-686-4201, E-mail: admissions@brescia.edu.

BRIAR CLIFF UNIVERSITY, Sioux City, IA 51104-0100

General Information Independent-religious, coed, comprehensive institution. *Graduate housing:* Room and/or apartments available on a first-come, first-served basis to single students; on-campus housing not available to married students. Housing application deadline: 6/1.

GRADUATE UNITS

Program in Human Resource Management ***Degree program information:*** Part-time and evening/weekend programs available. Part-time, evening/weekend. Offers human resource management (MA). Electronic applications accepted.

Program in Nursing ***Degree program information:*** Part-time and evening/weekend programs available. Part-time, evening/weekend. Offers nursing (MSN).

BRIDGEWATER STATE UNIVERSITY, Bridgewater, MA 02325-0001

General Information State-supported, coed, comprehensive institution. CGS member. *Graduate housing:* On-campus housing not available.

GRADUATE UNITS

College of Graduate Studies ***Degree program information:*** Part-time and evening/weekend programs available. Part-time, evening/weekend.

School of Arts and Sciences Degree program information: Part-time and evening/weekend programs available. Part-time, evening/weekend. Offers art (MAT); arts and sciences (MA, MAT, MPA, MS, MSW); biological sciences (MAT); computer science (MS); criminal justice (MS); English (MA, MAT); history (MAT); mathematics (MAT); physical sciences (MAT); physics (MAT); psychology (MA); public administration (MPA); social work (MSW).

School of Business Degree program information: Part-time and evening/weekend programs available. Part-time, evening/weekend. Offers accounting and finance (MSM); business (MSM); management (MSM).

School of Education and Allied Studies Degree program information: Part-time and evening/weekend programs available. Part-time, evening/weekend. Offers counseling (M Ed, CAGS); early childhood education (M Ed); education and allied studies (M Ed, MAT, MS, CAGS); educational leadership (M Ed, CAGS); elementary education (M Ed); health promotion (M Ed); instructional technology (M Ed); physical education (MS); reading (M Ed, CAGS); secondary education (MAT); special education (M Ed).

BRIERCREST SEMINARY, Caronport, SK S0H 0S0, Canada

General Information Independent-religious, coed, graduate-only institution. *Graduate housing:* Rooms and/or apartments guaranteed to single students and available on a first-come, first-served basis to married students.

GRADUATE UNITS

Graduate Programs ***Degree program information:*** Part-time programs available. Part-time. Offers Biblical studies (M Div); leadership (MA); leadership and management (M Div); marriage and family counseling (MA); missions (MA); New Testament (MATS); Old Testament (MATS); organizational leadership (MA); pastoral counseling (M Div, MA); pastoral ministry (M Div); theological studies (M Div); theology (MATS); worship (M Div, MA); youth and family ministry (M Div, MA).

BRIGHAM YOUNG UNIVERSITY, Provo, UT 84602-1001

General Information Independent-religious, coed, university. CGS member. *Enrollment:* 33,469 graduate, professional, and undergraduate students; 2,024 full-time matriculated graduate/professional students (753 women), 1,160 part-time matriculated graduate/professional students (441 women). *Enrollment by degree level:* 2,173 master's, 967 doctoral, 44 other advanced degrees. *Graduate faculty:* 1,018 full-time (172 women), 6 part-time/adjunct (0 women). *Graduate housing:* Rooms and/or apartments available on a first-come, first-served basis to single and married students. Housing application deadline: 2/1. *Student services:* Campus employment opportunities, campus safety program, career counseling, exercise/wellness program, free psychological counseling, grant writing training, international student services, low-cost health insurance, multicultural affairs office, services for students with disabilities, teacher training, writing training. *Library:* Harold B. Lee Library plus 2 others.

Computer facilities: Computer purchase and lease plans are available. A campuswide network can be accessed from student residence rooms and from off campus. Online class registration is available.
Website: http://www.byu.edu/

General Application Contact: Graduate Studies, 801-422-4091, Fax: 801-422-0270, E-mail: gradstudies@byu.edu.

GRADUATE UNITS

Graduate Studies Students: 2,024 full-time (753 women), 1,160 part-time (441 women); includes 362 minority (17 Black or African American, non-Hispanic/Latino; 11 American Indian or Alaska Native, non-Hispanic/Latino; 68 Asian, non-Hispanic/Latino; 158 Hispanic/Latino; 19 Native Hawaiian or other Pacific Islander, non-Hispanic/Latino; 89 Two or more races, non-Hispanic/Latino), 303 international. Average age 30. 2,270 applicants, 60% accepted, 1081 enrolled. *Faculty:* 1,018 full-time (172 women), 6 part-time/adjunct (0 women). *Financial support:* In 2015–16, 53 students received support, including 35 fellowships (averaging $12,000 per year), 13 research assistantships (averaging $30,000 per year), 5 teaching assistantships (averaging $4,000 per year); career-related internships or fieldwork, institutionally sponsored loans, scholarships/grants, health care benefits, and tuition waivers (full and partial) also available. Support available to part-time students. Financial award applicants required to submit FAFSA. In 2015, 1,037 master's, 218 doctorates, 7 other advanced degrees awarded. *Degree program information:* Part-time and evening/weekend programs available. Part-time, evening/weekend. *Application deadline:* For fall admission, 12/1 priority date for domestic and international students; for winter admission, 6/30 priority date for domestic and international students; for spring admission, 1/15 priority date for domestic and international students; for summer admission, 2/1 for domestic and international students. Applications are processed on a rolling basis. *Application fee:* $50. Electronic applications accepted. *Application Contact:* Dr. Kevin Green, Advisor, 801-422-7308, Fax: 801-422-0270, E-mail: gradstudies@byu.edu. *Dean*, Dr. Wynn Stirling, 801-422-4465, Fax: 801-422-0270, E-mail: gradstudies@byu.edu.

College of Family, Home, and Social Sciences Students: 226 full-time (153 women); includes 53 minority (3 Black or African American, non-Hispanic/Latino; 14 Asian, non-Hispanic/Latino; 30 Hispanic/Latino; 3 Native Hawaiian or other Pacific Islander, non-Hispanic/Latino; 3 Two or more races, non-Hispanic/Latino), 6 international. Average age 26. 3 applicants, 10500% accepted, 85 enrolled. *Faculty:* 96 full-time (20 women), 21 part-time/adjunct (12 women). *Financial support:* In 2015–16, 168 students received support, including 56 fellowships with tuition reimbursements available (averaging $1,850 per year), 120 research assistantships with tuition reimbursements available (averaging $12,804 per year), 7 teaching assistantships with tuition reimbursements available (averaging $6,050 per year); career-related internships or fieldwork, institutionally sponsored loans, scholarships/grants, tuition waivers (partial), unspecified assistantships, and administrative aides, paid field practicum, AmeriCorps education awards also available. Financial award application deadline: 3/27; financial award applicants required to submit FAFSA. In 2015, 72 master's, 19 doctorates awarded. Offers anthropology (MA); behavioral neuroscience (PhD); clinical psychology (PhD); family, home, and social sciences (MA, MS, MSW, PhD); marriage and family therapy (MS, PhD); marriage, family and human development (MS, PhD); social work (MSW); sociology (MS). *Application deadline:* For fall admission, 1/15 for domestic and international students. *Application fee:* $50. Electronic applications accepted. *Application Contact:* Adviser, 801-422-4541, Fax: 801-378-5238, E-mail: gradstudies@byu.edu. *Dean*, Dr. Benjamin M. Ogles, 801-422-2083, Fax: 801-422-2084, E-mail: ben_ogles@byu.edu.

College of Fine Arts and Communications Students: 79 full-time (49 women), 49 part-time (29 women); includes 17 minority (1 Black or African American, non-Hispanic/Latino; 1 American Indian or Alaska Native, non-Hispanic/Latino; 7 Asian, non-Hispanic/Latino; 6 Hispanic/Latino; 2 Native Hawaiian or other Pacific Islander, non-Hispanic/Latino), 6 international. Average age 29. 94 applicants, 59% accepted, 41 enrolled. *Faculty:* 96 full-time (18 women), 58 part-time/adjunct (33 women). *Financial support:* In 2015–16, 106 students received support, including 70 research assistantships (averaging $7,229 per year), 53 teaching assistantships (averaging $7,315 per year); career-related internships or fieldwork, institutionally sponsored loans, scholarships/grants, tuition waivers (partial), unspecified assistantships, and administrative aides, supplementary awards also available. Support available to part-time students. Financial award applicants required to submit FAFSA. In 2015, 43 master's awarded. Offers art education (MA); composition (MM); conducting (MM); fine arts and communications (MA, MFA, MM); mass communications (MA); music education (MA, MM); musicology (MA); performance (MM); studio arts (MFA); theatre and media arts (MA). *Application deadline:* Applications are processed on a rolling basis. *Application fee:* $50. Electronic applications accepted. *Application Contact:* Adviser, 801-422-4541, Fax: 801-378-5238, E-mail: gradstudies@byu.edu. *Dean*, Edward E. Adams, 801-422-8271, Fax: 801-422-0253, E-mail: amber_louw@byu.edu.

College of Humanities Students: 180 full-time (118 women), 83 part-time (33 women); includes 33 minority (15 Asian, non-Hispanic/Latino; 16 Hispanic/Latino; 2 Native Hawaiian or other Pacific Islander, non-Hispanic/Latino). Average age 30. 159 applicants, 67% accepted, 84 enrolled. *Faculty:* 172 full-time (41 women), 49 part-time/adjunct (29 women). *Financial support:* In 2015–16, 51 fellowships with partial tuition reimbursements (averaging $1,751 per year), 23 research assistantships with partial tuition reimbursements (averaging $2,285 per year), 175 teaching assistantships with partial tuition reimbursements (averaging $3,164 per year) were awarded; career-related internships or fieldwork, institutionally sponsored loans, scholarships/grants, tuition waivers (full and partial), unspecified assistantships, and student instructorships also available. Support available to part-time students. In 2015, 74 master's awarded. *Degree program information:* Part-time programs available. Part-time. Offers comparative studies (MA); creative writing (MFA); French studies (MA); humanities (MA, MFA); linguistics (MA); literature (MA); Portuguese (MA); rhetoric/composition (MA); second language teaching (MA); Spanish (MA); teaching English as a second language (MA). *Application fee:* $50. Electronic applications accepted. *Application Contact:* Adviser, 801-422-4541, Fax: 801-378-5238, E-mail: gradstudies@byu.edu. *Dean*, Scott J. Miller, 801-422-2779, Fax: 801-422-0308, E-mail: scott_miller@byu.edu.

College of Life Sciences Students: 184 full-time (101 women), 57 part-time (22 women); includes 39 minority (2 Black or African American, non-Hispanic/Latino; 1 American Indian or Alaska Native, non-Hispanic/Latino; 16 Asian, non-Hispanic/Latino; 14 Hispanic/Latino; 3 Native Hawaiian or other Pacific Islander, non-Hispanic/Latino; 3 Two or more races, non-Hispanic/Latino), 19 international. Average age 27. 155 applicants, 51% accepted, 69 enrolled. *Faculty:* 133 full-time (20 women), 5 part-time/adjunct (4 women). *Financial support:* In 2015–16, 216 students received support, including 38 fellowships with tuition reimbursements available (averaging $10,700 per year), 181 research assistantships with tuition reimbursements available (averaging $12,578 per year), 136 teaching assistantships with tuition reimbursements available (averaging $12,310 per year); career-related internships or fieldwork, institutionally sponsored loans, scholarships/grants, health care benefits, tuition waivers (full and partial), and unspecified assistantships also available. Financial award application deadline: 2/1; financial award applicants required to submit FAFSA. In 2015, 56 master's, 14 doctorates awarded. Offers athletic training (MS); biological science education (MS); biology (MS, PhD); environmental science (MS); exercise physiology (MS, PhD); exercise sciences (MS); food science (MS); genetics and biotechnology (MS); health promotion (MS, PhD); health science (MPH); life sciences (MPH, MS, PhD); microbiology and molecular biology (MS, PhD); neuroscience (MS, PhD); nutrition (MS); physical medicine and rehabilitation (PhD); physiology and developmental biology (MS, PhD); wildlife and wildlands conservation (MS, PhD). *Application deadline:* For fall admission, 2/1 for domestic and international students; for winter admission, 2/1 for international students. *Application fee:* $50. Electronic applications accepted. *Application Contact:* Sue Pratley, Application Contact, 801-422-3963, Fax: 801-422-0050, E-mail: sue_pratley@byu.edu. *Dean*, James P. Porter, 801-422-3963, Fax: 801-422-0050.

College of Nursing Students: 29 full-time (19 women); includes 1 minority (Hispanic/Latino). Average age 35. 48 applicants, 31% accepted, 15 enrolled. *Faculty:* 10 full-time (7 women), 1 part-time/adjunct (0 women). *Financial support:* In 2015–16, 29 students received support, including 2 research assistantships with tuition reimbursements available (averaging $10,000 per year), 3 teaching assistantships with tuition reimbursements available (averaging $10,000 per year); institutionally sponsored loans, scholarships/grants, tuition waivers (full), and unspecified assistantships also available. Support available to part-time students. Financial award application deadline: 2/1; financial award applicants required to submit FAFSA. In 2015, 12 master's awarded. Offers family nurse practitioner (MS). *Application deadline:* For spring admission, 12/1 for domestic students. Applications are processed on a rolling basis. *Application fee:* $50. Electronic applications accepted. *Application Contact:* Lynette Jakins, Graduate Secretary, 801-422-4142, Fax: 801-422-0538, E-mail: lynette-jakins@byu.edu. *Dean*, Dr. Patricia Ravert, 801-422-1167, Fax: 801-422-0536, E-mail: patricia_ravert@byu.edu.

College of Physical and Mathematical Sciences Students: 294 full-time (62 women), 38 part-time (11 women); includes 40 minority (28 Asian, non-Hispanic/Latino; 9 Hispanic/Latino; 3 Native Hawaiian or other Pacific Islander, non-Hispanic/Latino), 51 international. Average age 27. 229 applicants, 53% accepted, 97 enrolled. *Faculty:* 159 full-time (11 women), 8 part-time/adjunct (2 women). *Financial support:* In 2015–16, 316 students received support, including 14 fellowships with full tuition reimbursements available (averaging $21,660 per year), 162 research assistantships with tuition reimbursements available (averaging $16,778 per year), 140 teaching assistantships with tuition reimbursements available (averaging $16,191 per year); career-related internships or fieldwork, institutionally sponsored loans, scholarships/grants, health care benefits, tuition waivers (full and partial), and unspecified assistantships also available. Support available to part-time students. In 2015, 59 master's, 23 doctorates awarded. *Degree program information:* Part-time programs available. Part-time. Offers applied statistics (MS); biochemistry (MS, PhD); chemistry (MS, PhD); computer science (MS, PhD); geological sciences (MS); mathematics (MS, PhD); mathematics education (MA); physical and mathematical sciences (MA, MS, PhD); physics (MS, PhD); physics and astronomy (PhD). *Application deadline:* Applications are processed on a rolling basis. *Application fee:* $50. Electronic applications accepted. *Application Contact:* Lynn Patten, Executive Secretary, 801-422-4022, Fax: 801-422-0550, E-mail: lynn_patten@byu.edu. *Dean*, Dr. Scott D. Sommerfeldt, 801-422-2205, Fax: 801-422-0550, E-mail: scott_sommerfeldt@byu.edu.

College of Religious Education Students: 19 full-time (0 women). Average age 32. 19 applicants, 84% accepted, 19 enrolled. *Faculty:* 46 full-time (5 women), 2 part-time/adjunct (0 women). *Financial support:* In 2015–16, 6 students received support. Scholarships/grants available. In 2015, 8 master's awarded. Offers religious education (MA). *Application deadline:* For fall admission, 12/1 for domestic and international students. *Application fee:* $50. Electronic applications accepted. *Application Contact:* Dr. Terry B. Ball, Professor of Ancient Scripture, 801-422-3357, Fax: 801-422-0616, E-mail: terry_ball@byu.edu. *Dean*, Dr. Brent L. Top, 801-422-2736, Fax: 801-422-0616, E-mail: brent_top@byu.edu.

David O. McKay School of Education Students: 205 full-time (130 women), 112 part-time (71 women); includes 31 minority (2 Black or African American, non-Hispanic/Latino; 2 American Indian or Alaska Native, non-Hispanic/Latino; 5 Asian, non-Hispanic/Latino; 15 Hispanic/Latino; 7 Native Hawaiian or other Pacific Islander, non-Hispanic/Latino), 3 international. Average age 33. 286 applicants, 43% accepted, 147 enrolled. *Faculty:* 78 full-time (28 women), 12 part-time/adjunct (5 women). *Financial support:* In 2015–16, 144 students received support, including 84 research assistantships with tuition reimbursements available (averaging $5,202 per year), 31 teaching assistantships with tuition reimbursements available (averaging $4,868 per year); fellowships, career-related internships or fieldwork, institutionally sponsored loans, scholarships/grants, tuition waivers (partial), and unspecified assistantships also available. Support available to part-time students. Financial award applicants required to submit FAFSA. In 2015, 72 master's, 22 doctorates, 11 other advanced degrees awarded. *Degree program information:* Part-time programs available. Part-time. Offers communication disorders (MS); counseling psychology (PhD); education (M Ed, MA, MS, Ed D, PhD, Ed S); educational leadership and foundations (M Ed, Ed D); instructional psychology and technology (MS, PhD); integrative science-technology-engineering-mathematics (STEM) (MA); literacy education (MA); physical education teacher education (MA); school psychology (Ed S); special education (MS); teacher education (MA). *Application deadline:* For fall admission, 2/1 for domestic and international students; for winter admission, 2/1 for domestic and international students; for spring admission, 1/15 for domestic and international students; for summer admission, 3/1 for domestic and international students. *Application fee:* $50. Electronic applications accepted. *Application Contact:* Jay Oliver, Director, Education Student Services, 801-422-1202, Fax: 801-422-0195. *Dean*, Dr. Mary Anne Prater, 801-422-1592, Fax: 801-422-0200, E-mail: prater@byu.edu.

Ira A. Fulton College of Engineering and Technology Offers chemical engineering (MS, PhD); civil engineering (MS, PhD); construction management (MS); electrical and computer engineering (MS, PhD); engineering and technology (MS, PhD); information technology (MS); manufacturing systems (MS); mechanical engineering (MS, PhD); technology and engineering education (MS). Electronic applications accepted.

J. Reuben Clark Law School Students: 392 full-time (148 women), 12 part-time (6 women); includes 55 minority (7 Black or African American, non-Hispanic/Latino; 7 American Indian or Alaska Native, non-Hispanic/Latino; 12 Asian, non-Hispanic/Latino; 18 Hispanic/Latino; 7 Native Hawaiian or other Pacific Islander, non-Hispanic/Latino; 4 Two or more races, non-Hispanic/Latino), 5 international. Average age 25. 461 applicants, 40% accepted, 128 enrolled. *Faculty:* 24 full-time (7 women), 37 part-time/adjunct (6 women). *Financial support:* In 2015–16, 221 students received support. Fellowships, research assistantships, teaching assistantships, career-related internships or fieldwork, institutionally sponsored loans, scholarships/grants, and health care benefits available. Financial award application deadline: 6/1; financial award applicants required to submit FAFSA. In 2015, 7 master's, 133 doctorates awarded. Offers law (LL M, JD). *Application deadline:* For fall admission, 3/1 priority date for domestic students, 3/1 for international students. Applications are processed on a rolling basis. *Application fee:* $50. Electronic applications accepted. *Application Contact:* Marie Kulbeth, Admissions Director, 801-422-4277, Fax: 801-422-0389, E-mail: kulbethm@law.byu.edu. *Dean*, Gordon Smith, 801-422-6383, Fax: 801-422-0389, E-mail: smithg@law.byu.edu.

Marriott School of Management Students: 411 full-time (109 women), 269 part-time (63 women); includes 63 minority (4 Black or African American, non-Hispanic/Latino; 18 Asian, non-Hispanic/Latino; 27 Hispanic/Latino; 14 Native Hawaiian or other Pacific Islander, non-Hispanic/Latino), 87 international. Average age 34. 676 applicants, 58% accepted, 338 enrolled. *Faculty:* 135 full-time (12 women), 83 part-time/adjunct (27 women). *Financial support:* In 2015–16, 385 students received support. Research assistantships, teaching assistantships, career-related internships or fieldwork, institutionally sponsored loans, scholarships/grants, and tuition waivers (full and partial) available. Financial award applicants required to submit FAFSA. In 2015, 285 master's awarded. *Degree program information:* Evening/weekend programs available. Evening/weekend. Offers business administration (MBA); entrepreneurship (MBA); federal government (MPA); finance (MBA); finance and management analysis (MPA); global supply chain management (MBA); local government management (MPA); management (EMBA, MBA, MPA); marketing (MBA); nonprofit management (MPA); organizational behavior/human resources management (MBA); public administration (MPA). *Application fee:* $50. Electronic applications accepted. *Dean*, Dr. Lee Perry, 801-422-4121, Fax: 801-422-4501.

BRISTOL UNIVERSITY, Anaheim, CA 92806

General Information Proprietary, coed, comprehensive institution.

GRADUATE UNITS

Program in Business Administration Offers business administration (MBA); international business (MBA); marketing (MBA); sports management (MBA).

BRITE DIVINITY SCHOOL, Fort Worth, TX 76109

General Information Independent-religious, coed, graduate-only institution.

GRADUATE UNITS

Graduate and Professional Programs *Degree program information:* Part-time and evening/weekend programs available. Part-time, evening/weekend. Offers Biblical interpretation (PhD); divinity (M Div); ministry (D Min); pastoral theology (PhD); theological studies (MTS, CTS); theology (Th M); theology and ministry (MA).

BROADVIEW UNIVERSITY–WEST JORDAN, West Jordan, UT 84088

General Information Proprietary, coed, comprehensive institution.

GRADUATE UNITS

Graduate Programs

BROCK UNIVERSITY, St. Catharines, ON L2S 3A1, Canada

General Information Province-supported, coed, university. *Graduate housing:* Room and/or apartments available on a first-come, first-served basis to single students; on-campus housing not available to married students. *Research affiliation:* Registered Nurses Association of Ontario (nursing best practices), Canadian Honey Council (agriculture, therapeutic product development), Fly Fishing Canada/Trout Unlimited Canada (fisheries management), Henry Ford Health Centre (cancer epidemiology).

GRADUATE UNITS

Faculty of Graduate Studies *Degree program information:* Part-time and evening/weekend programs available. Part-time, evening/weekend. Electronic applications accepted.

Faculty of Applied Health Sciences Offers applied health sciences (M Sc, MA, PhD). Electronic applications accepted.

Faculty of Business Degree program information: Part-time programs available. Part-time. Offers accountancy (M Acc); business (M Acc, M Sc, MBA); business administration (MBA); management (M Sc). Electronic applications accepted.

Faculty of Education Degree program information: Part-time and evening/weekend programs available. Part-time, evening/weekend. Offers education (M Ed, PhD). Electronic applications accepted.

Faculty of Humanities Degree program information: Part-time programs available. Part-time. Offers applied linguistics (MA); classics (MA); English (MA); history (MA); humanities (MA); philosophy (MA); studies in comparative literatures and arts (MA). Electronic applications accepted.

Faculty of Mathematics and Science Degree program information: Part-time programs available. Part-time. Offers biological sciences (M Sc, PhD); biotechnology (M Sc, PhD); chemistry (M Sc, PhD); computer science (M Sc); earth sciences (M Sc); mathematics and science (M Sc, PhD); mathematics and statistics (M Sc); physics (M Sc). Electronic applications accepted.

Faculty of Social Sciences Degree program information: Part-time programs available. Part-time. Offers applied disability studies (MA, MADS, Diploma); behavioral neuroscience (MA, PhD); business economics (MBE); Canadian politics (MA); child and youth studies (MA); comparative politics (MA); critical sociology (MA); geography (MA); international relations (MA); life span development (MA, PhD); political theory or philosophy (MA); popular culture (MA); public policy (MA); social justice and equity studies (MA); social personality (MA, PhD); social sciences (MA, MADS, MBE, PhD, Diploma). Electronic applications accepted.

BROOKLYN COLLEGE OF THE CITY UNIVERSITY OF NEW YORK, Brooklyn, NY 11210-2889

General Information State and locally supported, coed, comprehensive institution. *Graduate housing:* Room and/or apartments available on a first-come, first-served basis to single students; on-campus housing not available to married students. *Research affiliation:* Biothera Inc. (biology), Silicon Valley Community Foundation (computer and information science), Jessie Smith Noyes Foundation (sustainability), Sloan-Kettering Memorial Cancer Center (health/biology), Community Health Care Association of New York State (health and nutrition sciences), Welfare Research Inc. (education).

GRADUATE UNITS

School of Business *Degree program information:* Part-time and evening/weekend programs available. Part-time, evening/weekend. Offers accounting (MS); business administration (MS). Electronic applications accepted.

School of Education *Degree program information:* Part-time and evening/weekend programs available. Part-time, evening/weekend. Offers adolescence science education (MAT); art teacher (K-12) (MA); autism spectrum disorders (AC); bilingual education (MS Ed); biology (MA); biology teacher (7-12) (MA); birth-grade 2 (MS Ed); chemistry (MA); chemistry teacher (7-12) (MA); earth science (MA); earth science teacher (7-12) (MAT); education (MA, MAT, MS Ed, AC); English teacher (7-12) (MA); French teacher (7-12) (MA); general science (MA); liberal arts (MS Ed); mathematics (MS Ed); mathematics teacher (7-12) (MA); middle childhood mathematics education (MS Ed); music teacher (MA); physics (MA); physics teacher (7-12) (MA); play therapy (AC); school building leader (MS Ed); school counseling (MS Ed); school district leader (MS Ed); school psychologist (MS Ed); science and environmental education (MS Ed); social studies teacher (7-12) (MA); Spanish teacher (7-12) (MA); teacher of students with disabilities (MS Ed). Electronic applications accepted.

School of Humanities and Social Sciences *Degree program information:* Part-time and evening/weekend programs available. Part-time, evening/weekend. Offers audiology (Au D); creative writing (MFA); English (MA); French (MA); history (MA); humanities and social sciences (MA, MFA, MS, Au D, PhD); international affairs (MA); Judaic studies (MA); political science (MA); sociology (MA, PhD); Spanish (MA); speech (MA); speech-language pathology (MS); urban policy and administration (MA). Electronic applications accepted.

School of Natural and Behavioral Sciences *Degree program information:* Part-time and evening/weekend programs available. Part-time, evening/weekend. Offers biology (MA); chemistry (MA, MS, PhD); community health (MA); community health education (MA); computer science (MA); earth and environmental sciences (MA, PhD); exercise and sports science (MS); experimental psychology (MA); general public health (MPH); grief counseling (CAS); health care policy and administration (MPH); health informatics (MS); industrial and organizational psychology (MA); information systems (MS); mathematics (MA); mental health counseling (MA); natural and behavioral sciences (MA, MPH, MS, PhD, AC, Advanced Certificate); nutrition (MS); parallel and distributed computing (Advanced Certificate); physical education teacher (MS); physics (MA); psychology (PhD); public health (MPH); sport management (MS); thanatology (MA). Electronic applications accepted.

School of Visual, Media and Performing Arts *Degree program information:* Part-time and evening/weekend programs available. Part-time, evening/weekend. Offers acting (MFA); art history (MA); design and technical theater (MFA); digital art (MFA); directing (MFA); drawing and painting (MFA); media studies (MS); performance and interactive media arts (MFA); performing arts management (MFA); photography (MFA); printmaking (MFA); sculpture (MFA); television production (MFA); theater history and criticism (MA); visual, media and performing arts (M Mus, MA, MFA, MS). Electronic applications accepted.

Conservatory of Music Degree program information: Part-time programs available. Part-time. Offers composition (MM); music teacher (MA); musicology (MA); performance (MM). Electronic applications accepted.

BROOKLYN LAW SCHOOL, Brooklyn, NY 11201-3798

General Information Independent, coed, graduate-only institution. *Graduate housing:* Rooms and/or apartments available to single students and guaranteed to married students. Housing application deadline: 5/1.

GRADUATE UNITS

Graduate and Professional Programs *Degree program information:* Part-time and evening/weekend programs available. Part-time, evening/weekend. Offers law (LL M, JD). JD/MBA offered jointly with Bernard M. Baruch College of the City University of New York; JD/MS with Pratt Institute; JD/MUP with Hunter College of the City University of New York; and JD/MA with Brooklyn College of the City University of New York. Electronic applications accepted.

BROWN UNIVERSITY, Providence, RI 02912

General Information Independent, coed, university. CGS member. *Graduate housing:* Room and/or apartments available to single students; on-campus housing not available to married students. *Research affiliation:* Woods Hole Oceanographic Institution-Marine Biological Laboratory, Rhode Island Reactor, International Center for Numismatic Studies, Meeting Street School.

GRADUATE UNITS

Graduate School *Degree program information:* Part-time programs available. Part-time. Offers acting and directing (MFA); American studies (PhD); American studies for international students (MA); ancient western Asian studies (PhD); anthropology (MA, PhD); Asian religious traditions (PhD); Brazilian studies (AM); chemistry (PhD); classics (MA, PhD); cognitive science (Sc M, PhD); comparative literature (PhD); computer music and multimedia (PhD); computer science (Sc M, PhD); economics (PhD); Egyptology (PhD); elementary education (MAT); English (MAT, PhD); English as a second language and cross-cultural studies (AM); ethnomusicology (PhD); French studies (PhD); geological sciences (PhD); German (PhD); Hispanic studies (PhD);

history (MA, PhD); history of art and architecture (PhD); history of the exact sciences in antiquity (PhD); history/social studies (MAT); Italian studies (PhD); linguistics (AM, PhD); literary arts (MFA); mathematics (PhD); philosophy (PhD); physics (Sc M, PhD); playwriting (MFA); political science (PhD); Portuguese and Brazilian studies (AM, PhD); Portuguese bilingual education and cross-cultural studies (AM); psychology (PhD); public humanities (MA); religion and critical thought (PhD); religions of the ancient Mediterranean (PhD); Russian language and literature (AM); science (MAT); secondary education (MAT); Slavic linguistics (AM); Slavic studies (PhD); sociology (MA, PhD); teaching (MAT); theatre and performance studies (PhD); urban education policy (AM).

A. Alfred Taubman Center for Public Policy and American Institutions Offers public policy and American institutions (MPA, MPP).

Division of Applied Mathematics Offers applied mathematics (Sc M, PhD).

Division of Biology and Medicine Degree program information: Part-time programs available. Part-time. Offers behavioral and social sciences intervention (M Sc); biology and medicine (AM, M Sc, MA, MPH, Sc M, MD, PhD); biomedical engineering (Sc M, PhD); biostatistics (AM, Sc M, PhD); biotechnology (PhD); ecology and evolutionary biology (PhD); epidemiology (Sc M); health services, policy and practice (PhD); medicine (MD); molecular biology, cell biology, and biochemistry (MA, PhD); molecular pharmacology and physiology (PhD); neuroscience (PhD); pathology and laboratory medicine (Sc M, PhD); public health (MPH). Electronic applications accepted.

Joukowsky Institute for Archaeology and the Ancient World Offers archaeology and the ancient world (PhD).

School of Engineering Offers biomedical engineering (Sc M, PhD); chemical and biochemical engineering (Sc M, PhD); electrical sciences and computer engineering (Sc M, PhD); fluid and thermal sciences (Sc M, PhD); materials science and engineering (Sc M, PhD); mechanics of solids and structures (Sc M, PhD).

National Institutes of Health Sponsored Programs Offers neuroscience (PhD).

BRYAN COLLEGE, Dayton, TN 37321

General Information Independent-religious, coed, comprehensive institution.

GRADUATE UNITS

MBA Program Offers business administration (MBA).

BRYAN COLLEGE OF HEALTH SCIENCES, Lincoln, NE 68506-1398

General Information Independent, coed, comprehensive institution. CGS member.

GRADUATE UNITS

School of Nurse Anesthesia Offers nurse anesthesia (MS).

BRYANT UNIVERSITY, Smithfield, RI 02917

General Information Independent, coed, comprehensive institution. *Enrollment:* 3,670 graduate, professional, and undergraduate students; 118 full-time matriculated graduate/professional students (60 women), 93 part-time matriculated graduate/professional students (33 women). *Enrollment by degree level:* 211 master's. *Graduate faculty:* 54 full-time (18 women), 4 part-time/adjunct (0 women). *Tuition, area resident:* Full-time $26,832; part-time $1118 per credit hour. Tuition and fees vary according to degree level and program. *Graduate housing:* Room and/or apartments available on a first-come, first-served basis to single students; on-campus housing not available to married students. Typical cost: $10,392 per year ($16,120 including board). Room and board charges vary according to board plan and housing facility selected. Housing application deadline: 8/1. *Student services:* Campus employment opportunities, campus safety program, career counseling, exercise/wellness program, free psychological counseling, international student services, low-cost health insurance, multicultural affairs office, services for students with disabilities, teacher training, writing training. *Library:* Douglas and Judith Krupp Library plus 1 other. Students can reserve study rooms.

Computer facilities: Computer purchase and lease plans are available. 574 computers available on campus for general student use. A campuswide network can be accessed from student residence rooms and from off campus. Online class registration, e-mail, online library, student Web hosts are available.
Website: http://www.bryant.edu/

General Application Contact: Diane Ruotolo, Graduate Admissions Manager, 401-232-6230, E-mail: druotol@bryant.edu.

GRADUATE UNITS

College of Arts and Sciences Students: 2 full-time (1 woman), 13 part-time (9 women); includes 1 minority (Two or more races, non-Hispanic/Latino). Average age 34. 27 applicants, 41% accepted, 4 enrolled. *Faculty:* 12 full-time (7 women). *Financial support:* Fellowships and research assistantships available. Financial award applicants required to submit FAFSA. In 2015, 7 master's awarded. *Degree program information:* Part-time and evening/weekend programs available. Part-time, evening/weekend. Offers communication (MA); global environmental studies (MS). *Application deadline:* For fall admission, 8/15 for domestic and international students; for spring admission, 1/15 for domestic and international students; for summer admission, 5/15 for domestic and international students. Applications are processed on a rolling basis. *Application fee:* $80. Electronic applications accepted. *Application Contact:* Jeffrey G. Hunter, Graduate and Professional Studies, 401-480-8148, E-mail: gps@bryant.edu. *Dean, College of Arts and Sciences,* Wendy Samter, 401-232-6944, E-mail: wsamter@bryant.edu.

Graduate School of Business Students: 85 full-time (38 women), 80 part-time (24 women); includes 20 minority (7 Black or African American, non-Hispanic/Latino; 2 Asian, non-Hispanic/Latino; 5 Hispanic/Latino; 6 Two or more races, non-Hispanic/Latino), 14 international. Average age 26. 208 applicants, 70% accepted, 91 enrolled. *Faculty:* 38 full-time (10 women), 4 part-time/adjunct (0 women). *Financial support:* Research assistantships, scholarships/grants, and unspecified assistantships available. Support available to part-time students. Financial award application deadline: 2/15; financial award applicants required to submit FAFSA. In 2015, 87 master's awarded. *Degree program information:* Part-time and evening/weekend programs available. Part-time, evening/weekend. Offers business administration (MBA); professional accountancy (MPAC); taxation (MST). *Application deadline:* For fall admission, 7/15 for domestic and international students; for spring admission, 11/15 for domestic and international students; for summer admission, 4/15 for domestic and international students. Applications are processed on a rolling basis. *Application fee:* $80. Electronic applications accepted. *Application Contact:* Diane Ruotolo, Assistant Director of Graduate Admission, 401-232-6230, Fax: 401-232-6494, E-mail: druotol@bryant.edu. *Director of Operations for Graduate Programs, School of Business,* Richard S. Cheney, 401-232-6707, Fax: 401-232-6494, E-mail: rcheney@bryant.edu.

School of Health Sciences Students: 31 full-time (21 women); includes 2 minority (1 Asian, non-Hispanic/Latino; 1 Two or more races, non-Hispanic/Latino). Average age 28. 48 applicants, 100% accepted, 36 enrolled. *Faculty:* 4 full-time (1 woman). *Financial support:* Fund for a Healthy Rhode Island awards available. Offers health sciences (MS). *Application deadline:* For winter admission, 10/1 for domestic and international students. Applications are processed on a rolling basis. *Application fee:* $80. Electronic applications accepted. *Application Contact:* Kevin Whitworth, Program Coordinator, 401-232-6556, E-mail: pa_program@bryant.edu. *Program Director,* Jay Amrien, 401-232-6217, E-mail: jamrien@bryant.edu.

BRYAN UNIVERSITY, Springfield, MO 65804

General Information Proprietary, coed, comprehensive institution.

GRADUATE UNITS

Program in Business Administration Online learning. Offers business administration (MBA).

BRYN ATHYN COLLEGE OF THE NEW CHURCH, Bryn Athyn, PA 19009-0717

General Information Independent-religious, coed, comprehensive institution. *Graduate housing:* Room and/or apartments available on a first-come, first-served basis to single students; on-campus housing not available to married students. Housing application deadline: 1/31.

GRADUATE UNITS

Academy of the New Church Theological School *Degree program information:* Part-time programs available. Part-time, online learning. Offers divinity (M Div); religious studies (MA).

BRYN MAWR COLLEGE, Bryn Mawr, PA 19010-2899

General Information Independent, Undergraduate: women only; graduate: coed, university. CGS member. *Enrollment:* 1,692 graduate, professional, and undergraduate students; 284 full-time matriculated graduate/professional students (216 women), 59 part-time matriculated graduate/professional students (47 women). *Enrollment by degree level:* 160 master's, 110 doctoral, 73 other advanced degrees. *Graduate faculty:* 57 full-time (32 women), 14 part-time/adjunct (8 women). *Tuition, area resident:* Full-time $39,240; part-time $6540 per unit. *Graduate housing:* On-campus housing not available. *Student services:* Campus employment opportunities, career counseling, exercise/wellness program, international student services, low-cost health insurance, multicultural affairs office, services for students with disabilities, teacher training. *Library:* Canaday Library plus 3 others. *Collection:* Books: 732,312 (physical), 626,265 (digital/electronic); Serial titles: 9,634 (physical), 90,706 (digital/electronic); Databases: 134.

Computer facilities: 125 computers available on campus for general student use. A campuswide network can be accessed from student residence rooms and from off campus. Online class registration is available.
Website: http://www.brynmawr.edu/

General Application Contact: Office of Admissions, 610-526-5152, Fax: 610-526-7471, E-mail: admissions@brynmawr.edu.

GRADUATE UNITS

Graduate School of Arts and Sciences Students: 75 full-time (58 women), 14 part-time (9 women); includes 10 minority (3 Asian, non-Hispanic/Latino; 5 Hispanic/Latino; 1 Native Hawaiian or other Pacific Islander, non-Hispanic/Latino; 1 Two or more races, non-Hispanic/Latino), 2 international. Average age 30. 115 applicants, 26% accepted, 12 enrolled. *Faculty:* 45 full-time (25 women), 3 part-time/adjunct (0 women). *Financial support:* In 2015–16, 83 students received support, including 50 fellowships with tuition reimbursements available (averaging $15,951 per year), 2 research assistantships with tuition reimbursements available (averaging $20,850 per year), 24 teaching assistantships with tuition reimbursements available (averaging $17,151 per year); career-related internships or fieldwork, Federal Work-Study, institutionally sponsored loans, health care benefits, unspecified assistantships, and tuition awards also available. Support available to part-time students. Financial award application deadline: 1/3. In 2015, 18 master's, 9 doctorates awarded. *Degree program information:* Part-time programs available. Part-time. Offers arts and sciences (MA, PhD); chemistry (MA, PhD); classical and Near Eastern archaeology (MA, PhD); Greek, Latin, and classical studies (MA, PhD); history of art (MA, PhD); mathematics (MA, PhD); physics (MA, PhD). *Application deadline:* For fall admission, 1/4 for domestic and international students. Applications are processed on a rolling basis. *Application fee:* $50. Electronic applications accepted. *Application Contact:* Maria Dantis, Graduate Program Administrator, 610-526-5074, E-mail: gsas@brynmawr.edu. *Dean of Graduate Studies,* Sharon Burgmayer, E-mail: sburgmay@brynmawr.edu.

Graduate School of Social Work and Social Research Students: 136 full-time (115 women), 45 part-time (38 women); includes 50 minority (33 Black or African American, non-Hispanic/Latino; 5 Asian, non-Hispanic/Latino; 7 Hispanic/Latino; 5 Two or more races, non-Hispanic/Latino), 1 international. Average age 34. 157 applicants, 78% accepted, 76 enrolled. *Faculty:* 12 full-time (7 women), 11 part-time/adjunct (8 women). *Financial support:* In 2015–16, 157 students received support. Fellowships with tuition reimbursements available, research assistantships with tuition reimbursements available, teaching assistantships with tuition reimbursements available, career-related internships or fieldwork, Federal Work-Study, institutionally sponsored loans, scholarships/grants, tuition waivers (full and partial), and dissertation awards (for PhD) available. Support available to part-time students. Financial award application deadline: 3/15; financial award applicants required to submit FAFSA. In 2015, 105 master's, 2 doctorates awarded. *Degree program information:* Part-time and evening/weekend programs available. Part-time, evening/weekend. Offers social work and social research (MSS, PhD). *Application deadline:* For fall admission, 4/15 for domestic and international students. Applications are processed on a rolling basis. *Application fee:* $50. Electronic applications accepted. *Application Contact:* Tara Stasik, Assistant Dean, 610-520-2612, E-mail: tstasik@brynmawr.edu. *Dean,* Dr. Darlyne Bailey, 610-520-2610, Fax: 610-520-2613, E-mail: dbailey01@brynmawr.edu.

BUCKNELL UNIVERSITY, Lewisburg, PA 17837

General Information Independent, coed, comprehensive institution. CGS member. *Graduate housing:* On-campus housing not available.

GRADUATE UNITS

Graduate Studies *Degree program information:* Part-time programs available. Part-time.

College of Arts and Sciences Degree program information: Part-time programs available. Part-time. Offers animal behavior (MS); arts and sciences (MA, MS, MS Ed); biology (MS); chemistry (MA, MS); college student personnel (MS Ed); English (MA); mathematics (MA, MS); psychology (MS).

College of Engineering Degree program information: Part-time programs available. Part-time. Offers chemical engineering (MS Ch E); civil and environmental engineering (MSCE, MSEV); electrical engineering (MSEE); engineering (MS Ch E, MSCE, MSEE, MSEV, MSME); mechanical engineering (MSME).

BUENA VISTA UNIVERSITY, Storm Lake, IA 50588

General Information Independent-religious, coed, comprehensive institution. *Graduate housing:* Room and/or apartments available on a first-come, first-served basis to single students; on-campus housing not available to married students. Housing application deadline: 5/1.

GRADUATE UNITS

School of Education ***Degree program information:*** Part-time and evening/weekend programs available. Part-time, evening/weekend, online learning. Offers curriculum and instruction (M Ed); school guidance and counseling (MS Ed). Program offered in summer only. Electronic applications accepted.

BUFFALO STATE COLLEGE, STATE UNIVERSITY OF NEW YORK, Buffalo, NY 14222-1095

General Information State-supported, coed, comprehensive institution. CGS member. *Graduate housing:* Room and/or apartments available on a first-come, first-served basis to single students; on-campus housing not available to married students. Housing application deadline: 8/15. *Research affiliation:* Friends of Buffalo River, Research Institute on Addictions at the University of Buffalo, Roswell Park Memorial Institute, Hauptman-Woodward Medical Research Institute, Ecology and Environment Corporation, Phillip Morris Foundation.

GRADUATE UNITS

The Graduate School ***Degree program information:*** Part-time and evening/weekend programs available. Part-time, evening/weekend, online learning. Offers multidisciplinary studies (MA, MS).

Faculty of Applied Science and Education Degree program information: Part-time and evening/weekend programs available. Part-time, evening/weekend, online learning. Offers adult education (MS, Certificate); applied science and education (MPS, MS, MS Ed, CAS, Certificate); business and marketing education (MS Ed); career and technical education (MS Ed); childhood education (grades 1-6) (MS Ed); creative studies (MS); criminal justice (MS); early childhood and childhood curriculum and instruction (MS Ed); early childhood education (birth-grade 2) (MS Ed); educational computing (MS Ed); educational leadership (CAS); elementary education (MS Ed); human resources development (Certificate); industrial technology (MS); literacy specialist (MPS, MS Ed); literacy specialist (birth-grade 6) (MS Ed); literacy specialist (grades 5-12) (MPS); special education (MS Ed); special education: adolescents (MS Ed); special education: childhood (MS Ed); special education: early childhood (MS Ed); speech-language pathology (MS Ed); student personnel administration (MS); teaching bilingual exceptional individuals (MS Ed); technology education (MS Ed).

Faculty of Arts and Humanities Degree program information: Part-time and evening/weekend programs available. Part-time, evening/weekend. Offers art conservation (CAS); art education (MS Ed); arts and humanities (MA, MS Ed, CAS); conservation of historic works and art works (MA); English (MA); secondary education (MS Ed).

Faculty of Natural and Social Sciences Degree program information: Part-time and evening/weekend programs available. Part-time, evening/weekend. Offers applied economics (MA); biology (MA); chemistry (MA); history (MA); mathematics education (MS Ed); natural and social sciences (MA, MS Ed); secondary education (MS Ed); secondary education physics (MS Ed).

BUTLER UNIVERSITY, Indianapolis, IN 46208-3485

General Information Independent, coed, comprehensive institution. *Enrollment:* 4,798 graduate, professional, and undergraduate students; 382 full-time matriculated graduate/professional students (244 women), 345 part-time matriculated graduate/professional students (169 women). *Enrollment by degree level:* 478 master's, 249 doctoral. *Graduate faculty:* 126 full-time (64 women), 30 part-time/adjunct (12 women). Tuition and fees vary according to course level, program and student level. *Graduate housing:* Room and/or apartments available on a first-come, first-served basis to single students; on-campus housing not available to married students. Housing application deadline: 8/1. *Student services:* Campus employment opportunities, campus safety program, career counseling, exercise/wellness program, free psychological counseling, international student services, low-cost health insurance, multicultural affairs office, services for students with disabilities. *Library:* Irwin Library plus 2 others. *Collection:* Books: 203,150 (physical), 240,614 (digital/electronic); Serial titles: 3,849 (physical), 44,712 (digital/electronic); Databases: 201. Weekly public service hours: 106; students can reserve study rooms.

Computer facilities: Computer purchase and lease plans are available. 450 computers available on campus for general student use. A campuswide network can be accessed from student residence rooms and from off campus. Online class registration is available.
Website: http://www.butler.edu/

General Application Contact: Diane Dubord, Graduate Student Services Specialist, 317-940-8107, Fax: 317-940-8250, E-mail: ddubord@butler.edu.

GRADUATE UNITS

College of Business Administration Students: 32 full-time (9 women), 162 part-time (47 women); includes 8 minority (1 Asian, non-Hispanic/Latino; 6 Hispanic/Latino; 1 Two or more races, non-Hispanic/Latino), 4 international. Average age 31. 141 applicants, 58% accepted, 41 enrolled. *Faculty:* 16 full-time (5 women), 7 part-time/adjunct (0 women). *Financial support:* Career-related internships or fieldwork and institutionally sponsored loans available. Support available to part-time students. Financial award application deadline: 7/15; financial award applicants required to submit CSS PROFILE or FAFSA. In 2015, 80 master's awarded. *Degree program information:* Part-time and evening/weekend programs available. Part-time, evening/weekend. Offers finance (MBA); international business (MBA); leadership (MBA); marketing (MBA); professional accounting (MP Acc). *Application deadline:* For fall admission, 8/1 for domestic and international students; for spring admission, 12/1 for domestic and international students; for summer admission, 4/1 for domestic and international students. Applications are processed on a rolling basis. Electronic applications accepted. *Application Contact:* Diane Dubord, Graduate Student Service Specialist, 317-940-8107, Fax: 317-940-8250, E-mail: ddubord@butler.edu. *Dean,* Dr. Stephen Standifird.

College of Education Students: 21 full-time (18 women), 126 part-time (87 women); includes 20 minority (12 Black or African American, non-Hispanic/Latino; 1 Asian, non-Hispanic/Latino; 3 Hispanic/Latino; 4 Two or more races, non-Hispanic/Latino). Average age 32. 55 applicants, 84% accepted, 19 enrolled. *Faculty:* 5 full-time (3 women), 2 part-time/adjunct (1 woman). *Financial support:* Institutionally sponsored loans available. Support available to part-time students. Financial award application deadline: 7/15; financial award applicants required to submit FAFSA. In 2015, 42 master's awarded. *Degree program information:* Part-time programs available. Part-time. Offers educational administration (experiential program for preparing school principals) (MS); effective teaching and leadership (MS); school counseling (MS). *Application deadline:* For fall admission, 8/1 for domestic students; for spring admission, 12/1 for domestic students; for summer admission, 4/1 for domestic students. Applications are processed on a rolling basis. Electronic applications accepted. *Application Contact:* Diane Dubord, Graduate Student Services Specialist, 317-940-8100, Fax: 317-940-8250, E-mail: ddubord@butler.edu. *Dean,* Dr. Ena Shelley, 317-940-9752, Fax: 317-940-6481.

College of Liberal Arts and Sciences Students: 10 full-time (7 women), 49 part-time (27 women); includes 6 minority (5 Black or African American, non-Hispanic/Latino; 1 Two or more races, non-Hispanic/Latino), 2 international. Average age 32. 64 applicants, 59% accepted, 18 enrolled. *Faculty:* 19 full-time (6 women), 4 part-time/adjunct (2 women). *Financial support:* Career-related internships or fieldwork, institutionally sponsored loans, and tuition waivers (full and partial) available. Support available to part-time students. Financial award applicants required to submit FAFSA. In 2015, 26 master's awarded. *Degree program information:* Part-time and evening/weekend programs available. Part-time, evening/weekend. Offers creative writing (MFA); English (MA); history (MA); liberal arts and sciences (MA, MFA). *Application deadline:* For fall admission, 2/15 for domestic and international students; for spring admission, 9/15 for domestic and international students. Electronic applications accepted. *Application Contact:* Diane Dubord, Graduate Student Services Specialist, 317-940-8107, Fax: 317-940-8250, E-mail: ddubord@butler.edu. *Dean,* Dr. Jay Howard, 317-940-9874, E-mail: jrhoward@butler.edu.

College of Pharmacy and Health Sciences Students: 310 full-time (219 women), 5 part-time (3 women); includes 25 minority (1 Black or African American, non-Hispanic/Latino; 1 American Indian or Alaska Native, non-Hispanic/Latino; 14 Asian, non-Hispanic/Latino; 6 Hispanic/Latino; 3 Two or more races, non-Hispanic/Latino), 8 international. Average age 24. 42 applicants, 2% accepted. *Faculty:* 63 full-time (44 women). *Financial support:* Applicants required to submit FAFSA. In 2015, 59 master's, 132 doctorates awarded. Offers pharmaceutical science (MS); pharmacy (Pharm D); physician assistant studies (MS). *Application deadline:* For fall admission, 5/1 for domestic and international students. Electronic applications accepted. *Application Contact:* Diane Dubord, Graduate Student Services Specialist, 317-940-8107, E-mail: ddubord@butler.edu. *Dean,* Dr. Mary Graham, 317-940-8056, E-mail: mandritz@butler.edu.

Jordan College of Fine Arts Students: 19 full-time (7 women), 20 part-time (7 women); includes 4 minority (2 Black or African American, non-Hispanic/Latino; 1 Hispanic/Latino; 1 Two or more races, non-Hispanic/Latino). Average age 27. 35 applicants, 66% accepted, 7 enrolled. *Faculty:* 23 full-time (6 women), 17 part-time/adjunct (9 women). *Financial support:* Fellowships, teaching assistantships with tuition reimbursements, career-related internships or fieldwork, institutionally sponsored loans, and scholarships/grants available. Support available to part-time students. Financial award application deadline: 7/15; financial award applicants required to submit FAFSA. In 2015, 15 master's awarded. *Degree program information:* Part-time programs available. Part-time. Offers composition (MM); conducting (MM); music education (MM); music history (MM). *Application deadline:* For fall admission, 2/1 for domestic and international students. Electronic applications accepted. *Application Contact:* Diane Dubord, Graduate Student Services Specialist, 317-940-8107, E-mail: ddubord@butler.edu. *Dean,* Ronald Caltabiano, 317-940-9231, E-mail: rcalt@butler.edu.

CABARRUS COLLEGE OF HEALTH SCIENCES, Concord, NC 28025

General Information Independent, coed, primarily women, comprehensive institution.

GRADUATE UNITS

Program in Occupational Therapy Offers occupational therapy (MOT).

CABRINI UNIVERSITY, Radnor, PA 19087

General Information Independent-religious, coed, comprehensive institution. *Graduate housing:* On-campus housing not available.

GRADUATE UNITS

Graduate Studies ***Degree program information:*** Part-time and evening/weekend programs available. Part-time, evening/weekend. Offers accounting (M Acc); education (M Ed); leadership (MS). Electronic applications accepted.

CAIRN UNIVERSITY, Langhorne, PA 19047-2990

General Information Independent-religious, coed, comprehensive institution. *Enrollment:* 1,043 graduate, professional, and undergraduate students; 56 full-time matriculated graduate/professional students (25 women), 204 part-time matriculated graduate/professional students (101 women). *Enrollment by degree level:* 254 master's, 6 other advanced degrees. *Graduate faculty:* 14 full-time (3 women), 17 part-time/adjunct (7 women). *Tuition, area resident:* Full-time $11,610; part-time $645 per credit hour. Tuition and fees vary according to program. *Graduate housing:* Rooms and/or apartments available on a first-come, first-served basis to single and married students. Typical cost: $4895 per year ($9350 including board) for single students. Room and board charges vary according to housing facility selected. *Student services:* Campus employment opportunities, campus safety program, career counseling, exercise/wellness program, international student services, low-cost health insurance, services for students with disabilities, teacher training, writing training. *Library:* Masland Learning Resource Center. *Collection:* Books: 122,140 (physical), 41,098 (digital/electronic); Serial titles: 6,990 (physical), 180,093 (digital/electronic); Databases: 140. Weekly public service hours: 86; students can reserve study rooms.

Computer facilities: Computer purchase and lease plans are available. 68 computers available on campus for general student use. A campuswide network can be accessed from student residence rooms and from off campus. Online class registration is available.
Website: http://cairn.edu/

General Application Contact: Rebecca Lippert, Director, Admissions, 800-572-2472, Fax: 215-702-4241, E-mail: blippert@cairn.edu.

GRADUATE UNITS

Department of Counseling Students: 22 full-time (17 women), 50 part-time (37 women); includes 28 minority (20 Black or African American, non-Hispanic/Latino; 1 Asian, non-Hispanic/Latino; 7 Hispanic/Latino), 3 international. Average age 37. 23 applicants, 96% accepted, 19 enrolled. *Faculty:* 2 full-time (0 women), 6 part-time/adjunct (4 women). *Financial support:* Scholarships/grants available. Support available to part-time students. Financial award applicants required to submit FAFSA. In 2015, 41 master's awarded. *Degree program information:* Part-time and evening/weekend programs available. Part-time, evening/weekend. Offers counseling (MS). *Application deadline:* Applications are processed on a rolling basis. *Application fee:* $25. Electronic applications accepted. *Application Contact:* Gwen Dorsey, Enrollment Counselor, Graduate Counseling, 800-572-2472, Fax: 215-702-4248, E-mail: gdorsey@cairn.edu. *Chair,* Dr. Jeff Black, 215-702-4347, E-mail: jblack@cairn.edu.

School of Business Students: 6 full-time (4 women), 37 part-time (16 women); includes 14 minority (8 Black or African American, non-Hispanic/Latino; 2 Asian, non-Hispanic/Latino; 2 Hispanic/Latino; 2 Two or more races, non-Hispanic/Latino), 6 international. Average age 34. 24 applicants, 100% accepted, 21 enrolled. *Faculty:* 1 full-time (0 women), 7 part-time/adjunct (1 woman). *Financial support:* Scholarships/grants available. Support available to part-time students. Financial award applicants required to submit FAFSA. In 2015, 10 master's awarded. *Degree program information:* Part-time and evening/weekend programs available. Part-time, evening/weekend, blended/hybrid learning. Offers accounting (MBA); business administration (MBA); organizational leadership (MSOL, Postbaccalaureate Certificate). *Application deadline:* Applications are processed on a rolling basis. *Application fee:* $25. Electronic applications accepted. *Application Contact:* Gwen Dorsey, Assistant Director, Graduate Admissions, 800-572-2472, Fax: 215-702-4248, E-mail: gdorsey@cairn.edu. *Dean, School of Business*, Yunn Kang, 215-702-4461, Fax: 215-702-4248, E-mail: ykang@cairn.edu.

School of Divinity Students: 23 full-time (2 women), 57 part-time (9 women); includes 37 minority (31 Black or African American, non-Hispanic/Latino; 5 Asian, non-Hispanic/Latino; 1 Hispanic/Latino), 2 international. Average age 40. 28 applicants, 100% accepted, 16 enrolled. *Faculty:* 8 full-time (0 women). *Financial support:* Scholarships/grants available. Support available to part-time students. Financial award applicants required to submit FAFSA. In 2015, 12 master's awarded. *Degree program information:* Part-time and evening/weekend programs available. Part-time, evening/weekend. Offers divinity (M Div); religion (MA). *Application deadline:* Applications are processed on a rolling basis. *Application fee:* $25. Electronic applications accepted. *Application Contact:* Abigail Sattler, Assistant Director, Graduate Admissions, 800-572-2472, Fax: 215-702-4248, E-mail: asattler@cairn.edu. *Dean*, Dr. Jonathan L. Master, 215-702-4358, Fax: 215-702-4359, E-mail: divinity@cairn.edu.

School of Education Students: 5 full-time (2 women), 60 part-time (39 women); includes 9 minority (4 Black or African American, non-Hispanic/Latino; 3 Asian, non-Hispanic/Latino; 2 Hispanic/Latino), 18 international. Average age 38. 36 applicants, 100% accepted, 24 enrolled. *Faculty:* 2 full-time (both women), 4 part-time/adjunct (2 women). *Financial support:* Scholarships/grants available. Support available to part-time students. Financial award applicants required to submit FAFSA. In 2015, 24 master's awarded. *Degree program information:* Part-time and evening/weekend programs available. Part-time, evening/weekend. Offers educational leadership and administration (MS El); teacher education (MS Ed). *Application deadline:* Applications are processed on a rolling basis. *Application fee:* $25. Electronic applications accepted. *Application Contact:* Abigail Simon, Enrollment Counselor, Graduate Education, 800-572-2472, Fax: 215-702-4248, E-mail: asimon@cairn.edu. *Dean*, Dr. Paula Gossard, 215-702-4264, E-mail: teacher.ed@cairn.edu.

CALDWELL UNIVERSITY, Caldwell, NJ 07006-6195

General Information Independent-religious, coed, comprehensive institution. CGS member.

GRADUATE UNITS

Graduate Studies ***Degree program information:*** Part-time and evening/weekend programs available. Part-time, evening/weekend. Offers art therapy (MA); counseling (MA); director of school counseling (Post-Master's Certificate); professional counselor (Post-Master's Certificate); school counselor (Post-Master's Certificate). Electronic applications accepted.

Division of Applied Behavior Analysis Degree program information: Part-time programs available. Part-time. Offers applied behavior analysis (MA, PhD, Post-Master's Certificate). Electronic applications accepted.

Division of Business Degree program information: Part-time programs available. Part-time. Offers accounting (MS); business administration (MBA). Electronic applications accepted.

Division of Education Degree program information: Part-time and evening/weekend programs available. Part-time, evening/weekend. Offers curriculum and instruction (MA); education (Ed D, Postbaccalaureate Certificate); educational administration (MA); learning disabilities teacher-consultant (Post-Master's Certificate); literacy instruction (MA); principal (Post-Master's Certificate); reading specialist (Post-Master's Certificate); special education (MA); superintendent (Post-Master's Certificate); supervisor (Post-Master's Certificate). Electronic applications accepted.

CALIFORNIA BAPTIST UNIVERSITY, Riverside, CA 92504-3206

General Information Independent-religious, coed, comprehensive institution. *Enrollment:* 8,541 graduate, professional, and undergraduate students; 932 full-time matriculated graduate/professional students (697 women), 979 part-time matriculated graduate/professional students (711 women). *Enrollment by degree level:* 1,908 master's, 3 doctoral. *Graduate faculty:* 120 full-time (70 women), 89 part-time/adjunct (51 women). *Tuition, area resident:* Full-time $11,232; part-time $624 per unit. *Required fees:* $175 per semester. One-time fee: $45. Tuition and fees vary according to course load, degree level and program. *Graduate housing:* Rooms and/or apartments available on a first-come, first-served basis to single and married students. Typical cost: $5110 per year ($9540 including board) for single students. Room and board charges vary according to board plan and housing facility selected. Housing application deadline: 8/1. *Student services:* Campus employment opportunities, campus safety program, career counseling, exercise/wellness program, free psychological counseling, international student services, low-cost health insurance, multicultural affairs office, services for students with disabilities, teacher training, writing training. *Library:* Annie Gabriel Library. *Collection:* Books: 116,792 (physical), 190,918 (digital/electronic); Serial titles: 261 (physical), 34,696 (digital/electronic); Databases: 83. Weekly public service hours: 101; students can reserve study rooms.

Computer facilities: Computer purchase and lease plans are available. 279 computers available on campus for general student use. A campuswide network can be accessed from student residence rooms and from off campus. Online class registration, online course evaluations are available.
Website: http://www.calbaptist.edu/

General Application Contact: Taylor Neece, Director of Graduate Admissions, 951-343-4871, Fax: 877-228-8877, E-mail: graduateadmissions@calbaptist.edu.

GRADUATE UNITS

Doctor of Nursing Practice Program Students: 2 part-time (both women). Average age 49. 9 applicants, 33% accepted, 2 enrolled. *Faculty:* 5 full-time (4 women). *Financial support:* Federal Work-Study and scholarships/grants available. Financial award applicants required to submit CSS PROFILE or FAFSA. *Degree program information:* Part-time programs available. Part-time. Offers nursing (DNP). *Application deadline:* For fall admission, 8/1 priority date for domestic students, 7/1 priority date for international students; for spring admission, 12/1 priority date for domestic students, 11/1 priority date for international students. Applications are processed on a rolling basis. *Application fee:* $45. Electronic applications accepted. *Application Contact:* Dr. Lisa Bursch, DNP Program Director, 951-343-4940, E-mail: lbursch@calbaptist.edu. *Dean, School of Nursing*, Dr. Geneva Oaks, 951-343-4702, E-mail: goaks@calbaptist.edu.

Program in Accounting Students: 5 full-time (3 women), 8 part-time (4 women); includes 7 minority (3 Black or African American, non-Hispanic/Latino; 1 Asian, non-Hispanic/Latino; 3 Hispanic/Latino). Average age 34. *Faculty:* 9 full-time (3 women), 1 part-time/adjunct (0 women). *Financial support:* Federal Work-Study and scholarships/grants available. Financial award applicants required to submit CSS PROFILE or FAFSA. *Degree program information:* Part-time and evening/weekend programs available. Part-time, evening/weekend, online only. Offers accounting (MS). *Application deadline:* For fall admission, 8/1 priority date for domestic students, 7/1 priority date for international students; for spring admission, 12/1 priority date for domestic students, 11/1 priority date for international students. Applications are processed on a rolling basis. *Application fee:* $45. Electronic applications accepted. *Application Contact:* Karin Nelson, Program Director, Accounting, 951-552-8777, E-mail: knelson@calbaptist.edu. *Vice President, Online and Professional Studies*, Dr. David Poole, 951-343-3902, E-mail: dpoole@calbaptist.edu.

Program in Applied Mathematics Students: 2 full-time (1 woman), 6 part-time (2 women); includes 3 minority (1 Black or African American, non-Hispanic/Latino; 2 Hispanic/Latino), 1 international. Average age 25. 8 applicants, 100% accepted, 7 enrolled. *Faculty:* 4 full-time (1 woman). *Financial support:* Applicants required to submit CSS PROFILE or FAFSA. *Degree program information:* Part-time programs available. Part-time. Offers applied mathematics (MS). *Application deadline:* For fall admission, 8/1 priority date for domestic students, 7/1 priority date for international students; for spring admission, 12/1 priority date for domestic students, 11/1 priority date for international students. Applications are processed on a rolling basis. *Application fee:* $45. Electronic applications accepted. *Application Contact:* Taylor Neece, Director of Graduate Admissions, 951-343-4871, Fax: 877-228-8877, E-mail: graduateadmissions@calbaptist.edu.

Program in Architecture Students: 60 full-time (24 women), 2 part-time (0 women); includes 29 minority (3 Black or African American, non-Hispanic/Latino; 4 Asian, non-Hispanic/Latino; 20 Hispanic/Latino; 1 Native Hawaiian or other Pacific Islander, non-Hispanic/Latino; 1 Two or more races, non-Hispanic/Latino), 15 international. Average age 21. *Faculty:* 6 full-time (3 women), 3 part-time/adjunct (0 women). *Financial support:* Federal Work-Study and scholarships/grants available. Financial award applicants required to submit CSS PROFILE or FAFSA. Offers architecture (M Arch). *Application deadline:* For fall admission, 8/1 priority date for domestic students, 7/1 for international students; for spring admission, 12/1 priority date for domestic students, 11/1 for international students. Applications are processed on a rolling basis. *Application fee:* $45. Electronic applications accepted. *Application Contact:* Mark Roberson, Dean, College of Architecture, Visual Arts, and Design, 951-552-8652, E-mail: mroberson@calbaptist.edu. *Dean, College of Architecture, Visual Arts, and Design*, Mark Roberson, 951-552-8652, E-mail: maroberson@calbaptist.edu.

Program in Athletic Training Students: 40 full-time (23 women); includes 16 minority (3 Black or African American, non-Hispanic/Latino; 5 Asian, non-Hispanic/Latino; 8 Hispanic/Latino). Average age 26. 8 applicants, 100% accepted, 7 enrolled. *Faculty:* 3 full-time (all women). *Financial support:* Research assistantships, Federal Work-Study, and scholarships/grants available. Financial award applicants required to submit CSS PROFILE or FAFSA. In 2015, 19 master's awarded. *Degree program information:* Part-time programs available. Part-time. Offers athletic training (MS). *Application deadline:* For fall admission, 8/1 priority date for domestic students, 7/1 for international students; for spring admission, 12/1 priority date for domestic students, 11/1 for international students. Applications are processed on a rolling basis. *Application fee:* $45. Electronic applications accepted. *Application Contact:* Dr. Nicole MacDonald, Director, Athletic Training Program, 951-343-4379, E-mail: nmacdona@calbaptist.edu. *Dean of the College of Health Science*, Dr. David Pearson, 951-343-4298, E-mail: dpearson@calbaptist.edu.

Program in Business Administration Students: 56 full-time (26 women), 115 part-time (55 women); includes 80 minority (20 Black or African American, non-Hispanic/Latino; 2 Asian, non-Hispanic/Latino; 55 Hispanic/Latino; 3 Two or more races, non-Hispanic/Latino), 26 international. Average age 30. 232 applicants, 71% accepted, 63 enrolled. *Faculty:* 18 full-time (5 women), 9 part-time/adjunct (1 woman). *Financial support:* Federal Work-Study and scholarships/grants available. Financial award applicants required to submit CSS PROFILE or FAFSA. In 2015, 48 master's awarded. *Degree program information:* Part-time and evening/weekend programs available. Part-time, evening/weekend, 100% online, blended/hybrid learning. Offers accounting (MBA); construction management (MBA); healthcare management (MBA); management (MBA). *Application deadline:* For fall admission, 8/1 priority date for domestic students, 7/1 for international students; for spring admission, 12/1 priority date for domestic students, 11/1 for international students. Applications are processed on a rolling basis. *Application fee:* $45. Electronic applications accepted. *Application Contact:* Stephanie Fluitt, Graduate Admissions Counselor, 951-343-4696, E-mail: sfluitt@calbaptist.edu. *Interim Dean, School of Business*, Dr. Steve Strombeck, 951-343-4701, Fax: 951-343-4361, E-mail: sstrombeck@calbaptist.edu.

Program in Civil Engineering Students: 1 full-time (0 women), 2 part-time (1 woman), 1 international. Average age 22. 21 applicants, 38% accepted, 2 enrolled. *Faculty:* 4 full-time (0 women), 1 part-time/adjunct (0 women). *Financial support:* Applicants required to submit CSS PROFILE or FAFSA. *Degree program information:* Part-time programs available. Part-time. Offers civil engineering (MS). *Application deadline:* For fall admission, 12/1 priority date for domestic students, 11/1 priority date for international students; for spring admission, 8/1 priority date for domestic students, 7/1 priority date for international students. Applications are processed on a rolling basis. *Application fee:* $45. Electronic applications accepted. *Application Contact:* Taylor Neece, Director of Graduate Admissions, 951-343-4871, Fax: 877-228-8877, E-mail: graduateadmissions@calbaptist.edu.

Program in Communication Students: 11 full-time (6 women), 7 part-time (4 women); includes 10 minority (3 Black or African American, non-Hispanic/Latino; 1 Asian, non-Hispanic/Latino; 6 Hispanic/Latino). Average age 29. *Faculty:* 3 full-time (all women), 1 (woman) part-time/adjunct. *Financial support:* Federal Work-Study and scholarships/grants available. Financial award applicants required to submit CSS PROFILE or FAFSA. In 2015, 6 master's awarded. *Degree program information:* Part-time and evening/weekend programs available. Part-time, evening/weekend, online only, 100% online. Offers communication (MA). *Application deadline:* For fall admission, 8/1 priority date for domestic students, 7/1 priority date for international students; for spring admission, 12/1 priority date for domestic students, 11/1 priority date for international students. Applications are processed on a rolling basis. *Application fee:* $45. Electronic applications accepted. *Application Contact:* Dr. MaryAnn Pearson, Program Director of MA in Communication, 951-343-3967, E-mail: mpearson@calbaptist.edu. *Vice President of Online and Professional Studies*, Dr. David Poole, 951-343-3901, E-mail: dpoole@calbaptist.edu.

Program in Counseling Ministry Students: 4 full-time (2 women), 8 part-time (6 women); includes 6 minority (2 Black or African American, non-Hispanic/Latino; 1 Asian, non-Hispanic/Latino; 3 Hispanic/Latino). Average age 35. 10 applicants, 70% accepted, 6 enrolled. *Faculty:* 5 full-time (2 women), 1 (woman) part-time/adjunct. *Financial support:* Federal Work-Study and scholarships/grants available. Financial award applicants required to submit CSS PROFILE or FAFSA. In 2015, 4 master's awarded. *Degree program information:* Part-time and evening/weekend programs available. Part-time, evening/weekend. Offers professional ministry (MA); research in counseling ministry (MA). *Application deadline:* For fall admission, 8/1 priority date for domestic students, 7/1 for international students; for spring admission, 12/1 priority date for domestic students, 11/1 for international students. Applications are processed on a rolling basis. *Application fee:* $45. Electronic applications accepted. *Application Contact:* Dr. Nathan Lewis, Program Director of Counseling Ministry, 951-343-4348, E-mail: nlewis@calbaptist.edu. *Dean, School of Behavioral Sciences*, Dr. Jacqueline Gustafson, 951-343-4487, E-mail: jcraig@calbaptist.edu.

Program in Counseling Ministry and Counseling Psychology (Dual Master's) Students: 9 full-time (6 women), 2 part-time (1 woman); includes 8 minority (2 Asian, non-Hispanic/Latino; 6 Hispanic/Latino). Average age 30. 18 applicants, 33% accepted, 5 enrolled. *Faculty:* 17 full-time (10 women), 7 part-time/adjunct (4 women). *Financial support:* Federal Work-Study and scholarships/grants available. Financial award applicants required to submit CSS PROFILE or FAFSA. *Degree program information:* Part-time and evening/weekend programs available. Part-time, evening/weekend. *Application deadline:* For fall admission, 8/1 priority date for domestic students, 7/1 for international students; for spring admission, 12/1 priority date for domestic students, 11/1 for international students. Applications are processed on a rolling basis. *Application fee:* $45. Electronic applications accepted. *Application Contact:* Mischa Routon, Director of Counseling Psychology Program, 951-343-4206, Fax: 877-228-8877, E-mail: mrouton@calbaptist.edu. *Dean, School of Behavioral Sciences*, Dr. Jacqueline Gustafson, 951-343-4487, E-mail: jcraig@calbaptist.edu.

Program in Counseling Psychology Students: 244 full-time (209 women), 94 part-time (76 women); includes 209 minority (52 Black or African American, non-Hispanic/Latino; 2 American Indian or Alaska Native, non-Hispanic/Latino; 11 Asian, non-Hispanic/Latino; 135 Hispanic/Latino; 9 Two or more races, non-Hispanic/Latino), 2 international. Average age 32. 125 applicants, 65% accepted, 59 enrolled. *Faculty:* 17 full-time (10 women), 6 part-time/adjunct (3 women). *Financial support:* Federal Work-Study and scholarships/grants available. Financial award applicants required to submit CSS PROFILE or FAFSA. In 2015, 98 master's awarded. *Degree program information:* Part-time and evening/weekend programs available. Part-time, evening/weekend, 100% online, blended/hybrid learning. Offers counseling psychology (MS); forensic psychology (MS); professional clinical counselor (MS). *Application deadline:* For fall admission, 8/1 priority date for domestic students, 7/1 for international students; for spring admission, 12/1 priority date for domestic students, 11/1 for international students. Applications are processed on a rolling basis. *Application fee:* $45. Electronic applications accepted. *Application Contact:* Mischa Routon, Associate Dean of Graduate Programs, 951-343-4206, Fax: 951-343-4569, E-mail: mrouton@calbaptist.edu. *Dean, School of Behavioral Sciences*, Dr. Jacqueline Gustafson, 951-343-4487, E-mail: jcraig@calbaptist.edu.

Program in Disability Studies Students: 16 part-time (14 women); includes 5 minority (2 Black or African American, non-Hispanic/Latino; 2 Hispanic/Latino; 1 Two or more races, non-Hispanic/Latino). Average age 41. 25 applicants, 64% accepted, 9 enrolled. *Faculty:* 3 full-time (1 woman), 3 part-time/adjunct (1 woman). *Financial support:* Federal Work-Study and scholarships/grants available. Financial award applicants required to submit CSS PROFILE or FAFSA. In 2015, 9 master's awarded. *Degree program information:* Part-time and evening/weekend programs available. Part-time, evening/weekend, 100% online. Offers disability ministry (MA); disability policy (MA). *Application deadline:* For fall admission, 8/1 priority date for domestic students, 7/1 for international students; for spring admission, 12/1 priority date for domestic students, 11/1 for international students. Applications are processed on a rolling basis. *Application fee:* $45. Electronic applications accepted. *Application Contact:* Dr. Jeff McNair, Program Director, MA in Disability Studies, 951-343-4489, E-mail: jmcnair@calbaptist.edu. *Vice President, Online and Professional Studies*, Dr. David Poole, 951-343-3901, E-mail: dpoole@calbaptist.edu.

Program in Education Students: 168 full-time (139 women), 292 part-time (229 women); includes 183 minority (22 Black or African American, non-Hispanic/Latino; 2 American Indian or Alaska Native, non-Hispanic/Latino; 12 Asian, non-Hispanic/Latino; 133 Hispanic/Latino; 1 Native Hawaiian or other Pacific Islander, non-Hispanic/Latino; 13 Two or more races, non-Hispanic/Latino), 4 international. Average age 31. 219 applicants, 75% accepted, 151 enrolled. *Faculty:* 19 full-time (9 women), 13 part-time/adjunct (8 women). *Financial support:* Federal Work-Study and scholarships/grants available. Financial award applicants required to submit FAFSA. In 2015, 124 master's awarded. *Degree program information:* Part-time and evening/weekend programs available. Part-time, evening/weekend, 100% online. Offers educational leadership (MS); educational leadership for faith-based institutions (MS); educational leadership for public institutions (MS); educational technology (MS); instructional computer applications (MS); international education (MS); leadership and adult learning (MS); leadership and organizational studies (MS); online teaching and learning (MS); reading (MS); science education (MA); special education in mild/moderate disabilities (MS); special education in moderate/severe disabilities (MS); teacher leadership (MS); teaching (MS); teaching and learning (MS). *Application deadline:* For fall admission, 8/1 priority date for domestic students, 7/1 for international students; for spring admission, 12/1 priority date for domestic students, 11/1 for international students. Applications are processed on a rolling basis. *Application fee:* $45. Electronic applications accepted. *Application Contact:* Dr. John Shoup, Dean, School of Education, 951-343-4516, E-mail: jshoup@calbaptist.edu. *Dean, School of Education*, Dr. John Shoup, 951-343-4205, Fax: 951-343-4516, E-mail: jshoup@calbaptist.edu.

Program in English Students: 2 full-time (1 woman), 30 part-time (23 women); includes 15 minority (4 Black or African American, non-Hispanic/Latino; 2 Asian, non-Hispanic/Latino; 9 Hispanic/Latino), 2 international. Average age 30. 17 applicants, 76% accepted, 11 enrolled. *Faculty:* 11 full-time (5 women). *Financial support:* Federal Work-Study and scholarships/grants available. Financial award applicants required to submit CSS PROFILE or FAFSA. *Degree program information:* Part-time and evening/weekend programs available. Part-time, evening/weekend. Offers English pedagogy (MA); literature (MA); teaching English to speakers of other languages (TESOL) (MA). *Application deadline:* For fall admission, 8/1 priority date for domestic students, 7/1 for international students; for spring admission, 12/1 priority date for domestic students, 11/1 for international students. Applications are processed on a rolling basis. *Application fee:* $45. Electronic applications accepted. *Application Contact:* Dr. Laura Veltman, Director, Master of Arts Program in English, 951-343-4276, Fax: 951-343-4661, E-mail: lveltman@calbaptist.edu. *Dean, College of Arts and Sciences*, Dr. Gayne Anacker, 951-343-4682, E-mail: ganacker@calbaptist.edu.

Program in Forensic Psychology Students: 52 full-time (42 women), 11 part-time (7 women); includes 34 minority (7 Black or African American, non-Hispanic/Latino; 2 American Indian or Alaska Native, non-Hispanic/Latino; 1 Asian, non-Hispanic/Latino; 24 Hispanic/Latino). Average age 28. 32 applicants, 59% accepted, 19 enrolled. *Faculty:* 9 full-time (5 women), 1 (woman) part-time/adjunct. *Financial support:* Federal Work-Study and scholarships/grants available. Financial award applicants required to submit CSS PROFILE or FAFSA. In 2015, 26 master's awarded. *Degree program information:* Part-time and evening/weekend programs available. Part-time, evening/weekend. Offers forensic psychology (MA). *Application deadline:* For fall admission, 8/1 priority date for domestic students, 7/1 for international students; for spring admission, 12/1 priority date for domestic students, 11/1 for international students. Applications are processed on a rolling basis. *Application fee:* $45. Electronic applications accepted. *Application Contact:* Dr. Anne-Marie Larsen, Director, Graduate Program in Forensic Psychology, 951-343-4761, E-mail: alarsen@calbaptist.edu. *Dean, School of Behavioral Sciences*, Dr. Jacqueline Gustafson, 951-343-4487, E-mail: jcraig@calbaptist.edu.

Program in Higher Education Leadership and Student Development Students: 1 (woman) full-time, 21 part-time (17 women); includes 10 minority (1 Black or African American, non-Hispanic/Latino; 9 Hispanic/Latino), 1 international. Average age 29. 21 applicants, 90% accepted, 14 enrolled. *Faculty:* 5 full-time (3 women), 2 part-time/adjunct (0 women). *Financial support:* Federal Work-Study and scholarships/grants available. *Degree program information:* Part-time and evening/weekend programs available. Part-time, evening/weekend. Offers higher education leadership and student development (MS). *Application deadline:* For fall admission, 8/1 priority date for domestic students, 7/1 for international students; for spring admission, 12/1 priority date for domestic students, 11/1 for international students. Applications are processed on a rolling basis. *Application fee:* $45. Electronic applications accepted. *Application Contact:* Dr. Shana Matamala, Associate Dean, School of Education, 951-343-4760, E-mail: smatamala@calbaptist.edu. *Dean, School of Education*, Dr. John Shoup, 951-343-4205, E-mail: jshoup@calbaptist.edu.

Program in Kinesiology Students: 47 full-time (21 women), 30 part-time (13 women); includes 33 minority (10 Black or African American, non-Hispanic/Latino; 6 Asian, non-Hispanic/Latino; 14 Hispanic/Latino; 3 Two or more races, non-Hispanic/Latino), 13 international. Average age 26. 42 applicants, 83% accepted, 33 enrolled. *Faculty:* 13 full-time (5 women), 7 part-time/adjunct (2 women). *Financial support:* Federal Work-Study, scholarships/grants, and unspecified assistantships available. Financial award applicants required to submit CSS PROFILE or FAFSA. In 2015, 19 master's awarded. *Degree program information:* Part-time programs available. Part-time, 100% online, blended/hybrid learning. Offers exercise science (MS); physical education (MS); sport management (MS). *Application deadline:* For fall admission, 8/1 priority date for domestic students, 7/1 for international students; for spring admission, 12/1 priority date for domestic students, 11/1 for international students. Applications are processed on a rolling basis. *Application fee:* $45. Electronic applications accepted. *Application Contact:* Dr. Sean Sullivan, Chair, Department of Kinesiology, 951-343-4528, Fax: 951-343-5095, E-mail: ssullivan@calbaptist.edu. *Dean, College of Allied Health*, Dr. David Pearson, 951-343-4298, E-mail: dpearson@calbaptist.edu.

Program in Leadership and Adult Learning 1 applicant. *Financial support:* Applicants required to submit CSS PROFILE or FAFSA. *Degree program information:* Part-time and evening/weekend programs available. Part-time, evening/weekend. Offers leadership and adult learning (MA). *Application deadline:* For fall admission, 8/1 priority date for domestic students, 7/1 priority date for international students; for spring admission, 12/1 priority date for domestic students, 11/1 priority date for international students. Applications are processed on a rolling basis. *Application fee:* $45. Electronic applications accepted. *Application Contact:* 877-228-8877. *Dean, School of Education*, Dr. John Shoup, 951-343-4205, E-mail: jshoup@calbaptist.edu.

Program in Leadership and Community Development Students: 2 part-time; includes 1 minority (Hispanic/Latino). Average age 24. 3 applicants, 67% accepted, 2 enrolled. *Faculty:* 5 full-time (2 women), 1 part-time/adjunct (0 women). *Financial support:* Applicants required to submit CSS PROFILE or FAFSA. *Degree program information:* Part-time and evening/weekend programs available. Part-time, evening/weekend. Offers leadership and community development (MA). *Application deadline:* For fall admission, 8/1 priority date for domestic students, 7/1 priority date for international students; for spring admission, 12/1 for domestic students, 11/1 priority date for international students. Applications are processed on a rolling basis. *Application fee:* $45. Electronic applications accepted. *Application Contact:* Taylor Neece, Director of Graduate Admissions, 951-343-4871, Fax: 877-228-8877, E-mail: graduateadmissions@calbaptist.edu. *Dean, School of Education*, Dr. John Shoup, 951-343-4205, E-mail: jshoup@calbaptist.edu.

Program in Leadership and Organizational Studies Students: 15 part-time (6 women); includes 8 minority (2 Black or African American, non-Hispanic/Latino; 5 Hispanic/Latino; 1 Two or more races, non-Hispanic/Latino). Average age 36. 20 applicants, 45% accepted, 6 enrolled. *Faculty:* 4 full-time (1 woman), 3 part-time/adjunct (1 woman). *Financial support:* Applicants required to submit CSS PROFILE or FAFSA. *Degree program information:* Part-time and evening/weekend programs available. Part-time, evening/weekend. Offers leadership and organizational studies (MA). *Application deadline:* For fall admission, 8/1 priority date for domestic students, 7/1 for international students; for spring admission, 11/1 priority date for domestic students, 11/1 for international students. Applications are processed on a rolling basis. *Application fee:* $45. Electronic applications accepted. *Application Contact:* Dr. Shana Matamala, Associate Dean, School of Education, 951-343-4760, E-mail: smatamala@calbaptist.edu. *Dean, School of Education*, Dr. John Shoup, 951-343-4205, E-mail: jshoup@calbaptist.edu.

Program in Music Students: 12 full-time (9 women), 7 part-time (3 women); includes 7 minority (2 Black or African American, non-Hispanic/Latino; 1 Asian, non-Hispanic/Latino; 4 Hispanic/Latino), 5 international. Average age 25. 8 applicants, 88% accepted, 6 enrolled. *Faculty:* 11 full-time (5 women), 5 part-time/adjunct (2 women). *Financial support:* Federal Work-Study and scholarships/grants available. Financial award applicants required to submit CSS PROFILE or FAFSA. In 2015, 6 master's awarded. *Degree program information:* Part-time and evening/weekend programs available. Part-time, evening/weekend. Offers conducting (MM); music education (MM); performance (MM). *Application deadline:* For fall admission, 8/1 priority date for domestic students, 7/1 for international students; for spring admission, 12/1 priority date for domestic students, 11/1 for international students. Applications are processed on a rolling basis. *Application fee:* $45. Electronic applications accepted. *Application Contact:* Stephanie Fluitt, Graduate Admissions Counselor, 952-343-4696, E-mail: sfluitt@calbaptist.edu. *Dean, School of Music*, Dr. Judd Bonner, 951-343-4256, Fax: 951-343-4570, E-mail: jbonner@calbaptist.edu.

Program in Nursing Students: 77 full-time (63 women), 143 part-time (117 women); includes 111 minority (26 Black or African American, non-Hispanic/Latino; 3 American Indian or Alaska Native, non-Hispanic/Latino; 38 Asian, non-Hispanic/Latino; 39 Hispanic/Latino; 1 Native Hawaiian or other Pacific Islander, non-Hispanic/Latino; 4 Two or more races, non-Hispanic/Latino), 5 international. Average age 33. 44 applicants, 64% accepted, 23 enrolled. *Faculty:* 18 full-time (17 women), 14 part-time/adjunct (11 women). *Financial support:* Federal Work-Study and scholarships/grants available. Financial award applicants required to submit CSS PROFILE or FAFSA. In 2015, 19 master's awarded. *Degree program information:* Part-time programs available. Part-time. Offers clinical nurse specialist (MSN); family nurse practitioner (MSN); healthcare systems management (MSN); teaching-learning (MSN). *Application deadline:* For fall admission, 8/1 priority date for domestic students, 7/1 for international students; for spring admission, 12/1 priority date for domestic students, 11/1 for international students. Applications are processed on a rolling basis. *Application fee:* $45. Electronic applications accepted. *Application Contact:* Dr. Rebecca Meyer, Director, Graduate Program in Nursing, 951-343-4952, Fax: 951-343-5095, E-mail: rmeyer@calbaptist.edu. *Dean, School of Nursing*, Dr. Geneva Oaks, 951-343-4702, E-mail: goaks@calbaptist.edu.

Program in Organizational Leadership Students: 29 full-time (17 women), 23 part-time (16 women); includes 28 minority (10 Black or African American, non-Hispanic/Latino; 4 Asian, non-Hispanic/Latino; 13 Hispanic/Latino; 1 Two or more races, non-Hispanic/Latino). Average age 38. *Faculty:* 5 full-time (1 woman). *Financial support:* Federal Work-Study and scholarships/grants available. Financial award applicants required to submit CSS PROFILE or FAFSA. In 2015, 4 master's awarded. *Degree program information:* Part-time and evening/weekend programs available. Part-time, evening/weekend, 100% online. Offers organizational leadership (MA). *Application deadline:* For fall admission, 8/1 for domestic students. Applications are processed on a rolling basis. Electronic applications accepted. *Application Contact:* Dr. Greg Bowden, Director of Master's in Organizational Leadership, 951-343-5560, E-mail: abowden@calbaptist.edu. *Vice President, Online and Professional Studies*, Dr. David Poole, 951-343-3902, E-mail: dpoole@calbaptist.edu.

Program in Physician Assistant Studies ***Financial support:*** Applicants required to submit CSS PROFILE or FAFSA. Offers physician assistant studies (MS). *Application deadline:* For fall admission, 12/1 priority date for domestic students, 11/1 priority date for international students; for spring admission, 8/1 priority date for domestic students, 7/1 priority date for international students. Applications are processed on a rolling basis. *Application fee:* $45. Electronic applications accepted. *Application Contact:* Taylor Neece, Director of Graduate Admissions, 951-343-4871, Fax: 877-228-8877, E-mail: graduateadmissions@calbaptist.edu. *Director*, Dr. Allan M. Bedashi, 951-552-8838, E-mail: abedashi@calbaptist.edu.

Program in Public Administration Students: 54 full-time (35 women), 32 part-time (21 women); includes 60 minority (14 Black or African American, non-Hispanic/Latino; 1 American Indian or Alaska Native, non-Hispanic/Latino; 41 Hispanic/Latino; 4 Two or more races, non-Hispanic/Latino). Average age 34. 86 applicants, 64% accepted, 33 enrolled. *Faculty:* 5 full-time (3 women), 3 part-time/adjunct (all women). *Financial support:* Federal Work-Study and scholarships/grants available. Financial award applicants required to submit CSS PROFILE or FAFSA. In 2015, 82 master's awarded. *Degree program information:* Part-time and evening/weekend programs available. Part-time, evening/weekend, 100% online, blended/hybrid learning. Offers public administration (MPA); strategic innovation (MPA). *Application deadline:* For fall admission, 8/1 priority date for domestic students, 7/1 for international students; for spring admission, 12/1 priority date for domestic students, 11/1 for international students. Applications are processed on a rolling basis. *Application fee:* $45. Electronic applications accepted. *Application Contact:* Dr. Elaine Ahumada, Director, MPA Program, 951-343-3929, Fax: 951-343-4661, E-mail: eahumada@calbaptist.edu. *Vice President, Online and Professional Studies*, Dr. David Poole, 951-343-3902, E-mail: dpoole@calbaptist.edu.

Program in Public Health Students: 41 full-time (36 women), 9 part-time (8 women); includes 33 minority (4 Black or African American, non-Hispanic/Latino; 1 Asian, non-Hispanic/Latino; 26 Hispanic/Latino; 2 Two or more races, non-Hispanic/Latino), 2 international. Average age 25. 41 applicants, 71% accepted, 26 enrolled. *Faculty:* 7 full-time (4 women), 3 part-time/adjunct (2 women). *Financial support:* Federal Work-Study and scholarships/grants available. Financial award applicants required to submit CSS PROFILE or FAFSA. *Degree program information:* Part-time and evening/weekend programs available. Part-time, evening/weekend. Offers health education and promotion (MPH); health policy and administration (MPH). *Application deadline:* For fall admission, 8/1 priority date for domestic students, 7/1 for international students; for spring admission, 12/1 priority date for domestic students, 11/1 for international students. Applications are processed on a rolling basis. *Application fee:* $45. Electronic applications accepted. *Application Contact:* Dr. Robert LaChausse, Chair, Department of Public Health Sciences, 951-552-8484, E-mail: rlachausse@calbaptist.edu. *Dean, College of Health Science*, Dr. David Pearson, 951-343-4298, E-mail: dpearson@calbaptist.edu.

Program in Public Relations Students: 9 full-time (7 women), 8 part-time (7 women); includes 12 minority (7 Black or African American, non-Hispanic/Latino; 4 Hispanic/Latino; 1 Two or more races, non-Hispanic/Latino). Average age 31. *Faculty:* 2 full-time (both women), 2 part-time/adjunct (both women). *Financial support:* Applicants required to submit CSS PROFILE or FAFSA. In 2015, 20 master's awarded. *Degree program information:* Part-time and evening/weekend programs available. Part-time, evening/weekend, online learning. Offers public relations (MA). *Application deadline:* For fall admission, 8/1 priority date for domestic students, 7/1 for international students; for spring admission, 12/1 priority date for domestic students, 11/1 priority date for international students. Applications are processed on a rolling basis. *Application fee:* $45. Electronic applications accepted. *Application Contact:* Dr. Maryann Pearson, Program Director, MA in Public Relations, 951-343-3967, E-mail: mpearson@calbaptist.edu. *Vice President of Online and Professional Studies*, Dr. David Poole, 951-343-3902, E-mail: dpoole@calbaptist.edu.

Program in School Counseling Students: 27 part-time (24 women); includes 19 minority (3 Black or African American, non-Hispanic/Latino; 1 American Indian or Alaska Native, non-Hispanic/Latino; 15 Hispanic/Latino). Average age 33. 38 applicants, 61% accepted, 21 enrolled. *Faculty:* 2 full-time (both women), 2 part-time/adjunct (1 woman). *Financial support:* Applicants required to submit CSS PROFILE or FAFSA. In 2015, 2 master's awarded. *Degree program information:* Part-time and evening/weekend programs available. Part-time, evening/weekend. Offers school counseling (MS). *Application deadline:* For fall admission, 8/1 priority date for domestic students, 7/7 priority date for international students; for spring admission, 12/1 priority date for domestic students, 11/1 priority date for international students. Applications are processed on a rolling basis. *Application fee:* $45. Electronic applications accepted. *Application Contact:* Dr. Nona Cabral, Program Coordinator, School Counseling, 951-343-4804, E-mail: ncabral@calbaptist.edu. *Dean, School of Education*, Dr. John Shoup, 951-343-4205, E-mail: jshoup@calbaptist.edu.

Program in School Psychology Students: 13 full-time (12 women), 22 part-time (19 women); includes 17 minority (3 Black or African American, non-Hispanic/Latino; 3 Asian, non-Hispanic/Latino; 11 Hispanic/Latino). Average age 33. 29 applicants, 66% accepted, 17 enrolled. *Faculty:* 2 full-time (both women), 5 part-time/adjunct (2 women). *Financial support:* Applicants required to submit CSS PROFILE or FAFSA. In 2015, 1 master's awarded. *Degree program information:* Part-time and evening/weekend programs available. Part-time, evening/weekend. Offers school psychology (MS). *Application deadline:* For fall admission, 7/1 priority date for domestic and international students; for spring admission, 12/1 priority date for domestic students, 11/1 priority date for international students. Applications are processed on a rolling basis. *Application fee:* $45. Electronic applications accepted. *Application Contact:* Dr. Jane McGuire, Program Coordinator, School Psychology, 951-343-4707, E-mail: jmcguire@calbaptiat.edu. *Dean, School of Education*, Dr. John Shoup, 951-343-4205, E-mail: jshoup@calbaptist.edu.

Program in Software Engineering Students: 4 full-time, 1 part-time; includes 1 minority (Asian, non-Hispanic/Latino), 3 international. Average age 23. 99 applicants, 47% accepted, 7 enrolled. *Faculty:* 3 full-time. *Financial support:* Applicants required to submit CSS PROFILE or FAFSA. *Degree program information:* Part-time programs available. Part-time. Offers software engineering (MS). *Application deadline:* For fall admission, 8/1 priority date for domestic students, 7/1 priority date for international students; for spring admission, 12/1 priority date for domestic students, 11/1 priority date for international students. Applications are processed on a rolling basis. *Application fee:* $45. Electronic applications accepted. *Application Contact:* Taylor Neece, Director of Graduate Admissions, 951-343-4871, Fax: 877-228-8877, E-mail: graduateadmissions@calbaptist.edu.

Program in Speech Language Pathology ***Financial support:*** Applicants required to submit CSS PROFILE or FAFSA. Offers speech language pathology (MS). *Application deadline:* For fall admission, 12/1 priority date for domestic students, 11/1 priority date for international students; for spring admission, 8/1 priority date for domestic students, 7/1 priority date for international students. Applications are processed on a rolling basis. *Application fee:* $45. Electronic applications accepted. *Application Contact:* Taylor Neece, Director of Graduate Admissions, 951-343-4871, Fax: 877-228-8877, E-mail: graduateadmissions@calbaptist.edu. *Director*, Dr. Candace Vickers, 951-552-8129, E-mail: cvickers@calbaptist.edu.

CALIFORNIA COAST UNIVERSITY, Santa Ana, CA 92701

General Information Proprietary, coed, comprehensive institution.

GRADUATE UNITS

School of Administration and Management Online learning. Offers business marketing (MBA); health care management (MBA); human resource management (MBA); management (MBA, MS). Electronic applications accepted.

School of Behavioral Science Online learning. Offers psychology (MS).

School of Criminal Justice Offers criminal justice (MS).

School of Education Online learning. Offers administration (M Ed); curriculum and instruction (M Ed); educational administration (Ed D); educational psychology (Ed D); organizational leadership (Ed D).

CALIFORNIA COLLEGE OF THE ARTS, San Francisco, CA 94107

General Information Independent, coed, comprehensive institution. *Enrollment:* 1,988 graduate, professional, and undergraduate students; 419 full-time matriculated graduate/professional students (273 women), 35 part-time matriculated graduate/professional students (23 women). *Enrollment by degree level:* 455 master's. *Graduate faculty:* 56 full-time (32 women), 131 part-time/adjunct (68 women). *Required fees:* $230. *Graduate housing:* Room and/or apartments available on a first-come, first-served basis to single students; on-campus housing not available to married students. Housing application deadline: 4/1. *Student services:* Campus employment opportunities, campus safety program, career counseling, exercise/wellness program, free psychological counseling, grant writing training, international student services, low-cost health insurance, services for students with disabilities, writing training. *Library:* Meyer Library plus 1 other.

Computer facilities: Computer purchase and lease plans are available. 400 computers available on campus for general student use. A campuswide network can be accessed from student residence rooms and from off campus. Online class registration, online course evaluations, Learning Management System, VoiceThread, Lynda.com,print payments are available.
Website: http://www.cca.edu/

General Application Contact: Wes Fanelli, Assistant Director of Graduate Admissions, 415-703-9533, Fax: 415-703-9539, E-mail: graduateprograms@cca.edu.

GRADUATE UNITS

Graduate Programs Students: 438 full-time (270 women), 25 part-time (16 women); includes 136 minority (30 Black or African American, non-Hispanic/Latino; 4 American Indian or Alaska Native, non-Hispanic/Latino; 57 Asian, non-Hispanic/Latino; 45 Hispanic/Latino), 72 international. Average age 31. *Financial support:* Fellowships, teaching assistantships, Federal Work-Study, scholarships/grants, and unspecified assistantships available. Financial award applicants required to submit FAFSA. Offers advanced architecture design (MAAD); architecture (M Arch); ceramics (MFA); creative non-fiction (MFA); curatorial practice (MA); design strategy (MBA); fiction (MFA); film/video/performance (MFA); glass (MFA); graphic design (MFA); industrial design (MFA); interaction design (MFA); interdisciplinary studies (MFA); jewelry/metal arts (MFA); media studies (MFA); painting/drawing (MFA); photography (MFA); poetry (MFA); printmaking (MFA); sculpture (MFA); textiles (MFA); visual and critical studies (MA); wood/furniture (MFA). *Application deadline:* For fall admission, 1/5 for domestic and international students. *Application fee:* $70. *Application Contact:* Wes Fanelli, Assistant Director of Graduate Admissions, 415-703-9533, Fax: 415-703-9539, E-mail: wfanelli@cca.edu. *Director of Graduate Admissions*, Noel Dahl, 415-703-9537, Fax: 415-703-9539, E-mail: ndahl@cca.edu.

CALIFORNIA INSTITUTE OF INTEGRAL STUDIES, San Francisco, CA 94103

General Information Independent, coed, upper-level institution. CGS member. *Enrollment:* 1,495 graduate, professional, and undergraduate students; 1,100 full-time matriculated graduate/professional students (801 women), 308 part-time matriculated graduate/professional students (227 women). *Enrollment by degree level:* 807 master's, 601 doctoral. *Graduate housing:* On-campus housing not available. *Student services:* Campus employment opportunities, campus safety program, career counseling, grant writing training, international student services, low-cost health insurance, multicultural affairs office, services for students with disabilities, writing training. *Library:* The Laurance S. Rockefeller Library plus 1 other. *Research affiliation:* Bay Area Reference Service.

Computer facilities: 25 computers available on campus for general student use. A campuswide network can be accessed from off campus. Online class registration is available.
Website: http://www.ciis.edu/

General Application Contact: Ellen Durst, Interim Director of Admissions, 415-575-6153, Fax: 415-575-1264, E-mail: admissions@ciis.edu.

GRADUATE UNITS

American College of Traditional Chinese Medicine Students: 170 full-time (127 women), 64 part-time (44 women); includes 91 minority (5 Black or African American, non-Hispanic/Latino; 2 American Indian or Alaska Native, non-Hispanic/Latino; 66 Asian, non-Hispanic/Latino; 12 Hispanic/Latino; 6 Native Hawaiian or other Pacific Islander, non-Hispanic/Latino), 8 international. Average age 37. 55 applicants, 91% accepted, 34 enrolled. Offers acupuncture and Chinese medicine (DACM, tDACM); acupuncture and Oriental medicine (DAOM); traditional Chinese medicine (MSTCM). *Application deadline:* For fall admission, 8/1 priority date for domestic students. *Application fee:* $65. Electronic applications accepted. *Application Contact:* Yuwen Chiu, Associate Director of Admissions, 415-828-7600, E-mail: yuwenchiu@actcm.edu. *Academic Dean,* Dr. Bingzen Zou, 415-8287600, E-mail: bingzou@actcm.edu.

School of Consciousness and Transformation Students: 386 full-time (263 women), 111 part-time (80 women); includes 127 minority (31 Black or African American, non-Hispanic/Latino; 3 American Indian or Alaska Native, non-Hispanic/Latino; 18 Asian, non-Hispanic/Latino; 43 Hispanic/Latino; 2 Native Hawaiian or other Pacific Islander, non-Hispanic/Latino; 30 Two or more races, non-Hispanic/Latino), 39 international. Average age 38. 188 applicants, 91% accepted, 107 enrolled. *Financial support:* Research assistantships, teaching assistantships, career-related internships or fieldwork, Federal Work-Study, and scholarships/grants available. Support available to part-time students. Financial award application deadline: 4/15; financial award applicants required to submit FAFSA. In 2015, 75 master's, 41 doctorates awarded. *Degree program information:* Part-time and evening/weekend programs available. Part-time, evening/weekend, 100% online, blended/hybrid learning. Offers anthropology and social change (MA, PhD); Asian philosophies and cultures (MA, PhD); creative inquiry/interdisciplinary arts (MFA); East-West psychology (MA, PhD); integral and transpersonal psychology (PhD); philosophy and religion (MA, PhD); theater and performance making (MFA); transformative leadership (MA); transformative studies (PhD); women, gender, spirituality and social justice (MA); writing and consciousness (MFA). *Application deadline:* For fall admission, 2/1 priority date for domestic and international students; for spring admission, 10/15 priority date for domestic and international students. Applications are processed on a rolling basis. *Application fee:* $65. Electronic applications accepted. *Application Contact:* Ellen Durst, Interim Director of Admissions, 415-575-6100, Fax: 415-575-1268, E-mail: admissions@ciis.edu.

School of Professional Psychology and Health Students: 544 full-time (411 women), 133 part-time (103 women); includes 179 minority (27 Black or African American, non-Hispanic/Latino; 6 American Indian or Alaska Native, non-Hispanic/Latino; 34 Asian, non-Hispanic/Latino; 71 Hispanic/Latino; 4 Native Hawaiian or other Pacific Islander, non-Hispanic/Latino; 37 Two or more races, non-Hispanic/Latino), 60 international. Average age 38. 392 applicants, 85% accepted, 191 enrolled. *Financial support:* Research assistantships with tuition reimbursements, teaching assistantships with tuition reimbursements, career-related internships or fieldwork, Federal Work-Study, and scholarships/grants available. Support available to part-time students. Financial award application deadline: 4/15; financial award applicants required to submit FAFSA. In 2015, 177 master's, 17 doctorates awarded. *Degree program information:* Part-time and evening/weekend programs available. Part-time, evening/weekend, blended/hybrid learning. Offers clinical psychology (Psy D); community mental health (MA); drama therapy (MA); expressive arts therapy (MA); human sexuality (PhD); integral counseling psychology (MA); integrative health studies (MA); psychological studies (MA); somatic psychology (MA). *Application deadline:* For fall admission, 2/1 priority date for domestic and international students; for spring admission, 10/15 priority date for domestic and international students. Applications are processed on a rolling basis. *Application fee:* $65. Electronic applications accepted. *Application Contact:* Ellen Durst, Interim Director of Admissions, 415-575-6100, Fax: 415-575-1268, E-mail: admissions@ciis.edu.

CALIFORNIA INSTITUTE OF TECHNOLOGY, Pasadena, CA 91125-0001

General Information Independent, coed, university. CGS member. *Graduate housing:* Rooms and/or apartments available on a first-come, first-served basis to single students and available to married students. Housing application deadline: 5/1. *Research affiliation:* Scripps Institute of Oceanography, Stanford Linear Accelerator Center (high-energy physics), European Center for Nuclear Research (high-energy physics), National Science Foundation Center for Research in Parallel Computing, Cosmic Gravitational Waves Observatory (laser interferometer gravitational waves).

GRADUATE UNITS

Division of Biology Offers biochemistry and molecular biophysics (PhD); cell biology and biophysics (PhD); developmental biology (PhD); genetics (PhD); immunology (PhD); molecular biology (PhD); neurobiology (PhD). Electronic applications accepted.

Division of Chemistry and Chemical Engineering Students: 309 full-time (98 women); includes 1 minority (Black or African American, non-Hispanic/Latino). Average age 26. 710 applicants, 21% accepted, 59 enrolled. *Faculty:* 41 full-time (7 women). *Financial support:* In 2015–16, 309 students received support, including fellowships (averaging $31,000 per year), research assistantships (averaging $25,900 per year), teaching assistantships (averaging $5,100 per year); Federal Work-Study, institutionally sponsored loans, scholarships/grants, traineeships, health care benefits, and unspecified assistantships also available. Financial award application deadline: 12/15. In 2015, 14 master's, 59 doctorates awarded. Offers biochemistry and molecular biophysics (MS, PhD); chemical engineering (MS, PhD); chemistry (MS, PhD). *Application deadline:* For fall admission, 12/15 for domestic and international students. *Application fee:* $100. Electronic applications accepted. *Application Contact:* Natalie Gilmore, Graduate Office, 626-395-3812, Fax: 626-577-9246, E-mail: ngilmore@its.caltech.edu. *Chair, Division of Chemistry and Chemical Engineering,* Prof. Jacqueline K. Barton, 626-395-3646, Fax: 626-395-6948, E-mail: jkbarton@caltech.edu.

Division of Engineering and Applied Science Offers aeronautics (MS, PhD, Engr); applied and computational mathematics (MS, PhD); applied mechanics (MS, PhD); applied physics (MS, PhD); bioengineering (MS, PhD); civil engineering (MS, PhD, Engr); computation and neural systems (MS, PhD); computer science (MS, PhD); control and dynamical systems (MS, PhD); electrical engineering (MS, PhD, Engr); environmental science and engineering (MS, PhD); materials science (MS, PhD); mechanical engineering (MS, PhD, Engr). Electronic applications accepted.

Division of Geological and Planetary Sciences Offers environmental science and engineering (MS, PhD); geobiology (MS, PhD); geochemistry (MS, PhD); geology (MS, PhD); geophysics (MS, PhD); planetary science (MS, PhD). Electronic applications accepted.

Division of Physics, Mathematics and Astronomy Offers astronomy (PhD); mathematics (PhD); physics (PhD).

Division of the Humanities and Social Sciences Students: 32 full-time (10 women), 29 international. Average age 27. 308 applicants, 8% accepted, 5 enrolled. *Faculty:* 32 full-time (4 women). *Financial support:* In 2015–16, 32 students received support, including 12 fellowships with tuition reimbursements available (averaging $30,500 per year), 5 research assistantships with tuition reimbursements available (averaging $30,500 per year), 13 teaching assistantships with tuition reimbursements available (averaging $30,500 per year); Federal Work-Study, institutionally sponsored loans, and scholarships/grants also available. In 2015, 3 master's, 9 doctorates awarded. Offers humanities and social sciences (MS, PhD); social science (MS, PhD). *Application deadline:* For fall admission, 12/15 for domestic and international students. *Application fee:* $100. Electronic applications accepted. *Application Contact:* Division Option Manager, HSS Social Sciences Graduate Programs, 626-395-4206, Fax: 626-405-9841, E-mail: gradsec@hss.caltech.edu. *Chair,* Dr. Jean Laurent Rosenthal, 626-395-4082, E-mail: jlr@hss.caltech.edu.

CALIFORNIA INSTITUTE OF THE ARTS, Valencia, CA 91355-2340

General Information Independent, coed, comprehensive institution. *Graduate housing:* Room and/or apartments available on a first-come, first-served basis to single students; on-campus housing not available to married students. Housing application deadline: 7/1.

GRADUATE UNITS

School of Art Offers art (MFA, Adv C); graphic design (MFA, Adv C); photography (MFA, Adv C). Electronic applications accepted.

School of Critical Studies Offers writing (MFA, Adv C).

School of Dance Offers dance (MFA, Adv C).

School of Film/Video Offers experimental animation (MFA); film directing (MFA, Adv C); film/video (Adv C). Electronic applications accepted.

School of Music ***Degree program information:*** Part-time programs available. Part-time. Offers African music (MFA, Adv C); composition (MFA, Adv C); composition/new media (MFA, Adv C); Indonesian music (MFA, Adv C); jazz (MFA, Adv C); North Indian music (MFA, Adv C); performance (MFA, Adv C); performer/composer (MFA, Adv C); voice (MFA, Adv C); world music performance (MFA). Electronic applications accepted.

School of Theatre Offers acting (MFA, Adv C); design and technology (Adv C); directing (MFA); performing arts design and technology (MFA); theater management (MFA, Adv C); writing for performance (MFA). Electronic applications accepted.

CALIFORNIA INTERCONTINENTAL UNIVERSITY, Irvine, CA 92614

General Information Proprietary, coed, comprehensive institution.

GRADUATE UNITS

Hollywood College of the Entertainment Industry Offers Hollywood and entertainment management (MBA).

School of Business Offers banking and finance (MBA); entrepreneurship and business management (DBA); global business leadership (DBA); international management and marketing (MBA); organizational management and human resource management (MBA).

School of Healthcare Offers healthcare management and leadership (MBA, DBA).

School of Information Technology Offers information systems and enterprise resource management (DBA); information systems and knowledge management (MBA); project and quality management (MBA).

CALIFORNIA INTERNATIONAL BUSINESS UNIVERSITY, San Diego, CA 92101

General Information Independent, coed, graduate-only institution.

GRADUATE UNITS

Graduate Programs Offers business (MBA, MSIM, DBA).

CALIFORNIA LUTHERAN UNIVERSITY, Thousand Oaks, CA 91360-2787

General Information Independent-religious, coed, comprehensive institution. CGS member. *Graduate housing:* Room and/or apartments available on a first-come, first-served basis to single students; on-campus housing not available to married students.

GRADUATE UNITS

Graduate Studies ***Degree program information:*** Part-time and evening/weekend programs available. Part-time, evening/weekend. Offers clinical psychology (MS, Psy D); marital and family therapy (MS); public policy and administration (MPPA). Electronic applications accepted.

Graduate School of Education Degree program information: Part-time and evening/weekend programs available. Part-time, evening/weekend. Offers counseling and guidance (MS); educational leadership (MA, Ed D); special education (MS); teacher leadership (M Ed); teaching (M Ed).

Pacific Lutheran Theological Seminary Degree program information: Part-time programs available. Part-time. Offers theology (M Div, MA, MCM, MTS, PhD, Th D, Certificate). MA, Th D, PhD offered jointly with Graduate Theological Union; PhD with University of California, Berkeley.

School of Management Degree program information: Part-time and evening/weekend programs available. Part-time, evening/weekend, online learning. Offers business (IMBA); computer science (MS); econometrics (MBA); economics (MS); entrepreneurship (MBA, Certificate); finance (MBA, Certificate); financial planning (MBA, Certificate); information systems and technology (MS); information technology management (MBA, Certificate); international business (MBA, Certificate); management and organization behavior (MBA); management and organizational behavior (Certificate); marketing (MBA, Certificate); microeconomics (MBA); nonprofit and social enterprise (MBA).

CALIFORNIA MARITIME ACADEMY, Vallejo, CA 94590

General Information State-supported, coed, comprehensive institution. *Enrollment:* 1,149 graduate, professional, and undergraduate students; 49 full-time matriculated graduate/professional students (10 women). *Enrollment by degree level:* 49 master's. *Graduate faculty:* 16 part-time/adjunct (2 women). *Student services:* Career counseling, services for students with disabilities.

Computer facilities: 75 computers available on campus for general student use. A campuswide network can be accessed from student residence rooms and from off campus. Online class registration is available.
Website: http://www.csum.edu/

General Application Contact: Kathy Arnold, Graduate Program Coordinator, 707-654-1271, Fax: 707-654-1158, E-mail: karnold@csum.edu.

GRADUATE UNITS

Graduate Studies Students: 49 full-time (10 women); includes 11 minority (2 Black or African American, non-Hispanic/Latino; 5 Asian, non-Hispanic/Latino; 2 Hispanic/Latino; 2 Native Hawaiian or other Pacific Islander, non-Hispanic/Latino), 1 international. 29 applicants, 93% accepted, 26 enrolled. *Faculty:* 16 part-time/adjunct (2 women). In 2015, 24 master's awarded. *Degree program information:* Evening/weekend programs available. Evening/weekend, online only, 100% online. Offers transportation and engineering management (MS). *Application deadline:* Applications are processed on a rolling basis. *Application fee:* $55. Electronic applications accepted. *Application Contact:* Kathy Arnold, Program Coordinator, 707-654-1271, Fax: 707-654-1158, E-mail: karnold@csum.edu. *Dean, Graduate Studies*, Dr. Jim Burns.

CALIFORNIA MIRAMAR UNIVERSITY, San Diego, CA 92108

General Information Proprietary, coed, comprehensive institution.

GRADUATE UNITS

Program in Business Administration Offers business administration (MBA).

Program in Strategic Leadership Offers strategic leadership (MS).

Program in Taxation and Trade for Executives Offers taxation and trade for executives (MT).

Program in Telecommunications Management Offers telecommunications management (MST).

CALIFORNIA NATIONAL UNIVERSITY FOR ADVANCED STUDIES, Northridge, CA 91325

General Information Proprietary, coed, comprehensive institution.

GRADUATE UNITS

College of Business Administration ***Degree program information:*** Part-time programs available. Part-time, online learning. Offers business administration (MBA, MHRM). Electronic applications accepted.

College of Engineering ***Degree program information:*** Part-time programs available. Part-time, online learning. Offers engineering (MS Eng). Electronic applications accepted.

College of Quality and Engineering Management ***Degree program information:*** Part-time programs available. Part-time. Offers quality and engineering management (MEM).

CALIFORNIA POLYTECHNIC STATE UNIVERSITY, SAN LUIS OBISPO, San Luis Obispo, CA 93407

General Information State-supported, coed, comprehensive institution. CGS member. *Enrollment:* 20,944 graduate, professional, and undergraduate students; 540 full-time matriculated graduate/professional students (242 women), 220 part-time matriculated graduate/professional students (100 women). *Enrollment by degree level:* 760 master's. *Graduate faculty:* 153 full-time (45 women), 24 part-time/adjunct (12 women). Tuition, state resident: full-time $6738; part-time $3906 per year. Tuition, nonresident: full-time $15,666; part-time $8370 per year. *Required fees:* $3528; $3075 per unit. $1025 per term. *Graduate housing:* Room and/or apartments available on a first-come, first-served basis to single students; on-campus housing not available to married students. Typical cost: $7176 per year ($12,009 including board). *Student services:* Campus employment opportunities, campus safety program, career counseling, exercise/wellness program, free psychological counseling, grant writing training, international student services, low-cost health insurance, multicultural affairs office, services for students with disabilities, teacher training, writing training. *Library:* Robert E. Kennedy Library.

Computer facilities: A campuswide network can be accessed from student residence rooms and from off campus. Online class registration is available.
Website: http://www.calpoly.edu/

General Application Contact: Dr. James Maraviglia, Associate Vice Provost for Marketing and Enrollment Development, 805-756-2311, Fax: 805-756-5400, E-mail: admissions@calpoly.edu.

GRADUATE UNITS

College of Agriculture, Food and Environmental Sciences Students: 44 full-time (34 women), 27 part-time (19 women); includes 15 minority (4 Asian, non-Hispanic/Latino; 8 Hispanic/Latino; 3 Two or more races, non-Hispanic/Latino), 6 international. Average age 26. 96 applicants, 42% accepted, 32 enrolled. *Faculty:* 27 full-time (12 women), 3 part-time/adjunct (2 women). *Financial support:* Fellowships, research assistantships, teaching assistantships, career-related internships or fieldwork, Federal Work-Study, institutionally sponsored loans, scholarships/grants, and health care benefits available. Support available to part-time students. Financial award application deadline: 3/2; financial award applicants required to submit FAFSA. In 2015, 49 master's awarded. *Degree program information:* Part-time programs available. Part-time. Offers agribusiness (MS); agricultural education and communication (MAE); agriculture (MS); agriculture, food and environmental sciences (MAE, MS); forestry sciences (MS). *Application deadline:* For fall admission, 4/1 for domestic students, 11/30 for international students; for winter admission, 10/1 for domestic students, 6/30 for international students; for spring admission, 10/1 for domestic students. Applications are processed on a rolling basis. *Application fee:* $55. Electronic applications accepted. *Application Contact:* Dr. Chris Dicus, Interim Associate Dean, Research and Graduate Programs, 805-756-5104, E-mail: cdicus@calpoly.edu. *Dean*, Dr. Andrew Thulin, 805-756-2161, Fax: 805-756-6577, E-mail: athulin@calpoly.edu.

College of Architecture and Environmental Design Students: 52 full-time (24 women), 8 part-time (5 women); includes 18 minority (1 Black or African American, non-Hispanic/Latino; 3 Asian, non-Hispanic/Latino; 13 Hispanic/Latino; 1 Two or more races, non-Hispanic/Latino), 10 international. Average age 25. 93 applicants, 59% accepted, 24 enrolled. *Faculty:* 10 full-time (4 women). *Financial support:* Research assistantships, teaching assistantships, career-related internships or fieldwork, Federal Work-Study, and institutionally sponsored loans available. Support available to part-time students. Financial award application deadline: 3/2; financial award applicants required to submit FAFSA. In 2015, 38 master's awarded. *Degree program information:* Part-time programs available. Part-time. Offers architecture (MS); architecture and environmental design (MCRP, MS); city and regional planning (MCRP). *Application deadline:* For fall admission, 6/1 for domestic students, 11/30 for international students; for winter admission, 11/1 for domestic students, 6/30 for international students. Applications are processed on a rolling basis. *Application fee:* $55. Electronic applications accepted. *Graduate Coordinator*, Thomas Fowler, 805-756-2981, Fax: 805-756-1500, E-mail: tfowler@calpoly.edu.

College of Engineering Students: 251 full-time (57 women), 81 part-time (18 women); includes 118 minority (3 Black or African American, non-Hispanic/Latino; 51 Asian, non-Hispanic/Latino; 38 Hispanic/Latino; 26 Two or more races, non-Hispanic/Latino), 33 international. Average age 24. 468 applicants, 42% accepted, 138 enrolled. *Faculty:* 66 full-time (12 women), 3 part-time/adjunct (0 women). *Financial support:* Fellowships, research assistantships, teaching assistantships, career-related internships or fieldwork, Federal Work-Study, institutionally sponsored loans, and unspecified assistantships available. Support available to part-time students. Financial award application deadline: 3/2; financial award applicants required to submit FAFSA. In 2015, 219 master's awarded. *Degree program information:* Part-time programs available. Part-time. Offers aerospace engineering (MS); biomedical and general engineering (MS); civil and environmental engineering (MS); computer science (MS); electrical engineering (MS); engineering (MS); industrial engineering (MS); mechanical engineering (MS). *Application deadline:* For fall admission, 7/1 for domestic students, 11/30 for international students; for winter admission, 11/1 for domestic students, 6/30 for international students; for spring admission, 2/1 for domestic students. Applications are processed on a rolling basis. *Application fee:* $55. Electronic applications accepted. *Dean*, Dr. Debra Larson, E-mail: dslarson@calpoly.edu.

College of Liberal Arts Students: 45 full-time (35 women), 55 part-time (33 women); includes 29 minority (1 Black or African American, non-Hispanic/Latino; 4 Asian, non-Hispanic/Latino; 18 Hispanic/Latino; 1 Native Hawaiian or other Pacific Islander, non-Hispanic/Latino; 5 Two or more races, non-Hispanic/Latino). Average age 27. 113 applicants, 50% accepted, 38 enrolled. *Faculty:* 15 full-time (7 women), 6 part-time/adjunct (3 women). *Financial support:* Fellowships, teaching assistantships, career-related internships or fieldwork, Federal Work-Study, institutionally sponsored loans, scholarships/grants, and tutorships, writing laboratory assistantships available. Support available to part-time students. Financial award application deadline: 3/2; financial award applicants required to submit FAFSA. In 2015, 27 master's awarded. *Degree program information:* Part-time programs available. Part-time. Offers English (MA); history (MA); liberal arts (MA, MPP, MS); political science (MPP); psychology (MS). *Application deadline:* For fall admission, 5/1 for domestic students, 11/30 for international students; for winter admission, 11/1 for domestic students, 6/30 for international students; for spring admission, 2/1 for domestic students. *Application fee:* $55. *Dean*, Dr. Douglas Epperson, 805-756-2706, Fax: 805-756-5748, E-mail: dleppers@calpoly.edu.

College of Science and Mathematics Students: 121 full-time (82 women), 41 part-time (22 women); includes 46 minority (12 Asian, non-Hispanic/Latino; 26 Hispanic/Latino; 8 Two or more races, non-Hispanic/Latino), 4 international. Average age 26. 277 applicants, 41% accepted, 89 enrolled. *Faculty:* 32 full-time (10 women), 10 part-time/adjunct (6 women). *Financial support:* Fellowships, research assistantships, teaching assistantships, career-related internships or fieldwork, and Federal Work-Study available. Support available to part-time students. Financial award application deadline: 3/2; financial award applicants required to submit FAFSA. In 2015, 89 master's awarded. *Degree program information:* Part-time programs available. Part-time. Offers biological sciences (MA, MS); kinesiology (MS); mathematics (MS); polymers and coating science (MS); science and mathematics (MA, MS). *Application deadline:* For fall admission, 7/1 for domestic students, 11/30 for international students; for winter admission, 11/1 for domestic students, 6/30 for international students; for spring admission, 2/1 for domestic students. Applications are processed on a rolling basis. *Application fee:* $55. Electronic applications accepted. *Dean*, Dr. Philip S. Bailey, 805-756-2226, Fax: 805-756-1670, E-mail: pbailey@calpoly.edu.

School of Education Students: 68 full-time (55 women), 2 part-time (both women); includes 20 minority (3 Asian, non-Hispanic/Latino; 13 Hispanic/Latino; 4 Two or more races, non-Hispanic/Latino). Average age 28. 136 applicants, 40% accepted, 50 enrolled. *Faculty:* 7 full-time (4 women), 8 part-time/adjunct (5 women). *Financial support:* Fellowships, research assistantships, career-related internships or fieldwork, Federal Work-Study, and institutionally sponsored loans available. Support available to part-time students. Financial award application deadline: 3/2; financial award applicants required to submit FAFSA. In 2015, 56 master's awarded. *Degree program information:* Part-time and evening/weekend programs available. Part-time, evening/weekend. Offers education (MA). *Application deadline:* For fall admission, 2/1 for domestic students, 11/30 for international students. *Application fee:* $55. *Application Contact:* E-mail: soe@calpoly.edu. *Director*, Dr. Kevin Taylor, 805-756-1503, E-mail: jktaylor@calpoly.edu.

Orfalea College of Business Students: 27 full-time (10 women), 8 part-time (3 women); includes 11 minority (2 Asian, non-Hispanic/Latino; 3 Hispanic/Latino; 6 Two or more races, non-Hispanic/Latino), 2 international. Average age 26. 100 applicants, 42% accepted, 27 enrolled. *Faculty:* 3 full-time (0 women), 2 part-time/adjunct (1 woman). *Financial support:* Fellowships, career-related internships or fieldwork, Federal Work-Study, institutionally sponsored loans, scholarships/grants, and unspecified assistantships available. Support available to part-time students. Financial award application deadline: 3/2; financial award applicants required to submit FAFSA. In 2015, 92 master's awarded. Offers business (MBA); taxation (MSA). *Application deadline:* For fall admission, 4/1 for domestic and international students. Applications are processed on a rolling basis. *Application fee:* $55. Electronic applications accepted. *Application Contact:* Dr. Sanjiv Jaggia, Associate Dean, Graduate Programs, 805-756-7519, E-mail: sjaggia@calpoly.edu. *Dean*, Dr. Scott Dawson, 805-756-2705, E-mail: scdawson@calpoly.edu.

CALIFORNIA SCHOOL OF PODIATRIC MEDICINE AT SAMUEL MERRITT UNIVERSITY, Oakland, CA 94609

General Information Independent, coed, graduate-only institution. *Research affiliation:* University of Southern California–Los Angeles County Medical Center, University of California, San Francisco Health Sciences Center, The University of Texas Health Science Center at San Antonio (biology).

GRADUATE UNITS

Professional Program Offers podiatric medicine (DPM).

CALIFORNIA STATE POLYTECHNIC UNIVERSITY, POMONA, Pomona, CA 91768-2557

General Information State-supported, coed, comprehensive institution. *Enrollment:* 23,717 graduate, professional, and undergraduate students; 397 full-time matriculated graduate/professional students (192 women), 882 part-time matriculated graduate/professional students (404 women). *Enrollment by degree level:* 1,229 master's, 50 doctoral. *Graduate faculty:* 573 full-time (251 women), 652 part-time/adjunct (245 women). Tuition, state resident: full-time $6738. Tuition, nonresident: full-time $13,434. *Required fees:* $1504. Tuition and fees vary according to course load, degree level and program. *Graduate housing:* Room and/or apartments available on a first-come, first-served basis to single students; on-campus housing not available to married students. Typical cost: $9858 per year ($15,238 including board). Room and board charges vary according to board plan and housing facility selected. Housing application deadline: 5/1. *Student services:* Campus employment opportunities, campus safety program, career counseling, child daycare facilities, free psychological counseling, international student services, low-cost health insurance, multicultural affairs office, services for students with disabilities. *Library:* University Library. *Collection:* Books: 851,411 (physical), 12,830 (digital/electronic); Serial titles: 103,658 (physical), 13,480 (digital/electronic); Databases: 151. Weekly public service hours: 92; study areas open 24 hours, 5–7 days a week; students can reserve study rooms.

Computer facilities: Computer purchase and lease plans are available. 2,117 computers available on campus for general student use. A campuswide network can be accessed from student residence rooms and from off campus. Online class registration is available.
Website: http://www.cpp.edu/

General Application Contact: Andrew M. Wright, Director of Admissions, 909-869-3130, Fax: 909-869-4529, E-mail: awright@cpp.edu.

GRADUATE UNITS

Ed D Program in Educational Leadership Students: 50 part-time (35 women); includes 34 minority (7 Black or African American, non-Hispanic/Latino; 5 Asian, non-Hispanic/Latino; 21 Hispanic/Latino; 1 Two or more races, non-Hispanic/Latino). Average age 40. 23 applicants, 65% accepted, 11 enrolled. Offers educational leadership (Ed D). *Application fee:* $55. *Doctoral Studies Coordinator,* Michael M. Bandoni, 909-869-3060, Fax: 909-869-5416, E-mail: mmbandoni@cpp.edu.

John T. Lyle Center for Regenerative Studies Students: 10 full-time (8 women), 8 part-time (5 women); includes 10 minority (3 Asian, non-Hispanic/Latino; 5 Hispanic/Latino; 2 Two or more races, non-Hispanic/Latino), 1 international. Average age 28. 14 applicants, 9 enrolled. *Financial support:* Application deadline: 3/2; applicants required to submit FAFSA. In 2015, 12 master's awarded. *Degree program information:* Part-time programs available. Part-time. Offers regenerative studies (MS). *Application deadline:* For fall admission, 5/1 priority date for domestic students; for winter admission, 10/15 priority date for domestic students; for spring admission, 1/20 priority date for domestic students. Applications are processed on a rolling basis. *Application fee:* $55. Electronic applications accepted. *Graduate Coordinator,* Dr. Denise L. Lawrence, 909-869-2674, Fax: 909-869-4331, E-mail: dllawrence@cpp.edu.

Master of Science in Business Administration Program Students: 7 part-time (2 women); includes 4 minority (3 Asian, non-Hispanic/Latino; 1 Hispanic/Latino), 1 international. Average age 28. 17 applicants, 29% accepted, 4 enrolled. In 2015, 1 master's awarded. Offers information systems auditing (MS). *Application deadline:* Applications are processed on a rolling basis. *Application fee:* $55. Electronic applications accepted. *Interim Dean,* Dr. Cheryl R. Wyrick, 909-869-2400, Fax: 909-869-6799, E-mail: crwyrick@cpp.edu.

Master's Programs in Education Students: 19 full-time (11 women), 104 part-time (76 women); includes 63 minority (8 Black or African American, non-Hispanic/Latino; 2 American Indian or Alaska Native, non-Hispanic/Latino; 7 Asian, non-Hispanic/Latino; 45 Hispanic/Latino; 1 Two or more races, non-Hispanic/Latino), 4 international. Average age 33. 56 applicants, 68% accepted, 28 enrolled. In 2015, 60 master's awarded. Offers curriculum and instruction (MA); educational leadership (MA); educational multimedia (MA); special education (MA). *Application fee:* $55. *Graduate Studies Coordinator,* Kelly Mitchell, 909-869-2358, Fax: 909-869-2722, E-mail: klmitchell@cpp.edu.

MBA Program Students: 3 full-time (1 woman), 39 part-time (22 women); includes 24 minority (1 Black or African American, non-Hispanic/Latino; 13 Asian, non-Hispanic/Latino; 7 Hispanic/Latino; 3 Two or more races, non-Hispanic/Latino), 6 international. Average age 28. 86 applicants, 20% accepted, 13 enrolled. *Financial support:* Applicants required to submit FAFSA. In 2015, 32 master's awarded. Offers business administration (MBA). *Application deadline:* Applications are processed on a rolling basis. *Application fee:* $55. *Interim Dean,* Dr. Cheryl R. Wyrick, 909-869-2400, E-mail: crwyrick@cpp.edu.

Program in Accountancy Students: 10 full-time (4 women), 4 part-time (3 women); includes 8 minority (4 Asian, non-Hispanic/Latino; 4 Hispanic/Latino), 3 international. Average age 25. 64 applicants, 45% accepted, 13 enrolled. *Financial support:* Applicants required to submit FAFSA. Offers accountancy (MS). *Application deadline:* Applications are processed on a rolling basis. *Application fee:* $55. Electronic applications accepted. *Program Coordinator,* Dr. Meihua Koo, 909-869-4531, Fax: 909-869-4511, E-mail: mkoo@cpp.edu.

Program in Agriculture Students: 13 full-time (9 women), 23 part-time (15 women); includes 16 minority (3 Black or African American, non-Hispanic/Latino; 4 Asian, non-Hispanic/Latino; 9 Hispanic/Latino), 3 international. Average age 28. 64 applicants, 42% accepted, 13 enrolled. *Financial support:* Career-related internships or fieldwork, Federal Work-Study, and institutionally sponsored loans available. Support available to part-time students. Financial award application deadline: 3/2; financial award applicants required to submit FAFSA. In 2015, 12 master's awarded. *Degree program information:* Part-time programs available. Part-time. Offers agricultural science (MS); nutrition and food science (MS). *Application deadline:* For fall admission, 5/1 priority date for domestic students; for winter admission, 10/15 priority date for domestic students; for spring admission, 1/2 priority date for domestic students. Applications are processed on a rolling basis. *Application fee:* $55. Electronic applications accepted. *Director of Research and Graduate Studies,* Dr. Harmit Singh, 909-869-3023, Fax: 909-869-5078, E-mail: harmitsingh@cpp.edu.

Program in Applied Biotechnology Students: 6 full-time (2 women), 17 part-time (9 women); includes 4 minority (1 Black or African American, non-Hispanic/Latino; 3 Asian, non-Hispanic/Latino), 9 international. Average age 25. 12 applicants. *Financial support:* Applicants required to submit FAFSA. In 2015, 2 master's awarded. Offers applied biotechnology (MBT). *Application deadline:* Applications are processed on a rolling basis. *Application fee:* $55. Electronic applications accepted. *Program Director,* Dr. David L. Dyer, 909-869-5508, Fax: 909-869-4078, E-mail: dldyer@cpp.edu.

Program in Architecture Students: 43 full-time (24 women), 3 part-time (1 woman); includes 16 minority (3 Black or African American, non-Hispanic/Latino; 4 Asian, non-Hispanic/Latino; 9 Hispanic/Latino), 3 international. Average age 26. 68 applicants, 62% accepted, 17 enrolled. *Financial support:* Career-related internships or fieldwork, Federal Work-Study, and institutionally sponsored loans available. Support available to part-time students. Financial award application deadline: 3/2; financial award applicants required to submit FAFSA. In 2015, 8 master's awarded. *Degree program information:* Part-time programs available. Part-time. Offers architecture (M Arch). *Application deadline:* For fall admission, 5/1 for domestic students; for winter admission, 10/15 priority date for domestic students; for spring admission, 1/20 priority date for domestic students. Applications are processed on a rolling basis. *Application fee:* $55. Electronic applications accepted. *Graduate Coordinator,* Kip A. Dickson, 909-869-2682, Fax: 909-869-4331, E-mail: kadickson@cpp.edu.

Program in Biological Sciences Students: 24 full-time (16 women), 50 part-time (28 women); includes 41 minority (2 Black or African American, non-Hispanic/Latino; 13 Asian, non-Hispanic/Latino; 24 Hispanic/Latino; 2 Two or more races, non-Hispanic/Latino), 5 international. Average age 25. 39 applicants, 44% accepted, 13 enrolled. *Financial support:* Career-related internships or fieldwork, Federal Work-Study, and institutionally sponsored loans available. Support available to part-time students. Financial award application deadline: 3/2; financial award applicants required to submit FAFSA. In 2015, 15 master's awarded. *Degree program information:* Part-time programs available. Part-time. Offers biological sciences (MS). *Application deadline:* For fall admission, 5/1 priority date for domestic students; for winter admission, 10/15 priority date for domestic students; for spring admission, 1/20 priority date for domestic students. Applications are processed on a rolling basis. *Application fee:* $55. Electronic applications accepted. *Graduate Coordinator,* Dr. Robert J. Talmadge, 909-869-3025, Fax: 909-869-4078, E-mail: rjtalmadge@cpp.edu.

Program in Chemistry Students: 4 full-time (2 women), 17 part-time (6 women); includes 7 minority (4 Asian, non-Hispanic/Latino; 3 Hispanic/Latino), 7 international. Average age 25. 36 applicants, 42% accepted, 6 enrolled. *Financial support:* In 2015–16, 2 students received support. Career-related internships or fieldwork, Federal Work-Study, and institutionally sponsored loans available. Support available to part-time students. Financial award application deadline: 3/2; financial award applicants required to submit FAFSA. In 2015, 3 master's awarded. *Degree program information:* Part-time programs available. Part-time. Offers chemistry (MS). *Application deadline:* For fall admission, 5/1 priority date for domestic students; for winter admission, 10/15 priority date for domestic students; for spring admission, 1/20 priority date for domestic students. Applications are processed on a rolling basis. *Application fee:* $55. Electronic applications accepted. *Graduate Coordinator,* Dr. Timothy C. Corcoran, 909-869-3672, Fax: 909-869-4344, E-mail: tccorcoran@cpp.edu.

Program in Civil Engineering Students: 28 full-time (6 women), 86 part-time (19 women); includes 61 minority (2 Black or African American, non-Hispanic/Latino; 34 Asian, non-Hispanic/Latino; 22 Hispanic/Latino; 3 Two or more races, non-Hispanic/Latino), 14 international. Average age 25. 112 applicants, 62% accepted, 36 enrolled. *Financial support:* Applicants required to submit FAFSA. In 2015, 24 master's awarded. *Degree program information:* Part-time programs available. Part-time. Offers civil engineering (MS). *Application deadline:* Applications are processed on a rolling basis. *Application fee:* $55. Electronic applications accepted. *Graduate Coordinator,* Dr. Ronald Yeung, 909-869-2640, Fax: 909-869-4342, E-mail: mryeung@cpp.edu.

Program in Computer Science Students: 8 full-time (2 women), 62 part-time (15 women); includes 28 minority (2 Black or African American, non-Hispanic/Latino; 20 Asian, non-Hispanic/Latino; 5 Hispanic/Latino; 1 Two or more races, non-Hispanic/Latino), 26 international. Average age 27. 193 applicants, 33% accepted, 16 enrolled. *Financial support:* Career-related internships or fieldwork, Federal Work-Study, and institutionally sponsored loans available. Support available to part-time students. Financial award application deadline: 3/2; financial award applicants required to submit FAFSA. In 2015, 14 master's awarded. *Degree program information:* Part-time programs available. Part-time. Offers computer science (MS). *Application deadline:* For fall admission, 5/1 priority date for domestic students; for winter admission, 10/15 priority date for domestic students; for spring admission, 1/20 priority date for domestic students. Applications are processed on a rolling basis. *Application fee:* $55. Electronic applications accepted. *Graduate Coordinator,* Dr. Gilbert Young, 909-869-4413, Fax: 909-869-4733, E-mail: gsyoung@cpp.edu.

Program in Economics Students: 8 full-time (1 woman), 26 part-time (11 women); includes 13 minority (1 Black or African American, non-Hispanic/Latino; 1 American Indian or Alaska Native, non-Hispanic/Latino; 5 Asian, non-Hispanic/Latino; 6 Hispanic/Latino), 12 international. Average age 27. 44 applicants, 77% accepted, 13 enrolled. *Financial support:* In 2015–16, 9 students received support. Federal Work-Study and institutionally sponsored loans available. Support available to part-time students. Financial award application deadline: 3/2; financial award applicants required to submit FAFSA. In 2015, 11 master's awarded. *Degree program information:* Part-time programs available. Part-time. Offers economics (MS). *Application deadline:* For fall admission, 5/1 priority date for domestic students; for winter admission, 10/15 priority date for domestic students; for spring admission, 1/20 priority date for domestic students. Applications are processed on a rolling basis. *Application fee:* $55. Electronic applications accepted. *Graduate Coordinator,* Dr. Gregory Hunter, 909-869-4888, Fax: 909-869-6987, E-mail: gwhunter@cpp.edu.

Program in Electrical Engineering Students: 28 full-time (4 women), 62 part-time (8 women); includes 45 minority (1 American Indian or Alaska Native, non-Hispanic/Latino; 30 Asian, non-Hispanic/Latino; 13 Hispanic/Latino; 1 Two or more races, non-Hispanic/Latino), 14 international. Average age 26. 115 applicants, 37% accepted, 16 enrolled. In 2015, 29 master's awarded. Offers communication systems (MSEE); computer systems (MSEE); control and robotics systems (MSEE). *Application deadline:* Applications are processed on a rolling basis. *Application fee:* $55. Electronic applications accepted. *Graduate Coordinator,* Dr. Halima M. El Naga, 909-869-2515, Fax: 909-869-4687, E-mail: helnaga@cpp.edu.

Program in Engineering Students: 1 full-time (0 women), 14 part-time (2 women); includes 6 minority (3 Asian, non-Hispanic/Latino; 3 Hispanic/Latino). Average age 27. 13 applicants, 15% accepted, 1 enrolled. *Financial support:* Applicants required to submit FAFSA. In 2015, 4 master's awarded. *Degree program information:* Part-time programs available. Part-time. Offers engineering (MSE). *Application deadline:* Applications are processed on a rolling basis. *Application fee:* $55. Electronic applications accepted. *Department Chair,* Dr. Ali R. Ahmadi, 909-869-2470, Fax: 909-869-6920, E-mail: arahmadi@cpp.edu.

Program in Engineering Management Students: 3 full-time (1 woman), 25 part-time (5 women); includes 18 minority (1 Black or African American, non-Hispanic/Latino; 10 Asian, non-Hispanic/Latino; 6 Hispanic/Latino; 1 Two or more races, non-Hispanic/Latino), 4 international. Average age 24. 46 applicants, 37% accepted, 4 enrolled. *Financial support:* Applicants required to submit FAFSA. In 2015, 10 master's awarded. *Degree program information:* Part-time programs available. Part-time. Offers engineering management (MS). *Application deadline:* Applications are processed on a rolling basis. *Application fee:* $55. Electronic applications accepted. *Chair/Graduate Coordinator,* Dr. Kamran Abedini, 909-869-2569, Fax: 909-869-2564, E-mail: kabedini@cpp.edu.

Program in English Students: 27 full-time (17 women), 43 part-time (28 women); includes 40 minority (2 Black or African American, non-Hispanic/Latino; 2 American Indian or Alaska Native, non-Hispanic/Latino; 10 Asian, non-Hispanic/Latino; 24 Hispanic/Latino; 2 Two or more races, non-Hispanic/Latino), 3 international. Average age 28. 40 applicants, 75% accepted, 14 enrolled. *Financial support:* In 2015–16, 2 fellowships were awarded; Federal Work-Study and institutionally sponsored loans also available. Support available to part-time students. Financial award application deadline: 3/2; financial award applicants required to submit FAFSA. In 2015, 22 master's awarded. *Degree program information:* Part-time programs available. Part-time. Offers English (MA). *Application deadline:* For fall admission, 5/1 priority date for domestic students; for winter admission, 10/15 priority date for domestic students; for spring admission, 1/20 priority date for domestic students. Applications are processed on a rolling basis. *Application fee:* $55. Electronic applications accepted. *Graduate Coordinator,* Dr. Lise-Hlne DeRosa, 909-869-3979, Fax: 909-869-4896, E-mail: lvtrouilloud@cpp.edu.

Program in Geology Students: 9 full-time (0 women), 18 part-time (8 women); includes 13 minority (1 Black or African American, non-Hispanic/Latino; 5 Asian, non-Hispanic/Latino; 6 Hispanic/Latino; 1 Two or more races, non-Hispanic/Latino). Average age 28. 12 applicants, 92% accepted, 6 enrolled. *Financial support:* Applicants required to submit FAFSA. In 2015, 6 master's awarded. *Degree program information:* Part-time programs available. Part-time. Offers geology (MS). *Department Chair/Graduate Coordinator*, Dr. Jonathan A. Nourse, 909-869-3460, Fax: 909-869-2920, E-mail: janourse@cpp.edu.

Program in History Students: 14 part-time (5 women); includes 8 minority (1 Black or African American, non-Hispanic/Latino; 6 Hispanic/Latino; 1 Two or more races, non-Hispanic/Latino). Average age 29. 14 applicants, 71% accepted, 6 enrolled. *Financial support:* Applicants required to submit FAFSA. In 2015, 6 master's awarded. *Degree program information:* Part-time programs available. Part-time. Offers history (MA). *Application deadline:* For fall admission, 5/1 priority date for domestic students; for winter admission, 10/15 priority date for domestic students; for spring admission, 1/20 priority date for domestic students. Applications are processed on a rolling basis. *Application fee:* $55. Electronic applications accepted. *Graduate Coordinator*, Dr. Amanda H. Podany, 909-869-3875, Fax: 909-869-4724, E-mail: ahpodany@cpp.edu.

Program in Hospitality Management Students: 9 full-time (all women), 43 part-time (28 women); includes 11 minority (1 Black or African American, non-Hispanic/Latino; 8 Asian, non-Hispanic/Latino; 1 Hispanic/Latino; 1 Two or more races, non-Hispanic/Latino), 34 international. Average age 27. 36 applicants, 53% accepted, 16 enrolled. *Financial support:* Applicants required to submit FAFSA. In 2015, 12 master's awarded. *Degree program information:* Part-time programs available. Part-time. Offers hospitality management (MS). *Program Director*, Dr. Neha Singh, 909-869-4565, Fax: 909-869-4805, E-mail: nsingh@cpp.edu.

Program in Interior Architecture Students: 21 full-time (14 women), 35 part-time (31 women); includes 11 minority (2 Black or African American, non-Hispanic/Latino; 7 Asian, non-Hispanic/Latino; 2 Hispanic/Latino), 24 international. Average age 28. 53 applicants, 75% accepted, 22 enrolled. *Financial support:* Applicants required to submit FAFSA. In 2015, 44 master's awarded. *Degree program information:* Part-time programs available. Part-time. Offers interior architecture (MIA). Program held jointly with UCLA Extension. *Application deadline:* Applications are processed on a rolling basis. Electronic applications accepted. *Program Coordinator*, George R. Proctor, 909-869-4728, Fax: 909-869-4331, E-mail: grproctor@cpp.edu.

Program in Kinesiology Students: 6 full-time (2 women), 8 part-time (7 women); includes 7 minority (4 Asian, non-Hispanic/Latino; 3 Hispanic/Latino). Average age 25. 19 applicants, 63% accepted, 8 enrolled. *Financial support:* Federal Work-Study and institutionally sponsored loans available. Support available to part-time students. Financial award application deadline: 3/2; financial award applicants required to submit FAFSA. In 2015, 4 master's awarded. *Degree program information:* Part-time programs available. Part-time. Offers kinesiology (MS). *Application deadline:* For fall admission, 5/1 priority date for domestic students; for winter admission, 10/15 priority date for domestic students; for spring admission, 1/20 priority date for domestic students. Applications are processed on a rolling basis. *Application fee:* $55. Electronic applications accepted. *Graduate Coordinator*, Dr. Ken Hansen, 909-869-4638, Fax: 909-869-4797, E-mail: kahansen@cpp.edu.

Program in Landscape Architecture Students: 24 full-time (11 women), 5 part-time (2 women); includes 6 minority (2 Asian, non-Hispanic/Latino; 3 Hispanic/Latino; 1 Two or more races, non-Hispanic/Latino), 8 international. Average age 29. 41 applicants, 32% accepted, 9 enrolled. *Financial support:* Career-related internships or fieldwork, Federal Work-Study, and institutionally sponsored loans available. Support available to part-time students. Financial award application deadline: 3/2; financial award applicants required to submit FAFSA. In 2015, 12 master's awarded. *Degree program information:* Part-time programs available. Part-time. Offers landscape architecture (M Land Arch). *Application deadline:* For fall admission, 5/1 priority date for domestic students; for winter admission, 10/15 priority date for domestic students; for spring admission, 1/20 priority date for domestic students. Applications are processed on a rolling basis. *Application fee:* $55. Electronic applications accepted. *Graduate Coordinator*, Gerald O. Taylor, Jr., 909-869-6891, Fax: 909-869-4460, E-mail: jotaylor@cpp.edu.

Program in Mathematics Students: 13 full-time (4 women), 26 part-time (7 women); includes 25 minority (3 Black or African American, non-Hispanic/Latino; 8 Asian, non-Hispanic/Latino; 13 Hispanic/Latino; 1 Two or more races, non-Hispanic/Latino), 2 international. Average age 26. 66 applicants, 38% accepted, 11 enrolled. *Financial support:* Career-related internships or fieldwork, Federal Work-Study, and institutionally sponsored loans available. Support available to part-time students. Financial award application deadline: 3/2; financial award applicants required to submit FAFSA. In 2015, 17 master's awarded. *Degree program information:* Part-time programs available. Part-time. Offers applied mathematics (MS); pure mathematics (MS). *Application deadline:* For fall admission, 5/1 priority date for domestic students; for winter admission, 10/15 priority date for domestic students; for spring admission, 1/20 priority date for domestic students. Applications are processed on a rolling basis. *Application fee:* $55. Electronic applications accepted. *Graduate Coordinator*, Dr. John Rock, 909-869-2404, Fax: 909-869-4904, E-mail: jarock@cpp.edu.

Program in Mechanical Engineering Students: 12 full-time (3 women), 52 part-time (6 women); includes 36 minority (2 Black or African American, non-Hispanic/Latino; 20 Asian, non-Hispanic/Latino; 12 Hispanic/Latino; 2 Two or more races, non-Hispanic/Latino), 13 international. Average age 25. 69 applicants, 62% accepted, 22 enrolled. *Financial support:* Applicants required to submit FAFSA. In 2015, 19 master's awarded. *Degree program information:* Part-time programs available. Part-time. Offers mechanical engineering (MS). *Application deadline:* Applications are processed on a rolling basis. *Application fee:* $55. Electronic applications accepted. *Graduate Coordinator*, Dr. Henry Xue, 909-869-4304, Fax: 909-869-4341, E-mail: hxue@cpp.edu.

Program in Psychology Students: 29 full-time (24 women); includes 22 minority (1 Black or African American, non-Hispanic/Latino; 1 American Indian or Alaska Native, non-Hispanic/Latino; 2 Asian, non-Hispanic/Latino; 14 Hispanic/Latino; 4 Two or more races, non-Hispanic/Latino). Average age 23. 126 applicants, 12% accepted, 15 enrolled. *Financial support:* Application deadline: 3/2; applicants required to submit FAFSA. In 2015, 17 master's awarded. *Degree program information:* Part-time programs available. Part-time. Offers psychology (MS). *Application deadline:* For fall admission, 4/15 for domestic students. Applications are processed on a rolling basis. *Application fee:* $55. Electronic applications accepted. *Director of Graduate Studies*, Dr. Jeffery Mio, 909-869-3899, Fax: 909-869-4930, E-mail: jsmio@cpp.edu.

Program in Public Administration Students: 6 full-time (3 women), 27 part-time (13 women); includes 20 minority (2 Black or African American, non-Hispanic/Latino; 1 Asian, non-Hispanic/Latino; 17 Hispanic/Latino), 2 international. Average age 30. 30 applicants, 60% accepted, 9 enrolled. *Financial support:* Applicants required to submit FAFSA. In 2015, 17 master's awarded. *Degree program information:* Part-time programs available. Part-time. Offers public administration (MPA). *Application deadline:* For fall admission, 5/1 priority date for domestic students; for winter admission, 10/15 priority date for domestic students; for spring admission, 1/20 priority date for domestic students. Applications are processed on a rolling basis. *Application fee:* $55. Electronic applications accepted. *MPA Director/Interim Chair*, Dr. Sandra M. Emerson, 909-869-3879, Fax: 909-869-6995, E-mail: smemerson@cpp.edu.

Program in Urban and Regional Planning Students: 33 full-time (14 women), 14 part-time (7 women); includes 34 minority (3 Black or African American, non-Hispanic/Latino; 7 Asian, non-Hispanic/Latino; 24 Hispanic/Latino), 2 international. Average age 27. 62 applicants, 74% accepted, 21 enrolled. *Financial support:* Career-related internships or fieldwork, Federal Work-Study, and institutionally sponsored loans available. Support available to part-time students. Financial award application deadline: 3/2; financial award applicants required to submit FAFSA. In 2015, 9 master's awarded. *Degree program information:* Part-time programs available. Part-time. Offers urban and regional planning (MURP). *Application deadline:* For fall admission, 5/1 priority date for domestic students; for winter admission, 10/15 priority date for domestic students; for spring admission, 1/20 priority date for domestic students. Applications are processed on a rolling basis. *Application fee:* $55. Electronic applications accepted. *Graduate Coordinator*, Dr. Do-Hyung Kim, 909-869-4645, Fax: 909-869-4688, E-mail: dohyungkim@cpp.edu.

CALIFORNIA STATE UNIVERSITY, BAKERSFIELD, Bakersfield, CA 93311

General Information State-supported, coed, comprehensive institution. CGS member. *Enrollment:* 9,225 graduate, professional, and undergraduate students; 500 full-time matriculated graduate/professional students (365 women), 218 part-time matriculated graduate/professional students (126 women). *Enrollment by degree level:* 718 master's. *Graduate faculty:* 48 full-time (23 women), 39 part-time/adjunct (23 women). *Tuition, area resident:* Full-time $2246; part-time $1302 per semester. Tuition, state resident: full-time $2246; part-time $1302 per semester. *Graduate housing:* Room and/or apartments available on a first-come, first-served basis to single students; on-campus housing not available to married students. Typical cost: $4411 per year ($6410 including board). Room and board charges vary according to board plan. Housing application deadline: 8/1. *Student services:* Campus employment opportunities, campus safety program, career counseling, child daycare facilities, exercise/wellness program, free psychological counseling, grant writing training, international student services, multicultural affairs office, services for students with disabilities, teacher training, writing training. *Library:* Walter W. Stiern Library.

Computer facilities: A campuswide network can be accessed from student residence rooms and from off campus. Online class registration is available.
Website: http://www.csub.edu/

General Application Contact: Dr. Vandana Kohli, Director, Graduate Programs, 661-664-2786, E-mail: vkohli@csub.edu.

GRADUATE UNITS

Division of Graduate Studies *Financial support:* Fellowships, research assistantships with partial tuition reimbursements, teaching assistantships with partial tuition reimbursements, career-related internships or fieldwork, Federal Work-Study, institutionally sponsored loans, scholarships/grants, and traineeships available. Support available to part-time students. Financial award application deadline: 1/15; financial award applicants required to submit CSS PROFILE. *Degree program information:* Part-time and evening/weekend programs available. Part-time, evening/weekend, online learning. Offers administration (MS); curriculum and instruction (MA Ed); interdisciplinary studies (MA). *Application deadline:* For fall admission, 8/1 priority date for domestic students; for winter admission, 11/1 priority date for domestic students; for spring admission, 3/1 priority date for domestic students. Applications are processed on a rolling basis. *Application fee:* $55. *Application Contact:* Thomas Wallace, Vice President, Student Affairs, 661-664-2161, E-mail: twallace4@csub.edu. *Associate Vice President for Academic Affairs*, Carl Kemnitz, 661-664-3420, Fax: 661-664-3342, E-mail: ckemnitz@csub.edu.

School of Arts and Humanities *Financial support:* Fellowships, career-related internships or fieldwork, institutionally sponsored loans, scholarships/grants, and traineeships available. *Degree program information:* Part-time and evening/weekend programs available. Part-time, evening/weekend. Offers arts and humanities (MA); English (MA); history (MA); Spanish (MA). *Application deadline:* Applications are processed on a rolling basis. *Application fee:* $55. *Application Contact:* Debbie Blowers, Assistant Director of Admissions, 661-664-3381, E-mail: dblowers@csub.edu. *Dean*, Dr. Richard Collins, 661-654-2221, E-mail: rcollins6@csub.edu.

School of Business and Public Administration *Financial support:* Career-related internships or fieldwork available. Offers business administration (MBA); business and public administration (MBA, MPA, MS); health care administration (MS); public administration (MPA). *Application deadline:* Applications are processed on a rolling basis. *Application fee:* $55. *Application Contact:* Debbie Blowers, Assistant Director of Admissions, 661-664-3381, E-mail: dblowers@csub.edu. *Dean*, Dr. Garo Kalfayan, 661-654-2023, Fax: 661-654-2027, E-mail: gkalfayan@csub.edu.

School of Natural Sciences, Mathematics, and Engineering Offers biology (MS); geological sciences (MS); hydrogeology (MS); natural sciences, mathematics, and engineering (MA, MS); petroleum geology (MS); science education (MS); teaching mathematics (MA). *Application fee:* $55. *Application Contact:* Debbie Blowers, Assistant Director of Admissions, 661-664-3381, E-mail: dblowers@csub.edu. *Dean*, Anne M. Houtman, 661-654-3450, E-mail: ahoutman@csub.edu.

School of Social Sciences and Education Offers anthropology (MA); counseling psychology (MS); educational administration (MA); school counseling (MS); social sciences and education (MA, MS, MSW); social work (MSW); sociology (MA); special education (MA). *Application deadline:* Applications are processed on a rolling basis. *Application fee:* $55. *Application Contact:* Debbie Blowers, Assistant Director of Admissions, 661-664-3381, E-mail: dblowers@csub.edu. *Dean*, Dr. Kathleen M. Knutzen, 661-664-2210, Fax: 661-664-2016, E-mail: kknutzen@csub.edu.

CALIFORNIA STATE UNIVERSITY CHANNEL ISLANDS, Camarillo, CA 93012

General Information State-supported, coed, comprehensive institution. *Graduate housing:* Room and/or apartments available on a first-come, first-served basis to single students; on-campus housing not available to married students. Housing application deadline: 6/1.

GRADUATE UNITS

Extended University and International Programs *Degree program information:* Part-time and evening/weekend programs available. Part-time, evening/weekend. Offers biotechnology and bioinformatics (MS); business administration (MBA); computer science (MS); mathematics (MS).

CALIFORNIA STATE UNIVERSITY, CHICO, Chico, CA 95929-0722

General Information State-supported, coed, comprehensive institution. *Enrollment:* 17,462 graduate, professional, and undergraduate students; 885 full-time matriculated graduate/professional students (594 women), 321 part-time matriculated graduate/professional students (200 women). *Enrollment by degree level:* 1,154 master's. *Graduate faculty:* 13 full-time (3 women), 30 part-time/adjunct (11 women). *Tuition, area resident:* Full-time $4146; part-time $2730. *Graduate housing:* Room and/or apartments available on a first-come, first-served basis to single students; on-campus housing not available to married students. Typical cost: $12,234 (including board). Housing application deadline: 3/22. *Student services:* Campus employment opportunities, campus safety program, career counseling, child daycare facilities, exercise/wellness program, free psychological counseling, grant writing training, international student services, low-cost health insurance, multicultural affairs office, services for students with disabilities, teacher training, writing training. *Library:* Meriam Library plus 1 other. *Collection:* Books: 923,470 (physical), 180,505 (digital/electronic); Serial titles: 660 (physical). Study areas open 24 hours, 5–7 days a week; students can reserve study rooms. *Research affiliation:* Sierra Nevada Brewery (nutrition, food sciences, agriculture), Lawrence Livermore Labs - Inspection and Surveillance Robots (engineering and computer science), U.S. Navy Office of Naval Research (engineering), California Department of Transportation Pavement Preservation and Recycling (engineering, computer science, construction management), U.S. Navy Office of Naval Research (engineering), Verizon Wireless/Samsung (business).

Computer facilities: Computer purchase and lease plans are available. 243 computers available on campus for general student use. A campuswide network can be accessed from student residence rooms and from off campus. Online class registration, student account information, calendar, transcripts are available.
Website: http://www.csuchico.edu/

General Application Contact: Judy L. Rice, Admissions Counselor, 530-898-6880, Fax: 530-898-3342, E-mail: graduatestudies@csuchico.edu.

GRADUATE UNITS

Office of Graduate Studies Students: 324 full-time (199 women), 192 part-time (115 women); includes 259 minority (11 Black or African American, non-Hispanic/Latino; 8 American Indian or Alaska Native, non-Hispanic/Latino; 32 Asian, non-Hispanic/Latino; 152 Hispanic/Latino; 1 Native Hawaiian or other Pacific Islander, non-Hispanic/Latino; 55 Two or more races, non-Hispanic/Latino), 149 international. Average age 29. 1,200 applicants, 47% accepted, 318 enrolled. *Faculty:* 131 full-time (66 women), 56 part-time/adjunct (36 women). *Financial support:* Fellowships, research assistantships, teaching assistantships, career-related internships or fieldwork, Federal Work-Study, scholarships/grants, unspecified assistantships, and stipends available. Support available to part-time students. Financial award application deadline: 3/1; financial award applicants required to submit FAFSA. *Degree program information:* Part-time programs available. Part-time, online learning. *Application deadline:* For fall admission, 3/1 priority date for domestic students, 3/1 for international students; for spring admission, 9/15 priority date for domestic students, 9/15 for international students. *Application fee:* $55. Electronic applications accepted. *Application Contact:* Judy L. Rice, Graduate Admissions Coordinator, 530-898-5416, Fax: 530-898-3342, E-mail: jlrice@csuchico.edu. *Office of Graduate Studies*, Dr. E. K. Parks, 530-898-6880, Fax: 530-898-6889, E-mail: ekpark@csuchico.edu.

College of Behavioral and Social Sciences Financial support: Fellowships, teaching assistantships, career-related internships or fieldwork, Federal Work-Study, scholarships/grants, and unspecified assistantships available. Support available to part-time students. Financial award application deadline: 3/1; financial award applicants required to submit FAFSA. Offers anthropology (MA); applied/school psychology (MA); behavioral and social sciences (MA, MPA, MS, MSW); health administration (MPA); local government management (MPA); marriage and family therapy (MS); museum studies (MA); political science (MA); psychological science (MA); public administration (MPA); social science (MA); social work (MSW). *Application deadline:* For fall admission, 3/1 for domestic and international students. *Application fee:* $55. Electronic applications accepted. *Application Contact:* Judy L. Rice, Graduate Admissions Coordinator, 530-898-6880, Fax: 530-898-6889, E-mail: jlrice@csuchico.edu. *Dean*, Dr. Eddie Vela, 530-898-6171, Fax: 530-898-5986, E-mail: bss@csuchico.edu.

College of Business Financial support: Career-related internships or fieldwork, institutionally sponsored loans, scholarships/grants, traineeships, and unspecified assistantships available. Financial award application deadline: 3/1; financial award applicants required to submit FAFSA. *Degree program information:* Part-time programs available. Part-time. Offers business (MBA). *Application deadline:* For fall admission, 3/1 for domestic and international students; for spring admission, 9/15 for domestic and international students. *Application fee:* $55. Electronic applications accepted. *Application Contact:* Dr. Matthew Meuter, MBA Director, 530-898-5880, Fax: 530-898-4584, E-mail: mmeuter@csuchico.edu. *Dean*, Dr. Judy Hennessey, 530-898-6272, Fax: 530-898-4584, E-mail: jehennessey@csuchico.edu.

College of Communication and Education Financial support: Fellowships, teaching assistantships, career-related internships or fieldwork, Federal Work-Study, and stipends available. Support available to part-time students. *Degree program information:* Part-time programs available. Part-time. Offers communication and education (MA, MS); communication sciences and disorders (MA); communication studies (MA); curriculum and instruction (MA); kinesiology (MA); recreation, parks, and tourism (MS); special education (MA); teaching English learners (MA); teaching English learners and special education advising patterns (MA). *Application deadline:* For fall admission, 3/1 for domestic and international students; for spring admission, 9/15 for domestic and international students. *Application fee:* $55. Electronic applications accepted. *Application Contact:* Judy L. Rice, School of Graduate, International, and Interdisciplinary Studies, 530-898-5416, Fax: 530-898-3342, E-mail: jlrice@csuchico.edu. *Dean*, Dr. Angela Trethewey, 530-898-4015, Fax: 530-898-4345, E-mail: cme@csuchico.edu.

College of Engineering, Computer Science, and Construction Management Financial support: Fellowships, research assistantships, teaching assistantships, career-related internships or fieldwork, Federal Work-Study, scholarships/grants, and traineeships available. Support available to part-time students. Financial award application deadline: 3/1; financial award applicants required to submit FAFSA. *Degree program information:* Part-time programs available. Part-time, online learning. Offers computer engineering (MS); computer science (MS); electronics engineering (MS); engineering, computer science, and construction management (MS). *Application deadline:* For fall admission, 3/1 priority date for domestic students, 3/1 for international students; for spring admission, 9/15 priority date for domestic students, 9/15 for international students. *Application fee:* $55. Electronic applications accepted. *Application Contact:* Judy L. Rice, Graduate Admissions Counselor, 530-898-5416, Fax: 530-898-3342, E-mail: jlrice@csuchico.edu. *Dean*, Ricardo Jacquez, 530-898-5963, Fax: 530-898-4070, E-mail: ecc@csuchico.edu.

College of Humanities and Fine Arts Financial support: Teaching assistantships, career-related internships or fieldwork, Federal Work-Study, scholarships/grants, and unspecified assistantships available. Support available to part-time students. Financial award application deadline: 3/1; financial award applicants required to submit FAFSA. Offers art history (MA); art studio (MFA); English (MA); fine arts (MFA); history (MA); humanities and fine arts (MA, MFA). *Application deadline:* For fall admission, 3/1 priority date for domestic students, 3/1 for international students; for spring admission, 9/15 priority date for domestic students, 9/15 for international students. *Application fee:* $55. Electronic applications accepted. *Application Contact:* Judy L. Rice, Graduate Admissions Coordinator, 530-898-5416, Fax: 530-898-3342, E-mail: jlrice@csuchico.edu. *Dean*, Dr. Robert M. Knight, 530-898-5351, Fax: 530-898-5581, E-mail: hfa@csuchico.edu.

College of Natural Sciences Financial support: Fellowships, research assistantships, teaching assistantships, career-related internships or fieldwork, and Federal Work-Study available. Support available to part-time students. Financial award application deadline: 3/1; financial award applicants required to submit FAFSA. *Degree program information:* Part-time programs available. Part-time. Offers biological sciences (MS); environmental science (MS, PSM); general nutritional science (MS); geosciences (MS); hydrology/hydrogeology (MS); math education (MS); natural sciences (MS, MSN, PSM); nursing (MSN); nutrition education (MS). *Application deadline:* For fall admission, 3/1 priority date for domestic students, 3/1 for international students; for spring admission, 9/15 priority date for domestic students, 9/15 for international students. *Application fee:* $55. Electronic applications accepted. *Application Contact:* Judy L. Rice, Graduate Admissions Coordinator, 530-898-5416, Fax: 530-898-3342, E-mail: jlrice@csuchico.edu. *Dean*, Dr. David Hassenzahl, 530-898-6121, Fax: 530-898-4363, E-mail: ns@csuchico.edu.

CALIFORNIA STATE UNIVERSITY, DOMINGUEZ HILLS, Carson, CA 90747-0001

General Information State-supported, coed, comprehensive institution. CGS member. *Enrollment:* 14,635 graduate, professional, and undergraduate students; 916 full-time matriculated graduate/professional students (637 women), 1,755 part-time matriculated graduate/professional students (1,181 women). *Enrollment by degree level:* 2,473 master's, 198 other advanced degrees. *Graduate faculty:* 76 full-time (49 women), 107 part-time/adjunct (78 women). *Graduate housing:* Rooms and/or apartments available on a first-come, first-served basis to single and married students. Housing application deadline: 4/15. *Student services:* Campus employment opportunities, campus safety program, career counseling, child daycare facilities, exercise/wellness program, free psychological counseling, international student services, low-cost health insurance, multicultural affairs office, services for students with disabilities, writing training. *Library:* Leo F. Cain Educational Resource Center. *Collection:* Books: 457,885 (physical), 300,523 (digital/electronic); Serial titles: 6,542 (physical), 75,366 (digital/electronic); Databases: 94. Weekly public service hours: 81; students can reserve study rooms. *Research affiliation:* Los Angeles Biomedical Research Institute at Harbor UCLA Medical Center (biomedical science), Hewlett Packard (catalyst initiative grants).

Computer facilities: 1,100 computers available on campus for general student use. A campuswide network can be accessed from student residence rooms and from off campus. Online class registration is available.
Website: http://www.csudh.edu/

General Application Contact: Brandy McLelland, Director of Student Records and Student Information Services, 310-243-3645, E-mail: bmclelland@csudh.edu.

GRADUATE UNITS

College of Arts and Humanities *Financial support:* Institutionally sponsored loans available. Support available to part-time students. *Degree program information:* Part-time and evening/weekend programs available. Part-time, evening/weekend. Offers arts and humanities (MA, Certificate); English literature (MA); negotiation, conflict resolution and peacebuilding (MA); rhetoric and composition (Certificate); teaching English as a second language (MA, Certificate). *Application deadline:* For fall admission, 6/1 for domestic students. *Application fee:* $55. *Application Contact:* Brandy McLelland, Director of Student Information Services/Registrar, 310-243-3645, E-mail: bmclelland@csudh.edu. *Dean*, Dr. Mitch Avila, 310-243-3389, E-mail: mitchavila@csudh.edu.

College of Business Administration and Public Policy *Degree program information:* Part-time and evening/weekend programs available. Part-time, evening/weekend, online learning. Offers business administration (MBA); business administration and public policy (MBA, MPA); public administration (MPA). *Application deadline:* For fall admission, 4/1 for domestic and international students; for spring admission, 11/1 for domestic students, 10/1 for international students. *Application fee:* $55. *Application Contact:* Betty Vu, Assistant Dean, Graduate and Professional Programs, 310-243-3165, E-mail: bvu@csudh.edu. *Dean*, Dr. Joseph Wen, 310-243-2124, E-mail: jwen@csudh.edu.

College of Education *Degree program information:* Part-time and evening/weekend programs available. Part-time, evening/weekend. Offers education (MA, MS). *Application deadline:* For fall admission, 6/1 priority date for domestic students; for spring admission, 10/1 priority date for domestic students. Applications are processed on a rolling basis. *Application fee:* $55. *Application Contact:* Brandy McLelland, Director of Student Information Services/Registrar, 310-243-3645, E-mail: bmclelland@csudh.edu. *Dean*, Dr. John Davis, 310-243-3510, Fax: 310-243-3518, E-mail: jdavis@csudh.edu.

Division of Graduate Education Degree program information: Part-time and evening/weekend programs available. Part-time, evening/weekend. Offers college counseling (MS); counseling (MS); curriculum and instruction (MA); curriculum and instruction: science education (MA); individualized education (MA); school counseling (MS); school leadership (MA). *Application deadline:* For fall admission, 6/1 for domestic students. *Application fee:* $55. *Application Contact:* Admissions Office, 310-243-3530. *Chair*, Anthony Normore, 310-243-3925, E-mail: anormore@csudh.edu.

Division of Teacher Education Degree program information: Part-time and evening/weekend programs available. Part-time, evening/weekend. Offers early childhood special education (MA); mild/moderate disabilities (MA); moderate/severe disabilities (MA); special education (MA). *Application deadline:* For fall admission, 6/1 for domestic students. *Application fee:* $55. *Application Contact:* Admissions Office, 310-243-3530. *Chair*, Dr. Deandrea Nelson, 310-243-2489, E-mail: dnelson@csudh.edu.

College of Extended and International Education *Faculty:* 17 part-time/adjunct. *Degree program information:* Part-time and evening/weekend programs available. Part-time, evening/weekend, online learning. Offers extended and international education (MA, MS); humanities (MA); quality assurance (MS). *Application fee:* $55. Electronic applications accepted. *Application Contact:* Jackie McKenzie, Extended Education

Registrar, 310-243-3741, E-mail: jmckenzie@csudh.edu. *Dean*, Dr. Kim McNutt, 310-243-3737, Fax: 310-516-4423, E-mail: kmncnutt@csudh.edu.

College of Health, Human Services and Nursing Offers health, human services and nursing (MA, MS, MSN, MSW); marital and family therapy (MS); nursing (MSN); occupational therapy (MS); physical education administration (MA); social work (MSW). *Application fee:* $55. Electronic applications accepted. *Application Contact:* Brandy McLelland, Director of Student Information Services/Registrar, 310-243-3645, E-mail: bmclelland@csudh.edu. *Dean*, Dr. Gary Sayed, 301-243-2046, Fax: 310-217-6800, E-mail: gsayed@csudh.edu.

College of Natural and Behavioral Sciences Offers biology (MS); clinical psychology (MA); computer science (MSCS); health psychology (MA); natural and behavioral sciences (MA, MS, MSCS, Certificate); social research (Certificate); sociology (MA); teaching of mathematics (MA). *Application Contact:* Brandy McLelland, Director of Student Information Services/Registrar, 310-243-3645, E-mail: bmclelland@csudh.edu. *Dean*, Dr. Rodrick Hay, 310-243-2547, E-mail: rhay@csudh.edu.

CALIFORNIA STATE UNIVERSITY, EAST BAY, Hayward, CA 94542-3000

General Information State-supported, coed, comprehensive institution. *Enrollment:* 15,528 graduate, professional, and undergraduate students; 923 full-time matriculated graduate/professional students (612 women), 1,236 part-time matriculated graduate/professional students (703 women). *Enrollment by degree level:* 2,104 master's, 55 doctoral. *Graduate faculty:* 354 full-time (179 women), 485 part-time/adjunct (205 women). *Graduate housing:* On-campus housing not available. *Student services:* Campus employment opportunities, campus safety program, career counseling, exercise/wellness program, free psychological counseling, international student services, low-cost health insurance, services for students with disabilities. *Library:* Hayward Campus Library. *Research affiliation:* Bayer USA Foundation (STEM), Chevron (STEM), Hearst Foundation (STEM), NASA (earth and environmental sciences), Irvine Foundation (education: teacher preparation), Carnegie Foundation (statistics for non-STEM majors).

Computer facilities: Computer purchase and lease plans are available. 700 computers available on campus for general student use. A campuswide network can be accessed from student residence rooms and from off campus. Online class registration is available.
Website: http://www.csueastbay.edu/

General Application Contact: Dr. Donna Wiley, Senior Director of Graduate Studies and Academic Programs, 510-885-2928, Fax: 510-885-4777, E-mail: donna.wiley@csueastbay.edu.

GRADUATE UNITS

Office of Graduate Studies Students: 923 full-time (612 women), 1,236 part-time (703 women); includes 953 minority (219 Black or African American, non-Hispanic/Latino; 5 American Indian or Alaska Native, non-Hispanic/Latino; 338 Asian, non-Hispanic/Latino; 289 Hispanic/Latino; 19 Native Hawaiian or other Pacific Islander, non-Hispanic/Latino; 83 Two or more races, non-Hispanic/Latino), 579 international. *Financial support:* Fellowships, teaching assistantships, career-related internships or fieldwork, Federal Work-Study, institutionally sponsored loans, and scholarships/grants available. Support available to part-time students. Financial award application deadline: 3/2; financial award applicants required to submit FAFSA. *Degree program information:* Part-time and evening/weekend programs available. Part-time, evening/weekend, online learning. Offers interdisciplinary studies (MA, MS). *Application deadline:* For fall admission, 6/30 for domestic and international students. Applications are processed on a rolling basis. *Application fee:* $55. Electronic applications accepted. *Interim Associate Vice President*, Dr. Donna Wiley, 510-885-3716, Fax: 510-885-4777, E-mail: donna.wiley@csueastbay.edu.

College of Business and Economics Students: 143 full-time (68 women), 191 part-time (91 women); includes 130 minority (22 Black or African American, non-Hispanic/Latino; 75 Asian, non-Hispanic/Latino; 24 Hispanic/Latino; 4 Native Hawaiian or other Pacific Islander, non-Hispanic/Latino; 5 Two or more races, non-Hispanic/Latino), 130 international. Average age 30. 691 applicants, 38% accepted, 123 enrolled. *Financial support:* Fellowships, career-related internships or fieldwork, Federal Work-Study, institutionally sponsored loans, and scholarships/grants available. Support available to part-time students. Financial award application deadline: 3/2; financial award applicants required to submit FAFSA. In 2015, 129 master's awarded. *Degree program information:* Part-time and evening/weekend programs available. Part-time, evening/weekend, online learning. Offers business and economics (MA, MBA); economics (MA); entrepreneurship (MBA); finance (MBA); global innovators (MBA); human resources and organizational behavior (MBA); information technology management (MBA); marketing management (MBA); operations and supply chain management (MBA); strategy and international business (MBA). *Application deadline:* For fall admission, 6/30 for domestic and international students. Applications are processed on a rolling basis. *Application fee:* $55. Electronic applications accepted. *Application Contact:* Dr. Donna Wiley, Interim Associate Vice President for Academic Programs and Graduate Studies, 510-885-3716, Fax: 510-885-4777, E-mail: donna.wiley@csueastbay.edu. *Dean*, Jagdish Agrawal, 510-885-3291, E-mail: jagdish.agrawal@csueastbay.edu.

College of Education and Allied Studies Students: 270 full-time (201 women), 142 part-time (91 women); includes 199 minority (45 Black or African American, non-Hispanic/Latino; 1 American Indian or Alaska Native, non-Hispanic/Latino; 43 Asian, non-Hispanic/Latino; 81 Hispanic/Latino; 6 Native Hawaiian or other Pacific Islander, non-Hispanic/Latino; 23 Two or more races, non-Hispanic/Latino), 8 international. Average age 36. 451 applicants, 60% accepted, 166 enrolled. *Financial support:* Career-related internships or fieldwork, Federal Work-Study, and institutionally sponsored loans available. Support available to part-time students. Financial award application deadline: 3/2; financial award applicants required to submit FAFSA. *Degree program information:* Part-time and evening/weekend programs available. Part-time, evening/weekend, online learning. Offers counseling (MS); education (MS); education and allied studies (MS, Ed D); educational leadership (MS, Ed D); kinesiology (MS); marriage and family therapy (MS); mild-moderate disabilities (MS); moderate-severe disabilities (MS); recreation and tourism (MS); school counseling (MS); school psychology (MS); special education (MS). *Application deadline:* For fall admission, 6/30 for domestic and international students. *Application fee:* $55. Electronic applications accepted. *Application Contact:* Dr. Donna Wiley, Interim Associate Vice President for Academic Programs and Graduate Studies, 510-885-3716, Fax: 510-885-4777, E-mail: donna.wiley@csueastbay.edu. *Dean*, Dr. Carolyn Nelson, 510-885-3942, Fax: 510-885-2283, E-mail: carolyn.nelson@csueastbay.edu.

College of Letters, Arts, and Social Sciences Students: 306 full-time (249 women), 469 part-time (339 women); includes 471 minority (134 Black or African American, non-Hispanic/Latino; 3 American Indian or Alaska Native, non-Hispanic/Latino; 136 Asian, non-Hispanic/Latino; 149 Hispanic/Latino; 6 Native Hawaiian or other Pacific Islander, non-Hispanic/Latino; 43 Two or more races, non-Hispanic/Latino), 79 international. Average age 32. 1,463 applicants, 35% accepted, 258 enrolled. *Financial support:* Fellowships, research assistantships, teaching assistantships, career-related internships or fieldwork, Federal Work-Study, institutionally sponsored loans, and scholarships/grants available. Support available to part-time students. Financial award application deadline: 3/2; financial award applicants required to submit FAFSA. *Degree program information:* Part-time and evening/weekend programs available. Part-time, evening/weekend, online learning. Offers anthropology (MA); children, youth, and family services (MSW); communication (MA); community mental health services (MSW); creative writing (MA); geography (MA); health care administration (MPA, MS); history (MA); letters, arts, and social sciences (MA, MPA, MS, MSW); literary studies (MA); management and change in health care (MS); multimedia (MA); music (MA); public administration (MPA); public history (MA); public management and policy analysis (MPA); speech-language pathology (MS); teaching (MA); teaching English to speakers of other languages (MA). *Application deadline:* For fall admission, 6/30 for domestic and international students. Applications are processed on a rolling basis. *Application fee:* $55. Electronic applications accepted. *Application Contact:* Dr. Donna Wiley, Interim Associate Vice President for Academic Programs and Graduate Studies, 510-885-3716, Fax: 510-885-4777, E-mail: donna.wiley@csueastbay.edu. *Dean*, Dr. Kathleen Rountree, 510-885-3161, Fax: 510-885-3164, E-mail: kathleen.rountree@csueastbay.edu.

College of Science Students: 203 full-time (94 women), 432 part-time (180 women); includes 151 minority (17 Black or African American, non-Hispanic/Latino; 1 American Indian or Alaska Native, non-Hispanic/Latino; 84 Asian, non-Hispanic/Latino; 34 Hispanic/Latino; 3 Native Hawaiian or other Pacific Islander, non-Hispanic/Latino; 12 Two or more races, non-Hispanic/Latino), 362 international. Average age 28. 1,867 applicants, 25% accepted, 189 enrolled. *Financial support:* Career-related internships or fieldwork, Federal Work-Study, and institutionally sponsored loans available. Support available to part-time students. Financial award application deadline: 3/2; financial award applicants required to submit FAFSA. In 2015, 217 master's awarded. *Degree program information:* Part-time and evening/weekend programs available. Part-time, evening/weekend. Offers actuarial science (MS); applied mathematics (MS); applied statistics (MS); biological sciences (MS); biostatistics (MS); chemistry (MS); computational statistics (MS); computer networks (MS); computer science (MS); construction management (MS); engineering management (MS); geology (MS); marine science (MS); mathematical statistics (MS); mathematics (MS); mathematics teaching (MS); science (MS); statistics (MS). *Application deadline:* For fall admission, 6/30 for domestic and international students. *Application fee:* $55. Electronic applications accepted. *Application Contact:* Dr. Donna Wiley, Interim Associate Vice President for Academic Programs and Graduate Studies, 510-885-3716, Fax: 510-885-4777, E-mail: donna.wiley@csueastbay.edu. *Dean*, Dr. Jason Singley, 510-885-3441, Fax: 510-885-2035, E-mail: jason.singley@csueastbay.edu.

CALIFORNIA STATE UNIVERSITY, FRESNO, Fresno, CA 93740-8027

General Information State-supported, coed, comprehensive institution. CGS member. *Graduate housing:* Room and/or apartments available on a first-come, first-served basis to single students; on-campus housing not available to married students. Housing application deadline: 4/1. *Research affiliation:* Coleman Foundation (administration), Starburst Foundation (engineering), Garabedian Foundation (agribusiness), California Endowment (arts and humanities).

GRADUATE UNITS

Division of Graduate Studies ***Degree program information:*** Part-time and evening/weekend programs available. Part-time, evening/weekend. Electronic applications accepted.

College of Agricultural Sciences and Technology Degree program information: Part-time and evening/weekend programs available. Part-time, evening/weekend. Offers agricultural sciences and technology (MS); animal science (MS); family and consumer sciences (MS); food science and nutritional sciences (MS); industrial technology (MS); plant science (MS); viticulture and enology (MS). Electronic applications accepted.

College of Arts and Humanities Degree program information: Part-time and evening/weekend programs available. Part-time, evening/weekend. Offers art (MA); arts and humanities (MA, MFA); communication (MA); composition theory (MA); creative writing (MFA); linguistics (MA); literature (MA); mass communication and journalism (MA); music (MA); music education (MA); performance (MA); Spanish (MA). Electronic applications accepted.

College of Engineering and Computer Science Degree program information: Part-time and evening/weekend programs available. Part-time, evening/weekend. Offers civil engineering (MS); electrical engineering (MS); engineering and computer science (MS); mechanical engineering (MS). Electronic applications accepted.

College of Health and Human Services Degree program information: Part-time and evening/weekend programs available. Part-time, evening/weekend. Offers communicative disorders (MA); exercise science (MA); health and human services (MA, MPH, MPT, MS, MSW, DPT); health policy and management (MPH); health promotion (MPH); nursing (MS); physical therapy (MPT, DPT); social work education (MSW); sport psychology (MA). Electronic applications accepted.

College of Science and Mathematics Degree program information: Part-time and evening/weekend programs available. Part-time, evening/weekend. Offers biology (MA); biotechnology (MBT); chemistry (MS); computer science (MS); geology (MS); marine sciences (MS); mathematics (MA); physics (MS); psychology (MA, MS); science and mathematics (MA, MBT, MS); teaching (MA). Electronic applications accepted.

College of Social Sciences Degree program information: Part-time and evening/weekend programs available. Part-time, evening/weekend. Offers criminology (MS); history-teaching option (MA); history-traditional track (MA); international relations (MA); public administration (MPA); social sciences (MA, MPA, MS). Electronic applications accepted.

Craig School of Business Degree program information: Part-time programs available. Part-time. Offers accountancy (MS); business (MBA, MS); business administration (MBA). Electronic applications accepted.

School of Education and Human Development Degree program information: Part-time and evening/weekend programs available. Part-time, evening/weekend. Offers counseling and student services (MS); education (MA); education and human development (MA, MS, Ed D); educational leadership (Ed D); marriage and family therapy (MS); rehabilitation counseling (MS); special education (MA). Electronic applications accepted.

CALIFORNIA STATE UNIVERSITY, FULLERTON, Fullerton, CA 92834-9480

General Information State-supported, coed, comprehensive institution. CGS member. *Enrollment:* 38,128 graduate, professional, and undergraduate students; 2,151 full-time matriculated graduate/professional students (1,213 women), 2,793 part-time matriculated graduate/professional students (1,428 women). *Enrollment by degree level:* 4,794 master's, 150 doctoral. *Graduate housing:* Rooms and/or apartments available on a first-come, first-served basis to single and married students. Typical cost: $13,000 per year ($13,000 including board) for single students; $13,000 per year ($13,000 including board) for married students. Room and board charges vary according to board plan, campus/location and housing facility selected. Housing application deadline: 6/30. *Student services:* Campus employment opportunities, campus safety program, career counseling, child daycare facilities, exercise/wellness program, free psychological counseling, international student services, low-cost health insurance, multicultural affairs office, services for students with disabilities, teacher training, writing training. *Library:* Pollak Library.

Computer facilities: 2,000 computers available on campus for general student use. A campuswide network can be accessed from student residence rooms and from off campus. Online class registration is available.
Website: http://www.fullerton.edu/

General Application Contact: Admissions/Applications, 657-278-2371, E-mail: admissions@fullerton.edu.

GRADUATE UNITS

Graduate Studies ***Degree program information:*** Part-time and evening/weekend programs available. Part-time, evening/weekend, online learning. Electronic applications accepted.

College of Business and Economics Degree program information: Part-time programs available. Part-time. Offers accounting (MBA, MS); business and economics (MA, MBA, MS); business intelligence (MBA); decision science (MBA); economics (MA, MBA); entrepreneurship (MBA); finance (MBA); general (MBA); information systems (MBA, MS); information systems and decision sciences (MS); information systems and e-commerce (MS); information technology (MS); international business (MBA); management (MBA); marketing (MBA); organizational leadership (MBA); risk management and insurance (MBA); taxation (MS). Electronic applications accepted.

College of Communications Degree program information: Part-time programs available. Part-time. Offers advertising (MA); communication studies (MA); communications (MA, MFA); communicative disorders (MA); mass communications research and theory (MA); professional communications (MA); screenwriting (MFA); tourism and entertainment (MA).

College of Education Offers bilingual/bicultural education (MS); community college educational leadership (Ed D); education (MS, Ed D); educational administration (MS); educational technology (MS); elementary curriculum and instruction (MS); higher education (MS); instructional design and technology (MS); pre K-12 educational leadership (Ed D); reading (MS); secondary education (MS); special education (MS); teaching foundational mathematics (MS).

College of Engineering and Computer Science Degree program information: Part-time programs available. Part-time. Offers civil engineering (MS); computer engineering (MS); computer science (MS); electrical engineering (MS); engineering and computer science (MS); environmental engineering (MS); mechanical engineering (MS); software engineering (MS); systems engineering (MS).

College of Health and Human Development Degree program information: Part-time programs available. Part-time. Offers counseling (MS); health and human development (MPH, MS, MSN, MSW, DNP); kinesiology (MS); leadership (MSN); nurse anesthesia (MSN); nurse educator (MSN); nursing (DNP); public health (MPH); social work (MSW); women's health care (MSN).

College of Humanities and Social Sciences Degree program information: Part-time programs available. Part-time. Offers American studies (MA); analysis of specific language structures (MA); anthropological linguistics (MA); anthropology (MA); applied linguistics (MA); clinical/community psychology (MS); communication and semantics (MA); disorders of communication (MA); English (MA); environmental studies (MS); experimental phonetics (MA); French (MA); geography (MA); German (MA); gerontology (MS); history (MA); humanities and social sciences (MA, MPA, MS); linguistics (MA); political science (MA); psychology (MA); public administration (MPA); sociology (MA); Spanish (MA); teaching English to speakers of other languages (MS).

College of Natural Science and Mathematics Degree program information: Part-time programs available. Part-time. Offers applied mathematics (MA); biology (MS); biotechnology (MBT); chemistry (MA, MS); geochemistry (MS); geological sciences (MS); mathematics (MA); natural science and mathematics (MA, MAT, MBT, MS); physics (MS); teaching (MA); teaching science (MAT).

College of the Arts Degree program information: Part-time programs available. Part-time. Offers art (MA, MFA); arts (MA, MFA, MM); music education (MA); music history and literature (MA); performance (MM); piano pedagogy (MA); theatre arts (MFA); theory-composition (MM).

CALIFORNIA STATE UNIVERSITY, LONG BEACH, Long Beach, CA 90840

General Information State-supported, coed, comprehensive institution. *Graduate housing:* Room and/or apartments available on a first-come, first-served basis to single students; on-campus housing not available to married students. Housing application deadline: 4/1. *Research affiliation:* Boeing Company (aerospace engineering and manufacturing).

GRADUATE UNITS

Graduate Studies ***Degree program information:*** Part-time and evening/weekend programs available. Part-time, evening/weekend, online learning. Offers interdisciplinary studies (MA, MS). Electronic applications accepted.

College of Business Administration Degree program information: Part-time and evening/weekend programs available. Part-time, evening/weekend. Offers business administration (MBA). Electronic applications accepted.

College of Education Degree program information: Part-time and evening/weekend programs available. Part-time, evening/weekend. Offers counseling (MS); education (MA, Ed D); educational administration (MA, Ed D); educational psychology (MA); elementary education (MA); marriage and family therapy (MS); school counseling (MS); secondary education (MA); special education (MS); student development in higher education (MS). Electronic applications accepted.

College of Engineering Degree program information: Part-time and evening/weekend programs available. Part-time, evening/weekend. Offers aerospace engineering (MSAE); chemical engineering (MS); civil engineering (MSCE); computer engineering (MSCS); computer science (MSCS); electrical engineering (MSEE); engineering (MS, MSAE, MSCE, MSCS, MSE, MSEE, MSME, PhD); engineering and industrial applied mathematics (PhD); interdisciplinary engineering (MSE); management engineering (MSE); mechanical engineering (MSME). Electronic applications accepted.

College of Health and Human Services Degree program information: Part-time and evening/weekend programs available. Part-time, evening/weekend, online learning. Offers adapted physical education (MA); coaching and student athlete development (MA); communicative disorders (MA); criminal justice (MS); emergency services administration (MS); exercise physiology and nutrition (MS); exercise science (MS); family and consumer sciences (MA); food science (MS); gerontology (MS); health and human services (MA, MPA, MPH, MS, MSN, MSW, DNP, DPT); health care administration (MS); health science (MPH, MS); hospitality foodservice and hotel management (MS); individualized studies (MA); kinesiology (MA); nursing (MSN, DNP); nutritional science (MS); pedagogical studies (MA); physical therapy (DPT); public policy and administration (MPA); recreation administration (MS); social work (MSW); sport and exercise psychology (MS); sport management (MA); sports medicine and injury studies (MS). Electronic applications accepted.

College of Liberal Arts Degree program information: Part-time and evening/weekend programs available. Part-time, evening/weekend. Offers Africa and the Middle East (MA); ancient/medieval Europe (MA); anthropology (MA); applied anthropology (MA); Asia (MA); Asian studies (MA); communication studies (MA); creative writing (MFA); economics (MA); English (MA); French and Francophone studies (MA); general linguistics (MA); geography (MA); German (MA); global logistics (MA); human factors (MS); industrial/organizational psychology (MS); language and culture (MA); Latin America (MA); liberal arts (MA, MFA, MS); modern Europe (MA); philosophy (MA); political science (MA); psychology (MA); religious studies (MA); Spanish (MA); special concentration (MA); teaching English to speakers of other languages (MA); United States (MA); world history (MA). Electronic applications accepted.

College of Natural Sciences and Mathematics Degree program information: Part-time programs available. Part-time. Offers biochemistry (MS); biology (MS); chemistry (MS); geology (MS); geophysics (MS); mathematics (MS); microbiology (MS); natural sciences and mathematics (MS); physics (MS); science education (MS). Electronic applications accepted.

College of the Arts Degree program information: Part-time programs available. Part-time. Offers acting (MFA); art education (MA); art history (MA); arts (MA, MFA, MM); composition (MM); conducting-choral (MM); conducting-instrumental (MM); dance (MA, MFA); design (MFA); instrument/vocal performance (MM); jazz studies (MM); music (MA); opera performance (MM); studio art (MA, MFA); theatre management (MFA). Electronic applications accepted.

CALIFORNIA STATE UNIVERSITY, LOS ANGELES, Los Angeles, CA 90032-8530

General Information State-supported, coed, comprehensive institution. CGS member. *Graduate housing:* Room and/or apartments available on a first-come, first-served basis to single students; on-campus housing not available to married students. *Research affiliation:* NASA (engineering), General Motors (engineering).

GRADUATE UNITS

Graduate Studies ***Degree program information:*** Part-time and evening/weekend programs available. Part-time, evening/weekend. Electronic applications accepted.

Charter College of Education Financial support: Career-related internships or fieldwork and Federal Work-Study available. Support available to part-time students. Financial award application deadline: 3/1. *Degree program information:* Part-time and evening/weekend programs available. Part-time, evening/weekend. Offers applied and advanced studies in education (Graduate Certificate); counseling (MS); education (MA, MS, Ed D, PhD, Graduate Certificate); elementary teaching (MA); special education (MA, PhD). *Application deadline:* For fall admission, 5/1 for domestic and international students. Applications are processed on a rolling basis. *Application fee:* $55. Electronic applications accepted.

College of Arts and Letters Financial support: Career-related internships or fieldwork and Federal Work-Study available. Support available to part-time students. Financial award application deadline: 3/1. *Degree program information:* Part-time and evening/weekend programs available. Part-time, evening/weekend. Offers art (MA); arts and letters (MA, MFA, MM, Certificate, Graduate Certificate); communication studies (MA, MFA); English (MA, Certificate); fine arts (MFA); French (MA); music composition (MM); music education (MA); musicology (MA); performance (MM); philosophy (MA, Graduate Certificate); Spanish (MA); theater arts (MA). *Application deadline:* For fall admission, 5/1 for domestic and international students. Applications are processed on a rolling basis. *Application fee:* $55. Electronic applications accepted.

College of Business and Economics Financial support: Fellowships, career-related internships or fieldwork, and Federal Work-Study available. Support available to part-time students. Financial award application deadline: 3/1. *Degree program information:* Part-time and evening/weekend programs available. Part-time, evening/weekend. Offers accounting (MBA); business and economics (MA, MBA, MS, Postbaccalaureate Certificate); finance and banking (MBA, MS); financial economics (MA); global economics (MA); health care management (MS); international business (MBA, MS); management (MBA, MS). *Application deadline:* For fall admission, 5/1 for international students. Applications are processed on a rolling basis. *Application fee:* $55. Electronic applications accepted.

College of Engineering, Computer Science, and Technology Degree program information: Part-time and evening/weekend programs available. Part-time, evening/weekend. Offers civil engineering (MS); computer science (MS); electrical engineering (MS); engineering, computer science, and technology (MA, MS); industrial and technical studies (MA); mechanical engineering (MS). Electronic applications accepted.

College of Health and Human Services Financial support: Career-related internships or fieldwork and Federal Work-Study available. Support available to part-time students. Financial award application deadline: 3/1. *Degree program information:* Part-time and evening/weekend programs available. Part-time, evening/weekend. Offers child development (MA); criminal justice (MS); criminalistics (MS); health and human services (MA, MS, MSW, Certificate, Post Master's Certificate); nursing (MS); nutritional science (MS); physical education and kinesiology (MA); social work (MSW); speech and hearing (MA); speech-language pathology (MA). *Application deadline:* For fall admission, 5/1 for domestic and international students. Applications are processed on a rolling basis. *Application fee:* $55. Electronic applications accepted.

College of Natural and Social Sciences Degree program information: Part-time and evening/weekend programs available. Part-time, evening/weekend. Offers analytical chemistry (MS); anthropology (MA); biology (MS); geography (MA); geological sciences (MS); history (MA); Latin American studies (MA); mathematics (MS); Mexican-American studies (MA); natural and social sciences (MA, MS); physics (MS); political science (MA); psychology (MA, MS); public administration (MS); sociology (MA).

CALIFORNIA STATE UNIVERSITY, MONTEREY BAY, Seaside, CA 93955-8001

General Information State-supported, coed, comprehensive institution. *Graduate housing:* Rooms and/or apartments available on a first-come, first-served basis to single and married students.

GRADUATE UNITS

College of Business ***Degree program information:*** Part-time and evening/weekend programs available. Part-time, evening/weekend, online learning. Offers business (MBA). Electronic applications accepted.

College of Education ***Degree program information:*** Part-time and evening/weekend programs available. Part-time, evening/weekend. Offers education (MAE). Electronic applications accepted.

College of Health Sciences and Human Services ***Degree program information:*** Part-time programs available. Part-time. Offers social work (MSW). Electronic applications accepted.

College of Science ***Degree program information:*** Part-time programs available. Part-time. Offers applied marine and watershed science (MS); marine science (MS); science (MS, MSMIT). Electronic applications accepted.

School of Computing and Design Offers computing and design (MS, MSMIT). MSMIT offered in conjunction with College of Business. Electronic applications accepted.

CALIFORNIA STATE UNIVERSITY, NORTHRIDGE, Northridge, CA 91330

General Information State-supported, coed, comprehensive institution. CGS member. *Enrollment:* 41,548 graduate, professional, and undergraduate students; 1,986 full-time matriculated graduate/professional students (1,231 women), 1,774 part-time matriculated graduate/professional students (1,071 women). *Enrollment by degree level:* 3,612 master's, 148 doctoral. *Graduate housing:* Room and/or apartments available to single students; on-campus housing not available to married students. *Student services:* Campus employment opportunities, campus safety program, career counseling, child daycare facilities, free psychological counseling, international student services, low-cost health insurance, multicultural affairs office, services for students with disabilities, teacher training. *Library:* Oviatt Library plus 1 other. *Collection:* Books: 1.3 million (physical), 583,651 (digital/electronic); Databases: 234. Students can reserve study rooms. *Research affiliation:* Haagen Company (archaeology), Northridge Hospital (biology), Warner Center Institute (child care), Jet Propulsion Laboratory (engineering), Hughes Aircraft Corporation (engineering), California Institute of Technology (science).

Computer facilities: A campuswide network can be accessed from student residence rooms and from off campus. Online class registration is available.
Website: http://www.csun.edu/

General Application Contact: Dr. Crist Khachikian, Associate Vice President, 818-677-2138.

GRADUATE UNITS

Graduate Studies Students: 1,837 full-time (1,163 women), 1,717 part-time (1,007 women); includes 1,451 minority (135 Black or African American, non-Hispanic/Latino; 11 American Indian or Alaska Native, non-Hispanic/Latino; 311 Asian, non-Hispanic/Latino; 880 Hispanic/Latino; 5 Native Hawaiian or other Pacific Islander, non-Hispanic/Latino; 109 Two or more races, non-Hispanic/Latino), 574 international. Average age 30. 5,937 applicants, 41% accepted, 1173 enrolled. *Faculty:* 717 full-time (306 women), 1,330 part-time/adjunct (688 women). *Financial support:* Fellowships, research assistantships, teaching assistantships, career-related internships or fieldwork, Federal Work-Study, institutionally sponsored loans, scholarships/grants, tuition waivers (partial), and unspecified assistantships available. Support available to part-time students. Financial award applicants required to submit FAFSA. In 2015, 1,992 master's, 11 doctorates awarded. *Degree program information:* Part-time and evening/weekend programs available. Part-time, evening/weekend. *Application deadline:* For fall admission, 3/31 for domestic students; for spring admission, 10/31 for domestic students. Applications are processed on a rolling basis. *Application fee:* $55. *Application Contact:* 818-677-3755. *Associate Vice President*, Dr. Crist Khachikian, 818-677-2138.

College of Arts, Media, and Communication Students: 142 full-time (91 women), 92 part-time (62 women); includes 76 minority (13 Black or African American, non-Hispanic/Latino; 3 American Indian or Alaska Native, non-Hispanic/Latino; 12 Asian, non-Hispanic/Latino; 38 Hispanic/Latino; 10 Two or more races, non-Hispanic/Latino), 45 international. Average age 30. 468 applicants, 39% accepted, 100 enrolled. *Faculty:* 85 full-time (36 women), 206 part-time/adjunct (91 women). *Financial support:* Teaching assistantships, career-related internships or fieldwork, Federal Work-Study, and unspecified assistantships available. Support available to part-time students. Financial award application deadline: 3/1. *Degree program information:* Part-time and evening/weekend programs available. Part-time, evening/weekend. Offers art education (MA); art history (MA); arts, media, and communication (MA, MFA, MM); communication studies (MA); composition (MM); conducting (MM); mass communication (MA); music education (MA); performance (MM); screenwriting (MA); studio art (MA, MFA); theatre (MA); visual communications (MA, MFA). *Application deadline:* For fall admission, 11/30 for domestic students. *Application fee:* $55. *Interim Dean*, Dan Hosken, 818-677-2246, E-mail: dan.hosken@csun.edu.

College of Business and Economics Students: 49 full-time (22 women), 100 part-time (41 women); includes 55 minority (4 Black or African American, non-Hispanic/Latino; 25 Asian, non-Hispanic/Latino; 21 Hispanic/Latino; 5 Two or more races, non-Hispanic/Latino), 23 international. Average age 32. 455 applicants, 30% accepted, 40 enrolled. *Faculty:* 89 full-time (21 women), 72 part-time/adjunct (15 women). *Financial support:* Teaching assistantships and Federal Work-Study available. Support available to part-time students. Financial award application deadline: 3/1. *Degree program information:* Part-time programs available. Part-time. Offers business and economics (MBA). *Application deadline:* For fall admission, 11/30 for domestic students. *Application fee:* $55. *Application Contact:* Dr. Deborah Heisley, Director of Graduate Programs, 818-677-2467, E-mail: deborah.heisley@csun.edu. *Dean*, Dr. Kenneth Lord, 818-677-2455.

College of Engineering and Computer Science Students: 353 full-time (66 women), 289 part-time (54 women); includes 96 minority (1 Black or African American, non-Hispanic/Latino; 1 American Indian or Alaska Native, non-Hispanic/Latino; 37 Asian, non-Hispanic/Latino; 46 Hispanic/Latino; 11 Two or more races, non-Hispanic/Latino), 371 international. Average age 27. 1,451 applicants, 32% accepted, 194 enrolled. *Faculty:* 52 full-time (9 women), 76 part-time/adjunct (16 women). *Financial support:* Teaching assistantships, career-related internships or fieldwork, and Federal Work-Study available. Support available to part-time students. Financial award application deadline: 3/1. *Degree program information:* Part-time and evening/weekend programs available. Part-time, evening/weekend. Offers computer science (MS); electrical engineering (MS); engineering (MS); engineering and computer science (MS); engineering automation (MS); engineering management (MS); manufacturing systems engineering (MS); materials engineering (MS); mechanical engineering (MS); software engineering (MS). *Application deadline:* For fall admission, 11/30 for domestic students. *Application fee:* $55. *Dean*, Dr. S. K. Ramesh, 818-677-4501, E-mail: s.ramesh@csun.edu.

College of Health and Human Development Students: 490 full-time (378 women), 247 part-time (184 women); includes 353 minority (43 Black or African American, non-Hispanic/Latino; 1 American Indian or Alaska Native, non-Hispanic/Latino; 106 Asian, non-Hispanic/Latino; 172 Hispanic/Latino; 4 Native Hawaiian or other Pacific Islander, non-Hispanic/Latino; 27 Two or more races, non-Hispanic/Latino), 60 international. Average age 29. 1,067 applicants, 38% accepted, 186 enrolled. *Faculty:* 83 full-time (49 women), 193 part-time/adjunct (125 women). *Financial support:* Teaching assistantships, career-related internships or fieldwork, Federal Work-Study, and institutionally sponsored loans available. Support available to part-time students. Financial award application deadline: 3/1. *Degree program information:* Part-time and evening/weekend programs available. Part-time, evening/weekend. Offers audiology (MS); environmental and occupational health (MS); family and consumer sciences (MS); health administration (MS); health and human development (MPH, MPT, MS); hospitality and tourism (MS); industrial hygiene (MS); kinesiology (MS); physical therapy (MPT); public health (MPH); recreational sport management/campus recreation (MS); speech language pathology (MS). *Application deadline:* For fall admission, 11/30 for domestic students. *Application fee:* $55. *Application Contact:* 818-677-3755. *Interim Dean*, Tami Abourezk, 818-677-3001.

College of Humanities Students: 75 full-time (45 women), 143 part-time (89 women); includes 353 minority (43 Black or African American, non-Hispanic/Latino; 1 American Indian or Alaska Native, non-Hispanic/Latino; 106 Asian, non-Hispanic/Latino; 172 Hispanic/Latino; 4 Native Hawaiian or other Pacific Islander, non-Hispanic/Latino; 27 Two or more races, non-Hispanic/Latino), 60 international. Average age 32. 166 applicants, 71% accepted, 66 enrolled. *Faculty:* 109 full-time (56 women), 207 part-time/adjunct (128 women). *Financial support:* Teaching assistantships and Federal Work-Study available. Support available to part-time students. Financial award application deadline: 3/1. *Degree program information:* Part-time and evening/weekend programs available. Part-time, evening/weekend. Offers Chicana and Chicano studies (MA); creative writing (MA); humanities (MA); linguistics (MA); literature (MA); rhetoric and composition theory (MA); Spanish (MA). *Application deadline:* For fall admission, 11/30 for domestic students. *Application fee:* $55. *Dean*, Dr. Elizabeth Say, 818-677-3301.

College of Science and Mathematics Students: 70 full-time (38 women), 142 part-time (57 women); includes 61 minority (3 Black or African American, non-Hispanic/Latino; 1 American Indian or Alaska Native, non-Hispanic/Latino; 24 Asian, non-Hispanic/Latino; 27 Hispanic/Latino; 6 Two or more races, non-Hispanic/Latino), 21 international. Average age 28. 267 applicants, 41% accepted, 64 enrolled. *Faculty:* 98 full-time (29 women), 193 part-time/adjunct (93 women). *Financial support:* Research assistantships, teaching assistantships, Federal Work-Study, institutionally sponsored loans, tuition waivers (partial), and unspecified assistantships available. Support available to part-time students. Financial award applicants required to submit FAFSA. *Degree program information:* Part-time and evening/weekend programs available. Part-time, evening/weekend. Offers applied mathematics (MS); biochemistry (MS); biology (MS); chemistry (MS); geology (MS); mathematics (MS); physics (MS); science and mathematics (MS). *Application fee:* $55. *Dean*, Dr. Jerry Stinner, 818-677-2004, E-mail: jerry.stinner@csun.edu.

College of Social and Behavioral Sciences Students: 315 full-time (236 women), 157 part-time (92 women); includes 270 minority (24 Black or African American, non-Hispanic/Latino; 1 American Indian or Alaska Native, non-Hispanic/Latino; 27 Asian, non-Hispanic/Latino; 208 Hispanic/Latino; 10 Two or more races, non-Hispanic/Latino), 18 international. Average age 31. 1,400 applicants, 45% accepted, 197 enrolled. *Faculty:* 120 full-time (56 women), 139 part-time/adjunct (66 women). *Financial support:* Teaching assistantships, career-related internships or fieldwork, Federal Work-Study, and institutionally sponsored loans available. Support available to part-time students. Financial award application deadline: 3/1. *Degree program information:* Part-time and evening/weekend programs available. Part-time, evening/weekend. Offers clinical psychology (MA); general anthropology (MA); general experimental psychology (MA); geography (MA); history (MA); political science (MA); public archaeology (MA); social and behavioral sciences (MA, MSW); social work (MSW); sociology (MA). *Application deadline:* For fall admission, 11/30 for domestic students. *Application fee:* $55. *Dean*, Dr. Stella Z. Theodoulou, 818-677-3317.

Michael D. Eisner College of Education Students: 343 full-time (287 women), 542 part-time (425 women); includes 164 minority (40 Black or African American, non-Hispanic/Latino; 2 American Indian or Alaska Native, non-Hispanic/Latino; 67 Asian, non-Hispanic/Latino; 22 Hispanic/Latino; 1 Native Hawaiian or other Pacific Islander, non-Hispanic/Latino; 32 Two or more races, non-Hispanic/Latino), 20 international. Average age 34. 662 applicants, 55% accepted, 300 enrolled. *Faculty:* 81 full-time (50 women), 210 part-time/adjunct (128 women). *Financial support:* Fellowships, career-related internships or fieldwork, Federal Work-Study, institutionally sponsored loans, scholarships/grants, and tuition waivers (partial) available. Support available to part-time students. Financial award application deadline: 3/1. *Degree program information:* Part-time and evening/weekend programs available. Part-time, evening/weekend. Offers counseling (MS); curriculum and instruction (MA); early childhood special education (MA); education (MA, MA Ed, MS, Ed D); education of the deaf and hard of hearing (MA); educational administration (MA); educational leadership (Ed D); educational psychology (MA Ed); educational technology (MA); educational therapy (MA); English education (MA); language and literacy (MA); mathematics education (MA); mild/moderate disabilities (MA); moderate/severe disabilities (MA); multilingual/multicultural education (MA); secondary science education (MA); teaching and learning (MA). *Application deadline:* For fall admission, 11/30 for domestic students. *Application fee:* $55. *Dean*, Dr. Michael E. Spagna, 818-677-2590.

The Tseng College of Extended Learning Offers business administration (Graduate Certificate); health administration (MPA); health education (MPH); knowledge management (MKM); music industry administration (MA); nonprofit-sector management (Graduate Certificate); public administration (MPA); public sector management and leadership (MPA); social work (MSW); taxation (MS); tourism, hospitality and recreation management (MS).

CALIFORNIA STATE UNIVERSITY, SACRAMENTO, Sacramento, CA 95819

General Information State-supported, coed, comprehensive institution. *Graduate housing:* Room and/or apartments available on a first-come, first-served basis to single students; on-campus housing not available to married students.

GRADUATE UNITS

Office of Graduate Studies ***Degree program information:*** Part-time and evening/weekend programs available. Part-time, evening/weekend. Electronic applications accepted.

College of Arts and Letters Degree program information: Part-time and evening/weekend programs available. Part-time, evening/weekend. Offers arts and letters (MA, MM); communication studies (MA); composition (MA); creative writing (MA); foreign languages (MA); history (MA); literature (MA); music (MM); public historical studies (PhD); public history (MA); studio art (MA); teaching English to speakers of other languages (MA). Electronic applications accepted.

College of Business Administration Degree program information: Part-time and evening/weekend programs available. Part-time, evening/weekend. Offers accountancy (MS); business administration (IMBA, MBA); human resources (MBA); urban land development (MBA). Electronic applications accepted.

College of Education Degree program information: Part-time programs available. Part-time. Offers behavioral sciences (MA); career counseling (MS); curriculum and instruction (MA); education (MA, MS); educational technology (MA); higher education leadership (MA); language and literacy (MA); marriage and family therapy (MS); multicultural education (MA); school counseling (MS); school psychology (MA); special education (MA); vocational rehabilitation counseling (MS). Electronic applications accepted.

College of Engineering and Computer Science Degree program information: Part-time and evening/weekend programs available. Part-time, evening/weekend. Offers civil engineering (MS); computer science (MS); electrical and electronic engineering (MS); engineering and computer science (MS); mechanical engineering (MS); software engineering (MS). Electronic applications accepted.

College of Health and Human Services Degree program information: Part-time programs available. Part-time. Offers criminal justice (MS); family and children's services (MSW); health and human services (MS, MSW); health care (MSW); kinesiology and health science (MS); mental health (MSW); nursing (MS); recreation, parks and tourism administration (MS); social justice and corrections (MSW); speech pathology (MS). Electronic applications accepted.

College of Natural Sciences and Mathematics Degree program information: Part-time programs available. Part-time. Offers biological conservation (MS); chemistry (MS); mathematics (MA); molecular and cellular biology (MS); natural sciences and mathematics (MA, MS); stem cell (MA). Electronic applications accepted.

College of Social Sciences and Interdisciplinary Studies Degree program information: Part-time programs available. Part-time. Offers anthropology (MA); applied behavior analysis (MA); counseling psychology (MA); government (MA); industrial/organizational psychology (MA); public policy and administration (MPPA); social sciences and interdisciplinary studies (MA, MPPA); sociology (MA). Electronic applications accepted.

CALIFORNIA STATE UNIVERSITY, SAN BERNARDINO, San Bernardino, CA 92407

General Information State-supported, coed, comprehensive institution. *Enrollment:* 20,024 graduate, professional, and undergraduate students; 747 full-time matriculated graduate/professional students (498 women), 1,131 part-time matriculated graduate/professional students (668 women). *Enrollment by degree level:* 1,813 master's, 65 doctoral. *Graduate faculty:* 157 full-time (70 women), 67 part-time/adjunct (39 women). Tuition, state resident: full-time $7843; part-time $5011.20 per year. Tuition and fees vary according to course load, degree level, program and reciprocity agreements. *Graduate housing:* Room and/or apartments available on a first-come, first-served basis to single students; on-campus housing not available to married students. *Student services:* Campus employment opportunities, campus safety program, career counseling, child daycare facilities, exercise/wellness program, free psychological counseling, international student services, low-cost health insurance, multicultural affairs office, services for students with disabilities, teacher training. *Library:* Pfau Library.

Computer facilities: Computer purchase and lease plans are available. A campuswide network can be accessed from student residence rooms and from off campus. Online class registration is available.
Website: http://www.csusb.edu/

General Application Contact: Dr. Jeffrey Thompson, Dean of Graduate Studies, 909-537-5058, Fax: 909-537-5078, E-mail: gradstud@csusb.edu.

GRADUATE UNITS

Graduate Studies Students: 747 full-time (498 women), 1,131 part-time (668 women); includes 914 minority (149 Black or African American, non-Hispanic/Latino; 6 American Indian or Alaska Native, non-Hispanic/Latino; 85 Asian, non-Hispanic/Latino; 629 Hispanic/Latino; 2 Native Hawaiian or other Pacific Islander, non-Hispanic/Latino; 43 Two or more races, non-Hispanic/Latino), 262 international. 2,262 applicants, 44% accepted, 665 enrolled. In 2015, 604 master's, 10 doctorates awarded. *Degree program information:* Part-time and evening/weekend programs available. Part-time, evening/weekend. Offers integrative studies (MA). *Application deadline:* For fall admission, 7/17 for domestic students. *Application fee:* $55. *Application Contact:* Olivia Rosas, Director of Admissions, 909-537-7577, Fax: 909-537-7034, E-mail: orosas@csusb.edu. *Dean*, Dr. Jeffrey Thompson, 909-537-5058, Fax: 909-537-5078, E-mail: jthompso@csusb.edu.

College of Arts and Letters Students: 50 full-time (28 women), 101 part-time (76 women); includes 86 minority (11 Black or African American, non-Hispanic/Latino; 2 Asian, non-Hispanic/Latino; 67 Hispanic/Latino; 6 Two or more races, non-Hispanic/Latino), 8 international. 94 applicants, 59% accepted, 44 enrolled. *Financial support:* Application deadline: 3/1. In 2015, 39 master's awarded. *Degree program information:* Part-time and evening/weekend programs available. Part-time, evening/weekend. Offers arts and letters (MA, MFA); communication studies (MA); creative writing (MFA); English composition (MA); integrated marketing communication (MA); Spanish (MA); studio art (MA). *Application deadline:* For fall admission, 7/17 priority date for domestic students. Applications are processed on a rolling basis. *Application fee:* $55. Electronic applications accepted. *Application Contact:* Dr. Jeffrey Thompson, Dean of Graduate Studies, 909-537-5058, Fax: 909-537-5078, E-mail: jthompso@csusb.edu. *Dean*, Dr. Terry L. Ballman, 909-537-5800, Fax: 909-537-5926, E-mail: tballman@csusb.edu.

College of Business and Public Administration Students: 102 full-time (40 women), 398 part-time (197 women); includes 233 minority (45 Black or African American, non-Hispanic/Latino; 2 American Indian or Alaska Native, non-Hispanic/Latino; 34 Asian, non-Hispanic/Latino; 142 Hispanic/Latino; 1 Native Hawaiian or other Pacific Islander, non-Hispanic/Latino; 9 Two or more races, non-Hispanic/Latino), 107 international. 608 applicants, 44% accepted, 150 enrolled. *Financial support:* Application deadline: 3/1. In 2015, 202 master's awarded. *Degree program information:* Part-time and evening/weekend programs available. Part-time, evening/weekend. Offers accountancy (MSA); accounting (MBA); business and public administration (MBA, MPA, MSA); entrepreneurship (MBA); finance (MBA); global business (MBA); information management (MBA); information security (MBA); management (MBA); public administration (MPA); supply chain management (MBA). *Application deadline:* For fall admission, 7/17 for domestic students. Applications are processed on a rolling basis. *Application fee:* $55. *Application Contact:* Dr. Jeffrey Thompson, Dean of Graduate Studies, 909-537-5058, Fax: 909-537-5078, E-mail: jthompso@csusb.edu. *Dean*, Dr. Lawrence C. Rose, 909-537-3703, E-mail: lrose@csusb.edu.

College of Education Students: 295 full-time (219 women), 365 part-time (254 women); includes 313 minority (50 Black or African American, non-Hispanic/Latino; 1 American Indian or Alaska Native, non-Hispanic/Latino; 29 Asian, non-Hispanic/Latino; 220 Hispanic/Latino; 13 Two or more races, non-Hispanic/Latino), 71 international. 402 applicants, 76% accepted, 252 enrolled. In 2015, 188 master's, 10 doctorates awarded. *Degree program information:* Part-time and evening/weekend programs available. Part-time, evening/weekend. Offers counseling and guidance (MS); education (MA, MS, Ed D); educational administration (MA); educational leadership: community college (MA); educational leadership: P-12 (Ed D); rehabilitation counseling (MA). *Application deadline:* For fall admission, 7/17 for domestic students. *Application fee:* $55. *Application Contact:* Dr. Jeffrey Thompson, Dean of Graduate Studies, 909-537-5808, E-mail: jthompso@csusb.edu. *Dean*, Dr. Jay Fiene, 909-537-5600, Fax: 909-537-7011, E-mail: jfiene@csusb.edu.

College of Natural Sciences Students: 44 full-time (16 women), 148 part-time (68 women); includes 69 minority (7 Black or African American, non-Hispanic/Latino; 1 American Indian or Alaska Native, non-Hispanic/Latino; 12 Asian, non-Hispanic/Latino; 47 Hispanic/Latino; 2 Two or more races, non-Hispanic/Latino), 72 international. 549 applicants, 26% accepted, 56 enrolled. *Financial support:* Fellowships, research assistantships, and teaching assistantships available. In 2015, 54 master's awarded. *Degree program information:* Part-time programs available. Part-time. Offers biology (MS); computer science (MS); earth and environmental sciences (MS); health services administration (MS); mathematics (MA); natural sciences (MA, MAT, MPH, MS, MSN); nursing (MSN); public health (MPH); teaching mathematics (MAT). *Application fee:* $55. *Application Contact:* Dr. Jeffrey Thompson, Dean of Graduate Studies, 909-537-5052, E-mail: jthompso@csusb.edu. *Dean*, Dr. Kirsten Fleming, 909-537-5300, Fax: 909-537-7005, E-mail: kfleming@csusb.edu.

College of Social and Behavioral Sciences Students: 251 full-time (192 women), 111 part-time (69 women); includes 207 minority (32 Black or African American, non-Hispanic/Latino; 2 American Indian or Alaska Native, non-Hispanic/Latino; 8 Asian, non-Hispanic/Latino; 151 Hispanic/Latino; 1 Native Hawaiian or other Pacific Islander, non-Hispanic/Latino; 13 Two or more races, non-Hispanic/Latino), 9 international. 601 applicants, 37% accepted, 156 enrolled. *Financial support:* Career-related internships or fieldwork, Federal Work-Study, institutionally sponsored loans, and unspecified assistantships available. Support available to part-time students. In 2015, 121 master's awarded. *Degree program information:* Part-time and evening/weekend programs available. Part-time, evening/weekend. Offers child development (MA); clinical psychology (MS); clinical/counseling psychology (MS); criminal justice (MA); general/experimental psychology (MA); industrial/organizational psychology (MS); national cyber security studies (MA); national security studies (MA); psychology-life span (MA); social and behavioral sciences (MA, MS, MSW); social sciences and globalization (MA); social work (MSW). *Application deadline:* For fall admission, 7/17 for domestic students. *Application fee:* $55. *Application Contact:* Dr. Jeffrey Thompson, Dean of Graduate Studies, 909-537-5058, E-mail: jthompso@csusb.edu. *Dean*, Dr. Jamal Nassar, 909-537-7500, Fax: 909-537-7107, E-mail: jnassar@csusb.edu.

CALIFORNIA STATE UNIVERSITY, SAN MARCOS, San Marcos, CA 92096-0001

General Information State-supported, coed, comprehensive institution. CGS member. *Enrollment:* 12,793 graduate, professional, and undergraduate students; 403 full-time matriculated graduate/professional students (277 women), 213 part-time matriculated graduate/professional students (144 women). *Enrollment by degree level:* 616 master's. *Graduate housing:* Room and/or apartments available on a first-come, first-served basis to single students; on-campus housing not available to married students. Typical cost: $13,240 (including board). Housing application deadline: 10/1. *Student services:* Campus employment opportunities, campus safety program, career counseling, child daycare facilities, exercise/wellness program, free psychological counseling, international student services, low-cost health insurance, multicultural affairs office, services for students with disabilities, teacher training, writing training. *Library:* Kellogg Library.

Computer facilities: A campuswide network can be accessed from student residence rooms and from off campus. Online class registration is available.
Website: http://www.csusm.edu/

General Application Contact: Admissions, 760-750-4848, Fax: 760-750-3248, E-mail: apply@csusm.edu.

GRADUATE UNITS

College of Business Administration ***Degree program information:*** Evening/weekend programs available. Evening/weekend. Offers business administration (MBA).

College of Education, Health and Human Services Offers behavioral health (MSW); children, youth and families (MSW); education, health and human services (MA, MSW, Ed D); speech-language pathology (MA).

School of Education Degree program information: Part-time and evening/weekend programs available. Part-time, evening/weekend. Offers educational administration (MA); educational leadership (Ed D); general education (MA); literacy education (MA); special education (MA).

College of Humanities, Arts, Behavioral and Social Sciences ***Degree program information:*** Part-time and evening/weekend programs available. Part-time, evening/weekend. Offers Hispanic cultures and society (MA); Hispanic language and linguistics (MA); Hispanic literatures and literary theory (MA); history (MA); humanities, arts, behavioral and social sciences (MA); literature and writing studies (MA); psychology (MA); sociological practice (MA). Electronic applications accepted.

College of Science and Mathematics Offers biological sciences (MS); computer science (MS); mathematics (MS); science and mathematics (MS).

CALIFORNIA STATE UNIVERSITY, STANISLAUS, Turlock, CA 95382

General Information State-supported, coed, comprehensive institution. CGS member. *Graduate housing:* Room and/or apartments available on a first-come, first-served basis to single students; on-campus housing not available to married students. Housing application deadline: 7/15. *Research affiliation:* Kaiser Permanente (health care), California Campus Compact–Carnegie Fellowship Program (teaching development for faculty), Valley Mountain Regional Center (development disability), Friends of Turlock Library, EDAW, Inc. (environmental sustainable development), Mathematical Association of America (mathematics).

GRADUATE UNITS

College of Business Administration ***Degree program information:*** Part-time and evening/weekend programs available. Part-time, evening/weekend. Offers business administration (EMBA, MBA).

College of Education ***Degree program information:*** Part-time and evening/weekend programs available. Part-time, evening/weekend. Offers community college leadership (Ed D); curriculum and instruction (MA); education (MA, Ed D, Graduate Certificate); P-12 leadership (Ed D); school administration (MA); school counseling (MA).

College of Human and Health Sciences Offers behavior analysis (MS); counseling psychology (MS); gerontological nursing (MS); human and health sciences (MA, MS, MSW, Graduate Certificate); nursing education (MS); psychology (MA); social work (MSW).

College of Humanities and Social Sciences Offers criminal justice (MA); history (MA); humanities and social sciences (MA, MPA, MS, Certificate); interdisciplinary studies (MA, MS); international relations (MA); literature (Certificate); public administration (MPA); rhetoric and teaching writing (MA); secondary school teachers (MA); teaching English to speakers of other languages (MA).

College of Natural Sciences Offers ecological conservation (MS); ecological economics (MS); genetic counseling (MS); natural sciences (MS).

CALIFORNIA UNIVERSITY OF MANAGEMENT AND SCIENCES, Anaheim, CA 92801

General Information Independent, coed, comprehensive institution.

GRADUATE UNITS

Graduate Programs Offers business administration (MBA, DBA); computer information systems (MS); economics (MS); international business (MS); sports management (MS).

CALIFORNIA UNIVERSITY OF PENNSYLVANIA, California, PA 15419-1394

General Information State-supported, coed, comprehensive institution. CGS member. *Enrollment:* 7,854 graduate, professional, and undergraduate students; 862 full-time matriculated graduate/professional students (558 women), 1,207 part-time matriculated graduate/professional students (747 women). *Enrollment by degree level:* 1,962 master's, 107 other advanced degrees. *Graduate faculty:* 79 full-time (46 women), 62 part-time/adjunct (24 women). Tuition, state resident: full-time $11,280; part-time $5640 per semester. Tuition, nonresident: full-time $16,920; part-time $8460 per semester. *Required fees:* $2876. Tuition and fees vary according to course load, degree level, campus/location and reciprocity agreements. *Graduate housing:* Room and/or apartments available on a first-come, first-served basis to single students; on-campus housing not available to married students. Typical cost: $6596 per year ($10,238 including board). Room and board charges vary according to board plan and housing facility selected. *Student services:* Campus employment opportunities, campus safety program, career counseling, exercise/wellness program, free psychological counseling, grant writing training, international student services, low-cost health insurance, services for students with disabilities, teacher training, writing training. *Library:* Manderino Library. *Collection:* Books: 236,664 (physical), 83,157 (digital/electronic); Databases: 107. Students can reserve study rooms. *Research affiliation:* The Center for Rural Pennsylvania (agriculture), The Technology Collaborative (robotics), International Technical Education Association (curricular development), National Collegiate Athletic Association (NCAA) (tobacco use), Gettysburg Travel Council (travel and tourism), NASA.

Computer facilities: 1,300 computers available on campus for general student use. A campuswide network can be accessed from student residence rooms and from off campus. Online class registration is available.
Website: http://www.calu.edu/

General Application Contact: Nicole Popielarcheck, Assistant Director of Graduate Admissions and Recruitment, 724-938-4029, Fax: 724-938-5712, E-mail: popielarcheck@calu.edu.

GRADUATE UNITS

School of Graduate Studies and Research Students: 1,011 full-time (620 women), 916 part-time (561 women); includes 252 minority (150 Black or African American, non-Hispanic/Latino; 6 American Indian or Alaska Native, non-Hispanic/Latino; 16 Asian, non-Hispanic/Latino; 49 Hispanic/Latino; 3 Native Hawaiian or other Pacific Islander, non-Hispanic/Latino; 28 Two or more races, non-Hispanic/Latino), 12 international. Average age 31. 715 applicants, 77% accepted, 355 enrolled. *Faculty:* 135 full-time (63 women), 29 part-time/adjunct (7 women). *Financial support:* Career-related internships or fieldwork, scholarships/grants, traineeships, tuition waivers (partial), and unspecified assistantships available. Financial award applicants required to submit FAFSA. In 2015, 955 master's awarded. *Degree program information:* Part-time and evening/weekend programs available. Part-time, evening/weekend, online learning. *Application deadline:* For fall admission, 8/1 priority date for domestic and international students; for winter admission, 12/1 priority date for domestic and international students; for spring admission, 5/1 priority date for domestic and international students. Applications are processed on a rolling basis. *Application fee:* $25. Electronic applications accepted. *Application Contact:* Suzanne C. Powers, Director of Graduate Admissions and Recruitment, 724-938-4029, Fax: 724-938-5712, E-mail: powers_s@cup.edu. *Dean,* Dr. Stan Komacek, 724-938-1589, Fax: 724-938-5712, E-mail: komacek@calu.edu.

College of Education and Human Services Financial support: Career-related internships or fieldwork, scholarships/grants, traineeships, and unspecified assistantships available. Financial award applicants required to submit FAFSA. *Degree program information:* Part-time and evening/weekend programs available. Part-time, evening/weekend, online learning. Offers athletic training (MS); clinical mental health counseling (MS); communication disorders (MS); education and human services (M Ed, MAT, MS, MSW); intercollegiate athletic administration (MS); mentally and/or physically handicapped education (M Ed); performance enhancement and injury prevention (MS); reading specialist (M Ed); rehabilitation science (MS); school administration (M Ed); school counseling (M Ed); secondary education (MAT); social work (MSW); sport management (MS); sport psychology (MS); sports counseling (MS); technology education (M Ed); wellness and fitness (MS). *Application deadline:* For fall admission, 8/1 priority date for domestic and international students; for winter admission, 12/1 priority date for domestic and international students; for spring admission, 5/1 priority date for domestic and international students. Applications are processed on a rolling basis. *Application fee:* $25. Electronic applications accepted. *Application Contact:* Suzanne C. Powers, Director of Graduate Admissions and Recruitment, 724-938-4029, Fax: 724-938-5712, E-mail: powers_s@cup.edu. *Dean,* Geraldine Jones, 724-938-4125, E-mail: jones_gm@cup.edu.

College of Liberal Arts Financial support: Career-related internships or fieldwork, scholarships/grants, traineeships, and unspecified assistantships available. *Degree program information:* Part-time and evening/weekend programs available. Part-time, evening/weekend. Offers applied criminology (MA); liberal arts (MA, MS); school psychology (MS). *Application deadline:* For fall admission, 8/1 priority date for domestic and international students; for winter admission, 12/1 priority date for domestic and international students; for spring admission, 5/1 priority date for domestic and international students. Applications are processed on a rolling basis. *Application fee:* $25. Electronic applications accepted. *Application Contact:* Suzanne C. Powers, Director of Graduate Admissions and Recruitment, 724-938-4029, Fax: 724-938-5712, E-mail: powers_s@cup.edu. *Dean,* Dr. Mohamed Yamba, 724-938-4058, E-mail: yamba@calu.edu.

Eberly College of Science and Technology Financial support: Career-related internships or fieldwork, scholarships/grants, traineeships, and unspecified assistantships available. *Degree program information:* Part-time and evening/weekend programs available. Part-time, evening/weekend, online learning. Offers business administration (MBA); business analytics (MBA); entrepreneurship (MBA); legal studies (MS); nursing administration and leadership (MBA); science and technology (MBA, MS). *Application deadline:* For fall admission, 8/1 priority date for domestic and international students; for winter admission, 12/1 priority date for domestic and international students; for spring admission, 5/1 priority date for domestic and international students. Applications are processed on a rolling basis. *Application fee:* $25. Electronic applications accepted. *Application Contact:* Suzanne C. Powers, Director of Graduate Admissions and Recruitment, 724-938-4029, Fax: 724-938-5712, E-mail: powers_s@cup.edu. *Dean,* Dr. Leonard Colelli, 724-938-4169, Fax: 724-938-5743, E-mail: colelli@cup.edu.

CALIFORNIA WESTERN SCHOOL OF LAW, San Diego, CA 92101-3090

General Information Independent, coed, graduate-only institution. *Graduate housing:* On-campus housing not available.

GRADUATE UNITS

Graduate and Professional Programs ***Degree program information:*** Part-time programs available. Part-time. Offers law (JD); trial advocacy (LL M). JD/MSW and JD/MBA offered jointly with San Diego State University. Electronic applications accepted.

CALUMET COLLEGE OF SAINT JOSEPH, Whiting, IN 46394-2195

General Information Independent-religious, coed, comprehensive institution.

GRADUATE UNITS

Program in Leadership in Teaching Offers leadership in teaching (MS Ed).

Program in Public Safety Administration Offers public safety administration (MS).

Program in Quality Assurance Offers quality assurance (MS).

CALVARY BIBLE COLLEGE AND THEOLOGICAL SEMINARY, Kansas City, MO 64147-1341

General Information Independent-religious, coed, comprehensive institution. *Graduate housing:* Rooms and/or apartments available on a first-come, first-served basis to single and married students.

GRADUATE UNITS

Calvary Theological Seminary ***Degree program information:*** Part-time and evening/weekend programs available. Part-time, evening/weekend. Offers Bible and theology (MS); Biblical counseling (MA); Biblical studies (MA); Christian ministry (MA); Christian studies (MS); Christian theology (MA); New Testament (MA); Old Testament (MA); pastoral studies (M Div).

CALVIN COLLEGE, Grand Rapids, MI 49546-4388

General Information Independent-religious, coed, comprehensive institution. *Enrollment:* 3,990 graduate, professional, and undergraduate students; 8 full-time matriculated graduate/professional students (5 women), 120 part-time matriculated graduate/professional students (83 women). *Enrollment by degree level:* 128 master's. *Graduate faculty:* 12 full-time (5 women). *Graduate housing:* Room and/or apartments available on a first-come, first-served basis to single students; on-campus housing not available to married students. Housing application deadline: 4/1. *Student services:* Campus employment opportunities, campus safety program, career counseling, exercise/wellness program, free psychological counseling, international student services, low-cost health insurance, multicultural affairs office, services for students with disabilities, writing training. *Library:* Hekman Library. *Collection:* Books: 714,950 (physical), 346,117 (digital/electronic); Serial titles: 5,893 (physical), 34,583 (digital/electronic); Databases: 137. Weekly public service hours: 90.

Computer facilities: Computer purchase and lease plans are available. 1,025 computers available on campus for general student use. A campuswide network can be accessed from student residence rooms and from off campus. Online class registration is available.
Website: http://www.calvin.edu/

General Application Contact: Cindi Hoekstra, Graduate Program Coordinator, 616-516-6158, Fax: 616-526-6505, E-mail: choekstr@calvin.edu.

GRADUATE UNITS

Graduate Programs in Education Students: 8 full-time (5 women), 120 part-time (83 women); includes 7 minority (1 Black or African American, non-Hispanic/Latino; 1 American Indian or Alaska Native, non-Hispanic/Latino; 2 Asian, non-Hispanic/Latino; 1 Hispanic/Latino; 2 Two or more races, non-Hispanic/Latino), 18 international. Average age 29. 21 applicants, 76% accepted, 16 enrolled. *Faculty:* 12 full-time (5 women). *Financial support:* Federal Work-Study, scholarships/grants, and tuition waivers (full and partial) available. Financial award application deadline: 4/3; financial award applicants required to submit FAFSA. In 2015, 27 master's awarded. *Degree program information:* Part-time programs available. Part-time. Offers curriculum and instruction (M Ed); educational leadership (M Ed); inclusion specialist (M Ed); literacy (M Ed). *Application deadline:* For fall admission, 8/1 priority date for domestic students, 5/1 priority date for international students; for spring admission, 1/1 priority date for domestic students, 12/1 priority date for international students; for summer admission, 5/18 for domestic students. Applications are processed on a rolling basis. *Application fee:* $0. Electronic applications accepted. *Application Contact:* Cindi Hoekstra, Program Coordinator, 616-526-6158, Fax: 616-526-6505, E-mail: choekstr@calvin.edu. *Graduate Program Director,* Dr. David Smith, 616-526-6158, Fax: 616-526-6505, E-mail: dsmith@calvin.edu.

CALVIN THEOLOGICAL SEMINARY, Grand Rapids, MI 49546-4387

General Information Independent-religious, coed, graduate-only institution. *Graduate housing:* Rooms and/or apartments available on a first-come, first-served basis to single and married students. Housing application deadline: 4/1.

GRADUATE UNITS

Graduate and Professional Programs ***Degree program information:*** Part-time programs available. Part-time. Offers Bible and theology (MA); divinity (M Div); educational ministry (MA); historical theology (PhD); missions and evangelism (MA); pastoral care (MA); philosophical and moral theology (PhD); systematic theology (PhD); theological studies (MTS); theology (Th M); worship (MA); youth and family ministries (MA). Electronic applications accepted.

CAMBRIDGE COLLEGE, Cambridge, MA 02138-5304

General Information Independent, coed, comprehensive institution. CGS member. *Graduate housing:* On-campus housing not available.

GRADUATE UNITS

School of Education ***Degree program information:*** Part-time and evening/weekend programs available. Part-time, evening/weekend, online learning. Offers autism specialist (M Ed); autism/behavior analyst (M Ed); behavior analyst (Post-Master's Certificate); behavioral management (M Ed); early childhood teacher (M Ed); education specialist in curriculum and instruction (CAGS); educational leadership (Ed D); elementary teacher (M Ed); English as a second language (M Ed, Certificate); general science (M Ed); health education (Post-Master's Certificate); health/family and consumer sciences (M Ed); history (M Ed); individualized (M Ed); information technology literacy (M Ed); instructional technology (M Ed); interdisciplinary studies (M Ed); library teacher (M Ed); literacy education (M Ed); mathematics (M Ed); mathematics specialist (Certificate); middle school mathematics and science (M Ed); school administration (M Ed, CAGS); school guidance counselor (M Ed); school nurse education (M Ed); school social worker/school adjustment counselor (M Ed); special education administrator (CAGS); special education/moderate disabilities (M Ed); teaching skills and methodologies (M Ed). Electronic applications accepted.

School of Management ***Degree program information:*** Part-time and evening/weekend programs available. Part-time, evening/weekend. Offers business negotiation and conflict resolution (M Mgt); general business (M Mgt); health care informatics (M Mgt); health care management (M Mgt); leadership in human and organizational dynamics (M Mgt); non-profit and public organization management (M Mgt); small business development (M Mgt); technology management (M Mgt). Electronic applications accepted.

School of Psychology and Counseling ***Degree program information:*** Part-time and evening/weekend programs available. Part-time, evening/weekend. Offers addiction counseling (M Ed); alcohol and drug counseling (Certificate); counseling psychology (M Ed, CAGS); counseling psychology: forensic counseling (M Ed); marriage and family therapy (M Ed); mental health and addiction counseling (M Ed); mental health counseling (M Ed); mental health counseling for school guidance counselors (Post Master's Certificate); psychological studies (M Ed); school adjustment and mental health counseling (M Ed); school adjustment, mental health and addiction counseling (M Ed); school guidance counselor (M Ed); trauma studies (Certificate). Electronic applications accepted.

CAMERON UNIVERSITY, Lawton, OK 73505-6377

General Information State-supported, coed, comprehensive institution. *Graduate housing:* Room and/or apartments available on a first-come, first-served basis to single students; on-campus housing not available to married students. *Research affiliation:* Telos-Ok (simulations), Army Research Institute (human factors), Advanced Systems Technology, Inc. (informational systems), Dynamics Research Corporation (multimedia systems), Eagle Systems, Inc. (multimedia systems), Halliburton (energy systems).

GRADUATE UNITS

Office of Graduate Studies ***Degree program information:*** Part-time and evening/weekend programs available. Part-time, evening/weekend, online learning. Offers behavioral sciences (MS); business administration (MBA); education (M Ed); educational leadership (MS); entrepreneurial studies (MS); teaching (MAT). Electronic applications accepted.

CAMPBELLSVILLE UNIVERSITY, Campbellsville, KY 42718-2799

General Information Independent-religious, coed, comprehensive institution. *Enrollment:* 3,128 graduate, professional, and undergraduate students; 235 full-time matriculated graduate/professional students (168 women), 196 part-time matriculated graduate/professional students (118 women). *Enrollment by degree level:* 431 master's. *Graduate faculty:* 55 full-time (25 women), 29 part-time/adjunct (18 women). *Tuition, area resident:* Full-time $13,200; part-time $399 per credit. *Required fees:* $75 per term. Tuition and fees vary according to program. *Graduate housing:* Rooms and/or apartments available on a first-come, first-served basis to single and married students. Typical cost: $7770 (including board) for single students; $7770 (including board) for married students. Room and board charges vary according to housing facility selected. Housing application deadline: 6/30. *Student services:* Campus employment opportunities, campus safety program, career counseling, exercise/wellness program, international student services, teacher training, writing training. *Library:* Montgomery Library. *Collection:* Books: 167,938 (physical), 202,225 (digital/electronic); Serial titles: 185 (physical), 26,515 (digital/electronic); Databases: 80. Weekly public service hours: 77; students can reserve study rooms.

Computer facilities: 220 computers available on campus for general student use. A campuswide network can be accessed from student residence rooms and from off campus. Online class registration is available.
Website: http://www.campbellsville.edu/

General Application Contact: Monica Bamwine, Assistant Director of Admissions, 270-789-5221, Fax: 270-789-5071, E-mail: mkbamwine@campbellsville.edu.

GRADUATE UNITS

Carver School of Social Work Students: 41 full-time (38 women), 42 part-time (37 women); includes 11 minority (10 Black or African American, non-Hispanic/Latino; 1 Hispanic/Latino). Average age 32. 73 applicants, 79% accepted, 42 enrolled. *Faculty:* 8 full-time (6 women), 3 part-time/adjunct (all women). *Financial support:* Applicants required to submit FAFSA. In 2015, 45 master's awarded. *Degree program information:* Part-time and evening/weekend programs available. Part-time, evening/weekend, 100% online, blended/hybrid learning. Offers social work (MA). *Application deadline:* Applications are processed on a rolling basis. *Application fee:* $25. Electronic applications accepted. *Application Contact:* Monica Bamwine, Assistant Director of Admissions, 270-789-5221, Fax: 270-789-5071, E-mail: mkbamwine@campbellsville.edu. *Program Director,* Dr. Helen K. Mudd, 270-789-5045, Fax: 270-789-5542, E-mail: hkmudd@campbellsville.edu.

College of Arts and Sciences Students: 5 full-time (2 women), 4 part-time (1 woman); includes 3 minority (1 Black or African American, non-Hispanic/Latino; 1 Hispanic/Latino; 1 Two or more races, non-Hispanic/Latino). Average age 26. 11 applicants, 73% accepted, 7 enrolled. *Faculty:* 5 full-time (2 women), 3 part-time/adjunct (2 women). *Financial support:* Unspecified assistantships available. Financial award application deadline: 6/1; financial award applicants required to submit FAFSA. *Degree program information:* Part-time and evening/weekend programs available. Part-time, evening/weekend. Offers social science (MA). *Application deadline:* Applications are processed on a rolling basis. *Application fee:* $25. Electronic applications accepted. *Application Contact:* Monica Bamwine, Assistant Director of Admissions, 270-789-5221, Fax: 270-789-5071, E-mail: mkbamwine@campbellsville.edu. *Dean,* Dr. Mike Page, 270-789-5394.

School of Business and Economics Students: 19 full-time (9 women), 82 part-time (46 women); includes 13 minority (10 Black or African American, non-Hispanic/Latino; 3 Hispanic/Latino), 19 international. Average age 32. 119 applicants, 40% accepted, 40 enrolled. *Faculty:* 7 full-time (1 woman), 4 part-time/adjunct (3 women). *Financial support:* Tuition waivers (full) and unspecified assistantships available. Financial award application deadline: 6/1; financial award applicants required to submit FAFSA. In 2015, 55 master's awarded. *Degree program information:* Part-time and evening/weekend programs available. Part-time, evening/weekend, 100% online, blended/hybrid learning. Offers business administration (MBA). *Application deadline:* For fall admission, 9/14 priority date for domestic and international students; for winter admission, 1/18 priority date for domestic and international students; for spring admission, 4/4 priority date for domestic and international students. Applications are processed on a rolling basis. *Application fee:* $25. Electronic applications accepted. *Application Contact:* Monica Bamwine, Assistant Director of Admissions, 270-789-5221, Fax: 270-789-5071, E-mail: mkbamwine@campbellsville.edu. *Dean,* Dr. Patricia H. Cowherd, 270-789-5553, Fax: 270-789-5066, E-mail: phcowherd@campbellsville.edu.

School of Education Students: 20 full-time (15 women), 116 part-time (85 women); includes 14 minority (all Black or African American, non-Hispanic/Latino). Average age 37. 167 applicants, 54% accepted, 76 enrolled. *Faculty:* 13 full-time (10 women), 8 part-time/adjunct (6 women). *Financial support:* Scholarships/grants and unspecified assistantships available. Support available to part-time students. Financial award application deadline: 6/1; financial award applicants required to submit FAFSA. In 2015, 65 master's awarded. *Degree program information:* Part-time and evening/weekend programs available. Part-time, evening/weekend, 100% online, blended/hybrid learning. Offers special education (MASE). *Application deadline:* For fall admission, 6/1 priority date for domestic students, 5/1 priority date for international students; for spring admission, 11/1 priority date for domestic students, 10/1 priority date for international students. Applications are processed on a rolling basis. *Application fee:* $25. Electronic applications accepted. *Application Contact:* Monica Bamwine, Assistant Director of Admissions, 270-789-5221, Fax: 270-789-5071, E-mail: redeaton@campbellsville.edu. *Dean,* Dr. Beverly Ennis, 270-789-5344, Fax: 270-789-5206, E-mail: bcennis@campbellsville.edu.

School of Music Students: 1 (woman) full-time, 18 part-time (9 women), 10 international. Average age 28. 7 applicants, 86% accepted, 6 enrolled. *Faculty:* 13 full-time (5 women), 8 part-time/adjunct (3 women). *Financial support:* In 2015–16, 19 students received support. Scholarships/grants available. Support available to part-time students. Financial award application deadline: 6/1; financial award applicants required to submit FAFSA. In 2015, 12 master's awarded. *Degree program information:* Part-time programs available. Part-time. Offers church music (MM); conducting (MM); instrumental performance (MM); music (MA); music education (MM); musicology (MA); pedagogy and performance (MM); worship (MA). *Application deadline:* For fall admission, 6/1 priority date for domestic students, 5/1 priority date for international students; for spring admission, 11/1 priority date for domestic students, 10/1 priority date for international students. Applications are processed on a rolling basis. *Application fee:* $25. Electronic applications accepted. *Application Contact:* Monica Bamwine, Assistant Director of Admissions, 270-789-5221, Fax: 270-789-5071, E-mail: mkbamwine@campbellsville.edu. *Dean,* Dr. Tony Cunha, 270-789-5240, Fax: 270-789-5524, E-mail: accunha@campbellsville.edu.

School of Theology Students: 1 full-time (0 women), 60 part-time (26 women); includes 28 minority (25 Black or African American, non-Hispanic/Latino; 1 American Indian or Alaska Native, non-Hispanic/Latino; 1 Asian, non-Hispanic/Latino; 1 Two or more races, non-Hispanic/Latino), 1 international. Average age 43. 65 applicants, 45% accepted, 25 enrolled. *Faculty:* 10 full-time (2 women), 4 part-time/adjunct (2 women). *Financial support:* Scholarships/grants and unspecified assistantships available. Financial award application deadline: 6/1; financial award applicants required to submit FAFSA. In 2015, 24 master's awarded. *Degree program information:* Part-time and evening/weekend programs available. Part-time, evening/weekend, 100% online, blended/hybrid learning. Offers marriage and family therapy (MMFT); theology (M Th). *Application deadline:* For fall admission, 8/25 priority date for domestic students; for spring admission, 1/25 for domestic students. Applications are processed on a rolling basis. *Application fee:* $25. Electronic applications accepted. *Application Contact:* Monica Bamwine, Assistant Director of Admissions, 270-789-5221, Fax: 270-789-5071, E-mail: mkbamwine@campbellsville.edu. *Dean,* Dr. John E. Hurtgen, 270-789-5077, Fax: 270-789-5050, E-mail: jehurtgen@campbellsville.edu.

CAMPBELL UNIVERSITY, Buies Creek, NC 27506

General Information Independent-religious, coed, university. *Graduate housing:* Rooms and/or apartments available on a first-come, first-served basis to single and married students. Housing application deadline: 6/2.

GRADUATE UNITS

Graduate and Professional Programs ***Degree program information:*** Part-time and evening/weekend programs available. Part-time, evening/weekend.

College of Pharmacy and Health Sciences Degree program information: Part-time and evening/weekend programs available. Part-time, evening/weekend. Offers clinical research (MS); pharmaceutical sciences (MS); pharmacy (Pharm D); physician assistant (MPAP); public health (MS). Electronic applications accepted.

Divinity School Offers Christian ministry (MA); divinity (M Div); ministry (D Min).

Lundy-Fetterman School of Business Degree program information: Part-time and evening/weekend programs available. Part-time, evening/weekend. Offers business (MBA, MTWM).

Norman Adrian Wiggins School of Law Offers law (JD). JD/MPA offered in partnership with North Carolina State University. Electronic applications accepted.

School of Education Degree program information: Part-time and evening/weekend programs available. Part-time, evening/weekend. Offers elementary education (M Ed); interdisciplinary studies (M Ed); middle grades education (M Ed); physical education (M Ed); school administration (MSA); school counseling (M Ed); secondary education (M Ed).

CANADIAN COLLEGE OF NATUROPATHIC MEDICINE, Toronto, ON M2K 1E2, Canada

General Information Independent, coed, primarily women, graduate-only institution. *Graduate housing:* Room and/or apartments available on a first-come, first-served basis to single students; on-campus housing not available to married students. Housing application deadline: 4/30. *Research affiliation:* Ottawa Regional Cancer Centre, McMaster University, University of Oxford, Hospital for Sick Children, Mayo Clinic, Johns Hopkins University.

GRADUATE UNITS

Bachelor of Naturopathy Program Offers naturopathy (BN). Electronic applications accepted.

CANADIAN MEMORIAL CHIROPRACTIC COLLEGE, Toronto, ON M2H 3J1, Canada

General Information Independent, coed, graduate-only institution. *Graduate housing:* On-campus housing not available. *Research affiliation:* University of Waterloo, University of Calgary, University of Toronto.

GRADUATE UNITS

Certificate Programs Offers chiropractic clinical sciences (Certificate); chiropractic radiology (Certificate); chiropractic sports sciences (Certificate); clinical acupuncture (Certificate).

Professional Program Offers chiropractic (DC).

CANADIAN SOUTHERN BAPTIST SEMINARY, Cochrane, AB T4C 2G1, Canada

General Information Independent-religious, coed, graduate-only institution. *Enrollment by degree level:* 36 master's. *Graduate faculty:* 6 full-time (0 women), 3 part-time/adjunct (0 women). Tuition and fees vary according to course load. *Graduate housing:* Rooms and/or apartments available on a first-come, first-served basis to single and married students. Housing application deadline: 7/1. *Student services:* Campus employment opportunities, free psychological counseling, international student services. *Library:* Keith C. Wills Library. *Collection:* Books: 40,100 (physical), 1,970 (digital/electronic). Weekly public service hours: 65.

Computer facilities: 6 computers available on campus for general student use. Online class registration is available.
Website: http://www.csbs.ca/

General Application Contact: Mike Sharkey, Admissions Counselor, 403-932-6622 Ext. 251, Fax: 403-932-7049, E-mail: admissions@csbs.ca.

GRADUATE UNITS

Graduate Programs Students: 10 full-time (1 woman), 26 part-time (10 women); includes 12 minority (2 Black or African American, non-Hispanic/Latino; 8 Asian, non-Hispanic/Latino; 2 Hispanic/Latino). Average age 29. 10 applicants, 100% accepted, 10 enrolled. *Faculty:* 6 full-time (0 women), 3 part-time/adjunct (0 women). *Financial support:* Scholarships/grants available. Financial award application deadline: 7/1. In 2015, 15 master's awarded. *Degree program information:* Part-time programs available. Part-time, 100% online, blended/hybrid learning. Offers Biblical studies (MBS); Christian ministry (MCMin); Christian studies (MCS); ministry (M Div). *Application deadline:* For fall admission, 7/1 priority date for domestic and international students; for winter admission, 11/15 priority date for domestic and international students. Applications are processed on a rolling basis. *Application fee:* $50 ($150 for international students). *Application Contact:* Kathleen McNaughton, Registrar, 403-932-6622 Ext. 221, E-mail: kathleen.mcnaughton@csbs.ca. *Academic Dean*, Dr. Steve Booth, 403-932-6622 Ext. 232, E-mail: steve.booth@csbs.ca.

CANISIUS COLLEGE, Buffalo, NY 14208-1098

General Information Independent-religious, coed, comprehensive institution. *Enrollment:* 3,904 graduate, professional, and undergraduate students; 499 full-time matriculated graduate/professional students (308 women), 716 part-time matriculated graduate/professional students (433 women). *Enrollment by degree level:* 1,095 master's. *Graduate faculty:* 65 full-time (30 women), 97 part-time/adjunct (54 women). *Tuition, area resident:* Full-time $14,040; part-time $9360 per semester. *Required fees:* $644; $161 per term. *Graduate housing:* Room and/or apartments available on a first-come, first-served basis to single students; on-campus housing not available to married students. Typical cost: $7500 per year ($12,766 including board). Room and board charges vary according to board plan, campus/location and housing facility selected. Housing application deadline: 5/1. *Student services:* Campus employment opportunities, campus safety program, career counseling, exercise/wellness program, free psychological counseling, international student services, multicultural affairs office, services for students with disabilities, teacher training. *Library:* Andrew L. Bouwhuis Library plus 1 other. *Collection:* Books: 313,916 (physical), 74,353 (digital/electronic); Serial titles: 1,558 (physical), 51,960 (digital/electronic); Databases: 106. Weekly public service hours: 158; students can reserve study rooms. *Research affiliation:* Eduventures (enrollment management).

Computer facilities: Computer purchase and lease plans are available. 700 computers available on campus for general student use. A campuswide network can be accessed from student residence rooms and from off campus. Online class registration, online accounts are available.
Website: http://www.canisius.edu/

General Application Contact: Arveal L. Drummer, Director of Graduate Admissions, 716-888-2210, Fax: 716-888-3290, E-mail: drummera@canisius.edu.

GRADUATE UNITS

Graduate Division Students: 499 full-time (308 women), 716 part-time (433 women); includes 152 minority (71 Black or African American, non-Hispanic/Latino; 4 American Indian or Alaska Native, non-Hispanic/Latino; 18 Asian, non-Hispanic/Latino; 46 Hispanic/Latino; 13 Two or more races, non-Hispanic/Latino), 50 international. Average age 29. 905 applicants, 76% accepted, 394 enrolled. *Faculty:* 65 full-time (30 women), 97 part-time/adjunct (54 women). *Financial support:* Career-related internships or fieldwork, Federal Work-Study, scholarships/grants, tuition waivers (partial), and unspecified assistantships available. Support available to part-time students. Financial award application deadline: 4/30; financial award applicants required to submit FAFSA. In 2015, 594 master's, 66 other advanced degrees awarded. *Degree program information:* Part-time and evening/weekend programs available. Part-time, evening/weekend, 100% online, blended/hybrid learning. *Application deadline:* Applications are processed on a rolling basis. *Application fee:* $25. Electronic applications accepted. *Application Contact:* Kathleen B. Davis, Vice President for Enrollment Management, 716-888-2500, Fax: 716-888-3195, E-mail: daviskb@canisius.edu. *Vice President for Academic Affairs*, Dr. Margaret C. McCarthy, 716-888-2120, Fax: 716-888-2120, E-mail: mmccarth@canisius.edu.

College of Arts and Sciences Students: 21 full-time (19 women), 43 part-time (30 women); includes 6 minority (2 Black or African American, non-Hispanic/Latino; 1 Asian, non-Hispanic/Latino; 3 Hispanic/Latino), 4 international. Average age 31. 97 applicants, 34% accepted, 24 enrolled. *Faculty:* 6 full-time (4 women), 6 part-time/adjunct (4 women). *Financial support:* Career-related internships or fieldwork, Federal Work-Study, scholarships/grants, tuition waivers (partial), and unspecified assistantships available. Financial award application deadline: 4/30; financial award applicants required to submit FAFSA. In 2015, 33 master's awarded. *Degree program information:* Part-time and evening/weekend programs available. Part-time, evening/weekend, 100% online, blended/hybrid learning. Offers anthrozoology (MS); arts and sciences (MS); communication and leadership (MS). *Application deadline:* For fall admission, 7/15 priority date for domestic students; for spring admission, 4/15 priority date for domestic students. Applications are processed on a rolling basis. *Application fee:* $25. Electronic applications accepted. *Application Contact:* Kathleen B. Davis, Vice President for Enrollment Management, 716-888-2500, Fax: 716-888-3195, E-mail: daviskb@canisius.edu. *Interim Dean of Arts and Sciences*, Dr. Patricia E. Erickson, 716-888-2793, E-mail: ericksop@canisius.edu.

Richard J. Wehle School of Business Students: 134 full-time (56 women), 154 part-time (62 women); includes 38 minority (13 Black or African American, non-Hispanic/Latino; 1 American Indian or Alaska Native, non-Hispanic/Latino; 12 Asian, non-Hispanic/Latino; 11 Hispanic/Latino; 1 Two or more races, non-Hispanic/Latino), 13 international. Average age 28. 214 applicants, 77% accepted, 118 enrolled. *Faculty:* 26 full-time (5 women), 14 part-time/adjunct (4 women). *Financial support:* Career-related internships or fieldwork, Federal Work-Study, scholarships/grants, tuition waivers (partial), and unspecified assistantships available. Support available to part-time students. Financial award application deadline: 4/30; financial award applicants required to submit FAFSA. In 2015, 141 master's awarded. *Degree program information:* Part-time and evening/weekend programs available. Part-time, evening/weekend. Offers accounting (MBA); business (MBA, MS); business administration (MBA); forensic accounting (MS); international business (MS); professional accounting (MBA). *Application deadline:* For fall admission, 7/1 priority date for domestic students; for spring admission, 11/1 priority date for domestic students. Applications are processed on a rolling basis. *Application fee:* $25. Electronic applications accepted. *Application Contact:* Kathleen B. Davis, Vice President of Enrollment Management, 716-888-2500, Fax: 716-888-3195, E-mail: daviskb@canisius.edu. *Interim Dean*, Dr. Richard A. Shick, 716-888-2160, Fax: 716-888-2145, E-mail: gradubus@canisius.edu.

School of Education and Human Services Students: 344 full-time (233 women), 519 part-time (341 women); includes 108 minority (56 Black or African American, non-Hispanic/Latino; 3 American Indian or Alaska Native, non-Hispanic/Latino; 5 Asian, non-Hispanic/Latino; 32 Hispanic/Latino; 12 Two or more races, non-Hispanic/Latino), 33 international. Average age 30. 594 applicants, 82% accepted, 252 enrolled. *Faculty:* 33 full-time (21 women), 77 part-time/adjunct (46 women). *Financial support:* Career-related internships or fieldwork, Federal Work-Study, scholarships/grants, tuition waivers (partial), and unspecified assistantships available. Support available to part-time students. Financial award application deadline: 4/30; financial award applicants required to submit FAFSA. In 2015, 420 master's awarded. *Degree program information:* Part-time and evening/weekend programs available. Part-time, evening/weekend, 100% online, blended/hybrid learning. Offers adolescence education (MS Ed); applied nutrition (MS, Certificate); business and marketing education (MS Ed); childhood education (MS Ed); college student personnel (MS Ed); community and school health (MS); community mental health counseling (MS); counseling and human services (MS); deaf education (MS Ed); deaf/adolescent education, grades 7-12 (MS Ed); deaf/childhood education, grades 1-6 (MS Ed); differentiated instruction (MS Ed); education administration (MS); education and human services (MS, MS Ed, MSA, Certificate); educational administration (MS Ed); educational technologies (Certificate); general education (MS Ed); gifted education extension (Certificate); health and human performance (MS); health information technology (MS); literacy (MS Ed); physical education (MS Ed); physical education birth - 12 (MS Ed); reading (Certificate); respiratory care (MS); school agency counseling (MS); school building leadership (MS Ed, Certificate); school district leadership (Certificate); special education (MS); sport administration (MSA); teacher leader (Certificate); TESOL (MS Ed). *Application deadline:* Applications are processed on a rolling basis. *Application fee:* $25. Electronic applications accepted. *Application Contact:* Kathleen B. Davis, Vice President of Enrollment Management, 716-888-2500, Fax: 716-888-3195, E-mail: daviskb@canisius.edu. *Dean*, Dr. Jeffrey R. Lindauer, 716-888-3294, Fax: 716-888-3164, E-mail: lindauej@canisius.edu.

CAPE BRETON UNIVERSITY, Sydney, NS B1P 6L2, Canada

General Information Province-supported, coed, comprehensive institution. *Graduate housing:* Room and/or apartments available on a first-come, first-served basis to single students; on-campus housing not available to married students. Housing application deadline: 3/31. *Research affiliation:* Hyperspectral Data International (marine remote sensing), Sable Offshore Energy, Inc. (petroleum resources), Fortress Louisbourg National Historic Park (museum/heritage projects), Dynagen Industrial Mine Technology (mining industry equipment), Atlantic Geomatics (computer networking and software development), Advanced Glazing, Limited (transparent insulation).

GRADUATE UNITS

Shannon School of Business ***Degree program information:*** Part-time programs available. Part-time. Offers business (MBA). Electronic applications accepted.

CAPELLA UNIVERSITY, Minneapolis, MN 55402

General Information Proprietary, coed, upper-level institution. CGS member.

GRADUATE UNITS

Harold Abel School of Social and Behavioral Science ***Degree program information:*** Part-time and evening/weekend programs available. Part-time, evening/weekend, online learning. Offers addiction psychology (PhD); applied behavior analysis (MS); child and adolescent development (MS); clinical psychology (MS, Psy D); counseling psychology (MS); educational psychology (MS, PhD); evaluation, research, and measurement (MS); general addiction counseling (MS); general advanced studies in human behavior (MS, PhD); general counselor education and supervision (PhD); general marriage and family counseling/therapy (MS); general mental health counseling

(MS); general psychology (MS, PhD); general school counseling (MS); general social work (DSW); industrial/organizational psychology (MS, PhD); leadership coaching psychology (MS); school psychology (MS, Psy D); social and behavioral science (MS, PhD, Psy D); sport psychology (MS). Electronic applications accepted.

School of Business and Technology ***Degree program information:*** Part-time and evening/weekend programs available. Part-time, evening/weekend, online learning. Offers accounting (MBA, DBA, PhD); business analysis (MS); business and technology (MBA, MS, DBA, PhD); business intelligence (MBA, DBA); enterprise software architecture (MS); entrepreneurship (MBA); finance (MBA, DBA, PhD); general business administration (MBA); general business management (PhD); general human resource management (MS); general information systems and technology management (MS); general information technology (PhD); general leadership (MS); global operations and supply chain management (MBA, DBA); health care management (MBA); human resource management (MBA, DBA, PhD); information assurance and security (MS, PhD); information technology education (PhD); information technology management (MBA, DBA, PhD); leadership (DBA, PhD); management education (PhD); marketing (MBA, DBA, PhD); network management (MS); project management (MBA, MS, DBA, PhD); strategy and innovation (DBA, PhD). Electronic applications accepted.

School of Education ***Degree program information:*** Part-time and evening/weekend programs available. Part-time, evening/weekend, online learning. Offers adult education (MS); curriculum and instruction (MS, PhD); early childhood education (MS); education (MS, Ed D, PhD); educational leadership and management (Ed D); enrollment management (MS); higher education leadership and management (MS); instructional design for online learning (MS, PhD); integrative studies (MS); K-12 studies in education (MS, PhD); leadership for higher education (PhD); leadership in educational administration (MS, PhD); postsecondary and adult education (PhD); professional studies in education (PhD); reading and literacy (MS, Ed D); special education leadership (PhD); special education teaching (MS); training and performance improvement (PhD). Electronic applications accepted.

School of Public Service Leadership Offers criminal justice (MS, PhD); diabetes nursing (MSN); emergency management (MS, PhD); epidemiology (Dr PH); general health administration (DHA); general nursing (MSN); general public administration (DPA); general public health (MPH); gerontology (MS); gerontology nursing (MSN); health administration (MHA); health advocacy and leadership (Dr PH); health care administration (PhD); health care leadership (DHA); health care operations (MHA); health information management (MS); health management policy (MPH); health policy (MHA); health policy advocacy (DHA); homeland security (MS); multidisciplinary human services (MS, PhD); nonprofit management and leadership (PhD); nurse educator (MSN); nursing education (PhD); nursing leadership and administration (MSN); nursing practice (DNP); public administration (MPA); public safety leadership (MS, PhD); public service leadership (MHA, MPA, MPH, MS, DHA, DPA, Dr PH, PhD); social and community services (MS, PhD); social behavioral sciences (MPH).

CAPITAL UNIVERSITY, Columbus, OH 43209-2394

General Information Independent-religious, coed, comprehensive institution. *Graduate housing:* On-campus housing not available.

GRADUATE UNITS

Conservatory of Music ***Degree program information:*** Part-time programs available. Part-time. Offers music education (MM). Program offered only in summer. Electronic applications accepted.

Law School ***Degree program information:*** Part-time and evening/weekend programs available. Part-time, evening/weekend. Offers business (LL M); business and taxation (LL M); law (LL M, MT, JD); taxation (LL M, MT). Electronic applications accepted.

School of Management Students: 165 (70 women); includes 16 minority (8 Black or African American, non-Hispanic/Latino; 6 Asian, non-Hispanic/Latino; 2 Hispanic/Latino), 6 international. Average age 32. 71 applicants, 56% accepted, 32 enrolled. *Faculty:* 17 full-time (7 women), 23 part-time/adjunct (1 woman). *Financial support:* Unspecified assistantships available. Financial award application deadline: 8/1; financial award applicants required to submit FAFSA. In 2015, 1 master's awarded. *Degree program information:* Part-time and evening/weekend programs available. Part-time, evening/weekend. Offers leadership (MBA). *Application deadline:* For fall admission, 7/1 priority date for domestic and international students; for winter admission, 11/1 for domestic students; for spring admission, 11/1 priority date for domestic and international students; for summer admission, 4/1 priority date for domestic and international students. Applications are processed on a rolling basis. Electronic applications accepted. *Application Contact:* Carli Isgrigg, Assistant Director of Adult and Graduate Education Recruitment, 614-236-6546, Fax: 614-236-6923, E-mail: cisgrigg@capital.edu. *MBA Director,* John Gentner, 614-236-6544, Fax: 614-236-6923, E-mail: jgentner@capital.edu.

School of Nursing ***Degree program information:*** Part-time and evening/weekend programs available. Part-time, evening/weekend. Offers administration (MSN); legal studies (MSN); theological studies (MSN).

CAPITOL TECHNOLOGY UNIVERSITY, Laurel, MD 20708-9759

General Information Independent, coed, comprehensive institution. *Graduate housing:* On-campus housing not available.

GRADUATE UNITS

Graduate Programs ***Degree program information:*** Part-time and evening/weekend programs available. Part-time, evening/weekend, online learning. Offers business administration (MBA); computer science (MS); electrical engineering (MS); information and telecommunications systems management (MS); information architecture (MS); network security (MS). Electronic applications accepted.

CARDINAL STRITCH UNIVERSITY, Milwaukee, WI 53217-3985

General Information Independent-religious, coed, university. *Enrollment:* 3,177 graduate, professional, and undergraduate students; 622 full-time matriculated graduate/professional students (396 women), 545 part-time matriculated graduate/professional students (334 women). *Enrollment by degree level:* 1,015 master's, 152 doctoral. *Tuition, area resident:* Full-time $11,500; part-time $740 per credit hour. *Required fees:* $380; $380 per unit. Tuition and fees vary according to class time, course load, degree level, program and student's religious affiliation. *Graduate housing:* Room and/or apartments available on a first-come, first-served basis to single students; on-campus housing not available to married students. Typical cost: $7700 (including board). Room and board charges vary according to board plan and housing facility selected. *Student services:* Campus employment opportunities, career counseling, exercise/wellness program, free psychological counseling, international student services, multicultural affairs office, services for students with disabilities, teacher training, writing training. *Library:* Cardinal Stritch University Library. *Collection:* Books: 148,847 (physical), 9,704 (digital/electronic); Serial titles: 164 (physical), 69 (digital/electronic); Databases: 76. Weekly public service hours: 85.

Computer facilities: Computer purchase and lease plans are available. 441 computers available on campus for general student use. A campuswide network can be accessed from student residence rooms and from off campus. Online class registration is available.
Website: http://www.stritch.edu/

General Application Contact: 800-347-8822 Ext. 4042, E-mail: gradadm@stritch.edu.

GRADUATE UNITS

College of Arts and Sciences ***Financial support:*** Research assistantships with partial tuition reimbursements, career-related internships or fieldwork, Federal Work-Study, and scholarships/grants available. Financial award applicants required to submit FAFSA. *Degree program information:* Part-time and evening/weekend programs available. Part-time, evening/weekend. Offers arts and sciences (MA, MS); clinical psychology (MA); ministry (MA); religious studies (MA); sport management (MS). *Application deadline:* For fall admission, 7/15 priority date for domestic students; for spring admission, 12/15 priority date for domestic students. Applications are processed on a rolling basis. *Application fee:* $25. *Application Contact:* 800-347-8822 Ext. 4042, E-mail: gradadm@stritch.edu. *Dean,* Dr. Dickson K. Smith, 414-410-4010.

College of Business and Management ***Financial support:*** Career-related internships or fieldwork, Federal Work-Study, and scholarships/grants available. Financial award applicants required to submit FAFSA. *Degree program information:* Part-time and evening/weekend programs available. Part-time, evening/weekend. Offers business and management (MBA, MSM). Programs also offered in Madison, WI and Minneapolis-St. Paul, MN. *Application deadline:* Applications are processed on a rolling basis. *Application fee:* $25. *Application Contact:* Shirley Hansen, Director of Marketing, 414-410-4315. *Dean,* 414-410-4437.

College of Education and Leadership ***Financial support:*** Fellowships, research assistantships with partial tuition reimbursements, career-related internships or fieldwork, Federal Work-Study, and scholarships/grants available. Financial award applicants required to submit FAFSA. *Degree program information:* Part-time and evening/weekend programs available. Part-time, evening/weekend. Offers education and leadership (MA, MAT, MS, Ed D, PhD); educational leadership (MS); language and literacy (MA, PhD); leadership for the advancement of learning and service (Ed D, PhD); special education (MA, PhD); teaching (MAT); urban education (MA). *Application deadline:* For fall admission, 7/15 priority date for domestic students; for spring admission, 12/15 priority date for domestic students. Applications are processed on a rolling basis. *Application fee:* $25. *Application Contact:* 800-347-8822 Ext. 4042, E-mail: gradamd@stritch.edu. *Dean,* Dr. Tia Bojar, 414-410-4434.

Ruth S. Coleman College of Nursing and Health Sciences ***Financial support:*** Federal Work-Study and scholarships/grants available. Financial award applicants required to submit FAFSA. *Degree program information:* Part-time and evening/weekend programs available. Part-time, evening/weekend. Offers nursing and health sciences (MSN). *Application deadline:* For fall admission, 6/15 priority date for domestic students; for spring admission, 11/15 priority date for domestic students. Applications are processed on a rolling basis. *Application fee:* $25. Electronic applications accepted. *Application Contact:* 800-347-8822 Ext. 4042, E-mail: gradadm@stritch.edu. *Dean,* Kelly J. Dries, 414-410-4397.

CAREY THEOLOGICAL COLLEGE, Vancouver, BC V6T 1J6, Canada

General Information Independent-religious, coed, graduate-only institution. *Graduate housing:* Rooms and/or apartments available on a first-come, first-served basis to single and married students. Housing application deadline: 5/31.

GRADUATE UNITS

Graduate Programs ***Degree program information:*** Part-time programs available. Part-time. Offers theology (M Div, MASF, D Min). Electronic applications accepted.

CARIBBEAN UNIVERSITY, Bayamón, PR 00960-0493

General Information Independent, coed, comprehensive institution.

GRADUATE UNITS

Graduate School

CARLETON UNIVERSITY, Ottawa, ON K1S 5B6, Canada

General Information Province-supported, coed, university. *Graduate housing:* Room and/or apartments guaranteed to single students; on-campus housing not available to married students. Housing application deadline: 5/31.

GRADUATE UNITS

Faculty of Graduate Studies ***Degree program information:*** Part-time and evening/weekend programs available. Part-time, evening/weekend. Electronic applications accepted.

Faculty of Arts and Social Sciences Degree program information: Part-time and evening/weekend programs available. Part-time, evening/weekend. Offers anthropology (MA); applied language studies (MA); art history: art and its institutions (MA); arts and social sciences (M Sc, MA, PhD); Canadian studies (MA, PhD); cognitive science (PhD); cultural mediations (PhD); English (MA, PhD); film studies (MA); French (MA); geography (M Sc, MA, PhD); history (MA, PhD); music and culture (MA); neuroscience (M Sc); philosophy (MA); psychology (MA, PhD); sociology (MA, PhD).

Faculty of Business Offers business (MBA, PhD); business administration (MBA); management (PhD).

Faculty of Engineering and Design Offers aerospace engineering (M Eng, MA Sc, PhD); biomedical engineering (MA Sc); civil and environmental engineering (M Eng, MA Sc, PhD); design studies (M Arch); electrical engineering (M Eng, M Sc, MA Sc, PhD); engineering and design (M Arch, M Des, M Eng, M Sc, MA Sc, PhD); industrial design (M Des); information and systems science (M Sc); materials engineering (M Eng, MA Sc); mechanical engineering (M Eng, MA Sc, PhD); technology innovation management (M Eng, MA Sc).

Faculty of Public Affairs and Management Degree program information: Part-time programs available. Part-time. Offers communication (MA, PhD); conflict resolution (Certificate); economics (MA, PhD); European and European Union studies (MA); European integration studies (Diploma); international affairs (MA, PhD); journalism (MJ); legal studies (MA); political economy (MA, PhD); political science (MA, PhD); public administration (MA, DPA); public affairs and management (MA, MJ, MSW, DPA, PhD, Certificate, Diploma); public policy (PhD); Russian, Eurasian and transition studies (MA); social work (MSW).

Faculty of Science Degree program information: Part-time and evening/weekend programs available. Part-time, evening/weekend. Offers biology (M Sc, PhD); chemistry (M Sc, PhD); computer science (MCS, PhD); earth sciences (M Sc, PhD);

information and system science (M Sc); information and systems science (M Sc); mathematics (M Sc, PhD); physics (M Sc, PhD); science (M Sc, MCS, PhD).

CARLOS ALBIZU UNIVERSITY, San Juan, PR 00901

General Information Independent, coed, university. *Graduate housing:* On-campus housing not available.

GRADUATE UNITS

Graduate Programs ***Degree program information:*** Part-time and evening/weekend programs available. Part-time, evening/weekend. Offers clinical psychology (MS, PhD, Psy D); general psychology (PhD); industrial/organizational psychology (MS, PhD); speech and language pathology (MS).

CARLOS ALBIZU UNIVERSITY, MIAMI CAMPUS, Miami, FL 33172-2209

General Information Independent, coed, comprehensive institution. *Enrollment:* 1,046 graduate, professional, and undergraduate students; 431 full-time matriculated graduate/professional students (343 women), 264 part-time matriculated graduate/professional students (225 women). *Enrollment by degree level:* 352 master's, 329 doctoral, 14 other advanced degrees. *Graduate faculty:* 25 full-time (20 women), 29 part-time/adjunct (15 women). *Graduate housing:* On-campus housing not available. *Student services:* Campus employment opportunities, campus safety program, career counseling, international student services, services for students with disabilities, teacher training, writing training. *Library:* Albizu Library. *Collection:* Books: 27,760 (physical), 22,900 (digital/electronic); Serial titles: 295 (physical), 17,034 (digital/electronic); Databases: 73. Weekly public service hours: 66.

Computer facilities: 268 computers available on campus for general student use. A campuswide network can be accessed from off campus. Online class registration, Campus Portal; Virtual Library; 24/7 Support; Cloud Computing; Learning Center are available.
Website: http://www.albizu.edu/

General Application Contact: Vanessa Almendarez, Administrative Assistant, 305-593-1223 Ext. 3137, Fax: 305-593-1854, E-mail: valmendarez@albizu.edu.

GRADUATE UNITS

Graduate Programs Students: 519 full-time (426 women), 171 part-time (143 women); includes 583 minority (55 Black or African American, non-Hispanic/Latino; 1 American Indian or Alaska Native, non-Hispanic/Latino; 8 Asian, non-Hispanic/Latino; 514 Hispanic/Latino; 5 Two or more races, non-Hispanic/Latino), 15 international. Average age 34. 189 applicants, 86% accepted, 142 enrolled. *Faculty:* 31 full-time (22 women), 37 part-time/adjunct (17 women). *Financial support:* In 2015–16, 158 students received support. Federal Work-Study, scholarships/grants, and tuition discounts available. Financial award application deadline: 6/1; financial award applicants required to submit FAFSA. In 2015, 147 master's, 36 doctorates awarded. *Degree program information:* Part-time and evening/weekend programs available. Part-time, evening/weekend, 100% online. Offers clinical psychology (PhD, Psy D); entrepreneurship (MBA); exceptional student education (MS); human services (PhD); industrial/organizational psychology (MS); marriage and family therapy (MS); mental health counseling (MS); nonprofit management (MBA); organizational management (MBA); psychology (MS); school counseling (MS); speech and language pathology (MS); teaching English for speakers of other languages (MS). *Application deadline:* For fall admission, 4/1 priority date for domestic students, 5/1 priority date for international students; for spring admission, 11/1 priority date for domestic students, 9/1 priority date for international students. Applications are processed on a rolling basis. *Application fee:* $50. Electronic applications accepted. *Application Contact:* Sonia Feliciano, Institutional Director of Student Recruitment, 305-593-1223 Ext. 3108, Fax: 305-477-8983, E-mail: sfeliciano@albizu.edu. *Provost,* Dr. Etiony Aldarondo, 305-593-1223 Ext. 3138, Fax: 305-592-7930, E-mail: ealdarondo@albizu.edu.

CARLOW UNIVERSITY, Pittsburgh, PA 15213-3165

General Information Independent-religious, coed, primarily women, comprehensive institution. CGS member. *Enrollment:* 2,272 graduate, professional, and undergraduate students; 653 full-time matriculated graduate/professional students (559 women), 210 part-time matriculated graduate/professional students (178 women). *Enrollment by degree level:* 762 master's, 79 doctoral, 22 other advanced degrees. *Graduate faculty:* 23 full-time, 78 part-time/adjunct. *Tuition, area resident:* Full-time $11,147; part-time $801 per credit. Tuition and fees vary according to course load, degree level and program. *Graduate housing:* On-campus housing not available. *Student services:* Campus employment opportunities, campus safety program, career counseling, child daycare facilities, exercise/wellness program, free psychological counseling, international student services, multicultural affairs office, services for students with disabilities, teacher training, writing training. *Library:* Grace Library.

Computer facilities: A campuswide network can be accessed from student residence rooms and from off campus. Online class registration is available.
Website: http://www.carlow.edu/

General Application Contact: Kimberly Lipniskis, Associate Director, Graduate and International Admissions, 412-578-6671, Fax: 412-578-6321, E-mail: gradstudies@carlow.edu.

GRADUATE UNITS

College of Health and Wellness Students: 281 full-time (253 women), 71 part-time (66 women); includes 26 minority (10 Black or African American, non-Hispanic/Latino; 2 American Indian or Alaska Native, non-Hispanic/Latino; 6 Asian, non-Hispanic/Latino; 6 Hispanic/Latino; 2 Two or more races, non-Hispanic/Latino), 1 international. Average age 35. 135 applicants, 92% accepted, 83 enrolled. *Financial support:* Application deadline: 4/1; applicants required to submit FAFSA. In 2015, 83 master's, 16 doctorates, 3 other advanced degrees awarded. *Degree program information:* Part-time and evening/weekend programs available. Part-time, evening/weekend, 100% online, blended/hybrid learning, low-residency. Offers family nurse practitioner (MSN, Certificate); health and wellness (MSN, DNP, Certificate); nursing leadership and education (MSN); nursing practice (DNP). *Application deadline:* For fall admission, 6/15 priority date for domestic and international students; for spring admission, 11/15 priority date for domestic and international students. Applications are processed on a rolling basis. Electronic applications accepted. *Application Contact:* E-mail: gradstudies@carlow.edu. *Dean,* Dr. Lynn George, Fax: 412-578-6114.

College of Leadership and Social Change Students: 301 full-time (244 women), 78 part-time (58 women); includes 95 minority (73 Black or African American, non-Hispanic/Latino; 1 American Indian or Alaska Native, non-Hispanic/Latino; 5 Asian, non-Hispanic/Latino; 9 Hispanic/Latino; 7 Two or more races, non-Hispanic/Latino), 1 international. Average age 32. 219 applicants, 91% accepted, 123 enrolled. *Financial support:* Federal Work-Study available. Financial award application deadline: 4/1; financial award applicants required to submit FAFSA. In 2015, 135 master's, 5 doctorates, 2 other advanced degrees awarded. *Degree program information:* Part-time and evening/weekend programs available. Part-time, evening/weekend, 100% online. Offers addictions (MS); adult/generalist (MS); alcohol and drug counseling (Certificate); child and family (MS); counseling psychology (Psy D); fraud and forensics (MS); healthcare management (MBA); human resource management (MBA); leadership and management (MBA); leadership and social change (MBA, MS, Psy D, Certificate); professional counseling (Certificate); project management (MBA); school counseling (Certificate). *Application deadline:* For fall admission, 6/15 priority date for domestic and international students; for spring admission, 11/15 priority date for domestic and international students. Applications are processed on a rolling basis. *Application fee:* $0. Electronic applications accepted. *Application Contact:* 412-578-6059, Fax: 412-578-6321, E-mail: gradstudies@carlow.edu. *Dean,* Dr. Allyson M. Lowe, 412-578-6663, Fax: 412-578-6357, E-mail: amlowe@carlow.edu.

College of Learning and Innovation Students: 71 full-time (62 women), 61 part-time (54 women); includes 23 minority (16 Black or African American, non-Hispanic/Latino; 1 American Indian or Alaska Native, non-Hispanic/Latino; 1 Asian, non-Hispanic/Latino; 1 Hispanic/Latino; 4 Two or more races, non-Hispanic/Latino). Average age 34. 61 applicants, 93% accepted, 46 enrolled. *Financial support:* Application deadline: 4/1; applicants required to submit FAFSA. In 2015, 52 master's awarded. *Degree program information:* Part-time and evening/weekend programs available. Part-time, evening/weekend, 100% online, blended/hybrid learning. Offers art education (M Ed); early childhood education (M Ed); early childhood supervision (M Ed); educational leadership for high performance learning (MS); fiction (MFA); learning and innovation (M Ed, MFA, MS); non-fiction (MFA); poetry (MFA); principal certification (MS); special education (M Ed). *Application deadline:* For fall admission, 6/15 priority date for domestic and international students; for spring admission, 11/15 priority date for domestic and international students. Applications are processed on a rolling basis. *Application fee:* $0. Electronic applications accepted. *Application Contact:* 412-578-6059, Fax: 412-578-6321, E-mail: gradstudies@carlow.edu. *Dean,* Dr. Matthew Gordley, 412-578-6262, E-mail: megordley@carlow.edu.

CARNEGIE MELLON UNIVERSITY, Pittsburgh, PA 15213-3891

General Information Independent, coed, university. CGS member. *Graduate housing:* On-campus housing not available. *Research affiliation:* National Census Data Research Center (public policy), Robotics Engineering Consortium (computer science and engineering), Software Engineering Institute (computer science and engineering), Carnegie Bosch Institute for Applied Studies in International Management (business and management), Pittsburgh Supercomputer Center.

GRADUATE UNITS

Carnegie Institute of Technology ***Degree program information:*** Part-time and evening/weekend programs available. Part-time, evening/weekend. Offers advanced infrastructure systems (MS, PhD); advanced infrastructure systems technology development and application (MS); air quality engineering and science (MS); bioengineering (MS, PhD); chemical engineering (M Ch E, MS, PhD); civil and environmental engineering (MS, PhD); civil and environmental engineering/engineering and public policy (PhD); civil engineering (MS, PhD); colloids, polymers and surfaces (MS); computational mechanics (MS, PhD); computational modeling and monitoring for resilient structural and material systems (MS); electrical and computer engineering (MS, PhD); energy infrastructure systems (MS); engineering and public policy (PhD); environmental engineering (MS, PhD); environmental management and science (MS, PhD); IT-based sustainable global infrastructure and construction management (MS); materials science and engineering (MS, PhD); mechanical engineering (MS, PhD); product development (MPD); sustainability and green design (MS); technology (M Ch E, MPD, MS, PhD); water quality engineering and science (MS).

Information Networking Institute Offers information networking (MS); information security (MS); information technology - information security (MS); information technology - mobility (MS); information technology - software management (MS).

Center for the Neural Basis of Cognition Offers neural basis of cognition (PhD).

College of Fine Arts ***Degree program information:*** Part-time programs available. Part-time. Offers fine arts (M Des, M Sc, MAM, MET, MFA, MM, MPD, MS, MSA, MTID, MUD, D Des, PhD). Electronic applications accepted.

School of Architecture Offers architecture (MSA); architecture, engineering, and construction management (PhD); building performance and diagnostics (MS, PhD); computational design (MS, PhD); engineering construction management (MSA); tangible interaction design (MTID); urban design (MUD).

School of Art Offers art (MFA).

School of Design Offers design (M Des, MA, MPD, D Des, PhD); design for interaction (M Des); design for interactions (M Des); design theory (PhD); new product development (PhD); product development (MPD); typography and information design (PhD).

School of Drama Offers design (MFA); directing (MFA); dramatic writing (MFA); production technology and management (MFA); video and media design (MFA).

School of Music Degree program information: Part-time programs available. Part-time. Offers collaborative piano (MM); composition (MM); instrumental performance (MM); music and technology (MS); music education (MM); vocal performance (MM).

Dietrich College of Humanities and Social Sciences ***Degree program information:*** Part-time programs available. Part-time. Offers African and African-American diaspora (PhD); behavioral decision research (PhD); cognitive neuroscience (PhD); cognitive psychology (PhD); communication planning and design (M Des); culture and power (PhD); developmental psychology (PhD); editing and publishing (MAPW); humanities and social sciences (M Des, MA, MAPW, MS, PhD); labor, politics and social movements (PhD); literary and cultural studies (MA, PhD); logic, computation and methodology (MS, PhD); machine learning and statistics (PhD); mathematical finance (PhD); philosophy (MA, PhD); policy and non-profit communication (MAPW); professional writing (MAPW); public and media relations/corporate communications (MAPW); pure and applied logic (PhD); rhetoric (MA, PhD); science or healthcare communication (MAPW); second language acquisition (MA, PhD); social and decision science (PhD); social/personality/health psychology (PhD); statistics (MS, PhD); statistics and public policy (PhD); strategy, entrepreneurship, and technological change (PhD); technical writing (MAPW); technology, environment, science and health (PhD); women, gender and the family (PhD); writing for new media (MAPW); writing for print media (MAPW). Electronic applications accepted.

Heinz College Australia Offers information technology (MSIT); public policy and management (MS).

H. John Heinz III College ***Degree program information:*** Part-time and evening/weekend programs available. Part-time, evening/weekend. Offers public policy and information systems (MAM, MEIM, MISM, MMM, MPM, MSBTM, MSHCPM, MSISPM, MSIT, MSPPM, PhD). Electronic applications accepted.

School of Information Systems and Management Offers information security policy and management (MSISPM); information systems and management (MISM, MSISPM, MSIT); information systems management (MISM); information technology (MSIT).

School of Public Policy and Management Offers arts management (MAM); biotechnology and management (MS); entertainment industry management (MEIM); health care policy and management (MSHCPM); medical management (MMM); public management (MPM); public policy and management (MMM, MPM, MS, MSHCPM, PhD).

Joint CMU-Pitt PhD Program in Computational Biology Offers computational biology (PhD).

Mellon College of Science *Degree program information:* Part-time programs available. Part-time. Offers algorithms, combinatorics, and optimization (PhD); applied physics (PhD); atmospheric chemistry (PhD); biochemistry (PhD); bioinorganic chemistry (PhD); bioorganic chemistry and chemical biology (PhD); biophysical chemistry (PhD); biophysics (PhD); catalysis (PhD); cell and developmental biology (PhD); computational biology (MS, PhD); computational finance (MS); genetics (PhD); green and environmental chemistry (PhD); materials and nanoscience (PhD); mathematical finance (PhD); mathematical sciences (DA, PhD); molecular biology (PhD); molecular biophysics and structural biology (PhD); neuroscience (PhD); physics (MS, PhD); pure and applied logic (PhD); renewable energy (PhD); science (MS, DA, PhD); sensors, probes, and imaging (PhD); spectroscopy and single molecule analysis (PhD); structural biology (PhD); theoretical and computational chemistry (PhD). Electronic applications accepted.

School of Computer Science Offers algorithms, combinatorics, and optimization (PhD); computer science (MS, PhD); entertainment technology (MET); human-computer interaction (MHCI, PhD); machine learning (MS, PhD); pure and applied logic (PhD); software engineering (MSE, PhD).

Language Technologies Institute Offers language technologies (MLT, MS, PhD).

Robotics Institute Offers computer vision (MS); robotic systems development (MS); robotics (MS, PhD); robotics technology (MS).

Tepper School of Business *Degree program information:* Part-time programs available. Part-time. Offers accounting (PhD); business management and software engineering (MBMSE); business technologies (PhD); civil engineering and industrial management (MS); computational finance (MSCF); economics (PhD); environmental engineering and management (MEEM); financial economics (PhD); industrial administration (MBA); marketing (PhD); mathematical finance (PhD); operations management (PhD); operations research (PhD); organizational behavior and theory (PhD); production and operations management (PhD); public policy and management (MS, MSED); software engineering and business management (MS). JD/MSIA offered jointly with University of Pittsburgh.

CAROLINA CHRISTIAN COLLEGE, Winston-Salem, NC 27102-0777

General Information Independent-religious, coed, comprehensive institution.

GRADUATE UNITS

Program in Religious Education Offers Christian education (MRE); pastoral care (MRE).

CAROLINA GRADUATE SCHOOL OF DIVINITY, Greensboro, NC 27403

General Information Independent-religious, coed, graduate-only institution.

GRADUATE UNITS

Divinity Program Offers divinity (M Div).

Ministry Program Offers ministry (D Min).

Program in Theological Studies Offers theological studies (MA).

CARROLL UNIVERSITY, Waukesha, WI 53186-5593

General Information Independent-religious, coed, comprehensive institution. *Enrollment:* 275 full-time matriculated graduate/professional students (175 women), 199 part-time matriculated graduate/professional students (144 women). *Enrollment by degree level:* 274 master's, 157 doctoral, 44 other advanced degrees. *Graduate faculty:* 18 full-time (12 women), 19 part-time/adjunct (18 women). *Tuition, area resident:* Full-time $10,548; part-time $586 per credit. *Required fees:* $520 per semester. Tuition and fees vary according to course load, degree level and program. *Graduate housing:* On-campus housing not available. *Student services:* Campus employment opportunities, campus safety program, career counseling, exercise/wellness program, free psychological counseling, international student services, multicultural affairs office, services for students with disabilities. *Library:* Todd Wehr Memorial Library.

Computer facilities: Computer purchase and lease plans are available. 400 computers available on campus for general student use. A campuswide network can be accessed from student residence rooms and from off campus. Online class registration is available.
Website: http://www.carrollu.edu/

General Application Contact: Lori Aliota, Graduate Admission Counselor, 262-524-7226, E-mail: laliota@carrollu.edu.

GRADUATE UNITS

Graduate Program in Education Students: 11 full-time (10 women), 163 part-time (125 women); includes 11 minority (3 Black or African American, non-Hispanic/Latino; 3 American Indian or Alaska Native, non-Hispanic/Latino; 2 Asian, non-Hispanic/Latino; 3 Hispanic/Latino), 1 international. Average age 34. 96 applicants, 38% accepted, 18 enrolled. *Faculty:* 7 full-time (5 women), 14 part-time/adjunct (all women). *Financial support:* Available to part-time students. Application deadline: 3/15; applicants required to submit FAFSA. In 2015, 43 master's awarded. *Degree program information:* Part-time and evening/weekend programs available. Part-time, evening/weekend. Offers education (M Ed); learning and teaching (M Ed). *Application deadline:* For fall admission, 8/15 priority date for domestic students. Applications are processed on a rolling basis. *Application fee:* $0. Electronic applications accepted. *Application Contact:* Lori Aliota, Graduate Admission Counselor, 262-524-7226, E-mail: laliota@carrollu.edu. *Chair,* Dr. Kim White, 262-650-4920, E-mail: whitek@carrollu.edu.

Program in Business Administration Students: 15 part-time (6 women). Average age 28. 54 applicants, 43% accepted. *Faculty:* 2 full-time (both women). *Degree program information:* Part-time programs available. Part-time. Offers business administration (MBA). *Application deadline:* Applications are processed on a rolling basis. Electronic applications accepted. *Application Contact:* Tami Bartunek, Graduate Admission Counselor, 262-524-7643, E-mail: tbartune@carrollu.edu. *Professor,* Dr. Richard J. Penlesky, 262-951-3023, E-mail: rpenlesk@carrollu.edu.

Program in Physical Therapy Students: 78 full-time (59 women); includes 4 minority (2 Asian, non-Hispanic/Latino; 2 Hispanic/Latino). Average age 24. 150 applicants, 69% accepted, 57 enrolled. *Faculty:* 6 full-time (3 women), 5 part-time/adjunct (4 women). *Financial support:* Available to part-time students. Application deadline: 3/15; applicants required to submit FAFSA. In 2015, 33 doctorates awarded. Offers physical therapy (MPT, DPT). *Application deadline:* For fall admission, 7/14 for domestic students. Applications are processed on a rolling basis. *Application fee:* $25. *Application Contact:* Tami Bartunek, Graduate Admission Counselor, 262-524-7643, E-mail: tbartune@carrollu.edu. *Dean, Natural and Health Sciences,* Dr. Jane F. Hopp, 262-524-7294, E-mail: jhopp@carrollu.edu.

Program in Physician Assistant Studies 167 applicants, 16% accepted, 22 enrolled. *Financial support:* Applicants required to submit FAFSA. Offers physician assistant studies (MS). *Application fee:* $0. *Application Contact:* Tami Bartunek, Graduate Admission Counselor, 262-524-7643, E-mail: tbartune@carrollu.edu. *Director,* Dr. Russell W. Harland, 262-524-7399, E-mail: rharland@carrollu.edu.

Program in Software Engineering *Financial support:* Institutionally sponsored loans available. Support available to part-time students. *Degree program information:* Part-time and evening/weekend programs available. Part-time, evening/weekend. Offers software engineering (MSE). *Application deadline:* For fall admission, 9/15 priority date for domestic students. Applications are processed on a rolling basis. *Application fee:* $0. Electronic applications accepted. *Application Contact:* Lori Aliota, Director of Graduate Admission, 262-524-7226, E-mail: laliota@carrollu.edu. *Professor/Director,* Dr. Chenglie Hu, 262-524-7170, E-mail: chu@carrollu.edu.

CARSON-NEWMAN UNIVERSITY, Jefferson City, TN 37760

General Information Independent-religious, coed, comprehensive institution. *Enrollment:* 2,528 graduate, professional, and undergraduate students; 114 full-time matriculated graduate/professional students (78 women), 658 part-time matriculated graduate/professional students (466 women). *Enrollment by degree level:* 580 master's, 149 doctoral, 43 other advanced degrees. *Graduate faculty:* 38 full-time (20 women), 14 part-time/adjunct (10 women). *Tuition, area resident:* Full-time $10,142; part-time $461 per credit hour. *Required fees:* $300; $461 per credit hour. $150 per semester. One-time fee: $150. *Graduate housing:* Room and/or apartments available to single students. Housing application deadline: 7/15. *Student services:* Campus employment opportunities, career counseling, free psychological counseling, international student services, low-cost health insurance, services for students with disabilities. *Library:* Stephens-Burnett Library plus 3 others. *Collection:* Books: 216,676 (physical), 435,957 (digital/electronic); Serial titles: 315 (physical); Databases: 143. Weekly public service hours: 90; study areas open 24 hours, 5–7 days a week; students can reserve study rooms.

Computer facilities: 200 computers available on campus for general student use. A campuswide network can be accessed from student residence rooms and from off campus. Online class registration is available.
Website: http://www.cn.edu/

General Application Contact: Nilma Stewart, Graduate Admissions and Services Adviser, 865-471-3230, Fax: 865-471-3875, E-mail: adults@cn.edu.

GRADUATE UNITS

Department of Nursing Students: 9 full-time (8 women), 34 part-time (31 women); includes 1 minority (Black or African American, non-Hispanic/Latino). Average age 33. 14 applicants, 100% accepted, 9 enrolled. *Faculty:* 4 full-time (3 women), 1 (woman) part-time/adjunct. *Financial support:* Federal Work-Study and tuition waivers (full and partial) available. Financial award applicants required to submit FAFSA. In 2015, 19 master's awarded. *Degree program information:* Part-time programs available. Part-time. Offers family nurse practitioner (MSN); nurse educator (MSN). *Application deadline:* For fall admission, 3/15 for domestic students; for spring admission, 10/15 for domestic students. Applications are processed on a rolling basis. *Application fee:* $50. *Application Contact:* Nilma Stewart, Graduate Admissions and Services Adviser, 865-471-3230, Fax: 865-471-3875, E-mail: adults@cn.edu. *Director,* Dr. Kimberly Bolton, 865-471-4056, E-mail: kbolton@cn.edu.

Graduate Program in Education Students: 53 full-time (27 women), 533 part-time (388 women); includes 51 minority (31 Black or African American, non-Hispanic/Latino; 1 American Indian or Alaska Native, non-Hispanic/Latino; 1 Asian, non-Hispanic/Latino; 17 Hispanic/Latino; 1 Two or more races, non-Hispanic/Latino), 7 international. Average age 35. 294 applicants, 100% accepted, 252 enrolled. *Faculty:* 20 full-time (12 women), 10 part-time/adjunct (8 women). *Financial support:* Federal Work-Study and unspecified assistantships available. Financial award applicants required to submit FAFSA. In 2015, 63 master's awarded. *Degree program information:* Part-time and evening/weekend programs available. Part-time, evening/weekend, 100% online, blended/hybrid learning. Offers curriculum and instruction (M Ed); educational leadership (M Ed); elementary education (MAT); school counseling (MS); secondary education (MAT); teaching English as a second language (MATESL). *Application deadline:* For fall admission, 7/15 priority date for domestic students. Applications are processed on a rolling basis. *Application fee:* $50. *Application Contact:* Nilma Stewart, Graduate Admissions and Services Adviser, 865-471-3230, Fax: 865-471-3875, E-mail: adults@cn.edu. *Chair,* Dr. Kim Hawkins, 865-471-3314, E-mail: khawkins@cn.edu.

Program in Applied Theology Students: 3 part-time (2 women). Average age 35. 1 applicant, 100% accepted. *Faculty:* 1 full-time (0 women), 1 part-time/adjunct (0 women). *Financial support:* Federal Work-Study and tuition waivers (full and partial) available. Financial award applicants required to submit FAFSA. *Degree program information:* Part-time and evening/weekend programs available. Part-time, evening/weekend. Offers applied theology (MAAT). *Application deadline:* For fall admission, 7/15 priority date for domestic students. Applications are processed on a rolling basis. *Application fee:* $50. *Application Contact:* Nilma Stewart, Graduate Admissions and Services Adviser, 865-473-3468, Fax: 865-471-3875, E-mail: adults@cn.edu. *Dean, School of Religion,* Dr. David E. Crutchley, 865-471-3277, E-mail: dcruthley@cn.edu.

Program in Business Administration Students: 4 full-time (2 women), 62 part-time (23 women); includes 4 minority (all Black or African American, non-Hispanic/Latino), 15 international. Average age 30. 31 applicants, 100% accepted, 24 enrolled. *Faculty:* 7 full-time (2 women). *Financial support:* Federal Work-Study and tuition waivers (full and partial) available. Financial award applicants required to submit FAFSA. In 2015, 36 master's awarded. *Degree program information:* Part-time and evening/weekend programs available. Part-time, evening/weekend, 100% online, blended/hybrid learning. Offers business administration (MBA). *Application deadline:* For fall admission, 7/15 priority date for domestic students. Applications are processed on a rolling basis. *Application fee:* $50. *Application Contact:* Nilma Stewart, Graduate Admissions and Services Adviser, 865-471-3230, Fax: 865-471-3875, E-mail: adults@cn.edu. *Director,* Dr. Kyle J. Kaplan, 865-471-7124, E-mail: kkaplan@cn.edu.

Program in Counseling Students: 46 full-time (39 women), 17 part-time (15 women); includes 5 minority (2 Black or African American, non-Hispanic/Latino; 3 Hispanic/Latino), 1 international. Average age 31. 21 applicants, 100% accepted, 17 enrolled. *Faculty:* 4 full-time (3 women), 2 part-time/adjunct (1 woman). *Financial support:* Federal Work-Study and tuition waivers (full and partial) available. Financial award applicants required to submit FAFSA. In 2015, 11 master's awarded. *Degree program information:* Part-time and evening/weekend programs available. Part-time, evening/weekend. Offers counseling (MSC). *Application deadline:* Applications are processed on a rolling basis. *Application fee:* $50. *Application Contact:* Nilma Stewart, Graduate Admissions and Services Adviser, 865-471-3230, Fax: 865-471-3875, E-mail: adults@cn.edu. *Director*, Dr. Michael L. Bundy, 865-471-2087, E-mail: mbundy@cn.edu.

Program in Social Entrepreneurship Students: 2 full-time (both women), 9 part-time (7 women); includes 1 minority (Black or African American, non-Hispanic/Latino). Average age 28. 3 applicants, 100% accepted, 3 enrolled. *Faculty:* 1 full-time (0 women). *Financial support:* Federal Work-Study and tuition waivers (full and partial) available. Financial award applicants required to submit FAFSA. In 2015, 1 master's awarded. *Degree program information:* Part-time and evening/weekend programs available. Part-time, evening/weekend, 100% online, blended/hybrid learning. Offers social entrepreneurship (MAASJ). *Application deadline:* For fall admission, 7/15 for domestic students. Applications are processed on a rolling basis. *Application fee:* $50. *Application Contact:* Nilma Stewart, Graduate Admissions and Services Adviser, 865-471-3223, Fax: 865-471-3875, E-mail: adults@cn.edu. *Department Chair*, Dr. Laura Wadlington, 865-471-3270.

CARTHAGE COLLEGE, Kenosha, WI 53140

General Information Independent-religious, coed, comprehensive institution. *Graduate housing:* On-campus housing not available.

GRADUATE UNITS

Division of Teacher Education ***Degree program information:*** Part-time and evening/weekend programs available. Part-time, evening/weekend. Offers classroom guidance and counseling (M Ed); creative arts (M Ed); gifted and talented children (M Ed); language arts (M Ed); modern language (M Ed); natural sciences (M Ed); reading (M Ed, Certificate); social sciences (M Ed); teacher leadership (M Ed).

CASE WESTERN RESERVE UNIVERSITY, Cleveland, OH 44106

General Information Independent, coed, university. CGS member. *Enrollment:* 11,340 graduate, professional, and undergraduate students; 5,144 full-time matriculated graduate/professional students (2,699 women), 870 part-time matriculated graduate/professional students (511 women). *Enrollment by degree level:* 2,912 master's, 3,054 doctoral, 48 other advanced degrees. *Graduate faculty:* 3,360 full-time (1,234 women). *Tuition, area resident:* Full-time $41,137; part-time $1714 per credit hour. *Required fees:* $32. Tuition and fees vary according to course load and program. *Graduate housing:* On-campus housing not available. *Student services:* Campus employment opportunities, campus safety program, career counseling, exercise/wellness program, free psychological counseling, grant writing training, international student services, low-cost health insurance, multicultural affairs office, services for students with disabilities, teacher training, writing training. *Library:* Kelvin Smith Library plus 6 others. *Collection:* Databases: 400. Students can reserve study rooms. *Research affiliation:* Bayer Materials Science (wind materials research), Cleveland Clinic Foundation (biomedical science), Johnson & Johnson Services, Inc. (human health), Cleveland Botanical Garden (plant sciences and ecology), Swagelok Company (surface analysis and materials technology), University Hospitals of Cleveland (biomedical science).

Computer facilities: Computer purchase and lease plans are available. 307 computers available on campus for general student use. A campuswide network can be accessed from student residence rooms and from off campus. Online class registration, software library, online reference databases, electronic books and journals, research computing, training are available.
Website: http://www.case.edu/

General Application Contact: Susan M. Benedict, Admissions Manager and Recruiter, 216-368-4402, Fax: 216-368-4250, E-mail: susan.benedict@case.edu.

GRADUATE UNITS

Frances Payne Bolton School of Nursing Students: 254 full-time (217 women), 225 part-time (184 women); includes 82 minority (28 Black or African American, non-Hispanic/Latino; 33 Asian, non-Hispanic/Latino; 15 Hispanic/Latino; 6 Two or more races, non-Hispanic/Latino), 29 international. Average age 37. 227 applicants, 67% accepted, 96 enrolled. *Faculty:* 31 full-time (27 women). *Financial support:* In 2015–16, 120 students received support, including 16 fellowships with full tuition reimbursements available (averaging $30,852 per year), 16 research assistantships with partial tuition reimbursements available (averaging $17,019 per year), 19 teaching assistantships with partial tuition reimbursements available (averaging $17,019 per year); traineeships, unspecified assistantships, and Nurse Faculty Loan Program also available. Financial award application deadline: 5/15; financial award applicants required to submit FAFSA. In 2015, 125 master's, 45 doctorates awarded. *Degree program information:* Part-time programs available. Part-time. Offers acute care cardiovascular nursing (MSN); acute care nurse practitioner (MSN); acute care pediatric nurse practitioner (MSN); acute care/flight nurse (MSN); adult gerontology acute care nurse practitioner (MSN); adult gerontology oncology and palliative care (MSN); adult gerontology primary care nurse practitioner (MSN); family nurse practitioner (MSN); family systems psychiatric mental health nursing (MSN); neonatal nurse practitioner (MSN); nurse anesthesia (MSN); nurse educator (MSN); nurse midwifery (MSN); nurse practitioner (MSN); nursing (MN); nursing practice (DNP); pediatric nurse practitioner (MSN); women's health nurse practitioner (MSN). *Application deadline:* For fall admission, 6/1 for domestic and international students; for spring admission, 10/1 for domestic and international students; for summer admission, 3/1 for domestic and international students. Applications are processed on a rolling basis. *Application fee:* $75. *Application Contact:* Donna Hassik, Admissions Coordinator, Graduate Programs, 216-368-5253, Fax: 216-368-0124, E-mail: donna.hassik@case.edu. *Dean/Professor*, Dr. Mary E. Kerr, 216-368-2545, Fax: 216-368-5050, E-mail: mek55@case.edu.

Jack, Joseph and Morton Mandel School of Applied Social Sciences ***Degree program information:*** Evening/weekend programs available. Evening/weekend, online learning. Offers nonprofit management (MNO); social welfare (PhD); social work (MSSA). Electronic applications accepted.

School of Dental Medicine Offers advanced general dentistry (Certificate); dental medicine (MSD, DMD, Certificate); dentistry (MSD, DMD, Certificate); endodontics (MSD, Certificate); oral surgery (Certificate); orthodontics (MSD, Certificate); pedodontics (MSD, Certificate); periodontics (MSD, Certificate). Electronic applications accepted.

School of Graduate Studies Students: 2,083 full-time (960 women), 307 part-time (140 women); includes 445 minority (112 Black or African American, non-Hispanic/Latino; 1 American Indian or Alaska Native, non-Hispanic/Latino; 211 Asian, non-Hispanic/Latino; 80 Hispanic/Latino; 1 Native Hawaiian or other Pacific Islander, non-Hispanic/Latino; 40 Two or more races, non-Hispanic/Latino), 758 international. Average age 28. 4,877 applicants, 37% accepted, 750 enrolled. *Faculty:* 3,360 full-time (1,234 women). *Financial support:* Fellowships with tuition reimbursements, research assistantships with tuition reimbursements, teaching assistantships with tuition reimbursements, career-related internships or fieldwork, Federal Work-Study, institutionally sponsored loans, scholarships/grants, traineeships, health care benefits, tuition waivers (full and partial), and unspecified assistantships available. Support available to part-time students. Financial award applicants required to submit CSS PROFILE or FAFSA. In 2015, 507 master's, 185 doctorates awarded. *Degree program information:* Part-time and evening/weekend programs available. Part-time, evening/weekend, online learning. Offers acting (MFA); anthropology (MA, PhD); applied mathematics (MS, PhD); art education (MA); art history (MA, PhD); art history and museum studies (MA); astronomy (MS, PhD); biology (MS, PhD); chemistry (MS, PhD); clinical psychology (PhD); cognitive linguistics (MA); communication sciences (MA, PhD); dance (MA, MFA); early music (MA, D Mus A); earth, environmental, and planetary sciences (MS, PhD); English (MA, PhD); experimental psychology (PhD); French (MA); historical musicology (MA, PhD); historical performance practice (DMA, PhD); history (MA, PhD); mathematics (MS, PhD); music education (MA, PhD); music history (MA); physician assistant (MA); physics (MS, PhD); political science (MA, PhD); sociology (MA, PhD); speech-language pathology (MA, PhD); theater (MA); world literature (MA). *Application deadline:* For fall admission, 3/1 for domestic students; for spring admission, 11/1 for domestic students. *Application fee:* $50. Electronic applications accepted. *Application Contact:* Susan M. Benedict, Admissions Manager and Recruiter, 216-368-4400, Fax: 216-368-4250, E-mail: susan.benedict@case.edu. *Vice Provost and Dean*, Dr. Charles E. Rozek, 216-368-4400, Fax: 216-368-4250, E-mail: charles.rozek@case.edu.

Case School of Engineering Students: 607 full-time (172 women), 64 part-time (11 women); includes 67 minority (10 Black or African American, non-Hispanic/Latino; 43 Asian, non-Hispanic/Latino; 9 Hispanic/Latino; 1 Native Hawaiian or other Pacific Islander, non-Hispanic/Latino; 4 Two or more races, non-Hispanic/Latino), 415 international. 1,382 applicants, 34% accepted, 129 enrolled. *Faculty:* 112 full-time (15 women). *Financial support:* In 2015–16, 358 students received support, including 46 fellowships with tuition reimbursements available, 276 research assistantships with tuition reimbursements available, 33 teaching assistantships; career-related internships or fieldwork, Federal Work-Study, and institutionally sponsored loans also available. Support available to part-time students. Financial award applicants required to submit FAFSA. In 2015, 133 master's, 64 doctorates awarded. *Degree program information:* Part-time and evening/weekend programs available. Part-time, evening/weekend, 100% online, blended/hybrid learning. Offers biomedical engineering (MS, PhD); chemical and biomolecular engineering (MS, PhD); civil engineering (MS, PhD); computer engineering (MS, PhD); computing and information sciences (MS, PhD); electrical engineering (MS, PhD); engineering (ME, MEM, MS, PhD); macromolecular science and engineering (MS, PhD); management and engineering (MEM); materials science and engineering (MS, PhD); mechanical and aerospace engineering (MS, PhD); systems and control engineering (MS, PhD). *Application deadline:* Applications are processed on a rolling basis. *Application fee:* $50. Electronic applications accepted. *Application Contact:* Dr. Marc Buchner, Associate Dean, Academics, 216-368-4096, Fax: 216-368-6939, E-mail: marc.buchner@case.edu. *Dean/Professor*, Jeffrey L. Duerk, 216-368-4436, Fax: 216-368-6939, E-mail: duerk@case.edu.

Cleveland Clinic Lerner Research Institute–Molecular Medicine PhD Program Offers molecular medicine (PhD). Electronic applications accepted.

School of Law Students: 380 full-time (191 women), 1 (woman) part-time; includes 74 minority (32 Black or African American, non-Hispanic/Latino; 20 Asian, non-Hispanic/Latino; 16 Hispanic/Latino; 6 Two or more races, non-Hispanic/Latino), 31 international. Average age 24. 1,678 applicants, 42% accepted, 122 enrolled. *Faculty:* 41 full-time (15 women), 23 part-time/adjunct (6 women). *Financial support:* In 2015–16, 355 students received support. Career-related internships or fieldwork, Federal Work-Study, institutionally sponsored loans, and scholarships/grants available. Financial award application deadline: 5/1; financial award applicants required to submit FAFSA. In 2015, 76 master's, 144 doctorates awarded. Offers intellectual property (LL M); international business law (LL M); international criminal law (LL M); law (JD, SJD); patent practice (MA); U.S. legal studies (LL M). *Application deadline:* For fall admission, 4/1 priority date for domestic and international students. Applications are processed on a rolling basis. *Application fee:* $40. Electronic applications accepted. *Application Contact:* Kelli Curtis, Associate Dean for Admissions, 216-368-3600, Fax: 216-368-0185, E-mail: lawadmissions@case.edu. *Co-Dean*, Jessica Berg, 216-368-3283.

School of Medicine ***Degree program information:*** Part-time programs available. Part-time. Offers clinical research (MS); medicine (MA, MPH, MS, MD, PhD).

Graduate Programs in Medicine Degree program information: Part-time programs available. Part-time. Offers anesthesiology (MS); applied anatomy (MS); biochemical research (MS); biochemistry (MS, PhD); bioethics (MA); biological anthropology (MS); biomedical sciences (PhD); biostatistics (MS, PhD); cancer biology (PhD); cell and molecular physiology (MS); cell biology (MS, PhD); cell physiology (PhD); cellular biology (MS, PhD); dietetics (MS); epidemiology (MS, PhD); genetic and molecular epidemiology (MS, PhD); genetic counseling (MS); health services research (MS, PhD); human, molecular, and developmental genetics and genomics (PhD); immunology (MS, PhD); medicine (MA, MPH, MS, PhD); microbiology (PhD); molecular biology (PhD); molecular medicine (PhD); molecular virology (PhD); molecular/cellular biophysics (PhD); neuroscience (PhD); nutrition (MS, PhD); pathology (MS, PhD); pharmacology (PhD); physiology and biophysics (PhD); public health (MPH); public health nutrition (MS); RNA biology (PhD); systems physiology (PhD). Electronic applications accepted.

Weatherhead School of Management ***Degree program information:*** Part-time and evening/weekend programs available. Part-time, evening/weekend. Offers accountancy (M Acc, PhD); business administration (EMBA, MBA); business analytics (MSM); designing sustainable systems (PhD); finance (MSM); healthcare (MSM); management (EMBA, M Acc, MBA, MNO, MPOD, MS, MSM, EDM, PhD, CNM); operations and supply chain management (MSM); operations research (PhD); organizational behavior (PhD); positive organization development and change (MS). Electronic applications accepted.

Mandel Center for Nonprofit Organizations Offers nonprofit management (MNO, CNM).

CASTLETON UNIVERSITY, Castleton, VT 05735

General Information State-supported, coed, comprehensive institution. *Graduate housing:* Room and/or apartments available on a first-come, first-served basis to single students; on-campus housing not available to married students. Housing application deadline: 5/19.

GRADUATE UNITS

Division of Graduate Studies ***Degree program information:*** Part-time and evening/weekend programs available. Part-time, evening/weekend. Offers curriculum and instruction (MA Ed); educational leadership (MA Ed, CAGS); forensic psychology (MA); language arts and reading (MA Ed, CAGS); special education (MA Ed, CAGS).

CATAWBA COLLEGE, Salisbury, NC 28144-2488

General Information Independent-religious, coed, comprehensive institution. *Enrollment:* 1,275 graduate, professional, and undergraduate students; 5 part-time matriculated graduate/professional students (all women). *Enrollment by degree level:* 5 master's. *Graduate faculty:* 4 full-time (3 women). *Tuition, area resident:* Part-time $180 per semester hour. *Required fees:* $25 per unit. *Graduate housing:* On-campus housing not available. *Student services:* Campus safety program, career counseling, exercise/wellness program, teacher training. *Library:* Corriher-Linn-Black Memorial Library plus 1 other. *Collection:* Books: 151,650 (physical), 184,548 (digital/electronic); Serial titles: 95 (physical), 32,589 (digital/electronic); Databases: 102. Weekly public service hours: 83; students can reserve study rooms.

Computer facilities: 173 computers available on campus for general student use. A campuswide network can be accessed from student residence rooms and from off campus. Online class registration is available.
Website: http://www.catawba.edu/

General Application Contact: Dr. Rhonda L. Truitt, Director, Graduate Program, 704-637-4468, Fax: 704-637-4732, E-mail: rltruitt@catawba.edu.

GRADUATE UNITS

Department of Teacher Education Average age 30. *Faculty:* 4 full-time (3 women). *Financial support:* In 2015–16, 1 student received support. Scholarships/grants available. In 2015, 2 master's awarded. *Degree program information:* Part-time and evening/weekend programs available. Part-time, evening/weekend. Offers elementary education (M Ed); STEM education (M Ed). *Application deadline:* For fall admission, 7/1 for domestic students; for spring admission, 12/1 for domestic students. Applications are processed on a rolling basis. *Application fee:* $25. *Chair/Director, Graduate Program,* Dr. Rhonda L. Truitt, 704-637-4468, Fax: 704-637-4732, E-mail: rltruitt@catawba.edu.

CATHOLIC DISTANCE UNIVERSITY, Hamilton, VA 20158

General Information Independent-religious, coed, graduate-only institution. *Graduate housing:* On-campus housing not available.

GRADUATE UNITS

Graduate Programs ***Degree program information:*** Part-time and evening/weekend programs available. Part-time, evening/weekend, online learning. Offers religious studies (MRS); theology (MA).

CATHOLIC THEOLOGICAL UNION, Chicago, IL 60615-5698

General Information Independent-religious, coed, graduate-only institution. *Graduate housing:* Rooms and/or apartments available on a first-come, first-served basis to single and married students. Housing application deadline: 7/1.

GRADUATE UNITS

Graduate and Professional Programs ***Degree program information:*** Part-time and evening/weekend programs available. Part-time, evening/weekend. Offers biblical spirituality (Certificate); cross-cultural ministries (D Min); cross-cultural missions (Certificate); divinity (M Div); liturgical studies (Certificate); liturgy (D Min); pastoral studies (MAPS, Certificate); spiritual formation (Certificate); spirituality (D Min); theology (MA). M Div/PhD offered jointly with University of Chicago; M Div/MSW with Loyola University Chicago and University of Chicago.

THE CATHOLIC UNIVERSITY OF AMERICA, Washington, DC 20064

General Information Independent-religious, coed, university. CGS member. *Enrollment:* 6,521 graduate, professional, and undergraduate students; 1,164 full-time matriculated graduate/professional students (511 women), 1,836 part-time matriculated graduate/professional students (1,054 women). *Enrollment by degree level:* 1,603 master's, 1,345 doctoral, 52 other advanced degrees. *Graduate faculty:* 399 full-time (153 women), 367 part-time/adjunct (163 women). *Tuition, area resident:* Full-time $41,400; part-time $1650 per credit. *Required fees:* $400; $290 per semester. $145 per semester. Part-time tuition and fees vary according to course load and program. *Graduate housing:* Room and/or apartments available on a first-come, first-served basis to single students; on-campus housing not available to married students. Typical cost: $15,822 (including board). Room and board charges vary according to board plan. Housing application deadline: 5/15. *Student services:* Campus employment opportunities, campus safety program, career counseling, exercise/wellness program, free psychological counseling, international student services, low-cost health insurance, multicultural affairs office, services for students with disabilities, teacher training, writing training. *Library:* Mullen Library plus 7 others. *Research affiliation:* EnergySolutions (waste vitrification research), National Rehabilitation Hospital (rehabilitation engineering research), Samsung (building environmental control), Space Telescope Science Institute (astronomy and space physics research), Better Way Foundation (early childhood education), Eco-Convergence Group, Inc. (concrete materials research).

Computer facilities: Computer purchase and lease plans are available. 366 computers available on campus for general student use. A campuswide network can be accessed from student residence rooms and from off campus. Online class registration, Internet2, video streaming, online voting, pedagogical software are available.
Website: http://www.cua.edu/

General Application Contact: Director of Graduate Admissions, 202-319-5057, Fax: 202-319-6533, E-mail: cua-admissions@cua.edu.

GRADUATE UNITS

Benjamin T. Rome School of Music Students: 31 full-time (13 women), 76 part-time (38 women); includes 29 minority (8 Black or African American, non-Hispanic/Latino; 14 Asian, non-Hispanic/Latino; 7 Hispanic/Latino), 16 international. Average age 33. 101 applicants, 69% accepted, 27 enrolled. *Faculty:* 18 full-time (3 women), 53 part-time/adjunct (22 women). *Financial support:* Fellowships, research assistantships, teaching assistantships, Federal Work-Study, scholarships/grants, tuition waivers (full and partial), and unspecified assistantships available. Financial award application deadline: 2/1; financial award applicants required to submit FAFSA. In 2015, 6 master's, 18 doctorates awarded. *Degree program information:* Part-time programs available. Part-time. Offers chamber music (piano) (MM, DMA); composition (MM, DMA); music (MAT); music teacher certification (Certificate); musicology (MA, PhD); orchestral conducting (MM, DMA); orchestral instruments (DMA); orchestral instruments/guitar (MM); piano pedagogy (MM, DMA); piano performance (MM, DMA); sacred music (MMSM, DMA); vocal accompanying (MM, DMA); vocal pedagogy (MM, DMA); vocal performance (MM, DMA). *Application deadline:* For fall admission, 7/15 priority date for domestic students, 7/1 for international students; for spring admission, 11/15 priority date for domestic students, 11/1 for international students. Applications are processed on a rolling basis. *Application fee:* $55. Electronic applications accepted. *Application Contact:* Director of Graduate Admissions, 202-319-5057, Fax: 202-319-6533, E-mail: cua-admissions@cua.edu. *Dean,* Dr. Grayson Wagstaff, 202-319-5417, Fax: 202-319-6280, E-mail: cua-music@cua.edu.

Columbus School of Law Students: 291 full-time (149 women), 164 part-time (73 women); includes 21 minority (11 Black or African American, non-Hispanic/Latino; 2 Asian, non-Hispanic/Latino; 7 Hispanic/Latino; 1 Two or more races, non-Hispanic/Latino), 3 international. Average age 26. 1,562 applicants, 56% accepted, 140 enrolled. *Faculty:* 45 full-time (21 women), 98 part-time/adjunct (21 women). *Financial support:* In 2015–16, 318 students received support. Career-related internships or fieldwork, Federal Work-Study, institutionally sponsored loans, and scholarships/grants available. Support available to part-time students. Financial award application deadline: 8/15; financial award applicants required to submit FAFSA. *Degree program information:* Part-time and evening/weekend programs available. Part-time, evening/weekend. Offers law (MLS, JD). *Application deadline:* For fall admission, 3/16 priority date for domestic students, 3/16 for international students. Applications are processed on a rolling basis. *Application fee:* $65. Electronic applications accepted. *Application Contact:* Shani J. P. Butts, Director of Admissions, 202-319-5151, Fax: 202-319-4462, E-mail: butts@law.edu. *Dean,* Daniel F. Attridge, 202-319-5139, Fax: 202-319-5473.

Metropolitan School of Professional Studies Students: 29 full-time (17 women), 214 part-time (133 women); includes 131 minority (76 Black or African American, non-Hispanic/Latino; 8 Asian, non-Hispanic/Latino; 24 Hispanic/Latino; 23 Two or more races, non-Hispanic/Latino), 9 international. Average age 37. 112 applicants, 74% accepted, 62 enrolled. *Faculty:* 39 part-time/adjunct (18 women). *Financial support:* Application deadline: 3/15; applicants required to submit FAFSA. In 2015, 92 master's awarded. *Degree program information:* Part-time and evening/weekend programs available. Part-time, evening/weekend, 100% online. Offers management (MSM). *Application deadline:* For fall admission, 7/15 priority date for domestic students, 7/1 for international students; for spring admission, 11/15 priority date for domestic students, 11/1 for international students. Applications are processed on a rolling basis. *Application fee:* $55. Electronic applications accepted. *Application Contact:* Director of Graduate Admissions, 202-319-5057, Fax: 202-319-6533, E-mail: cua-admissions@cua.edu. *Interim Dean,* Dr. Will C. Rainford, 202-319-5256, Fax: 202-319-6032, E-mail: rainford@cua.edu.

National Catholic School of Social Service Students: 131 full-time (108 women), 342 part-time (288 women); includes 208 minority (124 Black or African American, non-Hispanic/Latino; 2 American Indian or Alaska Native, non-Hispanic/Latino; 11 Asian, non-Hispanic/Latino; 40 Hispanic/Latino; 1 Native Hawaiian or other Pacific Islander, non-Hispanic/Latino; 30 Two or more races, non-Hispanic/Latino), 6 international. Average age 34. 419 applicants, 66% accepted, 185 enrolled. *Faculty:* 17 full-time (14 women), 23 part-time/adjunct (17 women). *Financial support:* Fellowships, research assistantships, teaching assistantships, Federal Work-Study, scholarships/grants, tuition waivers (full and partial), and unspecified assistantships available. Financial award application deadline: 3/15; financial award applicants required to submit FAFSA. In 2015, 106 master's, 9 doctorates awarded. *Degree program information:* Part-time programs available. Part-time, 100% online. Offers clinical (MSW); combined (clinical and social change) (MSW); social change (MSW); social work (PhD). *Application deadline:* For fall admission, 7/15 priority date for domestic students, 7/1 for international students; for spring admission, 11/15 priority date for domestic students, 11/1 for international students. Applications are processed on a rolling basis. *Application fee:* $55. Electronic applications accepted. *Application Contact:* Director of Graduate Admissions, 202-319-5057, Fax: 202-319-6533, E-mail: cua-admissions@cua.edu. *Dean,* Dr. Will Rainford, 202-319-5454, Fax: 202-319-5093, E-mail: rainford@cua.edu.

School of Architecture and Planning Students: 88 full-time (35 women), 30 part-time (16 women); includes 41 minority (11 Black or African American, non-Hispanic/Latino; 7 Asian, non-Hispanic/Latino; 11 Hispanic/Latino; 12 Two or more races, non-Hispanic/Latino), 15 international. Average age 29. 99 applicants, 96% accepted, 49 enrolled. *Faculty:* 21 full-time (8 women), 15 part-time/adjunct (2 women). *Financial support:* Fellowships, research assistantships, teaching assistantships, Federal Work-Study, scholarships/grants, tuition waivers (full and partial), and unspecified assistantships available. Financial award application deadline: 2/1; financial award applicants required to submit FAFSA. In 2015, 56 master's awarded. *Degree program information:* Part-time programs available. Part-time. Offers architecture and planning (M Arch, MS Arch St). *Application deadline:* For fall admission, 1/15 priority date for domestic students, 7/1 for international students; for spring admission, 10/15 priority date for domestic students, 11/1 for international students. Applications are processed on a rolling basis. *Application fee:* $55. Electronic applications accepted. *Application Contact:* Director of Graduate Admissions, 202-319-5057, Fax: 202-319-6533, E-mail: cua-admissions@cua.edu. *Dean,* Randall Ott, 202-319-5784, Fax: 202-319-2023, E-mail: ott@cua.edu.

School of Arts and Sciences Students: 165 full-time (90 women), 382 part-time (212 women); includes 94 minority (27 Black or African American, non-Hispanic/Latino; 1 American Indian or Alaska Native, non-Hispanic/Latino; 18 Asian, non-Hispanic/Latino; 23 Hispanic/Latino; 25 Two or more races, non-Hispanic/Latino), 93 international. Average age 31. 635 applicants, 43% accepted, 130 enrolled. *Faculty:* 161 full-time (70 women), 79 part-time/adjunct (40 women). *Financial support:* Fellowships, research assistantships, teaching assistantships, Federal Work-Study, scholarships/grants, tuition waivers (full and partial), and unspecified assistantships available. Financial award application deadline: 2/1; financial award applicants required to submit FAFSA. In 2015, 212 master's, 32 doctorates awarded. *Degree program information:* Part-time programs available. Part-time. Offers acting, directing, and playwriting (MFA); American government (MA, PhD); ancient near East (Biblical Hebrew/Aramaic) (MA, PhD); anthropology (MA); applied experimental psychology (PhD); Arabic (PhD); arts and sciences (MA, MFA, MS, MSBA, MSLS, PhD, Certificate); biotechnology (MS); Byzantine and Orthodox studies (MA); Catholic educational leadership and policy studies (PhD); Catholic school leadership (MA); cell and microbial biology (MS, PhD); Christian near East (Biblical Hebrew/Aramaic) (MA); clinical laboratory science (MS, PhD); clinical psychology (PhD); Congressional and Presidential studies (MA); Coptic (MA, PhD); crime and justice studies (MA); early Christian studies (MA, PhD); education (Certificate); English language and literature (MA, PhD); general psychology (MA); global and comparative sociology (MA); Greek (MA, Certificate); Greek and Latin (MA, PhD, Certificate); Hispanic studies (MA, PhD); history (MA, PhD); human development psychology (PhD); human factors (MA); international affairs (MA); international political economics (MA); Latin (MA, Certificate); library and information science (MSLS, Certificate); Medieval and Byzantine studies (PhD, Certificate); physics (MS, PhD); political theory (MA, PhD); public policy (MA); religion and society in the late medieval and early modern world (MA); rhetoric (Certificate); secondary education (MA); special education (MA); Syriac (MA, PhD); the Islamic world (MA); the Medieval West (MA); theatre education (MA); theatre history and criticism (MA); world politics (MA, PhD). *Application deadline:* For fall admission, 2/1 priority date for domestic students, 7/1 for international students; for spring admission, 11/15 priority date for domestic students, 11/1 for international students. Applications are processed on a rolling basis.

Application fee: $55. Electronic applications accepted. *Application Contact:* Director of Graduate Admissions, 202-319-5057, Fax: 202-319-6533, E-mail: cua-admissions@cua.edu. *Acting Dean*, Dr. Claudia Bornholdt, 202-319-5115, Fax: 202-319-6076, E-mail: bornholdt@cua.edu.

School of Business and Economics Students: 56 full-time (34 women), 8 part-time (6 women); includes 20 minority (6 Black or African American, non-Hispanic/Latino; 5 Asian, non-Hispanic/Latino; 8 Hispanic/Latino; 1 Two or more races, non-Hispanic/Latino), 22 international. Average age 26. 95 applicants, 67% accepted, 41 enrolled. *Faculty:* 23 full-time (6 women), 34 part-time/adjunct (6 women). *Financial support:* Fellowships, research assistantships, teaching assistantships, Federal Work-Study, scholarships/grants, tuition waivers (full and partial), and unspecified assistantships available. Financial award application deadline: 2/1; financial award applicants required to submit FAFSA. In 2015, 38 master's awarded. *Degree program information:* Part-time programs available. Part-time. Offers accounting (MS); business analysis (MSBA); integral economic development management (MA); integral economic development policy (MA); international political economics (MA); management (MS). *Application deadline:* For fall admission, 7/15 priority date for domestic students, 7/1 for international students; for spring admission, 11/15 priority date for domestic students, 11/1 for international students. Applications are processed on a rolling basis. *Application fee:* $55. Electronic applications accepted. *Application Contact:* Director of Graduate Admissions, 202-319-5057, Fax: 202-319-6533, E-mail: cua-admissions@cua.edu. *Interim Dean*, Dr. Brian Engelland, 202-319-6729, Fax: 202-319-4426, E-mail: engellab@cua.edu.

School of Canon Law Students: 34 full-time (2 women), 42 part-time (7 women); includes 8 minority (1 Black or African American, non-Hispanic/Latino; 2 Asian, non-Hispanic/Latino; 4 Hispanic/Latino; 1 Two or more races, non-Hispanic/Latino), 13 international. Average age 39. 41 applicants, 88% accepted, 26 enrolled. *Faculty:* 6 full-time (1 woman), 1 part-time/adjunct (0 women). *Financial support:* Fellowships, research assistantships, teaching assistantships, Federal Work-Study, scholarships/grants, tuition waivers (full and partial), and unspecified assistantships available. Financial award application deadline: 2/1; financial award applicants required to submit FAFSA. In 2015, 17 master's, 1 doctorate awarded. *Degree program information:* Part-time programs available. Part-time. Offers Canon law (JCD, JCL); church administration (MCA). *Application deadline:* For fall admission, 7/15 priority date for domestic students, 7/1 for international students; for spring admission, 11/15 priority date for domestic students, 11/1 for international students. Applications are processed on a rolling basis. *Application fee:* $55. Electronic applications accepted. *Application Contact:* Director of Graduate Admissions, 202-319-5057, Fax: 202-319-6533, E-mail: cua-admissions@cua.edu. *Dean*, Rev. Robert Kaslyn, SJ, 202-319-5492, Fax: 202-319-4187, E-mail: cua-canonlaw@cua.edu.

School of Engineering Students: 80 full-time (17 women), 111 part-time (29 women); includes 36 minority (19 Black or African American, non-Hispanic/Latino; 5 Asian, non-Hispanic/Latino; 2 Hispanic/Latino; 10 Two or more races, non-Hispanic/Latino), 113 international. Average age 32. 187 applicants, 69% accepted, 60 enrolled. *Faculty:* 31 full-time (3 women), 33 part-time/adjunct (4 women). *Financial support:* Fellowships, research assistantships, teaching assistantships, Federal Work-Study, scholarships/grants, tuition waivers (full and partial), and unspecified assistantships available. Financial award application deadline: 2/1; financial award applicants required to submit FAFSA. In 2015, 72 master's, 10 doctorates awarded. *Degree program information:* Part-time programs available. Part-time. Offers biomedical engineering (MBE, PhD); civil engineering (MS, PhD); computer science (PhD); electrical engineering (PhD); electrical engineering and computer science (MEE, MSCS); energy and environment (MME); engineering (MBE, MCE, MEE, MME, MS, MSCS, MSE, PhD, Certificate); engineering management (MSE, Certificate); general (MME); materials science and engineering (MS); mechanical engineering (MSE, PhD); program management (Certificate); systems engineering and management of information technology (Certificate); transportation and infrastructure systems (Certificate). *Application deadline:* For fall admission, 7/15 priority date for domestic students, 7/1 for international students; for spring admission, 11/15 priority date for domestic students, 11/1 for international students. Applications are processed on a rolling basis. *Application fee:* $55. Electronic applications accepted. *Application Contact:* Director of Graduate Admissions, 202-319-5057, Fax: 202-319-6533, E-mail: cua-admissions@cua.edu. *Dean*, Dr. Charles C. Nguyen, 202-319-5160, Fax: 202-319-4499, E-mail: nguyen@cua.edu.

School of Nursing Students: 35 full-time (33 women), 212 part-time (197 women); includes 82 minority (59 Black or African American, non-Hispanic/Latino; 10 Asian, non-Hispanic/Latino; 7 Hispanic/Latino; 6 Two or more races, non-Hispanic/Latino), 10 international. Average age 40. 144 applicants, 67% accepted, 60 enrolled. *Faculty:* 19 full-time (all women), 48 part-time/adjunct (43 women). *Financial support:* Fellowships, research assistantships, teaching assistantships, Federal Work-Study, scholarships/grants, tuition waivers (full and partial), and unspecified assistantships available. Financial award application deadline: 2/1; financial award applicants required to submit FAFSA. In 2015, 12 master's, 4 doctorates, 3 other advanced degrees awarded. *Degree program information:* Part-time programs available. Part-time. Offers nursing (MSN, DNP, PhD, Certificate). *Application deadline:* For fall admission, 7/15 priority date for domestic students, 7/1 for international students; for spring admission, 11/15 priority date for domestic students, 11/1 for international students. Applications are processed on a rolling basis. *Application fee:* $55. Electronic applications accepted. *Application Contact:* Director of Graduate Admissions, 202-319-5057, Fax: 202-319-6533, E-mail: cua-admissions@cua.edu. *Dean*, Dr. Patricia McMullen, 202-319-5403, Fax: 202-319-6485, E-mail: mcmullep@cua.edu.

School of Philosophy Students: 69 full-time (10 women), 75 part-time (10 women); includes 18 minority (1 Black or African American, non-Hispanic/Latino; 4 Asian, non-Hispanic/Latino; 9 Hispanic/Latino; 4 Two or more races, non-Hispanic/Latino), 8 international. Average age 32. 87 applicants, 63% accepted, 40 enrolled. *Faculty:* 21 full-time (5 women), 7 part-time/adjunct (3 women). *Financial support:* Fellowships, research assistantships, teaching assistantships, Federal Work-Study, scholarships/grants, tuition waivers (full and partial), and unspecified assistantships available. Financial award application deadline: 2/1; financial award applicants required to submit FAFSA. In 2015, 10 master's, 5 doctorates awarded. *Degree program information:* Part-time programs available. Part-time. Offers philosophy (MA, PhD, Ph L). *Application deadline:* For fall admission, 7/15 priority date for domestic students, 7/1 for international students; for spring admission, 11/15 priority date for domestic students, 11/1 for international students. Applications are processed on a rolling basis. *Application fee:* $55. Electronic applications accepted. *Application Contact:* Director of Graduate Admissions, 202-319-5057, Fax: 202-319-6533, E-mail: cua-admissions@cua.edu. *Dean*, Dr. John McCarthy, 202-319-6649, Fax: 202-319-4731, E-mail: mccartjc@cua.edu.

School of Theology and Religious Studies Students: 149 full-time (8 women), 189 part-time (47 women); includes 69 minority (8 Black or African American, non-Hispanic/Latino; 2 American Indian or Alaska Native, non-Hispanic/Latino; 11 Asian, non-Hispanic/Latino; 17 Hispanic/Latino; 1 Native Hawaiian or other Pacific Islander, non-Hispanic/Latino; 30 Two or more races, non-Hispanic/Latino), 53 international. Average age 35. 191 applicants, 70% accepted, 70 enrolled. *Faculty:* 39 full-time (3 women), 7 part-time/adjunct (1 woman). *Financial support:* Fellowships, research assistantships, teaching assistantships, Federal Work-Study, scholarships/grants, tuition waivers (full and partial), and unspecified assistantships available. Financial award application deadline: 2/1; financial award applicants required to submit FAFSA. In 2015, 41 master's, 25 doctorates awarded. *Degree program information:* Part-time programs available. Part-time. Offers theology and religious studies (M Cat, M Div, MA, D Min, PhD, STD, Certificate, STB, STL). *Application deadline:* For fall admission, 7/15 priority date for domestic students, 7/1 for international students; for spring admission, 11/15 priority date for domestic students, 11/1 for international students. Applications are processed on a rolling basis. *Application fee:* $55. Electronic applications accepted. *Application Contact:* Director of Graduate Admissions, 202-319-5057, Fax: 202-319-6533, E-mail: cua-admissions@cua.edu. *Interim Dean*, Dr. William Mattison, III, 202-319-5684, Fax: 202-319-5704, E-mail: mattison@cua.edu.

CEDAR CREST COLLEGE, Allentown, PA 18104-6196

General Information Independent-religious, coed, primarily women, comprehensive institution. *Enrollment:* 1,591 graduate, professional, and undergraduate students; 50 full-time matriculated graduate/professional students (43 women), 153 part-time matriculated graduate/professional students (140 women). *Enrollment by degree level:* 172 master's, 31 other advanced degrees. *Graduate faculty:* 20 full-time (15 women), 20 part-time/adjunct (11 women). *Tuition, area resident:* Part-time $772 per credit. *Required fees:* $50 per unit. *Graduate housing:* On-campus housing not available. *Student services:* Campus employment opportunities, campus safety program, career counseling, exercise/wellness program, free psychological counseling, international student services, multicultural affairs office, services for students with disabilities, teacher training. *Library:* Frank M. Cressman Library.

Computer facilities: Computer purchase and lease plans are available. 285 computers available on campus for general student use. A campuswide network can be accessed from student residence rooms and from off campus. Online class registration is available.
Website: http://www.cedarcrest.edu/

General Application Contact: Mary Ellen Hickes, Director of School of Adult and Graduate Education, 610-437-4471, E-mail: sage@cedarcrest.edu.

GRADUATE UNITS

Department of Education Students: 7 full-time (all women), 52 part-time (48 women); includes 9 minority (4 Black or African American, non-Hispanic/Latino; 5 Hispanic/Latino). Average age 34. *Faculty:* 4 full-time (all women), 5 part-time/adjunct (4 women). *Financial support:* In 2015–16, 60 students received support. Available to part-time students. Applicants required to submit FAFSA. In 2015, 28 master's awarded. *Degree program information:* Part-time and evening/weekend programs available. Part-time, evening/weekend. Offers education (M Ed). *Application deadline:* For fall admission, 8/7 priority date for domestic and international students; for winter admission, 11/7 priority date for domestic and international students; for spring admission, 1/8 priority date for domestic and international students. Applications are processed on a rolling basis. Electronic applications accepted. *Application Contact:* Mary Ellen Hickes, Director of School of Adult and Graduate Education, 610-606-4666, E-mail: sage@cedarcrest.edu. *Graduate Program Director*, Dr. Jill Purdy, 610-606-4666 Ext. 3419, E-mail: jepurdy@cedarcrest.edu.

Dietetic Internship Certificate Program Students: 26 part-time (24 women); includes 1 minority (Hispanic/Latino). Average age 26. *Faculty:* 1 (woman) full-time, 2 part-time/adjunct (1 woman). In 2015, 23 Graduate Certificates awarded. *Degree program information:* Part-time and evening/weekend programs available. Part-time, evening/weekend, blended/hybrid learning. Offers dietetic internship (Graduate Certificate). *Application deadline:* Applications are processed on a rolling basis. Electronic applications accepted. *Application Contact:* Mary Ellen Hickes, Director of School of Adult and Graduate Education, 610-437-4471, E-mail: sage@cedarcrest.edu. *Director*, Kati Fosselius, 610-606-4666 Ext. 3445, E-mail: kdfossel@cedarcrest.edu.

Program in Art Therapy Students: 17 full-time (all women), 10 part-time (all women); includes 2 minority (1 Asian, non-Hispanic/Latino; 1 Hispanic/Latino). Average age 31. *Faculty:* 2 full-time (both women), 3 part-time/adjunct (all women). *Degree program information:* Part-time and evening/weekend programs available. Part-time, evening/weekend, blended/hybrid learning. Offers art therapy (MA). *Application deadline:* Applications are processed on a rolling basis. Electronic applications accepted. *Application Contact:* Mary Ellen Hickes, Director of School of Adult and Graduate Education, 610-437-4471, E-mail: sage@cedarcrest.edu. *Director*, Rebecca Arnold, 610-437-4471 Ext. 3594, E-mail: rarnold@cedarcrest.edu.

Program in Business Administration Students: 13 full-time (9 women), 10 part-time (0 women); includes 13 minority (6 Black or African American, non-Hispanic/Latino; 1 Asian, non-Hispanic/Latino; 6 Hispanic/Latino). Average age 41. *Faculty:* 2 full-time (0 women), 2 part-time/adjunct (1 woman). *Degree program information:* Part-time and evening/weekend programs available. Part-time, evening/weekend. Offers business administration (MBA). *Application deadline:* Applications are processed on a rolling basis. Electronic applications accepted. *Application Contact:* Mary Ellen Hickes, Director of School of Adult and Graduate Education, 610-437-4471, E-mail: sage@cedarcrest.edu. *Chair*, Ibolya Balog, 610-437-4471 Ext. 4453, E-mail: ibalog@cedarcrest.edu.

Program in Creative Writing Students: 15 part-time (13 women). Average age 38. *Faculty:* 1 full-time (0 women), 5 part-time/adjunct (1 woman). *Degree program information:* Part-time and evening/weekend programs available. Part-time, evening/weekend, blended/hybrid learning. Offers creative writing (MFA). *Application deadline:* Applications are processed on a rolling basis. Electronic applications accepted. *Application Contact:* Mary Ellen Hickes, Director of School of Adult and Graduate Education, 610-437-4471, E-mail: sage@cedarcrest.edu. *Director of Writing Program*, Dr. Robert Wilson, 610-606-4666 Ext. 3474, E-mail: rawilson@cedarcrest.edu.

Program in Forensic Science Students: 112 full-time (10 women), 14 part-time (13 women); includes 6 minority (2 Black or African American, non-Hispanic/Latino; 1 American Indian or Alaska Native, non-Hispanic/Latino; 3 Asian, non-Hispanic/Latino). Average age 25. *Faculty:* 6 full-time (4 women), 2 part-time/adjunct (1 woman). *Financial support:* In 2015–16, 4 students received support. Unspecified assistantships available. In 2015, 6 master's awarded. Offers forensic science (MS). *Application deadline:* For fall admission, 1/2 priority date for domestic students. Applications are processed on a rolling basis. Electronic applications accepted. *Application Contact:* Mary Ellen Hickes, Director of School of Adult and Graduate Education, 610-606-4666, E-mail: sage@cedarcrest.edu. *Director and Associate Professor*, Dr. Lawrence A. Quarino, 610-606-4666 Ext. 3507, Fax: 610-740-3787, E-mail: laquarin@cedarcrest.edu.

Program in Nursing Students: 12 part-time (all women); includes 1 minority (Hispanic/Latino). Average age 35. *Faculty:* 4 full-time (all women), 1 part-time/adjunct (0 women). In 2015, 15 master's awarded. *Degree program information:* Part-time programs available. Part-time. Offers nursing administration (MS); nursing education (MS). *Application deadline:* Applications are processed on a rolling basis. Electronic applications accepted. *Application Contact:* Mary Ellen Hickes, Director of School of Adult and Graduate Education, 610-606-4666, E-mail: sage@cedarcrest.edu. *Director,* Dr. Wendy Robb, 610-606-4666, E-mail: wjrobb@cedarcrest.edu.

CEDARS-SINAI MEDICAL CENTER, Los Angeles, CA 90048

General Information Independent, coed, graduate-only institution. *Graduate housing:* On-campus housing not available.

GRADUATE UNITS

Graduate Program in Biomedical Sciences and Translational Medicine Offers biomedical sciences and translational medicine (PhD). Electronic applications accepted.

CEDARVILLE UNIVERSITY, Cedarville, OH 45314-0601

General Information Independent-religious, coed, comprehensive institution. *Enrollment:* 3,654 graduate, professional, and undergraduate students; 201 full-time matriculated graduate/professional students (116 women), 100 part-time matriculated graduate/professional students (71 women). *Enrollment by degree level:* 125 master's, 171 doctoral, 5 other advanced degrees. *Graduate faculty:* 61 full-time (26 women), 7 part-time/adjunct (2 women). *Tuition, area resident:* Full-time $12,594; part-time $566 per credit. Tuition and fees vary according to degree level and program. *Graduate housing:* Rooms and/or apartments available on a first-come, first-served basis to single and married students. Typical cost: $5582 per year ($8680 including board) for single students; $5250 per year ($8348 including board) for married students. Room and board charges vary according to board plan and housing facility selected. Housing application deadline: 3/15. *Student services:* Campus employment opportunities, campus safety program, career counseling, exercise/wellness program, free psychological counseling, international student services, low-cost health insurance, services for students with disabilities, writing training. *Library:* Centennial Library. *Collection:* Books: 185,200 (physical), 106,197 (digital/electronic); Serial titles: 768 (physical), 25,330 (digital/electronic); Databases: 199. Weekly public service hours: 87; students can reserve study rooms.

Computer facilities: 2,100 computers available on campus for general student use. A campuswide network can be accessed from student residence rooms and from off campus. Online class registration, over 70 software packages are available.
Website: http://www.cedarville.edu/

General Application Contact: Joel Tomkinson, Director of Graduate and Adult Admissions, 937-766-7700, E-mail: admissions@cedarville.edu.

GRADUATE UNITS

Graduate Programs Students: 201 full-time (116 women), 100 part-time (71 women); includes 53 minority (32 Black or African American, non-Hispanic/Latino; 3 American Indian or Alaska Native, non-Hispanic/Latino; 15 Asian, non-Hispanic/Latino; 2 Hispanic/Latino; 1 Native Hawaiian or other Pacific Islander, non-Hispanic/Latino), 5 international. Average age 30. 142 applicants, 58% accepted, 57 enrolled. *Faculty:* 61 full-time (26 women), 7 part-time/adjunct (2 women). *Financial support:* In 2015–16, 129 students received support. Scholarships/grants and unspecified assistantships available. Support available to part-time students. Financial award applicants required to submit FAFSA. In 2015, 41 degrees awarded. *Degree program information:* Part-time and evening/weekend programs available. Part-time, evening/weekend, online learning. Offers business administration (MBA); curriculum (M Ed); educational administration (M Ed); family nurse practitioner (MSN); global health ministries (MSN); instruction (M Ed); ministry (M Min); pharmacy (Pharm D). *Application deadline:* For fall admission, 5/1 priority date for domestic and international students; for spring admission, 11/1 priority date for domestic and international students. Applications are processed on a rolling basis. *Application fee:* $0. Electronic applications accepted. *Application Contact:* Roscoe Smith, Associate Vice President for University Admissions, 937-766-7700, Fax: 937-766-7575, E-mail: smithr@cedarville.edu. *Dean of Graduate Studies,* Dr. Mark McClain, 937-766-7700, E-mail: mcclain@cedarville.edu.

CENTENARY COLLEGE, Hackettstown, NJ 07840-2100

General Information Independent-religious, coed, comprehensive institution. *Graduate housing:* Room and/or apartments available on a first-come, first-served basis to single students; on-campus housing not available to married students. Housing application deadline: 6/1.

GRADUATE UNITS

Program in Business Administration ***Degree program information:*** Part-time and evening/weekend programs available. Part-time, evening/weekend, online learning. Offers business administration (MBA).

Program in Counseling Psychology ***Degree program information:*** Part-time and evening/weekend programs available. Part-time, evening/weekend, online learning. Offers counseling (MA); counseling psychology (MA).

Program in Education ***Degree program information:*** Part-time and evening/weekend programs available. Part-time, evening/weekend, online learning. Offers educational leadership (MA); instructional leadership (MA); special education (MA).

Program in Professional Accounting ***Degree program information:*** Part-time and evening/weekend programs available. Part-time, evening/weekend, online learning. Offers professional accounting (MS).

CENTENARY COLLEGE OF LOUISIANA, Shreveport, LA 71104

General Information Independent-religious, coed, comprehensive institution. *Graduate housing:* Rooms and/or apartments available on a first-come, first-served basis to single students and available to married students.

GRADUATE UNITS

Graduate Programs ***Degree program information:*** Part-time and evening/weekend programs available. Part-time, evening/weekend. Offers elementary education (MAT); secondary education (MAT).

Frost School of Business ***Degree program information:*** Part-time and evening/weekend programs available. Part-time, evening/weekend. Offers business (MBA).

CENTRAL BAPTIST THEOLOGICAL SEMINARY, Shawnee, KS 66226

General Information Independent-religious, coed, graduate-only institution. *Graduate housing:* On-campus housing not available.

GRADUATE UNITS

Graduate and Professional Programs ***Degree program information:*** Part-time programs available. Part-time. Offers missional church studies (MA); theological studies (MA); theology (M Div, Diploma). Electronic applications accepted.

CENTRAL CONNECTICUT STATE UNIVERSITY, New Britain, CT 06050-4010

General Information State-supported, coed, comprehensive institution. *Enrollment:* 12,086 graduate, professional, and undergraduate students; 496 full-time matriculated graduate/professional students (324 women), 1,474 part-time matriculated graduate/professional students (953 women). *Enrollment by degree level:* 1,614 master's, 54 doctoral, 302 other advanced degrees. *Graduate faculty:* 176 full-time (77 women), 69 part-time/adjunct (44 women). *Tuition, area resident:* Full-time $6188. Tuition, state resident: full-time $9284; part-time $577 per credit. Tuition, nonresident: full-time $17,240; part-time $592 per credit. *Required fees:* $4266; $234 per credit. *Graduate housing:* Room and/or apartments available on a first-come, first-served basis to single students; on-campus housing not available to married students. Typical cost: $7708 per year ($12,394 including board). Housing application deadline: 5/1. *Student services:* Campus employment opportunities, campus safety program, career counseling, child daycare facilities, exercise/wellness program, free psychological counseling, international student services, low-cost health insurance, multicultural affairs office, services for students with disabilities, teacher training, writing training. *Library:* Elihu Burritt Library plus 1 other. *Collection:* Books: 644,720 (physical), 10,422 (digital/electronic); Serial titles: 53,518 (digital/electronic); Databases: 84,568. Weekly public service hours: 84; students can reserve study rooms.

Computer facilities: 750 computers available on campus for general student use. A campuswide network can be accessed from student residence rooms and from off campus. Online class registration is available.
Website: http://www.ccsu.edu/

General Application Contact: Patricia Gardner, Associate Director of Graduate Studies, 860-832-2350, Fax: 860-832-2362, E-mail: graduateadmissions@ccsu.edu.

GRADUATE UNITS

School of Graduate Studies Students: 496 full-time (324 women), 1,474 part-time (953 women); includes 355 minority (151 Black or African American, non-Hispanic/Latino; 2 American Indian or Alaska Native, non-Hispanic/Latino; 64 Asian, non-Hispanic/Latino; 105 Hispanic/Latino; 1 Native Hawaiian or other Pacific Islander, non-Hispanic/Latino; 32 Two or more races, non-Hispanic/Latino), 113 international. Average age 33. 1,140 applicants, 70% accepted, 523 enrolled. *Faculty:* 176 full-time (77 women), 69 part-time/adjunct (44 women). *Financial support:* In 2015–16, 189 students received support, including 55 research assistantships; career-related internships or fieldwork, Federal Work-Study, scholarships/grants, and unspecified assistantships also available. Support available to part-time students. Financial award application deadline: 3/1; financial award applicants required to submit FAFSA. In 2015, 564 master's, 7 doctorates, 93 other advanced degrees awarded. *Degree program information:* Part-time and evening/weekend programs available. Part-time, evening/weekend. *Application deadline:* For fall admission, 6/1 for domestic students, 5/1 for international students; for spring admission, 11/1 for domestic and international students. Applications are processed on a rolling basis. *Application fee:* $50. Electronic applications accepted. *Associate Director of Graduate Studies,* Patricia Gardner, 860-832-2350, Fax: 860-832-2362, E-mail: graduateadmissions@ccsu.edu.

College of Liberal Arts and Social Sciences Students: 84 full-time (54 women), 224 part-time (147 women); includes 53 minority (23 Black or African American, non-Hispanic/Latino; 3 Asian, non-Hispanic/Latino; 21 Hispanic/Latino; 1 Native Hawaiian or other Pacific Islander, non-Hispanic/Latino; 5 Two or more races, non-Hispanic/Latino), 9 international. Average age 32. 241 applicants, 74% accepted, 107 enrolled. *Faculty:* 66 full-time (30 women), 5 part-time/adjunct (4 women). *Financial support:* In 2015–16, 32 students received support, including 23 research assistantships; career-related internships or fieldwork, Federal Work-Study, scholarships/grants, and unspecified assistantships also available. Support available to part-time students. Financial award application deadline: 3/1; financial award applicants required to submit FAFSA. In 2015, 90 master's, 17 other advanced degrees awarded. *Degree program information:* Part-time and evening/weekend programs available. Part-time, evening/weekend. Offers art education (MS, Certificate); community psychology (MA); criminal justice (MS); English (MA, Certificate); general psychology (MA); geography (MS); health psychology (MA); history (MA, Certificate); information design (MA); international studies (MS); liberal arts and social sciences (MA, MS, Certificate); modern language (MA, Certificate); music education (MS, Certificate); organizational communication (MS); public history (MA); public relations/promotions (Certificate); social studies (Certificate); Spanish (MS, Certificate); teaching English to speakers of other languages (MS, Certificate). *Application deadline:* For fall admission, 6/1 for domestic students, 5/1 for international students; for spring admission, 11/1 for domestic and international students. Applications are processed on a rolling basis. *Application fee:* $50. Electronic applications accepted. *Application Contact:* Patricia Gardner, Associate Director of Graduate Studies, 860-832-2350, Fax: 860-832-2362, E-mail: graduateadmissions@ccsu.edu. *Dean,* Dr. Susan Pease, 860-832-2600, E-mail: pease@ccsu.edu.

School of Business Students: 12 full-time (5 women), 125 part-time (56 women); includes 41 minority (15 Black or African American, non-Hispanic/Latino; 11 Asian, non-Hispanic/Latino; 11 Hispanic/Latino; 4 Two or more races, non-Hispanic/Latino). Average age 30. 118 applicants, 76% accepted, 59 enrolled. *Faculty:* 8 full-time (2 women), 1 part-time/adjunct (0 women). *Financial support:* In 2015–16, 12 students received support. Career-related internships or fieldwork, Federal Work-Study, and scholarships/grants available. Support available to part-time students. Financial award application deadline: 3/1; financial award applicants required to submit FAFSA. *Degree program information:* Part-time and evening/weekend programs available. Part-time, evening/weekend. Offers business (MBA). *Application deadline:* For fall admission, 6/1 for domestic students, 5/1 for international students; for spring admission, 11/1 for domestic and international students. Applications are processed on a rolling basis. *Application fee:* $50. Electronic applications accepted. *Application Contact:* Patricia Gardner, Associate Director of Graduate Admissions, 860-832-2350, Fax: 860-832-2362, E-mail: graduateadmissions@ccsu.edu. *MBA Director,* Dr. Jason Snyder, 860-832-3207, E-mail: mba@ccsu.edu.

School of Education and Professional Studies Students: 183 full-time (146 women), 830 part-time (635 women); includes 149 minority (73 Black or African American, non-Hispanic/Latino; 11 Asian, non-Hispanic/Latino; 49 Hispanic/Latino; 16 Two or more races, non-Hispanic/Latino), 38 international. Average age 34. 480 applicants, 68% accepted, 229 enrolled. *Faculty:* 50 full-time (29 women), 56 part-time/adjunct (38 women). *Financial support:* In 2015–16, 85 students received support, including

23 research assistantships; career-related internships or fieldwork, Federal Work-Study, scholarships/grants, and unspecified assistantships also available. Support available to part-time students. Financial award application deadline: 3/1; financial award applicants required to submit FAFSA. In 2015, 317 master's, 7 doctorates, 65 other advanced degrees awarded. *Degree program information:* Part-time and evening/weekend programs available. Part-time, evening/weekend. Offers education and professional studies (MAT, MS, Ed D, AC, Certificate, Sixth Year Certificate); educational leadership (MS, Ed D, AC, Sixth Year Certificate); educational technology and media (MS); literacy, elementary, and early childhood education (MS, AC, Sixth Year Certificate); marriage and family therapy (MS); physical education (MS, Certificate); professional counseling (MS, AC, Certificate); school counseling (MS); special education and interventions (MS, Certificate); student development in higher education (MS). *Application deadline:* For fall admission, 6/1 for domestic students, 5/1 for international students; for spring admission, 11/1 for domestic and international students. Applications are processed on a rolling basis. *Application fee:* $50. Electronic applications accepted. *Application Contact:* Patricia Gardner, Associate Director of Graduate Studies, 860-832-2350, Fax: 860-832-2362, E-mail: graduateadmissions@ccsu.edu. *Dean,* Dr. Michael Alfano, 860-832-2101, E-mail: malfano@ccsu.edu.

School of Engineering, Science and Technology Students: 217 full-time (119 women), 295 part-time (115 women); includes 112 minority (40 Black or African American, non-Hispanic/Latino; 2 American Indian or Alaska Native, non-Hispanic/Latino; 39 Asian, non-Hispanic/Latino; 24 Hispanic/Latino; 7 Two or more races, non-Hispanic/Latino), 66 international. Average age 31. 301 applicants, 68% accepted, 128 enrolled. *Faculty:* 52 full-time (16 women), 7 part-time/adjunct (2 women). *Financial support:* In 2015–16, 60 students received support, including 9 research assistantships; career-related internships or fieldwork, Federal Work-Study, scholarships/grants, and unspecified assistantships also available. Support available to part-time students. Financial award application deadline: 3/1; financial award applicants required to submit FAFSA. In 2015, 157 master's, 11 other advanced degrees awarded. *Degree program information:* Part-time and evening/weekend programs available. Part-time, evening/weekend. Offers biological sciences (MA, MS); biology (Certificate); biomolecular sciences (MS, Certificate); computer information technology (MS); construction management (MS, Certificate); data mining (MS, Certificate); engineering (MS); engineering, science and technology (MA, MS, Certificate, Sixth Year Certificate); lean manufacturing and Six Sigma (Certificate); mathematics (MA, MS, Certificate, Sixth Year Certificate); STEM education (MS); supply chain and logistics (Certificate); technology and engineering education (MS); technology management (MS). *Application deadline:* For fall admission, 6/1 for domestic students, 5/1 for international students; for spring admission, 11/1 for domestic and international students. Applications are processed on a rolling basis. *Application fee:* $50. Electronic applications accepted. *Application Contact:* Patricia Gardner, Associate Director of Graduate Studies, 860-832-2350, Fax: 860-832-2362, E-mail: graduateadmissions@ccsu.edu. *Dean,* Dr. Faris Malhas, 860-832-1800, E-mail: fmalhas@ccsu.edu.

CENTRAL EUROPEAN UNIVERSITY, H-1051 Budapest, Hungary

General Information Independent, coed, graduate-only institution. CGS member. *Enrollment by degree level:* 866 master's, 453 doctoral. *Graduate faculty:* 187 full-time (53 women), 107 part-time/adjunct (29 women). *Tuition, area resident:* Full-time 12,000 euros. Tuition and fees vary according to degree level, program and student level. *Graduate housing:* Room and/or apartments guaranteed to single students; on-campus housing not available to married students. Housing application deadline: 2/4. *Student services:* Campus employment opportunities, campus safety program, career counseling, exercise/wellness program, free psychological counseling, grant writing training, international student services, low-cost health insurance, multicultural affairs office, services for students with disabilities, teacher training, writing training. *Library:* CEU Library plus 1 other. *Collection:* Books: 188,883 (physical), 23,289 (digital/electronic); Serial titles: 334 (physical), 43,442 (digital/electronic); Databases: 103. Weekly public service hours: 80. *Research affiliation:* Institute of Human Sciences Vienna (social sciences), Open Society Institute (social sciences), Open Society Archives (social sciences).

Computer facilities: 286 computers available on campus for general student use. A campuswide network can be accessed from student residence rooms and from off campus. Online class registration is available.
Website: http://www.ceu.hu/

General Application Contact: Zsuzsanna Jaszberenyi, Admissions Officer, 361-327-3009, Fax: 361-327-3211, E-mail: admissions@ceu.edu.

GRADUATE UNITS

CEU Business School Students: 45 full-time (20 women), 110 part-time (30 women). Average age 33. 335 applicants, 30% accepted, 59 enrolled. *Faculty:* 17 full-time (4 women), 7 part-time/adjunct (1 woman). *Financial support:* Scholarships/grants, health care benefits, and tuition waivers (full and partial) available. In 2015, 67 master's awarded. *Degree program information:* Evening/weekend programs available. Evening/weekend. Offers business administration (PhD); business analytics (M Sc); executive business administration (EMBA); finance (M Sc); general management (MBA); information technology management (M Sc); international executive (MBA). *Application deadline:* For fall admission, 2/4 for domestic and international students. Applications are processed on a rolling basis. *Application fee:* $40. Electronic applications accepted. *Application Contact:* Miao Tan, Recruitment Coordinator, 361-887-5061, Fax: 361-887-5133, E-mail: tanm@ceubusiness.org. *Dean/Managing Director,* Dr. Mel Horwitch, 361-887-5050, E-mail: mhorwitch@ceubusiness.com.

Graduate Studies Students: 1,156 full-time (601 women), 8 part-time (6 women). Average age 28. 4,513 applicants, 21% accepted, 601 enrolled. *Faculty:* 170 full-time (49 women), 100 part-time/adjunct (28 women). *Financial support:* Fellowships, career-related internships or fieldwork, institutionally sponsored loans, scholarships/grants, health care benefits, and tuition waivers (full and partial) available. In 2015, 434 master's, 51 doctorates awarded. Offers applied mathematics (MS); business analytics (M Sc); cognitive science (PhD); comparative Constitutional law (LL M); comparative history: interdisciplinary Medieval studies (MA); cultural heritage studies (MA); economic policy in global markets (MA); economics (MA, PhD); environmental sciences and policy (MS, PhD); gender studies (MA, PhD); global economic relations (MA); history (MA, PhD); human rights (LL M, MA); international business law (LL M); international relations (MA, PhD); law and economics (LL M, MA); legal studies (SJD); mathematics and its applications (PhD); Medieval studies (MA, PhD); nationalism studies (MA); philosophy (MA, PhD); political science (MA, PhD); sociology and social anthropology (MA, PhD). *Application deadline:* For fall admission, 2/4 for domestic and international students. *Application fee:* $40. Electronic applications accepted. *Application Contact:* Zsuzsanna Jaszberenyi, Admissions Officer, 361-324-3009, Fax: 367-327-3211, E-mail: admissions@ceu.edu. *Provost/Academic Pro Rector,* Dr. Liviu Matei, 36 1 327-3000, Fax: 361-327-3211, E-mail: provost@ceu.edu.

School of Public Policy Students: 143 full-time (92 women). Average age 27. 847 applicants, 28% accepted, 82 enrolled. *Faculty:* 23 full-time (7 women), 11 part-time/adjunct (7 women). *Financial support:* In 2015–16, 97 students received support. Fellowships, career-related internships or fieldwork, scholarships/grants, health care benefits, and tuition waivers (full and partial) available. In 2015, 62 master's, 1 doctorate awarded. Offers public administration (MPA); public policy (MA, PhD). *Application deadline:* For fall admission, 2/4 for domestic and international students. *Application fee:* $40. Electronic applications accepted. *Application Contact:* Zsuzsanna Jaszberenyi, Admissions Officer, 361-324-3009, Fax: 367-327-3211, E-mail: admissions@ceu.edu. *Head,* Dr. Wolfang Reinicke, 361-327-3110, E-mail: spp@ceu.edu.

CENTRAL METHODIST UNIVERSITY, Fayette, MO 65248-1198

General Information Independent-religious, coed, comprehensive institution. *Graduate housing:* Rooms and/or apartments available on a first-come, first-served basis to single and married students.

GRADUATE UNITS

College of Graduate and Extended Studies ***Degree program information:*** Part-time and evening/weekend programs available. Part-time, evening/weekend, online learning. Offers clinical counseling (MS); clinical nurse leader (MSN); education (M Ed); music education (MME); nurse educator (MSN). Electronic applications accepted.

CENTRAL MICHIGAN UNIVERSITY, Mount Pleasant, MI 48859

General Information State-supported, coed, university. *Graduate housing:* Rooms and/or apartments available on a first-come, first-served basis to single and married students. *Research affiliation:* IBM (information technology), Dendritic Nanotechnologies, Inc. (chemistry, physics), Dow Corning Corporation (silicon-based technology), Dow Chemical Company (chemicals and plastics), SAS Business Analytics (business analysis), SAP (information technology).

GRADUATE UNITS

Central Michigan University Global Campus ***Degree program information:*** Part-time and evening/weekend programs available. Part-time, evening/weekend, online learning. Offers acquisitions administration (MSA, Certificate); college teaching (Graduate Certificate); community college (MA); curriculum and instruction (MA); cybersecurity (Certificate); educational technology (MA, DET); engineering management administration (MSA, Certificate); enterprise resource planning (MBA, Certificate); general administration (MSA, Certificate); general public administration (MPA); health administration (DHA); health services administration (MSA, Certificate); human resource management (MBA); human resources administration (MSA, Certificate); information resource management (MSA); information resource management administration (Certificate); international administration (MSA, Certificate); international health (Certificate); K-12 leadership (Ed D); leadership (MSA, Certificate); logistics management (MBA, Certificate); marketing (MBA); nutrition and dietetics (MS); philanthropy and fundraising administration (MSA, Certificate); professional counseling (MA); public administration (MSA, Certificate); public management (MPA); reading and literacy K-12 (MA); recreation and park administration (MSA); research administration (MSA, Certificate); school counseling (MA); school principalship (MA); state and local government (MPA); training and development (MA); value-driven organization (MBA). Electronic applications accepted.

College of Graduate Studies ***Degree program information:*** Part-time and evening/weekend programs available. Part-time, evening/weekend, online learning. Offers acquisitions administration (MSA, Graduate Certificate); general administration (MSA, Graduate Certificate); health services administration (MSA, Graduate Certificate); human resource administration (Graduate Certificate); human resources administration (MSA); information resource management (MSA, Graduate Certificate); international administration (MSA, Graduate Certificate); leadership (MSA, Graduate Certificate); public administration (MSA, Graduate Certificate); research administration (Graduate Certificate); sport administration (MSA). Electronic applications accepted.

College of Business Administration Degree program information: Part-time and evening/weekend programs available. Part-time, evening/weekend. Offers accounting (MBA); business administration (MA, MBA, MS, Graduate Certificate); business computing (Graduate Certificate); business economics (MBA); consulting (MBA); economics (MA); finance (MBA); general business (MBA); human resource management (MBA); information systems (MBA, MS); international business (MBA); logistics management (MBA); marketing (MBA); value-driven organization (MBA). Electronic applications accepted.

College of Communication and Fine Arts Degree program information: Part-time programs available. Part-time. Offers communication (MA); communication and fine arts (MA, MM); composition (MM); conducting (MM); electronic media management (MA); electronic media production (MA); electronic media studies (MA); film theory and criticism (MA); music education (MM); performance (MM). Electronic applications accepted.

College of Education and Human Services Degree program information: Part-time and evening/weekend programs available. Part-time, evening/weekend. Offers apparel product development and merchandising technology (MS); autism (Graduate Certificate); counseling (MA); education and human services (MA, MS, Ed D, Ed S, Graduate Certificate); educational leadership (Ed D); educational technology (MA, Graduate Certificate); elementary education (MA); general educational administration (Ed S); gerontology (Graduate Certificate); human development and family studies (MA); nutrition and dietetics (MS); reading and literacy K-12 (MA); school principalship (MA); secondary education (MA); special education (MA, Graduate Certificate); student affairs administration (MA); teacher leadership (MA). Electronic applications accepted.

College of Humanities and Social and Behavioral Sciences Degree program information: Part-time and evening/weekend programs available. Part-time, evening/weekend. Offers American politics (MA); applied experimental psychology (PhD); clinical psychology (PhD); English composition and communication (MA); English language and literature (MA); European history (Graduate Certificate); experimental psychology (MS, PhD); history (MA); humanities (MA); humanities and social and behavioral sciences (MA, MPA, MS, PhD, Graduate Certificate, S Psy S); industrial and organizational psychology (MA, PhD); modern history (Graduate Certificate); neuroscience (MS, PhD); occupational health psychology (PhD); political science (MA); professional development in public administration (Graduate Certificate); public administration (MPA, Graduate Certificate); public management (MPA); school psychology (PhD, S Psy S); Spanish (MA); state and local government (MPA); TESOL: teaching English to speakers of other languages (MA); United States history (Graduate Certificate). Electronic applications accepted.

College of Science and Technology Degree program information: Part-time and evening/weekend programs available. Part-time, evening/weekend. Offers biology (MS); chemistry (MS); computer science (MS); conservation biology (MS); geographic information sciences (MS); industrial management and technology (MA); mathematics (MA, PhD); physics (MS); science and technology (MA, MAT, MS, PhD, Graduate Certificate); science of advanced materials (PhD); teaching chemistry (MA). Electronic applications accepted.

The Herbert H. and Grace A. Dow College of Health Professions Degree program information: Part-time programs available. Part-time. Offers audiology (Au D); exercise science (MA); health administration (DHA); health professions (MA, MS, Au D, DHA, DPT, Graduate Certificate); physical therapy (DPT); physician assistant (MS); speech-language pathology (MA); sport administration (MA). Electronic applications accepted.

CENTRAL PENN COLLEGE, Summerdale, PA 17093-0309

General Information Proprietary, coed, comprehensive institution.

GRADUATE UNITS

Graduate Programs ***Degree program information:*** Evening/weekend programs available. Evening/weekend. Offers information systems management (MPS); organizational development (MPS). Programs offered in Harrisburg, PA.

CENTRAL WASHINGTON UNIVERSITY, Ellensburg, WA 98926

General Information State-supported, coed, comprehensive institution. CGS member. *Graduate housing:* Rooms and/or apartments available on a first-come, first-served basis to single and married students. *Research affiliation:* East-West Center (Pacific area studies), Associated Western Universities (science and engineering), Jet Propulsion Laboratory (engineering).

GRADUATE UNITS

Graduate Studies and Research ***Degree program information:*** Part-time and evening/weekend programs available. Part-time, evening/weekend. Offers individual studies (M Ed, MA, MS). Electronic applications accepted.

College of Arts and Humanities Degree program information: Part-time programs available. Part-time. Offers art (MA, MFA); arts and humanities (MA, MFA, MM); English (MA); history (MA); music (MM); teaching English as a second language (MA); theatre production (MA); theatre studies (MA). Electronic applications accepted.

College of Business Degree program information: Part-time programs available. Part-time. Offers accounting (MPA); business (MPA). Electronic applications accepted.

College of Education and Professional Studies Degree program information: Part-time programs available. Part-time. Offers athletic administration (MS); career and technical education (MS); education and professional studies (M Ed, MS); engineering technology (MS); exercise science (MS); family and consumer sciences education (MS); family studies (MS); health and physical education (MS); higher education (M Ed); master teacher (M Ed); nutrition (MS); reading education (M Ed); school administration (M Ed); school instructional leadership (M Ed); special education (M Ed). Electronic applications accepted.

College of the Sciences Degree program information: Part-time and evening/weekend programs available. Part-time, evening/weekend. Offers biological sciences (MS); chemistry (MS); experimental psychology (MS); geological sciences (MS); mathematics (MAT); mental health counseling (MS); resource management (MS); school counseling (M Ed); school psychology (M Ed); sciences (M Ed, MAT, MS). Electronic applications accepted.

CENTRAL YESHIVA TOMCHEI TMIMIM-LUBAVITCH, Brooklyn, NY 11230

General Information Independent-religious, men only, comprehensive institution.

GRADUATE UNITS

Graduate Programs Offers Jewish/Judaic studies (MA); Talmudic studies (MA).

CENTRO DE ESTUDIOS AVANZADOS DE PUERTO RICO Y EL CARIBE, Old San Juan, PR 00902-3970

General Information Independent, coed, graduate-only institution. *Graduate housing:* On-campus housing not available. *Research affiliation:* Museo de las Americas, Museo Hombre Dominicano, Archivo General, Museo Universidad del Turabo.

GRADUATE UNITS

Graduate Program in Puerto Rican and Caribbean Studies ***Degree program information:*** Part-time and evening/weekend programs available. Part-time, evening/weekend. Offers Puerto Rican and Caribbean history (MA, PhD); Puerto Rican and Caribbean literature (MA, PhD); Puerto Rican studies (MA).

CHADRON STATE COLLEGE, Chadron, NE 69337

General Information State-supported, coed, comprehensive institution. *Graduate housing:* Rooms and/or apartments available on a first-come, first-served basis to single and married students. Housing application deadline: 6/1.

GRADUATE UNITS

School of Professional and Graduate Studies ***Degree program information:*** Part-time and evening/weekend programs available. Part-time, evening/weekend, online learning. Offers business (MA Ed); business and economics (MBA); community counseling (MA Ed); educational administration (MS Ed, Sp Ed); elementary education (MS Ed); history (MA Ed); language and literature (MA Ed); secondary administration (MS Ed); secondary education (MS Ed). Electronic applications accepted.

CHAMINADE UNIVERSITY OF HONOLULU, Honolulu, HI 96816-1578

General Information Independent-religious, coed, comprehensive institution. *Enrollment:* 1,865 graduate, professional, and undergraduate students; 423 full-time matriculated graduate/professional students (307 women), 227 part-time matriculated graduate/professional students (155 women). *Enrollment by degree level:* 650 master's. *Graduate faculty:* 29 full-time (13 women), 41 part-time/adjunct (18 women). *Tuition, area resident:* Full-time $17,640; part-time $735 per credit. Tuition and fees vary according to campus/location. *Graduate housing:* On-campus housing not available. *Student services:* Campus safety program, career counseling, free psychological counseling, international student services, services for students with disabilities, teacher training, writing training. *Library:* Sullivan Library. *Collection:* Books: 48,643 (physical), 71,803 (digital/electronic); Databases: 83.

Computer facilities: 200 computers available on campus for general student use. A campuswide network can be accessed from student residence rooms and from off campus. Online class registration is available.
Website: http://www.chaminade.edu/

General Application Contact: 808-735-4755, E-mail: gradserv@chaminade.edu.

GRADUATE UNITS

Office of Professional and Continuing Education Students: 423 full-time (307 women), 227 part-time (155 women); includes 371 minority (25 Black or African American, non-Hispanic/Latino; 4 American Indian or Alaska Native, non-Hispanic/Latino; 159 Asian, non-Hispanic/Latino; 29 Hispanic/Latino; 139 Native Hawaiian or other Pacific Islander, non-Hispanic/Latino; 15 Two or more races, non-Hispanic/Latino), 5 international. Average age 33. 164 applicants, 91% accepted, 108 enrolled. *Faculty:* 29 full-time (13 women), 41 part-time/adjunct (18 women). *Financial support:* Applicants required to submit FAFSA. In 2015, 215 master's awarded. *Degree program information:* Part-time and evening/weekend programs available. Part-time, evening/weekend, 100% online, blended/hybrid learning. Offers accounting (MBA); business (MBA); child development (M Ed); criminal justice administration (MSCJA); educational leadership (M Ed); elementary education (MAT); forensic science (MSFS, Certificate); homeland security leadership development (Certificate); instructional leadership (M Ed); law enforcement (MSCJA); marriage and family counseling (MSCP); mental health counseling (MSCP); Montessori education (M Ed); not-for-profit (MBA); pastoral theology (MPT); school counseling (MSCP); secondary education (MAT); special education (MAT). *Application deadline:* Applications are processed on a rolling basis. *Application fee:* $25. Electronic applications accepted. *Application Contact:* 808-739-4664, Fax: 808-739-4766, E-mail: gradserv@chaminade.edu. *Director,* Cindy Janus, 808-739-4664, Fax: 808-735-4766, E-mail: gradserv@chaminade.edu.

CHAMPLAIN COLLEGE, Burlington, VT 05402-0670

General Information Independent, coed, comprehensive institution. CGS member. *Graduate housing:* Rooms and/or apartments available on a first-come, first-served basis to single and married students.

GRADUATE UNITS

Graduate Studies ***Degree program information:*** Part-time programs available. Part-time, online learning. Offers business (MBA); digital forensic science (MS); early childhood education (M Ed); emergent media (MFA, MS); executive leadership (MS); health care administration (MS); information security operations (MS); law (MS); mediation and applied conflict studies (MS). MS in emergent media program held in Shanghai. Electronic applications accepted.

CHAPMAN UNIVERSITY, Orange, CA 92866

General Information Independent-religious, coed, comprehensive institution. *Enrollment:* 8,305 graduate, professional, and undergraduate students; 1,422 full-time matriculated graduate/professional students (804 women), 517 part-time matriculated graduate/professional students (329 women). *Enrollment by degree level:* 1,062 master's, 856 doctoral, 21 other advanced degrees. *Graduate faculty:* 276 full-time (103 women), 265 part-time/adjunct (120 women). Tuition and fees vary according to program. *Graduate housing:* Rooms and/or apartments available on a first-come, first-served basis to single and married students. Housing application deadline: 6/1. *Student services:* Campus employment opportunities, campus safety program, career counseling, exercise/wellness program, free psychological counseling, grant writing training, international student services, low-cost health insurance, services for students with disabilities, teacher training, writing training. *Library:* Leatherby Libraries plus 1 other. *Collection:* Books: 329,477 (physical), 16,255 (digital/electronic); Serial titles: 373 (physical), 75,377 (digital/electronic); Databases: 267. Weekly public service hours: 127; students can reserve study rooms. *Research affiliation:* National Science Foundation (science, engineering), National Endowment for the Arts (NEA) (art), U.S. Department of Education (DOE) (education), U.S. Geological Survey (USGS) (earth sciences), U.S. Department of Agriculture (USDA) (agriculture, food, nutrition).

Computer facilities: Computer purchase and lease plans are available. A campuswide network can be accessed from student residence rooms and from off campus. Online class registration is available.
Website: http://www.chapman.edu/

General Application Contact: Eva Yen, Director of Graduate Admissions, 888-CU-APPLY, Fax: 714-997-6713, E-mail: eyen@chapman.edu.

GRADUATE UNITS

College of Educational Studies Students: 186 full-time (148 women), 186 part-time (134 women); includes 144 minority (9 Black or African American, non-Hispanic/Latino; 39 Asian, non-Hispanic/Latino; 78 Hispanic/Latino; 2 Native Hawaiian or other Pacific Islander, non-Hispanic/Latino; 16 Two or more races, non-Hispanic/Latino), 8 international. Average age 29. 233 applicants, 58% accepted, 86 enrolled. *Faculty:* 29 full-time (14 women), 36 part-time/adjunct (28 women). *Financial support:* Fellowships and scholarships/grants available. Financial award application deadline: 3/2; financial award applicants required to submit FAFSA. In 2015, 141 master's, 12 doctorates awarded. *Degree program information:* Part-time and evening/weekend programs available. Part-time, evening/weekend. Offers counseling (MA); education (PhD); educational psychology (MA); leadership development (MA); multiple subjects (Credential); pupil personnel services (Credential); school psychology (Ed S); single subject (Credential); special education (MA, Credential); teaching (MA). *Application deadline:* Applications are processed on a rolling basis. *Application fee:* $60. Electronic applications accepted. *Application Contact:* Sara Simon, Graduate Admission Counselor, 714-997-6770, E-mail: simon@chapman.edu. *Dean,* Dr. Margaret Grogan, 714-516-5968, E-mail: grogan@chapman.edu.

Crean College of Health and Behavioral Sciences Offers athletic training (MS); communication sciences and disorders (MS); health and behavioral sciences (MA, MS, DPT, TDPT); marriage and family therapy (MA); physical therapy (DPT, TDPT); physician assistant studies (MMS). *Application Contact:* Monica Chen, Graduate Admission Counselor, 714-289-3590, Fax: 714-997-6713, E-mail: mchen@chapman.edu. *Dean,* Dr. Janeen Hill, 714-628-7223, E-mail: jhill@chapman.edu.

Dodge College of Film and Media Arts Students: 226 full-time (99 women), 2 part-time (0 women); includes 45 minority (13 Black or African American, non-Hispanic/Latino; 11 Asian, non-Hispanic/Latino; 19 Hispanic/Latino; 2 Two or more races, non-Hispanic/Latino), 84 international. Average age 26. 453 applicants, 47% accepted, 97 enrolled. *Faculty:* 43 full-time (10 women), 77 part-time/adjunct (29 women). *Financial support:* Fellowships, Federal Work-Study, and scholarships/grants available. Financial award applicants required to submit FAFSA. In 2015, 84 master's awarded. Offers documentary filmmaking (MFA); film and television producing (MFA); film production (MFA); film studies (MA); production design (MFA); screenwriting (MFA). *Application deadline:* For fall admission, 12/1 for domestic students. *Application fee:* $60. Electronic applications accepted. *Application Contact:* Lauren Kacura, Assistant Director of Admissions, 714-744-7856, E-mail: kacura@chapman.edu. *Dean,* Robert Bassett, 714-997-6715, E-mail: bassett@chapman.edu.

Fowler School of Law Students: 453 full-time (223 women), 45 part-time (25 women); includes 172 minority (3 Black or African American, non-Hispanic/Latino; 1 American Indian or Alaska Native, non-Hispanic/Latino; 78 Asian, non-Hispanic/Latino; 61 Hispanic/Latino; 29 Two or more races, non-Hispanic/Latino), 23 international. Average age 26. 1,543 applicants, 47% accepted, 149 enrolled. *Faculty:* 44 full-time (19 women), 36 part-time/adjunct (7 women). *Financial support:* Fellowships, Federal Work-Study, and scholarships/grants available. Financial award applicants required to submit FAFSA. In 2015, 55 master's, 132 doctorates awarded. *Degree program information:* Part-time programs available. Part-time. Offers advocacy and dispute resolution (JD); business law (LL M, JD); criminal law (JD); entertainment and media law (LL M); entertainment law (JD); environmental, land use, and real estate law (JD); international and comparative law (LL M); international law (JD); law (JD); prosecutorial science (LL M); tax law (JD); taxation (LL M); trial advocacy (LL M). *Application deadline:* For fall admission, 4/15 priority date for domestic students. Applications are processed on a rolling basis. Electronic applications accepted. *Application Contact:* Karman Hsu, Assistant Dean of Admissions and Diversity Initiatives, 714-628-2500, E-mail: lawadmission@chapman.edu. *Interim Dean*, Dr. Scott Howe, 714-628-2526, E-mail: swhowe@chapman.edu.

The George L. Argyros School of Business and Economics Students: 143 full-time (69 women), 94 part-time (47 women); includes 65 minority (6 Black or African American, non-Hispanic/Latino; 23 Asian, non-Hispanic/Latino; 28 Hispanic/Latino; 2 Native Hawaiian or other Pacific Islander, non-Hispanic/Latino; 6 Two or more races, non-Hispanic/Latino), 66 international. Average age 29. 259 applicants, 69% accepted, 93 enrolled. *Faculty:* 53 full-time (11 women), 38 part-time/adjunct (7 women). *Financial support:* Fellowships, Federal Work-Study, and scholarships/grants available. Financial award applicants required to submit FAFSA. In 2015, 103 master's awarded. *Degree program information:* Part-time and evening/weekend programs available. Part-time, evening/weekend. Offers accounting (MS); business administration (Exec MBA, MBA); economic systems design (MS). *Application fee:* $60. Electronic applications accepted. *Application Contact:* Debra Gonda, Associate Dean, 714-997-6894, E-mail: gonda@chapman.edu. *Dean*, Reginald Gilyard, 714-997-6684.

Schmid College of Science and Technology ***Degree program information:*** Part-time programs available. Part-time. Offers computational and data sciences (MS, PhD); food science (MS); science and technology (MS, PhD). *Dean*, Dr. Andrew Lyon, 714-997-6730, E-mail: lyon@chapman.edu.

School of Pharmacy Students: 94 full-time (57 women), 1 (woman) part-time; includes 53 minority (5 Black or African American, non-Hispanic/Latino; 39 Asian, non-Hispanic/Latino; 7 Hispanic/Latino; 2 Two or more races, non-Hispanic/Latino), 8 international. Average age 28. *Faculty:* 20 full-time (8 women), 1 part-time/adjunct (0 women). *Financial support:* Fellowships, research assistantships, Federal Work-Study, and scholarships/grants available. Offers pharmaceutical sciences (MS); pharmacy (Pharm D). *Application deadline:* For fall admission, 3/1 for domestic students. Applications are processed on a rolling basis. Electronic applications accepted. *Application Contact:* Dr. Lawrence Brown, Associate Dean of Student and Academic Affairs, 714-516-5600, E-mail: pharmacyadmissions@chapman.edu. *Dean*, Ronald P. Jordan, 714-516-5486, E-mail: rpjordan@chapman.edu.

Wilkinson College of Arts, Humanities, and Social Sciences ***Degree program information:*** Part-time and evening/weekend programs available. Part-time, evening/weekend. Offers arts, humanities, and social sciences (MA, MFA, MS); creative writing (MFA); English (MA); health and strategic communication (MS); international studies (MA); war and society (MA). *Dean*, Dr. Patrick Fuery, 714-516-4580, E-mail: fuery@chapman.edu.

CHARLES R. DREW UNIVERSITY OF MEDICINE AND SCIENCE, Los Angeles, CA 90059

General Information Independent, coed, comprehensive institution. *Graduate housing:* On-campus housing not available.

GRADUATE UNITS

College of Science and Health

Professional Program in Medicine Offers medicine (MD).

CHARLESTON SOUTHERN UNIVERSITY, Charleston, SC 29423-8087

General Information Independent-religious, coed, comprehensive institution. *Graduate housing:* On-campus housing not available. *Research affiliation:* Santee Lynches Council of Governments (economic forecasting), Waccamaw Regional Planning and Development Council (economic forecasting), Metro Charleston Chamber of Commerce (economic forecasting).

GRADUATE UNITS

Department of Criminal Justice ***Degree program information:*** Part-time and evening/weekend programs available. Part-time, evening/weekend. Offers criminal justice (MSCJ).

School of Business ***Degree program information:*** Part-time and evening/weekend programs available. Part-time, evening/weekend. Offers accounting (MBA); finance (MBA); general management (MBA); leadership (MBA); management information systems (MBA).

School of Education ***Degree program information:*** Part-time and evening/weekend programs available. Part-time, evening/weekend. Offers elementary administration and supervision (M Ed); elementary education (M Ed).

CHARLOTTE CHRISTIAN COLLEGE AND THEOLOGICAL SEMINARY, Charlotte, NC 28205

General Information Independent-religious, coed, comprehensive institution.

GRADUATE UNITS

Graduate Program ***Degree program information:*** Part-time and evening/weekend programs available. Part-time, evening/weekend. Offers urban Christian ministry (MA). Electronic applications accepted.

CHARLOTTE SCHOOL OF LAW, Charlotte, NC 28204

General Information Independent, coed, graduate-only institution.

GRADUATE UNITS

Professional Program Offers law (JD).

CHATHAM UNIVERSITY, Pittsburgh, PA 15232-2826

General Information Independent, coed, primarily women, university. CGS member. *Enrollment:* 2,224 graduate, professional, and undergraduate students; 848 full-time matriculated graduate/professional students (678 women), 328 part-time matriculated graduate/professional students (284 women). *Enrollment by degree level:* 810 master's, 366 doctoral. *Graduate faculty:* 66 full-time (49 women), 97 part-time/adjunct (80 women). *Tuition, area resident:* Full-time $15,786; part-time $877 per credit hour. *Required fees:* $468; $26 per credit hour. *Graduate housing:* Rooms and/or apartments available on a first-come, first-served basis to single and married students. Typical cost: $5470 per year ($10,720 including board) for single students; $6440 per year ($11,690 including board) for married students. Housing application deadline: 3/26. *Student services:* Campus employment opportunities, campus safety program, career counseling, exercise/wellness program, free psychological counseling, international student services, low-cost health insurance, services for students with disabilities, teacher training, writing training. *Library:* Jennie King Mellon Library. *Collection:* Books: 143,723 (physical), 136,404 (digital/electronic); Serial titles: 106 (physical), 326,403 (digital/electronic); Databases: 63. Weekly public service hours: 99; study areas open 24 hours, 5–7 days a week; students can reserve study rooms.

Computer facilities: Computer purchase and lease plans are available. 180 computers available on campus for general student use. A campuswide network can be accessed from student residence rooms and from off campus. Online class registration is available.
Website: http://www.chatham.edu/

General Application Contact: Katie Noel, Assistant Director of Graduate Admission, 412-365-1695, Fax: 412-365-1609, E-mail: knoel@chatham.edu.

GRADUATE UNITS

Nursing Programs Students: 64 full-time (58 women), 80 part-time (73 women); includes 50 minority (31 Black or African American, non-Hispanic/Latino; 9 Asian, non-Hispanic/Latino; 5 Hispanic/Latino; 1 Native Hawaiian or other Pacific Islander, non-Hispanic/Latino; 4 Two or more races, non-Hispanic/Latino), 10 international. Average age 44. 181 applicants, 50% accepted, 61 enrolled. *Faculty:* 11 full-time (10 women), 23 part-time/adjunct (18 women). *Financial support:* Applicants required to submit FAFSA. In 2015, 9 master's, 76 doctorates awarded. Online learning. Offers education/leadership (MSN); nursing (DNP). *Application deadline:* For fall admission, 5/1 priority date for domestic and international students. Applications are processed on a rolling basis. *Application fee:* $0. Electronic applications accepted. *Application Contact:* Patricia Golla, Assistant Director of Graduate Admissions, 412-365-1386, Fax: 412-365-1720, E-mail: pgolla@chatham.edu. *Director*, Dr. Diane Hunker, 412-365-1738, E-mail: dhunker@chatham.edu.

Program in Accounting Students: 3 full-time (all women), 20 part-time (15 women); includes 5 minority (2 Black or African American, non-Hispanic/Latino; 2 Asian, non-Hispanic/Latino; 1 Hispanic/Latino), 1 international. Average age 32. 23 applicants, 70% accepted, 11 enrolled. *Faculty:* 1 full-time (0 women), 1 part-time/adjunct (0 women). *Financial support:* Applicants required to submit FAFSA. In 2015, 18 master's awarded. *Degree program information:* Part-time and evening/weekend programs available. Part-time, evening/weekend. Offers accounting (M Acc, MAC). *Application deadline:* For fall admission, 4/1 for domestic and international students; for spring admission, 11/1 for domestic students, 10/1 for international students. Applications are processed on a rolling basis. *Application fee:* $45. Electronic applications accepted. *Application Contact:* 412-365-1141, Fax: 412-365-1609, E-mail: gradadmissions@chatham.edu. *Director of Business and Entrepreneurship Program*, Dr. Rachel Chung, 412-365-2433, E-mail: rchung@chatham.edu.

Program in Biology Students: 52 full-time (33 women), 11 part-time (7 women); includes 20 minority (11 Black or African American, non-Hispanic/Latino; 4 Asian, non-Hispanic/Latino; 5 Hispanic/Latino), 7 international. Average age 25. 149 applicants, 66% accepted, 42 enrolled. *Faculty:* 1 (woman) full-time, 1 (woman) part-time/adjunct. *Financial support:* Applicants required to submit FAFSA. In 2015, 35 master's awarded. *Degree program information:* Part-time programs available. Part-time. Offers environmental biology (MS); human biology (MS). *Application deadline:* For fall admission, 4/1 priority date for domestic and international students; for spring admission, 11/1 priority date for domestic students, 10/1 priority date for international students. Applications are processed on a rolling basis. *Application fee:* $45. Electronic applications accepted. *Application Contact:* Ashlee Bartko, Senior Assistant Director of Graduate Admission, 412-365-1115, Fax: 412-365-1609, E-mail: gradadmissions@chatham.edu. *Director*, Dr. Lisa Lambert, 412-365-1217, E-mail: lambert@chatham.edu.

Program in Business Administration Students: 18 full-time (15 women), 30 part-time (27 women); includes 6 minority (4 Black or African American, non-Hispanic/Latino; 1 Asian, non-Hispanic/Latino; 1 Two or more races, non-Hispanic/Latino), 14 international. Average age 30. 56 applicants, 54% accepted, 22 enrolled. *Faculty:* 1 full-time (0 women), 2 part-time/adjunct (both women). *Financial support:* Applicants required to submit FAFSA. In 2015, 12 master's awarded. *Degree program information:* Part-time and evening/weekend programs available. Part-time, evening/weekend. Offers business administration (MBA); healthcare management (MBA); sustainability (MBA); women's leadership (MBA). *Application deadline:* For fall admission, 4/1 for domestic and international students; for spring admission, 11/1 for domestic students, 10/1 for international students. Applications are processed on a rolling basis. *Application fee:* $45. Electronic applications accepted. *Application Contact:* Katie Noel, Assistant Director of Graduate Admission, 412-365-2758, Fax: 412-365-1609, E-mail: gradadmissions@chatham.edu. *Director of Business and Entrepreneurship Program*, Dr. Rachel Chung, 412-365-2433.

Program in Communication Online learning. Offers environmental communication (M Comm); health communication (M Comm); strategic communication (M Comm).

Program in Counseling Psychology Students: 90 full-time (75 women), 29 part-time (28 women); includes 16 minority (9 Black or African American, non-Hispanic/Latino; 2 Asian, non-Hispanic/Latino; 3 Hispanic/Latino; 2 Two or more races, non-Hispanic/Latino), 7 international. Average age 30. 73 applicants, 70% accepted, 30 enrolled. *Faculty:* 12 full-time (8 women), 3 part-time/adjunct (2 women). *Financial support:* Career-related internships or fieldwork available. Financial award applicants required to submit FAFSA. In 2015, 58 master's awarded. *Degree program information:* Part-time and evening/weekend programs available. Part-time, evening/weekend. Offers child, adolescent and family (MSCP); counseling psychology (Psy D); health and holistic (MSCP); infant mental health (MSCP); organization and supervision (MSCP); sport and exercise (MSCP). *Application deadline:* For fall admission, 4/1 priority date for domestic and international students; for spring admission, 11/1 for domestic students, 10/1 for international students. Applications are processed on a rolling basis. *Application fee:* $45. Electronic applications accepted. *Application Contact:* Katie Noel, Assistant Director of Graduate Admission, 412-365-2758, Fax: 412-365-1609, E-mail: gradadmissions@chatham.edu. *Director*, Dr. Mary Beth Mannarino, 412-365-1196, Fax: 412-365-1505, E-mail: mmannarino@chatham.edu.

Program in Education Students: 31 full-time (24 women), 10 part-time (9 women); includes 12 minority (7 Black or African American, non-Hispanic/Latino; 2 Hispanic/Latino; 3 Two or more races, non-Hispanic/Latino), 2 international. Average age 30. 54 applicants, 46% accepted, 14 enrolled. *Faculty:* 1 (woman) full-time, 1 part-time/adjunct (0 women). *Financial support:* Career-related internships or fieldwork available. Financial award applicants required to submit FAFSA. In 2015, 9 master's awarded. Offers early childhood education (MAT); elementary education (MAT); environmental education (K-12) (MAT); secondary art (MAT); secondary biology education (MAT); secondary chemistry education (MAT); secondary English education (MAT); secondary math education (MAT); secondary physics education (MAT); secondary social studies education (MAT); special education (MAT). *Application deadline:* For fall admission, 4/1 priority date for domestic and international students; for spring admission, 11/1 priority date for domestic students, 10/1 priority date for international students. Applications are processed on a rolling basis. *Application fee:* $45. Electronic applications accepted. *Application Contact:* Katie Noel, Assistant Director of Graduate Admission, 412-365-2758, Fax: 412-365-1609, E-mail: gradadmissions@chatham.edu. *Director of Education Programs*, Dr. Edward Donovan, 412-365-2773, E-mail: edonovan@chatham.edu.

Program in Film and Digital Technology Students: 10 full-time (3 women), 1 part-time (0 women); includes 4 minority (all Black or African American, non-Hispanic/Latino), 3 international. Average age 26. 15 applicants, 87% accepted, 7 enrolled. *Faculty:* 1 (woman) part-time/adjunct. *Financial support:* Applicants required to submit FAFSA. In 2015, 6 master's awarded. *Degree program information:* Part-time and evening/weekend programs available. Part-time, evening/weekend. Offers film and digital technology (MFA). *Application deadline:* For fall admission, 4/1 priority date for domestic and international students; for spring admission, 11/1 priority date for domestic students, 10/1 priority date for international students. Applications are processed on a rolling basis. *Application fee:* $45. Electronic applications accepted. *Application Contact:* Katie Noel, Assistant Director of Graduate Admission, 412-365-2758, Fax: 412-365-1609, E-mail: gradadmissions@chatham.edu. *Director*, Dr. Prajna Parasher, 412-365-1182, E-mail: parasher@chatham.edu.

Program in Healthcare Informatics Online learning. Offers healthcare informatics (MHI).

Program in Interior Architecture Students: 21 full-time (20 women), 8 part-time (all women); includes 4 minority (2 Black or African American, non-Hispanic/Latino; 1 Asian, non-Hispanic/Latino; 1 Two or more races, non-Hispanic/Latino), 6 international. Average age 30. 35 applicants, 66% accepted, 11 enrolled. *Faculty:* 2 full-time (0 women), 6 part-time/adjunct (5 women). *Financial support:* Applicants required to submit FAFSA. In 2015, 7 master's awarded. *Degree program information:* Part-time and evening/weekend programs available. Part-time, evening/weekend, online learning. Offers interior architecture (MIA). *Application deadline:* For fall admission, 4/1 priority date for domestic and international students; for spring admission, 11/1 priority date for domestic students, 10/1 priority date for international students. Applications are processed on a rolling basis. *Application fee:* $45. Electronic applications accepted. *Director*, Dr. Thelma Lazo-Flores, 412-365-2977, E-mail: tlazoflores@chatham.edu.

Program in Landscape Architecture Students: 2 full-time (0 women), both international. Average age 27. *Faculty:* 1 (woman) full-time, 2 part-time/adjunct (0 women). *Financial support:* Career-related internships or fieldwork available. Financial award applicants required to submit FAFSA. In 2015, 7 master's awarded. *Degree program information:* Part-time and evening/weekend programs available. Part-time, evening/weekend. Offers landscape architecture (ML Arch); landscape design and development (MA). *Application deadline:* For fall admission, 4/1 priority date for domestic and international students; for spring admission, 11/1 priority date for domestic students, 10/1 priority date for international students. Applications are processed on a rolling basis. *Application fee:* $45. Electronic applications accepted. *Application Contact:* Katie Noel, Assistant Director of Graduate Admission, 412-365-2758, Fax: 412-365-1609, E-mail: gradadmissions@chatham.edu. *Director*, Dr. Thelma Lazo-Flores, 412-365-2977, E-mail: tlazoflores@chatham.edu.

Program in Occupational Therapy Students: 114 full-time (105 women), 29 part-time (24 women); includes 22 minority (8 Black or African American, non-Hispanic/Latino; 6 Asian, non-Hispanic/Latino; 7 Hispanic/Latino; 1 Two or more races, non-Hispanic/Latino). Average age 31. 509 applicants, 20% accepted, 66 enrolled. *Faculty:* 7 full-time (all women), 10 part-time/adjunct (all women). *Financial support:* Applicants required to submit FAFSA. In 2015, 38 master's, 40 doctorates awarded. Offers occupational therapy (MOT, OTD). *Application deadline:* For fall admission, 12/5 priority date for domestic and international students. Applications are processed on a rolling basis. *Application fee:* $45. Electronic applications accepted. *Application Contact:* Ashlee Bartko, Senior Assistant Director of Graduate Admission, 412-365-1115, Fax: 412-365-1609, E-mail: gradadmissions@chatham.edu. *Director*, Dr. Joyce Salls, 412-365-1177, E-mail: salls@chatham.edu.

Program in Physical Therapy Students: 117 full-time (87 women), 1 (woman) part-time; includes 11 minority (2 Black or African American, non-Hispanic/Latino; 5 Asian, non-Hispanic/Latino; 4 Hispanic/Latino). Average age 25. 409 applicants, 18% accepted, 39 enrolled. *Faculty:* 8 full-time (5 women), 1 (woman) part-time/adjunct. *Financial support:* Career-related internships or fieldwork available. Financial award applicants required to submit FAFSA. In 2015, 37 doctorates awarded. Offers physical therapy (DPT, TDPT). *Application deadline:* For fall admission, 12/1 priority date for domestic and international students. *Application fee:* $45. Electronic applications accepted. *Application Contact:* Ashlee Bartko, Senior Assistant Director of Graduate Admission, 412-365-2988, Fax: 412-365-1609, E-mail: gradadmissions@chatham.edu. *Director*, Dr. Patricia Downey, 412-365-1199, Fax: 412-365-1505, E-mail: downey@chatham.edu.

Program in Physician Assistant Studies Students: 147 full-time (118 women), 1 part-time (0 women); includes 16 minority (4 Black or African American, non-Hispanic/Latino; 1 American Indian or Alaska Native, non-Hispanic/Latino; 5 Asian, non-Hispanic/Latino; 5 Hispanic/Latino; 1 Two or more races, non-Hispanic/Latino). Average age 26. 592 applicants, 25% accepted, 77 enrolled. *Faculty:* 10 full-time (8 women), 12 part-time/adjunct (all women). *Financial support:* Career-related internships or fieldwork available. Financial award applicants required to submit FAFSA. In 2015, 72 master's awarded. Offers physician assistant studies (MPAS). *Application deadline:* For fall admission, 10/1 priority date for domestic and international students. *Application fee:* $0. Electronic applications accepted. *Application Contact:* Maureen Stokan, Assistant Director of Graduate Admission, 412-365-2988, Fax: 412-365-1609, E-mail: gradadmissions@chatham.edu. *Director*, Carl Garrubba, 412-365-1425, Fax: 412-365-1213, E-mail: cgarrubba@chatham.edu.

Program in Writing Students: 53 full-time (41 women), 64 part-time (58 women); includes 16 minority (10 Black or African American, non-Hispanic/Latino; 1 Asian, non-Hispanic/Latino; 4 Hispanic/Latino; 1 Two or more races, non-Hispanic/Latino), 2 international. Average age 32. 127 applicants, 81% accepted, 44 enrolled. *Faculty:* 3 full-time (2 women), 21 part-time/adjunct (17 women). *Financial support:* Career-related internships or fieldwork available. Financial award applicants required to submit FAFSA. In 2015, 54 master's awarded. *Degree program information:* Part-time and evening/weekend programs available. Part-time, evening/weekend, online learning. Offers children's writing (MFA); fiction (MFA); non-fiction (MFA); poetry (MFA); professional writing (MPW); screenwriting (MFA). *Application deadline:* For fall admission, 1/15 priority date for domestic and international students; for spring admission, 11/1 priority date for domestic students, 10/1 priority date for international students. Applications are processed on a rolling basis. *Application fee:* $45. Electronic applications accepted. *Application Contact:* Katie Noel, Assistant Director of Graduate Admission, 412-365-2758, Fax: 412-365-1609, E-mail: gradadmissions@chatham.edu. *Director*, Dr. Sheryl St. Germain, 412-365-1190, Fax: 412-365-1505, E-mail: sstgermain@chatham.edu.

CHESTNUT HILL COLLEGE, Philadelphia, PA 19118-2693

General Information Independent-religious, coed, comprehensive institution. *Enrollment:* 1,951 graduate, professional, and undergraduate students; 221 full-time matriculated graduate/professional students (177 women), 287 part-time matriculated graduate/professional students (235 women). *Enrollment by degree level:* 336 master's, 110 doctoral, 62 other advanced degrees. *Graduate faculty:* 18 full-time (9 women), 66 part-time/adjunct (48 women). *Tuition, area resident:* Full-time $12,420; part-time $690 per credit hour. One-time fee: $450. Tuition and fees vary according to degree level and program. *Graduate housing:* On-campus housing not available. *Student services:* Campus employment opportunities, campus safety program, career counseling, free psychological counseling, international student services, low-cost health insurance, services for students with disabilities, teacher training, writing training. *Library:* Logue Library. *Collection:* Books: 130,880 (physical), 173,931 (digital/electronic); Serial titles: 380 (physical), 87 (digital/electronic); Databases: 40. Weekly public service hours: 99; students can reserve study rooms.

Computer facilities: 70 computers available on campus for general student use. A campuswide network can be accessed from student residence rooms. Online class registration is available.
Website: http://www.chc.edu/

General Application Contact: Amy Boorse, Assistant Director of Graduate Admissions, 215-248-7097, Fax: 215-248-7161, E-mail: gradadmissions@chc.edu.

GRADUATE UNITS

School of Graduate Studies Students: 221 full-time (177 women), 287 part-time (235 women); includes 143 minority (100 Black or African American, non-Hispanic/Latino; 9 Asian, non-Hispanic/Latino; 29 Hispanic/Latino; 5 Two or more races, non-Hispanic/Latino), 16 international. Average age 32. 201 applicants, 80% accepted, 79 enrolled. *Faculty:* 26 full-time (15 women), 66 part-time/adjunct (48 women). *Financial support:* Unspecified assistantships available. In 2015, 203 master's, 20 doctorates, 9 other advanced degrees awarded. *Degree program information:* Part-time and evening/weekend programs available. Part-time, evening/weekend. Offers administration of human services (MS, CAS); early education (M Ed); educational leadership (M Ed); elementary/middle education (M Ed); instructional technology (MS, CAS); reading (M Ed); reading specialist (M Ed); secondary education (M Ed); special education (M Ed). *Application deadline:* For fall admission, 7/1 for domestic and international students; for spring admission, 11/1 for domestic and international students; for summer admission, 4/1 for domestic and international students. Applications are processed on a rolling basis. *Application fee:* $55. Electronic applications accepted. *Application Contact:* Amy Boorse, Assistant Director of Graduate Admissions, 215-248-7097, Fax: 215-248-7161, E-mail: gradadmissions@chc.edu. *Acting Dean of the School of Graduate Studies*, Dr. Barbara Hogan, 215-248-7120, Fax: 215-248-7161, E-mail: hoganb@chc.edu.

Division of Psychology Students: 188 full-time (148 women), 127 part-time (110 women); includes 71 minority (41 Black or African American, non-Hispanic/Latino; 6 Asian, non-Hispanic/Latino; 20 Hispanic/Latino; 4 Two or more races, non-Hispanic/Latino), 5 international. Average age 30. 153 applicants, 76% accepted, 46 enrolled. *Faculty:* 15 full-time (8 women), 33 part-time/adjunct (27 women). *Financial support:* Unspecified assistantships available. In 2015, 88 master's, 20 doctorates, 8 other advanced degrees awarded. *Degree program information:* Part-time and evening/weekend programs available. Part-time, evening/weekend. Offers clinical and counseling psychology (MS, CAS); clinical psychology (Psy D). *Application deadline:* For fall admission, 7/1 for domestic and international students; for spring admission, 11/1 for domestic and international students; for summer admission, 4/1 for domestic and international students. Applications are processed on a rolling basis. *Application fee:* $55. *Application Contact:* Amy Boorse, Assistant Director of Graduate Admissions, 215-248-7097, Fax: 215-248-7161, E-mail: gradadmissions@chc.edu. *Chair*, Dr. Cheryll Rothery, 215-248-7023, Fax: 215-248-3619, E-mail: rotheryc@chc.edu.

CHEYNEY UNIVERSITY OF PENNSYLVANIA, Cheyney, PA 19319

General Information State-supported, coed, comprehensive institution. *Graduate housing:* On-campus housing not available.

GRADUATE UNITS

Graduate Programs ***Degree program information:*** Part-time and evening/weekend programs available. Part-time, evening/weekend. Offers educational leadership (M Ed, Certificate); elementary education (M Ed); principal certification (Certificate); public administration (MPA); special education (M Ed); urban education (M Ed). Electronic applications accepted.

THE CHICAGO SCHOOL OF PROFESSIONAL PSYCHOLOGY, Chicago, IL 60610

General Information Independent, coed, primarily women, graduate-only institution. CGS member. *Graduate housing:* On-campus housing not available.

GRADUATE UNITS

Program in Applied Behavior Analysis Offers applied behavior analysis (MS, PhD).

Program in Business Psychology Offers business psychology (PhD); industrial and organizational business psychology (Psy D); industrial and organizational psychology (MA); organizational leadership (MA, PhD).

Program in Clinical Forensic Psychology Offers clinical forensic psychology (Psy D).

Program in Clinical Psychology Offers clinical psychology (Psy D). Electronic applications accepted.

Program in Forensic Psychology Offers forensic psychology (MA).

Program in Industrial and Organizational Psychology ***Degree program information:*** Part-time and evening/weekend programs available. Part-time, evening/weekend. Offers business psychology (Psy D); industrial and organizational psychology (MA).

Program in School Psychology ***Degree program information:*** Part-time programs available. Part-time. Offers school psychology (Ed D, Ed S).

THE CHICAGO SCHOOL OF PROFESSIONAL PSYCHOLOGY AT DOWNTOWN LOS ANGELES, Los Angeles, CA 90017

General Information Independent, coed, graduate-only institution.

GRADUATE UNITS

Program in Applied Behavior Analysis Offers applied behavior analysis (Psy D).

Program in Clinical Forensic Psychology Offers clinical forensic psychology (Psy D).

Program in Clinical Psychology Offers applied behavior analysis (MA); clinical psychology (Psy D); marital and family therapy (MA).

Program in Industrial and Organizational Psychology Offers industrial and organizational psychology (MA).

THE CHICAGO SCHOOL OF PROFESSIONAL PSYCHOLOGY AT IRVINE, Irvine, CA 92612

General Information Independent, coed, graduate-only institution.

GRADUATE UNITS

Program in Clinical Forensic Psychology Offers clinical forensic psychology (Psy D).

Program in Marital and Family Therapy Offers clinical psychology (MA); management practice (Psy D); psychodynamic psychotherapy (Psy D).

Program in Psychology Offers generalist (Psy D); psychodynamic psychotherapy (Psy D).

THE CHICAGO SCHOOL OF PROFESSIONAL PSYCHOLOGY: ONLINE, Chicago, IL 60654

General Information Independent, coed, graduate-only institution. *Graduate housing:* On-campus housing not available.

GRADUATE UNITS

PhD Program in Organizational Leadership Offers organizational leadership (PhD).

Program in Applied Industrial and Organizational Psychology Offers applied industrial and organizational psychology (MA, Certificate).

Program in Forensic Psychology Offers forensic psychology (MA, Certificate).

Program in International Psychology Offers international psychology (PhD).

Program in Psychology Offers child and adolescent psychology (MA); generalist (MA); gerontology (MA); international psychology (MA); organizational leadership (MA); sport and exercise psychology (MA).

CHICAGO STATE UNIVERSITY, Chicago, IL 60628

General Information State-supported, coed, comprehensive institution. *Graduate housing:* Room and/or apartments available on a first-come, first-served basis to single students; on-campus housing not available to married students.

GRADUATE UNITS

College of Pharmacy Offers pharmacy (Pharm D).

School of Graduate and Professional Studies ***Degree program information:*** Part-time and evening/weekend programs available. Part-time, evening/weekend. Electronic applications accepted.

College of Arts and Sciences ***Degree program information:*** Part-time and evening/weekend programs available. Part-time, evening/weekend. Offers arts and sciences (MA, MFA, MS, MSW); biological sciences (MS); computer science (MS); counseling (MA); creative writing (MFA); criminal justice (MS); English (MA); geographic information systems (MA); geography (MA); history (MA); mathematics (MS); social work (MSW).

College of Education ***Degree program information:*** Part-time programs available. Part-time. Offers bilingual education (M Ed); curriculum and instruction (MS Ed); early childhood education (MAT, MS Ed); education (M Ed, MA, MAT, MS Ed, Ed D); educational leadership (MA, Ed D); elementary education (MAT); general administration (MA); higher education administration (MA); instructional foundations (MS Ed); library information and media studies (MS Ed); middle school education (MAT); physical education (MS Ed); reading (MS Ed); secondary education (MAT); special education (M Ed); teaching of reading (MS Ed); technology and education (MS Ed).

College of Health Sciences Offers health sciences (MOT, MPH, MSN); nursing (MSN); occupational therapy (MOT); public health (MPH).

CHICAGO THEOLOGICAL SEMINARY, Chicago, IL 60637-1507

General Information Independent-religious, coed, graduate-only institution. *Graduate housing:* On-campus housing not available.

GRADUATE UNITS

Graduate and Professional Programs ***Degree program information:*** Part-time programs available. Part-time. Offers Bible, culture and hermeneutics (PhD); preaching (D Min); religion and health (D Min); religious studies (MA); spirituality and spiritual direction (D Min); theology (M Div); theology, ethics and the human sciences (PhD).

CHOWAN UNIVERSITY, Murfreesboro, NC 27855

General Information Independent-religious, coed, comprehensive institution. *Enrollment:* 1,532 graduate, professional, and undergraduate students; 10 full-time matriculated graduate/professional students (8 women). *Enrollment by degree level:* 10 master's. *Graduate faculty:* 3 full-time (all women). *Tuition, area resident:* Full-time $4620. *Graduate housing:* Room and/or apartments available to single students; on-campus housing not available to married students. *Student services:* Campus employment opportunities, campus safety program, career counseling, exercise/wellness program, free psychological counseling, international student services, low-cost health insurance, multicultural affairs office, services for students with disabilities, teacher training, writing training. *Library:* Whitaker Library plus 1 other. *Collection:* Books: 102,595 (physical), 44,795 (digital/electronic); Serial titles: 20,791 (physical), 2,601 (digital/electronic); Databases: 115. Weekly public service hours: 105; students can reserve study rooms.

Computer facilities: Computer purchase and lease plans are available. 215 computers available on campus for general student use. A campuswide network can be accessed from student residence rooms. Online class registration is available.
Website: http://www.chowan.edu/

General Application Contact: Sharon W. Rose, Director of Financial Aid, 252-398-6299, Fax: 252-398-6513, E-mail: roses1@chowan.edu.

GRADUATE UNITS

School of Graduate Studies Students: 10 full-time (8 women); includes 7 minority (6 Black or African American, non-Hispanic/Latino; 1 Hispanic/Latino), 2 international. Average age 30. *Faculty:* 3 full-time (all women). Offers education (M Ed). *Application fee:* $50. Electronic applications accepted. *Application Contact:* Shellie Saxby, Graduate Admissions Contact, 252-398-6214, E-mail: saxbys@chowan.edu.

CHRISTENDOM COLLEGE, Front Royal, VA 22630-5103

General Information Independent-religious, coed, comprehensive institution. *Graduate housing:* On-campus housing not available.

GRADUATE UNITS

Notre Dame Graduate School ***Degree program information:*** Part-time and evening/weekend programs available. Part-time, evening/weekend, online learning. Offers theological studies (MA). Electronic applications accepted.

CHRISTIAN BROTHERS UNIVERSITY, Memphis, TN 38104-5581

General Information Independent-religious, coed, comprehensive institution. *Graduate housing:* On-campus housing not available.

GRADUATE UNITS

School of Arts ***Degree program information:*** Part-time and evening/weekend programs available. Part-time, evening/weekend. Offers Catholic studies (MACS); educational leadership (MSEL); teacher-leadership (M Ed); teaching (MAT).

School of Business ***Degree program information:*** Part-time and evening/weekend programs available. Part-time, evening/weekend. Offers accountancy (M Acc); business (MBA); international business (MIB); project management (Certificate).

School of Engineering ***Degree program information:*** Part-time and evening/weekend programs available. Part-time, evening/weekend, online learning. Offers engineering (MEM, MSEM).

School of Sciences Offers physician assistant studies (MS).

CHRISTIAN THEOLOGICAL SEMINARY, Indianapolis, IN 46208-3301

General Information Independent-religious, coed, graduate-only institution. *Graduate housing:* Rooms and/or apartments available on a first-come, first-served basis to single and married students.

GRADUATE UNITS

Graduate and Professional Programs ***Degree program information:*** Part-time programs available. Part-time. Offers educational and arts ministries (MA); marriage and family therapy (MA); pastoral care and counseling (D Min); psychotherapy and faith (MA); theological studies (MTS); theology (M Div). Electronic applications accepted.

CHRISTIE'S EDUCATION, New York, NY 10020

General Information Proprietary, coed, primarily women, graduate-only institution. *Enrollment by degree level:* 60 master's, 4 other advanced degrees. *Graduate faculty:* 5 full-time (4 women). *Tuition, area resident:* Full-time $46,410; part-time $30,345 per year. *Required fees:* $1079; $1079 per year. *Graduate housing:* On-campus housing not available. *Student services:* Campus employment opportunities, career counseling, international student services, services for students with disabilities, writing training. *Library:* Christie's Education Library. *Collection:* Books: 6,000 (physical); Databases: 20.

Computer facilities: 11 computers available on campus for general student use. A campuswide network can be accessed.
Website: http://www.christies.edu/

General Application Contact: Hilary Smith, Recruitment and Admissions Officer, 212-355-1501 Ext. 3309, Fax: 212-355-7370, E-mail: hsmith@christies.edu.

GRADUATE UNITS

ART NOW: Contemporary Art Since the 1980s Certificate Program Offers contemporary art since the 1980s (Certificate). *Application deadline:* Applications are processed on a rolling basis. Electronic applications accepted. *Application Contact:* Catherine Warden, Academic and Financial Aid Administrator, 212-355-1501 Ext. 3300, Fax: 212-355-7370, E-mail: cwarden@christies.edu. *Director of Continuing Education,* Dr. Marisa Kayyem, 212-355-1501 Ext. 3303.

Certificate Program in Art Business Offers art business (Certificate). *Application deadline:* Applications are processed on a rolling basis. Electronic applications accepted. *Application Contact:* Catherine Warden, Academic Coordinator, 212-355-1501, Fax: 212-355-7370, E-mail: shortcoursesus@christies.edu. *Director of Continuing Education,* Dr. Marisa Kayyem, 212-355-1501, Fax: 212-355-7370, E-mail: mkayyem@christies.edu.

Certificate Program in Modern and Contemporary Art in New York Students: 4 (all women). *Faculty:* 5 full-time (4 women). *Degree program information:* Part-time programs available. Part-time. Offers modern and contemporary art (Certificate). *Application deadline:* Applications are processed on a rolling basis. *Application Contact:* Margaret Conklin, Business Manager, 212-355-1501 Ext. 302, Fax: 212-355-7370, E-mail: mconklin@christies.edu.

MA Program in Art, Law and Business ***Financial support:*** Scholarships/grants and unspecified assistantships available. *Degree program information:* Part-time programs available. Part-time. Offers art, law and business (MA). *Application deadline:* For fall admission, 1/15 priority date for domestic and international students. Applications are processed on a rolling basis. *Application fee:* $95. *Application Contact:* Hilary Smith, Recruitment and Admissions Officer, 212-355-1501 Ext. 3309, Fax: 212-355-7370, E-mail: hsmith@christies.edu. *Program Director,* Noah Kupferman, 212-355-1501 Ext. 7101, E-mail: nkupferman@christies.edu.

MA Program in Modern and Contemporary Art and the Market Students: 23 full-time (19 women), 37 part-time (35 women). *Faculty:* 5 full-time (4 women). *Financial support:* Scholarships/grants and unspecified assistantships available. Financial award applicants required to submit FAFSA. In 2015, 31 master's awarded. *Degree program information:* Part-time programs available. Part-time. Offers modern and contemporary art and the market (MA). *Application deadline:* For fall admission, 1/15 priority date for domestic and international students. Applications are processed on a rolling basis. *Application fee:* $90. *Application Contact:* Margaret Conklin, Business Manager, 212-355-1501 Ext. 302, Fax: 212-355-7370, E-mail: mconklin@christies.edu. *Program Director,* Dr. Julie Reiss, 212-355-1501 Ext. 3307, Fax: 212-355-7370, E-mail: jreiss@christies.edu.

CHRISTOPHER NEWPORT UNIVERSITY, Newport News, VA 23606-3072

General Information State-supported, coed, comprehensive institution. *Enrollment:* 5,172 graduate, professional, and undergraduate students; 80 full-time matriculated graduate/professional students (66 women), 33 part-time matriculated graduate/professional students (16 women). *Enrollment by degree level:* 113 master's. *Graduate faculty:* 52 full-time (19 women), 17 part-time/adjunct (14 women). Tuition, state resident: full-time $6444; part-time $358 per credit hour. Tuition, nonresident: full-time $14,706; part-time $817 per credit hour. *Required fees:* $3690; $205 per credit hour. Tuition and fees vary according to course load. *Graduate housing:* On-campus housing not available. *Student services:* Campus employment opportunities, campus safety program, career counseling, exercise/wellness program, free psychological counseling, grant writing training, international student services, multicultural affairs office, services for students with disabilities, teacher training, writing training. *Library:* Paul and Rosemary Trible Library. *Collection:* Books: 223,632 (physical), 547,263 (digital/electronic); Serial titles: 808 (physical), 61,981 (digital/electronic); Databases: 282. Weekly public service hours: 101; study areas open 24 hours, 5–7 days a week; students can reserve study rooms. *Research affiliation:* Thomas Jefferson National Accelerator Facility (instrument and nuclear physics), Applied Research Center (biology, engineering, physics), National Science Foundation (science), Langley Research Center, Center for Distance Learning (flow visualization), National Science Foundation (science).

Computer facilities: 540 computers available on campus for general student use. A campuswide network can be accessed from student residence rooms and from off campus. Online class registration is available.
Website: http://www.cnu.edu/

General Application Contact: Lyn Sawyer, Associate Director, Graduate Admissions, 757-594-7544, Fax: 757-594-7649, E-mail: gradstdy@cnu.edu.

GRADUATE UNITS

Graduate Studies Students: 80 full-time (66 women), 33 part-time (16 women); includes 14 minority (4 Black or African American, non-Hispanic/Latino; 1 Asian, non-Hispanic/Latino; 5 Hispanic/Latino; 4 Two or more races, non-Hispanic/Latino). Average age 24. 108 applicants, 83% accepted, 76 enrolled. *Faculty:* 52 full-time (19 women), 17 part-time/adjunct (14 women). *Financial support:* In 2015–16, 25 students received support, including 9 fellowships with full tuition reimbursements available (averaging $30,000 per year), 5 research assistantships with full tuition reimbursements available (averaging $2,000 per year), 8 teaching assistantships (averaging $1,500 per year); scholarships/grants and unspecified assistantships also available. Financial award application deadline: 3/1; financial award applicants required to submit FAFSA. In 2015, 94 master's awarded. *Degree program information:* Part-time programs available. Part-time. Offers applied physics and computer science (MS); environmental science (MS); teacher preparation (MAT). *Application deadline:* For fall admission, 7/15 for domestic students, 4/1 for international students; for spring admission, 10/15 for domestic students, 10/1 for international students; for summer admission, 12/1 for domestic students, 3/1 for international students. Applications are processed on a rolling basis. *Application fee:* $50. Electronic applications accepted. *Application Contact:* Lyn Sawyer, Associate Director, Graduate Admissions and Records, 757-594-7544, Fax: 757-594-7649, E-mail: gradstdy@cnu.edu. *Vice Provost for Research, Graduate Studies, and Assessment*, Dr. Geoffrey C. Klein, 757-594-7477, E-mail: geoffrey.klein@cnu.edu.

CHRIST THE KING SEMINARY, East Aurora, NY 14052

General Information Independent-religious, coed, graduate-only institution. *Graduate housing:* On-campus housing not available.

GRADUATE UNITS

Graduate and Professional Programs *Degree program information:* Part-time and evening/weekend programs available. Part-time, evening/weekend. Offers divinity (M Div); pastoral ministry (MA); theology (MA).

CHURCH DIVINITY SCHOOL OF THE PACIFIC, Berkeley, CA 94709-1217

General Information Independent-religious, coed, graduate-only institution. *Graduate housing:* Rooms and/or apartments available on a first-come, first-served basis to single and married students. Housing application deadline: 5/1.

GRADUATE UNITS

Graduate and Professional Programs *Degree program information:* Part-time programs available. Part-time. Offers theology (M Div, MA, MTS, D Min, Certificate). MA program offered jointly with Graduate Theological Union. Electronic applications accepted.

CINCINNATI CHRISTIAN UNIVERSITY, Cincinnati, OH 45204-3200

General Information Independent-religious, coed, comprehensive institution. *Graduate housing:* On-campus housing not available.

GRADUATE UNITS

Graduate School *Degree program information:* Part-time programs available. Part-time. Offers biblical studies (MA); church history (MA); counseling (MAC); divinity (M Div); ministry (M Min); practical ministries (MA); theological studies (MA). Electronic applications accepted.

THE CITADEL, THE MILITARY COLLEGE OF SOUTH CAROLINA, Charleston, SC 29409

General Information State-supported, coed, primarily men, comprehensive institution. *Enrollment:* 3,506 graduate, professional, and undergraduate students; 165 full-time matriculated graduate/professional students (102 women), 670 part-time matriculated graduate/professional students (377 women). *Enrollment by degree level:* 792 master's, 43 other advanced degrees. *Graduate faculty:* 74 full-time (22 women), 20 part-time/adjunct (6 women). Tuition, state resident: part-time $551 per credit hour. Tuition, nonresident: part-time $927 per credit hour. *Required fees:* $90 per term. *Graduate housing:* On-campus housing not available. *Student services:* Campus employment opportunities, career counseling, exercise/wellness program, free psychological counseling, international student services, low-cost health insurance, multicultural affairs office, services for students with disabilities, teacher training, writing training. *Library:* Daniel Library. *Collection:* Books: 187,399 (digital/electronic). Students can reserve study rooms.

Computer facilities: 350 computers available on campus for general student use. A campuswide network can be accessed from student residence rooms and from off campus. Online class registration is available.
Website: http://www.citadel.edu/

General Application Contact: Dr. Robert H. McNamara, Associate Provost, The Citadel Graduate College, 843-953-5089, Fax: 843-953-7630, E-mail: cgc@citadel.edu.

GRADUATE UNITS

Citadel Graduate College Students: 165 full-time (102 women), 627 part-time (344 women); includes 163 minority (115 Black or African American, non-Hispanic/Latino; 2 American Indian or Alaska Native, non-Hispanic/Latino; 7 Asian, non-Hispanic/Latino; 20 Hispanic/Latino; 2 Native Hawaiian or other Pacific Islander, non-Hispanic/Latino; 17 Two or more races, non-Hispanic/Latino), 2 international. Average age 32. 502 applicants, 74% accepted, 188 enrolled. *Faculty:* 77 full-time (25 women), 19 part-time/adjunct (6 women). *Financial support:* Fellowships, research assistantships, career-related internships or fieldwork, health care benefits, and unspecified assistantships available. Support available to part-time students. Financial award application deadline: 7/1; financial award applicants required to submit FAFSA. In 2015, 272 master's, 13 other advanced degrees awarded. *Degree program information:* Part-time and evening/weekend programs available. Part-time, evening/weekend. Offers biology (MA); computer science (MS); English (MA); health, exercise, and sport science (MS); history (MA); intelligence and security studies (MA); international politics and military affairs (MA); mathematics education (MAE); physical education (MAT); project management (MS); psychology (MA); school psychology (Ed S); social science (MA). *Application deadline:* For fall admission, 8/1 priority date for domestic students. Applications are processed on a rolling basis. *Application fee:* $40. Electronic applications accepted. *Application Contact:* Dr. Robert H. McNamara, Associate Provost, The Citadel Graduate College, 843-953-5089, Fax: 843-953-7630, E-mail: cgc@citadel.edu. *Provost and Dean of the College*, Connie Ledoux Book, 843-953-5007, Fax: 843-953-7240, E-mail: cbook1@citadel.edu.

School of Business Administration Students: 29 full-time (4 women), 194 part-time (78 women); includes 27 minority (18 Black or African American, non-Hispanic/Latino; 1 American Indian or Alaska Native, non-Hispanic/Latino; 3 Asian, non-Hispanic/Latino; 3 Hispanic/Latino; 2 Two or more races, non-Hispanic/Latino), 1 international. Average age 31. *Faculty:* 19 full-time (3 women), 3 part-time/adjunct (0 women). *Financial support:* Fellowships, career-related internships or fieldwork, health care benefits, and unspecified assistantships available. Support available to part-time students. Financial award application deadline: 3/15; financial award applicants required to submit FAFSA. In 2015, 109 master's awarded. *Degree program information:* Part-time and evening/weekend programs available. Part-time, evening/weekend. Offers business administration (MBA). *Application deadline:* For fall admission, 7/15 for domestic students; for spring admission, 11/15 for domestic students. Applications are processed on a rolling basis. *Application fee:* $40. Electronic applications accepted. *Application Contact:* Morgan LaForge, MBA Academic Advisor, 843-953-5257, Fax: 843-953-6764, E-mail: mlaforge@citadel.edu. *Interim MBA Program Director*, Dr. Wes Jones, 843-953-5056, Fax: 843-953-6764, E-mail: jonesw1@citadel.edu.

Zucker Family School of Education Students: 50 full-time (39 women), 220 part-time (166 women); includes 74 minority (62 Black or African American, non-Hispanic/Latino; 1 American Indian or Alaska Native, non-Hispanic/Latino; 1 Asian, non-Hispanic/Latino; 3 Hispanic/Latino; 1 Native Hawaiian or other Pacific Islander, non-Hispanic/Latino; 6 Two or more races, non-Hispanic/Latino). Average age 33. *Faculty:* 11 full-time (7 women), 6 part-time/adjunct (2 women). *Financial support:* Fellowships, career-related internships or fieldwork, health care benefits, and unspecified assistantships available. Support available to part-time students. Financial award application deadline: 3/15; financial award applicants required to submit FAFSA. In 2015, 73 master's, 13 other advanced degrees awarded. *Degree program information:* Part-time and evening/weekend programs available. Part-time, evening/weekend. Offers biology (MAT); education (M Ed, MAT, Certificate, Ed S); elementary/secondary school administration and supervision (M Ed); elementary/secondary school counseling (M Ed, Certificate); English language arts (MAT); literacy education (M Ed, Certificate); mathematics (MAT); middle grades education (MAT); physical education (MAT); school superintendency (Ed S); social studies (MAT); student affairs and college counseling (M Ed). *Application deadline:* Applications are processed on a rolling basis. *Application fee:* $40. Electronic applications accepted. *Application Contact:* Maj. Kathryn A. Richardson-Jones, Associate Dean/Teacher Education Program Coordinator, 843-953-3163, Fax: 843-953-7258, E-mail: kathryn.jones@citadel.edu. *Dean of the Zucker Family School of Education*, Dr. Larry G. Daniel, 843-953-5097, Fax: 843-953-7258, E-mail: ldaniel@citadel.edu.

CITY COLLEGE OF THE CITY UNIVERSITY OF NEW YORK, New York, NY 10031-9198

General Information State and locally supported, coed, comprehensive institution. CGS member. *Enrollment:* 16,027 graduate, professional, and undergraduate students; 178 full-time matriculated graduate/professional students (87 women), 579 part-time matriculated graduate/professional students (359 women). *Enrollment by degree level:* 2,340 master's, 641 doctoral, 54 other advanced degrees. *Graduate faculty:* 519 full-time (199 women), 610 part-time/adjunct (291 women). Tuition and fees vary according to course load, degree level and program. *Graduate housing:* Room and/or apartments available on a first-come, first-served basis to single students; on-campus housing not available to married students. *Student services:* Campus employment opportunities, campus safety program, career counseling, child daycare facilities, exercise/wellness program, free psychological counseling, international student services, multicultural affairs office, services for students with disabilities. *Library:* Morris Raphael Cohen Library plus 8 others. *Research affiliation:* New York Center for Biological Structures, Lucent Laboratories (engineering), Hospital for Joint Diseases (biomedical engineering), Museum of Natural History.

Computer facilities: Computer purchase and lease plans are available. 3,000 computers available on campus for general student use. A campuswide network can be accessed from off campus. Online class registration is available.
Website: http://www.ccny.cuny.edu/

General Application Contact: Pauline Pabon, Assistant Director of Graduate Admissions, 212-650-6977, Fax: 212-650-6417, E-mail: graduateadmissions@ccny.cuny.edu.

GRADUATE UNITS

Graduate School Students: 373 full-time (194 women), 2,975 part-time (1,817 women); includes 2,470 minority (885 Black or African American, non-Hispanic/Latino; 1 American Indian or Alaska Native, non-Hispanic/Latino; 577 Asian, non-Hispanic/Latino; 1,007 Hispanic/Latino), 462 international. 1,723 applicants, 70% accepted. *Financial support:* Fellowships, research assistantships, teaching assistantships, career-related internships or fieldwork, Federal Work-Study, institutionally sponsored loans, scholarships/grants, health care benefits, tuition waivers (full and partial), and unspecified assistantships available. Support available to part-time students. Financial award applicants required to submit FAFSA. In 2015, 953 master's awarded. *Degree program information:* Part-time and evening/weekend programs available. Part-time, evening/weekend. Offers sustainability in the urban environment (MS). *Application deadline:* Applications are processed on a rolling basis. *Application fee:* $125. *Application Contact:* 212-650-6977, Fax: 212-650-6417, E-mail: graduateadmissions@ccny.cuny.edu.

The Bernard and Anne Spitzer School of Architecture *Financial support:* Fellowships, career-related internships or fieldwork, and Federal Work-Study available. Support available to part-time students. *Degree program information:* Part-time programs available. Part-time. Offers architecture (M Arch); landscape architecture (MLA); urban design (MUP). *Application fee:* $125. *Application Contact:* Sarah Morales, Advisor, 212-650-8748, E-mail: archgrad@ccny.cuny.edu. *Acting Dean*, Gordon A. Gebert, 212-650-7284, Fax: 212-650-6566.

Colin Powell School for Civic and Global Leadership Financial support: Fellowships, research assistantships, teaching assistantships, career-related internships or fieldwork, Federal Work-Study, institutionally sponsored loans, scholarships/grants, and tuition waivers (full and partial) available. Support available to part-time students. Financial award applicants required to submit FAFSA. *Degree program information:* Part-time programs available. Part-time. Offers clinical psychology (PhD); economics (MA); economics and business (MA); general psychology (MA); international relations (MA); mental health counseling (MA); psychology (MA, PhD); public service management (MPA); sociology (MA). *Application deadline:* For fall admission, 3/15 priority date for domestic and international students; for spring admission, 11/15 priority date for domestic and international students. Applications are processed on a rolling basis. *Application fee:* $125. Electronic applications accepted. *Application Contact:* 212-650-6977, Fax: 212-650-6417, E-mail: gradadm@ccny.cuny.edu. *Dean*, Vincent Boudreau, 212-650-5967, E-mail: vboudreau@ccny.cuny.edu.

Division of Humanities and the Arts Financial support: Fellowships, teaching assistantships, career-related internships or fieldwork, Federal Work-Study, institutionally sponsored loans, scholarships/grants, tuition waivers (full and partial), and unspecified assistantships available. Support available to part-time students. Financial award applicants required to submit FAFSA. *Degree program information:* Part-time programs available. Part-time. Offers advertising design (MFA); art history (MA); art history and museum studies (MA); art museum education (MA); branding and integrated communications (MPS); ceramic design (MFA); creative writing (MFA); digital and interdisciplinary art practice (MFA); film (MFA); fine arts (MFA); history (MA); humanities and the arts (MA, MFA, MPS); language and literacy (MA); literature (MA); museum studies (MA); painting (MFA); printmaking (MFA); sculpture (MFA); Spanish (MA); wood and metal design (MFA). *Application deadline:* For fall admission, 5/1 for domestic and international students; for spring admission, 11/15 for domestic and international students. Applications are processed on a rolling basis. *Application fee:* $125. Electronic applications accepted. *Application Contact:* 212-650-6977, Fax: 212-650-6417, E-mail: graduateadmissions@ccny.cuny.edu. *Acting Dean*, Doris Cintron, 212-650-8166, Fax: 212-650-7649, E-mail: humanities@ccny.cuny.edu.

Division of Science Financial support: Fellowships, research assistantships, teaching assistantships, career-related internships or fieldwork, Federal Work-Study, and scholarships/grants available. Support available to part-time students. Financial award applicants required to submit FAFSA. *Degree program information:* Part-time programs available. Part-time. Offers biochemistry (MS, PhD); biology (MS, PhD); chemistry (MS, PhD); geology (MS); mathematics (MS); physics (MS, PhD); science (MS, PhD). *Application deadline:* For fall admission, 5/1 for domestic and international students; for spring admission, 11/15 for domestic and international students. Applications are processed on a rolling basis. *Application fee:* $125. Electronic applications accepted. *Application Contact:* 216-650-6977, E-mail: gradadm@ccny.cuny.edu. *Dean*, Dr. Tony M. Liss, 212-650-6849.

Grove School of Engineering Financial support: Fellowships with partial tuition reimbursements, research assistantships with full tuition reimbursements, teaching assistantships, Federal Work-Study, institutionally sponsored loans, and tuition waivers (full and partial) available. Support available to part-time students. Financial award applicants required to submit CSS PROFILE or FAFSA. *Degree program information:* Part-time programs available. Part-time. Offers biomedical engineering (MS, PhD); chemical engineering (ME, PhD); civil engineering (ME, MS, PhD); computer science (MS, PhD); electrical engineering (ME, MS, PhD); engineering (ME, MIS, MS, PhD); information systems (MIS); mechanical engineering (ME, MS, PhD). *Application deadline:* For fall admission, 5/1 for domestic and international students; for spring admission, 11/15 for domestic and international students. Applications are processed on a rolling basis. *Application fee:* $125. *Application Contact:* 212-650-6977, Fax: 212-650-6417, E-mail: gradadm@ccny.cuny.edu. *Dean*, Dr. Gilda A. Barabino, 212-650-8030, Fax: 212-650-8024.

School of Education Financial support: Fellowships, research assistantships, teaching assistantships, career-related internships or fieldwork, Federal Work-Study, and tuition waivers (full and partial) available. Support available to part-time students. *Degree program information:* Part-time and evening/weekend programs available. Part-time, evening/weekend. Offers adolescent mathematics education (MA, AC); bilingual education (MS); childhood education (MS); early childhood education (MS); education (MA, MS, MS Ed, AC); educational leadership (MS, AC); educational theatre (MS); English education (MA); literacy (MS); middle school mathematics education (MS); science education (MA); social studies education (AC); teacher of students with disabilities in adolescent education (MS Ed); teacher of students with disabilities in childhood education (MS Ed); TESOL (MS). *Application deadline:* For fall admission, 3/15 for domestic students; for spring admission, 10/15 for domestic students. *Application fee:* $125. *Application Contact:* Stacia Pusey, Graduate Admissions Adviser, 212-650-5345, E-mail: spusey@ccny.cuny.edu. *Dean*, Mary E. Driscoll, 212-650-5354.

CITY UNIVERSITY OF NEW YORK SCHOOL OF LAW, Long Island City, NY 11101-4356

General Information State and locally supported, coed, graduate-only institution. *Enrollment by degree level:* 353 doctoral. *Graduate faculty:* 52 full-time (35 women), 1 part-time/adjunct (0 women). Tuition, state resident: full-time $14,663; part-time $10,028. Tuition, nonresident: full-time $23,983; part-time $16,448. *Required fees:* $563; $173.95 per term. *Graduate housing:* On-campus housing not available. *Student services:* Campus employment opportunities, campus safety program, career counseling, exercise/wellness program, free psychological counseling, low-cost health insurance, services for students with disabilities, writing training. *Library:* CUNY School of Law Library. *Collection:* Books: 82,776 (physical), 45,885 (digital/electronic); Serial titles: 2,540 (physical), 103,557 (digital/electronic); Databases: 373. Weekly public service hours: 61; study areas open 24 hours, 5–7 days a week; students can reserve study rooms.

Computer facilities: 103 computers available on campus for general student use. A campuswide network can be accessed from off campus. Online class registration is available.
Website: http://www.law.cuny.edu/

General Application Contact: Degna P. Levister, Clinical Law Professor/Assistant Dean of Admissions and Enrollment Management, 718-340-4210, Fax: 718-340-4435, E-mail: admissions@law.cuny.edu.

GRADUATE UNITS

Professional Program Students: 307 full-time (197 women), 46 part-time (31 women); includes 161 minority (40 Black or African American, non-Hispanic/Latino; 1 American Indian or Alaska Native, non-Hispanic/Latino; 43 Asian, non-Hispanic/Latino; 56 Hispanic/Latino; 21 Two or more races, non-Hispanic/Latino), 10 international. Average age 27. 1,356 applicants, 45% accepted, 151 enrolled. *Faculty:* 52 full-time (35 women), 1 part-time/adjunct (0 women). *Financial support:* In 2015–16, 104 students received support, including 37 fellowships (averaging $14,100 per year), 17 research assistantships (averaging $664 per year); teaching assistantships, career-related internships or fieldwork, Federal Work-Study, scholarships/grants, and tuition waivers (full and partial) also available. Support available to part-time students. Financial award application deadline: 5/2; financial award applicants required to submit FAFSA. In 2015, 111 doctorates awarded. *Degree program information:* Part-time and evening/weekend programs available. Part-time, evening/weekend. Offers law (JD). *Application deadline:* For fall admission, 6/15 priority date for domestic students. Applications are processed on a rolling basis. *Application fee:* $60. Electronic applications accepted. *Application Contact:* Degna P. Levister, Clinical Law Professor/Assistant Dean of Admissions and Enrollment Management, 718-340-4210, Fax: 718-340-4435, E-mail: admissions@law.cuny.edu. *Dean/Professor of Law*, Michelle J. Anderson, 718-340-4201, Fax: 718-340-4482.

CITY UNIVERSITY OF SEATTLE, Seattle, WA 98121

General Information Independent, coed, comprehensive institution. *Graduate housing:* Room and/or apartments available on a first-come, first-served basis to single students; on-campus housing not available to married students.

GRADUATE UNITS

Graduate Division ***Degree program information:*** Part-time and evening/weekend programs available. Part-time, evening/weekend, online learning. Electronic applications accepted.

Albright School of Education Degree program information: Part-time and evening/weekend programs available. Part-time, evening/weekend, online learning. Offers administrator certification (Certificate); curriculum and instruction (M Ed); elementary education (MIT); guidance and counseling (M Ed); leadership (M Ed); reading and literacy (M Ed); school counseling (M Ed); special education (MIT); superintendent certification (Certificate). Electronic applications accepted.

Division of Arts and Sciences Degree program information: Part-time and evening/weekend programs available. Part-time, evening/weekend, online learning. Offers counseling psychology (MA). Electronic applications accepted.

Division of Doctoral Studies Online learning. Offers leadership (Ed D).

School of Management Degree program information: Part-time and evening/weekend programs available. Part-time, evening/weekend, online learning. Offers accounting (Certificate); change leadership (MBA, Certificate); computer systems (MS); finance (Certificate); financial management (MBA); general management (MBA); general management-Europe (MBA); global marketing (MBA); human resources management (Certificate); individualized study (MBA); information security (MS); information systems (MBA); leadership (MA); marketing (MBA, Certificate); project management (MBA, MS, Certificate); sustainable business (Certificate); technology management (MBA, Certificate). Electronic applications accepted.

CITY VISION UNIVERSITY, Kansas City, MO 64109-1845

General Information Independent-religious, coed, comprehensive institution.

GRADUATE UNITS

Program in Technology and Ministry Online learning. Offers technology and ministry (MS).

CLAFLIN UNIVERSITY, Orangeburg, SC 29115

General Information Independent-religious, coed, comprehensive institution. *Graduate housing:* Room and/or apartments available on a first-come, first-served basis to single students; on-campus housing not available to married students. Housing application deadline: 4/15.

GRADUATE UNITS

Graduate Programs ***Degree program information:*** Part-time programs available. Part-time. Offers biotechnology (MS); business administration (MBA).

CLAREMONT GRADUATE UNIVERSITY, Claremont, CA 91711-6160

General Information Independent, coed, graduate-only institution. CGS member. *Enrollment by degree level:* 783 master's, 1,286 doctoral, 43 other advanced degrees. *Graduate faculty:* 117 full-time (49 women), 13 part-time/adjunct (0 women). *Tuition, area resident:* Full-time $43,032; part-time $1793 per unit. *Required fees:* $600; $300 per semester. $300 per semester. Tuition and fees vary according to course load and program. *Graduate housing:* Rooms and/or apartments available on a first-come, first-served basis to single and married students. Typical cost: $8676 per year for single students; $16,368 per year for married students. Room charges vary according to housing facility selected. *Student services:* Campus employment opportunities, campus safety program, career counseling, exercise/wellness program, free psychological counseling, grant writing training, international student services, low-cost health insurance, multicultural affairs office, services for students with disabilities, teacher training, writing training. *Library:* Honnold/Mudd Library plus 3 others. Students can reserve study rooms. *Research affiliation:* Claremont School of Theology (religion), Rancho Santa Ana Botanic Garden (botany, native plants).

Computer facilities: 136 computers available on campus for general student use. A campuswide network can be accessed from student residence rooms and from off campus. Online class registration is available.
Website: http://www.cgu.edu/

General Application Contact: Loren Bryant, Admissions Coordinator, 909-607-7811, Fax: 909-607-7285, E-mail: admissions@cgu.edu.

GRADUATE UNITS

Graduate Programs Students: 1,428 full-time (776 women), 708 part-time (392 women); includes 697 minority (126 Black or African American, non-Hispanic/Latino; 10 American Indian or Alaska Native, non-Hispanic/Latino; 203 Asian, non-Hispanic/Latino; 284 Hispanic/Latino; 7 Native Hawaiian or other Pacific Islander, non-Hispanic/Latino; 67 Two or more races, non-Hispanic/Latino), 445 international. Average age 34. *Faculty:* 117 full-time (49 women), 13 part-time/adjunct (0 women). *Financial support:* Fellowships, research assistantships, teaching assistantships, career-related internships or fieldwork, Federal Work-Study, institutionally sponsored loans, scholarships/grants, tuition waivers (full and partial), and unspecified assistantships available. Support available to part-time students. Financial award application deadline: 2/15; financial award applicants required to submit FAFSA. In 2015, 447 master's, 132 doctorates, 57 other advanced degrees awarded. *Degree program information:* Part-time and evening/weekend programs available. Part-time, evening/weekend. Offers arts management (MA); botany (MS, PhD); financial engineering (MSFE). *Application deadline:* For fall admission, 2/1 priority date for domestic and international students; for spring admission, 11/1 priority date for domestic and international students. Applications are processed on a rolling basis. *Application fee:* $80. Electronic applications accepted. *Application Contact:* Loren Bryant, Admissions Coordinator, 909-607-7811, Fax: 909-607-7285, E-mail: admissions@cgu.edu. *President*, Robert Schult, 909-621-8025, Fax: 909-607-9103, E-mail: rwschult@cgu.edu.

Center for Information Systems and Technology Students: 63 full-time (22 women), 78 part-time (19 women); includes 29 minority (8 Black or African American, non-Hispanic/Latino; 15 Asian, non-Hispanic/Latino; 4 Hispanic/Latino; 1 Native Hawaiian or other Pacific Islander, non-Hispanic/Latino; 1 Two or more races, non-Hispanic/Latino), 81 international. Average age 35. *Faculty:* 8 full-time (1 woman), 1 part-time/adjunct (0 women). *Financial support:* Fellowships, research assistantships, teaching assistantships, Federal Work-Study, institutionally sponsored loans, and scholarships/grants available. Support available to part-time students. Financial award application deadline: 2/15; financial award applicants required to submit FAFSA. In 2015, 18 master's, 7 doctorates awarded. *Degree program information:* Part-time programs available. Part-time. Offers cybersecurity and networking (MS); data science and analytics (MS); electronic commerce (PhD); geographic information systems (MS); health informatics (MS); information systems (Certificate); IT strategy and innovation (MS); knowledge management (PhD); systems development (PhD); telecommunications and networking (PhD). *Application deadline:* For fall admission, 2/1 priority date for domestic and international students. Applications are processed on a rolling basis. *Application fee:* $80. Electronic applications accepted. *Application Contact:* Jake Campbell, Assistant Director of Admissions, 909-607-3024, E-mail: jake.campbell@cgu.edu. *Director*, Tom Horan, 909-607-9302, Fax: 909-621-8564, E-mail: tom.horan@cgu.edu.

Institute of Mathematical Sciences Students: 74 full-time (19 women), 35 part-time (12 women); includes 23 minority (2 Black or African American, non-Hispanic/Latino; 12 Asian, non-Hispanic/Latino; 8 Hispanic/Latino; 1 Two or more races, non-Hispanic/Latino), 51 international. Average age 30. *Faculty:* 6 full-time (1 woman), 2 part-time/adjunct (0 women). *Financial support:* Fellowships, research assistantships, Federal Work-Study, institutionally sponsored loans, scholarships/grants, and tuition waivers (full and partial) available. Support available to part-time students. Financial award application deadline: 2/15; financial award applicants required to submit FAFSA. In 2015, 25 master's, 10 doctorates awarded. *Degree program information:* Part-time programs available. Part-time. Offers computational and systems biology (PhD); computational mathematics and numerical analysis (MA, MS); computational science (PhD); engineering and industrial applied mathematics (PhD); mathematics (PhD); operations research and statistics (MA, MS); physical applied mathematics (MA, MS); pure mathematics (MA, MS); scientific computing (MA, MS); systems and control theory (MA, MS). *Application deadline:* For fall admission, 2/1 priority date for domestic and international students. Applications are processed on a rolling basis. *Application fee:* $80. Electronic applications accepted. *Application Contact:* Jake Campbell, Assistant Director of Admissions, 909-607-3024, E-mail: jake.campbell@cgu.edu. *Director*, Ali Nadim, 909-607-9413, E-mail: ali.nadim@cgu.edu.

Peter F. Drucker and Masatoshi Ito Graduate School of Management Students: 150 full-time (88 women), 104 part-time (45 women); includes 89 minority (12 Black or African American, non-Hispanic/Latino; 27 Asian, non-Hispanic/Latino; 36 Hispanic/Latino; 1 Native Hawaiian or other Pacific Islander, non-Hispanic/Latino; 13 Two or more races, non-Hispanic/Latino), 68 international. Average age 32. *Faculty:* 14 full-time (5 women), 1 part-time/adjunct (0 women). *Financial support:* Fellowships, research assistantships, teaching assistantships, Federal Work-Study, institutionally sponsored loans, and scholarships/grants available. Support available to part-time students. Financial award application deadline: 2/15; financial award applicants required to submit FAFSA. In 2015, 102 master's, 49 other advanced degrees awarded. *Degree program information:* Part-time programs available. Part-time. Offers advanced management (MS); art business (MA); executive management (EMBA); leadership (Certificate); management (EMBA, MA, MBA, MS, PhD, Certificate); strategy (Certificate). MS/MBA offered jointly with Art Center College of Design. *Application deadline:* For fall admission, 2/15 for domestic students. Applications are processed on a rolling basis. *Application fee:* $80. Electronic applications accepted. *Application Contact:* Andrew Henkes, Assistant Director of Admissions, 909-607-4999, E-mail: andrew.henkes@cgu.edu. *Dean*, Thomas Horan, E-mail: thomas.horan@cgu.edu.

School of Arts and Humanities Students: 385 full-time (198 women), 114 part-time (61 women); includes 139 minority (29 Black or African American, non-Hispanic/Latino; 3 American Indian or Alaska Native, non-Hispanic/Latino; 42 Asian, non-Hispanic/Latino; 48 Hispanic/Latino; 2 Native Hawaiian or other Pacific Islander, non-Hispanic/Latino; 15 Two or more races, non-Hispanic/Latino), 55 international. Average age 36. *Faculty:* 28 full-time (14 women), 4 part-time/adjunct (0 women). *Financial support:* Fellowships, research assistantships, teaching assistantships, Federal Work-Study, institutionally sponsored loans, and scholarships/grants available. Support available to part-time students. Financial award application deadline: 2/15; financial award applicants required to submit FAFSA. In 2015, 72 master's, 28 doctorates, 3 other advanced degrees awarded. *Degree program information:* Part-time programs available. Part-time. Offers Africana history (Certificate); Africana studies (Certificate); American studies (MA, PhD); American studies and U.S. history (MA, PhD); applied women's studies (MA); archival studies (MA); arts and humanities (M Phil, MA, MFA, DCM, DMA, PhD, Certificate); church music (MA, DCM); composition (MA, DMA); critical theory (MA, PhD); cultural studies (MA, PhD); digital media (MFA); drawing (MFA); early modern studies (MA, PhD); English (M Phil, MA, PhD); European studies (MA, PhD); Hebrew Bible (MA, PhD); historical performance practices (MA, DMA); history of Christianity and religions of North America (MA, PhD); installation (MFA); literary theory (PhD); literature (MA, PhD); literature and creative writing (MA); literature and film (MA); media studies (MA, PhD); museum studies (MA); musicology (MA, PhD); New Testament (MA, PhD); oral history (MA, PhD); painting (MFA); performance (MA, MFA, DMA); philosophy (MA, PhD); philosophy of religion and theology (MA, PhD); photography (MFA); sculpture (MFA); studio (MFA); theology, ethics and culture (MA, PhD); women's studies in religion (MA, PhD). *Application deadline:* For fall admission, 2/1 priority date for domestic and international students. Applications are processed on a rolling basis. *Application fee:* $80. Electronic applications accepted. *Application Contact:* Erma Cross, Admissions Coordinator, 909-607-9843, Fax: 909-607-9587, E-mail: erminia.cross@cgu.edu. *Dean/Professor*, Tammi Schneider, 909-607-3217, E-mail: tammi.schneider@cgu.edu.

School of Community and Global Health Students: 48 full-time (27 women), 46 part-time (36 women); includes 47 minority (8 Black or African American, non-Hispanic/Latino; 19 Asian, non-Hispanic/Latino; 16 Hispanic/Latino; 4 Two or more races, non-Hispanic/Latino), 14 international. Average age 30. *Faculty:* 8 full-time (3 women). *Financial support:* Fellowships, research assistantships, teaching assistantships, Federal Work-Study, institutionally sponsored loans, and scholarships/grants available. Support available to part-time students. Financial award application deadline: 2/15; financial award applicants required to submit FAFSA. In 2015, 23 master's, 1 doctorate awarded. Offers health promotion science (PhD); public health (MPH). *Application deadline:* For fall admission, 2/1 priority date for domestic and international students; for spring admission, 11/1 priority date for domestic students. Applications are processed on a rolling basis. *Application fee:* $80. Electronic applications accepted. *Application Contact:* Paige Piontkowsky, Assistant Director of Admissions, 909-607-3240, E-mail: paige.piontkowsky@cgu.edu. *Dean*, Stewart Donaldson, 909-607-8235, E-mail: stewart.donaldson@cgu.edu.

School of Educational Studies Students: 212 full-time (151 women), 196 part-time (138 women); includes 229 minority (48 Black or African American, non-Hispanic/Latino; 3 American Indian or Alaska Native, non-Hispanic/Latino; 37 Asian, non-Hispanic/Latino; 123 Hispanic/Latino; 2 Native Hawaiian or other Pacific Islander, non-Hispanic/Latino; 16 Two or more races, non-Hispanic/Latino), 13 international. Average age 39. *Faculty:* 14 full-time (8 women), 1 part-time/adjunct (0 women). *Financial support:* Fellowships, research assistantships, Federal Work-Study, institutionally sponsored loans, and scholarships/grants available. Support available to part-time students. Financial award application deadline: 2/15; financial award applicants required to submit FAFSA. In 2015, 44 master's, 35 doctorates, 13 other advanced degrees awarded. *Degree program information:* Part-time programs available. Part-time. Offers Africana education (Certificate); education and policy (MA, PhD); higher education/student affairs (MA, PhD); human development (MA, PhD); public school administration (MA, PhD); quantitative evaluation (MA, PhD); special education (MA, PhD); teacher education (MA); teaching and learning (MA, PhD); urban leadership (PhD). PhD program offered jointly with San Diego State University. *Application deadline:* For fall admission, 4/1 priority date for domestic and international students. Applications are processed on a rolling basis. *Application fee:* $80. Electronic applications accepted. *Application Contact:* Rachel Camacho, Assistant Director of Admission, 909-607-9418, E-mail: camacho@cgu.edu. *Dean*, Scott Thomas, 909-621-8075, Fax: 909-621-8734, E-mail: scott.thomas@cgu.edu.

School of Social Science, Policy and Evaluation Students: 488 full-time (260 women), 160 part-time (84 women); includes 170 minority (28 Black or African American, non-Hispanic/Latino; 3 American Indian or Alaska Native, non-Hispanic/Latino; 60 Asian, non-Hispanic/Latino; 56 Hispanic/Latino; 1 Native Hawaiian or other Pacific Islander, non-Hispanic/Latino; 22 Two or more races, non-Hispanic/Latino), 148 international. Average age 32. *Faculty:* 33 full-time (14 women), 4 part-time/adjunct (0 women). In 2015, 102 master's, 45 doctorates, 4 other advanced degrees awarded. Offers advanced study in evaluation (Certificate); American politics (MA, PhD); behavioral economics and neuroeconomics (PhD); business and financial economics (MA, PhD); cognitive psychology (MA, PhD); comparative politics (PhD); developmental psychology (MA, PhD); economic development (Certificate); evaluation and applied research methods (MA, PhD); health behavior research and evaluation (MA, PhD); human resource development and evaluation (MA); human resources design (MS); industrial/organizational psychology (MA, PhD); international economic and development policy (PhD); international economics policy and development (MA); international money and finance (PhD); international political economy (MA); international studies (MA); organizational behavior (MA, PhD); organizational psychology (MA, PhD); political economy and public economics (PhD); political economy and public policy (MA); political philosophy (PhD); political science (PhD); politics, economics and business (MA); politics, economics, and business (MA); public policy (MA, PhD); public policy and evaluation (MA); social psychology (MA, PhD); social science, policy and evaluation (MA, MS, PhD, Certificate); world politics (PhD). *Application fee:* $80. *Application Contact:* Paige Piontkowsky, Assistant Director of Admissions, 909-607-3240, E-mail: paige.piontkowsky@cgu.edu. *Dean*, Stewart Donaldson.

CLAREMONT LINCOLN UNIVERSITY, Claremont, CA 91711

General Information Independent, coed, graduate-only institution.

GRADUATE UNITS

Graduate Programs Offers ethical leadership (MA); interfaith action (MA); social impact (MA).

CLAREMONT MCKENNA COLLEGE, Claremont, CA 91711

General Information Independent, coed, comprehensive institution. *Enrollment:* 1,349 graduate, professional, and undergraduate students. *Graduate housing:* On-campus housing not available. *Library:* Honnold Library. *Collection:* Books: 1.1 million (physical).

Computer facilities: 220 computers available on campus for general student use. A campuswide network can be accessed from student residence rooms and from off campus. Online class registration is available.
Website: http://www.claremontmckenna.edu/

General Application Contact: Georgette DeVeres, Associate Vice President and Dean of Admission and Financial Aid, 909-607-3347, E-mail: gdeveres@cmc.edu.

GRADUATE UNITS

Robert Day School of Economics and Finance Students: 20 full-time (7 women); includes 4 minority (3 Asian, non-Hispanic/Latino; 1 Hispanic/Latino), 7 international. Average age 23. 296 applicants, 11% accepted, 20 enrolled. *Financial support:* In 2015–16, 20 students received support, including 20 fellowships with full and partial tuition reimbursements available. Financial award applicants required to submit FAFSA. In 2015, 17 master's awarded. Offers finance (MA). *Application deadline:* For fall admission, 11/2 for domestic and international students; for winter admission, 1/15 for domestic students; for spring admission, 3/9 for domestic students, 2/10 for international students. *Application fee:* $70. Electronic applications accepted. *Application Contact:* Kevin Arnold, Director of Graduate Admission, 909-607-3347, E-mail: karnold@cmc.edu. *Dean*, Brock Blomberg, 909-607-9597, E-mail: bblomberg@cmc.edu.

CLAREMONT SCHOOL OF THEOLOGY, Claremont, CA 91711-3199

General Information Independent-religious, coed, graduate-only institution. *Graduate housing:* Rooms and/or apartments guaranteed to single and married students. Housing application deadline: 6/1. *Research affiliation:* Moore Multicultural Resource and Research Center, Institute for Antiquity and Christianity, Center for Process Studies, National United Methodist Native American Center, Center for Pacific and Asian-American Ministries, Ancient Biblical Manuscript Center.

GRADUATE UNITS

Graduate and Professional Programs ***Degree program information:*** Part-time programs available. Part-time. Offers divinity (M Div); ministry (D Min); practical theology (PhD); religion (PhD); religion and theology (MA); religious education (MARE). Electronic applications accepted.

CLARION UNIVERSITY OF PENNSYLVANIA, Clarion, PA 16214

General Information State-supported, coed, comprehensive institution. *Graduate housing:* Room and/or apartments available on a first-come, first-served basis to single students; on-campus housing not available to married students. Housing application deadline: 6/28.

GRADUATE UNITS

Office of Transfer, Adult and Graduate Admissions ***Degree program information:*** Part-time and evening/weekend programs available. Part-time, evening/weekend. Offers business administration (MBA); curriculum and instruction (M Ed); data analytics (MS); early childhood (M Ed); family nurse practitioner (MSN, Post-Master's Certificate); library science (MSLS, CAS); mass media arts and journalism (MS); math education (M Ed); nurse educator (MSN, Post-Master's Certificate); public relations (Certificate); reading (M Ed); rehabilitative sciences (MS); science education (M Ed); special education (M Ed, MS); speech language pathology (MS); technology (M Ed). Electronic applications accepted.

CLARK ATLANTA UNIVERSITY, Atlanta, GA 30314

General Information Independent-religious, coed, university. CGS member. *Enrollment:* 3,661 graduate, professional, and undergraduate students; 657 full-time matriculated graduate/professional students (459 women), 263 part-time matriculated graduate/professional students (176 women). *Enrollment by degree level:* 684 master's, 233 doctoral, 3 other advanced degrees. *Graduate faculty:* 99 full-time (37 women), 47 part-time/adjunct (30 women). *Tuition, area resident:* Full-time $15,498; part-time $861 per credit hour. *Required fees:* $1006; $1006 per unit. Tuition and fees vary according to course load. *Graduate housing:* Room and/or apartments available on a first-come, first-served basis to single students; on-campus housing not available to married students. Housing application deadline: 6/1. *Student services:* Campus employment opportunities, campus safety program, career counseling, free psychological counseling, international student services, low-cost health insurance, services for students with disabilities. *Library:* Robert W. Woodruff Library.

Computer facilities: 741 computers available on campus for general student use. A campuswide network can be accessed from student residence rooms. Online class registration is available.
Website: http://www.cau.edu/

General Application Contact: Graduate Program Admissions, 404-880-8483, E-mail: graduateadmissions@cau.edu.

GRADUATE UNITS

School of Arts and Sciences Students: 172 full-time (88 women), 137 part-time (82 women); includes 195 minority (185 Black or African American, non-Hispanic/Latino; 9 Asian, non-Hispanic/Latino; 1 Hispanic/Latino), 77 international. Average age 32. 302 applicants, 42% accepted, 56 enrolled. *Faculty:* 62 full-time (18 women), 5 part-time/adjunct (1 woman). *Financial support:* Fellowships, research assistantships, teaching assistantships, career-related internships or fieldwork, Federal Work-Study, institutionally sponsored loans, scholarships/grants, and unspecified assistantships available. Support available to part-time students. Financial award application deadline: 4/30; financial award applicants required to submit FAFSA. In 2015, 41 master's, 7 doctorates awarded. *Degree program information:* Part-time programs available. Part-time. Offers African-American studies (MA, DAH); Africana women's studies (MA, DAH); arts and sciences (MA, MPA, MS, DAH, PhD); biology (MS, PhD); chemistry (MS, PhD); computer and information science (MS); criminal justice (MA); English (MA, DAH); history (MA, DAH); mathematical sciences (MS); physics (MS); political science (MA, PhD); public administration (MPA); Romance languages (MA, DAH); sociology (MA). *Application deadline:* For fall admission, 4/1 for domestic and international students; for spring admission, 11/1 for domestic and international students. Applications are processed on a rolling basis. *Application fee:* $40 ($55 for international students). *Application Contact:* Graduate Program Admissions, 404-880-8483, E-mail: graduateadmissions@cau.edu. *Dean*, Dr. Danille K. Taylor, 404-880-6774, E-mail: dtaylor3@cau.edu.

School of Business Administration Students: 84 full-time (46 women), 4 part-time (2 women); includes 49 minority (all Black or African American, non-Hispanic/Latino), 19 international. Average age 27. 263 applicants, 23% accepted, 34 enrolled. *Faculty:* 14 full-time (7 women), 1 part-time/adjunct (0 women). *Financial support:* Career-related internships or fieldwork, scholarships/grants, and unspecified assistantships available. Support available to part-time students. Financial award application deadline: 4/30; financial award applicants required to submit FAFSA. In 2015, 29 master's awarded. *Degree program information:* Part-time programs available. Part-time. Offers accounting (MA); business administration (MA, MBA); economics (MA). *Application deadline:* For fall admission, 4/1 for domestic and international students; for spring admission, 11/1 for domestic and international students. Applications are processed on a rolling basis. *Application fee:* $40 ($55 for international students). Electronic applications accepted. *Application Contact:* Graduate Program Admissions, 404-880-8483, E-mail: graduateadmissions@cau.edu. *Interim Dean*, Dr. Edward L. Davis, 404-880-8475, E-mail: edavis@cau.edu.

School of Education Students: 93 full-time (66 women), 71 part-time (49 women); includes 127 minority (124 Black or African American, non-Hispanic/Latino; 3 Asian, non-Hispanic/Latino), 15 international. Average age 33. 141 applicants, 40% accepted, 40 enrolled. *Faculty:* 13 full-time (8 women), 15 part-time/adjunct (10 women). *Financial support:* Career-related internships or fieldwork, Federal Work-Study, scholarships/grants, and unspecified assistantships available. Support available to part-time students. Financial award application deadline: 4/30; financial award applicants required to submit FAFSA. In 2015, 23 master's, 5 doctorates, 1 other advanced degree awarded. *Degree program information:* Part-time and evening/weekend programs available. Part-time, evening/weekend. Offers counseling and psychological studies (MA); education (MA, MAT, Ed D, Ed S); educational leadership (MA, Ed D, Ed S); special education general curriculum (MA); teaching math and science (MAT). *Application deadline:* For fall admission, 4/1 for domestic and international students; for spring admission, 11/1 for domestic and international students. Applications are processed on a rolling basis. *Application fee:* $40 ($55 for international students). Electronic applications accepted. *Application Contact:* Graduate Program Admissions, 404-880-8483, E-mail: graduateadmissions@cau.edu. *Dean*, Dr. Moses C. Norman, 404-880-8495, E-mail: mnorman@cau.edu.

School of Social Work Students: 308 full-time (259 women), 51 part-time (43 women); includes 312 minority (309 Black or African American, non-Hispanic/Latino; 2 American Indian or Alaska Native, non-Hispanic/Latino; 1 Hispanic/Latino), 7 international. Average age 31. 328 applicants, 44% accepted, 116 enrolled. *Faculty:* 10 full-time (4 women), 26 part-time/adjunct (19 women). *Financial support:* Career-related internships or fieldwork, Federal Work-Study, scholarships/grants, and unspecified assistantships available. Support available to part-time students. Financial award application deadline: 4/30; financial award applicants required to submit FAFSA. In 2015, 130 master's, 9 doctorates awarded. *Degree program information:* Part-time programs available. Part-time. Offers social work (MSW, PhD). *Application deadline:* For fall admission, 4/1 for domestic and international students; for spring admission, 11/1 for domestic and international students. Applications are processed on a rolling basis. *Application fee:* $40 ($55 for international students). Electronic applications accepted. *Application Contact:* Graduate Program Admissions, 404-880-8483, E-mail: graduateadmissions@cau.edu. *Dean*, Dr. Dorcas Bowles, 404-880-8578, E-mail: dbowles@cau.edu.

CLARKE UNIVERSITY, Dubuque, IA 52001-3198

General Information Independent-religious, coed, comprehensive institution. *Enrollment:* 1,075 graduate, professional, and undergraduate students; 148 full-time matriculated graduate/professional students (118 women), 59 part-time matriculated graduate/professional students (49 women). *Enrollment by degree level:* 80 master's, 127 doctoral. *Graduate faculty:* 29 full-time (23 women), 9 part-time/adjunct (5 women). *Tuition, area resident:* Part-time $535 per credit hour. *Required fees:* $35 per credit hour. Tuition and fees vary according to degree level and program. *Graduate housing:* On-campus housing not available. *Student services:* Campus employment opportunities, career counseling, exercise/wellness program, free psychological counseling, low-cost health insurance, multicultural affairs office, services for students with disabilities, writing training. *Library:* Nicholas J. Schrupp Library. *Collection:* Books: 98,480 (physical), 128,000 (digital/electronic); Serial titles: 240 (physical), 68,000 (digital/electronic); Databases: 62. Weekly public service hours: 89.

Computer facilities: 237 computers available on campus for general student use. A campuswide network can be accessed from student residence rooms and from off campus. Online class registration is available.
Website: http://www.clarke.edu/

General Application Contact: Kara Schroeder, Graduate Studies Coordinator, 563-588-6635, Fax: 563-588-6789, E-mail: graduate@clarke.edu.

GRADUATE UNITS

Department of Nursing and Health Students: 54 full-time (53 women), 9 part-time (8 women); includes 1 minority (Asian, non-Hispanic/Latino). Average age 36. 45 applicants, 58% accepted, 20 enrolled. *Faculty:* 6 full-time (all women), 1 (woman) part-time/adjunct. *Financial support:* In 2015–16, 7 students received support. Scholarships/grants and tuition waivers available. Financial award applicants required to submit FAFSA. In 2015, 8 doctorates awarded. *Degree program information:* Part-time programs available. Part-time. Offers family nurse practitioner (DNP). *Application deadline:* For fall admission, 2/1 priority date for domestic students. *Application fee:* $35. Electronic applications accepted. *Application Contact:* Kara Shroeder, Graduate Studies Coordinator, 563-588-6635, Fax: 563-588-6789, E-mail: graduate@clarke.edu. *Chair*, Dr. Jan Lee, 563-588-6339, Fax: 319-584-8684.

Department of Social Work Students: 14 full-time (12 women), 1 (woman) part-time; includes 2 minority (1 American Indian or Alaska Native, non-Hispanic/Latino; 1 Hispanic/Latino). Average age 33. 25 applicants, 52% accepted, 8 enrolled. *Faculty:* 6 full-time (all women). *Financial support:* Applicants required to submit FAFSA. In 2015, 4 master's awarded. *Degree program information:* Part-time programs available. Part-time. Offers social work (MSW). *Application deadline:* For fall admission, 2/1 priority date for domestic students. *Application fee:* $35. Electronic applications accepted. *Application Contact:* Kara Schroeder, Graduate Studies Coordinator, 563-588-6635, Fax: 563-588-6789, E-mail: graduate@clarke.edu. *Chair*, Regina Boarman, 888-825-2753 Ext. 6583, E-mail: regina.boarman@clarke.edu.

Graduate Business Programs Students: 11 full-time (7 women), 34 part-time (26 women); includes 2 minority (both Asian, non-Hispanic/Latino), 1 international. Average age 35. 22 applicants, 68% accepted, 7 enrolled. *Faculty:* 6 full-time (3 women). *Financial support:* In 2015–16, 2 students received support. Scholarships/grants and tuition waivers available. Financial award application deadline: 6/1; financial award applicants required to submit FAFSA. In 2015, 16 master's awarded. *Degree program information:* Part-time and evening/weekend programs available. Part-time, evening/weekend, blended/hybrid learning. Offers business (MBA). *Application deadline:* Applications are processed on a rolling basis. *Application fee:* $35. *Application Contact:* Kara Schroeder, Graduate Studies Coordinator, 563-588-6635, Fax: 563-588-6789, E-mail: graduate@clarke.edu. *Director of Graduate Business Studies*, B'Ann Dittmar, 563-588-6419, Fax: 563-588-6789, E-mail: bann.dittmar@clarke.edu.

Physical Therapy Program Students: 63 full-time (42 women), 1 (woman) part-time. Average age 24. 167 applicants, 28% accepted, 33 enrolled. *Faculty:* 6 full-time (4 women), 6 part-time/adjunct (3 women). *Financial support:* In 2015–16, 6 students received support. Scholarships/grants and tuition waivers available. Financial award applicants required to submit FAFSA. In 2015, 30 doctorates awarded. Offers physical therapy (DPT). *Application deadline:* For fall admission, 11/2 for domestic students. *Application fee:* $0. Electronic applications accepted. *Application Contact:* Kara Shroeder, Academic Program Coordinator, 563-588-6354, Fax: 563-588-6789, E-mail: graduate@clarke.edu. *Chair*, Dr. Bill O'Dell, 319-588-6382, Fax: 319-588-8684.

Program in Education Students: 6 full-time (4 women), 13 part-time (12 women). Average age 30. 19 applicants, 84% accepted, 11 enrolled. *Faculty:* 4 full-time (all women), 2 part-time/adjunct (1 woman). *Financial support:* In 2015–16, 6 students received support. Scholarships/grants and tuition waivers available. Financial award applicants required to submit FAFSA. In 2015, 6 master's awarded. *Degree program information:* Part-time and evening/weekend programs available. Part-time, evening/weekend, 100% online, blended/hybrid learning. Offers instructional leadership (MAE). *Application deadline:* Applications are processed on a rolling basis. *Application fee:* $35. Electronic applications accepted. *Application Contact:* Kara Shroeder, Graduate Studies Coordinator, 563-588-6635, Fax: 563-588-6789, E-mail: graduate@clarke.edu. *Director of Graduate Education*, Dr. Deb Fordice, 563-588-6407, Fax: 563-588-6789, E-mail: deb.fordice@clarke.edu.

CLARKSON COLLEGE, Omaha, NE 68131-2739

General Information Independent, coed, primarily women, comprehensive institution. *Graduate housing:* Room and/or apartments available on a first-come, first-served basis to single students; on-campus housing not available to married students. Housing application deadline: 6/30.

GRADUATE UNITS

Master of Science in Nursing Program ***Degree program information:*** Part-time and evening/weekend programs available. Part-time, evening/weekend, online learning. Offers adult nurse practitioner (MSN, Post-Master's Certificate); family nurse practitioner (MSN, Post-Master's Certificate); nursing education (MSN, Post-Master's Certificate); nursing health care leadership (MSN, Post-Master's Certificate). Electronic applications accepted.

Program in Health Care Administration *Degree program information:* Part-time and evening/weekend programs available. Part-time, evening/weekend, online learning. Offers health care administration (MHCA). Electronic applications accepted.

CLARKSON UNIVERSITY, Potsdam, NY 13699

General Information Independent, coed, university. *Enrollment:* 3,910 graduate, professional, and undergraduate students; 457 full-time matriculated graduate/professional students (178 women), 150 part-time matriculated graduate/professional students (43 women). *Enrollment by degree level:* 352 master's, 255 doctoral. *Graduate faculty:* 236 full-time (64 women), 39 part-time/adjunct (16 women). *Graduate housing:* On-campus housing not available. *Student services:* Campus employment opportunities, campus safety program, career counseling, free psychological counseling, international student services, low-cost health insurance, multicultural affairs office, services for students with disabilities. *Library:* Harriet Call Burnap Memorial Library plus 1 other. *Collection:* Books: 199,436 (physical), 183,844 (digital/electronic); Serial titles: 2,209 (physical), 59,830 (digital/electronic); Databases: 140. Weekly public service hours: 99; students can reserve study rooms. *Research affiliation:* Trudeau Institute (biomedical sciences).

Computer facilities: Computer purchase and lease plans are available. 350 computers available on campus for general student use. A campuswide network can be accessed from student residence rooms and from off campus. Online class registration is available.
Website: http://www.clarkson.edu/

GRADUATE UNITS

Graduate School Students: 444 full-time (186 women), 196 part-time (38 women); includes 65 minority (13 Black or African American, non-Hispanic/Latino; 2 American Indian or Alaska Native, non-Hispanic/Latino; 24 Asian, non-Hispanic/Latino; 20 Hispanic/Latino; 6 Two or more races, non-Hispanic/Latino), 188 international. Average age 29. 1,991 applicants, 24% accepted, 252 enrolled. *Faculty:* 229 full-time (60 women), 62 part-time/adjunct (28 women). *Financial support:* In 2015–16, 475 students received support, including 15 fellowships with full tuition reimbursements available (averaging $24,510 per year), 78 research assistantships with full tuition reimbursements available (averaging $24,510 per year), 102 teaching assistantships with full tuition reimbursements available (averaging $24,510 per year); scholarships/grants, tuition waivers (partial), and unspecified assistantships also available. In 2015, 147 master's, 48 doctorates awarded. *Degree program information:* Part-time and evening/weekend programs available. Part-time, evening/weekend. Offers bioethics (MS, AC); biology (MAT); chemistry (MAT); Chinese (MAT); data analytics (MS); earth science (MAT); engineering management (MS); English (MA, MAT); English and history (MA); French (MAT); general science (MAT); German (MAT); history (MA); Latin (MAT); life sciences (MS); mathematics (MAT); mathematics and computer technology (MS); mentoring and teacher leadership (AC); middle childhood extension (AC); national board certification and teacher leadership (AC); physical sciences (MS); physics (MAT); social studies (MAT); Spanish (MAT); technology (MAT). *Application deadline:* For fall admission, 1/30 priority date for domestic and international students; for spring admission, 9/1 priority date for domestic and international students. Applications are processed on a rolling basis. *Application fee:* $25 ($35 for international students). Electronic applications accepted.

Institute for a Sustainable Environment Students: 22 full-time (9 women), 1 part-time (0 women), 13 international. Average age 26. 30 applicants, 53% accepted, 8 enrolled. *Faculty:* 9 full-time (2 women), 3 part-time/adjunct (1 woman). *Financial support:* In 2015–16, 19 students received support, including fellowships with full tuition reimbursements available (averaging $24,510 per year), 10 research assistantships with full tuition reimbursements available (averaging $24,510 per year), 4 teaching assistantships with full tuition reimbursements available (averaging $24,510 per year); scholarships/grants, tuition waivers (partial), and unspecified assistantships also available. In 2015, 4 master's, 1 doctorate awarded. *Degree program information:* Part-time programs available. Part-time. Offers environmental politics and governance (MS); environmental science and engineering (MS, PhD); sustainable environment (MS, PhD). *Application deadline:* For fall admission, 1/30 priority date for domestic and international students; for spring admission, 9/1 priority date for domestic and international students. Applications are processed on a rolling basis. *Application fee:* $25 ($35 for international students). Electronic applications accepted. *Application Contact:* Carmen Camp, Administrative Assistant, 315-268-2318, Fax: 315-268-4291, E-mail: isegrad@clarkson.edu. *Interim Director of the Institute for a Sustainable Environment/Associate Director of Sustainability,* Dr. Susan Powers, 315-268-6542, Fax: 315-268-4291, E-mail: spowers@clarkson.edu.

School of Arts and Sciences Students: 222 full-time (120 women), 6 part-time (1 woman); includes 27 minority (4 Black or African American, non-Hispanic/Latino; 2 American Indian or Alaska Native, non-Hispanic/Latino; 11 Asian, non-Hispanic/Latino; 7 Hispanic/Latino; 3 Two or more races, non-Hispanic/Latino), 53 international. Average age 27. 1,238 applicants, 10% accepted, 85 enrolled. *Faculty:* 74 full-time (26 women), 42 part-time/adjunct (23 women). *Financial support:* In 2015–16, 158 students received support, including 4 fellowships with full tuition reimbursements available (averaging $24,510 per year), 12 research assistantships with full tuition reimbursements available (averaging $24,510 per year), 59 teaching assistantships with full tuition reimbursements available (averaging $24,510 per year); scholarships/grants, tuition waivers (partial), and unspecified assistantships also available. In 2015, 41 master's, 26 doctorates awarded. *Degree program information:* Part-time programs available. Part-time. Offers arts and sciences (MS, DPT, PhD); basic science (MS); chemistry (MS, PhD); computer science (MS, PhD); information technology (MS); interdisciplinary bioscience and biotechnology (PhD); mathematics (MS, PhD); occupational therapy (MS); physical therapy (DPT); physician assistant studies (MS); physics (MS, PhD). *Application deadline:* For fall admission, 1/30 priority date for domestic and international students; for spring admission, 9/1 priority date for domestic and international students. Applications are processed on a rolling basis. *Application fee:* $25 ($35 for international students). Electronic applications accepted. *Application Contact:* Jennifer Reed, Graduate School Coordinator, Provost's Office, 315-268-3802, Fax: 315-268-3989, E-mail: sciencegrad@clarkson.edu. *Dean,* Dr. Peter Turner, 315-268-2365, Fax: 315-268-3989, E-mail: pturner@clarkson.edu.

School of Business Students: 121 full-time (58 women), 155 part-time (65 women); includes 35 minority (7 Black or African American, non-Hispanic/Latino; 23 Asian, non-Hispanic/Latino; 3 Hispanic/Latino; 2 Two or more races, non-Hispanic/Latino), 30 international. Average age 30. 355 applicants, 29% accepted, 42 enrolled. *Faculty:* 48 full-time (11 women), 19 part-time/adjunct (2 women). *Financial support:* In 2015–16, 81 students received support. Scholarships/grants available. In 2015, 121 master's, 4 other advanced degrees awarded. *Degree program information:* Part-time and evening/weekend programs available. Part-time, evening/weekend, blended/hybrid learning. Offers business administration (MBA); general management (Certificate); health data analytics (MS); health systems administration (MBA, Certificate); human resources (Certificate). *Application deadline:* For fall admission, 1/30 priority date for domestic and international students; for spring admission, 9/1 priority date for domestic and international students. Applications are processed on a rolling basis. Electronic applications accepted. *Application Contact:* Erin Dumers, Program Coordinator, 315-268-6613, Fax: 315-268-3810, E-mail: busgrad@clarkson.edu. *Dean,* Dr. Dayle M. Smith, 315-268-2300, Fax: 315-268-3810, E-mail: dsmith@clarkson.edu.

Wallace H. Coulter School of Engineering Students: 142 full-time (30 women), 143 part-time (23 women); includes 34 minority (8 Black or African American, non-Hispanic/Latino; 15 Asian, non-Hispanic/Latino; 11 Hispanic/Latino), 93 international. Average age 30. 186 applicants, 68% accepted, 28 enrolled. *Faculty:* 116 full-time (25 women), 32 part-time/adjunct (6 women). *Financial support:* In 2015–16, 129 students received support, including 10 fellowships with full tuition reimbursements available (averaging $24,510 per year), 56 research assistantships with full tuition reimbursements available (averaging $24,510 per year), 39 teaching assistantships with full tuition reimbursements available (averaging $24,510 per year); scholarships/grants, tuition waivers (partial), and unspecified assistantships also available. In 2015, 73 master's, 21 doctorates awarded. *Degree program information:* Part-time programs available. Part-time. Offers chemical engineering (ME, MS, PhD); civil and environmental engineering (ME, MS, PhD); electrical and computer engineering (PhD); electrical engineering (ME, MS); engineering (ME, MS, PhD); interdisciplinary engineering science (MS, PhD); materials science and engineering (PhD); mechanical engineering (ME, MS, PhD). *Application deadline:* For fall admission, 1/30 priority date for domestic and international students; for spring admission, 9/1 priority date for domestic and international students. Applications are processed on a rolling basis. Electronic applications accepted. *Application Contact:* Jennifer Reed, Graduate School Coordinator, Provost's Office, 315-268-3802, Fax: 315-268-3989, E-mail: jreed@clarkson.edu. *Dean,* Dr. William Jemison, 315-268-6446, Fax: 315-268-4494, E-mail: wjemison@clarkson.edu.

CLARK UNIVERSITY, Worcester, MA 01610-1477

General Information Independent, coed, university. CGS member. *Enrollment:* 3,485 graduate, professional, and undergraduate students; 831 full-time matriculated graduate/professional students (491 women), 233 part-time matriculated graduate/professional students (123 women). *Enrollment by degree level:* 854 master's, 210 doctoral. *Graduate faculty:* 205 full-time (92 women), 146 part-time/adjunct (60 women). *Tuition, area resident:* Full-time $41,590; part-time $1300 per credit hour. *Required fees:* $80. Tuition and fees vary according to course load and program. *Graduate housing:* Rooms and/or apartments available on a first-come, first-served basis to single and married students. Typical cost: $7750 per year ($9530 including board) for single students. Room and board charges vary according to board plan and housing facility selected. *Student services:* Campus employment opportunities, campus safety program, career counseling, exercise/wellness program, free psychological counseling, grant writing training, international student services, low-cost health insurance, multicultural affairs office, services for students with disabilities, teacher training, writing training. *Library:* Robert Hutchings Goddard Library plus 8 others. *Collection:* Books: 661,744 (physical), 46,250 (digital/electronic); Serial titles: 2,443 (physical), 105,990 (digital/electronic); Databases: 82. Weekly public service hours: 151; students can reserve study rooms. *Research affiliation:* Worcester Area Computation Center, Worcester Foundation for Experimental Biology, Massachusetts Biotechnology Research Institute.

Computer facilities: 322 computers available on campus for general student use. A campuswide network can be accessed from student residence rooms and from off campus. Online class registration, online course support are available.
Website: http://www.clarku.edu/

General Application Contact: Ethan Bernstein, Director of Graduate Admissions, 508-793-7676, Fax: 508-793-8834, E-mail: graduateadmissions@clarku.edu.

GRADUATE UNITS

Graduate School Students: 831 full-time (491 women), 233 part-time (123 women); includes 107 minority (35 Black or African American, non-Hispanic/Latino; 2 American Indian or Alaska Native, non-Hispanic/Latino; 26 Asian, non-Hispanic/Latino; 34 Hispanic/Latino; 1 Native Hawaiian or other Pacific Islander, non-Hispanic/Latino; 9 Two or more races, non-Hispanic/Latino), 509 international. Average age 28. 2,387 applicants, 66% accepted, 476 enrolled. *Faculty:* 205 full-time (92 women), 146 part-time/adjunct (60 women). *Financial support:* In 2015–16, 10 fellowships with tuition reimbursements (averaging $1,700 per year), 39 research assistantships with tuition reimbursements (averaging $17,000 per year), 84 teaching assistantships with tuition reimbursements (averaging $17,000 per year) were awarded; career-related internships or fieldwork, Federal Work-Study, institutionally sponsored loans, scholarships/grants, and tuition waivers (full and partial) also available. Support available to part-time students. In 2015, 467 master's, 24 doctorates, 2 other advanced degrees awarded. *Degree program information:* Part-time and evening/weekend programs available. Part-time, evening/weekend. Offers American history (MA, PhD); biology (MS, PhD); community development and planning (MA); economics (PhD); English (MA); environmental science and policy (MS); geographic information science for development and environment (MS); history (MA, CAGS); Holocaust history (PhD); international development and social change (MA); physics (PhD). *Application deadline:* Applications are processed on a rolling basis. *Application fee:* $75. Electronic applications accepted. *Application Contact:* Ethan Bernstein, Director of Graduate Admission, 508-793-7373, E-mail: gradadmissions@clarku.edu. *Associate Provost and Dean of Graduate Studies,* Dr. William Fisher, 508-793-7676.

Adam Institute for Urban Teaching and School Practice Students: 24 full-time (18 women), 6 part-time (4 women); includes 8 minority (1 Black or African American, non-Hispanic/Latino; 3 Asian, non-Hispanic/Latino; 3 Hispanic/Latino; 1 Two or more races, non-Hispanic/Latino). Average age 26. 48 applicants, 69% accepted, 29 enrolled. *Faculty:* 9 full-time (6 women), 5 part-time/adjunct (3 women). *Financial support:* Fellowships with tuition reimbursements, research assistantships with tuition reimbursements, teaching assistantships with tuition reimbursements, institutionally sponsored loans, and tuition waivers (partial) available. Financial award application deadline: 5/1. In 2015, 29 master's awarded. Offers urban teaching and school practice (MAT). *Application deadline:* For fall admission, 1/15 priority date for domestic students. Applications are processed on a rolling basis. *Application fee:* $75. *Application Contact:* Andrea Allen, Program Coordinator, 508-793-7658, E-mail: aallen@clarku.edu. *Director,* Dr. Thomas Del Prete, 508-793-7197.

College of Professional and Continuing Education Students: 93 full-time (64 women), 65 part-time (38 women); includes 15 minority (8 Black or African American, non-Hispanic/Latino; 4 Hispanic/Latino; 3 Two or more races, non-Hispanic/Latino), 94 international. Average age 29. 245 applicants, 80% accepted, 82 enrolled. *Faculty:* 36 part-time/adjunct (14 women). *Financial support:* Career-related internships or fieldwork available. Support available to part-time students. In 2015, 88 master's awarded. *Degree program information:* Part-time and evening/weekend programs available. Part-time, evening/weekend. Offers information technology (MSIT); professional communication (MSPC); public administration (MPA, Certificate). *Application deadline:* Applications are processed on a rolling basis. *Application fee:* $75. Electronic applications accepted. *Application Contact:* Ethan Bernstein, Director of Graduate Admissions, 508-793-7373, E-mail: gradadmissions@clarku.edu. *Associate Dean*, Dr. John Chetro-Szivos.

Graduate School of Management Students: 307 full-time (169 women), 120 part-time (58 women); includes 27 minority (9 Black or African American, non-Hispanic/Latino; 7 Asian, non-Hispanic/Latino; 10 Hispanic/Latino; 1 Native Hawaiian or other Pacific Islander, non-Hispanic/Latino), 259 international. Average age 28. 1,183 applicants, 79% accepted, 183 enrolled. *Faculty:* 27 full-time (12 women), 19 part-time/adjunct (6 women). *Financial support:* In 2015–16, research assistantships with partial tuition reimbursements (averaging $4,800 per year), teaching assistantships with partial tuition reimbursements (averaging $4,800 per year) were awarded; fellowships, career-related internships or fieldwork, Federal Work-Study, institutionally sponsored loans, and tuition waivers (partial) also available. Support available to part-time students. Financial award application deadline: 5/31. In 2015, 214 master's awarded. *Degree program information:* Part-time and evening/weekend programs available. Part-time, evening/weekend. Offers accounting (MSA); finance (MBA); global business (MBA); information systems (MBA); management (MBA); marketing (MBA); social change (MBA); sustainability (MBA). *Application deadline:* For fall admission, 6/1 priority date for domestic students; for spring admission, 12/1 priority date for domestic students. Applications are processed on a rolling basis. *Application fee:* $75. Electronic applications accepted. *Application Contact:* Ethan Bernstein, Director of Admissions, E-mail: graduateadmissions@clarku.edu. *Dean*, Dr. Catherine Usoff, 508-793-8822, Fax: 508-793-8822, E-mail: cusoff@clarku.edu.

Gustav H. Carlson School of Chemistry Students: 17 full-time (6 women), 2 part-time (1 woman); includes 4 minority (2 Asian, non-Hispanic/Latino; 2 Hispanic/Latino), 9 international. Average age 27. 52 applicants, 23% accepted, 5 enrolled. *Faculty:* 10 full-time (1 woman), 1 (woman) part-time/adjunct. *Financial support:* In 2015–16, fellowships with tuition reimbursements (averaging $21,875 per year), 11 teaching assistantships with full tuition reimbursements (averaging $21,875 per year) were awarded; research assistantships with full tuition reimbursements and tuition waivers (full) also available. In 2015, 5 master's awarded. Offers biochemistry (MS, PhD); chemistry (MS, PhD). *Application deadline:* For fall admission, 1/15 priority date for domestic students. Applications are processed on a rolling basis. *Application fee:* $75. *Application Contact:* Rene Baril, Managerial Secretary, 508-793-7130, Fax: 528-793-7117, E-mail: mbaril@clarku.edu. *Chair*, Dr. Luis Smith, 508-793-7753.

Hiatt School of Psychology Students: 35 full-time (31 women), 3 part-time (1 woman); includes 8 minority (1 Black or African American, non-Hispanic/Latino; 1 American Indian or Alaska Native, non-Hispanic/Latino; 2 Asian, non-Hispanic/Latino; 4 Hispanic/Latino), 5 international. Average age 29. 243 applicants, 9% accepted, 10 enrolled. *Faculty:* 16 full-time (11 women), 2 part-time/adjunct (both women). *Financial support:* In 2015–16, 8 fellowships with full tuition reimbursements (averaging $17,325 per year), 6 research assistantships with full tuition reimbursements (averaging $17,325 per year), 16 teaching assistantships with full tuition reimbursements (averaging $17,325 per year) were awarded; career-related internships or fieldwork and tuition waivers (full and partial) also available. In 2015, 9 doctorates awarded. Offers clinical psychology (PhD); developmental psychology (PhD); social psychology (PhD). *Application deadline:* For fall admission, 12/15 priority date for domestic and international students. Applications are processed on a rolling basis. *Application fee:* $75. *Application Contact:* Kelly Boulay, Departmental Administrator, 508-793-7274, Fax: 508-793-7265, E-mail: psychology@clarku.edu. *Chair*, Dr. James Cordova, 508-793-7274.

School of Geography Students: 56 full-time (27 women), 1 (woman) part-time; includes 7 minority (2 Black or African American, non-Hispanic/Latino; 2 Asian, non-Hispanic/Latino; 3 Hispanic/Latino), 23 international. Average age 31. 103 applicants, 28% accepted, 20 enrolled. *Faculty:* 17 full-time (6 women). *Financial support:* In 2015–16, 3 fellowships with full tuition reimbursements (averaging $17,325 per year), 12 research assistantships with full tuition reimbursements (averaging $17,325 per year), 16 teaching assistantships with full tuition reimbursements (averaging $17,325 per year) were awarded; career-related internships or fieldwork and tuition waivers (full) also available. In 2015, 7 master's, 7 doctorates awarded. Offers geography (MS, PhD). *Application deadline:* For fall admission, 12/31 priority date for domestic and international students. Applications are processed on a rolling basis. *Application fee:* $75. *Application Contact:* Brenda Nikas-Hayes, Admission Coordinator, 508-793-7336, Fax: 508-793-8881, E-mail: geography@clarku.edu. *Director*, Dr. Anthony Bebbington, 508-793-7336.

CLAYTON STATE UNIVERSITY, Morrow, GA 30260-0285

General Information State-supported, coed, comprehensive institution. *Enrollment:* 7,012 graduate, professional, and undergraduate students; 135 full-time matriculated graduate/professional students (92 women), 290 part-time matriculated graduate/professional students (195 women). *Enrollment by degree level:* 425 master's. *Graduate faculty:* 71 full-time (31 women), 3 part-time/adjunct (all women). Tuition, state resident: full-time $3528; part-time $196 per credit hour. Tuition, nonresident: full-time $13,176; part-time $732 per credit hour. *Required fees:* $1454; $1454 per semester. $727 per semester. Tuition and fees vary according to campus/location and program. *Graduate housing:* On-campus housing not available. *Student services:* Campus employment opportunities, career counseling, exercise/wellness program, free psychological counseling, international student services, low-cost health insurance, multicultural affairs office, services for students with disabilities. *Library:* Clayton State University Library.

Computer facilities: 3,500 computers available on campus for general student use. A campuswide network can be accessed from student residence rooms and from off campus. Online class registration is available.
Website: http://www.clayton.edu/

General Application Contact: Elizabeth Taylor, Assistant to the Dean of Graduate Studies, 678-466-4113, Fax: 678-466-4119, E-mail: elizabethtaylor@clayton.edu.

GRADUATE UNITS

School of Graduate Studies ***Financial support:*** Application deadline: 7/1; applicants required to submit FAFSA. *Application deadline:* For fall admission, 6/15 priority date for domestic students, 5/1 for international students; for spring admission, 10/15 priority date for domestic students, 9/1 for international students. Applications are processed on a rolling basis. *Application fee:* $75. Electronic applications accepted. *Application Contact:* Elizabeth Taylor. *Dean*, Dr. Gwendolyn Jones-Harold, 678-466-4113, Fax: 678-466-4119, E-mail: graduate@clayton.edu.

College of Arts and Sciences Offers applied developmental psychology (MS); arts and sciences (MA, MAT, MS); biology (MAT); clinical/counseling psychology (MS); English (MAT); history (MAT); liberal studies (MA); mathematics (MAT). *Application Contact:* Elizabeth Taylor, Assistant to the Dean of Graduate Studies, 678-466-4113, Fax: 678-466-4119, E-mail: elizabethtaylor@clayton.edu. *Dean*, Dr. Nasser Momayezi, 678-466-4705.

College of Business Students: 32 full-time (18 women), 119 part-time (61 women). In 2015, 63 master's awarded. Offers accounting (MBA); business (MBA); human resource leadership (MBA); international business (MBA); sports and entertainment management (MBA); supply chain management (MBA). *Application Contact:* Heather Chaney, MBA Program Manager, 678-466-4520, Fax: 678-466-4599, E-mail: heatherchaney@clayton.edu. *Assistant Dean/MBA Director*, Dr. Judith Ogden, 678-466-4509, E-mail: jogden@clayton.edu.

College of Health Offers family nurse practitioner (MSN); health (MHA, MSN). *Application Contact:* Elizabeth Taylor, Assistant to the Dean of Graduate Studies, 678-466-4113, Fax: 678-466-4119, E-mail: elizabethtaylor@clayton.edu. *Dean*, Dr. Lisa Eichelberger, 678-4664951, Fax: 678-466-4119, E-mail: graduate@clayton.edu.

College of Information and Mathematical Sciences Offers archival studies (MAS); information and mathematical sciences (MAS). *Application Contact:* Elizabeth Taylor, Assistant to the Dean of Graduate Studies, 678-466-4113, Fax: 678-466-4119, E-mail: elizabethtaylor@clayton.edu. *Dean*, Dr. Lila F. Roberts, 678-466-4400, Fax: 678-466-4459, E-mail: lilaroberts@clayton.edu.

CLEARY UNIVERSITY, Howell, MI 48843

General Information Independent, coed, comprehensive institution. *Graduate housing:* On-campus housing not available.

GRADUATE UNITS

Online Program in Business Administration ***Degree program information:*** Part-time and evening/weekend programs available. Part-time, evening/weekend, online learning. Offers accounting (MBA); financial planning (MBA); financial planning (Graduate Certificate); green business strategy (MBA, Graduate Certificate); health care leadership (MBA); management (MBA); nonprofit management (MBA, Graduate Certificate); organizational leadership (MBA). Electronic applications accepted.

CLEMSON UNIVERSITY, Clemson, SC 29634

General Information State-supported, coed, university. CGS member. *Enrollment:* 22,698 graduate, professional, and undergraduate students; 2,870 full-time matriculated graduate/professional students (1,183 women), 1,494 part-time matriculated graduate/professional students (760 women). *Enrollment by degree level:* 2,830 master's, 1,469 doctoral, 65 other advanced degrees. *Graduate faculty:* 1,025 full-time (362 women), 124 part-time/adjunct (47 women). Tuition, state resident: full-time $9220; part-time $582 per credit hour. Tuition, nonresident: full-time $18,406; part-time $1166 per credit hour. *Required fees:* $816; $650 per semester. $325 per semester. Tuition and fees vary according to course load and program. *Graduate housing:* On-campus housing not available. *Student services:* Campus employment opportunities, campus safety program, career counseling, exercise/wellness program, free psychological counseling, grant writing training, international student services, low-cost health insurance, multicultural affairs office, services for students with disabilities, teacher training, writing training. *Library:* Robert Muldrow Cooper Library plus 1 other. *Research affiliation:* Savannah National Research Lab (energy), Fluor Corporation (supply chain logistics), Greenville Hospital System (biological sciences), South Carolina Universities Research and Education Foundation (energy), Oak Ridge National Laboratory (materials science, physics), BMW (automotive, electrical and mechanical engineering).

Computer facilities: Computer purchase and lease plans are available. 1,250 computers available on campus for general student use. A campuswide network can be accessed from student residence rooms and from off campus. Online class registration is available.
Website: http://www.clemson.edu/

General Application Contact: Laura Kinard, Admissions Coordinator, 864-656-5336, E-mail: lkinard@clemson.edu.

GRADUATE UNITS

Graduate School Students: 2,870 full-time (1,183 women), 1,494 part-time (760 women); includes 449 minority (211 Black or African American, non-Hispanic/Latino; 5 American Indian or Alaska Native, non-Hispanic/Latino; 60 Asian, non-Hispanic/Latino; 102 Hispanic/Latino; 4 Native Hawaiian or other Pacific Islander, non-Hispanic/Latino; 67 Two or more races, non-Hispanic/Latino), 1,389 international. Average age 30. 7,965 applicants, 43% accepted, 1545 enrolled. *Faculty:* 1,025 full-time (362 women), 124 part-time/adjunct (47 women). *Financial support:* In 2015–16, 2,193 students received support, including 234 fellowships with partial tuition reimbursements available (averaging $4,205 per year), 665 research assistantships with partial tuition reimbursements available (averaging $17,932 per year), 585 teaching assistantships with partial tuition reimbursements available (averaging $16,423 per year); career-related internships or fieldwork, health care benefits, and unspecified assistantships also available. In 2015, 1,226 master's, 242 doctorates, 93 other advanced degrees awarded. *Degree program information:* Part-time and evening/weekend programs available. Part-time, evening/weekend, 100% online. Offers policy studies (PhD, Certificate). *Application deadline:* For fall admission, 4/15 for international students; for spring admission, 10/15 for international students. Applications are processed on a rolling basis. *Application fee:* $80 ($90 for international students). Electronic applications accepted. *Application Contact:* Kathleen Costello, Director of Graduate Admissions and Recruitment, 864-656-2561, Fax: 864-656-5344, E-mail: kcostel@clemson.edu. *Associate Provost and Dean of the Graduate School*, Dr. Jason Osborne, 864-656-4172, Fax: 864-656-5344, E-mail: jwo@clemson.edu.

College of Agriculture, Forestry and Life Sciences Students: 263 full-time (153 women), 273 part-time (171 women); includes 26 minority (7 Black or African American, non-Hispanic/Latino; 2 Asian, non-Hispanic/Latino; 8 Hispanic/Latino; 9 Two or more races, non-Hispanic/Latino), 61 international. Average age 31. 201 applicants, 39% accepted, 57 enrolled. *Faculty:* 112 full-time (35 women), 7 part-time/adjunct (3 women). *Financial support:* In 2015–16, 174 students received support, including 9 fellowships with partial tuition reimbursements available (averaging $4,444 per year), 106 research assistantships with partial tuition reimbursements available (averaging $16,306 per year), 54 teaching assistantships with partial tuition reimbursements available (averaging $13,864 per year); career-related internships or fieldwork, health care benefits, and unspecified assistantships also available. In 2015, 69 master's, 22 doctorates awarded. *Degree program information:* Part-time programs available. Part-time. Offers agricultural education (M Ag Ed); agriculture, forestry and life sciences (M Ag Ed, MFR, MS, PhD); animal and veterinary sciences (MS, PhD); entomology (MS, PhD); environmental toxicology (MS, PhD); food technology (PhD); food, nutrition and culinary sciences (MS); forest resources (MFR, MS, PhD); packaging science (MS); plant and environmental sciences (MS, PhD); wildlife and fisheries biology (MS, PhD). *Application deadline:* Applications are processed on a rolling basis. *Application fee:* $80 ($90 for international students). Electronic applications accepted. *Application Contact:* Dr. Joseph Culin, Associate Dean for Research and Graduate Studies, 864-656-2810, E-mail: jculin@clemson.edu. *Dean*, Dr. George Askew, 864-656-3013, Fax: 864-656-1286, E-mail: caflsdean-l@clemson.edu.

College of Architecture, Arts, and Humanities Students: 342 full-time (187 women), 29 part-time (16 women); includes 26 minority (8 Black or African American, non-Hispanic/Latino; 3 Asian, non-Hispanic/Latino; 13 Hispanic/Latino; 2 Two or more races, non-Hispanic/Latino), 87 international. Average age 27. 681 applicants, 61% accepted, 160 enrolled. *Faculty:* 230 full-time (90 women), 31 part-time/adjunct (13 women). *Financial support:* In 2015–16, 145 students received support, including 77 fellowships with partial tuition reimbursements available (averaging $2,037 per year), 35 research assistantships with partial tuition reimbursements available (averaging $6,449 per year), 80 teaching assistantships with partial tuition reimbursements available (averaging $15,821 per year); career-related internships or fieldwork, health care benefits, and unspecified assistantships also available. In 2015, 136 master's, 10 doctorates awarded. *Degree program information:* Part-time programs available. Part-time, 100% online. Offers architecture (M Arch, MS, Certificate); architecture, arts, and humanities (M Arch, MA, MCRP, MCSM, MFA, MLA, MRED, MS, PhD, Certificate); city and regional planning (MCRP); construction science and management (MCSM); English (MA); historic preservation (MS); history (MA); landscape architecture (MLA); planning, design and the built environment (PhD); professional communication (MA); real estate development (MRED); rhetorics, communication and information design (PhD); visual arts (MFA). *Application deadline:* For fall admission, 4/15 for international students; for spring admission, 9/15 for international students. Applications are processed on a rolling basis. *Application fee:* $80 ($90 for international students). Electronic applications accepted. *Application Contact:* Dr. James London, Associate Dean for Research and Graduate Studies, 864-656-3927, E-mail: london1@clemson.edu. *Dean*, Dr. Richard Goodstein, 864-656-3084, Fax: 864-656-0204, E-mail: regst@clemson.edu.

College of Behavioral, Social and Health Sciences Students: 180 full-time (127 women), 263 part-time (175 women); includes 55 minority (31 Black or African American, non-Hispanic/Latino; 1 American Indian or Alaska Native, non-Hispanic/Latino; 5 Asian, non-Hispanic/Latino; 8 Hispanic/Latino; 10 Two or more races, non-Hispanic/Latino), 39 international. Average age 33. 491 applicants, 37% accepted, 129 enrolled. *Faculty:* 168 full-time (92 women), 17 part-time/adjunct (11 women). *Financial support:* In 2015–16, 181 students received support, including 8 fellowships with partial tuition reimbursements available (averaging $5,924 per year), 22 research assistantships with partial tuition reimbursements available (averaging $17,178 per year), 132 teaching assistantships with partial tuition reimbursements available (averaging $11,150 per year); health care benefits and unspecified assistantships also available. In 2015, 114 master's, 29 doctorates, 12 other advanced degrees awarded. *Degree program information:* Part-time and evening/weekend programs available. Part-time, evening/weekend, 100% online, blended/hybrid learning. Offers applied health research and evaluation (MS, PhD); applied psychology (MS); applied sociology (MS); behavioral, social and health sciences (MA, MPA, MS, PhD, Certificate); clinical and translational research (Certificate); communication, technology and society (MA); healthcare genetics (PhD); human factors psychology (PhD); industrial-organizational psychology (PhD); international family and community studies (PhD, Certificate); nursing (MS); parks, recreation, and tourism management (MPA, MS, PhD, Certificate); public administration (MPA, Certificate); youth development leadership (MS, Certificate). *Application deadline:* Applications are processed on a rolling basis. *Application fee:* $80 ($90 for international students). Electronic applications accepted. *Application Contact:* Dr. Eric Muth, Associate Dean for Research and Graduate Programs, 864-656-6741, Fax: 864-656-7641, E-mail: muth@clemson.edu. *Interim Dean*, Dr. Brett Wright, 864-656-7640, Fax: 864-656-7641, E-mail: wright@clemson.edu.

College of Business Students: 333 full-time (130 women), 306 part-time (101 women); includes 73 minority (33 Black or African American, non-Hispanic/Latino; 12 Asian, non-Hispanic/Latino; 21 Hispanic/Latino; 2 Native Hawaiian or other Pacific Islander, non-Hispanic/Latino; 5 Two or more races, non-Hispanic/Latino), 124 international. Average age 29. 732 applicants, 59% accepted, 239 enrolled. *Faculty:* 125 full-time (37 women), 28 part-time/adjunct (6 women). *Financial support:* In 2015–16, 126 students received support, including 16 fellowships with partial tuition reimbursements available (averaging $3,188 per year), 13 research assistantships with partial tuition reimbursements available (averaging $17,527 per year), 37 teaching assistantships with partial tuition reimbursements available (averaging $19,951 per year); career-related internships or fieldwork, health care benefits, and unspecified assistantships also available. In 2015, 226 master's, 14 doctorates awarded. *Degree program information:* Part-time and evening/weekend programs available. Part-time, evening/weekend. Offers accountancy (MP Acc); applied economics (PhD); applied economics and statistics (MS); business (MA, MBA, MP Acc, MS, PhD); business administration (MBA); business analytics (MBA); economics (MA, PhD); entrepreneurship and innovation (MBA); graphic communications (MS); management (MS, PhD); marketing (MS). *Application deadline:* Applications are processed on a rolling basis. *Application fee:* $80 ($90 for international students). Electronic applications accepted. *Application Contact:* Dr. Gregory Pickett, Senior Associate Dean, 864-656-3975, E-mail: pgregor@clemson.edu. *Interim Dean*, Dr. Robert McCormick, 864-656-3178, E-mail: sixmile@clemson.edu.

College of Education Students: 255 full-time (182 women), 356 part-time (243 women); includes 127 minority (86 Black or African American, non-Hispanic/Latino; 3 American Indian or Alaska Native, non-Hispanic/Latino; 6 Asian, non-Hispanic/Latino; 22 Hispanic/Latino; 10 Two or more races, non-Hispanic/Latino), 10 international. Average age 34. 578 applicants, 76% accepted, 336 enrolled. *Faculty:* 71 full-time (48 women), 5 part-time/adjunct (all women). *Financial support:* In 2015–16, 147 students received support, including 22 fellowships with partial tuition reimbursements available (averaging $5,403 per year), 8 research assistantships with partial tuition reimbursements available (averaging $13,739 per year), 25 teaching assistantships with partial tuition reimbursements available (averaging $13,131 per year); health care benefits and unspecified assistantships also available. In 2015, 167 master's, 19 doctorates, 37 other advanced degrees awarded. *Degree program information:* Part-time and evening/weekend programs available. Part-time, evening/weekend, 100% online. Offers administration and supervision (M Ed, Ed S); administration and supervision (K-12) (M Ed, Ed S); athletic leadership (MS, Certificate); clinical mental health counseling (M Ed); counselor education (M Ed, Ed S); curriculum and instruction (PhD); education and organizational leadership (MS, Certificate); educational leadership (PhD); higher education (PhD); human resource development (MHRD); leadership (Certificate); learning sciences (PhD); literacy (M Ed); literacy, language and culture (PhD); middle level education (MAT); middle-level education (MAT); P-12 (PhD); school counseling (M Ed); secondary education: math and science (MAT); secondary math and science (MAT); secondary mathematics (MAT); secondary science (MAT); special education (M Ed, MAT, PhD); STEAM education (Certificate); student affairs (M Ed); teaching and learning (M Ed). *Application deadline:* Applications are processed on a rolling basis. *Application fee:* $80 ($90 for international students). Electronic applications accepted. *Application Contact:* Dr. David Fleming, Graduate Programs Coordinator, 864-656-1881, Fax: 864-656-0311, E-mail: dflemin@clemson.edu. *Dean*, Dr. George Petersen, 864-656-4444, Fax: 864-656-0311, E-mail: soedean@clemson.edu.

College of Engineering, Computing and Applied Sciences Students: 1,200 full-time (301 women), 272 part-time (66 women); includes 91 minority (31 Black or African American, non-Hispanic/Latino; 1 American Indian or Alaska Native, non-Hispanic/Latino; 19 Asian, non-Hispanic/Latino; 20 Hispanic/Latino; 1 Native Hawaiian or other Pacific Islander, non-Hispanic/Latino; 19 Two or more races, non-Hispanic/Latino), 883 international. Average age 27. 3,853 applicants, 29% accepted, 401 enrolled. *Faculty:* 236 full-time (48 women), 37 part-time/adjunct (7 women). *Financial support:* In 2015–16, 890 students received support, including 85 fellowships with partial tuition reimbursements available (averaging $5,816 per year), 391 research assistantships with partial tuition reimbursements available (averaging $18,871 per year), 209 teaching assistantships with partial tuition reimbursements available (averaging $16,921 per year); career-related internships or fieldwork, health care benefits, and unspecified assistantships also available. In 2015, 386 master's, 104 doctorates, 7 other advanced degrees awarded. *Degree program information:* Part-time programs available. Part-time, 100% online. Offers automotive engineering (MS, PhD); bioengineering (MS, PhD); biomedical engineering (M Eng); biosystems engineering (MS, PhD); chemical and biomolecular engineering (MS, PhD); civil engineering (MS, PhD); computer engineering (MS, PhD); computer science (MS, PhD); digital production arts (MFA); electrical engineering (M Engr, MS, PhD); engineering, computing and applied sciences (M Eng, M Engr, MFA, MS, PhD, Certificate); environmental engineering and science (MS, PhD); environmental health physics (MS); human-centered computing (PhD); hydrogeology (MS); industrial engineering (M Eng, MS, PhD); materials science and engineering (MS, PhD); mechanical engineering (MS, PhD); medical device recycling and reprocessing (Certificate). *Application deadline:* Applications are processed on a rolling basis. *Application fee:* $80 ($90 for international students). Electronic applications accepted. *Application Contact:* Dr. Douglas Hirt, Interim Associate Dean for Research and Graduate Studies, 864-656-1899, E-mail: hirtd@clemson.edu. *Dean*, Dr. Anand Gramopadhye, 864-656-3200, E-mail: agrampo@clemson.edu.

College of Science Students: 351 full-time (151 women), 208 part-time (140 women); includes 49 minority (14 Black or African American, non-Hispanic/Latino; 13 Asian, non-Hispanic/Latino; 10 Hispanic/Latino; 1 Native Hawaiian or other Pacific Islander, non-Hispanic/Latino; 11 Two or more races, non-Hispanic/Latino), 173 international. Average age 27. 502 applicants, 48% accepted, 107 enrolled. *Faculty:* 160 full-time (48 women), 17 part-time/adjunct (10 women). *Financial support:* In 2015–16, 17 fellowships with partial tuition reimbursements (averaging $4,443 per year), 64 research assistantships with partial tuition reimbursements (averaging $21,069 per year), 185 teaching assistantships with partial tuition reimbursements (averaging $20,721 per year) were awarded; career-related internships or fieldwork and health care benefits also available. In 2015, 130 master's, 41 doctorates awarded. *Degree program information:* Part-time programs available. Part-time, 100% online. Offers biochemistry and molecular biology (PhD); biological sciences (MS, PhD); biological sciences for science educators (MBS); chemistry (MS, PhD); genetics (PhD); mathematical sciences (MS, PhD); microbiology (MS, PhD); physics and astronomy (MS, PhD); science (MBS, MS, PhD). *Application deadline:* Applications are processed on a rolling basis. *Application fee:* $80 ($90 for international students). Electronic applications accepted. *Application Contact:* Dr. Brian Dominy, Interim Associate Dean for Academic Affairs, 864-656-7702, E-mail: dominy@clemson.edu. *Interim Dean*, Dr. Mark Leising, 864-656-7137, E-mail: lmark@clemson.edu.

CLEVELAND INSTITUTE OF MUSIC, Cleveland, OH 44106-1776

General Information Independent, coed, comprehensive institution. *Graduate housing:* Room and/or apartments available on a first-come, first-served basis to single students; on-campus housing not available to married students. Housing application deadline: 5/30.

GRADUATE UNITS

Graduate Programs Offers performance (MM, DMA, AD, CPS). DMA and MM programs offered jointly with Case Western Reserve University. Electronic applications accepted.

CLEVELAND STATE UNIVERSITY, Cleveland, OH 44115

General Information State-supported, coed, university. CGS member. *Enrollment:* 17,260 graduate, professional, and undergraduate students; 1,818 full-time matriculated graduate/professional students (1,060 women), 3,309 part-time matriculated graduate/professional students (1,890 women). *Enrollment by degree level:* 4,204 master's, 923 doctoral. *Graduate faculty:* 369 full-time (142 women), 201 part-time/adjunct (96 women). Tuition, state resident: full-time $9565. Tuition, nonresident: full-time $17,980. Tuition and fees vary according to program. *Graduate housing:* Room and/or apartments available on a first-come, first-served basis to single students; on-campus housing not available to married students. Housing application deadline: 7/15. *Student services:* Campus employment opportunities, campus safety program, career counseling, exercise/wellness program, free psychological counseling, international student services, low-cost health insurance, multicultural affairs office, services for students with disabilities, teacher training, writing training. *Library:* Michael Schwartz Library plus 1 other. *Collection:* Books: 541,904 (physical), 137,302 (digital/electronic); Serial titles: 6,156 (physical), 203 (digital/electronic); Databases: 733. Students can reserve study rooms. *Research affiliation:* Cleveland Clinic Foundation, Metro Health System.

Computer facilities: Computer purchase and lease plans are available. 736 computers available on campus for general student use. A campuswide network can be accessed from student residence rooms and from off campus. Online class registration, each general purpose computer lab has a scanner and printer; students are allowed free black and white printing up to 2,000 pages per semester are available.
Website: http://www.csuohio.edu/

General Application Contact: Dianne C. Oloff, Graduate Student Services Specialist, 216-687-5230, Fax: 216-875-9933, E-mail: d.oloff@csuohio.edu.

GRADUATE UNITS

Cleveland-Marshall College of Law Students: 247 full-time (109 women), 181 part-time (111 women); includes 83 minority (40 Black or African American, non-Hispanic/Latino; 2 American Indian or Alaska Native, non-Hispanic/Latino; 10 Asian, non-Hispanic/Latino; 21 Hispanic/Latino; 10 Two or more races, non-Hispanic/Latino), 6 international. Average age 29. 711 applicants, 44% accepted, 118 enrolled. *Faculty:* 34 full-time (17 women), 61 part-time/adjunct (16 women). *Financial support:* In 2015–16, 198 students received support, including 17 fellowships (averaging $2,500 per year), 34 research assistantships, 7 teaching assistantships with partial tuition reimbursements available (averaging $6,700 per year); career-related internships or fieldwork, Federal Work-Study, scholarships/grants, and unspecified assistantships also available. Support available to part-time students. Financial award application deadline: 5/1; financial award applicants required to submit FAFSA. In 2015, 2 master's, 110 doctorates, 5 Certificates awarded. *Degree program information:* Part-time and evening/weekend programs available. Part-time, evening/weekend. Offers business law (JD); civil litigation and dispute resolution (JD); criminal law (JD); employment labor law (JD); health care compliance (Certificate); health law (Certificate); international and comparative law (JD); law (LL M, MLS). *Application deadline:* For fall admission, 5/1 for domestic and international students. Applications are processed on a rolling basis. *Application fee:* $0. Electronic applications accepted. *Application Contact:* Christopher Lucak, Assistant Dean for Admission and Financial Aid, 216-687-2304, Fax: 216-687-6881, E-mail: law.admissions@csuohio.edu. *Dean*, Craig M. Boise, 216-687-2300, Fax: 216-687-6881, E-mail: c.boise@csuohio.edu.

College of Graduate Studies Students: 2,022 full-time (1,128 women), 2,373 part-time (1,418 women); includes 1,009 minority (701 Black or African American, non-Hispanic/Latino; 3 American Indian or Alaska Native, non-Hispanic/Latino; 113 Asian, non-Hispanic/Latino; 129 Hispanic/Latino; 2 Native Hawaiian or other Pacific Islander, non-Hispanic/Latino; 61 Two or more races, non-Hispanic/Latino), 895 international. Average age 31. 4,931 applicants, 46% accepted, 966 enrolled. *Faculty:* 383 full-time (145 women), 151 part-time/adjunct (55 women). *Financial support:* In 2015–16, 306 research assistantships with tuition reimbursements (averaging $3,480 per year), 123 teaching assistantships with tuition reimbursements (averaging $3,480 per year) were awarded; career-related internships or fieldwork, scholarships/grants, tuition waivers (full and partial), and unspecified assistantships also available. Financial award applicants required to submit FAFSA. In 2015, 1,458 master's, 97 doctorates, 15 other advanced degrees awarded. *Degree program information:* Part-time and evening/weekend programs available. Part-time, evening/weekend, 100% online, blended/hybrid learning. *Application deadline:* For fall admission, 7/1 priority date for domestic students, 5/15 priority date for international students; for spring admission, 11/15 priority date for domestic students, 11/1 priority date for international students; for summer admission, 4/1 for domestic students, 3/15 for international students. Applications are processed on a rolling basis. *Application fee:* $30. Electronic applications accepted. *Application Contact:* Dianne C. Oloff, Graduate Student Services Specialist, 216-523-7572, Fax: 216-875-9933, E-mail: d.oloff@csuohio.edu. *Dean, College of Graduate Studies*, Dr. Jianping Zhu, 216-687-3595, Fax: 216-875-9933, E-mail: j.zhu94@csuohio.edu.

College of Education and Human Services Students: 231 full-time (175 women), 677 part-time (522 women); includes 286 minority (229 Black or African American, non-Hispanic/Latino; 1 American Indian or Alaska Native, non-Hispanic/Latino; 11 Asian, non-Hispanic/Latino; 29 Hispanic/Latino; 1 Native Hawaiian or other Pacific Islander, non-Hispanic/Latino; 15 Two or more races, non-Hispanic/Latino), 86 international. Average age 33. 487 applicants, 58% accepted, 178 enrolled. *Faculty:* 86 full-time (60 women), 106 part-time/adjunct (81 women). *Financial support:* In 2015–16, 64 students received support, including 38 research assistantships with full tuition reimbursements available (averaging $6,960 per year), 2 teaching assistantships with full tuition reimbursements available (averaging $7,800 per year); career-related internships or fieldwork, Federal Work-Study, scholarships/grants, tuition waivers (partial), and unspecified assistantships also available. Support available to part-time students. Financial award application deadline: 8/1; financial award applicants required to submit FAFSA. In 2015, 325 master's, 12 doctorates, 4 other advanced degrees awarded. *Degree program information:* Part-time and evening/weekend programs available. Part-time, evening/weekend, 100% online, blended/hybrid learning. Offers adult learning and development (M Ed); adult, continuing, and higher education (PhD); art education (M Ed); chemical dependency counseling (Certificate); clinical mental health counseling (M Ed); community health education (M Ed); counseling psychology (PhD); counselor education (PhD); early childhood education (M Ed); early childhood mental health counseling (Certificate); education and human services (M Ed, MPH, PhD, Certificate, Ed S); educational administration and supervision (M Ed); exercise science (M Ed); foreign language education (M Ed); human performance (M Ed); learning and development (PhD); middle childhood education (M Ed); middle childhood mathematics and science education (M Ed); nursing education (PhD); organizational leadership (M Ed); physical education pedagogy (M Ed); policy studies (PhD); public health (MPH); school administration (PhD, Ed S); school counseling (M Ed); school health education (M Ed); special education (M Ed); sport and exercise psychology (M Ed); sports management (M Ed); teaching English to speakers of other languages (M Ed). *Application deadline:* For fall admission, 7/1 priority date for domestic students, 5/15 for international students; for spring admission, 11/15 priority date for domestic students, 11/1 for international students; for summer admission, 4/1 for domestic students, 3/15 for international students. Applications are processed on a rolling basis. *Application fee:* $30. Electronic applications accepted. *Application Contact:* Patricia Sokolowski, Office Coordinator/Assistant to the Dean, 216-523-7143, Fax: 216-687-5415, E-mail: p.sokolowski@csuohio.edu. *Dean*, Dr. Sajit Zachariah, 216-523-7143, Fax: 216-687-5415, E-mail: sajit.zachariah@csuohio.edu.

College of Liberal Arts and Social Sciences Students: 266 full-time (191 women), 215 part-time (146 women); includes 174 minority (134 Black or African American, non-Hispanic/Latino; 4 Asian, non-Hispanic/Latino; 25 Hispanic/Latino; 11 Two or more races, non-Hispanic/Latino), 25 international. Average age 34. 499 applicants, 46% accepted, 123 enrolled. *Faculty:* 156 full-time (64 women), 184 part-time/adjunct (79 women). *Financial support:* In 2015–16, 99 research assistantships with tuition reimbursements (averaging $4,172 per year), 67 teaching assistantships with tuition reimbursements (averaging $4,657 per year) were awarded; fellowships, career-related internships or fieldwork, Federal Work-Study, institutionally sponsored loans, tuition waivers (full and partial), and unspecified assistantships also available. Support available to part-time students. Financial award applicants required to submit FAFSA. In 2015, 180 master's awarded. *Degree program information:* Part-time and evening/weekend programs available. Part-time, evening/weekend. Offers applied communication theory and methodology (MA); art history (MA); bioethics (MA, Certificate); composition (MM); creative writing (MA, MFA); culture, communication and health care (Certificate); economics (MA); French (M Ed); global interactions (MA); history (MA); liberal arts and social sciences (M Ed, MA, MFA, MM, MSW, Certificate); literature (MA); museum studies (MA); music education (MM); performance (MM); philosophy (MA); social work (MSW); sociology (MA); Spanish (M Ed, MA). *Application deadline:* For fall admission, 7/1 priority date for domestic students, 5/15 for international students; for spring admission, 11/15 priority date for domestic students, 11/1 for international students; for summer admission, 4/1 for domestic students, 3/15 for international students. Applications are processed on a rolling basis. *Application fee:* $30. Electronic applications accepted. *Application Contact:* Deborah L. Brown, Interim Assistant Director, Graduate Admissions, 216-523-7572, Fax: 216-687-5400, E-mail: d.l.brown@csuohio.edu. *Dean*, Dr. Gregory M. Sadlek, 216-687-3660.

College of Sciences and Health Professions Students: 595 full-time (412 women), 225 part-time (153 women); includes 113 minority (56 Black or African American, non-Hispanic/Latino; 1 American Indian or Alaska Native, non-Hispanic/Latino; 24 Asian, non-Hispanic/Latino; 24 Hispanic/Latino; 8 Two or more races, non-Hispanic/Latino), 107 international. Average age 28. 912 applicants, 34% accepted, 204 enrolled. *Faculty:* 107 full-time (35 women), 76 part-time/adjunct (43 women). *Financial support:* In 2015–16, 174 students received support, including 47 research assistantships with full tuition reimbursements available (averaging $17,000 per year), 127 teaching assistantships with tuition reimbursements available (averaging $10,700 per year); unspecified assistantships also available. Financial award applicants required to submit FAFSA. In 2015, 195 master's, 50 doctorates, 14 other advanced degrees awarded. *Degree program information:* Part-time and evening/weekend programs available. Part-time, evening/weekend, online learning. Offers analytical chemistry (MS); applied optics (MS); applied statistics (MS); biology (MS); clinical chemistry (PhD); condensed matter physics (MS); environmental science (MS); health sciences (MS); inorganic chemistry (MS); mathematics (MS); medical physics (MS); occupational therapy (MOT); optics and materials (MS); optics and medical imaging (MS); organic chemistry (MS); physical chemistry (MS); physical therapy (DPT); physician assistant science (MS); psychology (MA, PhD, Psy S); regulatory biology (PhD); sciences and health professions (MA, MOT, MS, DPT, PhD, Psy S); speech pathology and audiology (MA). *Application deadline:* For fall admission, 7/1 priority date for domestic students, 5/15 priority date for international students; for spring admission, 11/15 priority date for domestic students, 11/1 priority date for international students; for summer admission, 4/1 for domestic students, 3/15 for international students. Applications are processed on a rolling basis. *Application fee:* $30. Electronic applications accepted. *Application Contact:* Dianne C. Oloff, Graduate Student Services Specialist, 216-687-5230, Fax: 216-875-9933, E-mail: d.oloff@csuohio.edu. *Dean of the College of Graduate Studies*, Dr. Jianping Zhu, 216-687-3595, Fax: 216-875-9933, E-mail: j.zhu94@csuohio.edu.

Fenn College of Engineering Students: 479 full-time (98 women), 239 part-time (45 women); includes 37 minority (13 Black or African American, non-Hispanic/Latino; 17 Asian, non-Hispanic/Latino; 3 Hispanic/Latino; 4 Two or more races, non-Hispanic/Latino), 502 international. Average age 26. 1,037 applicants, 48% accepted, 143 enrolled. *Faculty:* 54 full-time (5 women), 12 part-time/adjunct (0 women). *Financial support:* In 2015–16, 93 students received support, including 1 fellowship with full tuition reimbursement available, 120 research assistantships with tuition reimbursements available (averaging $8,694 per year), 20 teaching assistantships with tuition reimbursements available (averaging $8,082 per year); career-related internships or fieldwork, institutionally sponsored loans, scholarships/grants, tuition waivers (full and partial), and unspecified assistantships also available. Support available to part-time students. Financial award application deadline: 3/30; financial award applicants required to submit FAFSA. In 2015, 131 master's, 5 doctorates awarded. *Degree program information:* Part-time and evening/weekend programs available. Part-time, evening/weekend. Offers accelerated civil engineering (MS); accelerated environmental engineering (MS); applied biomedical engineering (D Eng); chemical engineering (MS, D Eng); civil engineering (MS, D Eng); electrical engineering (MS, D Eng); engineering (MS, D Eng); engineering mechanics (MS); environmental engineering (MS); industrial engineering (MS, D Eng); mechanical engineering (MS, D Eng); software engineering (MS). *Application deadline:* For fall admission, 7/15 for domestic students, 5/15 for international students; for spring admission, 12/5 for domestic students, 11/1 for international students. Applications are processed on a rolling basis. *Application fee:* $30. Electronic applications accepted. *Application Contact:* Deborah L. Brown, Interim Assistant Director, Graduate Admissions, 216-523-7572, Fax: 216-687-9214, E-mail: d.l.brown@csuohio.edu. *Associate Dean*, Dr. Paul P. Lin, 216-687-2556, Fax: 216-687-9280, E-mail: p.lin@csuohio.edu.

Maxine Goodman Levin College of Urban Affairs Students: 53 full-time (30 women), 142 part-time (79 women); includes 52 minority (40 Black or African American, non-Hispanic/Latino; 1 American Indian or Alaska Native, non-Hispanic/Latino; 4 Asian, non-Hispanic/Latino; 5 Hispanic/Latino; 2 Two or more races, non-Hispanic/Latino), 14 international. Average age 33. 195 applicants, 47% accepted, 38 enrolled. *Faculty:* 22 full-time (9 women), 8 part-time/adjunct (4 women). *Financial support:* In 2015–16, 60 students received support, including 40 research assistantships with full tuition reimbursements available (averaging $8,000 per year), 15 teaching assistantships with tuition reimbursements available (averaging $7,000 per year); career-related internships or fieldwork, Federal Work-Study, institutionally sponsored loans, scholarships/grants, and unspecified assistantships also available. Support available to part-time students. Financial award application deadline: 3/1; financial award applicants required to submit FAFSA. In 2015, 75 master's, 3 doctorates awarded. *Degree program information:* Part-time and evening/weekend programs available. Part-time, evening/weekend. Offers city management (MPA); communication (PhD); community and neighborhood development (MS); economic development (MPA, MS, MUPDD); environmental nonprofit management (MAES); environmental planning (MAES); environmental sustainability (MUPDD); geographic information systems (MUPDD, Certificate); healthcare administration (MPA); historic preservation (MUPDD); housing and neighborhood development (MUPDD); local and urban management (Certificate); non-profit management (MPA, Certificate); nonprofit administration and leadership (MNAL); nonprofit management (Certificate); policy and administration (MAES); public administration (PhD); public finance (MS); public financial management (MPA); public management (MPA); sustainable economic development (MAES); urban affairs (MAES, MNAL, MPA, MS, MUPDD, PhD, Certificate); urban economic development (Certificate); urban policy analysis (MS); urban policy and development (PhD); urban real estate development and finance (MS, MUPDD, Certificate). *Application deadline:* For fall admission, 7/1 priority date for domestic students, 5/15 for international students; for spring admission, 11/15 for domestic students, 11/1 for international students; for summer admission, 4/1 for domestic students, 3/15 for international students. Applications are processed on a rolling basis. *Application fee:* $30. Electronic applications accepted. *Application Contact:* Graduate Program Coordinator, 216-523-7522, Fax: 216-687-5398, E-mail: urbanprograms@csuohio.edu. *Dean*, Dr. Roland V. Anglin, 216-687-2135, E-mail: r.anglin@csuohio.edu.

Monte Ahuja College of Business Students: 305 full-time (144 women), 553 part-time (256 women); includes 185 minority (97 Black or African American, non-Hispanic/Latino; 50 Asian, non-Hispanic/Latino; 25 Hispanic/Latino; 13 Two or more races, non-Hispanic/Latino), 152 international. Average age 31. 1,052 applicants,

46% accepted, 258 enrolled. *Faculty:* 48 full-time (16 women), 33 part-time/adjunct (12 women). *Financial support:* In 2015–16, 110 students received support, including 45 research assistantships with full tuition reimbursements available (averaging $6,960 per year), 1 teaching assistantship with full tuition reimbursement available (averaging $7,800 per year); career-related internships or fieldwork, scholarships/grants, tuition waivers (full), and unspecified assistantships also available. Financial award application deadline: 5/15; financial award applicants required to submit FAFSA. In 2015, 428 master's, 5 doctorates awarded. *Degree program information:* Part-time and evening/weekend programs available. Part-time, evening/weekend. Offers business (AMBA, EMBA, M Acc, MBA, MCIS, MLRHR, DBA, Graduate Certificate); business administration (AMBA, MBA); computer and information science (MCIS); executive business administration (EMBA); finance (DBA); financial accounting/audit (M Acc); global business (DBA, Graduate Certificate); health care administration (MBA); information systems (DBA); labor relations and human resources (MLRHR); marketing (MBA, DBA); marketing analytics (Graduate Certificate); operations management (DBA); taxation (M Acc). *Application deadline:* For fall admission, 7/1 priority date for domestic students, 5/15 for international students; for spring admission, 11/15 priority date for domestic students, 11/1 for international students; for summer admission, 4/1 for domestic students, 3/15 for international students. Applications are processed on a rolling basis. *Application fee:* $30. Electronic applications accepted. *Application Contact:* Kenneth Dippong, Director, Student Services, 216-523-7545, Fax: 216-687-9354, E-mail: k.dippong@csuohio.edu. *Dean,* Dr. Robert F. Scherer, 216-687-3786, Fax: 216-687-9354, E-mail: r.scherer@csuohio.edu.

School of Nursing Students: 7 full-time (all women), 43 part-time (42 women); includes 14 minority (12 Black or African American, non-Hispanic/Latino; 1 Asian, non-Hispanic/Latino; 1 Hispanic/Latino). Average age 37. 60 applicants, 62% accepted, 26 enrolled. *Faculty:* 7 full-time (all women). *Financial support:* Tuition waivers (full) and unspecified assistantships available. Financial award application deadline: 5/1; financial award applicants required to submit FAFSA. In 2015, 11 master's awarded. *Degree program information:* Part-time programs available. Part-time, 100% online. Offers clinical nurse leader (MSN); forensic nursing (MSN); nursing education (MSN); specialized population (MSN); urban education (PhD). *Application deadline:* For fall admission, 3/1 priority date for domestic and international students. *Application fee:* $55. Electronic applications accepted. *Application Contact:* Maureen Mitchell, Assistant Professor and Graduate Program Director, 216-523-7128, Fax: 216-687-3556, E-mail: m.m.mitchell1@csuohio.edu. *Dean,* Dr. Vida Lock, 216-523-7237, Fax: 216-687-3556, E-mail: v.lock@csuohio.edu.

CLEVELAND UNIVERSITY–KANSAS CITY, Overland Park, KS 66210

General Information Independent, coed, comprehensive institution. *Graduate housing:* On-campus housing not available.

GRADUATE UNITS

Professional Program ***Degree program information:*** Part-time programs available. Part-time. Offers chiropractic (DC). Electronic applications accepted.

Program in Health Promotion ***Degree program information:*** Part-time programs available. Part-time. Offers health promotion (MSHP). Electronic applications accepted.

COASTAL CAROLINA UNIVERSITY, Conway, SC 29528-6054

General Information State-supported, coed, comprehensive institution. *Enrollment:* 10,263 graduate, professional, and undergraduate students; 195 full-time matriculated graduate/professional students (113 women), 344 part-time matriculated graduate/professional students (246 women). *Enrollment by degree level:* 489 master's, 4 doctoral, 46 other advanced degrees. *Graduate faculty:* 66 full-time (26 women), 18 part-time/adjunct (6 women). Tuition, state resident: full-time $9666; part-time $537 per credit hour. Tuition, nonresident: full-time $17,532; part-time $974 per credit hour. *Required fees:* $90; $5 per credit hour. *Graduate housing:* Room and/or apartments available on a first-come, first-served basis to single students; on-campus housing not available to married students. Typical cost: $8690 (including board). Room and board charges vary according to board plan and housing facility selected. Housing application deadline: 5/1. *Student services:* Campus employment opportunities, campus safety program, career counseling, exercise/wellness program, free psychological counseling, grant writing training, international student services, low-cost health insurance, multicultural affairs office, services for students with disabilities, teacher training, writing training. *Library:* Kimbel Library. *Collection:* Books: 130,794 (physical), 349,735 (digital/electronic); Serial titles: 555 (physical), 45,000 (digital/electronic); Databases: 202. Weekly public service hours: 168; study areas open 24 hours, 5–7 days a week.

Computer facilities: Computer purchase and lease plans are available. 1,200 computers available on campus for general student use. A campuswide network can be accessed from student residence rooms and from off campus. Online class registration is available.
Website: http://www.coastal.edu/

General Application Contact: Dr. James O. Luken, Associate Provost/Director of Graduate Studies, 843-349-2235, Fax: 843-349-6444, E-mail: joluken@coastal.edu.

GRADUATE UNITS

College of Science Students: 29 full-time (16 women), 12 part-time (8 women), 2 international. Average age 25. 32 applicants, 63% accepted, 19 enrolled. *Faculty:* 21 full-time (5 women), 1 part-time/adjunct (0 women). *Financial support:* Fellowships, research assistantships, and unspecified assistantships available. Support available to part-time students. Financial award application deadline: 3/1; financial award applicants required to submit FAFSA. In 2015, 11 master's awarded. *Degree program information:* Part-time and evening/weekend programs available. Part-time, evening/weekend. Offers applied computing and information systems (Certificate); coastal marine and wetland studies (MS); marine science (PhD); sports management (MS). *Application deadline:* For fall admission, 1/15 priority date for domestic and international students; for spring admission, 11/1 priority date for domestic and international students. Applications are processed on a rolling basis. *Application fee:* $45. Electronic applications accepted. *Application Contact:* Dr. James O. Luken, Associate Provost/Director of Graduate Studies, 843-349-2235, Fax: 843-349-6444, E-mail: joluken@coastal.edu. *Dean,* Dr. Michael H. Roberts, 843-349-2282, Fax: 843-349-2545, E-mail: mroberts@coastal.edu.

E. Craig Wall, Sr. College of Business Administration Students: 56 full-time (19 women), 34 part-time (14 women); includes 17 minority (14 Black or African American, non-Hispanic/Latino; 1 Asian, non-Hispanic/Latino; 1 Hispanic/Latino; 1 Two or more races, non-Hispanic/Latino), 10 international. Average age 28. 80 applicants, 84% accepted, 51 enrolled. *Faculty:* 12 full-time (5 women), 3 part-time/adjunct (0 women). *Financial support:* Fellowships, research assistantships, and unspecified assistantships available. Support available to part-time students. Financial award application deadline: 3/1; financial award applicants required to submit FAFSA. In 2015, 61 master's, 6 other advanced degrees awarded. *Degree program information:* Part-time and evening/weekend programs available. Part-time, evening/weekend. Offers accounting (M Acc); business administration (MBA); business foundations (Certificate); fraud examination (Certificate). *Application deadline:* For fall admission, 6/15 priority date for domestic and international students; for spring admission, 11/15 priority date for domestic and international students; for summer admission, 4/15 priority date for domestic and international students. Applications are processed on a rolling basis. *Application fee:* $45. Electronic applications accepted. *Application Contact:* Dr. James O. Luken, Associate Provost/Director of Graduate Studies, 843-349-2235, Fax: 843-349-6444, E-mail: joluken@coastal.edu. *Associate Professor/Director of Graduate Programs and Executive Education,* Dr. Arlise P. McKinney, 843-349-2390, Fax: 843-349-2455, E-mail: amckinney@coastal.edu.

Thomas W. and Robin W. Edwards College of Humanities and Fine Arts Students: 26 full-time (21 women), 11 part-time (7 women); includes 4 minority (2 Black or African American, non-Hispanic/Latino; 2 Hispanic/Latino). Average age 33. 19 applicants, 79% accepted, 12 enrolled. *Faculty:* 14 full-time (7 women), 1 part-time/adjunct (0 women). *Financial support:* Fellowships, research assistantships, and unspecified assistantships available. Support available to part-time students. Financial award application deadline: 3/1; financial award applicants required to submit FAFSA. In 2015, 6 master's awarded. *Degree program information:* Part-time and evening/weekend programs available. Part-time, evening/weekend. Offers liberal studies (MA); writing (MA). *Application deadline:* For fall admission, 5/15 priority date for domestic and international students; for spring admission, 11/15 priority date for domestic and international students. Applications are processed on a rolling basis. *Application fee:* $45. Electronic applications accepted. *Application Contact:* Dr. James O. Luken, Associate Provost/Director of Graduate Studies, 843-349-2235, Fax: 843-349-6444, E-mail: joluken@coastal.edu. *Associate Professor/Coordinator of Graduate Study,* Joseph R. Oestreich, 843-349-2433, E-mail: joeo@coastal.edu.

William L. Spadoni College of Education Students: 84 full-time (57 women), 287 part-time (217 women); includes 68 minority (59 Black or African American, non-Hispanic/Latino; 1 American Indian or Alaska Native, non-Hispanic/Latino; 1 Asian, non-Hispanic/Latino; 4 Hispanic/Latino; 1 Native Hawaiian or other Pacific Islander, non-Hispanic/Latino; 2 Two or more races, non-Hispanic/Latino), 1 international. Average age 33. 314 applicants, 95% accepted, 175 enrolled. *Faculty:* 17 full-time (8 women), 13 part-time/adjunct (6 women). *Financial support:* Fellowships, research assistantships, and unspecified assistantships available. Support available to part-time students. Financial award application deadline: 3/1; financial award applicants required to submit FAFSA. In 2015, 169 master's, 1 other advanced degree awarded. *Degree program information:* Part-time and evening/weekend programs available. Part-time, evening/weekend. Offers education (MAT); educational leadership (M Ed, Ed S); English for speakers of other languages (Certificate); instructional technology (Ed S); learning and teaching (M Ed); online teaching and training (Certificate). *Application deadline:* For fall admission, 7/1 priority date for domestic and international students; for spring admission, 11/1 priority date for domestic and international students; for summer admission, 3/1 priority date for domestic and international students. Applications are processed on a rolling basis. *Application fee:* $45. Electronic applications accepted. *Application Contact:* Dr. James O. Luken, Associate Provost/Director of Graduate Studies, 843-349-2235, Fax: 843-349-6444, E-mail: joluken@coastal.edu. *Dean,* Dr. Edward Jadallah, 843-349-2773, Fax: 843-349-2106, E-mail: ejadalla@coastal.edu.

COGSWELL POLYTECHNICAL COLLEGE, San Jose, CA 95134

General Information Proprietary, coed, comprehensive institution.

GRADUATE UNITS

Program in Entrepreneurship and Innovation Offers entrepreneurship and innovation (MA).

COKER COLLEGE, Hartsville, SC 29550

General Information Independent, coed, comprehensive institution. *Enrollment:* 79 part-time matriculated graduate/professional students (43 women). *Enrollment by degree level:* 79 master's. *Graduate faculty:* 9 part-time/adjunct (5 women). *Library:* The Charles W. and Joan S. Coker Library-Information Technology Center plus 1 other.

Computer facilities: 116 computers available on campus for general student use. A campuswide network can be accessed from student residence rooms. Online class registration is available.
Website: http://www.coker.edu/

General Application Contact: Benjamin Beetch, Manager of Special Program Marketing, 843-857-4226, E-mail: bbeetch@coker.edu.

GRADUATE UNITS

Graduate Programs Students: 79 part-time (43 women); includes 21 minority (15 Black or African American, non-Hispanic/Latino; 1 American Indian or Alaska Native, non-Hispanic/Latino; 1 Hispanic/Latino; 4 Two or more races, non-Hispanic/Latino), 1 international. Average age 30. *Faculty:* 9 part-time/adjunct (5 women). *Financial support:* In 2015–16, 3 students received support. Unspecified assistantships available. Financial award application deadline: 6/30; financial award applicants required to submit FAFSA. In 2015, 42 master's awarded. *Degree program information:* Part-time programs available. Part-time, 100% online. Offers athletic administration (MS); literacy studies (M Ed). *Application deadline:* Applications are processed on a rolling basis. *Application fee:* $25. Electronic applications accepted. *Application Contact:* Benjamin Beetch, Manager of Special Program Marketing, 843-857-4226, E-mail: bbeetch@coker.edu.

THE COLBURN SCHOOL CONSERVATORY OF MUSIC, Los Angeles, CA 90012

General Information Independent, coed, comprehensive institution.

GRADUATE UNITS

Graduate Programs Offers music (AD); performance (MM).

COLD SPRING HARBOR LABORATORY, Cold Spring Harbor, NY 11724

General Information Independent, coed, graduate-only institution. *Enrollment by degree level:* 42 doctoral. *Graduate faculty:* 59 full-time (11 women). *Graduate housing:* Rooms and/or apartments guaranteed to single students and available on a first-come, first-served basis to married students. Housing application deadline: 8/1. *Student services:* Campus safety program, career counseling, child daycare facilities, exercise/wellness program, free psychological counseling, grant writing training, international student services, low-cost health insurance, services for students with disabilities, teacher training, writing training. *Library:* Cold Spring Harbor Laboratory Library. Study areas open 24 hours, 5–7 days a week; students can reserve study rooms.

Computer facilities: A campuswide network can be accessed from student residence rooms and from off campus.
Website: http://www.cshl.edu/gradschool/

General Application Contact: Kimberly Creteur, Admissions and Recruitment Manager, 516-367-6890, Fax: 516-367-6919, E-mail: gradschool@cshl.edu.

GRADUATE UNITS

Watson School of Biological Sciences Students: 42 full-time (22 women); includes 4 minority (1 Black or African American, non-Hispanic/Latino; 1 Asian, non-Hispanic/Latino; 2 Hispanic/Latino), 25 international. Average age 27. 310 applicants, 9% accepted, 7 enrolled. *Faculty:* 48 full-time (11 women). *Financial support:* In 2015–16, 42 students received support, including 42 fellowships with full tuition reimbursements available (averaging $33,000 per year); health care benefits and tuition waivers (full) also available. Financial award application deadline: 12/1. In 2015, 7 doctorates awarded. Offers biological sciences (PhD). *Application deadline:* For fall admission, 12/1 for domestic and international students. *Application fee:* $60. Electronic applications accepted. *Application Contact:* E-mail: gradschool@cshl.edu.

COLEMAN UNIVERSITY, San Diego, CA 92123

General Information Independent, coed, comprehensive institution. *Graduate housing:* On-campus housing not available.

GRADUATE UNITS

Program in Business and Technology Management ***Degree program information:*** Evening/weekend programs available. Evening/weekend, online learning. Offers business and technology management (MS).

Program in Information Technology ***Degree program information:*** Evening/weekend programs available. Evening/weekend. Offers information technology (MSIT).

COLGATE ROCHESTER CROZER DIVINITY SCHOOL, Rochester, NY 14620-2530

General Information Independent-religious, coed, graduate-only institution. *Enrollment by degree level:* 57 master's, 38 doctoral, 8 other advanced degrees. *Graduate faculty:* 8 full-time (4 women), 3 part-time/adjunct (1 woman). *Tuition, area resident:* Full-time $14,360; part-time $1795 per course. *Required fees:* $330; $35 per course. $70 per semester. One-time fee: $225. Tuition and fees vary according to course load. *Graduate housing:* Rooms and/or apartments available on a first-come, first-served basis to single and married students. Typical cost: $6525 per year for single students; $6525 per year for married students. Room charges vary according to housing facility selected. Housing application deadline: 7/1. *Student services:* Campus employment opportunities, campus safety program, services for students with disabilities. *Library:* Ambrose Swasey Library plus 1 other. *Collection:* Books: 19,115 (physical), 765 (digital/electronic); Databases: 23. Weekly public service hours: 41.

Computer facilities: 8 computers available on campus for general student use. A campuswide network can be accessed from student residence rooms and from off campus.
Website: http://www.crcds.edu/

General Application Contact: Melissa M. Morral, Vice President for Enrollment Services, 585-340-9500, Fax: 585-340-9644, E-mail: mmorral@crcds.edu.

GRADUATE UNITS

Graduate and Professional Programs Students: 79 full-time, 24 part-time; includes 54 minority (49 Black or African American, non-Hispanic/Latino; 3 Asian, non-Hispanic/Latino; 1 Hispanic/Latino; 1 Two or more races, non-Hispanic/Latino), 1 international. Average age 43. 33 applicants, 91% accepted, 27 enrolled. *Faculty:* 8 full-time (4 women), 3 part-time/adjunct (1 woman). *Financial support:* In 2015–16, 52 students received support. Scholarships/grants available. Financial award application deadline: 9/1; financial award applicants required to submit FAFSA. In 2015, 18 master's, 2 doctorates awarded. *Degree program information:* Part-time and evening/weekend programs available. Part-time, evening/weekend, blended/hybrid learning. Offers divinity (M Div, MA, Certificate); peace building and interfaith dialogue (D Min); prophetic preaching (D Min); transformative leadership (D Min). *Application deadline:* For fall admission, 7/1 priority date for domestic students, 3/1 for international students; for spring admission, 12/1 priority date for domestic students, 9/1 for international students. Applications are processed on a rolling basis. *Application fee:* $35. Electronic applications accepted. *Application Contact:* Melissa M. Morral, Vice President for Enrollment Services, 585-340-9633, Fax: 585-340-9644, E-mail: mmorral@crcds.edu. *President,* Marvin A. McMickle, PhD, 585-271-1320 Ext. 680, Fax: 585-271-8013.

COLGATE UNIVERSITY, Hamilton, NY 13346-1386

General Information Independent, coed, comprehensive institution. *Enrollment:* 2,861 graduate, professional, and undergraduate students; 9 full-time matriculated graduate/professional students (6 women). *Enrollment by degree level:* 9 master's. *Graduate faculty:* 6 full-time (4 women), 1 (woman) part-time/adjunct. *Graduate housing:* On-campus housing not available. *Student services:* Campus safety program, career counseling, exercise/wellness program, free psychological counseling, international student services, low-cost health insurance, multicultural affairs office, services for students with disabilities, teacher training, writing training. *Library:* Case Library and Geyer Center for Information Technology plus 1 other. *Collection:* Books: 813,245 (physical), 569,245 (digital/electronic); Serial titles: 5,948 (digital/electronic); Databases: 479. Students can reserve study rooms.

Computer facilities: Computer purchase and lease plans are available. 300 computers available on campus for general student use. A campuswide network can be accessed from student residence rooms and from off campus. Online class registration, software applications are available.
Website: http://www.colgate.edu/

General Application Contact: Meg Gardner, Director, Teacher Preparation and MAT Programs, 315-228-6385, Fax: 315-228-7857, E-mail: mgardner@colgate.edu.

GRADUATE UNITS

Master of Arts in Teaching Program Students: 9 full-time (6 women); includes 1 minority (American Indian or Alaska Native, non-Hispanic/Latino). Average age 27. 9 applicants, 89% accepted, 4 enrolled. *Faculty:* 6 full-time (4 women), 1 (woman) part-time/adjunct. *Financial support:* In 2015–16, 9 students received support. Scholarships/grants and unspecified assistantships available. Financial award application deadline: 2/15; financial award applicants required to submit FAFSA. In 2015, 3 master's awarded. Offers teaching (MAT). *Application deadline:* For fall admission, 2/15 for domestic students. *Application fee:* $50. *Application Contact:* Meg Gardner, Director, Teacher Preparation and MAT Programs, 315-228-6385, Fax: 315-228-7857, E-mail: mgardner@colgate.edu. *Administrative Coordinator of Teacher Education,* Stefanie Lints, 315-228-6385.

THE COLLEGE AT BROCKPORT, STATE UNIVERSITY OF NEW YORK, Brockport, NY 14420-2997

General Information State-supported, coed, comprehensive institution. CGS member. *Enrollment:* 8,161 graduate, professional, and undergraduate students; 354 full-time matriculated graduate/professional students (223 women), 659 part-time matriculated graduate/professional students (452 women). *Graduate faculty:* 121 full-time (62 women), 39 part-time/adjunct (23 women). *Graduate housing:* On-campus housing not available. *Student services:* Campus employment opportunities, campus safety program, career counseling, child daycare facilities, exercise/wellness program, free psychological counseling, grant writing training, international student services, low-cost health insurance, multicultural affairs office, services for students with disabilities, teacher training, writing training. *Library:* Drake Memorial Library. *Collection:* Books: 500,461 (physical), 185,000 (digital/electronic); Serial titles: 4,747 (physical), 113,396 (digital/electronic); Databases: 270. Weekly public service hours: 93; students can reserve study rooms.

Computer facilities: 1,000 computers available on campus for general student use. A campuswide network can be accessed from student residence rooms and from off campus. Online class registration is available.
Website: http://www.brockport.edu/

General Application Contact: Danielle A. Welch, Graduate Admissions Counselor, 585-395-2525, Fax: 585-395-2515, E-mail: dwelch@brockport.edu.

GRADUATE UNITS

General Education Division Students: 6 full-time (4 women), 20 part-time (12 women); includes 12 minority (6 Black or African American, non-Hispanic/Latino; 3 Asian, non-Hispanic/Latino; 2 Hispanic/Latino; 1 Two or more races, non-Hispanic/Latino). 13 applicants, 85% accepted, 10 enrolled. *Financial support:* Federal Work-Study, scholarships/grants, and unspecified assistantships available. Support available to part-time students. Financial award application deadline: 3/15; financial award applicants required to submit FAFSA. In 2015, 8 master's awarded. *Degree program information:* Part-time programs available. Part-time, 100% online. Offers liberal studies (MA). *Application deadline:* For fall admission, 6/15 priority date for domestic and international students; for spring admission, 10/15 priority date for domestic and international students; for summer admission, 3/15 priority date for domestic and international students. *Application fee:* $50. Electronic applications accepted. *Application Contact:* Danielle A. Welch, Graduate Admissions Counselor, 585-395-5465, Fax: 585-395-2515. *Vice Provost,* Dr. P. Michael Fox, 585-395-2524, Fax: 585-395-2401, E-mail: mmallory@brockport.edu.

School of Business Administration and Economics Students: 13 full-time (5 women), 8 part-time (5 women); includes 4 minority (3 Black or African American, non-Hispanic/Latino; 1 Asian, non-Hispanic/Latino). 29 applicants, 79% accepted, 19 enrolled. *Faculty:* 5 full-time (1 woman), 1 part-time/adjunct (0 women). *Financial support:* Career-related internships or fieldwork, Federal Work-Study, scholarships/grants, and unspecified assistantships available. Financial award application deadline: 3/15; financial award applicants required to submit FAFSA. In 2015, 11 master's awarded. *Degree program information:* Part-time programs available. Part-time. Offers forensic accounting (MS). *Application deadline:* For fall admission, 7/1 priority date for domestic and international students; for spring admission, 12/1 priority date for domestic and international students. *Application fee:* $50. Electronic applications accepted. *Application Contact:* Dr. Donald A. Kent, Graduate Director, 585-395-5521, Fax: 585-395-2515, E-mail: dkent@brockport.edu. *Department Chair,* Dr. James Cordeiro, 585-395-5793, Fax: 585-395-2542.

School of Education and Human Services Students: 201 full-time (147 women), 532 part-time (407 women); includes 120 minority (60 Black or African American, non-Hispanic/Latino; 3 American Indian or Alaska Native, non-Hispanic/Latino; 9 Asian, non-Hispanic/Latino; 21 Hispanic/Latino; 27 Two or more races, non-Hispanic/Latino). 514 applicants, 64% accepted, 256 enrolled. *Faculty:* 28 full-time (16 women), 37 part-time/adjunct (26 women). *Financial support:* In 2015–16, 3 teaching assistantships with full tuition reimbursements (averaging $3,000 per year) were awarded; institutionally sponsored loans, scholarships/grants, and unspecified assistantships also available. Financial award applicants required to submit FAFSA. In 2015, 227 master's, 49 other advanced degrees awarded. Offers adolescence biology education (MS Ed); adolescence chemistry education (MS Ed); adolescence earth science education (MS Ed); adolescence education (MS Ed); adolescence English education (MS Ed); adolescence mathematics education (MS Ed); adolescence physics education (MS Ed); adolescence social studies education (MS Ed); arts administration (AGC); bilingual education (MS Ed, AGC); biology (MS Ed, AGC); chemistry (MS Ed, AGC); childhood curriculum specialist (MS Ed); college counseling (MS Ed, CAS); education and human services (MPA, MS, MS Ed, MSW, AGC, Advanced Certificate, CAS, Graduate Certificate); English (MS Ed, Advanced Certificate); family and community practice (MSW); gerontology (AGC); inclusive generalist education (MS Ed, AGC, Advanced Certificate); interdisciplinary health practice (MSW); literacy education B-12 (MS Ed); mathematics (MS Ed, Advanced Certificate); mental health counseling (MS, CAS); nonprofit management (AGC); public administration (MPA); school building leader (CAS); school building leader/school district leader (CAS); school counseling (MS Ed, CAS); school counselor supervision (CAS); school district business leader (CAS); school district leader (CAS); science (MS Ed, Advanced Certificate); social studies (MS Ed, Advanced Certificate); teacher leadership (Graduate Certificate). *Application Contact:* Danielle A. Welch, Graduate Admissions Counselor, 585-395-2525, Fax: 585-395-2515. *Dean, School of Education and Human Services,* Dr. Thomas Hernandez, 585-395-2510, Fax: 585-395-2172, E-mail: thernandez@brockport.edu.

School of Health and Human Performance Students: 39 full-time (11 women), 46 part-time (17 women); includes 5 minority (3 Black or African American, non-Hispanic/Latino; 2 Hispanic/Latino), 1 international. 47 applicants, 81% accepted, 26 enrolled. *Faculty:* 11 full-time (6 women), 5 part-time/adjunct (3 women). *Financial support:* In 2015–16, 6 teaching assistantships with full tuition reimbursements (averaging $6,000 per year) were awarded; scholarships/grants and unspecified assistantships also available. Support available to part-time students. In 2015, 46 master's awarded. Offers adapted physical education (AGC); health and human performance (MS Ed, AGC); health education (MS Ed); physical education (MS Ed). *Application Contact:* Danielle A. Welch, Graduate Admissions Counselor, 585-395-5465, Fax: 585-395-2515. *Dean, School of Health and Human Performance,* Dr. Mark Kettleson, Fax: 585-395-2585, E-mail: mkittleson@brockport.edu.

School of Science and Mathematics Students: 43 full-time (25 women), 32 part-time (14 women); includes 10 minority (2 Black or African American, non-Hispanic/Latino; 3 Asian, non-Hispanic/Latino; 2 Hispanic/Latino; 3 Two or more races, non-Hispanic/Latino). 65 applicants, 60% accepted, 26 enrolled. *Faculty:* 32 full-time (15 women), 4 part-time/adjunct (all women). In 2015, 13 master's awarded. Offers biology (MS, PSM); environmental science and biology (MS); mathematics (MA); psychology (MA); science and mathematics (MA, MS, PSM). *Application Contact:* Danielle A. Welch,

Graduate Admissions Counselor, 585-395-2525, Fax: 585-395-2515. *Dean, School of Science and Mathematics*, Dr. Jose A. Maliekal, 585-395-2394, Fax: 585-395-2172, E-mail: kkifer@brockport.edu.

School of the Arts, Humanities and Social Sciences Students: 58 full-time (36 women), 42 part-time (25 women); includes 13 minority (6 Black or African American, non-Hispanic/Latino; 1 American Indian or Alaska Native, non-Hispanic/Latino; 1 Asian, non-Hispanic/Latino; 2 Hispanic/Latino; 3 Two or more races, non-Hispanic/Latino), 7 international. 98 applicants, 64% accepted, 41 enrolled. *Faculty:* 37 full-time (19 women), 5 part-time/adjunct (4 women). In 2015, 50 master's awarded. Offers arts, humanities and social sciences (MA, MFA, AGC); communication (MA); creative writing (AGC); dance (MA, MFA); English (MA); history (MA); visual studies (MFA). *Application Contact:* Danielle A. Welch, Graduate Admissions Counselor, 585-395-2525, Fax: 585-395-2515. *Dean*, Dr. Darwin Prioleau, 585-395-5806, Fax: 585-395-5808, E-mail: dprioleau@brockport.edu.

COLLÈGE DOMINICAIN DE PHILOSOPHIE ET DE THÉOLOGIE, Ottawa, ON K1R 7G3, Canada

General Information Independent-religious, coed, university. *Graduate housing:* Room and/or apartments available on a first-come, first-served basis to single students; on-campus housing not available to married students.

GRADUATE UNITS

Graduate Programs ***Degree program information:*** Part-time and evening/weekend programs available. Part-time, evening/weekend.

Faculty of Philosophy Offers philosophy (MA Ph, PhD).

Faculty of Theology Degree program information: Part-time and evening/weekend programs available. Part-time, evening/weekend. Offers theology (M Th, MA Th, PhD, Th D, L Th).

COLLEGE FOR CREATIVE STUDIES, Detroit, MI 48202-4034

General Information Independent, coed, comprehensive institution.

GRADUATE UNITS

Graduate Programs

COLLEGE FOR FINANCIAL PLANNING, Centennial, CO 80112

General Information Proprietary, coed, primarily men, graduate-only institution. *Graduate housing:* On-campus housing not available.

GRADUATE UNITS

Graduate Programs ***Degree program information:*** Part-time and evening/weekend programs available. Part-time, evening/weekend, online learning. Offers finance (MSF); financial analysis (MSF); personal financial planning (MS). Electronic applications accepted.

COLLEGE OF CHARLESTON, Charleston, SC 29424-0001

General Information State-supported, coed, comprehensive institution. CGS member. *Graduate housing:* On-campus housing not available. *Research affiliation:* Oak Ridge Associated Universities (science), South Carolina Department of Natural Resources, Marine Resources Division (marine biology, environmental studies), National Institute of Standards and Technology (NIST) (marine biology, environmental studies), National Oceanic and Atmospheric Administration (NOAA) (marine biology, environmental studies), U.S. Department of Agriculture (USDA) (environmental studies), South Carolina Aquarium (marine biology, environmental studies).

GRADUATE UNITS

Graduate School ***Degree program information:*** Part-time and evening/weekend programs available. Part-time, evening/weekend. Electronic applications accepted.

School of Business Offers accountancy (MS); business (MBA, MS); business administration (MBA). Electronic applications accepted.

School of Education, Health, and Human Performance Degree program information: Part-time and evening/weekend programs available. Part-time, evening/weekend. Offers early childhood education (MAT); education, health, and human performance (M Ed, MAT, Certificate); elementary education (MAT); English to speakers of other languages (Certificate); languages (M Ed); performing arts education (MAT); science and mathematics for teachers (M Ed); special education (MAT); teaching, learning and advocacy (M Ed). Electronic applications accepted.

School of Humanities and Social Sciences Degree program information: Part-time and evening/weekend programs available. Part-time, evening/weekend. Offers communication (MA); English (MA); history (MA); humanities and social sciences (MA, MPA, Certificate); public administration (MPA); urban and regional planning (Certificate). Electronic applications accepted.

School of Sciences and Mathematics Degree program information: Part-time and evening/weekend programs available. Part-time, evening/weekend. Offers computer and information sciences (MS); environmental studies (MS); marine biology (MS); mathematics (MS); sciences and mathematics (MS, Certificate). Electronic applications accepted.

School of the Arts Offers arts (MPA, MS, Certificate); arts management (MPA, Certificate); historic preservation (MS).

COLLEGE OF EMMANUEL AND ST. CHAD, Saskatoon, SK S7N 0W6, Canada

General Information Independent-religious, coed, graduate-only institution.

GRADUATE UNITS

Bachelor of Theology Program ***Degree program information:*** Part-time programs available. Part-time, online learning. Offers theology (B Th).

Graduate Programs ***Degree program information:*** Part-time programs available. Part-time. Offers theology (M Div, MTS, STM, L Th). STM program offered jointly with Lutheran Theological Seminary and St. Andrew's College.

THE COLLEGE OF IDAHO, Caldwell, ID 83605

General Information Independent, coed, comprehensive institution. *Enrollment:* 1,070 graduate, professional, and undergraduate students; 7 full-time matriculated graduate/professional students (5 women), 8 part-time matriculated graduate/professional students (all women). *Enrollment by degree level:* 31 master's. *Graduate faculty:* 4 full-time (3 women), 4 part-time/adjunct (3 women). *Tuition, area resident:* Full-time $18,575; part-time $525 per credit. *Required fees:* $75. *Graduate housing:* Room and/or apartments available on a first-come, first-served basis to single students; on-campus housing not available to married students. Typical cost: $8990 (including board). Housing application deadline: 5/1. *Student services:* Campus employment opportunities, campus safety program, career counseling, free psychological counseling, low-cost health insurance, multicultural affairs office, services for students with disabilities. *Library:* Terteling Library. *Collection:* Books: 132,423 (physical), 17,119 (digital/electronic); Serial titles: 4,026 (physical), 17,180 (digital/electronic); Databases: 61.

Computer facilities: 475 computers available on campus for general student use. A campuswide network can be accessed from student residence rooms and from off campus. Online class registration, online course syllabi, course assignments, course discussion are available.

Website: http://www.collegeofidaho.edu/

General Application Contact: Dr. Terah Moore, Assistant Professor of Education, 208-459-5815, E-mail: tmoore@collegeofidaho.edu.

GRADUATE UNITS

Department of Education Students: 7 full-time (5 women), 8 part-time (all women); includes 2 minority (1 Black or African American, non-Hispanic/Latino; 1 Asian, non-Hispanic/Latino). *Faculty:* 4 full-time (3 women), 4 part-time/adjunct (3 women). *Financial support:* Applicants required to submit FAFSA. Offers curriculum and instruction (M Ed); teaching (MAT). *Application deadline:* For fall admission, 3/15 priority date for domestic students. *Application fee:* $0. *Application Contact:* Dr. Terah Moore, Assistant Professor of Education, 208-459-5815, E-mail: tmoore@collegeofidaho.edu.

★ COLLEGE OF MOUNT SAINT VINCENT, Riverdale, NY 10471-1093

General Information Independent, coed, comprehensive institution. *Graduate housing:* On-campus housing not available.

GRADUATE UNITS

School of Professional and Continuing Studies Offers adult nurse practitioner (MSN, PMC); family nurse practitioner (MSN, PMC); instructional technology and global perspectives (Certificate); middle level education (Certificate); multicultural studies (Certificate); nurse educator (PMC); nursing administration (MSN); nursing for the adult and aged (MSN); urban and multicultural education (MS Ed).

See Display on next page and Close-Up on page 867.

★ THE COLLEGE OF NEW JERSEY, Ewing, NJ 08628

General Information State-supported, coed, comprehensive institution. CGS member. *Enrollment:* 7,406 graduate, professional, and undergraduate students; 413 full-time matriculated graduate/professional students (311 women), 867 part-time matriculated graduate/professional students (720 women). *Enrollment by degree level:* 724 master's, 274 other advanced degrees. *Student services:* Campus employment opportunities, campus safety program, career counseling, exercise/wellness program, free psychological counseling, international student services, low-cost health insurance, services for students with disabilities, teacher training. *Collection:* Books: 697,123 (physical), 5,467 (digital/electronic); Serial titles: 43,388 (physical), 8,812 (digital/electronic); Databases: 113. Students can reserve study rooms.

Computer facilities: Computer purchase and lease plans are available. 631 computers available on campus for general student use. A campuswide network can be accessed from student residence rooms and from off campus. Online class registration is available.

Website: http://www.tcnj.edu/

General Application Contact: Susan L. Hydro, Director of Graduate and Intersession Programs, 609-771-2300, Fax: 609-637-5105, E-mail: graduate@tcnj.edu.

GRADUATE UNITS

Graduate Studies Students: 413 full-time (311 women), 867 part-time (720 women); includes 207 minority (64 Black or African American, non-Hispanic/Latino; 3 American Indian or Alaska Native, non-Hispanic/Latino; 63 Asian, non-Hispanic/Latino; 71 Hispanic/Latino; 2 Native Hawaiian or other Pacific Islander, non-Hispanic/Latino; 4 Two or more races, non-Hispanic/Latino). 694 applicants, 79% accepted, 499 enrolled. *Financial support:* Tuition waivers (partial) and unspecified assistantships available. Financial award application deadline: 5/1; financial award applicants required to submit FAFSA. In 2015, 375 master's, 129 other advanced degrees awarded. *Degree program information:* Part-time and evening/weekend programs available. Part-time, evening/weekend. Offers overseas education (M Ed, Certificate). *Application deadline:* For fall admission, 2/1 priority date for domestic students; for spring admission, 10/1 priority date for domestic students. *Application fee:* $75. Electronic applications accepted. *Application Contact:* Susan L. Hydro, Director of Graduate and Intersession Programs, 609-771-2300, Fax: 609-637-5105, E-mail: graduate@tcnj.edu.

School of Education Students: 265 full-time (219 women), 629 part-time (555 women); includes 137 minority (44 Black or African American, non-Hispanic/Latino; 3 American Indian or Alaska Native, non-Hispanic/Latino; 29 Asian, non-Hispanic/Latino; 58 Hispanic/Latino; 2 Native Hawaiian or other Pacific Islander, non-Hispanic/Latino; 1 Two or more races, non-Hispanic/Latino). 506 applicants, 79% accepted, 357 enrolled. *Financial support:* Tuition waivers (partial) and unspecified assistantships available. Financial award application deadline: 5/1; financial award applicants required to submit FAFSA. In 2015, 282 master's, 47 other advanced degrees awarded. *Degree program information:* Part-time and evening/weekend programs available. Part-time, evening/weekend. Offers community counseling: human services (MA); community counseling: substance abuse and addiction (MA, Certificate); developmental reading (M Ed); early childhood education (M Ed, MAT); education (M Ed, MA, MAT, Certificate, Ed S); educational leadership (M Ed, Certificate); elementary education (M Ed, MAT); elementary teaching (MAT); English as a second language (M Ed); marriage and family therapy (Ed S); reading certification (Certificate); school counseling (MA); school personnel: preschool-grade 3 (M Ed); secondary education (MAT); special education (M Ed, MAT); special education with learning disabilities (Certificate); teaching English as a second language (M Ed, Certificate). *Application deadline:* For fall admission, 2/1 priority date for domestic students; for spring admission, 10/1 priority date for domestic students. *Application fee:* $75. Electronic applications accepted. *Application Contact:* Susan L. Hydro, Director of Graduate and Intersession Programs, 609-771-2300, Fax: 609-637-5105, E-mail: graduate@tcnj.edu. *Dean*, Dr. Jeff Passe, 609-771-3177, Fax: 609-637-5117, E-mail: passej@tcnj.edu.

School of Humanities and Social Sciences Students: 6 full-time (2 women), 31 part-time (21 women); includes 3 minority (2 Black or African American, non-Hispanic/Latino; 1 Two or more races, non-Hispanic/Latino). 23 applicants, 70% accepted, 14 enrolled. *Financial support:* Tuition waivers (partial) and unspecified assistantships available. Financial award application deadline: 5/1; financial award applicants required to submit FAFSA. In 2015, 11 master's awarded. *Degree program information:* Part-time programs available. Part-time. Offers English (MA); gender studies (Certificate); humanities and social sciences (MA, Certificate). *Application deadline:* For fall admission, 2/1 priority date for domestic students; for spring admission, 10/1 priority date for domestic students. *Application fee:* $75. Electronic applications accepted. *Application Contact:* Susan L. Hydro, Director of Graduate and Intersession Programs, 609-771-2300, Fax: 609-637-5105, E-mail: graduate@tcnj.edu. *Dean*, Dr. John Sisko, 609-771-3434, Fax: 609-637-5173, E-mail: sisko@tcnj.edu.

School of Nursing, Health and Exercise Science Students: 5 full-time (2 women), 41 part-time (37 women); includes 15 minority (7 Black or African American, non-Hispanic/Latino; 6 Asian, non-Hispanic/Latino; 1 Hispanic/Latino; 1 Two or more races, non-Hispanic/Latino). 37 applicants, 76% accepted, 23 enrolled. *Financial support:* Tuition waivers (partial) and unspecified assistantships available. Financial award application deadline: 5/1; financial award applicants required to submit FAFSA. In 2015, 9 master's awarded. *Degree program information:* Part-time programs available. Part-time. Offers health (MAT); health education (M Ed, MAT); nursing (MSN, Certificate); nursing, health and exercise science (M Ed, MAT, MSN, Certificate); physical education (M Ed, MAT). *Application deadline:* For fall admission, 2/1 priority date for domestic students; for spring admission, 10/1 priority date for domestic students. *Application fee:* $75. Electronic applications accepted. *Application Contact:* Susan L. Hydro, Director of Graduate and Intersession Programs, 609-771-2300, Fax: 609-637-5105, E-mail: graduate@tcnj.edu. *Dean*, Dr. Carole Kenner, 609-771-2591, Fax: 609-637-5159, E-mail: kennerc@tcnj.edu.

See Display on next page and Close-Up on page 869.

THE COLLEGE OF NEW ROCHELLE, New Rochelle, NY 10805-2308

General Information Independent, coed, primarily women, comprehensive institution. CGS member. *Enrollment:* 1,551 graduate, professional, and undergraduate students; 105 full-time matriculated graduate/professional students (97 women), 510 part-time matriculated graduate/professional students (432 women). *Enrollment by degree level:* 615 master's. *Graduate faculty:* 18 full-time (12 women), 45 part-time/adjunct (31 women). *Tuition, area resident:* Part-time $894 per credit. *Required fees:* $350 per semester. *Graduate housing:* Room and/or apartments available on a first-come, first-served basis to single students; on-campus housing not available to married students. Typical cost: $12,700 (including board). Housing application deadline: 8/1. *Student services:* Campus employment opportunities, campus safety program, career counseling, free psychological counseling, international student services, services for students with disabilities, teacher training, writing training. *Library:* Gill Library. *Collection:* Books: 90,490 (physical), 116,155 (digital/electronic); Databases: 96.

Computer facilities: Computer purchase and lease plans are available. 120 computers available on campus for general student use. A campuswide network can be accessed from student residence rooms and from off campus. Online class registration is available.
Website: http://www.cnr.edu/

General Application Contact: Michael Petri, Interim Director of Graduate Admission, 914-654-5256, E-mail: mpetri@cnr.edu.

GRADUATE UNITS

Graduate School Students: 105 full-time (97 women), 394 part-time (328 women); includes 332 minority (234 Black or African American, non-Hispanic/Latino; 6 American Indian or Alaska Native, non-Hispanic/Latino; 8 Asian, non-Hispanic/Latino; 81 Hispanic/Latino; 2 Native Hawaiian or other Pacific Islander, non-Hispanic/Latino; 1 Two or more races, non-Hispanic/Latino), 4 international. Average age 38. *Faculty:* 18 full-time (12 women), 34 part-time/adjunct (26 women). *Financial support:* Career-related internships or fieldwork, Federal Work-Study, scholarships/grants, traineeships, tuition waivers (partial), and unspecified assistantships available. Support available to part-time students. Financial award applicants required to submit FAFSA. In 2015, 237 master's, 24 other advanced degrees awarded. *Degree program information:* Part-time and evening/weekend programs available. Part-time, evening/weekend. Offers acute care nurse practitioner (MS, Certificate); clinical specialist in holistic nursing (MS, Certificate); family nurse practitioner (MS, Certificate); nursing and health care management (MS); nursing education (Certificate). *Application deadline:* Applications are processed on a rolling basis. *Application fee:* $35. Electronic applications accepted. *Application Contact:* Michael Petri, Interim Director of Admission for the Graduate School, 914-654-5256, E-mail: mpetri@cnr.edu. *Interim Dean of the Graduate School*, Dr. David Donnelly, 914-654-5321, E-mail: ddonnelly@cnr.edu.

Division of Art and Communication Studies Degree program information: Part-time and evening/weekend programs available. Part-time, evening/weekend. Offers art therapy (MS); art therapy/counseling (MS); communication studies (MS, Certificate).

Division of Education Degree program information: Part-time and evening/weekend programs available. Part-time, evening/weekend. Offers art education (MS); bilingual education (Certificate); childhood education (MS Ed); childhood education/early childhood education (MS Ed); early childhood education (MS Ed); educational leadership (MS, Advanced Certificate, Advanced Diploma); gifted education (Certificate); literacy education (MS Ed); multilingual/multicultural education (MS Ed, Certificate); school building leader (MS, Advanced Certificate); school district leader (MS, Advanced Diploma); special education (MS Ed); teaching English to speakers of other languages (MS Ed, Certificate). Electronic applications accepted.

Division of Human Services Degree program information: Part-time and evening/weekend programs available. Part-time, evening/weekend. Offers career development (MS, Advanced Certificate); guidance and counseling (MS, Advanced Certificate); long term care administration (MPA); marriage and family therapy (MMFT); mental health counseling (MS, Certificate); public administration (MPA); school psychology (MS); thanatology (Certificate). Electronic applications accepted.

COLLEGE OF SAINT ELIZABETH, Morristown, NJ 07960-6989

General Information Independent-religious, coed, primarily women, comprehensive institution. *Enrollment:* 1,247 graduate, professional, and undergraduate students; 94 full-time matriculated graduate/professional students (88 women), 348 part-time matriculated graduate/professional students (276 women). *Enrollment by degree level:* 317 master's, 81 doctoral, 44 other advanced degrees. *Graduate faculty:* 10 full-time (4 women), 58 part-time/adjunct (36 women). *Tuition, area resident:* Part-time $1001 per credit hour. *Required fees:* $325 per semester. $325 per semester. One-time fee: $175. Tuition and fees vary according to course load, degree level, program and student level. *Graduate housing:* Room and/or apartments available on a first-come, first-served basis to single students; on-campus housing not available to married students. Typical cost: $12,744 (including board). Room and board charges vary according to board plan. Housing application deadline: 7/1. *Student services:* Campus employment opportunities, campus safety program, career counseling, exercise/wellness program, free psychological counseling, international student services, low-cost health insurance, multicultural affairs office, services for students with disabilities, teacher training, writing training. *Library:* Mahoney Library plus 1 other. *Research affiliation:* National Figure Skating Association (sports nutrition), National Institute of Mental Health (NIMH) (mental

health service), Cornell University, The University of Texas at Houston (food biotechnology (attitude research)).

Computer facilities: 138 computers available on campus for general student use. A campuswide network can be accessed from student residence rooms and from off campus. Online class registration is available.
Website: http://www.cse.edu/

General Application Contact: Deborah S. Cobo, Associate Director for Graduate Admissions, 973-290-4194, Fax: 973-290-4710, E-mail: apply@cse.edu.

GRADUATE UNITS

Department of Business Administration and Management Students: 5 full-time (4 women), 45 part-time (35 women); includes 11 minority (8 Black or African American, non-Hispanic/Latino; 3 Hispanic/Latino), 1 international. Average age 41. 13 applicants, 54% accepted, 5 enrolled. *Faculty:* 2 part-time/adjunct (1 woman). *Financial support:* Career-related internships or fieldwork, scholarships/grants, tuition waivers (partial), and unspecified assistantships available. Financial award applicants required to submit FAFSA. In 2015, 47 master's awarded. *Degree program information:* Part-time programs available. Part-time. Offers human resource management (MS); organizational change (MS). *Application deadline:* For fall admission, 5/1 for international students. Applications are processed on a rolling basis. *Application fee:* $35. Electronic applications accepted. *Application Contact:* Marie Scolavino, Admissions Director of Graduate and Continuing Studies, 973-290-4413, Fax: 973-290-4710, E-mail: apply@cse.edu. *Program Chair and Director,* Dr. David B. Tataw, 973-290-4271, E-mail: dtataw@cse.edu.

Department of Educational Leadership Students: 18 full-time (16 women), 107 part-time (75 women); includes 34 minority (20 Black or African American, non-Hispanic/Latino; 1 Asian, non-Hispanic/Latino; 12 Hispanic/Latino; 1 Two or more races, non-Hispanic/Latino), 1 international. Average age 40. 71 applicants, 80% accepted, 47 enrolled. *Faculty:* 4 full-time (0 women), 25 part-time/adjunct (15 women). *Financial support:* Career-related internships or fieldwork, scholarships/grants, and unspecified assistantships available. Financial award applicants required to submit FAFSA. In 2015, 50 master's, 2 doctorates awarded. *Degree program information:* Part-time programs available. Part-time. Offers assistive technology (Certificate); education (MA); educational leadership (MA, Ed D). *Application deadline:* For fall admission, 5/1 for international students. Applications are processed on a rolling basis. *Application fee:* $35. Electronic applications accepted. *Application Contact:* Marie Scolavino, Admissions Director of Graduate and Continuing Studies, 973-290-4413, Fax: 973-290-4710, E-mail: apply@cse.edu. *Associate Professor/Course of Study Coordinator,* Dr. Joseph Ciccone, 973-290-4383, Fax: 973-290-4389, E-mail: jciccone@cse.edu.

Department of Foods and Nutrition Students: 35 full-time (34 women), 32 part-time (31 women); includes 11 minority (2 Black or African American, non-Hispanic/Latino; 5 Asian, non-Hispanic/Latino; 3 Hispanic/Latino; 1 Two or more races, non-Hispanic/Latino). Average age 28. 45 applicants, 73% accepted, 29 enrolled. *Faculty:* 1 (woman) full-time, 2 part-time/adjunct (both women). *Financial support:* Career-related internships or fieldwork, scholarships/grants, and unspecified assistantships available. Financial award applicants required to submit FAFSA. In 2015, 7 master's awarded. *Degree program information:* Part-time programs available. Part-time, blended/hybrid learning. Offers dietetic internship (Certificate); dietetics verification (Certificate); nutrition (MS); sports nutrition and wellness (Certificate). *Application deadline:* For fall admission, 5/1 for international students. Applications are processed on a rolling basis. *Application fee:* $35. Electronic applications accepted. *Application Contact:* Scolavino Marie, Admissions Director of Graduate and Continuing Studies, 973-290-4413, Fax: 973-290-4710, E-mail: apply@cse.edu. *Program Chair,* Dr. Marie Boyle, 973-290-4127, Fax: 973-290-4167, E-mail: mboyle01@cse.edu.

Department of Nursing Students: 2 full-time (1 woman), 40 part-time (34 women); includes 21 minority (6 Black or African American, non-Hispanic/Latino; 8 Asian, non-Hispanic/Latino; 7 Hispanic/Latino). Average age 44. 18 applicants, 89% accepted, 14 enrolled. *Faculty:* 5 part-time/adjunct (all women). *Financial support:* Career-related internships or fieldwork, scholarships/grants, tuition waivers (partial), and unspecified assistantships available. Financial award applicants required to submit FAFSA. In 2015, 16 master's awarded. *Degree program information:* Part-time programs available. Part-time. Offers nursing (MSN). *Application fee:* $35. Electronic applications accepted. *Application Contact:* Deborah S. Cobo, Associate Director for Graduate Admissions, 973-290-4194, Fax: 973-290-4710, E-mail: dscobo@cse.edu. *Interim Nursing Administrator,* Dr. Sarah Arnold, 973-290-4037, E-mail: sarnold@cse.edu.

Department of Psychology Students: 30 full-time (29 women), 48 part-time (40 women); includes 25 minority (11 Black or African American, non-Hispanic/Latino; 1 Asian, non-Hispanic/Latino; 11 Hispanic/Latino; 2 Two or more races, non-Hispanic/Latino). Average age 32. 76 applicants, 43% accepted, 21 enrolled. *Faculty:* 2 full-time (1 woman), 4 part-time/adjunct (3 women). *Financial support:* Career-related internships or fieldwork, scholarships/grants, tuition waivers (partial), and unspecified assistantships available. Support available to part-time students. Financial award applicants required to submit FAFSA. In 2015, 34 master's awarded. *Degree program information:* Part-time programs available. Part-time. Offers counseling psychology (MA); forensic psychology (MA); mental health counseling (Certificate); psychology (Psy D); student affairs in higher education (Certificate). *Application deadline:* For fall admission, 5/1 for international students. Applications are processed on a rolling basis. *Application fee:* $35. Electronic applications accepted. *Application Contact:* Marie Scolavino, Admissions Director of Graduate and Continuing Studies, 973-290-4413, Fax: 973-290-4710, E-mail: apply@cse.edu. *Director, Graduate and Doctoral Programs in Psychology,* Dr. Michelle M. Barrett, 973-290-4106, Fax: 973-290-4676, E-mail: tbarrett@cse.edu.

Department of Theology and Philosophy Students: 7 full-time (all women), 2 part-time (both women); includes 2 minority (1 Black or African American, non-Hispanic/Latino; 1 Asian, non-Hispanic/Latino), 1 international. Average age 46. 4 applicants, 75% accepted, 1 enrolled. *Faculty:* 4 part-time/adjunct (all women). *Financial support:* Career-related internships or fieldwork, scholarships/grants, tuition waivers (partial), and unspecified assistantships available. Financial award applicants required to submit FAFSA. In 2015, 2 degrees awarded. *Degree program information:* Part-time programs available. Part-time. Offers theology (MA). *Application deadline:* For fall admission, 5/1 for international students. Applications are processed on a rolling basis. *Application fee:* $35. Electronic applications accepted. *Application Contact:* Marie Scolavino, Admissions Director of Graduate and Continuing Studies, 973-290-4413, Fax: 973-290-4710, E-mail: apply@cse.edu. *Chairperson,* Dr. Anthony Santamaria, 973-290-4338, Fax: 973-290-4312, E-mail: asantamaria@cse.edu.

Health Administration Program Students: 5 full-time (4 women), 45 part-time (35 women); includes 15 minority (8 Black or African American, non-Hispanic/Latino; 4 Asian, non-Hispanic/Latino; 3 Hispanic/Latino), 1 international. Average age 41. 31 applicants, 68% accepted, 14 enrolled. *Faculty:* 3 full-time (2 women), 4 part-time/adjunct (0 women). *Financial support:* Career-related internships or fieldwork, scholarships/grants, tuition waivers (partial), and unspecified assistantships available. Financial award applicants required to submit FAFSA. In 2015, 47 degrees awarded.

Degree program information: Part-time programs available. Part-time. Offers health administration (MS). *Application deadline:* For fall admission, 5/1 for international students. Applications are processed on a rolling basis. *Application fee:* $35. Electronic applications accepted. *Application Contact:* Marie Scolavino, Admissions Director of Graduate and Continuing Studies, 973-290-4413, Fax: 973-290-4710, E-mail: apply@cse.edu. *Program Chair and Director, Health Care Administration,* Dr. David B. Tataw, 973-290-4271, Fax: 973-290-4167, E-mail: dtataw@cse.edu.

Program in Justice Administration and Public Service Students: 4 full-time (all women), 23 part-time (13 women); includes 11 minority (5 Black or African American, non-Hispanic/Latino; 6 Hispanic/Latino). Average age 29. 17 applicants, 88% accepted, 13 enrolled. *Faculty:* 1 full-time (0 women), 1 (woman) part-time/adjunct. *Financial support:* Career-related internships or fieldwork, scholarships/grants, and unspecified assistantships available. Support available to part-time students. Financial award applicants required to submit FAFSA. In 2015, 5 master's awarded. *Degree program information:* Part-time programs available. Part-time. Offers justice administration and public service (MA). *Application deadline:* For fall admission, 5/1 for international students. Applications are processed on a rolling basis. *Application fee:* $35. Electronic applications accepted. *Application Contact:* Marie Scolavino, Admissions Director of Graduate and Continuing Studies, 973-290-4413, Fax: 973-290-4710, E-mail: apply@cse.edu. *Associate Professor,* Dr. James Ford, 973-290-4324, E-mail: jford@cse.edu.

COLLEGE OF ST. JOSEPH, Rutland, VT 05701-3899

General Information Independent-religious, coed, comprehensive institution. *Graduate housing:* Room and/or apartments guaranteed to single students; on-campus housing not available to married students. Housing application deadline: 7/1.

GRADUATE UNITS

Graduate Programs ***Degree program information:*** Part-time and evening/weekend programs available. Part-time, evening/weekend. Electronic applications accepted.

Division of Business Degree program information: Part-time and evening/weekend programs available. Part-time, evening/weekend. Offers business administration (MBA). Electronic applications accepted.

Division of Education Degree program information: Part-time and evening/weekend programs available. Part-time, evening/weekend. Offers elementary education (M Ed); English (M Ed); general education (M Ed); reading (M Ed); secondary education (M Ed); social studies (M Ed); special education (M Ed). Electronic applications accepted.

Division of Psychology and Human Services Degree program information: Part-time and evening/weekend programs available. Part-time, evening/weekend. Offers alcohol and substance abuse counseling (MS); clinical mental health counseling (MS); clinical psychology (MS); community counseling (MS); school guidance counseling (MS). Electronic applications accepted.

COLLEGE OF SAINT MARY, Omaha, NE 68106

General Information Independent-religious, women only, comprehensive institution.

GRADUATE UNITS

Program in Education ***Degree program information:*** Part-time programs available. Part-time. Offers assessment leadership (MSE); English as a second language (MSE).

Program in Health Professions Education ***Degree program information:*** Part-time programs available. Part-time. Offers health professions education (Ed D).

Program in Nursing ***Degree program information:*** Part-time programs available. Part-time. Offers nursing (MSN).

Program in Occupational Therapy Offers occupational therapy (MOT).

Program in Organizational Leadership ***Degree program information:*** Part-time and evening/weekend programs available. Part-time, evening/weekend. Offers organizational leadership (MOL). Electronic applications accepted.

Program in Teaching ***Degree program information:*** Evening/weekend programs available. Evening/weekend. Offers teaching (MAT).

THE COLLEGE OF SAINT ROSE, Albany, NY 12203-1419

General Information Independent, coed, comprehensive institution. CGS member. *Enrollment:* 4,411 graduate, professional, and undergraduate students; 644 full-time matriculated graduate/professional students (462 women), 1,013 part-time matriculated graduate/professional students (713 women). *Enrollment by degree level:* 856 master's, 801 other advanced degrees. *Graduate faculty:* 93 full-time (48 women), 9 part-time/adjunct (7 women). *Tuition, area resident:* Full-time $13,968; part-time $776 per credit. *Required fees:* $790; $32 per credit hour. $85 per semester. Tuition and fees vary according to course load. *Graduate housing:* Room and/or apartments available on a first-come, first-served basis to single students; on-campus housing not available to married students. Typical cost: $7994 per year. Room charges vary according to board plan. *Student services:* Campus employment opportunities, campus safety program, career counseling, child daycare facilities, exercise/wellness program, free psychological counseling, international student services, multicultural affairs office, services for students with disabilities, teacher training, writing training. *Library:* Neil Hellman Library plus 2 others. *Collection:* Books: 240,000 (physical), 115,000 (digital/electronic); Serial titles: 1,200 (physical), 10 (digital/electronic); Databases: 104. Study areas open 24 hours, 5–7 days a week; students can reserve study rooms.

Computer facilities: 755 computers available on campus for general student use. A campuswide network can be accessed from student residence rooms and from off campus. Online class registration is available.
Website: http://www.strose.edu/

General Application Contact: Cris Murray, Assistant Vice President for Recruitment and Enrollment, 518-485-3390, Fax: 518-458-5479, E-mail: grad@strose.edu.

GRADUATE UNITS

Graduate Studies Students: 644 full-time (462 women), 1,013 part-time (713 women); includes 292 minority (137 Black or African American, non-Hispanic/Latino; 2 American Indian or Alaska Native, non-Hispanic/Latino; 28 Asian, non-Hispanic/Latino; 95 Hispanic/Latino; 1 Native Hawaiian or other Pacific Islander, non-Hispanic/Latino; 29 Two or more races, non-Hispanic/Latino), 155 international. Average age 32. 1,912 applicants, 64% accepted, 698 enrolled. *Faculty:* 93 full-time (48 women), 9 part-time/adjunct (7 women). *Financial support:* Career-related internships or fieldwork, scholarships/grants, tuition waivers (partial), and unspecified assistantships available. Support available to part-time students. Financial award application deadline: 3/1; financial award applicants required to submit FAFSA. In 2015, 445 master's, 474 other advanced degrees awarded. *Degree program information:* Part-time and evening/weekend programs available. Part-time, evening/weekend. *Application deadline:* For fall admission, 4/1 priority date for domestic and international students; for spring admission, 10/15 priority date for domestic and international students. Applications are processed on a rolling basis. Electronic applications accepted. *Application Contact:* Cris Murray, Assistant Vice President for Recruitment and Enrollment, 518-485-3390, Fax: 518-458-5479, E-mail: grad@strose.edu.

Huether School of Business Students: 66 full-time (30 women), 78 part-time (32 women); includes 25 minority (15 Black or African American, non-Hispanic/Latino; 4 Asian, non-Hispanic/Latino; 5 Hispanic/Latino; 1 Two or more races, non-Hispanic/Latino), 18 international. Average age 29. *Financial support:* Career-related internships or fieldwork, scholarships/grants, tuition waivers (partial), and unspecified assistantships available. Support available to part-time students. Financial award application deadline: 4/15; financial award applicants required to submit FAFSA. In 2015, 79 master's, 13 other advanced degrees awarded. *Degree program information:* Part-time and evening/weekend programs available. Part-time, evening/weekend. Offers accounting (MS); business administration (MBA); financial planning (Advanced Certificate); organizational leadership and change management (Advanced Certificate). *Application deadline:* For fall admission, 4/1 priority date for domestic and international students; for spring admission, 10/15 priority date for domestic and international students; for summer admission, 3/15 priority date for domestic and international students. Applications are processed on a rolling basis. *Application fee:* $40. Electronic applications accepted. *Application Contact:* Cris Murray, Assistant Vice President for Graduate Recruitment and Enrollment, 518-485-3390, Fax: 518-458-5479, E-mail: grad@strose.edu. *Dean,* Suzanne Wilhelm, 518-454-2122, E-mail: wilhelms@strose.edu.

School of Education Students: 459 full-time (391 women), 891 part-time (652 women); includes 257 minority (119 Black or African American, non-Hispanic/Latino; 2 American Indian or Alaska Native, non-Hispanic/Latino; 24 Asian, non-Hispanic/Latino; 85 Hispanic/Latino; 1 Native Hawaiian or other Pacific Islander, non-Hispanic/Latino; 26 Two or more races, non-Hispanic/Latino), 32 international. Average age 33. *Financial support:* Career-related internships or fieldwork, scholarships/grants, tuition waivers (partial), and unspecified assistantships available. Support available to part-time students. Financial award application deadline: 4/15; financial award applicants required to submit FAFSA. In 2015, 324 master's, 457 other advanced degrees awarded. *Degree program information:* Part-time and evening/weekend programs available. Part-time, evening/weekend, 100% online. Offers adolescence education (MS Ed, Advanced Certificate); adolescence education and special education (MS Ed); adolescence education/special education (Advanced Certificate); childhood education (MS Ed); childhood education and special education (MS Ed); childhood special education (MS Ed); clinical mental health counseling (Certificate); college student services administration (MS Ed); communication sciences and disorders (MS Ed); curriculum and instruction (MS Ed); early childhood education (MS Ed); early childhood special education (MS Ed); education (MS, MS Ed, Advanced Certificate, Certificate); educational leadership (MS Ed); educational psychology (MS Ed, Certificate); higher education leadership and administration (MS Ed, Advanced Certificate); literacy: birth-grade 6 (MS Ed, Advanced Certificate); literacy: grades 5-12 (MS Ed, Advanced Certificate); school building leader (Certificate); school counseling (MS Ed, Certificate); school district business leader (Certificate); school district leader (Certificate); school psychology (MS Ed); special education (Certificate); special education professional (MS Ed). *Application deadline:* For fall admission, 4/1 priority date for domestic and international students; for spring admission, 10/15 priority date for domestic and international students; for summer admission, 3/15 priority date for domestic and international students. Applications are processed on a rolling basis. *Application fee:* $40. Electronic applications accepted. *Application Contact:* Cris Murray, Assistant Vice President for Graduate Recruitment and Enrollment, 518-454-5136, Fax: 518-458-5479, E-mail: grad@strose.edu. *Dean,* Dr. Margaret McLane, 518-454-2147.

School of Mathematics and Sciences Students: 98 full-time (31 women), 19 part-time (10 women); includes 5 minority (2 Black or African American, non-Hispanic/Latino; 3 Hispanic/Latino), 102 international. Average age 25. *Financial support:* Career-related internships or fieldwork, scholarships/grants, tuition waivers (partial), and unspecified assistantships available. Support available to part-time students. Financial award application deadline: 4/15; financial award applicants required to submit FAFSA. In 2015, 34 master's, 4 other advanced degrees awarded. *Degree program information:* Part-time and evening/weekend programs available. Part-time, evening/weekend, 100% online. Offers computer information systems (MS, Advanced Certificate). *Application deadline:* For fall admission, 4/1 priority date for domestic and international students; for spring admission, 10/15 priority date for domestic and international students; for summer admission, 3/15 priority date for domestic and international students. Applications are processed on a rolling basis. *Application fee:* $40. Electronic applications accepted. *Application Contact:* Cris Murray, Assistant Vice President for Graduate Recruitment and Enrollment, 518-485-3390, Fax: 518-458-5479, E-mail: grad@strose.edu. *Dean,* Dr. Richard J. Thompson, Jr., 518-337-4853, E-mail: thompsor@strose.edu.

THE COLLEGE OF ST. SCHOLASTICA, Duluth, MN 55811-4199

General Information Independent-religious, coed, comprehensive institution. *Graduate housing:* On-campus housing not available.

GRADUATE UNITS

Graduate Studies ***Degree program information:*** Part-time and evening/weekend programs available. Part-time, evening/weekend, online learning. Offers athletic training (MS); computer information systems (MA, Certificate); education (M Ed, MS, Certificate); exercise physiology (MA); health information management (MA, Certificate); management (MA, Certificate); nursing (MA, PMC); occupational therapy (MA); physical therapy (DPT); social work (MSW). Electronic applications accepted.

COLLEGE OF STATEN ISLAND OF THE CITY UNIVERSITY OF NEW YORK, Staten Island, NY 10314-6600

General Information State and locally supported, coed, comprehensive institution. *Enrollment:* 13,775 graduate, professional, and undergraduate students; 200 full-time matriculated graduate/professional students (145 women), 662 part-time matriculated graduate/professional students (479 women). *Enrollment by degree level:* 778 master's, 37 doctoral, 47 other advanced degrees. *Graduate faculty:* 90 full-time (51 women), 76 part-time/adjunct (47 women). Tuition, state resident: full-time $10,130; part-time $425 per credit. Tuition, nonresident: full-time $18,720; part-time $780 per credit. *Required fees:* $181.10 per semester. Tuition and fees vary according to program. *Graduate housing:* Room and/or apartments available on a first-come, first-served basis to single students; on-campus housing not available to married students. Typical cost: $13,332 per year. Room charges vary according to board plan and housing facility selected. *Student services:* Campus employment opportunities, campus safety program, career counseling, child daycare facilities, exercise/wellness program, free psychological counseling, international student services, services for students with disabilities. *Library:* College of Staten Island Library. Students can reserve study rooms. *Research affiliation:* Massachusetts Clean Energy Technology Center (field survey for off shore wind),

National Science Foundation (analysis of Oxytocin regulation of naked mole rat and Hippocampal neuron interactions), National Science Foundation (spatial temporal information fusion and real-time sensor data assimilation using sequential Monte Carlo methods), New York State Department of Health (spinal cord injury), IEC (environmental science), National Institute on Minority Health and Health Disparities (cancer and Alzheimer's disease).

Computer facilities: 1,600 computers available on campus for general student use. A campuswide network can be accessed from off campus. Online class registration is available. Website: http://www.csi.cuny.edu/

General Application Contact: Sasha Spence, Associate Director for Graduate Admissions, 718-982-2019, Fax: 718-982-2500, E-mail: sasha.spence@csi.cuny.edu.

GRADUATE UNITS

Graduate Programs Average age 30. In 2015, 268 master's, 25 other advanced degrees awarded. *Application fee:* $125. *Application Contact:* Sasha Spence, Associate Director for Graduate Admissions, 718-982-2019, Fax: 718-982-2500, E-mail: sasha.spence@csi.cuny.edu. *Provost/Senior Vice President for Academic Affairs*, Dr. Gary Reichard, 718-982-2440, Fax: 718-982-2442, E-mail: provost@csi.cuny.edu.

Division of Humanities and Social Sciences Students: 104 full-time, 95 part-time. Average age 31. *Faculty:* 16 full-time (11 women), 24 part-time/adjunct (16 women). In 2015, 62 master's, 8 other advanced degrees awarded. Offers autism spectrum disorders (Advanced Certificate); cinema and media studies (MA); English (MA); history (MA); liberal studies (MA); mental health counseling (MA); social work (MSW). *Application Contact:* Sasha Spence, Associate Director for Graduate Recruitment and Admissions, 718-982-2019, Fax: 718-982-2500, E-mail: sasha.spence@csi.cuny.edu. *Dean of Humanities and Social Sciences*, Dr. Nan Sussman, 718-982-2315, Fax: 718-982-2316, E-mail: nan.sussman@csi.cuny.edu.

Division of Science and Technology Students: 24 full-time, 90 part-time. Average age 27. *Faculty:* 20 full-time, 9 part-time/adjunct. In 2015, 35 master's awarded. Offers biology (MS); computer science (MS); environmental science (MS); neuroscience and developmental disabilities (MS). *Application Contact:* Sasha Spence, Associate Director for Graduate Recruitment and Admissions, 718-982-2019, Fax: 718-982-2500, E-mail: sasha.spence@csi.cuny.edu. *Acting Dean of Science and Technology*, Dr. Alfred Levine, 718-982-2430, E-mail: alfred.levine@csi.cuny.edu.

School of Business Students: 6 full-time, 57 part-time. Average age 30. *Faculty:* 6 full-time, 21 part-time/adjunct (1 woman). *Financial support:* Applicants required to submit FAFSA. In 2015, 23 master's awarded. Offers accounting (MS); business (MS, Advanced Certificate); business analytics of large-scale data (Advanced Certificate); business management (MS). *Application Contact:* Sasha Spence, Associate Director for Graduate Recruitment and Admissions, 718-982-2019, Fax: 718-982-2500, E-mail: sasha.spence@csi.cuny.edu. *Dean of the School of Business*, Dr. Susan L. Holak, 718-982-2920, Fax: 718-982-3183, E-mail: susan.holak@csi.cuny.edu.

School of Education Students: 29 full-time, 343 part-time. Average age 28. 125 applicants. *Faculty:* 29 full-time, 27 part-time/adjunct. In 2015, 130 master's, 13 Advanced Certificates awarded. Offers biology (MS Ed); childhood education (MS Ed); education (MS Ed, Advanced Certificate, Post-Master's Certificate); leadership in education (Post-Master's Certificate); special education (MS Ed); teaching of English to speakers of other languages (MS Ed, Advanced Certificate). *Application Contact:* Sasha Spence, Associate Director for Graduate Admissions, 718-982-2019, Fax: 718-982-2500, E-mail: sasha.spence@csi.cuny.edu. *Interim Dean of School of Education*, Dr. Kenneth Gold, 718-982-3720, Fax: 718-982-3743, E-mail: education@csi.cuny.edu.

School of Health Sciences Students: 37 full-time, 77 part-time. Average age 34. *Faculty:* 11 full-time, 16 part-time/adjunct. In 2015, 18 master's, 4 other advanced degrees awarded. Offers adult-gerontological nursing (MS, Advanced Certificate); clinical nurse practitioner (MS, Advanced Certificate); clinical nurse specialist (MS, Advanced Certificate); cultural competence (Advanced Certificate); nursing practice (DNP); physical therapy (DPT). *Application Contact:* Sasha Spence, Associate Director for Graduate Recruitment and Admissions, 718-982-2019, Fax: 718-982-2500, E-mail: sasha.spence@csi.cuny.edu. *Interim Founding Dean*, Dr. Maureen Becker, 718-982-3690, Fax: 718-982-3813, E-mail: schoolhealthscience@csi.cuny.edu.

See Display on next page and Close-Up on page 871.

COLLEGE OF THE ATLANTIC, Bar Harbor, ME 04609-1198

General Information Independent, coed, comprehensive institution. *Graduate housing:* Room and/or apartments available to single students; on-campus housing not available to married students. Housing application deadline: 6/1. *Research affiliation:* Acadia National Park, National Park Service (research management, environmental education), Mount Desert Island Biological Laboratory, Jackson Laboratory (genetics), Society for Human Ecology (ecological decision making in society).

GRADUATE UNITS

Program in Human Ecology Offers human ecology (M Phil).

THE COLLEGE OF WILLIAM AND MARY, Williamsburg, VA 23187-8795

General Information State-supported, coed, university. CGS member. *Enrollment:* 8,484 graduate, professional, and undergraduate students; 1,665 full-time matriculated graduate/professional students (833 women), 402 part-time matriculated graduate/professional students (212 women). *Enrollment by degree level:* 965 master's, 1,087 doctoral, 15 other advanced degrees. *Graduate faculty:* 713 full-time (279 women), 159 part-time/adjunct (61 women). Tuition, state resident: full-time $8009; part-time $450 per credit hour. Tuition, nonresident: full-time $23,752; part-time $1160 per credit hour. *Required fees:* $4162. One-time fee: $400 full-time. *Graduate housing:* Room and/or apartments available on a first-come, first-served basis to single students; on-campus housing not available to married students. Housing application deadline: 2/14. *Student services:* Campus employment opportunities, campus safety program, career counseling, child daycare facilities, exercise/wellness program, free psychological counseling, grant writing training, international student services, low-cost health insurance, multicultural affairs office, services for students with disabilities, teacher training, writing training. *Library:* Earl Gregg Swem Library plus 4 others. *Collection:* Books: 1.1 million (physical), 1.5 million (digital/electronic); Serial titles: 36,153 (physical), 154,538 (digital/electronic); Databases: 476. Weekly public service hours: 110; students can reserve study rooms. *Research affiliation:* Center for Excellence in Aging and Geriatric Health (public policy, kinesiology), Colonial Williamsburg (archaeology, history), Thomas Jefferson National Accelerator Facility (nuclear physics), Court Records Solutions (law and technology), AidData (global aid flows and development finance), James City County Business and Technology Incubator (economic development).

Computer facilities: Computer purchase and lease plans are available. 275 computers available on campus for general student use. A campuswide network can be accessed from student residence rooms. Online class registration is available. Website: http://www.wm.edu/

General Application Contact: Evan Davies, Director of Institutional Research, 757-221-2147, Fax: 757-221-2080, E-mail: esdav2@wm.edu.

GRADUATE UNITS

Faculty of Arts and Sciences Students: 384 full-time (166 women), 15 part-time (7 women); includes 43 minority (9 Black or African American, non-Hispanic/Latino; 1 American Indian or Alaska Native, non-Hispanic/Latino; 11 Asian, non-Hispanic/Latino; 14 Hispanic/Latino; 8 Two or more races, non-Hispanic/Latino), 116 international. Average age 28. 747 applicants, 32% accepted, 117 enrolled. *Faculty:* 485 full-time (188 women), 100 part-time/adjunct (46 women). *Financial support:* Fellowships, research assistantships, teaching assistantships, career-related internships or fieldwork, Federal Work-Study, institutionally sponsored loans, and unspecified assistantships available. Financial award applicants required to submit FAFSA. In 2015, 110 master's, 30 doctorates awarded. *Degree program information:* Part-time programs available. Part-time. Offers accelerator science (PhD); American studies (MA, PhD); anthropology (MA, PhD); applied mathematics (PhD); applied mechanics (PhD); applied robotics (PhD); applied science (MS); arts and sciences (MA, MPP, MS, PhD); atmospheric and environmental science (PhD); biology (MS); chemistry (MA, MS); computational neuroscience (PhD); computational operations research (MS); computer science (MS, PhD); history (MA, PhD); interface, thin film and surface science (PhD); lasers and optics (PhD); magnetic resonance (PhD); materials science and engineering (PhD); mathematical and computational biology (PhD); medical imaging (PhD); nanotechnology (PhD); neuroscience (PhD); non-destructive evaluation (PhD); physics (MS, PhD); polymer chemistry (PhD); psychology (MA); public policy (MPP); remote sensing (PhD). *Application fee:* $45. *Application Contact:* Wanda Carter, Graduate Registrar, 757-221-2467, Fax: 757-221-4874, E-mail: wdcart@wm.edu. *Dean of Graduate Studies and Research*, Dr. Virginia Torczon, 757-221-2468, E-mail: vjtorc@wm.edu.

Raymond A. Mason School of Business Students: 342 full-time (114 women), 217 part-time (82 women); includes 122 minority (52 Black or African American, non-Hispanic/Latino; 30 Asian, non-Hispanic/Latino; 27 Hispanic/Latino; 13 Two or more races, non-Hispanic/Latino), 106 international. Average age 30. 348 applicants, 60% accepted, 99 enrolled. *Faculty:* 50 full-time (13 women), 7 part-time/adjunct (0 women). *Financial support:* In 2015–16, 141 students received support. Scholarships/grants and unspecified assistantships available. Financial award applicants required to submit FAFSA. In 2015, 292 master's awarded. *Degree program information:* Part-time and evening/weekend programs available. Part-time, evening/weekend, online learning. Offers accounting (M Acc); business (EMBA, M Acc, MBA, MS). *Application deadline:* For fall admission, 11/16 for domestic and international students; for winter admission, 1/18 for domestic and international students; for spring admission, 5/16 for domestic and international students; for summer admission, 7/15 for domestic students. *Application fee:* $100. Electronic applications accepted. *Application Contact:* Amanda K. Barth, Director, Full-time MBA Admissions, 757-221-2944, Fax: 757-221-2958, E-mail: amanda.barth@mason.wm.edu. *Dean*, Dr. Lawrence Pulley, 757-221-2891, Fax: 757-221-2937, E-mail: larry.pulley@mason.wm.edu.

School of Education Students: 206 full-time (164 women), 181 part-time (135 women); includes 81 minority (44 Black or African American, non-Hispanic/Latino; 13 Asian, non-Hispanic/Latino; 16 Hispanic/Latino; 8 Two or more races, non-Hispanic/Latino), 13 international. Average age 33. 452 applicants, 63% accepted, 183 enrolled. *Faculty:* 39 full-time (23 women), 94 part-time/adjunct (75 women). *Financial support:* In 2015–16, 150 students received support, including 1 fellowship with full tuition reimbursement available (averaging $20,000 per year), 93 research assistantships with tuition reimbursements available (averaging $17,647 per year); career-related internships or fieldwork, scholarships/grants, and unspecified assistantships also available. Financial award application deadline: 1/15; financial award applicants required to submit FAFSA. In 2015, 140 master's, 34 doctorates, 10 other advanced degrees awarded. *Degree program information:* Part-time and evening/weekend programs available. Part-time, evening/weekend. Offers community counseling (M Ed); curriculum and educational technology (PhD); curriculum and instruction (MA Ed); curriculum leadership (Ed D, PhD); education (M Ed, MA Ed, Ed D, PhD, Ed S); educational leadership (M Ed); educational policy, planning, and leadership (Ed D, PhD); school counseling (M Ed); school psychology (M Ed, Ed S). *Application deadline:* For fall admission, 1/15 for domestic and international students; for spring admission, 10/1 for domestic and international students. *Application fee:* $50. Electronic applications accepted. *Application Contact:* Dorothy Smith Osborne, Assistant Dean for Academic Programs and Student Services, 757-221-2317, Fax: 757-221-2293, E-mail: dsosbo@wm.edu. *Dean*, Dr. Spencer G. Niles, 757-221-2317, E-mail: sgniles@wm.edu.

Virginia Institute of Marine Science Students: 82 full-time (48 women), 2 part-time (0 women); includes 7 minority (2 Black or African American, non-Hispanic/Latino; 2 Asian, non-Hispanic/Latino; 1 Hispanic/Latino; 2 Two or more races, non-Hispanic/Latino), 19 international. Average age 28. 116 applicants, 28% accepted, 21 enrolled. *Faculty:* 65 full-time (20 women), 1 part-time/adjunct (0 women). *Financial support:* In 2015–16, 56 students received support, including fellowships with full tuition reimbursements available (averaging $25,000 per year), research assistantships with full tuition reimbursements available (averaging $20,452 per year), teaching assistantships with full tuition reimbursements available (averaging $20,452 per year); career-related internships or fieldwork, scholarships/grants, health care benefits, and unspecified assistantships also available. Financial award application deadline: 1/5; financial award applicants required to submit FAFSA. In 2015, 11 master's, 9 doctorates awarded. Offers marine science (MS, PhD). *Application deadline:* For fall admission, 1/5 for domestic and international students. *Application fee:* $53. Electronic applications accepted. *Application Contact:* Dr. Linda C. Schaffner, Associate Dean of Academic Studies, 804-684-7105, Fax: 804-684-7881, E-mail: admissions@vims.edu. *Dean/Director*, Dr. John T. Wells, 804-684-7102, Fax: 804-684-7009, E-mail: wells@vims.edu.

William and Mary Law School Students: 654 full-time (351 women), 15 part-time (10 women); includes 76 minority (24 Black or African American, non-Hispanic/Latino; 11 Asian, non-Hispanic/Latino; 27 Hispanic/Latino; 14 Two or more races, non-Hispanic/Latino), 49 international. Average age 25. 4,833 applicants, 38% accepted, 238 enrolled. *Faculty:* 44 full-time (19 women), 41 part-time/adjunct (10 women). *Financial support:* In 2015–16, 604 students received support, including 242 fellowships (averaging $4,000 per year), 62 research assistantships (averaging $2,419 per year), 35 teaching assistantships (averaging $5,391 per year); career-related internships or fieldwork, Federal Work-Study, and scholarships/grants also available. Financial award application deadline: 2/15; financial award applicants required to submit FAFSA. In 2015, 33 master's, 178 doctorates awarded. Offers law (LL M, JD). *Application deadline:* For fall admission, 3/1 priority date for domestic and international students. *Application fee:* $50. Electronic applications accepted. *Application Contact:* Faye F. Shealy, Associate Dean for Admission, 757-221-3785, Fax: 757-221-3261, E-mail: ffshea@wm.edu. *Dean/Professor*, Davison M. Douglas, 757-221-3790, Fax: 757-221-3261, E-mail: dmdoug@wm.edu.

COLORADO CHRISTIAN UNIVERSITY, Lakewood, CO 80226

General Information Independent-religious, coed, comprehensive institution. *Graduate housing:* On-campus housing not available.

GRADUATE UNITS

Program in Business Administration ***Degree program information:*** Part-time and evening/weekend programs available. Part-time, evening/weekend, online learning. Offers corporate training (MBA); information security (MA); leadership (MBA); project management (MBA). Electronic applications accepted.

Program in Counseling ***Degree program information:*** Part-time and evening/weekend programs available. Part-time, evening/weekend. Offers counseling (MAC). Electronic applications accepted.

Program in Curriculum and Instruction ***Degree program information:*** Part-time and evening/weekend programs available. Part-time, evening/weekend. Offers corporate education (MACI); early childhood educator (MACI); elementary educator (MACI); instructional technology (MACI); master educator (MACI); online course developer (MACI); online teaching and learning (MACI); special education generalist (MACI). Electronic applications accepted.

THE COLORADO COLLEGE, Colorado Springs, CO 80903-3294

General Information Independent, coed, comprehensive institution. *Graduate housing:* On-campus housing not available.

GRADUATE UNITS

Education Department Offers art teaching (K-12) (MAT); arts and humanities (MAT); elementary education (MAT); elementary school teaching (MAT); English teaching (MAT); foreign language teaching (MAT); integrated natural sciences (MAT); liberal arts (MAT); mathematics teaching (MAT); music teaching (MAT); science teaching (MAT); secondary education (MAT); social studies teaching (MAT); Southwest studies (MAT); teaching (MAT). Electronic applications accepted.

COLORADO HEIGHTS UNIVERSITY, Denver, CO 80236-2711

General Information Independent, coed, comprehensive institution.

GRADUATE UNITS

Program in International Business Offers accounting (MBA); corporate finance (MBA); environmental management (MBA); healthcare management (MBA).

COLORADO MESA UNIVERSITY, Grand Junction, CO 81501-3122

General Information State-supported, coed, comprehensive institution. *Graduate housing:* Room and/or apartments available on a first-come, first-served basis to single students; on-campus housing not available to married students. Housing application deadline: 6/1.

GRADUATE UNITS

Center for Teacher Education ***Degree program information:*** Part-time programs available. Part-time, online learning. Offers educational leadership (MAEd); English for speakers of other languages (MAEd); exceptional learner/special education (MAEd); teacher leader (MAEd). Electronic applications accepted.

Department of Business ***Degree program information:*** Part-time and evening/weekend programs available. Part-time, evening/weekend. Offers business (MBA). Electronic applications accepted.

Department of Health Sciences ***Degree program information:*** Part-time and evening/weekend programs available. Part-time, evening/weekend, online learning. Offers advanced nursing practice (MSN); family nurse practitioner (DNP); health information technology systems (Graduate Certificate); nursing education (MSN). Electronic applications accepted.

★ COLORADO SCHOOL OF MINES, Golden, CO 80401-1887

General Information State-supported, coed, university. CGS member. *Enrollment:* 5,924 graduate, professional, and undergraduate students; 1,162 full-time matriculated graduate/professional students (338 women), 159 part-time matriculated graduate/professional students (44 women). *Enrollment by degree level:* 729 master's, 592 doctoral. *Graduate faculty:* 404 full-time (121 women), 194 part-time/adjunct (54 women). Tuition, state resident: full-time $15,225. Tuition, nonresident: full-time $32,700. *Graduate housing:* Rooms and/or apartments available on a first-come, first-served basis to single and married students. Typical cost: $968 per year for single students; $1200 per year for married students. Room charges vary according to campus/location and housing facility selected. Housing application deadline: 5/15. *Student services:* Campus employment opportunities, campus safety program, career counseling, exercise/wellness program, free psychological counseling, international student services, low-cost health insurance, services for students with disabilities, teacher training, writing training. *Library:* Arthur Lakes Library. *Collection:* Books: 488,713 (physical), 105,000 (digital/electronic); Serial titles: 618 (physical), 106,092 (digital/electronic); Databases: 134. Weekly public service hours: 107; students can reserve study rooms.

Computer facilities: Computer purchase and lease plans are available. 1,330 computers available on campus for general student use. A campuswide network can be accessed from student residence rooms and from off campus. Online class registration is available.
Website: http://www.mines.edu/

General Application Contact: Angel Dotson, Graduate Admissions Coordinator, 303-273-3348, E-mail: grad-app@mines.edu.

GRADUATE UNITS

Office of Graduate Studies Students: 1,162 full-time (338 women), 159 part-time (44 women); includes 150 minority (10 Black or African American, non-Hispanic/Latino; 3 American Indian or Alaska Native, non-Hispanic/Latino; 33 Asian, non-Hispanic/Latino; 76 Hispanic/Latino; 1 Native Hawaiian or other Pacific Islander, non-Hispanic/Latino; 27 Two or more races, non-Hispanic/Latino), 409 international. Average age 28. 2,424 applicants, 38% accepted, 380 enrolled. *Faculty:* 404 full-time (283 women), 194 part-time/adjunct (140 women). *Financial support:* In 2015–16, 72 fellowships with full tuition reimbursements, 508 research assistantships with full tuition reimbursements, 177 teaching assistantships with full tuition reimbursements were awarded; career-related internships or fieldwork, Federal Work-Study, institutionally sponsored loans, scholarships/grants, health care benefits, and unspecified assistantships also available. Financial award application deadline: 12/15; financial award applicants required to submit FAFSA. In 2015, 345 master's, 124 doctorates awarded. *Degree program information:* Part-time programs available. Part-time. Offers applied physics (MS, PhD); chemical and biological engineering (MS, PhD); chemistry (MS, PhD); civil and environmental engineering (MS, PhD); computer science (MS, PhD); electrical engineering (MS, PhD); engineering and technology management (MS); environmental engineering science (MS, PhD); geochemistry (MS, PMS, PhD); geological engineering

(ME, MS, PhD); geology (MS, PhD); geophysical engineering (ME, MS, PhD); geophysics (MS, PhD); hydrology (MS, PhD); international political economy (Graduate Certificate); materials science (MS, PhD); mechanical engineering (MS, PhD); metallurgical and materials engineering (ME, MS, PhD); mineral economics (PhD); mineral exploration and mining geosciences (PMS); mining and earth systems engineering (MS); mining engineering (PhD); nuclear engineering (ME, MS, PhD); operations research and engineering (PhD); petroleum engineering (ME, MS, PhD); petroleum reservoir systems (PMS); science and technology policy (Graduate Certificate); underground construction and tunneling (MS, PhD). *Application deadline:* For fall admission, 12/15 priority date for domestic and international students; for spring admission, 9/1 priority date for domestic and international students. *Application fee:* $50 ($70 for international students). Electronic applications accepted. *Application Contact:* Angel Dotson, Graduate Admissions Coordinator, 303-273-3348, Fax: 303-273-3247, E-mail: grad-app@mines.edu. *Dean of Graduate Studies*, Dr. Tina Voelker, E-mail: bvoelker@mines.edu.

See Display below and Close-Up on page 873.

COLORADO SCHOOL OF TRADITIONAL CHINESE MEDICINE, Denver, CO 80206-2127

General Information Independent, coed, graduate-only institution. *Enrollment by degree level:* 92 master's. *Graduate faculty:* 52 part-time/adjunct (20 women). *Tuition, area resident:* Full-time $17,000; part-time $9000 per year. *Required fees:* $450; $1020 per unit. $340 per trimester. Part-time tuition and fees vary according to course load and program. *Graduate housing:* On-campus housing not available. *Student services:* Campus employment opportunities. *Library:* CSTCM Library.

Computer facilities: 4 computers available on campus for general student use. Website: http://www.cstcm.edu/

General Application Contact: Chris Duxbury-Edwards, Recruiting Director, 303-329-6355 Ext. 21, Fax: 303-388-8165, E-mail: recruiting@cstcm.edu.

GRADUATE UNITS

Graduate Programs Students: 92 full-time (67 women). Average age 33. 72 applicants, 88% accepted, 60 enrolled. *Faculty:* 52 part-time/adjunct (20 women). *Financial support:* Scholarships/grants available. Financial award applicants required to submit FAFSA. In 2015, 1 master's awarded. *Degree program information:* Part-time programs available. Part-time. Offers acupuncture (MS); traditional Chinese medicine (MS). *Application deadline:* For fall admission, 8/19 for domestic and international students; for winter admission, 12/23 for domestic and international students; for summer admission, 4/22 for domestic and international students. Applications are processed on a rolling basis. *Application fee:* $50. *Application Contact:* Chris Duxbury-Edwards, Recruiting Director, 303-329-6355 Ext. 21, Fax: 303-388-8165, E-mail: recruiting@cstcm.edu. *Administrative Director*, Vladimir Dibrigida, 303-329-6355 Ext. 11, Fax: 303-388-8165, E-mail: director@cstcm.edu.

COLORADO STATE UNIVERSITY, Fort Collins, CO 80523-0015

General Information State-supported, coed, university. CGS member. *Enrollment:* 31,943 graduate, professional, and undergraduate students; 2,820 full-time matriculated graduate/professional students (1,651 women), 4,041 part-time matriculated graduate/professional students (1,846 women). *Enrollment by degree level:* 4,625 master's, 2,219 doctoral, 17 other advanced degrees. *Graduate faculty:* 1,049 full-time (416 women), 237 part-time/adjunct (125 women). Tuition, state resident: full-time $9348. Tuition, nonresident: full-time $22,916. *Required fees:* $2174; $473.72 per credit hour. $236.86 per semester. Tuition and fees vary according to course load and program. *Graduate housing:* Room and/or apartments available on a first-come, first-served basis to single students; on-campus housing not available to married students. Typical cost: $5258 per year ($10,794 including board). Room and board charges vary according to board plan and housing facility selected. *Student services:* Campus employment opportunities, campus safety program, career counseling, child daycare facilities, exercise/wellness program, free psychological counseling, grant writing training, international student services, low-cost health insurance, multicultural affairs office, services for students with disabilities, teacher training, writing training. *Library:* William E. Morgan Library plus 2 others. *Collection:* Books: 1.2 million (physical), 511,081 (digital/electronic); Serial titles: 52,468 (physical), 91,932 (digital/electronic); Databases: 398. Weekly public service hours: 108; study areas open 24 hours, 5–7 days a week; students can reserve study rooms. *Research affiliation:* Department of Commerce/National Oceanic and Atmospheric Administration (NOAA) Joint Institutes (meteorological satellite imagery), Natural Resources Research Center/Agencies of U.S. Departments of Agriculture (USDA) and Interior (infectious disease), National Center for Genetic Resources Preservation (genetic resources of crops), National Wildlife Research Center (interactions of wild animals and society), National Centers for Atmospheric Research (climate, meteorology), Solix (algae-produced biofuels).

Computer facilities: Computer purchase and lease plans are available. 2,000 computers available on campus for general student use. A campuswide network can be accessed from student residence rooms and from off campus. Online class registration, personalized portal services including transcripts and financials (billing, financial aid) are available.
Website: http://www.colostate.edu/

General Application Contact: Sandra Dailey, Academic Progress and Special Admissions Coordinator, Graduate School, 970-491-6817, Fax: 970-491-2194, E-mail: gradschool@colostate.edu.

GRADUATE UNITS

College of Agricultural Sciences Students: 123 full-time (64 women), 221 part-time (121 women); includes 20 minority (1 Black or African American, non-Hispanic/Latino; 1 American Indian or Alaska Native, non-Hispanic/Latino; 9 Hispanic/Latino; 9 Two or more races, non-Hispanic/Latino), 64 international. Average age 32. 168 applicants, 65% accepted, 72 enrolled. *Faculty:* 84 full-time (22 women), 16 part-time/adjunct (9 women). *Financial support:* In 2015–16, 9 fellowships with full tuition reimbursements (averaging $49,223 per year), 75 research assistantships with tuition reimbursements (averaging $19,688 per year), 34 teaching assistantships (averaging $16,031 per year) were awarded; Federal Work-Study, scholarships/grants, tuition waivers, and unspecified assistantships also available. Financial award application deadline: 1/15; financial award applicants required to submit FAFSA. In 2015, 81 master's, 15 doctorates awarded. *Degree program information:* Part-time and evening/weekend programs available. Part-time, evening/weekend. Offers agricultural and resource economics (MS, PhD); agricultural sciences (M Agr, MAEE, MLA, MS, PhD); animal sciences (MS, PhD); entomology (MS, PhD); horticulture (MS, PhD); landscape architecture (MLA); pest management (MS); plant pathology and weed science (MS, PhD); soil and crop sciences (MS, PhD). *Application deadline:* Applications are processed on a rolling basis. *Application fee:* $60 ($70 for international students). Electronic applications accepted. *Application Contact:* Pam Schell, Administrative Assistant III, 970-491-2410, Fax: 970-

491-4895, E-mail: pam.schell@colostate.edu. *Dean,* Dr. Ajay Menon, 970-491-6274, Fax: 970-491-4895, E-mail: ajay.menon@colostate.edu.

College of Business Students: 243 full-time (108 women), 1,123 part-time (371 women); includes 269 minority (47 Black or African American, non-Hispanic/Latino; 9 American Indian or Alaska Native, non-Hispanic/Latino; 89 Asian, non-Hispanic/Latino; 94 Hispanic/Latino; 2 Native Hawaiian or other Pacific Islander, non-Hispanic/Latino; 28 Two or more races, non-Hispanic/Latino), 132 international. Average age 35. 814 applicants, 72% accepted, 417 enrolled. *Faculty:* 44 full-time (11 women), 7 part-time/adjunct (1 woman). *Financial support:* In 2015–16, 1 student received support. Career-related internships or fieldwork, scholarships/grants, and unspecified assistantships available. Financial award application deadline: 2/1; financial award applicants required to submit FAFSA. In 2015, 551 master's awarded. *Degree program information:* Part-time and evening/weekend programs available. Part-time, evening/weekend, 100% online, blended/hybrid learning. Offers accounting (M Acc); business (M Acc, MBA, MCIS, MS, MSBA); business administration (MBA); computer information systems (MCIS); financial risk management (MSBA); global social and sustainable enterprise (MBA). *Application fee:* $60 ($70 for international students). Electronic applications accepted. *Application Contact:* Graduate Programs Admissions Contact, 970-491-4622, E-mail: cobgradinfo@colostate.edu. *Dean,* Dr. Beth Walker, 970-491-6471, E-mail: beth.walker@colostate.edu.

College of Engineering Students: 372 full-time (98 women), 612 part-time (142 women); includes 91 minority (13 Black or African American, non-Hispanic/Latino; 1 American Indian or Alaska Native, non-Hispanic/Latino; 34 Asian, non-Hispanic/Latino; 32 Hispanic/Latino; 11 Two or more races, non-Hispanic/Latino), 395 international. Average age 29. 1,001 applicants, 60% accepted, 224 enrolled. *Faculty:* 160 full-time (33 women), 43 part-time/adjunct (9 women). *Financial support:* In 2015–16, 33 fellowships with full tuition reimbursements (averaging $46,011 per year), 236 research assistantships with tuition reimbursements (averaging $23,747 per year), 44 teaching assistantships with tuition reimbursements (averaging $16,137 per year) were awarded; scholarships/grants, traineeships, health care benefits, and unspecified assistantships also available. Financial award application deadline: 1/15; financial award applicants required to submit FAFSA. In 2015, 189 master's, 48 doctorates awarded. *Degree program information:* Part-time and evening/weekend programs available. Part-time, evening/weekend, 100% online, blended/hybrid learning. Offers atmospheric science (MS, PhD); chemical engineering (MS, PhD); civil engineering (ME, MS, PhD); electrical engineering (MEE, MS, PhD); engineering (ME, MEE, MS, PhD); mechanical engineering (ME, MS, PhD). *Application fee:* $60 ($70 for international students). Electronic applications accepted. *Application Contact:* Dr. Anthony Marchese, Associate Dean, 970-491-6220, Fax: 970-491-3429, E-mail: anthony.marchese@colostate.edu. *Dean,* Dr. David McLean, 970-491-3366, E-mail: david.mclean@colostate.edu.

College of Health and Human Sciences Students: 386 full-time (297 women), 712 part-time (507 women); includes 206 minority (38 Black or African American, non-Hispanic/Latino; 5 American Indian or Alaska Native, non-Hispanic/Latino; 20 Asian, non-Hispanic/Latino; 114 Hispanic/Latino; 1 Native Hawaiian or other Pacific Islander, non-Hispanic/Latino; 28 Two or more races, non-Hispanic/Latino), 41 international. Average age 34. 1,363 applicants, 26% accepted, 258 enrolled. *Faculty:* 100 full-time (65 women), 31 part-time/adjunct (24 women). *Financial support:* In 2015–16, 2 fellowships with full tuition reimbursements (averaging $41,520 per year), 58 research assistantships with tuition reimbursements (averaging $13,872 per year), 66 teaching assistantships with tuition reimbursements (averaging $11,019 per year) were awarded; Federal Work-Study, scholarships/grants, and unspecified assistantships also available. Financial award application deadline: 3/1; financial award applicants required to submit FAFSA. In 2015, 342 master's, 49 doctorates awarded. *Degree program information:* Part-time and evening/weekend programs available. Part-time, evening/weekend, 100% online, blended/hybrid learning. Offers construction management (MS); design and merchandising (MS); exercise science and nutrition (MS); family and developmental studies (MS); food science and human nutrition (MS, PhD); health and exercise science (MS); health and human sciences (M Ed, MOT, MS, MSW, PhD); human bioenergetics (PhD); human development and family studies (PhD); marriage and family therapy (MS); occupational therapy (MOT, MS, PhD). *Application fee:* $60 ($70 for international students). Electronic applications accepted. *Application Contact:* Patricia Davies, Associate Dean for Research and Graduate Programs, 970-491-7294, E-mail: patricia.davies@colostate.edu. *Dean,* Dr. Jeff McCubbin, 970-491-5841, E-mail: jeff.mccubbin@colostate.edu.

School of Education Students: 82 full-time (57 women), 544 part-time (372 women); includes 141 minority (29 Black or African American, non-Hispanic/Latino; 3 American Indian or Alaska Native, non-Hispanic/Latino; 15 Asian, non-Hispanic/Latino; 72 Hispanic/Latino; 1 Native Hawaiian or other Pacific Islander, non-Hispanic/Latino; 21 Two or more races, non-Hispanic/Latino), 15 international. Average age 37. 453 applicants, 28% accepted, 110 enrolled. *Faculty:* 29 full-time (19 women), 20 part-time/adjunct (14 women). *Financial support:* In 2015–16, 3 research assistantships with full tuition reimbursements (averaging $16,720 per year), 6 teaching assistantships with full tuition reimbursements (averaging $9,976 per year) were awarded; fellowships with partial tuition reimbursements, Federal Work-Study, scholarships/grants, and unspecified assistantships also available. Financial award application deadline: 3/1; financial award applicants required to submit FAFSA. In 2015, 151 master's, 40 doctorates awarded. *Degree program information:* Part-time and evening/weekend programs available. Part-time, evening/weekend, 100% online, blended/hybrid learning. Offers adult education and training (M Ed); counseling and career development (M Ed); education sciences (M Ed, PhD); educational leadership (M Ed, PhD); higher education leadership (PhD); organizational learning, performance and change (M Ed, PhD); student affairs in higher education (MS). *Application deadline:* For fall admission, 1/2 for domestic and international students; for summer admission, 3/1 for domestic and international students. Applications are processed on a rolling basis. *Application fee:* $60 ($70 for international students). Electronic applications accepted. *Application Contact:* Kelli Clark, Graduate Programs Coordinator, 970-491-2093, Fax: 970-491-1317, E-mail: kelli.clark@colostate.edu. *Director,* Dr. George Kamberelis, 970-491-6317, Fax: 970-491-1317, E-mail: george.kamberelis@colostate.edu.

School of Social Work Students: 71 full-time (56 women), 61 part-time (52 women); includes 28 minority (9 Black or African American, non-Hispanic/Latino; 1 American Indian or Alaska Native, non-Hispanic/Latino; 18 Hispanic/Latino), 3 international. Average age 32. 50 applicants, 98% accepted, 29 enrolled. *Faculty:* 8 full-time (7 women), 8 part-time/adjunct (7 women). *Financial support:* In 2015–16, 6 students received support, including 5 research assistantships with partial tuition reimbursements available (averaging $13,595 per year), 3 teaching assistantships with partial tuition reimbursements available (averaging $6,840 per year); career-related internships or fieldwork, scholarships/grants, and unspecified assistantships also available. Financial award application deadline: 3/1; financial award applicants required to submit FAFSA. In 2015, 72 master's, 1 doctorate awarded. *Degree program information:* Part-time and evening/weekend programs available. Part-time, evening/weekend, 100% online, blended/hybrid learning. Offers social work (MSW, PhD). *Application deadline:* For fall admission, 1/2 priority date for domestic and international students. *Application fee:* $60 ($70 for international students). Electronic applications accepted. *Application Contact:* Tim Frank, MSW Program Coordinator, 970-491-2536, Fax: 970-491-7280, E-mail: timothy.frank@colostate.edu. *Director,* Dr. Audrey Shillington, 970-491-6612, Fax: 970-491-7280, E-mail: audrey.shillington@colostate.edu.

College of Liberal Arts Students: 359 full-time (227 women), 339 part-time (233 women); includes 67 minority (7 Black or African American, non-Hispanic/Latino; 4 American Indian or Alaska Native, non-Hispanic/Latino; 9 Asian, non-Hispanic/Latino; 33 Hispanic/Latino; 1 Native Hawaiian or other Pacific Islander, non-Hispanic/Latino; 13 Two or more races, non-Hispanic/Latino), 77 international. Average age 30. 608 applicants, 63% accepted, 197 enrolled. *Faculty:* 173 full-time (90 women), 56 part-time/adjunct (46 women). *Financial support:* In 2015–16, 7 research assistantships with tuition reimbursements (averaging $16,994 per year), 261 teaching assistantships with tuition reimbursements (averaging $13,757 per year) were awarded; career-related internships or fieldwork, Federal Work-Study, scholarships/grants, and unspecified assistantships also available. Support available to part-time students. Financial award application deadline: 1/1; financial award applicants required to submit FAFSA. In 2015, 180 master's, 11 doctorates awarded. *Degree program information:* Part-time programs available. Part-time. Offers anthropology (MA); art and art history (MFA); communication studies (MA); creative writing (MFA); economics (MA, PhD); English (MA); ethnic studies (MA); history (MA); languages, literatures and cultures (MA); liberal arts (MA, MALA, MFA, MM, MS, PhD); philosophy (MA); political science (MA, PhD); public communication and technology (MS, PhD); sociology (MA, PhD). *Application fee:* $60 ($70 for international students). Electronic applications accepted. *Application Contact:* Dr. Bruce Ronda, Associate Dean for Faculty and Graduate Studies, 970-491-5421, Fax: 970-491-0528, E-mail: bruce.ronda@colostate.edu. *Dean,* Dr. Ann Gill, 970-491-5421, Fax: 970-491-0528, E-mail: ann.gill@colostate.edu.

LEAP Institute for the Arts Students: 11 full-time (10 women), 19 part-time (16 women); includes 3 minority (2 American Indian or Alaska Native, non-Hispanic/Latino; 1 Two or more races, non-Hispanic/Latino), 2 international. Average age 29. 36 applicants, 97% accepted, 17 enrolled. *Faculty:* 1 part-time/adjunct. *Financial support:* In 2015–16, 3 students received support. Fellowships, research assistantships, teaching assistantships, career-related internships or fieldwork, scholarships/grants, and tuition waivers available. Financial award application deadline: 3/1; financial award applicants required to submit FAFSA. In 2015, 4 master's awarded. *Degree program information:* Part-time and evening/weekend programs available. Part-time, evening/weekend, 100% online. Offers arts leadership and administration (MALA). *Application deadline:* For fall admission, 4/15 for domestic and international students; for spring admission, 9/15 for domestic and international students; for summer admission, 2/15 for domestic and international students. Applications are processed on a rolling basis. *Application fee:* $60 ($70 for international students). Electronic applications accepted. *Application Contact:* Dulcie Willis, Office Coordinator, 970-491-3746, Fax: 970-491-7541, E-mail: dulcie.willis@colostate.edu. *Director,* Dr. Constance DeVereaux, 970-491-3902, Fax: 970-491-7541, E-mail: constance.devereaux@colostate.edu.

School of Music, Theatre and Dance Students: 55 full-time (38 women), 112 part-time (90 women); includes 19 minority (1 Black or African American, non-Hispanic/Latino; 5 Asian, non-Hispanic/Latino; 11 Hispanic/Latino; 2 Two or more races, non-Hispanic/Latino), 12 international. Average age 30. 92 applicants, 72% accepted, 35 enrolled. *Faculty:* 24 full-time (7 women), 10 part-time/adjunct (5 women). *Financial support:* In 2015–16, 25 students received support, including 26 teaching assistantships with full tuition reimbursements available (averaging $8,418 per year); research assistantships, scholarships/grants, traineeships, and unspecified assistantships also available. Financial award application deadline: 2/15; financial award applicants required to submit FAFSA. In 2015, 40 master's awarded. *Degree program information:* Part-time programs available. Part-time. Offers choral conducting (MM); instrumental conducting (MM); music education (MM); music performance (MM); music therapy (MM). *Application deadline:* For fall admission, 2/15 for domestic and international students. Applications are processed on a rolling basis. *Application fee:* $60 ($70 for international students). Electronic applications accepted. *Application Contact:* Dr. G. Murray Oliver, Director of Graduate Studies/Assistant Professor, 970-491-5193, E-mail: murray.oliver@colostate.edu. *Director,* Dr. Daniel Goble, 970-491-5533, E-mail: dan.goble@colostate.edu.

College of Natural Sciences Students: 308 full-time (119 women), 499 part-time (189 women); includes 94 minority (1 Black or African American, non-Hispanic/Latino; 2 American Indian or Alaska Native, non-Hispanic/Latino; 30 Asian, non-Hispanic/Latino; 40 Hispanic/Latino; 21 Two or more races, non-Hispanic/Latino), 171 international. Average age 29. 529 applicants, 59% accepted, 202 enrolled. *Faculty:* 190 full-time (64 women), 24 part-time/adjunct (12 women). *Financial support:* In 2015–16, 58 fellowships (averaging $39,618 per year), 184 research assistantships with full tuition reimbursements (averaging $21,410 per year), 325 teaching assistantships with full tuition reimbursements (averaging $18,783 per year) were awarded; scholarships/grants also available. Financial award application deadline: 2/1; financial award applicants required to submit FAFSA. In 2015, 146 master's, 67 doctorates awarded. *Degree program information:* Part-time programs available. Part-time, 100% online. Offers biochemistry (MS, PhD); botany (MS, PhD); chemistry (MS, PhD); computer science (MCS, MS, PhD); industrial/organizational psychology (MAIOP); mathematics (MS, PhD); natural sciences (MAIOP, MAS, MCS, MS, PhD); physics (MS, PhD); psychology (MS, PhD); statistics (MAS, MS, PhD); zoology (MS, PhD). *Application fee:* $60 ($70 for international students). Electronic applications accepted. *Application Contact:* Dr. Simon Tavener, Associate Dean for Academics, 970-491-1300, E-mail: cns@colostate.edu. *Dean,* Dr. Janice Nerger, 970-491-1300, Fax: 970-491-6639, E-mail: janice.nerger@colostate.edu.

College of Veterinary Medicine and Biomedical Sciences Students: 836 full-time (627 women), 151 part-time (92 women); includes 174 minority (6 Black or African American, non-Hispanic/Latino; 7 American Indian or Alaska Native, non-Hispanic/Latino; 49 Asian, non-Hispanic/Latino; 78 Hispanic/Latino; 34 Two or more races, non-Hispanic/Latino), 49 international. Average age 27. 1,985 applicants, 20% accepted, 363 enrolled. *Faculty:* 235 full-time (113 women), 31 part-time/adjunct (16 women). *Financial support:* In 2015–16, 230 students received support, including 121 fellowships with full tuition reimbursements available (averaging $39,665 per year), 94 research assistantships with tuition reimbursements available (averaging $21,923 per year), 15 teaching assistantships with tuition reimbursements available (averaging $18,206 per year); scholarships/grants, traineeships, and unspecified assistantships also available. Financial award applicants required to submit FAFSA. In 2015, 142 master's, 19 doctorates awarded. Offers biomedical sciences (MS, PhD); clinical sciences (MS, PhD); environmental health (MS, PhD); microbiology (MS, PhD);

pathology (PhD); radiological health sciences (MS, PhD); toxicology (MS, PhD); veterinary medicine (DVM); veterinary medicine and biomedical sciences (MS, DVM, PhD). *Application fee:* $60 ($70 for international students). Electronic applications accepted. *Application Contact:* Dr. Sherry Stewart, Assistant Dean for Admissions and Student Affairs, 970-491-7051, Fax: 970-491-2250, E-mail: sherry.stewart@colostate.edu. *Dean*, Dr. Mark Stetter, 970-491-7051, Fax: 970-491-2250, E-mail: mark.stetter@colostate.edu.

Interdisciplinary College Students: 77 full-time (50 women), 152 part-time (82 women); includes 21 minority (4 Black or African American, non-Hispanic/Latino; 6 Asian, non-Hispanic/Latino; 9 Hispanic/Latino; 2 Two or more races, non-Hispanic/Latino), 41 international. Average age 31. 167 applicants, 19% accepted, 29 enrolled. In 2015, 27 master's, 36 doctorates awarded. Offers cell and molecular biology (MS, PhD); ecology (MS, PhD); molecular, cellular and integrative neurosciences (PhD). *Application fee:* $60 ($70 for international students). Electronic applications accepted. *Application Contact:* Sandra Dailey, Graduate School Administrative Assistant III, 970-491-6817, Fax: 970-491-2194, E-mail: gschool@grad.colostate.edu.

School of Biomedical Engineering Students: 12 full-time (5 women), 20 part-time (9 women); includes 3 minority (2 Asian, non-Hispanic/Latino; 1 Hispanic/Latino), 14 international. Average age 28. 49 applicants, 8% accepted, 3 enrolled. *Financial support:* In 2015–16, 18 students received support, including 15 research assistantships with full tuition reimbursements available (averaging $22,514 per year), 3 teaching assistantships with full tuition reimbursements available (averaging $16,200 per year); fellowships and unspecified assistantships also available. Financial award application deadline: 1/15; financial award applicants required to submit FAFSA. In 2015, 4 master's, 6 doctorates awarded. *Degree program information:* Part-time and evening/weekend programs available. Part-time, evening/weekend, 100% online. Offers biomedical engineering (ME, MS, PhD). *Application deadline:* For fall admission, 1/15 priority date for domestic and international students; for spring admission, 9/1 priority date for domestic and international students. *Application fee:* $60 ($70 for international students). Electronic applications accepted. *Application Contact:* Sara Mattern, Graduate Program Coordinator, 970-491-7157, E-mail: sara.mattern@colostate.edu. *Director*, Dr. Stu Tobet, 970-491-1672, Fax: 970-491-7907, E-mail: stuart.tobet@colostate.edu.

Warner College of Natural Resources Students: 116 full-time (61 women), 232 part-time (109 women); includes 41 minority (3 Black or African American, non-Hispanic/Latino; 1 American Indian or Alaska Native, non-Hispanic/Latino; 1 Asian, non-Hispanic/Latino; 27 Hispanic/Latino; 9 Two or more races, non-Hispanic/Latino), 34 international. Average age 31. 301 applicants, 63% accepted, 141 enrolled. *Faculty:* 63 full-time (18 women), 29 part-time/adjunct (8 women). *Financial support:* In 2015–16, 29 fellowships with full tuition reimbursements (averaging $47,674 per year), 96 research assistantships with partial tuition reimbursements (averaging $22,631 per year), 39 teaching assistantships with partial tuition reimbursements (averaging $13,208 per year) were awarded; career-related internships or fieldwork, Federal Work-Study, scholarships/grants, and unspecified assistantships also available. Financial award application deadline: 3/1; financial award applicants required to submit FAFSA. In 2015, 97 master's, 6 doctorates awarded. *Degree program information:* Part-time and evening/weekend programs available. Part-time, evening/weekend, 100% online. Offers conservation leadership (MS); fish, wildlife, and conservation biology (MFWCB, MS, PhD); forest sciences (MS, PhD); geosciences (MS, PhD); human dimensions of natural resources (MS, PhD); natural resources (MFWCB, MNRS, MS, MTM, PhD); natural resources stewardship (MNRS); rangeland ecosystem science (MS, PhD); tourism management (MTM). *Application fee:* $60 ($70 for international students). Electronic applications accepted. *Application Contact:* Dr. Rich Conant, Associate Dean for Academic Affairs, 970-491-1919, Fax: 970-491-0279, E-mail: conant@nrel.colostate.edu. *Dean*, John P. Hayes, 970-491-6675, Fax: 970-491-0279, E-mail: wcnr_deans_office@mail.colostate.edu.

COLORADO STATE UNIVERSITY–GLOBAL CAMPUS, Greenwood Village, CO 80111

General Information State-supported, coed, comprehensive institution.

GRADUATE UNITS

Graduate Programs Online learning.

COLORADO STATE UNIVERSITY–PUEBLO, Pueblo, CO 81001-4901

General Information State-supported, coed, comprehensive institution. *Graduate housing:* Room and/or apartments available on a first-come, first-served basis to single students; on-campus housing not available to married students. Housing application deadline: 8/1.

GRADUATE UNITS

College of Education, Engineering and Professional Studies ***Degree program information:*** Part-time and evening/weekend programs available. Part-time, evening/weekend. Offers art education (M Ed); education, engineering and professional studies (M Ed, MS); foreign language education (M Ed); health and physical education (M Ed); industrial and systems engineering (MS); instructional technology (M Ed); linguistically diverse education (M Ed); music education (M Ed); nursing (MS); special education (M Ed). Electronic applications accepted.

College of Science and Mathematics ***Degree program information:*** Part-time and evening/weekend programs available. Part-time, evening/weekend. Offers applied natural science (MS).

Malik and Seeme Hasan School of Business ***Degree program information:*** Part-time and evening/weekend programs available. Part-time, evening/weekend. Offers business (MBA).

COLORADO TECHNICAL UNIVERSITY COLORADO SPRINGS, Colorado Springs, CO 80907

General Information Proprietary, coed, university. *Graduate housing:* On-campus housing not available.

GRADUATE UNITS

Graduate Studies ***Degree program information:*** Part-time and evening/weekend programs available. Part-time, evening/weekend. Offers accounting (MBA, MSA); business administration (MBA); computer engineering (MSCE); computer science (DCS); computer systems security (MSCS); criminal justice (MSM); database systems (MSCS); electrical engineering (MSEE); finance (MBA); human resources management (MBA); information systems security (MSM); logistics/supply chain management (MBA); management (DM); marketing (MBA); mediation and dispute resolution (MBA); operations management (MBA); project management (MBA); software engineering (MSCS); systems engineering (MS); technology management (MBA).

COLORADO TECHNICAL UNIVERSITY DENVER SOUTH, Aurora, CO 80014

General Information Proprietary, coed, comprehensive institution. *Graduate housing:* On-campus housing not available.

GRADUATE UNITS

Program in Computer Engineering Offers computer engineering (MS).

Program in Computer Science ***Degree program information:*** Part-time and evening/weekend programs available. Part-time, evening/weekend. Offers computer systems security (MSCS); database systems (MSCS); software engineering (MSCS).

Program in Electrical Engineering Offers electrical engineering (MS).

Program in Information Science Offers information systems security (MSM).

Program in Systems Engineering Offers systems engineering (MS).

Programs in Business Administration and Management ***Degree program information:*** Part-time and evening/weekend programs available. Part-time, evening/weekend. Offers accounting (MBA); business administration (MBA); business administration and management (EMBA); finance (MBA); human resource management (MBA); marketing (MBA); mediation and dispute resolution (MBA); operations management (MBA); project management (MBA); technology management (MBA).

COLUMBIA COLLEGE, Columbia, MO 65216-0002

General Information Independent-religious, coed, comprehensive institution. *Enrollment:* 152 full-time matriculated graduate/professional students (99 women), 903 part-time matriculated graduate/professional students (543 women). *Graduate faculty:* 32 full-time (14 women), 74 part-time/adjunct (32 women). *Tuition, area resident:* Part-time $350 per credit hour. *Graduate housing:* On-campus housing not available. *Student services:* Campus employment opportunities, campus safety program, career counseling, exercise/wellness program, free psychological counseling, international student services, low-cost health insurance, services for students with disabilities, teacher training, writing training. *Library:* J. W. and Lois Stafford Library. *Collection:* Books: 61,653 (physical), 2 million (digital/electronic); Serial titles: 144 (physical), 165,979 (digital/electronic); Databases: 69. Weekly public service hours: 94; students can reserve study rooms.

Computer facilities: Computer purchase and lease plans are available. 128 computers available on campus for general student use. A campuswide network can be accessed from student residence rooms and from off campus. Online class registration is available.
Website: http://www.ccis.edu/

General Application Contact: Stephanie Johnson, Director of Admissions, 573-875-7352, Fax: 573-875-7506, E-mail: sjohnson@ccis.edu.

GRADUATE UNITS

Master of Arts in Teaching Program Students: 19 full-time (13 women), 82 part-time (60 women); includes 21 minority (11 Black or African American, non-Hispanic/Latino; 2 American Indian or Alaska Native, non-Hispanic/Latino; 1 Asian, non-Hispanic/Latino; 4 Hispanic/Latino; 3 Two or more races, non-Hispanic/Latino), 2 international. Average age 35. 105 applicants, 97% accepted, 68 enrolled. *Faculty:* 19 full-time (13 women), 13 part-time/adjunct (8 women). *Financial support:* Career-related internships or fieldwork, Federal Work-Study, and scholarships/grants available. Financial award application deadline: 3/15; financial award applicants required to submit FAFSA. In 2015, 45 master's awarded. *Degree program information:* Part-time and evening/weekend programs available. Part-time, evening/weekend, 100% online, blended/hybrid learning. Offers teaching (MAT). *Application deadline:* For fall admission, 8/9 priority date for domestic and international students; for spring admission, 12/27 priority date for domestic and international students. Applications are processed on a rolling basis. *Application fee:* $55. Electronic applications accepted. *Application Contact:* Stephanie Johnson, Director of Admissions, 573-875-7352, Fax: 573-875-7506, E-mail: sjohnson@ccis.edu. *Graduate Program Coordinator*, Dr. Karen Weston, 573-875-7637, Fax: 573-876-4493, E-mail: kjweston@ccis.edu.

Master of Business Administration Program Students: 52 full-time (28 women), 399 part-time (224 women); includes 99 minority (60 Black or African American, non-Hispanic/Latino; 3 American Indian or Alaska Native, non-Hispanic/Latino; 7 Asian, non-Hispanic/Latino; 20 Hispanic/Latino; 1 Native Hawaiian or other Pacific Islander, non-Hispanic/Latino; 8 Two or more races, non-Hispanic/Latino), 13 international. Average age 36. 383 applicants, 96% accepted, 145 enrolled. *Faculty:* 8 full-time (3 women), 38 part-time/adjunct (13 women). *Financial support:* Federal Work-Study and scholarships/grants available. Financial award application deadline: 3/1; financial award applicants required to submit FAFSA. In 2015, 194 master's awarded. *Degree program information:* Part-time and evening/weekend programs available. Part-time, evening/weekend, 100% online, blended/hybrid learning. Offers business administration (MBA). *Application deadline:* For fall admission, 8/9 priority date for domestic and international students; for spring admission, 12/27 priority date for domestic and international students. Applications are processed on a rolling basis. *Application fee:* $55. Electronic applications accepted. *Application Contact:* Stephanie Johnson, Director of Admissions, 573-875-7352, Fax: 573-875-7506, E-mail: sjohnson@ccis.edu. *MBA Program Coordinator*, Dr. Tim Ireland, 573-875-7587, Fax: 573-876-4493, E-mail: tireland@ccis.edu.

Master of Education in Educational Leadership Program Students: 7 full-time (4 women), 29 part-time (22 women); includes 4 minority (all Black or African American, non-Hispanic/Latino). Average age 33. 33 applicants, 100% accepted, 19 enrolled. *Faculty:* 19 full-time (13 women), 13 part-time/adjunct (8 women). *Financial support:* Federal Work-Study and scholarships/grants available. Financial award application deadline: 3/1; financial award applicants required to submit FAFSA. In 2015, 4 master's awarded. *Degree program information:* Part-time and evening/weekend programs available. Part-time, evening/weekend, 100% online, blended/hybrid learning. Offers educational leadership (M Ed). *Application deadline:* For fall admission, 8/9 priority date for domestic and international students; for spring admission, 12/27 priority date for domestic and international students. Applications are processed on a rolling basis. *Application fee:* $55. Electronic applications accepted. *Application Contact:* Stephanie Johnson, Director of Admissions, 573-875-7352, Fax: 573-875-7506, E-mail: sjohnson@ccis.edu. *M Ed Coordinator*, Teresa VanDover, 573-875-7794, E-mail: tmvandover@ccis.edu.

Master of Science in Criminal Justice Program Students: 9 full-time (5 women), 117 part-time (70 women); includes 38 minority (25 Black or African American, non-Hispanic/Latino; 9 Hispanic/Latino; 4 Two or more races, non-Hispanic/Latino), 1 international. Average age 38. 91 applicants, 92% accepted, 45 enrolled. *Faculty:* 4 full-time (1 woman), 13 part-time/adjunct (6 women). *Financial support:* Federal Work-Study and scholarships/grants available. Financial award application deadline: 3/1; financial award applicants required to submit FAFSA. In 2015, 59 master's awarded. *Degree program information:* Part-time and evening/weekend programs available. Part-time, evening/weekend, 100% online, blended/hybrid learning. Offers criminal justice (MSCJ). *Application deadline:* For fall admission, 8/9 priority date for domestic and international students; for spring admission, 12/27 priority date for domestic and international students. Applications are processed on a rolling basis. *Application fee:* $55. Electronic applications accepted. *Application Contact:* Stephanie Johnson, Director of Admissions, 573-875-7352, Fax: 573-875-7506, E-mail: sjohnson@ccis.edu. *Graduate Program Coordinator*, Dr. Mike Lyman, 573-875-7472, E-mail: mlyman@ccis.edu.

COLUMBIA COLLEGE, Columbia, SC 29203-5998

General Information Independent-religious, coed, primarily women, comprehensive institution. *Enrollment:* 1,650 graduate, professional, and undergraduate students; 95 full-time matriculated graduate/professional students (88 women), 2 part-time matriculated graduate/professional students (1 woman). *Enrollment by degree level:* 97 master's. *Graduate faculty:* 3 full-time (1 woman), 18 part-time/adjunct (10 women). *Tuition, area resident:* Full-time $4230; part-time $470 per semester hour. *Graduate housing:* On-campus housing not available. *Student services:* Campus safety program, career counseling. *Library:* J. Edens Drake Library plus 1 other.

Computer facilities: Computer purchase and lease plans are available. A campuswide network can be accessed from student residence rooms. Online class registration is available.
Website: http://www.columbiasc.edu/

General Application Contact: Diane Peaks, Director of Graduate School and Evening College Admissions, 803-786-3766, Fax: 803-786-3674, E-mail: dpeaks@columbiasc.edu.

GRADUATE UNITS

Graduate Programs Students: 95 full-time (88 women), 2 part-time (1 woman); includes 38 minority (36 Black or African American, non-Hispanic/Latino; 1 Asian, non-Hispanic/Latino; 1 Hispanic/Latino). Average age 26. 66 applicants, 98% accepted, 65 enrolled. *Faculty:* 3 full-time (1 woman), 18 part-time/adjunct (10 women). *Financial support:* Available to part-time students. Application deadline: 7/1; applicants required to submit FAFSA. In 2015, 141 master's awarded. *Degree program information:* Part-time and evening/weekend programs available. Part-time, evening/weekend. Offers organizational change and leadership (MA). *Application deadline:* For fall admission, 8/22 priority date for domestic students, 8/22 for international students. Applications are processed on a rolling basis. *Application fee:* $50. Electronic applications accepted. *Application Contact:* Diane Peaks, Director of Graduate School and Evening College Admissions, 803-786-3766, Fax: 803-786-3674, E-mail: dpeaks@columbiasc.edu. *Provost and Vice President for Academic Affairs*, Dr. Laurie B. Hopkins, 803-786-3669, Fax: 803-754-3178, E-mail: lhopkins@colacoll.edu.

Education Division Students: 76 full-time (69 women), 1 part-time (0 women); includes 28 minority (26 Black or African American, non-Hispanic/Latino; 1 Asian, non-Hispanic/Latino; 1 Hispanic/Latino). Average age 27. 108 applicants, 81% accepted, 77 enrolled. *Faculty:* 3 full-time (1 woman), 18 part-time/adjunct (10 women). *Financial support:* Available to part-time students. Application deadline: 7/1; applicants required to submit FAFSA. In 2015, 111 master's awarded. *Degree program information:* Part-time and evening/weekend programs available. Part-time, evening/weekend, online learning. Offers divergent learning (M Ed); higher education administration (M Ed). *Application deadline:* For fall admission, 8/22 for domestic students. *Application fee:* $50. Electronic applications accepted. *Application Contact:* Diane Peaks, Director of Graduate School and Evening College Admissions, 803-786-3766, Fax: 803-786-3674, E-mail: dpeaks@columbiasc.edu. *Chair*, Dr. Chris Burkett, 803-786-3782, Fax: 803-786-3034, E-mail: chrisburkett@colacoll.edu.

COLUMBIA COLLEGE CHICAGO, Chicago, IL 60605-1996

General Information Independent, coed, comprehensive institution. *Graduate housing:* Room and/or apartments available on a first-come, first-served basis to single students; on-campus housing not available to married students. Housing application deadline: 5/1.

GRADUATE UNITS

Graduate School ***Degree program information:*** Part-time and evening/weekend programs available. Part-time, evening/weekend, online learning. Offers arts, entertainment and media management (MA); cinema directing (MFA); creative producing (MFA); dance/movement therapy and counseling (MA, Certificate); drama therapy and counseling (MA); fiction (MFA); interdisciplinary arts (MA); interdisciplinary arts and media (MFA); interdisciplinary book and paper arts (MFA); journalism (MA); Laban movement analysis (Certificate); movement pattern analysis (Certificate); music composition for the screen (MFA); nonfiction (MFA); photography (MFA); poetry (MFA). Electronic applications accepted.

COLUMBIA INTERNATIONAL UNIVERSITY, Columbia, SC 29230-3122

General Information Independent-religious, coed, university. *Enrollment:* 1,003 graduate, professional, and undergraduate students; 187 full-time matriculated graduate/professional students (87 women), 267 part-time matriculated graduate/professional students (112 women). *Enrollment by degree level:* 419 master's, 15 doctoral, 20 other advanced degrees. *Graduate faculty:* 24 full-time (4 women), 10 part-time/adjunct (4 women). *Tuition, area resident:* Full-time $9540; part-time $530 per credit hour. *Required fees:* $240 per semester. One-time fee: $50. Tuition and fees vary according to program. *Graduate housing:* Rooms and/or apartments available on a first-come, first-served basis to single and married students. Typical cost: $7800 per year for single students; $10,560 per year for married students. Room charges vary according to housing facility selected. Housing application deadline: 8/1. *Student services:* Campus employment opportunities, campus safety program, career counseling, child daycare facilities, international student services, low-cost health insurance, services for students with disabilities, teacher training. *Library:* G. Allen Fleece Library. *Collection:* Books: 32,000 (physical), 100,000 (digital/electronic); Databases: 133. Weekly public service hours: 81; students can reserve study rooms.

Computer facilities: 106 computers available on campus for general student use. A campuswide network can be accessed from student residence rooms and from off campus. Online class registration is available.
Website: http://www.ciu.edu/

General Application Contact: Alan Lovell, Graduate Admissions Counselor, 803-807-5024, E-mail: yesgrad@ciu.edu.

GRADUATE UNITS

Columbia Graduate School Students: 231 full-time (127 women), 312 part-time (118 women); includes 167 minority (125 Black or African American, non-Hispanic/Latino; 1 American Indian or Alaska Native, non-Hispanic/Latino; 23 Asian, non-Hispanic/Latino; 8 Hispanic/Latino; 10 Two or more races, non-Hispanic/Latino), 43 international. Average age 35. 107 applicants, 56% accepted, 41 enrolled. *Faculty:* 11 full-time (4 women), 7 part-time/adjunct (5 women). *Financial support:* Career-related internships or fieldwork, Federal Work-Study, institutionally sponsored loans, and scholarships/grants available. Financial award application deadline: 3/17; financial award applicants required to submit FAFSA. *Degree program information:* Part-time and evening/weekend programs available. Part-time, evening/weekend, online learning. Offers Bible teaching (MABT); counseling (MACN); early childhood and elementary education (MAT); educational administration (M Ed); educational leadership (PhD); instruction and learning (M Ed); teaching English as a foreign language (Certificate); teaching English as a foreign language and intercultural studies (MATF). *Application deadline:* For fall admission, 8/1 priority date for domestic and international students; for winter admission, 12/1 priority date for domestic students, 11/1 priority date for international students; for spring admission, 12/1 priority date for domestic students, 11/1 priority date for international students. Applications are processed on a rolling basis. *Application fee:* $45. Electronic applications accepted. *Application Contact:* Dori Beach, Associate Director of Graduate Admissions, 803-807-5088, Fax: 803-786-4209, E-mail: dbeach@ciu.edu. *Dean*, Dr. John Harvey, 803-807-5363, Fax: 803-786-4209, E-mail: jharvey@ciu.edu.

Seminary and School of Ministry Students: 180 full-time (59 women), 218 part-time (61 women); includes 81 minority (58 Black or African American, non-Hispanic/Latino; 1 American Indian or Alaska Native, non-Hispanic/Latino; 18 Asian, non-Hispanic/Latino; 4 Hispanic/Latino), 22 international. Average age 36. 277 applicants, 81% accepted, 117 enrolled. *Faculty:* 14 full-time (1 woman), 9 part-time/adjunct (1 woman). *Financial support:* In 2015–16, 120 students received support. Career-related internships or fieldwork, Federal Work-Study, institutionally sponsored loans, and scholarships/grants available. Financial award application deadline: 3/15; financial award applicants required to submit FAFSA. In 2015, 74 master's, 3 doctorates, 15 other advanced degrees awarded. *Degree program information:* Part-time and evening/weekend programs available. Part-time, evening/weekend. Offers academic ministries (M Div); Bible and theology (Certificate); bible exposition (M Div, MABE); Biblical ministry (Certificate); chaplaincy (M Div); intercultural studies (MAIS); leadership (D Min); member care (D Min); missions (D Min); preaching (D Min); theological studies (MA). *Application deadline:* For fall admission, 8/1 priority date for domestic and international students; for winter admission, 12/15 priority date for domestic and international students; for spring admission, 1/15 priority date for domestic and international students. Applications are processed on a rolling basis. *Application fee:* $45. Electronic applications accepted. *Application Contact:* Michelle MacGregor, Director of Admissions, 800-777-2227 Ext. 5335, Fax: 803-786-4209, E-mail: yescbs@ciu.edu. *Dean*, Dr. Junias Venugopal, 803-754-4100 Ext. 5330, Fax: 803-786-4209, E-mail: jvenugopal@ciu.edu.

COLUMBIA SOUTHERN UNIVERSITY, Orange Beach, AL 36561

General Information Proprietary, coed, comprehensive institution. *Graduate housing:* On-campus housing not available.

GRADUATE UNITS

College of Safety and Emergency Services ***Degree program information:*** Part-time and evening/weekend programs available. Part-time, evening/weekend, online learning. Offers criminal justice administration (MS); emergency services management (MS); occupational safety and health (MS). Electronic applications accepted.

DBA Program ***Degree program information:*** Part-time and evening/weekend programs available. Part-time, evening/weekend, online learning. Offers business administration (DBA). Electronic applications accepted.

MBA Program ***Degree program information:*** Part-time and evening/weekend programs available. Part-time, evening/weekend, online learning. Offers finance (MBA); health care management (MBA); human resource management (MBA); marketing (MBA); project management (MBA); public administration (MBA). Electronic applications accepted.

Program in Organizational Leadership Offers organizational leadership (MS).

COLUMBIA THEOLOGICAL SEMINARY, Decatur, GA 30031-0520

General Information Independent-religious, coed, graduate-only institution. *Graduate housing:* Rooms and/or apartments available on a first-come, first-served basis to single students and available to married students. Housing application deadline: 4/30.

GRADUATE UNITS

Graduate and Professional Programs Offers theology (M Div, MATS, Th M, D Min, Th D). Th D program offered jointly with Emory University; D Min with Interdenominational Theological Center.

COLUMBIA UNIVERSITY, New York, NY 10027

General Information Independent, coed, university. CGS member. *Graduate housing:* Rooms and/or apartments available on a first-come, first-served basis to single and married students. Housing application deadline: 7/10. *Research affiliation:* Long Island Biological Laboratory, Brookhaven National Laboratory, New York Botanical Gardens, American Museum of Natural History, Marine Biological Laboratory, Goddard Space Flight Center.

GRADUATE UNITS

College of Dental Medicine Offers advanced education in general dentistry (Certificate); biomedical informatics (MA, PhD); dental and oral surgery (DDS); dental medicine (MA, MS, DDS, PhD, Certificate); endodontics (Certificate); orthodontics (MS, Certificate); periodontics (MS, Certificate); prosthodontics (MS, Certificate); science education (MA).

College of Physicians and Surgeons ***Degree program information:*** Part-time programs available. Part-time. Offers anatomy (M Phil, MA, PhD); anatomy and cell biology (PhD); biochemistry and molecular biophysics (M Phil, PhD); biomedical informatics (M Phil, MA, PhD); biomedical sciences (M Phil, MA, PhD); biophysics (PhD); cellular, molecular, structural and genetic studies (PhD); genetics (M Phil, MA, PhD); medicine (M Phil, MA, MS, DN Sc, DPT, Ed D, MD, PhD, Adv C); movement science (Ed D); neurobiology and behavior (PhD); occupational therapy (professional) (MS); occupational therapy administration or education (post-professional) (MS); pathobiology (M Phil, MA, PhD); pharmacology (M Phil, MA, PhD); pharmacology-toxicology (M Phil, MA, PhD); physical therapy (DPT); physiology and cellular biophysics (M Phil, MA, PhD).

Institute of Human Nutrition Students: 80 full-time (40 women), 2 part-time (1 woman); includes 37 minority (7 Black or African American, non-Hispanic/Latino; 27 Asian, non-Hispanic/Latino; 3 Hispanic/Latino), 8 international. Average age 23. 200 applicants, 63% accepted, 75 enrolled. *Faculty:* 46 full-time (22 women). *Financial support:* In 2015–16, 65 students received support, including 12 fellowships (averaging $28,164 per year), 17 research assistantships (averaging $28,164 per year); Federal Work-Study, institutionally sponsored loans, and traineeships also available. Support available to part-time students. Financial award application deadline: 1/4; financial award applicants required to submit FAFSA. In 2015, 85 master's, 3 doctorates awarded. *Degree program information:* Part-time programs available. Part-time. Offers nutrition (MS, PhD). *Application deadline:* For fall and spring admission, 7/15 priority date for domestic and international students. Applications are processed on a rolling basis. *Application fee:* $95. Electronic applications accepted. *Application Contact:* Dr. Sharon R. Akabas, Director, MS Program in Human Nutrition, 212-305-4808, Fax: 212-305-3079, E-mail: sa109@cumc.columbia.edu. *Director,* Dr. Richard J. Deckelbaum, 212-305-4808, Fax: 212-305-3079, E-mail: nutrition@cumc.columbia.edu.

Columbia University Mailman School of Public Health Students: 521 full-time (359 women), 912 part-time (727 women); includes 505 minority (97 Black or African American, non-Hispanic/Latino; 4 American Indian or Alaska Native, non-Hispanic/Latino; 245 Asian, non-Hispanic/Latino; 123 Hispanic/Latino; 1 Native Hawaiian or other Pacific Islander, non-Hispanic/Latino; 35 Two or more races, non-Hispanic/Latino), 281 international. Average age 28. 2,927 applicants, 58% accepted, 668 enrolled. *Faculty:* 235 full-time (118 women), 233 part-time/adjunct (105 women). *Financial support:* In 2015–16, 619 students received support. Fellowships, research assistantships, teaching assistantships, career-related internships or fieldwork, Federal Work-Study, and traineeships available. Support available to part-time students. Financial award application deadline: 2/1; financial award applicants required to submit FAFSA. In 2015, 582 master's, 29 doctorates awarded. *Degree program information:* Part-time and evening/weekend programs available. Part-time, evening/weekend. Offers biostatistics (MPH, MS, Dr PH, PhD); environmental health sciences (MPH, Dr PH, PhD); epidemiology (MPH, MS, Dr PH, PhD); health policy and management (Exec MHA, Exec MPH, MHA, MPH); population and family health (MPH, Dr PH); public health (Exec MHA, Exec MPH, MHA, MPH, MS, Dr PH, PhD). PhD offered in cooperation with the Graduate School of Arts and Sciences. *Application deadline:* For fall admission, 12/1 priority date for domestic and international students. *Application fee:* $120. Electronic applications accepted. *Application Contact:* Dr. Joseph Korevec, Senior Director of Admissions and Financial Aid, 212-305-8698, Fax: 212-342-1861, E-mail: ph-admit@columbia.edu. *Dean/Professor,* Dr. Linda P. Fried, 212-305-9300, Fax: 212-305-9342, E-mail: lpfried@columbia.edu.

Division of Sociomedical Sciences Students: 58 full-time (45 women), 205 part-time (170 women); includes 107 minority (25 Black or African American, non-Hispanic/Latino; 1 American Indian or Alaska Native, non-Hispanic/Latino; 46 Asian, non-Hispanic/Latino; 27 Hispanic/Latino; 8 Two or more races, non-Hispanic/Latino), 28 international. Average age 26. 517 applicants, 57% accepted, 116 enrolled. *Financial support:* Research assistantships, teaching assistantships, career-related internships or fieldwork, and Federal Work-Study available. Support available to part-time students. Financial award application deadline: 2/1; financial award applicants required to submit FAFSA. In 2015, 104 master's, 10 doctorates awarded. *Degree program information:* Part-time programs available. Part-time. Offers sociomedical sciences (MPH, MS, Dr PH, PhD). PhD offered in cooperation with the Graduate School of Arts and Sciences. *Application deadline:* For fall admission, 12/1 priority date for domestic and international students. *Application fee:* $120. Electronic applications accepted. *Application Contact:* Dr. Joseph Korevec, Senior Director of Admissions and Financial Aid, 212-305-8698, Fax: 212-342-1861, E-mail: ph-admit@columbia.edu. *Chair,* Dr. Lisa Metsch, 212-305-5656.

Fu Foundation School of Engineering and Applied Science ***Degree program information:*** Part-time programs available. Part-time, online learning. Offers applied mathematics (MS, Eng Sc D, PhD); applied physics (MS, Eng Sc D, PhD); biomedical engineering (MS, Eng Sc D, PhD); chemical engineering (MS, Eng Sc D, PhD); civil engineering (MS, Eng Sc D, PhD); computer engineering (MS); computer science (MS, Eng Sc D, PhD); computer science and journalism (MS); construction engineering and management (MS); earth and environmental engineering (MS, Eng Sc D, PhD); electrical engineering (MS, Eng Sc D, PhD); engineering and applied science (MS, Eng Sc D, PhD); engineering mechanics (MS, Eng Sc D, PhD); financial engineering (MS); industrial engineering and operations research (MS, Eng Sc D, PhD); management science and engineering (MS); materials science and engineering (MS, Eng Sc D, PhD); mechanical engineering (MS, Eng Sc D, PhD); medical physics (MS). Electronic applications accepted.

Data Science Institute Degree program information: Part-time programs available. Part-time. Offers data science (MS).

Graduate School of Architecture, Planning, and Preservation Offers advanced architectural design (MS); architecture (M Arch, PhD); architecture, planning, and preservation (M Arch, MS, PhD, Certificate); historic preservation (MS, Certificate); real estate development (MS); urban planning (MS, PhD). PhD offered through the Graduate School of Arts and Sciences.

Graduate School of Arts and Sciences Students: 3,030 full-time, 235 part-time; includes 861 minority (88 Black or African American, non-Hispanic/Latino; 5 American Indian or Alaska Native, non-Hispanic/Latino; 517 Asian, non-Hispanic/Latino; 159 Hispanic/Latino; 4 Native Hawaiian or other Pacific Islander, non-Hispanic/Latino; 88 Two or more races, non-Hispanic/Latino), 1,697 international. 13,288 applicants, 21% accepted, 1162 enrolled. *Financial support:* Fellowships, research assistantships, teaching assistantships, career-related internships or fieldwork, Federal Work-Study, institutionally sponsored loans, scholarships/grants, traineeships, health care benefits, tuition waivers, and unspecified assistantships available. Support available to part-time students. Financial award application deadline: 12/15. In 2015, 1,061 master's, 553 doctorates awarded. *Degree program information:* Part-time programs available. Part-time. Offers African-American studies (MA); American studies (MA); anthropology (MA, PhD); art history and archaeology (MA, PhD); astronomy (PhD); biological sciences (PhD); biotechnology (MA); chemical physics (PhD); chemistry (PhD); classical studies (MA, PhD); classics (MA, PhD); climate and society (MA); conservation biology (MA); earth and environmental sciences (PhD); East Asia: regional studies (MA); East Asian languages and cultures (MA, PhD); ecology, evolution and environmental biology (MA); ecology, evolution, and environmental biology (PhD); economics (MA, PhD); English and comparative literature (MA, PhD); French and Romance philology (MA, PhD); Germanic languages (MA, PhD); global French studies (MA); global thought (MA); Hispanic cultural studies (MA); history (PhD); history and literature (MA); human rights studies (MA); Islamic studies (MA); Italian (MA, PhD); Japanese pedagogy (MA); Jewish studies (MA); Latin America and the Caribbean: regional studies (MA); Latin American and Iberian cultures (PhD); mathematics (MA, PhD); medieval and Renaissance studies (MA); Middle Eastern, South Asian, and African studies (MA, PhD); modern art: critical and curatorial studies (MA); modern European studies (MA); museum anthropology (MA); music (DMA, PhD); oral history (MA); philosophical foundations of physics (MA); philosophy (MA, PhD); physics (PhD); political science (MA, PhD); psychology (PhD); quantitative methods in the social sciences (MA); religion (MA, PhD); Russia, Eurasia and East Europe: regional studies (MA); Russian translation (MA); Slavic cultures (MA); Slavic languages (MA, PhD); sociology (MA, PhD); South Asian studies (MA); statistics (MA, PhD); theatre (PhD). Dual-degree programs require admission to both Graduate School of Arts and Sciences and another Columbia school. *Application fee:* $105. Electronic applications accepted. *Application Contact:* GSAS Office of Admissions, 212-854-8903, E-mail: gsas-admissions@columbia.edu. *Dean of the Graduate School of Arts and Sciences,* Carlos J. Alonso, 212-854-5177.

Graduate School of Business Offers accounting (MBA); business (EMBA, MBA, PhD); business administration (EMBA, MBA); decision, risk, and operations (MBA); entrepreneurship (MBA); finance and economics (MBA); global business administration (EMBA); healthcare and pharmaceutical management (MBA); human resource management (MBA); international business (MBA); leadership and ethics (MBA); management (MBA); marketing (MBA); media (MBA); private equity (MBA); real estate (MBA); social enterprise (MBA); value investing (MBA). Electronic applications accepted.

Graduate School of Journalism ***Degree program information:*** Part-time programs available. Part-time. Offers journalism (MA, MS, PhD).

School of Continuing Education ***Degree program information:*** Part-time and evening/weekend programs available. Part-time, evening/weekend. Offers actuarial science (MS); bioethics (MS); communications practice (MS); construction administration (MS); fundraising management (MS); information and archive management (MS); landscape design (MS); narrative medicine (MS); negotiation and conflict resolution (MS); sports management (MS); strategic communications (MS); sustainability management (MS); technology management (Exec MS). Electronic applications accepted.

School of International and Public Affairs Offers development practice (MPA); environmental science and policy (MPA); international affairs (MIA); international and public affairs (MA, MIA, MPA, Certificate); public policy and administration (MPA). Electronic applications accepted.

School of Law Offers law (LL M, JD, JSD). Electronic applications accepted.

School of Nursing ***Degree program information:*** Part-time programs available. Part-time. Offers adult-gerontology acute care nurse practitioner (MS, Adv C); adult-gerontology primary care nurse practitioner (MS, Adv C); family nurse practitioner (MS, Adv C); nurse anesthesia (MS, Adv C); nurse midwifery (MS); nursing (MS, DNP, PhD, Adv C); pediatric nurse practitioner (MS, Adv C); psychiatric mental health nursing (MS, Adv C). Electronic applications accepted.

School of Social Work Students: 930 full-time (805 women), 38 part-time (30 women); includes 322 minority (89 Black or African American, non-Hispanic/Latino; 1 American Indian or Alaska Native, non-Hispanic/Latino; 84 Asian, non-Hispanic/Latino; 115 Hispanic/Latino; 1 Native Hawaiian or other Pacific Islander, non-Hispanic/Latino; 32 Two or more races, non-Hispanic/Latino), 122 international. Average age 26. 1,305 applicants, 54% accepted, 400 enrolled. *Faculty:* 44 full-time (25 women), 129 part-time/adjunct (90 women). *Financial support:* In 2015–16, 668 students received support, including 3 fellowships (averaging $5,000 per year), 5 research assistantships with partial tuition reimbursements available, 2 teaching assistantships with partial tuition reimbursements available; career-related internships or fieldwork, Federal Work-Study, institutionally sponsored loans, scholarships/grants, health care benefits, and unspecified assistantships also available. Support available to part-time students. Financial award application deadline: 2/1; financial award applicants required to submit FAFSA. In 2015, 418 master's, 16 doctorates awarded. 100% online. Offers social work (MSSW, PhD). MS/MS Ed offered jointly with Bank Street College of Education; MS/M Div with Union Theological Seminary in New York; MS/MA with The Jewish Theological Seminary; MS/MS dual degree with the Graduate School of Architecture, Planning, and Preservation. *Application deadline:* For fall admission, 1/4 for domestic students, 1/4 priority date for international students; for spring admission, 10/15 for domestic students, 10/15 priority date for international students. Applications are processed on a rolling basis. *Application fee:* $75. Electronic applications accepted. *Application Contact:* Debbie Lesperance, Director of Admissions, 212-851-2211, Fax: 212-851-2305, E-mail: dl635@columbia.edu. *Dean,* Dr. Jeanette Takamura, 212-851-2289.

School of the Arts Offers acting (MFA); arts (MA, MFA); creative producing (MFA); directing (MFA); dramaturgy (MFA); fiction (MFA); film studies (MA); new genres (MFA); nonfiction (MFA); painting (MFA); photography (MFA); playwriting (MFA); poetry (MFA); printmaking (MFA); screenwriting (MFA); sculpture (MFA); stage management (MFA); theater management and producing (MFA). Electronic applications accepted.

South Asia Institute Offers South Asia studies (MA, Certificate). Students must be enrolled in a separate graduate degree program at Columbia University. Electronic applications accepted.

COLUMBUS COLLEGE OF ART & DESIGN, Columbus, OH 43215-1758

General Information Independent, coed, comprehensive institution.

GRADUATE UNITS

Program in Visual Arts: New Projects Offers visual arts: new projects (MFA). Electronic applications accepted.

COLUMBUS STATE UNIVERSITY, Columbus, GA 31907-5645

General Information State-supported, coed, comprehensive institution. CGS member. *Enrollment:* 8,440 graduate, professional, and undergraduate students; 507 full-time matriculated graduate/professional students (287 women), 988 part-time matriculated graduate/professional students (576 women). *Enrollment by degree level:* 1,066 master's, 108 doctoral, 321 other advanced degrees. *Graduate faculty:* 113 full-time (46 women), 58 part-time/adjunct (34 women). Tuition, state resident: full-time $4804; part-time $2412 per semester hour. Tuition, nonresident: full-time $19,218; part-time $9612 per semester hour. *Required fees:* $1830; $1830 per unit. Tuition and fees vary according to program. *Graduate housing:* Room and/or apartments available on a first-come, first-served basis to single students; on-campus housing not available to married students. Typical cost: $4800 per year ($7350 including board). Room and board charges vary according to board plan, campus/location and housing facility selected. Housing application deadline: 6/30. *Student services:* Campus employment opportunities, campus safety program, career counseling, exercise/wellness program, free psychological counseling, international student services, low-cost health insurance, multicultural affairs office, services for students with disabilities, teacher training. *Library:* Simon Schwob Memorial Library plus 1 other. *Collection:* Books: 386,523 (physical), 35,632 (digital/electronic); Serial titles: 101 (physical), 24,569 (digital/electronic); Databases: 366. Weekly public service hours: 105.

Computer facilities: A campuswide network can be accessed from student residence rooms and from off campus. Online class registration is available.
Website: http://www.columbusstate.edu/

General Application Contact: Kristin Williams, Director of International and Graduate Admissions, 706-507-8848, Fax: 706-568-5091, E-mail: williams_kristin@columbusstate.edu.

GRADUATE UNITS

Graduate Studies Students: 507 full-time (287 women), 988 part-time (576 women); includes 607 minority (486 Black or African American, non-Hispanic/Latino; 5 American Indian or Alaska Native, non-Hispanic/Latino; 25 Asian, non-Hispanic/Latino; 57 Hispanic/Latino; 1 Native Hawaiian or other Pacific Islander, non-Hispanic/Latino; 33 Two or more races, non-Hispanic/Latino), 43 international. Average age 36. 960 applicants, 53% accepted, 391 enrolled. *Faculty:* 113 full-time (46 women), 58 part-time/adjunct (34 women). *Financial support:* In 2015–16, 792 students received support, including 96 research assistantships with partial tuition reimbursements available (averaging $3,000 per year); career-related internships or fieldwork, Federal Work-Study, institutionally sponsored loans, scholarships/grants, tuition waivers (partial), and unspecified assistantships also available. Support available to part-time students. Financial award application deadline: 5/1; financial award applicants required to submit FAFSA. In 2015, 369 master's, 9 doctorates, 55 other advanced degrees awarded. *Degree program information:* Part-time and evening/weekend programs available. Part-time, evening/weekend, online learning. *Application deadline:* For fall admission, 6/30 for domestic and international students; for spring admission, 11/1 for domestic and international students; for summer admission, 5/1 for domestic and international students. Applications are processed on a rolling basis. *Application fee:* $50. Electronic applications accepted. *Application Contact:* Kristin Williams, Director of International and Graduate Admissions, 706-507-8848, Fax: 706-568-5091, E-mail: williams_kristin@columbusstate.edu. *Assistant Vice President for Academic Affairs*, Dr. Ellen Roberts, 706-507-8573, Fax: 706-569-3168, E-mail: roberts_ellen@columbusstate.edu.

College of Education and Health Professions Students: 310 full-time (222 women), 531 part-time (411 women); includes 394 minority (347 Black or African American, non-Hispanic/Latino; 1 American Indian or Alaska Native, non-Hispanic/Latino; 7 Asian, non-Hispanic/Latino; 24 Hispanic/Latino; 15 Two or more races, non-Hispanic/Latino), 6 international. Average age 37. 514 applicants, 52% accepted, 245 enrolled. *Faculty:* 40 full-time (23 women), 44 part-time/adjunct (32 women). *Financial support:* In 2015–16, 591 students received support, including 35 research assistantships with partial tuition reimbursements available (averaging $3,000 per year); career-related internships or fieldwork, Federal Work-Study, institutionally sponsored loans, scholarships/grants, tuition waivers (partial), and unspecified assistantships also available. Support available to part-time students. Financial award application deadline: 5/1; financial award applicants required to submit FAFSA. In 2015, 132 master's, 9 doctorates, 55 other advanced degrees awarded. *Degree program information:* Part-time and evening/weekend programs available. Part-time, evening/weekend, 100% online. Offers clinical mental health counseling (MS); curriculum and instruction in accomplished teaching (M Ed); curriculum and leadership (Ed D); early childhood education (M Ed, MAT, Ed S); education and health professions (M Ed, MAT, MS, MSN, Ed D, Ed S); educational leadership (M Ed, Ed S); exercise science (MS); family nurse practitioner (MSN); health and physical education (M Ed); higher education (M Ed); middle grades education (M Ed, MAT, Ed S); nursing (MSN); school counseling (M Ed, Ed S); secondary education (M Ed, MAT, Ed S); special education (M Ed, MAT, Ed S); teacher leadership (M Ed). *Application deadline:* For fall admission, 6/30 for domestic students, 5/1 for international students; for spring admission, 11/1 for domestic and international students; for summer admission, 3/1 for domestic and international students. Applications are processed on a rolling basis. *Application fee:* $50. Electronic applications accepted. *Application Contact:* Kristin Williams, Director of International and Graduate Recruitment, 706-507-8848, Fax: 706-568-5091, E-mail: williams_kristin@columbusstate.edu. *Dean*, Dr. Deirdre Greer, 706-507-8505, Fax: 706-569-3134, E-mail: greer_deirdre@columbusstate.edu.

College of Letters and Sciences Students: 77 full-time (34 women), 298 part-time (105 women); includes 126 minority (99 Black or African American, non-Hispanic/Latino; 4 American Indian or Alaska Native, non-Hispanic/Latino; 4 Asian, non-Hispanic/Latino; 11 Hispanic/Latino; 8 Two or more races, non-Hispanic/Latino), 2 international. Average age 39. 141 applicants, 55% accepted, 69 enrolled. *Faculty:* 13 full-time (2 women), 7 part-time/adjunct (0 women). *Financial support:* In 2015–16, 97 students received support, including 20 research assistantships with tuition reimbursements available (averaging $3,000 per year); career-related internships or fieldwork, Federal Work-Study, institutionally sponsored loans, scholarships/grants, tuition waivers (partial), and unspecified assistantships also available. Support available to part-time students. Financial award application deadline: 5/1; financial award applicants required to submit FAFSA. In 2015, 104 master's awarded. *Degree program information:* Part-time and evening/weekend programs available. Part-time, evening/weekend, 100% online, blended/hybrid learning. Offers history (MA); letters and sciences (MA, MPA, MPSA, MS, Certificate); natural sciences (MS); public administration (MPA); public safety administration (MPSA); teaching English to speakers of other languages (Certificate). *Application deadline:* For fall admission, 6/30 for domestic students, 5/1 for international students; for spring admission, 11/1 for domestic students, 4/1 for international students; for summer admission, 3/1 for domestic and international students. Applications are processed on a rolling basis. *Application fee:* $50. Electronic applications accepted. *Application Contact:* Kristin Williams, Director of International and Graduate Recruitment, 706-507-8848, Fax: 706-568-5091, E-mail: williams_kristin@columbusstate.edu. *Dean*, Dr. Dennis Rome, 706-568-2056, E-mail: rome_dennis@columbusstate.edu.

College of the Arts Students: 25 full-time (11 women), 18 part-time (15 women); includes 12 minority (4 Black or African American, non-Hispanic/Latino; 5 Hispanic/Latino; 1 Native Hawaiian or other Pacific Islander, non-Hispanic/Latino; 2 Two or more races, non-Hispanic/Latino), 7 international. Average age 31. 47 applicants, 23% accepted, 9 enrolled. *Faculty:* 25 full-time (9 women), 5 part-time/adjunct (2 women). *Financial support:* In 2015–16, 28 students received support, including 16 research assistantships with partial tuition reimbursements available (averaging $3,000 per year); career-related internships or fieldwork, Federal Work-Study, institutionally sponsored loans, scholarships/grants, tuition waivers (partial), and unspecified assistantships also available. Support available to part-time students. Financial award application deadline: 5/1; financial award applicants required to submit FAFSA. In 2015, 11 master's awarded. *Degree program information:* Part-time and evening/weekend programs available. Part-time, evening/weekend, online learning. Offers art education (M Ed, MAT); arts (M Ed, MAT, MM, Artist Diploma); music (Artist Diploma); music education (MM); music performance (MM); theatre education (M Ed, MAT). *Application deadline:* For fall admission, 6/30 for domestic students, 5/1 for international students; for spring admission, 11/1 for domestic and international students; for summer admission, 3/1 for domestic and international students. Applications are processed on a rolling basis. *Application fee:* $50. Electronic applications accepted. *Application Contact:* Kristin Williams, Director of International and Graduate Recruitment, 706-507-8848, Fax: 706-568-5091, E-mail: williams_kristin@columbusstate.edu. *Dean*, Dr. Richard Baxter, 706-507-8043, E-mail: baxter_richard@columbusstate.edu.

Turner College of Business and Computer Science Students: 84 full-time (14 women), 132 part-time (43 women); includes 70 minority (36 Black or African American, non-Hispanic/Latino; 12 Asian, non-Hispanic/Latino; 14 Hispanic/Latino; 8 Two or more races, non-Hispanic/Latino), 21 international. Average age 32. 232 applicants, 41% accepted, 57 enrolled. *Faculty:* 11 full-time (4 women), 1 part-time/adjunct (0 women). *Financial support:* In 2015–16, 52 students received support, including 14 research assistantships (averaging $3,000 per year); Federal Work-Study also available. Financial award application deadline: 5/1; financial award applicants required to submit FAFSA. In 2015, 121 master's awarded. *Degree program information:* Part-time and evening/weekend programs available. Part-time, evening/weekend, 100% online, blended/hybrid learning. Offers applied computer science (MS); business administration (MBA); information systems security (Certificate); modeling and simulation (Certificate); organizational leadership (MS); servant leadership (Certificate). *Application deadline:* For fall admission, 6/30 for domestic students, 5/1 for international students; for spring admission, 11/1 for domestic and international students; for summer admission, 3/1 for domestic and international students. Applications are processed on a rolling basis. *Application fee:* $50. Electronic applications accepted. *Application Contact:* Kristin Williams, Director of International and Graduate Recruitment, 706-507-8848, Fax: 706-568-5091, E-mail: thornton_katie@colstate.edu. *Dean*, Dr. Linda U. Hadley, 706-507-8153, Fax: 706-568-2184, E-mail: hadley_linda@columbusstate.edu.

THE COMMONWEALTH MEDICAL COLLEGE, Scranton, PA 18509

General Information Independent, coed, graduate-only institution. *Enrollment by degree level:* 76 master's, 366 doctoral. *Graduate faculty:* 33 full-time (15 women), 35 part-time/adjunct (13 women). *Student services:* Campus safety program, career counseling, exercise/wellness program, free psychological counseling, low-cost health insurance, multicultural affairs office, services for students with disabilities. *Library:* Medical Library.

Computer facilities: 18 computers available on campus for general student use. Website: http://www.tcmc.edu/

General Application Contact: Jillian Golaszewski, Director of Admissions, Master's Programs, 570-504-7000, Fax: 570-504-2794, E-mail: jgolaszewski@tcmc.edu.

GRADUATE UNITS

Graduate Programs in Medicine Students: 55 full-time (26 women), 3 part-time (0 women). *Financial support:* Application deadline: 3/1; applicants required to submit FAFSA. *Degree program information:* Part-time and evening/weekend programs available. Part-time, evening/weekend. Offers biomedical sciences (MBS). *Application deadline:* Applications are processed on a rolling basis. *Application fee:* $55. Electronic applications accepted. *Application Contact:* Jillian Golaszewski, Enrollment Management Recruiter, 570-504-7000, Fax: 570-504-2794, E-mail: jgolaszewski@tcmc.edu.

Professional Program in Medicine Offers medicine (MD). *Application fee:* $100. *Application Contact:* Jillian Golaszewski, Enrollment Management Recruiter, 570-504-7000, Fax: 570-504-2794, E-mail: jgolaszewski@tcmc.edu.

CONCORDIA COLLEGE, Moorhead, MN 56562

General Information Independent-religious, coed, comprehensive institution.

GRADUATE UNITS

Program in Education Offers world language instruction (M Ed).

CONCORDIA COLLEGE–NEW YORK, Bronxville, NY 10708-1998

General Information Independent-religious, coed, comprehensive institution.

GRADUATE UNITS

Program in Business Leadership Offers business leadership (MS).

Program in Childhood Special Education Offers childhood special education (MS Ed).

CONCORDIA LUTHERAN SEMINARY, Edmonton, AB T5B 4E3, Canada

General Information Independent-religious, coed, primarily men, graduate-only institution. *Graduate housing:* On-campus housing not available.

GRADUATE UNITS

Graduate and Professional Programs ***Degree program information:*** Part-time programs available. Part-time. Offers theology (M Div, Graduate Certificate).

CONCORDIA SEMINARY, St. Louis, MO 63105-3199

General Information Independent-religious, coed, primarily men, graduate-only institution. *Graduate housing:* Rooms and/or apartments guaranteed to single students and available to married students. Housing application deadline: 3/4. *Research affiliation:* Center for Reformation Research, Concordia Historical Institute.

GRADUATE UNITS

Graduate Programs Offers theology (M Div, MA, STM, D Min, PhD, Certificate).

CONCORDIA THEOLOGICAL SEMINARY, Fort Wayne, IN 46825-4996

General Information Independent-religious, coed, primarily men, graduate-only institution. *Graduate housing:* Room and/or apartments available to single students; on-campus housing not available to married students.

GRADUATE UNITS

Graduate and Professional Programs ***Degree program information:*** Part-time programs available. Part-time. Offers theology (M Div, MA, STM, D Min, PhD).

CONCORDIA UNIVERSITY, Montréal, QC H3G 1M8, Canada

General Information Province-supported, coed, university. CGS member. *Enrollment:* 37,256 graduate, professional, and undergraduate students; 8,000 matriculated graduate/professional students. Tuition and fees vary according to course load, degree level and program. *Graduate housing:* Room and/or apartments available on a first-come, first-served basis to single students; on-campus housing not available to married students. *Student services:* Campus employment opportunities, campus safety program, career counseling, child daycare facilities, exercise/wellness program, free psychological counseling, grant writing training, international student services, multicultural affairs office, services for students with disabilities, writing training. *Library:* Webster Library plus 1 other. *Collection:* Books: 1.1 million (physical), 512,133 (digital/electronic); Serial titles: 19,550 (physical), 98,723 (digital/electronic); Databases: 1,000. Weekly public service hours: 70; study areas open 24 hours, 5–7 days a week; students can reserve study rooms. *Research affiliation:* Canadian Rural Revitalization Foundation (sociology), Blue Metropolis Literary Series (English), Canadian Journalism Project (journalism),

Centre de Recherche en Plasturgie et Composites (CREPEC) (mechanical and industrial engineering), Centre de Recherche Informatique de Montreal (CRIM) (computer science), Center d'experise et de services en application Multimedia (multimedia).

Computer facilities: 350 computers available on campus for general student use. A campuswide network can be accessed from student residence rooms and from off campus. Online class registration, specialized software applications are available.
Website: http://www.concordia.ca/

General Application Contact: Lorena Marzitelli, Graduate Recruitment Officer, 514-848-2424 Ext. 7325.

GRADUATE UNITS

School of Graduate Studies ***Financial support:*** Fellowships, research assistantships, teaching assistantships, career-related internships or fieldwork, and institutionally sponsored loans available. *Degree program information:* Part-time and evening/weekend programs available. Part-time, evening/weekend. Offers individualized research (M Sc, MA, PhD). *Application fee:* $50. *Application Contact:* Lorena Marzitelli, Advisor, Recruitment and Registration, 514-848-2424 Ext. 7325. *Dean*, Paula Wood-Adams, 514-848-2424, Fax: 514-848-2812.

Faculty of Arts and Science Financial support: Fellowships, research assistantships, teaching assistantships, career-related internships or fieldwork, institutionally sponsored loans, and scholarships/grants available. Offers adult education (Certificate, Diploma); Anglais-Franlfcais en langue et techniques de localization (Certificate); applied linguistics (MA, Certificate); arts and science (M Env, M Sc, MA, MTM, PhD, Certificate, Diploma, Graduate Diploma); biology (M Sc, PhD); biotechnology and genomics (Diploma); chemistry (M Sc, PhD); child studies (MA); communication (PhD); communication studies (Diploma); community economic development (Diploma); creative writing (MA); economics (MA, PhD, Diploma); educational studies (MA); educational technology (MA); English (MA, PhD); environmental assessment (M Env, Diploma); exercise science (M Sc); geography, urban and environmental studies (M Sc, PhD); history (MA, PhD); human systems intervention (MA); humanities (PhD); instructional technology (Diploma); journalism (Graduate Diploma); journalism studies (MA); Judaic studies (MA); littératures Francophones et résonances médiatiques (MA); mathematics (PhD); mathematics and statistics (M Sc, MA); media studies (MA); philosophy (MA); physics (M Sc, PhD); political science (PhD); psychology (MA, PhD, Certificate); public policy and public administration (MA); religion (MA, PhD); social and cultural analysis (PhD); social and cultural anthropology (MA); sociology (MA); teaching English as a second language (Certificate); teaching of mathematics (MTM); theological studies (MA); translation (Diploma); translation studies (MA); visual journalism (Diploma); youth work (Graduate Diploma). *Application fee:* $50. *Dean*, Andre Roy, 514-848-2424, Fax: 514-848-2877.

Faculty of Engineering and Computer Science Offers 3D graphics and game development (Certificate); aerospace engineering (M Eng); building engineering (M Eng, MA Sc, PhD, Certificate); civil engineering (M Eng, MA Sc, PhD); computer science (M App Comp Sc, M Comp Sc, PhD, Diploma); electrical and computer engineering (M Eng, MA Sc, PhD); engineering and computer science (M App Comp Sc, M Comp Sc, M Eng, MA Sc, PhD, Certificate, Diploma); environmental engineering (Certificate); industrial engineering (M Eng, MA Sc, PhD); information and systems engineering (PhD); information systems security (M Eng, MA Sc); mechanical engineering (M Eng, MA Sc, PhD, Certificate); quality systems engineering (M Eng, MA Sc); service engineering and network management (Certificate); software engineering (M Eng, MA Sc). *Application fee:* $50. *Dean*, Amir Asif, 514-848-2424, Fax: 514-848-4509.

Faculty of Fine Arts Financial support: Fellowships, research assistantships, teaching assistantships, and career-related internships or fieldwork available. *Degree program information:* Part-time programs available. Part-time. Offers advanced music performance studies (Diploma); art education (MA, PhD); art history (MA, PhD); art therapy (MA); design (M Des); digital technologies in design art practice (Certificate); drama therapy (MA); film and moving image studies (PhD); film production (MFA); film studies (MA); fine arts (M Des, MA, MFA, PhD, Certificate, Diploma); music therapy (MA); studio arts (MFA). *Application fee:* $50. *Dean*, Rebecca Duclos, 514-848-2424, Fax: 514-848-4599.

John Molson School of Business Financial support: Career-related internships or fieldwork, scholarships/grants, and health care benefits available. *Degree program information:* Part-time and evening/weekend programs available. Part-time, evening/weekend. Offers administration (M Sc); business administration (MBA, PhD, Certificate, Diploma); executive business administration (EMBA); supply chain management (MSCM). PhD program offered jointly with HEC Montreal, McGill University, and Université du Québec à Montréal. *Application deadline:* For fall admission, 6/1 for domestic students, 2/15 for international students; for winter admission, 10/1 for domestic students, 6/15 for international students. *Application fee:* $100. Electronic applications accepted. *Application Contact:* Anne-Marie Croteau, Associate Dean, Professional Graduate Programs and External Relations, 514-848-2424 Ext. 2983, E-mail: anne-marie.croteau@concordia.ca. *Interim Dean*, Stephane Brutus, 514-848-2424.

CONCORDIA UNIVERSITY, Portland, OR 97211-6099

General Information Independent-religious, coed, comprehensive institution. *Graduate housing:* Room and/or apartments available on a first-come, first-served basis to single students; on-campus housing not available to married students. Housing application deadline: 8/1.

GRADUATE UNITS

College of Education ***Degree program information:*** Part-time programs available. Part-time, online learning. Offers career and technical education (M Ed); curriculum and instruction (M Ed); early childhood (MAT); education leadership (Ed D); educational administration (M Ed); elementary education (MAT); secondary education (MAT); special education (M Ed); teacher leadership (Ed D). Electronic applications accepted.

School of Management ***Degree program information:*** Evening/weekend programs available. Evening/weekend. Offers management (MBA).

CONCORDIA UNIVERSITY ANN ARBOR, Ann Arbor, MI 48105-2797

General Information Independent-religious, coed, comprehensive institution. *Graduate housing:* On-campus housing not available.

GRADUATE UNITS

Graduate Programs ***Degree program information:*** Part-time and evening/weekend programs available. Part-time, evening/weekend. Offers curriculum and instruction (MS); educational leadership (MS); organizational leadership and administration (MS). Electronic applications accepted.

CONCORDIA UNIVERSITY CHICAGO, River Forest, IL 60305-1499

General Information Independent-religious, coed, comprehensive institution. CGS member. *Graduate housing:* Rooms and/or apartments available on a first-come, first-served basis to single and married students.

GRADUATE UNITS

College of Education Offers Christian education (MA); curriculum and instruction (MA); early childhood education (MA, Ed D); elementary education (MAT); reading education (MA); school leadership (MA, Ed D, CAS); secondary education (MAT).

College of Graduate and Innovative Programs Offers business administration (MBA); church music (MCM); community counseling (MA); educational technology (MA); gerontology (MA); human services (MA); liberal studies (MA); music (MA); psychology (MA); religion (MA); school counseling (MA, CAS).

CONCORDIA UNIVERSITY IRVINE, Irvine, CA 92612-3299

General Information Independent-religious, coed, comprehensive institution. *Graduate housing:* Room and/or apartments available on a first-come, first-served basis to single students; on-campus housing not available to married students. Housing application deadline: 6/1.

GRADUATE UNITS

School of Arts and Sciences ***Degree program information:*** Part-time and evening/weekend programs available. Part-time, evening/weekend, online learning. Offers coaching and athletic administration (MA). Electronic applications accepted.

School of Business and Professional Studies ***Degree program information:*** Part-time and evening/weekend programs available. Part-time, evening/weekend. Offers business administration: business practice (MBA); international studies (MA). Electronic applications accepted.

School of Education ***Degree program information:*** Part-time and evening/weekend programs available. Part-time, evening/weekend, online learning. Offers curriculum and instruction (MA); education and preliminary teaching credential (M Ed); educational administration and preliminary administrative services credential (MA); educational technology (MA); school counseling with pupil personnel services credential (MA). Electronic applications accepted.

School of Theology ***Degree program information:*** Part-time and evening/weekend programs available. Part-time, evening/weekend. Offers Christian leadership (MA); research in theology (MA); theology and culture (MA). Electronic applications accepted.

CONCORDIA UNIVERSITY, NEBRASKA, Seward, NE 68434-1556

General Information Independent-religious, coed, comprehensive institution. *Graduate housing:* Rooms and/or apartments available on a first-come, first-served basis to single and married students.

GRADUATE UNITS

Graduate Programs in Education ***Degree program information:*** Part-time and evening/weekend programs available. Part-time, evening/weekend. Offers early childhood education (M Ed); education (M Ed, MPE, MS); elementary and secondary education (M Ed); elementary education (M Ed); family life ministry (MS); parish education (MPE); reading education (M Ed); secondary education (M Ed). Electronic applications accepted.

Program in Computer Science Online learning. Offers cyber operations (MS).

CONCORDIA UNIVERSITY OF EDMONTON, Edmonton, AB T5B 4E4, Canada

General Information Independent-religious, coed, comprehensive institution.

GRADUATE UNITS

Program in Biblical and Christian Studies Offers Biblical and Christian studies (MA).

Program in Information Systems Security Management Offers information systems security management (MA).

CONCORDIA UNIVERSITY, ST. PAUL, St. Paul, MN 55104-5494

General Information Independent-religious, coed, comprehensive institution. CGS member. *Enrollment:* 4,380 graduate, professional, and undergraduate students; 1,721 full-time matriculated graduate/professional students (1,196 women), 92 part-time matriculated graduate/professional students (58 women). *Enrollment by degree level:* 1,624 master's, 71 doctoral, 118 other advanced degrees. *Graduate faculty:* 26 full-time (9 women), 147 part-time/adjunct (79 women). *International tuition:* $13,500 full-time. *Tuition, area resident:* Full-time $4536; part-time $378 per credit. Tuition and fees vary according to degree level and program. *Graduate housing:* Rooms and/or apartments available on a first-come, first-served basis to single and married students. Typical cost: $10,600 (including board) for single students; $6300 per year for married students. Room and board charges vary according to housing facility selected. Housing application deadline: 6/1. *Student services:* Campus employment opportunities, campus safety program, career counseling, child daycare facilities, exercise/wellness program, free psychological counseling, international student services, multicultural affairs office, services for students with disabilities, teacher training, writing training. *Library:* Library Technology Center. *Collection:* Books: 100,719 (physical), 156,975 (digital/electronic); Serial titles: 726 (physical), 119,903 (digital/electronic); Databases: 60. Weekly public service hours: 74; students can reserve study rooms.

Computer facilities: 10 computers available on campus for general student use. A campuswide network can be accessed from student residence rooms and from off campus. Online class registration is available.
Website: http://www.csp.edu/

General Application Contact: Kimberly Craig, Associate Vice President, Cohort Enrollment Management, 651-603-6223, Fax: 651-603-6320, E-mail: craig@csp.edu.

GRADUATE UNITS

College of Business and Technology Students: 392 full-time (252 women), 28 part-time (20 women); includes 104 minority (51 Black or African American, non-Hispanic/Latino; 1 American Indian or Alaska Native, non-Hispanic/Latino; 27 Asian, non-Hispanic/Latino; 11 Hispanic/Latino; 1 Native Hawaiian or other Pacific Islander, non-Hispanic/Latino; 13 Two or more races, non-Hispanic/Latino), 7 international. Average age 34. 417 applicants, 45% accepted, 152 enrolled. *Faculty:* 11 full-time (3 women), 29 part-time/adjunct (13 women). *Financial support:* Applicants required to submit FAFSA. In 2015, 225 master's awarded. *Degree program information:* Evening/weekend programs available. Evening/weekend, 100% online, blended/hybrid learning. Offers business administration (MBA); business and organizational leadership (MBA); health care management (MBA); human resource management (MA); leadership and management (MA); strategic communication management (MA). *Application deadline:* For fall admission, 8/1 for domestic and international students; for spring admission, 12/1 for domestic and international students; for summer admission, 5/1 for domestic and international students. Applications are processed on a rolling basis.

Application fee: $50. Electronic applications accepted. *Application Contact:* Kimberly Craig, Associate Vice President, Cohort Enrollment Management, 651-603-6223, Fax: 651-603-6320, E-mail: craig@csp.edu. *Dean*, Dr. Kevin Hall, 651-603-6165, Fax: 651-641-8807, E-mail: khall@csp.edu.

College of Education and Science Students: 1,327 full-time (944 women), 66 part-time (38 women); includes 168 minority (77 Black or African American, non-Hispanic/Latino; 12 American Indian or Alaska Native, non-Hispanic/Latino; 27 Asian, non-Hispanic/Latino; 25 Hispanic/Latino; 2 Native Hawaiian or other Pacific Islander, non-Hispanic/Latino; 25 Two or more races, non-Hispanic/Latino), 32 international. Average age 33. 924 applicants, 62% accepted, 473 enrolled. *Faculty:* 15 full-time (6 women), 119 part-time/adjunct (67 women). *Financial support:* Applicants required to submit FAFSA. In 2015, 583 master's, 116 other advanced degrees awarded. *Degree program information:* Part-time and evening/weekend programs available. Part-time, evening/weekend, 100% online, blended/hybrid learning. Offers classroom instruction (MA Ed); criminal justice (MA); differentiated instruction (MA Ed); early childhood education (MA Ed); educational leadership (MA Ed, Ed D); educational technology (MA Ed); exercise science (MS); family science (MA); forensic mental health (MA); K-12 principal licensure (Ed S); K-12 reading (Certificate); orthotics and prosthetics (MS); physical therapy (DPT); special education (MA Ed, Certificate); sports management (MA); superintendent (Ed S); teaching (MAT). *Application deadline:* For fall admission, 8/1 for domestic and international students; for spring admission, 12/1 for domestic and international students; for summer admission, 5/1 for domestic and international students. Applications are processed on a rolling basis. *Application fee:* $50. Electronic applications accepted. *Application Contact:* Kimberly Craig, Associate Vice President, Cohort Enrollment Management, 651-603-6223, Fax: 651-603-6320, E-mail: craig@csp.edu. *Dean*, Lonn Maly, 651-641-8203, E-mail: maly@csp.edu.

CONCORDIA UNIVERSITY TEXAS, Austin, TX 78726

General Information Independent-religious, coed, comprehensive institution.

GRADUATE UNITS

College of Education ***Degree program information:*** Part-time and evening/weekend programs available. Part-time, evening/weekend. Offers education (M Ed).

CONCORDIA UNIVERSITY WISCONSIN, Mequon, WI 53097-2402

General Information Independent-religious, coed, comprehensive institution. *Graduate housing:* Room and/or apartments available to single students; on-campus housing not available to married students. Housing application deadline: 8/1.

GRADUATE UNITS

Graduate Programs ***Degree program information:*** Part-time and evening/weekend programs available. Part-time, evening/weekend, online learning. Offers art education (MS Ed); curriculum and instruction (MS Ed); early childhood (MS Ed); educational administration (MS Ed); environmental education (MS Ed); family studies (MS Ed); professional counseling (MPC); reading (MS Ed); school counseling (MS Ed); special education (MS Ed). Electronic applications accepted.

School of Arts and Sciences Offers arts and sciences (MCM); church music (MCM).

School of Business and Legal Studies Offers business and legal studies (MBA, MSSPA); finance (MBA); health care administration (MBA); human resource management (MBA); international business (MBA); international business-bilingual English/Chinese (MBA); management (MBA); management information systems (MBA); managerial communications (MBA); marketing (MBA); public administration (MBA); risk management (MBA); student personnel administration (MSSPA).

School of Human Services Offers family nurse practitioner (MSN); geriatric nurse practitioner (MSN); human services (MOT, MSN, MSPT, MSRS, DPT); nurse educator (MSN); occupational therapy (MOT); physical therapy (MSPT, DPT); rehabilitation science (MSRS).

CONCORD LAW SCHOOL, Los Angeles, CA 90024

General Information Proprietary, coed, graduate-only institution.

GRADUATE UNITS

Program in Law ***Degree program information:*** Part-time and evening/weekend programs available. Part-time, evening/weekend, online learning. Offers law (EJD, JD). Electronic applications accepted.

CONCORD UNIVERSITY, Athens, WV 24712-1000

General Information State-supported, coed, comprehensive institution. *Enrollment:* 2,507 graduate, professional, and undergraduate students; 109 full-time matriculated graduate/professional students (91 women), 256 part-time matriculated graduate/professional students (195 women). *Enrollment by degree level:* 344 master's, 21 other advanced degrees. *Graduate faculty:* 20 full-time (13 women), 5 part-time/adjunct (3 women). Tuition, state resident: full-time $3619; part-time $2418 per semester. Tuition, nonresident: full-time $6311; part-time $4206 per semester. Tuition and fees vary according to course load. *Graduate housing:* Room and/or apartments available on a first-come, first-served basis to single students; on-campus housing not available to married students. Typical cost: $4182 per year ($8350 including board). Room and board charges vary according to board plan. *Student services:* Campus employment opportunities, career counseling, child daycare facilities, free psychological counseling, international student services, multicultural affairs office, services for students with disabilities. *Library:* J. Frank Marsh Library. *Collection:* Books: 156,138 (physical), 3,029 (digital/electronic); Databases: 21.

Computer facilities: 350 computers available on campus for general student use. A campuswide network can be accessed from student residence rooms and from off campus. Online class registration is available.
Website: http://www.concord.edu/

General Application Contact: Debra Moore, Special Events Assistant, 304-384-5113, E-mail: dlm@concord.edu.

GRADUATE UNITS

Graduate Studies Students: 109 full-time (91 women), 256 part-time (195 women); includes 28 minority (26 Black or African American, non-Hispanic/Latino; 1 American Indian or Alaska Native, non-Hispanic/Latino; 1 Hispanic/Latino), 2 international. Average age 34. *Faculty:* 20 full-time (13 women), 5 part-time/adjunct (3 women). *Financial support:* Tuition waivers and unspecified assistantships available. Financial award applicants required to submit FAFSA. *Degree program information:* Part-time and evening/weekend programs available. Part-time, evening/weekend, online learning. Offers educational leadership and supervision (M Ed); geography (M Ed); health promotion (MA); reading specialist (M Ed); social work (MSW); special education (M Ed); teaching (MAT). *Application deadline:* Applications are processed on a rolling basis. *Application fee:* $25. Electronic applications accepted. *Application Contact:* Debra Moore, Special Events Assistant, 304-384-5113, E-mail: dlm@concord.edu. *Director*, Dr. Cheryl Barnes, 304-384-6306, E-mail: cbarnes@concord.edu.

CONNECTICUT COLLEGE, New London, CT 06320

General Information Independent, coed, comprehensive institution. *Graduate housing:* On-campus housing not available. *Research affiliation:* Hartford Hospital (neuropsychology and clinical psychology).

GRADUATE UNITS

Department of Psychology ***Degree program information:*** Part-time programs available. Part-time. Offers behavioral medicine/health psychology (MA); clinical psychology (MA); neuroscience/psychobiology (MA); social/personality psychology (MA).

CONSERVATORIO DE MUSICA DE PUERTO RICO, San Juan, PR 00907

General Information Commonwealth-supported, coed, comprehensive institution.

GRADUATE UNITS

Program in Musical Performance Offers guitar (Diploma); orchestral instruments (Diploma); piano (Diploma); vocal performance (Diploma).

Program in Music Education Offers music education (MM Ed).

CONVERSE COLLEGE, Spartanburg, SC 29302-0006

General Information Independent, Undergraduate: women only; graduate: coed, comprehensive institution. *Graduate housing:* Room and/or apartments available to single students; on-campus housing not available to married students. *Student services:* Campus employment opportunities, campus safety program, career counseling, international student services, teacher training. *Library:* Mickel Library. *Collection:* Books: 165,873 (physical), 252,047 (digital/electronic); Databases: 30.

Computer facilities: 140 computers available on campus for general student use. A campuswide network can be accessed from student residence rooms and from off campus. Online class registration is available.
Website: http://www.converse.edu/

General Application Contact: Graduate Admissions, 864-596-9404, E-mail: graduate@converse.edu.

GRADUATE UNITS

School of Education and Graduate Studies ***Financial support:*** Research assistantships, career-related internships or fieldwork, and scholarships/grants available. Support available to part-time students. Financial award applicants required to submit FAFSA. *Degree program information:* Part-time and evening/weekend programs available. Part-time, evening/weekend. Offers administration and leadership (Ed S); administration and supervision (M Ed, Ed S); art education (M Ed, MAT); biology (MAT); chemistry (MAT); creative writing (MFA); education (M Ed, M Mus, MAT, MFA, MLA, MMFT, Ed S); elementary education (M Ed, MAT); English (M Ed, MAT, MLA); gifted education (M Ed); history (MLA); intellectual disabilities (MAT); language arts/English (MAT); learning disabilities (MAT); literacy (Ed S); marriage and family therapy (MMFT); mathematics (M Ed, MAT); middle level education (M Ed); natural sciences (M Ed); political science (MLA); science (MAT); social sciences (M Ed, MAT); social studies (MAT); special education (M Ed). *Application deadline:* For fall admission, 8/1 for domestic and international students; for winter admission, 11/15 for domestic and international students; for spring admission, 1/15 for domestic and international students. Applications are processed on a rolling basis. *Application fee:* $40. Electronic applications accepted. *Application Contact:* 864-596-9404, E-mail: graduate@converse.edu.

Petrie School of Music ***Financial support:*** Career-related internships or fieldwork, Federal Work-Study, institutionally sponsored loans, and unspecified assistantships available. Support available to part-time students. Financial award application deadline: 4/15. *Degree program information:* Part-time and evening/weekend programs available. Part-time, evening/weekend. Offers music education (M Mus); performance (M Mus). *Application deadline:* For spring admission, 3/1 priority date for domestic and international students. Applications are processed on a rolling basis. *Application fee:* $40. Electronic applications accepted. *Application Contact:* 864-596-9404, E-mail: graduate@converse.edu. *Director*, Patricia S. Foy, 864-596-9172, E-mail: patti.foy@converse.edu.

THE CONWAY SCHOOL, Conway, MA 01341-0179

General Information Independent, coed, graduate-only institution. *Enrollment by degree level:* 22 master's. *Graduate faculty:* 2 full-time (1 woman), 10 part-time/adjunct (6 women). *Tuition, area resident:* Full-time $27,375. *Required fees:* $4075. *Graduate housing:* On-campus housing not available. *Student services:* Career counseling. *Collection:* Books: 4,000 (physical). Study areas open 24 hours, 5–7 days a week; students can reserve study rooms.

Computer facilities: 4 computers available on campus for general student use. A campuswide network can be accessed.
Website: http://www.csld.edu/

General Application Contact: Adrian K. Dahlin, Director of Admissions, 413-369-4044 Ext. 5, Fax: 413-369-4032, E-mail: adrian@csld.edu.

GRADUATE UNITS

Program in Ecological Design Students: 22 full-time (13 women). Average age 41. *Faculty:* 2 full-time (1 woman), 10 part-time/adjunct (6 women). *Financial support:* Career-related internships or fieldwork, institutionally sponsored loans, and scholarships/grants available. Financial award application deadline: 11/9; financial award applicants required to submit FAFSA. Offers ecological design (MS). *Application deadline:* For fall admission, 2/1 priority date for domestic students. Applications are processed on a rolling basis. *Application fee:* $50. *Application Contact:* Adrian K. Dahlin, Director of Admissions, 413-369-4044 Ext. 5, Fax: 413-369-4032, E-mail: adrian@csld.edu. *Academic Coordinator*, Ken Byrne, 413-369-4044 Ext. 2.

COOPER UNION FOR THE ADVANCEMENT OF SCIENCE AND ART, New York, NY 10003-7120

General Information Independent, coed, comprehensive institution. *Enrollment:* 972 graduate, professional, and undergraduate students; 45 full-time matriculated graduate/professional students (10 women), 28 part-time matriculated graduate/professional students (4 women). *Enrollment by degree level:* 73 master's. *Graduate faculty:* 29 full-time (3 women), 19 part-time/adjunct (6 women). *Tuition, area resident:* Part-time $1200 per credit. *Required fees:* $925 per semester. One-time fee: $250. *Graduate housing:* On-campus housing not available. *Student services:* Campus employment opportunities, campus safety program, career counseling, international student services, low-cost health insurance, services for students with disabilities, writing training. *Library:* Cooper Union Library. *Collection:* Books: 96,957 (physical), 18,641 (digital/electronic); Serial titles: 75 (physical), 43,219 (digital/electronic); Databases: 58. Weekly public service hours: 69. *Research affiliation:* ITT (electrical engineering), Albert Einstein College of Medicine (child obesity and sleep apnea), Hotseat Chassis Inc. (enhanced driver's education through simulation), edX (STEM education), New York State Energy Research and Development Authority (energy efficiency and power regeneration), Maxentric (wireless communications).

Computer facilities: Computer purchase and lease plans are available. 100 computers available on campus for general student use. A campuswide network can be accessed from student residence rooms and from off campus. Online class registration is available.
Website: http://www.cooper.edu/

General Application Contact: Admissions Office, 212-353-4120, E-mail: admissions@cooper.edu.

GRADUATE UNITS

Albert Nerken School of Engineering Students: 33 full-time (4 women), 28 part-time (4 women); includes 25 minority (2 Black or African American, non-Hispanic/Latino; 18 Asian, non-Hispanic/Latino; 2 Hispanic/Latino; 3 Two or more races, non-Hispanic/Latino), 3 international. Average age 24. 56 applicants, 70% accepted, 27 enrolled. *Faculty:* 27 full-time (1 woman), 15 part-time/adjunct (2 women). *Financial support:* In 2015–16, 61 students received support, including 4 fellowships with tuition reimbursements available (averaging $11,000 per year); career-related internships or fieldwork, Federal Work-Study, tuition waivers (full and partial), and tuition scholarships offered to exceptional students also available. Support available to part-time students. Financial award application deadline: 5/1; financial award applicants required to submit FAFSA. In 2015, 25 master's awarded. *Degree program information:* Part-time programs available. Part-time. Offers chemical engineering (ME); civil engineering (ME); electrical engineering (ME); mechanical engineering (ME). *Application deadline:* For fall admission, 4/1 for domestic and international students. *Application fee:* $75. Electronic applications accepted. *Application Contact:* Student Contact, 212-353-4120, E-mail: admissions@cooper.edu. *Acting Dean of Albert Nerken School of Engineering*, Richard Stock, 212-353-4285, E-mail: stock@cooper.edu.

Irwin S. Chanin School of Architecture Students: 12 full-time (6 women); includes 1 minority (Asian, non-Hispanic/Latino), 11 international. Average age 27. 65 applicants, 37% accepted, 11 enrolled. *Faculty:* 14 full-time (3 women), 19 part-time/adjunct (6 women). *Financial support:* In 2015–16, 11 students received support. Tuition waivers (partial) and tuition scholarships offered to exceptional students available. Financial award application deadline: 5/1; financial award applicants required to submit FAFSA. In 2015, 9 master's awarded. Offers architecture (M Arch II). *Application deadline:* For fall admission, 3/2 for domestic and international students. *Application fee:* $75. Electronic applications accepted. *Application Contact:* Student Contact, 212-353-4120, E-mail: admissions@cooper.edu. *Dean*, Nader Tehrani, 212-353-4220, E-mail: ntehrani@cooper.edu.

COPPIN STATE UNIVERSITY, Baltimore, MD 21216-3698

General Information State-supported, coed, comprehensive institution. CGS member. *Graduate housing:* On-campus housing not available.

GRADUATE UNITS

Division of Graduate Studies ***Degree program information:*** Part-time and evening/weekend programs available. Part-time, evening/weekend, online learning.

Division of Arts and Sciences Degree program information: Part-time and evening/weekend programs available. Part-time, evening/weekend. Offers alcohol and substance abuse counseling (MS); arts and sciences (M Ed, MA, MS); criminal justice (MS); human services administration (MS); rehabilitation counseling (M Ed).

Division of Education Degree program information: Part-time and evening/weekend programs available. Part-time, evening/weekend, online learning. Offers adult and general education (MS); curriculum and instruction (M Ed); education (M Ed, MAT, MS); reading education (MS); special education (M Ed); teacher education (MAT); teaching (MAT).

Helene Fuld School of Nursing Degree program information: Part-time and evening/weekend programs available. Part-time, evening/weekend. Offers family nurse practitioner (PMC); nursing (MSN).

CORBAN UNIVERSITY, Salem, OR 97301-9392

General Information Independent-religious, coed, comprehensive institution.

GRADUATE UNITS

Graduate School Offers counseling (MA); education (MS Ed); management (MBA); non-profit management (MBA).

School of Ministry Degree program information: Part-time and evening/weekend programs available. Part-time, evening/weekend. Offers Biblical languages (M Div); Biblical leadership (Certificate); Christian leadership (MA); Church ministry (M Div); ministry (D Min).

CORNELL UNIVERSITY, Ithaca, NY 14853-0001

General Information Independent, coed, university. CGS member. *Graduate housing:* Rooms and/or apartments available on a first-come, first-served basis to single and married students. Housing application deadline: 7/1. *Research affiliation:* Brookhaven National Laboratory (physics, biology, medicine, chemistry, energy, engineering, environmental science), Fermi National Accelerator Laboratory, Boyce Thompson Institute for Plant Research (plant research).

GRADUATE UNITS

College of Veterinary Medicine Students: 398 full-time (320 women); includes 79 minority (12 Black or African American, non-Hispanic/Latino; 3 American Indian or Alaska Native, non-Hispanic/Latino; 26 Asian, non-Hispanic/Latino; 31 Hispanic/Latino; 7 Two or more races, non-Hispanic/Latino), 7 international. Average age 26. 948 applicants, 16% accepted, 102 enrolled. *Faculty:* 185 full-time (84 women). *Financial support:* In 2015–16, 326 students received support. Federal Work-Study, institutionally sponsored loans, and scholarships/grants available. Financial award application deadline: 2/1; financial award applicants required to submit CSS PROFILE or FAFSA. In 2015, 95 doctorates awarded. Offers veterinary medicine (DVM). *Application deadline:* For fall admission, 9/15 for domestic and international students. Electronic applications accepted. *Application Contact:* Jennifer A. Mailey, Director of Admissions, 607-253-3700, Fax: 607-253-3709, E-mail: jam333@cornell.edu. *Interim Dean*, Dr. Lorin Warnick, 607-253-3771, Fax: 607-253-3701.

Cornell Law School Offers law (LL M, JD, JSD). JD/MLLP offered jointly with Humboldt University, Berlin; JD/DESS offered jointly with Institut d'etudes Politiques de Paris ("Sciences Po") and Paris I. Electronic applications accepted.

Graduate School Students: 5,427 full-time (2,423 women); includes 837 minority (109 Black or African American, non-Hispanic/Latino; 8 American Indian or Alaska Native, non-Hispanic/Latino; 376 Asian, non-Hispanic/Latino; 227 Hispanic/Latino; 3 Native Hawaiian or other Pacific Islander, non-Hispanic/Latino; 114 Two or more races, non-Hispanic/Latino), 2,573 international. Average age 27. 19,807 applicants, 23% accepted, 2079 enrolled. *Faculty:* 1,902 full-time (530 women). *Financial support:* In 2015–16, 2,093 students received support, including 673 fellowships with full tuition reimbursements available, 1,013 research assistantships with full tuition reimbursements available, 1,133 teaching assistantships with full tuition reimbursements available; career-related internships or fieldwork, institutionally sponsored loans, scholarships/grants, traineeships, health care benefits, tuition waivers (full and partial), and unspecified assistantships also available. Financial award applicants required to submit FAFSA. In 2015, 1,735 master's, 487 doctorates awarded. Offers 19th century art (PhD); acarology (MS, PhD); adult and extension education (MPS, MS, PhD); advanced composites and structures (M Eng); advanced materials processing (M Eng, MS, PhD); aerospace engineering (M Eng, MS, PhD); African history (MA, PhD); African studies (MPS); African, African American and African diaspora (PhD); African-American literature (PhD); African-American studies (MPS); Africana studies (PhD); agricultural finance (MS, PhD); agriculture and life sciences (M Eng, MFS, MLA, MPS, MS, PhD); agronomy (MS, PhD); algorithms (M Eng, PhD); American art (PhD); American history (MA, PhD); American literature after 1865 (PhD); American literature to 1865 (PhD); American politics (PhD); American studies (PhD); analytical chemistry (PhD); ancient art and archaeology (PhD); ancient Greek history (PhD); ancient history (MA, PhD); ancient Near Eastern studies (MA, PhD); ancient philosophy (PhD); ancient Roman history (PhD); animal cytology (PhD); animal genetics (MPS, MS, PhD); animal genomics (MPS, MS, PhD); animal nutrition (MPS, MS, PhD); animal science (MPS, MS); apiculture (MS, PhD); apparel design (MA, MPS); applied econometrics and qualitative analysis (MS, PhD); applied economics (PhD); applied entomology (MS, PhD); applied linguistics (MA, PhD); applied logic and automated reasoning (M Eng, PhD); applied mathematics (PhD); applied mathematics and computational methods (M Eng, MS, PhD); applied physics (PhD); applied probability and statistics (PhD); applied research in human-environment relations (MS); applied statistics (MPS); aquatic entomology (MS, PhD); Arabic and Islamic studies (MA, PhD); archaeological anthropology (PhD); architectural design (M Arch); architectural science (MS); architecture, art and planning (M Arch, MA, MFA, MPS, MRP, MS, PhD); artificial intelligence (M Eng, PhD); arts and sciences (MA, MFA, MPA, MPS, MS, DMA, PhD); Asian American art (PhD); Asian religions (MA, PhD); astronomy (PhD); astrophysics (PhD); atmospheric science (MS, PhD); Baroque art (PhD); basic analytical economics (PhD); behavioral biology (PhD); behavioral physiology (MS, PhD); biblical studies (MA, PhD); bio-organic chemistry (PhD); biochemical engineering (M Eng, MS, PhD); biochemistry (PhD); bioenergy and integrated energy systems (M Eng, MPS, MS, PhD); biological anthropology (PhD); biological control (MS, PhD); biological engineering (M Eng, MPS, MS, PhD); biomechanical engineering (M Eng, MS, PhD); biomedical engineering (M Eng, MS, PhD); biometry (MS, PhD); biophysical chemistry (PhD); biophysics (PhD); bioprocess engineering (M Eng, MPS, MS, PhD); biopsychology (PhD); breeding of horticultural crops (MPS); cardiovascular and respiratory physiology (MS, PhD); cell biology (PhD); cellular and molecular medicine (MS, PhD); cellular and molecular toxicology (MS, PhD); cellular immunology (MS, PhD); chemical biology (PhD); chemical physics (PhD); chemical reaction engineering (M Eng, MS, PhD); Chinese philosophy (PhD); city and regional planning (MRP, PhD); classical and statistical thermodynamics (M Eng, MS, PhD); classical archaeology (PhD); classical Chinese literature (PhD); classical Japanese literature (PhD); classical literature and philology (PhD); classical myth (PhD); classical rhetoric (PhD); cognition (PhD); collective bargaining, labor law and labor history (MILR, MPS, MS, PhD); colonial and postcolonial literatures (PhD); combustion (M Eng, MS, PhD); communication (MS, PhD); community nutrition (MPS, PhD); community-based natural resources management (MS, PhD); comparative and functional anatomy (PhD); comparative biomedical sciences (MS, PhD); comparative literature (PhD); comparative modernities (PhD); comparative politics (PhD); composition (DMA); computational behavioral biology (PhD); computational biology (PhD); computational cell biology (PhD); computational ecology (PhD); computational genetics (PhD); computational macromolecular biology (PhD); computational organismal biology (PhD); computer engineering (M Eng, PhD); computer graphics (M Eng, MS, PhD); computer science (M Eng, PhD); computer vision (M Eng, PhD); concurrency and distributed computing (M Eng, PhD); conservation biology (MS, PhD); consumer policy (PhD); creative visual arts (MFA); creative writing (MFA); cultural studies (PhD); cytology (MS, PhD); dairy science (MPS, MS, PhD); decision theory (MS, PhD); development policy (MPS); developmental and reproductive biology (MS, PhD); developmental biology (PhD); developmental psychology (MA, PhD); digital art (PhD); drama and the theatre (PhD); dramatic literature (PhD); dynamics and space mechanics (MS, PhD); early modern European history (MA, PhD); East Asian art (PhD); East Asian linguistics (MA, PhD); East Asian literature and culture (PhD); East Asian studies (MA); ecohydrology (M Eng, MPS, MS, PhD); ecology (PhD); econometrics and economic statistics (PhD); economic and social statistics (MILR, MS, PhD); economic development and planning (PhD); economic geology (M Eng, MS, PhD); economic theory (PhD); economics of development (MS, PhD); economy and society (MA, PhD); ecosystem biology and biogeochemistry (MPS, MS, PhD); ecotoxicology and environmental chemistry (MS, PhD); electrical engineering (M Eng, PhD); electrical systems (M Eng, PhD); electrophysics (M Eng, PhD); endocrinology (MS, PhD); energy and power systems (M Eng, MS, PhD); engineering (M Eng, MPS, MS, PhD); engineering geology (M Eng, MS, PhD); engineering management (M Eng, MS, PhD); engineering physics (M Eng); engineering statistics (MS, PhD); English history (MA, PhD); English linguistics (MA, PhD); English poetry (PhD); English Renaissance to 1660 (PhD); enology (MS, PhD); environmental and comparative physiology (MS, PhD); environmental archaeology (MA); environmental economics (MS, PhD); environmental engineering (M Eng, MPS, MS, PhD); environmental fluid mechanics and hydrology (M Eng, MS, PhD); environmental geophysics (M Eng, MS, PhD); environmental information science (MS, PhD); environmental management (MPS); environmental planning and design (MRP, PhD); environmental studies (MA, MS, PhD); environmental systems engineering (M Eng, MS, PhD); evolutionary biology (PhD); experimental design (MS, PhD); experimental physics (MS, PhD); facilities planning and management (MS); family and social welfare policy (PhD); farm management and production economics (MS, PhD); fiber science (MS, PhD); field crop science (MS, PhD); fishery and aquatic science (MPS, MS, PhD); fluid dynamics, rheology and biorheology (M Eng, MS, PhD); fluid mechanics (M Eng, MS, PhD); food chemistry (MPS, MS, PhD); food engineering (M Eng, MPS, MS, PhD); food microbiology (MPS, MS, PhD); food processing waste technology (MPS, MS, PhD); food science (MFS, MPS, MS, PhD); forest science (MPS, MS, PhD); French history (MA, PhD); French linguistics (PhD); French literature (PhD); fungal and oomycete biology (MPS, MS, PhD); gastrointestinal and metabolic physiology (MS, PhD); gender and life course (MA, PhD); general geology (M Eng, MS, PhD); general linguistics (MA, PhD); general space sciences (PhD); genetics (PhD); genomics (PhD); geobiology (M Eng, MS, PhD); geochemistry and isotope geology (M Eng, MS, PhD); geohydrology (M Eng, MS, PhD); geomorphology (M Eng, MS, PhD); geophysics (M Eng, MS, PhD); geotechnical engineering (M Eng, MS, PhD); geotectonics (M Eng, MS, PhD); German area studies (MA, PhD); German history (MA, PhD); German intellectual history (MA, PhD); Germanic linguistics (MA, PhD); Germanic literature (MA,

PhD); Greek and Latin language and linguistics (PhD); health administration (MHA); health management and policy (PhD); heat and mass transfer (M Eng, MS, PhD); heat transfer (M Eng, MS, PhD); Hebrew and Judaic studies (MA, PhD); Hispanic literature (PhD); histology (PhD); historic preservation planning (MA); historical archaeology (MA); history and philosophy of science and technology (MA, PhD); history of architecture (MA, PhD); history of photography (PhD); history of science (MA, PhD); history of urban development (MA, PhD); horticultural crop management systems (MPS); housing and design (MS); human computer interaction (PhD); human development and family studies (MA, PhD); human dimensions of natural resources management (MPS, MS, PhD); human ecology (MA, MHA, MPA, MPS, MS, PhD); human experimental psychology (PhD); human factors and ergonomics (MS); human nutrition (MPS, PhD); human resource studies (MILR, MPS, MS, PhD); human-computer interaction (MS, PhD); human-environment relations (MS); human-plant interactions (MPS, PhD); immunochemistry (MS, PhD); immunogenetics (MS, PhD); immunopathology (MS, PhD); Indo-European linguistics (MA, PhD); industrial and labor relations problems (MILR, MPS, MS, PhD); industrial biotechnology (M Eng, MPS, MS, PhD); industrial organization and control (PhD); infection and immunity (MS, PhD); infectious diseases (MS, PhD); information organization and retrieval (M Eng, PhD); information science (PhD); information systems (PhD); infrared astronomy (PhD); inorganic chemistry (PhD); insect behavior (MS, PhD); insect biochemistry (MS, PhD); insect ecology (MS, PhD); insect genetics (MS, PhD); insect morphology (MS, PhD); insect pathology (MS, PhD); insect physiology (MS, PhD); insect systematics (MS, PhD); insect toxicology and insecticide chemistry (MS, PhD); integrated pest management (MS, PhD); interior design (MA, MPS); international agriculture and development (MPS); international and comparative labor (MILR, MPS, MS, PhD); international development (MPS); international development planning (MRP, PhD); international economics (PhD); international food science (MPS, MS, PhD); international nutrition (MPS, PhD); international planning (MPS); international population (MPS); international relations (PhD); international spatial problems (MA, MS, PhD); Islamic art (PhD); Italian linguistics (PhD); Italian literature (PhD); kinetics and catalysis (M Eng, MS, PhD); Korean history (PhD); Korean literature (PhD); labor economics (MILR, MPS, MS, PhD); landscape architecture (MLA, MPS); language and communication (MS, PhD); Latin American archaeology (MA); Latin American art (PhD); Latin American history (MA, PhD); learning, teaching, and social policy (MPS, MS, PhD); lesbian, bisexual, and gay literary studies (PhD); literary criticism and theory (PhD); location theory (MA, MS, PhD); manufacturing systems engineering (PhD); marine geology (MS, PhD); marketing and food distribution (MS, PhD); materials and manufacturing engineering (M Eng, MS, PhD); materials chemistry (PhD); materials engineering (M Eng, PhD); materials science (M Eng, PhD); mathematical programming (PhD); mathematical statistics (MS, PhD); mathematics (PhD); mathematics 7-12 (MS); mechanical systems and design (M Eng, MS, PhD); mechanics of materials (MS, PhD); media communication and society (MS, PhD); medical and veterinary entomology (MS, PhD); medieval and Renaissance Latin literature (PhD); medieval archaeology (MA, PhD); medieval art (PhD); medieval Chinese history (MA, PhD); medieval history (MA, PhD); medieval literature (PhD); medieval music (PhD); medieval philology and linguistics (PhD); medieval philosophy (PhD); Mediterranean and Near Eastern archaeology (MA); membrane and epithelial physiology (MS, PhD); methodology (MA, PhD); microbiology (PhD); mineralogy (M Eng, MS, PhD); modern art (PhD); modern Chinese history (MA, PhD); modern Chinese literature (PhD); modern European history (MA, PhD); modern Japanese history (MA, PhD); modern Japanese literature (PhD); modern Middle Eastern history (PhD); molecular and cellular physiology (MS, PhD); molecular biochemistry (MPS, PhD); molecular biology (PhD); monetary and macro economics (PhD); multiphase flows (M Eng, MS, PhD); multiregional economic analysis (MA, MS, PhD); musicology (PhD); nanobiotechnology (M Eng, MPS, MS, PhD); neural and sensory physiology (MS, PhD); neurobiology (PhD); nutritional and food toxicology (MS, PhD); Old and Middle English (PhD); old Norse (MA, PhD); operating systems (M Eng, PhD); operations research and industrial engineering (M Eng); organic chemistry (PhD); organizational behavior (MILR, MPS, MS, PhD); organizational communication (MS, PhD); organizations (MA, PhD); organometallic chemistry (PhD); paleobotany (MS, PhD); paleontology (M Eng, MS, PhD); parallel computing (M Eng, PhD); peace science (MA, MS, PhD); performance practice (DMA); personality and social psychology (PhD); petroleum geology (M Eng, MS, PhD); petrology (M Eng, MS, PhD); pharmacology (MS, PhD); philosophy (PhD); phonetics (MA, PhD); phonological theory (MA, PhD); physical chemistry (PhD); physics (MS, PhD); physiological genomics (MS, PhD); physiology and ecology of horticultural crops (MPS, MS, PhD); physiology of reproduction (MPS, MS, PhD); planetary geology (M Eng, MS, PhD); planetary studies (PhD); planning methods (MA, MS, PhD); planning theory and systems analysis (MRP, PhD); plant biochemistry (MS, PhD); plant breeding (MPS, MS, PhD); plant cell biology (MS, PhD); plant ecology (MS, PhD); plant genetics (MPS, MS, PhD); plant microbe pathology (MPS, MS, PhD); plant molecular biology (MS, PhD); plant morphology, anatomy and biomechanics (MS, PhD); plant pathology (MPS, MS, PhD); plant physiology (MS, PhD); plant protection (MPS); policy analysis (MA, PhD); policy and institutional analysis (MS, PhD); political methodology (PhD); political sociology/social movements (MA, PhD); political thought (PhD); polymer chemistry (PhD); polymer science (MS, PhD); polymers (M Eng, MS, PhD); population and development (MS, PhD); population medicine and epidemiology (MS, PhD); Precambrian geology (M Eng, MS, PhD); premodern Islamic history (MA, PhD); premodern Japanese history (MA, PhD); probability (MS, PhD); program development and evaluation (MPS, MS, PhD); programming environments (M Eng, PhD); programming languages and methodology (M Eng, PhD); prose fiction (PhD); public affairs (MPA); public finance (PhD); public policy (PhD); public policy analysis (MS, PhD); quantitative ecology (MS, PhD); Quaternary geology (M Eng, MS, PhD); racial and ethnic relations (MA, PhD); radio astronomy (PhD); radiophysics (PhD); real estate (MPS); regional economics and development planning (MRP, PhD); regional science (MRP, PhD); remote sensing (M Eng, MS, PhD); Renaissance art (PhD); Renaissance history (MA, PhD); reproductive physiology (MS, PhD); resource economics (PhD); Restoration and the eighteenth-century (PhD); risk assessment, management and public policy (MS, PhD); robotics (M Eng, PhD); rock mechanics (M Eng, MS, PhD); Romance linguistics (MA, PhD); rural and environmental sociology (MS, PhD); Russian history (MA, PhD); sampling (MS, PhD); science and technology policy (MPS); science, environment and health communication (MS, PhD); scientific computing (M Eng, PhD); second language acquisition (MA, PhD); sedimentology (M Eng, MS, PhD); seismology (M Eng, MS, PhD); semantics (MA, PhD); sensory evaluation (MPS, MS, PhD); Slavic linguistics (MA, PhD); social and health systems planning (MRP, PhD); social aspects of information (PhD); social networks (MA, PhD); social psychology (MA, PhD); social psychology of communication (MS, PhD); social stratification (MA, PhD); social studies of science and technology (MA, PhD); sociocultural anthropology (PhD); sociolinguistics (MA, PhD); soil science (MS, PhD); solid mechanics (MS, PhD); South Asian history (PhD); South Asian linguistics (MA, PhD); South Asian literature and culture (PhD); South Asian studies (MA); Southeast Asian art (PhD); Southeast Asian history (MA, PhD); Southeast Asian linguistics (MA, PhD); Southeast Asian literature and culture (PhD); Southeast Asian studies (MA); Spanish linguistics (PhD); state, economy, and society (MS, PhD); statistical computing (MS, PhD); stochastic processes (MS, PhD); Stone Age archaeology (MA); stratigraphy (M Eng, MS, PhD); structural and functional biology (MS, PhD); structural engineering (M Eng, MS, PhD); structural geology (M Eng, MS, PhD); structural mechanics (M Eng, MS); surface science (M Eng, MS, PhD); sustainable systems (M Eng, MPS, MS, PhD); syntactic theory (MA, PhD); synthetic biology (MS); syntheticbiology (M Eng, MPS, PhD); systematic botany (MS, PhD); systems engineering (M Eng); textile science (MS, PhD); the nineteenth century (PhD); the twentieth century (PhD); theatre history (PhD); theatre theory and aesthetics (PhD); theoretical astrophysics (PhD); theoretical chemistry (PhD); theoretical physics (MS, PhD); theory and criticism (PhD); theory and criticism of architecture (M Arch); theory of computation (M Eng, PhD); theory of music (MA); transportation engineering (MS, PhD); transportation systems engineering (M Eng); urban and regional economics (MA, MS, PhD); urban and regional theory (MRP, PhD); urban design (M Arch); urban planning history (MRP, PhD); visual studies (PhD); water resource systems (M Eng, MS, PhD); wildlife conservation (PhD); wildlife science (MPS, MS, PhD); women's literature (PhD). *Application deadline:* For fall admission, 1/15 for domestic and international students; for spring admission, 11/1 for domestic and international students. *Application fee:* $95. Electronic applications accepted. *Application Contact:* Graduate School Application Requests, 607-255-5816, E-mail: gradadmissions@cornell.edu. *Dean,* Dr. Barbara Knuth, 607-255-5417.

Field of Hotel Administration Offers hospitality management (MMH); hotel administration (MS, PhD). Electronic applications accepted.

Graduate Field in the Law School Offers law (JSD). Electronic applications accepted.

Graduate Field of Management Offers accounting (PhD); finance (PhD); marketing (PhD); organizational behavior (PhD); production and operations management (PhD). Electronic applications accepted.

Samuel Curtis Johnson Graduate School of Management Students: 535 full-time (147 women); includes 143 minority (25 Black or African American, non-Hispanic/Latino; 2 American Indian or Alaska Native, non-Hispanic/Latino; 69 Asian, non-Hispanic/Latino; 25 Hispanic/Latino; 1 Native Hawaiian or other Pacific Islander, non-Hispanic/Latino; 21 Two or more races, non-Hispanic/Latino), 179 international. Average age 27. 1,704 applicants, 32% accepted, 274 enrolled. *Faculty:* 67 full-time (15 women), 58 part-time/adjunct (7 women). *Financial support:* Fellowships, research assistantships, career-related internships or fieldwork, Federal Work-Study, institutionally sponsored loans, and tuition waivers (full and partial) available. Financial award applicants required to submit FAFSA. Offers management (Exec MBA, MBA, PhD). *Application deadline:* For fall admission, 10/1 for domestic and international students; for winter admission, 11/17 for domestic and international students; for spring admission, 1/15 for domestic and international students; for summer admission, 3/17 for domestic and international students. *Application fee:* $200. Electronic applications accepted. *Application Contact:* Admissions Office, 800-847-2082, Fax: 607-255-0065, E-mail: mba@johnson.cornell.edu. *Dean,* Dr. Soumitra Dutta, 607-255-6418, E-mail: dean@johnson.cornell.edu.

CORNERSTONE UNIVERSITY, Grand Rapids, MI 49525-5897

General Information Independent-religious, coed, comprehensive institution. *Graduate housing:* Rooms and/or apartments available on a first-come, first-served basis to single and married students.

GRADUATE UNITS

Graduate Programs ***Degree program information:*** Part-time programs available. Part-time, online learning. Offers business administration (MBA); education (MA Ed); management (MSM); teaching English to speakers of other languages (MA, Graduate Certificate). Programs also offered at Holland, Kalamazoo, and Troy, MI campuses. Electronic applications accepted.

COVENANT COLLEGE, Lookout Mountain, GA 30750

General Information Independent-religious, coed, comprehensive institution. *Graduate housing:* Room and/or apartments available on a first-come, first-served basis to single students; on-campus housing not available to married students. Housing application deadline: 5/1.

GRADUATE UNITS

Program in Education ***Degree program information:*** Part-time programs available. Part-time. Offers education (M Ed, MAT).

COVENANT THEOLOGICAL SEMINARY, St. Louis, MO 63141-8697

General Information Independent-religious, coed, graduate-only institution. *Graduate housing:* Rooms and/or apartments available on a first-come, first-served basis to single and married students.

GRADUATE UNITS

Graduate and Professional Programs ***Degree program information:*** Part-time and evening/weekend programs available. Part-time, evening/weekend, online learning. Offers theology (M Div, MA, MAC, MAEM, Th M, D Min, Certificate). Electronic applications accepted.

COX COLLEGE, Springfield, MO 65802

General Information Independent, coed, primarily women, comprehensive institution.

GRADUATE UNITS

Programs in Nursing Offers clinical nurse leader (MSN); family nurse practitioner (MSN); nurse educator (MSN). Electronic applications accepted.

CRANBROOK ACADEMY OF ART, Bloomfield Hills, MI 48303-0801

General Information Independent, coed, graduate-only institution. *Enrollment by degree level:* 152 master's. *Graduate faculty:* 10 full-time (3 women). *Tuition, area resident:* Full-time $33,406. *Required fees:* $1278. One-time fee: $175 full-time. *Graduate housing:* Room and/or apartments available on a first-come, first-served basis to single students; on-campus housing not available to married students. Typical cost: $3175 per year. Housing application deadline: 4/1. *Student services:* Campus employment opportunities. *Library:* Cranbrook Academy of Art Library. *Collection:* Books: 39,349 (physical); Serial titles: 4,343 (physical); Databases: 40.

Computer facilities: 20 computers available on campus for general student use. A campuswide network can be accessed from student residence rooms.
Website: http://www.cranbrookart.edu/

General Application Contact: Leslie Tobakos, Registrar/Financial Aid and Admissions Manager, 248-645-3360, Fax: 248-645-3591, E-mail: ltobakos@cranbrook.edu.

GRADUATE UNITS

Graduate School Students: 152 full-time (106 women); includes 36 minority (8 Black or African American, non-Hispanic/Latino; 16 Asian, non-Hispanic/Latino; 7 Hispanic/Latino; 1 Native Hawaiian or other Pacific Islander, non-Hispanic/Latino; 4 Two or more races, non-Hispanic/Latino), 22 international. Average age 27. 390 applicants,

37% accepted, 79 enrolled. *Faculty:* 10 full-time (3 women). *Financial support:* Federal Work-Study and scholarships/grants available. Financial award application deadline: 2/1; financial award applicants required to submit FAFSA. Offers 2D design (MFA); architecture (M Arch); ceramics (MFA); fiber (MFA); metalsmithing (MFA); painting (MFA); photography (MFA); print media (MFA); sculpture (MFA). *Application deadline:* For fall admission, 2/1 priority date for domestic and international students; for spring admission, 11/1 for domestic students, 11/1 priority date for international students. *Application fee:* $85. Electronic applications accepted. *Application Contact:* Leslie Tobakos, Registrar/Financial Aid and Admissions Manager, 248-645-3360, Fax: 248-646-0046, E-mail: ltobakos@cranbrook.edu. *Director,* Christopher Scoates, 248-645-3300, Fax: 248-646-0046.

CRANDALL UNIVERSITY, Moncton, NB E1C 9L7, Canada

General Information Independent-religious, coed, comprehensive institution.

GRADUATE UNITS

Graduate Programs

CREIGHTON UNIVERSITY, Omaha, NE 68178-0001

General Information Independent-religious, coed, university. CGS member. *Enrollment:* 8,435 graduate, professional, and undergraduate students; 2,875 full-time matriculated graduate/professional students (1,676 women), 1,370 part-time matriculated graduate/professional students (807 women). *Enrollment by degree level:* 1,009 master's, 3,099 doctoral, 137 other advanced degrees. *Graduate faculty:* 325 full-time (110 women). *Tuition, area resident:* Full-time $14,400; part-time $800 per credit hour. *Required fees:* $158 per semester. Tuition and fees vary according to course load, campus/location, program, reciprocity agreements and student's religious affiliation. *Graduate housing:* Rooms and/or apartments available on a first-come, first-served basis to single and married students. Typical cost: $10,620 per year for single students; $10,620 per year for married students. Room charges vary according to board plan, campus/location and housing facility selected. Housing application deadline: 5/1. *Student services:* Campus employment opportunities, campus safety program, career counseling, child daycare facilities, exercise/wellness program, free psychological counseling, grant writing training, international student services, low-cost health insurance, multicultural affairs office, services for students with disabilities, teacher training, writing training. *Library:* Reinert Alumni Memorial Library plus 2 others. *Collection:* Books: 360,420 (physical), 275,427 (digital/electronic); Serial titles: 4,089 (physical), 87,926 (digital/electronic); Databases: 789. Weekly public service hours: 121; study areas open 24 hours, 5–7 days a week. *Research affiliation:* U.S. Department of Education (DOE) (student support services), National Institutes of Health (asthma), U.S. Department of Commerce (atmospheric science), National Science Foundation (business and education).

Computer facilities: Computer purchase and lease plans are available. 402 computers available on campus for general student use. A campuswide network can be accessed from student residence rooms and from off campus. Online class registration, financial aid information are available.
Website: http://www.creighton.edu/

General Application Contact: Lindsay Johnson, Director of Graduate and Adult Recruitment, 402-280-2703, Fax: 402-280-2423, E-mail: gradschool@creighton.edu.

GRADUATE UNITS

College of Nursing Students: 132 full-time (120 women), 228 part-time (212 women); includes 38 minority (10 Black or African American, non-Hispanic/Latino; 3 American Indian or Alaska Native, non-Hispanic/Latino; 11 Asian, non-Hispanic/Latino; 1 Hispanic/Latino; 2 Native Hawaiian or other Pacific Islander, non-Hispanic/Latino; 11 Two or more races, non-Hispanic/Latino). Average age 31. 66 applicants, 91% accepted, 43 enrolled. *Faculty:* 10 full-time (all women), 48 part-time/adjunct (45 women). *Financial support:* In 2015–16, 7 students received support. Scholarships/grants available. Financial award applicants required to submit FAFSA. In 2015, 54 master's, 17 doctorates, 1 other advanced degree awarded. *Degree program information:* Part-time programs available. Part-time, blended/hybrid learning. Offers adult acute care nurse practitioner (Post-Master's Certificate); adult gerontology acute care nurse practitioner (DNP); adult gerontology nurse practitioner (DNP); clinical nurse leader (MSN, Post-Graduate Certificate); clinical systems administration (MSN, DNP); family nurse practitioner (DNP, Post-Master's Certificate); neonatal nurse practitioner (DNP, Post-Master's Certificate); pediatric acute care nurse practitioner (DNP, Post-Master's Certificate); psychiatric mental health nurse practitioner (DNP). *Application deadline:* For fall admission, 6/15 priority date for domestic and international students; for spring admission, 11/15 priority date for domestic and international students; for summer admission, 4/15 for domestic and international students. Applications are processed on a rolling basis. *Application fee:* $50. Electronic applications accepted. *Application Contact:* Shannon Cox, Enrollment Specialist, 402-280-2067, Fax: 402-280-2045, E-mail: shannoncox@creighton.edu. *Dean,* Dr. Catherine Todero, 402-280-2004, Fax: 402-280-2045.

Graduate School Students: 2,875 full-time (1,676 women), 1,370 part-time (807 women); includes 193 minority (103 Black or African American, non-Hispanic/Latino; 15 American Indian or Alaska Native, non-Hispanic/Latino; 45 Asian, non-Hispanic/Latino; 26 Hispanic/Latino; 4 Native Hawaiian or other Pacific Islander, non-Hispanic/Latino), 77 international. Average age 35. 687 applicants, 74% accepted. *Faculty:* 325 full-time (110 women). *Financial support:* In 2015–16, fellowships with tuition reimbursements (averaging $23,000 per year), research assistantships with tuition reimbursements (averaging $15,700 per year), teaching assistantships with tuition reimbursements (averaging $15,700 per year) were awarded; career-related internships or fieldwork, institutionally sponsored loans, scholarships/grants, tuition waivers (partial), and unspecified assistantships also available. Support available to part-time students. Financial award application deadline: 3/1; financial award applicants required to submit FAFSA. In 2015, 394 master's, 36 doctorates awarded. *Degree program information:* Part-time and evening/weekend programs available. Part-time, evening/weekend, 100% online, blended/hybrid learning. Offers emergency medical services (MS); leadership (MS, Ed D). *Application deadline:* For fall admission, 3/1 priority date for domestic and international students; for winter admission, 10/1 for domestic students, 7/1 for international students; for spring admission, 4/1 for domestic students, 10/1 for international students. Applications are processed on a rolling basis. *Application fee:* $50. Electronic applications accepted. *Application Contact:* Lindsay Johnson, Director of Graduate and Adult Recruitment, 402-280-2703, Fax: 402-280-2423, E-mail: gradschool@creighton.edu. *Dean,* Dr. Gail M. Jensen, 402-280-2424, Fax: 402-280-2423, E-mail: gjensen@creighton.edu.

College of Arts and Sciences Students: 66 full-time (30 women), 225 part-time (145 women); includes 14 minority (6 Black or African American, non-Hispanic/Latino; 5 American Indian or Alaska Native, non-Hispanic/Latino; 1 Asian, non-Hispanic/Latino; 1 Hispanic/Latino; 1 Native Hawaiian or other Pacific Islander, non-Hispanic/Latino), 14 international. Average age 35. 102 applicants, 84% accepted, 78 enrolled. *Faculty:* 119 full-time (37 women). *Financial support:* In 2015–16, teaching assistantships with full tuition reimbursements (averaging $11,465 per year) were awarded; fellowships, scholarships/grants, and tuition waivers (partial) also available. Financial award applicants required to submit FAFSA. In 2015, 82 master's awarded. *Degree program information:* Part-time and evening/weekend programs available. Part-time, evening/weekend, 100% online, blended/hybrid learning. Offers arts and sciences (M Ed, MA, MFA, MS); creative writing (MA, MFA); East-West studies (MA); educational leadership (MS); elementary school guidance (MS); elementary teaching (M Ed); international relations (MA); medical anthropology (MA); physics (MS); school counseling and preventive mental health (MS); secondary school guidance (MS); secondary teaching (M Ed); teaching (M Ed); theology (MA). *Application deadline:* For fall admission, 3/1 for domestic and international students; for winter admission, 10/1 for domestic students, 7/1 for international students; for spring admission, 4/1 for domestic students, 10/1 for international students. Applications are processed on a rolling basis. *Application fee:* $50. Electronic applications accepted. *Application Contact:* Lindsay Johnson, Director of Graduate and Adult Recruitment, 402-280-2703, Fax: 402-280-2423, E-mail: gradschool@creighton.edu. *Dean,* Dr. Bridget M. Keegan, 402-280-4015, E-mail: bridgetkeegan@creighton.edu.

Heider College of Business Students: 28 full-time (9 women), 285 part-time (61 women); includes 43 minority (24 Black or African American, non-Hispanic/Latino; 2 American Indian or Alaska Native, non-Hispanic/Latino; 7 Asian, non-Hispanic/Latino; 9 Hispanic/Latino; 1 Native Hawaiian or other Pacific Islander, non-Hispanic/Latino), 19 international. Average age 31. 94 applicants, 93% accepted, 71 enrolled. *Faculty:* 37 full-time (7 women). *Financial support:* In 2015–16, 10 fellowships with partial tuition reimbursements (averaging $8,448 per year) were awarded; career-related internships or fieldwork, tuition waivers (partial), and unspecified assistantships also available. Financial award application deadline: 3/1. In 2015, 144 master's awarded. *Degree program information:* Part-time and evening/weekend programs available. Part-time, evening/weekend, 100% online, blended/hybrid learning. Offers business (MBA, MS, MSAPM). *Application deadline:* For fall admission, 7/1 priority date for domestic students, 3/1 for international students; for winter admission, 10/1 priority date for domestic students, 7/1 for international students; for spring admission, 4/1 priority date for domestic students, 10/1 for international students; for summer admission, 5/1 for domestic and international students. Applications are processed on a rolling basis. *Application fee:* $50. Electronic applications accepted. *Application Contact:* Chris Karasek, Assistant Dean, 402-280-2829, Fax: 402-280-2172, E-mail: chriskarasek@creighton.edu. *Associate Dean for Graduate Programs,* Dr. Deborah Wells, 402-280-2841, E-mail: deborahwells@creighton.edu.

School of Dentistry Offers dentistry (DDS).

School of Law ***Degree program information:*** Part-time programs available. Part-time. Offers law (MS, JD, Certificate); negotiation and conflict resolution (MS, Certificate). Electronic applications accepted.

School of Medicine Offers biomedical sciences (MS, PhD); clinical anatomy (MS); medical microbiology and immunology (MS, PhD); medicine (MS, MD, PhD); pharmaceutical sciences (MS); pharmacology (MS, PhD). Electronic applications accepted.

School of Pharmacy and Health Professions Online learning. Offers occupational therapy (OTD); pharmaceutical sciences (MS); pharmacy (Pharm D); pharmacy and health professions (MS, DPT, OTD, Pharm D); physical therapy (DPT). Electronic applications accepted.

CRISWELL COLLEGE, Dallas, TX 75246-1537

General Information Independent-religious, coed, comprehensive institution. *Graduate housing:* On-campus housing not available.

GRADUATE UNITS

Graduate School of the Bible ***Degree program information:*** Part-time programs available. Part-time. Offers biblical studies (M Div); Christian leadership (MA); counseling (MA); Jewish studies (MA); ministry (MA); theological and biblical studies (MA). Electronic applications accepted.

CROWN COLLEGE, St. Bonifacius, MN 55375-9001

General Information Independent-religious, coed, comprehensive institution. *Graduate housing:* Room and/or apartments available on a first-come, first-served basis to married students; on-campus housing not available to single students. Housing application deadline: 7/1.

GRADUATE UNITS

Adult and Graduate Studies ***Degree program information:*** Part-time and evening/weekend programs available. Part-time, evening/weekend, online learning. Offers Christian studies (MA); instructional leadership (MA); international leadership (MA); ministry leadership (MA); organizational leadership (MA). Electronic applications accepted.

CUMBERLAND UNIVERSITY, Lebanon, TN 37087

General Information Independent, coed, comprehensive institution. *Graduate housing:* Room and/or apartments available on a first-come, first-served basis to single students; on-campus housing not available to married students.

GRADUATE UNITS

Program in Business Administration ***Degree program information:*** Part-time and evening/weekend programs available. Part-time, evening/weekend. Offers business administration (MBA).

Program in Education ***Degree program information:*** Part-time and evening/weekend programs available. Part-time, evening/weekend, online learning. Offers education (MAE).

Program in Public Service Administration ***Degree program information:*** Part-time and evening/weekend programs available. Part-time, evening/weekend. Offers public service administration (MS).

CUNY GRADUATE SCHOOL OF JOURNALISM, New York, NY 10018

General Information City-supported, coed, graduate-only institution. *Graduate faculty:* 105. *Student services:* Campus employment opportunities, career counseling, free psychological counseling, international student services, low-cost health insurance, services for students with disabilities, writing training. *Library:* Research Center.

Computer facilities: 80 computers available on campus for general student use.
Website: http://www.journalism.cuny.edu

General Application Contact: Colleen Marshall, Director of Admissions, 646-758-7852, Fax: 646-758-7709, E-mail: colleen.marshall@journalism.cuny.edu.

GRADUATE UNITS

Graduate Program Students: 199 full-time (123 women); includes 107 minority (36 Black or African American, non-Hispanic/Latino; 30 Asian, non-Hispanic/Latino; 38 Hispanic/Latino; 3 Two or more races, non-Hispanic/Latino). Average age 27. 290 applicants, 100 enrolled. *Faculty:* 105. *Financial support:* Career-related internships or fieldwork, Federal Work-Study, institutionally sponsored loans, and scholarships/grants available. Financial award application deadline: 3/1; financial award applicants required to submit FAFSA. In 2015, 86 master's awarded. Offers entrepreneurial journalism (MA, Advanced Certificate); journalism (MA); social journalism (MA). *Application deadline:* For fall admission, 1/9 for domestic and international students. *Application fee:* $125. Electronic applications accepted. *Application Contact:* Maximo Patino, Associate Director of Admissions, 646-758-7704, Fax: 646-758-7709, E-mail: maximo.patino@journalism.cuny.edu. *Director of Admissions*, Colleen Leigh, 646-758-7852, Fax: 646-758-7709, E-mail: colleen.leigh@journalism.cuny.edu.

CURRY COLLEGE, Milton, MA 02186-9984

General Information Independent, coed, comprehensive institution. *Graduate housing:* On-campus housing not available. *Research affiliation:* Literacy Centers/GED Programs.

GRADUATE UNITS

Graduate Studies *Degree program information:* Part-time and evening/weekend programs available. Part-time, evening/weekend. Offers business administration (MBA); criminal justice (MA); elementary education (M Ed); finance (Certificate); foundations (non-license) (M Ed); nursing (MSN); reading (M Ed, Certificate); special education (M Ed).

CURTIS INSTITUTE OF MUSIC, Philadelphia, PA 19103-6107

General Information Independent, coed, comprehensive institution. *Graduate housing:* On-campus housing not available.

GRADUATE UNITS

Graduate Studies Offers opera (MM).

DAEMEN COLLEGE, Amherst, NY 14226-3592

General Information Independent, coed, comprehensive institution. *Graduate housing:* Room and/or apartments available on a first-come, first-served basis to single students; on-campus housing not available to married students. Housing application deadline: 7/15.

GRADUATE UNITS

Department of Accounting/Information Systems *Degree program information:* Part-time and evening/weekend programs available. Part-time, evening/weekend. Offers global business (MS). Electronic applications accepted.

Department of Nursing *Degree program information:* Part-time programs available. Part-time. Offers adult nurse practitioner (MS, Post Master's Certificate); nurse executive leadership (Post Master's Certificate); nursing education (MS, Post Master's Certificate); nursing executive leadership (MS); nursing practice (DNP); palliative care nursing (Post Master's Certificate). Electronic applications accepted.

Department of Physical Therapy *Degree program information:* Part-time programs available. Part-time. Offers orthopedic manual physical therapy (Advanced Certificate); physical therapy-direct entry (DPT); transitional (DPT). Electronic applications accepted.

Department of Visual and Performing Arts Offers arts administration (MS).

Education Department *Degree program information:* Part-time programs available. Part-time. Offers adolescence education (MS); childhood education (MS); childhood special education (MS); childhood special-alternative certification (MS); early childhood special-alternative certification (MS). Electronic applications accepted.

Physician Assistant Department Offers physician assistant (MS). Electronic applications accepted.

Program in Executive Leadership and Change *Degree program information:* Part-time and evening/weekend programs available. Part-time, evening/weekend. Offers business (MS); health professions (MS); not-for-profit organizations (MS). Electronic applications accepted.

Program in Public Health *Degree program information:* Part-time programs available. Part-time, online learning. Offers community health education (MPH); epidemiology (MPH); generalist (MPH).

Program in Social Work Offers social work (MSW).

DAKOTA STATE UNIVERSITY, Madison, SD 57042-1799

General Information State-supported, coed, comprehensive institution. CGS member. *Enrollment:* 3,145 graduate, professional, and undergraduate students; 83 full-time matriculated graduate/professional students (19 women), 211 part-time matriculated graduate/professional students (57 women). *Enrollment by degree level:* 203 master's, 78 doctoral, 13 other advanced degrees. *Graduate faculty:* 24 full-time (6 women), 2 part-time/adjunct (0 women). Tuition, state resident: full-time $5059; part-time $210.80 per credit hour. Tuition, nonresident: full-time $10,710; part-time $446.25 per credit hour. *Required fees:* $3043; $126.80 per credit hour. Tuition and fees vary according to program and reciprocity agreements. *Graduate housing:* Room and/or apartments available on a first-come, first-served basis to single students; on-campus housing not available to married students. Typical cost: $3281 per year ($6060 including board). Room and board charges vary according to board plan. *Student services:* Campus employment opportunities, campus safety program, career counseling, exercise/wellness program, free psychological counseling, grant writing training, international student services, low-cost health insurance, multicultural affairs office, services for students with disabilities, teacher training, writing training. *Library:* Karl E. Mundt Library & Learning Commons plus 1 other. *Collection:* Books: 65,796 (physical), 106,897 (digital/electronic); Serial titles: 243 (physical), 103,584 (digital/electronic); Databases: 115. Weekly public service hours: 77. *Research affiliation:* SBS–Secure Banking Solutions, LLC (information security), Secure Healthcare Solutions (information security), Chenega Logistics (information security).

Computer facilities: Computer purchase and lease plans are available. 165 computers available on campus for general student use. A campuswide network can be accessed from student residence rooms and from off campus. Online class registration is available.
Website: http://www.dsu.edu/

General Application Contact: Erin Blankespoor, Senior Secretary, Office of Graduate Studies and Research, 605-256-5799, E-mail: erin.blankespoor@dsu.edu.

GRADUATE UNITS

College of Business and Information Systems Students: 83 full-time (19 women), 198 part-time (49 women); includes 61 minority (21 Black or African American, non-Hispanic/Latino; 3 American Indian or Alaska Native, non-Hispanic/Latino; 21 Asian, non-Hispanic/Latino; 9 Hispanic/Latino; 7 Two or more races, non-Hispanic/Latino), 74 international. Average age 34. 271 applicants, 62% accepted, 95 enrolled. *Faculty:* 20 full-time (5 women), 1 part-time/adjunct (0 women). *Financial support:* In 2015–16, 27 students received support, including 10 fellowships with partial tuition reimbursements available (averaging $13,932 per year), 11 research assistantships with partial tuition reimbursements available (averaging $33,765 per year), 2 teaching assistantships with partial tuition reimbursements available (averaging $33,765 per year); career-related internships or fieldwork, Federal Work-Study, scholarships/grants, and unspecified assistantships also available. Support available to part-time students. Financial award applicants required to submit FAFSA. In 2015, 86 master's, 5 doctorates, 9 other advanced degrees awarded. *Degree program information:* Part-time and evening/weekend programs available. Part-time, evening/weekend, 100% online, blended/hybrid learning. Offers analytics (MSA); applied computer science (MSACS); business and information systems (Graduate Certificate); cyber security (D Sc); general management (MBA); health informatics (MSHI); information assurance (MSIA); information systems (MSIS, D Sc IS). *Application deadline:* For fall admission, 6/15 for domestic students, 4/15 for international students; for spring admission, 11/15 for domestic students, 9/15 priority date for international students; for summer admission, 4/15 for domestic and international students. Applications are processed on a rolling basis. *Application fee:* $35. *Application Contact:* Erin Blankespoor, Secretary, Office of Graduate Studies and Research, 605-256-5799, Fax: 605-256-5093, E-mail: erin.blankespoor@dsu.edu. *Dean of Graduate Studies and Research*, Dr. Omar El-Gayar, 605-256-5799, Fax: 605-256-5093, E-mail: omar.el-gayar@dsu.edu.

College of Education Students: 13 part-time (8 women). Average age 30. 7 applicants, 86% accepted, 5 enrolled. *Faculty:* 4 full-time (1 woman), 1 part-time/adjunct (0 women). *Financial support:* In 2015–16, 3 students received support, including 3 fellowships with partial tuition reimbursements available (averaging $13,992 per year); career-related internships or fieldwork, Federal Work-Study, scholarships/grants, unspecified assistantships, and administrative assistantships also available. Support available to part-time students. Financial award applicants required to submit FAFSA. In 2015, 5 master's awarded. *Degree program information:* Part-time and evening/weekend programs available. Part-time-only, evening/weekend, online only, 100% online. Offers educational technology (MSET). *Application deadline:* For fall admission, 6/15 for domestic students; for spring admission, 11/15 for domestic students; for summer admission, 4/15 for domestic students. Applications are processed on a rolling basis. *Application fee:* $35. *Application Contact:* Erin Blankespoor, Senior Secretary, Office of Graduate Studies and Research, 605-256-5799, E-mail: erin.blankespoor@dsu.edu. *Dean*, Dr. Omar El-Gayar, 605-256-5799, Fax: 605-256-5093, E-mail: omar.el-gayar@dsu.edu.

DAKOTA WESLEYAN UNIVERSITY, Mitchell, SD 57301-4398

General Information Independent-religious, coed, comprehensive institution.

GRADUATE UNITS

Program in Education *Degree program information:* Part-time and evening/weekend programs available. Part-time, evening/weekend. Offers curriculum and instruction (MA Ed); educational policy and administration (MA Ed); preK-12 principal certification (MA Ed); secondary certification (MA Ed). Electronic applications accepted.

DALHOUSIE UNIVERSITY, Halifax, NS B3H 4R2, Canada

General Information Province-supported, coed, university. *Graduate housing:* Rooms and/or apartments available on a first-come, first-served basis to single and married students. Housing application deadline: 8/1.

GRADUATE UNITS

Faculty of Agriculture *Degree program information:* Part-time programs available. Part-time. Offers agriculture (M Sc).

Faculty of Architecture and Planning Offers architecture and planning (M Arch, M Eng, M Plan, MEDS, MPS). Electronic applications accepted.

School of Planning Offers planning (M Eng, M Plan, MPS). Electronic applications accepted.

Faculty of Arts and Social Science *Degree program information:* Part-time programs available. Part-time. Offers arts and social science (MA, PhD); classics (MA, PhD); English (MA, PhD); French (MA, PhD); German (MA); history (MA, PhD); international development studies (MA); musicology (MA); philosophy (MA, PhD); political science (MA, PhD); social anthropology (MA, PhD); sociology (MA, PhD). Electronic applications accepted.

Faculty of Computer Science Offers computational biology and bioinformatics (M Sc); computer science (MA Sc, MC Sc, PhD); electronic commerce (MEC); health informatics (MHI). Electronic applications accepted.

Faculty of Dentistry Offers dentistryoral and maxillofacial surgery.

Faculty of Engineering Offers biological engineering (M Eng, MA Sc, PhD); biomedical engineering (MA Sc, PhD); chemical engineering (M Eng, MA Sc, PhD); civil and resource engineering (M Eng, MA Sc, PhD); electrical and computer engineering (M Eng, MA Sc, PhD); engineering (M Eng, M Sc, MA Sc, PhD); engineering mathematics (M Sc, PhD); environmental engineering (M Eng, MA Sc, PhD); food science and technology (M Sc, PhD); industrial engineering (M Eng, MA Sc, PhD); internetworking (M Eng); materials engineering (M Eng, MA Sc, PhD); mechanical engineering (M Eng, MA Sc, PhD); mineral resource engineering (M Eng, MA Sc, PhD).

Faculty of Graduate Studies *Degree program information:* Part-time programs available. Part-time, online learning. Offers anatomy and neurobiology (M Sc, PhD); interdisciplinary studies (PhD); medicine (M Sc, PhD); neuroscience (M Sc, PhD); pathology (M Sc, PhD); pharmacology (M Sc, PhD). Electronic applications accepted.

Dalhousie Law School ***Degree program information:*** Part-time programs available. Part-time. Offers law (LL M, JSD). Electronic applications accepted.

Faculty of Health Professions *Degree program information:* Part-time programs available. Part-time, online learning. Offers health professions (M Sc, MA, MAHSR, MHA, MN, MPH, MSW, PhD).

School of Health Administration ***Degree program information:*** Part-time programs available. Part-time, online learning. Offers health administration (MAHSR, MHA, MPH, PhD). Electronic applications accepted.

School of Health and Human Performance ***Degree program information:*** Part-time programs available. Part-time. Offers health and human performance (M Sc, MA); health promotion (MA); kinesiology (M Sc); leisure studies (MA). Electronic applications accepted.

School of Human Communication Disorders Offers audiology (M Sc); speech-language pathology (M Sc). Electronic applications accepted.

School of Nursing ***Degree program information:*** Part-time programs available. Part-time, online learning. Offers nursing (MN, PhD). Electronic applications accepted.

School of Occupational Therapy ***Degree program information:*** Part-time and evening/weekend programs available. Part-time, evening/weekend, online learning.

Offers occupational therapy (entry to profession) (M Sc); occupational therapy (post-professional) (M Sc). Electronic applications accepted.

School of Physiotherapy Offers physiotherapy (entry to profession) (M Sc); physiotherapy (rehabilitation research) (M Sc). Electronic applications accepted.

School of Social Work Degree program information: Part-time programs available. Part-time, online learning. Offers social work (MSW). Electronic applications accepted.

Faculty of Management ***Degree program information:*** Part-time programs available. Part-time. Offers management (MBA, MEC, MES, MIM, MLIS, MMM, MPA, MREM, GDPA); marine affairs (MMM). Electronic applications accepted.

Centre for Advanced Management Education Degree program information: Part-time programs available. Part-time, online learning. Offers financial services (MBA); information management (MIM); management (MPA); natural resources (MBA). Electronic applications accepted.

School for Resource and Environmental Studies Degree program information: Part-time programs available. Part-time. Offers resource and environmental studies (MES, MREM). Electronic applications accepted.

School of Business Administration Degree program information: Part-time programs available. Part-time. Offers business administration (MBA); financial services (MBA). Electronic applications accepted.

School of Information Management Degree program information: Part-time programs available. Part-time. Offers information management (MIM, MLIS). Electronic applications accepted.

School of Public Administration Degree program information: Part-time programs available. Part-time. Offers management (MPA); public administration (MPA, GDPA). Electronic applications accepted.

Faculty of Medicine Offers biochemistry and molecular biology (M Sc, PhD); community health and epidemiology (M Sc); medicine (M Sc, MD, PhD); microbiology and immunology (M Sc, PhD); physiology and biophysics (M Sc, PhD). Electronic applications accepted.

Faculty of Science Offers biology (M Sc, PhD); chemistry (M Sc, PhD); clinical psychology (PhD); earth sciences (M Sc, PhD); economics (MA, MDE, PhD); mathematics (M Sc, PhD); oceanography (M Sc, PhD); physics and atmospheric science (M Sc, PhD); psychology (M Sc, PhD); psychology/neuroscience (M Sc, PhD); science (M Sc, MA, MDE, PhD); statistics (M Sc, PhD). Electronic applications accepted.

DALLAS BAPTIST UNIVERSITY, Dallas, TX 75211-9299

General Information Independent-religious, coed, comprehensive institution. *Enrollment:* 5,319 graduate, professional, and undergraduate students; 707 full-time matriculated graduate/professional students (437 women), 1,297 part-time matriculated graduate/professional students (862 women). *Enrollment by degree level:* 1,727 master's, 277 doctoral. *Graduate faculty:* 66 full-time (26 women), 192 part-time/adjunct (75 women). *Tuition, area resident:* Full-time $14,814; part-time $823 per credit hour. *Required fees:* $250 per semester. Tuition and fees vary according to course load and degree level. *Graduate housing:* Room and/or apartments available on a first-come, first-served basis to single students; on-campus housing not available to married students. Typical cost: $3590 per year ($7326 including board). Room and board charges vary according to board plan and housing facility selected. Housing application deadline: 5/1. *Student services:* Campus employment opportunities, campus safety program, career counseling, exercise/wellness program, free psychological counseling, international student services, low-cost health insurance, services for students with disabilities, writing training. *Library:* Vance Memorial Library plus 2 others. *Collection:* Books: 237,167 (physical), 65,000 (digital/electronic); Serial titles: 302 (physical), 31,557 (digital/electronic); Databases: 157. Weekly public service hours: 108.

Computer facilities: 296 computers available on campus for general student use. A campuswide network can be accessed from student residence rooms and from off campus. Online class registration is available.
Website: http://www.dbu.edu/

General Application Contact: Kit Montgomery, Director of Graduate Programs, 214-333-5242, Fax: 214-333-5579, E-mail: graduate@dbu.edu.

GRADUATE UNITS

College of Business ***Financial support:*** Federal Work-Study, institutionally sponsored loans, scholarships/grants, and tuition waivers (full and partial) available. Support available to part-time students. Financial award applicants required to submit FAFSA. *Degree program information:* Part-time and evening/weekend programs available. Part-time, evening/weekend, online learning. Offers accounting (MBA); business (MA, MBA, MS); business communication (MBA); conflict resolution management (MA, MBA); entrepreneurship (MBA); finance (MBA); general management (MA); health care management (MA, MBA); human resource management (MA); international business (MBA); leading the non-profit organization (MBA); management (MBA, MS); management information systems (MBA); marketing (MBA); organizational communication (MA); performance management (MA); professional sales and management optimization (MA); project management (MBA); technology and engineering (MBA). *Application deadline:* Applications are processed on a rolling basis. *Application fee:* $25. Electronic applications accepted. *Application Contact:* Kit P. Montgomery, Director of Graduate Programs, 214-333-5242, Fax: 214-333-5579, E-mail: graduate@dbu.edu. *Dean*, Dr. Dale B. Sims, 214-333-5244, Fax: 214-333-8857, E-mail: graduate@dbu.edu.

Dorothy M. Bush College of Education ***Financial support;*** Federal Work-Study, institutionally sponsored loans, scholarships/grants, and tuition waivers (full and partial) available. Support available to part-time students. Financial award applicants required to submit FAFSA. *Degree program information:* Part-time and evening/weekend programs available. Part-time, evening/weekend. Offers bilingual education (M Ed); counseling (MA); curriculum and instruction (M Ed); distance learning (MAT); early childhood (MAT); education (M Ed, MA, MAT, Advanced Certificate); educational leadership (M Ed); elementary (MAT); English as a second language (M Ed, MAT); kinesiology (M Ed); master reading teacher (M Ed); Montessori (MAT); multisensory (MAT); reading specialist (M Ed); school counseling (M Ed, Advanced Certificate); secondary (MAT); special education (M Ed). *Application deadline:* Applications are processed on a rolling basis. *Application fee:* $25. Electronic applications accepted. *Application Contact:* Kit P. Montgomery, Director of Graduate Programs, 214-333-5242, Fax: 214-333-5579, E-mail: graduate@dbu.edu. *Dean*, Dr. Neil Dugger, 214-333-5413, E-mail: graduate@dbu.edu.

Gary Cook School of Leadership ***Financial support:*** Federal Work-Study, institutionally sponsored loans, scholarships/grants, and tuition waivers (full and partial) available. Support available to part-time students. Financial award applicants required to submit FAFSA. *Degree program information:* Part-time and evening/weekend programs available. Part-time, evening/weekend. Offers higher education (M Ed); leadership (M Ed, MA, MATS, Ed D, PhD); leadership studies (PhD). *Application deadline:* Applications are processed on a rolling basis. *Application fee:* $25. Electronic applications accepted. *Application Contact:* Kit P. Montgomery, Director of Graduate Programs, 214-333-5242, Fax: 214-333-5579, E-mail: graduate@dbu.edu. *Dean*, Dr. Adam Wright, 214-333-5597, E-mail: graduate@dbu.edu.

Graduate School of Ministry Offers adult ministry (MA); business communication (MA); business ministry (MA); children's ministry (MA); Christian heritage (MATS); Christian ministry (MA); Christian scriptures (MATS); Christian studies (MA); collegiate ministry (MA); communication ministry (MA); counseling ministry (MA); East Asian studies (MA); ESL (MA); family ministry (MA); general ministry (MA); general studies (MA); global leadership (MA); global studies (MA); international business (MA); leading the nonprofit organization (MA); ministry (MA, MATS); missions (MA); missions ministry (MA); small group ministry (MA); student ministry (MA); worship leadership (MA); worship ministry (MA); worship music (MA).

Liberal Arts Program ***Financial support:*** Federal Work-Study, institutionally sponsored loans, scholarships/grants, and tuition waivers (full and partial) available. Support available to part-time students. Financial award applicants required to submit FAFSA. *Degree program information:* Part-time and evening/weekend programs available. Part-time, evening/weekend. Offers art (MLA); Christian studies (MLA); commercial art (MLA); East Asian studies (MLA); English (MLA); English as a second language (MLA); fine arts (MLA); history (MLA); missions (MLA); political science (MLA). *Application deadline:* Applications are processed on a rolling basis. *Application fee:* $25. Electronic applications accepted. *Application Contact:* Kit P. Montgomery, Director of Graduate Programs, 214-333-5242, Fax: 214-333-5579, E-mail: graduate@dbu.edu. *Director*, Sena Baker, 214-333-6830, Fax: 214-333-5558, E-mail: graduate@dbu.edu.

Professional Development Program ***Financial support:*** Federal Work-Study, institutionally sponsored loans, scholarships/grants, and tuition waivers (full and partial) available. Support available to part-time students. Financial award applicants required to submit FAFSA. *Degree program information:* Part-time and evening/weekend programs available. Part-time, evening/weekend. Offers business (MA); counseling (MA); criminal justice (MA); English as a second language (MA); higher education (MA); interdisciplinary (MA); leadership studies (MA); missions (MA); professional life coaching (MA); training and development (MA). *Application fee:* $25. *Application Contact:* Kit P. Montgomery, Director of Graduate Programs, 214-333-5242, Fax: 214-333-5579, E-mail: graduate@dbu.edu. *Director*, Sena Baker, 214-333-6830, E-mail: graduate@dbu.edu.

DALLAS THEOLOGICAL SEMINARY, Dallas, TX 75204-6499

General Information Independent, coed, graduate-only institution. *Graduate housing:* Rooms and/or apartments available on a first-come, first-served basis to single and married students.

GRADUATE UNITS

Graduate Programs ***Degree program information:*** Part-time programs available. Part-time, online learning. Offers adult education (Th M); apologetics (Th M); Bible backgrounds (Th M); Bible translation (Th M); Biblical and theological studies (Certificate); biblical counseling (MA); biblical exegesis and linguistics (MA); biblical exposition (PhD); biblical studies (MA); Biblical theology (Th M); children's education (Th M); Christian education (MA, D Min); Christian leadership (MA); cross-cultural ministries (MA); educational administration (Th M); educational leadership (Th M); evangelism and discipleship (Th M); exposition of Biblical books (Th M); family life education (Th M); general studies (Th M); Hebrew and cognate studies (Th M); hermeneutics (Th M); historical theology (Th M); homiletics (Th M); intercultural ministries (Th M); Jesus studies (Th M); leadership studies (Th M); media and communication (MA); media arts (Th M); ministry (D Min); ministry with women (Th M); New Testament studies (Th M, PhD); Old Testament studies (Th M, PhD); parachurch ministries (Th M); pastoral care and counseling (Th M); pastoral theology and practice (Th M); philosophy (Th M); sacred theology (STM); spiritual formation (Th M); systematic theology (Th M); teaching in Christian institutions (Th M); theological studies (PhD); urban ministries (Th M); worship studies (Th M); youth education (Th M). Electronic applications accepted.

DANIEL WEBSTER COLLEGE, Nashua, NH 03063-1300

General Information Proprietary, coed, comprehensive institution. *Enrollment:* 686 graduate, professional, and undergraduate students; 63 full-time matriculated graduate/professional students (38 women). *Enrollment by degree level:* 63 master's. *International tuition:* $15,696 full-time. *Tuition, area resident:* Full-time $15,696; part-time $7848 per quarter hour. *Graduate housing:* On-campus housing not available. *Student services:* Career counseling, free psychological counseling, services for students with disabilities, writing training. *Library:* Veterans Memorial Library. *Collection:* Books: 24,000 (physical), 150,000 (digital/electronic); Serial titles: 70 (physical), 40,000 (digital/electronic); Databases: 62. Weekly public service hours: 81; students can reserve study rooms.

Computer facilities: 182 computers available on campus for general student use. A campuswide network can be accessed from student residence rooms and from off campus. Online class registration is available.
Website: http://www.dwc.edu/

General Application Contact: Jenn O'Neal, Director of Admissions, 800-325-6876, Fax: 603-577-6001, E-mail: admissions@dwc.edu.

GRADUATE UNITS

MBA Program ***Degree program information:*** Part-time and evening/weekend programs available. Part-time, evening/weekend, online learning. Offers management (MBA). *Application deadline:* Applications are processed on a rolling basis. *Application fee:* $25. Electronic applications accepted. *Application Contact:* Chrissy Harrington, Graduate Admissions Specialist, 866-458-7525, Fax: 603-577-6503, E-mail: mba@dwc.edu. *Dean, School of Business and Management*, Neil Parmenter, 603-577-6650, Fax: 603-577-6503, E-mail: parmenter@dwc.edu.

★ DARTMOUTH COLLEGE, Hanover, NH 03755

General Information Independent, coed, university. CGS member. *Enrollment:* 6,350 graduate, professional, and undergraduate students; 1,875 full-time matriculated graduate/professional students (796 women), 78 part-time matriculated graduate/professional students (40 women). *Enrollment by degree level:* 984 master's, 925 doctoral, 44 other advanced degrees. *Graduate faculty:* 570 full-time (195 women), 162 part-time/adjunct (65 women). *Tuition, area resident:* Full-time $48,120. *Required fees:* $296. One-time fee: $50 full-time. *Graduate housing:* Rooms and/or apartments available on a first-come, first-served basis to single students and available to married students. Housing application deadline: 5/15. *Student services:* Campus safety program, career counseling, free psychological counseling, international student services, low-cost health insurance, services for students with disabilities, teacher training, writing training. *Library:* Baker-Berry Library plus 9 others. *Collection:* Books: 2.6 million (physical); Serial titles: 68,862 (physical). Study areas open 24 hours, 5–7 days a week; students can reserve study rooms.

Computer facilities: Computer purchase and lease plans are available. 200 computers available on campus for general student use. A campuswide network can be accessed from student residence rooms and from off campus. Online class registration is available.
Website: http://www.dartmouth.edu/

General Application Contact: Jane Seibel, Assistant Dean of Recruiting and Diversity, Graduate Studies Office, 603-646-6578, Fax: 603-646-3488, E-mail: jane.b.seibel@dartmouth.edu.

GRADUATE UNITS

Arts and Sciences Graduate Programs Students: 578 full-time (264 women), 27 part-time (15 women); includes 71 minority (7 Black or African American, non-Hispanic/Latino; 5 American Indian or Alaska Native, non-Hispanic/Latino; 34 Asian, non-Hispanic/Latino; 13 Hispanic/Latino; 12 Two or more races, non-Hispanic/Latino), 214 international. Average age 30. *Faculty:* 164 full-time (49 women), 47 part-time/adjunct (18 women). *Financial support:* In 2015–16, fellowships with full tuition reimbursements (averaging $23,832 per year), research assistantships with full tuition reimbursements (averaging $23,832 per year), teaching assistantships with full tuition reimbursements (averaging $23,832 per year) were awarded; career-related internships or fieldwork, institutionally sponsored loans, scholarships/grants, traineeships, tuition waivers (full and partial), and unspecified assistantships also available. Support available to part-time students. Financial award application deadline: 4/1; financial award applicants required to submit CSS PROFILE or FAFSA. In 2015, 131 master's, 48 doctorates awarded. Offers arts and sciences (AM, MA, MALS, MS, PhD); biophysical chemistry (MS); chemistry (PhD); cognitive neuroscience (PhD); comparative literature (MA); computer science (MS, PhD); digital music (MA); earth sciences (MS, PhD); ecology and evolutionary biology (PhD); liberal studies (MALS); mathematics (AM, PhD); physics and astronomy (PhD); psychology (PhD). *Application deadline:* For fall admission, 1/15 for domestic students. Electronic applications accepted. *Application Contact:* Gary Hutchins, Assistant Dean, School of Arts and Sciences, 603-646-2107, Fax: 603-646-3488, E-mail: g.hutchins@dartmouth.edu. *Dean of Graduate Studies,* Dr. Jon Kull, 603-646-1552, E-mail: f.jon.kull@dartmouth.edu.

Institute for Quantitative Biomedical Sciences Students: 16 full-time (9 women); includes 3 minority (1 Black or African American, non-Hispanic/Latino; 2 Asian, non-Hispanic/Latino), 3 international. Average age 28. 39 applicants, 31% accepted, 5 enrolled. *Financial support:* In 2015–16, fellowships with tuition reimbursements (averaging $28,200 per year) were awarded. In 2015, 1 doctorate awarded. Offers quantitative biomedical sciences (PhD). Program offered in collaboration with the Department of Genetics and the Department of Community and Family Medicine. *Application deadline:* For fall admission, 3/1 for domestic students. *Application fee:* $75. Electronic applications accepted. *Application Contact:* Gary Hutchins, Assistant Dean, School of Arts and Sciences, 603-646-2107, Fax: 603-646-3488, E-mail: g.hutchins@dartmouth.edu. *Director,* Krissy Giffin.

The Dartmouth Institute Students: 40 full-time (26 women), 37 part-time (17 women); includes 15 minority (2 Black or African American, non-Hispanic/Latino; 6 Asian, non-Hispanic/Latino; 4 Hispanic/Latino; 3 Two or more races, non-Hispanic/Latino), 7 international. Average age 33. *Faculty:* 60 full-time (28 women), 99 part-time/adjunct (39 women). *Financial support:* In 2015–16, fellowships with full tuition reimbursements (averaging $28,200 per year) were awarded; scholarships/grants also available. In 2015, 51 master's awarded. *Degree program information:* Part-time programs available. Part-time. Offers evaluative clinical sciences (MS, PhD); public health (MPH). *Application deadline:* For fall admission, 1/15 for domestic students. *Application fee:* $75. *Application Contact:* Courtney Theroux, Director of Recruitment and Admissions, 603-653-3234, Fax: 603-650-1900. *Director,* Dr. Elliot S. Fisher, 603-653-0802, Fax: 603-650-1900.

Geisel School of Medicine Students: 363 full-time (212 women), 6 part-time (2 women); includes 166 minority (29 Black or African American, non-Hispanic/Latino; 6 American Indian or Alaska Native, non-Hispanic/Latino; 73 Asian, non-Hispanic/Latino; 53 Hispanic/Latino; 1 Native Hawaiian or other Pacific Islander, non-Hispanic/Latino; 4 Two or more races, non-Hispanic/Latino), 42 international. Average age 26. 6,112 applicants, 5% accepted, 92 enrolled. *Faculty:* 251 full-time (106 women), 88 part-time/adjunct (42 women). *Financial support:* Institutionally sponsored loans and scholarships/grants available. In 2015, 88 doctorates awarded. Offers medicine (MD). *Application deadline:* For fall admission, 11/1 for domestic students. *Application fee:* $130. Electronic applications accepted. *Application Contact:* Andrew Welch, Director, DMS Admissions, 603-650-1505, Fax: 603-650-1560, E-mail: geisel.admissions@dartmouth.edu. *Senior Associate Dean for Faculty Affairs,* Dr. Leslie Henderson, 603-650-1312, E-mail: leslie.p.henderson@dartmouth.edu.

Graduate Program in Molecular and Cellular Biology Students: 98 full-time (52 women); includes 17 minority (7 Asian, non-Hispanic/Latino; 9 Hispanic/Latino; 1 Two or more races, non-Hispanic/Latino), 28 international. Average age 27. 193 applicants, 38% accepted, 30 enrolled. *Faculty:* 72 full-time (19 women), 4 part-time/adjunct (1 woman). *Financial support:* In 2015–16, fellowships with full tuition reimbursements (averaging $28,200 per year) were awarded; health care benefits also available. In 2015, 16 doctorates awarded. Offers biochemistry (PhD); biological sciences (PhD); genetics (PhD); immunology (PhD); microbiology and immunology (PhD); molecular and cellular biology (PhD); molecular pathogenesis (PhD). *Application deadline:* For fall admission, 12/1 for domestic students. Applications are processed on a rolling basis. *Application fee:* $75. Electronic applications accepted. *Application Contact:* Janet Cheney, Program Coordinator, 603-650-1612, Fax: 603-650-1006, E-mail: mcb@dartmouth.edu. *Chair,* Dr. Patrick J. Dolph, 603-650-1092, E-mail: mcb@dartmouth.edu.

Program in Experimental and Molecular Medicine Students: 52 full-time (31 women); includes 6 minority (4 Asian, non-Hispanic/Latino; 2 Hispanic/Latino), 8 international. Average age 26. 127 applicants, 15% accepted, 10 enrolled. *Faculty:* 29 full-time (10 women), 11 part-time/adjunct (3 women). *Financial support:* In 2015–16, fellowships with full tuition reimbursements (averaging $28,200 per year) were awarded; health care benefits also available. Offers experimental and molecular medicine. *Application deadline:* For fall admission, 1/1 for domestic and international students. *Application fee:* $75. Electronic applications accepted. *Application Contact:* Gail L. Paige, Program Coordinator, 603-650-4933, Fax: 603-650-4932, E-mail: molecular.medicine@dartmouth.edu. *Director,* Dr. Michael Spinella, 603-650-4933, Fax: 603-650-4932.

Thayer School of Engineering Students: 193 full-time (54 women); includes 23 minority (3 Black or African American, non-Hispanic/Latino; 15 Asian, non-Hispanic/Latino; 3 Hispanic/Latino; 2 Two or more races, non-Hispanic/Latino), 110 international. Average age 24. 717 applicants, 21% accepted, 84 enrolled. *Faculty:* 56 full-time (10 women), 39 part-time/adjunct (3 women). *Financial support:* In 2015–16, 190 students received support, including 32 fellowships with full tuition reimbursements available (averaging $25,920 per year), 70 research assistantships with full tuition reimbursements available (averaging $25,920 per year), 20 teaching assistantships with partial tuition reimbursements available (averaging $7,800 per year); career-related internships or fieldwork, institutionally sponsored loans, scholarships/grants, and tuition waivers (full and partial) also available. Financial award application deadline: 2/15; financial award applicants required to submit CSS PROFILE. In 2015, 59 master's, 12 doctorates awarded. Offers biomedical engineering (M Eng, MS, PhD); biotechnology and biochemical engineering (MS, PhD); computer engineering (MS, PhD); engineering (M Eng, MEM, MS, PhD); engineering management (MEM); environmental engineering (MS, PhD); innovation (PhD); materials sciences and engineering (MS, PhD); mechanical engineering (MS, PhD). *Application deadline:* For fall admission, 1/1 priority date for domestic and international students. Applications are processed on a rolling basis. *Application fee:* $45. Electronic applications accepted. *Application Contact:* Candace S. Potter, Graduate Admissions and Financial Aid Administrator, 603-646-3844, Fax: 603-646-1620, E-mail: candace.s.potter@dartmouth.edu. *Dean,* Dr. Joseph J. Helbie, 603-646-2238, Fax: 603-646-2580, E-mail: joseph.j.helbie@dartmouth.edu.

Tuck School of Business at Dartmouth Students: 563 full-time (209 women); includes 94 minority (22 Black or African American, non-Hispanic/Latino; 6 American Indian or Alaska Native, non-Hispanic/Latino; 49 Asian, non-Hispanic/Latino; 11 Hispanic/Latino; 6 Two or more races, non-Hispanic/Latino), 186 international. Average age 28. 2,585 applicants, 23% accepted, 286 enrolled. *Faculty:* 52 full-time (11 women). *Financial support:* Institutionally sponsored loans and scholarships/grants available. Financial award applicants required to submit FAFSA. In 2015, 276 master's awarded. Offers business (MBA). *Application fee:* $225. Electronic applications accepted. *Application Contact:* Dawna Clarke, Director of Admissions, 603-646-3162, Fax: 603-646-1441, E-mail: tuck.admissions@tuck.dartmouth.edu. *Dean,* Matthew J. Slaughter, 603-646-2460, Fax: 603-646-1308, E-mail: tuck.public.relations@tuck.dartmouth.edu.

See Close-Up on page 875.

DAVENPORT UNIVERSITY, Grand Rapids, MI 49512

General Information Independent, coed, comprehensive institution. *Graduate housing:* Room and/or apartments available on a first-come, first-served basis to single students; on-campus housing not available to married students. *Research affiliation:* Human Synergistic Center for Applied Research, Inc. (leadership, organizational culture, strategy).

GRADUATE UNITS

Sneden Graduate School ***Degree program information:*** Evening/weekend programs available. Evening/weekend. Offers accounting (MBA); business administration (EMBA); finance (MBA); health care management (MBA); human resources (MBA); information assurance (MS); public health (MPH); strategic management (MBA). Electronic applications accepted.

DEFIANCE COLLEGE, Defiance, OH 43512-1610

General Information Independent-religious, coed, comprehensive institution. *Graduate housing:* On-campus housing not available.

GRADUATE UNITS

Program in Business Administration ***Degree program information:*** Part-time and evening/weekend programs available. Part-time, evening/weekend. Offers criminal justice (MBA); health care (MBA); leadership (MBA); sport management (MBA).

Program in Education ***Degree program information:*** Part-time programs available. Part-time. Offers adolescent and young adult licensure (MA); mild and moderate intervention specialist (MA).

DELAWARE STATE UNIVERSITY, Dover, DE 19901-2277

General Information State-supported, coed, university. *Graduate housing:* Room and/or apartments available on a first-come, first-served basis to single students; on-campus housing not available to married students.

GRADUATE UNITS

Graduate Programs ***Degree program information:*** Part-time and evening/weekend programs available. Part-time, evening/weekend. Offers applied chemistry (MS, PhD); applied mathematics (MS); applied mathematics and theoretical physics (PhD); applied optics (MS); biological sciences (MA, MS, PhD); biology education (MS); chemistry (MS); French (MA); historic preservation (MA); mathematics (MS); mathematics education (MS); molecular and cellular neuroscience (MS); natural resources (MS); neuroscience (PhD); optics (PhD); physics (MS); physics teaching (MS); plant science (MS); Spanish (MA).

College of Business Degree program information: Part-time and evening/weekend programs available. Part-time, evening/weekend. Offers business administration (MBA). Electronic applications accepted.

College of Education, Health and Public Policy Degree program information: Part-time and evening/weekend programs available. Part-time, evening/weekend. Offers adult literacy and basic education (MA); art education (MA); curriculum and instruction (MA); education, health and public policy (MA, MS, MSW, Ed D); educational leadership (MA, Ed D); nursing (MS); science education (MA); social work (MSW); special education (MA); sport administration (MS); teaching (MA). Electronic applications accepted.

DELAWARE VALLEY UNIVERSITY, Doylestown, PA 18901-2697

General Information Independent, coed, comprehensive institution. *Graduate housing:* On-campus housing not available.

GRADUATE UNITS

MBA Program ***Degree program information:*** Part-time and evening/weekend programs available. Part-time, evening/weekend, online learning. Offers accounting (MBA); entrepreneurship (MBA); finance (MBA); food and agribusiness (MBA); general business (MBA); global executive leadership (MBA); human resource management (MBA); supply chain management (MBA). Electronic applications accepted.

Program in Counseling Psychology Offers child and adolescent therapy (MA); social justice community counseling (MA).

Program in Educational Leadership ***Degree program information:*** Part-time and evening/weekend programs available. Part-time, evening/weekend. Offers instruction, curriculum and technology (MS); school administration and leadership (MS).

DELL'ARTE INTERNATIONAL SCHOOL OF PHYSICAL THEATRE, Blue Lake, CA 95525

General Information Independent, coed, graduate-only institution. *Graduate housing:* Rooms and/or apartments available on a first-come, first-served basis to single and married students.

GRADUATE UNITS

MFA Program Offers ensemble based physical theatre (MFA). Electronic applications accepted.

DELTA STATE UNIVERSITY, Cleveland, MS 38733-0001

General Information State-supported, coed, comprehensive institution. *Graduate housing:* Rooms and/or apartments available on a first-come, first-served basis to single and married students. Housing application deadline: 6/1.

GRADUATE UNITS

Graduate Programs ***Degree program information:*** Part-time and evening/weekend programs available. Part-time, evening/weekend, online learning. Electronic applications accepted.

College of Arts and Sciences Degree program information: Part-time programs available. Part-time. Offers arts and sciences (M Ed, MALS, MSCD, MSCJ, MSJC, MSNS); community development (MS); evolving human voices (MALS); gender and diversity studies (MALS); globalization studies (MALS); Mississippi Delta studies (MALS); natural sciences (MSNS); philosophy (MALS); religious studies (MALS); secondary education (M Ed); social justice and criminology (MSJC); social science secondary education (M Ed).

College of Business Degree program information: Part-time and evening/weekend programs available. Part-time, evening/weekend, online learning. Offers accountancy (MPA); business (MBA, MCA, MPA); business administration (MBA); commercial aviation (MCA).

College of Education Degree program information: Part-time and evening/weekend programs available. Part-time, evening/weekend. Offers counseling (M Ed); counselor education (Ed D); education (M Ed, MAT, MS, Ed D, Ed S); educational administration and supervision (M Ed, Ed S); elementary education (M Ed, MAT, Ed D, Ed S); health, physical education, and recreation (M Ed); higher education (Ed D); professional studies (Ed D); secondary education (MAT); special education (M Ed); sport and human performance (MS).

School of Nursing Degree program information: Part-time programs available. Part-time. Offers family nurse practitioner (MSN); nurse administrator (MSN); nurse educator (MSN). Electronic applications accepted.

DENVER SEMINARY, Littleton, CO 80120

General Information Independent-religious, coed, graduate-only institution. *Graduate housing:* Rooms and/or apartments available on a first-come, first-served basis to single and married students. Housing application deadline: 6/1.

GRADUATE UNITS

Graduate and Professional Programs ***Degree program information:*** Part-time and evening/weekend programs available. Part-time, evening/weekend, online learning. Offers apologetics (Certificate); biblical studies (MA); Christian formation and soul care (MA, Certificate); Christian studies (MA, Certificate); church and parachurch leadership (D Min); counseling licensure (MA); counseling ministry (MA); intercultural ministry (Certificate); leadership (MA, Certificate); marriage and family counseling (D Min); pastoral ministry (D Min); philosophy of religion (MA); spiritual guidance (Certificate); theology (M Div, Certificate); worship (Certificate); youth and family ministry (MA). Electronic applications accepted.

DEPAUL UNIVERSITY, Chicago, IL 60604-2287

General Information Independent-religious, coed, university. CGS member. *Graduate housing:* Room and/or apartments available on a first-come, first-served basis to single students; on-campus housing not available to married students. *Research affiliation:* Civic Federation (public services), Metro Chicago Information Center (public services), International Institute of Higher Studies in the Criminal Sciences (law).

GRADUATE UNITS

Charles H. Kellstadt Graduate School of Business ***Degree program information:*** Part-time and evening/weekend programs available. Part-time, evening/weekend, online learning. Offers accountancy (M Acc, MS, MSA); applied economics (MBA); banking (MBA); behavioral finance (MBA); brand and product management (MBA); business development (MBA); business information technology (MS); business strategy and decision-making (MBA); computational finance (MS); consumer insights (MBA); corporate finance (MBA); economic policy analysis (MS); entrepreneurship (MBA, MS); finance (MBA, MS); financial analysis (MBA); general business (MBA); health sector management (MBA); hospitality leadership (MBA); hospitality leadership and operational performance (MS); human resource management (MBA); human resources (MS); investment management (MBA); leadership and change management (MBA); management accounting (MBA); marketing (MBA, MS); marketing analysis (MS); marketing strategy and planning (MBA); operations management (MBA); organizational diversity (MBA); real estate (MS); real estate finance and investment (MBA); revenue management (MBA); sports management (MBA); strategic global marketing (MBA); strategy, execution and valuation (MBA); sustainable management (MBA, MS); taxation (MS); wealth management (MS). Electronic applications accepted.

College of Communication ***Degree program information:*** Part-time and evening/weekend programs available. Part-time, evening/weekend. Offers digital communication and media arts (MA); health communication (MA); journalism (MA); media and cinema studies (MA); organizational and multicultural communication (MA); public relations and advertising (MA); relational communication (MA). Electronic applications accepted.

College of Computing and Digital Media ***Degree program information:*** Part-time and evening/weekend programs available. Part-time, evening/weekend, online learning. Offers animation (MA, MFA); business information technology (MS); cinema (MFA); cinema production (MS); computational finance (MS); computer and information sciences (PhD); computer game development (MS); computer information and network security (MS); computer science (MS); e-commerce technology (MS); health informatics (MS); human-computer interaction (MS); information systems (MS); information technology project management (MS); network engineering and management (MS); predictive analytics (MS); screenwriting (MFA); software engineering (MS). Electronic applications accepted.

College of Education ***Degree program information:*** Part-time and evening/weekend programs available. Part-time, evening/weekend, online learning. Offers bilingual bicultural education (M Ed, MA); counseling (M Ed, MA); curriculum studies (M Ed, MA, Ed D); early childhood education (M Ed, MA, Ed D); educating adults (MA); educational leadership (M Ed, MA, Ed D); elementary education (MA); mathematics education (MA); mathematics for teaching (MS); middle school mathematics education (MS); reading specialist (M Ed, MA); secondary education (M Ed); social and cultural foundations in education (MA); special education (M Ed, MA); world languages education (M Ed, MA). Electronic applications accepted.

College of Law ***Degree program information:*** Part-time and evening/weekend programs available. Part-time, evening/weekend. Offers health law (LL M); intellectual property law (LL M); international law (LL M); law (JD); taxation (LL M). Electronic applications accepted.

College of Liberal Arts and Social Sciences ***Degree program information:*** Part-time and evening/weekend programs available. Part-time, evening/weekend, online learning. Offers Arabic (MA); Chinese (MA); English (MA); French (MA); German (MA); history (MA); interdisciplinary studies (MA, MS); international public service (MS); international studies (MA); Italian (MA); Japanese (MA); leadership and policy studies (MS); liberal studies (MA); new media studies (MA); nonprofit management (MNM); public administration (MPA); public health (MPH); public service management (MS); social work (MSW); sociology (MA); Spanish (MA); sustainable urban development (MA); women and gender studies (MA); writing and publishing (MA); writing, rhetoric, and discourse (MA). Electronic applications accepted.

College of Science and Health Offers applied mathematics (MS); applied statistics (MS); biological sciences (MA, MS); chemistry (MS); mathematics education (MA); mathematics for teaching (MS); nursing (MS); nursing practice (DNP); physics (MS); psychology (MS); pure mathematics (MS); science education (MS). Electronic applications accepted.

School for New Learning ***Degree program information:*** Part-time and evening/weekend programs available. Part-time, evening/weekend. Offers applied professional studies (MA); applied technology (MS); educating adults (MA). Electronic applications accepted.

School of Music ***Degree program information:*** Part-time and evening/weekend programs available. Part-time, evening/weekend. Offers composition (MM); jazz studies (MM); music education (MM); music performance (MM); performance (Certificate). Electronic applications accepted.

The Theatre School Offers acting (MFA); arts leadership (MFA); directing (MFA). Electronic applications accepted.

DEREE - THE AMERICAN COLLEGE OF GREECE, GR-153-42 Aghia Paraskevi, Athens, Greece

General Information Independent, coed, comprehensive institution.

GRADUATE UNITS

Graduate Programs

DESALES UNIVERSITY, Center Valley, PA 18034-9568

General Information Independent-religious, coed, comprehensive institution. *Enrollment:* 3,136 graduate, professional, and undergraduate students; 349 full-time matriculated graduate/professional students (234 women), 496 part-time matriculated graduate/professional students (289 women). *Enrollment by degree level:* 760 master's, 77 doctoral, 8 other advanced degrees. *Graduate faculty:* 39 full-time (22 women), 51 part-time/adjunct (19 women). *Tuition, area resident:* Full-time $815; part-time $815 per credit hour. Tuition and fees vary according to degree level and program. *Graduate housing:* Room and/or apartments available on a first-come, first-served basis to single students; on-campus housing not available to married students. Typical cost: $7800 per year. Housing application deadline: 3/15. *Student services:* Campus safety program, career counseling, free psychological counseling, international student services, low-cost health insurance, multicultural affairs office, services for students with disabilities, teacher training. *Library:* Trexler Library. *Collection:* Books: 142,001 (physical), 132,682 (digital/electronic); Serial titles: 260 (physical), 12,117 (digital/electronic); Databases: 87. Weekly public service hours: 52; students can reserve study rooms.

Computer facilities: 245 computers available on campus for general student use. A campuswide network can be accessed from student residence rooms and from off campus. Online class registration is available.
Website: http://www.desales.edu/

General Application Contact: Abigail Wernicki, Director of Graduate Admissions, 610-282-1100 Ext. 1768, Fax: 610-282-0525, E-mail: gradadmissions@desales.edu.

GRADUATE UNITS

Division of Business Students: 61 full-time (29 women), 346 part-time (181 women); includes 65 minority (17 Black or African American, non-Hispanic/Latino; 22 Asian, non-Hispanic/Latino; 20 Hispanic/Latino; 6 Two or more races, non-Hispanic/Latino). Average age 38. *Faculty:* 13 full-time (5 women), 31 part-time/adjunct (7 women). *Financial support:* Applicants required to submit FAFSA. In 2015, 120 master's awarded. *Degree program information:* Part-time and evening/weekend programs available. Part-time, evening/weekend, 100% online, blended/hybrid learning. Offers accounting (MBA); computer information systems (MBA); finance (MBA); health care systems management (MBA); human resources management (MBA); management (MBA); marketing (MBA); project management (MBA); self-design (MBA); supply chain management (MBA). *Application deadline:* Applications are processed on a rolling basis. *Application fee:* $50. Electronic applications accepted. *Application Contact:* Abigail Wernicki, Director of Graduate Admissions, 610-282-1100 Ext. 1768, E-mail: gradadmissions@desales.edu. *Director, MBA Program*, Dr. David M. Gilfoil, 610-282-1100 Ext. 1828, Fax: 610-282-2869, E-mail: david.gilfoil@desales.edu.

Division of Healthcare Students: 244 full-time (178 women), 55 part-time (50 women); includes 24 minority (7 Black or African American, non-Hispanic/Latino; 9 Asian, non-Hispanic/Latino; 6 Hispanic/Latino; 2 Two or more races, non-Hispanic/Latino). Average age 31. 68 applicants, 85% accepted, 52 enrolled. *Faculty:* 22 full-time (14 women), 37 part-time/adjunct (29 women). *Financial support:* Applicants required to submit FAFSA. In 2015, 73 master's awarded. *Degree program information:* Part-time programs available. Part-time. Offers adult-gerontology acute care (Post Master's Certificate); adult-gerontology acute care nurse practitioner (MSN); adult-gerontology acute certified nurse practitioner (Post Master's Certificate); adult-gerontology clinical nurse specialist (MSN, Post Master's Certificate); clinical leadership (DNP); family nurse practitioner (MSN, Post Master's Certificate); general nursing practice (DNP); health care information management (MSIS); network security (MSIS); nurse anesthetists (MSN); nurse educator (Post Master's Certificate, Postbaccalaureate Certificate); nurse midwives (MSN); nurse practitioner (MSN); project management (MSIS); psychiatric-mental health nurse practitioner (MSN, Post Master's Certificate). *Application deadline:* Applications are processed on a rolling basis. *Application fee:* $50. Electronic applications accepted. *Application Contact:* Abigail Wernicki, Director of Graduate Admissions, 610-282-1100 Ext. 1768, Fax: 610-282-2869, E-mail: gradadmissions@desales.edu. *Dean of Graduate Education*, Fr. Dr. Peter Leonard, OSFS, 610-282-1100 Ext. 1289, E-mail: peter.leonard@desales.edu.

Division of Liberal Arts and Social Sciences Students: 37 full-time (25 women), 83 part-time (55 women); includes 23 minority (5 Black or African American, non-Hispanic/Latino; 14 Hispanic/Latino; 4 Two or more races, non-Hispanic/Latino). Average age 33. *Faculty:* 6 full-time (3 women), 9 part-time/adjunct (5 women). *Financial support:* Applicants required to submit FAFSA. In 2015, 34 master's awarded. *Degree* *program information:* Part-time programs available. Part-time, 100% online, blended/hybrid learning. Offers cyber security (Postbaccalaureate Certificate); digital forensics (Postbaccalaureate Certificate); education (M Ed). *Application deadline:* Applications are processed on a rolling basis. *Application fee:* $50. Electronic applications accepted. *Application Contact:* Abigail Wernicki, Director of Graduate Admissions, 610-282-1100 Ext. 1768, Fax: 610-282-0525, E-mail: gradadmissions@desales.edu. *Division Head of Liberal Arts and Social Studies*, Dr. Brain Kane, 610-282-1100 Ext. 1274, E-mail: brian.kane@desales.edu.

Division of Science and Mathematics Students: 5 full-time (0 women), 14 part-time (6 women); includes 2 minority (1 Black or African American, non-Hispanic/Latino; 1 Asian, non-Hispanic/Latino). Average age 36. *Faculty:* 1 (woman) full-time, 3 part-time/adjunct (0 women). *Financial support:* Applicants required to submit FAFSA. In 2015, 6 master's awarded. *Degree program information:* Part-time and evening/weekend programs available. Part-time, evening/weekend, 100% online, blended/hybrid learning. Offers information systems (MS). *Application deadline:* Applications are processed on a rolling basis. *Application fee:* $50. Electronic applications accepted. *Application Contact:* Abigail Wernicki, Director of Graduate Admissions, 610-282-1100 Ext. 1768, Fax: 610-282-2869, E-mail: gradadmissions@desales.edu. *MSIS Director/Assistant Professor of Computer Science*, Dr. Patricia Riola, 610-282-1100 Ext. 1647, E-mail: patricia.riola@desales.edu.

DES MOINES UNIVERSITY, Des Moines, IA 50312-4104

General Information Independent, coed, graduate-only institution. *Graduate housing:* On-campus housing not available.

GRADUATE UNITS

College of Health Sciences ***Degree program information:*** Part-time and evening/weekend programs available. Part-time, evening/weekend. Offers health sciences (MHA, MPH, MS, DPT); healthcare administration (MHA); physical therapy (DPT); physician assistant (MS); public health (MPH). Electronic applications accepted.

College of Osteopathic Medicine Offers anatomy (MS); biomedical sciences (MS); osteopathic medicine (DO). Electronic applications accepted.

College of Podiatric Medicine and Surgery Offers podiatric medicine and surgery (DPM). Electronic applications accepted.

DEVRY COLLEGE OF NEW YORK, New York, NY 10016-5267

General Information Proprietary, coed, comprehensive institution. *Enrollment:* 1,495 graduate, professional, and undergraduate students; 169 full-time matriculated graduate/professional students (74 women), 408 part-time matriculated graduate/professional students (193 women). *Enrollment by degree level:* 577 master's. *Student services:* Campus employment opportunities. *Library:* Learning Resource Center.
Website: http://www.devry.edu/

GRADUATE UNITS

Keller Graduate School of Management Students: 169 full-time (74 women), 408 part-time (193 women). In 2015, 121 master's awarded. Offers management (M Acc, MAFM, MBA, MHRM, MISM, MNCM, MPA, MPM).

DEVRY UNIVERSITY, Columbus, OH 43209

General Information Proprietary, coed, comprehensive institution. *Enrollment:* 1,567 graduate, professional, and undergraduate students; 36 full-time matriculated graduate/professional students (18 women), 210 part-time matriculated graduate/professional students (115 women). *Enrollment by degree level:* 246 master's.
Website: http://www.devry.edu/

GRADUATE UNITS

Keller Graduate School of Management Students: 36 full-time (18 women), 210 part-time (115 women). In 2015, 123 master's awarded. Offers management (MAFM, MBA, MHRM, MISM, MNCM, MPA, MPM). *Application Contact:* Student Application Contact, 614-253-7291.

DEVRY UNIVERSITY, Chicago, IL 60618

General Information Proprietary, coed, comprehensive institution. *Enrollment:* 1,168 graduate, professional, and undergraduate students; 44 full-time matriculated graduate/professional students (23 women), 109 part-time matriculated graduate/professional students (49 women). *Enrollment by degree level:* 153 master's. *Library:* Learning Resource Center.
Website: http://www.devry.edu/

GRADUATE UNITS

Graduate Programs Students: 44 full-time (23 women), 109 part-time (49 women). In 2015, 47 master's awarded.

DEVRY UNIVERSITY, Seven Hills, OH 44131

General Information Proprietary, coed, comprehensive institution.

GRADUATE UNITS

Keller Graduate School of Management Offers management (MAFM, MBA, MHRM, MISM, MNCM, MPA, MPM, Graduate Certificate).

DEVRY UNIVERSITY, Orlando, FL 32819

General Information Proprietary, coed, comprehensive institution. *Enrollment:* 1,064 graduate, professional, and undergraduate students; 63 full-time matriculated graduate/professional students (34 women), 232 part-time matriculated graduate/professional students (130 women). *Enrollment by degree level:* 295 master's. *Library:* Learning Resource Center.

Computer facilities: Online class registration is available.
Website: http://www.devry.edu/

GRADUATE UNITS

Graduate Programs Students: 63 full-time (34 women), 232 part-time (130 women). In 2015, 95 master's awarded. *Application Contact:* Student Application Contact, 407-345-2800.

DEVRY UNIVERSITY, Glendale, AZ 85305

General Information Proprietary, coed, graduate-only institution.

GRADUATE UNITS

Keller Graduate School of Management Offers management (MAFM, MBA, MHRM, MISM, MNCM, MPA, MPM, Graduate Certificate).

DEVRY UNIVERSITY, Mesa, AZ 85210-2011

General Information Proprietary, coed, comprehensive institution.

GRADUATE UNITS

Keller Graduate School of Management Offers management (MAFM, MBA, MHRM, MISM, MNCM, MPA, MPM, Graduate Certificate).

DEVRY UNIVERSITY, Phoenix, AZ 85021

General Information Proprietary, coed, comprehensive institution. *Enrollment:* 755 graduate, professional, and undergraduate students; 12 full-time matriculated graduate/professional students (4 women), 98 part-time matriculated graduate/professional students (44 women). *Enrollment by degree level:* 110 master's. *Library:* Learning Resource Center.

Computer facilities: Online class registration is available.
Website: http://www.devry.edu/

General Application Contact: Student Application Contact, 602-870-9222.

GRADUATE UNITS

Keller Graduate School of Management Students: 12 full-time (4 women), 98 part-time (44 women). In 2015, 52 master's awarded. Offers management (MAFM, MBA, MHRM, MISM, MNCM, MPA, MPM, MSA). *Application Contact:* Student Application Contact, 602-870-9222.

DEVRY UNIVERSITY, Alhambra, CA 91803

General Information Proprietary, coed, comprehensive institution.

GRADUATE UNITS

Keller Graduate School of Management Offers management (MAFM, MBA, MHRM, MISM, MNCM, MPA, MPM).

DEVRY UNIVERSITY, Anaheim, CA 92806-6136

General Information Proprietary, coed, comprehensive institution.

GRADUATE UNITS

Keller Graduate School of Management Offers management (MAFM, MBA, MHRM, MISM, MNCM, MPA, MPM).

DEVRY UNIVERSITY, Fremont, CA 94555

General Information Proprietary, coed, comprehensive institution.

GRADUATE UNITS

Keller Graduate School of Management Offers management (MAFM, MBA, MHRM, MISM, MNCM, MPA, MPM).

DEVRY UNIVERSITY, Long Beach, CA 90806

General Information Proprietary, coed, comprehensive institution.

GRADUATE UNITS

Keller Graduate School of Management Offers management (MAFM, MBA, MHRM, MISM, MNCM, MPA, MPM).

DEVRY UNIVERSITY, Oakland, CA 94612

General Information Proprietary, coed, comprehensive institution.

GRADUATE UNITS

Keller Graduate School of Management Offers management (MAFM, MBA, MHRM, MISM, MNCM, MPA, MPM).

DEVRY UNIVERSITY, Oxnard, CA 93036

General Information Proprietary, coed, comprehensive institution.

GRADUATE UNITS

Keller Graduate School of Management Offers management (MAFM, MBA, MHRM, MISM, MNCM, MPA, MPM, Graduate Certificate).

DEVRY UNIVERSITY, Palmdale, CA 93551

General Information Proprietary, coed, comprehensive institution.

GRADUATE UNITS

Keller Graduate School of Management Offers management (MAFM, MBA, MHRM, MPM, Graduate Certificate).

DEVRY UNIVERSITY, Pomona, CA 91768

General Information Proprietary, coed, comprehensive institution. *Enrollment:* 1,358 graduate, professional, and undergraduate students; 43 full-time matriculated graduate/professional students (17 women), 181 part-time matriculated graduate/professional students (81 women). *Enrollment by degree level:* 224 master's.

Computer facilities: Online class registration is available.
Website: http://www.devry.edu/

GRADUATE UNITS

Graduate Programs Students: 43 full-time (17 women), 181 part-time (81 women). In 2015, 83 master's awarded. *Application Contact:* Student Application Contact, 909-622-8866.

DEVRY UNIVERSITY, San Diego, CA 92108-1633

General Information Proprietary, coed, comprehensive institution.

GRADUATE UNITS

Keller Graduate School of Management Offers management (MAFM, MBA, MHRM, MISM, MNCM, MPA, MPM, Graduate Certificate).

DEVRY UNIVERSITY, Kansas City, MO 64105-2112

General Information Proprietary, coed, comprehensive institution.

GRADUATE UNITS

Keller Graduate School of Management Offers management (MAFM, MBA, MHRM, MISM, MNCM, MPA, MPM).

DEVRY UNIVERSITY, Colorado Springs, CO 80920

General Information Proprietary, coed, comprehensive institution.

GRADUATE UNITS

Keller Graduate School of Management Offers management (MAFM, MBA, MHRM, MISM, MNCM, MPA, MPM, Graduate Certificate).

DEVRY UNIVERSITY, Jacksonville, FL 32256-6040

General Information Proprietary, coed, comprehensive institution.

GRADUATE UNITS

Keller Graduate School of Management Offers management (MAFM, MBA, MHRM, MISM, MNCM, MPA, MPM).

DEVRY UNIVERSITY, Miramar, FL 33027

General Information Proprietary, coed, comprehensive institution. *Enrollment:* 581 graduate, professional, and undergraduate students; 55 full-time matriculated graduate/professional students (26 women), 121 part-time matriculated graduate/professional students (49 women). *Enrollment by degree level:* 176 master's. Website: http://www.devry.edu/

GRADUATE UNITS

Graduate Programs Students: 55 full-time (26 women), 121 part-time (49 women). In 2015, 54 master's awarded. *Application Contact:* Student Application Contact, 954-499-9775.

DEVRY UNIVERSITY, Alpharetta, GA 30009

General Information Proprietary, coed, comprehensive institution.

GRADUATE UNITS

Keller Graduate School of Management Offers management (MAFM, MBA, MHRM, MISM, MNCM, MPA, MPM).

DEVRY UNIVERSITY, Decatur, GA 30030

General Information Proprietary, coed, comprehensive institution. *Enrollment:* 1,468 graduate, professional, and undergraduate students; 26 full-time matriculated graduate/professional students (13 women), 212 part-time matriculated graduate/professional students (139 women). *Enrollment by degree level:* 238 master's. *Library:* Learning Resource Center.
Website: http://www.devry.edu/

GRADUATE UNITS

Keller Graduate School of Management Students: 26 full-time (13 women), 212 part-time (139 women). In 2015, 75 master's awarded. Offers management (MAFM, MBA, MHRM, MISM, MNCM, MPA, MPM, MSA). *Application Contact:* Student Application Contact, 404-270-2700.

DEVRY UNIVERSITY, Duluth, GA 30096-7671

General Information Proprietary, coed, comprehensive institution.

GRADUATE UNITS

Keller Graduate School of Management Offers management (MAFM, MBA, MHRM, MISM, MNCM, MPA, MPM, Graduate Certificate).

DEVRY UNIVERSITY, Downers Grove, IL 60515

General Information Proprietary, coed, comprehensive institution. *Graduate housing:* On-campus housing not available.

GRADUATE UNITS

Graduate Programs Offers accounting and financial management (MAFM); business administration (MBA); education (MS); educational technology (MS); electrical engineering (MS); human resources management (MHRM); information systems management (MISM); network and communications management (MNCM); project management (MPM); public administration (MPA).

DEVRY UNIVERSITY, Elgin, IL 60123

General Information Proprietary, coed, comprehensive institution.

GRADUATE UNITS

Keller Graduate School of Management Offers management (MAFM, MBA, MHRM, MISM, MNCM, MPA, MPM, Graduate Certificate).

DEVRY UNIVERSITY, Gurnee, IL 60031-9126

General Information Proprietary, coed, comprehensive institution.

GRADUATE UNITS

Keller Graduate School of Management Offers management (MAFM, MBA, MHRM, MISM, MNCM, MPA, MPM, Graduate Certificate).

DEVRY UNIVERSITY, Naperville, IL 60563-2361

General Information Proprietary, coed, comprehensive institution.

GRADUATE UNITS

Keller Graduate School of Management Offers management (MAFM, MBA, MHRM, MISM, MNCM, MPA, MPM, Graduate Certificate).

DEVRY UNIVERSITY, Tinley Park, IL 60477

General Information Proprietary, coed, comprehensive institution.

GRADUATE UNITS

Keller Graduate School of Management Offers management (MAFM, MBA, MHRM, MISM, MNCM, MPA, MPM).

DEVRY UNIVERSITY, Merrillville, IN 46410-5673

General Information Proprietary, coed, comprehensive institution.

GRADUATE UNITS

Keller Graduate School of Management Offers management (MAFM, MBA, MHRM, MISM, MNCM, MPA, MPM, Graduate Certificate).

DEVRY UNIVERSITY, Henderson, NV 89074-7120

General Information Proprietary, coed, comprehensive institution.

GRADUATE UNITS

Keller Graduate School of Management Offers management (MAFM, MBA, MHRM, MISM, MNCM, MPA, MPM).

DEVRY UNIVERSITY, North Brunswick, NJ 08902

General Information Proprietary, coed, comprehensive institution. *Enrollment:* 842 graduate, professional, and undergraduate students; 36 full-time matriculated graduate/professional students (18 women), 87 part-time matriculated graduate/professional students (41 women). *Enrollment by degree level:* 123 master's. *Library:* Learning Resource Center.

Computer facilities: Online class registration is available.
Website: http://www.devry.edu/

GRADUATE UNITS

Keller Graduate School of Management Students: 36 full-time (18 women), 87 part-time (41 women). In 2015, 37 master's awarded. Offers management (MBA).

DEVRY UNIVERSITY, Paramus, NJ 07652

General Information Proprietary, coed, comprehensive institution.

GRADUATE UNITS

Keller Graduate School of Management Offers management (MBA).

DEVRY UNIVERSITY, Charlotte, NC 28273-4068

General Information Proprietary, coed, comprehensive institution.

GRADUATE UNITS

Keller Graduate School of Management Offers management (MAFM, MBA, MHRM, MISM, MNCM, MPA, MPM).

DEVRY UNIVERSITY, Fort Washington, PA 19034

General Information Proprietary, coed, comprehensive institution.

GRADUATE UNITS

Keller Graduate School of Management Offers management (MAFM, MBA, MHRM, MISM, MNCM, MPA, MPM).

DEVRY UNIVERSITY, King of Prussia, PA 19406-2926

General Information Proprietary, coed, comprehensive institution.

GRADUATE UNITS

Keller Graduate School of Management Offers management (MAFM, MBA, MHRM, MISM, MNCM, MPA, MPM, Graduate Certificate).

DEVRY UNIVERSITY, Nashville, TN 37211-4147

General Information Proprietary, coed, comprehensive institution.

GRADUATE UNITS

Keller Graduate School of Management Offers management (MAFM, MBA, MHRM, MISM, MNCM, MPA, MPM).

DEVRY UNIVERSITY, Irving, TX 75063

General Information Proprietary, coed, comprehensive institution. *Enrollment:* 728 graduate, professional, and undergraduate students; 48 full-time matriculated graduate/professional students (23 women), 181 part-time matriculated graduate/professional students (84 women). *Enrollment by degree level:* 229 master's. *Library:* Learning Resource Center.
Website: http://www.devry.edu/

GRADUATE UNITS

Keller Graduate School of Management Students: 48 full-time (23 women), 181 part-time (84 women). In 2015, 77 master's awarded. Offers management (M Acc, MAFM, MBA, MHRM, MISM, MPM). *Application Contact:* Student Application Contact, 972-929-6777.

DEVRY UNIVERSITY, Arlington, VA 22202

General Information Proprietary, coed, comprehensive institution. *Enrollment:* 590 graduate, professional, and undergraduate students; 47 full-time matriculated graduate/professional students (15 women), 252 part-time matriculated graduate/professional students (108 women). *Enrollment by degree level:* 299 master's. *Library:* Learning Resource Center.

Computer facilities: Online class registration is available.
Website: http://www.devry.edu/

GRADUATE UNITS

Keller Graduate School of Management Students: 47 full-time (15 women), 252 part-time (108 women). In 2015, 104 master's awarded. Offers management (M Acc, MAFM, MBA, MHRM, MISM, MNCM, MPA, MPM). *Application Contact:* Student Application Contact, 703-414-4000.

DEVRY UNIVERSITY, Chesapeake, VA 23320-3671

General Information Proprietary, coed, comprehensive institution.

GRADUATE UNITS

Keller Graduate School of Management Offers management (MAFM, MBA, MHRM, MISM, MNCM, MPA, MPM).

DEVRY UNIVERSITY, Manassas, VA 20109-3173

General Information Proprietary, coed, comprehensive institution.

GRADUATE UNITS

Keller Graduate School of Management Offers management (MAFM, MBA, MHRM, MISM, MNCM, MPA, MPM, Graduate Certificate).

DEVRY UNIVERSITY ONLINE, Addison, IL 60101

General Information Proprietary, coed, comprehensive institution. *Enrollment:* 17,582 graduate, professional, and undergraduate students; 643 full-time matriculated graduate/professional students (380 women), 3,439 part-time matriculated graduate/professional students (2,093 women). *Enrollment by degree level:* 4,082 master's.
Website: http://www.devry.edu/

GRADUATE UNITS

Graduate Programs Students: 643 full-time (380 women), 3,439 part-time (2,093 women). In 2015, 1,462 master's awarded.

DIGIPEN INSTITUTE OF TECHNOLOGY, Redmond, WA 98052

General Information Proprietary, coed, comprehensive institution. *Enrollment:* 1,062 graduate, professional, and undergraduate students; 62 full-time matriculated graduate/professional students (8 women), 18 part-time matriculated graduate/professional students (2 women). *Enrollment by degree level:* 80 master's. *Graduate faculty:* 19 full-time (4 women), 3 part-time/adjunct (0 women). *Tuition, area resident:* Full-time $17,100; part-time $950 per credit. *Required fees:* $100 per semester. Tuition and fees vary according to program. *Graduate housing:* Room and/or apartments available on a first-come, first-served basis to single students; on-campus housing not available to married students. Typical cost: $10,754 (including board). Housing application deadline: 6/1. *Student services:* Campus employment opportunities, career counseling, free psychological counseling, international student services, multicultural affairs office, services for students with disabilities. *Library:* DigiPen Library. *Collection:* Books: 5,024 (physical), 138,729 (digital/electronic); Serial titles: 29 (physical); Databases: 10. Weekly public service hours: 81. *Research affiliation:* Andretti (software development), Boeing (simulations), Lotus Formula 1 (software development).

Computer facilities: 794 computers available on campus for general student use. A campuswide network can be accessed. Online class registration is available.
Website: http://www.digipen.edu/

General Application Contact: Danial Powers, Director of Admissions, 425-629-5071, Fax: 425-558-0378, E-mail: dpowers@digipen.edu.

GRADUATE UNITS

Graduate Programs Students: 62 full-time (8 women), 18 part-time (2 women); includes 31 minority (2 Black or African American, non-Hispanic/Latino; 20 Asian, non-Hispanic/Latino; 9 Hispanic/Latino), 25 international. Average age 26. 161 applicants, 37% accepted, 35 enrolled. *Faculty:* 19 full-time (4 women), 3 part-time/adjunct (0 women). *Financial support:* In 2015–16, 2 students received support, including 2 fellowships (averaging $15,450 per year); career-related internships or fieldwork and scholarships/grants also available. Financial award application deadline: 5/1; financial award applicants required to submit FAFSA. In 2015, 17 master's awarded. *Degree program information:* Part-time programs available. Part-time. Offers computer science (MS); digital art and animation (MFA). *Application deadline:* For fall admission, 2/1 priority date for domestic and international students; for spring admission, 7/1 for domestic and international students. Applications are processed on a rolling basis. *Application fee:* $35. Electronic applications accepted. *Application Contact:* Danial Powers, Director of Admissions, 425-629-5071, Fax: 425-558-0378, E-mail: dpowers@digipen.edu. *Senior Vice President*, Angela Kugler, 425-895-4438, Fax: 425-558-0378, E-mail: akugler@digipen.edu.

DIGITAL MEDIA ARTS COLLEGE, Boca Raton, FL 33487

General Information Proprietary, coed, comprehensive institution.

GRADUATE UNITS

Graduate Programs Offers graphic design (MFA); special FX animation (MFA).

DOANE UNIVERSITY, Crete, NE 68333-2430

General Information Independent-religious, coed, comprehensive institution. *Enrollment:* 1,057 graduate, professional, and undergraduate students; 427 full-time matriculated graduate/professional students (300 women), 549 part-time matriculated graduate/professional students (429 women). *Enrollment by degree level:* 869 master's, 30 doctoral, 77 other advanced degrees. *Graduate faculty:* 5 full-time (3 women), 121 part-time/adjunct (79 women). *Graduate housing:* On-campus housing not available. *Student services:* Career counseling, teacher training. *Library:* Perkins Library plus 1 other.

Computer facilities: Computer purchase and lease plans are available. 250 computers available on campus for general student use. A campuswide network can be accessed from student residence rooms and from off campus. Online class registration is available.
Website: http://www.doane.edu/

General Application Contact: Wilma Daddario, Assistant Dean, 402-466-4774, Fax: 404-466-4228, E-mail: wilma.daddario@doane.edu.

GRADUATE UNITS

Program in Counseling Students: 78 full-time (57 women), 29 part-time (22 women); includes 12 minority (1 Black or African American, non-Hispanic/Latino; 1 American Indian or Alaska Native, non-Hispanic/Latino; 10 Hispanic/Latino). Average age 34. *Faculty:* 2 full-time (1 woman), 14 part-time/adjunct (9 women). *Financial support:* Unspecified assistantships available. Financial award application deadline: 6/1; financial award applicants required to submit FAFSA. In 2015, 31 master's awarded. *Degree program information:* Evening/weekend programs available. Evening/weekend. Offers counseling (MAC). *Application deadline:* Applications are processed on a rolling basis. *Application fee:* $25. Electronic applications accepted. *Application Contact:* Jean Kilnoski, Assistant Dean, 402-466-4774, Fax: 404-466-4228, E-mail: jean.kilnoski@doane.edu. *Associate Dean/Director of the Counseling Program*, Dr. Donald Belau, 402-466-4774, Fax: 402-466-4228, E-mail: donald.belau@doane.edu.

Program in Education Students: 225 full-time (169 women), 502 part-time (396 women); includes 25 minority (7 Black or African American, non-Hispanic/Latino; 1 Asian, non-Hispanic/Latino; 14 Hispanic/Latino; 3 Two or more races, non-Hispanic/Latino). Average age 32. *Financial support:* Applicants required to submit FAFSA. In 2015, 366 master's awarded. *Degree program information:* Part-time and evening/weekend programs available. Part-time, evening/weekend. Offers curriculum and instruction (M Ed); educational leadership (M Ed). *Application deadline:* Applications are processed on a rolling basis. Electronic applications accepted. *Application Contact:* Wilma Daddario, Assistant Dean, 402-464-1223, Fax: 402-466-4228, E-mail: wdaddario@doane.edu. *Dean*, Lyn C. Forester, 402-826-8604, Fax: 402-826-8278.

Program in Management Students: 123 full-time (73 women), 18 part-time (11 women); includes 23 minority (10 Black or African American, non-Hispanic/Latino; 4 American Indian or Alaska Native, non-Hispanic/Latino; 3 Asian, non-Hispanic/Latino; 5 Hispanic/Latino; 1 Two or more races, non-Hispanic/Latino). Average age 35. *Faculty:* 2 full-time (1 woman), 21 part-time/adjunct (9 women). *Financial support:* Application deadline: 6/1; applicants required to submit FAFSA. In 2015, 69 master's awarded. *Degree program information:* Part-time and evening/weekend programs available. Part-time, evening/weekend. Offers management (MA). *Application deadline:* Applications are processed on a rolling basis. *Application fee:* $25. Electronic applications accepted. *Application Contact:* Kerry Fina, 402-466-4774, Fax: 404-466-4228, E-mail: kerry.fina@doane.edu. *Dean*, Janice Hedfield, 880-333-6263, E-mail: janice.hedfield@doane.edu.

DOMINICAN COLLEGE, Orangeburg, NY 10962-1210

General Information Independent, coed, comprehensive institution. *Graduate housing:* Room and/or apartments available on a first-come, first-served basis to single students; on-campus housing not available to married students.

GRADUATE UNITS

Division of Allied Health ***Degree program information:*** Part-time and evening/weekend programs available. Part-time, evening/weekend, online learning. Offers allied health (MS, DPT); occupational therapy (MS); physical therapy (MS, DPT).

Division of Nursing ***Degree program information:*** Part-time and evening/weekend programs available. Part-time, evening/weekend. Offers nursing (MSN, DNP).

Division of Teacher Education ***Degree program information:*** Part-time and evening/weekend programs available. Part-time, evening/weekend, online learning. Offers teacher education (MS Ed).

MBA Program ***Degree program information:*** Evening/weekend programs available. Evening/weekend. Offers accounting (MBA); healthcare management (MBA); management (MBA). Electronic applications accepted.

DOMINICAN HOUSE OF STUDIES, PONTIFICAL FACULTY OF THE IMMACULATE CONCEPTION, Washington, DC 20017-1585

General Information Independent-religious, coed, primarily men, graduate-only institution. *Graduate housing:* On-campus housing not available. *Research affiliation:* Washington Theological Consortium (theology, ecumenism), The Thomist (theology).

GRADUATE UNITS

Graduate and Professional Programs in Theology ***Degree program information:*** Part-time programs available. Part-time. Offers moral theology (STL); sacred scripture (STL); systematic theology (STL); theology (M Div, MA, STB); Thomistic studies (MA, STD, STL).

DOMINICAN SCHOOL OF PHILOSOPHY AND THEOLOGY, Berkeley, CA 94708

General Information Independent-religious, coed, graduate-only institution. *Enrollment:* 32 full-time matriculated graduate/professional students (5 women), 25 part-time matriculated graduate/professional students (13 women). *Enrollment by degree level:* 36 master's, 3 other advanced degrees. *Graduate faculty:* 12 full-time (3 women), 5 part-time/adjunct (0 women). *Tuition, area resident:* Full-time $16,560; part-time $690 per credit. *Required fees:* $50; $50 per unit. *Graduate housing:* Rooms and/or apartments available on a first-come, first-served basis to single and married students. Housing application deadline: 5/1. *Student services:* Campus employment opportunities, career counseling, international student services. *Library:* Flora Lamson Hewlett Library of the Graduate Theological Union. Students can reserve study rooms.

Computer facilities: 3 computers available on campus for general student use. A campuswide network can be accessed. Online class registration is available.
Website: http://www.dspt.edu/

General Application Contact: Jamie L. Martos, Director of Admissions and Recruitment, 510-883-2073, Fax: 510-849-1372, E-mail: admissions@dspt.edu.

GRADUATE UNITS

Graduate Programs Students: 32 full-time (5 women), 25 part-time (13 women); includes 24 minority (2 Black or African American, non-Hispanic/Latino; 1 American Indian or Alaska Native, non-Hispanic/Latino; 12 Asian, non-Hispanic/Latino; 5 Hispanic/Latino; 4 Two or more races, non-Hispanic/Latino), 3 international. *Faculty:* 12 full-time (3 women), 5 part-time/adjunct (0 women). *Financial support:* Institutionally sponsored loans, scholarships/grants, and tuition waivers (partial) available. Financial award application deadline: 3/4. *Degree program information:* Part-time programs available. Part-time. Offers philosophy (MA); theology (M Div, MA, MTS, Certificate). *Application deadline:* For fall admission, 3/1 priority date for domestic and international students; for spring admission, 11/1 priority date for domestic and international students. Applications are processed on a rolling basis. *Application fee:* $50. Electronic applications accepted. *Application Contact:* Jamie L. Martos, Director of Admissions and Recruitment, 510-883-2073, Fax: 510-849-1372, E-mail: admissions@dspt.edu. *Academic Dean*, Fr. Christopher Renz, OP, 510-883-2084, Fax: 510-849-1372, E-mail: crenz@dspt.edu.

DOMINICAN UNIVERSITY, River Forest, IL 60305-1099

General Information Independent-religious, coed, comprehensive institution. *Enrollment:* 3,696 graduate, professional, and undergraduate students; 354 full-time matriculated graduate/professional students (275 women), 790 part-time matriculated graduate/professional students (589 women). *Enrollment by degree level:* 1,129 master's, 11 doctoral, 4 other advanced degrees. *Graduate faculty:* 61 full-time (35 women), 128 part-time/adjunct (95 women). *Tuition, area resident:* Full-time $24,480; part-time $816 per credit hour. *Required fees:* $540; $18 per credit hour. Tuition and fees vary according to course load, degree level and program. *Graduate housing:* Room and/or apartments available on a first-come, first-served basis to single students; on-campus housing not available to married students. Typical cost: $5980 per year ($9380 including board). Room and board charges vary according to housing facility selected. Housing application deadline: 7/1. *Student services:* Campus employment opportunities, campus safety program, career counseling, child daycare facilities, exercise/wellness program, free psychological counseling, international student services, low-cost health insurance, multicultural affairs office, services for students with disabilities, teacher training, writing training. *Library:* Rebecca Crown Library. *Collection:* Books: 206,808 (physical), 9,389 (digital/electronic); Serial titles: 280 (physical), 53,047 (digital/electronic); Databases: 154. Weekly public service hours: 104; students can reserve study rooms.

Computer facilities: Computer purchase and lease plans are available. 550 computers available on campus for general student use. A campuswide network can be accessed from student residence rooms and from off campus. Online class registration is available.
Website: http://www.dom.edu/

General Application Contact: Ann Hurley, Director of Graduate Admissions, 708-524-6829, E-mail: ahurley@dom.edu.

GRADUATE UNITS

Edward A. and Lois L. Brennan School of Business Students: 80 full-time (60 women), 102 part-time (59 women); includes 42 minority (13 Black or African American, non-Hispanic/Latino; 12 Asian, non-Hispanic/Latino; 16 Hispanic/Latino; 1 Native Hawaiian or other Pacific Islander, non-Hispanic/Latino), 18 international. Average age 29. 113 applicants, 73% accepted, 53 enrolled. *Faculty:* 22 full-time (9 women), 18 part-time/adjunct (7 women). *Financial support:* Career-related internships or fieldwork, Federal Work-Study, tuition waivers (partial), and unspecified assistantships available. Support available to part-time students. Financial award application deadline: 3/1; financial award applicants required to submit FAFSA. In 2015, 86 master's awarded. *Degree program information:* Part-time and evening/weekend programs available. Part-time, evening/weekend, 100% online, blended/hybrid learning. Offers business (MBA, MSA). JD/MBA offered jointly with John Marshall Law School. *Application deadline:* Applications are processed on a rolling basis. *Application fee:* $25. Electronic applications accepted. *Application Contact:* Dr. Kathleen Odell, Associate Dean, Brennan School of Business, 708-524-6507, Fax: 708-524-6939, E-mail: mquilty@dom.edu. *Dean*, Dr. Roberto Curci, 708-524-6321, Fax: 708-524-6939, E-mail: rcurci@dom.edu.

Graduate School of Library and Information Science Students: 97 full-time (70 women), 165 part-time (134 women); includes 61 minority (29 Black or African American, non-Hispanic/Latino; 4 Asian, non-Hispanic/Latino; 27 Hispanic/Latino; 1 Native Hawaiian or other Pacific Islander, non-Hispanic/Latino), 2 international. Average age 34. 140 applicants, 79% accepted, 81 enrolled. *Faculty:* 11 full-time (7 women), 17 part-time/adjunct (11 women). *Financial support:* Fellowships, research assistantships, career-related internships or fieldwork, Federal Work-Study, scholarships/grants, and tuition waivers (partial) available. Support available to part-time students. Financial award application deadline: 4/15; financial award applicants required to submit FAFSA. In 2015, 125 master's, 2 doctorates, 4 other advanced degrees awarded. *Degree program information:* Part-time and evening/weekend programs available. Part-time, evening/weekend, 100% online, blended/hybrid learning. Offers knowledge management (Certificate); library and information science (MLIS, MPS, PhD); special studies (CSS). MLIS/M Div offered jointly with McCormick Theological Seminary,

MLIS/MA with Loyola University Chicago, MLIS/MM with Northwestern University. *Application deadline:* For fall admission, 6/1 priority date for domestic students; for winter admission, 3/1 priority date for domestic students; for spring admission, 10/1 priority date for domestic students. Applications are processed on a rolling basis. *Application fee:* $25. *Application Contact:* Ann Hurley, Director of Graduate Admissions, 708-524-6829, E-mail: ahurley@dom.edu. *Dean*, Dr. Kate Marek, 708-524-6648, Fax: 708-524-6657, E-mail: kmarek@dom.edu.

Graduate School of Social Work Students: 133 full-time (114 women), 105 part-time (91 women); includes 112 minority (50 Black or African American, non-Hispanic/Latino; 1 American Indian or Alaska Native, non-Hispanic/Latino; 4 Asian, non-Hispanic/Latino; 55 Hispanic/Latino; 2 Native Hawaiian or other Pacific Islander, non-Hispanic/Latino), 4 international. Average age 32. *Faculty:* 9 full-time (6 women), 19 part-time/adjunct (17 women). *Financial support:* Research assistantships with partial tuition reimbursements, Federal Work-Study, scholarships/grants, and unspecified assistantships available. Financial award applicants required to submit FAFSA. In 2015, 59 master's awarded. *Degree program information:* Part-time programs available. Part-time. Offers social work (MSW). *Application deadline:* For fall admission, 7/1 for domestic and international students; for spring admission, 11/1 for domestic and international students. Applications are processed on a rolling basis. *Application fee:* $25. Electronic applications accepted. *Application Contact:* Kathy Clyburn, Assistant Dean, 708-771-5298, Fax: 708-366-3446, E-mail: kclyburn@dom.edu. *Dean*, Dr. Charles Stoops, 708-366-3316, E-mail: cstoops@dom.edu.

School of Education Students: 16 full-time (12 women), 398 part-time (291 women); includes 106 minority (39 Black or African American, non-Hispanic/Latino; 1 American Indian or Alaska Native, non-Hispanic/Latino; 18 Asian, non-Hispanic/Latino; 39 Hispanic/Latino; 1 Native Hawaiian or other Pacific Islander, non-Hispanic/Latino; 8 Two or more races, non-Hispanic/Latino), 1 international. Average age 27. 24 applicants, 67% accepted, 11 enrolled. *Faculty:* 19 full-time (13 women), 64 part-time/adjunct (57 women). *Financial support:* Career-related internships or fieldwork, scholarships/grants, and tuition waivers (partial) available. Support available to part-time students. Financial award application deadline: 8/15; financial award applicants required to submit FAFSA. *Degree program information:* Part-time and evening/weekend programs available. Part-time, evening/weekend, 100% online. Offers curriculum and instruction (MA Ed); early childhood education (MS); education (MAT); educational administration (MA); elementary education (MA Ed); English as a second language (MA Ed); reading (MA Ed); special education (MS). *Application deadline:* Applications are processed on a rolling basis. *Application fee:* $25. *Application Contact:* Keven Hansen, Coordinator of Recruitment and Admissions, 708-524-6921, Fax: 708-524-6665, E-mail: educate@dom.edu. *Dean*, Dr. Vicki Chou, 718-524-6643, Fax: 708-524-6665, E-mail: vchou@dom.edu.

School of Professional and Continuing Studies Students: 31 full-time (27 women), 18 part-time (13 women); includes 24 minority (19 Black or African American, non-Hispanic/Latino; 5 Hispanic/Latino). Average age 32. 19 applicants, 89% accepted, 15 enrolled. *Faculty:* 13 part-time/adjunct (4 women). *Financial support:* Applicants required to submit FAFSA. In 2015, 12 master's awarded. *Degree program information:* Part-time and evening/weekend programs available. Part-time, evening/weekend, 100% online, blended/hybrid learning. Offers conflict resolution (MA). *Application deadline:* Applications are processed on a rolling basis. *Application fee:* $25. *Application Contact:* Monica Halloran, Associate Director of Academic Advising, 708-714-9007, Fax: 708-714-9126, E-mail: mhallora@dom.edu. *Assistant Provost for Continuing Studies and Special Initiatives*, Dr. Matthew Hlinak, 708-714-9056, E-mail: mhlinak@dom.edu.

DOMINICAN UNIVERSITY OF CALIFORNIA, San Rafael, CA 94901-2298

General Information Independent-religious, coed, comprehensive institution. *Enrollment:* 1,863 graduate, professional, and undergraduate students; 265 full-time matriculated graduate/professional students (207 women), 198 part-time matriculated graduate/professional students (146 women). *Enrollment by degree level:* 463 master's. *Graduate faculty:* 52 full-time (34 women), 63 part-time/adjunct (43 women). *Required fees:* $300. Tuition and fees vary according to course load and program. *Graduate housing:* On-campus housing not available. *Student services:* Campus employment opportunities, career counseling, free psychological counseling, international student services, low-cost health insurance, services for students with disabilities. *Library:* Archbishop Alemany Library. *Collection:* Books: 110,523 (physical); Databases: 84.

Computer facilities: 195 computers available on campus for general student use. A campuswide network can be accessed from student residence rooms. Online class registration, office software are available.
Website: http://www.dominican.edu/

General Application Contact: 415-485-3204, Fax: 415-485-3214, E-mail: graduateprograms@dominican.edu.

GRADUATE UNITS

Barowsky School of Business Students: 16 full-time (10 women), 43 part-time (18 women); includes 17 minority (6 Black or African American, non-Hispanic/Latino; 3 Asian, non-Hispanic/Latino; 5 Hispanic/Latino; 1 Native Hawaiian or other Pacific Islander, non-Hispanic/Latino; 2 Two or more races, non-Hispanic/Latino), 9 international. Average age 34. 53 applicants, 68% accepted, 18 enrolled. *Faculty:* 9 full-time (3 women), 15 part-time/adjunct (5 women). *Financial support:* Scholarships/grants available. Support available to part-time students. Financial award application deadline: 3/2; financial award applicants required to submit FAFSA. In 2015, 47 master's awarded. *Degree program information:* Part-time and evening/weekend programs available. Part-time, evening/weekend. Offers global business (MBA); strategic leadership (MBA); sustainable enterprise (MBA). *Application deadline:* For fall admission, 5/15 priority date for domestic and international students; for spring admission, 11/15 priority date for domestic and international students. Applications are processed on a rolling basis. Electronic applications accepted. *Application Contact:* Robbie Hayes, Associate Director, Graduate Admissions, 415-458-3771, Fax: 415-485-3214, E-mail: robbie.hayes@dominican.edu. *Dean*, Dr. Sam Beldona, 415-458-3786, E-mail: sriam.beldona@dominican.edu.

School of Arts, Humanities and Social Sciences Students: 2 full-time (both women), 25 part-time (20 women); includes 3 minority (1 Black or African American, non-Hispanic/Latino; 2 Two or more races, non-Hispanic/Latino). Average age 48. 11 applicants, 91% accepted, 5 enrolled. *Faculty:* 11 full-time (5 women), 5 part-time/adjunct (2 women). *Financial support:* Scholarships/grants available. Support available to part-time students. Financial award application deadline: 3/2; financial award applicants required to submit FAFSA. In 2015, 6 master's awarded. *Degree program information:* Part-time and evening/weekend programs available. Part-time, evening/weekend. Offers applied music (MA); art history (MA); arts, humanities and social sciences (MA); creative writing (MA); gender studies (MA); history (MA); literature (MA); philosophy (MA); political theory (MA); religion (MA). *Application deadline:* For fall admission, 5/15 for domestic and international students; for spring admission, 11/15 for domestic and international students. Applications are processed on a rolling basis. Electronic applications accepted. *Application Contact:* Ryan Purtill, Admissions Counselor, 415-458-3748, Fax: 415-485-3214, E-mail: ryan.purtill@dominican.edu. *Dean*, Dr. Nicola Pitchford, 415-485-1880, Fax: 415-257-0120, E-mail: nicola.pitchford@dominican.edu.

School of Education and Counseling Psychology Students: 107 full-time (81 women), 63 part-time (53 women); includes 35 minority (4 Black or African American, non-Hispanic/Latino; 2 American Indian or Alaska Native, non-Hispanic/Latino; 6 Asian, non-Hispanic/Latino; 18 Hispanic/Latino; 5 Two or more races, non-Hispanic/Latino). Average age 34. 108 applicants, 81% accepted, 70 enrolled. *Faculty:* 16 full-time (14 women), 28 part-time/adjunct (23 women). *Financial support:* Scholarships/grants available. Support available to part-time students. Financial award application deadline: 3/2; financial award applicants required to submit FAFSA. In 2015, 34 master's awarded. *Degree program information:* Part-time and evening/weekend programs available. Part-time, evening/weekend. Offers education and counseling psychology (MFT, MS); general (MS); marriage and family therapy (MS); multiple subject (MS); single subject (MS). *Application deadline:* Applications are processed on a rolling basis. Electronic applications accepted. *Application Contact:* Shana Friedman, Assistant Director, Graduate Admissions, 415-485-3246, Fax: 415-485-3214, E-mail: shana.friedman@dominican.edu. *Dean*, Dr. Rande Webster, 415-257-1305, Fax: 415-458-3790, E-mail: rande.webster@dominican.edu.

School of Health and Natural Sciences Students: 98 full-time (78 women), 36 part-time (29 women); includes 68 minority (5 Black or African American, non-Hispanic/Latino; 39 Asian, non-Hispanic/Latino; 14 Hispanic/Latino; 3 Native Hawaiian or other Pacific Islander, non-Hispanic/Latino; 7 Two or more races, non-Hispanic/Latino), 3 international. Average age 28. 175 applicants, 41% accepted, 46 enrolled. *Faculty:* 12 full-time (8 women), 12 part-time/adjunct (10 women). *Financial support:* Application deadline: 3/2; applicants required to submit FAFSA. In 2015, 66 master's awarded. Offers biological sciences (MS); clinical laboratory sciences (MS); health and natural sciences (MS); occupational therapy (MS). *Application deadline:* For fall admission, 3/15 for domestic and international students. Applications are processed on a rolling basis. Electronic applications accepted. *Application Contact:* Shannon Lovelace-White, Associate Vice President, Graduate and Adult Admissions, 415-485-3204, Fax: 415-485-3214, E-mail: shannon.lovelace-white@dominican.edu. *Dean*, Dr. Ching-Hua Wang, 415-457-4440.

DONGGUK UNIVERSITY LOS ANGELES, Los Angeles, CA 90020

General Information Independent, coed, graduate-only institution. *Graduate housing:* On-campus housing not available.

GRADUATE UNITS

Program in Oriental Medicine ***Degree program information:*** Part-time and evening/weekend programs available. Part-time, evening/weekend. Offers Oriental medicine (MS).

DORDT COLLEGE, Sioux Center, IA 51250-1697

General Information Independent-religious, coed, comprehensive institution. *Graduate housing:* Rooms and/or apartments available to single and married students.

GRADUATE UNITS

Program in Education ***Degree program information:*** Part-time programs available. Part-time, online learning. Offers education (M Ed). Electronic applications accepted.

DRAKE UNIVERSITY, Des Moines, IA 50311-4516

General Information Independent, coed, university. *Enrollment:* 4,991 graduate, professional, and undergraduate students; 856 full-time matriculated graduate/professional students (508 women), 752 part-time matriculated graduate/professional students (517 women). *Enrollment by degree level:* 736 master's, 821 doctoral, 47 other advanced degrees. *Graduate faculty:* 107 full-time (60 women), 70 part-time/adjunct (43 women). *Tuition, area resident:* Full-time $37,942; part-time $540 per credit hour. *Required fees:* $146; $73 per semester. Tuition and fees vary according to course load and program. *Graduate housing:* Room and/or apartments available on a first-come, first-served basis to single students; on-campus housing not available to married students. Typical cost: $5150 per year ($9596 including board). Housing application deadline: 8/1. *Student services:* Campus employment opportunities, campus safety program, career counseling, exercise/wellness program, free psychological counseling, international student services, low-cost health insurance, services for students with disabilities, teacher training, writing training. *Library:* Cowles Library plus 1 other. *Collection:* Books: 4,389 (physical), 129,239 (digital/electronic); Serial titles: 745 (physical), 121,135 (digital/electronic); Databases: 344. Weekly public service hours: 108; study areas open 24 hours, 5–7 days a week; students can reserve study rooms. *Research affiliation:* NASA through Iowa State University of Science and Technology (arts and sciences), Albertson's Inc. (pharmacy), U.S. Department of Agriculture (USDA) (agriculture), U.S. Department of Education (DOE) (education), Iowa Department of Education (education), National Science Foundation (biology, physics).

Computer facilities: 1,000 computers available on campus for general student use. A campuswide network can be accessed from student residence rooms and from off campus. Online class registration is available.
Website: http://www.drake.edu/

General Application Contact: Jennifer Reitano, Director, Graduate Student Programs, 515-271-2188, Fax: 515-271-2831, E-mail: jennifer.reitano@drake.edu.

GRADUATE UNITS

College of Business and Public Administration Students: 31 full-time (12 women), 206 part-time (106 women); includes 24 minority (9 Black or African American, non-Hispanic/Latino; 1 Asian, non-Hispanic/Latino; 8 Hispanic/Latino; 6 Two or more races, non-Hispanic/Latino), 15 international. Average age 31. 131 applicants, 76% accepted, 75 enrolled. *Faculty:* 15 full-time (5 women). *Financial support:* Fellowships with tuition reimbursements, teaching assistantships, career-related internships or fieldwork, and institutionally sponsored loans available. Support available to part-time students. Financial award application deadline: 3/1; financial award applicants required to submit FAFSA. In 2015, 202 master's awarded. *Degree program information:* Part-time and evening/weekend programs available. Part-time, evening/weekend. Offers business and public administration (M Acc, MBA, MFM, MPA). *Application deadline:* For fall admission, 8/15 priority date for domestic students; for winter admission, 12/20 priority date for domestic students; for spring admission, 12/1 priority date for domestic students. Applications are processed on a rolling basis. *Application fee:* $25. Electronic applications accepted. *Application Contact:* Danette Kenne, Assistant Dean, 515-271-2188, Fax: 515-271-4518, E-mail: cbpa.gradprograms@drake.edu. *Dean*, Dr. Terri Vaughan, 515-271-2871, Fax: 515-271-4518, E-mail: terri.vaughan@drake.edu.

College of Pharmacy and Health Sciences Students: 432 full-time (285 women), 4 part-time (1 woman); includes 62 minority (4 Black or African American, non-Hispanic/Latino; 1 American Indian or Alaska Native, non-Hispanic/Latino; 46 Asian, non-Hispanic/Latino; 5 Hispanic/Latino; 6 Two or more races, non-Hispanic/Latino), 1 international. Average age 22. 54 applicants, 31% accepted, 17 enrolled. *Faculty:* 36 full-time (18 women). *Financial support:* In 2015–16, 10 teaching assistantships (averaging $3,200 per year) were awarded; career-related internships or fieldwork, Federal Work-Study, institutionally sponsored loans, and scholarships/grants also available. Support available to part-time students. Financial award application deadline: 3/1; financial award applicants required to submit FAFSA. In 2015, 122 doctorates awarded. Offers pharmacy (Pharm D). *Application deadline:* For fall admission, 2/1 priority date for domestic students. *Application fee:* $135. Electronic applications accepted. *Dean*, Dr. Renae Chesnut, 515-271-3018, Fax: 515-271-4171, E-mail: renae.chesnut@drake.edu.

Law School Students: 310 full-time (150 women), 20 part-time (12 women); includes 51 minority (21 Black or African American, non-Hispanic/Latino; 1 American Indian or Alaska Native, non-Hispanic/Latino; 5 Asian, non-Hispanic/Latino; 16 Hispanic/Latino; 8 Two or more races, non-Hispanic/Latino), 6 international. Average age 26. 521 applicants, 44% accepted, 117 enrolled. *Faculty:* 28 full-time (10 women), 18 part-time/adjunct (5 women). *Financial support:* In 2015–16, 20 research assistantships (averaging $757 per year), 6 teaching assistantships (averaging $2,142 per year) were awarded; career-related internships or fieldwork, Federal Work-Study, institutionally sponsored loans, scholarships/grants, and tuition waivers (full and partial) also available. Support available to part-time students. Financial award application deadline: 3/1; financial award applicants required to submit FAFSA. In 2015, 7 master's, 116 doctorates awarded. Offers law (LL M, MJ, JD). *Application deadline:* For fall admission, 4/1 priority date for domestic and international students. Applications are processed on a rolling basis. *Application fee:* $40. Electronic applications accepted. *Application Contact:* Kara Blanchard, Director of Admission, 515-271-2953, Fax: 515-271-2530, E-mail: kara.blanchard@drake.edu. *Dean*, Ben Ullem, 515-271-3985, Fax: 515-271-4118, E-mail: ben.ullem@drake.edu.

School of Education Students: 83 full-time (61 women), 545 part-time (410 women); includes 41 minority (18 Black or African American, non-Hispanic/Latino; 1 American Indian or Alaska Native, non-Hispanic/Latino; 3 Asian, non-Hispanic/Latino; 13 Hispanic/Latino; 6 Two or more races, non-Hispanic/Latino), 2 international. Average age 34. 328 applicants, 87% accepted, 219 enrolled. *Faculty:* 24 full-time (11 women), 48 part-time/adjunct (37 women). *Financial support:* In 2015–16, 14 research assistantships were awarded; career-related internships or fieldwork and unspecified assistantships also available. Support available to part-time students. In 2015, 196 master's, 8 doctorates, 23 other advanced degrees awarded. *Degree program information:* Part-time and evening/weekend programs available. Part-time, evening/weekend. Offers education (MAT, MS, MSE, MST, Ed D, Ed S). *Application deadline:* For fall admission, 7/1 priority date for domestic students, 6/1 priority date for international students; for spring admission, 11/1 priority date for domestic students, 10/1 priority date for international students. Applications are processed on a rolling basis. *Application fee:* $25. Electronic applications accepted. *Dean*, Dr. Janet McMahill, 515-271-3829, E-mail: janet.mcmahill@drake.edu.

School of Journalism and Mass Communication Students: 20 part-time (17 women); includes 2 minority (1 Black or African American, non-Hispanic/Latino; 1 Asian, non-Hispanic/Latino). Average age 30. 5 applicants, 100% accepted, 5 enrolled. *Faculty:* 4 full-time (3 women). *Degree program information:* Part-time and evening/weekend programs available. Part-time, evening/weekend. Offers journalism and mass communication (MCL). *Dean*, Dr. Kathleen Richardson, 515-271-2295, Fax: 515-271-4518, E-mail: kathleen.richardson@drake.edu.

DREW UNIVERSITY, Madison, NJ 07940-1493

General Information Independent-religious, coed, university. CGS member. *Enrollment:* 2,082 graduate, professional, and undergraduate students; 279 full-time matriculated graduate/professional students (154 women), 353 part-time matriculated graduate/professional students (187 women). *Enrollment by degree level:* 286 master's, 330 doctoral. *Graduate faculty:* 25 full-time (11 women), 50 part-time/adjunct (26 women). Tuition and fees vary according to program. *Graduate housing:* Rooms and/or apartments available on a first-come, first-served basis to single and married students. Housing application deadline: 7/1. *Student services:* Campus employment opportunities, campus safety program, career counseling, child daycare facilities, exercise/wellness program, free psychological counseling, international student services, low-cost health insurance, multicultural affairs office, services for students with disabilities, teacher training, writing training. *Library:* Rose Memorial Library plus 1 other. *Collection:* Books: 649,118 (physical), 5,821 (digital/electronic); Databases: 315. Weekly public service hours: 83. *Research affiliation:* Center for Research Libraries (humanities), Dana Rise Institute (science), St. Barnabas Medical Center (medical humanities), Overlook Hospital (medical humanities), Methodist Archives (religion).

Computer facilities: Computer purchase and lease plans are available. A campuswide network can be accessed from student residence rooms and from off campus. Online class registration is available.
Website: http://www.drew.edu/

General Application Contact: Carla J. Burns, Director of Graduate Admissions, 973-408-3110, Fax: 973-408-3242, E-mail: gradm@drew.edu.

GRADUATE UNITS

Caspersen School of Graduate Studies Students: 125 full-time (82 women), 261 part-time (164 women); includes 34 minority (17 Black or African American, non-Hispanic/Latino; 6 Asian, non-Hispanic/Latino; 11 Hispanic/Latino), 6 international. Average age 42. 120 applicants, 90% accepted, 76 enrolled. *Faculty:* 1 full-time, 26 part-time/adjunct. *Financial support:* In 2015–16, 214 students received support. Fellowships, research assistantships, teaching assistantships, career-related internships or fieldwork, Federal Work-Study, scholarships/grants, and unspecified assistantships available. Support available to part-time students. Financial award applicants required to submit FAFSA. In 2015, 54 master's, 36 doctorates, 9 other advanced degrees awarded. *Degree program information:* Part-time and evening/weekend programs available. Part-time, evening/weekend. Offers conflict resolution and leadership (Certificate); history and culture (MA, PhD); K-12 education (MAT); liberal studies (M Litt, D Litt); medical humanities (MMH, DMH, CMH); poetry and poetry in translation (MFA). *Application deadline:* Applications are processed on a rolling basis. *Application fee:* $35. *Application Contact:* Leanne Horinko, Interim Director of Admissions, 973-408-3110, Fax: 973-408-3110, E-mail: gradm@drew.edu. *Dean*, Dr. Robert Ready, 973-408-3285, Fax: 973-408-3040, E-mail: gsdean@drew.edu.

Theological School *Degree program information:* Part-time programs available. Part-time, online learning. Offers theology (M Div, MA, MA Min, STM, D Min, PhD, Certificate). Electronic applications accepted.

DREXEL UNIVERSITY, Philadelphia, PA 19104-2875

General Information Independent, coed, university. CGS member. *Graduate housing:* On-campus housing not available.

GRADUATE UNITS

College of Arts and Sciences *Degree program information:* Part-time and evening/weekend programs available. Part-time, evening/weekend. Offers arts and sciences (MA, MS, PhD); biological sciences (MS, PhD); chemistry (MS, PhD); clinical psychology (PhD); communication (MS); environmental policy (MS); environmental science (MS, PhD); forensic psychology (PhD); health psychology (PhD); human nutrition (MS); law-psychologymathematics (MS, PhD); neuropsychology (PhD); physics (MS, PhD); psychology (MS); public communication (MS); publication management (MS); science communication (MS); science, technology and society (MS); technical communication (MS). Electronic applications accepted.

College of Computing and Informatics Students: 151 full-time (86 women), 444 part-time (248 women); includes 97 minority (26 Black or African American, non-Hispanic/Latino; 28 Asian, non-Hispanic/Latino; 24 Hispanic/Latino; 19 Two or more races, non-Hispanic/Latino), 81 international. Average age 33. 634 applicants, 57% accepted, 147 enrolled. *Faculty:* 47 full-time (21 women), 10 part-time/adjunct (6 women). *Financial support:* In 2015–16, 110 students received support, including 40 research assistantships with full tuition reimbursements available (averaging $26,730 per year), 19 teaching assistantships with full tuition reimbursements available (averaging $26,730 per year); career-related internships or fieldwork, institutionally sponsored loans, scholarships/grants, health care benefits, and tuition waivers (partial) also available. Support available to part-time students. Financial award application deadline: 3/1; financial award applicants required to submit FAFSA. In 2015, 270 master's, 11 doctorates, 28 other advanced degrees awarded. *Degree program information:* Part-time and evening/weekend programs available. Part-time, evening/weekend, 100% online. Offers competitive intelligence and knowledge management (MS); computer science (MS, PhD); computing and informatics (MS, MSHI, MSIS, MSSE, PhD, Advanced Certificate, Certificate, PMC); health informatics (MSHI); information studies (PhD); information systems (MSIS); national security management (MS). *Application deadline:* For fall admission, 8/15 for domestic students, 8/1 for international students; for spring admission, 3/1 for domestic students, 2/1 for international students. Applications are processed on a rolling basis. *Application fee:* $0. Electronic applications accepted. *Application Contact:* Matthew Lechtenberg, Director, Recruitment, 215-895-1951, Fax: 215-895-2303, E-mail: ml333@drexel.edu. *Interim Dean/Professor of Computer Science*, Dr. Spiros Mancoridis, 215-895-6824, Fax: 215-895-0545, E-mail: spiros@drexel.edu.

College of Engineering *Degree program information:* Part-time and evening/weekend programs available. Part-time, evening/weekend. Offers architectural / building systems engineering (PhD); architectural/building systems engineering (MS); biochemical engineering (MS); chemical engineering (MS, PhD); civil engineering (MS, PhD); computer engineering (MS); electrical and computer engineering (PhD); electrical engineering (MSEE); engineering (MS, MSEE, MSSE, PhD, Certificate); engineering management (MS, Certificate); environmental engineering (MS, PhD); geotechnical, geoenvironmental and geosynthetics (MS, PhD); geotechnical, geoenvironmental and geosynthetics engineering (MS, PhD); hydraulics, hydrology and water resources engineering (MS, PhD); materials engineering (MS, PhD); mechanical engineering (MS, PhD); software engineering (MSSE); structures (MS); telecommunications engineering (MSEE). Electronic applications accepted.

College of Medicine *Degree program information:* Part-time programs available. Part-time. Offers medicine (MLAS, MMS, MS, MD, PhD, Certificate). Electronic applications accepted.

Biomedical Graduate Programs *Degree program information:* Part-time programs available. Part-time. Offers biochemistry (MS, PhD); biomedical sciences (MLAS, MMS, MS, PhD, Certificate); drug discovery and development (MS); laboratory animal science (MLAS); medical science (MMS, Certificate); microbiology and immunology (MS, PhD); molecular and cell biology and genetics (MS, PhD); molecular medicine (MS); molecular pathobiology (MS, PhD); neuroscience (MS, PhD); pharmacology and physiology (MS, PhD). Electronic applications accepted.

College of Nursing and Health Professions *Degree program information:* Part-time and evening/weekend programs available. Part-time, evening/weekend. Offers art therapy (MA, PMC); clinical biomechanics and orthopedics (PhD); couple and family therapy (MFT, PhD); creative arts therapies (PhD); dance/movement therapy (MA, PMC); emergency and public safety services (MS); hand and upper quarter rehabilitation (Certificate); hand therapy (MHS, PPDPT); music therapy (MA, PMC); nurse anesthesia (MSN); nursing and health professions (MA, MFT, MHS, MS, MSN, DPT, Dr NP, PPDPT, PhD, Certificate, PMC); nursing studies (Dr NP); orthopedics (MHS, PPDPT); pediatric rehabilitation (Certificate); pediatrics (MHS, PPDPT, PhD); physical therapy (DPT); physician assistant (MHS). Electronic applications accepted.

Division of Graduate Nursing Offers adult acute care (MSN); adult psychiatric/mental health (MSN); advanced practice nursing (MSN); clinical trials research (MSN); family nurse practitioner (MSN); leadership in health systems management (MSN); nursing education (MSN); pediatric primary care (MSN); women's health (MSN). Electronic applications accepted.

Goodwin College of Professional Studies

School of Education *Degree program information:* Part-time and evening/weekend programs available. Part-time, evening/weekend, online learning. Offers applied behavior analysis (MS); creativity and innovation (MS); education improvement and transformation (MS); educational administration (MS); educational leadership and management (Ed D); educational leadership development and learning technologies (PhD); global and international education (MS); higher education (MS); human resources development (MS); learning technologies (MS); mathematics, learning and teaching (MS); special education (MS); teaching, learning and curriculum (MS). Electronic applications accepted.

School of Technology and Professional Studies *Degree program information:* Part-time and evening/weekend programs available. Part-time, evening/weekend. Offers construction management (MS); creativity and innovation (MS); engineering technology (MS); food science (MS); hospitality management (MS); professional studies: creativity studies (MS); professional studies: e-learning leadership (MS); professional studies: homeland security management (MS); project management (MS); property management (MS); sport management (MS). Electronic applications accepted.

LeBow College of Business *Degree program information:* Part-time and evening/weekend programs available. Part-time, evening/weekend. Offers accounting (MS); business (MBA, MS, PhD, APC); business administration (MBA, PhD, APC); finance (MS). Electronic applications accepted.

School of Biomedical Engineering, Science and Health Systems Offers biomedical engineering (MS, PhD); biomedical science (MS, PhD); biostatistics (MS); clinical/rehabilitation engineering (MS). Electronic applications accepted.

School of Journalism Offers journalism (MA).

School of Public Health Offers biostatistics (MS); epidemiology (PhD); epidemiology and biostatistics (Certificate); public health (MPH, MS, PhD, Certificate). Electronic applications accepted.

Westphal College of Media Arts and Design *Degree program information:* Part-time and evening/weekend programs available. Part-time, evening/weekend. Offers arts administration (MS); design research (MS); digital media (MS); fashion design (MS); interior architecture and design (MS); museum leadership (MS); television management (MS). Electronic applications accepted.

DRURY UNIVERSITY, Springfield, MO 65802

General Information Independent, coed, comprehensive institution. *Graduate housing:* Rooms and/or apartments available on a first-come, first-served basis to single and married students. *Research affiliation:* Yale University (child development).

GRADUATE UNITS

Breech School of Business Administration *Degree program information:* Part-time and evening/weekend programs available. Part-time, evening/weekend. Offers business administration (MBA). Electronic applications accepted.

Graduate Programs in Education *Degree program information:* Part-time and evening/weekend programs available. Part-time, evening/weekend. Offers elementary education (M Ed); gifted education (M Ed); human services (M Ed); instructional mathematics K-8 (M Ed); instructional technology (M Ed); middle school teaching (M Ed); secondary education (M Ed); special education (M Ed); special reading (M Ed). Electronic applications accepted.

Hammons School of Architecture Offers architecture (M Arch).

Program in Communication *Degree program information:* Part-time and evening/weekend programs available. Part-time, evening/weekend. Offers communication (MA). Electronic applications accepted.

Program in Criminology/Criminal Justice *Degree program information:* Part-time and evening/weekend programs available. Part-time, evening/weekend. Offers criminal justice (MS); criminology (MA). Electronic applications accepted.

Program in Studio Art and Theory Offers studio art and theory (MA). Electronic applications accepted.

DUKE UNIVERSITY, Durham, NC 27708-0586

General Information Independent-religious, coed, university. CGS member. *Graduate housing:* Rooms and/or apartments available on a first-come, first-served basis to single and married students. Housing application deadline: 5/8. *Research affiliation:* Highlands Biological Station, U.S. Forest Sciences Laboratory, Organization for Tropical Studies.

GRADUATE UNITS

Divinity School *Degree program information:* Part-time programs available. Part-time, online learning. Offers theology (M Div, MACP, MACS, MTS, Th M, D Min, Th D). Electronic applications accepted.

The Fuqua School of Business Students: 1,560 full-time (535 women); includes 348 minority (64 Black or African American, non-Hispanic/Latino; 6 American Indian or Alaska Native, non-Hispanic/Latino; 203 Asian, non-Hispanic/Latino; 71 Hispanic/Latino; 2 Native Hawaiian or other Pacific Islander, non-Hispanic/Latino; 2 Two or more races, non-Hispanic/Latino), 555 international. *Faculty:* 87 full-time (17 women), 47 part-time/adjunct (7 women). *Financial support:* In 2015–16, 641 students received support. Applicants required to submit FAFSA. In 2015, 820 master's, 10 doctorates awarded. Offers academic excellence in finance (Certificate); accounting (PhD); business (EMBA, GEMBA, MBA, MMS, WEMBA, PhD, Certificate); business administration (MBA); decision sciences (MBA, PhD); energy and environment (MBA); energy finance (MBA); entrepreneurship and innovation (MBA); finance (MBA, PhD); financial analysis (MBA); foundations of business (MMS); health sector management (Certificate); leadership and ethics (MBA); management (MBA); management and organizations (PhD); management studies (MMS); marketing (MBA, PhD); operations management (MBA, PhD); social entrepreneurship (MBA); strategy (MBA, PhD). Electronic applications accepted. *Application Contact:* Liz Riley Hargrove, Associate Dean for Admissions, 919-660-7705, Fax: 919-681-8026, E-mail: admissions-info@fuqua.duke.edu. *Dean,* William Boulding, 919-660-7822, Fax: 919-684-8742, E-mail: bb1@duke.edu.

Graduate School *Degree program information:* Part-time and evening/weekend programs available. Part-time, evening/weekend. Offers bioethics and science policy (MA); biological psychology (PhD); biology (PhD); business administration (PhD); cell and molecular biology (Certificate); cell biology (PhD); cellular and molecular biology (PhD); chemistry (PhD); classical studies (PhD); clinical psychology (PhD); cognitive neuroscience (PhD, Certificate); cognitive psychology (PhD); computational biology and bioinformatics (PhD, Certificate); computer science (MS, PhD); crystallography of macromolecules (PhD); developmental and stem cell biology (Certificate); developmental psychology (PhD); East Asian studies (AM, Certificate); ecology (PhD, Certificate); econometrics (MS); economics (AM, PhD); economics and computation (MS); English (PhD); environment (PhD); environmental policy (PhD); enzyme mechanisms (PhD); experimental and documentary arts (MFA); experimental psychology (PhD); financial economics (MS); French (PhD); genetics and genomics (PhD); German studies (PhD); gross anatomy and physical anthropology (PhD); health psychology (PhD); historical and cultural visualization (MA); history (AM, PhD); history of art (PhD); human social development (PhD); humanities (AM); immunology (PhD); integrated toxicology and environmental health (Certificate); Italian (PhD); Latin American studies (PhD); liberal studies (AM); lipid biochemistry (PhD); literature (PhD); marine science and conservation (PhD); mathematics (PhD); medical physics (MS, PhD); membrane structure and function (PhD); molecular cancer biology (PhD); molecular genetics (PhD); molecular genetics and microbiology (PhD); music composition (PhD); musicology (PhD); neuroanatomy (PhD); neurobiology (PhD); neurochemistry (PhD); nucleic acid structure and function (PhD); pathology (PhD); performance practice (PhD); pharmacology (PhD); philosophy (PhD); physical anthropology (PhD); physics (PhD); political science (AM, PhD); protein structure and function (PhD); public policy (PhD); religion (MA, PhD); Slavic and Eurasian studies (AM, Certificate); social/cultural anthropology (PhD); sociology (AM, PhD); Spanish (PhD); statistical science (MSS, PhD); structural biology and biophysics (Certificate); teaching (MAT). Electronic applications accepted.

Division of Earth and Ocean Sciences *Degree program information:* Part-time programs available. Part-time. Offers earth and ocean sciences (MS, PhD). Electronic applications accepted.

Duke Global Health Institute Offers global health (MS).

Pratt School of Engineering *Degree program information:* Part-time programs available. Part-time, online learning. Offers biomedical engineering (MS, PhD); civil and environmental engineering (MS, PhD); civil engineering (M Eng); electrical and computer engineering (M Eng); engineering (M Eng, MEM, MS, PhD); engineering management (MEM); environmental engineering (M Eng, MS, PhD); materials science (MS, PhD); materials science and engineering (M Eng); mechanical engineering (M Eng, MS, PhD); photonics and optical sciences (M Eng).

Nicholas School of the Environment Online learning. Offers environment (PhD); environmental management (MEM); forestry (MF). Application deadline for PhD program is December 8. Electronic applications accepted.

Sanford School of Public Policy Offers international development policy (MIDP); public policy (MIDP, MPP). Electronic applications accepted.

School of Law Students: 668 full-time, 18 part-time; includes 164 minority (46 Black or African American, non-Hispanic/Latino; 2 American Indian or Alaska Native, non-Hispanic/Latino; 75 Asian, non-Hispanic/Latino; 34 Hispanic/Latino; 2 Native Hawaiian or other Pacific Islander, non-Hispanic/Latino; 5 Two or more races, non-Hispanic/Latino), 49 international. Average age 24. 4,819 applicants, 23% accepted, 225 enrolled. *Faculty:* 86 full-time (40 women), 31 part-time/adjunct (10 women). *Financial support:* In 2015–16, 560 students received support. Institutionally sponsored loans, scholarships/grants, and unspecified assistantships available. Financial award application deadline: 3/15; financial award applicants required to submit FAFSA. In 2015, 139 master's, 210 doctorates awarded. Offers law (LL M, MJS, MLS, JD, SJD). LL M and SJD offered only to international students; MJS offered only to sitting judges. *Application deadline:* For fall admission, 2/15 for domestic and international students. Applications are processed on a rolling basis. *Application fee:* $70. Electronic applications accepted. *Application Contact:* William J. Hoye, Associate Dean for Admissions and Student Affairs, 919-613-7020, Fax: 919-613-7257, E-mail: hoye@law.duke.edu. *Dean/Professor of Law,* David F. Levi, 919-613-7001, Fax: 919-613-7158.

School of Medicine Students: 974 full-time (561 women), 82 part-time (43 women); includes 359 minority (86 Black or African American, non-Hispanic/Latino; 16 American Indian or Alaska Native, non-Hispanic/Latino; 210 Asian, non-Hispanic/Latino; 42 Hispanic/Latino; 5 Two or more races, non-Hispanic/Latino), 39 international. 9,766 applicants, 7% accepted, 433 enrolled. *Faculty:* 1,530 full-time (528 women), 96 part-time/adjunct (44 women). *Financial support:* In 2015–16, 409 students received support. Institutionally sponsored loans and scholarships/grants available. Financial award application deadline: 5/1; financial award applicants required to submit FAFSA. In 2015, 131 master's, 150 doctorates awarded. *Degree program information:* Part-time programs available. Part-time. Offers biomedical sciences (MS); biostatistics (MS); clinical informatics (MS); clinical leadership (MHS); clinical research (MHS); medicine (MHS, MS, DPT, MD); pathologists' assistant (MHS); physician assistant (MHS). *Application Contact:* Andrea Lanahan, Director of Admissions, 919-684-2985, Fax: 919-684-8893, E-mail: medadm@mc.duke.edu. *Vice Dean, Medical Education,* Dr. Edward G. Buckley, 919-668-3381, Fax: 919-660-7040, E-mail: buckl002@mc.duke.edu.

Physical Therapy Division Students: 212 full-time (148 women); includes 24 minority (6 Black or African American, non-Hispanic/Latino; 1 American Indian or Alaska Native, non-Hispanic/Latino; 8 Asian, non-Hispanic/Latino; 9 Hispanic/Latino), 2 international. 964 applicants, 13% accepted, 74 enrolled. *Faculty:* 17 full-time (9 women), 6 part-time/adjunct (5 women). *Financial support:* In 2015–16, 11 students received support. Application deadline: 5/1; applicants required to submit FAFSA. In 2015, 61 doctorates awarded. Offers physical therapy (DPT). *Application deadline:* For fall admission, 11/1 priority date for domestic and international students. Applications are processed on a rolling basis. *Application fee:* $50. Electronic applications accepted. *Application Contact:* Mya Shackleford, Admissions Coordinator, 919-668-5206, Fax: 919-684-1846, E-mail: mya.shackleford@duke.edu. *Program Director,* Dr. Chad Cook, 919-684-8905, Fax: 919-684-1846, E-mail: chad.cook@duke.edu.

School of Nursing Students: 179 full-time (152 women), 528 part-time (466 women); includes 145 minority (42 Black or African American, non-Hispanic/Latino; 3 American Indian or Alaska Native, non-Hispanic/Latino; 44 Asian, non-Hispanic/Latino; 35 Hispanic/Latino; 1 Native Hawaiian or other Pacific Islander, non-Hispanic/Latino; 20 Two or more races, non-Hispanic/Latino), 7 international. Average age 33. 619 applicants, 46% accepted, 201 enrolled. *Faculty:* 74 full-time (63 women). *Financial support:* Career-related internships or fieldwork, institutionally sponsored loans, scholarships/grants, traineeships, and tuition waivers (partial) available. Support available to part-time students. Financial award applicants required to submit FAFSA. In 2015, 243 master's, 62 doctorates, 26 other advanced degrees awarded. *Degree program information:* Part-time and evening/weekend programs available. Part-time, evening/weekend, online learning. Offers acute care pediatric nurse practitioner (MSN, Post Master's Certificate); adult-gerontology nurse practitioner (MSN, Post Master's Certificate); family nurse practitioner (MSN, Post Master's Certificate); neonatal nurse practitioner (MSN, Post Master's Certificate); nurse anesthesia (DNP); nurse practitioner (DNP); nursing (MSN, DNP, PhD, Post Master's Certificate); nursing and health care leadership (MSN); nursing education (MSN); nursing informatics (MSN, Post Master's Certificate); pediatric nurse practitioner (MSN, Post Master's Certificate); women's health nurse practitioner (MSN, Post Master's Certificate). *Application deadline:* For fall admission, 12/1 for domestic and international students; for spring admission, 5/1 for domestic and international students. *Application fee:* $50. Electronic applications accepted. *Application Contact:* Dr. Ernie Rushing, Director of Admissions and Recruitment, 919-668-6274, Fax: 919-668-4693, E-mail: ernie.rushing@dm.duke.edu. *Dean/Vice Chancellor for Nursing Affairs/Associate Vice President for Academic Affairs for Nursing,* Dr. Marion E. Broome, 919-684-9446, Fax: 919-684-9414, E-mail: marion.broome@duke.edu.

DUNLAP-STONE UNIVERSITY, Phoenix, AZ 85024

General Information Proprietary, coed, comprehensive institution.

GRADUATE UNITS

Graduate Law Center Offers regulatory trade compliance (M Sc); U.S. regulatory trade law (LL M).

DUQUESNE UNIVERSITY, Pittsburgh, PA 15282-0001

General Information Independent-religious, coed, university. CGS member. *Enrollment:* 9,404 graduate, professional, and undergraduate students; 2,846 full-time matriculated graduate/professional students (1,737 women), 573 part-time matriculated graduate/professional students (342 women). *Enrollment by degree level:* 1,443 master's, 1,927 doctoral, 49 other advanced degrees. *Graduate faculty:* 447 full-time (191 women), 496 part-time/adjunct (214 women). *Tuition, area resident:* Full-time $21,402; part-time $1189 per credit. Tuition and fees vary according to program. *Graduate housing:* Rooms and/or apartments available on a first-come, first-served basis to single and married students. Housing application deadline: 5/1. *Student services:* Campus employment opportunities, campus safety program, career counseling, child daycare facilities, exercise/wellness program, free psychological counseling, international student services, low-cost health insurance, multicultural affairs office, services for students with disabilities, teacher training, writing training. *Library:* Gumberg Library. *Collection:* Books: 648,583 (physical), 162,924 (digital/electronic); Serial titles: 107,061 (physical), 203 (digital/electronic); Databases: 201. Weekly public service hours: 111; students can reserve study rooms.

Computer facilities: Computer purchase and lease plans are available. 1,000 computers available on campus for general student use. A campuswide network can be accessed from student residence rooms and from off campus. Online class registration is available.
Website: http://www.duq.edu/

General Application Contact: Todd Eicker, Director of Graduate Admission, 412-396-6219, E-mail: eickert@duq.edu.

GRADUATE UNITS

Bayer School of Natural and Environmental Sciences Students: 112 full-time (58 women), 24 part-time (16 women); includes 12 minority (1 Black or African American, non-Hispanic/Latino; 5 Asian, non-Hispanic/Latino; 2 Hispanic/Latino; 4 Two or more races, non-Hispanic/Latino), 28 international. Average age 27. 174 applicants, 43% accepted, 39 enrolled. *Faculty:* 39 full-time (12 women), 29 part-time/adjunct (11 women). *Financial support:* In 2015–16, 119 students received support, including 3 fellowships with full tuition reimbursements available, 18 research assistantships with full tuition reimbursements available, 54 teaching assistantships with full tuition reimbursements available; career-related internships or fieldwork, scholarships/grants, tuition waivers (partial), and unspecified assistantships also available. Financial award application deadline: 5/31. In 2015, 42 master's, 15 doctorates awarded. *Degree program information:* Part-time programs available. Part-time. Offers biological sciences (PhD); biotechnology (MS); chemistry (PhD); environmental science and management (MS, Certificate); forensic science and law (MS); natural and environmental sciences (MS, PhD, Certificate). *Application deadline:* For fall admission, 2/15 priority date for domestic students, 2/15 for international students; for spring admission, 10/1 priority date for domestic students, 10/1 for international students. Applications are processed on a rolling basis. *Application fee:* $0. Electronic applications accepted. *Application Contact:* Heather Costello, Senior Graduate Academic Advisor, 412-396-6339, Fax: 412-396-4881, E-mail: costelloh@duq.edu. *Dean,* Dr. Philip Reeder, 412-396-4877, Fax: 412-396-4881, E-mail: reederp@duq.edu.

Graduate School of Liberal Arts Students: 539 full-time (270 women), 143 part-time (79 women); includes 119 minority (74 Black or African American, non-Hispanic/Latino; 11 Asian, non-Hispanic/Latino; 16 Hispanic/Latino; 1 Native Hawaiian or other Pacific Islander, non-Hispanic/Latino; 17 Two or more races, non-Hispanic/Latino), 95 international. Average age 33. 664 applicants, 44% accepted, 149 enrolled. *Faculty:* 134 full-time (49 women), 37 part-time/adjunct (18 women). *Financial support:* In 2015–16, 14 research assistantships with tuition reimbursements (averaging $11,000 per year), 121 teaching assistantships with tuition reimbursements (averaging $13,600 per year) were awarded; career-related internships or fieldwork, Federal Work-Study, institutionally sponsored loans, scholarships/grants, and tuition waivers (full and partial) also available. Support available to part-time students. Financial award application deadline: 5/1. In 2015, 304 master's, 36 doctorates, 1 other advanced degree awarded. *Degree program information:* Part-time and evening/weekend programs available. Part-time, evening/weekend. Offers clinical psychology (PhD); communication (MA); computational mathematics (MA, MS); English (MA, PhD); historical studies (MA); journalism and media arts (MS, Certificate); leadership (MS); liberal arts (MA, MS, DHCE, PhD, Certificate); pastoral ministry (MA); philosophy (MA, PhD); public history (MA); religious education (MA); rhetoric (PhD); systematic theology (PhD); theology (MA). *Application deadline:* For fall admission, 8/1 for domestic students, 5/1 for international students; for spring admission, 11/1 for domestic students, 9/1 for international students. Applications are processed on a rolling basis. *Application fee:* $0. Electronic applications accepted. *Application Contact:* Linda Rendulic, Assistant to the Dean, 412-396-6400, Fax: 412-396-5197, E-mail: rendulic@duq.edu. *Dean,* Dr. James Swindal, 412-396-6400.

Center for Healthcare Ethics Students: 47 full-time (24 women), 4 part-time (all women); includes 9 minority (6 Black or African American, non-Hispanic/Latino; 3 Asian, non-Hispanic/Latino), 16 international. Average age 38. 21 applicants, 67% accepted, 10 enrolled. *Faculty:* 3 full-time (0 women). *Financial support:* In 2015–16, 6 teaching assistantships (averaging $18,000 per year) were awarded; Federal Work-Study and tuition waivers (full and partial) also available. Support available to part-time students. Financial award application deadline: 5/1. In 2015, 8 doctorates awarded. *Degree program information:* Part-time programs available. Part-time, 100% online. Offers healthcare ethics (MA, DHCE, PhD, Certificate). *Application deadline:* For fall admission, 8/1 for domestic students, 5/1 for international students. *Application fee:* $0. Electronic applications accepted. *Application Contact:* Linda Rendulic, Assistant to the Dean, 412-396-6400, Fax: 412-396-5197, E-mail: rendulic@duq.edu. *Director,* Dr. Henk Ten Have, 412-396-1585, E-mail: tenhaveh@duq.edu.

Graduate Center for Social and Public Policy Students: 17 full-time (13 women), 3 part-time (2 women); includes 6 minority (2 Black or African American, non-Hispanic/Latino; 1 Asian, non-Hispanic/Latino; 1 Hispanic/Latino; 2 Two or more races, non-Hispanic/Latino). Average age 28. 36 applicants, 33% accepted, 5 enrolled. *Faculty:* 6 full-time (2 women), 1 (woman) part-time/adjunct. *Financial support:* In 2015–16, 20 students received support, including 8 teaching assistantships with tuition reimbursements available (averaging $10,000 per year); career-related internships or fieldwork, institutionally sponsored loans, scholarships/grants, tuition waivers (full and partial), and unspecified assistantships also available. Support available to part-time students. Financial award application deadline: 5/1. In 2015, 9 master's awarded. *Degree program information:* Part-time and evening/weekend programs available. Part-time, evening/weekend. Offers conflict resolution and peace studies (Certificate); social and public policy (MA, Certificate). *Application deadline:* For fall admission, 4/30 priority date for domestic and international students; for spring admission, 11/1 priority date for domestic and international students. Applications are processed on a rolling basis. *Application fee:* $0. Electronic applications accepted. *Application Contact:* Linda Rendulic, Assistant to the Dean, 412-396-6400, Fax: 412-396-5197, E-mail: rendulic@duq.edu. *Director,* Dr. Michael Irwin, 412-396-6488, E-mail: irwinm@duq.edu.

John F. Donahue Graduate School of Business Students: 82 full-time (33 women), 163 part-time (63 women); includes 13 minority (5 Black or African American, non-Hispanic/Latino; 4 Asian, non-Hispanic/Latino; 3 Hispanic/Latino; 1 Two or more races, non-Hispanic/Latino), 31 international. Average age 28. 331 applicants, 56% accepted, 100 enrolled. *Faculty:* 54 full-time (19 women), 35 part-time/adjunct (10 women). *Financial support:* In 2015–16, 211 students received support, including 12 fellowships with partial tuition reimbursements available (averaging $14,200 per year), 20 research assistantships with partial tuition reimbursements available (averaging $19,853 per year); career-related internships or fieldwork, scholarships/grants, and unspecified assistantships also available. Support available to part-time students. Financial award application deadline: 7/1; financial award applicants required to submit FAFSA. In 2015, 131 master's awarded. *Degree program information:* Part-time and evening/weekend programs available. Part-time, evening/weekend, minimal on-campus study. Offers accounting (M Acc); finance (MBA); information systems management (MSISM); management (MBA); marketing (MBA); sustainability (MBA). *Application deadline:* For fall admission, 7/1 priority date for domestic and international students; for spring admission, 12/1 for domestic and international students; for summer admission, 4/1 for domestic and international students. Applications are processed on a rolling basis. *Application fee:* $0. Electronic applications accepted. *Application Contact:* Maria DeCrosta, Enrollment Manager, 412-396-5529, Fax: 412-396-1726, E-mail: decrostam@duq.edu. *Associate Dean of Graduate Programs and Executive Education,* Dr. Karen Donovan, 412-396-6276, Fax: 412-396-1726, E-mail: donovan6@duq.edu.

John G. Rangos, Sr. School of Health Sciences Students: 230 full-time (180 women), 11 part-time (5 women); includes 15 minority (1 Black or African American, non-Hispanic/Latino; 3 Asian, non-Hispanic/Latino; 7 Hispanic/Latino; 4 Two or more races, non-Hispanic/Latino), 20 international. Average age 23. 685 applicants, 9% accepted, 24 enrolled. *Faculty:* 45 full-time (32 women), 33 part-time/adjunct (17 women). *Financial support:* Federal Work-Study available. Financial award applicants required to submit FAFSA. In 2015, 132 master's, 32 doctorates awarded. Minimal on-campus study. Offers health management systems (MHMS); occupational therapy (MS, OTD); physical therapy (DPT); physician assistant studies (MPAS); rehabilitation science (MS, PhD); speech-language pathology (MS). *Application deadline:* For fall admission, 2/1 for domestic and international students; for spring admission, 7/1 for domestic and international students. Applications are processed on a rolling basis. *Application fee:* $0. Electronic applications accepted. *Application Contact:* Christopher R. Hilf, Recruiter/Academic Advisor, 412-396-5653, Fax: 412-396-5554, E-mail: hilfc@duq.edu. *Dean,* Dr. Gregory H. Frazer, 412-396-5303, Fax: 412-396-5554, E-mail: frazer@duq.edu.

Mary Pappert School of Music Students: 68 full-time (28 women), 14 part-time (5 women); includes 9 minority (1 Black or African American, non-Hispanic/Latino; 1 Asian, non-Hispanic/Latino; 4 Hispanic/Latino; 3 Two or more races, non-Hispanic/Latino), 23 international. Average age 26. 137 applicants, 65% accepted, 42 enrolled. *Faculty:* 26 full-time (9 women), 80 part-time/adjunct (23 women). *Financial support:* In 2015–16, 61 students received support, including 56 fellowships with tuition reimbursements available (averaging $16,007 per year); scholarships/grants, tuition waivers (full and partial), and unspecified assistantships also available. Financial award application deadline: 4/1. In 2015, 22 master's, 8 ADs awarded. *Degree program information:* Part-time programs available. Part-time. Offers music education (MM). *Application deadline:* For fall admission, 7/1 priority date for domestic and international students; for spring admission, 12/1 priority date for domestic and international students; for summer admission, 6/1 priority date for domestic students, 5/1 priority date for international students. Applications are processed on a rolling basis. *Application fee:* $50. Electronic applications accepted. *Application Contact:* Peggy Eiseman, Administrative Assistant of Admissions, 412-396-5064, Fax: 412-396-5719, E-mail: eiseman@duq.edu. *Dean,* Dr. Seth Beckman, 412-396-6082, Fax: 412-396-1524, E-mail: beckmans@duq.edu.

Mylan School of Pharmacy Students: 769 full-time (468 women), 41 part-time (22 women); includes 66 minority (17 Black or African American, non-Hispanic/Latino; 31 Asian, non-Hispanic/Latino; 10 Hispanic/Latino; 8 Two or more races, non-Hispanic/Latino), 52 international. Average age 23. 523 applicants, 45% accepted, 203 enrolled. *Faculty:* 48 full-time (22 women), 4 part-time/adjunct (0 women). *Financial support:* In 2015–16, 927 students received support, including 14 research assistantships with full tuition reimbursements available, 43 teaching assistantships with full tuition reimbursements available; Federal Work-Study also available. In 2015, 2 master's, 177 doctorates awarded. *Degree program information:* Evening/weekend programs available. Evening/weekend. Offers pharmacy (MS, PhD, Pharm D). *Application deadline:* For fall admission, 2/1 for domestic and international students; for spring admission, 10/1 for domestic and international students. Applications are processed on a rolling basis. *Application fee:* $50. Electronic applications accepted. *Dean,* Dr. J. Douglas Bricker, 412-396-6377, Fax: 412-396-5130.

Graduate School of Pharmaceutical Sciences Students: 62 full-time (28 women), 1 part-time (0 women); includes 2 minority (1 Asian, non-Hispanic/Latino; 1 Hispanic/Latino), 43 international. Average age 27. 215 applicants, 23% accepted, 8 enrolled. *Faculty:* 22 full-time (7 women). *Financial support:* In 2015–16, 57 students received support, including 14 research assistantships with full tuition reimbursements available, 43 teaching assistantships with full tuition reimbursements available; unspecified assistantships also available. In 2015, 2 master's, 8 doctorates awarded. Offers medicinal chemistry (MS, PhD); pharmaceutics (MS, PhD); pharmacology (MS, PhD); pharmacy administration (MS). *Application deadline:* For fall admission, 2/1 priority date for domestic and international students; for spring admission, 10/1 priority date for domestic and international students. Applications are processed on a rolling basis. *Application fee:* $50. Electronic applications accepted. *Application Contact:* Information Contact, 412-396-1172, E-mail: gsps-adm@duq.edu. *Associate Dean for Research and Graduate Programs,* Dr. James K. Drennen, III, 412-396-5520.

Post-Baccalaureate Pre-Medical and Health Professions Program Offers pre-medical studies and health professions (Postbaccalaureate Certificate).

School of Education Students: 487 full-time (352 women), 63 part-time (51 women); includes 75 minority (47 Black or African American, non-Hispanic/Latino; 4 Asian, non-Hispanic/Latino; 9 Hispanic/Latino; 15 Two or more races, non-Hispanic/Latino), 49 international. Average age 31. 577 applicants, 54% accepted, 159 enrolled. *Faculty:* 52 full-time (31 women), 83 part-time/adjunct (63 women). *Financial support:* Research assistantships, teaching assistantships with tuition reimbursements, career-related internships or fieldwork, Federal Work-Study, institutionally sponsored loans, and tuition waivers available. Support available to part-time students. In 2015, 191 master's, 39 doctorates awarded. *Degree program information:* Part-time and evening/weekend programs available. Part-time, evening/weekend, 100% online. Offers biology (MS Ed); chemistry (MS Ed); child psychology (MS Ed); clinical mental health counseling (MS Ed, Post-Master's Certificate); cognitive, behavior, physical/health disabilities (MS Ed); community and special education support (MS Ed); counselor education (MS Ed, Ed D, Post-Master's Certificate); counselor education and supervision (Ed D); counselor licensure (Post-Master's Certificate); curriculum and instruction (Post-Master's Certificate); early level (PreK-4) education (MS Ed); education (MS Ed, Ed D, PhD, Psy D, CAGS, Post-Master's Certificate); educational leadership (Ed D); educational studies (MS Ed); English (MS Ed); English as a second language (MS Ed); instructional technology (MS Ed, Ed D, Post-Master's Certificate); K-12 education (MS Ed); marriage and family counseling (MS Ed); mathematics (MS Ed); middle level (4-8) education (MS Ed); physics (MS Ed); program evaluation (MS Ed); reading and language arts (MS Ed); school administration and supervision (MS Ed, Post-Master's Certificate); school administration K-12 (MS Ed, Post-Master's Certificate); school counseling

(MS Ed); school psychology (MS Ed, PhD, Psy D); school supervision (MS Ed); secondary education (MS Ed); social studies (MS Ed); special education (MS Ed, PhD); special education 7-12 (MS Ed); special education PreK-8 (MS Ed). *Application deadline:* For fall admission, 3/1 for domestic students; for spring admission, 9/1 for domestic students. Applications are processed on a rolling basis. *Application fee:* $0. Electronic applications accepted. *Application Contact:* Michael Dolinger, Director of Student and Academic Services, 412-396-6647, Fax: 412-396-5585, E-mail: dolingerm@duq.edu. *Dean*, Dr. Olga Welch, 412-396-6102, Fax: 412-396-5585.

School of Law Students: 307 full-time (160 women), 96 part-time (50 women); includes 26 minority (5 Black or African American, non-Hispanic/Latino; 5 Asian, non-Hispanic/Latino; 7 Hispanic/Latino; 9 Two or more races, non-Hispanic/Latino), 3 international. Average age 26. 718 applicants, 64% accepted, 130 enrolled. *Faculty:* 28 full-time (13 women), 32 part-time/adjunct (9 women). *Financial support:* Research assistantships with partial tuition reimbursements, teaching assistantships with partial tuition reimbursements, career-related internships or fieldwork, scholarships/grants, and tuition waivers (partial) available. Support available to part-time students. Financial award application deadline: 5/31; financial award applicants required to submit FAFSA. In 2015, 5 master's, 145 doctorates awarded. *Degree program information:* Part-time and evening/weekend programs available. Part-time, evening/weekend. Offers American law for foreign lawyers (LL M); law (JD). JD/M Div offered jointly with Pittsburgh Theological Seminary. *Application deadline:* For fall admission, 3/1 priority date for domestic and international students. Applications are processed on a rolling basis. *Application fee:* $0. Electronic applications accepted. *Application Contact:* Office of Admissions, 412-396-6296, Fax: 412-396-6659, E-mail: lawadmissions@duq.edu. *Interim Dean*, Nancy Perkins, 412-396-6285, Fax: 412-396-6283, E-mail: perkins@duq.edu.

School of Nursing Students: 148 full-time (135 women), 114 part-time (101 women); includes 49 minority (28 Black or African American, non-Hispanic/Latino; 5 Asian, non-Hispanic/Latino; 11 Hispanic/Latino; 5 Two or more races, non-Hispanic/Latino), 4 international. Average age 38. 383 applicants, 33% accepted, 97 enrolled. *Faculty:* 17 full-time (14 women), 10 part-time/adjunct (9 women). *Financial support:* In 2015–16, 60 students received support, including 5 research assistantships with partial tuition reimbursements available (averaging $2,200 per year), 8 teaching assistantships with partial tuition reimbursements available (averaging $1,100 per year); institutionally sponsored loans, scholarships/grants, traineeships, tuition waivers (partial), and unspecified assistantships also available. Support available to part-time students. Financial award application deadline: 7/1; financial award applicants required to submit FAFSA. In 2015, 39 master's, 37 doctorates, 1 other advanced degree awarded. *Degree program information:* Part-time and evening/weekend programs available. Part-time, evening/weekend, minimal on-campus study. Offers family (individual across the life span) nurse practitioner (MSN, Post-Master's Certificate); forensic nursing (MSN, Post-Master's Certificate); nursing (MSN, DNP, PhD, Post-Master's Certificate); nursing education (MSN); nursing education and faculty role (Post-Master's Certificate); nursing practice (DNP). *Application deadline:* For summer admission, 3/1 for domestic and international students. *Application fee:* $0. Electronic applications accepted. *Application Contact:* Susan Hardner, Nurse Recruiter, 412-396-4945, Fax: 412-396-6346, E-mail: nursing@duq.edu. *Dean/Professor*, Dr. Mary Ellen Glasgow, 412-396-6554, Fax: 412-396-5974, E-mail: glasgowm@duq.edu.

D'YOUVILLE COLLEGE, Buffalo, NY 14201-1084

General Information Independent, coed, comprehensive institution. *Enrollment:* 2,909 graduate, professional, and undergraduate students; 837 full-time matriculated graduate/professional students (522 women), 257 part-time matriculated graduate/professional students (199 women). *Enrollment by degree level:* 481 master's, 538 doctoral, 25 other advanced degrees. *Tuition, area resident:* Full-time $21,120; part-time $880 per credit hour. *Required fees:* $235; $96. One-time fee: $100. *Graduate housing:* Room and/or apartments available on a first-come, first-served basis to single students. Housing application deadline: 8/1. *Student services:* Campus employment opportunities, campus safety program, career counseling, exercise/wellness program, free psychological counseling, grant writing training, international student services, low-cost health insurance, multicultural affairs office, services for students with disabilities, writing training. *Library:* Montante Family Library.

Computer facilities: 120 computers available on campus for general student use. A campuswide network can be accessed from student residence rooms and from off campus. Online class registration is available.
Website: http://www.dyc.edu/

General Application Contact: Mark Pavone, Graduate Admissions Director, 716-829-8400, Fax: 716-829-7900, E-mail: graduateadmissions@dyc.edu.

GRADUATE UNITS

Department of Business Students: 58 full-time (23 women), 18 part-time (7 women); includes 19 minority (8 Black or African American, non-Hispanic/Latino; 5 Asian, non-Hispanic/Latino; 6 Hispanic/Latino), 9 international. Average age 29. 47 applicants, 94% accepted, 25 enrolled. *Faculty:* 5 full-time (2 women), 12 part-time/adjunct (5 women). *Financial support:* Career-related internships or fieldwork, Federal Work-Study, and scholarships/grants available. Support available to part-time students. Financial award application deadline: 3/1; financial award applicants required to submit FAFSA. In 2015, 27 master's awarded. *Degree program information:* Part-time and evening/weekend programs available. Part-time, evening/weekend. Offers business administration (MBA); international business (MS). *Application deadline:* For fall admission, 5/1 priority date for international students; for spring admission, 9/1 priority date for international students. Applications are processed on a rolling basis. Electronic applications accepted. *Application Contact:* Mark Pavone, Graduate Admissions Director, 716-829-8400, Fax: 716-829-7900, E-mail: graduateadmissions@dyc.edu. *Chair/Associate Professor*, Dr. Susan Kowalewski, 716-829-7839, Fax: 716-829-7660, E-mail: kowalews@dyc.edu.

Department of Chiropractic Students: 80 full-time (32 women), 3 part-time (1 woman); includes 5 minority (1 Black or African American, non-Hispanic/Latino; 1 Asian, non-Hispanic/Latino; 3 Hispanic/Latino), 22 international. Average age 26. 74 applicants, 77% accepted, 28 enrolled. In 2015, 27 doctorates awarded. Offers chiropractic (DC). *Application deadline:* Applications are processed on a rolling basis. Electronic applications accepted. *Application Contact:* Mark Pavone, Graduate Admissions Director, 716-829-8400, Fax: 716-829-7900, E-mail: graduateadmissions@dyc.edu. *Acting Executive Director, Chiropractic Department*, Dr. Jeffrey Ware, 716-829-8448, Fax: 716-829-7893.

Department of Dietetics Students: 92 full-time (82 women), 16 part-time (15 women); includes 13 minority (4 Black or African American, non-Hispanic/Latino; 4 Asian, non-Hispanic/Latino; 1 Hispanic/Latino; 4 Two or more races, non-Hispanic/Latino), 10 international. Average age 24. 69 applicants, 90% accepted, 31 enrolled. In 2015, 22 master's awarded. Offers dietetics (MS). Five-year program begins at freshman entry. *Application deadline:* For fall admission, 5/1 priority date for international students; for spring admission, 9/1 priority date for international students. Applications are processed on a rolling basis. Electronic applications accepted. *Application Contact:* Dr. Steven Smith, Director of Admissions, 716-829-7600, Fax: 716-829-7900, E-mail: admissons@dyc.edu. *Chair*, Dr. Charlotte Baumgart, 716-829-7752, Fax: 716-829-8137.

Department of Education Students: 73 full-time (61 women), 26 part-time (17 women); includes 12 minority (9 Black or African American, non-Hispanic/Latino; 1 American Indian or Alaska Native, non-Hispanic/Latino; 1 Asian, non-Hispanic/Latino; 1 Hispanic/Latino), 33 international. Average age 31. 116 applicants, 96% accepted, 48 enrolled. *Financial support:* Career-related internships or fieldwork, Federal Work-Study, institutionally sponsored loans, scholarships/grants, tuition waivers (full and partial), and unspecified assistantships available. Support available to part-time students. Financial award application deadline: 3/1; financial award applicants required to submit FAFSA. In 2015, 61 master's, 8 doctorates awarded. *Degree program information:* Part-time and evening/weekend programs available. Part-time, evening/weekend. Offers educational leadership (Ed D); elementary education (MS Ed); secondary education (MS Ed); special education (MS Ed). *Application deadline:* For fall admission, 5/1 priority date for international students; for spring admission, 9/1 priority date for international students. Applications are processed on a rolling basis. Electronic applications accepted. *Application Contact:* Mark Pavone, Graduate Admissions Director, 716-829-8400, Fax: 716-829-7900, E-mail: graduateadmissions@dyc.edu. *Chair*, Dr. Hilary Lochte, 716-829-8110, Fax: 716-829-7660.

Department of Health Services Administration Students: 17 full-time (9 women), 68 part-time (50 women); includes 25 minority (20 Black or African American, non-Hispanic/Latino; 2 American Indian or Alaska Native, non-Hispanic/Latino; 1 Asian, non-Hispanic/Latino; 2 Hispanic/Latino), 13 international. Average age 37. 51 applicants, 84% accepted, 25 enrolled. *Financial support:* Career-related internships or fieldwork, Federal Work-Study, and scholarships/grants available. Support available to part-time students. Financial award application deadline: 3/1; financial award applicants required to submit FAFSA. In 2015, 10 master's, 2 doctorates awarded. *Degree program information:* Part-time and evening/weekend programs available. Part-time, evening/weekend. Offers clinical research associate (Certificate); health administration (Ed D); health services administration (MS, Certificate); long term care administration (Certificate). *Application deadline:* For fall admission, 5/1 priority date for international students; for spring admission, 9/1 priority date for international students. Applications are processed on a rolling basis. Electronic applications accepted. *Application Contact:* Mark Pavone, Graduate Admissions Director, 716-829-8400, Fax: 716-829-7900, E-mail: graduateadmissions@dyc.edu. *Chair*, Dr. Lisa Rafalson, 716-829-8489, Fax: 716-829-8184.

Department of Physical Therapy Students: 160 full-time (91 women), 4 part-time (2 women); includes 20 minority (6 Black or African American, non-Hispanic/Latino; 1 American Indian or Alaska Native, non-Hispanic/Latino; 9 Asian, non-Hispanic/Latino; 3 Hispanic/Latino; 1 Two or more races, non-Hispanic/Latino), 27 international. Average age 25. 368 applicants, 26% accepted, 57 enrolled. *Financial support:* Federal Work-Study and scholarships/grants available. Financial award application deadline: 3/1; financial award applicants required to submit FAFSA. In 2015, 49 doctorates awarded. *Degree program information:* Part-time programs available. Part-time, online learning. Offers advanced orthopedic physical therapy (Certificate); manual physical therapy (Certificate); physical therapy (DPT). *Application deadline:* For fall admission, 5/1 priority date for international students; for spring admission, 9/1 priority date for international students. Applications are processed on a rolling basis. Electronic applications accepted. *Application Contact:* Mark Pavone, Graduate Admissions Director, 716-829-8400, Fax: 716-829-7900, E-mail: graduateadmissions@dyc.edu. *Chair*, Dr. Lynn Rivers, 716-829-7708, Fax: 716-829-8137, E-mail: riversl@dyc.edu.

Occupational Therapy Department Students: 262 full-time (242 women), 29 part-time (26 women); includes 33 minority (11 Black or African American, non-Hispanic/Latino; 1 American Indian or Alaska Native, non-Hispanic/Latino; 9 Asian, non-Hispanic/Latino; 7 Hispanic/Latino; 5 Two or more races, non-Hispanic/Latino), 9 international. Average age 23. 361 applicants, 44% accepted, 81 enrolled. *Financial support:* Scholarships/grants, tuition waivers (partial), and unspecified assistantships available. In 2015, 70 master's awarded. Offers occupational therapy (MS). *Application deadline:* For fall admission, 5/1 priority date for international students; for spring admission, 9/1 priority date for international students. Applications are processed on a rolling basis. Electronic applications accepted. *Application Contact:* Mark Pavone, Graduate Admissions Director, 716-829-8400, Fax: 716-829-7900, E-mail: graduateadmissions@dyc.edu. *Chair*, Dr. Theresa Vallone, 716-829-7831, Fax: 716-829-8137.

Physician Assistant Department Students: 154 full-time (95 women), 15 part-time (10 women); includes 20 minority (5 Black or African American, non-Hispanic/Latino; 2 American Indian or Alaska Native, non-Hispanic/Latino; 3 Asian, non-Hispanic/Latino; 7 Hispanic/Latino; 3 Two or more races, non-Hispanic/Latino), 4 international. Average age 25. 230 applicants, 29% accepted, 55 enrolled. In 2015, 35 master's awarded. Offers physician assistant (MS). *Application deadline:* For fall admission, 5/1 priority date for international students; for spring admission, 9/1 priority date for international students. Applications are processed on a rolling basis. Electronic applications accepted. *Application Contact:* Dr. Stephen Smith, Admissions Director, 716-829-7600, Fax: 716-829-7900, E-mail: admissions@dyc.edu. *Chair*, Dr. Maureen F. Finney, 716-829-7712, E-mail: andreeff@dyc.edu.

School of Nursing Students: 75 full-time (70 women), 136 part-time (119 women); includes 21 minority (12 Black or African American, non-Hispanic/Latino; 1 American Indian or Alaska Native, non-Hispanic/Latino; 6 Asian, non-Hispanic/Latino; 2 Hispanic/Latino), 64 international. Average age 35. 197 applicants, 88% accepted, 119 enrolled. *Faculty:* 36 full-time (35 women), 15 part-time/adjunct (13 women). *Financial support:* Federal Work-Study, scholarships/grants, traineeships, and unspecified assistantships available. Support available to part-time students. Financial award application deadline: 3/1; financial award applicants required to submit FAFSA. In 2015, 48 master's, 1 doctorate, 2 other advanced degrees awarded. *Degree program information:* Part-time programs available. Part-time. Offers advanced practice nursing (DNP); family nurse practitioner (MSN, Certificate); nursing and health-related professions education (Certificate). *Application deadline:* For fall admission, 5/1 priority date for international students; for spring admission, 9/1 priority date for international students. Applications are processed on a rolling basis. Electronic applications accepted. *Application Contact:* Mark Pavone, Graduate Admissions Director, 716-829-8400, Fax: 716-829-7900, E-mail: graduateadmissions@dyc.edu. *Chair*, Dr. Ann Caughill, 716-829-7892, Fax: 716-829-8159.

School of Pharmacy Students: 281 full-time (143 women), 4 part-time (3 women); includes 45 minority (6 Black or African American, non-Hispanic/Latino; 1 American Indian or Alaska Native, non-Hispanic/Latino; 26 Asian, non-Hispanic/Latino; 4 Hispanic/Latino; 8 Two or more races, non-Hispanic/Latino), 29 international. Average age 23. 523 applicants, 23% accepted, 76 enrolled. *Faculty:* 29 full-time (13 women), 2 part-time/adjunct (1 woman). *Financial support:* In 2015–16, 62 students received support. Application deadline: 4/15; applicants required to submit FAFSA. In 2015, 60 doctorates awarded. Offers pharmacy (Pharm D). *Application deadline:* For fall admission, 3/1 for domestic and international students. Applications are processed on a rolling basis. Electronic applications accepted. *Application Contact:* Kathryn Stricker, School of Pharmacy Admission Counselor, 716-829-8324, Fax: 716-829-7904, E-mail: pharmacyadmissions@dyc.edu. *Assistant Dean of Faculty and Student Affairs,* Dr. Canio Marasco, 716-829-7846, Fax: 716-829-7760, E-mail: pharmacyadmissions@dyc.edu.

EARLHAM COLLEGE, Richmond, IN 47374-4095

General Information Independent-religious, coed, comprehensive institution. *Graduate housing:* On-campus housing not available.

GRADUATE UNITS

Graduate Programs Offers education (M Ed, MAT).

EARLHAM SCHOOL OF RELIGION, Richmond, IN 47374-5360

General Information Independent-religious, coed, graduate-only institution. *Enrollment by degree level:* 53 master's, 4 other advanced degrees. *Graduate faculty:* 8 full-time (3 women), 4 part-time/adjunct (2 women). *Tuition, area resident:* Full-time $14,391; part-time $1599 per course. *Required fees:* $200 per semester. *Graduate housing:* On-campus housing not available. *Student services:* Campus employment opportunities, campus safety program, career counseling, exercise/wellness program, international student services, teacher training, writing training. *Library:* Lilly Library plus 2 others. *Collection:* Books: 351,561 (physical); Serial titles: 292 (physical). Weekly public service hours: 112; students can reserve study rooms.

Computer facilities: 125 computers available on campus for general student use. Online class registration is available.
Website: http://www.esr.earlham.edu/

General Application Contact: Matthew Hisrich, Director of Recruitment and Admissions, 765-983-1523, Fax: 765-983-1688, E-mail: hisrima@earlham.edu.

GRADUATE UNITS

Graduate Programs Students: 35 full-time (19 women), 27 part-time (22 women). *Faculty:* 8 full-time (3 women), 4 part-time/adjunct (2 women). *Financial support:* Scholarships/grants and tuition waivers (full and partial) available. Financial award application deadline: 4/15; financial award applicants required to submit FAFSA. *Degree program information:* Part-time programs available. Part-time, online learning. Offers religion (MA); theology (M Div, M Min). *Application deadline:* For fall admission, 7/15 priority date for domestic students; for winter admission, 12/15 priority date for domestic students. Applications are processed on a rolling basis. *Application fee:* $35. Electronic applications accepted. *Application Contact:* Matthew Hisrich, Director of Recruitment and Admissions, 765-983-1523, Fax: 765-983-1688, E-mail: hisrima@earlham.edu. *Dean,* Jay W. Marshall, 800-432-1377, Fax: 765-983-1688, E-mail: marshja@earlham.edu.

EAST CAROLINA UNIVERSITY, Greenville, NC 27858-4353

General Information State-supported, coed, university. CGS member. *Enrollment:* 28,289 graduate, professional, and undergraduate students; 2,466 full-time matriculated graduate/professional students (1,556 women), 2,463 part-time matriculated graduate/professional students (1,589 women). *Enrollment by degree level:* 3,726 master's, 1,144 doctoral, 59 other advanced degrees. *Graduate faculty:* 975 full-time (427 women), 64 part-time/adjunct (39 women). *Graduate housing:* Room and/or apartments available on a first-come, first-served basis to single students; on-campus housing not available to married students. Housing application deadline: 5/1. *Student services:* Campus employment opportunities, campus safety program, career counseling, exercise/wellness program, free psychological counseling, grant writing training, international student services, low-cost health insurance, multicultural affairs office, services for students with disabilities, teacher training, writing training. *Library:* Joyner Library plus 1 other. *Collection:* Books: 1.3 million (physical), 1.6 million (digital/electronic); Serial titles: 8,391 (physical), 89,781 (digital/electronic); Databases: 428. Weekly public service hours: 142; study areas open 24 hours, 5–7 days a week; students can reserve study rooms.

Computer facilities: Computer purchase and lease plans are available. 2,375 computers available on campus for general student use. A campuswide network can be accessed from student residence rooms and from off campus. Online class registration is available.
Website: http://www.ecu.edu/

General Application Contact: Dr. Heidi Puckett, Director of Admissions, 252-328-5400, Fax: 252-328-6071, E-mail: gradschool@ecu.edu.

GRADUATE UNITS

Brody School of Medicine Students: 169 full-time (105 women), 23 part-time (19 women); includes 58 minority (26 Black or African American, non-Hispanic/Latino; 2 American Indian or Alaska Native, non-Hispanic/Latino; 18 Asian, non-Hispanic/Latino; 7 Hispanic/Latino; 5 Two or more races, non-Hispanic/Latino), 18 international. Average age 27. 174 applicants, 61% accepted, 70 enrolled. *Financial support:* Fellowships with partial tuition reimbursements and institutionally sponsored loans available. Financial award application deadline: 6/1. In 2015, 40 master's, 92 doctorates awarded. Offers anatomy and cell biology (PhD); biochemistry and molecular biology (PhD); biomedical science (MS); medicine (MPH, MS, MD, PhD); microbiology and immunology (MS, MD, PhD); pharmacology and toxicology (PhD); physiology (PhD); public health (MPH). *Application fee:* $50. *Application Contact:* Contact Center, 252-744-1020.

Graduate School ***Financial support:*** Fellowships with partial tuition reimbursements, research assistantships with partial tuition reimbursements, teaching assistantships with partial tuition reimbursements, career-related internships or fieldwork, Federal Work-Study, scholarships/grants, traineeships, and unspecified assistantships available. Support available to part-time students. Financial award application deadline: 6/1; financial award applicants required to submit FAFSA. *Degree program information:* Part-time and evening/weekend programs available. Part-time, evening/weekend, online learning. *Application deadline:* Applications are processed on a rolling basis. *Application fee:* $60. *Dean of Graduate School,* Dr. Paul Gemperline, 252-328-6073, E-mail: gemperlinep@ecu.edu.

College of Allied Health Sciences Students: 466 full-time (379 women), 109 part-time (89 women); includes 70 minority (33 Black or African American, non-Hispanic/Latino; 1 American Indian or Alaska Native, non-Hispanic/Latino; 13 Asian, non-Hispanic/Latino; 14 Hispanic/Latino; 9 Two or more races, non-Hispanic/Latino), 2 international. Average age 28. 903 applicants, 31% accepted, 213 enrolled. *Financial support:* Research assistantships with partial tuition reimbursements, teaching assistantships with partial tuition reimbursements, career-related internships or fieldwork, Federal Work-Study, and scholarships/grants available. Support available to part-time students. Financial award application deadline: 6/1; financial award applicants required to submit FAFSA. In 2015, 127 master's, 38 doctorates awarded. *Degree program information:* Part-time and evening/weekend programs available. Part-time, evening/weekend, online learning. Offers allied health sciences (MS, MSOT, DPT, PhD, Certificate); communication sciences and disorders (MS, PhD); health informatics and information management (MS); military and trauma counseling (Certificate); nutrition science (MS); occupational therapy (MSOT); physical therapy (DPT); physician assistant studies (MS); rehabilitation and career counseling (MS); rehabilitation counseling (Certificate); rehabilitation counseling and administration (PhD); substance abuse and clinical counseling (MS); substance abuse counseling (Certificate); vocational evaluation (Certificate). *Application fee:* $70. *Application Contact:* Dean of Graduate School, 252-328-6012, Fax: 252-328-6071, E-mail: gradschool@ecu.edu. *Interim Dean,* Dr. Greg Hassler, 252-744-6010, E-mail: hasslerg@ecu.edu.

College of Business Students: 234 full-time (93 women), 621 part-time (268 women); includes 184 minority (108 Black or African American, non-Hispanic/Latino; 4 American Indian or Alaska Native, non-Hispanic/Latino; 29 Asian, non-Hispanic/Latino; 26 Hispanic/Latino; 1 Native Hawaiian or other Pacific Islander, non-Hispanic/Latino; 16 Two or more races, non-Hispanic/Latino), 13 international. Average age 32. 449 applicants, 83% accepted, 267 enrolled. *Financial support:* Research assistantships with partial tuition reimbursements, teaching assistantships with partial tuition reimbursements, and Federal Work-Study available. Support available to part-time students. Financial award application deadline: 6/1. In 2015, 200 master's awarded. *Degree program information:* Part-time and evening/weekend programs available. Part-time, evening/weekend. Offers accounting (MSA); business (MBA, MSA); hospitality management (MBA); management (MBA). *Application deadline:* For fall admission, 6/1 priority date for domestic students. Applications are processed on a rolling basis. *Application fee:* $70. Electronic applications accepted. *Interim Director of Graduate Programs,* Paul Russell, 252-328-6970, E-mail: gradbus@ecu.edu.

College of Education Students: 153 full-time (124 women), 767 part-time (607 women); includes 189 minority (123 Black or African American, non-Hispanic/Latino; 15 American Indian or Alaska Native, non-Hispanic/Latino; 6 Asian, non-Hispanic/Latino; 31 Hispanic/Latino; 1 Native Hawaiian or other Pacific Islander, non-Hispanic/Latino; 13 Two or more races, non-Hispanic/Latino), 4 international. Average age 37. 453 applicants, 91% accepted, 342 enrolled. *Financial support:* Research assistantships with partial tuition reimbursements, teaching assistantships with partial tuition reimbursements, and Federal Work-Study available. Support available to part-time students. Financial award application deadline: 6/1. In 2015, 254 master's, 37 doctorates, 2 other advanced degrees awarded. *Degree program information:* Part-time and evening/weekend programs available. Part-time, evening/weekend, online learning. Offers adult education (MA Ed); assistive technology (Certificate); autism (Certificate); business and marketing education (MA); career and technical education (MA Ed); counselor education (MS); education (MA, MA Ed, MAT, MLS, MS, MSA, Ed D, Certificate, Ed S); educational administration and supervision (Ed S); educational leadership (Ed D); elementary education (MA Ed, MAT); elementary mathematics (Certificate); English education (MAT); family and consumer science (MAT); health education (MAT); Hispanic studies (MAT); history education (MA Ed, MAT); instructional technology (MA Ed, MS); library science (MLS); mathematics education (MA Ed); middle grades education (MA Ed, MAT); music education (MAT); reading education (MA Ed); school administration (MSA); science education (MA Ed, MAT); special education (MA Ed, MAT); vocational education (MAT, MS). *Application deadline:* For fall admission, 6/1 priority date for domestic students. Applications are processed on a rolling basis. *Application fee:* $50. *Application Contact:* Dean of Graduate School, 252-328-6012, Fax: 252-328-6071, E-mail: gradschool@ecu.edu. *Dean,* Dr. Linda Ann Patriarca, 252-328-1000, Fax: 252-328-4219, E-mail: patriarcal@ecu.edu.

College of Engineering and Technology Students: 60 full-time (17 women), 195 part-time (40 women); includes 60 minority (33 Black or African American, non-Hispanic/Latino; 2 American Indian or Alaska Native, non-Hispanic/Latino; 11 Asian, non-Hispanic/Latino; 8 Hispanic/Latino; 1 Native Hawaiian or other Pacific Islander, non-Hispanic/Latino; 5 Two or more races, non-Hispanic/Latino), 40 international. Average age 37. 124 applicants, 82% accepted, 75 enrolled. *Financial support:* Fellowships, research assistantships, teaching assistantships, and Federal Work-Study available. Support available to part-time students. Financial award application deadline: 6/1. In 2015, 49 master's awarded. *Degree program information:* Part-time programs available. Part-time. Offers biomedical engineering (MS); computer network professional (Certificate); computer science (MS); construction management (MCM); engineering and technology (MCM, MS, PhD, Certificate); information assurance (Certificate); Lean Six Sigma Black Belt (Certificate); network technology (MS); occupational safety (MS); software engineering (MS); technology management (PhD); technology systems (MS); Website developer (Certificate). *Application deadline:* For fall admission, 6/1 priority date for domestic students. Applications are processed on a rolling basis. *Application fee:* $50. *Application Contact:* Dean of Graduate School, 252-328-6012, Fax: 252-328-6071, E-mail: gradschool@ecu.edu. *Dean,* Dr. David White, 252-328-9604.

College of Fine Arts and Communication Students: 59 full-time (42 women), 56 part-time (40 women); includes 21 minority (12 Black or African American, non-Hispanic/Latino; 1 American Indian or Alaska Native, non-Hispanic/Latino; 1 Asian, non-Hispanic/Latino; 4 Hispanic/Latino; 3 Two or more races, non-Hispanic/Latino), 2 international. Average age 31. 90 applicants, 69% accepted, 42 enrolled. In 2015, 35 master's awarded. Offers advanced performance studies (Certificate); art education (MA Ed); ceramics (MFA); fine arts and communication (MA, MA Ed, MFA, MM, Certificate); graphic design (MFA); health communication (MA); illustration (MFA); metal design (MFA); music education (MM); music therapy (MM); painting and drawing (MFA); performance (MM); photography (MFA); printmaking (MFA); sculpture (MFA); Suzuki pedagogy (Certificate); textile design (MFA); theory and composition (MM); wood design (MFA). *Application fee:* $50. *Application Contact:* 252-328-6012, Fax: 252-328-6071, E-mail: gradschool@ecu.edu. *Dean,* J. Christopher Buddo, 252-328-1283, E-mail: buddoj@ecu.edu.

College of Health and Human Performance Students: 334 full-time (250 women), 147 part-time (103 women); includes 125 minority (96 Black or African American, non-Hispanic/Latino; 2 American Indian or Alaska Native, non-Hispanic/Latino; 6 Asian, non-Hispanic/Latino; 13 Hispanic/Latino; 8 Two or more races, non-Hispanic/Latino), 2 international. Average age 29. 474 applicants, 69% accepted, 266 enrolled. *Financial support:* Research assistantships, teaching assistantships, and Federal Work-Study available. Support available to part-time students. Financial award application deadline: 6/1. In 2015, 167 master's, 2 doctorates awarded. *Degree program information:* Part-time and evening/weekend programs available. Part-time, evening/weekend. Offers adapted physical education (MS); aquatic therapy (Certificate); bioenergetics and exercise science (PhD); biofeedback (Certificate); biomechanics (MS); birth through kindergarten education (MA Ed); child development and family relations (MS); environmental health (MS); exercise physiology (MS);

gerontology (Certificate); health and human performance (MA, MA Ed, MAT, MS, MSW, PhD, Certificate); health education (MA Ed); health education and promotion (MA); marriage and family therapy (MS); medical family therapy (PhD); physical activity promotion (MS); physical education (MA Ed, MAT); physical education pedagogy (MS); recreation and park administration (MS); social work (MSW); sport and exercise psychology (MS); sport management (MS, Certificate); substance abuse (Certificate). *Application deadline:* For fall admission, 6/1 priority date for domestic students. Applications are processed on a rolling basis. *Application fee:* $50. *Dean*, Dr. Glen Gilbert, 252-328-0038, E-mail: gilbertg@ecu.edu.

College of Nursing Students: 138 full-time (120 women), 379 part-time (351 women); includes 111 minority (72 Black or African American, non-Hispanic/Latino; 5 American Indian or Alaska Native, non-Hispanic/Latino; 12 Asian, non-Hispanic/Latino; 13 Hispanic/Latino; 9 Two or more races, non-Hispanic/Latino). Average age 38. 221 applicants, 89% accepted, 172 enrolled. *Financial support:* Research assistantships with partial tuition reimbursements, teaching assistantships with partial tuition reimbursements, and Federal Work-Study available. Support available to part-time students. Financial award application deadline: 6/1. In 2015, 108 master's, 11 doctorates, 7 other advanced degrees awarded. *Degree program information:* Part-time programs available. Part-time. Offers nursing (MSN, DNP, PhD, PMC). *Application deadline:* For fall admission, 6/1 priority date for domestic students. Applications are processed on a rolling basis. *Application fee:* $70. *Application Contact:* Dean of Graduate School, 252-328-6012, Fax: 252-328-6071, E-mail: gradschool@ecu.edu. *Dean*, Dr. Sylvia Brown, 252-744-6372, E-mail: brownsy@ecu.edu.

Thomas Harriot College of Arts and Sciences Students: 429 full-time (229 women), 306 part-time (157 women); includes 122 minority (60 Black or African American, non-Hispanic/Latino; 2 American Indian or Alaska Native, non-Hispanic/Latino; 15 Asian, non-Hispanic/Latino; 21 Hispanic/Latino; 24 Two or more races, non-Hispanic/Latino), 23 international. Average age 29. 754 applicants, 54% accepted, 252 enrolled. *Financial support:* Fellowships with partial tuition reimbursements, research assistantships with partial tuition reimbursements, teaching assistantships with partial tuition reimbursements, career-related internships or fieldwork, Federal Work-Study, scholarships/grants, traineeships, and unspecified assistantships available. Support available to part-time students. Financial award application deadline: 6/1. In 2015, 169 master's, 8 doctorates, 4 other advanced degrees awarded. *Degree program information:* Part-time and evening/weekend programs available. Part-time, evening/weekend. Offers American history (MA); anthropology (MA); applied and resource economics (MS); applied physics (MS); arts and sciences (MA, MA Ed, MPA, MS, PhD, Certificate); Atlantic world (MA); biology (MS); biomedical physics (PhD); chemistry (MS); community health administration (Certificate); creative writing (MA); criminal justice (MS); criminal justice education (Certificate); economic development (Certificate); English studies (MA); European history (MA); geographic information science and technology (Certificate); geography (MA); geology (MS); health physics (MS); health psychology (PhD); history education (MA Ed); hydrogeology and environmental geology (Certificate); industrial and organizational psychology (MA); international studies (MA); linguistics (MA); literature (MA); maritime studies (MA); mathematics (MA); mathematics in the community college (MA); medical physics (MS); military history (MA); molecular biology and biotechnology (MS); multicultural and transnational literatures (MA, Certificate); public administration (MPA); public history (MA); public management and leadership (Certificate); rhetoric and composition (MA); rhetoric, writing, and professional communication (PhD); security studies (Certificate); sociology (MA); statistics (MA, Certificate); teaching English in the two-year college (Certificate); teaching English to speakers of other languages (MA, Certificate); technical and professional communication (MA). *Application deadline:* Applications are processed on a rolling basis. *Application fee:* $50. *Application Contact:* Dean of Graduate School, 252-328-6012, Fax: 252-328-6071, E-mail: gradschool@ecu.edu. *Dean*, Dr. William M. Downs, 252-328-6249, E-mail: downsw14@ecu.edu.

School of Dental Medicine Offers dental medicine (DMD). *Application Contact:* Student Admissions, E-mail: sodmadmissions@ecu.edu. *Dean*, Dr. Greg Chadwick, 252-737-7030.

EAST CENTRAL UNIVERSITY, Ada, OK 74820

General Information State-supported, coed, comprehensive institution. CGS member. *Graduate housing:* Rooms and/or apartments available on a first-come, first-served basis to single and married students.

GRADUATE UNITS

School of Graduate Studies ***Degree program information:*** Part-time and evening/weekend programs available. Part-time, evening/weekend. Offers administration (MSHR); counseling (MSHR); criminal justice (MSHR); education (M Ed); human services (MSHR); psychology (MSPS); rehabilitation counseling (MSHR). Electronic applications accepted.

EASTERN CONNECTICUT STATE UNIVERSITY, Willimantic, CT 06226-2295

General Information State-supported, coed, comprehensive institution. *Graduate housing:* On-campus housing not available. *Research affiliation:* Department of Education (early childhood education, mathematics and science education).

GRADUATE UNITS

School of Education and Professional Studies/Graduate Division ***Degree program information:*** Part-time and evening/weekend programs available. Part-time, evening/weekend. Offers early childhood education (MS); education and professional studies (MS); educational technology (MS); elementary education (MS); organizational management (MS); reading and language arts (MS); science education (MS); secondary education (MS).

EASTERN ILLINOIS UNIVERSITY, Charleston, IL 61920

General Information State-supported, coed, comprehensive institution. CGS member. *Graduate housing:* Rooms and/or apartments available on a first-come, first-served basis to single and married students.

GRADUATE UNITS

Graduate School ***Degree program information:*** Part-time and evening/weekend programs available. Part-time, evening/weekend, online learning. Electronic applications accepted.

College of Arts and Humanities Degree program information: Part-time and evening/weekend programs available. Part-time, evening/weekend, online learning. Offers art (MA); art education (MA); arts and humanities (MA); community arts (MA); community college pedagogy (MA); English (MA); historical administration (MA); history (MA); music (MA). Electronic applications accepted.

College of Education and Professional Studies Degree program information: Part-time and evening/weekend programs available. Part-time, evening/weekend. Offers college student affairs (MS); counseling (MS); education and professional studies (MS, MS Ed, Ed S); educational leadership (MS Ed, Ed S); elementary education (MS Ed); kinesiology and sports studies (MS); special education (MS Ed). Electronic applications accepted.

College of Sciences Degree program information: Part-time and evening/weekend programs available. Part-time, evening/weekend, online learning. Offers biological sciences (MS); chemistry (MS); clinical psychology (MA); communication disorders and sciences (MS); economics (MA); elementary/middle school mathematics education (MA); geology/geography (MS); mathematics (MA); political science (MA); school psychology (SSP); sciences (MA, MS, SSP). Electronic applications accepted.

Lumpkin College of Business and Applied Sciences Degree program information: Part-time and evening/weekend programs available. Part-time, evening/weekend, online learning. Offers accountancy (MBA); aging studies (MA); applied management (MBA); business administration (MBA); business and applied sciences (MA, MBA, MS, Certificate); computer technology (Certificate); family and consumer sciences (MA, MS); nutrition and dietetics (MS); quality systems (Certificate); research (MBA); sustainable energy (MS); technology (MS, Certificate); technology security (Certificate); work performance improvement (Certificate). Electronic applications accepted.

EASTERN KENTUCKY UNIVERSITY, Richmond, KY 40475-3102

General Information State-supported, coed, comprehensive institution. CGS member. *Graduate housing:* Rooms and/or apartments guaranteed to single students and available to married students.

GRADUATE UNITS

The Graduate School ***Degree program information:*** Part-time and evening/weekend programs available. Part-time, evening/weekend, online learning. Electronic applications accepted.

College of Arts and Sciences Degree program information: Part-time and evening/weekend programs available. Part-time, evening/weekend. Offers arts and sciences (MA, MFA, MM, MPA, MS, PhD, Psy S); biological sciences (MS); chemistry (MS); choral conducting (MM); clinical psychology (MS); community development (MPA); community health administration (MPA); creative writing (MFA); ecology (MS); English (MA); general public administration (MPA); geology (MS, PhD); history (MA); industrial/organizational psychology (MS); mathematical sciences (MS); performance (MM); political science (MA); school psychology (Psy S); theory/composition (MM).

College of Business and Technology Degree program information: Part-time programs available. Part-time. Offers business administration (MBA); business and technology (MBA, MS); industrial education (MS); industrial technology (MS); occupational training and development (MS); technical administration (MS); technology education (MS).

College of Education Degree program information: Part-time programs available. Part-time, online learning. Offers communication disorders (MA Ed); education (MA, MA Ed, MAT); elementary education (MA Ed); human services (MA); instructional leadership (MA Ed); library science (MA Ed); mental health counseling (MA); music education (MA Ed); school counseling (MA Ed); secondary and higher education (MA Ed); secondary education (MA Ed); teaching (MAT).

College of Health Sciences Degree program information: Part-time programs available. Part-time. Offers community health (MPH); community nutrition (MS); environmental health science (MPH); exercise and sport science (MS); exercise and wellness (MS); health sciences (MPH, MS, MSN); occupational therapy (MS); recreation and park administration (MS); rural community health care (MSN); rural health family nurse practitioner (MSN); sports administration (MS).

College of Justice and Safety Degree program information: Part-time programs available. Part-time. Offers correctional and juvenile justice studies (MS); criminal justice (MS); criminal justice education (MS); justice and safety (MS); loss prevention and safety (MS); police studies (MS).

EASTERN MENNONITE UNIVERSITY, Harrisonburg, VA 22802-2462

General Information Independent-religious, coed, comprehensive institution. *Enrollment:* 133 full-time matriculated graduate/professional students (66 women), 204 part-time matriculated graduate/professional students (148 women). *Enrollment by degree level:* 311 master's, 11 other advanced degrees. *Graduate faculty:* 42 full-time (20 women), 25 part-time/adjunct (13 women). *Tuition, area resident:* Part-time $600 per credit hour. *Required fees:* $25 per unit. Part-time tuition and fees vary according to course load and program. *Graduate housing:* Rooms and/or apartments available on a first-come, first-served basis to single and married students. Housing application deadline: 4/15. *Student services:* Campus employment opportunities, campus safety program, career counseling, exercise/wellness program, free psychological counseling, international student services, low-cost health insurance, multicultural affairs office, services for students with disabilities, teacher training, writing training. *Library:* Sadie Hartzler Library.

Computer facilities: 154 computers available on campus for general student use. A campuswide network can be accessed from student residence rooms and from off campus. Online class registration is available.
Website: http://www.emu.edu/

General Application Contact: Shirley Ewald, Assistant to the Dean of Graduate Studies, 540-432-4026, Fax: 540-432-4444, E-mail: shirley.ewald@emu.edu.

GRADUATE UNITS

Eastern Mennonite Seminary Students: 44 full-time (19 women), 77 part-time (42 women); includes 6 minority (2 Black or African American, non-Hispanic/Latino; 4 Hispanic/Latino), 4 international. Average age 42. *Faculty:* 9 full-time (2 women), 20 part-time/adjunct (6 women). *Financial support:* Application deadline: 6/30; applicants required to submit FAFSA. *Degree program information:* Part-time programs available. Part-time. Offers church leadership (MA); divinity (M Div); ministry studies (Certificate); religion (MA); theological studies (Certificate). *Application deadline:* For fall admission, 6/15 priority date for domestic and international students; for winter admission, 11/15 priority date for domestic and international students; for spring admission, 3/15 priority date for domestic and international students. Applications are processed on a rolling basis. *Application fee:* $25. *Application Contact:* Laura Lehman, Director of Seminary Admissions, 540-432-4268, Fax: 540-432-4598, E-mail: semadmiss@emu.edu. *Dean*, Dr. Michael A. King, 540-432-4261, Fax: 540-432-4444, E-mail: michael.king@emu.edu.

Master of Arts in Counseling Program ***Financial support:*** Scholarships/grants available. Financial award application deadline: 6/30; financial award applicants required to submit FAFSA. *Degree program information:* Part-time programs available. Part-time. Offers counseling (MA). *Application deadline:* For fall admission, 3/1 for domestic and international students. *Application fee:* $50. Electronic applications accepted. *Application Contact:* Amanda Williams, Administrative Assistant, 540-432-4243, Fax: 540-432-4444, E-mail: amanda.k.williams@emu.edu. *Director,* Dr. Teresa J. Haase, 540-432-4248, Fax: 540-432-4444, E-mail: teresa.haase@emu.edu.

Program in Biomedicine Offers biomedicine (MA). *Application deadline:* For fall admission, 7/31 for domestic students; for spring admission, 11/30 for domestic students. Applications are processed on a rolling basis. *Application fee:* $50. Electronic applications accepted. *Application Contact:* Don A. Yoder, Director of Seminary and Graduate Admissions, 540-432-4257, Fax: 540-432-4598, E-mail: yoderda@emu.edu. *Director,* Dr. Roman J. Miller, 540-432-4412, E-mail: millerrj@emu.edu.

Program in Business Administration Students: 10 part-time. *Faculty:* 1 part-time/adjunct. *Financial support:* Application deadline: 6/30; applicants required to submit FAFSA. *Degree program information:* Part-time and evening/weekend programs available. Part-time, evening/weekend. Offers general management (MBA); health services administration (MBA); non-profit leadership (MBA). *Application deadline:* For fall admission, 3/1 priority date for domestic and international students. Applications are processed on a rolling basis. *Application fee:* $25. Electronic applications accepted. *Application Contact:* Patricia S. Eckard, Administrative Coordinator, 540-432-4150, Fax: 540-432-4071, E-mail: eckardp@emu.edu. *Department Chair,* Dr. James M. Leaman, 540-432-4152, Fax: 540-432-4071, E-mail: james.leaman@emu.edu.

Program in Conflict Transformation ***Financial support:*** Scholarships/grants available. Financial award application deadline: 6/30; financial award applicants required to submit FAFSA. *Degree program information:* Part-time programs available. Part-time. Offers conflict transformation (MA, Graduate Certificate). *Application deadline:* For fall admission, 2/15 priority date for domestic and international students. Applications are processed on a rolling basis. *Application fee:* $25. Electronic applications accepted. *Application Contact:* Lora Steiner, Coordinator of Admissions and Marketing, 540-432-4689, Fax: 540-432-4449, E-mail: lora.steiner@emu.edu. *Program Director,* Dr. Jayne Docherty, 540-432-4627, Fax: 540-432-4449, E-mail: jayne.docherty@emu.edu.

Program in Education ***Financial support:*** Federal Work-Study and scholarships/grants available. Financial award application deadline: 6/30; financial award applicants required to submit FAFSA. *Degree program information:* Part-time programs available. Part-time. Offers education (MA). *Application deadline:* Applications are processed on a rolling basis. *Application fee:* $25. Electronic applications accepted. *Application Contact:* Yvonne Martin, Office Assistant, 540-432-4350, Fax: 540-432-4071, E-mail: yvonne.martin@emu.edu. *Director,* Sarah Armstrong, 434-760-8930.

Program in Nursing ***Financial support:*** Federal Work-Study and scholarships/grants available. Financial award applicants required to submit FAFSA. *Degree program information:* Part-time programs available. Part-time, online learning. Offers leadership and management (MSN); leadership and school nursing (MSN). *Application deadline:* For fall admission, 6/1 for domestic students. Applications are processed on a rolling basis. *Application fee:* $25. *Application Contact:* Don A. Yoder, Director of Seminary and Graduate Admissions, 540-432-4257, Fax: 540-432-4598, E-mail: yoderda@emu.edu. *Coordinator,* Ann Hershberger, 540-432-4192, E-mail: hershbea@emu.edu.

Program in Organizational Leadership Offers organizational leadership (MA). *Application Contact:* Lois Shank, Assistant to the Provost, 540-432-4105, Fax: 540-432-4444, E-mail: graduate@emu.edu. *Director,* Sue Cockley, 540-432-4984, E-mail: mol@emu.edu.

EASTERN MICHIGAN UNIVERSITY, Ypsilanti, MI 48197

General Information State-supported, coed, comprehensive institution. CGS member. *Enrollment:* 21,634 graduate, professional, and undergraduate students; 1,029 full-time matriculated graduate/professional students (681 women), 2,786 part-time matriculated graduate/professional students (1,748 women). *Enrollment by degree level:* 3,078 master's, 274 doctoral, 377 other advanced degrees. *Graduate faculty:* 742 full-time (379 women). *Graduate housing:* Rooms and/or apartments available on a first-come, first-served basis to single and married students. *Student services:* Campus employment opportunities, campus safety program, career counseling, child daycare facilities, exercise/wellness program, free psychological counseling, grant writing training, international student services, low-cost health insurance, multicultural affairs office, services for students with disabilities, teacher training, writing training. *Library:* Bruce T. Halle Library. *Research affiliation:* 3M Corporation (coatings research), Toyota (coatings research), Beckers-Fusion (coatings research), Dima-Shield (coatings research), Signal Medical Corporation (textiles research), TRACO (coatings research).

Computer facilities: 1,600 computers available on campus for general student use. A campuswide network can be accessed from student residence rooms. Online class registration is available.
Website: http://www.emich.edu/

General Application Contact: Graduate Admissions, 734-487-2400, Fax: 734-487-6559, E-mail: graduate.admissions@emich.edu.

GRADUATE UNITS

Graduate School Students: 1,029 full-time (681 women), 2,786 part-time (1,748 women); includes 774 minority (484 Black or African American, non-Hispanic/Latino; 13 American Indian or Alaska Native, non-Hispanic/Latino; 117 Asian, non-Hispanic/Latino; 98 Hispanic/Latino; 2 Native Hawaiian or other Pacific Islander, non-Hispanic/Latino; 60 Two or more races, non-Hispanic/Latino), 342 international. Average age 32. 3,430 applicants, 53% accepted, 1267 enrolled. *Faculty:* 742 full-time (379 women). *Financial support:* Fellowships, research assistantships with full tuition reimbursements, teaching assistantships with full tuition reimbursements, career-related internships or fieldwork, Federal Work-Study, institutionally sponsored loans, scholarships/grants, tuition waivers (partial), and unspecified assistantships available. Support available to part-time students. Financial award applicants required to submit FAFSA. In 2015, 1,177 master's, 25 doctorates, 215 other advanced degrees awarded. *Degree program information:* Part-time and evening/weekend programs available. Part-time, evening/weekend, online learning. *Application deadline:* For fall admission, 5/15 priority date for domestic students, 2/15 priority date for international students; for winter admission, 10/15 priority date for domestic students, 9/1 priority date for international students; for summer admission, 3/15 priority date for domestic students, 3/1 priority date for international students. Applications are processed on a rolling basis. *Application fee:* $45. Electronic applications accepted. *Application Contact:* Graduate Admissions, 734-487-2400, Fax: 734-487-6559, E-mail: graduate.admissions@emich.edu. *Interim Dean, Graduate School,* Dr. Wade Tornquist, 734-487-0042, Fax: 734-487-0050, E-mail: wade.tornquist@emich.edu.

Academic Affairs Division Students: 14 full-time (7 women), 88 part-time (63 women); includes 19 minority (10 Black or African American, non-Hispanic/Latino; 5 Asian, non-Hispanic/Latino; 1 Hispanic/Latino; 3 Two or more races, non-Hispanic/Latino), 4 international. Average age 39. 109 applicants, 85% accepted, 67 enrolled. In 2015, 2 master's awarded. Offers individualized studies (MA, MS); integrated marketing communications (MS). *Application fee:* $45. *Application Contact:* Graduate Admissions, 734-487-2400, Fax: 734-487-6559, E-mail: graduate.admissions@emich.edu. *Interim Dean,* Dr. Wade Tornquist, 734-487-0042, Fax: 734-487-0050, E-mail: wade.tornquist@emich.edu.

College of Arts and Sciences Students: 283 full-time (179 women), 570 part-time (324 women); includes 152 minority (72 Black or African American, non-Hispanic/Latino; 3 American Indian or Alaska Native, non-Hispanic/Latino; 30 Asian, non-Hispanic/Latino; 24 Hispanic/Latino; 23 Two or more races, non-Hispanic/Latino), 98 international. Average age 30. 1,010 applicants, 48% accepted, 328 enrolled. *Faculty:* 404 full-time (181 women). *Financial support:* Fellowships, research assistantships with full tuition reimbursements, teaching assistantships with full tuition reimbursements, career-related internships or fieldwork, Federal Work-Study, institutionally sponsored loans, and tuition waivers (partial) available. Support available to part-time students. Financial award applicants required to submit FAFSA. In 2015, 277 master's, 6 doctorates, 15 other advanced degrees awarded. *Degree program information:* Part-time and evening/weekend programs available. Part-time, evening/weekend. Offers Africology and African-American studies (Graduate Certificate); applied drama/theatre for the young (MA, MFA); art education (MA); arts administration (MA); arts and sciences (MA, MFA, MLS, MM, MPA, MS, PhD, Graduate Certificate); cell and molecular biology (MS); chemistry (MS); children's literature (MA); clinical psychology (MS); communication (MA); community college biology teaching (MS); computer science (MS); creative writing (MA); criminology and criminal justice (MA); cultural museum studies (Graduate Certificate); earth science education (MS); ecology and organismal biology (MS); economics (MA, Graduate Certificate); English linguistics (MA, Graduate Certificate); English studies for teachers (MA); experimental psychology (MS); fine arts (MFA); general biology (MS); general public management (Graduate Certificate); general science (MS); geographic information systems (MS, Graduate Certificate); geography and geology (Graduate Certificate); GIS educator (Graduate Certificate); GIS planning (MS); GIS professional (Graduate Certificate); heritage interpretation and museum practice (MS); historic preservation (MS, Graduate Certificate); history (MA); interpretation/performance studies (MA); language and international trade (MA); language technology (Graduate Certificate); literature (MA); local government management (Graduate Certificate); management of public healthcare services (Graduate Certificate); mathematics (MA); music (MM); nonprofit management (Graduate Certificate); philosophy (MA); physics (MS); preservation planning and administration (MS); public administration (MPA, Graduate Certificate); public budget management (Graduate Certificate); public land planning and development management (Graduate Certificate); public personnel management (Graduate Certificate); public policy analysis (Graduate Certificate); recording, documentation and digital cultural heritage (MS); schools, society and violence (MA); social science (MA); sociology (MA); sociology - applied research specialty (MA); studio art (MA); teaching English to speakers of other languages (MA); teaching of writing (Graduate Certificate); technical communications (MA, Graduate Certificate); theatre arts (MA); transportation planning and modeling (Graduate Certificate); urban and regional planning (MS, Graduate Certificate); water resources (MS); women's and gender studies (MA, Graduate Certificate); world languages (MA, Graduate Certificate); written communication (MA, Graduate Certificate); written communications (MA). *Application deadline:* Applications are processed on a rolling basis. *Application fee:* $45. *Dean,* Dr. Thomas Venner, 734-487-4344, Fax: 734-485-9592, E-mail: tom.venner@emich.edu.

College of Business Students: 204 full-time (111 women), 508 part-time (296 women); includes 192 minority (117 Black or African American, non-Hispanic/Latino; 6 American Indian or Alaska Native, non-Hispanic/Latino; 31 Asian, non-Hispanic/Latino; 27 Hispanic/Latino; 11 Two or more races, non-Hispanic/Latino), 101 international. Average age 31. 608 applicants, 62% accepted, 313 enrolled. *Faculty:* 83 full-time (32 women). *Financial support:* Fellowships, research assistantships with full tuition reimbursements, teaching assistantships with full tuition reimbursements, career-related internships or fieldwork, Federal Work-Study, institutionally sponsored loans, traineeships, tuition waivers (partial), and unspecified assistantships available. Support available to part-time students. Financial award applicants required to submit FAFSA. In 2015, 242 master's, 70 other advanced degrees awarded. *Degree program information:* Part-time and evening/weekend programs available. Part-time, evening/weekend, online learning. Offers accounting (MS); accounting information systems (MS); business (MBA, MS, MSHROD, Graduate Certificate, Postbaccalaureate Certificate); business administration (MBA, Graduate Certificate); computer information systems (Graduate Certificate); e-business (MBA, Graduate Certificate); enterprise business intelligence (MBA); entrepreneurship (MBA, Graduate Certificate, Postbaccalaureate Certificate); finance (MBA, Graduate Certificate); human resources (MBA); human resources management (Graduate Certificate); human resources management and organizational development (MSHROD); information systems (MBA); integrated marketing communications (MS, Postbaccalaureate Certificate); internal auditing (MBA); international business (MBA, Graduate Certificate); marketing management (MBA, Graduate Certificate); nonprofit management (MBA); organizational development (Graduate Certificate); supply chain management (MBA, Graduate Certificate). *Application deadline:* Applications are processed on a rolling basis. *Application fee:* $45. *Application Contact:* K. Michelle Henry, Director, Graduate Business Programs, 734-487-4444, Fax: 734-483-1316, E-mail: cob.graduate@emich.edu. *Dean,* Dr. Michael Tidwell, 734-487-4140, Fax: 734-487-7099, E-mail: cob_dean@emich.edu.

College of Education Students: 201 full-time (169 women), 842 part-time (635 women); includes 202 minority (147 Black or African American, non-Hispanic/Latino; 2 American Indian or Alaska Native, non-Hispanic/Latino; 18 Asian, non-Hispanic/Latino; 22 Hispanic/Latino; 1 Native Hawaiian or other Pacific Islander, non-Hispanic/Latino; 12 Two or more races, non-Hispanic/Latino), 19 international. Average age 34. 714 applicants, 56% accepted, 236 enrolled. *Faculty:* 71 full-time (49 women). *Financial support:* Fellowships, research assistantships with full tuition reimbursements, teaching assistantships with full tuition reimbursements, career-related internships or fieldwork, Federal Work-Study, institutionally sponsored loans, scholarships/grants, tuition waivers (partial), and unspecified assistantships available. Support available to part-time students. Financial award applicants required to submit FAFSA. In 2015, 282 master's, 14 doctorates, 99 other advanced degrees awarded. *Degree program information:* Part-time and evening/weekend programs available. Part-time, evening/weekend, online learning. Offers administration and supervision (SPA); autism spectrum disorders (MA); clinical mental health counseling (MA); cognitive impairment (MA); college counseling (MA); community college leadership (Graduate Certificate); counseling (MA, Graduate Certificate, Post Master's Certificate); curriculum and instruction (MA); curriculum development (SPA); early childhood education (MA); education (MA, Ed D, PhD, Graduate Certificate, Post Master's Certificate, SPA); educational assessment (Graduate Certificate); educational leadership (MA, Ed D, Graduate Certificate, Post Master's Certificate, SPA); educational media and technology (MA); educational psychology (MA); educational psychology and assessment (MA, Graduate Certificate); educational studies (PhD); elementary education (MA); emotional impairment (MA); hearing impairment (MA); helping interventions in a multicultural society (Graduate Certificate); higher education/general administration (MA); higher education/student affairs (MA); K-12 administration (MA); K-12 basic administration (Post Master's Certificate); K-12 education (MA); learning disabilities (MA); mentally impaired (MA); middle school education (MA); physical/other health impairment (MA); reading (MA); school counseling (MA); school counselor licensure (Post Master's Certificate); secondary school education (MA); social foundations (MA); special education (MA, SPA); speech-language pathology (MA); urban/diversity education (MA); visual impairment (MA). *Application deadline:* Applications are processed on a rolling basis. *Application fee:* $45. *Dean*, Dr. Michael Sayler, 734-487-1414, Fax: 734-484-6471, E-mail: msayler@emich.edu.

College of Health and Human Services Students: 246 full-time (184 women), 447 part-time (332 women); includes 144 minority (99 Black or African American, non-Hispanic/Latino; 1 American Indian or Alaska Native, non-Hispanic/Latino; 19 Asian, non-Hispanic/Latino; 17 Hispanic/Latino; 1 Native Hawaiian or other Pacific Islander, non-Hispanic/Latino; 7 Two or more races, non-Hispanic/Latino), 28 international. Average age 32. 675 applicants, 42% accepted, 212 enrolled. *Faculty:* 126 full-time (98 women). *Financial support:* Fellowships, research assistantships with full tuition reimbursements, teaching assistantships with full tuition reimbursements, career-related internships or fieldwork, Federal Work-Study, institutionally sponsored loans, scholarships/grants, tuition waivers (partial), and unspecified assistantships available. Support available to part-time students. Financial award applicants required to submit FAFSA. In 2015, 260 master's, 23 other advanced degrees awarded. *Degree program information:* Part-time and evening/weekend programs available. Part-time, evening/weekend, online learning. Offers adapted physical education (MS); clinical research administration (MS, Graduate Certificate); community building (Graduate Certificate); dementia (Graduate Certificate); dietetics (MS); exercise physiology (MS); gerontology (Graduate Certificate); health administration (MHA, MS, Graduate Certificate); health and human services (MHA, MOT, MS, MSN, MSW, Graduate Certificate); health education (MS, Graduate Certificate); health promotion and human performance (MS, Graduate Certificate); health sciences (MHA, MOT, MS, Graduate Certificate); human nutrition (MS); non-profit management (Graduate Certificate); nursing (MSN); occupational therapy (MOT, MS); orthotics (Graduate Certificate); orthotics/prosthetics (MS); physical education pedagogy (MS); physician assistant studies (MS); prosthetics (Graduate Certificate); social work (MSW); sports management (MS); sports medicine-biomechanics (MS); sports medicine-corporate adult fitness (MS); sports medicine-exercise physiology (MS); teaching in health care systems (MSN, Graduate Certificate). *Application deadline:* For fall admission, 5/15 priority date for domestic students, 2/15 priority date for international students; for winter admission, 10/15 priority date for domestic students, 9/1 priority date for international students; for summer admission, 3/15 priority date for domestic students, 3/1 priority date for international students. Applications are processed on a rolling basis. *Application fee:* $45. *Dean*, Dr. Murali Nair, 734-487-0077, Fax: 734-487-8536, E-mail: mnair@emich.edu.

College of Technology Students: 86 full-time (33 women), 342 part-time (106 women); includes 70 minority (40 Black or African American, non-Hispanic/Latino; 1 American Indian or Alaska Native, non-Hispanic/Latino; 14 Asian, non-Hispanic/Latino; 7 Hispanic/Latino; 8 Two or more races, non-Hispanic/Latino), 96 international. Average age 36. 314 applicants, 59% accepted, 111 enrolled. *Faculty:* 58 full-time (19 women). *Financial support:* Fellowships, research assistantships with full tuition reimbursements, teaching assistantships with full tuition reimbursements, career-related internships or fieldwork, Federal Work-Study, institutionally sponsored loans, scholarships/grants, tuition waivers (partial), and unspecified assistantships available. Support available to part-time students. Financial award applicants required to submit FAFSA. In 2015, 114 master's, 5 doctorates, 8 other advanced degrees awarded. *Degree program information:* Part-time and evening/weekend programs available. Part-time, evening/weekend, online learning. Offers apparel textiles and merchandising (MS); CAD/CAM (MS); computer-aided technology (MS); construction management (MS); engineering management (MS); engineering technology (MS, Graduate Certificate, Postbaccalaureate Certificate); hotel and restaurant management (MS, Graduate Certificate); information assurance (Graduate Certificate); information security and applied computing (Graduate Certificate); interior design (MS); polymers and coatings technology (MS, Postbaccalaureate Certificate); quality (MS, Graduate Certificate); quality management (MS); technology (MLS, MS, PhD, Graduate Certificate); technology studies (MS); visual and built environments (MS, Graduate Certificate). *Application deadline:* For fall admission, 5/15 priority date for domestic students, 2/15 priority date for international students; for winter admission, 10/15 priority date for domestic students, 9/1 priority date for international students; for summer admission, 3/15 priority date for domestic students, 3/1 priority date for international students. Applications are processed on a rolling basis. *Application fee:* $45. *Dean*, Dr. Mohamad Qatu, 734-487-0354, Fax: 734-487-0843, E-mail: cot_dean@emich.edu.

EASTERN NAZARENE COLLEGE, Quincy, MA 02170

General Information Independent-religious, coed, comprehensive institution. *Graduate housing:* Rooms and/or apartments available to single students and available on a first-come, first-served basis to married students.

GRADUATE UNITS

Adult and Graduate Studies ***Degree program information:*** Part-time and evening/weekend programs available. Part-time, evening/weekend. Offers management (MSM); marriage and family therapy (MS).

Division of Teacher Education Degree program information: Part-time and evening/weekend programs available. Part-time, evening/weekend. Offers administration (M Ed); early childhood education (M Ed, Certificate); elementary education (M Ed, Certificate); English as a second language (Certificate); instructional enrichment and development (Certificate); middle school education (M Ed, Certificate); moderate special needs education (Certificate); principal (Certificate); program development and supervision (Certificate); secondary education (M Ed, Certificate); special education administrator (Certificate); special needs (M Ed); supervisor (Certificate); teacher of reading (M Ed, Certificate). M Ed also available through weekend program for administration, special needs, and teacher of reading only.

EASTERN NEW MEXICO UNIVERSITY, Portales, NM 88130

General Information State-supported, coed, comprehensive institution. *Graduate housing:* Rooms and/or apartments available on a first-come, first-served basis to single and married students. Housing application deadline: 8/1. *Research affiliation:* National Institutes of Health.

GRADUATE UNITS

Graduate School ***Degree program information:*** Part-time and evening/weekend programs available. Part-time, evening/weekend, online learning. Electronic applications accepted.

College of Business Degree program information: Part-time and evening/weekend programs available. Part-time, evening/weekend, online learning. Offers business (MBA). Electronic applications accepted.

College of Education and Technology Degree program information: Part-time programs available. Part-time, online learning. Offers bilingual education (M Ed); counseling (MA); early childhood special education (M Sp Ed); education (M Ed); education and technology (M Ed, M Sp Ed, MA, MS); educational technology (M Ed); elementary education (M Ed); English as a second language (M Ed); general (M Sp Ed); pedagogy and learning (M Ed); physical education (MS); professional technical education (M Ed); reading/literacy (M Ed); school counseling (M Ed); special education (M Sp Ed). Electronic applications accepted.

College of Fine Arts Degree program information: Part-time programs available. Part-time, online learning. Offers communicative arts and sciences (MA). Electronic applications accepted.

College of Liberal Arts and Sciences Degree program information: Part-time and evening/weekend programs available. Part-time, evening/weekend, online learning. Offers anthropology (MA); applied ecology (MS); botany (MS); cell, molecular biology and biotechnology (MS); chemistry (MS); English (MA); liberal arts and sciences (MA, MS, MSN); microbiology (MS); nursing (MSN); speech pathology and audiology (MS); zoology (MS). Electronic applications accepted.

EASTERN OREGON UNIVERSITY, La Grande, OR 97850-2899

General Information State-supported, coed, comprehensive institution. *Enrollment:* 3,488 graduate, professional, and undergraduate students; 85 full-time matriculated graduate/professional students (55 women), 148 part-time matriculated graduate/professional students (111 women). *Enrollment by degree level:* 233 master's. *Graduate faculty:* 23 full-time (13 women), 16 part-time/adjunct (8 women). Tuition, state resident: full-time $11,934; part-time $316 per credit. Tuition, nonresident: full-time $15,030; part-time $398 per credit. *Required fees:* $1434; $201 per credit. $255 per quarter. Tuition and fees vary according to course load, campus/location and program. *Graduate housing:* Rooms and/or apartments available on a first-come, first-served basis to single and married students. Typical cost: $9642 (including board) for single students; $4200 per year for married students. Room and board charges vary according to board plan and housing facility selected. *Student services:* Campus employment opportunities, campus safety program, career counseling, free psychological counseling, low-cost health insurance, multicultural affairs office, services for students with disabilities. *Library:* Pierce Library. *Collection:* Books: 169,456 (physical), 6,790 (digital/electronic); Serial titles: 996 (physical), 1,454 (digital/electronic); Databases: 158. Weekly public service hours: 89; students can reserve study rooms.

Computer facilities: Computer purchase and lease plans are available. 120 computers available on campus for general student use. A campuswide network can be accessed from student residence rooms and from off campus. Online class registration is available.
Website: http://www.eou.edu/

General Application Contact: Dr. Danny Ray Mielke, Coordinator of Graduate Studies, 541-962-3399, Fax: 541-962-3701, E-mail: danny.mielke@eou.edu.

GRADUATE UNITS

Master of Arts in Teaching Program Students: 35 full-time (23 women), 3 part-time (1 woman); includes 4 minority (1 Asian, non-Hispanic/Latino; 2 Hispanic/Latino; 1 Native Hawaiian or other Pacific Islander, non-Hispanic/Latino). Average age 28. *Faculty:* 11 full-time (7 women), 7 part-time/adjunct (4 women). *Financial support:* Federal Work-Study and tuition waivers (full and partial) available. Support available to part-time students. In 2015, 8 master's awarded. *Degree program information:* Part-time programs available. Part-time, online learning. Offers elementary education (MAT); secondary education (MAT). *Application deadline:* For fall admission, 1/1 priority date for domestic students. Applications are processed on a rolling basis. *Application fee:* $50. *Application Contact:* Janet Frye, Administrative Support, MAT/MS Graduate Admission, 541-962-3772, Fax: 541-962-3701, E-mail: jfrye@eou.edu. *Dean of College of Business and Education*, Dr. Danny Ray Mielke, 541-962-3399, Fax: 541-962-3701, E-mail: dmeilke@eou.edu.

Master of Science Program Students: 6 full-time (4 women), 79 part-time (69 women); includes 5 minority (1 American Indian or Alaska Native, non-Hispanic/Latino; 2 Asian, non-Hispanic/Latino; 1 Hispanic/Latino; 1 Native Hawaiian or other Pacific Islander, non-Hispanic/Latino). Average age 36. *Faculty:* 11 full-time (7 women), 5 part-time/adjunct (3 women). In 2015, 21 master's awarded. *Degree program information:* Part-time programs available. Part-time, online learning. Offers education (MS). *Application deadline:* Applications are processed on a rolling basis. Electronic applications accepted. *Application Contact:* Dr. Danny Ray Mielke, Coordinator of Graduate Studies, 541-962-3399, Fax: 541-962-3701, E-mail: danny.mielke@eou.edu. *Coordinator*, Dr. Danny Ray Mielke, 541-962-3349, Fax: 541-962-3701, E-mail: danny.mielke@eou.edu.

Program in Business Administration Students: 28 full-time (17 women), 40 part-time (20 women); includes 12 minority (1 American Indian or Alaska Native, non-Hispanic/Latino; 6 Asian, non-Hispanic/Latino; 5 Hispanic/Latino), 2 international. Average age 34. *Faculty:* 8 full-time (3 women), 3 part-time/adjunct (1 woman). *Financial support:* Federal Work-Study, scholarships/grants, and tuition waivers (full and partial) available. Support available to part-time students. Financial award applicants required to submit FAFSA. In 2015, 17 master's awarded. *Degree program information:* Part-time programs available. Part-time, online learning. Offers business administration (MBA). *Application deadline:* For fall admission, 1/1 priority date for domestic students. Applications are processed on a rolling basis. *Application fee:* $50. *Application Contact:* Dr. Danny Ray Mielke, Coordinator of Graduate Studies, 541-962-3399, Fax: 541-962-3701, E-mail: danny.mielke@eou.edu. *Program Coordinator*, Les Mueller, 541-962-3225, E-mail: lmueller@eou.edu.

EASTERN UNIVERSITY, St. Davids, PA 19087-3696

General Information Independent-religious, coed, comprehensive institution. *Enrollment:* 630 full-time matriculated graduate/professional students (387 women), 706 part-time matriculated graduate/professional students (487 women). *Enrollment by degree level:* 1,003 master's, 167 doctoral, 166 other advanced degrees. *Graduate faculty:* 54 full-time (23 women), 137 part-time/adjunct (64 women). *Graduate housing:* Room and/or apartments available on a first-come, first-served basis to single students; on-campus housing not available to married students. *Student services:* Campus employment opportunities, campus safety program, career counseling, international student services, low-cost health insurance, services for students with disabilities. *Library:* Warner Memorial Library plus 4 others.

Computer facilities: 98 computers available on campus for general student use. A campuswide network can be accessed from student residence rooms and from off campus. Online class registration is available.
Website: http://www.eastern.edu/

General Application Contact: Casey Malone, Director of Enrollment, 610-225-5462, E-mail: cmalone2@eastern.edu.

GRADUATE UNITS

Department of Counseling Psychology Students: 99 full-time (83 women), 76 part-time (63 women); includes 65 minority (56 Black or African American, non-Hispanic/Latino; 1 American Indian or Alaska Native, non-Hispanic/Latino; 1 Asian, non-Hispanic/Latino; 5 Hispanic/Latino; 2 Two or more races, non-Hispanic/Latino), 2 international. Average age 29. 117 applicants, 77% accepted, 68 enrolled. *Faculty:* 6 full-time (3 women), 8 part-time/adjunct (6 women). *Financial support:* In 2015–16, 21 students received support. Research assistantships with partial tuition reimbursements available, scholarships/grants, and unspecified assistantships available. Financial award application deadline: 3/15. In 2015, 44 master's awarded. *Degree program information:* Part-time programs available. Part-time. Offers applied behavior analysis (MA); counseling (MA); school counseling (MA, Certificate); school psychology (MS, Certificate). *Application deadline:* For fall admission, 6/15 for domestic students, 5/30 for international students. Applications are processed on a rolling basis. *Application fee:* $35. Electronic applications accepted. *Executive Director of Enrollment*, Michael Dziedziak, 800-732-7669, Fax: 610-225-5601, E-mail: gpsadm@eastern.edu.

Department of Urban Studies Students: 10 full-time (9 women), 41 part-time (37 women); includes 30 minority (25 Black or African American, non-Hispanic/Latino; 1 Asian, non-Hispanic/Latino; 3 Hispanic/Latino; 1 Two or more races, non-Hispanic/Latino), 2 international. Average age 31. 38 applicants, 97% accepted, 19 enrolled. *Faculty:* 3 full-time (1 woman), 4 part-time/adjunct (1 woman). *Financial support:* In 2015–16, 34 students received support. Scholarships/grants available. Financial award application deadline: 3/15; financial award applicants required to submit FAFSA. In 2015, 18 master's awarded. *Degree program information:* Part-time and evening/weekend programs available. Part-time, evening/weekend, online learning. Offers urban studies (MA). *Application deadline:* For fall admission, 8/14 for domestic students; for spring admission, 12/20 for domestic students. Applications are processed on a rolling basis. *Application fee:* $35. *Executive Director of Enrollment*, Michael Dziedziak, 800-732-7669, Fax: 610-225-5601, E-mail: gpsadm@eastern.edu.

Loeb School of Education Students: 50 full-time (39 women), 96 part-time (75 women); includes 51 minority (32 Black or African American, non-Hispanic/Latino; 2 Asian, non-Hispanic/Latino; 13 Hispanic/Latino; 4 Two or more races, non-Hispanic/Latino), 2 international. Average age 39. 109 applicants, 95% accepted, 85 enrolled. *Faculty:* 22 full-time (11 women), 26 part-time/adjunct (18 women). *Financial support:* In 2015–16, 84 students received support, including 6 research assistantships with partial tuition reimbursements available (averaging $7,710 per year); scholarships/grants and unspecified assistantships also available. Financial award application deadline: 3/15; financial award applicants required to submit FAFSA. In 2015, 72 master's awarded. *Degree program information:* Part-time and evening/weekend programs available. Part-time, evening/weekend, online learning. Offers ESL program specialist (K-12) (Certificate); general supervisor (PreK-12) (Certificate); health and physical education (K-12) (Certificate); middle level (4-8) (Certificate); multicultural education (M Ed); pre K-4 (Certificate); pre K-4 with special education (Certificate); reading (M Ed); reading specialist (K-12) (Certificate); reading supervisor (K-12) (Certificate); school health services (M Ed); school health supervisor (Certificate); school nurse (Certificate); school principalship (K-12) (Certificate); secondary biology education (7-12) (Certificate); secondary chemistry education (7-12) (Certificate); secondary communication education (7-12) (Certificate); secondary education (7-12) (Certificate); secondary English education (7-12) (Certificate); secondary math education (7-12) (Certificate); secondary social studies education (7-12) (Certificate); special education (M Ed); special education (7-12) (Certificate); special education (Pre K-8) (Certificate); special education supervisor (N-12) (Certificate); TESOL (M Ed); world language (Certificate). *Application deadline:* For fall admission, 8/14 for domestic students; for spring admission, 12/20 for domestic students. Applications are processed on a rolling basis. *Application fee:* $35. *Executive Director of Enrollment*, Michael Dziedziak, 800-732-7669, Fax: 610-225-5601, E-mail: gpsadm@eastern.edu.

Palmer Theological Seminary Students: 107 full-time (56 women), 104 part-time (51 women); includes 115 minority (110 Black or African American, non-Hispanic/Latino; 1 Asian, non-Hispanic/Latino; 3 Hispanic/Latino; 1 Two or more races, non-Hispanic/Latino), 4 international. Average age 47. 117 applicants, 56% accepted, 61 enrolled. *Faculty:* 14 full-time (7 women), 17 part-time/adjunct (7 women). *Financial support:* In 2015–16, 130 students received support, including 2 fellowships (averaging $4,000 per year), 15 teaching assistantships (averaging $1,200 per year); career-related internships or fieldwork, Federal Work-Study, and scholarships/grants also available. Financial award application deadline: 8/1; financial award applicants required to submit FAFSA. In 2015, 45 master's, 9 doctorates awarded. *Degree program information:* Part-time programs available. Part-time, online learning. Offers Biblical studies and theology (MTS); Christian counseling (MTS); Christian faith and public policy (MTS); contextual leadership (D Min); divinity (M Div); general studies (MTS). *Application deadline:* For fall admission, 8/1 priority date for domestic students, 3/31 for international students; for spring admission, 1/15 for domestic students, 10/31 for international students. Applications are processed on a rolling basis. *Application fee:* $30. Electronic applications accepted.

Program in Marriage and Family Therapy Studies Students: 52 full-time (39 women); includes 36 minority (30 Black or African American, non-Hispanic/Latino; 1 Asian, non-Hispanic/Latino; 5 Hispanic/Latino). Average age 42. 17 applicants, 76% accepted, 12 enrolled. *Faculty:* 1 (woman) full-time, 3 part-time/adjunct (2 women). In 2015, 7 doctorates awarded. *Degree program information:* Evening/weekend programs available. Evening/weekend, online learning. Offers marriage and family therapy studies (DA). *Application deadline:* For spring admission, 1/15 for domestic students. *Application fee:* $75. *Application Contact:* Deb Berghuis. *Executive Director of Enrollment*, Dr. Gwen White, 800-732-7669, Fax: 610-225-5601, E-mail: gpsadm@eastern.edu.

Program in Organizational Leadership Students: 82 full-time (48 women); includes 22 minority (16 Black or African American, non-Hispanic/Latino; 3 Asian, non-Hispanic/Latino; 3 Hispanic/Latino), 4 international. Average age 46. In 2015, 5 doctorates awarded. Offers organizational leadership (PhD). *Director*, Dr. Gwen White, 610-341-1596.

Program in Theological and Cultural Anthropology Students: 7 full-time (5 women), 3 part-time (1 woman); includes 3 minority (1 Black or African American, non-Hispanic/Latino; 2 Hispanic/Latino). Average age 28. 6 applicants, 100% accepted, 5 enrolled. Offers theological and cultural anthropology (MA). *Application deadline:* For fall admission, 8/14 for domestic students. Applications are processed on a rolling basis. *Application fee:* $35. Electronic applications accepted. *Executive Director of Enrollment*, Michael Dziedziak, 800-732-7669, Fax: 610-225-5601, E-mail: gpsadm@eastern.edu.

School of Leadership and Development Students: 83 full-time (47 women), 56 part-time (30 women); includes 40 minority (25 Black or African American, non-Hispanic/Latino; 1 American Indian or Alaska Native, non-Hispanic/Latino; 2 Asian, non-Hispanic/Latino; 8 Hispanic/Latino; 1 Native Hawaiian or other Pacific Islander, non-Hispanic/Latino; 3 Two or more races, non-Hispanic/Latino), 23 international. Average age 33. 62 applicants, 90% accepted, 46 enrolled. *Faculty:* 6 full-time (3 women), 19 part-time/adjunct (8 women). *Financial support:* In 2015–16, 131 students received support, including 3 fellowships with partial tuition reimbursements available (averaging $2,500 per year), 7 research assistantships with partial tuition reimbursements available (averaging $1,500 per year); scholarships/grants and unspecified assistantships also available. Financial award application deadline: 3/15; financial award applicants required to submit FAFSA. In 2015, 83 master's awarded. *Degree program information:* Part-time and evening/weekend programs available. Part-time, evening/weekend, online learning. Offers economic development (MBA); international development (MA); nonprofit management (MS); organizational leadership (MA). *Application deadline:* For fall admission, 8/14 for domestic students. Applications are processed on a rolling basis. *Application fee:* $35. *Executive Director of Enrollment*, Michael Dziedziak, 800-732-7669, Fax: 610-225-5601, E-mail: gpsadm@eastern.edu.

School of Management Studies Students: 38 full-time (29 women), 176 part-time (114 women); includes 101 minority (86 Black or African American, non-Hispanic/Latino; 7 Asian, non-Hispanic/Latino; 7 Hispanic/Latino; 1 Two or more races, non-Hispanic/Latino), 23 international. Average age 35. 84 applicants, 96% accepted, 64 enrolled. *Faculty:* 7 full-time (5 women), 40 part-time/adjunct (13 women). *Financial support:* In 2015–16, 34 students received support. Scholarships/grants available. Financial award applicants required to submit FAFSA. In 2015, 143 master's awarded. *Degree program information:* Part-time and evening/weekend programs available. Part-time, evening/weekend, online learning. Offers health administration (MBA); health services management (MS); management (MBA). Programs also offered at Harrisburg location. *Application deadline:* For fall admission, 8/16 for domestic students; for spring admission, 3/14 for domestic students. Applications are processed on a rolling basis. *Application fee:* $35. *Executive Director of Enrollment*, Michael Dziedziak, 800-732-7669, Fax: 610-225-5601, E-mail: gpsadm@eastern.edu.

EASTERN VIRGINIA MEDICAL SCHOOL, Norfolk, VA 23501-1980

General Information Independent, coed, graduate-only institution. *Graduate housing:* On-campus housing not available.

GRADUATE UNITS

Biotechnology Program Offers biotechnology (MS). Electronic applications accepted.

Doctoral Program in Biomedical Sciences Offers biomedical sciences (PhD). Electronic applications accepted.

Graduate Art Therapy and Counseling Program Offers art therapy and counseling (MS). Electronic applications accepted.

Master of Physician Assistant Program Offers physician assistant (MPA). Electronic applications accepted.

Master of Public Health Program ***Degree program information:*** Evening/weekend programs available. Evening/weekend. Offers public health (MPH). Program offered jointly with Old Dominion University. Electronic applications accepted.

Master of Surgical Assisting Program Offers surgical assisting (MSA). Electronic applications accepted.

Master's Program in Biomedical Sciences Research Offers biomedical sciences research (MS). Electronic applications accepted.

Master's Program in Clinical Embryology and Andrology Online learning. Offers clinical embryology and andrology (MS). Electronic applications accepted.

Medical Master's Program in Biomedical Sciences Offers biomedical sciences (MS). Electronic applications accepted.

Ophthalmic Technology Program Offers ophthalmic technology (Certificate). Electronic applications accepted.

Professional Program in Medicine Offers medicine (MD). Electronic applications accepted.

The Virginia Consortium Program in Clinical Psychology Offers clinical psychology (Psy D). Program offered jointly with The College of William and Mary, Norfolk State University, and Old Dominion University.

EASTERN WASHINGTON UNIVERSITY, Cheney, WA 99004-2431

General Information State-supported, coed, comprehensive institution. CGS member. *Enrollment:* 12,361 graduate, professional, and undergraduate students; 694 full-time matriculated graduate/professional students (443 women), 258 part-time matriculated graduate/professional students (184 women). *Enrollment by degree level:* 799 master's, 114 doctoral, 39 other advanced degrees. *Graduate faculty:* 576. *Graduate housing:* Rooms and/or apartments available on a first-come, first-served basis to single and married students. Housing application deadline: 5/1. *Student services:* Campus employment opportunities, campus safety program, career counseling, child daycare facilities, exercise/wellness program, free psychological counseling, grant writing training, international student services, low-cost health insurance, multicultural affairs office, services for students with disabilities, teacher training, writing training. *Library:* John F. Kennedy Library. *Collection:* Books: 776,002 (physical), 122,696 (digital/electronic); Databases: 185. Students can reserve study rooms.

Computer facilities: Computer purchase and lease plans are available. 1,012 computers available on campus for general student use. A campuswide network can be accessed from student residence rooms and from off campus. Online class registration, network disk storage; discounted software; laptops, still and video cameras, projectors for checkout; print credit; black white laser, color laser, and color photo options, large format print service are available.
Website: http://www.ewu.edu/

General Application Contact: Roberta Brooke, Interim Director of Graduate Programs, 509-359-6297, Fax: 509-359-6044, E-mail: gradprograms@ewu.edu.

GRADUATE UNITS

Graduate Studies Students: 877 full-time (596 women), 301 part-time (203 women); includes 184 minority (23 Black or African American, non-Hispanic/Latino; 33 American Indian or Alaska Native, non-Hispanic/Latino; 58 Asian, non-Hispanic/Latino; 66 Hispanic/Latino; 2 Native Hawaiian or other Pacific Islander, non-Hispanic/Latino; 2 Two or more races, non-Hispanic/Latino). Average age 32. 1,587 applicants, 25% accepted, 359 enrolled. *Faculty:* 576. *Financial support:* In 2015–16, 183 teaching assistantships with partial tuition reimbursements (averaging $7,000 per year) were awarded; career-related internships or fieldwork, Federal Work-Study, institutionally sponsored loans, scholarships/grants, health care benefits, tuition waivers (full and partial), and unspecified assistantships also available. Support available to part-time students. Financial award application deadline: 2/1. In 2015, 1,604 master's, 38 doctorates awarded. *Degree program information:* Part-time and evening/weekend programs available. Part-time, evening/weekend. Offers interdisciplinary studies (MA, MS). *Application deadline:* For fall admission, 3/1 priority date for domestic students. *Application fee:* $50. *Vice Provost of Academic Planning, Graduate Programs, Grants and Institutional Research*, Colin Ormsby, PhD, 509-359-4217, E-mail: cormsby@ewu.edu.

College of Arts, Letters and Education Students: 695 full-time (444 women), 256 part-time (182 women); includes 110 minority (1 Black or African American, non-Hispanic/Latino; 8 American Indian or Alaska Native, non-Hispanic/Latino; 10 Asian, non-Hispanic/Latino; 91 Hispanic/Latino), 34 international. Average age 32. 227 applicants, 43% accepted, 72 enrolled. *Faculty:* 111 full-time, 40 part-time/adjunct. *Financial support:* In 2015–16, 27 teaching assistantships with partial tuition reimbursements (averaging $7,000 per year) were awarded; career-related internships or fieldwork, Federal Work-Study, institutionally sponsored loans, scholarships/grants, health care benefits, tuition waivers (partial), and unspecified assistantships also available. Support available to part-time students. In 2015, 120 master's awarded. *Degree program information:* Part-time programs available. Part-time. Offers adult education (M Ed); arts, letters and education (M Ed, MA, MFA, MS); composition (MA); creative writing (MFA); curriculum development (M Ed); early childhood education (M Ed); education (M Ed); elementary teaching (M Ed); exercise science (MS); general (MA); history (MA); instrumental/vocal performance (MA); jazz pedagogy (MA); literacy (M Ed); literature (MA); music education (MA); rhetoric, composition, and technical communication (MA); secondary teaching (M Ed); special education (M Ed); sports and recreation administration (MS); teaching English as a second language (MA); teaching K-8 (M Ed). *Application deadline:* Applications are processed on a rolling basis. *Application fee:* $50. *Application Contact:* Julie Marr, Advisor/Recruiter for Graduate Studies, 509-359-2491, Fax: 509-359-6044, E-mail: gradprograms@ewu.edu. *Dean*, Dr. Lynn C. Briggs, 509-359-2328.

College of Business and Public Administration Degree program information: Part-time and evening/weekend programs available. Part-time, evening/weekend. Offers business administration (MBA); business and public administration (MBA, MPA, MURP); public administration (MPA); urban and regional planning (MURP).

College of Science, Health and Engineering Degree program information: Part-time programs available. Part-time. Offers biology (MS); communication disorders (MS); computer and technology-supported education (M Ed); computer science (MS); dental hygiene (MS); mathematics (MS); occupational therapy (MOT); physical therapy (DPT); science, health and engineering (M Ed, MA, MOT, MS, DPT); teaching mathematics (MA).

College of Social and Behavioral Sciences and Social Work Degree program information: Part-time and evening/weekend programs available. Part-time, evening/weekend. Offers applied psychology (MS); clinical psychology (MS); communication studies (MSC); experimental psychology (MS); mental health counseling (MS); psychology (MS); school counseling (MS); school psychology (MS); social and behavioral sciences and social work (MS, MSC, MSW); social work (MSW).

EAST STROUDSBURG UNIVERSITY OF PENNSYLVANIA, East Stroudsburg, PA 18301-2999

General Information State-supported, coed, comprehensive institution. CGS member. *Enrollment:* 6,828 graduate, professional, and undergraduate students; 327 full-time matriculated graduate/professional students (189 women), 267 part-time matriculated graduate/professional students (187 women). *Enrollment by degree level:* 535 master's, 55 doctoral, 4 other advanced degrees. *Graduate faculty:* 83 full-time (40 women), 12 part-time/adjunct (7 women). *International tuition:* $15,368 full-time. *Tuition, area resident:* Full-time $8460; part-time $5640 per year. Tuition, state resident: full-time $8460; part-time $5640 per year. Tuition, nonresident: full-time $12,690; part-time $8460 per year. *Required fees:* $2462; $1630 per unit. $815 per semester. Tuition and fees vary according to course load, campus/location and program. *Graduate housing:* Room and/or apartments available on a first-come, first-served basis to single students; on-campus housing not available to married students. Typical cost: $7320 per year ($9848 including board). Room and board charges vary according to board plan and housing facility selected. Housing application deadline: 6/1. *Student services:* Campus employment opportunities, campus safety program, career counseling, child daycare facilities, exercise/wellness program, free psychological counseling, international student services, low-cost health insurance, multicultural affairs office, services for students with disabilities. *Library:* Kemp Library. *Collection:* Books: 599,041 (physical), 81,119 (digital/electronic); Serial titles: 73,801 (physical); Databases: 82. Weekly public service hours: 99.

Computer facilities: 500 computers available on campus for general student use. A campuswide network can be accessed from student residence rooms and from off campus. Online class registration, online classes are available.
Website: http://www.esu.edu/

General Application Contact: Kevin Quintero, Coordinator of Graduate Admissions, 570-422-3536, Fax: 570-422-3711, E-mail: kquintero@esu.edu.

GRADUATE UNITS

Graduate College Students: 327 full-time (189 women), 267 part-time (187 women); includes 101 minority (46 Black or African American, non-Hispanic/Latino; 1 American Indian or Alaska Native, non-Hispanic/Latino; 2 Asian, non-Hispanic/Latino; 33 Hispanic/Latino; 1 Native Hawaiian or other Pacific Islander, non-Hispanic/Latino; 18 Two or more races, non-Hispanic/Latino), 36 international. Average age 30. 742 applicants, 47% accepted, 206 enrolled. *Faculty:* 83 full-time (40 women), 12 part-time/adjunct (7 women). *Financial support:* Research assistantships with tuition reimbursements, teaching assistantships, career-related internships or fieldwork, Federal Work-Study, scholarships/grants, and unspecified assistantships available. Support available to part-time students. Financial award application deadline: 6/30; financial award applicants required to submit FAFSA. In 2015, 223 master's awarded. *Degree program information:* Part-time and evening/weekend programs available. Part-time, evening/weekend, 100% online, blended/hybrid learning. *Application deadline:* For fall admission, 7/31 priority date for domestic students, 6/30 priority date for international students; for spring admission, 11/30 for domestic students, 10/31 for international students. Applications are processed on a rolling basis. *Application fee:* $50. Electronic applications accepted. *Application Contact:* Kevin Quintero, Graduate Admissions Coordinator, 570-422-3536, Fax: 570-422-3711, E-mail: kquintero@esu.edu. *Faculty Liaison to the Provost*, Dr. Shala Davis, 570-422-3536, Fax: 570-422-3711, E-mail: sdavis@esu.edu.

College of Arts and Sciences Students: 83 full-time (28 women), 44 part-time (23 women); includes 20 minority (9 Black or African American, non-Hispanic/Latino; 2 Asian, non-Hispanic/Latino; 5 Hispanic/Latino; 1 Native Hawaiian or other Pacific Islander, non-Hispanic/Latino; 3 Two or more races, non-Hispanic/Latino), 30 international. Average age 27. 100 applicants, 65% accepted, 35 enrolled. *Faculty:* 34 full-time (11 women), 2 part-time/adjunct (1 woman). *Financial support:* Research assistantships with tuition reimbursements, career-related internships or fieldwork, Federal Work-Study, and institutionally sponsored loans available. Financial award application deadline: 3/1; financial award applicants required to submit FAFSA. *Degree program information:* Part-time and evening/weekend programs available. Part-time, evening/weekend. Offers arts and sciences (M Ed, MA, MS); biology (M Ed, MS); computer science (MS); GIS and remote sensing in environmental science (MS); history (M Ed, MA); information security (MS); management and leadership in public administration (MS); political science (M Ed, MA). *Application deadline:* For fall admission, 7/31 for domestic students, 6/30 priority date for international students; for spring admission, 11/30 for domestic students, 10/31 for international students. Applications are processed on a rolling basis. *Application fee:* $50. Electronic applications accepted. *Application Contact:* Kevin Quintero, Graduate Admissions Coordinator, 570-422-3536, Fax: 570-422-3711, E-mail: kquintero@esu.edu. *Dean of Arts and Sciences*, Dr. Peter Hawkes, 570-422-3494.

College of Business and Management Financial support: Research assistantships, career-related internships or fieldwork, Federal Work-Study, and institutionally sponsored loans available. Financial award application deadline: 3/1; financial award applicants required to submit FAFSA. *Degree program information:* Part-time and evening/weekend programs available. Part-time, evening/weekend, online learning. Offers business and management (MS); management and leadership in sport management (MS); sport management (MS). *Application deadline:* For fall admission, 7/31 for domestic students, 6/30 priority date for international students; for spring admission, 11/30 for domestic students, 10/31 for international students. Applications are processed on a rolling basis. *Application fee:* $50. Electronic applications accepted. *Application Contact:* Kevin Quintero, Graduate Admissions Coordinator, 570-422-3536, Fax: 570-422-2711, E-mail: kquintero@esu.edu. *Dean*, Tribhuvan Puri, 570-422-3589, Fax: 570-422-3506, E-mail: tpuri@esu.edu.

College of Education Financial support: Research assistantships with tuition reimbursements, career-related internships or fieldwork, Federal Work-Study, and institutionally sponsored loans available. Financial award application deadline: 3/1; financial award applicants required to submit FAFSA. *Degree program information:* Part-time and evening/weekend programs available. Part-time, evening/weekend, online learning. Offers education (M Ed, Ed D); educational leadership and administration (Ed D); instructional technology (M Ed); reading (M Ed); secondary education (M Ed); special education (M Ed); special education: applied behavior analysis (M Ed); teaching the developing child (M Ed). *Application deadline:* For fall admission, 7/31 priority date for domestic students, 6/30 priority date for international students; for spring admission, 11/30 for domestic students, 10/31 for international students. Applications are processed on a rolling basis. *Application fee:* $50. Electronic applications accepted. *Application Contact:* Kevin Quintero, Graduate Admissions Coordinator, 570-422-3536, Fax: 570-422-3711, E-mail: kquintero@esu.edu. *Dean*, Terry Barry, 570-422-3377, Fax: 570-422-3506, E-mail: tbarry1@esu.edu.

College of Health Sciences Financial support: Research assistantships with tuition reimbursements, career-related internships or fieldwork, Federal Work-Study, and institutionally sponsored loans available. Financial award application deadline: 3/1; financial award applicants required to submit FAFSA. *Degree program information:* Part-time and evening/weekend programs available. Part-time, evening/weekend, online learning. Offers athletic training (MS); clinical exercise physiology (MS); exercise science (MS); health education (MS); health sciences (MPH, MS); public health (MPH); speech-language pathology (MS). *Application deadline:* For fall admission, 7/31 priority date for domestic students, 6/30 priority date for international students; for spring admission, 11/30 for domestic students, 10/31 for international students. Applications are processed on a rolling basis. *Application fee:* $50. Electronic applications accepted. *Application Contact:* Kevin Quintero, Graduate Admissions Coordinator, 570-422-3536, Fax: 570-422-2711, E-mail: kquintero@esu.edu. *Interim Dean*, Dr. Shala Davis, 570-422-3425, Fax: 570-422-3347, E-mail: sdavis@esu.edu.

EAST TENNESSEE STATE UNIVERSITY, Johnson City, TN 37614

General Information State-supported, coed, university. *Enrollment:* 14,334 graduate, professional, and undergraduate students; 1,864 full-time matriculated graduate/professional students (1,058 women), 1,093 part-time matriculated graduate/professional students (797 women). *Enrollment by degree level:* 1,614 master's, 1,197 doctoral, 146 other advanced degrees. *Graduate faculty:* 588 full-time (260 women), 32 part-time/adjunct (22 women). *Graduate housing:* Rooms and/or apartments available on a first-come, first-served basis to single and married students. Housing application deadline: 8/1. *Student services:* Campus employment opportunities, campus safety program, career counseling, child daycare facilities, exercise/wellness program, free psychological counseling, grant writing training, international student services, low-cost health insurance, multicultural affairs office, services for students with disabilities, teacher training. *Library:* Charles C. Sherrod Library plus 2 others. *Collection:* Books: 731,960 (physical), 98,312 (digital/electronic); Databases: 158. *Research affiliation:* Puckett Institute (education), Cyberonics (biomedical science), Mountain Home VA Medical Center (clinical and biomedical science), Mountain States Health Alliance; Wellmont Health System; State of Franklin Healthcare Associates (clinical, nursing, and biomedical science), Oak Ridge National Laboratory (biomedical physical science and computer science), Frontier Health, Inc.; Cherokee Health Systems (clinical and education).

Computer facilities: Computer purchase and lease plans are available. 1,400 computers available on campus for general student use. A campuswide network can be accessed from student residence rooms. Online class registration is available.
Website: http://www.etsu.edu/

General Application Contact: Dr. Karin Bartoszuk, Associate Dean, 423-439-4221, Fax: 423-439-5624, E-mail: gradsch@etsu.edu.

GRADUATE UNITS

Bill Gatton College of Pharmacy Students: 323 full-time (164 women); includes 26 minority (9 Black or African American, non-Hispanic/Latino; 10 Asian, non-Hispanic/Latino; 4 Hispanic/Latino; 3 Two or more races, non-Hispanic/Latino). Average age 25. 630 applicants, 27% accepted, 78 enrolled. In 2015, 76 doctorates awarded. *Degree program information:* Part-time programs available. Part-time. Offers pharmacy (Pharm D). *Application Contact:* Admissions and Records Office, 423-439-6300, Fax: 423-439-6320, E-mail: pharmacy@etsu.edu. *Dean*, Dr. Larry D. Calhoun, 423-439-2068, Fax: 423-439-6310, E-mail: calhoun@etsu.edu.

James H. Quillen College of Medicine Students: 319 full-time (136 women), 2 part-time (1 woman); includes 49 minority (9 Black or African American, non-Hispanic/Latino;

3 American Indian or Alaska Native, non-Hispanic/Latino; 27 Asian, non-Hispanic/Latino; 8 Hispanic/Latino; 2 Two or more races, non-Hispanic/Latino), 13 international. Average age 26. 2,187 applicants, 6% accepted, 72 enrolled. *Financial support:* Career-related internships or fieldwork, Federal Work-Study, institutionally sponsored loans, scholarships/grants, and tuition waivers (full) available. Financial award applicants required to submit FAFSA. In 2015, 76 doctorates awarded. *Degree program information:* Part-time programs available. Part-time. Offers anatomy (PhD); biochemistry (PhD); medicine (MD, PhD); microbiology (PhD); pharmaceutical sciences (PhD); pharmacology (PhD); physiology (PhD); quantitative biosciences (PhD). *Application Contact:* E. Doug Taylor, Assistant Dean for Admissions and Records, 423-439-2033, Fax: 423-439-2110, E-mail: dougt@etsu.edu. *Dean*, Dr. Philip Bagnell, 423-439-6316, Fax: 423-439-8090, E-mail: bagnell@etsu.edu.

School of Graduate Studies Students: 1,834 full-time (1,024 women), 1,097 part-time (818 women); includes 327 minority (138 Black or African American, non-Hispanic/Latino; 9 American Indian or Alaska Native, non-Hispanic/Latino; 81 Asian, non-Hispanic/Latino; 45 Hispanic/Latino; 54 Two or more races, non-Hispanic/Latino), 149 international. Average age 31. 2,622 applicants, 41% accepted, 727 enrolled. *Faculty:* 588 full-time (260 women), 32 part-time/adjunct (22 women). *Financial support:* In 2015–16, 811 students received support, including 21 fellowships with tuition reimbursements available (averaging $15,600 per year), 573 research assistantships with tuition reimbursements available (averaging $9,300 per year), 219 teaching assistantships with tuition reimbursements available (averaging $7,900 per year). Financial award application deadline: 7/1; financial award applicants required to submit FAFSA. In 2015, 660 master's, 118 doctorates, 55 other advanced degrees awarded. *Application deadline:* For fall admission, 6/1 for domestic students, 4/30 for international students; for spring admission, 11/1 for domestic students, 9/30 for international students. *Application fee:* $35 ($45 for international students). *Application Contact:* Graduate Specialist, 423-439-4221, Fax: 423-439-5624, E-mail: gradsch@etsu.edu. *Dean*, Dr. Cecilia McIntosh, 423-439-4221, Fax: 423-439-5624, E-mail: gradsch@etsu.edu.

College of Arts and Sciences Students: 326 full-time (185 women), 112 part-time (46 women); includes 46 minority (21 Black or African American, non-Hispanic/Latino; 1 American Indian or Alaska Native, non-Hispanic/Latino; 7 Asian, non-Hispanic/Latino; 5 Hispanic/Latino; 1 Native Hawaiian or other Pacific Islander, non-Hispanic/Latino; 11 Two or more races, non-Hispanic/Latino), 66 international. Average age 30. 547 applicants, 45% accepted, 139 enrolled. *Faculty:* 200 full-time (74 women), 8 part-time/adjunct (2 women). *Financial support:* In 2015–16, 265 students received support, including 120 research assistantships with tuition reimbursements available (averaging $8,300 per year), 144 teaching assistantships with tuition reimbursements available (averaging $7,600 per year); career-related internships or fieldwork, institutionally sponsored loans, traineeships, and unspecified assistantships also available. Financial award application deadline: 7/1; financial award applicants required to submit FAFSA. In 2015, 146 master's, 9 doctorates, 17 other advanced degrees awarded. Offers Appalachian studies (MA, Postbaccalaureate Certificate); arts and sciences (MA, MCM, MFA, MPA, MS, MSW, PhD, Postbaccalaureate Certificate); chemistry (MS); criminal justice and criminology (MA, Postbaccalaureate Certificate); economic development (Postbaccalaureate Certificate); geospatial analysis (MS); history (MA); literature and language (MA, Postbaccalaureate Certificate); mathematical sciences (MS); not-for-profit administration (MPA); paleontology (MS); planning and development (MPA); professional communication (MA); psychology (PhD); public financial management (MPA); social work (MSW); sociology and anthropology (MA); studio art (MFA); urban planning (Postbaccalaureate Certificate). *Application fee:* $35 ($45 for international students). *Application Contact:* School of Graduate Studies, 423-439-4221, Fax: 423-439-5624, E-mail: gradsch@etsu.edu. *Dean*, Dr. Gordon K. Anderson, 423-439-5671, Fax: 423-439-4645, E-mail: andersgk@etsu.edu.

College of Business and Technology Students: 155 full-time (57 women), 76 part-time (24 women); includes 20 minority (9 Black or African American, non-Hispanic/Latino; 5 Asian, non-Hispanic/Latino; 3 Hispanic/Latino; 3 Two or more races, non-Hispanic/Latino), 39 international. Average age 30. 365 applicants, 39% accepted, 95 enrolled. *Faculty:* 55 full-time (11 women), 1 part-time/adjunct (0 women). *Financial support:* In 2015–16, 117 students received support, including 92 research assistantships with tuition reimbursements available (averaging $5,700 per year), 18 teaching assistantships with tuition reimbursements available (averaging $10,000 per year). Financial award application deadline: 7/1; financial award applicants required to submit FAFSA. In 2015, 96 master's, 6 other advanced degrees awarded. Offers accountancy (M Acc); business administration (MBA, Postbaccalaureate Certificate); business and technology (M Acc, MBA, MS, Postbaccalaureate Certificate); computing (MS, Postbaccalaureate Certificate); digital marketing (MS); engineering technology, surveying and digital media (MS, Postbaccalaureate Certificate); entrepreneurial leadership (Postbaccalaureate Certificate); health care management (Postbaccalaureate Certificate). *Application fee:* $35 ($45 for international students). *Application Contact:* School of Graduate Studies, 423-439-4221, Fax: 423-439-5624, E-mail: gradsch@etsu.edu. *Dean*, Dr. Dennis Depew, 423-439-4289, Fax: 423-439-5274, E-mail: depewd@etsu.edu.

College of Clinical and Rehabilitative Health Sciences Students: 220 full-time (164 women), 25 part-time (21 women); includes 11 minority (1 Black or African American, non-Hispanic/Latino; 4 Asian, non-Hispanic/Latino; 5 Hispanic/Latino; 1 Two or more races, non-Hispanic/Latino). Average age 26. 425 applicants, 27% accepted, 51 enrolled. *Faculty:* 57 full-time (41 women). *Financial support:* In 2015–16, 97 students received support, including 97 research assistantships with tuition reimbursements available (averaging $3,400 per year), 6 teaching assistantships with tuition reimbursements available (averaging $4,500 per year). In 2015, 47 master's, 44 doctorates awarded. Offers allied health (MSAH); clinical and rehabilitative health sciences (MS, MSAH, Au D, DPT); clinical nutrition (MS); communicative disorders (MS); physical therapy (DPT). *Application Contact:* School of Graduate Studies, 423-439-4221, Fax: 423-439-5624, E-mail: gradsch@etsu.edu. *Dean*, Dr. Don Samples, 423-439-7454, Fax: 423-439-4240, E-mail: carhs@etsu.edu.

College of Education Students: 288 full-time (175 women), 349 part-time (250 women); includes 70 minority (47 Black or African American, non-Hispanic/Latino; 1 American Indian or Alaska Native, non-Hispanic/Latino; 5 Asian, non-Hispanic/Latino; 5 Hispanic/Latino; 12 Two or more races, non-Hispanic/Latino), 21 international. Average age 34. 427 applicants, 52% accepted, 187 enrolled. *Faculty:* 114 full-time (74 women), 8 part-time/adjunct (all women). *Financial support:* In 2015–16, 216 students received support, including 21 fellowships with full tuition reimbursements available (averaging $15,000 per year), 146 research assistantships with full tuition reimbursements available (averaging $6,000 per year), 47 teaching assistantships with full tuition reimbursements available (averaging $6,000 per year); career-related internships or fieldwork, institutionally sponsored loans, scholarships/grants, and unspecified assistantships also available. Financial award application deadline: 7/1; financial award applicants required to submit FAFSA. In 2015, 172 master's, 43 doctorates, 8 other advanced degrees awarded. Offers counseling and human services (MA); early childhood education (MA, PhD); early childhood education emergent inquiry (Post-Master's Certificate); education (M Ed, MA, MAT, Ed D, PhD, Ed S, Post-Master's Certificate, Postbaccalaureate Certificate); educational leadership and policy analysis (M Ed, Ed D, Ed S); educational technology (M Ed); elementary education (M Ed); exercise physiology and performance (MA); kinesiology, sport and recreation management (Post-Master's Certificate); reading (MA); school library professional (Post-Master's Certificate); secondary education (M Ed); special education (M Ed); sport management (MA); sport physiology and performance (PhD); teacher education with multiple levels (MAT). *Application Contact:* School of Graduate Studies, 423-439-4221, Fax: 423-439-5624, E-mail: gradsch@etsu.edu. *Dean*, Dr. Terrance Hicks, 423-439-7626, Fax: 423-439-7560, E-mail: lewisar@etsu.edu.

College of Nursing Students: 107 full-time (91 women), 331 part-time (294 women); includes 37 minority (18 Black or African American, non-Hispanic/Latino; 1 American Indian or Alaska Native, non-Hispanic/Latino; 6 Asian, non-Hispanic/Latino; 4 Hispanic/Latino; 2 Native Hawaiian or other Pacific Islander, non-Hispanic/Latino; 6 Two or more races, non-Hispanic/Latino). Average age 36. 280 applicants, 42% accepted, 83 enrolled. *Faculty:* 27 full-time (26 women), 7 part-time/adjunct (all women). *Financial support:* In 2015–16, 3 students received support, including 9 research assistantships with tuition reimbursements available (averaging $4,500 per year), 1 teaching assistantship (averaging $6,000 per year); career-related internships or fieldwork, institutionally sponsored loans, scholarships/grants, and unspecified assistantships also available. Financial award application deadline: 7/1; financial award applicants required to submit FAFSA. In 2015, 80 master's, 13 doctorates, 10 other advanced degrees awarded. *Degree program information:* Part-time and evening/weekend programs available. Part-time, evening/weekend, online learning. Offers family nurse practitioner (DNP); nursing (MSN, PhD, Post-Master's Certificate). *Application deadline:* For fall admission, 2/1 for domestic and international students; for spring admission, 7/1 for domestic students. *Application fee:* $35 ($45 for international students). Electronic applications accepted. *Application Contact:* Linda Raines, School of Graduate Studies, 423-439-6158, Fax: 423-439-5624, E-mail: rainesIt@etsu.edu. *Dean*, Dr. Wendy Nehring, 423-439-7051, Fax: 423-439-4522, E-mail: nursing@etsu.edu.

College of Public Health Students: 105 full-time (74 women), 89 part-time (75 women); includes 45 minority (29 Black or African American, non-Hispanic/Latino; 10 Asian, non-Hispanic/Latino; 3 Hispanic/Latino; 3 Two or more races, non-Hispanic/Latino), 24 international. Average age 30. 147 applicants, 71% accepted, 60 enrolled. *Faculty:* 43 full-time (14 women), 4 part-time/adjunct (3 women). *Financial support:* In 2015–16, 57 students received support, including 54 research assistantships with tuition reimbursements available (averaging $6,750 per year), 3 teaching assistantships with tuition reimbursements available (averaging $14,000 per year); career-related internships or fieldwork, institutionally sponsored loans, scholarships/grants, and unspecified assistantships also available. Financial award application deadline: 7/1; financial award applicants required to submit FAFSA. In 2015, 26 master's, 6 doctorates, 9 other advanced degrees awarded. *Degree program information:* Part-time programs available. Part-time, online learning. Offers environmental health (MSEH, PhD); public health (MPH, MSEH, DPH, PhD, Postbaccalaureate Certificate). *Application fee:* $35 ($45 for international students). Electronic applications accepted. *Application Contact:* Mary Duncan, Graduate Specialist, 423-439-4302, Fax: 423-439-5624, E-mail: duncanm@etsu.edu. *Dean*, Dr. Randy Wykoff, 423-439-4243, Fax: 423-439-5238, E-mail: wykoff@etsu.edu.

School of Continuing Studies and Academic Outreach Students: 11 full-time (7 women), 27 part-time (21 women); includes 4 minority (2 Black or African American, non-Hispanic/Latino; 1 American Indian or Alaska Native, non-Hispanic/Latino; 1 Hispanic/Latino), 3 international. Average age 41. 42 applicants, 50% accepted, 19 enrolled. *Faculty:* 12 full-time (6 women). *Financial support:* In 2015–16, 14 students received support, including 7 research assistantships with full tuition reimbursements available (averaging $7,000 per year), 1 teaching assistantship with full tuition reimbursement available (averaging $6,000 per year); institutionally sponsored loans, scholarships/grants, tuition waivers, and unspecified assistantships also available. Financial award application deadline: 7/1; financial award applicants required to submit FAFSA. In 2015, 12 master's, 2 other advanced degrees awarded. *Degree program information:* Part-time programs available. Part-time, online learning. *Application deadline:* For fall admission, 6/1 for domestic students, 4/30 for international students; for spring admission, 11/1 for domestic students, 9/30 for international students. *Application fee:* $35 ($45 for international students). Electronic applications accepted. *Application Contact:* Mary Duncan, Graduate Specialist, 423-439-4302, Fax: 423-439-5624, E-mail: duncanm@etsu.edu. *Dean*, Dr. Rick E. Osborn, 423-439-4223, Fax: 423-439-7091, E-mail: osbornr@etsu.edu.

EAST TEXAS BAPTIST UNIVERSITY, Marshall, TX 75670-1498

General Information Independent-religious, coed, comprehensive institution.

GRADUATE UNITS

Master of Arts in Counseling Program ***Degree program information:*** Part-time programs available. Part-time. Offers counseling (MA). Electronic applications accepted.

Master of Business Administration Program ***Degree program information:*** Part-time programs available. Part-time. Offers entrepreneurial leadership (MBA). Electronic applications accepted.

Master of Education Program ***Degree program information:*** Part-time programs available. Part-time. Offers curriculum and instruction (M Ed); principal certification (M Ed); sports and exercise leadership (M Ed); teacher certification (M Ed). Electronic applications accepted.

School of Christian Studies ***Degree program information:*** Part-time programs available. Part-time. Offers Christian ministry (MACM); religion (MA). Electronic applications accepted.

EAST WEST COLLEGE OF NATURAL MEDICINE, Sarasota, FL 34234

General Information Proprietary, coed, graduate-only institution.

GRADUATE UNITS

Graduate Programs Offers Oriental medicine (MSOM).

EC-COUNCIL UNIVERSITY, Albuquerque, NM 87109

General Information Proprietary, coed, upper-level institution.

GRADUATE UNITS

Program in Security Science Online learning. Offers security science (MSS).

ECOLE HÔTELIÈRE DE LAUSANNE, CH-1000 Lausanne 25, Switzerland

General Information Independent, coed, comprehensive institution.

GRADUATE UNITS

Program in Hospitality Administration Offers hospitality administration (MHA).

ÉCOLE POLYTECHNIQUE DE MONTRÉAL, Montréal, QC H3C 3A7, Canada

General Information Province-supported, coed, university. *Graduate housing:* Room and/or apartments available on a first-come, first-served basis to single students; on-campus housing not available to married students. Housing application deadline: 2/1. *Research affiliation:* Hydro-Quebec (energy), Bell Canada (telecommunications), Bombardier, Inc. (aircraft and aviation), IBM (computer research), Pratt and Whitney (aircraft and aviation), Ubisoft (video games).

GRADUATE UNITS

Graduate Programs ***Degree program information:*** Part-time and evening/weekend programs available. Part-time, evening/weekend. Offers aerothermics (M Eng, M Sc A, PhD); applied mechanics (M Eng, M Sc A, PhD); automation (M Eng, M Sc A, PhD); chemical engineering (M Eng, M Sc A, PhD, DESS); civil, geological and mining engineering (DESS); computer science (M Eng, M Sc A, PhD); electrical engineering (DESS); electrotechnology (M Eng, M Sc A, PhD); environmental engineering (M Eng, M Sc A, PhD); ergonomy (M Eng, M Sc A, DESS); geotechnical engineering (M Eng, M Sc A, PhD); hydraulics engineering (M Eng, M Sc A, PhD); mathematical method in CA engineering (M Eng, M Sc A, PhD); microelectronics (M Eng, M Sc A, PhD); microwave technology (M Eng, M Sc A, PhD); operational research (M Eng, M Sc A, PhD); optical engineering (M Eng, M Sc A, PhD); production (M Eng, M Sc A); solid-state physics and engineering (M Eng, M Sc A, PhD); structural engineering (M Eng, M Sc A, PhD); technology management (M Eng, M Sc A); tool design (M Eng, M Sc A, PhD); transportation engineering (M Eng, M Sc A, PhD). Electronic applications accepted.

Institute of Biomedical Engineering ***Degree program information:*** Part-time programs available. Part-time. Offers biomedical engineering (M Sc A, PhD, DESS). M Sc A and PhD programs offered jointly with Université de Montréal.

Institute of Nuclear Engineering Offers nuclear engineering (M Eng, PhD, DESS); nuclear engineering, socio-economics of energy (M Sc A).

ECUMENICAL THEOLOGICAL SEMINARY, Detroit, MI 48201

General Information Independent-religious, coed, graduate-only institution. *Graduate housing:* On-campus housing not available.

GRADUATE UNITS

Professional Program Offers theology (M Div).

Program in Ministry Offers ministry (D Min).

EDEN THEOLOGICAL SEMINARY, St. Louis, MO 63119-3192

General Information Independent-religious, coed, graduate-only institution. *Enrollment by degree level:* 118 master's, 25 doctoral. *Graduate faculty:* 10 full-time (6 women), 7 part-time/adjunct (2 women). *Graduate housing:* Rooms and/or apartments available on a first-come, first-served basis to single and married students. Housing application deadline: 7/30. *Student services:* Campus employment opportunities, international student services, services for students with disabilities, writing training. *Library:* Luhr Reading and Reference Library plus 1 other.

Computer facilities: 5 computers available on campus for general student use.
Website: http://www.eden.edu/

General Application Contact: Tiffany Pittman, Admissions Office, 314-918-2501, Fax: 314-918-2640, E-mail: tpittman@eden.edu.

GRADUATE UNITS

Graduate and Professional Programs Students: 97 full-time (56 women), 46 part-time (24 women); includes 28 minority (all Black or African American, non-Hispanic/Latino), 8 international. *Faculty:* 10 full-time (6 women), 7 part-time/adjunct (2 women). *Financial support:* Career-related internships or fieldwork and scholarships/grants available. Financial award application deadline: 6/15; financial award applicants required to submit FAFSA. Offers theology (M Div, MAPS, MTS, D Min). *Application deadline:* For fall admission, 8/10 for domestic students, 11/15 for international students; for winter admission, 12/15 for domestic students; for spring admission, 1/15 for domestic students. Applications are processed on a rolling basis. *Application fee:* $25. Electronic applications accepted. *Application Contact:* Tiffany Pittman, Admissions Office, 314-918-2501, Fax: 314-918-2640, E-mail: tpittman@eden.edu. *President*, Dr. David M. Greenhaw, 314-961-2620.

EDGEWOOD COLLEGE, Madison, WI 53711-1997

General Information Independent-religious, coed, comprehensive institution. *Enrollment:* 2,678 graduate, professional, and undergraduate students; 225 full-time matriculated graduate/professional students (144 women), 415 part-time matriculated graduate/professional students (309 women). *Enrollment by degree level:* 476 master's, 164 doctoral. *Graduate housing:* On-campus housing not available. *Student services:* Campus employment opportunities, career counseling, free psychological counseling, international student services, low-cost health insurance, multicultural affairs office, services for students with disabilities, writing training. *Library:* Oscar Rennebohm Library. *Collection:* Books: 93,406 (physical), 123,136 (digital/electronic); Serial titles: 279 (physical), 30,300 (digital/electronic); Databases: 76. Weekly public service hours: 98.

Computer facilities: Computer purchase and lease plans are available. 100 computers available on campus for general student use. A campuswide network can be accessed from student residence rooms and from off campus. Online class registration, online library are available.
Website: http://www.edgewood.edu/

General Application Contact: Joann Eastman, Admissions Counselor, 608-663-3250, Fax: 608-663-2214, E-mail: gps@edgewood.edu.

GRADUATE UNITS

Henry Predolin School of Nursing Students: 11 full-time (10 women), 60 part-time (55 women); includes 4 minority (1 Asian, non-Hispanic/Latino; 3 Hispanic/Latino). Average age 39. In 2015, 25 master's, 5 doctorates awarded. Offers administration (MSN); education (MSN); nursing (DNP). *Application deadline:* For fall admission, 8/15 priority date for domestic students, 5/1 for international students; for spring admission, 1/8 priority date for domestic students, 11/1 for international students. Applications are processed on a rolling basis. *Application fee:* $30. Electronic applications accepted. *Application Contact:* Tracy Kantor, Enrollment and Applications Manager, 608-663-3297, Fax: 608-663-3496, E-mail: gps@edgewood.edu. *Dean*, Dr. Margaret Noreuil, 608-663-2820, Fax: 608-663-3291, E-mail: mnoreuil@edgewood.edu.

Program in Business Students: 18 full-time (11 women), 98 part-time (48 women); includes 13 minority (2 Black or African American, non-Hispanic/Latino; 1 American Indian or Alaska Native, non-Hispanic/Latino; 5 Asian, non-Hispanic/Latino; 2 Hispanic/Latino; 1 Native Hawaiian or other Pacific Islander, non-Hispanic/Latino; 2 Two or more races, non-Hispanic/Latino), 10 international. Average age 32. *Financial support:* Career-related internships or fieldwork and scholarships/grants available. In 2015, 37 master's awarded. *Degree program information:* Part-time and evening/weekend programs available. Part-time, evening/weekend. Offers accountancy (MS); accounting (MBA); business administration (MBA); finance (MBA); management (MBA); marketing (MBA); sustainability leadership (MBA). *Application deadline:* For fall admission, 8/15 for domestic students, 5/1 for international students; for spring admission, 1/8 for domestic students, 11/1 for international students. Applications are processed on a rolling basis. *Application fee:* $30. Electronic applications accepted. *Application Contact:* Joann Eastman, Admissions Counselor, 608-663-3250, Fax: 608-663-2214, E-mail: gps@edgewood.edu. *Dean*, Dr. Amy Gannon, 608-663-2898, Fax: 608-663-3291, E-mail: agannon@edgewood.edu.

Program in Education Students: 156 full-time (101 women), 175 part-time (136 women); includes 51 minority (21 Black or African American, non-Hispanic/Latino; 2 American Indian or Alaska Native, non-Hispanic/Latino; 9 Asian, non-Hispanic/Latino; 15 Hispanic/Latino; 4 Two or more races, non-Hispanic/Latino), 24 international. Average age 37. *Faculty:* 13 full-time (9 women), 15 part-time/adjunct (10 women). In 2015, 76 master's, 27 doctorates awarded. *Degree program information:* Part-time and evening/weekend programs available. Part-time, evening/weekend. Offers adult learning (MA Ed); bilingual teaching and learning (MA Ed); director of instruction (Certificate); director of special education and pupil services (Certificate); education (MA Ed); educational administration (MA Ed); educational leadership (Ed D); professional studies (MA Ed); program coordinator (Certificate); reading administration (MA Ed); school business administration (Certificate); school principalship K-12 (Certificate); special education (MA Ed); sustainability leadership (MA Ed); teaching and learning (MA Ed); teaching English to speakers of other languages (TESOL) (MA Ed). *Application deadline:* For fall admission, 8/15 for domestic students, 5/1 for international students; for spring admission, 1/8 for domestic students, 11/1 for international students. Applications are processed on a rolling basis. *Application fee:* $30. Electronic applications accepted. *Application Contact:* Joann Eastman, Admissions Counselor, 608-663-3250, Fax: 608-663-2214, E-mail: gps@edgewood.edu. *Dean*, Dr. Timothy D. Slekar, E-mail: tslekar@edgewood.edu.

Program in Marriage and Family Therapy Students: 23 full-time (20 women), 24 part-time (21 women); includes 5 minority (4 Black or African American, non-Hispanic/Latino; 1 Hispanic/Latino), 2 international. Average age 32. 34 applicants, 44% accepted, 12 enrolled. *Faculty:* 2 full-time (both women), 8 part-time/adjunct (5 women). In 2015, 32 master's awarded. *Degree program information:* Part-time and evening/weekend programs available. Part-time, evening/weekend. Offers marriage and family therapy (MS). *Application deadline:* For fall admission, 2/15 for domestic students; for spring admission, 10/15 for domestic students. *Application fee:* $30. Electronic applications accepted. *Application Contact:* Jenna Alsteen, Admissions Counselor, 608-663-3250, Fax: 608-663-2214, E-mail: gps@edgewood.edu. *Associate Dean*, Dr. William Hutter, 608-663-3211, Fax: 608-663-3291, E-mail: whutter@edgewood.edu.

Program in Organization Development Students: 29 part-time (20 women); includes 2 minority (1 Hispanic/Latino; 1 Two or more races, non-Hispanic/Latino), 2 international. Average age 34. In 2015, 15 master's awarded. *Degree program information:* Part-time and evening/weekend programs available. Part-time, evening/weekend, online learning. Offers organization development (MS). *Application deadline:* For fall admission, 8/15 for domestic students, 5/1 for international students; for spring admission, 1/8 for domestic students, 11/1 for international students. *Application fee:* $30. Electronic applications accepted. *Application Contact:* Jenna Alsteen, Program Representative, 608-663-4255, Fax: 608-663-3496, E-mail: jalsteen@edgewood.edu. *Program Director*, Dr. Daniel A. Schroeder, 608-663-4255, E-mail: schroeder@edgewood.edu.

Program in Sustainability Leadership Students: 21 part-time (15 women); includes 4 minority (3 Black or African American, non-Hispanic/Latino; 1 Hispanic/Latino). Average age 35. 15 applicants, 100% accepted, 14 enrolled. *Faculty:* 1 full-time (0 women), 2 part-time/adjunct (1 woman). *Financial support:* In 2015–16, 14 students received support. Scholarships/grants available. Support available to part-time students. Financial award application deadline: 5/1. In 2015, 1 master's awarded. *Degree program information:* Part-time and evening/weekend programs available. Part-time, evening/weekend. Offers sustainability leadership (MA). *Application deadline:* For fall admission, 7/1 for domestic students. *Application fee:* $30. *Director*, Dr. Stephan Gilchrist, 608-663-6991, E-mail: sgilchrist@edgewood.edu.

EDINBORO UNIVERSITY OF PENNSYLVANIA, Edinboro, PA 16444

General Information State-supported, coed, comprehensive institution. *Enrollment:* 568 full-time matriculated graduate/professional students (447 women), 722 part-time matriculated graduate/professional students (556 women). *Enrollment by degree level:* 1,152 master's, 11 doctoral, 127 other advanced degrees. *Graduate faculty:* 40 full-time (20 women). *International tuition:* $16,920 full-time. Tuition, state resident: full-time $11,280; part-time $470 per credit hour. Tuition, nonresident: full-time $16,920; part-time $705 per credit hour. *Required fees:* $3247.20; $135.30 per credit hour. *Graduate housing:* Room and/or apartments available on a first-come, first-served basis to single students; on-campus housing not available to married students. Typical cost: $8560 per year ($11,154 including board). Housing application deadline: 4/3. *Student services:* Campus employment opportunities, campus safety program, career counseling, exercise/wellness program, free psychological counseling, international student services, low-cost health insurance, multicultural affairs office, services for students with disabilities, teacher training. *Library:* Baron-Forness Library plus 1 other. *Research affiliation:* Arts Erie (art), State Higher Education Executive Officers Association (education and learning), Preventative Aftercare, Inc. (social work), CampusEAI (computing), Northwest Institute of Research (training and education), College Board (disability education).

Computer facilities: Computer purchase and lease plans are available. 1,157 computers available on campus for general student use. A campuswide network can be accessed from student residence rooms. Online class registration, We have a staffed help desk for technology issues. New students receive technology instruction during orientation. An open 24 hour computer lab. Some software is available are available.
Website: http://www.edinboro.edu/

General Application Contact: Dr. Alan Biel, Dean of Graduate Studies and Research, 814-732-2856, Fax: 814-732-2611, E-mail: abiel@edinboro.edu.

GRADUATE UNITS

Department of Art ***Financial support:*** Research assistantships with tuition reimbursements, Federal Work-Study, scholarships/grants, and unspecified assistantships available. Financial award application deadline: 2/15; financial award applicants required to submit FAFSA. *Degree program information:* Evening/weekend programs available. Evening/weekend. Offers art education (MA); fine arts (MFA); studio art (MA). *Application deadline:* Applications are processed on a rolling basis. *Application fee:* $30. Electronic applications accepted. *Application Contact:* James Parlin, Chairperson, 814-732-2406, E-mail: jparlin@edinboro.edu. *Chairperson*, James Parlin, 814-732-2406, E-mail: jparlin@edinboro.edu.

Department of Communication Studies ***Financial support:*** Research assistantships with tuition reimbursements, career-related internships or fieldwork, Federal Work-Study, scholarships/grants, and unspecified assistantships available. Support available to part-time students. Financial award application deadline: 2/15; financial award applicants required to submit FAFSA. *Degree program information:* Part-time and evening/weekend programs available. Part-time, evening/weekend. Offers communication studies (MA). *Application deadline:* Applications are processed on a rolling basis. *Application fee:* $30. Electronic applications accepted. *Application Contact:* Dr. Kathleen M. Golden, Chairperson, 814-732-2528, E-mail: kgolden@edinboro.edu. *Chairperson*, Dr. Kathleen M. Golden, 814-732-2528, E-mail: kgolden@edinboro.edu.

Department of Counseling, School Psychology and Special Education ***Financial support:*** Research assistantships with tuition reimbursements, career-related internships or fieldwork, Federal Work-Study, scholarships/grants, and unspecified assistantships available. Support available to part-time students. Financial award application deadline: 2/15; financial award applicants required to submit FAFSA. *Degree program information:* Part-time and evening/weekend programs available. Part-time, evening/weekend. Offers counseling (MA); educational psychology (M Ed); school psychology (Ed S); special education (M Ed). *Application deadline:* Applications are processed on a rolling basis. *Application fee:* $30. Electronic applications accepted. *Application Contact:* Jennifer Gardner, Secretary, 814-732-1326, E-mail: jsgardner@edinboro.edu. *Chairperson*, Dr. Joel Erion, 814-732-2287, E-mail: jerion@edinboro.edu.

Department of Early Childhood and Reading ***Financial support:*** Research assistantships with tuition reimbursements, career-related internships or fieldwork, Federal Work-Study, scholarships/grants, and unspecified assistantships available. Support available to part-time students. Financial award application deadline: 2/15; financial award applicants required to submit FAFSA. *Degree program information:* Part-time and evening/weekend programs available. Part-time, evening/weekend. Offers arts infusion (Graduate Certificate); early childhood education (M Ed); reading (M Ed); reading specialist (Graduate Certificate). *Application deadline:* Applications are processed on a rolling basis. *Application fee:* $30. Electronic applications accepted. *Application Contact:* Dr. Mary Melvin, Chairperson, 814-732-2154, E-mail: mmelvin@edinboro.edu. *Chairperson*, Dr. Mary Melvin, 814-732-2154, E-mail: mmelvin@edinboro.edu.

Department of History, Politics, Languages, and Cultures ***Financial support:*** Research assistantships with tuition reimbursements, career-related internships or fieldwork, Federal Work-Study, institutionally sponsored loans, scholarships/grants, and unspecified assistantships available. Support available to part-time students. Financial award application deadline: 2/15; financial award applicants required to submit FAFSA. *Degree program information:* Part-time and evening/weekend programs available. Part-time, evening/weekend. Offers social sciences (MA). *Application deadline:* Applications are processed on a rolling basis. *Application fee:* $30. Electronic applications accepted. *Application Contact:* Andre Smith, Chairperson, 814-732-1231. *Chairperson*, Andre Smith, 814-732-1231.

Department of Middle and Secondary Education and Educational Leadership ***Financial support:*** Research assistantships with tuition reimbursements, career-related internships or fieldwork, Federal Work-Study, scholarships/grants, and unspecified assistantships available. Support available to part-time students. Financial award application deadline: 2/15; financial award applicants required to submit FAFSA. *Degree program information:* Part-time and evening/weekend programs available. Part-time, evening/weekend. Offers educational leadership (M Ed); middle and secondary instruction (M Ed). *Application deadline:* Applications are processed on a rolling basis. *Application fee:* $30. Electronic applications accepted. *Application Contact:* Dr. Stacie Wolbert, Chair, 814-732-1719, E-mail: swolbert@edinboro.edu. *Chair*, Dr. Stacie Wolbert, 814-732-1719, E-mail: swolbert@edinboro.edu.

Department of Nursing ***Financial support:*** Research assistantships with tuition reimbursements, career-related internships or fieldwork, Federal Work-Study, scholarships/grants, and unspecified assistantships available. Support available to part-time students. Financial award application deadline: 2/15; financial award applicants required to submit FAFSA. *Degree program information:* Part-time and evening/weekend programs available. Part-time, evening/weekend. Offers advanced practice nursing (DNP); family nurse practitioner (MSN); nurse educator (MSN). *Application deadline:* Applications are processed on a rolling basis. *Application fee:* $30. Electronic applications accepted. *Application Contact:* Dr. Amy McClune, Chair, 814-732-2619, E-mail: amcclune@edinboro.edu. *Chair*, Dr. Amy McClune, 814-732-2619, E-mail: amcclune@edinboro.edu.

Department of Social Work ***Financial support:*** Research assistantships with tuition reimbursements, career-related internships or fieldwork, Federal Work-Study, scholarships/grants, and unspecified assistantships available. Support available to part-time students. Financial award application deadline: 2/15; financial award applicants required to submit FAFSA. *Degree program information:* Evening/weekend programs available. Evening/weekend. Offers social work (MSW). *Application deadline:* Applications are processed on a rolling basis. *Application fee:* $30. Electronic applications accepted. *Application Contact:* Dr. David Pugh, Chairperson, 814-732-2022, E-mail: dpugh@edinboro.edu. *Chairperson*, Dr. David Pugh, 814-732-2022, E-mail: dpugh@edinboro.edu.

Department of Speech, Language and Hearing ***Financial support:*** Research assistantships with tuition reimbursements, career-related internships or fieldwork, Federal Work-Study, scholarships/grants, and unspecified assistantships available. Support available to part-time students. Financial award application deadline: 2/15; financial award applicants required to submit FAFSA. *Degree program information:* Part-time and evening/weekend programs available. Part-time, evening/weekend. Offers speech language pathology (MA). *Application deadline:* Applications are processed on a rolling basis. *Application fee:* $30. Electronic applications accepted. *Application Contact:* Dr. Mary Mason-Baughman, Chairperson, 814-732-1287, E-mail: mmasonbaughman@edinboro.edu. *Chairperson*, Dr. Mary Mason-Baughman, 814-732-1287, E-mail: mmasonbaughman@edinboro.edu.

EDP UNIVERSITY OF PUERTO RICO–SAN SEBASTIAN, San Sebastian, PR 00685

General Information Independent, coed, comprehensive institution.

GRADUATE UNITS

Graduate School

EDWARD VIA COLLEGE OF OSTEOPAHTIC MEDICINE–VIRGINIA CAMPUS, Blacksburg, VA 24060

General Information Independent, coed, graduate-only institution. *Research affiliation:* Virginia Polytechnic Institute and State University (biomedical research).

GRADUATE UNITS

Graduate Program Offers osteopathic medicine (DO).

EDWARD VIA COLLEGE OF OSTEOPATHIC MEDICINE–CAROLINAS CAMPUS, Spartanburg, SC 29303

General Information Independent, coed, graduate-only institution.

GRADUATE UNITS

Graduate Program Offers osteopathic medicine (DO).

ELIZABETH CITY STATE UNIVERSITY, Elizabeth City, NC 27909-7806

General Information State-supported, coed, comprehensive institution. CGS member. *Graduate housing:* Room and/or apartments available on a first-come, first-served basis to single students; on-campus housing not available to married students. Housing application deadline: 5/31.

GRADUATE UNITS

School of Education and Psychology ***Degree program information:*** Part-time and evening/weekend programs available. Part-time, evening/weekend. Offers education and psychology (M Ed, MSA); elementary education (M Ed); school administration (MSA). Electronic applications accepted.

School of Mathematics, Science and Technology ***Degree program information:*** Part-time and evening/weekend programs available. Part-time, evening/weekend. Offers applied mathematics (MS); biological sciences (MS); biology education (MS); community college teaching (MS); mathematics education (MS); mathematics, science and technology (MS); remote sensing (MS). Electronic applications accepted.

ELIZABETHTOWN COLLEGE, Elizabethtown, PA 17022-2298

General Information Independent-religious, coed, comprehensive institution.

GRADUATE UNITS

Department of Occupational Therapy Offers occupational therapy (MS).

ELLIS UNIVERSITY, Oakbrook Terrace, IL 60181

General Information Proprietary, coed, comprehensive institution.

GRADUATE UNITS

MBA Program Offers e-commerce (MBA); finance (MBA); general business (MBA); global management (MBA); health care administration (MBA); leadership (MBA); management of information systems (MBA); marketing (MBA); professional accounting (MBA); project management (MBA); public accounting (MBA); risk management (MBA).

Program in Education Offers early childhood education (MA Ed); education (MA Ed); teacher as a leader (MA Ed).

Program in Instructional Technology Offers instructional technology (MS).

Program in Management Offers management (MS).

ELMEZZI GRADUATE SCHOOL OF MOLECULAR MEDICINE, Manhasset, NY 11030

General Information Independent, coed, graduate-only institution. *Enrollment by degree level:* 8 doctoral. *Graduate faculty:* 41 full-time (13 women). *Graduate housing:* On-campus housing not available. *Student services:* Campus employment opportunities, campus safety program, career counseling, exercise/wellness program, free psychological counseling, grant writing training, low-cost health insurance. *Library:* North Shore University Hospital Library plus 3 others. *Research affiliation:* Feinstein Institute for Medical Research (biomedical research), North Shore Long Island Jewish Health System (medicine).

Computer facilities: 20 computers available on campus for general student use. A campuswide network can be accessed from student residence rooms.
Website: http://www.elmezzigraduateschool.org/

General Application Contact: Emilia C. Hristis, Education Coordinator, 516-562-3405, Fax: 516-562-1022, E-mail: ehristis@nshs.edu.

GRADUATE UNITS

Graduate Program Students: 8 full-time (2 women), 7 international. *Faculty:* 41 full-time (13 women). *Financial support:* In 2015–16, 8 students received support. Fellowships with full tuition reimbursements available, health care benefits, and tuition waivers (full) available. Offers molecular medicine (PhD). *Application deadline:* Applications are processed on a rolling basis. *Application fee:* $25. *Application Contact:* Emilia C. Hristis, Education Coordinator, 516-562-3405, Fax: 516-562-1022, E-mail: ehristis@nshs.edu. *Chief Scientific Officer*, Dr. Bettie M. Steinberg, 516-562-1159, Fax: 516-562-1022, E-mail: bsteinbe@lij.edu.

ELMHURST COLLEGE, Elmhurst, IL 60126-3296

General Information Independent-religious, coed, comprehensive institution. *Enrollment:* 3,298 graduate, professional, and undergraduate students; 83 full-time matriculated graduate/professional students (77 women), 375 part-time matriculated graduate/professional students (225 women). *Enrollment by degree level:* 458 master's. *Graduate faculty:* 28 full-time (21 women), 38 part-time/adjunct (23 women). *Tuition, area resident:* Part-time $750 per semester hour. *Graduate housing:* On-campus housing not available. *Student services:* Campus employment opportunities, campus safety program, career counseling, exercise/wellness program, free psychological counseling, international student services, low-cost health insurance, multicultural affairs office, services for students with disabilities, teacher training, writing training. *Library:* Buehler Library.

Computer facilities: 800 computers available on campus for general student use. A campuswide network can be accessed from student residence rooms and from off campus. Online class registration is available.
Website: http://www.elmhurst.edu/

General Application Contact: Timothy J. Panfil, Director of Enrollment Management, School for Professional Studies, 630-617-3300 Ext. 3256, Fax: 630-617-6471, E-mail: panfilt@elmhurst.edu.

GRADUATE UNITS

Graduate Programs Students: 83 full-time (77 women), 375 part-time (225 women); includes 102 minority (26 Black or African American, non-Hispanic/Latino; 27 Asian, non-Hispanic/Latino; 42 Hispanic/Latino; 1 Native Hawaiian or other Pacific Islander, non-Hispanic/Latino; 6 Two or more races, non-Hispanic/Latino), 9 international. Average age 31. 479 applicants, 63% accepted, 229 enrolled. *Faculty:* 28 full-time (21 women), 38 part-time/adjunct (23 women). *Financial support:* In 2015–16, 181 students received support. Scholarships/grants available. Support available to part-time students. Financial award application deadline: 6/1; financial award applicants required to submit FAFSA. In 2015, 155 master's awarded. *Degree program information:* Part-time and evening/weekend programs available. Part-time, evening/weekend, 100% online. Offers applied geospatial sciences (MS); business administration (MBA); communication sciences and disorders (MS); computer information systems (MS); data science (MS); early childhood special education (M Ed); industrial/organizational psychology (MA); nursing (MS, MSN); professional accountancy (MPA); public health (MPH); supply chain management (MS); teacher leadership (M Ed). *Application deadline:* For fall admission, 7/1 priority date for domestic and international students. Applications are processed on a rolling basis. *Application fee:* $0. Electronic applications accepted. *Application Contact:* Timothy J. Panfil, Director of Enrollment Management, School for Professional Studies, 630-617-3300 Ext. 3256, Fax: 630-617-6471, E-mail: panfilt@elmhurst.edu.

ELMS COLLEGE, Chicopee, MA 01013-2839

General Information Independent-religious, coed, comprehensive institution. *Enrollment:* 1,712 graduate, professional, and undergraduate students; 60 full-time matriculated graduate/professional students (41 women), 320 part-time matriculated graduate/professional students (265 women). *Enrollment by degree level:* 238 master's, 61 doctoral, 81 other advanced degrees. *Graduate faculty:* 20 full-time (11 women), 26 part-time/adjunct (20 women). *Graduate housing:* On-campus housing not available. *Student services:* Career counseling, low-cost health insurance. *Library:* Alumnae Library.

Computer facilities: A campuswide network can be accessed from student residence rooms and from off campus.
Website: http://www.elms.edu/

General Application Contact: Dr. Elizabeth Teahan Hukowicz, Dean, School of Graduate and Professional Studies, 413-265-2360 Ext. 238, Fax: 413-265-2459, E-mail: hukowicze@elms.edu.

GRADUATE UNITS

Division of Business Students: 42 part-time (27 women); includes 5 minority (4 Black or African American, non-Hispanic/Latino; 1 Hispanic/Latino), 1 international. Average age 34. 7 applicants, 100% accepted, 5 enrolled. *Faculty:* 2 full-time (both women), 6 part-time/adjunct (4 women). In 2015, 30 master's awarded. *Degree program information:* Part-time and evening/weekend programs available. Part-time, evening/weekend. Offers accounting (MBA); healthcare leadership (MBA); management (MBA). *Application deadline:* Applications are processed on a rolling basis. *Application fee:* $30. *Application Contact:* Dr. Elizabeth Teahan Hukowicz, Dean, School of Graduate and Professional Studies, 413-265-2360 Ext. 238, Fax: 413-265-2459, E-mail: hukowicze@elms.edu. *Chair, Division of Business*, Dr. David Kimball, 413-265-2300, E-mail: kimballd@elms.edu.

Division of Communication Sciences and Disorders Students: 2 full-time (1 woman), 43 part-time (38 women); includes 5 minority (3 Black or African American, non-Hispanic/Latino; 2 Hispanic/Latino). Average age 36. 20 applicants, 95% accepted, 14 enrolled. *Faculty:* 6 part-time/adjunct (5 women). *Financial support:* Applicants required to submit FAFSA. In 2015, 9 master's, 12 other advanced degrees awarded. *Degree program information:* Part-time programs available. Part-time. Offers autism spectrum disorders (MS, CAGS); communication sciences and disorders (CAGS). *Application deadline:* For fall admission, 7/1 priority date for domestic students; for spring admission, 11/1 priority date for domestic students. Applications are processed on a rolling basis. *Application fee:* $30. *Application Contact:* Dr. Elizabeth Teahan Hukowicz, Dean, School of Graduate and Professional Studies, 413-265-2360, Fax: 413-265-2459, E-mail: hukowicze@elms.edu. *Chair, Division of Communication Sciences and Disorders*, Dr. Kathryn James, 413-265-2253, E-mail: jamesk@elms.edu.

Division of Education Students: 17 full-time (13 women), 122 part-time (97 women); includes 9 minority (2 Black or African American, non-Hispanic/Latino; 1 Asian, non-Hispanic/Latino; 6 Hispanic/Latino). Average age 33. 56 applicants, 86% accepted, 44 enrolled. *Faculty:* 5 full-time (4 women), 5 part-time/adjunct (all women). *Financial support:* In 2015–16, 2 teaching assistantships with partial tuition reimbursements were awarded; tuition waivers (partial) also available. Support available to part-time students. Financial award applicants required to submit FAFSA. In 2015, 38 master's awarded. *Degree program information:* Part-time and evening/weekend programs available. Part-time, evening/weekend. Offers early childhood education (MAT); education (M Ed, CAGS); elementary education (MAT); English as a second language (MAT); reading (MAT); secondary education (MAT); special education (MAT). *Application deadline:* For fall admission, 7/1 priority date for domestic students; for spring admission, 11/1 priority date for domestic students. Applications are processed on a rolling basis. *Application fee:* $30. *Application Contact:* Dr. Elizabeth Teahan Hukowicz, Dean, School of Graduate and Professional Studies, 413-265-2360, Fax: 413-265-2459, E-mail: hukowicze@elms.edu. *Chair, Division of Education*, Dr. Mary Janeczek, 413-594-2761, Fax: 413-592-4871, E-mail: janeczeke@elms.edu.

Religious Studies Department Students: 4 part-time (3 women). Average age 57. 3 applicants, 100% accepted, 3 enrolled. *Faculty:* 2 full-time (0 women), 3 part-time/adjunct (2 women). *Financial support:* Tuition waivers (partial) available. Financial award applicants required to submit FAFSA. In 2015, 4 master's awarded. *Degree program information:* Part-time and evening/weekend programs available. Part-time, evening/weekend. Offers religious studies (MAAT). *Application deadline:* For fall admission, 7/1 priority date for domestic students; for spring admission, 11/1 priority date for domestic students. Applications are processed on a rolling basis. *Application fee:* $30. *Application Contact:* Dr. Elizabeth Teahan Hukowicz, Dean, School of Graduate and Professional Studies, 413-265-2360, Fax: 413-265-2459, E-mail: hukowicze@elms.edu. *Director of Religious Studies*, Dr. Martin Pion, 413-265-3581, Fax: 413-594-3951, E-mail: pionm@elms.edu.

School of Nursing Students: 99 part-time (91 women); includes 6 minority (2 Black or African American, non-Hispanic/Latino; 1 American Indian or Alaska Native, non-Hispanic/Latino; 3 Hispanic/Latino). Average age 40. 43 applicants, 81% accepted, 27 enrolled. *Faculty:* 4 full-time (all women), 5 part-time/adjunct (4 women). *Financial support:* Applicants required to submit FAFSA. In 2015, 16 master's awarded. *Degree program information:* Part-time and evening/weekend programs available. Part-time, evening/weekend. Offers nursing and health services management (MSN); nursing education (MSN). *Application deadline:* For fall admission, 7/1 priority date for domestic students; for spring admission, 11/1 priority date for domestic students. Applications are processed on a rolling basis. *Application fee:* $30. *Application Contact:* Dr. Cynthia L. Dakin, Director of Graduate Nursing Studies, 413-265-2455, Fax: 413-265-2335, E-mail: dakinc@elms.edu. *Dean, School of Nursing*, Dr. Kathleen Scoble, 413-265-2204, E-mail: scoblek@elms.edu.

ELON UNIVERSITY, Elon, NC 27244-2010

General Information Independent-religious, coed, comprehensive institution. *Enrollment:* 6,631 graduate, professional, and undergraduate students; 631 full-time matriculated graduate/professional students (389 women), 97 part-time matriculated graduate/professional students (47 women). *Enrollment by degree level:* 271 master's, 457 doctoral. *Graduate faculty:* 84 full-time (34 women), 49 part-time/adjunct (27 women). *Graduate housing:* On-campus housing not available. *Student services:* Campus employment opportunities, campus safety program, career counseling, exercise/wellness program, free psychological counseling, international student services, low-cost health insurance, multicultural affairs office, services for students with disabilities, teacher training, writing training. *Library:* Carol Grotnes Belk. *Collection:* Books: 396,632 (physical), 196,192 (digital/electronic); Serial titles: 59,199 (digital/electronic); Databases: 168. Weekly public service hours: 143; study areas open 24 hours, 5–7 days a week; students can reserve study rooms.

Computer facilities: Computer purchase and lease plans are available. 1,200 computers available on campus for general student use. A campuswide network can be accessed from student residence rooms and from off campus. Online class registration is available.
Website: http://www.elon.edu/

General Application Contact: Art Fadde, Director of Graduate Admissions, 800-334-8448 Ext. 3, Fax: 336-278-7699, E-mail: afadde@elon.edu.

GRADUATE UNITS

Program in Business Administration Students: 16 full-time (9 women), 124 part-time (45 women); includes 34 minority (17 Black or African American, non-Hispanic/Latino; 4 American Indian or Alaska Native, non-Hispanic/Latino; 11 Asian, non-Hispanic/Latino; 1 Hispanic/Latino; 1 Two or more races, non-Hispanic/Latino), 3 international. Average age 33. 71 applicants, 85% accepted, 55 enrolled. *Faculty:* 21 full-time (9 women), 4 part-time/adjunct (2 women). *Financial support:* Federal Work-Study and scholarships/grants available. Support available to part-time students. Financial award application deadline: 3/15; financial award applicants required to submit FAFSA. In 2015, 47 master's awarded. *Degree program information:* Part-time and evening/weekend programs available. Part-time, evening/weekend. Offers business administration (MBA, MSM). *Application deadline:* For fall admission, 8/15 priority date for domestic students; for spring admission, 2/15 priority date for domestic students. Applications are processed on a rolling basis. *Application fee:* $50. Electronic applications accepted. *Application Contact:* Art Fadde, Director of Graduate Admissions, 800-334-8448 Ext. 3, Fax: 336-278-7699, E-mail: afadde@elon.edu. *Director*, Dr. William Burpitt, 336-278-5949, Fax: 336-278-5952, E-mail: wburpitt@elon.edu.

Program in Education Students: 20 part-time (19 women); includes 7 minority (3 Black or African American, non-Hispanic/Latino; 1 American Indian or Alaska Native, non-Hispanic/Latino; 1 Asian, non-Hispanic/Latino; 2 Hispanic/Latino). Average age 33. 30 applicants, 80% accepted, 20 enrolled. *Faculty:* 6 full-time (2 women), 9 part-time/adjunct (8 women). *Financial support:* Federal Work-Study and scholarships/grants available. Support available to part-time students. Financial award application deadline: 6/1; financial award applicants required to submit FAFSA. In 2015, 2 master's awarded. *Degree program information:* Part-time programs available. Part-time. Offers elementary education (M Ed); gifted education (M Ed); special education (M Ed). *Application deadline:* For fall admission, 5/1 for domestic students; for winter admission, 6/1 priority date for domestic students. Applications are processed on a rolling basis. *Application fee:* $50. Electronic applications accepted. *Application Contact:* Art Fadde, Director of Graduate Admissions, 800-334-8448 Ext. 3, Fax: 336-278-7699, E-mail: afadde@elon.edu. *Interim Dean of the School of Education/Professor*, Dr. Ayesha Delpish, 336-278-5859, E-mail: adelpish@elon.edu.

Program in Interactive Media Students: 36 full-time (23 women); includes 11 minority (10 Black or African American, non-Hispanic/Latino; 1 American Indian or Alaska Native, non-Hispanic/Latino), 3 international. Average age 24. 60 applicants, 77% accepted, 36 enrolled. *Faculty:* 13 full-time (3 women). *Financial support:* Federal Work-Study and scholarships/grants available. Financial award application deadline: 3/15; financial award applicants required to submit FAFSA. In 2015, 31 master's awarded. Offers interactive media (MA). *Application deadline:* For fall admission, 5/1 priority date for domestic students. Applications are processed on a rolling basis. *Application fee:* $50. Electronic applications accepted. *Application Contact:* Art Fadde, Director of Graduate Admissions, 800-334-8448 Ext. 3, Fax: 336-278-7699, E-mail: afadde@elon.edu. *Dean of the School of Communications*, Dr. Paul Parsons, 336-278-5724, E-mail: pparsons@elon.edu.

Program in Law Students: 309 full-time (179 women); includes 70 minority (53 Black or African American, non-Hispanic/Latino; 2 American Indian or Alaska Native, non-Hispanic/Latino; 2 Asian, non-Hispanic/Latino; 13 Hispanic/Latino). Average age 26. 691 applicants, 47% accepted, 133 enrolled. *Faculty:* 22 full-time (5 women), 20 part-time/adjunct (7 women). *Financial support:* In 2015–16, 215 students received support. Federal Work-Study and scholarships/grants available. Financial award applicants required to submit FAFSA. In 2015, 76 doctorates awarded. Offers law (JD). *Application deadline:* For fall admission, 7/30 for domestic students; for spring admission, 4/1 priority date for domestic students. Applications are processed on a rolling basis. *Application fee:* $50. Electronic applications accepted. *Application Contact:* Alan Woodlief, Associate Dean of School of Law/Director of Law School Admissions, 336-279-9203, E-mail: awoodlief@elon.edu. *Dean*, Dr. Luke Bierman, 336-279-9201, E-mail: lbierman@elon.edu.

Program in Physical Therapy Students: 148 full-time (102 women); includes 9 minority (1 Black or African American, non-Hispanic/Latino; 2 Hispanic/Latino; 6 Two or more races, non-Hispanic/Latino). Average age 26. 992 applicants, 8% accepted, 46 enrolled. *Faculty:* 14 full-time (8 women), 10 part-time/adjunct (7 women). *Financial support:* Federal Work-Study and scholarships/grants available. Financial award application deadline: 10/1; financial award applicants required to submit FAFSA. In 2015, 58 doctorates awarded. Offers physical therapy (DPT). *Application deadline:* For fall admission, 11/2 for domestic students; for winter admission, 12/1 priority date for domestic students. Applications are processed on a rolling basis. *Application fee:* $50. Electronic applications accepted. *Application Contact:* Art Fadde, Director of Graduate Admissions, 800-334-8448 Ext. 3, Fax: 336-278-7699, E-mail: afadde@elon.edu. *Chair*, Dr. Stephen Folger, 336-278-6347, Fax: 336-278-6414, E-mail: folgers@elon.edu.

Program in Physician Assistant Studies Students: 75 full-time (59 women); includes 4 minority (3 Asian, non-Hispanic/Latino; 1 Two or more races, non-Hispanic/Latino). Average age 27. 1,825 applicants, 3% accepted, 40 enrolled. *Faculty:* 8 full-time (7 women), 6 part-time/adjunct (3 women). *Financial support:* Federal Work-Study and scholarships/grants available. Financial award application deadline: 10/1; financial award applicants required to submit FAFSA. In 2015, 37 master's awarded. Offers physician assistant studies (MS). *Application deadline:* For fall admission, 10/1 for domestic students. Applications are processed on a rolling basis. *Application fee:* $50. Electronic applications accepted. *Application Contact:* Art Fadde, Director of Graduate Admissions, 800-334-8448 Ext. 3, Fax: 336-278-7699, E-mail: afadde@elon.edu. *Deptartment Chair/Program Director of the School of Physician Assistant Studies*, Dr. Patti Ragan, 336-278-6850, E-mail: pragan@elon.edu.

EMBRY-RIDDLE AERONAUTICAL UNIVERSITY–DAYTONA, Daytona Beach, FL 32114-3900

General Information Independent, coed, university. *Enrollment:* 5,806 graduate, professional, and undergraduate students; 425 full-time matriculated graduate/professional students (112 women), 103 part-time matriculated graduate/professional students (28 women). *Enrollment by degree level:* 462 master's, 66 doctoral. *Graduate faculty:* 89 full-time (13 women), 2 part-time/adjunct (1 woman). *Tuition, area resident:* Full-time $15,972; part-time $1331 per credit hour. *Required fees:* $1334; $667 per semester. Tuition and fees vary according to program. *Graduate housing:* Room and/or apartments available on a first-come, first-served basis to single students; on-campus housing not available to married students. Typical cost: $8170 per year. Room charges vary according to board plan and housing facility selected. Housing application deadline: 6/1. *Student services:* Campus employment opportunities, campus safety program, career counseling, exercise/wellness program, free psychological counseling, international student services, low-cost health insurance, multicultural affairs office, services for students with disabilities. *Library:* Jack R. Hunt Memorial Library. *Research affiliation:* Federal Aviation Administration, Marinvent Corporation, Lockheed Martin Corporation, Gulfstream Aerospace, Larsen Motorsports (high-performance vehicles research and development; jet-propulsion), Lockheed Martin, ENSCO, Transtech Airport Solutions Inc., Mosaic ATM, Daytona Beach Int'l Airport (teaching airport advanced integrated technology).

Computer facilities: 1,049 computers available on campus for general student use. A campuswide network can be accessed from student residence rooms and from off campus. Online class registration is available.
Website: http://www.embryriddle.edu/

General Application Contact: Graduate Admissions, 800-388-3728, Fax: 386-226-7070, E-mail: graduate.admissions@erau.edu.

GRADUATE UNITS

Department of Aerospace Engineering Students: 148 full-time (28 women), 16 part-time (3 women); includes 9 minority (1 American Indian or Alaska Native, non-Hispanic/Latino; 3 Asian, non-Hispanic/Latino; 1 Hispanic/Latino; 4 Two or more races, non-Hispanic/Latino), 123 international. Average age 25. 214 applicants, 36% accepted, 41 enrolled. *Faculty:* 29 full-time (3 women), 1 (woman) part-time/adjunct. *Financial support:* Research assistantships, career-related internships or fieldwork, and unspecified assistantships available. Financial award application deadline: 3/15; financial award applicants required to submit FAFSA. In 2015, 36 master's awarded. *Degree program information:* Part-time programs available. Part-time. Offers aerospace engineering (MAE, MS, MSAE, PhD); unmanned and autonomous systems engineering (MSUASE). *Application deadline:* Applications are processed on a rolling basis. *Application fee:* $50. Electronic applications accepted. *Application Contact:* Graduate Admissions, 386-226-6176, E-mail: graduate.admissions@erau.edu. *Professor and Chair, Aerospace Engineering*, Dr. Anastasios Lyrintzis, 386-226-7007, Fax: 386-226-6747, E-mail: lyrintzi@erau.edu.

Department of Applied Aviation Sciences Students: 35 full-time (6 women), 15 part-time (0 women); includes 8 minority (2 Black or African American, non-Hispanic/Latino; 1 American Indian or Alaska Native, non-Hispanic/Latino; 3 Asian, non-Hispanic/Latino; 1 Hispanic/Latino; 1 Two or more races, non-Hispanic/Latino), 23 international. Average age 28. 54 applicants, 28% accepted, 11 enrolled. *Faculty:* 9 full-time (1 woman), 1 part-time/adjunct (0 women). *Financial support:* Research assistantships with tuition reimbursements, career-related internships or fieldwork, scholarships/grants, and unspecified assistantships available. Financial award application deadline: 3/15; financial award applicants required to submit FAFSA. In 2015, 20 master's awarded. *Degree program information:* Part-time and evening/weekend programs available. Part-time, evening/weekend. Offers aeronautics (MSA). *Application deadline:* Applications are processed on a rolling basis. *Application fee:* $50. Electronic applications accepted. *Application Contact:* Applied Aviation Sciences Department, 386-226-6100, E-mail: daytonabeach@erau.edu. *Associate Professor and Chair, Department of Applied Aviation Sciences*, Antonio I. Cortes, PhD, 386-226-6100, E-mail: antonio.cortes@erau.edu.

Department of Business Administration Students: 82 full-time (34 women), 14 part-time (8 women); includes 11 minority (1 Black or African American, non-Hispanic/Latino; 5 Asian, non-Hispanic/Latino; 1 Hispanic/Latino; 4 Two or more races, non-Hispanic/Latino), 66 international. Average age 26. 95 applicants, 36% accepted, 27 enrolled. *Faculty:* 13 full-time (2 women). *Financial support:* Research assistantships, career-related internships or fieldwork, tuition waivers, and unspecified assistantships available. Financial award application deadline: 3/15; financial award applicants required to submit FAFSA. In 2015, 33 master's awarded. *Degree program information:* Part-time programs available. Part-time. Offers aviation business administration (PhD); aviation finance (MSAF); aviation management (MBA-AM); business administration (MBA). *Application deadline:* Applications are processed on a rolling basis. *Application fee:* $50. Electronic applications accepted. *Application Contact:* Graduate Admissions, 386-226-6176, Fax: 386-226-7070, E-mail: graduate.admissions@erau.edu. *Professor of Management/Dean, College of Business*, Michael J. Williams, PhD, 386-226-6293, E-mail: michael.williams@erau.edu.

Department of Electrical, Computer, Software and Systems Engineering Students: 49 full-time (14 women), 10 part-time (3 women); includes 7 minority (3 Black or African American, non-Hispanic/Latino; 2 Asian, non-Hispanic/Latino; 2 Two or more races, non-Hispanic/Latino), 34 international. Average age 26. 57 applicants, 56% accepted, 20 enrolled. *Faculty:* 14 full-time (1 woman). *Financial support:* Research assistantships, career-related internships or fieldwork, scholarships/grants, and unspecified assistantships available. Financial award application deadline: 3/15; financial award applicants required to submit FAFSA. In 2015, 24 master's awarded. *Degree program information:* Part-time and evening/weekend programs available. Part-time, evening/weekend. Offers cybersecurity engineering (MS); electrical and computer engineering (MSECE); electrical, computer, software, and systems engineering (PhD); software engineering (MSE). *Application deadline:* Applications are processed on a rolling basis. *Application fee:* $50. Electronic applications accepted. *Application Contact:* Graduate Admissions, 386-226-6176, Fax: 386-226-7070, E-mail: graduate.admissions@erau.edu. *Professor of Electrical and Computer Engineering/Chair, Department of Electrical, Computer, Software and Systems Engineering*, Dr. Timothy Wilson, 386-226-6100, E-mail: timothy.wilson@erau.edu.

Department of Human Factors Students: 33 full-time (18 women), 5 part-time (4 women); includes 4 minority (2 Black or African American, non-Hispanic/Latino; 1 American Indian or Alaska Native, non-Hispanic/Latino; 1 Two or more races, non-Hispanic/Latino), 7 international. Average age 27. 63 applicants, 41% accepted, 21 enrolled. *Faculty:* 7 full-time (2 women). *Financial support:* Research assistantships, teaching assistantships, career-related internships or fieldwork, scholarships/grants, and unspecified assistantships available. Financial award application deadline: 3/15; financial award applicants required to submit FAFSA. In 2015, 16 master's awarded. *Degree program information:* Part-time and evening/weekend programs available. Part-time, evening/weekend. Offers human factors (PhD); human factors engineering (MSHFS); systems engineering (MSHFS). *Application deadline:* Applications are processed on a rolling basis. *Application fee:* $50. Electronic applications accepted. *Application Contact:* Graduate Admissions, 386-226-6176, Fax: 386-226-7070, E-mail: graduate.admissions@erau.edu. *Professor and Chair, Department of Human Factors and Systems*, Scott Shappell, PhD, 386-226-6100, E-mail: scott.shappell@erau.edu.

Department of Mechanical Engineering Students: 46 full-time (3 women), 15 part-time (6 women); includes 11 minority (4 Black or African American, non-Hispanic/Latino; 2 Asian, non-Hispanic/Latino; 1 Hispanic/Latino; 4 Two or more races, non-Hispanic/Latino), 24 international. Average age 25. 56 applicants, 41% accepted, 12 enrolled. *Faculty:* 11 full-time (4 women). *Financial support:* Research assistantships, teaching assistantships, career-related internships or fieldwork, and unspecified assistantships available. Financial award application deadline: 3/15. In 2015, 33 master's awarded. *Degree program information:* Part-time and evening/weekend programs available. Part-time, evening/weekend. Offers mechanical engineering (MSME, PhD). *Application deadline:* Applications are processed on a rolling basis. *Application fee:* $50. Electronic applications accepted. *Application Contact:* Graduate Admissions, 386-226-6176, Fax: 386-226-7070, E-mail: graduate.admissions@erau.edu. *Professor and Chair, Department of Mechanical Engineering*, Charles Reinholtz, PhD, 386-323-8848, E-mail: charles.reinholtz@erau.edu.

Department of Physical Sciences Students: 32 full-time (9 women), 1 part-time (0 women); includes 9 minority (1 Black or African American, non-Hispanic/Latino; 1 Asian, non-Hispanic/Latino; 3 Hispanic/Latino; 4 Two or more races, non-Hispanic/Latino), 10 international. Average age 26. 18 applicants, 50% accepted, 5 enrolled. *Faculty:* 10 full-time (1 woman). *Financial support:* Research assistantships, teaching assistantships, career-related internships or fieldwork, and unspecified assistantships available. Financial award application deadline: 3/15; financial award applicants required to submit FAFSA. In 2015, 6 master's, 1 doctorate awarded. *Degree program information:* Part-time and evening/weekend programs available. Part-time, evening/weekend. Offers engineering physics (MS, PhD). *Application deadline:* Applications are processed on a rolling basis. *Application fee:* $50. Electronic applications accepted. *Application Contact:* Graduate Admissions, 386-226-6176, Fax: 386-226-7070, E-mail: graduate.admissions@erau.edu. *Professor of Engineering Physics/Chair, Department of Physical Sciences*, Terry Oswalt, PhD, 386-226-6100, E-mail: terry.oswalt@erau.edu.

EMBRY-RIDDLE AERONAUTICAL UNIVERSITY–PRESCOTT, Prescott, AZ 86301-3720

General Information Independent, coed, comprehensive institution. *Enrollment:* 2,265 graduate, professional, and undergraduate students; 51 full-time matriculated graduate/professional students (11 women), 9 part-time matriculated graduate/professional students. *Enrollment by degree level:* 60 master's. *Graduate faculty:* 10 full-time (1 woman), 1 (woman) part-time/adjunct. *Tuition, area resident:* Full-time $15,972; part-time $7986 per credit hour. *Required fees:* $1200; $600 per semester. *Graduate housing:* On-campus housing not available. *Student services:* Campus employment opportunities, campus safety program, career counseling, exercise/wellness program, free psychological counseling, international student services, low-cost health insurance, services for students with disabilities. *Library:* Christine & Steven F. Udvar-Hazy Library & Learning Center. *Research affiliation:* Boeing, Intelligent Light, and Pointwise (CFD analysis on aerospace vehicles and energy systems), University of Alaska, Anchorage (development of field deployed multi-spectral computer vision systems), NASA (optimization ideas for aircraft design), Federal Aviation Administration (human factors, air traffic control interoperability, air traffic management, low-altitude operations, wake separation and noise reduction), NATO Modelling & Simulation Centre of Excellence (operational requirements, training and interoperability), Flight Research Inc. (production of world-class training and curriculum programs for aircraft loss-of-control situations).

Computer facilities: 730 computers available on campus for general student use. A campuswide network can be accessed from student residence rooms and from off campus. Online class registration is available.
Website: http://www.embryriddle.edu/

General Application Contact: Graduate Admissions, 928-777-6600, E-mail: prescottgradinfo@erau.edu.

GRADUATE UNITS

College of Security and Intelligence Students: 23 full-time (6 women), 2 part-time (0 women); includes 4 minority (1 Black or African American, non-Hispanic/Latino; 1 Asian, non-Hispanic/Latino; 1 Hispanic/Latino; 1 Two or more races, non-Hispanic/Latino), 2 international. Average age 25. 50 applicants, 72% accepted, 15 enrolled. *Faculty:* 5 full-time (0 women). *Financial support:* In 2015–16, 7 students received support, including 6 research assistantships (averaging $5,666 per year); career-related internships or fieldwork, scholarships/grants, and administrative assistantships also available. Financial award application deadline: 3/15; financial award applicants required to submit FAFSA. *Degree program information:* Part-time programs available. Part-time. Offers security and intelligence studies (MSSIS). *Application deadline:* Applications are processed on a rolling basis. *Application fee:* $50. Electronic applications accepted. *Application Contact:* Graduate Admissions, 928-777-6600, E-mail: prescottgradinfo@erau.edu. *Dean and Professor, College of Security and Intelligence*, Philip Jones, PhD, 928-777-6992, E-mail: philip.e.jones@erau.edu.

Department of Behavioral and Safety Sciences Students: 28 full-time (5 women), 7 part-time (0 women); includes 6 minority (1 Black or African American, non-Hispanic/Latino; 2 Hispanic/Latino; 3 Two or more races, non-Hispanic/Latino), 10 international. Average age 31. 32 applicants, 59% accepted, 8 enrolled. *Faculty:* 5 full-time (0 women). *Financial support:* In 2015–16, 12 students received support, including 6 research assistantships (averaging $5,666 per year); career-related internships or fieldwork and unspecified assistantships also available. Financial award application deadline: 3/15; financial award applicants required to submit FAFSA. In 2015, 10 master's awarded. *Degree program information:* Part-time programs available. Part-time. Offers aviation safety (MSSS); occupational health and safety (MSSS). *Application deadline:* Applications are processed on a rolling basis. *Application fee:* $50. Electronic applications accepted. *Application Contact:* Graduate Admissions, 928-777-6600, E-mail: prescottgradinfo@erau.edu. *Department Chair/Associate Professor, Safety Science*, Erin E. Bowen, PhD, 928-777-6960, E-mail: erin.bowen@erau.edu.

EMBRY-RIDDLE AERONAUTICAL UNIVERSITY–WORLDWIDE, Daytona Beach, FL 32114-3900

General Information Independent, coed, comprehensive institution. *Enrollment:* 14,701 graduate, professional, and undergraduate students; 2,072 full-time matriculated graduate/professional students (455 women), 2,143 part-time matriculated graduate/professional students (400 women). *Enrollment by degree level:* 4,149 master's, 64 doctoral, 2 other advanced degrees. *Tuition, area resident:* Full-time $6960; part-time $580 per credit hour. Tuition and fees vary according to degree level and program. *Student services:* Campus employment opportunities, career counseling, international student services. *Library:* Jack R. Hunt Memorial Library. *Research affiliation:* The Society for Protective Coatings and Honda Aircraft (creation of standards for training and certification program for higher paint quality).

Computer facilities: Online class registration is available.
Website: http://www.embryriddle.edu/

General Application Contact: Student Help Center, 800-522-6787 Ext. 2, E-mail: worldwide@erau.edu.

GRADUATE UNITS

College of Business Students: 1,119 full-time (290 women), 998 part-time (218 women); includes 563 minority (261 Black or African American, non-Hispanic/Latino; 7 American Indian or Alaska Native, non-Hispanic/Latino; 72 Asian, non-Hispanic/Latino; 73 Hispanic/Latino; 5 Native Hawaiian or other Pacific Islander, non-Hispanic/Latino; 145 Two or more races, non-Hispanic/Latino), 79 international. Average age 37. *Financial support:* Career-related internships or fieldwork and scholarships/grants available. Financial award applicants required to submit FAFSA. In 2015, 488 master's awarded. *Degree program information:* Part-time and evening/weekend programs available. Part-time, evening/weekend, 100% online, blended/hybrid learning, EagleVision Classroom (between classrooms), EagleVision Home (faculty and students at home), and a blend of Classroom or Home. Offers aviation (MBAA); aviation finance (MSAF); engineering management (MSEM); information security assurance (MSISA); leadership (MSL); logistics and supply chain management (MSLSCM); management (MSM); management information systems (MSMIS); project management (MSPM). *Application deadline:* Applications are processed on a rolling basis. *Application fee:* $50. Electronic applications accepted. *Application Contact:* Admissions, 800-522-6787, E-mail: worldwide@erau.edu. *Interim Dean, Worldwide College of Business,* Bobby McMasters, EdD.

Department of Aeronautics, Graduate Studies Students: 882 full-time (145 women), 1,072 part-time (163 women); includes 435 minority (163 Black or African American, non-Hispanic/Latino; 9 American Indian or Alaska Native, non-Hispanic/Latino; 58 Asian, non-Hispanic/Latino; 68 Hispanic/Latino; 6 Native Hawaiian or other Pacific Islander, non-Hispanic/Latino; 131 Two or more races, non-Hispanic/Latino), 114 international. Average age 37. *Financial support:* Career-related internships or fieldwork available. Financial award applicants required to submit FAFSA. In 2015, 691 master's awarded. *Degree program information:* Part-time and evening/weekend programs available. Part-time, evening/weekend, 100% online, blended/hybrid learning, EagleVision Classroom (between classrooms), EagleVision Home (faculty and students at home), and a blend of Classroom or Home. Offers aeronautical science (MAS); aviation maintenance (MS); human factors (MS); occupational safety management (MS); unmanned systems (MS). *Application deadline:* Applications are processed on a rolling basis. *Application fee:* $50. Electronic applications accepted. *Application Contact:* Admissions Department, 800-522-6787, Fax: 386-226-6894, E-mail: worldwide@erau.edu. *Professor and Chair, Aeronautics,* Dr. Ian McAndrew, 011-441638542916, E-mail: ian.mcandrew@erau.edu.

Department of Security, Emergency Response and Interdisciplinary Studies Students: 2 full-time (both women), 5 part-time (2 women); includes 1 minority (Two or more races, non-Hispanic/Latino). Average age 34. *Financial support:* Career-related internships or fieldwork and scholarships/grants available. Financial award applicants required to submit FAFSA. *Degree program information:* Part-time and evening/weekend programs available. Part-time, evening/weekend, 100% online, blended/hybrid learning, EagleVision Classroom (between classrooms), EagleVision Home (faculty and students at home), and a blend of Classroom or Home. Offers security, emergency response and interdisciplinary studies (MS, MSCMP, MSHSR). *Application deadline:* Applications are processed on a rolling basis. *Application fee:* $50. Electronic applications accepted. *Application Contact:* Student Help Center, 800-522-6787, Fax: 386-226-6984, E-mail: worldwide@erau.edu. *Department Chair/Assistant Professor,* Dr. Ron Wakeham, 800-522-6787, E-mail: worldwide@erau.edu.

PhD in Aviation Program Students: 27 full-time (9 women), 37 part-time (9 women); includes 10 minority (1 Black or African American, non-Hispanic/Latino; 1 American Indian or Alaska Native, non-Hispanic/Latino; 4 Asian, non-Hispanic/Latino; 4 Two or more races, non-Hispanic/Latino), 7 international. Average age 45. In 2015, 4 doctorates awarded. *Degree program information:* Part-time and evening/weekend programs available. Part-time, evening/weekend, online learning. Offers aviation (PhD). *Application deadline:* For fall admission, 2/1 for domestic students. Applications are processed on a rolling basis. *Application fee:* $50. Electronic applications accepted. *Application Contact:* PhD in Aviation Program, 386-226-7499, Fax: 386-226-7279, E-mail: haywardk@erau.edu. *Dean/Professor,* Dr. Tim Brady, 386-226-7499, Fax: 386-226-7279.

EMERSON COLLEGE, Boston, MA 02116-4624

General Information Independent, coed, comprehensive institution. CGS member. *Enrollment:* 4,467 graduate, professional, and undergraduate students; 598 full-time matriculated graduate/professional students (464 women), 80 part-time matriculated graduate/professional students (59 women). *Enrollment by degree level:* 678 master's. *Graduate faculty:* 202 full-time (91 women), 35 part-time/adjunct (16 women). *Graduate housing:* On-campus housing not available. *Student services:* Campus employment opportunities, campus safety program, career counseling, exercise/wellness program, free psychological counseling, grant writing training, international student services, low-cost health insurance, multicultural affairs office, services for students with disabilities, writing training. *Library:* Iwasaki Library plus 1 other. *Collection:* Books: 336,669 (physical), 2,484 (digital/electronic); Serial titles: 67,760 (digital/electronic); Databases: 125. Weekly public service hours: 93; students can reserve study rooms.

Computer facilities: Computer purchase and lease plans are available. 480 computers available on campus for general student use. A campuswide network can be accessed from student residence rooms and from off campus. Online class registration is available.
Website: http://www.emerson.edu/

General Application Contact: Office of Graduate Admission, 617-824-8610, Fax: 617-824-8614, E-mail: gradapp@emerson.edu.

GRADUATE UNITS

Graduate Studies Students: 598 full-time (464 women), 80 part-time (59 women); includes 118 minority (31 Black or African American, non-Hispanic/Latino; 18 Asian, non-Hispanic/Latino; 56 Hispanic/Latino; 1 Native Hawaiian or other Pacific Islander, non-Hispanic/Latino; 12 Two or more races, non-Hispanic/Latino), 147 international. Average age 25. 1,641 applicants, 45% accepted, 271 enrolled. *Faculty:* 202 full-time (91 women), 35 part-time/adjunct (16 women). *Financial support:* In 2015–16, 175 students received support, including 175 fellowships with partial tuition reimbursements available (averaging $11,378 per year); research assistantships with partial tuition reimbursements available, Federal Work-Study, scholarships/grants, and unspecified assistantships also available. Financial award application deadline: 3/1; financial award applicants required to submit FAFSA. In 2015, 350 master's awarded. *Degree program information:* Part-time and evening/weekend programs available. Part-time, evening/weekend. *Application deadline:* Applications are processed on a rolling basis. *Application fee:* $60 ($75 for international students). Electronic applications accepted. *Application Contact:* Leanda Ferland, Director of Graduate Admission, 617-824-8610, Fax: 617-824-8614, E-mail: gradapp@emerson.edu. *Dean of Graduate Studies,* Jan Roberts-Breslin, 617-824-8612.

School of Communication Students: 273 full-time (232 women), 31 part-time (24 women); includes 32 minority (11 Black or African American, non-Hispanic/Latino; 12 Asian, non-Hispanic/Latino; 5 Hispanic/Latino; 4 Two or more races, non-Hispanic/Latino), 100 international. Average age 26. 1,077 applicants, 37% accepted, 135 enrolled. *Faculty:* 59 full-time (27 women), 14 part-time/adjunct (4 women). *Financial support:* In 2015–16, 75 students received support, including 75 fellowships (averaging $9,449 per year); Federal Work-Study, scholarships/grants, and unspecified assistantships also available. Financial award application deadline: 3/1; financial award applicants required to submit FAFSA. In 2015, 197 master's awarded. Offers communication (MA, MS); communication disorders (MS); communication management (MA); global marketing communication and advertising (MA); health communication (MA); integrated marketing communication (MA); journalism (MA). *Application deadline:* Applications are processed on a rolling basis. *Application fee:* $60 ($75 for international students). Electronic applications accepted. *Application Contact:* Leanda Ferland, Director of Graduate Admission, 617-824-8610, Fax: 617-824-8614, E-mail: gradapp@emerson.edu. *Interim Dean/Professor,* Phillip Glenn, 617-824-8739, E-mail: phillip_glenn@emerson.edu.

School of the Arts Students: 355 full-time (247 women), 45 part-time (13 women); includes 68 minority (22 Black or African American, non-Hispanic/Latino; 5 Asian, non-Hispanic/Latino; 32 Hispanic/Latino; 9 Two or more races, non-Hispanic/Latino), 40 international. Average age 27. 784 applicants, 48% accepted, 144 enrolled. *Faculty:* 122 full-time (52 women), 19 part-time/adjunct (11 women). *Financial support:* In 2015–16, 100 students received support, including 100 fellowships (averaging $12,824 per year); research assistantships, Federal Work-Study, scholarships/grants, and unspecified assistantships also available. Financial award application deadline: 3/1; financial award applicants required to submit FAFSA. In 2015, 139 master's awarded. *Degree program information:* Part-time programs available. Part-time. Offers arts (MA, MFA); creative writing (MFA); media art (MFA); publishing and writing (MA); theatre education (MA); visual and media arts (MFA). *Application deadline:* Applications are processed on a rolling basis. *Application fee:* $60 ($75 for international students). Electronic applications accepted. *Application Contact:* Leanda Ferland, Director of Graduate Admission, 617-824-8610, Fax: 617-824-8614, E-mail: gradapp@emerson.edu. *Interim Dean/Professor,* Robert Sabal, 617-824-8983, E-mail: robert_sabal@emerson.edu.

EMILY CARR UNIVERSITY OF ART + DESIGN, Vancouver, BC V6H 3R9, Canada

General Information Province-supported, coed, comprehensive institution. *Graduate housing:* On-campus housing not available. *Research affiliation:* Children's Hospital, Vancouver BC (health care research), Aldrich Pears and Associates (experience design), Kodak Communications Group (interaction design), Donat Group (e-learning), Paperny Films (television and film production), Fuel Cell Research Centre, National Research Council (clean technology).

GRADUATE UNITS

Program in Applied Arts Offers design (M Des); media arts (MAA); visual arts (MAA). Electronic applications accepted.

Program in Digital Media Offers digital media (MDM). Electronic applications accepted.

EMMANUEL COLLEGE, Boston, MA 02115

General Information Independent-religious, coed, comprehensive institution. *Enrollment:* 2,201 graduate, professional, and undergraduate students; 12 full-time matriculated graduate/professional students (10 women), 178 part-time matriculated graduate/professional students (139 women). *Enrollment by degree level:* 184 master's, 6 other advanced degrees. *Graduate faculty:* 7 full-time (all women), 28 part-time/adjunct (16 women). Tuition and fees vary according to program. *Graduate housing:* On-campus housing not available. *Student services:* Campus safety program, career counseling, services for students with disabilities, writing training. *Library:* Cardinal Cushing Library. *Collection:* Books: 94,000 (physical), 263,181 (digital/electronic); Serial titles: 114 (physical), 3,772 (digital/electronic); Databases: 64. Weekly public service hours: 107; students can reserve study rooms.

Computer facilities: 284 computers available on campus for general student use. A campuswide network can be accessed from student residence rooms. Online class registration, software/applications are available.
Website: http://www.emmanuel.edu/

General Application Contact: Helen Muterperl, Assistant Director of Admissions for Graduate Studies and Nursing, 617-735-9700, Fax: 617-507-0434, E-mail: gpp@emmanuel.edu.

GRADUATE UNITS

Graduate and Professional Programs Students: 12 full-time (10 women), 178 part-time (139 women); includes 41 minority (24 Black or African American, non-Hispanic/Latino; 4 Asian, non-Hispanic/Latino; 12 Hispanic/Latino; 1 Two or more races, non-Hispanic/Latino), 1 international. Average age 37. *Faculty:* 7 full-time (all women), 28 part-time/adjunct (16 women). *Financial support:* Applicants required to submit FAFSA. In 2015, 104 master's, 17 other advanced degrees awarded. *Degree program information:* Part-time and evening/weekend programs available. Part-time, evening/weekend, online learning. Offers education (MSN, Graduate Certificate); elementary education (MAT); human resource management (MS, Graduate Certificate); management (MSM, MSN, Graduate Certificate); management and leadership (Graduate Certificate); research administration (MSM, Graduate Certificate); secondary education (MAT). *Application deadline:* For fall admission, 7/31 priority date for domestic students; for spring admission, 11/30 priority date for domestic students. Applications are processed on a rolling basis. *Application fee:* $0. Electronic applications accepted. *Application Contact:* Helen Muterperl, Assistant Director of Graduate Admissions, 617-735-9700, Fax: 617-507-0434, E-mail: gpp@emmanuel.edu. *Dean of Enrollment,* Sandy Robbins, 617-735-9700, Fax: 617-507-0434, E-mail: gpp@emmanuel.edu.

EMORY & HENRY COLLEGE, Emory, VA 24327-0947

General Information Independent-religious, coed, comprehensive institution. *Graduate housing:* Room and/or apartments available on a first-come, first-served basis to single students; on-campus housing not available to married students.

GRADUATE UNITS

Graduate Programs ***Degree program information:*** Part-time and evening/weekend programs available. Part-time, evening/weekend. Offers American history (MA Ed); organizational leadership (MCOL); professional studies (M Ed); reading specialist (MA Ed).

EMORY UNIVERSITY, Atlanta, GA 30322-1100

General Information Independent-religious, coed, university. CGS member. *Graduate housing:* Rooms and/or apartments available on a first-come, first-served basis to single and married students. *Research affiliation:* Bill and Melinda Gates Foundation, Children's Pediatric Research Trust, International AIDS Vaccine Initiative, Garden City Group, Georgia Cancer Coalition, The Wistar Institute.

GRADUATE UNITS

Candler School of Theology ***Degree program information:*** Part-time programs available. Part-time. Offers formation and witness (M Div); history, scripture and tradition (MTS); leadership in church and community (M Div); modern religious thought and experience (MTS); pastoral counseling (Th D); religion and race (M Div); religion, health and science (M Div); scripture and interpretation (M Div); society and personality (M Div); theology (Th M); theology and ethics (M Div); theology and the arts (M Div); traditions of the church (M Div); women and religion (M Div). Electronic applications accepted.

Goizueta Business School Students: 528 full-time (144 women), 263 part-time (78 women); includes 200 minority (81 Black or African American, non-Hispanic/Latino; 69 Asian, non-Hispanic/Latino; 44 Hispanic/Latino; 6 Two or more races, non-Hispanic/Latino), 193 international. Average age 30. 1,761 applicants, 36% accepted, 336 enrolled. *Faculty:* 73 full-time (14 women), 23 part-time/adjunct (3 women). *Financial support:* In 2015–16, 456 students received support. Fellowships with full tuition reimbursements available, research assistantships, teaching assistantships, career-related internships or fieldwork, Federal Work-Study, institutionally sponsored loans, and scholarships/grants available. Support available to part-time students. Financial award application deadline: 4/1; financial award applicants required to submit FAFSA. In 2015, 345 master's, 1 doctorate awarded. *Degree program information:* Part-time and evening/weekend programs available. Part-time, evening/weekend. Offers accounting (MBA, PhD); alternative investments (MBA); business (MBA, PhD); business administration (MBA); capitol markets (MBA); corporate finance (MBA); customer relationship management (MBA); finance (MBA, PhD); information systems and operations management (MBA, PhD); investment banking (MBA); marketing (MBA, PhD); organization and management (MBA, PhD); product and brand management (MBA); real estate (MBA). *Application deadline:* For fall admission, 10/5 for domestic and international students; for winter admission, 11/30 for domestic and international students; for spring admission, 1/18 for domestic and international students. Applications are processed on a rolling basis. Electronic applications accepted. *Application Contact:* Julie Barefoot, Associate Dean, 404-727-6311, Fax: 404-727-4612, E-mail: mbaadmissions@emory.edu. *Interim Dean*, Dr. Robert Kazanjian, 404-727-6377, Fax: 404-727-0868, E-mail: kazanjian@emory.edu.

Laney Graduate School Offers anthropology (PhD); art history (PhD); biophysics (PhD); chemistry (PhD); choral conducting (MM, MSM); clinical psychology (PhD); clinical research (MS); cognition and development (PhD); comparative literature (PhD, Certificate); computer science (MS); computer science and informatics (PhD); development practice (MDP); economics (PhD); English (PhD, Graduate Certificate); experimental condensed matter physics (PhD); film studies (MA); French (PhD); French and educational studies (PhD); history (PhD); mathematics (MS, PhD); neuroscience and animal behavior (PhD); nursing (PhD); organ performance (MM, MSM); philosophy (PhD); political science (PhD); psychoanalytic studies (PhD); sociology (PhD); Spanish (PhD); theoretical and computational statistical physics (PhD); women's studies (Certificate); women's, gender, and sexuality studies (PhD). Electronic applications accepted.

Division of Biological and Biomedical Sciences Offers biochemistry, cell and developmental biology (PhD); biological and biomedical sciences (PhD); cancer biology (PhD); genetics and molecular biology (PhD); immunology and molecular pathogenesis (PhD); microbiology and molecular genetics (PhD); molecular and systems pharmacology (PhD); neuroscience (PhD); nutrition and health sciences (PhD); population biology, ecology and evolution (PhD). Electronic applications accepted.

Division of Educational Studies Offers educational studies (MA, PhD); middle grades teaching (MAT); secondary teaching (MAT). Electronic applications accepted.

Division of Religion Offers religion (PhD). Electronic applications accepted.

Emory Center for Ethics Offers bioethics (MA). Electronic applications accepted.

Graduate Institute of the Liberal Arts Offers liberal arts (PhD). Electronic applications accepted.

Nell Hodgson Woodruff School of Nursing ***Degree program information:*** Part-time programs available. Part-time. Offers adult nurse practitioner (MSN); emergency nurse practitioner (MSN); family nurse practitioner (MSN); family nurse-midwife (MSN); health systems leadership (MSN); nurse-midwifery (MSN); pediatric nurse practitioner acute and primary care (MSN); women's health care (Title X) (MSN); women's health nurse practitioner (MSN). Electronic applications accepted.

Rollins School of Public Health ***Degree program information:*** Part-time and evening/weekend programs available. Part-time, evening/weekend, online learning. Offers applied epidemiology (MPH); applied public health informatics (MPH); behavioral sciences and health education (MPH, PhD); bioinformatics (PhD); biostatistics (MPH, MSPH); environmental health (MPH); environmental health and epidemiology (MSPH); environmental health sciences (PhD); epidemiology (MPH, MSPH, PhD); global environmental health (MPH); global health (MPH); health policy (MPH); health policy research (MSPH); health services management (MPH); health services research and health policy (PhD); prevention science (MPH); public health (MPH, MSPH, PhD); public health informatics (MSPH); public nutrition (MSPH). Electronic applications accepted.

School of Law Offers law (LL M, JD, Certificate). Electronic applications accepted.

School of Medicine Offers anesthesiology assistant (MM Sc); genetic counseling (MM Sc); medicine (MM Sc, DPT, MD); physical therapy (DPT); physician assistant (MM Sc). Electronic applications accepted.

EMPEROR'S COLLEGE OF TRADITIONAL ORIENTAL MEDICINE, Santa Monica, CA 90403

General Information Private, coed, graduate-only institution. *Graduate housing:* On-campus housing not available. *Research affiliation:* Lotus Herbs (herbs), LA Free Clinic (herbs), UCLA Ashe Center (student health).

GRADUATE UNITS

Graduate Programs ***Degree program information:*** Part-time and evening/weekend programs available. Part-time, evening/weekend. Offers oriental medicine (MTOM, DAOM).

EMPIRE COLLEGE, Santa Rosa, CA 95403

General Information Proprietary, coed.

GRADUATE UNITS

School of Law Offers law (MLS, JD).

EMPORIA STATE UNIVERSITY, Emporia, KS 66801-5415

General Information State-supported, coed, comprehensive institution. CGS member. *Enrollment:* 6,094 graduate, professional, and undergraduate students; 480 full-time matriculated graduate/professional students (310 women), 1,494 part-time matriculated graduate/professional students (1,041 women). *Enrollment by degree level:* 1,953 master's, 15 doctoral, 6 other advanced degrees. *Graduate faculty:* 205 full-time (89 women), 20 part-time/adjunct (11 women). Tuition, state resident: full-time $5640; part-time $235 per credit hour. Tuition, nonresident: full-time $17,544; part-time $731 per credit hour. *Required fees:* $1848; $77 per credit hour. *Graduate housing:* Room and/or apartments available on a first-come, first-served basis to single students; on-campus housing not available to married students. Typical cost: $4500 per year ($7968 including board). Room and board charges vary according to board plan and housing facility selected. Housing application deadline: 8/25. *Student services:* Campus employment opportunities, campus safety program, career counseling, child daycare facilities, exercise/wellness program, free psychological counseling, grant writing training, international student services, low-cost health insurance, multicultural affairs office, services for students with disabilities, teacher training, writing training. *Library:* William Allen White Library plus 1 other. *Collection:* Books: 408,235 (physical), 118,878 (digital/electronic); Serial titles: 24,348 (physical); Databases: 135. Weekly public service hours: 79; study areas open 24 hours, 5–7 days a week; students can reserve study rooms.

Computer facilities: 410 computers available on campus for general student use. A campuswide network can be accessed from student residence rooms and from off campus. Online class registration is available.
Website: http://www.emporia.edu/

General Application Contact: April Huddleston, Recruitment and Development Specialist, 800-950-GRAD, Fax: 620-341-5909, E-mail: ahuddles@emporia.edu.

GRADUATE UNITS

Department of Biological Sciences Students: 26 full-time (13 women), 15 part-time (7 women); includes 1 minority (Two or more races, non-Hispanic/Latino), 24 international. 16 applicants, 100% accepted, 11 enrolled. *Faculty:* 14 full-time (3 women), 1 part-time/adjunct (0 women). *Financial support:* In 2015–16, 7 research assistantships with full tuition reimbursements (averaging $7,344 per year), 12 teaching assistantships with full tuition reimbursements (averaging $7,844 per year) were awarded; career-related internships or fieldwork, Federal Work-Study, institutionally sponsored loans, health care benefits, and unspecified assistantships also available. Financial award application deadline: 3/15; financial award applicants required to submit FAFSA. In 2015, 17 master's awarded. *Degree program information:* Part-time programs available. Part-time. Offers botany (MS); environmental biology (MS); general biology (MS); microbial and cellular biology (MS); zoology (MS). *Application deadline:* For fall admission, 8/15 priority date for domestic students. Applications are processed on a rolling basis. *Application fee:* $30 ($75 for international students). Electronic applications accepted. *Chair*, Dr. Yixin Eric Yang, 620-341-5311, Fax: 620-341-5608, E-mail: yyang@emporia.edu.

Department of Health, Physical Education and Recreation Students: 28 full-time (13 women), 167 part-time (66 women); includes 11 minority (8 Black or African American, non-Hispanic/Latino; 1 Asian, non-Hispanic/Latino; 1 Hispanic/Latino; 1 Two or more races, non-Hispanic/Latino). 30 applicants, 100% accepted, 27 enrolled. *Faculty:* 17 full-time (12 women), 2 part-time/adjunct (both women). *Financial support:* In 2015–16, 5 teaching assistantships with full tuition reimbursements (averaging $7,353 per year) were awarded; research assistantships, career-related internships or fieldwork, Federal Work-Study, institutionally sponsored loans, health care benefits, and unspecified assistantships also available. Financial award application deadline: 3/15; financial award applicants required to submit FAFSA. In 2015, 71 master's awarded. *Degree program information:* Part-time programs available. Part-time, online learning. Offers health, physical education and recreation (MS). *Application deadline:* For fall admission, 8/15 priority date for domestic students. Applications are processed on a rolling basis. *Application fee:* $30 ($75 for international students). Electronic applications accepted. *Application Contact:* Mary Sewell, Admissions Coordinator, 800-950-GRAD, Fax: 620-341-5909, E-mail: msewell@emporia.edu. *Chair*, Dr. Shawna Shane, 620-341-5848, E-mail: sshane@emporia.edu.

Department of Instructional Design and Technology Students: 38 full-time (18 women), 59 part-time (41 women); includes 13 minority (7 Black or African American, non-Hispanic/Latino; 2 Asian, non-Hispanic/Latino; 3 Hispanic/Latino; 1 Two or more races, non-Hispanic/Latino), 28 international. 30 applicants, 100% accepted, 17 enrolled. *Faculty:* 7 full-time (5 women), 1 part-time/adjunct (0 women). *Financial support:* In 2015–16, 8 teaching assistantships with full tuition reimbursements (averaging $7,344 per year) were awarded; Federal Work-Study, institutionally sponsored loans, health care benefits, and unspecified assistantships also available. Financial award application deadline: 3/15; financial award applicants required to submit FAFSA. In 2015, 44 master's awarded. *Degree program information:* Part-time programs available. Part-time, online learning. Offers instructional design and technology (MS). *Application deadline:* For fall admission, 8/15 priority date for domestic students. Applications are processed on a rolling basis. *Application fee:* $30 ($75 for international students). Electronic applications accepted. *Application Contact:* Mary Sewell, Admissions Coordinator, 800-950-GRAD, Fax: 620-341-5909, E-mail: msewell@emporia.edu. *Chair*, Dr. Zeni Colorado, 620-341-5477, E-mail: jcolorad@emporia.edu.

Department of Mathematics and Economics Students: 15 full-time (9 women), 112 part-time (53 women); includes 18 minority (5 Black or African American, non-Hispanic/Latino; 3 Asian, non-Hispanic/Latino; 6 Hispanic/Latino; 1 Native Hawaiian or other Pacific Islander, non-Hispanic/Latino; 3 Two or more races, non-Hispanic/Latino), 9 international. 39 applicants, 79% accepted, 25 enrolled. *Faculty:* 14 full-time (3 women). *Financial support:* In 2015–16, 5 teaching assistantships with full tuition reimbursements (averaging $7,844 per year) were awarded; research assistantships, career-related internships or fieldwork, Federal Work-Study, institutionally sponsored loans, health care benefits, and unspecified assistantships also available. Financial award application deadline: 3/15; financial award applicants required to submit FAFSA. In 2015, 14 master's awarded. *Degree program information:* Part-time and evening/weekend programs available. Part-time, evening/weekend, online learning. Offers mathematics (MS). *Application deadline:* For fall admission, 8/15 priority date for domestic students. Applications are processed on a rolling basis. *Application fee:* $30 ($75 for international students). Electronic applications accepted. *Application Contact:* Mary Sewell, Admissions Coordinator, 800-950-GRAD, Fax: 620-341-5909, E-mail: msewell@emporia.edu. *Chair,* Dr. H. Joe Yanik, 620-341-5281, Fax: 620-341-6055, E-mail: hyanik@emporia.edu.

Department of Music Students: 7 full-time (5 women), 7 part-time (4 women); includes 2 minority (1 Black or African American, non-Hispanic/Latino; 1 Hispanic/Latino), 7 international. 5 applicants, 100% accepted, 5 enrolled. *Faculty:* 13 full-time (4 women), 3 part-time/adjunct (all women). *Financial support:* In 2015–16, 5 teaching assistantships with full tuition reimbursements (averaging $7,344 per year) were awarded; Federal Work-Study, institutionally sponsored loans, health care benefits, and unspecified assistantships also available. Financial award application deadline: 3/15; financial award applicants required to submit FAFSA. In 2015, 12 master's awarded. *Degree program information:* Part-time programs available. Part-time. Offers music (MM). *Application deadline:* For fall admission, 8/15 priority date for domestic students. Applications are processed on a rolling basis. *Application fee:* $30 ($75 for international students). Electronic applications accepted. *Application Contact:* Dr. Andrew Houchins, Graduate Coordinator, 620-341-6089, E-mail: ahouchin@emporia.edu. *Chair,* Dr. Allan D. Comstock, 620-341-5431, E-mail: acomstoc@emporia.edu.

Department of Physical Sciences Students: 16 full-time (7 women), 21 part-time (9 women); includes 1 minority (Two or more races, non-Hispanic/Latino), 17 international. 9 applicants, 100% accepted, 6 enrolled. *Faculty:* 15 full-time (5 women). *Financial support:* In 2015–16, 2 research assistantships with full tuition reimbursements (averaging $7,344 per year), 8 teaching assistantships with full tuition reimbursements (averaging $7,844 per year) were awarded; Federal Work-Study, institutionally sponsored loans, health care benefits, and unspecified assistantships also available. Financial award application deadline: 3/15; financial award applicants required to submit FAFSA. In 2015, 12 master's, 2 other advanced degrees awarded. *Degree program information:* Part-time programs available. Part-time, online learning. Offers physical sciences (MS, Postbaccalaureate Certificate). *Application deadline:* For fall admission, 8/15 priority date for domestic students. Applications are processed on a rolling basis. *Application fee:* $30 ($75 for international students). Electronic applications accepted. *Application Contact:* Mary Sewell, Admissions Coordinator, 800-950-GRAD, Fax: 620-341-5909, E-mail: msewell@emporia.edu. *Chair,* Dr. Kim Simons, 620-341-5330, Fax: 620-341-6055, E-mail: ksimons@emporia.edu.

Program in Accountancy Students: 12 full-time (10 women), 23 part-time (14 women); includes 2 minority (1 Hispanic/Latino; 1 Two or more races, non-Hispanic/Latino), 10 international. 19 applicants, 100% accepted, 12 enrolled. *Faculty:* 30 full-time (5 women), 1 part-time/adjunct (0 women). *Financial support:* In 2015–16, 1 teaching assistantship with full tuition reimbursement (averaging $7,335 per year) was awarded; research assistantships and unspecified assistantships also available. Financial award applicants required to submit FAFSA. *Degree program information:* Part-time programs available. Part-time, 100% online, blended/hybrid learning. Offers accountancy (M Acc). *Application deadline:* Applications are processed on a rolling basis. *Application fee:* $40. Electronic applications accepted. *Application Contact:* April Huddleston, Recruitment and Development Specialist, 800-950-GRAD, Fax: 620-341-5909, E-mail: ahuddles@emporia.edu. *Chair of the Faculty,* Dr. Shawn Keough, 620-341-5408, E-mail: skeough@emporia.edu.

Program in Art Therapy Students: 29 full-time (27 women), 5 part-time (all women); includes 5 minority (2 American Indian or Alaska Native, non-Hispanic/Latino; 3 Hispanic/Latino), 2 international. 18 applicants, 94% accepted, 11 enrolled. *Faculty:* 11 full-time (7 women), 1 (woman) part-time/adjunct. *Financial support:* Career-related internships or fieldwork, Federal Work-Study, institutionally sponsored loans, health care benefits, and unspecified assistantships available. Financial award application deadline: 3/15; financial award applicants required to submit FAFSA. In 2015, 8 master's awarded. *Degree program information:* Part-time programs available. Part-time. Offers art therapy (MS). *Application deadline:* For fall admission, 6/1 for domestic students; for spring admission, 10/1 for domestic students. Applications are processed on a rolling basis. *Application fee:* $30 ($75 for international students). Electronic applications accepted. *Application Contact:* Mary Sewell, Admissions Coordinator, 800-950-GRAD, Fax: 620-341-5909, E-mail: msewell@emporia.edu. *Chair,* Dr. James Costello, 620-341-5791, E-mail: jcostell@emporia.edu.

Program in Business Administration Students: 74 full-time (33 women), 47 part-time (27 women); includes 11 minority (3 Black or African American, non-Hispanic/Latino; 4 Asian, non-Hispanic/Latino; 3 Hispanic/Latino; 1 Two or more races, non-Hispanic/Latino), 49 international. 60 applicants, 80% accepted, 27 enrolled. *Faculty:* 30 full-time (5 women), 1 part-time/adjunct (0 women). *Financial support:* In 2015–16, 3 research assistantships with full tuition reimbursements (averaging $7,344 per year), 11 teaching assistantships with full tuition reimbursements (averaging $7,344 per year) were awarded; career-related internships or fieldwork, health care benefits, and unspecified assistantships also available. Financial award applicants required to submit FAFSA. In 2015, 26 master's awarded. *Degree program information:* Part-time and evening/weekend programs available. Part-time, evening/weekend, blended/hybrid learning. Offers business administration (MBA). *Application deadline:* For fall admission, 8/15 for domestic students. Applications are processed on a rolling basis. *Application fee:* $30 ($75 for international students). Electronic applications accepted. *Application Contact:* Mary Sewell, Admissions Coordinator, 800-950-GRAD, Fax: 620-341-5909, E-mail: msewell@emporia.edu. *Coordinator, Graduate and Career Services,* Alisha Lyon, 620-341-5456, E-mail: alyon1@emporia.edu.

Program in Business Education Students: 4 full-time (2 women), 12 part-time (8 women); includes 1 minority (Asian, non-Hispanic/Latino). *Faculty:* 30 full-time (5 women), 1 part-time/adjunct. *Financial support:* Career-related internships or fieldwork, institutionally sponsored loans, health care benefits, and unspecified assistantships available. Financial award application deadline: 3/15; financial award applicants required to submit FAFSA. In 2015, 4 master's awarded. *Degree program information:* Part-time and evening/weekend programs available. Part-time, evening/weekend, online learning. Offers business education (MS). *Application deadline:* For fall admission, 8/15 priority date for domestic students. Applications are processed on a rolling basis. *Application fee:* $30 ($75 for international students). Electronic applications accepted. *Coordinator, Graduate and Career Services,* Alisha Lyon, 620-341-5456, E-mail: alyon1@emporia.edu.

Program in Clinical Counseling Students: 28 full-time (24 women), 4 part-time (3 women); includes 9 minority (4 Black or African American, non-Hispanic/Latino; 1 Asian, non-Hispanic/Latino; 2 Hispanic/Latino; 2 Two or more races, non-Hispanic/Latino), 2 international. 20 applicants, 100% accepted, 9 enrolled. *Faculty:* 11 full-time (7 women), 1 (woman) part-time/adjunct. *Financial support:* In 2015–16, 7 research assistantships with full tuition reimbursements (averaging $7,344 per year) were awarded; Federal Work-Study, institutionally sponsored loans, health care benefits, and unspecified assistantships also available. Financial award application deadline: 3/15; financial award applicants required to submit FAFSA. In 2015, 13 master's awarded. *Degree program information:* Part-time programs available. Part-time. Offers clinical counseling (MS). *Application deadline:* For fall admission, 8/15 for domestic students. Applications are processed on a rolling basis. *Application fee:* $30 ($75 for international students). Electronic applications accepted. *Application Contact:* Mary Sewell, Admissions Coordinator, 800-950-GRAD, Fax: 620-341-5909, E-mail: msewell@emporia.edu. *Chair,* Dr. James Costello, 620-341-5791, E-mail: jcostell@emporia.edu.

Program in Clinical Psychology Students: 16 full-time (9 women), 4 part-time (3 women); includes 4 minority (2 Black or African American, non-Hispanic/Latino; 1 Asian, non-Hispanic/Latino; 1 Two or more races, non-Hispanic/Latino), 1 international. 11 applicants, 100% accepted, 5 enrolled. *Faculty:* 7 full-time (3 women). *Financial support:* Career-related internships or fieldwork, Federal Work-Study, institutionally sponsored loans, health care benefits, and unspecified assistantships available. Support available to part-time students. Financial award application deadline: 3/15; financial award applicants required to submit FAFSA. In 2015, 12 master's awarded. *Degree program information:* Part-time programs available. Part-time. Offers clinical psychology (MS). *Application deadline:* For fall admission, 8/15 for domestic students. Applications are processed on a rolling basis. *Application fee:* $30 ($75 for international students). Electronic applications accepted. *Application Contact:* Mary Sewell, Admissions Coordinator, 800-950-GRAD, Fax: 620-341-5909, E-mail: msewell@emporia.edu. *Chair,* Dr. Jim Persinger, 620-341-5317, E-mail: jpersing@emporia.edu.

Program in Curriculum and Instruction Students: 10 full-time (all women), 125 part-time (115 women); includes 11 minority (1 American Indian or Alaska Native, non-Hispanic/Latino; 1 Asian, non-Hispanic/Latino; 6 Hispanic/Latino; 3 Two or more races, non-Hispanic/Latino). 51 applicants, 100% accepted, 40 enrolled. *Faculty:* 10 full-time (3 women). *Financial support:* Research assistantships, career-related internships or fieldwork, Federal Work-Study, institutionally sponsored loans, health care benefits, and unspecified assistantships available. Financial award application deadline: 3/15; financial award applicants required to submit FAFSA. In 2015, 42 master's awarded. *Degree program information:* Part-time programs available. Part-time. Offers curriculum leadership (MS); effective practitioner (MS); national board certification (MS). *Application deadline:* For fall admission, 8/15 priority date for domestic students. Applications are processed on a rolling basis. *Application fee:* $30 ($75 for international students). Electronic applications accepted. *Application Contact:* Mary Sewell, Admissions Coordinator, 800-950-GRAD, Fax: 620-341-5909, E-mail: msewell@emporia.edu. *Chair,* Dr. Daniel Stiffler, 620-341-5776, E-mail: dstiffle@emporia.edu.

Program in Early Childhood Education Students: 1 (woman) full-time, 69 part-time (67 women); includes 5 minority (1 Black or African American, non-Hispanic/Latino; 4 Hispanic/Latino). 14 applicants, 100% accepted, 8 enrolled. *Faculty:* 31 full-time (23 women), 3 part-time/adjunct (2 women). *Financial support:* Teaching assistantships, Federal Work-Study, institutionally sponsored loans, health care benefits, and unspecified assistantships available. Financial award application deadline: 3/15; financial award applicants required to submit FAFSA. In 2015, 23 master's awarded. *Degree program information:* Part-time programs available. Part-time, online learning. Offers early childhood education (MS). *Application deadline:* For fall admission, 8/15 priority date for domestic students. Applications are processed on a rolling basis. *Application fee:* $30 ($75 for international students). Electronic applications accepted. *Application Contact:* Mary Sewell, Admissions Coordinator, 800-950-GRAD, Fax: 620-341-5909, E-mail: msewell@emporia.edu. *Chair,* Dr. Matt Siemears, 620-341-6057, E-mail: mseimear@emporia.edu.

Program in Educational Administration Students: 11 full-time (7 women), 114 part-time (52 women); includes 8 minority (3 Black or African American, non-Hispanic/Latino; 1 American Indian or Alaska Native, non-Hispanic/Latino; 1 Asian, non-Hispanic/Latino; 2 Hispanic/Latino; 1 Two or more races, non-Hispanic/Latino). 27 applicants, 100% accepted, 15 enrolled. *Faculty:* 10 full-time (3 women). *Financial support:* Research assistantships, career-related internships or fieldwork, Federal Work-Study, institutionally sponsored loans, health care benefits, and unspecified assistantships available. Financial award application deadline: 3/15; financial award applicants required to submit FAFSA. In 2015, 58 master's awarded. *Degree program information:* Part-time programs available. Part-time. Offers elementary administration (MS); elementary/secondary administration (MS); secondary administration (MS). *Application deadline:* For fall admission, 8/15 priority date for domestic students. Applications are processed on a rolling basis. *Application fee:* $30 ($75 for international students). Electronic applications accepted. *Application Contact:* Mary Sewell, Admissions Coordinator, 800-950-GRAD, Fax: 620-341-5909, E-mail: msewell@emporia.edu. *Chair,* Dr. Daniel Stiffler, 620-341-5776, E-mail: dstiffle@emporia.edu.

Program in English Students: 15 full-time (5 women), 14 part-time (10 women); includes 1 minority (Two or more races, non-Hispanic/Latino), 8 international. 12 applicants, 100% accepted, 8 enrolled. *Faculty:* 17 full-time (7 women), 4 part-time/adjunct (3 women). *Financial support:* In 2015–16, 14 teaching assistantships with full tuition reimbursements (averaging $8,244 per year) were awarded; Federal Work-Study, health care benefits, and unspecified assistantships also available. Financial award application deadline: 2/15; financial award applicants required to submit FAFSA. In 2015, 5 master's awarded. *Degree program information:* Part-time programs available. Part-time. Offers English (MA). *Application deadline:* For fall admission, 8/15 for domestic students. *Application fee:* $30 ($75 for international students). *Application Contact:* Mary Sewell, Admissions Coordinator, 800-950-GRAD, Fax: 620-341-5909, E-mail: msewell@emporia.edu. *Chair,* Dr. Kevin Rabas, 620-341-5216, E-mail: krabas@emporia.edu.

Program in Forensic Science Students: 17 full-time (11 women); includes 2 minority (1 Black or African American, non-Hispanic/Latino; 1 Hispanic/Latino), 4 international. 22 applicants, 95% accepted, 15 enrolled. *Faculty:* 14 full-time (3 women), 1 part-time/adjunct (0 women). *Financial support:* Unspecified assistantships available. Financial award applicants required to submit FAFSA. *Degree program information:* Part-time programs available. Part-time. Offers forensic science (MS). *Application deadline:* For fall admission, 4/15 for domestic students. Applications are processed on a rolling basis. *Application fee:* $40. Electronic applications accepted. *Application Contact:* April Huddleston, Recruitment and Development Specialist, 800-950-GRAD, Fax: 620-341-5909, E-mail: ahuddles@emporia.edu. *Interim Director,* Dr. Melissa M. Bailey, 620-341-5619, E-mail: mbailey4@emporia.edu.

Program in History Students: 6 full-time (1 woman), 16 part-time (5 women); includes 1 minority (Two or more races, non-Hispanic/Latino). 5 applicants, 100% accepted, 4 enrolled. *Faculty:* 14 full-time (6 women), 1 (woman) part-time/adjunct. *Financial support:* In 2015–16, 1 research assistantship with full tuition reimbursement (averaging $7,344 per year), 6 teaching assistantships with full tuition reimbursements (averaging $7,344 per year) were awarded; Federal Work-Study, institutionally sponsored loans, health care benefits, and unspecified assistantships also available. Financial award application deadline: 3/15; financial award applicants required to submit FAFSA. In 2015, 1 master's awarded. *Degree program information:* Part-time programs available. Part-time. Offers American history (MA); world history (MA). *Application deadline:* For fall admission, 8/15 priority date for domestic students. Applications are processed on a rolling basis. *Application fee:* $30 ($75 for international students). Electronic applications accepted. *Chair,* Dr. Michael Smith, 620-341-5566, E-mail: msmith3@emporia.edu.

Program in Informatics Students: 8 part-time (7 women); includes 3 minority (2 Black or African American, non-Hispanic/Latino; 1 Hispanic/Latino). 8 applicants, 100% accepted, 8 enrolled. *Faculty:* 9 full-time (5 women). *Degree program information:* Part-time programs available. Part-time, 100% online. Offers nursing (MS). *Application deadline:* Applications are processed on a rolling basis. *Application fee:* $40. Electronic applications accepted. *Application Contact:* April Huddleston, Recruitment and Development Specialist, 800-950-GRAD, Fax: 620-341-5909, E-mail: ahuddles@emporia.edu. *Interim Dean,* Dr. Mirah Dow, 620-341-5203, E-mail: mdow@emporia.edu.

Program in Instructional Specialist Students: 6 full-time (all women), 58 part-time (56 women); includes 2 minority (both Hispanic/Latino). 16 applicants, 100% accepted, 11 enrolled. *Faculty:* 31 full-time (23 women), 3 part-time/adjunct (2 women). *Financial support:* Federal Work-Study, institutionally sponsored loans, health care benefits, and unspecified assistantships available. Financial award application deadline: 3/15; financial award applicants required to submit FAFSA. In 2015, 28 master's awarded. *Degree program information:* Part-time programs available. Part-time. Offers elementary subject matter (MS); reading (MS). *Application deadline:* For fall admission, 8/15 priority date for domestic students. Applications are processed on a rolling basis. *Application fee:* $30 ($75 for international students). Electronic applications accepted. *Application Contact:* Mary Sewell, Admissions Coordinator, 800-950-GRAD, Fax: 620-341-5909, E-mail: msewell@emporia.edu. *Chair,* Dr. Matt Siemears, 620-341-6057, E-mail: msiemear@emporia.edu.

Program in Psychology Students: 15 full-time (10 women), 8 part-time (6 women); includes 5 minority (3 Black or African American, non-Hispanic/Latino; 1 American Indian or Alaska Native, non-Hispanic/Latino; 1 Hispanic/Latino), 2 international. 9 applicants, 100% accepted, 6 enrolled. *Faculty:* 7 full-time (3 women). *Financial support:* In 2015–16, 13 teaching assistantships with full tuition reimbursements (averaging $7,344 per year) were awarded; career-related internships or fieldwork, Federal Work-Study, institutionally sponsored loans, health care benefits, and unspecified assistantships also available. Financial award application deadline: 3/15; financial award applicants required to submit FAFSA. In 2015, 6 master's awarded. *Degree program information:* Part-time programs available. Part-time. Offers general psychology (MS); industrial/organizational psychology (MS). *Application deadline:* For fall admission, 6/1 priority date for domestic students; for spring admission, 10/1 for domestic students. Applications are processed on a rolling basis. *Application fee:* $30 ($75 for international students). Electronic applications accepted. *Application Contact:* Mary Sewell, Admissions Coordinator, 800-950-GRAD, Fax: 620-341-5909, E-mail: msewell@emporia.edu. *Chair,* Dr. Jim Persinger, 620-341-5317, E-mail: jpersing@emporia.edu.

Program in Rehabilitation Counseling Students: 22 full-time (19 women), 4 part-time (1 woman); includes 5 minority (2 Black or African American, non-Hispanic/Latino; 1 Asian, non-Hispanic/Latino; 2 Hispanic/Latino). 4 applicants, 100% accepted, 2 enrolled. *Faculty:* 11 full-time (7 women), 1 (woman) part-time/adjunct. *Financial support:* Career-related internships or fieldwork, Federal Work-Study, institutionally sponsored loans, health care benefits, and unspecified assistantships available. Financial award application deadline: 3/15; financial award applicants required to submit FAFSA. In 2015, 8 master's awarded. *Degree program information:* Part-time programs available. Part-time. Offers rehabilitation counseling (MS). *Application deadline:* For fall admission, 8/15 priority date for domestic students. Applications are processed on a rolling basis. *Application fee:* $30 ($75 for international students). Electronic applications accepted. *Application Contact:* Mary Sewell, Admissions Coordinator, 800-950-GRAD, Fax: 620-341-5909, E-mail: msewell@emporia.edu. *Chair/Graduate Co-Coordinator,* Dr. James Costello, 620-341-5791, E-mail: jcostell@emporia.edu.

Program in School Counseling Students: 19 full-time (18 women), 86 part-time (75 women); includes 9 minority (2 Black or African American, non-Hispanic/Latino; 5 Hispanic/Latino; 2 Two or more races, non-Hispanic/Latino), 1 international. 13 applicants, 100% accepted, 13 enrolled. *Faculty:* 11 full-time (7 women), 1 (woman) part-time/adjunct. *Financial support:* Career-related internships or fieldwork, Federal Work-Study, institutionally sponsored loans, health care benefits, and unspecified assistantships available. Financial award application deadline: 3/15; financial award applicants required to submit FAFSA. In 2015, 14 master's awarded. *Degree program information:* Part-time programs available. Part-time. Offers school counseling (MS). *Application deadline:* For fall admission, 8/15 priority date for domestic students. Applications are processed on a rolling basis. *Application fee:* $30 ($75 for international students). Electronic applications accepted. *Application Contact:* Mary Sewell, Admissions Coordinator, 800-950-GRAD, Fax: 620-341-5909, E-mail: msewell@emporia.edu. *Chair,* Dr. James Costello, 620-341-5791, E-mail: jcostell@emporia.edu.

Program in School Psychology Students: 14 full-time (12 women), 4 part-time (all women); includes 3 minority (2 Black or African American, non-Hispanic/Latino; 1 Two or more races, non-Hispanic/Latino), 1 international. 7 applicants, 100% accepted, 6 enrolled. *Faculty:* 7 full-time (3 women). *Financial support:* Career-related internships or fieldwork, Federal Work-Study, institutionally sponsored loans, health care benefits, and unspecified assistantships available. Financial award application deadline: 3/15; financial award applicants required to submit FAFSA. In 2015, 5 master's, 12 other advanced degrees awarded. *Degree program information:* Part-time programs available. Part-time. Offers school psychology (MS, Ed S). *Application deadline:* For fall admission, 8/15 priority date for domestic students. Applications are processed on a rolling basis. *Application fee:* $30 ($75 for international students). Electronic applications accepted. *Application Contact:* Mary Sewell, Admissions Coordinator, 800-950-GRAD, Fax: 620-341-5909, E-mail: msewell@emporia.edu. *Chair,* Dr. Jim Persinger, 620-341-5317, E-mail: jpersing@emporia.edu.

Program in Social Sciences Students: 1 part-time (0 women). *Faculty:* 14 full-time (6 women), 1 (woman) part-time/adjunct. *Financial support:* Federal Work-Study, institutionally sponsored loans, health care benefits, and unspecified assistantships available. Financial award application deadline: 3/15; financial award applicants required to submit FAFSA. In 2015, 1 master's awarded. *Degree program information:* Part-time programs available. Part-time. Offers American history (MAT); anthropology (MAT); economics (MAT); geography (MAT); political science (MAT); social studies education (MAT); sociology (MAT); world history (MAT). *Application deadline:* For fall admission, 8/15 priority date for domestic students. Applications are processed on a rolling basis. *Application fee:* $30 ($75 for international students). Electronic applications accepted. *Application Contact:* Dr. Christopher Lovett, Associate Professor, 620-341-5577, E-mail: clovett@emporia.edu. *Chair,* Dr. Michael Smith, 620-341-5461, E-mail: msmith3@emporia.edu.

Program in Special Education Students: 6 full-time (5 women), 158 part-time (130 women); includes 11 minority (4 Black or African American, non-Hispanic/Latino; 2 Asian, non-Hispanic/Latino; 3 Hispanic/Latino; 2 Two or more races, non-Hispanic/Latino). 22 applicants, 100% accepted, 22 enrolled. *Faculty:* 31 full-time (23 women), 3 part-time/adjunct (2 women). *Financial support:* Federal Work-Study, institutionally sponsored loans, health care benefits, and unspecified assistantships available. Financial award application deadline: 3/15; financial award applicants required to submit FAFSA. In 2015, 44 master's awarded. *Degree program information:* Part-time programs available. Part-time. Offers behavior disorders (MS); gifted, talented, and creative (MS); interrelated special education (MS). *Application deadline:* For fall admission, 8/15 priority date for domestic students. Applications are processed on a rolling basis. *Application fee:* $30 ($75 for international students). Electronic applications accepted. *Application Contact:* Mary Sewell, Admissions Coordinator, 800-950-GRAD, Fax: 620-341-5909, E-mail: msewell@emporia.edu. *Chair,* Dr. Matt Siemears, 620-341-6057, E-mail: msiemear@emporia.edu.

Program in Teaching Students: 4 full-time (2 women), 31 part-time (21 women); includes 8 minority (2 Black or African American, non-Hispanic/Latino; 6 Hispanic/Latino). 8 applicants, 100% accepted, 3 enrolled. *Faculty:* 10 full-time (3 women). In 2015, 5 master's awarded. *Degree program information:* Part-time programs available. Part-time, online learning. Offers teaching (M Ed). *Application Contact:* Mary Sewell, Admissions Coordinator, 800-950-GRAD, Fax: 620-341-5909, E-mail: msewell@emporia.edu. *Chair,* Dr. Daniel Stiffler, 620-341-5776, E-mail: dstiffle@emporia.edu.

Program in Teaching English to Speakers of Other Languages Students: 5 full-time (4 women), 20 part-time (15 women); includes 4 minority (all Hispanic/Latino), 2 international. 4 applicants, 100% accepted. *Faculty:* 7 full-time (5 women), 1 part-time/adjunct (0 women). *Financial support:* Federal Work-Study, institutionally sponsored loans, health care benefits, and unspecified assistantships available. Financial award application deadline: 2/15. In 2015, 9 master's awarded. *Degree program information:* Part-time programs available. Part-time. Offers teaching English to speakers of other languages (MA). *Application deadline:* For fall admission, 8/15 priority date for domestic students. Applications are processed on a rolling basis. *Application fee:* $30 ($75 for international students). Electronic applications accepted. *Application Contact:* Mary Sewell, Admissions Coordinator, 800-950-GRAD, Fax: 620-341-5909, E-mail: msewell@emporia.edu. *Associate Professor,* Dr. Abdelilah Salim Sehlaoui, 620-341-5237, E-mail: asehlaou@emporia.edu.

School of Library and Information Management Students: 36 full-time (29 women), 299 part-time (234 women); includes 37 minority (4 Black or African American, non-Hispanic/Latino; 2 American Indian or Alaska Native, non-Hispanic/Latino; 3 Asian, non-Hispanic/Latino; 20 Hispanic/Latino; 1 Native Hawaiian or other Pacific Islander, non-Hispanic/Latino; 7 Two or more races, non-Hispanic/Latino), 4 international. 68 applicants, 96% accepted, 53 enrolled. *Faculty:* 9 full-time (5 women). *Financial support:* In 2015–16, 17 research assistantships with full tuition reimbursements (averaging $7,500 per year) were awarded; Federal Work-Study, institutionally sponsored loans, and unspecified assistantships also available. Financial award application deadline: 3/15; financial award applicants required to submit FAFSA. In 2015, 122 master's, 3 doctorates, 4 other advanced degrees awarded. *Degree program information:* Part-time and evening/weekend programs available. Part-time, evening/weekend, online learning. Offers archives studies (Certificate); library and information management (MLS, PhD). *Application deadline:* For fall admission, 8/15 priority date for domestic students. Applications are processed on a rolling basis. *Application fee:* $30 ($75 for international students). Electronic applications accepted. *Application Contact:* Candace Boardman, Director, Kansas MLS Program, 620-341-6159, E-mail: cboardma@emporia.edu. *Interim Dean,* Dr. Mirah Down, 620-341-5203, Fax: 620-341-5233, E-mail: mdow@emporia.edu.

ENDICOTT COLLEGE, Beverly, MA 01915-2096

General Information Independent, coed, comprehensive institution. *Enrollment:* 4,879 graduate, professional, and undergraduate students; 462 full-time matriculated graduate/professional students (286 women), 471 part-time matriculated graduate/professional students (363 women). *Enrollment by degree level:* 866 master's, 42 doctoral, 25 other advanced degrees. *Graduate faculty:* 31 full-time (18 women), 103 part-time/adjunct (50 women). Tuition and fees vary according to program. *Graduate housing:* Room and/or apartments available on a first-come, first-served basis to single students; on-campus housing not available to married students. *Student services:* Campus employment opportunities, campus safety program, career counseling, free psychological counseling, international student services, low-cost health insurance, multicultural affairs office, services for students with disabilities, teacher training, writing training. *Library:* Diane M. Halle Library. *Collection:* Books: 115,917 (physical), 148,320 (digital/electronic); Databases: 160. Weekly public service hours: 97. *Research affiliation:* Peabody Essex Museum (history), North Shore Consortium (special needs).

Computer facilities: Computer purchase and lease plans are available. 285 computers available on campus for general student use. A campuswide network can be accessed from student residence rooms and from off campus. Online class registration is available.
Website: http://www.endicott.edu/

General Application Contact: Dr. Mary Huegel, Vice President and Dean of the School of Graduate and Professional Studies, 978-232-2084, Fax: 978-232-3000, E-mail: mhuegel@endicott.edu.

GRADUATE UNITS

Van Loan School of Graduate and Professional Studies Students: 462 full-time (286 women), 471 part-time (363 women); includes 105 minority (32 Black or African American, non-Hispanic/Latino; 19 Asian, non-Hispanic/Latino; 43 Hispanic/Latino; 1 Native Hawaiian or other Pacific Islander, non-Hispanic/Latino; 10 Two or more races, non-Hispanic/Latino), 23 international. Average age 32. 328 applicants, 99% accepted, 264 enrolled. *Faculty:* 31 full-time (18 women), 103 part-time/adjunct (50 women). *Financial support:* Fellowships, research assistantships, teaching assistantships, career-related internships or fieldwork, Federal Work-Study, tuition waivers (partial), and unspecified assistantships available. Financial award applicants required to submit FAFSA. In 2015, 405 master's awarded. *Degree program information:* Part-time and evening/weekend programs available. Part-time, evening/weekend, 100% online, blended/hybrid learning. Offers administrative leadership (M Ed); athletic administration (M Ed); autism and applied behavior analysis (M Ed, PhD); business administration (MBA); early childhood and elementary education (M Ed); educational leadership (Ed D); homeland security (MS); information technology (MSIT); integrative education (M Ed); interior architecture (MA, MFA); nursing (MSN, PhD); organizational management (M Ed); reading and literacy (M Ed); secondary education (M Ed); special needs and applied behavior analysis (M Ed). *Application deadline:* Applications are processed on a rolling basis. *Application fee:* $50. Electronic applications accepted. *Application Contact:* Ian Menchini, Director, Graduate Enrollment and Advising, 978-232-5292. *Dean,* Dr. Mary Huegel, 978-232-2084, Fax: 978-232-3000, E-mail: mhuegel@endicott.edu.

EPISCOPAL DIVINITY SCHOOL, Cambridge, MA 02138-3494

General Information Independent-religious, coed, graduate-only institution. *Graduate housing:* Rooms and/or apartments available on a first-come, first-served basis to single and married students. Housing application deadline: 7/31. *Research affiliation:* Boston Theological Institute.

GRADUATE UNITS

Graduate and Professional Programs ***Degree program information:*** Part-time programs available. Part-time.

ERIKSON INSTITUTE, Chicago, IL 60654

General Information Independent, coed, primarily women, graduate-only institution.

GRADUATE UNITS

Academic Programs ***Degree program information:*** Part-time and evening/weekend programs available. Part-time, evening/weekend. Offers administration (Certificate); bilingual/ESL (Certificate); child development (MS); early childhood education (MS); infant mental health (Certificate); infant studies (Certificate). MS/MSW offered jointly with Loyola University Chicago.

ERSKINE THEOLOGICAL SEMINARY, Due West, SC 29639-0668

General Information Independent-religious, coed, graduate-only institution. *Graduate housing:* Room and/or apartments available on a first-come, first-served basis to single students; on-campus housing not available to married students. Housing application deadline: 6/1.

GRADUATE UNITS

Graduate and Professional Programs ***Degree program information:*** Part-time and evening/weekend programs available. Part-time, evening/weekend. Offers theology (M Div, MAPM, MATS, Th M, D Min). Electronic applications accepted.

EVANGELICAL SEMINARY, Myerstown, PA 17067-1212

General Information Independent-religious, coed, graduate-only institution. *Graduate housing:* Rooms and/or apartments available on a first-come, first-served basis to single and married students. Housing application deadline: 6/1.

GRADUATE UNITS

Graduate and Professional Programs ***Degree program information:*** Part-time programs available. Part-time, online learning. Offers Biblical studies (MAR); congregational ministry (M Div); global and contextual studies (M Div, MAR); historical and theological studies (MAR); interdisciplinary studies (MAR); marriage and family counseling (M Div); marriage and family therapy (MA); New Testament (MAR); Old Testament (MAR); spiritual formation (MAR); teaching ministry (M Div); youth ministry (M Div).

EVANGELICAL SEMINARY OF PUERTO RICO, San Juan, PR 00925-2207

General Information Independent-religious, coed, graduate-only institution. *Graduate housing:* Rooms and/or apartments available on a first-come, first-served basis to single and married students. Housing application deadline: 12/15.

GRADUATE UNITS

Graduate and Professional Programs ***Degree program information:*** Part-time programs available. Part-time. Offers theology (M Div, MAR, D Min).

EVANGEL UNIVERSITY, Springfield, MO 65802

General Information Independent-religious, coed, comprehensive institution. *Enrollment:* 1,958 graduate, professional, and undergraduate students; 118 full-time matriculated graduate/professional students (82 women), 117 part-time matriculated graduate/professional students (86 women). *Enrollment by degree level:* 197 master's, 26 doctoral, 12 other advanced degrees. *Graduate faculty:* 26 full-time (10 women), 28 part-time/adjunct (17 women). *Graduate housing:* Rooms and/or apartments available on a first-come, first-served basis to single and married students. Housing application deadline: 5/1. *Student services:* Campus employment opportunities, campus safety program, career counseling, exercise/wellness program, free psychological counseling, international student services, multicultural affairs office, services for students with disabilities, teacher training, writing training. *Library:* Claude Kendrick Library.

Computer facilities: A campuswide network can be accessed from student residence rooms. Online class registration, online payment are available.
Website: http://www.evangel.edu/

General Application Contact: Karen Benitez, Admissions Representative, Graduate Studies, 417-865-2811 Ext. 7416, Fax: 417-575-5484, E-mail: benitezk@evangel.edu.

GRADUATE UNITS

Department of Behavioral Sciences Students: 37 full-time (29 women), 19 part-time (10 women); includes 8 minority (2 Black or African American, non-Hispanic/Latino; 2 Asian, non-Hispanic/Latino; 4 Hispanic/Latino). Average age 33. 51 applicants, 59% accepted, 30 enrolled. *Faculty:* 5 full-time (3 women), 3 part-time/adjunct (2 women). *Financial support:* In 2015–16, 6 students received support. Unspecified assistantships available. Financial award application deadline: 4/1; financial award applicants required to submit FAFSA. In 2015, 16 master's awarded. *Degree program information:* Part-time programs available. Part-time. Offers clinical mental health counseling (MS). *Application deadline:* For fall admission, 7/15 priority date for domestic students, 8/1 for international students; for spring admission, 11/15 priority date for domestic students, 12/1 for international students. Applications are processed on a rolling basis. *Application fee:* $25. Electronic applications accepted. *Application Contact:* Matt Petry, Admissions Representative, Graduate Studies, 417-865-2815 Ext. 7229, Fax: 417-575-5484, E-mail: petrym@evangel.edu. *Program Coordinator,* Christine Arnzen, 417-865-2815 Ext. 8618, E-mail: arnzenc@evangel.edu.

Department of Education Students: 5 full-time (4 women), 39 part-time (31 women); includes 4 minority (2 Asian, non-Hispanic/Latino; 2 Hispanic/Latino). Average age 34. 15 applicants, 80% accepted, 12 enrolled. *Faculty:* 7 full-time (5 women), 6 part-time/adjunct (3 women). *Financial support:* In 2015–16, 8 students received support. Scholarships/grants and unspecified assistantships available. Financial award application deadline: 4/1; financial award applicants required to submit FAFSA. In 2015, 29 master's awarded. *Degree program information:* Part-time and evening/weekend programs available. Part-time, evening/weekend, 100% online, blended/hybrid learning. Offers curriculum and instruction (M Ed); educational leadership (M Ed); literacy (M Ed); secondary teaching (M Ed). *Application deadline:* For fall admission, 7/15 priority date for domestic students, 8/1 for international students; for spring admission, 11/15 priority date for domestic students, 12/1 for international students. Applications are processed on a rolling basis. *Application fee:* $25. Electronic applications accepted. *Application Contact:* Matt Petry, Admissions Representative, Graduate Studies, 417-865-2815 Ext. 7416, Fax: 417-575-5484, E-mail: benitezk@evangel.edu. *Program Coordinator,* Dr. Gordon Pace, 417-865-2815 Ext. 8564, E-mail: paceg@evangel.edu.

Doctor of Educational Leadership in Curriculum and Instruction Program Students: 22 full-time (17 women), 4 part-time (2 women); includes 1 minority (American Indian or Alaska Native, non-Hispanic/Latino). Average age 40. 2 applicants, 100% accepted, 2 enrolled. *Faculty:* 5 full-time (3 women), 4 part-time/adjunct (2 women). *Financial support:* In 2015–16, 5 students received support. Scholarships/grants available. Support available to part-time students. Financial award application deadline: 4/1; financial award applicants required to submit FAFSA. *Degree program information:* Part-time and evening/weekend programs available. Part-time, evening/weekend, 100% online, blended/hybrid learning. Offers educational leadership in curriculum and instruction (Ed D). *Application deadline:* For fall admission, 7/15 priority date for domestic students, 8/1 for international students; for spring admission, 11/15 priority date for domestic students, 12/1 for international students. Applications are processed on a rolling basis. *Application fee:* $25. Electronic applications accepted. *Application Contact:* Karen Benitez, Admissions Representative, Graduate Studies, 417-865-2811 Ext. 7416, Fax: 417-575-5484, E-mail: benitezk@evangel.edu. *Program Coordinator,* Dr. Gordon Pace, 417-865-2815 Ext. 8564, E-mail: paceg@evangel.edu.

Organizational Leadership Program Students: 43 full-time (22 women), 4 part-time (2 women); includes 8 minority (4 Black or African American, non-Hispanic/Latino; 1 American Indian or Alaska Native, non-Hispanic/Latino; 1 Asian, non-Hispanic/Latino; 1 Hispanic/Latino; 1 Native Hawaiian or other Pacific Islander, non-Hispanic/Latino). Average age 34. 4 applicants, 100% accepted, 4 enrolled. *Faculty:* 4 full-time (0 women), 6 part-time/adjunct (2 women). *Financial support:* In 2015–16, 11 students received support. Research assistantships and scholarships/grants available. Support available to part-time students. Financial award application deadline: 4/1; financial award applicants required to submit FAFSA. In 2015, 23 master's awarded. *Degree program information:* Part-time and evening/weekend programs available. Part-time, evening/weekend, 100% online, blended/hybrid learning. Offers organizational leadership (MOL). *Application deadline:* For fall admission, 7/15 priority date for domestic students, 8/1 for international students; for spring admission, 11/15 priority date for domestic students, 12/1 for international students. Applications are processed on a rolling basis. *Application fee:* $25. Electronic applications accepted. *Application Contact:* Karen Benitez, Admissions Representative, Graduate Studies, 417-865-2815 Ext. 7416, Fax: 417-575-5484, E-mail: benitezk@evangel.edu. *Program Coordinator,* Dr. Duane Praschan, 417-865-2815 Ext. 8118, Fax: 417-575-5484, E-mail: praschand@evangel.edu.

School Counseling Program Students: 8 full-time (all women), 50 part-time (40 women); includes 2 minority (1 Black or African American, non-Hispanic/Latino; 1 Two or more races, non-Hispanic/Latino). Average age 34. 20 applicants, 85% accepted, 17 enrolled. *Faculty:* 2 full-time (both women), 5 part-time/adjunct (3 women). *Financial support:* In 2015–16, 8 students received support. Scholarships/grants and unspecified assistantships available. Support available to part-time students. Financial award application deadline: 4/1; financial award applicants required to submit FAFSA. In 2015, 16 master's awarded. *Degree program information:* Part-time and evening/weekend programs available. Part-time, evening/weekend. Offers school counseling (MS). *Application deadline:* For fall admission, 7/15 priority date for domestic students, 7/1 for international students; for spring admission, 11/15 priority date for domestic students, 12/1 for international students. Applications are processed on a rolling basis. *Application fee:* $25. Electronic applications accepted. *Application Contact:* Karen Benitez, Admissions Representative, Graduate Studies, 417-865-2815 Ext. 7416, Fax: 417-575-5484, E-mail: benitezk@evangel.edu. *Program Coordinator,* Debbie Bicket, 417-865-2815 Ext. 8567, Fax: 417-575-5484, E-mail: bicketd@evangel.edu.

EVEREST UNIVERSITY, Tampa, FL 33614

General Information Independent, coed, comprehensive institution. *Graduate housing:* On-campus housing not available.

GRADUATE UNITS

Department of Business Administration ***Degree program information:*** Part-time and evening/weekend programs available. Part-time, evening/weekend. Offers accounting (MBA); human resources (MBA); international business (MBA).

EVEREST UNIVERSITY, Orlando, FL 32819

General Information Independent, coed, comprehensive institution. *Graduate housing:* On-campus housing not available.

GRADUATE UNITS

Program in Business Administration Offers accounting (MBA); general management (MBA); human resources (MBA); international management (MBA).

EVEREST UNIVERSITY, Largo, FL 33770

General Information Independent, coed, comprehensive institution.

GRADUATE UNITS

Program in Business Administration Offers accounting (MBA); human resources management (MBA); international business (MBA).

EVERGLADES UNIVERSITY, Boca Raton, FL 33431

General Information Independent, coed, comprehensive institution. *Enrollment:* 1,451 graduate, professional, and undergraduate students; 112 full-time matriculated graduate/professional students (73 women), 97 part-time matriculated graduate/professional students (36 women). *Enrollment by degree level:* 209 master's. *Graduate faculty:* 22 full-time (5 women), 19 part-time/adjunct (4 women). *Tuition, area resident:* Full-time $15,696; part-time $7848 per credit. *Required fees:* $1600; $800 per semester. One-time fee: $195. *Graduate housing:* On-campus housing not available. *Student services:* Career counseling, writing training. *Library:* Everglades University Library. *Collection:* Books: 19,974 (physical), 122,000 (digital/electronic); Serial titles: 48 (physical), 5,180 (digital/electronic); Databases: 55. Weekly public service hours: 6.

Computer facilities: 19 computers available on campus for general student use.
Website: http://www.evergladesuniversity.edu/

General Application Contact: Patricia Ramirez, Director of Admissions, 561-912-1211, Fax: 561-912-1191, E-mail: pramirez@evergladesuniversity.edu.

GRADUATE UNITS

Graduate Programs Students: 112 full-time (73 women), 97 part-time (36 women); includes 100 minority (41 Black or African American, non-Hispanic/Latino; 8 Asian, non-Hispanic/Latino; 43 Hispanic/Latino; 1 Native Hawaiian or other Pacific Islander, non-Hispanic/Latino; 7 Two or more races, non-Hispanic/Latino), 1 international. Average age 40. 100 applicants, 87 enrolled. *Faculty:* 22 full-time (5 women), 19 part-time/adjunct (4 women). *Financial support:* In 2015–16, 17 students received support. Scholarships/grants available. Financial award applicants required to submit FAFSA. In 2015, 4 master's awarded. *Degree program information:* Part-time and evening/weekend programs available. Part-time, evening/weekend, 100% online. Offers accounting for managers (MBA); aviation management (MBA); aviation operations management (MSA); aviation security (MSA); business administration (MSA); complementary and alternative medicine (MPH); entrepreneurship (MS); human resource management (MBA); project management (MBA). *Application deadline:* Applications are processed on a rolling basis. *Application fee:* $50. Electronic applications accepted. *Application Contact:* Patricia Ramirez, Director of Admissions, 561-912-1211, Fax: 561-912-1191, E-mail: pramirez@evergladesuniversity.edu.

THE EVERGREEN STATE COLLEGE, Olympia, WA 98505

General Information State-supported, coed, comprehensive institution. *Enrollment:* 4,190 graduate, professional, and undergraduate students; 209 full-time matriculated graduate/professional students (141 women), 102 part-time matriculated graduate/professional students (69 women). *Enrollment by degree level:* 311 master's. *Graduate faculty:* 15 full-time (11 women), 18 part-time/adjunct (10 women). Tuition, state resident: full-time $9138; part-time $305 per credit. Tuition, nonresident: full-time $21,501; part-time $717 per credit. *Required fees:* $9 per credit. Tuition and fees vary according to course load. *Graduate housing:* Rooms and/or apartments available on a first-come, first-served basis to single and married students. Typical cost: $6222 per year ($9492 including board) for single students; $6222 per year ($9492 including board) for married students. Housing application deadline: 6/15. *Student services:* Campus employment opportunities, campus safety program, career counseling, child daycare facilities, exercise/wellness program, free psychological counseling, grant writing training, international student services, multicultural affairs office, services for students with disabilities, teacher training, writing training. *Library:* Daniel J. Evans Library. *Collection:* Books: 325,606 (physical), 147,328 (digital/electronic); Serial titles: 80 (physical), 43,081 (digital/electronic); Databases: 58. Weekly public service hours: 83; students can reserve study rooms. *Research affiliation:* Washington State Institute for Public Policy (public policy).

Computer facilities: 556 computers available on campus for general student use. A campuswide network can be accessed from student residence rooms and from off campus. Online class registration, online payment, student accounts history, financial aid records, academic history, housing application, evaluations are available.
Website: http://www.evergreen.edu/

General Application Contact: Admissions, 360-867-6170, E-mail: admissions@evergreen.edu.

GRADUATE UNITS

Graduate Programs Students: 209 full-time (141 women), 102 part-time (69 women); includes 86 minority (15 Black or African American, non-Hispanic/Latino; 21 American Indian or Alaska Native, non-Hispanic/Latino; 6 Asian, non-Hispanic/Latino; 24 Hispanic/Latino; 20 Two or more races, non-Hispanic/Latino), 3 international. Average age 33. 267 applicants, 67% accepted, 129 enrolled. *Faculty:* 15 full-time (11 women), 18 part-time/adjunct (10 women). *Financial support:* In 2015–16, 202 students received support, including 34 fellowships with partial tuition reimbursements available (averaging $2,293 per year); career-related internships or fieldwork, Federal Work-Study, institutionally sponsored loans, scholarships/grants, health care benefits, and tuition waivers (partial) also available. Support available to part-time students. Financial award application deadline: 3/1; financial award applicants required to submit FAFSA. In 2015, 121 master's awarded. *Degree program information:* Part-time and evening/weekend programs available. Part-time, evening/weekend. Offers environmental studies (MES); public administration (MPA); teaching (MIT). *Application deadline:* For fall admission, 2/1 priority date for domestic and international students; for winter admission, 10/1 priority date for domestic and international students; for spring admission, 12/1 priority date for domestic and international students. Applications are processed on a rolling basis. *Application fee:* $50. Electronic applications accepted. *Application Contact:* 360-867-6170, E-mail: admissions@evergreen.edu. *Vice President and Provost,* Dr. Michael Zimmerman, 360-867-6400, Fax: 360-867-6745, E-mail: zimmermm@evergreen.edu.

EXCELSIOR COLLEGE, Albany, NY 12203-5159

General Information Independent, coed, comprehensive institution. *Enrollment:* 40,103 graduate, professional, and undergraduate students; 3,176 part-time matriculated graduate/professional students (1,525 women). *Enrollment by degree level:* 3,134 master's, 42 other advanced degrees. *Graduate faculty:* 81 part-time/adjunct (48 women). *Tuition, area resident:* Part-time $645 per credit. *Required fees:* $265 per unit. *Student services:* Services for students with disabilities, writing training. *Library:* Excelsior College Library.

Computer facilities: A campuswide network can be accessed. Online class registration is available.
Website: http://www.excelsior.edu/

General Application Contact: Admissions Counselor, 518-464-8500, Fax: 518-464-8777, E-mail: admissions@excelsior.edu.

GRADUATE UNITS

School of Business and Technology Students: 1,698 part-time (490 women); includes 720 minority (388 Black or African American, non-Hispanic/Latino; 5 American Indian or Alaska Native, non-Hispanic/Latino; 53 Asian, non-Hispanic/Latino; 200 Hispanic/Latino; 9 Native Hawaiian or other Pacific Islander, non-Hispanic/Latino; 65 Two or more races, non-Hispanic/Latino), 11 international. Average age 39. *Faculty:* 27 part-time/adjunct (10 women). *Financial support:* Scholarships/grants available. In 2015, 153 master's awarded. *Degree program information:* Part-time and evening/weekend programs available. Part-time, evening/weekend, online learning. Offers business administration (MBA); cybersecurity (MS); cybersecurity management (MBA, Graduate Certificate); health care management (MBA); human performance technology (MBA); human resources management (MBA); leadership (MBA); mediation and arbitration (MBA); social media management (MBA); technology management (MBA). *Application deadline:* Applications are processed on a rolling basis. *Application fee:* $110. Electronic applications accepted. *Application Contact:* Admissions, 888-647-2388 Ext. 133, Fax: 518-464-8777, E-mail: admissions@excelsior.edu. *Dean,* Dr. Karl Lawrence, 888-647-2388.

School of Health Sciences Students: 256 part-time (183 women); includes 148 minority (83 Black or African American, non-Hispanic/Latino; 2 American Indian or Alaska Native, non-Hispanic/Latino; 18 Asian, non-Hispanic/Latino; 30 Hispanic/Latino; 6 Native Hawaiian or other Pacific Islander, non-Hispanic/Latino; 9 Two or more races, non-Hispanic/Latino), 1 international. Average age 39. *Faculty:* 9 part-time/adjunct (8 women). *Financial support:* Scholarships/grants available. In 2015, 2 master's awarded. *Degree program information:* Part-time and evening/weekend programs available. Part-time, evening/weekend, online learning. Offers health care informatics (Certificate); health professions education (MSHS); healthcare informatics (MS); public health (MSHS). *Application deadline:* Applications are processed on a rolling basis. *Application fee:* $110. Electronic applications accepted. *Application Contact:* Admissions Counselor, 518-464-8500, Fax: 518-464-8777, E-mail: admissions@excelsior.edu. *Dean,* Dr. Deborah Sopczyk, 518-464-8500, Fax: 518-464-8777.

School of Liberal Arts Students: 124 part-time (42 women); includes 53 minority (34 Black or African American, non-Hispanic/Latino; 2 American Indian or Alaska Native, non-Hispanic/Latino; 1 Asian, non-Hispanic/Latino; 10 Hispanic/Latino; 1 Native Hawaiian or other Pacific Islander, non-Hispanic/Latino; 5 Two or more races, non-Hispanic/Latino). Average age 47. *Faculty:* 25 part-time/adjunct (15 women). *Financial support:* Scholarships/grants available. In 2015, 14 master's awarded. *Degree program information:* Part-time and evening/weekend programs available. Part-time, evening/weekend, online learning. Offers liberal studies (MA). *Application deadline:* Applications are processed on a rolling basis. *Application fee:* $110. Electronic applications accepted. *Application Contact:* Admissions Counselor, 518-464-8500, Fax: 518-464-8777, E-mail: admissions@excelsior.edu. *Dean,* Dr. George Timmons, 518-464-8500, Fax: 518-464-8777, E-mail: mlsadmin@excelsior.edu.

School of Nursing Students: 938 part-time (770 women); includes 295 minority (166 Black or African American, non-Hispanic/Latino; 8 American Indian or Alaska Native, non-Hispanic/Latino; 36 Asian, non-Hispanic/Latino; 60 Hispanic/Latino; 8 Native Hawaiian or other Pacific Islander, non-Hispanic/Latino; 17 Two or more races, non-Hispanic/Latino), 2 international. Average age 45. *Faculty:* 18 part-time/adjunct (14 women). *Financial support:* Scholarships/grants available. In 2015, 200 master's awarded. *Degree program information:* Part-time and evening/weekend programs available. Part-time, evening/weekend, online learning. Offers nursing (MS); nursing education (MS); nursing informatics (MS); nursing leadership and administration of health care systems (MS). *Application deadline:* Applications are processed on a rolling basis. *Application fee:* $110. Electronic applications accepted. *Application Contact:* Admissions Counselor, 518-464-8500, Fax: 518-464-8777, E-mail: admissions@excelsior.edu. *Associate Dean, Graduate Program in Nursing,* Dr. Barbara Pieper, 518-464-8500, Fax: 518-464-8777, E-mail: msn@excelsior.edu.

School of Public Service Students: 160 part-time (40 women); includes 76 minority (42 Black or African American, non-Hispanic/Latino; 2 Asian, non-Hispanic/Latino; 24 Hispanic/Latino; 1 Native Hawaiian or other Pacific Islander, non-Hispanic/Latino; 7 Two or more races, non-Hispanic/Latino). Average age 42. *Faculty:* 2 part-time/adjunct (1 woman). *Financial support:* Scholarships/grants available. In 2015, 30 master's awarded. *Degree program information:* Part-time and evening/weekend programs available. Part-time, evening/weekend, online learning. Offers homeland security and emergency management (MSCJ); justice administration (MSCJ); public administration (MPA). *Application deadline:* Applications are processed on a rolling basis. *Application fee:* $110. Electronic applications accepted. *Application Contact:* Admissions Counselor, 518-464-8500, Fax: 518-464-8777, E-mail: admissions@excelsior.edu. *Dean, School of Public Service,* Dr. Robert Waters, 518-464-8500, Fax: 518-464-8777.

FAIRFIELD UNIVERSITY, Fairfield, CT 06824

General Information Independent-religious, coed, comprehensive institution. *Enrollment:* 5,138 graduate, professional, and undergraduate students; 493 full-time matriculated graduate/professional students (274 women), 675 part-time matriculated graduate/professional students (471 women). *Enrollment by degree level:* 977 master's, 123 doctoral, 68 other advanced degrees. *Graduate faculty:* 72 full-time (47 women), 70 part-time/adjunct (34 women). *Tuition, area resident:* Part-time $725 per credit hour. Tuition and fees vary according to degree level and program. *Graduate housing:* Room and/or apartments available on a first-come, first-served basis to single students; on-campus housing not available to married students. Typical cost: $11,620 per year ($13,860 including board). Room and board charges vary according to housing facility selected. *Student services:* Campus employment opportunities, campus safety program, career counseling, child daycare facilities, exercise/wellness program, free psychological counseling, international student services, low-cost health insurance, multicultural affairs office, services for students with disabilities, teacher training, writing training. *Library:* DiMenna-Nyselius Library. *Collection:* Books: 374,586 (physical), 653,659 (digital/electronic); Serial titles: 2,645 (physical), 32,695 (digital/electronic); Databases: 169. Weekly public service hours: 105; study areas open 24 hours, 5–7 days a week; students can reserve study rooms.

Computer facilities: Computer purchase and lease plans are available. 68 computers available on campus for general student use. A campuswide network can be accessed from student residence rooms and from off campus. Online class registration is available.
Website: http://www.fairfield.edu/

General Application Contact: Marianne Gumpper, Director of Graduate Admission, 203-254-4184, Fax: 203-254-4073, E-mail: gradadmis@fairfield.edu.

GRADUATE UNITS

College of Arts and Sciences Students: 22 full-time (7 women), 87 part-time (42 women); includes 12 minority (3 Black or African American, non-Hispanic/Latino; 1 Asian, non-Hispanic/Latino; 4 Hispanic/Latino; 1 Native Hawaiian or other Pacific Islander, non-Hispanic/Latino; 3 Two or more races, non-Hispanic/Latino), 10 international. Average age 34. 77 applicants, 69% accepted, 27 enrolled. *Faculty:* 16 full-time (10 women), 3 part-time/adjunct (0 women). *Financial support:* In 2015–16, 14 students received support. Scholarships/grants and unspecified assistantships available. Financial award applicants required to submit FAFSA. In 2015, 44 master's awarded. *Degree program information:* Part-time and evening/weekend programs available. Part-time, evening/weekend, online learning. Offers American studies (MA); communication (MA); creative writing (MFA); mathematics (MS); public administration (MPA). *Application deadline:* For fall admission, 5/15 for international students; for spring admission, 10/15 for international students. Applications are processed on a rolling basis. *Application fee:* $60. Electronic applications accepted. *Application Contact:* Marianne Gumpper, Director of Graduate Admission, 203-254-4184, Fax: 203-254-4073, E-mail: gradadmis@fairfield.edu. *Dean,* Dr. Yohuru Williams, 203-254-4000 Ext. 2221, Fax: 203-254-4119, E-mail: ywilliams@fairfield.edu.

Dolan School of Business Students: 94 full-time (45 women), 48 part-time (17 women); includes 13 minority (3 Black or African American, non-Hispanic/Latino; 1 Asian, non-Hispanic/Latino; 7 Hispanic/Latino; 2 Two or more races, non-Hispanic/Latino), 31 international. Average age 26. 90 applicants, 41% accepted, 29 enrolled. *Faculty:* 18 full-time (8 women), 5 part-time/adjunct (0 women). *Financial support:* In 2015–16, 30 students received support. Scholarships/grants and unspecified assistantships available. Financial award applicants required to submit FAFSA. In 2015, 95 master's awarded. *Degree program information:* Part-time and evening/weekend programs available. Part-time, evening/weekend. Offers accounting (MBA, MS, CAS); accounting information systems (MBA, CAS); business analytics (MS); entrepreneurship (MBA, CAS); finance (MBA, MS, CAS); general management (MBA, CAS); human resource management (MBA, CAS); information systems and operations (MBA); information systems and operations management (CAS); marketing (MBA, CAS); taxation (MBA, CAS). *Application deadline:* For fall admission, 5/15 for international students; for spring admission, 10/15 for international students.

Applications are processed on a rolling basis. *Application fee:* $60. Electronic applications accepted. *Application Contact:* Marianne Gumpper, Director of Graduate and Continuing Studies Admission, 203-254-4184, Fax: 203-254-4073, E-mail: gradadmis@fairfield.edu. *Dean,* Dr. Donald Gibson, 203-254-4070, Fax: 203-254-4105, E-mail: dgibson@fairfield.edu.

Graduate School of Education and Allied Professions Students: 154 full-time (137 women), 293 part-time (237 women); includes 83 minority (26 Black or African American, non-Hispanic/Latino; 1 American Indian or Alaska Native, non-Hispanic/Latino; 14 Asian, non-Hispanic/Latino; 35 Hispanic/Latino; 7 Two or more races, non-Hispanic/Latino), 9 international. Average age 32. 291 applicants, 68% accepted, 88 enrolled. *Faculty:* 23 full-time (19 women), 31 part-time/adjunct (24 women). *Financial support:* In 2015–16, 43 students received support. Career-related internships or fieldwork and unspecified assistantships available. Support available to part-time students. Financial award applicants required to submit FAFSA. In 2015, 151 master's awarded. *Degree program information:* Part-time and evening/weekend programs available. Part-time, evening/weekend. Offers applied behavior analysis (ATC); applied psychology (MA); clinical mental health counseling (MA, CAS); educational technology (MA); elementary education (MA, CAS); family studies (MA); integration of spirituality and religion in counseling (ATC); marriage and family therapy (MA); school counseling (MA, CAS); school psychology (MA, CAS); school-based marriage and family therapy (ATC); secondary education (MA); special education (MA, CAS); substance abuse counseling (ATC); teaching (Certificate); teaching and foundations (MA, CAS); TESOL, world languages, and bilingual education (MA, CAS). *Application deadline:* For fall admission, 2/15 for international students; for spring admission, 10/1 for international students. *Application fee:* $60. Electronic applications accepted. *Application Contact:* Marianne Gumpper, Director of Graduate Admission, 203-254-4184, Fax: 203-254-4073, E-mail: gradadmis@fairfield.edu. *Dean,* Dr. Robert D. Hannafin, 203-254-4250, Fax: 203-254-4241, E-mail: rhannafin@fairfield.edu.

Marion Peckham Egan School of Nursing and Health Studies Students: 43 full-time (35 women), 181 part-time (163 women); includes 52 minority (20 Black or African American, non-Hispanic/Latino; 1 American Indian or Alaska Native, non-Hispanic/Latino; 11 Asian, non-Hispanic/Latino; 16 Hispanic/Latino; 4 Two or more races, non-Hispanic/Latino), 1 international. Average age 36. 103 applicants, 67% accepted, 43 enrolled. *Faculty:* 8 full-time (all women), 9 part-time/adjunct (7 women). *Financial support:* In 2015–16, 51 students received support. Unspecified assistantships available. Financial award applicants required to submit FAFSA. In 2015, 12 master's, 21 doctorates awarded. *Degree program information:* Part-time and evening/weekend programs available. Part-time, evening/weekend. Offers advanced practice (DNP); family nurse practitioner (MSN, DNP); nurse anesthesia (DNP); nursing leadership (MSN); psychiatric nurse practitioner (MSN, DNP). *Application deadline:* For fall admission, 5/15 for international students; for spring admission, 10/15 for international students. Applications are processed on a rolling basis. *Application fee:* $60. Electronic applications accepted. *Application Contact:* Marianne Gumpper, Director of Graduate and Continuing Studies Admission, 203-254-4184, Fax: 203-254-4073, E-mail: gradadmis@fairfield.edu. *Dean,* Dr. Meredith Wallace Kazer, 203-254-4000 Ext. 2701, Fax: 203-254-4126, E-mail: mkazer@fairfield.edu.

School of Engineering Students: 180 full-time (50 women), 66 part-time (12 women); includes 15 minority (6 Black or African American, non-Hispanic/Latino; 3 Asian, non-Hispanic/Latino; 5 Hispanic/Latino; 1 Two or more races, non-Hispanic/Latino), 189 international. Average age 27. 421 applicants, 49% accepted, 51 enrolled. *Faculty:* 7 full-time (2 women), 22 part-time/adjunct (3 women). *Financial support:* In 2015–16, 46 students received support. Scholarships/grants and unspecified assistantships available. Financial award applicants required to submit FAFSA. In 2015, 65 degrees awarded. *Degree program information:* Part-time and evening/weekend programs available. Part-time, evening/weekend. Offers automated manufacturing (CAS); database management (CAS); electrical and computer engineering (MS); information security (CAS); management of technology (MS); mechanical engineering (MS); network technology (CAS); software engineering (MS); Web application development (CAS). *Application deadline:* For fall admission, 5/15 for international students; for spring admission, 10/15 for international students. Applications are processed on a rolling basis. *Application fee:* $60. Electronic applications accepted. *Application Contact:* Marianne Gumpper, Director of Graduate and Continuing Studies Admission, 203-254-4184, Fax: 203-254-4073, E-mail: gradadmis@fairfield.edu. *Dean,* Dr. Bruce Berdanier, 203-254-4147, Fax: 203-254-4013, E-mail: bberdanier@fairfield.edu.

FAIRLEIGH DICKINSON UNIVERSITY, COLLEGE AT FLORHAM, Madison, NJ 07940-1099

General Information Independent, coed, comprehensive institution. *Graduate housing:* Room and/or apartments available on a first-come, first-served basis to single students; on-campus housing not available to married students.

GRADUATE UNITS

Anthony J. Petrocelli College of Continuing Studies Offers continuing studies (MAS, MPA, MS, MSA); sports administration (MSA).

International School of Hospitality and Tourism Management Offers hospitality management studies (MS).

Public Administration Institute Offers public administration (MPA).

School of Administrative Science Offers administrative science (MAS).

Maxwell Becton College of Arts and Sciences Offers arts and sciences (MA, MFA, MS, Certificate); biology (MS); chemistry (MS); clinical mental health counseling (MA); computer science (MS); corporate and organizational communication (MA); counseling (MA); creative writing (MFA); creative writing and literature for educators (MA); industrial/organizational psychology (MA); organizational behavior (MA, Certificate); organizational leadership (Certificate).

Silberman College of Business *Degree program information:* Part-time and evening/weekend programs available. Part-time, evening/weekend. Offers accounting (MS); business (EMBA, MBA, MS, Certificate); business administration (MBA); entrepreneurial studies (MBA, Certificate); evolving technology (Certificate); finance (MBA, Certificate); health care and life sciences (EMBA); international business (MBA, Certificate); international taxation (Certificate); management (EMBA, MBA, Certificate); managing sustainability (Certificate); marketing (MBA, Certificate); pharmaceutical studies (MBA, Certificate); taxation (MS, Certificate).

Center for Human Resource Management Studies Offers human resource management (MBA); human resource management studies (MBA).

University College: Arts, Sciences, and Professional Studies Offers arts, sciences, and professional studies (MA, MAT, Certificate).

Peter Sammartino School of Education Offers education for certified teachers (MA, Certificate); educational leadership (MA); instructional technology (Certificate); literacy/reading (Certificate); teaching (MAT).

FAIRLEIGH DICKINSON UNIVERSITY, METROPOLITAN CAMPUS, Teaneck, NJ 07666-1914

General Information Independent, coed, comprehensive institution. *Graduate housing:* Room and/or apartments available on a first-come, first-served basis to single students; on-campus housing not available to married students.

GRADUATE UNITS

Anthony J. Petrocelli College of Continuing Studies Offers continuing studies (MAS, MPA, MS, MSA, MSHS, Certificate); sports administration (MSA).

International School of Hospitality and Tourism Management Offers hospitality management (MS).

Public Administration Institute Offers public administration (MPA, Certificate); public non-profit management (Certificate).

School of Administrative Science Offers administrative science (MAS, MSHS, Certificate); homeland security (MSHS).

Silberman College of Business Offers accounting (MBA, MS, Certificate); business (EMBA, MBA, MS, Certificate); business administration (MBA); chemical studies (Certificate); entrepreneurial studies (MBA, Certificate); executive management (EMBA); finance (MBA, Certificate); healthcare and life sciences (EMBA); international business (MBA); management (MBA, Certificate); management information systems (Certificate); marketing (MBA, Certificate); pharmaceutical studies (MBA, Certificate); taxation (MS).

Center for Human Resources Management Studies Offers human resource management (MBA, Certificate).

University College: Arts, Sciences, and Professional Studies Offers arts, sciences, and professional studies (MA, MAT, MS, MSEE, MSN, DNP, PhD, Psy D, Certificate); English and literature (MA); systems science (MS).

Henry P. Becton School of Nursing and Allied Health Offers medical technology (MS); nursing (MSN, Certificate); nursing practice (DNP).

Peter Sammartino School of Education Degree program information: Part-time programs available. Part-time. Offers dyslexia specialist (Certificate); education for certified teachers (MA); educational leadership (MA); instructional technology (Certificate); learning disabilities (MA); literacy/reading (Certificate); multilingual education (MA); teacher of the handicapped (Certificate); teaching (MAT).

School of Art and Media Studies Offers art and media studies (MA); media and communications (MA).

School of Computer Sciences and Engineering Offers computer engineering (MS); computer science (MS); e-commerce (MS); electrical engineering (MSEE); management information systems (MS); mathematical foundation (MS).

School of Criminal Justice and Legal Studies Offers criminal justice (MA).

School of History, Political and International Studies Offers history (MA); international studies (MA); political science (MA).

School of Natural Sciences Offers biology (MS); chemistry (MS); cosmetic science (MS); science (MA).

School of Psychology Offers clinical psychology (MA, PhD); clinical psychopharmacology (MA); forensic psychology (MA); general-theoretical psychology (MA, Certificate); school psychology (MA, Psy D).

FAIRMONT STATE UNIVERSITY, Fairmont, WV 26554

General Information State-supported, coed, comprehensive institution. CGS member. *Enrollment:* 4,041 graduate, professional, and undergraduate students; 96 full-time matriculated graduate/professional students (58 women), 132 part-time matriculated graduate/professional students (97 women). *Enrollment by degree level:* 228 master's. *Graduate faculty:* 34 part-time/adjunct (16 women). Tuition, state resident: full-time $7148; part-time $385 per credit hour. Tuition, nonresident: full-time $15,296; part-time $837 per credit hour. Part-time tuition and fees vary according to course load. *Graduate housing:* Rooms and/or apartments available on a first-come, first-served basis to single and married students. Typical cost: $4878 per year ($8766 including board) for single students; $4878 per year ($8766 including board) for married students. Room and board charges vary according to board plan and housing facility selected. Housing application deadline: 7/18. *Student services:* Campus employment opportunities, campus safety program, career counseling, child daycare facilities, free psychological counseling, international student services, multicultural affairs office, services for students with disabilities. *Library:* Musick Library. Study areas open 24 hours, 5–7 days a week.

Computer facilities: Computer purchase and lease plans are available. 1,350 computers available on campus for general student use. A campuswide network can be accessed from student residence rooms and from off campus. Online class registration is available.
Website: http://www.fairmontstate.edu/

General Application Contact: Jack Kirby, Director of Graduate Studies, 304-367-4101, E-mail: jack.kirby@fairmontstate.edu.

GRADUATE UNITS

Program in Business Administration Students: 17 full-time (7 women), 13 part-time (7 women); includes 1 minority (Black or African American, non-Hispanic/Latino), 2 international. Average age 28. 50 applicants, 74% accepted, 26 enrolled. *Faculty:* 5 part-time/adjunct (2 women). *Financial support:* In 2015–16, 11 students received support. Federal Work-Study, scholarships/grants, and tuition waivers (full and partial) available. Financial award applicants required to submit FAFSA. In 2015, 14 master's awarded. *Degree program information:* Part-time and evening/weekend programs available. Part-time, evening/weekend. Offers business administration (MBA). *Application deadline:* For fall admission, 5/1 for domestic and international students. Applications are processed on a rolling basis. *Application fee:* $40. Electronic applications accepted. *Application Contact:* Jack Kirby, Director of Graduate Studies, 304-367-4101, E-mail: jack.kirby@fairmontstate.edu. *Director,* Dr. Edward Gailey, 304-367-4728, Fax: 304-367-4613, E-mail: edward.gailey@fairmontstate.edu.

Program in Criminal Justice Students: 17 full-time (13 women), 15 part-time (9 women); includes 6 minority (1 Black or African American, non-Hispanic/Latino; 1 Asian, non-Hispanic/Latino; 1 Hispanic/Latino; 3 Two or more races, non-Hispanic/Latino). Average age 28. 21 applicants, 62% accepted, 12 enrolled. *Faculty:* 4 part-time/adjunct (2 women). *Financial support:* In 2015–16, 4 students received support. Applicants required to submit FAFSA. In 2015, 13 master's awarded. *Degree program information:* Part-time and evening/weekend programs available. Part-time, evening/weekend, online learning. Offers criminal justice (MS). *Application deadline:* For fall admission, 5/1 for domestic and international students. Applications are processed on a rolling basis. *Application fee:* $40. Electronic applications accepted. *Application Contact:* Jack Kirby, Director of Graduate Studies, 304-367-4101, E-mail: jack.kirby@fairmontstate.edu. *Director, Graduate Program in Criminal Justice,* Dr. Jennifer Myers, 304-367-4936, Fax: 304-367-4785, E-mail: jennifer.myers@fairmontstate.edu.

Programs in Education Students: 59 full-time (37 women), 103 part-time (80 women); includes 8 minority (4 Black or African American, non-Hispanic/Latino; 2 Hispanic/Latino; 2 Two or more races, non-Hispanic/Latino). Average age 32. 85 applicants, 79% accepted, 50 enrolled. *Faculty:* 22 part-time/adjunct (14 women). *Financial support:* In 2015–16, 25 students received support. Applicants required to submit FAFSA. In 2015, 58 master's awarded. *Degree program information:* Part-time and evening/weekend programs available. Part-time, evening/weekend, online learning. Offers digital media, new literacies and learning (M Ed); education (MAT); exercise science, fitness and wellness (M Ed); online learning (M Ed); professional studies (M Ed); reading (M Ed); special education (M Ed). *Application deadline:* For fall admission, 5/1 for domestic and international students. Applications are processed on a rolling basis. *Application fee:* $40. Electronic applications accepted. *Application Contact:* Jack Kirby, Director of Graduate Studies, 304-367-4101, E-mail: jack.kirby@fairmontstate.edu. *Interim Dean, School of Education,* Dr. Carolyn Crislip-Tacy, 304-367-4143, Fax: 304-367-4599, E-mail: carolyn.crislip-tacy@fairmontstate.edu.

FAITH BAPTIST BIBLE COLLEGE AND THEOLOGICAL SEMINARY, Ankeny, IA 50023

General Information Independent-religious, coed, comprehensive institution. *Enrollment:* 279 graduate, professional, and undergraduate students; 12 full-time matriculated graduate/professional students, 27 part-time matriculated graduate/professional students (4 women). *Enrollment by degree level:* 39 master's. *Graduate faculty:* 3 full-time (0 women), 4 part-time/adjunct (0 women). *Graduate housing:* Rooms and/or apartments available on a first-come, first-served basis to single and married students. Housing application deadline: 8/1. *Student services:* Campus employment opportunities, career counseling, free psychological counseling, international student services, low-cost health insurance. *Library:* John L. Patten Library.

Computer facilities: 45 computers available on campus for general student use. A campuswide network can be accessed from student residence rooms and from off campus. Online class registration is available.
Website: http://www.faith.edu/

General Application Contact: Mark Davis, Director of Admissions, 888-FAITH4U, Fax: 515-964-1638, E-mail: admissions@faith.edu.

GRADUATE UNITS

Graduate Program Students: 12 full-time (0 women), 27 part-time (4 women); includes 4 minority (1 Black or African American, non-Hispanic/Latino; 1 Asian, non-Hispanic/Latino; 1 Hispanic/Latino; 1 Two or more races, non-Hispanic/Latino). Average age 33. *Faculty:* 3 full-time (0 women), 4 part-time/adjunct (0 women). *Financial support:* Career-related internships or fieldwork and scholarships/grants available. Support available to part-time students. Financial award application deadline: 3/1; financial award applicants required to submit FAFSA. In 2015, 13 master's awarded. *Degree program information:* Part-time programs available. Part-time. Offers Biblical studies (MA); pastoral studies (M Div); pastoral training (MA); religion (MA); theological studies (MA). *Application deadline:* For fall admission, 8/1 priority date for domestic students, 8/1 for international students; for spring admission, 12/15 for domestic and international students. Applications are processed on a rolling basis. *Application fee:* $25. Electronic applications accepted. *Application Contact:* Stacy Lansdown, Admissions Administrative Assistant, 888-FAITH4U, Fax: 515-964-1638, E-mail: admissions@faith.edu. *President,* Rev. Jim Tillotson, 515-964-0601, E-mail: tillotsonj@faith.edu.

FAITH EVANGELICAL COLLEGE & SEMINARY, Tacoma, WA 98407

General Information Independent-religious, coed, graduate-only institution.

GRADUATE UNITS

Graduate and Professional Programs *Degree program information:* Part-time and evening/weekend programs available. Part-time, evening/weekend, online learning. Offers theology (M Div, MACM, MTS, D Min).

FAITH THEOLOGICAL SEMINARY, Baltimore, MD 21212

General Information Independent-religious, coed, comprehensive institution.

GRADUATE UNITS

Graduate Programs Offers theology (M Div, D Min, Th D).

FASHION INSTITUTE OF TECHNOLOGY, New York, NY 10001-5992

General Information State and locally supported, coed, primarily women, comprehensive institution. *Enrollment:* 9,571 graduate, professional, and undergraduate students; 116 full-time matriculated graduate/professional students (91 women), 63 part-time matriculated graduate/professional students (56 women). *Enrollment by degree level:* 179 master's. *Graduate faculty:* 8 full-time (6 women), 27 part-time/adjunct (17 women). *International tuition:* $22,210 full-time. *Tuition, area resident:* Full-time $10,870; part-time $453 per credit. Tuition, state resident: full-time $10,870; part-time $453 per credit. Tuition, nonresident: full-time $22,210; part-time $925 per credit. *Required fees:* $730. *Graduate housing:* Room and/or apartments available on a first-come, first-served basis to single students; on-campus housing not available to married students. Typical cost: $13,280 per year ($17,626 including board). Room and board charges vary according to board plan and housing facility selected. *Student services:* Career counseling, exercise/wellness program, free psychological counseling, international student services, services for students with disabilities. *Library:* Gladys Marcus Library. *Research affiliation:* Grove Dictionary of Art, Oxford University Press (costume history), Exhibition Designers and Producers Association (exhibition design), Society for Environmental Graphic Design (exhibition design), Lolita S. A. (global fashion management), IDEO (design and management innovation).

Computer facilities: Computer purchase and lease plans are available. 1,700 computers available on campus for general student use. A campuswide network can be accessed from student residence rooms and from off campus. Online class registration is available.
Website: http://www.fitnyc.edu/

GRADUATE UNITS

School of Graduate Studies ***Financial support:*** Federal Work-Study and scholarships/grants available. Financial award applicants required to submit FAFSA. *Degree program information:* Part-time and evening/weekend programs available. Part-time, evening/weekend. Offers art market (MA); cosmetics and fragrance marketing and management (MPS); exhibition design (MA); fashion and textile studies: history, theory, museum practice (MA); global fashion management (MPS); illustration (MFA); sustainable interior environments (MA). *Application deadline:* For fall admission, 2/15 priority date for domestic and international students. Applications are processed on a rolling basis. *Application fee:* $50. Electronic applications accepted. *Application Contact:* Carole deSantis, Administrative Secretary, Graduate Admissions, 212-217-4314, Fax: 212-217-5156, E-mail: carole_desantis@fitnyc.edu. *Dean,* Dr. Mary Davis, 212-217-4300.

FAULKNER UNIVERSITY, Montgomery, AL 36109-3398

General Information Independent-religious, coed, university. *Graduate housing:* On-campus housing not available.

GRADUATE UNITS

Alabama Christian College of Arts and Sciences Offers arts and sciences (M Ed, MJA, MLA, MS); counseling (MS); criminal justice (MJA); liberal arts (MLA).

College of Biblical Studies Offers ministry (MABS); missions (MABS); New Testament (MABS); Old Testament (MABS); youth and family ministry (MABS).

College of Education Offers education (M Ed).

Great Books Honors College Offers Western civilization (M Litt).

Harris College of Business and Executive Education Offers management (MSM).

Thomas Goode Jones School of Law Offers law (JD). Electronic applications accepted.

FAYETTEVILLE STATE UNIVERSITY, Fayetteville, NC 28301-4298

General Information State-supported, coed, comprehensive institution. *Enrollment:* 6,104 graduate, professional, and undergraduate students; 240 full-time matriculated graduate/professional students (174 women), 160 part-time matriculated graduate/professional students (104 women). *Enrollment by degree level:* 341 master's, 59 doctoral. *Graduate faculty:* 131 full-time (59 women), 20 part-time/adjunct (9 women). *Graduate housing:* On-campus housing not available. *Student services:* Campus employment opportunities, career counseling, child daycare facilities, free psychological counseling, low-cost health insurance. *Library:* Charles W. Chestnut Library. *Collection:* Books: 213,496 (physical), 161,887 (digital/electronic); Serial titles: 284 (physical), 28,173 (digital/electronic); Databases: 380. Weekly public service hours: 97; students can reserve study rooms. *Research affiliation:* Research Triangle Park.

Computer facilities: Computer purchase and lease plans are available. 600 computers available on campus for general student use. A campuswide network can be accessed from student residence rooms and from off campus. Online class registration is available.
Website: http://www.uncfsu.edu/

General Application Contact: Dr. Samuel Adu-Mireku, Associate Dean, 910-672-1042, Fax: 910-672-1083, E-mail: sadu-mireku@uncfsu.edu.

GRADUATE UNITS

Graduate School Students: 247 full-time (178 women), 172 part-time (114 women); includes 265 minority (217 Black or African American, non-Hispanic/Latino; 6 American Indian or Alaska Native, non-Hispanic/Latino; 14 Asian, non-Hispanic/Latino; 18 Hispanic/Latino; 10 Two or more races, non-Hispanic/Latino), 5 international. Average age 35. 189 applicants, 88% accepted, 134 enrolled. *Faculty:* 131 full-time (59 women), 20 part-time/adjunct (9 women). *Financial support:* In 2015–16, 19 research assistantships (averaging $4,000 per year) were awarded; institutionally sponsored loans and unspecified assistantships also available. Support available to part-time students. Financial award application deadline: 3/1; financial award applicants required to submit FAFSA. In 2015, 169 master's, 8 doctorates awarded. *Degree program information:* Part-time and evening/weekend programs available. Part-time, evening/weekend. Offers biological sciences (MS); business administration (MBA); criminal justice (MA); elementary education (MA Ed); English (MA); mathematics (MA Ed); mathematics and computer science (MS); middle grades (MA Ed); political science (MA Ed); psychology (MA); school administration (MSA); social work (MSW); sociology (MA); special education (MA Ed). *Application deadline:* For fall admission, 4/1 for domestic students, 3/1 for international students; for spring admission, 10/15 for domestic students. Applications are processed on a rolling basis. *Application fee:* $40. *Application Contact:* Office of Admissions, 910-672-1374, Fax: 910-672-1470. *Office of Admissions,* 910-672-1374, Fax: 910-672-1470.

FELICIAN UNIVERSITY, Lodi, NJ 07644-2117

General Information Independent-religious, coed, comprehensive institution. CGS member. *Enrollment:* 1,957 graduate, professional, and undergraduate students; 41 full-time matriculated graduate/professional students (26 women), 307 part-time matriculated graduate/professional students (256 women). *Enrollment by degree level:* 312 master's, 16 doctoral, 20 other advanced degrees. *Graduate faculty:* 26 full-time (17 women), 12 part-time/adjunct (6 women). *Tuition, area resident:* Part-time $965 per credit. Tuition and fees vary according to course load and program. *Graduate housing:* Room and/or apartments available on a first-come, first-served basis to single students; on-campus housing not available to married students. Typical cost: $15,200 (including board). Housing application deadline: 5/1. *Student services:* Campus employment opportunities, campus safety program, career counseling, child daycare facilities, free psychological counseling, international student services, low-cost health insurance, services for students with disabilities, teacher training, writing training. *Library:* Felician University Library plus 1 other. *Collection:* Books: 80,365 (physical), 126,239 (digital/electronic); Serial titles: 264 (physical), 48,745 (digital/electronic); Databases: 32. Weekly public service hours: 144; students can reserve study rooms.

Computer facilities: 170 computers available on campus for general student use. A campuswide network can be accessed from student residence rooms and from off campus. Online class registration is available.
Website: http://www.felician.edu/

General Application Contact: Margaret Smolin, Director, Graduate Admissions, 201-559-1451, E-mail: graduate@felician.edu.

GRADUATE UNITS

Doctor of Nursing Practice Program Students: 16 part-time (14 women); includes 9 minority (5 Black or African American, non-Hispanic/Latino; 2 Asian, non-Hispanic/Latino; 1 Hispanic/Latino; 1 Native Hawaiian or other Pacific Islander, non-Hispanic/Latino). Average age 53. 16 applicants, 75% accepted, 8 enrolled. *Faculty:* 1 (woman) full-time, 1 (woman) part-time/adjunct. *Financial support:* Applicants required to submit FAFSA. In 2015, 6 doctorates awarded. *Degree program information:* Evening/weekend programs available. Evening/weekend, online learning. Offers advanced practice (DNP); executive leadership (DNP). *Application deadline:* Applications are processed on a rolling basis. *Application fee:* $40. Electronic applications accepted. *Application Contact:* Dr. Margaret Smolin, Director, Graduate Admissions, 201-559-1451, E-mail: graduate@felician.edu. *Associate Dean, Department of Graduate Nursing,* Dr. Ann Tritak, 201-559-6151, E-mail: tritaka@felician.edu.

Master of Science in Nursing Program Students: 1 (woman) full-time, 121 part-time (112 women); includes 60 minority (23 Black or African American, non-Hispanic/Latino; 1 American Indian or Alaska Native, non-Hispanic/Latino; 19 Asian, non-

Hispanic/Latino; 17 Hispanic/Latino). Average age 40. 111 applicants, 83% accepted, 52 enrolled. *Faculty:* 11 full-time (9 women), 2 part-time/adjunct (both women). *Financial support:* In 2015–16, 10 students received support. Traineeships available. Financial award applicants required to submit FAFSA. In 2015, 18 master's awarded. *Degree program information:* Part-time and evening/weekend programs available. Part-time, evening/weekend, online learning. Offers adult-gerontology nurse practitioner (MSN, PMC); executive leadership (MSN, PMC); family nurse practitioner (MSN, PMC); nursing education (MSN, PMC). *Application deadline:* Applications are processed on a rolling basis. *Application fee:* $40. Electronic applications accepted. *Application Contact:* Dr. Margaret Smolin, Director, Graduate Admissions, 201-559-1451, E-mail: graduate@felician.edu. *Associate Dean, Department of Graduate Nursing*, Dr. Ann Tritak, 201-201-559-6151, E-mail: tritaka@felician.edu.

Program in Business Students: 5 full-time (3 women), 36 part-time (22 women); includes 23 minority (10 Black or African American, non-Hispanic/Latino; 3 Asian, non-Hispanic/Latino; 10 Hispanic/Latino), 6 international. Average age 41. 35 applicants, 89% accepted, 17 enrolled. *Faculty:* 4 full-time (0 women), 2 part-time/adjunct (0 women). *Financial support:* Applicants required to submit FAFSA. In 2015, 14 master's awarded. *Degree program information:* Part-time and evening/weekend programs available. Part-time-only, evening/weekend. Offers innovation and entrepreneurship (MBA). *Application deadline:* Applications are processed on a rolling basis. *Application fee:* $40. Electronic applications accepted. *Application Contact:* Dr. Margaret Smolin, Director, Graduate Admissions, 201-559-1451, E-mail: graduate@felician.edu. *Associate Dean/Associate Professor, School of Business*, Dr. David M. Turi, 201-559-3327, E-mail: turid@felician.edu.

Program in Counseling Psychology Students: 26 full-time (15 women), 21 part-time (17 women); includes 29 minority (5 Black or African American, non-Hispanic/Latino; 2 Asian, non-Hispanic/Latino; 21 Hispanic/Latino; 1 Native Hawaiian or other Pacific Islander, non-Hispanic/Latino), 2 international. Average age 47. 32 applicants, 81% accepted, 10 enrolled. *Faculty:* 5 full-time (2 women). *Financial support:* Applicants required to submit FAFSA. In 2015, 14 master's awarded. Offers counseling psychology (MA). *Application deadline:* Applications are processed on a rolling basis. *Application fee:* $40. Electronic applications accepted. *Application Contact:* Dr. Margaret Smolin, Director, Graduate Admissions, 201-559-1451, E-mail: graduate@felician.edu. *Director of the Master's in Counseling Program*, Dr. Daniel Mahoney, 201-559-6161, E-mail: mahoneyd@felician.edu.

Program in Education Students: 6 full-time (4 women), 72 part-time (66 women); includes 22 minority (5 Black or African American, non-Hispanic/Latino; 6 Asian, non-Hispanic/Latino; 11 Hispanic/Latino), 3 international. Average age 35. 50 applicants, 72% accepted, 19 enrolled. *Faculty:* 6 full-time (4 women), 8 part-time/adjunct (4 women). *Financial support:* Federal Work-Study available. Financial award applicants required to submit FAFSA. In 2015, 21 master's awarded. *Degree program information:* Part-time and evening/weekend programs available. Part-time, evening/weekend. Offers education (MA); educational leadership (principal/supervision) (MA); educational supervision (PMC); principal (PMC); school nursing and health education (MA, Certificate). *Application deadline:* Applications are processed on a rolling basis. *Application fee:* $40. Electronic applications accepted. *Application Contact:* Dr. Margaret Smolin, Director, Graduate Admissions, 201-559-1451, E-mail: graduate@felician.edu. *Dean and Professor, School of Education*, Dr. Rose Rudnitski, 201-559-3551, E-mail: rudnitskir@felician.edu.

Program in Health Care Administration Students: 3 full-time (all women), 20 part-time (8 women); includes 8 minority (5 Black or African American, non-Hispanic/Latino; 2 Hispanic/Latino; 1 Two or more races, non-Hispanic/Latino). Average age 29. 20 applicants, 95% accepted, 10 enrolled. *Faculty:* 5 full-time (3 women). *Financial support:* Applicants required to submit FAFSA. In 2015, 7 master's awarded. *Degree program information:* Part-time and evening/weekend programs available. Part-time, evening/weekend. Offers health care administration (MSHA). *Application deadline:* Applications are processed on a rolling basis. *Application fee:* $40. Electronic applications accepted. *Application Contact:* Dr. Margaret Smolin, Director, Graduate Admissions, 201-559-1451, E-mail: graduate@felician.edu. *Associate Dean/Associate Professor, School of Business*, Dr. David M. Turi, 201-559-3327, E-mail: turid@felician.edu.

Program in Religious Education Students: 20 part-time (16 women); includes 6 minority (3 Asian, non-Hispanic/Latino; 2 Hispanic/Latino; 1 Native Hawaiian or other Pacific Islander, non-Hispanic/Latino). Average age 46. *Faculty:* 2 full-time (1 woman). *Financial support:* Scholarships/grants and tuition waivers (partial) available. Financial award applicants required to submit FAFSA. In 2015, 10 master's awarded. *Degree program information:* Part-time and evening/weekend programs available. Part-time, evening/weekend, online only. Offers religious education (MA, Certificate). *Application deadline:* Applications are processed on a rolling basis. *Application fee:* $40. Electronic applications accepted. *Application Contact:* Michael Szarek, Assistant Vice-President for Graduate and International Enrollment Services, 201-559-6047, Fax: 201-559-6047, E-mail: adultandgraduate@felician.edu. *Director of the Online Institute for Religious Studies and Education Ministry*, Dr. Dolores M. Henchy, 201-559-1451, E-mail: kravatzm@felician.edu.

FERRIS STATE UNIVERSITY, Big Rapids, MI 49307

General Information State-supported, coed, comprehensive institution. CGS member. *Enrollment:* 14,715 graduate, professional, and undergraduate students; 966 full-time matriculated graduate/professional students (516 women), 334 part-time matriculated graduate/professional students (190 women). *Enrollment by degree level:* 486 master's, 744 doctoral, 70 other advanced degrees. *Graduate faculty:* 98 full-time (57 women), 199 part-time/adjunct (85 women). Tuition and fees vary according to degree level and program. *Graduate housing:* Rooms and/or apartments available on a first-come, first-served basis to single and married students. Typical cost: $9434 (including board) for single students. *Student services:* Campus employment opportunities, campus safety program, career counseling, child daycare facilities, exercise/wellness program, free psychological counseling, international student services, low-cost health insurance, multicultural affairs office, services for students with disabilities, teacher training. *Library:* Ferris Library for Information, Technology and Education. *Collection:* Books: 264,567 (physical), 204,657 (digital/electronic); Serial titles: 1,778 (physical), 81,484 (digital/electronic); Databases: 146. Weekly public service hours: 93; study areas open 24 hours, 5–7 days a week. *Research affiliation:* Vistakon-Johnson & Johnson (optometry), Allergan-Hydron (optometry), Bausch & Lomb (optometry), Ciba Vision (optometry), American Education Research Association (education).

Computer facilities: 1,875 computers available on campus for general student use. A campuswide network can be accessed from student residence rooms and from off campus. Online class registration is available.
Website: http://www.ferris.edu/

General Application Contact: Dr. Kristen Salomonson, Dean, Enrollment Services/Director, Admissions and Records, 231-591-2100, Fax: 231-591-3944, E-mail: admissions@ferris.edu.

GRADUATE UNITS

College of Business Students: 113 full-time (28 women), 99 part-time (34 women); includes 18 minority (4 Black or African American, non-Hispanic/Latino; 1 American Indian or Alaska Native, non-Hispanic/Latino; 3 Asian, non-Hispanic/Latino; 5 Hispanic/Latino; 5 Two or more races, non-Hispanic/Latino), 109 international. Average age 29. 367 applicants, 18% accepted, 39 enrolled. *Faculty:* 8 full-time (3 women), 6 part-time/adjunct (2 women). *Financial support:* Career-related internships or fieldwork, Federal Work-Study, scholarships/grants, and unspecified assistantships available. Support available to part-time students. Financial award application deadline: 3/15; financial award applicants required to submit FAFSA. In 2015, 43 master's awarded. *Degree program information:* Part-time and evening/weekend programs available. Part-time, evening/weekend, 100% online, blended/hybrid learning. Offers business intelligence (MBA); design and innovation management (MBA); incident response (MBA); information security and intelligence (MS); lean systems and leadership (MBA); performance metrics (MBA); project management (MBA); supply chain management and lean logistics (MBA). *Application deadline:* For fall admission, 7/1 priority date for domestic students, 6/15 for international students; for winter admission, 11/1 priority date for domestic students, 10/15 for international students; for spring admission, 3/1 priority date for domestic students, 2/15 for international students. Applications are processed on a rolling basis. *Application fee:* $0 ($30 for international students). Electronic applications accepted. *Application Contact:* Shannon Yost, Department Secretary, 231-591-2168, Fax: 231-591-3521, E-mail: yosts@ferris.edu. *College of Business Dean*, Dr. David Nicol, 231-591-2168, Fax: 231-591-3521, E-mail: davidnicol@ferris.edu.

College of Education and Human Services Students: 23 full-time (16 women), 112 part-time (59 women); includes 32 minority (13 Black or African American, non-Hispanic/Latino; 1 American Indian or Alaska Native, non-Hispanic/Latino; 1 Asian, non-Hispanic/Latino; 12 Hispanic/Latino; 5 Two or more races, non-Hispanic/Latino), 11 international. Average age 35. 44 applicants, 93% accepted, 34 enrolled. *Faculty:* 14 full-time (6 women), 9 part-time/adjunct (6 women). *Financial support:* In 2015–16, 1 research assistantship (averaging $4,850 per year) was awarded; career-related internships or fieldwork, Federal Work-Study, scholarships/grants, and unspecified assistantships also available. Support available to part-time students. Financial award applicants required to submit FAFSA. In 2015, 65 master's awarded. *Degree program information:* Part-time and evening/weekend programs available. Part-time, evening/weekend, blended/hybrid learning. Offers education and human services (M Ed, MS, MSCJ, MSCTE). *Application deadline:* For fall admission, 7/1 priority date for domestic and international students; for winter admission, 12/15 for domestic and international students; for spring admission, 11/1 priority date for domestic and international students; for summer admission, 3/1 priority date for domestic and international students. Applications are processed on a rolling basis. *Application fee:* $30. Electronic applications accepted. *Application Contact:* Dr. Kristen Salomonson, Dean, Enrollment Services/Director, Admissions and Records, 231-591-2100, Fax: 231-591-3944, E-mail: admissions@ferris.edu. *Interim Dean*, Steven Reifert, 231-591-5080, Fax: 231-592-3792, E-mail: feifers@ferris.edu.

School of Criminal Justice Students: 13 full-time (7 women), 52 part-time (22 women); includes 26 minority (11 Black or African American, non-Hispanic/Latino; 1 American Indian or Alaska Native, non-Hispanic/Latino; 1 Asian, non-Hispanic/Latino; 10 Hispanic/Latino; 1 Native Hawaiian or other Pacific Islander, non-Hispanic/Latino; 2 Two or more races, non-Hispanic/Latino). Average age 35. 26 applicants, 92% accepted, 20 enrolled. *Faculty:* 7 full-time (2 women). *Financial support:* In 2015–16, 1 research assistantship (averaging $4,850 per year) was awarded; Federal Work-Study and unspecified assistantships also available. Support available to part-time students. Financial award applicants required to submit FAFSA. In 2015, 19 master's awarded. *Degree program information:* Part-time and evening/weekend programs available. Part-time, evening/weekend. Offers criminal justice administration (MSCJ). *Application deadline:* For fall admission, 8/15 for domestic students; for winter admission, 12/15 for domestic students; for spring admission, 3/15 for domestic students. Applications are processed on a rolling basis. *Application fee:* $0. Electronic applications accepted. *Application Contact:* Sara P. Rasmussen, Secretary, 231-591-3652, Fax: 231-591-3792, E-mail: sararasmussen@ferris.edu. *Professor/Graduate Program Coordinator*, Dr. Gregory P. Vanderkooi, 231-591-2458, Fax: 231-591-3792, E-mail: vanderkg@ferris.edu.

School of Education Students: 10 full-time (9 women), 60 part-time (37 women); includes 7 minority (2 Black or African American, non-Hispanic/Latino; 2 Hispanic/Latino; 3 Two or more races, non-Hispanic/Latino), 11 international. Average age 35. 18 applicants, 94% accepted, 14 enrolled. *Faculty:* 7 full-time (4 women), 9 part-time/adjunct (6 women). *Financial support:* Career-related internships or fieldwork and scholarships/grants available. Support available to part-time students. Financial award applicants required to submit FAFSA. In 2015, 46 master's awarded. *Degree program information:* Part-time and evening/weekend programs available. Part-time, evening/weekend, blended/hybrid learning. Offers curriculum and instruction (M Ed); educational leadership (MS); instructor (MSCTE); post-secondary administration (MSCTE); training and development (MSCTE). *Application deadline:* For fall admission, 7/1 priority date for domestic and international students; for spring admission, 11/1 priority date for domestic and international students; for summer admission, 3/1 priority date for domestic and international students. Applications are processed on a rolling basis. *Application fee:* $30. Electronic applications accepted. *Application Contact:* Liza Ing, Graduate Program Coordinator, 231-591-5362, Fax: 231-591-2043, E-mail: lizalng@ferris.edu. *Director*, Dr. Usman Adamu, 231-591-3512, Fax: 231-591-2043, E-mail: usmanadamu@ferris.edu.

College of Health Professions Students: 95 part-time (84 women); includes 11 minority (4 Black or African American, non-Hispanic/Latino; 1 American Indian or Alaska Native, non-Hispanic/Latino; 3 Asian, non-Hispanic/Latino; 1 Hispanic/Latino; 1 Native Hawaiian or other Pacific Islander, non-Hispanic/Latino; 1 Two or more races, non-Hispanic/Latino). Average age 39. 23 applicants, 117% accepted, 13 enrolled. *Faculty:* 5 full-time (all women), 2 part-time/adjunct (both women). *Financial support:* In 2015–16, 3 students received support. Career-related internships or fieldwork, Federal Work-Study, and scholarships/grants available. Support available to part-time students. Financial award application deadline: 4/15; financial award applicants required to submit FAFSA. In 2015, 15 master's awarded. *Degree program information:* Part-time and evening/weekend programs available. Part-time, evening/weekend, 100% online. Offers health professions (MSN). *Application deadline:* For fall admission, 4/15 priority date for domestic students; for spring admission, 10/15 for domestic students. Applications are processed on a rolling basis. *Application fee:* $0. Electronic applications accepted. *Application Contact:* Debby Buck, Off-Campus Student Support, 231-591-2094, Fax:

231-591-3788, E-mail: buckd@ferris.edu. *Chair, School of Nursing*, Dr. Susan Owens, 231-591-2267, Fax: 231-591-3788, E-mail: owenss3@ferris.edu.

School of Nursing Students: 95 part-time (84 women); includes 11 minority (4 Black or African American, non-Hispanic/Latino; 1 American Indian or Alaska Native, non-Hispanic/Latino; 3 Asian, non-Hispanic/Latino; 1 Hispanic/Latino; 1 Native Hawaiian or other Pacific Islander, non-Hispanic/Latino; 1 Two or more races, non-Hispanic/Latino). Average age 39. 23 applicants, 74% accepted, 13 enrolled. *Faculty:* 5 full-time (all women), 2 part-time/adjunct (both women). *Financial support:* In 2015–16, 3 students received support. Fellowships, research assistantships, teaching assistantships, career-related internships or fieldwork, and scholarships/grants available. Financial award application deadline: 4/15; financial award applicants required to submit FAFSA. In 2015, 15 master's awarded. *Degree program information:* Part-time and evening/weekend programs available. Part-time, evening/weekend, 100% online. Offers nursing (MSN); nursing administration (MSN); nursing education (MSN); nursing informatics (MSN). *Application deadline:* For fall admission, 4/15 priority date for domestic students; for spring admission, 10/15 for domestic students. *Application fee:* $0. Electronic applications accepted. *Application Contact:* Debby Buck, Off-Campus Program Secretary, 231-591-2270, Fax: 231-591-3788, E-mail: buckd@ferris.edu. *Chair, School of Nursing*, Dr. Susan Owens, 231-591-2267, Fax: 231-591-2325, E-mail: owenss3@ferris.edu.

College of Pharmacy Students: 580 full-time (321 women), 18 part-time (9 women); includes 40 minority (6 Black or African American, non-Hispanic/Latino; 2 American Indian or Alaska Native, non-Hispanic/Latino; 9 Asian, non-Hispanic/Latino; 17 Hispanic/Latino; 6 Two or more races, non-Hispanic/Latino), 20 international. Average age 24. 468 applicants, 39% accepted, 152 enrolled. *Faculty:* 35 full-time (24 women), 4 part-time/adjunct (2 women). *Financial support:* Career-related internships or fieldwork, Federal Work-Study, institutionally sponsored loans, and scholarships/grants available. Financial award applicants required to submit FAFSA. In 2015, 126 doctorates awarded. Offers pharmacy (Pharm D). *Application deadline:* For fall admission, 2/2 for domestic and international students. *Application fee:* $150. *Application Contact:* Tara M. Lee, Administrative Specialist, Admissions, 231-591-3780, Fax: 231-591-3829, E-mail: leet@ferris.edu. *Dean*, Dr. Stephen Durst, 231-591-2254, Fax: 231-591-3829, E-mail: dursts@ferris.edu.

Extended and International Operations Students: 67 full-time (44 women), 3 part-time (2 women); includes 14 minority (12 Black or African American, non-Hispanic/Latino; 1 Asian, non-Hispanic/Latino; 1 Hispanic/Latino). Average age 35. 30 applicants, 80% accepted, 23 enrolled. *Faculty:* 23 part-time/adjunct (13 women). *Financial support:* In 2015–16, 4 teaching assistantships (averaging $1,000 per year) were awarded. Financial award application deadline: 5/1; financial award applicants required to submit FAFSA. In 2015, 24 doctorates awarded. *Degree program information:* Evening/weekend programs available. Evening/weekend, blended/hybrid learning. Offers community college leadership (Ed D). *Application deadline:* For fall admission, 12/15 for domestic and international students; for winter admission, 1/27 for domestic and international students; for spring admission, 4/15 for domestic students, 4/18 for international students. Applications are processed on a rolling basis. *Application fee:* $0. Electronic applications accepted. *Application Contact:* Megan Biller, DCCL Coordinator, 231-591-2710, Fax: 231-591-3539, E-mail: meganbiller@ferris.edu. *Director*, Dr. Roberta Teahen, 231-591-3805, E-mail: robertateahen@ferris.edu.

Kendall College of Art and Design Students: 37 full-time (28 women), 7 part-time (2 women); includes 5 minority (1 Black or African American, non-Hispanic/Latino; 4 Hispanic/Latino), 6 international. Average age 31. 25 applicants, 60% accepted, 11 enrolled. *Faculty:* 17 full-time (12 women), 5 part-time/adjunct (2 women). *Financial support:* In 2015–16, 32 students received support, including 11 fellowships (averaging $18,313 per year); scholarships/grants and unspecified assistantships also available. Financial award application deadline: 2/1; financial award applicants required to submit FAFSA. In 2015, 18 master's awarded. *Degree program information:* Part-time programs available. Part-time. Offers architecture (M Arch); art education (MAE); design (MA); design and innovation management (MBA); drawing (MFA); painting (MFA); photography (MFA); printmaking (MFA); visual and critical studies (MA). *Application deadline:* For fall admission, 2/1 priority date for domestic and international students; for spring admission, 11/1 priority date for domestic and international students. Applications are processed on a rolling basis. *Application fee:* $0. Electronic applications accepted. *Application Contact:* Thomas Post, Graduate Student Recruitment Specialist, 616-451-2787, Fax: 616-831-9689, E-mail: thomaspost@ferris.edu. *President*, Leslie Bellavance, 616-451-2787.

Michigan College of Optometry Students: 146 full-time (79 women); includes 14 minority (1 Black or African American, non-Hispanic/Latino; 3 Asian, non-Hispanic/Latino; 8 Hispanic/Latino; 2 Two or more races, non-Hispanic/Latino), 2 international. Average age 24. 264 applicants, 23% accepted, 38 enrolled. *Faculty:* 19 full-time (7 women), 143 part-time/adjunct (51 women). *Financial support:* In 2015–16, 68 students received support. Career-related internships or fieldwork, Federal Work-Study, and scholarships/grants available. Financial award application deadline: 3/15; financial award applicants required to submit FAFSA. In 2015, 37 doctorates awarded. Offers optometry (OD). *Application deadline:* For fall admission, 2/15 for domestic and international students. Applications are processed on a rolling basis. *Application fee:* $155. Electronic applications accepted. *Application Contact:* Amy Parks, Health College Administrative Specialist, 231-591-3703, Fax: 231-591-2394, E-mail: amyparks@ferris.edu. *Dean*, Dr. David Damari, 231-591-3706, Fax: 231-591-2394, E-mail: damarid@ferris.edu.

FIELDING GRADUATE UNIVERSITY, Santa Barbara, CA 93105-3814

General Information Independent, coed, graduate-only institution. CGS member. *Enrollment by degree level:* 106 master's, 891 doctoral, 204 other advanced degrees. *Graduate faculty:* 58 full-time (38 women), 120 part-time/adjunct (68 women). *Tuition, area resident:* Full-time $26,640; part-time $720 per credit. Tuition and fees vary according to course load, degree level and program. *Graduate housing:* On-campus housing not available. *Student services:* Grant writing training, international student services, services for students with disabilities, writing training. *Library:* Fielding Graduate University Library Services. *Collection:* Books: 100,000 (digital/electronic); Serial titles: 40,000 (digital/electronic); Databases: 80.

Computer facilities: A campuswide network can be accessed from off campus. Online class registration is available.
Website: http://www.fielding.edu/

General Application Contact: Admission Office, 800-340-1099, Fax: 805-687-9793, E-mail: admission@fielding.edu.

GRADUATE UNITS

Graduate Programs Students: 973 full-time (713 women), 228 part-time (168 women); includes 381 minority (162 Black or African American, non-Hispanic/Latino; 20 American Indian or Alaska Native, non-Hispanic/Latino; 45 Asian, non-Hispanic/Latino; 105 Hispanic/Latino; 5 Native Hawaiian or other Pacific Islander, non-Hispanic/Latino; 44 Two or more races, non-Hispanic/Latino), 5 international. Average age 45. 375 applicants, 70% accepted, 194 enrolled. *Faculty:* 58 full-time (38 women), 120 part-time/adjunct (68 women). *Financial support:* In 2015–16, 215 students received support, including 14 teaching assistantships (averaging $1,200 per year). Support available to part-time students. Financial award applicants required to submit FAFSA. In 2015, 62 master's, 138 doctorates, 147 other advanced degrees awarded. *Degree program information:* Part-time programs available. Part-time, 100% online, blended/hybrid learning. *Application deadline:* For fall admission, 7/15 for domestic students, 7/1 for international students; for spring admission, 11/1 for domestic and international students; for summer admission, 3/1 for domestic and international students. *Application fee:* $75. Electronic applications accepted. *Application Contact:* Enrollment Coordinator, 800-340-1099 Ext. 4098, Fax: 805-687-9793, E-mail: admission@fielding.edu. *President*, Dr. Katrina Rogers, 805-898-2924, Fax: 805-687-9793, E-mail: krogers@fielding.edu.

School of Leadership Studies Students: 437 full-time (326 women), 125 part-time (98 women); includes 192 minority (86 Black or African American, non-Hispanic/Latino; 16 American Indian or Alaska Native, non-Hispanic/Latino; 26 Asian, non-Hispanic/Latino; 41 Hispanic/Latino; 4 Native Hawaiian or other Pacific Islander, non-Hispanic/Latino; 19 Two or more races, non-Hispanic/Latino), 1 international. Average age 48. 97 applicants, 96% accepted, 64 enrolled. *Faculty:* 26 full-time (17 women), 78 part-time/adjunct (49 women). *Financial support:* In 2015–16, 125 students received support. Scholarships/grants and tuition waivers (partial) available. Support available to part-time students. Financial award applicants required to submit FAFSA. In 2015, 43 master's, 75 doctorates, 109 other advanced degrees awarded. *Degree program information:* Part-time programs available. Part-time, 100% online, blended/hybrid learning. Offers comprehensive evidence based coaching (Graduate Certificate); digital teaching and learning (MA); educational administration (Graduate Certificate); evidence based coaching for organization leadership (Graduate Certificate); human development (PhD); infant and early childhood development (PhD); leadership for change (Ed D); nonprofit leadership (Graduate Certificate); organization consulting (Graduate Certificate); organizational development and change (PhD); organizational development and leadership (MA, Graduate Certificate). *Application deadline:* For fall admission, 7/1 for domestic and international students; for spring admission, 9/1 for domestic and international students; for summer admission, 3/1 for domestic and international students. *Application fee:* $75. Electronic applications accepted. *Application Contact:* Enrollment Coordinator, 800-340-1099 Ext. 4098, Fax: 805-687-9793, E-mail: hodadmission@fielding.edu. *Provost and Senior Vice President*, Dr. Gerald Porter, 805-898-2940, Fax: 805-687-9793, E-mail: gporter@fielding.edu.

School of Psychology Students: 521 full-time (380 women), 75 part-time (55 women); includes 189 minority (76 Black or African American, non-Hispanic/Latino; 4 American Indian or Alaska Native, non-Hispanic/Latino; 19 Asian, non-Hispanic/Latino; 64 Hispanic/Latino; 1 Native Hawaiian or other Pacific Islander, non-Hispanic/Latino; 25 Two or more races, non-Hispanic/Latino), 4 international. Average age 41. 278 applicants, 61% accepted, 130 enrolled. *Faculty:* 32 full-time (21 women), 42 part-time/adjunct (19 women). *Financial support:* In 2015–16, 82 students received support, including 11 teaching assistantships (averaging $1,600 per year); scholarships/grants also available. Support available to part-time students. Financial award applicants required to submit FAFSA. In 2015, 19 master's, 63 doctorates, 38 other advanced degrees awarded. *Degree program information:* Part-time programs available. Part-time, 100% online, blended/hybrid learning. Offers clinical psychology (PhD, Graduate Certificate); clinical psychology respecialization (Post-Doctoral Certificate); media psychology (MA, PhD, Graduate Certificate); neuropsychology (Post-Doctoral Certificate). *Application deadline:* For fall admission, 1/24 for domestic and international students; for spring admission, 11/1 for domestic and international students; for summer admission, 3/1 for domestic and international students. *Application fee:* $75. Electronic applications accepted. *Application Contact:* Enrollment Coordinator, 800-340-1099 Ext. 4098, Fax: 805-687-9793, E-mail: psyadmission@fielding.edu. *Provost and Senior Vice President*, Dr. Gerald Porter, 805-898-2940, E-mail: gporter@fielding.edu.

FISHER COLLEGE, Boston, MA 02116-1500

General Information Independent, coed, comprehensive institution.

GRADUATE UNITS

Master of Business Administration Program Online learning. Offers business administration (MBA). Electronic applications accepted.

FISK UNIVERSITY, Nashville, TN 37208-3051

General Information Independent-religious, coed, comprehensive institution. *Graduate housing:* Rooms and/or apartments available on a first-come, first-served basis to single and married students. Housing application deadline: 4/6. *Research affiliation:* Oak Ridge Associated Universities (physics).

GRADUATE UNITS

Division of Graduate Studies ***Degree program information:*** Part-time programs available. Part-time. Offers biology (MA); chemistry (MA); clinical psychology (MA); physics (MA); psychology (MA). Electronic applications accepted.

FITCHBURG STATE UNIVERSITY, Fitchburg, MA 01420-2697

General Information State-supported, coed, comprehensive institution. *Enrollment:* 160 full-time matriculated graduate/professional students (99 women), 750 part-time matriculated graduate/professional students (562 women). *Enrollment by degree level:* 820 master's, 90 other advanced degrees. Tuition, state resident: full-time $3006; part-time $1002 per year. Tuition, nonresident: full-time $3006; part-time $1002 per year. *Required fees:* $2468. *Graduate housing:* On-campus housing not available. *Student services:* Campus employment opportunities, campus safety program, career counseling, exercise/wellness program, free psychological counseling, international student services, low-cost health insurance, multicultural affairs office, services for students with disabilities, teacher training, writing training. *Library:* Amelia V. Galucci-Cirio Library.

Computer facilities: Computer purchase and lease plans are available. 500 computers available on campus for general student use. A campuswide network can be accessed from student residence rooms and from off campus. Online class registration is available.
Website: http://www.fitchburgstate.edu/

General Application Contact: Sean Ganas, Director of Admissions, 978-665-3144, Fax: 978-665-4540, E-mail: admissions@fitchburgstate.edu.

GRADUATE UNITS

Division of Graduate and Continuing Education Students: 160 full-time (99 women), 750 part-time (562 women); includes 115 minority (16 Black or African American, non-Hispanic/Latino; 3 American Indian or Alaska Native, non-Hispanic/Latino; 55 Asian, non-Hispanic/Latino; 26 Hispanic/Latino; 15 Two or more races, non-Hispanic/Latino). Average age 35. 271 applicants, 98% accepted, 197 enrolled. *Faculty:* 58 full-time (28 women), 176 part-time/adjunct (130 women). *Financial support:* In 2015–16, research assistantships with partial tuition reimbursements (averaging $5,500 per year) were awarded; Federal Work-Study, scholarships/grants, and unspecified assistantships also available. Support available to part-time students. Financial award application deadline: 3/1; financial award applicants required to submit FAFSA. In 2015, 506 master's, 51 other advanced degrees awarded. *Degree program information:* Part-time and evening/weekend programs available. Part-time, evening/weekend, online learning. Offers accounting (MBA); applied communications (MS, CAGS, Certificate); arts education (M Ed); biology and teaching biology (secondary level) (MA, MAT, Certificate); computer science (MS); counseling/psychology (CAGS); curriculum and teaching (M Ed); early childhood education (M Ed); educational leadership and management (M Ed, CAGS); educational technology (Certificate); elementary education (M Ed); elementary school guidance counseling (MS); English and teaching English (secondary level) (MA, MAT, Certificate); fine arts director (Certificate); forensic nursing (MS, Certificate); guided studies (M Ed); health communication (MS); history and teaching history (secondary level) (MA, MAT, Certificate); human resource management (MBA); individualized track (CAGS); library media (MS); management (MBA); mental health counseling (MS); middle school education (M Ed); occupational education (M Ed); reading specialist (M Ed, CAGS); school principal (M Ed, CAGS); science education (M Ed); secondary school guidance counseling (MS); supervisor/director (M Ed, CAGS); teaching students with moderate disabilities (M Ed); teaching students with severe disabilities (M Ed); technical and professional writing (MS); technology education (M Ed); technology leader (M Ed, CAGS). *Application deadline:* For fall admission, 7/15 for international students; for spring admission, 12/1 for international students. Applications are processed on a rolling basis. *Application fee:* $25 ($50 for international students). Electronic applications accepted. *Application Contact:* Sean Ganas, Director of Admissions, 978-665-3144, Fax: 978-665-4540, E-mail: admissions@fitchburgstate.edu. *Interim Dean,* Brian Bercier, 978-665-3182, Fax: 978-665-3658, E-mail: gce@fitchburgstate.edu.

FIVE BRANCHES UNIVERSITY, Santa Cruz, CA 95062

General Information Independent, coed, graduate-only institution. *Enrollment by degree level:* 100 master's, 300 doctoral. *Graduate faculty:* 10 full-time (5 women), 90 part-time/adjunct (45 women). *Tuition, area resident:* Full-time $16,000; part-time $9600 per credit. *Required fees:* $200; $200 per credit. $50 per trimester. Tuition and fees vary according to degree level. *Graduate housing:* On-campus housing not available. *Student services:* Campus employment opportunities, campus safety program, career counseling, international student services. *Library:* Five Branches University Library plus 1 other. *Collection:* Books: 2,000 (physical); Serial titles: 6,000 (physical); Databases: 3. Weekly public service hours: 40. *Research affiliation:* Highland Hospital (healthcare).

Computer facilities: 4 computers available on campus for general student use. Online class registration is available.
Website: http://www.fivebranches.edu/

General Application Contact: Eleonor Mendelson, Admissions Director, 831-476-9424, Fax: 831-476-8928, E-mail: tcm@fivebranches.com.

GRADUATE UNITS

Graduate School of Traditional Chinese Medicine Students: 400 full-time (320 women). Average age 35. *Faculty:* 10 full-time (5 women), 90 part-time/adjunct (45 women). *Financial support:* In 2015–16, 80 students received support. Career-related internships or fieldwork and scholarships/grants available. Financial award application deadline: 4/15; financial award applicants required to submit FAFSA. Offers acupuncture (M Ac); acupuncture and Oriental medicine (DAOM); traditional Chinese medicine (MTCM, PhD). *Application deadline:* For fall admission, 6/1 priority date for domestic students; for spring admission, 11/1 priority date for domestic students. Applications are processed on a rolling basis. *Application fee:* $30. Electronic applications accepted. *Application Contact:* Eleonor Mendelson, Admissions Director, 831-476-9424, Fax: 831-476-8928, E-mail: tcm@fivebranches.com. *Vice President, Academic Affairs,* Joanna Zhao, 831-476-9424 Ext. 42, Fax: 831-476-8928, E-mail: dean@fivebranches.edu.

FIVE TOWNS COLLEGE, Dix Hills, NY 11746-6055

General Information Independent, coed, comprehensive institution. *Enrollment:* 681 graduate, professional, and undergraduate students; 21 full-time matriculated graduate/professional students (7 women), 6 part-time matriculated graduate/professional students (2 women). *Enrollment by degree level:* 10 master's, 14 doctoral, 3 other advanced degrees. *Graduate faculty:* 12 full-time (3 women), 6 part-time/adjunct (0 women). *Tuition, area resident:* Full-time $15,000; part-time $625 per credit. *Required fees:* $600; $150 per semester. Tuition and fees vary according to degree level. *Graduate housing:* Room and/or apartments available on a first-come, first-served basis to single students; on-campus housing not available to married students. Typical cost: $8800 per year ($13,800 including board). *Student services:* Campus employment opportunities, campus safety program, career counseling, international student services, low-cost health insurance, services for students with disabilities, teacher training, writing training. *Library:* Five Towns College Library plus 1 other.

Computer facilities: 110 computers available on campus for general student use. A campuswide network can be accessed from student residence rooms.
Website: http://www.ftc.edu/

General Application Contact: Ronnie MacDonald, Director of Admissions, 631-656-2110, Fax: 631-656-2172, E-mail: admissions@ftc.edu.

GRADUATE UNITS

Graduate Programs Students: 18 full-time (7 women), 6 part-time (2 women); includes 9 minority (3 Black or African American, non-Hispanic/Latino; 4 Asian, non-Hispanic/Latino; 1 Hispanic/Latino; 1 Two or more races, non-Hispanic/Latino), 1 international. Average age 35. 63 applicants, 11% accepted, 7 enrolled. *Faculty:* 12 full-time (3 women), 6 part-time/adjunct (0 women). *Financial support:* Fellowships with tuition reimbursements, teaching assistantships with tuition reimbursements, and tuition waivers (partial) available. Financial award applicants required to submit FAFSA. *Degree program information:* Part-time programs available. Part-time. Offers childhood education (MS Ed); composition and arranging (DMA); jazz/commercial music (MM); music education (MM, DMA); music history and literature (DMA); music performance (DMA). *Application deadline:* For fall admission, 9/1 for domestic and international students; for spring admission, 1/25 for domestic and international students. Applications are processed on a rolling basis. *Application fee:* $50. Electronic applications accepted. *Application Contact:* Ronnie MacDonald, Director of Admissions, 631-656-2110, Fax: 631-656-2172, E-mail: admissions@ftc.edu.

FLORIDA AGRICULTURAL AND MECHANICAL UNIVERSITY, Tallahassee, FL 32307-3200

General Information State-supported, coed, university. CGS member. *Graduate housing:* Rooms and/or apartments available on a first-come, first-served basis to single and married students. Housing application deadline: 6/1. *Research affiliation:* Boeing Company (aerospace science), Minority Health Professions Foundation (health science), Pfizer, Inc.

GRADUATE UNITS

College of Law ***Degree program information:*** Part-time and evening/weekend programs available. Part-time, evening/weekend. Offers law (JD).

Division of Graduate Studies, Research, and Continuing Education ***Degree program information:*** Part-time and evening/weekend programs available. Part-time, evening/weekend.

College of Education Degree program information: Part-time and evening/weekend programs available. Part-time, evening/weekend. Offers administration and supervision (M Ed, MS, PhD); adult education (M Ed, MS); biology (M Ed); business education (MBE); chemistry (MS Ed); education (M Ed, MBE, MS, MS Ed, PhD); educational leadership (PhD); elementary education (M Ed, MS); English (MS Ed); guidance and counseling (M Ed, MS); history (MS Ed); industrial education (MS Ed); math (MS Ed); physics (MS Ed); sport management (MS); technology education (M Ed).

College of Pharmacy and Pharmaceutical Sciences Offers environmental toxicology (PhD); health outcomes research and pharmacoeconomics (PhD); medicinal chemistry (MS, PhD); pharmaceutics (MS, PhD); pharmacology/toxicology (MS, PhD); pharmacy administration (MS); pharmacy and pharmaceutical sciences (MPH, MS, DPH, PhD, Pharm D); public health (MPH, DPH).

College of Science and Technology Offers chemistry (MS); physics (MS, PhD); science and technology (MS, PhD); software engineering (MS).

College of Social Sciences, Arts and Humanities Degree program information: Part-time programs available. Part-time. Offers community psychology (MS); criminal justice (MASS); history (MASS); history and political science (MASS, MSW); political science (MASS); public administration (MASS); social sciences, arts and humanities (MASS, MS, MSW); social work (MSW).

FAMU-FSU College of Engineering Offers biomedical engineering (MS, PhD); chemical engineering (MS, PhD); civil engineering (M Eng, MS, PhD); electrical engineering (MS, PhD); engineering (M Eng, MS, PhD); industrial engineering (MS, PhD); mechanical engineering (MS, PhD). College administered jointly by Florida State University.

School of Allied Health Sciences Offers health administration (MS); occupational therapy (MOT); physical therapy (DPT).

School of Architecture Degree program information: Part-time programs available. Part-time. Offers architectural studies (MS Arch); architecture (professional) (M Arch); landscape architecture (MLA).

School of Business and Industry Offers accounting (MBA); finance (MBA); management information systems (MBA); marketing (MBA).

School of Journalism and Graphic Communication Offers journalism (MS).

School of Nursing Offers nursing (MSN, PhD).

School of the Environment Offers the environment (MS, PhD).

FLORIDA ATLANTIC UNIVERSITY, Boca Raton, FL 33431-0991

General Information State-supported, coed, university. CGS member. *Enrollment:* 1,998 full-time matriculated graduate/professional students (1,147 women), 2,658 part-time matriculated graduate/professional students (1,680 women). *Enrollment by degree level:* 3,501 master's, 1,118 doctoral, 37 other advanced degrees. *Graduate faculty:* 791 full-time (342 women), 541 part-time/adjunct (275 women). *Tuition, area resident:* Full-time $7392; part-time $369.82 per credit hour. Tuition, state resident: full-time $7392; part-time $369.82 per credit hour. Tuition, nonresident: full-time $19,432; part-time $1024.81 per credit hour. *Graduate housing:* Room and/or apartments available on a first-come, first-served basis to single students; on-campus housing not available to married students. Housing application deadline: 5/1. *Student services:* Campus employment opportunities, campus safety program, career counseling, exercise/wellness program, free psychological counseling, international student services, low-cost health insurance, multicultural affairs office, services for students with disabilities, teacher training. *Library:* S. E. Wimberly Library plus 2 others. *Research affiliation:* The Scripps Research Institute (biomedical sciences), The Vaccine and Gene Institute of Florida (biomedical sciences), Torrey Pines Institute for Molecular Studies (medical research), Max Planck Florida Institute for Neuroscience (neuroscience), Max Planck Florida Institute for Neuroscience (neuroscience).

Computer facilities: 1,350 computers available on campus for general student use. A campuswide network can be accessed from student residence rooms and from off campus. Online class registration is available.
Website: http://www.fau.edu/

General Application Contact: Amanda Frederick, Coordinator, Graduate Recruitment, 561-297-1213, Fax: 561-297-1212, E-mail: afrede11@fau.edu.

GRADUATE UNITS

Charles E. Schmidt College of Medicine ***Financial support:*** Fellowships and research assistantships available. Financial award applicants required to submit FAFSA. *Degree program information:* Part-time programs available. Part-time. Offers biomedical science (MS). *Application deadline:* For fall admission, 5/1 for domestic students, 3/15 for international students; for spring admission, 10/1 for domestic and international students. *Application fee:* $30. Electronic applications accepted.

Charles E. Schmidt College of Science ***Financial support:*** Fellowships with partial tuition reimbursements, research assistantships with partial tuition reimbursements, teaching assistantships with partial tuition reimbursements, career-related internships or fieldwork, Federal Work-Study, institutionally sponsored loans, scholarships/grants, tuition waivers (partial), and unspecified assistantships available. Financial award applicants required to submit FAFSA. *Degree program information:* Part-time programs available. Part-time. Offers applied mathematics and statistics (MS); biology (MS, MST); chemistry (MS, MST, PhD); geology (MS); geosciences (PhD); mathematics (MST, PhD); physics (MS, MST, PhD); psychology (MA); science (MA, MS, MSMP, MST, PhD). *Application deadline:* For fall admission, 6/1 for domestic students, 2/15 for international students; for spring admission, 11/1 for domestic students, 8/15 for international students. Applications are processed on a rolling basis. *Application fee:* $30. Electronic applications accepted.

Center for Complex Systems and Brain Sciences Financial support: Fellowships with full tuition reimbursements, research assistantships with partial tuition reimbursements, teaching assistantships with partial tuition reimbursements, Federal Work-Study, and traineeships available. Offers complex systems and brain sciences (PhD). *Application deadline:* For fall admission, 1/15 priority date for domestic and international students. *Application fee:* $30.

Christine E. Lynn College of Nursing *Financial support:* Research assistantships with partial tuition reimbursements, teaching assistantships with partial tuition reimbursements, career-related internships or fieldwork, Federal Work-Study, institutionally sponsored loans, scholarships/grants, and traineeships available. Support available to part-time students. *Degree program information:* Part-time programs available. Part-time. Offers administrative and financial leadership in nursing and health care (Post Master's Certificate); nursing (PhD); nursing practice (DNP). *Application deadline:* For fall admission, 6/1 for domestic students, 2/15 for international students; for spring admission, 10/1 for domestic students, 7/15 for international students. Applications are processed on a rolling basis. *Application fee:* $30.

College of Business *Financial support:* Fellowships with partial tuition reimbursements, research assistantships with partial tuition reimbursements, teaching assistantships with full tuition reimbursements, career-related internships or fieldwork, Federal Work-Study, institutionally sponsored loans, tuition waivers (full and partial), and unspecified assistantships available. Support available to part-time students. Financial award application deadline: 3/1. *Degree program information:* Part-time and evening/weekend programs available. Part-time, evening/weekend, online learning. Offers business (M Tax, MAC, MBA, MHA, MS, PhD); business administration (MBA); economics (MS); finance (MS); information technology management (MS); marketing (MBA); music business administration (MS). *Application deadline:* For fall admission, 5/1 priority date for domestic students, 2/15 priority date for international students; for spring admission, 4/1 priority date for domestic students, 1/15 priority date for international students. Applications are processed on a rolling basis. *Application fee:* $30.

School of Accounting Financial support: Fellowships, research assistantships with partial tuition reimbursements, teaching assistantships, career-related internships or fieldwork, Federal Work-Study, institutionally sponsored loans, scholarships/grants, and tuition waivers (partial) available. Support available to part-time students. Financial award application deadline: 3/1. *Degree program information:* Part-time and evening/weekend programs available. Part-time, evening/weekend, online learning. Offers accounting (MAC). *Application deadline:* For fall admission, 7/1 priority date for domestic students, 2/15 priority date for international students; for spring admission, 11/1 priority date for domestic students, 7/15 priority date for international students. Applications are processed on a rolling basis. *Application fee:* $30.

College of Design and Social Inquiry *Financial support:* Fellowships with partial tuition reimbursements, research assistantships with partial tuition reimbursements, teaching assistantships with partial tuition reimbursements, career-related internships or fieldwork, Federal Work-Study, and institutionally sponsored loans available. Support available to part-time students. Financial award application deadline: 4/1. *Degree program information:* Part-time and evening/weekend programs available. Part-time, evening/weekend. Offers design and social inquiry (MNM, MPA, MS, MSW, MURP, DSW, PhD). *Application deadline:* For fall admission, 5/1 for domestic students, 2/15 for international students; for spring admission, 11/1 for domestic students, 7/15 for international students. Applications are processed on a rolling basis. *Application fee:* $30.

School of Criminology and Criminal Justice Financial support: Research assistantships with partial tuition reimbursements, institutionally sponsored loans, scholarships/grants, and unspecified assistantships available. Financial award application deadline: 4/1. *Degree program information:* Part-time and evening/weekend programs available. Part-time, evening/weekend, online learning. Offers criminology and criminal justice (MS). *Application deadline:* For fall admission, 5/1 priority date for domestic students, 2/15 for international students; for spring admission, 11/1 priority date for domestic students, 7/15 for international students. Applications are processed on a rolling basis. *Application fee:* $30. Electronic applications accepted. *Application Contact:* Sigal Altman, 561-297-4936, E-mail: saltman2013@fau.edu.

School of Public Administration Financial support: Fellowships with full tuition reimbursements, research assistantships with partial tuition reimbursements, teaching assistantships with partial tuition reimbursements, career-related internships or fieldwork, Federal Work-Study, institutionally sponsored loans, and tuition waivers (partial) available. Support available to part-time students. Financial award application deadline: 4/1. *Degree program information:* Part-time and evening/weekend programs available. Part-time, evening/weekend. Offers public administration (MPA, PhD). *Application deadline:* For fall admission, 5/1 priority date for domestic students, 2/15 for international students; for spring admission, 11/1 for domestic students, 7/15 for international students. Applications are processed on a rolling basis. *Application fee:* $30. *Application Contact:* Kelly Roy, 561-297.4532, E-mail: kroy7@fau.edu.

School of Social Work Financial support: Fellowships with tuition reimbursements, research assistantships with tuition reimbursements, career-related internships or fieldwork, Federal Work-Study, institutionally sponsored loans, and tuition waivers (partial) available. Financial award application deadline: 4/1. *Degree program information:* Part-time and evening/weekend programs available. Part-time, evening/weekend. Offers social work (MSW, DSW). *Application deadline:* For fall admission, 5/1 priority date for domestic students, 2/15 for international students. Applications are processed on a rolling basis. *Application fee:* $30. *Application Contact:* Joy McClellan, 561-297-3234, E-mail: jmcclel2@fau.edu.

School of Urban and Regional Planning Financial support: Fellowships with full tuition reimbursements, research assistantships, career-related internships or fieldwork, Federal Work-Study, institutionally sponsored loans, and tuition waivers (partial) available. Financial award application deadline: 4/1. *Degree program information:* Part-time and evening/weekend programs available. Part-time, evening/weekend. Offers urban and regional planning (MURP). *Application deadline:* For fall admission, 5/1 priority date for domestic students, 2/15 for international students; for spring admission, 11/1 priority date for domestic students, 7/15 for international students. Applications are processed on a rolling basis. *Application fee:* $30.

College of Education *Financial support:* Fellowships with partial tuition reimbursements, research assistantships with partial tuition reimbursements, teaching assistantships with partial tuition reimbursements, career-related internships or fieldwork, Federal Work-Study, and unspecified assistantships available. *Degree program information:* Part-time and evening/weekend programs available. Part-time, evening/weekend. Offers adult and community education (M Ed, PhD, Ed S); counselor education (PhD); curriculum and instruction (M Ed, PhD, Ed S); early childhood education (M Ed); education (M Ed, MA, MS, Ed D, PhD, Ed S); educational leadership (M Ed, PhD, Ed S); elementary education (M Ed); environmental education (M Ed); exceptional student education (M Ed, Ed D); exercise science and health promotion (MS); higher education (M Ed, PhD); K-12 school leadership (M Ed, PhD, Ed S); multicultural education (M Ed); reading education (M Ed); social foundations of education (M Ed); speech-language pathology (MS); TESOL and bilingual education (MA). *Application deadline:* For fall admission, 5/1 for domestic students. Applications are processed on a rolling basis. *Application fee:* $30. Electronic applications accepted. *Application Contact:* Dr. Paul Peluso, 561-297-3625, E-mail: ppeluso@fau.edu.

College of Engineering and Computer Science *Financial support:* Fellowships, research assistantships with partial tuition reimbursements, teaching assistantships with partial tuition reimbursements, career-related internships or fieldwork, Federal Work-Study, and unspecified assistantships available. Support available to part-time students. Financial award applicants required to submit FAFSA. *Degree program information:* Part-time and evening/weekend programs available. Part-time, evening/weekend, online learning. Offers bioengineering (MS); civil engineering (MS); computer engineering (PhD); engineering and computer science (MS, PhD); environmental engineering (MS); mechanical engineering (MS, PhD). *Application deadline:* For fall admission, 7/1 for domestic students, 2/15 for international students; for spring admission, 11/1 for domestic students, 7/15 for international students. Applications are processed on a rolling basis. *Application fee:* $30.

Dorothy F. Schmidt College of Arts and Letters *Financial support:* Fellowships with partial tuition reimbursements, research assistantships, teaching assistantships, career-related internships or fieldwork, Federal Work-Study, institutionally sponsored loans, and tuition waivers (partial) available. Support available to part-time students. *Degree program information:* Part-time programs available. Part-time. Offers acting (MFA); American literature (MA); anthropology (MA, MAT); arts and letters (MA, MAT, MFA, MM, PhD); comparative literature (MA); comparative studies (MA); design and technology (MFA); French (MA); history (MA); liberal studies (MA); linguistics (MA); music (MM); political science (MA); sociology (MA); Spanish (MA); visual art (MFA). *Application deadline:* For fall admission, 6/1 priority date for domestic students. Applications are processed on a rolling basis. *Application fee:* $30. Electronic applications accepted.

Center for Women, Gender and Sexuality Studies Financial support: Fellowships with tuition reimbursements, teaching assistantships with tuition reimbursements, career-related internships or fieldwork, Federal Work-Study, institutionally sponsored loans, scholarships/grants, and unspecified assistantships available. Support available to part-time students. Financial award applicants required to submit FAFSA. *Degree program information:* Part-time programs available. Part-time. Offers women, gender and sexuality studies (MA). *Application deadline:* For fall admission, 7/1 for domestic students, 2/15 for international students; for spring admission, 11/1 for domestic students, 7/15 for international students. Applications are processed on a rolling basis. *Application fee:* $30. Electronic applications accepted. *Application Contact:* Regina Gloncalves, Senior Secretary, 561-297-3865, E-mail: rgoncal@fau.edu. *Senior Secretary,* Regina Gloncalves, 561-297-3865, E-mail: rgoncal@fau.edu.

School of Communication and Multimedia Studies Students: 22 full-time (13 women), 14 part-time (5 women); includes 14 minority (7 Black or African American, non-Hispanic/Latino; 1 Asian, non-Hispanic/Latino; 6 Hispanic/Latino), 3 international. Average age 33. 28 applicants, 75% accepted, 15 enrolled. *Faculty:* 25 full-time (8 women). *Financial support:* Teaching assistantships with partial tuition reimbursements, Federal Work-Study, institutionally sponsored loans, scholarships/grants, and unspecified assistantships available. Support available to part-time students. Financial award application deadline: 3/1; financial award applicants required to submit FAFSA. In 2015, 10 master's awarded. *Degree program information:* Part-time programs available. Part-time. Offers communication studies (MA); film and video (Certificate); media, technology and entertainment (MFA). *Application deadline:* For fall admission, 7/1 priority date for domestic students, 4/1 for international students; for spring admission, 11/1 for domestic students, 10/1 for international students. Applications are processed on a rolling basis. *Application fee:* $30. Electronic applications accepted. *Application Contact:* Dr. Eric M. Freedman, Graduate Coordinator, 561-297-2534, Fax: 561-297-2615, E-mail: efreedma@fau.edu. *Director,* Dr. David Williams, 561-297-0045, Fax: 561-297-2615, E-mail: dcwill@fau.edu.

FLORIDA COASTAL SCHOOL OF LAW, Jacksonville, FL 32256

General Information Proprietary, coed, graduate-only institution.

GRADUATE UNITS

Professional Program *Degree program information:* Part-time programs available. Part-time. Offers law (JD). Electronic applications accepted.

FLORIDA COLLEGE OF INTEGRATIVE MEDICINE, Orlando, FL 32809

General Information Proprietary, coed, graduate-only institution. *Graduate housing:* On-campus housing not available.

GRADUATE UNITS

Graduate Program *Degree program information:* Evening/weekend programs available. Evening/weekend. Offers Oriental medicine (MSOM). Electronic applications accepted.

FLORIDA GULF COAST UNIVERSITY, Fort Myers, FL 33965-6565

General Information State-supported, coed, comprehensive institution. CGS member. *Enrollment:* 14,860 graduate, professional, and undergraduate students; 388 full-time matriculated graduate/professional students (239 women), 755 part-time matriculated graduate/professional students (514 women). *Enrollment by degree level:* 834 master's, 146 doctoral. *Graduate faculty:* 456 full-time (207 women), 343 part-time/adjunct (170 women). Tuition, state resident: full-time $6974. Tuition, nonresident: full-time $28,170. *Required fees:* $1987. One-time fee: $10 full-time. Tuition and fees vary according to course load and degree level. *Graduate housing:* Room and/or apartments available on a first-come, first-served basis to single students; on-campus housing not available to married students. Typical cost: $4820 per year ($8320 including board). Room and board charges vary according to board plan. Housing application deadline: 4/1. *Student services:* Campus employment opportunities, campus safety program, career counseling, child daycare facilities, exercise/wellness program, free psychological counseling, international student services, low-cost health insurance, multicultural affairs office, services for students with disabilities, teacher training. *Library:* Library Services plus 1 other. *Research affiliation:* Women's Fund of Southwest Florida (human trafficking), Florida Department of Health (Tice Connectivity), Louisiana University Marine Consortium (effect of Macondo oil spill), United States Department of Commerce (Ecohab Ciguahab: Ciguatera Investigations), Community Housing and Resources Inc. (Sanibel CHR Community Needs), Fl Department of Environmental Protection.

Computer facilities: Computer purchase and lease plans are available. 942 computers available on campus for general student use. A campuswide network can be accessed

from student residence rooms and from off campus. Online class registration, online admissions and advising are available.
Website: http://www.fgcu.edu/

General Application Contact: Francisco Marquez, Graduate Studies Admissions, 239-590-7908, E-mail: graduate@fgcu.edu.

GRADUATE UNITS

College of Arts and Sciences Students: 78 full-time (51 women), 150 part-time (97 women); includes 41 minority (12 Black or African American, non-Hispanic/Latino; 2 Asian, non-Hispanic/Latino; 24 Hispanic/Latino; 3 Two or more races, non-Hispanic/Latino), 4 international. Average age 32. 123 applicants, 82% accepted, 80 enrolled. *Faculty:* 235 full-time (96 women), 142 part-time/adjunct (60 women). *Financial support:* In 2015–16, 37 students received support. Application deadline: 3/1; applicants required to submit FAFSA. In 2015, 55 master's awarded. *Degree program information:* Part-time programs available. Part-time, blended/hybrid learning. Offers arts and sciences (MA, MPA, MS); criminal forensic studies (MS); criminal justice studies (MS); English (MA); environmental policy (MPA); environmental science (MS); history (MA); management (MPA); mathematics (MS). *Application deadline:* For fall admission, 2/15 priority date for domestic students; for spring admission, 10/1 for domestic students. Applications are processed on a rolling basis. *Application fee:* $30. Electronic applications accepted. *Application Contact:* Patricia Rice, Executive Secretary, 239-590-7196, Fax: 239-590-7200, E-mail: price@fgcu.edu. *Dean*, Dr. Robert Gregerson, 239-590-7156, Fax: 239-590-7200, E-mail: rgregerson@fgcu.edu.

College of Education Students: 22 full-time (19 women), 165 part-time (124 women); includes 41 minority (14 Black or African American, non-Hispanic/Latino; 1 American Indian or Alaska Native, non-Hispanic/Latino; 1 Asian, non-Hispanic/Latino; 24 Hispanic/Latino; 1 Two or more races, non-Hispanic/Latino), 2 international. Average age 36. 74 applicants, 80% accepted, 44 enrolled. *Faculty:* 31 full-time (22 women), 40 part-time/adjunct (29 women). *Financial support:* In 2015–16, 16 students received support. Application deadline: 6/30; applicants required to submit FAFSA. In 2015, 72 master's awarded. *Degree program information:* Part-time and evening/weekend programs available. Part-time, evening/weekend, online learning. Offers behavior disorders (M Ed); education (M Ed, MA); educational leadership (M Ed, MA); English education (M Ed); mental retardation (M Ed); specific learning disabilities (M Ed); varying exceptionalities (M Ed). *Application deadline:* For fall admission, 7/1 priority date for domestic students; for spring admission, 10/15 for domestic students. Applications are processed on a rolling basis. *Application fee:* $30. Electronic applications accepted. *Application Contact:* Shannon Acosta, Graduate Studies Admissions, 239-590-7027, Fax: 239-590-7843, E-mail: sacosta@fgcu.edu. *Interim Dean*, Dr. Ivan Banks, 239-590-7791, Fax: 239-590-7801, E-mail: ibanks@fgcu.edu.

College of Health Professions and Social Work Students: 225 full-time (143 women), 158 part-time (123 women); includes 94 minority (29 Black or African American, non-Hispanic/Latino; 14 Asian, non-Hispanic/Latino; 44 Hispanic/Latino; 7 Two or more races, non-Hispanic/Latino), 1 international. Average age 31. 476 applicants, 42% accepted, 153 enrolled. *Faculty:* 58 full-time (42 women), 43 part-time/adjunct (28 women). *Financial support:* In 2015–16, 111 students received support. Career-related internships or fieldwork, Federal Work-Study, and institutionally sponsored loans available. Financial award application deadline: 6/30; financial award applicants required to submit FAFSA. In 2015, 86 master's, 36 doctorates awarded. *Degree program information:* Part-time and evening/weekend programs available. Part-time, evening/weekend, online learning. Offers health professions and social work (M Ed, MA, MS, MSN, MSW, DNP, DPT); health sciences (MS); nurse anesthesia (MSN); occupational therapy (MS); physical therapy (DPT); social work (MSW). *Application deadline:* Applications are processed on a rolling basis. *Application fee:* $30. Electronic applications accepted. *Application Contact:* Lynn O'Hare, Administrative Assistant, 239-590-7451, Fax: 239-590-7474, E-mail: lohare@fgcu.edu. *Dean*, Dr. Mitchell Cordova, 239-590-7451, Fax: 239-590-7474.

Lutgert College of Business Students: 41 full-time (13 women), 132 part-time (58 women); includes 30 minority (4 Black or African American, non-Hispanic/Latino; 9 Asian, non-Hispanic/Latino; 15 Hispanic/Latino; 1 Native Hawaiian or other Pacific Islander, non-Hispanic/Latino; 1 Two or more races, non-Hispanic/Latino), 5 international. Average age 29. 144 applicants, 67% accepted, 63 enrolled. *Faculty:* 57 full-time (20 women), 31 part-time/adjunct (7 women). *Financial support:* In 2015–16, 21 students received support. Application deadline: 6/30; applicants required to submit FAFSA. In 2015, 79 master's awarded. *Degree program information:* Part-time and evening/weekend programs available. Part-time, evening/weekend. Offers accounting and taxation (MS); business (MBA, MS); business administration (MBA). *Application deadline:* For fall admission, 7/1 priority date for domestic students; for spring admission, 10/1 for domestic students. Applications are processed on a rolling basis. *Application fee:* $30. Electronic applications accepted. *Application Contact:* Judy Wynekoop, Associate Dean and Professor of Computer Information Systems, 239-590-7387, Fax: 239-590-7330, E-mail: jwynekoo@fgcu.edu. *Dean, Lutgert College of Business*, Robert Beatty, 239-590-7300, Fax: 239-590-7330, E-mail: rbeatty@fgcu.edu.

FLORIDA INSTITUTE OF TECHNOLOGY, Melbourne, FL 32901-6975

General Information Independent, coed, university. *Enrollment:* 6,631 graduate, professional, and undergraduate students; 1,515 full-time matriculated graduate/professional students (642 women), 1,516 part-time matriculated graduate/professional students (520 women). *Enrollment by degree level:* 2,475 master's, 556 doctoral. *Graduate faculty:* 288 full-time (63 women), 209 part-time/adjunct (53 women). *Tuition, area resident:* Full-time $21,690; part-time $1205 per credit hour. *Required fees:* $500. Tuition and fees vary according to degree level, campus/location and program. *Graduate housing:* Room and/or apartments available on a first-come, first-served basis to single students; on-campus housing not available to married students. Typical cost: $14,000 (including board). Room and board charges vary according to board plan and housing facility selected. Housing application deadline: 6/1. *Student services:* Campus employment opportunities, campus safety program, career counseling, exercise/wellness program, free psychological counseling, international student services, low-cost health insurance, multicultural affairs office, services for students with disabilities, writing training. *Library:* Evans Library. *Collection:* Books: 272,871 (physical), 525,512 (digital/electronic); Serial titles: 1,596 (physical), 66,427 (digital/electronic); Databases: 172. Weekly public service hours: 96; students can reserve study rooms. *Research affiliation:* Siemens (mechanical and aerospace engineering), Boeing Corporation (digital signal processing aeronautics), General Electric-Harris (software testing), IBM (software technology, information assurance), Microsoft Corporation (simulation software development), Lockheed Martin Corporation (biological sciences).

Computer facilities: 254 computers available on campus for general student use. A campuswide network can be accessed from student residence rooms and from off campus. Online class registration is available.
Website: http://www.fit.edu/

General Application Contact: Cheryl A. Brown, Associate Director of Graduate Admissions, 321-674-7581, Fax: 321-723-9468, E-mail: cbrown@fit.edu.

GRADUATE UNITS

College of Aeronautics Students: 53 full-time (12 women), 76 part-time (16 women); includes 12 minority (6 Black or African American, non-Hispanic/Latino; 4 Asian, non-Hispanic/Latino; 2 Hispanic/Latino), 47 international. Average age 33. 144 applicants, 47% accepted, 42 enrolled. *Faculty:* 19 full-time (7 women), 9 part-time/adjunct (0 women). *Financial support:* In 2015–16, 1 research assistantship with partial tuition reimbursement (averaging $4,800 per year), 2 teaching assistantships with partial tuition reimbursements (averaging $13,328 per year) were awarded; career-related internships or fieldwork, institutionally sponsored loans, tuition waivers (partial), and tuition remissions also available. Support available to part-time students. Financial award application deadline: 3/1; financial award applicants required to submit FAFSA. In 2015, 34 master's awarded. *Degree program information:* Part-time and evening/weekend programs available. Part-time, evening/weekend, 100% online. Offers airport development and management (MSA); applied aviation safety (MSA); aviation human factors (MS); aviation safety (MSA); aviation sciences (PhD); human factors in aeronautics (MS). *Application deadline:* For fall admission, 4/1 for international students; for spring admission, 9/30 for international students. Applications are processed on a rolling basis. Electronic applications accepted. *Application Contact:* Cheryl A. Brown, Associate Director of Graduate Admissions, 321-674-7581, Fax: 321-723-9468, E-mail: cbrown@fit.edu. *Dean*, Dr. Korhan Oyman, 321-674-8971, Fax: 321-674-7368, E-mail: koyman@fit.edu.

College of Engineering Students: 722 full-time (171 women), 250 part-time (40 women); includes 50 minority (12 Black or African American, non-Hispanic/Latino; 18 Asian, non-Hispanic/Latino; 15 Hispanic/Latino; 5 Two or more races, non-Hispanic/Latino), 754 international. Average age 27. 2,952 applicants, 42% accepted, 252 enrolled. *Faculty:* 110 full-time (13 women), 37 part-time/adjunct (5 women). *Financial support:* In 2015–16, 35 research assistantships with partial tuition reimbursements (averaging $6,289 per year), 69 teaching assistantships with partial tuition reimbursements (averaging $4,809 per year) were awarded; career-related internships or fieldwork, institutionally sponsored loans, unspecified assistantships, and tuition remissions also available. Support available to part-time students. Financial award application deadline: 3/1; financial award applicants required to submit FAFSA. In 2015, 236 master's, 19 doctorates awarded. *Degree program information:* Part-time programs available. Part-time. Offers aerospace engineering (MS, PhD); biological oceanography (MS); biomedical engineering (MS, PhD); chemical engineering (MS, PhD); chemical oceanography (MS); civil engineering (MS, PhD); coastal management (MS); computer engineering (MS, PhD); computer information systems (MS); computer science (MS, PhD); earth remote sensing (MS); electrical engineering (MS, PhD); engineering (MS, PhD); engineering management (MS); environmental resource management (MS); environmental science (MS, PhD); flight test engineering (MS); geological oceanography (MS); information assurance and cybersecurity (MS); mechanical engineering (MS, PhD); meteorology (MS); ocean engineering (MS, PhD); oceanography (PhD); physical oceanography (MS); software engineering (MS); systems engineering (MS, PhD). *Application deadline:* For fall admission, 4/1 for international students; for spring admission, 9/30 for international students. Applications are processed on a rolling basis. Electronic applications accepted. *Application Contact:* Cheryl A. Brown, Associate Director of Graduate Admissions, 321-674-7581, Fax: 321-723-9468, E-mail: cbrown@fit.edu. *Dean*, Dr. Martin Glicksman, 321-674-8020, Fax: 321-674-7270, E-mail: coe@fit.edu.

College of Psychology and Liberal Arts Students: 355 full-time (286 women), 28 part-time (24 women); includes 96 minority (15 Black or African American, non-Hispanic/Latino; 1 American Indian or Alaska Native, non-Hispanic/Latino; 14 Asian, non-Hispanic/Latino; 51 Hispanic/Latino; 1 Native Hawaiian or other Pacific Islander, non-Hispanic/Latino; 14 Two or more races, non-Hispanic/Latino), 24 international. Average age 28. 735 applicants, 36% accepted, 138 enrolled. *Faculty:* 45 full-time (23 women), 15 part-time/adjunct (12 women). *Financial support:* In 2015–16, 4 fellowships (averaging $2,285 per year), 31 research assistantships with partial tuition reimbursements (averaging $8,241 per year), 2 teaching assistantships with partial tuition reimbursements (averaging $8,002 per year) were awarded; career-related internships or fieldwork, institutionally sponsored loans, tuition waivers (partial), unspecified assistantships, and tuition remissions also available. Support available to part-time students. Financial award application deadline: 3/1; financial award applicants required to submit FAFSA. In 2015, 54 master's, 17 doctorates awarded. *Degree program information:* Part-time and evening/weekend programs available. Part-time, evening/weekend, 100% online. Offers applied behavior analysis (MS); applied behavior analysis and organizational behavior management (MS); behavior analysis (PhD); clinical psychology (Psy D); global strategic communication (MS); industrial/organizational psychology (MS, PhD); organizational behavior management (MS); professional behavior analysis (MA); psychology and liberal arts (MA, MS, PhD, Psy D). *Application deadline:* For fall admission, 4/1 for international students; for spring admission, 9/30 for international students. Applications are processed on a rolling basis. Electronic applications accepted. *Application Contact:* Cheryl A. Brown, Associate Director of Graduate Admissions, 321-674-7581, Fax: 321-723-9468, E-mail: cbrown@fit.edu. *Dean*, Dr. Mary Beth Kenkel, 321-674-8142, Fax: 321-674-7105, E-mail: mkenkel@fit.edu.

College of Science Students: 212 full-time (106 women), 76 part-time (38 women); includes 27 minority (10 Black or African American, non-Hispanic/Latino; 6 Asian, non-Hispanic/Latino; 10 Hispanic/Latino; 1 Two or more races, non-Hispanic/Latino), 157 international. Average age 29. 715 applicants, 41% accepted, 85 enrolled. *Faculty:* 78 full-time (11 women), 14 part-time/adjunct (2 women). *Financial support:* In 2015–16, 7 research assistantships with partial tuition reimbursements (averaging $14,110 per year), 68 teaching assistantships with partial tuition reimbursements (averaging $14,428 per year) were awarded; career-related internships or fieldwork, institutionally sponsored loans, tuition waivers (partial), unspecified assistantships, and tuition remissions also available. Support available to part-time students. Financial award application deadline: 3/1; financial award applicants required to submit FAFSA. In 2015, 81 master's, 15 doctorates awarded. *Degree program information:* Part-time and evening/weekend programs available. Part-time, evening/weekend. Offers applied mathematics (MS, PhD); biochemistry (MS); biological science (PhD); biotechnology (MS); cell and molecular biology (MS); chemistry (MS, PhD); computer education (MS); conservation technology (MS); ecology (MS); educational technology (MS); elementary science education (M Ed); environmental education (MS); interdisciplinary science (MS); marine biology (MS); mathematics education (MS, PhD, Ed S); operations research (MS, PhD); physics (MS, PhD); science (M Ed, MAT, MS, PhD, Ed S); science education (MS, PhD, Ed S); science education: informal science education (MS); space sciences (MS, PhD); teaching (MAT). *Application deadline:* For fall admission, 3/1 for domestic students, 4/1 for international students; for spring admission, 9/1 for domestic students, 9/30 for international students. Applications are processed on a rolling basis. Electronic applications accepted. *Application Contact:* Cheryl A. Brown, Associate Director of Graduate Admissions, 321-674-7581, Fax: 321-723-9468, E-mail: cbrown@fit.edu. *Dean*, Dr. Hamid K. Rassoul, 321-674-7273, Fax: 321-674-8864, E-mail: rassoul@fit.edu.

Extended Studies Division Students: 128 full-time (48 women), 1,058 part-time (393 women); includes 439 minority (282 Black or African American, non-Hispanic/Latino; 10 American Indian or Alaska Native, non-Hispanic/Latino; 30 Asian, non-Hispanic/Latino; 92 Hispanic/Latino; 1 Native Hawaiian or other Pacific Islander, non-Hispanic/Latino; 24 Two or more races, non-Hispanic/Latino), 44 international. Average age 36. 962 applicants, 48% accepted, 323 enrolled. *Faculty:* 10 full-time (3 women), 123 part-time/adjunct (30 women). *Financial support:* Application deadline: 3/1; applicants required to submit FAFSA. In 2015, 434 master's awarded. *Degree program information:* Part-time and evening/weekend programs available. Part-time, evening/weekend, online learning. Offers acquisition and contract management (MS); aerospace engineering (MS); business administration (MBA, DBA); computer information systems (MS); computer science (MS); electrical engineering (MS); engineering management (MS); human resources management (MS); logistics management (MS); management (MS); material acquisition management (MS); mechanical engineering (MS); operations research (MS); project management (MS); public administration (MPA); quality management (MS); software engineering (MS); space systems (MS); space systems management (MS); supply chain management (MS); systems management (MS); technology management (MS). *Application deadline:* For fall admission, 4/1 for international students; for spring admission, 9/30 for international students. Applications are processed on a rolling basis. Electronic applications accepted. *Application Contact:* Carolyn Farrior, Director of Graduate Admissions, Online Learning and Off-Campus Programs, 321-674-7118, Fax: 321-674-8216, E-mail: cfarrior@fit.edu. *Senior Associate Dean*, Dr. Theodore R. Richardson, III, 321-674-8123, Fax: 321-674-7597, E-mail: trichardson@fit.edu.

Nathan M. Bisk College of Business Students: 31 full-time (14 women), 23 part-time (8 women); includes 7 minority (3 Black or African American, non-Hispanic/Latino; 2 Asian, non-Hispanic/Latino; 1 Hispanic/Latino; 1 Two or more races, non-Hispanic/Latino), 26 international. Average age 29. 206 applicants, 40% accepted, 18 enrolled. *Faculty:* 23 full-time (6 women), 11 part-time/adjunct (4 women). *Financial support:* In 2015–16, 7 research assistantships with partial tuition reimbursements (averaging $1,779 per year) were awarded; career-related internships or fieldwork, institutionally sponsored loans, and unspecified assistantships also available. Support available to part-time students. Financial award application deadline: 3/1; financial award applicants required to submit FAFSA. In 2015, 27 master's awarded. *Degree program information:* Part-time programs available. Part-time, online learning. Offers business (MBA, MS); business administration (MBA); healthcare management (MBA); innovation and entrepreneurship (MS). *Application deadline:* For fall admission, 4/1 for international students; for spring admission, 9/30 for international students. Applications are processed on a rolling basis. Electronic applications accepted. *Application Contact:* Cheryl A. Brown, Associate Director of Graduate Admissions, 321-674-7581, Fax: 321-723-9468, E-mail: cbrown@fit.edu. *Dean*, Dr. S. Ann Becker, 321-674-7327, Fax: 321-674-8896, E-mail: abecker@fit.edu.

School of Human-Centered Design, Innovation and Art Students: 14 full-time (5 women), 5 part-time (1 woman); includes 1 minority (Black or African American, non-Hispanic/Latino), 12 international. Average age 33. 21 applicants, 57% accepted, 4 enrolled. *Faculty:* 3 full-time (0 women). *Financial support:* In 2015–16, 2 research assistantships with partial tuition reimbursements (averaging $14,729 per year) were awarded; career-related internships or fieldwork, institutionally sponsored loans, tuition waivers (partial), unspecified assistantships, and tuition remissions also available. Financial award application deadline: 3/1; financial award applicants required to submit FAFSA. *Degree program information:* Part-time and evening/weekend programs available. Part-time, evening/weekend. Offers human-centered design, innovation and art (MS, PhD). *Application deadline:* For fall admission, 4/1 for international students; for spring admission, 9/30 for international students. Applications are processed on a rolling basis. Electronic applications accepted. *Application Contact:* Cheryl A. Brown, Associate Director of Graduate Admissions, 321-674-7581, Fax: 321-723-9468, E-mail: cbrown@fit.edu. *Director*, Dr. Guy Boy, 321-674-7631, Fax: 321-984-8461, E-mail: gboy@fit.edu.

★ FLORIDA INTERNATIONAL UNIVERSITY, Miami, FL 33199

General Information State-supported, coed, university. CGS member. *Enrollment:* 49,892 graduate, professional, and undergraduate students; 6,107 full-time matriculated graduate/professional students (3,471 women), 2,353 part-time matriculated graduate/professional students (1,432 women). *Enrollment by degree level:* 6,030 master's, 2,430 doctoral. *Graduate faculty:* 1,000 full-time (408 women), 981 part-time/adjunct (450 women). Tuition, state resident: full-time $10,708; part-time $455.64 per credit hour. Tuition, nonresident: full-time $23,816; part-time $1001.69 per credit hour. *Required fees:* $390; $195 per semester. Tuition and fees vary according to program. *Graduate housing:* Rooms and/or apartments available on a first-come, first-served basis to single and married students. *Student services:* Campus employment opportunities, campus safety program, career counseling, child daycare facilities, exercise/wellness program, free psychological counseling, international student services, low-cost health insurance, multicultural affairs office, services for students with disabilities, writing training. *Library:* Steven and Dorothea Green Library plus 4 others. *Collection:* Books: 1.8 million (physical), 373,895 (digital/electronic); Serial titles: 64,879 (physical), 106,509 (digital/electronic); Databases: 693. Weekly public service hours: 112; students can reserve study rooms. *Research affiliation:* National Institute of Justice (chemistry), National Science Foundation (biological sciences), Howard Hughes Medical Institute (physics), National Institute of Child Health and Human Development (social work), The Boeing Company (mechanical engineering), American Heart Association (biomedical engineering).

Computer facilities: A campuswide network can be accessed from student residence rooms and from off campus. Online class registration, online financial and cashier's information; class schedule, financial, campus maps information available on cell phones are available.
Website: http://www.fiu.edu/

General Application Contact: Nanett Rojas, Assistant Director of Graduate Admissions, 305-348-7442, Fax: 305-348-7441, E-mail: gradadm@fiu.edu.

GRADUATE UNITS

Chapman Graduate School of Business Students: 1,453 full-time (765 women), 543 part-time (290 women); includes 1,395 minority (250 Black or African American, non-Hispanic/Latino; 1 American Indian or Alaska Native, non-Hispanic/Latino; 63 Asian, non-Hispanic/Latino; 1,054 Hispanic/Latino; 1 Native Hawaiian or other Pacific Islander, non-Hispanic/Latino; 26 Two or more races, non-Hispanic/Latino), 333 international. Average age 31. 2,705 applicants, 45% accepted, 790 enrolled. *Faculty:* 131 full-time (40 women), 102 part-time/adjunct (27 women). *Financial support:* Institutionally sponsored loans and scholarships/grants available. Financial award application deadline: 3/1; financial award applicants required to submit FAFSA. In 2015, 1,302 master's, 9 doctorates awarded. *Degree program information:* Part-time and evening/weekend programs available. Part-time, evening/weekend. Offers business (EMBA, IMBA, M Acc, MBA, MIB, MS, MSF, MSHRM, MST, PMBA, PhD); business administration (EMBA, IMBA, MBA, PMBA, PhD); decision sciences and information systems (PhD); finance (MSF); health information management systems (MS); human resources management (MSHRM); international business (MIB, PhD); management and international business (PhD); systems management (MS). *Application deadline:* For fall admission, 6/1 for domestic students, 4/1 for international students; for spring admission, 10/1 for domestic students, 9/1 for international students. Applications are processed on a rolling basis. *Application fee:* $30. Electronic applications accepted. *Application Contact:* Nanett Rojas, Manager, Admissions Operations, 305-348-7464, Fax: 305-348-7441, E-mail: gradadm@fiu.edu. *Acting Dean*, Jose M. Aldrich, 305-348-2751, Fax: 305-919-5478, E-mail: jose.aldrich@fiu.edu.

Hollo School of Real Estate Students: 68 full-time (26 women), 6 part-time (3 women); includes 55 minority (11 Black or African American, non-Hispanic/Latino; 4 Asian, non-Hispanic/Latino; 40 Hispanic/Latino), 6 international. Average age 37. 137 applicants, 58% accepted, 49 enrolled. *Faculty:* 5 full-time (1 woman), 4 part-time/adjunct (2 women). *Financial support:* Institutionally sponsored loans and scholarships/grants available. Financial award application deadline: 3/1; financial award applicants required to submit FAFSA. In 2015, 68 master's awarded. *Degree program information:* Part-time and evening/weekend programs available. Part-time, evening/weekend. Offers international real estate (MS). *Application deadline:* For fall admission, 4/1 for domestic and international students. *Application fee:* $30. Electronic applications accepted. *Application Contact:* Isabel Lopez, Associate Director for Academic Support Services, 305-348-4198, E-mail: isabel.lopez@fiu.edu. *Director*, Willam Hardin, 305-779-7898, E-mail: hardinw@fiu.edu.

School of Accounting Students: 123 full-time (64 women), 42 part-time (23 women); includes 140 minority (5 Black or African American, non-Hispanic/Latino; 9 Asian, non-Hispanic/Latino; 126 Hispanic/Latino), 4 international. Average age 26. 268 applicants, 53% accepted, 111 enrolled. *Faculty:* 27 full-time (9 women), 15 part-time/adjunct (2 women). *Financial support:* Institutionally sponsored loans and scholarships/grants available. Financial award application deadline: 3/1; financial award applicants required to submit FAFSA. In 2015, 148 master's awarded. *Degree program information:* Part-time and evening/weekend programs available. Part-time, evening/weekend. Offers accounting (M Acc). *Application deadline:* For fall admission, 6/1 for domestic students, 4/1 for international students; for spring admission, 10/1 for domestic students, 9/1 for international students. Applications are processed on a rolling basis. *Application fee:* $30. Electronic applications accepted. *Application Contact:* Cynthia Teijeiro, Program Manager, 305-348-7564, E-mail: cteijeir@fiu.edu. *Director*, Ruth Ann McEewen, 305-348-2581, E-mail: rmcewen@fiu.edu.

College of Arts, Sciences, and Education Students: 953 full-time (619 women), 711 part-time (527 women); includes 1,064 minority (218 Black or African American, non-Hispanic/Latino; 1 American Indian or Alaska Native, non-Hispanic/Latino; 26 Asian, non-Hispanic/Latino; 790 Hispanic/Latino; 3 Native Hawaiian or other Pacific Islander, non-Hispanic/Latino; 26 Two or more races, non-Hispanic/Latino), 179 international. Average age 31. 1,373 applicants, 41% accepted, 388 enrolled. *Faculty:* 230 full-time (112 women), 190 part-time/adjunct (95 women). *Financial support:* Career-related internships or fieldwork, Federal Work-Study, institutionally sponsored loans, and scholarships/grants available. Financial award application deadline: 3/1; financial award applicants required to submit FAFSA. In 2015, 438 master's, 81 doctorates awarded. *Degree program information:* Part-time and evening/weekend programs available. Part-time, evening/weekend. Offers adult education and human resource development (MS, Ed D); arts, sciences, and education (MA, MFA, MS, Ed D, PhD, Certificate, Ed S); behavioral analysis (MS); biological sciences (MS, PhD); chemistry (MS, PhD); clinical science (PhD); cognitive neuroscience (PhD); counseling (MS); counseling psychology (MS); counselor education (MS); creative writing (MFA); developmental science (MS, PhD); economics (MA, PhD); educational administration and supervision (Ed D); educational leadership (MS, Certificate, Ed S); English (MA); environmental studies (MS); forensic science (MS, PhD); geosciences (MS, PhD); higher education (Ed D); higher education administration (MS); legal psychology (PhD); liberal studies (MA); linguistics (MA); literature (MA); mathematical sciences (MS); organizational psychology (MS, PhD); physics (MS, PhD); recreation and sport management (MS); school psychology (Ed S); statistics (MS); urban education (MS). *Application deadline:* For fall admission, 6/1 for domestic students, 4/1 for international students; for spring admission, 10/1 for domestic students, 9/1 for international students. Applications are processed on a rolling basis. *Application fee:* $30. Electronic applications accepted. *Application Contact:* Nanett Rojas, Manager, Graduate Operations, 305-348-7464, Fax: 305-348-7441, E-mail: gradadm@fiu.edu. *Dean*, Dr. Michael Heithaus, 305-348-2866, Fax: 305-348-4172, E-mail: casdean@fiu.edu.

School of Education and Human Development Students: 410 full-time (312 women), 579 part-time (453 women); includes 774 minority (187 Black or African American, non-Hispanic/Latino; 1 American Indian or Alaska Native, non-Hispanic/Latino; 13 Asian, non-Hispanic/Latino; 555 Hispanic/Latino; 3 Native Hawaiian or other Pacific Islander, non-Hispanic/Latino; 15 Two or more races, non-Hispanic/Latino), 41 international. Average age 33. 645 applicants, 55% accepted, 229 enrolled. *Faculty:* 60 full-time (42 women), 108 part-time/adjunct (77 women). *Financial support:* Career-related internships or fieldwork, Federal Work-Study, institutionally sponsored loans, and tuition waivers (full and partial) available. Support available to part-time students. In 2015, 126 master's, 16 doctorates awarded. *Degree program information:* Part-time and evening/weekend programs available. Part-time, evening/weekend. Offers art education (MA, MS); curriculum and instruction (MS, Ed D, PhD, Ed S); early childhood education (MS); education and human development (MA, MS, Ed D, PhD, Certificate, Ed S); exceptional student education (Ed D); foreign language education (MS); international/intercultural education (MS); language, literacy and culture (PhD); mathematics, science, and learning technologies (PhD); physical education (MS); reading education (MS). *Application deadline:* For fall admission, 6/1 priority date for domestic students, 4/1 for international students; for winter admission, 10/1 priority date for domestic students, 9/1 for international students; for spring admission, 3/1 priority date for domestic students, 2/1 for international students. Applications are processed on a rolling basis. *Application fee:* $30. Electronic applications accepted. *Application Contact:* Nanett Rojas, Manager, Admissions Operations, 305-348-7464, Fax: 305-348-7441, E-mail: gradadm@fiu.edu. *Executive Director*, Dr. Laura Dinehart, 305-348-3790, Fax: 305-348-3205.

College of Communication, Architecture and The Arts Students: 340 full-time (232 women), 86 part-time (39 women); includes 295 minority (44 Black or African American, non-Hispanic/Latino; 5 Asian, non-Hispanic/Latino; 237 Hispanic/Latino; 9 Two or more races, non-Hispanic/Latino), 53 international. Average age 29. 368 applicants, 53%

accepted, 122 enrolled. *Faculty:* 88 full-time (35 women), 136 part-time/adjunct (60 women). *Financial support:* Institutionally sponsored loans and scholarships/grants available. Financial award application deadline: 3/1; financial award applicants required to submit FAFSA. In 2015, 198 master's awarded. *Degree program information:* Part-time and evening/weekend programs available. Part-time, evening/weekend. Offers communication, architecture and the arts (M Arch, MA, MFA, MIA, MLA, MM, MS, Certificate, Graduate Certificate); museum studies (Graduate Certificate); studio art (MFA). *Application deadline:* For fall admission, 6/1 for domestic students, 4/1 for international students; for spring admission, 10/1 for domestic students, 9/1 for international students. Applications are processed on a rolling basis. *Application fee:* $30. Electronic applications accepted. *Application Contact:* Nanett Rojas, Manager of Admissions Operations, 305-348-7464, Fax: 305-348-7441, E-mail: gradadm@fiu.edu. *Dean*, Dr. Brian Schriner, 305-348-3176, Fax: 305-348-6716, E-mail: schriner@fiu.edu.

School of Architecture Students: 212 full-time (145 women), 11 part-time (1 woman); includes 153 minority (19 Black or African American, non-Hispanic/Latino; 2 Asian, non-Hispanic/Latino; 126 Hispanic/Latino; 6 Two or more races, non-Hispanic/Latino), 33 international. Average age 29. 154 applicants, 45% accepted, 32 enrolled. *Faculty:* 17 full-time (5 women), 27 part-time/adjunct (15 women). *Financial support:* Institutionally sponsored loans and scholarships/grants available. Financial award application deadline: 3/1; financial award applicants required to submit FAFSA. In 2015, 122 master's awarded. *Degree program information:* Part-time and evening/weekend programs available. Part-time, evening/weekend. Offers architecture (M Arch, MA, MIA, MLA, Certificate); interior architecture (MA, MIA, Certificate); landscape architecture (MLA). *Application deadline:* For fall admission, 2/1 for domestic and international students. *Application fee:* $30. Electronic applications accepted. *Application Contact:* Nanett Rojas, Manager, Admissions Operations, 305-348-7464, Fax: 305-348-7441, E-mail: gradadm@fiu.edu. *Chair*, John Stuart, 305-348-3178, E-mail: stuartj@fiu.edu.

School of Communication and Journalism Students: 68 full-time (52 women), 51 part-time (31 women); includes 85 minority (17 Black or African American, non-Hispanic/Latino; 2 Asian, non-Hispanic/Latino; 65 Hispanic/Latino; 1 Two or more races, non-Hispanic/Latino), 16 international. Average age 29. 137 applicants, 60% accepted, 62 enrolled. *Faculty:* 22 full-time (14 women), 19 part-time/adjunct (9 women). *Financial support:* Institutionally sponsored loans and scholarships/grants available. Financial award application deadline: 3/1; financial award applicants required to submit FAFSA. In 2015, 46 master's awarded. *Degree program information:* Part-time and evening/weekend programs available. Part-time, evening/weekend. Offers mass communication (MS). *Application deadline:* For fall admission, 6/1 for domestic students, 4/1 for international students; for spring admission, 10/1 for domestic students, 9/1 for international students. Applications are processed on a rolling basis. *Application fee:* $30. Electronic applications accepted. *Application Contact:* Nanett Rojas, Assistant Director of Graduate Admissions, 305-348-7442, Fax: 305-348-7441, E-mail: gradadm@fiu.edu. *Interim Executive Director*, Dr. Juliet Pinto, 305-919-4404, E-mail: juliet.pinto@fiu.edu.

School of Music Students: 33 full-time (15 women), 19 part-time (7 women); includes 35 minority (4 Black or African American, non-Hispanic/Latino; 1 Asian, non-Hispanic/Latino; 29 Hispanic/Latino; 1 Two or more races, non-Hispanic/Latino), 2 international. Average age 29. 40 applicants, 68% accepted, 18 enrolled. *Faculty:* 22 full-time (3 women), 33 part-time/adjunct (9 women). *Financial support:* Institutionally sponsored loans and scholarships/grants available. Financial award application deadline: 3/1; financial award applicants required to submit FAFSA. In 2015, 22 master's awarded. *Degree program information:* Part-time and evening/weekend programs available. Part-time, evening/weekend. Offers music (MM); music education (MS). *Application deadline:* For fall admission, 6/1 for domestic students, 4/1 for international students; for spring admission, 10/1 for domestic students, 9/1 for international students. Applications are processed on a rolling basis. *Application fee:* $30. Electronic applications accepted. *Application Contact:* Joel Galand, Graduate Program Director, 305-348-7078, E-mail: galandj@fiu.edu. *Interim Chair*, Robert Dundas, 305-348-3587, E-mail: robert.dundas@fiu.edu.

College of Engineering and Computing Students: 606 full-time (169 women), 281 part-time (65 women); includes 337 minority (56 Black or African American, non-Hispanic/Latino; 1 American Indian or Alaska Native, non-Hispanic/Latino; 27 Asian, non-Hispanic/Latino; 240 Hispanic/Latino; 1 Native Hawaiian or other Pacific Islander, non-Hispanic/Latino; 12 Two or more races, non-Hispanic/Latino), 476 international. Average age 29. 1,446 applicants, 41% accepted, 214 enrolled. *Faculty:* 134 full-time (22 women), 72 part-time/adjunct (9 women). *Financial support:* Career-related internships or fieldwork, Federal Work-Study, institutionally sponsored loans, scholarships/grants, and unspecified assistantships available. Financial award application deadline: 3/1; financial award applicants required to submit FAFSA. In 2015, 345 master's, 45 doctorates awarded. *Degree program information:* Part-time and evening/weekend programs available. Part-time, evening/weekend, online learning. Offers biomedical engineering (MS, PhD); civil engineering (MS, PhD); computer engineering (MS); electrical engineering (MS, PhD); engineering and computing (MS, PMS, PhD); engineering management (MS); environmental engineering (MS); materials science and engineering (MS, PhD); mechanical engineering (MS, PhD). *Application deadline:* For fall admission, 6/1 for domestic students, 4/1 for international students; for spring admission, 10/1 for domestic students, 9/1 for international students. Applications are processed on a rolling basis. *Application fee:* $30. Electronic applications accepted. *Application Contact:* Sara-Michelle Lemus, Engineering Admissions Officer, 305-348-1890, E-mail: grad_eng@fiu.edu. *Dean*, Dr. Ranu Jung, 305-348-2522, Fax: 305-348-1401, E-mail: rjung@fiu.edu.

School of Computing and Information Sciences Students: 163 full-time (37 women), 70 part-time (13 women); includes 86 minority (6 Black or African American, non-Hispanic/Latino; 1 American Indian or Alaska Native, non-Hispanic/Latino; 9 Asian, non-Hispanic/Latino; 68 Hispanic/Latino; 2 Two or more races, non-Hispanic/Latino), 136 international. Average age 29. 519 applicants, 38% accepted, 71 enrolled. *Faculty:* 44 full-time (9 women), 30 part-time/adjunct (6 women). *Financial support:* Research assistantships, teaching assistantships, institutionally sponsored loans, scholarships/grants, and unspecified assistantships available. Financial award application deadline: 3/1; financial award applicants required to submit FAFSA. In 2015, 82 master's, 15 doctorates awarded. *Degree program information:* Part-time and evening/weekend programs available. Part-time, evening/weekend. Offers computer science (MS, PhD); information technology (MS); telecommunications and networking (MS). *Application deadline:* For fall admission, 6/1 for domestic students, 4/1 for international students; for spring admission, 10/1 for domestic students, 9/1 for international students. Applications are processed on a rolling basis. *Application fee:* $30. Electronic applications accepted. *Application Contact:* Sara-Michelle Lemus, Engineering Admissions Officer, 305-348-1890, E-mail: grad_eng@fiu.edu. *Director*, Dr. S. S. Iyengar, 305-348-3947, E-mail: iyengar@cis.fiu.edu.

School of Construction Students: 32 full-time (12 women), 47 part-time (19 women); includes 40 minority (9 Black or African American, non-Hispanic/Latino; 3 Asian, non-Hispanic/Latino; 27 Hispanic/Latino; 1 Two or more races, non-Hispanic/Latino), 19 international. Average age 33. 108 applicants, 35% accepted, 15 enrolled. *Financial support:* In 2015–16, 5 students received support. Institutionally sponsored loans, scholarships/grants, and unspecified assistantships available. Financial award application deadline: 3/1; financial award applicants required to submit FAFSA. In 2015, 64 master's awarded. *Degree program information:* Part-time and evening/weekend programs available. Part-time, evening/weekend. Offers construction management (MS, PMS). *Application deadline:* For fall admission, 6/1 for domestic students, 4/1 for international students; for spring admission, 10/1 for domestic students, 9/1 for international students. Applications are processed on a rolling basis. *Application fee:* $30. Electronic applications accepted. *Application Contact:* Sara-Michelle Lemus, Engineering Admissions Officer, 305-348-1890, Fax: 305-348-7441, E-mail: grad_eng@fiu.edu. *Director*, Dr. Irtishad Ahmad, 305-348-3172, Fax: 305-348-6255, E-mail: ahmadi@fiu.edu.

College of Law Students: 479 full-time (255 women), 25 part-time (12 women); includes 319 minority (31 Black or African American, non-Hispanic/Latino; 1 American Indian or Alaska Native, non-Hispanic/Latino; 11 Asian, non-Hispanic/Latino; 272 Hispanic/Latino; 1 Native Hawaiian or other Pacific Islander, non-Hispanic/Latino; 3 Two or more races, non-Hispanic/Latino), 15 international. Average age 27. 2,042 applicants, 31% accepted, 194 enrolled. *Faculty:* 33 full-time (15 women), 46 part-time/adjunct (12 women). *Financial support:* Application deadline: 3/1; applicants required to submit FAFSA. In 2015, 9 master's, 145 doctorates awarded. *Degree program information:* Part-time and evening/weekend programs available. Part-time, evening/weekend. Offers American law for foreign lawyers (LL M); law (JD). *Application deadline:* For fall admission, 5/1 for domestic and international students. Applications are processed on a rolling basis. *Application fee:* $20. Electronic applications accepted. *Application Contact:* Prof. Manuel Gomez, Associate Dean for International and Graduate Studies, 305-348-1158, Fax: 305-348-2282, E-mail: manuel.gomez1@fiu.edu. *Dean*, Dr. R. Alex Acosta, 305-348-1118, Fax: 305-348-1159, E-mail: acosta@fiu.edu.

College of Nursing and Health Sciences Students: 694 full-time (508 women), 127 part-time (111 women); includes 603 minority (108 Black or African American, non-Hispanic/Latino; 52 Asian, non-Hispanic/Latino; 426 Hispanic/Latino; 2 Native Hawaiian or other Pacific Islander, non-Hispanic/Latino; 15 Two or more races, non-Hispanic/Latino), 8 international. Average age 30. 1,760 applicants, 19% accepted, 282 enrolled. *Faculty:* 60 full-time (44 women), 136 part-time/adjunct (98 women). *Financial support:* Career-related internships or fieldwork, Federal Work-Study, institutionally sponsored loans, and scholarships/grants available. Financial award application deadline: 3/1; financial award applicants required to submit FAFSA. In 2015, 287 master's, 62 doctorates awarded. *Degree program information:* Part-time and evening/weekend programs available. Part-time, evening/weekend. Offers athletic training (MS); nursing (MSN, DNP, PhD); nursing and health sciences (MS, MSN, MSOT, DNP, DPT, PhD); occupational therapy (MSOT); physical therapy (DPT); speech-language pathology (MS). *Application fee:* $30. Electronic applications accepted. *Application Contact:* Nanett Rojas, Manager, Admissions Operations, 305-348-7464, Fax: 305-348-7441, E-mail: gradadm@fiu.edu. *Dean*, Dr. Ora Strickland, 305-348-0407, E-mail: olstrick@fiu.edu.

Herbert Wertheim College of Medicine Students: 532 full-time (273 women); includes 316 minority (35 Black or African American, non-Hispanic/Latino; 95 Asian, non-Hispanic/Latino; 172 Hispanic/Latino; 14 Two or more races, non-Hispanic/Latino), 10 international. Average age 25. 4,966 applicants, 7% accepted, 170 enrolled. *Faculty:* 66 full-time (29 women), 69 part-time/adjunct (23 women). *Financial support:* Institutionally sponsored loans and scholarships/grants available. Financial award application deadline: 3/1; financial award applicants required to submit FAFSA. In 2015, 80 doctorates awarded. Offers medicine (MPA, MD, PhD); physician assistant studies (MPA). *Application deadline:* For fall admission, 12/15 for domestic students. *Application fee:* $160. Electronic applications accepted. *Application Contact:* Nanett Rojas, Manager, Admissions Operations, 305-348-7464, Fax: 305-348-7441, E-mail: gradadm@fiu.edu. *Dean*, Dr. John Rock, 305-348-0570, E-mail: med.admissions@fiu.edu.

Robert Stempel College of Public Health and Social Work Students: 337 full-time (255 women), 178 part-time (147 women); includes 378 minority (104 Black or African American, non-Hispanic/Latino; 17 Asian, non-Hispanic/Latino; 246 Hispanic/Latino; 11 Two or more races, non-Hispanic/Latino), 52 international. Average age 30. 519 applicants, 38% accepted, 137 enrolled. *Faculty:* 60 full-time (35 women), 19 part-time/adjunct (14 women). *Financial support:* Institutionally sponsored loans, scholarships/grants, and unspecified assistantships available. Financial award application deadline: 3/1; financial award applicants required to submit FAFSA. In 2015, 187 master's, 18 doctorates awarded. *Degree program information:* Part-time and evening/weekend programs available. Part-time, evening/weekend, online learning. Offers biostatistics (MPH); dietetics and nutrition (MS, PhD); environmental and occupational health (MPH, PhD); epidemiology (MPH, PhD); health policy and management (MPH); health promotion and disease prevention (MPH, PhD); public health and social work (MPH, MS, MSW, PhD). *Application deadline:* For fall admission, 6/1 for domestic students, 4/1 for international students; for spring admission, 10/1 for domestic students, 9/1 for international students. Applications are processed on a rolling basis. *Application fee:* $30. Electronic applications accepted. *Application Contact:* Nanett Rojas, Manager, Admissions Operations, 305-348-7464, Fax: 305-348-7441, E-mail: gradadm@fiu.edu. *Dean*, Dr. Tomas Guilarte, 305-348-1158, Fax: 305-348-1691, E-mail: tomas.guilarte@fiu.edu.

School of Social Work Students: 152 full-time (123 women), 76 part-time (65 women); includes 193 minority (52 Black or African American, non-Hispanic/Latino; 1 Asian, non-Hispanic/Latino; 133 Hispanic/Latino; 7 Two or more races, non-Hispanic/Latino), 4 international. Average age 31. 141 applicants, 46% accepted, 52 enrolled. *Faculty:* 22 full-time (13 women), 9 part-time/adjunct (5 women). *Financial support:* Institutionally sponsored loans and scholarships/grants available. Financial award application deadline: 3/1; financial award applicants required to submit FAFSA. In 2015, 84 master's, 3 doctorates awarded. *Degree program information:* Part-time and evening/weekend programs available. Part-time, evening/weekend. Offers social welfare (PhD); social work (MSW). *Application deadline:* For fall admission, 6/1 for domestic students, 4/1 for international students; for spring admission, 10/1 for domestic students, 9/1 for international students. Applications are processed on a rolling basis. *Application fee:* $30. Electronic applications accepted. *Application Contact:* Gladys Ramos, Program Assistant, 305-348-5887, E-mail: gladys.ramos@fiu.edu. *Director*, Dr. Mary Helen Hayden, 305-348-1208, E-mail: haydenm@fiu.edu.

School of Hospitality and Tourism Management Students: 224 full-time (162 women), 88 part-time (66 women); includes 101 minority (24 Black or African American, non-Hispanic/Latino; 7 Asian, non-Hispanic/Latino; 65 Hispanic/Latino; 5 Two or more races, non-Hispanic/Latino), 169 international. Average age 26. 232 applicants, 73%

accepted, 109 enrolled. *Faculty:* 20 full-time (8 women), 31 part-time/adjunct (10 women). *Financial support:* Institutionally sponsored loans and scholarships/grants available. Financial award application deadline: 3/1; financial award applicants required to submit FAFSA. In 2015, 208 master's awarded. *Degree program information:* Part-time and evening/weekend programs available. Part-time, evening/weekend, online learning. Offers hospitality and tourism management (MS); hospitality management (MS). *Application deadline:* For fall admission, 6/1 for domestic students, 4/1 for international students; for spring admission, 10/1 for domestic students, 9/1 for international students. Applications are processed on a rolling basis. *Application fee:* $30. Electronic applications accepted. *Application Contact:* Nanett Rojas, Manager, Admissions Operations, 305-348-7464, Fax: 305-348-7441, E-mail: gradadm@fiu.edu. *Dean*, Dr. Mike Hampton, 305-919-4018, E-mail: mhampton@fiu.edu.

Steven J. Green School of International and Public Affairs Students: 489 full-time (233 women), 314 part-time (175 women); includes 101 minority (24 Black or African American, non-Hispanic/Latino; 7 Asian, non-Hispanic/Latino; 65 Hispanic/Latino; 5 Two or more races, non-Hispanic/Latino), 169 international. 519 applicants, 38% accepted, 137 enrolled. *Faculty:* 233 full-time, 175 part-time/adjunct. In 2015, 240 master's, 33 doctorates awarded. Offers African and African diaspora studies (MA); Asian studies (MA); criminal justice (MS); disaster management (MA); global affairs (MA); global and sociocultural studies (MA, PhD); history (MA, PhD); international and public affairs (MA, MPA, MS, PhD); international relations (MA, PhD); international studies (MA); Latin American and Caribbean studies (MA); political science (MA, PhD); public administration (MPA); public affairs (PhD); religious studies (MA); Spanish (MA, PhD). *Application Contact:* Nanett Rojas, Assistant Director of Graduate Admissions, 305-348-7442, Fax: 305-348-7441, E-mail: gradadm@fiu.edu. *Dean*, John F. Stack, Jr., 305-348-7266.

See Display on next page and Close-Up on page 877.

FLORIDA MEMORIAL UNIVERSITY, Miami-Dade, FL 33054

General Information Independent-religious, coed, comprehensive institution.

GRADUATE UNITS

School of Business ***Degree program information:*** Part-time programs available. Part-time. Offers business (MBA).

School of Education Offers elementary education (MS); exceptional student education (MS); reading (MS).

FLORIDA NATIONAL UNIVERSITY, Hialeah, FL 33012

General Information Proprietary, coed, comprehensive institution. *Enrollment:* 2,492 graduate, professional, and undergraduate students; 34 full-time matriculated graduate/professional students (23 women), 2 part-time matriculated graduate/professional students (1 woman). *Enrollment by degree level:* 36 master's. *Graduate faculty:* 6 full-time (2 women), 3 part-time/adjunct (1 woman). *Tuition, area resident:* Full-time $15,600. *Required fees:* $650. *Student services:* Campus employment opportunities, campus safety program, career counseling, child daycare facilities, international student services. *Library:* Hialeah Campus Library plus 1 other. *Collection:* Books: 23,840 (physical), 132,699 (digital/electronic); Serial titles: 56 (physical), 28,122 (digital/electronic); Databases: 32. Weekly public service hours: 69; students can reserve study rooms.

Computer facilities: 300 computers available on campus for general student use. A campuswide network can be accessed from off campus. Online class registration is available.
Website: http://www.fnu.edu/

General Application Contact: Olga Rodriguez, Assistant Campus Dean, 305-821-3333 Ext. 1044, Fax: 305-362-0595, E-mail: orodriguez@fnu.edu.

GRADUATE UNITS

Program in Business Administration Students: 21 full-time (12 women), 2 part-time (1 woman); includes 17 minority (2 Black or African American, non-Hispanic/Latino; 15 Hispanic/Latino), 2 international. Average age 32. 8 applicants, 100% accepted, 8 enrolled. *Faculty:* 6 full-time (2 women), 2 part-time/adjunct (0 women). *Financial support:* Federal Work-Study, institutionally sponsored loans, scholarships/grants, and tuition waivers available. Financial award applicants required to submit FAFSA. In 2015, 15 master's awarded. *Degree program information:* Part-time programs available. Part-time, blended/hybrid learning. Offers finance (MBA); general management (MBA); health services administration (MBA); marketing (MBA); public management and leadership (MBA). *Application deadline:* Applications are processed on a rolling basis. Electronic applications accepted. *Application Contact:* Olga Rodriguez, Assistant Campus Dean, 305-821-3333 Ext. 1044, Fax: 305-362-0595, E-mail: orodriguez@fnu.edu. *Business Department Head*, Dr. Ernesto Gonzalez, 305-821-3333 Ext. 1070, Fax: 305-362-0595, E-mail: egonzalez@fnu.edu.

Program in Health Services Administration Students: 18 full-time (14 women); all minorities (1 Black or African American, non-Hispanic/Latino; 17 Hispanic/Latino). Average age 32. 6 applicants, 100% accepted, 6 enrolled. *Faculty:* 2 full-time (both women), 1 part-time/adjunct (0 women). *Financial support:* Scholarships/grants available. Financial award applicants required to submit FAFSA. *Degree program information:* Part-time and evening/weekend programs available. Part-time, evening/weekend, 100% online, blended/hybrid learning. Offers health services administration (MHSA). *Application deadline:* Applications are processed on a rolling basis. Electronic applications accepted. *Application Contact:* Virginia Rabelo, Admissions supervisor, 305-821-3333 Ext. 1016, Fax: 305-362-0595, E-mail: vrabelo@fnu.edu. *Allied Health Division Head*, Dr. Loreto Almonte, 305-821-3333 Ext. 1074, Fax: 305-362-0595, E-mail: lalmonte@fnu.edu.

Program in Nursing Offers family nurse practitioner (MSN); nurse educator (MSN); nurse leadership and management (MSN).

FLORIDA SOUTHERN COLLEGE, Lakeland, FL 33801-5698

General Information Independent-religious, coed, comprehensive institution. *Graduate housing:* On-campus housing not available.

GRADUATE UNITS

Program in Business Administration ***Degree program information:*** Part-time and evening/weekend programs available. Part-time, evening/weekend. Offers business administration (MBA).

Program in Nursing ***Degree program information:*** Part-time and evening/weekend programs available. Part-time, evening/weekend. Offers adult gerontology clinical nurse specialist (MSN); adult gerontology primary care nurse practitioner (MSN); nurse educator (MSN); nursing administration (MSN).

Programs in Teaching ***Degree program information:*** Part-time and evening/weekend programs available. Part-time, evening/weekend. Offers teaching (M Ed, MAT).

FLORIDA STATE UNIVERSITY, Tallahassee, FL 32306

General Information State-supported, coed, university. CGS member. *Enrollment:* 40,920 graduate, professional, and undergraduate students; 5,913 full-time matriculated graduate/professional students (3,058 women), 1,906 part-time matriculated graduate/professional students (1,187 women). *Enrollment by degree level:* 3,892 master's, 3,804 doctoral, 123 other advanced degrees. *Graduate faculty:* 1,915 full-time (782 women), 75 part-time/adjunct (34 women). *Tuition, area resident:* Full-time $7263; part-time $403.50 per credit hour. Tuition, nonresident: full-time $18,087; part-time $1004.85 per credit hour. *Required fees:* $1365; $75.81 per credit hour. $20 per semester. Tuition and fees vary according to campus/location. *Graduate housing:* Room and/or apartments available on a first-come, first-served basis to single students; on-campus housing not available to married students. Typical cost: $2610 per year ($4609 including board). Room and board charges vary according to housing facility selected. Housing application deadline: 9/5. *Student services:* Campus employment opportunities, campus safety program, career counseling, child daycare facilities, exercise/wellness program, free psychological counseling, grant writing training, international student services, low-cost health insurance, multicultural affairs office, services for students with disabilities, teacher training, writing training. *Library:* Robert Manning Strozier Library plus 8 others. *Collection:* Books: 3.3 million (physical), 1.2 million (digital/electronic); Serial titles: 38,445 (physical), 119,385 (digital/electronic); Databases: 1,064. Weekly public service hours: 134; study areas open 24 hours, 5–7 days a week; students can reserve study rooms. *Research affiliation:* University Corporation for Atmospheric Research (atmospheric research), Oak Ridge National Laboratory (materials science), Southeastern Universities Research Association (energy), University Research Association (energy), Bruker, Inc. (nuclear magnetic resonance), Oak Ridge Associated Universities (education, environmental assessment).

Computer facilities: 3,821 computers available on campus for general student use. A campuswide network can be accessed from student residence rooms and from off campus. Online class registration, course home pages, course search, online fee payment are available.
Website: http://www.fsu.edu/

General Application Contact: Melanie Booker, Associate Director for Graduate Admissions, 850-644-7145, Fax: 850-644-0197, E-mail: mbooker@admin.fsu.edu.

GRADUATE UNITS

College of Law Students: 626 full-time (265 women), 40 part-time (20 women); includes 160 minority (52 Black or African American, non-Hispanic/Latino; 10 American Indian or Alaska Native, non-Hispanic/Latino; 20 Asian, non-Hispanic/Latino; 69 Hispanic/Latino; 1 Native Hawaiian or other Pacific Islander, non-Hispanic/Latino; 8 Two or more races, non-Hispanic/Latino), 20 international. Average age 25. 1,992 applicants, 43% accepted, 211 enrolled. *Faculty:* 55 full-time (25 women), 24 part-time/adjunct (7 women). *Financial support:* In 2015–16, 326 students received support, including 3 fellowships with full tuition reimbursements available (averaging $20,683 per year), 27 research assistantships (averaging $1,025 per year), 12 teaching assistantships (averaging $1,604 per year); scholarships/grants and unspecified assistantships also available. Financial award application deadline: 3/1; financial award applicants required to submit FAFSA. In 2015, 14 master's, 267 doctorates awarded. Offers American law for foreign lawyers (LL M); business law (LL M); environmental law and policy (LL M); law (JM, JD). *Application deadline:* For fall admission, 5/15 for domestic and international students. Applications are processed on a rolling basis. *Application fee:* $30. Electronic applications accepted. *Application Contact:* Jennifer L. Kessinger, Director of Admissions and Records, 850-644-3787, Fax: 850-644-7284, E-mail: jkessing@law.fsu.edu. *Dean*, Donald J. Weidner, 850-644-3400, Fax: 850-644-5487, E-mail: dweidner@law.fsu.edu.

College of Medicine Students: 488 full-time (240 women); includes 223 minority (64 Black or African American, non-Hispanic/Latino; 47 Asian, non-Hispanic/Latino; 82 Hispanic/Latino; 30 Two or more races, non-Hispanic/Latino). Average age 26. *Faculty:* 150 full-time (71 women), 73 part-time/adjunct (23 women). *Financial support:* In 2015–16, 322 students received support. Scholarships/grants available. Financial award application deadline: 6/30; financial award applicants required to submit FAFSA. In 2015, 115 doctorates awarded. Offers biomedical sciences (PhD); medicine (MD, PhD); neuroscience (PhD). *Application deadline:* Applications are processed on a rolling basis. Electronic applications accepted. *Application Contact:* Dana Urrutia, Admissions Coordinator, 850-644-1857, Fax: 850-645-2846, E-mail: medadmissions@med.fsu.edu. *Dean*, Dr. John Patrick Fogarty, MD, 850-644-1346, Fax: 850-645-1420, E-mail: john.fogarty@med.fsu.edu.

The Graduate School Students: 5,913 full-time (3,058 women), 1,906 part-time (1,187 women); includes 1,388 minority (525 Black or African American, non-Hispanic/Latino; 11 American Indian or Alaska Native, non-Hispanic/Latino; 162 Asian, non-Hispanic/Latino; 560 Hispanic/Latino; 4 Native Hawaiian or other Pacific Islander, non-Hispanic/Latino; 126 Two or more races, non-Hispanic/Latino), 1,285 international. Average age 29. 8,965 applicants, 43% accepted, 1893 enrolled. *Faculty:* 1,915 full-time (782 women), 75 part-time/adjunct (34 women). *Financial support:* In 2015–16, 39 fellowships with full tuition reimbursements (averaging $8,949 per year), 1,892 research assistantships with full tuition reimbursements, 3,605 teaching assistantships with full tuition reimbursements were awarded; career-related internships or fieldwork, Federal Work-Study, institutionally sponsored loans, scholarships/grants, traineeships, health care benefits, tuition waivers (full and partial), and unspecified assistantships also available. Support available to part-time students. Financial award applicants required to submit FAFSA. In 2015, 2,153 master's, 444 doctorates, 49 other advanced degrees awarded. *Degree program information:* Part-time and evening/weekend programs available. Part-time, evening/weekend, online learning. Offers materials science and engineering (MS, PhD). *Application deadline:* For fall admission, 7/1 for domestic and international students; for spring admission, 11/1 for domestic and international students. *Application fee:* $35. Electronic applications accepted. *Application Contact:* Melanie Booker, Associate Director for Graduate Admissions, 850-644-7145, Fax: 850-644-0197, E-mail: mbooker@admin.fsu.edu. *Dean*, Dr. Nancy Marcus, 850-644-3501, Fax: 850-644-2969, E-mail: nmarcus@fsu.edu.

College of Arts and Sciences Students: 1,591 full-time, 179 part-time; includes 227 minority (50 Black or African American, non-Hispanic/Latino; 2 American Indian or Alaska Native, non-Hispanic/Latino; 48 Asian, non-Hispanic/Latino; 98 Hispanic/Latino; 1 Native Hawaiian or other Pacific Islander, non-Hispanic/Latino; 28 Two or more races, non-Hispanic/Latino), 571 international. Average age 29. *Faculty:* 443 full-time (115 women), 6 part-time/adjunct (3 women). *Financial support:* Fellowships, research assistantships, teaching assistantships, career-related internships or fieldwork, institutionally sponsored loans, scholarships/grants, traineeships, and unspecified assistantships available. Support available to part-time students. Financial award applicants required to submit FAFSA. In 2015, 349 master's, 191 doctorates awarded. *Degree program information:* Part-time programs available. Part-time. Offers analytical chemistry (MS, PhD); ancient history (MA);

applied behavior analysis (MS); applied computational mathematics (MS, PhD); applied statistics (MS); aquatic environmental science (MS, PSM); arts and sciences (MA, MFA, MS, MST, PhD); biochemistry (MS, PhD); biomathematics (MS, PhD); biostatistics (MS, PhD); cell and molecular biology (MS, PhD); classical archaeology (MA); classical civilization (MA); classics (PhD); clinical psychology (PhD); cognitive psychology (PhD); community college science teaching (MST); computational science (MS, PhD); computer criminology (MS); computer network and system administration (MS); computer science (MS, PhD); creative writing (MFA); cyber security (MS); developmental psychology (PhD); ecology and evolutionary biology (MS, PhD); English (PhD); financial mathematics (MS, PhD); French (MA, PhD); geological sciences (MS, PhD); geophysical fluid dynamics (PhD); German (MA); Greek (MA); Greek and Latin (MA); historical administration and public history (MA); history (MA, MS, PhD); history and philosophy of science (MA); humanities (PhD); inorganic chemistry (MS, PhD); Italian (MA); Italian studies (MA); Latin (MA); literature (MA); materials chemistry (PhD); mathematical statistics (MS, PhD); meteorology (MS, PhD); molecular biophysics (PhD); neuroscience (MS, PhD); oceanography (MS, PSM, PhD); organic chemistry (MS, PhD); philosophy (MA, PhD); physical chemistry (MS, PhD); physics (MS, PhD); plant biology (MS, PhD); pure mathematics (MS, PhD); religion (MA, PhD); rhetoric and composition (MA); science teaching (MST); Slavic languages and literatures (MA); Slavic languages/Russian (MA); social psychology (PhD); Spanish (MA, PhD); statistical data science (MS); structural biology (MS, PhD); structural biology and computational biophysics (PhD). *Application fee:* $30. *Application Contact:* Ginger Martin, Graduate Academic Coordinator, 850-644-1081, Fax: 850-644-9656, E-mail: vmartin@fsu.edu. *Dean*, Dr. Sam Huckaba, 850-644-1081.

College of Business Students: 241 full-time (95 women), 294 part-time (92 women); includes 139 minority (36 Black or African American, non-Hispanic/Latino; 1 American Indian or Alaska Native, non-Hispanic/Latino; 51 Asian, non-Hispanic/Latino; 37 Hispanic/Latino; 1 Native Hawaiian or other Pacific Islander, non-Hispanic/Latino; 13 Two or more races, non-Hispanic/Latino), 45 international. Average age 30. 773 applicants, 66% accepted, 323 enrolled. *Faculty:* 101 full-time (27 women), 4 part-time/adjunct (2 women). *Financial support:* In 2015–16, 115 students received support, including 9 fellowships (averaging $1,500 per year), 38 research assistantships with full tuition reimbursements available (averaging $20,000 per year), 26 teaching assistantships with full tuition reimbursements available (averaging $20,000 per year); career-related internships or fieldwork, scholarships/grants, health care benefits, and unspecified assistantships also available. Financial award application deadline: 1/1. In 2015, 257 master's, 13 doctorates awarded. *Degree program information:* Part-time programs available. Part-time, online learning. Offers accounting (M Acc); business administration (MBA, PhD); finance (MS); management information systems (MS); marketing (MS); risk management and insurance (MS). *Application deadline:* For fall admission, 6/1 for domestic and international students; for spring admission, 10/1 for domestic and international students. Applications are processed on a rolling basis. *Application fee:* $30. Electronic applications accepted. *Application Contact:* Jack Tyndall, Inquiry Specialist, 850-644-6458, E-mail: gradprograms@business.fsu.edu. *Dean*, Dr. Michael Hartline, 850-644-4405, Fax: 850-644-0915, E-mail: mhartline@business.fsu.edu.

College of Communication and Information Students: 240 full-time (190 women), 359 part-time (279 women); includes 186 minority (47 Black or African American, non-Hispanic/Latino; 54 Asian, non-Hispanic/Latino; 79 Hispanic/Latino; 6 Two or more races, non-Hispanic/Latino), 12 international. Average age 29. 684 applicants, 39% accepted, 154 enrolled. *Faculty:* 72 full-time (40 women), 14 part-time/adjunct (9 women). *Financial support:* In 2015–16, 244 students received support, including 2 fellowships with full tuition reimbursements available (averaging $14,000 per year), 43 research assistantships with full tuition reimbursements available (averaging $15,255 per year), 147 teaching assistantships with full tuition reimbursements available (averaging $16,503 per year); career-related internships or fieldwork, Federal Work-Study, institutionally sponsored loans, scholarships/grants, health care benefits, tuition waivers (full and partial), and unspecified assistantships also available. Support available to part-time students. Financial award application deadline: 1/1; financial award applicants required to submit FAFSA. In 2015, 329 master's, 24 doctorates, 5 other advanced degrees awarded. *Degree program information:* Part-time and evening/weekend programs available. Part-time, evening/weekend, 100% online. Offers communication and information (MA, MS, PhD, Specialist); communication science and disorders (MS, PhD); communication theory and research (PhD); information studies (MA, MS, PhD, Specialist); information technology (MS); integrated marketing communication (MA, MS); media and communication studies (MA, MS); public interest media and communication (MA, MS). *Application deadline:* For fall admission, 7/1 for domestic students, 5/1 for international students; for spring admission, 11/1 for domestic and international students. Applications are processed on a rolling basis. *Application fee:* $30. Electronic applications accepted. *Application Contact:* Betsy Crawford, Development and Recruiting Coordinator, 850-645-9661, Fax: 850-644-0611, E-mail: betsy.crawford@cci.fsu.edu. *Dean*, Dr. Lawrence C. Dennis, 850-644-9698, Fax: 850-644-0611, E-mail: larry.dennis@cci.fsu.edu.

College of Criminology and Criminal Justice Students: 137 full-time (90 women), 115 part-time (64 women); includes 84 minority (41 Black or African American, non-Hispanic/Latino; 2 American Indian or Alaska Native, non-Hispanic/Latino; 8 Asian, non-Hispanic/Latino; 29 Hispanic/Latino; 4 Two or more races, non-Hispanic/Latino). 214 applicants, 64% accepted, 84 enrolled. *Faculty:* 18 full-time (5 women). *Financial support:* In 2015–16, 5 fellowships with full tuition reimbursements (averaging $15,000 per year), 31 research assistantships with full tuition reimbursements (averaging $14,500 per year), 15 teaching assistantships with full tuition reimbursements (averaging $14,500 per year) were awarded; Federal Work-Study, institutionally sponsored loans, scholarships/grants, tuition waivers (full), and unspecified assistantships also available. Financial award application deadline: 1/15; financial award applicants required to submit FAFSA. In 2015, 67 master's, 6 doctorates awarded. *Degree program information:* Part-time programs available. Part-time, 100% online. Offers criminology and criminal justice (MA, MSC, PhD). *Application deadline:* For fall admission, 7/1 for domestic and international students; for spring admission, 11/1 for domestic and international students. Applications are processed on a rolling basis. *Application fee:* $30. Electronic applications accepted. *Application Contact:* Margarita Frankeberger, Program Director, 850-644-7373, Fax: 850-644-9614, E-mail: mfrankeberger@fsu.edu. *Dean*, Dr. Thomas G. Blomberg, 850-644-7365, Fax: 850-644-9614.

College of Education Students: 657 full-time (427 women), 345 part-time (222 women); includes 229 minority (105 Black or African American, non-Hispanic/Latino; 2 American Indian or Alaska Native, non-Hispanic/Latino; 22 Asian, non-Hispanic/Latino; 79 Hispanic/Latino; 21 Two or more races, non-Hispanic/Latino), 189 international. Average age 31. 939 applicants, 57% accepted, 282 enrolled. *Faculty:* 84 full-time (55 women), 73 part-time/adjunct (50 women). *Financial support:* In

2015–16, 292 students received support, including 23 fellowships with tuition reimbursements available, 297 research assistantships with tuition reimbursements available, 305 teaching assistantships with tuition reimbursements available; scholarships/grants, tuition waivers (full and partial), and unspecified assistantships also available. Financial award application deadline: 1/15; financial award applicants required to submit FAFSA. In 2015, 323 master's, 58 doctorates, 44 other advanced degrees awarded. *Degree program information:* Part-time and evening/weekend programs available. Part-time, evening/weekend, blended/hybrid learning, asynchronous, minimal on-campus study. Offers coaching (Certificate); counseling and human systemscounseling psychology and school psychology (PhD); curriculum and instruction (MS, PhD, Ed S); education (MS, Ed D, PhD, Certificate, Ed S); education policy and evaluation (MS, Ed D, PhD); educational leadership/administration (MS, Ed D, PhD, Certificate, Ed S); higher education (MS, PhD); human performance technology (Certificate); instructional systems and learning technologies (MS, PhD); learning and cognition (MS, PhD); measurement and statistics (MS, PhD, Certificate); online instructional development (Certificate); program evaluation (Certificate); social, historical and philosophical foundations of education (MS, PhD); sociocultural and international development education studies (MS, Ed D, PhD); sport management (MS, PhD); sport psychology (MS, PhD). *Application fee:* $30. Electronic applications accepted. *Application Contact:* Jennie H. Kroeger, Assistant Director, Office of Communication and Recruitment, 850-644-6885, Fax: 850-644-2725, E-mail: jennie.kroeger@fsu.edu.

College of Fine Arts Students: 265 full-time (198 women), 33 part-time (29 women); includes 51 minority (16 Black or African American, non-Hispanic/Latino; 1 American Indian or Alaska Native, non-Hispanic/Latino; 4 Asian, non-Hispanic/Latino; 30 Hispanic/Latino), 18 international. Average age 24. 370 applicants, 86% accepted, 301 enrolled. *Faculty:* 67 full-time (40 women), 17 part-time/adjunct (12 women). *Financial support:* In 2015–16, 5 fellowships with partial tuition reimbursements (averaging $18,000 per year), 90 research assistantships with partial tuition reimbursements (averaging $4,957 per year), 78 teaching assistantships with partial tuition reimbursements (averaging $8,001 per year) were awarded; career-related internships or fieldwork, Federal Work-Study, institutionally sponsored loans, scholarships/grants, and unspecified assistantships also available. Support available to part-time students. Financial award applicants required to submit FAFSA. In 2015, 95 master's, 5 doctorates awarded. *Degree program information:* Part-time programs available. Part-time. Offers acting (MFA); American dance studies (MA); art (MFA); art education (MA, MS, Ed D, PhD); art history (MA, PhD); costume design (MFA); dance (MFA); directing (MFA); fine arts (MA, MFA, MS, Ed D, PhD, Certificate, Graduate Certificate); interior architecture and design (MFA, MS); museum and cultural heritage studies (MA); museum studies (Certificate); studio and related studies (MA); technical production (MFA); theatre (MA, PhD); theatre management (MFA). *Application deadline:* For fall admission, 7/1 priority date for domestic students; for spring admission, 11/1 priority date for domestic students. Applications are processed on a rolling basis. *Application fee:* $30. Electronic applications accepted. *Application Contact:* Melanie Booker, Associate Director for Graduate Admissions, 850-644-3420, Fax: 850-644-0197, E-mail: mbooker@admin.fsu.edu. *Dean*, Peter Weisher, 850-664-5244, Fax: 850-644-2604, E-mail: pweishar@fsu.edu.

College of Human Sciences Students: 128 full-time (79 women), 7 part-time (5 women); includes 29 minority (12 Black or African American, non-Hispanic/Latino; 1 Asian, non-Hispanic/Latino; 9 Hispanic/Latino; 7 Two or more races, non-Hispanic/Latino), 19 international. Average age 27. 234 applicants, 43% accepted, 46 enrolled. *Faculty:* 39 full-time (23 women). *Financial support:* In 2015–16, 91 students received support, including 26 research assistantships with full tuition reimbursements available (averaging $6,665 per year), 75 teaching assistantships with full tuition reimbursements available (averaging $10,706 per year); career-related internships or fieldwork, Federal Work-Study, institutionally sponsored loans, scholarships/grants, and unspecified assistantships also available. Financial award application deadline: 1/15; financial award applicants required to submit FAFSA. In 2015, 54 master's, 14 doctorates awarded. *Degree program information:* Part-time programs available. Part-time. Offers exercise physiology (MS, PhD); family and child sciences (MS); family relations (PhD); human sciences (MS, PhD); marriage and family therapy (PhD); nutrition and food science (MS, PhD); retail, merchandising and product development (MS); sports nutrition (MS); sports sciences (MS). *Application deadline:* For fall admission, 4/1 for domestic and international students; for spring admission, 10/1 for domestic and international students. Applications are processed on a rolling basis. *Application fee:* $30. Electronic applications accepted. *Application Contact:* Tara L. Hartman, Academic Program Specialist, 850-644-7221, Fax: 850-644-0700, E-mail: thartman@fsu.edu. *Dean*, Dr. Michael D. Delp, 850-644-1281, Fax: 850-644-0700, E-mail: mdelp@fsu.edu.

College of Motion Picture Arts Students: 57 full-time (28 women); includes 27 minority (5 Black or African American, non-Hispanic/Latino; 10 Asian, non-Hispanic/Latino; 8 Hispanic/Latino; 4 Two or more races, non-Hispanic/Latino). Average age 25. 187 applicants, 16% accepted, 30 enrolled. *Faculty:* 24 full-time (9 women), 3 part-time/adjunct (1 woman). *Financial support:* In 2015–16, 20 students received support, including 20 teaching assistantships with partial tuition reimbursements available (averaging $5,500 per year); institutionally sponsored loans and unspecified assistantships also available. Financial award application deadline: 12/1; financial award applicants required to submit FAFSA. In 2015, 30 master's awarded. Offers film production (MFA); screenwriting (MFA). *Application deadline:* For fall admission, 12/1 for domestic and international students. *Application fee:* $30. Electronic applications accepted. *Application Contact:* Gloria McElroy, Staff Director of Admissions and Recruitment, 850-644-8524, Fax: 850-644-2626, E-mail: gmcelroy@fsu.edu. *Dean*, Frank Patterson, 850-644-0453, Fax: 850-644-2626.

College of Music Students: 368 full-time (191 women); includes 86 minority (31 Black or African American, non-Hispanic/Latino; 2 American Indian or Alaska Native, non-Hispanic/Latino; 18 Asian, non-Hispanic/Latino; 25 Hispanic/Latino; 1 Native Hawaiian or other Pacific Islander, non-Hispanic/Latino; 9 Two or more races, non-Hispanic/Latino). Average age 26. 737 applicants, 42% accepted, 138 enrolled. *Faculty:* 87 full-time, 13 part-time/adjunct. *Financial support:* In 2015–16, 222 students received support, including 2 fellowships with full tuition reimbursements available (averaging $15,000 per year), 14 research assistantships (averaging $5,540 per year), 201 teaching assistantships (averaging $5,540 per year); career-related internships or fieldwork, Federal Work-Study, scholarships/grants, tuition waivers (full and partial), and unspecified assistantships also available. Support available to part-time students. Financial award application deadline: 2/28; financial award applicants required to submit FAFSA. In 2015, 108 master's, 42 doctorates awarded. Offers accompanying (MM); arts administration (MA); choral conducting (MM); composition (MM, DM); ethnomusicology (MM); general music (MA); instrumental accompanying (MM); instrumental conducting (MM); jazz studies (MM); music education (MM Ed, PhD); music theory (MM, PhD); music therapy (MM); musicology (MM, PhD); opera (MM); performance (MM, DM); piano pedagogy (MM); piano technology (MA); vocal accompanying (MM). *Application deadline:* For fall admission, 7/1 for domestic and international students; for spring admission, 11/1 for domestic and international students; for summer admission, 3/1 for domestic students. Applications are processed on a rolling basis. *Application fee:* $30. Electronic applications accepted. *Application Contact:* Dr. James Mathes, Interim Associate Dean for Academic Affairs/Director of Graduate Studies in Music, 850-644-5848, Fax: 850-644-2033, E-mail: jmathes@fsu.edu. *Dean*, Dr. Patricia Flowers, 850-644-4361, Fax: 850-644-2033, E-mail: pjflowers@fsu.edu.

College of Nursing Students: 56 full-time (49 women), 25 part-time (23 women); includes 25 minority (13 Black or African American, non-Hispanic/Latino; 4 Asian, non-Hispanic/Latino; 7 Hispanic/Latino; 1 Two or more races, non-Hispanic/Latino). Average age 38. 90 applicants, 50% accepted, 44 enrolled. *Faculty:* 13 full-time (12 women). *Financial support:* In 2015–16, 75 students received support, including fellowships with partial tuition reimbursements available (averaging $6,300 per year), research assistantships with partial tuition reimbursements available (averaging $3,000 per year), 3 teaching assistantships with partial tuition reimbursements available (averaging $3,000 per year); career-related internships or fieldwork, Federal Work-Study, institutionally sponsored loans, scholarships/grants, traineeships, and tuition waivers (partial) also available. Financial award application deadline: 4/15; financial award applicants required to submit FAFSA. In 2015, 2 master's, 20 doctorates awarded. *Degree program information:* Part-time programs available. Part-time, online learning. Offers family nurse practitioner (DNP); nurse educator (MSN, Certificate); nurse leader (MSN); nursing leadership (Certificate). *Application deadline:* For fall admission, 4/15 for domestic and international students. *Application fee:* $30. Electronic applications accepted. *Application Contact:* Carlos Urrutia, Assistant Director for Student Services, 850-644-5638, Fax: 850-645-7249, E-mail: currutia@fsu.edu. *Dean*, Dr. Judith McFetridge-Durdle, 850-644-6846, Fax: 850-644-7660, E-mail: jdurdle@nursing.fsu.edu.

College of Social Sciences and Public Policy Students: 443 full-time (216 women), 183 part-time (95 women); includes 182 minority (66 Black or African American, non-Hispanic/Latino; 29 Asian, non-Hispanic/Latino; 69 Hispanic/Latino; 18 Two or more races, non-Hispanic/Latino), 100 international. Average age 26. 743 applicants, 64% accepted, 225 enrolled. *Faculty:* 134 full-time (47 women), 44 part-time/adjunct (7 women). *Financial support:* In 2015–16, 273 students received support, including 33 fellowships with full tuition reimbursements available (averaging $21,828 per year), 85 research assistantships with full tuition reimbursements available (averaging $13,487 per year), 126 teaching assistantships with full tuition reimbursements available (averaging $18,710 per year); career-related internships or fieldwork, Federal Work-Study, institutionally sponsored loans, scholarships/grants, health care benefits, tuition waivers (full and partial), and unspecified assistantships also available. Support available to part-time students. Financial award application deadline: 1/15; financial award applicants required to submit FAFSA. In 2015, 294 master's, 31 doctorates awarded. *Degree program information:* Part-time and evening/weekend programs available. Part-time, evening/weekend. Offers applied economics (MS); Asian studies (MA, MS); demography (MS); economics (PhD); geographic information science (MS); geography (MA, MS, PhD); international affairs (MA, MS); political science (MA, MS, PhD); public administration and policy (MPA, PhD, Certificate); public health (MPH); Russian and East European studies (MA, MS); social sciences and public policy (MA, MPA, MPH, MS, MSP, PhD, Certificate); sociology (MA, MS, PhD); urban and regional planning (MSP, PhD). *Application deadline:* For fall admission, 7/1 priority date for domestic and international students; for spring admission, 11/1 priority date for domestic and international students; for summer admission, 3/1 priority date for domestic and international students. Applications are processed on a rolling basis. *Application fee:* $30. Electronic applications accepted. *Application Contact:* Melanie Booker, Associate Director for Graduate Admissions, 850-644-3420, Fax: 850-644-0197, E-mail: mbooker@admin.fsu.edu. *Interim Dean*, Dr. Timothy Chapin, 850-644-5488, Fax: 850-645-4923, E-mail: tchapin@fsu.edu.

College of Social Work Students: 236 full-time (206 women), 263 part-time (240 women); includes 173 minority (88 Black or African American, non-Hispanic/Latino; 1 American Indian or Alaska Native, non-Hispanic/Latino; 16 Asian, non-Hispanic/Latino; 48 Hispanic/Latino; 1 Native Hawaiian or other Pacific Islander, non-Hispanic/Latino; 19 Two or more races, non-Hispanic/Latino). Average age 30. 257 applicants, 88% accepted, 141 enrolled. *Faculty:* 35 full-time (23 women), 17 part-time/adjunct (9 women). *Financial support:* In 2015–16, 114 students received support, including 1 fellowship with full tuition reimbursement available (averaging $22,000 per year), 26 research assistantships with full tuition reimbursements available (averaging $4,000 per year), 14 teaching assistantships with full tuition reimbursements available (averaging $16,000 per year); career-related internships or fieldwork, scholarships/grants, health care benefits, tuition waivers (partial), and unspecified assistantships also available. Financial award application deadline: 5/1; financial award applicants required to submit FAFSA. In 2015, 249 master's, 5 doctorates awarded. *Degree program information:* Part-time and evening/weekend programs available. Part-time, evening/weekend, 100% online coursework in specified areas with mandatory in-person internships. Offers clinical social work (MSW); social leadership (MSW); social work (PhD). *Application deadline:* For fall admission, 5/1 for domestic and international students; for winter admission, 3/1 for domestic and international students; for spring admission, 10/1 for domestic and international students; for summer admission, 3/1 for domestic and international students. Applications are processed on a rolling basis. *Application fee:* $30. Electronic applications accepted. *Application Contact:* Dana DeBoer, Coordinator of MSW Admissions, 800-378-9550, Fax: 850-644-9591, E-mail: ddeboer2@admin.fsu.edu. *Dean*, Dr. James Clark, 850-644-4752, Fax: 850-644-9750, E-mail: nfmazza@fsu.edu.

FAMU-FSU College of Engineering Students: 331 full-time (72 women); includes 61 minority (31 Black or African American, non-Hispanic/Latino; 10 Asian, non-Hispanic/Latino; 18 Hispanic/Latino; 2 Two or more races, non-Hispanic/Latino), 185 international. Average age 25. 538 applicants, 43% accepted, 84 enrolled. *Faculty:* 86 full-time (10 women), 15 part-time/adjunct (2 women). *Financial support:* In 2015–16, 22 fellowships with full tuition reimbursements, 125 research assistantships with full tuition reimbursements, 94 teaching assistantships with full tuition reimbursements were awarded; career-related internships or fieldwork, scholarships/grants, tuition waivers (full), and unspecified assistantships also available. Financial award application deadline: 1/15; financial award applicants required to submit FAFSA. In 2015, 49 master's, 20 doctorates awarded. *Degree program information:* Part-time programs available. Part-time. Offers biomedical engineering (MS, PhD); chemical engineering (MS, PhD); civil and environmental engineering (M Eng, MS, PhD); electrical engineering (MS, PhD); engineering (M Eng, MS, PhD); industrial engineering (MS, PhD); mechanical engineering (MS, PhD); sustainable energy (MS). *Application deadline:* For fall admission, 3/1 for domestic and international students;

for spring admission, 10/1 for domestic and international students. Applications are processed on a rolling basis. *Application fee:* $30. Electronic applications accepted. *Interim Dean/Professor,* Dr. Bruce R. Locke, 850-410-6161, Fax: 850-410-6546, E-mail: dean@eng.fsu.edu.

FONTBONNE UNIVERSITY, St. Louis, MO 63105-3098

General Information Independent-religious, coed, comprehensive institution. *Graduate housing:* Room and/or apartments available on a first-come, first-served basis to single students; on-campus housing not available to married students. Housing application deadline: 3/8.

GRADUATE UNITS

Graduate Programs ***Degree program information:*** Part-time and evening/weekend programs available. Part-time, evening/weekend, online learning. Offers accounting (MS); art (MA); art (K-12) (MAT); business (MBA); computer science (MS); deaf education (MA); early intervention in deaf education (MA); education (MA); elementary education (MAT); family and consumer sciences (MA, MAT); fine arts (MFA); instructional design and technology (MS); learning technologies (MS); management (MM); middle school education (MAT); nonprofit management (MS); secondary education (MAT); special education (MAT); speech-language pathology (MS); supply chain management (MS); theatre (MA). Electronic applications accepted.

FORDHAM UNIVERSITY, New York, NY 10458

General Information Independent-religious, coed, university. CGS member. *Enrollment:* 15,286 graduate, professional, and undergraduate students; 4,220 full-time matriculated graduate/professional students (2,544 women), 2,284 part-time matriculated graduate/professional students (1,403 women). *Enrollment by degree level:* 4,131 master's, 2,267 doctoral, 106 other advanced degrees. *Graduate faculty:* 617 full-time (257 women), 922 part-time/adjunct (447 women). *Graduate housing:* Room and/or apartments available on a first-come, first-served basis to single students; on-campus housing not available to married students. Housing application deadline: 4/10. *Student services:* Campus employment opportunities, campus safety program, career counseling, free psychological counseling, international student services, low-cost health insurance, services for students with disabilities, teacher training, writing training. *Library:* Walsh Library plus 3 others. *Collection:* Books: 2.3 million (physical), 600,000 (digital/electronic); Serial titles: 9,200 (physical), 76,000 (digital/electronic); Databases: 275. Weekly public service hours: 108; study areas open 24 hours, 5–7 days a week. *Research affiliation:* Equator Initiative /United Nations Development Programme, Folger Shakespeare Library, New York Botanical Gardens, New York Ocean Science Library, Wildlife Conservation Society, Memorial Sloan-Kettering Cancer Center.

Computer facilities: Computer purchase and lease plans are available. 1,400 computers available on campus for general student use. A campuswide network can be accessed from student residence rooms and from off campus. Online class registration is available. Website: http://www.fordham.edu/

General Application Contact: Office of Admission, 718-817-1000.

GRADUATE UNITS

Gabelli School of Business Students: 1,271 full-time (711 women), 550 part-time (285 women); includes 185 minority (47 Black or African American, non-Hispanic/Latino; 1 American Indian or Alaska Native, non-Hispanic/Latino; 69 Asian, non-Hispanic/Latino; 61 Hispanic/Latino; 1 Native Hawaiian or other Pacific Islander, non-Hispanic/Latino; 6 Two or more races, non-Hispanic/Latino), 1,193 international. Average age 26. 4,554 applicants, 46% accepted, 803 enrolled. *Faculty:* 128 full-time (44 women), 52 part-time/adjunct (9 women). *Financial support:* In 2015–16, 71 students received support. Career-related internships or fieldwork, institutionally sponsored loans, scholarships/grants, and unspecified assistantships available. Support available to part-time students. Financial award application deadline: 6/15; financial award applicants required to submit FAFSA. In 2015, 1,023 master's awarded. *Degree program information:* Part-time and evening/weekend programs available. Part-time, evening/weekend. Offers accounting (MBA, MS); applied statistics and decision-making (MS); business analytics (MS); communications and media management (MBA); finance (MBA); global finance (MS); information systems (MBA, MS); investor relations (MS); management (EMBA); management systems (MBA); marketing (MBA); marketing intelligence (MS); media management (MS); nonprofit leadership (MS); quantitative finance (MS); taxation (MS). *Application deadline:* For fall admission, 6/1 for domestic students, 5/1 for international students; for spring admission, 12/1 for domestic students, 11/1 for international students; for summer admission, 3/1 for domestic students. Applications are processed on a rolling basis. *Application fee:* $130. Electronic applications accepted. *Application Contact:* Lawrence Murray, Senior Assistant Dean of Graduate Admissions and Advising, 212-636-6200, Fax: 212-636-7076, E-mail: admissionsgb@fordham.edu. *Dean,* Dr. Donna Rapaccioli, 212-636-6165, Fax: 212-307-1779, E-mail: rapaccioli@fordham.edu.

Graduate School of Arts and Sciences Students: 475 full-time (232 women), 206 part-time (104 women); includes 119 minority (19 Black or African American, non-Hispanic/Latino; 2 American Indian or Alaska Native, non-Hispanic/Latino; 71 Asian, non-Hispanic/Latino; 27 Hispanic/Latino), 138 international. Average age 31. 1,883 applicants, 31% accepted, 210 enrolled. *Faculty:* 249 full-time (81 women). *Financial support:* In 2015–16, 29 fellowships with tuition reimbursements (averaging $22,844 per year), 106 research assistantships with tuition reimbursements (averaging $16,516 per year), 280 teaching assistantships with tuition reimbursements (averaging $19,927 per year) were awarded; career-related internships or fieldwork, Federal Work-Study, institutionally sponsored loans, scholarships/grants, health care benefits, tuition waivers (full and partial), and unspecified assistantships also available. Support available to part-time students. Financial award application deadline: 1/4; financial award applicants required to submit FAFSA. In 2015, 145 master's, 56 doctorates, 87 other advanced degrees awarded. *Degree program information:* Part-time and evening/weekend programs available. Part-time, evening/weekend. Offers applied developmental psychology (PhD); applied psychological methods (MS); arts and sciences (MA, MFA, MS, PhD, Advanced Certificate, Certificate, Graduate Certificate); biological sciences (MS, PhD); classical Greek and Latin literature (MA); classics (PhD); clinical psychology (PhD); clinical research methodology (MS); computer science (MS); conservation biology (Graduate Certificate); cybersecurity (MS); data analytics (MS); economics (MA, PhD); elections and campaign management (MA); English language and literature (MA, PhD); history (MA, PhD); international humanitarian action (MA); international political economy and development (MA, Certificate); philosophical resources (MA); philosophy (MA, PhD); playwriting (MFA); psychometrics (PhD); theology (MA, PhD); urban studies (MA). *Application deadline:* For fall admission, 1/4 priority date for domestic and international students; for spring admission, 10/31 for domestic and international students. Applications are processed on a rolling basis. *Application fee:* $70. Electronic applications accepted. *Application Contact:* Bernadette Valentino-Morrison, Director of Graduate Admissions, 718-817-4419, Fax: 718-817-3566, E-mail: valentinomor@fordham.edu. *Dean,* Dr. Eva Badowska, 718-817-4400, Fax: 718-817-4474, E-mail: badowska@fordham.edu.

Program in Ethics and Society Students: 8 full-time (7 women), 5 part-time (3 women); includes 3 minority (2 Black or African American, non-Hispanic/Latino; 1 Asian, non-Hispanic/Latino), 1 international. Average age 34. 39 applicants, 28% accepted, 7 enrolled. *Financial support:* In 2015–16, 1 student received support. Teaching assistantships, Federal Work-Study, institutionally sponsored loans, scholarships/grants, tuition waivers (partial), and unspecified assistantships available. Financial award application deadline: 1/4. In 2015, 6 master's awarded. *Degree program information:* Part-time programs available. Part-time. Offers ethics and society (MA); health care ethics (Certificate). *Application deadline:* For fall admission, 1/4 priority date for domestic students; for spring admission, 10/31 for domestic students. Applications are processed on a rolling basis. *Application fee:* $70. Electronic applications accepted. *Application Contact:* Bernadette Valentino-Morrison, Director of Graduate Admissions, 718-817-4419, Fax: 718-817-3566, E-mail: valentinomor@fordham.edu. *Assistant Director, Fordham University Center for Ethics Education,* Dr. Adam Fried, 718-817-0926, Fax: 212-759-2009, E-mail: afried@fordham.edu.

Program in Medieval Studies Students: 8 full-time (7 women), 5 part-time (3 women); includes 3 minority (2 Black or African American, non-Hispanic/Latino; 1 Asian, non-Hispanic/Latino), 1 international. Average age 27. 36 applicants, 53% accepted, 7 enrolled. *Financial support:* In 2015–16, 4 students received support. Institutionally sponsored loans, tuition waivers (full and partial), and unspecified assistantships available. Financial award application deadline: 1/4; financial award applicants required to submit FAFSA. In 2015, 6 master's, 2 other advanced degrees awarded. *Degree program information:* Part-time and evening/weekend programs available. Part-time, evening/weekend. Offers medieval studies (MA, Certificate). *Application deadline:* For fall admission, 1/4 priority date for domestic students; for spring admission, 11/1 for domestic students. Applications are processed on a rolling basis. *Application fee:* $70. Electronic applications accepted. *Application Contact:* Bernadette Valentino-Morrison, Director of Graduate Admissions, 718-817-4419, Fax: 718-817-3566, E-mail: valentinomor@fordham.edu. *Director,* Dr. Susanne Hafner, 718-817-4655, E-mail: hafner@fordham.edu.

Graduate School of Education Students: 273 full-time (222 women), 657 part-time (497 women); includes 317 minority (106 Black or African American, non-Hispanic/Latino; 2 American Indian or Alaska Native, non-Hispanic/Latino; 44 Asian, non-Hispanic/Latino; 139 Hispanic/Latino; 3 Native Hawaiian or other Pacific Islander, non-Hispanic/Latino; 23 Two or more races, non-Hispanic/Latino), 99 international. Average age 32. 1,077 applicants, 68% accepted, 330 enrolled. *Faculty:* 38 full-time (26 women), 81 part-time/adjunct (54 women). *Financial support:* In 2015–16, 700 students received support, including 131 fellowships with partial tuition reimbursements available (averaging $3,500 per year), 91 research assistantships with partial tuition reimbursements available (averaging $8,250 per year); career-related internships or fieldwork, Federal Work-Study, scholarships/grants, and unspecified assistantships also available. Support available to part-time students. Financial award applicants required to submit FAFSA. In 2015, 573 master's, 45 doctorates, 6 other advanced degrees awarded. *Degree program information:* Part-time and evening/weekend programs available. Part-time, evening/weekend. Offers education (MSE, MST, Ed D, PhD, Adv C). *Application fee:* $70. Electronic applications accepted. *Application Contact:* Graduate School of Education Admissions Office, 212-636-6400, Fax: 347-842-3082, E-mail: gse_admiss@fordham.edu. *Dean,* Dr. Virginia Roach, 212-636-6400, E-mail: vroach@fordham.edu.

Division of Curriculum and Teaching Students: 120 full-time (93 women), 296 part-time (249 women); includes 152 minority (53 Black or African American, non-Hispanic/Latino; 20 Asian, non-Hispanic/Latino; 66 Hispanic/Latino; 1 Native Hawaiian or other Pacific Islander, non-Hispanic/Latino; 12 Two or more races, non-Hispanic/Latino), 50 international. Average age 24. 657 applicants, 49% accepted, 138 enrolled. *Faculty:* 22 full-time (18 women), 38 part-time/adjunct (28 women). *Financial support:* Scholarships/grants and unspecified assistantships available. Support available to part-time students. Financial award applicants required to submit FAFSA. In 2015, 351 master's awarded. *Degree program information:* Part-time and evening/weekend programs available. Part-time, evening/weekend. Offers curriculum and teaching (MSE); early childhood education (MSE); elementary education (MST); special education (MSE, Adv C); teaching English as a second language (MSE). *Application deadline:* For fall admission, 6/30 for domestic students, 4/14 for international students; for spring admission, 11/15 for domestic students; for summer admission, 4/15 for domestic students. Applications are processed on a rolling basis. *Application fee:* $70. Electronic applications accepted. *Application Contact:* Linda Horisk, Assistant Dean of Admissions, 212-636-6400, E-mail: horisk@fordham.edu. *Chair,* Dr. Chun Zhang, 212-636-6400.

Division of Educational Leadership, Administration and Policy Students: 15 full-time (11 women), 213 part-time (123 women); includes 75 minority (33 Black or African American, non-Hispanic/Latino; 7 Asian, non-Hispanic/Latino; 32 Hispanic/Latino; 1 Native Hawaiian or other Pacific Islander, non-Hispanic/Latino; 2 Two or more races, non-Hispanic/Latino), 23 international. Average age 41. 140 applicants, 69% accepted, 89 enrolled. *Faculty:* 8 full-time (3 women), 20 part-time/adjunct (12 women). *Financial support:* Career-related internships or fieldwork, scholarships/grants, and unspecified assistantships available. Financial award applicants required to submit FAFSA. In 2015, 105 master's, 19 doctorates awarded. *Degree program information:* Part-time and evening/weekend programs available. Part-time, evening/weekend. Offers administration and supervision (MSE, Adv C); administration and supervision for church leaders (PhD); educational administration and supervision (Ed D, PhD). *Application fee:* $70. Electronic applications accepted. *Application Contact:* Linda Horisk, Assistant Dean of Admissions, 212-636-6400, E-mail: horisk@fordham.edu. *Chairperson,* Dr. John Craven, 212-636-6400.

Division of Psychological and Educational Services Students: 141 full-time (122 women), 143 part-time (122 women); includes 95 minority (20 Black or African American, non-Hispanic/Latino; 2 American Indian or Alaska Native, non-Hispanic/Latino; 20 Asian, non-Hispanic/Latino; 42 Hispanic/Latino; 11 Two or more races, non-Hispanic/Latino), 27 international. Average age 29. 500 applicants, 33% accepted, 104 enrolled. *Faculty:* 18 full-time (11 women), 23 part-time/adjunct (14 women). *Financial support:* Research assistantships, scholarships/grants, and unspecified assistantships available. Support available to part-time students. Financial award applicants required to submit FAFSA. In 2015, 117 master's, 18 doctorates awarded. *Degree program information:* Part-time and evening/weekend programs available. Part-time, evening/weekend. Offers counseling and personnel services (MSE); counseling psychology (PhD); school psychology (PhD). *Application fee:* $70. Electronic applications accepted. *Application Contact:* Linda Horisk,

Assistant Dean of Admissions, 212-636-6400, E-mail: horisk@fordham.edu. *Chairman*, Dr. Mitch Rabinowitz, 212-636-6461.

Graduate School of Religion and Religious Education ***Degree program information:*** Part-time programs available. Part-time. Offers pastoral counseling and spiritual care (MA); pastoral ministry/spirituality/pastoral counseling (D Min); religion and religious education (MA); religious education (MS, PhD, PD); spiritual direction (Certificate). Electronic applications accepted.

Graduate School of Social Service ***Degree program information:*** Part-time and evening/weekend programs available. Part-time, evening/weekend, online learning. Offers nonprofit leadership (MS); social work (MSW, PhD). MS jointly sponsored with Graduate School of Business and conducted through the Fordham Center for Nonprofit Leaders. Electronic applications accepted.

School of Law ***Degree program information:*** Part-time and evening/weekend programs available. Part-time, evening/weekend. Offers banking, corporate and finance law (LL M); corporate compliance (MSL); fashion law (MSL); intellectual property and information law (LL M); international business and trade law (LL M); law (JD). Electronic applications accepted.

FORT HAYS STATE UNIVERSITY, Hays, KS 67601-4099

General Information State-supported, coed, comprehensive institution. CGS member. *Graduate housing:* Rooms and/or apartments available to single and married students. Housing application deadline: 8/1.

GRADUATE UNITS

Graduate School ***Degree program information:*** Part-time programs available. Part-time. Electronic applications accepted.

College of Arts and Sciences Degree program information: Part-time programs available. Part-time. Offers arts and sciences (MA, MFA, MLS, MS, Ed S); communication (MS); English (MA); geography (MS); geology (MS); geosciences (MS); history (MA); liberal studies (MLS); psychology (MS); school psychology (Ed S); studio art (MFA). Electronic applications accepted.

College of Business and Leadership Degree program information: Part-time programs available. Part-time. Offers business and leadership (MBA); management (MBA). Electronic applications accepted.

College of Education and Technology Degree program information: Part-time programs available. Part-time. Offers counseling (MS); education (MSE); education and technology (MS, MSE, Ed S); educational administration (MS, Ed S); instructional technology (MS); special education (MS). Electronic applications accepted.

College of Health and Life Sciences Degree program information: Part-time programs available. Part-time. Offers biology (MS); health and human performance (MS); health and life sciences (MS, MSN); nursing (MSN); speech-language pathology (MS). Electronic applications accepted.

FORT LEWIS COLLEGE, Durango, CO 81301-3999

General Information State-supported, coed, comprehensive institution.

GRADUATE UNITS

Program in Teacher Leadership Offers teacher leadership (MA, Certificate).

FORT VALLEY STATE UNIVERSITY, Fort Valley, GA 31030

General Information State-supported, coed, comprehensive institution. *Enrollment:* 175 full-time matriculated graduate/professional students (123 women), 254 part-time matriculated graduate/professional students (206 women). *Enrollment by degree level:* 420 master's, 9 other advanced degrees. *Graduate faculty:* 15 full-time (2 women), 3 part-time/adjunct (1 woman). *Graduate housing:* Room and/or apartments available on a first-come, first-served basis to single students; on-campus housing not available to married students. Typical cost: $2469 per year ($4219 including board). Room and board charges vary according to board plan and housing facility selected. Housing application deadline: 7/1. *Student services:* Campus employment opportunities, campus safety program, career counseling, free psychological counseling, international student services, low-cost health insurance, multicultural affairs office, services for students with disabilities. *Library:* Henry A. Hunt Memorial Library.

Computer facilities: A campuswide network can be accessed from off campus. Online grade reports available.
Website: http://www.fvsu.edu/

General Application Contact: Calandria Wright, Director of Admissions, 478-825-6672, E-mail: wrightc@fvsu.edu.

GRADUATE UNITS

College of Graduate Studies and Extended Education ***Financial support:*** Federal Work-Study and unspecified assistantships available. Support available to part-time students. Financial award application deadline: 5/1; financial award applicants required to submit FAFSA. *Degree program information:* Part-time programs available. Part-time. Offers animal science (MS); environmental health (MPH); guidance and counseling (Ed S); mental health counseling (MS); rehabilitation counseling (MS). *Application deadline:* For fall admission, 8/23 for domestic students. *Application fee:* $20.

FRAMINGHAM STATE UNIVERSITY, Framingham, MA 01701-9101

General Information State-supported, coed, comprehensive institution. CGS member. *Graduate housing:* On-campus housing not available.

GRADUATE UNITS

Continuing Education ***Degree program information:*** Part-time and evening/weekend programs available. Part-time, evening/weekend, online learning. Offers art (M Ed); business administration (MBA); counseling psychology (MA); curriculum and instructional technology (M Ed); dietetics (MS); early childhood education (M Ed); educational leadership (MA); elementary education (M Ed); English (M Ed); food science and nutrition science (MS); health care administration (MA); history (M Ed); human nutrition: education and media technologies (MS); human resource management (MA); literacy and language (M Ed); mathematics (M Ed); nursing education (MSN); nursing leadership (MSN); public administration (MA); Spanish (M Ed); special education (M Ed); teaching of English as a second language (M Ed).

FRANCISCAN SCHOOL OF THEOLOGY, Berkeley, CA 94709-1294

General Information Independent-religious, coed, graduate-only institution. *Graduate housing:* Rooms and/or apartments available on a first-come, first-served basis to single and married students. Housing application deadline: 5/15.

GRADUATE UNITS

Graduate and Professional Programs ***Degree program information:*** Part-time programs available. Part-time. Offers theology (M Div, MA, MAMC, MTS).

FRANCISCAN UNIVERSITY OF STEUBENVILLE, Steubenville, OH 43952-1763

General Information Independent-religious, coed, comprehensive institution. *Enrollment:* 2,716 graduate, professional, and undergraduate students; 141 full-time matriculated graduate/professional students (71 women), 472 part-time matriculated graduate/professional students (265 women). *Enrollment by degree level:* 613 master's. *Graduate faculty:* 8 full-time (3 women), 45 part-time/adjunct (13 women). *Tuition, area resident:* Full-time $12,330; part-time $685 per credit hour. *Required fees:* $288; $16 per credit hour. Tuition and fees vary according to course level and program. *Graduate housing:* On-campus housing not available. *Student services:* Campus employment opportunities, career counseling, exercise/wellness program, free psychological counseling, international student services, services for students with disabilities. *Library:* John Paul II Library.

Computer facilities: Computer purchase and lease plans are available. A campuswide network can be accessed from student residence rooms. Online class registration is available.
Website: http://www.franciscan.edu/

General Application Contact: Mark McGuire, Director of Graduate Enrollment, 800-783-6220, Fax: 740-284-5456, E-mail: mmcguire@franciscan.edu.

GRADUATE UNITS

Graduate Programs ***Degree program information:*** Part-time and evening/weekend programs available. Part-time, evening/weekend, online learning. Offers administration (MS Ed); business (MBA); clinical mental health counseling (MA); nursing (MSN); philosophy (MA); teaching (MS Ed); theology and Christian ministry (MA). Electronic applications accepted.

FRANCIS MARION UNIVERSITY, Florence, SC 29502-0547

General Information State-supported, coed, comprehensive institution. *Enrollment:* 3,947 graduate, professional, and undergraduate students; 102 full-time matriculated graduate/professional students (82 women), 156 part-time matriculated graduate/professional students (118 women). *Enrollment by degree level:* 246 master's, 12 other advanced degrees. *Graduate faculty:* 32 full-time (25 women). *Tuition, area resident:* Full-time $9780; part-time $489 per credit hour. Tuition, nonresident: full-time $19,560; part-time $978 per credit hour. *Required fees:* $14.40 per credit hour. $141 per semester. Tuition and fees vary according to course load and program. *Graduate housing:* Room and/or apartments available on a first-come, first-served basis to single students; on-campus housing not available to married students. Typical cost: $4222 per year ($7472 including board). Room and board charges vary according to board plan and housing facility selected. Housing application deadline: 5/1. *Student services:* Campus employment opportunities, campus safety program, career counseling, child daycare facilities, free psychological counseling, international student services, low-cost health insurance, multicultural affairs office, services for students with disabilities, teacher training, writing training. *Library:* James A. Rogers Library plus 1 other. *Collection:* Books: 343,000 (digital/electronic).

Computer facilities: 634 computers available on campus for general student use. A campuswide network can be accessed from student residence rooms. Online class registration, Blackboard are available.
Website: http://www.fmarion.edu/

General Application Contact: Jennifer Taylor, Administrative Manager, Provost's Office, 843-661-1286, Fax: 843-661-4688, E-mail: jtaylor@fmarion.edu.

GRADUATE UNITS

Graduate Programs Students: 192 full-time (152 women), 55 part-time (44 women); includes 16 minority (5 Black or African American, non-Hispanic/Latino; 1 American Indian or Alaska Native, non-Hispanic/Latino; 9 Asian, non-Hispanic/Latino; 1 Two or more races, non-Hispanic/Latino), 3 international. Average age 34. 276 applicants, 100% accepted, 98 enrolled. *Faculty:* 28 full-time (17 women), 4 part-time/adjunct (all women). *Financial support:* Unspecified assistantships available. Support available to part-time students. Financial award application deadline: 3/1; financial award applicants required to submit FAFSA. In 2015, 93 master's, 6 other advanced degrees awarded. *Degree program information:* Part-time and evening/weekend programs available. Part-time, evening/weekend. Offers applied psychology (MS); family nurse practitioner (MSN); family nurse practitioner with nurse educator certificate (MSN); nurse educator (MSN); physician assistant (MPAS); school psychology (SSP). *Application deadline:* For fall admission, 3/15 for domestic and international students; for spring admission, 10/15 for domestic and international students. Applications are processed on a rolling basis. *Application fee:* $37. Electronic applications accepted. *Application Contact:* Jennifer Taylor, Administrative Manager, Provost's Office, 843-661-1286, Fax: 843-661-4688, E-mail: jtaylor@fmarion.edu. *Provost's Office*, 843-661-1284, Fax: 843-661-4688.

School of Business Students: 4 full-time (2 women), 34 part-time (13 women); includes 10 minority (7 Black or African American, non-Hispanic/Latino; 2 Asian, non-Hispanic/Latino; 1 Hispanic/Latino), 2 international. Average age 34. 18 applicants, 67% accepted, 12 enrolled. *Faculty:* 4 full-time (2 women). *Financial support:* Research assistantships available. Support available to part-time students. Financial award application deadline: 3/1; financial award applicants required to submit FAFSA. In 2015, 15 master's awarded. *Degree program information:* Part-time and evening/weekend programs available. Part-time, evening/weekend. Offers business (MBA); health executive management (MBA). *Application deadline:* For fall admission, 3/15 for domestic and international students; for spring admission, 10/15 for domestic and international students. Applications are processed on a rolling basis. *Application fee:* $37. *Application Contact:* Jennifer Taylor, Administrative Manager, 843-661-1286, Fax: 843-661-4688, E-mail: jtaylor@fmarion.edu. *Dean*, Dr. M. Barry O'Brien, 843-661-1419, Fax: 843-661-1432, E-mail: mobrien@fmarion.edu.

School of Education Students: 20 full-time (17 women), 80 part-time (69 women); includes 37 minority (32 Black or African American, non-Hispanic/Latino; 3 Asian, non-Hispanic/Latino; 1 Hispanic/Latino; 1 Two or more races, non-Hispanic/Latino). Average age 32. 18 applicants, 100% accepted, 18 enrolled. *Faculty:* 5 full-time (4 women). *Financial support:* Research assistantships and unspecified assistantships available. Support available to part-time students. Financial award application deadline: 3/1; financial award applicants required to submit FAFSA. In 2015, 37 master's awarded. *Degree program information:* Part-time programs available. Part-time. Offers learning disabilities (M Ed, MAT). *Application deadline:* For fall admission, 3/15 priority date for domestic students, 3/15 for international students; for spring admission, 10/15 priority date for domestic students, 10/15 for international students. Applications are processed on a rolling basis. *Application fee:* $37. *Application Contact:* Jennifer Taylor, Administrative Manager, 843-661-1286, Fax: 843-661-4688, E-mail: jtaylor@fmarion.edu. *Dean*, Dr. Shirley Carr Bausmith, 843-661-1460, Fax: 843-661-4647.

FRANKLIN COLLEGE, Franklin, IN 46131

General Information Independent-religious, coed, comprehensive institution.

GRADUATE UNITS

Program in Athletic Training Offers athletic training (MSAT).

FRANKLIN PIERCE UNIVERSITY, Rindge, NH 03461-0060

General Information Independent, coed, university. *Tuition, area resident:* Part-time $660 per credit hour. Tuition and fees vary according to program. *Graduate housing:* On-campus housing not available. *Student services:* Campus employment opportunities, career counseling, exercise/wellness program, low-cost health insurance, services for students with disabilities. *Library:* Frank S. DiPietro Library plus 1 other. *Collection:* Books: 115,351 (physical), 189,962 (digital/electronic); Serial titles: 40 (physical), 42 (digital/electronic); Databases: 58. Weekly public service hours: 95.

Computer facilities: Computer purchase and lease plans are available. 100 computers available on campus for general student use. A campuswide network can be accessed from student residence rooms and from off campus. Online class registration is available.
Website: http://www.franklinpierce.edu/

General Application Contact: Linda Quimby, Assistant Vice President of Enrollment, 800-437-0048, Fax: 603-626-4815, E-mail: cgps@franklinpierce.edu.

GRADUATE UNITS

Graduate and Professional Studies ***Financial support:*** Teaching assistantships with tuition reimbursements, career-related internships or fieldwork, and unspecified assistantships available. Support available to part-time students. Financial award applicants required to submit FAFSA. *Degree program information:* Part-time programs available. Part-time, online learning. Offers curriculum and instruction (M Ed); elementary education (MS Ed); emerging network technologies (Graduate Certificate); energy and sustainability studies (MBA, Graduate Certificate); health administration (MBA, Graduate Certificate); human resource management (MBA, Graduate Certificate); information technology (MBA); leadership (MBA); nursing education (MS); nursing leadership (MS); physical therapy (DPT); physician assistant studies (MPAS); special education (M Ed); sports management (MBA). *Application deadline:* Applications are processed on a rolling basis. *Application fee:* $0. Electronic applications accepted. *Application Contact:* Graduate Studies, 800-325-1090, Fax: 603-626-4815, E-mail: cgps@franklinpierce.edu. *Dean,* Dr. Maria Altobello, 603-647-3509, Fax: 603-229-4580, E-mail: altobellom@franklinpierce.edu.

FRANKLIN UNIVERSITY, Columbus, OH 43215-5399

General Information Independent, coed, comprehensive institution. *Graduate housing:* On-campus housing not available.

GRADUATE UNITS

Accounting Program Online learning. Offers accounting (MSA).

Computer Science Program ***Degree program information:*** Part-time and evening/weekend programs available. Part-time, evening/weekend. Offers computer science (MS). Electronic applications accepted.

Instructional Design and Performance Technology Program Offers instructional design and performance technology (MS).

Marketing and Communication Program ***Degree program information:*** Part-time and evening/weekend programs available. Part-time, evening/weekend. Offers marketing and communication (MS). Electronic applications accepted.

MBA Program ***Degree program information:*** Part-time and evening/weekend programs available. Part-time, evening/weekend, online learning. Offers business administration (MBA). Electronic applications accepted.

FRANKLIN UNIVERSITY SWITZERLAND, CH-6924 Sorengo, Switzerland

General Information Independent, coed, comprehensive institution.

GRADUATE UNITS

The Taylor Institute for Global Enterprise Management Offers international management (MS).

FRANK LLOYD WRIGHT SCHOOL OF ARCHITECTURE, Scottsdale, AZ 85261-4430

General Information Independent, coed, graduate-only institution. *Graduate housing:* Rooms and/or apartments guaranteed to single students and available on a first-come, first-served basis to married students. Housing application deadline: 3/20.

GRADUATE UNITS

Graduate Program Offers architecture (M Arch). Summer session held in Spring Green, WI.

FREDERICK S. PARDEE RAND GRADUATE SCHOOL, Santa Monica, CA 90407-2138

General Information Independent, coed, graduate-only institution. *Enrollment by degree level:* 107 doctoral. *Graduate faculty:* 263 part-time/adjunct (101 women). *Tuition, area resident:* Full-time $26,500. Full-time tuition and fees vary according to student level. *Graduate housing:* On-campus housing not available. *Student services:* Campus employment opportunities, career counseling, exercise/wellness program, free psychological counseling, grant writing training, international student services, low-cost health insurance, writing training. *Library:* RAND Corporation Library plus 1 other. *Collection:* Books: 17,327 (physical), 46,457 (digital/electronic); Serial titles: 1,271 (physical), 55,438 (digital/electronic); Databases: 61. Weekly public service hours: 65; study areas open 24 hours, 5–7 days a week; students can reserve study rooms. *Research affiliation:* RAND Corporation (not-for-profit research).

Computer facilities: 107 computers available on campus for general student use. A campuswide network can be accessed from off campus. Online class registration is available. Website: http://www.prgs.edu/

General Application Contact: Stefanie Howard, Director of Admissions, 310-393-0411 Ext. 8224, Fax: 310-451-6978, E-mail: sstern@rand.org.

GRADUATE UNITS

Program in Policy Analysis ***Financial support:*** Fellowships with tuition reimbursements, research assistantships, teaching assistantships, career-related internships or fieldwork, scholarships/grants, and health care benefits available. Offers policy analysis (PhD). *Application deadline:* For fall admission, 1/5 for domestic and international students. *Application fee:* $50. Electronic applications accepted. *Application Contact:* Mary Parker, Registrar/Admissions Manager, 310-393-0411 Ext. 7690, Fax: 310-451-6978, E-mail: mfparker@prgs.edu. *Dean,* Dr. Susan L. Marquis, 310-393-0411 Ext. 7075, Fax: 310-451-6978.

FREED-HARDEMAN UNIVERSITY, Henderson, TN 38340-2399

General Information Independent-religious, coed, comprehensive institution. *Graduate housing:* Room and/or apartments available on a first-come, first-served basis to single students; on-campus housing not available to married students. Housing application deadline: 8/22.

GRADUATE UNITS

Program in Business Administration ***Degree program information:*** Part-time and evening/weekend programs available. Part-time, evening/weekend, online learning. Offers accounting (MBA); corporate responsibility (MBA); leadership (MBA).

Program in Counseling ***Degree program information:*** Part-time and evening/weekend programs available. Part-time, evening/weekend. Offers counseling (MS).

Program in Education ***Degree program information:*** Part-time and evening/weekend programs available. Part-time, evening/weekend. Offers curriculum and instruction (M Ed); school counseling (M Ed); school leadership (Ed S).

School of Biblical Studies ***Degree program information:*** Part-time programs available. Part-time. Offers biblical studies (M Div, M Min, MA); divinity (M Div); ministry (M Min); New Testament (MA).

FRESNO PACIFIC UNIVERSITY, Fresno, CA 93702-4709

General Information Independent-religious, coed, comprehensive institution. *Graduate housing:* Rooms and/or apartments available on a first-come, first-served basis to single and married students. Housing application deadline: 4/20.

GRADUATE UNITS

Biblical Seminary ***Degree program information:*** Part-time programs available. Part-time, online learning. Offers Christian ministry (MA); divinity (M Div); marriage and family therapy (MA); New Testament (MA); Old Testament (MA); theology (MA); urban mission (MA).

Graduate Programs ***Degree program information:*** Part-time and evening/weekend programs available. Part-time, evening/weekend. Offers business administration (MBA); church conflict and peacemaking (Certificate); family nurse practitioner (MSN); individualized study (MA); kinesiology (MA); leadership and organizational studies (MA); mediation (Certificate); peacemaking and conflict studies (MA); restorative justice (Certificate). Electronic applications accepted.

School of Education ***Degree program information:*** Part-time and evening/weekend programs available. Part-time, evening/weekend. Offers administrative services (MA); board certified associate behavior analyst (Certificate); curriculum and teaching (MA); education (MA, MA Ed, Certificate); educational technology (MA); reading (Certificate); reading/English as a second language (MA Ed); reading/language arts (MA Ed); school counseling (MA); school library and information technology (MA Ed); school psychology (MA); special education (MA); STEM education (MA Ed). Electronic applications accepted.

FRIENDS UNIVERSITY, Wichita, KS 67213

General Information Independent-religious, coed, comprehensive institution.

GRADUATE UNITS

Graduate School ***Degree program information:*** Part-time and evening/weekend programs available. Part-time, evening/weekend, online learning. Offers family therapy (MSFT); global business administration (MBA); health care leadership (MHCL); management information systems (MMIS); professional business administration (MBA). Electronic applications accepted.

FRONTIER NURSING UNIVERSITY, Hyden, KY 41749

General Information Independent, coed, primarily women, graduate-only institution.

GRADUATE UNITS

Graduate Programs Offers family nurse practitioner (MSN, DNP, Post Master's Certificate); nurse-midwifery (MSN, DNP, Post Master's Certificate); women's health care nurse practitioner (MSN, DNP, Post Master's Certificate).

FROSTBURG STATE UNIVERSITY, Frostburg, MD 21532-1099

General Information State-supported, coed, comprehensive institution. *Graduate housing:* Room and/or apartments available to single students; on-campus housing not available to married students. Housing application deadline: 6/1.

GRADUATE UNITS

Graduate School ***Degree program information:*** Part-time and evening/weekend programs available. Part-time, evening/weekend. Electronic applications accepted.

College of Business ***Degree program information:*** Part-time and evening/weekend programs available. Part-time, evening/weekend. Offers business (MBA); business administration (MBA). Electronic applications accepted.

College of Education ***Degree program information:*** Part-time and evening/weekend programs available. Part-time, evening/weekend. Offers curriculum and instruction (M Ed); education (M Ed, MAT, MS); educational administration and supervision (M Ed); educational technology (M Ed); elementary (M Ed); elementary education (M Ed); elementary teaching (MAT); interdisciplinary education (M Ed); parks and recreational management (MS); reading (M Ed); school counseling (M Ed); secondary (M Ed); secondary education (M Ed); secondary teaching (MAT); special education (M Ed). Electronic applications accepted.

College of Liberal Arts and Sciences ***Degree program information:*** Part-time and evening/weekend programs available. Part-time, evening/weekend. Offers applied computer science (MS); applied ecology and conservation biology (MS); counseling psychology (MS); fisheries and wildlife management (MS); liberal arts and sciences (MS, MSN); nursing administration (MSN); nursing education (MSN). Electronic applications accepted.

FULLER THEOLOGICAL SEMINARY, Pasadena, CA 91182

General Information Independent-religious, coed, graduate-only institution. *Graduate housing:* Rooms and/or apartments available on a first-come, first-served basis to single and married students.

GRADUATE UNITS

Graduate Programs Offers Christian leadership (MACL); clinical psychology (PhD, Psy D); family studies (MA); global leadership (MA); global ministries (D Min); global ministries (Korean language) (D Min); intercultural studies (MA, Th M, PhD); intercultural studies (Korean language) (MA); marital and family therapy (MS); marriage and family enrichment (Certificate); ministry (M Div, D Min); missiology (D Miss); missiology (Korean language) (Th M); theology (MA, Th M, PhD); theology and ministry (MA).

FULL SAIL UNIVERSITY, Winter Park, FL 32792-7437

General Information Proprietary, coed, primarily men, comprehensive institution. *Graduate housing:* On-campus housing not available.

GRADUATE UNITS

Creative Writing Master of Fine Arts Program - Online Online learning. Offers creative writing (MFA).

Education Media Design and Technology Master of Science Program - Online Online learning. Offers education media design and technology (MS).

Entertainment Business Master of Science Program - Campus Offers entertainment business (MS).

Entertainment Business Master of Science Program - Online Online learning. Offers entertainment business (MS).

Game Design Master of Science Program - Campus Offers game design (MS).

Internet Marketing Master of Science Program - Online Online learning. Offers Internet marketing (MS).

Media Design Master of Fine Arts Program - Online Online learning. Offers media design (MFA).

New Media Journalism Master of Arts Program - Online Offers new media journalism (MA).

FURMAN UNIVERSITY, Greenville, SC 29613

General Information Independent, coed, comprehensive institution. CGS member. *Graduate housing:* On-campus housing not available.

GRADUATE UNITS

Graduate Division ***Degree program information:*** Part-time programs available. Part-time, online learning. Offers chemistry (MS); curriculum and instruction (MA); early childhood education (MA); educational leadership (Ed S); English as a second language (MA); literacy (MA); school leadership (MA); special education (MA).

FUTURE GENERATIONS GRADUATE SCHOOL, Franklin, WV 26807

General Information Independent, coed, graduate-only institution. *Enrollment by degree level:* 16 master's. *Graduate faculty:* 4 full-time (1 woman), 4 part-time/adjunct (2 women). *Tuition, area resident:* Full-time $17,500. *Graduate housing:* On-campus housing not available. *Student services:* Campus safety program, international student services, services for students with disabilities.

Computer facilities: Online class registration is available.
Website: http://www.future.edu/

General Application Contact: Christie Hand, Director of Student Success, 304-358-2000, E-mail: christie@future.edu.

GRADUATE UNITS

Program in Applied Community Change Students: 16 full-time (7 women); includes 13 minority (6 Black or African American, non-Hispanic/Latino; 4 Asian, non-Hispanic/Latino; 3 Hispanic/Latino). *Faculty:* 4 full-time (1 woman), 4 part-time/adjunct (2 women). *Financial support:* Scholarships/grants and tuition waivers (partial) available. Financial award application deadline: 10/1; financial award applicants required to submit FAFSA. Blended/hybrid learning. Offers conservation (MA). *Application deadline:* For winter admission, 10/11 for domestic and international students. *Application fee:* $0. Electronic applications accepted. *Application Contact:* Christie Hand, Director of Student Success, 304-358-2000, E-mail: christie@future.edu. *Chair of Dean's Council*, Daniel Robison, 304-358-2000.

GALLAUDET UNIVERSITY, Washington, DC 20002-3625

General Information Independent, coed, university. CGS member. *Enrollment:* 1,477 graduate, professional, and undergraduate students; 295 full-time matriculated graduate/professional students (229 women), 149 part-time matriculated graduate/professional students (104 women). *Enrollment by degree level:* 266 master's, 155 doctoral, 23 other advanced degrees. *International tuition:* $33,192 full-time. *Tuition, area resident:* Full-time $16,596; part-time $922 per credit hour. *Required fees:* $3047; $263 per semester. *Graduate housing:* Rooms and/or apartments available on a first-come, first-served basis to single and married students. Typical cost: $7080 per year ($12,630 including board) for single students; $1780 per year ($12,630 including board) for married students. Room and board charges vary according to housing facility selected. Housing application deadline: 4/1. *Student services:* Campus employment opportunities, campus safety program, career counseling, exercise/wellness program, free psychological counseling, grant writing training, international student services, low-cost health insurance, multicultural affairs office, services for students with disabilities, teacher training, writing training. *Library:* Merrill Learning Center. *Collection:* Books: 162,331 (physical), 972 (digital/electronic); Serial titles: 5,637 (physical), 25 (digital/electronic); Databases: 39. Weekly public service hours: 90; students can reserve study rooms. *Research affiliation:* Spencer Foundation (deaf legal discourse), University of Wisconsin-Madison/U.S. Department of Education (DOE) (telecommunications access), University of California Los Angeles/National Institutes of Health (cancer genetics), National Science Foundation/Howard University (linguistics, visual language and visual learning, integrated quantum materials), Maryland Sea Grant/University of Maryland/National Oceanic and Atmospheric Administration (NOAA) (advanced recruitment and retention in geosciences), U.S. Department of Education/Vcom3D Inc. (signing math dictionaries with mouth morphemes; accessibility and usability technologies for deaf and hard of hearing).

Computer facilities: 400 computers available on campus for general student use. A campuswide network can be accessed from student residence rooms and from off campus. Online class registration is available.
Website: http://www.gallaudet.edu/

General Application Contact: Wednesday Luria, Coordinator of Prospective Graduate Student Services, 202-651-5400, Fax: 202-651-5295, E-mail: graduate.school@gallaudet.edu.

GRADUATE UNITS

The Graduate School Students: 295 full-time (229 women), 149 part-time (104 women); includes 127 minority (32 Black or African American, non-Hispanic/Latino; 2 American Indian or Alaska Native, non-Hispanic/Latino; 14 Asian, non-Hispanic/Latino; 35 Hispanic/Latino; 44 Two or more races, non-Hispanic/Latino), 26 international. Average age 31. 598 applicants, 47% accepted, 158 enrolled. *Financial support:* In 2015–16, 229 students received support. Fellowships, research assistantships, teaching assistantships, career-related internships or fieldwork, Federal Work-Study, scholarships/grants, tuition waivers (partial), and unspecified assistantships available. Support available to part-time students. Financial award application deadline: 7/1; financial award applicants required to submit FAFSA. In 2015, 140 master's, 17 doctorates, 8 other advanced degrees awarded. *Degree program information:* Part-time programs available. Part-time. Offers American Sign Language/English bilingual early childhood deaf education: birth to 5 (Certificate); audiology (Au D); clinical psychology (PhD); deaf and hard of hearing infants, toddlers, and their families (Certificate); deaf education (MA, Ed S); deaf history (Certificate); deaf studies (Certificate); educating deaf students with disabilities (Certificate); education: teacher preparation (MA); educational neuroscience (PhD); hearing, speech and language sciences (MS, PhD); international development (MA); interpretation (MA, PhD); linguistics (MA, PhD); mental health counseling (MA); peer mentoring (Certificate); public administration (MPA); school counseling (MA); school psychology (Psy S); sign language teaching (MA); social work (MSW); speech-language pathology (MS). *Application deadline:* For fall admission, 2/15 for domestic students. Applications are processed on a rolling basis. *Application fee:* $75. Electronic applications accepted. *Application Contact:* Wednesday Luria, Coordinator of Prospective Graduate Student Services, 202-651-5400, Fax: 202-651-5295, E-mail: graduate.school@gallaudet.edu. *Dean, Graduate School and Continuing Studies*, Dr. Gaurav Mathur, 202-250-2380, Fax: 202-651-5027, E-mail: gaurav.mathur@gallaudet.edu.

GANNON UNIVERSITY, Erie, PA 16541-0001

General Information Independent-religious, coed, university. *Enrollment:* 4,416 graduate, professional, and undergraduate students; 555 full-time matriculated graduate/professional students (280 women), 538 part-time matriculated graduate/professional students (339 women). *Enrollment by degree level:* 851 master's, 199 doctoral, 43 other advanced degrees. *Graduate faculty:* 79 full-time (34 women), 41 part-time/adjunct (15 women). *Graduate housing:* Rooms and/or apartments available on a first-come, first-served basis to single and married students. *Student services:* Campus employment opportunities, campus safety program, career counseling, exercise/wellness program, free psychological counseling, international student services, low-cost health insurance, multicultural affairs office, services for students with disabilities, teacher training, writing training. *Library:* Nash Library. *Collection:* Books: 260,865 (physical); Serial titles: 56,251 (physical); Databases: 50. Weekly public service hours: 97. *Research affiliation:* Precision Rehabilitation Manufacturing (software development), AirBorn (PPS software enhancer), Department of Environmental Protection (baseline human health risk assessment), Precision Rehabilitation Manufacturing (software development), AirBorn (PPS software enhancer), AirBorn (PPS software enhancer).

Computer facilities: 386 computers available on campus for general student use. A campuswide network can be accessed from student residence rooms and from off campus. Online class registration is available.
Website: http://www.gannon.edu/

General Application Contact: Kara Morgan, Director of Graduate Admissions, 814-871-5831, Fax: 814-871-5827, E-mail: graduate@gannon.edu.

GRADUATE UNITS

School of Graduate Studies Students: 752 full-time (333 women), 537 part-time (282 women); includes 45 minority (19 Black or African American, non-Hispanic/Latino; 1 American Indian or Alaska Native, non-Hispanic/Latino; 9 Asian, non-Hispanic/Latino; 9 Hispanic/Latino; 1 Native Hawaiian or other Pacific Islander, non-Hispanic/Latino; 6 Two or more races, non-Hispanic/Latino), 492 international. Average age 27. 4,348 applicants, 56% accepted, 423 enrolled. *Faculty:* 93 full-time (49 women), 44 part-time/adjunct (25 women). *Financial support:* In 2015–16, 7 teaching assistantships (averaging $6,079 per year) were awarded; Federal Work-Study, scholarships/grants, and unspecified assistantships also available. Support available to part-time students. Financial award application deadline: 7/1; financial award applicants required to submit FAFSA. In 2015, 470 master's, 49 doctorates, 51 other advanced degrees awarded. *Degree program information:* Part-time and evening/weekend programs available. Part-time, evening/weekend, 100% online, blended/hybrid learning. *Application deadline:* Applications are processed on a rolling basis. *Application fee:* $25. Electronic applications accepted. *Application Contact:* Bridget Philip, Director of Graduate Admissions, 814-871-7412, E-mail: graduate@gannon.edu.

College of Engineering and Business Students: 379 full-time (75 women), 264 part-time (85 women); includes 17 minority (11 Black or African American, non-Hispanic/Latino; 4 Asian, non-Hispanic/Latino; 1 Hispanic/Latino; 1 Two or more races, non-Hispanic/Latino), 480 international. Average age 26. 3,812 applicants, 57% accepted, 273 enrolled. *Faculty:* 37 full-time (8 women), 16 part-time/adjunct (5 women). *Financial support:* Federal Work-Study and unspecified assistantships available. Financial award application deadline: 7/1; financial award applicants required to submit FAFSA. In 2015, 254 master's awarded. *Degree program information:* Part-time and evening/weekend programs available. Part-time, evening/weekend, 100% online, blended/hybrid learning. Offers applied computer science (MSCIS); business administration (MBA, MPA); computer and information science (MSCIS); computer and information sciences (MSCIS); electrical and computer engineering (MSEE, MSES); engineering and business (MBA, MPA, MS, MSCIS, MSEE, MSEM, MSES, MSME, Certificate); engineering management (MSEM); environmental health and engineering (MS); environmental science and engineering (MS); finance (MBA); human resources management (MBA); information analytics (MSCIS); information systems (MSCIS); marketing (MBA); mechanical engineering (MSME); public administration (MPA); software engineering (MSCIS); Web development (MSCIS). *Application deadline:* Applications are processed on a rolling basis. *Application fee:* $25. Electronic applications accepted. *Application Contact:* Bridget Philip, Director of Graduate Admissions, 814-871-7412, E-mail: graduate@gannon.edu. *Dean*, Dr. WIlliam L. Scheller, II, 814-871-7582, E-mail: scheller002@gannon.edu.

College of Humanities, Education, and Social Sciences Students: 51 full-time (37 women), 199 part-time (147 women); includes 5 minority (3 Black or African American, non-Hispanic/Latino; 1 Hispanic/Latino; 1 Native Hawaiian or other Pacific Islander, non-Hispanic/Latino), 5 international. Average age 33. 200 applicants, 60% accepted, 75 enrolled. *Faculty:* 20 full-time (10 women), 17 part-time/adjunct (12 women). *Financial support:* In 2015–16, 5 teaching assistantships (averaging $7,131 per year) were awarded; Federal Work-Study and unspecified assistantships also available. Financial award application deadline: 7/1; financial award applicants required to submit FAFSA. In 2015, 98 master's, 4 doctorates, 50 other advanced degrees awarded. *Degree program information:* Part-time and evening/weekend programs available. Part-time, evening/weekend, 100% online, blended/hybrid learning. Offers clinical mental health counseling (MS); criminalistics (MS); curriculum and instruction (M Ed); curriculum supervisor (Certificate); English (MA); English as a second language (Certificate); health communication (MA); humanities, education, and social sciences (M Ed, MA, MS, PhD, Certificate); organizational learning and leadership (PhD); pastoral studies (MA, Certificate); principal certification (Certificate); reading (M Ed); reading specialist (Certificate); special education supervisor (Certificate); superintendent letter of eligibility (Certificate); theological studies (Certificate). *Application deadline:* Applications are processed on a rolling basis. *Application fee:* $25. Electronic applications accepted. *Application Contact:* Bridget Philip, Director of Graduate Admissions, 814-871-7412, E-mail: graduate@gannon.edu. *Dean*, Dr. Linda Fleming, 814-871-7549, E-mail: fleming006@gannon.edu.

Morosky College of Health Professions and Sciences Students: 322 full-time (221 women), 74 part-time (50 women); includes 23 minority (5 Black or African American, non-Hispanic/Latino; 1 American Indian or Alaska Native, non-Hispanic/Latino; 5 Asian, non-Hispanic/Latino; 7 Hispanic/Latino; 5 Two or more races, non-Hispanic/Latino), 7 international. Average age 25. 336 applicants, 42% accepted, 75 enrolled. *Faculty:* 36 full-time (31 women), 11 part-time/adjunct (8 women). *Financial support:* In 2015–16, 2 teaching assistantships (averaging $3,452 per year) were awarded; Federal Work-Study, scholarships/grants, and unspecified assistantships also available. Financial award application deadline: 7/1; financial award applicants required to submit FAFSA. In 2015, 118 master's, 45 doctorates, 1 other advanced degree awarded. *Degree program information:* Part-time and evening/weekend programs available. Part-time, evening/weekend, 100% online. Offers athletic training (MAT); family nurse practitioner (MSN, Certificate); health professions and sciences (MAT, MPAS, MS, MSN, DNP, DPT, OTD, Certificate); human performance (MS); nurse anesthesia (MSN, Certificate); nursing administration (MSN); nursing practice (DNP); occupational therapy (MS, OTD); physical therapy (DPT); physician assistant science (MPAS); sport and exercise science (MS). *Application deadline:* Applications are processed on a rolling basis. *Application fee:* $25. Electronic applications accepted. *Application Contact:* Bridget Philip, Director of Graduate Admissions, 814-871-7412, E-mail: graduate@gannon.edu. *Dean*, Dr. Carolyn Master, 814-871-7568, E-mail: masters004@gannon.edu.

GARDNER-WEBB UNIVERSITY, Boiling Springs, NC 28017

General Information Independent-religious, coed, university. *Enrollment:* 4,305 graduate, professional, and undergraduate students; 222 full-time matriculated graduate/professional students (127 women), 1,473 part-time matriculated graduate/professional students (1,079 women). *Enrollment by degree level:* 1,259 master's, 398 doctoral, 38 other advanced degrees. *Graduate faculty:* 64 full-time (34 women), 70 part-time/adjunct (31 women). *Graduate housing:* Room and/or apartments available on a first-come, first-served basis to single students; on-campus housing not available to married students. *Student services:* Campus employment opportunities, campus safety program, career counseling, exercise/wellness program, free psychological counseling, international student services, low-cost health insurance, services for students with disabilities, teacher training, writing training. *Library:* Dover Memorial Library plus 1 other.

Computer facilities: Computer purchase and lease plans are available. 121 computers available on campus for general student use. A campuswide network can be accessed from student residence rooms and from off campus. Online class registration is available.
Website: http://www.gardner-webb.edu/

General Application Contact: Brandon Beach, Office of Graduate Admissions, 877-498-4723, Fax: 704-406-3895, E-mail: gradinfo@gardner-webb.edu.

GRADUATE UNITS

Graduate School Students: 71 full-time (48 women), 1,118 part-time (898 women); includes 371 minority (330 Black or African American, non-Hispanic/Latino; 8 American Indian or Alaska Native, non-Hispanic/Latino; 15 Asian, non-Hispanic/Latino; 18 Hispanic/Latino), 1 international. Average age 37. 1,064 applicants, 45% accepted, 401 enrolled. *Faculty:* 27 full-time (14 women), 50 part-time/adjunct (26 women). *Financial support:* Fellowships, Federal Work-Study, institutionally sponsored loans, and unspecified assistantships available. Support available to part-time students. In 2015, 180 master's, 23 doctorates, 45 other advanced degrees awarded. *Degree program information:* Part-time and evening/weekend programs available. Part-time, evening/weekend. Offers English (MA); English education (MA); physician assistant studies (MPAS); sport science and pedagogy (MA). *Application deadline:* Applications are processed on a rolling basis. *Application fee:* $0. Electronic applications accepted. *Application Contact:* Lamont Reeves, Office of Graduate Admissions, 877-498-4723, Fax: 704-406-3895, E-mail: gradinfo@gardner-webb.edu. *Dean*, Dr. Franki Burch, 704-406-4723, E-mail: gradschool@gardner-webb.edu.

Graduate School of Business Students: 27 full-time (12 women), 276 part-time (148 women); includes 92 minority (77 Black or African American, non-Hispanic/Latino; 6 Asian, non-Hispanic/Latino; 9 Hispanic/Latino), 2 international. Average age 33. 277 applicants, 59% accepted, 123 enrolled. *Faculty:* 10 full-time (1 woman), 6 part-time/adjunct (2 women). *Financial support:* In 2015–16, 23 students received support. Unspecified assistantships available. Support available to part-time students. Financial award applicants required to submit FAFSA. In 2015, 112 master's awarded. *Degree program information:* Part-time and evening/weekend programs available. Part-time, evening/weekend, online learning. Offers business (IMBA, M Acc, MBA). *Application deadline:* For spring admission, 1/15 for domestic students. Applications are processed on a rolling basis. Electronic applications accepted. *Application Contact:* Mischia Taylor, Director of Admissions, 877-498-4723, Fax: 704-406-3895, E-mail: mataylor@gardner-webb.edu. *Dean*, Dr. Van Graham, 704-406-4622, E-mail: vgraham@gardner-webb.edu.

School of Education Students: 19 full-time (14 women), 789 part-time (607 women); includes 313 minority (290 Black or African American, non-Hispanic/Latino; 5 American Indian or Alaska Native, non-Hispanic/Latino; 6 Asian, non-Hispanic/Latino; 12 Hispanic/Latino), 1 international. Average age 38. 584 applicants, 56% accepted, 269 enrolled. *Faculty:* 17 full-time (6 women), 50 part-time/adjunct (26 women). *Financial support:* Unspecified assistantships available. In 2015, 160 master's, 23 doctorates, 45 other advanced degrees awarded. *Degree program information:* Part-time and evening/weekend programs available. Part-time, evening/weekend. Offers curriculum and instruction (Ed D); educational leadership (Ed D); elementary education (MA); executive leadership studies (MA, Ed S); middle grades education (MA); organizational leadership (Ed D); school administration (MA). *Application deadline:* For fall admission, 8/1 priority date for domestic students. Applications are processed on a rolling basis. Electronic applications accepted. *Application Contact:* Office of Graduate Admissions, 877-498-4723, Fax: 704-406-3895, E-mail: gradinfo@gardner-webb.edu. *Dean*, Dr. Alan D. Eury, 704-406-4402, Fax: 704-406-3921, E-mail: dsimmons@gardner-webb.edu.

School of Nursing Students: 1 (woman) full-time, 241 part-time (224 women); includes 38 minority (28 Black or African American, non-Hispanic/Latino; 3 American Indian or Alaska Native, non-Hispanic/Latino; 5 Asian, non-Hispanic/Latino; 2 Hispanic/Latino). Average age 40. 263 applicants, 39% accepted, 89 enrolled. *Faculty:* 10 full-time (9 women), 11 part-time/adjunct (9 women). In 2015, 51 master's, 11 doctorates awarded. *Degree program information:* Part-time programs available. Part-time, online learning. Offers nursing (MSN, DNP). *Application Contact:* Office of Graduate Admissions, 877-498-4723, Fax: 704-406-3895, E-mail: gradinfo@gardner-webb.edu. *Dean*, Dr. Sharon Starr, 704-406-4358, Fax: 704-406-4329, E-mail: gradschool@gardner-webb.edu.

School of Psychology Students: 53 part-time (45 women); includes 12 minority (10 Black or African American, non-Hispanic/Latino; 2 Hispanic/Latino). Average age 32. 135 applicants, 20% accepted, 24 enrolled. *Faculty:* 5 full-time (4 women). *Financial support:* Unspecified assistantships available. In 2015, 29 master's awarded. *Degree program information:* Part-time and evening/weekend programs available. Part-time, evening/weekend. Offers mental health counseling (MA); school counseling (MA). *Application deadline:* For fall admission, 7/1 priority date for domestic students. Applications are processed on a rolling basis. Electronic applications accepted. *Application Contact:* Office of Graduate Admissions, 877-498-4723, Fax: 704-406-3895, E-mail: gradinfo@gardner-webb.edu. *Chair*, Dr. David Carscaddon, 704-406-4437, Fax: 704-406-4329, E-mail: dcarscaddon@gardner-webb.edu.

School of Divinity Students: 124 full-time (67 women), 79 part-time (33 women); includes 97 minority (85 Black or African American, non-Hispanic/Latino; 7 Asian, non-Hispanic/Latino; 5 Hispanic/Latino). Average age 40. 85 applicants, 52% accepted, 44 enrolled. *Faculty:* 12 full-time (2 women), 3 part-time/adjunct (1 woman). *Financial support:* Fellowships, institutionally sponsored loans, and unspecified assistantships available. Support available to part-time students. Financial award application deadline: 5/15. In 2015, 36 master's, 9 doctorates awarded. *Degree program information:* Part-time programs available. Part-time. Offers biblical studies (M Div); Christian education and formation (M Div); intercultural studies (M Div); ministry (D Min); missiology (M Div); pastoral care and counseling (M Div); pastoral care and counseling/member care for missionaries (D Min); pastoral studies (M Div). *Application deadline:* Applications are processed on a rolling basis. Electronic applications accepted. *Application Contact:* Kheresa Harmon, Director of Admissions, 704-406-3205, Fax: 704-406-3895, E-mail: kharmon@gardner-webb.edu. *Dean*, Dr. Robert W. Canoy, Sr., 704-406-4400, Fax: 704-406-3935, E-mail: rcanoy@gardner-webb.edu.

GARRETT-EVANGELICAL THEOLOGICAL SEMINARY, Evanston, IL 60201-3298

General Information Independent-religious, coed, graduate-only institution. *Graduate housing:* Rooms and/or apartments guaranteed to single students and available to married students. Housing application deadline: 4/1.

GRADUATE UNITS

Graduate and Professional Programs ***Degree program information:*** Part-time programs available. Part-time. Offers Bible and culture (PhD); Christian education (MA); Christian education and congregational studies (PhD); contemporary theology and culture (PhD); divinity (M Div); ethics, church, and society (MA); liturgical studies (PhD); ministry (D Min); music ministry (MA); pastoral care and counseling (MA); pastoral theology, personality, and culture (PhD); spiritual formation and evangelism (MA); theological studies (MTS). M Div/MSW offered jointly with Loyola University Chicago. Electronic applications accepted.

GATEWAY SEMINARY, Ontario, CA 91761-8642

General Information Independent-religious, coed, graduate-only institution. *Graduate housing:* Rooms and/or apartments available on a first-come, first-served basis to single and married students. Housing application deadline: 6/15.

GRADUATE UNITS

Graduate and Professional Programs ***Degree program information:*** Part-time and evening/weekend programs available. Part-time, evening/weekend. Offers divinity (M Div); early childhood education (Certificate); education leadership (MAEL, Diploma); ministry (D Min); theological studies (MTS); theology (Th M); youth ministry (Certificate). Electronic applications accepted.

GENERAL THEOLOGICAL SEMINARY, New York, NY 10011-4977

General Information Independent-religious, coed, graduate-only institution. *Graduate housing:* Rooms and/or apartments available to single and married students. Housing application deadline: 6/1.

GRADUATE UNITS

Graduate and Professional Programs ***Degree program information:*** Part-time and evening/weekend programs available. Part-time, evening/weekend. Offers Anglican studies (STM, Th D, Certificate); ascetical theology (Certificate); biblical studies (Certificate); congregational development (Certificate); divinity (M Div); historical and theological studies (Certificate); spiritual direction (MASD, STM, Certificate); theology (MA).

GENEVA COLLEGE, Beaver Falls, PA 15010-3599

General Information Independent-religious, coed, comprehensive institution. *Enrollment:* 1,512 graduate, professional, and undergraduate students; 171 full-time matriculated graduate/professional students (112 women), 79 part-time matriculated graduate/professional students (51 women). *Enrollment by degree level:* 250 master's. *Graduate faculty:* 32 full-time (13 women), 33 part-time/adjunct (15 women). *Tuition, area resident:* Full-time $11,520. *Graduate housing:* On-campus housing not available. *Student services:* Campus employment opportunities, campus safety program, career counseling, free psychological counseling, international student services, low-cost health insurance, multicultural affairs office, services for students with disabilities, teacher training. *Library:* McCartney Library plus 3 others. *Research affiliation:* INOVA Fairfax Hospital (cardiovascular science).

Computer facilities: 150 computers available on campus for general student use. A campuswide network can be accessed from student residence rooms and from off campus. Online class registration is available.
Website: http://www.geneva.edu/

General Application Contact: Information Contact, 724-846-5100.

GRADUATE UNITS

Master of Arts in Counseling Program Students: 44 full-time (34 women), 36 part-time (26 women); includes 14 minority (12 Black or African American, non-Hispanic/Latino; 1 Hispanic/Latino; 1 Two or more races, non-Hispanic/Latino). Average age 36. 61 applicants, 59% accepted, 31 enrolled. *Faculty:* 6 full-time (2 women), 7 part-time/adjunct (6 women). *Financial support:* In 2015–16, 3 students received support. Research assistantships, teaching assistantships, career-related internships or fieldwork, and unspecified assistantships available. Financial award application deadline: 8/1; financial award applicants required to submit FAFSA. In 2015, 29 master's awarded. *Degree program information:* Part-time and evening/weekend programs available. Part-time, evening/weekend. Offers clinical mental health counseling (MA); marriage and family counseling (MA); school counseling (MA). *Application deadline:* For fall admission, 9/1 for domestic students; for spring admission, 1/10 for domestic students. Applications are processed on a rolling basis. Electronic applications accepted. *Application Contact:* Marina Frazier, Graduate Program Manager, 724-847-

6697, E-mail: counseling@geneva.edu. *Program Director*, Dr. Shannon Shiderly, 724-847-6649, Fax: 724-847-6101, E-mail: slshider@geneva.edu.

Master of Arts in Higher Education Program Students: 48 full-time (30 women), 4 part-time (2 women); includes 6 minority (1 Black or African American, non-Hispanic/Latino; 3 Hispanic/Latino; 2 Two or more races, non-Hispanic/Latino), 1 international. Average age 26. 51 applicants, 71% accepted, 23 enrolled. *Faculty:* 1 full-time (0 women), 11 part-time/adjunct (5 women). *Financial support:* In 2015–16, 37 students received support. Unspecified assistantships available. Financial award application deadline: 8/1; financial award applicants required to submit FAFSA. In 2015, 39 master's awarded. *Degree program information:* Part-time and evening/weekend programs available. Part-time, evening/weekend, online learning. Offers campus ministry (MA); college teaching (MA); educational leadership (MA); student affairs administration (MA). *Application deadline:* For fall admission, 9/1 priority date for domestic students; for winter admission, 1/2 priority date for domestic students; for spring admission, 3/11 priority date for domestic students. Applications are processed on a rolling basis. Electronic applications accepted. *Application Contact:* Jerryn S. Carson, Program Coordinator, 724-847-6510, Fax: 724-847-6696, E-mail: hed@geneva.edu. *Program Director*, Dr. Keith Martel, 724-847-6884, Fax: 724-847-6107, E-mail: hed@geneva.edu.

Master of Education in Reading Program Students: 2 full-time (both women), 4 part-time (all women). Average age 30. 1 applicant, 100% accepted. *Faculty:* 5 full-time (all women). *Financial support:* In 2015–16, 4 students received support. Scholarships/grants available. Financial award application deadline: 9/1; financial award applicants required to submit FAFSA. In 2015, 1 master's awarded. *Degree program information:* Part-time and evening/weekend programs available. Part-time, evening/weekend. Offers reading (M Ed). *Application deadline:* Applications are processed on a rolling basis. Electronic applications accepted. *Application Contact:* Marina Frazier, Director of Graduate Enrollment, 724-846-6697, E-mail: reading@geneva.edu. *Program Director*, Dr. Adel Aiken, 724-847-5002, E-mail: reading@geneva.edu.

Master of Education in Special Education Program Average age 34. 1 applicant. *Faculty:* 5 full-time (all women). *Financial support:* In 2015–16, 1 student received support. Scholarships/grants available. Financial award applicants required to submit FAFSA. In 2015, 1 master's awarded. *Degree program information:* Part-time and evening/weekend programs available. Part-time, evening/weekend. Offers special education (M Ed). *Application deadline:* For fall admission, 8/1 priority date for domestic students; for spring admission, 12/1 priority date for domestic students. Applications are processed on a rolling basis. *Application fee:* $0. Electronic applications accepted. *Application Contact:* Marina Frazier, Director of Graduate Enrollment, 724-847-6697, E-mail: speced@geneva.edu. *Program Head*, Dr. Karen Schmalz, 724-847-6125, E-mail: kschmalz@geneva.edu.

Master of Science in Cardiovascular Science Program Students: 3 full-time (0 women), 1 international. Average age 28. *Faculty:* 1 full-time (0 women), 2 part-time/adjunct (1 woman). *Financial support:* Application deadline: 8/1; applicants required to submit FAFSA. In 2015, 1 master's awarded. Offers cardiovascular science (MS). *Application deadline:* For fall admission, 5/30 for domestic students. Applications are processed on a rolling basis. Electronic applications accepted. *Program Coordinator*, Dr. David A. Essig, 724-847-6900, E-mail: dessig@geneva.edu.

Program in Business Administration Students: 20 full-time (7 women), 15 part-time (4 women); includes 2 minority (1 Black or African American, non-Hispanic/Latino; 1 Asian, non-Hispanic/Latino), 1 international. Average age 34. 27 applicants, 70% accepted, 10 enrolled. *Faculty:* 9 full-time (2 women), 1 part-time/adjunct (0 women). *Financial support:* In 2015–16, 1 student received support. Scholarships/grants available. Financial award application deadline: 8/1; financial award applicants required to submit FAFSA. *Degree program information:* Part-time and evening/weekend programs available. Part-time, evening/weekend. Offers business administration (MBA); finance (MBA); marketing (MBA); operations (MBA). *Application deadline:* For fall admission, 3/1 priority date for domestic students; for spring admission, 11/1 priority date for domestic students. Applications are processed on a rolling basis. Electronic applications accepted. *Application Contact:* Marina Frazier, Director of Graduate Enrollment, 724-847-6697, E-mail: mba@geneva.edu. *Director of the MBA Program*, Dr. Gary Vander Plaats, 724-847-6619, E-mail: gpvander@geneva.edu.

Program in Organizational Leadership Students: 54 full-time (39 women), 18 part-time (14 women); includes 19 minority (16 Black or African American, non-Hispanic/Latino; 2 Hispanic/Latino; 1 Two or more races, non-Hispanic/Latino). Average age 44. 40 applicants, 60% accepted, 21 enrolled. *Faculty:* 1 (woman) full-time, 11 part-time/adjunct (2 women). *Financial support:* In 2015–16, 50 students received support. Scholarships/grants available. Financial award application deadline: 8/1; financial award applicants required to submit FAFSA. In 2015, 33 master's awarded. *Degree program information:* Evening/weekend programs available. Evening/weekend. Offers organizational leadership (MS). *Application deadline:* For fall admission, 9/21 for domestic students; for spring admission, 2/23 for domestic students; for summer admission, 7/22 for domestic students. Applications are processed on a rolling basis. *Application fee:* $15. Electronic applications accepted. *Application Contact:* Linda Roundtree, Enrollment Counselor, 724-847-6856, Fax: 724-847-4198, E-mail: lroundtr@geneva.edu. *Chair*, Dr. James K. Dittmar, 724-847-6853, Fax: 724-847-4198, E-mail: jkd@geneva.edu.

GEORGE FOX UNIVERSITY, Newberg, OR 97132-2697

General Information Independent-religious, coed, university. *Enrollment:* 3,899 graduate, professional, and undergraduate students; 385 full-time matriculated graduate/professional students (241 women), 818 part-time matriculated graduate/professional students (420 women). *Enrollment by degree level:* 795 master's, 302 doctoral, 106 other advanced degrees. *Graduate faculty:* 58 full-time (25 women), 79 part-time/adjunct (39 women). *Graduate housing:* On-campus housing not available. *Student services:* Campus employment opportunities, career counseling, international student services, low-cost health insurance, services for students with disabilities, writing training. *Library:* Murdock Learning Resource Center.

Computer facilities: A campuswide network can be accessed from student residence rooms and from off campus. Online class registration, online acceptance of financial aid are available.
Website: http://www.georgefox.edu/

General Application Contact: Patrick Kelley, Director for Graduate Admissions, 503-554-6026, Fax: 503-554-3110, E-mail: pkelley@georgefox.edu.

GRADUATE UNITS

College of Business ***Financial support:*** Applicants required to submit FAFSA. *Degree program information:* Part-time and evening/weekend programs available. Part-time, evening/weekend, online learning. Offers accounting (DBA); finance (MBA); management (DBA); management and leadership (MBA); marketing (DBA); organizational strategy (MBA); strategic human resource management (MBA). MBA offered in Newberg, OR and in Portland, OR. *Application deadline:* For fall admission, 8/1 for domestic and international students; for spring admission, 12/1 for domestic and international students. Applications are processed on a rolling basis. *Application fee:* $40. Electronic applications accepted. *Application Contact:* Patrick Kelley, Director of Graduate Admissions, 800-493-4937, Fax: 503-554-6111, E-mail: business@georgefox.edu.

College of Education Offers administrative leadership (Ed S); clinical mental health counseling (MA); continuing administrator license (Certificate); education (M Ed, MA, MAT, Ed D, Certificate, Ed S); educational leadership (M Ed); educational technology (M Ed); English for speakers of other languages (M Ed); ESOL (Certificate); initial administrator license (Certificate); marriage, couple and family counseling (MA, Certificate); reading (M Ed, Certificate); school counseling (MA, Certificate); school psychology (Ed S); special education (M Ed); teaching (MAT). *Application Contact:* Kipp Wilfong, Graduate Admissions Counselor, 800-631-0921, Fax: 503-554-3110, E-mail: kwilfong@georgefox.edu.

George Fox Evangelical Seminary ***Financial support:*** Career-related internships or fieldwork and scholarships/grants available. Financial award application deadline: 5/1; financial award applicants required to submit FAFSA. *Degree program information:* Part-time and evening/weekend programs available. Part-time, evening/weekend, online learning. Offers Biblical studies (M Div); chaplaincy studies (M Div); Christian earthkeeping (M Div); Christian history and theology (M Div); intercultural studies (MA); leadership and spiritual formation (D Min); leadership and the emerging culture (D Min); ministry leadership (MA); partners in ministry (Certificate); pastoral studies (M Div); spiritual formation (MA, Certificate); spiritual formation and discipleship (M Div); theological studies (MA). *Application deadline:* For fall admission, 7/1 for domestic and international students; for winter admission, 11/1 for domestic and international students; for spring admission, 4/1 for domestic and international students. Applications are processed on a rolling basis. *Application fee:* $40. Electronic applications accepted. *Application Contact:* Ty Sohlman, Admissions Counselor, 503-554-6122, E-mail: tsohlman@georgefox.edu. *Vice President and Dean*, Dr. Chuck Conniry, 503-554-6152, E-mail: cconniry@georgefox.edu.

Program in Clinical Psychology ***Financial support:*** Scholarships/grants available. Financial award application deadline: 5/15; financial award applicants required to submit FAFSA. Offers clinical psychology (Psy D). *Application deadline:* For fall admission, 12/15 for domestic and international students. *Application fee:* $40. Electronic applications accepted. *Application Contact:* Megan Janes, Admissions Counselor, 503-554-6168, Fax: 503-554-6026, E-mail: psyd@georgefox.edu. *Chairperson*, Dr. Mary Peterson, 503-554-2377, E-mail: mpeterso@georgefox.edu.

Program in Physical Therapy ***Financial support:*** Applicants required to submit FAFSA. Offers physical therapy (DPT). *Application deadline:* For fall admission, 12/1 for domestic and international students. *Application fee:* $40. Electronic applications accepted. *Application Contact:* Cristina Schmitt, Director of Graduate Admissions, 503-554-6097, Fax: 503-554-3110, E-mail: dpt@georgefox.edu. *Director*, Dr. Tyler Cuddeford, 503-554-2452, E-mail: tcuddeford@georgefox.edu.

School of Social Work Offers social work (MSW). *Application Contact:* Patrick Kelley, Director for Graduate Admissions, 503-554-6026, Fax: 503-554-3110, E-mail: pkelley@georgefox.edu. *Director*, Cliff Rosenbohm, 503-554-2748, E-mail: crosenbo@georgefox.edu.

GEORGE MASON UNIVERSITY, Fairfax, VA 22030

General Information State-supported, coed, university. CGS member. *Enrollment:* 33,925 graduate, professional, and undergraduate students; 4,009 full-time matriculated graduate/professional students (2,127 women), 5,988 part-time matriculated graduate/professional students (3,536 women). *Enrollment by degree level:* 6,807 master's, 2,728 doctoral, 462 other advanced degrees. *Graduate faculty:* 1,402 full-time (584 women), 1,172 part-time/adjunct (553 women). *Graduate housing:* Room and/or apartments available on a first-come, first-served basis to single students; on-campus housing not available to married students. Housing application deadline: 5/1. *Student services:* Campus employment opportunities, campus safety program, career counseling, child daycare facilities, exercise/wellness program, free psychological counseling, grant writing training, international student services, low-cost health insurance, multicultural affairs office, services for students with disabilities, teacher training, writing training. *Library:* Fenwick Library plus 3 others. *Collection:* Books: 1.3 million (physical), 1.5 million (digital/electronic); Serial titles: 1,244 (physical), 102,222 (digital/electronic); Databases: 793. Weekly public service hours: 87; study areas open 24 hours, 5–7 days a week; students can reserve study rooms. *Research affiliation:* L3 Communications (high-tech communication technology), Alion Science and Technology Corporation (science and technology research), Northrop Grumman Corporation (high-tech communication technology), Science Applications International Corporation (science and technology), Lockheed Martin Corporation (science and technology), Inova Health System (health care and medical research).

Computer facilities: Computer purchase and lease plans are available. 622 computers available on campus for general student use. A campuswide network can be accessed from student residence rooms and from off campus. Online class registration is available.
Website: http://www.gmu.edu/

General Application Contact: Graduate Admissions Office, 703-993-9700, Fax: 703-993-2392, E-mail: masongrad@gmu.edu.

GRADUATE UNITS

Antonin Scalia Law School Students: 329 full-time (145 women), 155 part-time (65 women); includes 108 minority (15 Black or African American, non-Hispanic/Latino; 50 Asian, non-Hispanic/Latino; 31 Hispanic/Latino; 1 Native Hawaiian or other Pacific Islander, non-Hispanic/Latino; 11 Two or more races, non-Hispanic/Latino), 9 international. 2,059 applicants, 35% accepted, 157 enrolled. *Faculty:* 31 full-time (7 women), 113 part-time/adjunct (32 women). *Financial support:* Fellowships, research assistantships, career-related internships or fieldwork, scholarships/grants, and tuition waivers (full and partial) available. Support available to part-time students. *Degree program information:* Part-time and evening/weekend programs available. Part-time, evening/weekend. Offers intellectual property (LL M); law (JD); law and economics (LL M); U.S. law (LL M). *Application deadline:* For fall admission, 4/1 for domestic and international students. Applications are processed on a rolling basis. *Application fee:* $0. Electronic applications accepted. *Application Contact:* Alison H. Price, Associate Dean for Admissions and Enrollment Management, 703-993-8010, Fax: 703-993-8088, E-mail: lawadmit@gmu.edu. *Dean*, Henry N. Butler, 703-993-8644, Fax: 703-993-8088.

College of Education and Human Development Students: 384 full-time (307 women), 2,129 part-time (1,706 women); includes 635 minority (243 Black or African American, non-Hispanic/Latino; 9 American Indian or Alaska Native, non-Hispanic/Latino; 142 Asian, non-Hispanic/Latino; 187 Hispanic/Latino; 5 Native Hawaiian or other Pacific Islander, non-Hispanic/Latino; 49 Two or more races, non-Hispanic/Latino), 59 international. Average age 34. 1,392 applicants, 74% accepted, 773 enrolled. *Faculty:* 120 full-time (80 women), 198 part-time/adjunct (131 women). *Financial support:* In 2015–16, 108 students received support, including 15 fellowships (averaging $11,750 per year), 72 research assistantships with tuition reimbursements available (averaging $13,483 per year), 32 teaching assistantships with tuition reimbursements available (averaging $3,978 per year); career-related internships or fieldwork, Federal Work-Study, scholarships/grants, unspecified assistantships, and health care benefits (for full-time research or teaching assistantship recipients) also available. Support available to part-time students. Financial award application deadline: 3/1; financial award applicants required to submit FAFSA. In 2015, 826 master's, 36 doctorates, 196 other advanced degrees awarded. *Degree program information:* Part-time and evening/weekend programs available. Part-time, evening/weekend, online learning. Offers advanced international baccalaureate (M Ed); assistive technology (M Ed); community agency counseling (M Ed); counseling and development (PhD, Certificate); designing digital learning in schools (M Ed); early childhood education (M Ed); early childhood education for diverse learners (M Ed); education and human development (M Ed, MS, PhD, Certificate); education leadership (M Ed, PhD, Certificate); educational psychology (MS, PhD, Certificate); elementary education (M Ed); English as a second language (M Ed); exercise, fitness, and health promotion (MS); gifted child education (M Ed); higher education (PhD); history (M Ed); literacy (M Ed); literacy leadership for diverse schools (M Ed); physical education (M Ed); school counseling PK-12 (M Ed); science K-12 (M Ed); secondary education (M Ed); special education (M Ed); teacher leadership (M Ed); teaching culturally, linguistically diverse and exceptional learners (M Ed); transformative teaching (M Ed). *Application fee:* $75 ($80 for international students). Electronic applications accepted. *Application Contact:* Nicole Mariam, Graduate Admissions Coordinator, 703-993-3832, Fax: 703-993-2020, E-mail: nwhite5@gmu.edu. *Dean*, Mark Ginsberg, 703-993-2004, Fax: 703-993-2001, E-mail: mginsber@gmu.edu.

College of Health and Human Services Students: 353 full-time (295 women), 416 part-time (349 women); includes 310 minority (128 Black or African American, non-Hispanic/Latino; 2 American Indian or Alaska Native, non-Hispanic/Latino; 100 Asian, non-Hispanic/Latino; 67 Hispanic/Latino; 2 Native Hawaiian or other Pacific Islander, non-Hispanic/Latino; 11 Two or more races, non-Hispanic/Latino), 44 international. Average age 33. 769 applicants, 65% accepted, 266 enrolled. *Faculty:* 93 full-time (66 women), 121 part-time/adjunct (100 women). *Financial support:* In 2015–16, 52 students received support, including 2 fellowships (averaging $15,000 per year), 51 research assistantships with tuition reimbursements available (averaging $15,971 per year), 7 teaching assistantships with tuition reimbursements available (averaging $4,412 per year); career-related internships or fieldwork, Federal Work-Study, scholarships/grants, unspecified assistantships, and health care benefits (for full-time research or teaching assistantship recipients) also available. Support available to part-time students. Financial award application deadline: 3/1; financial award applicants required to submit FAFSA. In 2015, 252 master's, 28 doctorates, 21 other advanced degrees awarded. *Degree program information:* Part-time and evening/weekend programs available. Part-time, evening/weekend, online learning. Offers global and community health (Certificate); global health (MS); health and human services (MHA, MPH, MS, MSN, MSW, DNP, PhD, Certificate); health and medical policy (MS); health systems management (MHA); nursing (PhD); nutrition (MS); public health (MPH); rehabilitation science (PhD, Certificate); social work (MSW). *Application fee:* $75 ($80 for international students). Electronic applications accepted. *Application Contact:* Kelly Benedicto, Administrative Office Specialist, Graduate Admissions, 703-993-8246, Fax: 703-993-3606, E-mail: kbenedi2@gmu.edu. *Dean*, Dr. Thomas Prohaska, 703-993-1918, Fax: 703-993-1943, E-mail: tprohask@gmu.edu.

College of Humanities and Social Sciences Students: 786 full-time (471 women), 731 part-time (409 women); includes 266 minority (86 Black or African American, non-Hispanic/Latino; 2 American Indian or Alaska Native, non-Hispanic/Latino; 46 Asian, non-Hispanic/Latino; 96 Hispanic/Latino; 2 Native Hawaiian or other Pacific Islander, non-Hispanic/Latino; 34 Two or more races, non-Hispanic/Latino), 106 international. Average age 32. 2,004 applicants, 45% accepted, 440 enrolled. *Faculty:* 385 full-time (186 women), 242 part-time/adjunct (139 women). *Financial support:* In 2015–16, 456 students received support, including 42 fellowships (averaging $6,921 per year), 211 research assistantships with tuition reimbursements available (averaging $14,079 per year), 274 teaching assistantships with tuition reimbursements available (averaging $9,550 per year); career-related internships or fieldwork, Federal Work-Study, scholarships/grants, unspecified assistantships, and health care benefits (for full-time research or teaching assistantship recipients) also available. Support available to part-time students. Financial award application deadline: 3/1; financial award applicants required to submit FAFSA. In 2015, 394 master's, 64 doctorates, 31 other advanced degrees awarded. *Degree program information:* Part-time and evening/weekend programs available. Part-time, evening/weekend. Offers anthropology (MA); applied developmental psychology (Certificate); art history (MA); cognitive and behavioral neuroscience (MA); communication (MA, PhD, Certificate); community college education (DA); community college teaching (MAIS); creative writing (MFA); criminology, law and society (MA, PhD); cultural studies (PhD); economics (MA, PhD, Graduate Certificate); English (MA, Certificate); ethics and public affairs (MA); foreign languages (MA); global affairs (MA); higher education (Certificate); history (PhD); humanities and social sciences (MA, MAIS, MFA, DA, PhD, Certificate, Graduate Certificate); industrial/organizational psychology (PhD); linguistics (PhD); Middle East and Islamic studies (MA, Certificate); sociology (PhD). *Application deadline:* For fall admission, 2/1 for domestic and international students. *Application fee:* $75 ($80 for international students). Electronic applications accepted. *Application Contact:* Nicollette Williams, Graduate Admissions Specialist, 703-993-6144, E-mail: nwilli16@gmu.edu. *Dean*, Deborah A. Boehm-Davis, 703-993-8715, Fax: 703-993-8714, E-mail: dbdavis@gmu.edu.

College of Science Students: 471 full-time (240 women), 462 part-time (203 women); includes 252 minority (77 Black or African American, non-Hispanic/Latino; 3 American Indian or Alaska Native, non-Hispanic/Latino; 92 Asian, non-Hispanic/Latino; 61 Hispanic/Latino; 1 Native Hawaiian or other Pacific Islander, non-Hispanic/Latino; 18 Two or more races, non-Hispanic/Latino), 131 international. Average age 32. 941 applicants, 58% accepted, 263 enrolled. *Faculty:* 299 full-time (97 women), 80 part-time/adjunct (25 women). *Financial support:* In 2015–16, 278 students received support, including 27 fellowships (averaging $7,419 per year), 145 research assistantships with tuition reimbursements available (averaging $17,202 per year), 133 teaching assistantships with tuition reimbursements available (averaging $15,156 per year); career-related internships or fieldwork, Federal Work-Study, scholarships/grants, and health care benefits (for full-time research or teaching assistantship recipients) also available. Support available to part-time students. Financial award application deadline: 3/1; financial award applicants required to submit FAFSA. In 2015, 158 master's, 53 doctorates, 73 other advanced degrees awarded. *Degree program information:* Part-time and evening/weekend programs available. Part-time, evening/weekend. Offers applied and engineering physics (MS); aquatic ecology (MS); chemistry (MS); chemistry and biochemistry (PhD); climate dynamics (PhD); computational science and informatics (PhD); computational techniques and applications (Certificate); earth system science (MS); earth systems and geoinformation sciences (PhD); forensic science (MS); geography and geoinformation science (Certificate); mathematical sciences (MS, PhD, Certificate); neuroscience (MAIS, PhD); science (MAIS, MS, PhD, Certificate); systems biology (PhD). *Application fee:* $75 ($80 for international students). Electronic applications accepted. *Application Contact:* Melissa C. Hayes, Graduate Programs Director, 703-993-3430, Fax: 703-993-9033, E-mail: mhayes5@gmu.edu. *Dean*, Peggy Agouris, 703-993-1362, Fax: 703-993-9614, E-mail: pagouris@gmu.edu.

College of Visual and Performing Arts Students: 99 full-time (68 women), 138 part-time (81 women); includes 51 minority (15 Black or African American, non-Hispanic/Latino; 12 Asian, non-Hispanic/Latino; 17 Hispanic/Latino; 1 Native Hawaiian or other Pacific Islander, non-Hispanic/Latino; 6 Two or more races, non-Hispanic/Latino), 19 international. Average age 31. 179 applicants, 56% accepted, 53 enrolled. *Faculty:* 71 full-time (30 women), 149 part-time/adjunct (80 women). *Financial support:* In 2015–16, 8 students received support, including 1 fellowship (averaging $10,000 per year), 2 research assistantships with tuition reimbursements available (averaging $20,000 per year), 8 teaching assistantships with tuition reimbursements available (averaging $5,674 per year); career-related internships or fieldwork, Federal Work-Study, scholarships/grants, unspecified assistantships, and health care benefits (for full-time research or teaching assistantship recipients) also available. Support available to part-time students. Financial award application deadline: 3/1; financial award applicants required to submit FAFSA. In 2015, 60 master's, 6 other advanced degrees awarded. *Degree program information:* Part-time and evening/weekend programs available. Part-time, evening/weekend. Offers art education (MAT); arts management (MA, Certificate); drawing (MFA); graphic design (MA); visual and performing arts (MA, MAT, MFA, MM, DMA, PhD, Certificate). *Application fee:* $75 ($80 for international students). Electronic applications accepted. *Application Contact:* Dena Hudson, Assistant Director, Admissions and Student Outreach, 703-993-5572, Fax: 703-993-9037, E-mail: dbarbour@gmu.edu. *Dean*, Davis Rick, 703-993-8624, Fax: 703-993-8883, E-mail: rdavi4@gmu.edu.

School of Music Students: 37 full-time (19 women), 52 part-time (20 women); includes 20 minority (6 Black or African American, non-Hispanic/Latino; 6 Asian, non-Hispanic/Latino; 7 Hispanic/Latino; 1 Native Hawaiian or other Pacific Islander, non-Hispanic/Latino), 4 international. Average age 33. 65 applicants, 63% accepted, 23 enrolled. *Faculty:* 19 full-time (8 women), 66 part-time/adjunct (24 women). *Financial support:* In 2015–16, 4 students received support, including 1 fellowship (averaging $10,000 per year), 2 research assistantships with tuition reimbursements available (averaging $20,000 per year), 8 teaching assistantships with tuition reimbursements available (averaging $5,674 per year); career-related internships or fieldwork, Federal Work-Study, scholarships/grants, unspecified assistantships, and health care benefits (for full-time research or teaching assistantship recipients) also available. Support available to part-time students. Financial award application deadline: 3/1; financial award applicants required to submit FAFSA. In 2015, 1 other advanced degree awarded. Offers composition (MM, DMA); instrumental performance artist (Certificate); music education (PhD); musical arts (DMA). *Application fee:* $75 ($80 for international students). Electronic applications accepted. *Application Contact:* Dr. Lisa A. Billingham, Director of Graduate Studies, 703-993-3778, Fax: 703-993-1394, E-mail: lbillin1@gmu.edu. *Managing Director*, Dr. Linda Apple Monson, 703-993-3580, Fax: 703-993-1394, E-mail: lmonson@gmu.edu.

School for Conflict Analysis and Resolution Students: 139 full-time (79 women), 167 part-time (96 women); includes 83 minority (41 Black or African American, non-Hispanic/Latino; 16 Asian, non-Hispanic/Latino; 18 Hispanic/Latino; 1 Native Hawaiian or other Pacific Islander, non-Hispanic/Latino; 7 Two or more races, non-Hispanic/Latino), 34 international. Average age 34. 346 applicants, 52% accepted, 80 enrolled. *Faculty:* 19 full-time (10 women), 17 part-time/adjunct (7 women). *Financial support:* In 2015–16, 43 students received support, including 14 fellowships (averaging $6,774 per year), 24 research assistantships with tuition reimbursements available (averaging $16,120 per year), 10 teaching assistantships with tuition reimbursements available (averaging $6,478 per year); career-related internships or fieldwork, Federal Work-Study, scholarships/grants, unspecified assistantships, and health care benefits (for full-time research or teaching assistantship recipients) also available. Support available to part-time students. Financial award application deadline: 3/1; financial award applicants required to submit FAFSA. In 2015, 70 master's, 6 doctorates, 5 other advanced degrees awarded. *Degree program information:* Part-time and evening/weekend programs available. Part-time, evening/weekend. Offers conflict analysis and resolution (MS, PhD, Certificate). *Application fee:* $75 ($80 for international students). Electronic applications accepted. *Application Contact:* Monique Barner, Assistant Director for Graduate Admissions, 703-993-3655, Fax: 703-993-1302, E-mail: mwilli43@gmu.edu. *Dean*, Kevin Avruch, 703-993-3607, Fax: 703-993-1302, E-mail: kavruch@gmu.edu.

School of Business Students: 391 full-time (146 women), 121 part-time (49 women); includes 175 minority (60 Black or African American, non-Hispanic/Latino; 64 Asian, non-Hispanic/Latino; 36 Hispanic/Latino; 1 Native Hawaiian or other Pacific Islander, non-Hispanic/Latino; 14 Two or more races, non-Hispanic/Latino), 37 international. Average age 33. 683 applicants, 59% accepted, 254 enrolled. *Faculty:* 93 full-time (31 women), 61 part-time/adjunct (19 women). *Financial support:* In 2015–16, 19 students received support, including 13 research assistantships with tuition reimbursements available (averaging $7,591 per year), 8 teaching assistantships with tuition reimbursements available (averaging $7,668 per year); career-related internships or fieldwork, Federal Work-Study, scholarships/grants, unspecified assistantships, and health care benefits (for full-time research or teaching assistantship recipients) also available. Support available to part-time students. Financial award application deadline: 3/1; financial award applicants required to submit FAFSA. In 2015, 253 master's, 8 other advanced degrees awarded. *Degree program information:* Part-time and evening/weekend programs available. Part-time, evening/weekend, online learning. Offers accounting (MS, Certificate); business (EMBA, MBA, MS, Certificate); business administration (MBA); management of secure information systems (MS); technology management (MS). *Application fee:* $75 ($80 for international students). Electronic applications accepted. *Application Contact:* Kevin Rockmann, Associate Dean of Graduate Programs, 703-993-4988, Fax: 703-993-1870, E-mail: krockman@gmu.edu. *Dean*, Sarah E. Nutter, 703-993-1807, Fax: 703-993-1867, E-mail: snutter@gmu.edu.

School of Policy, Government, and International Affairs Students: 306 full-time (146 women), 737 part-time (373 women); includes 302 minority (111 Black or African American, non-Hispanic/Latino; 1 American Indian or Alaska Native, non-Hispanic/Latino; 64 Asian, non-Hispanic/Latino; 98 Hispanic/Latino; 1 Native Hawaiian or other Pacific Islander, non-Hispanic/Latino; 27 Two or more races, non-Hispanic/Latino), 66 international. Average age 32. 792 applicants, 65% accepted, 262 enrolled. *Faculty:* 79 full-time (26 women), 40 part-time/adjunct (10 women). *Financial support:* In 2015–16, 69 students received support, including 8 fellowships (averaging $9,106 per year), 37 research assistantships with tuition reimbursements available (averaging $17,639 per year), 13 teaching assistantships (averaging $14,113 per year); career-related internships or fieldwork, Federal Work-Study, scholarships/grants, unspecified assistantships, and health care benefits (for full-time research or teaching assistantship recipients) also available. Support available to part-time students. Financial award application deadline: 3/1; financial award applicants required to submit FAFSA. In 2015, 434 master's, 21 doctorates, 25 other advanced degrees awarded. *Degree program information:* Part-time and evening/weekend programs available. Part-time, evening/weekend. Offers administration of justice (Certificate); biodefense (MS, PhD); international commerce and policy (MA); organization development and knowledge management (MS); peace operations (MS); policy, government, and international affairs (MA, MPA, MPP, MS, PhD, Certificate); political science (MA, PhD); public administration (MPA); public policy (MPP, PhD); transportation policy, operations and logistics (MA, Certificate). *Application fee:* $75 ($80 for international students). Electronic applications accepted. *Application Contact:* Travis Major, Director of Graduate Admissions, 703-993-3183, Fax: 703-993-4876, E-mail: tmajor@gmu.edu. *Dean*, Mark Rozell, 703-993-8171, Fax: 703-993-8215, E-mail: mrozell@gmu.edu.

Volgenau School of Engineering Students: 726 full-time (223 women), 893 part-time (194 women); includes 388 minority (82 Black or African American, non-Hispanic/Latino; 214 Asian, non-Hispanic/Latino; 62 Hispanic/Latino; 3 Native Hawaiian or other Pacific Islander, non-Hispanic/Latino; 27 Two or more races, non-Hispanic/Latino), 615 international. Average age 30. 2,219 applicants, 54% accepted, 482 enrolled. *Faculty:* 167 full-time (40 women), 166 part-time/adjunct (16 women). *Financial support:* In 2015–16, 260 students received support, including 8 fellowships (averaging $11,215 per year), 110 research assistantships with tuition reimbursements available (averaging $15,911 per year), 179 teaching assistantships with tuition reimbursements available (averaging $11,074 per year); career-related internships or fieldwork, Federal Work-Study, scholarships/grants, unspecified assistantships, and health care benefits (for full-time research or teaching assistantship recipients) also available. Support available to part-time students. Financial award application deadline: 3/1; financial award applicants required to submit FAFSA. In 2015, 492 master's, 40 doctorates, 82 other advanced degrees awarded. *Degree program information:* Part-time and evening/weekend programs available. Part-time, evening/weekend, online learning. Offers applied information technology (MS); bioengineering (PhD); biostatistics (MS); computer engineering (MS); computer science (MS, PhD, Certificate); construction project management (MS); data analytics engineering (MS); electrical and computer engineering (PhD, Certificate); engineering (M Eng, MS, PhD, Certificate); geotechnical, construction, and structural engineering (M Eng); information sciences and technology (Certificate); information technology (PhD); operations research (MS); statistical science (MS, PhD); statistics (Certificate); systems engineering and operations research (PhD, Certificate); transportation engineering (PhD). *Application fee:* $75 ($80 for international students). Electronic applications accepted. *Application Contact:* Shukri Abdi, Graduate Admissions Specialist, 703-993-1830, Fax: 703-993-1242, E-mail: sabdi2@gmu.edu. *Dean*, Kenneth S. Ball, 703-993-1498, Fax: 703-993-1734, E-mail: vsdean@gmu.edu.

GEORGETOWN COLLEGE, Georgetown, KY 40324-1696

General Information Independent-religious, coed, comprehensive institution. *Graduate housing:* On-campus housing not available.

GRADUATE UNITS

Department of Education ***Degree program information:*** Part-time programs available. Part-time. Offers reading and writing (MA Ed); special education (MA Ed); teaching (MA Ed).

GEORGETOWN UNIVERSITY, Washington, DC 20057

General Information Independent-religious, coed, university. CGS member. *Graduate housing:* On-campus housing not available.

GRADUATE UNITS

GeorgeSquared Special Master's Program Offers biomedical sciences (MS). Program offered jointly with George Mason University.

Graduate School of Arts and Sciences Offers American government (MA); analytical chemistry (PhD); arts and sciences (EMBA, EML, GEMBA, MA, MAE, MALS, MAT, MBA, MIPM, MPM, MPP, MPS, MS, DLS, DNP, PhD, Certificate); biochemistry (PhD); biochemistry and molecular and cellular biology (MS, PhD); bioethics (MA); biohazardous threat agents and emerging infectious diseases (MS); biology (PhD); biomedical science policy and advocacy (MS); biostatistics (MS, Certificate); British and American literature (MA); communication, culture, and technology (MA); computational chemistry (PhD); computer science (MS, PhD); conflict resolution (MA); democracy and governance (MA); development, management and policy (MA); econometrics (PhD); economic development (PhD); economic theory (PhD); epidemiology (Certificate); general microbiology and immunology (MS); German (MA, PhD); global history (MA); global infectious diseases (PhD); global, international and comparative history (MA); government (PhD); health physics (MS); history (MA, PhD); industrial organization (PhD); inorganic chemistry (PhD); international macro and finance (PhD); international trade (PhD); labor economics (PhD); language and communication (MA); linguistics (MS, PhD); macroeconomics (PhD); materials chemistry (PhD); mathematics and statistics (MS); microbiology and immunology (PhD); neuroscience (PhD); nuclear nonproliferation (MS); organic chemistry (PhD); pharmacology (MS, PhD); philosophy (PhD); physiology (MS); psychology (PhD); public economics and political economy (PhD); Spanish (MS, PhD); theology (PhD); theoretical chemistry (PhD).

Edmund A. Walsh School of Foreign Service Offers Asian studies (MA); contemporary Arab studies (MA, Certificate); Eurasian, Russian and East European studies (MA); foreign service (MA, MS, Certificate); German and European studies (MA); global business and finance (MS); global human development (MA); global politics and security (MS); international development (MS); Latin American studies (MA); security studies (MA); self design (MS).

McCourt School of Public Policy Offers policy management (MPM); public policy (MPP).

McDonough School of Business Offers business administration (EMBA, GEMBA, MBA); finance (MS); leadership (EML).

School of Continuing Studies Offers American studies (MALS); Catholic studies (MALS); classical civilizations (MALS); emergency and disaster management (MPS); ethics and the professions (MALS); global strategic communications (MPS); hospitality management (MPS); human resources management (MPS); humanities (MALS); individualized study (MALS); integrated marketing communications (MPS); international affairs (MALS); Islam and Muslim-Christian relations (MALS); journalism (MPS); liberal studies (DLS); literature and society (MALS); medieval and early modern European studies (MALS); public relations and corporate communications (MPS); real estate (MPS); religious studies (MALS); social and public policy (MALS); sports industry management (MPS); systems engineering management (MPS); technology management (MPS); the theory and practice of American democracy (MALS); urban and regional planning (MPS); visual culture (MALS). MPS in systems engineering management offered jointly with Stevens Institute of Technology.

School of Nursing and Health Studies Offers acute care nurse practitioner (MS); clinical nurse specialist (MS); family nurse practitioner (MS); nurse anesthesia (MS); nurse-midwifery (MS); nursing (DNP); nursing education (MS).

Law Center ***Degree program information:*** Part-time and evening/weekend programs available. Part-time, evening/weekend. Offers environmental law (LL M); global health law (LL M); global health law and international institutions (LL M); individualized study (LL M); international business and economic law (LL M); law (JD, SJD); national security law (LL M); securities and financial regulation (LL M); taxation (LL M).

National Institutes of Health Sponsored Programs Offers biomedical sciences (MS, PhD).

School of Medicine Offers medicine (MD).

THE GEORGE WASHINGTON UNIVERSITY, Washington, DC 20052

General Information Independent, coed, university. CGS member. *Enrollment:* 26,212 graduate, professional, and undergraduate students; 7,407 full-time matriculated graduate/professional students (4,185 women), 7,181 part-time matriculated graduate/professional students (4,257 women). *Enrollment by degree level:* 9,398 master's, 4,525 doctoral, 665 other advanced degrees. *Graduate faculty:* 1,268 full-time (543 women), 1,344 part-time/adjunct (564 women). *Graduate housing:* Room and/or apartments available on a first-come, first-served basis to single students; on-campus housing not available to married students. *Student services:* Campus employment opportunities, campus safety program, career counseling, exercise/wellness program, free psychological counseling, international student services, low-cost health insurance, multicultural affairs office, services for students with disabilities, teacher training, writing training. *Library:* Gelman Library. *Research affiliation:* Goddard Space Flight Center (radar modeling analysis, space systems technologies), Library of Congress, Smithsonian Institution, National Institutes of Health (biostatistics), NASA-Langley Research Center (aeroacoustics, aeronautics, astronautics), Children's Hospital National Medical Center.

Computer facilities: A campuswide network can be accessed from student residence rooms and from off campus.
Website: http://www.gwu.edu/

General Application Contact: Kristin Williams, Associate Provost for Graduate and Special Enrollment Management, 202-994-0467, Fax: 202-994-0371, E-mail: ksw@gwu.edu.

GRADUATE UNITS

College of Professional Studies Students: 273 full-time (99 women), 759 part-time (457 women); includes 300 minority (142 Black or African American, non-Hispanic/Latino; 2 American Indian or Alaska Native, non-Hispanic/Latino; 38 Asian, non-Hispanic/Latino; 81 Hispanic/Latino; 5 Native Hawaiian or other Pacific Islander, non-Hispanic/Latino; 32 Two or more races, non-Hispanic/Latino), 80 international. Average age 35. 877 applicants, 84% accepted, 452 enrolled. *Faculty:* 23 full-time (6 women), 91 part-time/adjunct (25 women). In 2015, 418 master's, 84 other advanced degrees awarded. Offers healthcare corporate compliance (Graduate Certificate); law firm management (MPS, Graduate Certificate); paralegal studies (MPS, Graduate Certificate); publishing (MPS). *Application Contact:* Kristin Williams, Associate Provost, Graduate Enrollment, 202-994-0467, Fax: 202-994-0371, E-mail: ksw@gwu.edu. *Dean*, Dr. Ali Eskandarian, 202-994-8192, E-mail: ea1102@gwu.edu.

Graduate School of Political Management Students: 53 full-time (25 women), 178 part-time (78 women); includes 56 minority (25 Black or African American, non-Hispanic/Latino; 2 Asian, non-Hispanic/Latino; 27 Hispanic/Latino; 2 Two or more races, non-Hispanic/Latino), 50 international. Average age 31. 180 applicants, 79% accepted, 93 enrolled. *Financial support:* In 2015–16, 18 students received support. Fellowships with tuition reimbursements available, scholarships/grants, and tuition waivers available. Financial award application deadline: 2/1. In 2015, 102 master's, 4 other advanced degrees awarded. Offers community advocacy (Graduate Certificate); legislative affairs (MPS); PACs and political management (Graduate Certificate); political management (MPS). *Application deadline:* For fall admission, 6/15 priority date for domestic students, 4/1 priority date for international students; for spring admission, 11/15 priority date for domestic students, 10/1 priority date for international students. Applications are processed on a rolling basis. *Application fee:* $75. Electronic applications accepted. *Application Contact:* Information Contact, 202-994-6000, Fax: 202-994-6006. *Director*, Mark Kennedy, 202-994-6000, Fax: 202-994-6006, E-mail: gspmmail@gwu.edu.

Columbian College of Arts and Sciences Students: 1,506 full-time (992 women), 1,045 part-time (653 women); includes 489 minority (145 Black or African American, non-Hispanic/Latino; 7 American Indian or Alaska Native, non-Hispanic/Latino; 146 Asian, non-Hispanic/Latino; 144 Hispanic/Latino; 2 Native Hawaiian or other Pacific Islander, non-Hispanic/Latino; 45 Two or more races, non-Hispanic/Latino), 676 international. Average age 28. 6,283 applicants, 46% accepted, 990 enrolled. *Faculty:* 836 full-time (242 women), 770 part-time/adjunct (488 women). *Financial support:* Fellowships with tuition reimbursements, research assistantships, teaching assistantships with tuition reimbursements, career-related internships or fieldwork, Federal Work-Study, scholarships/grants, tuition waivers, and unspecified assistantships available. Support available to part-time students. Financial award application deadline: 2/1. In 2015, 782 master's, 118 doctorates, 105 other advanced degrees awarded. *Degree program information:* Part-time and evening/weekend programs available. Part-time, evening/weekend. Offers American studies (PhD); analytical chemistry (MS, PhD); anthropology (MA, PhD); applied mathematics (MS); applied social psychology (PhD); art and the book (MA); art education (MA, MAT); art history (MA); art therapy (MA, Graduate Certificate); arts and sciences (MA, MAT, MFA, MFS, MPA, MPP, MS, PhD, Psy D, Certificate, Graduate Certificate); biological sciences (MS, PhD); biostatistics (MS, PhD); ceramics (MFA); classical acting (MFA); clinical psychology (PhD); cognitive neuroscience (PhD); crime scene investigation (MFS); criminology (MA); dance (MFA); drawing/painting (MFA); economics (MA, PhD); English (MA, PhD); environmental and resource policy (MA); exhibit design (Graduate Certificate); exhibition design (MA); financial mathematics (Graduate Certificate); folk life (MA); forensic chemistry (MFS); forensic molecular biology (MFS); forensic toxicology (MFS); geography (MA, Graduate Certificate); high-technology crime investigation (MS); historic preservation (MA); history (MA, PhD); human resources management (MA); inorganic chemistry (MS, PhD); interior design (MA, MFA); international development (MA); Islam (MA); legal institutions and theory (MA); material culture (MA); materials science (MS, PhD); mathematics (MA, PhD, Graduate Certificate); medical anthropology (MA); museum collections management and care (Graduate Certificate); museum studies (MA); museum training (MA); new media (MFA); new media photojournalism (MA); non-profit management (Graduate Certificate); organic chemistry (MS, PhD); organizational management (Graduate Certificate); philosophy and social policy (MA); photography (MFA); physical chemistry (MS, PhD); physics (MA, PhD); political science (MA); production design (MFA); professional psychology (MA, Psy D, Graduate Certificate); sculpture (MFA); security management (MFS); sociology (MA); speech-language pathology (MA); statistics (MS, PhD); survey design and data analysis (Graduate Certificate); women's studies (MA, Certificate). *Application deadline:* For fall admission, 1/15 priority date for domestic and international students; for spring admission, 10/1 priority date for domestic and international students. Applications are processed on a rolling basis. *Application fee:* $75. Electronic applications accepted. *Application Contact:* Linda Wilkerson, Executive Assistant, 202-994-6210, Fax: 202-994-6213, E-mail: askccas@gwu.edu. *Dean*, Ben Vinson, III, 202-994-6130, E-mail: bvinson3@gwu.edu.

Institute for Biomedical Sciences Students: 103 full-time (67 women), 86 part-time (52 women); includes 62 minority (6 Black or African American, non-Hispanic/Latino; 1 American Indian or Alaska Native, non-Hispanic/Latino; 31 Asian, non-Hispanic/Latino; 13 Hispanic/Latino; 11 Two or more races, non-Hispanic/Latino), 47 international. Average age 28. 673 applicants, 31% accepted, 83 enrolled. *Faculty:* 26 full-time (8 women), 5 part-time/adjunct (1 woman). *Financial support:* In 2015–16, 24 students received support. Fellowships with full tuition reimbursements available, Federal Work-Study, institutionally sponsored loans, and tuition waivers available. In 2015, 11 doctorates awarded. *Degree program information:* Part-time and evening/weekend programs available. Part-time, evening/weekend. Offers biochemistry and systems biology (PhD); microbiology and immunology (PhD); molecular and cellular oncology (PhD); molecular medicine (PhD); neurosciences (PhD); pharmacology and physiology (PhD). *Application deadline:* For fall admission, 12/15 priority date for domestic and international students. Applications are processed on a rolling basis. *Application fee:* $60. Electronic applications accepted. *Application Contact:* 202-994-2179, Fax: 202-994-0967, E-mail: gwibs@gwu.edu. *Director*, Dr. Linda L. Werling, 202-994-2918, Fax: 202-994-0967, E-mail: lwerling@gwu.edu.

School of Media and Public Affairs Students: 31 full-time (19 women), 15 part-time (12 women); includes 12 minority (4 Black or African American, non-Hispanic/Latino; 1 Asian, non-Hispanic/Latino; 5 Hispanic/Latino; 1 Native Hawaiian or other Pacific Islander, non-Hispanic/Latino; 1 Two or more races, non-Hispanic/Latino), 6 international. Average age 26. 75 applicants, 68% accepted, 21 enrolled. *Faculty:* 23 full-time (10 women), 18 part-time/adjunct (4 women). *Financial support:* In 2015–16, fellowships with tuition reimbursements (averaging $10,000 per year), teaching assistantships with tuition reimbursements (averaging $5,000 per year) were awarded. Financial award application deadline: 1/15. In 2015, 14 master's, 14 other advanced degrees awarded. Offers media and public affairs (MA, Graduate Certificate). *Application deadline:* For fall admission, 4/1 priority date for domestic students, 1/15 priority date for international students; for spring admission, 10/1 priority date for domestic students, 9/1 priority date for international students. Applications are processed on a rolling basis. *Application fee:* $75. Electronic applications accepted. *Application Contact:* Information Contact, 202-994-6227, Fax: 202-994-5806, E-mail: smpa@gwu.edu. *Director*, Frank Sesno, 202-994-9553, E-mail: sesno@gwu.edu.

Trachtenberg School of Public Policy and Public Administration Students: 165 full-time (112 women), 192 part-time (118 women); includes 77 minority (22 Black or African American, non-Hispanic/Latino; 2 American Indian or Alaska Native, non-Hispanic/Latino; 21 Asian, non-Hispanic/Latino; 24 Hispanic/Latino; 8 Two or more races, non-Hispanic/Latino), 48 international. Average age 28. 815 applicants, 68% accepted, 155 enrolled. *Faculty:* 20 full-time (11 women), 12 part-time/adjunct (5 women). *Financial support:* In 2015–16, 92 students received support. Fellowships, research assistantships, teaching assistantships, Federal Work-Study, scholarships/grants, health care benefits, and unspecified assistantships available. Financial award application deadline: 1/5; financial award applicants required to submit FAFSA. In 2015, 127 master's, 15 doctorates awarded. *Degree program information:* Part-time and evening/weekend programs available. Part-time, evening/weekend. Offers public administration (MPA); public policy (MPP); public policy and administration (PhD). *Application deadline:* For fall admission, 1/5 priority date for domestic and international students. *Application fee:* $75. Electronic applications accepted. *Application Contact:* Denee Bottoms, Assistant Director of Graduate Studies, 202-994-6295, Fax: 202-994-6792, E-mail: tspppa@gwu.edu. *Director*, Dr. Kathyrn E. Newcomer, 202-994-3959, Fax: 202-994-3959, E-mail: newcomer@gwu.edu.

Elliott School of International Affairs Students: 548 full-time (321 women), 302 part-time (172 women); includes 221 minority (43 Black or African American, non-Hispanic/Latino; 68 Asian, non-Hispanic/Latino; 81 Hispanic/Latino; 29 Two or more races, non-Hispanic/Latino), 145 international. Average age 27. 1,681 applicants, 76% accepted, 352 enrolled. *Faculty:* 77 full-time (25 women), 112 part-time/adjunct (45 women). *Financial support:* In 2015–16, 155 students received support. Fellowships with partial tuition reimbursements available and Federal Work-Study available. Financial award application deadline: 1/15; financial award applicants required to submit FAFSA. In 2015, 383 master's, 2 other advanced degrees awarded. *Degree program information:* Part-time programs available. Part-time. Offers Asian studies (MA); European and Eurasian studies (MA); global communication (MA); global gender policy (Graduate Certificate); international affairs (MA, MIPP, MIS, Graduate Certificate); international development studies (MA); international policy and practice (MIPP); international science and technology policy (MA, Graduate Certificate); international studies (MIS); international trade and investment policy (MA); Latin American and hemispheric studies (MA); Middle East studies (MA); security policy studies (MA). *Application deadline:* For fall admission, 1/15 priority date for domestic students, 1/15 for international students; for spring admission, 10/1 for domestic and international students. *Application fee:* $75. Electronic applications accepted. *Application Contact:* Nicole A. Campbell, Director of Graduate Admissions, 202-994-7050, Fax: 202-994-9537, E-mail: esiagrad@gwu.edu. *Dean*, Rueben E. Brigety, 202-994-6240, Fax: 202-994-0335, E-mail: esiadean@gwu.edu.

Graduate School of Education and Human Development Students: 414 full-time (328 women), 971 part-time (712 women); includes 478 minority (286 Black or African American, non-Hispanic/Latino; 4 American Indian or Alaska Native, non-Hispanic/Latino; 60 Asian, non-Hispanic/Latino; 90 Hispanic/Latino; 1 Native Hawaiian or other Pacific Islander, non-Hispanic/Latino; 37 Two or more races, non-Hispanic/Latino), 89 international. Average age 36. 1,405 applicants, 73% accepted, 526 enrolled. *Faculty:* 68 full-time (36 women), 100 part-time/adjunct (73 women). *Financial support:* In 2015–16, 279 students received support. Fellowships with tuition reimbursements available, research assistantships with tuition reimbursements available, teaching assistantships with tuition reimbursements available, career-related internships or fieldwork, Federal Work-Study, and tuition waivers (full and partial) available. Support available to part-time students. Financial award application deadline: 1/15. In 2015, 297 master's, 80 doctorates, 135 other advanced degrees awarded. *Degree program information:* Part-time and evening/weekend programs available. Part-time, evening/weekend, online learning. Offers adolescents with emotional and behavioral disabilities (MA Ed/HD); adolescents with learning disabilities (MA Ed/HD); Arabic (M Ed); art education (MA); autism spectrum disorder (MA Ed/HD); bilingual special education (MA Ed, Certificate); brain injury special education (MA Ed/HD); brain injury specialist (MA Ed/HD); clinical mental health counseling (MA); college teaching and academic leadership (MA Ed/HD, Ed S); counseling (PhD, Ed S); counseling culturally and linguistically diverse persons (MA Ed/HD, Certificate); curriculum and instruction (MA Ed, Ed D, Ed S, Graduate Certificate); design and assessment of adult learning (Graduate Certificate); e-learning (Graduate Certificate); early childhood special education (MA Ed/HD); early childhood special education (MA Ed/HD); education and human development (M Ed, MA, MA Ed, MA Ed/HD, MAT, Ed D, PhD, Certificate, Ed S, Graduate Certificate, Teaching Certificate); education policy (Ed D); education policy studies (MA Ed); educational administration (Ed D); educational administration and policy studies (Ed D); educational leadership and administration (MA Ed, Certificate, Ed S); educational technology leadership (MA Ed); elementary education (MA Ed/HD); forensic rehabilitation counseling (Graduate Certificate); general administration (MA Ed/HD, Ed S); higher education administration (MA Ed/HD, Ed D, Ed S); higher education finance (MA Ed/HD, Ed S); human and organizational learning (Ed D, Ed S); human resource development (MA); infant special education (MA Ed/HD); instructional design (Graduate Certificate); integrating technology into education (Graduate Certificate); interdisciplinary transition services (MA Ed/HD); international education (MA Ed); Italian (M Ed); job development and placement (Graduate Certificate); leadership development (Graduate Certificate); leadership in educational technology (Graduate Certificate); math (M Ed); multimedia development (Graduate Certificate); museum education (MAT); organizational learning and change (Graduate Certificate); physics (M Ed); policy (MA Ed/HD, Ed S); rehabilitation counseling (MA Ed/HD); Russian (M Ed); school counseling (MA Ed, Graduate Certificate); secondary education (M Ed); secondary special education and transition services (MA Ed/HD); special education (Ed D, Ed S); special education and transition services (Certificate); special education for children with emotional and behavioral disabilities (MA Ed/HD); special education for culturally and linguistically diverse persons (MA Ed/HD, Certificate); student affairs administration (MA Ed/HD, Ed S); substance abuse and psychiatric disabilities (MA Ed/HD); training and educational technology (Graduate Certificate); transition special education (Teaching Certificate); traumatic brain injury (MA Ed/HD). *Application deadline:* For fall admission, 1/15 priority date for domestic students; for spring admission, 10/1 for domestic students. Applications are processed on a rolling basis. *Application fee:* $75. Electronic applications accepted. *Application Contact:* Sarah Lang, Director of Graduate Admissions, 202-994-1447, Fax: 202-994-7207, E-mail: slang@gwu.edu. *Dean*, Michael Feuer, 202-994-6161, Fax: 202-994-7207, E-mail: mjfeuer@gwu.edu.

Law School Students: 1,620 full-time (865 women), 356 part-time (152 women); includes 488 minority (177 Black or African American, non-Hispanic/Latino; 12 American Indian or Alaska Native, non-Hispanic/Latino; 237 Asian, non-Hispanic/Latino; 50 Hispanic/Latino; 3 Native Hawaiian or other Pacific Islander, non-Hispanic/Latino; 9 Two or more races, non-Hispanic/Latino), 185 international. Average age 27. 219 applicants, 100% accepted, 131 enrolled. *Faculty:* 82 full-time (31 women), 238 part-time/adjunct (73 women). *Financial support:* Research assistantships, career-related internships or fieldwork, Federal Work-Study, institutionally sponsored loans, scholarships/grants, and tuition waivers (full and partial) available. Support available to part-time students. Financial award application deadline: 3/1; financial award applicants required to submit CSS PROFILE or FAFSA. In 2015, 171 master's awarded. *Degree program information:* Part-time and evening/weekend programs available. Part-time, evening/weekend. Offers law (SJD); national security and U.S. foreign relations (LL M). *Application deadline:* For fall admission, 3/1 for domestic students. Applications are processed on a rolling basis. *Application fee:* $75. *Application Contact:* Sophia Sim, Assistant Dean of Admissions and Financial Aid, 202-994-7235, Fax: 202-739-0624, E-mail: ssim@law.gwu.edu. *Dean*, Blake D. Morant, E-mail: bmorant@law.gwu.edu.

Milken Institute School of Public Health Students: 442 full-time (346 women), 1,173 part-time (894 women); includes 637 minority (269 Black or African American, non-Hispanic/Latino; 6 American Indian or Alaska Native, non-Hispanic/Latino; 207 Asian, non-Hispanic/Latino; 108 Hispanic/Latino; 3 Native Hawaiian or other Pacific Islander, non-Hispanic/Latino; 44 Two or more races, non-Hispanic/Latino), 46 international. Average age 31. 2,808 applicants, 68% accepted, 653 enrolled. *Faculty:* 124 full-time (78 women). *Financial support:* In 2015–16, 71 students received support. Career-related internships or fieldwork, Federal Work-Study, institutionally sponsored loans, scholarships/grants, and tuition waivers (partial) available. Support available to part-time students. Financial award application deadline: 2/15. In 2015, 381 master's, 9 doctorates, 13 other advanced degrees awarded. *Degree program information:* Part-time and evening/weekend programs available. Part-time, evening/weekend. Offers biostatistics (MPH); environmental and occupational health (Dr PH); epidemiology (MPH); exercise science (MS); global health (Dr PH); global health communication (MPH); health policy (EMHA, MHA, MPH, MS, Graduate Certificate); microbiology and emerging infectious diseases (MSPH); prevention and community health (MPH, Dr PH); public health (EMHA, MHA, MPH, MS, MSPH, Dr PH, Graduate Certificate). *Application deadline:* For fall admission, 2/15 priority date for domestic students, 2/15 for international students. Applications are processed on a rolling basis. *Application Contact:* Director of Admissions, 202-994-2160, Fax: 202-994-1860, E-mail: sphhsinfo@gwumc.edu. *Dean*, Dr. Lynn Goldman, 202-994-5179, E-mail: goldmanl@gwu.edu.

School of Business Students: 1,030 full-time (509 women), 852 part-time (368 women); includes 513 minority (196 Black or African American, non-Hispanic/Latino; 4 American Indian or Alaska Native, non-Hispanic/Latino; 163 Asian, non-Hispanic/Latino; 112 Hispanic/Latino; 4 Native Hawaiian or other Pacific Islander, non-Hispanic/Latino; 34 Two or more races, non-Hispanic/Latino), 690 international. Average age 32. 3,671 applicants, 41% accepted, 675 enrolled. *Faculty:* 124 full-time (36 women), 67 part-time/adjunct (18 women). *Financial support:* In 2015–16, 194 students received support. Fellowships with tuition reimbursements available, teaching assistantships with tuition reimbursements available, career-related internships or fieldwork, Federal Work-Study, institutionally sponsored loans, and tuition waivers (partial) available. Financial award application deadline: 4/1. In 2015, 812 master's, 8 doctorates, 7 other advanced degrees awarded. *Degree program information:* Part-time and evening/weekend programs available. Part-time, evening/weekend, online learning. Offers accountancy (M Accy); business (M Accy, MBA, MS, MSF, MSIST, MTA, PMBA, PhD, Certificate, Professional Certificate); business administration (MBA); business analytics (MS, Certificate); destination management (Professional Certificate); event and meeting management (MTA); event management (Professional Certificate); finance (MSF, PhD); finance and investments (MBA); government contracts (MS); hospitality management (MTA); individualized studies (MTA); information and decision systems (PhD); information systems (MSIST); information systems development (MSIST); information systems management (MBA); information systems project management (MSIST); international business (PhD); management information systems (MSIST); management of science, technology, and innovation (MBA, PhD); marketing (MBA, PhD); project management (MS); sport management (MTA); strategic management and public policy (MBA, PhD); sustainable tourism destination management (MTA); tourism and hospitality management (MBA); walkable urban real estate development (Professional Certificate). PMBA also offered in Alexandria and Ashburn, VA. *Application deadline:* For fall admission, 4/1 priority date for domestic students; for spring admission, 10/1 for domestic students. Applications are processed on a rolling basis. *Application fee:* $75. Electronic applications accepted. *Application Contact:* Christopher Storer, Executive Director, Graduate Admissions, 202-994-1212, E-mail: gwmba@gwu.edu. *Dean*, Dr. Linda Livingstone.

School of Engineering and Applied Science Students: 613 full-time (172 women), 1,000 part-time (259 women); includes 349 minority (173 Black or African American, non-Hispanic/Latino; 2 American Indian or Alaska Native, non-Hispanic/Latino; 123 Asian, non-Hispanic/Latino; 39 Hispanic/Latino; 5 Native Hawaiian or other Pacific Islander, non-Hispanic/Latino; 7 Two or more races, non-Hispanic/Latino), 653 international. Average age 32. 2,188 applicants, 67% accepted, 484 enrolled. *Faculty:* 94 full-time (18 women), 95 part-time/adjunct (12 women). *Financial support:* In 2015–16, 216 students received support. Fellowships with tuition reimbursements available, research assistantships with tuition reimbursements available, teaching assistantships with tuition reimbursements available, career-related internships or fieldwork, Federal Work-Study, institutionally sponsored loans, and tuition waivers (full and partial) available. Financial award application deadline: 3/1; financial award applicants required to submit FAFSA. In 2015, 494 master's, 66 doctorates, 37 other advanced degrees awarded. *Degree program information:* Part-time and evening/weekend programs available. Part-time, evening/weekend. Offers biomedical engineering (MS, PhD); civil and environmental engineering (MS, PhD, App Sc, Engr, Graduate Certificate); computer science (MS, D Sc); cybersecurity (MS); electrical engineering (MS, PhD); engineering and applied science (MS, D Sc, PhD, App Sc, Engr, Graduate Certificate); mechanical and aerospace engineering (Engr); regulatory biomedical engineering (MS); system engineering (PhD); telecommunication and computers (MS). *Application deadline:* For fall admission, 3/1 for domestic students; for spring admission, 10/1 for domestic students. Applications are processed on a rolling basis. *Application fee:* $75. *Application Contact:* Adina Lav, Marketing, Recruiting and Admissions, 202-994-5827, Fax: 202-994-0909, E-mail: engineering@gwu.edu. *Dean*, David S. Dolling, 202-994-6080, E-mail: dolling@gwu.edu.

School of Medicine and Health Sciences Students: 1,004 full-time (609 women), 347 part-time (256 women); includes 507 minority (128 Black or African American, non-Hispanic/Latino; 4 American Indian or Alaska Native, non-Hispanic/Latino; 257 Asian, non-Hispanic/Latino; 97 Hispanic/Latino; 7 Native Hawaiian or other Pacific Islander, non-Hispanic/Latino; 14 Two or more races, non-Hispanic/Latino), 46 international. Average age 30. 2,003 applicants, 22% accepted, 251 enrolled. *Faculty:* 127 full-time (64 women), 113 part-time/adjunct (73 women). *Financial support:* Career-related internships or fieldwork, Federal Work-Study, and institutionally sponsored loans available. In 2015, 158 master's, 35 doctorates, 160 other advanced degrees awarded. Offers clinical practice management (MSHS); clinical research administration (MSHS); emergency services management (MSHS); end-of-life care (MSHS); immunohematology (MSHS); immunohematology and biotechnology (MSHS); medicine (MD); medicine and health sciences (MSHS, DPT, MD, OTD, Graduate Certificate); physical therapy (DPT); physician assistant (MSHS). *Application deadline:* Applications are processed on a rolling basis. *Application fee:* $75. *Application Contact:* Admissions, 202-994-3748, Fax: 202-994-1753, E-mail: medadmit@gwu.edu. *Dean*, Dr. Jeffrey Akman, 202-994-3727, E-mail: akman@gwu.edu.

School of Nursing Students: 52 full-time (48 women), 519 part-time (463 women); includes 162 minority (72 Black or African American, non-Hispanic/Latino; 4 American Indian or Alaska Native, non-Hispanic/Latino; 52 Asian, non-Hispanic/Latino; 31 Hispanic/Latino; 3 Two or more races, non-Hispanic/Latino), 2 international. Average age 37. 465 applicants, 69% accepted, 187 enrolled. *Faculty:* 42 full-time (all women), 71 part-time/adjunct (66 women). In 2015, 121 master's, 35 doctorates, 1 other advanced degree awarded. Offers adult nurse practitioner (MSN, DNP, Post-Master's Certificate); clinical research administration (MSN); family nurse practitioner (MSN, Post-Master's Certificate); health care quality (MSN, Post-Master's Certificate); nursing leadership and management (MSN); nursing practice (DNP); palliative care nurse practitioner (Post-Master's Certificate). *Application Contact:* Kristin Williams, Associate Provost for Graduate Enrollment Management, 202-994-0467, Fax: 202-994-0371, E-mail: ksw@gwu.edu. *Dean*, Pamela R. Jeffries, 202-994-3725, E-mail: pjeffries@gwu.edu.

GEORGIA CAMPUS–PHILADELPHIA COLLEGE OF OSTEOPATHIC MEDICINE, Suwanee, GA 30024

General Information Independent, coed, graduate-only institution. *Enrollment by degree level:* 139 master's, 931 doctoral. *Graduate faculty:* 29 full-time (12 women), 174 part-time/adjunct (99 women). *Graduate housing:* On-campus housing not available. *Student services:* Campus employment opportunities, campus safety program, career counseling, exercise/wellness program, free psychological counseling, multicultural affairs office. Study areas open 24 hours, 5–7 days a week.

Computer facilities: A campuswide network can be accessed from off campus.
Website: http://www.pcom.edu/General_Information/georgia/georgia.html

General Application Contact: Craig Brown, Director of Admissions, 678-225-7500, E-mail: craigbro@pcom.edu.

GRADUATE UNITS

Doctor of Osteopathic Medicine Program Students: 526 full-time (261 women); includes 280 minority (65 Black or African American, non-Hispanic/Latino; 62 Asian, non-Hispanic/Latino; 16 Hispanic/Latino; 137 Two or more races, non-Hispanic/Latino), 6 international. 4,919 applicants, 5% accepted, 135 enrolled. *Financial support:* Application deadline: 3/15; applicants required to submit FAFSA. In 2015, 77 doctorates awarded. Offers osteopathic medicine (DO). *Application deadline:* For fall admission, 3/1 for domestic and international students. Applications are processed on a rolling basis. *Application fee:* $75. Electronic applications accepted. *Application Contact:* Deborah Benvenger, Chief Admissions Officer, 678-225-7500.

School of Pharmacy Students: 405 full-time (216 women); includes 270 minority (85 Black or African American, non-Hispanic/Latino; 17 Asian, non-Hispanic/Latino; 1 Hispanic/Latino; 167 Two or more races, non-Hispanic/Latino), 17 international. Average age 27. 931 applicants, 23% accepted, 103 enrolled. *Faculty:* 29 full-time (12 women), 174 part-time/adjunct (99 women). *Financial support:* Federal Work-Study, institutionally sponsored loans, and scholarships/grants available. Financial award application deadline: 3/15; financial award applicants required to submit FAFSA. In 2015, 78 doctorates awarded. Offers pharmacy (Pharm D). *Application deadline:* For fall admission, 3/1 for domestic students. Applications are processed on a rolling basis. Electronic applications accepted. *Application Contact:* Marsha Williams, Associate Director of Admissions, 215-871-6700, E-mail: marshawi@pcom.edu. *Dean*, Dr. Mark Okamoto, 678-407-7330, Fax: 678-407-7339.

GEORGIA CHRISTIAN UNIVERSITY, Atlanta, GA 30360

General Information Independent-religious, coed, comprehensive institution.

GRADUATE UNITS

School of Business Offers business (MBA).

School of Divinity Offers Christian education (MA); divinity (M Div); ministry (D Min); mission studies and world Christianity (MA); theological studies (MA).

School of Music Offers music (MA).

GEORGIA COLLEGE & STATE UNIVERSITY, Milledgeville, GA 31061

General Information State-supported, coed, comprehensive institution. *Enrollment:* 6,889 graduate, professional, and undergraduate students; 312 full-time matriculated graduate/professional students (212 women), 526 part-time matriculated graduate/professional students (346 women). *Enrollment by degree level:* 677 master's, 22 doctoral, 139 other advanced degrees. *Tuition, area resident:* Full-time $5184; part-time $288 per credit hour. Tuition, nonresident: full-time $18,486; part-time $1027 per credit hour. Tuition and fees vary according to degree level and program. *Graduate housing:* Room and/or apartments available on a first-come, first-served basis to single students; on-campus housing not available to married students. Typical cost: $6124 per year ($11,612 including board). Room and board charges vary according to board plan, campus/location and housing facility selected. Housing application deadline: 5/1. *Student services:* Campus employment opportunities, campus safety program, career counseling, child daycare facilities, exercise/wellness program, free psychological counseling, international student services, low-cost health insurance, multicultural affairs office, services for students with disabilities, teacher training. *Library:* Ina Dillard Russell Library plus 1 other. *Collection:* Books: 175,679 (physical), 161,259 (digital/electronic); Serial titles: 1,755 (physical), 20,623 (digital/electronic); Databases: 369. Weekly public service hours: 108; study areas open 24 hours, 5–7 days a week; students can reserve study rooms.

Computer facilities: 900 computers available on campus for general student use. A campuswide network can be accessed from student residence rooms and from off campus. Online class registration is available.
Website: http://www.gcsu.edu/

General Application Contact: Kate Marshall, Graduate Admissions Coordinator, 478-445-1184, Fax: 478-445-1336, E-mail: grad-admit@gcsu.edu.

GRADUATE UNITS

Graduate School Students: 312 full-time (212 women), 526 part-time (346 women); includes 271 minority (203 Black or African American, non-Hispanic/Latino; 19 Asian, non-Hispanic/Latino; 33 Hispanic/Latino; 16 Two or more races, non-Hispanic/Latino), 22 international. Average age 32. 449 applicants, 84% accepted, 222 enrolled. *Financial support:* Scholarships/grants and unspecified assistantships available. Financial award application deadline: 3/1; financial award applicants required to submit FAFSA. In 2015, 348 master's, 9 doctorates, 78 other advanced degrees awarded. *Degree program information:* Part-time and evening/weekend programs available. Part-time, evening/weekend, 100% online. *Application deadline:* For fall admission, 7/1 priority date for domestic students, 4/1 priority date for international students; for spring admission, 11/1 priority date for domestic students, 9/1 priority date for international students; for summer admission, 4/1 priority date for domestic students. Applications are processed on a rolling basis. *Application fee:* $40. Electronic applications accepted. *Application Contact:* Kate Marshall, Graduate Admissions Coordinator, 478-445-1184, Fax: 478-445-1336, E-mail: grad-admit@gcsu.edu. *Interim Associate Provost/Dean of Graduate Studies*, Dr. Costas Spirou, 478-445-4715, Fax: 478-445-5151, E-mail: costas.spirou@gcsu.edu.

College of Arts and Sciences Students: 65 full-time (43 women), 67 part-time (39 women); includes 42 minority (27 Black or African American, non-Hispanic/Latino; 2 Asian, non-Hispanic/Latino; 7 Hispanic/Latino; 6 Two or more races, non-Hispanic/Latino), 5 international. Average age 30. 143 applicants, 68% accepted, 43 enrolled. *Financial support:* Unspecified assistantships available. Support available to part-time students. Financial award application deadline: 3/1; financial award applicants required to submit FAFSA. In 2015, 56 master's awarded. *Degree program information:* Part-time and evening/weekend programs available. Part-time, evening/weekend, 100% online. Offers arts and sciences (MA, MFA, MM Ed, MPA, MS, MSCJ); biology (MS); creative writing (MFA); criminal justice (MSCJ); English (MA); history, geography, and philosophy (MA); music (MM Ed); public administration (MPA); public history (MA). *Application deadline:* For fall admission, 7/1 priority date for domestic students, 4/1 priority date for international students; for spring admission, 11/1 priority date for domestic students, 9/1 priority date for international students; for summer admission, 4/1 priority date for domestic students. Applications are processed on a rolling basis. *Application fee:* $40. Electronic applications accepted. *Application Contact:* Kate Marshall, Graduate Admissions Coordinator, 478-445-1184, Fax: 478-445-1336, E-mail: grad-admit@gcsu.edu. *Dean*, Kenneth Proctor, 478-445-4441, E-mail: ken.proctor@gcsu.edu.

College of Health Sciences Students: 50 full-time (32 women), 131 part-time (119 women); includes 47 minority (31 Black or African American, non-Hispanic/Latino; 5 Asian, non-Hispanic/Latino; 7 Hispanic/Latino; 4 Two or more races, non-Hispanic/Latino), 2 international. Average age 33. 46 applicants, 98% accepted, 29 enrolled. *Financial support:* Unspecified assistantships available. Support available to part-time students. Financial award application deadline: 3/1; financial award applicants required to submit FAFSA. In 2015, 50 master's, 9 doctorates awarded. *Degree program information:* Part-time and evening/weekend programs available. Part-time, evening/weekend, 100% online. Offers art therapy (MA); health and human performance (MS); health sciences (M Ed, MA, MAT, MMT, MS, MSN, DNP); kinesiology/health education (MAT); music therapy (MMT); nursing (MSN); nursing practice (DNP). *Application deadline:* For fall admission, 7/1 priority date for domestic students, 4/1 priority date for international students; for spring admission, 11/1 priority date for domestic students, 9/1 priority date for international students; for summer admission, 4/1 priority date for domestic students. Applications are processed on a rolling basis. *Application fee:* $40. Electronic applications accepted. *Application Contact:* Kate Marshall, Graduate Admissions Coordinator, 478-445-1184, Fax: 478-445-1336, E-mail: grad-admit@gcsu.edu. *Dean*, Dr. Sandra Gangstead, 478-445-4092, E-mail: sandra.gangstead@gcsu.edu.

The John H. Lounsbury College of Education Students: 158 full-time (116 women), 156 part-time (127 women); includes 135 minority (117 Black or African American, non-Hispanic/Latino; 2 Asian, non-Hispanic/Latino; 11 Hispanic/Latino; 5 Two or more races, non-Hispanic/Latino). Average age 33. 130 applicants, 99% accepted, 76 enrolled. *Financial support:* Unspecified assistantships available. Support available to part-time students. Financial award application deadline: 3/1; financial award applicants required to submit FAFSA. In 2015, 147 master's, 78 other advanced degrees awarded. *Degree program information:* Part-time programs available. Part-time, 100% online, blended/hybrid learning. Offers curriculum and instruction (Ed S); early childhood education (M Ed); education (M Ed, MAT, Ed S); education/instructional technology (M Ed); educational leadership (Ed S); library media (M Ed); reading, literacy, and language (M Ed); secondary education (MAT); special education (M Ed, MAT, Ed S). *Application deadline:* For fall admission, 7/1 priority date for domestic students; for spring admission, 11/1 priority date for domestic students; for summer admission, 4/1 priority date for domestic students. Applications are processed on a rolling basis. *Application fee:* $40. Electronic applications accepted. *Application Contact:* Shanda Brand, Graduate Admissions Advisor, 478-445-1383, Fax: 478-445-6582, E-mail: shanda.brand@gcsu.edu.

The J. Whitney Bunting School of Business Students: 39 full-time (21 women), 172 part-time (61 women); includes 47 minority (28 Black or African American, non-Hispanic/Latino; 10 Asian, non-Hispanic/Latino; 8 Hispanic/Latino; 1 Two or more races, non-Hispanic/Latino), 15 international. Average age 32. 126 applicants, 82% accepted, 72 enrolled. *Financial support:* Unspecified assistantships available. Financial award application deadline: 3/1; financial award applicants required to submit FAFSA. In 2015, 113 master's awarded. *Degree program information:* Part-time and evening/weekend programs available. Part-time, evening/weekend, 100% online. Offers accounting (M Acc); business (M Acc, MBA, MLSCM, MMIS); business administration (MBA); logistics (MLSCM); management information systems (MMIS). *Application deadline:* For fall admission, 7/1 priority date for domestic students, 4/1 priority date for international students; for spring admission, 11/1 priority date for domestic students, 8/1 priority date for international students; for summer admission, 4/1 priority date for domestic students. Applications are processed on a rolling basis. *Application fee:* $40. Electronic applications accepted. *Application Contact:* Lynn Hanson, Director of Graduate Programs, 478-445-5115, E-mail: lynn.hanson@gcsu.edu. *Dean, School of Business,* Dr. James Payne, 478-445-5497, E-mail: james.payne@gcsu.edu.

GEORGIA INSTITUTE OF TECHNOLOGY, Atlanta, GA 30332-0001

General Information State-supported, coed, university. CGS member. *Graduate housing:* Rooms and/or apartments available on a first-come, first-served basis to single and married students. Housing application deadline: 6/1. *Research affiliation:* Oak Ridge National Laboratory (energy, health, environment), Children's Healthcare of Atlanta (pediatric biomedical and device research), Georgia State University (brain imaging), Southeastern Universities Research Association (high-energy physics), Emory University Medical School (biomedical engineering), Zoo Atlanta (environmental design, environmental psychology).

GRADUATE UNITS

Graduate Studies *Financial support:* Fellowships, research assistantships, teaching assistantships, career-related internships or fieldwork, Federal Work-Study, institutionally sponsored loans, traineeships, tuition waivers (partial), and unspecified assistantships available. Support available to part-time students. Financial award application deadline: 5/1; financial award applicants required to submit FAFSA. *Degree program information:* Part-time and evening/weekend programs available. Part-time, evening/weekend, online learning. Offers algorithms, combinatorics, and optimization (PhD); analytics (MS); bioengineering (MS, PhD); bioinformatics (MS, PhD); computational science and engineering (MS, PhD); human computer interaction (MS); paper science and engineering (MS, PhD); quantitative and computational finance (MS); statistics (MS). *Application deadline:* Applications are processed on a rolling basis. *Application fee:* $75. Electronic applications accepted.

College of Architecture Offers architecture (M Arch, MCRP, MS, PhD); building construction (PhD); city and regional planning (PhD); economic development (MCRP); environmental planning and management (MCRP); geographic information systems (MCRP); industrial design (MID); integrated facility and property management (MS); integrated project delivery systems (MS); land and community development (MCRP); land use planning (MCRP); music technology (MS, PhD); program management (MS); residential construction development (MS); transportation (MCRP); urban design (MCRP). Electronic applications accepted.

College of Computing Financial support: Fellowships, research assistantships, teaching assistantships, career-related internships or fieldwork, Federal Work-Study, institutionally sponsored loans, tuition waivers (partial), and unspecified assistantships available. Support available to part-time students. Financial award application deadline: 5/1. *Degree program information:* Part-time programs available. Part-time, online learning. Offers computer science (MS, PhD); computing (MS, PhD); human-centered computing (MS, PhD); information security (MS); robotics (PhD). *Application deadline:* For fall admission, 12/15 for domestic and international students. Applications are processed on a rolling basis. *Application fee:* $75. Electronic applications accepted. *Application Contact:* Graduate Coordinator, 404-894-1610, E-mail: gradinfo@mail.gatech.edu. *Director,* Jennifer Whitlow, E-mail: jwhitlow@cc.gatech.edu.

College of Engineering Financial support: Fellowships, research assistantships, teaching assistantships, career-related internships or fieldwork, Federal Work-Study, institutionally sponsored loans, tuition waivers (partial), and unspecified assistantships available. Support available to part-time students. Financial award application deadline: 5/1. *Degree program information:* Part-time programs available. Part-time, online learning. Offers aerospace engineering (MS, PhD); applied systems engineering (PMS); biomedical engineering (PhD); chemical engineering (MS, PhD); civil engineering (MS, PhD); electrical and computer engineering (MS, PhD); engineering (MS, MSMP, MSNE, PhD); engineering science and mechanics (MS, PhD); environmental engineering (MS); health systems (MS); industrial and systems engineering (MS, PhD); industrial engineering (MS, PhD); international logistics (MS); materials science and engineering (MS, PhD); mechanical engineering (MS, MSME, PhD); medical physics (MS, MSMP); nuclear and radiological engineering (PhD); nuclear and radiological engineering and medical physics (MS, MSMP, MSNE, PhD); nuclear engineering (MSNE); operations research (MS, PhD). *Application deadline:* Applications are processed on a rolling basis. *Application fee:* $75. Electronic applications accepted. *Application Contact:* Laurence Jocobs, Associate Dean, 404-894-2344, E-mail: laurence.jacobs@coe.gatech.edu. *Associate Dean,* Laurence Jocobs, 404-894-2344, E-mail: laurence.jacobs@coe.gatech.edu.

College of Sciences Financial support: Fellowships, research assistantships, teaching assistantships, career-related internships or fieldwork, Federal Work-Study, institutionally sponsored loans, tuition waivers (partial), and unspecified assistantships available. Support available to part-time students. Financial award application deadline: 5/1. *Degree program information:* Part-time programs available. Part-time. Offers applied physiology (PhD); biology (MS, PhD); chemistry and biochemistry (MS, PhD); earth and atmospheric sciences (MS, PhD); mathematics (MS, PhD); physics (MS, PhD); prosthetics and orthotics (MS); psychology (MS, PhD); sciences (MS, PMASE, PhD). *Application deadline:* Applications are processed on a rolling basis. *Application fee:* $75. Electronic applications accepted. *Application Contact:* Graduate Coordinator, 404-894-1610, E-mail: gradinfo@mail.gatech.edu. *Director, Graduate Studies,* David Bamburowski, 404-894-1610, E-mail: david.bamburowski@grad.gatech.edu.

Ivan Allen College of Liberal Arts Financial support: Fellowships, research assistantships, teaching assistantships, career-related internships or fieldwork, Federal Work-Study, institutionally sponsored loans, tuition waivers (partial), and unspecified assistantships available. Support available to part-time students. Financial award application deadline: 5/1. *Degree program information:* Part-time programs available. Part-time. Offers digital media (MS, PhD); economics (MS, PhD); history and sociology of technology and science (MS); international affairs (MS); liberal arts (MS, PhD); public policy (MS, PhD). *Application deadline:* Applications are processed on a rolling basis. *Application fee:* $75. Electronic applications accepted.

Scheller College of Business Financial support: Fellowships, research assistantships, teaching assistantships, career-related internships or fieldwork, Federal Work-Study, institutionally sponsored loans, tuition waivers (partial), and unspecified assistantships available. Support available to part-time students. Financial award application deadline: 5/1. *Degree program information:* Part-time and evening/weekend programs available. Part-time, evening/weekend. Offers business (MBA, MS, PhD); business administration (MBA); global business (MBA); management (MS, PhD); management of technology (MBA). *Application deadline:* For fall admission, 3/15 for domestic students, 1/15 for international students. Applications are processed on a rolling basis. *Application fee:* $75. Electronic applications accepted.

GEORGIAN COURT UNIVERSITY, Lakewood, NJ 08701-2697

General Information Independent-religious, coed, comprehensive institution. *Enrollment:* 2,122 graduate, professional, and undergraduate students; 157 full-time matriculated graduate/professional students (123 women), 437 part-time matriculated graduate/professional students (360 women). *Enrollment by degree level:* 421 master's, 173 other advanced degrees. *Graduate faculty:* 43 full-time (24 women), 29 part-time/adjunct (16 women). *Tuition, area resident:* Full-time $15,102; part-time $839 per credit. *Required fees:* $968; $566 per unit. Tuition and fees vary according to campus/location and program. *Graduate housing:* On-campus housing not available. *Student services:* Campus employment opportunities, campus safety program, career counseling, exercise/wellness program, free psychological counseling, low-cost health insurance, services for students with disabilities, teacher training. *Library:* The Sister Mary Joseph Cunningham Library. *Collection:* Books: 128,663 (physical), 80,878 (digital/electronic). Weekly public service hours: 85; students can reserve study rooms.

Computer facilities: 198 computers available on campus for general student use. A campuswide network can be accessed from student residence rooms and from off campus. Online class registration is available.
Website: http://www.georgian.edu/

General Application Contact: Patrick Givens, Director of Graduate Admissions, 732-987-2736, Fax: 732-987-2084, E-mail: graduateadmissions@georgian.edu.

GRADUATE UNITS

School of Arts and Sciences Students: 84 full-time (72 women), 121 part-time (95 women); includes 34 minority (10 Black or African American, non-Hispanic/Latino; 19 Hispanic/Latino; 5 Two or more races, non-Hispanic/Latino). Average age 35. 164 applicants, 54% accepted, 58 enrolled. *Faculty:* 19 full-time (10 women), 7 part-time/adjunct (2 women). *Financial support:* Scholarships/grants, health care benefits, and unspecified assistantships available. Financial award application deadline: 4/15; financial award applicants required to submit FAFSA. In 2015, 58 master's, 7 other advanced degrees awarded. *Degree program information:* Part-time and evening/weekend programs available. Part-time, evening/weekend. Offers applied behavior analysis (MA); clinical mental health counseling (MA); holistic health studies (MA, Certificate); homeland security (MS, Certificate); mercy spirituality (Certificate); parish business management (Certificate); professional counselor (Certificate); school psychology (MA, Certificate); theology (MA, Certificate). *Application deadline:* For fall admission, 8/1 priority date for domestic students, 4/1 for international students; for spring admission, 1/1 priority date for domestic students, 7/1 for international students. Applications are processed on a rolling basis. *Application fee:* $40. Electronic applications accepted. *Application Contact:* Patrick Givens, Director of Graduate Admissions, 732-987-2736, Fax: 732-987-2084, E-mail: graduateadmissions@georgian.edu. *Dean,* Dr. Rita Kipp, 732-987-2493, Fax: 732-987-2007, E-mail: rkipp@georgian.edu.

School of Business and Digital Media Students: 30 full-time (20 women), 44 part-time (31 women); includes 13 minority (5 Black or African American, non-Hispanic/Latino; 1 Asian, non-Hispanic/Latino; 5 Hispanic/Latino; 2 Two or more races, non-Hispanic/Latino), 2 international. Average age 32. 70 applicants, 59% accepted, 32 enrolled. *Faculty:* 6 full-time (2 women), 8 part-time/adjunct (3 women). *Financial support:* Scholarships/grants, health care benefits, and unspecified assistantships available. Financial award application deadline: 4/15; financial award applicants required to submit FAFSA. In 2015, 31 master's, 2 other advanced degrees awarded. *Degree program information:* Part-time and evening/weekend programs available. Part-time, evening/weekend. Offers business (MBA); business essentials (Certificate); nonprofit management (Certificate). *Application deadline:* For fall admission, 8/1 priority date for domestic students, 4/1 for international students; for spring admission, 1/1 priority date for domestic students, 7/1 for international students. Applications are processed on a rolling basis. *Application fee:* $40. Electronic applications accepted. *Application Contact:* Patrick Givens, Director of Graduate Admissions, 732-987-2736, Fax: 732-987-2084, E-mail: graduateadmissions@georgian.edu. *Dean,* Dr. Janice Warner, 732-987-2662, Fax: 732-987-2024, E-mail: jwarner@georgian.edu.

School of Education Students: 43 full-time (31 women), 272 part-time (234 women); includes 38 minority (8 Black or African American, non-Hispanic/Latino; 1 Asian, non-Hispanic/Latino; 25 Hispanic/Latino; 4 Two or more races, non-Hispanic/Latino). Average age 31. 288 applicants, 53% accepted, 103 enrolled. *Faculty:* 18 full-time (12 women), 14 part-time/adjunct (11 women). *Financial support:* Scholarships/grants, health care benefits, and unspecified assistantships available. Financial award application deadline: 4/15; financial award applicants required to submit FAFSA. In 2015, 94 master's awarded. *Degree program information:* Part-time and evening/weekend programs available. Part-time, evening/weekend. Offers administration and leadership (MA); autism spectrum disorders (Certificate); education (MA); instructional technology (Certificate). *Application deadline:* For fall admission, 8/1 priority date for domestic students, 4/1 for international students; for spring admission, 1/1 priority date for domestic students, 7/1 for international students. Applications are processed on a rolling basis. *Application fee:* $40. Electronic applications accepted. *Application Contact:* Patrick Givens, Director of Graduate Admissions, 732-987-2736,

Fax: 732-987-2084, E-mail: graduateadmissions@georgian.edu. *Dean*, Dr. Lynn DeCapua, 732-987-2729, E-mail: ldecapua@georgian.edu.

GEORGIA SOUTHERN UNIVERSITY, Statesboro, GA 30458

General Information State-supported, coed, university. CGS member. *Enrollment:* 20,459 graduate, professional, and undergraduate students; 1,016 full-time matriculated graduate/professional students (630 women), 1,418 part-time matriculated graduate/professional students (975 women). *Enrollment by degree level:* 1,755 master's, 473 doctoral, 206 other advanced degrees. *Graduate faculty:* 662 full-time (279 women), 23 part-time/adjunct (10 women). Tuition, state resident: full-time $7236; part-time $277 per semester hour. Tuition, nonresident: full-time $27,118; part-time $1105 per semester hour. *Required fees:* $2092. *Graduate housing:* Room and/or apartments available to single students; on-campus housing not available to married students. Typical cost: $6050 per year ($9800 including board). Housing application deadline: 5/1. *Student services:* Campus employment opportunities, campus safety program, career counseling, exercise/wellness program, free psychological counseling, grant writing training, international student services, low-cost health insurance, multicultural affairs office, services for students with disabilities, teacher training, writing training. *Library:* Henderson Library. *Collection:* Books: 657,965 (physical), 30,602 (digital/electronic); Serial titles: 435 (physical), 84,081 (digital/electronic); Databases: 369. Study areas open 24 hours, 5–7 days a week; students can reserve study rooms. *Research affiliation:* Oak Ridge National Laboratory (physical sciences), Mount Desert Island Biological Laboratory (marine biology), Space Telescope Science Institute (astronomy, physics), St. Catherine's Island Foundation (marine science, life sciences), Skidaway Institute of Oceanography (marine sciences).

Computer facilities: Computer purchase and lease plans are available. 3,872 computers available on campus for general student use. A campuswide network can be accessed from student residence rooms and from off campus. Online class registration, online degree audit, online career services, and online healthcare are available. Website: http://www.georgiasouthern.edu/

General Application Contact: Office of Graduate Admissions, 912-478-5384, Fax: 912-478-0740, E-mail: gradadmissions@georgiasouthern.edu.

GRADUATE UNITS

Jack N. Averitt College of Graduate Studies Students: 1,016 full-time (630 women), 1,418 part-time (975 women); includes 748 minority (546 Black or African American, non-Hispanic/Latino; 4 American Indian or Alaska Native, non-Hispanic/Latino; 48 Asian, non-Hispanic/Latino; 99 Hispanic/Latino; 51 Two or more races, non-Hispanic/Latino), 106 international. Average age 31. 1,658 applicants, 64% accepted, 563 enrolled. *Faculty:* 662 full-time (279 women), 23 part-time/adjunct (10 women). *Financial support:* In 2015–16, 670 students received support, including 192 research assistantships with partial tuition reimbursements available (averaging $7,200 per year), teaching assistantships with partial tuition reimbursements available (averaging $7,200 per year); career-related internships or fieldwork, Federal Work-Study, scholarships/grants, traineeships, tuition waivers (partial), unspecified assistantships, and doctoral stipends also available. Support available to part-time students. Financial award application deadline: 4/15; financial award applicants required to submit FAFSA. In 2015, 831 master's, 43 doctorates, 101 other advanced degrees awarded. *Degree program information:* Part-time and evening/weekend programs available. Part-time, evening/weekend, online learning. *Application deadline:* For fall admission, 4/1 priority date for domestic and international students; for spring admission, 10/1 priority date for domestic students, 10/1 for international students. Applications are processed on a rolling basis. *Application fee:* $50. Electronic applications accepted. *Application Contact:* Samuel T. Aldridge, Director, Graduate Admissions, 912-478-5384, Fax: 912-478-0740, E-mail: gradadmissions@georgiasouthern.edu. *Dean, College of Graduate Studies*, Dr. Devon Jensen, 912-478-0851, Fax: 912-478-8642, E-mail: devonjensen@georgiasouthern.edu.

Allen E. Paulson College of Engineering and Information Technology Students: 54 full-time (10 women), 62 part-time (9 women); includes 44 minority (28 Black or African American, non-Hispanic/Latino; 4 Asian, non-Hispanic/Latino; 7 Hispanic/Latino; 5 Two or more races, non-Hispanic/Latino), 22 international. Average age 30. 148 applicants, 65% accepted, 17 enrolled. *Faculty:* 52 full-time (5 women), 1 part-time/adjunct (0 women). *Financial support:* In 2015–16, 39 students received support, including 3 research assistantships with full tuition reimbursements available (averaging $7,750 per year), 4 teaching assistantships with full tuition reimbursements available (averaging $7,750 per year); Federal Work-Study, scholarships/grants, tuition waivers (full), and unspecified assistantships also available. Financial award applicants required to submit FAFSA. In 2015, 34 master's awarded. *Degree program information:* Part-time programs available. Part-time, online learning. Offers civil engineering and construction management (MSAE); computer science (MS); electrical and electronic systems (MSAE); engineering and information technology (MS, MSAE, Graduate Certificate); engineering and manufacturing management (Graduate Certificate); engineering/energy science (MSAE); engineering/engineering management (MSAE); engineering/mechatronics (MSAE); information technology (MSAE); occupational safety and environmental compliance (Graduate Certificate); occupational safety and environmental science (Graduate Certificate). *Application fee:* $50. *Dean*, Dr. Mohammad S. Davoud, 912-478-8046, E-mail: mdavoud@georgiasouthern.edu.

College of Business Administration Students: 100 full-time (39 women), 184 part-time (71 women); includes 78 minority (48 Black or African American, non-Hispanic/Latino; 8 Asian, non-Hispanic/Latino; 17 Hispanic/Latino; 5 Two or more races, non-Hispanic/Latino), 21 international. Average age 31. 254 applicants, 67% accepted, 65 enrolled. *Faculty:* 82 full-time (22 women), 1 part-time/adjunct (0 women). *Financial support:* In 2015–16, 58 students received support. Research assistantships with partial tuition reimbursements available, teaching assistantships with partial tuition reimbursements available, career-related internships or fieldwork, Federal Work-Study, scholarships/grants, tuition waivers (partial), and unspecified assistantships also available. Support available to part-time students. Financial award application deadline: 4/15; financial award applicants required to submit FAFSA. In 2015, 165 master's, 7 doctorates, 12 other advanced degrees awarded. *Degree program information:* Part-time and evening/weekend programs available. Part-time, evening/weekend, blended/hybrid learning. Offers applied economics (MS); business administration (M Acc, MBA, MS, PhD, Graduate Certificate); enterprise resource planning (Graduate Certificate); forensic accounting (M Acc); information systems (Graduate Certificate); logistics and supply chain management (PhD). *Application deadline:* For fall admission, 3/1 priority date for domestic and international students; for spring admission, 10/1 priority date for domestic students, 10/1 for international students. Applications are processed on a rolling basis. *Application fee:* $50. Electronic applications accepted. *Dean*, Dr. Allen Amason, 912-478-2622, Fax: 912-478-0292, E-mail: aamason@georgiasouthern.edu.

College of Education Students: 317 full-time (244 women), 904 part-time (723 women); includes 372 minority (303 Black or African American, non-Hispanic/Latino; 3 American Indian or Alaska Native, non-Hispanic/Latino; 10 Asian, non-Hispanic/Latino; 35 Hispanic/Latino; 21 Two or more races, non-Hispanic/Latino), 7 international. Average age 33. 382 applicants, 77% accepted, 163 enrolled. *Faculty:* 86 full-time (57 women), 12 part-time/adjunct (6 women). *Financial support:* In 2015–16, 103 students received support, including 1 teaching assistantship with full tuition reimbursement available (averaging $7,750 per year); research assistantships with partial tuition reimbursements available, career-related internships or fieldwork, Federal Work-Study, scholarships/grants, tuition waivers (full), unspecified assistantships, and doctoral stipends also available. Support available to part-time students. Financial award application deadline: 4/15; financial award applicants required to submit FAFSA. In 2015, 362 master's, 34 doctorates, 73 other advanced degrees awarded. *Degree program information:* Part-time and evening/weekend programs available. Part-time, evening/weekend, blended/hybrid learning. Offers counselor education (M Ed, Ed S); curriculum and instruction - accomplished teaching (M Ed); curriculum studies (Ed D); early childhood education (M Ed, Ed S); education (M Ed, MAT, Ed D, Ed S); educational administration (Ed D); educational leadership (M Ed, Ed D, Ed S); English education (MAT); higher education (M Ed); higher education administration (M Ed); higher education leadership (Ed D); instructional technology (M Ed, Ed S); middle grades education (Ed S); P-12 education (MAT); P-12 leadership (M Ed, Ed S); reading education (M Ed, Ed S); school library media (M Ed, Ed S); school psychology (M Ed, Ed S); secondary education (M Ed, MAT, Ed S); special education (M Ed, MAT, Ed S). *Application deadline:* For fall admission, 3/1 priority date for domestic and international students; for spring admission, 10/1 priority date for domestic students, 10/1 for international students. Applications are processed on a rolling basis. *Application fee:* $50. Electronic applications accepted. *Dean*, Dr. Thomas Koballa, 912-478-5648, Fax: 912-478-5093, E-mail: tkoballa@georgiasouthern.edu.

College of Health and Human Sciences Students: 110 full-time (74 women), 120 part-time (76 women); includes 60 minority (33 Black or African American, non-Hispanic/Latino; 1 American Indian or Alaska Native, non-Hispanic/Latino; 8 Asian, non-Hispanic/Latino; 10 Hispanic/Latino; 8 Two or more races, non-Hispanic/Latino), 2 international. Average age 29. 309 applicants, 49% accepted, 50 enrolled. *Faculty:* 76 full-time (51 women), 1 (woman) part-time/adjunct. *Financial support:* In 2015–16, 118 students received support, including 24 fellowships with full tuition reimbursements available (averaging $7,750 per year), 9 research assistantships with full tuition reimbursements available (averaging $7,750 per year), 33 teaching assistantships with full tuition reimbursements available (averaging $7,750 per year); career-related internships or fieldwork, Federal Work-Study, scholarships/grants, traineeships, tuition waivers (full), and unspecified assistantships also available. Support available to part-time students. Financial award application deadline: 4/15; financial award applicants required to submit FAFSA. In 2015, 98 master's, 10 doctorates, 2 other advanced degrees awarded. *Degree program information:* Part-time and evening/weekend programs available. Part-time, evening/weekend, blended/hybrid learning. Offers dietetics (Certificate); family nurse practitioner (MSN); health and human sciences (MS, MSN, DNP, Certificate); kinesiology (MS); nurse educator (Certificate); nurse practitioner (MSN); nursing science (DNP); psychiatric mental health nurse practitioner (MSN); sport management (MS). *Application deadline:* For fall admission, 3/1 priority date for domestic students, 3/1 for international students; for spring admission, 10/1 priority date for domestic students, 10/1 for international students. Applications are processed on a rolling basis. *Application fee:* $50. Electronic applications accepted. *Dean*, Dr. Barry Joyner, 912-478-5322, Fax: 912-478-5349, E-mail: joyner@georgiasouthern.edu.

College of Liberal Arts and Social Sciences Students: 195 full-time (125 women), 82 part-time (54 women); includes 77 minority (47 Black or African American, non-Hispanic/Latino; 5 Asian, non-Hispanic/Latino; 16 Hispanic/Latino; 9 Two or more races, non-Hispanic/Latino), 17 international. Average age 28. 239 applicants, 66% accepted, 73 enrolled. *Faculty:* 179 full-time (79 women), 5 part-time/adjunct (1 woman). *Financial support:* In 2015–16, 153 students received support, including 72 fellowships with full tuition reimbursements available (averaging $7,750 per year), 10 research assistantships with full tuition reimbursements available (averaging $7,750 per year), 26 teaching assistantships with full tuition reimbursements available (averaging $7,750 per year); career-related internships or fieldwork, Federal Work-Study, scholarships/grants, tuition waivers (full), and unspecified assistantships also available. Support available to part-time students. Financial award application deadline: 4/15; financial award applicants required to submit FAFSA. In 2015, 88 master's, 9 doctorates, 9 other advanced degrees awarded. *Degree program information:* Part-time programs available. Part-time. Offers clinical psychology (Psy D); composition (MM); conducting (MM); English (MA); fine arts (MFA); history (MA); liberal arts and social sciences (MA, MFA, MM, MPA, MS, Psy D, Graduate Certificate); music education (MM); music technology (MM); performance (MM); psychology (MS); public administration (MPA); public and nonprofit management (Graduate Certificate); public history (Graduate Certificate); social science (MA); Spanish (MA). *Application deadline:* For fall admission, 3/1 priority date for domestic and international students; for spring admission, 10/1 priority date for domestic students, 10/1 for international students. Applications are processed on a rolling basis. *Application fee:* $50. Electronic applications accepted. *Dean*, Dr. Curtis Ricker, 912-478-2527, Fax: 912-478-5346, E-mail: cricker@georgiasouthern.edu.

College of Science and Mathematics Students: 82 full-time (33 women), 23 part-time (10 women); includes 20 minority (7 Black or African American, non-Hispanic/Latino; 6 Asian, non-Hispanic/Latino; 4 Hispanic/Latino; 3 Two or more races, non-Hispanic/Latino), 7 international. Average age 25. 70 applicants, 63% accepted, 30 enrolled. *Faculty:* 114 full-time (35 women), 2 part-time/adjunct (1 woman). *Financial support:* In 2015–16, 105 students received support, including 4 fellowships with full tuition reimbursements available (averaging $7,750 per year), 22 research assistantships with full tuition reimbursements available (averaging $7,750 per year), 79 teaching assistantships with full tuition reimbursements available (averaging $7,750 per year); career-related internships or fieldwork, Federal Work-Study, scholarships/grants, tuition waivers (full), and unspecified assistantships also available. Support available to part-time students. Financial award application deadline: 4/15; financial award applicants required to submit FAFSA. In 2015, 37 master's awarded. *Degree program information:* Part-time programs available. Part-time. Offers applied physical science (MS); biology (MS); mathematics (MS); science and mathematics (MS, Certificate). *Application deadline:* For fall admission, 3/1 priority date for domestic and international students; for spring admission, 10/1 priority date for domestic students, 10/1 for international students. Applications are processed on a rolling basis. *Application fee:* $50. Electronic applications accepted. *Application Contact:* Samuel T. Aldridge, Director, Graduate Admissions, 912-478-5384, Fax: 912-478-0740, E-mail: gradadmissions@georgiasouthern.edu. *Dean*, Dr. Martha Abell, 912-478-5132, Fax: 912-478-0836, E-mail: martha@georgiasouthern.edu.

Jiann-Ping Hsu College of Public Health Students: 158 full-time (105 women), 43 part-time (32 women); includes 104 minority (80 Black or African American, non-Hispanic/Latino; 7 Asian, non-Hispanic/Latino; 10 Hispanic/Latino; 7 Two or more races, non-Hispanic/Latino), 30 international. Average age 30. 256 applicants, 60% accepted, 55 enrolled. *Faculty:* 36 full-time (15 women), 1 (woman) part-time/adjunct. *Financial support:* In 2015–16, 113 students received support, including 53 fellowships with full tuition reimbursements available (averaging $7,750 per year), 3 research assistantships with full tuition reimbursements available (averaging $7,750 per year), 1 teaching assistantship with full tuition reimbursement available (averaging $7,750 per year); career-related internships or fieldwork, Federal Work-Study, scholarships/grants, tuition waivers (full), and unspecified assistantships also available. Support available to part-time students. Financial award application deadline: 4/15; financial award applicants required to submit FAFSA. In 2015, 52 master's, 8 doctorates awarded. *Degree program information:* Part-time programs available. Part-time. Offers biostatistics (MPH, Dr PH); community health behavior and education (Dr PH); community health education (MPH); environmental health sciences (MPH); epidemiology (MPH); health policy and management (MPH, Dr PH); healthcare administration (MHA); public health (MHA, MPH, Dr PH). *Application deadline:* For fall admission, 6/1 priority date for domestic and international students; for spring admission, 10/1 priority date for domestic students, 10/1 for international students. Applications are processed on a rolling basis. *Application fee:* $50. Electronic applications accepted. *Dean*, Dr. Greg Evans, 912-478-2676, Fax: 912-478-5605, E-mail: rgevans@georgiasouthern.edu.

GEORGIA SOUTHWESTERN STATE UNIVERSITY, Americus, GA 31709-4693

General Information State-supported, coed, comprehensive institution. *Enrollment:* 2,755 graduate, professional, and undergraduate students; 234 full-time matriculated graduate/professional students (207 women), 82 part-time matriculated graduate/professional students (56 women). *Enrollment by degree level:* 209 master's, 107 other advanced degrees. *Graduate faculty:* 34 full-time (18 women), 9 part-time/adjunct (8 women). Tuition, state resident: full-time $3330; part-time $185 per credit hour. Tuition, nonresident: full-time $13,248; part-time $736 per credit hour. *Required fees:* $1376. Tuition and fees vary according to course load, campus/location and program. *Graduate housing:* Room and/or apartments available on a first-come, first-served basis to single students; on-campus housing not available to married students. Typical cost: $4980 per year ($8640 including board). Room and board charges vary according to board plan and housing facility selected. *Student services:* Campus employment opportunities, campus safety program, career counseling, exercise/wellness program, international student services, low-cost health insurance, services for students with disabilities. *Library:* James Earl Carter Library. *Collection:* Books: 171,317 (physical), 2,639 (digital/electronic); Serial titles: 76 (physical), 71 (digital/electronic); Databases: 275. Weekly public service hours: 71; students can reserve study rooms.

Computer facilities: 260 computers available on campus for general student use. A campuswide network can be accessed from student residence rooms and from off campus. Online class registration is available.
Website: http://www.gsw.edu/

General Application Contact: Whitney Ford, Office of Graduate Admissions, 800-338-0082, Fax: 229-931-4206, E-mail: graduateadmissions@gsw.edu.

GRADUATE UNITS

School of Business Administration Students: 6 full-time (4 women), 28 part-time (18 women); includes 8 minority (7 Black or African American, non-Hispanic/Latino; 1 Asian, non-Hispanic/Latino), 1 international. Average age 29. 12 applicants, 67% accepted, 5 enrolled. *Faculty:* 11 full-time (4 women). *Financial support:* Application deadline: 6/1; applicants required to submit FAFSA. In 2015, 26 master's awarded. *Degree program information:* Part-time programs available. Part-time, online only, 100% online. Offers business administration (MBA). *Application deadline:* For fall admission, 6/30 for domestic students; for spring admission, 11/30 for domestic students; for summer admission, 4/30 for domestic students. Applications are processed on a rolling basis. *Application fee:* $25. Electronic applications accepted. *Application Contact:* Whitney Ford, Office of Graduate Admissions, 800-338-0082, Fax: 229-931-2983, E-mail: graduateadmissions@gsw.edu. *Dean*, Dr. Liz Wilson, 229-931-2090.

School of Computing and Mathematics Students: 10 full-time (3 women), 11 part-time (5 women); includes 5 minority (1 Black or African American, non-Hispanic/Latino; 1 American Indian or Alaska Native, non-Hispanic/Latino; 3 Asian, non-Hispanic/Latino), 11 international. Average age 33. 13 applicants, 100% accepted, 8 enrolled. *Faculty:* 2 full-time (0 women), 1 part-time/adjunct (0 women). *Financial support:* Application deadline: 6/1; applicants required to submit FAFSA. In 2015, 16 master's, 3 other advanced degrees awarded. *Degree program information:* Part-time programs available. Part-time, 100% online. Offers computer information systems (Graduate Certificate); computer science (MS). *Application deadline:* For fall admission, 5/31 for domestic students; for spring admission, 10/15 for domestic students; for summer admission, 3/15 for domestic students. Applications are processed on a rolling basis. *Application fee:* $25. Electronic applications accepted. *Application Contact:* Whitney Ford, Office of Graduate Admission, 800-338-0082, Fax: 229-931-2983. *Dean*, Dr. Boris V. Peltsverger, 229-931-2100.

School of Education Students: 203 full-time (186 women), 2 part-time (1 woman); includes 44 minority (40 Black or African American, non-Hispanic/Latino; 4 Hispanic/Latino). Average age 34. *Faculty:* 15 full-time (8 women), 6 part-time/adjunct (all women). *Financial support:* Application deadline: 6/1; applicants required to submit FAFSA. In 2015, 45 master's awarded. Offers early childhood education (M Ed, Ed S); middle grades education (Ed S); middle grades language arts (M Ed); middle grades mathematics (M Ed); special education (M Ed). *Application deadline:* For summer admission, 4/15 for domestic students. *Application fee:* $25. Electronic applications accepted. *Application Contact:* Whitney Ford, Office of Graduate Admissions, 800-338-0082, Fax: 229-931-2983. *Dean*, Dr. Rachel Abbott, 229-931-2145.

GEORGIA STATE UNIVERSITY, Atlanta, GA 30302-3083

General Information State-supported, coed, university. CGS member. *Enrollment:* 32,080 graduate, professional, and undergraduate students; 5,048 full-time matriculated graduate/professional students (2,936 women), 1,669 part-time matriculated graduate/professional students (1,122 women). *Enrollment by degree level:* 4,118 master's, 2,508 doctoral, 97 other advanced degrees. *Graduate faculty:* 816 full-time (340 women). Tuition, state resident: full-time $6876; part-time $382 per credit hour. Tuition, nonresident: full-time $22,374; part-time $1243 per credit hour. *Required fees:* $2128; $2128 per term. $1064 per term. Part-time tuition and fees vary according to course load and program. *Graduate housing:* Rooms and/or apartments available on a first-come, first-served basis to single and married students. Typical cost: $9850 per year ($13,646 including board) for single students. Room and board charges vary according to board plan and housing facility selected. *Student services:* Campus employment opportunities, campus safety program, career counseling, child daycare facilities, exercise/wellness program, international student services, services for students with disabilities. *Library:* University Library plus 1 other. *Collection:* Books: 1.7 million (physical), 465,205 (digital/electronic); Serial titles: 13,194 (digital/electronic). Students can reserve study rooms. *Research affiliation:* Cerro Tololo Interamerican Observatory (astronomy), Research Atlanta, Inc. (policy studies), Oak Ridge National Laboratory (environmental policy), Lowell Observatory (astronomy), Brookhaven National Laboratory (physics), Argonne National Laboratory, Advanced Photon Source (crystallography).

Computer facilities: 935 computers available on campus for general student use. A campuswide network can be accessed from student residence rooms and from off campus. Online class registration is available.
Website: http://www.gsu.edu/

GRADUATE UNITS

Andrew Young School of Policy Studies Students: 377 full-time (247 women), 115 part-time (70 women); includes 187 minority (139 Black or African American, non-Hispanic/Latino; 12 Asian, non-Hispanic/Latino; 26 Hispanic/Latino; 2 Native Hawaiian or other Pacific Islander, non-Hispanic/Latino; 8 Two or more races, non-Hispanic/Latino), 97 international. Average age 29. 575 applicants, 59% accepted, 158 enrolled. *Faculty:* 63 full-time (22 women). *Financial support:* Unspecified assistantships available. Financial award application deadline: 2/15; financial award applicants required to submit FAFSA. In 2015, 156 master's, 17 doctorates, 7 other advanced degrees awarded. *Degree program information:* Part-time and evening/weekend programs available. Part-time, evening/weekend. Offers criminal justice (MPA, MS, PhD); disaster management (Certificate); disaster policy (MPA); economics (MA); environmental economics (PhD); environmental policy (PhD); experimental economics (PhD); health policy (PhD); labor economics (PhD); management and finance (MPA); nonprofit management (MPA, Certificate); nonprofit policy (MPA); planning and economic development (MPP, Certificate); policy (MA); policy analysis and evaluation (MPA); policy studies (MA, MPA, MPP, MS, MSW, PhD, Certificate); public administration (MS); public and nonprofit management (PhD); public finance (PhD); public finance and budgeting (PhD); public finance policy (MPA); public health (MPA); urban and regional economics (PhD). *Application deadline:* For fall admission, 1/15 for domestic and international students. *Application fee:* $50. Electronic applications accepted. *Dean*, Dr. Mary Beth Walker, 404-413-0000, Fax: 404-413-0004.

School of Social Work Students: 104 full-time (94 women), 10 part-time (9 women); includes 71 minority (62 Black or African American, non-Hispanic/Latino; 4 Hispanic/Latino; 2 Native Hawaiian or other Pacific Islander, non-Hispanic/Latino; 3 Two or more races, non-Hispanic/Latino), 1 international. Average age 28. 119 applicants, 75% accepted, 43 enrolled. *Faculty:* 12 full-time (8 women). *Financial support:* In 2015–16, research assistantships with tuition reimbursements (averaging $4,000 per year), teaching assistantships with tuition reimbursements (averaging $4,000 per year) were awarded; career-related internships or fieldwork, institutionally sponsored loans, scholarships/grants, tuition waivers, and unspecified assistantships also available. Financial award application deadline: 2/1; financial award applicants required to submit FAFSA. In 2015, 40 master's, 1 other advanced degree awarded. *Degree program information:* Part-time programs available. Part-time. Offers child welfare leadership (Certificate); community partnerships (MSW); forensic social work (Certificate). *Application deadline:* For fall admission, 2/1 priority date for domestic and international students. *Application fee:* $50. Electronic applications accepted. *Director of School of Social Work*, Brian Bride, 404-413-1052, Fax: 404-413-1075, E-mail: bbride@gsu.edu.

Byrdine F. Lewis School of Nursing Students: 275 full-time (195 women), 230 part-time (204 women); includes 192 minority (123 Black or African American, non-Hispanic/Latino; 49 Asian, non-Hispanic/Latino; 12 Hispanic/Latino; 2 Native Hawaiian or other Pacific Islander, non-Hispanic/Latino; 6 Two or more races, non-Hispanic/Latino), 35 international. Average age 33. 240 applicants, 61% accepted, 95 enrolled. *Faculty:* 18 full-time (11 women). *Financial support:* In 2015–16, research assistantships with tuition reimbursements (averaging $1,666 per year), teaching assistantships with tuition reimbursements (averaging $1,920 per year) were awarded; scholarships/grants, tuition waivers (full and partial), and unspecified assistantships also available. Support available to part-time students. Financial award application deadline: 8/1; financial award applicants required to submit FAFSA. In 2015, 115 master's, 40 doctorates, 19 other advanced degrees awarded. *Degree program information:* Part-time programs available. Part-time, blended/hybrid learning. Offers adult health clinical nurse specialist/nurse practitioner (MS, Certificate); child health clinical nurse specialist/pediatric nurse practitioner (MS, Certificate); family nurse practitioner (MS, Certificate); family psychiatric mental health nurse practitioner (MS, Certificate); nursing (PhD); nursing leadership in healthcare innovations (MS); nutrition (MS); perinatal clinical nurse specialist/women's health nurse practitioner (MS, Certificate); physical therapy (DPT); respiratory therapy (MS). *Application deadline:* For fall admission, 2/1 priority date for domestic and international students; for spring admission, 9/15 for domestic and international students. Applications are processed on a rolling basis. *Application fee:* $50. Electronic applications accepted. *Dean of Nursing*, Nancy Kropf, 404-413-1101, Fax: 404-413-1090, E-mail: nkropf@gsu.edu.

Division of Nutrition Students: 34 full-time (29 women), 3 part-time (all women); includes 5 minority (3 Asian, non-Hispanic/Latino; 2 Two or more races, non-Hispanic/Latino), 1 international. Average age 28. 49 applicants, 37% accepted, 12 enrolled. *Faculty:* 7 full-time (4 women). *Financial support:* In 2015–16, research assistantships with tuition reimbursements (averaging $1,647 per year), teaching assistantships with full tuition reimbursements (averaging $2,666 per year) were awarded. Financial award application deadline: 4/1. In 2015, 23 master's awarded. *Degree program information:* Part-time programs available. Part-time. Offers nutrition (MS). *Application deadline:* For fall admission, 5/15 for domestic and international students; for spring admission, 10/1 for domestic and international students. *Application fee:* $50. Electronic applications accepted. *Department Head*, Dr. Anita Nucci, 404-413-1234, Fax: 404-413-1228.

Division of Physical Therapy Students: 107 full-time (61 women), 1 part-time (0 women); includes 29 minority (12 Black or African American, non-Hispanic/Latino; 15 Asian, non-Hispanic/Latino; 1 Native Hawaiian or other Pacific Islander, non-Hispanic/Latino; 1 Two or more races, non-Hispanic/Latino), 2 international. Average age 26. 343 applicants, 15% accepted, 36 enrolled. *Faculty:* 4 full-time (1 woman). *Financial support:* In 2015–16, research assistantships with full tuition reimbursements (averaging $2,000 per year), teaching assistantships with full tuition reimbursements (averaging $2,000 per year) were awarded; scholarships/grants, tuition waivers (partial), and unspecified assistantships also available. Financial award application deadline: 4/1; financial award applicants required to submit FAFSA. In 2015, 33 doctorates awarded. Offers physical therapy (DPT). *Application deadline:* For fall admission, 11/15 for domestic and international students. *Application fee:*

$50. Electronic applications accepted. *Department Head,* Dr. Andrew Butler, 404-413-1415, Fax: 404-413-1230, E-mail: andrewbutler@gsu.edu.

Division of Respiratory Therapy Students: 25 full-time (13 women), 5 part-time (2 women); includes 9 minority (5 Black or African American, non-Hispanic/Latino; 2 Asian, non-Hispanic/Latino; 2 Two or more races, non-Hispanic/Latino), 12 international. Average age 27. 49 applicants, 67% accepted, 30 enrolled. *Faculty:* 3 full-time (2 women). *Financial support:* In 2015–16, research assistantships with full tuition reimbursements (averaging $2,000 per year), teaching assistantships with full tuition reimbursements (averaging $2,000 per year) were awarded; scholarships/grants and unspecified assistantships also available. Financial award application deadline: 6/1; financial award applicants required to submit FAFSA. In 2015, 9 master's awarded. Offers respiratory therapy (MS). *Application deadline:* For fall admission, 5/1 for domestic and international students; for spring admission, 9/15 for domestic and international students. *Application fee:* $50. Electronic applications accepted. *Department Head,* Dr. Douglas Gardenhire, 404-413-1270, Fax: 404-413-1230, E-mail: dgardenhire@gsu.edu.

College of Arts and Sciences Students: 1,741 full-time (958 women), 414 part-time (260 women); includes 579 minority (298 Black or African American, non-Hispanic/Latino; 2 American Indian or Alaska Native, non-Hispanic/Latino; 124 Asian, non-Hispanic/Latino; 83 Hispanic/Latino; 1 Native Hawaiian or other Pacific Islander, non-Hispanic/Latino; 71 Two or more races, non-Hispanic/Latino), 478 international. Average age 32. 2,477 applicants, 38% accepted, 539 enrolled. *Faculty:* 444 full-time (180 women). *Financial support:* Fellowships with tuition reimbursements, research assistantships with tuition reimbursements, teaching assistantships with tuition reimbursements, career-related internships or fieldwork, scholarships/grants, health care benefits, tuition waivers (partial), and unspecified assistantships available. Support available to part-time students. Financial award application deadline: 4/15; financial award applicants required to submit FAFSA. In 2015, 448 master's, 124 doctorates, 22 other advanced degrees awarded. *Degree program information:* Part-time and evening/weekend programs available. Part-time, evening/weekend. Offers African-American studies (MA); analytical chemistry (MS, PhD); anthropology (MA); applied and environmental microbiology (MS, PhD); applied linguistics (MA, PhD); applied linguistics and pedagogy (MA); arts and sciences (MA, MA Ed, MFA, MHP, MM, MS, PhD, Certificate, Graduate Certificate); astronomy (PhD); biochemistry (MS, PhD); bioinformatics (MS, PhD); biophysical chemistry (PhD); biostatistics (MS, PhD); cellular and molecular biology and physiology (MS, PhD); clinical (PhD); cognitive sciences (PhD); community (PhD); computational chemistry (MS, PhD); computer science (MS, PhD); creative writing (MA, MFA, PhD); developmental (PhD); discrete mathematics (MS); English (MA, PhD); fiction (MA, MFA); film, video, and digital imaging (MA); French (MA); French studies (MA); geochemistry (PhD); geographic information systems (Certificate); geography (MS); geology (MS); heritage preservation (MHP); historic preservation (MA); history (MA, PhD); human communication and social influence (MA); interpretation (Certificate); Latin American studies (Certificate); literary studies (MA, PhD); literature and culture (MA); mass communication (MA); mathematics (MS, PhD); media and society (PhD); molecular genetics and biochemistry (MS, PhD); moving image studies (PhD); neurobiology and behavior (MS, PhD); neuropsychology and behavioral neuroscience (PhD); organic/medicinal chemistry (MS, PhD); philosophy (MA); physical chemistry (MS); physics (MS, PhD); poetry (MA, MFA); political science (MA, PhD); public communication (PhD); public history (MA); religious studies (MA); rhetoric and composition (MA, PhD); rhetoric and politics (PhD); scientific computing (MS); sociology (MA, PhD); Spanish (MA); statistics (MS); translation (Certificate); translation and interpretation (Certificate); world history (MA). *Application deadline:* For fall admission, 7/1 for domestic and international students; for spring admission, 11/15 for domestic and international students. *Application fee:* $50. Electronic applications accepted. *Application Contact:* Amber Amari, Director, Graduate and Scheduling Services, 404-413-5037, E-mail: aamari@gsu.edu. *Dean,* Dr. William J. Long, 404-413-5114, Fax: 404-413-5117, E-mail: long@gsu.edu.

Ernest G. Welch School of Art and Design Students: 55 full-time (39 women), 6 part-time (4 women); includes 10 minority (4 Black or African American, non-Hispanic/Latino; 2 Asian, non-Hispanic/Latino; 1 Hispanic/Latino; 3 Two or more races, non-Hispanic/Latino), 4 international. Average age 32. 89 applicants, 30% accepted, 21 enrolled. *Faculty:* 26 full-time (15 women). *Financial support:* In 2015–16, fellowships with full tuition reimbursements (averaging $11,000 per year), research assistantships with full tuition reimbursements (averaging $6,000 per year), teaching assistantships with full tuition reimbursements (averaging $7,000 per year) were awarded; scholarships/grants and unspecified assistantships also available. Financial award application deadline: 4/15; financial award applicants required to submit FAFSA. In 2015, 25 master's awarded. Offers art and design (MA, MA Ed, MFA); art education (MA Ed); art history (MA); ceramics (MFA); drawing and painting (MFA); graphic design (MFA); interior design (MFA); photography (MFA); printmaking (MFA); sculpture (MFA); textiles (MFA). *Application deadline:* For fall admission, 1/6 for domestic and international students; for spring admission, 1/15 priority date for domestic and international students. *Application fee:* $50. Electronic applications accepted. *Application Contact:* Hubert Stanley Anderson, Director of Graduate Studies, 404-413-5229, Fax: 404-413-5261, E-mail: artgrad@gsu.edu. *Director, Welch School of Art and Design,* Michael White, 404-413-5228, E-mail: mwhite@gsu.edu.

Gerontology Institute Students: 13 full-time (11 women), 19 part-time (17 women); includes 23 minority (19 Black or African American, non-Hispanic/Latino; 2 Asian, non-Hispanic/Latino; 1 Hispanic/Latino; 1 Two or more races, non-Hispanic/Latino), 1 international. Average age 46. 10 applicants, 80% accepted, 7 enrolled. *Faculty:* 4 full-time (all women). *Financial support:* In 2015–16, research assistantships with full tuition reimbursements (averaging $6,000 per year) were awarded; career-related internships or fieldwork, scholarships/grants, and unspecified assistantships also available. Financial award application deadline: 4/15; financial award applicants required to submit FAFSA. In 2015, 10 master's, 3 other advanced degrees awarded. *Degree program information:* Part-time programs available. Part-time. Offers gerontology (MA, Certificate). *Application deadline:* For fall admission, 4/15 for domestic and international students; for spring admission, 10/15 for domestic and international students. Applications are processed on a rolling basis. *Application fee:* $50. Electronic applications accepted. *Application Contact:* Dr. Candace L. Kemp, Director of Graduate Studies, 404-413-5210, Fax: 404-413-5219, E-mail: ckemp@gsu.edu. *Director,* Dr. Elizabeth O. Burgess, 404-413-5210, Fax: 404-413-5219, E-mail: eburgess@gsu.edu.

Institute for Women's, Gender, and Sexuality Studies Students: 15 full-time (13 women), 5 part-time (all women); includes 10 minority (6 Black or African American, non-Hispanic/Latino; 3 Asian, non-Hispanic/Latino; 1 Two or more races, non-Hispanic/Latino), 1 international. Average age 33. 20 applicants, 85% accepted, 7 enrolled. *Faculty:* 4 full-time (all women). *Financial support:* In 2015–16, research assistantships with full tuition reimbursements (averaging $7,000 per year), teaching assistantships with full tuition reimbursements (averaging $7,500 per year) were awarded; career-related internships or fieldwork, health care benefits, and unspecified assistantships also available. Financial award application deadline: 2/15. In 2015, 1 other advanced degree awarded. *Degree program information:* Part-time programs available. Part-time. Offers women's, gender, and sexuality studies (MA, Graduate Certificate). *Application deadline:* For fall admission, 2/15 for domestic and international students. *Application fee:* $50. Electronic applications accepted. *Application Contact:* Dr. Amira Jarmakani, Director of Graduate Studies, 404-413-6583, Fax: 404-413-6585, E-mail: amira@gsu.edu. *Director,* Dr. Susan Talburt, 404-413-6581, Fax: 404-413-6585, E-mail: stalburt@gsu.edu.

Neuroscience Institute Students: 51 full-time (27 women); includes 9 minority (1 Black or African American, non-Hispanic/Latino; 2 Asian, non-Hispanic/Latino; 2 Hispanic/Latino; 2 Native Hawaiian or other Pacific Islander, non-Hispanic/Latino; 2 Two or more races, non-Hispanic/Latino), 9 international. Average age 29. 53 applicants, 30% accepted, 11 enrolled. *Faculty:* 18 full-time (7 women). *Financial support:* In 2015–16, fellowships (averaging $22,000 per year), research assistantships (averaging $22,000 per year) were awarded. Financial award applicants required to submit FAFSA. In 2015, 10 doctorates awarded. Offers neuroscience (PhD). *Application deadline:* For fall admission, 12/10 for domestic and international students. *Application fee:* $50. Electronic applications accepted. *Application Contact:* Dr. Laura L. Carruth, Director of Graduate Studies, 404-413-5340, E-mail: lcarruth@gsu.edu. *Director,* Prof. Walter Wilczynski, 404-413-6307, E-mail: wwilczynski@gsu.edu.

School of Music Students: 65 full-time (30 women), 7 part-time (3 women); includes 25 minority (19 Black or African American, non-Hispanic/Latino; 3 Asian, non-Hispanic/Latino; 3 Hispanic/Latino), 8 international. Average age 30. 88 applicants, 64% accepted, 35 enrolled. *Faculty:* 29 full-time (7 women). *Financial support:* In 2015–16, research assistantships with full tuition reimbursements (averaging $4,000 per year) were awarded; Federal Work-Study, scholarships/grants, health care benefits, tuition waivers (partial), and unspecified assistantships also available. Financial award application deadline: 3/1; financial award applicants required to submit FAFSA. In 2015, 26 master's, 1 other advanced degree awarded. *Degree program information:* Part-time and evening/weekend programs available. Part-time, evening/weekend. Offers choral conducting (MM); jazz studies (MM); music (Certificate); music composition (MM); music education (PhD); orchestral conducting (MM); performance (MM); piano pedagogy (MM); wind band conducting (MM). *Application deadline:* For fall admission, 3/1 priority date for domestic and international students; for spring admission, 10/1 priority date for domestic and international students. Applications are processed on a rolling basis. *Application fee:* $50. Electronic applications accepted. *Application Contact:* Dr. Steven Andrew Harper, Graduate Director, 404-413-5943, Fax: 404-413-5910, E-mail: sharper@gsu.edu. *Director, School of Music,* William Dwight Coleman, 404-413-5953, Fax: 404-413-5910, E-mail: wcoleman@gsu.edu.

College of Education Students: 768 full-time (576 women), 415 part-time (305 women); includes 518 minority (382 Black or African American, non-Hispanic/Latino; 1 American Indian or Alaska Native, non-Hispanic/Latino; 36 Asian, non-Hispanic/Latino; 75 Hispanic/Latino; 24 Two or more races, non-Hispanic/Latino), 41 international. Average age 32. 380 applicants, 80% accepted, 232 enrolled. *Faculty:* 118 full-time (77 women). *Financial support:* In 2015–16, fellowships with full tuition reimbursements (averaging $25,000 per year), research assistantships with tuition reimbursements (averaging $4,867 per year), teaching assistantships with tuition reimbursements (averaging $4,683 per year) were awarded; career-related internships or fieldwork, Federal Work-Study, scholarships/grants, tuition waivers (partial), and unspecified assistantships also available. Support available to part-time students. Financial award applicants required to submit FAFSA. In 2015, 434 master's, 69 doctorates, 27 other advanced degrees awarded. *Degree program information:* Part-time and evening/weekend programs available. Part-time, evening/weekend, online learning. Offers autism spectrum disorders (PhD); behavior and learning disabilities (M Ed); behavior disorders (PhD); communication disorders (M Ed, PhD); counseling psychology (PhD); counselor education and practice (PhD); curriculum and instruction (Ed D); early childhood and elementary education (PhD); early childhood education (M Ed, Ed S); early childhood special education (M Ed, PhD); education (M Ed, MAT, MS, Ed D, PhD, Ed S); education of students with exceptionalities (PhD); educational leadership (M Ed, Ed D, Ed S); educational psychology (MS, PhD); educational research (MS, PhD); English education (MAT); exercise science (MS); health and physical education (M Ed); kinesiology (PhD); learning disabilities (PhD); mathematics education (M Ed, MAT); mental health counseling (MS, Ed S); mental retardation (PhD); middle level education (MAT); multiple and severe disabilities (M Ed); orthopedic impairments (PhD); reading, language and literacy education (M Ed, MAT); rehabilitation counseling (MS); school counseling (M Ed, Ed S); school psychology (M Ed, PhD, Ed S); science education (M Ed, MAT); sensory impairments (PhD); social foundations of education (MS, PhD); social studies education (M Ed, MAT); special education adapted curriculum (intellectual disabilities) (M Ed); special education deaf education (M Ed); special education general and adapted curriculum (autism spectrum disorders) (M Ed); special education physical and health disabilities (orthopedic impairments) (M Ed); sports administration (MS); sports medicine (MS); teaching and learning (PhD); urban education (M Ed); urban teacher leadership (M Ed). *Application fee:* $50. Electronic applications accepted. *Application Contact:* Nancy Keita, Director, Office of Academic Assistance and Graduate Admissions, 404-413-8001, E-mail: nkeita@gsu.edu. *Interim Dean,* Dr. Paul A. Alberto, 404-413-8100, Fax: 404-413-8103, E-mail: palberto@gsu.edu.

Learning Technologies Division Students: 16 full-time (12 women), 32 part-time (20 women); includes 22 minority (17 Black or African American, non-Hispanic/Latino; 3 Asian, non-Hispanic/Latino; 2 Two or more races, non-Hispanic/Latino). Average age 37. 13 applicants, 77% accepted, 9 enrolled. *Faculty:* 4 full-time (1 woman). *Financial support:* Federal Work-Study and institutionally sponsored loans available. In 2015, 1 master's awarded. *Degree program information:* Part-time and evening/weekend programs available. Part-time, evening/weekend. Offers instructional design and technology (MS); instructional technology (PhD). *Application fee:* $50. Electronic applications accepted. *Application Contact:* Nancy Keita, Director, Office of Academic Assistance and Graduate Admissions, 404-413-8001, E-mail: nkeita@gsu.edu. *Interim Dean,* Dr. Paul A. Alberto, 404-413-8100, Fax: 404-413-8103, E-mail: palberto@gsu.edu.

College of Law Students: 637 full-time (302 women), 18 part-time (14 women); includes 190 minority (80 Black or African American, non-Hispanic/Latino; 3 American Indian or Alaska Native, non-Hispanic/Latino; 50 Asian, non-Hispanic/Latino; 46 Hispanic/Latino; 2 Native Hawaiian or other Pacific Islander, non-Hispanic/Latino; 9 Two or more races, non-Hispanic/Latino), 9 international. Average age 29. 1,520 applicants, 36% accepted, 235 enrolled. *Faculty:* 40 full-time (16 women). *Financial support:* In 2015–16, research assistantships with tuition reimbursements (averaging $2,500 per year), teaching assistantships (averaging $2,500 per year) were awarded; scholarships/grants, tuition waivers, and unspecified assistantships also available. Financial award application deadline: 4/1; financial award applicants required to submit FAFSA. In 2015, 193 doctorates awarded. *Degree program information:* Part-time and evening/weekend programs available. Part-time, evening/weekend. Offers law (JD). *Application deadline:* For fall admission, 3/15 for domestic students, 3/15 priority date for international students. Applications are processed on a rolling basis. *Application fee:* $50. Electronic applications accepted. *Application Contact:* Dr. Cheryl Jester-George, Senior Director of Admissions, 404-413-9004, Fax: 404-413-9203, E-mail: cjgeorge@gsu.edu. *Dean, College of Law*, Dr. Steven J. Kaminshine, 404-413-9035, Fax: 404-413-9227, E-mail: skaminshine@gsu.edu.

J. Mack Robinson College of Business Students: 1,058 full-time (506 women), 367 part-time (179 women); includes 515 minority (287 Black or African American, non-Hispanic/Latino; 1 American Indian or Alaska Native, non-Hispanic/Latino; 145 Asian, non-Hispanic/Latino; 56 Hispanic/Latino; 2 Native Hawaiian or other Pacific Islander, non-Hispanic/Latino; 24 Two or more races, non-Hispanic/Latino), 392 international. Average age 31. 1,774 applicants, 49% accepted, 451 enrolled. *Faculty:* 120 full-time (29 women). *Financial support:* Research assistantships, teaching assistantships, scholarships/grants, tuition waivers, and unspecified assistantships available. Financial award applicants required to submit FAFSA. In 2015, 868 master's, 28 doctorates, 20 other advanced degrees awarded. *Degree program information:* Part-time and evening/weekend programs available. Part-time, evening/weekend. Offers actuarial science (MAS); business (EMBA, Exec MS, GMBA, M Tax, MAS, MBA, MIB, MPA, MPA, MS, MSCIS, MSHA, MSIS, MSRE, PMBA, EDB, PhD, Certificate); business administration (MBA); business analysis (MBA, MS); computer information systems (PhD); enterprise risk management (MBA, Certificate); entrepreneurship (MBA); executive business administration (EMBA); finance (MBA, MS, PhD); financial risk management (MBA); global business administration (GMBA); health informatics (MBA, MS); hotel real estate (MBA); human resources management (MBA, MS); information systems (MSIS, Certificate); information systems development and project management (MBA); information systems management (MBA); managing information technology (Exec MS); marketing (MBA, MS, PhD); mathematical risk management (MS); operations management (MBA, MS); organization behavior/human resource management (PhD); organization management (MBA); organizational change (MS); professional business administration (PMBA); real estate (MBA, MS, PhD, Certificate); risk and insurance (MS); risk management and insurance (MBA, MS, PhD, Certificate); strategic management (PhD); the wireless organization (MBA). *Application deadline:* For fall admission, 5/1 priority date for domestic students, 2/1 priority date for international students; for spring admission, 9/15 priority date for domestic students, 4/1 priority date for international students. Applications are processed on a rolling basis. *Application fee:* $50. Electronic applications accepted. *Application Contact:* Toby McChesney, Assistant Dean for Graduate Recruiting and Student Services, 404-413-7167, Fax: 404-413-7162, E-mail: rcbgradadmissions@gsu.edu. *Dean of the J. Mack Robinson College of Business*, Dr. Richard D. Phillips, 404-413-7000, Fax: 404-413-7035.

Institute of Health Administration Degree program information: Part-time and evening/weekend programs available. Part-time, evening/weekend. Offers health administration (MBA, MSHA); health informatics (MBA, MSCIS). Electronic applications accepted.

Institute of International Business Students: 38 full-time (20 women), 15 part-time (8 women); includes 31 minority (18 Black or African American, non-Hispanic/Latino; 2 Asian, non-Hispanic/Latino; 10 Hispanic/Latino; 1 Two or more races, non-Hispanic/Latino), 9 international. Average age 30. 39 applicants, 69% accepted, 16 enrolled. *Faculty:* 7 full-time (3 women). *Financial support:* Research assistantships, teaching assistantships, scholarships/grants, tuition waivers (partial), and unspecified assistantships available. Financial award application deadline: 5/1. In 2015, 42 master's awarded. *Degree program information:* Part-time and evening/weekend programs available. Part-time, evening/weekend. Offers international business (GMBA, MBA, MIB); international business and information technology (MBA); international entrepreneurship (MBA). *Application deadline:* For fall admission, 5/1 priority date for domestic students, 2/1 priority date for international students; for spring admission, 9/15 priority date for domestic students, 5/1 priority date for international students. Applications are processed on a rolling basis. *Application fee:* $50. Electronic applications accepted. *Application Contact:* Toby McChesney, Assistant Dean for Graduate Recruiting and Student Services, 404-413-7167, Fax: 404-413-7162, E-mail: rcbgradadmissions@gsu.edu. *Professor/Director of the Institute of International Business*, Dr. Daniel Bello, 404-413-7275, Fax: 404-413-7276.

School of Accountancy Students: 172 full-time (100 women), 103 part-time (60 women); includes 117 minority (53 Black or African American, non-Hispanic/Latino; 48 Asian, non-Hispanic/Latino; 10 Hispanic/Latino; 1 Native Hawaiian or other Pacific Islander, non-Hispanic/Latino; 5 Two or more races, non-Hispanic/Latino), 52 international. Average age 29. 244 applicants, 67% accepted, 117 enrolled. *Faculty:* 15 full-time (2 women). *Financial support:* Research assistantships, teaching assistantships, scholarships/grants, tuition waivers, and unspecified assistantships available. Financial award applicants required to submit FAFSA. In 2015, 176 master's, 2 doctorates awarded. *Degree program information:* Part-time and evening/weekend programs available. Part-time, evening/weekend. Offers accounting (MBA, PhD); information systems audit and control (MS); professional accountancy (MPA); taxation (M Tax). *Application deadline:* For fall admission, 5/1 priority date for domestic students, 2/1 priority date for international students; for spring admission, 9/15 priority date for domestic students, 4/1 priority date for international students. Applications are processed on a rolling basis. *Application fee:* $50. Electronic applications accepted. *Application Contact:* Toby McChesney, Assistant Dean for Graduate Recruiting and Student Services, 404-413-7167, Fax: 404-413-7162, E-mail: rcbgradadmissions@gsu.edu. *Director of the School of Accountancy*, Dr. Galen R. Sevcik, 404-413-7200, Fax: 404-413-7203.

School of Public Health Students: 192 full-time (152 women), 106 part-time (86 women); includes 156 minority (112 Black or African American, non-Hispanic/Latino; 2 American Indian or Alaska Native, non-Hispanic/Latino; 29 Asian, non-Hispanic/Latino; 9 Hispanic/Latino; 4 Two or more races, non-Hispanic/Latino), 38 international. Average age 30. 524 applicants, 41% accepted, 90 enrolled. *Faculty:* 21 full-time (13 women). *Financial support:* In 2015–16, fellowships (averaging $2,500 per year), research assistantships with full tuition reimbursements (averaging $22,000 per year), teaching assistantships with full tuition reimbursements (averaging $22,000 per year) were awarded; career-related internships or fieldwork, scholarships/grants, health care benefits, unspecified assistantships, and out-of-state tuition waivers also available. In 2015, 60 master's, 4 doctorates, 9 other advanced degrees awarded. *Degree program information:* Part-time programs available. Part-time. Offers public health (MPH, PhD, Certificate). *Application deadline:* For fall admission, 2/1 for domestic and international students; for spring admission, 10/1 for domestic and international students. *Application fee:* $50. Electronic applications accepted. *Application Contact:* Courtney M. Burton, Graduate Coordinator, 404-413-1143, E-mail: cmburton@gsu.edu. *Dean*, Dr. Michael P. Eriksen, 404-413-1132, Fax: 404-413-1140, E-mail: meriksen@gsu.edu.

GERSTNER SLOAN KETTERING GRADUATE SCHOOL OF BIOMEDICAL SCIENCES, New York, NY 10021

General Information Independent, coed, graduate-only institution. *Graduate housing:* Rooms and/or apartments available on a first-come, first-served basis to single and married students. *Research affiliation:* Memorial Sloan-Kettering Cancer Center (biomedical sciences).

GRADUATE UNITS

Program in Cancer Biology Offers cancer biology (PhD). Electronic applications accepted.

GLION INSTITUTE OF HIGHER EDUCATION, CH-1823 Glion-sur-Montreux, Switzerland

General Information Proprietary, coed, comprehensive institution.

GRADUATE UNITS

Graduate Programs *Degree program information:* Evening/weekend programs available. Evening/weekend.

GLOBAL UNIVERSITY, Springfield, MO 65804

General Information Independent-religious, coed, comprehensive institution. *Graduate housing:* On-campus housing not available.

GRADUATE UNITS

Graduate School of Theology *Degree program information:* Part-time and evening/weekend programs available. Part-time, evening/weekend, online learning. Offers bible and theology (D Min); biblical language (M Div); biblical studies (MA); Christian ministry (M Div, D Min); ministerial studies (MA). Electronic applications accepted.

GLOBE UNIVERSITY–WOODBURY, Woodbury, MN 55125

General Information Proprietary, coed, comprehensive institution.

GRADUATE UNITS

Minnesota School of Business Offers business administration (MBA); health care management (MSM); information technology (MSM); managerial leadership (MSM).

★ GODDARD COLLEGE, Plainfield, VT 05667-9432

General Information Independent, coed, comprehensive institution. *Graduate housing:* On-campus housing not available. *Student services:* Services for students with disabilities, teacher training, writing training. *Library:* Eliot Pratt Center. *Collection:* Books: 34,000 (physical), 151,000 (digital/electronic); Databases: 21.

Computer facilities: 55 computers available on campus for general student use. A campuswide network can be accessed from student residence rooms and from off campus. Online class registration, library services are available.
Website: http://www.goddard.edu/

General Application Contact: Gariot Louima, Dean of Enrollment and External Affairs, 800-468-4888 Ext. 266, Fax: 802-454-1029, E-mail: gariot.louima@goddard.edu.

GRADUATE UNITS

Graduate Division Students: 317 full-time (243 women), 11 part-time (9 women); includes 40 minority (13 Black or African American, non-Hispanic/Latino; 1 American Indian or Alaska Native, non-Hispanic/Latino; 5 Asian, non-Hispanic/Latino; 14 Hispanic/Latino; 1 Native Hawaiian or other Pacific Islander, non-Hispanic/Latino; 6 Two or more races, non-Hispanic/Latino), 1 international. Average age 37. *Faculty:* 12 full-time (11 women), 60 part-time/adjunct (47 women). *Financial support:* In 2015–16, 84 students received support. Scholarships/grants and tuition waivers (full and partial) available. Financial award applicants required to submit FAFSA. In 2015, 163 master's awarded. *Degree program information:* Part-time programs available. Part-time, online learning. Offers community education (MA); consciousness studies (MA); creative writing (MFA); expressive arts therapy (MA); health arts and sciences (MA); interdisciplinary arts (MFA); psychology (MA); sexual orientation (MA); social innovation and sustainability (MA); teacher licensure (MA); transformative language arts (MA). *Application deadline:* Applications are processed on a rolling basis. *Application fee:* $65. Electronic applications accepted. *Application Contact:* Gariot Louima, Dean of Enrollment and External Affairs, 800-906-8312, Fax: 802-454-1029, E-mail: admissions@goddard.edu. *Academic Dean and Chief Academic Officer*, Dr. Lewis Jones, 802-322-1655, Fax: 802-454-1451, E-mail: lewis.jones@goddard.edu.

See Display on next page and Close-Up on page 879.

GOLDEN GATE UNIVERSITY, San Francisco, CA 94105-2968

General Information Independent, coed, university. *Graduate housing:* On-campus housing not available.

GRADUATE UNITS

Ageno School of Business *Degree program information:* Part-time and evening/weekend programs available. Part-time, evening/weekend. Offers accounting (MBA); business administration (EMBA, MBA, PMBA, DBA); finance (MBA, MS, Certificate); financial planning (MS, Certificate); healthcare information systems (Certificate); human resource management (MBA, MS); human resources management (Certificate); information systems (MS); information technology (MBA); information technology management (Certificate); integrated marketing and communications (MS, Certificate); international business (MBA); management (MBA); marketing (MBA, MS, Certificate); operations supply chain management (Certificate); psychology (MA, Certificate); public administration (EMPA); public relations (MS, Certificate); technical market analysis (Certificate). Electronic applications accepted.

School of Accounting *Degree program information:* Part-time and evening/weekend programs available. Part-time, evening/weekend. Offers accounting (M Ac, MSA, Graduate Certificate); forensic accounting (M Ac, MSA, Graduate Certificate); taxation (M Ac). Electronic applications accepted.

School of Law *Degree program information:* Part-time and evening/weekend programs available. Part-time, evening/weekend. Offers environmental law (LL M); intellectual property law (LL M); international legal studies (LL M, SJD); law (JD); taxation (LL M); U. S. legal studies (LL M). Electronic applications accepted.

School of Taxation *Degree program information:* Part-time and evening/weekend programs available. Part-time, evening/weekend. Offers advanced studies in taxation (Certificate); estate planning (Certificate); international tax (Certificate); tax (Certificate); taxation (MS). Electronic applications accepted.

GOLDEY-BEACOM COLLEGE, Wilmington, DE 19808-1999

General Information Independent, coed, comprehensive institution. *Graduate housing:* Room and/or apartments available on a first-come, first-served basis to single students; on-campus housing not available to married students.

GRADUATE UNITS

Graduate Program ***Degree program information:*** Part-time and evening/weekend programs available. Part-time, evening/weekend. Offers business administration (MBA); finance (MS); financial management (MBA); health care management (MBA); human resource management (MBA); information technology (MBA); international business management (MBA); major finance (MBA); major taxation (MBA); management (MM); marketing management (MBA); taxation (MBA, MS). Electronic applications accepted.

GOLDFARB SCHOOL OF NURSING AT BARNES-JEWISH COLLEGE, St. Louis, MO 63110

General Information Independent, coed, primarily women, comprehensive institution. *Enrollment:* 722 graduate, professional, and undergraduate students; 89 full-time matriculated graduate/professional students (76 women), 32 part-time matriculated graduate/professional students (all women). *Enrollment by degree level:* 112 master's, 9 doctoral. *Graduate faculty:* 42 full-time (39 women), 6 part-time/adjunct (all women). *Graduate housing:* On-campus housing not available. *Student services:* Campus employment opportunities, campus safety program, international student services, services for students with disabilities. *Library:* Goldfarb School of Nursing Library plus 2 others. *Collection:* Books: 1,100 (physical), 20,000 (digital/electronic); Serial titles: 40 (digital/electronic); Databases: 11.

Computer facilities: 160 computers available on campus for general student use. A campuswide network can be accessed from off campus. Software, research databases available.
Website: http://www.barnesjewishcollege.edu/

General Application Contact: Margaret Anne O'Connor, Program Officer, 314-454-7557, Fax: 314-362-0984, E-mail: maoconnor@bjc.org.

GRADUATE UNITS

Graduate Programs Students: 58 full-time (57 women), 29 part-time (24 women); includes 17 minority (11 Black or African American, non-Hispanic/Latino; 2 Asian, non-Hispanic/Latino; 2 Hispanic/Latino; 2 Two or more races, non-Hispanic/Latino). Average age 26. 41 applicants, 22% accepted, 8 enrolled. *Faculty:* 51 full-time (47 women), 6 part-time/adjunct (all women). *Financial support:* Fellowships, research assistantships, Federal Work-Study, institutionally sponsored loans, and scholarships/grants available. Support available to part-time students. Financial award applicants required to submit FAFSA. In 2015, 56 master's awarded. *Degree program information:* Part-time programs available. Part-time, online learning. Offers adult-gerontology acute care nurse practitioner (MSN); adult-gerontology nurse practitioner (MSN); nurse anesthesia (MSN); nurse educator (MSN); nurse executive (MSN). *Application deadline:* For fall admission, 2/1 priority date for international students; for spring admission, 10/1 priority date for international students. Applications are processed on a rolling basis. *Application fee:* $50. *Application Contact:* Karen Sartorius, Admissions Specialist, 314-454-7057, Fax: 314-362-9250, E-mail: ksartorius@bjc.org. *Dean*, Dr. Gretchen Drinkard, 314-454-7540, Fax: 314-362-9222, E-mail: gld9643@bjc.org.

GONZAGA UNIVERSITY, Spokane, WA 99258

General Information Independent-religious, coed, comprehensive institution. *Enrollment:* 7,491 graduate, professional, and undergraduate students; 597 full-time matriculated graduate/professional students (300 women), 1,771 part-time matriculated graduate/professional students (1,201 women). *Enrollment by degree level:* 1,840 master's, 528 doctoral. *Graduate faculty:* 109 full-time (62 women), 118 part-time/adjunct (59 women). *Graduate housing:* Rooms and/or apartments available on a first-come, first-served basis to single and married students. Housing application deadline: 5/1. *Student services:* Campus employment opportunities, career counseling, exercise/wellness program, free psychological counseling, grant writing training, international student services, low-cost health insurance, multicultural affairs office, services for students with disabilities, writing training. *Library:* Ralph E. and Helen Higgins Foley Center plus 1 other. *Collection:* Books: 284,484 (physical), 27,422 (digital/electronic); Serial titles: 3,590 (physical), 69,824 (digital/electronic); Databases: 254. Weekly public service hours: 112; study areas open 24 hours, 5–7 days a week; students can reserve study rooms.

Computer facilities: Computer purchase and lease plans are available. 576 computers available on campus for general student use. A campuswide network can be accessed from student residence rooms and from off campus. Online class registration is available.
Website: http://www.gonzaga.edu/

General Application Contact: Julie McCulloh, Dean of Admissions, 509-313-6592, Fax: 509-313-5780, E-mail: admissions@gonzaga.edu.

GRADUATE UNITS

College of Arts and Sciences Students: 1 full-time (0 women), 23 part-time (8 women); includes 3 minority (1 Asian, non-Hispanic/Latino; 2 Hispanic/Latino). Average age 33. *Faculty:* 10 full-time (2 women). *Financial support:* Fellowships, teaching assistantships, and Federal Work-Study available. Support available to part-time students. Financial award application deadline: 2/1; financial award applicants required to submit FAFSA. *Degree program information:* Part-time programs available. Part-time. Offers philosophy (MA); theology and leadership (MA). *Application deadline:* For fall admission, 7/20 priority date for domestic students; for spring admission, 11/1 for domestic students. Applications are processed on a rolling basis. *Application fee:* $50. Electronic applications accepted. *Application Contact:* Carolyn Von Muller, Assistant to the Dean, 509-313-5522, E-mail: vonmuller@gonzaga.edu. *Dean*, Dr. Elisabeth Mermann-Jozwiak, 509-313-6603, Fax: 509-313-6684, E-mail: merrmann-jozwiak@gonzaga.edu.

English Language Center Students: 9 full-time (6 women), 23 part-time (16 women); includes 3 minority (1 Black or African American, non-Hispanic/Latino; 2 Hispanic/Latino), 13 international. Average age 32. *Faculty:* 4 full-time (3 women), 3 part-time/adjunct (all women). Offers teaching English as a second language (MA); teaching English as a second language: studies in language and culture (MA). Teaching English as a second language: studies in language and culture program offered jointly with Peace Corps. *Application fee:* $50. Electronic applications accepted. *Manager of Student Services*, Melissa Heid, 509-313-6560, E-mail: heid@gonzaga.edu.

School of Business Administration Students: 64 full-time (25 women), 106 part-time (40 women); includes 25 minority (3 Black or African American, non-Hispanic/Latino; 5 American Indian or Alaska Native, non-Hispanic/Latino; 3 Asian, non-Hispanic/Latino; 7 Hispanic/Latino; 7 Two or more races, non-Hispanic/Latino), 17 international. Average age 29. *Faculty:* 18 full-time (6 women), 10 part-time/adjunct (3 women). *Financial support:* In 2015–16, 65 students received support. Teaching assistantships and

Federal Work-Study available. Support available to part-time students. Financial award application deadline: 2/1; financial award applicants required to submit FAFSA. *Degree program information:* Part-time and evening/weekend programs available. Part-time, evening/weekend. Offers American Indian entrepreneurship (MBA); business administration (M Acc, MBA); taxation (MS). *Application deadline:* For fall admission, 7/20 priority date for domestic students; for spring admission, 11/1 for domestic students. Applications are processed on a rolling basis. *Application fee:* $50. Electronic applications accepted. *Application Contact:* Stacey Chatman, Assistant Director for Admissions, 509-313-4622, E-mail: chatman@gonzaga.edu. *Interim Dean*, Dr. Ken Anderson, 509-313-5991, E-mail: anderson@gem.gonzaga.edu.

School of Education Students: 117 full-time (90 women), 251 part-time (166 women); includes 29 minority (4 Black or African American, non-Hispanic/Latino; 2 American Indian or Alaska Native, non-Hispanic/Latino; 4 Asian, non-Hispanic/Latino; 12 Hispanic/Latino; 7 Two or more races, non-Hispanic/Latino), 125 international. Average age 32. *Faculty:* 23 full-time (17 women), 43 part-time/adjunct (24 women). *Financial support:* Teaching assistantships, Federal Work-Study, and tuition waivers (full and partial) available. Support available to part-time students. Financial award application deadline: 2/1; financial award applicants required to submit FAFSA. *Degree program information:* Part-time and evening/weekend programs available. Part-time, evening/weekend, online learning. Offers clinical mental health counseling (MA); elementary education (MIT); leadership and administration (MA); marriage and family counseling (MA); school counseling (MA); secondary education (MIT); special education (M Ed, MIT); sport and athletic administration (MA). *Application deadline:* Applications are processed on a rolling basis. *Application fee:* $50. Electronic applications accepted. *Application Contact:* Luke Cairney, Graduate Admissions Program Specialist, 509-313-3821, E-mail: cairney@gonzaga.edu. *Dean*, Dr. Vincent Alfonso, 509-313-3594, Fax: 509-313-5821, E-mail: alfonso@gonzaga.edu.

School of Law Students: 335 full-time (136 women), 1 (woman) part-time; includes 57 minority (8 Black or African American, non-Hispanic/Latino; 6 American Indian or Alaska Native, non-Hispanic/Latino; 9 Asian, non-Hispanic/Latino; 20 Hispanic/Latino; 3 Native Hawaiian or other Pacific Islander, non-Hispanic/Latino; 11 Two or more races, non-Hispanic/Latino), 5 international. Average age 27. *Faculty:* 20 full-time (13 women), 15 part-time/adjunct (4 women). *Financial support:* Career-related internships or fieldwork, Federal Work-Study, institutionally sponsored loans, and scholarships/grants available. Support available to part-time students. Financial award application deadline: 2/1; financial award applicants required to submit FAFSA. *Degree program information:* Part-time programs available. Part-time. Offers law (JD). *Application deadline:* For fall admission, 4/15 priority date for domestic students. Applications are processed on a rolling basis. *Application fee:* $50. Electronic applications accepted. *Application Contact:* Susan Lee, Director of Admissions, 509-313-3734, E-mail: slee@lawschool.gonzaga.edu. *Dean*, Jane Korn, 509-313-3700.

School of Nursing and Human Physiology Students: 36 full-time (22 women), 705 part-time (590 women); includes 123 minority (19 Black or African American, non-Hispanic/Latino; 6 American Indian or Alaska Native, non-Hispanic/Latino; 26 Asian, non-Hispanic/Latino; 34 Hispanic/Latino; 7 Native Hawaiian or other Pacific Islander, non-Hispanic/Latino; 31 Two or more races, non-Hispanic/Latino), 2 international. Average age 38. *Faculty:* 16 full-time (14 women), 23 part-time/adjunct (18 women). *Financial support:* Application deadline: 2/1; applicants required to submit FAFSA. *Degree program information:* Part-time and evening/weekend programs available. Part-time, evening/weekend, online learning. Offers nursing and human physiology (MSN, DNP, DNP-A). *Application deadline:* For fall admission, 7/20 priority date for domestic students; for spring admission, 11/1 for domestic students. Applications are processed on a rolling basis. *Application fee:* $50. Electronic applications accepted. *Application Contact:* Shannon Zaranski, Assistant to the Dean, 509-313-3569, E-mail: zaranski@gu.gonzaga.edu. *Dean*, Dr. Brenda Stevenson Marshall, 509-313-3569, E-mail: stevenson-marshall@gonzaga.edu.

School of Professional Studies Students: 35 full-time (21 women), 647 part-time (378 women); includes 119 minority (31 Black or African American, non-Hispanic/Latino; 10 American Indian or Alaska Native, non-Hispanic/Latino; 11 Asian, non-Hispanic/Latino; 44 Hispanic/Latino; 7 Native Hawaiian or other Pacific Islander, non-Hispanic/Latino; 16 Two or more races, non-Hispanic/Latino), 16 international. Average age 38. *Faculty:* 17 full-time (7 women), 20 part-time/adjunct (7 women). *Financial support:* Application deadline: 2/1; applicants required to submit FAFSA. In 2015, 387 master's, 12 doctorates awarded. *Degree program information:* Part-time and evening/weekend programs available. Part-time, evening/weekend. Offers communication and leadership (MA); leadership studies (PhD); organizational leadership (MA). *Application deadline:* For fall admission, 7/20 priority date for domestic students; for spring admission, 11/1 for domestic students. Applications are processed on a rolling basis. *Application fee:* $50. Electronic applications accepted. *Application Contact:* Teresa Crane, Program Specialist, 509-313-6645, E-mail: guonlinestudentservices@gonzaga.edu. *Dean*, Dr. Joe Albert, 509-313-6645, E-mail: albert@gonzaga.edu.

GORDON COLLEGE, Wenham, MA 01984-1899

General Information Independent-religious, coed, comprehensive institution. *Enrollment:* 2,045 graduate, professional, and undergraduate students; 91 full-time matriculated graduate/professional students (67 women), 163 part-time matriculated graduate/professional students (143 women). *Enrollment by degree level:* 254 master's. *Graduate faculty:* 15 full-time (5 women), 36 part-time/adjunct (28 women). *Tuition, area resident:* Full-time $5850; part-time $325 per credit. *Required fees:* $100. Tuition and fees vary according to course load and program. *Graduate housing:* On-campus housing not available. *Student services:* Campus safety program, career counseling, exercise/wellness program, international student services, low-cost health insurance, multicultural affairs office, services for students with disabilities, teacher training, writing training. *Library:* Jenks Learning Resource Center. *Collection:* Books: 132,221 (physical); Serial titles: 1,537 (physical). Weekly public service hours: 103. *Research affiliation:* National Association for Music Education (music education), Feierabend Association for Music Education (early childhood music education), American Choral Directors Association (choral music education), Embracing the New Music Educators Association (mentoring for new music teaching professionals).

Computer facilities: Computer purchase and lease plans are available. 100 computers available on campus for general student use. A campuswide network can be accessed from student residence rooms and from off campus. Online class registration is available.
Website: http://www.gordon.edu/

General Application Contact: Julie Lenocker, Program Administrator, 978-867-4322, Fax: 978-867-4663, E-mail: graduate-education@gordon.edu.

GRADUATE UNITS

Graduate Education Program Students: 83 full-time (62 women), 126 part-time (116 women); includes 17 minority (2 Black or African American, non-Hispanic/Latino; 3 Asian, non-Hispanic/Latino; 11 Hispanic/Latino; 1 Two or more races, non-Hispanic/Latino), 11 international. Average age 34. 136 applicants, 100% accepted, 101 enrolled. *Faculty:* 13 full-time (4 women), 29 part-time/adjunct (24 women). *Financial support:* Applicants required to submit FAFSA. In 2015, 96 master's, 12 Ed Ss awarded. *Degree program information:* Part-time programs available. Part-time. Offers early childhood (M Ed); educational leadership (M Ed, Ed S); elementary education (M Ed); English as a second language (M Ed, Ed S); math specialist (M Ed); mathematics specialist (Ed S); middle school education (M Ed); moderate disabilities (M Ed); Montessori education (M Ed); reading (M Ed, Ed S); secondary education (M Ed). *Application deadline:* Applications are processed on a rolling basis. *Application fee:* $50. *Application Contact:* Julie Lenocker, Program Administrator, 978-867-4322, Fax: 978-867-4663, E-mail: graduate-education@gordon.edu. *Director of Graduate Studies*, Dr. Janet Arndt, 978-867-4355, Fax: 978-867-4663.

Graduate Music Education Program Students: 8 full-time (5 women), 37 part-time (27 women); includes 3 minority (2 Hispanic/Latino; 1 Two or more races, non-Hispanic/Latino). Average age 29. 13 applicants, 92% accepted, 10 enrolled. *Faculty:* 2 full-time (1 woman), 7 part-time/adjunct (4 women). *Financial support:* Applicants required to submit FAFSA. In 2015, 16 master's awarded. *Degree program information:* Part-time programs available. Part-time. Offers music education (MM Ed). *Application deadline:* For summer admission, 4/1 for domestic and international students. Applications are processed on a rolling basis. *Application fee:* $50. *Application Contact:* Kristen Harrington, Program Administrator, 978-867-4429, Fax: 978-867-4663, E-mail: kristen.harrington@gordon.edu. *Associate Professor*, Dr. Sandra Doneski, 978-867-4818, E-mail: sandra.doneski@gordon.edu.

GORDON-CONWELL THEOLOGICAL SEMINARY, South Hamilton, MA 01982-2395

General Information Independent-religious, coed, graduate-only institution. *Graduate housing:* Rooms and/or apartments available to single and married students. Housing application deadline: 4/1.

GRADUATE UNITS

Graduate and Professional Programs ***Degree program information:*** Part-time and evening/weekend programs available. Part-time, evening/weekend. Offers Biblical languages (MABL); church history (MACH); counseling (MACO); ministry (D Min); missions/evangelism (MAME); New Testament (MANT); Old Testament (MAOT); religion (MAR); theology (M Div, MATH, Th M, Th D).

GOSHEN COLLEGE, Goshen, IN 46526-4794

General Information Independent-religious, coed, comprehensive institution. *Enrollment:* 839 graduate, professional, and undergraduate students; 60 full-time matriculated graduate/professional students (55 women), 6 part-time matriculated graduate/professional students (3 women). *Enrollment by degree level:* 66 master's. *Graduate faculty:* 15 full-time (6 women), 6 part-time/adjunct (1 woman). *Graduate housing:* Rooms and/or apartments available on a first-come, first-served basis to single and married students. Housing application deadline: 5/1. *Student services:* Child daycare facilities, exercise/wellness program, international student services, multicultural affairs office, services for students with disabilities, writing training. *Library:* The Harold and Wilma Good Library plus 1 other. *Collection:* Books: 219,000 (physical), 110,000 (digital/electronic); Serial titles: 960 (physical), 210 (digital/electronic); Databases: 95. Weekly public service hours: 81; students can reserve study rooms.

Computer facilities: 160 computers available on campus for general student use. A campuswide network can be accessed from student residence rooms and from off campus. Online class registration is available.
Website: http://www.goshen.edu/

General Application Contact: Kendra Ramseyer, Graduate and Continuing Studies Recruitment and Outreach Specialist, 574-535-7458, Fax: 574-535-7245, E-mail: kendramr@goshen.edu.

GRADUATE UNITS

Merry Lea Environmental Learning Center ***Faculty:*** 1 part-time/adjunct. *Financial support:* Application deadline: 9/10. Offers environmental education (MA). *Application deadline:* For fall admission, 3/1 for domestic students. *Application Contact:* Dr. David Ostergren, Director of the Graduate Program in Environmental Education, 260-799-5869, E-mail: daveo@goshen.edu. *Executive Director*, Dr. Luke Gascho, 260-799-5869, E-mail: lukeag@goshen.edu.

Program in Nursing ***Financial support:*** Scholarships/grants available. *Degree program information:* Part-time and evening/weekend programs available. Part-time, evening/weekend. Offers family nurse practitioner (MSN). *Application deadline:* For fall admission, 3/15 priority date for domestic students. Electronic applications accepted. *Application Contact:* Ruth Stoltzfus, Director, 574-535-7973, E-mail: ruthas@goshen.edu. *Director*, Ruth Stoltzfus, 574-535-7973, E-mail: ruthas@goshen.edu.

GOUCHER COLLEGE, Baltimore, MD 21204-2794

General Information Independent, coed, comprehensive institution. *Enrollment:* 2,148 graduate, professional, and undergraduate students; 133 full-time matriculated graduate/professional students (98 women), 323 part-time matriculated graduate/professional students (251 women). *Enrollment by degree level:* 377 master's, 79 other advanced degrees. *Graduate faculty:* 7 full-time (5 women), 242 part-time/adjunct (165 women). *Graduate housing:* On-campus housing not available. *Student services:* Career counseling. *Library:* Goucher College Library plus 1 other. *Collection:* Books: 252,958 (physical), 287,067 (digital/electronic); Serial titles: 96,275 (digital/electronic); Databases: 135. Weekly public service hours: 168; study areas open 24 hours, 5–7 days a week. *Research affiliation:* Sheppard-Pratt Hospital (education).

Computer facilities: Computer purchase and lease plans are available. 246 computers available on campus for general student use. A campuswide network can be accessed from student residence rooms and from off campus. Online class registration, transcripts, financial aid information, billing, ePortfolios, academic progress reports, study abroad plans are available.
Website: http://www.goucher.edu/

General Application Contact: Kathea Smith, Director of Admissions and Recruitment, Welch Center for Graduate and Professional Studies, 410-337-6200, Fax: 410-337-6085, E-mail: kathea.smith@goucher.edu.

GRADUATE UNITS

Graduate Programs in Education Students: 29 full-time (20 women), 285 part-time (217 women); includes 54 minority (41 Black or African American, non-Hispanic/Latino; 3 Asian, non-Hispanic/Latino; 7 Hispanic/Latino; 3 Two or more races, non-Hispanic/Latino), 1 international. Average age 34. 85 applicants, 100% accepted, 61 enrolled. *Faculty:* 3 full-time (all women), 52 part-time/adjunct (40 women). *Financial support:* Career-related internships or fieldwork and unspecified assistantships available. Support available to part-time students. Financial award application deadline: 4/15; financial award applicants required to submit FAFSA. In 2015, 207 master's awarded. *Degree program information:* Part-time and evening/weekend programs available. Part-time, evening/weekend. Offers at-risk and diverse learners (M Ed, Certificate); athletic program leadership and administration (M Ed, Certificate); elementary and special education (MAT); elementary education (MAT); literacy strategies for content learning (M Ed, Certificate); middle school (M Ed, Certificate); Montessori studies (M Ed); reading instruction (M Ed, Certificate); school improvement leadership (M Ed, Certificate); school mediation (M Ed, Certificate); secondary and special education (MAT); secondary education (MAT); special education (MAT); special education for certified teachers (M Ed, Certificate); teacher as leader in technology (M Ed, Certificate). *Application deadline:* For fall admission, 9/1 for domestic students; for spring admission, 1/15 for domestic students. Applications are processed on a rolling basis. *Application fee:* $75. Electronic applications accepted. *Application Contact:* Kathea Smith, Director of Admissions and Recruitment, 410-337-6163, Fax: 410-337-6085, E-mail: kathea.smith@goucher.edu. *Assistant Provost*, Dr. Phyllis Sunshine, 410-337-6047, Fax: 410-337-6394, E-mail: psunshin@goucher.edu.

MA and MFA Programs Students: 70 full-time (50 women), 69 part-time (52 women); includes 15 minority (7 Black or African American, non-Hispanic/Latino; 1 American Indian or Alaska Native, non-Hispanic/Latino; 1 Asian, non-Hispanic/Latino; 4 Hispanic/Latino; 2 Two or more races, non-Hispanic/Latino), 2 international. 74 applicants, 88% accepted, 42 enrolled. *Faculty:* 6 full-time (4 women), 100 part-time/adjunct (56 women). *Financial support:* Scholarships/grants and unspecified assistantships available. Financial award application deadline: 4/15; financial award applicants required to submit FAFSA. In 2015, 83 master's awarded. *Degree program information:* Part-time and evening/weekend programs available. Part-time, evening/weekend, blended/hybrid learning. Offers arts administration (MA); creative nonfiction (MFA); cultural sustainability (MA); digital arts (MA, MFA); environmental studies (MA); historic preservation (MA); management (MA). *Application deadline:* Applications are processed on a rolling basis. *Application fee:* $75. Electronic applications accepted. *Application Contact:* Kathea Smith, Director of Admissions and Recruitment, 410-337-6163, Fax: 410-337-6085, E-mail: kathea.smith@goucher.edu. *Assistant Provost*, Tiffany Espinosa, 410-337-6296, E-mail: tiffany.espinosa@goucher.edu.

Post-Baccalaureate Premedical Program Students: 31 full-time (18 women); includes 5 minority (1 Black or African American, non-Hispanic/Latino; 3 Asian, non-Hispanic/Latino; 1 Hispanic/Latino). Average age 25. 339 applicants, 12% accepted, 30 enrolled. *Faculty:* 11 full-time (5 women). *Financial support:* In 2015–16, 6 students received support, including 8 fellowships (averaging $4,000 per year); institutionally sponsored loans and scholarships/grants also available. Financial award application deadline: 3/1; financial award applicants required to submit FAFSA. Offers premedical studies (Certificate). *Application deadline:* Applications are processed on a rolling basis. *Application fee:* $60. Electronic applications accepted. *Application Contact:* Theresa Reifsnider, Program Assistant, 800-414-3437, Fax: 410-337-6461, E-mail: pbpm@goucher.edu. *Director*, Betsy Merideth, 800-414-3437, Fax: 410-337-6461, E-mail: bmerideth@goucher.edu.

GOVERNORS STATE UNIVERSITY, University Park, IL 60484

General Information State-supported, coed, university. CGS member. *Graduate housing:* On-campus housing not available.

GRADUATE UNITS

College of Arts and Sciences ***Degree program information:*** Part-time and evening/weekend programs available. Part-time, evening/weekend. Offers analytical chemistry (MS); art (MA); arts and sciences (MA, MS); communication studies (MA); computer science (MS); English (MA); environmental biology (MS); instructional and training technology (MA); media communication (MA); political and justice studies (MA).

College of Business and Public Administration ***Degree program information:*** Part-time and evening/weekend programs available. Part-time, evening/weekend. Offers accounting (MS); business administration (MBA); business and public administration (MBA, MPA, MS); management information systems (MS); public administration (MPA).

College of Education ***Degree program information:*** Part-time and evening/weekend programs available. Part-time, evening/weekend. Offers counseling (MA); early childhood education (MA); education (MA); educational administration and supervision (MA); multi-categorical special education (MA); psychology (MA); reading (MA).

College of Health Professions ***Degree program information:*** Part-time and evening/weekend programs available. Part-time, evening/weekend. Offers addictions studies (MHS); communication disorders (MHS); health administration (MHA); health professions (MHA, MHS, MOT, MPT, MSN, MSW, DPT); nursing (MSN); occupational therapy (MOT); physical therapy (MPT, DPT); social work (MSW).

GRACE COLLEGE, Winona Lake, IN 46590-1294

General Information Independent-religious, coed, comprehensive institution. *Enrollment:* 2,303 graduate, professional, and undergraduate students; 53 full-time matriculated graduate/professional students (39 women), 26 part-time matriculated graduate/professional students (20 women). *Enrollment by degree level:* 79 master's. *Graduate faculty:* 5 full-time (2 women), 5 part-time/adjunct (1 woman). *Graduate housing:* On-campus housing not available. *Student services:* Campus employment opportunities, campus safety program, career counseling, exercise/wellness program, free psychological counseling. *Library:* Morgan Library.

Computer facilities: 150 computers available on campus for general student use. A campuswide network can be accessed from student residence rooms and from off campus. Online class registration is available.
Website: http://www.grace.edu/

General Application Contact: Zachary Parrott, Graduate Admissions Counselor, 800-823-8533, E-mail: graceonline@grace.edu.

GRADUATE UNITS

Department of Graduate Counseling Students: 68 full-time (46 women), 23 part-time (16 women); includes 9 minority (6 Black or African American, non-Hispanic/Latino; 2 Hispanic/Latino; 1 Native Hawaiian or other Pacific Islander, non-Hispanic/Latino). Average age 32. *Faculty:* 5 full-time (2 women), 5 part-time/adjunct (1 woman). *Financial support:* Teaching assistantships with partial tuition reimbursements, career-related internships or fieldwork, and unspecified assistantships available. Financial award application deadline: 3/10; financial award applicants required to submit FAFSA. In 2015, 23 master's awarded. *Degree program information:* Part-time programs available. Part-time. Offers clinical mental health counseling (MA). *Application deadline:* For fall admission, 8/1 priority date for domestic students; for spring admission, 12/1 priority date for domestic students. Applications are processed on a rolling basis. *Application fee:* $250. Electronic applications accepted. *Application Contact:* Zachary Parrott, 800-823.8533, E-mail: graceonline@grace.edu. *Chair, Department of Graduate Counseling*, Amy Gilbert, 574-322-5100 Ext. 6064, Fax: 574-372-5143, E-mail: gilberal@grace.edu.

GRACELAND UNIVERSITY, Lamoni, IA 50140

General Information Independent-religious, coed, comprehensive institution. *Enrollment:* 2,292 graduate, professional, and undergraduate students; 682 full-time matriculated graduate/professional students (610 women). *Enrollment by degree level:* 680 master's, 2 doctoral. *Graduate faculty:* 20 full-time (17 women), 35 part-time/adjunct (25 women). *Graduate housing:* On-campus housing not available. *Student services:* Campus safety program, career counseling, free psychological counseling, services for students with disabilities, teacher training, writing training. *Library:* F. M. Smith Library.

Computer facilities: A campuswide network can be accessed from student residence rooms and from off campus. Online class registration is available.
Website: http://www.graceland.edu/

General Application Contact: Lisa Libich, Director of Retention Operations for College of Graduate and Continuing Studies, 816-423-4730, Fax: 816-833-2990, E-mail: libich@graceland.edu.

GRADUATE UNITS

Community of Christ Seminary Students: 33 full-time (21 women); includes 2 minority (1 Asian, non-Hispanic/Latino; 1 Native Hawaiian or other Pacific Islander, non-Hispanic/Latino), 5 international. Average age 45. 12 applicants, 100% accepted, 9 enrolled. *Faculty:* 2 full-time (1 woman), 5 part-time/adjunct (0 women). *Financial support:* Scholarships/grants available. Financial award application deadline: 12/15; financial award applicants required to submit FAFSA. In 2015, 4 master's awarded. *Degree program information:* Part-time programs available. Part-time, online learning. Offers theology (MAR). *Application deadline:* For fall admission, 8/15 priority date for domestic students; for winter admission, 10/15 priority date for domestic students; for spring admission, 4/15 priority date for domestic students. Applications are processed on a rolling basis. *Application fee:* $50. *Application Contact:* Sharon Ward, Administrative Assistant, 816-423-4676, Fax: 816-423-4753, E-mail: ward@graceland.edu. *Dean*, Dr. Stassi Cramm, 816-833-0524 Ext. 5276, Fax: 816-833-2990, E-mail: frizzell@graceland.edu.

Gleazer School of Education Students: 160 full-time (148 women); includes 2 minority (1 Black or African American, non-Hispanic/Latino; 1 Two or more races, non-Hispanic/Latino). Average age 35. 29 applicants, 48% accepted, 14 enrolled. *Faculty:* 4 full-time (all women), 9 part-time/adjunct (5 women). *Financial support:* Institutionally sponsored loans and scholarships/grants available. Financial award application deadline: 12/15; financial award applicants required to submit FAFSA. In 2015, 86 master's awarded. *Degree program information:* Part-time and evening/weekend programs available. Part-time, evening/weekend, online learning. Offers curriculum and instruction (M Ed); differentiated instruction (M Ed); instructional leadership (M Ed); literacy and instruction (M Ed); management in the inclusive classroom (M Ed); mild/moderate special education (M Ed); technology integration (M Ed). *Application deadline:* For fall admission, 10/1 for domestic students; for winter admission, 11/15 for domestic students; for spring admission, 2/15 priority date for domestic students; for summer admission, 6/1 for domestic students. *Application fee:* $50. Electronic applications accepted. *Application Contact:* Jeanette Calipetro, Admissions Representative, 816-423-4716, Fax: 816-833-2990, E-mail: jcali1@graceland.edu. *Dean*, Dr. Scott Huddleston, 641-784-5000 Ext. 4744, E-mail: huddlest@graceland.edu.

School of Nursing Students: 489 full-time (441 women); includes 75 minority (41 Black or African American, non-Hispanic/Latino; 5 American Indian or Alaska Native, non-Hispanic/Latino; 15 Asian, non-Hispanic/Latino; 2 Native Hawaiian or other Pacific Islander, non-Hispanic/Latino; 12 Two or more races, non-Hispanic/Latino), 1 international. Average age 39. 140 applicants, 69% accepted, 69 enrolled. *Faculty:* 14 full-time (12 women), 21 part-time/adjunct (20 women). *Financial support:* Institutionally sponsored loans available. Support available to part-time students. Financial award applicants required to submit FAFSA. In 2015, 137 master's, 11 doctorates awarded. *Degree program information:* Part-time programs available. Part-time, online learning. Offers family nurse practitioner (MSN, PMC); nurse educator (MSN, PMC); organizational leadership (DNP). *Application deadline:* For fall admission, 6/1 priority date for domestic students; for winter admission, 10/1 priority date for domestic students; for spring admission, 10/1 priority date for domestic students; for summer admission, 2/1 for domestic students. *Application fee:* $50. Electronic applications accepted. *Application Contact:* Nick Walker, Admissions Representative, 816-423-4717, Fax: 816-833-2990, E-mail: nowalker@graceland.edu. *Dean*, Dr. Claudia D. Horton, 816-423-4670, Fax: 816-423-4753, E-mail: horton@graceland.edu.

GRACE MISSION UNIVERSITY, Fullerton, CA 92833

General Information Independent, coed, comprehensive institution.

GRADUATE UNITS

Graduate School Offers missions (M Div, MACE, MAICS, D Miss).

GRACE THEOLOGICAL SEMINARY, Winona Lake, IN 46590-9907

General Information Independent-religious, coed, primarily men, graduate-only institution. *Graduate faculty:* 4 full-time (0 women), 5 part-time/adjunct (0 women). *Graduate housing:* On-campus housing not available. *Student services:* Campus employment opportunities, career counseling, low-cost health insurance. *Library:* Morgan Library.

Computer facilities: 36 computers available on campus for general student use.
Website: http://www.grace.edu/academics/seminary

General Application Contact: Dr. Jeffrey A. Gill, Vice President and Dean, 574-372-5100 Ext. 6438, Fax: 574-372-5113, E-mail: gillja@grace.edu.

GRADUATE UNITS

Graduate and Professional Programs ***Financial support:*** Career-related internships or fieldwork, Federal Work-Study, scholarships/grants, and tuition waivers (partial) available. Support available to part-time students. Financial award application deadline: 4/1; financial award applicants required to submit FAFSA. *Degree program information:* Part-time programs available. Part-time, online learning. Offers biblical studies (Certificate); chaplaincy (M Div); exegetical studies (M Div); intercultural studies (M Div, MA, D Min); local church ministry (MA); pastoral counseling (M Div); pastoral studies (M Div, D Min); theology (Diploma). *Application deadline:* For fall admission, 4/1 priority date for domestic students. Applications are processed on a rolling basis. *Application fee:* $25. Electronic applications accepted. *Application Contact:* Mark Pohl, Director of Admissions, 574-372-5100 Ext. 6431, Fax: 574-372-5117, E-mail: mark.pohl@grace.edu. *Executive Assistant for Academic Affairs*, Elma Sherman, 574-372-5100 Ext. 6134, Fax: 574-372-5117, E-mail: shermaec@grace.edu.

GRACE UNIVERSITY, Omaha, NE 68108

General Information Independent-religious, coed, comprehensive institution. *Graduate housing:* Rooms and/or apartments available on a first-come, first-served basis to single and married students.

GRADUATE UNITS

College of Graduate Studies *Degree program information:* Part-time and evening/weekend programs available. Part-time, evening/weekend. Offers Bible (MA); counseling (MA). Electronic applications accepted.

THE GRADUATE CENTER, CITY UNIVERSITY OF NEW YORK, New York, NY 10016-4039

General Information State and locally supported, coed, graduate-only institution. CGS member. *Graduate housing:* Rooms and/or apartments available to single and married students. Housing application deadline: 5/1. *Research affiliation:* American Museum of Natural History (anthropology), Roche Institute of Molecular Biology (biological sciences), New York Botanical Gardens (biological sciences).

GRADUATE UNITS

Graduate Studies Offers accounting (PhD); anthropological linguistics (PhD); archaeology (PhD); architecture (PhD); audiology (Au D); basic applied neurocognition (PhD); behavioral science (PhD); biochemistry (PhD); biology (PhD); biomedical engineering (PhD); biopsychology (PhD); chemical engineering (PhD); chemistry (PhD); civil engineering (PhD); classics (MA, PhD); clinical psychology (PhD); comparative literature (MA, PhD); computer science (PhD); criminal justice (PhD); cultural anthropology (PhD); developmental psychology (PhD); earth and environmental sciences (PhD); economics (PhD); educational psychology (PhD); electrical engineering (PhD); English (PhD); environmental psychology (PhD); experimental psychology (PhD); finance (PhD); French (PhD); Germanic languages and literatures (MA, PhD); graphic arts (PhD); Hispanic and Luso-Brazilian literatures and languages (PhD); history (PhD); industrial psychology (PhD); learning processes (PhD); liberal studies (MA); linguistics (MA, PhD); management planning systems (PhD); mathematics (PhD); mechanical engineering (PhD); music (DMA, PhD); neuropsychology (PhD); nursing science (DNS); painting (PhD); philosophy (MA, PhD); photography (PhD); physical anthropology (PhD); physical therapy (DPT); physics (PhD); political science (MA, PhD); psychology (PhD); public health (DPH); sculpture (PhD); social personality (PhD); social welfare (DSW, PhD); sociology (PhD); speech and hearing sciences (PhD); theatre (PhD); urban education (PhD). Electronic applications accepted.

Interdisciplinary Studies Offers language in social context (PhD); medieval studies (PhD); public policy (MA, PhD); urban studies (MA, PhD); women's studies (MA, PhD).

GRADUATE INSTITUTE OF APPLIED LINGUISTICS, Dallas, TX 75236

General Information Independent, coed, graduate-only institution.

GRADUATE UNITS

Graduate Programs *Degree program information:* Part-time programs available. Part-time. Offers applied linguistics (MA, Certificate); language development (MA). Electronic applications accepted.

GRADUATE THEOLOGICAL UNION, Berkeley, CA 94709-1212

General Information Independent-religious, coed, graduate-only institution. *Graduate housing:* Rooms and/or apartments available on a first-come, first-served basis to single and married students. Housing application deadline: 6/1.

GRADUATE UNITS

Graduate Programs Offers art and religion (MA, PhD, Th D); biblical languages (MA); biblical studies (MA); Biblical studies (PhD, Th D); Buddhist studies (MA); Christian spirituality (MA, PhD, Th D); cultural and historical studies of religions (MA, PhD, Th D); ethics and social theory (PhD, Th D); history (MA, PhD, Th D); homiletics (MA, PhD, Th D); interdisciplinary studies (PhD, Th D); Jewish studies (MA, PhD, Th D, Certificate); liturgical studies (MA, PhD, Th D); Near Eastern religions (PhD, Th D); Orthodox Christian studies (MA); religion and psychology (MA, PhD, Th D); religion and society/ethics and social theory (MA); systematic and philosophical theology (MA, PhD, Th D). PhD programs in Jewish studies and Near Eastern religions offered jointly with University of California, Berkeley. Electronic applications accepted.

GRAMBLING STATE UNIVERSITY, Grambling, LA 71245

General Information State-supported, coed, university. CGS member. *Graduate housing:* On-campus housing not available. *Research affiliation:* U.S. Department of Defense (cyberspace technology, materials and manufacturing), National Institutes of Justice (technology and equipment in forensic science), U.S. Housing and Urban Development (housing preservation in low-income areas), National Science Foundation (science and engineering), NASA (aeronautics research), National Institutes of Health (biomedical sciences).

GRADUATE UNITS

School of Graduate Studies and Research *Degree program information:* Part-time and evening/weekend programs available. Part-time, evening/weekend. Electronic applications accepted.

College of Arts and Sciences Degree program information: Part-time programs available. Part-time. Offers arts and sciences (MA, MPA); health services administration (MPA); human resource management (MPA); public management (MPA); social sciences (MA); state and local government (MPA). Electronic applications accepted.

College of Education Degree program information: Part-time and evening/weekend programs available. Part-time, evening/weekend. Offers curriculum and instruction (MS); developmental education (MS, Ed D, PMC); education (M Ed, MAT, MS, Ed D, PMC); educational leadership (M Ed); special education (M Ed); sports administration (MS). Electronic applications accepted.

College of Professional Studies Degree program information: Part-time programs available. Part-time. Offers criminal justice (MS); family nurse practitioner (PMC); mass communication (MA); nursing (MSN); social work (MSW). Electronic applications accepted.

GRAND CANYON UNIVERSITY, Phoenix, AZ 85017-1097

General Information Independent-religious, coed, comprehensive institution. *Graduate housing:* Rooms and/or apartments available on a first-come, first-served basis to single and married students.

GRADUATE UNITS

College of Business *Degree program information:* Part-time and evening/weekend programs available. Part-time, evening/weekend, online learning. Offers accounting (MBA); corporate business administration (MBA); disaster preparedness and crisis management (MBA); executive fire service leadership (MS); finance (MBA); general management (MBA); government and policy (MPA); health care management (MPA); health systems management (MBA); human resource management (MBA); innovation (MBA); leadership (MBA, MS); management of information system (MBA); marketing (MBA); project-based (MBA); six sigma (MBA); strategic human resource management (MBA). Electronic applications accepted.

College of Doctoral Studies Offers business administration (DBA); general psychology (PhD); organizational leadership (Ed D, PhD).

College of Education *Degree program information:* Part-time and evening/weekend programs available. Part-time, evening/weekend, online learning. Offers curriculum and instruction (M Ed); education administration (M Ed); elementary education (M Ed); secondary education (M Ed); special education (M Ed); teaching (MA). Electronic applications accepted.

College of Nursing *Degree program information:* Part-time and evening/weekend programs available. Part-time, evening/weekend, online learning. Offers acute care nurse practitioner (MS, PMC); clinical nurse specialist (PMC); family nurse practitioner (MS); leadership in health care systems (MS); nurse education (MS).

College of Nursing and Health Sciences *Degree program information:* Part-time and evening/weekend programs available. Part-time, evening/weekend, online learning. Offers addiction counseling (MS); health care administration (MS); health care informatics (MS); marriage and family therapy (MS); professional counseling (MS); public health (MS).

GRAND RAPIDS THEOLOGICAL SEMINARY OF CORNERSTONE UNIVERSITY, Grand Rapids, MI 49525-5897

General Information Independent-religious, coed, graduate-only institution. *Graduate housing:* Rooms and/or apartments available on a first-come, first-served basis to single and married students. Housing application deadline: 6/1.

GRADUATE UNITS

Graduate Programs *Degree program information:* Part-time programs available. Part-time, online learning. Offers Biblical counseling (M Div); biblical counseling (MA); chaplaincy (M Div); Christian education (M Div, MA); intercultural studies (M Div, MA); New Testament (MA, Th M); Old Testament (MA, Th M); pastoral studies (M Div); systematic theology (MA); theology (Th M). Electronic applications accepted.

GRAND VALLEY STATE UNIVERSITY, Allendale, MI 49401-9403

General Information State-supported, coed, comprehensive institution. CGS member. *Enrollment:* 25,325 graduate, professional, and undergraduate students; 1,391 full-time matriculated graduate/professional students (973 women), 1,755 part-time matriculated graduate/professional students (1,163 women). *Enrollment by degree level:* 2,839 master's, 271 doctoral, 33 other advanced degrees. *Graduate faculty:* 278 full-time (145 women), 102 part-time/adjunct (64 women). *Graduate housing:* Rooms and/or apartments available on a first-come, first-served basis to single and married students. Housing application deadline: 2/1. *Student services:* Campus employment opportunities, campus safety program, career counseling, child daycare facilities, exercise/wellness program, free psychological counseling, grant writing training, international student services, low-cost health insurance, multicultural affairs office, services for students with disabilities, teacher training, writing training. *Library:* Mary Idema Pew Library Learning and Information Commons plus 5 others. *Collection:* Books: 567,197 (physical), 1 million (digital/electronic). Students can reserve study rooms. *Research affiliation:* Elkins Innovations (life sciences), Progressive AE (water quality).

Computer facilities: 2,600 computers available on campus for general student use. A campuswide network can be accessed from student residence rooms and from off campus. Online class registration, transcript, degree audit, credit card payments are available.

Website: http://www.gvsu.edu/

General Application Contact: Tracey James-Heer, Associate Director for Graduate Recruitment, 616-331-2025, Fax: 616-486-6476, E-mail: james-ht@gvsu.edu.

GRADUATE UNITS

College of Community and Public Service Students: 288 full-time (224 women), 320 part-time (234 women); includes 105 minority (38 Black or African American, non-Hispanic/Latino; 7 American Indian or Alaska Native, non-Hispanic/Latino; 13 Asian, non-Hispanic/Latino; 29 Hispanic/Latino; 18 Two or more races, non-Hispanic/Latino), 24 international. Average age 30. 323 applicants, 90% accepted, 163 enrolled. *Faculty:* 32 full-time (19 women), 32 part-time/adjunct (21 women). *Financial support:* In 2015–16, 99 students received support, including 48 research assistantships with tuition reimbursements available (averaging $7,554 per year); teaching assistantships, career-related internships or fieldwork, Federal Work-Study, institutionally sponsored loans, scholarships/grants, and unspecified assistantships also available. Financial award application deadline: 5/1. In 2015, 263 master's awarded. *Degree program information:* Part-time and evening/weekend programs available. Part-time, evening/weekend, online learning. Offers community and public service (MHA, MPA, MPNL, MS, MSW). *Application deadline:* For fall admission, 5/1 priority date for domestic students; for winter admission, 11/1 priority date for domestic students; for spring admission, 4/10 priority date for domestic students. Applications are processed on a rolling basis. *Application fee:* $30. Electronic applications accepted. *Application Contact:* Tracey James-Heer, Associate Director for Graduate Recruitment, 616-331-2025, Fax: 616-486-6476, E-mail: james-ht@gvsu.edu. *Dean,* George Grant, 616-331-6550.

School of Criminal Justice Students: 29 full-time (17 women), 19 part-time (14 women); includes 10 minority (4 Black or African American, non-Hispanic/Latino; 1 Asian, non-Hispanic/Latino; 4 Hispanic/Latino; 1 Two or more races, non-Hispanic/Latino), 1 international. Average age 27. 23 applicants, 96% accepted, 21 enrolled. *Faculty:* 3 full-time (1 woman). *Financial support:* In 2015–16, 17 students received support, including 5 fellowships (averaging $750 per year), 14 research assistantships with full tuition reimbursements available (averaging $5,588 per year); career-related internships or fieldwork, Federal Work-Study, scholarships/grants, and unspecified assistantships also available. Support available to part-time students. Financial award application deadline: 5/1. In 2015, 6 master's awarded. *Degree program information:* Part-time and evening/weekend programs available. Part-time, evening/weekend. Offers criminal justice (MS). *Application deadline:* For fall admission, 7/30 priority date for domestic students; for winter admission, 12/10 priority date for domestic students; for spring admission, 4/10 priority date for domestic students. *Application fee:* $30. *Application Contact:* Tracey James-Heer, Associate Director for Graduate Recruitment, 616-331-2025, Fax: 616-486-6476, E-mail: james-ht@gvsu.edu. *Director,* Dr. Kathleen Bailey, 616-331-7148, Fax: 616-331-7155, E-mail: baileyk@gvsu.edu.

School of Public and Nonprofit Administration Students: 65 full-time (41 women), 123 part-time (87 women); includes 34 minority (13 Black or African American, non-Hispanic/Latino; 1 American Indian or Alaska Native, non-Hispanic/Latino; 8 Asian, non-Hispanic/Latino; 8 Hispanic/Latino; 4 Two or more races, non-Hispanic/Latino), 3 international. Average age 31. 69 applicants, 91% accepted, 50 enrolled. *Faculty:* 15 full-time (8 women), 4 part-time/adjunct (1 woman). *Financial support:* In 2015–16, 30 students received support, including 17 fellowships (averaging $4,631 per year),

16 research assistantships with tuition reimbursements available (averaging $9,140 per year); career-related internships or fieldwork, Federal Work-Study, scholarships/grants, and unspecified assistantships also available. Financial award application deadline: 5/1. In 2015, 70 master's awarded. *Degree program information:* Part-time and evening/weekend programs available. Part-time, evening/weekend. Offers health administration (MHA); philanthropy and nonprofit leadership (MPNL); public and nonprofit administration (MHA, MPA, MPNL). *Application deadline:* For fall admission, 5/1 priority date for domestic students; for winter admission, 11/1 priority date for domestic students. Applications are processed on a rolling basis. *Application fee:* $30. Electronic applications accepted. *Application Contact:* Tracey James-Heer, Associate Director for Graduate Recruitment, 616-331-2025, Fax: 616-486-6476, E-mail: james-ht@gvsu.edu. *Director*, Dr. Richard Jelier, 616-331-6575, Fax: 616-331-7120, E-mail: jelierr@gvsu.edu.

School of Social Work Students: 206 full-time (170 women), 144 part-time (119 women); includes 57 minority (22 Black or African American, non-Hispanic/Latino; 5 American Indian or Alaska Native, non-Hispanic/Latino; 5 Asian, non-Hispanic/Latino; 13 Hispanic/Latino; 12 Two or more races, non-Hispanic/Latino), 9 international. Average age 29. 182 applicants, 92% accepted, 116 enrolled. *Faculty:* 14 full-time (10 women), 28 part-time/adjunct (20 women). *Financial support:* In 2015–16, 50 students received support, including 35 fellowships (averaging $3,295 per year), 16 research assistantships with tuition reimbursements available (averaging $6,615 per year); career-related internships or fieldwork, Federal Work-Study, institutionally sponsored loans, and unspecified assistantships also available. In 2015, 167 master's awarded. *Degree program information:* Part-time programs available. Part-time. Offers social work (MSW). *Application deadline:* For fall admission, 5/1 priority date for domestic students; for winter admission, 10/1 priority date for domestic students; for spring admission, 3/15 priority date for domestic students. Applications are processed on a rolling basis. *Application fee:* $30. Electronic applications accepted. *Application Contact:* Salvator Lopez-Arias, Graduate Program Director, 616-331-6553, E-mail: lopezars@gvsu.edu. *Chair*, Dr. Dianne Green-Smith, 616-331-6565, Fax: 616-331-6550, E-mail: greensmd@gvsu.edu.

College of Education Students: 154 full-time (105 women), 900 part-time (673 women); includes 147 minority (85 Black or African American, non-Hispanic/Latino; 4 American Indian or Alaska Native, non-Hispanic/Latino; 13 Asian, non-Hispanic/Latino; 25 Hispanic/Latino; 20 Two or more races, non-Hispanic/Latino), 15 international. Average age 33. 269 applicants, 99% accepted, 145 enrolled. *Faculty:* 42 full-time (27 women), 21 part-time/adjunct (10 women). *Financial support:* In 2015–16, 121 students received support, including 58 fellowships (averaging $2,867 per year), 68 research assistantships with tuition reimbursements available (averaging $12,169 per year); career-related internships or fieldwork, Federal Work-Study, scholarships/grants, and unspecified assistantships also available. In 2015, 324 master's, 22 Ed Ss awarded. *Degree program information:* Part-time and evening/weekend programs available. Part-time, evening/weekend, online learning. Offers adult and higher education (M Ed); cognitive impairment (M Ed); college student affairs leadership (M Ed); early childhood developmental delay (M Ed); early childhood education (M Ed); education (M Ed, Ed S); educational differentiation (M Ed); educational leadership (M Ed); educational technology (M Ed); educational technology integration (M Ed); elementary education (M Ed); emotional impairment (M Ed); higher education (M Ed); instruction and curriculum (M Ed); leadership (Ed S); learning disabilities (M Ed); literacy studies (M Ed); middle level education (M Ed); reading and language arts (M Ed); school counseling (M Ed); school library media services (M Ed); secondary level education (M Ed); special education (M Ed); teaching English to speakers of other languages (M Ed). *Application deadline:* Applications are processed on a rolling basis. *Application fee:* $30. Electronic applications accepted. *Application Contact:* Thomas Owens, Admissions Office, 616-331-6282, Fax: 616-331-2000, E-mail: owenst@gvsu.edu. *Dean*, Dr. Elaine C. Collins, 616-331-6821, Fax: 616-331-6515, E-mail: collinse@gvsu.edu.

College of Health Professions Students: 592 full-time (452 women), 33 part-time (27 women); includes 62 minority (14 Black or African American, non-Hispanic/Latino; 1 American Indian or Alaska Native, non-Hispanic/Latino; 12 Asian, non-Hispanic/Latino; 18 Hispanic/Latino; 17 Two or more races, non-Hispanic/Latino), 4 international. Average age 26. 1,332 applicants, 27% accepted, 246 enrolled. *Faculty:* 57 full-time (41 women), 20 part-time/adjunct (18 women). *Financial support:* In 2015–16, 106 students received support, including 74 fellowships (averaging $8,745 per year), 41 research assistantships with partial tuition reimbursements available (averaging $4,439 per year); career-related internships or fieldwork, Federal Work-Study, institutionally sponsored loans, and scholarships/grants also available. Financial award application deadline: 2/15. In 2015, 174 master's, 47 doctorates awarded. Offers health professions (MPAS, MPH, MS, DPT); occupational therapy (MS); physical therapy (DPT); physician assistant studies (MPAS); public health (MPH); speech-language pathology (MS). *Application deadline:* For winter admission, 1/15 priority date for domestic and international students. Applications are processed on a rolling basis. Electronic applications accepted. *Application Contact:* Darlene Zwart, Student Services Coordinator, 616-331-3958, E-mail: zwartda@gvsu.edu. *Dean*, Dr. Roy Olsson, 616-331-3356, Fax: 616-331-3350, E-mail: olssonr@gvsu.edu.

College of Liberal Arts and Sciences Students: 101 full-time (61 women), 122 part-time (76 women); includes 22 minority (10 Black or African American, non-Hispanic/Latino; 1 American Indian or Alaska Native, non-Hispanic/Latino; 2 Asian, non-Hispanic/Latino; 6 Hispanic/Latino; 3 Two or more races, non-Hispanic/Latino), 24 international. Average age 28. 197 applicants, 65% accepted, 76 enrolled. *Faculty:* 61 full-time (25 women), 2 part-time/adjunct (1 woman). *Financial support:* In 2015–16, 89 students received support, including 11 fellowships (averaging $3,948 per year), 81 research assistantships with tuition reimbursements available (averaging $7,862 per year), teaching assistantships with tuition reimbursements available (averaging $8,000 per year); career-related internships or fieldwork, Federal Work-Study, institutionally sponsored loans, scholarships/grants, and unspecified assistantships also available. In 2015, 73 master's awarded. *Degree program information:* Part-time and evening/weekend programs available. Part-time, evening/weekend. Offers biology (MS); biomedical sciences (MHS); biostatistics (MS); cell and molecular biology (MS); English (MA); liberal arts and sciences (MA, MHS, MS, Psy S); school psychology (MS, Psy S). *Application fee:* $30. Electronic applications accepted. *Application Contact:* Tracey James-Heer, Associate Director for Graduate Recruitment, 616-331-2025, Fax: 616-486-6476, E-mail: james-ht@gvsu.edu. *Dean*, Dr. Frederick Antczak, 616-331-2261.

School of Communications Students: 25 full-time (12 women), 41 part-time (29 women); includes 10 minority (4 Black or African American, non-Hispanic/Latino; 1 Asian, non-Hispanic/Latino; 4 Hispanic/Latino; 1 Two or more races, non-Hispanic/Latino), 5 international. Average age 30. 28 applicants, 82% accepted, 22 enrolled. *Faculty:* 2 full-time (0 women), 1 part-time/adjunct (0 women). *Financial support:* In 2015–16, 13 students received support, including 8 fellowships (averaging $7,383 per year), 5 research assistantships with tuition reimbursements available (averaging $7,587 per year); career-related internships or fieldwork, Federal Work-Study, and institutionally sponsored loans also available. Support available to part-time students. Financial award application deadline: 4/15. In 2015, 21 master's awarded. *Degree program information:* Part-time and evening/weekend programs available. Part-time, evening/weekend. Offers communications (MS). *Application deadline:* For fall admission, 8/15 priority date for domestic students; for winter admission, 12/15 priority date for domestic students; for spring admission, 4/15 priority date for domestic students. Applications are processed on a rolling basis. *Application fee:* $30. Electronic applications accepted. *Application Contact:* Dr. Alex Nesterenko, Coordinator, 616-331-3668, Fax: 616-331-2700, E-mail: nesterea@gvsu.edu. *Director*, Dr. Anthony Thompson, 616-331-3606, Fax: 616-895-2700, E-mail: thompsoa@gvsu.edu.

Kirkhof College of Nursing Students: 71 full-time (59 women), 53 part-time (45 women); includes 16 minority (10 Black or African American, non-Hispanic/Latino; 2 Asian, non-Hispanic/Latino; 3 Hispanic/Latino; 1 Two or more races, non-Hispanic/Latino), 3 international. Average age 33. 64 applicants, 94% accepted, 31 enrolled. *Faculty:* 17 full-time (16 women), 6 part-time/adjunct (5 women). *Financial support:* In 2015–16, 58 students received support, including 39 fellowships (averaging $11,141 per year), 33 research assistantships with tuition reimbursements available (averaging $7,339 per year); career-related internships or fieldwork, Federal Work-Study, institutionally sponsored loans, and traineeships also available. Financial award application deadline: 2/15. In 2015, 1 master's, 11 doctorates awarded. *Degree program information:* Part-time programs available. Part-time. Offers advanced practice (MSN); case management (MSN); nursing administration (MSN); nursing education (MSN); nursing practice (DNP). *Application deadline:* For fall admission, 3/15 priority date for domestic students. Applications are processed on a rolling basis. *Application fee:* $30. Electronic applications accepted. *Application Contact:* Dr. Cynthia Coviak, Associate Dean of Nursing Research and Faculty Development, 616-331-7170, Fax: 616-331-7362, E-mail: coviakc@gvsu.edu. *Dean*, Dr. Cynthia McCurren, 616-331-7161, Fax: 616-331-7362.

Padnos College of Engineering and Computing Students: 69 full-time (16 women), 91 part-time (19 women); includes 13 minority (3 Black or African American, non-Hispanic/Latino; 5 Asian, non-Hispanic/Latino; 5 Hispanic/Latino), 69 international. Average age 29. 140 applicants, 66% accepted, 41 enrolled. *Faculty:* 29 full-time (5 women). *Financial support:* In 2015–16, 52 students received support, including 12 fellowships (averaging $2,633 per year), 46 research assistantships with tuition reimbursements available (averaging $9,707 per year); unspecified assistantships also available. In 2015, 44 master's awarded. *Degree program information:* Part-time programs available. Part-time. Offers engineering and computing (MS, MSE); medical and bioinformatics (MS). *Application deadline:* For fall admission, 2/1 for domestic students. Applications are processed on a rolling basis. *Application fee:* $30. Electronic applications accepted. *Application Contact:* Tracey James-Heer, Associate Director for Graduate Recruitment, 616-331-2025, Fax: 616-486-6476, E-mail: james-ht@gvsu.edu. *Dean*, Dr. Paul Plotkowski, 616-331-6260, Fax: 616-331-6770, E-mail: plotkowp@gvsu.edu.

School of Computing and Information Systems Students: 42 full-time (14 women), 54 part-time (16 women); includes 10 minority (3 Black or African American, non-Hispanic/Latino; 5 Asian, non-Hispanic/Latino; 2 Hispanic/Latino), 22 international. Average age 30. 54 applicants, 65% accepted, 34 enrolled. *Faculty:* 8 full-time (all women). *Financial support:* In 2015–16, 11 students received support, including 4 fellowships (averaging $1,856 per year), 7 research assistantships with tuition reimbursements available (averaging $10,134 per year). In 2015, 26 master's awarded. *Degree program information:* Part-time and evening/weekend programs available. Part-time, evening/weekend. Offers computer information systems (MS). *Application deadline:* For fall admission, 6/1 for international students; for winter admission, 9/1 for international students. Applications are processed on a rolling basis. *Application fee:* $30. Electronic applications accepted. *Application Contact:* D. Robert Adams, Graduate Program Chair, 616-331-3885, Fax: 616-331-2106, E-mail: adams@cis.gvsu.edu. *Director*, Paul Leidig, 616-331-2038, Fax: 616-331-2106, E-mail: leidigp@gvsu.edu.

School of Engineering Students: 40 full-time (11 women), 38 part-time (7 women); includes 5 minority (2 Black or African American, non-Hispanic/Latino; 1 Asian, non-Hispanic/Latino; 2 Hispanic/Latino), 28 international. Average age 27. 65 applicants, 58% accepted, 30 enrolled. *Faculty:* 20 full-time (5 women). *Financial support:* In 2015–16, 38 students received support, including 9 fellowships (averaging $3,049 per year), 35 research assistantships with full tuition reimbursements available (averaging $10,237 per year); career-related internships or fieldwork, Federal Work-Study, institutionally sponsored loans, scholarships/grants, and unspecified assistantships also available. In 2015, 13 master's awarded. *Degree program information:* Part-time and evening/weekend programs available. Part-time, evening/weekend. Offers electrical and computer engineering (MSE); manufacturing operations (MSE); mechanical engineering (MSE); product design and manufacturing engineering (MSE). *Application deadline:* Applications are processed on a rolling basis. *Application fee:* $30. Electronic applications accepted. *Application Contact:* Dr. Pranod Chaphalkar, Graduate Director, 616-331-6843, Fax: 616-331-7215, E-mail: chaphalp@gvsu.edu. *Acting Director*, Dr. Charles Standridge, 616-331-6750, Fax: 616-331-7215, E-mail: standric@gvsu.edu.

Seidman College of Business Students: 102 full-time (48 women), 230 part-time (84 women); includes 25 minority (3 Black or African American, non-Hispanic/Latino; 9 Asian, non-Hispanic/Latino; 8 Hispanic/Latino; 5 Two or more races, non-Hispanic/Latino), 13 international. Average age 31. 118 applicants, 86% accepted, 68 enrolled. *Faculty:* 28 full-time (10 women), 7 part-time/adjunct (1 woman). *Financial support:* In 2015–16, 77 students received support, including 61 fellowships (averaging $7,239 per year), 22 research assistantships with tuition reimbursements available (averaging $7,809 per year); Federal Work-Study, institutionally sponsored loans, and unspecified assistantships also available. Support available to part-time students. Financial award application deadline: 2/15; financial award applicants required to submit FAFSA. In 2015, 129 master's awarded. *Degree program information:* Part-time and evening/weekend programs available. Part-time, evening/weekend. Offers accounting (MSA); business (MBA, MSA, MST); business administration (MBA); taxation (MST). *Application deadline:* For fall admission, 8/1 priority date for domestic students, 5/1 priority date for international students; for winter admission, 12/1 priority date for domestic students, 11/1 priority date for international students; for spring admission, 4/1 priority date for domestic students, 3/1 priority date for international students. Applications are processed on a rolling basis. *Application fee:* $30. Electronic applications accepted. *Application Contact:* Claudia J. Bajema, Director, Graduate Business Programs, 616-331-7387, Fax: 616-331-7389, E-mail: bajemac@gvsu.edu. *Dean*, Dr. Diana Lawson, 616-331-7385, Fax: 616-331-7380, E-mail: lawsond1@gvsu.edu.

GRAND VIEW UNIVERSITY, Des Moines, IA 50316-1599

General Information Independent-religious, coed, comprehensive institution.

GRADUATE UNITS

Master of Science in Innovative Leadership Program ***Degree program information:*** Part-time and evening/weekend programs available. Part-time, evening/weekend. Offers business (MS); education (MS); nursing (MS). Electronic applications accepted.

GRANITE STATE COLLEGE, Concord, NH 03301

General Information State and locally supported, coed, comprehensive institution. *Enrollment:* 2,180 graduate, professional, and undergraduate students; 51 full-time matriculated graduate/professional students (20 women), 55 part-time matriculated graduate/professional students (33 women). *Enrollment by degree level:* 106 master's. *Graduate faculty:* 3 full-time (2 women), 36 part-time/adjunct (18 women). *Tuition, area resident:* Full-time $9000; part-time $512 per credit. Tuition, nonresident: full-time $9630; part-time $545 per credit. *Graduate housing:* On-campus housing not available. *Student services:* Campus employment opportunities, campus safety program, career counseling, free psychological counseling, services for students with disabilities. *Library:* GSC Library and Research Commons plus 1 other. *Collection:* Books: 187,000 (digital/electronic); Serial titles: 18,000 (digital/electronic); Databases: 14. Weekly public service hours: 126.

Computer facilities: 139 computers available on campus for general student use. A campuswide network can be accessed. Online class registration is available.
Website: http://www.granite.edu/

General Application Contact: Ana Gonzalez, Administrative Assistant, Office of Graduate Studies, 603-513-1334, Fax: 603-513-1387, E-mail: gsc.graduatestudies@granite.edu.

GRADUATE UNITS

Program in Leadership Students: 32 full-time (12 women), 21 part-time (17 women); includes 2 minority (1 American Indian or Alaska Native, non-Hispanic/Latino; 1 Hispanic/Latino). Average age 39. 22 applicants, 100% accepted, 18 enrolled. *Faculty:* 1 (woman) full-time, 18 part-time/adjunct (10 women). *Financial support:* Federal Work-Study and National Guard course waivers available. Financial award applicants required to submit FAFSA. In 2015, 16 master's awarded. *Degree program information:* Part-time programs available. Part-time, 100% online, blended/hybrid learning. Offers leadership (MS). *Application deadline:* Applications are processed on a rolling basis. *Application fee:* $0. Electronic applications accepted. *Application Contact:* Ana Gonzalez, Administrative Assistant, Office of Graduate Studies, 603-513-1334, Fax: 603-513-1387, E-mail: gsc.graduatestudies@granite.edu. *Vice Provost of Academic Affairs*, Dr. Johnna Herrick-Phelps, 603-228-3000, E-mail: johnna.herrick-phelps@granite.edu.

Program in Management Students: 5 full-time (2 women), 10 part-time (5 women); includes 2 minority (1 Hispanic/Latino; 1 Two or more races, non-Hispanic/Latino). Average age 32. 4 applicants, 100% accepted, 3 enrolled. *Faculty:* 1 (woman) full-time, 10 part-time/adjunct (3 women). *Financial support:* Federal Work-Study and National Guard course waivers available. Financial award applicants required to submit FAFSA. In 2015, 1 master's awarded. *Degree program information:* Part-time programs available. Part-time, 100% online, blended/hybrid learning. Offers management (MS). *Application deadline:* Applications are processed on a rolling basis. *Application fee:* $0. Electronic applications accepted. *Application Contact:* Ana Gonzalez, Administrative Assistant, Office of Graduate Studies, 603-513-1334, Fax: 603-513-1387, E-mail: gsc.graduatestudies@granite.edu. *Vice Provost of Academic Affairs*, Dr. Johnna Herrick-Phelps, 855-228-3000, E-mail: johnna.herrick-phelps@granite.edu.

Program in Project Management Students: 14 full-time (6 women), 24 part-time (11 women); includes 2 minority (1 Black or African American, non-Hispanic/Latino; 1 American Indian or Alaska Native, non-Hispanic/Latino). Average age 40. 12 applicants, 100% accepted, 11 enrolled. *Faculty:* 1 full-time (0 women), 15 part-time/adjunct (7 women). *Financial support:* Federal Work-Study and National Guard course waivers available. Financial award applicants required to submit FAFSA. In 2015, 25 master's awarded. *Degree program information:* Part-time programs available. Part-time, 100% online, blended/hybrid learning. Offers project management (MS). *Application deadline:* Applications are processed on a rolling basis. *Application fee:* $0. Electronic applications accepted. *Application Contact:* Ana Gonzalez, Administrative Assistant, Office of Graduate Studies, 603-513-1334, Fax: 603-513-1387, E-mail: gsc.graduatestudies@granite.edu. *Vice Provost for Academic Affairs*, Dr. Johnna Herrick-Phelps, 855-228-3000, E-mail: johnna.herrick-phelps@granite.edu.

Program in School Leadership Offers school leadership (MS). *Application Contact:* Ana Gonzalez, Administrative Assistant, Office of Graduate Studies, 603-513-1334, Fax: 603-513-1387, E-mail: gsc.graduatestudies@granite.edu.

GRANTHAM UNIVERSITY, Lenexa, KS 66219

General Information Proprietary, coed, comprehensive institution. *Enrollment:* 188 full-time matriculated graduate/professional students (93 women), 1,837 part-time matriculated graduate/professional students (815 women). *Enrollment by degree level:* 1,937 master's, 27 other advanced degrees. *Graduate faculty:* 2 full-time (1 woman), 56 part-time/adjunct (28 women). *Tuition, area resident:* Full-time $3900; part-time $325 per credit hour. *Required fees:* $45 per term. One-time fee: $100. *Student services:* Career counseling, international student services, services for students with disabilities, writing training. *Library:* Grantham Online Library.

Computer facilities: Online class registration is available.
Website: http://www.grantham.edu/

General Application Contact: Jared Parlette, Vice President of Student Enrollment, 800-955-2527, Fax: 866-908-2360, E-mail: admissions@grantham.edu.

GRADUATE UNITS

College of Engineering and Computer Science Students: 21 full-time (3 women), 265 part-time (63 women); includes 114 minority (80 Black or African American, non-Hispanic/Latino; 4 American Indian or Alaska Native, non-Hispanic/Latino; 9 Asian, non-Hispanic/Latino; 14 Hispanic/Latino; 2 Native Hawaiian or other Pacific Islander, non-Hispanic/Latino; 5 Two or more races, non-Hispanic/Latino). Average age 39. 325 applicants, 95% accepted, 286 enrolled. *Faculty:* 8 part-time/adjunct (1 woman). *Financial support:* Scholarships/grants available. In 2015, 59 master's awarded. *Degree program information:* Part-time and evening/weekend programs available. Part-time, evening/weekend, online only, 100% online. Offers information management (MS); information management technology (MS); information technology (MS). *Application deadline:* Applications are processed on a rolling basis. Electronic applications accepted. *Application Contact:* Jared Parlette, Vice President of Student Enrollment, 888-947-2684, Fax: 866-908-2360, E-mail: admissions@grantham.edu. *Dean of the College of Engineering and Computer Sciences*, Dr. Nancy Miller, 913-309-4738, Fax: 855-681-5201, E-mail: nmiller@grantham.edu.

College of Nursing and Allied Health Students: 59 full-time (42 women), 368 part-time (277 women); includes 181 minority (119 Black or African American, non-Hispanic/Latino; 2 American Indian or Alaska Native, non-Hispanic/Latino; 23 Asian, non-Hispanic/Latino; 21 Hispanic/Latino; 4 Native Hawaiian or other Pacific Islander, non-Hispanic/Latino; 12 Two or more races, non-Hispanic/Latino). Average age 41. 498 applicants, 94% accepted, 427 enrolled. *Faculty:* 1 (woman) full-time, 15 part-time/adjunct (11 women). *Financial support:* Scholarships/grants available. In 2015, 119 master's awarded. *Degree program information:* Part-time and evening/weekend programs available. Part-time, evening/weekend, online only, 100% online. Offers case management (MSN); health systems management (MHSM, MSN); healthcare administration (MHA); nursing education (MSN); nursing informatics (MSN); nursing management and organizational leadership (MSN). *Application deadline:* Applications are processed on a rolling basis. Electronic applications accepted. *Application Contact:* Jared Parlette, Vice President of Student Enrollment, 888-947-2684, Fax: 866-908-2360, E-mail: admissions@grantham.edu. *Dean, College of Nursing and Allied Health*, Dana Basara, 913-309-4783, Fax: 844-897-6490, E-mail: dbasara@grantham.edu.

Mark Skousen School of Business Students: 107 full-time (48 women), 1,144 part-time (460 women); includes 440 minority (316 Black or African American, non-Hispanic/Latino; 9 American Indian or Alaska Native, non-Hispanic/Latino; 20 Asian, non-Hispanic/Latino; 72 Hispanic/Latino; 6 Native Hawaiian or other Pacific Islander, non-Hispanic/Latino; 17 Two or more races, non-Hispanic/Latino). Average age 40. 1,467 applicants, 95% accepted, 1251 enrolled. *Faculty:* 2 full-time (1 woman), 39 part-time/adjunct (16 women). *Financial support:* Scholarships/grants available. In 2015, 283 master's awarded. *Degree program information:* Part-time and evening/weekend programs available. Part-time, evening/weekend, online only, 100% online. Offers business administration (MBA); business intelligence (MS); human resources management (Certificate); information management (MBA); performance improvement (MS); project management (MBA, Certificate). *Application deadline:* Applications are processed on a rolling basis. Electronic applications accepted. *Application Contact:* Jared Parlette, Vice President of Student Enrollment, 888-947-2684, Fax: 866-908-2360, E-mail: admissions@grantham.edu. *Dean, Mark Skousen School of Business*, Dr. Niccole Buckley, 913-309-4747, Fax: 844-260-6287, E-mail: dmarker@grantham.edu.

GRATZ COLLEGE, Melrose Park, PA 19027

General Information Independent-religious, coed, graduate-only institution. *Graduate housing:* On-campus housing not available.

GRADUATE UNITS

Graduate Programs ***Degree program information:*** Part-time and evening/weekend programs available. Part-time, evening/weekend, online learning. Offers education (MA); educational technology (Graduate Certificate); Holocaust and genocide studies (MA, Graduate Certificate); Jewish communal service (MA, Certificate); Jewish education (MA, Ed D, Certificate); Jewish non-profit management (Graduate Certificate); Jewish studies (MA, Certificate); Jewish-Christian studies (Graduate Certificate).

GREEN MOUNTAIN COLLEGE, Poultney, VT 05764-1199

General Information Independent, coed, comprehensive institution.

GRADUATE UNITS

Program in Business Administration Online learning. Offers business administration (MBA). Distance learning only. Electronic applications accepted.

Program in Environmental Studies ***Degree program information:*** Part-time and evening/weekend programs available. Part-time, evening/weekend, online learning. Offers environmental studies (MS). Distance learning only. Electronic applications accepted.

GREENSBORO COLLEGE, Greensboro, NC 27401-1875

General Information Independent-religious, coed, comprehensive institution. *Graduate housing:* Rooms and/or apartments guaranteed to single students and available on a first-come, first-served basis to married students. Housing application deadline: 6/1.

GRADUATE UNITS

Program in Education ***Degree program information:*** Part-time and evening/weekend programs available. Part-time, evening/weekend. Offers elementary education (M Ed); special education (M Ed). Electronic applications accepted.

Program in Teaching English to Speakers of Other Languages ***Degree program information:*** Part-time and evening/weekend programs available. Part-time, evening/weekend. Offers teaching English to speakers of other languages (MA). Electronic applications accepted.

GREENVILLE COLLEGE, Greenville, IL 62246-0159

General Information Independent-religious, coed, comprehensive institution. *Graduate housing:* On-campus housing not available.

GRADUATE UNITS

Program in Education Offers education (MAT); elementary education (MAE); secondary education (MAE). Electronic applications accepted.

Program in Leadership and Ministry ***Degree program information:*** Part-time programs available. Part-time. Offers leadership and ministry (MA). Electronic applications accepted.

GWYNEDD MERCY UNIVERSITY, Gwynedd Valley, PA 19437-0901

General Information Independent-religious, coed, comprehensive institution. *Enrollment:* 2,582 graduate, professional, and undergraduate students; 503 full-time matriculated graduate/professional students (382 women), 79 part-time matriculated graduate/professional students (68 women). *Enrollment by degree level:* 454 master's, 96 doctoral, 32 other advanced degrees. *Graduate faculty:* 9 full-time (7 women), 17 part-time/adjunct (11 women). *Tuition, area resident:* Part-time $500 per credit. One-time fee: $165. Tuition and fees vary according to degree level and program. *Graduate housing:* On-campus housing not available. *Student services:* Campus employment opportunities, campus safety program, career counseling, free psychological counseling, international student services, low-cost health insurance, services for students with disabilities, teacher training. *Library:* Lourdes Library plus 1 other. *Collection:* Books: 86,674 (physical), 138,950 (digital/electronic); Serial titles: 132 (physical), 32,373 (digital/electronic); Databases: 43. Students can reserve study rooms.

Computer facilities: 218 computers available on campus for general student use. A campuswide network can be accessed from student residence rooms and from off campus. Online class registration is available.
Website: http://www.gmercyu.edu/

General Application Contact: Admission Counselor, 877-499-6333, E-mail: graduate@gmercyu.edu.

GRADUATE UNITS

Frances M. Maguire School of Nursing and Health Professions Students: 28 full-time (23 women), 68 part-time (62 women); includes 27 minority (18 Black or African American, non-Hispanic/Latino; 7 Asian, non-Hispanic/Latino; 2 Hispanic/Latino). Average age 37. 72 applicants, 25% accepted, 16 enrolled. *Faculty:* 3 full-time (all women), 2 part-time/adjunct (both women). *Financial support:* In 2015–16, 21 students received support. Scholarships/grants, traineeships, and unspecified assistantships available. Financial award application deadline: 8/30. In 2015, 7 master's awarded. *Degree program information:* Part-time programs available. Part-time, online learning. Offers clinical nurse specialist (MSN); nurse educator (MSN); nurse practitioner (MSN); nursing (DNP). *Application deadline:* For fall admission, 8/1 priority date for domestic students; for winter admission, 12/1 priority date for domestic students. Applications are processed on a rolling basis. Electronic applications accepted. *Application Contact:* Dr. Barbara A. Jones, Director, 215-646-7300 Ext. 407, Fax: 215-641-5564, E-mail: jones.b@gmc.edu. *Dean,* Dr. Andrea D. Hollingsworth, 215-646-7300 Ext. 539, Fax: 215-641-5517, E-mail: hollingsworth.a@gmc.edu.

School of Education Students: 377 full-time (285 women); includes 77 minority (55 Black or African American, non-Hispanic/Latino; 10 Asian, non-Hispanic/Latino; 12 Hispanic/Latino). Average age 30. 127 applicants, 18% accepted, 9 enrolled. *Faculty:* 8 full-time (5 women), 38 part-time/adjunct (24 women). *Financial support:* In 2015–16, 2 research assistantships were awarded; career-related internships or fieldwork, Federal Work-Study, institutionally sponsored loans, tuition waivers (full and partial), and unspecified assistantships also available. Financial award applicants required to submit FAFSA. In 2015, 100 master's awarded. *Degree program information:* Part-time and evening/weekend programs available. Part-time, evening/weekend. Offers educational administration (MS); master teacher (MS); school counseling (MS); special education (MS). *Application deadline:* Applications are processed on a rolling basis. *Application Contact:* Graduate Program Coordinator, 877-499-6333, E-mail: graduate@gmercyu.edu. *Dean,* Dr. Heather Pfleger, 215-646-7300 Ext. 21581, E-mail: pfleger.h@gmercyu.edu.

School of Graduate and Professional Studies Students: 97 full-time (73 women); includes 51 minority (44 Black or African American, non-Hispanic/Latino; 2 Asian, non-Hispanic/Latino; 5 Hispanic/Latino). Average age 36. *Faculty:* 7 part-time/adjunct (1 woman). *Financial support:* Career-related internships or fieldwork, Federal Work-Study, tuition waivers (full and partial), and unspecified assistantships available. Financial award applicants required to submit FAFSA. In 2015, 80 master's awarded. *Degree program information:* Part-time and evening/weekend programs available. Part-time, evening/weekend. Offers health care administration (MBA); management (MSM); strategic management and leadership (MBA). *Application deadline:* Applications are processed on a rolling basis. *Application Contact:* Information Contact, 800-342-5462, Fax: 215-641-5556. *Dean,* Dr. Mary Sortino, 215-646-7300, E-mail: sortino.m@gmercyu.edu.

HALLMARK UNIVERSITY, San Antonio, TX 78230

General Information Independent, coed, comprehensive institution. *Enrollment:* 615 graduate, professional, and undergraduate students; 3 part-time matriculated graduate/professional students (2 women). *Graduate faculty:* 3 full-time (1 woman), 2 part-time/adjunct (1 woman). *Tuition, area resident:* Full-time $13,650. *Required fees:* $540. *Graduate housing:* On-campus housing not available. *Library:* Randall K. Williams Assessment Center/ Virtual Library plus 1 other.

Computer facilities: 250 computers available on campus for general student use. A campuswide network can be accessed from off campus. Online class registration is available.
Website: http://www.hallmarkuniversity.edu/

General Application Contact: Sal Ross, Vice President of Admissions, 210-690-9000 Ext. 214, Fax: 210-699-1807, E-mail: slross@hallmarkuniversity.edu.

GRADUATE UNITS

School of Business Students: 3 part-time (2 women); includes 2 minority (1 Hispanic/Latino; 1 Two or more races, non-Hispanic/Latino). *Faculty:* 3 full-time (1 woman), 2 part-time/adjunct (1 woman). *Financial support:* Applicants required to submit FAFSA. In 2015, 1 master's awarded. Offers global management (MBA). *Application deadline:* Applications are processed on a rolling basis. *Application fee:* $60 ($0 for international students). *Application Contact:* Sal Ross, Vice President of Admissions, 210-690-9000 Ext. 214, Fax: 210-899-1807, E-mail: slross@hallmarkuniversity.edu. *Dean of Academics,* Dr. Darla Kenward, 210-690-9000 Ext. 242, Fax: 210-697-8225, E-mail: dkenward@hallmarkuniversity.edu.

HAMLINE UNIVERSITY, St. Paul, MN 55104-1284

General Information Independent-religious, coed, comprehensive institution. *Enrollment:* 4,258 graduate, professional, and undergraduate students; 842 full-time matriculated graduate/professional students (502 women), 1,187 part-time matriculated graduate/professional students (845 women). *Enrollment by degree level:* 1,509 master's, 340 doctoral, 39 other advanced degrees. *Graduate faculty:* 50 full-time (26 women), 168 part-time/adjunct (111 women). Tuition and fees vary according to degree level and program. *Graduate housing:* Rooms and/or apartments available on a first-come, first-served basis to single and married students. *Student services:* Campus employment opportunities, campus safety program, career counseling, exercise/wellness program, international student services, low-cost health insurance, multicultural affairs office, services for students with disabilities, teacher training, writing training. *Library:* Bush Library. *Research affiliation:* Minnesota Women Elected Officials.

Computer facilities: 300 computers available on campus for general student use. A campuswide network can be accessed from student residence rooms and from off campus. Online class registration is available.
Website: http://www.hamline.edu/

General Application Contact: Shawn Skoog, Director of Graduate Recruitment and Admission, 651-523-2900, Fax: 651-523-3058, E-mail: sskoog03@hamline.edu.

GRADUATE UNITS

College of Liberal Arts Students: 71 full-time (54 women), 92 part-time (57 women); includes 11 minority (1 Black or African American, non-Hispanic/Latino; 4 Asian, non-Hispanic/Latino; 2 Hispanic/Latino; 4 Two or more races, non-Hispanic/Latino), 1 international. Average age 37. 48 applicants, 65% accepted, 16 enrolled. *Faculty:* 8 full-time (6 women), 16 part-time/adjunct (9 women). *Financial support:* Federal Work-Study and scholarships/grants available. Support available to part-time students. Financial award applicants required to submit FAFSA. In 2015, 54 master's awarded. *Degree program information:* Part-time and evening/weekend programs available. Part-time, evening/weekend, online learning. Offers writing (MFA); writing for children and young adults (MFA). *Application deadline:* For fall admission, 6/1 for domestic and international students; for spring admission, 11/1 for domestic and international students. Applications are processed on a rolling basis. *Application fee:* $0 ($100 for international students). Electronic applications accepted. *Application Contact:* Shawn Skoog, Director of Graduate Admission and Recruitment, 651-523-2900, Fax: 651-523-3058, E-mail: gradprog@hamline.edu. *Interim Dean,* Dr. Marcela Kostihova, 651-523-2206, Fax: 651-523-3055, E-mail: cladean@hamline.edu.

Mitchell Hamline School of Law *Degree program information:* Part-time and evening/weekend programs available. Part-time, evening/weekend, online learning. Offers law (LL M, JD). Electronic applications accepted.

School of Business Students: 297 full-time (148 women), 88 part-time (49 women); includes 61 minority (37 Black or African American, non-Hispanic/Latino; 1 American Indian or Alaska Native, non-Hispanic/Latino; 17 Asian, non-Hispanic/Latino; 6 Hispanic/Latino), 19 international. Average age 34. 252 applicants, 54% accepted, 54 enrolled. *Faculty:* 12 full-time (3 women), 25 part-time/adjunct (7 women). *Financial support:* Career-related internships or fieldwork, Federal Work-Study, scholarships/grants, and unspecified assistantships available. Support available to part-time students. Financial award applicants required to submit FAFSA. In 2015, 159 master's, 3 doctorates awarded. *Degree program information:* Part-time and evening/weekend programs available. Part-time, evening/weekend, online learning. Offers business administration (MBA); nonprofit management (MNM); public administration (MPA, DPA). *Application deadline:* Applications are processed on a rolling basis. *Application fee:* $0 ($100 for international students). Electronic applications accepted. *Application Contact:* Shawn Skoog, Director of Graduate Recruitment and Admission, 651-523-2900, Fax: 651-523-3058, E-mail: gradprog@hamline.edu. *Dean,* Dr. Anne McCarthy, 651-523-2284, Fax: 651-523-3098, E-mail: hsb@hamline.edu.

School of Education Students: 291 full-time (208 women), 762 part-time (597 women); includes 101 minority (19 Black or African American, non-Hispanic/Latino; 5 American Indian or Alaska Native, non-Hispanic/Latino; 41 Asian, non-Hispanic/Latino; 23 Hispanic/Latino; 13 Two or more races, non-Hispanic/Latino), 14 international. Average age 34. 496 applicants, 70% accepted, 230 enrolled. *Faculty:* 19 full-time (14 women), 110 part-time/adjunct (86 women). *Financial support:* Career-related internships or fieldwork, Federal Work-Study, and scholarships/grants available. Support available to part-time students. Financial award applicants required to submit FAFSA. In 2015, 211 master's, 18 doctorates awarded. *Degree program information:* Part-time and evening/weekend programs available. Part-time, evening/weekend, online learning. Offers education (MA Ed, Ed D); English as a second language (MA); literacy education (MA); natural science and environmental education (MA Ed); teaching (MAT); teaching English to speakers of other languages (MA). *Application deadline:* Applications are processed on a rolling basis. *Application fee:* $0 ($100 for international students). Electronic applications accepted. *Application Contact:* Shawn Skoog, Director of Graduate Recruitment and Admission, 651-523-2900, Fax: 651-523-3058, E-mail: gradprog@hamline.edu. *Dean,* Dr. Nancy Sorenson, 651-523-2600, Fax: 651-523-2489, E-mail: education@hamline.edu.

HAMPTON UNIVERSITY, Hampton, VA 23668

General Information Independent, coed, comprehensive institution. CGS member. *Enrollment:* 4,269 graduate, professional, and undergraduate students; 633 full-time matriculated graduate/professional students (439 women), 217 part-time matriculated graduate/professional students (140 women). *Enrollment by degree level:* 286 master's, 489 doctoral, 75 other advanced degrees. *Graduate faculty:* 146 full-time (66 women), 26 part-time/adjunct (19 women). *Tuition, area resident:* Full-time $10,263; part-time $522 per credit hour. *Required fees:* $35. Tuition and fees vary according to course load and program. *Graduate housing:* Rooms and/or apartments available on a first-come, first-served basis to single and married students. Typical cost: $5292 per year ($10,176 including board) for single students. Room and board charges vary according to board plan. Housing application deadline: 6/1. *Student services:* Campus employment opportunities, campus safety program, career counseling, child daycare facilities, exercise/wellness program, free psychological counseling, international student services, services for students with disabilities, teacher training, writing training. *Library:* William R. and Norma B. Harvey Library plus 4 others. *Collection:* Books: 307,143 (physical), 91,991 (digital/electronic); Serial titles: 8,240 (physical); Databases: 115. Study areas open 24 hours, 5–7 days a week; students can reserve study rooms. *Research affiliation:* NASA-Langley Research Center (physical sciences), Southeastern Universities Research Association (science), Continuous Electron Beam Accelerator Facility (science).

Computer facilities: Computer purchase and lease plans are available. 1,500 computers available on campus for general student use. A campuswide network can be accessed from student residence rooms and from off campus. Online class registration, Banner Systems are available.
Website: http://www.hamptonu.edu/

General Application Contact: Dr. Michelle Penn-Marshall, Dean, Graduate College, 757-727-5454, E-mail: hugrad@hamptonu.edu.

GRADUATE UNITS

Program in Business Administration ***Degree program information:*** Part-time programs available. Part-time, online learning. Offers business administration (MBA, PhD). Electronic applications accepted.

School of Education and Human Development ***Degree program information:*** Part-time and evening/weekend programs available. Part-time, evening/weekend. Offers college student development (MA); community agency counseling (MA); counseling (Ed S); counselor education and supervision (PhD); education and human development (MA, MS, MT, PhD, Ed S); educational leadership (MA); educational management (PhD); elementary education (MA); music education (MT); pastoral counseling (MA); school counseling (MA); secondary education (MT); sport administration (MS). Electronic applications accepted.

School of Engineering and Technology Offers architecture (M Arch). Students enter program as freshmen. Electronic applications accepted.

School of Liberal Arts ***Degree program information:*** Part-time programs available. Part-time. Offers liberal arts (MS). Electronic applications accepted.

School of Nursing ***Degree program information:*** Part-time programs available. Part-time, online learning. Offers advanced adult nursing (MS); community health nursing (MS); community mental health/psychiatric nursing (MS); family nursing (MS); gerontological nursing for the nurse practitioner (MS); nursing (PhD); women's health nursing (MS). Electronic applications accepted.

School of Pharmacy Offers pharmacy (Pharm D).

School of Science ***Degree program information:*** Part-time and evening/weekend programs available. Part-time, evening/weekend, online learning. Offers atmospheric science (MS, PhD); biology (MS); chemistry and biochemistry (MS); computational mathematics (MS); computer science (MS); environmental science (MS); information assurance (MS); medical physics (MS, PhD); medical science (MS); nonlinear science (MS); nuclear physics (MS, PhD); optical physics (MS, PhD); physical therapy (DPT);

planetary science (MS, PhD); science (MA, MS, MT, DPT, PhD); speech-language pathology (MA); statistics and probability (MS). Electronic applications accepted.

HANNIBAL-LAGRANGE UNIVERSITY, Hannibal, MO 63401-1999

General Information Independent-religious, coed, comprehensive institution.

GRADUATE UNITS

Program in Education ***Degree program information:*** Part-time and evening/weekend programs available. Part-time, evening/weekend. Offers literacy (MS Ed); teaching and learning (MS Ed).

HARDING SCHOOL OF THEOLOGY, Memphis, TN 38117-5499

General Information Independent-religious, coed, primarily men, graduate-only institution. *Graduate housing:* Rooms and/or apartments available to single and married students.

GRADUATE UNITS

Graduate Programs ***Degree program information:*** Part-time programs available. Part-time, online learning. Offers Christian ministry (MA); counseling (MA); ministry (M Div, D Min); religion (MA). Electronic applications accepted.

HARDING UNIVERSITY, Searcy, AR 72149-0001

General Information Independent-religious, coed, university. *Enrollment:* 6,009 graduate, professional, and undergraduate students; 667 full-time matriculated graduate/professional students (424 women), 892 part-time matriculated graduate/professional students (583 women). *Enrollment by degree level:* 884 master's, 376 doctoral, 36 other advanced degrees. *Graduate faculty:* 77 full-time (37 women), 146 part-time/adjunct (40 women). *Graduate housing:* Rooms and/or apartments available on a first-come, first-served basis to single and married students. *Student services:* Campus employment opportunities, campus safety program, career counseling, exercise/wellness program, free psychological counseling, international student services, services for students with disabilities, writing training. *Library:* Brackett Library plus 1 other.

Computer facilities: 512 computers available on campus for general student use. A campuswide network can be accessed from student residence rooms and from off campus. Online class registration is available.
Website: http://www.harding.edu/

GRADUATE UNITS

Cannon-Clary College of Education Students: 121 full-time (88 women), 351 part-time (247 women); includes 100 minority (63 Black or African American, non-Hispanic/Latino; 7 American Indian or Alaska Native, non-Hispanic/Latino; 1 Asian, non-Hispanic/Latino; 13 Hispanic/Latino; 16 Two or more races, non-Hispanic/Latino), 8 international. Average age 36. 144 applicants, 87% accepted, 123 enrolled. *Faculty:* 16 full-time (5 women), 43 part-time/adjunct (27 women). *Financial support:* In 2015–16, 31 students received support. Unspecified assistantships available. In 2015, 132 master's, 34 other advanced degrees awarded. *Degree program information:* Part-time and evening/weekend programs available. Part-time, evening/weekend. Offers advanced studies in teaching and learning (M Ed); art (MSE); behavioral science (MSE); counseling (MS, Ed S); early childhood special education (M Ed, MSE); education (MSE); educational leadership (M Ed, Ed S); elementary education (M Ed); English (MSE); French (MSE); history/social science (MSE); kinesiology (MSE); math (MSE); reading (M Ed); secondary education (M Ed); Spanish (MSE); teaching (MAT); teaching English as a second language (MSE). *Application deadline:* For fall admission, 8/1 for domestic and international students; for spring admission, 1/1 for domestic and international students. Applications are processed on a rolling basis. *Application fee:* $35. *Application Contact:* Information Contact, 501-279-4315, E-mail: gradstudiesedu@harding.edu. *Chair,* Dr. Clara Carroll, 501-279-4501, Fax: 501-279-4083, E-mail: ccarroll@harding.edu.

College of Allied Health Students: 240 full-time (163 women); includes 32 minority (9 Black or African American, non-Hispanic/Latino; 4 American Indian or Alaska Native, non-Hispanic/Latino; 8 Asian, non-Hispanic/Latino; 8 Hispanic/Latino; 3 Two or more races, non-Hispanic/Latino), 1 international. Average age 27. 825 applicants, 16% accepted, 92 enrolled. *Faculty:* 27 full-time (16 women), 4 part-time/adjunct (2 women). *Financial support:* In 2015–16, 6 students received support. In 2015, 47 master's, 26 doctorates awarded. Offers allied health (MS, DPT); communication sciences and disorders (MS); physical therapy (DPT); physician assistant (MS). *Application Contact:* Dr. Julie Hixson-Wallace, Vice Provost, 501-279-5205, Fax: 501-279-5192, E-mail: jahixson@harding.edu.

College of Bible and Ministry Students: 21 full-time (14 women), 21 part-time (3 women); includes 3 minority (2 Black or African American, non-Hispanic/Latino; 1 American Indian or Alaska Native, non-Hispanic/Latino), 1 international. Average age 37. 20 applicants, 80% accepted, 16 enrolled. *Faculty:* 7 full-time (1 woman), 14 part-time/adjunct (1 woman). *Financial support:* In 2015–16, 23 students received support. Scholarships/grants and unspecified assistantships available. Financial award applicants required to submit FAFSA. In 2015, 17 master's awarded. *Degree program information:* Part-time programs available. Part-time, online learning. Offers Bible and ministry (M Min, MS); marriage and family therapy (MS); mental health counseling (MS); ministry (M Min). *Application Contact:* 501-279-4448, Fax: 501-279-5192, E-mail: bible@harding.edu. *Dean,* Dr. Monte Cox, 501-279-4448, Fax: 501-279-4042, E-mail: mcox@harding.edu.

College of Pharmacy Students: 221 full-time (134 women), 3 part-time (2 women); includes 65 minority (22 Black or African American, non-Hispanic/Latino; 4 American Indian or Alaska Native, non-Hispanic/Latino; 35 Asian, non-Hispanic/Latino; 4 Hispanic/Latino), 8 international. Average age 27. 208 applicants, 37% accepted, 48 enrolled. *Faculty:* 34 full-time (18 women), 1 part-time/adjunct (0 women). *Financial support:* In 2015–16, 35 students received support. Scholarships/grants available. Financial award applicants required to submit FAFSA. In 2015, 43 doctorates awarded. Offers pharmacy (Pharm D). *Application deadline:* For fall admission, 3/1 priority date for domestic and international students. Applications are processed on a rolling basis. *Application fee:* $50. Electronic applications accepted. *Application Contact:* Carol Jones, Director of Admissions, 501-279-5523, Fax: 501-279-5525, E-mail: ccjones@harding.edu. *Vice Provost,* Dr. Julie Ann Hixson-Wallace, 501-279-5205, Fax: 501-279-5525, E-mail: jahixson@harding.edu.

Paul R. Carter College of Business Administration Students: 37 full-time (19 women), 116 part-time (48 women); includes 23 minority (16 Black or African American, non-Hispanic/Latino; 1 American Indian or Alaska Native, non-Hispanic/Latino; 4 Asian, non-Hispanic/Latino; 2 Hispanic/Latino), 13 international. Average age 37. 45 applicants, 98% accepted, 44 enrolled. *Faculty:* 26 part-time/adjunct (6 women). *Financial support:* Unspecified assistantships available. Financial award application deadline: 7/30; financial award applicants required to submit FAFSA. In 2015, 78 master's awarded. *Degree program information:* Part-time and evening/weekend programs available. Part-time, evening/weekend, online learning. Offers health care management (MBA); information technology management (MBA); international business (MBA); leadership and organizational management (MBA). *Application deadline:* For fall admission, 8/1 priority date for domestic and international students; for spring admission, 12/1 priority date for domestic and international students. Applications are processed on a rolling basis. *Application fee:* $40. *Application Contact:* Melanie Kiihnl, Recruiting Manager/Director of Marketing, 501-279-4523, Fax: 501-279-4805, E-mail: mba@harding.edu. *Director of Graduate Studies,* Glen Metheny, 501-279-5851, Fax: 501-279-4805, E-mail: gmetheny@harding.edu.

HARDIN-SIMMONS UNIVERSITY, Abilene, TX 79698-0001

General Information Independent-religious, coed, comprehensive institution. *Enrollment:* 2,112 graduate, professional, and undergraduate students; 238 full-time matriculated graduate/professional students (126 women), 235 part-time matriculated graduate/professional students (126 women). *Enrollment by degree level:* 326 master's, 147 doctoral. *Graduate faculty:* 87 full-time (32 women), 33 part-time/adjunct (6 women). *Tuition, area resident:* Full-time $12,060; part-time $670 per credit hour. *Required fees:* $325; $110 per semester. *Graduate housing:* Rooms and/or apartments available on a first-come, first-served basis to single and married students. Typical cost: $3600 per year ($7740 including board) for single students. Room and board charges vary according to board plan and housing facility selected. *Student services:* Campus employment opportunities, career counseling, free psychological counseling, services for students with disabilities. *Library:* Richardson Library plus 1 other. *Collection:* Books: 355,463 (physical), 4,956 (digital/electronic); Serial titles: 259 (physical), 53,455 (digital/electronic); Databases: 125. Weekly public service hours: 89.

Computer facilities: 258 computers available on campus for general student use. A campuswide network can be accessed from student residence rooms and from off campus. Online class registration is available.
Website: http://www.hsutx.edu/

General Application Contact: Dr. Nancy Kucinski, Dean of Graduate Studies, 325-670-1298, Fax: 325-670-1564, E-mail: gradoff@hsutx.edu.

GRADUATE UNITS

Graduate School Students: 134 full-time (67 women), 232 part-time (123 women); includes 94 minority (37 Black or African American, non-Hispanic/Latino; 1 American Indian or Alaska Native, non-Hispanic/Latino; 2 Asian, non-Hispanic/Latino; 45 Hispanic/Latino; 9 Two or more races, non-Hispanic/Latino), 13 international. Average age 31. *Faculty:* 78 full-time (27 women), 33 part-time/adjunct (6 women). *Financial support:* In 2015–16, 281 students received support, including 32 fellowships (averaging $1,980 per year); career-related internships or fieldwork, scholarships/grants, and recreation assistantships, coaching assistantships also available. Support available to part-time students. Financial award application deadline: 6/30; financial award applicants required to submit FAFSA. In 2015, 95 master's, 6 doctorates awarded. *Degree program information:* Part-time programs available. Part-time. *Application deadline:* For fall admission, 8/15 priority date for domestic students, 4/1 for international students; for spring admission, 1/5 priority date for domestic students, 9/1 for international students. Applications are processed on a rolling basis. *Application fee:* $50. Electronic applications accepted. *Dean of Graduate Studies,* Dr. Nancy Kucinski, 325-670-1298, Fax: 325-670-1564, E-mail: gradoff@hsutx.edu.

College of Fine Arts Students: 8 full-time (5 women), 3 part-time (1 woman); includes 5 minority (2 Black or African American, non-Hispanic/Latino; 2 Hispanic/Latino; 1 Two or more races, non-Hispanic/Latino), 1 international. Average age 26. *Faculty:* 9 full-time (4 women), 3 part-time/adjunct (1 woman). *Financial support:* In 2015–16, 17 students received support, including 3 fellowships (averaging $3,000 per year); career-related internships or fieldwork and scholarships/grants also available. Support available to part-time students. Financial award application deadline: 6/30; financial award applicants required to submit FAFSA. In 2015, 1 master's awarded. *Degree program information:* Part-time programs available. Part-time. Offers church music (MM); music education (MM); music performance (MM); theory and composition (MM). *Application deadline:* For fall admission, 8/15 priority date for domestic students, 4/1 for international students; for spring admission, 1/5 priority date for domestic students, 9/1 for international students. Applications are processed on a rolling basis. *Application fee:* $50. Electronic applications accepted. *Application Contact:* Dr. Nancy Kucinski, Dean of Graduate Studies, 325-670-1298, Fax: 325-670-1564, E-mail: gradoff@hsutx.edu. *Program Director,* Dr. Lynnette Chambers, 325-670-1430, Fax: 325-670-5873, E-mail: lchambers@hsutx.edu.

Cynthia Ann Parker College of Liberal Arts Students: 19 full-time (all women), 5 part-time (2 women); includes 4 minority (3 Hispanic/Latino; 1 Two or more races, non-Hispanic/Latino). Average age 28. *Faculty:* 12 full-time (5 women), 1 part-time/adjunct (0 women). *Financial support:* In 2015–16, 17 students received support, including 14 fellowships (averaging $1,508 per year); scholarships/grants also available. Support available to part-time students. Financial award application deadline: 6/30; financial award applicants required to submit FAFSA. In 2015, 12 master's awarded. *Degree program information:* Part-time programs available. Part-time. Offers clinical counseling and marriage and family therapy (MA); English (MA); history (MA); liberal arts (MA). *Application deadline:* For fall admission, 8/15 priority date for domestic students, 4/1 for international students; for spring admission, 1/5 priority date for domestic students, 9/1 for international students. Applications are processed on a rolling basis. *Application fee:* $50. Electronic applications accepted. *Application Contact:* Dr. Nancy Kucinski, Dean of Graduate Studies, 325-670-1298, Fax: 325-670-1564, E-mail: gradoff@hsutx.edu. *Dean,* Dr. Alan R. Stafford, 325-670-1487, E-mail: stafford@hsutx.edu.

Holland School of Sciences and Mathematics Students: 5 full-time (2 women), 9 part-time (6 women); includes 2 minority (1 Hispanic/Latino; 1 Two or more races, non-Hispanic/Latino). Average age 33. *Faculty:* 7 full-time (2 women). *Financial support:* In 2015–16, 11 students received support. Fellowships, career-related internships or fieldwork, and scholarships/grants available. Support available to part-time students. Financial award application deadline: 6/30; financial award applicants required to submit FAFSA. In 2015, 4 master's awarded. *Degree program information:* Part-time programs available. Part-time. Offers environmental management (MS); mathematics (MS); physical therapy (DPT); sciences and mathematics (MS, DPT). *Application deadline:* For fall admission, 8/15 priority date for domestic students, 4/1 for international students; for spring admission, 1/5 priority date for domestic students, 9/1 for international students. Applications are processed on a rolling basis. *Application fee:* $50. Electronic applications accepted. *Application Contact:* Dr. Nancy Kucinski, Dean of Graduate Studies, 325-670-1298, Fax: 325-670-1564, E-mail: gradoff@hsutx.edu. *Dean,* Dr. Christopher McNair, 325-670-1401, Fax: 325-670-1385, E-mail: cmcnair@hsutx.edu.

Irvin School of Education Students: 26 full-time (12 women), 84 part-time (68 women); includes 24 minority (12 Black or African American, non-Hispanic/Latino; 10 Hispanic/Latino; 2 Two or more races, non-Hispanic/Latino), 3 international. Average

age 33. *Faculty:* 15 full-time (7 women), 8 part-time/adjunct (3 women). *Financial support:* In 2015–16, 60 students received support, including 14 fellowships (averaging $2,550 per year); career-related internships or fieldwork, scholarships/grants, and coaching assistantships also available. Support available to part-time students. Financial award application deadline: 6/30; financial award applicants required to submit FAFSA. In 2015, 36 master's awarded. *Degree program information:* Part-time programs available. Part-time. Offers counseling and human development (M Ed); education (M Ed, Ed D); education leadership (Ed D); gifted education (M Ed); kinesiology, sport, and recreation (M Ed); reading specialist education (M Ed). *Application deadline:* For fall admission, 8/15 priority date for domestic students, 4/1 for international students; for spring admission, 1/5 priority date for domestic students, 9/1 for international students. Applications are processed on a rolling basis. *Application fee:* $50. Electronic applications accepted. *Application Contact:* Dr. Nancy Kucinski, Dean of Graduate Studies, 325-670-1298, Fax: 325-670-1564, E-mail: gradoff@hsutx.edu. *Dean*, Dr. Perry Kay Brown, 325-670-1021, Fax: 325-670-5859, E-mail: pkbrown@hsutx.edu.

Kelley College of Business Students: 17 full-time (9 women), 7 part-time (2 women); includes 5 minority (2 Black or African American, non-Hispanic/Latino; 1 Hispanic/Latino; 2 Two or more races, non-Hispanic/Latino), 5 international. Average age 24. *Faculty:* 9 full-time (3 women), 1 part-time/adjunct (0 women). *Financial support:* In 2015–16, 19 students received support, including 1 fellowship (averaging $2,400 per year); scholarships/grants also available. Support available to part-time students. Financial award application deadline: 6/30; financial award applicants required to submit FAFSA. In 2015, 14 master's awarded. *Degree program information:* Part-time programs available. Part-time. Offers business administration (MBA); sports management (MBA). *Application deadline:* For fall admission, 8/15 priority date for domestic students, 4/1 for international students; for spring admission, 1/5 priority date for domestic students, 9/1 for international students. Applications are processed on a rolling basis. *Application fee:* $50. Electronic applications accepted. *Application Contact:* Dr. Nancy Kucinski, Dean of Graduate Studies, 325-670-1298, Fax: 325-670-1564, E-mail: gradoff@hsutx.edu. *Program Director*, Dr. Jennifer Plantier, 325-671-2166, Fax: 325-670-1523, E-mail: jplantier@hsutx.edu.

Logsdon School of Theology Students: 59 full-time (20 women), 106 part-time (29 women); includes 49 minority (19 Black or African American, non-Hispanic/Latino; 2 Asian, non-Hispanic/Latino; 26 Hispanic/Latino; 2 Two or more races, non-Hispanic/Latino), 4 international. Average age 36. *Faculty:* 21 full-time (1 woman), 19 part-time/adjunct (1 woman). *Financial support:* In 2015–16, 150 students received support. Fellowships and scholarships/grants available. Support available to part-time students. Financial award application deadline: 6/30; financial award applicants required to submit FAFSA. In 2015, 24 master's, 6 doctorates awarded. *Degree program information:* Part-time and evening/weekend programs available. Part-time, evening/weekend. Offers family ministry (MA); ministry (D Min); religion (MA); theology (M Div, MA, D Min). *Application deadline:* For fall admission, 8/15 priority date for domestic students, 4/1 for international students; for spring admission, 1/5 priority date for domestic students, 9/1 for international students. Applications are processed on a rolling basis. *Application fee:* $50. Electronic applications accepted. *Application Contact:* Dr. Nancy Kucinski, Dean of Graduate Studies, 325-670-1298, Fax: 325-670-1564, E-mail: gradoff@hsutx.edu. *Dean*, Dr. Don Williford, 325-670-1491, Fax: 325-671-2157, E-mail: willifrd@hsutx.edu.

Patty Hanks Shelton School of Nursing Students: 18 part-time (15 women); includes 5 minority (2 Black or African American, non-Hispanic/Latino; 1 American Indian or Alaska Native, non-Hispanic/Latino; 2 Hispanic/Latino). Average age 33. *Faculty:* 5 full-time (all women), 1 (woman) part-time/adjunct. *Financial support:* In 2015–16, 17 students received support. Career-related internships or fieldwork and scholarships/grants available. Support available to part-time students. Financial award application deadline: 6/30; financial award applicants required to submit FAFSA. In 2015, 4 master's awarded. *Degree program information:* Part-time programs available. Part-time. Offers advanced healthcare delivery (MSN); family nurse practitioner (MSN). Programs offered jointly with Abilene Christian University and McMurry University. *Application deadline:* For fall admission, 8/15 priority date for domestic students, 4/1 for international students; for spring admission, 1/5 priority date for domestic students, 9/1 for international students. Applications are processed on a rolling basis. *Application fee:* $50. Electronic applications accepted. *Application Contact:* Dr. Nancy Kucinski, Dean of Graduate Studies, 325-670-1298, Fax: 325-670-1564, E-mail: gradoff@hsutx.edu. *Dean*, Dr. Nina Ouimette, 325-671-2357, Fax: 325-671-2386, E-mail: nouimette@phssn.edu.

HARRISBURG UNIVERSITY OF SCIENCE AND TECHNOLOGY, Harrisburg, PA 17101

General Information Independent, coed, comprehensive institution. *Graduate housing:* On-campus housing not available.

GRADUATE UNITS

Program in Information Systems Engineering and Management ***Degree program information:*** Part-time programs available. Part-time. Offers digital government (MS); digital health (MS); entrepreneurship (MS). Electronic applications accepted.

Program in Learning Technologies ***Degree program information:*** Part-time and evening/weekend programs available. Part-time, evening/weekend. Offers learning technologies (MS). Electronic applications accepted.

Program in Project Management ***Degree program information:*** Part-time and evening/weekend programs available. Part-time, evening/weekend. Offers construction services (MS); governmental services (MS); information technology (MS). Electronic applications accepted.

HARRISON MIDDLETON UNIVERSITY, Tempe, AZ 85282

General Information Independent, coed, comprehensive institution.

GRADUATE UNITS

Graduate Program ***Degree program information:*** Part-time and evening/weekend programs available. Part-time, evening/weekend, online learning. Offers education (MA, Ed D); humanities (MA); imaginative literature (MA); interdisciplinary studies (DA); jurisprudence (MA); natural science (MA); philosophy and religion (MA); social science (MA). Electronic applications accepted.

HARTFORD SEMINARY, Hartford, CT 06105-2279

General Information Independent-religious, coed, graduate-only institution. *Graduate housing:* Rooms and/or apartments available on a first-come, first-served basis to single and married students. Housing application deadline: 7/15.

GRADUATE UNITS

Graduate Programs ***Degree program information:*** Part-time and evening/weekend programs available. Part-time, evening/weekend, online learning. Offers Islamic studies (MA); ministry (D Min); religious studies (MA); spirituality (Certificate).

HARVARD UNIVERSITY, Cambridge, MA 02138

General Information Independent, coed, university. CGS member. *Graduate housing:* Rooms and/or apartments available on a first-come, first-served basis to single and married students. *Research affiliation:* Woods Hole Oceanographic Institution (biology).

GRADUATE UNITS

Cyprus International Institute for the Environment and Public Health in Association with Harvard School of Public Health Offers environmental health (MS); environmental/public health (PhD); epidemiology and biostatistics (MS). Electronic applications accepted.

Extension School ***Degree program information:*** Part-time and evening/weekend programs available. Part-time, evening/weekend. Offers applied sciences (CAS); biotechnology (ALM); educational technologies (ALM); educational technology (CET); English for graduate and professional studies (DGP); environmental management (ALM, CEM); information technology (ALM); journalism (ALM); liberal arts (ALM); management (ALM, CM); mathematics for teaching (ALM); museum studies (ALM); premedical studies (Diploma); publication and communication (CPC).

Graduate School of Arts and Sciences Offers African and African American studies (PhD); African history (PhD); Akkadian and Sumerian (AM, PhD); American history (PhD); ancient art (PhD); ancient Near Eastern art (PhD); ancient, medieval, early modern, and modern Europe (PhD); anthropology and Middle Eastern studies (PhD); Arabic (AM, PhD); archaeology (PhD); architecture (PhD); Armenian (AM, PhD); arts and sciences (AM, MDE, ME, MFS, SM, PhD); astronomy (PhD); astrophysics (PhD); Baroque art (PhD); biblical history (AM, PhD); biochemical chemistry (PhD); biological anthropology (PhD); biological sciences in dental medicine (PhD); biology (PhD); biophysics (PhD); biostatistics (PhD); business economics (PhD); Byzantine art (PhD); Byzantine Greek (PhD); chemical biology (PhD); chemical physics (PhD); Chinese (PhD); Chinese studies (AM); classical archaeology (PhD); classical art (PhD); classical philology (PhD); classical philosophy (PhD); comparative literature (PhD); composition (AM, PhD); critical theory (PhD); descriptive linguistics (PhD); diplomatic history (PhD); earth and planetary sciences (AM, PhD); East Asian history (PhD); economic and social history (PhD); economics (PhD); economics and Middle Eastern studies (PhD); eighteenth-century literature (PhD); experimental physics (PhD); fine arts and Middle Eastern studies (PhD); forest science (MFS); French (AM, PhD); German (PhD); health policy (PhD); Hebrew (AM, PhD); historical linguistics (PhD); history and Middle Eastern studies (PhD); history of American civilization (PhD); history of science (AM, PhD); Indian art (PhD); Indian philosophy (AM, PhD); Indo-Muslim culture (AM, PhD); information, technology and management (PhD); Inner Asian and Altaic studies (PhD); inorganic chemistry (PhD); intellectual history (PhD); Iranian (AM, PhD); Irish (PhD); Islamic art (PhD); Italian (AM, PhD); Japanese (PhD); Japanese and Chinese art (PhD); Japanese studies (AM); Jewish history and literature (AM, PhD); Korean (PhD); Korean studies (AM); landscape architecture (PhD); Latin American history (PhD); legal anthropology (AM); literature: nineteenth-century to the present (PhD); mathematics (PhD); medical anthropology (AM); medical engineering/medical physics (PhD); medieval art (PhD); medieval Latin (PhD); medieval literature and language (PhD); modern art (PhD); modern British and American literature (PhD); molecular and cellular biology (PhD); Mongolian (PhD); Mongolian studies (AM); musicology (AM); musicology and ethnomusicology (PhD); Near Eastern history (PhD); neurobiology (PhD); oceanic history (PhD); oral literature (PhD); organic chemistry (PhD); organizational behavior (PhD); Pali (AM, PhD); Persian (AM, PhD); philosophy (PhD); physical chemistry (PhD); Polish (PhD); political economy and government (PhD); political science (PhD); Portuguese (AM, PhD); psychology (PhD); public policy (PhD); regional studies–Middle East (AM); regional studies-Russia, Eastern Europe, and Central Asia (AM); Renaissance and modern architecture (PhD); Renaissance art (PhD); Renaissance literature (PhD); Russian (PhD); Sanskrit (AM, PhD); Scandinavian (PhD); Semitic philology (AM, PhD); Serbo-Croatian (PhD); Slavic philology (PhD); social anthropology (AM, PhD); social change and development (AM); social policy (PhD); social psychology (PhD); sociology (PhD); Spanish (AM, PhD); statistics (AM, PhD); study of religion (PhD); Syro-Palestinian archaeology (AM, PhD); systems biology (PhD); theoretical linguistics (PhD); theoretical physics (PhD); theory (AM, PhD); Tibetan (AM, PhD); Turkish (AM, PhD); Ukrainian (PhD); urban planning (PhD); Urdu (AM, PhD); Vietnamese (PhD); Vietnamese studies (AM); Welsh (PhD). Electronic applications accepted.

Division of Medical Sciences Offers biological chemistry and molecular pharmacology (PhD); cell biology (PhD); genetics (PhD); microbiology and molecular genetics (PhD); pathology (PhD).

Harvard John A. Paulson School of Engineering and Applied Sciences Students: 425 full-time (109 women), 12 part-time (1 woman); includes 70 minority (1 Black or African American, non-Hispanic/Latino; 44 Asian, non-Hispanic/Latino; 17 Hispanic/Latino; 8 Two or more races, non-Hispanic/Latino), 207 international. Average age 27. 2,116 applicants, 11% accepted, 132 enrolled. *Faculty:* 101 full-time (14 women), 10 part-time/adjunct (1 woman). *Financial support:* In 2015–16, 353 students received support, including 92 fellowships with full tuition reimbursements available (averaging $25,650 per year), 213 research assistantships with tuition reimbursements available (averaging $34,200 per year), 127 teaching assistantships with tuition reimbursements available (averaging $5,775 per year); health care benefits also available. In 2015, 88 master's, 64 doctorates awarded. *Degree program information:* Part-time programs available. Part-time. Offers applied mathematics (ME, SM, PhD); applied physics (ME, SM, PhD); computational science and engineering (ME, SM); computer science (ME, SM, PhD); design engineering (MDE); engineering science (ME); engineering sciences (SM, PhD). MDE offered in collaboration with Graduate School of Design. *Application deadline:* For fall admission, 12/15 priority date for domestic and international students. *Application fee:* $105. Electronic applications accepted. *Application Contact:* Office of Admissions and Financial Aid, 617-495-5315, E-mail: admissions@seas.harvard.edu. *Dean*, Francis J. Doyle, III, 617-495-5829, Fax: 617-495-5264, E-mail: dean@seas.harvard.edu.

Graduate School of Design Offers architecture (M Arch); design (M Arch, M Des S, MAUD, MLA, MLAUD, MUP, Dr DES); design studies (M Des S); landscape architecture (MLA); urban planning (MUP); urban planning and design (MAUD, MLAUD). Electronic applications accepted.

Harvard Business School Offers accounting and management (DBA); business (MBA, DBA, PhD); business administration (MBA); business economics (PhD); health policy management (PhD); management (DBA); marketing (DBA); organizational behavior (PhD); science, technology and management (PhD); strategy (DBA); technology and operations management (DBA).

Harvard Divinity School Offers divinity (M Div, MTS, Th M). Electronic applications accepted.

Harvard Graduate School of Education Students: 892 full-time (635 women), 74 part-time (52 women); includes 294 minority (88 Black or African American, non-Hispanic/Latino; 94 Asian, non-Hispanic/Latino; 75 Hispanic/Latino; 1 Native Hawaiian or other Pacific Islander, non-Hispanic/Latino; 36 Two or more races, non-Hispanic/Latino), 155 international. Average age 29. 2,723 applicants, 36% accepted, 717 enrolled. *Faculty:* 68 full-time (36 women), 92 part-time/adjunct (51 women). *Financial support:* In 2015–16, 641 students received support, including 247 fellowships with tuition reimbursements available (averaging $23,359 per year), 56 research assistantships (averaging $7,490 per year), 200 teaching assistantships (averaging $6,900 per year); career-related internships or fieldwork, Federal Work-Study, institutionally sponsored loans, scholarships/grants, health care benefits, tuition waivers (full and partial), and unspecified assistantships also available. Support available to part-time students. Financial award application deadline: 2/1; financial award applicants required to submit FAFSA. In 2015, 635 master's, 66 doctorates awarded. *Degree program information:* Part-time programs available. Part-time. Offers arts in education (Ed M); education (Ed M, Ed L D, PhD); education leadership (Ed L D); education policy and management (Ed M); higher education (Ed M); human development and psychology (Ed M); international education policy (Ed M); language and literacy (Ed M); learning and teaching (Ed M); mind, brain, and education (Ed M); prevention science and practice (Ed M); school leadership (Ed M); special studies (Ed M); teacher education (Ed M); technology, innovation, and education (Ed M). *Application deadline:* For fall admission, 12/1 for domestic and international students. *Application fee:* $85. Electronic applications accepted. *Application Contact:* Julie Deland, Director of Admissions, 617-495-3414, Fax: 617-496-3577, E-mail: gseadmissions@harvard.edu. *Dean of the Harvard Graduate School of Education*, James E. Ryan, 617-495-3401.

Harvard Medical School Offers medicine (M Eng, SM, MD, PhD, Sc D). Electronic applications accepted.

Harvard T.H. Chan School of Public Health Students: 1,105 full-time (660 women), 119 part-time (70 women); includes 343 minority (51 Black or African American, non-Hispanic/Latino; 1 American Indian or Alaska Native, non-Hispanic/Latino; 185 Asian, non-Hispanic/Latino; 66 Hispanic/Latino; 1 Native Hawaiian or other Pacific Islander, non-Hispanic/Latino; 39 Two or more races, non-Hispanic/Latino), 431 international. Average age 27. 2,653 applicants, 29% accepted, 607 enrolled. *Faculty:* 347 full-time (125 women), 133 part-time/adjunct (45 women). *Financial support:* Fellowships, research assistantships, teaching assistantships, career-related internships or fieldwork, Federal Work-Study, scholarships/grants, traineeships, and unspecified assistantships available. Support available to part-time students. Financial award application deadline: 2/15; financial award applicants required to submit FAFSA. In 2015, 299 master's, 13 doctorates awarded. *Degree program information:* Part-time programs available. Part-time. Offers biological sciences in public health (PhD); biostatistics (SM, PhD); cancer epidemiology (SM); cardiovascular epidemiology (SM, SD); clinical effectiveness (MPH); clinical epidemiology (SM, SD); computational biology and quantitative genetics (SM); environmental and occupational epidemiology (SM, SD); environmental health (SM, PhD, SD); epidemiologic methods (SD); epidemiology of aging (SM, SD); exposure, epidemiology, and risk (SM, SD); genetic epidemiology and statistical genetics (SD); global health (MPH); global health and population (SM, SD); health and social behavior (MPH); health management (MPH); health policy (MPH); health policy and management (SM); infectious disease epidemiology (SM, SD); neuroepidemiology (SD); nutrition (SD); nutritional epidemiology (SD); occupational and environmental health (MPH); occupational health (SM, SD); pharmacoepidemiology (SM, SD); physiology (PhD, SD); psychiatric epidemiology (SM); public health (MPH, SM, Dr PH, PhD, SD); public health nutrition (SD); quantitative methods (MPH); reproductive epidemiology (SM, SD); social and behavioral sciences (SM, SD). SM program offered jointly with Simmons College. *Application deadline:* For fall admission, 12/15 for domestic and international students. *Application fee:* $120. Electronic applications accepted. *Application Contact:* Vincent W. James, Director of Admissions, 617-432-1031, Fax: 617-432-7080, E-mail: admissions@hsph.harvard.edu. *Dean of the Faculty*, Dr. David Hunter, 617-432-1025, Fax: 617-277-5320, E-mail: deansoff@hsph.harvard.edu.

John F. Kennedy School of Government Students: 897 full-time (392 women), 21 part-time (12 women); includes 159 minority (34 Black or African American, non-Hispanic/Latino; 1 American Indian or Alaska Native, non-Hispanic/Latino; 69 Asian, non-Hispanic/Latino; 37 Hispanic/Latino; 1 Native Hawaiian or other Pacific Islander, non-Hispanic/Latino; 17 Two or more races, non-Hispanic/Latino), 430 international. Average age 31. 2,805 applicants, 35% accepted, 593 enrolled. *Financial support:* Fellowships, research assistantships, teaching assistantships, career-related internships or fieldwork, Federal Work-Study, institutionally sponsored loans, scholarships/grants, and unspecified assistantships available. Support available to part-time students. Financial award application deadline: 2/26; financial award applicants required to submit CSS PROFILE or FAFSA. In 2015, 569 master's awarded. Offers government (MPA, MPAID, MPP, PhD); political economy and government (PhD); public administration (MPA); public administration/international development (MPAID); public policy (MPP, PhD). *Application deadline:* For fall admission, 12/2 for domestic students. *Application fee:* $100. Electronic applications accepted. *Application Contact:* 617-495-1155, Fax: 617-496-1165, E-mail: hks_admissions@harvard.edu. *Dean*, Dr. David Ellwood, 617-495-1122.

Law School Offers international and comparative law (JD); law (LL M, JD, SJD); law and business (JD); law and government (JD); law and social change (JD); law, science and technology (JD).

School of Dental Medicine Offers advanced general dentistry (Certificate); dental medicine (M Med Sc, D Med Sc, DMD, Certificate); dental public health (Certificate); endodontics (Certificate); general practice residency (Certificate); oral biology (M Med Sc, D Med Sc); oral implantology (Certificate); oral medicine (Certificate); oral pathology (Certificate); oral surgery (Certificate); orthodontics (Certificate); pediatric dentistry (Certificate); periodontics (Certificate); prosthodontics (Certificate).

HASTINGS COLLEGE, Hastings, NE 68901

General Information Independent-religious, coed, comprehensive institution. *Graduate housing:* On-campus housing not available.

GRADUATE UNITS

Department of Teacher Education ***Degree program information:*** Part-time programs available. Part-time. Offers teacher education (MAT). Electronic applications accepted.

HAWAI`I PACIFIC UNIVERSITY, Honolulu, HI 96813

General Information Independent, coed, comprehensive institution. *Enrollment:* 4,781 graduate, professional, and undergraduate students; 509 full-time matriculated graduate/professional students (300 women), 273 part-time matriculated graduate/professional students (147 women). *Enrollment by degree level:* 768 master's, 14 other advanced degrees. *Graduate faculty:* 70 full-time (28 women), 32 part-time/adjunct (9 women). *Tuition, area resident:* Full-time $16,470; part-time $915 per credit. *Required fees:* $130; $26 per unit. Tuition and fees vary according to course load and program. *Graduate housing:* Rooms and/or apartments available on a first-come, first-served basis to single and married students. Typical cost: $13,899 (including board) for single students. Room and board charges vary according to board plan, campus/location and housing facility selected. *Student services:* Campus employment opportunities, campus safety program, career counseling, exercise/wellness program, free psychological counseling, international student services, low-cost health insurance, multicultural affairs office, services for students with disabilities, writing training. *Library:* Meader Library plus 2 others. *Collection:* Books: 104,039 (physical), 183,444 (digital/electronic); Serial titles: 94 (physical), 4,649 (digital/electronic); Databases: 82. Students can reserve study rooms. *Research affiliation:* Oceanic Institute (marine science).

Computer facilities: 200 computers available on campus for general student use. A campuswide network can be accessed from student residence rooms and from off campus. Online class registration is available.
Website: http://www.hpu.edu/

General Application Contact: Danny Lam, Assistant Director of Graduate Admissions, 808-544-1135, Fax: 808-544-0280, E-mail: graduate@hpu.edu.

GRADUATE UNITS

College of Business Students: 163 full-time (80 women), 117 part-time (48 women); includes 126 minority (11 Black or African American, non-Hispanic/Latino; 1 American Indian or Alaska Native, non-Hispanic/Latino; 34 Asian, non-Hispanic/Latino; 26 Hispanic/Latino; 8 Native Hawaiian or other Pacific Islander, non-Hispanic/Latino; 46 Two or more races, non-Hispanic/Latino), 83 international. Average age 32. 170 applicants, 79% accepted, 83 enrolled. *Faculty:* 18 full-time (7 women), 11 part-time/adjunct (0 women). *Financial support:* In 2015–16, 109 students received support. Research assistantships, teaching assistantships, career-related internships or fieldwork, Federal Work-Study, scholarships/grants, tuition waivers, and unspecified assistantships available. Financial award application deadline: 3/1; financial award applicants required to submit FAFSA. In 2015, 213 master's awarded. *Degree program information:* Part-time and evening/weekend programs available. Part-time, evening/weekend, online learning. Offers accounting (MBA); business (MA, MBA, MSIS); economics (MBA); finance (MBA); hospitality and tourism management (MBA); human resource management (MA); information systems (MBA); international business (MBA); management (MBA); marketing (MBA); organizational change (MA); organizational change and development (MBA). *Application deadline:* For fall admission, 2/15 priority date for domestic students; for spring admission, 10/15 priority date for domestic students. Applications are processed on a rolling basis. *Application fee:* $50. Electronic applications accepted. *Application Contact:* Danny Lam, Assistant Director of Graduate Admissions, 808-544-1135, Fax: 808-544-0280, E-mail: graduate@hpu.edu. *Dean*, Dr. Deborah Crown, 808-544-0275, Fax: 808-566-2403, E-mail: dcrown@hpu.edu.

College of Health and Society Students: 97 full-time (80 women), 31 part-time (26 women); includes 71 minority (11 Black or African American, non-Hispanic/Latino; 24 Asian, non-Hispanic/Latino; 16 Hispanic/Latino; 4 Native Hawaiian or other Pacific Islander, non-Hispanic/Latino; 16 Two or more races, non-Hispanic/Latino), 8 international. Average age 33. 96 applicants, 82% accepted, 50 enrolled. *Faculty:* 8 full-time (7 women), 4 part-time/adjunct (2 women). *Financial support:* In 2015–16, 74 students received support. Career-related internships or fieldwork, Federal Work-Study, scholarships/grants, traineeships, tuition waivers, and unspecified assistantships available. Financial award application deadline: 3/1; financial award applicants required to submit FAFSA. In 2015, 42 master's awarded. *Degree program information:* Part-time and evening/weekend programs available. Part-time, evening/weekend. Offers health and society (MSN, MSW); nursing (MSN); social work (MSW). *Application deadline:* For fall admission, 2/15 priority date for domestic students; for spring admission, 10/15 priority date for domestic students. Applications are processed on a rolling basis. *Application fee:* $50. Electronic applications accepted. *Application Contact:* Danny Lam, Assistant Director of Graduate Admissions, 808-544-1135, Fax: 808-544-0280, E-mail: graduate@hpu.edu. *Dean*, Dr. Lynette Landry, 808-236-5811, Fax: 808-236-3524, E-mail: llandry@hpu.edu.

College of Liberal Arts Students: 188 full-time (103 women), 106 part-time (57 women); includes 112 minority (11 Black or African American, non-Hispanic/Latino; 1 American Indian or Alaska Native, non-Hispanic/Latino; 34 Asian, non-Hispanic/Latino; 28 Hispanic/Latino; 1 Native Hawaiian or other Pacific Islander, non-Hispanic/Latino; 37 Two or more races, non-Hispanic/Latino), 47 international. Average age 32. 202 applicants, 85% accepted, 103 enrolled. *Faculty:* 28 full-time (9 women), 14 part-time/adjunct (5 women). *Financial support:* In 2015–16, 121 students received support. Career-related internships or fieldwork, Federal Work-Study, scholarships/grants, tuition waivers, and unspecified assistantships available. Financial award application deadline: 3/1; financial award applicants required to submit FAFSA. In 2015, 125 master's awarded. *Degree program information:* Part-time and evening/weekend programs available. Part-time, evening/weekend. Offers clinical mental health counseling (MA); communication (MA); diplomacy and military studies (MA); elementary education (M Ed); global leadership and sustainable development (MA); liberal arts (M Ed, MA); secondary education (M Ed); teaching English to speakers of other languages (MA). *Application deadline:* For fall admission, 2/15 priority date for domestic students; for spring admission, 10/15 priority date for domestic students. Applications are processed on a rolling basis. *Application fee:* $50. Electronic applications accepted. *Application Contact:* Danny Lam, Assistant Director of Graduate Admissions, 808-544-1135, Fax: 808-544-0280, E-mail: graduate@hpu.edu. *Dean*, Dr. David Lanoue, 808-544-0828, Fax: 808-544-1424, E-mail: dlanoue@hpu.edu.

College of Natural and Computational Sciences Students: 15 full-time (11 women), 19 part-time (15 women); includes 6 minority (2 Asian, non-Hispanic/Latino; 1 Hispanic/Latino; 3 Two or more races, non-Hispanic/Latino), 3 international. Average age 27. 36 applicants, 83% accepted, 5 enrolled. *Faculty:* 8 full-time (7 women), 4 part-time/adjunct (2 women). *Financial support:* In 2015–16, 13 students received support. Career-related internships or fieldwork, Federal Work-Study, scholarships/grants, tuition waivers, and unspecified assistantships available. Financial award application deadline: 3/1; financial award applicants required to submit FAFSA. In 2015, 17 master's awarded. *Degree program information:* Part-time programs available. Part-time. Offers marine science (MS); natural and computational sciences (MS). *Application deadline:* For fall admission, 1/15 for domestic students. *Application fee:* $50. Electronic applications accepted. *Application Contact:* Danny Lam, Assistant Director of Graduate Admissions, 808-544-1135, Fax: 808-544-0280, E-mail: graduate@hpu.edu. *Interim Dean*, Roland L. Jenkins, 808-687-7028, Fax: 808-236-5880, E-mail: rjenkins@hpu.edu.

HAZELDEN GRADUATE SCHOOL OF ADDICTION STUDIES, Center City, MN 55012

General Information Independent, coed, graduate-only institution. CGS member. *Graduate housing:* On-campus housing not available.

GRADUATE UNITS

Graduate Programs ***Degree program information:*** Part-time programs available. Part-time. Offers addiction counseling (MA, Certificate).

HEBREW COLLEGE, Newton Centre, MA 02459

General Information Independent-religious, coed, graduate-only institution. *Graduate housing:* On-campus housing not available.

GRADUATE UNITS

Cantor Educator Program Offers cantor educator (MJ Ed).

Program in Jewish Studies ***Degree program information:*** Part-time and evening/weekend programs available. Part-time, evening/weekend, online learning. Offers Jewish liturgical music (Certificate); Jewish music education (Certificate); Jewish studies (MA).

Rabbinical School Offers rabbinics (MA).

Shoolman Graduate School of Jewish Education ***Degree program information:*** Part-time and evening/weekend programs available. Part-time, evening/weekend, online learning. Offers early childhood Jewish education (Certificate); Jewish day school education (Certificate); Jewish education (MJ Ed); Jewish family education (Certificate); Jewish special education (Certificate); Jewish youth education, informal education and camping (Certificate).

HEBREW UNION COLLEGE–JEWISH INSTITUTE OF RELIGION, New York, NY 10012-1186

General Information Independent-religious, coed, graduate-only institution. *Graduate housing:* On-campus housing not available.

GRADUATE UNITS

Rabbinical School Offers rabbinical studies (MAHL).

School of Education ***Degree program information:*** Part-time programs available. Part-time. Offers education (MARE).

School of Graduate Studies ***Degree program information:*** Part-time programs available. Part-time. Offers Hebrew letters (DHL); Judaic studies (MAJS); pastoral counseling (D Min).

School of Jewish Nonprofit Management Offers Jewish nonprofit management (MA).

School of Sacred Music Offers sacred music (MSM).

HEC MONTREAL, Montréal, QC H3T 2A7, Canada

General Information Province-supported, coed, comprehensive institution. *Enrollment:* 13,705 graduate, professional, and undergraduate students; 1,596 full-time matriculated graduate/professional students (787 women), 1,336 part-time matriculated graduate/professional students (746 women). *Enrollment by degree level:* 1,561 master's, 130 doctoral, 1,241 other advanced degrees. *Graduate faculty:* 289 full-time (96 women), 422 part-time/adjunct (136 women). *International tuition:* $18,849 Canadian dollars full-time. *Tuition, area resident:* Part-time $76.45 Canadian dollars per credit. Tuition, province resident: full-time $2752 Canadian dollars; part-time $234.35 Canadian dollars per credit. Tuition, Canadian resident: full-time $8437 Canadian dollars; part-time $523.57 Canadian dollars per credit. *Required fees:* $1626 Canadian dollars; $38.75 Canadian dollars per credit. $66.66 Canadian dollars per term. Tuition and fees vary according to degree level and program. *Graduate housing:* Rooms and/or apartments available on a first-come, first-served basis to single and married students. Typical cost: $3850 Canadian dollars per year for single students; $6270 Canadian dollars per year for married students. *Student services:* Campus employment opportunities, campus safety program, career counseling, child daycare facilities, exercise/wellness program, free psychological counseling, grant writing training, international student services, low-cost health insurance, multicultural affairs office, services for students with disabilities. *Library:* Myriam et J.-Robert Ouimet Library plus 1 other. *Collection:* Books: 115,341 (physical), 279,804 (digital/electronic); Serial titles: 4,648 (physical), 82,608 (digital/electronic); Databases: 139. Weekly public service hours: 82; students can reserve study rooms. *Research affiliation:* CIRANO (Centre for Interuniversity Research and Analysis of Organizations) (research and transfer), CEFRIO (research and digital expertise), ACFAS (Association francophone pour le savoir), ASAC (Administrative Sciences Administration of Canada) (administrative sciences), CRIAQ (Consortium of Synergetic Research and Innovation in Aerospace) (research in aerospace), PROMPT Institute (research in information and communications technologies).

Computer facilities: Computer purchase and lease plans are available. 154 computers available on campus for general student use. A campuswide network can be accessed from student residence rooms. Online class registration, Complete Learning Management System, corporate calendar and Web sites for resources available for classes are available.
Website: http://www.hec.ca/

General Application Contact: Louise Champagne, Registrar, 514-340-6110, Fax: 514-340-6411, E-mail: registraire.info@hec.ca.

GRADUATE UNITS

School of Business Administration Students: 1,596 full-time (787 women), 1,336 part-time (746 women). Average age 29. 1,690 applicants, 62% accepted, 792 enrolled. *Faculty:* 289 full-time (96 women), 422 part-time/adjunct (136 women). *Financial support:* In 2015–16, 955 students received support. Research assistantships, teaching assistantships, and scholarships/grants available. Financial award application deadline: 9/2. In 2015, 588 master's, 22 doctorates, 868 other advanced degrees awarded. Offers administration (LL M, M Sc, MM, PhD, Graduate Diploma); applied economics (M Sc); applied financial economics (M Sc); business administration (LL M, M Sc, MBA, MM, PhD, Graduate Certificate); business administration and management (MBA); business analytics (M Sc); business intelligence (M Sc); cultural enterprises (MM); e-business (Graduate Diploma); electronic commerce (M Sc); energy management (Graduate Diploma); finance (M Sc); financial engineering (M Sc); financial professions (Graduate Diploma); global supply chain management (M Sc); human resources management (M Sc); information technologies (M Sc); international business (M Sc); international logistics (M Sc); management (M Sc, Graduate Diploma); management and social innovations (M Sc); management and sustainable development (Graduate Diploma); management control (M Sc); management in cultural enterprises (MM); management of cultural organizations (Graduate Diploma); marketing (M Sc); marketing communication (Graduate Diploma); operations management (M Sc); organizational development (M Sc); professional accounting (M Sc, Graduate Diploma); strategy (M Sc); supply chain management (Graduate Diploma); taxation (LL M, Graduate Diploma). Most courses are given in French. *Application fee:* $85 Canadian dollars. Electronic applications accepted. *Application Contact:* Louise Champagne, Registrar, 514-340-6110, Fax: 514-340-6411, E-mail: registraire.info@hec.ca. *Director*, Dr. Michel Patry, 514-340-6110, Fax: 514-340-5640.

HEIDELBERG UNIVERSITY, Tiffin, OH 44883-2462

General Information Independent-religious, coed, comprehensive institution. *Graduate housing:* On-campus housing not available.

GRADUATE UNITS

Program in Business Administration ***Degree program information:*** Part-time and evening/weekend programs available. Part-time, evening/weekend. Offers business administration (MBA).

Program in Counseling ***Degree program information:*** Part-time and evening/weekend programs available. Part-time, evening/weekend. Offers community mental health counseling (MA); school counseling (MA).

Program in Education ***Degree program information:*** Part-time and evening/weekend programs available. Part-time, evening/weekend. Offers education (MAE).

Program in Music Education ***Degree program information:*** Part-time programs available. Part-time. Offers music education (MME). Summer program only. Electronic applications accepted.

HENDERSON STATE UNIVERSITY, Arkadelphia, AR 71999-0001

General Information State-supported, coed, comprehensive institution. CGS member. *Enrollment:* 3,527 graduate, professional, and undergraduate students; 75 full-time matriculated graduate/professional students (53 women), 353 part-time matriculated graduate/professional students (246 women). *Enrollment by degree level:* 401 master's, 27 other advanced degrees. *Graduate faculty:* 42 full-time (16 women), 7 part-time/adjunct (3 women). Tuition, state resident: full-time $6096; part-time $3048 per credit hour. Tuition, nonresident: full-time $12,504; part-time $6252 per credit hour. *Required fees:* $1447; $1024 per unit. Tuition and fees vary according to course load and student level. *Graduate housing:* Room and/or apartments available on a first-come, first-served basis to single students; on-campus housing not available to married students. Typical cost: $4200 (including board). Room and board charges vary according to board plan and housing facility selected. *Student services:* Campus employment opportunities, career counseling, free psychological counseling, international student services, services for students with disabilities. *Library:* Huie Library plus 1 other. *Collection:* Books: 225,000 (physical), 132,000 (digital/electronic); Databases: 150. Weekly public service hours: 80; students can reserve study rooms.

Computer facilities: 125 computers available on campus for general student use. A campuswide network can be accessed from student residence rooms and from off campus. Online class registration is available.
Website: http://www.hsu.edu/

General Application Contact: Dr. Ken Taylor, Graduate Dean, 870-230-5126, Fax: 870-230-5479, E-mail: taylorke@hsu.edu.

GRADUATE UNITS

Graduate Studies Students: 75 full-time (53 women), 353 part-time (246 women); includes 115 minority (88 Black or African American, non-Hispanic/Latino; 2 American Indian or Alaska Native, non-Hispanic/Latino; 3 Asian, non-Hispanic/Latino; 13 Hispanic/Latino; 9 Two or more races, non-Hispanic/Latino), 7 international. Average age 32. 115 applicants, 100% accepted, 101 enrolled. *Faculty:* 42 full-time (16 women), 7 part-time/adjunct (3 women). *Financial support:* In 2015–16, 60 teaching assistantships with partial tuition reimbursements (averaging $4,000 per year) were awarded; scholarships/grants and unspecified assistantships also available. Financial award application deadline: 4/15; financial award applicants required to submit FAFSA. In 2015, 134 master's, 3 other advanced degrees awarded. *Degree program information:* Part-time programs available. Part-time, 100% online. *Application deadline:* For fall admission, 8/1 priority date for domestic students, 6/30 priority date for international students; for spring admission, 1/1 priority date for domestic students, 11/30 priority date for international students. Applications are processed on a rolling basis. *Application fee:* $25 ($75 for international students). *Application Contact:* Yvette Bragg, Administrative Assistant I, 870-230-5126, Fax: 870-230-5479, E-mail: braggy@hsu.edu. *Graduate Dean*, Dr. Ken Taylor, 870-230-5126, Fax: 870-230-5479, E-mail: taylorke@hsu.edu.

Ellis College of Arts and Sciences Students: 5 full-time (2 women), 20 part-time (10 women); includes 10 minority (5 Black or African American, non-Hispanic/Latino; 1 Asian, non-Hispanic/Latino; 2 Hispanic/Latino; 2 Two or more races, non-Hispanic/Latino). Average age 33. 10 applicants, 100% accepted, 10 enrolled. *Faculty:* 14 full-time (4 women), 2 part-time/adjunct (1 woman). *Financial support:* In 2015–16, 10 teaching assistantships with partial tuition reimbursements (averaging $4,000 per year) were awarded; scholarships/grants and unspecified assistantships also available. Financial award application deadline: 4/15; financial award applicants required to submit FAFSA. In 2015, 3 master's awarded. *Degree program information:* Part-time programs available. Part-time. Offers arts and sciences (MLA). *Application deadline:* For fall admission, 8/1 priority date for domestic students, 6/30 priority date for international students; for spring admission, 1/1 priority date for domestic students, 11/30 priority date for international students. Applications are processed on a rolling basis. *Application fee:* $25 ($75 for international students). *Application Contact:* Dr. Ken Taylor, Graduate Dean, 870-230-5126, Fax: 870-230-5479, E-mail: taylorke@hsu.edu. *MLA Director*, Dr. Clinton Atchley, 870-230-5276, Fax: 870-230-5144, E-mail: atchlec@hsu.edu.

School of Business Administration Students: 19 full-time (13 women), 27 part-time (10 women); includes 7 minority (5 Black or African American, non-Hispanic/Latino; 1 Asian, non-Hispanic/Latino; 1 Hispanic/Latino), 3 international. Average age 29. 10 applicants, 100% accepted, 10 enrolled. *Faculty:* 3 full-time (1 woman), 2 part-time/adjunct (0 women). *Financial support:* In 2015–16, 5 teaching assistantships with partial tuition reimbursements (averaging $4,000 per year) were awarded; scholarships/grants and unspecified assistantships also available. Financial award application deadline: 4/15; financial award applicants required to submit FAFSA. In 2015, 22 master's awarded. *Degree program information:* Part-time programs available. Part-time. Offers business administration (MBA). *Application deadline:* For fall admission, 8/1 priority date for domestic students, 6/30 priority date for international students; for spring admission, 1/1 priority date for domestic students, 11/30 priority date for international students. Applications are processed on a rolling basis. *Application fee:* $25 ($75 for international students). *Application Contact:* Dr. Ken Taylor, Graduate Dean, 870-230-5126, Fax: 870-230-5479, E-mail: taylorke@hsu.edu. *MBA Director*, Dr. Lonnie Jackson, 870-230-5311, Fax: 870-230-5286, E-mail: jacksol@hsu.edu.

Teachers College Students: 51 full-time (38 women), 287 part-time (209 women); includes 97 minority (77 Black or African American, non-Hispanic/Latino; 2 American Indian or Alaska Native, non-Hispanic/Latino; 1 Asian, non-Hispanic/Latino; 10

Hispanic/Latino; 7 Two or more races, non-Hispanic/Latino), 4 international. Average age 34. 42 applicants, 100% accepted, 42 enrolled. *Faculty:* 20 full-time (11 women), 3 part-time/adjunct (2 women). *Financial support:* In 2015–16, 17 teaching assistantships with partial tuition reimbursements (averaging $4,000 per year) were awarded; scholarships/grants and unspecified assistantships also available. Financial award application deadline: 4/15; financial award applicants required to submit FAFSA. In 2015, 94 master's, 9 other advanced degrees awarded. *Degree program information:* Part-time programs available. Part-time, online learning. Offers clinical mental health counseling (MS); curriculum leadership (Ed S); developmental therapy (MS, MSE, Graduate Certificate); dyslexia therapy (Graduate Certificate); education (MAT); educational leadership (MSE, Graduate Certificate); educational leadership district (Ed S); educational technology leadership (Graduate Certificate); English as a second language (Graduate Certificate); English as second language (MSE); instructional facilitator (MSE, Graduate Certificate); middle level education (MAT); secondary school counseling (MSE); special education (K-12) (MAT, MSE); special education/early childhood (MAT); sports administration (MS). *Application deadline:* For fall admission, 8/1 priority date for domestic students, 6/30 priority date for international students; for spring admission, 1/1 priority date for domestic students, 11/30 priority date for international students. Applications are processed on a rolling basis. *Application fee:* $25 ($75 for international students). *Application Contact:* Dr. Ken Taylor, Graduate Dean, 870-230-5126, Fax: 870-230-5479, E-mail: taylorke@hsu.edu. *Dean,* Dr. Celya Taylor, 870-230-5363, Fax: 870-230-5455, E-mail: taylorc@hsu.edu.

HENDRIX COLLEGE, Conway, AR 72032-3080

General Information Independent-religious, coed, comprehensive institution. *Graduate housing:* Room and/or apartments available on a first-come, first-served basis to single students. Housing application deadline: 6/1.

GRADUATE UNITS

Program in Accounting ***Degree program information:*** Part-time programs available. Part-time. Offers accounting (MA).

HENLEY-PUTNAM UNIVERSITY, San Jose, CA 95131

General Information Proprietary, coed, comprehensive institution.

GRADUATE UNITS

Doctorate Program in Strategic Security ***Degree program information:*** Part-time programs available. Part-time, online learning. Offers strategic security (DSS).

Master of Science Program in Intelligence Management ***Degree program information:*** Part-time programs available. Part-time, online learning. Offers intelligence management (MS).

Master of Science Program in Strategic Security and Protection Management ***Degree program information:*** Part-time programs available. Part-time, online learning. Offers extremist organizations (MS).

Master of Science Program in Terrorism and Counterterrorism Studies ***Degree program information:*** Part-time programs available. Part-time, online learning. Offers intelligence operations (MS); protective intelligence (MS).

HERITAGE CHRISTIAN UNIVERSITY, Florence, AL 35630

General Information Independent-religious, coed, primarily men, comprehensive institution.

GRADUATE UNITS

Graduate Programs Offers counseling (MM); Greek (MA); ministry (MM); New Testament (MA).

HERITAGE COLLEGE AND SEMINARY, Cambridge, ON N3C 3T2, Canada

General Information Independent-religious, coed, comprehensive institution.

GRADUATE UNITS

Graduate and Professional Programs Offers general (M Div); intercultural studies (M Div); pastoral (M Div); research (M Div); theological studies (MTS, CTS).

HERITAGE UNIVERSITY, Toppenish, WA 98948-9599

General Information Independent, coed, comprehensive institution. *Graduate housing:* On-campus housing not available.

GRADUATE UNITS

Graduate Programs in Education ***Degree program information:*** Part-time and evening/weekend programs available. Part-time, evening/weekend. Offers bilingual education/ESL (M Ed); biology (M Ed); counseling (M Ed); educational administration (M Ed); English and literature (M Ed); professional studies (M Ed); reading/literacy (M Ed); special education (M Ed); teaching (MIT).

HERZING UNIVERSITY ONLINE, Menomonee Falls, WI 53051

General Information Independent, coed, comprehensive institution. CGS member.

GRADUATE UNITS

Program in Business Administration Online learning. Offers accounting (MBA); business administration (MBA); business management (MBA); healthcare management (MBA); human resources (MBA); marketing (MBA); project management (MBA); technology management (MBA).

Program in Nursing Online learning. Offers nursing (MSN); nursing education (MSN); nursing management (MSN).

HIGH POINT UNIVERSITY, High Point, NC 27268

General Information Independent-religious, coed, comprehensive institution. CGS member. *Graduate housing:* On-campus housing not available.

GRADUATE UNITS

Norcross Graduate School ***Degree program information:*** Part-time and evening/weekend programs available. Part-time, evening/weekend. Offers business administration (MBA); educational leadership (M Ed); elementary education (M Ed); history (MA); nonprofit management (MA); secondary math (M Ed); special education (M Ed); strategic communication (MA); teaching elementary education k-6 (MAT); teaching secondary mathematics 9-12 (MAT). Electronic applications accepted.

HILBERT COLLEGE, Hamburg, NY 14075-1597

General Information Independent-religious, coed, comprehensive institution. *Enrollment:* 933 graduate, professional, and undergraduate students; 32 full-time matriculated graduate/professional students (19 women), 13 part-time matriculated graduate/professional students (11 women). *Enrollment by degree level:* 45 master's. *Graduate faculty:* 6 full-time (2 women), 14 part-time/adjunct (3 women). *Tuition, area resident:* Full-time $17,400; part-time $725 per credit. *Required fees:* $160; $20 per course. One-time fee: $50. *Graduate housing:* On-campus housing not available. *Student services:* Campus safety program, career counseling, exercise/wellness program, free psychological counseling, multicultural affairs office, services for students with disabilities, writing training. *Library:* McGrath Library. *Collection:* Books: 34,500 (physical), 8,700 (digital/electronic); Serial titles: 130 (physical), 70,000 (digital/electronic); Databases: 26. Weekly public service hours: 78; students can reserve study rooms.

Computer facilities: 146 computers available on campus for general student use. A campuswide network can be accessed from student residence rooms. Online class registration is available.
Website: http://www.hilbert.edu/

General Application Contact: Kim Chiarmonte, Director of the Office of Adult and Graduate Studies, 716-926-8949, Fax: 716-649-0702, E-mail: graduatestudies@hilbert.edu.

GRADUATE UNITS

Program in Criminal Justice Administration Students: 18 full-time (10 women), 5 part-time (3 women); includes 2 minority (1 Black or African American, non-Hispanic/Latino; 1 Two or more races, non-Hispanic/Latino). Average age 30. 16 applicants, 44% accepted, 7 enrolled. *Faculty:* 4 full-time (1 woman), 3 part-time/adjunct (1 woman). *Financial support:* In 2015–16, 21 students received support. Scholarships/grants and tuition waivers (partial) available. Financial award application deadline: 7/1; financial award applicants required to submit FAFSA. In 2015, 3 master's awarded. *Degree program information:* Evening/weekend programs available. Evening/weekend, 100% online. Offers criminal justice administration (MS). *Application deadline:* Applications are processed on a rolling basis. *Application fee:* $25. Electronic applications accepted. *Application Contact:* Kim Chiarmonte, Director, Center for Adult and Graduate Studies, 716-926-8948, Fax: 716-649-0702, E-mail: kchiarmonte@hilbert.edu. *Chair,* Dr. Martin Floss, 716-649-7900 Ext. 307, Fax: 716-649-0702, E-mail: mfloss@hilbert.edu.

Program in Public Administration Students: 24 full-time (17 women), 11 part-time (10 women); includes 11 minority (5 Black or African American, non-Hispanic/Latino; 2 American Indian or Alaska Native, non-Hispanic/Latino; 1 Hispanic/Latino; 3 Two or more races, non-Hispanic/Latino), 1 international. Average age 34. 24 applicants, 33% accepted, 8 enrolled. *Faculty:* 1 full-time (0 women), 4 part-time/adjunct (2 women). *Financial support:* In 2015–16, 25 students received support. Scholarships/grants and tuition waivers (partial) available. Financial award application deadline: 7/1; financial award applicants required to submit FAFSA. In 2015, 16 master's awarded. *Degree program information:* Evening/weekend programs available. Evening/weekend. Offers health administration (MPA); public administration (MPA). *Application deadline:* Applications are processed on a rolling basis. *Application fee:* $25. Electronic applications accepted. *Application Contact:* Kim Chiarmonte, Director, Center for Adult and Graduate Studies, 716-926-8948, Fax: 716-649-0702, E-mail: kchiarmonte@hilbert.edu. *Dean of Graduate Studies/Professor of Public Administration,* Dr. Walter Iwanenko, 716-649-7900 Ext. 331, E-mail: wiwanenko@hilbert.edu.

HILLSDALE COLLEGE, Hillsdale, MI 49242-1298

General Information Independent, coed, comprehensive institution.

GRADUATE UNITS

Graduate School

HILLSDALE FREE WILL BAPTIST COLLEGE, Moore, OK 73160-1208

General Information Independent-religious, coed, comprehensive institution. *Graduate housing:* Room and/or apartments available on a first-come, first-served basis to single students.

GRADUATE UNITS

Department of Bible Studies ***Degree program information:*** Part-time and evening/weekend programs available. Part-time, evening/weekend. Offers ministry (MA).

HIRAM COLLEGE, Hiram, OH 44234-0067

General Information Independent, coed, comprehensive institution.

GRADUATE UNITS

Graduate Studies ***Degree program information:*** Part-time and evening/weekend programs available. Part-time, evening/weekend. Offers interdisciplinary studies (MAIS).

HODGES UNIVERSITY, Naples, FL 34119

General Information Independent, coed, comprehensive institution. *Enrollment:* 1,724 graduate, professional, and undergraduate students; 47 full-time matriculated graduate/professional students (30 women), 190 part-time matriculated graduate/professional students (122 women). *Enrollment by degree level:* 237 master's. *Graduate faculty:* 13 full-time (8 women), 7 part-time/adjunct (0 women). *Tuition, area resident:* Part-time $660 per credit hour. *Graduate housing:* On-campus housing not available. *Student services:* Career counseling, services for students with disabilities. *Library:* Terry P. McMahan Libraries plus 1 other.

Computer facilities: 1,500 computers available on campus for general student use. A campuswide network can be accessed. Online class registration, Our campus intranet takes the form of a student portal that is accessible via the internet. The portal provides single sign on access to all of the above as well as our Learning Management System, online storage, library resources, and a student calendar are available.
Website: http://www.hodges.edu/

General Application Contact: Brent Passey, Chief Admissions Officer, 239-513-1122 Ext. 6104, Fax: 239-598-6253, E-mail: bpassey@hodges.edu.

GRADUATE UNITS

Graduate Programs Students: 47 full-time (30 women), 190 part-time (122 women); includes 99 minority (27 Black or African American, non-Hispanic/Latino; 6 Asian, non-Hispanic/Latino; 63 Hispanic/Latino; 3 Two or more races, non-Hispanic/Latino). Average age 38. 79 applicants, 100% accepted, 79 enrolled. *Faculty:* 13 full-time (8 women), 7 part-time/adjunct (0 women). *Financial support:* Federal Work-Study and scholarships/grants available. Financial award application deadline: 7/9; financial award applicants required to submit FAFSA. In 2015, 77 master's awarded. *Degree program information:* Part-time and evening/weekend programs available. Part-time, evening/weekend, 100% online, blended/hybrid learning. Offers accounting (M Acc); business administration (MBA); clinical mental health counseling (MS); health services administration (MS); information systems management (MIS); legal studies (MS); management (MSM). *Application deadline:* Applications are processed on a rolling basis. *Application fee:* $50. Electronic applications accepted. *Application Contact:* Brent Passey, Chief Admissions Officer, 239-513-1122, Fax: 239-598-6253, E-mail: bpassey@hodges.edu. *President,* Dr. David Borofsky, 239-513-1122, Fax: 239-598-6253, E-mail: dwortham@hodges.edu.

HOFSTRA UNIVERSITY, Hempstead, NY 11549

General Information Independent, coed, university. CGS member. *Enrollment:* 10,814 graduate, professional, and undergraduate students; 2,943 full-time matriculated graduate/professional students (1,760 women), 962 part-time matriculated graduate/professional students (583 women). *Enrollment by degree level:* 2,445 master's, 1,376 doctoral, 84 other advanced degrees. *Graduate faculty:* 268 full-time (120 women), 243 part-time/adjunct (110 women). *Graduate housing:* Room and/or apartments available on a first-come, first-served basis to single students; on-campus housing not available to married students. Housing application deadline: 5/1. *Student services:* Campus employment opportunities, career counseling, exercise/wellness program, free psychological counseling, grant writing training, international student services, low-cost health insurance, multicultural affairs office, services for students with disabilities, teacher training, writing training. *Library:* Axinn Library plus 2 others. *Collection:* Books: 1 million (physical), 168,505 (digital/electronic); Serial titles: 2,315 (physical), 13,825 (digital/electronic); Databases: 153. Weekly public service hours: 102; study areas open 24 hours, 5–7 days a week; students can reserve study rooms.

Computer facilities: Computer purchase and lease plans are available. 1,501 computers available on campus for general student use. A campuswide network can be accessed from student residence rooms and from off campus. Online class registration, online course management system, online card services balance update, online e-portfolio, software tutoring, support for specific tech-enhanced assignments, repair and rebuilding-after-virus services, printing services are available.
Website: http://www.hofstra.edu/

General Application Contact: Sunil Samuel, Assistant Vice President of Admissions, 516-463-4723, Fax: 516-463-4664, E-mail: graduateadmission@hofstra.edu.

GRADUATE UNITS

College of Liberal Arts and Sciences Students: 299 full-time (195 women), 47 part-time (33 women); includes 60 minority (14 Black or African American, non-Hispanic/Latino; 2 American Indian or Alaska Native, non-Hispanic/Latino; 14 Asian, non-Hispanic/Latino; 24 Hispanic/Latino; 1 Native Hawaiian or other Pacific Islander, non-Hispanic/Latino; 5 Two or more races, non-Hispanic/Latino), 28 international. Average age 28. 416 applicants, 50% accepted, 108 enrolled. *Faculty:* 59 full-time (20 women), 52 part-time/adjunct (20 women). *Financial support:* In 2015–16, 181 students received support, including 142 fellowships with tuition reimbursements available (averaging $6,929 per year), 8 research assistantships with tuition reimbursements available (averaging $6,183 per year); career-related internships or fieldwork, Federal Work-Study, institutionally sponsored loans, health care benefits, tuition waivers (full and partial), unspecified assistantships, and limited diversity and endowed scholarships also available. Support available to part-time students. Financial award applicants required to submit FAFSA. In 2015, 85 master's, 30 doctorates awarded. *Degree program information:* Part-time and evening/weekend programs available. Part-time, evening/weekend. Offers applied linguistics (TESOL) (MA); applied organizational psychology (PhD); biology (MA, MS); clinical psychology (PhD); creative writing (MFA); industrial/organizational psychology (MA); liberal arts and sciences (MA, MFA, MS, PhD, Psy D); linguistics (MA); medical physics (MS); school-community psychology (Psy D); sustainability studies (MA); urban ecology (MA, MS). *Application deadline:* Applications are processed on a rolling basis. *Application fee:* $70 ($75 for international students). Electronic applications accepted. *Application Contact:* Sunil Samuel, Assistant Vice President of Admissions, 516-463-4723, Fax: 516-463-4664, E-mail: graduateadmission@hofstra.edu. *Dean*, Dr. Bernard J. Firestone, 516-463-5411, Fax: 516-463-4861, E-mail: lasbjf@hofstra.edu.

Frank G. Zarb School of Business Students: 752 full-time (375 women), 300 part-time (129 women); includes 127 minority (34 Black or African American, non-Hispanic/Latino; 1 American Indian or Alaska Native, non-Hispanic/Latino; 55 Asian, non-Hispanic/Latino; 29 Hispanic/Latino; 2 Native Hawaiian or other Pacific Islander, non-Hispanic/Latino; 6 Two or more races, non-Hispanic/Latino), 611 international. Average age 27. 1,637 applicants, 75% accepted, 330 enrolled. *Faculty:* 56 full-time (14 women), 28 part-time/adjunct (5 women). *Financial support:* In 2015–16, 130 students received support, including 108 fellowships with tuition reimbursements available (averaging $5,352 per year), 5 research assistantships with tuition reimbursements available (averaging $7,216 per year); Federal Work-Study, institutionally sponsored loans, scholarships/grants, tuition waivers (full and partial), and unspecified assistantships also available. Support available to part-time students. Financial award applicants required to submit FAFSA. In 2015, 509 master's awarded. *Degree program information:* Part-time and evening/weekend programs available. Part-time, evening/weekend, online learning. Offers accounting (MS, Advanced Certificate); business (EMBA, MBA, MS, Advanced Certificate); business administration (MBA); corporate finance (Advanced Certificate); finance (MS); general management (Advanced Certificate); human resource management (MS, Advanced Certificate); information systems (MS, Advanced Certificate); international business (Advanced Certificate); investment management (Advanced Certificate); management (EMBA); marketing (MS, Advanced Certificate); marketing research (MS); quantitative finance (MS); taxation (MS, Advanced Certificate). *Application deadline:* Applications are processed on a rolling basis. *Application fee:* $70 ($75 for international students). Electronic applications accepted. *Application Contact:* Sunil Samuel, Assistant Vice President of Admissions, 516-463-4723, Fax: 516-463-4664, E-mail: graduateadmission@hofstra.edu. *Dean*, Dr. Herman Berliner, 516-463-5676, Fax: 516-463-5268, E-mail: prohab@hofstra.edu.

Lawrence Herbert School of Communication Students: 66 full-time (48 women), 38 part-time (23 women); includes 47 minority (23 Black or African American, non-Hispanic/Latino; 2 American Indian or Alaska Native, non-Hispanic/Latino; 2 Asian, non-Hispanic/Latino; 18 Hispanic/Latino; 2 Two or more races, non-Hispanic/Latino), 17 international. Average age 28. 129 applicants, 67% accepted, 34 enrolled. *Faculty:* 21 full-time (8 women), 10 part-time/adjunct (5 women). *Financial support:* In 2015–16, 46 students received support, including 20 fellowships with tuition reimbursements available (averaging $3,725 per year), 9 research assistantships with tuition reimbursements available (averaging $4,757 per year); Federal Work-Study, institutionally sponsored loans, scholarships/grants, tuition waivers (full and partial), and unspecified assistantships also available. Support available to part-time students. Financial award applicants required to submit FAFSA. In 2015, 17 master's awarded. *Degree program information:* Part-time and evening/weekend programs available. Part-time, evening/weekend. Offers documentary studies and production (MFA); journalism (MA); journalism and public relations (MA); public relations (MA); rhetorical studies (MA). *Application deadline:* Applications are processed on a rolling basis. *Application fee:* $70 ($75 for international students). Electronic applications accepted. *Application Contact:* Sunil Samuel, Assistant Vice President of Admissions, 516-463-4723, Fax: 516-463-4664, E-mail: graduateadmission@hofstra.edu. *Dean*, Dr. Evan W. Cornog, 516-463-5215, Fax: 516-463-4866, E-mail: comewc@hofstra.edu.

School of Education Students: 255 full-time (201 women), 367 part-time (258 women); includes 148 minority (66 Black or African American, non-Hispanic/Latino; 2 American Indian or Alaska Native, non-Hispanic/Latino; 20 Asian, non-Hispanic/Latino; 55 Hispanic/Latino; 1 Native Hawaiian or other Pacific Islander, non-Hispanic/Latino; 4 Two or more races, non-Hispanic/Latino), 20 international. Average age 31. 530 applicants, 89% accepted, 213 enrolled. *Faculty:* 35 full-time (25 women), 46 part-time/adjunct (34 women). *Financial support:* In 2015–16, 373 students received support, including 159 fellowships with tuition reimbursements available (averaging $4,155 per year), 10 research assistantships with tuition reimbursements available (averaging $9,697 per year); Federal Work-Study, institutionally sponsored loans, scholarships/grants, health care benefits, and tuition waivers (full and partial) also available. Support available to part-time students. Financial award applicants required to submit FAFSA. In 2015, 259 master's, 13 doctorates, 70 other advanced degrees awarded. *Degree program information:* Part-time and evening/weekend programs available. Part-time, evening/weekend, online learning. Offers applied behavior analysis (Advanced Certificate); bilingual education (MA); business education (MS Ed); early childhood and childhood education (MS Ed); early childhood education (MA); early childhood special education (MS Ed, Advanced Certificate); education (MA, MS, MS Ed, Ed D, PhD, Advanced Certificate); education technology (Advanced Certificate); elementary education (MA); English education (MS Ed); fine arts education (MS Ed); foreign language and TESOL (MS Ed); gifted education (Advanced Certificate); inclusive early childhood special education (MS Ed); inclusive elementary special education (MS Ed); inclusive secondary special education (MS Ed); learning and teaching (Ed D); mathematics education (MA, MS Ed); secondary education (Advanced Certificate); secondary education generalist (MS Ed); social studies education (MA, MS Ed); special education (MS Ed, Advanced Certificate); special education assessment and diagnosis (Advanced Certificate); special education generalist (MS Ed); teaching students with severe or multiple disabilities (Advanced Certificate). *Application deadline:* Applications are processed on a rolling basis. *Application fee:* $70 ($75 for international students). Electronic applications accepted. *Application Contact:* Sunil Samuel, Assistant Vice President of Admissions, 516-463-4723, Fax: 516-463-4664, E-mail: graduateadmission@hofstra.edu. *Interim Dean*, Dr. Sean Fanelli, 516-463-5741, Fax: 516-463-6461, E-mail: edasaf@hofstra.edu.

School of Engineering and Applied Science Students: 13 full-time (3 women), 17 part-time (3 women); includes 4 minority (all Asian, non-Hispanic/Latino), 8 international. Average age 30. 27 applicants, 59% accepted, 12 enrolled. *Faculty:* 7 full-time (2 women), 3 part-time/adjunct (0 women). *Financial support:* In 2015–16, 10 students received support, including 4 fellowships with tuition reimbursements available (averaging $4,300 per year), 1 research assistantship with tuition reimbursement available (averaging $8,147 per year); Federal Work-Study, institutionally sponsored loans, scholarships/grants, tuition waivers (full and partial), and unspecified assistantships also available. Support available to part-time students. Financial award applicants required to submit FAFSA. In 2015, 6 master's awarded. *Degree program information:* Part-time and evening/weekend programs available. Part-time, evening/weekend, online learning. Offers computer science (MS). *Application deadline:* Applications are processed on a rolling basis. *Application fee:* $70 ($75 for international students). Electronic applications accepted. *Application Contact:* Sunil Samuel, Assistant Vice President of Admissions, 516-463-4723, Fax: 516-463-4664, E-mail: graduateadmission@hofstra.edu. *Acting Dean*, Dr. Sina Rabbany, 516-463-6672, E-mail: eggsyr@hofstra.edu.

School of Health Sciences and Human Services Students: 380 full-time (321 women), 152 part-time (113 women); includes 167 minority (69 Black or African American, non-Hispanic/Latino; 1 American Indian or Alaska Native, non-Hispanic/Latino; 53 Asian, non-Hispanic/Latino; 39 Hispanic/Latino; 2 Native Hawaiian or other Pacific Islander, non-Hispanic/Latino; 3 Two or more races, non-Hispanic/Latino), 27 international. Average age 28. 697 applicants, 54% accepted, 184 enrolled. *Faculty:* 33 full-time (24 women), 52 part-time/adjunct (30 women). *Financial support:* In 2015–16, 219 students received support, including 94 fellowships with tuition reimbursements available (averaging $4,535 per year), 8 research assistantships with tuition reimbursements available (averaging $8,079 per year); Federal Work-Study, institutionally sponsored loans, scholarships/grants, tuition waivers (full and partial), and unspecified assistantships also available. Support available to part-time students. Financial award applicants required to submit FAFSA. In 2015, 171 master's, 8 doctorates, 6 other advanced degrees awarded. *Degree program information:* Part-time and evening/weekend programs available. Part-time, evening/weekend. Offers audiology (Au D); community health (MS); counseling (MS Ed, PD); creative arts therapy (MA); health administration (MHA); health sciences and human services (MA, MHA, MPH, MS, MS Ed, Au D, Advanced Certificate, PD); interdisciplinary transition specialist (Advanced Certificate); marriage and family therapy (MA); mental health counseling (MA); physician assistant (MS); public health (MPH); rehabilitation administration (PD); rehabilitation counseling (MS Ed, Advanced Certificate); rehabilitation counseling in mental health (MS Ed, Advanced Certificate); school counselor bilingual extension (Advanced Certificate); speech-language pathology (MA). *Application deadline:* Applications are processed on a rolling basis. *Application fee:* $70 ($75 for international students). Electronic applications accepted. *Application Contact:* Sunil Samuel, Assistant Vice President of Admissions, 516-463-4723, Fax: 516-463-4664, E-mail: graduateadmission@hofstra.edu. *Vice Dean*, Dr. Holly Seirup, 516-463-5348, E-mail: vpshjs@hofstra.edu.

School of Law Students: 777 full-time (391 women), 41 part-time (24 women); includes 222 minority (79 Black or African American, non-Hispanic/Latino; 3 American Indian or Alaska Native, non-Hispanic/Latino; 57 Asian, non-Hispanic/Latino; 71 Hispanic/Latino; 2 Native Hawaiian or other Pacific Islander, non-Hispanic/Latino; 10 Two or more races, non-Hispanic/Latino), 37 international. Average age 26. 2,343 applicants, 63% accepted, 310 enrolled. *Faculty:* 45 full-time (21 women), 43 part-time/adjunct (11 women). *Financial support:* In 2015–16, 521 students received support, including 509 fellowships with tuition reimbursements available (averaging $27,715 per year), 2 research assistantships with tuition reimbursements available (averaging $6,125 per year); Federal Work-Study, institutionally sponsored loans, scholarships/grants, tuition waivers (full and partial), and unspecified assistantships also available. Support available to part-time students. Financial award applicants required to submit FAFSA. In 2015, 14 master's, 314 doctorates awarded. *Degree program information:* Part-time programs available. Part-time, online learning. Offers American legal studies (LL M); family law (LL M); health law and policy (MA); law (JD). *Application deadline:* For fall admission, 4/15 priority date for domestic students, 4/15 for international students. Applications are processed on a rolling basis. *Application fee:* $70 ($75 for international students). Electronic applications accepted. *Application Contact:* Sunil Samuel, Assistant Vice President of Admissions, 516-463-4723, Fax: 516-463-4664. *Interim Dean*, Eric Lane, 516-463-5854, Fax: 516-463-6264, E-mail: lawezl@hofstra.edu.

School of Medicine Students: 277 full-time (130 women); includes 104 minority (14 Black or African American, non-Hispanic/Latino; 50 Asian, non-Hispanic/Latino; 30 Hispanic/Latino; 2 Native Hawaiian or other Pacific Islander, non-Hispanic/Latino; 8 Two or more races, non-Hispanic/Latino), 1 international. Average age 25. 6,199 applicants,

4% accepted, 99 enrolled. *Faculty:* 12 full-time (6 women), 9 part-time/adjunct (5 women). *Financial support:* In 2015–16, 239 students received support, including 222 fellowships with tuition reimbursements available (averaging $23,020 per year); research assistantships with tuition reimbursements available, Federal Work-Study, institutionally sponsored loans, scholarships/grants, and tuition waivers (full and partial) also available. Support available to part-time students. Financial award applicants required to submit FAFSA. Offers medicine (MD); molecular basis of medicine (PhD). *Application deadline:* For fall admission, 12/1 priority date for domestic students. *Application fee:* $100. Electronic applications accepted. *Application Contact:* Sunil Samuel, Assistant Vice President of Admissions, 516-463-4723, Fax: 516-463-4664. *Vice Dean*, Dr. Veronica Catanese, 516-463-7517, Fax: 516-463-7543, E-mail: medvmc@hofstra.edu.

HOLLINS UNIVERSITY, Roanoke, VA 24020

General Information Independent, Undergraduate: women only; graduate: coed, comprehensive institution. *Enrollment:* 802 graduate, professional, and undergraduate students; 155 full-time matriculated graduate/professional students (109 women), 68 part-time matriculated graduate/professional students (59 women). *Enrollment by degree level:* 220 master's, 3 other advanced degrees. *Graduate faculty:* 15 full-time (10 women), 34 part-time/adjunct (19 women). *Graduate housing:* Room and/or apartments available on a first-come, first-served basis to single students; on-campus housing not available to married students. Housing application deadline: 8/1. *Student services:* Campus safety program, career counseling, international student services, low-cost health insurance, multicultural affairs office, services for students with disabilities, teacher training, writing training. *Library:* Wyndham Robertson Library plus 1 other. *Collection:* Books: 314,781 (physical), 57,842 (digital/electronic); Serial titles: 2,386 (physical), 52,399 (digital/electronic); Databases: 126. Weekly public service hours: 94.

Computer facilities: Computer purchase and lease plans are available. 120 computers available on campus for general student use. A campuswide network can be accessed from student residence rooms. Online class registration is available.
Website: http://www.hollins.edu/

General Application Contact: Cathy S. Koon, Manager of Graduate Services, 540-362-6326, Fax: 540-362-6288, E-mail: ckoon@hollins.edu.

GRADUATE UNITS

Graduate Programs Students: 155 full-time (109 women), 68 part-time (59 women); includes 30 minority (16 Black or African American, non-Hispanic/Latino; 1 American Indian or Alaska Native, non-Hispanic/Latino; 4 Asian, non-Hispanic/Latino; 6 Hispanic/Latino; 3 Two or more races, non-Hispanic/Latino), 6 international. Average age 33. 355 applicants, 50% accepted, 100 enrolled. *Faculty:* 15 full-time (10 women), 34 part-time/adjunct (19 women). *Financial support:* In 2015–16, 106 students received support, including 106 fellowships, 4 teaching assistantships; Federal Work-Study and scholarships/grants also available. Support available to part-time students. Financial award application deadline: 7/15; financial award applicants required to submit FAFSA. In 2015, 77 master's awarded. *Degree program information:* Part-time and evening/weekend programs available. Part-time, evening/weekend. Offers children's book writing and illustrating (MFA); children's literature (MA, MFA); creative writing (MFA); dance (MFA); humanities (MALS); interdisciplinary studies (MALS); leadership (MALS); new play directing (Certificate); new play performance (Certificate); playwriting (MFA); screenwriting (MFA); screenwriting and film studies (MA); social sciences (MALS); teaching (MAT); visual and performing arts (MALS). *Application deadline:* For fall admission, 1/6 priority date for domestic and international students. Applications are processed on a rolling basis. *Application fee:* $40. Electronic applications accepted. *Application Contact:* Cathy S. Koon, Manager of Graduate Services, 540-362-6326, Fax: 540-362-6288, E-mail: ckoon@hollins.edu.

HOLMES INSTITUTE, Burbank, CA 91505

General Information Independent-religious, coed, graduate-only institution. *Enrollment by degree level:* 89 master's, 36 other advanced degrees. *Graduate faculty:* 25 part-time/adjunct (4 women). One-time fee: $300 part-time. *Graduate housing:* On-campus housing not available.

Computer facilities: Online class registration is available.
Website: http://www.holmesinstitute.org/

General Application Contact: Maureen Thurston, Administrative Registrar, 720-279-8992, Fax: 303-526-0913, E-mail: mthurston@csl.org.

GRADUATE UNITS

Graduate Program Students: 125 part-time (101 women); includes 5 minority (all Black or African American, non-Hispanic/Latino). *Faculty:* 25 part-time/adjunct (4 women). Online learning. Offers consciousness studies (MS). *Application deadline:* Applications are processed on a rolling basis. *Application fee:* $200. *Application Contact:* Maureen Thurston, Administrative Registrar, 720-279-8992, Fax: 303-526-0913, E-mail: mthurston@csl.org. *Director of Education*, Rev. Bob Deen, 720-279-8990, Fax: 303-526-0913, E-mail: bdeen@csl.org.

HOLY APOSTLES COLLEGE AND SEMINARY, Cromwell, CT 06416-2005

General Information Independent-religious, coed, comprehensive institution. *Graduate housing:* On-campus housing not available.

GRADUATE UNITS

Department of Theology ***Degree program information:*** Part-time and evening/weekend programs available. Part-time, evening/weekend, online learning. Offers bioethics (MA, Certificate, Post Master's Certificate); church history (MA, Certificate, Post Master's Certificate); dogmatic theology (MA, Certificate, Post Master's Certificate); liturgical music (MA, Certificate, Post Master's Certificate); liturgy (MA, Certificate, Post Master's Certificate); moral theology (MA, Certificate, Post Master's Certificate); philosophical theology (MA, Certificate, Post Master's Certificate); religious education (MA, Certificate, Post Master's Certificate); sacred scripture (MA, Post Master's Certificate); sacred scriptures (Certificate); theology (M Div). Electronic applications accepted.

HOLY CROSS GREEK ORTHODOX SCHOOL OF THEOLOGY, Brookline, MA 02445-7496

General Information Independent-religious, coed, primarily men, graduate-only institution. *Graduate housing:* Rooms and/or apartments available on a first-come, first-served basis to single and married students.

GRADUATE UNITS

Theological Programs ***Degree program information:*** Part-time programs available. Part-time. Offers theology (M Div, MTS, Th M).

HOLY FAMILY UNIVERSITY, Philadelphia, PA 19114

General Information Independent-religious, coed, comprehensive institution. *Enrollment:* 2,712 graduate, professional, and undergraduate students; 202 full-time matriculated graduate/professional students (162 women), 465 part-time matriculated graduate/professional students (346 women). *Enrollment by degree level:* 747 master's, 27 doctoral. *Graduate faculty:* 34 full-time (25 women), 70 part-time/adjunct (35 women). *Graduate housing:* On-campus housing not available. *Student services:* Campus employment opportunities, campus safety program, career counseling, free psychological counseling, low-cost health insurance, services for students with disabilities, teacher training. *Library:* Holy Family University Library plus 1 other. *Collection:* Books: 124,616 (physical), 18,080 (digital/electronic); Databases: 42. Weekly public service hours: 113; students can reserve study rooms.

Computer facilities: 300 computers available on campus for general student use. A campuswide network can be accessed from student residence rooms and from off campus. Online class registration, online course syllabi, online course evaluations are available.
Website: http://www.holyfamily.edu/

General Application Contact: Robert McIntyre, Associate Director of Graduate Admissions, 267-341-3555, Fax: 215-637-1478, E-mail: rmcintyre01@holyfamily.edu.

GRADUATE UNITS

Division of Extended Learning Students: 116 part-time (59 women); includes 4 minority (2 Black or African American, non-Hispanic/Latino; 1 Asian, non-Hispanic/Latino; 1 Hispanic/Latino). Average age 34. 25 applicants, 96% accepted, 6 enrolled. *Faculty:* 13 part-time/adjunct (3 women). *Financial support:* In 2015–16, 3 students received support. Available to part-time students. Applicants required to submit FAFSA. In 2015, 52 master's awarded. *Degree program information:* Part-time and evening/weekend programs available. Part-time, evening/weekend. Offers business administration (MBA); finance (MBA); health care administration (MBA); human resources management (MBA). *Application deadline:* For fall admission, 7/1 priority date for domestic and international students; for spring admission, 11/1 priority date for domestic and international students; for summer admission, 4/1 priority date for domestic and international students. Applications are processed on a rolling basis. *Application fee:* $50. Electronic applications accepted. *Application Contact:* Don Reinmold, Director of Admissions, 267-341-5001 Ext. 3230, Fax: 215-633-0558, E-mail: dreinmold@holyfamily.edu. *Director of Academic Services*, Chris Quinn, 267-341-5006, Fax: 215-633-0558, E-mail: cquinn1@holyfamily.edu.

Graduate and Professional Programs ***Financial support:*** Research assistantships with partial tuition reimbursements and unspecified assistantships available. Support available to part-time students. Financial award application deadline: 2/15; financial award applicants required to submit FAFSA. *Degree program information:* Part-time and evening/weekend programs available. Part-time, evening/weekend. *Application deadline:* For fall admission, 7/1 priority date for domestic and international students; for spring admission, 11/1 priority date for domestic and international students; for summer admission, 4/1 priority date for domestic and international students. Applications are processed on a rolling basis. *Application fee:* $25. Electronic applications accepted. *Application Contact:* Robert McIntyre, Associate Director of Graduate Admissions, 267-341-3555, Fax: 215-637-1478, E-mail: rmcintyre01@holyfamily.edu. *Executive Director of Admissions*, Lauren Campbell, 215-637-3050, Fax: 215-281-1022, E-mail: lcampbell@holyfamily.edu.

School of Arts and Sciences Students: 202 full-time (162 women), 358 part-time (290 women); includes 80 minority (37 Black or African American, non-Hispanic/Latino; 1 American Indian or Alaska Native, non-Hispanic/Latino; 15 Asian, non-Hispanic/Latino; 27 Hispanic/Latino), 2 international. Average age 29. 85 applicants, 71% accepted, 45 enrolled. *Faculty:* 9 full-time (6 women), 12 part-time/adjunct (9 women). *Financial support:* Available to part-time students. Application deadline: 5/1; applicants required to submit FAFSA. *Degree program information:* Part-time and evening/weekend programs available. Part-time, evening/weekend. Offers counseling psychology (MS); criminal justice (MA). *Application deadline:* For fall admission, 7/1 priority date for domestic and international students; for winter admission, 1/1 for domestic students; for spring admission, 11/1 priority date for domestic and international students; for summer admission, 4/1 priority date for domestic and international students. Applications are processed on a rolling basis. *Application fee:* $25. Electronic applications accepted. *Application Contact:* Robert McIntyre, Associate Director of Graduate Admissions, 267-341-3555, Fax: 215-637-1478, E-mail: rmcIntyre01@holyfamily.edu. *Dean*, Dr. Rochelle Robbins, 267-341-3238, Fax: 215-827-0492, E-mail: srobbins@holyfamily.edu.

School of Business Administration Financial support: Available to part-time students. Application deadline: 5/1; applicants required to submit FAFSA. *Degree program information:* Part-time and evening/weekend programs available. Part-time, evening/weekend. Offers accountancy (MS); finance (MBA); health care administration (MBA); human resource management (MBA); information systems management (MBA). *Application deadline:* For fall admission, 7/1 priority date for domestic and international students; for winter admission, 1/1 for domestic students; for spring admission, 11/1 priority date for domestic and international students; for summer admission, 4/1 priority date for domestic and international students. Applications are processed on a rolling basis. *Application fee:* $25. Electronic applications accepted. *Application Contact:* Gidget Marie Montelibano, Associate Director of Graduate Admissions, 267-341-3558, Fax: 215-637-1478, E-mail: gmontelibano@holyfamily.edu. *Dean*, Dr. Barry Dickinson, 267-341-3440, Fax: 215-637-5937, E-mail: jdickinson@holyfamily.edu.

School of Education Financial support: Research assistantships with partial tuition reimbursements available. Support available to part-time students. Financial award application deadline: 2/15; financial award applicants required to submit FAFSA. *Degree program information:* Part-time and evening/weekend programs available. Part-time, evening/weekend. Offers early elementary education (PreK-Grade 4) (M Ed); education (M Ed, Ed D); education leadership (M Ed); educational leadership and professional studies (Ed D); general education (M Ed); reading specialist (M Ed); special education (M Ed); TESOL and literacy (M Ed). *Application deadline:* For fall admission, 7/1 priority date for domestic and international students; for winter admission, 1/1 for domestic students; for spring admission, 11/1 priority date for domestic and international students; for summer admission, 4/1 priority date for domestic and international students. Applications are processed on a rolling basis. *Application fee:* $25. Electronic applications accepted. *Application Contact:* Gidget Marie Montelibano, Associate Director of Graduate Admissions, 267-341-3358, Fax: 215-637-1478, E-mail: gmontelibano@holyfamily.edu. *Dean*, Dr. Kevin Zook, 267-341-3565, Fax: 215-824-2438, E-mail: kzook@holyfamily.edu.

School of Nursing and Allied Health Professions Students: 42 part-time (39 women); includes 9 minority (4 Black or African American, non-Hispanic/Latino; 4 Asian, non-Hispanic/Latino; 1 Hispanic/Latino). Average age 36. 17 applicants, 82% accepted, 6 enrolled. *Faculty:* 7 full-time (all women). *Financial support:* In 2015–16, 1 student received support. Available to part-time students. Application deadline: 2/15; applicants required to submit FAFSA. In 2015, 12 master's awarded. *Degree program information:* Part-time and evening/weekend programs available. Part-time, evening/weekend. Offers nursing administration (MSN); nursing education (MSN). *Application deadline:* For fall admission, 7/1 priority date for domestic and international students; for winter admission, 1/1 for domestic students; for spring admission, 11/1 priority date for domestic and international students; for summer admission, 4/1 priority date for domestic and international students. Applications are processed on a rolling basis. *Application fee:* $25. Electronic applications accepted. *Application Contact:* Gidget Matie Montelibano, Associate Director of Graduate Admissions, 267-341-3558, Fax: 215-637-1478, E-mail: gmontelibano@holyfamily.edu. *Dean*, Dr. Ana Maria Catanzaro, 267-341-3292, Fax: 215-637-6598, E-mail: acatanzaro@holyfamily.edu.

HOLY NAMES UNIVERSITY, Oakland, CA 94619-1699

General Information Independent-religious, coed, comprehensive institution. *Enrollment:* 1,049 graduate, professional, and undergraduate students; 107 full-time matriculated graduate/professional students (88 women), 286 part-time matriculated graduate/professional students (216 women). *Enrollment by degree level:* 343 master's, 50 other advanced degrees. *Graduate faculty:* 70. *Tuition, area resident:* Full-time $25,272; part-time $936 per credit hour. *Required fees:* $500; $250 per credit hour. *Graduate housing:* Room and/or apartments available on a first-come, first-served basis to single students; on-campus housing not available to married students. Typical cost: $11,870 (including board). Room and board charges vary according to board plan. Housing application deadline: 8/15. *Student services:* Campus employment opportunities, campus safety program, career counseling, exercise/wellness program, free psychological counseling, international student services, low-cost health insurance, services for students with disabilities, writing training. *Library:* Cushing Library.

Computer facilities: 92 computers available on campus for general student use. A campuswide network can be accessed from student residence rooms. Online class registration is available.
Website: http://www.hnu.edu/

General Application Contact: Graduate Admissions Office, 510-436-1351, Fax: 510-436-1325, E-mail: graduateadmissions@hnu.edu.

GRADUATE UNITS

Graduate Division ***Degree program information:*** Part-time and evening/weekend programs available. Part-time, evening/weekend. Offers administration/management (MSN, PMC); clinical faculty (MSN, PMC); community health nursing/case manager (MSN); counseling psychology (MA); creative writing (MA); educational therapy (Certificate); energy and environment management (MBA); family nurse practitioner (MSN, PMC); finance (MBA); forensic psychology (MA, Certificate); Kodaly (Certificate); management and leadership (MBA); marketing (MBA); mild/moderate disabilities (Ed S); multiple subject teaching (Credential); music education with Kodaly emphasis (MM); pastoral counseling (MA, Certificate); pastoral ministries (MA, Certificate); piano pedagogy (MM); piano pedagogy with Suzuki emphasis (MM); single subject teaching (Credential); sports management (MBA); teaching English as a second language (TESL) (M Ed); urban education: educational therapy (M Ed); urban education: K-12 education (M Ed); urban education: special education (M Ed); vocal pedagogy (MM). Electronic applications accepted.

Sophia Center in Culture and Spirituality Offers culture and spirituality (MA, Certificate). Electronic applications accepted.

HOOD COLLEGE, Frederick, MD 21701-8575

General Information Independent, coed, comprehensive institution. CGS member. *Enrollment:* 2,288 graduate, professional, and undergraduate students; 140 full-time matriculated graduate/professional students (69 women), 850 part-time matriculated graduate/professional students (580 women). *Enrollment by degree level:* 862 master's, 128 other advanced degrees. *Graduate faculty:* 37 full-time (16 women), 77 part-time/adjunct (41 women). *Tuition, area resident:* Part-time $450 per credit hour. *Required fees:* $105 per term. Part-time tuition and fees vary according to degree level, campus/location and program. *Graduate housing:* On-campus housing not available. *Student services:* Campus employment opportunities, campus safety program, career counseling, international student services, multicultural affairs office, services for students with disabilities, teacher training. *Library:* Beneficial-Hodson Library and Information Technology Center plus 1 other. *Collection:* Books: 172,311 (physical), 295,531 (digital/electronic); Serial titles: 235 (physical), 42,000 (digital/electronic); Databases: 96. Students can reserve study rooms. *Research affiliation:* U.S. Department of Agriculture (USDA) (biomedical science and environmental biology), United States Army Medical Research Institute of Infectious Diseases (USAMRID) (biomedical science), National Cancer Institute (biomedical science).

Computer facilities: Computer purchase and lease plans are available. 500 computers available on campus for general student use. A campuswide network can be accessed from student residence rooms and from off campus. Online class registration is available.
Website: http://www.hood.edu/

General Application Contact: Dr. Maria Green Cowles, Dean of Graduate School, 301-696-3811, Fax: 301-696-3597, E-mail: gofurther@hood.edu.

GRADUATE UNITS

Graduate School ***Financial support:*** Research assistantships with full tuition reimbursements, tuition waivers (partial), and unspecified assistantships available. Financial award applicants required to submit FAFSA. *Degree program information:* Part-time and evening/weekend programs available. Part-time, evening/weekend. Offers accounting (MBA); administration and management (MBA); bioinformatics (Certificate); biomedical science (MS); ceramic arts (Certificate); ceramics (MA, MFA); computer and information sciences (MS); computer science (MS); curriculum and instruction (MS); educational leadership (MS, Certificate); environmental biology (MS); finance (MBA); human resource management (MBA); human sciences (MA); humanities (MA); information security (Certificate); information systems (MBA); management of information technology (MS); marketing (MBA); public management (MBA); reading specialization (MS); secondary mathematics education (Certificate); STEM (Certificate). *Application deadline:* For fall admission, 7/15 for domestic and international students; for spring admission, 12/1 for domestic and international students. Applications are processed on a rolling basis. *Application fee:* $35. Electronic applications accepted.

HOOD THEOLOGICAL SEMINARY, Salisbury, NC 28144

General Information Independent-religious, coed, graduate-only institution. *Graduate housing:* Rooms and/or apartments guaranteed to single students and available on a first-come, first-served basis to married students. Housing application deadline: 8/15.

GRADUATE UNITS

Graduate and Professional Programs ***Degree program information:*** Part-time and evening/weekend programs available. Part-time, evening/weekend, online learning. Offers theology (M Div, MTS, D Min).

HOPE INTERNATIONAL UNIVERSITY, Fullerton, CA 92831-3138

General Information Independent-religious, coed, comprehensive institution. *Graduate housing:* Room and/or apartments available on a first-come, first-served basis to single students; on-campus housing not available to married students. Housing application deadline: 7/1.

GRADUATE UNITS

School of Graduate and Professional Studies ***Degree program information:*** Part-time and evening/weekend programs available. Part-time, evening/weekend, online learning. Offers Christian leadership (MCM); church music (MA); church music (Korean track) (MCM); church planting (MCM); education administration (MA); elementary education (ME); general management (MBA, MSM); intercultural studies (MCM); international development (MBA, MSM); marketing management (MBA, MSM); marriage and family therapy (MA, MFT); non-profit management (MBA, MSM); secondary education (ME); worship (MCM). Electronic applications accepted.

HOUGHTON COLLEGE, Houghton, NY 14744

General Information Independent-religious, coed, comprehensive institution. *Graduate housing:* On-campus housing not available.

GRADUATE UNITS

Greatbatch School of Music Offers collaborative performance (MMus); composition (MMus); conducting (MMus); music (MA); performance (MMus); world music with theology and intercultural studies (MA). Electronic applications accepted.

HOUSTON BAPTIST UNIVERSITY, Houston, TX 77074-3298

General Information Independent-religious, coed, comprehensive institution. *Enrollment:* 3,160 graduate, professional, and undergraduate students; 338 full-time matriculated graduate/professional students (235 women), 572 part-time matriculated graduate/professional students (417 women). *Enrollment by degree level:* 857 master's, 53 other advanced degrees. *Graduate faculty:* 56 full-time (26 women), 30 part-time/adjunct (9 women). *Tuition, area resident:* Full-time $12,500; part-time $12,500 per year. *Required fees:* $2500; $2500 per unit. Tuition and fees vary according to campus/location and program. *Graduate housing:* Rooms and/or apartments available on a first-come, first-served basis to single and married students. Housing application deadline: 4/1. *Student services:* Campus employment opportunities, career counseling, exercise/wellness program, free psychological counseling, international student services, low-cost health insurance, services for students with disabilities, teacher training, writing training. *Library:* Moody Library. *Collection:* Books: 154,036 (physical), 264,873 (digital/electronic); Serial titles: 6,041 (physical); Databases: 96. Weekly public service hours: 88; students can reserve study rooms.

Computer facilities: 52 computers available on campus for general student use. A campuswide network can be accessed from student residence rooms. Online class registration, office software for 5 devices for each student are available.
Website: http://www.hbu.edu/

General Application Contact: Allyson Cates, Director of Admissions, Graduate School, 281-649-3099, Fax: 281-649-3390, E-mail: acates@hbu.edu.

GRADUATE UNITS

Archie W. Dunham College of Business Students: 148 full-time (91 women), 85 part-time (56 women); includes 135 minority (79 Black or African American, non-Hispanic/Latino; 17 Asian, non-Hispanic/Latino; 38 Hispanic/Latino; 1 Two or more races, non-Hispanic/Latino), 31 international. Average age 30. 502 applicants, 23% accepted, 70 enrolled. *Financial support:* In 2015–16, 18 students received support. Federal Work-Study and scholarships/grants available. Support available to part-time students. Financial award application deadline: 4/1; financial award applicants required to submit FAFSA. In 2015, 86 master's awarded. *Degree program information:* Part-time and evening/weekend programs available. Part-time, evening/weekend. Offers business (MACCT, MBA, MIB, MSHRM); business administration (MBA); human resources management (MSHRM); international business (MIB). *Application deadline:* For fall admission, 8/1 for domestic students, 6/1 for international students; for spring admission, 12/1 for domestic students, 10/1 for international students; for summer admission, 5/1 for domestic students, 3/1 for international students. Applications are processed on a rolling basis. *Application fee:* $0 ($100 for international students). Electronic applications accepted. *Application Contact:* Laurel Motal, Secretary, 281-649-3306, Fax: 281-649-3436, E-mail: lmotal@hbu.edu. *Dean, Archie W. Dunham College of Business*, Dr. Michael Weeks, 281-649-3014, E-mail: mweeks@hbu.edu.

College of Education and Behavioral Sciences Students: 136 full-time (113 women), 356 part-time (306 women); includes 314 minority (182 Black or African American, non-Hispanic/Latino; 2 American Indian or Alaska Native, non-Hispanic/Latino; 23 Asian, non-Hispanic/Latino; 99 Hispanic/Latino; 8 Two or more races, non-Hispanic/Latino), 15 international. Average age 32. 596 applicants, 30% accepted, 128 enrolled. *Faculty:* 24 full-time (20 women), 19 part-time/adjunct (16 women). *Financial support:* In 2015–16, 7 students received support. Career-related internships or fieldwork, Federal Work-Study, and scholarships/grants available. Support available to part-time students. Financial award application deadline: 4/1; financial award applicants required to submit FAFSA. In 2015, 128 master's awarded. *Degree program information:* Part-time and evening/weekend programs available. Part-time, evening/weekend. Offers bilingual education (M Ed); Christian counseling (MACC); counseling (MAC); counselor education (M Ed); curriculum and instruction (M Ed); education and behavioral sciences (M Ed, MAC, MACC, MAP); educational administration (M Ed); educational diagnostician (M Ed); general psychology (MAP); reading education (M Ed); school psychology (MAP). *Application deadline:* For fall admission, 8/1 for domestic students, 6/1 for international students; for spring admission, 12/1 for domestic students, 10/1 for international students; for summer admission, 5/1 for domestic students, 3/1 for international students. Applications are processed on a rolling basis. *Application fee:* $0 ($100 for international students). Electronic applications accepted. *Application Contact:* Kristy Wright, Secretary, 281-649-3094 Ext. 3241, Fax: 281-649-3361, E-mail: kwright@hbu.edu. *Acting Dean*, Dr. Carol McGaughey, 281-649-3667, Fax: 281-649-3361, E-mail: cmchaughey@hbu.edu.

Program in Liberal Arts Students: 8 full-time (6 women), 26 part-time (17 women); includes 14 minority (8 Black or African American, non-Hispanic/Latino; 1 American Indian or Alaska Native, non-Hispanic/Latino; 5 Hispanic/Latino), 1 international. Average age 32. 37 applicants, 32% accepted, 8 enrolled. *Faculty:* 50 full-time (15 women), 12 part-time/adjunct (8 women). *Financial support:* In 2015–16, 3 students received support. Federal Work-Study and scholarships/grants available. Support available to part-time students. Financial award application deadline: 4/1; financial award applicants required to submit FAFSA. In 2015, 8 master's awarded. *Degree program information:* Part-time and evening/weekend programs available. Part-time, evening/weekend. Offers liberal arts (MLA). *Application deadline:* For fall admission, 8/1 for domestic students, 6/1 for international students; for spring admission, 12/1 for domestic students, 10/1 for international students; for summer admission, 5/1 for domestic students, 3/1 for international students. Applications are processed on a rolling basis. *Application fee:* $0 ($100 for international students). Electronic applications accepted. *Application Contact:* Kathy Holston, Administrative Assistant to the Dean, 281-649-3404, E-mail: kholston@hbu.edu. *Director, Master of Liberal Arts*, Dr. David Davis, 281-649-3638, E-mail: ddavis@hbu.edu.

School of Christian Thought Students: 25 full-time (9 women), 103 part-time (37 women); includes 46 minority (29 Black or African American, non-Hispanic/Latino; 1 American Indian or Alaska Native, non-Hispanic/Latino; 4 Asian, non-Hispanic/Latino; 9 Hispanic/Latino; 3 Two or more races, non-Hispanic/Latino), 3 international. Average age 37. 176 applicants, 53% accepted, 54 enrolled. *Faculty:* 19 full-time (2 women), 22 part-time/adjunct (3 women). *Financial support:* In 2015–16, 15 students received support. Federal Work-Study and scholarships/grants available. Support available to part-time students. Financial award application deadline: 4/1; financial award applicants required to submit FAFSA. In 2015, 11 master's awarded. *Degree program information:* Part-time and evening/weekend programs available. Part-time, evening/weekend. Offers apologetics (MA); Biblical languages (MA); philosophy (MA); theological studies (MA). *Application deadline:* For fall admission, 8/1 for domestic students, 6/1 for international students; for spring admission, 12/1 for domestic students, 10/1 for international students; for summer admission, 5/1 for domestic students, 3/1 for international students. Applications are processed on a rolling basis. *Application fee:* $0 ($100 for international students). Electronic applications accepted. *Application Contact:* Celeste Risteski, Administrative Assistant to the Dean, 281-649-3383, Fax: 281-649-3012, E-mail: cristeski@hbu.edu. *Dean*, Dr. Craig Evans, 281-649-3383, Fax: 281-649-3012, E-mail: cevans@hbu.edu.

School of Fine Arts Students: 21 full-time (16 women), 2 part-time (1 woman); includes 11 minority (2 Black or African American, non-Hispanic/Latino; 2 Asian, non-Hispanic/Latino; 5 Hispanic/Latino; 2 Two or more races, non-Hispanic/Latino). Average age 34. 41 applicants, 34% accepted, 12 enrolled. *Faculty:* 21 full-time (3 women), 13 part-time/adjunct (6 women). *Financial support:* In 2015–16, 5 students received support. Federal Work-Study and scholarships/grants available. Support available to part-time students. Financial award application deadline: 4/1; financial award applicants required to submit FAFSA. In 2015, 8 master's awarded. *Degree program information:* Part-time and evening/weekend programs available. Part-time, evening/weekend. Offers fine arts (MFA). *Application deadline:* For fall admission, 4/1 for domestic students, 2/1 for international students. Applications are processed on a rolling basis. *Application fee:* $0 ($100 for international students). Electronic applications accepted. *Application Contact:* Dr. Michael Collins, Program Director, E-mail: mcollins@hbu.edu. *Dean*, Dr. Jason Lester, 281-649-3339, E-mail: jlester@hbu.edu.

HOUSTON COLLEGE OF LAW, Houston, TX 77002-7000

General Information Independent, coed, graduate-only institution.

GRADUATE UNITS

Professional Program ***Degree program information:*** Part-time and evening/weekend programs available. Part-time, evening/weekend. Offers law (JD). Electronic applications accepted.

HOUSTON GRADUATE SCHOOL OF THEOLOGY, Houston, TX 77092

General Information Independent-religious, coed, graduate-only institution. *Graduate housing:* On-campus housing not available.

GRADUATE UNITS

Graduate Programs ***Degree program information:*** Part-time and evening/weekend programs available. Part-time, evening/weekend. Offers counseling (MA); pastoral ministry (M Div, D Min); theology (MA).

HOWARD PAYNE UNIVERSITY, Brownwood, TX 76801-2715

General Information Independent-religious, coed, comprehensive institution. *Enrollment:* 1,163 graduate, professional, and undergraduate students; 27 full-time matriculated graduate/professional students (9 women), 57 part-time matriculated graduate/professional students (18 women). *Enrollment by degree level:* 84 master's. *Graduate faculty:* 12 full-time (2 women), 7 part-time/adjunct (1 woman). *Graduate housing:* Room and/or apartments available on a first-come, first-served basis to single students; on-campus housing not available to married students. *Student services:* Campus employment opportunities, career counseling, exercise/wellness program, free psychological counseling, services for students with disabilities, writing training. *Library:* Walker Memorial Library.

Computer facilities: 260 computers available on campus for general student use. A campuswide network can be accessed from student residence rooms and from off campus.
Website: http://www.hputx.edu/

General Application Contact: Dr. Gary Gramling, Director of Graduate Programs/Professor of Christian Studies, 325-649-8404, Fax: 325-649-8949, E-mail: ggramling@hputx.edu.

GRADUATE UNITS

Program in Business Administration Students: 15 full-time (6 women), 20 part-time (8 women); includes 12 minority (all Hispanic/Latino), 1 international. Average age 31. 14 applicants, 100% accepted, 10 enrolled. *Faculty:* 7 full-time (2 women), 5 part-time/adjunct (0 women). *Financial support:* Application deadline: 3/15; applicants required to submit FAFSA. In 2015, 16 master's awarded. *Degree program information:* Part-time and evening/weekend programs available. Part-time, evening/weekend. Offers business administration (MBA). *Application deadline:* For fall admission, 7/1 for domestic students; for spring admission, 12/1 for domestic students. Applications are processed on a rolling basis. *Application fee:* $0. Electronic applications accepted. *Application Contact:* Mary Hill, Administrative Assistant, School of Business, 325-649-8704, E-mail: mhill@hputx.edu. *Director*, Dr. Brad Lemler, 325-649-8149, E-mail: blemler@hputx.edu.

Program in Instructional Leadership Students: 3 full-time (2 women), 5 part-time (4 women); includes 2 minority (1 Black or African American, non-Hispanic/Latino; 1 Hispanic/Latino). Average age 40. 6 applicants, 100% accepted, 6 enrolled. *Faculty:* 1 full-time (0 women), 3 part-time/adjunct (1 woman). *Financial support:* Application deadline: 3/15; applicants required to submit FAFSA. In 2015, 6 master's awarded. *Degree program information:* Part-time and evening/weekend programs available. Part-time, evening/weekend, online only. Offers instructional leadership (M Ed). *Application deadline:* For fall admission, 7/1 for domestic students; for spring admission, 12/1 for domestic students. Applications are processed on a rolling basis. *Application fee:* $0. Electronic applications accepted. *Application Contact:* Susan Sharp, Administrative Assistant, School of Education/Certification Officer, 325-649-8144, E-mail: ssharp@hputx.edu. *Director of Instructional Leadership Graduate Program/Professor of Education*, Dr. Joe Robinson, 325-649-8205, E-mail: jrobinson@hputx.edu.

Program in Sport and Wellness Leadership Students: 19 part-time (5 women); includes 5 minority (1 Black or African American, non-Hispanic/Latino; 3 Hispanic/Latino; 1 Two or more races, non-Hispanic/Latino). Average age 29. 36 applicants, 67% accepted, 19 enrolled. *Faculty:* 2 full-time (0 women), 2 part-time/adjunct (1 woman). *Financial support:* Unspecified assistantships available. Financial award applicants required to submit FAFSA. *Degree program information:* Part-time programs available. Part-time. Offers sport and wellness leadership (M Ed). Electronic applications accepted. *Professor and Chair, Exercise and Sport Science/Director, Graduate Program in Sport and Recreation Leadership*, Dr. Graham Hatcher, 325-649-8966, E-mail: ghatcher@hputx.edu.

Program in Theology and Ministry Students: 3 full-time (0 women), 8 part-time (0 women); includes 1 minority (Two or more races, non-Hispanic/Latino). Average age 28. 4 applicants, 75% accepted, 3 enrolled. *Faculty:* 6 full-time (1 woman), 1 part-time/adjunct (0 women). *Financial support:* Applicants required to submit FAFSA. In 2015, 3 master's awarded. *Degree program information:* Part-time programs available. Part-time. Offers theology and ministry (MA). *Application deadline:* For fall admission, 7/1 for domestic students; for spring admission, 12/1 for domestic students. Applications are processed on a rolling basis. *Application fee:* $0. Electronic applications accepted. *Application Contact:* Kristian Simpson, Administrative Assistant for Christian Studies Graduate Programs, 325-649-8039, E-mail: ksimpson@hputx.edu. *Director of Graduate Programs/Professor of Christian Studies*, Dr. Gary Gramling, 325-649-8404, E-mail: ggramling@hputx.edu.

Program in Youth Ministry Students: 6 full-time (1 woman), 5 part-time (1 woman); includes 1 minority (Hispanic/Latino). Average age 26. 1 applicant, 100% accepted. *Faculty:* 4 full-time (0 women), 1 part-time/adjunct (0 women). *Financial support:* Application deadline: 3/15; applicants required to submit FAFSA. In 2015, 4 master's awarded. *Degree program information:* Part-time programs available. Part-time. Offers youth ministry (MA). *Application deadline:* For fall admission, 7/1 for domestic students; for spring admission, 12/1 for domestic students. Applications are processed on a rolling basis. *Application fee:* $0. Electronic applications accepted. *Application Contact:* Kristian Simpson, Administrative Assistant for Christian Studies Graduate Programs, 325-649-8039, E-mail: ksimpson@hputx.edu. *Director*, Dr. Gary Gramling, 325-649-8404, E-mail: ggramling@hputx.edu.

HOWARD UNIVERSITY, Washington, DC 20059-0002

General Information Independent, coed, university. CGS member. *Graduate housing:* Rooms and/or apartments available on a first-come, first-served basis to single and married students. Housing application deadline: 4/1. *Research affiliation:* Ewing Marion Kauffman Foundation (science education), The Tokyo Foundation (women's studies, international affairs), National Oceanic and Atmospheric Administration (NOAA) (atmospheric science and nanotechnology), National Institute of Mental Health (NIMH) (genomics), Akilu Lamma Institute of Pathobiology (HIV/AIDS infection, water resources development, population movement), Labor Research Laboratories and Medical Center in Benin City, Nigeria (infectious diseases).

GRADUATE UNITS

College of Dentistry Offers advanced education program general dentistry (Certificate); dentistry (DDS); general dentistry (Certificate); oral and maxillofacial surgery (Certificate); orthodontics (Certificate); pediatric dentistry (Certificate).

College of Engineering, Architecture, and Computer Sciences ***Degree program information:*** Part-time programs available. Part-time. Offers engineering, architecture, and computer sciences (M Eng, MCS, MS, PhD). Electronic applications accepted.

School of Engineering and Computer Science ***Degree program information:*** Part-time programs available. Part-time. Offers chemical engineering (MS); civil engineering (M Eng); electrical engineering (M Eng, PhD); engineering and computer science (M Eng, MCS, MS, PhD); mechanical engineering (M Eng, PhD); systems and computer science (MCS). Electronic applications accepted.

College of Medicine Offers biochemistry and molecular biology (PhD); biotechnology (MS); medicine (MPH, MS, MD, PhD); microbiology (PhD); pharmacology (MS, PhD); public health (MPH).

College of Nursing and Allied Health Sciences ***Degree program information:*** Part-time programs available. Part-time. Offers nursing and allied health sciences (MSN, Certificate). Electronic applications accepted.

Division of Nursing ***Degree program information:*** Part-time programs available. Part-time. Offers nurse practitioner (Certificate); primary family health nursing (MSN).

College of Pharmacy Online learning. Offers pharmacy (Pharm D). Electronic applications accepted.

Graduate School ***Degree program information:*** Part-time and evening/weekend programs available. Part-time, evening/weekend. Offers African diaspora (MA, PhD); African history (MA, PhD); African studies (MA, PhD); analytical chemistry (MS, PhD); anatomy (MS, PhD); applied mathematics (MS, PhD); atmospheric (MS, PhD); atmospheric sciences (MS, PhD); biochemistry (MS, PhD); biology (MS, PhD); biophysics (PhD); clinical psychology (PhD); developmental psychology (PhD); economics (MA, PhD); English (MA, PhD); environmental (MS, PhD); exercise physiology (MS); experimental psychology (PhD); French (MA); health education (MS); inorganic chemistry (MS, PhD); Latin America and the Caribbean (MA, PhD); mathematics (MS, PhD); neuropsychology (PhD); nutrition (MS, PhD); organic chemistry (MS, PhD); personality psychology (PhD); philosophy (MA); physical chemistry (MS, PhD); physics (MS, PhD); physiology (PhD); political science (MA, MAPA, PhD); psychology (MS); public administration (MAPA); public history (MA); social psychology (PhD); sociology (MA, PhD); Spanish (MA); sports studies (MS); United States history (MA, PhD); urban recreation (MS). Electronic applications accepted.

Division of Fine Arts ***Degree program information:*** Part-time programs available. Part-time. Offers 3D reality (sculpture and ceramics) (MFA); applied music (MM); art history (MA); design (MFA); electronic studio (MFA); fine arts (MFA); history of art and visual culture (MA); instrument (MM Ed); jazz studies (MM); organ (MM Ed); painting (MFA); photography (MFA); piano (MM Ed); voice (MM Ed).

School of Business ***Degree program information:*** Part-time and evening/weekend programs available. Part-time, evening/weekend, online learning. Offers accounting (MBA); business (MBA); entrepreneurship (MBA); finance (MBA); general management (MBA); human resources management (MBA); information systems (MBA); international business (MBA); marketing (MBA); supply chain management (MBA).

School of Communications ***Degree program information:*** Part-time and evening/weekend programs available. Part-time, evening/weekend. Offers communication sciences (PhD); communications (MA, MFA, MS, PhD); film (MFA);

intercultural communication (MA, PhD); organizational communication (MA, PhD); speech pathology (MS). Electronic applications accepted.

Division of Mass Communication and Media Studies Degree program information: Part-time and evening/weekend programs available. Part-time, evening/weekend. Offers mass communication (MA, PhD); media studies (MA, PhD). Electronic applications accepted.

School of Divinity ***Degree program information:*** Part-time and evening/weekend programs available. Part-time, evening/weekend. Offers theology (M Div, MARS, D Min). Electronic applications accepted.

School of Education Offers counseling psychology (PhD); education (M Ed, Ed D, PhD, CAGS); educational administration (Ed D); educational administration and supervision (M Ed, CAGS); educational psychology (PhD); elementary education (M Ed); school psychology (PhD); school psychology and counseling services (M Ed); secondary education (M Ed); special education (M Ed). Electronic applications accepted.

School of Law Offers law (LL M, JD). Electronic applications accepted.

School of Social Work ***Degree program information:*** Part-time programs available. Part-time. Offers social work (MSW, PhD).

HULT INTERNATIONAL BUSINESS SCHOOL, Cambridge, MA 02141

General Information Independent, coed, comprehensive institution. *Graduate housing:* On-campus housing not available.

GRADUATE UNITS

MBA Program Offers business administration (MBA). Electronic applications accepted.

Program in Business Administration - Hult London Campus ***Degree program information:*** Part-time programs available. Part-time. Offers entrepreneurship (MBA); international business (MBA); international finance (MBA); marketing (MBA). Electronic applications accepted.

Program in Finance Offers finance (MF).

Program in Finance - Hult Dubai Campus Offers finance (MF).

Program in Finance - Hult London Campus Offers finance (MF). Electronic applications accepted.

Program in International Business Offers international business (MIB).

Program in International Business - Hult Dubai Campus Offers international business (MIB).

Program in International Business - Hult London Campus Offers international business (MIB).

Program in International Business - Hult San Francisco Campus Offers international business (MIB).

Program in International Relations - Hult London Campus ***Degree program information:*** Part-time programs available. Part-time. Offers conflict resolution (MA); diplomacy (MA); international public law (MA); international relations (MA); Middle East international security (MA); politics (MA); security studies (MA); terrorism (MA); U.S. foreign policy (MA). Electronic applications accepted.

Program in International Relations - Hult San Francisco Campus Offers international relations (MA).

HUMBOLDT STATE UNIVERSITY, Arcata, CA 95521-8299

General Information State-supported, coed, comprehensive institution. *Graduate housing:* Room and/or apartments available on a first-come, first-served basis to single students; on-campus housing not available to married students. Housing application deadline: 2/1. *Research affiliation:* McIntire-Stennis (forestry), National Sea Grant, U.S. Fish and Wildlife Service–Wildlife Field Station, Redwood Sciences Laboratory of the Pacific Southwest Forest and Range Experiment Station, California Cooperative Fisheries Research Unit.

GRADUATE UNITS

Academic Programs ***Financial support:*** Fellowships, research assistantships, teaching assistantships, career-related internships or fieldwork, Federal Work-Study, and institutionally sponsored loans available. Support available to part-time students. Financial award application deadline: 3/1; financial award applicants required to submit FAFSA. *Degree program information:* Part-time and evening/weekend programs available. Part-time, evening/weekend. *Application deadline:* Applications are processed on a rolling basis. *Application fee:* $55. Electronic applications accepted.

College of Arts, Humanities, and Social Sciences Financial support: Fellowships, teaching assistantships, career-related internships or fieldwork, Federal Work-Study, and institutionally sponsored loans available. Support available to part-time students. Financial award application deadline: 3/1; financial award applicants required to submit FAFSA. *Degree program information:* Part-time programs available. Part-time. Offers applied anthropology (MA); arts, humanities, and social sciences (MA); English (MA); environment and community (MA); sociology (MA). *Application deadline:* Applications are processed on a rolling basis. *Application fee:* $55. Electronic applications accepted.

College of Natural Resources and Sciences Financial support: Fellowships, career-related internships or fieldwork, and Federal Work-Study available. Support available to part-time students. Financial award application deadline: 3/1; financial award applicants required to submit FAFSA. *Degree program information:* Part-time programs available. Part-time. Offers biological sciences (MS); environmental systems (MS); natural resources (MS); natural resources and sciences (MA, MS, Certificate). *Application deadline:* Applications are processed on a rolling basis. *Application fee:* $55.

College of Professional Studies Financial support: Fellowships, teaching assistantships, career-related internships or fieldwork, Federal Work-Study, and institutionally sponsored loans available. Support available to part-time students. Financial award application deadline: 3/1; financial award applicants required to submit FAFSA. *Degree program information:* Part-time and evening/weekend programs available. Part-time, evening/weekend. Offers business (MBA); education (MA); kinesiology (MS); psychology (MA); social work (MSW). *Application deadline:* Applications are processed on a rolling basis. *Application fee:* $55.

HUMPHREYS COLLEGE, Stockton, CA 95207-3896

General Information Independent, coed, comprehensive institution. *Graduate housing:* Room and/or apartments available on a first-come, first-served basis to single students; on-campus housing not available to married students.

GRADUATE UNITS

Laurence Drivon School of Law ***Degree program information:*** Part-time and evening/weekend programs available. Part-time, evening/weekend. Offers law (JD). Electronic applications accepted.

HUNTER COLLEGE OF THE CITY UNIVERSITY OF NEW YORK, New York, NY 10065-5085

General Information State and locally supported, coed, comprehensive institution. *Graduate housing:* Room and/or apartments available on a first-come, first-served basis to single students; on-campus housing not available to married students. *Research affiliation:* New York Hospital, Mount Sinai Medical Center, Bellevue Hospital Center, Cornell University Medical Center.

GRADUATE UNITS

Graduate School 5,255 applicants, 64% accepted, 1399 enrolled. *Financial support:* Fellowships with tuition reimbursements, research assistantships with partial tuition reimbursements, teaching assistantships, career-related internships or fieldwork, Federal Work-Study, institutionally sponsored loans, scholarships/grants, traineeships, tuition waivers (full and partial), unspecified assistantships, and lesson stipends available. Support available to part-time students. Financial award applicants required to submit FAFSA. In 2015, 4,284 master's, 273 other advanced degrees awarded. *Degree program information:* Part-time and evening/weekend programs available. Part-time, evening/weekend. *Application deadline:* For fall admission, 4/1 for domestic students; for spring admission, 11/1 for domestic students. *Application fee:* $125. *Application Contact:* Milena Solo, Director for Graduate Admissions, 212-772-4288, E-mail: milena.solo@hunter.cuny.edu.

School of Arts and Sciences 1,979 applicants, 27% accepted, 273 enrolled. *Financial support:* Fellowships, research assistantships, teaching assistantships, career-related internships or fieldwork, Federal Work-Study, institutionally sponsored loans, scholarships/grants, tuition waivers (full and partial), unspecified assistantships, and lesson stipends available. Support available to part-time students. In 2015, 394 master's, 8 other advanced degrees awarded. *Degree program information:* Part-time and evening/weekend programs available. Part-time, evening/weekend. Offers accounting (MS); adolescent mathematics education (MA); anthropology (MA); applied mathematics (MA); applied social research (MS); art (MA, MFA); art history (MA); arts and sciences (MA, MFA, MS, MUP, PhD, Certificate); biochemistry (MA, PhD); biological sciences (MA, PhD); British and American literature (MA); creative writing (MFA); economics (MA, PhD); fiction (MFA); French (MA); geography (MA, Certificate); history (MA); integrated media arts (MFA); Italian (MA); memoir (MFA); music (MA); physics (MA, PhD); playwriting (MFA); poetry (MFA); psychology (MA); pure mathematics (MA); Romance languages (MA); Spanish (MA); statistics (MA); studio art (MFA); teaching Chinese (MA); teaching Latin (MA); theatre (MA); urban affairs (MS); urban affairs and planning (MS, MUP); urban planning (MUP). *Application deadline:* For fall admission, 2/1 for domestic and international students; for spring admission, 11/1 for domestic students, 9/1 for international students. *Application Contact:* Milena Solo, Director of Graduate Admissions, 212-772-4288, E-mail: milena.solo@hunter.cuny.edu. *Acting Dean of the School of Arts and Sciences,* Dr. Andrew J. Polsky, 212-772-5121, Fax: 212-772-5148, E-mail: apolsky@hunter.cuny.edu.

School of Education Degree program information: Part-time and evening/weekend programs available. Part-time, evening/weekend. Offers bilingual education (MS); biology education (MA); blind or visually impaired (MS Ed); chemistry education (MA); early childhood education (MS); earth science (MA); education (MA, MS, MS Ed, AC); educational supervision and administration (AC); elementary education (MS); English education (MA); French education (MA); Italian education (MA); mathematics education (MA); music education (MA); physics education (MA); rehabilitation counseling (MS Ed); school counseling (MS Ed); severe/multiple disabilities (MS Ed); social studies education (MA); Spanish education (MA); teaching English as a second language (MA). Electronic applications accepted.

School of Social Work Students: 745 full-time (593 women), 226 part-time (181 women); includes 483 minority (216 Black or African American, non-Hispanic/Latino; 4 American Indian or Alaska Native, non-Hispanic/Latino; 53 Asian, non-Hispanic/Latino; 210 Hispanic/Latino), 14 international. Average age 30. 1,362 applicants, 38% accepted, 311 enrolled. *Financial support:* In 2015–16, 120 fellowships (averaging $1,000 per year) were awarded; career-related internships or fieldwork, Federal Work-Study, and tuition waivers (partial) also available. Support available to part-time students. In 2015, 501 master's awarded. Offers social work (MSW, DSW). DSW offered jointly with The Graduate Center, City University of New York. *Application deadline:* For fall admission, 1/15 for domestic and international students. Applications are processed on a rolling basis. *Application Contact:* Raymond Montero, Coordinator of Admissions, 212-452-7005, E-mail: grad.socworkadvisor@hunter.cuny.edu. *Dean/Professor,* Dr. Jacqueline B. Mondros, 212-452-7085, Fax: 212-452-7150, E-mail: jmondros@hunter.cuny.edu.

Schools of the Health Professions Financial support: Federal Work-Study and tuition waivers (partial) available. Support available to part-time students. In 2015, 102 master's awarded. *Degree program information:* Part-time and evening/weekend programs available. Part-time, evening/weekend. Offers adult nurse practitioner (MS); community health education (MPH); community health nursing (MS); environmental and occupational health sciences (MPH); epidemiology and biostatistics (MPH); gerontological nurse practitioner (MS); health policy management (MPH); health professions (MPH, MS, AC); health sciences (MPH, MS); nursing (MS, AC); nutrition (MPH); psychiatric nursing (MS, AC); speech-language pathology (MS). *Application deadline:* For fall admission, 4/1 for domestic students, 2/1 for international students; for spring admission, 11/1 for domestic students, 9/1 for international students. *Application Contact:* Milena Solo, Director for Graduate Admissions, 212-772-4288, E-mail: milena.solo@hunter.cuny.edu. *Dean,* Lauren N. Sherwen, 212-481-4314.

HUNTINGTON COLLEGE OF HEALTH SCIENCES, Knoxville, TN 37918

General Information Proprietary, coed, comprehensive institution.

GRADUATE UNITS

Program in Nutrition ***Degree program information:*** Part-time and evening/weekend programs available. Part-time, evening/weekend, online learning. Offers clinical nutrition (DHS); nutrition (MS); personalized option (DHS). Electronic applications accepted.

HUNTINGTON UNIVERSITY, Huntington, IN 46750-1299

General Information Independent-religious, coed, comprehensive institution. *Graduate housing:* On-campus housing not available. *Research affiliation:* Link Institute (youth ministry).

GRADUATE UNITS

Graduate School ***Degree program information:*** Part-time programs available. Part-time, online learning. Offers counseling (MA); early adolescent education (M Ed); education (M Ed); global missions leadership (MA); global youth ministry (MA); TESOL education (M Ed); youth ministry leadership (MA). Electronic applications accepted.

HUSSON UNIVERSITY, Bangor, ME 04401-2999

General Information Independent, coed, comprehensive institution. *Enrollment:* 3,418 graduate, professional, and undergraduate students; 559 full-time matriculated graduate/professional students (340 women), 145 part-time matriculated graduate/professional students (89 women). *Enrollment by degree level:* 417 master's, 287 doctoral. *Graduate faculty:* 67 full-time (35 women), 33 part-time/adjunct (19 women). *Tuition, area resident:* Full-time $22,914; part-time $547 per credit. *Required fees:* $600. Tuition and fees vary according to degree level and program. *Graduate housing:* Room and/or apartments available on a first-come, first-served basis to single students; on-campus housing not available to married students. Typical cost: $5226 per year ($9676 including board). Room and board charges vary according to board plan and housing facility selected. Housing application deadline: 6/1. *Student services:* Campus employment opportunities, campus safety program, career counseling, exercise/wellness program, free psychological counseling, international student services, writing training. *Library:* Sawyer Library. *Collection:* Books: 42,921 (physical), 11,606 (digital/electronic); Serial titles: 347 (physical), 38,699 (digital/electronic); Databases: 78. Weekly public service hours: 98; study areas open 24 hours, 5–7 days a week; students can reserve study rooms.

Computer facilities: 131 computers available on campus for general student use. A campuswide network can be accessed from student residence rooms and from off campus. Online class registration is available.
Website: http://www.husson.edu/

General Application Contact: Kristen Card, Director of Graduate Admissions, 207-404-5660, Fax: 207-941-7850, E-mail: cardk@husson.edu.

GRADUATE UNITS

Doctorate in Physical Therapy Program Students: 74 full-time (42 women); includes 1 minority (Black or African American, non-Hispanic/Latino), 1 international. Average age 24. 428 applicants, 4% accepted, 10 enrolled. *Faculty:* 10 full-time (6 women), 9 part-time/adjunct (6 women). *Financial support:* Federal Work-Study and unspecified assistantships available. Financial award application deadline: 4/15; financial award applicants required to submit FAFSA. In 2015, 33 doctorates awarded. Offers physical therapy (DPT). *Application deadline:* For fall admission, 4/15 for domestic and international students. *Application fee:* $50. Electronic applications accepted. *Application Contact:* Cecile Ferguson, Administrative Assistant, 207-941-7101, E-mail: pt@fc.husson.edu. *Director*, Dr. Suzanne Gordon, 207-941-7797, E-mail: gordons@husson.edu.

Graduate Nursing Program Students: 27 full-time (26 women), 10 part-time (9 women); includes 4 minority (2 Asian, non-Hispanic/Latino; 2 Two or more races, non-Hispanic/Latino). Average age 39. 70 applicants, 27% accepted, 13 enrolled. *Faculty:* 6 full-time (all women), 2 part-time/adjunct (1 woman). *Financial support:* Research assistantships, Federal Work-Study, institutionally sponsored loans, traineeships, and unspecified assistantships available. Financial award application deadline: 3/31; financial award applicants required to submit FAFSA. In 2015, 9 master's awarded. *Degree program information:* Part-time programs available. Part-time. Offers advanced practice psychiatric nursing (MSN, PMC); family and community nurse practitioner (MSN, PMC); nursing education (MSN, PMC). *Application deadline:* For fall admission, 3/31 for domestic students; for spring admission, 10/30 for domestic students. *Application fee:* $40. Electronic applications accepted. *Application Contact:* Kristen Card, Director of Graduate Admissions, 207-404-5660, Fax: 207-941-7935, E-mail: cardk@husson.edu. *Director, Graduate Nursing*, Prof. Mary Jude, 207-941-7769, Fax: 207-941-7198, E-mail: judem@husson.edu.

Graduate Programs in Counseling and Human Relations Students: 46 full-time (40 women), 24 part-time (21 women); includes 2 minority (1 Black or African American, non-Hispanic/Latino; 1 American Indian or Alaska Native, non-Hispanic/Latino), 2 international. Average age 34. 52 applicants, 67% accepted, 17 enrolled. *Faculty:* 3 full-time (2 women), 2 part-time/adjunct (both women). *Financial support:* Federal Work-Study, scholarships/grants, and unspecified assistantships available. Financial award application deadline: 4/15; financial award applicants required to submit FAFSA. In 2015, 13 master's awarded. *Degree program information:* Part-time and evening/weekend programs available. Part-time, evening/weekend. Offers clinical mental health counseling (MS); human relations (MS); school counseling (MS). *Application deadline:* For fall admission, 4/15 for domestic students. Applications are processed on a rolling basis. *Application fee:* $50. Electronic applications accepted. *Application Contact:* Kristen Card, Director of Graduate Admissions, 207-404-5660, Fax: 207-941-7935, E-mail: cardk@husson.edu. *Director, Graduate Counseling Programs*, Dr. Deborah Drew, 207-992-4912, Fax: 207-992-4952, E-mail: drewd@husson.edu.

Master of Business Administration Program Students: 125 full-time (54 women), 97 part-time (56 women); includes 18 minority (4 Black or African American, non-Hispanic/Latino; 2 American Indian or Alaska Native, non-Hispanic/Latino; 7 Asian, non-Hispanic/Latino; 2 Hispanic/Latino; 3 Two or more races, non-Hispanic/Latino), 6 international. Average age 34. 143 applicants, 76% accepted, 53 enrolled. *Faculty:* 9 full-time (5 women), 11 part-time/adjunct (2 women). *Financial support:* Career-related internships or fieldwork, Federal Work-Study, scholarships/grants, and unspecified assistantships available. Financial award application deadline: 4/15; financial award applicants required to submit FAFSA. In 2015, 108 master's awarded. *Degree program information:* Part-time and evening/weekend programs available. Part-time, evening/weekend. Offers biotechnology and innovation (MBA); general business administration (MBA); healthcare management (MBA); hospitality and tourism management (MBA); organizational management (MBA); risk management (MBA). *Application deadline:* Applications are processed on a rolling basis. *Application fee:* $50. Electronic applications accepted. *Application Contact:* Kristen Card, Director of Graduate Admissions, 207-404-5660, Fax: 207-941-7935, E-mail: cardk@husson.edu. *Director, Graduate and Online Programs*, Prof. Stephanie Shayne, 207-404-5632, Fax: 207-992-4987, E-mail: shaynes@husson.edu.

Master of Science in Criminal Justice Administration Program Students: 7 full-time (3 women), 5 part-time (1 woman); includes 1 minority (Hispanic/Latino). Average age 28. 6 applicants, 100% accepted, 1 enrolled. *Faculty:* 4 full-time (2 women), 2 part-time/adjunct (0 women). *Financial support:* Career-related internships or fieldwork and unspecified assistantships available. Financial award application deadline: 4/15; financial award applicants required to submit FAFSA. In 2015, 5 master's awarded. *Degree program information:* Part-time programs available. Part-time. Offers criminal justice administration (MS). *Application deadline:* For fall admission, 8/1 for domestic students. Applications are processed on a rolling basis. *Application fee:* $50 ($0 for international students). Electronic applications accepted. *Application Contact:* Kristen Card, Director of Graduate Admissions, 207-404-5660, E-mail: cardk@husson.edu. *Director, School of Legal Studies*, John Michaud, 207-941-7037, E-mail: michaudj@husson.edu.

Master of Science in Occupational Therapy Program Students: 57 full-time (53 women); includes 5 minority (2 Hispanic/Latino; 1 Native Hawaiian or other Pacific Islander, non-Hispanic/Latino; 2 Two or more races, non-Hispanic/Latino). Average age 25. 64 applicants, 23% accepted, 9 enrolled. *Faculty:* 6 full-time (5 women), 1 part-time/adjunct (0 women). *Financial support:* Federal Work-Study, scholarships/grants, and unspecified assistantships available. Financial award application deadline: 4/15; financial award applicants required to submit FAFSA. In 2015, 35 master's awarded. Offers occupational therapy (MSOT). *Application deadline:* For fall admission, 5/1 for domestic students. *Application fee:* $50 ($0 for international students). Electronic applications accepted. *Application Contact:* Kristen Card, Director of Graduate Admissions, 207-404-5660, E-mail: cardk@husson.edu. *Program Director*, Dr. Laurie Mouradian, 207-404-5630, E-mail: mouradianl@husson.edu.

School of Pharmacy Students: 213 full-time (117 women); includes 83 minority (36 Black or African American, non-Hispanic/Latino; 2 American Indian or Alaska Native, non-Hispanic/Latino; 37 Asian, non-Hispanic/Latino; 5 Hispanic/Latino; 1 Native Hawaiian or other Pacific Islander, non-Hispanic/Latino; 2 Two or more races, non-Hispanic/Latino), 8 international. Average age 27. 268 applicants, 31% accepted, 44 enrolled. *Faculty:* 30 full-time (10 women), 1 part-time/adjunct (0 women). *Financial support:* Federal Work-Study, scholarships/grants, and unspecified assistantships available. Financial award application deadline: 3/1; financial award applicants required to submit FAFSA. In 2015, 65 doctorates awarded. Offers pharmacy (Pharm D). *Application deadline:* For fall admission, 3/1 for domestic students. *Application fee:* $50 ($0 for international students). *Application Contact:* Kristen Card, Director of Graduate Admissions, 207-404-5660, E-mail: cardk@husson.edu. *Dean*, Dr. Rodney A. Larson, 207-941-7122, E-mail: larsonr@husson.edu.

HUSTON-TILLOTSON UNIVERSITY, Austin, TX 78702-2795

General Information Independent-religious, coed, comprehensive institution.

GRADUATE UNITS

Graduate Programs

ICAHN SCHOOL OF MEDICINE AT MOUNT SINAI, New York, NY 10029-6504

General Information Independent, coed, graduate-only institution. *Graduate housing:* Rooms and/or apartments guaranteed to single and married students. Housing application deadline: 6/1.

GRADUATE UNITS

The Bioethics Program Offers bioethics (MS). Program offered jointly with Union Graduate College.

Department of Medical Education Offers medical education (MD). Electronic applications accepted.

Graduate School of Biomedical Sciences Offers biomedical sciences (MS, PhD); clinical research education (MS, PhD); community medicine (MPH); genetic counseling (MS); neurosciences (PhD). Electronic applications accepted.

IDAHO STATE UNIVERSITY, Pocatello, ID 83209

General Information State-supported, coed, university. CGS member. *Graduate housing:* Rooms and/or apartments available on a first-come, first-served basis to single and married students. Housing application deadline: 5/1. *Research affiliation:* S.M. Stoller Corporation (ecology, waste management), ON Semiconductor (computer sciences, environmental management), Inland Northwest Research Alliance (INRA) (science), J.R. Simplot Company (plant sciences, environmental studies), Bechtel BWXT Idaho, LLC (environmental management, nuclear sciences), Environmental Science and Research Foundation (waste management, ecology).

GRADUATE UNITS

Office of Graduate Studies *Degree program information:* Part-time programs available. Part-time. Offers general interdisciplinary (M Ed, MA, MNS); waste management and environmental science (MS). Electronic applications accepted.

College of Arts and Letters *Degree program information:* Part-time programs available. Part-time. Offers anthropology (MA, MS); art (MFA); arts and letters (MA, MFA, MNS, MPA, MS, DA, PhD, Post-Master's Certificate, Postbaccalaureate Certificate); clinical psychology (PhD); communication and rhetorical studies (MA); English (MA, DA); English and the teaching of English (PhD); experimental psychology (PhD); historical resources management (MA); political science (MA, DA); public administration (MPA); sociology (MA); TESOL (Post-Master's Certificate); theatre (MA). Electronic applications accepted.

College of Business *Degree program information:* Part-time programs available. Part-time. Offers business administration (MBA, Postbaccalaureate Certificate); computer information systems (MS, Postbaccalaureate Certificate). Electronic applications accepted.

College of Education *Degree program information:* Part-time programs available. Part-time. Offers child and family studies (M Ed); curriculum leadership (M Ed); deaf education (M Ed); education (M Ed, MPE, Ed D, PhD, 5th Year Certificate, 6th Year Certificate, Ed S); educational administration (M Ed, 6th Year Certificate, Ed S); educational foundations (5th Year Certificate); educational leadership (Ed D); educational leadership and instructional design (PhD); elementary education (M Ed); human exceptionality (M Ed); instructional design (PhD); instructional technology (M Ed); literacy (M Ed); physical education (MPE); school psychology (Ed S); special education (Ed S). Electronic applications accepted.

College of Pharmacy *Degree program information:* Part-time programs available. Part-time. Offers biopharmaceutical analysis (PhD); drug delivery (PhD); medicinal chemistry (PhD); pharmaceutical sciences (MS); pharmacology (PhD); pharmacy (MS, PhD, Pharm D); pharmacy administration (MS, PhD). Electronic applications accepted.

College of Science and Engineering *Degree program information:* Part-time programs available. Part-time. Offers applied physics (PhD); biology (MNS, MS, DA, PhD); chemistry (MNS, MS); civil engineering (MS); clinical laboratory science (MS); environmental engineering (MS); environmental science and management (MS); geographic information science (MS); geology (MNS, MS); geology with emphasis in environmental geoscience (MS); geophysics/hydrology/geology (MS); geotechnology (Postbaccalaureate Certificate); health physics (MS); mathematics (MS, DA); mathematics for secondary teachers (MA); measurement and control engineering (MS); mechanical engineering (MS); microbiology (MS); nuclear science and engineering (MS, PhD); physics (MNS); science and engineering (MA, MNS, MS, DA, PhD, Postbaccalaureate Certificate). Electronic applications accepted.

College of Technology *Degree program information:* Part-time and evening/weekend programs available. Part-time, evening/weekend. Offers human resource training and development (MTD); technology (MTD). Electronic applications accepted.

Kasiska College of Health Professions *Degree program information:* Part-time programs available. Part-time. Offers advanced general dentistry (Post-Doctoral Certificate); audiology (MS, Au D); communication sciences and disorders

(Postbaccalaureate Certificate); communication sciences and disorders and education of the deaf (Certificate); counseling (M Coun, Ed S); counselor education and counseling (PhD); deaf education (MS); dental hygiene (MS); dietetics (Certificate); family medicine (Post-Master's Certificate); health education (MHE); health professions (M Coun, MHE, MOT, MPAS, MPH, MS, Au D, DPT, PhD, Certificate, Ed S, Post-Doctoral Certificate, Post-Master's Certificate, Postbaccalaureate Certificate); nursing (MS, Post-Master's Certificate); occupational therapy (MOT); physical therapy (DPT); physician assistant studies (MPAS); public health (MPH); speech language pathology (MS). Electronic applications accepted.

ILIFF SCHOOL OF THEOLOGY, Denver, CO 80210-4798

General Information Independent-religious, coed, graduate-only institution. *Graduate housing:* Rooms and/or apartments available on a first-come, first-served basis to single and married students.

GRADUATE UNITS

Graduate and Professional Programs ***Degree program information:*** Part-time and evening/weekend programs available. Part-time, evening/weekend. Offers biblical studies (MA); church history (MA); religion (MA); religion and social change (MA); specialized ministry (MASM); theology (M Div, MTS, D Min, PhD); theology/ethics (MA). PhD offered jointly with University of Denver. Electronic applications accepted.

ILLINOIS COLLEGE, Jacksonville, IL 62650-2299

General Information Independent-religious, coed, comprehensive institution.

GRADUATE UNITS

Program in Education ***Degree program information:*** Part-time and evening/weekend programs available. Part-time, evening/weekend. Offers education (MA Ed). Electronic applications accepted.

ILLINOIS COLLEGE OF OPTOMETRY, Chicago, IL 60616-3878

General Information Independent, coed, graduate-only institution. *Graduate housing:* Rooms and/or apartments guaranteed to single students and available on a first-come, first-served basis to married students. Housing application deadline: 6/1. *Research affiliation:* University of Chicago (vision science), Rush University (cataract development), Ocular Science (contact lenses), University of Illinois at Chicago (neuropharmacology), Vision Service Plan (pediatric optometry), Ciba Vision (contact lenses).

GRADUATE UNITS

Professional Program Offers optometry (OD). Electronic applications accepted.

ILLINOIS INSTITUTE OF TECHNOLOGY, Chicago, IL 60616-3793

General Information Independent, coed, university. CGS member. *Graduate housing:* Rooms and/or apartments available on a first-come, first-served basis to single and married students. Housing application deadline: 6/1.

GRADUATE UNITS

Chicago-Kent College of Law ***Degree program information:*** Part-time and evening/weekend programs available. Part-time, evening/weekend. Offers family law (LL M); financial services law (LL M); international intellectual property law (LL M); law (JD); legal studies (JSD); taxation (LL M); U.S., international, and transnational law (LL M). Electronic applications accepted.

Graduate College ***Degree program information:*** Part-time and evening/weekend programs available. Part-time, evening/weekend, online learning. Electronic applications accepted.

Armour College of Engineering Degree program information: Part-time and evening/weekend programs available. Part-time, evening/weekend, online learning. Offers architectural engineering (M Arch E); biological engineering (MAS); biomedical engineering (MAS, MS, PhD); biomedical imaging and signals (MAS); chemical engineering (MAS, MS, PhD); civil engineering (MS, PhD); computer engineering (MS, PhD); construction engineering and management (MCEM); electrical engineering (MS, PhD); electricity markets (MAS); engineering (M Arch E, M Env E, M Geoenv E, M Trans E, MAS, MCEM, MGE, MPW, MS, MSE, PhD); environmental engineering (M Env E, MS, PhD); geoenvironmental engineering (M Geoenv E); geotechnical engineering (MGE); infrastructure engineering and management (MPW); manufacturing engineering (MAS, MS); materials science and engineering (MAS, MS, PhD); mechanical and aerospace engineering (MAS, MS, PhD); network engineering (MAS); power engineering (MAS); structural engineering (MSE); telecommunications and software engineering (MAS); transportation engineering (M Trans E); VLSI and microelectronics (MAS). Electronic applications accepted.

College of Architecture Degree program information: Part-time programs available. Part-time. Offers architecture (M Arch, MLA, MS Arch, PhD). Electronic applications accepted.

College of Science Degree program information: Part-time and evening/weekend programs available. Part-time, evening/weekend, online learning. Offers analytical chemistry (MAS); applied mathematics (MS, PhD); applied physics (MS); biochemistry (MS); biology (MS, PhD); business (MCS); cell and molecular biology (MS); chemistry (MAS, MS, PhD); computational intelligence (MCS); computer science (MCS, MS, PhD); cyber-physical systems (MCS); data analytics (MCS); data science (MAS); database systems (MCS); distributed and cloud computing (MCS); education (MCS); finance (MCS); health physics (MAS); information security and assurance (MCS); materials chemistry (MAS); mathematical finance (MAS); mathematics education (MAS, PhD); microbiology (MS); molecular biochemistry and biophysics (MS, PhD); networking and communications (MCS); physics (MS, PhD); science (MAS, MCS, MS, PhD); science education (MAS, PhD); software engineering (MCS); telecommunications and software engineering (MAS). Electronic applications accepted.

Institute of Design Degree program information: Part-time programs available. Part-time. Offers design (M Des, MDM, PhD). Electronic applications accepted.

Lewis College of Human Sciences Offers clinical psychology (PhD); human sciences (MS, PhD); industrial and organizational psychology (PhD); information architecture (MS); personnel and human resource development (MS); rehabilitation and mental health counseling (MS); rehabilitation counseling education (PhD); technical communication (PhD); technical communication and information design (MS).

School of Applied Technology Degree program information: Part-time and evening/weekend programs available. Part-time, evening/weekend, online learning. Offers applied technology (MAS, MFPE, MFST, MS); cyber forensics and security (MAS); food process engineering (MFPE, MS); food safety and technology (MFST, MS); industrial technology and management (MAS); information technology and management (MAS). Electronic applications accepted.

Stuart School of Business ***Degree program information:*** Part-time and evening/weekend programs available. Part-time, evening/weekend. Offers business (MBA, MMF, MPA, MS, PhD); environmental management and sustainability (MS); finance (MS); management science (PhD); marketing analytics and communication (MS); mathematical finance (MMF); public administration (MPA); sustainability (MBA); technological entrepreneurship (MTE). Electronic applications accepted.

ILLINOIS STATE UNIVERSITY, Normal, IL 61790-2200

General Information State-supported, coed, university. CGS member. *Graduate housing:* Rooms and/or apartments available to single and married students. Housing application deadline: 4/1.

GRADUATE UNITS

Graduate School ***Degree program information:*** Part-time programs available. Part-time.

College of Applied Science and Technology Financial support: Fellowships, research assistantships, teaching assistantships, career-related internships or fieldwork, Federal Work-Study, institutionally sponsored loans, tuition waivers (full and partial), and unspecified assistantships available. Support available to part-time students. Financial award application deadline: 4/1. *Degree program information:* Part-time programs available. Part-time. Offers agribusiness (MS); applied science and technology (MA, MS, Certificate, Graduate Certificate); criminal justice sciences (MA, MS); family and consumer sciences (MA, MS); health education (MS); information technology (MS); technology (MS). *Application deadline:* Applications are processed on a rolling basis. *Application fee:* $40.

College of Arts and Sciences Degree program information: Part-time programs available. Part-time. Offers animal behavior (MS); arts and sciences (MA, MS, MSW, PhD, SSP); bacteriology (MS); biochemistry (MS); biological sciences (MS); biology (PhD); biophysics (MS); biotechnology (MS); botany (MS, PhD); cell biology (MS); chemistry (MCE, MS, MSCE); communication (MA, MS); communication sciences and disorders (MA, MS); conservation biology (MS); developmental biology (MS); ecology (MS, PhD); economics (MA, MS); English (MA, MS, PhD); English studies (PhD); entomology (MS); evolutionary biology (MS); French (MA); French and German (MA); French and Spanish (MA); genetics (MS, PhD); geography-geology (Graduate Certificate); German (MA); German and Spanish (MA); historical archaeology (MA, MS); history (MA, MS); immunology (MS); mathematics (MA, MS); mathematics education (MA, PhD); microbiology (MS, PhD); molecular biology (MS); molecular genetics (MS); neurobiology (MS); neuroscience (MS); parasitology (MS); physiology (MS, PhD); plant biology (MS); plant molecular biology (MS); plant sciences (MS); politics and government (MA, MS); psychology (MA, MS); school psychology (PhD, SSP); social work (MSW); sociology (MA, MS); Spanish (MA); structural biology (MS); writing (MA, MS); zoology (MS, PhD).

College of Business Degree program information: Part-time programs available. Part-time. Offers accounting (MPA, MS); business (MBA, MPA, MS); business administration (MBA).

College of Education Degree program information: Part-time programs available. Part-time. Offers college student personnel administration (MS); curriculum and instruction (MS, MS Ed, Ed D); education (MS, MS Ed, Ed D, PhD, Certificate); educational administration (MS, MS Ed, Ed D, PhD); educational policies (Ed D); postsecondary education (Ed D); reading (MS Ed); special education (MS, MS Ed, Ed D, Certificate); supervision (Ed D).

College of Fine Arts Degree program information: Part-time programs available. Part-time. Offers art history (MA, MS); arts technology (MS); ceramics (MFA, MS); drawing (MFA, MS); fibers (MFA, MS); fine arts (MA, MFA, MM, MM Ed, MS); glass (MFA, MS); graphic design (MFA, MS); metals (MFA, MS); music (MM, MM Ed); painting (MFA, MS); photography (MFA, MS); printmaking (MFA, MS); sculpture (MFA, MS); theatre (MA, MFA, MS).

Mennonite College of Nursing Offers family nurse practitioner (PMC); nursing (MSN, PhD). *Application fee:* $40. *Application Contact:* Caroline Mallory, 309-438-2659, E-mail: cmmallo@ilstu.edu.

IMCA–INTERNATIONAL MANAGEMENT CENTRES ASSOCIATION, Buckingham MK18 1BP, United Kingdom

General Information Independent, coed, graduate-only institution.

GRADUATE UNITS

Programs in Business Administration Online learning. Offers business administration (M Mgt, M Phil, MBA, MS).

IMMACULATA UNIVERSITY, Immaculata, PA 19345

General Information Independent-religious, coed, university. CGS member. *Graduate housing:* Rooms and/or apartments available on a first-come, first-served basis to single and married students.

GRADUATE UNITS

College of Graduate Studies ***Degree program information:*** Part-time and evening/weekend programs available. Part-time, evening/weekend. Offers bilingual studies (MA); clinical mental health counseling (MA); clinical psychology (Psy D); educational leadership (MA, Ed D); forensic psychology (Graduate Certificate); integrative psychotherapy (Graduate Certificate); music therapy (MA); neuropsychology (Graduate Certificate); nutrition education for the registered dietitian (MA); nutrition education with dietetic internship (MA); nutrition education with wellness promotion (MA); organization leadership (MA); principal (Certificate); psychodynamic psychotherapy (Graduate Certificate); psychological testing (Graduate Certificate); school counseling (MA, Graduate Certificate); school psychology (MA); secondary education (Certificate); supervisor of special education (Certificate); TESOL (MA). Electronic applications accepted.

Division of Nursing Degree program information: Part-time and evening/weekend programs available. Part-time, evening/weekend. Offers nursing administration (MSN); nursing education (MSN).

INDEPENDENCE UNIVERSITY, Salt Lake City, UT 84107

General Information Proprietary, coed, comprehensive institution. *Graduate housing:* On-campus housing not available.

GRADUATE UNITS

Program in Business Administration Offers business administration (MBA).

Program in Business Administration in Health Care ***Degree program information:*** Part-time and evening/weekend programs available. Part-time, evening/weekend, online learning. Offers health care administration (MBA).

Program in Health Care Administration ***Degree program information:*** Part-time and evening/weekend programs available. Part-time, evening/weekend, online learning. Offers health care administration (MSHCA).

Program in Health Services ***Degree program information:*** Part-time and evening/weekend programs available. Part-time, evening/weekend, online learning. Offers community health (MSHS); wellness promotion (MSHS).

Program in Nursing Offers community health (MSN); gerontology (MSN); nursing administration (MSN); wellness promotion (MSN).

Program in Public Health ***Degree program information:*** Part-time and evening/weekend programs available. Part-time, evening/weekend, online learning. Offers public health (MPH).

INDIANA STATE UNIVERSITY, Terre Haute, IN 47809

General Information State-supported, coed, university. CGS member. *Graduate housing:* Rooms and/or apartments available on a first-come, first-served basis to single and married students. Housing application deadline: 4/18. *Research affiliation:* Indiana Space Grant (remote sensing), Indiana University School of Medicine (cancer and Lupus research), Cranberry Lake Biological Station (psychosocial impacts of cancer), Boston Museum of Science (remote sensing, biology), Great Lakes Northern Forest Cooperative Ecosystem Study Unit (biology, life sciences).

GRADUATE UNITS

College of Graduate and Professional Studies ***Degree program information:*** Part-time and evening/weekend programs available. Part-time, evening/weekend, online learning. Offers technology management (PhD). Electronic applications accepted.

Bayh College of Education Degree program information: Part-time and evening/weekend programs available. Part-time, evening/weekend. Offers clinical mental health counseling (MS); communication disorders (MS); curriculum and instruction (M Ed, PhD); education (M Ed, MS, PhD, Ed S); educational administration (PhD); educational technology (MS); higher education leadership (PhD); K-12 district leadership (PhD); school administration (Ed S); school administration and supervision (M Ed); school counseling (M Ed); school psychology (PhD, Ed S); student affairs and higher education (MS). Electronic applications accepted.

College of Arts and Sciences Degree program information: Part-time and evening/weekend programs available. Part-time, evening/weekend. Offers applied linguistics/teaching English as a second language (MA); arts and sciences (MA, MFA, MM, MPA, MS, PhD, Psy D, CAS); British and American literature (MA); cellular and molecular biology (PhD); ceramics (MA, MFA); clinical psychology (Psy D); communication studies (MA); computer science (MS); conducting (MM); criminology and criminal justice (MA, MS); drawing (MA, MFA); ecology, systematics and evolution (PhD); English (MA); general psychology (MA, MS); graphic design (MA, MFA); history (MA, MS); language education (PhD); life sciences (MS); mathematics (MA, MS); music education (MM); music performance (MM); painting (MA, MFA); photography (MA, MFA); physiology (PhD); printmaking (MA, MFA); public administration (MPA); radio, television and film (MA); science education (MS); sculpture (MA, MFA); Spanish/teaching english as a second language (MA); TESL/TEFL (CAS); writing (MA). Electronic applications accepted.

College of Nursing, Health, and Human Services Offers advanced practice nursing (DNP); applied health sciences (MS, DHS); athletic training (MS, DAT); family nurse practitioner (MS); nursing administration (MS); nursing education (MS); nursing, health, and human services (MA, MS, MSW, DAT, DNP, DPT, PhD); occupational therapy (MS); physical education (MS); physical therapy (DPT); physician assistant (MS); recreation and sport management (MS); social work (MSW); sport management (PhD). Electronic applications accepted.

College of Technology Offers career and technical education (MS); electronics and computer technology (MS); human resource development (MS); occupational safety management (MS); technology (MS); technology management (MS). Electronic applications accepted.

Scott College of Business Degree program information: Part-time and evening/weekend programs available. Part-time, evening/weekend. Offers business (MBA). Electronic applications accepted.

See Display below and Close-Up on page 881.

INDIANA TECH, Fort Wayne, IN 46803-1297

General Information Independent, coed, comprehensive institution. *Enrollment:* 408 full-time matriculated graduate/professional students (204 women), 231 part-time matriculated graduate/professional students (124 women). *Enrollment by degree level:* 445 master's, 194 doctoral. *Graduate faculty:* 23 full-time (8 women), 76 part-time/adjunct (16 women). *Tuition, area resident:* Part-time $495 per credit. Part-time tuition and fees vary according to degree level and program. *Graduate housing:* Room and/or apartments available on a first-come, first-served basis to single students; on-campus housing not available to married students. Housing application deadline: 8/15. *Student services:* Career counseling, exercise/wellness program, free psychological counseling, low-cost health insurance, services for students with disabilities. *Library:* McMillen Library plus 1 other.

Computer facilities: 460 computers available on campus for general student use. A campuswide network can be accessed from student residence rooms and from off campus. Online class registration is available.
Website: https://www.indianatech.edu/

General Application Contact: Steven A. Herendeen, Vice President for Enrollment Management, 260-422-5561 Ext. 2121, Fax: 260-422-1518, E-mail: saherendeen@indianatech.edu.

GRADUATE UNITS

Program in Business Administration Students: 160 full-time (94 women), 97 part-time (53 women); includes 69 minority (58 Black or African American, non-Hispanic/Latino; 1 Asian, non-Hispanic/Latino; 8 Hispanic/Latino; 2 Two or more races, non-Hispanic/Latino), 11 international. Average age 36. *Financial support:* Applicants required to submit FAFSA. *Degree program information:* Part-time and evening/weekend programs available. Part-time, evening/weekend, online learning. Offers accounting (MBA); health care management (MBA); human resources (MBA); management (MBA); marketing (MBA). *Application deadline:* Applications are processed on a rolling basis. *Application fee:* $25. Electronic applications accepted. *Application Contact:* Dr. Andrew I. Nwanne, Associate Dean of Business/Academic Coordinator, 260-422-5561 Ext. 2214, E-mail: ainwanne@indianatech.edu. *Associate Dean of Business/Academic Coordinator*, Dr. Andrew I. Nwanne, 260-422-5561 Ext. 2214, E-mail: ainwanne@indianatech.edu.

Program in Engineering Management ***Financial support:*** Applicants required to submit FAFSA. *Degree program information:* Part-time and evening/weekend programs available. Part-time, evening/weekend, online only, 100% online. Offers engineering management (MSE). *Application deadline:* Applications are processed on a rolling basis. *Application fee:* $25. Electronic applications accepted. *Application Contact:* David A. Aschliman, Dean of Engineering and Computer Sciences, 260-422-5561 Ext. 2102,

E-mail: daaschliman@indianatech.edu. *Dean of Engineering and Computer Sciences*, David A. Aschliman, 260-422-5561 Ext. 2102, E-mail: daaschliman@indianatech.edu.

Program in Global Leadership ***Degree program information:*** Part-time and evening/weekend programs available. Part-time, evening/weekend, online only, 100% online. Offers global leadership (PhD). *Application deadline:* Applications are processed on a rolling basis. *Application fee:* $50. Electronic applications accepted. *Application Contact:* Dr. Kenneth E. Rauch, Director, 260-422-5561 Ext. 2446, E-mail: kerauch@indianatech.edu. *Director*, Dr. Kenneth E. Rauch, 260-422-5561 Ext. 2446, E-mail: kerauch@indianatech.edu.

Program in Management ***Financial support:*** Applicants required to submit FAFSA. *Degree program information:* Part-time and evening/weekend programs available. Part-time, evening/weekend, 100% online. Offers management (MSM). *Application deadline:* Applications are processed on a rolling basis. *Application fee:* $25. Electronic applications accepted. *Application Contact:* Dr. Jeffrey A. Zimmerman, Dean of Business, 260-422-5561 Ext. 2117, E-mail: jazimmerman@indianatech.edu. *Dean of Business*, Dr. Jeffrey A. Zimmerman, 260-422-5561 Ext. 2117, E-mail: jazimmerman@indianatech.edu.

Program in Organizational Leadership ***Financial support:*** Applicants required to submit FAFSA. *Degree program information:* Part-time and evening/weekend programs available. Part-time, evening/weekend, online only, 100% online. Offers organizational leadership (MS). *Application deadline:* Applications are processed on a rolling basis. *Application fee:* $25. Electronic applications accepted. *Application Contact:* Dr. Jeffrey A. Zimmerman, Dean of Business, 260-422-5561 Ext. 2117, E-mail: jazimmerman@indianatech.edu. *Dean of Business*, Dr. Jeffrey A. Zimmerman, 260-422-5561 Ext. 2117, E-mail: jazimmerman@indianatech.edu.

INDIANA UNIVERSITY BLOOMINGTON, Bloomington, IN 47405-7000

General Information State-supported, coed, university. CGS member. *Graduate housing:* Rooms and/or apartments available to single and married students.

GRADUATE UNITS

Jacobs School of Music Offers church music (DM); music (MA, MM, MME, MS, DM, DME, PhD, AD, Performance Diploma, Spec); music literature and performance (DM); performance (MM); performance and church music (MM). Electronic applications accepted.

Kelley School of Business Offers business (MBA, MPA, MS, DBA, PhD). PhD offered through University Graduate School. Electronic applications accepted.

Maurer School of Law Offers comparative law (MCL); juridical science (SJD); law (LL M, JD); law and social sciences (PhD); legal studies (Certificate). PhD offered through University Graduate School. Electronic applications accepted.

School of Education ***Degree program information:*** Part-time programs available. Part-time, online learning. Offers art education (MS, Ed D, PhD); counseling (MS, PhD, Ed S); counselor education (MS, Ed S); curriculum studies (Ed D, PhD); education (MS, Ed D, PhD, Ed S); education policy studies (PhD); educational leadership (MS, Ed D, Ed S); educational psychology (MS, PhD); elementary education (MS, Ed D, PhD, Ed S); higher education (MS, Ed D, PhD); history and philosophy of education (MS); history of education (PhD); inquiry methodology (PhD); instructional systems technology (MS, PhD); international and comparative education (MS, PhD); learning and developmental sciences (MS, PhD); literacy, culture, and language education (MS, Ed D, PhD, Ed S); mathematics education (MS, Ed D, PhD); philosophy of education (PhD); school psychology (PhD, Ed S); science education (MS, Ed D, PhD); secondary education (MS, Ed D, PhD); social studies education (MS, PhD); special education (PhD, Ed S); student affairs administration (MS). Electronic applications accepted.

School of Informatics and Computing ***Degree program information:*** Part-time programs available. Part-time, online learning. Offers computer science (MS, PhD); data science (MS, Graduate Certificate); informatics (MS, PhD); information and library science (MIS, MLS, MS, PhD, Graduate Certificate, Sp LIS); information architecture (Graduate Certificate); information science (MIS, PhD); intelligent systems engineering (PhD); library and information science (Sp LIS); library science (MLS); media arts and science (MS). PhD offered through University Graduate School. Electronic applications accepted.

School of Optometry Offers optometry (MS, OD, PhD). Electronic applications accepted.

School of Public and Environmental Affairs ***Degree program information:*** Part-time programs available. Part-time. Offers applied ecology (MSES); arts administration (MAAA); economic development (MPA); energy (MPA, MSES); environmental chemistry, toxicology, and risk assessment (MSES); environmental policy (PhD); environmental policy and natural resource management (MPA); environmental science (PhD); hazardous materials management (Certificate); information systems (MPA); international development (MPA); local government management (MPA); nonprofit management (MPA, Certificate); policy analysis (MPA); public and environmental affairs (MAAA, MPA, MSES, PhD, Certificate); public budgeting and financial management (Certificate); public finance (PhD); public financial administration (MPA); public management (MPA, PhD, Certificate); public policy analysis (PhD); social entrepreneurship (Certificate); specialized environmental science (MSES); specialized public affairs (MPA); sustainability and sustainable development (MPA); water resources (MSES). Electronic applications accepted.

School of Public Health ***Degree program information:*** Part-time programs available. Part-time, online learning. Offers applied sport science (MS); athletic administration/sport management (MS); athletic training (MS); behavioral, social, and community health (MPH); biomechanics (MS); biostatistics (MPH); environmental health (MPH, PhD); epidemiology (MPH, PhD); ergonomics (MS); exercise physiology (MS); family health (MPH); health behavior (PhD); human performance (PhD); leisure behavior (PhD); motor learning/control (MS); nutrition science (MS); outdoor recreation (MS); park and public lands management (MS); physical activity (MPH); physical activity, fitness and wellness (MS); professional health education (MPH); public health (MPH, MS, PhD); public health administration (MPH); recreation administration (MS); recreational sports administration (MS); recreational therapy (MS); safety management (MS); school and college health education (MS); tourism management (MS). Electronic applications accepted.

University Graduate School ***Degree program information:*** Part-time programs available. Part-time. Electronic applications accepted.

College of Arts and Sciences ***Degree program information:*** Part-time programs available. Part-time. Offers acting (MFA); African American and African diaspora studies (MA); African languages and linguistics (PhD); African studies (MA); analytical chemistry (PhD); anthropology (MA, PhD); applied mathematics (MA); applied statistics (MS); arts and sciences (MA, MAT, MFA, MS, Au D, PhD, Certificate); astronomy (MA, PhD); astrophysics (PhD); audiology (Au D); auditory sciences (Au D, PhD); biochemistry (PhD); biogeochemistry (MS, PhD); biology teaching (MAT); biotechnology (MA); Central Eurasian studies (MA, PhD); chemical biology (PhD); chemistry (MAT); Chinese (MA, PhD); Chinese language pedagogy (MA); classical studies (MA, MAT, PhD); clinical science (PhD); cognitive neuroscience (PhD); cognitive psychology (PhD); cognitive science (PhD); communication and culture (MA); comparative literature (MA, MAT, PhD); composition, literacy, and culture (PhD); computational linguistics (MA, PhD); creative writing (MA, MFA); crime and youth development (MA, PhD); crime, law and psychology (MA, PhD); criminal justice (MA, PhD); criminal justice institutions and practices (MA, PhD); criminology (MA, PhD); design and technology (MFA); developmental criminology (MA, PhD); developmental psychology (PhD); directing (MFA); East Asian studies (MA); economic geology (MS, PhD); economics (PhD); European studies (MA); evolution, ecology, and behavior (MA, PhD); film and media studies (PhD); fine arts (MA, MFA, PhD); folklore (MA, PhD); French (MA, PhD); gender studies (PhD); genetics (PhD); geobiology (MS, PhD); geography (MA, MS, PhD); geophysics, structural geology and tectonics (MS, PhD); German philology and linguistics (PhD); German studies (MA, PhD); global and international studies (MA, MS, PhD, Certificate); history (MA, MAT, PhD); history and philosophy of science (MA, PhD); history of art (MA, PhD); hydrogeology (MS, PhD); inorganic chemistry (PhD); interdisciplinary studies in crime and punishment (PhD); interdisciplinary studies of crime and punishment (MA); international studies (MA, MS); Italian (MA, PhD); Japanese (MA, PhD); Japanese language pedagogy (MA); Jewish studies (MA); journalism (MA, MAT); language (MA); language sciences (PhD); Latin American and Caribbean studies (MA); linguistics (MA, PhD); literature (MA, PhD); mass communication (PhD); mass communications (PhD); materials chemistry (PhD); mathematical physics (PhD); mathematics education (MAT); media (MA, MAT, MS, PhD); medical physics (MS); medieval German studies (PhD); methods of behavior (PhD); microbiology (MA, PhD); mineralogy (MS, PhD); molecular systems neuroscience (PhD); molecular, cellular, and developmental biology (PhD); Near Eastern languages and cultures (MA, PhD); neuroscience (PhD); organic chemistry (PhD); performance and ethnography (PhD); philosophy (MA, PhD); physical chemistry (PhD); physics (MAT, MS, PhD); plant sciences (MA, PhD); playwriting (MFA); political science (MA, PhD); Portuguese (MA, PhD); pure mathematics (MA, PhD); religious studies (MA, PhD); rhetoric and public culture (PhD); Russian and East European studies (MA, Certificate); second language studies (MA, PhD); Slavic languages and literatures (MA, MAT, PhD); social psychology (PhD); sociology (MA, PhD); Spanish (MA, PhD); speech and hearing sciences (MA, Au D, PhD); speech and voice sciences (PhD); speech-language pathology (MA); statistical science (MS, PhD); stratigraphy and sedimentology (MS, PhD); teaching German (MAT); telecommunications (MA, MS, PhD); TESOL and applied linguistics (MA); the relationship between crime and gender, race and ethnicity (MA, PhD); theatre history, theory, and literature (MA, PhD); theoretical analyses of criminology (MA, PhD); writing (MA); zoology (MA, PhD). Electronic applications accepted.

INDIANA UNIVERSITY EAST, Richmond, IN 47374-1289

General Information State-supported, coed, comprehensive institution.

GRADUATE UNITS

School of Education Offers education (MS Ed).

School of Nursing Offers nursing (MSN).

School of Social Work Offers social work (MSW).

INDIANA UNIVERSITY KOKOMO, Kokomo, IN 46904-9003

General Information State-supported, coed, comprehensive institution. *Graduate housing:* On-campus housing not available.

GRADUATE UNITS

Department of Public Administration and Health Management Offers public administration and health management (MPM, Graduate Certificate).

School of Business ***Degree program information:*** Part-time and evening/weekend programs available. Part-time, evening/weekend. Offers business (MBA).

School of Nursing Offers nurse administrator (MSN); nurse educator (MSN).

INDIANA UNIVERSITY NORTHWEST, Gary, IN 46408-1197

General Information State-supported, coed, comprehensive institution. *Graduate housing:* On-campus housing not available.

GRADUATE UNITS

College of Arts and Sciences Offers clinical counseling (MS); liberal studies (MLS).

School of Business and Economics ***Degree program information:*** Part-time and evening/weekend programs available. Part-time, evening/weekend. Offers management (Certificate); management and administrative studies (MBA).

School of Education ***Degree program information:*** Part-time and evening/weekend programs available. Part-time, evening/weekend. Offers educational leadership (MS Ed); elementary education (MS Ed); secondary education (MS Ed).

School of Public and Environmental Affairs ***Degree program information:*** Part-time programs available. Part-time. Offers criminal justice (MPA); environmental affairs (Graduate Certificate); health services (MPA); nonprofit management (Certificate); public management (MPA).

School of Social Work ***Degree program information:*** Part-time and evening/weekend programs available. Part-time, evening/weekend. Offers social work (MSW).

INDIANA UNIVERSITY OF PENNSYLVANIA, Indiana, PA 15705-1087

General Information State-supported, coed, university. CGS member. *Enrollment:* 13,775 graduate, professional, and undergraduate students; 877 full-time matriculated graduate/professional students (488 women), 1,362 part-time matriculated graduate/professional students (813 women). *Enrollment by degree level:* 1,293 master's, 822 doctoral, 124 other advanced degrees. *Graduate faculty:* 280 full-time (125 women), 14 part-time/adjunct (8 women). *Graduate housing:* Room and/or apartments available on a first-come, first-served basis to single students; on-campus housing not available to married students. Housing application deadline: 4/15. *Student services:* Campus employment opportunities, campus safety program, career counseling, free psychological counseling, international student services, low-cost health insurance, multicultural affairs office, services for students with disabilities. *Library:* Stapleton Library. *Collection:* Books: 702,503 (physical), 76,900 (digital/electronic); Serial titles: 175,942 (physical). Weekly public service hours: 134; study areas open 24 hours, 5–7 days a week; students can reserve study rooms.

Computer facilities: Computer purchase and lease plans are available. 2,363 computers available on campus for general student use. A campuswide network can be accessed from student residence rooms and from off campus. Online class registration is available.

Website: http://www.iup.edu/

General Application Contact: Paula Stossel, Assistant Dean for Administration, 724-357-2222, Fax: 724-357-4862, E-mail: graduate-admissions@iup.edu.

GRADUATE UNITS

School of Graduate Studies and Research Students: 958 full-time (528 women), 1,280 part-time (801 women); includes 223 minority (105 Black or African American, non-Hispanic/Latino; 4 American Indian or Alaska Native, non-Hispanic/Latino; 32 Asian, non-Hispanic/Latino; 46 Hispanic/Latino; 1 Native Hawaiian or other Pacific Islander, non-Hispanic/Latino; 35 Two or more races, non-Hispanic/Latino), 483 international. Average age 32. 2,489 applicants, 52% accepted, 749 enrolled. *Faculty:* 282 full-time (131 women), 12 part-time/adjunct (9 women). *Financial support:* In 2015–16, 65 fellowships with full tuition reimbursements (averaging $830 per year), 414 research assistantships with tuition reimbursements (averaging $4,070 per year), 29 teaching assistantships with partial tuition reimbursements (averaging $21,229 per year) were awarded; career-related internships or fieldwork, Federal Work-Study, scholarships/grants, tuition waivers (full and partial), and unspecified assistantships also available. Support available to part-time students. Financial award application deadline: 3/15; financial award applicants required to submit FAFSA. In 2015, 561 master's, 126 doctorates, 15 other advanced degrees awarded. *Degree program information:* Part-time and evening/weekend programs available. Part-time, evening/weekend, online learning. *Application deadline:* Applications are processed on a rolling basis. *Application fee:* $50. Electronic applications accepted. *Application Contact:* Paula Stossel, Assistant Dean for Administration, 724-357-4511, Fax: 724-357-4862, E-mail: graduate-admissions@iup.edu. *Director of Graduate Marketing*, Simon Stuchlik, 724-357-2127, Fax: 724-357-4862, E-mail: stuchlik@iup.edu.

College of Education and Educational Technology Students: 251 full-time (191 women), 465 part-time (328 women); includes 74 minority (41 Black or African American, non-Hispanic/Latino; 1 American Indian or Alaska Native, non-Hispanic/Latino; 2 Asian, non-Hispanic/Latino; 14 Hispanic/Latino; 1 Native Hawaiian or other Pacific Islander, non-Hispanic/Latino; 15 Two or more races, non-Hispanic/Latino), 26 international. Average age 32. 794 applicants, 46% accepted, 234 enrolled. *Faculty:* 64 full-time (39 women), 9 part-time/adjunct (8 women). *Financial support:* In 2015–16, 16 fellowships (averaging $1,043 per year), 126 research assistantships with tuition reimbursements (averaging $4,343 per year), 8 teaching assistantships with tuition reimbursements (averaging $17,236 per year) were awarded; career-related internships or fieldwork, Federal Work-Study, scholarships/grants, and unspecified assistantships also available. Support available to part-time students. Financial award application deadline: 4/15; financial award applicants required to submit FAFSA. In 2015, 152 master's, 65 doctorates, 14 other advanced degrees awarded. *Degree program information:* Part-time and evening/weekend programs available. Part-time, evening/weekend. Offers administration and leadership studies (D Ed); adult and community education (M Ed, MA); adult and community education/communications technology (MA); adult education and communications technology (MA); business/administrative (M Ed); business/business specialist (M Ed); business/workforce development (M Ed); clinical mental health counseling (MA); communications media and instructional technology (PhD); community counseling (MA); curriculum and instruction (D Ed); education (M Ed); education and educational technology (M Ed, MA, MS, D Ed, PhD, Certificate); education of exceptional persons (M Ed); educational psychology (M Ed, Certificate); literacy (M Ed, Certificate); principal (Certificate); reading (Certificate); school counseling (M Ed); school psychology (D Ed, Certificate); special education (Certificate); speech-language pathology (MS); student affairs in higher education (MA). *Application deadline:* Applications are processed on a rolling basis. *Application fee:* $50. Electronic applications accepted. *Application Contact:* Paula Stossel, Assistant Dean for Administration, 724-357-4511, Fax: 724-357-4862, E-mail: graduate-admissions@iup.edu. *Dean*, Dr. Lara Luetkehans, 724-357-2480, Fax: 724-357-5595.

College of Fine Arts Students: 22 full-time (12 women), 20 part-time (13 women); includes 6 minority (2 Black or African American, non-Hispanic/Latino; 1 Hispanic/Latino; 3 Two or more races, non-Hispanic/Latino), 4 international. Average age 27. 42 applicants, 76% accepted, 20 enrolled. *Faculty:* 22 full-time (9 women), 1 part-time/adjunct (0 women). *Financial support:* In 2015–16, 3 fellowships with full tuition reimbursements (averaging $230 per year), 22 research assistantships with tuition reimbursements (averaging $2,375 per year) were awarded; career-related internships or fieldwork, Federal Work-Study, scholarships/grants, and unspecified assistantships also available. Support available to part-time students. Financial award application deadline: 4/15; financial award applicants required to submit FAFSA. In 2015, 12 master's awarded. *Degree program information:* Part-time programs available. Part-time. Offers art (MA, MFA); fine arts (MA, MFA); music (MA); music education (MA); performance (MA). *Application deadline:* Applications are processed on a rolling basis. *Application fee:* $50. Electronic applications accepted. *Application Contact:* Dr. Susan Palmisano, Graduate Coordinator, 724-357-2536, E-mail: palmisan@iup.edu. *Dean*, Michael Hood, 724-357-2397, E-mail: mhood@iup.edu.

College of Health and Human Services Students: 197 full-time (108 women), 250 part-time (166 women); includes 53 minority (24 Black or African American, non-Hispanic/Latino; 1 American Indian or Alaska Native, non-Hispanic/Latino; 7 Asian, non-Hispanic/Latino; 14 Hispanic/Latino; 7 Two or more races, non-Hispanic/Latino), 45 international. Average age 31. 503 applicants, 64% accepted, 196 enrolled. *Faculty:* 52 full-time (31 women). *Financial support:* In 2015–16, 17 fellowships with full tuition reimbursements (averaging $936 per year), 82 research assistantships with tuition reimbursements (averaging $4,982 per year), 7 teaching assistantships with partial tuition reimbursements (averaging $21,640 per year) were awarded; career-related internships or fieldwork, Federal Work-Study, scholarships/grants, and unspecified assistantships also available. Support available to part-time students. Financial award application deadline: 4/15; financial award applicants required to submit FAFSA. In 2015, 146 master's, 7 doctorates, 1 other advanced degree awarded. *Degree program information:* Part-time and evening/weekend programs available. Part-time, evening/weekend, online learning. Offers criminology (MA, PhD); employment and labor relations (MA); food and nutrition (MS); health and human services (M Ed, MA, MS, PhD, Certificate); health and physical education (M Ed); health service administration (MS); health services administration (MS); nursing (PhD); nursing administration (MS); nursing education (MS); safety sciences (MS, PhD); sport science/exercise science (MS); sport science/sport management (MS); sport science/sport studies (MS). *Application deadline:* Applications are processed on a rolling basis. *Application fee:* $50. Electronic applications accepted. *Application Contact:* Paula Stossel, Assistant Dean, 724-357-4511, Fax: 724-357-4862, E-mail: graduate-admissions@iup.edu. *Acting Dean*, Dr. Mary Williams, 724-357-2560, Fax: 724-357-6205, E-mail: mary.e.williams@iup.edu.

College of Humanities and Social Sciences Students: 159 full-time (85 women), 313 part-time (190 women); includes 54 minority (26 Black or African American, non-Hispanic/Latino; 1 American Indian or Alaska Native, non-Hispanic/Latino; 8 Asian, non-Hispanic/Latino; 13 Hispanic/Latino; 6 Two or more races, non-Hispanic/Latino), 100 international. Average age 36. 446 applicants, 45% accepted, 90 enrolled. *Faculty:* 68 full-time (31 women), 1 (woman) part-time/adjunct. *Financial support:* In 2015–16, 24 fellowships with full tuition reimbursements (averaging $714 per year), 84 research assistantships with tuition reimbursements (averaging $4,623 per year), 12 teaching assistantships with partial tuition reimbursements (averaging $23,305 per year) were awarded; career-related internships or fieldwork, Federal Work-Study, scholarships/grants, and unspecified assistantships also available. Support available to part-time students. Financial award application deadline: 4/15; financial award applicants required to submit FAFSA. In 2015, 63 master's, 45 doctorates awarded. *Degree program information:* Part-time and evening/weekend programs available. Part-time, evening/weekend. Offers administration and leadership studies (PhD); applied archaeology (MA); composition and literature (MA); composition and teaching English to speakers of other languages (PhD); English: generalist (MA); English: literature (MA); English: TESOL (MA); environmental planning (MS); geographic information science and geospatial techniques (Certificate); geographic information science/cartography (MS); geography (MA); history (MA); humanities and social sciences (MA, MS, PhD, Certificate); literature and criticism (PhD); public affairs (MA); public history (MA); regional planning (MS); sociology (MA, PhD); Spanish/applied linguistics and teaching methodology (MA); Spanish/Hispanic literatures and cultures (MA); teaching English (MA). *Application deadline:* Applications are processed on a rolling basis. *Application fee:* $50. Electronic applications accepted. *Application Contact:* Paula Stossel, Assistant Dean, 724-357-4511, E-mail: graduate-admissions@iup.edu. *Dean*, Dr. Yaw Asamoah, 724-357-5764.

College of Natural Sciences and Mathematics Students: 89 full-time (54 women), 59 part-time (39 women); includes 15 minority (4 Black or African American, non-Hispanic/Latino; 4 Asian, non-Hispanic/Latino; 4 Hispanic/Latino; 3 Two or more races, non-Hispanic/Latino), 18 international. Average age 27. 375 applicants, 30% accepted, 39 enrolled. *Faculty:* 45 full-time (17 women). *Financial support:* In 2015–16, 5 fellowships with full tuition reimbursements (averaging $696 per year), 66 research assistantships with tuition reimbursements (averaging $3,468 per year), 2 teaching assistantships (averaging $23,305 per year) were awarded; career-related internships or fieldwork, Federal Work-Study, scholarships/grants, and unspecified assistantships also available. Support available to part-time students. Financial award application deadline: 4/15; financial award applicants required to submit FAFSA. In 2015, 46 master's, 9 doctorates awarded. *Degree program information:* Part-time programs available. Part-time. Offers applied and industrial chemistry (PSM); applied mathematics (MS); biology (MS); chemistry (MA); clinical psychology (Psy D); elementary and middle school mathematics education (M Ed); nanoscience/industrial materials (PSM); natural sciences and mathematics (M Ed, MA, MS, PSM, Psy D); physics (MA, PSM); psychology (MA); science for disaster response (MS); secondary mathematics education (M Ed). *Application deadline:* Applications are processed on a rolling basis. *Application fee:* $50. Electronic applications accepted. *Application Contact:* Paula Stossel, Assistant Dean of Administration, 724-357-4511, Fax: 724-357-4862, E-mail: graduate-admissions@iup.edu. *Dean*, Dr. Deanne Snavely, 724-357-2609, Fax: 724-357-5700, E-mail: snavely@iup.edu.

Eberly College of Business and Information Technology Students: 238 full-time (77 women), 149 part-time (54 women); includes 20 minority (8 Black or African American, non-Hispanic/Latino; 1 American Indian or Alaska Native, non-Hispanic/Latino; 10 Asian, non-Hispanic/Latino; 1 Two or more races, non-Hispanic/Latino), 273 international. Average age 28. 253 applicants, 75% accepted, 158 enrolled. *Faculty:* 30 full-time (3 women), 1 part-time/adjunct (0 women). *Financial support:* In 2015–16, 30 research assistantships with tuition reimbursements (averaging $1,623 per year) were awarded; fellowships with full tuition reimbursements, career-related internships or fieldwork, Federal Work-Study, scholarships/grants, and unspecified assistantships also available. Support available to part-time students. Financial award application deadline: 4/15; financial award applicants required to submit FAFSA. In 2015, 142 master's awarded. *Degree program information:* Part-time and evening/weekend programs available. Part-time, evening/weekend. Offers business administration (MBA); business and information technology (M Ed, MBA). *Application deadline:* Applications are processed on a rolling basis. *Application fee:* $50. Electronic applications accepted. *Application Contact:* Paula Stossel, Assistant Dean, 724-357-4511, Fax: 724-357-4862, E-mail: graduate-admissions@iup.edu. *Dean*, Dr. Robert Camp, 724-357-7889, E-mail: bobcamp@iup.edu.

INDIANA UNIVERSITY–PURDUE UNIVERSITY FORT WAYNE, Fort Wayne, IN 46805-1499

General Information State-supported, coed, comprehensive institution. CGS member. *Enrollment:* 137 full-time matriculated graduate/professional students (61 women), 394 part-time matriculated graduate/professional students (244 women). *Enrollment by degree level:* 505 master's, 2 doctoral, 24 other advanced degrees. *Graduate faculty:* 155 full-time (57 women), 1 (woman) part-time/adjunct. *Graduate housing:* Room and/or apartments available on a first-come, first-served basis to single students; on-campus housing not available to married students. *Student services:* Campus employment opportunities, campus safety program, career counseling, exercise/wellness program, free psychological counseling, international student services, low-cost health insurance, multicultural affairs office, services for students with disabilities, teacher training, writing training. *Library:* Helmke Library. *Research affiliation:* Regenstrief Institute, Inc. (nursing), Earthwatch (biology), PHD, Inc. (engineering), Bendix Commercial Vehicle Systems, LLC (engineering, technology, and computer science), Northeast Indiana Fund (education and public policy), Fort Wayne Metals (geosciences).

Computer facilities: Computer purchase and lease plans are available. 642 computers available on campus for general student use. A campuswide network can be accessed from student residence rooms and from off campus. Online class registration, student academic records are available.
Website: http://www.ipfw.edu/

General Application Contact: Susan Humphrey, Graduate Applications Coordinator, 260-481-6145, Fax: 260-481-0347, E-mail: graduate@ipfw.edu.

GRADUATE UNITS

College of Arts and Sciences Students: 32 full-time (20 women), 63 part-time (37 women); includes 17 minority (6 Black or African American, non-Hispanic/Latino; 1 American Indian or Alaska Native, non-Hispanic/Latino; 3 Asian, non-Hispanic/Latino; 3 Hispanic/Latino; 4 Two or more races, non-Hispanic/Latino), 10 international. Average age 30. 35 applicants, 100% accepted, 24 enrolled. *Faculty:* 61 full-time (19 women), 1 (woman) part-time/adjunct. *Financial support:* In 2015–16, 10 research assistantships with partial tuition reimbursements (averaging $13,522 per year), 39 teaching assistantships with partial tuition reimbursements (averaging $13,522 per year) were awarded; career-related internships or fieldwork, institutionally sponsored loans, and scholarships/grants also available. Support available to part-time students. Financial award application deadline: 3/1; financial award applicants required to submit FAFSA. In 2015, 38 master's, 1 other advanced degree awarded. *Degree program information:* Part-time and evening/weekend programs available. Part-time, evening/weekend. Offers applied mathematics (MS); applied statistics (Certificate); arts and sciences (MA, MAT, MS, Certificate); biology (MS); English (MA, MAT); mathematics (MS); operations research (MS); professional communication (MA, MS); teaching (MAT); TENL (teaching English as a new language) (Certificate). *Application deadline:* Applications are processed on a rolling basis. *Application fee:* $55 ($60 for international students). *Application Contact:* Susan Humphrey, Graduate Applications Coordinator, 260-481-6145, Fax: 260-481-6880, E-mail: graduate@ipfw.edu. *Dean*, Dr. Eric Carl Link, 260-481-5750, Fax: 260-481-6985, E-mail: eric.link@ipfw.edu.

College of Education and Public Policy Students: 9 full-time (5 women), 148 part-time (102 women); includes 30 minority (12 Black or African American, non-Hispanic/Latino; 2 Asian, non-Hispanic/Latino; 12 Hispanic/Latino; 4 Two or more races, non-Hispanic/Latino), 3 international. Average age 32. 46 applicants, 100% accepted, 39 enrolled. *Faculty:* 19 full-time (11 women). *Financial support:* In 2015–16, 2 teaching assistantships with partial tuition reimbursements (averaging $13,522 per year) were awarded; scholarships/grants also available. Support available to part-time students. Financial award application deadline: 3/1; financial award applicants required to submit FAFSA. In 2015, 53 master's, 1 Certificate awarded. *Degree program information:* Part-time programs available. Part-time. Offers couple and family counseling (MS Ed); education and public policy (MPM, MS Ed, Certificate); educational leadership (MS Ed); elementary education (MS Ed); public management (MPM, Certificate); school counseling (MS Ed); secondary education (MS Ed); special education (MS Ed, Certificate). *Application deadline:* For fall admission, 4/1 priority date for domestic and international students. Applications are processed on a rolling basis. *Application fee:* $55. *Application Contact:* Vicky L. Schmidt, Graduate Recorder, 260-481-6450, Fax: 260-481-5408, E-mail: schmidt@ipfw.edu. *Dean*, Dr. James Burg, 260-481-5406, Fax: 260-481-5408, E-mail: burgj@ipfw.edu.

College of Engineering, Technology, and Computer Science Students: 32 full-time (12 women), 80 part-time (29 women); includes 18 minority (7 Black or African American, non-Hispanic/Latino; 1 American Indian or Alaska Native, non-Hispanic/Latino; 7 Asian, non-Hispanic/Latino; 2 Hispanic/Latino; 1 Two or more races, non-Hispanic/Latino), 29 international. Average age 31. 57 applicants, 100% accepted, 46 enrolled. *Faculty:* 43 full-time (8 women). *Financial support:* In 2015–16, 2 research assistantships with partial tuition reimbursements (averaging $13,522 per year), 10 teaching assistantships with partial tuition reimbursements (averaging $13,522 per year) were awarded; career-related internships or fieldwork, scholarships/grants, and unspecified assistantships also available. Support available to part-time students. Financial award application deadline: 3/1; financial award applicants required to submit FAFSA. In 2015, 10 master's awarded. *Degree program information:* Part-time programs available. Part-time. Offers applied computer science (MS); civil engineering (MSE); computer engineering (MSE); electrical engineering (MSE); engineering, technology, and computer science (MS, MSE, Certificate); facilities/construction management (MS); human resources (MS); industrial technology/manufacturing (MS); information technology/advanced computer applications (MS); leadership (MS); mechanical engineering (MSE); organizational leadership and supervision (Certificate); systems engineering (MSE). *Application deadline:* For fall admission, 7/15 for domestic students, 5/15 for international students; for spring admission, 12/1 for domestic students, 10/15 for international students. Applications are processed on a rolling basis. *Application fee:* $55 ($60 for international students). Electronic applications accepted. *Interim Dean*, Dr. Carlos Pomalaza-Raez, 260-481-6839, Fax: 260-481-5734, E-mail: raez@ipfw.edu.

College of Health and Human Services Students: 6 full-time (all women), 79 part-time (70 women); includes 8 minority (2 Black or African American, non-Hispanic/Latino; 3 Asian, non-Hispanic/Latino; 3 Hispanic/Latino). Average age 36. 14 applicants, 100% accepted, 10 enrolled. *Faculty:* 8 full-time (all women). *Financial support:* In 2015–16, 12 teaching assistantships with partial tuition reimbursements (averaging $13,522 per year) were awarded; scholarships/grants also available. Support available to part-time students. Financial award application deadline: 3/1; financial award applicants required to submit FAFSA. In 2015, 11 master's awarded. *Degree program information:* Part-time programs available. Part-time. Offers adult-gerontology primary care nurse practitioner (MS); family nurse practitioner (MS); health and human services (MS, DNP, Certificate); nurse executive (MS); nursing administration (Certificate); nursing education (MS). *Application deadline:* For fall admission, 5/15 priority date for domestic students, 5/1 priority date for international students; for spring admission, 11/15 for domestic students. Applications are processed on a rolling basis. *Application fee:* $55 ($60 for international students). Electronic applications accepted. *Application Contact:* Dr. Deb Poling, Chair/Director of Graduate Nursing Program, 260-481-6276, Fax: 260-481-5767, E-mail: polingd@ipfw.edu. *Dean*, Dr. Ann Obergfell, 260-481-0512, Fax: 260-481-5767, E-mail: obergfea@ipfw.edu.

Doermer School of Business Students: 58 full-time (18 women), 24 part-time (6 women); includes 20 minority (7 Black or African American, non-Hispanic/Latino; 5 Asian, non-Hispanic/Latino; 5 Hispanic/Latino; 3 Two or more races, non-Hispanic/Latino), 6 international. Average age 33. 64 applicants, 100% accepted, 54 enrolled. *Faculty:* 24 full-time (11 women). *Financial support:* In 2015–16, 8 teaching assistantships with partial tuition reimbursements (averaging $13,522 per year) were awarded; scholarships/grants and unspecified assistantships also available. Support available to part-time students. Financial award application deadline: 3/1; financial award applicants required to submit FAFSA. In 2015, 47 master's awarded. *Degree program information:* Part-time programs available. Part-time. Offers business (MBA). *Application deadline:* For fall admission, 7/15 for domestic students, 5/1 for international students; for spring admission, 11/15 for domestic students, 10/1 for international students. Applications are processed on a rolling basis. *Application fee:* $55. *Application Contact:* James Cashdollar, 260-481-6118, Fax: 260-481-6879, E-mail: cashdolj@ipfw.edu. *Interim Dean*, Dr. Joseph Khamalah, 260-481-6481, Fax: 260-481-6879, E-mail: khamaljn@ipfw.edu.

INDIANA UNIVERSITY–PURDUE UNIVERSITY INDIANAPOLIS, Indianapolis, IN 46202

General Information State-supported, coed, university. *Graduate housing:* Rooms and/or apartments available on a first-come, first-served basis to single and married students.

GRADUATE UNITS

Herron School of Art and Design Offers art education (MAE); art therapy (MA); furniture design (MFA); printmaking (MFA); sculpture (MFA); visual communication (MFA). Electronic applications accepted.

Indiana University School of Medicine Offers anatomy and cell biology (MS, PhD); biochemistry and molecular biology (MS, PhD); biostatistics (PhD); genetic counseling (MS); medical and molecular genetics (MS, PhD); medicine (MS, MD, PhD); microbiology and immunology (MS, PhD); pathology and laboratory medicine (MS, PhD); pharmacology (MS, PhD); toxicology (MS, PhD).

Stark Neurosciences Research Institute Offers neurosciences (PhD).

Kelley School of Business *Degree program information:* Part-time and evening/weekend programs available. Part-time, evening/weekend, online learning. Offers accounting (MSA); business (MBA). Electronic applications accepted.

Lilly Family School of Philanthropy Offers philanthropy (MA, XMA, PhD).

Robert H. McKinney School of Law Offers law (LL M, JD, SJD).

School of Dentistry Offers dentistry (MS, MSD, DDS, PhD, Certificate). Electronic applications accepted.

School of Education *Degree program information:* Part-time and evening/weekend programs available. Part-time, evening/weekend. Offers computer education (Certificate); curriculum and instruction (MS); early childhood (MS); educational leadership (MS, Certificate); English as a second language (Certificate); higher education and student affairs (MS); kindergarten (Certificate); language education (MS); reading (Certificate); school counseling (MS); special education (MS, Certificate).

School of Engineering and Technology *Degree program information:* Part-time and evening/weekend programs available. Part-time, evening/weekend. Offers biomedical engineering (MS, MS Bm E, PhD); computer-aided mechanical engineering (Certificate); electrical and computer engineering (MS, PhD); engineering (interdisciplinary) (MSE); engineering and technology (MS, MS Bm E, MSE, MSME, PhD, Certificate); mechanical engineering (MSME, PhD); music technology (MS); music therapy (MS).

School of Health and Rehabilitation Sciences *Degree program information:* Part-time and evening/weekend programs available. Part-time, evening/weekend. Offers health and rehabilitation sciences (PhD); health sciences (MS); nutrition and dietetics (MS); occupational therapy (MS); physical therapy (DPT); physician assistant (MPAS). Electronic applications accepted.

School of Informatics and Computing *Degree program information:* Part-time and evening/weekend programs available. Part-time, evening/weekend. Offers bioinformatics (MS, PhD); health informatics (MS, PhD); human-computer interaction (MS, PhD); information and library science (MLS); media arts and science (MS). Electronic applications accepted.

School of Liberal Arts Offers American philosophy (Certificate); applied communication (MA); bioethics (Certificate); economics (MA); English (MA); family/gender studies (MA); geographic information systems (MS, Certificate); health communication (PhD); history (MA); liberal arts (MA, MS, PhD, Certificate); medical sociology (MA); museum studies (MS, Certificate); philosophy (MA); political science (MA, Certificate); public history (MA); teaching English to speakers of other languages (TESOL) (Certificate); teaching writing (Certificate); work/occupations (MA).

School of Nursing *Degree program information:* Part-time programs available. Part-time. Offers nursing (MSN, DNP, PhD, Post-Master's Certificate); nursing education (MSN); nursing leadership in health systems (MSN); nursing science (PhD).

School of Physical Education and Tourism Management Offers physical education (MS).

School of Public and Environmental Affairs *Degree program information:* Part-time and evening/weekend programs available. Part-time, evening/weekend, online learning. Offers criminal justice and public safety (MS); homeland security and emergency management (Graduate Certificate); library management (Graduate Certificate); nonprofit management (Graduate Certificate); public affairs (MPA); public management (Graduate Certificate); social entrepreneurship: nonprofit and public benefit organizations (Graduate Certificate). Electronic applications accepted.

School of Public Health Offers biostatistics (MPH); environmental health science (MPH); epidemiology (MPH, PhD); health administration (MHA); health policy and management (MPH, PhD); social and behavioral sciences (MPH).

School of Science *Degree program information:* Part-time and evening/weekend programs available. Part-time, evening/weekend. Offers applied earth sciences (PhD); biology (MS, PhD); chemistry and chemical biology (MS, PhD); clinical psychology (MS); computer science (MS, PhD); forensic and investigative sciences (MS); geology (MS); industrial/organizational psychology (MS); mathematics (MS, PhD); physics (MS, PhD); psychobiology of addictions (PhD); science (MS, PhD, Graduate Certificate). Electronic applications accepted.

School of Social Work *Degree program information:* Part-time and evening/weekend programs available. Part-time, evening/weekend. Offers social work (MSW, PhD, Certificate).

INDIANA UNIVERSITY SOUTH BEND, South Bend, IN 46634-7111

General Information State-supported, coed, comprehensive institution. *Graduate housing:* On-campus housing not available.

GRADUATE UNITS

College of Liberal Arts and Sciences *Degree program information:* Part-time and evening/weekend programs available. Part-time, evening/weekend. Offers applied mathematics and computer science (MS); English (MA); liberal studies (MLS); public affairs (MPA).

Judd Leighton School of Business and Economics *Degree program information:* Part-time and evening/weekend programs available. Part-time, evening/weekend. Offers accounting (MSA); business administration (MBA); management of information technologies (MS).

Raclin School of the Arts *Degree program information:* Part-time programs available. Part-time. Offers music (MM); studio teaching (MM).

School of Education *Degree program information:* Part-time and evening/weekend programs available. Part-time, evening/weekend. Offers counseling and human services (MS Ed); elementary and secondary education leadership (MS Ed); elementary education (MS Ed); secondary education (MS Ed); special education (MAT, MS Ed). Electronic applications accepted.

Vera Z. Dwyer College of Health Sciences Offers health sciences (MSN, MSW).

School of Nursing *Degree program information:* Part-time and evening/weekend programs available. Part-time, evening/weekend. Offers family nurse practitioner (MSN).

School of Social Work *Degree program information:* Part-time and evening/weekend programs available. Part-time, evening/weekend. Offers social work (MSW).

INDIANA UNIVERSITY SOUTHEAST, New Albany, IN 47150-6405

General Information State-supported, coed, comprehensive institution. *Graduate housing:* On-campus housing not available.

GRADUATE UNITS

Master of Interdisciplinary Studies Program Offers interdisciplinary studies (MIS, MIS, Graduate Certificate).

School of Business Offers business administration (MBA); strategic finance (MS).

School of Education *Degree program information:* Part-time and evening/weekend programs available. Part-time, evening/weekend. Offers counselor education (MS Ed); elementary education (MS Ed); secondary education (MS Ed).

INDIANA WESLEYAN UNIVERSITY, Marion, IN 46953-4974

General Information Independent-religious, coed, comprehensive institution. *Enrollment:* 3,573 full-time matriculated graduate/professional students (2,425 women), 482 part-time matriculated graduate/professional students (279 women). *Enrollment by degree level:* 3,894 master's, 154 doctoral, 7 other advanced degrees. *Graduate faculty:* 92 full-time (37 women), 529 part-time/adjunct (248 women). *Graduate housing:* On-campus housing not available. *Student services:* Campus employment opportunities, campus safety program, career counseling, free psychological counseling, multicultural affairs office, services for students with disabilities, teacher training, writing training. *Library:* Lewis A. Jackson Library. Students can reserve study rooms. *Research affiliation:* Eli Lilly and Company (student internships).

Computer facilities: A campuswide network can be accessed from student residence rooms and from off campus. Online class registration is available.
Website: http://www.indwes.edu/

General Application Contact: Graduate School, 866-IWU-4-YOU, Fax: 765-677-2541, E-mail: graduate@indwes.edu.

GRADUATE UNITS

College of Adult and Professional Studies Students: 2,033 full-time (1,287 women), 313 part-time (152 women); includes 978 minority (761 Black or African American, non-Hispanic/Latino; 7 American Indian or Alaska Native, non-Hispanic/Latino; 43 Asian, non-Hispanic/Latino; 126 Hispanic/Latino; 41 Two or more races, non-Hispanic/Latino), 17 international. Average age 37. *Faculty:* 266 full-time (114 women), 22 part-time/adjunct (7 women). *Financial support:* Available to part-time students. Applicants required to submit FAFSA. *Degree program information:* Part-time and evening/weekend programs available. Part-time, evening/weekend, online learning. Offers accounting (MBA, Graduate Certificate); applied management (MBA); business administration (MBA); health care (MBA, Graduate Certificate); human resources (MBA, Graduate Certificate); management (MS); organizational leadership (MA, Ed D). *Application deadline:* Applications are processed on a rolling basis. *Application fee:* $25. Electronic applications accepted. *Application Contact:* Graduate School, 866-IWU-4-YOU, Fax: 765-677-2541, E-mail: graduate@indwes.edu. *Interim Vice President*, Audrey Hahn, 765-677-2762, E-mail: audrey.hahn@indwes.edu.

School of Educational Leadership Students: 195 full-time (131 women), 36 part-time (21 women); includes 65 minority (20 Black or African American, non-Hispanic/Latino; 11 Asian, non-Hispanic/Latino; 30 Hispanic/Latino; 4 Two or more races, non-Hispanic/Latino), 7 international. Average age 35. *Faculty:* 25 full-time (15 women), 5 part-time/adjunct (4 women). *Financial support:* Available to part-time students. Applicants required to submit FAFSA. *Degree program information:* Part-time and evening/weekend programs available. Part-time, evening/weekend, online learning. Offers educational leadership (M Ed, Ed S). *Application deadline:* Applications are processed on a rolling basis. *Application fee:* $25. Electronic applications accepted. *Application Contact:* Graduate School, 866-IWU-4-YOU, Fax: 765-677-2541, E-mail: graduate@indwes.edu. *Associate Dean*, Dr. Sally Ingles, 765-677-1536, Fax: 765-677-1456, E-mail: sally.ingles@indwes.edu.

Graduate School Students: 1,468 full-time (1,083 women), 169 part-time (127 women); includes 357 minority (243 Black or African American, non-Hispanic/Latino; 8 American Indian or Alaska Native, non-Hispanic/Latino; 21 Asian, non-Hispanic/Latino; 54 Hispanic/Latino; 1 Native Hawaiian or other Pacific Islander, non-Hispanic/Latino; 30 Two or more races, non-Hispanic/Latino), 42 international. Average age 37. *Financial support:* Fellowships, career-related internships or fieldwork, Federal Work-Study, scholarships/grants, and traineeships available. Support available to part-time students. Financial award applicants required to submit FAFSA. *Degree program information:* Part-time and evening/weekend programs available. Part-time, evening/weekend, online learning. *Application deadline:* Applications are processed on a rolling basis. *Application fee:* $25. Electronic applications accepted. *Application Contact:* Graduate School, 866-IWU-4-YOU, Fax: 765-677-2541, E-mail: graduate@indwes.edu. *Dean*, Dr. Jim Fuller, 765-677-2090, Fax: 765-677-2380.

College of Arts and Sciences Students: 114 full-time (81 women), 117 part-time (95 women); includes 11 minority (1 American Indian or Alaska Native, non-Hispanic/Latino; 1 Asian, non-Hispanic/Latino; 6 Hispanic/Latino; 3 Two or more races, non-Hispanic/Latino), 1 international. Average age 34. *Financial support:* In 2015–16, 1 research assistantship with partial tuition reimbursement, 1 teaching assistantship with partial tuition reimbursement were awarded. Support available to part-time students. Financial award application deadline: 3/1; financial award applicants required to submit FAFSA. *Degree program information:* Part-time programs available. Part-time. Offers addictions counseling (MS); clinical mental health counseling (MS); community counseling (MS); marriage and family therapy (MS); school counseling (MS); student development counseling and administration (MS). *Application deadline:* For fall admission, 6/14 priority date for domestic students. *Application fee:* $25. Electronic applications accepted. *Application Contact:* Graduate School, 866-IWU-4-YOU, Fax: 765-677-2541, E-mail: graduate@indwes.edu. *Director of Graduate Counseling Studies*, Dr. Mark Gerig, 765-677-2995, Fax: 765-677-1456, E-mail: mark.gerig@indwes.edu.

School of Nursing Students: 884 full-time (818 women), 27 part-time (all women); includes 148 minority (92 Black or African American, non-Hispanic/Latino; 5 American Indian or Alaska Native, non-Hispanic/Latino; 18 Asian, non-Hispanic/Latino; 16 Hispanic/Latino; 17 Two or more races, non-Hispanic/Latino), 2 international. Average age 38. *Financial support:* Fellowships, career-related internships or fieldwork, scholarships/grants, and traineeships available. Support available to part-time students. Financial award application deadline: 3/15; financial award applicants required to submit FAFSA. *Degree program information:* Part-time programs available. Part-time, online learning. Offers nursing administration (MS); nursing education (MS); primary care nursing (MS). *Application deadline:* Applications are processed on a rolling basis. *Application Contact:* Graduate School, 866-IWU-4-YOU, Fax: 765-677-2541, E-mail: graduate@indwes.edu. *Dean*, Dr. Barbara Ihrke, 765-677-2813, Fax: 765-677-1768, E-mail: barbara.ihrke@indwes.edu.

Wesley Seminary Students: 470 full-time (184 women), 25 part-time (5 women); includes 159 minority (112 Black or African American, non-Hispanic/Latino; 2 American Indian or Alaska Native, non-Hispanic/Latino; 2 Asian, non-Hispanic/Latino; 32 Hispanic/Latino; 1 Native Hawaiian or other Pacific Islander, non-Hispanic/Latino; 10 Two or more races, non-Hispanic/Latino), 39 international. Average age 41. Offers children, youth and family ministry (MA); divinity (M Div); ministerial leadership (MA); ministry (MA). *Dean*, Dr. David Smith, 765-677-4406, E-mail: david.smith@indwes.edu.

INSTITUTE FOR CHRISTIAN STUDIES, Toronto, ON M5T 1R4, Canada

General Information Independent-religious, coed, graduate-only institution. *Graduate housing:* On-campus housing not available.

GRADUATE UNITS

Graduate Programs *Degree program information:* Part-time programs available. Part-time, online learning. Offers education (M Phil F, PhD); history of philosophy (M Phil F, PhD); philosophical aesthetics (M Phil F, PhD); philosophy of religion (M Phil F, PhD); political theory (M Phil F, PhD); systematic philosophy (M Phil F, PhD); theology (M Phil F, PhD); worldview studies (MWS).

INSTITUTE FOR CLINICAL SOCIAL WORK, Chicago, IL 60601

General Information Independent, coed, primarily women, graduate-only institution. *Graduate housing:* On-campus housing not available.

GRADUATE UNITS

Graduate Programs *Degree program information:* Part-time programs available. Part-time. Offers clinical social work (PhD).

INSTITUTE FOR DOCTORAL STUDIES IN THE VISUAL ARTS, Portland, ME 04102

General Information Independent, coed, graduate-only institution.

GRADUATE UNITS

PhD Program in Visual Art: Philosophy, Aesthetics, and Art Theory Online learning. Offers aesthetics (PhD); art theory (PhD); philosophy (PhD). Electronic applications accepted.

THE INSTITUTE FOR THE PSYCHOLOGICAL SCIENCES, Arlington, VA 30327

General Information Independent-religious, coed, graduate-only institution.

GRADUATE UNITS

Program in Clinical Psychology *Degree program information:* Part-time programs available. Part-time. Offers clinical psychology (MS, Psy D).

INSTITUTE OF AMERICAN INDIAN ARTS, Santa Fe, NM 87508

General Information Federally supported, coed, comprehensive institution. *Enrollment:* 524 graduate, professional, and undergraduate students; 53 full-time matriculated graduate/professional students (32 women), 5 part-time matriculated graduate/professional students (4 women). *Enrollment by degree level:* 58 master's. Tuition, state resident: full-time $9360; part-time $390 per credit hour. Tuition, nonresident: full-time $9360; part-time $390 per credit hour. *Required fees:* $600; $300 per semester. *Graduate housing:* On-campus housing not available. *Student services:* Campus safety program, career counseling, exercise/wellness program, services for students with disabilities. *Library:* Fogelson Library plus 1 other. Students can reserve study rooms.

Computer facilities: 50 computers available on campus for general student use. A campuswide network can be accessed from student residence rooms. Online class registration is available.
Website: http://www.iaia.edu/

General Application Contact: Jon Davis, Director, Low Residency MFA in Creative Writing, 505-424-2365, Fax: 505-424-3030, E-mail: jdavis@iaia.edu.

GRADUATE UNITS

Low Residency MFA in Creative Writing Program Students: 53 full-time (32 women), 5 part-time (4 women); includes 35 minority (28 American Indian or Alaska Native, non-Hispanic/Latino; 2 Asian, non-Hispanic/Latino; 2 Hispanic/Latino; 3 Two or more races, non-Hispanic/Latino), 2 international. *Financial support:* Scholarships/grants available. Financial award application deadline: 1/31; financial award applicants required to submit FAFSA. In 2015, 15 master's awarded. Low-residency. Offers creative writing (MFA). *Application deadline:* For fall admission, 1/31 for domestic and international students. *Application fee:* $25. Electronic applications accepted. *Director, Low Residency MFA in Creative Writing*, Jon Davis, 505-424-2365, Fax: 505-424-3030, E-mail: mfa@iaia.edu.

INSTITUTE OF CLINICAL ACUPUNCTURE AND ORIENTAL MEDICINE, Honolulu, HI 96817

General Information Proprietary, coed, graduate-only institution.

GRADUATE UNITS

Program in Oriental Medicine Offers Oriental medicine (MSOM).

INSTITUTE OF PUBLIC ADMINISTRATION, Dublin 4, Ireland

General Information Proprietary, coed, comprehensive institution.

GRADUATE UNITS

Programs in Public Administration Offers healthcare management (MA); local government management (MA); public management (MA, Diploma).

THE INSTITUTE OF WORLD POLITICS, Washington, DC 20036

General Information Independent, coed, graduate-only institution. *Graduate housing:* On-campus housing not available.

GRADUATE UNITS

Graduate Programs in National Security, Intelligence, and International Affairs *Degree program information:* Part-time and evening/weekend programs available. Part-time, evening/weekend. Offers American foreign policy (Certificate); comparative political culture (Certificate); counterintelligence (Certificate); democracy building (Certificate); intelligence (Certificate); international politics (Certificate); national security affairs (Certificate); public diplomacy and political warfare (Certificate); statecraft and national security affairs (MA); statecraft and world politics (MA); strategic intelligence studies (MA). Electronic applications accepted.

INSTITUT FRANCO-EUROPEN DE CHIROPRAXIE, F-94200 Ivry-sur-Seine, France

General Information Independent, coed, graduate-only institution.

GRADUATE UNITS

Professional Program Offers chiropractic (DC).

INSTITUTO CENTROAMERICANO DE ADMINISTRACIÓN DE EMPRESAS, La Garita, Alajuela, Costa Rica

General Information Independent, coed, graduate-only institution. *Graduate housing:* Rooms and/or apartments guaranteed to single students and available to married students. *Research affiliation:* Tropical Agricultural Research and Higher Education Center (agribusiness), Harvard Institute for International Development (macroeconomics and environment), Earth University (agribusiness), Inter-American Institute for Cooperation on Agriculture (agribusiness), David Rockefeller Center for Latin American Studies (competitiveness), Zamarano (agribusiness).

GRADUATE UNITS

Graduate Programs Offers agribusiness management (MIAM); business administration (EMBA); finance (MBA); real estate management (MGREM); sustainable development (MBA); technology (MBA). Electronic applications accepted.

INSTITUTO TECNOLÓGICO Y DE ESTUDIOS SUPERIORES DE MONTERREY, CAMPUS CENTRAL DE VERACRUZ, 94500 Córdoba, Veracruz, Mexico

General Information Independent, coed, comprehensive institution.

GRADUATE UNITS

Graduate Programs ***Degree program information:*** Part-time and evening/weekend programs available. Part-time, evening/weekend, online learning. Electronic applications accepted.

INSTITUTO TECNOLÓGICO Y DE ESTUDIOS SUPERIORES DE MONTERREY, CAMPUS CHIAPAS, 29000 Tuxtla Gutiérrez, Chiapas, Mexico

General Information Independent, coed, comprehensive institution.

INSTITUTO TECNOLÓGICO Y DE ESTUDIOS SUPERIORES DE MONTERREY, CAMPUS CHIHUAHUA, 31300 Chihuahua, Chihuahua, Mexico

General Information Independent, coed, comprehensive institution.

GRADUATE UNITS

Graduate Programs Offers computer systems engineering (Ingeniero); electrical engineering (Ingeniero); electromechanical engineering (Ingeniero); electronic engineering (Ingeniero); engineering administration (MEA); industrial engineering (MIE, Ingeniero); international trade (MIT); mechanical engineering (Ingeniero).

INSTITUTO TECNOLÓGICO Y DE ESTUDIOS SUPERIORES DE MONTERREY, CAMPUS CIUDAD DE MÉXICO, 14380 Ciudad de Mexico, DF, Mexico

General Information Independent, coed, comprehensive institution. *Graduate housing:* On-campus housing not available. *Research affiliation:* McGill University (management), Concordia University (business and management), Eli Lilly S. A. de C. U. (technological development), Ford Motor Company (industrial organizations), German Research Center on Artificial Intelligence (informatics), Brent University (telecommunications).

GRADUATE UNITS

School of Business Administration ***Degree program information:*** Part-time and evening/weekend programs available. Part-time, evening/weekend, online learning. Offers business administration (EMBA, MBA, PhD); economy (MBA); finance (MBA). EMBA program offered jointly with The University of Texas at Austin.

School of Design, Engineering and Architecture ***Degree program information:*** Part-time and evening/weekend programs available. Part-time, evening/weekend, online learning. Offers management (MA); telecommunications (MA).

School of Humanities and Social Sciences ***Degree program information:*** Part-time and evening/weekend programs available. Part-time, evening/weekend. Offers humanities and social sciences (LL B).

Virtual University Division ***Degree program information:*** Part-time and evening/weekend programs available. Part-time, evening/weekend, online learning.

INSTITUTO TECNOLÓGICO Y DE ESTUDIOS SUPERIORES DE MONTERREY, CAMPUS CIUDAD JUÁREZ, 32320 Ciudad Juárez, Chihuahua, Mexico

General Information Independent, coed, comprehensive institution.

GRADUATE UNITS

Program in Administration of Information Technology Offers administration of information technology (MAIT).

Program in Applied Public Management Offers applied public management (MPM).

Program in Business Administration ***Degree program information:*** Part-time programs available. Part-time, online learning. Offers business administration (MBA).

Program in Education Offers education (M Ed).

Program in Educational Administration Offers educational administration (MEA).

Program in Educational Innovation Offers educational innovation (DE).

Program in Educational Technology Offers educational technology (MTE).

Program in Electronic Commerce Offers electronic commerce (MEC).

Program in Humanistic Studies Offers humanistic studies (MEH).

Program in Quality Management Offers quality management (MQM).

INSTITUTO TECNOLÓGICO Y DE ESTUDIOS SUPERIORES DE MONTERREY, CAMPUS CIUDAD OBREGÓN, 85000 Ciudad Obregón, Sonora, Mexico

General Information Independent, coed, comprehensive institution.

GRADUATE UNITS

Program in Administration Offers administration (MA).

Program in Administration of Information Technology Offers administration of information technology (MATI).

Program in Administration of Telecommunications Offers administration of telecommunications (MAT).

Program in Engineering Offers engineering (ME).

Program in Finance Offers finance (MF).

Program in International Relations Offers international relations (MIR).

Program in Marketing Technology Offers marketing technology (MMT).

Programs in Education Offers cognitive development (ME); communications (ME); mathematics (ME).

INSTITUTO TECNOLÓGICO Y DE ESTUDIOS SUPERIORES DE MONTERREY, CAMPUS COLIMA, 28010 Colima, Colima, Mexico

General Information Independent, coed, comprehensive institution.

INSTITUTO TECNOLÓGICO Y DE ESTUDIOS SUPERIORES DE MONTERREY, CAMPUS CUERNAVACA, 62000 Temixco, Morelos, Mexico

General Information Independent, coed, comprehensive institution.

GRADUATE UNITS

Programs in Business Administration Offers finance (MA); human resources management (MA); international business (MA); marketing (MA).

Programs in Information Science Offers administration of information technology (MATI); computer science (MCC, DCC); information technology (MTI).

INSTITUTO TECNOLÓGICO Y DE ESTUDIOS SUPERIORES DE MONTERREY, CAMPUS ESTADO DE MÉXICO, Estado de Mexico 52926, Mexico

General Information Independent, coed, comprehensive institution. *Graduate housing:* On-campus housing not available. *Research affiliation:* Transportadora San Marcos, S. A. de C. V. (quality control), Microsoft Visual Studio (computer science), Trinity (new products), Texas Instruments (semiconductors), Sony Electronics (new products), Kaltex (quality control).

GRADUATE UNITS

Professional and Graduate Division ***Degree program information:*** Part-time programs available. Part-time, online learning. Offers administration of information technologies (MITA); architecture (M Arch); business administration (GMBA, MBA); computer sciences (MCS, PhD); education (M Ed); educational institution administration (MAD); educational technology and innovation (PhD); electronic commerce (MEC); environmental systems (MS); finance (MAF); humanistic studies (MHS); information sciences and knowledge management (MISKM); information systems (MS); manufacturing systems (MS); marketing (MEM); quality systems and productivity (MS); science and materials engineering (PhD); telecommunications management (MTM).

INSTITUTO TECNOLÓGICO Y DE ESTUDIOS SUPERIORES DE MONTERREY, CAMPUS GUADALAJARA, 45140 Zapopan, Jalisco, Mexico

General Information Independent, coed, comprehensive institution. *Graduate housing:* Rooms and/or apartments available to single and married students. Housing application deadline: 8/30.

GRADUATE UNITS

Program in Business Administration ***Degree program information:*** Part-time and evening/weekend programs available. Part-time, evening/weekend, online learning. Offers business administration (IEMBA, M Ad).

Program in Finance Offers finance (MF).

INSTITUTO TECNOLÓGICO Y DE ESTUDIOS SUPERIORES DE MONTERREY, CAMPUS HIDALGO, 42090 Pachuca, Hidalgo, Mexico

General Information Independent, coed, comprehensive institution.

INSTITUTO TECNOLÓGICO Y DE ESTUDIOS SUPERIORES DE MONTERREY, CAMPUS IRAPUATO, 36660 Irapuato, Guanajuato, Mexico

General Information Independent, coed, comprehensive institution.

GRADUATE UNITS

Graduate Programs Offers administration (MBA); administration of information technology (MAIT); administration of telecommunications (MAT); architecture (M Arch); computer science (MCS); education (M Ed); educational administration (MEA); educational innovation and technology (DEIT); educational technology (MET); electronic commerce (MBA); environmental administration and planning (MEAP); environmental systems (MES); finances (MBA); humanistic studies (MHS); international management for Latin American executives (MIMLAE); library and information science (MLIS); manufacturing quality management (MMQM); marketing research (MBA).

INSTITUTO TECNOLÓGICO Y DE ESTUDIOS SUPERIORES DE MONTERREY, CAMPUS LAGUNA, 27250 Torreón, Coahuila, Mexico

General Information Independent, coed, comprehensive institution. *Graduate housing:* On-campus housing not available.

GRADUATE UNITS

Graduate School ***Degree program information:*** Part-time programs available. Part-time. Offers business administration (MBA); industrial engineering (MIE); management information systems (MS).

INSTITUTO TECNOLÓGICO Y DE ESTUDIOS SUPERIORES DE MONTERREY, CAMPUS LEÓN, 37120 León, Guanajuato, Mexico

General Information Independent, coed, comprehensive institution.

GRADUATE UNITS

Program in Business Administration ***Degree program information:*** Part-time programs available. Part-time. Offers business administration (MBA).

INSTITUTO TECNOLÓGICO Y DE ESTUDIOS SUPERIORES DE MONTERREY, CAMPUS MONTERREY, 64849 Monterrey, Nuevo León, Mexico

General Information Independent, coed, comprehensive institution. *Graduate housing:* Room and/or apartments available to single students; on-campus housing not available to married students. *Research affiliation:* IBM de Mexico (computer science), Southwest Research Institute (environment), Hylsa (steel), Vitro (glass products), Cydsa (petrochemicals), Cemex (cement).

GRADUATE UNITS

Graduate and Research Division ***Degree program information:*** Part-time and evening/weekend programs available. Part-time, evening/weekend. Offers agricultural parasitology (PhD); agricultural sciences (MS); applied statistics (M Eng); artificial intelligence (PhD); automation engineering (M Eng); biotechnology (MS); chemical engineering (M Eng); chemistry (MS, PhD); civil engineering (M Eng); communications

(MS); computer science (MS); education (MA); electrical engineering (M Eng); electronic engineering (M Eng); environmental engineering (M Eng); farming productivity (MS); food processing engineering (MS); industrial engineering (M Eng, PhD); informatics (PhD); information systems (MS); information technology (MS); manufacturing engineering (M Eng); mechanical engineering (M Eng); phytopathology (MS); systems and quality engineering (M Eng).

Graduate School of Business Administration and Leadership ***Degree program information:*** Part-time programs available. Part-time. Offers business administration (MA, MBA); finance (M Sc); international business (M Sc); management (PhD); management and leadership (M Sc, MA, MBA, PhD); marketing (M Sc).

INSTITUTO TECNOLÓGICO Y DE ESTUDIOS SUPERIORES DE MONTERREY, CAMPUS QUERÉTARO, 76130 Querétaro, Querétaro, Mexico

General Information Independent, coed, comprehensive institution. *Graduate housing:* Room and/or apartments guaranteed to single students; on-campus housing not available to married students. Housing application deadline: 6/15. *Research affiliation:* Transmisiones y Equipos Mecanicos (manufacturing design).

GRADUATE UNITS

School of Business Offers business (MBA).

INSTITUTO TECNOLÓGICO Y DE ESTUDIOS SUPERIORES DE MONTERREY, CAMPUS SALTILLO, 25270 Saltillo, Coahuila, Mexico

General Information Independent, coed, comprehensive institution.

INSTITUTO TECNOLÓGICO Y DE ESTUDIOS SUPERIORES DE MONTERREY, CAMPUS SAN LUIS POTOSÍ, 78140 San Luis Potosí, SLP, Mexico

General Information Independent, coed, comprehensive institution.

INSTITUTO TECNOLÓGICO Y DE ESTUDIOS SUPERIORES DE MONTERREY, CAMPUS SINALOA, 80800 Culiacán, Sinaloa, Mexico

General Information Independent, coed, comprehensive institution.

INSTITUTO TECNOLÓGICO Y DE ESTUDIOS SUPERIORES DE MONTERREY, CAMPUS SONORA NORTE, 83000 Hermosillo, Sonora, Mexico

General Information Independent, coed, comprehensive institution. *Graduate housing:* On-campus housing not available. *Research affiliation:* National Council for Science and Technology (engineering).

GRADUATE UNITS

Program in Business Offers business (MA).

Program in Education Offers education (MA).

Program in Technological Information Management Offers technological information management (MA).

INSTITUTO TECNOLÓGICO Y DE ESTUDIOS SUPERIORES DE MONTERREY, CAMPUS TAMPICO, 89120 Altimira, Tamaulipas, Mexico

General Information Independent, coed, comprehensive institution.

INSTITUTO TECNOLÓGICO Y DE ESTUDIOS SUPERIORES DE MONTERREY, CAMPUS TOLUCA, 50252 Toluca, Estado de Mexico, Mexico

General Information Independent, coed, comprehensive institution.

GRADUATE UNITS

Graduate Programs ***Degree program information:*** Part-time and evening/weekend programs available. Part-time, evening/weekend.

INSTITUTO TECNOLÓGICO Y DE ESTUDIOS SUPERIORES DE MONTERREY, CAMPUS ZACATECAS, 98000 Zacatecas, Zacatecas, Mexico

General Information Independent, coed, comprehensive institution.

INTER AMERICAN UNIVERSITY OF PUERTO RICO, AGUADILLA CAMPUS, Aguadilla, PR 00605

General Information Independent, coed, comprehensive institution.

GRADUATE UNITS

Graduate School ***Degree program information:*** Part-time and evening/weekend programs available. Part-time, evening/weekend. Electronic applications accepted.

INTER AMERICAN UNIVERSITY OF PUERTO RICO, ARECIBO CAMPUS, Arecibo, PR 00614-4050

General Information Independent, coed, comprehensive institution.

GRADUATE UNITS

Program in Anesthesia Offers anesthesia (MS).

Program in Business Administration Offers accounting (MBA); finance (MBA); human resources (MBA).

Program in Nursing Offers critical care nursing (MSN); surgical nursing (MSN).

Programs in Education Offers administration and educational supervision (MA Ed); counseling and guidance (MA Ed); curriculum and teaching (MA Ed); elementary education (MA Ed).

INTER AMERICAN UNIVERSITY OF PUERTO RICO, BARRANQUITAS CAMPUS, Barranquitas, PR 00794

General Information Independent, coed, comprehensive institution. *Graduate housing:* Rooms and/or apartments available to single and married students.

GRADUATE UNITS

Program in Business Administration Offers accounting (IMBA); finance (IMBA).

Program in Education Offers curriculum and teaching (M Ed); educational leadership and management (MA); elementary education (M Ed); information and library service technology (M Ed); special education (MA). Electronic applications accepted.

INTER AMERICAN UNIVERSITY OF PUERTO RICO, BAYAMÓN CAMPUS, Bayamón, PR 00957

General Information Independent, coed, comprehensive institution. *Enrollment:* 4,630 graduate, professional, and undergraduate students; 6 full-time matriculated graduate/professional students (4 women), 117 part-time matriculated graduate/professional students (68 women). *Enrollment by degree level:* 123 master's. *Graduate faculty:* 14 full-time (3 women), 5 part-time/adjunct (3 women). *Tuition, area resident:* Part-time $207 per credit. *Required fees:* $328 per semester. *Graduate housing:* Room and/or apartments available on a first-come, first-served basis to single students; on-campus housing not available to married students. Typical cost: $3113 per year ($6114 including board). *Student services:* Career counseling, free psychological counseling, international student services, services for students with disabilities. *Library:* Centro de Acceso a la Informacion plus 1 other. *Collection:* Books: 33,328 (physical), 203,163 (digital/electronic); Serial titles: 1,623 (physical), 2 (digital/electronic); Databases: 37. Weekly public service hours: 79; students can reserve study rooms. *Research affiliation:* Bayamon Central University.

Computer facilities: Computer purchase and lease plans are available. 660 computers available on campus for general student use. A campuswide network can be accessed from student residence rooms and from off campus. Online class registration is available.
Website: http://bayamon.inter.edu/

General Application Contact: Hector Vargas, Interim Director of Admissions, 787-279-1912 Ext. 2017, Fax: 787-279-2205, E-mail: hvargas@bayamon.inter.edu.

GRADUATE UNITS

Graduate School Students: 6 full-time (4 women), 117 part-time (68 women); includes 122 minority (1 Asian, non-Hispanic/Latino; 121 Hispanic/Latino). *Faculty:* 14 full-time (3 women), 5 part-time/adjunct (3 women). *Degree program information:* Part-time and evening/weekend programs available. Part-time, evening/weekend. Offers biology (MS); human resources (MBA). *Application deadline:* For fall admission, 7/1 for domestic students, 5/1 priority date for international students; for winter admission, 11/15 priority date for domestic and international students; for spring admission, 2/15 priority date for domestic and international students. *Application fee:* $31. *Application Contact:* Hector Vargas, Interim Director of Admissions, 787-279-1912 Ext. 2017, Fax: 787-279-2205, E-mail: hvargas@bayamon.inter.edu. *Chancellor,* Prof. Juan F. Martinez, 787-279-1200 Ext. 2295, Fax: 787-279-2205, E-mail: jmartinez@bayamon.inter.edu.

INTER AMERICAN UNIVERSITY OF PUERTO RICO, FAJARDO CAMPUS, Fajardo, PR 00738-7003

General Information Independent, coed, comprehensive institution.

GRADUATE UNITS

Graduate Programs

INTER AMERICAN UNIVERSITY OF PUERTO RICO, GUAYAMA CAMPUS, Guayama, PR 00785

General Information Independent, coed, comprehensive institution.

GRADUATE UNITS

Department of Business Administration Offers marketing (MBA).

Department of Education and Social Sciences ***Degree program information:*** Part-time programs available. Part-time. Offers early childhood education (0-4 years) (M Ed); elementary education (M Ed). Electronic applications accepted.

Department of Natural and Applied Sciences Offers computer security and networks (MS); networking and security (MCS).

INTER AMERICAN UNIVERSITY OF PUERTO RICO, METROPOLITAN CAMPUS, San Juan, PR 00919-1293

General Information Independent, coed, comprehensive institution. CGS member. *Graduate housing:* On-campus housing not available. *Research affiliation:* Innovation Technology (electronics).

GRADUATE UNITS

Graduate Programs ***Degree program information:*** Part-time and evening/weekend programs available. Part-time, evening/weekend. Offers accounting (MBA); administration of clinical laboratories (MS); advanced clinical services (MSW); advanced social work administration (MSW); American history (PhD); Christian education (PhD); clinical services (MSW); commercial education (MA); counseling psychology (MA, PhD); criminal justice (MA); curriculum and instruction (Ed D); educational administration (Ed D); educational computing (MA); elementary education (MA); English (MA); environmental evaluation and protection (MS); finance (MBA); general business (MBA); guidance and counseling (MA, Ed D); higher education administration (MA); history (MA, PhD); history education (MA); human resources (MBA); industrial management (MBA); industrial/organizational psychology (MA, PhD); international business (MIB); interregional and international business (PhD); labor relations (MA); management information systems (MBA); marketing (MBA); molecular microbiology (MS); music education (MM); occupational education (MA); open information systems (MS); pastoral theology (PhD); school psychology (MA, PhD); social work administration (MSW); Spanish (MA); Spanish education (MA); special education (MA); special education administration (Ed D); teaching English as a second language (MA); teaching of math (MA); teaching of physical education (MA); teaching of science (MA); theological studies (PhD); training and sport performance (MA); women's and gender studies (MA). Electronic applications accepted.

INTER AMERICAN UNIVERSITY OF PUERTO RICO, PONCE CAMPUS, Mercedita, PR 00715-1602

General Information Independent, coed, comprehensive institution.

GRADUATE UNITS

Graduate School

INTER AMERICAN UNIVERSITY OF PUERTO RICO, SAN GERMÁN CAMPUS, San Germán, PR 00683-5008

General Information Independent, coed, university. *Graduate housing:* Room and/or apartments available on a first-come, first-served basis to single students; on-campus housing not available to married students. Housing application deadline: 6/15.

GRADUATE UNITS

Graduate Studies Center ***Degree program information:*** Part-time and evening/weekend programs available. Part-time, evening/weekend. Offers accounting (MBA); applied mathematics (MA); business education (MA); counseling psychology (MA, PhD); curriculum and instruction (Ed D); drawing (MFA); education: counseling (MA, PhD); elementary education (MA); environmental sciences (MS); finance (MBA);

general business administration (MBA); graphic design (MFA); health and physical education (MA); human resources (MBA, PhD); industrial relations (MBA); information systems (MBA); international and interregional business (PhD); library sciences (MLS); management (MBA); marketing (MBA); music (MA); music teacher education (MA); painting (MFA); photography (MFA); printmaking (MFA); school psychology (MA, PhD); science education (MA); sculpture (MFA); special education (MA); teaching English as a second language (MA).

INTER AMERICAN UNIVERSITY OF PUERTO RICO SCHOOL OF LAW, San Juan, PR 00936-8351

General Information Independent, coed, graduate-only institution.

GRADUATE UNITS

Professional Program ***Degree program information:*** Part-time and evening/weekend programs available. Part-time, evening/weekend. Offers law (JD).

INTER AMERICAN UNIVERSITY OF PUERTO RICO SCHOOL OF OPTOMETRY, Bayamn, PR 00957

General Information Independent, coed, graduate-only institution. *Graduate housing:* Room and/or apartments available on a first-come, first-served basis to single students; on-campus housing not available to married students.

GRADUATE UNITS

Professional Program Offers optometry (OD). Electronic applications accepted.

INTERDENOMINATIONAL THEOLOGICAL CENTER, Atlanta, GA 30314-4112

General Information Independent-religious, coed, graduate-only institution. *Enrollment by degree level:* 237 master's, 28 doctoral. *Graduate faculty:* 15 full-time (6 women), 11 part-time/adjunct (4 women). *Tuition, area resident:* Full-time $13,000; part-time $9324 per credit. *Required fees:* $938; $938 per credit. Full-time tuition and fees vary according to course load. *Graduate housing:* Room and/or apartments available on a first-come, first-served basis to single students; on-campus housing not available to married students. Typical cost: $2525 per year. Room charges vary according to housing facility selected. Housing application deadline: 8/1. *Student services:* Campus employment opportunities, campus safety program, career counseling, exercise/wellness program, free psychological counseling, international student services, low-cost health insurance, services for students with disabilities. *Library:* Robert W. Woodruff Library. *Collection:* Books: 364,010 (physical). Students can reserve study rooms. *Research affiliation:* Atlanta University Center, Inc., Columbia Theological Seminary Library, Candler School of Theology Library, Emory University Library.

Computer facilities: 50 computers available on campus for general student use. A campuswide network can be accessed from student residence rooms. Online class registration is available.
Website: http://www.itc.edu/

General Application Contact: Michelle Davis, Office of Admission and Recruitment, 404-527-7793, E-mail: lmdavis@itc.edu.

GRADUATE UNITS

Graduate and Professional Programs Students: 131 full-time (53 women), 134 part-time (54 women); includes 258 minority (257 Black or African American, non-Hispanic/Latino; 1 Two or more races, non-Hispanic/Latino), 2 international. Average age 41. 218 applicants, 43% accepted, 68 enrolled. *Faculty:* 17 full-time (8 women), 10 part-time/adjunct (4 women). *Financial support:* Research assistantships, career-related internships or fieldwork, and Federal Work-Study available. Support available to part-time students. Financial award application deadline: 6/15; financial award applicants required to submit FAFSA. In 2015, 75 master's, 6 doctorates awarded. *Degree program information:* Part-time and evening/weekend programs available. Part-time, evening/weekend, blended/hybrid learning. Offers theology (M Div, MACE, D Min, Th D). D Min and Th D programs offered in collaboration with the Atlanta Theological Association. *Application deadline:* For fall admission, 7/1 for domestic and international students; for spring admission, 10/1 for domestic and international students. Applications are processed on a rolling basis. *Application fee:* $50. Electronic applications accepted. *Application Contact:* Michelle Davis, Office of Admission and Recruitment, 404-527-7793, E-mail: lmdavis@itc.edu. *President*, Edward Lorenza Wheeler, 404-527-7702, Fax: 404-527-7770.

INTERIOR DESIGNERS INSTITUTE, Newport Beach, CA 92660

General Information Proprietary, coed, comprehensive institution.

GRADUATE UNITS

Graduate Program Offers interior design (MA).

INTERNATIONAL BAPTIST COLLEGE AND SEMINARY, Chandler, AZ 85286

General Information Independent-religious, coed, comprehensive institution. *Graduate housing:* Room and/or apartments available on a first-come, first-served basis to single students; on-campus housing not available to married students.

GRADUATE UNITS

Program in Biblical Studies Offers Biblical studies (MA).

Program in Education Offers education (M Ed).

Program in Ministry Offers ministry (M Min, D Min).

INTERNATIONAL COLLEGE OF THE CAYMAN ISLANDS, Newlands, Grand Cayman, Cayman Islands

General Information Independent, coed, comprehensive institution. *Graduate housing:* Room and/or apartments available on a first-come, first-served basis to single students; on-campus housing not available to married students.

GRADUATE UNITS

Graduate Program in Management ***Degree program information:*** Part-time and evening/weekend programs available. Part-time, evening/weekend. Offers business administration (MBA); management (MS).

INTERNATIONAL INSTITUTE FOR RESTORATIVE PRACTICES, Bethlehem, PA 18018

General Information Independent, coed, graduate-only institution. *Enrollment by degree level:* 67 master's. *Graduate faculty:* 5 full-time (4 women). *Tuition, area resident:* Part-time $587 per credit.
Website: http://www.iirp.org/

General Application Contact: Jamie Kaintz, Registrar, 610-807-9221, Fax: 610-807-0423, E-mail: registrar@iirp.edu.

GRADUATE UNITS

Graduate Programs Students: 1 (woman) full-time, 66 part-time (49 women). *Faculty:* 5 full-time (4 women), 5 part-time/adjunct (2 women). *Financial support:* Institutionally sponsored loans and scholarships/grants available. Online learning. Offers restorative practices (MS, Certificate). *Application Contact:* Jamie Kaintz, Registrar, 610-807-9221, E-mail: registrar@iirp.edu.

INTERNATIONAL TECHNOLOGICAL UNIVERSITY, San Jose, CA 95113

General Information Independent, coed, graduate-only institution. CGS member. *Research affiliation:* Linux Works, Inc. (software), @Channel (software), New Trends Technology, Inc. (hardware), Pico Turbo, Inc. (hardware).

GRADUATE UNITS

Program in Business Administration ***Degree program information:*** Part-time and evening/weekend programs available. Part-time, evening/weekend. Offers business administration (MBA, DBA). Electronic applications accepted.

Program in Computer Engineering ***Degree program information:*** Part-time and evening/weekend programs available. Part-time, evening/weekend. Offers computer engineering (MSCE). Electronic applications accepted.

Program in Digital Arts ***Degree program information:*** Part-time programs available. Part-time. Offers digital arts (MA). Electronic applications accepted.

Program in Electrical Engineering ***Degree program information:*** Part-time and evening/weekend programs available. Part-time, evening/weekend. Offers electrical engineering (MSEE, PhD). Electronic applications accepted.

Program in Engineering Management ***Degree program information:*** Part-time and evening/weekend programs available. Part-time, evening/weekend. Offers engineering management (MSEM). Electronic applications accepted.

Program in Software Engineering ***Degree program information:*** Part-time and evening/weekend programs available. Part-time, evening/weekend. Offers software engineering (MSSE). Electronic applications accepted.

INTERNATIONAL UNIVERSITY IN GENEVA, CH-1215 Geneva 15, Switzerland

General Information Private, coed, comprehensive institution. *Graduate housing:* Room and/or apartments available on a first-come, first-served basis to single students; on-campus housing not available to married students. Housing application deadline: 7/31.

GRADUATE UNITS

Business Programs ***Degree program information:*** Part-time and evening/weekend programs available. Part-time, evening/weekend. Offers business administration (MBA, DBA); entrepreneurship (MBA); international business (MIB); international trade (MIT); sales and marketing (MBA). Electronic applications accepted.

Leadership Programs Offers international relations and diplomacy (MIRD); media and communication (MA); public administration (DPA). Electronic applications accepted.

THE INTERNATIONAL UNIVERSITY OF MONACO, MC-98000 Principality of Monaco, Monaco

General Information Independent, coed, comprehensive institution. *Graduate housing:* Rooms and/or apartments guaranteed to single and married students. *Research affiliation:* Alpstar (hedge funds).

GRADUATE UNITS

Graduate Programs ***Degree program information:*** Part-time programs available. Part-time. Offers entrepreneurship (EMBA, MBA); financial engineering (M Sc); hedge fund and private equity (M Sc); international marketing (EMBA, MBA); international wealth management (M Sc); luxury goods and services (EMBA, M Sc, MBA); wealth and asset management (EMBA, MBA). Electronic applications accepted.

IONA COLLEGE, New Rochelle, NY 10801-1890

General Information Independent-religious, coed, comprehensive institution. *Graduate housing:* On-campus housing not available. *Research affiliation:* IBM (teacher preparation).

GRADUATE UNITS

Hagan School of Business ***Degree program information:*** Part-time and evening/weekend programs available. Part-time, evening/weekend. Offers business (MBA, MS, AC, PMC); business administration (MBA); business continuity and risk management (AC); financial management (MBA); financial services (MS); general accounting (MBA, AC); health care management (MBA, AC); human resource management (PMC); information systems (PMC); international business (AC, PMC); international finance (MS); long term care services management (AC); management (MBA, PMC); public accounting (MBA, MS, AC); sports and entertainment management (AC). Electronic applications accepted.

School of Arts and Science ***Degree program information:*** Part-time and evening/weekend programs available. Part-time, evening/weekend. Offers adolescence education: biology (MS Ed, MST); adolescence education: English (MS Ed); adolescence education: mathematics (MST); adolescence education: social studies (MS Ed, MST); adolescence education: Spanish (MS Ed); adolescence special education 5-12 (MST); arts and science (MA, MS, MS Ed, MST, Certificate); childhood and special education (MST); communication sciences and disorders (MA); computer science (MS); cyber security (MS); early childhood and childhood (MST); educational leadership (MS Ed); English (MA); forensic criminology (Certificate); general-experimental psychology (MA); history (MA); human resources (Certificate); industrial-organizational psychology (MA); marriage and family therapy (MS); mental health counseling (MA); non-profit public relations (Certificate); organizational behavior (Certificate); psychology (MA); school psychology (MA); Spanish literature (MA). Electronic applications accepted.

IOWA STATE UNIVERSITY OF SCIENCE AND TECHNOLOGY, Ames, IA 50011

General Information State-supported, coed, university. CGS member. *Graduate housing:* Rooms and/or apartments available on a first-come, first-served basis to single and married students. Housing application deadline: 6/15. *Research affiliation:* National Veterinary Services Laboratories, National Animal Disease Center, National Soil Tilth Laboratory, North Central Regional Center for Rural Development, U.S. Department of Energy–Ames Laboratory.

GRADUATE UNITS

Bioinformatics and Computational Biology Program Offers bioinformatics and computational biology (MS, PhD). Electronic applications accepted.

Department of Accounting Offers accounting (M Acc). Electronic applications accepted.

Department of Aerospace Engineering and Engineering Mechanics Offers aerospace engineering (M Eng, MS, PhD); engineering mechanics (M Eng, MS, PhD). Electronic applications accepted.

Department of Agricultural Education and Studies Offers agricultural education and studies (MS, PhD). Electronic applications accepted.

Department of Agronomy Offers agricultural meteorology (MS, PhD); agronomy (MS); crop production and physiology (MS, PhD); plant breeding (MS, PhD); soil science (MS, PhD). Electronic applications accepted.

Department of Animal Science Offers animal breeding and genetics (MS, PhD); animal physiology (MS); animal psychology (PhD); animal science (MS, PhD); meat science (MS, PhD). Electronic applications accepted.

Department of Anthropology Offers anthropology (MA). Electronic applications accepted.

Department of Apparel, Education Studies, and Hospitality Management Offers family and consumer sciences education and studies (M Ed, MS, PhD); foodservice and lodging management (MFCS, MS, PhD); textiles and clothing (MFCS, MS, PhD). Electronic applications accepted.

Department of Architecture Offers architectural studies (MSAS); architecture (M Arch). Electronic applications accepted.

Department of Biomedical Sciences Offers biomedical sciences (MS, PhD). Electronic applications accepted.

Department of Chemical and Biological Engineering Offers chemical and biological engineering (M Eng, MS, PhD). Electronic applications accepted.

Department of Chemistry Offers chemistry (MS, PhD). Electronic applications accepted.

Department of Civil and Construction Engineering Offers civil engineering (MS, PhD). Electronic applications accepted.

Department of Community and Regional Planning Offers community and regional planning (MCRP); transportation (MS). Electronic applications accepted.

Department of Computer Science Offers computer science (MS, PhD). Electronic applications accepted.

Department of Curriculum and Instruction Offers curriculum and instructional technology (M Ed, MS, PhD); elementary education (M Ed, MS); historical, philosophical, and comparative studies in education (M Ed, MS); special education (M Ed, MS, PhD). Electronic applications accepted.

Department of Economics Offers agricultural economics (MS, PhD); economics (MS, PhD). JD/MS and JD/PhD offered jointly with Drake University and The University of Iowa. Electronic applications accepted.

Department of Educational Leadership and Policy Studies Offers counselor education (M Ed, MS); educational administration (M Ed, MS); educational leadership (PhD); higher education (M Ed, MS); organizational learning and human resource development (M Ed, MS); research and evaluation (MS); student affairs (MS). Electronic applications accepted.

Department of Electrical and Computer Engineering Offers computer engineering (M Eng, MS, PhD); electrical engineering (M Eng, MS, PhD). Electronic applications accepted.

Department of English Offers creative writing (MFA); English (MA); rhetoric and professional communication (PhD). Electronic applications accepted.

Department of Entomology Offers entomology (MS, PhD). Electronic applications accepted.

Department of Food Science and Human Nutrition Offers food science and technology (MS, PhD); nutrition (MS, PhD). Electronic applications accepted.

Department of Geological and Atmospheric Sciences Offers earth science (MS, PhD); environmental science (MS, PhD); geology (MS, PhD); meteorology (MS, PhD). Electronic applications accepted.

Department of History Offers agricultural history and rural studies (PhD); history (MA); history of technology and science (MA, PhD). Electronic applications accepted.

Department of Horticulture Offers horticulture (MS, PhD). Electronic applications accepted.

Department of Human Development and Family Studies Offers human development and family studies (MFCS, MS, PhD). Electronic applications accepted.

Department of Industrial and Manufacturing Systems Engineering Offers industrial engineering (M Eng, MS, PhD); operations research (MS); systems engineering (M Eng). Electronic applications accepted.

Department of Kinesiology Offers kinesiology (MS, PhD). Electronic applications accepted.

Department of Landscape Architecture ***Degree program information:*** Part-time programs available. Part-time. Offers landscape architecture (MLA). Electronic applications accepted.

Department of Materials Science and Engineering Offers materials science and engineering (MS, PhD). Electronic applications accepted.

Department of Mathematics Offers applied mathematics (MS, PhD); mathematics (MS, PhD); school mathematics (MSM). Electronic applications accepted.

Department of Mechanical Engineering Offers mechanical engineering (M Eng, MS, PhD); systems engineering (M Eng). Electronic applications accepted.

Department of Natural Resource Ecology and Management Offers forestry (MS, PhD); wildlife ecology (MS). Electronic applications accepted.

Department of Physics and Astronomy Offers applied physics (MS, PhD); astrophysics (MS, PhD); condensed matter physics (MS, PhD); high energy physics (MS, PhD); nuclear physics (MS, PhD); physics (MS, PhD). Electronic applications accepted.

Department of Plant Pathology Offers plant pathology (MS, PhD). Electronic applications accepted.

Department of Political Science Offers political science (MA); public administration (MPA). JD/MA offered jointly with Drake University. Electronic applications accepted.

Department of Psychology Offers cognitive psychology (PhD); counseling psychology (PhD); social psychology (PhD). Electronic applications accepted.

Department of Sociology Offers rural sociology (MS, PhD); sociology (MS, PhD). Electronic applications accepted.

Department of Statistics Offers statistics (MS, PhD). Electronic applications accepted.

Department of Veterinary Clinical Sciences Offers veterinary clinical sciences (MS). Electronic applications accepted.

Department of Veterinary Diagnostic and Production Animal Medicine Offers veterinary preventative medicine (MS). Electronic applications accepted.

Department of Veterinary Microbiology and Preventive Medicine Offers veterinary microbiology (MS, PhD). Electronic applications accepted.

Department of Veterinary Pathology Offers veterinary pathology (MS, PhD). Electronic applications accepted.

Greenlee School of Journalism and Mass Communication Offers journalism and mass communication (MS). Electronic applications accepted.

Program in Agricultural and Biosystems Engineering Offers agricultural and biosystems engineering (M En, MS, PhD). Electronic applications accepted.

Program in Agricultural Economics Offers agricultural economics (MS, PhD). Electronic applications accepted.

Program in Agricultural History and Rural Studies Offers agricultural history and rural studies (PhD). Electronic applications accepted.

Program in Agricultural Meteorology Offers agricultural meteorology (MS, PhD). Electronic applications accepted.

Program in Analytical Chemistry Offers analytical chemistry (PhD). Electronic applications accepted.

Program in Animal Breeding and Genetics Offers animal breeding and genetics (MS); immunogenetics (PhD); molecular genetics (PhD); quantitative genetics (PhD). Electronic applications accepted.

Program in Animal Physiology Offers animal physiology (MS, PhD). Electronic applications accepted.

Program in Apparel, Merchandising, and Design Offers apparel, merchandising, and design (MS, PhD). Electronic applications accepted.

Program in Applied Linguistics and Technology Offers applied linguistics and technology (PhD). Electronic applications accepted.

Program in Applied Mathematics Offers applied mathematics (MS, PhD). Electronic applications accepted.

Program in Applied Physics Offers applied physics (MS, PhD). Electronic applications accepted.

Program in Astrophysics Offers astrophysics (MS, PhD).

Program in Biophysics Offers biophysics (MS, PhD). Electronic applications accepted.

Program in Biorenewable Resources and Technology Offers biorenewable resources and technology (MS, PhD). Electronic applications accepted.

Program in Business Administration Offers business administration (MBA, MS); business and technology (PhD). Electronic applications accepted.

Program in Business and Technology Offers business and technology (PhD). Electronic applications accepted.

Program in Computer Engineering Offers computer engineering (M Eng, MS, PhD). Electronic applications accepted.

Program in Condensed Matter Physics Offers condensed matter physics (MS, PhD). Electronic applications accepted.

Program in Creative Writing and Environment Offers creative writing and environment (MFA). Electronic applications accepted.

Program in Crop Production and Physiology Offers crop production and physiology (MS, PhD). Electronic applications accepted.

Program in Diet and Exercise Offers diet and exercise (MS). Electronic applications accepted.

Program in Earth Science Offers earth science (MS, PhD). Electronic applications accepted.

Program in Ecology and Evolutionary Biology Offers ecology and evolutionary biology (MS, PhD). Electronic applications accepted.

Program in Engineering Mechanics Offers engineering mechanics (M Eng, MS, PhD). Electronic applications accepted.

Program in Environmental Sciences Offers environmental sciences (MS, PhD). Electronic applications accepted.

Program in Family and Consumer Sciences Offers family and consumer sciences (MFCS). Electronic applications accepted.

Program in Finance Offers finance (M Fin).

Program in Fisheries Biology Offers fisheries biology (MS, PhD). Electronic applications accepted.

Program in Forestry Offers forestry (MS, PhD). Electronic applications accepted.

Program in Genetics Offers genetics (MS, PhD). Electronic applications accepted.

Program in Graphic Design Offers graphic design (MFA). Electronic applications accepted.

Program in High Energy Physics Offers high energy physics (MS, PhD). Electronic applications accepted.

Program in History of Technology and Science Offers history of technology and science (MS, PhD). Electronic applications accepted.

Program in Human-Computer Interaction Offers human-computer interaction (MS, PhD). Electronic applications accepted.

Program in Immunobiology Offers immunobiology (MS, PhD). Electronic applications accepted.

Program in Industrial Agriculture and Technology Offers industrial agriculture and technology (MS, PhD). Electronic applications accepted.

Program in Industrial Design Offers industrial design (MID). Electronic applications accepted.

Program in Information Assurance Offers information assurance (MS). Electronic applications accepted.

Program in Inorganic Chemistry Offers inorganic chemistry (MS, PhD). Electronic applications accepted.

Program in Integrated Visual Arts Offers integrated visual arts (MFA).

Program in Interdisciplinary Graduate Studies Offers interdisciplinary graduate studies (MA, MS). Electronic applications accepted.

Program in Interior Design Offers interior design (MFA). Electronic applications accepted.

Program in Logistics, Operations, and Management Information Systems Offers information systems (MS). Electronic applications accepted.

Program in Meat Science Offers meat science (MS, PhD). Electronic applications accepted.

Program in Meteorology Offers meteorology (MS, PhD). Electronic applications accepted.

Program in Microbiology Offers microbiology (MS, PhD). Electronic applications accepted.

Program in Molecular, Cellular, and Developmental Biology Offers molecular, cellular, and developmental biology (MS, PhD). Electronic applications accepted.

Program in Neuroscience Offers neuroscience (MS, PhD). Electronic applications accepted.

Program in Nuclear Physics Offers nuclear physics (MS, PhD). Electronic applications accepted.

Program in Nutritional Sciences Offers nutritional sciences (MS, PhD). Electronic applications accepted.

Program in Organic Chemistry Offers organic chemistry (MS, PhD). Electronic applications accepted.

Program in Physical Chemistry Offers physical chemistry (MS, PhD). Electronic applications accepted.

Program in Plant Biology Offers plant biology (MS, PhD). Electronic applications accepted.

Program in Plant Breeding Offers plant breeding (MS, PhD). Electronic applications accepted.

Program in Professional Agriculture Online learning. Offers professional agriculture (M Ag). Electronic applications accepted.

Program in Rhetoric and Professional Communication Offers rhetoric and professional communication (PhD). Electronic applications accepted.

Program in Rhetoric, Composition, and Professional Communication Offers rhetoric, composition, and professional communication (MA). Electronic applications accepted.

Program in Rural Sociology Offers rural sociology (MS, PhD). Electronic applications accepted.

Program in School Mathematics Offers school mathematics (MSM). Electronic applications accepted.

Program in Science Education Offers science education (MAT). Electronic applications accepted.

Program in Seed Technology and Business Offers seed technology and business (MS). Electronic applications accepted.

Program in Soil Science Offers soil science (MS, PhD). Electronic applications accepted.

Program in Sustainable Agriculture Offers sustainable agriculture (MS, PhD). Electronic applications accepted.

Program in Systems Engineering Offers systems engineering (M Eng). Electronic applications accepted.

Program in Teaching English as a Second Language/Applied Linguistics Offers teaching English as a second language/applied linguistics (MA). Electronic applications accepted.

Program in Toxicology Offers toxicology (MS, PhD). Electronic applications accepted.

Program in Transportation Offers transportation (MS). Electronic applications accepted.

IRELL & MANELLA GRADUATE SCHOOL OF BIOLOGICAL SCIENCES, Duarte, CA 91010

General Information Independent, coed, graduate-only institution. *Enrollment by degree level:* 79 doctoral. *Graduate faculty:* 75 full-time (40 women). Full-time tuition and fees vary according to class time, course level, course load, degree level, campus/location, program and student level. *Graduate housing:* Room and/or apartments available on a first-come, first-served basis to single students; on-campus housing not available to married students. Housing application deadline: 7/31. *Student services:* Campus employment opportunities, campus safety program, career counseling, exercise/wellness program, free psychological counseling, grant writing training, international student services, low-cost health insurance, multicultural affairs office, writing training. *Library:* Lee Graff Medical and Scientific Library. Study areas open 24 hours, 5–7 days a week; students can reserve study rooms.

Computer facilities: 100 computers available on campus for general student use. A campuswide network can be accessed from student residence rooms and from off campus. Online class registration is available.
Website: http://www.cityofhope.org/grad-school

General Application Contact: Dr. Kate Sleeth, Interim Associate Dean of Administration and Student Development, 626-218-1742, Fax: 626-471-3901, E-mail: gradschool@coh.org.

GRADUATE UNITS

Graduate Program Students: 75 full-time (40 women); includes 28 minority (2 Black or African American, non-Hispanic/Latino; 10 Asian, non-Hispanic/Latino; 10 Hispanic/Latino; 2 Native Hawaiian or other Pacific Islander, non-Hispanic/Latino; 4 Two or more races, non-Hispanic/Latino), 15 international. Average age 26. 197 applicants, 12% accepted, 19 enrolled. *Faculty:* 70 full-time (18 women). *Financial support:* In 2015–16, 12 students received support, including 35 fellowships with full tuition reimbursements available (averaging $32,000 per year); teaching assistantships, health care benefits, and tuition waivers (full) also available. Financial award applicants required to submit FAFSA. In 2015, 12 doctorates awarded. Offers brain metastatic cancer (PhD); cancer and stem cell metabolism (PhD); cancer biology (PhD); cancer biology and developmental therapeutics (PhD); cell biology (PhD); chemical biology (PhD); chromosomal break repair (PhD); diabetes and pancreatic progenitor cell biology (PhD); DNA repair and cancer biology (PhD); germline epigenetic remodeling and endocrine disruptors (PhD); hematology and hematopoietic cell transplantation (PhD); hematology and immunology (PhD); inflammation and cancer (PhD); micrornas and gene regulation in cardiovascular disease (PhD); mixed chimrism for reversal of autoimmunity (PhD); molecular and cellular biology (PhD); molecular biology and genetics (PhD); nanoparticle mediated twist1 silencing in metastatic cancer (PhD); neuro-oncology and stem cell biology (PhD); neuroscience (PhD); rna directed therapies for hiv-1 (PhD); small rna-induced transcriptional gene activation (PhD); stem cell regulation by the microenvironment (PhD); translational oncology and pharmaceutical sciences (PhD); tumor biology (PhD). *Application deadline:* For fall admission, 1/1 priority date for domestic and international students. *Application fee:* $0. Electronic applications accepted. *Application Contact:* Dr. Kate Sleeth, Interim Associate Dean of Administration and Student Development, 626-218-1742, Fax: 626-471-3901, E-mail: gradschool@coh.org. *Dean*, Dr. John J. Rossi, 877-715-GRAD, Fax: 626-471-3901, E-mail: gradschool@coh.org.

ITHACA COLLEGE, Ithaca, NY 14850

General Information Independent, coed, comprehensive institution. *Enrollment:* 6,769 graduate, professional, and undergraduate students; 370 full-time matriculated graduate/professional students (277 women), 73 part-time matriculated graduate/professional students (46 women). *Enrollment by degree level:* 275 master's, 168 doctoral. *Graduate faculty:* 173 full-time (81 women), 5 part-time/adjunct (4 women). Tuition and fees vary according to program. *Graduate housing:* On-campus housing not available. *Student services:* Campus employment opportunities, campus safety program, career counseling, exercise/wellness program, free psychological counseling, international student services, low-cost health insurance, multicultural affairs office, services for students with disabilities, teacher training, writing training. *Library:* Ithaca College Library. *Collection:* Books: 306,820 (physical), 126,138 (digital/electronic); Databases: 151. Weekly public service hours: 148; study areas open 24 hours, 5–7 days a week. *Research affiliation:* National Science Foundation (physics), National Science Foundation (Noyce Teacher Scholarship Program for students in STEM), National Science Foundation (computer science), NASA (physics and astronomy), National Science Foundation (health sciences), Department of Health and Human Services/National Institutes of Health (biology).

Computer facilities: Computer purchase and lease plans are available. 640 computers available on campus for general student use. A campuswide network can be accessed from student residence rooms and from off campus. Online class registration is available.
Website: http://www.ithaca.edu/

General Application Contact: Nicole Eversley Bradwell, Interim Director, Office of Admission, 607-274-3124, Fax: 607-274-1263, E-mail: admission@ithaca.edu.

GRADUATE UNITS

Roy H. Park School of Communications Students: 2 full-time (1 woman), 17 part-time (11 women); includes 2 minority (both Black or African American, non-Hispanic/Latino), 3 international. Average age 31. 12 applicants, 58% accepted, 5 enrolled. *Faculty:* 9 full-time (2 women). *Financial support:* In 2015–16, 16 students received support, including 8 teaching assistantships (averaging $9,659 per year); career-related internships or fieldwork, Federal Work-Study, scholarships/grants, and unspecified assistantships also available. Support available to part-time students. Financial award application deadline: 3/1; financial award applicants required to submit CSS PROFILE or FAFSA. In 2015, 14 master's awarded. *Degree program information:* Part-time programs available. Part-time. Offers communications innovation (MS). *Application deadline:* For fall admission, 3/15 priority date for domestic and international students; for spring admission, 12/1 for domestic and international students. Applications are processed on a rolling basis. *Application fee:* $40. Electronic applications accepted. *Application Contact:* Nicole Eversley Bradwell, Interim Director, Office of Admission, 607-274-3124, Fax: 607-274-1263, E-mail: admission@ithaca.edu. *Dean*, Dr. Diane Gayeski, 607-274-3895, E-mail: gayeski@ithaca.edu.

School of Business Students: 31 full-time (13 women), 5 part-time (2 women); includes 2 minority (both Hispanic/Latino), 2 international. Average age 24. 48 applicants, 77% accepted, 29 enrolled. *Faculty:* 25 full-time (9 women), 1 (woman) part-time/adjunct. *Financial support:* In 2015–16, 21 students received support, including 20 fellowships (averaging $11,520 per year); career-related internships or fieldwork, Federal Work-Study, and scholarships/grants also available. Support available to part-time students. Financial award application deadline: 3/1; financial award applicants required to submit CSS PROFILE or FAFSA. In 2015, 25 master's awarded. *Degree program information:* Part-time programs available. Part-time. Offers business administration (MBA); professional accountancy (MBA). *Application deadline:* For fall admission, 5/15 for domestic and international students; for spring admission, 11/1 for domestic and international students. Applications are processed on a rolling basis. *Application fee:* $40. Electronic applications accepted. *Application Contact:* Nicole Eversley Bradwell, Interim Director, Office of Admission, 607-274-3124, Fax: 607-274-1263, E-mail: admission@ithaca.edu. *Dean*, Sean Reid, 607-274-3341, E-mail: sreid@ithaca.edu.

School of Health Sciences and Human Performance Students: 305 full-time (241 women), 21 part-time (17 women); includes 33 minority (7 Black or African American, non-Hispanic/Latino; 12 Asian, non-Hispanic/Latino; 8 Hispanic/Latino; 6 Two or more races, non-Hispanic/Latino), 5 international. Average age 23. *Faculty:* 60 full-time (42 women). *Financial support:* In 2015–16, 216 students received support, including 61 teaching assistantships (averaging $11,982 per year); career-related internships or fieldwork, Federal Work-Study, scholarships/grants, and unspecified assistantships also available. Support available to part-time students. Financial award applicants required to submit CSS PROFILE or FAFSA. In 2015, 97 master's, 82 doctorates awarded. *Degree program information:* Part-time programs available. Part-time. Offers exercise and sport sciences (MS); health education (MS); health sciences and human performance (MS, DPT); occupational therapy (MS); physical education (MS); physical therapy (DPT); speech-language pathology (MS); speech-language pathology with teacher certification (MS). *Application deadline:* Applications are processed on a rolling basis. *Application fee:* $40. Electronic applications accepted. *Application Contact:* Nicole Eversley Bradwell, Interim Director, Office of Admission, 607-274-3124, Fax: 607-274-1263, E-mail: admission@ithaca.edu. *Dean*, Dr. Linda Petrosino, 607-274-3265, Fax: 607-274-1263, E-mail: lpetrosino@ithaca.edu.

School of Humanities and Sciences Students: 13 full-time (11 women), 1 (woman) part-time. Average age 24. 37 applicants, 70% accepted, 14 enrolled. *Faculty:* 29 full-time (10 women). *Financial support:* In 2015–16, 13 students received support, including 13 teaching assistantships (averaging $9,420 per year); career-related internships or fieldwork, Federal Work-Study, scholarships/grants, and unspecified assistantships also available. Support available to part-time students. Financial award applicants required to submit CSS PROFILE or FAFSA. In 2015, 22 master's awarded. *Degree program information:* Part-time programs available. Part-time. Offers agriculture education (MAT); biology 7-12 (MAT); chemistry 7-12 (MAT); childhood education (MS); earth science 7-12 (MAT); English 7-12 (MAT); French 7-12 (MAT); humanities and sciences (MAT, MS); math 7-12 (MAT); physics 7-12 (MAT); social studies 7-12 (MAT); Spanish 7-12 (MAT). *Application deadline:* For fall admission, 2/15 priority date for domestic and international students; for spring admission, 12/1 for domestic and international students. Applications are processed on a rolling basis. *Application fee:* $40. Electronic applications accepted. *Application Contact:* Nicole Eversley Bradwell, Interim Director, Office of Admission, 607-274-3124, Fax: 607-274-1263, E-mail: admission@ithaca.edu. *Interim Dean*, Dr. Michael Richardson, 607-274-3102, E-mail: mrichardson@ithaca.edu.

School of Music Students: 19 full-time (11 women), 29 part-time (15 women); includes 6 minority (1 Black or African American, non-Hispanic/Latino; 2 Asian, non-Hispanic/Latino; 2 Hispanic/Latino; 1 Two or more races, non-Hispanic/Latino), 9 international. Average age 25. 145 applicants, 38% accepted, 31 enrolled. *Faculty:* 50 full-time (18 women), 4 part-time/adjunct (3 women). *Financial support:* In 2015–16, 43 students received support, including 43 teaching assistantships (averaging $10,052 per year); career-related internships or fieldwork, Federal Work-Study, scholarships/grants, and unspecified assistantships also available. Support available to part-time students. Financial award application deadline: 3/1; financial award applicants required to submit CSS PROFILE or FAFSA. In 2015, 50 master's awarded. *Degree program information:* Part-time programs available. Part-time. Offers composition (MM); conducting (MM); music (MM, MS); music education (MM, MS); performance (MM); Suzuki pedagogy (MM). *Application deadline:* For fall admission, 1/15 for domestic and international students; for spring admission, 12/1 for domestic and international students. Applications are processed on a rolling basis. *Application fee:* $40. Electronic applications accepted. *Application Contact:* Nicole Eversley Bradwell, Interim Director, Office of Admission, 607-274-3124, Fax: 607-274-1263, E-mail: admission@ithaca.edu. *Dean, School of Music,* Dr. Karl Paulnack, 607-274-3343, E-mail: kpaulnack@ithaca.edu.

JACKSON STATE UNIVERSITY, Jackson, MS 39217

General Information State-supported, coed, university. CGS member. *Graduate housing:* Room and/or apartments available on a first-come, first-served basis to single students; on-campus housing not available to married students. Housing application deadline: 7/15. *Research affiliation:* Lawrence A. Berkeley Laboratories (biology, chemistry), U.S. Department of Energy (biology), National Science Foundation (biology, chemistry), U.S. Environmental Protection Agency, Oak Ridge Associated Universities (science), Raytheon Systems Company (computer science).

GRADUATE UNITS

Graduate School ***Degree program information:*** Part-time and evening/weekend programs available. Part-time, evening/weekend, online learning.

College of Business Degree program information: Part-time and evening/weekend programs available. Part-time, evening/weekend. Offers accounting (MPA); business (MBA, MPA, PhD); business administration (MBA, PhD).

College of Education and Human Development Degree program information: Part-time and evening/weekend programs available. Part-time, evening/weekend. Offers community and agency counseling (MS); early childhood education (MS Ed, Ed D); education administration (Ed S); education and human development (MS, MS Ed, Ed D, PhD, Ed S); educational administration (MS Ed, PhD); elementary education (MS Ed, Ed S); guidance and counseling (MS, MS Ed); health, physical education and recreation (MS Ed); rehabilitation counseling (MS Ed); secondary education (MS Ed, Ed S); special education (MS Ed, Ed S).

College of Liberal Arts Degree program information: Part-time and evening/weekend programs available. Part-time, evening/weekend. Offers clinical psychology (PhD); criminology and justice services (MA); English (MA); history (MA); liberal arts (MA, MAT, MM Ed, MS, PhD); mass communications (MS); music education (MM Ed); political science (MA); sociology (MA); teaching English (MAT).

College of Public Service Offers communicative disorders (MS); public policy and administration (MPPA, PhD); public service (MPPA, MS, PhD); urban and regional planning (MS, PhD).

College of Science, Engineering and Technology Degree program information: Part-time and evening/weekend programs available. Part-time, evening/weekend. Offers chemistry and biochemistry (MS, PhD); computer science (MS); environmental science (MS, PhD); hazardous materials management (MS); mathematics (MS); science and mathematics teaching (MST); science, engineering and technology (MS, MS Ed, MST, PhD); technology education (MS Ed).

School of Social Work Degree program information: Evening/weekend programs available. Evening/weekend. Offers social work (MSW, PhD).

JACKSONVILLE STATE UNIVERSITY, Jacksonville, AL 36265-1602

General Information State-supported, coed, comprehensive institution. *Enrollment:* 8,314 graduate, professional, and undergraduate students; 203 full-time matriculated graduate/professional students (124 women), 809 part-time matriculated graduate/professional students (492 women). *Enrollment by degree level:* 884 master's, 19 doctoral, 109 other advanced degrees. *Graduate faculty:* 149 full-time (58 women), 24 part-time/adjunct (10 women). *Graduate housing:* Rooms and/or apartments available on a first-come, first-served basis to single and married students. *Student services:* Campus employment opportunities, campus safety program, career counseling, child daycare facilities, exercise/wellness program, free psychological counseling, international student services, multicultural affairs office, services for students with disabilities. *Library:* Houston Cole Library.

Computer facilities: 350 computers available on campus for general student use. A campuswide network can be accessed from student residence rooms and from off campus. Online class registration is available.
Website: http://www.jsu.edu/

General Application Contact: Dr. Joe Delap, Associate Vice President for Academic Affairs, 256-782-5284, E-mail: jdelap@jsu.edu.

GRADUATE UNITS

College of Graduate Studies and Continuing Education Students: 179 full-time (123 women), 752 part-time (465 women); includes 156 minority (147 Black or African American, non-Hispanic/Latino; 4 American Indian or Alaska Native, non-Hispanic/Latino; 1 Asian, non-Hispanic/Latino; 4 Hispanic/Latino), 37 international. Average age 33. 677 applicants, 43% accepted, 164 enrolled. *Faculty:* 148 full-time (56 women), 23 part-time/adjunct (8 women). *Financial support:* In 2015–16, 216 students received support. Available to part-time students. Application deadline: 3/15; applicants required to submit FAFSA. In 2015, 274 master's, 44 other advanced degrees awarded. *Degree program information:* Part-time and evening/weekend programs available. Part-time, evening/weekend. *Application deadline:* Applications are processed on a rolling basis. *Application fee:* $35. Electronic applications accepted. *Application Contact:* Dr. Jean Pugliese, Associate Dean, 256-782-8278, Fax: 256-782-5321, E-mail: pugliese@jsu.edu. *Vice Provost and Dean of Graduate Studies,* Dr. Joe Delap, 256-782-8186, E-mail: jdelap@jsu.edu.

College of Arts and Sciences Students: 56 full-time (35 women), 236 part-time (115 women); includes 45 minority (41 Black or African American, non-Hispanic/Latino; 1 American Indian or Alaska Native, non-Hispanic/Latino; 1 Asian, non-Hispanic/Latino; 2 Hispanic/Latino), 17 international. Average age 33. 333 applicants, 45% accepted, 66 enrolled. *Faculty:* 95 full-time (29 women), 10 part-time/adjunct (4 women). *Financial support:* In 2015–16, 108 students received support. Available to part-time students. Application deadline: 4/1; applicants required to submit FAFSA. In 2015, 84 master's awarded. *Degree program information:* Part-time and evening/weekend programs available. Part-time, evening/weekend, 100% online, blended/hybrid learning. Offers arts and sciences (MA, MPA, MS, D Sc); biology (MS); computer systems and software design (MS); criminal justice (MS); emergency management (MS, D Sc); English (MA); history (MA); liberal studies (MA); mathematics (MS); music (MA); political science (MPA); psychology (MS). *Application deadline:* Applications are processed on a rolling basis. *Application fee:* $35. *Application Contact:* Dr. Jean Pugliese, Associate Dean, 256-782-8278, Fax: 256-782-5321, E-mail: pugliese@jsu.edu. *Dean,* Dr. Earl Wade, 256-782-5649, E-mail: jwade@jsu.edu.

College of Commerce and Business Administration Students: 12 full-time (3 women), 48 part-time (21 women); includes 1 minority (Black or African American, non-Hispanic/Latino), 10 international. Average age 29. 68 applicants, 41% accepted, 22 enrolled. *Faculty:* 9 full-time (1 woman). *Financial support:* In 2015–16, 12 students received support. Available to part-time students. Application deadline: 4/1; applicants required to submit FAFSA. In 2015, 17 master's awarded. *Degree program information:* Part-time and evening/weekend programs available. Part-time, evening/weekend. Offers commerce and business administration (MBA). *Application deadline:* Applications are processed on a rolling basis. *Application fee:* $35. Electronic applications accepted. *Application Contact:* Dr. Jean Pugliese, Associate Dean, 256-782-8278, Fax: 256-782-5321, E-mail: pugliese@jsu.edu. *Dean,* Dr. William Fielding, 256-782-5508, E-mail: fielding@jsu.edu.

College of Education and Professional Studies Students: 101 full-time (75 women), 412 part-time (277 women); includes 98 minority (93 Black or African American, non-Hispanic/Latino; 3 American Indian or Alaska Native, non-Hispanic/Latino; 2 Hispanic/Latino), 9 international. Average age 32. 256 applicants, 35% accepted, 70 enrolled. *Faculty:* 40 full-time (23 women), 12 part-time/adjunct (4 women). *Financial support:* In 2015–16, 90 students received support. Available to part-time students. Application deadline: 4/1; applicants required to submit FAFSA. In 2015, 198 master's, 47 other advanced degrees awarded. *Degree program information:* Part-time and evening/weekend programs available. Part-time, evening/weekend. Offers early childhood education (MS Ed); education (Ed S); education and professional studies (MS, MS Ed, Ed S); educational administration (MS Ed, Ed S); elementary education (MS Ed); guidance and counseling (MS); instructional media (MS Ed); physical education (MS Ed, Ed S); reading specialist (MS Ed); secondary education (MS Ed); special education (MS Ed). *Application deadline:* Applications are processed on a rolling basis. *Application fee:* $35. Electronic applications accepted. *Application Contact:* Dr. Jean Pugliese, Associate Dean, 256-782-8278, Fax: 256-782-5321, E-mail: pugliese@jsu.edu. *Dean,* Dr. John Hammett, 256-782-8212, E-mail: jhammett@jsu.edu.

College of Nursing Students: 10 full-time (all women), 43 part-time (41 women); includes 6 minority (all Black or African American, non-Hispanic/Latino). Average age 41. 19 applicants, 63% accepted, 10 enrolled. *Faculty:* 3 full-time (all women), 1 part-time/adjunct (0 women). *Financial support:* Available to part-time students. Application deadline: 4/1; applicants required to submit FAFSA. In 2015, 14 master's awarded. *Degree program information:* Part-time and evening/weekend programs available. Part-time, evening/weekend. Offers nursing (MSN). *Application deadline:* Applications are processed on a rolling basis. *Application fee:* $35. Electronic applications accepted. *Application Contact:* Dr. Jean Pugliese, Associate Dean, 256-782-8278, Fax: 256-782-5321, E-mail: pugliese@jsu.edu. *Dean,* Dr. Sarah Latham, 256-782-5431, E-mail: slatham@jsu.edu.

JACKSONVILLE UNIVERSITY, Jacksonville, FL 32211

General Information Independent, coed, comprehensive institution. *Enrollment:* 4,048 graduate, professional, and undergraduate students; 300 full-time matriculated graduate/professional students (193 women), 716 part-time matriculated graduate/professional students (552 women). *Enrollment by degree level:* 873 master's, 85 doctoral, 35 other advanced degrees. *Graduate faculty:* 14 full-time (8 women), 19 part-time/adjunct (10 women). *Tuition, area resident:* Full-time $12,960; part-time $8640 per credit hour. One-time fee: $50. Tuition and fees vary according to course load, degree level, campus/location and program. *Graduate housing:* Room and/or apartments available on a first-come, first-served basis to single students; on-campus housing not available to married students. Typical cost: $8800 per year ($13,320 including board). Room and board charges vary according to board plan and housing facility selected. Housing application deadline: 8/1. *Student services:* Campus employment opportunities, campus safety program, career counseling, exercise/wellness program, free psychological counseling, international student services, low-cost health insurance, multicultural affairs office, services for students with disabilities, teacher training, writing training. *Library:* Carl S. Swisher Library. *Collection:* Books: 156,688 (physical), 148,457 (digital/electronic); Serial titles: 183,530 (physical); Databases: 2. Weekly public service hours: 88; students can reserve study rooms.

Computer facilities: Computer purchase and lease plans are available. 400 computers available on campus for general student use. A campuswide network can be accessed from student residence rooms and from off campus. Online class registration, Blackboard and Web Advisor are available.
Website: http://www.ju.edu/

General Application Contact: Allana Forte, Director of Admissions and Recruitment, 904-256-7000, E-mail: admissions@ju.edu.

GRADUATE UNITS

College of Fine Arts Offers choreography (MFA); visual arts (MFA). *Application Contact:* Cari Coble, MFA Coordinator, 904-256-7398, E-mail: ccoble@ju.edu.

Davis College of Business Students: 149 full-time (61 women), 43 part-time (20 women); includes 62 minority (33 Black or African American, non-Hispanic/Latino; 1 American Indian or Alaska Native, non-Hispanic/Latino; 10 Asian, non-Hispanic/Latino; 17 Hispanic/Latino; 1 Native Hawaiian or other Pacific Islander, non-Hispanic/Latino), 25 international. Average age 31. 152 applicants, 54% accepted, 63 enrolled. *Faculty:* 22 full-time (5 women), 1 part-time/adjunct (0 women). *Financial support:* Unspecified assistantships available. Financial award application deadline: 7/1; financial award applicants required to submit FAFSA. In 2015, 124 master's awarded. *Degree program information:* Part-time and evening/weekend programs available. Part-time, evening/weekend. Offers accounting and finance (MBA); business (MBA, MS); consumer goods and services marketing (MBA); leadership development (MBA); management (MBA); management accounting (MBA); organizational leadership (MS). *Application deadline:* For fall admission, 8/1 priority date for domestic students, 7/15 priority date for international students; for spring admission, 12/1 priority date for domestic students, 11/15 priority date for international students; for summer admission, 4/1 priority date for domestic students, 3/15 priority date for international students. Applications are processed on a rolling basis. *Application fee:* $50. Electronic applications accepted. *Application Contact:* AnnaMaria Murphy, Admissions Counselor, 904-256-7426, Fax: 904-256-7168, E-mail: mba@ju.edu. *Dean,* Dr. Don Capener, 904-256-7431, Fax: 904-256-7467, E-mail: dcapene@ju.edu.

Marine Science Research Institute Offers marine science (MA, MS). *Application Contact:* Marisol Preston, Chief Admissions Officer, 904-256-7000, E-mail:

admissions@ju.edu. *Executive Director*, Dr. A. Quinton White, Jr., 904-256-7100, E-mail: qwhite@ju.edu.

School of Applied Health Sciences Offers health informatics (MS); kinesiological sciences (MS); mental health counseling (MS); speech language pathology (MS). *Application Contact:* Marisol Preston, Chief Admissions Officer, 904-256-7000, E-mail: admissions@ju.edu.

School of Nursing ***Financial support:*** Federal Work-Study, institutionally sponsored loans, and scholarships/grants available. Support available to part-time students. Financial award application deadline: 3/15. *Degree program information:* Part-time programs available. Part-time. Offers nursing (MSN, DNP). *Application fee:* $50. *Application Contact:* Marisol Preston, Chief Admissions Officer, 904-256-7000, E-mail: admissions@ju.edu. *Assistant Dean*, Dr. Leigh B. Hart, 904-256-7600, E-mail: lhart@ju.edu.

School of Orthodontics Offers orthodontics (Certificate). *Application deadline:* For fall admission, 9/30 for domestic students. Applications are processed on a rolling basis. *Application fee:* $175. *Application Contact:* Marisol Preston, Chief Admissions Officer, 904-256-7000, E-mail: admissions@ju.edu. *Dean*, Dr. Laurance Jerrold, 904-256-7847, E-mail: ljerrol@ju.edu.

★ JAMES MADISON UNIVERSITY, Harrisonburg, VA 22807

General Information State-supported, coed, comprehensive institution. CGS member. *Enrollment:* 21,227 graduate, professional, and undergraduate students; 1,110 full-time matriculated graduate/professional students (810 women), 484 part-time matriculated graduate/professional students (297 women). *Enrollment by degree level:* 1,361 master's, 164 doctoral, 69 other advanced degrees. *Graduate faculty:* 539 full-time (261 women), 54 part-time/adjunct (29 women). *Graduate housing:* On-campus housing not available. *Student services:* Campus employment opportunities, campus safety program, career counseling, exercise/wellness program, free psychological counseling, international student services, multicultural affairs office, services for students with disabilities, teacher training, writing training. *Library:* Carrier Library. *Research affiliation:* National Institute of Standards and Technology (NIST) through George Mason University (network risk assessment), National Science Foundation (science, technology, engineering, and math (STEM)), National Oceanic and Atmospheric Administration (NOAA) (applied meteorological research), National Science Foundation (quantitative skills in biology), National Science Foundation (development of a detector array for Compton Scattering using polarized beams and targets).

Computer facilities: Computer purchase and lease plans are available. A campuswide network can be accessed from student residence rooms and from off campus. Online class registration is available.
Website: http://www.jmu.edu/

General Application Contact: Dr. Jie Chen, Dean, The Graduate School, 540-568-4213, Fax: 540-568-7860, E-mail: grad@jmu.edu.

GRADUATE UNITS

The Graduate School Students: 1,110 full-time (810 women), 484 part-time (297 women); includes 208 minority (68 Black or African American, non-Hispanic/Latino; 3 American Indian or Alaska Native, non-Hispanic/Latino; 42 Asian, non-Hispanic/Latino; 53 Hispanic/Latino; 42 Two or more races, non-Hispanic/Latino), 45 international. Average age 30. 2,418 applicants, 47% accepted, 827 enrolled. *Faculty:* 539 full-time (261 women), 54 part-time/adjunct (29 women). *Financial support:* In 2015–16, 425 students received support, including 55 fellowships, 44 teaching assistantships with full tuition reimbursements available (averaging $8,837 per year); career-related internships or fieldwork, Federal Work-Study, unspecified assistantships, and 25 athletic assistantships (averaging $8837), 7 service assistantships (averaging $7530), 76 doctoral assistantships also available. Financial award application deadline: 3/1; financial award applicants required to submit FAFSA. In 2015, 729 master's, 38 doctorates, 19 other advanced degrees awarded. *Degree program information:* Part-time and evening/weekend programs available. Part-time, evening/weekend, 100% online, blended/hybrid learning. *Application fee:* $55. Electronic applications accepted. *Application Contact:* Lynette D. Michael, Director of Graduate Admissions, 540-568-6131 Ext. 6395, Fax: 540-568-7860, E-mail: michaeld@jmu.edu. *Dean, The Graduate School*, Dr. Jie Chen, 540-568-4213, Fax: 540-568-7860, E-mail: grad@jmu.edu.

College of Arts and Letters Students: 97 full-time (60 women), 36 part-time (16 women); includes 17 minority (7 Black or African American, non-Hispanic/Latino; 1 Asian, non-Hispanic/Latino; 2 Hispanic/Latino; 7 Two or more races, non-Hispanic/Latino), 2 international. Average age 30. 117 applicants, 90% accepted, 58 enrolled. *Faculty:* 110 full-time (54 women), 4 part-time/adjunct (all women). *Financial support:* In 2015–16, 40 students received support, including 17 teaching assistantships with full tuition reimbursements available (averaging $8,837 per year); Federal Work-Study, unspecified assistantships, and 46 assistantships (averaging $7530) also available. Financial award application deadline: 3/1; financial award applicants required to submit FAFSA. In 2015, 59 master's awarded. *Degree program information:* Part-time programs available. Part-time. Offers arts and letters (MA, MPA, MS); English (MA); environmental communication (MA); health communication (MA); individualized (MPA); local/regional/public history (MA); political science (MA); public management (MPA); United States history (MA); world history (MA); writing, rhetoric and technical communication (MA, MS). *Application fee:* $55. Electronic applications accepted. *Application Contact:* Lynette D. Michael, Director of Graduate Admissions, 540-568-6131 Ext. 6395, Fax: 540-568-7860, E-mail: michaeld@jmu.edu. *Dean*, Dr. David K. Jeffrey, 540-568-7044.

College of Business Students: 116 full-time (42 women), 102 part-time (37 women); includes 35 minority (15 Black or African American, non-Hispanic/Latino; 12 Asian, non-Hispanic/Latino; 4 Hispanic/Latino; 4 Two or more races, non-Hispanic/Latino), 7 international. Average age 30. 164 applicants, 80% accepted, 109 enrolled. *Faculty:* 48 full-time (12 women), 2 part-time/adjunct (1 woman). *Financial support:* In 2015–16, 32 students received support. Career-related internships or fieldwork, Federal Work-Study, unspecified assistantships, and assistantships (averaging $7530), athletic assistantships, doctoral assistantships available. Financial award application deadline: 3/1; financial award applicants required to submit FAFSA. In 2015, 89 master's, 8 doctorates awarded. *Degree program information:* Part-time and evening/weekend programs available. Part-time, evening/weekend, blended/hybrid learning. Offers accounting information systems (MS); business (MBA, MS, PhD); executive leadership (MBA); postsecondary analysis and leadership (PhD); taxation (MS). *Application fee:* $55. Electronic applications accepted. *Application Contact:* Lynette D. Michael, Director of Graduate Admissions, 540-568-6395, Fax: 540-568-7860, E-mail: michaeld@jmu.edu. *Dean*, Dr. Mary A. Gowan, 540-568-3254, E-mail: gowanma@jmu.edu.

College of Education Students: 337 full-time (302 women), 113 part-time (82 women); includes 54 minority (10 Black or African American, non-Hispanic/Latino; 1 American Indian or Alaska Native, non-Hispanic/Latino; 8 Asian, non-Hispanic/Latino; 22 Hispanic/Latino; 13 Two or more races, non-Hispanic/Latino), 4 international. Average age 30. 415 applicants, 97% accepted, 360 enrolled. *Faculty:* 62 full-time (42 women), 14 part-time/adjunct (10 women). *Financial support:* In 2015–16, 38 students received support. Career-related internships or fieldwork, Federal Work-Study, unspecified assistantships, and assistantships (averaging $7530), athletic assistantship (averaging $8837) available. Financial award application deadline: 3/1; financial award applicants required to submit FAFSA. In 2015, 347 master's awarded. *Degree program information:* Part-time and evening/weekend programs available. Part-time, evening/weekend, 100% online, blended/hybrid learning. Offers adapted curriculum (MAT); autism (M Ed); behavior specialist (M Ed); early childhood education (MAT); early childhood education (preK-3) (MAT); early childhood special edication (MAT); education (M Ed, MAT, MS Ed); educational leadership (M Ed); educational technology (M Ed); elementary education (MAT); equity and cultural diversity (M Ed); general curriculum K-12 special education (MAT); gifted education (M Ed); higher education (MS Ed); human resource management (MS Ed); inclusive early childhood education (MAT); inclusive early childhood special education (MAT); individualized (MS Ed); instructional design (MS Ed); instructional specialist (M Ed); K-12 special education (MAT); K-8 math specialist (M Ed); K-8 mathematics specialist (M Ed); leadership and facilitation (MS Ed); mathematics (M Ed); middle education (MAT); program evaluation and measurement (MS Ed); reading education (M Ed); secondary education (MAT); Spanish language and culture for educators (M Ed); TESOL (MAT); visual impairments (MAT). *Application fee:* $55. Electronic applications accepted. *Application Contact:* Lynette D. Michael, Director of Graduate Admissions, 540-568-6131 Ext. 6395, Fax: 540-568-7860, E-mail: michaeld@jmu.edu. *Dean*, Dr. Phillip M. Wishon, 540-568-6572, E-mail: wishonpm@jmu.edu.

College of Health and Behavioral Sciences Students: 457 full-time (352 women), 150 part-time (121 women); includes 74 minority (27 Black or African American, non-Hispanic/Latino; 2 American Indian or Alaska Native, non-Hispanic/Latino; 16 Asian, non-Hispanic/Latino; 15 Hispanic/Latino; 14 Two or more races, non-Hispanic/Latino), 9 international. Average age 30. 1,566 applicants, 25% accepted, 246 enrolled. *Faculty:* 177 full-time (99 women), 28 part-time/adjunct (14 women). *Financial support:* In 2015–16, 222 students received support, including 18 teaching assistantships with full tuition reimbursements available (averaging $8,837 per year); career-related internships or fieldwork, Federal Work-Study, unspecified assistantships, and athletic assistantships (averaging $8837), service assistantships (averaging $7,530), doctoral assistantships also available. Financial award application deadline: 3/1; financial award applicants required to submit FAFSA. In 2015, 183 master's, 23 doctorates, 19 other advanced degrees awarded. *Degree program information:* Part-time and evening/weekend programs available. Part-time, evening/weekend, 100% online, blended/hybrid learning. Offers adult/gerontology primary care nurse practitioner (MSN); applied research (MA); assessment and measurement (PhD); audiology (Au D); behavior analysis (MA); clinical and school psychology (Psy D); clinical exercise physiology (MS); clinical mental health counseling (MA, Ed S); clinical nurse leader (MSN); communication sciences and disorders (PhD); counseling and supervision (PhD); exercise physiology (MS); experimental psychology (MA); family nurse practitioner (MSN); health and behavioral sciences (M Ed, MA, MAT, MOT, MPAS, MS, MSN, Au D, DNP, PhD, Psy D, Ed S); kinesiology (MAT, MS); nurse administrator (MSN); nurse midwifery (MSN); nursing (MSN, DNP); nutrition and exercise (MS); nutrition and physical activity (MS); occupational therapy (MOT); physical and health education (MAT); physician assistant studies (MPAS); quantitative psychology (MA); school psychology (MA, Ed S); speech-language pathology (MS); sport and recreation leadership (MS). *Application fee:* $55. Electronic applications accepted. *Application Contact:* Lynette D. Michael, Director of Graduate Admissions, 540-568-6131 Ext. 6395, Fax: 540-568-7860, E-mail: michaeld@jmu.edu. *Dean*, Dr. Sharon E. Lovell, 540-568-2705, Fax: 540-568-2747, E-mail: lovellse@jmu.edu.

College of Integrated Science and Engineering Students: 32 full-time (18 women), 26 part-time (4 women); includes 13 minority (5 Black or African American, non-Hispanic/Latino; 2 Asian, non-Hispanic/Latino; 5 Hispanic/Latino; 1 Two or more races, non-Hispanic/Latino), 6 international. Average age 30. 29 applicants, 97% accepted, 18 enrolled. *Faculty:* 52 full-time (14 women), 4 part-time/adjunct (0 women). *Financial support:* In 2015–16, 4 students received support. Career-related internships or fieldwork, Federal Work-Study, unspecified assistantships, and assistantships (averaging $7530) available. Financial award application deadline: 3/1; financial award applicants required to submit FAFSA. In 2015, 22 master's awarded. *Degree program information:* Part-time and evening/weekend programs available. Part-time, evening/weekend, 100% online, blended/hybrid learning, study abroad. Offers digital forensics (MS); environmental management and sustainability (MS); information security (MS); integrated science and engineering (MS). *Application fee:* $55. Electronic applications accepted. *Application Contact:* Lynette D. Michael, Director of Graduate Admissions, 540-568-6395, Fax: 540-568-7860, E-mail: michaeld@jmu.edu. *Dean*, Dr. Robert A. Kolvoord, 540-568-2752, E-mail: kolvoora@jmu.edu.

College of Science and Mathematics Students: 16 full-time (8 women), 6 part-time (1 woman); includes 4 minority (1 Black or African American, non-Hispanic/Latino; 2 Asian, non-Hispanic/Latino; 1 Hispanic/Latino). Average age 30. 30 applicants, 47% accepted, 9 enrolled. *Faculty:* 63 full-time (25 women), 1 part-time/adjunct (0 women). *Financial support:* In 2015–16, 14 students received support, including 4 fellowships; Federal Work-Study, unspecified assistantships, and 14 assistantships (averaging $11,194) also available. Financial award application deadline: 3/1; financial award applicants required to submit FAFSA. In 2015, 11 master's awarded. *Degree program information:* Part-time programs available. Part-time. Offers biology (MS); mathematics (M Ed); science and mathematics (M Ed, MS). *Application fee:* $55. Electronic applications accepted. *Application Contact:* Lynette D. Michael, Director of Graduate Admissions, 540-568-6131 Ext. 6395, Fax: 540-568-7860, E-mail: michaeld@jmu.edu. *Dean*, Dr. David F. Brakke, 540-568-3508, E-mail: brakkedf@jmu.edu.

College of Visual and Performing Arts Students: 55 full-time (28 women), 18 part-time (11 women); includes 8 minority (3 Black or African American, non-Hispanic/Latino; 4 Hispanic/Latino; 1 Two or more races, non-Hispanic/Latino), 17 international. Average age 30. 83 applicants, 65% accepted, 27 enrolled. *Faculty:* 64 full-time (27 women), 9 part-time/adjunct (3 women). *Financial support:* In 2015–16, 49 students received support, including 18 fellowships, teaching assistantships with full tuition reimbursements available (averaging $8,837 per year); Federal Work-Study and assistantships (averaging $7530), doctoral assistantships (averaging $12,935) also available. Financial award application deadline: 3/1; financial award applicants required to submit FAFSA. In 2015, 18 master's, 7 doctorates awarded. *Degree program information:* Part-time programs available. Part-time. Offers art education (MA); composition (MM); conducting (MM, DMA); music education (MM);

performance (MM, DMA); studio art (MA, MFA); visual and performing arts (MA, MFA, MM, DMA). *Application fee:* $55. Electronic applications accepted. *Application Contact:* Lynette D. Michael, Director of Graduate Admissions and Student Records, 540-568-6131 Ext. 6395, Fax: 540-568-7860, E-mail: michaeld@jmu.edu. *Dean*, Dr. George Sparks, 540-568-6247, E-mail: sparksge@jmu.edu.

See Display below and Close-Up on page 883.

JEFFERSON COLLEGE OF HEALTH SCIENCES, Roanoke, VA 24013

General Information Independent, coed, comprehensive institution. *Graduate housing:* Room and/or apartments available on a first-come, first-served basis to single students; on-campus housing not available to married students. *Research affiliation:* Carilion Clinic (hospital and medical services), Virginia Polytechnic Institute and State University/Carilion Medical School (medicine).

GRADUATE UNITS

Program in Nursing ***Degree program information:*** Part-time programs available. Part-time. Offers nursing education (MSN); nursing management (MSN). Electronic applications accepted.

Program in Occupational Therapy ***Degree program information:*** Part-time programs available. Part-time. Offers occupational therapy (MS). Electronic applications accepted.

Program in Physician Assistant Offers physician assistant (MS). Electronic applications accepted.

THE JEWISH THEOLOGICAL SEMINARY, New York, NY 10027-4649

General Information Independent-religious, coed, university. *Graduate housing:* Rooms and/or apartments available on a first-come, first-served basis to single and married students. Housing application deadline: 5/15.

GRADUATE UNITS

The Graduate School ***Degree program information:*** Part-time programs available. Part-time. Offers ancient Judaism (MA, DHL, PhD); Bible and ancient Semitic languages (MA, DHL, PhD); interdepartmental studies (MA); Jewish art and visual culture (MA); Jewish gender and women's studies (MA); Jewish history (MA, DHL, PhD); Jewish literature (MA, DHL, PhD); Jewish philosophy (DHL); Jewish thought (MA, PhD); liturgy (MA, DHL, PhD); medieval Jewish studies (MA, DHL, PhD); Midrash (DHL); Midrash and scriptural interpretation (MA, PhD); modern Jewish studies (MA, DHL, PhD); Talmud and rabbinics (MA, DHL, PhD). MA/MSW offered jointly with Columbia University.

H. L. Miller Cantorial School and College of Jewish Music Offers Jewish music (MSM).

The Rabbinical School Offers theology (MA, Rabbi).

William Davidson Graduate School of Jewish Education ***Degree program information:*** Part-time programs available. Part-time, online learning. Offers Jewish education (MA, Ed D). Offered in conjunction with Rabbinical School; H. L. Miller Cantorial School and College of Jewish Music; Teacher's College, Columbia University; and Union Theological Seminary.

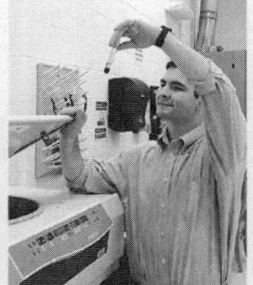

JOHN BROWN UNIVERSITY, Siloam Springs, AR 72761-2121

General Information Independent-religious, coed, comprehensive institution. *Graduate housing:* Rooms and/or apartments available on a first-come, first-served basis to single and married students.

GRADUATE UNITS

Graduate Counseling Programs ***Degree program information:*** Part-time and evening/weekend programs available. Part-time, evening/weekend. Offers clinical mental health counseling (MS); marriage and family therapy (MS); play therapy (Graduate Certificate); school counseling (MS). Electronic applications accepted.

Graduate Education Programs ***Degree program information:*** Part-time and evening/weekend programs available. Part-time, evening/weekend. Offers curriculum and instruction (M Ed); secondary education (MAT).

Soderquist College of Business ***Degree program information:*** Part-time and evening/weekend programs available. Part-time, evening/weekend, online learning. Offers higher education leadership (MS); international business (MBA); leadership and ethics (MBA, MS). Electronic applications accepted.

JOHN CARROLL UNIVERSITY, University Heights, OH 44118-4581

General Information Independent-religious, coed, comprehensive institution. CGS member. *Graduate housing:* On-campus housing not available.

GRADUATE UNITS

Graduate School ***Degree program information:*** Part-time and evening/weekend programs available. Part-time, evening/weekend. Offers administration (M Ed, MA); biology (MA, MS); clinical counseling (Certificate); communications management (MA); community counseling (MA); educational and school psychology (M Ed, MA); English (MA); history (MA); humanities (MA); integrated science (MA); mathematics (MA, MS); nonprofit administration (MA); professional teacher education (M Ed, MA); religious studies (MA); school based adolescent-young adult education (M Ed); school based early childhood education (M Ed); school based middle childhood education (M Ed); school based multi-age education (M Ed); school counseling (M Ed, MA). Electronic applications accepted.

John M. and Mary Jo Boler School of Business Degree program information: Part-time and evening/weekend programs available. Part-time, evening/weekend. Offers accountancy (MS); business (MBA). Electronic applications accepted.

JOHN F. KENNEDY UNIVERSITY, Pleasant Hill, CA 94523-4817

General Information Independent, coed, primarily women, upper-level institution. *Graduate housing:* On-campus housing not available.

GRADUATE UNITS

Graduate School of Holistic Studies ***Degree program information:*** Part-time and evening/weekend programs available. Part-time, evening/weekend. Offers consciousness and transformative studies (MA); counseling psychology (MA); dream studies (Certificate); holistic health education (MA); holistic studies (MA, MFA, Certificate); integral psychology (MA, Certificate); life coaching (Certificate); somatic psychology (MA); studio arts (MFA); transformative arts (MA); transpersonal psychology (MA).

Graduate School of Professional Psychology ***Degree program information:*** Part-time and evening/weekend programs available. Part-time, evening/weekend. Offers counseling psychology (MA); organizational psychology (MA, Certificate); professional psychology (MA, Psy D, Certificate); psychology (Psy D); sport psychology (MA).

School of Education and Liberal Arts *Degree program information:* Part-time and evening/weekend programs available. Part-time, evening/weekend. Offers education (MAT); education and liberal arts (MA, MAT, Certificate); museum studies (MA, Certificate).

School of Law *Degree program information:* Part-time and evening/weekend programs available. Part-time, evening/weekend. Offers law (JD).

School of Management *Degree program information:* Part-time and evening/weekend programs available. Part-time, evening/weekend. Offers business administration (MBA); career coaching (Certificate); career development (MA, Certificate); management (MA, MBA, Certificate); organizational leadership (Certificate).

JOHN JAY COLLEGE OF CRIMINAL JUSTICE OF THE CITY UNIVERSITY OF NEW YORK, New York, NY 10019-1093

General Information State and locally supported, coed, comprehensive institution. CGS member. *Graduate housing:* On-campus housing not available. *Research affiliation:* Criminal Justice Center, Criminal Justice Research and Evaluation Center, Center on Violence and Human Survival, Center for Dispute Resolution, The Fire Science Institute, The Institute For Criminal Justice Ethics.

GRADUATE UNITS

Graduate Studies *Degree program information:* Part-time and evening/weekend programs available. Part-time, evening/weekend. Offers criminal justice (MA, PhD); criminology and deviance (PhD); forensic computing (MS); forensic psychology (PhD); forensic science (PhD); international crime and justice (MA); law and philosophy (PhD); organizational behavior (PhD); protection management (MS); public administration (MPA); public policy (PhD).

JOHN MARSHALL LAW SCHOOL, Chicago, IL 60604-3968

General Information Independent, coed, graduate-only institution. *Enrollment by degree level:* 166 master's, 1,038 doctoral. *Graduate faculty:* 62 full-time (25 women), 152 part-time/adjunct (50 women). *Graduate housing:* On-campus housing not available. *Student services:* Campus employment opportunities, career counseling, exercise/wellness program, free psychological counseling, international student services, low-cost health insurance, multicultural affairs office, services for students with disabilities, writing training. *Library:* Louis L. Biro Law Library.

Computer facilities: 28 computers available on campus for general student use. Online class registration is available.
Website: http://www.jmls.edu/

General Application Contact: William B. Powers, Associate Dean of Admission and Student Affairs, 800-537-4280, Fax: 312-427-5136, E-mail: admission@jmls.edu.

GRADUATE UNITS

Graduate and Professional Programs Students: 839 full-time (415 women), 365 part-time (170 women); includes 396 minority (163 Black or African American, non-Hispanic/Latino; 4 American Indian or Alaska Native, non-Hispanic/Latino; 79 Asian, non-Hispanic/Latino; 119 Hispanic/Latino; 2 Native Hawaiian or other Pacific Islander, non-Hispanic/Latino; 29 Two or more races, non-Hispanic/Latino), 56 international. Average age 27. 1,764 applicants, 73% accepted, 334 enrolled. *Faculty:* 62 full-time (25 women), 152 part-time/adjunct (50 women). *Financial support:* In 2015–16, 798 students received support. Research assistantships, Federal Work-Study, scholarships/grants, and tuition waivers (full and partial) available. Support available to part-time students. Financial award application deadline: 4/1; financial award applicants required to submit FAFSA. In 2015, 89 master's, 381 doctorates awarded. *Degree program information:* Part-time and evening/weekend programs available. Part-time, evening/weekend, 100% online, blended/hybrid learning. Offers employee benefits (LL M); estate planning (LL M); information technology and privacy law (LL M); intellectual property (LL M); international business and trade (LL M); law (JD); real estate (LL M); taxation (LL M); trial advocacy (LL M); U.S. legal studies (LL M). *Application deadline:* For fall admission, 3/1 priority date for domestic and international students; for spring admission, 10/15 priority date for domestic and international students. Applications are processed on a rolling basis. *Application fee:* $0. Electronic applications accepted. *Application Contact:* William B. Powers, Associate Dean for Admission and Student Affairs, 800-537-4280, Fax: 312-427-5136, E-mail: admission@jmls.edu. *Dean*, John E. Corkery, 312-427-2737 Ext. 426, E-mail: 7corkery@jmls.edu.

JOHN PAUL THE GREAT CATHOLIC UNIVERSITY, Escondido, CA 92025

General Information Independent-religious, coed, comprehensive institution.

GRADUATE UNITS

School of Theology Offers biblical theology (MA).

JOHNS HOPKINS UNIVERSITY, Baltimore, MD 21218

General Information Independent, coed, university. CGS member. *Graduate housing:* On-campus housing not available. *Research affiliation:* General Electric Company (GE) (medical technology), Carnegie Institution of Washington (biological sciences), SmithKline Beecham (asthma and allergy), Bristol-Myers Squibb (human nutrition), Howard Hughes Medical Institute (biomedical sciences), Space Telescope Science Institute (astronomy).

GRADUATE UNITS

Bloomberg School of Public Health *Degree program information:* Part-time programs available. Part-time, online learning. Offers biochemistry and molecular biology (MHS, Sc M, PhD); bioethics and policy (PhD); bioinformatics (MHS); biostatistics (MHS, Sc M, PhD); cancer etiology and prevention (MHS, Sc M, PhD, Sc D); cardiovascular diseases (MHS, Sc M, PhD, Sc D); child and adolescent health and development (MHS, Dr PH, PhD); children's mental health services (PhD); clinical epidemiology (MHS, Sc M, PhD, Sc D); clinical investigation (MHS, Sc M, PhD); clinical trials (PhD, Sc D); demography (MHS); drug dependence epidemiology (PhD); environmental health engineering (PhD); environmental health sciences (MHS, Dr PH); epidemiology (MHS, Sc M, Dr PH, PhD, Sc D); epidemiology of aging (MHS, Sc M, PhD, Sc D); genetic counseling (Sc M); genetic epidemiology (MHS, Sc M, PhD, Sc D); global disease epidemiology and control (MHS, PhD); health and public policy (PhD); health care management and leadership (Dr PH); health economics (MHS); health economics and policy (PhD); health education and health communication (MSPH); health finance and management (MHA); health policy (MSPH); health services research and policy (PhD); health systems (MHS, PhD); human nutrition (MHS, PhD); infectious disease epidemiology (MHS, Sc M, PhD, Sc D); international health (MSPH, Dr PH); mental health (MHS, Dr PH); molecular microbiology and immunology (MHS, Sc M, PhD); occupational and environmental epidemiology (MHS, Sc M, PhD, Sc D); occupational and environmental health (PhD); physiology (PhD); population and health (Dr PH, PhD); psychiatric epidemiology (PhD); public health (MBE, MHA, MHS, MPH, MPP, MSPH, Sc M, Dr PH, PhD, Sc D); public policy (MPP); registered dietician (MSPH); reproductive, perinatal and women's health (MHS, Dr PH, PhD); social and behavioral interventions (MHS, PhD); social and behavioral sciences (Dr PH, PhD); social factors in health (MHS); toxicology (PhD). Electronic applications accepted.

Berman Institute of Bioethics Offers bioethics (MBE).

Carey Business School *Degree program information:* Part-time and evening/weekend programs available. Part-time, evening/weekend, online learning. Offers business (Exec MBA, MBA, MS, Certificate); business administration (Exec MBA, MBA); business of health care (Certificate); finance (MS); financial management (Certificate); health care management (MS); information systems (MS); investments (Certificate); marketing (MS); real estate and infrastructure (MS). Electronic applications accepted.

Engineering Program for Professionals *Degree program information:* Part-time and evening/weekend programs available. Part-time, evening/weekend. Offers applied and computational mathematics (MS, Post-Master's Certificate); applied biomedical engineering (MS, Post-Master's Certificate); applied physics (MS, Post-Master's Certificate); bioinformatics (MS); chemical and biomolecular engineering (M Ch E); civil engineering (MCE); computer science (MS, Post-Master's Certificate); cybersecurity (MS, Post-Master's Certificate); electrical and computer engineering (MS, Post-Master's Certificate); engineering (M Ch E, M Mat SE, MCE, MEE, MME, MS, MSE, Graduate Certificate, Post-Master's Certificate); environmental engineering (MS, Graduate Certificate, Post-Master's Certificate); environmental engineering and science (MEE, MS, Graduate Certificate, Post-Master's Certificate); environmental planning and management (MS, Post-Master's Certificate); information assurance (MS); information systems and technology (MS, Post-Master's Certificate); materials science and engineering (M Mat SE, MSE); mechanical engineering (MME); space systems engineering (MS, Post-Master's Certificate); systems engineering (MS, Graduate Certificate, Post-Master's Certificate); technical management (MS, Graduate Certificate, Post-Master's Certificate); telecommunications and networking (MS). Electronic applications accepted.

G. W. C. Whiting School of Engineering Offers bioengineering innovation and design (MSE); biomaterials (MSEM); biomedical engineering (MSE, PhD); chemical and biomolecular engineering (MSE, PhD); civil engineering (MSE, PhD); communications science (MSEM); computational medicine (PhD); computer science (MSE, MSSI, PhD); discrete mathematics (MA, MSE, PhD); electrical and computer engineering (MSE, PhD); engineering (M Ch E, M Mat SE, MA, MEE, MME, MS, MSE, MSEM, MSSI, PhD, Certificate, Post-Master's Certificate); environmental systems analysis, economics and public policy (MSEM); financial mathematics (MSE); fluid mechanics (MSEM); geography and environmental engineering (MA, MS, MSE, PhD); materials science and engineering (MSEM); mechanical engineering (MSEM); mechanics and materials (MSEM); nano-biotechnology (MSEM); nanomaterials and nanotechnology (MSEM); operations research (MSEM); operations research/optimization (MA, MSE, PhD); probability and statistics (MSEM); robotics (MSE); smart product and device design (MSEM); statistics/probability (MA, MSE, PhD). Electronic applications accepted.

Information Security Institute *Degree program information:* Part-time programs available. Part-time. Offers information security (MSSI). Electronic applications accepted.

National Institutes of Health Sponsored Programs Offers biology (PhD); cell, molecular, and developmental biology and biophysics (PhD). Electronic applications accepted.

Peabody Conservatory Offers music (MA, MM, DMA, AD, GPD). Electronic applications accepted.

School of Advanced International Studies Offers global risk (MA); international development (MA, Certificate); international economics and finance (MA); international public policy (MIPP); international relations (PhD); international studies (Certificate); Japan studies (MA); Korea studies (MA); South Asia studies (MA); Southeast Asia studies (MA). Electronic applications accepted.

School of Education Students: 322 full-time (254 women), 1,839 part-time (1,390 women); includes 830 minority (373 Black or African American, non-Hispanic/Latino; 6 American Indian or Alaska Native, non-Hispanic/Latino; 153 Asian, non-Hispanic/Latino; 199 Hispanic/Latino; 11 Native Hawaiian or other Pacific Islander, non-Hispanic/Latino; 88 Two or more races, non-Hispanic/Latino), 74 international. Average age 30. 2,648 applicants, 59% accepted, 1193 enrolled. *Faculty:* 75 full-time (53 women), 235 part-time/adjunct (164 women). *Financial support:* In 2015–16, 84 students received support. Fellowships, research assistantships, teaching assistantships, Federal Work-Study, and scholarships/grants available. Support available to part-time students. Financial award applicants required to submit FAFSA. In 2015, 623 master's, 13 doctorates, 217 other advanced degrees awarded. *Degree program information:* Part-time and evening/weekend programs available. Part-time, evening/weekend, 100% online, blended/hybrid learning. Offers advanced methods for differentiated instruction and inclusive education (Graduate Certificate); applied behavior analysis (Post-Master's Certificate); clinical mental health counseling (Post-Master's Certificate); counseling (MS, Advanced Certificate); data-based decision making and organizational improvement (Graduate Certificate); early intervention/preschool special education specialist (Graduate Certificate); education (M Ed, MAT, MS, Ed D, PhD, Advanced Certificate, Graduate Certificate, Post-Master's Certificate); education of students with autism and other pervasive developmental disorders (Graduate Certificate); elementary education (MAT); evidence-based teaching in the health professions (Post-Master's Certificate); health professions (M Ed); intelligence analysis (MS); organizational leadership (MS); secondary education (MAT); special education (MS). *Application deadline:* For fall admission, 4/1 for domestic and international students; for spring admission, 10/1 for domestic and international students; for summer admission, 2/1 for domestic and international students. *Application fee:* $80. Electronic applications accepted. *Application Contact:* Rhodri Evans, Director of Enrollment Services, 410-516-0741, Fax: 410-516-6697, E-mail: revans@jhu.edu. *Interim Dean*, Dr. Mariale M. Hardiman, 410-516-7820, Fax: 410-516-6697, E-mail: mmhardiman@jhu.edu.

School of Medicine Offers medicine (MA, MS, MD, PhD, Certificate). Electronic applications accepted.

Division of Health Sciences Informatics Offers applied health sciences informatics (MS); clinical informatics (Certificate); health sciences informatics (PhD); health sciences informatics research (MS). Electronic applications accepted.

Graduate Programs in Medicine Offers biochemistry, cellular and molecular biology (PhD); biological chemistry (PhD); cellular and molecular medicine (PhD); cellular and molecular physiology (PhD); functional anatomy and evolution (PhD); human genetics (PhD); immunology (PhD); medical and biological illustration (MA); medicine (MA, PhD); neuroscience (PhD); pathobiology (PhD); pharmacology and molecular sciences (PhD); physiology (PhD). Electronic applications accepted.

School of Nursing ***Degree program information:*** Part-time programs available. Part-time. Offers nursing (MSN, DNP, PhD, Certificate). Electronic applications accepted.

Zanvyl Krieger School of Arts and Sciences Offers anthropology (PhD); archaeology (PhD); arts and sciences (MA, MBEE, MFA, MS, PhD, Certificate); Assyriology (PhD); astronomy (PhD); biology (PhD); biophysics (PhD); chemistry (PhD); chemistry-biology (PhD); classics (PhD); cognitive science (PhD); earth and planetary sciences (MA, PhD); economics (PhD); Egyptology (PhD); English and American literature (PhD); fiction writing (MFA); French (PhD); German (PhD); Hebrew Bible/Northwest Semitics (PhD); history (PhD); history of art (MA, PhD); history of science and technology (MA, PhD); Italian (PhD); mathematics (PhD); philosophy (MA, PhD); physics (PhD); poetry (MFA); political science (MA, PhD); psychological and brain sciences (PhD); sociology (PhD); Spanish (PhD). Electronic applications accepted.

Advanced Academic Programs Degree program information: Part-time and evening/weekend programs available. Part-time, evening/weekend, online learning. Offers applied economics (MA); bioinformatics (MS); biotechnology (MS); biotechnology enterprise and entrepreneurship (MBEE); communication (MA); digital curation (Certificate); energy policy and climate (MS); environmental sciences (MS); film and media (MA); geographic information systems (MS, Certificate); global security studies (MA); government (MA); liberal arts (MA, Certificate); museum studies (MA); national securities study (Certificate); nonprofit management (Certificate); public management (MA); regulatory science (MS); research administration (MS); science writing (MA, Certificate); writing (MA). Electronic applications accepted.

Humanities Center Offers comparative literature (PhD); intellectual history (PhD). Electronic applications accepted.

JOHNSON & WALES UNIVERSITY, Providence, RI 02903-3703

General Information Independent, coed, comprehensive institution. *Enrollment:* 9,454 graduate, professional, and undergraduate students; 596 full-time matriculated graduate/professional students (362 women), 90 part-time matriculated graduate/professional students (52 women). *Enrollment by degree level:* 621 master's, 65 doctoral. *Graduate faculty:* 20 full-time (6 women), 20 part-time/adjunct (6 women). *Tuition, area resident:* Full-time $11,826; part-time $5913 per credit hour. *Graduate housing:* On-campus housing not available. *Student services:* Campus employment opportunities, campus safety program, career counseling, free psychological counseling, international student services, low-cost health insurance. *Library:* Johnson & Wales University Library. *Research affiliation:* Consortium of Rhode Island Academic and Research Libraries, Association of Institutional Research.

Computer facilities: A campuswide network can be accessed from student residence rooms and from off campus. Online class registration is available.
Website: http://www.jwu.edu/providence/

General Application Contact: Graduate School Admissions, 401-598-1015, Fax: 401-598-1286, E-mail: gradadm@jwu.edu.

GRADUATE UNITS

Graduate Studies Students: 807 full-time (484 women), 438 part-time (282 women); includes 49 minority (18 Black or African American, non-Hispanic/Latino; 7 Asian, non-Hispanic/Latino; 23 Hispanic/Latino; 1 Native Hawaiian or other Pacific Islander, non-Hispanic/Latino), 640 international. *Faculty:* 26 full-time (9 women), 24 part-time/adjunct (8 women). *Financial support:* Career-related internships or fieldwork, institutionally sponsored loans, tuition waivers (partial), and unspecified assistantships available. Support available to part-time students. Financial award application deadline: 5/1. *Degree program information:* Part-time and evening/weekend programs available. Part-time, evening/weekend. Offers business administration (MBA); business education and secondary special education (MAT); criminal justice (MS); culinary arts education (MAT); educational leadership (Ed D); elementary education and elementary special education (MAT); elementary education and elementary/secondary special education (MAT); elementary education and secondary special education (MAT); food service education (MAT); physician assistant studies (MS). *Application deadline:* Applications are processed on a rolling basis. *Application fee:* $0. *Application Contact:* Graduate School Admissions, 401-598-1015, Fax: 401-598-1286, E-mail: pvdgrad@admissions.jwu.edu.

JOHNSON C. SMITH UNIVERSITY, Charlotte, NC 28216-5398

General Information Independent, coed, comprehensive institution.

GRADUATE UNITS

Program in Social Work Offers social work (MSW).

JOHNSON STATE COLLEGE, Johnson, VT 05656

General Information State-supported, coed, comprehensive institution. *Enrollment:* 1,662 graduate, professional, and undergraduate students; 40 full-time matriculated graduate/professional students (32 women), 105 part-time matriculated graduate/professional students (82 women). *Enrollment by degree level:* 145 master's. *Graduate faculty:* 10 full-time (5 women), 7 part-time/adjunct (4 women). Tuition, state resident: part-time $537 per credit. Tuition, nonresident: part-time $1158 per credit. *Graduate housing:* Rooms and/or apartments available on a first-come, first-served basis to single and married students. Housing application deadline: 3/15. *Student services:* Campus employment opportunities, career counseling, exercise/wellness program, free psychological counseling, international student services, services for students with disabilities. *Library:* Willey Library plus 1 other. *Collection:* Books: 111,100 (physical), 6,500 (digital/electronic). Study areas open 24 hours, 5–7 days a week.

Computer facilities: 160 computers available on campus for general student use. A campuswide network can be accessed from student residence rooms and from off campus. Online class registration is available.
Website: http://www.jsc.edu/

General Application Contact: Catherine H. Higley, Administrative Assistant for Graduate Programs, 800-635-2356 Ext. 1244, Fax: 802-635-1230, E-mail: catherine.higley@jsc.edu.

GRADUATE UNITS

Graduate Program in Education Students: 3 full-time (all women), 51 part-time (37 women). Average age 29. *Faculty:* 3 full-time (1 woman), 1 (woman) part-time/adjunct. *Financial support:* Scholarships/grants and unspecified assistantships available. Financial award application deadline: 3/1; financial award applicants required to submit FAFSA. In 2015, 39 master's awarded. *Degree program information:* Part-time programs available. Part-time. Offers applied behavior analysis (MA Ed); curriculum and instruction (MA Ed); foundations of education (MA Ed); literacy (MA Ed); secondary education (MA Ed); special education (MA Ed). *Application deadline:* For fall admission, 4/1 priority date for domestic students, 1/15 priority date for international students; for spring admission, 11/1 for domestic students, 8/15 priority date for international students. Applications are processed on a rolling basis. Electronic applications accepted. *Application Contact:* Catherine H. Higley, Administrative Assistant, 800-635-2356 Ext. 1244, Fax: 802-635-1248, E-mail: catherine.higley@jsc.edu. *Chair, Department of Education*, Dr. Kathleen Brinegar, 802-635-1472, Fax: 802-635-1465, E-mail: kathleen.brinegar@jsc.edu.

Program in Counseling Students: 35 full-time (28 women), 50 part-time (41 women). Average age 31. *Faculty:* 2 full-time (1 woman), 6 part-time/adjunct (3 women). *Financial support:* Career-related internships or fieldwork and unspecified assistantships available. Support available to part-time students. Financial award application deadline: 3/1; financial award applicants required to submit FAFSA. In 2015, 30 master's awarded. *Degree program information:* Part-time programs available. Part-time. Offers clinical mental health counseling (MA); general counseling (MA); school guidance counseling (MA). *Application deadline:* For fall admission, 3/15 priority date for domestic students, 2/15 priority date for international students; for spring admission, 10/1 priority date for domestic students, 7/15 priority date for international students. Applications are processed on a rolling basis. Electronic applications accepted. *Application Contact:* Catherine H. Higley, Administrative Assistant, 800-635-2356 Ext. 1244, Fax: 802-635-1248, E-mail: catherine.higley@jsc.edu. *Counseling Program Coordinator*, Dr. David Fink, 802-635-1383, Fax: 802-635-1465, E-mail: david.fink@jsc.edu.

Program in Studio Arts Students: 3 full-time (1 woman). Average age 41. *Faculty:* 3 full-time (1 woman). *Financial support:* Teaching assistantships and unspecified assistantships available. Support available to part-time students. Financial award application deadline: 3/1; financial award applicants required to submit FAFSA. In 2015, 1 master's awarded. *Degree program information:* Part-time programs available. Part-time, online learning. Offers drawing (MFA); mixed media (MFA); painting (MFA); printmaking (MFA); sculpture (MFA). *Application deadline:* For fall admission, 3/15 for domestic students, 1/15 for international students. Applications are processed on a rolling basis. Electronic applications accepted. *Application Contact:* Catherine H. Higley, Administrative Assistant, 800-635-2356 Ext. 1244, Fax: 802-635-1248, E-mail: catherine.higley@jsc.edu.

JOHNSON UNIVERSITY, Knoxville, TN 37998-1001

General Information Independent-religious, coed, comprehensive institution. *Graduate housing:* Rooms and/or apartments available on a first-come, first-served basis to single students and available to married students. Housing application deadline: 8/1.

GRADUATE UNITS

Graduate and Professional Programs ***Degree program information:*** Part-time and evening/weekend programs available. Part-time, evening/weekend, online learning. Offers educational technology (MA); intercultural studies (MA); leadership studies (PhD); marriage and family therapy/professional counseling (MA); New Testament (MA); school counseling (MA); teacher education (MA). Electronic applications accepted.

JOHN WESLEY UNIVERSITY, High Point, NC 27265

General Information Independent-religious, coed, comprehensive institution.

GRADUATE UNITS

School of Management Offers management (MBA).

JOSE MARIA VARGAS UNIVERSITY, Pembroke Pines, FL 33026

General Information Proprietary, coed, comprehensive institution.

GRADUATE UNITS

Program in Preschool Education Offers preschool education (MS).

THE JUDGE ADVOCATE GENERAL'S SCHOOL, U.S. ARMY, Charlottesville, VA 22903-1781

General Information Federally supported, coed, primarily men, graduate-only institution. *Enrollment by degree level:* 111 doctoral. *Graduate faculty:* 40 full-time (10 women). *Graduate housing:* On-campus housing not available. *Student services:* Campus safety program, career counseling, exercise/wellness program, free psychological counseling, international student services, low-cost health insurance, multicultural affairs office, teacher training, writing training. *Library:* JAG Law Library plus 3 others. Weekly public service hours: 40; study areas open 24 hours, 5–7 days a week; students can reserve study rooms.

Computer facilities: 150 computers available on campus for general student use. A campuswide network can be accessed.
Website: http://www.jagcnet.army.mil/

General Application Contact: Maurice A. Lescault, Jr., Associate Dean, 434-971-3303, Fax: 434-971-3295, E-mail: maurice.e.lescault.civ@mail.mil.

GRADUATE UNITS

Graduate Programs Students: 111 full-time (30 women); includes 13 minority (8 Black or African American, non-Hispanic/Latino; 2 Asian, non-Hispanic/Latino; 3 Hispanic/Latino), 3 international. Average age 34. *Faculty:* 40 full-time (10 women). Offers military law (LL M). Program available only to active duty military lawyers. *Application fee:* $0. *Application Contact:* Maurice A. Lescault, Jr., Associate Dean, 434-971-3303, Fax: 434-971-3295, E-mail: maurice.a.lescault.civ@mail.mil. *Commandant*, Brig. Gen. Scott C. Black, 434-971-3301, Fax: 434-972-6203, E-mail: scott.black@us.army.mil.

JUDSON UNIVERSITY, Elgin, IL 60123-1498

General Information Independent-religious, coed, comprehensive institution. *Enrollment:* 1,274 graduate, professional, and undergraduate students. *Enrollment by degree level:* 37 doctoral. *Graduate housing:* Rooms and/or apartments available on a first-come, first-served basis to single and married students. Housing application deadline: 8/1. *Student services:* Campus employment opportunities, campus safety program, career counseling, exercise/wellness program, international student services, low-cost health insurance, multicultural affairs office, services for students with disabilities, writing training. *Library:* Benjamin P. Browne Library. *Collection:* Books: 138,580 (physical), 2,243 (digital/electronic); Serial titles: 291 (physical), 15 (digital/electronic); Databases: 60. Weekly public service hours: 83; students can reserve study rooms.

Computer facilities: 90 computers available on campus for general student use. A campuswide network can be accessed from student residence rooms and from off campus. Online class registration is available.
Website: http://www.judsonu.edu/

General Application Contact: Maria Aguirre, Student Academic Advisor, 847-628-1160, E-mail: maguirre@judsonu.edu.

GRADUATE UNITS

Doctor of Education in Literacy Program Students: 37 full-time (32 women); includes 2 minority (1 Black or African American, non-Hispanic/Latino; 1 Two or more races, non-Hispanic/Latino). Average age 40. 10 applicants, 90% accepted, 8 enrolled. *Faculty:* 6 full-time, 8 part-time/adjunct. *Financial support:* Application deadline: 4/1; applicants required to submit FAFSA. *Degree program information:* Evening/weekend programs available. Evening/weekend. Offers literacy (Ed D). *Application deadline:* For fall admission, 11/1 for domestic and international students. *Application fee:* $200. *Application Contact:* Maria Aguirre, Student Academic Advisor, 847-628-1160, E-mail: maguirre@judsonu.edu. *Director*, Dr. Steven L. Layne, 847-628-1093, E-mail: slayne@judsonu.edu.

Master of Architecture Program Students: 19 full-time (5 women); includes 5 minority (1 Black or African American, non-Hispanic/Latino; 3 Hispanic/Latino; 1 Two or more races, non-Hispanic/Latino). Average age 22. 24 applicants, 83% accepted, 19 enrolled. *Faculty:* 9 full-time (3 women), 3 part-time/adjunct (1 woman). *Financial support:* In 2015–16, 19 students received support, including 1 fellowship with partial tuition reimbursement available (averaging $5,000 per year), 1 research assistantship with partial tuition reimbursement available (averaging $5,000 per year), 12 teaching assistantships with partial tuition reimbursements available (averaging $2,500 per year); unspecified assistantships also available. Financial award application deadline: 7/1; financial award applicants required to submit FAFSA. In 2015, 16 master's awarded. *Degree program information:* Part-time programs available. Part-time. Offers architecture (M Arch); sustainable design (M Arch); traditional architecture and urbanism (M Arch). *Application deadline:* For fall admission, 2/15 priority date for domestic and international students; for winter admission, 11/15 for domestic students; for spring admission, 11/15 for domestic and international students. Applications are processed on a rolling basis. *Application fee:* $100. Electronic applications accepted. *Application Contact:* Nathan McNeely, Director of Admissions, 847-628-2510, E-mail: nmcneely@judsonu.edu. *Chair*, Ian Hoffman, 847-628-1014, E-mail: ihoffman@judsonu.edu.

Master of Arts in Clinical Mental Health Counseling Program *Faculty:* 1 (woman) full-time. *Degree program information:* Evening/weekend programs available. Evening/weekend. Offers clinical mental health counseling (MA). *Application deadline:* Applications are processed on a rolling basis. Electronic applications accepted. *Application Contact:* Maria Aguirre, Student Academic Advisor, 847-628-1160, E-mail: maguirre@judsonu.edu. *Chair, Professional Studies*, Dr. Susan Wesner, 847-628-1544, E-mail: susan.wesner@judsonu.edu.

Master of Arts in Human Services Administration Program *Faculty:* 1 (woman) full-time. Offers human services administration (MA). *Application deadline:* Applications are processed on a rolling basis. Electronic applications accepted. *Application Contact:* Maria Aguirre, Student Academic Advisor, 847-628-1160, E-mail: maguirre@judsonu.edu.

Master of Arts in Organizational Leadership Program Students: 40 full-time (20 women); includes 14 minority (6 Black or African American, non-Hispanic/Latino; 2 Asian, non-Hispanic/Latino; 6 Hispanic/Latino), 2 international. Average age 37. *Faculty:* 4 full-time (2 women), 20 part-time/adjunct (10 women). *Financial support:* Institutionally sponsored loans and scholarships/grants available. Financial award applicants required to submit FAFSA. *Degree program information:* Part-time and evening/weekend programs available. Part-time, evening/weekend, 100% online, blended/hybrid learning. Offers organizational leadership (MA). *Application deadline:* For fall admission, 8/1 for domestic students, 7/1 for international students; for spring admission, 3/1 for domestic students, 1/2 for international students. Applications are processed on a rolling basis. *Application fee:* $35. Electronic applications accepted. *Application Contact:* Eric Downs, Enrollment Manager, 847-628-5026, Fax: 847-628-1007, E-mail: eric.downs@info.judsonu.edu. *Dean*, Dr. David Cook, 847-628-1518, Fax: 847-628-1007, E-mail: dcook@judsonu.edu.

Master of Business Administration Program 25 applicants, 80% accepted, 18 enrolled. *Financial support:* Applicants required to submit FAFSA. *Degree program information:* Evening/weekend programs available. Evening/weekend, 100% online. Offers business administration (MBA). *Application deadline:* Applications are processed on a rolling basis. *Application fee:* $35. Electronic applications accepted. *Application Contact:* Maria Aguirre, Student Academic Advisor, 847-628-1160, E-mail: maguirre@judsonu.edu. *Chair*, Dr. Michelle L. Kilbourne, 847-268-1515, E-mail: mkilbourne@judsonu.edu.

Master of Education in Literacy Program Students: 17 full-time (13 women); includes 1 minority (Hispanic/Latino). Average age 33. 17 applicants, 100% accepted, 17 enrolled. *Faculty:* 4 full-time (2 women), 9 part-time/adjunct (all women). *Financial support:* Application deadline: 4/15; applicants required to submit FAFSA. In 2015, 17 master's awarded. Offers literacy (M Ed). *Application deadline:* Applications are processed on a rolling basis. *Application fee:* $40. *Application Contact:* Maria Aguirre, Student Academic Advisor, 847-628-1160, E-mail: maguirre@judsonu.edu. *Director*, Dr. Steven L. Layne, 847-628-1093, E-mail: slayne@judsonu.edu.

Master of Leadership in Ministry Program Students: 7 full-time (4 women); includes 3 minority (all Black or African American, non-Hispanic/Latino). Average age 37. *Faculty:* 3 full-time (1 woman), 5 part-time/adjunct (2 women). *Financial support:* In 2015–16, 5 students received support. Scholarships/grants available. Financial award application deadline: 10/31; financial award applicants required to submit FAFSA. *Degree program information:* Evening/weekend programs available. Evening/weekend, online only, blended/hybrid learning. Offers leadership in ministry (MLM). *Application deadline:* Applications are processed on a rolling basis. *Application fee:* $35. Electronic applications accepted. *Application Contact:* Debbie Sanders, Assistant, Department of Christian Ministries, 847-628-1124, E-mail: deborah.sanders@judsonu.edu. *Director*, Dr. Keith Krispin, Jr., 847-628-1057, E-mail: kkrispin@judsonu.edu.

THE JUILLIARD SCHOOL, New York, NY 10023-6588

General Information Independent, coed, comprehensive institution. *Graduate housing:* Room and/or apartments available on a first-come, first-served basis to single students; on-campus housing not available to married students. Housing application deadline: 5/1.

GRADUATE UNITS

Program in Music Offers music (MM, DMA, Artist Diploma, Diploma). Electronic applications accepted.

JUNIATA COLLEGE, Huntingdon, PA 16652-2119

General Information Independent-religious, coed, comprehensive institution. *Enrollment:* 1,583 graduate, professional, and undergraduate students; 8 full-time matriculated graduate/professional students (3 women), 5 part-time matriculated graduate/professional students (3 women). *Enrollment by degree level:* 13 master's. *Tuition, area resident:* Full-time $24,800; part-time $775 per credit. *Required fees:* $560. *Graduate housing:* On-campus housing not available. *Library:* Beeghly Library. *Collection:* Books: 51,000 (physical); Serial titles: 11,500 (physical). Weekly public service hours: 105.

Computer facilities: 170 computers available on campus for general student use. A campuswide network can be accessed from student residence rooms and from off campus. Online class registration is available.
Website: http://www.juniata.edu/

GRADUATE UNITS

Department of Accounting, Business, and Economics Students: 8 full-time (3 women), 5 part-time (3 women). Offers accounting (M Acc). *Chair*, Dr. Dom Peruso, 814-641-3661, E-mail: peruso@juniata.edu.

KANSAS CITY UNIVERSITY OF MEDICINE AND BIOSCIENCES, Kansas City, MO 64106-1453

General Information Independent, coed, graduate-only institution. CGS member. *Graduate housing:* On-campus housing not available. *Research affiliation:* Boehringer Ingelheim (HIV/AIDS), Mylanta-Bertek (hypertension), Covance (hypertension), Novartis Pharmaceuticals (Chronic Obstructive Pulmonary Disease (COPD)).

GRADUATE UNITS

College of Biosciences ***Degree program information:*** Part-time programs available. Part-time. Offers bioethics (MA); biomedical sciences (MS).

College of Osteopathic Medicine Offers osteopathic medicine (DO).

KANSAS STATE UNIVERSITY, Manhattan, KS 66506

General Information State-supported, coed, university. CGS member. *Graduate housing:* Rooms and/or apartments available on a first-come, first-served basis to single and married students. Housing application deadline: 2/1. *Research affiliation:* Visteon Corporation, Midwest Research Institute, NASA–Research Center, U.S. Grain Marketing Research Laboratory.

GRADUATE UNITS

Graduate School ***Degree program information:*** Part-time and evening/weekend programs available. Part-time, evening/weekend, online learning. Electronic applications accepted.

College of Agriculture Degree program information: Part-time programs available. Part-time, online learning. Offers agricultural economics (MAB, MS, PhD); agricultural education and communication (MS); agriculture (MAB, MS, PhD, Certificate); crop science (MS, PhD); entomology (MS, PhD); food science (MS, PhD); genetics (MS, PhD); grain science and industry (MS, PhD); horticulture (MS, PhD); meat science (PhD); monogastric nutrition (PhD); plant breeding and genetics (MS); plant pathology (MS, PhD); range and forage science (MS, PhD); ruminant nutrition (MS, PhD); soil and environmental science (PhD); weed science (MS, PhD). Electronic applications accepted.

College of Architecture, Planning and Design Degree program information: Part-time and evening/weekend programs available. Part-time, evening/weekend, online learning. Offers architecture (M Arch, MS Arch); architecture, planning and design (M Arch, MIAPD, MLA, MRCP, MS, MS Arch, PhD); community development (MS); environmental design and planning (PhD); interior architecture and product design (MIAPD); landscape architecture (MLA); regional and community planning (MRCP). Electronic applications accepted.

College of Arts and Sciences Degree program information: Part-time programs available. Part-time, online learning. Offers advertising (MS); analytical chemistry (MS); art (MFA); arts and sciences (MA, MFA, MM, MPA, MS, PhD, Graduate Certificate); biochemistry and molecular biophysics (MS, PhD); biological chemistry (MS); biology (MS); communication studies (MA); community journalism (MS); economics (MA, PhD); English (MA, Graduate Certificate); geography (MA, PhD, Graduate Certificate); geology (MS); global communication (MS); health communication (MS); history (MA, PhD); inorganic chemistry (MS); materials chemistry (MS); mathematics (MS, PhD, Graduate Certificate); media management (MS); modern languages (MA); music, theatre and dance (MA, MM); organic chemistry (MS); physical chemistry (MS); physics (MS, PhD); political science (MA); psychological sciences (MS, PhD); public administration (MPA); public relations (MS); security studies (MA, PhD); sociology (MA, PhD); statistics (MS, PhD, Graduate Certificate); women's studies (Graduate Certificate). Electronic applications accepted.

College of Business Administration Degree program information: Part-time programs available. Part-time. Offers accounting (M Acc); business administration (M Acc, MBA, Certificate); finance (MBA); management (MBA); supply chain management (MBA). Electronic applications accepted.

College of Education Degree program information: Part-time and evening/weekend programs available. Part-time, evening/weekend, online learning. Offers counseling and student development (MS); curriculum and instruction (Ed D, PhD); digital teaching and learning (MS); education (MS, Ed D, PhD); educational computing, design and online learning (MS); educational leadership (MS, Ed D, PhD); elementary/middle level curriculum and instruction (MS); reading specialist endorsement (MS); reading/language arts (MS); special education (MS, Ed D); teacher leader/school improvement (MS). Electronic applications accepted.

College of Engineering Degree program information: Part-time programs available. Part-time, online learning. Offers architectural engineering and construction science (MS); biological and agricultural engineering (MS, PhD); chemical engineering (MS, PhD, Graduate Certificate); civil engineering (MS, PhD); computing and information sciences (MS, MSE, PhD); electrical engineering (MS); engineering (MEM, MS, MSE, PhD, Graduate Certificate); engineering management (MEM); environmental engineering (MS, PhD); geotechnical engineering (MS, PhD); industrial engineering (MS); mechanical engineering (MS); nuclear engineering (PhD); operations research (MS); structural engineering (MS, PhD); transportation engineering (MS, PhD); water resources engineering (MS, PhD). Electronic applications accepted.

College of Human Ecology Degree program information: Part-time programs available. Part-time, online learning. Offers apparel and textiles (MS, PhD); communication sciences and disorders (MS); conflict resolution (Graduate Certificate); dietetics (MS); early childhood education (MS); family and community service (MS); family life education and consultation (PhD); family studies (MS); food service and hospitality management (PhD); gerontology (MS, Graduate Certificate); hospitality and dietetics administration (MS); human ecology (MS, PhD, Graduate Certificate); human nutrition (MS, PhD); kinesiology (MS); life span human development (MS); lifespan and human development (PhD); marriage and family therapy (MS, PhD); nutritional sciences (PhD); personal financial planning (MS, PhD, Graduate Certificate); public health nutrition (PhD); public health physical activity (PhD); sensory analysis and consumer behavior (PhD); youth development (MS, Graduate Certificate). Electronic applications accepted.

College of Technology and Aviation Offers technology and aviation (MT). Electronic applications accepted.

College of Veterinary Medicine Offers biomedical science (MS); clinical sciences (MPH, Graduate Certificate); diagnostic medicine/pathobiology (PhD); physiology (PhD); veterinary medicine (MPH, MS, DVM, PhD, Graduate Certificate). Electronic applications accepted.

See Display on next page and Close-Up on page 885.

KANSAS WESLEYAN UNIVERSITY, Salina, KS 67401-6196

General Information Independent-religious, coed, comprehensive institution. *Graduate housing:* Rooms and/or apartments available to single and married students.

GRADUATE UNITS

Program in Business Administration *Degree program information:* Part-time and evening/weekend programs available. Part-time, evening/weekend. Offers business administration (MBA); sports management (MBA).

KAPLAN UNIVERSITY, DAVENPORT CAMPUS, Davenport, IA 52807-2095

General Information Proprietary, coed, comprehensive institution.

GRADUATE UNITS

School of Business *Degree program information:* Part-time and evening/weekend programs available. Part-time, evening/weekend, online learning. Offers business administration (MBA); change leadership (MS); entrepreneurship (MBA); finance (MBA); health care management (MBA, MS); human resource (MBA); international business (MBA); management (MS); marketing (MBA); project management (MBA, MS); supply chain management and logistics (MBA, MS). Electronic applications accepted.

School of Criminal Justice *Degree program information:* Part-time and evening/weekend programs available. Part-time, evening/weekend, online learning. Offers corrections (MSCJ); global issues in criminal justice (MSCJ); law (MSCJ); leadership and executive management (MSCJ); policing (MSCJ). Electronic applications accepted.

School of Higher Education Studies *Degree program information:* Part-time and evening/weekend programs available. Part-time, evening/weekend, online learning. Offers college administration and leadership (MS); college teaching and learning (MS); student services (MS).

School of Information Technology *Degree program information:* Part-time and evening/weekend programs available. Part-time, evening/weekend, online learning. Offers decision support systems (MS); information security and assurance (MS).

School of Legal Studies *Degree program information:* Part-time and evening/weekend programs available. Part-time, evening/weekend, online learning. Offers health care delivery (MS); pathway to paralegal (Postbaccalaureate Certificate); state and local government (MS).

School of Nursing *Degree program information:* Part-time and evening/weekend programs available. Part-time, evening/weekend, online learning. Offers nurse administrator (MS); nurse educator (MS).

School of Teacher Education *Degree program information:* Part-time and evening/weekend programs available. Part-time, evening/weekend, online learning. Offers education (M Ed); secondary education (M Ed); teaching and learning (MA); teaching literacy and language: grades 6-12 (MA); teaching literacy and language: grades K-6 (MA); teaching mathematics: grades 6-8 (MA); teaching mathematics: grades 9-12 (MA); teaching mathematics: grades K-5 (MA); teaching science: grades 6-12 (MA); teaching science: grades K-6 (MA); teaching students with special needs (MA); teaching with technology (MA).

KEAN UNIVERSITY, Union, NJ 07083

General Information State-supported, coed, comprehensive institution. CGS member. *Enrollment:* 14,112 graduate, professional, and undergraduate students; 848 full-time matriculated graduate/professional students (674 women), 1,287 part-time matriculated graduate/professional students (996 women). *Enrollment by degree level:* 1,993 master's, 110 doctoral, 32 other advanced degrees. *Graduate faculty:* 251 full-time (133 women). Tuition, state resident: full-time $12,835; part-time $625 per credit. Tuition, nonresident: full-time $17,396; part-time $766 per credit. *Required fees:* $3235; $147 per credit. Tuition and fees vary according to course level, course load, degree level and program. *Graduate housing:* Room and/or apartments available on a first-come, first-served basis to single students; on-campus housing not available to married students. Housing application deadline: 5/1. *Student services:* Campus employment opportunities, campus safety program, career counseling, child daycare facilities, exercise/wellness program, free psychological counseling, grant writing training, international student services, low-cost health insurance, multicultural affairs office, services for students with disabilities, teacher training, writing training. *Library:* Nancy Thompson Library. *Collection:* Books: 207,300 (physical), 21,392 (digital/electronic); Serial titles: 32,785 (digital/electronic); Databases: 243. Weekly public service hours: 102. *Research affiliation:* Robert Wood Johnson Foundation (the effect of tobacco control policy), Institute of Vertebrate Paleontology and Paleoanthropology (paleoanthropology), Shodor Foundation (intelligent Internet search engines for science research and education), New Jersey Institute of Technology (partitioning to support auditing and extending the UMLS), National Bureau of Economic Research (alcoholic advertising and youth).

Computer facilities: 1,700 computers available on campus for general student use. A campuswide network can be accessed from student residence rooms and from off campus. Online class registration is available.
Website: http://www.kean.edu/

General Application Contact: Helen Ramirez, Associate Director, 908-737-7137, E-mail: hramirez@kean.edu.

GRADUATE UNITS

College of Business and Public Management Students: 157 full-time (93 women), 130 part-time (73 women); includes 176 minority (99 Black or African American, non-Hispanic/Latino; 17 Asian, non-Hispanic/Latino; 57 Hispanic/Latino; 3 Two or more races, non-Hispanic/Latino), 20 international. Average age 32. 119 applicants, 56% accepted, 62 enrolled. *Faculty:* 31 full-time (8 women). *Financial support:* In 2015–16, 29 research assistantships with full tuition reimbursements (averaging $3,771 per year) were awarded; scholarships/grants and unspecified assistantships also available. Financial award applicants required to submit FAFSA. In 2015, 86 master's awarded. *Degree program information:* Part-time programs available. Part-time. Offers accounting (MS); business and public management (MA, MBA, MPA, MS); criminal justice (MA); executive management (MBA); global management (MBA); health services administration (MPA); non-profit management (MPA); public administration (MPA). *Application deadline:* For fall admission, 6/1 for domestic and international students; for spring admission, 12/1 for domestic and international students. Applications are processed on a rolling basis. *Application fee:* $75. Electronic applications accepted. *Application Contact:* Pedro Lopes, Admissions Counselor, 908-737-7100, E-mail: plopes@kean.edu. *Dean*, Dr. Michael Cooper, 908-737-4707, Fax: 908-737-4765, E-mail: mrcooper@kean.edu.

College of Education Students: 42 full-time (31 women), 386 part-time (325 women); includes 179 minority (56 Black or African American, non-Hispanic/Latino; 7 Asian, non-Hispanic/Latino; 113 Hispanic/Latino; 1 Native Hawaiian or other Pacific Islander, non-Hispanic/Latino; 2 Two or more races, non-Hispanic/Latino), 1 international. Average age 35. 702 applicants, 34% accepted, 240 enrolled. *Faculty:* 48 full-time (33 women).

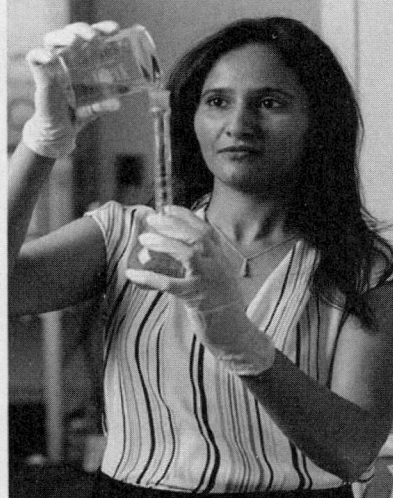

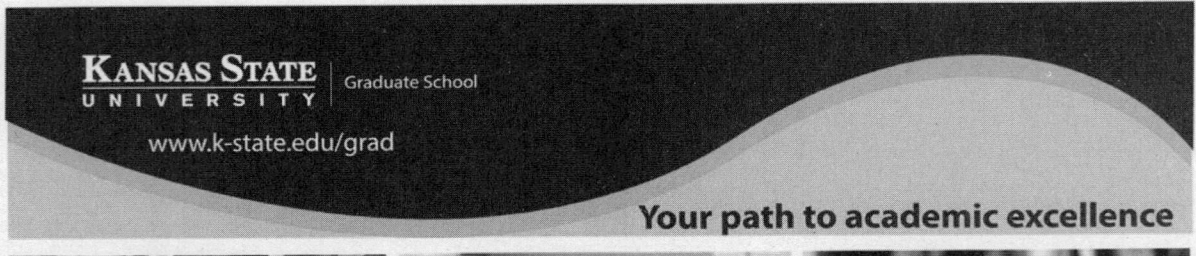

Financial support: In 2015–16, 11 research assistantships with full tuition reimbursements (averaging $3,771 per year) were awarded; scholarships/grants and unspecified assistantships also available. Financial award applicants required to submit FAFSA. In 2015, 105 master's awarded. *Degree program information:* Part-time programs available. Part-time. Offers administration in early childhood and family studies (MA); adult literacy (MA); advanced curriculum and teaching (MA); autism and development disabilities (MA); basic skills (MA); bilingual/bicultural education (MA); classroom instruction (MA); earth science (MA); education (MA, MS); exercise science (MS); learning and behavioral disabilities (MA); mathematics/science/computer education (MA); reading specialization (MA); teaching (MA); teaching English as a second language (MA); world languages (Spanish) (MA). *Application deadline:* For fall admission, 6/1 for domestic and international students; for spring admission, 12/1 for domestic and international students. Applications are processed on a rolling basis. *Application fee:* $75. Electronic applications accepted. *Application Contact:* Brittany Gerstenhaber, Admissions Counselor, 908-737-7100, E-mail: grad-adm@kean.edu. *Acting Dean*, Dr. Anthony Pitmann, 908-737-3750, Fax: 908-737-3760, E-mail: polirsts@kean.edu.

College of Humanities and Social Sciences Students: 88 full-time (74 women), 94 part-time (62 women); includes 83 minority (44 Black or African American, non-Hispanic/Latino; 4 Asian, non-Hispanic/Latino; 31 Hispanic/Latino; 4 Two or more races, non-Hispanic/Latino), 4 international. Average age 31. 129 applicants, 47% accepted, 58 enrolled. *Faculty:* 72 full-time (34 women). *Financial support:* In 2015–16, 17 research assistantships with full tuition reimbursements (averaging $3,771 per year) were awarded; scholarships/grants and unspecified assistantships also available. Financial award applicants required to submit FAFSA. In 2015, 65 master's, 10 other advanced degrees awarded. *Degree program information:* Part-time programs available. Part-time. Offers communication studies (MA); English writing studies (MA); Holocaust and genocide studies (MA); human behavior and organizational psychology (MA); humanities and social sciences (MA, Diploma); marriage and family therapy (MA, Diploma); psychological services (MA). *Application deadline:* For fall admission, 6/1 for domestic and international students; for spring admission, 12/1 for domestic and international students. Applications are processed on a rolling basis. *Application fee:* $75. Electronic applications accepted. *Application Contact:* Amy Hadjusek, Program Assistant, 908-737-7100, E-mail: grad-adm@kean.edu. *Dean*, Dr. Susan Bousequet, 908-737-0430, Fax: 908-737-0435, E-mail: sbousque@kean.edu.

College of Natural, Applied and Health Sciences Students: 22 full-time (17 women), 161 part-time (148 women); includes 81 minority (59 Black or African American, non-Hispanic/Latino; 15 Asian, non-Hispanic/Latino; 5 Hispanic/Latino; 2 Two or more races, non-Hispanic/Latino), 10 international. Average age 43. 90 applicants, 58% accepted, 47 enrolled. *Faculty:* 34 full-time (17 women). *Financial support:* In 2015–16, research assistantships with full tuition reimbursements (averaging $3,771 per year) were awarded; scholarships/grants and unspecified assistantships also available. Financial award applicants required to submit FAFSA. In 2015, 63 master's awarded. *Degree program information:* Part-time programs available. Part-time. Offers clinical management (MSN); community health nursing (MSN); computer information systems (MS); natural, applied and health sciences (MS, MSN, PhD); nursing educational leadership (PhD); school nursing (MSN). *Application deadline:* For fall admission, 6/1 for domestic and international students; for spring admission, 12/1 for domestic and international students. Applications are processed on a rolling basis. *Application fee:* $75. Electronic applications accepted. *Application Contact:* Pedro Lopes, Admissions Counselor, 908-737-7100, E-mail: grad-adm@kean.edu. *Dean*, Dr. George Chang, 908-737-3600, Fax: 908-737-3606, E-mail: gchang@kean.edu.

College of Visual and Performing Arts Students: 11 full-time (10 women), 26 part-time (20 women); includes 9 minority (3 Black or African American, non-Hispanic/Latino; 6 Hispanic/Latino). Average age 35. 17 applicants, 76% accepted, 13 enrolled. *Faculty:* 9 full-time (4 women). *Financial support:* In 2015–16, 5 research assistantships with full tuition reimbursements (averaging $3,771 per year) were awarded; scholarships/grants and unspecified assistantships also available. Financial award applicants required to submit FAFSA. In 2015, 11 master's awarded. *Degree program information:* Part-time programs available. Part-time. Offers initial teaching certification (MA); studio (MA); supervision (MA); visual and performing arts (MA). *Application deadline:* For fall admission, 6/1 for domestic and international students; for spring admission, 12/1 for domestic and international students. Applications are processed on a rolling basis. *Application fee:* $75. Electronic applications accepted. *Application Contact:* Amy Hadjusek, Program Assistant, 908-737-7100, E-mail: grad-adm@kean.edu. *Acting Dean*, Dr. Suzanne Bousquet, 908-737-4376, Fax: 908-737-4377, E-mail: sbousque@kean.edu.

Nathan Weiss Graduate College Students: 503 full-time (432 women), 482 part-time (364 women); includes 392 minority (164 Black or African American, non-Hispanic/Latino; 1 American Indian or Alaska Native, non-Hispanic/Latino; 33 Asian, non-Hispanic/Latino; 180 Hispanic/Latino; 2 Native Hawaiian or other Pacific Islander, non-Hispanic/Latino; 12 Two or more races, non-Hispanic/Latino), 5 international. Average age 31. 1,045 applicants, 40% accepted, 268 enrolled. *Faculty:* 40 full-time (31 women). *Financial support:* In 2015–16, 60 research assistantships with full tuition reimbursements (averaging $3,771 per year) were awarded; scholarships/grants and unspecified assistantships also available. Financial award applicants required to submit FAFSA. In 2015, 238 master's, 19 doctorates, 10 other advanced degrees awarded. *Degree program information:* Part-time programs available. Part-time. Offers alcohol and drug abuse counseling (MA); clinical mental health counseling (MA); combined school and clinical psychology (Psy D); educational leadership (Ed D); occupational therapy (MS); school business administration (MA); school counseling (MA); school psychology (MA, Diploma); social work (MSW); speech language pathology (MA); supervisors and principals (MA); supervisors, principals and school business administrators (MA). *Application deadline:* For fall admission, 6/1 for domestic and international students; for spring admission, 12/1 for domestic and international students. Applications are processed on a rolling basis. *Application fee:* $75. Electronic applications accepted. *Application Contact:* Ann-Marie Kay, Assistant Director of Graduate Admissions, 908-737-7132, Fax: 908-737-7135, E-mail: akay@kean.edu. *Dean*, Dr. Jeffrey Beck, 908-737-5902, Fax: 908-737-5905, E-mail: jbeck@kean.edu.

New Jersey Center for Science, Technology and Mathematics Students: 25 full-time (17 women), 7 part-time (4 women); includes 15 minority (1 Black or African American, non-Hispanic/Latino; 8 Asian, non-Hispanic/Latino; 6 Hispanic/Latino), 4 international. Average age 25. 20 applicants, 45% accepted, 8 enrolled. *Faculty:* 7 full-time (1 woman). *Financial support:* In 2015–16, 4 research assistantships with full tuition reimbursements (averaging $3,771 per year) were awarded; scholarships/grants and unspecified assistantships also available. Financial award applicants required to submit FAFSA. In 2015, 34 master's awarded. Offers biotechnology science (MS); instruction and curriculum (MA). *Application deadline:* For fall admission, 6/1 for domestic and international students; for spring admission, 12/1 for domestic and international students. Applications are processed on a rolling basis. *Application fee:* $75. Electronic applications accepted. *Application Contact:* Helen Ramirez, Associate Director of Graduate Admissions, 908-737-7100, E-mail: grad-adm@kean.edu. *Dean*, Dr. Keith Bostian, 908-737-7200, Fax: 908-737-7205, E-mail: kbostian@kean.edu.

KECK GRADUATE INSTITUTE, Claremont, CA 91711

General Information Independent, coed, graduate-only institution. CGS member.

GRADUATE UNITS

KGI School of Pharmacy Offers pharmacy (Pharm D).

School of Applied Life Sciences Offers applied life sciences (PhD); bioscience (MBS); bioscience management (Certificate). Electronic applications accepted.

KEENE STATE COLLEGE, Keene, NH 03435

General Information State-supported, coed, comprehensive institution. *Enrollment:* 4,383 graduate, professional, and undergraduate students; 28 full-time matriculated graduate/professional students (22 women), 67 part-time matriculated graduate/professional students (47 women). *Enrollment by degree level:* 95 master's. *Graduate faculty:* 11 full-time (6 women), 9 part-time/adjunct (5 women). Tuition, state resident: full-time $4500; part-time $500 per credit. Tuition, nonresident: full-time $4905; part-time $545 per credit. *Required fees:* $909; $101 per credit. Tuition and fees vary according to course load. *Graduate housing:* On-campus housing not available. *Student services:* Campus employment opportunities, campus safety program, career counseling, exercise/wellness program, free psychological counseling, grant writing training, international student services, multicultural affairs office, services for students with disabilities, teacher training, writing training. *Library:* Mason Library. *Collection:* Books: 315,880 (physical), 245,217 (digital/electronic); Serial titles: 207 (physical), 61,114 (digital/electronic); Databases: 86. Weekly public service hours: 104; students can reserve study rooms.

Computer facilities: Computer purchase and lease plans are available. 600 computers available on campus for general student use. A campuswide network can be accessed from student residence rooms and from off campus. Online class registration is available.
Website: http://www.keene.edu/

General Application Contact: Peggy Richmond, Director of Admissions, 603-358-2276, Fax: 603-358-2767, E-mail: admissions@keene.edu.

GRADUATE UNITS

School of Professional and Graduate Studies Students: 28 full-time (22 women), 67 part-time (47 women); includes 5 minority (3 Hispanic/Latino; 2 Two or more races, non-Hispanic/Latino). Average age 32. 40 applicants, 75% accepted, 24 enrolled. *Faculty:* 11 full-time (6 women), 9 part-time/adjunct (5 women). *Financial support:* In 2015–16, 27 students received support. Career-related internships or fieldwork, Federal Work-Study, institutionally sponsored loans, scholarships/grants, and unspecified assistantships available. Support available to part-time students. Financial award application deadline: 3/1; financial award applicants required to submit FAFSA. In 2015, 38 master's awarded. *Degree program information:* Part-time and evening/weekend programs available. Part-time, evening/weekend. Offers curriculum and instruction (M Ed); education leadership (PMC); educational leadership (M Ed); safety and occupational health applied science (MS); school counselor (M Ed, PMC); special education (M Ed). *Application deadline:* For fall admission, 4/1 for domestic and international students; for spring admission, 11/1 for domestic and international students; for summer admission, 3/1 for domestic and international students. Applications are processed on a rolling basis. *Application fee:* $50. Electronic applications accepted. *Application Contact:* Graduate Studies Office, 603-358-2497, E-mail: kscgraduatestudies@keene.edu. *Dean of Professional and Graduate Studies*, Dr. Rebecca Lytle, 603-358-2220, E-mail: rebecca.lytle@keene.edu.

KEHILATH YAKOV RABBINICAL SEMINARY, Ossining, NY 10562

General Information Independent-religious, men only, comprehensive institution.

GRADUATE UNITS

Graduate Programs

KEISER UNIVERSITY, Fort Lauderdale, FL 33309

General Information Independent, coed, university.

GRADUATE UNITS

Doctor of Business Administration Program Offers global business (DBA); global organizational leadership (DBA); marketing (DBA).

EdS in Educational Leadership Program Offers educational leadership (Ed S).

EdS in Instructional Design and Technology Program Offers instructional design and technology (Ed S).

Joint MS Ed/MBA Program

MA in Criminal Justice-Homeland Security Program Offers criminal justice-homeland security (MA).

MA in Criminal Justice Program ***Degree program information:*** Part-time programs available. Part-time, online learning. Offers criminal justice (MA).

Master of Accountancy Program Offers forensic accounting (M Acc); general accounting (M Acc).

Master of Business Administration Program ***Degree program information:*** Part-time programs available. Part-time, online learning. Offers accounting (MBA); health services management (MBA); information security management (MBA); international business (MBA); leadership for managers (MBA); marketing (MBA). All concentrations except information security management also offered in Mandarin; leadership for managers and international business also offered in Spanish.

Master of Science in Education Program ***Degree program information:*** Part-time programs available. Part-time, online learning. Offers allied health teaching and leadership (MS Ed); career college administration (MS Ed); leadership (MS Ed); online teaching and learning (MS Ed); teaching and learning (MS Ed).

Master of Science in Nursing Program Offers nursing (MSN).

MS in Information Security Program Offers information security (MS).

MS in Information Technology Leadership Program Offers information technology leadership (MS).

MS in Management Program Offers management (MS). Program also offered in Spanish.

MS in Organizational Psychology Program Offers organizational psychology (MS).

MS in Physician Assistant Program Offers physician assistant (MS).

MS in Psychology Program Offers psychology (MS).

PhD in Educational Leadership Program Offers educational leadership (PhD).

PhD in Industrial and Organizational Psychology Program Offers industrial and organizational psychology (PhD).

PhD in Instructional Design and Technology Program Offers instructional design and technology (PhD).
PhD in Psychology Program Offers psychology (PhD).

KENNESAW STATE UNIVERSITY, Kennesaw, GA 30144

General Information State-supported, coed, comprehensive institution. CGS member. *Graduate housing:* Room and/or apartments available on a first-come, first-served basis to single students; on-campus housing not available to married students.

GRADUATE UNITS

College of Architecture and Construction Management *Degree program information:* Part-time and evening/weekend programs available. Part-time, evening/weekend. Offers architecture (MS Arch); architecture and construction management (MS, MS Arch); construction management (MS). Electronic applications accepted.

College of Computing and Software Engineering *Degree program information:* Part-time and evening/weekend programs available. Part-time, evening/weekend, online learning. Offers computer science (MS); computing and software engineering (MS, MSIT, MSSWE, Graduate Certificate, Graduate Transition Certificate, Postbaccalaureate Certificate); health information technology (Postbaccalaureate Certificate); information security and assurance (Graduate Certificate); information technology (MSIT, Graduate Certificate); information technology fundamentals (Postbaccalaureate Certificate); software engineering (MSSWE, Graduate Certificate); software engineering foundations (Graduate Certificate). Electronic applications accepted.

College of Humanities and Social Sciences *Degree program information:* Part-time and evening/weekend programs available. Part-time, evening/weekend. Offers American studies (MA); conflict management (MSCM); criminal justice (MS); humanities and social sciences (MA, MAPW, MPA, MS, MSCM, PhD); integrated global communication (MA); international conflict management (PhD); international policy management (MS); professional writing (MAPW); public administration (MPA). Electronic applications accepted.

College of Science and Mathematics *Degree program information:* Part-time programs available. Part-time, online learning. Offers applied statistics (MSAS); biochemistry (MS); chemistry (MS); integrative biology (MS); science and mathematics (MS, MSAS). Electronic applications accepted.

Leland and Clarice C. Bagwell College of Education *Degree program information:* Part-time programs available. Part-time. Offers art education (MAT); biology (MAT); chemistry (MAT); education (M Ed, MAT, Ed D, Ed S); educational leadership (M Ed); educational leadership technology (M Ed); elementary and early childhood education (M Ed); foreign language education (Chinese and Spanish) (MAT); instructional technology (M Ed); leadership for learning (Ed D, Ed S); middle grades education (M Ed); physics (MAT); reading (M Ed); secondary education (M Ed); secondary English (MAT); secondary mathematics (MAT); special education (M Ed, MAT); teaching English to speakers of other languages (M Ed, MAT). Electronic applications accepted.

Michael J. Coles College of Business *Degree program information:* Part-time and evening/weekend programs available. Part-time, evening/weekend. Offers accounting (M Acc); business (M Acc, MBA, MSIS, DBA); business administration (MBA, DBA); information systems (MSIS). Electronic applications accepted.

Siegel Institute for Leadership, Ethics and Character *Degree program information:* Part-time and evening/weekend programs available. Part-time, evening/weekend, online learning. Offers leadership and ethics (Graduate Certificate). Electronic applications accepted.

Southern Polytechnic College of Engineering and Engineering Technology *Degree program information:* Part-time and evening/weekend programs available. Part-time, evening/weekend, online learning. Offers electrical engineering technology (MS); engineering and engineering technology (MBA, MS, MSA, Graduate Certificate, Graduate Transition Certificate); quality assurance (MS); systems engineering (MS, Graduate Certificate). Electronic applications accepted.

WellStar College of Health and Human Services *Degree program information:* Part-time and evening/weekend programs available. Part-time, evening/weekend, online learning. Offers advanced care management and leadership (MSN); applied exercise and health science (MS); health and human services (MS, MSN, MSW, DNS); nursing science (DNS); primary care nurse practitioner (MSN); social work (MSW). Electronic applications accepted.

KENRICK-GLENNON SEMINARY, St. Louis, MO 63119-4330

General Information Independent-religious, men only, graduate-only institution. *Graduate housing:* Room and/or apartments available to single students; on-campus housing not available to married students.

GRADUATE UNITS

Graduate and Professional Programs Offers theology (M Div, MA).

KENT STATE UNIVERSITY, Kent, OH 44242-0001

General Information State-supported, coed, university. CGS member. *Enrollment:* 29,762 graduate, professional, and undergraduate students; 3,769 full-time matriculated graduate/professional students (2,036 women), 2,494 part-time matriculated graduate/professional students (1,747 women). *Enrollment by degree level:* 4,402 master's, 1,732 doctoral, 129 other advanced degrees. *Graduate faculty:* 856. Tuition, state resident: full-time $10,864; part-time $495 per credit hour. Tuition, nonresident: full-time $18,380; part-time $837 per credit hour. *Graduate housing:* Room and/or apartments available on a first-come, first-served basis to single students; on-campus housing not available to married students. *Student services:* Campus employment opportunities, campus safety program, career counseling, child daycare facilities, exercise/wellness program, free psychological counseling, grant writing training, international student services, multicultural affairs office, services for students with disabilities, teacher training, writing training. *Library:* Kent State University Libraries and Media Services plus 4 others. *Collection:* Books: 2.4 million (physical), 844 (digital/electronic); Serial titles: 45,499 (physical), 520 (digital/electronic); Databases: 344. Study areas open 24 hours, 5–7 days a week; students can reserve study rooms.

Computer facilities: Computer purchase and lease plans are available. 2,000 computers available on campus for general student use. A campuswide network can be accessed from student residence rooms and from off campus. Online class registration is available.
Website: http://www.kent.edu/

General Application Contact: Lana Whitehead, Director, Graduate Admissions, 330-672-2661, Fax: 330-672-6262, E-mail: gradapps@kent.edu.

GRADUATE UNITS

College of Applied Engineering, Sustainability and Technology Students: 38 full-time (12 women), 30 part-time (9 women); includes 5 minority (2 Black or African American, non-Hispanic/Latino; 2 Asian, non-Hispanic/Latino; 1 Hispanic/Latino), 33 international. Average age 32. 95 applicants, 68% accepted, 38 enrolled. *Faculty:* 19 full-time (0 women). *Financial support:* Research assistantships with full tuition reimbursements, teaching assistantships with full tuition reimbursements, career-related internships or fieldwork, Federal Work-Study, and unspecified assistantships available. Financial award application deadline: 2/1. In 2015, 18 master's awarded. *Degree program information:* Part-time programs available. Part-time, online learning. Offers applied engineering, sustainability and technology (MT). *Application deadline:* For fall admission, 7/12 for domestic students, 5/15 for international students; for spring admission, 11/29 for domestic students, 10/15 for international students. Applications are processed on a rolling basis. *Application fee:* $45 ($70 for international students). Electronic applications accepted. *Application Contact:* Dr. John Duncan, Assistant Professor/Coordinator, Graduate Program, 330-672-2892, E-mail: caest@kent.edu. *Interim Dean*, Robert Sines, Jr., 330-672-0790, E-mail: rsines@kent.edu.

College of Architecture and Environmental Design Students: 455 full-time (31 women), 8 part-time (3 women); includes 6 minority (2 Black or African American, non-Hispanic/Latino; 1 American Indian or Alaska Native, non-Hispanic/Latino; 2 Hispanic/Latino; 1 Two or more races, non-Hispanic/Latino), 8 international. Average age 26. 242 applicants, 67% accepted, 116 enrolled. *Faculty:* 24 full-time (5 women). *Financial support:* Research assistantships with full tuition reimbursements, teaching assistantships with full tuition reimbursements, career-related internships or fieldwork, Federal Work-Study, scholarships/grants, and unspecified assistantships available. Financial award application deadline: 2/1. In 2015, 45 master's awarded. *Degree program information:* Part-time programs available. Part-time. Offers architecture (M Arch); architecture and environmental design (MS); health care design (MHCD); landscape architecture (ML Arch); urban design (MUD). *Application deadline:* For fall admission, 1/15 for domestic and international students. *Application fee:* $45 ($70 for international students). Electronic applications accepted. *Application Contact:* Johnathan Fleming, Assistant Professor and Director, Master of Architecture, 330-672-2917, Fax: 330-672-3809, E-mail: caed_info@kent.edu. *Dean*, Douglas Steidl, 330-672-2917, Fax: 330-672-3809, E-mail: dsteidl@kent.edu.

College of Arts and Sciences Students: 1,063 full-time (507 women), 271 part-time (146 women); includes 113 minority (37 Black or African American, non-Hispanic/Latino; 1 American Indian or Alaska Native, non-Hispanic/Latino; 17 Asian, non-Hispanic/Latino; 31 Hispanic/Latino; 27 Two or more races, non-Hispanic/Latino), 552 international. Average age 29. 4,202 applicants, 27% accepted, 617 enrolled. *Faculty:* 380 full-time (161 women). *Financial support:* Fellowships with full tuition reimbursements, research assistantships with full tuition reimbursements, teaching assistantships with full tuition reimbursements, career-related internships or fieldwork, Federal Work-Study, institutionally sponsored loans, scholarships/grants, and unspecified assistantships available. In 2015, 232 master's, 91 doctorates, 1 other advanced degree awarded. *Degree program information:* Part-time programs available. Part-time, online learning. Offers anthropology (MA); applied geology (PhD); applied mathematics (MA, MS, PhD); arts and sciences (MA, MFA, MLS, MPA, MS, PhD, Certificate); biological sciences (MS, PhD); chemical physics (MS, PhD); chemistry (MA); clinical psychology (MA, PhD); computer science (MA, MS, PhD); creative writing (MFA); English (PhD); English for teachers (MA); experimental psychology (MA, PhD); geography (MA, PhD); history (PhD); literature and writing (MA); philosophy (MA); physics (MA, MS, PhD); public administration (MPA); pure mathematics (MA, MS, PhD); rhetoric and composition (PhD); sociology (MA, PhD); teaching English as a second language (MA); TESL/TEFL (Certificate); translation (MA); translation studies (PhD). *Application fee:* $45 ($70 for international students). Electronic applications accepted. *Application Contact:* 330-672-2062, E-mail: asadvise@kent.edu. *Interim Dean*, Dr. James L. Blank, 330-672-2650, Fax: 330-672-2938, E-mail: jblank@kent.edu.

Center for Comparative and Integrative Programs Students: 2 full-time (both women), 12 part-time (8 women); includes 3 minority (all Black or African American, non-Hispanic/Latino). Average age 40. 27 applicants, 59% accepted, 11 enrolled. *Financial support:* Career-related internships or fieldwork and Federal Work-Study available. In 2015, 4 master's awarded. *Degree program information:* Part-time and evening/weekend programs available. Part-time, evening/weekend, online learning. Offers comparative and integrative programs (MLS). *Application deadline:* For fall admission, 5/1 for domestic students; for spring admission, 11/29 for domestic students. Applications are processed on a rolling basis. *Application fee:* $45 ($70 for international students). Electronic applications accepted. *Application Contact:* Richard M. Berrong, Director of Liberal Studies, E-mail: rberrong@kent.edu. *Associate Dean*, Dr. David W. Odell-Scott, 330-672-0271, E-mail: dodellsc@kent.edu.

School of Biomedical Sciences Students: 76 full-time (46 women), 1 (woman) part-time; includes 6 minority (1 Black or African American, non-Hispanic/Latino; 2 Asian, non-Hispanic/Latino; 1 Hispanic/Latino; 2 Two or more races, non-Hispanic/Latino), 28 international. Average age 29. 223 applicants, 13% accepted, 22 enrolled. *Financial support:* In 2015–16, 76 students received support. Research assistantships with full tuition reimbursements available, teaching assistantships, career-related internships or fieldwork, Federal Work-Study, and unspecified assistantships available. Financial award application deadline: 1/1. In 2015, 5 master's, 7 doctorates awarded. Offers biological anthropology (PhD); cellular and molecular biology (PhD); neurosciences (PhD); pharmacology (MS); physiology (PhD). *Application deadline:* For fall admission, 1/1 for domestic students. *Application fee:* $45 ($70 for international students). Electronic applications accepted. *Application Contact:* 330-672-2263, Fax: 330-672-9391, E-mail: jwearden@kent.edu. *Director*, Dr. Eric Mintz, 330-672-2263, E-mail: emintz@kent.edu.

College of Business Administration Students: 284 (113 women); includes 22 minority (9 Black or African American, non-Hispanic/Latino; 1 American Indian or Alaska Native, non-Hispanic/Latino; 4 Asian, non-Hispanic/Latino; 2 Hispanic/Latino; 6 Two or more races, non-Hispanic/Latino), 102 international. Average age 27. 222 applicants, 55% accepted, 77 enrolled. *Faculty:* 75 full-time (30 women). *Financial support:* In 2015–16, 71 students received support, including 34 research assistantships with full tuition reimbursements available (averaging $4,500 per year), 46 teaching assistantships with full tuition reimbursements available (averaging $23,000 per year); fellowships with full tuition reimbursements available, career-related internships or fieldwork, Federal Work-Study, and unspecified assistantships also available. Financial award applicants required to submit FAFSA. In 2015, 53 master's, 6 doctorates awarded. *Degree program information:* Part-time and evening/weekend programs available. Part-time, evening/weekend. Offers accounting (MS, PhD); business administration (MA, MBA, MS, MSBA, PhD); economics (MA); finance (PhD); management systems (PhD); marketing (PhD). *Application fee:* $45 ($70 for international students). Electronic applications accepted. *Application Contact:* Louise M. Ditchey, Administrative Director, 330-672-2282, Fax: 330-672-7303, E-mail: gradbus@kent.edu. *Associate Dean*, Dr. Robert D. Hisrich, 330-672-2772, Fax: 330-672-1231, E-mail: rhisric1@kent.edu.

College of Communication and Information Students: 299 full-time (215 women), 779 part-time (562 women); includes 128 minority (50 Black or African American, non-

Hispanic/Latino; 3 American Indian or Alaska Native, non-Hispanic/Latino; 17 Asian, non-Hispanic/Latino; 33 Hispanic/Latino; 1 Native Hawaiian or other Pacific Islander, non-Hispanic/Latino; 24 Two or more races, non-Hispanic/Latino), 39 international. Average age 33. 950 applicants, 79% accepted, 563 enrolled. *Faculty:* 80 full-time (47 women). *Financial support:* Research assistantships with full tuition reimbursements, teaching assistantships with full tuition reimbursements, career-related internships or fieldwork, Federal Work-Study, scholarships/grants, and unspecified assistantships available. In 2015, 386 master's, 5 doctorates, 5 other advanced degrees awarded. *Degree program information:* Part-time programs available. Part-time, online learning. Offers communication and information (MA, MFA, MLIS, MS, PhD, Certificate). *Application deadline:* For fall admission, 2/1 for domestic and international students. *Application fee:* $45 ($70 for international students). Electronic applications accepted. *Application Contact:* Dr. Paul Haridakis, Professor/Coordinator of Doctoral Education, 330-672-0180, Fax: 330-672-7965, E-mail: pharidak@kent.edu. *Professor and Dean*, Amy Reynolds, 330-672-2950, E-mail: areyno24@kent.edu.

School of Communication Studies Students: 28 full-time (20 women), 12 part-time (10 women); includes 3 minority (2 Asian, non-Hispanic/Latino; 1 Hispanic/Latino), 12 international. Average age 29. 92 applicants, 52% accepted, 36 enrolled. *Faculty:* 16 full-time (12 women). *Financial support:* Research assistantships with full tuition reimbursements, teaching assistantships with full tuition reimbursements, career-related internships or fieldwork, Federal Work-Study, scholarships/grants, and unspecified assistantships available. Financial award application deadline: 2/1. In 2015, 7 master's awarded. *Degree program information:* Part-time programs available. Part-time. Offers communication and information (PhD); communication studies (MA). *Application deadline:* For fall admission, 1/15 for domestic students; for spring admission, 11/15 for domestic students. *Application fee:* $45 ($70 for international students). Electronic applications accepted. *Application Contact:* Dr. Nichole Egbert, Professor and Graduate Coordinator, 330-672-3314, Fax: 330-672-3510, E-mail: negbert@kent.edu. *Associate Professor/Interim Director*, Dr. Jeffrey T. Child, 330-672-2659, E-mail: jchild@kent.edu.

School of Journalism and Mass Communication Students: 14 full-time (10 women), 124 part-time (84 women); includes 21 minority (13 Black or African American, non-Hispanic/Latino; 1 American Indian or Alaska Native, non-Hispanic/Latino; 1 Asian, non-Hispanic/Latino; 1 Hispanic/Latino; 5 Two or more races, non-Hispanic/Latino), 5 international. Average age 36. 112 applicants, 68% accepted, 50 enrolled. *Faculty:* 28 full-time (13 women). *Financial support:* Research assistantships with full tuition reimbursements, teaching assistantships with full tuition reimbursements, career-related internships or fieldwork, Federal Work-Study, scholarships/grants, and unspecified assistantships available. Financial award application deadline: 2/1. In 2015, 117 master's awarded. *Degree program information:* Part-time programs available. Part-time. Offers media management (MA); public relations (MA); reporting and editing (MA). *Application deadline:* For fall admission, 7/1 for domestic students, 3/1 for international students; for spring admission, 12/1 for domestic students, 10/30 for international students; for summer admission, 5/1 for domestic students. *Application fee:* $45 ($70 for international students). Electronic applications accepted. *Application Contact:* Dr. Danielle Coombs, Graduate Coordinator and Associate Professor, 330-672-8876, E-mail: dcoombs@kent.edu. *Director and Professor*, Thor Wasbotten, 330-672-4066, E-mail: thor@kent.edu.

School of Library and Information Science Students: 208 full-time (163 women), 633 part-time (459 women); includes 95 minority (32 Black or African American, non-Hispanic/Latino; 2 American Indian or Alaska Native, non-Hispanic/Latino; 11 Asian, non-Hispanic/Latino; 31 Hispanic/Latino; 19 Two or more races, non-Hispanic/Latino), 9 international. Average age 33. 652 applicants, 90% accepted, 445 enrolled. *Faculty:* 22 full-time (16 women). *Financial support:* Research assistantships with full tuition reimbursements, teaching assistantships with full tuition reimbursements, career-related internships or fieldwork, Federal Work-Study, scholarships/grants, and unspecified assistantships available. Financial award application deadline: 2/1. In 2015, 257 master's, 5 other advanced degrees awarded. *Degree program information:* Part-time and evening/weekend programs available. Part-time, evening/weekend, online learning. Offers library and information science (MLIS, MS, Certificate). *Application deadline:* For fall admission, 3/15 for domestic students; for spring admission, 9/15 for domestic students; for summer admission, 1/15 for domestic students. *Application fee:* $45 ($70 for international students). Electronic applications accepted. *Application Contact:* 330-672-2782, E-mail: slisinform@kent.edu. *Professor and Interim Director*, Jeff Fruit, 330-672-0890, E-mail: jfruit@kent.edu.

School of Visual Communication Design Students: 32 full-time (13 women), 3 part-time (all women); includes 5 minority (4 Black or African American, non-Hispanic/Latino; 1 Asian, non-Hispanic/Latino), 8 international. Average age 28. 50 applicants, 60% accepted, 26 enrolled. *Faculty:* 13 full-time (6 women). *Financial support:* Research assistantships with tuition reimbursements, teaching assistantships with tuition reimbursements, career-related internships or fieldwork, Federal Work-Study, scholarships/grants, and unspecified assistantships available. Financial award application deadline: 2/1. In 2015, 5 master's awarded. *Degree program information:* Part-time programs available. Part-time. Offers visual communication design (MA, MFA). *Application deadline:* For fall admission, 3/1 for domestic and international students; for spring admission, 10/1 for domestic and international students. *Application fee:* $45 ($70 for international students). Electronic applications accepted. *Application Contact:* Ken Visocky O'Grady, Graduate Coordinator and Associate Professor, 330-672-7856, E-mail: kogrady@kent.edu. *Associate Professor/Acting Director*, Jaime Kennedy, 330-672-9724, E-mail: jkenned8@kent.edu.

College of Education, Health and Human Services ***Degree program information:*** Part-time and evening/weekend programs available. Part-time, evening/weekend, online learning. Offers education, health and human services (M Ed, MA, MAT, MS, Au D, PhD, Ed S). Electronic applications accepted.

School of Foundations, Leadership and Administration Offers cultural foundations (M Ed, MA, PhD); evaluation and measurement (M Ed, PhD); higher education (PhD, Ed S); higher education and student personnel (M Ed); hospitality and tourism management (MS); K-12 leadership (M Ed, PhD, Ed S); sport and recreation management (MA); sports recreation and management (MA); sports studies (MA). Electronic applications accepted.

School of Health Sciences Degree program information: Part-time and evening/weekend programs available. Part-time, evening/weekend. Offers athletic training (MS); audiology (Au D, PhD); exercise physiology (MS, PhD); health education and promotion (M Ed, PhD); nutrition (MS); speech language pathology (MA, PhD). Electronic applications accepted.

School of Lifespan Development and Educational Sciences Degree program information: Part-time and evening/weekend programs available. Part-time, evening/weekend. Offers clinical mental health counseling (M Ed); computer technology (M Ed); counseling (Ed S); counseling and human development services (PhD); deaf education (M Ed); early childhood education (M Ed); educational interpreter K-12 (M Ed); educational psychology (M Ed, MA, PhD); general instructional technology (M Ed); general special education (M Ed); human development and family studies (MA); instructional technology (M Ed, PhD); mild/moderate intervention (M Ed); rehabilitation counseling (M Ed); school counseling (M Ed); school psychology (PhD, Ed S); special education (M Ed, PhD, Ed S); transition to work (M Ed). Electronic applications accepted.

School of Teaching, Learning and Curriculum Studies Degree program information: Part-time and evening/weekend programs available. Part-time, evening/weekend. Offers career technical teacher education (M Ed); curriculum and instruction (M Ed, PhD, Ed S); early childhood education (M Ed, MA, MAT); junior high/middle school (M Ed, MA); math specialization (M Ed, MA); reading specialization (M Ed, MA); secondary education (MAT). Electronic applications accepted.

College of Nursing Students: 78 full-time (56 women), 414 part-time (365 women); includes 63 minority (34 Black or African American, non-Hispanic/Latino; 1 American Indian or Alaska Native, non-Hispanic/Latino; 12 Asian, non-Hispanic/Latino; 12 Hispanic/Latino; 4 Two or more races, non-Hispanic/Latino), 16 international. Average age 37. 653 applicants, 54% accepted, 309 enrolled. *Faculty:* 52 full-time (48 women). *Financial support:* Research assistantships with full tuition reimbursements, teaching assistantships with full tuition reimbursements, career-related internships or fieldwork, Federal Work-Study, traineeships, and unspecified assistantships available. Financial award application deadline: 2/1. In 2015, 140 master's, 1 doctorate, 13 other advanced degrees awarded. *Degree program information:* Part-time programs available. Part-time, online learning. Offers advanced nursing practice (DNP); nursing (MSN, PhD); nursing education (Certificate); primary care pediatric nurse practitioner (Certificate); women's health nurse practitioner (Certificate). PhD program offered jointly with The University of Akron. *Application deadline:* For fall admission, 2/1 for domestic students; for spring admission, 11/1 for domestic students. *Application fee:* $45 ($70 for international students). Electronic applications accepted. *Application Contact:* Dr. Wendy A. Umberger, Associate Dean for Graduate Programs/Professor, 330-672-8813, E-mail: wlewando@kent.edu. *Dean*, Dr. Barbara Broome, 330-672-3777, E-mail: bbroome1@kent.edu.

College of Podiatric Medicine Offers podiatric medicine (DPM). Electronic applications accepted.

College of Public Health Students: 139 full-time (101 women), 100 part-time (76 women); includes 56 minority (33 Black or African American, non-Hispanic/Latino; 1 American Indian or Alaska Native, non-Hispanic/Latino; 9 Asian, non-Hispanic/Latino; 9 Hispanic/Latino; 1 Native Hawaiian or other Pacific Islander, non-Hispanic/Latino; 3 Two or more races, non-Hispanic/Latino), 22 international. Average age 33. 291 applicants, 65% accepted, 137 enrolled. *Faculty:* 23 full-time (11 women). *Financial support:* Research assistantships with full tuition reimbursements, teaching assistantships with full tuition reimbursements, career-related internships or fieldwork, Federal Work-Study, and unspecified assistantships available. In 2015, 29 master's, 1 doctorate awarded. *Degree program information:* Part-time and evening/weekend programs available. Part-time, evening/weekend, online learning. Offers public health (MPH, PhD). *Application deadline:* For fall admission, 7/1 priority date for domestic students, 3/1 for international students; for spring admission, 11/15 priority date for domestic students; for summer admission, 4/15 priority date for domestic students. Applications are processed on a rolling basis. *Application fee:* $45 ($70 for international students). Electronic applications accepted. *Application Contact:* 330-325-6500, E-mail: publichealth@kent.edu. *Dean*, Dr. Sonia Alemagno, 330-672-6500, E-mail: salemagn@kent.edu.

College of the Arts Students: 116 full-time (63 women), 199 part-time (136 women); includes 22 minority (11 Black or African American, non-Hispanic/Latino; 1 American Indian or Alaska Native, non-Hispanic/Latino; 2 Asian, non-Hispanic/Latino; 3 Hispanic/Latino; 1 Native Hawaiian or other Pacific Islander, non-Hispanic/Latino; 4 Two or more races, non-Hispanic/Latino), 35 international. Average age 31. 372 applicants, 64% accepted, 175 enrolled. *Faculty:* 99 full-time (58 women). *Financial support:* Research assistantships with full tuition reimbursements, teaching assistantships with full tuition reimbursements, Federal Work-Study, scholarships/grants, and unspecified assistantships available. In 2015, 121 master's, 5 doctorates awarded. *Degree program information:* Part-time programs available. Part-time, online learning. Offers arts (MA, MFA, MM, PhD). *Application deadline:* For fall admission, 2/2 for domestic students; for spring admission, 9/15 for domestic students. *Application fee:* $45 ($70 for international students). Electronic applications accepted. *Application Contact:* 330-672-2760, E-mail: collegeofthearts@kent.edu. *Dean and Professor*, John R. Crawford, 330-672-2760, Fax: 330-672-4706, E-mail: jcrawfo1@kent.edu.

Hugh A. Glauser School of Music Students: 54 full-time (28 women), 193 part-time (107 women); includes 11 minority (5 Black or African American, non-Hispanic/Latino; 1 Asian, non-Hispanic/Latino; 3 Hispanic/Latino; 2 Two or more races, non-Hispanic/Latino), 20 international. Average age 31. 195 applicants, 76% accepted, 115 enrolled. *Faculty:* 32 full-time (9 women). *Financial support:* Research assistantships with full tuition reimbursements, teaching assistantships with full tuition reimbursements, Federal Work-Study, scholarships/grants, and unspecified assistantships available. Financial award application deadline: 2/1. In 2015, 98 master's, 5 doctorates, 1 other advanced degree awarded. *Degree program information:* Part-time programs available. Part-time, online learning. Offers conducting (MM); ethnomusicology (MA); music composition (MA, Certificate); music conducting (Certificate); music education (MM, PhD); music performance (Certificate); music theory (MA, PhD); performance (MM). *Application deadline:* For fall admission, 8/1 for domestic students; for spring admission, 12/1 for domestic students. *Application fee:* $45 ($70 for international students). Electronic applications accepted. *Application Contact:* Michael W. Chunn, Coordinator of Graduate Studies, 330-672-2172, Fax: 330-672-7837, E-mail: mchunn@kent.edu. *Acting Director*, Ralph Lorenz, 330-672-2172, E-mail: rlorenz@kent.edu.

School of Art Students: 38 full-time (25 women), 31 part-time (23 women); includes 5 minority (1 Black or African American, non-Hispanic/Latino; 2 Hispanic/Latino; 2 Two or more races, non-Hispanic/Latino), 6 international. Average age 33. 106 applicants, 49% accepted, 24 enrolled. *Faculty:* 22 full-time (14 women). *Financial support:* Research assistantships with full tuition reimbursements, teaching assistantships with full tuition reimbursements, career-related internships or fieldwork, Federal Work-Study, scholarships/grants, and unspecified assistantships available. Financial award application deadline: 2/15. In 2015, 21 master's awarded. *Degree program information:* Part-time programs available. Part-time. Offers art education (MA); art history (MA); crafts (MA, MFA). *Application deadline:* For fall admission, 2/2 priority date for domestic students; for spring admission, 9/15 priority date for domestic students. Applications are processed on a rolling basis. *Application fee:* $45 ($70 for international students). Electronic applications accepted. *Application Contact:* Linda A. Hoeptner-Poling, Associate Professor and Graduate Coordinator, 330-672-7895,

E-mail: lhoeptne@kent.edu. *Director*, Dr. Christine Havice, 330-672-2192, Fax: 330-672-4729, E-mail: chavice@kent.edu.

School of Theatre and Dance Students: 13 full-time (5 women); includes 2 minority (both Black or African American, non-Hispanic/Latino), 1 international. Average age 33. 10 applicants, 60% accepted, 6 enrolled. *Faculty:* 19 full-time (13 women). *Financial support:* In 2015–16, 13 students received support. Career-related internships or fieldwork, Federal Work-Study, and scholarships/grants available. Financial award application deadline: 2/1. In 2015, 2 master's awarded. *Degree program information:* Part-time programs available. Part-time. Offers acting (MFA); design and technology (MFA). *Application deadline:* For fall admission, 7/12 for domestic students; for spring admission, 11/29 for domestic students. Applications are processed on a rolling basis. *Application fee:* $45 ($70 for international students). Electronic applications accepted. *Application Contact:* Yuko Kurahashi, Associate Professor and Graduate Coordinator, 330-672-2082, E-mail: theatre@kent.edu. *Associate Professor/Acting Director*, Eric Van Baars, 330-672-0102, E-mail: fvanbaar@kent.edu.

School of Digital Sciences Students: 457 full-time (156 women), 80 part-time (24 women); includes 4 minority (1 Black or African American, non-Hispanic/Latino; 2 Asian, non-Hispanic/Latino; 1 Hispanic/Latino), 504 international. Average age 25. 465 applicants, 69% accepted, 162 enrolled. *Financial support:* Research assistantships with full tuition reimbursements, teaching assistantships with full tuition reimbursements, career-related internships or fieldwork, Federal Work-Study, and unspecified assistantships available. In 2015, 9 master's awarded. *Degree program information:* Part-time programs available. Part-time, online learning. Offers digital sciences (MDS); enterprise architecture (Certificate). *Application deadline:* For fall admission, 7/1 for domestic students; for spring admission, 11/15 for domestic students; for summer admission, 4/15 priority date for domestic students. Applications are processed on a rolling basis. *Application fee:* $45 ($70 for international students). Electronic applications accepted. *Application Contact:* 330-672-9069, E-mail: digital-sciences@kent.edu. *Director*, Dr. Robert A. Walker, 330-672-9105, E-mail: rawalke1@kent.edu.

KENT STATE UNIVERSITY AT STARK, Canton, OH 44720-7599

General Information State-supported, coed, comprehensive institution.

GRADUATE UNITS

Graduate School of Education, Health and Human Services Offers curriculum and instruction studies (M Ed, MA).

Professional MBA Program Offers business administration (MBA).

KENTUCKY CHRISTIAN UNIVERSITY, Grayson, KY 41143-2205

General Information Independent-religious, coed, comprehensive institution. *Graduate housing:* Rooms and/or apartments available on a first-come, first-served basis to single and married students.

GRADUATE UNITS

Graduate School ***Degree program information:*** Part-time programs available. Part-time. Offers Biblical studies (MA); Christian leadership (MA). Electronic applications accepted.

KENTUCKY STATE UNIVERSITY, Frankfort, KY 40601

General Information State-related, coed, comprehensive institution. *Enrollment:* 1,586 graduate, professional, and undergraduate students; 91 full-time matriculated graduate/professional students (48 women), 59 part-time matriculated graduate/professional students (34 women). *Enrollment by degree level:* 138 master's, 12 doctoral. *Graduate faculty:* 31 full-time (9 women), 3 part-time/adjunct (2 women). Tuition, state resident: full-time $7524; part-time $418 per credit hour. Tuition, nonresident: full-time $11,322; part-time $629 per credit hour. Tuition and fees vary according to course load. *Graduate housing:* Room and/or apartments available on a first-come, first-served basis to single students; on-campus housing not available to married students. Typical cost: $3340 per year ($6690 including board). Room and board charges vary according to board plan and housing facility selected. Housing application deadline: 6/3. *Student services:* Campus employment opportunities, campus safety program, career counseling, child daycare facilities, exercise/wellness program, free psychological counseling, grant writing training, international student services, low-cost health insurance, multicultural affairs office, services for students with disabilities, teacher training, writing training. *Library:* Paul G. Blazer Library. *Collection:* Books: 331,660 (physical), 23,427 (digital/electronic); Serial titles: 16,649 (physical), 13,303 (digital/electronic); Databases: 60. Weekly public service hours: 101; study areas open 24 hours, 5–7 days a week. *Research affiliation:* Alltech Biotechnology Center (animal nutrition).

Computer facilities: 127 computers available on campus for general student use. A campuswide network can be accessed from student residence rooms and from off campus. Online class registration, student bill-pay, address verification, ability to accept financial aid awards are available.
Website: http://www.kysu.edu/

General Application Contact: Dr. James Obielodan, Director of Graduate Studies, 502-597-4723, E-mail: james.obielodan@kysu.edu.

GRADUATE UNITS

College of Agriculture, Food Science and Sustainable Systems Students: 24 full-time (10 women), 9 part-time (6 women); includes 9 minority (6 Black or African American, non-Hispanic/Latino; 1 Asian, non-Hispanic/Latino; 1 Hispanic/Latino; 1 Two or more races, non-Hispanic/Latino), 1 international. Average age 30. 25 applicants, 84% accepted, 17 enrolled. *Faculty:* 11 full-time (1 woman). *Financial support:* In 2015–16, 11 students received support, including 24 research assistantships (averaging $21,061 per year); scholarships/grants, tuition waivers (partial), and unspecified assistantships also available. Financial award application deadline: 4/15; financial award applicants required to submit FAFSA. In 2015, 12 master's awarded. *Degree program information:* Part-time and evening/weekend programs available. Part-time, evening/weekend. Offers aquaculture (MS); environmental studies (MS). *Application deadline:* Applications are processed on a rolling basis. *Application fee:* $30 ($100 for international students). Electronic applications accepted. *Application Contact:* Dr. James Obielodan, Director of Graduate Studies, 502-597-4723, E-mail: james.obielodan@kysu.edu. *Interim Director of Land Grant Programs*, Dr. Kirk Pomper, 502-597-5942, E-mail: kirk.pomper@kysu.edu.

College of Business and Computer Science Students: 24 full-time (9 women), 16 part-time (4 women); includes 13 minority (10 Black or African American, non-Hispanic/Latino; 2 Asian, non-Hispanic/Latino; 1 Two or more races, non-Hispanic/Latino), 9 international. Average age 32. 23 applicants, 74% accepted, 14 enrolled. *Faculty:* 9 full-time (1 woman), 1 part-time/adjunct (0 women). *Financial support:* In 2015–16, 12 students received support, including 3 research assistantships (averaging $12,393 per year); scholarships/grants, tuition waivers (partial), and unspecified assistantships also available. Financial award application deadline: 4/15; financial award applicants required to submit FAFSA. In 2015, 17 master's awarded. *Degree program information:* Part-time and evening/weekend programs available. Part-time, evening/weekend. Offers business administration (MBA); computer science technology (MS). *Application deadline:* Applications are processed on a rolling basis. *Application fee:* $30 ($100 for international students). Electronic applications accepted. *Application Contact:* Dr. James Obielodan, Director of Graduate Studies, 502-597-4723, E-mail: james.obielodan@kysu.edu. *Vice President of Academic Affairs*, Dr. Lynda Brown-Wright, 502-597-6442, E-mail: lynda.brownwright@kysu.edu.

College of Professional Studies Students: 34 full-time (22 women), 34 part-time (24 women); includes 47 minority (45 Black or African American, non-Hispanic/Latino; 1 Asian, non-Hispanic/Latino; 1 Two or more races, non-Hispanic/Latino), 3 international. Average age 36. 35 applicants, 83% accepted, 22 enrolled. *Faculty:* 7 full-time (3 women), 2 part-time/adjunct (both women). *Financial support:* In 2015–16, 34 students received support, including 1 research assistantship (averaging $15,599 per year); scholarships/grants, tuition waivers (partial), and unspecified assistantships also available. Financial award application deadline: 4/15; financial award applicants required to submit FAFSA. In 2015, 23 master's awarded. *Degree program information:* Part-time and evening/weekend programs available. Part-time, evening/weekend, blended/hybrid learning. Offers nursing (DNP); public administration (MPA); special education (MA). *Application deadline:* Applications are processed on a rolling basis. *Application fee:* $30 ($100 for international students). Electronic applications accepted. *Application Contact:* Dr. James Obielodan, Director of Graduate Studies, 502-597-4723, E-mail: james.obielodan@kysu.edu. *Vice President of Academic Affairs*, Dr. Lynda Brown-Wright, 502-597-6442, E-mail: lynda.brownwright@kysu.edu.

KETTERING COLLEGE, Kettering, OH 45429-1299

General Information Independent-religious, coed, primarily women, comprehensive institution.

GRADUATE UNITS

Program in Physician Assistant Studies Offers physician assistant studies (MPAS).

KETTERING UNIVERSITY, Flint, MI 48504

General Information Independent, coed, comprehensive institution. *Graduate housing:* Rooms and/or apartments available on a first-come, first-served basis to single students and available to married students. Housing application deadline: 7/15. *Research affiliation:* McLaren Foundation (orthopedic surgery biomechanics), Shin-Estu Chemical Company (atmospheric plasma technology), Broad-Ocean Technologies (electric vehicle battery systems), Landaal Packaging Systems (space utilization and process flow of operations), Mahindra Tractor Assembly, dba Mahindra GenZe (electric power and control boards), TRW (crash safety).

GRADUATE UNITS

Graduate School ***Degree program information:*** Part-time and evening/weekend programs available. Part-time, evening/weekend, online learning. Offers business (MBA, MS); engineering (MS). Electronic applications accepted.

KEUKA COLLEGE, Keuka Park, NY 14478-0098

General Information Independent-religious, coed, comprehensive institution. *Enrollment:* 1,933 graduate, professional, and undergraduate students; 203 full-time matriculated graduate/professional students (164 women), 6 part-time matriculated graduate/professional students (3 women). *Enrollment by degree level:* 209 master's. *Graduate faculty:* 29 full-time (20 women), 124 part-time/adjunct (50 women). *Graduate housing:* Room and/or apartments available on a first-come, first-served basis to single students; on-campus housing not available to married students. Typical cost: $5258 per year ($11,070 including board). *Student services:* Career counseling, grant writing training, services for students with disabilities, teacher training, writing training. *Library:* Lightner Library plus 1 other. *Collection:* Books: 118,107 (physical), 1,068 (digital/electronic); Serial titles: 107 (physical), 115 (digital/electronic); Databases: 120,000. Weekly public service hours: 96.

Computer facilities: 185 computers available on campus for general student use. A campuswide network can be accessed from student residence rooms and from off campus. Online class registration, phone app for registration, cancellations are available.
Website: http://www.keuka.edu/

General Application Contact: Megan Perkins, Director of Admissions, 315-279-5254, Fax: 315-279-5386, E-mail: admissions@keuka.edu.

GRADUATE UNITS

Program in Childhood Education/Literacy Students: 9 full-time (7 women); includes 1 minority (American Indian or Alaska Native, non-Hispanic/Latino). Average age 24. 9 applicants, 100% accepted, 9 enrolled. *Faculty:* 5 full-time (4 women), 1 part-time/adjunct (0 women). *Financial support:* In 2015–16, 8 students received support. Scholarships/grants and tuition waivers available. Financial award applicants required to submit FAFSA. In 2015, 7 master's awarded. Offers childhood education/literacy (MS). *Application deadline:* For fall admission, 8/15 priority date for domestic students; for winter admission, 12/15 priority date for domestic students; for spring admission, 4/15 priority date for domestic students. Applications are processed on a rolling basis. *Application fee:* $50. Electronic applications accepted. *Application Contact:* Anna Decker, Secretary, Graduate Education, 315-279-5510, E-mail: adecker@keuka.edu. *Director of Graduate Program in Education*, Dr. Andrew Beigel, 315-279-5442 Ext. 5662, E-mail: abeigel@keuka.edu.

Program in Criminal Justice Administration Students: 13 full-time (9 women); includes 6 minority (5 Black or African American, non-Hispanic/Latino; 1 Two or more races, non-Hispanic/Latino). Average age 36. *Faculty:* 4 full-time (1 woman), 33 part-time/adjunct (9 women). *Financial support:* In 2015–16, 6 students received support. Scholarships/grants and tuition waivers available. Financial award applicants required to submit FAFSA. In 2015, 16 master's awarded. Offers criminal justice administration (MS). *Application deadline:* For fall admission, 8/15 for domestic students; for winter admission, 12/15 for domestic students; for spring admission, 4/15 for domestic students. Applications are processed on a rolling basis. *Application fee:* $50. Electronic applications accepted. *Application Contact:* Fred Hoyle, Dean of Enrollment, 315-279-5413, Fax: 315-279-5386, E-mail: admissions@mail.keuka.edu. *Program Director*, Dr. Tom Tremer, 315-279-5672, E-mail: ttremer@mail.keuka.edu.

Program in Management Students: 64 full-time (42 women); includes 19 minority (5 Black or African American, non-Hispanic/Latino; 2 American Indian or Alaska Native, non-Hispanic/Latino; 9 Asian, non-Hispanic/Latino; 2 Hispanic/Latino; 1 Two or more races, non-Hispanic/Latino). Average age 32. 90 applicants, 18% accepted, 21 enrolled. *Faculty:* 7 full-time (2 women), 66 part-time/adjunct (16 women). *Financial support:* In 2015–16, 18 students received support. Scholarships/grants and tuition waivers available. Financial award applicants required to submit FAFSA. In 2015, 54 master's awarded. *Degree program information:* Evening/weekend programs available.

Evening/weekend. Offers management (MS). *Application deadline:* For fall admission, 8/15 priority date for domestic students; for winter admission, 12/15 priority date for domestic students; for spring admission, 4/15 priority date for domestic students. Applications are processed on a rolling basis. *Application fee:* $50. *Application Contact:* Graduate Admissions, 866-255-3852, Fax: 315-279-5386, E-mail: asapadvisor@keuka.edu. *Chair, Division of Business and Management,* Daniel Robeson, 315-279-5008, E-mail: drobeson@keuka.edu.

Program in Nursing Students: 68 full-time (62 women); includes 8 minority (6 Black or African American, non-Hispanic/Latino; 1 Asian, non-Hispanic/Latino; 1 Hispanic/Latino). Average age 36. *Faculty:* 8 full-time (all women), 23 part-time/adjunct (22 women). *Financial support:* Scholarships/grants and tuition waivers available. Financial award applicants required to submit FAFSA. In 2015, 20 master's awarded. Offers adult gerontology nurse practitioner (MS); nursing (MS). *Application deadline:* Applications are processed on a rolling basis. *Application fee:* $50. Electronic applications accepted. *Application Contact:* Graduate Admissions, 866-255-3852, Fax: 315-279-5386, E-mail: asapadvisor@keuka.edu. *Chair,* Dr. Debra Gates, 315-279-5115 Ext. 5273, E-mail: dgates@keuka.edu.

Program in Occupational Therapy Students: 38 full-time (32 women); includes 4 minority (2 Black or African American, non-Hispanic/Latino; 2 Asian, non-Hispanic/Latino). Average age 24. 38 applicants, 97% accepted, 37 enrolled. *Faculty:* 6 full-time (all women), 2 part-time/adjunct (0 women). *Financial support:* In 2015–16, 3 students received support. Scholarships/grants and tuition waivers available. Financial award applicants required to submit FAFSA. In 2015, 37 master's awarded. Offers occupational therapy (MS). *Application deadline:* For fall admission, 8/15 priority date for domestic students; for winter admission, 12/15 priority date for domestic students; for spring admission, 4/15 priority date for domestic students. Applications are processed on a rolling basis. *Application fee:* $50. Electronic applications accepted. *Application Contact:* Jennifer Nielsen, Transfer Counselor, Admissions, 315-279-5203, Fax: 315-279-5386, E-mail: jnielsen@keuka.edu. *Associate Professor/Chair/Program Director,* Dr. Dianne Trickey-Rokenbrok, 315-279-5608, Fax: 315-279-5439, E-mail: dtrickey@keuka.edu.

KEYSTONE COLLEGE, La Plume, PA 18440

General Information Independent, coed, comprehensive institution. *Enrollment:* 20 full-time matriculated graduate/professional students (11 women), 30 part-time matriculated graduate/professional students (all women). *Enrollment by degree level:* 50 master's. *Graduate faculty:* 7 full-time (5 women), 8 part-time/adjunct (5 women). *Tuition, area resident:* Part-time $650 per credit. One-time fee: $175. *Graduate housing:* On-campus housing not available. *Student services:* Campus employment opportunities, campus safety program, career counseling, child daycare facilities, exercise/wellness program, free psychological counseling, grant writing training, international student services, services for students with disabilities, writing training. *Library:* Miller Library.

Computer facilities: 100 computers available on campus for general student use. A campuswide network can be accessed from student residence rooms and from off campus. Online class registration is available.
Website: http://www.keystone.edu/

General Application Contact: Jennifer Sekol, Director of Admissions, 570-945-8117, Fax: 570-945-7916, E-mail: jennifer.sekol@keystone.edu.

GRADUATE UNITS

Program in Accountancy Students: 9 full-time, 2 part-time. 5 applicants, 80% accepted, 3 enrolled. *Faculty:* 2 full-time (1 woman), 3 part-time/adjunct (1 woman). *Financial support:* Application deadline: 5/2; applicants required to submit FAFSA. *Degree program information:* Part-time programs available. Part-time, online only, 100% online. Offers accountancy (M Acc). *Application deadline:* For fall admission, 8/1 for domestic students; for spring admission, 12/1 for domestic students; for summer admission, 5/1 for domestic students. Applications are processed on a rolling basis. *Application fee:* $50. Electronic applications accepted. *Application Contact:* Jennifer Sekol, Director of Admissions, 570-945-8117, Fax: 570-945-7916, E-mail: jennifer.sekol@keystone.edu. *Professor,* Patricia Davis, PhD, 570-945-8424, E-mail: patricia.davis@keystone.edu.

Program in Early Childhood Education Leadership Students: 37 part-time. 24 applicants, 88% accepted, 19 enrolled. *Faculty:* 3 full-time (all women), 2 part-time/adjunct (both women). *Financial support:* Application deadline: 5/1; applicants required to submit FAFSA. *Degree program information:* Part-time programs available. Part-time, blended/hybrid learning. Offers early childhood education leadership (M Ed). *Application deadline:* For fall admission, 8/1 for domestic students; for spring admission, 12/1 for domestic students; for summer admission, 5/1 for domestic students. Applications are processed on a rolling basis. *Application fee:* $50. Electronic applications accepted. *Application Contact:* Jennifer Sekol, Director of Admissions, 570-945-8117, Fax: 570-945-7916, E-mail: jennifer.sekol@keystone.edu. *Dean, School of Professional Studies,* Fran Langan, PhD, 570-945-8472, E-mail: fran.langan@keystone.edu.

Program in Sport Leadership and Management Students: 7 full-time, 2 part-time. 10 applicants, 100% accepted, 9 enrolled. *Faculty:* 2 full-time (1 woman), 3 part-time/adjunct (2 women). *Financial support:* Application deadline: 5/1; applicants required to submit FAFSA. *Degree program information:* Part-time programs available. Part-time, online only, 100% online. Offers sport leadership and management (MS). *Application deadline:* For fall admission, 8/1 for domestic students; for spring admission, 12/1 for domestic students; for summer admission, 5/1 for domestic students. Applications are processed on a rolling basis. *Application fee:* $50. Electronic applications accepted. *Application Contact:* Jennifer Sekol, Director of Admissions, 570-945-8117, Fax: 570-945-7916, E-mail: jennifer.sekol@keystone.edu. *Assistant Professor,* Bradley Congelio, PhD, 570-945-8432, E-mail: bradley.congelio@keystone.edu.

KING'S COLLEGE, Wilkes-Barre, PA 18711-0801

General Information Independent-religious, coed, comprehensive institution. *Graduate housing:* On-campus housing not available.

GRADUATE UNITS

Program in Education ***Degree program information:*** Part-time and evening/weekend programs available. Part-time, evening/weekend. Offers education (M Ed).

Program in Physician Assistant Studies Offers physician assistant studies (MSPAS). Electronic applications accepted.

William G. McGowan School of Business ***Degree program information:*** Part-time programs available. Part-time. Offers business (MS).

THE KING'S UNIVERSITY, Southlake, TX 76092

General Information Independent-religious, coed, comprehensive institution.

GRADUATE UNITS

Graduate and Professional Programs Offers Biblical studies (Graduate Certificate); Christian ministry (Graduate Certificate); ministry (M Div, MPT, D Min).

KINGSWOOD UNIVERSITY, Sussex, NB E4E 5L2, Canada

General Information Independent-religious, coed, comprehensive institution.

GRADUATE UNITS

Program in Pastoral Theology Offers pastoral theology (MA).

KING UNIVERSITY, Bristol, TN 37620-2699

General Information Independent-religious, coed, comprehensive institution. *Graduate housing:* Room and/or apartments available on a first-come, first-served basis to single students; on-campus housing not available to married students.

GRADUATE UNITS

School of Business and Economics ***Degree program information:*** Part-time and evening/weekend programs available. Part-time, evening/weekend, online learning. Offers accounting (MBA); finance (MBA); healthcare management (MBA); human resources management (MBA); leadership (MBA); management (MBA); marketing (MBA); project management (MBA). Electronic applications accepted.

KNOWLEDGE SYSTEMS INSTITUTE, Skokie, IL 60076

General Information Independent, coed, graduate-only institution. *Graduate housing:* On-campus housing not available.

GRADUATE UNITS

Program in Computer and Information Sciences ***Degree program information:*** Part-time and evening/weekend programs available. Part-time, evening/weekend, online learning. Offers computer and information sciences (MS). Electronic applications accepted.

KNOX COLLEGE, Toronto, ON M5S 2E6, Canada

General Information Independent-religious, coed, graduate-only institution. *Graduate housing:* Room and/or apartments available on a first-come, first-served basis to single students; on-campus housing not available to married students. Housing application deadline: 5/31.

GRADUATE UNITS

College of Theology ***Degree program information:*** Part-time programs available. Part-time. Offers theology (M Div, MRE, MTS, Th M, D Min, Th D). Applicants for D Min, Th M, and Th D must apply to Toronto School of Theology; MRE, M Div, MTS, Th D, and Th M programs offered jointly with University of Toronto.

KNOX THEOLOGICAL SEMINARY, Fort Lauderdale, FL 33308

General Information Independent-religious, coed, primarily men, graduate-only institution. *Graduate faculty:* 4 full-time (0 women), 2 part-time/adjunct (0 women). *Graduate housing:* On-campus housing not available. *Student services:* Campus employment opportunities, career counseling, international student services. *Library:* Anthony and Beverly Hartig Knox Memorial Library.

Computer facilities: 9 computers available on campus for general student use. Online class registration is available.
Website: http://www.knoxseminary.edu/

General Application Contact: Russell Norris, Senior Admissions Advisor, 800-344-5669, Fax: 954-351-3343, E-mail: rnorris@knoxseminary.edu.

GRADUATE UNITS

Graduate Programs ***Financial support:*** Scholarships/grants available. Support available to part-time students. *Degree program information:* Part-time programs available. Part-time, blended/hybrid learning. Offers Biblical and theological studies (MA); Christian and classical studies (MA); divinity (M Div); ministry (D Min). *Application deadline:* For fall admission, 7/1 priority date for domestic students, 6/1 priority date for international students; for winter admission, 12/1 priority date for domestic students, 10/1 priority date for international students; for spring admission, 1/1 priority date for domestic students, 11/1 priority date for international students. Applications are processed on a rolling basis. *Application fee:* $100. *Application Contact:* Russell Norris, Senior Admissions Advisor, 800-344-5669, Fax: 954-351-3343, E-mail: rnorris@knoxseminary.edu.

KUTZTOWN UNIVERSITY OF PENNSYLVANIA, Kutztown, PA 19530-0730

General Information State-supported, coed, comprehensive institution. CGS member. *Enrollment:* 9,000 graduate, professional, and undergraduate students; 285 full-time matriculated graduate/professional students (226 women), 401 part-time matriculated graduate/professional students (313 women). *Enrollment by degree level:* 678 master's. *Graduate faculty:* 80 full-time (53 women), 1 part-time/adjunct (0 women). *Tuition, area resident:* Part-time $470 per credit. Tuition, nonresident: part-time $705 per credit. *Required fees:* $98 per credit. *Graduate housing:* Rooms and/or apartments available on a first-come, first-served basis to single and married students. Typical cost: $5552 per year for single students; $5552 per year for married students. *Student services:* Campus employment opportunities, campus safety program, career counseling, exercise/wellness program, free psychological counseling, international student services, low-cost health insurance, multicultural affairs office, services for students with disabilities. *Library:* Rohrbach Library. *Collection:* Books: 379,570 (physical), 385,501 (digital/electronic); Serial titles: 5,277 (physical), 142,078 (digital/electronic); Databases: 119. Weekly public service hours: 92; students can reserve study rooms.

Computer facilities: Computer purchase and lease plans are available. 1,075 computers available on campus for general student use. A campuswide network can be accessed from student residence rooms. Online class registration is available.
Website: http://www.kutztown.edu/

General Application Contact: Kelly Hish, Admissions Clerk, 610-683-4200, Fax: 610-683-1393, E-mail: graduate@kutztown.edu.

GRADUATE UNITS

College of Business Students: 20 full-time (7 women), 14 part-time (7 women); includes 4 minority (2 Black or African American, non-Hispanic/Latino; 2 Asian, non-Hispanic/Latino), 1 international. Average age 29. 30 applicants, 87% accepted, 13 enrolled. *Faculty:* 7 full-time (4 women). *Financial support:* Career-related internships or fieldwork, Federal Work-Study, scholarships/grants, tuition waivers (full), and unspecified assistantships available. Financial award application deadline: 3/1; financial award applicants required to submit FAFSA. In 2015, 15 master's awarded. *Degree program information:* Part-time and evening/weekend programs available. Part-time, evening/weekend. Offers business (MBA); business administration (MBA). *Application deadline:* For fall admission, 8/1 priority date for domestic and international students; for spring admission, 12/1 priority date for domestic and international students. Applications are processed on a rolling basis. *Application fee:* $35. Electronic applications accepted. *Dean*, Dr. Martha Geaney, 610-683-4575, Fax: 610-683-4573, E-mail: mba@kutztown.edu.

College of Education Students: 164 full-time (140 women), 290 part-time (229 women); includes 54 minority (18 Black or African American, non-Hispanic/Latino; 3 Asian, non-Hispanic/Latino; 30 Hispanic/Latino; 3 Two or more races, non-Hispanic/Latino), 1 international. Average age 30. 268 applicants, 82% accepted, 140 enrolled. *Faculty:* 24 full-time (18 women), 1 part-time/adjunct (0 women). *Financial support:* Career-related internships or fieldwork, Federal Work-Study, scholarships/grants, and unspecified assistantships available. Financial award application deadline: 3/1; financial award applicants required to submit FAFSA. In 2015, 145 master's awarded. *Degree program information:* Part-time and evening/weekend programs available. Part-time, evening/weekend. Offers agency counseling (MA); biology (M Ed); counselor education (M Ed); curriculum and instruction (M Ed); education (M Ed, MA, MLS); elementary education (M Ed); English (M Ed); instructional technology (M Ed); library science (MLS); marital and family therapy (MA); mathematics (M Ed); reading (M Ed); social studies (M Ed); student affairs in higher education (M Ed). *Application deadline:* For fall admission, 8/1 priority date for domestic and international students; for spring admission, 12/1 priority date for domestic and international students. Applications are processed on a rolling basis. *Application fee:* $35. Electronic applications accepted. *Application Contact:* Kelly Hish, Admissions Clerk, 610-683-4200, Fax: 610-683-1393, E-mail: graduate@kutztown.edu. *Acting Dean*, Dr. Michelle Kiec, 610-683-4253, Fax: 610-683-4255, E-mail: tfaust@kutztown.edu.

College of Liberal Arts and Sciences Students: 82 full-time (64 women), 64 part-time (47 women); includes 29 minority (14 Black or African American, non-Hispanic/Latino; 3 Asian, non-Hispanic/Latino; 10 Hispanic/Latino; 2 Two or more races, non-Hispanic/Latino), 5 international. Average age 29. 106 applicants, 85% accepted, 64 enrolled. *Faculty:* 32 full-time (19 women). *Financial support:* Career-related internships or fieldwork, Federal Work-Study, scholarships/grants, and unspecified assistantships available. Financial award application deadline: 3/1; financial award applicants required to submit FAFSA. In 2015, 67 master's awarded. *Degree program information:* Part-time and evening/weekend programs available. Part-time, evening/weekend. Offers computer science (MS); English (MA); liberal arts and sciences (MA, MPA, MS, MSW); public administration (MPA); social work (MSW). *Application deadline:* For fall admission, 8/1 priority date for domestic and international students; for spring admission, 12/1 priority date for domestic and international students. Applications are processed on a rolling basis. *Application fee:* $35. Electronic applications accepted. *Acting Dean*, Dr. David Beougher, 610-683-4305, Fax: 610-683-4633, E-mail: clas@kutztown.edu.

College of Visual and Performing Arts Students: 19 full-time (15 women), 33 part-time (30 women), 2 international. Average age 33. 27 applicants, 89% accepted, 22 enrolled. *Faculty:* 17 full-time (12 women). *Financial support:* Career-related internships or fieldwork, Federal Work-Study, scholarships/grants, and unspecified assistantships available. Financial award application deadline: 3/1; financial award applicants required to submit FAFSA. In 2015, 26 master's awarded. *Degree program information:* Part-time programs available. Part-time. Offers art education (M Ed); communication design (MFA); visual and performing arts (M Ed, MFA, MS). *Application deadline:* For fall admission, 8/1 priority date for domestic and international students; for spring admission, 12/1 priority date for domestic and international students. Applications are processed on a rolling basis. *Application fee:* $35. Electronic applications accepted. *Application Contact:* Kelly Hish, Admissions Clerk, 610-683-4200, Fax: 610-683-1393, E-mail: graduate@kutztown.edu. *Dean*, Dr. William Mowder, 610-683-4500, Fax: 610-683-4547, E-mail: mowder@kutztown.edu.

LAGRANGE COLLEGE, LaGrange, GA 30240-2999

General Information Independent-religious, coed, comprehensive institution. *Graduate housing:* Room and/or apartments available on a first-come, first-served basis to single students; on-campus housing not available to married students. Housing application deadline: 5/1.

GRADUATE UNITS

Graduate Programs ***Degree program information:*** Part-time and evening/weekend programs available. Part-time, evening/weekend. Offers clinical mental health counseling (MS); curriculum and instruction (M Ed, Ed S); middle grades (MAT); organizational leadership (MA); secondary education (MAT). Electronic applications accepted.

LAGUNA COLLEGE OF ART & DESIGN, Laguna Beach, CA 92651-1136

General Information Independent, coed, comprehensive institution.

GRADUATE UNITS

Graduate Program Electronic applications accepted.

LAKE ERIE COLLEGE, Painesville, OH 44077-3389

General Information Independent, coed, comprehensive institution. *Enrollment:* 1,244 graduate, professional, and undergraduate students; 85 full-time matriculated graduate/professional students (51 women), 161 part-time matriculated graduate/professional students (74 women). *Enrollment by degree level:* 246 master's. *Graduate faculty:* 6 full-time (2 women), 12 part-time/adjunct (5 women). *Tuition, area resident:* Full-time $5072. *Required fees:* $504. Tuition and fees vary according to course load and program. *Graduate housing:* On-campus housing not available. *Student services:* Campus employment opportunities, campus safety program, career counseling, exercise/wellness program, international student services, services for students with disabilities, teacher training, writing training. *Library:* Lincoln Library. *Collection:* Books: 40,569 (physical), 108,846 (digital/electronic); Serial titles: 11,525 (digital/electronic); Databases: 75. Weekly public service hours: 56.

Computer facilities: 78 computers available on campus for general student use. A campuswide network can be accessed from student residence rooms and from off campus. Online class registration is available.
Website: http://www.lec.edu/

General Application Contact: Marco Gaudio, Assistant Director of International Recruitment and Graduate Programs, 440-375-7060, Fax: 440-375-7103, E-mail: admissions@lec.edu.

GRADUATE UNITS

School of Business Students: 34 full-time (17 women), 144 part-time (66 women); includes 19 minority (12 Black or African American, non-Hispanic/Latino; 3 Asian, non-Hispanic/Latino; 2 Hispanic/Latino; 2 Two or more races, non-Hispanic/Latino), 6 international. Average age 33. 57 applicants, 82% accepted, 37 enrolled. *Faculty:* 2 full-time (1 woman), 8 part-time/adjunct (1 woman). *Financial support:* Career-related internships or fieldwork, tuition waivers (full and partial), and unspecified assistantships available. Financial award applicants required to submit FAFSA. In 2015, 53 master's awarded. *Degree program information:* Part-time and evening/weekend programs available. Part-time, evening/weekend. Offers general management (MBA); health care administration (MBA); information technology management (MBA). *Application deadline:* For fall admission, 8/1 priority date for domestic students, 6/1 for international students; for spring admission, 12/15 for domestic students, 10/1 for international students. Applications are processed on a rolling basis. *Application fee:* $30. Electronic applications accepted. *Application Contact:* Marco Gaudio, Senior Assistant Director of International Recruitment, 800-533-4996, Fax: 440-375-7060, E-mail: mgaudio@lec.edu. *Dean*, Dr. Robert Trebar, 440-375-7115, Fax: 440-375-7005, E-mail: rtrebar@lec.edu.

School of Education and Professional Studies Students: 1 (woman) full-time, 17 part-time (8 women); includes 4 minority (3 Black or African American, non-Hispanic/Latino; 1 Hispanic/Latino), 3 international. Average age 29. 11 applicants, 82% accepted, 7 enrolled. *Faculty:* 3 part-time/adjunct (all women). *Financial support:* Tuition waivers (full and partial) and unspecified assistantships available. Financial award applicants required to submit FAFSA. In 2015, 1 master's awarded. *Degree program information:* Part-time and evening/weekend programs available. Part-time, evening/weekend. Offers education and professional studies (M Ed). *Application deadline:* For fall admission, 8/1 priority date for domestic students, 6/1 for international students; for spring admission, 12/15 for domestic students, 10/1 for international students. Applications are processed on a rolling basis. *Application fee:* $30. Electronic applications accepted. *Application Contact:* Kaitlyn Holland, Admissions Counselor, 800-916-0904, Fax: 440-375-7112, E-mail: kholland@lec.edu. *Dean*, Dr. Katharine Delavan, 440-375-7389, E-mail: kdelavan@lec.edu.

LAKE ERIE COLLEGE OF OSTEOPATHIC MEDICINE, Erie, PA 16509-1025

General Information Independent, coed, graduate-only institution. *Graduate housing:* On-campus housing not available. *Research affiliation:* West Virginia University (neurology), Neuro Structural Research Laboratories (neurology), Cornelli Consulting (CORCON) (neurology), University of Maryland (neurology), Duke University (neurology).

GRADUATE UNITS

Professional Programs Offers biomedical sciences (Postbaccalaureate Certificate); medical education (MS); osteopathic medicine (DO); pharmacy (Pharm D). Electronic applications accepted.

LAKE FOREST COLLEGE, Lake Forest, IL 60045

General Information Independent, coed, comprehensive institution. *Graduate housing:* On-campus housing not available. *Research affiliation:* Argonne National Laboratory (physics), Merck & Company, Inc., Chicago History Museum (Chicago history), Lake Forest Hospital (genomes), The Art Institute of Chicago (Asian art), Newberry Library (medieval and Renaissance history, American West).

GRADUATE UNITS

Graduate Program in Liberal Studies Students: 41 part-time (20 women); includes 5 minority (2 Asian, non-Hispanic/Latino; 3 Hispanic/Latino). Average age 37. 23 applicants, 52% accepted, 8 enrolled. *Faculty:* 9 full-time (4 women). *Financial support:* In 2015–16, 6 students received support. Partial tuition grants (for full-time teachers) available. In 2015, 5 master's awarded. *Degree program information:* Part-time and evening/weekend programs available. Part-time, evening/weekend. Offers American studies (MLS); environmental studies (MLS); history (MLS); Medieval and Renaissance art (MLS); philosophy (MLS); writing (MLS). *Application deadline:* For fall admission, 7/15 priority date for domestic students, 6/1 priority date for international students; for spring admission, 12/1 priority date for domestic students, 10/1 priority date for international students. Applications are processed on a rolling basis. *Application fee:* $30. *Application Contact:* Prof. Carol Gayle, Associate Director, 847-735-5083, Fax: 847-735-6291, E-mail: gayle@lakeforest.edu. *Director*, Prof. D. L. LeMahieu, 847-735-5133, Fax: 847-735-6291, E-mail: lemahieu@lakeforest.edu.

Master of Arts in Teaching Program Offers elementary education (MAT); K-12 French (MAT); K-12 music (MAT); K-12 Spanish (MAT); K-12 visual art (MAT); secondary biology (MAT); secondary chemistry (MAT); secondary English (MAT); secondary history (MAT); secondary mathematics (MAT).

LAKE FOREST GRADUATE SCHOOL OF MANAGEMENT, Lake Forest, IL 60045

General Information Independent, coed, graduate-only institution. *Graduate housing:* On-campus housing not available.

GRADUATE UNITS

The Immersion MBA Program (iMBA) Online learning. Offers global business (MBA).

The Leadership MBA Program ***Degree program information:*** Part-time and evening/weekend programs available. Part-time, evening/weekend. Offers finance (MBA); global business (MBA); healthcare management (MBA); management (MBA); marketing (MBA); organizational behavior (MBA). Electronic applications accepted.

LAKEHEAD UNIVERSITY, Thunder Bay, ON P7B 5E1, Canada

General Information Province-supported, coed, comprehensive institution. *Graduate housing:* Rooms and/or apartments available to single students and available on a first-come, first-served basis to married students. Housing application deadline: 3/10. *Research affiliation:* Falcon Bridge (biology), Placer Dome (biology), Bowater Inc. (engineering), Centre for Northern Forest Ecosystem Research (biology, forestry, tourism), Thunder Bay Regional Cancer Centre (psychosocial oncology), Bowater Inc. (chemistry).

GRADUATE UNITS

Graduate Studies ***Degree program information:*** Part-time and evening/weekend programs available. Part-time, evening/weekend. Offers clinical psychology (PhD); experimental psychology (MA); geology (M Sc); gerontology (M Ed, M Sc, MA, MSW); history (MA); physics (M Sc); women's studies (MA).

Faculty of Education Degree program information: Part-time and evening/weekend programs available. Part-time, evening/weekend. Offers educational studies (PhD); gerontology (M Ed); women's studies (M Ed).

Faculty of Engineering Degree program information: Part-time programs available. Part-time. Offers control engineering (M Sc Engr); electrical/computer engineering (M Sc Engr); environmental engineering (M Sc Engr).

Faculty of Natural Resources Management Degree program information: Part-time programs available. Part-time. Offers forest sciences (PhD); forestry (M Sc F).

Faculty of Social Sciences and Humanities Degree program information: Part-time and evening/weekend programs available. Part-time, evening/weekend. Offers biology (M Sc); chemistry (M Sc); economics (MA); English (MA); gerontology (MA); health services and policy research (MA); social sciences and humanities (M Sc, MA, MSW, PhD); sociology (MA); women's studies (MA).

School of Kinesiology Degree program information: Part-time programs available. Part-time. Offers kinesiology (M Sc); kinesiology and gerontology (M Sc).

School of Mathematical Sciences Degree program information: Part-time and evening/weekend programs available. Part-time, evening/weekend. Offers computer science (M Sc); mathematical science (MA).

School of Social Work Degree program information: Part-time programs available. Part-time. Offers gerontology (MSW); social work (MSW); women's studies (MSW).

LAKEHEAD UNIVERSITY–ORILLIA, Orillia, ON L3V 0B9, Canada

General Information Public, coed, comprehensive institution.

GRADUATE UNITS

MBA Program ***Degree program information:*** Part-time programs available. Part-time. Offers business administration (MBA).

LAKELAND UNIVERSITY, Plymouth, WI 53073

General Information Independent-religious, coed, comprehensive institution. *Graduate housing:* On-campus housing not available.

GRADUATE UNITS

Graduate Studies Division ***Degree program information:*** Part-time and evening/weekend programs available. Part-time, evening/weekend. Offers accounting (MBA); counseling (MA); education (M Ed); finance (MBA); healthcare management (MBA); project management (MBA); theology (MAT).

LAMAR UNIVERSITY, Beaumont, TX 77710

General Information State-supported, coed, university. CGS member. *Enrollment:* 14,965 graduate, professional, and undergraduate students; 1,090 full-time matriculated graduate/professional students (351 women), 4,090 part-time matriculated graduate/professional students (2,952 women). *Enrollment by degree level:* 4,796 master's, 384 doctoral. *Graduate faculty:* 235 full-time (108 women), 73 part-time/adjunct (42 women). *Tuition, area resident:* Full-time $6720; part-time $4032. Tuition, nonresident: full-time $14,880; part-time $8928. *Required fees:* $1900; $950 $784. *Graduate housing:* Rooms and/or apartments available to single students and available on a first-come, first-served basis to married students. Typical cost: $5252 (including board) for single students; $7878 (including board) for married students. Room and board charges vary according to board plan. Housing application deadline: 6/30. *Student services:* Campus employment opportunities, campus safety program, career counseling, exercise/wellness program, free psychological counseling, grant writing training, international student services, low-cost health insurance, multicultural affairs office, services for students with disabilities, teacher training, writing training. *Library:* Mary and John Gray Library plus 1 other. *Collection:* Books: 431,367 (physical), 37,218 (digital/electronic); Serial titles: 431 (physical), 828 (digital/electronic); Databases: 66. Weekly public service hours: 93; students can reserve study rooms. *Research affiliation:* Grants Resource Center, National Council of Research Administrators, BASF.

Computer facilities: 644 computers available on campus for general student use. A campuswide network can be accessed from student residence rooms and from off campus. Online class registration is available.
Website: http://www.lamar.edu/

General Application Contact: Melissa Gallien, Director, Admissions and Academic Services, 409-880-8888, Fax: 409-880-7419, E-mail: gradmissions@lamar.edu.

GRADUATE UNITS

College of Graduate Studies Students: 1,090 full-time (351 women), 4,090 part-time (2,952 women); includes 1,648 minority (774 Black or African American, non-Hispanic/Latino; 20 American Indian or Alaska Native, non-Hispanic/Latino; 77 Asian, non-Hispanic/Latino; 700 Hispanic/Latino; 77 Two or more races, non-Hispanic/Latino), 1,139 international. Average age 29. 3,747 applicants, 67% accepted, 1202 enrolled. *Faculty:* 235 full-time (108 women), 73 part-time/adjunct (42 women). *Financial support:* Fellowships with partial tuition reimbursements, research assistantships, teaching assistantships, career-related internships or fieldwork, Federal Work-Study, institutionally sponsored loans, scholarships/grants, and tuition waivers (partial) available. Support available to part-time students. Financial award application deadline: 4/1; financial award applicants required to submit FAFSA. In 2015, 2,305 master's, 96 doctorates awarded. *Degree program information:* Part-time and evening/weekend programs available. Part-time, evening/weekend. *Application deadline:* For fall admission, 8/1 for domestic students, 7/1 for international students; for spring admission, 1/5 for domestic students, 12/5 for international students. Applications are processed on a rolling basis. *Application fee:* $25 ($50 for international students). Electronic applications accepted. *Application Contact:* Melissa Gallien, Director, Admissions and Academic Services, 409-880-8888, Fax: 409-880-7419, E-mail: gradmissions@lamar.edu. *Dean*, Dr. William E. Harn, 409-880-8229, Fax: 409-880-1723, E-mail: lugradstudies@lamar.edu.

College of Arts and Sciences Students: 11 full-time (9 women), 232 part-time (161 women); includes 126 minority (70 Black or African American, non-Hispanic/Latino; 1 American Indian or Alaska Native, non-Hispanic/Latino; 8 Asian, non-Hispanic/Latino; 44 Hispanic/Latino; 3 Two or more races, non-Hispanic/Latino), 3 international. Average age 34. 578 applicants, 73% accepted, 231 enrolled. *Faculty:* 65 full-time (31 women), 7 part-time/adjunct (5 women). *Financial support:* Fellowships, research assistantships, teaching assistantships with tuition reimbursements, career-related internships or fieldwork, Federal Work-Study, institutionally sponsored loans, scholarships/grants, and tuition waivers (partial) available. Support available to part-time students. Financial award application deadline: 4/1; financial award applicants required to submit FAFSA. In 2015, 196 master's awarded. *Degree program information:* Part-time and evening/weekend programs available. Part-time, evening/weekend. Offers arts and sciences (MA, MPA, MS, MSN); biology (MS); chemistry (MS); clinical psychology (MS); computer science (MS); criminal justice (MS); English (MA); history (MA); industrial/organizational psychology (MS); mathematics (MS); nursing administration (MSN); nursing education (MSN); public administration (MPA); teaching Spanish (MA). *Application deadline:* For fall admission, 8/10 for domestic students, 7/1 for international students; for spring admission, 1/15 for domestic students, 12/1 for international students. Applications are processed on a rolling basis. *Application fee:* $25 ($50 for international students). Electronic applications accepted. *Application Contact:* Melissa Gallien, Director, Admissions and Academic Services, 409-880-8888, E-mail: gradmissions@lamar.edu. *Interim Dean*, Dr. Joe Nordgren, 409-880-8508, Fax: 409-880-8007.

College of Business Students: 35 full-time (20 women), 167 part-time (95 women); includes 70 minority (43 Black or African American, non-Hispanic/Latino; 11 Asian, non-Hispanic/Latino; 16 Hispanic/Latino), 51 international. Average age 31. 156 applicants, 91% accepted, 52 enrolled. *Faculty:* 24 full-time (7 women), 2 part-time/adjunct (0 women). *Financial support:* Fellowships with tuition reimbursements, research assistantships with partial tuition reimbursements, career-related internships or fieldwork, Federal Work-Study, institutionally sponsored loans, scholarships/grants, and tuition waivers (partial) available. Support available to part-time students. Financial award application deadline: 4/1; financial award applicants required to submit FAFSA. In 2015, 93 master's awarded. *Degree program information:* Part-time and evening/weekend programs available. Part-time, evening/weekend. Offers accounting (MBA); experiential business and entrepreneurship (MBA); healthcare administration (MBA). *Application deadline:* For fall admission, 8/10 for domestic students, 7/1 for international students; for spring admission, 1/5 for domestic students, 12/1 for international students. Applications are processed on a rolling basis. *Application fee:* $25 ($50 for international students). Electronic applications accepted. *Application Contact:* Melissa Gallien, Director, Admissions and Academic Services, 409-880-8888, Fax: 409-880-7419, E-mail: gradmissions@lamar.edu. *Dean*, Dr. Enrique R. Venta, 409-880-8604, Fax: 409-880-8088, E-mail: henry.venta@lamar.edu.

College of Education and Human Development Students: 93 full-time (61 women), 3,305 part-time (2,597 women); includes 1,332 minority (610 Black or African American, non-Hispanic/Latino; 17 American Indian or Alaska Native, non-Hispanic/Latino; 33 Asian, non-Hispanic/Latino; 607 Hispanic/Latino; 65 Two or more races, non-Hispanic/Latino), 22 international. Average age 37. 2,038 applicants, 94% accepted, 615 enrolled. *Faculty:* 71 full-time (51 women), 55 part-time/adjunct (34 women). *Financial support:* Fellowships, research assistantships, teaching assistantships, career-related internships or fieldwork, Federal Work-Study, institutionally sponsored loans, and scholarships/grants available. Support available to part-time students. Financial award application deadline: 4/1; financial award applicants required to submit FAFSA. In 2015, 1,791 master's, 60 doctorates awarded. *Degree program information:* Part-time and evening/weekend programs available. Part-time, evening/weekend, online learning. Offers clinical mental health counseling (M Ed); digital learning and leading (M Ed); education administration (M Ed); education and human development (M Ed, MS, Ed D, Certificate); educational leadership (Ed D); educational technology (M Ed); family and consumer sciences (MS); public health (MS); school counseling (M Ed); science of kinesiology promotion (MS); special education (M Ed); teacher education (M Ed). *Application deadline:* For fall admission, 8/10 for domestic students, 7/1 for international students; for spring admission, 1/5 for domestic students, 12/1 for international students. Applications are processed on a rolling basis. *Application fee:* $25 ($50 for international students). Electronic applications accepted. *Application Contact:* Melissa Gallien, Director, Admissions and Academic Services, 409-880-8888, Fax: 409-880-7419, E-mail: gradmissions@lamar.edu. *Dean*, Dr. Robert Spina, 409-880-8661.

College of Engineering Students: 486 full-time (54 women), 250 part-time (39 women); includes 32 minority (9 Black or African American, non-Hispanic/Latino; 1 American Indian or Alaska Native, non-Hispanic/Latino; 16 Asian, non-Hispanic/Latino; 5 Hispanic/Latino; 1 Two or more races, non-Hispanic/Latino), 685 international. Average age 25. 922 applicants, 53% accepted, 246 enrolled. *Faculty:* 49 full-time (6 women), 4 part-time/adjunct (0 women). *Financial support:* Fellowships with partial tuition reimbursements, research assistantships with partial tuition reimbursements, teaching assistantships with partial tuition reimbursements, career-related internships or fieldwork, Federal Work-Study, institutionally sponsored loans, scholarships/grants, tuition waivers (full and partial), and laboratory assistantships available. Support available to part-time students. Financial award application deadline: 4/1; financial award applicants required to submit FAFSA. In 2015, 184 master's, 21 doctorates awarded. *Degree program information:* Part-time and evening/weekend programs available. Part-time, evening/weekend. Offers chemical engineering (ME, PhD); civil engineering (ME, MES); electrical engineering (ME, MES, DE); engineering (ME, MEM, MES, MS, DE, PhD); engineering management (MEM); environmental engineering (MS); environmental studies (MS, DE); industrial engineering (ME, MES, DE); mechanical engineering (ME, MES, DE). *Application deadline:* For fall admission, 8/1 for domestic students, 7/1 for international students; for spring admission, 1/5 for domestic students, 12/1 for international students. Applications are processed on a rolling basis. *Application fee:* $25 ($50 for international students). Electronic applications accepted. *Application Contact:* Melissa Gallien, Director, Admissions and Academic Services, 409-880-8888, Fax: 409-880-7419, E-mail: gradmissions@lamar.edu. *Dean*, Dr. Srinivas Palanki, 409-880-8784, Fax: 409-880-2197.

College of Fine Arts and Communication Students: 119 full-time (95 women), 31 part-time (26 women); includes 48 minority (12 Black or African American, non-Hispanic/Latino; 1 American Indian or Alaska Native, non-Hispanic/Latino; 5 Asian, non-Hispanic/Latino; 26 Hispanic/Latino; 4 Two or more races, non-Hispanic/Latino), 9 international. Average age 31. 85 applicants, 85% accepted, 58 enrolled. *Faculty:* 27 full-time (13 women), 4 part-time/adjunct (3 women). *Financial support:* Fellowships, research assistantships, teaching assistantships, career-related internships or fieldwork, Federal Work-Study, institutionally sponsored loans, and tuition waivers (partial) available. Support available to part-time students. Financial award application deadline: 4/1; financial award applicants required to submit FAFSA. In 2015, 41 master's, 15 doctorates awarded. *Degree program information:* Part-time and evening/weekend programs available. Part-time, evening/weekend. Offers audiology (Au D); deaf studies and deaf education (MS, Ed D); fine arts and communication (MM, MS, Au D, Ed D); music (MM); speech language pathology (MS). *Application deadline:* For fall admission, 8/10 for domestic students, 7/1 for international students; for spring admission, 1/5 for domestic students, 12/1 for international students. Applications are processed on a rolling basis. *Application fee:* $25 ($50 for international students). Electronic applications accepted. *Application Contact:* Melissa Gallien, Director, Admissions and Academic Services, 409-880-8888, Fax: 409-880-7419, E-mail: gradmissions@lamar.edu. *Dean*, Dr. Derina Holtzhauser, 409-880-8137, Fax: 409-880-2286.

LANCASTER BIBLE COLLEGE, Lancaster, PA 17601

General Information Independent-religious, coed, comprehensive institution. *Graduate housing:* On-campus housing not available.

GRADUATE UNITS

Capital Bible Seminary ***Degree program information:*** Part-time and evening/weekend programs available. Part-time, evening/weekend. Offers biblical studies (MA, Certificate); Christian counseling and discipleship (MA, Certificate); ministry (MA); theology (M Div).

Graduate School ***Degree program information:*** Part-time and evening/weekend programs available. Part-time, evening/weekend. Offers adult ministries (MA); Bible (MA); children and family ministry (MA); church planting (MA); consulting resource teacher (M Ed); elementary school counseling (M Ed); leadership (PhD); leadership studies (MA); marriage and family counseling (MA); mental health counseling (MA); pastoral studies (MA); secondary school counseling (M Ed); sports ministry (MA); student ministry (MA); town and country ministry (MA).

LANCASTER THEOLOGICAL SEMINARY, Lancaster, PA 17603-2812

General Information Independent-religious, coed, graduate-only institution. *Graduate housing:* Rooms and/or apartments available on a first-come, first-served basis to single and married students. Housing application deadline: 8/1.

GRADUATE UNITS

Graduate and Professional Programs Offers biblical studies (MAR); Christian education (MAR); Christianity and the arts (MAR); church history (MAR); congregational life (MAR); lay leadership (Certificate); theological studies (M Div); theology (D Min); theology and ethics (MAR).

LANDER UNIVERSITY, Greenwood, SC 29649-2099

General Information State-supported, coed, comprehensive institution. *Graduate housing:* Room and/or apartments available on a first-come, first-served basis to single students; on-campus housing not available to married students.

GRADUATE UNITS

Graduate Studies ***Degree program information:*** Part-time programs available. Part-time, online learning. Offers clinical nurse leader (MSN); emergency management (MS); Montessori education (M Ed); teaching and learning (M Ed). Electronic applications accepted.

LANGSTON UNIVERSITY, Langston, OK 73050

General Information State-supported, coed, comprehensive institution. CGS member. *Graduate housing:* Rooms and/or apartments available on a first-come, first-served basis to single and married students.

GRADUATE UNITS

School of Education and Behavioral Sciences ***Degree program information:*** Part-time programs available. Part-time. Offers bilingual/multicultural (M Ed); elementary education (M Ed); English as a second language (M Ed); rehabilitation counseling (M Sc); urban education (M Ed).

School of Physical Therapy Offers physical therapy (DPT).

LA ROCHE COLLEGE, Pittsburgh, PA 15237-5898

General Information Independent-religious, coed, comprehensive institution. *Enrollment:* 1,523 graduate, professional, and undergraduate students; 76 full-time matriculated graduate/professional students (52 women), 49 part-time matriculated graduate/professional students (34 women). *Enrollment by degree level:* 108 master's, 17 other advanced degrees. *Graduate faculty:* 10 full-time (7 women), 19 part-time/adjunct (6 women). *Tuition, area resident:* Full-time $12,240; part-time $680 per credit. *Required fees:* $25 per semester. *Graduate housing:* On-campus housing not available. *Student services:* Campus employment opportunities, career counseling, free psychological counseling, international student services, low-cost health insurance, multicultural affairs office, services for students with disabilities. *Library:* John J. Wright Library plus 1 other. *Collection:* Books: 75,803 (physical), 221,000 (digital/electronic); Databases: 1,248.

Computer facilities: Computer purchase and lease plans are available. 200 computers available on campus for general student use. A campuswide network can be accessed. Online class registration is available.
Website: http://www.laroche.edu/

General Application Contact: Hope Schiffgens, Director of Graduate Studies and Adult Education, 412-536-1266, Fax: 412-536-1283, E-mail: schombh1@laroche.edu.

GRADUATE UNITS

School of Graduate Studies and Adult Education Students: 76 full-time (52 women), 49 part-time (34 women); includes 4 minority (3 Black or African American, non-Hispanic/Latino; 1 Hispanic/Latino), 17 international. Average age 35. *Faculty:* 10 full-time (7 women), 19 part-time/adjunct (6 women). *Financial support:* Unspecified assistantships available. Financial award application deadline: 3/31; financial award applicants required to submit FAFSA. In 2015, 45 master's awarded. *Degree program information:* Part-time and evening/weekend programs available. Part-time, evening/weekend. Offers accounting (MS); human resources management (MS, Certificate); nurse anesthesia (MS); nursing education (MSN); nursing management (MSN). *Application deadline:* For fall admission, 8/15 for domestic and international students; for spring admission, 12/15 for domestic and international students. Applications are processed on a rolling basis. *Application fee:* $50. Electronic applications accepted. *Application Contact:* Hope Schiffgens, Director of Graduate Studies and Adult Education, 412-536-1266, Fax: 412-536-1283, E-mail: schombh1@laroche.edu. *Dean,* Dr. Rosemary McCarthy, 412-536-1193, Fax: 412-536-1763, E-mail: rosemary.mccarthy@laroche.edu.

LA SALLE UNIVERSITY, Philadelphia, PA 19141-1199

General Information Independent-religious, coed, comprehensive institution. CGS member. *Enrollment:* 5,675 graduate, professional, and undergraduate students; 331 full-time matriculated graduate/professional students (249 women), 1,397 part-time matriculated graduate/professional students (993 women). *Enrollment by degree level:* 1,462 master's, 173 doctoral, 93 other advanced degrees. *Graduate faculty:* 81 full-time (45 women), 100 part-time/adjunct (58 women). *Tuition, area resident:* Full-time $13,500; part-time $750 per credit. *Required fees:* $570; $210 per semester. Tuition and fees vary according to course load, degree level, program and reciprocity agreements. *Graduate housing:* Room and/or apartments available on a first-come, first-served basis to single students; on-campus housing not available to married students. Typical cost: $9410 per year. Room charges vary according to board plan and housing facility selected. *Student services:* Campus employment opportunities, campus safety program, career counseling, child daycare facilities, exercise/wellness program, free psychological counseling, international student services, multicultural affairs office, services for students with disabilities, teacher training, writing training. *Library:* Connelly Library. *Collection:* Books: 349,395 (physical), 437,494 (digital/electronic); Serial titles: 2,095 (physical), 124,278 (digital/electronic); Databases: 125. Weekly public service hours: 96; students can reserve study rooms.

Computer facilities: Computer purchase and lease plans are available. 1,100 computers available on campus for general student use. A campuswide network can be accessed from student residence rooms and from off campus. Online class registration, Canvas Course Management System are available.
Website: http://www.lasalle.edu/

General Application Contact: Alison McAnespey Target, Director, Graduate and Adult Enrollment, 215-951-1100, Fax: 215-951-1462, E-mail: target@lasalle.edu.

GRADUATE UNITS

School of Arts and Sciences Students: 215 full-time (168 women), 626 part-time (445 women); includes 212 minority (118 Black or African American, non-Hispanic/Latino; 2 American Indian or Alaska Native, non-Hispanic/Latino; 23 Asian, non-Hispanic/Latino; 52 Hispanic/Latino; 17 Two or more races, non-Hispanic/Latino), 32 international. Average age 32. 510 applicants, 70% accepted, 188 enrolled. *Faculty:* 40 full-time (20 women), 67 part-time/adjunct (37 women). *Financial support:* In 2015–16, 159 students received support. Career-related internships or fieldwork, Federal Work-Study, scholarships/grants, and unspecified assistantships available. Support available to part-time students. Financial award application deadline: 8/31; financial award applicants required to submit FAFSA. In 2015, 251 master's, 17 doctorates, 15 other advanced degrees awarded. *Degree program information:* Part-time and evening/weekend programs available. Part-time, evening/weekend, online learning. Offers American history (Certificate); American studies (MA, Certificate); application development (Certificate); arts and sciences (MA, MS, Psy D, Th D, Certificate); autism spectrum disorders (MA, Certificate); bilingual/bicultural studies (MA); Catholic studies (Th D); Central and Eastern European studies (MA); child clinical psychology (Psy D); Christian spirituality (Th D); church ministry (Th D, Certificate); classroom management (MA); clinical health psychology (Psy D); clinical psychology (MA); communication consulting and development (MA); communication management (MA); computer information science (MS); corporate fraud (MS); dual early childhood and special education (MA); dual middle-level science and math and special education (MA); education (MA); English (MA); English as a second language (Certificate); English for educators (MA); English in literary and cultural studies (MA); European history (Certificate); founder's studies (Th D); fraud and forensic accounting (Certificate); general practice psychology (Psy D); general professional communication (MA); global literature (Certificate); history (MA); history for educators (MA); industrial/organizational management and human resources (MA); information technology leadership (MS); instructional coach (Certificate); instructional leadership (MA); instructional technology management (MS, Certificate); intelligence and security studies (Certificate); liturgy (Certificate); marriage and family therapy (MA); media studies and the performing and visual arts (Certificate); network security (MS); pastoral care (Certificate); pastoral counseling (MA); pastoral studies (MA); Philadelphia and regional studies (Certificate); professional and business communication (Certificate); professional clinical counseling (MA); public history (MA); public relations (MA); reading specialist (MA, Certificate); religion (MA); religious education (Certificate); secondary education (MA); social and new media (Certificate); software project leadership (Certificate); special education (MA, Certificate); teaching advanced placement history (Certificate); theological studies (MA, Certificate); world history (Certificate). *Application fee:* $35. Electronic applications accepted. *Application Contact:* Alison McAnespey Target, Director, Graduate and Adult Enrollment, 215-951-1100, Fax: 215-951-1886, E-mail: target@lasalle.edu. *Dean,* Dr. Thomas A. Keagy, 215-951-1042, E-mail: keagy@lasalle.edu.

Hispanic Institute Students: 1 (woman) full-time, 33 part-time (27 women); includes 15 minority (5 Black or African American, non-Hispanic/Latino; 1 American Indian or Alaska Native, non-Hispanic/Latino; 7 Hispanic/Latino; 2 Two or more races, non-Hispanic/Latino), 1 international. Average age 35. 14 applicants, 79% accepted, 8 enrolled. *Faculty:* 2 full-time (1 woman), 5 part-time/adjunct (2 women). *Financial support:* In 2015–16, 11 students received support. Scholarships/grants available. Support available to part-time students. Financial award application deadline: 8/31; financial award applicants required to submit FAFSA. In 2015, 7 master's, 4 other advanced degrees awarded. *Degree program information:* Part-time and evening/weekend programs available. Part-time, evening/weekend. Offers bilingual/bicultural studies (MA); ESL program specialist (Certificate); interpretation: English/Spanish-Spanish-English (Certificate); teaching English to speakers of other languages (MA); translation and interpretation (MA); translation: English/Spanish-Spanish/English (Certificate). *Application deadline:* For fall admission, 8/15 priority date for domestic students, 7/15 for international students; for spring admission, 12/15 priority date for domestic students, 11/15 for international students; for summer admission, 4/15 priority date for domestic students, 3/15 for international students. Applications are processed on a rolling basis. *Application fee:* $35. Electronic applications accepted. *Application Contact:* Alison McAnespey Target, Director, Graduate and Adult Enrollment, 215-951-1100, Fax: 215-951-1462, E-mail: target@lasalle.edu. *Director,* Dr. Carmen Lamas, 215-951-1209, Fax: 215-991-3506, E-mail: lamas@lasalle.edu.

School of Business Students: 57 full-time (26 women), 366 part-time (206 women); includes 127 minority (75 Black or African American, non-Hispanic/Latino; 21 Asian, non-Hispanic/Latino; 20 Hispanic/Latino; 11 Two or more races, non-Hispanic/Latino), 16 international. Average age 32. 186 applicants, 86% accepted, 78 enrolled. *Faculty:* 18 full-time (5 women), 16 part-time/adjunct (7 women). *Financial support:* In 2015–16, 81 students received support. Scholarships/grants and unspecified assistantships available. Support available to part-time students. Financial award application deadline: 8/31; financial award applicants required to submit FAFSA. In 2015, 182 master's, 1 other advanced degree awarded. *Degree program information:* Part-time and evening/weekend programs available. Part-time, evening/weekend, 100% online, blended/hybrid learning. Offers accounting (MBA, Post-MBA Certificate); business administration (MBA, Post-MBA Certificate); business systems and analytics (MBA, Post-MBA Certificate); finance (MBA, Post-MBA Certificate); general business administration (MBA, Post-MBA Certificate); human capital development (MS, Certificate); human resource management (MBA, Post-MBA Certificate); international business (Post-MBA Certificate); management (MBA, Post-MBA Certificate); marketing (Post-MBA Certificate); nonprofit leadership (MS). *Application deadline:* For fall admission, 8/15 priority date for domestic students, 7/15 for international students; for spring admission, 12/15 priority date for domestic students, 11/15 for international students; for summer admission, 4/15 priority date for domestic students, 3/15 for international students. Applications are processed on a rolling basis. *Application fee:* $35. Electronic applications accepted. *Application Contact:* Alison McAnespey Target, Director, Graduate and Adult Enrollment, 215-951-1100, Fax: 215-951-1462, E-mail: target@lasalle.edu. *Dean,* Dr. Gary Giamartino, 215-951-1040, Fax: 215-951-1886, E-mail: giamartino@lasalle.edu.

School of Nursing and Health Sciences Students: 57 full-time (54 women), 418 part-time (350 women); includes 123 minority (73 Black or African American, non-Hispanic/Latino; 1 American Indian or Alaska Native, non-Hispanic/Latino; 29 Asian, non-Hispanic/Latino; 13 Hispanic/Latino; 7 Two or more races, non-Hispanic/Latino), 6 international. Average age 36. 422 applicants, 38% accepted, 75 enrolled. *Faculty:* 23 full-time (20 women), 15 part-time/adjunct (13 women). *Financial support:* In 2015–16, 35 students received support. Scholarships/grants, tuition waivers (partial), and unspecified assistantships available. Support available to part-time students. Financial award application deadline: 8/31; financial award applicants required to submit FAFSA. In 2015, 134 master's, 3 doctorates, 10 other advanced degrees awarded. *Degree program information:* Part-time and evening/weekend programs available. Part-time, evening/weekend. Offers adult gerontology primary care nurse practitioner (MSN,

Certificate); adult health and illness clinical nurse specialist (MSN); adult-gerontology clinical nurse specialist (MSN, Certificate); clinical nurse leader (MSN); family primary care nurse practitioner (MSN, Certificate); gerontology (Certificate); nurse anesthetist (MSN, Certificate); nursing (MSN, Certificate); nursing administration (MSN, Certificate); nursing and health sciences (MPH, MS, MSN, DNP, Certificate); nursing education (Certificate); nursing practice (DNP); nursing service administration (MSN); public health (MPH); public health nursing (MSN, Certificate); school nursing (Certificate); speech-language pathology (MS). *Application deadline:* Applications are processed on a rolling basis. *Application fee:* $35. Electronic applications accepted. *Application Contact:* Alison McAnespey Target, Director, Graduate and Adult Enrollment, 215-951-1100, Fax: 215-951-1462, E-mail: target@lasalle.edu. *Dean*, Dr. Kathleen Czekanski, 215-951-1430, Fax: 215-951-1896, E-mail: czekanski@lasalle.edu.

LASELL COLLEGE, Newton, MA 02466-2709

General Information Independent, coed, comprehensive institution. *Enrollment:* 2,209 graduate, professional, and undergraduate students; 143 full-time matriculated graduate/professional students (100 women), 241 part-time matriculated graduate/professional students (177 women). *Enrollment by degree level:* 379 master's, 5 other advanced degrees. *Graduate faculty:* 16 full-time (10 women), 37 part-time/adjunct (22 women). *Tuition, area resident:* Full-time $10,710; part-time $595 per credit hour. *Required fees:* $160; $160 per unit. One-time fee: $40. *Graduate housing:* On-campus housing not available. *Student services:* Campus employment opportunities, career counseling, international student services, multicultural affairs office, services for students with disabilities. *Library:* Brennan Library. *Collection:* Books: 45,000 (physical), 1,500 (digital/electronic); Serial titles: 50 (physical); Databases: 85. Weekly public service hours: 76; study areas open 24 hours, 5–7 days a week. *Research affiliation:* Lasell Village (elder care).

Computer facilities: Computer purchase and lease plans are available. 219 computers available on campus for general student use. A campuswide network can be accessed from student residence rooms and from off campus. Online class registration, online tutoring are available.
Website: http://www.lasell.edu/

General Application Contact: Adrienne Franciosi, Director of Graduate Enrollment, 617-243-2400, Fax: 617-243-2450, E-mail: gradinfo@lasell.edu.

GRADUATE UNITS

Graduate and Professional Studies in Communication Students: 44 full-time (35 women), 69 part-time (56 women); includes 22 minority (17 Black or African American, non-Hispanic/Latino; 2 Asian, non-Hispanic/Latino; 3 Hispanic/Latino), 31 international. Average age 32. 75 applicants, 35% accepted, 17 enrolled. *Faculty:* 6 full-time (4 women), 10 part-time/adjunct (4 women). *Financial support:* Federal Work-Study and scholarships/grants available. Support available to part-time students. Financial award application deadline: 8/31; financial award applicants required to submit FAFSA. In 2015, 66 master's, 2 other advanced degrees awarded. *Degree program information:* Part-time and evening/weekend programs available. Part-time, evening/weekend, 100% online, blended/hybrid learning. Offers health communication (MSC, Graduate Certificate); integrated marketing communication (MSC, Graduate Certificate); public relations (MSC, Graduate Certificate). *Application deadline:* For fall admission, 8/31 priority date for domestic students, 6/30 priority date for international students; for spring admission, 12/31 priority date for domestic students, 10/31 priority date for international students. Applications are processed on a rolling basis. Electronic applications accepted. *Application Contact:* Adrienne Franciosi, Director of Graduate Admission, 617-243-2214, Fax: 617-243-2450, E-mail: gradinfo@lasell.edu. *Dean of Graduate and Professional Studies*, Dr. Joan Dolamore, 617-243-2485, Fax: 617-243-2450, E-mail: gradinfo@lasell.edu.

Graduate and Professional Studies in Criminal Justice Students: 4 full-time (2 women), 11 part-time (5 women); includes 2 minority (both Black or African American, non-Hispanic/Latino). Average age 27. 33 applicants, 58% accepted, 15 enrolled. *Faculty:* 2 full-time (both women). *Financial support:* Federal Work-Study and scholarships/grants available. Support available to part-time students. Financial award application deadline: 8/31; financial award applicants required to submit FAFSA. *Degree program information:* Part-time and evening/weekend programs available. Part-time, evening/weekend, 100% online. Offers emergency and crisis management (MS); homeland security and global justice (MS); violence prevention and advocacy (MS). *Application deadline:* For fall admission, 8/31 priority date for domestic students, 6/30 priority date for international students; for spring admission, 12/31 priority date for domestic students, 10/31 priority date for international students. Applications are processed on a rolling basis. Electronic applications accepted. *Application Contact:* Adrienne Franciosi, Director of Graduate Enrollment, 617-243-2400, Fax: 617-243-2450, E-mail: gradinfo@lasell.edu. *Dean of Graduate and Professional Studies*, Dr. Joan Dolamore, 617-243-2485, Fax: 617-243-2450, E-mail: gradinfo@lasell.edu.

Graduate and Professional Studies in Education Students: 8 full-time (7 women), 42 part-time (37 women); includes 2 minority (1 Asian, non-Hispanic/Latino; 1 Hispanic/Latino). Average age 29. 20 applicants, 35% accepted, 6 enrolled. *Faculty:* 3 full-time (all women), 5 part-time/adjunct (all women). *Financial support:* Federal Work-Study and scholarships/grants available. Support available to part-time students. Financial award application deadline: 8/31; financial award applicants required to submit FAFSA. In 2015, 13 master's awarded. *Degree program information:* Part-time and evening/weekend programs available. Part-time-only, evening/weekend. Offers elementary education (M Ed); special education (M Ed). *Application deadline:* For fall admission, 8/31 priority date for domestic students, 6/30 priority date for international students; for spring admission, 12/31 priority date for domestic students, 10/31 priority date for international students. Applications are processed on a rolling basis. Electronic applications accepted. *Application Contact:* Adrienne Franciosi, Director of Graduate Admission, 617-243-2214, Fax: 617-243-2450, E-mail: gradinfo@lasell.edu. *Dean of Graduate and Professional Studies*, Dr. Joan Dolamore, 617-243-2485, Fax: 617-243-2450, E-mail: gradinfo@lasell.edu.

Graduate and Professional Studies in Management Students: 69 full-time (48 women), 84 part-time (68 women); includes 37 minority (26 Black or African American, non-Hispanic/Latino; 6 Asian, non-Hispanic/Latino; 2 Hispanic/Latino; 3 Two or more races, non-Hispanic/Latino), 23 international. Average age 32. 81 applicants, 60% accepted, 34 enrolled. *Faculty:* 3 full-time (1 woman), 16 part-time/adjunct (9 women). *Financial support:* Federal Work-Study and scholarships/grants available. Support available to part-time students. Financial award application deadline: 8/31; financial award applicants required to submit FAFSA. In 2015, 68 master's, 4 other advanced degrees awarded. *Degree program information:* Part-time and evening/weekend programs available. Part-time, evening/weekend, 100% online, blended/hybrid learning. Offers business administration (PMBA); elder care management (MSM, Graduate Certificate); hospitality and event management (MSM, Graduate Certificate); human resources management (MSM, Graduate Certificate); management (MSM, Graduate Certificate); marketing (MSM, Graduate Certificate); non-profit management (MSM, Graduate Certificate); project management (MSM, Graduate Certificate). *Application deadline:* For fall admission, 8/31 priority date for domestic students, 6/30 priority date for international students; for spring admission, 12/31 priority date for domestic students, 10/31 priority date for international students. Applications are processed on a rolling basis. Electronic applications accepted. *Application Contact:* Adrienne Franciosi, Director of Graduate Admission, 617-243-2214, Fax: 617-243-2450, E-mail: gradinfo@lasell.edu. *Dean of Graduate and Professional Studies*, Dr. Joan Dolamore, 617-243-2485, Fax: 617-243-2450, E-mail: gradinfo@lasell.edu.

Graduate and Professional Studies in Rehabilitation Science ***Financial support:*** Federal Work-Study and scholarships/grants available. Support available to part-time students. Financial award application deadline: 8/31; financial award applicants required to submit FAFSA. *Degree program information:* Part-time and evening/weekend programs available. Part-time, evening/weekend, online learning. Offers rehabilitation science (MS). *Application deadline:* For fall admission, 8/31 priority date for domestic students, 6/30 priority date for international students; for spring admission, 12/31 priority date for domestic students, 10/31 priority date for international students. Applications are processed on a rolling basis. Electronic applications accepted. *Application Contact:* Adrienne Franciosi, Director of Graduate Enrollment, 617-243-2400, Fax: 617-243-2450, E-mail: gradinfo@lasell.edu. *Dean of Graduate and Professional Studies*, Dr. Joan Dolamore, 617-243-2485, Fax: 617-243-2450, E-mail: gradinfo@lasell.edu.

Graduate and Professional Studies in Sport Management Students: 18 full-time (8 women), 35 part-time (11 women); includes 12 minority (9 Black or African American, non-Hispanic/Latino; 1 American Indian or Alaska Native, non-Hispanic/Latino; 1 Hispanic/Latino; 1 Two or more races, non-Hispanic/Latino). Average age 30. 28 applicants, 68% accepted, 14 enrolled. *Faculty:* 2 full-time (0 women), 4 part-time/adjunct (2 women). *Financial support:* Federal Work-Study and scholarships/grants available. Support available to part-time students. Financial award application deadline: 8/31; financial award applicants required to submit FAFSA. In 2015, 25 master's, 1 other advanced degree awarded. *Degree program information:* Part-time and evening/weekend programs available. Part-time, evening/weekend, 100% online. Offers sport hospitality management (MS, Graduate Certificate); sport leadership (MS, Graduate Certificate); sport non-profit management (MS, Graduate Certificate). *Application deadline:* For fall admission, 8/31 priority date for domestic students, 6/30 priority date for international students; for spring admission, 12/31 priority date for domestic students, 10/31 priority date for international students. Applications are processed on a rolling basis. Electronic applications accepted. *Application Contact:* Adrienne Franciosi, Director of Graduate Admission, 617-243-2214, Fax: 617-243-2450, E-mail: gradinfo@lasell.edu. *Dean of Graduate and Professional Studies*, Dr. Joan Dolamore, 617-243-2485, Fax: 617-243-2450, E-mail: gradinfo@lasell.edu.

LA SIERRA UNIVERSITY, Riverside, CA 92515

General Information Independent-religious, coed, comprehensive institution. CGS member. *Graduate housing:* Rooms and/or apartments available on a first-come, first-served basis to single students and available to married students.

GRADUATE UNITS

College of Arts and Sciences ***Degree program information:*** Part-time programs available. Part-time. Offers arts and sciences (MA); communication (MA); English (MA).

School of Business and Management Offers accounting (MBA); finance (MBA); general management (MBA); human resources management (MBA); leadership, values, and ethics for business and management (Certificate); marketing (MBA).

School of Education ***Degree program information:*** Part-time and evening/weekend programs available. Part-time, evening/weekend. Offers administration and leadership (MA, Ed D, Ed S); counseling (MA); curriculum and instruction (MA, Ed D, Ed S); education (MA, MAT, Ed D, Ed S); educational psychology (Ed S); school psychology (Ed S); teaching (MAT).

School of Religion ***Degree program information:*** Part-time programs available. Part-time. Offers pastoral ministry (M Div); religion (MA); religious education (MA); religious studies (MA).

LAURENTIAN UNIVERSITY, Sudbury, ON P3E 2C6, Canada

General Information Province-supported, coed, comprehensive institution. *Graduate housing:* Rooms and/or apartments available on a first-come, first-served basis to single and married students.

GRADUATE UNITS

School of Graduate Studies and Research ***Degree program information:*** Part-time and evening/weekend programs available. Part-time, evening/weekend. Offers analytical chemistry (M Sc); applied psychology (MA); applied social research (MA); biochemistry (M Sc); biology (M Sc); boreal ecology (PhD); environmental chemistry (M Sc); European history (MA); experimental psychology (MA); geology (M Sc); history of Northern Ontario (MA); human development (M Sc, MA); humanities: interpretation and values (MA); mineral deposits and precambrian geology (PhD); mineral exploration (M Sc); North American history (MA); nursing (M Sc N); organic chemistry (M Sc); physical/theoretical chemistry (M Sc); physics (M Sc); rural and Northern health (PhD); science communication (G Dip).

School of Commerce and Administration Degree program information: Part-time and evening/weekend programs available. Part-time, evening/weekend. Offers commerce and administration (MBA).

School of Engineering Degree program information: Part-time programs available. Part-time. Offers mineral resources engineering (M Eng, MA Sc); natural resources engineering (PhD).

School of Social Work Degree program information: Part-time programs available. Part-time. Offers social work (MSW). Open only to French-speaking students.

LAWRENCE TECHNOLOGICAL UNIVERSITY, Southfield, MI 48075-1058

General Information Independent, coed, university. *Enrollment:* 4,161 graduate, professional, and undergraduate students; 67 full-time matriculated graduate/professional students (17 women), 1,315 part-time matriculated graduate/professional students (323 women). *Enrollment by degree level:* 1,299 master's, 61 doctoral, 22 other advanced degrees. *Graduate faculty:* 60 full-time (17 women), 76 part-time/adjunct (16 women). *Tuition, area resident:* Full-time $14,700; part-time $1050 per credit. *Required fees:* $150; $150 per unit. One-time fee: $150. *Graduate housing:* Rooms and/or apartments available on a first-come, first-served basis to single and married students. Typical cost: $5552 per year ($9470 including board) for single students; $5552 per year ($9470 including board) for married students. Housing application deadline: 5/1. *Student services:* Campus employment opportunities, campus safety program, career counseling, exercise/wellness program, free psychological counseling, international student services, low-cost health insurance, multicultural affairs office, services for students with disabilities, writing training. *Library:*

Lawrence Technological University Library plus 1 other. *Collection:* Books: 61,504 (physical), 227,308 (digital/electronic); Serial titles: 143,348 (digital/electronic); Databases: 171. Weekly public service hours: 73; study areas open 24 hours, 5–7 days a week. *Research affiliation:* William Beaumont Hospital (biomedical engineering), Clinton River Watershed Council (storm water analysis), Detroit Economic Growth Association (Great Lakes Shoreline Cities Green Infrastructure Project), Hyundai-KIA America Technical Center, Inc. (improvement of built-in hands-free cell phone performance), Johnson Controls Battery Group, Inc. (vehicle system power management testing), National Renewable Energy Laboratory (NREL) (solar design).

Computer facilities: Computer purchase and lease plans are available. 126 computers available on campus for general student use. A campuswide network can be accessed from student residence rooms and from off campus. Online class registration, degree audit, Blackboard, SCT Banner (student information), personal websites, document collection are available.
Website: http://www.ltu.edu/

General Application Contact: Jane Rohrback, Director of Admissions, 248-204-3160, Fax: 248-204-2228, E-mail: admissions@ltu.edu.

GRADUATE UNITS

College of Architecture and Design Students: 7 full-time (4 women), 177 part-time (75 women); includes 16 minority (3 Black or African American, non-Hispanic/Latino; 4 Asian, non-Hispanic/Latino; 7 Hispanic/Latino; 2 Two or more races, non-Hispanic/Latino), 59 international. Average age 30. 129 applicants, 37% accepted, 34 enrolled. *Faculty:* 16 full-time (4 women), 23 part-time/adjunct (7 women). *Financial support:* In 2015–16, 58 students received support, including 8 research assistantships with partial tuition reimbursements available (averaging $6,000 per year); teaching assistantships, career-related internships or fieldwork, scholarships/grants, and unspecified assistantships also available. Financial award application deadline: 4/1; financial award applicants required to submit FAFSA. In 2015, 86 master's awarded. *Degree program information:* Part-time and evening/weekend programs available. Part-time, evening/weekend. Offers architecture (M Arch); environmental graphic design (MA); interior design (MID); urban design (MUD, Graduate Certificate). *Application deadline:* For fall admission, 5/22 for international students; for spring admission, 10/11 for international students; for summer admission, 2/16 for international students. Applications are processed on a rolling basis. *Application fee:* $50. Electronic applications accepted. *Application Contact:* Jane Rohrback, Director of Admissions, 248-204-3160, Fax: 248-204-2228, E-mail: admissions@ltu.edu. *Interim Dean*, Prof. Amy Deines, 248-204-2802, Fax: 248-204-2900, E-mail: archdean@ltu.edu.

College of Arts and Sciences Students: 1 (woman) full-time, 51 part-time (24 women); includes 8 minority (6 Black or African American, non-Hispanic/Latino; 1 Hispanic/Latino; 1 Two or more races, non-Hispanic/Latino), 21 international. Average age 33. 399 applicants, 23% accepted, 5 enrolled. *Faculty:* 6 full-time (3 women), 14 part-time/adjunct (5 women). *Financial support:* In 2015–16, 7 students received support. Scholarships/grants and tuition reduction available. Financial award application deadline: 4/1; financial award applicants required to submit FAFSA. In 2015, 20 master's awarded. *Degree program information:* Part-time and evening/weekend programs available. Part-time, evening/weekend. Offers computer science (MS); educational technology (MA); science education (MA); technical and professional communication (MS). *Application deadline:* For fall admission, 5/22 for international students; for spring admission, 10/11 for international students; for summer admission, 2/16 for international students. Applications are processed on a rolling basis. *Application fee:* $50. Electronic applications accepted. *Application Contact:* Jane Rohrback, Director of Admissions, 248-204-3160, Fax: 248-204-2228, E-mail: admissions@ltu.edu. *Dean*, Dr. Hsiao-Ping Moore, 248-204-3500, Fax: 248-204-3518, E-mail: scidean@itu.edu.

College of Engineering Students: 57 full-time (11 women), 680 part-time (88 women); includes 22 minority (8 Black or African American, non-Hispanic/Latino; 7 Asian, non-Hispanic/Latino; 5 Hispanic/Latino; 2 Two or more races, non-Hispanic/Latino), 579 international. Average age 27. 1,601 applicants, 41% accepted, 187 enrolled. *Faculty:* 25 full-time (4 women), 24 part-time/adjunct (2 women). *Financial support:* In 2015–16, 34 students received support, including 5 research assistantships with full tuition reimbursements available; unspecified assistantships also available. Financial award application deadline: 4/1; financial award applicants required to submit FAFSA. In 2015, 106 master's, 1 doctorate awarded. *Degree program information:* Part-time and evening/weekend programs available. Part-time, evening/weekend. Offers architectural engineering (MS); automotive engineering (MS); biomedical engineering (MS); civil engineering (MA, MS, PhD); construction engineering management (MA); electrical and computer engineering (MS); engineering management (MEM); engineering technology (MS); fire engineering (MS); industrial engineering (MS); mechanical engineering (MS, DE); mechatronic systems engineering (MS). *Application deadline:* For fall admission, 5/22 for international students; for spring admission, 10/11 for international students; for summer admission, 2/16 for international students. Applications are processed on a rolling basis. *Application fee:* $50. Electronic applications accepted. *Application Contact:* Jane Rohrback, Director of Admissions, 248-204-3160, Fax: 248-204-2228, E-mail: admissions@ltu.edu. *Dean*, Dr. Nabil Grace, 248-204-2500, Fax: 248-204-2509, E-mail: engrdean@ltu.edu.

College of Management Students: 2 full-time (1 woman), 407 part-time (136 women); includes 85 minority (45 Black or African American, non-Hispanic/Latino; 2 American Indian or Alaska Native, non-Hispanic/Latino; 18 Asian, non-Hispanic/Latino; 12 Hispanic/Latino; 8 Two or more races, non-Hispanic/Latino), 157 international. Average age 33. 318 applicants, 53% accepted, 84 enrolled. *Faculty:* 16 full-time (6 women), 16 part-time/adjunct (2 women). *Financial support:* In 2015–16, 33 students received support, including 8 research assistantships with partial tuition reimbursements available (averaging $3,250 per year); unspecified assistantships also available. Financial award application deadline: 4/1; financial award applicants required to submit FAFSA. In 2015, 106 master's, 3 doctorates awarded. *Degree program information:* Part-time and evening/weekend programs available. Part-time, evening/weekend. Offers business administration (MBA, DBA); information technology (MS). *Application deadline:* For fall admission, 5/22 for international students; for spring admission, 10/11 for international students; for summer admission, 2/16 for international students. Applications are processed on a rolling basis. *Application fee:* $50. Electronic applications accepted. *Application Contact:* Jane Rohrback, Director of Admissions, 248-204-3160, Fax: 248-204-2228, E-mail: admissions@ltu.edu. *Dean*, Dr. Bahman Mirshab, 248-204-3050, E-mail: mgtdean@ltu.edu.

LEBANESE AMERICAN UNIVERSITY, Beirut, Lebanon

General Information Private, coed, comprehensive institution.

GRADUATE UNITS

School of Arts and Sciences Offers computer science (MS); international affairs (MA).

School of Business Offers business (MBA).

School of Pharmacy Offers pharmacy (Pharm D).

LEBANON VALLEY COLLEGE, Annville, PA 17003-1400

General Information Independent-religious, coed, comprehensive institution. *Enrollment:* 1,918 graduate, professional, and undergraduate students; 93 full-time matriculated graduate/professional students (67 women), 98 part-time matriculated graduate/professional students (56 women). *Enrollment by degree level:* 114 master's, 77 doctoral. *Graduate faculty:* 14 full-time (5 women), 16 part-time/adjunct (6 women). Tuition and fees vary according to program. *Graduate housing:* Room and/or apartments available on a first-come, first-served basis to single students; on-campus housing not available to married students. Typical cost: $6240 per year. *Student services:* Campus safety program, career counseling, exercise/wellness program, free psychological counseling, international student services, multicultural affairs office, services for students with disabilities, teacher training, writing training. *Library:* Vernon and Doris Bishop Library. *Collection:* Books: 181,747 (physical), 187,609 (digital/electronic); Databases: 116. Weekly public service hours: 101; students can reserve study rooms.

Computer facilities: Computer purchase and lease plans are available. 199 computers available on campus for general student use. A campuswide network can be accessed from student residence rooms and from off campus. Online class registration is available.
Website: http://www.lvc.edu/

General Application Contact: Tami S Morgan, Senior Assistant for Admissions and Financial Aid, 717-867-6181, E-mail: tmorgan@lvc.edu.

GRADUATE UNITS

Program in Athletic Training ***Faculty:*** 1 full-time (0 women), 3 part-time/adjunct (1 woman). *Financial support:* Applicants required to submit FAFSA. Offers athletic training (MAT). Electronic applications accepted. *Application Contact:* EJ Smith, Assistant Director of Admission, 717-867-6183, Fax: 717-867-6849, E-mail: ejsmith@lvc.edu. *Director of Athletic Training*, Dr. Joseph Murphy, 717-867-6845, Fax: 717-867-6849, E-mail: jmurphy@lvc.edu.

Program in Business Administration Students: 17 full-time (13 women), 85 part-time (46 women); includes 11 minority (4 Black or African American, non-Hispanic/Latino; 2 Asian, non-Hispanic/Latino; 4 Hispanic/Latino; 1 Two or more races, non-Hispanic/Latino), 2 international. Average age 33. 17 applicants, 94% accepted, 14 enrolled. *Faculty:* 7 full-time (1 woman), 10 part-time/adjunct (1 woman). *Financial support:* Scholarships/grants available. Financial award application deadline: 3/1; financial award applicants required to submit FAFSA. In 2015, 51 master's awarded. *Degree program information:* Part-time and evening/weekend programs available. Part-time, evening/weekend. Offers business administration (MBA); healthcare management (MBA). *Application deadline:* Applications are processed on a rolling basis. *Application fee:* $0. Electronic applications accepted. *Application Contact:* Christine M. Martin, Enrollment and Operations Specialist, 717-867-6486, Fax: 717-867-6013, E-mail: cmartin@lvc.edu. *Chair of the Department of Business and Economics/MBA Director*, Dr. David Setley, 717-867-6104, Fax: 717-867-6018, E-mail: setley@lvc.edu.

Program in Music Education Students: 5 part-time (2 women); includes 2 minority (1 Black or African American, non-Hispanic/Latino; 1 Hispanic/Latino). Average age 34. 4 applicants, 75% accepted, 2 enrolled. *Faculty:* 9 part-time/adjunct (2 women). *Financial support:* Scholarships/grants available. Financial award application deadline: 5/1; financial award applicants required to submit FAFSA. In 2015, 37 master's awarded. *Degree program information:* Part-time and evening/weekend programs available. Part-time-only, evening/weekend, blended/hybrid learning. Offers music education (MME). *Application deadline:* Applications are processed on a rolling basis. *Application fee:* $0. Electronic applications accepted. *Application Contact:* Cherie VanZant, Administrator of the Master of Music Education Program, 717-867-6383, Fax: 717-867-6383, E-mail: vanzant@lvc.edu. *Director of Graduate and Community Music Programs*, Cherie VanZant, 717-867-6383, E-mail: vanzant@lvc.edu.

Program in Physical Therapy Students: 76 full-time (54 women), 1 (woman) part-time; includes 9 minority (1 Black or African American, non-Hispanic/Latino; 1 American Indian or Alaska Native, non-Hispanic/Latino; 2 Hispanic/Latino; 5 Two or more races, non-Hispanic/Latino). Average age 23. 188 applicants, 27% accepted, 46 enrolled. *Faculty:* 9 full-time (4 women), 3 part-time/adjunct (0 women). *Financial support:* In 2015–16, 100 students received support. Scholarships/grants available. Financial award application deadline: 3/1; financial award applicants required to submit FAFSA. In 2015, 30 doctorates awarded. Offers physical therapy (DPT). *Application deadline:* For winter admission, 2/1 for domestic students. Electronic applications accepted. *Application Contact:* EJ Smith, Assistant Director of Admission, 866-582-4236, Fax: 717-867-6026, E-mail: ejsmith@lvc.edu. *Chair of Physical Therapy*, Dr. Stan M. Dacko, 717-867-6843, Fax: 717-867-6849, E-mail: dacko@lvc.edu.

Program in Science Education Students: 7 part-time (all women). Average age 33. 3 applicants, 33% accepted. *Faculty:* 16 part-time/adjunct (7 women). *Financial support:* Scholarships/grants available. Financial award application deadline: 5/1; financial award applicants required to submit FAFSA. In 2015, 4 master's awarded. *Degree program information:* Part-time and evening/weekend programs available. Part-time-only, evening/weekend. Offers science education (MSE); STEM education (MSE). *Application deadline:* Applications are processed on a rolling basis. *Application fee:* $0. Electronic applications accepted. *Director of MSE and STEM-based programs*, Carrie Coryer, 717-867-6190, Fax: 717-867-6018, E-mail: coryer@lvc.edu.

LEE UNIVERSITY, Cleveland, TN 37320-3450

General Information Independent-religious, coed, comprehensive institution. *Enrollment:* 5,041 graduate, professional, and undergraduate students; 227 full-time matriculated graduate/professional students (128 women), 227 part-time matriculated graduate/professional students (109 women). *Enrollment by degree level:* 447 master's, 7 other advanced degrees. *Graduate faculty:* 53 full-time (16 women), 15 part-time/adjunct (2 women). *Tuition, area resident:* Full-time $10,800; part-time $600 per credit hour. *Required fees:* $35 per term. One-time fee: $25. Tuition and fees vary according to program. *Graduate housing:* Rooms and/or apartments available on a first-come, first-served basis to single and married students. Typical cost: $4330 per year ($7880 including board) for single students; $7200 per year ($10,750 including board) for married students. Room and board charges vary according to board plan, campus/location and housing facility selected. Housing application deadline: 9/1. *Student services:* Campus employment opportunities, campus safety program, career counseling, exercise/wellness program, free psychological counseling, international student services, services for students with disabilities, teacher training, writing training. *Library:* William G. Squires Library plus 2 others. *Collection:* Books: 154,127 (physical), 312,014 (digital/electronic); Serial titles: 273 (physical), 23,861 (digital/electronic); Databases: 131. Weekly public service hours: 91; students can reserve study rooms.

Computer facilities: 410 computers available on campus for general student use. A campuswide network can be accessed from student residence rooms and from off campus. Online class registration is available.
Website: http://www.leeuniversity.edu/

General Application Contact: Director of Graduate Enrollment, 423-614-8691.

GRADUATE UNITS

Graduate Studies in Counseling Students: 51 full-time (41 women), 13 part-time (11 women); includes 14 minority (7 Black or African American, non-Hispanic/Latino; 1 American Indian or Alaska Native, non-Hispanic/Latino; 1 Asian, non-Hispanic/Latino; 4 Hispanic/Latino; 1 Two or more races, non-Hispanic/Latino), 1 international. Average age 27. 49 applicants, 67% accepted, 25 enrolled. *Faculty:* 9 full-time (3 women), 3 part-time/adjunct (0 women). *Financial support:* In 2015–16, 29 students received support. Career-related internships or fieldwork, Federal Work-Study, institutionally sponsored loans, scholarships/grants, and unspecified assistantships available. Financial award application deadline: 3/1; financial award applicants required to submit FAFSA. In 2015, 47 master's awarded. *Degree program information:* Part-time programs available. Part-time. Offers holistic child development (MS); marriage and family studies (MS); marriage and family therapy (MS); school counseling (MS). *Application deadline:* For fall admission, 4/1 priority date for domestic and international students; for spring admission, 11/1 priority date for domestic and international students. Applications are processed on a rolling basis. *Application fee:* $25. Electronic applications accepted. *Director*, Dr. Trevor Milliron, 423-614-8126, Fax: 423-614-8124, E-mail: tmilliron@leeuniversity.edu.

MBA Program Students: 7 full-time (4 women), 41 part-time (24 women); includes 3 minority (2 Black or African American, non-Hispanic/Latino; 1 Hispanic/Latino), 6 international. Average age 28. 34 applicants, 79% accepted, 24 enrolled. *Faculty:* 5 full-time (1 woman). *Financial support:* In 2015–16, 18 students received support. Scholarships/grants available. Financial award application deadline: 3/1; financial award applicants required to submit FAFSA. *Degree program information:* Part-time and evening/weekend programs available. Part-time, evening/weekend. Offers business administration (MBA). *Application deadline:* For fall admission, 4/1 priority date for domestic and international students; for spring admission, 10/1 priority date for domestic and international students. Applications are processed on a rolling basis. *Application fee:* $25. Electronic applications accepted. *Director*, Dr. Shane Griffith, 423-614-8694, E-mail: mba@leeuniversity.edu.

Program in Education Students: 39 full-time (28 women), 57 part-time (37 women); includes 13 minority (7 Black or African American, non-Hispanic/Latino; 4 Hispanic/Latino; 1 Native Hawaiian or other Pacific Islander, non-Hispanic/Latino; 1 Two or more races, non-Hispanic/Latino), 5 international. Average age 30. 46 applicants, 76% accepted, 29 enrolled. *Faculty:* 12 full-time (6 women), 7 part-time/adjunct (2 women). *Financial support:* In 2015–16, 52 students received support. Career-related internships or fieldwork, Federal Work-Study, institutionally sponsored loans, scholarships/grants, and unspecified assistantships available. Financial award application deadline: 3/1; financial award applicants required to submit FAFSA. In 2015, 45 master's, 10 other advanced degrees awarded. *Degree program information:* Part-time programs available. Part-time. Offers art (MAT); curriculum and instruction (M Ed, Ed S); early childhood (MAT); educational leadership (M Ed, Ed S); elementary education (MAT); English and math (MAT); English and science (MAT); English and social studies (MAT); higher education administration (MS); history (MAT); history and economics (MAT); math and science (MAT); math and social studies (MAT); middle grades (MAT); science and social studies (MASW); secondary education (MAT); Spanish (MAT); special education (M Ed, MAT); TESOL (MAT). *Application deadline:* For fall admission, 6/1 priority date for domestic and international students; for spring admission, 11/1 priority date for domestic and international students; for summer admission, 4/1 priority date for domestic and international students. Applications are processed on a rolling basis. *Application fee:* $25. Electronic applications accepted. *Application Contact:* Crystal Keeter, Graduate Education Secretary, 423-614-8544, E-mail: ckeeter@leeuniversity.edu. *Director*, Dr. William Kamm, 423-614-8544, E-mail: wkamm@leeuniversity.edu.

Program in Music Students: 24 full-time (17 women), 15 part-time (8 women); includes 5 minority (3 Black or African American, non-Hispanic/Latino; 1 Asian, non-Hispanic/Latino; 1 Hispanic/Latino), 10 international. Average age 25. 27 applicants, 59% accepted, 11 enrolled. *Faculty:* 18 full-time (3 women), 2 part-time/adjunct (0 women). *Financial support:* In 2015–16, 34 students received support. Career-related internships or fieldwork, Federal Work-Study, institutionally sponsored loans, scholarships/grants, and unspecified assistantships available. Financial award application deadline: 3/1; financial award applicants required to submit FAFSA. In 2015, 11 master's awarded. *Degree program information:* Part-time programs available. Part-time. Offers conducting (MM); music education (MM); music performance (MM); religious/sacred music (MCM). *Application deadline:* For fall admission, 4/1 priority date for domestic and international students; for spring admission, 10/1 priority date for domestic and international students. Applications are processed on a rolling basis. *Application fee:* $25. Electronic applications accepted. *Director*, Dr. Brad J. Moffett, 423-614-8240, Fax: 423-614-8245, E-mail: gradmusic@leeuniversity.edu.

Programs in Religion Students: 47 full-time (14 women), 49 part-time (19 women); includes 20 minority (14 Black or African American, non-Hispanic/Latino; 1 American Indian or Alaska Native, non-Hispanic/Latino; 1 Asian, non-Hispanic/Latino; 4 Hispanic/Latino), 5 international. Average age 38. 54 applicants, 96% accepted, 51 enrolled. *Faculty:* 14 full-time (3 women), 14 part-time/adjunct (1 woman). *Financial support:* In 2015–16, 27 students received support, including 7 teaching assistantships (averaging $2,031 per year); career-related internships or fieldwork, Federal Work-Study, institutionally sponsored loans, scholarships/grants, and unspecified assistantships also available. Financial award application deadline: 3/1; financial award applicants required to submit FAFSA. In 2015, 19 master's awarded. *Degree program information:* Part-time programs available. Part-time, 100% online. Offers biblical studies (MA); ministry studies/leadership (MA); ministry studies/worship (MA); ministry studies/youth and family (MA); theological studies (MA). *Application deadline:* For fall admission, 4/1 priority date for domestic and international students; for spring admission, 10/1 priority date for domestic and international students. Applications are processed on a rolling basis. *Application fee:* $25. Electronic applications accepted. *Director*, Dr. Lisa Long, 423-303-5100 Ext. 5100, E-mail: llong@leeuniversity.edu.

LEHIGH UNIVERSITY, Bethlehem, PA 18015-3094

General Information Independent, coed, university. CGS member. *Enrollment:* 7,054 graduate, professional, and undergraduate students; 1,209 full-time matriculated graduate/professional students (512 women), 677 part-time matriculated graduate/professional students (326 women). *Enrollment by degree level:* 1,170 master's, 700 doctoral, 16 other advanced degrees. *Graduate faculty:* 389 full-time (112 women), 36 part-time/adjunct (19 women). *Graduate housing:* Rooms and/or apartments available on a first-come, first-served basis to single and married students. *Student services:* Campus employment opportunities, campus safety program, career counseling, child daycare facilities, exercise/wellness program, free psychological counseling, international student services, low-cost health insurance, multicultural affairs office, services for students with disabilities, teacher training, writing training. *Library:* E. W. Fairchild-Martindale Library plus 1 other. *Collection:* Books: 915,850 (physical), 348,262 (digital/electronic); Serial titles: 2,212 (physical), 52,787 (digital/electronic); Databases: 177. Weekly public service hours: 80; students can reserve study rooms.

Computer facilities: Computer purchase and lease plans are available. 586 computers available on campus for general student use. A campuswide network can be accessed from student residence rooms and from off campus. Online class registration is available.

Website: http://www.lehigh.edu/

GRADUATE UNITS

College of Arts and Sciences Students: 271 full-time (132 women), 93 part-time (50 women); includes 36 minority (11 Black or African American, non-Hispanic/Latino; 2 American Indian or Alaska Native, non-Hispanic/Latino; 8 Asian, non-Hispanic/Latino; 12 Hispanic/Latino; 3 Two or more races, non-Hispanic/Latino), 68 international. Average age 28. 544 applicants, 36% accepted, 76 enrolled. *Faculty:* 167 full-time (57 women), 7 part-time/adjunct (4 women). *Financial support:* In 2015–16, 26 fellowships with full tuition reimbursements (averaging $25,000 per year) were awarded; scholarships/grants, tuition waivers (full and partial), and unspecified assistantships also available. Financial award application deadline: 1/1. In 2015, 103 master's, 24 doctorates awarded. *Degree program information:* Part-time programs available. Part-time, online learning. Offers American studies (MA); applied mathematics (MS, PhD); arts and sciences (MA, MS, PhD, Graduate Certificate); Atlantic world (PhD); biochemistry (PhD); British history (PhD); cell and molecular biology (PhD); chemistry (MS, PhD); documentary film (Graduate Certificate); earth and environmental sciences (MS, PhD); English (MA, PhD); environmental policy and law (Graduate Certificate); environmental policy design (MA); history (MA); industrial and modern America (PhD); integrative biology (PhD); mathematics (MS, PhD); molecular biology (MS); photonics (MS); physics (MS, PhD); politics and policy (MA); psychology (MS, PhD); public history (MA); sociology (MA); statistics (MS); sustainable development (Graduate Certificate); urban environmental policy (Graduate Certificate). *Application deadline:* For fall admission, 7/1 for domestic students, 7/15 for international students; for spring admission, 12/1 for domestic and international students. *Application fee:* $75. Electronic applications accepted. *Application Contact:* Gary Burgess, Administrative Clerk, 610-758-4281, Fax: 610-758-6232, E-mail: glb215@lehigh.edu. *Associate Dean of Graduate Studies*, Dr. Dominic Packer, 610-758-4282, Fax: 610-758-6232, E-mail: dlp208@lehigh.edu.

College of Business and Economics Students: 209 full-time (117 women), 155 part-time (41 women); includes 43 minority (4 Black or African American, non-Hispanic/Latino; 1 American Indian or Alaska Native, non-Hispanic/Latino; 23 Asian, non-Hispanic/Latino; 9 Hispanic/Latino; 1 Native Hawaiian or other Pacific Islander, non-Hispanic/Latino; 5 Two or more races, non-Hispanic/Latino), 158 international. Average age 28. 737 applicants, 41% accepted, 126 enrolled. *Faculty:* 50 full-time (15 women), 4 part-time/adjunct (0 women). *Financial support:* In 2015–16, 93 students received support, including 10 fellowships with partial tuition reimbursements available, 1 research assistantship with full tuition reimbursement available (averaging $18,000 per year), 15 teaching assistantships with full tuition reimbursements available (averaging $18,000 per year); scholarships/grants, health care benefits, and tuition waivers (full and partial) also available. Support available to part-time students. Financial award application deadline: 1/15. In 2015, 160 master's, 4 doctorates awarded. *Degree program information:* Part-time and evening/weekend programs available. Part-time, evening/weekend, online learning. Offers accounting and information analysis (MS); analytical finance (MS); business administration (MBA); business and economics (MBA, MS, PhD); economics (MS); project management (MBA). *Application deadline:* For fall admission, 7/15 for domestic students, 5/1 for international students; for spring admission, 12/1 for domestic and international students. *Application fee:* $75. *Application Contact:* Michael Tarantino, Director of Recruitment and Admissions, 610-758-3418, Fax: 610-758-5283, E-mail: mgt215@lehigh.edu. *Dean*, Georgette Chapman-Phillips, 610-758-6725, Fax: 610-758-4499, E-mail: gcp214@lehigh.edu.

College of Education Students: 144 full-time (123 women), 275 part-time (199 women); includes 37 minority (11 Black or African American, non-Hispanic/Latino; 11 Asian, non-Hispanic/Latino; 14 Hispanic/Latino; 1 Native Hawaiian or other Pacific Islander, non-Hispanic/Latino), 47 international. Average age 32. 534 applicants, 58% accepted, 78 enrolled. *Faculty:* 33 full-time (18 women), 19 part-time/adjunct (15 women). *Financial support:* In 2015–16, 162 students received support, including 6 fellowships with tuition reimbursements available (averaging $15,632 per year), 40 research assistantships with tuition reimbursements available (averaging $9,548 per year); teaching assistantships, career-related internships or fieldwork, institutionally sponsored loans, scholarships/grants, tuition waivers (partial), and unspecified assistantships also available. Financial award application deadline: 3/1; financial award applicants required to submit FAFSA. In 2015, 147 master's, 16 doctorates, 7 other advanced degrees awarded. *Degree program information:* Part-time and evening/weekend programs available. Part-time, evening/weekend, blended/hybrid learning. Offers comparative and international education (MA, PhD); counseling and human services (M Ed); counseling psychology (PhD); education (M Ed, MA, MS, Ed D, PhD, Certificate, Ed S, Graduate Certificate); educational leadership (M Ed, Ed D, Certificate); globalization and educational change (M Ed); instructional technology (MS); international counseling (M Ed, Certificate); international development in education (Certificate); school counseling (M Ed); school psychology (PhD, Ed S); special education (M Ed, PhD); teaching, learning and technology (PhD); technology use in the schools (Graduate Certificate); TESOL (Certificate). *Application deadline:* For fall admission, 1/1 for domestic and international students; for spring admission, 11/1 for domestic and international students; for summer admission, 5/1 for domestic and international students. *Application fee:* $65. Electronic applications accepted. *Application Contact:* Donna M. Johnson, Manager of Admissions and Recruitment, 610-758-3231, Fax: 610-758-6223, E-mail: dmj4@lehigh.edu. *Dean*, Dr. Gary M. Sasso, 610-758-3221, Fax: 610-758-6223, E-mail: gary.sasso@lehigh.edu.

P.C. Rossin College of Engineering and Applied Science Students: 585 full-time (140 women), 154 part-time (36 women); includes 56 minority (10 Black or African American, non-Hispanic/Latino; 22 Asian, non-Hispanic/Latino; 19 Hispanic/Latino; 1 Native Hawaiian or other Pacific Islander, non-Hispanic/Latino; 4 Two or more races, non-Hispanic/Latino), 426 international. Average age 26. 2,538 applicants, 25% accepted, 187 enrolled. *Faculty:* 139 full-time (22 women), 6 part-time/adjunct (0 women). *Financial support:* In 2015–16, 312 students received support, including 29 fellowships with tuition reimbursements available (averaging $21,105 per year), 103 research assistantships with tuition reimbursements available (averaging $28,140 per year), 62 teaching assistantships with tuition reimbursements available (averaging $21,530 per year); career-related internships or fieldwork, scholarships/grants, tuition waivers (full and partial), and unspecified assistantships also available. Financial award application deadline: 1/15. In 2015, 214 master's, 61 doctorates awarded. *Degree program information:* Part-time programs available. Part-time, 100% online, blended/hybrid learning. Offers analytical finance (MS); bioengineering (MS, PhD);

biological chemical engineering (M Eng); chemical and biomolecular engineering (M Eng, MS, PhD); chemical energy engineering (M Eng); civil and environmental engineering (M Eng, MS, PhD); computational and engineering mechanics (MS, PhD); computer engineering (M Eng, MS, PhD); computer science (M Eng, MS, PhD); electrical engineering (MS, PhD); energy systems engineering (M Eng); engineering and applied science (M Eng, MS, PhD); healthcare systems engineering (M Eng); industrial and systems engineering (M Eng, MS); industrial engineering (PhD); management science and engineering (M Eng, MS); manufacturing systems engineering (MS); materials science and engineering (M Eng, MS, PhD); mechanical engineering (M Eng, MS, PhD); photonics (MS); polymer science/engineering (M Eng, MS, PhD); technical entrepreneurship (M Eng); wireless network engineering (MS). *Application deadline:* For fall admission, 7/15 for domestic and international students; for spring admission, 12/1 for domestic and international students. Applications are processed on a rolling basis. *Application fee:* $75. Electronic applications accepted. *Application Contact:* Brianne Lisk, Manager of Graduate Programs, 610-758-6310, Fax: 610-758-5623, E-mail: brie.lisk@lehigh.edu. *Interim Associate Dean of Graduate Studies and Research,* Dr. Raymond A. Pearson, 610-758-6310, Fax: 610-758-5623, E-mail: rp02@lehigh.edu.

Center for Polymer Science and Engineering Students: 4 full-time (2 women), 14 part-time (3 women); includes 2 minority (1 Asian, non-Hispanic/Latino; 1 Native Hawaiian or other Pacific Islander, non-Hispanic/Latino), 1 international. Average age 30. 51 applicants, 16% accepted, 5 enrolled. *Faculty:* 18 full-time (0 women), 1 part-time/adjunct (0 women). *Financial support:* In 2015–16, 1 student received support, including 1 research assistantship (averaging $1,000 per year); teaching assistantships, scholarships/grants, and health care benefits also available. Financial award application deadline: 1/15. In 2015, 4 master's awarded. *Degree program information:* Part-time and evening/weekend programs available. Part-time, evening/weekend, 100% online, blended/hybrid learning. Offers polymer science and engineering (M Eng, MS, PhD). *Application deadline:* For fall admission, 7/15 for domestic students, 1/15 for international students; for spring admission, 12/1 for domestic and international students. Applications are processed on a rolling basis. *Application fee:* $75. Electronic applications accepted. *Application Contact:* James E. Roberts, Chair, Polymer Education Committee, 610-758-4841, Fax: 610-758-6536, E-mail: jer1@lehigh.edu. *Director,* Dr. Raymond A. Pearson, 610-758-3857, Fax: 610-758-3526, E-mail: rp02@lehigh.edu.

LEHMAN COLLEGE OF THE CITY UNIVERSITY OF NEW YORK, Bronx, NY 10468-1589

General Information State and locally supported, coed, comprehensive institution. *Graduate housing:* On-campus housing not available. *Research affiliation:* New York Botanical Gardens, Montefiore Hospital and Medical Center.

GRADUATE UNITS

Division of Arts and Humanities ***Degree program information:*** Part-time and evening/weekend programs available. Part-time, evening/weekend. Offers art (MA, MFA); arts and humanities (MA, MAT, MFA); English (MA); history (MA); music (MAT); Spanish (MA); speech-language pathology and audiology (MA).

Division of Education ***Degree program information:*** Part-time and evening/weekend programs available. Part-time, evening/weekend. Offers bilingual special education (MS Ed); business education (MS Ed); early childhood education (MS Ed); early special education (MS Ed); education (MA, MS Ed); elementary education (MS Ed); emotional handicaps (MS Ed); English education (MS Ed); guidance and counseling (MS Ed); learning disabilities (MS Ed); mathematics 7–12 (MS Ed); mental retardation (MS Ed); music education (MS Ed); reading teacher (MS Ed); science education (MS Ed); social studies 7–12 (MA); teachers of special education (MS Ed); teaching English to speakers of other languages (MS Ed).

School of Natural and Social Sciences ***Degree program information:*** Part-time and evening/weekend programs available. Part-time, evening/weekend. Offers accounting (MS); adult health nursing (MS); biology (MA); businessclinical nutrition (MS); community nutrition (MS); computer science (MS); dietetic internship (MS); health education and promotion (MA); health N–12 teacher (MS Ed); mathematics (MA); natural and social sciences (MA, MS, MS Ed, PhD); nursing of older adults (MS); nutrition (MS); parent-child nursing (MS); pediatric nurse practitioner (MS); plant sciences (PhD); recreation (MA, MS Ed); recreation education (MA, MS Ed).

LE MOYNE COLLEGE, Syracuse, NY 13214

General Information Independent-religious, coed, comprehensive institution. *Graduate housing:* On-campus housing not available. *Research affiliation:* Blue Highway, Inc. (medical technology).

GRADUATE UNITS

Department of Education ***Degree program information:*** Part-time and evening/weekend programs available. Part-time, evening/weekend. Offers adolescent education (MS Ed, MST); adolescent education/special education (MS Ed, MST); adolescent English (MST); adolescent English/special education (MST); adolescent foreign language (MST); adolescent history (MST); childhood education (MS Ed); childhood education/special education (MS Ed); elementary education (MS Ed); general education (MS Ed); inclusive childhood education (MST); literacy education (MS Ed); school building leader (MS Ed); school building leadership (CAS); school district business leader (MS Ed, CAS); school district leader (MS Ed); school district leadership (CAS); secondary education (MS Ed); special education (MS Ed); teaching English to speakers of other languages (MS Ed); urban studies (MS Ed).

Department of Nursing ***Degree program information:*** Part-time and evening/weekend programs available. Part-time, evening/weekend. Offers informatics (MS, CAS); nursing administration (MS, CAS); nursing education (MS, CAS); nursing gerontology (MS, CAS); palliative care (MS, CAS).

Department of Occupational Therapy Offers occupational therapy (MS).

Department of Physician Assistant Studies Offers physician assistant studies (MS). Electronic applications accepted.

Madden School of Business ***Degree program information:*** Part-time and evening/weekend programs available. Part-time, evening/weekend. Offers business (MBA, MS).

Program in Arts Administration Offers arts administration (MS, Graduate Certificate).

LENOIR-RHYNE UNIVERSITY, Hickory, NC 28601

General Information Independent-religious, coed, comprehensive institution. *Enrollment:* 2,303 graduate, professional, and undergraduate students; 348 full-time matriculated graduate/professional students (247 women), 355 part-time matriculated graduate/professional students (255 women). *Enrollment by degree level:* 703 master's. *Graduate faculty:* 56 full-time (33 women), 29 part-time/adjunct (17 women). *Tuition, area resident:* Full-time $4950; part-time $550 per credit hour. Tuition and fees vary according to program. *Graduate housing:* Room and/or apartments available on a first-come, first-served basis to single students; on-campus housing not available to married students. Housing application deadline: 5/1. *Student services:* Campus employment opportunities, campus safety program, career counseling, exercise/wellness program, free psychological counseling, international student services, multicultural affairs office, services for students with disabilities, teacher training, writing training. *Library:* Carl Rudisill Library. *Collection:* Books: 140,480 (physical), 427,580 (digital/electronic); Serial titles: 60 (physical), 28,308 (digital/electronic); Databases: 134. Weekly public service hours: 89.

Computer facilities: Computer purchase and lease plans are available. 150 computers available on campus for general student use. A campuswide network can be accessed from student residence rooms and from off campus. Online class registration is available.
Website: http://www.lr.edu/

General Application Contact: Mary Ann Gosnell, Director of Graduate Recruiting, 828-328-7111, Fax: 828-328-7378, E-mail: admission@lr.edu.

GRADUATE UNITS

Graduate Programs Students: 348 full-time (247 women), 355 part-time (255 women); includes 108 minority (63 Black or African American, non-Hispanic/Latino; 1 American Indian or Alaska Native, non-Hispanic/Latino; 5 Asian, non-Hispanic/Latino; 30 Hispanic/Latino; 9 Two or more races, non-Hispanic/Latino), 14 international. Average age 33. *Faculty:* 56 full-time (33 women), 29 part-time/adjunct (17 women). *Financial support:* In 2015–16, 34 research assistantships were awarded; scholarships/grants and unspecified assistantships also available. Financial award application deadline: 3/1; financial award applicants required to submit FAFSA. In 2015, 133 master's awarded. *Degree program information:* Part-time and evening/weekend programs available. Part-time, evening/weekend, online learning. *Application deadline:* Applications are processed on a rolling basis. *Application fee:* $35. Electronic applications accepted. *Application Contact:* Mary Ann Gosnell, Director of Graduate Recruiting, 828-328-7300, E-mail: admission@lr.edu. *Assistant Provost and Dean of Graduate Studies,* Dr. Amy Wood, 828-328-7728, Fax: 828-328-7368, E-mail: amy.wood@lr.edu.

Charles M. Snipes School of Business Students: 38 full-time (13 women), 47 part-time (19 women); includes 15 minority (6 Black or African American, non-Hispanic/Latino; 1 Asian, non-Hispanic/Latino; 8 Hispanic/Latino), 7 international. Average age 30. *Faculty:* 7 full-time (2 women). *Financial support:* Scholarships/grants available. Financial award application deadline: 3/1; financial award applicants required to submit FAFSA. In 2015, 18 master's awarded. *Degree program information:* Part-time and evening/weekend programs available. Part-time, evening/weekend, online learning. Offers accounting (MBA); business analytics and information technology (MBA); entrepreneurship (MBA); global business (MBA); healthcare administration (MBA); innovation and change management (MBA); leadership development (MBA). *Application deadline:* Applications are processed on a rolling basis. *Application fee:* $35. Electronic applications accepted. *Application Contact:* Mary Ann Gosnell, Director of Graduate Recruitment, 828-328-7111, Fax: 828-328-7378, E-mail: admission@lr.edu. *Dean,* Dr. Mary Lesser, 828-328-7078, Fax: 828-328-7368, E-mail: mary.lesser@lr.edu.

Lutheran Theological Southern Seminary Students: 49 full-time (21 women), 28 part-time (12 women); includes 15 minority (14 Black or African American, non-Hispanic/Latino; 1 Hispanic/Latino). Average age 37. *Faculty:* 9 full-time (4 women), 8 part-time/adjunct (2 women). *Financial support:* In 2015–16, 94 students received support. Career-related internships or fieldwork, institutionally sponsored loans, scholarships/grants, tuition waivers (partial), and on-campus employment available. Support available to part-time students. Financial award application deadline: 3/15; financial award applicants required to submit FAFSA. In 2015, 12 degrees awarded. *Degree program information:* Part-time programs available. Part-time. Offers theology (M Div, MACM, MAR, STM). *Application deadline:* For fall admission, 5/15 priority date for domestic students, 10/1 for international students; for spring admission, 12/1 priority date for domestic students. Applications are processed on a rolling basis. *Application fee:* $35. *Application Contact:* Jenny Tomalka, Director of Admissions, 800-804-5233, E-mail: jtomalka@ltss.edu. *Provost, School of Theology,* Rev. Dr. Clay Schmit, 803-786-5150, E-mail: clay.schmit@lr.edu.

School of Arts and Letters Students: 1 (woman) full-time, 19 part-time (13 women); includes 3 minority (1 Black or African American, non-Hispanic/Latino; 1 Hispanic/Latino; 1 Two or more races, non-Hispanic/Latino). Average age 40. *Faculty:* 1 (woman) full-time. In 2015, 1 master's awarded. Offers arts and letters (MA); writing (MA). *Application fee:* $35. Electronic applications accepted. *Application Contact:* Mary Ann Gosnell, Director of Graduate Recruitment, 828-328-7300, E-mail: admission@lr.edu. *Assistant Provost and Dean of Graduate Studies,* Dr. Amy Wood, 828-328-7728, Fax: 828-328-7368, E-mail: amy.wood@lr.edu.

School of Counseling and Human Services Students: 62 full-time (48 women), 82 part-time (64 women); includes 24 minority (14 Black or African American, non-Hispanic/Latino; 2 Asian, non-Hispanic/Latino; 6 Hispanic/Latino; 2 Two or more races, non-Hispanic/Latino). Average age 33. *Faculty:* 8 full-time (5 women), 8 part-time/adjunct (5 women). *Financial support:* Application deadline: 3/1; applicants required to submit FAFSA. In 2015, 17 degrees awarded. *Degree program information:* Part-time and evening/weekend programs available. Part-time, evening/weekend. Offers clinical mental health counseling (MA); counseling and human services (MA); school counseling (MA). *Application deadline:* Applications are processed on a rolling basis. *Application fee:* $35. Electronic applications accepted. *Application Contact:* Mary Ann Gosnell, Director of Graduate Recruiting, 828-328-7111, Fax: 828-328-7378, E-mail: admission@lr.edu. *Chair, School of Counseling,* Dr. Neal Gray, 828-328-7918, E-mail: neal.gray@lr.edu.

School of Education Students: 30 full-time (17 women), 45 part-time (32 women); includes 11 minority (3 Black or African American, non-Hispanic/Latino; 1 American Indian or Alaska Native, non-Hispanic/Latino; 5 Hispanic/Latino; 2 Two or more races, non-Hispanic/Latino). Average age 36. *Faculty:* 7 full-time (5 women), 5 part-time/adjunct (2 women). *Financial support:* Application deadline: 3/1; applicants required to submit FAFSA. In 2015, 11 master's awarded. *Degree program information:* Part-time and evening/weekend programs available. Part-time, evening/weekend, online learning. Offers community and nonprofit leadership (MA); community college administration (MA); education (MA, MAT, MS); general management (MA); higher education leadership (MA); management (MA); online teaching and instructional design (MS); second language community services (MA); secondary education (MAT); substance abuse (MA); vocational strategies (MA). *Application deadline:* Applications are processed on a rolling basis. *Application fee:* $35. Electronic applications accepted. *Application Contact:* Mary Ann Gosnell, Director of Graduate Recruiting, 828-328-7111, E-mail: admission@lr.edu. *Chair, School of Education,* Dr. David Temple, 828-328-7451, E-mail: david.temple@lr.edu.

School of Health, Exercise and Sport Science Students: 28 full-time (18 women), 32 part-time (26 women); includes 15 minority (10 Black or African American, non-

Hispanic/Latino; 2 Asian, non-Hispanic/Latino; 2 Hispanic/Latino; 1 Two or more races, non-Hispanic/Latino), 6 international. Average age 27. *Faculty:* 10 full-time (6 women), 2 part-time/adjunct (1 woman). *Financial support:* Research assistantships available. Financial award applicants required to submit FAFSA. In 2015, 20 master's awarded. *Degree program information:* Part-time programs available. Part-time. Offers athletic training (MS); public health (MPH). *Application fee:* $35. *Application Contact:* Mary Ann Gosnell, Director, Graduate Recruiting, 828-328-7111, E-mail: admission@lr.edu. *Chair, School of Health, Exercise and Sport Science*, Stephanie Stadden, 828-328-7297, E-mail: stephanie.stadden@lr.edu.

School of Natural Sciences Students: 4 full-time (2 women), 7 part-time (3 women). Average age 35. *Faculty:* 1 full-time (0 women). *Degree program information:* Part-time and evening/weekend programs available. Part-time, evening/weekend, online learning. Offers natural sciences (MS); sustainability studies (MS). *Application fee:* $35. Electronic applications accepted. *Application Contact:* Mary Ann Gosnell, Director of Graduate Recruiting, 828-328-7300, E-mail: admission@lr.edu. *Assistant Provost and Dean of Graduate Studies*, Dr. Amy Wood, 828-328-7728, Fax: 828-328-7368, E-mail: amy.wood@lr.edu.

School of Nursing Students: 4 full-time (all women), 46 part-time (45 women); includes 4 minority (2 Black or African American, non-Hispanic/Latino; 2 Hispanic/Latino). Average age 39. *Faculty:* 7 full-time (all women). Online only. Offers nursing (MSN); nursing administration (MSN); nursing education (MSN). *Application fee:* $35. Electronic applications accepted. *Application Contact:* Mary Ann Gosnell, Director of Graduate Recruiting, 828-328-7300, E-mail: admission@lr.edu. *Chair, School of Nursing*, Dr. Kerry Thompson, 828-328-7282, Fax: 828-328-7368, E-mail: thompsonk@lr.edu.

School of Occupational Therapy Students: 61 full-time (59 women), 1 (woman) part-time; includes 4 minority (2 Hispanic/Latino; 2 Two or more races, non-Hispanic/Latino). Average age 25. *Faculty:* 4 full-time (all women). *Financial support:* Research assistantships available. Financial award applicants required to submit FAFSA. In 2015, 19 master's awarded. Offers occupational therapy (MS). *Application deadline:* For summer admission, 1/31 for domestic students. *Application fee:* $35. *Application Contact:* Mary Ann Gosnell, Director of Graduate Recruiting, 828-328-3711, E-mail: maryann.gosnell@lr.edu. *Coordinator*, Dr. Toni Oakes, 828-328-7366, E-mail: oakes@lrc.edu.

School of Physician Assistant Studies Faculty: 4 full-time (1 woman). Offers physician assistant studies (MS). *Application Contact:* Mary Ann Gosnell, Director of Graduate Recruiting, 828-328-7111, E-mail: admission@lr.edu. *Chair, School of Physician Assistant Studies*, Richard Ball, 828-328-7764, E-mail: richard.ball@lr.edu.

LESLEY UNIVERSITY, Cambridge, MA 02138-2790

General Information Independent, coed, primarily women, comprehensive institution. *Graduate housing:* Room and/or apartments available to single students; on-campus housing not available to married students. *Research affiliation:* TERC (education research and development).

GRADUATE UNITS

College of Art and Design ***Degree program information:*** Part-time programs available. Part-time. Offers photography (MFA); visual arts (MFA). Electronic applications accepted.

Graduate School of Arts and Social Sciences ***Degree program information:*** Part-time programs available. Part-time, online learning. Offers clinical mental health counseling (MA); counseling psychology (MA, CAGS); creative writing (MFA); expressive therapies (MA, PhD, CAGS); independent studies (CAGS); independent study (MA); intercultural relations (MA, CAGS); interdisciplinary studies (MA); urban environmental leadership (MA). Electronic applications accepted.

Graduate School of Education ***Degree program information:*** Part-time and evening/weekend programs available. Part-time, evening/weekend, online learning. Offers arts, community, and education (M Ed); autism studies (Certificate); curriculum and instruction (M Ed, CAGS); early childhood education (M Ed); ecological teaching and learning (MS); educational studies (PhD); elementary education (M Ed); emergent technologies for educators (Certificate); ESLArts: language learning through the arts (M Ed); high school education (M Ed); individually designed (M Ed); integrated teaching through the arts (M Ed); literacy for K-8 classroom teachers (M Ed); mathematics education (M Ed); middle school education (M Ed); moderate disabilities (M Ed); online learning (Certificate); reading (CAGS); science in education (M Ed); severe disabilities (M Ed); special needs (CAGS); specialist teacher of reading (M Ed); teacher of visual art (M Ed); technology in education (M Ed, CAGS). Electronic applications accepted.

LES ROCHES INTERNATIONAL SCHOOL OF HOTEL MANAGEMENT, CH-3975 Bluche, Switzerland

General Information Private, coed, comprehensive institution.

GRADUATE UNITS

Program in Hospitality Management Offers hospitality management (MBA). Available only at Switzerland campus.

LETOURNEAU UNIVERSITY, Longview, TX 75607-7001

General Information Independent-religious, coed, comprehensive institution. *Enrollment:* 2,796 graduate, professional, and undergraduate students; 82 full-time matriculated graduate/professional students (48 women), 428 part-time matriculated graduate/professional students (331 women). *Enrollment by degree level:* 510 master's. *Graduate faculty:* 24 full-time (7 women), 40 part-time/adjunct (15 women). *Graduate housing:* Rooms and/or apartments available on a first-come, first-served basis to single and married students. *Student services:* Campus employment opportunities, campus safety program, career counseling, exercise/wellness program, free psychological counseling, international student services, low-cost health insurance, multicultural affairs office, services for students with disabilities, writing training. *Library:* Margaret Estes Library plus 1 other.

Computer facilities: Computer purchase and lease plans are available. A campuswide network can be accessed from student residence rooms and from off campus. Online class registration is available.
Website: http://www.letu.edu/

General Application Contact: Chris Fontaine, Assistant Vice President, Enrollment Services and Global Admissions, 903-233-4312, E-mail: chrisfontaine@letu.edu.

GRADUATE UNITS

Graduate Programs Students: 82 full-time (48 women), 428 part-time (331 women); includes 234 minority (138 Black or African American, non-Hispanic/Latino; 5 American Indian or Alaska Native, non-Hispanic/Latino; 5 Asian, non-Hispanic/Latino; 50 Hispanic/Latino; 36 Two or more races, non-Hispanic/Latino), 15 international. Average age 37. 257 applicants, 60% accepted, 141 enrolled. *Faculty:* 24 full-time (7 women), 40 part-time/adjunct (15 women). *Financial support:* Research assistantships, institutionally sponsored loans, and unspecified assistantships available. Financial award applicants required to submit FAFSA. In 2015, 136 master's awarded. *Degree program information:* Part-time programs available. Part-time, 100% online, blended/hybrid learning. Offers business administration (MBA); counseling (MA); curriculum and instruction (M Ed); education administration (M Ed); engineering (ME, MS); engineering management (MEM); health care administration (MS); marriage and family therapy (MA); psychology (MA); strategic leadership (MSL); teacher leadership (M Ed); teaching and learning (M Ed). *Application deadline:* For fall admission, 8/22 for domestic students, 8/29 for international students; for winter admission, 10/10 for domestic students; for spring admission, 1/2 for domestic students, 1/10 for international students; for summer admission, 5/1 for domestic and international students. Applications are processed on a rolling basis. Electronic applications accepted. *Application Contact:* Chris Fontaine, Assistant Vice President for Global Campus Admissions, 903-233-4312, E-mail: chrisfontaine@letu.edu.

LEWIS & CLARK COLLEGE, Portland, OR 97219-7899

General Information Independent, coed, comprehensive institution. *Graduate housing:* On-campus housing not available.

GRADUATE UNITS

Graduate School of Education and Counseling ***Degree program information:*** Part-time and evening/weekend programs available. Part-time, evening/weekend. Offers curriculum and instruction (M Ed); early childhood/elementary education (MAT); education and counseling (M Ed, MA, MAT, MS, Ed D, Ed S); educational leadership (Ed D, Ed S); educational studies (M Ed); marriage, couple and family therapy (MA, MS); middle level/high school education (MAT); professional mental health counseling (MA, MS); professional mental health counseling–addictions (MA, MS); psychological and cultural studies (MA, MS); school counseling (M Ed); school psychology (Ed S); special education (M Ed). Electronic applications accepted.

Lewis & Clark Law School ***Degree program information:*** Part-time and evening/weekend programs available. Part-time, evening/weekend. Offers environmental and natural resources law (LL M); law (JD). Electronic applications accepted.

LEWIS UNIVERSITY, Romeoville, IL 60446

General Information Independent-religious, coed, comprehensive institution. CGS member. *Graduate housing:* Room and/or apartments available on a first-come, first-served basis to single students; on-campus housing not available to married students. Housing application deadline: 7/1.

GRADUATE UNITS

College of Arts and Sciences ***Degree program information:*** Part-time and evening/weekend programs available. Part-time, evening/weekend, online learning. Offers administration (MS); arts and sciences (MA, MS); child and adolescent counseling (MA); coaching (MA); criminal/social justice (MS); higher education/student services (MA); management (MS); mental health counseling (MA); non-for-profit management (MA); organizational management (MA); public safety administration (MS); safety and security (MS); school counseling (MA); technical (MS); training and development (MA). Electronic applications accepted.

College of Business ***Degree program information:*** Part-time and evening/weekend programs available. Part-time, evening/weekend, online learning. Offers business (MBA, MS). Electronic applications accepted.

Graduate School of Management Degree program information: Part-time and evening/weekend programs available. Part-time, evening/weekend, online learning. Offers accounting (MBA); business administration (MBA); business analytics (MS); custom elective option (MBA); e-business (MBA); finance (MS); financial analytics (MS); healthcare analytics (MS); healthcare management (MBA); human resources management (MBA); international business (MBA); management information systems (MBA); marketing (MBA); marketing analytics (MS); operations analytics (MS); project management (MBA, MS); technology and operations management (MBA).

College of Education ***Degree program information:*** Part-time and evening/weekend programs available. Part-time, evening/weekend. Offers advanced study in education (CAS); biology (MA); chemistry (MA); curriculum and instruction: instructional technology (M Ed); early childhood education (MA); educational leadership (M Ed, MA); educational leadership for teaching and learning (Ed D); elementary education (MA); English (MA); English as a second language (M Ed); history (MA); instructional technology (M Ed); math (MA); physics (MA); psychology and social science (MA); reading and literacy (M Ed, MA); secondary education (MA); special education (MA). Electronic applications accepted.

College of Nursing and Health Professions ***Degree program information:*** Part-time and evening/weekend programs available. Part-time, evening/weekend, online learning. Offers adult nurse practitioner (MSN); nursing administration (MSN); nursing and health professions (MSN, DNP); nursing education (MSN). Electronic applications accepted.

LEXINGTON THEOLOGICAL SEMINARY, Lexington, KY 40508-3218

General Information Independent-religious, coed, graduate-only institution. *Graduate housing:* Rooms and/or apartments available on a first-come, first-served basis to single and married students. Housing application deadline: 6/15.

GRADUATE UNITS

Graduate and Professional Programs ***Degree program information:*** Part-time and evening/weekend programs available. Part-time, evening/weekend. Offers theology (M Div, MA, MAPS, D Min). M Div/MSW offered jointly with University of Kentucky.

LIBERTY UNIVERSITY, Lynchburg, VA 24515

General Information Independent-religious, coed, comprehensive institution. *Enrollment:* 10,220 full-time matriculated graduate/professional students (6,068 women), 20,061 part-time matriculated graduate/professional students (12,131 women). *Enrollment by degree level:* 26,743 master's, 2,050 doctoral, 1,488 other advanced degrees. *Graduate housing:* Room and/or apartments guaranteed to single students; on-campus housing not available to married students. *Student services:* Campus employment opportunities, career counseling, exercise/wellness program, free psychological counseling, international student services, multicultural affairs office, services for students with disabilities, writing training. *Library:* Jerry Falwell Library plus 1 other.

Computer facilities: 820 computers available on campus for general student use. A campuswide network can be accessed from student residence rooms and from off campus. Online class registration is available.
Website: http://www.liberty.edu/

General Application Contact: Jay Bridge, Director of Admissions, 800-424-9595, Fax: 800-628-7977, E-mail: gradadmissions@liberty.edu.

GRADUATE UNITS

College of Arts and Sciences Students: 48 full-time (20 women), 21 part-time (8 women); includes 4 minority (1 Black or African American, non-Hispanic/Latino; 2 Hispanic/Latino; 1 Two or more races, non-Hispanic/Latino), 3 international. Average age 26. 72 applicants, 44% accepted, 22 enrolled. *Financial support:* Teaching assistantships with tuition reimbursements and Federal Work-Study available. In 2015, 25 master's awarded. *Degree program information:* Part-time programs available. Part-time, online learning. Offers English (MA); history (MA); philosophical studies (MA). *Application deadline:* For fall admission, 6/1 for domestic students; for spring admission, 11/1 for domestic students. Applications are processed on a rolling basis. *Application fee:* $50. Electronic applications accepted. *Application Contact:* Dr. Terry Elam, Director of Graduate Admissions, 434-592-3966, Fax: 434-522-0430, E-mail: gradadmissions@liberty.edu. *Dean*, Dr. Roger Schultz, 434-592-4031, Fax: 434-522-0430, E-mail: rschultz@liberty.edu.

College of Osteopathic Medicine Students: 317 full-time (153 women); includes 19 minority (3 Black or African American, non-Hispanic/Latino; 9 Asian, non-Hispanic/Latino; 2 Hispanic/Latino; 5 Two or more races, non-Hispanic/Latino), 16 international. Average age 26. 3,959 applicants, 4% accepted, 161 enrolled. Offers osteopathic medicine (DO). *Application deadline:* Applications are processed on a rolling basis. Electronic applications accepted. *Application Contact:* Jay Bridge, Director of Admissions, 800-424-9595, Fax: 800-628-7977, E-mail: gradadmissions@liberty.edu. *Dean*, Dr. Ronnie B. Martin, 434-592-6400.

Helms School of Government Students: 257 full-time (126 women), 615 part-time (251 women); includes 202 minority (151 Black or African American, non-Hispanic/Latino; 4 American Indian or Alaska Native, non-Hispanic/Latino; 7 Asian, non-Hispanic/Latino; 8 Hispanic/Latino; 3 Native Hawaiian or other Pacific Islander, non-Hispanic/Latino; 29 Two or more races, non-Hispanic/Latino), 9 international. Average age 35. 784 applicants, 53% accepted, 203 enrolled. In 2015, 65 master's awarded. *Degree program information:* Part-time programs available. Part-time, online learning. Offers criminal justice (MS); public policy (MA). *Application deadline:* Applications are processed on a rolling basis. *Application fee:* $50. Electronic applications accepted. *Application Contact:* Jay Bridge, Director of Admissions, 800-424-9595, Fax: 800-628-7977, E-mail: gradadmissions@liberty.edu. *Dean*, Shawn D. Akers, 434-592-4986.

School of Behavioral Sciences Students: 2,717 full-time (2,135 women), 5,745 part-time (4,465 women); includes 2,407 minority (2,049 Black or African American, non-Hispanic/Latino; 33 American Indian or Alaska Native, non-Hispanic/Latino; 53 Asian, non-Hispanic/Latino; 77 Hispanic/Latino; 8 Native Hawaiian or other Pacific Islander, non-Hispanic/Latino; 187 Two or more races, non-Hispanic/Latino), 170 international. Average age 39. 6,318 applicants, 47% accepted, 1620 enrolled. *Financial support:* Applicants required to submit FAFSA. In 2015, 2,601 master's, 11 doctorates, 2 other advanced degrees awarded. *Degree program information:* Part-time programs available. Part-time, online learning. Offers advanced clinical skills (PhD); clinical mental health counseling (MA); counselor education and supervision (PhD); human services counseling (MA); marriage and family therapy (MA); military resilience (Certificate); professional counseling (MA). *Application deadline:* Applications are processed on a rolling basis. *Application fee:* $50. Electronic applications accepted. *Application Contact:* Jay Bridge, Director of Admissions, 800-424-9595, Fax: 800-628-7977, E-mail: gradadmissions@liberty.edu. *Founding Dean, School of Behavioral Sciences*, Dr. Ronald Hawkins.

School of Business Students: 1,488 full-time (825 women), 4,187 part-time (1,957 women); includes 1,252 minority (987 Black or African American, non-Hispanic/Latino; 24 American Indian or Alaska Native, non-Hispanic/Latino; 72 Asian, non-Hispanic/Latino; 53 Hispanic/Latino; 5 Native Hawaiian or other Pacific Islander, non-Hispanic/Latino; 111 Two or more races, non-Hispanic/Latino), 136 international. Average age 35. 5,375 applicants, 44% accepted, 1245 enrolled. In 2015, 1,474 master's, 63 other advanced degrees awarded. *Degree program information:* Part-time programs available. Part-time, online learning. Offers accounting (MBA, MS, DBA); business administration (MBA); criminal justice (MBA); cyber security (MS); executive leadership (MA); healthcare (MBA); human resources (DBA); information systems (MS); international business (MBA, DBA); leadership (MBA, DBA); marketing (MBA, MS, DBA); project management (MBA, DBA); public administration (MBA); public relations (MBA). *Application deadline:* Applications are processed on a rolling basis. *Application fee:* $50. Electronic applications accepted. *Application Contact:* Jay Bridge, Director of Graduate Admissions, 800-424-9595, Fax: 800-628-7977, E-mail: gradadmissions@liberty.edu. *Dean*, Dr. Scott Hicks, 434-592-4808, Fax: 434-582-2366, E-mail: smhicks@liberty.edu.

School of Communication and Creative Arts Students: 110 full-time (70 women), 115 part-time (72 women); includes 45 minority (36 Black or African American, non-Hispanic/Latino; 1 Asian, non-Hispanic/Latino; 2 Hispanic/Latino; 6 Two or more races, non-Hispanic/Latino), 15 international. Average age 30. 44 applicants, 241% accepted, 70 enrolled. *Financial support:* Federal Work-Study and unspecified assistantships available. Financial award applicants required to submit FAFSA. In 2015, 15 master's awarded. *Degree program information:* Part-time programs available. Part-time. Offers strategic communication (MA); studio and digital arts (MFA). *Application deadline:* For fall admission, 6/1 for domestic students; for spring admission, 11/1 for domestic students. Applications are processed on a rolling basis. *Application fee:* $50. Electronic applications accepted. *Application Contact:* Dr. Terry Elam, Director of Graduate Admissions, 434-582-2111, Fax: 434-582-7836, E-mail: gradadmissions@liberty.edu. *Dean*, Dr. Norman Mintle, 434-582-2077, E-mail: cvkramer@liberty.edu.

School of Divinity Students: 2,433 full-time (713 women), 3,418 part-time (949 women); includes 1,363 minority (1,093 Black or African American, non-Hispanic/Latino; 18 American Indian or Alaska Native, non-Hispanic/Latino; 64 Asian, non-Hispanic/Latino; 90 Hispanic/Latino; 4 Native Hawaiian or other Pacific Islander, non-Hispanic/Latino; 94 Two or more races, non-Hispanic/Latino), 303 international. Average age 41. 4,301 applicants, 38% accepted, 1026 enrolled. *Financial support:* Teaching assistantships with tuition reimbursements, career-related internships or fieldwork, and Federal Work-Study available. Financial award applicants required to submit FAFSA. In 2015, 1,779 master's, 126 doctorates, 75 other advanced degrees awarded. *Degree program information:* Part-time programs available. Part-time, online learning. Offers Biblical studies (M Div, MAR, MTS, Th M); church history (M Div, MAR, MTS, Th M); discipleship (D Min); discipleship and church ministry (M Div, MAR, MCM); evangelism and church planting (M Div, MAR, MCM, D Min); global studies (M Div, MAR, MCM, MGS, Th M); homiletics (M Div, MAR, MCM, Th M, D Min); leadership (M Div, MAR, MCM, D Min); marketplace chaplaincy (M Div, MAR, MCM); ministry (D Min); pastoral counseling (M Div, MA, MAR, MCM, D Min); pastoral ministries (M Div, MAR, MCM); religious education (MRE); theology (M Div, MAR, MTS, Th M); theology and apologetics (PhD); worship (M Div, MAR, MCM, D Min). *Application deadline:* For fall admission, 6/1 for domestic students; for spring admission, 11/1 for domestic students. Applications are processed on a rolling basis. *Application fee:* $50. Electronic applications accepted. *Application Contact:* Jay Bridge, Director of Graduate Admissions, 800-424-9595, Fax: 800-628-7977, E-mail: gradadmissions@liberty.edu. *Acting Dean*, Dr. Ed Hindson, 434-592-4140, Fax: 434-522-0415, E-mail: ehindson@liberty.edu.

School of Education Students: 2,020 full-time (1,469 women), 4,544 part-time (3,384 women); includes 1,451 minority (1,182 Black or African American, non-Hispanic/Latino; 33 American Indian or Alaska Native, non-Hispanic/Latino; 44 Asian, non-Hispanic/Latino; 46 Hispanic/Latino; 11 Native Hawaiian or other Pacific Islander, non-Hispanic/Latino; 135 Two or more races, non-Hispanic/Latino), 87 international. Average age 37. 5,314 applicants, 44% accepted, 1241 enrolled. *Financial support:* Federal Work-Study and tuition waivers (partial) available. In 2015, 1,199 master's, 118 doctorates, 539 other advanced degrees awarded. *Degree program information:* Part-time programs available. Part-time, online learning. Offers administration and supervision (M Ed); curriculum and instruction (Ed D, Ed S); early childhood education (M Ed); educational leadership (Ed D, Ed S); educational technology and online instruction (M Ed); elementary education (M Ed, MAT); English (M Ed); gifted education (M Ed, Certificate); history (M Ed); leadership (M Ed); math specialist (M Ed); middle grades (M Ed, MAT, Certificate); outdoor adventure sport (MS); preschool (Certificate); reading specialist (M Ed); school counseling (M Ed); school leadership (Certificate); secondary education (MAT); special education (M Ed, MAT); sport administration (MS); sport management (MS, Certificate); student service (M Ed); teaching and learning (M Ed); tourism (MS). *Application deadline:* For fall admission, 6/1 for domestic students; for spring admission, 11/1 for domestic students. Applications are processed on a rolling basis. *Application fee:* $50. Electronic applications accepted. *Application Contact:* Jay Bridge, Director of Graduate Admissions, 800-424-9595, Fax: 800-628-7977, E-mail: gradadmissions@liberty.edu. *Dean*, Dr. Karen L. Parker, 434-582-2195, Fax: 434-582-2468, E-mail: kparker@liberty.edu.

School of Engineering and Computational Sciences Students: 45 full-time (9 women), 112 part-time (22 women); includes 46 minority (40 Black or African American, non-Hispanic/Latino; 3 Asian, non-Hispanic/Latino; 1 Hispanic/Latino; 2 Two or more races, non-Hispanic/Latino), 2 international. Average age 36. 206 applicants, 30% accepted, 35 enrolled. *Degree program information:* Part-time programs available. Part-time, online learning. Offers cyber security (MS). *Application deadline:* Applications are processed on a rolling basis. *Application fee:* $50. Electronic applications accepted. *Application Contact:* Jay Bridge, Director of Admissions, 800-424-9595, Fax: 800-628-7977, E-mail: gradadmissions@liberty.edu. *Dean*, David Donahoo, 434-592-7150.

School of Health Sciences Students: 435 full-time (342 women), 609 part-time (489 women); includes 301 minority (238 Black or African American, non-Hispanic/Latino; 6 American Indian or Alaska Native, non-Hispanic/Latino; 25 Asian, non-Hispanic/Latino; 12 Hispanic/Latino; 1 Native Hawaiian or other Pacific Islander, non-Hispanic/Latino; 19 Two or more races, non-Hispanic/Latino), 71 international. Average age 33. 1,433 applicants, 43% accepted, 295 enrolled. In 2015, 50 master's, 8 other advanced degrees awarded. *Degree program information:* Part-time programs available. Part-time, online learning. Offers biomedical sciences (MS); global health (MPH); health promotion (MPH); healthcare management (Certificate); nutrition (MPH). *Application fee:* $50. *Application Contact:* Jay Bridge, Director of Admissions, 800-424-9595, Fax: 800-628-7977, E-mail: gradadmissions@liberty.edu. *Dean*, Dr. Ralph Linstra.

School of Law Students: 173 full-time (71 women); includes 22 minority (7 Black or African American, non-Hispanic/Latino; 1 American Indian or Alaska Native, non-Hispanic/Latino; 4 Asian, non-Hispanic/Latino; 7 Hispanic/Latino; 3 Two or more races, non-Hispanic/Latino), 8 international. Average age 26. 172 applicants, 20% accepted, 30 enrolled. In 2015, 77 doctorates awarded. Offers law (JD). *Application deadline:* For fall admission, 6/1 for domestic students. *Application Contact:* Joleen Thaxton, Assistant Director of Admissions, 434-592-5300, Fax: 434-592-5400, E-mail: lawadmissions@liberty.edu. *Interim Dean*, Rena M. Lindevaldsen, 434-592-5300, Fax: 434-592-5400, E-mail: law@liberty.edu.

School of Music Students: 69 full-time (35 women), 187 part-time (80 women); includes 46 minority (35 Black or African American, non-Hispanic/Latino; 2 Asian, non-Hispanic/Latino; 1 Hispanic/Latino; 8 Two or more races, non-Hispanic/Latino), 17 international. Average age 37. 323 applicants, 26% accepted, 52 enrolled. In 2015, 41 master's awarded. *Degree program information:* Part-time programs available. Part-time, online learning. Offers ethnomusicology (MA); music and worship (MA); music education (MA); worship studies (MA, DWS). *Application deadline:* Applications are processed on a rolling basis. *Application fee:* $50. Electronic applications accepted. *Application Contact:* Jay Bridge, Director of Admissions, 800-424-9595, Fax: 800-628-7977, E-mail: gradadmissions@liberty.edu. *Dean*, Dr. Vernon Whaley, 434-592-3463, E-mail: vwhaley@liberty.edu.

School of Nursing Students: 108 full-time (100 women), 508 part-time (454 women); includes 106 minority (84 Black or African American, non-Hispanic/Latino; 3 American Indian or Alaska Native, non-Hispanic/Latino; 8 Asian, non-Hispanic/Latino; 1 Hispanic/Latino; 10 Two or more races, non-Hispanic/Latino), 7 international. Average age 39. 577 applicants, 30% accepted, 119 enrolled. In 2015, 161 master's awarded. *Degree program information:* Part-time programs available. Part-time, online learning. Offers family nurse practitioner (DNP); nurse educator (MSN); nursing administration (MSN). *Application deadline:* Applications are processed on a rolling basis. *Application fee:* $50. Electronic applications accepted. *Application Contact:* Jay Bridge, Director of Admissions, 800-424-9595, Fax: 800-628-7977, E-mail: gradadmissions@liberty.edu. *Dean*, Dr. Deanna Britt, 434-582-2519, E-mail: dbritt@liberty.edu.

LIFE CHIROPRACTIC COLLEGE WEST, Hayward, CA 94545

General Information Independent, coed, graduate-only institution. *Graduate housing:* On-campus housing not available. *Research affiliation:* National Center for Complimentary Medicine, National Center for Complementary and Alternative Medicine/University Cancer Research Fund, Advanced Orthogonality, San Jose State University, University of Calgary, Bay Area Research Roundtable (BAER).

GRADUATE UNITS

Professional Program Offers chiropractic (DC). Electronic applications accepted.

LIFE UNIVERSITY, Marietta, GA 30060-2903

General Information Independent, coed, comprehensive institution. *Enrollment:* 2,708 graduate, professional, and undergraduate students; 1,786 full-time matriculated graduate/professional students (848 women), 204 part-time matriculated graduate/professional students (117 women). *Enrollment by degree level:* 207 master's, 1,783 doctoral. *Graduate faculty:* 92 full-time (36 women), 31 part-time/adjunct (12 women). *Tuition, area resident:* Part-time $329 per quarter hour. *Graduate housing:* Rooms and/or apartments available on a first-come, first-served basis to single and married students. Typical cost: $12,450 (including board) for single students; $12,450 (including board) for married students. Room and board charges vary according to campus/location and housing facility selected. *Student services:* Campus employment opportunities, campus safety program, career counseling, exercise/wellness program, free psychological counseling, international student services, services for students with disabilities. *Library:* Library & Learning Services.

Computer facilities: A campuswide network can be accessed from student residence rooms and from off campus. Online class registration is available.
Website: http://www.life.edu/

General Application Contact: Robyn Stanley, Director of Enrollment Services, 800-543-3202, Fax: 770-426-2741, E-mail: robyn.stanley@life.edu.

GRADUATE UNITS

College of Chiropractic Students: 1,686 full-time (788 women), 97 part-time (49 women); includes 494 minority (196 Black or African American, non-Hispanic/Latino; 10 American Indian or Alaska Native, non-Hispanic/Latino; 45 Asian, non-Hispanic/Latino; 243 Hispanic/Latino), 64 international. Average age 28. *Faculty:* 103 full-time (47 women), 33 part-time/adjunct (13 women). *Financial support:* Research assistantships, Federal Work-Study, institutionally sponsored loans, scholarships/grants, and tuition waivers (partial) available. Support available to part-time students. Financial award application deadline: 9/1; financial award applicants required to submit FAFSA. In 2015, 346 doctorates awarded. *Degree program information:* Part-time programs available. Part-time. Offers chiropractic (DC). *Application deadline:* Applications are processed on a rolling basis. *Application fee:* $50. Electronic applications accepted. *Application Contact:* Jana Holwick, Director of Enrollment, 770-426-2889, Fax: 770-426-2895, E-mail: jana.holwick@life.edu. *Dean*, Dr. Leslie King, 770-426-2713, E-mail: lesliek@life.edu.

Graduate Programs Students: 100 full-time (60 women), 107 part-time (68 women); includes 104 minority (88 Black or African American, non-Hispanic/Latino; 2 American Indian or Alaska Native, non-Hispanic/Latino; 6 Asian, non-Hispanic/Latino; 8 Hispanic/Latino), 8 international. Average age 30. *Faculty:* 6 full-time (1 woman), 7 part-time/adjunct (2 women). *Financial support:* Career-related internships or fieldwork, Federal Work-Study, and tuition waivers (full and partial) available. Support available to part-time students. Financial award application deadline: 9/1; financial award applicants required to submit FAFSA. *Degree program information:* Part-time programs available. Part-time, 100% online, blended/hybrid learning. Offers athletic training (MAT); chiropractic sport science (MS); clinical nutrition (MS); nutrition and sport science (MS); sport coaching (MS); sport injury management (MS); sports health science (MS). *Application deadline:* For fall admission, 4/1 priority date for domestic and international students; for winter admission, 12/1 priority date for domestic and international students; for spring admission, 3/1 priority date for domestic and international students. Applications are processed on a rolling basis. *Application fee:* $50. Electronic applications accepted. *Application Contact:* Robyn Stanley, Director of Enrollment, 770-426-2889, E-mail: robin.stanley@life.edu. *Dean of Graduate and Undergraduate Studies*, Dr. Jana Holwick, 678-331-4407, Fax: 770-426-2699, E-mail: jana.holwick@life.edu.

LIM COLLEGE, New York, NY 10022-5268

General Information Proprietary, coed, primarily women, comprehensive institution. *Graduate housing:* Room and/or apartments available on a first-come, first-served basis to single students; on-campus housing not available to married students.

GRADUATE UNITS

MBA Program Offers entrepreneurship (MBA); fashion management (MBA).

MPS Program Offers fashion marketing (MPS); fashion merchandising and retail management (MPS); visual merchandising (MPS).

LIMESTONE COLLEGE, Gaffney, SC 29340-3799

General Information Independent, coed, comprehensive institution. *Enrollment:* 1,280 graduate, professional, and undergraduate students; 4 full-time matriculated graduate/professional students (2 women), 73 part-time matriculated graduate/professional students (45 women). *Enrollment by degree level:* 62 master's. *Graduate faculty:* 10 full-time (2 women), 1 (woman) part-time/adjunct. *Tuition, area resident:* Part-time $1875 per course. *Graduate housing:* On-campus housing not available. *Student services:* Career counseling, free psychological counseling, services for students with disabilities. *Library:* A. J. Eastwood Library plus 1 other. *Collection:* Books: 77,342 (physical), 477,167 (digital/electronic); Serial titles: 107 (physical), 277,716 (digital/electronic); Databases: 150.

Computer facilities: 137 computers available on campus for general student use. A campuswide network can be accessed from student residence rooms and from off campus. Online class registration is available.
Website: http://www.limestone.edu/

General Application Contact: Adair Haynes, Administrative Assistant, MBA Program, 800-795-7151 Ext. 4370, Fax: 864-487-8706, E-mail: ahaynes@limestone.edu.

GRADUATE UNITS

MBA Program Students: 4 full-time (2 women), 73 part-time (45 women); includes 32 minority (31 Black or African American, non-Hispanic/Latino; 1 Hispanic/Latino), 2 international. Average age 40. 91 applicants, 68% accepted, 42 enrolled. *Faculty:* 10 full-time (2 women), 1 (woman) part-time/adjunct. *Financial support:* In 2015–16, 8 students received support. Application deadline: 6/15; applicants required to submit FAFSA. In 2015, 8 master's awarded. *Degree program information:* Part-time and evening/weekend programs available. Part-time, evening/weekend, online learning. Offers business administration (MBA). *Application deadline:* For fall admission, 8/1 priority date for domestic and international students; for winter admission, 12/12 priority date for domestic and international students; for spring admission, 4/1 priority date for domestic and international students. Applications are processed on a rolling basis. *Application fee:* $25. Electronic applications accepted. *Application Contact:* Adair Haynes, Administrative Assistant, MBA Program, 800-795-7151 Ext. 4370, Fax: 864-467-8706, E-mail: ahaynes@limestone.edu. *Director, MBA Program*, Brandon Gibson, 864-488-4371, Fax: 864-487-8706, E-mail: bgibson@limestone.edu.

LINCOLN CHRISTIAN SEMINARY, Lincoln, IL 62656-2167

General Information Independent-religious, coed, graduate-only institution. *Graduate housing:* Rooms and/or apartments available on a first-come, first-served basis to single and married students.

GRADUATE UNITS

Graduate and Professional Programs ***Degree program information:*** Part-time programs available. Part-time. Offers Bible and theology (MA); Christian ministries (MA); counseling (MA); divinity (M Div); leadership ministry (D Min); religious education (MRE). Electronic applications accepted.

LINCOLN CHRISTIAN UNIVERSITY, Lincoln, IL 62656-2167

General Information Independent-religious, coed, comprehensive institution. *Enrollment:* 886 graduate, professional, and undergraduate students; 84 full-time matriculated graduate/professional students (36 women), 266 part-time matriculated graduate/professional students (102 women). *Enrollment by degree level:* 328 master's, 21 doctoral, 1 other advanced degree. *Graduate faculty:* 25 full-time (6 women), 14 part-time/adjunct (5 women). *Graduate housing:* Rooms and/or apartments available on a first-come, first-served basis to single and married students. Typical cost: $4722 per year ($6296 including board) for single students; $4722 per year ($6296 including board) for married students. *Student services:* Campus employment opportunities, campus safety program, international student services, services for students with disabilities. *Library:* Jessie Eury Library. *Collection:* Books: 94,521 (physical), 52,784 (digital/electronic); Serial titles: 719 (physical), 15,583 (digital/electronic); Databases: 63. Weekly public service hours: 82.

Computer facilities: 51 computers available on campus for general student use. A campuswide network can be accessed from student residence rooms and from off campus. Online class registration is available.
Website: http://www.lincolnchristian.edu/

General Application Contact: Lindsey Clark, Associate Director of Graduate and Seminary Enrollment, 217-732-3168 Ext. 2398, E-mail: lclark@lincolnchristian.edu.

GRADUATE UNITS

Hargrove School of Adult and Graduate Studies Students: 84 full-time (36 women), 266 part-time (102 women). Average age 39. *Faculty:* 25 full-time (6 women), 14 part-time/adjunct (5 women). *Financial support:* Applicants required to submit FAFSA. Online learning. Offers bible and theology (MA); intercultural studies (MA); marriage and family therapy (MA); organizational leadership (MA); spiritual formation (MA). MA in marriage and family therapy offered in Las Vegas, NV; MA in spiritual formation offered in Bloomington-Normal, IL. *Application deadline:* For fall admission, 8/1 for domestic students, 3/1 for international students; for spring admission, 11/15 for domestic students, 11/1 for international students. *Application fee:* $25 ($50 for international students). *Application Contact:* Lindsey Clark, Associate Director of Graduate and Seminary Enrollment, 217-732-3168 Ext. 2398, E-mail: lclark@lincolnchristian.edu.

LINCOLN MEMORIAL UNIVERSITY, Harrogate, TN 37752-1901

General Information Independent, coed, comprehensive institution. *Graduate housing:* Rooms and/or apartments available on a first-come, first-served basis to single and married students.

GRADUATE UNITS

Carter and Moyers School of Education ***Degree program information:*** Part-time and evening/weekend programs available. Part-time, evening/weekend, online learning. Offers administration and supervision (M Ed, Ed S); counseling and guidance (M Ed); curriculum and instruction (M Ed, Ed D, Ed S); English (M Ed); executive leadership (Ed D); higher education administration (Ed D); human resource development (Ed D); leadership and administration (Ed D).

Caylor School of Nursing ***Degree program information:*** Part-time programs available. Part-time. Offers family nurse practitioner (MSN); nurse anesthesia (MSN); psychiatric mental health nurse practitioner (MSN).

DeBusk College of Osteopathic Medicine Offers osteopathic medicine (DO).

Duncan School of Law ***Degree program information:*** Part-time programs available. Part-time. Offers law (JD). Electronic applications accepted.

School of Business ***Degree program information:*** Part-time and evening/weekend programs available. Part-time, evening/weekend. Offers business (MBA).

LINCOLN UNIVERSITY, Oakland, CA 94612

General Information Independent, coed, comprehensive institution. *Enrollment:* 734 graduate, professional, and undergraduate students; 542 full-time matriculated graduate/professional students (215 women), 3 part-time matriculated graduate/professional students (1 woman). *Enrollment by degree level:* 514 master's, 31 doctoral. *Graduate faculty:* 13 full-time (1 woman), 16 part-time/adjunct (3 women). *Tuition, area resident:* Full-time $7650. *Required fees:* $400. Tuition and fees vary according to course level, course load, degree level and program. *Student services:* Campus employment opportunities, career counseling, international student services, low-cost health insurance, writing training. *Library:* Lincoln University Library. *Collection:* Books: 14,400 (physical), 128,000 (digital/electronic); Serial titles: 350 (physical), 5,050 (digital/electronic); Databases: 19.

Computer facilities: 39 computers available on campus for general student use. A campuswide network can be accessed.
Website: http://www.lincolnuca.edu/

General Application Contact: Peggy Au, Director of Admissions and Records, 510-628-8010, Fax: 510-628-8012, E-mail: admissions@lincolnuca.edu.

GRADUATE UNITS

Graduate Studies Students: 542 full-time (215 women), 3 part-time (1 woman); includes 10 minority (8 Asian, non-Hispanic/Latino; 1 Hispanic/Latino; 1 Two or more races, non-Hispanic/Latino), 531 international. Average age 26. 970 applicants, 52% accepted, 102 enrolled. *Faculty:* 13 full-time (1 woman), 16 part-time/adjunct (3 women). *Financial support:* Teaching assistantships, career-related internships or fieldwork, and scholarships/grants available. Financial award application deadline: 7/31; financial award applicants required to submit FAFSA. In 2015, 98 master's awarded. *Degree program information:* Part-time programs available. Part-time. Offers finance and investments (DBA); finance management (MS); finance management and investments (MBA); general business (MBA); human resource management (MBA, DBA); international business (MBA, MS); management information systems (MBA). *Application deadline:* For fall admission, 7/17 for domestic students, 6/17 for international students; for spring admission, 11/30 for domestic students, 10/31 for international students; for summer admission, 5/8 for domestic students, 4/8 for international students. Applications are processed on a rolling basis. *Application fee:* $75. Electronic applications accepted. *Application Contact:* Reenu Shrestha, Assistant to the President, 510-628-8017, Fax: 510-208-2826, E-mail: sreenu@lincolnuca.edu. *Director of Graduate Programs*, Dr. Marshall Burak, 510-628-8016, Fax: 510-628-8012, E-mail: mburak@lincolnuca.edu.

LINCOLN UNIVERSITY, Jefferson City, MO 65101

General Information State-supported, coed, comprehensive institution. *Enrollment:* 2,944 graduate, professional, and undergraduate students; 53 full-time matriculated graduate/professional students (29 women), 68 part-time matriculated graduate/professional students (45 women). *Enrollment by degree level:* 112 master's, 9 other advanced degrees. Tuition, state resident: full-time $6840; part-time $5130 per year. Tuition, nonresident: full-time $12,720; part-time $9540 per year. *Required fees:* $852; $811 per unit. Tuition and fees vary according to course load. *Graduate housing:* Room and/or apartments available on a first-come, first-served basis to single students; on-campus housing not available to married students. Typical cost: $4076 per year ($7080 including board). Room and board charges vary according to board plan and housing facility selected. Housing application deadline: 7/1. *Student services:* Campus employment opportunities, career counseling, international student services, services for students with disabilities. *Library:* Inman E. Page Library. *Collection:* Books: 117,214 (physical), 182,129 (digital/electronic); Serial titles: 140 (physical), 194 (digital/electronic); Databases: 149. Weekly public service hours: 93. *Research affiliation:* National Science Foundation (STEM research), Ceres Trust (agriculture), Missouri Department of Agriculture (agriculture), Center for Rural Affairs (sustainable agriculture), U.S. Department of Education (DOE) (defense, government), U.S. Department of Agriculture (USDA) (agriculture, government).

Computer facilities: Computer purchase and lease plans are available. 365 computers available on campus for general student use. A campuswide network can be accessed from student residence rooms and from off campus. Online class registration is available.
Website: http://www.lincolnu.edu/

General Application Contact: Dr. Linda S. Bickel, Dean, 573-681-5247, Fax: 573-681-5106, E-mail: gradschool@lincolnu.edu.

GRADUATE UNITS

Graduate Studies Students: 53 full-time (29 women), 68 part-time (45 women); includes 32 minority (30 Black or African American, non-Hispanic/Latino; 1 American Indian or Alaska Native, non-Hispanic/Latino; 1 Two or more races, non-Hispanic/Latino), 14 international. Average age 34. 53 applicants, 49% accepted, 18 enrolled. *Financial support:* In 2015–16, 4 fellowships with tuition reimbursements, 7 research assistantships with tuition reimbursements were awarded; Federal Work-Study and scholarships/grants also available. Support available to part-time students. Financial award application deadline: 3/1; financial award applicants required to submit FAFSA. In 2015, 35 master's awarded. *Degree program information:* Part-time and evening/weekend programs available. Part-time, evening/weekend, 100% online, blended/hybrid learning. Offers business administration (MBA); guidance and counseling (M Ed); history (MA); school teaching (M Ed); sociology (MA); sociology/criminal justice (MA). *Application deadline:* For fall admission, 7/1 priority date for domestic students, 5/1 priority date for international students; for spring admission, 11/1 priority date for domestic students, 10/1 priority date for international students; for summer admission, 6/1 priority date for domestic students. Applications are processed on a rolling basis. *Application fee:* $30. Electronic applications accepted. *Application Contact:* Irasema Steck, Administrative Assistant, 573-681-5247, Fax: 573-681-5106, E-mail: gradschool@lincolnu.edu. *Dean,* Dr. Linda S. Bickel, 573-681-5247, Fax: 573-681-5106, E-mail: gradschool@lincolnu.edu.

LINCOLN UNIVERSITY, Lincoln University, PA 19352

General Information State-related, coed, comprehensive institution. *Graduate housing:* On-campus housing not available. *Research affiliation:* The Treatment Research Institute (addictive disorders).

GRADUATE UNITS

Graduate Studies ***Degree program information:*** Part-time and evening/weekend programs available. Part-time, evening/weekend. Offers early childhood education (M Ed); educational leadership (M Ed); human resources (MSA); human services (MHS); reading (MSR).

LINDENWOOD UNIVERSITY, St. Charles, MO 63301-1695

General Information Independent-religious, coed, comprehensive institution. *Enrollment:* 11,620 graduate, professional, and undergraduate students; 1,409 full-time matriculated graduate/professional students (880 women), 1,878 part-time matriculated graduate/professional students (1,369 women). *Enrollment by degree level:* 2,764 master's, 348 doctoral, 175 other advanced degrees. *Graduate faculty:* 106 full-time (51 women), 338 part-time/adjunct (191 women). *Tuition, area resident:* Full-time $15,672; part-time $453 per credit hour. *Required fees:* $205 per semester. Tuition and fees vary according to course level, course load and degree level. *Graduate housing:* Rooms and/or apartments available on a first-come, first-served basis to single and married students. Housing application deadline: 8/24. *Student services:* Campus employment opportunities, campus safety program, career counseling, exercise/wellness program, free psychological counseling, international student services, services for students with disabilities, teacher training, writing training. *Library:* Butler Library plus 1 other. *Collection:* Books: 93,643 (physical), 187,346 (digital/electronic); Serial titles: 295 (physical), 137 (digital/electronic); Databases: 96. Study areas open 24 hours, 5–7 days a week.

Computer facilities: 286 computers available on campus for general student use. A campuswide network can be accessed from student residence rooms and from off campus. Online class registration is available.
Website: http://www.lindenwood.edu/

General Application Contact: Tyler Kostich, Director, Evening and Graduate Admissions, 636-949-4138, Fax: 636-949-4109, E-mail: adultadmissions@lindenwood.edu.

GRADUATE UNITS

Graduate Programs Students: 1,409 full-time (880 women), 1,878 part-time (1,369 women); includes 871 minority (709 Black or African American, non-Hispanic/Latino; 13 American Indian or Alaska Native, non-Hispanic/Latino; 18 Asian, non-Hispanic/Latino; 69 Hispanic/Latino; 3 Native Hawaiian or other Pacific Islander, non-Hispanic/Latino; 59 Two or more races, non-Hispanic/Latino), 146 international. Average age 35. 1,268 applicants, 69% accepted, 757 enrolled. *Faculty:* 106 full-time (51 women), 338 part-time/adjunct (191 women). *Financial support:* In 2015–16, 1,820 students received support. Career-related internships or fieldwork, Federal Work-Study, institutionally sponsored loans, scholarships/grants, tuition waivers (full), and unspecified assistantships available. Financial award application deadline: 6/30; financial award applicants required to submit FAFSA. In 2015, 1,270 master's, 59 doctorates, 74 other advanced degrees awarded. *Degree program information:* Part-time and evening/weekend programs available. Part-time, evening/weekend, 100% online. *Application deadline:* For fall admission, 8/22 priority date for domestic and international students; for spring admission, 1/9 priority date for domestic and international students; for summer admission, 5/16 priority date for domestic and international students. Applications are processed on a rolling basis. *Application fee:* $30 ($100 for international students). Electronic applications accepted. *Application Contact:* Tyler Kostich, Director, Evening and Graduate Admissions, 636-949-4138, Fax: 636-949-4109, E-mail: adultadmissions@lindenwood.edu. *Provost and Vice President of Academic Affairs,* Dr. Marilyn Abbott, 636-949-4846, Fax: 636-949-4912, E-mail: mabbott@lindenwood.edu.

Plaster School of Business and Entrepreneurship Students: 248 full-time (120 women), 98 part-time (53 women); includes 52 minority (32 Black or African American, non-Hispanic/Latino; 3 Asian, non-Hispanic/Latino; 9 Hispanic/Latino; 8 Two or more races, non-Hispanic/Latino), 93 international. Average age 28. 206 applicants, 60% accepted, 109 enrolled. *Faculty:* 12 full-time (4 women), 24 part-time/adjunct (5 women). *Financial support:* In 2015–16, 358 students received support. Career-related internships or fieldwork, Federal Work-Study, institutionally sponsored loans, scholarships/grants, tuition waivers (partial), and unspecified assistantships available. Financial award application deadline: 6/30; financial award applicants required to submit FAFSA. In 2015, 213 master's awarded. *Degree program information:* Part-time and evening/weekend programs available. Part-time, evening/weekend, 100% online. Offers accountancy (M Acc); accounting (MBA); business administration (MBA); entrepreneurial studies (MBA); finance (MBA, MS); human resource management (MBA); international business (MBA); leadership (MBA); management (MBA); marketing (MBA, MS); public administration (MBA); sport management (MA); supply chain management (MBA). *Application deadline:* For fall admission, 8/10 priority date for domestic and international students; for winter admission, 1/4 priority date for domestic and international students; for spring admission, 3/7 priority date for domestic and international students; for summer admission, 5/23 priority date for domestic and international students. Applications are processed on a rolling basis. *Application fee:* $30 ($100 for international students). Electronic applications accepted. *Application Contact:* Tyler Kostich, Director, Evening and Graduate Admissions, 636-949-4138, Fax: 636-949-4109, E-mail: adultadmissions@lindenwood.edu. *Dean, School of Business and Entrepreneurship,* Roger Ellis, 636-949-4839, E-mail: rellis@lindenwood.edu.

School of Accelerated Degree Programs Students: 707 full-time (442 women), 143 part-time (92 women); includes 286 minority (232 Black or African American, non-Hispanic/Latino; 5 American Indian or Alaska Native, non-Hispanic/Latino; 6 Asian, non-Hispanic/Latino; 27 Hispanic/Latino; 1 Native Hawaiian or other Pacific Islander, non-Hispanic/Latino; 15 Two or more races, non-Hispanic/Latino), 21 international. Average age 35. 337 applicants, 68% accepted, 190 enrolled. *Faculty:* 18 full-time (7 women), 72 part-time/adjunct (28 women). *Financial support:* In 2015–16, 852 students received support. Career-related internships or fieldwork, institutionally sponsored loans, scholarships/grants, tuition waivers (partial), and unspecified assistantships available. Financial award application deadline: 6/30; financial award applicants required to submit FAFSA. In 2015, 473 master's awarded. *Degree program information:* Part-time and evening/weekend programs available. Part-time, evening/weekend, 100% online. Offers administration (MSA); business administration (MBA); communications (MA); criminal justice and administration (MS); gerontology (MA); healthcare administration (MS); human resource management (MS); information technology (Certificate); managing information security (MS); managing information technology (MS); managing virtualization and cloud computing (MS); writing (MFA). *Application deadline:* For fall admission, 9/28 priority date for domestic and international students; for winter admission, 1/4 priority date for domestic and international students; for spring admission, 4/4 priority date for domestic and international students; for summer admission, 7/5 priority date for domestic and international students. Applications are processed on a rolling basis. *Application fee:* $30 ($100 for international students). Electronic applications accepted. *Application Contact:* Tyler Kostich, Director, Evening and Graduate Admissions, 636-949-4138, Fax: 636-949-4109, E-mail: adultadmissions@lindenwood.edu. *Dean, Accelerated Degree Programs,* Dr. Gina Ganahl, 636-949-4501, Fax: 636-949-4505, E-mail: gganahl@lindenwood.edu.

School of Communications Students: 14 full-time (9 women), 5 part-time (3 women); includes 2 minority (1 Asian, non-Hispanic/Latino; 1 Two or more races, non-Hispanic/Latino), 4 international. Average age 27. 16 applicants, 100% accepted, 9 enrolled. *Faculty:* 10 full-time (2 women), 4 part-time/adjunct (1 woman). *Financial support:* In 2015–16, 12 students received support. Career-related internships or fieldwork, Federal Work-Study, institutionally sponsored loans, scholarships/grants, tuition waivers (partial), and unspecified assistantships available. Financial award application deadline: 6/30; financial award applicants required to submit FAFSA. In 2015, 7 master's awarded. *Degree program information:* Part-time and evening/weekend programs available. Part-time, evening/weekend. Offers broadcast (MA); communications studies (MA); interactive media and Web design (MA); journalism (MA). *Application deadline:* For fall admission, 8/22 priority date for domestic and international students; for spring admission, 1/9 priority date for domestic and international students; for summer admission, 5/16 priority date for domestic and international students. Applications are processed on a rolling basis. *Application fee:* $30 ($100 for international students). Electronic applications accepted. *Application Contact:* Tyler Kostich, Director, Evening and Graduate Admissions, 636-949-4138, Fax: 636-949-4109, E-mail: adultadmissions@lindenwood.edu. *Dean, School of Communications,* Mike Wall, 636-949-4880, E-mail: mwall@lindenwood.edu.

School of Education Students: 359 full-time (267 women), 1,544 part-time (1,149 women); includes 479 minority (408 Black or African American, non-Hispanic/Latino; 7 American Indian or Alaska Native, non-Hispanic/Latino; 5 Asian, non-Hispanic/Latino; 27 Hispanic/Latino; 2 Native Hawaiian or other Pacific Islander, non-Hispanic/Latino; 30 Two or more races, non-Hispanic/Latino), 22 international. Average age 36. 609 applicants, 74% accepted, 402 enrolled. *Faculty:* 43 full-time (27 women), 234 part-time/adjunct (154 women). *Financial support:* In 2015–16, 442 students received support. Career-related internships or fieldwork, Federal Work-Study, institutionally sponsored loans, scholarships/grants, tuition waivers (partial), and unspecified assistantships available. Financial award application deadline: 6/30; financial award applicants required to submit FAFSA. In 2015, 519 master's, 59 doctorates, 74 other advanced degrees awarded. *Degree program information:* Part-time and evening/weekend programs available. Part-time, evening/weekend, 100% online. Offers education (MA); educational administration (MA, Ed D, Ed S); English to speakers of other languages (MA); instructional leadership (Ed D, Ed S); library media (MA); professional counseling (MA); school administration (MA, Ed S); school counseling (MA); teaching (MA). *Application deadline:* For fall admission, 8/22 priority date for domestic and international students; for spring admission, 1/9 priority date for domestic and international students; for summer admission, 5/16 priority date for domestic and international students. Applications are processed on a rolling basis. *Application fee:* $30 ($100 for international students). Electronic applications accepted. *Application Contact:* Tyler Kostich, Director, Evening and Graduate Admissions, 636-949-4138, Fax: 636-949-4109, E-mail: adultadmissions@lindenwood.edu. *Dean, School of Education,* Dr. Cynthia Bice, 636-949-4618, Fax: 636-949-4197, E-mail: cbice@lindenwood.edu.

School of Fine and Performing Arts Students: 5 full-time (3 women), 2 part-time (1 woman); includes 2 minority (both Hispanic/Latino). Average age 27. 11 applicants, 27% accepted, 3 enrolled. *Faculty:* 8 full-time (3 women), 2 part-time/adjunct (both women). *Financial support:* In 2015–16, 9 students received support. Career-related internships or fieldwork, institutionally sponsored loans, scholarships/grants, tuition waivers (partial), and unspecified assistantships available. Financial award application deadline: 6/30; financial award applicants required to submit FAFSA. In 2015, 13 master's awarded. *Degree program information:* Part-time programs available. Part-time. Offers arts management (MA); cinema and media arts (MFA); studio art (MA, MFA). *Application deadline:* For fall admission, 8/22 priority date for domestic and international students; for spring admission, 1/9 for domestic students, 1/9 priority date for international students; for summer admission, 5/16 priority date for domestic and international students. Applications are processed on a rolling basis. *Application fee:* $30 ($100 for international students). Electronic applications accepted. *Application Contact:* Tyler Kostich, Director, Evening and Graduate Admissions, 636-949-4138, Fax: 636-949-4109, E-mail: adultadmissions@lindenwood.edu. *Dean, School of Fine and Performing Arts*, Dr. Joseph Alsobrook, 636-949-4164, Fax: 636-949-4910, E-mail: jalsobrook@lindenwood.edu.

School of Humanities Students: 3 full-time (all women), 7 part-time (all women); includes 1 minority (Asian, non-Hispanic/Latino). Average age 35. *Faculty:* 1 (woman) full-time, 2 part-time/adjunct (1 woman). *Financial support:* In 2015–16, 3 students received support. Career-related internships or fieldwork, institutionally sponsored loans, scholarships/grants, tuition waivers (partial), and unspecified assistantships available. Financial award application deadline: 6/30; financial award applicants required to submit FAFSA. In 2015, 2 master's awarded. *Degree program information:* Part-time programs available. Part-time. Offers teaching English to speakers of other languages (MA). *Application deadline:* For fall admission, 8/22 priority date for domestic and international students; for spring admission, 1/9 priority date for domestic and international students; for summer admission, 5/16 priority date for domestic and international students. Applications are processed on a rolling basis. *Application fee:* $30 ($100 for international students). Electronic applications accepted. *Application Contact:* Tyler Kostich, Director, Evening and Graduate Admissions, 636-949-4138, Fax: 636-949-4109, E-mail: adultadmissions@lindenwood.edu. *Dean, School of Humanities*, Dr. Michael Whaley, 636-949-4561, E-mail: mwhaley@lindenwood.edu.

School of Human Services Students: 3 full-time (all women), 51 part-time (42 women); includes 28 minority (23 Black or African American, non-Hispanic/Latino; 1 American Indian or Alaska Native, non-Hispanic/Latino; 2 Hispanic/Latino; 2 Two or more races, non-Hispanic/Latino). Average age 36. 20 applicants, 75% accepted, 11 enrolled. *Faculty:* 3 full-time (1 woman), 2 part-time/adjunct (both women). *Financial support:* In 2015–16, 43 students received support. Career-related internships or fieldwork, institutionally sponsored loans, scholarships/grants, tuition waivers, and unspecified assistantships available. Financial award application deadline: 6/30; financial award applicants required to submit FAFSA. In 2015, 18 master's awarded. *Degree program information:* Part-time programs available. Part-time, 100% online. Offers nonprofit administration (MA). *Application deadline:* For fall admission, 8/22 priority date for domestic and international students; for spring admission, 1/9 priority date for domestic and international students; for summer admission, 5/16 priority date for domestic and international students. Applications are processed on a rolling basis. *Application fee:* $30 ($100 for international students). Electronic applications accepted. *Application Contact:* Tyler Kostich, Director, Evening and Graduate Admissions, 636-949-4138, Fax: 636-949-4109, E-mail: adultadmissions@lindenwood.edu. *Interim Dean, School of Human Services*, Dr. Billi Patzius, 636-949-4731, E-mail: bpatzius@lindenwood.edu.

School of Nursing and Allied Health Sciences Students: 1 (woman) full-time, 17 part-time (all women); includes 1 minority (Black or African American, non-Hispanic/Latino). Average age 45. 23 applicants, 61% accepted, 11 enrolled. *Faculty:* 2 full-time (both women). *Financial support:* In 2015–16, 30 students received support. Career-related internships or fieldwork, Federal Work-Study, institutionally sponsored loans, scholarships/grants, tuition waivers (partial), and unspecified assistantships available. Financial award application deadline: 6/30; financial award applicants required to submit FAFSA. *Degree program information:* Part-time programs available. Part-time, blended/hybrid learning. Offers nursing (MS). *Application deadline:* For fall admission, 8/22 priority date for domestic and international students; for spring admission, 1/9 priority date for domestic and international students; for summer admission, 5/16 priority date for domestic and international students. Applications are processed on a rolling basis. *Application fee:* $30 ($100 for international students). Electronic applications accepted. *Application Contact:* Tyler Kostich, Director, Evening and Graduate Admissions, 636-949-4138, Fax: 636-949-4109, E-mail: adultadmissions@lindenwood.edu. *Dean, School of Nursing and Allied Science*, Dr. Peggy Ellis, 636-949-2907, E-mail: pellis@lindenwood.edu.

School of Sport, Recreation, and Exercise Sciences Students: 42 full-time (15 women), 5 part-time (3 women); includes 4 minority (2 Asian, non-Hispanic/Latino; 1 Hispanic/Latino; 1 Two or more races, non-Hispanic/Latino), 6 international. Average age 25. 46 applicants, 48% accepted, 22 enrolled. *Faculty:* 8 full-time (4 women), 1 (woman) part-time/adjunct. *Financial support:* In 2015–16, 40 students received support. Career-related internships or fieldwork, institutionally sponsored loans, scholarships/grants, tuition waivers (partial), and unspecified assistantships available. Financial award application deadline: 6/30; financial award applicants required to submit FAFSA. In 2015, 20 master's awarded. *Degree program information:* Part-time and evening/weekend programs available. Part-time, evening/weekend. Offers human performance (MS). *Application deadline:* For fall admission, 8/22 priority date for domestic and international students; for spring admission, 1/9 priority date for domestic and international students; for summer admission, 5/16 priority date for domestic and international students. Applications are processed on a rolling basis. *Application fee:* $30 ($100 for international students). Electronic applications accepted. *Application Contact:* Tyler Kostich, Director, Evening and Graduate Admissions, 636-949-4138, Fax: 636-949-4109, E-mail: adultadmissions@lindenwood.edu. *Dean, School of Sport, Recreation, and Exercise Sciences*, Dr. Cynthia Schroeder, 636-949-4318, E-mail: cschroeder@lindenwood.edu.

LINDENWOOD UNIVERSITY–BELLEVILLE, Belleville, IL 62226

General Information Independent-religious, coed, comprehensive institution.

GRADUATE UNITS

Graduate Programs

LINDSEY WILSON COLLEGE, Columbia, KY 42728

General Information Independent-religious, coed, comprehensive institution. *Graduate housing:* Rooms and/or apartments available on a first-come, first-served basis to single and married students.

GRADUATE UNITS

Division of Education Online learning. Offers teacher as leader (M Ed).

Louisville Center for Design Online learning. Offers interactive design (MA).

School of Professional Counseling *Degree program information:* Part-time and evening/weekend programs available. Part-time, evening/weekend, online learning. Offers counseling and human development (M Ed); counselor education and supervision (PhD).

LIPSCOMB UNIVERSITY, Nashville, TN 37204-3951

General Information Independent-religious, coed, comprehensive institution. CGS member. *Enrollment:* 4,680 graduate, professional, and undergraduate students; 846 full-time matriculated graduate/professional students (516 women), 616 part-time matriculated graduate/professional students (376 women). *Enrollment by degree level:* 969 master's, 409 doctoral, 84 other advanced degrees. *Graduate faculty:* 111 full-time (44 women), 88 part-time/adjunct (35 women). *Tuition, area resident:* Full-time $18,432; part-time $1024 per credit hour. Tuition and fees vary according to degree level and program. *Graduate housing:* Room and/or apartments available on a first-come, first-served basis to single students; on-campus housing not available to married students. Typical cost: $6192 per year ($10,736 including board). Room and board charges vary according to board plan and housing facility selected. Housing application deadline: 7/15. *Student services:* Campus employment opportunities, campus safety program, career counseling, exercise/wellness program, free psychological counseling, international student services, multicultural affairs office, services for students with disabilities, teacher training. *Library:* Beaman Library plus 1 other. *Collection:* Books: 224,421 (physical). Students can reserve study rooms.

Computer facilities: 150 computers available on campus for general student use. A campuswide network can be accessed from student residence rooms and from off campus. Online class registration is available.
Website: http://www.lipscomb.edu/

General Application Contact: Barbara Blackman, Coordinator of Graduate Studies, 615-966-6287, Fax: 615-966-7619, E-mail: graduatestudies@lipscomb.edu.

GRADUATE UNITS

College of Business Students: 128 full-time (67 women), 114 part-time (53 women); includes 43 minority (27 Black or African American, non-Hispanic/Latino; 4 Asian, non-Hispanic/Latino; 7 Hispanic/Latino; 5 Two or more races, non-Hispanic/Latino), 2 international. Average age 32. 225 applicants, 62% accepted, 92 enrolled. *Faculty:* 15 full-time (1 woman), 10 part-time/adjunct (2 women). *Financial support:* Career-related internships or fieldwork, scholarships/grants, tuition waivers (partial), and unspecified assistantships available. Support available to part-time students. Financial award application deadline: 7/1; financial award applicants required to submit FAFSA. In 2015, 125 master's awarded. *Degree program information:* Part-time and evening/weekend programs available. Part-time, evening/weekend. Offers accountancy (M Acc); accounting (MBA); conflict management (MBA); financial services (MBA); health care informatics (MBA); healthcare management (MBA); human resources (MHR); information security (MBA); leadership (MBA); nonprofit management (MBA); professional accountancy (Certificate); sports management (MBA); strategic human resources (MBA); sustainability (MBA). *Application deadline:* For fall admission, 6/15 for domestic students, 2/1 for international students; for winter admission, 6/1 for international students; for spring admission, 11/15 for domestic students. Applications are processed on a rolling basis. *Application fee:* $50 ($75 for international students). Electronic applications accepted. *Application Contact:* Lisa Shacklett, Assistant Dean of Enrollment and Marketing, 615-966-5968, E-mail: lisa.shacklett@lipscomb.edu. *Associate Dean of Graduate Business Programs*, Allison Duke, 615-966-5732, Fax: 615-966-1818, E-mail: allison.duke@lipscomb.edu.

College of Computing and Technology Students: 32 full-time (12 women), 15 part-time (8 women); includes 14 minority (5 Black or African American, non-Hispanic/Latino; 1 American Indian or Alaska Native, non-Hispanic/Latino; 8 Asian, non-Hispanic/Latino). Average age 37. 46 applicants, 80% accepted, 21 enrolled. *Faculty:* 6 full-time (0 women), 9 part-time/adjunct (1 woman). *Financial support:* Scholarships/grants and employer agreements available. Financial award applicants required to submit FAFSA. In 2015, 13 master's awarded. *Degree program information:* Part-time and evening/weekend programs available. Part-time, evening/weekend. Offers data science (MS); information technology (MS); software engineering (MS). *Application deadline:* Applications are processed on a rolling basis. *Application fee:* $50 ($75 for international students). Electronic applications accepted. *Application Contact:* Finn Breland, Enrollment Management Specialist, 615-966-1193, E-mail: finn.breland@lipscomb.edu. *Dean*, Dr. Fortune S. Mhlanga, 615-966-5073, E-mail: fortune.mhlanga@lipscomb.edu.

College of Education Students: 150 full-time (113 women), 258 part-time (206 women); includes 64 minority (52 Black or African American, non-Hispanic/Latino; 3 Asian, non-Hispanic/Latino; 5 Hispanic/Latino; 2 Native Hawaiian or other Pacific Islander, non-Hispanic/Latino; 2 Two or more races, non-Hispanic/Latino). Average age 33. *Faculty:* 23 full-time (17 women), 27 part-time/adjunct (18 women). *Financial support:* Scholarships/grants, unspecified assistantships, and partnerships with local school districts available. Financial award applicants required to submit FAFSA. In 2015, 220 master's, 34 doctorates, 56 other advanced degrees awarded. *Degree program information:* Part-time and evening/weekend programs available. Part-time, evening/weekend, online learning. Offers applied behavior analysis (MS, Certificate); educational leadership (M Ed, Ed S); English language learning (M Ed, Ed S); instructional coaching (M Ed, Certificate, Ed S); instructional practice (M Ed); learning organizations and strategic change (Ed D); literacy coaching (Certificate); professional learning and coaching in mathematics (M Ed, Ed S); reading specialty (M Ed, Ed S); special education (M Ed); teaching, learning, and leading (M Ed); technology integration (M Ed); technology integration specialist (Certificate). *Application deadline:* For fall admission, 8/29 priority date for domestic students; for spring admission, 1/15 priority date for domestic students. Applications are processed on a rolling basis. *Application fee:* $50 ($75 for international students). Electronic applications accepted. *Application Contact:* Amanda Logsdon, Director of Enrollment and Outreach, 615-966-7199, E-mail: amanda.logsdon@lipscomb.edu. *Director of Graduate Studies*, Dr. Deborah Boyd, 615-966-6263, E-mail: deborah.boyd@lipscomb.edu.

College of Pharmacy Students: 292 full-time (167 women), 5 part-time (3 women); includes 70 minority (22 Black or African American, non-Hispanic/Latino; 4 American Indian or Alaska Native, non-Hispanic/Latino; 31 Asian, non-Hispanic/Latino; 7 Hispanic/Latino; 2 Native Hawaiian or other Pacific Islander, non-Hispanic/Latino; 4 Two or more races, non-Hispanic/Latino). Average age 27. *Faculty:* 32 full-time (16 women), 5 part-time/adjunct (1 woman). *Financial support:* Application deadline: 2/15; applicants required to submit FAFSA. In 2015, 3 master's, 78 doctorates awarded. Offers healthcare informatics (MS). *Application deadline:* For fall admission, 2/7 for domestic students. Applications are processed on a rolling basis. *Application fee:* $50 ($75 for international students). Electronic applications accepted. *Application Contact:* Laura Ward, Director of Admissions and Student Affairs, 615-966-7173, E-mail: laura.ward@lipscomb.edu. *Dean/Professor of Pharmacy Practice*, Dr. Roger Davis, 615-966-7161.

Department of Graduate Psychology and Counseling Students: 110 full-time (90 women), 35 part-time (28 women); includes 36 minority (24 Black or African American, non-Hispanic/Latino; 2 Asian, non-Hispanic/Latino; 8 Hispanic/Latino; 2 Two or more races, non-Hispanic/Latino). Average age 28. *Faculty:* 9 full-time (2 women), 10 part-time/adjunct (5 women). *Financial support:* Scholarships/grants and unspecified assistantships available. Financial award applicants required to submit FAFSA. In 2015,

52 master's awarded. *Degree program information:* Part-time and evening/weekend programs available. Part-time, evening/weekend. Offers clinical mental health counseling (MS); counseling psychology (Certificate); marriage and family therapy (MMFT); psychology (MS). *Application deadline:* For fall admission, 7/1 for domestic students; for spring admission, 11/1 for domestic students. Applications are processed on a rolling basis. *Application fee:* $50 ($75 for international students). Electronic applications accepted. *Application Contact:* Kathi Johnson, Recruiting and Marketing Coordinator, 615-966-5237, E-mail: kathi.johnson@lipscomb.edu. *Director/Professor of Psychology,* Dr. Shanna Ray, 615-966-5833, E-mail: shanna.ray@lipscomb.edu.

Hazelip School of Theology Students: 41 full-time (13 women), 86 part-time (19 women); includes 22 minority (19 Black or African American, non-Hispanic/Latino; 1 Asian, non-Hispanic/Latino; 1 Hispanic/Latino; 1 Two or more races, non-Hispanic/Latino). Average age 38. *Faculty:* 9 full-time (0 women), 4 part-time/adjunct (1 woman). *Financial support:* Scholarships/grants and unspecified assistantships available. Financial award application deadline: 3/1; financial award applicants required to submit FAFSA. In 2015, 9 master's, 6 doctorates awarded. *Degree program information:* Part-time and evening/weekend programs available. Part-time, evening/weekend, online learning. Offers Christian practice (MA); missional and spiritual formation (D Min); student ministry (Certificate); theology (M Div). *Application deadline:* For fall admission, 8/1 priority date for domestic students; for spring admission, 12/15 for domestic students. Applications are processed on a rolling basis. *Application fee:* $50 ($75 for international students). Electronic applications accepted. *Application Contact:* Kellye McCool, Coordinator of Student Services, 615-966-5458, Fax: 615-966-6052, E-mail: kellye.mccool@lipscomb.edu. *Director,* Dr. Mark Black, 615-966-5709, Fax: 615-966-6052, E-mail: mark.black@lipscomb.edu.

Institute for Conflict Management Students: 9 full-time (4 women), 19 part-time (16 women); includes 7 minority (all Black or African American, non-Hispanic/Latino). Average age 40. *Faculty:* 2 full-time (1 woman), 5 part-time/adjunct (2 women). *Financial support:* Tuition waivers (full) available. Financial award applicants required to submit FAFSA. In 2015, 9 master's, 7 other advanced degrees awarded. *Degree program information:* Part-time and evening/weekend programs available. Part-time, evening/weekend. Offers conflict management (MA, Certificate). *Application deadline:* For fall admission, 7/15 for domestic students; for spring admission, 12/15 for domestic students. Applications are processed on a rolling basis. *Application fee:* $50 ($75 for international students). Electronic applications accepted. *Application Contact:* Dr. Phyllis Hildreth. *Managing Director,* Dr. Steve Joiner, 615-966-7141, Fax: 615-966-7143, E-mail: steve.joiner@lipscomb.edu.

Institute for Sustainable Practice Students: 8 full-time (5 women), 9 part-time (1 woman); includes 3 minority (2 Black or African American, non-Hispanic/Latino; 1 Hispanic/Latino). Average age 33. 23 applicants, 43% accepted, 4 enrolled. *Faculty:* 2 full-time (1 woman), 5 part-time/adjunct (1 woman). *Financial support:* Unspecified assistantships available. Financial award applicants required to submit FAFSA. In 2015, 9 master's, 2 other advanced degrees awarded. *Degree program information:* Part-time and evening/weekend programs available. Part-time, evening/weekend, online learning. Offers sustainable practice (MS, Certificate). *Application deadline:* For fall admission, 7/15 for domestic students; for spring admission, 12/15 for domestic students. Applications are processed on a rolling basis. *Application fee:* $50 ($75 for international students). Electronic applications accepted. *Application Contact:* Emily Stutzman Jones, Academic Director, 615-966-5076, E-mail: emily.jones@lipscomb.edu. *Executive Director,* G. Dodd Galbreath, 615-966-1771, E-mail: dodd.galbreath@lipscomb.edu.

Nelson and Sue Andrews Institute for Civic Leadership Students: 17 full-time (11 women), 11 part-time (6 women); includes 14 minority (12 Black or African American, non-Hispanic/Latino; 1 Hispanic/Latino; 1 Two or more races, non-Hispanic/Latino). Average age 40. *Faculty:* 1 (woman) full-time, 2 part-time/adjunct (1 woman). *Financial support:* Applicants required to submit FAFSA. In 2015, 16 master's awarded. *Degree program information:* Part-time and evening/weekend programs available. Part-time, evening/weekend. Offers civic leadership (MA). *Application deadline:* Applications are processed on a rolling basis. *Application fee:* $50 ($75 for international students). Electronic applications accepted. *Application Contact:* Dr. MIchelle Steele, Academic Director, 615-966-5181, E-mail: michelle.steele@lipscomb.edu. *Executive Director,* Linda Peek Schacht, 615-966-1341, E-mail: linda.schacht@lipscomb.edu.

Program in Biomolecular Science Students: 21 full-time (9 women), 5 part-time (3 women); includes 6 minority (4 Black or African American, non-Hispanic/Latino; 1 Hispanic/Latino; 1 Two or more races, non-Hispanic/Latino). Average age 26. 75 applicants, 24% accepted, 13 enrolled. *Faculty:* 5 full-time (3 women), 1 part-time/adjunct (0 women). *Financial support:* Unspecified assistantships available. Financial award applicants required to submit FAFSA. In 2015, 18 master's awarded. *Degree program information:* Part-time and evening/weekend programs available. Part-time, evening/weekend. Offers biomolecular science (MS). *Application deadline:* For fall admission, 8/1 for domestic students; for winter admission, 12/14 for domestic students; for spring admission, 5/14 for domestic students. Applications are processed on a rolling basis. *Application fee:* $50 ($75 for international students). Electronic applications accepted. *Application Contact:* Tina Fulford, Administrative Assistant, 615-966-5330, E-mail: tina.fulford@lipscomb.edu. *Director,* Dr. Kent Gallaher, 615-966-5721, E-mail: kent.gallaher@lipscomb.edu.

Program in Engineering Management Students: 4 full-time (0 women), 2 part-time (1 woman); includes 3 minority (all Black or African American, non-Hispanic/Latino). Average age 29. 10 applicants, 10% accepted, 1 enrolled. *Faculty:* 1 full-time (0 women), 1 part-time/adjunct (0 women). *Financial support:* Applicants required to submit FAFSA. In 2015, 4 master's awarded. *Degree program information:* Part-time and evening/weekend programs available. Part-time, evening/weekend. Offers engineering management (MS). *Application deadline:* Applications are processed on a rolling basis. *Application fee:* $50 ($75 for international students). Electronic applications accepted. *Application Contact:* Laurie Winton, Recruiting and Marketing Coordinator, 615-966-5039, E-mail: laurie.winton@lipscomb.edu. *Director,* David Davidson, 615-966-5071, E-mail: david.davidson@lipscomb.edu.

Program in Exercise and Nutrition Science Students: 11 full-time (6 women), 37 part-time (21 women); includes 7 minority (3 Black or African American, non-Hispanic/Latino; 1 Asian, non-Hispanic/Latino; 3 Hispanic/Latino), 1 international. Average age 28. *Faculty:* 4 full-time (3 women), 3 part-time/adjunct (1 woman). *Financial support:* Unspecified assistantships available. Financial award applicants required to submit FAFSA. In 2015, 21 master's awarded. *Degree program information:* Part-time and evening/weekend programs available. Part-time, evening/weekend. Offers exercise and nutrition science (MS). *Application deadline:* For fall admission, 6/1 for domestic students; for spring admission, 12/1 for domestic students. Applications are processed on a rolling basis. *Application fee:* $50 ($75 for international students). Electronic applications accepted. *Application Contact:* Julie Lillicrap, Administrative Assistant, 615-966-5700, E-mail: julie.lillicrap@lipscomb.edu. *Director,* Dr. Karen Robichaud, 615-966-5602, E-mail: karen.robichaud@lipscomb.edu.

Program in Film and Creative Media Students: 16 full-time (12 women), 19 part-time (7 women); includes 17 minority (13 Black or African American, non-Hispanic/Latino; 1 Asian, non-Hispanic/Latino; 2 Hispanic/Latino; 1 Two or more races, non-Hispanic/Latino). Average age 33. 26 applicants, 77% accepted, 13 enrolled. *Faculty:* 3 full-time (0 women), 7 part-time/adjunct (1 woman). *Financial support:* Unspecified assistantships available. Financial award applicants required to submit FAFSA. *Degree program information:* Part-time and evening/weekend programs available. Part-time, evening/weekend. Offers film and creative media (MA, MFA). *Application deadline:* Applications are processed on a rolling basis. *Application fee:* $50 ($75 for international students). Electronic applications accepted. *Application Contact:* Tessa Bryant, Administrative Assistant, 615-966-7111, E-mail: tessa.bryant@lipscomb.edu. *Director,* David DeBorde, 615-966-7111, E-mail: david.deborde@lipscomb.edu.

LOCK HAVEN UNIVERSITY OF PENNSYLVANIA, Lock Haven, PA 17745-2390

General Information State-supported, coed, comprehensive institution. *Enrollment:* 4,607 graduate, professional, and undergraduate students; 216 full-time matriculated graduate/professional students (162 women), 171 part-time matriculated graduate/professional students (128 women). *Enrollment by degree level:* 378 master's. *Graduate faculty:* 13 full-time (9 women), 2 part-time/adjunct (1 woman). Tuition, state resident: part-time $470 per credit hour. Tuition, nonresident: part-time $705 per credit hour. *Required fees:* $203 per credit hour. $40 per semester. Tuition and fees vary according to program. *Graduate housing:* Room and/or apartments available on a first-come, first-served basis to single students; on-campus housing not available to married students. Typical cost: $5964 per year ($9344 including board). Room and board charges vary according to housing facility selected. Housing application deadline: 6/1. *Student services:* Campus employment opportunities, campus safety program, career counseling, exercise/wellness program, free psychological counseling, international student services, low-cost health insurance, multicultural affairs office, services for students with disabilities, writing training. *Library:* Stevenson Library plus 1 other. *Collection:* Books: 226,712 (physical), 18,288 (digital/electronic); Databases: 7. Weekly public service hours: 87; students can reserve study rooms.

Computer facilities: 290 computers available on campus for general student use. A campuswide network can be accessed from student residence rooms and from off campus. Online class registration is available.
Website: http://www.lhup.edu/

General Application Contact: Donna Tatarka, Director of Admissions, 570-484-2011, Fax: 570-484-2734, E-mail: drt831@lhup.edu.

GRADUATE UNITS

College of Liberal Arts and Education ***Financial support:*** Unspecified assistantships available. Financial award application deadline: 8/1. *Degree program information:* Part-time and evening/weekend programs available. Part-time, evening/weekend, online learning. Offers alternative education (M Ed); educational leadership (M Ed); teaching and learning (M Ed). *Application deadline:* Applications are processed on a rolling basis. *Application fee:* $25. Electronic applications accepted. *Application Contact:* Kelly Hibbler, Assistant to the Dean, 570-484-2147, Fax: 570-484-2734, E-mail: khibbler@lhup.edu. *Dean,* Dr. Susan Rimby, 570-484-2137, E-mail: ser1116@lhup.edu.

College of Natural, Behavioral and Health Sciences ***Financial support:*** Unspecified assistantships available. Financial award application deadline: 8/1. Offers actuarial science (PSM); athletic training (MS); health promotion/education (MHS); healthcare management (MHS); physician assistant (MHS). Program also offered at the Clearfield, Coudersport, and Harrisburg campuses. *Application deadline:* Applications are processed on a rolling basis. *Application fee:* $25. Electronic applications accepted. *Application Contact:* Cherie Dolan, Secretary to the Dean, 570-484-2204, Fax: 570-484-2734, E-mail: cdolan1@lhup.edu. *Dean,* Dr. Scott Carnicom, 570-484-2204, E-mail: carnicom@lhup.edu.

The Stephen Poorman College of Business, Information Systems, and Human Services ***Financial support:*** Unspecified assistantships available. Financial award application deadline: 8/1. Online learning. Offers clinical mental health counseling (MS); sport science (MS). *Application deadline:* Applications are processed on a rolling basis. *Application fee:* $25. Electronic applications accepted. *Application Contact:* Lucas A. Fanning, Assistant to the Dean, 570-484-2169, Fax: 570-484-2734, E-mail: laf1158@lhup.edu. *Dean,* Dr. Stephen Neun, 570-484-2136, E-mail: spn207@lhup.edu.

LOGAN UNIVERSITY, Chesterfield, MO 63017

General Information Independent, coed, upper-level institution. *Enrollment:* 915 graduate, professional, and undergraduate students; 762 full-time matriculated graduate/professional students (304 women), 97 part-time matriculated graduate/professional students (61 women). *Enrollment by degree level:* 115 master's, 744 doctoral. *Graduate faculty:* 53 full-time (23 women), 52 part-time/adjunct (21 women). *Graduate housing:* On-campus housing not available. *Student services:* Campus employment opportunities, campus safety program, career counseling, free psychological counseling, international student services, low-cost health insurance, multicultural affairs office, services for students with disabilities. *Library:* Learning Resources Center. *Collection:* Books: 12,567 (physical), 3,052 (digital/electronic); Serial titles: 20 (physical), 29,367 (digital/electronic); Databases: 87. Weekly public service hours: 84. *Research affiliation:* BTE-Multi-Cervical Unit (cervical spine analysis), Cadwell (electrophysiological diagnosis), Standard Process (nutrition and lipid management), Standard Process (nutrition), Biofreeze (topical analgesics), Foot Levelers, Inc. (orthotics).

Computer facilities: 100 computers available on campus for general student use. A campuswide network can be accessed. Online class registration, student portal, LMS, online storage, specialty health care software, high-speed printing are available.
Website: http://www.logan.edu/

General Application Contact: Dr. Boyd Bradshaw, Vice President, Enrollment Management, 636-227-2100 Ext. 1924, Fax: 636-207-2431, E-mail: admissions@logan.edu.

GRADUATE UNITS

College of Chiropractic Students: 743 full-time (289 women), 1 (woman) part-time; includes 71 minority (25 Black or African American, non-Hispanic/Latino; 4 American Indian or Alaska Native, non-Hispanic/Latino; 21 Asian, non-Hispanic/Latino; 13 Hispanic/Latino; 8 Two or more races, non-Hispanic/Latino), 11 international. Average age 26. 169 applicants, 73% accepted, 124 enrolled. *Faculty:* 50 full-time (21 women), 38 part-time/adjunct (16 women). *Financial support:* In 2015–16, 129 students received support. Federal Work-Study and scholarships/grants available. Financial award applicants required to submit FAFSA. In 2015, 221 doctorates awarded. Offers chiropractic (DC). *Application deadline:* Applications are processed on a rolling basis. *Application fee:* $50. Electronic applications accepted. *Application Contact:* Caitlin

Mueller, Assistant Director of Admissions, 636-227-2100 Ext. 1709, Fax: 636-207-2425, E-mail: admissions@logan.edu. *Dean of the College of Chiropractic*, Dr. Vincent DeBono, 636-227-2100 Ext. 2701, Fax: 636-207-2431, E-mail: vincent.debono@logan.edu.

College of Health Sciences Students: 19 full-time (15 women), 96 part-time (60 women); includes 12 minority (6 Black or African American, non-Hispanic/Latino; 1 Asian, non-Hispanic/Latino; 4 Hispanic/Latino; 1 Two or more races, non-Hispanic/Latino). Average age 31. 74 applicants, 85% accepted, 63 enrolled. *Faculty:* 3 full-time (2 women), 14 part-time/adjunct (5 women). *Financial support:* In 2015–16, 4 students received support. Federal Work-Study and scholarships/grants available. Support available to part-time students. Financial award applicants required to submit FAFSA. In 2015, 95 master's awarded. *Degree program information:* Part-time programs available. Part-time, 100% online, blended/hybrid learning. Offers health informatics (MS); health professionals education (DHPE); nutrition and human performance (MS); sports science and rehabilitation (MS). *Application deadline:* Applications are processed on a rolling basis. *Application fee:* $50. Electronic applications accepted. *Application Contact:* Jordan LaMarca, Assistant Director of Admissions, 636-227-2100 Ext. 1973, Fax: 636-207-2425, E-mail: admissions@logan.edu. *Dean, College of Health Sciences*, Dr. Sherri Cole, 636-227-2100 Ext. 2702, Fax: 636-207-2418, E-mail: sherri.cole@logan.edu.

LOGOS EVANGELICAL SEMINARY, El Monte, CA 91731

General Information Independent-religious, coed, graduate-only institution. *Graduate housing:* Rooms and/or apartments available on a first-come, first-served basis to single and married students. Housing application deadline: 7/15.

GRADUATE UNITS

Graduate Programs ***Degree program information:*** Part-time programs available. Part-time, online learning. Offers theology (M Div, MA, Th M, D Min). Electronic applications accepted.

LOMA LINDA UNIVERSITY, Loma Linda, CA 92350

General Information Independent-religious, coed, university. CGS member. *Enrollment:* 2,388 full-time matriculated graduate/professional students (1,288 women), 573 part-time matriculated graduate/professional students (399 women). *Enrollment by degree level:* 971 master's, 540 doctoral, 94 other advanced degrees. *Graduate faculty:* 1,063 full-time (367 women), 335 part-time/adjunct (121 women). *Graduate housing:* Room and/or apartments available on a first-come, first-served basis to single students; on-campus housing not available to married students. *Student services:* Campus employment opportunities, campus safety program, career counseling, child daycare facilities, exercise/wellness program, free psychological counseling, international student services, low-cost health insurance, multicultural affairs office, writing training. *Library:* Del E. Webb Memorial Library. *Research affiliation:* City of Hope Hospital (cancer research), Children's Hospital Los Angeles (cancer research), Children's Hospital Orange County (cancer research).

Computer facilities: 160 computers available on campus for general student use. A campuswide network can be accessed from student residence rooms and from off campus. Online class registration, online courses are available.
Website: http://www.llu.edu/

General Application Contact: Admissions Office, 909-651-5029, Fax: 909-558-4879, E-mail: admissions.app@llu.edu.

GRADUATE UNITS

School of Allied Health Professions Offers allied health professions (MOT, MPA, MS, DPT, OTD, PhD, SLPD); occupational therapy (MOT, OTD); physical therapy (DPT, PhD); physician assistant sciences (MPA); rehabilitation (MS); speech-language pathology (MS, SLPD). *Application deadline:* For fall admission, 8/1 for domestic and international students; for winter admission, 11/1 for domestic and international students; for spring admission, 2/1 for domestic and international students. Applications are processed on a rolling basis. *Application fee:* $60. Electronic applications accepted. *Application Contact:* Helen Greenwood, Director, Admissions and Records, 909-824-4599, Fax: 909-824-4809, E-mail: hgreenwood@sahp.llu.edu. *Dean*, Dr. Craig R. Jackson, 909-824-4545, Fax: 909-824-4809.

School of Behavioral Health Offers behavioral health (MS, MSW, DMFT, PhD, Psy D, Certificate); child life specialist (MS); clinical mediation (Certificate); clinical psychology (PhD, Psy D); counseling (MS); criminal justice (MS); drug and alcohol counseling (Certificate); family life education (Certificate); gerontology (MS); marital and family therapy (DMFT); school counseling (Certificate); social policy and social research (PhD); social work (MSW). *Application fee:* $60. Electronic applications accepted. *Application Contact:* Admissions Office, 909-651-5029, Fax: 909-558-4879, E-mail: admissions.app@llu.edu. *Dean*, Beverly J. Buckles, 909-558-4528.

School of Dentistry ***Financial support:*** Fellowships, career-related internships or fieldwork, Federal Work-Study, and institutionally sponsored loans available. Offers dentistry (MS, DDS, Certificate); endodontics (MS, Certificate); implant dentistry (MS, Certificate); oral and maxillofacial surgery (MS, Certificate); orthodontics and dentofacial orthopedics (MS, Certificate); periodontics (MS). *Application deadline:* Applications are processed on a rolling basis. *Application fee:* $75. *Application Contact:* Admissions Office, 909-651-5029, Fax: 909-558-4879, E-mail: admissions.app@llu.edu. *Dean*, Dr. Ronald J. Dailey, 909-558-4683, Fax: 909-824-4211.

School of Medicine ***Financial support:*** Fellowships, research assistantships, teaching assistantships, career-related internships or fieldwork, Federal Work-Study, institutionally sponsored loans, and tuition waivers (full and partial) available. Support available to part-time students. Offers biochemistry (MS, PhD); human anatomy (PhD); medicine (MS, MD, PhD); microbiology (PhD); pathology (PhD); pharmacology (PhD); physiology (PhD). *Application deadline:* For fall admission, 11/15 for domestic students. *Application fee:* $100. *Application Contact:* Admissions Office, 909-651-5029, Fax: 909-558-4879, E-mail: admissions.app@llu.edu. *Dean*, Dr. Roger Hadley, 909-558-4481, Fax: 909-824-4146.

School of Nursing ***Financial support:*** Career-related internships or fieldwork, Federal Work-Study, institutionally sponsored loans, and scholarships/grants available. Support available to part-time students. Financial award application deadline: 6/1. *Degree program information:* Part-time programs available. Part-time. Offers adult/gerontology (MS); nursing (MS, DNP, PhD); nursing administration (MS); obstetrics-pediatrics (MS). *Application deadline:* For fall admission, 8/1 for domestic students; for winter admission, 11/1 for domestic students; for spring admission, 2/1 for domestic students. *Application fee:* $60. Electronic applications accepted. *Application Contact:* Admissions Office, 909-651-5029, Fax: 909-558-4879, E-mail: admissions.app@llu.edu. *Dean*, Dr. Elizabeth Bossert, RN, 909-558-4923.

School of Pharmacy Offers pharmacy (Pharm D). *Application fee:* $75. *Application Contact:* Admissions Office, 909-651-5029, Fax: 909-558-4879, E-mail: admissions.app@llu.edu. *Interim Dean*, Dr. Marilyn M. Herrmann, 909-558-4745, Fax: 909-558-7973.

School of Public Health ***Financial support:*** Fellowships, research assistantships, teaching assistantships, career-related internships or fieldwork, Federal Work-Study, institutionally sponsored loans, tuition waivers (partial), and unspecified assistantships available. Support available to part-time students. Financial award application deadline: 5/15. *Degree program information:* Part-time programs available. Part-time. Offers biostatistics (MPH); environmental and occupational health (MPH); epidemiology (MPH, Dr PH, PhD); global health (MPH); health education (MPH, Dr PH); healthcare administration (MBA); public health (MBA, MPH, MS, Dr PH, PhD); public health nutrition (MPH, Dr PH). *Application deadline:* Applications are processed on a rolling basis. *Application fee:* $100. Electronic applications accepted. *Application Contact:* Wendy Genovez, Assistant Dan of Admissions and Records, 909-824-4694, Fax: 909-824-8087, E-mail: wgenovez@llu.edu. *Dean*, Helen Hopp Marshak, 909-558-4578, Fax: 909-824-4087.

School of Religion Offers bioethics (MA, Certificate); chaplaincy (MS); religion (MA, MS, Certificate); religion and society (MA). *Application deadline:* For fall admission, 8/1 for domestic and international students; for winter admission, 11/1 for domestic and international students; for spring admission, 2/1 for domestic and international students. *Application fee:* $60. Electronic applications accepted. *Application Contact:* Admissions Office, 909-651-5029, Fax: 909-558-4879, E-mail: admissions.app@llu.edu. *Dean*, Dr. Jon Paulien, 909-558-8434.

LONDON METROPOLITAN UNIVERSITY, London N7 8DB, United Kingdom

General Information Private, coed, university.

GRADUATE UNITS

Graduate Programs

LONG ISLAND UNIVERSITY–BRENTWOOD CAMPUS, Brentwood, NY 11717

General Information Independent, coed, upper-level institution. *Enrollment:* 89 full-time matriculated graduate/professional students (78 women), 93 part-time matriculated graduate/professional students (81 women). *Enrollment by degree level:* 165 master's, 17 other advanced degrees. *Graduate faculty:* 14 part-time/adjunct (4 women). *Tuition, area resident:* Part-time $1155 per credit. *Required fees:* $442 per term. Tuition and fees vary according to course load and program. *Graduate housing:* On-campus housing not available. *Student services:* Campus employment opportunities, career counseling, services for students with disabilities, teacher training. *Library:* Brentwood Campus Library.

Computer facilities: Computer purchase and lease plans are available. 50 computers available on campus for general student use. A campuswide network can be accessed from off campus. Online class registration is available.
Website: http://www.liu.edu/

General Application Contact: Christina Seifert, Director of Enrollment Management, 631-287-8500, Fax: 631-287-8575, E-mail: asma.malik@liu.edu.

GRADUATE UNITS

College of Education, Information and Technology Students: 89 full-time (78 women), 85 part-time (74 women); includes 26 minority (9 Black or African American, non-Hispanic/Latino; 2 Asian, non-Hispanic/Latino; 15 Hispanic/Latino). 85 applicants, 89% accepted, 43 enrolled. *Faculty:* 12 part-time/adjunct (6 women). *Financial support:* Scholarships/grants and unspecified assistantships available. Support available to part-time students. Financial award applicants required to submit FAFSA. In 2015, 99 master's, 11 other advanced degrees awarded. *Degree program information:* Part-time programs available. Part-time. Offers childhood education grades 1-6 (MS); childhood/childhood special education (MS); childhood/literacy b-6 (MS); clinical mental health counseling (Advanced Certificate); literacy B-6 (MS Ed); mental health counseling (MS); school counselor (MS); special education (MS Ed); students with disabilities 7-12 generalist (Advanced Certificate). *Application deadline:* Applications are processed on a rolling basis. *Application fee:* $50. *Application Contact:* Christina Seifert, Director of Enrollment Management, 631-287-8500, Fax: 631-287-8575, E-mail: asma.malik@liu.edu. *Dean and Chief Operating Officer, LIU Brentwood and LIU Riverhead*, Donna Di Donato, 631-287-8010, Fax: 631-287 8575, E-mail: donna.didonato@liu.edu.

LONG ISLAND UNIVERSITY–HUDSON AT ROCKLAND, Orangeburg, NY 10962

General Information Independent, coed, graduate-only institution. *Enrollment by degree level:* 215 master's, 51 other advanced degrees. *Graduate faculty:* 3 full-time (2 women), 26 part-time/adjunct (13 women). *Tuition, area resident:* Part-time $1155 per credit. *Required fees:* $442 per term. Tuition and fees vary according to degree level and program. *Graduate housing:* On-campus housing not available. *Student services:* Career counseling, low-cost health insurance, services for students with disabilities, teacher training. *Library:* Long Island University Library System. *Collection:* Books: 3,147 (physical), 155,850 (digital/electronic); Serial titles: 94,194 (digital/electronic); Databases: 168.

Computer facilities: A campuswide network can be accessed. Online class registration is available.
Website: http://liu.edu/Hudson

General Application Contact: Sylvia Blake, Dean/Chief Operating Officer, 845-450-5437, E-mail: sylvia.blake@liu.edu.

GRADUATE UNITS

Graduate School Students: 90 full-time (71 women), 176 part-time (134 women); includes 63 minority (26 Black or African American, non-Hispanic/Latino; 10 Asian, non-Hispanic/Latino; 24 Hispanic/Latino; 3 Two or more races, non-Hispanic/Latino). Average age 34. 140 applicants, 96% accepted, 103 enrolled. *Faculty:* 3 full-time (2 women). *Financial support:* Scholarships/grants available. In 2015, 89 master's, 17 other advanced degrees awarded. *Degree program information:* Part-time and evening/weekend programs available. Part-time, evening/weekend, online learning. Offers adolescence education (MS Ed); business (MBA); early childhood education (Advanced Certificate); early childhood/childhood education (MS Ed); early childhood/literacy b-6 (MS); early childhood/special education (MS Ed, Advanced Certificate); educational leadership (MS Ed); long term care (Advanced Certificate); mental health counseling (MS); pharmaceutics (MS); public administration (MPA); school counseling (Advanced Certificate). *Application deadline:* Applications are processed on a rolling basis. *Application fee:* $50. Electronic applications accepted. *Application Contact:* Jeffrey McDowell, Recruitment Manager, 845-450-5414, Fax: 845-359-7248, E-mail: jeffrey.mcdowell@liu.edu. *Dean and Chief Operating Officer*, Dr. Sylvia Blake, 845-450-5437, Fax: 845-359-7248, E-mail: sylvia.blake@liu.edu.

LONG ISLAND UNIVERSITY–HUDSON AT WESTCHESTER, Purchase, NY 10577

General Information Independent, coed, graduate-only institution. *Enrollment by degree level:* 156 master's, 20 other advanced degrees. *Graduate faculty:* 5 full-time (4 women), 27 part-time/adjunct (18 women). *Tuition, area resident:* Part-time $1155 per credit. *Required fees:* $442 per term. Tuition and fees vary according to degree level and program. *Graduate housing:* On-campus housing not available. *Student services:* Career counseling, exercise/wellness program, international student services, low-cost health insurance, teacher training, writing training. *Library:* Long Island University Library System. *Collection:* Books: 155,850 (digital/electronic); Serial titles: 94,194 (digital/electronic); Databases: 168.

Computer facilities: A campuswide network can be accessed. Online class registration is available.
Website: http://liu.edu/Hudson

General Application Contact: Sylvia Blake, Dean, 914-831-2701, Fax: 914-251-5959, E-mail: westchester@liu.edu.

GRADUATE UNITS

Graduate School Students: 50 full-time (35 women), 128 part-time (101 women); includes 40 minority (8 Black or African American, non-Hispanic/Latino; 1 Asian, non-Hispanic/Latino; 31 Hispanic/Latino). Average age 35. *Faculty:* 6 full-time (5 women). In 2015, 58 master's, 15 other advanced degrees awarded. *Degree program information:* Part-time and evening/weekend programs available. Part-time, evening/weekend, online learning. Offers adolescence education (MS Ed); autism (Advanced Certificate); childhood education (MS Ed); finance (MBA); healthcare sector management (MBA); literacy B-12 (MS Ed); management (MBA); mental health counseling (MS); school counselor (Advanced Certificate); school psychology (MS Ed); special education (MS Ed); TESOL (all grades) (MS Ed, Advanced Certificate). *Application deadline:* Applications are processed on a rolling basis. *Application fee:* $50. Electronic applications accepted. *Application Contact:* Cindy Pagnotta, Director of Marketing and Enrollment, 914-831-2701, Fax: 914-251-5959, E-mail: cindy.pagnotta@liu.edu. *Dean and Chief Operating Officer,* Dr. Sylvia Blake, 914-831-2704, Fax: 914-251-5959, E-mail: sylvia.blake@liu.edu.

LONG ISLAND UNIVERSITY–LIU BROOKLYN, Brooklyn, NY 11201-8423

General Information Independent, coed, university. *Enrollment:* 8,170 graduate, professional, and undergraduate students; 1,941 full-time matriculated graduate/professional students (1,295 women), 1,432 part-time matriculated graduate/professional students (1,065 women). *Enrollment by degree level:* 2,651 master's, 634 doctoral, 88 other advanced degrees. *Graduate faculty:* 153 full-time (83 women), 201 part-time/adjunct (108 women). *Tuition, area resident:* Part-time $1155 per credit. *Required fees:* $442 per term. Tuition and fees vary according to degree level, program and student level. *Graduate housing:* Room and/or apartments available on a first-come, first-served basis to single students; on-campus housing not available to married students. Typical cost: $20,248 (including board). Room and board charges vary according to board plan and housing facility selected. Housing application deadline: 5/1. *Student services:* Campus employment opportunities, career counseling, exercise/wellness program, international student services, low-cost health insurance, services for students with disabilities, teacher training, writing training. *Library:* Salena Library. *Collection:* Books: 217,633 (physical), 170,074 (digital/electronic); Serial titles: 327,932 (physical), 94,194 (digital/electronic); Databases: 396. *Research affiliation:* California Table Grape Commission (pharmacy), Latitude Pharmaceuticals, Inc. (pharmacy), National Institute for Pharmaceutical Technology and Education (pharmacy), Natoli Engineering Company (pharmacy), Onconova Therapeutics, Inc. (pharmacy), Transdermal Research Pharm Laboratories, LLC (pharmacy).

Computer facilities: 580 computers available on campus for general student use. A campuswide network can be accessed from student residence rooms and from off campus. Online class registration is available.
Website: http://www.liu.edu/

General Application Contact: Richard Sunday, Dean of Admissions, 718-488-1011, Fax: 718-780-6110, E-mail: bkln-admissions@liu.edu.

GRADUATE UNITS

Arnold and Marie Schwartz College of Pharmacy and Health Sciences Students: 579 full-time (346 women), 29 part-time (14 women); includes 191 minority (24 Black or African American, non-Hispanic/Latino; 1 American Indian or Alaska Native, non-Hispanic/Latino; 144 Asian, non-Hispanic/Latino; 19 Hispanic/Latino; 3 Two or more races, non-Hispanic/Latino), 193 international. Average age 27. 350 applicants, 63% accepted, 65 enrolled. *Faculty:* 49 full-time (25 women), 20 part-time/adjunct (9 women). *Financial support:* In 2015–16, 185 students received support, including 6 fellowships with full tuition reimbursements available (averaging $12,800 per year), 28 teaching assistantships with full tuition reimbursements available (averaging $6,000 per year); Federal Work-Study, institutionally sponsored loans, and scholarships/grants also available. Support available to part-time students. Financial award application deadline: 2/15; financial award applicants required to submit FAFSA. In 2015, 114 master's, 206 doctorates awarded. *Degree program information:* Part-time programs available. Part-time. Offers drug regulatory affairs (MS); pharmaceutics (MS, PhD); pharmacology and toxicology (MS); pharmacy (Pharm D). *Application deadline:* Applications are processed on a rolling basis. *Application fee:* $50. Electronic applications accepted. *Application Contact:* Dr. Anait Levinsont, Associate Dean of Research and Graduate Studies, 718-246-6323, E-mail: anait.levenson@liu.edu. *Dean,* Dr. John M. Pezzuto, 718-488-1004, Fax: 718-488-0628, E-mail: john.pezzuto@liu.edu.

Harriet Rothkopf Heilbrunn School of Nursing Students: 1 (woman) full-time, 215 part-time (192 women); includes 136 minority (89 Black or African American, non-Hispanic/Latino; 28 Asian, non-Hispanic/Latino; 13 Hispanic/Latino; 2 Native Hawaiian or other Pacific Islander, non-Hispanic/Latino; 4 Two or more races, non-Hispanic/Latino), 1 international. Average age 43. 167 applicants, 57% accepted, 63 enrolled. *Faculty:* 6 full-time (4 women), 5 part-time/adjunct (4 women). *Financial support:* In 2015–16, 24 students received support. Scholarships/grants and unspecified assistantships available. Support available to part-time students. Financial award application deadline: 2/15; financial award applicants required to submit FAFSA. In 2015, 23 master's, 5 other advanced degrees awarded. *Degree program information:* Part-time and evening/weekend programs available. Part-time, evening/weekend, blended/hybrid learning. Offers adult nurse practitioner (MS, Advanced Certificate); family nurse practitioner (MS, Advanced Certificate); nurse educator (MS). *Application deadline:* Applications are processed on a rolling basis. *Application fee:* $50. Electronic applications accepted. *Application Contact:* Richard Sunday, Dean of Admissions, 718-488-1011, Fax: 718-780-6110, E-mail: bkln-admissions@liu.edu. *Interim Dean,* Dr. Loretta Knapp, 718-488-1508, Fax: 718-780-4019, E-mail: lori.knapp@liu.edu.

Richard L. Conolly College of Liberal Arts and Sciences Students: 382 full-time (288 women), 223 part-time (154 women); includes 257 minority (129 Black or African American, non-Hispanic/Latino; 33 Asian, non-Hispanic/Latino; 80 Hispanic/Latino; 1 Native Hawaiian or other Pacific Islander, non-Hispanic/Latino; 14 Two or more races, non-Hispanic/Latino), 93 international. Average age 33. 801 applicants, 44% accepted, 169 enrolled. *Faculty:* 90 full-time (35 women), 125 part-time/adjunct (67 women). *Financial support:* In 2015–16, 221 students received support, including 135 fellowships with full tuition reimbursements available (averaging $23,986 per year), 29 research assistantships with partial tuition reimbursements available (averaging $13,860 per year), 185 teaching assistantships with full tuition reimbursements available (averaging $20,790 per year). Financial award application deadline: 2/15; financial award applicants required to submit FAFSA. In 2015, 163 master's, 16 doctorates, 9 other advanced degrees awarded. *Degree program information:* Part-time and evening/weekend programs available. Part-time, evening/weekend, blended/hybrid learning. Offers biology (MA); chemistry (MS); clinical psychology (PhD); communication sciences and disorders (MS); creative writing (MFA); English (MA); media arts (MA, MFA); political science (MA); psychology (MA); social science (MS); speech-language pathology (MS); United Nations (Advanced Certificate); urban studies (MA); writing and production for television (MFA). *Application deadline:* Applications are processed on a rolling basis. *Application fee:* $50. Electronic applications accepted. *Application Contact:* Richard Sunday, Dean of Admissions, 718-488-1011, Fax: 718-780-6110, E-mail: bkln-admissions@liu.edu. *Dean,* Dr. David Cohen, 718-488-1003, E-mail: david.cohen@liu.edu.

School of Business, Public Administration and Information Sciences Students: 298 full-time (178 women), 240 part-time (158 women); includes 319 minority (218 Black or African American, non-Hispanic/Latino; 2 American Indian or Alaska Native, non-Hispanic/Latino; 47 Asian, non-Hispanic/Latino; 46 Hispanic/Latino; 1 Native Hawaiian or other Pacific Islander, non-Hispanic/Latino; 5 Two or more races, non-Hispanic/Latino), 122 international. Average age 33. 756 applicants, 77% accepted, 195 enrolled. *Faculty:* 22 full-time (12 women), 46 part-time/adjunct (10 women). *Financial support:* In 2015–16, 94 students received support. Federal Work-Study, scholarships/grants, and unspecified assistantships available. Support available to part-time students. Financial award application deadline: 2/15; financial award applicants required to submit FAFSA. In 2015, 174 master's, 10 other advanced degrees awarded. *Degree program information:* Part-time and evening/weekend programs available. Part-time, evening/weekend. Offers accounting (MBA); accounting (MS); business administration (MBA); computer science (MS); gerontology (Advanced Certificate); health administration (MPA); human resource management (Advanced Certificate); human resources management (MS); not-for-profit management (Advanced Certificate); public administration (MPA); taxation (MS); United Nations (Advanced Certificate). *Application deadline:* Applications are processed on a rolling basis. *Application fee:* $50. Electronic applications accepted. *Application Contact:* Richard Sunday, Dean of Admissions, 718-488-1011, Fax: 718-780-6110, E-mail: bkln-admissions@liu.edu. *Dean,* Dr. Edward Rogoff, 718-488-1159, E-mail: edward.rogoff@liu.edu.

School of Education Students: 178 full-time (156 women), 613 part-time (465 women); includes 507 minority (265 Black or African American, non-Hispanic/Latino; 1 American Indian or Alaska Native, non-Hispanic/Latino; 32 Asian, non-Hispanic/Latino; 190 Hispanic/Latino; 1 Native Hawaiian or other Pacific Islander, non-Hispanic/Latino; 18 Two or more races, non-Hispanic/Latino), 12 international. Average age 35. 507 applicants, 83% accepted, 299 enrolled. *Faculty:* 21 full-time (14 women), 40 part-time/adjunct (29 women). *Financial support:* In 2015–16, 81 students received support. Research assistantships with partial tuition reimbursements available and teaching assistantships with partial tuition reimbursements available available. Financial award application deadline: 2/15; financial award applicants required to submit FAFSA. In 2015, 189 master's, 14 other advanced degrees awarded. *Degree program information:* Part-time and evening/weekend programs available. Part-time, evening/weekend. Offers adolescence urban education (MS Ed); applied behavior analysis (Advanced Certificate); bilingual education (Advanced Certificate); bilingual school counselor (MS Ed, Advanced Certificate); childhood urban education (MS Ed); childhood/early childhood urban education (MS Ed); early childhood urban education (MS Ed, Advanced Certificate); educational leadership (Advanced Certificate); marriage and family therapy (MS, Advanced Certificate); mental health counseling (MS, Advanced Certificate); school building district leader (Advanced Certificate); school counselor (MS Ed, Advanced Certificate); school psychologist (MS Ed); teaching urban children/adolescents with disabilities (MS Ed); TESOL (MS Ed). *Application deadline:* Applications are processed on a rolling basis. *Application fee:* $50. Electronic applications accepted. *Application Contact:* Richard Sunday, Dean of Admissions, 718-488-1555, Fax: 718-780-6110, E-mail: richard.sunday@liu.edu. *Acting Dean,* Dr. Amy Patraka Ginsberg, 718-488-1055, E-mail: amy.ginsberg@liu.edu.

School of Health Professions Students: 503 full-time (326 women), 112 part-time (82 women); includes 212 minority (117 Black or African American, non-Hispanic/Latino; 35 Asian, non-Hispanic/Latino; 48 Hispanic/Latino; 12 Two or more races, non-Hispanic/Latino), 59 international. Average age 31. 1,154 applicants, 38% accepted, 227 enrolled. *Faculty:* 36 full-time (26 women), 47 part-time/adjunct (19 women). *Financial support:* In 2015–16, 10 research assistantships with partial tuition reimbursements (averaging $12,660 per year), 40 teaching assistantships with partial tuition reimbursements (averaging $12,660 per year) were awarded. Financial award application deadline: 2/15; financial award applicants required to submit FAFSA. In 2015, 228 master's, 41 doctorates awarded. Offers athletic training and sport sciences (MS); exercise science (MS); occupational therapy (MS); physical therapy (DPT); physician assistant (MS); public health (MPH); social work (MSW). *Application deadline:* Applications are processed on a rolling basis. *Application fee:* $50. Electronic applications accepted. *Application Contact:* Richard Sunday, Dean of Admissions, 718-488-1011, Fax: 718-780-6110, E-mail: bkln-admissions@liu.edu. *Dean,* Dr. Barry S. Eckert, 718-780-6578, Fax: 718-780-4561, E-mail: barry.eckert@liu.edu.

LONG ISLAND UNIVERSITY–LIU POST, Brookville, NY 11548-1300

General Information Independent, coed, comprehensive institution. *Enrollment:* 8,623 graduate, professional, and undergraduate students; 1,152 full-time matriculated graduate/professional students (845 women), 1,173 part-time matriculated graduate/professional students (899 women). *Enrollment by degree level:* 1,821 master's, 257 doctoral, 247 other advanced degrees. *Graduate faculty:* 168 full-time (86 women), 199 part-time/adjunct (106 women). *Tuition, area resident:* Part-time $1155 per credit. *Required fees:* $442 per term. Tuition and fees vary according to degree level and program. *Graduate housing:* Room and/or apartments available on a first-come, first-served basis to single students; on-campus housing not available to married students. Typical cost: $17,838 (including board). Room and board charges vary according to board plan and housing facility selected. Housing application deadline: 5/1. *Student services:* Campus employment opportunities, career counseling, child daycare facilities, exercise/wellness program, international student services, low-cost health insurance, services for students with disabilities, teacher training, writing training. *Library:* B. Davis Schwartz Memorial Library. *Collection:* Books: 1.6 million (physical), 170,023 (digital/electronic); Serial titles: 459,188 (physical), 94,194 (digital/electronic); Databases: 383. *Research affiliation:* Structure-ase Inc. (biology).

Computer facilities: 580 computers available on campus for general student use. A campuswide network can be accessed from student residence rooms and from off campus. Online class registration is available.
Website: http://www.liu.edu/

General Application Contact: Marcelle Hicks, Director of Admissions, 516-299-2900 Ext. 3952, Fax: 516-299-2137, E-mail: post-enroll@liu.edu.

GRADUATE UNITS

College of Arts, Communications and Design Students: 130 full-time (93 women), 34 part-time (29 women); includes 30 minority (6 Black or African American, non-Hispanic/Latino; 1 American Indian or Alaska Native, non-Hispanic/Latino; 8 Asian, non-Hispanic/Latino; 13 Hispanic/Latino; 2 Two or more races, non-Hispanic/Latino), 39 international. Average age 29. 173 applicants, 84% accepted, 67 enrolled. *Faculty:* 38 full-time (19 women), 113 part-time/adjunct (67 women). *Financial support:* Fellowships, career-related internships or fieldwork, Federal Work-Study, institutionally sponsored loans, scholarships/grants, and unspecified assistantships available. Support available to part-time students. Financial award application deadline: 2/15; financial award applicants required to submit CSS PROFILE or FAFSA. In 2015, 52 master's awarded. *Degree program information:* Part-time and evening/weekend programs available. Part-time, evening/weekend. Offers art (MA); art education (MS); art therapy and counseling (MA); clinical art therapy (MA); clinical art therapy and counseling (MA); digital game design and development (MA); fine arts and design (MFA); interactive multimedia arts (MA); music education (MA); theatre (MFA). *Application deadline:* Applications are processed on a rolling basis. *Application fee:* $50. Electronic applications accepted. *Application Contact:* Carol Zerah, Director of Graduate Admissions, 516-299-3952, Fax: 516-299-2137, E-mail: post-enroll@liu.edu. *Dean*, Dr. Noel Zahler, 516-299-2395, Fax: 516-299-4180, E-mail: noel.zahler@liu.edu.

College of Education, Information and Technology Students: 440 full-time (373 women), 690 part-time (545 women); includes 250 minority (96 Black or African American, non-Hispanic/Latino; 39 Asian, non-Hispanic/Latino; 105 Hispanic/Latino; 1 Native Hawaiian or other Pacific Islander, non-Hispanic/Latino; 9 Two or more races, non-Hispanic/Latino), 36 international. Average age 32. 875 applicants, 76% accepted, 344 enrolled. *Faculty:* 54 full-time (31 women), 131 part-time/adjunct (49 women). *Financial support:* Career-related internships or fieldwork and Federal Work-Study available. Support available to part-time students. Financial award application deadline: 2/15; financial award applicants required to submit FAFSA. In 2015, 326 master's, 15 doctorates, 62 other advanced degrees awarded. *Degree program information:* Part-time and evening/weekend programs available. Part-time, evening/weekend. Offers adolescence education (MS); archives and records management (AC); art education (MS); childhood education (MS); childhood/special education (MS); clinical mental health counseling (AC); early childhood education (MS); early childhood education/childhood education (MS); educational leadership (AC); educational technology (MS); information studies (PhD); information technology education (MS); interdisciplinary educational studies (Ed D); literacy B-6 (MS); special education (MS Ed); students with disabilities, 7-12 generalist (AC); teaching students with speech language disabilities (MA); TESOL (MA). *Application deadline:* Applications are processed on a rolling basis. *Application fee:* $50. Electronic applications accepted. *Application Contact:* Carol Zerah, Director of Graduate and International Admissions, 516-299-2900 Ext. 3952, Fax: 516-299-3952, E-mail: enroll@cwpost.liu.edu. *Dean*, Dr. Barbara Garii, 516-299-2210, Fax: 516-299-4167, E-mail: barbara.garii@liu.edu.

College of Liberal Arts and Sciences Students: 254 full-time (178 women), 177 part-time (134 women); includes 104 minority (40 Black or African American, non-Hispanic/Latino; 27 Asian, non-Hispanic/Latino; 28 Hispanic/Latino; 1 Native Hawaiian or other Pacific Islander, non-Hispanic/Latino; 8 Two or more races, non-Hispanic/Latino), 44 international. Average age 31. 686 applicants, 47% accepted, 138 enrolled. *Faculty:* 77 full-time (35 women), 36 part-time/adjunct (17 women). *Financial support:* In 2015–16, 48 fellowships (averaging $12,637 per year), 5 research assistantships with full tuition reimbursements were awarded; Federal Work-Study and institutionally sponsored loans also available. Support available to part-time students. Financial award application deadline: 2/15; financial award applicants required to submit FAFSA. In 2015, 135 master's awarded. *Degree program information:* Part-time and evening/weekend programs available. Part-time, evening/weekend, online learning. Offers applied mathematics (MS); behavior analysis (MA); biology (MS); criminal justice (MS); earth science (MS); English (MA); environmental studies (MS); environmental sustainability (MS); genetic counseling (MS); gerontology (Advanced Certificate); health care administration (MPA); history (MA); interdisciplinary studies (MA, MS); mathematics for secondary school teachers (MS); mobile GIS application development (Advanced Certificate); non-profit management (Advanced Certificate); political science (MA); psychology (MA); public administration (MPA). *Application deadline:* Applications are processed on a rolling basis. *Application fee:* $50. Electronic applications accepted. *Application Contact:* Carol Zerah, Director of Graduate Admissions, 516-299-2900 Ext. 3952, Fax: 516-299-2137, E-mail: enroll@cwpost.liu.edu. *Acting Dean*, Dr. Nicholas J. Ramer, 516-299-2233, Fax: 516-299-4140, E-mail: nicholas.ramer@liu.edu.

College of Management Students: 138 full-time (62 women), 86 part-time (30 women); includes 41 minority (12 Black or African American, non-Hispanic/Latino; 16 Asian, non-Hispanic/Latino; 12 Hispanic/Latino; 1 Two or more races, non-Hispanic/Latino), 99 international. Average age 29. 512 applicants, 46% accepted, 64 enrolled. *Faculty:* 38 full-time (14 women), 28 part-time/adjunct (7 women). *Financial support:* In 2015–16, 68 students received support. Research assistantships, career-related internships or fieldwork, Federal Work-Study, institutionally sponsored loans, scholarships/grants, tuition waivers (partial), and unspecified assistantships available. Support available to part-time students. Financial award application deadline: 2/15; financial award applicants required to submit FAFSA. In 2015, 130 master's awarded. *Degree program information:* Part-time and evening/weekend programs available. Part-time, evening/weekend, 100% online, blended/hybrid learning. Offers accountancy (MS); finance (MBA); information systems (MS); international business (MBA); management (MBA); management engineering (MS); marketing (MBA); taxation (MS). *Application deadline:* Applications are processed on a rolling basis. *Application fee:* $50. Electronic applications accepted. *Application Contact:* Carol Zerah, Director of Graduate and International Admissions, 516-299-3952, Fax: 516-299-2137, E-mail: enroll@cwpost.liu.edu. *Dean*, Dr. Robert M. Valli, 516-299-3017, Fax: 516-299-2786, E-mail: rob.valli@liu.edu.

School of Health Professions and Nursing Students: 190 full-time (139 women), 181 part-time (157 women); includes 141 minority (51 Black or African American, non-Hispanic/Latino; 46 Asian, non-Hispanic/Latino; 41 Hispanic/Latino; 3 Two or more races, non-Hispanic/Latino), 47 international. Average age 36. 422 applicants, 64% accepted, 141 enrolled. *Faculty:* 16 full-time (14 women), 46 part-time/adjunct (33 women). *Financial support:* In 2015–16, 6 research assistantships with partial tuition reimbursements were awarded; career-related internships or fieldwork, Federal Work-Study, institutionally sponsored loans, tuition waivers (partial), and unspecified assistantships also available. Support available to part-time students. Financial award application deadline: 2/15; financial award applicants required to submit FAFSA. In 2015, 96 master's, 28 other advanced degrees awarded. *Degree program information:* Part-time and evening/weekend programs available. Part-time, evening/weekend, blended/hybrid learning. Offers biomedical sciences (MS); cardiovascular perfusion (MS); dietetic internship (Advanced Certificate); family nurse practitioner (MS); forensic social work (Advanced Certificate); nursing education (MS); social work (MSW). *Application deadline:* Applications are processed on a rolling basis. *Application fee:* $50. Electronic applications accepted. *Application Contact:* Carol Zerah, Director of Graduate and International Admissions, 516-299-2900 Ext. 3952, Fax: 516-299-2137, E-mail: post-enroll@liu.edu. *Acting Dean*, Dr. Stacy Gropack, 516-299-2486, Fax: 516-299-2527, E-mail: post-shpn@liu.edu.

LONG ISLAND UNIVERSITY–RIVERHEAD, Riverhead, NY 11901

General Information Independent, coed, graduate-only institution. *Enrollment by degree level:* 122 master's, 4 other advanced degrees. *Graduate faculty:* 6 full-time (2 women), 13 part-time/adjunct (8 women). *Graduate housing:* On-campus housing not available. *Student services:* Campus employment opportunities, campus safety program, career counseling, low-cost health insurance, services for students with disabilities. *Library:* LIU Riverhead Library.

Computer facilities: A campuswide network can be accessed from off campus. Online class registration, Online Bill Pay are available.
Website: http://www.liu.edu/Riverhead/

General Application Contact: Jean Conroy, Associate Dean, 631-287-8301, Fax: 631-287-8253, E-mail: jean.conroy@liu.edu.

GRADUATE UNITS

Education Division Students: 14 full-time (all women), 41 part-time (37 women); includes 7 minority (1 Black or African American, non-Hispanic/Latino; 6 Hispanic/Latino). Average age 32. 38 applicants, 84% accepted, 23 enrolled. *Faculty:* 4 full-time (1 woman), 19 part-time/adjunct (9 women). *Financial support:* Institutionally sponsored loans, scholarships/grants, tuition waivers (partial), and unspecified assistantships available. Support available to part-time students. Financial award application deadline: 2/15; financial award applicants required to submit FAFSA. In 2015, 37 master's awarded. *Degree program information:* Part-time programs available. Part-time. Offers childhood education (MS); teaching students with disabilities (MS); TESOL (Advanced Certificate). *Application deadline:* Applications are processed on a rolling basis. *Application fee:* $50. Electronic applications accepted. *Application Contact:* Christina Seifert, Director of Admission, LIU Brentwood and LIU Riverhead, 631-287-8505, Fax: 631-287-8253, E-mail: christina.seifert@liu.edu. *Dean and Chief Operating Officer, LIU Brentwood and LIU Riverhead*, Donna Di Donato, 631-287-8010, Fax: 631-287-8575, E-mail: donna.didonato@liu.edu.

Homeland Security and Terrorism Institute Students: 8 full-time (2 women), 46 part-time (15 women); includes 16 minority (5 Black or African American, non-Hispanic/Latino; 3 Asian, non-Hispanic/Latino; 8 Hispanic/Latino). Average age 42. 37 applicants, 95% accepted, 15 enrolled. *Faculty:* 4 full-time (1 woman), 19 part-time/adjunct (9 women). *Financial support:* Career-related internships or fieldwork and scholarships/grants available. Support available to part-time students. Financial award application deadline: 2/15; financial award applicants required to submit FAFSA. In 2015, 11 master's, 17 other advanced degrees awarded. *Degree program information:* Part-time and evening/weekend programs available. Part-time, evening/weekend, 100% online. Offers cyber security policy (Advanced Certificate); homeland security management (MS, Advanced Certificate). *Application deadline:* Applications are processed on a rolling basis. *Application fee:* $50. Electronic applications accepted. *Application Contact:* Christina Seifert, Director of Admissions, LIU Riverhead and LIU Brentwood, 631-287-8505, Fax: 631-287-8253, E-mail: christina.seifert@liu.edu. *Director of Homeland Security and Terrorism Institute*, Dr. Harvey Kushner, 516-299-2986, Fax: 516-299 2587, E-mail: harvey.kushner@liu.edu.

LONGWOOD UNIVERSITY, Farmville, VA 23909

General Information State-supported, coed, comprehensive institution. CGS member. *Enrollment:* 5,087 graduate, professional, and undergraduate students; 159 full-time matriculated graduate/professional students (140 women), 242 part-time matriculated graduate/professional students (211 women). *Enrollment by degree level:* 401 master's. *Graduate faculty:* 109 full-time (61 women), 20 part-time/adjunct (13 women). Tuition, state resident: part-time $442 per credit hour. Tuition, nonresident: part-time $1030 per credit hour. Tuition and fees vary according to campus/location and program. *Graduate housing:* On-campus housing not available. *Student services:* Campus employment opportunities, campus safety program, career counseling, exercise/wellness program, free psychological counseling, international student services, low-cost health insurance, multicultural affairs office, services for students with disabilities, teacher training, writing training. *Library:* The Janet D. Greenwood Library. *Collection:* Books: 240,059 (physical), 166,897 (digital/electronic); Serial titles: 1,211 (physical), 611 (digital/electronic); Databases: 273. Weekly public service hours: 93.

Computer facilities: 325 computers available on campus for general student use. A campuswide network can be accessed from student residence rooms. Online class registration is available.
Website: http://www.longwood.edu/

General Application Contact: Kathy E. K. Charleston, Assistant Dean of Graduate and Professional Studies, 434-395-2380, Fax: 434-395-2750, E-mail: graduate@longwood.edu.

GRADUATE UNITS

College of Graduate and Professional Studies Students: 159 full-time (140 women), 242 part-time (211 women); includes 54 minority (32 Black or African American, non-Hispanic/Latino; 8 Asian, non-Hispanic/Latino; 8 Hispanic/Latino; 6 Two or more races, non-Hispanic/Latino). 338 applicants, 51% accepted, 116 enrolled. *Faculty:* 109 full-time (61 women), 20 part-time/adjunct (13 women). *Financial support:* Fellowships, research assistantships, career-related internships or fieldwork, Federal Work-Study, and unspecified assistantships available. Support available to part-time students. Financial award applicants required to submit FAFSA. In 2015, 159 master's awarded. *Degree program information:* Part-time and evening/weekend programs available. Part-time, evening/weekend. *Application deadline:* For fall admission, 5/1 priority date for domestic students; for spring admission, 10/1 priority date for domestic students; for summer admission, 2/1 priority date for domestic students. Applications are processed on a rolling basis. *Application fee:* $50. Electronic applications accepted. *Application Contact:* Kathy E. K. Charleston, Assistant Dean, 434-395-2380, Fax: 434-395-2750, E-mail: graduate@longwood.edu. *Dean*, Dr. Jeannine Rajewski Perry, 434-395-2069, Fax: 434-395-2750, E-mail: perryjr@longwood.edu.

College of Business and Economics Students: 3 full-time (2 women), 24 part-time (17 women); includes 2 minority (1 Black or African American, non-Hispanic/Latino; 1 Asian, non-Hispanic/Latino). 24 applicants, 63% accepted, 8 enrolled. *Faculty:* 20 full-time (7 women). *Financial support:* Fellowships, research assistantships, career-related internships or fieldwork, Federal Work-Study, and unspecified assistantships available. Support available to part-time students. Financial award applicants required to submit FAFSA. In 2015, 9 master's awarded. *Degree program information:* Part-time programs available. Part-time, online only, 100% online. Offers general business (MBA); real estate (MBA); retail management (MBA). *Application deadline:* For fall admission, 5/1 priority date for domestic students; for summer admission, 2/1 priority date for domestic students. Applications are processed on a rolling basis. *Application fee:* $50. Electronic applications accepted. *Application Contact:* College of Graduate and Professional Studies, 434-395-2380, Fax: 434-395-2750, E-mail: graduate@longwood.edu. *Assistant Dean and MBA Program Coordinator*, Abigail H. O'Connor, 434-395-2043, E-mail: oconnorah@longwood.edu.

College of Education and Human Services Students: 106 full-time (90 women), 210 part-time (187 women); includes 44 minority (28 Black or African American, non-Hispanic/Latino; 6 Asian, non-Hispanic/Latino; 6 Hispanic/Latino; 4 Two or more races, non-Hispanic/Latino). 313 applicants, 50% accepted, 94 enrolled. *Faculty:* 52 full-time (38 women), 18 part-time/adjunct (13 women). *Financial support:* Fellowships, research assistantships, teaching assistantships, career-related internships or fieldwork, Federal Work-Study, and unspecified assistantships available. Financial award applicants required to submit FAFSA. In 2015, 138 master's awarded. *Degree program information:* Part-time and evening/weekend programs available. Part-time, evening/weekend. Offers communication sciences and disorders (MS); education (MS); reading, literacy and learning (M Ed); school librarianship (M Ed); social work and communication sciences and disorders (MS). *Application deadline:* For fall admission, 5/1 priority date for domestic students; for spring admission, 10/1 priority date for domestic students; for summer admission, 2/1 priority date for domestic students. Applications are processed on a rolling basis. *Application fee:* $50. Electronic applications accepted. *Application Contact:* College of Graduate and Professional Studies, 434-395-2380, Fax: 434-395-2750, E-mail: graduate@longwood.edu. *Dean, College of Education and Human Services*, Dr. Paul E. Chapman, 434-395-2051, E-mail: chapmanpe@longwood.edu.

LORAS COLLEGE, Dubuque, IA 52004-0178

General Information Independent-religious, coed, comprehensive institution. *Graduate housing:* On-campus housing not available.

GRADUATE UNITS

Graduate Division ***Degree program information:*** Part-time and evening/weekend programs available. Part-time, evening/weekend. Offers applied psychology (MA); educational leadership (MA); instructional strategist I K-6 and 7-12 (MA); ministry (MA); theology (MA).

LOUISIANA COLLEGE, Pineville, LA 71359-0001

General Information Independent-religious, coed, comprehensive institution.

GRADUATE UNITS

Caskey School of Divinity Offers biblical and theological studies (MA); pastoral ministry (MA).

Graduate Programs

LOUISIANA STATE UNIVERSITY AND AGRICULTURAL & MECHANICAL COLLEGE, Baton Rouge, LA 70803

General Information State-supported, coed, university. CGS member. *Graduate housing:* Rooms and/or apartments available on a first-come, first-served basis to single and married students. Housing application deadline: 3/15. *Student services:* Campus employment opportunities, campus safety program, career counseling, child daycare facilities, exercise/wellness program, free psychological counseling, grant writing training, international student services, low-cost health insurance, services for students with disabilities, teacher training, writing training. *Library:* Troy H. Middleton Library plus 4 others. *Collection:* Books: 3.1 million (physical), 502,101 (digital/electronic); Serial titles: 632,059 (physical), 191,565 (digital/electronic); Databases: 352. Study areas open 24 hours, 5–7 days a week; students can reserve study rooms. *Research affiliation:* Arctic Research Consortium of the U.S., Organization for Tropical Studies, Coalition for Academic Scientific Computing, Albert Einstein Institute, Inter-University Consortium for Political and Social Research, Laser Interferometer Gravitational Wave Observatory.

Computer facilities: 1,180 computers available on campus for general student use. A campuswide network can be accessed from student residence rooms and from off campus. Online class registration, free software for download, storage, discounts on hardware, virtual computer lab are available.
Website: http://www.lsu.edu/

General Application Contact: Dr. Renee Renegar, Director of Graduate School, 225-578-1128, Fax: 225-578-1370, E-mail: rreneg1@lsu.edu.

GRADUATE UNITS

Graduate School

College of Agriculture Offers agricultural economics and agribusiness (MS, PhD); agriculture (M App St, MS, PhD); animal sciences (MS, PhD); applied statistics (M App St); entomology (MS, PhD); fisheries (MS); food science (MS, PhD); forestry (MS, PhD); human ecology (MS, PhD); plant health (MS, PhD); plant, environmental and soil sciences (MS, PhD); wildlife (MS); wildlife and fisheries science (PhD).

College of Art and Design Offers architecture (M Arch); art and design (M Arch, M Sc, MA, MFA, MLA); art history (MA); ceramics (MFA); digital media arts and engineering (M Sc); graphic design (MFA); landscape architecture (MLA); painting and drawing (MFA); photography (MFA); printmaking (MFA); sculpture (MFA); studio art (MFA).

College of Engineering Offers biological and agricultural engineering (MSBAE); chemical engineering (MS Ch E, PhD); computer science (MSSS, PhD); construction management (MS, PhD); electrical and computer engineering (MSEE, PhD); engineering (MS, MS Ch E, MS Pet E, MSBAE, MSCE, MSEE, MSES, MSME, MSSS, PhD); engineering science (MS, PhD); environmental engineering (MSCE, PhD); geotechnical engineering (MSCE, PhD); mechanical and industrial engineering (MSME, PhD); petroleum engineering (MS Pet E, PhD); structural engineering and mechanics (MSCE, PhD); systems science (MSSS); transportation engineering (MSCE, PhD); water resources (MSCE, PhD).

College of Humanities and Social Sciences Offers biological psychology (MA, PhD); clinical psychology (MA, PhD); cognitive psychology (MA, PhD); communication sciences and disorders (MA, PhD); communication studies (MA, PhD); comparative literature (MA, PhD); creative writing (MFA); developmental psychology (MA, PhD); English (MA, PhD); French literature and linguistics (MA, PhD); geography (MA, MS); geography and anthropology (PhD); Hispanic studies (MA); history (MA, PhD); humanities and social sciences (MA, MALA, MFA, MS, PhD); liberal arts (MALA); philosophy (MA); political science (MA, PhD); school psychology (MA, PhD); sociology (MA, PhD).

College of Human Sciences and Education Offers agriculture and extension education and youth development (MS, PhD); career and technical education (MS, PhD); comprehensive vocational education (MS, PhD); counseling (M Ed, MA, Ed S); educational administration (M Ed, MA, PhD, Ed S); educational technology (MA); elementary education (M Ed, MAT); extension and international education (MS, PhD); higher education (PhD); human resource and leadership development (MS, PhD); human sciences and education (M Ed, MA, MAT, MLIS, MS, MSW, PhD, Ed S); industrial education (MS); kinesiology (MS, PhD); library and information science (MLIS); research methodology (PhD); secondary education (M Ed, MAT); social work (MSW, PhD); vocational agriculture education (MS, PhD); vocational business education (MS); vocational home economics education (MS).

College of Music and Dramatic Arts Offers acting (MFA); directing (MFA); music (MM, DMA, PhD); music and dramatic arts (MFA, MM, DMA, PhD); music education (PhD); theatre (PhD); theatre design/technology (MFA).

College of Science Offers astronomy (PhD); astrophysics (PhD); biochemistry (MS, PhD); biological science (MS, PhD); chemistry (MS, PhD); geology and geophysics (MS, PhD); mathematics (MS, PhD); medical physics (MS); natural sciences (MNS); physics (MS, PhD); science (MNS).

E. J. Ourso College of Business Offers accounting (MS, PhD); business (EMBA, MBA, MPA, MS, PMBA, PhD); business administration (PhD); economics (MS, PhD); finance (MS); information systems and decision sciences (MS, PhD); public administration (MPA).

Manship School of Mass Communication Offers mass communication (MMC, PhD).

School of the Coast and Environment Offers environmental planning and management (MS); environmental science (PhD); environmental toxicology (MS); oceanography and coastal sciences (MS, PhD); the coast and environment (MS, PhD).

Paul M. Hebert Law Center Offers law (LL M, JD). Electronic applications accepted.

School of Veterinary Medicine Offers comparative biomedical sciences (MS, PhD); pathobiological sciences (MS, PhD); veterinary clinical sciences (MS, PhD); veterinary medicine (MS, DVM, PhD).

LOUISIANA STATE UNIVERSITY HEALTH SCIENCES CENTER, New Orleans, LA 70112-2223

General Information State-supported, coed, university. CGS member. *Graduate housing:* Rooms and/or apartments available to single and married students. Housing application deadline: 6/1.

GRADUATE UNITS

School of Allied Health Professions Offers allied health professions (MCD, MHS, MOT, MPAS, Au D, DPT); audiology (Au D); clinical rehabilitation and counseling (MHS); occupational therapy (MOT); physical therapy (DPT); physician assistant studies (MPAS); speech pathology (MCD).

School of Dentistry Offers dentistry (DDS).

School of Graduate Studies in New Orleans Students: 70 full-time (36 women), 2 part-time (1 woman); includes 17 minority (5 Black or African American, non-Hispanic/Latino; 8 Asian, non-Hispanic/Latino; 4 Hispanic/Latino), 14 international. Average age 26. 75 applicants, 28% accepted, 15 enrolled. *Faculty:* 159 full-time (45 women). *Financial support:* Unspecified assistantships available. In 2015, 21 doctorates awarded. Offers cell biology and anatomy (PhD); human genetics (PhD); medicine (PhD); microbiology and immunology (PhD); neuroscience (PhD); pharmacology and experimental therapeutics (PhD); physiology (PhD). *Application deadline:* For fall admission, 4/1 for domestic and international students. Applications are processed on a rolling basis. *Application fee:* $30. *Application Contact:* Leigh A. Smith-Vaniz, Coordinator of Student Affairs, 504-568-2211, Fax: 504-568-5588, E-mail: lsmi30@lsuhsc.edu. *Head*, Dr. Joseph M. Moerschbaecher, III, 504-568-2211, Fax: 504-568-2361.

School of Medicine in New Orleans Offers medicine (MPH, MD). Open only to Louisiana residents. Electronic applications accepted.

School of Nursing Students: 254 (185 women); includes 68 minority (44 Black or African American, non-Hispanic/Latino; 12 Asian, non-Hispanic/Latino; 12 Hispanic/Latino). Average age 33. 144 applicants, 54% accepted, 73 enrolled. *Faculty:* 22 full-time (19 women), 21 part-time/adjunct (8 women). *Financial support:* Federal Work-Study, institutionally sponsored loans, scholarships/grants, and traineeships available. Financial award applicants required to submit FAFSA. In 2015, 84 master's, 6 doctorates awarded. *Degree program information:* Part-time programs available. Part-time. Offers adult gerontology clinical nurse specialist (Post-Master's Certificate); clinical nurse leader (MSN); executive nurse leader (Post-Master's Certificate); neonatal nurse practitioner (Post-Master's Certificate); nurse anesthesia (Post-Master's Certificate); nurse educator (MSN); nursing (DNS); primary care family nurse practitioner (Post-Master's Certificate); public/community health nursing (Post-Master's Certificate). *Application deadline:* Applications are processed on a rolling basis. *Application fee:* $250. Electronic applications accepted. *Application Contact:* Tracie Gravolet, Director, Office of Student Affairs, 504-568-4114, Fax: 504-568-5711, E-mail: tgravo@lsuhsc.edu. *Dean*, Dr. Demetrius James Porche, 504-568-4106, Fax: 504-599-0573, E-mail: dporch@lsuhsc.edu.

School of Public Health ***Degree program information:*** Part-time programs available. Part-time. Offers behavioral and community health sciences (MPH); biostatistics (MPH, MS, PhD); community health sciences (PhD); environmental and occupational health sciences (MPH); epidemiology (MPH, PhD); health policy and systems management (MPH).

LOUISIANA STATE UNIVERSITY HEALTH SCIENCES CENTER AT SHREVEPORT, Shreveport, LA 71130-3932

General Information State-supported, coed, university. *Research affiliation:* Pennington Biomedical Research Center (metabolic disorders/obesity).

GRADUATE UNITS

Department of Biochemistry and Molecular Biology Students: 12 full-time (6 women), 10 international. Average age 28. 16 applicants, 31% accepted, 3 enrolled. *Faculty:* 13 full-time (3 women). *Financial support:* In 2015–16, 3 fellowships (averaging $28,000 per year), 9 research assistantships (averaging $26,000 per year) were awarded. In 2015, 1 master's, 3 doctorates awarded. Offers biochemistry and molecular biology (MS, PhD). *Application deadline:* For fall admission, 3/15 for domestic and international students. Applications are processed on a rolling basis. Electronic applications accepted. *Application Contact:* April Coutee, Coordinator, 318-675-5160,

Fax: 318-675-5180, E-mail: admissions-bmb@lsuhsc.edu. *Interim Head*, Dr. Stephan N. Witt, 318-675-5161, Fax: 318-675-5180.

Department of Cellular Biology and Anatomy Offers cellular biology and anatomy (MS, PhD).

Department of Microbiology and Immunology Students: 17 full-time (9 women), 2 international. Average age 27. 9 applicants, 100% accepted, 7 enrolled. *Faculty:* 13 full-time (3 women). *Financial support:* In 2015–16, 20 students received support, including 20 fellowships with full tuition reimbursements available (averaging $26,000 per year); institutionally sponsored loans, scholarships/grants, and tuition waivers (for all full-time PhD students) also available. Financial award application deadline: 1/31. In 2015, 5 master's, 5 doctorates awarded. Offers microbiology and immunology (MS, PhD). *Application deadline:* For fall admission, 1/31 for domestic and international students. *Application fee:* $0. Electronic applications accepted. *Application Contact:* Marti Glass, Administrative Coordinator, 318-675-7851 Ext. 4781, Fax: 318-675-5764, E-mail: mglass@lsuhsc.edu. *Head*, Dr. Dennis J. O'Callaghan, 318-675-5750, Fax: 318-675-5764.

Department of Molecular and Cellular Physiology Students: 14 full-time (8 women); includes 8 minority (1 Black or African American, non-Hispanic/Latino; 7 Asian, non-Hispanic/Latino). Average age 29. 13 applicants, 46% accepted, 5 enrolled. *Faculty:* 8 full-time (4 women), 3 part-time/adjunct (1 woman). *Financial support:* Fellowships with full tuition reimbursements, institutionally sponsored loans, and unspecified assistantships available. In 2015, 1 master's, 1 doctorate awarded. Offers physiology (MS, PhD). *Application deadline:* For fall admission, 1/31 priority date for domestic and international students. *Application fee:* $0. *Application Contact:* Deborah Fausto, Coordinator, 318-675-6011, Fax: 318-675-6005, E-mail: dfaust1@lsuhsc.edu. *Head*, Dr. D. Neil Granger, 318-675-6011, Fax: 318-675-6005, E-mail: dgrang@lsuhsc.edu.

Department of Pharmacology, Toxicology and Neuroscience Students: 15 full-time (11 women); includes 2 minority (1 Black or African American, non-Hispanic/Latino; 1 Asian, non-Hispanic/Latino), 2 international. Average age 25. 16 applicants, 25% accepted, 4 enrolled. *Faculty:* 10 full-time (2 women), 5 part-time/adjunct (3 women). *Financial support:* In 2015–16, 3 fellowships with full tuition reimbursements (averaging $28,000 per year), 9 research assistantships with full tuition reimbursements (averaging $24,000 per year) were awarded; institutionally sponsored loans also available. Financial award application deadline: 5/1. In 2015, 1 master's, 1 doctorate awarded. Offers pharmacology (PhD). *Application deadline:* For fall admission, 2/1 priority date for domestic students, 2/1 for international students. *Application fee:* $0. *Application Contact:* Ty E. Martinez, Academic Coordinator, 318-675-7851, Fax: 318-675-7857, E-mail: tmoren@lsuhsc.edu. *Head*, Dr. Nicholas E. Goeders, 318-675-7850, Fax: 318-675-7857, E-mail: ngoede@lsuhsc.edu.

Master of Science in Biomedical Sciences Program Offers biomedical sciences (MS).

School of Medicine Offers medicine (MD).

LOUISIANA STATE UNIVERSITY IN SHREVEPORT, Shreveport, LA 71115-2399

General Information State-supported, coed, comprehensive institution. *Enrollment:* 4,428 graduate, professional, and undergraduate students; 404 full-time matriculated graduate/professional students (254 women), 1,189 part-time matriculated graduate/professional students (745 women). *Enrollment by degree level:* 1,529 master's, 47 doctoral, 17 other advanced degrees. Tuition, state resident: part-time $325 per credit hour. Tuition, nonresident: part-time $1019 per credit hour. *Required fees:* $52 per credit hour. Tuition and fees vary according to program. *Student services:* Campus employment opportunities, career counseling, exercise/wellness program, free psychological counseling, multicultural affairs office, services for students with disabilities, teacher training. *Library:* Noel Memorial Library. *Collection:* Databases: 142. Weekly public service hours: 71; students can reserve study rooms. *Research affiliation:* Micromanufacturing Institute (manufacturing technology), Department of Agriculture (crop science), Louisiana Manufacturing Science Center (robotics), Biomedical Research Institute, Cotton, Incorporated (plant physiology).

Computer facilities: A campuswide network can be accessed from off campus. Online class registration is available.
Website: http://www.lsus.edu/

General Application Contact: Jolie Banks, Data Coordinator, 318-798-4112, Fax: 318-798-4120, E-mail: jolie.banks@lsus.edu.

GRADUATE UNITS

College of Arts and Sciences Students: 51 full-time (33 women), 53 part-time (39 women); includes 32 minority (20 Black or African American, non-Hispanic/Latino; 4 Asian, non-Hispanic/Latino; 3 Hispanic/Latino; 5 Two or more races, non-Hispanic/Latino), 5 international. Average age 32. 172 applicants, 95% accepted, 33 enrolled. *Financial support:* Unspecified assistantships available. Financial award applicants required to submit FAFSA. In 2015, 40 master's awarded. *Degree program information:* Part-time and evening/weekend programs available. Part-time, evening/weekend. Offers arts and sciences (MA, MS); biological sciences (MS); computer systems technology (MS); liberal arts (MA); nonprofit administration (MS). *Application deadline:* For fall admission, 6/30 for domestic and international students; for spring admission, 11/30 for domestic and international students; for summer admission, 4/30 for domestic and international students. Applications are processed on a rolling basis. *Application fee:* $20 ($30 for international students). Electronic applications accepted. *Application Contact:* David Stanford, Director of Admissions, 318-795-2403, Fax: 318-797-5286, E-mail: david.stanford@lsus.edu. *Dean*, Dr. Larry Anderson, 318-797-5371, Fax: 318-797-5358, E-mail: larry.anderson@lsus.edu.

College of Business, Education, and Human Development Students: 353 full-time (221 women), 840 part-time (410 women); includes 533 minority (378 Black or African American, non-Hispanic/Latino; 7 American Indian or Alaska Native, non-Hispanic/Latino; 43 Asian, non-Hispanic/Latino; 65 Hispanic/Latino; 3 Native Hawaiian or other Pacific Islander, non-Hispanic/Latino; 37 Two or more races, non-Hispanic/Latino), 40 international. Average age 33. 1,106 applicants, 93% accepted, 341 enrolled. *Financial support:* Research assistantships available. Financial award applicants required to submit FAFSA. In 2015, 77 master's, 4 other advanced degrees awarded. *Degree program information:* Part-time programs available. Part-time. Offers business administration (MBA); business, education, and human development (M Ed, MBA, MHA, MPH, MS, Ed D, SSP); counseling (MS); curriculum and instruction (M Ed); educational leadership (M Ed); health administration (MHA); public health (MPH); school counseling (M Ed); school psychology (SSP). *Application deadline:* For fall admission, 6/30 for domestic and international students; for spring admission, 10/30 for domestic students, 11/30 for international students; for summer admission, 4/30 for domestic and international students. Applications are processed on a rolling basis. *Application fee:* $20 ($30 for international students). Electronic applications accepted. *Application Contact:* David Stanford, Director, Admissions, 318-795-2403, Fax: 318-797-5286, E-mail: david.stanford@lsus.edu. *Associate Dean*, Dr. Douglas Bible, 318-797-5383, Fax: 318-797-5176, E-mail: douglas.bible@lsus.edu.

LOUISIANA TECH UNIVERSITY, Ruston, LA 71272

General Information State-supported, coed, university. *Enrollment:* 12,371 graduate, professional, and undergraduate students; 928 full-time matriculated graduate/professional students (532 women), 403 part-time matriculated graduate/professional students (237 women). *Enrollment by degree level:* 1,185 master's, 146 doctoral. *Graduate housing:* Rooms and/or apartments guaranteed to single students and available on a first-come, first-served basis to married students. Housing application deadline: 7/15. *Student services:* Campus employment opportunities, career counseling, exercise/wellness program, free psychological counseling, international student services, low-cost health insurance, multicultural affairs office, services for students with disabilities. *Library:* Prescott Memorial Library.

Computer facilities: A campuswide network can be accessed from student residence rooms and from off campus.
Website: http://www.latech.edu/

General Application Contact: Dr. Sheryl S. Shoemaker, Dean of the Graduate School, 318-257-2924, Fax: 318-257-4487, E-mail: sshoemaker@latech.edu.

GRADUATE UNITS

Graduate School Students: 928 full-time (532 women), 403 part-time (237 women); includes 512 minority (436 Black or African American, non-Hispanic/Latino; 15 American Indian or Alaska Native, non-Hispanic/Latino; 48 Asian, non-Hispanic/Latino; 13 Hispanic/Latino), 206 international. *Financial support:* Fellowships, research assistantships, teaching assistantships, career-related internships or fieldwork, Federal Work-Study, institutionally sponsored loans, tuition waivers (partial), and unspecified assistantships available. In 2015, 434 master's, 41 doctorates awarded. *Degree program information:* Part-time programs available. Part-time. *Application deadline:* For fall admission, 8/1 for domestic students, 6/1 for international students; for winter admission, 11/1 for domestic students, 9/1 for international students; for spring admission, 2/1 for domestic students, 12/1 for international students; for summer admission, 5/1 for domestic students, 3/1 for international students. *Application fee:* $40. *Application Contact:* Marilyn J. Robinson, Assistant to the Dean, 318-257-2924, Fax: 318-257-4487. *Dean*, Dr. Sheryl S. Shoemaker, 318-257-2924, Fax: 318-257-4487, E-mail: sshoemaker@latech.edu.

College of Applied and Natural Sciences *Financial support:* Fellowships, research assistantships, teaching assistantships, career-related internships or fieldwork, and Federal Work-Study available. Financial award application deadline: 2/1. *Degree program information:* Part-time programs available. Part-time. Offers applied and natural sciences (MHI, MS); biology (MS); health informatics (MHI); molecular sciences and nanotechnology (MS); nutrition and dietetics (MS). *Application deadline:* For fall admission, 7/29 priority date for domestic students; for spring admission, 2/3 for domestic students. Applications are processed on a rolling basis. *Application fee:* $20 ($30 for international students). *Dean*, Dr. Gary A. Kennedy, 318-257-4287, Fax: 318-257-5060, E-mail: kennedy@latech.edu.

College of Business *Financial support:* Fellowships, research assistantships, and teaching assistantships available. *Degree program information:* Part-time programs available. Part-time. Offers accounting (MPA, DBA); business (MBA, MPA, DBA); finance (MBA, DBA); finance and economics (DBA). *Application deadline:* For fall admission, 7/29 for domestic students; for spring admission, 2/3 for domestic students. *Application fee:* $20 ($30 for international students). *Application Contact:* Marilyn J. Robinson, Assistant to the Dean, 318-257-2924, Fax: 318-257-4487. *Dean*, Dr. Christopher D. Martin, 318-257-4526, Fax: 318-257-4253.

College of Education *Financial support:* Fellowships, research assistantships, teaching assistantships, and career-related internships or fieldwork available. Financial award application deadline: 2/1. *Degree program information:* Part-time programs available. Part-time. Offers administration of sport and physical activity (MS); counseling and guidance (MA); counseling psychology (PhD); curriculum and instruction (M Ed); education (M Ed, MA, MS, Ed D, PhD); educational leadership (M Ed, Ed D); industrial and organizational psychology (MA, PhD); sports performance (MS). *Application deadline:* For fall admission, 7/29 for domestic students; for spring admission, 2/3 for domestic students. *Application fee:* $20 ($30 for international students). *Application Contact:* Dr. Cathy Stockton, Associate Dean of Graduate Studies, 318-257-3229, Fax: 318-257-2379, E-mail: cstock@latech.edu. *Dean*, Don Schillinger, 318-257-3712.

College of Engineering and Science *Financial support:* Fellowships, research assistantships, teaching assistantships, career-related internships or fieldwork, Federal Work-Study, tuition waivers (partial), and unspecified assistantships available. Financial award application deadline: 4/1. *Degree program information:* Part-time programs available. Part-time. Offers applied physics (MS); biomedical engineering (MS, PhD); chemical engineering (MS, PhD); chemistry (MS); civil engineering (MS, PhD); computational analysis and modeling (PhD); computer science (MS); electrical engineering (MS, PhD); engineering and science (MS, PhD); industrial engineering (MS); mathematics and statistics (MS); mechanical engineering (MS, PhD). *Application deadline:* For fall admission, 8/1 for domestic students; for spring admission, 2/1 for domestic students. Applications are processed on a rolling basis. *Application fee:* $20 ($30 for international students). *Application Contact:* Marilyn J. Robinson, Assistant to the Dean, 318-257-2924, Fax: 318-257-4487. *Dean*, Dr. Hisham Hegab, 318-257-4647, Fax: 318-257-2562, E-mail: hhegab@latech.edu.

College of Liberal Arts *Financial support:* Fellowships, research assistantships, teaching assistantships, career-related internships or fieldwork, Federal Work-Study, institutionally sponsored loans, tuition waivers (partial), and unspecified assistantships available. Financial award application deadline: 2/1. *Degree program information:* Part-time programs available. Part-time. Offers architecture (M Arch, D Arch); audiology (Au D); English (MA); graphic design (MFA); history (MA); liberal arts (M Arch, MA, MFA, Au D, D Arch, Graduate Certificate); photography (MFA); speech-language pathology (MA); studio (MFA); technical writing (Graduate Certificate); theatre (MA). *Application deadline:* For fall admission, 7/29 for domestic students; for spring admission, 2/3 for domestic students. Applications are processed on a rolling basis. *Application fee:* $40. *Application Contact:* Mary Green, Administrative Assistant, 318-257-2924, Fax: 318-257-4487, E-mail: meg@latech.edu. *Dean*, Dr. Donald P. Kaczvinsky, 318-257-4805, Fax: 318-257-3935, E-mail: dkaczv@latech.edu.

LOUISVILLE PRESBYTERIAN THEOLOGICAL SEMINARY, Louisville, KY 40205-1798

General Information Independent-religious, coed, graduate-only institution. *Enrollment by degree level:* 114 master's, 56 doctoral. *Graduate faculty:* 16 full-time (8 women), 13 part-time/adjunct (6 women). *Tuition, area resident:* Full-time $11,400; part-time $380 per credit hour. *Required fees:* $286; $286 per unit. $143 per semester. *Graduate housing:* Rooms and/or apartments available on a first-come, first-served basis to single and married students. Typical cost: $6132 per year for single students; $7644 per year for married students. Room charges vary according to housing facility selected. Housing application deadline: 4/15. *Student services:* Campus employment opportunities, career counseling, international student services, services for students with disabilities, writing training. *Library:* E.M. White Library. *Collection:* Books: 194,503 (physical), 100 (digital/electronic). Students can reserve study rooms. *Research affiliation:* Louisville Institute (American religion).

Computer facilities: 22 computers available on campus for general student use.
Website: http://www.lpts.edu/

General Application Contact: Rev. Emily Miller, Director of Admissions, 502-895-3411 Ext. 371, Fax: 502-895-1096, E-mail: emiller@lpts.edu.

GRADUATE UNITS

Graduate and Professional Programs Students: 105 full-time (63 women), 65 part-time (32 women); includes 49 minority (38 Black or African American, non-Hispanic/Latino; 1 American Indian or Alaska Native, non-Hispanic/Latino; 3 Asian, non-Hispanic/Latino; 7 Hispanic/Latino), 3 international. Average age 40. *Faculty:* 17 full-time (7 women), 20 part-time/adjunct (9 women). *Financial support:* Career-related internships or fieldwork, Federal Work-Study, institutionally sponsored loans, and scholarships/grants available. Financial award application deadline: 2/1; financial award applicants required to submit FAFSA. *Degree program information:* Part-time programs available. Part-time. Offers Bible (MAR); divinity (M Div); ministry (D Min); religious thought (MAR). JD/M Div, M Div/MBA, and M Div/MSSW offered jointly with University of Louisville. *Application deadline:* For fall admission, 6/15 priority date for domestic students, 2/1 priority date for international students; for spring admission, 11/15 priority date for domestic students, 11/15 for international students. Applications are processed on a rolling basis. *Application fee:* $50. Electronic applications accepted. *Application Contact:* Rev. Emily Miller, Director of Admissions, 502-895-3411, Fax: 502-895-1096, E-mail: emiller@lpts.edu. *Dean*, Dr. Susan R. Garrett, 502-895-3411, Fax: 502-895-1096, E-mail: sgarrett@lpts.edu.

LOURDES UNIVERSITY, Sylvania, OH 43560-2898

General Information Independent-religious, coed, comprehensive institution. CGS member. *Graduate housing:* Rooms and/or apartments available to single and married students. Housing application deadline: 5/1.

GRADUATE UNITS

Graduate School *Degree program information:* Evening/weekend programs available. Evening/weekend. Offers business (MBA); leadership (M Ed); nurse anesthesia (MSN); nurse educator (MSN); nurse leader (MSN); organizational leadership (MOL); reading (M Ed); teaching and curriculum (M Ed); theology (MA).

LOYOLA MARYMOUNT UNIVERSITY, Los Angeles, CA 90045-2659

General Information Independent-religious, coed, comprehensive institution. CGS member. *Enrollment:* 9,392 graduate, professional, and undergraduate students; 2,760 full-time matriculated graduate/professional students (1,701 women), 611 part-time matriculated graduate/professional students (351 women). *Enrollment by degree level:* 1,789 master's, 1,242 doctoral, 340 other advanced degrees. *Graduate faculty:* 331 full-time (133 women), 139 part-time/adjunct (86 women). *Graduate housing:* Room and/or apartments available on a first-come, first-served basis to single students; on-campus housing not available to married students. *Student services:* Campus employment opportunities, career counseling, child daycare facilities, exercise/wellness program, free psychological counseling, international student services, low-cost health insurance, multicultural affairs office, services for students with disabilities, teacher training. *Library:* William H. Hannon Library. *Collection:* Books: 648,576 (physical), 411,484 (digital/electronic); Serial titles: 964 (physical), 43,751 (digital/electronic); Databases: 188. Weekly public service hours: 146; study areas open 24 hours, 5–7 days a week; students can reserve study rooms.

Computer facilities: Computer purchase and lease plans are available. 820 computers available on campus for general student use. A campuswide network can be accessed from student residence rooms and from off campus. Online class registration is available.
Website: http://www.lmu.edu/

General Application Contact: Chake H. Kouyoumjian, Associate Dean of Graduate Studies, 310-338-2721, Fax: 310-338-6086, E-mail: ckouyoum@lmu.edu.

GRADUATE UNITS

College of Business Administration Offers accounting (MS); business administration (MBA, MS); executive business administration (MBA). *Application Contact:* Chake H Kouyoumjian, Associate Dean of Graduate Studies, 310-338-2721, E-mail: ckouyoum@lmu.edu. *Associate Dean, Graduate Programs*, Dr. Jack Gregg, 310-338-2848, Fax: 310-338-2899, E-mail: jack.gregg@lmu.edu.

College of Fine Arts Offers fine arts (MA); marital and family therapy (MA). *Application Contact:* Chake H. Kouyoumjian, Associate Dean of Graduate Studies, 310-338-2721, E-mail: ckouyoum@lmu.edu. *Dean*, Dr. Bryant Keith Alexander, 310-338-7430, E-mail: bryantkeithalexander@lmu.edu.

College of Liberal Arts Offers English (MA); liberal arts (MA); pastoral theology (MA); philosophy (MA); theology (MA); yoga studies (MA). *Application Contact:* Chake H. Kouyoumjian, Associate Dean of Graduate Studies, 310-338-2721, E-mail: ckouyoum@lmu.edu. *Dean*, Dr. Robin D. Crabtree, 310-338-2716, E-mail: rcrabtr1@lmu.edu.

The Bioethics Institute Offers bioethics (MA). *Application Contact:* Chake H. Kouyoumjian, Associate Dean of Graduate Studies, 310-338-2721, E-mail: ckouyoum@lmu.edu. *Director, Bioethics Institute*, Dr. Roberto Dell'Oro, 310-338-2752, E-mail: rdelloro@lmu.edu.

College of Science and Engineering Offers civil engineering (MSE); environmental science (MS); mechanical engineering (MSE); science and engineering (MAT, MS, MSE); system engineering leadership (MS); systems engineering (MS); teaching in mathematics (MAT). *Application Contact:* Chake H. Kouyoumjian, Associate Dean of Graduate Studies, 310-338-2721, E-mail: ckouyoum@lmu.edu. *Dean*, Dr. Tina Choe, 310-338-2834, E-mail: tchoe@lmu.edu.

Loyola Law School Los Angeles Students: 830 full-time (451 women), 197 part-time (100 women); includes 450 minority (43 Black or African American, non-Hispanic/Latino; 6 American Indian or Alaska Native, non-Hispanic/Latino; 144 Asian, non-Hispanic/Latino; 211 Hispanic/Latino; 46 Two or more races, non-Hispanic/Latino), 68 international. Average age 25. 3,627 applicants, 42% accepted, 268 enrolled. *Faculty:* 62 full-time (31 women), 62 part-time/adjunct (22 women). *Financial support:* Research assistantships, Federal Work-Study, and scholarships/grants available. Financial award application deadline: 3/15; financial award applicants required to submit FAFSA. In 2015, 45 master's, 407 doctorates awarded. *Degree program information:* Part-time and evening/weekend programs available. Part-time, evening/weekend. Offers law (LL M, MLS, JD, JSD); tax (LL M in Tax). *Application deadline:* For fall admission, 2/1 for domestic and international students. Applications are processed on a rolling basis. *Application fee:* $0. Electronic applications accepted. *Application Contact:* Jannell Lundy Roberts, Assistant Dean, Admissions, 213-736-1074, Fax: 213-736-6523, E-mail: admissions@lls.edu. *Interim Dean*, Paul Hayden, 213-736-1064, Fax: 213-487-6736, E-mail: paul.hayden@lls.edu.

School of Education Offers bilingual elementary education (MA); bilingual secondary education (MA); Catholic inclusive education (MA); Catholic school administration (MA); counseling (MA); education (MA, Ed D); educational leadership (MA); educational leadership for social justice (Ed D); educational studies (MA); elementary education (MA); guidance and counseling (MA); higher education administration (MA); literacy education (MA); literacy/language arts (MA); reading instruction (MA); school administration (MA); school counseling (MA); school psychology (MA); secondary education (MA); special education (MA); urban education (MA). *Application Contact:* Chake H. Kouyoumjian, Associate Dean of Graduate Studies, 310-338-2721, E-mail: ckouyoum@lmu.edu. *Dean*, Dr. Shane P. Martin, 310-338-7301, E-mail: smartin@lmu.edu.

School of Film and Television ***Financial support:*** Applicants required to submit FAFSA. Offers film and television (MFA); film and television production (MFA); writing and producing for television (MFA); writing for the screen (MFA). Electronic applications accepted. *Application Contact:* Chake H. Kouyoumjian, Associate Dean of Graduate Studies, 310-338-2721, E-mail: ckouyoum@lmu.edu. *Dean*, Stephen Ujlaki, 310-338-5800, E-mail: sujlaki@lmu.edu.

LOYOLA UNIVERSITY CHICAGO, Chicago, IL 60660

General Information Independent-religious, coed, university. CGS member. *Enrollment:* 16,437 graduate, professional, and undergraduate students; 3,955 full-time matriculated graduate/professional students (2,395 women), 1,352 part-time matriculated graduate/professional students (1,001 women). *Enrollment by degree level:* 3,174 master's, 2,027 doctoral, 106 other advanced degrees. *Graduate faculty:* 862 full-time (407 women), 876 part-time/adjunct (460 women). *Tuition, area resident:* Full-time $18,054; part-time $9027 per credit hour. *Required fees:* $832; $284 per credit hour. Part-time tuition and fees vary according to course load, degree level and program. *Graduate housing:* Room and/or apartments available on a first-come, first-served basis to single students; on-campus housing not available to married students. Typical cost: $13,310 (including board). Room and board charges vary according to housing facility selected. Housing application deadline: 5/1. *Student services:* Campus employment opportunities, campus safety program, career counseling, exercise/wellness program, free psychological counseling, international student services, low-cost health insurance, services for students with disabilities, teacher training, writing training. *Library:* Cudahy Library plus 7 others. *Collection:* Books: 1.9 million (physical); Serial titles: 57,795 (physical). *Research affiliation:* Center for Community Arts Partnerships (arts integration), Aspire of Illinois (inclusion of children with disabilities), Illinois Institutions of Higher Education Partnership (preservice educator program curricula), Center for School Evaluation, Intervention, and Training (Loyola) (classroom teachers addressing the varied needs of all learners), Collaboration for Effective Educator Development, Accountability, And Reform Center (CEEDAR Center) (improving core and specialized instruction in settings that enable students with disabilities to achieve college ready standards), Illinois School Board of Education (student behavior and learning).

Computer facilities: Computer purchase and lease plans are available. 1,300 computers available on campus for general student use. A campuswide network can be accessed from student residence rooms and from off campus. Online class registration is available.
Website: http://www.luc.edu/

General Application Contact: Ron Martin, Associate Director, Graduate and Professional Enrollment Management Operations, 312-915-8951, E-mail: rmarti7@luc.edu.

GRADUATE UNITS

Graduate School Students: 1,018 full-time (554 women), 276 part-time (153 women); includes 318 minority (93 Black or African American, non-Hispanic/Latino; 1 American Indian or Alaska Native, non-Hispanic/Latino; 97 Asian, non-Hispanic/Latino; 101 Hispanic/Latino; 3 Native Hawaiian or other Pacific Islander, non-Hispanic/Latino; 23 Two or more races, non-Hispanic/Latino), 168 international. Average age 31. 1,328 applicants, 48% accepted, 284 enrolled. *Financial support:* In 2015–16, 325 students received support, including 90 fellowships with full tuition reimbursements available (averaging $19,000 per year), 130 research assistantships with full tuition reimbursements available (averaging $18,000 per year), 105 teaching assistantships with tuition reimbursements available (averaging $13,000 per year); career-related internships or fieldwork, Federal Work-Study, institutionally sponsored loans, scholarships/grants, and unspecified assistantships also available. Support available to part-time students. Financial award application deadline: 2/1; financial award applicants required to submit FAFSA. In 2015, 361 master's, 107 doctorates, 16 other advanced degrees awarded. *Degree program information:* Part-time and evening/weekend programs available. Part-time, evening/weekend, 100% online, blended/hybrid learning. Offers applied statistics (MS); biochemistry and molecular biology (MS, PhD); bioethics (D Be); biology (MS); cell and molecular physiology (PhD); chemistry and biochemistry (MS, PhD); clinical psychology (MA, PhD); clinical research methods (MS); comparative politics (PhD); computer science (MS); criminal justice and criminology (MA); developmental psychology (MA, PhD); digital humanities (MA); English (MA, PhD); history (MA, PhD); infectious disease and immunology (MS); information technology (MS); integrative cell biology (PhD); international relations (PhD); mathematics (MS); medical physiology (MS); medical sciences (MA); microbiology and immunology (MS, PhD); molecular pharmacology and therapeutics (MS, PhD); neuroscience (MS, PhD); philosophy (MA, PhD); political science (MA); public health (MPH); public history (MA); public policy (MPP); social psychology (MA, PhD); sociology (MA, PhD); software engineering (MS); Spanish (MA); theology (MA, PhD); urban affairs (MA). *Application deadline:* Applications are processed on a rolling basis. *Application fee:* $50. Electronic applications accepted. *Application Contact:* Ron Martin, Associate Director of Enrollment Management, 312-915-8950, Fax: 312-915-8905, E-mail: gradapp@luc.edu. *Dean*, Dr. Samuel Attoh, 773-508-3459, Fax: 773-508-2460, E-mail: sattoh@luc.edu.

Marcella Niehoff School of Nursing Students: 174 full-time (161 women), 232 part-time (221 women); includes 95 minority (19 Black or African American, non-Hispanic/Latino; 2 American Indian or Alaska Native, non-Hispanic/Latino; 38 Asian, non-Hispanic/Latino; 28 Hispanic/Latino; 2 Native Hawaiian or other Pacific Islander, non-Hispanic/Latino; 6 Two or more races, non-Hispanic/Latino), 3 international. Average age 35. 209 applicants, 52% accepted, 83 enrolled. *Faculty:* 27 full-time (25 women), 12 part-time/adjunct (10 women). *Financial support:* In 2015–16, 10 students received support, including 3 research assistantships with full tuition reimbursements available (averaging $18,000 per year), 1 teaching assistantship with full tuition reimbursement available (averaging $18,000 per year); scholarships/grants, unspecified assistantships, and nurse faculty loan program also available. Financial award application deadline: 5/1; financial award applicants required to submit FAFSA. In 2015, 78 master's, 10 doctorates, 17 other advanced degrees awarded. *Degree program information:* Part-time programs available. Part-time, blended/hybrid learning. Offers adult gerontology acute care clinical nurse specialist (MSN); adult gerontology acute care nurse practitioner (MSN); adult gerontology clinical nurse specialist (MSN); adult gerontology nursing (Certificate); adult nurse practitioner (Certificate); dietetics (MS); family nurse practitioner (MSN, Certificate); informatics (MSN); leadership (DNP); nursing science (PhD); women's health nurse practitioner (MSN); women's health nursing (Certificate). *Application deadline:* For fall admission, 6/1 priority date for domestic and international students; for spring admission, 11/15 priority date for domestic and international students; for summer admission, 3/15 priority date for domestic and international students. Applications are processed on a rolling basis. *Application fee:* $50. Electronic applications accepted. *Application Contact:* Toni Topalova, Enrollment Advisor, 708-216-3751, Fax: 708-216-9555, E-mail: atopalova@luc.edu. *Dean*, Dr. Vicky Keough, 708-216-5448, Fax: 708-216-9555, E-mail: vkeough@luc.edu.

Neiswanger Institute for Bioethics Students: 25 full-time (13 women), 91 part-time (53 women); includes 24 minority (12 Black or African American, non-Hispanic/Latino; 4 Asian, non-Hispanic/Latino; 6 Hispanic/Latino; 1 Native Hawaiian or other Pacific Islander, non-Hispanic/Latino; 1 Two or more races, non-Hispanic/Latino). Average age 48. 21 applicants, 86% accepted, 17 enrolled. *Financial support:* Scholarships/grants available. In 2015, 10 doctorates, 13 Certificates awarded. Online learning. Offers bioethics (D Be, Certificate). *Application Contact:* Ron Martin, Assistant Director of Enrollment Management, 312-915-8950, Fax: 312-915-8905, E-mail: gradapp@luc.edu. *Dean*, Dr. Samuel Attoh, 773-508-8948, Fax: 773-508-2460, E-mail: sattoh@luc.edu.

School of Communication Students: 29 full-time (19 women), 8 part-time (5 women); includes 13 minority (10 Black or African American, non-Hispanic/Latino; 2 Hispanic/Latino; 1 Two or more races, non-Hispanic/Latino), 5 international. Average age 28. 75 applicants, 79% accepted, 30 enrolled. In 2015, 1 master's awarded. Offers digital storytelling (MC); global strategic communication (MS). *Application Contact:* Ron Martin, Associate Director of Enrollment Management, 312-915-8950, Fax: 312-915-8905, E-mail: gradapp@luc.edu. *Dean*, Dr. Don Heider, 312-915-6548, E-mail: dheider@luc.edu.

Institute of Pastoral Studies Students: 65 full-time (50 women), 137 part-time (99 women); includes 40 minority (17 Black or African American, non-Hispanic/Latino; 5 Asian, non-Hispanic/Latino; 15 Hispanic/Latino; 3 Two or more races, non-Hispanic/Latino), 19 international. Average age 45. 88 applicants, 99% accepted, 63 enrolled. *Faculty:* 6 full-time (1 woman), 33 part-time/adjunct (16 women). *Financial support:* In 2015–16, 84 students received support. Career-related internships or fieldwork, Federal Work-Study, institutionally sponsored loans, scholarships/grants, and tuition waivers (partial) available. Support available to part-time students. Financial award application deadline: 3/1; financial award applicants required to submit FAFSA. In 2015, 58 master's, 4 other advanced degrees awarded. *Degree program information:* Part-time and evening/weekend programs available. Part-time, evening/weekend. Offers counseling for ministry (MA); healthcare mission leadership (MA); pastoral counseling (MA); pastoral studies (M Div, MA); social justice (MA, Certificate); spirituality (MA). *Application deadline:* Applications are processed on a rolling basis. *Application fee:* $50. Electronic applications accepted. *Application Contact:* Dr. M. Therese Lysaught, Associate Director, 312-915-7485, Fax: 312-915-7410, E-mail: mlysaught@luc.edu. *Director*, Dr. Brian J. Schmisek, 312-915-7400, Fax: 312-915-7410, E-mail: bschmisek@luc.edu.

Quinlan School of Business Students: 487 full-time (264 women), 104 part-time (51 women); includes 101 minority (27 Black or African American, non-Hispanic/Latino; 41 Asian, non-Hispanic/Latino; 27 Hispanic/Latino; 6 Two or more races, non-Hispanic/Latino), 189 international. Average age 29. 845 applicants, 63% accepted, 166 enrolled. *Faculty:* 79 full-time (22 women), 10 part-time/adjunct (4 women). *Financial support:* Federal Work-Study, scholarships/grants, health care benefits, and unspecified assistantships available. Support available to part-time students. In 2015, 397 master's awarded. *Degree program information:* Part-time and evening/weekend programs available. Part-time, evening/weekend. Offers accountancy (MSA); accounting (MBA); asset management (MSF); business (MBA, MSA, MSF, MSHR, MSIMC, MSSCM); business ethics (MBA); corporate finance (MSF); derivative markets (MBA); economics (MBA); entrepreneurship (MBA); executive business administration (MBA); finance (MBA); healthcare management (MBA); human resources (MSHR); human resources management (MBA); information systems management (MBA); integrated marketing communications (MSIMC); intercontinental (MBA); international business (MBA); marketing (MBA); operations management (MBA); risk management (MBA, MSF); supply chain management (MSSCM). *Application deadline:* For fall admission, 7/15 for domestic and international students; for winter admission, 10/1 for domestic and international students; for spring admission, 1/15 for domestic and international students; for summer admission, 4/1 for domestic and international students. Applications are processed on a rolling basis. *Application fee:* $50. Electronic applications accepted. *Application Contact:* Lauren Griffin, Enrollment Advisor, Quinlan School of Business Graduate Programs, 312-915-8908, Fax: 312-915-7207, E-mail: lgriffin3@luc.edu. *Assistant Dean for Graduate Programs*, Katherine Acles, 312-915-6124, Fax: 312-915-7207, E-mail: kacles@luc.edu.

School of Education Students: 411 full-time (318 women), 255 part-time (188 women); includes 238 minority (104 Black or African American, non-Hispanic/Latino; 1 American Indian or Alaska Native, non-Hispanic/Latino; 31 Asian, non-Hispanic/Latino; 79 Hispanic/Latino; 23 Two or more races, non-Hispanic/Latino), 22 international. Average age 36. 798 applicants, 61% accepted, 236 enrolled. *Faculty:* 53 full-time (38 women), 72 part-time/adjunct (49 women). *Financial support:* In 2015–16, 392 students received support, including 160 fellowships with partial tuition reimbursements available, 87 research assistantships with full tuition reimbursements available (averaging $14,000 per year), 104 teaching assistantships (averaging $4,000 per year); career-related internships or fieldwork, Federal Work-Study, institutionally sponsored loans, scholarships/grants, traineeships, health care benefits, and unspecified assistantships also available. Support available to part-time students. Financial award application deadline: 2/1; financial award applicants required to submit FAFSA. In 2015, 164 master's, 39 doctorates, 20 other advanced degrees awarded. *Degree program information:* Part-time and evening/weekend programs available. Part-time, evening/weekend, blended/hybrid learning. Offers administration and supervision (M Ed, Ed D, Certificate); community counseling (M Ed, MA); community mental health counseling (Ed S); counseling psychology (PhD); cultural and educational policy studies (M Ed, MA, PhD); curriculum and instruction (M Ed, Ed D); education (M Ed, MA, Ed D, PhD, Certificate, Ed S); elementary education (M Ed); English as a second language (Certificate); English language teaching and learning (M Ed); higher education (M Ed); reading specialist (M Ed); reading teacher (Certificate); research methods (MA, PhD); school counseling (M Ed, Certificate); school psychology (Ed D, PhD, Ed S); secondary education (M Ed); special education (M Ed). *Application fee:* $50. Electronic applications accepted. *Application Contact:* Marie Hatland, Information Contact, 312-915-8600, E-mail: schleduc@luc.edu. *Dean*, Dr. Terri Pigott, 312-915-6992, Fax: 312-915-6980, E-mail: tpigott@luc.edu.

School of Law Students: 745 full-time (397 women), 304 part-time (234 women); includes 313 minority (143 Black or African American, non-Hispanic/Latino; 5 American Indian or Alaska Native, non-Hispanic/Latino; 49 Asian, non-Hispanic/Latino; 80 Hispanic/Latino; 2 Native Hawaiian or other Pacific Islander, non-Hispanic/Latino; 34 Two or more races, non-Hispanic/Latino), 48 international. Average age 32. 2,612 applicants, 57% accepted, 357 enrolled. *Faculty:* 56 full-time (28 women), 199 part-time/adjunct (98 women). *Financial support:* In 2015–16, 624 students received support, including 72 fellowships; Federal Work-Study and scholarships/grants also available. Financial award application deadline: 3/1; financial award applicants required to submit FAFSA. In 2015, 168 master's, 270 doctorates awarded. *Degree program information:* Part-time and evening/weekend programs available. Part-time, evening/weekend, 100% online, blended/hybrid learning. Offers advocacy (LL M); business law (LL M, MJ); child and family law (LL M); children's law and policy (MJ); global competition law (LL M, MJ); health law (LL M, MJ); health law and policy (SJD); law (JD); rule of law development (LL M); tax law (LL M); U.S. law for foreign lawyers (LL M). MJ in business law offered in partnership with Concord Law School. *Application deadline:* For fall admission, 4/1 for domestic and international students. Applications are processed on a rolling basis. *Application fee:* $0. Electronic applications accepted. *Application Contact:* Ron Martin, Associate Director, Graduate and Professional Enrollment Management Operations, 312-915-8951, E-mail: rmarti7@luc.edu. *Associate Dean for Administration, Law School*, James Faught, JD, 312-915-7131, Fax: 312-915-6911, E-mail: law-admissions@luc.edu.

School of Social Work ***Degree program information:*** Part-time programs available. Part-time. Offers social work (MSW, PhD, PGC).

LOYOLA UNIVERSITY MARYLAND, Baltimore, MD 21210-2699

General Information Independent-religious, coed, university. CGS member. *Enrollment:* 5,977 graduate, professional, and undergraduate students; 932 full-time matriculated graduate/professional students (728 women), 1,163 part-time matriculated graduate/professional students (927 women). *Enrollment by degree level:* 1,921 master's, 88 doctoral, 86 other advanced degrees. *Graduate faculty:* 58 full-time (34 women), 73 part-time/adjunct (43 women). *Graduate housing:* On-campus housing not available. *Student services:* Campus employment opportunities, campus safety program, career counseling, exercise/wellness program, free psychological counseling, international student services, low-cost health insurance, multicultural affairs office, services for students with disabilities. *Library:* Loyola/Notre Dame Library plus 1 other.

Computer facilities: Computer purchase and lease plans are available. 690 computers available on campus for general student use. A campuswide network can be accessed from student residence rooms and from off campus. Online class registration is available.
Website: http://www.loyola.edu/

General Application Contact: Maureen Faux, Executive Director, Graduate Admissions, 410-617-5020, Fax: 410-617-2002, E-mail: graduate@loyola.edu.

GRADUATE UNITS

Graduate Programs Students: 932 full-time (728 women), 1,163 part-time (927 women); includes 424 minority (238 Black or African American, non-Hispanic/Latino; 7 American Indian or Alaska Native, non-Hispanic/Latino; 63 Asian, non-Hispanic/Latino; 75 Hispanic/Latino; 3 Native Hawaiian or other Pacific Islander, non-Hispanic/Latino; 38 Two or more races, non-Hispanic/Latino), 45 international. Average age 32. *Faculty:* 58 full-time (34 women), 73 part-time/adjunct (43 women). *Financial support:* Research assistantships and unspecified assistantships available. Financial award application deadline: 4/15; financial award applicants required to submit FAFSA. In 2015, 787 master's, 27 doctorates, 32 other advanced degrees awarded. *Degree program information:* Part-time and evening/weekend programs available. Part-time, evening/weekend. *Application fee:* $50. Electronic applications accepted. *Application Contact:* Maureen Faux, Executive Director, Graduate Admissions, 410-617-5020, Fax: 410-617-2002, E-mail: graduate@loyola.edu. *Associate Dean for Graduate Programs*, Dr. Cindy Moore, 410-617-2830, E-mail: clmoore1@loyola.edu.

Loyola College of Arts and Sciences Financial support: Research assistantships and unspecified assistantships available. Financial award application deadline: 4/15; financial award applicants required to submit FAFSA. *Degree program information:* Part-time and evening/weekend programs available. Part-time, evening/weekend. Offers arts and sciences (MA, MS, MTS, PhD, Psy D, CAS, Certificate); chaplaincy (MA); clinical psychology (MS, Psy D, CAS); computer science (MS); counseling psychology (MS, CAS); emerging media (MA); faith and social justice (MA); liberal studies (MA); ministry (MA); pastoral counseling (MS, PhD, CAS); software engineering (MS); speech-language pathology (MS); spiritual and pastoral care (MA); spiritual direction (MA); spirituality and trauma (Certificate); theology (MTS, Certificate). *Application fee:* $50. Electronic applications accepted.

School of Education Financial support: Research assistantships and unspecified assistantships available. Financial award application deadline: 4/15; financial award applicants required to submit FAFSA. *Degree program information:* Part-time and evening/weekend programs available. Part-time, evening/weekend. Offers curriculum and instruction (MA); early childhood education (M Ed, CAS); education (M Ed, MA, MAT, CAS); educational leadership (M Ed, CAS); educational technology (M Ed, MA); elementary education (M Ed); elementary/middle education (M Ed, MAT, CAS); Kodaly music education (M Ed); literacy teacher (M Ed); Montessori education (CAS); school counseling (M Ed, MA, CAS); secondary education (M Ed, CAS). *Application deadline:* For fall admission, 6/15 for domestic students; for spring admission, 11/1 priority date for domestic students. *Application fee:* $50.

Sellinger School of Business Financial support: Research assistantships and unspecified assistantships available. Financial award applicants required to submit FAFSA. *Degree program information:* Part-time and evening/weekend programs available. Part-time, evening/weekend. Offers accounting (MBA); business (M Acc, MBA, MSF, Certificate); business administration (MBA); cyber security (Certificate); executive business administration (MBA); finance (MBA); general business (MBA); information systems operations management (MBA); international business (MBA); management (MBA); marketing (MBA). *Application fee:* $50. Electronic applications accepted. *Application Contact:* Maureen Faux, Executive Director, Graduate Admissions, 410-617-5020, Fax: 410-617-2002, E-mail: graduate@loyola.edu. *Dean*, Kathleen A. Getz, 410-617-2301.

LOYOLA UNIVERSITY NEW ORLEANS, New Orleans, LA 70118-6195

General Information Independent-religious, coed, comprehensive institution. CGS member. *Enrollment:* 4,087 graduate, professional, and undergraduate students; 587 full-time matriculated graduate/professional students (356 women), 809 part-time matriculated graduate/professional students (614 women). *Enrollment by degree level:* 756 master's, 640 doctoral. *Graduate faculty:* 111 full-time (61 women), 78 part-time/adjunct (29 women). *Graduate housing:* Room and/or apartments available on a first-come, first-served basis to single students; on-campus housing not available to married students. Housing application deadline: 8/1. *Student services:* Campus employment opportunities, campus safety program, career counseling, child daycare facilities, exercise/wellness program, free psychological counseling, international student services, low-cost health insurance, multicultural affairs office, services for students with disabilities. *Library:* Monroe Library plus 1 other. *Collection:* Books: 387,652 (physical), 42,637 (digital/electronic); Serial titles: 221,718 (physical). Weekly public service hours: 114; students can reserve study rooms. *Research affiliation:* New Orleans Museum of Art (communications, history, visual arts).

Computer facilities: Computer purchase and lease plans are available. 525 computers available on campus for general student use. A campuswide network can be accessed from student residence rooms and from off campus. Online class registration is available.
Website: http://www.loyno.edu/

General Application Contact: Melissa L. Lightell, Director, Office of Professional and Continuing Studies, 504-865-2157, Fax: 504-865-2787, E-mail: malandr2@loyno.edu.

GRADUATE UNITS

College of Law Students: 400 full-time (219 women), 143 part-time (62 women); includes 134 minority (58 Black or African American, non-Hispanic/Latino; 5 American Indian or Alaska Native, non-Hispanic/Latino; 13 Asian, non-Hispanic/Latino; 46 Hispanic/Latino; 1 Native Hawaiian or other Pacific Islander, non-Hispanic/Latino; 11 Two or more races, non-Hispanic/Latino), 9 international. Average age 28. 1,040 applicants, 57% accepted, 139 enrolled. *Faculty:* 49 full-time (26 women), 19 part-time/adjunct (1 woman). *Financial support:* Research assistantships, teaching assistantships, career-related internships or fieldwork, and scholarships/grants available. Support available to part-time students. Financial award application deadline: 5/1; financial award applicants required to submit FAFSA. In 2015, 201 doctorates awarded. *Degree program information:* Part-time and evening/weekend programs available. Part-time, evening/weekend. Offers law (LL M, JD). *Application deadline:* For fall admission, 2/1 priority date for domestic and international students. Applications are processed on a rolling basis. *Application fee:* $0. Electronic applications accepted. *Application Contact:* Forrest Stanford, Interim Director of Law Admissions, 504-861-5553, Fax: 504-861-5775, E-mail: ladmit@loyno.edu. *Interim Dean,* Dr. Lawrence W. Moore, SJ, 504-861-5575, Fax: 504-861-5739, E-mail: ladmit@loyno.edu.

College of Music and Fine Arts Students: 32 full-time (19 women), 6 part-time (3 women); includes 11 minority (6 Black or African American, non-Hispanic/Latino; 1 Asian, non-Hispanic/Latino; 4 Hispanic/Latino), 3 international. Average age 26. 44 applicants, 59% accepted, 18 enrolled. *Faculty:* 22 full-time (10 women), 19 part-time/adjunct (5 women). *Financial support:* Career-related internships or fieldwork, Federal Work-Study, institutionally sponsored loans, scholarships/grants, unspecified assistantships, and talent-based music scholarships available. Support available to part-time students. Financial award application deadline: 5/1; financial award applicants required to submit FAFSA. In 2015, 7 master's awarded. *Degree program information:* Part-time programs available. Part-time. Offers music therapy (MMT); performance (MM). *Application deadline:* For fall admission, 8/15 priority date for domestic and international students; for spring admission, 1/1 priority date for domestic and international students. Applications are processed on a rolling basis. *Application fee:* $20. Electronic applications accepted. *Application Contact:* Melissa L. Lightell, Director, Office of Professional and Continuing Studies, 504-865-3530, Fax: 504-865-2787, E-mail: evening@loyno.edu. *Associate Dean,* Dr. Victoria P. Vega, 504-865-3037, Fax: 504-865-2852, E-mail: vpvega@loyno.edu.

College of Social Sciences Students: 464 full-time (411 women), 263 part-time (207 women); includes 200 minority (119 Black or African American, non-Hispanic/Latino; 4 American Indian or Alaska Native, non-Hispanic/Latino; 28 Asian, non-Hispanic/Latino; 44 Hispanic/Latino; 1 Native Hawaiian or other Pacific Islander, non-Hispanic/Latino; 4 Two or more races, non-Hispanic/Latino). Average age 40. 331 applicants, 72% accepted, 162 enrolled. *Faculty:* 29 full-time (19 women), 37 part-time/adjunct (23 women). *Financial support:* Application deadline: 5/1; applicants required to submit FAFSA. In 2015, 241 master's, 28 doctorates, 1 other advanced degree awarded. *Degree program information:* Part-time and evening/weekend programs available. Part-time, evening/weekend. Offers clinical mental health counseling (MS); criminal justice (MCJ); social sciences (MCJ, MPS, MRE, MS, MSN, DNP, Certificate). *Application deadline:* For fall admission, 8/1 priority date for domestic and international students; for winter admission, 12/15 for international students; for spring admission, 1/5 priority date for domestic and international students. Applications are processed on a rolling basis. Electronic applications accepted. *Application Contact:* Melissa L. Lightell, Director, Office of Professional and Continuing Studies, 504-865-3530, Fax: 504-865-2787, E-mail: evening@loyno.edu. *Interim Dean,* Dr. Roger White, 504-865-3530, Fax: 504-865-2787, E-mail: rwhite@loyno.edu.

Loyola Institute for Ministry Students: 25 full-time (18 women), 134 part-time (94 women); includes 22 minority (8 Black or African American, non-Hispanic/Latino; 1 American Indian or Alaska Native, non-Hispanic/Latino; 2 Asian, non-Hispanic/Latino; 9 Hispanic/Latino; 2 Two or more races, non-Hispanic/Latino). Average age 47. 57 applicants, 68% accepted, 39 enrolled. *Faculty:* 4 full-time (1 woman), 7 part-time/adjunct (5 women). *Financial support:* Career-related internships or fieldwork, scholarships/grants, health care benefits, and tuition waivers (partial) available. Support available to part-time students. Financial award application deadline: 5/1; financial award applicants required to submit FAFSA. In 2015, 38 master's awarded. *Degree program information:* Part-time and evening/weekend programs available. Part-time, evening/weekend, online learning. Offers pastoral studies (MPS); religious education (MRE); theology and ministry (Certificate). *Application deadline:* Applications are processed on a rolling basis. *Application fee:* $20. Electronic applications accepted. *Application Contact:* Diane Blair, Manager of Admissions, 504-865-3728, Fax: 504-865-2066, E-mail: lim@loyno.edu. *Director,* Dr. Tom Ryan, 504-865-2069, Fax: 504-865-2066, E-mail: tfryan@loyno.edu.

School of Nursing Students: 350 full-time (321 women), 95 part-time (85 women); includes 139 minority (97 Black or African American, non-Hispanic/Latino; 2 American Indian or Alaska Native, non-Hispanic/Latino; 22 Asian, non-Hispanic/Latino; 15 Hispanic/Latino; 1 Native Hawaiian or other Pacific Islander, non-Hispanic/Latino; 2 Two or more races, non-Hispanic/Latino). Average age 41. 229 applicants, 76% accepted, 100 enrolled. *Faculty:* 14 full-time (13 women), 16 part-time/adjunct (12 women). *Financial support:* Traineeships and Incumbent Workers Training Program grants available. Financial award application deadline: 5/1; financial award applicants required to submit FAFSA. In 2015, 139 master's, 28 doctorates awarded. *Degree program information:* Part-time and evening/weekend programs available. Part-time, evening/weekend, online learning. Offers health care systems management (MSN); nursing (MSN, DNP). *Application deadline:* For fall admission, 8/1 priority date for domestic and international students; for winter admission, 12/15 priority date for domestic and international students; for spring admission, 5/15 priority date for domestic and international students. Applications are processed on a rolling basis. *Application fee:* $40. Electronic applications accepted. *Application Contact:* Deborah Smith, Executive Assistant to the Director, 504-865-2823, Fax: 504-865-3254, E-mail: dhsmith@loyno.edu. *Interim Director,* Dr. Patricia Pearce, 800-488-6257, Fax: 504-865-3254, E-mail: nursing@loyno.edu.

Joseph A. Butt, S.J., College of Business Students: 66 full-time (36 women), 13 part-time (8 women); includes 22 minority (6 Black or African American, non-Hispanic/Latino; 2 American Indian or Alaska Native, non-Hispanic/Latino; 3 Asian, non-Hispanic/Latino; 9 Hispanic/Latino; 2 Two or more races, non-Hispanic/Latino), 5 international. Average age 29. 52 applicants, 71% accepted, 35 enrolled. *Faculty:* 11 full-time (6 women), 3 part-time/adjunct (0 women). *Financial support:* Research assistantships, scholarships/grants, tuition waivers (partial), and unspecified assistantships available. Financial award application deadline: 5/1; financial award applicants required to submit FAFSA. In 2015, 25 master's awarded. *Degree program information:* Part-time and evening/weekend programs available. Part-time, evening/weekend, online learning. Offers business (MBA); entrepreneurship and marketing innovation (MBA); organizational performance excellence (MBA). *Application deadline:* For fall admission, 6/15 priority date for domestic students, 5/15 priority date for international students; for spring admission, 11/15 priority date for domestic students, 10/15 priority date for international students. Applications are processed on a rolling basis. *Application fee:* $50. Electronic applications accepted. *Application Contact:* Ashley Francis, Director of Graduate Programs, 504-864-7979, Fax: 504-864-7970, E-mail: mba@loyno.edu. *Dean,* Dr. William B. Locander, 504-864-7990, Fax: 504-864-7970, E-mail: mba@loyno.edu.

LUBBOCK CHRISTIAN UNIVERSITY, Lubbock, TX 79407-2099

General Information Independent-religious, coed, comprehensive institution. *Graduate housing:* Rooms and/or apartments available to single and married students. Housing application deadline: 8/15.

GRADUATE UNITS

Graduate Biblical Studies ***Degree program information:*** Part-time programs available. Part-time. Offers Bible and ministry (MS); biblical interpretation (MA).

LUTHERAN SCHOOL OF THEOLOGY AT CHICAGO, Chicago, IL 60615-5199

General Information Independent-religious, coed, graduate-only institution. *Enrollment by degree level:* 193 master's, 73 doctoral, 16 other advanced degrees. *Graduate faculty:* 20 full-time (6 women), 18 part-time/adjunct (5 women). *Tuition, area resident:* Full-time $16,200. *Required fees:* $220. *Graduate housing:* Rooms and/or apartments available on a first-come, first-served basis to single and married students. Typical cost: $4383 per year for single students; $7677 per year for married students. Room charges vary according to housing facility selected. Housing application deadline: 5/15. *Student services:* Campus employment opportunities, campus safety program, career counseling, international student services, multicultural affairs office. *Library:* JKM Library. Students can reserve study rooms. *Research affiliation:* Chicago Center for Public Ministry, Zygon Center for Religion and Science.

Computer facilities: Online class registration is available.
Website: http://www.lstc.edu/

General Application Contact: Dr. R. Scott Chalmers, Director of Admissions, 773-256-0727, Fax: 773-256-0782, E-mail: schalmers@lstc.edu.

GRADUATE UNITS

Graduate and Professional Programs Students: 195 full-time (96 women), 87 part-time (48 women). *Faculty:* 20 full-time (6 women), 18 part-time/adjunct (5 women). *Financial support:* Career-related internships or fieldwork and scholarships/grants available. Support available to part-time students. *Degree program information:* Part-time programs available. Part-time. Offers ministry (MAM, D Min); theological studies (MATS, PhD); theology (M Div). *Application deadline:* Applications are processed on a rolling basis. *Application fee:* $50. *Application Contact:* Dr. R. Scott Chalmers, Director of Admissions, 773-256-0727, Fax: 773-256-0782, E-mail: schalmers@lstc.edu. *Dean and Vice President for Academic Affairs,* Esther Menn, 773-256-0721, Fax: 773-256-0782, E-mail: emenn@lstc.edu.

LUTHERAN THEOLOGICAL SEMINARY AT GETTYSBURG, Gettysburg, PA 17325-1795

General Information Independent-religious, coed, graduate-only institution. *Graduate housing:* Rooms and/or apartments available on a first-come, first-served basis to single and married students. Housing application deadline: 4/1.

GRADUATE UNITS

Graduate and Professional Programs ***Degree program information:*** Part-time programs available. Part-time, online learning. Offers divinity (M Div); ministerial studies (MAMS); outdoor ministry (MAR); parish ministry (D Min); theology (STM). Electronic applications accepted.

THE LUTHERAN THEOLOGICAL SEMINARY AT PHILADELPHIA, Philadelphia, PA 19119-1794

General Information Independent-religious, coed, graduate-only institution. *Enrollment by degree level:* 176 master's, 72 doctoral, 20 other advanced degrees. *Graduate faculty:* 17 full-time (3 women), 10 part-time/adjunct (5 women). *Required fees:* $14,310; $1590 per course. $225 per semester. One-time fee: $350. Tuition and fees vary according to degree level and program. *Graduate housing:* Rooms and/or apartments available on a first-come, first-served basis to single and married students. Typical cost: $7200 per year for single students; $10,350 per year for married students. Housing application deadline: 5/15. *Student services:* Campus employment opportunities, campus safety program, multicultural affairs office. *Library:* Krauth Memorial Library. *Collection:* Books: 193,087 (physical); Databases: 4. Weekly public service hours: 58.

Computer facilities: 3 computers available on campus for general student use. Online class registration is available.
Website: http://www.ltsp.edu/

General Application Contact: Nate Preisinger, Associate Director of Admissions, 800-286-4616 Ext. 6321, Fax: 215-248-7315, E-mail: admissions@ltsp.edu.

GRADUATE UNITS

Graduate School Students: 78 full-time (40 women), 196 part-time (103 women); includes 92 minority (80 Black or African American, non-Hispanic/Latino; 2 Asian, non-Hispanic/Latino; 10 Hispanic/Latino), 14 international. *Faculty:* 17 full-time (3 women), 10 part-time/adjunct (5 women). *Financial support:* Research assistantships with tuition reimbursements, teaching assistantships with tuition reimbursements, career-related internships or fieldwork, and Federal Work-Study available. Financial award application deadline: 7/1; financial award applicants required to submit FAFSA. *Degree program information:* Part-time and evening/weekend programs available. Part-time, evening/weekend. Offers divinity (M Div); ministry (D Min); public leadership (MA); religion (MAR); social ministry and church (Certificate); theology (STM, PhD). *Application deadline:* For fall admission, 4/15 priority date for domestic students. Applications are processed on a rolling basis. *Application fee:* $40. Electronic applications accepted. *Application Contact:* Nate Preisinger, Associate Director of Admissions, 800-286-4616 Ext. 6321, Fax: 215-248-7315, E-mail: admissions@ltsp.edu. *Dean*, Rev. Dr. J. Jayakiran Sebastian, 215-248-7378, Fax: 215-248-4577, E-mail: jsebastian@ltsp.edu.

LUTHERAN THEOLOGICAL SEMINARY SASKATOON, Saskatoon, SK S7N 0X3, Canada

General Information Independent-religious, coed, graduate-only institution. *Graduate housing:* Room and/or apartments available to single students; on-campus housing not available to married students. Housing application deadline: 4/30.

GRADUATE UNITS

Graduate and Professional Programs ***Degree program information:*** Part-time programs available. Part-time. Offers Biblical studies (MTS); church history (MTS); ethics/church and society (MTS); history of Christianity (STM); New Testament (STM); Old Testament (STM); pastoral studies (STM); pastoral theology (MTS); systematic theology (MTS); systematic theology and philosophy of religion (STM); theology (M Div, D Div). STM programs offered jointly with College of Emmanuel and St. Chad and St. Andrew's College.

LUTHER RICE COLLEGE & SEMINARY, Lithonia, GA 30038-2454

General Information Independent-religious, coed, comprehensive institution. *Graduate housing:* On-campus housing not available.

GRADUATE UNITS

Graduate Programs ***Degree program information:*** Part-time and evening/weekend programs available. Part-time, evening/weekend, online learning. Offers apologetics (MA); Bible languages (M Div); Biblical counseling (MA); Christian ministry (M Div, D Min); Christian studies (MA); leadership (MA). Electronic applications accepted.

LUTHER SEMINARY, St. Paul, MN 55108-1445

General Information Independent-religious, coed, graduate-only institution. *Graduate housing:* Rooms and/or apartments available on a first-come, first-served basis to single and married students.

GRADUATE UNITS

Graduate and Professional Programs ***Degree program information:*** Part-time programs available. Part-time, online learning. Offers aging and health (MA); Biblical preaching (D Min); children, youth and family (M Div, MA); congregational mission and leadership (M Th, MA, D Min); history of Christianity (M Th, MA); missions and world religions (M Th); New Testament (M Th, MA); Old Testament (M Th, MA); pastoral care: clinical pastoral theology (M Th); pastoral theology and ministry (M Th); systematic theology (M Th, MA). Electronic applications accepted.

LYNCHBURG COLLEGE, Lynchburg, VA 24501-3199

General Information Independent-religious, coed, comprehensive institution. *Enrollment:* 2,794 graduate, professional, and undergraduate students; 283 full-time matriculated graduate/professional students (198 women), 370 part-time matriculated graduate/professional students (260 women). *Enrollment by degree level:* 355 master's, 170 doctoral, 23 other advanced degrees. *Graduate faculty:* 53 full-time (30 women), 21 part-time/adjunct (11 women). *Tuition, area resident:* Full-time $8550; part-time $475 per credit hour. *Required fees:* $120; $5.10 per credit hour. Tuition and fees vary according to course load, degree level and program. *Graduate housing:* On-campus housing not available. *Student services:* Campus employment opportunities, career counseling, exercise/wellness program, free psychological counseling, international student services, multicultural affairs office, services for students with disabilities, teacher training, writing training. *Library:* Knight-Capron Library.

Computer facilities: 300 computers available on campus for general student use. A campuswide network can be accessed from student residence rooms. Online class registration is available.
Website: http://www.lynchburg.edu/

General Application Contact: Dr. Atul Gupta, Associate Dean for Academic Affairs, Graduate Studies, 434-544-8651, E-mail: gupta@lynchburg.edu.

GRADUATE UNITS

Graduate Studies Students: 283 full-time (198 women), 370 part-time (260 women); includes 81 minority (48 Black or African American, non-Hispanic/Latino; 3 American Indian or Alaska Native, non-Hispanic/Latino; 6 Asian, non-Hispanic/Latino; 11 Hispanic/Latino; 13 Two or more races, non-Hispanic/Latino), 8 international. Average age 32. *Faculty:* 53 full-time (30 women), 21 part-time/adjunct (11 women). *Financial support:* Career-related internships or fieldwork, Federal Work-Study, scholarships/grants, and unspecified assistantships available. Financial award applicants required to submit FAFSA. In 2015, 105 master's, 54 doctorates awarded. *Degree program information:* Part-time and evening/weekend programs available. Part-time, evening/weekend. Offers business administration (MBA); clinical mental health counseling (M Ed); clinical nurse leader (MS); higher education (M Ed); history (MA); instructional leadership (M Ed); leadership studies (Ed D); music (MA); physical therapy (DPT); PK-12 administrative and supervisory (M Ed); reading instruction (M Ed); reading specialist (M Ed); school counseling (M Ed); science education (M Ed); special education (M Ed); teacher licensure (M Ed). *Application fee:* $30. *Dean of Graduate Studies*, Dr. Atul Gupta, 434-544-8651, E-mail: gupta@lynchburg.edu.

LYNDON STATE COLLEGE, Lyndonville, VT 05851-0919

General Information State-supported, coed, comprehensive institution. *Graduate housing:* On-campus housing not available.

GRADUATE UNITS

Graduate Programs in Education ***Degree program information:*** Part-time and evening/weekend programs available. Part-time, evening/weekend. Offers curriculum and instruction (M Ed); education (M Ed); natural sciences (MST); reading specialist (M Ed); science education (MST); special education (M Ed); teaching and counseling (M Ed).

LYNN UNIVERSITY, Boca Raton, FL 33431-5598

General Information Independent, coed, comprehensive institution. *Enrollment:* 2,693 graduate, professional, and undergraduate students; 581 full-time matriculated graduate/professional students (306 women), 109 part-time matriculated graduate/professional students (62 women). *Enrollment by degree level:* 600 master's, 61 doctoral, 29 other advanced degrees. *Graduate faculty:* 41 full-time (15 women), 31 part-time/adjunct (21 women). *Tuition, area resident:* Full-time $17,040; part-time $8520 per year. One-time fee: $100. Tuition and fees vary according to class time, course load and degree level. *Graduate housing:* Room and/or apartments available on a first-come, first-served basis to single students; on-campus housing not available to married students. *Student services:* Campus employment opportunities, campus safety program, career counseling, exercise/wellness program, free psychological counseling, international student services, low-cost health insurance, multicultural affairs office, services for students with disabilities. *Library:* Eugene M. and Christine E. Lynn Library. *Collection:* Books: 62,900 (physical), 174,794 (digital/electronic); Serial titles: 85 (physical), 131,431 (digital/electronic); Databases: 108. Weekly public service hours: 98.

Computer facilities: Computer purchase and lease plans are available. 250 computers available on campus for general student use. A campuswide network can be accessed from student residence rooms and from off campus. Online registration with advisor approval for juniors, seniors and MBA students available.
Website: http://www.lynn.edu/

General Application Contact: Steven Pruitt, Assistant Director of Graduate Admissions, 561-237-7834, Fax: 561-237-7100, E-mail: admission@lynn.edu.

GRADUATE UNITS

College of Arts and Sciences Students: 103 full-time (73 women), 31 part-time (17 women); includes 33 minority (23 Black or African American, non-Hispanic/Latino; 1 Asian, non-Hispanic/Latino; 7 Hispanic/Latino; 1 Native Hawaiian or other Pacific Islander, non-Hispanic/Latino; 1 Two or more races, non-Hispanic/Latino), 16 international. Average age 30. 78 applicants, 94% accepted, 54 enrolled. *Faculty:* 4 full-time (2 women), 10 part-time/adjunct (8 women). *Financial support:* In 2015–16, 37 students received support. Career-related internships or fieldwork, Federal Work-Study, scholarships/grants, tuition waivers (full and partial), and unspecified assistantships available. Support available to part-time students. Financial award application deadline: 3/1; financial award applicants required to submit FAFSA. In 2015, 41 master's awarded. *Degree program information:* Part-time and evening/weekend programs available. Part-time, evening/weekend, blended/hybrid learning. Offers administration (MS); applied psychology (MS); applied psychology and counseling (MS). *Application deadline:* For fall admission, 8/17 for domestic students, 8/3 for international students; for spring admission, 12/14 for domestic students, 11/30 for international students; for summer admission, 4/18 for domestic students, 4/4 for international students. Applications are processed on a rolling basis. *Application fee:* $45. Electronic applications accepted. *Application Contact:* Steven Pruitt, Director of Graduate Admission, 561-237-7834, Fax: 561-237-7100, E-mail: admissionpm@lynn.edu. *Dean*, Dr. Katrina Carter-Tellison, 561-237-7412, E-mail: kcartertellison@lynn.edu.

College of Business and Management Students: 343 full-time (157 women), 23 part-time (17 women); includes 80 minority (46 Black or African American, non-Hispanic/Latino; 2 Asian, non-Hispanic/Latino; 27 Hispanic/Latino; 5 Two or more races, non-Hispanic/Latino), 91 international. Average age 29. 235 applicants, 99% accepted, 165 enrolled. *Faculty:* 13 full-time (3 women), 12 part-time/adjunct (6 women). *Financial support:* In 2015–16, 97 students received support. Career-related internships or fieldwork, Federal Work-Study, scholarships/grants, tuition waivers (full and partial), and unspecified assistantships available. Support available to part-time students. Financial award application deadline: 3/1; financial award applicants required to submit FAFSA. In 2015, 179 master's awarded. *Degree program information:* Part-time and evening/weekend programs available. Part-time, evening/weekend, online learning. Offers business administration (MBA). *Application deadline:* For fall admission, 8/17 for domestic students, 8/3 for international students; for spring admission, 12/14 for domestic students, 11/30 for international students; for summer admission, 4/18 for domestic students, 4/1 for international students. Applications are processed on a rolling basis. *Application fee:* $45. Electronic applications accepted. *Application Contact:* Steven Pruitt, Director of Graduate and Undergraduate Evening Admission, 561-237-7834, Fax: 561-237-7100, E-mail: spruitt@lynn.edu. *Senior Associate Dean*, Dr. Ralph Norcio, 561-237-7010, Fax: 561-237-7014, E-mail: rnorcio@lynn.edu.

Conservatory of Music Students: 53 full-time (24 women); includes 10 minority (1 Black or African American, non-Hispanic/Latino; 4 Asian, non-Hispanic/Latino; 5 Hispanic/Latino), 26 international. Average age 25. 70 applicants, 100% accepted, 24 enrolled. *Faculty:* 17 full-time (3 women), 2 part-time/adjunct (1 woman). *Financial support:* In 2015–16, 53 students received support. Federal Work-Study, scholarships/grants, and unspecified assistantships available. Support available to part-time students. Financial award application deadline: 3/1; financial award applicants required to submit FAFSA. In 2015, 22 master's, 5 Certificates awarded. *Degree program information:* Part-time and evening/weekend programs available. Part-time, evening/weekend. Offers collaborative piano (MM); composition (MM); performance (MM); professional performance (Certificate). *Application deadline:* For fall admission, 8/17 for domestic students, 8/3 priority date for international students. Applications are processed on a rolling basis. *Application fee:* $50. Electronic applications accepted. *Application Contact:* Steven Pruitt, Director of Graduate Admissions, 561-237-7834, Fax: 561-237-7100, E-mail: admission@lynn.edu. *Dean*, Dr. Jon Robertson, 561-237-7702, Fax: 561-237-9002, E-mail: jrobertson@lynn.edu.

Donald E. and Helen L. Ross College of Education Students: 48 full-time (29 women), 51 part-time (36 women); includes 27 minority (17 Black or African American, non-Hispanic/Latino; 9 Hispanic/Latino; 1 Two or more races, non-Hispanic/Latino), 9 international. Average age 37. 31 applicants, 97% accepted, 25 enrolled. *Faculty:* 3 full-time (all women), 7 part-time/adjunct (6 women). *Financial support:* In 2015–16, 72 students received support. Career-related internships or fieldwork, Federal Work-Study, scholarships/grants, tuition waivers (partial), and unspecified assistantships available. Support available to part-time students. Financial award application deadline: 3/1; financial award applicants required to submit FAFSA. In 2015, 24 master's, 10 doctorates awarded. *Degree program information:* Part-time and evening/weekend programs available. Part-time, evening/weekend, online learning. Offers educational leadership (M Ed, Ed D); exceptional student education (M Ed). *Application deadline:* For fall admission, 8/17 for domestic students, 8/3 for international students; for spring admission, 12/14 for domestic students, 11/30 for international students; for summer admission, 4/18 for domestic students, 4/4 for international students. Applications are processed on a rolling basis. *Application fee:* $45. Electronic applications accepted. *Application Contact:* Steven Pruitt, Director of Graduate and Undergraduate Evening

Admission, 561-237-7834, Fax: 561-237-7100, E-mail: spruitt@lynn.edu. *Dean, College of Education*, Dr. Kathleen Weigel, 561-237-7441, E-mail: kweigel@lynn.edu.

Eugene M. and Christine E. Lynn College of International Communication Students: 34 full-time (23 women), 1 (woman) part-time; includes 8 minority (5 Black or African American, non-Hispanic/Latino; 2 Hispanic/Latino; 1 Two or more races, non-Hispanic/Latino), 10 international. Average age 27. 25 applicants, 100% accepted, 24 enrolled. *Faculty:* 5 full-time (4 women). *Financial support:* In 2015–16, 9 students received support. Career-related internships or fieldwork, Federal Work-Study, institutionally sponsored loans, scholarships/grants, tuition waivers (partial), and unspecified assistantships available. Support available to part-time students. Financial award application deadline: 8/1; financial award applicants required to submit FAFSA. In 2015, 14 master's awarded. *Degree program information:* Part-time and evening/weekend programs available. Part-time, evening/weekend. Offers communication and media (MS); digital media (Certificate). *Application deadline:* For fall admission, 8/17 for domestic students, 8/3 for international students; for spring admission, 12/14 for domestic students, 11/30 for international students; for summer admission, 4/18 for domestic students, 4/4 for international students. Applications are processed on a rolling basis. *Application fee:* $45. Electronic applications accepted. *Application Contact:* Steven Pruitt, Director of Graduate Admission, 561-237-7834, Fax: 561-237-7100, E-mail: admission@lynn.edu. *Dean*, Dr. David L. Jaffe, 561-237-7099, Fax: 561-237-7097, E-mail: djaffe@lynn.edu.

MAASTRICHT SCHOOL OF MANAGEMENT, 6201 BE Maastricht, Netherlands

General Information Private, coed, graduate-only institution.

GRADUATE UNITS

Graduate Programs Offers business administration (MBA, DBA, PhD); facility management (Exec MBA); management (M Sc); sustainability (Exec MBA).

MACHZIKEI HADATH RABBINICAL COLLEGE, Brooklyn, NY 11204-1805

General Information Independent-religious, men only, comprehensive institution. *Graduate housing:* Room and/or apartments available to single students; on-campus housing not available to married students.

GRADUATE UNITS

Graduate Programs

MADONNA UNIVERSITY, Livonia, MI 48150-1173

General Information Independent-religious, coed, comprehensive institution. *Graduate housing:* Room and/or apartments available on a first-come, first-served basis to single students; on-campus housing not available to married students. Housing application deadline: 4/29.

GRADUATE UNITS

Department of Psychology ***Degree program information:*** Part-time and evening/weekend programs available. Part-time, evening/weekend. Offers clinical psychology (MSCP). Electronic applications accepted.

Program in Health Services ***Degree program information:*** Part-time programs available. Part-time. Offers health services (MSHS). Electronic applications accepted.

Program in Hospice ***Degree program information:*** Part-time and evening/weekend programs available. Part-time, evening/weekend. Offers hospice (MSH). Electronic applications accepted.

Program in Liberal Studies Offers liberal studies (MALS).

Program in Nursing ***Degree program information:*** Part-time programs available. Part-time. Offers adult health: chronic health conditions (MSN); adult nurse practitioner (MSN); nursing administration (MSN). Electronic applications accepted.

Program in Religious Studies Offers pastoral ministry (MA).

Program in Teaching English to Speakers of Other Languages ***Degree program information:*** Part-time and evening/weekend programs available. Part-time, evening/weekend. Offers teaching English to speakers of other languages (MATESOL). Electronic applications accepted.

Programs in Education ***Degree program information:*** Part-time and evening/weekend programs available. Part-time, evening/weekend. Offers Catholic school leadership (MSA); educational leadership (MSA); learning disabilities (MAT); literacy education (MAT); teaching and learning (MAT). Electronic applications accepted.

School of Business ***Degree program information:*** Part-time and evening/weekend programs available. Part-time, evening/weekend, online learning. Offers business administration (MBA); international business (MSBA); leadership studies (MSBA); leadership studies in criminal justice (MSBA); quality and operations management (MSBA). Electronic applications accepted.

MAHARISHI UNIVERSITY OF MANAGEMENT, Fairfield, IA 52557

General Information Independent, coed, university. *Enrollment:* 1,530 graduate, professional, and undergraduate students; 802 full-time matriculated graduate/professional students (175 women), 375 part-time matriculated graduate/professional students (126 women). *Enrollment by degree level:* 720 master's, 24 doctoral. *Graduate faculty:* 118 full-time (33 women), 49 part-time/adjunct (12 women). *Tuition, area resident:* Full-time $27,000; part-time $450 per credit hour. *Required fees:* $530. *Graduate housing:* Room and/or apartments guaranteed to single students; on-campus housing not available to married students. Typical cost: $7400 (including board). Housing application deadline: 8/1. *Student services:* Campus employment opportunities, campus safety program, career counseling, child daycare facilities, exercise/wellness program, free psychological counseling, international student services, teacher training. *Library:* Maharishi University of Management Library. *Research affiliation:* National Institutes of Health (stress reduction/disease prevention), Department of Defense (therapy/education/PTSD in veterans), Columbia University Medical Center (natural medicine and prevention), Institute of Noetic Sciences (psychophysiological correlates of consciousness), San Diego VA Healthcare System (veterans' health/PTSD stress reduction), Howard University Medical Center (stress reduction/hypertension prevention).

Computer facilities: A campuswide network can be accessed from student residence rooms and from off campus.
Website: http://www.mum.edu/

General Application Contact: Gwen Stowe, Dean of Admissions, 641-472-1110, Fax: 641-472-1179, E-mail: admissions@mum.edu.

GRADUATE UNITS

Graduate Studies ***Financial support:*** Fellowships, research assistantships, teaching assistantships, career-related internships or fieldwork, Federal Work-Study, institutionally sponsored loans, scholarships/grants, tuition waivers (partial), and unspecified assistantships available. Support available to part-time students. Financial award applicants required to submit FAFSA. *Degree program information:* Evening/weekend programs available. Evening/weekend, online learning. Offers accounting (MBA); computer science (MS); Maharishi Vedic science (MA, PhD); management (PhD); sustainability (MBA). *Application deadline:* For fall admission, 4/15 priority date for domestic students, 5/15 priority date for international students. Applications are processed on a rolling basis. *Application fee:* $30. Electronic applications accepted. *Application Contact:* Barbara Rainbow, Director of Admissions, 641-472-1110, Fax: 641-472-1179, E-mail: admissions@mum.edu. *Dean of the Graduate School*, Dr. Frederick Travis, 641-472-7000 Ext. 3309, E-mail: ftravis@mum.edu.

MAINE COLLEGE OF ART, Portland, ME 04101

General Information Independent, coed, comprehensive institution.

GRADUATE UNITS

Program in Studio Art Offers studio art (MA, MFA). Electronic applications accepted.

MAINE MARITIME ACADEMY, Castine, ME 04420

General Information State-supported, coed, primarily men, comprehensive institution. *Graduate housing:* Rooms and/or apartments available on a first-come, first-served basis to single and married students. Housing application deadline: 4/15.

GRADUATE UNITS

Loeb-Sullivan School of International Business and Logistics ***Degree program information:*** Part-time programs available. Part-time. Offers global logistics and maritime management (MS); international logistics management (MS).

MALONE UNIVERSITY, Canton, OH 44709

General Information Independent-religious, coed, comprehensive institution. *Graduate housing:* On-campus housing not available.

GRADUATE UNITS

Graduate Program in Business ***Degree program information:*** Part-time and evening/weekend programs available. Part-time, evening/weekend, online learning. Offers business (MBA).

Graduate Program in Counseling and Human Development ***Degree program information:*** Part-time and evening/weekend programs available. Part-time, evening/weekend. Offers clinical counseling (MA); school counseling (MA).

Graduate Program in Education ***Degree program information:*** Part-time and evening/weekend programs available. Part-time, evening/weekend. Offers curriculum and instruction (MA); curriculum, instruction, and professional development (MA); educational leadership (principal license) (MA); intervention specialist (MA).

Graduate Program in Nursing ***Degree program information:*** Part-time and evening/weekend programs available. Part-time, evening/weekend. Offers family nurse practitioner (MSN).

Graduate Program in Organizational Leadership ***Degree program information:*** Part-time and evening/weekend programs available. Part-time, evening/weekend. Offers organizational leadership (MAOL).

Graduate Program in Theological Studies ***Degree program information:*** Part-time and evening/weekend programs available. Part-time, evening/weekend. Offers theological studies (MA).

MANCHESTER UNIVERSITY, North Manchester, IN 46962-1225

General Information Independent-religious, coed, comprehensive institution. *Enrollment:* 1,536 graduate, professional, and undergraduate students; 284 full-time matriculated graduate/professional students (174 women), 6 part-time matriculated graduate/professional students (4 women). *Enrollment by degree level:* 19 master's, 271 doctoral. *Graduate faculty:* 40 full-time (20 women), 1 part-time/adjunct (0 women). *Graduate housing:* On-campus housing not available. *Student services:* Campus safety program, career counseling, multicultural affairs office. *Library:* Funderburg Library.

Computer facilities: Computer purchase and lease plans are available. 226 computers available on campus for general student use. A campuswide network can be accessed from student residence rooms and from off campus. Online class registration is available.
Website: http://www.manchester.edu/

General Application Contact: Dr. Mark Huntington, Graduate Program Director, 260-982-5033, E-mail: mwhuntington@manchester.edu.

GRADUATE UNITS

Doctor of Pharmacy Program Students: 271 full-time (166 women), 6 part-time (4 women); includes 120 minority (41 Black or African American, non-Hispanic/Latino; 2 American Indian or Alaska Native, non-Hispanic/Latino; 71 Asian, non-Hispanic/Latino; 6 Hispanic/Latino). Average age 25. 667 applicants, 21% accepted, 72 enrolled. *Faculty:* 34 full-time (19 women). Offers pharmacy (Pharm D). *Application deadline:* For fall admission, 3/1 for domestic students. *Application fee:* $180. *Associate Dean for Student Affairs*, Dr. Joseph K. Bonnarens, 260-470-2655, E-mail: jkbonnarens@manchester.edu.

Program in Athletic Training Students: 13 full-time (8 women); includes 2 minority (1 Black or African American, non-Hispanic/Latino; 1 Asian, non-Hispanic/Latino). Average age 22. 28 applicants, 75% accepted, 6 enrolled. *Faculty:* 6 full-time (1 woman), 1 part-time/adjunct (0 women). *Financial support:* In 2015–16, 13 students received support, including 13 fellowships (averaging $7,400 per year). Financial award application deadline: 5/1; financial award applicants required to submit FAFSA. In 2015, 7 master's awarded. Offers athletic training (MAT). *Application deadline:* For fall admission, 2/1 priority date for domestic students. Applications are processed on a rolling basis. *Application fee:* $50. Electronic applications accepted. *Program Director, Graduate Athletic Training Education*, Mark Huntington, 260-982-5033, E-mail: mwhuntington@manchester.edu.

MANHATTAN COLLEGE, Riverdale, NY 10471

General Information Independent-religious, coed, comprehensive institution. *Graduate housing:* Rooms and/or apartments available on a first-come, first-served basis to single and married students.

GRADUATE UNITS

Graduate Programs ***Degree program information:*** Part-time and evening/weekend programs available. Part-time, evening/weekend.

School of Business Students: 45 full-time (24 women), 7 part-time (4 women). Average age 24. *Faculty:* 35 full-time (19 women), 2 part-time/adjunct (1 woman). *Financial support:* Research assistantships, career-related internships or fieldwork, scholarships/grants, and unspecified assistantships available. In 2015, 36 master's awarded. *Degree program information:* Part-time programs available. Part-time, 100%

online, blended/hybrid learning. Offers business (MBA). *Application deadline:* For fall admission, 8/1 for domestic and international students; for spring admission, 1/1 for domestic and international students; for summer admission, 4/1 for domestic and international students. Applications are processed on a rolling basis. *Application fee:* $75. Electronic applications accepted. *Application Contact:* Dr. Marc Waldman, MBA Program Director, 718-862-7872, E-mail: marc.waldman@manhattan.edu. *Dean*, Dr. Salwa Ammar, 718-862-8032.

School of Continuing and Professional Studies Offers organizational leadership (MS). Electronic applications accepted.

School of Education and Health Degree program information: Part-time and evening/weekend programs available. Part-time, evening/weekend, online learning. Offers autism spectrum disorder (Advanced Certificate); bilingual pupil personnel services (Professional Diploma); bilingual special education (Advanced Certificate); dual childhood/special education (MS Ed); education and health (MA, MS, MS Ed, Advanced Certificate, Certificate, Professional Diploma); instructional design and delivery (MS); mental health counseling (MS, Professional Diploma); school building leadership (MS Ed, Advanced Certificate); school counseling (MA, Professional Diploma); special education (MS Ed).

School of Engineering Degree program information: Part-time and evening/weekend programs available. Part-time, evening/weekend. Offers chemical engineering (MS); civil engineering (MS); computer engineering (MS); cosmetic engineering (MS); electrical engineering (MS); environmental engineering (ME, MS); mechanical engineering (MS).

School of Science Offers applied mathematics-data analytics (MS); mathematics (MS).

MANHATTAN SCHOOL OF MUSIC, New York, NY 10027-4698

General Information Independent, coed, comprehensive institution. *Graduate housing:* Room and/or apartments available on a first-come, first-served basis to single students; on-campus housing not available to married students. Housing application deadline: 6/15.

GRADUATE UNITS

Graduate Programs Offers composition (MM, DMA); jazz (MM, DMA); music performance (MM, DMA); orchestral performance (MM). Electronic applications accepted.

Professional Studies Certificate Program Offers instrumental music (CPS); vocal music (CPS). Electronic applications accepted.

MANHATTANVILLE COLLEGE, Purchase, NY 10577-2132

General Information Independent, coed, comprehensive institution. *Enrollment:* 2,921 graduate, professional, and undergraduate students; 181 full-time matriculated graduate/professional students (105 women), 730 part-time matriculated graduate/professional students (491 women). *Enrollment by degree level:* 755 master's, 79 doctoral, 77 other advanced degrees. *Graduate faculty:* 22 full-time (14 women), 118 part-time/adjunct (64 women). *Tuition, area resident:* Full-time $16,110; part-time $895 per credit. *Required fees:* $60 per semester. Part-time tuition and fees vary according to course load and program. *Graduate housing:* Room and/or apartments available on a first-come, first-served basis to single students; on-campus housing not available to married students. Typical cost: $8680 per year ($14,520 including board). Room and board charges vary according to board plan. Housing application deadline: 7/22. *Student services:* Campus employment opportunities, campus safety program, career counseling, exercise/wellness program, international student services, multicultural affairs office, services for students with disabilities, teacher training, writing training. *Library:* Manhattanville College Library. *Collection:* Books: 190,979 (physical), 151,519 (digital/electronic); Serial titles: 984 (physical), 57,840 (digital/electronic); Databases: 111. Weekly public service hours: 139.

Computer facilities: 150 computers available on campus for general student use. A campuswide network can be accessed from student residence rooms and from off campus. Online class registration is available.
Website: http://www.mville.edu/

GRADUATE UNITS

Master of Fine Art in Creative Writing Program Students: 11 full-time (7 women), 27 part-time (20 women). Average age 29. 64 applicants, 53% accepted, 8 enrolled. *Faculty:* 7 part-time/adjunct (5 women). *Financial support:* In 2015–16, 8 fellowships were awarded; Federal Work-Study, scholarships/grants, tuition waivers (partial), and unspecified assistantships also available. Financial award application deadline: 7/15; financial award applicants required to submit FAFSA. *Degree program information:* Part-time programs available. Part-time. Offers creative writing (MFA). *Application deadline:* Applications are processed on a rolling basis. *Application fee:* $0. Electronic applications accepted. *Application Contact:* Jeanine Pardey-Levine, Director of Graduate Enrollment Management, 914-323-3208, E-mail: jeanine.pardey@mville.edu. *Program Director*, Mark Nowak, 914-323-7157, Fax: 914-323-3122, E-mail: mfa@mville.edu.

School of Business Students: 38 full-time (12 women), 99 part-time (56 women); includes 60 minority (23 Black or African American, non-Hispanic/Latino; 9 Asian, non-Hispanic/Latino; 21 Hispanic/Latino; 7 Two or more races, non-Hispanic/Latino). Average age 29. 153 applicants, 47% accepted, 42 enrolled. *Faculty:* 29 part-time/adjunct (8 women). *Financial support:* Federal Work-Study, institutionally sponsored loans, scholarships/grants, and unspecified assistantships available. Financial award applicants required to submit FAFSA. In 2015, 115 master's awarded. *Degree program information:* Part-time and evening/weekend programs available. Part-time, evening/weekend. Offers accounting (MS); business (MS); business leadership (MS); corporate finance (MS); finance (MS); human resource management (MS); investment management (MS); marketing communication management (MS); organizational effectiveness (MS); sport business management (MS). *Application deadline:* Applications are processed on a rolling basis. *Application fee:* $75. Electronic applications accepted. *Application Contact:* Monika Pottgen, Assistant Director, Recruitment and Admissions, 914-323-5150, E-mail: business@mville.edu. *Dean*, Anthony Davidson, 914-323-5315, E-mail: anthony.davidson@mville.edu.

School of Education Students: 132 full-time (86 women), 604 part-time (415 women); includes 111 minority (32 Black or African American, non-Hispanic/Latino; 1 American Indian or Alaska Native, non-Hispanic/Latino; 10 Asian, non-Hispanic/Latino; 55 Hispanic/Latino; 13 Two or more races, non-Hispanic/Latino). Average age 32. 379 applicants, 58% accepted, 170 enrolled. *Faculty:* 22 full-time (14 women), 82 part-time/adjunct (51 women). *Financial support:* Teaching assistantships, career-related internships or fieldwork, Federal Work-Study, institutionally sponsored loans, scholarships/grants, and unspecified assistantships available. Financial award applicants required to submit FAFSA. In 2015, 190 master's, 4 doctorates, 18 other advanced degrees awarded. *Degree program information:* Part-time and evening/weekend programs available. Part-time, evening/weekend. Offers accelerated teacher certification (MAT, MPS, Advanced Certificate); adult and international settings (MPS); biology (MAT); biology and special education (MPS); chemistry (MAT); chemistry and special education (MPS); childhood education (MAT, MPS); childhood education (grades 1-6) (MAT); early childhood and special education (birth-grade 2) (MPS); early childhood education (birth-grade 2) (MAT); education (M Ed, MAT, MPS, Ed D, Advanced Certificate, PD); education entrepreneurship (M Ed); educational leadership (MPS, Ed D, PD); educational studies (M Ed); English (MAT); English and special education (MPS); health and wellness specialist (Advanced Certificate); literacy and special education (MPS); literacy education (MPS); literacy specialist (MPS); math and special education (MPS); mathematics (MAT); music education (MAT); physical education and sport pedagogy (MAT); physics (MAT); social studies (MAT); social studies and special education (MPS); special education (MPS, Advanced Certificate); special education (birth-grade 2) (MPS); special education (birth-grade 6) (MPS); special education generalist (MPS); teaching English as a second language (MPS); teaching languages other than English (MAT); visual arts education (MAT). *Application deadline:* For fall admission, 7/1 priority date for domestic and international students; for spring admission, 11/1 priority date for domestic students; for summer admission, 4/1 priority date for domestic and international students. Applications are processed on a rolling basis. *Application fee:* $75. Electronic applications accepted. *Application Contact:* Jeanine Pardey-Levine, Director of Graduate Enrollment Management, 914-323-3208, Fax: 914-694-1732, E-mail: edschool@mville.edu. *Dean*, Dr. Shelley Wepner, 914-323-3153, Fax: 914-694-2386, E-mail: shelley.wepner@mville.edu.

MANSFIELD UNIVERSITY OF PENNSYLVANIA, Mansfield, PA 16933

General Information State-supported, coed, comprehensive institution. *Graduate housing:* Room and/or apartments available on a first-come, first-served basis to single students; on-campus housing not available to married students.

GRADUATE UNITS

Graduate Studies *Degree program information:* Part-time and evening/weekend programs available. Part-time, evening/weekend, online learning. Offers art education (M Ed); band conducting (MA); choral conducting (MA); elementary education (M Ed); library science (M Ed); nursing (MSN); organizational leadership (MA); performance (MA); secondary education (MS); special education (M Ed). Electronic applications accepted.

MAPLE SPRINGS BAPTIST BIBLE COLLEGE AND SEMINARY, Capitol Heights, MD 20743

General Information Independent-religious, coed, comprehensive institution. *Graduate housing:* On-campus housing not available.

GRADUATE UNITS

Graduate and Professional Programs Offers biblical studies (MA, Certificate); Christian counseling (MA); church administration (MA); divinity (M Div); ministry (D Min); religious education (MRE).

MARANATHA BAPTIST UNIVERSITY, Watertown, WI 53094

General Information Independent-religious, coed, comprehensive institution. *Enrollment:* 1,035 graduate, professional, and undergraduate students; 27 full-time matriculated graduate/professional students (4 women), 65 part-time matriculated graduate/professional students (5 women). *Enrollment by degree level:* 92 master's. *Graduate faculty:* 7 full-time (1 woman), 9 part-time/adjunct (2 women). *Tuition, area resident:* Full-time $6300; part-time $3150 per credit. *Required fees:* $210; $35 per course. Tuition and fees vary according to course load and degree level. *Graduate housing:* Room and/or apartments available to single students; on-campus housing not available to married students. *Student services:* Campus employment opportunities, campus safety program, child daycare facilities, teacher training. *Library:* Cedarholm Library and Resource Center.

Computer facilities: A campuswide network can be accessed from student residence rooms and from off campus. Online class registration is available.
Website: http://www.mbu.edu/

General Application Contact: Dr. Jim Harrison, Director of Admissions, 920-206-2327, Fax: 920-261-9109, E-mail: admissions@mbbc.edu.

GRADUATE UNITS

Master of Arts in English Bible Program *Degree program information:* Part-time programs available. Part-time, online learning. Offers English Bible (MA).

Master of Arts in Intercultural Studies Program *Degree program information:* Part-time programs available. Part-time. Offers intercultural studies (MA).

Master of Divinity Program *Degree program information:* Part-time programs available. Part-time. Offers divinity (M Div).

Program in Biblical Counseling *Degree program information:* Part-time programs available. Part-time. Offers Biblical counseling (MA).

Program in Biblical Studies *Degree program information:* Part-time programs available. Part-time. Offers Biblical studies (MA).

Program in Teaching and Learning *Degree program information:* Part-time and evening/weekend programs available. Part-time, evening/weekend, online learning. Offers teaching and learning (M Ed).

MARCONI INTERNATIONAL UNIVERSITY, Pembroke Pines, FL 33028

General Information Proprietary, coed, comprehensive institution.

GRADUATE UNITS

Graduate Programs

MARIAN UNIVERSITY, Indianapolis, IN 46222-1997

General Information Independent-religious, coed, comprehensive institution. *Enrollment:* 2,900 graduate, professional, and undergraduate students; 502 full-time matriculated graduate/professional students (245 women), 299 part-time matriculated graduate/professional students (224 women). *Enrollment by degree level:* 303 master's, 472 doctoral. *Graduate faculty:* 37 full-time (14 women), 41 part-time/adjunct (32 women). *Tuition, area resident:* Full-time $46,300. *Required fees:* $1500. Tuition and fees vary according to degree level and program. *Graduate housing:* Rooms and/or apartments available on a first-come, first-served basis to single and married students. Typical cost: $4692 per year ($9436 including board) for single students; $6528 per year ($11,272 including board) for married students. Room and board charges vary according to housing facility selected. Housing application deadline: 3/1. *Student services:* Campus safety program, career counseling, exercise/wellness program, free psychological counseling, international student services, low-cost health insurance, services for students with disabilities, teacher training, writing training. *Library:* Mother

Theresa Hackelmeier Memorial Library. *Collection:* Books: 92,184 (physical); Serial titles: 100 (physical), 50 (digital/electronic). Weekly public service hours: 95.

Computer facilities: Computer purchase and lease plans are available. 118 computers available on campus for general student use. A campuswide network can be accessed from student residence rooms. Online class registration is available.
Website: http://www.marian.edu/

General Application Contact: Bryan Moody, Executive Director of Graduate Admission, 317-955-6284, E-mail: bmoody@marian.edu.

GRADUATE UNITS

College of Osteopathic Medicine Students: 472 full-time (225 women); includes 93 minority (9 Black or African American, non-Hispanic/Latino; 58 Asian, non-Hispanic/Latino; 18 Hispanic/Latino; 8 Two or more races, non-Hispanic/Latino), 12 international. Average age 25. 4,339 applicants, 8% accepted, 162 enrolled. *Faculty:* 29 full-time (8 women), 1 part-time/adjunct (0 women). *Financial support:* Applicants required to submit FAFSA. Offers osteopathic medicine (DO). *Application deadline:* For fall admission, 3/1 for domestic and international students. Applications are processed on a rolling basis. *Application fee:* $100. Electronic applications accepted. *Application Contact:* Bryan Moody, Director of Enrollment Management, 317-955-6284, E-mail: bmoody@marian.edu. *Vice President of Health Professions/Dean of the College of Osteopathic Medicine,* Dr. Donald Sefcik, 317-955-6289, E-mail: dsefcik@marian.edu.

School of Education Students: 29 full-time (21 women), 247 part-time (177 women); includes 63 minority (47 Black or African American, non-Hispanic/Latino; 12 Asian, non-Hispanic/Latino; 4 Two or more races, non-Hispanic/Latino). Average age 27. 192 applicants, 91% accepted, 169 enrolled. *Faculty:* 6 full-time (5 women), 23 part-time/adjunct (16 women). In 2015, 139 master's awarded. *Degree program information:* Part-time and evening/weekend programs available. Part-time, evening/weekend. Offers education (MA, MA Ed, MAT). *Application deadline:* For fall admission, 2/1 priority date for domestic students. Applications are processed on a rolling basis. *Application fee:* $35. Electronic applications accepted. *Application Contact:* Erika Wise, Graduate Education Program Director, 317-955-6286, Fax: 317-955-6406, E-mail: ewise@marian.edu. *Dean,* Dr. Diana Cheshire, 317-955-6096, Fax: 317-955-6406, E-mail: dcheshire@marian.edu.

MARIAN UNIVERSITY, Fond du Lac, WI 54935-4699

General Information Independent-religious, coed, comprehensive institution. CGS member. *Enrollment:* 2,099 graduate, professional, and undergraduate students; 44 full-time matriculated graduate/professional students (38 women), 449 part-time matriculated graduate/professional students (310 women). *Enrollment by degree level:* 307 master's, 70 doctoral, 116 other advanced degrees. *Graduate faculty:* 19 full-time (15 women), 24 part-time/adjunct (13 women). *Tuition, area resident:* Part-time $490 per credit hour. *Graduate housing:* On-campus housing not available. *Student services:* Campus employment opportunities, campus safety program, career counseling, child daycare facilities, exercise/wellness program, free psychological counseling, international student services, multicultural affairs office, services for students with disabilities, teacher training, writing training. *Library:* Cardinal Meyer Library. *Collection:* Books: 210,079 (physical), 147,236 (digital/electronic); Databases: 1,805.

Computer facilities: Computer purchase and lease plans are available. 500 computers available on campus for general student use. A campuswide network can be accessed from student residence rooms and from off campus. Online class registration is available.
Website: http://www.marianuniversity.edu/

General Application Contact: Dr. Sheryl Ayala, Interim Vice President for Academic Affairs, 920-923-7671, E-mail: sayala@marianuniversity.edu.

GRADUATE UNITS

School of Business and Public Safety Students: 1 (woman) full-time, 53 part-time (32 women); includes 5 minority (3 Black or African American, non-Hispanic/Latino; 1 Asian, non-Hispanic/Latino; 1 Hispanic/Latino). Average age 38. *Faculty:* 4 part-time/adjunct (2 women). *Financial support:* Institutionally sponsored loans available. Financial award application deadline: 3/1; financial award applicants required to submit FAFSA. In 2015, 27 master's awarded. *Degree program information:* Part-time and evening/weekend programs available. Part-time, evening/weekend. Offers criminal justice leadership (MS); organizational leadership (MS). *Application deadline:* Applications are processed on a rolling basis. *Application fee:* $25. Electronic applications accepted. *Dean, Marian School of Business,* Dr. Jeffrey G. Reed, 920-923-8759, Fax: 920-923-7167, E-mail: jreed@marianuniversity.edu.

School of Education Students: 22 full-time (17 women), 300 part-time (193 women); includes 35 minority (15 Black or African American, non-Hispanic/Latino; 7 American Indian or Alaska Native, non-Hispanic/Latino; 8 Asian, non-Hispanic/Latino; 4 Hispanic/Latino; 1 Two or more races, non-Hispanic/Latino). Average age 38. *Faculty:* 13 full-time (9 women), 14 part-time/adjunct (8 women). *Financial support:* In 2015–16, 3 students received support. Federal Work-Study and institutionally sponsored loans available. Support available to part-time students. Financial award application deadline: 3/1; financial award applicants required to submit FAFSA. In 2015, 75 master's, 12 doctorates awarded. *Degree program information:* Part-time and evening/weekend programs available. Part-time, evening/weekend, online learning. Offers curriculum and instruction leadership (PhD); educational administration (PhD); educational leadership (MAE); educational technology (MAE); leadership studies (PhD); special education (MAE); teacher education (MAE). PhD in leadership studies offered jointly with School of Business and Public Safety. *Application deadline:* Applications are processed on a rolling basis. *Application fee:* $50. *Application Contact:* Rachel Benike, Admissions Counselor, 920-923-8118, Fax: 920-923-7154, E-mail: rlbenike43@marianuniversity.edu. *Dean,* Dr. Sue Stoddart, 920-923-8099, Fax: 920-923-7663, E-mail: sstoddart@marianuniversity.edu.

School of Nursing and Health Professions Students: 21 full-time (20 women), 95 part-time (85 women); includes 10 minority (6 Black or African American, non-Hispanic/Latino; 2 Asian, non-Hispanic/Latino; 2 Hispanic/Latino). Average age 40. *Faculty:* 6 full-time (all women), 4 part-time/adjunct (2 women). *Financial support:* In 2015–16, 3 students received support. Institutionally sponsored loans and scholarships/grants available. Support available to part-time students. Financial award application deadline: 3/1; financial award applicants required to submit FAFSA. In 2015, 26 master's awarded. *Degree program information:* Part-time and evening/weekend programs available. Part-time, evening/weekend. Offers adult nurse practitioner (MSN); nurse educator (MSN). *Application deadline:* Applications are processed on a rolling basis. *Application fee:* $50. Electronic applications accepted. *Application Contact:* Selina Scoles, Admissions Counselor, 920-923-8938, Fax: 920-923-8770, E-mail: sascoles30@marianuniversity.edu. *Dean,* Dr. Linda Matheson, 920-923-7668, Fax: 920-923-8770, E-mail: lkmatheson85@marianuniversity.edu.

MARIETTA COLLEGE, Marietta, OH 45750-4000

General Information Independent, coed, comprehensive institution. *Enrollment:* 1,331 graduate, professional, and undergraduate students; 83 full-time matriculated graduate/professional students (62 women), 2 part-time matriculated graduate/professional students (both women). *Enrollment by degree level:* 85 master's. *Graduate faculty:* 5 full-time (2 women), 7 part-time/adjunct (2 women). *Tuition, area resident:* Full-time $36,841; part-time $750 per credit hour. One-time fee: $500 full-time. Tuition and fees vary according to program. *Graduate housing:* On-campus housing not available. *Student services:* Campus safety program, career counseling, free psychological counseling, international student services, services for students with disabilities, teacher training, writing training. *Library:* Legacy Library. *Collection:* Books: 242,208 (physical), 129,563 (digital/electronic); Serial titles: 245 (physical), 63,128 (digital/electronic); Databases: 186. Weekly public service hours: 94; students can reserve study rooms.

Computer facilities: 400 computers available on campus for general student use. A campuswide network can be accessed from student residence rooms and from off campus. Online class registration is available.
Website: http://www.marietta.edu/

General Application Contact: Scott McVicar, Director of Admissions, 740-376-4606, E-mail: scott.mcvicar@marietta.edu.

GRADUATE UNITS

Program in Physician Assistant Studies Students: 72 full-time (53 women); includes 12 minority (1 Black or African American, non-Hispanic/Latino; 1 American Indian or Alaska Native, non-Hispanic/Latino; 7 Asian, non-Hispanic/Latino; 2 Hispanic/Latino; 1 Two or more races, non-Hispanic/Latino). Average age 24. 877 applicants, 4% accepted, 36 enrolled. *Faculty:* 5 full-time (2 women), 2 part-time/adjunct (0 women). *Financial support:* Scholarships/grants available. In 2015, 36 master's awarded. Offers physician assistant studies (MS). *Application deadline:* For fall admission, 11/1 for domestic students. *Application fee:* $175. Electronic applications accepted. *Director,* Miranda Collins, 740-376-4953, E-mail: miranda.collins@marietta.edu.

Program in Psychology Students: 10 full-time (6 women), 1 (woman) part-time; includes 1 minority (Black or African American, non-Hispanic/Latino), 1 international. Average age 24. 16 applicants, 63% accepted, 6 enrolled. *Faculty:* 5 part-time/adjunct (2 women). *Financial support:* Unspecified assistantships available. In 2015, 1 master's awarded. *Degree program information:* Part-time programs available. Part-time. Offers psychology (MAP). *Application deadline:* Applications are processed on a rolling basis. *Application fee:* $25. *Director,* Dr. Chris Klein, 740-376-4795, E-mail: clk002@marietta.edu.

MARIST COLLEGE, Poughkeepsie, NY 12601-1387

General Information Independent, coed, comprehensive institution. *Graduate housing:* On-campus housing not available. *Research affiliation:* Center for Advanced Brain Imaging Psychology (psychology), New York State Office of Technology and Academic Research (NYSTAR) (technology), Hudson Valley Technology Development Corporation (HVTDC) (technology), Hudson River Psychiatric Center (psychology), St. Francis Hospital, Dutchess County Community Mental Health Center (mental health).

GRADUATE UNITS

Graduate Programs *Degree program information:* Part-time and evening/weekend programs available. Part-time, evening/weekend, online learning. Electronic applications accepted.

School of Communication and the Arts Degree program information: Part-time programs available. Part-time, online learning. Offers communication (MA); integrated marketing communication (MA); museum studies (MA). Electronic applications accepted.

School of Computer Science and Mathematics Degree program information: Part-time and evening/weekend programs available. Part-time, evening/weekend, online learning. Offers computer science/software development (MS); information systems (MS, Adv C); technology management (MS). Electronic applications accepted.

School of Management Degree program information: Part-time and evening/weekend programs available. Part-time, evening/weekend, online learning. Offers business administration (MBA, Adv C); executive leadership (Adv C); public administration (MPA); technology management (MS). Electronic applications accepted.

School of Social and Behavioral Sciences Degree program information: Part-time and evening/weekend programs available. Part-time, evening/weekend. Offers education (M Ed, MA); mental health counseling (MA); school psychology (MA, Adv C). Electronic applications accepted.

MARLBORO COLLEGE, Marlboro, VT 05344

General Information Independent, coed, comprehensive institution. *Enrollment:* 280 graduate, professional, and undergraduate students; 23 full-time matriculated graduate/professional students (9 women), 64 part-time matriculated graduate/professional students (39 women). *Enrollment by degree level:* 83 master's, 4 other advanced degrees. *Graduate faculty:* 3 full-time (2 women), 54 part-time/adjunct (33 women). *Tuition, area resident:* Part-time $765 per credit. Tuition and fees vary according to course load and program. *Graduate housing:* On-campus housing not available. *Student services:* Career counseling, international student services, services for students with disabilities, teacher training, writing training. *Library:* Rice-Aron Library. *Collection:* Books: 88,500 (physical), 137,548 (digital/electronic); Serial titles: 5,400 (physical), 150 (digital/electronic); Databases: 75. Study areas open 24 hours, 5–7 days a week.

Computer facilities: Computer purchase and lease plans are available. 47 computers available on campus for general student use. A campuswide network can be accessed from student residence rooms and from off campus. Online class registration is available.
Website: http://www.marlboro.edu/

General Application Contact: Brandon McNeice, Assistant Director of Graduate Admissions, 802-258-9209, Fax: 802-258-9201, E-mail: admissions@gradschool.marlboro.edu.

GRADUATE UNITS

Graduate and Professional Studies Students: 23 full-time (9 women), 64 part-time (39 women); includes 23 minority (8 Black or African American, non-Hispanic/Latino; 1 Asian, non-Hispanic/Latino; 9 Hispanic/Latino; 5 Two or more races, non-Hispanic/Latino), 1 international. Average age 38. 60 applicants, 52% accepted, 20 enrolled. *Faculty:* 3 full-time (2 women), 54 part-time/adjunct (33 women). *Financial support:* In 2015–16, 5 students received support. Scholarships/grants available. Financial award applicants required to submit FAFSA. In 2015, 44 master's awarded. *Degree program information:* Part-time and evening/weekend programs available. Part-time, evening/weekend, blended/hybrid learning. Offers business administration (MBA); collaborative leadership (MBA, MS); conscious business (MBA, MS); educational technology (Certificate); management (MS); mission driven organizations (MBA, MS); project management (MBA, MS, Certificate); social innovation (MBA, MS); sustainable food systems (MBA, MS); teaching English to speakers of other languages (MAT); teaching for social justice (MAT); teaching with technology (MAT, Certificate). *Application deadline:* For fall admission, 8/5 for domestic and international students; for winter admission, 12/5 for domestic and international students; for spring admission, 4/5 for domestic and international students. Applications are processed on a rolling basis. *Application fee:* $0. Electronic applications accepted. *Application Contact:* Kara Hamilton, Admissions Counselor, 802-451-7506, E-mail: khamilton@marlboro.edu. *Associate Dean for Graduate and Professional Studies*, Kate Jellema, 802-258-9203, Fax: 802-258-9201, E-mail: katej@marlboro.edu.

MARQUETTE UNIVERSITY, Milwaukee, WI 53201-1881

General Information Independent-religious, coed, university. CGS member. *Graduate housing:* Rooms and/or apartments available on a first-come, first-served basis to single and married students. *Student services:* Campus employment opportunities, campus safety program, career counseling, child daycare facilities, exercise/wellness program, free psychological counseling, grant writing training, international student services, low-cost health insurance, multicultural affairs office, services for students with disabilities, teacher training, writing training. *Library:* Raynor Memorial Libraries plus 1 other. *Collection:* Books: 1.8 million (physical), 3,492 (digital/electronic); Serial titles: 1,596 (physical), 46,519 (digital/electronic); Databases: 231. Weekly public service hours: 166; study areas open 24 hours, 5–7 days a week; students can reserve study rooms. *Research affiliation:* Shriners Hospital for Children in Chicago, Rehabilitation Institute of Chicago, Froedtert Memorial Lutheran Hospital, Children's Hospital of Wisconsin, Blood Center of Wisconsin, Department of Orthopedic Surgery, Medical College of Wisconsin.

Computer facilities: 1,720 computers available on campus for general student use. A campuswide network can be accessed from student residence rooms and from off campus. Online class registration, AV Software, MATLAB, Printwise are available. Website: http://www.marquette.edu/

GRADUATE UNITS

Graduate School Students: 1,001 full-time (615 women), 631 part-time (392 women); includes 195 minority (38 Black or African American, non-Hispanic/Latino; 2 American Indian or Alaska Native, non-Hispanic/Latino; 59 Asian, non-Hispanic/Latino; 70 Hispanic/Latino; 26 Two or more races, non-Hispanic/Latino), 180 international. Average age 28. 1,790 applicants, 53% accepted, 495 enrolled. *Faculty:* 429 full-time (186 women), 274 part-time/adjunct (155 women). *Financial support:* In 2015–16, 56 fellowships, 73 research assistantships with full tuition reimbursements, 217 teaching assistantships with full tuition reimbursements were awarded; career-related internships or fieldwork, Federal Work-Study, institutionally sponsored loans, scholarships/grants, and tuition waivers (full and partial) also available. Support available to part-time students. Financial award application deadline: 2/15. In 2015, 407 master's, 62 doctorates, 103 other advanced degrees awarded. *Degree program information:* Part-time and evening/weekend programs available. Part-time, evening/weekend, online learning. Offers interdisciplinary studies (PhD); transfusion medicine (MSTM). *Application deadline:* Applications are processed on a rolling basis. Electronic applications accepted. *Vice Provost for Research/Dean*, Dr. Douglas Woods, 414-288-1532, Fax: 414-288-1578.

College of Arts and Sciences Students: 332 full-time (136 women), 162 part-time (53 women); includes 54 minority (6 Black or African American, non-Hispanic/Latino; 18 Asian, non-Hispanic/Latino; 22 Hispanic/Latino; 8 Two or more races, non-Hispanic/Latino), 103 international. Average age 30. 651 applicants, 38% accepted, 127 enrolled. *Faculty:* 233 full-time (84 women), 76 part-time/adjunct (29 women). *Financial support:* In 2015–16, 309 students received support, including 33 fellowships with partial tuition reimbursements available, 43 research assistantships with full tuition reimbursements available, 166 teaching assistantships with full tuition reimbursements available; scholarships/grants, health care benefits, tuition waivers (full and partial), and unspecified assistantships also available. Support available to part-time students. Financial award application deadline: 2/15. In 2015, 95 master's, 38 doctorates awarded. *Degree program information:* Part-time programs available. Part-time. Offers American literature (PhD); analytical chemistry (MS, PhD); ancient philosophy (PhD); arts and sciences (MA, MACD, MS, PhD); bioanalytical chemistry (MS, PhD); bioinformatics (MS); biophysical chemistry (MS, PhD); British and American literature (MA); British empiricism and analytic philosophy (PhD); British literature (PhD); cell biology (MS, PhD); chemical physics (MS, PhD); Christian philosophy (PhD); computational sciences (MS, PhD); computing (MS); developmental biology (MS, PhD); early modern European philosophy (PhD); ecology (MS, PhD); epithelial physiology (MS, PhD); ethics (PhD); European history (MA, PhD); genetics (MS, PhD); German philosophy (PhD); global studies (MA); history of philosophy (MA); inorganic chemistry (MS, PhD); international affairs (MA); mathematics education (MS); medieval philosophy (PhD); microbiology (MS, PhD); molecular biology (MS, PhD); muscle and exercise physiology (MS, PhD); neuroscience (PhD); organic chemistry (MS, PhD); phenomenology and existentialism (PhD); philosophy of religion (PhD); physical chemistry (MS, PhD); political science (MA); psychology (PhD); social and applied philosophy (MA); Spanish (MA); theology (MA, PhD); United States history (MA, PhD). *Application deadline:* Applications are processed on a rolling basis. Electronic applications accepted. *Dean*, Dr. Richard Holz, 414-288-7230.

College of Communication Students: 26 full-time (21 women), 16 part-time (10 women); includes 8 minority (2 Black or African American, non-Hispanic/Latino; 1 American Indian or Alaska Native, non-Hispanic/Latino; 4 Hispanic/Latino; 1 Two or more races, non-Hispanic/Latino), 5 international. Average age 28. 69 applicants, 67% accepted, 21 enrolled. *Faculty:* 34 full-time (17 women), 46 part-time/adjunct (17 women). *Financial support:* In 2015–16, 41 students received support, including 2 fellowships with partial tuition reimbursements available (averaging $10,385 per year), 6 research assistantships with full tuition reimbursements available (averaging $13,285 per year), 12 teaching assistantships with full tuition reimbursements available (averaging $13,285 per year); career-related internships or fieldwork, scholarships/grants, health care benefits, tuition waivers (full and partial), and unspecified assistantships also available. Support available to part-time students. Financial award application deadline: 2/15. In 2015, 16 master's, 6 other advanced degrees awarded. *Degree program information:* Part-time and evening/weekend programs available. Part-time, evening/weekend. Offers advertising and public relations (MA); communication studies (MA); digital storytelling (Certificate); journalism (MA); mass communication (MA); science, health and environmental communication (MA). *Application deadline:* Applications are processed on a rolling basis. Electronic applications accepted. *Application Contact:* Dr. Sarah Bonewits Feldner, Professor and Associate Dean, 414-288-3497. *Associate Dean*, Dr. Joyce Wolburg, 414-288-7133, Fax: 414-288-1578.

College of Education Students: 108 full-time (87 women), 98 part-time (69 women); includes 32 minority (13 Black or African American, non-Hispanic/Latino; 1 American Indian or Alaska Native, non-Hispanic/Latino; 5 Asian, non-Hispanic/Latino; 8 Hispanic/Latino; 5 Two or more races, non-Hispanic/Latino), 2 international. Average age 29. 202 applicants, 63% accepted, 99 enrolled. *Faculty:* 23 full-time (16 women), 29 part-time/adjunct (19 women). *Financial support:* In 2015–16, 155 students received support, including 2 fellowships with tuition reimbursements available, 11 research assistantships with full tuition reimbursements available; scholarships/grants, health care benefits, tuition waivers (partial), and unspecified assistantships also available. Support available to part-time students. Financial award application deadline: 2/15. In 2015, 76 master's, 4 doctorates, 2 other advanced degrees awarded. *Degree program information:* Part-time programs available. Part-time. Offers clinical mental health counseling (MS); college student personnel administration (M Ed); community counseling (MA); counseling psychology (PhD); curriculum and instruction (MA); education (M Ed, MA, MS, PhD, Certificate); educational administration (M Ed); educational policy and foundations (MA); elementary education (Certificate); literacy (MA); principal (Certificate); reading specialist (Certificate); reading teacher (Certificate); school counseling (MA); secondary education (Certificate); superintendent (Certificate). *Application deadline:* For fall admission, 1/15 for domestic and international students. *Dean*, Dr. William Henk, 414-288-7376.

College of Engineering Students: 118 full-time (35 women), 77 part-time (17 women); includes 22 minority (3 Black or African American, non-Hispanic/Latino; 8 Asian, non-Hispanic/Latino; 8 Hispanic/Latino; 3 Two or more races, non-Hispanic/Latino), 62 international. Average age 27. 294 applicants, 61% accepted, 45 enrolled. *Faculty:* 61 full-time (9 women), 14 part-time/adjunct (4 women). *Financial support:* In 2015–16, 63 students received support, including 9 fellowships with partial tuition reimbursements available, 5 research assistantships with full tuition reimbursements available, 31 teaching assistantships with full tuition reimbursements available; scholarships/grants, health care benefits, tuition waivers (partial), and unspecified assistantships also available. Support available to part-time students. Financial award application deadline: 2/15. In 2015, 39 master's, 12 doctorates awarded. *Degree program information:* Part-time and evening/weekend programs available. Part-time, evening/weekend. Offers biocomputing (ME); bioimaging (ME); bioinstrumentation (ME); bioinstrumentation/computers (MS, PhD); biomechanics (ME); biomechanics/biomaterials (MS, PhD); biorehabilitation (ME); construction engineering and management (MS, PhD, Certificate); digital signal processing (Certificate); electric machines, drives, and controls (Certificate); electrical and computer engineering (MS, PhD); engineering (ME, MS, MSEM, PhD, Certificate); engineering innovation (Certificate); engineering management (MSEM); environmental engineering (MS, PhD); functional imaging (PhD); healthcare technologies management (MS); mechanical engineering (MS, PhD); microwaves and antennas (Certificate); new product and process development (Certificate); rehabilitation bioengineering (PhD); sensors and smart systems (Certificate); structural design (Certificate); structural engineering and structural mechanics (MS, PhD); systems physiology (MS, PhD); transportation (Certificate); transportation engineering and materials (MS, PhD); waste and wastewater treatment processes (Certificate); water resources engineering (Certificate). *Application deadline:* Applications are processed on a rolling basis. Electronic applications accepted. *Dean*, Dr. Kris Ropella, 414-288-6591, Fax: 414-288-7082, E-mail: robert.bishop@marquette.edu.

College of Health Sciences Students: 282 full-time (223 women), 28 part-time (18 women); includes 44 minority (4 Black or African American, non-Hispanic/Latino; 16 Asian, non-Hispanic/Latino; 18 Hispanic/Latino; 6 Two or more races, non-Hispanic/Latino), 3 international. Average age 24. 2,309 applicants, 15% accepted, 127 enrolled. *Faculty:* 41 full-time (24 women), 40 part-time/adjunct (25 women). *Financial support:* In 2015–16, 32 students received support, including 1 fellowship, 6 research assistantships. In 2015, 78 master's, 1 doctorate, 72 other advanced degrees awarded. Offers bilingual English/Spanish (Certificate); clinical and translational rehabilitation science (MS, PhD); health sciences (MPAS, MS, DPT, PhD, Certificate); physical therapy (DPT); physician assistant studies (MPAS); speech-language pathology (MS). Electronic applications accepted. *Dean*, Dr. William C. Cullinan, 414-288-5053, E-mail: jack.brooks@mu.edu.

College of Nursing Students: 123 full-time (112 women), 242 part-time (220 women); includes 34 minority (9 Black or African American, non-Hispanic/Latino; 12 Asian, non-Hispanic/Latino; 10 Hispanic/Latino; 3 Two or more races, non-Hispanic/Latino), 4 international. Average age 30. 269 applicants, 61% accepted, 98 enrolled. *Faculty:* 35 full-time (all women), 56 part-time/adjunct (55 women). *Financial support:* In 2015–16, 41 students received support, including 1 fellowship with partial tuition reimbursement available (averaging $17,500 per year), 2 research assistantships with full tuition reimbursements available (averaging $13,285 per year), 8 teaching assistantships with full tuition reimbursements available (averaging $13,912 per year); career-related internships or fieldwork, Federal Work-Study, scholarships/grants, health care benefits, tuition waivers (partial), and unspecified assistantships also available. Support available to part-time students. Financial award application deadline: 2/15. In 2015, 84 master's, 5 doctorates, 22 other advanced degrees awarded. Offers acute care nurse practitioner (Certificate); adult clinical nurse specialist (Certificate); adult nurse practitioner (Certificate); advanced practice nursing (MSN, DNP); family nurse practitioner (Certificate); nurse-midwifery (Certificate); nursing (PhD); pediatric acute care (Certificate); pediatric primary care (Certificate); systems leadership and healthcare quality (Certificate). *Application deadline:* For fall admission, 2/15 for domestic and international students. Electronic applications accepted. *Application Contact:* Dr. Maureen O'Brien, Associate Dean/Clinical Associate Professor, 414-288-3823. *Interim Chair*, Dr. Donna McCarthy, 414-288-3800, Fax: 414-288-1578.

Graduate School of Management Students: 150 full-time (85 women), 279 part-time (92 women); includes 24 minority (7 Black or African American, non-Hispanic/Latino; 8 Asian, non-Hispanic/Latino; 7 Hispanic/Latino; 2 Two or more races, non-Hispanic/Latino), 7 international. Average age 29. 477 applicants, 63% accepted, 212 enrolled. *Faculty:* 77 full-time (23 women), 32 part-time/adjunct (11 women). *Financial support:* In 2015–16, 6 fellowships, 24 teaching assistantships were awarded; research assistantships, Federal Work-Study, institutionally sponsored loans, scholarships/grants, and tuition waivers (full and partial) also available. Support available to part-time students. Financial award application deadline: 2/15. In 2015, 201 master's, 7 other advanced degrees awarded. *Degree program information:* Part-time and evening/weekend programs available. Part-time, evening/weekend. Offers accounting (MSA); business administration (MBA); business economics (MSAE); economics (MBA); entrepreneurship (Certificate); finance (MBA); financial economics (MSAE); human resources (MBA); international business (MBA); international economics (MSAE); management (MBA, MSA, MSAE, MSHR, Certificate); management information systems (MBA); marketing (MBA); marketing research (MSAE); operations and supply chain management (MBA); real estate economics (MSAE); sports business (MBA). *Application deadline:* For fall admission, 2/15 for domestic and international students. Applications are processed on a rolling basis. Electronic applications accepted. *Application Contact:* Dr. Jeanne Simmons. *Dean*, Dr. Brian Till, 414-288-5724.

Law School Students: 530 full-time (192 women), 69 part-time (39 women); includes 103 minority (23 Black or African American, non-Hispanic/Latino; 16 Asian, non-Hispanic/Latino; 48 Hispanic/Latino; 16 Two or more races, non-Hispanic/Latino), 3 international. Average age 26. 1,107 applicants, 76% accepted, 179 enrolled. *Faculty:* 34 full-time (13 women), 33 part-time/adjunct (16 women). *Financial support:* Career-related internships or fieldwork, Federal Work-Study, and scholarships/grants available. Support available to part-time students. Financial award application deadline: 3/1; financial award applicants required to submit FAFSA. *Degree program information:* Part-time and evening/weekend programs available. Part-time, evening/weekend. Offers law (JD). *Application deadline:* For fall admission, 4/1 for domestic students. Applications are processed on a rolling basis. *Application fee:* $50. Electronic applications accepted. *Dean*, Joseph D. Kearney, 414-288-7090, Fax: 414-288-6403, E-mail: joseph.kearney@marquette.edu.

School of Dentistry Students: 410 full-time (199 women), 5 part-time (3 women); includes 103 minority (11 Black or African American, non-Hispanic/Latino; 3 American Indian or Alaska Native, non-Hispanic/Latino; 44 Asian, non-Hispanic/Latino; 34 Hispanic/Latino; 11 Two or more races, non-Hispanic/Latino), 9 international. Average age 25. 2,465 applicants, 5% accepted, 104 enrolled. *Faculty:* 50 full-time (13 women), 159 part-time/adjunct (40 women). *Financial support:* In 2015–16, 320 students received support. Fellowships with partial tuition reimbursements available, career-related internships or fieldwork, Federal Work-Study, institutionally sponsored loans, scholarships/grants, and tuition waivers (full and partial) available. Support available to part-time students. Financial award application deadline: 3/1; financial award applicants required to submit FAFSA. In 2015, 10 master's, 88 other advanced degrees awarded. Offers advanced training in general dentistry (MS, Certificate); dental biomaterials (MS); dentistry (MS, DDS, Certificate); endodontics (MS, Certificate); orthodontics (MS, Certificate); prosthodontics (MS, Certificate). *Application deadline:* For spring admission, 3/1 priority date for domestic and international students. Applications are processed on a rolling basis. *Application Contact:* Dr. T. Gerry Bradley. *Dean*, Dr. William K. Lobb, 414-288-6546, Fax: 414-288-3586, E-mail: william.lobb@marquette.edu.

MARSHALL B. KETCHUM UNIVERSITY, Fullerton, CA 92831-1615

General Information Independent, coed, graduate-only institution. *Graduate housing:* On-campus housing not available. *Research affiliation:* Alcon Laboratories (ophthalmic products), Essilor (spectacle lenses), Allergan (ophthalmic products).

GRADUATE UNITS

Graduate and Professional Programs Offers optometry (OD); vision science (MS). Electronic applications accepted.

MARSHALL UNIVERSITY, Huntington, WV 25755

General Information State-supported, coed, university. *Enrollment:* 13,621 graduate, professional, and undergraduate students; 1,222 full-time matriculated graduate/professional students (706 women), 1,591 part-time matriculated graduate/professional students (940 women). *Enrollment by degree level:* 2,137 master's, 259 doctoral, 756 other advanced degrees. *Graduate faculty:* 249 full-time (98 women), 23 part-time/adjunct (11 women). *Graduate housing:* Rooms and/or apartments available on a first-come, first-served basis to single and married students. *Student services:* Campus employment opportunities, campus safety program, career counseling, child daycare facilities, exercise/wellness program, free psychological counseling, grant writing training, international student services, low-cost health insurance, multicultural affairs office, services for students with disabilities, teacher training, writing training. *Library:* John Deaver Drinko Library plus 1 other. *Collection:* Books: 442,352 (physical), 112,120 (digital/electronic); Serial titles: 1,946 (physical), 50,707 (digital/electronic); Databases: 107. Weekly public service hours: 133; study areas open 24 hours, 5–7 days a week; students can reserve study rooms. *Research affiliation:* Bayer Corporation, Kanawha Valley Local Port District, Greenbrier County Commission, Dominion Power, Wyeth-Ayerst (clinical pharmaceutical study).

Computer facilities: Computer purchase and lease plans are available. 1,461 computers available on campus for general student use. A campuswide network can be accessed from student residence rooms and from off campus. Online class registration, Virtual Computer Lab - MU Remote and Web Conferencing are available.
Website: http://www.marshall.edu/

General Application Contact: Dr. Tammy Johnson, Graduate Admissions, 304-746-1900, Fax: 304-746-1902, E-mail: services@marshall.edu.

GRADUATE UNITS

Academic Affairs Division Students: 1,222 full-time (706 women), 1,591 part-time (940 women); includes 244 minority (103 Black or African American, non-Hispanic/Latino; 7 American Indian or Alaska Native, non-Hispanic/Latino; 47 Asian, non-Hispanic/Latino; 44 Hispanic/Latino; 3 Native Hawaiian or other Pacific Islander, non-Hispanic/Latino; 40 Two or more races, non-Hispanic/Latino), 250 international. Average age 28. *Faculty:* 249 full-time (98 women), 23 part-time/adjunct (11 women). *Financial support:* Fellowships, research assistantships, teaching assistantships, career-related internships or fieldwork, Federal Work-Study, tuition waivers (full and partial), and unspecified assistantships available. Support available to part-time students. In 2015, 720 master's, 76 doctorates, 42 other advanced degrees awarded. *Degree program information:* Part-time and evening/weekend programs available. Part-time, evening/weekend. *Application deadline:* Applications are processed on a rolling basis. *Application fee:* $40 ($100 for international students). *Application Contact:* Information Contact, Graduate Admissions, 304-746-1900, Fax: 304-746-1902, E-mail: services@marshall.edu. *Provost/Senior Vice President*, Dr. Gayle Ormiston, 304-696-3716, E-mail: ormiston@marshall.edu.

College of Arts and Media Students: 23 full-time (8 women), 10 part-time (5 women); includes 6 minority (1 Black or African American, non-Hispanic/Latino; 1 Asian, non-Hispanic/Latino; 1 Hispanic/Latino; 3 Two or more races, non-Hispanic/Latino), 4 international. Average age 27. *Faculty:* 21 full-time (6 women), 1 (woman) part-time/adjunct. In 2015, 8 master's awarded. *Degree program information:* Evening/weekend programs available. Evening/weekend. Offers arts and media (MA, MAJ); journalism (MAJ); music (MA). *Application fee:* $40. *Application Contact:* Information Contact, 304-746-1900, Fax: 304-746-1902, E-mail: services@marshall.edu. *Dean*, Dr. Donald Van Horn, 304-696-2964, E-mail: vanhorn@marshall.edu.

College of Business Students: 346 full-time (150 women), 79 part-time (47 women); includes 46 minority (24 Black or African American, non-Hispanic/Latino; 2 American Indian or Alaska Native, non-Hispanic/Latino; 5 Asian, non-Hispanic/Latino; 6 Hispanic/Latino; 9 Two or more races, non-Hispanic/Latino), 111 international. Average age 29. *Faculty:* 26 full-time (7 women), 2 part-time/adjunct (1 woman). *Financial support:* Career-related internships or fieldwork and tuition waivers (full) available. Support available to part-time students. Financial award applicants required to submit FAFSA. In 2015, 122 master's, 26 doctorates awarded. *Degree program information:* Part-time and evening/weekend programs available. Part-time, evening/weekend. Offers accountancy (MS); business (MBA, MS, DMPNA, Graduate Certificate); business administration (MBA); health care administration (MS); human resource management (MS); nurse anesthesia (DMPNA). *Application deadline:* Applications are processed on a rolling basis. *Application fee:* $40. *Application Contact:* Wesley Spradlin, Information Contact, 304-746-8964, Fax: 304-746-1902, E-mail: spradlin2@marshall.edu. *Interim Dean*, Dr. Deanna Mader, 304-696-2862, Fax: 304-696-4344, E-mail: maderd@marshall.edu.

College of Education and Professional Development Students: 289 full-time (220 women), 792 part-time (509 women); includes 77 minority (36 Black or African American, non-Hispanic/Latino; 3 American Indian or Alaska Native, non-Hispanic/Latino; 3 Asian, non-Hispanic/Latino; 23 Hispanic/Latino; 2 Native Hawaiian or other Pacific Islander, non-Hispanic/Latino; 10 Two or more races, non-Hispanic/Latino), 3 international. Average age 35. *Faculty:* 42 full-time (20 women), 10 part-time/adjunct (7 women). *Financial support:* Career-related internships or fieldwork, Federal Work-Study, tuition waivers (full and partial), and unspecified assistantships available. Support available to part-time students. Financial award applicants required to submit FAFSA. In 2015, 312 master's, 14 doctorates, 42 other advanced degrees awarded. *Degree program information:* Part-time and evening/weekend programs available. Part-time, evening/weekend. Offers adult and technical education (MS); counseling (MA, Ed S, Graduate Certificate); early childhood education (MA); education and professional development (MA, MAT, MS, Ed D, Certificate, Ed S, Graduate Certificate); elementary education (MA, Graduate Certificate); leadership studies (MA, MS, Ed D, Certificate, Ed S); literacy education (MA, Ed S); school psychology (Ed S); secondary education (MA); special education (MA); teaching (MAT). *Application deadline:* For fall admission, 5/1 for domestic students; for spring admission, 12/1 for domestic students. Applications are processed on a rolling basis. *Application fee:* $40. Electronic applications accepted. *Application Contact:* Information Contact, 304-746-1900, Fax: 304-746-1902, E-mail: services@marshall.edu. *Dean*, Dr. Teresa Eagle, 304-746-8924, E-mail: thardman@marshall.edu.

College of Health Professions Students: 154 full-time (116 women), 230 part-time (151 women); includes 22 minority (11 Black or African American, non-Hispanic/Latino; 6 Asian, non-Hispanic/Latino; 2 Hispanic/Latino; 3 Two or more races, non-Hispanic/Latino), 14 international. Average age 27. *Faculty:* 22 full-time (11 women), 1 part-time/adjunct (0 women). In 2015, 103 master's, 25 doctorates awarded. Offers athletic training (MS); communication disorders (MS); dietetics (MS); exercise science (MS); health informatics (MS); health professions (MPH, MS, MSN, MSW, DPT); kinesiology (MS); nursing (MSN); physical therapy (DPT); public health (MPH); social work (MSW); sport administration (MS). *Application fee:* $40. *Application Contact:* Information Contact, 304-746-1900, Fax: 304-746-1902, E-mail: services@marshall.edu. *Dean*, Dr. Michael Prewitt, 304-696-3765, E-mail: prewittm@marshall.edu.

College of Information Technology and Engineering Students: 126 full-time (32 women), 109 part-time (25 women); includes 9 minority (5 Black or African American, non-Hispanic/Latino; 2 Asian, non-Hispanic/Latino; 1 Hispanic/Latino; 1 Two or more races, non-Hispanic/Latino), 95 international. Average age 30. *Faculty:* 12 full-time (1 woman), 7 part-time/adjunct (1 woman). *Financial support:* Fellowships and tuition waivers (full) available. Support available to part-time students. Financial award application deadline: 8/1; financial award applicants required to submit FAFSA. In 2015, 58 degrees awarded. *Degree program information:* Part-time and evening/weekend programs available. Part-time, evening/weekend. Offers applied science and technology (MS); computer science (MS); engineering (MSME); engineering management (MSE); environmental engineering (MSE); environmental science (MS); information systems (MS); information technology and engineering (MS, MSE, MSME); safety (MS); technology management (MS); transportation and infrastructure engineering (MSE). *Application fee:* $40. *Application Contact:* Information Contact, 304-746-1900, Fax: 304-746-1902, E-mail: services@marshall.edu. *Interim Dean*, Dr. Wael Zatar, 304-696-6043, E-mail: zatar@marshall.edu.

College of Liberal Arts Students: 197 full-time (127 women), 56 part-time (38 women); includes 17 minority (5 Black or African American, non-Hispanic/Latino; 1 American Indian or Alaska Native, non-Hispanic/Latino; 6 Hispanic/Latino; 5 Two or more races, non-Hispanic/Latino), 14 international. Average age 31. *Faculty:* 69 full-time (32 women), 2 part-time/adjunct (1 woman). *Financial support:* Fellowships and teaching assistantships with tuition reimbursements available. In 2015, 68 master's, 11 doctorates awarded. *Degree program information:* Evening/weekend programs available. Evening/weekend. Offers clinical psychology (Certificate); communication studies (MA); English (MA, Graduate Certificate); geography (MA, MS, Certificate); history (MA, Certificate); humanities (MA, Certificate); Latin (MA, Certificate); liberal arts (MA, MPA, MS, Psy D, Certificate, Graduate Certificate); political science (MA, MPA); psychology (MA, Psy D); sociology (MA). *Application fee:* $40. *Application Contact:* Graduate Admissions, 304-746-1900, Fax: 304-746-1902, E-mail: services@marshall.edu. *Interim Dean*, Dr. Robert Bookwalter, 304-696-2731, E-mail: bookwalt@marshall.edu.

College of Science Students: 54 full-time (25 women), 12 part-time (6 women); includes 5 minority (2 Black or African American, non-Hispanic/Latino; 1 Asian, non-Hispanic/Latino; 1 Native Hawaiian or other Pacific Islander, non-Hispanic/Latino; 1 Two or more races, non-Hispanic/Latino), 5 international. Average age 28. *Faculty:* 47 full-time (16 women). *Financial support:* Career-related internships or fieldwork available. In 2015, 30 master's awarded. Offers biological science (MA, MS); chemistry (MS); criminal justice (MS); mathematics (MA); physical and applied science (MS); science (MA, MS). *Application fee:* $40. *Application Contact:* Information Contact, Graduate Admissions, 304-746-1900, Fax: 304-746-1902, E-mail: services@marshall.edu. *Dean*, Dr. Charles Somerville, 304-696-2424, E-mail: somervil@marshall.edu.

Forensic Science Center Students: 33 full-time (28 women); includes 2 minority (1 Asian, non-Hispanic/Latino; 1 Two or more races, non-Hispanic/Latino), 1 international. Average age 23. *Financial support:* In 2015–16, 12 research assistantships with full tuition reimbursements (averaging $4,000 per year), teaching assistantships with full tuition reimbursements (averaging $6,000 per year) were awarded; career-related internships or fieldwork, Federal Work-Study, institutionally sponsored loans, tuition waivers (partial), and unspecified assistantships also available. Financial award application deadline: 8/27; financial award applicants required to submit FAFSA. In 2015, 19 master's awarded. Offers forensic science (MS, Graduate Certificate). *Application deadline:* For fall admission, 3/1 for domestic and international students. *Application fee:* $40. *Application Contact:* Kelly Preston, Senior Administrative Secretary, 304-690-4363 Ext. 248, Fax: 304-690-4371, E-mail: forensics@marshall.edu. *Director,* Dr. Terry W. Fenger, 304-690-4373, Fax: 304-690-4360, E-mail: fenger@marshall.edu.

School of Pharmacy Students: 303 part-time (159 women); includes 60 minority (19 Black or African American, non-Hispanic/Latino; 1 American Indian or Alaska Native, non-Hispanic/Latino; 28 Asian, non-Hispanic/Latino; 5 Hispanic/Latino; 7 Two or more races, non-Hispanic/Latino), 3 international. Average age 26. *Faculty:* 10 full-time (5 women). Offers pharmacy (Pharm D). *Application Contact:* Dr. Tammy Johnson, Graduate Admissions, 304-746-1900, Fax: 304-746-1902, E-mail: services@marshall.edu. *Founding Dean,* Dr. Kevin W. Yingling, 304-696-7302, E-mail: pharmacy@marshall.edu.

Joan C. Edwards School of Medicine Offers biomedical sciences (MS, PhD); medicine (MS, MD, PhD). Electronic applications accepted.

MARS HILL UNIVERSITY, Mars Hill, NC 28754

General Information Independent-religious, coed, comprehensive institution.

GRADUATE UNITS

Adult and Graduate Studies

MARTIN LUTHER COLLEGE, New Ulm, MN 56073

General Information Independent-religious, coed, comprehensive institution. *Enrollment:* 900 graduate, professional, and undergraduate students; 10 full-time matriculated graduate/professional students (5 women), 112 part-time matriculated graduate/professional students (38 women). *Enrollment by degree level:* 122 master's. *Graduate faculty:* 9 full-time (1 woman), 21 part-time/adjunct (10 women). *Tuition, area resident:* Full-time $5400; part-time $300 per credit. *Required fees:* $105; $105 per unit. $35 per semester. Tuition and fees vary according to course load. *Graduate housing:* On-campus housing not available. *Library:* Martin Luther College Library.

Computer facilities: A campuswide network can be accessed from student residence rooms. Website: http://www.mlc-wels.edu/

General Application Contact: John E. Meyer, Director of Graduate Studies, 507-354-8221 Ext. 398, Fax: 507-354-8225, E-mail: meyerjd@mlc-wels.edu.

GRADUATE UNITS

Graduate Studies Students: 10 full-time (5 women), 112 part-time (38 women); includes 6 minority (2 Black or African American, non-Hispanic/Latino; 1 American Indian or Alaska Native, non-Hispanic/Latino; 2 Asian, non-Hispanic/Latino; 1 Hispanic/Latino). Average age 32. 28 applicants, 100% accepted, 28 enrolled. *Faculty:* 6 full-time (2 women), 12 part-time/adjunct (2 women). *Financial support:* In 2015–16, 4 students received support. Scholarships/grants available. Financial award application deadline: 9/1; financial award applicants required to submit FAFSA. In 2015, 10 master's awarded. *Degree program information:* Part-time programs available. Part-time, online only, 100% online. Offers early childhood director (MS El); educational technology (MS Ed); instruction (MS Ed); leadership (MS Ed); principal (MS El); special education (MS Ed). *Application deadline:* Applications are processed on a rolling basis. *Application fee:* $35. Electronic applications accepted. *Director of Graduate Studies,* John E. Meyer, 507-354-8221 Ext. 398, E-mail: meyerjd@mlc-wels.edu.

MARTIN UNIVERSITY, Indianapolis, IN 46218-3867

General Information Independent, coed, comprehensive institution. *Graduate housing:* On-campus housing not available.

GRADUATE UNITS

Division of Psychology ***Degree program information:*** Part-time and evening/weekend programs available. Part-time, evening/weekend. Offers community psychology (MS).

Graduate School of Urban Ministry ***Degree program information:*** Part-time and evening/weekend programs available. Part-time, evening/weekend. Offers urban ministry studies (MA).

MARY BALDWIN COLLEGE, Staunton, VA 24401-3610

General Information Independent, coed, primarily women, comprehensive institution. *Graduate housing:* On-campus housing not available.

GRADUATE UNITS

Graduate Studies ***Degree program information:*** Part-time and evening/weekend programs available. Part-time, evening/weekend, online learning. Offers acting (M Litt); directing (M Litt); elementary education (MAT); middle grades education (MAT); Shakespeare and Renaissance literature in performance (M Litt, MFA); teaching (M Litt, MAT).

MARYGROVE COLLEGE, Detroit, MI 48221-2599

General Information Independent-religious, coed, primarily women, comprehensive institution. *Graduate housing:* Room and/or apartments available to single students; on-campus housing not available to married students.

GRADUATE UNITS

Graduate Division ***Degree program information:*** Part-time and evening/weekend programs available. Part-time, evening/weekend, online learning. Offers art of teaching (MAT); educational leadership (MA); educational technology (M Ed); English (MA); Griot (M Ed); human resource management (MA); modern language translation (Certificate); reading and literacy (M Ed); Sage (M Ed); social justice (MA). Electronic applications accepted.

MARYLAND INSTITUTE COLLEGE OF ART, Baltimore, MD 21217

General Information Independent, coed, comprehensive institution. *Graduate housing:* Room and/or apartments available on a first-come, first-served basis to single students; on-campus housing not available to married students. Housing application deadline: 5/1.

GRADUATE UNITS

Graduate Studies ***Degree program information:*** Part-time programs available. Part-time, online learning. Offers art education (MA); community arts (MFA); critical studies (MA); curatorial practice (MFA); filmmaking (MFA); fine arts (Postbaccalaureate Certificate); graphic design (MFA, Postbaccalaureate Certificate); illustration practice (MFA); information visualization (MPS); photographic and electronic media (MFA); social design (MA); studio art (MFA); teaching (MAT); the business of art and design (MPS). Electronic applications accepted.

Hoffberger School of Painting Offers painting (MFA).

Mount Royal School of Art Offers painting (MFA). Electronic applications accepted.

Rinehart School of Sculpture Offers sculpture (MFA).

MARYLAND UNIVERSITY OF INTEGRATIVE HEALTH, Laurel, MD 20723

General Information Independent, coed, primarily women, graduate-only institution. *Graduate housing:* On-campus housing not available. *Research affiliation:* Maryland State Department of Public Safety and Corrections (acupuncture detoxification services).

GRADUATE UNITS

Chinese Herb Certificate Program ***Degree program information:*** Part-time and evening/weekend programs available. Part-time, evening/weekend. Offers Chinese herb (Certificate).

Program in Acupuncture Offers acupuncture (M Ac).

Program in Applied Healing Arts Offers applied healing arts (MA).

Program in Herbal Medicine Offers herbal medicine (MS).

MARYLHURST UNIVERSITY, Marylhurst, OR 97036-0261

General Information Independent-religious, coed, comprehensive institution. *Enrollment:* 982 graduate, professional, and undergraduate students; 428 matriculated graduate/professional students (269 women). *Enrollment by degree level:* 428 master's. *Tuition, area resident:* Part-time $463 per credit hour. *Graduate housing:* On-campus housing not available. *Student services:* Career counseling, free psychological counseling, international student services, low-cost health insurance, services for students with disabilities, teacher training, writing training. *Library:* Shoen Library. *Collection:* Books: 105,004 (physical), 11,479 (digital/electronic); Serial titles: 156 (physical).

Computer facilities: A campuswide network can be accessed. Online class registration is available.
Website: http://www.marylhurst.edu/

General Application Contact: Office of Admissions, 503-699-6268, Fax: 503-699-6320, E-mail: admissions@marylhurst.edu.

GRADUATE UNITS

Applied Pastoral Theology Program ***Financial support:*** Scholarships/grants available. Support available to part-time students. Financial award applicants required to submit FAFSA. *Degree program information:* Part-time and evening/weekend programs available. Part-time, evening/weekend. Offers applied pastoral theology (MA). *Application deadline:* Applications are processed on a rolling basis. *Application fee:* $50. Electronic applications accepted. *Application Contact:* Maruksa Lynch, Graduate Admissions Counselor, 800-634-9982 Ext. 6322, Fax: 503-699-6320, E-mail: admissions@marylhurst.edu. *Chair,* Dr. Jerry Roussell, Jr., 503-636-8141, Fax: 503-697-5597, E-mail: jroussell@marylhurst.edu.

Department of Art Therapy Counseling Students: 40 (38 women); includes 6 minority (3 Hispanic/Latino; 3 Two or more races, non-Hispanic/Latino). Average age 34. *Financial support:* Scholarships/grants available. Support available to part-time students. Financial award applicants required to submit FAFSA. *Degree program information:* Part-time programs available. Part-time. Offers art therapy (PGC); art therapy counseling (MA); counseling (PGC). *Application deadline:* For fall admission, 1/31 priority date for domestic and international students. Applications are processed on a rolling basis. *Application fee:* $50. Electronic applications accepted. *Application Contact:* Maruska Lynch, Graduate Admissions Counselor, 800-634-9982 Ext. 6322, Fax: 503-699-6320, E-mail: admissions@marylhurst.edu. *Chair,* Christine Turner, 503-636-8141, Fax: 503-636-9526, E-mail: cturner@marylhurst.edu.

Department of Business Administration Students: 287 (155 women); includes 57 minority (31 Black or African American, non-Hispanic/Latino; 11 Asian, non-Hispanic/Latino; 9 Hispanic/Latino; 2 Native Hawaiian or other Pacific Islander, non-Hispanic/Latino; 4 Two or more races, non-Hispanic/Latino), 5 international. Average age 38. *Financial support:* Scholarships/grants available. Support available to part-time students. Financial award applicants required to submit FAFSA. *Degree program information:* Part-time and evening/weekend programs available. Part-time, evening/weekend, 100% online, blended/hybrid learning. Offers health care management (MBA); real estate (MBA); sustainable business (MBA). *Application deadline:* Applications are processed on a rolling basis. *Application fee:* $50. Electronic applications accepted. *Application Contact:* Maruska Lynch, Graduate Admissions Counselor, 800-634-9982 Ext. 6322, E-mail: admissions@marylhurst.edu. *School of Business Director,* Stuart Noble-Goodman, 503-699-6315, E-mail: snoblegoodman@marylhurst.edu.

Department of Education Students: 46 (37 women); includes 6 minority (1 Black or African American, non-Hispanic/Latino; 1 Asian, non-Hispanic/Latino; 3 Hispanic/Latino; 1 Two or more races, non-Hispanic/Latino), 1 international. Average age 33. *Financial support:* Scholarships/grants available. Support available to part-time students. Financial award applicants required to submit FAFSA. In 2015, 13 master's awarded. *Degree program information:* Part-time programs available. Part-time. Offers education (M Ed); teaching (MA). *Application deadline:* For fall admission, 3/1 priority date for domestic and international students. Applications are processed on a rolling basis. *Application fee:* $50. Electronic applications accepted. *Application Contact:* Maruska Lynch, Graduate Admissions Counselor, 800-634-9982 Ext. 6322, Fax: 503-699-6320, E-mail: admissions@marylhurst.edu. *Chair,* Dr. Jan Carpenter, 503-675.3975, E-mail: jcarpenter@marylhurst.edu.

Department of Food Systems and Society ***Financial support:*** Scholarships/grants available. Support available to part-time students. Financial award applicants required to submit FAFSA. *Degree program information:* Part-time programs available. Part-time. Offers food systems and society (MS). *Application deadline:* For fall admission, 3/15 for domestic students. Applications are processed on a rolling basis. *Application fee:* $50. Electronic applications accepted. *Application Contact:* Maruska Lynch, Graduate Admissions Counselor, 503-699-6268, Fax: 503-699-6320, E-mail: admissions@marylhurst.edu. *Chair,* Dr. Patricia Allen, 503-675-3977, E-mail: pallen@marylhurst.edu.

Department of Interdisciplinary Studies Students: 24 (17 women); includes 5 minority (1 Black or African American, non-Hispanic/Latino; 1 Hispanic/Latino; 1 Native Hawaiian or other Pacific Islander, non-Hispanic/Latino; 2 Two or more races, non-Hispanic/Latino), 1 international. Average age 49. *Financial support:* Scholarships/grants available. Support available to part-time students. Financial award applicants required to submit FAFSA. *Degree program information:* Part-time and evening/weekend programs available. Part-time, evening/weekend. Offers interdisciplinary studies (MA). *Application deadline:* Applications are processed on a rolling basis. *Application fee:* $50. Electronic applications accepted. *Application Contact:* Maruska Lynch, Graduate Admissions Counselor, 800-634-9982 Ext. 6322, E-mail: admissions@marylhurst.edu. *Provost,* Ann Marie Fallon, 503-699-6316, E-mail: amfallon@marylhurst.edu.

Divinity Program Students: 31 (22 women); includes 2 minority (1 Black or African American, non-Hispanic/Latino; 1 Two or more races, non-Hispanic/Latino). Average age

46. *Financial support:* Scholarships/grants available. Support available to part-time students. Financial award applicants required to submit FAFSA. *Degree program information:* Part-time and evening/weekend programs available. Part-time, evening/weekend. Offers divinity (M Div). *Application deadline:* Applications are processed on a rolling basis. *Application fee:* $50. Electronic applications accepted. *Application Contact:* Maruska Lynch, Graduate Admissions Counselor, 800-634-9982 Ext. 6322, Fax: 503-699-6320, E-mail: admissions@marylhurst.edu. *Chair,* Dr. Jerry Roussell, Jr., 503-636-8141, E-mail: jroussell@marylhurst.edu.

MARYMOUNT CALIFORNIA UNIVERSITY, Rancho Palos Verdes, CA 90275-6299

General Information Independent-religious, coed, comprehensive institution.

GRADUATE UNITS

Program in Business Administration Offers business administration (MBA).

Program in Community Psychology Offers community psychology (MS).

Program in Leadership and Global Development Offers leadership and global development (MS).

MARYMOUNT UNIVERSITY, Arlington, VA 22207-4299

General Information Independent-religious, coed, comprehensive institution. *Enrollment:* 3,363 graduate, professional, and undergraduate students; 544 full-time matriculated graduate/professional students (428 women), 475 part-time matriculated graduate/professional students (336 women). *Enrollment by degree level:* 842 master's, 147 doctoral, 30 other advanced degrees. *Graduate faculty:* 71 full-time (50 women), 60 part-time/adjunct (38 women). *Tuition, area resident:* Part-time $910 per credit hour. *Required fees:* $10 per credit hour. One-time fee: $230 part-time. Tuition and fees vary according to program. *Graduate housing:* Room and/or apartments available on a first-come, first-served basis to single students; on-campus housing not available to married students. Housing application deadline: 5/1. *Student services:* Campus employment opportunities, campus safety program, career counseling, free psychological counseling, international student services, low-cost health insurance, services for students with disabilities, teacher training. *Library:* Emerson C. Reinsch Library plus 1 other. *Collection:* Books: 242,042 (physical), 330,637 (digital/electronic); Serial titles: 1,527 (physical), 81,795 (digital/electronic); Databases: 227. Weekly public service hours: 104; students can reserve study rooms.

Computer facilities: 250 computers available on campus for general student use. A campuswide network can be accessed from student residence rooms and from off campus. Online class registration, online drive space are available.
Website: http://www.marymount.edu/

General Application Contact: Francesca Reed, Director, Graduate Admissions, 703-284-5901, Fax: 703-527-3815, E-mail: grad.admissions@marymount.edu.

GRADUATE UNITS

School of Arts and Sciences Students: 27 full-time (25 women), 27 part-time (22 women); includes 16 minority (11 Black or African American, non-Hispanic/Latino; 2 Asian, non-Hispanic/Latino; 2 Hispanic/Latino; 1 Two or more races, non-Hispanic/Latino), 10 international. Average age 32. 42 applicants, 98% accepted, 26 enrolled. *Faculty:* 9 full-time (6 women), 3 part-time/adjunct (1 woman). *Financial support:* In 2015–16, 13 students received support, including 4 research assistantships with tuition reimbursements available; teaching assistantships with tuition reimbursements available, career-related internships or fieldwork, Federal Work-Study, scholarships/grants, and unspecified assistantships also available. Support available to part-time students. Financial award applicants required to submit FAFSA. In 2015, 10 master's, 2 other advanced degrees awarded. *Degree program information:* Part-time and evening/weekend programs available. Part-time, evening/weekend. Offers arts and sciences (MA, Certificate); English and humanities (MA); interior design (MA); teaching English at the community college (Certificate). *Application deadline:* For fall admission, 7/1 for international students; for spring admission, 10/15 for international students. Applications are processed on a rolling basis. *Application fee:* $40. Electronic applications accepted. *Application Contact:* Francesca Reed, Director, Graduate Admissions, 703-284-5901, Fax: 703-527-3815, E-mail: grad.admissions@marymount.edu. *Dean,* Dr. Rosemary Hubbard, 703-284-1560, Fax: 703-284-3859, E-mail: rosemary.hubbard@marymount.edu.

School of Business Administration Students: 93 full-time (54 women), 206 part-time (115 women); includes 125 minority (58 Black or African American, non-Hispanic/Latino; 1 American Indian or Alaska Native, non-Hispanic/Latino; 33 Asian, non-Hispanic/Latino; 24 Hispanic/Latino; 3 Native Hawaiian or other Pacific Islander, non-Hispanic/Latino; 6 Two or more races, non-Hispanic/Latino), 46 international. Average age 32. 196 applicants, 96% accepted, 116 enrolled. *Faculty:* 24 full-time (16 women), 12 part-time/adjunct (2 women). *Financial support:* In 2015–16, 39 students received support, including 8 research assistantships with tuition reimbursements available, 3 teaching assistantships with tuition reimbursements available; career-related internships or fieldwork, Federal Work-Study, scholarships/grants, and unspecified assistantships also available. Support available to part-time students. Financial award applicants required to submit FAFSA. In 2015, 122 master's, 23 other advanced degrees awarded. *Degree program information:* Part-time and evening/weekend programs available. Part-time, evening/weekend. Offers business administration (MA, MBA, MS, Certificate); computer security and information assurance (Certificate); cybersecurity (MS, Certificate); health care informatics (Certificate); health care management (MS); human resource management (MA, Certificate); information technology (MS, Certificate); information technology project management and technology leadership (Certificate); leadership (Certificate); leadership and management (MS); non-profit management (Certificate); organization development (Certificate); project management (Certificate). *Application deadline:* For fall admission, 7/1 priority date for domestic students, 7/1 for international students; for spring admission, 11/15 for domestic students, 10/15 for international students. Applications are processed on a rolling basis. *Application fee:* $40. Electronic applications accepted. *Application Contact:* Francesca Reed, Director, Graduate Admissions, 703-284-5901, Fax: 703-527-3815, E-mail: grad.admissions@marymount.edu. *Dean,* James Ryerson, 703-284-5910, Fax: 703-527-3830, E-mail: james.ryerson@marymount.edu.

School of Education and Human Services Students: 289 full-time (254 women), 174 part-time (137 women); includes 127 minority (51 Black or African American, non-Hispanic/Latino; 3 American Indian or Alaska Native, non-Hispanic/Latino; 17 Asian, non-Hispanic/Latino; 42 Hispanic/Latino; 14 Two or more races, non-Hispanic/Latino), 18 international. Average age 29. 258 applicants, 84% accepted, 159 enrolled. *Faculty:* 23 full-time (16 women), 26 part-time/adjunct (19 women). *Financial support:* In 2015–16, 48 students received support, including 13 research assistantships with tuition reimbursements available, 11 teaching assistantships with tuition reimbursements available; career-related internships or fieldwork, Federal Work-Study, scholarships/grants, and unspecified assistantships also available. Support available to part-time students. Financial award applicants required to submit FAFSA. In 2015, 209 master's awarded. *Degree program information:* Part-time and evening/weekend programs available. Part-time, evening/weekend, online learning. Offers clinical mental health counseling (MA); counselor education and supervision (Ed D); education and human services (M Ed, MA, Ed D); elementary education (M Ed); English as a second language (M Ed); forensic and legal psychology (MA); intelligence studies (MA); pastoral and spiritual care (MA); pastoral counseling (MA); professional studies (M Ed); school counseling (MA); secondary education (M Ed); special education: general curriculum (M Ed). *Application deadline:* For fall admission, 7/1 for international students; for spring admission, 10/15 for international students. Applications are processed on a rolling basis. *Application fee:* $40. Electronic applications accepted. *Application Contact:* Francesca Reed, Director, Graduate Admissions, 703-284-5901, Fax: 703-527-3815, E-mail: grad.admissions@marymount.edu. *Dean,* Dr. Lois Stover, 703-284-1620, Fax: 703-284-1631, E-mail: lois.stover@marymount.edu.

School of Health Professions Students: 135 full-time (95 women), 68 part-time (62 women); includes 56 minority (26 Black or African American, non-Hispanic/Latino; 14 Asian, non-Hispanic/Latino; 10 Hispanic/Latino; 1 Native Hawaiian or other Pacific Islander, non-Hispanic/Latino; 5 Two or more races, non-Hispanic/Latino), 5 international. Average age 30. 773 applicants, 26% accepted, 71 enrolled. *Faculty:* 16 full-time (13 women), 19 part-time/adjunct (16 women). *Financial support:* In 2015–16, 34 students received support, including 3 research assistantships with tuition reimbursements available, 14 teaching assistantships with tuition reimbursements available; career-related internships or fieldwork, Federal Work-Study, scholarships/grants, and unspecified assistantships also available. Support available to part-time students. Financial award applicants required to submit FAFSA. In 2015, 25 master's, 34 doctorates awarded. *Degree program information:* Part-time and evening/weekend programs available. Part-time, evening/weekend. Offers family nurse practitioner (MSN, Certificate); health education and promotion (MS); health professions (MS, MSN, DNP, DPT, Certificate); nursing (DNP); physical therapy (DPT). *Application deadline:* For fall admission, 7/1 for international students; for spring admission, 10/15 for international students. Applications are processed on a rolling basis. *Application fee:* $40. Electronic applications accepted. *Application Contact:* Francesca Reed, Director, Graduate Admissions, 703-284-5901, Fax: 703-527-3815, E-mail: grad.admissions@marymount.edu. *Dean,* Dr. Jeanne Matthews, 703-284-1580, Fax: 703-284-3819, E-mail: jeanne.matthews@marymount.edu.

MARYVILLE UNIVERSITY OF SAINT LOUIS, St. Louis, MO 63141-7299

General Information Independent, coed, comprehensive institution. *Enrollment:* 6,414 graduate, professional, and undergraduate students; 274 full-time matriculated graduate/professional students (205 women), 3,345 part-time matriculated graduate/professional students (2,893 women). *Enrollment by degree level:* 3,176 master's, 443 doctoral. *Graduate faculty:* 78 full-time (59 women), 233 part-time/adjunct (176 women). *Tuition, area resident:* Full-time $25,558; part-time $781 per credit hour. *Required fees:* $2400. Part-time tuition and fees vary according to course load and degree level. *Graduate housing:* Room and/or apartments available on a first-come, first-served basis to single students; on-campus housing not available to married students. Typical cost: $11,868 (including board). Room and board charges vary according to board plan and housing facility selected. Housing application deadline: 5/1. *Student services:* Campus employment opportunities, campus safety program, career counseling, exercise/wellness program, free psychological counseling, international student services, low-cost health insurance, multicultural affairs office, services for students with disabilities, teacher training, writing training. *Library:* Maryville University Library. *Collection:* Books: 59,697 (physical), 214,601 (digital/electronic); Serial titles: 4,000 (physical), 95,068 (digital/electronic); Databases: 120. Weekly public service hours: 101; study areas open 24 hours, 5–7 days a week. *Research affiliation:* Monsanto Fund (early childhood, science, mathematics curriculum development and teacher enrichment), Southwestern Bell Foundation (secondary education curriculum and teacher education).

Computer facilities: Computer purchase and lease plans are available. 575 computers available on campus for general student use. A campuswide network can be accessed from student residence rooms and from off campus. Online class registration, specialized software, university catalog are available.
Website: http://www.maryville.edu/

General Application Contact: Crystal Jacobsmeyer, Assistant Director, Graduate Enrollment Advising, 314-529-9654, Fax: 314-529-9927, E-mail: cjacobsmeyer@maryville.edu.

GRADUATE UNITS

College of Arts and Sciences Students: 23 full-time (13 women), 34 part-time (27 women); includes 7 minority (2 Black or African American, non-Hispanic/Latino; 3 Asian, non-Hispanic/Latino; 1 Hispanic/Latino; 1 Two or more races, non-Hispanic/Latino), 15 international. Average age 31. *Faculty:* 9 full-time (6 women), 7 part-time/adjunct (5 women). *Financial support:* Application deadline: 3/1; applicants required to submit FAFSA. In 2015, 18 master's awarded. *Degree program information:* Part-time programs available. Part-time. Offers actuarial science (MS); organizational leadership and development (MA); strategic communication and leadership (MA). *Application deadline:* Applications are processed on a rolling basis. Electronic applications accepted. *Application Contact:* Crystal Jacobsmeyer, Assistant Director, Graduate Enrollment Advising, 314-529-9654, Fax: 314-529-9927, E-mail: cjacobsmeyer@maryville.edu. *Dean,* Cherie Fister, 314-529-9563, Fax: 314-529-9965, E-mail: cfister@maryville.edu.

The John E. Simon School of Business Students: 61 full-time (35 women), 131 part-time (76 women); includes 40 minority (24 Black or African American, non-Hispanic/Latino; 5 Asian, non-Hispanic/Latino; 5 Hispanic/Latino; 1 Native Hawaiian or other Pacific Islander, non-Hispanic/Latino; 5 Two or more races, non-Hispanic/Latino), 9 international. Average age 32. *Faculty:* 3 full-time (1 woman), 42 part-time/adjunct (11 women). *Financial support:* Career-related internships or fieldwork, Federal Work-Study, tuition waivers (partial), and campus employment available. Financial award application deadline: 3/1; financial award applicants required to submit FAFSA. In 2015, 43 master's awarded. *Degree program information:* Part-time and evening/weekend programs available. Part-time, evening/weekend, 100% online, blended/hybrid learning. Offers accounting (MBA, Certificate); business studies (Certificate); cyber security (MBA); cybersecurity (Certificate); financial services (MBA, Certificate); healthcare practice management (MBA, Certificate); human resource management (MBA); information technology (MBA, Certificate); management (MBA, Certificate); management and leadership (MA); marketing (MBA, Certificate); project management (MBA); sport business management (MBA); supply chain management/logistics (MBA). *Application deadline:* Applications are processed on a rolling basis. Electronic applications accepted. *Application Contact:* Dustin Loeffler, Director for Graduate Studies in Business, 314-529-9571, Fax: 314-529-9975, E-mail: dloeffler@maryville.edu. *Interim Dean,* 314-529-9680, Fax: 314-529-9975.

School of Education Students: 27 full-time (22 women), 262 part-time (183 women); includes 65 minority (52 Black or African American, non-Hispanic/Latino; 6 Asian, non-Hispanic/Latino; 2 Hispanic/Latino; 5 Two or more races, non-Hispanic/Latino), 4 international. Average age 37. *Faculty:* 14 full-time (9 women), 17 part-time/adjunct (12 women). *Financial support:* Career-related internships or fieldwork, Federal Work-Study, tuition waivers (partial), and professional educator discounts available. Financial award application deadline: 3/1; financial award applicants required to submit FAFSA. In 2015, 34 master's, 67 doctorates awarded. *Degree program information:* Part-time and evening/weekend programs available. Part-time, evening/weekend. Offers art education (MA Ed); early childhood education (MA Ed); educational leadership (Ed D); educational leadership: principal certification (MA Ed); elementary education (MA Ed); gifted education (MA Ed); higher education leadership (Ed D); literacy specialist (MA Ed); middle grades education (MA Ed); secondary teaching and inquiry (MA Ed); teacher as leader (MA Ed); teacher leadership (Ed D). *Application deadline:* Applications are processed on a rolling basis. Electronic applications accepted. *Application Contact:* Holly Stanwich, Graduate Admissions Coordinator, 314-529-9542, Fax: 314-529-9921, E-mail: teachered@maryville.edu. *Dean*, Dr. Cathy Bear, 314-529-9692, Fax: 314-529-9921, E-mail: cbear@maryville.edu.

Walker College of Health Professions Students: 136 full-time (113 women), 2,891 part-time (2,588 women); includes 692 minority (338 Black or African American, non-Hispanic/Latino; 40 American Indian or Alaska Native, non-Hispanic/Latino; 126 Asian, non-Hispanic/Latino; 129 Hispanic/Latino; 8 Native Hawaiian or other Pacific Islander, non-Hispanic/Latino; 51 Two or more races, non-Hispanic/Latino), 59 international. Average age 36. *Faculty:* 51 full-time (42 women), 168 part-time/adjunct (149 women). *Financial support:* Career-related internships or fieldwork, Federal Work-Study, and campus employment available. Financial award application deadline: 3/1; financial award applicants required to submit FAFSA. In 2015, 460 master's, 62 doctorates awarded. *Degree program information:* Part-time and evening/weekend programs available. Part-time, evening/weekend, 100% online. Offers health professions (MARC, MMT, MOT, MSN, DNP, DPT); marriage and family therapy (MARC); music therapy (MARC); occupational therapy (MOT); physical therapy (DPT); substance abuse (MARC). *Application deadline:* Applications are processed on a rolling basis. Electronic applications accepted. *Application Contact:* Crystal Jacobsmeyer, Assistant Director, Graduate Enrollment Advising, 314-529-9654, Fax: 314-529-9927, E-mail: cjacobsmeyer@maryville.edu. *Dean*, Dr. Charles Gulas, 314-529-9625, Fax: 314-529-9495, E-mail: hlthprofessions@maryville.edu.

The Catherine McAuley School of Nursing Students: 38 full-time (35 women), 2,802 part-time (2,511 women); includes 681 minority (332 Black or African American, non-Hispanic/Latino; 40 American Indian or Alaska Native, non-Hispanic/Latino; 126 Asian, non-Hispanic/Latino; 126 Hispanic/Latino; 8 Native Hawaiian or other Pacific Islander, non-Hispanic/Latino; 49 Two or more races, non-Hispanic/Latino), 58 international. Average age 37. *Faculty:* 18 full-time (all women), 158 part-time/adjunct (141 women). *Financial support:* Federal Work-Study and campus employment available. Support available to part-time students. Financial award application deadline: 3/1; financial award applicants required to submit FAFSA. In 2015, 413 master's, 33 doctorates awarded. 100% online. Offers acute care nurse practice (MSN); adult gerontology nurse practitioner (MSN); advanced practice nursing (DNP); family nurse practitioner (MSN); pediatric nurse practice (MSN). *Application deadline:* Applications are processed on a rolling basis. Electronic applications accepted. *Application Contact:* Crystal Jacobsmeyer, Assistant Director, Graduate Enrollment Advising, 314-929-9654, Fax: 314-529-9927, E-mail: cjacobsmeyer@maryville.edu. *Director*, Dr. Elizabeth Buck, 314-529-9453, Fax: 314-529-9139, E-mail: ebuck@maryville.edu.

MARYWOOD UNIVERSITY, Scranton, PA 18509-1598

General Information Independent-religious, coed, comprehensive institution. *Graduate housing:* Room and/or apartments available on a first-come, first-served basis to single students; on-campus housing not available to married students.

GRADUATE UNITS

Academic Affairs ***Degree program information:*** Part-time and evening/weekend programs available. Part-time, evening/weekend, online learning. Electronic applications accepted.

Center for Interdisciplinary Studies Degree program information: Part-time programs available. Part-time. Offers human development (PhD). Electronic applications accepted.

College of Health and Human Services Degree program information: Part-time programs available. Part-time, online learning. Offers dietetic internship (Certificate); gerontology (MS); health and human services (MHSA, MPA, MS, MSW, Certificate); health services administration (MHSA); nutrition (MS); physician assistant studies (MS); public administration (MPA); social work (MSW); sports nutrition and exercise science (MS). Electronic applications accepted.

Insalaco College of Creative and Performing Arts Degree program information: Part-time programs available. Part-time. Offers art (Graduate Certificate); art education (MA); art therapy (MA, Graduate Certificate); clay (MA, MFA); communication arts (MA); creative and performing arts (MA, MFA, MMT, Graduate Certificate); graphic design (MFA); illustration (MFA); music education (MA); painting (MA, MFA); photography (MA, MFA); printmaking (MA, MFA); sculpture (MA, MFA); studio art (MA); visual arts (MFA). Electronic applications accepted.

Munley College of Liberal Arts and Sciences Degree program information: Part-time programs available. Part-time, online learning. Offers biotechnology (MS); criminal justice (MS); finance/investment (MBA); general management (MBA); information security (MS); liberal arts and sciences (MBA, MS); management information systems (MBA, MS). Electronic applications accepted.

Reap College of Education and Human Development Degree program information: Part-time programs available. Part-time. Offers clinical psychology (Psy D); clinical services (MA); counselor education (MS); early childhood intervention (MS); education and human development (M Ed, MA, MAT, MS, Psy D, Certificate, Post-Master's Certificate); general theoretical psychology (MA); higher education administration (MS); instructional leadership (M Ed); mental health counseling (MA); PK-4 education (MAT); psychology (MA); reading education (MS); school leadership (MS); secondary/K-12 education (MAT); special education (MS); special education administration and supervision (MS); speech-language pathology (MS).

School of Architecture Degree program information: Part-time programs available. Part-time. Offers architecture (M Arch, MA); interior architecture/design (MA). Electronic applications accepted.

★ MASSACHUSETTS COLLEGE OF ART AND DESIGN, Boston, MA 02115-5882

General Information State-supported, coed, comprehensive institution. *Enrollment:* 1,990 graduate, professional, and undergraduate students; 92 full-time matriculated graduate/professional students (64 women), 20 part-time matriculated graduate/professional students (15 women). *Enrollment by degree level:* 108 master's, 4 other advanced degrees. *Graduate faculty:* 34 full-time (16 women), 37 part-time/adjunct (16 women). Tuition, state resident: full-time $23,400; part-time $780 per credit. Tuition, nonresident: full-time $23,400; part-time $780 per credit. Tuition and fees vary according to course load and degree level. *Graduate housing:* Room and/or apartments available on a first-come, first-served basis to single students; on-campus housing not available to married students. Typical cost: $12,630 per year ($15,756 including board). Room and board charges vary according to board plan and housing facility selected. Housing application deadline: 5/1. *Student services:* Campus employment opportunities, campus safety program, career counseling, exercise/wellness program, international student services, low-cost health insurance, services for students with disabilities, teacher training, writing training. *Library:* Morton R. Godine Library. *Collection:* Books: 105,776 (physical), 103,655 (digital/electronic); Databases: 31.

Computer facilities: Computer purchase and lease plans are available. 370 computers available on campus for general student use. A campuswide network can be accessed from student residence rooms and from off campus. Online class registration is available. Website: http://www.massart.edu/

General Application Contact: Graduate Admissions Counselor, 617-879-7203, Fax: 617-879-7250, E-mail: gradprogram@massart.edu.

GRADUATE UNITS

Graduate Programs Students: 92 full-time (64 women), 20 part-time (15 women); includes 17 minority (6 Black or African American, non-Hispanic/Latino; 4 Asian, non-Hispanic/Latino; 6 Hispanic/Latino; 1 Native Hawaiian or other Pacific Islander, non-Hispanic/Latino), 25 international. Average age 30. 346 applicants, 49% accepted, 59 enrolled. *Faculty:* 34 full-time (16 women), 37 part-time/adjunct (16 women). *Financial support:* In 2015–16, 81 students received support, including 50 teaching assistantships (averaging $2,160 per year); career-related internships or fieldwork, scholarships/grants, tuition waivers (partial), and 6 adjunct faculty co-teaching positions; 41 non-teaching assistantships also available. Support available to part-time students. Financial award application deadline: 1/6. In 2015, 64 master's, 5 other advanced degrees awarded. Offers 2D fine arts (MFA); 3D fine arts (MFA); architecture (M Arch); art education (MAT, Postbaccalaureate Certificate); design (MFA, Postbaccalaureate Certificate); fine arts (MFA); media arts (MFA, Postbaccalaureate Certificate). *Application deadline:* For fall admission, 1/6 priority date for domestic and international students; for summer admission, 1/6 priority date for domestic and international students. *Application fee:* $75. Electronic applications accepted. *Application Contact:* Graduate Admissions Counselor, 617-879-7203, Fax: 617-879-7250, E-mail: gradprogram@massart.edu. *Interim Dean of Graduate Studies*, Paul Paturzo, 617-879-7166, E-mail: pjpaturzo@massart.edu.

See Display on next page and Close-Up on page 887.

MASSACHUSETTS COLLEGE OF LIBERAL ARTS, North Adams, MA 01247-4100

General Information State-supported, coed, comprehensive institution. *Enrollment:* 1,641 graduate, professional, and undergraduate students; 14 full-time matriculated graduate/professional students (12 women), 170 part-time matriculated graduate/professional students (111 women). *Enrollment by degree level:* 97 master's, 87 other advanced degrees. Tuition and fees vary according to program. *Graduate housing:* On-campus housing not available. *Student services:* Campus safety program, career counseling, low-cost health insurance. *Library:* Eugene L. Freel Library.

Computer facilities: Computer purchase and lease plans are available. 140 computers available on campus for general student use. A campuswide network can be accessed from student residence rooms and from off campus. Online class registration is available. Website: http://www.mcla.edu/

General Application Contact: Joshua Mendel, Associate Director of Admissions, 413-662-5409.

GRADUATE UNITS

Graduate Programs Students: 55 full-time (35 women), 107 part-time (75 women). *Financial support:* Career-related internships or fieldwork available. Financial award application deadline: 5/1; financial award applicants required to submit FAFSA. *Degree program information:* Part-time and evening/weekend programs available. Part-time, evening/weekend. Offers business (MBA); educational administration (M Ed); educational leadership (CAGS); instruction and curriculum (M Ed); instructional technology (M Ed); physical education and health (M Ed); reading (M Ed); special education (M Ed). *Application deadline:* Applications are processed on a rolling basis. *Application Contact:* Joshua Mendel, Associate Director of Admissions, 413-662-5409. *Dean, Graduate and Continuing Education*, Dr. Howard Eberwein, 413-662-5543.

MASSACHUSETTS INSTITUTE OF TECHNOLOGY, Cambridge, MA 02139-4307

General Information Independent, coed, university. CGS member. *Enrollment:* 11,331 graduate, professional, and undergraduate students; 6,609 full-time matriculated graduate/professional students (2,200 women), 22 part-time matriculated graduate/professional students (7 women). *Enrollment by degree level:* 2,722 master's, 3,909 doctoral. *Graduate faculty:* 1,022 full-time (226 women), 14 part-time/adjunct (4 women). *Tuition:* Full-time $46,400; part-time $725 per credit. One-time fee: $304 full-time. Full-time tuition and fees vary according to course load and program. *Graduate housing:* Rooms and/or apartments available to single and married students. Housing application deadline: 5/15. *Student services:* Campus employment opportunities, campus safety program, career counseling, child daycare facilities, exercise/wellness program, free psychological counseling, grant writing training, international student services, low-cost health insurance, services for students with disabilities, teacher training, writing training. *Library:* MIT Libraries plus 5 others. *Collection:* Books: 1.5 million (physical), 6 million (digital/electronic); Serial titles: 51,454 (physical), 62,291 (digital/electronic); Databases: 301. Weekly public service hours: 95; study areas open 24 hours, 5–7 days a week; students can reserve study rooms. *Research affiliation:* Novartis Pharmaceuticals (pharmaceutical manufacturing), Singapore National Research Foundation (infectious diseases, environmental sensing, biosystems, urban transportation, low power electronics), Woods Hole Oceanographic Institution (applied ocean science and engineering), Broad Institute (genomics and biomedical research), Whitehead Institute for Biomedical Research (developmental biology), Eni S.p.A (renewable energy).

Computer facilities: Computer purchase and lease plans are available. 1,100 computers available on campus for general student use. A campuswide network can be accessed from student residence rooms and from off campus. Online class registration is available.
Website: http://web.mit.edu/

General Application Contact: Graduate Admissions, 617-324-6730, E-mail: mitgrad@mit.edu.

GRADUATE UNITS

MIT Sloan School of Management ***Financial support:*** Fellowships with tuition reimbursements, research assistantships with tuition reimbursements, teaching assistantships with tuition reimbursements, Federal Work-Study, institutionally sponsored loans, scholarships/grants, health care benefits, and unspecified assistantships available. Support available to part-time students. Offers management (M Fin, MBA, MS, SM, PhD). Electronic applications accepted. *Application Contact:* Rod Garcia, Director of Admissions, 617-253-5434, Fax: 617-253-6405, E-mail: mbaadmissions@sloan.mit.edu. *Dean*, David C. Schmittlein, 617-253-2804, Fax: 617-258-6617, E-mail: dschmitt@mit.edu.

Operations Research Center Students: 80 full-time (14 women); includes 7 minority (all Asian, non-Hispanic/Latino), 48 international. Average age 26. 387 applicants, 7% accepted, 18 enrolled. *Faculty:* 48 full-time (9 women). *Financial support:* In 2015–16, 69 students received support, including 16 fellowships (averaging $37,800 per year), 55 research assistantships (averaging $36,400 per year), 6 teaching assistantships (averaging $38,100 per year); Federal Work-Study, institutionally sponsored loans, scholarships/grants, traineeships, health care benefits, and unspecified assistantships also available. Support available to part-time students. Financial award application deadline: 4/15; financial award applicants required to submit FAFSA. In 2015, 10 master's, 11 doctorates awarded. Offers operations research (SM, PhD). *Application deadline:* For fall admission, 12/15 for domestic and international students. *Application fee:* $75. Electronic applications accepted. *Application Contact:* Laura A. Rose, Graduate Admissions Coordinator, 617-253-3601, Fax: 617-258-9214, E-mail: lrose@mit.edu. *Co-Director*, Dr. Dimitris J. Bertsimas, 617-253-3601, Fax: 617-258-9214, E-mail: orc-www@mit.edu.

School of Architecture and Planning Students: 592 full-time (278 women), 2 part-time (1 woman); includes 122 minority (17 Black or African American, non-Hispanic/Latino; 52 Asian, non-Hispanic/Latino; 38 Hispanic/Latino; 15 Two or more races, non-Hispanic/Latino), 258 international. Average age 29. 2,550 applicants, 14% accepted, 229 enrolled. *Faculty:* 83 full-time (24 women), 1 part-time/adjunct (0 women). *Financial support:* In 2015–16, 503 students received support, including 226 fellowships (averaging $25,900 per year), 248 research assistantships (averaging $32,100 per year), 40 teaching assistantships (averaging $35,800 per year); Federal Work-Study, institutionally sponsored loans, scholarships/grants, health care benefits, and unspecified assistantships also available. Financial award application deadline: 4/15; financial award applicants required to submit FAFSA. In 2015, 184 master's, 36 doctorates awarded. Offers architecture (M Arch, PhD); architecture and planning (M Arch, MCP, MSRED, SM, SM Arch S, SMACT, SMBT, PhD); architecture studies (SM Arch S); art, culture and technology (SMACT); building technology (SMBT); city planning (MCP); media arts and sciences (SM, PhD); media technology (SM); urban and regional planning (PhD); urban and regional studies (PhD); urban studies and planning (SM). *Application fee:* $75. Electronic applications accepted. *Application Contact:* Graduate Admissions, E-mail: mitgrad@mit.edu. *Dean*, Prof. Hashim Sarkis, 617-253-4401, Fax: 617-253-9417, E-mail: sap-info@mit.edu.

Center for Real Estate Students: 36 full-time (14 women); includes 2 minority (1 Asian, non-Hispanic/Latino; 1 Two or more races, non-Hispanic/Latino), 19 international. Average age 31. 75 applicants, 41% accepted, 25 enrolled. *Faculty:* 3 full-time (0 women), 8 part-time/adjunct (0 women). *Financial support:* In 2015–16, 10 students received support, including 11 fellowships (averaging $29,100 per year); research assistantships, teaching assistantships, Federal Work-Study, institutionally sponsored loans, scholarships/grants, health care benefits, and unspecified assistantships also available. Financial award application deadline: 4/15; financial award applicants required to submit FAFSA. In 2015, 26 master's awarded. Offers real estate development (MSRED). *Application deadline:* For fall admission, 1/5 for domestic and international students. *Application fee:* $75. Electronic applications accepted. *Application Contact:* 617-253-4373, Fax: 617-258-6991, E-mail: mit-msred_admissions@mit.edu. *Director*, Prof. Albert Saiz, 617-253-4373, Fax: 617-258-6991, E-mail: mit-cre@mit.edu.

School of Engineering Students: 3,106 full-time (883 women), 17 part-time (6 women); includes 655 minority (33 Black or African American, non-Hispanic/Latino; 4 American Indian or Alaska Native, non-Hispanic/Latino; 410 Asian, non-Hispanic/Latino; 136 Hispanic/Latino; 72 Two or more races, non-Hispanic/Latino), 1,352 international. Average age 27. 8,294 applicants, 16% accepted, 879 enrolled. *Faculty:* 376 full-time (67 women), 2 part-time/adjunct (0 women). *Financial support:* In 2015–16, 2,528 students received support, including 674 fellowships (averaging $39,900 per year), 1,636 research assistantships (averaging $35,600 per year), 301 teaching assistantships (averaging $37,200 per year); Federal Work-Study, institutionally sponsored loans, scholarships/grants, traineeships, health care benefits, and unspecified assistantships also available. Financial award application deadline: 4/15; financial award applicants required to submit FAFSA. In 2015, 698 master's, 348 doctorates, 15 other advanced degrees awarded. Offers aeronautics and astronautics (SM, PhD, Sc D, EAA); aerospace computational engineering (PhD, Sc D); air transportation systems (PhD, Sc D); air-breathing propulsion (PhD, Sc D); aircraft systems engineering (PhD, Sc D); applied biosciences (PhD, Sc D); archaeological materials (PhD, Sc D); autonomous systems (PhD, Sc D); bioengineering (PhD, Sc D); biological engineering (PhD, Sc D); biological oceanography (PhD, Sc D); biomedical engineering (M Eng); chemical engineering (PhD, Sc D); chemical engineering practice (SM, PhD); chemical oceanography (PhD, Sc D); civil and environmental engineering (M Eng, SM, PhD, Sc D); civil and environmental systems (PhD, Sc D); civil engineering (PhD, Sc D, CE); coastal engineering (PhD, Sc D); communications and networks (PhD, Sc D); computation for design and optimization (SM); computational and systems biology (PhD); computer science (PhD, Sc D, ECS); computer science and engineering (PhD, Sc D); construction engineering and management (PhD, Sc D); controls (PhD, Sc D); electrical engineering (PhD, Sc D, EE); electrical engineering and computer science (M Eng, SM, PhD, Sc D); engineering (M Eng, SM, PhD, Sc D, CE, EAA, ECS, EE, Mat E, Mech E, NE, Naval E); environmental biology (PhD, Sc D); environmental chemistry (PhD, Sc D); environmental engineering (PhD, Sc D); environmental fluid mechanics (PhD, Sc D); geotechnical and geoenvironmental engineering (PhD, Sc D); health sciences and technology (SM, PhD, Sc D); humans in aerospace (PhD, Sc D); hydrology (PhD, Sc D); information technology (PhD, Sc D); manufacturing (M Eng); materials and structures (PhD, Sc D); materials engineering (Mat E); materials science and engineering (SM, PhD, Sc D); mechanical engineering (SM, PhD, Sc D, Mech E); naval architecture and marine engineering (SM, PhD, Sc D); naval engineering (Naval E); nuclear science and engineering (SM, PhD, Sc D, NE); ocean engineering (SM, PhD, Sc D); oceanographic engineering (SM, PhD, Sc D); space propulsion (PhD, Sc D); space systems (PhD, Sc D); structures and materials (PhD, Sc D); toxicology (SM); transportation (PhD, Sc D). *Application fee:* $75. Electronic applications accepted.

Application Contact: Graduate Admissions, E-mail: mitgrad@mit.edu. *Dean*, Prof. Ian A. Waitz, 617-253-3291, Fax: 617-253-8549.

Institute for Data, Systems, and Society Students: 327 full-time (55 women); includes 18 minority (3 Black or African American, non-Hispanic/Latino; 8 Asian, non-Hispanic/Latino; 5 Hispanic/Latino; 2 Two or more races, non-Hispanic/Latino), 53 international. Average age 27. 406 applicants, 29% accepted, 92 enrolled. *Faculty:* 6 full-time (3 women). *Financial support:* In 2015–16, 110 students received support, including 31 fellowships (averaging $37,600 per year), 82 research assistantships (averaging $34,100 per year), 6 teaching assistantships (averaging $41,400 per year); Federal Work-Study, institutionally sponsored loans, scholarships/grants, traineeships, health care benefits, and unspecified assistantships also available. Support available to part-time students. Financial award application deadline: 4/15; financial award applicants required to submit FAFSA. In 2015, 157 master's awarded. Offers technology and policy (SM). *Application fee:* $75. Electronic applications accepted. *Application Contact:* Graduate Admissions, 617-253-1182, E-mail: idss_academic_office@mit.edu. *Director*, Munther A. Dahleh, 617-253-1764, E-mail: idss-info@mit.edu.

School of Humanities, Arts, and Social Sciences Students: 335 full-time (138 women), 2 part-time (0 women); includes 49 minority (4 Black or African American, non-Hispanic/Latino; 2 American Indian or Alaska Native, non-Hispanic/Latino; 21 Asian, non-Hispanic/Latino; 10 Hispanic/Latino; 12 Two or more races, non-Hispanic/Latino), 153 international. Average age 28. 1,888 applicants, 6% accepted, 68 enrolled. *Faculty:* 167 full-time (54 women), 7 part-time/adjunct (3 women). *Financial support:* In 2015–16, 288 students received support, including 129 fellowships (averaging $39,000 per year), 99 research assistantships (averaging $36,900 per year), 62 teaching assistantships (averaging $41,600 per year); Federal Work-Study, institutionally sponsored loans, scholarships/grants, traineeships, health care benefits, and unspecified assistantships also available. Support available to part-time students. Financial award application deadline: 4/15; financial award applicants required to submit FAFSA. In 2015, 24 master's, 29 doctorates awarded. Offers comparative media studies (SM); economics (SM, PhD); history, anthropology, and science, technology and society (PhD); humanities, arts, and social sciences (SM, PhD); linguistics (PhD); philosophy (PhD); political science (SM, PhD); science writing (SM). *Application fee:* $75. Electronic applications accepted. *Application Contact:* Graduate Admissions Office, E-mail: mitgrad@mit.edu. *Dean*, Prof. Melissa Nobles, 617-253-3450, Fax: 617-253-3451, E-mail: shass-www@mit.edu.

School of Science Students: 1,146 full-time (395 women), 1 part-time (0 women); includes 234 minority (9 Black or African American, non-Hispanic/Latino; 2 American Indian or Alaska Native, non-Hispanic/Latino; 110 Asian, non-Hispanic/Latino; 74 Hispanic/Latino; 39 Two or more races, non-Hispanic/Latino), 404 international. Average age 26. 3,209 applicants, 14% accepted, 196 enrolled. *Faculty:* 270 full-time (53 women), 3 part-time/adjunct (1 woman). *Financial support:* In 2015–16, 993 students received support, including 414 fellowships (averaging $40,600 per year), 570 research assistantships (averaging $38,800 per year), 153 teaching assistantships (averaging $39,600 per year); Federal Work-Study, institutionally sponsored loans, scholarships/grants, traineeships, health care benefits, and unspecified assistantships also available. Support available to part-time students. Financial award application deadline: 4/15; financial award applicants required to submit FAFSA. In 2015, 23 master's, 167 doctorates awarded. Offers atmospheric chemistry (PhD, Sc D); atmospheric science (SM, PhD, Sc D); biochemistry (PhD); biological chemistry (PhD); biological oceanography (PhD); biology (PhD); biophysical chemistry and molecular structure (PhD); cell biology (PhD); chemical oceanography (SM, PhD, Sc D); climate physics and chemistry (SM, PhD, Sc D); cognitive science (PhD); computational and systems biology (PhD); developmental biology (PhD); earth and planetary sciences (SM); genetics (PhD); geochemistry (PhD, Sc D); geology (PhD, Sc D); geophysics (PhD, Sc D); immunology (PhD); inorganic chemistry (PhD); marine geology and geophysics (SM, PhD, Sc D); mathematics (PhD); microbiology (PhD); molecular biology (PhD); neurobiology (PhD); neuroscience (PhD); organic chemistry (PhD); physical chemistry (PhD); physical oceanography (SM, PhD, Sc D); physics (SM, PhD); planetary sciences (PhD, Sc D); science (SM, PhD, Sc D). *Application fee:* $75. Electronic applications accepted. *Application Contact:* Graduate Admissions Office, E-mail: mitgrad@mit.edu. *Dean*, Michael Sipser, 617-253-8900, Fax: 617-253-8901, E-mail: scnc@mit.edu.

MASSACHUSETTS MARITIME ACADEMY, Buzzards Bay, MA 02532-1803

General Information State-supported, coed, primarily men, comprehensive institution. *Enrollment:* 1,674 graduate, professional, and undergraduate students; 70 part-time matriculated graduate/professional students (15 women). *Enrollment by degree level:* 70 master's. *Graduate faculty:* 21 part-time/adjunct (1 woman). *Student services:* Campus employment opportunities, career counseling, low-cost health insurance. *Library:* American Bureau of Shipping Information Commons plus 1 other. *Collection:* Books: 36,954 (physical), 141,440 (digital/electronic); Serial titles: 83 (physical), 52,621 (digital/electronic); Databases: 122. Weekly public service hours: 73; students can reserve study rooms.

Computer facilities: Computer purchase and lease plans are available. 130 computers available on campus for general student use. A campuswide network can be accessed from student residence rooms and from off campus. Online class registration, course-supported e-learning are available.
Website: http://www.maritime.edu/

General Application Contact: Kelly DeMello, Graduate Outreach Coordinator, 508-830-6492, Fax: 508-830-5018, E-mail: dce@maritime.edu.

GRADUATE UNITS

Program in Emergency Management Students: 25 part-time (10 women). Average age 34. *Faculty:* 13 part-time/adjunct (2 women). In 2015, 1 master's awarded. *Degree program information:* Part-time and evening/weekend programs available. Part-time-only, evening/weekend. Offers emergency management (MS). *Application deadline:* Applications are processed on a rolling basis. Electronic applications accepted. *Application Contact:* Kelly DeMello, Graduate Outreach Coordinator, 508-830-6492, Fax: 508-830-5018, E-mail: dce@maritime.edu. *Dean, Graduate and Continuing Education*, James McDonald, 508-830-5096, Fax: 508-830-5018, E-mail: dce@maritime.edu.

Program in Facilities Management Students: 46 (9 women). *Faculty:* 12 part-time/adjunct (1 woman). In 2015, 17 master's awarded. *Degree program information:* Part-time and evening/weekend programs available. Part-time-only, evening/weekend. Offers facilities management (MS). *Application deadline:* Applications are processed on a rolling basis. Electronic applications accepted. *Application Contact:* Kelly DeMello, Graduate Outreach Coordinator, 508-830-6492, Fax: 508-830-5018, E-mail: dce@maritime.edu. *Dean, Graduate and Continuing Education*, Dr. James McDonald, 508-830-5096, Fax: 508-830-5018, E-mail: dce@maritime.edu.

MASSACHUSETTS SCHOOL OF LAW AT ANDOVER, Andover, MA 01810

General Information Independent, coed, graduate-only institution. *Graduate housing:* On-campus housing not available.

GRADUATE UNITS

Professional Program ***Degree program information:*** Part-time and evening/weekend programs available. Part-time, evening/weekend. Offers law (JD). Electronic applications accepted.

THE MASTER'S COLLEGE AND SEMINARY, Santa Clarita, CA 91321-1200

General Information Independent-religious, coed, comprehensive institution. *Graduate housing:* On-campus housing not available.

GRADUATE UNITS

The Master's Seminary ***Degree program information:*** Part-time programs available. Part-time. Offers biblical counseling (MABC); New Testament (Th D); Old Testament (Th D); preaching (D Min); theology (M Div, M Th, Th D).

MAYO GRADUATE SCHOOL, Rochester, MN 55905

General Information Independent, coed, graduate-only institution. *Graduate housing:* On-campus housing not available.

GRADUATE UNITS

Graduate Programs in Biomedical Sciences Offers biochemistry and structural biology (PhD); biomedical engineering (PhD); biomedical sciences (PhD); cell biology and genetics (PhD); immunology (PhD); molecular biology (PhD); molecular neuroscience (PhD); molecular pharmacology and experimental therapeutics (PhD); tumor biology (PhD); virology and gene therapy (PhD). Electronic applications accepted.

MAYO MEDICAL SCHOOL, Rochester, MN 55905

General Information Independent, coed, graduate-only institution. *Graduate housing:* On-campus housing not available.

GRADUATE UNITS

Professional Program Offers medicine (MD). MD offered through the Mayo Foundation's Division of Education; MD/PhD, MD/Certificate with Mayo Graduate School. Electronic applications accepted.

MAYO SCHOOL OF HEALTH SCIENCES, Rochester, MN 55905

General Information Independent, coed, graduate-only institution. *Enrollment:* 246 full-time matriculated graduate/professional students (163 women). *Enrollment by degree level:* 77 master's, 169 doctoral. *Graduate faculty:* 18 full-time (9 women). Full-time tuition and fees vary according to course load and program. *Student services:* Campus employment opportunities, campus safety program, career counseling, exercise/wellness program, free psychological counseling, international student services, multicultural affairs office, services for students with disabilities. *Library:* Venables Health Sciences Library plus 1 other. Study areas open 24 hours, 5–7 days a week; students can reserve study rooms.

Computer facilities: A campuswide network can be accessed from student residence rooms and from off campus. Online class registration is available.
Website: http://www.mayo.edu/mshs/

General Application Contact: Kammi Englund, Education Coordinator, 507-284-3678, Fax: 507-284-0656, E-mail: englund.kammi@mayo.edu.

GRADUATE UNITS

Doctor of Nurse Anesthesia Practice Program ***Faculty:*** 3 part-time/adjunct. *Financial support:* Scholarships/grants, health care benefits, and stipends available. Financial award applicants required to submit FAFSA. Offers nurse anesthesia practice (DNAP). *Application deadline:* For fall admission, 9/1 for domestic students. *Application fee:* $50. Electronic applications accepted. *Application Contact:* Julie Predmore, Administrative Assistant, 507-286-4163, Fax: 507-284-2818, E-mail: predmore.julie@mayo.edu. *Director*, Dr. Mary E. Marienau, 507-284-8331, Fax: 507-284-2818, E-mail: marienau.mary@mayo.edu.

Program in Physical Therapy Students: 84 full-time (57 women); includes 6 minority (3 Black or African American, non-Hispanic/Latino; 1 American Indian or Alaska Native, non-Hispanic/Latino; 1 Asian, non-Hispanic/Latino; 1 Hispanic/Latino). Average age 25. 629 applicants, 9% accepted, 28 enrolled. *Faculty:* 5 full-time (0 women), 3 part-time/adjunct (all women). *Financial support:* In 2015–16, 75 students received support. Scholarships/grants available. Financial award applicants required to submit FAFSA. In 2015, 28 doctorates awarded. Offers physical therapy (DPT). *Application deadline:* For fall admission, 10/15 for domestic and international students. Applications are processed on a rolling basis. Electronic applications accepted. *Application Contact:* Carol Cooper, Administrative Assistant, 507-284-2054, Fax: 507-284-0656, E-mail: cooper.carol@mayo.edu. *Director*, Dr. John Hollman, 507-284-9547, Fax: 507-284-0656, E-mail: hollman.john@mayo.edu.

MCCORMICK THEOLOGICAL SEMINARY, Chicago, IL 60615

General Information Independent-religious, coed, graduate-only institution. *Graduate housing:* Rooms and/or apartments available on a first-come, first-served basis to single and married students. Housing application deadline: 7/1.

GRADUATE UNITS

Graduate and Professional Programs ***Degree program information:*** Part-time and evening/weekend programs available. Part-time, evening/weekend. Offers ministry (D Min); theological studies (MATS, Certificate); theology (M Div). M Div/MSW offered jointly with Loyola University Chicago, University of Chicago, and University of Illinois at Chicago.

MCDANIEL COLLEGE, Westminster, MD 21157-4390

General Information Independent, coed, comprehensive institution. *Enrollment:* 3,126 graduate, professional, and undergraduate students; 125 full-time matriculated graduate/professional students (85 women), 1,354 part-time matriculated graduate/professional students (1,066 women). *Enrollment by degree level:* 1,380 master's, 99 other advanced degrees. *Graduate faculty:* 24 full-time (15 women), 141 part-time/adjunct (86 women). *Tuition, area resident:* Full-time $8370; part-time $465 per credit. *Required fees:* $75 per semester. Tuition and fees vary according to course load, program and reciprocity agreements. *Graduate housing:* On-campus housing not available. *Student services:* Campus safety program, career counseling, free psychological counseling, international student services, multicultural affairs office, services for students with disabilities. *Library:* Hoover Library. *Collection:* Books: 378,679 (physical), 133,291 (digital/electronic); Serial titles: 15,639 (physical), 25,272 (digital/electronic); Databases: 87. Weekly public service hours: 135; study areas open 24 hours, 5–7 days a week; students can reserve study rooms.

Computer facilities: 138 computers available on campus for general student use. A campuswide network can be accessed from student residence rooms and from off campus. Online class registration, online billing summaries, financial aid letter, tax information are available.
Website: http://www.mcdaniel.edu/

General Application Contact: Crystal L. Perry, Assistant Director of Graduate Enrollment Management, 410-857-2516, Fax: 410-857-2515, E-mail: cperry@mcdaniel.edu.

GRADUATE UNITS

Graduate and Professional Studies Students: 120 full-time (80 women), 899 part-time (701 women); includes 177 minority (112 Black or African American, non-Hispanic/Latino; 5 American Indian or Alaska Native, non-Hispanic/Latino; 23 Asian, non-Hispanic/Latino; 33 Hispanic/Latino; 1 Native Hawaiian or other Pacific Islander, non-Hispanic/Latino; 3 Two or more races, non-Hispanic/Latino), 13 international. Average age 32. 436 applicants, 89% accepted. *Faculty:* 24 full-time (15 women), 141 part-time/adjunct (86 women). *Financial support:* In 2015–16, 1 student received support. Career-related internships or fieldwork, institutionally sponsored loans, and scholarships/grants available. Support available to part-time students. Financial award application deadline: 3/1; financial award applicants required to submit FAFSA. In 2015, 332 master's awarded. *Degree program information:* Part-time and evening/weekend programs available. Part-time, evening/weekend, 100% online, blended/hybrid learning. Offers counselor education (MS); curriculum and instruction (MS); deaf education (MS); educational leadership (MS); elementary education (MS); exercise science and physical education (MS); gerontology (MS, Graduate Certificate); human resources development (MS); human services management (MS); liberal arts (MLA); reading specialists: literacy leadership (MS); school librarianship (MS); secondary education (MS); special education (MS); teaching of English to speakers of other languages (MS). *Application deadline:* For fall admission, 6/1 priority date for domestic students; for spring admission, 11/1 priority date for domestic students; for summer admission, 3/1 priority date for domestic students. Applications are processed on a rolling basis. *Application fee:* $75. Electronic applications accepted. *Application Contact:* Penny Pfeiffer, Senior Graduate Enrollment Management Specialist, 410-857-2513, Fax: 410-857-2515, E-mail: ppfeiffer@mcdaniel.edu. *Dean, Graduate and Professional Studies*, Dr. J. Michael Tyler, 410-857-2525, Fax: 410-857-2515, E-mail: mtyler@mcdaniel.edu.

MCGILL UNIVERSITY, Montréal, QC H3A 2T5, Canada

General Information Province-supported, coed, university. CGS member. *Graduate housing:* Room and/or apartments available to married students; on-campus housing not available to single students.

GRADUATE UNITS

Faculty of Graduate and Postdoctoral Studies

Desautels Faculty of Management Offers administration (PhD); entrepreneurial studies (MBA); finance (MBA); general management (Post Master's Certificate); information systems (MBA); international business (MBA); international practicing management (MM); management (MBA); management for development (MBA); manufacturing management (MMM); marketing (MBA); operations management (MBA); public accountancy (Diploma); strategic management (MBA). MMM offered jointly with Faculty of Engineering; PhD with Concordia University, HEC Montreal, Université de Montréal, Université du Québec à Montréal.

Faculty of Agricultural and Environmental Sciences Offers agricultural and environmental sciences (M Sc, M Sc A, PhD, Certificate, Graduate Diploma); agricultural economics (M Sc); animal science (M Sc, M Sc A, PhD); biotechnology (M Sc A, Certificate); computer applications (M Sc, M Sc A, PhD); dietetics (M Sc A, Graduate Diploma); entomology (M Sc, PhD); environmental assessment (M Sc); food engineering (M Sc, M Sc A, PhD); food science and agricultural chemistry (M Sc, PhD); forest science (M Sc, PhD); grain drying (M Sc, M Sc A, PhD); human nutrition (M Sc, M Sc A, PhD); irrigation and drainage (M Sc, M Sc A, PhD); machinery (M Sc, M Sc A, PhD); microbiology (M Sc, PhD); micrometeorology (M Sc, PhD); neotropical environment (M Sc, PhD); parasitology (M Sc, PhD); plant science (M Sc, M Sc A, PhD, Certificate); pollution control (M Sc, M Sc A, PhD); post-harvest technology (M Sc, M Sc A, PhD); soil dynamics (M Sc, M Sc A, PhD); soil science (M Sc, PhD); structure and environment (M Sc, M Sc A, PhD); vegetable and fruit storage (M Sc, M Sc A, PhD); wildlife biology (M Sc, PhD).

Faculty of Arts Offers anthropology (MA, PhD); art history and communication studies (MA, PhD); arts (MA, MSW, PhD, Diploma); bioethics (MA); East Asian studies (MA, PhD); economics (MA, PhD); English (MA, PhD); French language and literature (MA, PhD); German studies (MA, PhD); Hispanic studies (MA, PhD); history (MA, PhD); history of medicine (MA); Islamic studies (MA, PhD, Diploma); Italian studies (MA, PhD); Jewish studies (MA); language acquisition (PhD); linguistics (MA, PhD); medical anthropology (MA); medical sociology (MA); neo-tropical environment (MA); philosophy (PhD); political science (MA, PhD); Russian literature (MA, PhD); social statistics (MA); social work (MSW, PhD, Diploma); sociology (MA, PhD, Diploma).

Faculty of Dentistry Offers forensic dentistry (Certificate); oral and maxillofacial surgery (M Sc, PhD).

Faculty of Education Offers counseling psychology (MA, PhD); culture and values in education (MA, PhD); curriculum studies (MA); education (M Ed, M Sc, MA, MLIS, PhD, Certificate, Diploma); educational leadership (MA, Certificate); educational psychology (M Ed, MA, PhD); educational studies (PhD); information studies (MLIS, PhD, Certificate, Diploma); integrated studies in education (M Ed); kinesiology and physical education (M Sc, MA, PhD, Certificate, Diploma); school/applied child psychology and applied developmental psychology (M Ed, MA, PhD, Diploma); second language education (MA, PhD).

Faculty of Engineering Offers aerospace (M Eng); affordable homes (M Arch II, Diploma); architectural history and theory (M Arch II); architecture (PhD); chemical engineering (M Eng, PhD); domestic environment (M Arch II); domestic environments (Diploma); electrical and computer engineering (M Eng, PhD); engineering (M Arch I, M Arch II, M Eng, M Sc, MMM, MUP, PhD, Diploma); environmental engineering (M Eng, M Sc, PhD); environmental planning (MUP); fluid mechanics (M Sc); fluid mechanics and hydraulic engineering (M Eng, PhD); housing (MUP); manufacturing management (MMM); materials engineering (M Eng, PhD); mechanical engineering (M Eng, M Sc, PhD); minimum cost housing in developing countries (M Arch II, Diploma); mining engineering (M Eng, M Sc, PhD, Diploma); professional architecture (M Arch I); rehabilitation of urban infrastructure (M Eng, PhD); soil behavior (M Eng, PhD); soil mechanics and foundations (M Eng, PhD); structures and structural mechanics (M Eng, PhD); transportation (MUP); urban design (MUP); urban planning, policy and design (PhD); water resources (M Sc); water resources engineering (M Eng, PhD).

Faculty of Law Offers air and space law (LL M, DCL, Graduate Certificate); bioethics (LL M); comparative law (LL M, DCL, Graduate Certificate); law (LL M, DCL). Applications for LL M with specialization in bioethics are made initially through the Biomedical Ethics Unit in the Faculty of Medicine.

Faculty of Medicine Offers anatomy and cell biology (M Sc, PhD); assessing driving capability (PGC); biochemistry (M Sc, PhD); biomedical engineering (M Eng, PhD); communication science and disorders (M Sc); communication sciences and disorders (PhD); community health (M Sc); environmental health (M Sc); epidemiology and biostatistics (M Sc, PhD, Diploma); experimental medicine (M Sc, PhD); genetic counseling (M Sc); health care evaluation (M Sc); human genetics (M Sc, PhD); medical anthropology (MA, PhD); medical history (MA, PhD); medical physics (M Sc, PhD); medical sociology (MA, PhD); medical statistics (M Sc); medicine (M Eng, M Sc, M Sc A, MA, PhD, Diploma, Graduate Diploma, PGC); microbiology and immunology (M Sc, M Sc A, PhD); neurology and neurosurgery (M Sc, PhD); nurse practitioner (Graduate Diploma); nursing (M Sc A, PhD); occupational health (M Sc, PhD); otolaryngology (M Sc); pathology (M Sc, PhD); pharmacology and therapeutics (M Sc, PhD); physiology (M Sc, PhD); psychiatry (M Sc); rehabilitation science (M Sc, PhD); speech-language pathology (M Sc A); surgery (M Sc, PhD).

Faculty of Religious Studies Offers religious studies (MA, STM, PhD).

Faculty of Science Offers atmospheric science (M Sc, PhD); bioinformatics (M Sc, PhD); chemical biology (M Sc, PhD); chemistry (M Sc, PhD); clinical psychology (PhD); computational science and engineering (M Sc); computer science (M Sc, PhD); earth and planetary sciences (M Sc, PhD); environment (M Sc, PhD); experimental psychology (M Sc, MA, PhD); geography (M Sc, MA, PhD); mathematics and statistics (M Sc, MA, PhD); neo-tropical environment (M Sc, MA, PhD); physical oceanography (M Sc, PhD); physics (M Sc, PhD); science (M Sc, MA, PhD); social statistics (MA).

Schulich School of Music Offers composition (M Mus, D Mus, PhD); music education (MA, PhD); music technology (MA, PhD); musicology (MA, PhD); performance (M Mus); performance studies (D Mus); sound recording (M Mus, PhD); theory (MA, PhD).

Professional Program in Dentistry Offers dentistry (DMD). Electronic applications accepted.

Professional Program in Medicine Offers medicine.

MCKENDREE UNIVERSITY, Lebanon, IL 62254-1299

General Information Independent-religious, coed, comprehensive institution. *Graduate housing:* On-campus housing not available.

GRADUATE UNITS

Graduate Programs ***Degree program information:*** Part-time and evening/weekend programs available. Part-time, evening/weekend. Offers business administration (MBA); clinical mental health counseling (MA); curriculum design and instruction (Ed D, Ed S); educational administration and leadership (MA Ed); educational studies (MA Ed); higher education administrative services (MA Ed); human resource management (MBA); international business (MBA); music education (MA Ed); nursing education (MSN); nursing management/administration (MSN); reading (MA Ed); special education (MA Ed); teacher leadership (MA Ed); teaching certification (MA Ed). Electronic applications accepted.

MCMASTER UNIVERSITY, Hamilton, ON L8S 4M2, Canada

General Information Province-supported, coed, university. CGS member. *Graduate housing:* Room and/or apartments available to single students; on-campus housing not available to married students. Housing application deadline: 6/30. *Research affiliation:* Commonwealth Development (telecommunications), Canadian Centre for Inland Waters (chemical and civil engineering).

GRADUATE UNITS

Faculty of Health Sciences ***Degree program information:*** Part-time programs available. Part-time, online learning. Offers biochemistry and biomedical sciences (M Sc, PhD); blood and vascular (M Sc, PhD); genetics and cancer (M Sc, PhD); health research methodology (course-based) (M Sc); health research methodology (thesis) (M Sc, PhD); health sciences (M Sc, PhD); immunity and infection (M Sc, PhD); metabolism and nutrition (M Sc, PhD); neurosciences and behavioral sciences (M Sc, PhD); nursing (M Sc, PhD); occupational therapy (M Sc); physiology/pharmacology (M Sc, PhD); physiotherapy (M Sc); rehabilitation science (M Sc, PhD); rehabilitation science (course-based) (M Sc).

McMaster Divinity College ***Degree program information:*** Part-time programs available. Part-time. Offers Biblical studies (MA, MTS, Diploma); biblical studies (M Div); Christian interpretation/history (M Div, MA, MTS, Diploma); Christian ministry (M Div, MA, MTS, Diploma); Christian Studies (Certificate); Christian theology (PhD). Affiliated with the Toronto School of Theology.

School of Graduate Studies ***Degree program information:*** Part-time programs available. Part-time.

Faculty of Business Degree program information: Part-time programs available. Part-time. Offers business (MBA, PhD); human resources and management (MBA, PhD); information systems (PhD).

Faculty of Engineering Degree program information: Part-time programs available. Part-time. Offers chemical engineering (M Eng, MA Sc, PhD); civil engineering (M Eng, MA Sc, PhD); computer science (M Sc, PhD); electrical engineering (M Eng, MA Sc, PhD); engineering (M Eng, M Sc, MA Sc, PhD); engineering physics (M Eng, MA Sc, PhD); materials engineering (M Eng, MA Sc, PhD); materials science (M Eng, PhD); mechanical engineering (M Eng, MA Sc, PhD); nuclear engineering (PhD); software engineering (M Eng, MA Sc, PhD).

Faculty of Humanities Degree program information: Part-time and evening/weekend programs available. Part-time, evening/weekend. Offers classics (MA, PhD); cultural studies and critical theory (MA); English (MA, PhD); French (MA); globalization studies (MA); history (MA, PhD); humanities (MA, PhD); philosophy (MA, PhD).

Faculty of Science Degree program information: Part-time and evening/weekend programs available. Part-time, evening/weekend. Offers analytical chemistry (M Sc, PhD); applied statistics (M Sc); astrophysics (PhD); biology (M Sc, PhD); chemical physics (M Sc, PhD); chemistry (M Sc, PhD); geochemistry (PhD); geology (M Sc, PhD); health and radiation physics (M Sc); human geography (MA, PhD); inorganic chemistry (M Sc, PhD); mathematics (M Sc, PhD); medical physics (M Sc, PhD); medical statistics (M Sc); organic chemistry (M Sc, PhD); physical chemistry (M Sc, PhD); physical geography (M Sc, PhD); physics (PhD); polymer chemistry (M Sc, PhD); psychology (M Sc, PhD); science (M Sc, MA, PhD); statistical theory (M Sc); statistics (M Sc).

Faculty of Social Sciences Degree program information: Part-time and evening/weekend programs available. Part-time, evening/weekend. Offers analysis of social welfare policy (MSW); analysis of social work practice (MSW); anthropology

(MA, PhD); economics (MA, PhD); human biodynamics (M Sc, PhD); international relations (PhD); political science (MA); public and the global economy (MA); public policy (PhD); public policy and administration (MA); religious studies (MA, PhD); social sciences (M Sc, MA, MSW, PhD); sociology (MA, PhD); work and society (MA).

MCMURRY UNIVERSITY, Abilene, TX 79697

General Information Independent-religious, coed, comprehensive institution.

GRADUATE UNITS

Graduate Studies

MCNALLY SMITH COLLEGE OF MUSIC, Saint Paul, MN 55101

General Information Proprietary, coed, comprehensive institution. *Graduate housing:* On-campus housing not available.

GRADUATE UNITS

Master of Music in Performance Program ***Degree program information:*** Part-time and evening/weekend programs available. Part-time, evening/weekend. Offers bass performance (MM); brass and woodwind performance (MM); guitar performance (MM); keyboard performance (MM); percussion performance (MM); string performance (MM); vocal performance (MM). Electronic applications accepted.

MCNEESE STATE UNIVERSITY, Lake Charles, LA 70609

General Information State-supported, coed, comprehensive institution. *Graduate housing:* Room and/or apartments available on a first-come, first-served basis to single students. Housing application deadline: 8/15.

GRADUATE UNITS

Doré School of Graduate Studies ***Degree program information:*** Part-time and evening/weekend programs available. Part-time, evening/weekend.

Burton College of Education Degree program information: Part-time and evening/weekend programs available. Part-time, evening/weekend. Offers addiction treatment (MA); advanced professional (M Ed); applied behavior analysis (MA); autism (M Ed); counseling psychology (MA); counseling, grades K-12 (Graduate Certificate); curriculum and instruction (M Ed); early childhood education (M Ed); early childhood education grades PK-3 (Postbaccalaureate Certificate); education (M Ed, MA, MAT, MS, Ed S, Graduate Certificate, Postbaccalaureate Certificate); educational diagnostician (M Ed, Graduate Certificate); educational leadership (M Ed, Ed S); educational technology (Ed S); educational technology leadership (M Ed); elementary education (M Ed, MAT); elementary education grades 1-5 (Postbaccalaureate Certificate); exercise physiology (MS); general/experimental psychology (MA); health promotion (MS); instructional technology (MS); middle school education grades 4-8 (Postbaccalaureate Certificate); multiple levels grades K-12 (Postbaccalaureate Certificate); nutrition and wellness (MS); reading (M Ed); reading specialist (Graduate Certificate); school counseling (M Ed); school librarian (Postbaccalaureate Certificate); secondary education (MAT); secondary education grades 6-12 (Postbaccalaureate Certificate); special education (M Ed); special education - mild/moderate grades 1-12 (MAT); special education intervention birth-5 (Postbaccalaureate Certificate); special education, mild/moderate for elementary education grades 1-5 (Postbaccalaureate Certificate); special education, mild/moderate for secondary education grades 6-12 (Postbaccalaureate Certificate).

College of Business Degree program information: Part-time and evening/weekend programs available. Part-time, evening/weekend. Offers business (MBA); business administration (MBA).

College of Engineering and Engineering Technology Degree program information: Part-time and evening/weekend programs available. Part-time, evening/weekend. Offers chemical engineering (M Eng); civil engineering (M Eng); electrical (M Eng); electrical engineering (M Eng); engineering (M Eng); engineering and engineering technology (M Eng, Graduate Certificate, Postbaccalaureate Certificate); engineering management (M Eng); mechanical engineering (M Eng); pump reliability engineering (Graduate Certificate, Postbaccalaureate Certificate).

College of Liberal Arts Degree program information: Part-time and evening/weekend programs available. Part-time, evening/weekend. Offers creative writing (MFA); criminal justice (MS); English (MA); liberal arts (MA, MFA, MS, Postbaccalaureate Certificate); music education (Postbaccalaureate Certificate).

College of Nursing Offers family nurse practitioner (PMC); family psychiatric/mental health nurse practitioner (PMC); nurse educator (MSN); nurse executive (MSN); nursing (MSN); nursing case management (Postbaccalaureate Certificate). Program offered jointly with Southeastern Louisiana University and Southern University and Agricultural and Mechanical College.

College of Science Degree program information: Part-time and evening/weekend programs available. Part-time, evening/weekend. Offers agricultural sciences (MS); chemistry (MS); chemistry/environmental science education (MS); computer science (MS); environmental and chemical sciences (MS); environmental science (MS); mathematics (MS); science (MS); statistics (MS).

MCPHERSON COLLEGE, McPherson, KS 67460-1402

General Information Independent-religious, coed, comprehensive institution. *Enrollment:* 21 full-time matriculated graduate/professional students (9 women), 13 part-time matriculated graduate/professional students (10 women). *Enrollment by degree level:* 21 master's, 13 other advanced degrees. *Graduate faculty:* 1 full-time (0 women), 8 part-time/adjunct (4 women). *Tuition, area resident:* Part-time $350 per credit hour. *Graduate housing:* On-campus housing not available. *Student services:* Campus employment opportunities, career counseling, free psychological counseling, services for students with disabilities. *Library:* Miller Library plus 1 other.

Computer facilities: A campuswide network can be accessed from student residence rooms and from off campus.
Website: http://www.mcpherson.edu/

GRADUATE UNITS

Program in Education Students: 21 full-time (9 women), 13 part-time (10 women). *Faculty:* 1 full-time (0 women), 8 part-time/adjunct (4 women). Offers education (M Ed). *Coordinator,* Dr. Bruce Carter, 620-242-0542, E-mail: carterb@mcpherson.edu.

MCPHS UNIVERSITY, Boston, MA 02115-5896

General Information Independent, coed, university. *Enrollment:* 7,074 graduate, professional, and undergraduate students; 2,665 full-time matriculated graduate/professional students (1,661 women), 462 part-time matriculated graduate/professional students (352 women). *Enrollment by degree level:* 1,019 master's, 2,054 doctoral, 54 other advanced degrees. *Graduate housing:* Room and/or apartments available on a first-come, first-served basis to single students; on-campus housing not available to married students. Housing application deadline: 5/1. *Student services:* Campus employment opportunities, campus safety program, career counseling, exercise/wellness program, free psychological counseling, grant writing training, international student services, low-cost health insurance, multicultural affairs office, services for students with disabilities, writing training. *Library:* Henrietta DeBenedictis Library plus 2 others. *Research affiliation:* Cephrim Biosciences, Inc. (pharmaceutics), Center for Analytical Science (analytical medicinal chemistry).

Computer facilities: 507 computers available on campus for general student use. A campuswide network can be accessed from student residence rooms and from off campus. Online class registration is available.
Website: http://www.mcphs.edu/

General Application Contact: Julie George, Director of Graduate, Transfer and Online Admission, 617-732-2988, E-mail: admissions@mcphs.edu.

GRADUATE UNITS

Graduate Studies ***Degree program information:*** Part-time programs available. Part-time. Offers drug regulatory affairs and health policy (MS); medicinal chemistry (MS, PhD); nursing (MS); pharmaceutics/industrial pharmacy (MS, PhD); pharmacology (MS, PhD); pharmacy (Pharm D); pharmacy and health sciences (MPAS, MS, PhD, Pharm D); physician assistant studies (MPAS).

New England School of Acupuncture ***Degree program information:*** Part-time programs available. Part-time. Offers acupuncture (M Ac); acupuncture and Oriental medicine (MAOM).

School of Pharmacy–Worcester/Manchester Offers pharmacy (Pharm D).

MEADVILLE LOMBARD THEOLOGICAL SCHOOL, Chicago, IL 60637-1602

General Information Independent-religious, coed, graduate-only institution. *Graduate housing:* Rooms and/or apartments available on a first-come, first-served basis to single and married students. Housing application deadline: 3/15.

GRADUATE UNITS

Graduate and Professional Programs ***Degree program information:*** Part-time programs available. Part-time, online learning. Offers divinity (M Div); ministry (D Min); religion (MA). M Div/MSW offered jointly with University of Chicago.

MEDAILLE COLLEGE, Buffalo, NY 14214-2695

General Information Independent, coed, comprehensive institution. *Graduate housing:* Rooms and/or apartments available on a first-come, first-served basis to single and married students. Housing application deadline: 8/15.

GRADUATE UNITS

Program in Business Administration - Amherst ***Degree program information:*** Evening/weekend programs available. Evening/weekend. Offers business administration (MBA); organizational leadership (MA). Electronic applications accepted.

Program in Business Administration - Rochester ***Degree program information:*** Evening/weekend programs available. Evening/weekend. Offers business administration (MBA); organizational leadership (MA).

Program in Education ***Degree program information:*** Part-time and evening/weekend programs available. Part-time, evening/weekend. Offers adolescent education (MS Ed); curriculum and instruction (MS Ed); education preparation (MS Ed); literacy (MS Ed); special education (MS). Electronic applications accepted.

Programs in Psychology ***Degree program information:*** Part-time and evening/weekend programs available. Part-time, evening/weekend. Offers clinical psychology (Psy D); marriage and family therapy (MA); mental health counseling (MA); psychology (MA). Electronic applications accepted.

MEDICAL COLLEGE OF WISCONSIN, Milwaukee, WI 53226-0509

General Information Independent, coed, graduate-only institution. CGS member. *Graduate housing:* On-campus housing not available. *Research affiliation:* General Electric Medical Systems (biophysics, radiology).

GRADUATE UNITS

Graduate School of Biomedical Sciences ***Degree program information:*** Part-time and evening/weekend programs available. Part-time, evening/weekend, online learning. Offers biochemistry (PhD); bioinformatics (MS); biomedical sciences (MA, MPH, MS, PhD, Graduate Certificate); biophysics (PhD); biostatistics (PhD); clinical and translational science (MS); epidemiology (MS); functional imaging (PhD); health care technologies management (MS); medical informatics (MS); microbiology and molecular genetics (MS, PhD); neuroscience (PhD); pharmacology and toxicology (PhD); physiology (PhD); public and community health (PhD); public health (MPH, PhD, Graduate Certificate); translational science (PhD). Electronic applications accepted.

Center for Bioethics and Medical Humanities Degree program information: Part-time programs available. Part-time. Offers bioethics (MA); clinical bioethics (Graduate Certificate); research ethics (Graduate Certificate).

Medical Scientist Training Program

Interdisciplinary Program in Biomedical Sciences Offers biomedical sciences (PhD).

Medical School ***Degree program information:*** Part-time programs available. Part-time, online learning. Offers medicine (MPH, MD).

MEDICAL UNIVERSITY OF SOUTH CAROLINA, Charleston, SC 29425

General Information State-supported, coed, upper-level institution. CGS member. *Research affiliation:* Novartis Pharmaceuticals (cancer), Boston Scientific Corporation (cardiovascular diseases), Genentech (Alzheimer's disease), AstraZeneca (cancer/cardiovascular diseases), Merck & Company, Inc. (neuroscience), Eli Lilly and Company (substance abuse).

GRADUATE UNITS

College of Dental Medicine Offers dental medicine (DMD). Electronic applications accepted.

College of Graduate Studies Offers biochemistry and molecular biology (MS, PhD); cancer biology (PhD); cardiovascular biology (PhD); cardiovascular imaging (PhD); cell and molecular pharmacology and experimental therapeutics (MS, PhD); cell injury and repair (PhD); cell regulation (PhD); craniofacial biology (PhD); drug discovery (PhD); genetics and development (PhD); marine biomedicine (PhD); medicinal chemistry (PhD); microbiology and immunology (MS, PhD); neurosciences (MS, PhD); pathology and laboratory medicine (MS, PhD); toxicology (PhD). Electronic applications accepted.

Division of Biostatistics and Epidemiology Offers biostatistics (MS, PhD); epidemiology (MS, PhD). Electronic applications accepted.

South Carolina Clinical and Translational Research Institute Online learning. Offers clinical and translational research (MS). Electronic applications accepted.

College of Health Professions ***Degree program information:*** Part-time programs available. Part-time. Offers anesthesia for nurses (MSNA); health administration (DHA);

health administration-executive (MHA); health administration-global (MHA); health administration-residential (MHA); health and rehabilitation science (PhD); health professions (MHA, MS, MSNA, MSOT, DHA, DPT, PhD); occupational therapy (MSOT); physical therapy (DPT); physician assistant studies (MS). Electronic applications accepted.

College of Medicine Offers medicine (MD). Electronic applications accepted.

College of Nursing *Degree program information:* Part-time programs available. Part-time, online learning. Offers adult-gerontology health nurse practitioner (MSN, DNP); advanced practice nursing (DNP); family nurse practitioner (MSN, DNP); nurse administrator (MSN); nurse educator (MSN); nursing (MSN, DNP, PhD); pediatric nurse practitioner (MSN, DNP). Electronic applications accepted.

South Carolina College of Pharmacy Offers pharmacy (Pharm D). Electronic applications accepted.

MEHARRY MEDICAL COLLEGE, Nashville, TN 37208-9989

General Information Independent-religious, coed, graduate-only institution. CGS member. *Graduate faculty:* 273 full-time (69 women), 46 part-time/adjunct (11 women). *Graduate housing:* Rooms and/or apartments available on a first-come, first-served basis to single and married students. *Student services:* Campus employment opportunities, campus safety program, career counseling, child daycare facilities, exercise/wellness program, free psychological counseling, international student services, low-cost health insurance. *Library:* Meharry Medical College Library.

Computer facilities: 100 computers available on campus for general student use. Website: http://www.mmc.edu/

General Application Contact: Roslyn M. White, Director of Admissions and Recruitment, 615-327-6453, Fax: 615-327-6228, E-mail: rwhite@mmc.edu.

GRADUATE UNITS

School of Dentistry *Financial support:* Career-related internships or fieldwork, Federal Work-Study, and institutionally sponsored loans available. Financial award application deadline: 4/15; financial award applicants required to submit FAFSA. Offers dentistry (DDS, PhD). *Application deadline:* For winter admission, 1/15 for domestic and international students. Applications are processed on a rolling basis. *Application fee:* $65.

School of Graduate Studies *Financial support:* Fellowships, research assistantships, teaching assistantships, career-related internships or fieldwork, Federal Work-Study, institutionally sponsored loans, scholarships/grants, and tuition waivers (full) available. Support available to part-time students. Financial award applicants required to submit FAFSA. Online learning. Offers cancer biology (PhD); microbiology and immunology (PhD); neuroscience (PhD); pharmacology (PhD). *Application deadline:* For fall admission, 6/1 for domestic students. Applications are processed on a rolling basis. *Application fee:* $65. Electronic applications accepted.

Division of Community Health Sciences Financial support: Career-related internships or fieldwork, Federal Work-Study, institutionally sponsored loans, and scholarships/grants available. Support available to part-time students. Financial award application deadline: 7/15; financial award applicants required to submit FAFSA. *Degree program information:* Part-time and evening/weekend programs available. Part-time, evening/weekend. Offers occupational medicine (MSPH); public health administration (MSPH). *Application deadline:* For fall admission, 6/1 for domestic students. Applications are processed on a rolling basis. *Application fee:* $65.

School of Medicine *Financial support:* Federal Work-Study, institutionally sponsored loans, and tuition waivers (partial) available. Financial award applicants required to submit FAFSA. Offers medicine (MD). *Application deadline:* For fall admission, 12/15 for domestic students. Applications are processed on a rolling basis. *Application fee:* $65. Electronic applications accepted.

MELBOURNE BUSINESS SCHOOL, Carlton, Victoria 3053, Australia

General Information Independent, coed, graduate-only institution.

GRADUATE UNITS

Graduate Programs Offers business administration (Exec MBA, MBA); management (PhD); management science (PhD); marketing (PhD); social impact (Graduate Certificate).

MEMORIAL UNIVERSITY OF NEWFOUNDLAND, St. John's, NL A1C 5S7, Canada

General Information Province-supported, coed, university. CGS member. *Enrollment:* 2,357 full-time matriculated graduate/professional students (1,074 women), 1,330 part-time matriculated graduate/professional students (842 women). *Enrollment by degree level:* 2,812 master's, 766 doctoral, 69 other advanced degrees. *Graduate faculty:* 800. *International tuition:* $2859 Canadian dollars full-time. *Tuition, area resident:* Full-time $2199 Canadian dollars. *Graduate housing:* Rooms and/or apartments available on a first-come, first-served basis to single and married students. Typical cost: $5466 Canadian dollars per year for single students; $10,500 Canadian dollars per year for married students. *Student services:* Campus employment opportunities, campus safety program, career counseling, child daycare facilities, exercise/wellness program, free psychological counseling, grant writing training, international student services, low-cost health insurance, multicultural affairs office, services for students with disabilities, teacher training, writing training. *Library:* Queen Elizabeth II Library plus 4 others. *Research affiliation:* Eastern Regional Health Authority (health research).

Computer facilities: 875 computers available on campus for general student use. A campuswide network can be accessed from student residence rooms and from off campus. Online class registration is available.
Website: http://www.mun.ca/

General Application Contact: Andrew Kim, Director, Graduate Enrolment Services, 709-864-8847, Fax: 709-864-4702, E-mail: akim@mun.ca.

GRADUATE UNITS

Faculty of Medicine *Degree program information:* Part-time programs available. Part-time, online learning. Offers medicine (M Sc, PhD, Diploma). Electronic applications accepted.

Graduate Programs in Medicine Degree program information: Part-time programs available. Part-time. Offers applied health services research (M Sc); cancer (M Sc, PhD); cardiovascular (M Sc, PhD); clinical epidemiology (M Sc, PhD, Diploma); community health (M Sc, PhD, Diploma); human genetics (M Sc, PhD); immunology (M Sc, PhD); medicine (M Sc, PhD, Diploma); neuroscience (M Sc, PhD). Electronic applications accepted.

School of Graduate Studies Students: 2,357 full-time (1,074 women), 1,330 part-time (842 women). 4,623 applicants, 26% accepted, 755 enrolled. *Financial support:* Fellowships, research assistantships, teaching assistantships, career-related internships or fieldwork, scholarships/grants, and unspecified assistantships available. In 2015, 836 master's, 84 doctorates, 22 other advanced degrees awarded. *Degree program information:* Part-time and evening/weekend programs available. Part-time, evening/weekend, 100% online, blended/hybrid learning. Offers applied psychological sciences (MAPS); aquaculture (M Sc); archaeology and physical anthropology (MA, PhD); atomic and molecular physics (PhD); biochemistry (M Sc, PhD); biology (M Sc, PhD); chemistry (M Sc, PhD); classics (MA); clinical psychology (Psy D); cognitive and behavioral ecology (M Sc, PhD); computer engineering (MA Sc); computer science (M Sc, PhD); condensed matter physics (PhD); economics (MA); employment relations (MER); English (MA, PhD); environmental science (M Env Sc, M Sc, PhD); environmental systems engineering and management (MA Sc); ethnomusicology (MA, PhD); experimental psychology (M Sc, PhD); fisheries resource management (MMS, Graduate Diploma); folklore (MA, PhD); food science (M Sc, PhD); French studies (MA); gender (PhD); gender studies (MGS); geography (M Sc, MA, PhD); geology (M Sc, PhD); geophysics (M Sc, PhD); German language and literature (M Phil, MA); history (MA, PhD); humanities (M Phil); instrumental analysis (M Sc); linguistics (MA, PhD); marine spatial planning and management (MMS); maritime sociology (PhD); mathematics (M Sc, PhD); philosophy (MA, PhD); physical oceanography (M Sc, PhD); physics (M Sc); political science (MA); religious studies (MA); scientific computing (M Sc); social and cultural anthropology (MA, PhD); sociology (M Phil, MA); statistics (M Sc, MAS, PhD); work and development (PhD). *Application deadline:* Applications are processed on a rolling basis. *Application fee:* $50 Canadian dollars. Electronic applications accepted. *Application Contact:* Andrew Kim, Director, Graduate Enrolment Services, 709-864-8847, Fax: 709-864-4702, E-mail: akim@mun.ca. *Acting Dean,* Dr. Faye Murrin, 709-737-2478, Fax: 709-737-4702, E-mail: sgs@mun.ca.

Faculty of Business Administration Financial support: Fellowships available. *Degree program information:* Part-time programs available. Part-time. Offers business administration (MBA). *Application deadline:* For fall admission, 5/1 for domestic students, 2/1 for international students; for winter admission, 10/15 for domestic students; for spring admission, 1/15 for domestic students. Applications are processed on a rolling basis. *Application fee:* $50 ($100 for international students). Electronic applications accepted. *Application Contact:* Dr. Peggy Coady, Associate Dean, 709-737-8522, Fax: 709-864-2467, E-mail: pacoady@mun.ca. *Dean,* Dr. Wilfred Xerbe, 709-864-8851, E-mail: wzerbe@mun.ca.

Faculty of Education Financial support: Fellowships, research assistantships, teaching assistantships, and career-related internships or fieldwork available. *Degree program information:* Part-time programs available. Part-time. Offers counseling psychology (M Ed); curriculum, teaching, and learning studies (M Ed); education (PhD); educational leadership studies (M Ed, Graduate Diploma); information technology (M Ed); post-secondary studies (M Ed, Diploma). *Application deadline:* For fall admission, 2/1 for domestic and international students; for winter admission, 9/15 for domestic and international students; for spring admission, 2/1 for domestic and international students. Applications are processed on a rolling basis. *Application fee:* $50 Canadian dollars ($100 Canadian dollars for international students). Electronic applications accepted. *Application Contact:* Dr. Rhonda Joy, Interim Associate Dean, 709-737-6402, Fax: 709-864-4379, E-mail: gradeduc@mun.ca. *Dean,* Dr. Kirk Anderson, 709-864-8588, Fax: 709-864-4379, E-mail: kirk.anderson@mun.ca.

Faculty of Engineering and Applied Science Financial support: Fellowships, research assistantships, and teaching assistantships available. *Degree program information:* Part-time programs available. Part-time. Offers civil engineering (M Eng, PhD); electrical and computer engineering (M Eng, PhD); mechanical engineering (M Eng, PhD); ocean and naval architecture engineering (M Eng, PhD). *Application deadline:* For fall admission, 12/1 for domestic students, 12/1 priority date for international students. Applications are processed on a rolling basis. *Application fee:* $50 Canadian dollars ($100 Canadian dollars for international students). Electronic applications accepted. *Application Contact:* Dr. Leonard Lye, Graduate Officer, 709-864-8900, Fax: 709-864-3480, E-mail: llye@mun.ca. *Dean,* Dr. Greg Naterer, 709-864-8810, Fax: 709-864-3480, E-mail: gnaterer@mun.ca.

School of Human Kinetics and Recreation Financial support: Fellowships, research assistantships, and teaching assistantships available. *Degree program information:* Part-time programs available. Part-time. Offers administration, curriculum and supervision (MPE); biomechanics/ergonomics (MS Kin); exercise and work physiology (MS Kin); psychology of sport, exercise and recreation (MS Kin); socio-cultural studies of physical activity and health (MS Kin). *Application deadline:* For fall admission, 5/1 priority date for domestic and international students. Applications are processed on a rolling basis. *Application fee:* $50 Canadian dollars ($100 Canadian dollars for international students). Electronic applications accepted. *Application Contact:* Scott MacKinnon, Graduate Officer, 709-864-6936, Fax: 709-864-3979, E-mail: smackinn@mun.ca. *Dean,* Dr. Heather Carnahan, 709-864-8129, Fax: 709-864-7531, E-mail: hkrdirec@mun.ca.

School of Music Financial support: Fellowships, research assistantships, and teaching assistantships available. Offers conducting (MMus); performance pedagogy (MMus); performing (MMus). *Application deadline:* For fall admission, 12/15 priority date for domestic and international students. Applications are processed on a rolling basis. *Application fee:* $50 Canadian dollars ($100 Canadian dollars for international students). Electronic applications accepted. *Application Contact:* Kristina Szutor, Graduate Officer, 709-864-3560, Fax: 709-864-2666, E-mail: kszutor@mun.ca. *Acting Dean,* Dr. Maureen Volk, 709-864-7486, Fax: 709-864-2666, E-mail: mvolk@mun.ca.

School of Nursing Financial support: Fellowships, research assistantships, and teaching assistantships available. Financial award application deadline: 12/31. *Degree program information:* Part-time programs available. Part-time. Offers nursing (MN, PhD). *Application deadline:* For fall admission, 2/15 priority date for domestic and international students. Applications are processed on a rolling basis. *Application fee:* $50 Canadian dollars ($100 Canadian dollars for international students). Electronic applications accepted. *Application Contact:* Dr. Donna Moralejo, Graduate Officer, 709-777-6527, E-mail: mnson@mun.ca. *Dean,* Dr. Alice Gaudine, 709-777-6972, Fax: 709-777-7037, E-mail: agaudine@mun.ca.

School of Pharmacy Financial support: Fellowships and research assistantships available. *Degree program information:* Part-time programs available. Part-time. Offers pharmacy (MSCPharm, PhD). *Application deadline:* For fall admission, 2/28 priority date for domestic and international students; for winter admission, 7/31 priority date for domestic and international students. Applications are processed on a rolling basis. *Application fee:* $50 Canadian dollars ($100 Canadian dollars for international students). Electronic applications accepted. *Application Contact:* Dr. John Weber, Graduate Officer, 709-777-7022, Fax: 709-777-7044, E-mail: jweber@mun.ca. *Dean,* Dr. Carlo Marra, 709-777-6571, Fax: 709-777-7044.

School of Social Work Financial support: Fellowships and career-related internships or fieldwork available. Offers social work (MSW, PhD). *Application deadline:* For fall admission, 1/15 priority date for domestic and international students. Applications are processed on a rolling basis. *Application fee:* $50 Canadian dollars ($100 Canadian dollars for international students). Electronic applications accepted. *Application Contact:* Dr. Mike Devine, Chair, MSW Program, 709-864-8152, Fax: 709-864-4512, E-mail: mdevine@mun.ca. *Dean*, Dr. Donna Hardy-Cox, 709-864-8044, Fax: 709-864-3503, E-mail: deansocialwork@mun.ca.

MEMPHIS COLLEGE OF ART, Memphis, TN 38104-2764

General Information Independent, coed, comprehensive institution. *Enrollment:* 29 full-time matriculated graduate/professional students (23 women), 23 part-time matriculated graduate/professional students (15 women). *Enrollment by degree level:* 43 master's, 9 other advanced degrees. *Graduate faculty:* 24 full-time (16 women), 35 part-time/adjunct (18 women). *Tuition, area resident:* Full-time $31,120. *Graduate housing:* Room and/or apartments available on a first-come, first-served basis to single students; on-campus housing not available to married students. Housing application deadline: 6/1. *Student services:* Campus employment opportunities, campus safety program, career counseling, international student services, services for students with disabilities. *Library:* G. Pillow Lewis Library.

Computer facilities: 100 computers available on campus for general student use. A campuswide network can be accessed from student residence rooms.
Website: http://www.mca.edu/

General Application Contact: Gail Massey, Director of Enrollment, 901-272-5153, Fax: 901-272-5158, E-mail: gmassey@mca.edu.

GRADUATE UNITS

Graduate Programs Students: 29 full-time (23 women), 23 part-time (15 women); includes 14 minority (9 Black or African American, non-Hispanic/Latino; 2 Asian, non-Hispanic/Latino; 3 Hispanic/Latino), 3 international. Average age 32. 57 applicants, 67% accepted, 19 enrolled. *Faculty:* 24 full-time (16 women), 35 part-time/adjunct (18 women). *Financial support:* In 2015–16, 52 students received support, including 10 fellowships (averaging $4,000 per year), 5 teaching assistantships (averaging $3,000 per year); career-related internships or fieldwork, Federal Work-Study, scholarships/grants, unspecified assistantships, and teaching professional tuition discount also available. Financial award application deadline: 7/1; financial award applicants required to submit FAFSA. In 2015, 14 master's awarded. *Degree program information:* Part-time and evening/weekend programs available. Part-time, evening/weekend. Offers art education (MA, MAT); illustration (MFA); metals (MFA); painting/drawing (MFA); photography (MFA); studio art (MFA). *Application deadline:* For fall admission, 2/1 for domestic students, 3/1 for international students; for spring admission, 11/1 for domestic and international students. *Application fee:* $50. Electronic applications accepted. *Application Contact:* Gail Massey, Director of Enrollment, 901-272-5153, Fax: 901-272-5158, E-mail: gmassey@mca.edu.

MEMPHIS THEOLOGICAL SEMINARY, Memphis, TN 38104-4395

General Information Independent-religious, coed, graduate-only institution. *Graduate housing:* Rooms and/or apartments available on a first-come, first-served basis to single and married students. Housing application deadline: 7/15. *Research affiliation:* Lilly Foundation (technology, religion), Wabash Center for Teaching and Learning (theology, religion).

GRADUATE UNITS

Graduate and Professional Programs ***Degree program information:*** Part-time programs available. Part-time. Offers theology (M Div, MAR, D Min).

MERCER UNIVERSITY, Macon, GA 31207

General Information Independent-religious, coed, university. *Enrollment:* 6,832 graduate, professional, and undergraduate students; 2,815 full-time matriculated graduate/professional students (1,719 women), 1,098 part-time matriculated graduate/professional students (807 women). *Enrollment by degree level:* 1,871 master's, 1,962 doctoral, 80 other advanced degrees. *Graduate faculty:* 258 full-time (123 women), 86 part-time/adjunct (46 women). Tuition and fees vary according to campus/location and program. *Graduate housing:* Rooms and/or apartments available on a first-come, first-served basis to single and married students. *Student services:* Campus employment opportunities, campus safety program, career counseling, exercise/wellness program, free psychological counseling, international student services, low-cost health insurance, services for students with disabilities. *Library:* Jack Tarver Library plus 3 others. *Research affiliation:* Total Therapeutic Management (pharmaceuticals), The Coca Cola Company (pharmaceutical research), Georgia Neurological Institute (medical research), Medical Center of Central Georgia (medical research), Memorial Health Care (medical research), Piedmont (medical research).

Computer facilities: A campuswide network can be accessed from student residence rooms and from off campus. Online class registration is available.
Website: http://www.mercer.edu/

General Application Contact: Tracey Wofford, Director of Graduate Admissions, 678-547-6422, Fax: 678-547-6422, E-mail: wofford_tm@mercer.edu.

GRADUATE UNITS

Graduate Studies, Cecil B. Day Campus Students: 1,670 full-time (1,144 women), 750 part-time (573 women); includes 1,201 minority (819 Black or African American, non-Hispanic/Latino; 9 American Indian or Alaska Native, non-Hispanic/Latino; 250 Asian, non-Hispanic/Latino; 76 Hispanic/Latino; 4 Native Hawaiian or other Pacific Islander, non-Hispanic/Latino; 43 Two or more races, non-Hispanic/Latino), 107 international. Average age 31. *Faculty:* 134 full-time (75 women), 42 part-time/adjunct (27 women). *Financial support:* Teaching assistantships, career-related internships or fieldwork, Federal Work-Study, and scholarships/grants available. Support available to part-time students. Financial award applicants required to submit FAFSA. In 2015, 457 master's, 194 doctorates, 18 other advanced degrees awarded. *Degree program information:* Part-time and evening/weekend programs available. Part-time, evening/weekend, online learning. *Application Contact:* Tracey M. Wofford, Director of Graduate Admissions, 678-547-6422, E-mail: wofford_tm@mercer.edu. *Senior Vice President*, Richard V. Swindle, 678-547-6397, E-mail: swindle_rv@mercer.edu.

College of Health Professions Students: 286 full-time (230 women), 4 part-time (all women); includes 94 minority (69 Black or African American, non-Hispanic/Latino; 14 Asian, non-Hispanic/Latino; 7 Hispanic/Latino; 4 Two or more races, non-Hispanic/Latino), 3 international. Average age 26. *Faculty:* 27 full-time (19 women), 14 part-time/adjunct (7 women). *Financial support:* Federal Work-Study, traineeships, and unspecified assistantships available. In 2015, 80 master's, 32 doctorates awarded. Offers physical therapy (DPT); physician assistant (MM Sc); public health (MPH). *Application Contact:* Laura Ellison, Director of Admissions and Student Affairs, 678-547-6391, E-mail: ellison_la@mercer.edu. *Dean/Clinical Professor*, Dr. Lisa Lundquist, 678-547-6308, E-mail: lundquist_lm@mercer.edu.

College of Pharmacy Students: 667 full-time (418 women), 3 part-time (1 woman); includes 355 minority (133 Black or African American, non-Hispanic/Latino; 2 American Indian or Alaska Native, non-Hispanic/Latino; 170 Asian, non-Hispanic/Latino; 22 Hispanic/Latino; 28 Two or more races, non-Hispanic/Latino), 42 international. Average age 26. 1,895 applicants, 18% accepted, 176 enrolled. *Faculty:* 24 full-time (14 women). *Financial support:* In 2015–16, 350 students received support. Teaching assistantships with tuition reimbursements available, career-related internships or fieldwork, Federal Work-Study, institutionally sponsored loans, scholarships/grants, tuition waivers, and unspecified assistantships available. Support available to part-time students. Financial award application deadline: 5/1; financial award applicants required to submit FAFSA. In 2015, 151 doctorates awarded. Offers pharmaceutical sciences (PhD); pharmacology (PhD); pharmacy (Pharm D). *Application deadline:* Applications are processed on a rolling basis. Electronic applications accepted. *Application Contact:* Dr. James W. Bartling, Associate Dean for Student Affairs and Admissions, 678-547-6181, Fax: 678-547-6518, E-mail: bartling_jw@mercer.edu. *Dean*, Dr. Hewitt W. Matthews, 678-547-6306, Fax: 678-547-6315, E-mail: matthews_h@mercer.edu.

Eugene W. Stetson School of Business and Economics (Atlanta) Students: 194 full-time (95 women), 102 part-time (45 women); includes 127 minority (96 Black or African American, non-Hispanic/Latino; 2 American Indian or Alaska Native, non-Hispanic/Latino; 23 Asian, non-Hispanic/Latino; 5 Hispanic/Latino; 1 Two or more races, non-Hispanic/Latino), 44 international. Average age 32. 141 applicants, 77% accepted, 80 enrolled. *Faculty:* 25 full-time (10 women), 5 part-time/adjunct (2 women). *Financial support:* Federal Work-Study available. Financial award application deadline: 5/1; financial award applicants required to submit FAFSA. In 2015, 164 master's awarded. *Degree program information:* Part-time and evening/weekend programs available. Part-time, evening/weekend, 100% online. Offers accounting (M Acc); business analytics (MS); innovation (PMBA); international business (MBA). *Application deadline:* For fall admission, 6/15 priority date for domestic and international students; for spring admission, 11/1 priority date for domestic and international students; for summer admission, 3/15 priority date for domestic and international students. Applications are processed on a rolling basis. *Application fee:* $50 ($100 for international students). Electronic applications accepted. *Application Contact:* Stevens VanDuzer, Director of Admissions, 678-547-6159, Fax: 678-547-6160, E-mail: vanduzer_sf@mercer.edu. *Dean*, Dr. Susan P. Gilbert, 678-547-6438, Fax: 678-547-6337, E-mail: gilbert_sp@mercer.edu.

Georgia Baptist College of Nursing Students: 78 full-time (71 women), 42 part-time (39 women); includes 44 minority (21 Black or African American, non-Hispanic/Latino; 16 Asian, non-Hispanic/Latino; 6 Hispanic/Latino; 1 Native Hawaiian or other Pacific Islander, non-Hispanic/Latino), 5 international. Average age 35. 65 applicants, 66% accepted, 30 enrolled. *Faculty:* 10 full-time (9 women), 1 (woman) part-time/adjunct. *Financial support:* In 2015–16, 59 students received support. Scholarships/grants and traineeships available. Financial award application deadline: 6/30; financial award applicants required to submit FAFSA. In 2015, 36 master's, 5 doctorates awarded. *Degree program information:* Part-time programs available. Part-time, blended/hybrid learning. Offers adult gerontology acute care nurse practitioner (MSN, Certificate); family nurse practitioner (MSN); nursing (PhD); nursing practice (DNP). *Application deadline:* For fall admission, 5/1 for domestic students, 3/1 for international students; for winter admission, 11/1 for domestic students, 9/1 for international students; for spring admission, 11/1 for domestic students, 10/1 for international students; for summer admission, 3/1 for domestic and international students. Applications are processed on a rolling basis. *Application fee:* $50. Electronic applications accepted. *Application Contact:* Janda Anderson, Director of Admissions, 678-547-6700, Fax: 678-547-6794, E-mail: anderson_j@mercer.edu. *Dean/Professor*, Dr. Linda Streit, 678-547-6793, Fax: 678-547-6796, E-mail: streit_la@mercer.edu.

James and Carolyn McAfee School of Theology Students: 128 full-time (70 women), 67 part-time (37 women); includes 98 minority (89 Black or African American, non-Hispanic/Latino; 1 American Indian or Alaska Native, non-Hispanic/Latino; 2 Asian, non-Hispanic/Latino; 5 Hispanic/Latino; 1 Two or more races, non-Hispanic/Latino), 5 international. Average age 37. 105 applicants, 74% accepted, 45 enrolled. *Faculty:* 14 full-time (5 women), 4 part-time/adjunct (3 women). *Financial support:* In 2015–16, 30 students received support. Career-related internships or fieldwork, Federal Work-Study, institutionally sponsored loans, and scholarships/grants available. Support available to part-time students. Financial award application deadline: 10/1; financial award applicants required to submit FAFSA. In 2015, 42 master's, 4 doctorates awarded. *Degree program information:* Part-time programs available. Part-time. Offers Christian ministry (MACM); Christian spirituality (D Min); divinity (M Div); preaching (D Min). *Application deadline:* For fall admission, 7/1 for domestic and international students; for spring admission, 11/15 for domestic and international students. Applications are processed on a rolling basis. *Application fee:* $50. Electronic applications accepted. *Application Contact:* L. Nikki Hardeman, Director of Admissions, 678-547-6357, Fax: 678-547-6478, E-mail: hardeman_ln@mercer.edu. *Dean*, Dr. Jeffrey Willetts, 678-547-6470, Fax: 678-547-6478.

Penfield College Students: 132 full-time (109 women), 249 part-time (211 women); includes 212 minority (173 Black or African American, non-Hispanic/Latino; 3 American Indian or Alaska Native, non-Hispanic/Latino; 14 Asian, non-Hispanic/Latino; 17 Hispanic/Latino; 2 Native Hawaiian or other Pacific Islander, non-Hispanic/Latino; 3 Two or more races, non-Hispanic/Latino), 4 international. Average age 32. 300 applicants, 45% accepted, 114 enrolled. *Faculty:* 17 full-time (9 women), 22 part-time/adjunct (18 women). *Financial support:* In 2015–16, 32 students received support. Federal Work-Study, scholarships/grants, and unspecified assistantships available. Financial award applicants required to submit FAFSA. In 2015, 115 master's, 3 doctorates awarded. *Degree program information:* Part-time and evening/weekend programs available. Part-time, evening/weekend, 100% online, blended/hybrid learning. Offers certified rehabilitation counseling (MS); clinical mental health (MS); counselor education and supervision (PhD); human services (MS); organizational leadership (MS); public safety leadership (MS); school counseling (MS). *Application deadline:* For fall admission, 7/1 priority date for domestic and international students; for spring admission, 11/1 priority date for domestic and international students; for summer admission, 4/1 priority date for domestic and international students. *Application fee:* $35. Electronic applications accepted. *Application Contact:* Carmen C. Jones, Director of Graduate Admissions, 678-547-6346, E-mail: jones_c@mercer.edu. *Dean*, Dr. Priscilla R. Danheiser, 678-547-6028, Fax: 678-547-6008, E-mail: danheiser_p@mercer.edu.

Tift College of Education (Atlanta) Students: 212 full-time (172 women), 358 part-time (298 women); includes 320 minority (284 Black or African American, non-Hispanic/Latino; 1 American Indian or Alaska Native, non-Hispanic/Latino; 14 Asian, non-Hispanic/Latino; 12 Hispanic/Latino; 1 Native Hawaiian or other Pacific Islander, non-Hispanic/Latino; 8 Two or more races, non-Hispanic/Latino), 3 international. Average age 35. *Faculty:* 39 full-time (22 women), 11 part-time/adjunct (5 women).

Financial support: Federal Work-Study and unspecified assistantships available. Support available to part-time students. Financial award application deadline: 5/1; financial award applicants required to submit FAFSA. In 2015, 136 master's, 31 doctorates, 50 other advanced degrees awarded. *Degree program information:* Part-time and evening/weekend programs available. Part-time, evening/weekend. Offers curriculum and instruction (PhD); early childhood education (M Ed, MAT, Ed S); educational leadership (PhD); educational leadership P-12 (M Ed, Ed S); higher education leadership (M Ed); independent and charter school leadership (M Ed); middle grades education (M Ed, MAT); reading specialist (M Ed); secondary education (M Ed, MAT); teacher leadership (Ed S). *Application deadline:* For fall admission, 8/1 for domestic and international students; for spring admission, 12/1 for domestic and international students; for summer admission, 5/1 for domestic and international students. Applications are processed on a rolling basis. *Application fee:* $25 ($50 for international students). Electronic applications accepted. *Application Contact:* Renee Slaton, Associate Director of Graduate Admissions, 678-547-6084, Fax: 678-547-6055, E-mail: mercereducation@mercer.edu. *Dean*, Dr. James Barta, 478-301-5355, Fax: 478-301-2280, E-mail: barta_jj@mercer.edu.

Graduate Studies, Macon Campus Students: 152 full-time (61 women), 151 part-time (72 women); includes 99 minority (81 Black or African American, non-Hispanic/Latino; 8 Asian, non-Hispanic/Latino; 4 Hispanic/Latino; 1 Native Hawaiian or other Pacific Islander, non-Hispanic/Latino; 5 Two or more races, non-Hispanic/Latino), 10 international. Average age 32. *Faculty:* 91 full-time (34 women), 13 part-time/adjunct (6 women). *Financial support:* Career-related internships or fieldwork, Federal Work-Study, and institutionally sponsored loans available. Support available to part-time students. In 2015, 136 master's, 13 doctorates, 5 other advanced degrees awarded. *Degree program information:* Part-time and evening/weekend programs available. Part-time, evening/weekend. *Application Contact:* Tracey Wofford, Director of Graduate Admissions, 678-547-6422, E-mail: wofford_tm@mercer.edu. *Senior Vice Provost and Dean of Graduate Studies*, Wayne Glasgow, 912-721-8201, E-mail: glasgow_wc@mercer.edu.

Eugene W. Stetson School of Business and Economics (Macon) Students: 49 full-time (17 women), 35 part-time (13 women); includes 35 minority (31 Black or African American, non-Hispanic/Latino; 2 Asian, non-Hispanic/Latino; 1 Hispanic/Latino; 1 Two or more races, non-Hispanic/Latino), 2 international. Average age 32. *Faculty:* 6 full-time (3 women), 1 part-time/adjunct (0 women). In 2015, 44 master's awarded. *Degree program information:* Part-time and evening/weekend programs available. Part-time, evening/weekend. Offers business and economics (MBA). *Application deadline:* For fall admission, 8/1 for domestic students; for spring admission, 12/1 for domestic students. Applications are processed on a rolling basis. *Application fee:* $50 ($100 for international students). *Application Contact:* Robert Holland, Jr., Director/Academic Administrator, 478-301-2835, Fax: 478-301-2635, E-mail: holland_r@mercer.edu. *Dean*, Dr. Susan P. Gilbert, 478-301-6438, E-mail: gilbert_sp@mercer.edu.

School of Engineering Students: 35 full-time (8 women), 59 part-time (12 women); includes 18 minority (9 Black or African American, non-Hispanic/Latino; 6 Asian, non-Hispanic/Latino; 1 Hispanic/Latino; 2 Two or more races, non-Hispanic/Latino), 5 international. Average age 30. *Faculty:* 20 full-time (5 women), 2 part-time/adjunct (0 women). *Financial support:* Federal Work-Study available. In 2015, 69 master's awarded. *Degree program information:* Part-time and evening/weekend programs available. Part-time-only, evening/weekend, online learning. Offers biomedical engineering (MSE); computer engineering (MSE); electrical engineering (MSE); engineering management (MSE); environmental engineering (MSE); environmental systems (MS); mechanical engineering (MSE); software engineering (MSE); software systems (MS); technical communications management (MS); technical management (MS). *Application deadline:* For fall admission, 4/1 priority date for domestic and international students; for spring admission, 11/1 priority date for domestic and international students. Applications are processed on a rolling basis. *Application fee:* $75. Electronic applications accepted. *Application Contact:* Dr. Richard O. Mines, Jr., Program Director, 478-301-2347, Fax: 478-301-5433, E-mail: mines_ro@mercer.edu. *Dean*, Dr. Wade H. Shaw, 478-301-2459, Fax: 478-301-5593, E-mail: shaw_wh@mercer.edu.

Tift College of Education (Macon) Students: 52 full-time (31 women), 56 part-time (47 women); includes 43 minority (39 Black or African American, non-Hispanic/Latino; 1 Asian, non-Hispanic/Latino; 1 Hispanic/Latino; 2 Two or more races, non-Hispanic/Latino), 1 international. Average age 35. *Faculty:* 14 full-time (9 women), 3 part-time/adjunct (2 women). *Financial support:* Federal Work-Study, institutionally sponsored loans, and unspecified assistantships available. Support available to part-time students. Financial award application deadline: 5/1; financial award applicants required to submit FAFSA. In 2015, 18 master's, 13 doctorates awarded. *Degree program information:* Part-time and evening/weekend programs available. Part-time, evening/weekend, 100% online, blended/hybrid learning. Offers curriculum and instruction (PhD); early childhood education (M Ed, Ed S); educational leadership (M Ed, PhD, Ed S); higher education leadership (M Ed); independent and charter school leadership (M Ed); secondary education (MAT); teacher leadership (Ed S). *Application deadline:* For fall admission, 8/1 for domestic and international students; for spring admission, 12/1 for domestic and international students. Applications are processed on a rolling basis. *Application fee:* $35. Electronic applications accepted. *Application Contact:* Tracey M. Wofford, Associate Director of Admissions, 678-547-6422, Fax: 678-547-6367, E-mail: wofford_tm@mercer.edu. *Dean*, Dr. James Barta, 478-301-5397, Fax: 478-301-2280, E-mail: barta_jj@mercer.edu.

Townsend School of Music Students: 16 full-time (5 women), 1 part-time (0 women); includes 3 minority (2 Black or African American, non-Hispanic/Latino; 1 Hispanic/Latino), 2 international. Average age 30. 25 applicants, 48% accepted, 9 enrolled. *Faculty:* 12 full-time (5 women), 14 part-time/adjunct (3 women). *Financial support:* In 2015–16, 14 students received support. Tuition waivers (full) and unspecified assistantships available. Financial award application deadline: 6/1; financial award applicants required to submit FAFSA. In 2015, 5 master's awarded. Offers choral conducting (MM); church music (MM); collaborative piano (MM); instrumental conducting (MM); performance (MM). *Application deadline:* For fall admission, 6/1 for domestic students, 5/1 for international students. Applications are processed on a rolling basis. *Application fee:* $100. *Application Contact:* Director, 912-301-2700. *Director of Graduate Studies*, Dr. Richard G. Kosowski, 478-301-4167, Fax: 478-301-5633, E-mail: keith_cd@mercer.edu.

School of Medicine Offers medicine (MFT, MPH, MSA, MD).

Walter F. George School of Law ***Degree program information:*** Part-time programs available. Part-time. Offers law (JD). Electronic applications accepted.

MERCY COLLEGE, Dobbs Ferry, NY 10522-1189

General Information Independent, coed, comprehensive institution. CGS member. *Enrollment:* 11,295 graduate, professional, and undergraduate students; 1,419 full-time matriculated graduate/professional students (1,124 women), 1,560 part-time matriculated graduate/professional students (1,286 women). *Enrollment by degree level:* 2,790 master's, 106 doctoral, 83 other advanced degrees. *Tuition, area resident:* Full-time $14,904; part-time $828 per credit hour. *Required fees:* $610; $153 per term. $153 per term. Tuition and fees vary according to course load and program. *Graduate housing:* Room and/or apartments available on a first-come, first-served basis to single students; on-campus housing not available to married students. Typical cost: $9350 per year ($13,700 including board). Housing application deadline: 7/1. *Student services:* Campus employment opportunities, campus safety program, career counseling, exercise/wellness program, free psychological counseling, international student services, services for students with disabilities, teacher training, writing training. *Library:* Mercy College Library plus 3 others. *Collection:* Books: 85,689 (digital/electronic); Serial titles: 21,126 (digital/electronic). Students can reserve study rooms.

Computer facilities: Computer purchase and lease plans are available. 972 computers available on campus for general student use. A campuswide network can be accessed from student residence rooms and from off campus. Online class registration is available.
Website: http://www.mercy.edu/

General Application Contact: Allison Gurdineer, Senior Director of Admissions, 877-637-2946, Fax: 914-674-7382, E-mail: admissions@mercy.edu.

GRADUATE UNITS

School of Business ***Degree program information:*** Part-time and evening/weekend programs available. Part-time, evening/weekend, online learning. Offers business administration (MBA); human resource management (MS); organizational leadership (MS); public accounting (MS). Electronic applications accepted.

School of Education ***Degree program information:*** Part-time and evening/weekend programs available. Part-time, evening/weekend, online learning. Offers adolescence education (MS); childhood education (MS); early childhood education (MS); school building leadership (MS, Advanced Certificate); teaching English to speakers of other languages (TESOL) (MS, Advanced Certificate); teaching literacy (MS, Advanced Certificate); teaching literacy, birth-6 (MS); teaching literacy/grades 5-12 (MS). Electronic applications accepted.

School of Health and Natural Sciences ***Degree program information:*** Part-time and evening/weekend programs available. Part-time, evening/weekend, online learning. Offers communication disorders (MS); nursing (MS); nursing administration (MS); nursing education (MS); occupational therapy (MS); physical therapy (DPT); physician assistant studies (MS). Electronic applications accepted.

School of Liberal Arts ***Degree program information:*** Part-time and evening/weekend programs available. Part-time, evening/weekend, online learning. Offers cybersecurity (MS); English literature (MA). Electronic applications accepted.

School of Social and Behavioral Sciences ***Degree program information:*** Part-time and evening/weekend programs available. Part-time, evening/weekend, online learning. Offers counseling (MS, Certificate); family counseling (Certificate); health services management (MPA, MS); marriage and family therapy (MS); mental health counseling (MS); psychology (MS); school counseling (Certificate); school psychology (MS). Electronic applications accepted.

MERCYHURST UNIVERSITY, Erie, PA 16546

General Information Independent-religious, coed, comprehensive institution. *Graduate housing:* On-campus housing not available.

GRADUATE UNITS

Graduate Studies ***Degree program information:*** Part-time and evening/weekend programs available. Part-time, evening/weekend. Offers accounting (MS); administration of justice (MS); applied behavior analysis (MS); applied intelligence (MS, Certificate); archaeology and geological archaeology (MS); autism (MS); data science (MS); forensic and biological anthropology (MS); generalist (MS); higher education administration (MS); higher education leadership and disabilities (MS); human resources (MS); organizational leadership (MS, Certificate); physician assistant studies (MS); secondary education: pedagogy and practice (MS); sports leadership (MS); strategy and innovation (MS). Electronic applications accepted.

MEREDITH COLLEGE, Raleigh, NC 27607-5298

General Information Independent, Undergraduate: women only; graduate: coed, comprehensive institution. *Enrollment:* 1,949 graduate, professional, and undergraduate students; 131 full-time matriculated graduate/professional students (120 women), 139 part-time matriculated graduate/professional students (121 women). *Enrollment by degree level:* 198 master's, 72 other advanced degrees. *Graduate faculty:* 26 full-time (22 women), 10 part-time/adjunct (7 women). Tuition and fees vary according to degree level and program. *Graduate housing:* On-campus housing not available. *Student services:* Campus safety program, career counseling, free psychological counseling, international student services, services for students with disabilities. *Library:* Carlyle Campbell Library.

Computer facilities: 140 computers available on campus for general student use. A campuswide network can be accessed from student residence rooms. Online class registration is available.
Website: http://www.meredith.edu/

General Application Contact: Sylvia Horton, Admissions Coordinator, 919-760-8423, Fax: 919-760-2898, E-mail: hortons@meredith.edu.

GRADUATE UNITS

Nutrition, Health and Human Performance Department Students: 75 full-time (71 women), 35 part-time (33 women); includes 7 minority (4 Black or African American, non-Hispanic/Latino; 1 American Indian or Alaska Native, non-Hispanic/Latino; 1 Asian, non-Hispanic/Latino; 1 Hispanic/Latino), 2 international. Average age 27. 252 applicants, 31% accepted, 72 enrolled. *Faculty:* 4 full-time (3 women), 6 part-time/adjunct (all women). *Financial support:* Application deadline: 2/15; applicants required to submit FAFSA. In 2015, 18 master's, 27 other advanced degrees awarded. Offers dietetic internship (Postbaccalaureate Certificate); nutrition (MS). *Application deadline:* For fall admission, 7/1 priority date for domestic and international students; for spring admission, 11/1 priority date for domestic and international students. Applications are processed on a rolling basis. *Application fee:* $50. Electronic applications accepted. *Application Contact:* Dr. William H. Landis, Director, 919-760-2355, Fax: 919-760-2819, E-mail: landisb@meredith.edu. *Head*, Dr. Judy Peel, 919-760-8014, E-mail: peeljudy@meredith.edu.

School of Business Students: 3 full-time (all women), 73 part-time (59 women); includes 23 minority (19 Black or African American, non-Hispanic/Latino; 2 American Indian or Alaska Native, non-Hispanic/Latino; 2 Asian, non-Hispanic/Latino), 6 international. Average age 37. 63 applicants, 78% accepted, 35 enrolled. *Faculty:* 11 full-time (8 women), 2 part-time/adjunct (0 women). *Financial support:* Career-related internships or fieldwork, institutionally sponsored loans, scholarships/grants, and tuition waivers (partial) available. Support available to part-time students. Financial award application deadline: 2/15; financial award applicants required to submit FAFSA. In 2015, 29 master's awarded. *Degree program information:* Part-time and evening/weekend programs available. Part-time, evening/weekend. Offers business administration (MBA). *Application deadline:* For fall admission, 7/1 priority date for domestic and international students; for spring admission, 11/1 priority date for domestic and international students. Applications are processed on a rolling basis. *Application fee:* $50. Electronic applications accepted. *Application Contact:* Page Midyette, Coordinator, 919-760-2281, Fax: 919-760-2898, E-mail: midyette@meredith.edu. *Dean*, Kristie Ogilvie, 919-760-8432, Fax: 919-760-8470.

School of Education Students: 25 full-time (24 women), 22 part-time (all women); includes 11 minority (8 Black or African American, non-Hispanic/Latino; 1 Asian, non-Hispanic/Latino; 1 Hispanic/Latino; 1 Two or more races, non-Hispanic/Latino), 3 international. Average age 30. 41 applicants, 85% accepted, 25 enrolled. *Faculty:* 10 full-time (all women), 2 part-time/adjunct (both women). *Financial support:* Career-related internships or fieldwork, institutionally sponsored loans, and tuition waivers (partial) available. Support available to part-time students. Financial award application deadline: 2/15; financial award applicants required to submit FAFSA. In 2015, 34 master's awarded. *Degree program information:* Part-time and evening/weekend programs available. Part-time, evening/weekend. Offers education (M Ed, MAT). *Application deadline:* For fall admission, 7/1 priority date for domestic students; for spring admission, 11/1 priority date for domestic students. Applications are processed on a rolling basis. *Application fee:* $50. Electronic applications accepted. *Graduate Program Manager*, Dr. Monica McKinney, 919-760-8056, Fax: 919-760-2303, E-mail: mckinneym@meredith.edu.

MERRIMACK COLLEGE, North Andover, MA 01845-5800

General Information Independent-religious, coed, comprehensive institution. CGS member. *Enrollment:* 3,644 graduate, professional, and undergraduate students; 206 full-time matriculated graduate/professional students (141 women), 81 part-time matriculated graduate/professional students (56 women). *Enrollment by degree level:* 285 master's, 2 other advanced degrees. *Graduate faculty:* 22 full-time, 34 part-time/adjunct. *Graduate housing:* On-campus housing not available. *Student services:* Campus employment opportunities, campus safety program, career counseling, exercise/wellness program, free psychological counseling, international student services, low-cost health insurance, multicultural affairs office, services for students with disabilities, teacher training, writing training. *Library:* McQuade Library.

Computer facilities: Computer purchase and lease plans are available. A campuswide network can be accessed from student residence rooms and from off campus. Online class registration is available.
Website: http://www.merrimack.edu/

General Application Contact: Rachael Tampone, Graduate Admission Counselor, 978-837-5196, E-mail: graduate@merrimack.edu.

GRADUATE UNITS

Girard School of Business Students: 81 full-time (38 women), 29 part-time (9 women); includes 3 minority (1 Hispanic/Latino; 2 Two or more races, non-Hispanic/Latino), 23 international. Average age 27. 125 applicants, 62% accepted, 57 enrolled. *Faculty:* 11 full-time, 9 part-time/adjunct. *Financial support:* Career-related internships or fieldwork, scholarships/grants, health care benefits, and unspecified assistantships available. Support available to part-time students. Financial award applicants required to submit FAFSA. In 2015, 30 master's awarded. *Degree program information:* Part-time and evening/weekend programs available. Part-time, evening/weekend. Offers accounting (MS); management (MS). *Application deadline:* For fall admission, 8/13 for domestic students, 7/13 for international students; for spring admission, 1/10 for domestic and international students; for summer admission, 5/10 for domestic students, 4/10 for international students. Applications are processed on a rolling basis. *Application fee:* $0. Electronic applications accepted. *Application Contact:* Allison Pena, Graduate Admissions Counselor, 978-837-5227, E-mail: penaa@merrimack.edu.

School of Education and Social Policy Students: 180 full-time (136 women), 57 part-time (52 women); includes 14 minority (1 Black or African American, non-Hispanic/Latino; 11 Hispanic/Latino; 2 Two or more races, non-Hispanic/Latino), 7 international. Average age 27. 323 applicants, 77% accepted, 168 enrolled. *Faculty:* 16 full-time, 26 part-time/adjunct. *Financial support:* Fellowships with full tuition reimbursements, career-related internships or fieldwork, scholarships/grants, and health care benefits available. Support available to part-time students. Financial award applicants required to submit FAFSA. In 2015, 154 master's awarded. *Degree program information:* Part-time and evening/weekend programs available. Part-time, evening/weekend, 100% online courses with immersion events and in-classroom practicum close to home. Offers community engagement (M Ed); criminology and criminal justice (MS); curriculum and instruction (M Ed); early childhood education (M Ed); educational leadership (CAGS); elementary education (M Ed); English as a second language (PreK-6) (M Ed); high school education (M Ed); higher education (M Ed); middle school education (M Ed); moderate disabilities (PreK-8) (M Ed); school counseling (M Ed). *Application deadline:* For fall admission, 8/13 for domestic students, 7/13 for international students; for spring admission, 1/10 for domestic and international students; for summer admission, 5/10 for domestic students, 4/10 for international students. Applications are processed on a rolling basis. *Application fee:* $0. Electronic applications accepted. *Application Contact:* Allison Pena, Graduate Admissions Counselor, 978-837-5227, E-mail: penaa@merrimack.edu.

School of Liberal Arts Students: 11 full-time (4 women), 1 part-time (0 women); includes 1 minority (Hispanic/Latino). Average age 26. 19 applicants, 95% accepted, 12 enrolled. *Faculty:* 6 full-time. *Financial support:* Career-related internships or fieldwork, scholarships/grants, and health care benefits available. Support available to part-time students. Financial award applicants required to submit FAFSA. *Degree program information:* Part-time programs available. Part-time. Offers clinical mental health counseling (MS); public affairs (MPA). *Application deadline:* For fall admission, 8/13 for domestic students, 7/13 for international students; for spring admission, 1/10 for domestic and international students; for summer admission, 5/10 for domestic students, 4/10 for international students. Applications are processed on a rolling basis. Electronic applications accepted. *Application Contact:* Allison Pena, Graduate Admissions Counselor, 978-837-5227, E-mail: graduate@merrimack.edu.

School of Science and Engineering Students: 62 full-time (25 women), 12 part-time (4 women); includes 5 minority (1 Asian, non-Hispanic/Latino; 4 Hispanic/Latino), 18 international. Average age 24. 141 applicants, 67% accepted, 62 enrolled. *Faculty:* 18 full-time, 4 part-time/adjunct. *Financial support:* Fellowships with partial tuition reimbursements, career-related internships or fieldwork, scholarships/grants, and health care benefits available. Support available to part-time students. Financial award applicants required to submit FAFSA. In 2015, 12 master's awarded. *Degree program information:* Part-time programs available. Part-time. Offers civil engineering (MS); community health education (MS); computer science (MS); exercise and sport science (MS); health and wellness management (MS); mechanical engineering (MS). *Application deadline:* For fall admission, 8/13 for domestic students, 7/13 for international students; for spring admission, 1/10 for domestic and international students; for summer admission, 5/10 for domestic students, 4/10 for international students. Applications are processed on a rolling basis. *Application fee:* $0. Electronic applications accepted. *Application Contact:* Allison Pena, Graduate Admissions Counselor, 978-837-5227, E-mail: penaa@merrimack.edu.

MESIVTA OF EASTERN PARKWAY–YESHIVA ZICHRON MEILECH, Brooklyn, NY 11218-5559

General Information Independent-religious, men only.

GRADUATE UNITS

Graduate Programs

MESIVTA TORAH VODAATH RABBINICAL SEMINARY, Brooklyn, NY 11218-5299

General Information Independent-religious, men only, comprehensive institution.

GRADUATE UNITS

Graduate Programs

MESIVTHA TIFERETH JERUSALEM OF AMERICA, New York, NY 10002-6301

General Information Independent-religious, men only, comprehensive institution.

GRADUATE UNITS

Graduate Programs

MESSIAH COLLEGE, Mechanicsburg, PA 17055

General Information Independent-religious, coed, comprehensive institution.

GRADUATE UNITS

Program in Business and Leadership Online learning. Offers leadership (MBA, Certificate); management (Certificate); strategic leadership (MA).

Program in Conducting ***Degree program information:*** Part-time programs available. Part-time, online learning. Offers choral conducting (MM); orchestral conducting (MM); wind conducting (MM). Electronic applications accepted.

Program in Counseling ***Degree program information:*** Part-time programs available. Part-time, online learning. Offers clinical mental health counseling (MAC); counseling (CAGS); marriage, couple, and family counseling (MAC); school counseling (MAC). Electronic applications accepted.

Program in Education ***Degree program information:*** Part-time programs available. Part-time, online learning. Offers curriculum and instruction (M Ed); special education (M Ed); teaching English to speakers of other languages (M Ed). Electronic applications accepted.

Program in Higher Education ***Degree program information:*** Part-time programs available. Part-time. Offers college athletics management (MA); self-designed concentration (MA); student affairs (MA). Electronic applications accepted.

Program in Nursing Offers nurse educator (MSN).

METHODIST THEOLOGICAL SCHOOL IN OHIO, Delaware, OH 43015-8004

General Information Independent-religious, coed, graduate-only institution. *Graduate housing:* Rooms and/or apartments available on a first-come, first-served basis to single students and available to married students. Housing application deadline: 8/15.

GRADUATE UNITS

Graduate and Professional Programs ***Degree program information:*** Part-time programs available. Part-time. Offers theology (M Div, MACE, MACM, MTS, D Min).

METHODIST UNIVERSITY, Fayetteville, NC 28311-1498

General Information Independent-religious, coed, comprehensive institution. *Graduate housing:* Room and/or apartments available on a first-come, first-served basis to single students; on-campus housing not available to married students. Housing application deadline: 6/1.

GRADUATE UNITS

School of Graduate Studies ***Degree program information:*** Part-time and evening/weekend programs available. Part-time, evening/weekend. Offers business administration (MBA); justice administration (MJA); physician assistant studies (MMS). Electronic applications accepted.

METROPOLITAN COLLEGE OF NEW YORK, New York, NY 10013

General Information Independent, coed, comprehensive institution. *Enrollment:* 1,195 graduate, professional, and undergraduate students; 370 full-time matriculated graduate/professional students (265 women), 46 part-time matriculated graduate/professional students (23 women). *Enrollment by degree level:* 416 master's. *Tuition, area resident:* Full-time $25,800; part-time $860 per credit hour. *Required fees:* $540; $270. One-time fee: $45. *Graduate housing:* On-campus housing not available. *Student services:* Career counseling, free psychological counseling, grant writing training, international student services. *Library:* Main Library plus 1 other. *Collection:* Books: 32,442 (physical), 136,723 (digital/electronic); Serial titles: 81 (physical), 50,762 (digital/electronic); Databases: 88. Weekly public service hours: 76. *Research affiliation:* U.S. Department of Homeland Security (homeland security), U.S. Federal Emergency Management Administration (higher education).

Computer facilities: 99 computers available on campus for general student use. A campuswide network can be accessed. Online class registration is available.
Website: http://www.metropolitan.edu/

General Application Contact: Steebo Varghese, Assistant Director of Admissions, 212-343-1234 Ext. 2708, Fax: 212-343-8470, E-mail: svarghese@mcny.edu.

GRADUATE UNITS

Program in Business Administration Students: 163 full-time (108 women), 33 part-time (16 women); includes 141 minority (106 Black or African American, non-Hispanic/Latino; 7 Asian, non-Hispanic/Latino; 26 Hispanic/Latino; 2 Two or more races, non-Hispanic/Latino), 27 international. Average age 35. 273 applicants, 65% accepted, 75 enrolled. *Financial support:* Scholarships/grants available. Financial award application deadline: 8/15; financial award applicants required to submit FAFSA. In 2015, 88 master's awarded. *Degree program information:* Evening/weekend programs available. Evening/weekend. Offers financial services (MBA); general management (MBA); health services and risk management (MBA); media management (MBA). *Application deadline:* For fall admission, 7/15 priority date for domestic students; for winter admission, 11/15 priority date for domestic students; for spring admission, 3/30 priority date for domestic students. Applications are processed on a rolling basis. *Application fee:* $45. Electronic applications accepted. *Application Contact:* Steebo Varghese, Assistant Director of Admissions, 212-343-1234 Ext. 2708, Fax: 212-343-8470. *Dean and Professor, School for Business*, Dr. Tilokie Depoo, 212-343-1234 Ext. 2204.

Program in Childhood/Special Education ***Financial support:*** Career-related internships or fieldwork, Federal Work-Study, institutionally sponsored loans, and scholarships/grants available. Financial award application deadline: 8/15; financial award applicants required to submit FAFSA. Offers childhood/special education (MS). *Application deadline:* Applications are processed on a rolling basis. *Application fee:* $45. *Application Contact:* Sylvia Cameron, Graduate Admissions Coordinator, 212-343-1234 Ext. 2704, Fax: 212-343-7900, E-mail: scameron@mcny.edu. *Director,* Dr. Patrick Ianniello, 212-343-1234 Ext. 2424, E-mail: pianniello@metropolitan.edu.

Program in Public Administration Students: 188 full-time (140 women), 11 part-time (5 women); includes 147 minority (115 Black or African American, non-Hispanic/Latino; 4 Asian, non-Hispanic/Latino; 28 Hispanic/Latino), 2 international. Average age 37. 211 applicants, 50% accepted, 86 enrolled. *Financial support:* Fellowships with tuition reimbursements, career-related internships or fieldwork, scholarships/grants, and tuition waivers (partial) available. Financial award application deadline: 8/15; financial award applicants required to submit FAFSA. In 2015, 91 master's awarded. *Degree program information:* Evening/weekend programs available. Evening/weekend. Offers emergency and disaster management (MPA); public affairs and administration (MPA). *Application deadline:* For fall admission, 7/30 priority date for domestic students, 7/1 for international students; for winter admission, 11/30 priority date for domestic students, 11/1 for international students; for spring admission, 3/30 priority date for domestic students, 3/1 for international students. Applications are processed on a rolling basis. *Application fee:* $45. Electronic applications accepted. *Application Contact:* Steebo Varghese, Assistant Director of Admissions, 212-343-1234 Ext. 2708, Fax: 212-343-8474, E-mail: svarghese@mcny.edu. *Dean, Graduate School for Public Affairs Administration,* Prof. Humphrey Crookendale, 212-343-1234 Ext. 2209, E-mail: hcrookendale@mcny.edu.

METROPOLITAN STATE UNIVERSITY, St. Paul, MN 55106-5000

General Information State-supported, coed, comprehensive institution. *Graduate housing:* On-campus housing not available.

GRADUATE UNITS

College of Arts and Sciences ***Degree program information:*** Part-time and evening/weekend programs available. Part-time, evening/weekend. Offers computer science (MS); liberal studies (MA); technical communication (MS). Electronic applications accepted.

College of Health, Community and Professional Studies ***Degree program information:*** Part-time programs available. Part-time. Offers advanced dental therapy (MS); leadership and management (MSN); nurse educator (MSN); nursing (DNP); psychology (MA).

College of Management ***Degree program information:*** Part-time and evening/weekend programs available. Part-time, evening/weekend. Offers business administration (MBA, DBA); database administration (Graduate Certificate); healthcare information technology management (Graduate Certificate); information assurance security (Graduate Certificate); management information systems (MMIS); MIS generalist (Graduate Certificate); MIS systems analysis and design (Graduate Certificate); project management (Graduate Certificate); public and nonprofit administration (MPNA). Electronic applications accepted.

School of Law Enforcement and Criminal Justice ***Degree program information:*** Part-time and evening/weekend programs available. Part-time, evening/weekend. Offers criminal justice (MS). Electronic applications accepted.

METROPOLITAN STATE UNIVERSITY OF DENVER, Denver, CO 80204

General Information State-supported, coed, comprehensive institution. CGS member.

GRADUATE UNITS

School of Business Offers accounting (MP Acc).

School of Letters, Arts and Sciences Offers social work (MSW).

School of Professional Studies Offers elementary education (MAT); special education (MAT).

MGH INSTITUTE OF HEALTH PROFESSIONS, Boston, MA 02129

General Information Independent, coed, primarily women, graduate-only institution. *Graduate housing:* On-campus housing not available. *Research affiliation:* Health and Disability Research Institute, Boston University (efficacy of a post-rehabilitation exercise intervention in patients after hip fracture), Eunice Kennedy Shriver National Institute of Child and Health Development (dyadic intervention for women at risk for postpartum depression and their infants), National Institutes of Health (postnatal parental depression family dynamics in early parenting), Robert Wood Johnson Foundation (mother-infant intervention for the prevention of postpartum depression and associated mother-infant relationship dysfunction), Department of Defense (robotic nursing assistant to Hstar technology), The American Academy of Nursing and the John W. Hartford Foundation (building academic geriatric nursing capacity).

GRADUATE UNITS

School of Health and Rehabilitation Sciences ***Degree program information:*** Part-time programs available. Part-time. Offers health and rehabilitation sciences (MPAS, MS, DPT, OTD, Certificate); occupational therapy (OTD); physical therapy (MS, DPT, Certificate); physician assistant studies (MPAS); reading (Certificate); speech-language pathology (MS). Electronic applications accepted.

School of Nursing Offers advanced practice nursing (MSN); gerontological nursing (MSN); nursing (DNP); pediatric nursing (MSN); psychiatric nursing (MSN); teaching and learning for health care education (Certificate); women's health nursing (MSN). Electronic applications accepted.

MIAMI INTERNATIONAL UNIVERSITY OF ART & DESIGN, Miami, FL 33132-1418

General Information Proprietary, coed, comprehensive institution.

GRADUATE UNITS

Program in Design and Media Management Offers design and media management (MA).

Program in Film Online learning. Offers film (MFA).

MIAMI UNIVERSITY, Oxford, OH 45056

General Information State-related, coed, university. CGS member. *Enrollment:* 19,076 graduate, professional, and undergraduate students; 983 full-time matriculated graduate/professional students (567 women), 1,131 part-time matriculated graduate/professional students (872 women). *Enrollment by degree level:* 1,782 master's, 332 doctoral. *Graduate faculty:* 648 full-time (291 women). Tuition, state resident: full-time $12,888; part-time $537 per credit hour. Tuition, nonresident: full-time $29,022; part-time $1209 per credit hour. *Required fees:* $530; $24 per credit hour. $30 per semester. Part-time tuition and fees vary according to course load and program. *Graduate housing:* Rooms and/or apartments available on a first-come, first-served basis to single and married students. *Student services:* Campus employment opportunities, campus safety program, career counseling, child daycare facilities, exercise/wellness program, free psychological counseling, grant writing training, international student services, low-cost health insurance, multicultural affairs office, services for students with disabilities, teacher training, writing training. *Library:* King Library plus 3 others. *Collection:* Books: 2.7 million (physical), 665,740 (digital/electronic); Serial titles: 1,139 (physical), 26,272 (digital/electronic); Databases: 750. Weekly public service hours: 168; study areas open 24 hours, 5–7 days a week; students can reserve study rooms.

Computer facilities: Computer purchase and lease plans are available. A campuswide network can be accessed from student residence rooms and from off campus. Online class registration is available.
Website: http://miamioh.edu/

General Application Contact: Graduate Admission Coordinator, 513-529-3734, E-mail: applygrad@miamioh.edu.

GRADUATE UNITS

College of Arts and Science ***Financial support:*** Application deadline: 3/1. *Degree program information:* Part-time programs available. Part-time. Offers arts and science (M Env, MA, MAT, MGS, MPSG, MS, MS Stat, PhD); biology (MA, MAT, MS, PhD); chemistry and biochemistry (MS, PhD); English (MA, MAT, PhD); French (MA); geography (MA); geology (MA, MS, PhD); gerontology (MGS); history (MA); mathematics (MA, MAT, MS); microbiology (MS, PhD); philosophy (MA); physics (MS); political science (MA); population and social gerontology (MPSG); psychology (MA, PhD); social gerontology (PhD); speech pathology and audiology (MA, MS); statistics (MS Stat). *Application Contact:* Admission Coordinator, 513-529-3734, E-mail: applygrad@miamioh.edu. *Dean,* Dr. Chris Makaroff, 513-529-1234, E-mail: cas@miamioh.edu.

College of Creative Arts Offers architecture and interior design (M Arch); art education (MA); creative arts (M Arch, MA, MFA, MM); music education (MM); music performance (MM); studio art (MFA); theatre (MA). *Application Contact:* Graduate Admission Coordinator, 513-529-3734, E-mail: applygrad@miamioh.edu. *Dean,* Dr. Liz Mullenix, 513-529-6010, E-mail: cca@miamioh.edu.

College of Education, Health and Society Offers education, health and society (M Ed, MA, MAT, MS, Ed D, PhD, Ed S); educational leadership (M Ed, MS, Ed D, PhD); educational psychology (M Ed, MA, MS, Ed S); family studies and social work (MA); kinesiology and health (MS); teacher education (M Ed, MAT). *Application Contact:* Graduate Admission Coordinator, 513-529-3734, E-mail: applygrad@miamioh.edu. *Dean,* Dr. Michael Dantley, 513-529-6317, E-mail: ehs@miamioh.edu.

College of Engineering and Computing Offers chemical, paper and biomedical engineering (MS); computer science (MCS); electrical and computer engineering (MS); engineering and computing (MCS, MS); mechanical and manufacturing engineering (MS). *Application Contact:* Graduate Admission Coordinator, 513-529-3734, E-mail: applygrad@miamioh.edu. *Dean,* Dr. Marek Dollar, 513-529-0700, E-mail: cec@miamioh.edu.

Farmer School of Business Offers accountancy (M Acc); business (M Acc, MA, MBA); business administration (MBA); economics (MA). *Application Contact:* Admission Coordinator, 513-529-3734, E-mail: applygrad@miamioh.edu. *Dean/Chair of Business Leadership,* Dr. Matthew Myers, 513-529-3631, E-mail: deanofbusiness@miamioh.edu.

Institute for the Environment and Sustainability Students: 44 full-time (25 women), 3 part-time (1 woman); includes 6 minority (4 Hispanic/Latino; 2 Two or more races, non-Hispanic/Latino), 2 international. Average age 28. *Financial support:* Application deadline: 2/15; applicants required to submit FAFSA. In 2015, 16 master's awarded. *Degree program information:* Part-time programs available. Part-time. Offers environment and sustainability (M Env). *Application deadline:* For fall admission, 2/1 for domestic and international students. *Application fee:* $50. Electronic applications accepted. *Application Contact:* 513-529-5811, E-mail: ies@miamioh.edu. *Director/Associate Professor of Geology and Environmental Earth Science,* Dr. Jonathan Levy, 513-529-1947, E-mail: levyj@miamioh.edu.

MICHIGAN SCHOOL OF PROFESSIONAL PSYCHOLOGY, Farmington Hills, MI 48334

General Information Independent, coed, graduate-only institution. *Enrollment by degree level:* 69 master's, 72 doctoral. *Graduate faculty:* 10 full-time (5 women), 16 part-time/adjunct (11 women). *Tuition, area resident:* Full-time $30,000; part-time $15,132 per year. *Required fees:* $625; $460 per semester. One-time fee: $75. Tuition and fees vary according to course load, degree level and program. *Graduate housing:* On-campus housing not available. *Student services:* Campus employment opportunities, campus safety program, international student services, multicultural affairs office, services for students with disabilities, writing training. *Library:* Moustakas Johnson Library plus 1 other. Weekly public service hours: 45.

Computer facilities: 16 computers available on campus for general student use.
Website: http://www.mispp.edu/

General Application Contact: Tori Holmes, Coordinator of Admissions and Student Engagement, 248-476-1122 Ext. 117, Fax: 248-476-1125, E-mail: tholmes@mispp.edu.

GRADUATE UNITS

MA and Psy D Programs in Clinical Psychology Students: 109 full-time (60 women), 32 part-time (20 women); includes 39 minority (28 Black or African American, non-Hispanic/Latino; 4 Asian, non-Hispanic/Latino; 2 Hispanic/Latino; 5 Two or more races, non-Hispanic/Latino), 1 international. Average age 25. 159 applicants, 53% accepted, 59 enrolled. *Faculty:* 10 full-time (5 women), 16 part-time/adjunct (11 women). *Financial support:* In 2015–16, 6 students received support, including 3 research assistantships, 4 teaching assistantships; career-related internships or fieldwork, institutionally sponsored loans, scholarships/grants, and unspecified assistantships also available. Support available to part-time students. Financial award application deadline: 8/30; financial award applicants required to submit FAFSA. In 2015, 47 master's, 19 doctorates awarded. *Degree program information:* Part-time programs available. Part-time. Offers clinical psychology (MA, Psy D). *Application deadline:* Applications are processed on a rolling basis. *Application fee:* $75. Electronic applications accepted.

Application Contact: Tori Holmes, Coordinator of Admissions and Student Engagement, 248-476-1122 Ext. 117, Fax: 248-476-1125, E-mail: tholmes@mispp.edu. *Program Director,* Dr. Frances Brown, 248-476-1122, Fax: 248-476-1125.

MICHIGAN STATE UNIVERSITY, East Lansing, MI 48824

General Information State-supported, coed, university. CGS member. *Graduate housing:* Rooms and/or apartments available on a first-come, first-served basis to single and married students. *Research affiliation:* Argonne National Laboratory (high-energy physics and structural biology), Association of Sea Grant Programs (fresh water ecosystems), Fraunhofer Center (manufacturing), Michigan Economic Development Corporation (life sciences, homeland security, automotive technologies), Oak Ridge Associated Universities (scientific research and education), Southern Astrophysical Research (SOAR) Telescope (astronomy).

GRADUATE UNITS

College of Human Medicine Offers biochemistry and molecular biology (MS, PhD); epidemiology (MS, PhD); human medicine (MD); human medicine/medical scientist training program (MD); microbiology (MS); microbiology and molecular genetics (PhD); pharmacology and toxicology (MS, PhD); physiology (MS, PhD); public health (MPH).

College of Osteopathic Medicine Offers biochemistry and molecular biology (MS, PhD); integrative pharmacology (MS); microbiology (MS); microbiology and molecular genetics (PhD); osteopathic medicine (MS, DO, PhD); pharmacology and toxicology (MS, PhD); pharmacology and toxicology-environmental toxicology (PhD); physiology (MS, PhD).

College of Veterinary Medicine Offers animal science–environmental toxicology (PhD); biochemistry and molecular biology–environmental toxicology (PhD); chemistry–environmental toxicology (PhD); comparative medicine and integrative biology (MS, PhD); comparative medicine and integrative biology–environmental toxicology (PhD); crop and soil sciences–environmental toxicology (PhD); environmental engineering–environmental toxicology (PhD); environmental geosciences–environmental toxicology (PhD); fisheries and wildlife–environmental toxicology (PhD); food safety (MS); food safety and toxicology (MS); food science–environmental toxicology (PhD); forestry–environmental toxicology (PhD); genetics–environmental toxicology (PhD); human nutrition–environmental toxicology (PhD); industrial microbiology (MS, PhD); integrative toxicology (PhD); large animal clinical sciences (MS, PhD); microbiology (MS, PhD); microbiology and molecular genetics (MS, PhD); microbiology–environmental toxicology (PhD); pathobiology and diagnostic investigation (MS, PhD); pathology (MS, PhD); pathology–environmental toxicology (PhD); pharmacology and toxicology (MS, PhD); pharmacology and toxicology–environmental toxicology (PhD); physiology (MS, PhD); small animal clinical sciences (MS); veterinary medicine (DVM); veterinary medicine/medical scientist training program (DVM); zoology–environmental toxicology (PhD).

The Graduate School ***Degree program information:*** Part-time and evening/weekend programs available. Part-time, evening/weekend, online learning. Electronic applications accepted.

College of Agriculture and Natural Resources Offers agricultural economics (MS, PhD); agricultural, food, and resource economics (MS, PhD); agriculture and natural resources (MA, MIPS, MS, MURP, PhD); animal science (MS, PhD); animal science-environmental toxicology (PhD); biochemistry and molecular biology (PhD); biosystems engineering (MS, PhD); cellular and molecular biology (PhD); community, agriculture, recreation, and resource studies (MS, PhD); construction management (MS, PhD); crop and soil sciences (MS, PhD); crop and soil sciences-environmental toxicology (PhD); entomology (MS, PhD); environmental design (MA); fisheries and wildlife (MS, PhD); fisheries and wildlife - environmental toxicology (PhD); food science (MS, PhD); food science - environmental toxicology (PhD); forestry (MS, PhD); forestry-environmental toxicology (PhD); genetics (PhD); horticulture (MS, PhD); human nutrition (MS, PhD); human nutrition-environmental toxicology (PhD); integrated pest management (MS); interior design and facilities management (MA); international planning studies (MIPS); microbiology and molecular genetics (PhD); packaging (MS, PhD); plant biology (PhD); plant breeding and genetics (MS, PhD); plant breeding and genetics-crop and soil sciences (MS); plant breeding, genetics and biotechnology-crop and soil sciences (PhD); plant breeding, genetics and biotechnology-forestry (MS, PhD); plant breeding, genetics and biotechnology-horticulture (MS, PhD); plant pathology (MS, PhD); plant physiology (PhD); urban and regional planning (MURP).

College of Arts and Letters Offers African American and African studies (MA, PhD); American studies (MA, PhD); applied Spanish linguistics (MA); arts and letters (MA, MFA, PhD); critical studies in literacy and pedagogy (MA); digital rhetoric and professional writing (MA); English (PhD); French (MA); French language and literature (PhD); German studies (MA, PhD); Hispanic cultural studies (PhD); Hispanic literatures (MA); linguistics (MA, PhD); literature in English (MA); philosophy (MA, PhD); rhetoric and writing (PhD); second language studies (PhD); studio art (MFA); teaching English to speakers of other languages (MA); theatre (MA, MFA). Electronic applications accepted.

College of Communication Arts and Sciences Offers advertising (MA); communication (MA, PhD); communication arts and sciences (MA, MS, PhD); communication arts and sciences–media and information studies (PhD); communicative sciences and disorders (MA, PhD); digital media arts and technology (MA); health communication (MA); information and telecommunication management (MA); information, policy and society (MA); journalism (MA); public relations (MA); retailing (MS, PhD); serious game design (MA).

College of Education Offers counseling (MA); curriculum, instruction and teacher education (PhD, Ed S); education (MA, MS, PhD, Ed S); educational policy (PhD); educational psychology and educational technology (PhD); educational technology (MA); higher, adult and lifelong education (MA, PhD); K–12 educational administration (MA, PhD, Ed S); kinesiology (MS, PhD); literacy instruction (MA); measurement and quantitative methods (PhD); rehabilitation counseling (MA); rehabilitation counselor education (PhD); school psychology (MA, PhD, Ed S); special education (MA, PhD); student affairs administration (MA); teaching and curriculum (MA). Electronic applications accepted.

College of Engineering Degree program information: Part-time programs available. Part-time. Offers chemical engineering (MS, PhD); civil engineering (MS, PhD); computer science (MS, PhD); electrical engineering (MS, PhD); engineering (MS, PhD); engineering mechanics (MS, PhD); environmental engineering (MS, PhD); environmental engineering-environmental toxicology (PhD); materials science and engineering (MS, PhD); mechanical engineering (MS, PhD). Electronic applications accepted.

College of Music Offers collaborative piano (M Mus); jazz studies (M Mus); music (PhD); music composition (M Mus, DMA); music conducting (M Mus, DMA); music education (M Mus); music performance (M Mus, DMA); music theory (M Mus); music therapy (M Mus); musicology (MA); piano pedagogy (M Mus). Electronic applications accepted.

College of Natural Science Offers applied mathematics (MS, PhD); applied statistics (MS); astrophysics and astronomy (MS, PhD); biochemistry and molecular biology (MS, PhD); biochemistry and molecular biology/environmental toxicology (PhD); biological, physical and general science for teachers (MAT, MS); biomedical laboratory operations (MS); cell and molecular biology (MS, PhD); cell and molecular biology/environmental toxicology (PhD); chemical physics (PhD); chemistry (MS, PhD); chemistry-environmental toxicology (PhD); clinical laboratory sciences (MS); computational chemistry (MS); ecology, evolutionary biology and behavior (PhD); environmental geosciences (MS, PhD); environmental geosciences-environmental toxicology (PhD); genetics (MS, PhD); genetics–environmental toxicology (PhD); geological sciences (MS, PhD); industrial mathematics (MS); mathematics (MAT, MS, PhD); mathematics education (MS, PhD); natural science (MAT, MS, PhD); neuroscience (MS, PhD); physics (MS, PhD); physiology (MS, PhD); plant biology (MS, PhD); plant breeding, genetics and biotechnology - plant biology (MS, PhD); quantitative biology (PhD); statistics (MS, PhD); zoo and aquarium management (MS); zoology (MS, PhD); zoology-environmental toxicology (PhD). Electronic applications accepted.

College of Nursing Degree program information: Part-time programs available. Part-time, online learning. Offers nursing (MSN, PhD). Electronic applications accepted.

College of Social Science Offers anthropology (MA, PhD); Chicano/Latino studies (PhD); child development (MA); clinical social work (MSW); community services (MS); criminal justice (MS, PhD); economics (MA, PhD); family and child ecology (PhD); family studies (MA); forensic science (MS); geographic information science (MS); geography (MS, PhD); history (MA, PhD); history-secondary school teaching (MA); human resources and labor relations (MLRHR); industrial relations and human resources (PhD); law enforcement intelligence and analysis (MS); marriage and family therapy (MA); organizational and community practice (MSW); political science (MA, PhD); professional applications in anthropology (MA); psychology (MA, PhD); public policy (MPP); social science (MA, MIPS, MLRHR, MPP, MS, MSW, MURP, PhD); social work (PhD); sociology (MA, PhD); youth development (MA). Electronic applications accepted.

Eli Broad College of Business Faculty: 113 full-time, 9 part-time/adjunct. *Financial support:* Fellowships, research assistantships with tuition reimbursements, teaching assistantships with tuition reimbursements, scholarships/grants, and unspecified assistantships available. Financial award applicants required to submit FAFSA. In 2015, 474 master's, 12 doctorates awarded. *Degree program information:* Evening/weekend programs available. Evening/weekend. Offers accounting (MS, PhD); business (MBA, MS, PhD); business analytics (MS); business information systems (PhD); finance (MS, PhD); foodservice business management (MS); hospitality business management (MS); human resource management (MBA); integrative management (MBA); logistics (PhD); management (PhD); management, strategy, and leadership (MS); marketing (MBA, PhD); marketing research (MS); operations and sourcing management (PhD); supply chain management (MBA, MS). Electronic applications accepted. *Application Contact:* Dr. Sanjay Gupta, Dean, 517-432-6488, Fax: 517-353-6395, E-mail: gupta@broad.msu.edu. *Dean,* Dr. Sanjay Gupta, 517-432-6488, Fax: 517-353-6395, E-mail: gupta@broad.msu.edu.

National Superconducting Cyclotron Laboratory Offers chemistry (PhD); physics (PhD).

MICHIGAN STATE UNIVERSITY COLLEGE OF LAW, East Lansing, MI 48824-1300

General Information Independent, coed, graduate-only institution. *Enrollment by degree level:* 89 master's, 801 doctoral. *Graduate faculty:* 57 full-time (25 women), 74 part-time/adjunct (17 women). *Graduate housing:* Rooms and/or apartments available on a first-come, first-served basis to single and married students. Housing application deadline: 4/1. *Student services:* Campus employment opportunities, campus safety program, career counseling, exercise/wellness program, international student services, low-cost health insurance, multicultural affairs office, services for students with disabilities, writing training. *Library:* John F. Schaefer Law Library plus 5 others. *Collection:* Books: 164,532 (physical), 37,863 (digital/electronic); Serial titles: 6,280 (physical), 14,667 (digital/electronic); Databases: 24. Weekly public service hours: 70; students can reserve study rooms.

Computer facilities: 100 computers available on campus for general student use. A campuswide network can be accessed from student residence rooms and from off campus. Online class registration is available.
Website: http://www.law.msu.edu/

General Application Contact: Charles Roboski, Assistant Dean of Admissions, 517-432-0222, Fax: 517-432-0098, E-mail: roboski@law.msu.edu.

GRADUATE UNITS

Professional Program Students: 758 full-time (373 women), 132 part-time (62 women); includes 178 minority (64 Black or African American, non-Hispanic/Latino; 11 American Indian or Alaska Native, non-Hispanic/Latino; 27 Asian, non-Hispanic/Latino; 46 Hispanic/Latino; 1 Native Hawaiian or other Pacific Islander, non-Hispanic/Latino; 29 Two or more races, non-Hispanic/Latino), 113 international. Average age 24. 2,406 applicants, 48% accepted, 280 enrolled. *Faculty:* 57 full-time (25 women), 74 part-time/adjunct (17 women). *Financial support:* In 2015–16, 521 students received support. Career-related internships or fieldwork, Federal Work-Study, scholarships/grants, and tuition waivers (full and partial) available. Support available to part-time students. Financial award application deadline: 4/15; financial award applicants required to submit FAFSA. In 2015, 40 master's, 291 doctorates awarded. *Degree program information:* Part-time programs available. Part-time. Offers American legal system (LL M, MJ); global food law (LL M, MJ); intellectual property (LL M, MJ); law (JD); legal doctrine and analysis (MJ). *Application deadline:* For fall admission, 4/30 priority date for domestic students, 7/1 priority date for international students. Applications are processed on a rolling basis. *Application fee:* $60. Electronic applications accepted. *Application Contact:* Charles Roboski, Assistant Dean of Admissions, 517-432-0222, Fax: 517-432-0098, E-mail: roboski@law.msu.edu. *Dean/Professor of Law,* Joan W. Howarth, 517-432-6993, Fax: 517-432-6801, E-mail: howarth@law.msu.edu.

MICHIGAN TECHNOLOGICAL UNIVERSITY, Houghton, MI 49931

General Information State-supported, coed, university. CGS member. *Enrollment:* 7,242 graduate, professional, and undergraduate students; 1,141 full-time matriculated graduate/professional students (319 women), 353 part-time matriculated graduate/professional students (92 women). *Enrollment by degree level:* 936 master's, 555 doctoral, 3 other advanced degrees. *Graduate faculty:* 517 full-time (133 women), 256 part-time/adjunct (49 women). Tuition, state resident: full-time $15,507; part-time $861.50 per credit. Tuition, nonresident: full-time $15,507; part-time $861.50 per credit. *Required fees:* $248; $248. Tuition and fees vary according to course load and program. *Graduate housing:* Rooms and/or apartments available on a first-come, first-served basis to single and married students. Typical cost: $5925 per year ($10,296 including board) for single students; $5925 per year ($10,296 including board) for married students. Room and board charges vary according to board plan and housing facility selected. *Student services:* Campus employment opportunities, campus safety program, career counseling, child daycare facilities, exercise/wellness program, free psychological counseling, grant writing training, international student services, low-cost health insurance, multicultural affairs office, services for students with disabilities, teacher training, writing training. *Library:* J. R. Van Pelt and John and Ruanne Opie Library. *Collection:* Books: 409,533 (physical), 98,139 (digital/electronic); Databases: 152. Weekly public service hours: 119; study areas open 24 hours, 5–7 days a week; students can reserve study rooms. *Research affiliation:* Southwestern Energy Co. (automotive technology and design), E3 Spark Plugs (automotive technology and design), ArcelorMittal (materials processing), Ford Motor Company (vehicle engine research), Nostrum Energy, LLC (control system design), Treamin Energy, Inc. (materials processing).

Computer facilities: 1,079 computers available on campus for general student use. A campuswide network can be accessed from student residence rooms and from off campus. Online class registration is available.
Website: http://www.mtu.edu/

General Application Contact: Carol T. Wingerson, Administrative Aide, 906-487-2328, Fax: 906-487-2284, E-mail: gradadms@mtu.edu.

GRADUATE UNITS

Graduate School Students: 1,141 full-time (319 women), 353 part-time (92 women); includes 68 minority (21 Black or African American, non-Hispanic/Latino; 1 American Indian or Alaska Native, non-Hispanic/Latino; 13 Asian, non-Hispanic/Latino; 16 Hispanic/Latino; 17 Two or more races, non-Hispanic/Latino), 918 international. Average age 28. 5,159 applicants, 29% accepted, 466 enrolled. *Faculty:* 517 full-time (133 women), 256 part-time/adjunct (49 women). *Financial support:* In 2015–16, 924 students received support, including 71 fellowships with tuition reimbursements available (averaging $14,516 per year), 205 research assistantships with tuition reimbursements available (averaging $14,516 per year), 224 teaching assistantships with tuition reimbursements available (averaging $14,516 per year); career-related internships or fieldwork, Federal Work-Study, scholarships/grants, traineeships, health care benefits, unspecified assistantships, and cooperative program also available. Financial award applicants required to submit FAFSA. In 2015, 358 master's, 75 doctorates, 34 other advanced degrees awarded. *Degree program information:* Part-time programs available. Part-time, 100% online, blended/hybrid learning. Offers atmospheric sciences (PhD); biochemistry and molecular biology (PhD); computational science and engineering (PhD); data science (MS, Graduate Certificate); engineering (M Eng); environmental engineering (PhD); international profile (Graduate Certificate); nanotechnology (Graduate Certificate); sustainability (Graduate Certificate); sustainable water resources systems (Graduate Certificate). *Application deadline:* Applications are processed on a rolling basis. Electronic applications accepted. *Application Contact:* Carol T. Wingerson, Administrative Aide, 906-487-2328, Fax: 906-487-2284, E-mail: gradadms@mtu.edu. *Provost and Vice President for Academic Affairs,* Dr. Jacqueline E. Huntoon, 906-487-2440, Fax: 906-487-2284, E-mail: jeh@mtu.edu.

College of Engineering Students: 758 full-time (162 women), 219 part-time (39 women); includes 41 minority (13 Black or African American, non-Hispanic/Latino; 7 Asian, non-Hispanic/Latino; 14 Hispanic/Latino; 7 Two or more races, non-Hispanic/Latino), 700 international. Average age 27. 3,505 applicants, 33% accepted, 329 enrolled. *Faculty:* 271 full-time (46 women), 125 part-time/adjunct (13 women). *Financial support:* In 2015–16, 574 students received support, including 45 fellowships with tuition reimbursements available (averaging $14,516 per year), 121 research assistantships with tuition reimbursements available (averaging $14,516 per year), 79 teaching assistantships with tuition reimbursements available (averaging $14,516 per year); career-related internships or fieldwork, Federal Work-Study, scholarships/grants, health care benefits, unspecified assistantships, and cooperative program also available. Financial award applicants required to submit FAFSA. In 2015, 261 master's, 41 doctorates, 30 other advanced degrees awarded. *Degree program information:* Part-time programs available. Part-time, online learning. Offers advanced electric power engineering (Graduate Certificate); biomedical engineering (MS, PhD); chemical engineering (MS, PhD); civil engineering (MS, PhD); computer engineering (MS, PhD); electrical engineering (MS, PhD); engineering (MS, PhD, Graduate Certificate); engineering mechanics (MS); environmental engineering (MS); environmental engineering science (MS); geological engineering (MS, PhD); geology (MS, PhD); geophysics (MS, PhD); hybrid electric drive vehicle engineering (Graduate Certificate); materials science and engineering (MS, PhD); mechanical engineering (MS); mechanical engineering-engineering mechanics (PhD); mining engineering (MS, PhD). *Application deadline:* Applications are processed on a rolling basis. Electronic applications accepted. *Application Contact:* Carol T. Wingerson, Administrative Aide, 906-487-2328, Fax: 906-487-2284, E-mail: gradadms@mtu.edu. *Dean,* Dr. Wayne D. Pennington, 906-487-2005, Fax: 906-487-2782, E-mail: wayne@mtu.edu.

College of Sciences and Arts Students: 236 full-time (99 women), 75 part-time (35 women); includes 18 minority (6 Black or African American, non-Hispanic/Latino; 1 American Indian or Alaska Native, non-Hispanic/Latino; 3 Asian, non-Hispanic/Latino; 1 Hispanic/Latino; 7 Two or more races, non-Hispanic/Latino), 135 international. Average age 31. 1,111 applicants, 19% accepted, 65 enrolled. *Faculty:* 257 full-time (87 women), 78 part-time/adjunct (20 women). *Financial support:* In 2015–16, 233 students received support, including 10 fellowships with tuition reimbursements available (averaging $14,516 per year), 51 research assistantships with tuition reimbursements available (averaging $14,516 per year), 127 teaching assistantships with tuition reimbursements available (averaging $14,516 per year); career-related internships or fieldwork, Federal Work-Study, scholarships/grants, traineeships, health care benefits, unspecified assistantships, and cooperative program also available. Financial award applicants required to submit FAFSA. In 2015, 51 master's, 22 doctorates awarded. *Degree program information:* Part-time programs available. Part-time, online learning. Offers applied cognitive science and human factors (MS, PhD); applied physics (MS); applied science education (MS); biological sciences (MS, PhD); chemistry (MS, PhD); computer science (MS, PhD); engineering physics (PhD); environmental and energy policy (MS, PhD); industrial archaeology (MS); industrial heritage and archeology (PhD); kinesiology (MS); mathematical sciences (MS, PhD); physics (MS, PhD); post-secondary STEM education (Graduate Certificate); rhetoric, theory and culture (MS, PhD); sciences and arts (MS, PhD, Graduate Certificate). *Application deadline:* For fall admission, 4/1 for domestic and international students; for spring admission, 9/1 for domestic and international students. Applications are processed on a rolling basis. Electronic applications accepted. *Application Contact:* Carol T. Wingerson, Administrative Aide, 906-487-2328, Fax: 906-487-2284, E-mail: gradadms@mtu.edu. *Dean,* Dr. Bruce E. Seely, 906-487-2156, Fax: 906-487-3347, E-mail: bseely@mtu.edu.

School of Business and Economics Students: 24 full-time (7 women), 19 part-time (9 women); includes 3 minority (1 Black or African American, non-Hispanic/Latino; 1 Asian, non-Hispanic/Latino; 1 Hispanic/Latino), 14 international. Average age 29. 115 applicants, 29% accepted, 17 enrolled. *Faculty:* 28 full-time (8 women), 1 part-time/adjunct. *Financial support:* In 2015–16, 19 students received support. Career-related internships or fieldwork, health care benefits, unspecified assistantships, and cooperative program available. Support available to part-time students. Financial award application deadline: 4/1; financial award applicants required to submit FAFSA. In 2015, 18 master's awarded. *Degree program information:* Part-time and evening/weekend programs available. Part-time, evening/weekend. Offers accounting (MS); applied natural resource economics (MS); business administration (MBA). *Application deadline:* For fall admission, 7/1 for domestic and international students; for spring admission, 12/1 for domestic and international students. Applications are processed on a rolling basis. Electronic applications accepted. *Application Contact:* Carol T. Wingerson, Administrative Aide, 906-487-2328, Fax: 906-487-2284, E-mail: gradadms@mtu.edu. *Interim Dean,* Dr. Dean Johnson, 906-487-2668, Fax: 906-487-1863, E-mail: dean@mtu.edu.

School of Forest Resources and Environmental Science Students: 58 full-time (24 women), 23 part-time (6 women); includes 2 minority (both Two or more races, non-Hispanic/Latino), 19 international. Average age 31. 92 applicants, 51% accepted, 32 enrolled. *Faculty:* 41 full-time (11 women), 52 part-time/adjunct (18 women). *Financial support:* In 2015–16, 51 students received support, including 6 fellowships with tuition reimbursements available (averaging $14,516 per year), 17 research assistantships with tuition reimbursements available (averaging $14,516 per year), 6 teaching assistantships with tuition reimbursements available (averaging $14,516 per year); career-related internships or fieldwork, Federal Work-Study, scholarships/grants, health care benefits, unspecified assistantships, and cooperative program also available. Financial award applicants required to submit FAFSA. In 2015, 16 master's, 5 doctorates awarded. *Degree program information:* Part-time programs available. Part-time. Offers applied ecology (MS); forest ecology and management (MS); forest molecular genetics and biotechnology (MS, PhD); forest science (PhD); forestry (MF, MS); geographic information science (MGIS). *Application deadline:* Applications are processed on a rolling basis. Electronic applications accepted. *Application Contact:* Dr. Andrew J. Storer, Associate Dean, 906-487-3470, Fax: 906-487-2915, E-mail: storer@mtu.edu. *Dean,* Dr. Terry Sharik, 906-487-2352, Fax: 906-487-2915, E-mail: tlsharik@mtu.edu.

School of Technology Students: 12 full-time (5 women), 7 part-time (2 women); includes 2 minority (1 Black or African American, non-Hispanic/Latino; 1 Asian, non-Hispanic/Latino), 6 international. Average age 35. 36 applicants, 44% accepted, 6 enrolled. *Faculty:* 27 full-time, 4 part-time/adjunct. *Financial support:* In 2015–16, 9 students received support, including 3 fellowships with tuition reimbursements available (averaging $14,516 per year); career-related internships or fieldwork, Federal Work-Study, scholarships/grants, and health care benefits also available. Financial award applicants required to submit FAFSA. In 2015, 9 master's awarded. *Degree program information:* Part-time programs available. Part-time. Offers integrated geospatial technology (MS); medical informatics (MS). *Application deadline:* Applications are processed on a rolling basis. Electronic applications accepted. *Application Contact:* Peggy A. Gorton, Executive Assistant, 906-487-2260, Fax: 906-487-2583, E-mail: pagorton@mtu.edu. *Dean,* Dr. James O. Frendewey, 906-487-2260, Fax: 906-487-2583, E-mail: jimf@mtu.edu.

MID-AMERICA BAPTIST THEOLOGICAL SEMINARY, Cordova, TN 38016

General Information Independent-religious, men only, comprehensive institution. *Graduate housing:* Rooms and/or apartments available on a first-come, first-served basis to single and married students.

GRADUATE UNITS

Graduate and Professional Programs Offers theology (M Div, MACE, MCE, MM, D Min, PhD). Electronic applications accepted.

MID-AMERICA BAPTIST THEOLOGICAL SEMINARY NORTHEAST BRANCH, Schenectady, NY 12303-3463

General Information Independent-religious, coed, primarily men, graduate-only institution. *Graduate housing:* Rooms and/or apartments available on a first-come, first-served basis to single and married students.

GRADUATE UNITS

Program in Theology ***Degree program information:*** Part-time and evening/weekend programs available. Part-time, evening/weekend. Offers theology (M Div). Electronic applications accepted.

MID-AMERICA CHRISTIAN UNIVERSITY, Oklahoma City, OK 73170-4504

General Information Independent-religious, coed, comprehensive institution.

GRADUATE UNITS

Program in Business Administration Offers business administration (MBA).

Program in Counseling Offers marital and family therapy (MS); pastoral/spiritual direction (MS); professional counselor (MS).

Program in Leadership Offers leadership (MA).

Program in Public Administration Offers public administration (MA).

MIDAMERICA NAZARENE UNIVERSITY, Olathe, KS 66062-1899

General Information Independent-religious, coed, comprehensive institution. *Enrollment:* 2,015 graduate, professional, and undergraduate students; 103 full-time matriculated graduate/professional students (90 women), 288 part-time matriculated graduate/professional students (222 women). *Enrollment by degree level:* 391 master's. *Graduate faculty:* 29 full-time (18 women), 55 part-time/adjunct (27 women). *Tuition, area resident:* Part-time $19,184 per degree program. *Required fees:* $1063 per degree program. Tuition and fees vary according to program. *Graduate housing:* On-campus housing not available. *Student services:* Campus safety program, exercise/wellness program, free psychological counseling, international student services, teacher training. *Library:* Mabee Library. *Collection:* Books: 106,000 (physical), 249,000 (digital/electronic); Serial titles: 412 (physical), 10 (digital/electronic); Databases: 35. Weekly public service hours: 81; study areas open 24 hours, 5–7 days a week; students can reserve study rooms.

Computer facilities: 85 computers available on campus for general student use. A campuswide network can be accessed from student residence rooms and from off campus. Online class registration is available.
Website: http://www.mnu.edu/

General Application Contact: E-mail: pgadmissions@mnu.edu.

GRADUATE UNITS

Post-Licensure and Graduate Nursing Education Program Students: 9 full-time (8 women), 103 part-time (100 women); includes 23 minority (14 Black or African American, non-Hispanic/Latino; 1 American Indian or Alaska Native, non-Hispanic/Latino; 4 Asian, non-Hispanic/Latino; 4 Hispanic/Latino). 50 applicants, 82% accepted. *Faculty:* 8 full-time (all women), 6 part-time/adjunct (3 women). *Financial support:* Unspecified assistantships available. Financial award applicants required to submit FAFSA. In 2015, 36 master's awarded. *Degree program information:* Part-time programs available. Part-time, 100% online, blended/hybrid learning. Offers healthcare administration (MSN); healthcare quality management (MSN); nursing education (MSN); public health (MSN). *Application deadline:* Applications are processed on a rolling basis. Electronic applications accepted. *Application Contact:* E-mail: pgadmissions@mnu.edu. *Dean*, Dr. Karen Wiegman, RN, 913-971-3839, E-mail: kdwiegman@mnu.edu.

Professional and Graduate Studies in Education Students: 23 full-time (19 women), 38 part-time (30 women); includes 3 minority (2 Black or African American, non-Hispanic/Latino; 1 Asian, non-Hispanic/Latino). 20 applicants, 30% accepted. *Faculty:* 6 full-time (4 women), 14 part-time/adjunct (8 women). *Financial support:* Applicants required to submit FAFSA. In 2015, 34 master's awarded. *Degree program information:* Part-time and evening/weekend programs available. Part-time, evening/weekend, 100% online, blended/hybrid learning. Offers ESOL (M Ed); professional teaching (M Ed); reading specialist (M Ed); special education (MA); technology enhanced teaching (M Ed). *Application deadline:* Applications are processed on a rolling basis. Electronic applications accepted. *Application Contact:* Glenna Murray, Administrative Assistant, 913-971-3292, Fax: 913-971-3002, E-mail: gkmurray@mnu.edu. *Director*, Dr. Ramona Stowe, 913-971-3524, Fax: 913-971-3407, E-mail: rsstowe@mnu.edu.

School of Behavioral Sciences and Counseling Students: 71 full-time (63 women), 54 part-time (42 women); includes 22 minority (16 Black or African American, non-Hispanic/Latino; 1 American Indian or Alaska Native, non-Hispanic/Latino; 3 Asian, non-Hispanic/Latino; 1 Hispanic/Latino; 1 Native Hawaiian or other Pacific Islander, non-Hispanic/Latino). 147 applicants, 46% accepted, 67 enrolled. *Faculty:* 9 full-time (4 women), 15 part-time/adjunct (9 women). *Financial support:* Applicants required to submit FAFSA. In 2015, 62 master's awarded. *Degree program information:* Evening/weekend programs available. Evening/weekend. Offers counseling (MAC); play therapy (PMC). *Application deadline:* For fall admission, 4/1 for domestic students. Applications are processed on a rolling basis. Electronic applications accepted. *Application Contact:* Aileen Douglas, Administrative Assistant, 913-971-3730, Fax: 913-791-3402, E-mail: jmblades@mnu.edu. *Director*, Dr. Todd Frye, 913-971-3731, Fax: 913-971-3402, E-mail: tmfrye@mnu.edu.

School of Business Students: 93 part-time (50 women); includes 26 minority (17 Black or African American, non-Hispanic/Latino; 2 American Indian or Alaska Native, non-Hispanic/Latino; 2 Asian, non-Hispanic/Latino; 4 Hispanic/Latino; 1 Two or more races, non-Hispanic/Latino). Average age 34. 77 applicants, 58% accepted, 45 enrolled. *Faculty:* 6 full-time (2 women), 20 part-time/adjunct (7 women). *Financial support:* In 2015–16, 20 students received support. Tuition waivers and unspecified assistantships available. Financial award applicants required to submit FAFSA. In 2015, 43 master's awarded. *Degree program information:* Part-time and evening/weekend programs available. Part-time, evening/weekend, 100% online, blended/hybrid learning. Offers management (MBA, MSM). *Application deadline:* Applications are processed on a rolling basis. Electronic applications accepted. *Application Contact:* Piper Childs, Director of School of Professional and Graduate Studies Enrollment Services, 913-971-3804, E-mail: pmchilds@mnu.edu. *Professor and Chair, Graduate Studies in Management*, Dr. Graydon Dawson, 913-971-3873, Fax: 913-791-3409, E-mail: rgdawson@mnu.edu.

MID-AMERICA REFORMED SEMINARY, Dyer, IN 46311

General Information Independent-religious, men only, graduate-only institution.

GRADUATE UNITS

Graduate Programs Offers theology (M Div, MTS).

MIDDLEBURY COLLEGE, Middlebury, VT 05753-6002

General Information Independent, coed, comprehensive institution. *Enrollment:* 2,558 graduate, professional, and undergraduate students; 805 full-time matriculated graduate/professional students (548 women). *Graduate faculty:* 302 full-time (162 women). Full-time tuition and fees vary according to program. *Graduate housing:* Room and/or apartments guaranteed to single students; on-campus housing not available to married students. Typical cost: $3215 (including board). *Student services:* Campus safety program, career counseling, free psychological counseling, international student services, services for students with disabilities, teacher training. *Library:* Davis Family Library plus 2 others. *Collection:* Books: 764,667 (physical), 644,056 (digital/electronic); Databases: 695. Weekly public service hours: 112; students can reserve study rooms.

Computer facilities: Computer purchase and lease plans are available. 250 computers available on campus for general student use. A campuswide network can be accessed from student residence rooms and from off campus. Online class registration, helpdesk, personal Web pages, file servers are available.
Website: http://www.middlebury.edu/

General Application Contact: Admissions Office, 802-443-3000, Fax: 802-443-2056, E-mail: admissions@middlebury.edu.

GRADUATE UNITS

Language Schools Students: 393 full-time (276 women); includes 101 minority (8 Black or African American, non-Hispanic/Latino; 29 Asian, non-Hispanic/Latino; 54 Hispanic/Latino; 10 Two or more races, non-Hispanic/Latino). Average age 33. 745 applicants, 74% accepted, 419 enrolled. *Faculty:* 257 full-time (142 women). *Financial support:* Fellowships and scholarships/grants available. Financial award applicants required to submit FAFSA. In 2015, 128 master's, 7 doctorates awarded. Offers language (MA, DML). *Application deadline:* For summer admission, 5/1 for domestic and international students. Applications are processed on a rolling basis. *Application fee:* $75. Electronic applications accepted. *Application Contact:* Kara Gennarelli, Technical and Lead Coordinator, Language Schools Office, 802-443-5727, Fax: 802-443-2075, E-mail: languages@middlebury.edu. *Dean of Language Schools*, Dr. Stephen B. Snyder, 802-443-5979, Fax: 802-443-2075, E-mail: ssnyder@middlebury.edu.

Arabic School Students: 27 full-time (11 women); includes 3 minority (2 Hispanic/Latino; 1 Two or more races, non-Hispanic/Latino). Average age 34. 54 applicants, 69% accepted, 28 enrolled. *Faculty:* 40 full-time (17 women). *Financial support:* Fellowships and scholarships/grants available. Financial award application deadline: 3/14; financial award applicants required to submit FAFSA. In 2015, 7 master's awarded. Offers Arabic language pedagogy (MA); Arabic studies (MA). *Application deadline:* For summer admission, 5/1 for domestic and international students. Applications are processed on a rolling basis. *Application fee:* $75. Electronic applications accepted. *Application Contact:* Barbara Walter, Coordinator, 802-443-5230, Fax: 802-443-2075, E-mail: bwalter@middlebury.edu. *Director*, Dr. Mahmoud Abdalla, 802-443-5230, Fax: 802-443-2075, E-mail: mabdalla@miis.edu.

Chinese School Students: 28 full-time (26 women); includes 25 minority (22 Asian, non-Hispanic/Latino; 3 Two or more races, non-Hispanic/Latino). Average age 35. 36 applicants, 94% accepted, 28 enrolled. *Faculty:* 37 full-time (28 women). *Financial support:* Fellowships and scholarships/grants available. Financial award application deadline: 3/15; financial award applicants required to submit FAFSA. In 2015, 10 master's awarded. Offers Chinese (MA). *Application deadline:* Applications are processed on a rolling basis. *Application fee:* $75. Electronic applications accepted. *Application Contact:* Anna Sun, Coordinator, 802-443-5520, Fax: 802-443-2075, E-mail: sun@middlebury.edu. *Director*, Dr. Jianhua Bai, 802-443-5520, Fax: 802-443-2075, E-mail: jbai@middlebury.edu.

French School Students: 86 full-time (63 women), 1 (woman) part-time; includes 19 minority (6 Black or African American, non-Hispanic/Latino; 1 Asian, non-Hispanic/Latino; 11 Hispanic/Latino; 1 Two or more races, non-Hispanic/Latino). Average age 32. 149 applicants, 85% accepted, 93 enrolled. *Faculty:* 36 full-time (14 women). *Financial support:* Fellowships and scholarships/grants available. Financial award application deadline: 3/10; financial award applicants required to submit FAFSA. In 2015, 27 master's, 1 doctorate awarded. Offers French (MA, DML). *Application deadline:* Applications are processed on a rolling basis. *Application fee:* $75. Electronic applications accepted. *Application Contact:* Sheila Schwaneflugel, Coordinator, 802-443-5526, Fax: 802-443-2075, E-mail: sschwaneflugel@middlebury.edu. *Director*, Dr. Phillipe France, 802-443-5526, Fax: 802-443-2075.

German School Students: 10 full-time (5 women). Average age 28. 23 applicants, 74% accepted, 11 enrolled. *Faculty:* 20 full-time (7 women). *Financial support:* Fellowships and scholarships/grants available. Financial award application deadline: 3/9; financial award applicants required to submit FAFSA. In 2015, 3 master's awarded. Offers German (MA, DML). *Application deadline:* Applications are processed on a rolling basis. *Application fee:* $75. Electronic applications accepted. *Application Contact:* Christina Ellison, Coordinator, 802-443-5203, Fax: 802-443-2075, E-mail: ccartwri@middlebury.edu. *Director*, Dr. Bettina Matthias, 802-443-3248, Fax: 802-443-2075, E-mail: bmatthia@middlebury.edu.

Hebrew School Students: 17 full-time (16 women). Average age 43. 24 applicants, 83% accepted, 19 enrolled. *Faculty:* 20 full-time (10 women). *Financial support:* Fellowships and scholarships/grants available. Financial award application deadline: 3/28; financial award applicants required to submit FAFSA. Blended/hybrid learning. Offers Hebrew (MA). *Application deadline:* Applications are processed on a rolling basis. *Application fee:* $75. Electronic applications accepted. *Application Contact:* Kara Gennarelli, Technical and Lead Coordinator, Language Schools Office, 802-443-5727, Fax: 802-443-2075, E-mail: languages@middlebury.edu. *Director*, Vardit Ringvald, 802-443-3574, E-mail: vringval@middlebury.edu.

Italian School Students: 29 full-time (23 women); includes 6 minority (1 Asian, non-Hispanic/Latino; 3 Hispanic/Latino; 2 Two or more races, non-Hispanic/Latino). Average age 34. 55 applicants, 84% accepted, 34 enrolled. *Faculty:* 20 full-time (11 women). *Financial support:* Fellowships and scholarships/grants available. Financial award application deadline: 3/10; financial award applicants required to submit FAFSA. In 2015, 13 master's, 4 doctorates awarded. Offers Italian (MA, DML). *Application deadline:* Applications are processed on a rolling basis. *Application fee:* $75. Electronic applications accepted. *Application Contact:* Kara Gennarelli, Coordinator, 802-443-5727, Fax: 802-443-2075, E-mail: kgennar@middlebury.edu. *Director*, Dr. Antonio Vitti, 802-443-5727, Fax: 802-443-2075, E-mail: acvitti@middlebury.edu.

Russian School Students: 23 full-time (12 women); includes 3 minority (all Hispanic/Latino). Average age 28. 44 applicants, 93% accepted, 26 enrolled. *Faculty:* 29 full-time (22 women). *Financial support:* Fellowships and scholarships/grants available. Financial award application deadline: 3/14; financial award applicants required to submit FAFSA. In 2015, 5 master's awarded. Offers Russian (MA, DML). *Application deadline:* Applications are processed on a rolling basis. *Application fee:* $75. Electronic applications accepted. *Application Contact:* Oliver Carling, Coordinator, 802-443-2006, Fax: 802-443-2075, E-mail: ocarling@middlebury.edu. *Director*, Dr. Jason Merrill, 802-443-5230, Fax: 802-443-2075, E-mail: jmerrill@middlebury.edu.

Spanish School Students: 176 full-time (123 women); includes 45 minority (2 Black or African American, non-Hispanic/Latino; 5 Asian, non-Hispanic/Latino; 35 Hispanic/Latino; 3 Two or more races, non-Hispanic/Latino). Average age 32. 260 applicants, 89% accepted, 180 enrolled. *Faculty:* 47 full-time (29 women). *Financial support:* Fellowships and scholarships/grants available. Financial award application deadline: 3/8; financial award applicants required to submit FAFSA. In 2015, 63 master's, 2 doctorates awarded. Offers Spanish (MA, DML). *Application deadline:* Applications are processed on a rolling basis. *Application fee:* $75. Electronic applications accepted. *Application Contact:* Audrey LaRock, Coordinator, 802-443-5539, Fax: 802-443-2075, E-mail: larock@middlebury.edu. *Director*, Dr. Jacobo Sefami, 802-443-5539, Fax: 802-443-2075, E-mail: jsefami@middlelbury.edu.

Middlebury Bread Loaf School of English Students: 412 full-time (272 women); includes 52 minority (8 Black or African American, non-Hispanic/Latino; 2 American Indian or Alaska Native, non-Hispanic/Latino; 10 Asian, non-Hispanic/Latino; 22 Hispanic/Latino; 10 Two or more races, non-Hispanic/Latino), 17 international. Average age 33. 179 applicants, 78% accepted, 110 enrolled. *Faculty:* 45 full-time (20 women). *Financial support:* In 2015–16, 216 students received support, including 28 fellowships; scholarships/grants also available. Support available to part-time students. In 2015, 86 master's awarded. *Degree program information:* Part-time programs available. Part-time. Offers English (M Litt, MA). Offered during summer only. *Application deadline:* For summer admission, 5/13 for domestic and international students. Applications are processed on a rolling basis. *Application fee:* $65. Electronic applications accepted. *Application Contact:* Dana Olsen, Budget and Communications Manager/Director of Admissions, 802-443-5049, Fax: 802-443-2060, E-mail: dolsen@middlebury.edu. *Professor*, Dr. Emily Bartels, 802-443-5418, Fax: 802-443-2060, E-mail: blse@breadnet.middlebury.edu.

MIDDLEBURY INSTITUTE OF INTERNATIONAL STUDIES AT MONTEREY, Monterey, CA 93940-2691

General Information Independent, coed, graduate-only institution. *Enrollment:* 617 full-time matriculated graduate/professional students (421 women), 79 part-time matriculated graduate/professional students (52 women). *Enrollment by degree level:* 693 master's, 3 other advanced degrees. *Graduate faculty:* 81 full-time (41 women), 73 part-time/adjunct (37 women). *Tuition, area resident:* Full-time $37,100; part-time $1776 per credit. *Required fees:* $78 per semester. *Graduate housing:* On-campus housing not available. *Student services:* Campus employment opportunities, career counseling, exercise/wellness program, international student services, low-cost health insurance, services for students with disabilities, writing training. *Library:* William Tell Coleman

Library. *Collection:* Books: 121,799 (digital/electronic); Serial titles: 18,658 (digital/electronic). Students can reserve study rooms.

Computer facilities: 90 computers available on campus for general student use. Online class registration is available.
Website: http://www.miis.edu/

General Application Contact: Madeline Aiello, Admissions Office, 831-647-4116, Fax: 831-647-4188, E-mail: info@miis.edu.

GRADUATE UNITS

Graduate School of International Policy and Management Offers corporate risk management and compliance (MBA); international education management (MA); international environmental policy (MA); international policy and development (MA); international policy and management (MA, MBA, MPA); international trade and economic diplomacy (MA); nonproliferation and terrorism studies (MA); public administration (MPA). Electronic applications accepted.

Graduate School of Translation, Interpretation and Language Education Offers conference interpretation (MA); teaching English to speakers of other languages (MATESOL); teaching foreign language (MATFL); translation (MA); translation and interpretation (MA); translation and localization management (MA); translation, interpretation and language education (MA, MATESOL, MATFL). Electronic applications accepted.

MIDDLE GEORGIA STATE UNIVERSITY, Macon, GA 31206

General Information State-supported, coed, comprehensive institution. *Tuition, area resident:* Full-time $1755; part-time $1170 per semester. Tuition, nonresident: full-time $1755; part-time $1170 per semester. *Required fees:* $596 per semester. Tuition and fees vary according to course load, campus/location and program. *Student services:* Campus safety program, career counseling, services for students with disabilities. *Library:* Macon State University Library. *Collection:* Books: 143,214 (physical), 164,854 (digital/electronic); Serial titles: 4,554 (physical), 23,764 (digital/electronic); Databases: 138. Weekly public service hours: 23; students can reserve study rooms.

Computer facilities: 500 computers available on campus for general student use. A campuswide network can be accessed from student residence rooms and from off campus. Online class registration is available.
Website: http://www.mga.edu/

General Application Contact: Melinda Rodgers, Graduate Admissions, 478-471-2312, Fax: 478-471-2469, E-mail: graduate.admissions@mga.edu.

GRADUATE UNITS

Office of Graduate Studies *Financial support:* Application deadline: 3/15; applicants required to submit FAFSA. Offers adult/gerontology acute care nurse practitioner (MSN); information technology (MS). *Application deadline:* For fall admission, 5/27 priority date for domestic students; for spring admission, 9/16 priority date for domestic students. *Application fee:* $40. *Application Contact:* Melinda Rodgers, Graduate Admissions, 478-471-2312, E-mail: graduate.admissions@mga.edu. *Interim Dean,* Dr. Loretta Clayton, 478-471-4762, Fax: 478-929-6714, E-mail: loretta.clayton@mga.edu.

MIDDLE TENNESSEE SCHOOL OF ANESTHESIA, Madison, TN 37116

General Information Independent-religious, coed, graduate-only institution. *Enrollment by degree level:* 136 master's, 8 doctoral. *Graduate faculty:* 6 full-time (2 women), 13 part-time/adjunct (4 women). *Graduate housing:* On-campus housing not available. *Library:* Nelda F. Ackerman Learning Resource Center.

Computer facilities: 10 computers available on campus for general student use.
Website: http://www.mtsa.edu/

General Application Contact: Pam Nimmo, Admission and Financial Aid Assistant, 615-868-6503, Fax: 615-732-7662, E-mail: pam@mtsa.edu.

GRADUATE UNITS

Graduate Programs Students: 144 full-time (72 women). *Faculty:* 6 full-time (2 women), 13 part-time/adjunct (4 women). *Financial support:* Traineeships available. Offers anesthesia (MS, DNAP). *Application deadline:* For fall admission, 10/31 for domestic students. Applications are processed on a rolling basis. *Application Contact:* Pam Nimmo, Admissions, 615-868-6503, Fax: 615-732-7662, E-mail: pam@mtsa.edu. *Dean and Program Administrator,* Dr. Chris Hulin, 615-732-7841, Fax: 615-732-7676, E-mail: chris.hulin@mtsa.edu.

MIDDLE TENNESSEE STATE UNIVERSITY, Murfreesboro, TN 37132

General Information State-supported, coed, university. CGS member. *Graduate housing:* Rooms and/or apartments available on a first-come, first-served basis to single and married students.

GRADUATE UNITS

College of Graduate Studies ***Degree program information:*** Part-time and evening/weekend programs available. Part-time, evening/weekend, online learning. Offers mathematics and science education (PhD). Electronic applications accepted.

College of Basic and Applied Sciences Degree program information: Part-time and evening/weekend programs available. Part-time, evening/weekend, online learning. Offers actuarial sciences (MS); aerospace education (M Ed); aviation administration (MS); basic and applied sciences (M Ed, MS, MSN, MST, PhD, Graduate Certificate); biology (MS); biostatistics (MS); biotechnology (MS); chemistry (MS); computational science (PhD); computer science (MS); engineering management (MS); engineering technology (MS); health care informatics (MS); horse science (MS); mathematics (MS, MST); molecular biosciences (PhD). Electronic applications accepted.

College of Behavioral and Health Sciences Offers behavioral and health sciences (MA, MCJ, MS, MSN, MSW, PhD, Ed S, Graduate Certificate); clinical psychology (MA); criminal justice administration (MCJ); exercise science (MS); experimental psychology (MA); family nurse practitioner (MSN, Graduate Certificate); health and human performance (MS); health, physical education and recreation (MS); human performance (PhD); industrial/organizational psychology (MA); leisure and sport management (MS); nursing (MSN, Graduate Certificate); psychology (MA, Ed S); quantitative psychology (MA); school psychology (MA); social work (MSW). Electronic applications accepted.

College of Education Degree program information: Part-time and evening/weekend programs available. Part-time, evening/weekend, online learning. Offers administration and supervision (M Ed, Ed S); curriculum and instruction (M Ed, Ed S); early childhood education (M Ed); education (M Ed, PhD, Ed S); elementary education (M Ed, Ed S); English as a second language (M Ed, Ed S); literacy studies (PhD); mental health counseling (M Ed); middle school education (M Ed); professional counseling (M Ed); reading (M Ed); school counseling (M Ed); secondary education (M Ed); special education (M Ed); technology and curriculum design (Ed S). Electronic applications accepted.

College of Liberal Arts Degree program information: Part-time and evening/weekend programs available. Part-time, evening/weekend, online learning. Offers archival management (Graduate Certificate); English (MA, PhD); foreign languages (MAT); geosciences (Graduate Certificate); gerontology (Graduate Certificate); history (MA); international affairs (MA); liberal arts (MA, MAT, MSW, PhD, Graduate Certificate); music (MA); public history (PhD); sociology (MA); women's and gender studies (Graduate Certificate). Electronic applications accepted.

College of Mass Communication Degree program information: Part-time and evening/weekend programs available. Part-time, evening/weekend, online learning. Offers mass communication (MFA, MS); recording arts and technologies (MFA). Electronic applications accepted.

Jennings A. Jones College of Business Degree program information: Part-time and evening/weekend programs available. Part-time, evening/weekend, online learning. Offers accounting (M Acc); business (M Acc, MA, MBA, MBE, MS, PhD); business administration (MBA); business education (MBE); computer information systems (MS); economics (MA, PhD); management (MS). Electronic applications accepted.

University College Degree program information: Part-time and evening/weekend programs available. Part-time, evening/weekend, online learning. Offers advanced studies in teaching and learning (M Ed); human resources leadership (MPS); nursing administration (MSN); nursing education (MSN); strategic leadership (MPS); training and development (MPS).

MIDWAY UNIVERSITY, Midway, KY 40347-1120

General Information Independent-religious, coed, comprehensive institution. *Graduate housing:* On-campus housing not available.

GRADUATE UNITS

Graduate Programs Offers education (MAT); leadership (MBA).

MIDWEST COLLEGE OF ORIENTAL MEDICINE, Racine, WI 53403-9747

General Information Proprietary, coed, graduate-only institution. *Graduate housing:* On-campus housing not available. *Research affiliation:* Guangzhou University of Traditional Chinese Medicine (pharmacology).

GRADUATE UNITS

Graduate Programs ***Degree program information:*** Part-time and evening/weekend programs available. Part-time, evening/weekend. Offers acupuncture (Certificate); oriental medicine (MSOM).

Graduate Programs-Chicago ***Degree program information:*** Part-time and evening/weekend programs available. Part-time, evening/weekend.

MIDWESTERN BAPTIST THEOLOGICAL SEMINARY, Kansas City, MO 64118-4697

General Information Independent-religious, coed, graduate-only institution. *Graduate housing:* Rooms and/or apartments guaranteed to single and married students.

GRADUATE UNITS

Graduate and Professional Programs ***Degree program information:*** Part-time programs available. Part-time, online learning. Offers Christian education (MACE); Christian foundations (Graduate Certificate); church music (MCM); counseling (MA); ministry (D Ed Min, D Min); Old or New Testament studies (PhD); theology (M Div). Electronic applications accepted.

MIDWESTERN STATE UNIVERSITY, Wichita Falls, TX 76308

General Information State-supported, coed, comprehensive institution. *Graduate housing:* Rooms and/or apartments available on a first-come, first-served basis to single and married students.

GRADUATE UNITS

Billie Doris McAda Graduate School ***Degree program information:*** Part-time and evening/weekend programs available. Part-time, evening/weekend. Electronic applications accepted.

College of Science and Mathematics Degree program information: Part-time and evening/weekend programs available. Part-time, evening/weekend. Offers biology (MS); computer science (MS); science and mathematics (MS). Electronic applications accepted.

Dillard College of Business Administration Degree program information: Part-time and evening/weekend programs available. Part-time, evening/weekend. Offers business administration (MBA). Electronic applications accepted.

Prothro-Yeager College of Humanities and Social Sciences Degree program information: Part-time and evening/weekend programs available. Part-time, evening/weekend. Offers clinical/counseling psychology (MA); English (MA); history (MA); humanities and social sciences (MA, PhD); philosophy (PhD); political science (MA). Electronic applications accepted.

Robert D. and Carol Gunn College of Health Sciences and Human Services Degree program information: Part-time and evening/weekend programs available. Part-time, evening/weekend. Offers criminal justice (MA); exercise physiology (MS); family nurse practitioner (MSN); family psychiatric mental health nurse practitioner (MSN); health information management (MHA); health sciences and human services (MA, MHA, MS, MSN, Graduate Certificate); health services administration (Graduate Certificate); medical practice management (MHA); nurse educator (MSN); public and community sector health care management (MHA); radiologic sciences (MS); rural and urban hospital management (MHA). Electronic applications accepted.

West College of Education Degree program information: Part-time and evening/weekend programs available. Part-time, evening/weekend. Offers counseling (MA); curriculum and instruction (M Ed); education (M Ed, MA); educational leadership (M Ed); educational technology (M Ed); human resource development (MA); reading (M Ed); school counseling (M Ed); special education (M Ed); sport administration (M Ed); training and development (MA). Electronic applications accepted.

MIDWESTERN UNIVERSITY, DOWNERS GROVE CAMPUS, Downers Grove, IL 60515-1235

General Information Independent, coed, graduate-only institution. *Graduate housing:* Rooms and/or apartments available on a first-come, first-served basis to single and married students.

GRADUATE UNITS

Chicago College of Osteopathic Medicine Offers osteopathic medicine (DO).

Chicago College of Pharmacy ***Degree program information:*** Part-time programs available. Part-time, online learning. Offers pharmacy (Pharm D).

College of Dental Medicine-Illinois Offers dental medicine (DMD).

College of Health Sciences, Illinois Campus Offers biomedical sciences (MA, MBS); clinical psychology (MA, Psy D); health science (DHS); health sciences (MA, MBS, MMS, MOT, DHS, DPT, Psy D); occupational therapy (MOT); physical therapy (DPT); physician assistant studies (MMS).

MIDWESTERN UNIVERSITY, GLENDALE CAMPUS, Glendale, AZ 85308

General Information Independent, coed, graduate-only institution. *Graduate housing:* Rooms and/or apartments available on a first-come, first-served basis to single and married students.

GRADUATE UNITS

Arizona College of Optometry Offers optometry (OD).

Arizona College of Osteopathic Medicine Offers osteopathic medicine (DO). Electronic applications accepted.

College of Dental Medicine Offers dental medicine (DMD).

College of Health Sciences, Arizona Campus ***Degree program information:*** Part-time programs available. Part-time. Offers biomedical sciences (MA, MBS); cardiovascular science (MCVS); clinical psychology (Psy D); health sciences (MA, MBS, MCVS, MMS, MOT, MS, DPM, DPT, Psy D); nurse anesthesia (MS); occupational therapy (MOT); physical therapy (DPT); physician assistant studies (MMS); podiatric medicine (DPM).

College of Pharmacy-Glendale Offers pharmacy (Pharm D).

MIDWEST UNIVERSITY, Wentzville, MO 63385

General Information Independent-religious, coed, university. *Graduate housing:* Rooms and/or apartments available on a first-come, first-served basis to single and married students. Housing application deadline: 1/21.

MIDWIVES COLLEGE OF UTAH, Salt Lake City, UT 84106

General Information Independent, women only, comprehensive institution.

GRADUATE UNITS

Graduate Program Offers midwifery (MS).

MILLENNIA ATLANTIC UNIVERSITY, Doral, FL 33178

General Information Proprietary, coed, comprehensive institution.

GRADUATE UNITS

Graduate Programs Online learning.

MILLERSVILLE UNIVERSITY OF PENNSYLVANIA, Millersville, PA 17551-0302

General Information State-supported, coed, comprehensive institution. CGS member. *Enrollment:* 7,988 graduate, professional, and undergraduate students; 178 full-time matriculated graduate/professional students (135 women), 513 part-time matriculated graduate/professional students (371 women). *Enrollment by degree level:* 681 master's, 13 doctoral. *Graduate faculty:* 177 full-time (93 women), 98 part-time/adjunct (69 women). Tuition, state resident: full-time $8460; part-time $470 per credit. Tuition, nonresident: full-time $12,690; part-time $705 per credit. *Required fees:* $2471; $133.75 per credit. Tuition and fees vary according to course load, degree level and program. *Graduate housing:* Room and/or apartments available on a first-come, first-served basis to single students; on-campus housing not available to married students. Typical cost: $8034 per year ($12,188 including board). Room and board charges vary according to board plan and housing facility selected. *Student services:* Campus employment opportunities, campus safety program, career counseling, exercise/wellness program, free psychological counseling, grant writing training, international student services, low-cost health insurance, multicultural affairs office, services for students with disabilities, teacher training, writing training. *Library:* The Francine G. McNairy Library and Learning Forum at Ganser Hall. *Collection:* Books: 321,557 (physical), 52,503 (digital/electronic); Serial titles: 4,191 (physical), 271,204 (digital/electronic); Databases: 181. Weekly public service hours: 94; students can reserve study rooms. *Research affiliation:* Chincoteague Bay Field Station of the Marine Science Consortium (biology).

Computer facilities: 430 computers available on campus for general student use. A campuswide network can be accessed from student residence rooms and from off campus. Online class registration is available.
Website: http://www.millersville.edu/

General Application Contact: Dr. Victor S. DeSantis, Dean of College of Graduate Studies and Adult Education/Associate Provost for Civic and Community Engagement, 717-871-7619, Fax: 717-871-7954, E-mail: victor.desantis@millersville.edu.

GRADUATE UNITS

College of Graduate Studies and Adult Learning Students: 178 full-time (135 women), 513 part-time (371 women); includes 87 minority (29 Black or African American, non-Hispanic/Latino; 1 American Indian or Alaska Native, non-Hispanic/Latino; 14 Asian, non-Hispanic/Latino; 33 Hispanic/Latino; 1 Native Hawaiian or other Pacific Islander, non-Hispanic/Latino; 9 Two or more races, non-Hispanic/Latino), 7 international. 358 applicants, 68% accepted, 243 enrolled. *Faculty:* 177 full-time (93 women), 98 part-time/adjunct (69 women). *Financial support:* Application deadline: 3/15; applicants required to submit FAFSA. In 2015, 242 master's awarded. *Degree program information:* Part-time and evening/weekend programs available. Part-time, evening/weekend, online learning. Offers graduate studies and adult learning (M Ed, MA, MS, MSN, MSW, DSW, Ed D). *Application deadline:* For fall admission, 2/1 for domestic and international students; for spring admission, 10/1 for domestic and international students. *Application fee:* $40. Electronic applications accepted. *Dean of College of Graduate Studies and Adult Learning/Associate Provost for Civic and Community Engagement,* Dr. Victor S. DeSantis, 717-871-7619, Fax: 717-871-7954, E-mail: victor.desantis@millersville.edu.

College of Arts, Humanities and Social Sciences Students: 24 full-time (11 women), 51 part-time (32 women); includes 14 minority (3 Black or African American, non-Hispanic/Latino; 5 Asian, non-Hispanic/Latino; 6 Hispanic/Latino), 1 international. 25 applicants, 76% accepted, 19 enrolled. *Faculty:* 52 full-time (31 women), 24 part-time/adjunct (17 women). *Financial support:* Application deadline: 3/15; applicants required to submit FAFSA. In 2015, 24 master's awarded. *Degree program information:* Part-time programs available. Part-time. Offers art education (M Ed); arts, humanities and social sciences (M Ed, MA); English (M Ed, MA); history (MA); languages and cultures: French (MA); languages and cultures: German (MA); languages and cultures: Spanish (MA); social work (MSW, DSW). *Application deadline:* Applications are processed on a rolling basis. *Application fee:* $40. Electronic applications accepted. *Application Contact:* Dr. Victor S. DeSantis, Dean of College of Graduate Studies and Adult Learning/Associate Provost for Civic and Community Engagement, 717-871-7619, Fax: 717-871-7954, E-mail: victor.desantis@millersville.edu. *Dean,* Dr. Diane M. Umble, 717-871-7160, Fax: 717-871-7947, E-mail: diane.umble@millersville.edu.

College of Education and Human Services Students: 132 full-time (117 women), 306 part-time (242 women); includes 48 minority (21 Black or African American, non-Hispanic/Latino; 1 American Indian or Alaska Native, non-Hispanic/Latino; 2 Asian, non-Hispanic/Latino; 17 Hispanic/Latino; 7 Two or more races, non-Hispanic/Latino), 3 international. 245 applicants, 67% accepted, 164 enrolled. *Faculty:* 71 full-time (43 women), 54 part-time/adjunct (42 women). *Financial support:* Application deadline: 3/15; applicants required to submit FAFSA. In 2015, 159 master's awarded. Online learning. Offers assessment, curriculum and teaching - online teaching (M Ed); assessment, curriculum and teaching - STEM education (M Ed); clinical psychology (MS); early childhood education (M Ed); education (M Ed, MS, MSW, DSW, Ed D); educational leadership (Ed D); gifted education (M Ed); language and literacy (M Ed); language and literacy: ESL (M Ed); leadership for teaching and learning (M Ed); school counseling (M Ed); school psychology (MS); special education (M Ed); special education: 7-12 (M Ed); special education: PreK-8 (M Ed); sport management: athletic coaching (M Ed); sport management: athletic management (M Ed). *Application fee:* $40. Electronic applications accepted. *Application Contact:* Dr. Victor S. DeSantis, Dean of College of Graduate Studies and Adult Learning/Associate Provost for Civic and Community Engagement, 717-871-7619, Fax: 717-871-7954, E-mail: victor.desantis@millersville.edu. *Dean,* Dr. George Drake, 717-871-7333, E-mail: george.drake@millersville.edu.

College of Science and Technology Students: 22 full-time (7 women), 159 part-time (98 women); includes 25 minority (5 Black or African American, non-Hispanic/Latino; 7 Asian, non-Hispanic/Latino; 10 Hispanic/Latino; 1 Native Hawaiian or other Pacific Islander, non-Hispanic/Latino; 2 Two or more races, non-Hispanic/Latino), 3 international. Average age 34. 88 applicants, 68% accepted, 60 enrolled. *Faculty:* 54 full-time (19 women), 20 part-time/adjunct (10 women). *Financial support:* Application deadline: 3/15; applicants required to submit FAFSA. In 2015, 58 master's awarded. *Degree program information:* Part-time programs available. Part-time, online learning. Offers emergency management (MS); family nurse practitioner (MSN); integrated scientific applications: climate science applications (MS); integrated scientific applications: environmental systems management (MS); integrated scientific applications: geoinformatics (MS); integrated scientific applications: weather intelligence and risk management (MS); mathematics (M Ed); nursing education (MSN); science and technology (M Ed, MS, MSN); technology and innovation (M Ed). *Application deadline:* Applications are processed on a rolling basis. *Application fee:* $40. Electronic applications accepted. *Application Contact:* Dr. Victor S. DeSantis, Dean of College of Graduate Studies and Adult Learning/Associate Provost for Civic and Community Engagement, 717-871-7619, Fax: 717-871-7954, E-mail: victor.desantis@millersville.edu. *Dean,* Dr. Michael Jackson, 717-871-4292, E-mail: michael.jackson@millersville.edu.

MILLIGAN COLLEGE, Milligan College, TN 37682

General Information Independent-religious, coed, comprehensive institution. *Graduate housing:* Rooms and/or apartments available on a first-come, first-served basis to single and married students. Housing application deadline: 4/1.

GRADUATE UNITS

Area of Teacher Education ***Degree program information:*** Part-time programs available. Part-time. Offers teacher education (M Ed). Electronic applications accepted.

Emmanuel Christian Seminary at Milligan College ***Degree program information:*** Part-time programs available. Part-time, online learning. Offers Christian care and counseling (M Div); Christian education (M Div); Christian ministries (MCM); Christian ministry (M Div); Christian theology (M Div, MAR); church history (MAR); church history/historical theology (M Div); general studies (M Div); ministry (D Min); New Testament (M Div, MAR); Old Testament (M Div, MAR); urban ministry (M Div); world missions (M Div). Electronic applications accepted.

Program in Business Administration Online learning. Offers business administration (MBA). Electronic applications accepted.

Program in Occupational Therapy Students: 92 full-time (82 women). Average age 30. 400 applicants, 10% accepted, 32 enrolled. *Faculty:* 6 full-time (4 women), 5 part-time/adjunct (4 women). *Financial support:* In 2015–16, 55 students received support. Career-related internships or fieldwork and institutionally sponsored loans available. Financial award application deadline: 4/15; financial award applicants required to submit FAFSA. In 2015, 31 master's awarded. Offers occupational therapy (MSOT). *Application deadline:* For spring admission, 11/15 for domestic and international students. *Application fee:* $120. Electronic applications accepted. *Application Contact:* Kristia Brown, Office Manager and Admissions Representative, 423-975-8010, Fax: 423-975-8019, E-mail: kngarland@milligan.edu. *Department Chair/Professor,* Dr. Jeff Snodgrass, 423-975-8010, Fax: 423-975-8019, E-mail: jsnodgrass@milligan.edu.

MILLIKIN UNIVERSITY, Decatur, IL 62522-2084

General Information Independent-religious, coed, comprehensive institution. *Enrollment:* 2,154 graduate, professional, and undergraduate students; 73 full-time matriculated graduate/professional students (42 women), 14 part-time matriculated graduate/professional students (13 women). *Enrollment by degree level:* 61 master's, 26 doctoral. *Graduate faculty:* 20 full-time (16 women), 15 part-time/adjunct (7 women). *Tuition, area resident:* Part-time $750 per credit hour. Tuition and fees vary according to course load, degree level and program. *Student services:* Campus employment opportunities, career counseling, exercise/wellness program, grant writing training, international student services, multicultural affairs office, services for students with disabilities, writing training. *Library:* Staley Library. *Collection:* Books: 189,000 (physical), 82,000 (digital/electronic); Serial titles: 1,000 (physical), 53,000 (digital/electronic); Databases: 80. Weekly public service hours: 89.

Computer facilities: 282 computers available on campus for general student use. A campuswide network can be accessed from student residence rooms. Online class registration, online degree audit, online financials (view and pay bills, financial aid) are available.
Website: http://www.millikin.edu/

General Application Contact: Marianne Taylor, Director of Graduate Admission, 217-420-6771, Fax: 217-425-4669, E-mail: mgtaylor@millikin.edu.

GRADUATE UNITS

School of Nursing Students: 44 full-time (27 women), 14 part-time (13 women); includes 9 minority (5 Black or African American, non-Hispanic/Latino; 1 American Indian or Alaska Native, non-Hispanic/Latino; 1 Asian, non-Hispanic/Latino; 1 Hispanic/Latino; 1 Two or more races, non-Hispanic/Latino), 1 international. Average

age 32. 117 applicants, 29% accepted, 26 enrolled. *Faculty:* 11 full-time (all women), 4 part-time/adjunct (3 women). *Financial support:* Traineeships and unspecified assistantships available. Financial award applicants required to submit FAFSA. In 2015, 15 master's awarded. *Degree program information:* Part-time programs available. Part-time. Offers entry into nursing practice (MSN); nurse anesthesia (DNP); nurse educator (MSN); nursing practice (DNP). *Application deadline:* For spring admission, 7/1 priority date for domestic and international students; for summer admission, 11/1 priority date for domestic and international students. Applications are processed on a rolling basis. *Application fee:* $0. Electronic applications accepted. *Application Contact:* Bonnie Niemeyer, Administrative Assistant, 800-373-7733 Ext. 5034, Fax: 217-420-6677, E-mail: bniemeyer@millikin.edu. *Director*, Dr. Pamela Lindsey, 217-424-6348, Fax: 217-420-6731, E-mail: plindsey@millikin.edu.

Tabor School of Business Students: 28 full-time (15 women), 1 part-time (0 women); includes 8 minority (3 Black or African American, non-Hispanic/Latino; 1 Asian, non-Hispanic/Latino; 1 Hispanic/Latino; 3 Two or more races, non-Hispanic/Latino). Average age 31. 25 applicants, 92% accepted, 18 enrolled. *Faculty:* 3 full-time (1 woman), 6 part-time/adjunct (2 women). *Financial support:* Research assistantships and teaching assistantships available. Financial award applicants required to submit FAFSA. In 2015, 20 master's awarded. *Degree program information:* Evening/weekend programs available. Evening/weekend. Offers business (MBA). *Application deadline:* For fall admission, 6/1 priority date for domestic students, 4/1 for international students; for spring admission, 11/1 priority date for domestic students, 8/1 priority date for international students. Applications are processed on a rolling basis. *Application fee:* $0. Electronic applications accepted. *MBA Director/Associate Professor*, Dr. Anthony Liberatore, 217-424-6338, E-mail: aliberatore@millikin.edu.

MILLSAPS COLLEGE, Jackson, MS 39210-0001

General Information Independent-religious, coed, comprehensive institution. *Graduate housing:* Room and/or apartments available to single students; on-campus housing not available to married students. Housing application deadline: 6/1. *Research affiliation:* Downtown Jackson Partners Group (real estate development), Oxbow Ventures (commercialization of renewable energy), Midtown Partners (economic development).

GRADUATE UNITS

Else School of Management ***Degree program information:*** Part-time programs available. Part-time. Offers accounting (M Acc); business administration (MBA). Electronic applications accepted.

MILLS COLLEGE, Oakland, CA 94613-1000

General Information Independent, Undergraduate: women only; graduate: coed, comprehensive institution. *Enrollment:* 1,397 graduate, professional, and undergraduate students; 426 full-time matriculated graduate/professional students (336 women), 111 part-time matriculated graduate/professional students (91 women). *Enrollment by degree level:* 431 master's, 39 doctoral, 67 other advanced degrees. *Graduate faculty:* 47 full-time (31 women), 56 part-time/adjunct (40 women). *Tuition, area resident:* Full-time $31,620; part-time $17,530 per credit. *Required fees:* $1118; $1118 per unit. $574 per semester. Tuition and fees vary according to course load, degree level and program. *Graduate housing:* Rooms and/or apartments available on a first-come, first-served basis to single and married students. Typical cost: $6790 per year ($13,100 including board) for single students; $9320 per year ($15,730 including board) for married students. Room and board charges vary according to board plan and housing facility selected. Housing application deadline: 6/15. *Student services:* Campus employment opportunities, campus safety program, career counseling, exercise/wellness program, free psychological counseling, international student services, low-cost health insurance, multicultural affairs office, services for students with disabilities, teacher training, writing training. *Library:* F. W. Olin Library. *Collection:* Books: 186,191 (physical), 128,868 (digital/electronic); Serial titles: 263 (physical), 43,312 (digital/electronic); Databases: 51. Weekly public service hours: 89; students can reserve study rooms.

Computer facilities: Computer purchase and lease plans are available. 335 computers available on campus for general student use. A campuswide network can be accessed from student residence rooms and from off campus. Online class registration, online degree audit are available.
Website: http://www.mills.edu/

General Application Contact: Shrim Bathey, Director of Graduate Admission, 510-430-3125, Fax: 510-430-2159, E-mail: grad-studies@mills.edu.

GRADUATE UNITS

Graduate Studies Students: 425 full-time (335 women), 113 part-time (93 women); includes 250 minority (73 Black or African American, non-Hispanic/Latino; 3 American Indian or Alaska Native, non-Hispanic/Latino; 59 Asian, non-Hispanic/Latino; 80 Hispanic/Latino; 2 Native Hawaiian or other Pacific Islander, non-Hispanic/Latino; 33 Two or more races, non-Hispanic/Latino), 19 international. Average age 33. 885 applicants, 72% accepted, 291 enrolled. *Faculty:* 47 full-time (31 women), 56 part-time/adjunct (40 women). *Financial support:* In 2015–16, 565 students received support, including 169 teaching assistantships with tuition reimbursements available (averaging $6,219 per year); fellowships with tuition reimbursements available, research assistantships, career-related internships or fieldwork, institutionally sponsored loans, scholarships/grants, and unspecified assistantships also available. Support available to part-time students. Financial award application deadline: 2/1; financial award applicants required to submit FAFSA. In 2015, 219 master's, 10 doctorates, 120 other advanced degrees awarded. *Degree program information:* Part-time and evening/weekend programs available. Part-time, evening/weekend. Offers art (MFA); book art and creative writing (MFA); ceramics (MFA); choreography (MFA); composition (MA); computer science (Certificate); dance (MA); electronic music and recording media (MFA); infant mental health (MA); interdisciplinary computer science (MA); intermedia (MFA); literature (MA); painting (MFA); performance and choreography (MFA); performance and literature (MFA); photography (MFA); poetry (MFA); pre-medical studies (Certificate); prose (MFA); public policy (MPP); sculpture (MFA); Spanish creative writing (Certificate); translation (MFA). *Application deadline:* For fall admission, 12/15 priority date for domestic students, 12/15 for international students; for spring admission, 11/1 priority date for domestic students, 10/1 for international students. Applications are processed on a rolling basis. *Application fee:* $50. Electronic applications accepted. *Director of Graduate Admission*, Shrim Bathey, 510-430-3309, Fax: 510-430-2159, E-mail: grad-admissions@mills.edu.

Lorry I. Lokey Graduate School of Business Students: 47 full-time (41 women), 20 part-time (18 women); includes 41 minority (17 Black or African American, non-Hispanic/Latino; 7 Asian, non-Hispanic/Latino; 11 Hispanic/Latino; 1 Native Hawaiian or other Pacific Islander, non-Hispanic/Latino; 5 Two or more races, non-Hispanic/Latino), 5 international. Average age 33. 43 applicants, 65% accepted, 19 enrolled. *Faculty:* 3 full-time (all women), 13 part-time/adjunct (9 women). *Financial support:* In 2015–16, 77 students received support, including 6 teaching assistantships with tuition reimbursements available (averaging $1,900 per year); fellowships, scholarships/grants, and unspecified assistantships also available. Support available to part-time students. Financial award application deadline: 2/1; financial award applicants required to submit FAFSA. In 2015, 28 master's awarded. *Degree program information:* Part-time programs available. Part-time. Offers applied economics (MA); management (MBA). *Application deadline:* For fall admission, 2/1 priority date for domestic students, 12/15 for international students; for spring admission, 10/1 for domestic students. Applications are processed on a rolling basis. *Application fee:* $50. *Application Contact:* Shrim Bathey, Director of Graduate Admission, 510-430-3309, Fax: 510-430-2159, E-mail: grad-admission@mills.edu. *Interim Department Chair*, Bruce Patton, 510-430-3345, Fax: 510-430-2159, E-mail: bpaton@mills.edu.

School of Education Students: 125 full-time (109 women), 64 part-time (50 women); includes 77 minority (15 Black or African American, non-Hispanic/Latino; 3 American Indian or Alaska Native, non-Hispanic/Latino; 20 Asian, non-Hispanic/Latino; 30 Hispanic/Latino; 9 Two or more races, non-Hispanic/Latino), 6 international. Average age 30. 248 applicants, 77% accepted, 83 enrolled. *Faculty:* 12 full-time (10 women), 12 part-time/adjunct (8 women). *Financial support:* In 2015–16, 130 students received support, including 33 teaching assistantships with tuition reimbursements available (averaging $7,174 per year); fellowships with tuition reimbursements available, career-related internships or fieldwork, and scholarships/grants also available. Support available to part-time students. Financial award application deadline: 2/1; financial award applicants required to submit FAFSA. In 2015, 71 master's, 10 doctorates, 42 other advanced degrees awarded. *Degree program information:* Part-time and evening/weekend programs available. Part-time, evening/weekend. Offers child life in hospitals (MA); early childhood education (MA); education (MA); educational leadership (MA, Ed D); educational leadership: community colleges (Ed D); educational leadership: independent schools (MA); language, culture, and trauma (Certificate). *Application deadline:* For fall admission, 12/31 priority date for domestic students, 12/15 for international students; for spring admission, 11/1 priority date for domestic students, 10/1 for international students. Applications are processed on a rolling basis. *Application fee:* $50. Electronic applications accepted. *Application Contact:* Shrim Bathey, Director of Graduate Admission, 510-430-3309, Fax: 510-430-2159, E-mail: grad-admission@mills.edu. *Department Head*, Dr. Diane Ketelle, 510-430-3190, Fax: 510-430-2159, E-mail: dketelle@mills.edu.

MILWAUKEE SCHOOL OF ENGINEERING, Milwaukee, WI 53202-3109

General Information Independent, coed, primarily men, comprehensive institution. *Enrollment:* 2,939 graduate, professional, and undergraduate students; 61 full-time matriculated graduate/professional students (22 women), 166 part-time matriculated graduate/professional students (42 women). *Enrollment by degree level:* 227 master's. *Graduate faculty:* 28 full-time (13 women), 48 part-time/adjunct (18 women). *Tuition, area resident:* Full-time $34,200; part-time $760 per credit. *Graduate housing:* Room and/or apartments available on a first-come, first-served basis to single students; on-campus housing not available to married students. Typical cost: $7824 per year ($11,109 including board). Room and board charges vary according to board plan. Housing application deadline: 7/1. *Student services:* Campus employment opportunities, campus safety program, career counseling, exercise/wellness program, international student services, multicultural affairs office, services for students with disabilities, writing training. *Collection:* Books: 68,970 (physical), 305,378 (digital/electronic); Serial titles: 2,000 (physical), 2,431 (digital/electronic); Databases: 98. Weekly public service hours: 96; students can reserve study rooms. *Research affiliation:* Keen Foundation (entrepreneurship and engineering education), National Fluid Power Association (hydraulics and pneumatics), 3dMD (biomolecular modeling), National Additine Manufacturing Innovation Institute (rapid prototyping), Caterpillar, Inc. (electrohydraulics), Clinical Translational Science Institute (medical/healthcare innovation and transfer).

Computer facilities: Computer purchase and lease plans are available. A campuswide network can be accessed from student residence rooms and from off campus. Online class registration is available.
Website: http://www.msoe.edu/

General Application Contact: Ian Dahlinghaus, Graduate Admissions Counselor, 414-277-7208, E-mail: dahlinghaus@msoe.edu.

GRADUATE UNITS

Civil and Architectural Engineering and Construction Management Department Students: 8 full-time (0 women), 1 international. 13 applicants, 38% accepted, 4 enrolled. *Faculty:* 3 full-time (0 women), 2 part-time/adjunct (0 women). *Financial support:* Research assistantships, career-related internships or fieldwork, institutionally sponsored loans, and scholarships/grants available. Financial award application deadline: 3/15; financial award applicants required to submit FAFSA. In 2015, 12 master's awarded. *Degree program information:* Part-time and evening/weekend programs available. Part-time, evening/weekend. Offers architectural engineering (MSAE); civil engineering (MS). *Application deadline:* Applications are processed on a rolling basis. *Application fee:* $0. Electronic applications accepted. *Application Contact:* Ian Dahlinghaus, Graduate Program Associate, 414-277-7208, E-mail: dahlinghaus@msoe.edu. *Chair*, Dr. Blake E. Wentz, 414-277-2204, E-mail: wentz@msoe.edu.

Department of Electrical Engineering and Computer Science Students: 22 full-time (8 women), 35 part-time (8 women); includes 6 minority (2 Black or African American, non-Hispanic/Latino; 1 American Indian or Alaska Native, non-Hispanic/Latino; 2 Asian, non-Hispanic/Latino; 1 Hispanic/Latino), 12 international. Average age 28. 87 applicants, 30% accepted, 19 enrolled. *Faculty:* 3 full-time (0 women), 12 part-time/adjunct (4 women). *Financial support:* In 2015–16, 10 students received support, including 3 research assistantships (averaging $8,043 per year); career-related internships or fieldwork, institutionally sponsored loans, scholarships/grants, and tuition waivers (partial) also available. Financial award application deadline: 3/15; financial award applicants required to submit FAFSA. In 2015, 26 master's awarded. *Degree program information:* Part-time and evening/weekend programs available. Part-time, evening/weekend. Offers engineering (MS); perfusion (MS). *Application deadline:* Applications are processed on a rolling basis. *Application fee:* $0. Electronic applications accepted. *Application Contact:* Ian Dahlinghaus, Graduate Program Associate, 414-277-7208, E-mail: dahlinghaus@msoe.edu. *Chairman*, Dr. Steven Williams, 414-277-7420, E-mail: williams@msoe.edu.

Program in Health Care Systems Management Students: 4 full-time (all women), 6 part-time (all women); includes 2 minority (both Hispanic/Latino). 8 applicants, 75% accepted, 4 enrolled. *Faculty:* 1 (woman) full-time, 1 (woman) part-time/adjunct. *Financial support:* In 2015–16, 2 students received support. Scholarships/grants available. Financial award application deadline: 3/15; financial award applicants required to submit FAFSA. Offers health care systems management (MSN). *Application deadline:* Applications are processed on a rolling basis. Electronic applications accepted.

Application Contact: Ian Dahlinghaus, Graduate Admissions Counselor, 414-277-7208, E-mail: dahlinghaus@msoe.edu. *Department Chair,* Dr. Debra Jenks, 414-277-4516, E-mail: jenks@msoe.edu.

Rader School of Business Students: 47 full-time (17 women), 109 part-time (20 women); includes 22 minority (5 Black or African American, non-Hispanic/Latino; 1 American Indian or Alaska Native, non-Hispanic/Latino; 6 Asian, non-Hispanic/Latino; 10 Hispanic/Latino), 5 international. Average age 31. 79 applicants, 46% accepted, 25 enrolled. *Faculty:* 8 full-time (5 women), 21 part-time/adjunct (8 women). *Financial support:* In 2015–16, 15 fellowships (averaging $45,552 per year) were awarded; career-related internships or fieldwork, institutionally sponsored loans, scholarships/grants, traineeships, and tuition waivers (partial) also available. Financial award application deadline: 3/15; financial award applicants required to submit FAFSA. In 2015, 36 master's awarded. *Degree program information:* Part-time and evening/weekend programs available. Part-time, evening/weekend. Offers business administration (MBA); construction and business management (MS); education leadership (MBA); engineering management (MS); marketing and export management (MS); medical informatics (MS); new product management (MS); STEM leadership (MBA). *Application deadline:* Applications are processed on a rolling basis. *Application fee:* $0. Electronic applications accepted. *Application Contact:* Ian Dahlinghaus, Graduate Program Associate, 414-277-7208, E-mail: dahlinghaus@msoe.edu. *Chairman,* Dr. Steven Bialek, 414-277-7364, Fax: 414-277-7479, E-mail: bialek@msoe.edu.

See Display on next page and Close-Up on page 889.

MINNEAPOLIS COLLEGE OF ART AND DESIGN, Minneapolis, MN 55404-4347

General Information Independent, coed, comprehensive institution. *Graduate housing:* On-campus housing not available.

GRADUATE UNITS

Certificate Programs *Degree program information:* Part-time programs available. Part-time, online learning. Offers design (Certificate); fine arts (Certificate); graphic design (Certificate); media (Certificate); sustainable design (Certificate). Electronic applications accepted.

Program in Visual Studies *Degree program information:* Part-time programs available. Part-time. Offers animation (MFA); comic art (MFA); drawing (MFA); filmmaking (MFA); fine arts (MFA); furniture design (MFA); graphic design (MFA); illustration (MFA); interactive media (MFA); painting (MFA); photography (MFA); printmaking (MFA); sculpture (MFA). Electronic applications accepted.

MINNESOTA STATE UNIVERSITY MANKATO, Mankato, MN 56001

General Information State-supported, coed, university. CGS member. *Enrollment:* 15,407 graduate, professional, and undergraduate students; 710 full-time matriculated graduate/professional students (417 women), 1,276 part-time matriculated graduate/professional students (821 women). *Graduate housing:* Room and/or apartments available on a first-come, first-served basis to single students; on-campus housing not available to married students. *Student services:* Campus employment opportunities, campus safety program, career counseling, child daycare facilities, exercise/wellness program, free psychological counseling, international student services, low-cost health insurance, multicultural affairs office, services for students with disabilities, teacher training, writing training. *Library:* Memorial Library.

Computer facilities: Computer purchase and lease plans are available. 900 computers available on campus for general student use. A campuswide network can be accessed from student residence rooms and from off campus. Online class registration is available.
Website: http://www.mnsu.edu/

General Application Contact: Joni H. Miller, Information Contact, 507-389-2321, E-mail: grad@mnsu.edu.

GRADUATE UNITS

College of Graduate Studies and Research ***Financial support:*** Fellowships with full tuition reimbursements, research assistantships with tuition reimbursements, teaching assistantships with tuition reimbursements, career-related internships or fieldwork, Federal Work-Study, institutionally sponsored loans, scholarships/grants, and unspecified assistantships available. Support available to part-time students. Financial award application deadline: 3/15; financial award applicants required to submit FAFSA. *Degree program information:* Part-time programs available. Part-time, online learning. Offers cross-disciplinary studies (MS). *Application deadline:* For fall admission, 7/1 for domestic students, 5/1 for international students; for spring admission, 11/1 for domestic students, 10/1 for international students. Applications are processed on a rolling basis. *Application fee:* $40. Electronic applications accepted.

College of Allied Health and Nursing Financial support: Research assistantships with full tuition reimbursements, teaching assistantships with full tuition reimbursements, career-related internships or fieldwork, Federal Work-Study, institutionally sponsored loans, and unspecified assistantships available. Support available to part-time students. Financial award application deadline: 3/15; financial award applicants required to submit FAFSA. *Degree program information:* Part-time programs available. Part-time. Offers allied health and nursing (MA, MS, MSN, DNP, Postbaccalaureate Certificate); communication disorders (MS); community health education (MS); human performance (MA, MS); rehabilitation counseling (MS); school health education (MS, Postbaccalaureate Certificate). *Application deadline:* Applications are processed on a rolling basis. *Application fee:* $40. Electronic applications accepted. *Chairperson,* Julia Hebenstreit.

College of Arts and Humanities Financial support: Research assistantships with full tuition reimbursements, teaching assistantships with full tuition reimbursements, career-related internships or fieldwork, Federal Work-Study, institutionally sponsored loans, and unspecified assistantships available. Support available to part-time students. Financial award application deadline: 3/15; financial award applicants required to submit FAFSA. *Degree program information:* Part-time and evening/weekend programs available. Part-time, evening/weekend. Offers arts and humanities (MA, MAT, MFA, MM, MS, Certificate); communication education (Certificate); communication studies (MA, MS); creative writing (MFA); English (MAT); English studies (MA); forensics (MFA); French (MS); music (MAT, MM); professional communication (Certificate); Spanish (MS); studio art (MA); teaching art (MAT); teaching English as a second language (MA, Certificate); technical communication (MA, Certificate); theatre arts (MA, MFA). *Application deadline:* For fall admission, 7/1 for domestic students, 5/1 for international students; for spring admission, 11/1 for domestic students, 10/1 for international students. Applications are processed on a rolling basis. *Application fee:* $40.

College of Business Offers business (MBA). *Application deadline:* For fall admission, 7/1 for domestic students, 5/1 for international students; for spring admission, 11/1 for domestic students, 10/1 for international students. Electronic applications accepted.

College of Education Financial support: Fellowships with partial tuition reimbursements, research assistantships with full tuition reimbursements, teaching assistantships with full tuition reimbursements, career-related internships or fieldwork, Federal Work-Study, institutionally sponsored loans, and unspecified assistantships available. Support available to part-time students. Financial award application deadline: 3/15; financial award applicants required to submit FAFSA. *Degree program information:* Part-time and evening/weekend programs available. Part-time, evening/weekend. Offers college student affairs (MS); counselor education and supervision (Ed D); education (MAT, MS, Ed D, Certificate); educational leadership (MS, Ed D); emotional/behavioral disorders (MS, Certificate); experiential education (MS); learning disabilities (MS, Certificate); mental health counseling (MS); professional school counseling (k-12) (MS). *Application deadline:* Applications are processed on a rolling basis. *Application fee:* $40. Electronic applications accepted.

College of Science, Engineering and Technology Financial support: Research assistantships with full tuition reimbursements, teaching assistantships with full tuition reimbursements, career-related internships or fieldwork, Federal Work-Study, institutionally sponsored loans, and unspecified assistantships available. Support available to part-time students. Financial award application deadline: 3/15; financial award applicants required to submit FAFSA. *Degree program information:* Part-time programs available. Part-time. Offers biology (MS); biology education (MS); environmental sciences (MS); information technology (MS); manufacturing engineering technology (MS); mathematics (MA, MS); mathematics education (MS); physics and astronomy (MA, MS); science, engineering and technology (MA, MAT, MS, Certificate); statistics (MS). *Application deadline:* For fall admission, 7/1 priority date for domestic students; for spring admission, 11/1 for domestic students. Applications are processed on a rolling basis. *Application fee:* $40. Electronic applications accepted.

College of Social and Behavioral Sciences Financial support: Fellowships with partial tuition reimbursements, research assistantships with full tuition reimbursements, teaching assistantships with full tuition reimbursements, career-related internships or fieldwork, Federal Work-Study, institutionally sponsored loans, and unspecified assistantships available. Support available to part-time students. Financial award application deadline: 3/15; financial award applicants required to submit FAFSA. *Degree program information:* Part-time programs available. Part-time. Offers aging studies (MS); anthropology (MS); clinical psychology (MA); ethnic and multicultural studies (MS); gender and women's studies (MS); geography (MS); history (MA, MS); industrial/organizational psychology (MA); local government management (Certificate); public administration (MPA); school psychology (Psy D); social and behavioral sciences (MA, MAT, MPA, MS, MSW, Psy D); social studies (MAT); social work (MSW); sociology (MA); sociology: college teaching (MA); sociology: corrections (MS); sociology: human services planning and administration (MS); urban and regional studies (MA); urban planning (MA, Certificate). *Application deadline:* Applications are processed on a rolling basis. *Application fee:* $40. Electronic applications accepted.

MINNESOTA STATE UNIVERSITY MOORHEAD, Moorhead, MN 56563

General Information State-supported, coed, comprehensive institution. *Enrollment:* 5,836 graduate, professional, and undergraduate students; 180 full-time matriculated graduate/professional students (149 women), 392 part-time matriculated graduate/professional students (296 women). *Enrollment by degree level:* 489 master's, 83 other advanced degrees. *Graduate faculty:* 211 full-time, 27 part-time/adjunct. Tuition, state resident: full-time $9000; part-time $4500 per credit. Tuition, nonresident: full-time $18,000; part-time $9000 per credit. *Required fees:* $942; $39.25 per credit. One-time fee: $90 full-time. Full-time tuition and fees vary according to course load, degree level, program and reciprocity agreements. *Graduate housing:* Room and/or apartments available on a first-come, first-served basis to single students; on-campus housing not available to married students. Typical cost: $5572 per year ($8522 including board). Room and board charges vary according to board plan and housing facility selected. Housing application deadline: 3/1. *Student services:* Campus employment opportunities, campus safety program, career counseling, child daycare facilities, exercise/wellness program, free psychological counseling, grant writing training, international student services, low-cost health insurance, multicultural affairs office, services for students with disabilities, teacher training, writing training. *Library:* Livingston Lord Library plus 1 other. *Collection:* Books: 561,220 (physical), 15,357 (digital/electronic); Databases: 558. Students can reserve study rooms. *Research affiliation:* West Central Minnesota Business Innovation Center.

Computer facilities: Computer purchase and lease plans are available. 2,200 computers available on campus for general student use. A campuswide network can be accessed from student residence rooms and from off campus. Online class registration is available.
Website: http://www.mnstate.edu/

General Application Contact: Karla Wenger, Graduate Studies Office, 218-477-2344, Fax: 218-477-2482, E-mail: wengerk@mnstate.edu.

GRADUATE UNITS

Graduate Studies Students: 174 full-time (137 women), 427 part-time (337 women). Average age 33. *Faculty:* 211 full-time, 27 part-time/adjunct. *Financial support:* Career-related internships or fieldwork, Federal Work-Study, scholarships/grants, and unspecified assistantships available. Support available to part-time students. Financial award application deadline: 7/15; financial award applicants required to submit FAFSA. In 2015, 165 master's, 17 other advanced degrees awarded. *Degree program information:* Part-time and evening/weekend programs available. Part-time, evening/weekend, 100% online, blended/hybrid learning. *Application deadline:* Applications are processed on a rolling basis. *Application fee:* $20. Electronic applications accepted. *Application Contact:* Karla Wenger, Graduate Studies Office, 218-236-2344, Fax: 218-236-2482, E-mail: wengerk@mnstate.edu. *Director of Graduate Studies,* Dr. Lisa Karch, 218-477-2699, Fax: 218-236-2482, E-mail: lisa.karch@mnstate.edu.

College of Business and Innovation Students: 2 full-time (0 women), 27 part-time (11 women); includes 1 minority (American Indian or Alaska Native, non-Hispanic/Latino), 4 international. Average age 27. 10 applicants, 100% accepted. *Faculty:* 12 full-time (3 women). *Financial support:* Federal Work-Study and unspecified assistantships available. Financial award application deadline: 7/15; financial award applicants required to submit FAFSA. In 2015, 4 master's awarded. *Degree program information:* Part-time and evening/weekend programs available. Part-time, evening/weekend, 100% online, blended/hybrid learning. Offers accounting and finance (MS); business administration (MBA); health care management (MBA). *Application deadline:* For fall admission, 5/1 priority date for domestic students; for spring admission, 9/1 for domestic students. Applications are processed on a rolling basis. *Application fee:* $20 ($35 for international students). Electronic applications accepted. *Application Contact:* Karla Wenger, Coordinator, 218-477-2344, E-mail: wengerk@mnstate.edu. *Dean*, Dr. Marsha Weber, 218-477-2076, E-mail: marsha.weber@mnstate.edu.

College of Education and Human Services Financial support: Career-related internships or fieldwork, Federal Work-Study, and unspecified assistantships available. Financial award application deadline: 7/15; financial award applicants required to submit FAFSA. *Degree program information:* Part-time and evening/weekend programs available. Part-time, evening/weekend, 100% online, blended/hybrid learning. Offers counseling and student affairs (MS); curriculum and instruction (MS); educational leadership (MS, Ed S); special education (MS); speech-language pathology (MS). *Application deadline:* For fall admission, 4/15 priority date for domestic students; for spring admission, 11/1 priority date for domestic students. Applications are processed on a rolling basis. *Application fee:* $20. Electronic applications accepted. *Application Contact:* Karla Wenger, Graduate Studies Office, 218-477-2344, Fax: 218-477-2482, E-mail: wengerk@mnstate.edu. *Interim Dean*, Dr. Boyd Bradbury, 218-477-2471.

College of Humanities and Social Sciences Financial support: Research assistantships, teaching assistantships, Federal Work-Study, and unspecified assistantships available. Financial award application deadline: 7/15; financial award applicants required to submit FAFSA. *Degree program information:* Part-time and evening/weekend programs available. Part-time, evening/weekend, 100% online, blended/hybrid learning. Offers teaching English as a second language (MA). *Application deadline:* Applications are processed on a rolling basis. *Application fee:* $20. Electronic applications accepted. *Application Contact:* Karla Wenger, Graduate Studies Office, 218-477-2344, Fax: 218-477-2482, E-mail: wengerk@mnstate.edu. *Dean*, Dr. Randy Cagle, 218-477-2477, E-mail: caglera@mnstate.edu.

College of Science, Health and the Environment Financial support: Research assistantships, career-related internships or fieldwork, Federal Work-Study, and unspecified assistantships available. Financial award application deadline: 7/15; financial award applicants required to submit FAFSA. *Degree program information:* Part-time and evening/weekend programs available. Part-time, evening/weekend, 100% online, blended/hybrid learning. Offers healthcare administration (MHA); nursing (MS); school psychology (MS, Psy S). *Application deadline:* Applications are processed on a rolling basis. *Application fee:* $20. Electronic applications accepted. *Application Contact:* Karla Wenger, Graduate Studies Office, 218-477-2344, Fax: 218-477-2482, E-mail: wengerk@mnstate.edu. *Acting Dean*, Jeffrey Bodwin, 218-477-5892, E-mail: bodwin@mnstate.edu.

MINOT STATE UNIVERSITY, Minot, ND 58707-0002

General Information State-supported, coed, comprehensive institution. *Enrollment:* 3,348 graduate, professional, and undergraduate students; 107 full-time matriculated graduate/professional students (75 women), 177 part-time matriculated graduate/professional students (108 women). *Enrollment by degree level:* 284 master's. Tuition, state resident: full-time $6018. Tuition, nonresident: full-time $6018. *Required fees:* $1325. *Graduate housing:* Rooms and/or apartments available on a first-come, first-served basis to single and married students. Housing application deadline: 6/30. *Student services:* Campus employment opportunities, campus safety program, career counseling, exercise/wellness program, free psychological counseling, international student services, multicultural affairs office, services for students with disabilities, writing training. *Library:* Gordon B. Olson Library. *Research affiliation:* Rural Crime and Justice Center (criminal justice research), North Dakota Center for Persons with Disabilities (NDCPD).

Computer facilities: Computer purchase and lease plans are available. A campuswide network can be accessed from student residence rooms and from off campus. Online class registration is available.
Website: http://www.minotstateu.edu/

General Application Contact: Penny Brandt, Graduate Admission Specialist, 701-858-3413, E-mail: graduate@minotstateu.edu.

GRADUATE UNITS

Graduate School Students: 107 full-time (75 women), 177 part-time (108 women); includes 19 minority (5 Black or African American, non-Hispanic/Latino; 4 American Indian or Alaska Native, non-Hispanic/Latino; 5 Asian, non-Hispanic/Latino; 3 Hispanic/Latino; 2 Two or more races, non-Hispanic/Latino), 93 international. *Faculty:* 86 full-time (41 women). *Financial support:* In 2015–16, 102 students received support, including 28 research assistantships with partial tuition reimbursements available (averaging $1,370 per year); scholarships/grants, tuition waivers (partial), and unspecified assistantships also available. Financial award application deadline: 4/1; financial award applicants required to submit FAFSA. In 2015, 112 master's awarded. *Degree program information:* Part-time programs available. Part-time, 100% online, blended/hybrid learning. Offers deaf/hard of hearing education (MS); elementary education (M Ed); information systems (MSIS); management (MSM); mathematics (MAT); school psychology (Ed Sp); science (MAT); specific learning disabilities (MS); speech-language pathology (MS). *Application deadline:* Applications are processed on a rolling basis. *Application fee:* $35. Electronic applications accepted. *Application Contact:* Penny Brandt, Graduate Admission Specialist, 701-858-3413, Fax: 701-858-4286, E-mail: graduate@minotstateu.edu. *Assistant Dean*, Dr. Lori Willoughby, 701-858-3314, E-mail: lori.willoughby@minotstateu.edu.

MIRRER YESHIVA, Brooklyn, NY 11223-2010

General Information Independent-religious, men only, comprehensive institution.

GRADUATE UNITS

Graduate Programs

MISERICORDIA UNIVERSITY, Dallas, PA 18612-1098

General Information Independent-religious, coed, comprehensive institution. *Enrollment:* 3,065 graduate, professional, and undergraduate students; 416 full-time matriculated graduate/professional students (297 women), 566 part-time matriculated graduate/professional students (414 women). *Enrollment by degree level:* 603 master's, 379 doctoral. *Graduate faculty:* 72 full-time (52 women), 65 part-time/adjunct (39 women). *Graduate housing:* On-campus housing not available. *Student services:* Campus employment opportunities, campus safety program, career counseling, exercise/wellness program, free psychological counseling, international student services, low-cost health insurance, multicultural affairs office, services for students with disabilities, writing training. *Library:* Mary Kintz Bevevino Library. *Collection:* Books: 79,890 (physical), 376 (digital/electronic); Serial titles: 640 (physical), 60,527 (digital/electronic); Databases: 112. Weekly public service hours: 90; students can reserve study rooms.

Computer facilities: Computer purchase and lease plans are available. 150 computers available on campus for general student use. A campuswide network can be accessed from student residence rooms and from off campus. Online class registration is available.
Website: http://www.misericordia.edu/

General Application Contact: David Pasquini, Assistant Director of Admissions, Part-Time and Graduate Programs, 570-674-8183, Fax: 570-674-6232, E-mail: dpasquin@misericordia.edu.

GRADUATE UNITS

College of Health Sciences Students: 228 full-time (167 women), 151 part-time (132 women); includes 21 minority (3 Black or African American, non-Hispanic/Latino; 5 Asian, non-Hispanic/Latino; 8 Hispanic/Latino; 5 Two or more races, non-Hispanic/Latino). Average age 28. *Faculty:* 33 full-time (27 women), 18 part-time/adjunct (14 women). *Financial support:* In 2015–16, 252 students received support. Teaching assistantships, career-related internships or fieldwork, Federal Work-Study, scholarships/grants, traineeships, and tuition waivers (partial) available. Support available to part-time students. Financial award application deadline: 6/30; financial award applicants required to submit FAFSA. In 2015, 91 master's, 70 doctorates awarded. *Degree program information:* Part-time and evening/weekend programs available. Part-time, evening/weekend. Offers health sciences (MSN, MSOT, MSSLP, DNP, DPT, OTD); nursing (MSN, DNP); occupational therapy (MSOT, OTD); physical therapy (DPT); speech-language pathology (MSSLP). *Application deadline:* Applications are processed on a rolling basis. *Application fee:* $35. Electronic applications accepted. *Application Contact:* Maureen Sheridan, Assistant Director of Admissions, Part-Time Undergraduate and Graduate Programs, 570-674-6451, Fax: 570-674-6232, E-mail: msherida@misericordia.edu. *Dean*, Dr. Leamor Kahanov, 570-674-8406, E-mail: lkahanov@misericordia.edu.

College of Professional Studies and Social Sciences Students: 188 part-time (105 women); includes 4 minority (1 Black or African American, non-Hispanic/Latino; 2 Hispanic/Latino; 1 Native Hawaiian or other Pacific Islander, non-Hispanic/Latino). Average age 33. *Faculty:* 10 full-time (2 women), 25 part-time/adjunct (11 women). *Financial support:* In 2015–16, 117 students received support. Career-related internships or fieldwork and scholarships/grants available. Support available to part-time students. Financial award application deadline: 6/30; financial award applicants required to submit FAFSA. In 2015, 65 master's awarded. *Degree program information:* Part-time and evening/weekend programs available. Part-time, evening/weekend. Offers accounting (MBA); healthcare management (MBA, MS); human resource management (MS); human resources (MBA); information technology management (MS); instructional technology (MS); management (MBA, MS); not-for-profit management (MS); professional studies and social sciences (MBA, MS); reading specialist (MS); special education (MS); sport management (MBA). *Application deadline:* Applications are processed on a rolling basis. *Application fee:* $35. Electronic applications accepted. *Application Contact:* David Pasquini, Assistant Director of Admissions, 570-674-8183, Fax: 570-674-6232, E-mail: dpasquin@misericordia.edu. *Dean,* Dr. Fred Croop, 570-674-6327, E-mail: fcroop@misericordia.edu.

MISSISSIPPI COLLEGE, Clinton, MS 39058

General Information Independent-religious, coed, comprehensive institution. *Graduate housing:* Room and/or apartments available on a first-come, first-served basis to single students; on-campus housing not available to married students. Housing application deadline: 8/15. *Research affiliation:* Gulf Coast Research Laboratory (marine biology).

GRADUATE UNITS

Graduate School *Degree program information:* Part-time and evening/weekend programs available. Part-time, evening/weekend, online learning. Offers health services administration (MHSA); liberal studies (MLS). Electronic applications accepted.

College of Arts and Sciences *Degree program information:* Part-time and evening/weekend programs available. Part-time, evening/weekend. Offers administration of justice (MSS); applied communication (MSC); applied music performance (MM); art (M Ed, MA, MFA); arts and sciences (M Ed, MA, MCS, MFA, MM, MS, MSC, MSS, Certificate); biological science (M Ed); biology (MCS); biology-biological sciences (MS); biology-medical sciences (MS); chemistry and biochemistry (MCS, MS); Christian studies and the arts (M Ed, MA, MFA, MM, MSC); computer science (M Ed, MS); conducting (MM); English (M Ed, MA); history (M Ed, MA, MSS); humanities and social sciences (M Ed, MA, MS, MSS, Certificate); mathematics (M Ed, MCS, MS); music education (MM); music performance: organ (MM); paralegal studies (Certificate); political science (MSS); public relations and corporate communication (MSC); science and mathematics (M Ed, MCS, MS); social sciences (M Ed, MSS); teaching English to speakers of other languages (MA, MS); vocal pedagogy (MM). Electronic applications accepted.

School of Business *Degree program information:* Part-time and evening/weekend programs available. Part-time, evening/weekend. Offers accounting (Certificate); business administration (MBA); business education (M Ed); finance (MBA, Certificate). Electronic applications accepted.

School of Education *Degree program information:* Part-time and evening/weekend programs available. Part-time, evening/weekend, online learning. Offers art (M Ed); athletic administration (MS); biological science (M Ed); business education (M Ed); computer science (M Ed); counseling (Ed S); dyslexia therapy (M Ed); education (M Ed, MS, Ed D, Ed S); educational leadership (M Ed, Ed D, Ed S); elementary education (M Ed, Ed S); English (M Ed); higher education administration (MS); marriage and family counseling (MS); mathematics (M Ed); mental health counseling (MS); school counseling (M Ed); secondary education (M Ed); social studies (history) (M Ed); teaching arts (M Ed). Electronic applications accepted.

School of Law Offers civil law studies (Certificate); law (JD). Electronic applications accepted.

MISSISSIPPI STATE UNIVERSITY, Mississippi State, MS 39762

General Information State-supported, coed, university. CGS member. *Enrollment:* 20,873 graduate, professional, and undergraduate students; 1,839 full-time matriculated graduate/professional students (926 women), 1,481 part-time matriculated graduate/professional students (708 women). *Enrollment by degree level:* 1,807 master's, 1,473 doctoral, 40 other advanced degrees. *Graduate faculty:* 839 full-time (261 women), 29 part-time/adjunct (9 women). *Tuition, area resident:* Full-time $7502; part-time $833.74 per credit hour. Tuition, nonresident: full-time $20,142; part-time $2238.24 per credit hour. *Graduate housing:* Room and/or apartments available on a first-come, first-served basis to single students; on-campus housing not available to married students. Typical cost: $5891 (including board). Housing application deadline: 8/1. *Student services:* Campus employment opportunities, campus safety program, career counseling, child daycare facilities, exercise/wellness program, free psychological counseling, grant writing training, international student services, low-cost health insurance, multicultural affairs office, services for students with disabilities, teacher training, writing training. *Library:* Mitchell Memorial Library plus 2 others. *Collection:* Books: 2.6 million (physical), 71,436 (digital/electronic); Serial titles: 2,417 (physical), 119,145 (digital/electronic); Databases: 97. Weekly public service hours: 110; students can reserve study rooms. *Research affiliation:* Southeastern Universities Research Association (interdisciplinary research), Oak Ridge Associated Universities (interdisciplinary energy-related research), Mississippi Research and Technology Park (interdisciplinary engineering), Mississippi Mineral Resources Institute (geology sciences and engineering), NASA-Stennis Space Center (interdisciplinary research), Mississippi Research Consortium (interdisciplinary research).

Computer facilities: 1,000 computers available on campus for general student use. A campuswide network can be accessed from student residence rooms and from off campus. Online class registration is available.
Website: http://www.msstate.edu/

General Application Contact: Forest Sparks, Admissions Manager, 662-325-7400, Fax: 662-325-1967, E-mail: grad@grad.msstate.edu.

GRADUATE UNITS

Bagley College of Engineering Students: 357 full-time (82 women), 269 part-time (45 women); includes 93 minority (41 Black or African American, non-Hispanic/Latino; 18 Asian, non-Hispanic/Latino; 29 Hispanic/Latino; 1 Native Hawaiian or other Pacific Islander, non-Hispanic/Latino; 4 Two or more races, non-Hispanic/Latino), 206 international. Average age 30. 690 applicants, 42% accepted, 157 enrolled. *Faculty:* 116 full-time (15 women), 8 part-time/adjunct (1 woman). *Financial support:* In 2015–16, 81 research assistantships with full tuition reimbursements (averaging $16,677 per year), 52 teaching assistantships with full tuition reimbursements (averaging $14,427 per year) were awarded; Federal Work-Study, institutionally sponsored loans, scholarships/grants, and unspecified assistantships also available. Financial award application deadline: 4/1; financial award applicants required to submit FAFSA. In 2015, 84 master's, 36 doctorates awarded. *Degree program information:* Part-time programs available. Part-time, online learning. Offers aerospace engineering (MS); civil engineering (MS); computer science (MS, PhD); electrical and computer engineering (MS, PhD); engineering (M Eng, MS, PhD); human factors and ergonomics (MS); industrial and systems engineering (PhD); industrial systems (MS); management systems (MS); manufacturing systems (MS); mechanical engineering (MS); operations research (MS). *Application deadline:* For fall admission, 7/1 for domestic students, 5/1 for international students; for spring admission, 11/1 for domestic students, 9/1 for international students. Applications are processed on a rolling basis. *Application fee:* $60. Electronic applications accepted. *Application Contact:* Doretta Martin, Senior Admissions Assistant, 662-325-9514, E-mail: dmartin@grad.msstate.edu. *Dean*, Dr. Jason Keith, 662-325-2270, Fax: 662-325-8573, E-mail: keith@bagley.msstate.edu.

Dave C. Swalm School of Chemical Engineering Students: 16 full-time (5 women), 2 part-time (1 woman), 15 international. Average age 29. 11 applicants, 45% accepted, 3 enrolled. *Faculty:* 9 full-time (2 women). *Financial support:* In 2015–16, 14 research assistantships with full tuition reimbursements (averaging $15,568 per year), 1 teaching assistantship with full tuition reimbursement (averaging $16,687 per year) were awarded; Federal Work-Study, institutionally sponsored loans, and unspecified assistantships also available. Financial award application deadline: 4/1; financial award applicants required to submit FAFSA. In 2015, 5 master's awarded. Offers chemical engineering (MS); engineering (PhD). *Application deadline:* For fall admission, 4/1 priority date for domestic students, 5/1 for international students; for spring admission, 8/1 priority date for domestic students, 9/1 for international students. Applications are processed on a rolling basis. *Application fee:* $60. Electronic applications accepted. *Application Contact:* Doretta Martin, Senior Admissions Assistant, 662-325-9514, E-mail: dmartin@grad.msstate.edu. *Interim Director/Associate Professor*, Dr. Bill Elmore, 662-325-2480, Fax: 662-325-2482, E-mail: elmore@che.msstate.edu.

College of Agriculture and Life Sciences Students: 240 full-time (129 women), 166 part-time (93 women); includes 57 minority (38 Black or African American, non-Hispanic/Latino; 1 American Indian or Alaska Native, non-Hispanic/Latino; 6 Asian, non-Hispanic/Latino; 9 Hispanic/Latino; 3 Two or more races, non-Hispanic/Latino), 95 international. Average age 31. 256 applicants, 52% accepted, 101 enrolled. *Faculty:* 187 full-time (49 women), 5 part-time/adjunct (3 women). *Financial support:* In 2015–16, 153 research assistantships with full tuition reimbursements (averaging $15,077 per year), 14 teaching assistantships with full tuition reimbursements (averaging $12,890 per year) were awarded; career-related internships or fieldwork, Federal Work-Study, institutionally sponsored loans, scholarships/grants, tuition waivers (partial), and unspecified assistantships also available. Financial award application deadline: 4/1; financial award applicants required to submit FAFSA. In 2015, 100 master's, 24 doctorates awarded. Online learning. Offers agribusiness management (MABM); agricultural life sciences (MS); agricultural science (PhD); agricultural sciences (PhD); agriculture (MS, PhD); agriculture and life sciences (MABM, MLA, MS, PhD); agriculture life sciences (MS); biological engineering (MS); biomedical engineering (MS, PhD); engineering (PhD); food science and technology (MS); food science and technology (PhD); health promotion (MS); landscape architecture (MLA); life science (PhD); life sciences (PhD); molecular biology (PhD); nutrition (MS, PhD). *Application deadline:* For fall admission, 7/1 for domestic students, 5/1 for international students; for spring admission, 11/1 for domestic students, 9/1 for international students. Applications are processed on a rolling basis. *Application fee:* $60. Electronic applications accepted. *Application Contact:* Marina Hunt, Admissions Assistant, 662-325-5188, Fax: 662-325-1967, E-mail: mhunt@grad.msstate.edu. *Dean of Agriculture and Life Sciences/Director of Mississippi Agricultural and Forestry Experiment Station*, Dr. George Hopper, 662-325-2110, Fax: 662-325-8580, E-mail: dean@cals.msstate.edu.

School of Human Sciences Students: 32 full-time (23 women), 63 part-time (42 women); includes 17 minority (15 Black or African American, non-Hispanic/Latino; 1 Hispanic/Latino; 1 Two or more races, non-Hispanic/Latino), 5 international. Average age 35. 18 applicants, 78% accepted, 11 enrolled. *Faculty:* 24 full-time (15 women), 1 part-time/adjunct (0 women). *Financial support:* In 2015–16, 15 research assistantships (averaging $13,002 per year) were awarded; Federal Work-Study, institutionally sponsored loans, and unspecified assistantships also available. Financial award application deadline: 4/1; financial award applicants required to submit FAFSA. In 2015, 16 master's, 1 doctorate awarded. *Degree program information:* Part-time programs available. Part-time. Offers agricultural sciences (PhD); agriculture and extension education (MS); human development and family studies (MS, PhD). *Application deadline:* For fall admission, 7/1 for domestic students, 5/1 for international students; for spring admission, 11/1 for domestic students, 9/1 for international students. Applications are processed on a rolling basis. *Application fee:* $60. Electronic applications accepted. *Application Contact:* Marina Hunt, Admissions Assistant, 662-325-5188, E-mail: mhunt@grad.msstate.edu. *Director and Professor,* Dr. Michael Newman, 662-325-2950, E-mail: mnewman@humansci.msstate.edu.

College of Arts and Sciences Students: 390 full-time (202 women), 325 part-time (167 women); includes 109 minority (63 Black or African American, non-Hispanic/Latino; 2 American Indian or Alaska Native, non-Hispanic/Latino; 10 Asian, non-Hispanic/Latino; 21 Hispanic/Latino; 1 Native Hawaiian or other Pacific Islander, non-Hispanic/Latino; 12 Two or more races, non-Hispanic/Latino), 110 international. Average age 31. 615 applicants, 50% accepted, 219 enrolled. *Faculty:* 232 full-time (79 women), 5 part-time/adjunct (0 women). *Financial support:* In 2015–16, 48 research assistantships with full tuition reimbursements (averaging $13,777 per year), 272 teaching assistantships with full tuition reimbursements (averaging $13,432 per year) were awarded; Federal Work-Study, institutionally sponsored loans, scholarships/grants, tuition waivers (partial), and unspecified assistantships also available. Financial award application deadline: 4/1; financial award applicants required to submit FAFSA. In 2015, 184 master's, 24 doctorates awarded. *Degree program information:* Part-time and evening/weekend programs available. Part-time, evening/weekend. Offers applied anthropology (MA); applied cognitive science (PhD); applied meteorology (MS); applied psychology (PhD); arts and sciences (MA, MPPA, MS, PhD); biological sciences (MS, PhD); broadcast meteorology (MS); chemistry (MA, MS, PhD); earth and atmospheric science (PhD); engineering (PhD); English (MA); environmental geosciences (MS); French (MA); geography (MS); geology (MS); geospatial sciences (MS); German (MA); mathematical sciences (PhD); mathematics (MS); physics (MS, PhD); political science (MA); professional meteorology/climatology (MS); psychology (MS); public policy and administration (MPPA, PhD); sociology (MS, PhD); Spanish (MA); statistics (MS); teachers in geosciences (MS); U.S. and European history (MA, PhD). *Application deadline:* For fall admission, 7/1 for domestic students, 5/1 for international students; for spring admission, 11/1 for domestic students, 9/1 for international students. Applications are processed on a rolling basis. *Application fee:* $60. Electronic applications accepted. *Application Contact:* Meredith Nagel, Admissions Assistant, 662-325-9077, E-mail: mnagel@grad.msstate.edu. *Dean*, Dr. R. Greg Dunaway, 662-325-7091, Fax: 662-325-8740, E-mail: dunaway@deanas.msstate.edu.

College of Business Students: 122 full-time (34 women), 189 part-time (47 women); includes 33 minority (14 Black or African American, non-Hispanic/Latino; 1 American Indian or Alaska Native, non-Hispanic/Latino; 7 Asian, non-Hispanic/Latino; 7 Hispanic/Latino; 4 Two or more races, non-Hispanic/Latino), 25 international. Average age 30. 339 applicants, 40% accepted, 99 enrolled. *Faculty:* 59 full-time (18 women), 1 part-time/adjunct (0 women). *Financial support:* In 2015–16, 39 teaching assistantships (averaging $11,884 per year) were awarded; career-related internships or fieldwork, Federal Work-Study, institutionally sponsored loans, scholarships/grants, and unspecified assistantships also available. Financial award application deadline: 4/1; financial award applicants required to submit FAFSA. In 2015, 144 master's, 9 doctorates awarded. *Degree program information:* Part-time and evening/weekend programs available. Part-time, evening/weekend, online learning. Offers applied economics (PhD); business (MA, MBA, MPA, MSIS, MTX, PhD); business administration (MBA, PhD); economics (MA); information systems (MSIS); project management (MBA). *Application deadline:* For fall admission, 3/1 priority date for domestic students, 5/1 for international students; for spring admission, 11/1 for domestic students, 9/1 for international students. Applications are processed on a rolling basis. *Application fee:* $60. Electronic applications accepted. *Application Contact:* Lakan Drinker, Admissions Assistant, 662-325-8951, E-mail: ldrinker@grad.msstate.edu. *Dean and Professor*, Dr. Sharon Oswald, 662-325-2580, Fax: 662-325-2410, E-mail: slo49@msstate.edu.

Adkerson School of Accountancy Students: 38 full-time (12 women), 2 part-time (1 woman); includes 1 minority (Hispanic/Latino), 3 international. Average age 23. 51 applicants, 45% accepted, 21 enrolled. *Faculty:* 10 full-time (2 women). *Financial support:* Career-related internships or fieldwork, Federal Work-Study, institutionally sponsored loans, scholarships/grants, and unspecified assistantships available. Support available to part-time students. Financial award application deadline: 4/1; financial award applicants required to submit FAFSA. In 2015, 35 master's awarded. Offers accounting (MPA); systems (MPA); taxation (MTX). *Application deadline:* For fall admission, 7/1 for domestic students, 5/1 for international students; for spring admission, 11/1 for domestic students, 9/1 for international students. Applications are processed on a rolling basis. *Application fee:* $60. Electronic applications accepted. *Application Contact:* Lakan Drinker, Admissions Assistant, 662-325-8951, E-mail: ldrinker@grad.msstate.edu. *Director and Professor*, Dr. Shawn Mauldin, 662-325-3710, Fax: 662-325-1646, E-mail: smauldin@business.msstate.edu.

College of Education Students: 272 full-time (173 women), 453 part-time (321 women); includes 249 minority (218 Black or African American, non-Hispanic/Latino; 5 American Indian or Alaska Native, non-Hispanic/Latino; 9 Asian, non-Hispanic/Latino; 7 Hispanic/Latino; 1 Native Hawaiian or other Pacific Islander, non-Hispanic/Latino; 9 Two or more races, non-Hispanic/Latino), 14 international. Average age 33. 419 applicants, 58% accepted, 191 enrolled. *Faculty:* 85 full-time (50 women), 4 part-time/adjunct (all women). *Financial support:* In 2015–16, 17 research assistantships (averaging $11,027 per year), 26 teaching assistantships (averaging $9,383 per year) were awarded; career-related internships or fieldwork, Federal Work-Study, institutionally sponsored loans, scholarships/grants, and unspecified assistantships also available. Financial award application deadline: 4/1; financial award applicants required to submit FAFSA. In 2015, 172 master's, 38 doctorates, 25 other advanced degrees awarded. *Degree program information:* Part-time and evening/weekend programs available. Part-time, evening/weekend, online learning. Offers college student counseling and personnel services (PhD); community college education (MAT); community college leadership (PhD); counselor education (MS); curriculum and instruction (PhD); education (Ed S); educational psychology (MS, PhD); elementary education (MS); elementary, middle and secondary education administration (PhD); exercise physiology (MS); exercise science (PhD); instructional design (MSIT); instructional systems and workforce development (PhD); middle level education (MAT); multimedia (MSIT); school administration (MS); school counseling (PhD); secondary education (MAT, MS); special education (MAT, MS); sport administration (MS); sport pedagogy (MS); sports studies (PhD); technology (MS); workforce education leadership (MS). *Application deadline:* For fall admission, 7/1 for domestic students, 5/1 for international students; for spring admission, 11/1 for domestic students, 9/1 for international students. Applications are processed on a rolling basis. *Application fee:* $60. Electronic applications accepted. *Application Contact:* Linda Bonner, Senior Admissions Assistant, 662-325-3363, E-mail: lbonner@grad.msstate.edu. *Dean*, Dr. Richard Blackbourn, 662-325-3717, Fax: 662-325-8784, E-mail: rlb277@msstate.edu.

College of Forest Resources Students: 93 full-time (30 women), 43 part-time (14 women); includes 6 minority (2 Black or African American, non-Hispanic/Latino; 1 American Indian or Alaska Native, non-Hispanic/Latino; 2 Asian, non-Hispanic/Latino; 1 Two or more races, non-Hispanic/Latino), 40 international. Average age 30. 56 applicants, 55% accepted, 27 enrolled. *Faculty:* 60 full-time (13 women), 2 part-time/adjunct (0 women). *Financial support:* In 2015–16, 82 research assistantships with full tuition reimbursements (averaging $15,102 per year) were awarded; career-related internships or fieldwork, Federal Work-Study, institutionally sponsored loans, and unspecified assistantships also available. Financial award application deadline: 4/1; financial award applicants required to submit FAFSA. In 2015, 23 master's, 14 doctorates awarded. *Degree program information:* Part-time programs available. Part-time. Offers forest products (MS); forest resources (PhD); forestry (MS); wildlife, fisheries and aquaculture (MS). *Application deadline:* For fall admission, 7/1 for domestic students, 5/1 for international students; for spring admission, 11/1 for domestic students, 9/1 for international students. Applications are processed on a rolling basis. *Application fee:* $60. Electronic applications accepted. *Application Contact:* Nathan Drake, Admissions Assistant, 662-325-3804, E-mail: ndrake@grad.msstate.edu. *Dean*, Dr. George Hopper, 662-325-2953, Fax: 662-325-8726, E-mail: ghopper@cfr.msstate.edu.

College of Veterinary Medicine Students: 365 full-time (276 women), 36 part-time (21 women); includes 30 minority (10 Black or African American, non-Hispanic/Latino; 1 American Indian or Alaska Native, non-Hispanic/Latino; 1 Asian, non-Hispanic/Latino; 10 Hispanic/Latino; 1 Native Hawaiian or other Pacific Islander, non-Hispanic/Latino; 7 Two or more races, non-Hispanic/Latino), 24 international. Average age 26. 132 applicants, 83% accepted, 105 enrolled. *Faculty:* 68 full-time (26 women), 4 part-time/adjunct (1 woman). *Financial support:* In 2015–16, 33 research assistantships with full tuition reimbursements (averaging $15,933 per year) were awarded; career-related internships or fieldwork, Federal Work-Study, and institutionally sponsored loans also available. Financial award application deadline: 6/30; financial award applicants required to submit FAFSA. In 2015, 8 master's, 86 doctorates awarded. Offers environmental toxicology (PhD); veterinary medical sciences (MS, PhD); veterinary medicine (MS, DVM, PhD). *Application deadline:* For fall admission, 7/1 for domestic students, 5/1 for international students; for spring admission, 11/1 for domestic students, 9/1 for international students. *Application fee:* $60. Electronic applications accepted. *Application Contact:* Missy Hadaway, Admissions and Student Affairs Coordinator, 662-325-9065, E-mail: missy.hadaway@msstate.edu. *Dean*, Dr. Kent H. Hoblet, 662-325-1131, Fax: 662-325-1498, E-mail: hoblet@cvm.msstate.edu.

MISSISSIPPI UNIVERSITY FOR WOMEN, Columbus, MS 39701-9998

General Information State-supported, coed, comprehensive institution. *Graduate housing:* Rooms and/or apartments available on a first-come, first-served basis to single and married students.

GRADUATE UNITS

Graduate School ***Degree program information:*** Part-time programs available. Part-time. Offers health education (MS).

College of Education and Human Sciences Degree program information: Part-time programs available. Part-time. Offers differentiated instruction (M Ed); educational leadership (M Ed); gifted studies (M Ed); reading/literacy (M Ed); teaching (MAT).

College of Nursing and Speech Language Pathology Degree program information: Part-time programs available. Part-time. Offers nursing (MSN, PMC); speech-language pathology (MS).

MISSISSIPPI VALLEY STATE UNIVERSITY, Itta Bena, MS 38941-1400

General Information State-supported, coed, comprehensive institution. *Enrollment:* 2,309 graduate, professional, and undergraduate students; 161 full-time matriculated graduate/professional students (127 women), 200 part-time matriculated graduate/professional students (134 women). *Enrollment by degree level:* 361 master's. *Graduate faculty:* 33 full-time (18 women), 2 part-time/adjunct (1 woman). Tuition, state resident: full-time $9990; part-time $6660 per credit hour. Tuition, nonresident: full-time $9990; part-time $6660 per credit hour. *Required fees:* $150; $150 per unit. $75 per semester. *Graduate housing:* On-campus housing not available. *Student services:* Career counseling, child daycare facilities, exercise/wellness program, international student services, low-cost health insurance, writing training. *Library:* James Herbert White Library. *Collection:* Books: 127,541 (physical), 52,564 (digital/electronic); Serial titles: 238 (physical), 9,415 (digital/electronic); Databases: 52. Weekly public service hours: 84; students can reserve study rooms.

Computer facilities: 285 computers available on campus for general student use. A campuswide network can be accessed from student residence rooms and from off campus. Online class registration is available.
Website: http://www.mvsu.edu/

General Application Contact: Office of Admissions, 601-254-3344.

GRADUATE UNITS

College of Education Students: 15. *Faculty:* 5. Offers education (MAT); special education (MS); teacher education (MS). *Application deadline:* Applications are processed on a rolling basis. *Application fee:* $0. *Application Contact:* Office of Admissions, 601-254-3344. *Chair*, Dr. O. Edward Jack, 601-254-3619.

Department of Criminal Justice Students: 8 full-time (5 women), 62 part-time (39 women); includes 66 minority (all Black or African American, non-Hispanic/Latino). Average age 33. 13 applicants, 100% accepted. *Faculty:* 5 full-time (2 women). *Financial support:* In 2015–16, 10 students received support, including research assistantships with full tuition reimbursements available (averaging $3,640 per year); Federal Work-Study and scholarships/grants also available. Support available to part-time students. Financial award application deadline: 4/15. *Degree program information:* Part-time and evening/weekend programs available. Part-time, evening/weekend. Offers criminal justice (MS). *Application deadline:* For fall admission, 4/1 priority date for domestic students; for spring admission, 12/15 priority date for domestic students. Applications are processed on a rolling basis. *Application fee:* $0. Electronic applications accepted. *Chair*, Dr. Emmanuel Amadi, 601-254-3363, Fax: 601-254-3646.

Department of Natural Science and Environmental Health Students: 33; includes 29 minority (all Black or African American, non-Hispanic/Latino). *Degree program information:* Part-time and evening/weekend programs available. Part-time, evening/weekend. Offers bioinformatics (MS). *Application deadline:* Applications are processed on a rolling basis. *Application fee:* $0. *Application Contact:* Office of Admissions, 601-254-3344. *Chair*, Louis Hall, 662-254-3377.

MISSOURI BAPTIST UNIVERSITY, St. Louis, MO 63141-8660

General Information Independent-religious, coed, comprehensive institution.

GRADUATE UNITS

Graduate Programs

MISSOURI SOUTHERN STATE UNIVERSITY, Joplin, MO 64801-1595

General Information State-supported, coed, comprehensive institution.

GRADUATE UNITS

Program in Business Administration Online learning. Offers business administration (MBA). Program offered jointly with Northwest Missouri State University.

Program in Criminal Justice Administration Online learning. Offers criminal justice administration (MS). Program offered jointly with Southeast Missouri State University.

Program in Dental Hygiene ***Degree program information:*** Part-time programs available. Part-time. Offers dental hygiene (MS). Program offered jointly with University of Missouri–Kansas City. Electronic applications accepted.

Program in Early Childhood Education Offers early childhood education (MS Ed). Program offered jointly with Northwest Missouri State University.

Program in Instructional Technology Offers instructional technology (MS Ed). Program offered jointly with Northwest Missouri State University.

Program in Nursing ***Degree program information:*** Part-time programs available. Part-time. Offers nursing (MSN). Program offered jointly with University of Missouri–Kansas City. Electronic applications accepted.

Program in Teaching Offers teaching (MAT). Program offered jointly with Missouri State University.

★ MISSOURI STATE UNIVERSITY, Springfield, MO 65897

General Information State-supported, coed, comprehensive institution. CGS member. *Enrollment:* 22,273 graduate, professional, and undergraduate students; 1,577 full-time matriculated graduate/professional students (962 women), 1,844 part-time matriculated graduate/professional students (1,187 women). *Enrollment by degree level:* 3,107 master's, 277 doctoral, 75 other advanced degrees. *Graduate faculty:* 370 full-time (150 women), 74 part-time/adjunct (36 women). Tuition, state resident: full-time $5500. Tuition, nonresident: full-time $10,108. *Required fees:* $1000. *Graduate housing:* Rooms and/or apartments available on a first-come, first-served basis to single and married students. Housing application deadline: 7/1. *Student services:* Campus employment opportunities, campus safety program, career counseling, child daycare facilities, exercise/wellness program, free psychological counseling, grant writing training, international student services, low-cost health insurance, multicultural affairs office, services for students with disabilities, teacher training, writing training. *Library:* Meyer Library.

Computer facilities: A campuswide network can be accessed from student residence rooms and from off campus. Online class registration is available.
Website: http://www.missouristate.edu/

General Application Contact: Michael Edwards, Coordinator of Graduate Admissions, 417-836-5330, Fax: 417-836-6200, E-mail: graduateadmissions@missouristate.edu.

GRADUATE UNITS

Graduate College Students: 1,577 full-time (962 women), 1,844 part-time (1,187 women); includes 299 minority (78 Black or African American, non-Hispanic/Latino; 19 American Indian or Alaska Native, non-Hispanic/Latino; 45 Asian, non-Hispanic/Latino; 76 Hispanic/Latino; 2 Native Hawaiian or other Pacific Islander, non-Hispanic/Latino; 79 Two or more races, non-Hispanic/Latino), 592 international. Average age 31. 1,368 applicants, 75% accepted, 762 enrolled. *Faculty:* 370 full-time (150 women), 74 part-time/adjunct (36 women). *Financial support:* In 2015–16, 44 research assistantships with full tuition reimbursements (averaging $8,600 per year), 195 teaching assistantships with full tuition reimbursements (averaging $8,600 per year) were awarded; Federal Work-Study, institutionally sponsored loans, scholarships/grants, and unspecified assistantships also available. Financial award application deadline: 3/31; financial award applicants required to submit FAFSA. In 2015, 1,080 master's, 62 doctorates, 12 other advanced degrees awarded. *Degree program information:* Part-time programs available. Part-time, 100% online, blended/hybrid learning. Offers administrative studies (Certificate); applied communication (MS); criminal justice (MS); environmental management (MS); homeland security (MS); individualized (MS); screenwriting and producing (MS); sports management (MS). *Application deadline:* For fall admission, 7/20 priority date for domestic students, 5/1 for international students; for spring admission, 12/20 priority date for domestic students, 9/1 for international students. Applications are processed on a rolling basis. *Application fee:* $35 ($50 for international students). Electronic applications accepted. *Application Contact:* Michael Edwards, Coordinator of Graduate Admissions, 417-836-5330, Fax: 417-836-6200, E-mail: michaeledwards@missouristate.edu. *Associate Provost/Dean,* Dr. Julie Masterson, 417-836-5335, Fax: 417-836-6888, E-mail: juliemasterson@missouristate.edu.

College of Arts and Letters Students: 109 full-time (71 women), 115 part-time (75 women); includes 22 minority (6 Black or African American, non-Hispanic/Latino; 1 American Indian or Alaska Native, non-Hispanic/Latino; 1 Asian, non-Hispanic/Latino; 5 Hispanic/Latino; 9 Two or more races, non-Hispanic/Latino), 34 international. Average age 34. 184 applicants, 61% accepted, 66 enrolled. *Faculty:* 74 full-time (32 women), 7 part-time/adjunct (5 women). *Financial support:* In 2015–16, 61 teaching assistantships with full tuition reimbursements (averaging $8,600 per year) were awarded; Federal Work-Study, institutionally sponsored loans, scholarships/grants, and unspecified assistantships also available. Financial award application deadline: 3/31; financial award applicants required to submit FAFSA. In 2015, 85 master's awarded. *Degree program information:* Part-time and evening/weekend programs available. Part-time, evening/weekend, 100% online, blended/hybrid learning. Offers applied second language acquisition (MASLA); arts and letters (MA, MASLA, MFA, MM, MS Ed, Certificate); communication and mass media (MA); English (MA); English education (MS Ed); music (MM, MS Ed); speech and theatre education (MS Ed); teaching English to speakers of other languages (Certificate); visual studies (MFA); writing (MA). *Application deadline:* For fall admission, 7/20 priority date for domestic students, 5/1 for international students; for spring admission, 12/20 priority date for domestic students, 9/1 for international students; for summer admission, 5/20 priority date for domestic students. Applications are processed on a rolling basis. *Application fee:* $35 ($50 for international students). Electronic applications accepted. *Application Contact:* Michael Edwards, Coordinator of Graduate Admissions, 417-836-5330, Fax: 417-836-6200, E-mail: michaeledwards@missouristate.edu. *Dean,* Dr. Gloria Galanes, 417-836-5247, Fax: 417-836-6940, E-mail: gloriagalanes@missouristate.edu.

College of Business Administration Students: 430 full-time (193 women), 320 part-time (124 women); includes 55 minority (13 Black or African American, non-Hispanic/Latino; 3 American Indian or Alaska Native, non-Hispanic/Latino; 9 Asian, non-Hispanic/Latino; 16 Hispanic/Latino; 14 Two or more races, non-Hispanic/Latino), 314 international. Average age 33. 581 applicants, 52% accepted, 195 enrolled. *Faculty:* 50 full-time (13 women), 8 part-time/adjunct (1 woman). *Financial support:* In 2015–16, 4 teaching assistantships with full tuition reimbursements (averaging $10,464 per year) were awarded; Federal Work-Study, institutionally sponsored loans, scholarships/grants, and unspecified assistantships also available. Financial award application deadline: 3/31; financial award applicants required to submit FAFSA. In 2015, 473 master's awarded. *Degree program information:* Part-time and evening/weekend programs available. Part-time, evening/weekend, 100% online, blended/hybrid learning. Offers accountancy (M Acc); business administration (M Acc, MBA, MHA, MS, MS Ed); cybersecurity (MS); health administration (MHA); project management (MS). *Application deadline:* For fall admission, 7/20 priority date for domestic students, 5/1 for international students; for spring admission, 12/20 priority date for domestic students, 9/1 for international students; for summer admission, 5/20 priority date for domestic students. Applications are processed on a rolling basis. *Application fee:* $35 ($50 for international students). Electronic applications accepted. *Application Contact:* Michael Edwards, Coordinator of Graduate Admissions, 417-836-5330, Fax: 417-836-6200, E-mail: michaeledwards@missouristate.edu. *Dean,* Dr. Stephanie Bryant, 417-836-5646, Fax: 417-836-4407, E-mail: coba@missouristate.edu.

College of Education Students: 215 full-time (169 women), 552 part-time (461 women); includes 59 minority (14 Black or African American, non-Hispanic/Latino; 4 American Indian or Alaska Native, non-Hispanic/Latino; 5 Asian, non-Hispanic/Latino; 21 Hispanic/Latino; 2 Native Hawaiian or other Pacific Islander, non-Hispanic/Latino; 13 Two or more races, non-Hispanic/Latino), 22 international. Average age 33. 266 applicants, 66% accepted, 126 enrolled. *Faculty:* 43 full-time (26 women), 11 part-time/adjunct (6 women). *Financial support:* Federal Work-Study, institutionally sponsored loans, scholarships/grants, and unspecified assistantships available. Financial award application deadline: 3/31; financial award applicants required to submit FAFSA. In 2015, 194 master's, 12 other advanced degrees awarded. *Degree program information:* Part-time programs available. Part-time. Offers alternative certification (MS Ed); autism spectrum disorder (MS Ed); blindness and low vision (MS Ed); counseling (MS); counseling and assessment (Ed S); early childhood and family development (MS); education (MAT, MS, MS Ed, Ed S); educational administration (MS Ed, Ed S); educational technology (MS Ed); elementary education (MS Ed); elementary principal (MS Ed, Ed S); elementary school counseling (MS); literacy (MS Ed); mental health counseling (MS); orientation and mobility (MS Ed); secondary principal (MS Ed, Ed S); secondary school counseling (MS); special education (MS Ed); student affairs in higher education (MS); superintendent (Ed S); teacher leadership (Certificate, Ed S); teaching (MAT); teaching and learning (MA, Certificate). *Application deadline:* For fall admission, 7/20 for domestic students, 5/1 for international students; for spring admission, 12/20 for domestic students, 9/1 for international students; for summer admission, 5/20 for domestic students. Applications are processed on a rolling basis. *Application fee:* $35 ($50 for international students). Electronic applications accepted. *Application Contact:* Michael Edwards, Coordinator of Graduate Admissions, 417-836-5330, Fax: 417-836-6200, E-mail: michaeledwards@missouristate.edu. *Dean,* Dr. David Hough, 417-836-5254, Fax: 417-836-4884, E-mail: collegeofeducation@missouristate.edu.

College of Health and Human Services Students: 549 full-time (392 women), 188 part-time (151 women); includes 75 minority (18 Black or African American, non-Hispanic/Latino; 6 American Indian or Alaska Native, non-Hispanic/Latino; 16 Asian, non-Hispanic/Latino; 12 Hispanic/Latino; 23 Two or more races, non-Hispanic/Latino), 31 international. Average age 28. 549 applicants, 42% accepted, 180 enrolled. *Faculty:* 89 full-time (58 women), 33 part-time/adjunct (21 women). *Financial support:* In 2015–16, 9 research assistantships with full tuition reimbursements (averaging $8,600 per year), 33 teaching assistantships with full tuition reimbursements (averaging $8,600 per year) were awarded; Federal Work-Study, institutionally sponsored loans, scholarships/grants, and unspecified assistantships also available. Financial award application deadline: 3/31; financial award applicants required to submit FAFSA. In 2015, 178 master's, 34 doctorates awarded. *Degree program information:* Part-time programs available. Part-time. Offers applied behavior analysis (MS); athletic training (MS); cell and molecular biology (MS); clinical psychology (MS); communication sciences and disorders (Au D); dietetic internship (Certificate); experimental psychology (MS); forensic child psychology (Certificate); health and human services (MOT, MPH, MS, MS Ed, MSN, MSW, Au D, DNAP, DNP, DPT, Certificate); health promotion and wellness management (MS); industrial/organizational psychology (MS); nurse anesthesia (DNAP); nursing (MSN); nursing practice (DNP); occupational therapy (MOT); physical therapy (DPT); physician assistant studies (MS); public health (MPH); secondary education (MS Ed); social work (MSW); speech language pathology (MS). *Application fee:* $35 ($50 for international students). Electronic applications accepted. *Application Contact:* Michael Edwards, Coordinator of Graduate Admissions, 417-836-5330, Fax: 417-836-6200, E-mail: michaeledwards@missouristate.edu. *Dean,* Dr. Helen Reid, 417-836-4176, Fax: 417-836-6905, E-mail: chhs@missouristate.edu.

College of Humanities and Public Affairs Students: 87 full-time (39 women), 164 part-time (54 women); includes 34 minority (13 Black or African American, non-Hispanic/Latino; 1 American Indian or Alaska Native, non-Hispanic/Latino; 4 Asian, non-Hispanic/Latino; 11 Hispanic/Latino; 5 Two or more races, non-Hispanic/Latino), 16 international. Average age 32. 157 applicants, 65% accepted, 69 enrolled. *Faculty:* 66 full-time (20 women), 21 part-time/adjunct (5 women). *Financial support:* In 2015–16, 3 teaching assistantships with partial tuition reimbursements (averaging $2,150 per year) were awarded; Federal Work-Study, institutionally sponsored loans, scholarships/grants, and unspecified assistantships also available. Financial award application deadline: 3/31; financial award applicants required to submit FAFSA. In 2015, 83 master's awarded. *Degree program information:* Part-time programs available. Part-time. Offers community corrections (Certificate); criminology and criminal justice (MS); defense and strategic studies (Certificate); general weapons of mass destruction (MS); global studies (MGS); history (MA, MS Ed); history for teachers (Certificate); homeland security and defense (Certificate); humanities and public affairs (MA, MGS, MIAA, MPA, MS, MS Ed, Certificate); public administration (MPA); public management (Certificate); religious studies (MA); religious studies for the professions (Certificate). *Application deadline:* For fall admission, 7/20 priority date for domestic students, 5/1 for international students; for spring admission, 12/20 priority date for domestic students, 9/1 for international students; for summer admission, 5/20 priority date for domestic students. Applications are processed on a rolling basis. *Application fee:* $35 ($50 for international students). Electronic applications accepted. *Application Contact:* Michael Edwards, Coordinator of Graduate Admissions, 417-836-5330, Fax: 417-836-6200, E-mail: michaeledwards@missouristate.edu. *Dean,* Dr. Victor Matthews, 417-836-5529, Fax: 417-836-8472, E-mail: victormatthews@missouristate.edu.

College of Natural and Applied Sciences Students: 74 full-time (29 women), 80 part-time (43 women); includes 7 minority (2 Black or African American, non-Hispanic/Latino; 2 Asian, non-Hispanic/Latino; 1 Hispanic/Latino; 2 Two or more races, non-Hispanic/Latino), 38 international. Average age 27. 161 applicants, 43% accepted, 43 enrolled. *Faculty:* 87 full-time (14 women), 8 part-time/adjunct (2 women). *Financial support:* In 2015–16, 11 research assistantships with full tuition reimbursements (averaging $10,464 per year), 81 teaching assistantships with full tuition reimbursements (averaging $9,483 per year) were awarded; Federal Work-

Study, institutionally sponsored loans, scholarships/grants, and unspecified assistantships also available. Financial award application deadline: 3/31; financial award applicants required to submit FAFSA. In 2015, 52 master's awarded. *Degree program information:* Part-time and evening/weekend programs available. Part-time, evening/weekend. Offers biology (MS); chemistry (MS); materials science (MS); mathematics (MS); natural and applied science (MNAS); natural and applied sciences (MNAS, MS, MS Ed); secondary education (MS Ed). *Application deadline:* For fall admission, 7/20 priority date for domestic students, 5/1 for international students; for spring admission, 12/20 priority date for domestic students, 9/1 for international students; for summer admission, 5/20 priority date for domestic students. Applications are processed on a rolling basis. *Application fee:* $35 ($50 for international students). Electronic applications accepted. *Application Contact:* Michael Edwards, Coordinator of Graduate Admissions, 417-836-5330, Fax: 417-836-6200, E-mail: michaeledwards@missouristate.edu. *Dean*, Dr. Tamera Jahnke, 417-836-5249, Fax: 417-836-6934.

William H. Darr School of Agriculture Students: 17 full-time (9 women), 26 part-time (17 women); includes 3 minority (1 Black or African American, non-Hispanic/Latino; 1 Hispanic/Latino; 1 Two or more races, non-Hispanic/Latino), 1 international. Average age 27. 28 applicants, 64% accepted, 17 enrolled. *Faculty:* 16 full-time (5 women), 1 part-time/adjunct (0 women). *Financial support:* In 2015–16, 7 research assistantships with full tuition reimbursements (averaging $9,365 per year), 6 teaching assistantships with full tuition reimbursements (averaging $8,450 per year) were awarded; Federal Work-Study, institutionally sponsored loans, scholarships/grants, and unspecified assistantships also available. Financial award application deadline: 3/31; financial award applicants required to submit FAFSA. In 2015, 21 master's awarded. *Degree program information:* Part-time programs available. Part-time. Offers plant science (MS); secondary education (MS Ed). *Application deadline:* For fall admission, 7/20 priority date for domestic students, 5/1 for international students; for spring admission, 12/20 priority date for domestic students, 9/1 for international students; for summer admission, 5/20 priority date for domestic students. Applications are processed on a rolling basis. *Application fee:* $35 ($50 for international students). Electronic applications accepted. *Application Contact:* Michael Edwards, Coordinator of Graduate Admissions, 417-836-5330, Fax: 417-836-6200, E-mail: michaeledwards@missouristate.edu. *Head*, Dr. W. Anson Elliott, 417-836-5638, E-mail: ansonelliot@missouristate.edu.

See Display below and Close-Up on page 891.

MISSOURI UNIVERSITY OF SCIENCE AND TECHNOLOGY, Rolla, MO 65409

General Information State-supported, coed, university. CGS member. *Enrollment:* 8,889 graduate, professional, and undergraduate students; 768 full-time matriculated graduate/professional students (183 women), 646 part-time matriculated graduate/professional students (155 women). *Enrollment by degree level:* 804 master's, 344 doctoral, 266 other advanced degrees. *Graduate faculty:* 291 full-time (42 women), 30 part-time/adjunct (2 women). Tuition, state resident: full-time $10,536. Tuition, nonresident: full-time $27,015. Full-time tuition and fees vary according to course load. *Graduate housing:* Rooms and/or apartments available on a first-come, first-served basis to single and married students. *Student services:* Campus employment opportunities, campus safety program, career counseling, exercise/wellness program, free psychological counseling, international student services, low-cost health insurance, multicultural affairs office. *Library:* Curtis Laws Wilson Library. *Collection:* Books: 295,079 (physical), 348,067 (digital/electronic); Serial titles: 14,178 (physical), 79,586 (digital/electronic); Databases: 180. Weekly public service hours: 112; students can reserve study rooms. *Research affiliation:* Geoengineers, Inc. (rock mechanics and explosives research), Caterpillar, Inc. (mining and nuclear engineering), Idaho National Laboratory (material research), Hussmann, Corp (mining and nuclear engineering), Samsung (material research), Cisco Sys, Inc. (material research).

Computer facilities: Computer purchase and lease plans are available. 959 computers available on campus for general student use. A campuswide network can be accessed from student residence rooms and from off campus. Online class registration is available.
Website: http://www.mst.edu/

General Application Contact: Debbie Schwertz, Admissions Coordinator, 573-341-6013, Fax: 573-341-6271, E-mail: schwertz@mst.edu.

GRADUATE UNITS

Graduate School Students: 1,235 full-time (271 women), 813 part-time (173 women); includes 198 minority (59 Black or African American, non-Hispanic/Latino; 4 American Indian or Alaska Native, non-Hispanic/Latino; 60 Asian, non-Hispanic/Latino; 61 Hispanic/Latino; 2 Native Hawaiian or other Pacific Islander, non-Hispanic/Latino; 12 Two or more races, non-Hispanic/Latino), 932 international. Average age 29. 2,088 applicants, 57% accepted, 518 enrolled. *Faculty:* 356 full-time (90 women), 51 part-time/adjunct (6 women). *Financial support:* In 2015–16, 68 fellowships with tuition reimbursements, 390 research assistantships with tuition reimbursements, 194 teaching assistantships with tuition reimbursements were awarded; career-related internships or fieldwork, Federal Work-Study, institutionally sponsored loans, traineeships, and tuition waivers (partial) also available. Support available to part-time students. Financial award application deadline: 3/1; financial award applicants required to submit FAFSA. In 2015, 675 master's, 95 doctorates awarded. *Degree program information:* Part-time and evening/weekend programs available. Part-time, evening/weekend. Offers aerospace engineering (MS, PhD); applied and environmental biology (MS); applied mathematics (MS); business and information technology (MBA); ceramic engineering (MS, DE, PhD); chemical engineering (MS, DE, PhD); chemistry (MS, MST, PhD); civil engineering (MS, DE, PhD); computer engineering (MS, DE, PhD); computer science (MS, PhD); construction engineering (MS, DE, PhD); electrical engineering (MS, DE, PhD); engineering management (MS, DE, PhD); environmental engineering (MS); fluid mechanics (MS, DE, PhD); geological engineering (MS, DE, PhD); geology and geophysics (MS, PhD); geotechnical engineering (MS, DE, PhD); hydrology and hydraulic engineering (MS, DE, PhD); information science and technology (MS); manufacturing engineering (M Eng, MS); mathematics (MST, PhD); mechanical engineering (MS, DE, PhD); metallurgical engineering (MS, PhD); mining engineering (MS, DE, PhD); nuclear engineering (MS, DE, PhD); petroleum engineering (MS, DE, PhD); physics (MS, MST, PhD); systems engineering (MS, PhD). *Application deadline:* For fall admission, 7/15 for domestic students, 5/15 for international students; for spring admission, 12/15 for domestic students, 10/15 for international students; for summer admission, 5/1 for domestic students, 3/1 for international students. Applications are processed on a rolling basis. *Application fee:* $55 ($75 for international students). Electronic applications accepted. *Application Contact:* Debbie Schwertz, Admissions Coordinator, 573-341-6013, Fax: 573-341-6271, E-mail: schwertz@mst.edu. *Vice Provost for Graduate Studies*, Dr. Venkat Allada, 573-341-4141, Fax: 573-341-6127, E-mail: mstgrad@mst.edu.

MISSOURI VALLEY COLLEGE, Marshall, MO 65340-3197

General Information Independent-religious, coed, comprehensive institution.

GRADUATE UNITS

Graduate Studies

MISSOURI WESTERN STATE UNIVERSITY, St. Joseph, MO 64507-2294

General Information State-supported, coed, comprehensive institution. CGS member. *Enrollment:* 5,513 graduate, professional, and undergraduate students; 68 full-time matriculated graduate/professional students (19 women), 147 part-time matriculated graduate/professional students (92 women). *Enrollment by degree level:* 208 master's, 7 other advanced degrees. *Graduate faculty:* 39 full-time (17 women), 9 part-time/adjunct (4 women). Tuition, state resident: full-time $6290; part-time $314 per credit hour. Tuition, nonresident: full-time $11,490; part-time $574 per credit hour. *Required fees:* $542; $99 per credit hour. $176 per semester. One-time fee: $45. Tuition and fees vary according to course load and program. *Graduate housing:* Room and/or apartments available on a first-come, first-served basis to single students; on-campus housing not available to married students. Typical cost: $6514 per year ($9728 including board). Room and board charges vary according to board plan and housing facility selected. *Student services:* Campus employment opportunities, campus safety program, career counseling, child daycare facilities, exercise/wellness program, free psychological counseling, international student services, low-cost health insurance, multicultural affairs office, services for students with disabilities. *Library:* Missouri Western State University Library. *Collection:* Books: 229,485 (physical), 140,698 (digital/electronic); Serial titles: 12,958 (physical), 6,056 (digital/electronic); Databases: 68.

Computer facilities: Computer purchase and lease plans are available. A campuswide network can be accessed from student residence rooms and from off campus. Online class registration, personal online storage are available.
Website: http://www.missouriwestern.edu/

General Application Contact: Dr. Benjamin D. Caldwell, Dean of the Graduate School, 816-271-4394, Fax: 816-271-4525, E-mail: graduate@missouriwestern.edu.

GRADUATE UNITS

Program in Applied Science Students: 40 full-time (14 women), 38 part-time (12 women); includes 9 minority (8 Black or African American, non-Hispanic/Latino; 1 Asian, non-Hispanic/Latino), 19 international. Average age 29. 36 applicants, 92% accepted, 25 enrolled. *Financial support:* Scholarships/grants and unspecified assistantships available. Support available to part-time students. In 2015, 28 master's awarded. *Degree program information:* Part-time programs available. Part-time. Offers chemistry (MAS); engineering technology management (MAS); human factors and usability testing (MAS); industrial life science (MAS); information technology management (MAS); sport and fitness management (MAS). *Application deadline:* For fall admission, 7/15 for domestic and international students; for spring admission, 11/1 for domestic students, 10/15 for international students; for summer admission, 4/29 for domestic students. Applications are processed on a rolling basis. *Application fee:* $45 ($50 for international students). Electronic applications accepted. *Dean of the Graduate School*, Dr. Benjamin D. Caldwell, 816-271-4394, Fax: 816-271-4525, E-mail: graduate@missouriwestern.edu.

Program in Assessment Students: 32 part-time (26 women); includes 3 minority (1 Black or African American, non-Hispanic/Latino; 1 American Indian or Alaska Native, non-Hispanic/Latino; 1 Hispanic/Latino). Average age 35. 5 applicants, 100% accepted, 5 enrolled. *Financial support:* Scholarships/grants and unspecified assistantships available. Support available to part-time students. In 2015, 13 master's, 3 other advanced degrees awarded. *Degree program information:* Part-time programs available. Part-time. Offers autism spectrum disorders (MAS, Graduate Certificate); TESOL (MAS, Graduate Certificate); writing (MAS). *Application deadline:* For fall admission, 7/15 for domestic and international students; for spring admission, 11/1 for domestic students, 10/15 for international students; for summer admission, 4/29 for domestic students. Applications are processed on a rolling basis. *Application fee:* $45 ($50 for international students). Electronic applications accepted. *Application Contact:* Dr. Benjamin D. Caldwell, Dean of the Graduate School, 816-271-4394, Fax: 816-271-4525, E-mail: graduate@missouriwestern.edu. *Director of Graduate Programs in Education*, Dr. Susan Bashinski, 816-271-5629, E-mail: sbashinski@missouriwestern.edu.

Program in Digital Media Students: 2 full-time (0 women), 12 part-time (3 women); includes 1 minority (Black or African American, non-Hispanic/Latino), 5 international. Average age 30. 4 applicants, 100% accepted, 3 enrolled. *Financial support:* Scholarships/grants and unspecified assistantships available. Support available to part-time students. In 2015, 2 master's awarded. *Degree program information:* Part-time programs available. Part-time. Offers digital media (MAA). *Application deadline:* For fall admission, 7/15 for domestic and international students; for spring admission, 11/1 for domestic students, 10/15 for international students; for summer admission, 4/29 for domestic students. Applications are processed on a rolling basis. *Application fee:* $45 ($50 for international students). Electronic applications accepted. *Application Contact:* Dr. Benjamin D. Caldwell, Dean of the Graduate School, 816-271-4394, Fax: 816-271-4525, E-mail: graduate@missouriwestern.edu. *Professor*, Dr. Bob Bergland, 816-271-4446, E-mail: bergland@missouriwestern.edu.

Program in Forensic Investigations Students: 2 full-time (1 woman), 8 part-time (5 women); includes 3 minority (2 Black or African American, non-Hispanic/Latino; 1 Two or more races, non-Hispanic/Latino). Average age 32. 2 applicants, 100% accepted, 1 enrolled. *Financial support:* Scholarships/grants and unspecified assistantships available. Support available to part-time students. In 2015, 9 master's awarded. *Degree program information:* Part-time programs available. Part-time. Offers forensic investigations (MAS, Graduate Certificate). *Application deadline:* For fall admission, 7/15 for domestic and international students; for spring admission, 11/1 for domestic students, 10/15 for international students; for summer admission, 4/29 for domestic students. Applications are processed on a rolling basis. *Application fee:* $45 ($50 for international students). Electronic applications accepted. *Application Contact:* Dr. Benjamin D. Caldwell, Dean of the Graduate School, 816-271-4394, Fax: 816-271-4525, E-mail: graduate@missouriwestern.edu. *Forensics Graduate Program Director*, Dr. Monty Smith, 816-271-4434, E-mail: msmith84@missouriwestern.edu.

Program in Information Management Students: 15 full-time (3 women), 14 part-time (8 women); includes 3 minority (2 Black or African American, non-Hispanic/Latino; 1 Two or more races, non-Hispanic/Latino), 13 international. Average age 31. 15 applicants, 87% accepted, 10 enrolled. *Financial support:* Scholarships/grants and unspecified assistantships available. Support available to part-time students. *Degree program information:* Part-time programs available. Part-time. Offers enterprise resource planning (MIM). *Application deadline:* For fall admission, 7/15 for domestic and international students; for spring admission, 11/1 for domestic students, 10/15 for international students; for summer admission, 4/29 for domestic students. Applications are processed on a rolling basis. *Application fee:* $45 ($50 for international students). Electronic applications accepted. *Application Contact:* Dr. Benjamin D. Caldwell, Dean of the Graduate School, 816-271-4394, Fax: 816-271-4525, E-mail: graduate@missouriwestern.edu. *Professor*, Dr. Peggy Lane, 816-271-5832, E-mail: plane3@missouriwestern.edu.

Program in Information Technology Assurance Administration Students: 11 full-time (4 women), 3 part-time (0 women), 12 international. Average age 27. 23 applicants, 65% accepted, 3 enrolled. *Financial support:* Scholarships/grants and unspecified assistantships available. Support available to part-time students. *Degree program information:* Part-time programs available. Part-time. Offers information technology assurance administration (MS). *Application deadline:* For fall admission, 7/15 for domestic and international students; for spring admission, 11/1 for domestic students, 10/15 for international students; for summer admission, 4/29 for domestic students. Applications are processed on a rolling basis. *Application fee:* $45 ($50 for international students). Electronic applications accepted. *Application Contact:* Dr. Benjamin D. Caldwell, Dean of the Graduate School, 816-271-4394, Fax: 816-271-4525, E-mail: graduate@missouriwestern.edu. *Associate Professor*, Dr. Baoqiang Yan, 816-271-4372, E-mail: byan@missouriwestern.edu.

Program in Nursing Students: 31 part-time (30 women). Average age 34. 17 applicants, 100% accepted, 14 enrolled. *Financial support:* Scholarships/grants and unspecified assistantships available. Support available to part-time students. In 2015, 2 master's awarded. *Degree program information:* Part-time programs available. Part-time. Offers health care leadership (MSN); nurse educator (MSN, Graduate Certificate). *Application deadline:* For fall admission, 7/15 for domestic and international students; for spring admission, 11/1 for domestic students, 10/15 for international students; for summer admission, 4/29 for domestic students. Applications are processed on a rolling basis. *Application fee:* $45 ($50 for international students). Electronic applications accepted. *Application Contact:* Dr. Benjamin D. Caldwell, Dean of the Graduate School, 816-271-4394, Fax: 816-271-4525, E-mail: graduate@missouriwestern.edu. *Associate Professor*, Dr. Carolyn Brose, 816-271-5912, E-mail: brose@missouriwestern.edu.

Program in Written Communication Students: 1 full-time (0 women), 11 part-time (9 women); includes 1 minority (American Indian or Alaska Native, non-Hispanic/Latino). Average age 38. 2 applicants, 100% accepted, 2 enrolled. *Financial support:* Scholarships/grants and unspecified assistantships available. Support available to part-time students. In 2015, 3 master's, 1 other advanced degree awarded. *Degree program information:* Part-time programs available. Part-time. Offers teaching of writing (Graduate Certificate); technical communication (MAA); writing studies (MAA). *Application deadline:* For fall admission, 7/15 for domestic and international students; for spring admission, 11/1 for domestic students, 10/15 for international students; for summer admission, 4/29 for domestic students. Applications are processed on a rolling basis. *Application fee:* $45 ($50 for international students). Electronic applications accepted. *Application Contact:* Dr. Benjamin D. Caldwell, Dean of the Graduate School, 816-271-4394, Fax: 816-271-4525, E-mail: graduate@missouriwestern.edu. *Associate Professor/Director of Graduate Studies*, Dr. Michael Charlton, 816-271-4323, E-mail: mcharlton@missouriwestern.edu.

See Display on next page and Close-Up on page 893.

MOLLOY COLLEGE, Rockville Centre, NY 11571-5002

General Information Independent, coed, comprehensive institution. *Enrollment:* 4,894 graduate, professional, and undergraduate students; 239 full-time matriculated graduate/professional students (192 women), 877 part-time matriculated graduate/professional students (741 women). *Enrollment by degree level:* 1,036 master's, 61 doctoral, 19 other advanced degrees. *Graduate faculty:* 66 full-time (58 women), 68 part-time/adjunct (53 women). *Tuition, area resident:* Full-time $18,450; part-time $1025 per credit. *Required fees:* $900; $740 per unit. Tuition and fees vary according to course load. *Graduate housing:* On-campus housing not available. *Student services:* Campus employment opportunities, campus safety program, career counseling, free psychological counseling, international student services, low-cost health insurance, services for students with disabilities, teacher training, writing training. *Library:* James Edward Tobin Library plus 1 other. *Collection:* Books: 51,424 (physical), 229,806 (digital/electronic); Serial titles: 50 (physical), 56,083 (digital/electronic); Databases: 161.

Computer facilities: 713 computers available on campus for general student use. A campuswide network can be accessed from student residence rooms and from off campus. Online class registration is available.
Website: http://www.molloy.edu/

General Application Contact: Jaclyn Machowicz, Assistant Director for Admissions, 516-323-4010, E-mail: jmachowicz@molloy.edu.

GRADUATE UNITS

Criminal Justice Program Students: 17 full-time (8 women), 9 part-time (5 women); includes 12 minority (6 Black or African American, non-Hispanic/Latino; 2 Asian, non-Hispanic/Latino; 4 Hispanic/Latino). Average age 32. 17 applicants, 88% accepted, 12 enrolled. *Faculty:* 4 full-time (2 women), 2 part-time/adjunct (1 woman). In 2015, 20 master's awarded. *Degree program information:* Part-time and evening/weekend programs available. Part-time, evening/weekend. Offers criminal justice (MS). *Application deadline:* Applications are processed on a rolling basis. *Application fee:* $60. Electronic applications accepted. *Application Contact:* Jaclyn Machowicz, Assistant Director for Admissions, 516-323-4010, E-mail: jmachowicz@molloy.edu. *Associate Dean/Graduate Program Director*, Dr. John Eterno, 516-323-3806, E-mail: jeterno@molloy.edu.

Division of Nursing Students: 13 full-time (all women), 550 part-time (515 women); includes 316 minority (169 Black or African American, non-Hispanic/Latino; 1 American Indian or Alaska Native, non-Hispanic/Latino; 88 Asian, non-Hispanic/Latino; 56 Hispanic/Latino; 2 Native Hawaiian or other Pacific Islander, non-Hispanic/Latino). Average age 43. 208 applicants, 69% accepted, 121 enrolled. *Faculty:* 26 full-time (all women), 12 part-time/adjunct (9 women). *Financial support:* Research assistantships with partial tuition reimbursements, teaching assistantships with partial tuition reimbursements, institutionally sponsored loans, scholarships/grants, and unspecified assistantships available. Support available to part-time students. Financial award application deadline: 4/1; financial award applicants required to submit FAFSA. In 2015, 116 master's, 1 doctorate, 6 other advanced degrees awarded. *Degree program information:* Part-time and evening/weekend programs available. Part-time, evening/weekend. Offers adult-gerontology primary care nurse practitioner (MS); clinical nurse specialist (MS); clinical nurse specialist: adult-gerontology (Advanced Certificate); family nurse practitioner (MS, Advanced Certificate); family psychiatric mental health nurse practitioner (MS); nursing (DNP, PhD); nursing administration (MS); nursing education (MS); pediatric nurse practitioner (MS). *Application deadline:* For fall admission, 9/2 priority date for domestic students; for spring admission, 1/20 priority date for domestic students. Applications are processed on a rolling basis. *Application* *fee:* $60. Electronic applications accepted. *Application Contact:* Jaclyn Machowicz, Assistant Director for Admissions, 516-323-4010, E-mail: jmachowicz@molloy.edu. *Dean of Nursing,* Dr. Jeannine Muldoon, 516-323-3651, E-mail: jmuldoon@molloy.edu.

Graduate Business Program Students: 46 full-time (25 women), 103 part-time (51 women); includes 48 minority (27 Black or African American, non-Hispanic/Latino; 8 Asian, non-Hispanic/Latino; 12 Hispanic/Latino; 1 Native Hawaiian or other Pacific Islander, non-Hispanic/Latino), 3 international. Average age 29. 64 applicants, 84% accepted, 46 enrolled. *Faculty:* 5 full-time (2 women), 14 part-time/adjunct (7 women). *Financial support:* Applicants required to submit FAFSA. In 2015, 55 master's awarded. *Degree program information:* Part-time and evening/weekend programs available. Part-time, evening/weekend. Offers accounting (MBA); finance (MBA); healthcare (MBA); management (MBA); marketing (MBA). *Application deadline:* Applications are processed on a rolling basis. *Application fee:* $60. Electronic applications accepted. *Application Contact:* Jaclyn Machowicz, Assistant Director for Admissions, 516-323-4010, E-mail: jmachowicz@molloy.edu. *Associate Dean/Director of Graduate Program,* Dr. Maureen Mackenzie, 516-323-3080, E-mail: mmackenzie@molloy.edu.

Graduate Education Program Students: 84 full-time (66 women), 176 part-time (133 women); includes 35 minority (8 Black or African American, non-Hispanic/Latino; 4 Asian, non-Hispanic/Latino; 23 Hispanic/Latino). Average age 27. 116 applicants, 79% accepted, 83 enrolled. *Faculty:* 18 full-time (16 women), 29 part-time/adjunct (26 women). *Financial support:* Applicants required to submit FAFSA. In 2015, 85 master's, 5 Advanced Certificates awarded. *Degree program information:* Part-time and evening/weekend programs available. Part-time, evening/weekend. Offers adolescent education in biology (MS Ed); adolescent special education (Advanced Certificate); bilingual extension (Advanced Certificate); childhood education (MS Ed); childhood special education (Advanced Certificate); early childhood education (MS Ed); English (MS Ed); mathematics (MS Ed); social studies (MS Ed); Spanish (MS Ed); special education on both childhood and adolescent levels (MS Ed); teaching English to speakers of other languages (TESOL) in grades Pre-K to 12 (MS Ed); TESOL (Advanced Certificate). *Application deadline:* Applications are processed on a rolling basis. *Application fee:* $60. Electronic applications accepted. *Application Contact:* Jaclyn Machowicz, Assistant Director for Admissions, 516-323-4010, E-mail: jmachowicz@molloy.edu. *Associate Dean/Director,* Joanne O'Brien, 516-323-3116, E-mail: jobrien@molloy.edu.

Graduate Music Therapy Program Students: 13 full-time (10 women), 19 part-time (11 women); includes 8 minority (2 Black or African American, non-Hispanic/Latino; 2 Asian, non-Hispanic/Latino; 4 Hispanic/Latino), 5 international. Average age 31. 48 applicants, 46% accepted, 12 enrolled. *Faculty:* 4 full-time (3 women), 8 part-time/adjunct (7 women). *Financial support:* Applicants required to submit FAFSA. In 2015, 9 master's awarded. *Degree program information:* Part-time and evening/weekend programs available. Part-time, evening/weekend. Offers music therapy (MS). *Application deadline:* Applications are processed on a rolling basis. *Application fee:* $60. Electronic applications accepted. *Application Contact:* Jaclyn Machowicz, Assistant Director for Admissions, 516-323-4010, E-mail: jmachowicz@molloy.edu. *Associate Dean/Director of Graduate Music Therapy,* Suzanne Sorel, 516-323-3322, E-mail: ssorel@molloy.edu.

Program in Clinical Mental Health Counseling Students: 18 part-time (15 women); includes 6 minority (2 Black or African American, non-Hispanic/Latino; 1 American Indian or Alaska Native, non-Hispanic/Latino; 1 Asian, non-Hispanic/Latino; 2 Hispanic/Latino). Average age 32. 32 applicants, 59% accepted, 18 enrolled. *Faculty:* 3 full-time (all women). *Financial support:* Applicants required to submit FAFSA. *Degree program information:* Part-time and evening/weekend programs available. Part-time-only, evening/weekend. Offers clinical mental health counseling (MS). *Application deadline:* Applications are processed on a rolling basis. *Application fee:* $60. Electronic applications accepted. *Application Contact:* Jaclyn Machowicz, Assistant Director for Admissions, 516-323-4010, E-mail: jmachowicz@molloy.edu. *Associate Dean and Director for Department of Clinical Mental Health Counseling,* Dr. Laura B. Kestemberg, 516-323-3842, E-mail: lkestemberg@molloy.edu.

Program in Speech Language Pathology Students: 52 full-time (51 women), 1 (woman) part-time; includes 8 minority (4 Asian, non-Hispanic/Latino; 3 Hispanic/Latino; 1 Two or more races, non-Hispanic/Latino), 1 international. Average age 24. 324 applicants, 24% accepted, 32 enrolled. *Faculty:* 7 full-time (all women), 3 part-time/adjunct (all women). *Financial support:* Applicants required to submit FAFSA. In 2015, 17 master's awarded. *Degree program information:* Part-time and evening/weekend programs available. Part-time, evening/weekend. Offers speech-language pathology (MS). *Application deadline:* Applications are processed on a rolling basis. *Application fee:* $60. Electronic applications accepted. *Application Contact:* Jaclyn Machowicz, Assistant Director for Admissions, 516-323-4010, E-mail: jmachowicz@molloy.edu. *Associate Dean of Speech-Language Pathology,* Dr. Barbara Schmidt, 516-323-3519, E-mail: bschmidt@molloy.edu.

MONMOUTH UNIVERSITY, West Long Branch, NJ 07764-1898

General Information Independent, coed, comprehensive institution. CGS member. *Enrollment:* 6,394 graduate, professional, and undergraduate students; 737 full-time matriculated graduate/professional students (566 women), 898 part-time matriculated graduate/professional students (673 women). *Enrollment by degree level:* 1,578 master's, 4 doctoral, 53 other advanced degrees. *Graduate faculty:* 119 full-time (69 women), 91 part-time/adjunct (50 women). *Tuition, area resident:* Part-time $1098 per credit hour. *Required fees:* $175 per semester. Tuition and fees vary according to program. *Graduate housing:* On-campus housing not available. *Student services:* Campus employment opportunities, campus safety program, career counseling, exercise/wellness program, free psychological counseling, international student services, low-cost health insurance, multicultural affairs office, services for students with disabilities, writing training. *Library:* Monmouth University Library. *Collection:* Books: 285,496 (physical), 31,870 (digital/electronic); Serial titles: 1,200 (physical), 71,277 (digital/electronic); Databases: 163. Weekly public service hours: 111; students can reserve study rooms. *Research affiliation:* The Nature Conservancy, Ecotrust (healthy oceans and coastal communities), National Institute of Standards and Technology (NIST), National Oceanic and Atmospheric Administration (NOAA), Substance Abuse and Mental Health Services Administration (SAMHSA) (campus suicide prevention), Gordon and Betty Moore Foundation (environmental conservation, patient care).

Computer facilities: Computer purchase and lease plans are available. 1,000 computers available on campus for general student use. A campuswide network can be accessed from student residence rooms and from off campus. Online class registration is available.
Website: http://www.monmouth.edu/

General Application Contact: Lauren Vento-Cifelli, Associate Vice President of Undergraduate and Graduate Admission, 732-571-3452, Fax: 732-263-5123, E-mail: gradadm@monmouth.edu.

GRADUATE UNITS

Graduate Studies Students: 737 full-time (566 women), 898 part-time (673 women); includes 317 minority (109 Black or African American, non-Hispanic/Latino; 3 American Indian or Alaska Native, non-Hispanic/Latino; 73 Asian, non-Hispanic/Latino; 113 Hispanic/Latino; 4 Native Hawaiian or other Pacific Islander, non-Hispanic/Latino; 15 Two or more races, non-Hispanic/Latino), 96 international. Average age 30. 1,739 applicants, 60% accepted, 633 enrolled. *Faculty:* 119 full-time (69 women), 91 part-time/adjunct (50 women). *Financial support:* In 2015–16, 1,573 students received support, including 1,432 fellowships (averaging $3,581 per year), 141 research assistantships (averaging $8,386 per year); career-related internships or fieldwork, institutionally sponsored loans, scholarships/grants, and unspecified assistantships also available. Support available to part-time students. Financial award applicants required to submit FAFSA. In 2015, 664 master's, 8 doctorates awarded. *Degree program information:* Part-time and evening/weekend programs available. Part-time, evening/weekend, 100% online, blended/hybrid learning. Offers anthropology (MA); computer science (MS); computer science software design and development (Certificate); corporate and public communication (MA); creative writing (MA); criminal justice (MA); criminal justice administration (Certificate); European history (MA); history of the U.S. (MA); homeland security (MS, Certificate); human resources management and communication (Certificate); information systems (MS); literature (MA); professional counseling (MS, PMC); psychological counseling (MA); public policy (MA); public service communication specialist (Certificate); rhetoric and writing (MA); software development (Certificate); software engineering (MS, Certificate); strategic public relations and new media (Certificate); world history (MA). *Application deadline:* For fall admission, 7/15 priority date for domestic students, 6/1 for international students; for spring admission, 11/15 priority date for domestic students, 11/1 for international students. Applications are processed on a rolling basis. *Application fee:* $50. Electronic applications accepted. *Application Contact:* Laurie Kuhn, Associate Director of Graduate Admission, 732-571-3452, Fax: 732-263-5123, E-mail: gradadm@monmouth.edu. *Vice Provost for Graduate Studies,* Dr. Michael A. Palladino, 732-571-7550, Fax: 732-263-5142.

Leon Hess Business School Students: 77 full-time (39 women), 105 part-time (48 women); includes 19 minority (5 Black or African American, non-Hispanic/Latino; 7 Asian, non-Hispanic/Latino; 3 Hispanic/Latino; 1 Native Hawaiian or other Pacific Islander, non-Hispanic/Latino; 3 Two or more races, non-Hispanic/Latino), 3 international. Average age 30. 130 applicants, 80% accepted, 76 enrolled. *Faculty:* 19 full-time (4 women), 11 part-time/adjunct (1 woman). *Financial support:* In 2015–16, 148 students received support, including 138 fellowships (averaging $3,075 per year), 10 research assistantships (averaging $12,977 per year); career-related internships or fieldwork, institutionally sponsored loans, scholarships/grants, and unspecified assistantships also available. Support available to part-time students. Financial award applicants required to submit FAFSA. In 2015, 107 master's, 2 other advanced degrees awarded. *Degree program information:* Part-time and evening/weekend programs available. Part-time, evening/weekend. Offers accounting (MBA, Post-Master's Certificate); business administration (MBA); finance (MBA); management (MBA); marketing (MBA); real estate (MBA). *Application deadline:* For fall admission, 7/15 priority date for domestic students, 6/1 for international students; for spring admission, 12/15 priority date for domestic students, 11/1 for international students. Applications are processed on a rolling basis. *Application fee:* $50. Electronic applications accepted. *Application Contact:* Laurie Kuhn, Associate Director of Graduate Admission, 732-571-3452, Fax: 732-263-5123, E-mail: gradadm@monmouth.edu. *MBA Program Director,* Dr. Susan Gupta, 732-571-3639, Fax: 732-263-5517, E-mail: sgupta@monmouth.edu.

The Marjorie K. Unterberg School of Nursing and Health Studies Students: 58 full-time (46 women), 271 part-time (252 women); includes 93 minority (31 Black or African American, non-Hispanic/Latino; 40 Asian, non-Hispanic/Latino; 18 Hispanic/Latino; 1 Native Hawaiian or other Pacific Islander, non-Hispanic/Latino; 3 Two or more races, non-Hispanic/Latino), 1 international. Average age 37. 450 applicants, 32% accepted, 103 enrolled. *Faculty:* 14 full-time (13 women), 10 part-time/adjunct (5 women). *Financial support:* In 2015–16, 241 students received support, including 220 fellowships (averaging $3,403 per year), 5 research assistantships (averaging $5,146 per year); career-related internships or fieldwork, scholarships/grants, and unspecified assistantships also available. Support available to part-time students. Financial award applicants required to submit FAFSA. In 2015, 68 master's, 8 doctorates, 11 other advanced degrees awarded. *Degree program information:* Part-time and evening/weekend programs available. Part-time, evening/weekend, 100% online, blended/hybrid learning. Offers adult and gerontological primary care nurse practitioner (MSN); adult-gerontological primary care nurse practitioner (Post-Master's Certificate); family nurse practitioner (MSN, Post-Master's Certificate); family psychiatric and mental health advanced practice nursing (MSN); family psychiatric and mental health nurse practitioner (Post-Master's Certificate); forensic nursing (MSN, Certificate); nursing (MSN); nursing administration (MSN, Post-Master's Certificate); nursing education (MSN, Post-Master's Certificate); nursing practice (DNP); physician assistant (MS); school nursing (MSN, Certificate). *Application deadline:* For fall admission, 7/15 priority date for domestic students, 6/1 for international students; for spring admission, 12/15 priority date for domestic students, 11/1 for international students; for summer admission, 5/1 for domestic students. Applications are processed on a rolling basis. *Application fee:* $50. Electronic applications accepted. *Application Contact:* Lucia Fedele, Graduate Admission Counselor, 732-571-3452, Fax: 732-263-5123, E-mail: gradadm@monmouth.edu. *Dean,* Dr. Janet Mahoney, 732-571-3443, Fax: 732-263-5131, E-mail: jmahoney@monmouth.edu.

School of Education Students: 195 full-time (173 women), 153 part-time (126 women); includes 42 minority (12 Black or African American, non-Hispanic/Latino; 6 Asian, non-Hispanic/Latino; 21 Hispanic/Latino; 1 Native Hawaiian or other Pacific Islander, non-Hispanic/Latino; 2 Two or more races, non-Hispanic/Latino). Average age 27. 471 applicants, 54% accepted, 147 enrolled. *Faculty:* 25 full-time (20 women), 28 part-time/adjunct (22 women). *Financial support:* In 2015–16, 303 students received support, including 274 fellowships (averaging $3,853 per year), 29 research assistantships (averaging $11,874 per year); institutionally sponsored loans, scholarships/grants, and unspecified assistantships also available. Support available to part-time students. Financial award applicants required to submit FAFSA. In 2015, 124 master's, 3 other advanced degrees awarded. *Degree program information:* Part-time and evening/weekend programs available. Part-time, evening/weekend, 100% online, blended/hybrid learning. Offers applied behavioral analysis (Certificate); autism (Certificate); director of school counseling services (Post-Master's Certificate); initial certification (MAT); learning disabilities teacher-consultant (Post-Master's Certificate); principal/school administrator (MS Ed); principal/supervisor (MS Ed); school counseling (MS Ed); special education (MS Ed); speech-language pathology (MS Ed); student affairs and college counseling (MS Ed); supervisor (Post-Master's Certificate); teaching English to speakers of other languages (TESOL) (Certificate). *Application deadline:* For fall admission, 7/15 priority date for domestic students, 7/1 for international students; for spring admission, 12/15 priority date for domestic students, 11/1 for international students. Applications are processed on a rolling basis. *Application fee:* $50. Electronic applications accepted. *Application Contact:* Laurie Kuhn, Associate Director of Graduate Admission, 732-571-3452, Fax: 732-263-5123, E-mail: gradadm@monmouth.edu. *Dean of The School of Education,* Dr. John E. Henning, 732-263-5513, Fax: 732-263-5277.

School of Social Work Students: 150 full-time (136 women), 99 part-time (84 women); includes 82 minority (36 Black or African American, non-Hispanic/Latino; 1 American Indian or Alaska Native, non-Hispanic/Latino; 5 Asian, non-Hispanic/Latino; 35 Hispanic/Latino; 1 Native Hawaiian or other Pacific Islander, non-Hispanic/Latino; 4 Two or more races, non-Hispanic/Latino), 1 international. Average age 30. 238 applicants, 95% accepted, 136 enrolled. *Faculty:* 14 full-time (11 women), 18 part-time/adjunct (14 women). *Financial support:* In 2015–16, 150 students received support, including 140 fellowships (averaging $4,591 per year), 10 research assistantships (averaging $10,836 per year); scholarships/grants and unspecified assistantships also available. Support available to part-time students. Financial award applicants required to submit FAFSA. In 2015, 131 master's, 2 other advanced degrees awarded. *Degree program information:* Part-time and evening/weekend programs available. Part-time, evening/weekend. Offers clinical practice with families and children (MSW); international and community development (MSW); play therapy (Post-Master's Certificate). *Application deadline:* For fall admission, 3/15 for domestic and international students. Applications are processed on a rolling basis. *Application fee:* $50. Electronic applications accepted. *Application Contact:* Lucia Fedele, Graduate Admission Counselor, 732-571-3452, Fax: 732-263-5123, E-mail: gradm@monmouth.edu. *Dean, School of Social Work,* Dr. Robin Mama, 732-571-3543, Fax: 732-263-5217, E-mail: swdept@monmouth.edu.

MONROE COLLEGE, Bronx, NY 10468-5407

General Information Proprietary, coed, comprehensive institution.

GRADUATE UNITS

King Graduate School Online learning. Offers business management (MBA); criminal justice (MS); executive leadership in hospitality management (MS); public health (MPH). Program also offered in New Rochelle, NY.

MONTANA STATE UNIVERSITY, Bozeman, MT 59717

General Information State-supported, coed, university. CGS member. *Graduate housing:* Rooms and/or apartments available on a first-come, first-served basis to single and married students. *Research affiliation:* Phillips Environmental (microbial technology), Microvision (information transmission systems), LigoCyte Pharmaceuticals, Inc. (pharmaceuticals), Eli Lilly and Company (antifungal technology), S2 Corporation (instrumentation), ILX Lightwave (laser diodes, electro-optical test equipment).

GRADUATE UNITS

The Graduate School ***Degree program information:*** Part-time programs available. Part-time, online learning. Electronic applications accepted.

College of Agriculture Degree program information: Part-time programs available. Part-time, online learning. Offers agricultural education (MS); agriculture (MS, PhD); animal and range sciences (MS, PhD); immunology and infectious diseases (MS, PhD); land rehabilitation (interdisciplinary) (MS); land resources and environmental sciences (MS); plant pathology (MS); plant sciences (MS, PhD). Electronic applications accepted.

College of Arts and Architecture Degree program information: Part-time programs available. Part-time. Offers architecture (M Arch); art (MFA); art history (MA); arts and architecture (M Arch, MA, MFA); science and natural history filmmaking (MFA). Electronic applications accepted.

College of Business Degree program information: Part-time programs available. Part-time. Offers professional accountancy (MP Ac). Electronic applications accepted.

College of Education, Health, and Human Development Degree program information: Part-time programs available. Part-time, online learning. Offers adult and higher education (Ed D); curriculum and instruction (M Ed, Ed D); education (M Ed); education, health, and human development (M Ed, MS, Ed D, Ed S); educational leadership (Ed D, Ed S); family and consumer sciences (MS). Electronic applications accepted.

College of Engineering Degree program information: Part-time programs available. Part-time. Offers chemical engineering (MS); civil engineering (MS); computer science (MS, PhD); construction engineering management (MCEM); electrical engineering (MS); engineering (PhD); environmental engineering (MS); industrial and management engineering (MS); mechanical engineering (MS). Electronic applications accepted.

College of Letters and Science Degree program information: Part-time programs available. Part-time, online learning. Offers biochemistry (MS, PhD); biological sciences (PhD); chemistry (MS, PhD); earth sciences (MS, PhD); ecological and environmental statistics (MS); ecology and environmental sciences (PhD); English (MA); fish and wildlife biology (PhD); fish and wildlife management (MS); history (MA, PhD); letters and science (MA, MPA, MS, PhD); mathematics (MS, PhD); microbiology (MS, PhD); Native American studies (MA); neuroscience (MS, PhD); physics (MS, PhD); psychology (MS); public administration (MPA); statistics (MS, PhD). Electronic applications accepted.

College of Nursing Degree program information: Part-time programs available. Part-time, online learning. Offers clinical nurse leader (MN); family and individual nurse practitioner (DNP); family nurse practitioner (MN, Post-Master's Certificate); nursing education (Certificate, Post-Master's Certificate); psychiatric mental health nurse practitioner (MN); psychiatric/mental health nurse practitioner (DNP). Electronic applications accepted.

MONTANA STATE UNIVERSITY BILLINGS, Billings, MT 59101

General Information State-supported, coed, comprehensive institution. *Graduate housing:* Rooms and/or apartments available on a first-come, first-served basis to single and married students. Housing application deadline: 5/1.

GRADUATE UNITS

College of Allied Health Professions ***Degree program information:*** Part-time and evening/weekend programs available. Part-time, evening/weekend, online learning. Offers allied health professions (MHA, MS); athletic training (MS); clinical rehabilitation and mental health counseling (MS); health administration (MHA).

College of Arts and Sciences ***Degree program information:*** Part-time programs available. Part-time, online learning. Offers arts and sciences (MPA, MS); psychology (MS); public administration (MPA); public relations (MS).

College of Education ***Degree program information:*** Part-time programs available. Part-time, online learning. Offers advanced studies (MS Sp Ed); education (M Ed, MS Sp Ed, Certificate); general curriculum (M Ed); generalist (MS Sp Ed);

interdisciplinary studies (M Ed); online instructional technologies (M Ed); reading (M Ed); school counseling (M Ed); special education (MS Sp Ed); teaching (Certificate).

MONTANA STATE UNIVERSITY–NORTHERN, Havre, MT 59501-7751

General Information State-supported, coed, comprehensive institution. *Graduate housing:* Rooms and/or apartments available on a first-come, first-served basis to single students and available to married students. Housing application deadline: 8/22.

GRADUATE UNITS

Graduate Programs ***Degree program information:*** Part-time and evening/weekend programs available. Part-time, evening/weekend, online learning. Offers counselor education (M Ed); learning development (M Ed). Electronic applications accepted.

MONTANA TECH OF THE UNIVERSITY OF MONTANA, Butte, MT 59701-8997

General Information State-supported, coed, comprehensive institution. CGS member. *Enrollment:* 2,980 graduate, professional, and undergraduate students; 80 full-time matriculated graduate/professional students (28 women), 130 part-time matriculated graduate/professional students (48 women). *Enrollment by degree level:* 180 master's, 9 doctoral, 5 other advanced degrees. *Graduate faculty:* 138 full-time (49 women), 78 part-time/adjunct (35 women). Tuition, state resident: full-time $2901; part-time $1450.68 per degree program. Tuition, nonresident: full-time $8432; part-time $4215.84 per degree program. *Required fees:* $668; $354 per degree program. Tuition and fees vary according to course load and program. *Graduate housing:* Rooms and/or apartments available on a first-come, first-served basis to single and married students. Typical cost: $4098 per year ($7128 including board) for single students; $4950 per year ($0 including board) for married students. Room and board charges vary according to board plan, campus/location and housing facility selected. Housing application deadline: 7/1. *Student services:* Campus employment opportunities, campus safety program, career counseling, exercise/wellness program, free psychological counseling, grant writing training, international student services, low-cost health insurance, multicultural affairs office, services for students with disabilities, writing training. *Library:* Montana Tech Library. *Research affiliation:* Newmont Mining (mining and mineral processing), Stillwater Mining (mineral production and training), NorthWestern Energy (electric efficiency), Edison Welding Institute (fuel cell design), Montana Resources, Inc. (mine reclamation and revegetation), QualTech, Inc. (battery monitor technology).

Computer facilities: 660 computers available on campus for general student use. A campuswide network can be accessed from student residence rooms and from off campus. Online class registration is available.
Website: http://www.mtech.edu/

General Application Contact: Daniel Stirling, Graduate School Program Manager, 406-496-4304, Fax: 406-496-4710, E-mail: gradschool@mtech.edu.

GRADUATE UNITS

Graduate School Students: 65 full-time (23 women), 96 part-time (37 women); includes 24 minority (8 Black or African American, non-Hispanic/Latino; 4 American Indian or Alaska Native, non-Hispanic/Latino; 4 Asian, non-Hispanic/Latino; 8 Hispanic/Latino), 6 international. Average age 28. 150 applicants, 47% accepted, 65 enrolled. *Faculty:* 134 full-time (46 women), 80 part-time/adjunct (35 women). *Financial support:* In 2015–16, 68 students received support, including 10 research assistantships with tuition reimbursements available (averaging $10,000 per year), 40 teaching assistantships with tuition reimbursements available (averaging $8,000 per year); career-related internships or fieldwork, tuition waivers (full and partial), and unspecified assistantships also available. Financial award application deadline: 4/1; financial award applicants required to submit FAFSA. In 2015, 44 master's awarded. *Degree program information:* Part-time and evening/weekend programs available. Part-time, evening/weekend, 100% online. Offers electrical engineering (MS); environmental engineering (MS); general engineering (MS); geochemistry (MS); geological engineering (MS); geology (MS); geophysical engineering (MS); health care informatics (Certificate); hydrogeological engineering (MS); hydrogeology (MS); industrial hygiene (MS); interdisciplinary studies (MS); materials science (PhD); metallurgical/mineral processing engineering (MS); mining engineering (MS); petroleum engineering (MS); project engineering and management (MPEM); technical communication (MS). *Application deadline:* For fall admission, 4/1 priority date for domestic students, 3/1 priority date for international students; for spring admission, 10/1 priority date for domestic students, 6/1 priority date for international students. Applications are processed on a rolling basis. *Application fee:* $50. Electronic applications accepted. *Application Contact:* Daniel Stirling, Administrator, Graduate School, 406-496-4304, Fax: 406-496-4723, E-mail: gradschool@mtech.edu. *Associate Vice Chancellor, Research and Graduate Studies,* Dr. Beverly Hartline, 406-496-4102, Fax: 406-496-4723, E-mail: graduatedean@mtech.edu.

MONTCLAIR STATE UNIVERSITY, Montclair, NJ 07043-1624

General Information State-supported, coed, university. CGS member. *Enrollment:* 20,465 graduate, professional, and undergraduate students; 1,373 full-time matriculated graduate/professional students (955 women), 2,194 part-time matriculated graduate/professional students (1,562 women). *Enrollment by degree level:* 3,068 master's, 231 doctoral, 268 other advanced degrees. *Graduate faculty:* 604 full-time (292 women), 1,210 part-time/adjunct (648 women). Tuition, state resident: part-time $553 per credit. Tuition, nonresident: part-time $854 per credit. *Required fees:* $91 per credit. Tuition and fees vary according to program. *Graduate housing:* Room and/or apartments available on a first-come, first-served basis to single students; on-campus housing not available to married students. Typical cost: $10,466 (including board). Housing application deadline: 3/1. *Student services:* Campus employment opportunities, campus safety program, career counseling, child daycare facilities, exercise/wellness program, free psychological counseling, grant writing training, international student services, low-cost health insurance, multicultural affairs office, services for students with disabilities, teacher training, writing training. *Library:* Sprague Library. *Collection:* Books: 540,337 (physical), 6,418 (digital/electronic); Databases: 201. Weekly public service hours: 93; students can reserve study rooms. *Research affiliation:* Spencer Foundation (education improvement), The International Society for Optical Engineering (optics and photonics), Deafness Research Foundation (heating science).

Computer facilities: Computer purchase and lease plans are available. 1,700 computers available on campus for general student use. A campuswide network can be accessed from student residence rooms and from off campus. Online class registration, online storage, online course delivery, online computing lab, student online portal are available.
Website: http://www.montclair.edu/

General Application Contact: Amy Aiello, Executive Director of The Graduate School, 973-655-5147, Fax: 973-655-7869, E-mail: aielloa@mail.montclair.edu.

GRADUATE UNITS

The Graduate School Students: 1,373 full-time (955 women), 2,194 part-time (1,562 women); includes 1,158 minority (363 Black or African American, non-Hispanic/Latino; 2 American Indian or Alaska Native, non-Hispanic/Latino; 153 Asian, non-Hispanic/Latino; 574 Hispanic/Latino; 4 Native Hawaiian or other Pacific Islander, non-Hispanic/Latino; 62 Two or more races, non-Hispanic/Latino), 203 international. Average age 31. 2,471 applicants, 53% accepted, 1012 enrolled. *Faculty:* 604 full-time (292 women), 1,210 part-time/adjunct (648 women). *Financial support:* In 2015–16, fellowships with full tuition reimbursements (averaging $15,000 per year), 208 research assistantships with full tuition reimbursements (averaging $7,000 per year), 32 teaching assistantships (averaging $7,000 per year) were awarded; Federal Work-Study, institutionally sponsored loans, scholarships/grants, and unspecified assistantships also available. Support available to part-time students. Financial award application deadline: 3/1; financial award applicants required to submit FAFSA. In 2015, 1,095 master's, 31 doctorates, 222 other advanced degrees awarded. *Degree program information:* Part-time and evening/weekend programs available. Part-time, evening/weekend. *Application deadline:* For fall admission, 6/1 for international students; for spring admission, 10/1 for international students. Applications are processed on a rolling basis. *Application fee:* $60. Electronic applications accepted. *Application Contact:* Amy Aiello, Executive Director of The Graduate School, 973-655-5147, Fax: 973-655-7869, E-mail: graduate.school@montclair.edu. *Dean,* Dr. Joan C. Ficke, 973-655-5147, Fax: 973-655-7869, E-mail: graduate.school@montclair.edu.

College of Education and Human Services Students: 695 full-time (527 women), 1,136 part-time (871 women); includes 567 minority (176 Black or African American, non-Hispanic/Latino; 2 American Indian or Alaska Native, non-Hispanic/Latino; 60 Asian, non-Hispanic/Latino; 298 Hispanic/Latino; 4 Native Hawaiian or other Pacific Islander, non-Hispanic/Latino; 27 Two or more races, non-Hispanic/Latino), 31 international. Average age 31. 839 applicants, 69% accepted, 487 enrolled. *Faculty:* 125 full-time (84 women), 236 part-time/adjunct (163 women). *Financial support:* In 2015–16, 78 research assistantships with full tuition reimbursements (averaging $7,727 per year), 1 teaching assistantship with full tuition reimbursement (averaging $7,000 per year) were awarded; Federal Work-Study, scholarships/grants, and unspecified assistantships also available. Support available to part-time students. Financial award application deadline: 3/1; financial award applicants required to submit FAFSA. In 2015, 873 master's, 8 doctorates, 63 other advanced degrees awarded. *Degree program information:* Part-time and evening/weekend programs available. Part-time, evening/weekend. Offers art (MAT); biology (MAT); certified alcohol and drug counselor (Certificate); chemistry (MAT); counseling (MA); counselor education (PhD); developmental models of autism intervention (Certificate); dietetics (Postbaccalaureate Certificate); earth science (MAT); education and human services (M Ed, MA, MAT, MPH, MS, Ed D, PhD, Certificate, Post Master's Certificate, Postbaccalaureate Certificate); educational leadership (MA); English (MAT); exercise science (MA); family and child studies (MA); family studies (PhD); French (MAT); health and physical education (MAT); health education (MAT); inclusive early childhood education (M Ed); infant and early childhood mental health (Certificate); learning disabilities (M Ed); mathematics (MAT); music (MAT); nutrition and exercise science (Certificate); nutrition and food science (MS); physical education (MAT); physical science (MAT); program evaluation (Certificate); public health (MPH); reading (MA); social studies (MAT); Spanish (MAT); sports administration and coaching (MA); teacher education and teacher development (PhD); teacher of English as a second language (MAT); teaching and supervision in physical education (MA). *Application deadline:* For fall admission, 6/1 for international students; for spring admission, 10/1 for international students. Applications are processed on a rolling basis. *Application fee:* $60. Electronic applications accepted. *Application Contact:* Amy Aiello, Executive Director of The Graduate School, 973-655-5147, E-mail: graduate.school@montclair.edu. *Dean,* Dr. Ada Beth Cutler, 973-655-5167, E-mail: cutler@mail.montclair.edu.

College of Humanities and Social Sciences Students: 313 full-time (245 women), 416 part-time (322 women); includes 285 minority (103 Black or African American, non-Hispanic/Latino; 20 Asian, non-Hispanic/Latino; 145 Hispanic/Latino; 17 Two or more races, non-Hispanic/Latino), 12 international. Average age 30. 966 applicants, 28% accepted, 228 enrolled. *Faculty:* 217 full-time (124 women), 393 part-time/adjunct (223 women). *Financial support:* In 2015–16, 46 research assistantships with tuition reimbursements (averaging $7,000 per year), 10 teaching assistantships with full tuition reimbursements (averaging $7,000 per year) were awarded; Federal Work-Study, scholarships/grants, and unspecified assistantships also available. Support available to part-time students. Financial award application deadline: 3/1; financial award applicants required to submit FAFSA. In 2015, 214 master's, 15 doctorates, 123 other advanced degrees awarded. *Degree program information:* Part-time and evening/weekend programs available. Part-time, evening/weekend. Offers adolescent advocacy (Certificate); applied linguistics (MA); audiology (Sc D); child advocacy and policy (MA, Certificate); clinical psychology (MA); communication sciences and disorders (MA); computational linguistics (Certificate); conflict management and peace studies (MA); conflict management in the workplace (Certificate); data collection and management (Certificate); English (MA); family/civil forensic psychology (Certificate); forensic psychology (Certificate); French literature (MA); French studies (MA); governance, compliance and regulation (MA); humanities and social sciences (MA, Sc D, Certificate); industrial and organizational psychology (MA); intellectual property (MA); law and governance (MA); legal management (MA); paralegal studies (Certificate); psychology (MA); Spanish (MA); teaching English to speakers of other languages (Certificate); teaching writing (Certificate); translation and interpreting in Spanish (Certificate). *Application deadline:* For fall admission, 6/1 for international students; for spring admission, 10/1 for international students. Applications are processed on a rolling basis. *Application fee:* $60. Electronic applications accepted. *Application Contact:* Amy Aiello, Executive Director of The Graduate School, 973-655-5147, Fax: 973-655-7869, E-mail: graduate.school@montclair.edu. *Dean,* Dr. Marietta Morrissey, 973-655-4314, E-mail: morrisseym@mail.montclair.edu.

College of Science and Mathematics Students: 174 full-time (83 women), 281 part-time (173 women); includes 122 minority (31 Black or African American, non-Hispanic/Latino; 34 Asian, non-Hispanic/Latino; 47 Hispanic/Latino; 10 Two or more races, non-Hispanic/Latino), 75 international. Average age 31. 237 applicants, 69% accepted, 114 enrolled. *Faculty:* 108 full-time (30 women), 90 part-time/adjunct (32 women). *Financial support:* In 2015–16, 65 research assistantships with full tuition reimbursements (averaging $7,000 per year), 3 teaching assistantships (averaging $7,000 per year) were awarded; Federal Work-Study, scholarships/grants, and unspecified assistantships also available. Support available to part-time students. Financial award application deadline: 3/1; financial award applicants required to submit FAFSA. In 2015, 107 master's, 3 doctorates, 9 other advanced degrees awarded. *Degree program information:* Part-time and evening/weekend programs available. Part-time, evening/weekend. Offers biological science/education (MS);

biology (MS); chemistry (MS); computer networking (Certificate); computer science (MS); earth and environmental science (MS); ecology and evolution (MS); environmental education (MA); environmental forensics (Certificate); environmental management (MA); environmental science (MA); geographic information science (Certificate); geoscience (MS); information technology (MS); marine biology and coastal sciences (MS); mathematics education (Ed D); molecular biology (MS, Certificate); pharmaceutical biochemistry (MS); physiology (MS); pure and applied mathematics (MS); science and mathematics (MA, MAT, MS, Ed D, PhD, Certificate); statistics (MS); sustainability science (MS); teaching middle grades mathematics (MA, Certificate); teaching physical education (MAT); water resource management (Certificate). *Application deadline:* For fall admission, 6/1 for international students; for spring admission, 10/1 for international students. Applications are processed on a rolling basis. *Application fee:* $60. Electronic applications accepted. *Application Contact:* Amy Aiello, Director of Graduate Admissions and Operations, 973-655-5147, Fax: 973-655-7869, E-mail: graduate.school@montclair.edu. *Dean*, Dr. Robert Prezant, 973-655-5108.

College of the Arts Students: 59 full-time (44 women), 135 part-time (84 women); includes 34 minority (11 Black or African American, non-Hispanic/Latino; 6 Asian, non-Hispanic/Latino; 15 Hispanic/Latino; 2 Two or more races, non-Hispanic/Latino), 45 international. Average age 31. 121 applicants, 67% accepted, 63 enrolled. *Faculty:* 76 full-time (34 women), 374 part-time/adjunct (191 women). *Financial support:* In 2015–16, 13 research assistantships with full tuition reimbursements (averaging $7,000 per year) were awarded; Federal Work-Study, scholarships/grants, and unspecified assistantships also available. Support available to part-time students. Financial award application deadline: 3/1; financial award applicants required to submit FAFSA. In 2015, 59 master's, 12 other advanced degrees awarded. *Degree program information:* Part-time and evening/weekend programs available. Part-time, evening/weekend. Offers arts (MA, MFA, AD, Performer's Certificate, Postbaccalaureate Certificate); arts management (MA); museum management (MA); music (MA, AD, Performer's Certificate); music education (MA); music therapy (MA, Postbaccalaureate Certificate); performance (MA); production/stage management (MA); public and organizational relations (MA); studio (MA); studio art (MFA); theatre studies (MA); theory/composition (MA). *Application deadline:* For fall admission, 6/1 for international students; for spring admission, 10/1 for international students. Applications are processed on a rolling basis. *Application fee:* $60. Electronic applications accepted. *Application Contact:* Amy Aiello, Director of Graduate Admissions and Operations, 973-655-5147, Fax: 973-655-7869, E-mail: graduate.school@montclair.edu. *Dean*, Dr. Geoffrey Newman, 973-655-5104, E-mail: newmang@mail.montclair.edu.

Feliciano School of Business Students: 132 full-time (56 women), 226 part-time (112 women); includes 150 minority (42 Black or African American, non-Hispanic/Latino; 33 Asian, non-Hispanic/Latino; 69 Hispanic/Latino; 6 Two or more races, non-Hispanic/Latino), 40 international. Average age 31. 208 applicants, 75% accepted, 120 enrolled. *Faculty:* 78 full-time (20 women), 96 part-time/adjunct (21 women). *Financial support:* In 2015–16, 28 students received support, including 17 research assistantships with full tuition reimbursements available (averaging $7,000 per year); Federal Work-Study, scholarships/grants, and unspecified assistantships also available. Support available to part-time students. Financial award application deadline: 3/1; financial award applicants required to submit FAFSA. In 2015, 153 master's, 1 other advanced degree awarded. *Degree program information:* Part-time and evening/weekend programs available. Part-time, evening/weekend. Offers accounting (MS, Post Master's Certificate); business (MBA, MS, Graduate Certificate, Post Master's Certificate); business administration (MBA); forensic accounting (Graduate Certificate). *Application deadline:* For fall admission, 6/1 for international students; for spring admission, 10/1 for international students. Applications are processed on a rolling basis. *Application fee:* $60. Electronic applications accepted. *Application Contact:* Amy Aiello, Executive Director of The Graduate School, 973-655-5147, Fax: 973-655-7869, E-mail: graduate.school@montclair.edu. *Dean*, Dr. E. LeBrent Chrite, 973-655-4304, E-mail: chritee@mail.montclair.edu.

MONTREAT COLLEGE, Montreat, NC 28757-1267

General Information Independent-religious, coed, comprehensive institution. *Graduate housing:* On-campus housing not available.

GRADUATE UNITS

School of Professional and Adult Studies ***Degree program information:*** Part-time and evening/weekend programs available. Part-time, evening/weekend, online learning. Electronic applications accepted.

MOODY BIBLE INSTITUTE, Chicago, IL 60610-3284

General Information Independent-religious, coed, comprehensive institution. *Graduate housing:* Rooms and/or apartments guaranteed to single students and available on a first-come, first-served basis to married students. Housing application deadline: 6/1.

GRADUATE UNITS

Graduate School ***Degree program information:*** Part-time programs available. Part-time. Offers biblical studies (MABS, Graduate Certificate); intercultural studies (MAIS, Graduate Certificate); ministry (M Div, M Min); spiritual formation and discipleship (MASF, Graduate Certificate); urban studies (MA, Graduate Certificate).

MOODY THEOLOGICAL SEMINARYMICHIGAN, Plymouth, MI 48170

General Information Independent-religious, coed, graduate-only institution. *Graduate housing:* On-campus housing not available.

GRADUATE UNITS

Graduate Programs ***Degree program information:*** Part-time and evening/weekend programs available. Part-time, evening/weekend. Offers Bible (Graduate Certificate); Christian education (MA); counseling psychology (MA); divinity (M Div); theological studies (MA).

MOORE COLLEGE OF ART & DESIGN, Philadelphia, PA 19103

General Information Independent, Undergraduate: women only; graduate: coed, comprehensive institution.

GRADUATE UNITS

Program in Art Education ***Degree program information:*** Part-time programs available. Part-time. Offers art education (MA).

Program in Community Practice Offers community practice (MFA).

Program in Interior Design ***Degree program information:*** Evening/weekend programs available. Evening/weekend. Offers interior design (MFA).

Program in Social Engagement ***Degree program information:*** Part-time programs available. Part-time. Offers social engagement (MA).

Program in Studio Art Offers studio art (MFA).

MORAVIAN COLLEGE, Bethlehem, PA 18018-6650

General Information Independent-religious, coed, comprehensive institution. *Graduate housing:* On-campus housing not available.

GRADUATE UNITS

Moravian College Comenius Center ***Degree program information:*** Part-time and evening/weekend programs available. Part-time, evening/weekend. Offers accounting (MBA); business analytics (MBA); curriculum and instruction (M Ed); education (MAT); general management (MBA); health administration (MHA); healthcare management (MBA); human resource management (MBA); leadership (MSHRM); learning and performance management (MSHRM); supply chain management (MBA).

St. Luke's School of Nursing Degree program information: Part-time and evening/weekend programs available. Part-time, evening/weekend. Offers clinical nurse leader (MS); nurse administrator (MS); nurse educator (MS).

MORAVIAN THEOLOGICAL SEMINARY, Bethlehem, PA 18018-6614

General Information Independent-religious, coed, graduate-only institution. *Enrollment by degree level:* 72 master's, 22 other advanced degrees. *Graduate faculty:* 7 full-time (3 women), 12 part-time/adjunct (5 women). *Tuition, area resident:* Full-time $12,816; part-time $7128 per year. *Required fees:* $430; $430 per unit. Tuition and fees vary according to course load. *Graduate housing:* Rooms and/or apartments available on a first-come, first-served basis to single and married students. Typical cost: $9912 per year for single students; $13,980 per year for married students. Room charges vary according to housing facility selected. Housing application deadline: 7/31. *Student services:* Campus employment opportunities, campus safety program, exercise/wellness program, international student services, low-cost health insurance, multicultural affairs office, services for students with disabilities, writing training. *Library:* Reeves Library. *Collection:* Books: 313,914 (physical), 31,184 (digital/electronic); Serial titles: 6,060 (physical), 262 (digital/electronic); Databases: 53. Weekly public service hours: 100; students can reserve study rooms.

Computer facilities: 227 computers available on campus for general student use. A campuswide network can be accessed from student residence rooms. Online class registration is available.
Website: http://www.moravianseminary.edu/

General Application Contact: Dr. David H. DeRemer, Director of Enrollment, 610-861-1512, Fax: 610-861-1569, E-mail: deremerd@moravian.edu.

GRADUATE UNITS

Graduate and Certificate Programs Students: 26 full-time (12 women), 68 part-time (51 women); includes 17 minority (11 Black or African American, non-Hispanic/Latino; 5 Hispanic/Latino; 1 Two or more races, non-Hispanic/Latino), 1 international. Average age 48. 41 applicants, 98% accepted, 29 enrolled. *Faculty:* 7 full-time (3 women), 12 part-time/adjunct (5 women). *Financial support:* In 2015–16, 71 students received support. Career-related internships or fieldwork, Federal Work-Study, and scholarships/grants available. Support available to part-time students. Financial award application deadline: 5/1; financial award applicants required to submit FAFSA. In 2015, 12 master's, 8 other advanced degrees awarded. *Degree program information:* Part-time programs available. Part-time. Offers divinity (M Div); formative spirituality (M Div, MATS, Graduate Certificate); spiritual direction (Graduate Certificate). *Application deadline:* For fall admission, 4/1 priority date for international students; for spring admission, 9/1 priority date for international students. Applications are processed on a rolling basis. *Application fee:* $50. Electronic applications accepted. *Application Contact:* Dr. David H. DeRemer, Director of Enrollment, 610-861-1512, Fax: 610-861-1569, E-mail: deremerd@moravian.edu. *Dean and Vice President*, Rev. Dr. Frank L. Crouch, 610-861-1516, E-mail: crouchf@moravian.edu.

MOREHEAD STATE UNIVERSITY, Morehead, KY 40351

General Information State-supported, coed, comprehensive institution. *Graduate housing:* Room and/or apartments available on a first-come, first-served basis to single students; on-campus housing not available to married students. Housing application deadline: 3/12.

GRADUATE UNITS

Graduate Programs ***Degree program information:*** Part-time and evening/weekend programs available. Part-time, evening/weekend, online learning. Electronic applications accepted.

Caudill College of Arts, Humanities and Social Sciences Degree program information: Part-time and evening/weekend programs available. Part-time, evening/weekend, online learning. Offers art education (MA); arts, humanities and social sciences (MA, MM); communication (MA); criminology (MA); English (MA); general sociology (MA); gerontology (MA); graphic design (MA); music education (MM); music performance (MM); sociology regional analysis (MA); sociology/chemical dependency (MA); studio art (MA). Electronic applications accepted.

College of Business and Public Affairs Degree program information: Part-time and evening/weekend programs available. Part-time, evening/weekend, online learning. Offers business administration (MA, MBA, MSIS); business and public affairs (MA, MBA, MPA, MSIS); information systems (MSIS); public policy (MPA); sport management (MA). Electronic applications accepted.

College of Education Degree program information: Part-time and evening/weekend programs available. Part-time, evening/weekend. Offers adult and higher education (MA, Ed S); business and marketing education (MAT); certified professional counselor (Ed S); counseling P-12 (MA); curriculum and instruction (Ed S); education (MA, MA Ed, MAT, Ed S); educational technology (MA Ed); elementary education (MA Ed); English/language arts 5-9 (MAT); French (MAT); health P-12 (MAT); instructional leadership (Ed S); learning and behavioral disorders P-12 (MAT); mathematics 5-9 (MAT); moderate and severe disabilities P-12 (MAT); physical education P-12 (MAT); school administration (MA); school counseling (Ed S); science 5-9 (MAT); secondary biology (MAT); secondary chemistry (MAT); secondary earth science (MAT); secondary education (MA Ed); secondary English (MAT); secondary math (MAT); secondary physics (MAT); secondary social studies (MAT); social studies 5-9 (MAT); Spanish (MAT); special education (MA Ed); teacher leader business and marketing content (MA Ed); teacher leader business and marketing technology (MA Ed); teacher leader educational technology (MA Ed); teacher leader English (MA Ed); teacher leader gifted education (MA Ed); teacher leader IECE certification (MA Ed); teacher leader interdisciplinary education P-5 (MA Ed); teacher leader middle grades (MA Ed); teacher leader non IECE certification (MA Ed); teacher leader reading/writing - non-certification (MA Ed); teacher leader reading/writing certification (MA Ed); teacher leader school communication - certification (MA Ed); teacher leader school communication - non-certification (MA Ed); teacher leader social studies

(MA Ed); teacher leader special education (MA Ed); teaching (MAT). Electronic applications accepted.

College of Science and Technology Degree program information: Part-time and evening/weekend programs available. Part-time, evening/weekend. Offers biology (MS); biology regional analysis (MS); career and technical agricultural education (MS); career and technical education (MS); clinical/counseling psychology (MS); engineering technology (MS); general/experimental psychology (MS); health/physical education (MA); science and technology (MA, MS). Electronic applications accepted.

Institute for Regional Analysis and Public Policy Offers public administration (MPA). Electronic applications accepted.

MOREHOUSE SCHOOL OF MEDICINE, Atlanta, GA 30310-1495

General Information Independent, coed, graduate-only institution. CGS member. *Enrollment by degree level:* 94 master's, 304 doctoral. *Graduate faculty:* 221 full-time (110 women), 55 part-time/adjunct (35 women). *Graduate housing:* On-campus housing not available. *Student services:* Campus employment opportunities, career counseling, exercise/wellness program, free psychological counseling, international student services. *Library:* MSM Library. *Research affiliation:* Merck & Company, Inc. (hypotension), CareStat (renal insufficiency), Wyeth (helicobacter pylori study), Bristol Myers Squibb (pharmacokinetics), Parke-Davis (cardiovascular risk factors), NitroMel, Inc. (heart failure).

Computer facilities: 200 computers available on campus for general student use. Online class registration is available.
Website: http://www.msm.edu/

General Application Contact: Director of Admissions, 404-752-1650, Fax: 404-752-1512.

GRADUATE UNITS

Graduate Programs in Biomedical Sciences *Financial support:* Fellowships with tuition reimbursements, career-related internships or fieldwork, institutionally sponsored loans, scholarships/grants, traineeships, health care benefits, and tuition waivers (full) available. Financial award application deadline: 5/1; financial award applicants required to submit FAFSA. Offers biomedical research (MS); biomedical sciences (PhD); biomedical technology (MS); medical sciences (MS). *Application deadline:* For fall admission, 10/1 for domestic and international students; for spring admission, 2/1 for domestic and international students. *Application fee:* $50. Electronic applications accepted. *Application Contact:* Brandon Hunter, Director of Admissions, 404-752-1650, Fax: 404-752-1512, E-mail: phdadmissions@msm.edu. *Associate Dean for Graduate Studies*, Dr. Douglas Paulsen, 404-752-1559.

Master of Public Health Program *Financial support:* Fellowships, research assistantships with partial tuition reimbursements, teaching assistantships, career-related internships or fieldwork, Federal Work-Study, institutionally sponsored loans, scholarships/grants, and unspecified assistantships available. Support available to part-time students. Financial award application deadline: 5/1; financial award applicants required to submit FAFSA. *Degree program information:* Part-time programs available. Part-time. Offers public health (MPH). *Application deadline:* For fall admission, 3/1 for domestic and international students. *Application fee:* $50. Electronic applications accepted. *Application Contact:* Brandon Hunter, Director of Admissions, 404-752-1650, Fax: 404-752-1512, E-mail: mphadmissions@msm.edu. *Director*, Dr. Stephanie Miles-Richardson, 404-752-1944, Fax: 404-752-1051, E-mail: smiles-richardson@msm.edu.

Master of Science in Clinical Research Program *Financial support:* Applicants required to submit FAFSA. *Degree program information:* Part-time programs available. Part-time. Offers clinical research (MS). *Application deadline:* For fall admission, 4/6 for domestic and international students. *Application fee:* $50. Electronic applications accepted. *Application Contact:* Brandon Hunter, Director of Admissions, 404-752-1650, Fax: 404-752-1512, E-mail: bhunter@msm.edu. *Co-Director*, Dr. Alexander Quarshie, 404-752-7681, E-mail: aquarshie@msm.edu.

Professional Program *Financial support:* Career-related internships or fieldwork, Federal Work-Study, institutionally sponsored loans, and scholarships/grants available. Financial award application deadline: 5/1; financial award applicants required to submit FAFSA. Offers medicine (MD). *Application deadline:* For fall admission, 12/1 for domestic students. Applications are processed on a rolling basis. *Application fee:* $50. Electronic applications accepted. *Application Contact:* Brandon Hunter, Director of Admissions, 404-752-1650, Fax: 404-752-1512, E-mail: mdadmission@msm.edu. *Associate Dean for Admissions and Student Affairs*, Dr. Ngozi Anachebe, 404-752-1650, Fax: 404-752-1594.

MORGAN STATE UNIVERSITY, Baltimore, MD 21251

General Information State-supported, coed, university. CGS member. *Graduate housing:* Rooms and/or apartments available on a first-come, first-served basis to single and married students.

GRADUATE UNITS

School of Graduate Studies *Degree program information:* Part-time and evening/weekend programs available. Part-time, evening/weekend.

Clarence M. Mitchell, Jr. School of Engineering Degree program information: Part-time and evening/weekend programs available. Part-time, evening/weekend. Offers civil engineering (M Eng, D Eng); electrical and computer engineering (M Eng, MS, D Eng); industrial and systems engineering (M Eng, D Eng); transportation (MS).

College of Liberal Arts Degree program information: Part-time programs available. Part-time. Offers African-American studies (MA); economics (MA); English (MA, PhD); fine and performing arts (MA); history (MA, PhD); international studies (MA); liberal arts (MA, MS, PhD); museum studies and historic preservation (MA); psychometrics (MS, PhD); sociology (MA, MS).

Earl G. Graves School of Business and Management Degree program information: Part-time and evening/weekend programs available. Part-time, evening/weekend. Offers business administration (MBA, PhD); business and management (MBA, PhD).

Institute of Architecture and Planning Offers architecture (M Arch); city and regional planning (MCRP); landscape architecture (MLA).

School of Community Health and Policy Offers nursing (MS); public health (MPH, Dr PH).

School of Computer, Mathematical, and Natural Sciences Offers bioenvironmental science (PhD); bioinformatics (MS); biology (MS); chemistry (MS); computer, mathematical, and natural sciences (MA, MS, PhD); mathematics (MA); science education (MS).

School of Education and Urban Studies Degree program information: Part-time programs available. Part-time. Offers community college leadership (Ed D); education and urban studies (MA, MAT, MS, Ed D, PhD); educational administration and supervision (Ed D); elementary education (MAT); high school education (MAT); higher education (PhD); higher education administration (MA, MA, PhD); mathematics education (MS, Ed D); middle school education (MAT); science education (MS, Ed D); urban educational leadership (Ed D).

School of Social Work Offers social work (MSW, PhD).

MORNINGSIDE COLLEGE, Sioux City, IA 51106

General Information Independent-religious, coed, comprehensive institution. CGS member. *Graduate housing:* Rooms and/or apartments available to single and married students. Housing application deadline: 7/1. *Research affiliation:* Iowa Public Service Company (biology, chemistry, physics).

GRADUATE UNITS

Graduate Division *Degree program information:* Part-time and evening/weekend programs available. Part-time, evening/weekend. Offers professional educator (MAT); special education: instructional strategist I: mild/moderate elementary (K-6) (MAT); special education: instructional strategist II-mild/moderate secondary (7-12) (MAT); special education: K-12 instructional strategist II-behavior disorders/learning disabilities (MAT); special education: K-12 instructional strategist II-mental disabilities (MAT).

MOUNT ALLISON UNIVERSITY, Sackville, NB E4L 1E4, Canada

General Information Province-supported, coed, comprehensive institution. *Graduate housing:* Room and/or apartments available to single students; on-campus housing not available to married students. Housing application deadline: 5/15. *Research affiliation:* Atlantic Cancer Institute (medical research), Moncton Hospital (medical research), Huntsman Marine Science Centre (marine biology).

GRADUATE UNITS

Department of Biology Offers biology (M Sc).

Department of Chemistry Offers chemistry (M Sc).

MOUNT ALOYSIUS COLLEGE, Cresson, PA 16630-1999

General Information Independent-religious, coed, comprehensive institution. *Enrollment:* 1,877 graduate, professional, and undergraduate students; 44 full-time matriculated graduate/professional students (26 women), 34 part-time matriculated graduate/professional students (22 women). *Enrollment by degree level:* 78 master's. *Graduate faculty:* 12 full-time (10 women), 18 part-time/adjunct (7 women). *Tuition, area resident:* Full-time $6390; part-time $710 per credit. *Graduate housing:* On-campus housing not available. *Student services:* Campus employment opportunities, campus safety program, career counseling, child daycare facilities, exercise/wellness program, free psychological counseling, international student services, services for students with disabilities, writing training. *Library:* Mount Aloysius College Library.

Computer facilities: Computer purchase and lease plans are available. A campuswide network can be accessed from student residence rooms and from off campus. Online class registration is available.
Website: http://www.mtaloy.edu/

General Application Contact: Matthew P Bodenschatz, Director of Graduate and Continuing Education Admissions, 814-886-6406, Fax: 814-886-6441, E-mail: mbodenschatz@mtaloy.edu.

GRADUATE UNITS

Program in Behavioral Specialist Consulting *Financial support:* Unspecified assistantships available. *Degree program information:* Evening/weekend programs available. Evening/weekend. Offers behavioral specialist consulting (MS). *Application deadline:* Applications are processed on a rolling basis. *Application fee:* $30. Electronic applications accepted. *Application Contact:* Matthew P Bodenschatz, Director of Graduate and Continuing Education Admissions, 814-886-6406, Fax: 814-886-6441, E-mail: mbodenschatz@mtaloy.edu.

Program in Business Administration *Financial support:* Unspecified assistantships available. Financial award applicants required to submit FAFSA. *Degree program information:* Part-time and evening/weekend programs available. Part-time, evening/weekend. Offers accounting (MBA); health and human services administration (MBA); non-profit management (MBA); project management (MBA). *Application deadline:* For fall admission, 8/1 for domestic students; for spring admission, 12/1 for domestic students. Applications are processed on a rolling basis. *Application fee:* $30. Electronic applications accepted. *Application Contact:* Matthew P. Bodenschatz, Director of Graduate and Continuing Education Admissions, 814-886-6406, Fax: 814-886-6441, E-mail: mbodenschatz@mtaloy.edu.

Program in Community Counseling *Financial support:* Unspecified assistantships available. *Degree program information:* Part-time programs available. Part-time. Offers community counseling (MS). *Application deadline:* Applications are processed on a rolling basis. Electronic applications accepted. *Application Contact:* Matthew P. Bodenschatz, Director of Graduate and Continuing Education Admissions, 814-886-6406, Fax: 814-886-6441, E-mail: mbodenschatz@mtaloy.edu.

Program in Psychology *Financial support:* Unspecified assistantships available. Offers psychology (MS). *Application deadline:* Applications are processed on a rolling basis. Electronic applications accepted. *Application Contact:* Matthew P. Bodenschatz, Director of Graduate and Continuing Education Admissions, 814-886-6406, Fax: 814-886-6441, E-mail: mbodenschatz@mtaloy.edu.

MOUNT ANGEL SEMINARY, Saint Benedict, OR 97373

General Information Independent-religious, Undergraduate: men only; graduate: coed, comprehensive institution. *Graduate housing:* Room and/or apartments guaranteed to single students; on-campus housing not available to married students.

GRADUATE UNITS

Program in Theology *Degree program information:* Part-time programs available. Part-time. Offers theology (M Div, MA).

MOUNT CARMEL COLLEGE OF NURSING, Columbus, OH 43222

General Information Independent, coed, primarily women, comprehensive institution. *Enrollment:* 1,063 graduate, professional, and undergraduate students; 73 full-time matriculated graduate/professional students (64 women), 92 part-time matriculated graduate/professional students (84 women). *Enrollment by degree level:* 153 master's, 6 doctoral, 6 other advanced degrees. *Graduate faculty:* 8 full-time (all women), 5 part-time/adjunct (4 women). *Tuition, area resident:* Full-time $9480; part-time $474 per credit. One-time fee: $120. Tuition and fees vary according to course load, degree level and program. *Graduate housing:* Room and/or apartments available on a first-come, first-served basis to single students; on-campus housing not available to married students. Typical cost: $4780 per year ($6380 including board). Housing application deadline: 6/15. *Student services:* Free psychological counseling, grant writing training, multicultural affairs office, teacher training, writing training. *Library:* The Mount Carmel Health Sciences Library plus 1 other. *Collection:* Books: 7,633 (physical), 78,102 (digital/electronic); Serial titles: 400 (physical), 48,954 (digital/electronic). Weekly public service hours: 65; study areas open 24 hours, 5–7 days a week; students can reserve study rooms.

Computer facilities: 80 computers available on campus for general student use. A campuswide network can be accessed from off campus. Online class registration is available.
Website: http://www.mccn.edu/

General Application Contact: Kim Campbell, Director of Recruitment and Admissions, 614-234-5144, Fax: 614-234-5427, E-mail: kcampbell@mccn.edu.

GRADUATE UNITS

Nursing Program Students: 72 full-time (63 women), 92 part-time (84 women); includes 15 minority (7 Black or African American, non-Hispanic/Latino; 3 Asian, non-Hispanic/Latino; 2 Hispanic/Latino; 3 Two or more races, non-Hispanic/Latino). Average age 37. 140 applicants, 45% accepted, 50 enrolled. *Faculty:* 8 full-time (all women), 5 part-time/adjunct (4 women). *Financial support:* In 2015–16, 5 students received support. Institutionally sponsored loans and scholarships/grants available. Financial award applicants required to submit FAFSA. In 2015, 50 master's awarded. *Degree program information:* Part-time programs available. Part-time. Offers adult gerontology acute care nurse practitioner (MS); adult health clinical nurse specialist (MS); family nurse practitioner (MS); nursing (DNP); nursing administration (MS); nursing education (MS). *Application deadline:* For fall admission, 6/1 priority date for domestic students; for winter admission, 11/1 for domestic students; for spring admission, 10/1 priority date for domestic students; for summer admission, 3/1 for domestic students. Applications are processed on a rolling basis. *Application fee:* $30. *Application Contact:* Dr. Kim Campbell, Director of Recruitment and Admissions, 614-234-5144, Fax: 614-234-5427, E-mail: kcampbell@mccn.edu.

MOUNT HOLYOKE COLLEGE, South Hadley, MA 01075

General Information Independent, women only, comprehensive institution. *Enrollment:* 2,215 graduate, professional, and undergraduate students; 26 full-time matriculated graduate/professional students (23 women), 37 part-time matriculated graduate/professional students (34 women). *Enrollment by degree level:* 63 master's. *Graduate faculty:* 24 full-time (13 women), 11 part-time/adjunct (8 women). *Tuition, area resident:* Full-time $24,500; part-time $770 per credit hour. *Required fees:* $117. Tuition and fees vary according to course load and program. *Graduate housing:* On-campus housing not available. *Student services:* Campus employment opportunities, career counseling, free psychological counseling, low-cost health insurance, services for students with disabilities. *Library:* Williston Memorial Library plus 2 others. *Collection:* Books: 557,528 (physical), 731,213 (digital/electronic); Serial titles: 672 (physical), 6,853 (digital/electronic); Databases: 223. Weekly public service hours: 115; students can reserve study rooms.

Computer facilities: Computer purchase and lease plans are available. 456 computers available on campus for general student use. A campuswide network can be accessed from student residence rooms and from off campus. Online class registration, personal Web pages are available.
Website: http://www.mtholyoke.edu/

General Application Contact: Lenore Reilly, Interim Director of Professional and Graduate Education, 413-538-3478, Fax: 413-538-3098.

GRADUATE UNITS

Professional and Graduate Education (PaGE) Students: 26 full-time (23 women), 35 part-time (32 women); includes 6 minority (2 Black or African American, non-Hispanic/Latino; 3 Hispanic/Latino; 1 Two or more races, non-Hispanic/Latino), 4 international. Average age 35. 2 applicants, 100% accepted, 2 enrolled. *Faculty:* 22 full-time (11 women), 11 part-time/adjunct (8 women). *Financial support:* In 2015–16, 65 students received support. Scholarships/grants available. Financial award applicants required to submit FAFSA. In 2015, 15 master's awarded. *Degree program information:* Part-time programs available. Part-time, 100% online, blended/hybrid learning. Offers mathematics teaching (MAMT); teacher leadership (MATL); teaching (MAT). *Application deadline:* Applications are processed on a rolling basis. *Application fee:* $0. Electronic applications accepted. *Interim Director,* Lenore Reilly, 413-538-3478, Fax: 413-538-3098.

MOUNT IDA COLLEGE, Newton, MA 02459-3310

General Information Independent, coed, comprehensive institution. *Enrollment:* 1,345 graduate, professional, and undergraduate students; 9 full-time matriculated graduate/professional students (5 women), 23 part-time matriculated graduate/professional students (13 women). *Enrollment by degree level:* 32 master's. *Graduate faculty:* 7 full-time (4 women), 2 part-time/adjunct (0 women). *Tuition, area resident:* Part-time $595 per credit. *Graduate housing:* On-campus housing not available. *Student services:* Campus employment opportunities, campus safety program, career counseling, exercise/wellness program, free psychological counseling, international student services, low-cost health insurance, multicultural affairs office, services for students with disabilities, writing training. *Library:* Wadsworth Learning Resource Center plus 1 other. Students can reserve study rooms.

Computer facilities: 82 computers available on campus for general student use. A campuswide network can be accessed from student residence rooms.
Website: http://www.mountida.edu/

General Application Contact: Trae Alston-Swan, Associate Director of Graduate Admissions, 617-928-4553, Fax: 617-928-4508, E-mail: taswan@mountida.edu.

GRADUATE UNITS

Program in Management Students: 9 full-time (5 women), 23 part-time (13 women). Average age 26. 46 applicants, 46% accepted, 18 enrolled. *Faculty:* 4 full-time (2 women), 2 part-time/adjunct (0 women). *Financial support:* Federal Work-Study and unspecified assistantships available. Support available to part-time students. Financial award application deadline: 8/15; financial award applicants required to submit FAFSA. *Degree program information:* Part-time and evening/weekend programs available. Part-time, evening/weekend, online learning. Offers healthcare management (MSM); human resource management (MSM); interior architecture (MSM); leadership in sport (MSM); management (MSM). *Application deadline:* For fall admission, 8/15 for domestic and international students; for spring admission, 1/10 for domestic and international students. Applications are processed on a rolling basis. *Application fee:* $0. Electronic applications accepted. *Application Contact:* Trae Alston-Swan, Associate Director of Graduate Admissions, 617-928-4508, Fax: 617-928-4507, E-mail: taswan@mountida.edu. *Dean, School of Business,* Sharon McKechnie, 617-928-7354, E-mail: smckechnie@mountida.edu.

MOUNT MARTY COLLEGE, Yankton, SD 57078-3724

General Information Independent-religious, coed, comprehensive institution. *Graduate housing:* On-campus housing not available.

GRADUATE UNITS

Graduate Studies Division Offers business administration (MBA); nurse anesthesia (MS); nursing (MSN); pastoral ministries (MPM). Electronic applications accepted.

MOUNT MARY UNIVERSITY, Milwaukee, WI 53222-4597

General Information Independent-religious, Undergraduate: women only; graduate: coed, comprehensive institution. CGS member. *Enrollment:* 1,313 graduate, professional, and undergraduate students; 317 full-time matriculated graduate/professional students (291 women), 124 part-time matriculated graduate/professional students (111 women). *Enrollment by degree level:* 404 master's, 27 doctoral, 10 other advanced degrees. *Graduate faculty:* 24 full-time (21 women), 44 part-time/adjunct (30 women). *Tuition, area resident:* Full-time $12,308; part-time $684 per credit. *Required fees:* $440; $220 per semester. Tuition and fees vary according to course load, degree level and program. *Graduate housing:* Room and/or apartments available on a first-come, first-served basis to single students; on-campus housing not available to married students. *Student services:* Campus employment opportunities, campus safety program, career counseling, child daycare facilities, exercise/wellness program, free psychological counseling, international student services, low-cost health insurance, services for students with disabilities, teacher training, writing training. *Library:* The Patrick and Beatrice Haggerty Library. *Collection:* Books: 65,458 (physical), 130,464 (digital/electronic); Serial titles: 2,838 (physical), 208,435 (digital/electronic); Databases: 89. Students can reserve study rooms.

Computer facilities: 240 computers available on campus for general student use. A campuswide network can be accessed from student residence rooms and from off campus. Online class registration is available.
Website: http://www.mtmary.edu/

General Application Contact: Kirk Heller de Messer, Director, Graduate Admissions, 414-930-3221, E-mail: hellerk@mtmary.edu.

GRADUATE UNITS

Graduate Division Students: 317 full-time (291 women), 124 part-time (111 women); includes 94 minority (40 Black or African American, non-Hispanic/Latino; 2 American Indian or Alaska Native, non-Hispanic/Latino; 10 Asian, non-Hispanic/Latino; 27 Hispanic/Latino; 1 Native Hawaiian or other Pacific Islander, non-Hispanic/Latino; 14 Two or more races, non-Hispanic/Latino), 4 international. Average age 33. 626 applicants, 36% accepted, 175 enrolled. *Faculty:* 28 full-time (25 women), 40 part-time/adjunct (26 women). *Financial support:* Career-related internships or fieldwork, Federal Work-Study, and unspecified assistantships available. Support available to part-time students. Financial award application deadline: 5/1; financial award applicants required to submit FAFSA. In 2015, 193 master's, 6 doctorates, 2 other advanced degrees awarded. *Degree program information:* Part-time and evening/weekend programs available. Part-time, evening/weekend, 100% online, blended/hybrid learning. Offers administrative dietetics (MS); art therapy (MS, DAT); clinical dietetics (MS); clinical mental health counseling (MS, Certificate); clinical rehabilitation counseling (MS, Certificate); creative writing (MA); education (MA); general management (MBA); health systems leadership (MBA); nutrition education (MS); occupational therapy (MS, OTD); professional and new media writing (MA); professional development (MA); school counseling (MS, Certificate); vocational rehabilitation counseling (MS, Certificate). *Application deadline:* For fall admission, 8/1 for domestic and international students; for winter admission, 8/15 for domestic students, 9/15 for international students; for spring admission, 12/1 for domestic and international students; for summer admission, 5/1 for domestic and international students. Applications are processed on a rolling basis. *Application fee:* $45. Electronic applications accepted. *Application Contact:* Kirk Heller de Messer, Director, Graduate Admissions, 414-930-3221, E-mail: hellerk@mtmary.edu.

MOUNT MERCY UNIVERSITY, Cedar Rapids, IA 52402-4797

General Information Independent-religious, coed, comprehensive institution.

GRADUATE UNITS

Program in Business Administration ***Degree program information:*** Evening/weekend programs available. Evening/weekend. Offers human resource (MBA); quality management (MBA). Electronic applications accepted.

Program in Criminal Justice ***Degree program information:*** Evening/weekend programs available. Evening/weekend, online learning. Offers criminal justice (MA).

Program in Education Offers reading (MA Ed); special education (MA Ed); teacher leadership (MA Ed). Electronic applications accepted.

Program in Marriage and Family Therapy ***Degree program information:*** Evening/weekend programs available. Evening/weekend. Offers marriage and family therapy (MA).

Program in Nursing ***Degree program information:*** Evening/weekend programs available. Evening/weekend. Offers health advocacy (MSN); nurse administration (MSN); nurse education (MSN).

Program in Strategic Leadership ***Degree program information:*** Evening/weekend programs available. Evening/weekend. Offers strategic leadership (MSL).

MOUNT ST. JOSEPH UNIVERSITY, Cincinnati, OH 45233-1670

General Information Independent-religious, coed, comprehensive institution. CGS member. *Enrollment:* 1,983 graduate, professional, and undergraduate students; 226 full-time matriculated graduate/professional students (159 women), 250 part-time matriculated graduate/professional students (189 women). *Enrollment by degree level:* 445 master's, 133 doctoral, 2 other advanced degrees. *Graduate faculty:* 88 full-time (73 women), 30 part-time/adjunct (23 women). *Tuition, area resident:* Full-time $15,255; part-time $565 per credit hour. *Required fees:* $500; $100 per term. $100 per semester. Full-time tuition and fees vary according to course load, degree level and program. *Graduate housing:* Room and/or apartments available on a first-come, first-served basis to single students; on-campus housing not available to married students. Typical cost: $5800 per year ($10,110 including board). Room and board charges vary according to board plan and housing facility selected. Housing application deadline: 4/1. *Student services:* Campus employment opportunities, campus safety program, career counseling, child daycare facilities, exercise/wellness program, free psychological counseling, international student services, low-cost health insurance, services for students with disabilities, teacher training, writing training. *Library:* Archbishop Alter Library.

Computer facilities: 190 computers available on campus for general student use. A campuswide network can be accessed from student residence rooms and from off campus. Online class registration is available.
Website: http://www.msj.edu/

General Application Contact: Mary Brigham, Assistant Director for Graduate Recruitment, 513-244-4233, Fax: 513-244-4629, E-mail: mary.brigham@msj.edu.

GRADUATE UNITS

Doctor of Nursing Practice Program Average age 51. *Faculty:* 12 full-time (11 women), 5 part-time/adjunct (all women). *Financial support:* Applicants required to submit FAFSA. *Degree program information:* Part-time programs available. Part-time. Offers health systems leadership (DNP). *Application fee:* $50. Electronic applications accepted. *Application Contact:* Mary Brigham, Assistant Director for Graduate Recruitment, 513-244-4233, Fax: 513-244-4629, E-mail: mary.brigham@msj.edu. *Director,* Dr. Nancy Hinzman, 513-244-4325, E-mail: nancy.hinzman@msj.edu.

Graduate Education Program Students: 37 full-time (27 women), 103 part-time (96 women); includes 22 minority (19 Black or African American, non-Hispanic/Latino; 1 Hispanic/Latino; 2 Two or more races, non-Hispanic/Latino). Average age 25. 51 applicants, 92% accepted, 36 enrolled. *Faculty:* 12 full-time (9 women), 8 part-time/adjunct (7 women). *Financial support:* In 2015–16, 96 students received support. Research assistantships available. Financial award applicants required to submit FAFSA. In 2015, 48 master's awarded. *Degree program information:* Part-time and evening/weekend programs available. Part-time, evening/weekend. Offers adolescent to young adult education (MA); dyslexia (Certificate); inclusive early childhood education (MA); instructional leadership (MA); middle childhood education (MA); multicultural special education (MA); Pre-K special needs (Certificate); reading (Certificate); reading science (MA). *Application deadline:* Applications are processed on a rolling basis. *Application fee:* $50. Electronic applications accepted. *Application Contact:* Mary Brigham, Assistant Director of Graduate Recruitment, 513-244-4233, Fax: 513-244-4629, E-mail: mary.brigham@msj.edu. *Chair,* Dr. Mary West, 513-244-3263, Fax: 513-244-4867, E-mail: mary.west@msj.edu.

Graduate Program in Religious Studies Students: 1 (woman) full-time, 10 part-time (all women); includes 1 minority (Black or African American, non-Hispanic/Latino). Average age 42. 3 applicants, 67% accepted, 3 enrolled. *Faculty:* 2 full-time (1 woman), 2 part-time/adjunct (1 woman). *Financial support:* In 2015–16, 6 students received support. Scholarships/grants available. Financial award application deadline: 3/1; financial award applicants required to submit FAFSA. In 2015, 4 master's awarded. *Degree program information:* Part-time and evening/weekend programs available. Part-time, evening/weekend. Offers pastoral administration (Certificate); religious studies (MA); spirituality and wellness (Certificate). *Application deadline:* Applications are processed on a rolling basis. *Application fee:* $50. Electronic applications accepted. *Application Contact:* Mary Brigham, Assistant Director of Graduate Recruitment, 513-244-4233, Fax: 513-244-4629, E-mail: mary.brigham@msj.edu. *Chair of Religious/Pastoral Studies,* Dr. John Trokan, 513-244-4272, Fax: 513-244-4222, E-mail: john.trokan@msj.edu.

Master of Business Administration Program Students: 17 full-time (9 women), 40 part-time (21 women); includes 6 minority (3 Black or African American, non-Hispanic/Latino; 2 Asian, non-Hispanic/Latino; 1 Two or more races, non-Hispanic/Latino). Average age 25. 6 applicants, 83% accepted, 5 enrolled. *Faculty:* 4 full-time (2 women), 6 part-time/adjunct (3 women). *Financial support:* In 2015–16, 23 students received support. Application deadline: 6/1; applicants required to submit FAFSA. In 2015, 12 master's awarded. *Degree program information:* Part-time and evening/weekend programs available. Part-time, evening/weekend. Offers business administration (MBA). *Application deadline:* Applications are processed on a rolling basis. *Application fee:* $50. Electronic applications accepted. *Application Contact:* Mary Brigham, Assistant Director for Graduate Recruitment, 513-244-4333, Fax: 513-745-4629, E-mail: mary.brigham@msj.edu. *Professor,* Dr. Nancy Waldeck, 513-244-4917, E-mail: nancy.waldeck@msj.edu.

Master of Science in Nursing Program Students: 53 full-time (all women), 2 part-time (both women); includes 4 minority (all Black or African American, non-Hispanic/Latino). Average age 44. 148 applicants, 68% accepted, 58 enrolled. *Faculty:* 12 full-time (11 women), 5 part-time/adjunct (all women). *Financial support:* In 2015–16, 3 students received support. Application deadline: 3/1; applicants required to submit FAFSA. In 2015, 65 master's awarded. *Degree program information:* Part-time programs available. Part-time. Offers administration (MSN); clinical nurse leader (MSN); education (MSN). *Application fee:* $50. Electronic applications accepted. *Application Contact:* Mary Brigham, Assistant Director for Graduate Recruitment, 513-244-4233, Fax: 513-244-4629, E-mail: mary.brigham@msj.edu. *MSN/DNP Director,* Dr. Nancy Hinzman, 513-244-4325, E-mail: nancy.hinzman@msj.edu.

Master of Science in Organizational Leadership Program Students: 1 full-time (0 women), 53 part-time (29 women); includes 6 minority (4 Black or African American, non-Hispanic/Latino; 1 Hispanic/Latino; 1 Two or more races, non-Hispanic/Latino). Average age 42. 6 applicants, 83% accepted, 5 enrolled. *Faculty:* 3 full-time (1 woman), 2 part-time/adjunct (both women). *Financial support:* In 2015–16, 9 students received support. Application deadline: 6/1; applicants required to submit FAFSA. In 2015, 22 master's awarded. *Degree program information:* Part-time and evening/weekend programs available. Part-time, evening/weekend. Offers organizational leadership (MS). *Application deadline:* Applications are processed on a rolling basis. *Application fee:* $50. Electronic applications accepted. *Application Contact:* Mary Brigham, Assistant Director of Graduate Recruitment, 513-244-4233, Fax: 513-244-4629, E-mail: mary.brigham@msj.edu. *Chair,* Daryl Smith, 513-244-4920, Fax: 513-244-4270, E-mail: daryl.smith@msj.edu.

Master's Graduate Entry-Level into Nursing (MAGELIN) Program Students: 96 full-time (78 women), 1 (woman) part-time; includes 19 minority (13 Black or African American, non-Hispanic/Latino; 3 Asian, non-Hispanic/Latino; 3 Two or more races, non-Hispanic/Latino). Average age 23. 36 applicants, 111% accepted, 34 enrolled. *Faculty:* 11 full-time (all women), 5 part-time/adjunct (4 women). *Financial support:* In 2015–16, 6 students received support. Scholarships/grants available. Financial award application deadline: 3/1; financial award applicants required to submit FAFSA. In 2015, 61 master's awarded. Offers nursing (MSN). *Application deadline:* Applications are processed on a rolling basis. *Application fee:* $50. Electronic applications accepted. *Application Contact:* Mary Brigham, Assistant Director of Graduate Recruitment, 513-244-4233, Fax: 513-244-4629, E-mail: mary.brigham@msj.edu. *Program Director,* Mary Kishman, 513-244-4726, Fax: 513-451-2547, E-mail: mary.kishman@msj.edu.

Physical Therapy Program Students: 66 full-time (45 women), 43 part-time (13 women); includes 2 minority (1 Black or African American, non-Hispanic/Latino; 1 Two or more races, non-Hispanic/Latino). Average age 24. 148 applicants, 43% accepted, 43 enrolled. *Faculty:* 7 full-time (6 women), 1 part-time/adjunct (0 women). *Financial support:* In 2015–16, 1 student received support. Application deadline: 6/1; applicants required to submit FAFSA. In 2015, 40 doctorates awarded. Offers physical therapy (DPT). *Application deadline:* For fall admission, 11/1 for domestic students. *Application fee:* $50. Electronic applications accepted. *Application Contact:* Mary Brigham, Assistant Director of Graduate Recruitment, 513-244-4233, Fax: 513-244-4629, E-mail: mary.brigham@msj.edu. *Chair,* Dr. Rosanne Thomas, 513-244-4519, Fax: 513-451-2547, E-mail: rosanne.thomas@msj.edu.

MOUNT SAINT MARY COLLEGE, Newburgh, NY 12550-3494

General Information Independent, coed, comprehensive institution. *Enrollment:* 2,508 graduate, professional, and undergraduate students; 82 full-time matriculated graduate/professional students (53 women), 265 part-time matriculated graduate/professional students (208 women). *Enrollment by degree level:* 343 master's, 4 other advanced degrees. *Graduate faculty:* 22 full-time (17 women), 11 part-time/adjunct (3 women). *Tuition, area resident:* Part-time $750 per credit. *Required fees:* $40 per semester. *Graduate housing:* Room and/or apartments guaranteed to single students; on-campus housing not available to married students. Typical cost: $9126 per year ($13,860 including board). Housing application deadline: 5/1. *Student services:* Campus employment opportunities, campus safety program, career counseling, free psychological counseling, international student services, services for students with disabilities. *Library:* Kaplan Family Library and Learning Center. *Collection:* Books: 85,305 (physical), 11,506 (digital/electronic); Serial titles: 213 (physical), 59,724 (digital/electronic); Databases: 84. Students can reserve study rooms.

Computer facilities: Computer purchase and lease plans are available. 470 computers available on campus for general student use. A campuswide network can be accessed from student residence rooms and from off campus. Online class registration, Intranet are available.
Website: http://www.msmc.edu/

General Application Contact: Lisa Gallina, Director of Admissions for Graduate Programs and Adult Degree Completion, 845-569-3166, Fax: 845-569-3450, E-mail: lisa.gallina@msmc.edu.

GRADUATE UNITS

Division of Education Students: 32 full-time (29 women), 107 part-time (84 women); includes 14 minority (3 Black or African American, non-Hispanic/Latino; 1 Asian, non-Hispanic/Latino; 9 Hispanic/Latino; 1 Two or more races, non-Hispanic/Latino). Average age 28. 44 applicants, 66% accepted, 21 enrolled. *Faculty:* 10 full-time (8 women), 2 part-time/adjunct (1 woman). *Financial support:* In 2015–16, 25 students received support. Unspecified assistantships available. Financial award application deadline: 4/15; financial award applicants required to submit FAFSA. In 2015, 46 master's awarded. *Degree program information:* Part-time and evening/weekend programs available. Part-time, evening/weekend. Offers adolescence and special education (MS Ed); adolescence education (MS Ed); childhood and special education (MS Ed); childhood education (MS Ed); literacy (5-12) (Advanced Certificate); literacy (birth-6) (Advanced Certificate); literacy and special education (MS Ed); literacy/childhood (MS Ed); middle school (5-6) (MS Ed); middle school (7-9) (MS Ed); special education (1-6) (MS Ed); special education (7-12) (MS Ed). *Application deadline:* Applications are processed on a rolling basis. *Application fee:* $45. Electronic applications accepted. *Application Contact:* Lisa Gallina, Director of Admissions for Graduate Programs and Adult Degree Completion, 845-569-3166, Fax: 845-569-3450, E-mail: lisa.gallina@msmc.edu. *Graduate Coordinator,* Dr. Monica Merritt, 845-569-3430, Fax: 845-569-3535, E-mail: monica.merritt@msmc.edu.

School of Business Students: 45 full-time (20 women), 41 part-time (19 women); includes 24 minority (7 Black or African American, non-Hispanic/Latino; 1 American Indian or Alaska Native, non-Hispanic/Latino; 3 Asian, non-Hispanic/Latino; 12 Hispanic/Latino; 1 Native Hawaiian or other Pacific Islander, non-Hispanic/Latino), 1 international. Average age 32. 21 applicants, 95% accepted, 19 enrolled. *Faculty:* 6 full-time (3 women), 8 part-time/adjunct (1 woman). *Financial support:* In 2015–16, 18 students received support. Unspecified assistantships available. Financial award application deadline: 4/15; financial award applicants required to submit FAFSA. In 2015, 34 master's awarded. *Degree program information:* Part-time and evening/weekend programs available. Part-time, evening/weekend. Offers business (MBA); financial planning (MBA). *Application deadline:* Applications are processed on a rolling basis. *Application fee:* $45. Electronic applications accepted. *Application Contact:* Lisa Gallina, Director of Admissions for Graduate Programs and Adult Degree Completion, 845-569-3166, Fax: 845-569-3450, E-mail: lisa.gallina@msmc.edu. *Graduate Coordinator,* Dr. Moira Tolan, 845-569-3121, Fax: 845-562-6762, E-mail: moira.tolan@msmc.edu.

School of Nursing Students: 5 full-time (4 women), 117 part-time (105 women); includes 42 minority (18 Black or African American, non-Hispanic/Latino; 2 American Indian or Alaska Native, non-Hispanic/Latino; 8 Asian, non-Hispanic/Latino; 12 Hispanic/Latino; 2 Native Hawaiian or other Pacific Islander, non-Hispanic/Latino). Average age 38. 44 applicants, 84% accepted, 25 enrolled. *Faculty:* 6 full-time (all women), 1 (woman) part-time/adjunct. *Financial support:* In 2015–16, 14 students received support. Unspecified assistantships available. Financial award application deadline: 4/15; financial award applicants required to submit FAFSA. In 2015, 25 master's, 4 other advanced degrees awarded. *Degree program information:* Part-time and evening/weekend programs available. Part-time, evening/weekend, blended/hybrid learning. Offers adult nurse practitioner (MS, Advanced Certificate); clinical nurse specialist-adult health (MS); family nurse practitioner (Advanced Certificate). *Application deadline:* For fall admission, 6/3 priority date for domestic students; for spring admission, 10/31 priority date for domestic students. Applications are processed on a rolling basis. *Application fee:* $45. Electronic applications accepted. *Application Contact:* Lisa Gallina, Director of Admissions for Graduate Programs and Adult Degree Completion, 845-569-3166, Fax: 845-569-3450, E-mail: lisa.gallina@msmc.edu. *Graduate Coordinator,* Christine Berte, 845-569-3141, Fax: 845-562-6762, E-mail: christine.berte@msmc.edu.

MOUNT SAINT MARY'S UNIVERSITY, Los Angeles, CA 90049

General Information Independent-religious, coed, primarily women, comprehensive institution. CGS member. *Enrollment:* 3,474 graduate, professional, and undergraduate students; 495 full-time matriculated graduate/professional students (369 women), 149 part-time matriculated graduate/professional students (121 women). *Enrollment by degree level:* 541 master's, 96 doctoral, 142 other advanced degrees. *Graduate faculty:* 115 full-time, 304 part-time/adjunct. One-time fee: $135. Tuition and fees vary according to degree level. *Graduate housing:* Room and/or apartments available on a first-come, first-served basis to single students; on-campus housing not available to married students. *Student services:* Campus employment opportunities, career counseling, exercise/wellness program, free psychological counseling, low-cost health insurance, services for students with disabilities, writing training. *Library:* Charles Willard Coe Library plus 2 others. *Collection:* Books: 310,130 (physical), 363,514 (digital/electronic); Serial titles: 615 (physical), 37,727 (digital/electronic); Databases: 217. Weekly public service hours: 89; study areas open 24 hours, 5–7 days a week. *Research affiliation:* John Tracy Clinic (education - deaf and hard of hearing teacher preparation).

Computer facilities: 170 computers available on campus for general student use. A campuswide network can be accessed from student residence rooms and from off campus. Online class registration is available.
Website: http://www.msmu.edu/

General Application Contact: Dr. Linda Moody, Graduate Dean, 213-477-2800, Fax: 213-477-2797, E-mail: gradprograms@msmu.edu.

GRADUATE UNITS

Graduate Division Students: 495 full-time (369 women), 149 part-time (121 women); includes 414 minority (73 Black or African American, non-Hispanic/Latino; 4 American Indian or Alaska Native, non-Hispanic/Latino; 60 Asian, non-Hispanic/Latino; 259 Hispanic/Latino; 7 Native Hawaiian or other Pacific Islander, non-Hispanic/Latino; 11 Two or more races, non-Hispanic/Latino), 4 international. Average age 33. 1,398 applicants, 21% accepted, 242 enrolled. *Faculty:* 115 full-time, 304 part-time/adjunct. *Financial support:* Career-related internships or fieldwork, Federal Work-Study, institutionally sponsored loans, and tuition waivers (full and partial) available. Support available to part-time students. Financial award application deadline: 3/15; financial award applicants required to submit FAFSA. In 2015, 172 master's, 26 doctorates, 23 other advanced degrees awarded. *Degree program information:* Part-time and evening/weekend programs available. Part-time, evening/weekend. Offers business administration (MBA); counseling psychology (MS); creative writing (MFA); education (MS, Certificate); film and television (MFA); health policy and management (MS); humanities (MA); nursing (MSN, Certificate); physical therapy (DPT); religious studies (MA). *Application deadline:* For fall admission, 6/30 priority date for domestic and international students; for spring admission, 10/30 priority date for domestic and international students; for summer admission, 3/30 priority date for domestic and international students. Applications are processed on a rolling basis. *Application fee:* $50. Electronic applications accepted. *Application Contact:* Tara Wessel, Assistant Director, Graduate Admission, 213-477-2799, E-mail: gradprograms@msmu.edu. *Graduate Dean*, Dr. Linda Moody, 213-477-2800, E-mail: gradprograms@msmu.edu.

MOUNT ST. MARY'S UNIVERSITY, Emmitsburg, MD 21727-7799

General Information Independent-religious, coed, comprehensive institution. *Enrollment:* 2,257 graduate, professional, and undergraduate students; 240 full-time matriculated graduate/professional students (36 women), 253 part-time matriculated graduate/professional students (141 women). *Enrollment by degree level:* 482 master's, 11 other advanced degrees. *Graduate faculty:* 33 full-time (12 women), 26 part-time/adjunct (9 women). *Graduate housing:* Room and/or apartments available on a first-come, first-served basis to single students; on-campus housing not available to married students. *Student services:* Campus employment opportunities, campus safety program, career counseling, exercise/wellness program, free psychological counseling, international student services, low-cost health insurance, multicultural affairs office, services for students with disabilities, teacher training, writing training. *Library:* Phillips Library. *Collection:* Books: 147,503 (physical), 199,373 (digital/electronic); Serial titles: 266 (physical), 24,866 (digital/electronic); Databases: 125.

Computer facilities: 80 computers available on campus for general student use. A campuswide network can be accessed from student residence rooms. Online class registration, tuition payment, course management system are available.
Website: http://www.msmary.edu/

General Application Contact: Joseph Lebherz, Director, Center for Professional and Continuing Studies, 301-682-8315, Fax: 301-682-5247, E-mail: lebherz@msmary.edu.

GRADUATE UNITS

Graduate Seminary Students: 122 full-time (0 women), 1 part-time (0 women); includes 7 minority (1 Black or African American, non-Hispanic/Latino; 2 Asian, non-Hispanic/Latino; 4 Hispanic/Latino), 5 international. Average age 29. 41 applicants, 88% accepted, 32 enrolled. *Faculty:* 10 full-time (2 women), 6 part-time/adjunct (2 women). *Financial support:* Career-related internships or fieldwork and scholarships/grants available. Financial award applicants required to submit FAFSA. In 2015, 49 master's awarded. Offers theology (M Div, MA). *Application deadline:* For fall admission, 8/1 for domestic and international students. *Application fee:* $0. *Application Contact:* Susan Nield, Seminary Admissions, 301-447-7423, Fax: 301-447-7402, E-mail: nield@msmary.edu. *Vice President/Rector*, Rev. Andrew R. Baker, 301-447-5295, Fax: 301-447-5636, E-mail: baker@msmary.edu.

Program in Biotechnology and Management Students: 1 full-time (0 women), 24 part-time (13 women); includes 8 minority (5 Black or African American, non-Hispanic/Latino; 3 Hispanic/Latino), 1 international. Average age 28. 30 applicants, 63% accepted, 14 enrolled. *Faculty:* 1 (woman) full-time, 1 part-time/adjunct (0 women). *Financial support:* Unspecified assistantships available. Financial award applicants required to submit FAFSA. *Degree program information:* Part-time and evening/weekend programs available. Part-time-only, evening/weekend. Offers biotechnology and management (MS). *Application deadline:* Applications are processed on a rolling basis. *Application fee:* $35. Electronic applications accepted. *Interim Director*, Paul Smock, 301-447-5716, E-mail: smock@msmary.edu.

Program in Business Administration Students: 59 full-time (24 women), 117 part-time (53 women); includes 45 minority (21 Black or African American, non-Hispanic/Latino; 3 American Indian or Alaska Native, non-Hispanic/Latino; 5 Asian, non-Hispanic/Latino; 11 Hispanic/Latino; 2 Native Hawaiian or other Pacific Islander, non-Hispanic/Latino; 3 Two or more races, non-Hispanic/Latino), 7 international. Average age 32. 113 applicants, 64% accepted, 46 enrolled. *Faculty:* 8 full-time (2 women), 16 part-time/adjunct (3 women). *Financial support:* Career-related internships or fieldwork and unspecified assistantships available. Financial award applicants required to submit FAFSA. In 2015, 110 master's awarded. *Degree program information:* Part-time and evening/weekend programs available. Part-time, evening/weekend. Offers business administration (MBA). *Application deadline:* Applications are processed on a rolling basis. *Application fee:* $35. *Assistant Director of Graduate and Adult Business Program*, Terry McCune, 301-447-5908, Fax: 301-447-5335, E-mail: mba@msmary.edu.

Program in Education Students: 16 full-time (12 women), 62 part-time (43 women); includes 10 minority (3 Black or African American, non-Hispanic/Latino; 3 American Indian or Alaska Native, non-Hispanic/Latino; 2 Asian, non-Hispanic/Latino; 2 Hispanic/Latino), 1 international. Average age 32. *Faculty:* 6 full-time (4 women), 8 part-time/adjunct (6 women). *Financial support:* Career-related internships or fieldwork and unspecified assistantships available. Financial award applicants required to submit FAFSA. In 2015, 20 master's awarded. *Degree program information:* Part-time and evening/weekend programs available. Part-time, evening/weekend. Offers education (M Ed, MAT). *Application deadline:* For fall admission, 8/15 for domestic and international students. Applications are processed on a rolling basis. *Application fee:* $35. *Dean of School of Education and Human Services*, Dr. Barbara Martin-Palmer, 301-447-5371, Fax: 301-447-5250, E-mail: palmer@msmary.edu.

Program in Health Administration Students: 1 full-time (0 women), 49 part-time (31 women); includes 19 minority (7 Black or African American, non-Hispanic/Latino; 1 American Indian or Alaska Native, non-Hispanic/Latino; 5 Asian, non-Hispanic/Latino; 6 Hispanic/Latino). Average age 31. 30 applicants, 73% accepted, 16 enrolled. *Faculty:* 6 part-time/adjunct (1 woman). *Financial support:* Applicants required to submit FAFSA. In 2015, 33 master's awarded. *Degree program information:* Part-time and evening/weekend programs available. Part-time, evening/weekend. Offers health administration (MHA). *Application deadline:* Applications are processed on a rolling basis. *Application fee:* $35. *Director*, Cyd Maubert, 301-447-5773.

Program in Philosophical Studies Students: 2 part-time (0 women). Average age 32. *Faculty:* 3 full-time (0 women), 1 part-time/adjunct (0 women). *Financial support:* Unspecified assistantships available. Financial award applicants required to submit FAFSA. In 2015, 2 master's awarded. *Degree program information:* Part-time programs available. Part-time. Offers philosophical studies (MA). *Application deadline:* For fall admission, 8/1 for domestic students; for spring admission, 12/1 for domestic students. *Director*, Dr. Christopher Anadale, 301-447-5368 Ext. 4307, E-mail: anadale@msmary.edu.

Program in Sport Management Students: 1 full-time (0 women), 7 part-time (4 women); includes 2 minority (1 Black or African American, non-Hispanic/Latino; 1 Hispanic/Latino). Average age 25. 10 applicants, 80% accepted, 8 enrolled. *Faculty:* 1 (woman) full-time, 1 part-time/adjunct (0 women). *Financial support:* Unspecified assistantships available. Financial award applicants required to submit FAFSA. *Degree program information:* Part-time and evening/weekend programs available. Part-time, evening/weekend. Offers sport management (MS). *Application deadline:* Applications are processed on a rolling basis. *Application fee:* $35. Electronic applications accepted. *Director*, Dr. Corinne Farneti, 301-447-5878, E-mail: farneti@msmary.edu.

MOUNT SAINT VINCENT UNIVERSITY, Halifax, NS B3M 2J6, Canada

General Information Province-supported, coed, primarily women, comprehensive institution. *Graduate housing:* Room and/or apartments available on a first-come, first-served basis to single students; on-campus housing not available to married students. Housing application deadline: 5/15.

GRADUATE UNITS

Graduate Programs ***Degree program information:*** Part-time and evening/weekend programs available. Part-time, evening/weekend, online learning. Offers applied human nutrition (M Sc AHN, MAHN); child and youth study (MA); family studies and gerontology (MA); women's studies (MA). Electronic applications accepted.

Faculty of Education Degree program information: Part-time and evening/weekend programs available. Part-time, evening/weekend, online learning. Offers adult education (M Ed, MA Ed, MA-R); curriculum studies (M Ed, MA Ed, MA-R); education of the blind or visually impaired (M Ed, MA Ed); education of the deaf or hard of hearing (M Ed, MA Ed); education of young adolescents (M Ed, MA Ed, MA-R); educational foundations (M Ed, MA Ed, MA-R); educational psychology (M Ed, MA Ed, MA-R); elementary education (M Ed, MA Ed, MA-R); general studies (M Ed, MA Ed, MA-R); human relations (M Ed, MA Ed); literacy education (M Ed, MA Ed, MA-R); school psychology (MASP); teaching English as a second language (M Ed, MA Ed, MA-R). Electronic applications accepted.

MOUNT VERNON NAZARENE UNIVERSITY, Mount Vernon, OH 43050-9500

General Information Independent-religious, coed, comprehensive institution. *Graduate housing:* On-campus housing not available.

GRADUATE UNITS

Department of Education ***Degree program information:*** Part-time and evening/weekend programs available. Part-time, evening/weekend. Offers education (MA Ed); professional educator's license (MA Ed).

Program in Management ***Degree program information:*** Part-time and evening/weekend programs available. Part-time, evening/weekend. Offers management (MSM).

Program in Ministry ***Degree program information:*** Part-time and evening/weekend programs available. Part-time, evening/weekend. Offers ministry (M Min).

MULTNOMAH UNIVERSITY, Portland, OR 97220-5898

General Information Independent-religious, coed, comprehensive institution. *Enrollment:* 736 graduate, professional, and undergraduate students; 244 full-time matriculated graduate/professional students (106 women), 85 part-time matriculated graduate/professional students (33 women). *Enrollment by degree level:* 302 master's, 27 doctoral. *Graduate faculty:* 20 full-time (9 women), 16 part-time/adjunct (3 women). *Tuition, area resident:* Full-time $10,000; part-time $6000 per semester. *Required fees:* $220; $110 per semester. Tuition and fees vary according to course load, degree level and program. *Graduate housing:* Rooms and/or apartments available on a first-come, first-served basis to single and married students. Typical cost: $5940 per year ($7820 including board) for single students; $8050 per year for married students. Room and board charges vary according to board plan and housing facility selected. Housing application deadline: 7/15. *Student services:* Campus employment opportunities, career counseling, free psychological counseling, low-cost health insurance, teacher training. *Library:* John Mitchell Library. *Collection:* Books: 109,611 (physical), 133,119 (digital/electronic); Serial titles: 19,107 (digital/electronic). Weekly public service hours: 88; students can reserve study rooms.

Computer facilities: 36 computers available on campus for general student use. A campuswide network can be accessed from student residence rooms and from off campus. Online class registration is available.
Website: http://www.multnomah.edu/

General Application Contact: Mindy Kate Hasenkamp, Director of Admissions, 503-251-6483, Fax: 503-254-1268, E-mail: admiss@multnomah.edu.

GRADUATE UNITS

Graduate Programs Students: 120 full-time (80 women), 31 part-time (23 women); includes 35 minority (15 Black or African American, non-Hispanic/Latino; 2 Asian, non-Hispanic/Latino; 9 Hispanic/Latino; 1 Native Hawaiian or other Pacific Islander, non-Hispanic/Latino; 8 Two or more races, non-Hispanic/Latino), 3 international. Average age 30. 95 applicants, 69% accepted, 54 enrolled. *Faculty:* 11 full-time (6 women), 10 part-time/adjunct (3 women). *Financial support:* Career-related internships or fieldwork and scholarships/grants available. Support available to part-time students. Financial award application deadline: 7/1; financial award applicants required to submit FAFSA. In 2015, 50 master's awarded. *Degree program information:* Part-time and evening/weekend programs available. Part-time, evening/weekend. Offers counseling (MA); global development and justice (MA); teaching (MA); TESOL (MA). *Application deadline:* For fall admission, 8/1 for domestic students, 12/1 for international students; for spring admission, 12/1 for domestic and international students. *Application fee:* $40. Electronic applications accepted. *Application Contact:* Mindy Kate Hasenkamp, Director of Admissions, 503-251-6483, Fax: 503-254-1268, E-mail: admiss@multnomah.edu. *Academic Dean*, Dr. Daniel Scalberg, 503-251-6441, E-mail: dscalberg@multnomah.edu.

Multnomah Biblical Seminary Students: 95 full-time (27 women), 56 part-time (10 women); includes 26 minority (3 Black or African American, non-Hispanic/Latino; 1 American Indian or Alaska Native, non-Hispanic/Latino; 8 Asian, non-Hispanic/Latino; 8 Hispanic/Latino; 2 Native Hawaiian or other Pacific Islander, non-Hispanic/Latino; 4 Two or more races, non-Hispanic/Latino), 2 international. Average age 35. 75 applicants, 79% accepted, 50 enrolled. *Faculty:* 9 full-time (3 women), 6 part-time/adjunct (0 women). *Financial support:* Career-related internships or fieldwork and scholarships/grants available. Support available to part-time students. Financial award application deadline: 7/1; financial award applicants required to submit FAFSA. In 2015, 51 master's awarded. *Degree program information:* Part-time programs available. Part-time. Offers theology (M Div, MABS, MACL, MATS, Th M, D Min). *Application deadline:* For fall and spring admission, 12/1 priority date for domestic and international students. Applications are processed on a rolling basis. *Application fee:* $40. *Application Contact:* Mindy Kate Hasenkamp, Director of Admissions, 503-251-6483, Fax: 503-254-1268, E-mail: admiss@multnomah.edu. *Dean*, Dr. Roy Andrews, 503-252-6731, Fax: 503-251-6444, E-mail: randrews@multnomah.edu.

MURRAY STATE UNIVERSITY, Murray, KY 42071

General Information State-supported, coed, university. *Graduate housing:* Rooms and/or apartments available on a first-come, first-served basis to single and married students.

GRADUATE UNITS

College of Business and Public Affairs ***Degree program information:*** Part-time and evening/weekend programs available. Part-time, evening/weekend. Offers business administration (MBA); business and public affairs (MA, MBA, MPAC, MS); economics (MS); mass communications (MA, MS); organizational communication (MA, MS); professional accountancy (MPAC); telecommunications systems management (MS).

College of Education ***Degree program information:*** Part-time programs available. Part-time. Offers advanced learning behavior disorders (MA Ed); community and agency counseling (Ed S); early childhood education (MA Ed); education (MA Ed, MS, Ed D, PhD, Ed S); elementary education (MA Ed, Ed S); elementary education/reading and writing (MA Ed, Ed S); health, physical education, and recreation (MA); human development and leadership (MS); industrial and technical education (MS); learning disabilities (MA Ed); middle school education (MA Ed, Ed S); moderate/severe disorders (MA Ed); reading and writing (MA Ed); school administration (MA Ed, Ed S); school guidance and counseling (MA Ed, Ed S); secondary education (MA Ed, Ed S); special education (MA Ed). PhD, Ed D offered jointly with University of Kentucky.

College of Health Sciences and Human Services ***Degree program information:*** Part-time programs available. Part-time. Offers clinical nurse specialist (MSN); environmental science (MS); exercise and leisure studies (MS); family nurse practitioner (MSN); health sciences and human services (MS, MSN); industrial hygiene (MS); nurse anesthesia (MSN); safety management (MS); speech-language pathology (MS).

College of Humanities and Fine Arts ***Degree program information:*** Part-time programs available. Part-time. Offers clinical psychology (MA, MS); creative writing (MFA); English (MA); history (MA); humanities and fine arts (MA, MFA, MME, MPA, MS); music education (MME); psychology (MA, MS); public administration (MPA); public affairs (MPA); teaching English to speakers of other languages (MA).

College of Science, Engineering and Technology ***Degree program information:*** Part-time programs available. Part-time. Offers biological sciences (MAT, MS, PhD); chemistry (MS); geosciences (MS); management of technology (MS); mathematics (MA, MAT, MS); science, engineering and technology (MA, MAT, MS, PhD); water science (MS).

School of Agriculture ***Degree program information:*** Evening/weekend programs available. Evening/weekend, online learning. Offers agriculture (MS); agriculture education (MS).

MUSKINGUM UNIVERSITY, New Concord, OH 43762

General Information Independent-religious, coed, comprehensive institution. *Graduate housing:* On-campus housing not available.

GRADUATE UNITS

Graduate Programs in Education ***Degree program information:*** Part-time programs available. Part-time. Offers education (MAE, MAT).

NAROPA UNIVERSITY, Boulder, CO 80302-6697

General Information Independent, coed, comprehensive institution. *Enrollment:* 942 graduate, professional, and undergraduate students; 371 full-time matriculated graduate/professional students (254 women), 174 part-time matriculated graduate/professional students (136 women). *Enrollment by degree level:* 545 master's. *Graduate faculty:* 34 full-time (19 women), 57 part-time/adjunct (44 women). *Tuition, area resident:* Full-time $23,880; part-time $995 per credit hour. *Required fees:* $335 per semester. Tuition and fees vary according to course load. *Graduate housing:* Room and/or apartments available on a first-come, first-served basis to single students; on-campus housing not available to married students. Typical cost: $9465 (including board). Housing application deadline: 6/15. *Student services:* Campus employment opportunities, campus safety program, career counseling, free psychological counseling, international student services, low-cost health insurance, multicultural affairs office, services for students with disabilities, writing training. *Library:* Allen Ginsberg Library plus 2 others. *Collection:* Books: 34,909 (physical), 150,000 (digital/electronic); Serial titles: 47 (physical), 12 (digital/electronic); Databases: 29. Weekly public service hours: 69.

Computer facilities: 48 computers available on campus for general student use. A campuswide network can be accessed from student residence rooms and from off campus. Online class registration is available.
Website: http://www.naropa.edu/

General Application Contact: Office of Admissions, 303-546-3572, Fax: 303-546-3583, E-mail: admissions@naropa.edu.

GRADUATE UNITS

Graduate Programs Students: 371 full-time (254 women), 174 part-time (136 women); includes 88 minority (4 Black or African American, non-Hispanic/Latino; 4 American Indian or Alaska Native, non-Hispanic/Latino; 9 Asian, non-Hispanic/Latino; 38 Hispanic/Latino; 33 Two or more races, non-Hispanic/Latino), 19 international. Average age 32. 505 applicants, 68% accepted, 205 enrolled. *Faculty:* 34 full-time (19 women), 57 part-time/adjunct (44 women). *Financial support:* In 2015–16, 240 students received support, including 41 research assistantships (averaging $3,561 per year); fellowships, teaching assistantships, career-related internships or fieldwork, Federal Work-Study, scholarships/grants, tuition waivers (partial), and unspecified assistantships also available. Support available to part-time students. Financial award application deadline: 3/1; financial award applicants required to submit FAFSA. In 2015, 180 master's awarded. *Degree program information:* Part-time programs available. Part-time, blended/hybrid learning. Offers contemplative education (MA); contemplative psychotherapy and Buddhist psychology (MA); creative writing (MFA); creative writing and poetics (MFA); divinity (M Div); ecopsychology (MA); environmental leadership (MA); mindfulness-based transpersonal counseling (MA); religious studies (MA); religious studies with language (MA); somatic counseling: body psychotherapy (MA); somatic counseling: dance/movement therapy (MA); theater: contemporary performance (MFA); transpersonal art therapy (MA); transpersonal wilderness therapy (MA). *Application deadline:* For fall admission, 1/15 priority date for domestic and international students; for spring admission, 10/15 priority date for domestic and international students. Applications are processed on a rolling basis. *Application fee:* $60. Electronic applications accepted. *Application Contact:* Office of Admissions, 303-546-3572, Fax: 303-546-3583, E-mail: admissions@naropa.edu. *Dean of Admissions*, Janet Erickson, 303-245-4725, Fax: 303-546-3583, E-mail: jerickson@naropa.edu.

NASHOTAH HOUSE THEOLOGICAL SEMINARY, Nashotah, WI 53058-9793

General Information Independent-religious, coed, primarily men, graduate-only institution. *Enrollment by degree level:* 8 master's, 45 doctoral, 3 other advanced degrees. *Graduate faculty:* 8 full-time (0 women), 6 part-time/adjunct (0 women). *Graduate housing:* Rooms and/or apartments available on a first-come, first-served basis to single and married students. Housing application deadline: 5/1. *Student services:* Campus employment opportunities, career counseling. *Library:* Frances Donaldson Library. Study areas open 24 hours, 5–7 days a week.

Computer facilities: 6 computers available on campus for general student use. Online class registration is available.
Website: http://www.nashotah.edu/

General Application Contact: Fr. Dr. Rick Hartley, Associate Dean of Students/Registrar, 262-646-6547, Fax: 262-646-6504, E-mail: rhartley@nashotah.edu.

GRADUATE UNITS

Graduate Programs Students: 78 full-time (14 women), 5 part-time (2 women); includes 3 minority (2 Black or African American, non-Hispanic/Latino; 1 Asian, non-Hispanic/Latino). Average age 37. *Faculty:* 8 full-time (0 women), 6 part-time/adjunct (0 women). *Financial support:* Teaching assistantships, career-related internships or fieldwork, scholarships/grants, and tuition waivers (partial) available. Support available to part-time students. Financial award application deadline: 9/15; financial award applicants required to submit FAFSA. *Degree program information:* Part-time programs available. Part-time. Offers theology (M Div, MM, MTS, STM, D Min, Certificate). *Application deadline:* For fall admission, 7/1 priority date for domestic students. Applications are processed on a rolling basis. *Application fee:* $0. *Application Contact:* Fr. Dr. Rick Hartley, Associate Dean of Students/Registrar, 262-646-6547, Fax: 262-646-6504, E-mail: rhartley@nashotah.edu. *Dean/President*, Very Rev. Steven A. Peay, 262-646-6512, Fax: 262-646-6504, E-mail: speay@nashotah.edu.

NATIONAL AMERICAN UNIVERSITY, Rapid City, SD 57701

General Information Proprietary, coed, comprehensive institution. *Graduate housing:* Room and/or apartments available on a first-come, first-served basis to single students. Housing application deadline: 6/1.

GRADUATE UNITS

Graduate Programs ***Degree program information:*** Part-time and evening/weekend programs available. Part-time, evening/weekend, online learning. Offers business (MBA, MM). Programs also offered in Wichita, KS; Albuquerque, NM; Bloomington, MN; Brooklyn Center, MN; Colorado Springs, CO; Denver, CO; Independence, MO; Overland Park, KS; Rio Rancho, NM; Roseville, MN; Zona Rosa, MO. Electronic applications accepted.

NATIONAL COLLEGE OF MIDWIFERY, Taos, NM 87571

General Information Independent, women only, comprehensive institution.

GRADUATE UNITS

Graduate Programs ***Degree program information:*** Part-time and evening/weekend programs available. Part-time, evening/weekend, online learning. Offers midwifery (MS, PhD). Electronic applications accepted.

NATIONAL COLLEGE OF NATURAL MEDICINE, Portland, OR 97201

General Information Independent, coed, primarily women, graduate-only institution. *Graduate housing:* On-campus housing not available. *Research affiliation:* Kaiser Center for Health Research, Oregon Health and Science University, Bob's Red Mill, Oregon College of Oriental Medicine.

GRADUATE UNITS

School of Classical Chinese Medicine ***Degree program information:*** Evening/weekend programs available. Evening/weekend. Offers classical Chinese medicine (M Ac, MSOM).

School of Naturopathic Medicine Offers integrative medicine research (MS); naturopathic medicine (ND).

NATIONAL DEFENSE UNIVERSITY, Washington, DC 20319-5066

General Information Federally supported, coed, graduate-only institution. *Graduate housing:* On-campus housing not available.

GRADUATE UNITS

College of International Security Affairs ***Degree program information:*** Part-time and evening/weekend programs available. Part-time, evening/weekend. Offers strategic security studies (MA).

The Dwight D. Eisenhower School for National Security and Resource Strategy Offers national resource strategy (MS). Open only to Department of Defense employees and specific federal agencies.

Joint Advanced Warfighting School Offers joint campaign planning and strategy (MS). Open only to Department of Defense employees and specific federal agencies.

National War College Offers national security strategy (MS). Open only to Department of Defense employees and specific federal agencies.

THE NATIONAL GRADUATE SCHOOL OF QUALITY MANAGEMENT, Falmouth, MA 02541

General Information Independent, coed, graduate-only institution.

GRADUATE UNITS

Graduate Programs Offers homeland security (MS); quality systems management (MS, DBA).

NATIONAL INTELLIGENCE UNIVERSITY, Washington, DC 20340-5100

General Information Federally supported, coed, graduate-only institution. *Graduate housing:* On-campus housing not available.

GRADUATE UNITS

Graduate Program ***Degree program information:*** Part-time and evening/weekend programs available. Part-time, evening/weekend. Offers strategic intelligence (MSSI). Open only to federal government employees.

NATIONAL LOUIS UNIVERSITY, Chicago, IL 60603

General Information Independent, coed, university.

GRADUATE UNITS

College of Arts and Sciences ***Degree program information:*** Part-time and evening/weekend programs available. Part-time, evening/weekend, online learning. Offers adult education (Ed D); counseling and human services (MS); language and academic development (M Ed, Certificate); psychology (MA, PhD, Certificate); public policy (MA); written communication (MS, Certificate). Electronic applications accepted.

College of Management and Business ***Degree program information:*** Part-time and evening/weekend programs available. Part-time, evening/weekend. Offers business administration (MBA); human resource management and development (MS); management (MS).

National College of Education ***Degree program information:*** Part-time and evening/weekend programs available. Part-time, evening/weekend. Offers administration and supervision (M Ed, Ed D, CAS, Ed S); curriculum and instruction (M Ed, MS Ed, CAS); early childhood administration (M Ed, CAS); early childhood education (M Ed, MAT, MS Ed, CAS); education (Ed D); educational psychology/human learning and development (M Ed, MS Ed, CAS, Ed S); elementary education (MAT); interdisciplinary curriculum and instruction (M Ed); mathematics education (M Ed, MS Ed, CAS); reading and language (M Ed, MS Ed, CAS); school psychology (M Ed, Ed S); science education (M Ed, MS Ed, CAS); secondary education (MAT); special education (M Ed, MAT, CAS); technology in education (M Ed, CAS).

NATIONAL PARALEGAL COLLEGE, Phoenix, AZ 85014

General Information Proprietary, coed, comprehensive institution. *Library:* Jones eGlobal Library.
Website: http://nationalparalegal.edu/

General Application Contact: Danielle Backman, Registrar, E-mail: danielle@nationalparalegal.edu.

GRADUATE UNITS

Graduate Programs In 2015, 3 master's awarded. *Degree program information:* Part-time programs available. Part-time. Offers compliance law (MS); legal studies (MS); taxation (MS). *Application deadline:* Applications are processed on a rolling basis. Electronic applications accepted. *Dean*, Jeremy A. Rovinsky, E-mail: jeremy@nationalparalegal.edu.

NATIONAL UNIVERSITY, La Jolla, CA 92037-1011

General Information Independent, coed, comprehensive institution. CGS member. *Enrollment:* 17,488 graduate, professional, and undergraduate students; 5,245 full-time matriculated graduate/professional students (3,412 women), 3,238 part-time matriculated graduate/professional students (2,122 women). *Enrollment by degree level:* 7,411 master's, 1,072 other advanced degrees. *Graduate faculty:* 269 full-time (128 women), 625 part-time/adjunct (319 women). *Graduate housing:* On-campus housing not available. *Student services:* Campus employment opportunities, campus safety program, career counseling, international student services, services for students with disabilities, teacher training, writing training. *Library:* National University Library. *Collection:* Books: 216,825 (physical), 242,163 (digital/electronic); Serial titles: 1,630 (physical), 76,410 (digital/electronic); Databases: 190. Weekly public service hours: 72; students can reserve study rooms.

Computer facilities: 2,800 computers available on campus for general student use. A campuswide network can be accessed. Online class registration is available.
Website: http://www.nu.edu/

General Application Contact: Frank Rojas, Vice President for Enrollment Services, 800-628-8648, E-mail: advisor@nu.edu.

GRADUATE UNITS

Academic Affairs Students: 5,245 full-time (3,412 women), 3,238 part-time (2,122 women); includes 4,068 minority (854 Black or African American, non-Hispanic/Latino; 33 American Indian or Alaska Native, non-Hispanic/Latino; 647 Asian, non-Hispanic/Latino; 2,120 Hispanic/Latino; 69 Native Hawaiian or other Pacific Islander, non-Hispanic/Latino; 345 Two or more races, non-Hispanic/Latino), 318 international. Average age 34. *Faculty:* 253 full-time (120 women), 561 part-time/adjunct (299 women). *Financial support:* Career-related internships or fieldwork, institutionally sponsored loans, scholarships/grants, and tuition waivers (partial) available. Support available to part-time students. Financial award application deadline: 6/30; financial award applicants required to submit FAFSA. In 2015, 4,902 master's awarded. *Degree program information:* Part-time and evening/weekend programs available. Part-time, evening/weekend, 100% online, blended/hybrid learning. *Application deadline:* Applications are processed on a rolling basis. *Application fee:* $60 ($65 for international students). Electronic applications accepted. *Application Contact:* Brandon Jouganatos, Vice President for Enrollment Services, E-mail: advisor@nu.edu. *Provost*, Gangaram Singh, 858-642-8130, E-mail: instresearch@nu.edu.

College of Letters and Sciences Students: 689 full-time (493 women), 318 part-time (230 women); includes 508 minority (137 Black or African American, non-Hispanic/Latino; 5 American Indian or Alaska Native, non-Hispanic/Latino; 50 Asian, non-Hispanic/Latino; 248 Hispanic/Latino; 10 Native Hawaiian or other Pacific Islander, non-Hispanic/Latino; 58 Two or more races, non-Hispanic/Latino), 5 international. Average age 34. *Faculty:* 75 full-time (39 women), 87 part-time/adjunct (39 women). *Financial support:* Career-related internships or fieldwork, institutionally sponsored loans, scholarships/grants, and tuition waivers (partial) available. Support available to part-time students. Financial award application deadline: 6/30; financial award applicants required to submit FAFSA. In 2015, 470 master's awarded. *Degree program information:* Part-time and evening/weekend programs available. Part-time, evening/weekend, 100% online, blended/hybrid learning. Offers applied linguistics (MA); biology (MS); counseling psychology (MA); creative writing (MFA); English (MA); film studies (MA); forensic and crime science (Certificate); forensic studies (MFS); history (MA); human behavior (MA); mathematics for educators (MS); performance psychology (MA); strategic communications (MA). *Application deadline:* Applications are processed on a rolling basis. *Application fee:* $60 ($65 for international students). Electronic applications accepted. *Application Contact:* Brandon Jouganatos, Interim Vice President for Enrollment Services, 800-628-8648, E-mail: advisor@nu.edu. *College of Letters and Sciences*, 800-628-8648, E-mail: cols@nu.edu.

School of Business and Management Students: 652 full-time (316 women), 303 part-time (161 women); includes 462 minority (115 Black or African American, non-Hispanic/Latino; 6 American Indian or Alaska Native, non-Hispanic/Latino; 107 Asian, non-Hispanic/Latino; 171 Hispanic/Latino; 13 Native Hawaiian or other Pacific Islander, non-Hispanic/Latino; 50 Two or more races, non-Hispanic/Latino), 159 international. Average age 33. *Faculty:* 37 full-time (9 women), 74 part-time/adjunct (20 women). *Financial support:* Career-related internships or fieldwork, scholarships/grants, and tuition waivers (partial) available. Support available to part-time students. Financial award application deadline: 6/30; financial award applicants required to submit FAFSA. In 2015, 691 master's awarded. *Degree program information:* Part-time and evening/weekend programs available. Part-time, evening/weekend, 100% online, blended/hybrid learning. Offers business administration (MBA); global management (MGM). *Application deadline:* Applications are processed on a rolling basis. *Application fee:* $60 ($65 for international students). Electronic applications accepted. *Application Contact:* Brandon Jouganatos, Vice President for Enrollment Services, 800-628-8648, E-mail: advisor@nu.edu. *School of Business and Management*, 800-628-8648, Fax: 858-642-8719, E-mail: sobm@nu.edu.

School of Education Students: 3,029 full-time (2,147 women), 2,210 part-time (1,524 women); includes 2,391 minority (367 Black or African American, non-Hispanic/Latino; 21 American Indian or Alaska Native, non-Hispanic/Latino; 301 Asian, non-Hispanic/Latino; 1,489 Hispanic/Latino; 31 Native Hawaiian or other Pacific Islander, non-Hispanic/Latino; 182 Two or more races, non-Hispanic/Latino). Average age 33. *Faculty:* 81 full-time (51 women), 371 part-time/adjunct (227 women). *Financial support:* Career-related internships or fieldwork, institutionally sponsored loans, scholarships/grants, and tuition waivers (partial) available. Support available to part-time students. Financial award application deadline: 6/30. In 2015, 3,396 master's awarded. *Degree program information:* Part-time and evening/weekend programs available. Part-time, evening/weekend, 100% online, blended/hybrid learning. Offers applied behavior analysis (Certificate); applied school leadership (MS); autism (Certificate); best practices (Certificate); e-teaching and learning (Certificate); early childhood education (Certificate); education (MA); education with preliminary multiple or single subject (M Ed); educational administration (MS); educational and instructional technology (MS); educational counseling (MS); educational technology (Certificate); higher education administration (MS); innovative school leadership (MS); instructional leadership (MS); juvenile justice special education (MS); reading (Certificate); school psychology (MS); special education (MS); teacher leadership (Certificate); teaching (MA); teaching mathematics (Certificate). *Application deadline:* Applications are processed on a rolling basis. *Application fee:* $60 ($65 for international students). Electronic applications accepted. *Application Contact:* Brandon Jouganatos, Vice President for Enrollment Services, 800-628-8648, E-mail: advisor@nu.edu. *School of Education*, 800-628-8648, E-mail: soe@nu.edu.

School of Engineering and Computing Students: 286 full-time (69 women), 116 part-time (31 women); includes 143 minority (41 Black or African American, non-Hispanic/Latino; 48 Asian, non-Hispanic/Latino; 35 Hispanic/Latino; 5 Native Hawaiian or other Pacific Islander, non-Hispanic/Latino; 14 Two or more races, non-Hispanic/Latino), 120 international. Average age 32. *Faculty:* 20 full-time (3 women), 28 part-time/adjunct (5 women). *Financial support:* Career-related internships or fieldwork, institutionally sponsored loans, scholarships/grants, and tuition waivers (partial) available. Support available to part-time students. Financial award application deadline: 6/30; financial award applicants required to submit FAFSA. In 2015, 232 master's awarded. *Degree program information:* Part-time and evening/weekend programs available. Part-time, evening/weekend, 100% online, blended/hybrid learning. Offers computer science (MS); cyber security and information assurance (MS); data analytics (MS); engineering management (MS); environmental engineering (MS); homeland security and emergency management (MS); management information systems (MS); project management (Certificate); sustainability management (MS); wireless communications (MS). *Application deadline:* Applications are processed on a rolling basis. *Application fee:* $60 ($65 for international students). Electronic applications accepted. *Application Contact:* Brandon Jouganatos, Vice President for Enrollment Services, 800-628-8648, E-mail: advisor@nu.edu. *School of Engineering and Computing*, 800-628-8648, E-mail: soec@nu.edu.

School of Health and Human Services Students: 353 full-time (263 women), 136 part-time (87 women); includes 322 minority (111 Black or African American, non-Hispanic/Latino; 1 American Indian or Alaska Native, non-Hispanic/Latino; 105 Asian, non-Hispanic/Latino; 72 Hispanic/Latino; 7 Native Hawaiian or other Pacific Islander, non-Hispanic/Latino; 26 Two or more races, non-Hispanic/Latino), 31 international. Average age 32. *Faculty:* 31 full-time (18 women), 33 part-time/adjunct (20 women). *Financial support:* Career-related internships or fieldwork, institutionally sponsored loans, scholarships/grants, and tuition waivers (partial) available. Support available to part-time students. Financial award application deadline: 6/30; financial award applicants required to submit FAFSA. In 2015, 103 master's awarded. *Degree program information:* Part-time and evening/weekend programs available. Part-time, evening/weekend, 100% online, blended/hybrid learning. Offers clinical affairs (MS); clinical informatics (Certificate); clinical regulatory affairs (MS); health and life science analytics (MS); health coaching (Certificate); health informatics (MS); healthcare administration (MHA); nurse anesthesia (MS); nursing (MS); nursing administration (Certificate); nursing informatics (Certificate); nursing practice (DNP); public health (MPH). *Application deadline:* Applications are processed on a rolling basis. *Application fee:* $60 ($65 for international students). Electronic applications accepted. *Application Contact:* Frank Rojas, Vice President for Enrollment Services, 800-628-8648, E-mail: advisor@nu.edu. *School of Health and Human Services*, 800-628-8648, E-mail: shhs@nu.edu.

School of Professional Studies Students: 236 full-time (124 women), 155 part-time (89 women); includes 236 minority (83 Black or African American, non-Hispanic/Latino; 30 Asian, non-Hispanic/Latino; 105 Hispanic/Latino; 3 Native Hawaiian or other Pacific Islander, non-Hispanic/Latino; 15 Two or more races, non-Hispanic/Latino), 3 international. Average age 37. *Faculty:* 25 full-time (8 women), 32 part-time/adjunct (8 women). *Financial support:* Career-related internships or fieldwork, institutionally sponsored loans, scholarships/grants, and tuition waivers (partial) available. Support available to part-time students. Financial award application deadline: 6/30; financial award applicants required to submit FAFSA. In 2015, 9 master's awarded. *Degree program information:* Part-time and evening/weekend programs available. Part-time, evening/weekend, 100% online, blended/hybrid learning. Offers criminal justice (MCJ); digital cinema (MFA); digital journalism (MA);

juvenile justice (MS); professional screen writing (MFA); public administration (MPA). *Application deadline:* Applications are processed on a rolling basis. *Application fee:* $60 ($65 for international students). Electronic applications accepted. *Application Contact:* Brandon Jouganatos, Vice President for Enrollment Services, 800-628-8648, E-mail: advisor@nu.edu. *School of Professional Studies*, 800-628-8648, E-mail: sops@nu.edu.

NATIONAL UNIVERSITY COLLEGE, Bayamón, PR 00960

General Information Proprietary, coed, comprehensive institution.

GRADUATE UNITS

Graduate Programs

NATIONAL UNIVERSITY OF HEALTH SCIENCES, Lombard, IL 60148-4583

General Information Independent, coed, graduate-only institution. *Graduate housing:* Rooms and/or apartments available on a first-come, first-served basis to single and married students. *Research affiliation:* University of Illinois at Chicago (public health), Canadian Memorial Chiropractic College (mechanisms of CAM), Cox Technic F/D Enterprise LLC (mechanisms of CAM), Logan Chiropractic College (behavior research), Foot Levelers, Inc. (orthotics/biomechanics), Auburn University (mechanisms of CAM).

GRADUATE UNITS

Graduate Programs

NAVAJO TECHNICAL UNIVERSITY, Crownpoint, NM 87313

General Information Independent, coed, comprehensive institution.

GRADUATE UNITS

Program in Dine Studies Offers dine studies (MA).

NAVAL POSTGRADUATE SCHOOL, Monterey, CA 93943

General Information Federally supported, coed, graduate-only institution. *Graduate housing:* Rooms and/or apartments available to single and married students. *Research affiliation:* Department of Homeland Security, National Reconnaissance Office, National Oceanic and Atmospheric Administration (NOAA), National Security Agency, Federal Law Enforcement Training.

GRADUATE UNITS

Departments and Academic Groups ***Degree program information:*** Part-time programs available. Part-time, online learning. Offers applied mathematics (MS); applied physics (MS, PhD); applied science (MS); astronautical engineer (AstE); astronautical engineering (MS); combat systems technology (MS); command and control (MS); communications (MS); computer engineering (MS); computer science (MS, PhD); cost estimating analysis (MS); defense analysis (MS); electrical engineer (EE); electrical engineering (MS, PhD); electronic warfare systems engineering (MS); engineering acoustics (MS, PhD); engineering science (MS); engineering systems (MS); financial management (MS); human systems integration (MS); identity management and cyber security (MA); information operations (MS); information sciences (PhD); information systems and operations (MS); information technology management (MS); information warfare systems engineering (MS); irregular warfare (MS); knowledge superiority (Certificate); mechanical and aerospace engineering (PhD); mechanical engineer (ME); mechanical engineering (MS, MSME); meteorology (MS, PhD); meteorology and physical oceanography (MS); modeling of virtual environments and simulations (MS, PhD); national security affairs (MA, MS); operations analysis (MS); operations research (MS, PhD); physical oceanography (MS, PhD); physics (MS, PhD); product development (MS); remote sensing intelligence (MS); security studies (MA); software engineering (MS, PhD); space systems (Engr); space systems operations (MS); special operations (MA, MS); stability, security, and development in complex operations (Certificate); system technology (command, control and communications) (MS); systems analysis (MS); systems engineering (MS, PhD, Certificate); systems engineering analysis (MS, PhD); systems engineering management (MS, PhD); tactile missiles (MS); terrorist operations and financing (MS). Programs only open to commissioned officers of the United States and friendly nations and selected United States federal civilian employees.

Graduate School of Business and Public Policy Degree program information: Part-time programs available. Part-time, online learning. Offers acquisition and contract management (MBA); business administration (EMBA, MBA); contract management (MS); defense business management (MBA); defense systems analysis (MS); defense systems management (international) (MBA); financial management (MBA); information management (MBA); manpower systems analysis (MS); material logistics support management (MBA); program management (MS); resource planning and management for international defense (MBA); supply chain management (MBA); systems acquisition management (MBA); transportation management (MBA). Program only open to commissioned officers of the United States and friendly nations and selected United States federal civilian employees.

NAVAL WAR COLLEGE, Newport, RI 02841-1207

General Information Federally supported, coed, primarily men, graduate-only institution.

GRADUATE UNITS

Program in National Security and Strategic Studies Offers national security and strategic studies (MA). Program open only to full-time military personnel.

NAZARENE THEOLOGICAL SEMINARY, Kansas City, MO 64131-1263

General Information Independent-religious, coed, graduate-only institution. *Enrollment by degree level:* 221 master's, 23 doctoral. *Graduate faculty:* 11 full-time (1 woman), 26 part-time/adjunct (4 women). *Graduate housing:* Rooms and/or apartments available on a first-come, first-served basis to single and married students. *Student services:* Campus employment opportunities, career counseling, free psychological counseling, international student services, low-cost health insurance. *Library:* William Broadhurst Library. Students can reserve study rooms. *Research affiliation:* University of Missouri-Kansas City (religious studies).

Computer facilities: 14 computers available on campus for general student use. A campuswide network can be accessed.
Website: http://www.nts.edu/

General Application Contact: Pamala J. Asher, Registrar/Director of Admissions, 816-268-5442, Fax: 816-268-5500, E-mail: pjasher@nts.edu.

GRADUATE UNITS

Graduate and Professional Programs Students: 95 full-time (28 women), 174 part-time (55 women); includes 22 minority (7 Black or African American, non-Hispanic/Latino; 1 American Indian or Alaska Native, non-Hispanic/Latino; 1 Asian, non-Hispanic/Latino; 9 Hispanic/Latino; 4 Two or more races, non-Hispanic/Latino), 29 international. Average age 33. *Faculty:* 11 full-time (1 woman), 26 part-time/adjunct (4 women). *Financial support:* Teaching assistantships, institutionally sponsored loans, and scholarships/grants available. Support available to part-time students. Financial award application deadline: 3/1; financial award applicants required to submit FAFSA. *Degree program information:* Part-time programs available. Part-time. Offers Christian formation and discipleship (MA); intercultural studies (MA); theological studies (MA); theology (M Div, D Min). *Application deadline:* For fall admission, 3/1 priority date for domestic and international students; for spring admission, 11/1 priority date for domestic and international students. Applications are processed on a rolling basis. *Application fee:* $50. Electronic applications accepted. *Application Contact:* Pamala J. Asher, Registrar/Director of Admissions, 816-268-5442, Fax: 816-268-5500, E-mail: pjasher@nts.edu. *Dean of the Faculty*, Dr. Roger L. Hahn, 816-268-5412, Fax: 816-268-5500, E-mail: rlhahn@nts.edu.

NAZARETH COLLEGE OF ROCHESTER, Rochester, NY 14618-3790

General Information Independent, coed, comprehensive institution. *Graduate housing:* Room and/or apartments available on a first-come, first-served basis to single students; on-campus housing not available to married students. Housing application deadline: 5/15.

GRADUATE UNITS

Graduate Studies ***Financial support:*** Research assistantships with partial tuition reimbursements, career-related internships or fieldwork, and scholarships/grants available. Support available to part-time students. Financial award application deadline: 3/1; financial award applicants required to submit FAFSA. *Degree program information:* Part-time and evening/weekend programs available. Part-time, evening/weekend, online learning. Offers art education (MS Ed); communication sciences and disorders (MS); creative arts therapy (MS Ed); educational technology (MS Ed); human resource management (MS); inclusive adolescence education (MS Ed); inclusive childhood education (MS Ed); inclusive early childhood education (MS Ed); literacy education (MS Ed); management (MS); music education (MS Ed); physical therapy (DPT); social work (MSW); teaching English to speakers of other languages (MS Ed). *Application deadline:* For fall admission, 4/1 for domestic students; for spring admission, 10/1 for domestic students. Applications are processed on a rolling basis. *Application fee:* $40.

NEBRASKA METHODIST COLLEGE, Omaha, NE 68114

General Information Independent-religious, coed, comprehensive institution. *Graduate housing:* Rooms and/or apartments available on a first-come, first-served basis to single students and available to married students. Housing application deadline: 4/1.

GRADUATE UNITS

Program in Healthcare Operations Management ***Degree program information:*** Part-time and evening/weekend programs available. Part-time, evening/weekend, online learning. Offers healthcare operations management (MS).

Program in Health Promotion Management ***Degree program information:*** Part-time and evening/weekend programs available. Part-time, evening/weekend, online learning. Offers health promotion management (MS).

Program in Nursing ***Degree program information:*** Evening/weekend programs available. Evening/weekend, online learning. Offers nurse educator (MSN); nurse executive (MSN).

NEBRASKA WESLEYAN UNIVERSITY, Lincoln, NE 68504-2796

General Information Independent-religious, coed, comprehensive institution.

GRADUATE UNITS

University College ***Degree program information:*** Part-time programs available. Part-time. Offers forensic science (MFS); historical studies (MA); nursing (MSN).

NER ISRAEL RABBINICAL COLLEGE, Baltimore, MD 21208

General Information Independent-religious, men only, comprehensive institution. *Graduate housing:* Rooms and/or apartments guaranteed to single students and available on a first-come, first-served basis to married students.

GRADUATE UNITS

Graduate Programs Offers rabbinics (MTL, DTL, Professional Certificate).

NER ISRAEL YESHIVA COLLEGE OF TORONTO, Thornhill, ON L4J 8A7, Canada

General Information Independent-religious, men only, comprehensive institution.

GRADUATE UNITS

Graduate Programs

NEUMANN UNIVERSITY, Aston, PA 19014-1298

General Information Independent-religious, coed, comprehensive institution. *Enrollment:* 2,901 graduate, professional, and undergraduate students; 133 full-time matriculated graduate/professional students (82 women), 342 part-time matriculated graduate/professional students (238 women). *Enrollment by degree level:* 307 master's, 147 doctoral. *Graduate faculty:* 27 full-time (19 women), 48 part-time/adjunct (22 women). *Tuition, area resident:* Part-time $660 per credit. Tuition and fees vary according to degree level and program. *Graduate housing:* On-campus housing not available. *Student services:* Campus safety program, career counseling, child daycare facilities, exercise/wellness program, free psychological counseling, international student services, services for students with disabilities, teacher training, writing training. *Library:* Neumann University Library plus 1 other. *Collection:* Books: 50,667 (physical), 160,882 (digital/electronic); Serial titles: 53 (physical), 100,000 (digital/electronic); Databases: 46. Weekly public service hours: 80; students can reserve study rooms.

Computer facilities: Computer purchase and lease plans are available. 550 computers available on campus for general student use. A campuswide network can be accessed from student residence rooms and from off campus. Online class registration is available.
Website: http://www.neumann.edu/

General Application Contact: Kittie D. Pain, Associate Director of Admissions, Graduate and Adult Programs, 610-558-5613, Fax: 610-361-2548, E-mail: paink@neumann.edu.

GRADUATE UNITS

Master of Science in Education Program ***Financial support:*** Available to part-time students. Application deadline: 3/15; applicants required to submit FAFSA. *Degree program information:* Part-time programs available. Part-time, online learning. Offers education (MS); social emotional learning (MS); special education (MS). *Application deadline:* Applications are processed on a rolling basis. *Application fee:* $50. Electronic applications accepted. *Application Contact:* Kittie D. Pain, Associate Director, Graduate and Adult Admissions, 610-558-5613, Fax: 610-361-2548, E-mail: paink@neumann.edu. *Director of Graduate Education*, Dr. Stephanie Smith-Budhai, 610-358-4249, E-mail: budhais@neumann.edu.

Program in Educational Leadership Students: 1 (woman) full-time, 46 part-time (24 women); includes 4 minority (3 Black or African American, non-Hispanic/Latino; 1 Asian, non-Hispanic/Latino). Average age 39. *Faculty:* 4 full-time (2 women), 1 (woman) part-time/adjunct. Offers educational leadership (Ed D). *Application Contact:* Kittie D. Pain, Associate Director of Admissions, Graduate and Adult Programs, 610-558-5613, Fax: 610-361-2548, E-mail: paink@neumann.edu. *Director of EdD Program*, Cynthia Speace, 610-358-4243, E-mail: speacec@neumann.edu.

Program in Nursing Students: 18 part-time. *Financial support:* Available to part-time students. Application deadline: 3/15; applicants required to submit FAFSA. *Degree program information:* Part-time programs available. Part-time. Offers adult-gerontology nurse practitioner (MS); nurse educator (MS). *Application deadline:* Applications are processed on a rolling basis. *Application fee:* $50. *Application Contact:* Kittie D. Pain, Associate Director, Graduate and Adult Admissions, 610-558-5613, Fax: 610-558-5652, E-mail: paink@neumann.edu. *Dean, Division of Nursing and Health Sciences*, Dr. Kathleen Hoover, 610-558-5560, Fax: 610-459-1370, E-mail: hooverk@neumann.edu.

Program in Organizational and Strategic Leadership ***Financial support:*** Available to part-time students. Application deadline: 3/15; applicants required to submit FAFSA. Online learning. Offers organizational and strategic leadership (MS). *Application deadline:* Applications are processed on a rolling basis. *Application fee:* $50. Electronic applications accepted. *Application Contact:* Kittie D. Pain, Associate Director, Graduate and Adult Admissions, 610-558-5613, Fax: 610-558-5652, E-mail: paink@neumann.edu. *Coordinator, Division of Continuing Adult and Professional Studies*, Dr. Fredenick Loomis, 610-361-5292, E-mail: loomisf@neumann.edu.

Program in Pastoral Clinical Mental Health Counseling ***Financial support:*** Available to part-time students. Application deadline: 3/15; applicants required to submit FAFSA. *Degree program information:* Part-time and evening/weekend programs available. Part-time, evening/weekend. Offers pastoral clinical mental health counseling (MS); pastoral counseling (PhD); spiritual formation and direction (CSD). *Application deadline:* For fall admission, 8/1 for domestic students; for spring admission, 12/1 for domestic students. Applications are processed on a rolling basis. *Application fee:* $50. Electronic applications accepted. *Application Contact:* Kittie D. Pain, Associate Director, Graduate and Adult Admissions, 610-558-5613, Fax: 610-558-5652, E-mail: paink@neumann.edu. *Coordinator*, Sr. Suzanne Mayer, 610-361-2292, Fax: 610-459-1370, E-mail: mayers@neumann.edu.

Program in Physical Therapy ***Financial support:*** Available to part-time students. Application deadline: 3/15; applicants required to submit FAFSA. *Degree program information:* Evening/weekend programs available. Evening/weekend. Offers physical therapy (DPT). *Application deadline:* For fall admission, 11/1 for domestic students. Applications are processed on a rolling basis. *Application fee:* $50. Electronic applications accepted. *Application Contact:* Kittie D. Pain, Associate Director, Graduate and Adult Admissions, 610-558-5613, Fax: 610-558-5652, E-mail: paink@neumann.edu. *Director*, Dr. Robert Post, 610-558-5233, Fax: 610-459-1370, E-mail: postr@neumann.edu.

Program in Sport and Entertainment Management ***Financial support:*** Available to part-time students. Application deadline: 3/15; applicants required to submit FAFSA. *Degree program information:* Part-time programs available. Part-time. Offers sports and entertainment management (MS). *Application deadline:* Applications are processed on a rolling basis. *Application fee:* $50. Electronic applications accepted. *Application Contact:* Kittie D. Pain, Associate Director of Admissions, Graduate and Adult Programs, 610-558-5613, Fax: 610-558-5652, E-mail: paink@neumann.edu. *Coordinator*, Dr. Sandra L. Slabik, 610-361-5291, Fax: 610-558-5574, E-mail: slabiks@neumann.edu.

NEW BRUNSWICK THEOLOGICAL SEMINARY, New Brunswick, NJ 08901-1196

General Information Independent-religious, coed, graduate-only institution. *Graduate housing:* Rooms and/or apartments available on a first-come, first-served basis to single and married students. Housing application deadline: 6/30.

GRADUATE UNITS

Graduate and Professional Programs ***Degree program information:*** Part-time and evening/weekend programs available. Part-time, evening/weekend. Offers pastoral care and counseling (D Min). Electronic applications accepted.

NEW CHARTER UNIVERSITY, San Francisco, CA 94105

General Information Proprietary, coed, comprehensive institution. *Graduate housing:* On-campus housing not available.

GRADUATE UNITS

College of Business ***Degree program information:*** Part-time and evening/weekend programs available. Part-time, evening/weekend, online learning. Offers finance (MBA); health care management (MBA); management (MBA). Electronic applications accepted.

College of Public Policy and Administration ***Degree program information:*** Part-time and evening/weekend programs available. Part-time, evening/weekend, online learning. Offers criminal justice (MS); public administration (MPA); public policy and administration (MPA, MS). Electronic applications accepted.

NEW COLLEGE OF FLORIDA, Sarasota, FL 34243

General Information State-supported, coed, comprehensive institution.

GRADUATE UNITS

Program in Data Science Offers data science (MDS).

NEW ENGLAND COLLEGE, Henniker, NH 03242-3293

General Information Independent, coed, comprehensive institution. *Graduate housing:* Room and/or apartments available on a first-come, first-served basis to single students; on-campus housing not available to married students. Housing application deadline: 5/1.

GRADUATE UNITS

Program in Community Mental Health Counseling ***Degree program information:*** Part-time and evening/weekend programs available. Part-time, evening/weekend. Offers human services (MS); mental health counseling (MS).

Program in Education ***Degree program information:*** Part-time and evening/weekend programs available. Part-time, evening/weekend. Offers higher education administration (MS, Ed D); K-12 leadership (Ed D); literacy and language arts (M Ed); meeting the needs of all learners/special education (M Ed); teacher leadership/school reform (M Ed).

Program in Management ***Degree program information:*** Part-time and evening/weekend programs available. Part-time, evening/weekend. Offers accounting (MSA); healthcare administration (MS); international relations (MA); marketing management (MS); nonprofit leadership (MS); project management (MS); strategic leadership (MS). Electronic applications accepted.

Program in Public Policy ***Degree program information:*** Part-time and evening/weekend programs available. Part-time, evening/weekend, online learning. Offers public policy (MA). Electronic applications accepted.

Program in Sports and Recreation Management: Coaching Offers sports and recreation management: coaching (MS).

Programs in Writing ***Degree program information:*** Part-time and evening/weekend programs available. Part-time, evening/weekend. Offers poetry (MFA); professional writing (MA). Electronic applications accepted.

NEW ENGLAND COLLEGE OF BUSINESS AND FINANCE, Boston, MA 02111-2645

General Information Independent, coed, primarily women, comprehensive institution.

GRADUATE UNITS

Program in Business Ethics and Compliance Online learning. Offers business ethics and compliance (MS).

Program in Finance Online learning. Offers finance (MSF).

NEW ENGLAND COLLEGE OF OPTOMETRY, Boston, MA 02115-1100

General Information Independent, coed, graduate-only institution. *Graduate housing:* On-campus housing not available. *Research affiliation:* Vistakon-Johnson & Johnson (contact lenses), Boston University School of Medicine (vision science).

GRADUATE UNITS

Graduate and Professional Programs Offers optometry (OD); vision science (MS). Electronic applications accepted.

NEW ENGLAND CONSERVATORY OF MUSIC, Boston, MA 02115-5000

General Information Independent, coed, comprehensive institution. *Enrollment:* 788 graduate, professional, and undergraduate students; 359 full-time matriculated graduate/professional students (178 women), 23 part-time matriculated graduate/professional students (8 women). *Enrollment by degree level:* 293 master's, 28 doctoral, 61 other advanced degrees. *Graduate faculty:* 102 full-time (35 women), 133 part-time/adjunct (42 women). *Tuition, area resident:* Full-time $44,300. *Graduate housing:* Room and/or apartments available on a first-come, first-served basis to single students; on-campus housing not available to married students. Housing application deadline: 6/15. *Student services:* Campus employment opportunities, career counseling, free psychological counseling, international student services, low-cost health insurance, services for students with disabilities. *Library:* Spaulding Library plus 3 others. *Collection:* Books: 103,097 (physical), 248,432 (digital/electronic); Serial titles: 161 (physical), 98 (digital/electronic); Databases: 109. Weekly public service hours: 85.

Computer facilities: 70 computers available on campus for general student use. A campuswide network can be accessed. Online class registration is available.
Website: http://necmusic.edu/

General Application Contact: Alex Powell, Assistant Dean for Admissions, 617-585-1101, Fax: 617-585-1115, E-mail: alex.powell@necmusic.edu.

GRADUATE UNITS

Graduate Program in Music Students: 359 full-time (178 women), 23 part-time (8 women); includes 49 minority (2 Black or African American, non-Hispanic/Latino; 22 Asian, non-Hispanic/Latino; 19 Hispanic/Latino; 6 Two or more races, non-Hispanic/Latino), 174 international. Average age 22. 1,467 applicants, 30% accepted, 185 enrolled. *Faculty:* 102 full-time (35 women), 133 part-time/adjunct (42 women). *Financial support:* Fellowships with partial tuition reimbursements, teaching assistantships, Federal Work-Study, scholarships/grants, and tuition waivers (partial) available. Support available to part-time students. Financial award application deadline: 12/1; financial award applicants required to submit FAFSA. In 2015, 129 master's, 6 doctorates awarded. Offers music (MM, DMA, Diploma). *Application deadline:* For fall admission, 12/1 priority date for domestic and international students; for spring admission, 10/15 for domestic and international students. Applications are processed on a rolling basis. *Application fee:* $115. *Application Contact:* Alex Powell, Assistant Dean for Admissions, 617-585-1101, Fax: 617-585-1115, E-mail: alex.powell@newenglandconservatory.edu. *Provost/Dean of the College*, Tom Novak, 617-585-1308, Fax: 617-585-1303, E-mail: tom.novak@necmusic.edu.

NEW ENGLAND INSTITUTE OF TECHNOLOGY, East Greenwich, RI 02818

General Information Independent, coed, comprehensive institution. *Enrollment:* 2,919 graduate, professional, and undergraduate students; 55 full-time matriculated graduate/professional students (47 women), 51 part-time matriculated graduate/professional students (14 women). *Student services:* Campus safety program, career counseling. *Library:* New England Institute of Technology Library. *Collection:* Books: 46,744 (physical), 15,492 (digital/electronic); Serial titles: 142 (physical), 34,780 (digital/electronic); Databases: 82. Weekly public service hours: 67; students can reserve study rooms.

Computer facilities: 1,000 computers available on campus for general student use. A campuswide network can be accessed. Online class registration is available.
Website: http://www.neit.edu/

General Application Contact: James Jessup, Director of Admissions, 401-467-7744 Ext. 3339, Fax: 401-886-0868, E-mail: neitadmissions@neit.edu.

GRADUATE UNITS

Program in Construction Management Students: 11 part-time (3 women); includes 3 minority (1 Black or African American, non-Hispanic/Latino; 1 American Indian or Alaska Native, non-Hispanic/Latino; 1 Hispanic/Latino), 3 international. Average age 38. *Financial support:* Applicants required to submit FAFSA. *Degree program information:* Part-time and evening/weekend programs available. Part-time-only, evening/weekend, 100% online, blended/hybrid learning. Offers construction management (MS). *Application deadline:* Applications are processed on a rolling basis. *Application fee:* $25. Electronic applications accepted. *Application Contact:* Michael Caruso, Director of Admissions, 401-467-7744 Ext. 3411, Fax: 401-886-0868, E-mail: mcaruso@neit.edu. *Director of Admissions*, Michael Caruso, 401-467-7744 Ext. 3411, Fax: 401-886-0868, E-mail: mcaruso@neit.edu.

Program in Information Technology Students: 31 part-time (5 women); includes 3 minority (1 Black or African American, non-Hispanic/Latino; 1 Asian, non-Hispanic/Latino; 1 Hispanic/Latino), 19 international. Average age 29. *Financial support:* Applicants required to submit FAFSA. *Degree program information:* Part-time and evening/weekend programs available. Part-time-only, evening/weekend, 100% online, blended/hybrid learning. Offers information technology (MS). *Application deadline:* Applications are processed on a rolling basis. *Application fee:* $25. Electronic applications accepted. *Application Contact:* Michael Caruso, Director of Admissions, 401-467-7744 Ext. 3411, Fax: 401-886-0868, E-mail: mcaruso@neit.edu. *Director of Admissions*, Michael Caruso, 401-467-7744 Ext. 3411, Fax: 401-886-0868, E-mail: mcaruso@neit.edu.

Program in Occupational Therapy Students: 55 full-time (47 women), 9 part-time (6 women); includes 4 minority (1 Black or African American, non-Hispanic/Latino; 2 Asian, non-Hispanic/Latino; 1 Two or more races, non-Hispanic/Latino), 6 international. Average age 33. *Financial support:* Applicants required to submit FAFSA. *Degree program information:* Part-time and evening/weekend programs available. Part-time-only, evening/weekend, blended/hybrid learning. Offers occupational therapy (MS). *Application deadline:* Applications are processed on a rolling basis. *Application fee:* $25. Electronic applications accepted. *Application Contact:* Michael Caruso, Director of Admissions, 401-467-7744 Ext. 3411, Fax: 401-886-0868, E-mail: mcaruso@neit.edu. *Director of Admissions*, Michael Caruso, 401-467-7744 Ext. 3411, Fax: 401-886-0868, E-mail: mcaruso@neit.edu.

NEW ENGLAND LAW–BOSTON, Boston, MA 02116-5687

General Information Independent, coed, graduate-only institution. *Enrollment by degree level:* 683 doctoral. *Graduate faculty:* 42 full-time (16 women), 85 part-time/adjunct (38 women). *Tuition, area resident:* Full-time $45,606; part-time $34,204 per year. *Required fees:* $80; $80 per unit. Tuition and fees vary according to class time, course load and degree level. *Graduate housing:* On-campus housing not available. *Student services:* Campus employment opportunities, career counseling, low-cost health insurance, services for students with disabilities, writing training. *Library:* New England Law | Boston Law Library. *Collection:* Books: 100,889 (physical), 42,701 (digital/electronic); Serial titles: 2,157 (physical), 21,704 (digital/electronic); Databases: 96. Weekly public service hours: 104; students can reserve study rooms.

Computer facilities: 36 computers available on campus for general student use. A campuswide network can be accessed from off campus. Online class registration is available.
Website: http://www.nesl.edu/

General Application Contact: Michelle L'Etoile, Director of Admissions, 617-422-7210, Fax: 617-422-7201, E-mail: admit@nesl.edu.

GRADUATE UNITS

Professional Program Students: 466 full-time (263 women), 217 part-time (110 women); includes 195 minority (65 Black or African American, non-Hispanic/Latino; 1 American Indian or Alaska Native, non-Hispanic/Latino; 32 Asian, non-Hispanic/Latino; 69 Hispanic/Latino; 28 Two or more races, non-Hispanic/Latino), 15 international. Average age 27. 2,934 applicants, 72% accepted, 385 enrolled. *Faculty:* 42 full-time (16 women), 85 part-time/adjunct (38 women). *Financial support:* In 2015–16, 644 students received support, including 80 fellowships (averaging $3,500 per year); Federal Work-Study, scholarships/grants, and tuition waivers (full and partial) also available. Financial award application deadline: 3/20; financial award applicants required to submit FAFSA. In 2015, 335 doctorates awarded. *Degree program information:* Part-time and evening/weekend programs available. Part-time, evening/weekend. Offers advanced legal studies (LL M); law (JD). *Application deadline:* For fall admission, 3/15 for domestic students. Applications are processed on a rolling basis. *Application fee:* $65. Electronic applications accepted. *Application Contact:* Michelle L'Etoile, Director of Admissions, 617-422-7210, Fax: 617-422-7201, E-mail: admit@nesl.edu. *Dean*, John F. O'Brien, 617-422-7221, Fax: 617-422-7333.

NEW HAMPSHIRE INSTITUTE OF ART, Manchester, NH 03104

General Information Independent, coed, comprehensive institution. *Enrollment:* 468 graduate, professional, and undergraduate students; 60 full-time matriculated graduate/professional students (39 women), 12 part-time matriculated graduate/professional students (all women). *Enrollment by degree level:* 78 master's. *Graduate faculty:* 31 part-time/adjunct (14 women). *Tuition, area resident:* Full-time $18,990; part-time $2395 per course. *Required fees:* $1390. One-time fee: $300. *Graduate housing:* Room and/or apartments available on a first-come, first-served basis to single students; on-campus housing not available to married students. Typical cost: $1350 per year. Housing application deadline: 6/15. *Student services:* Campus employment opportunities, career counseling, free psychological counseling, services for students with disabilities, teacher training. *Library:* Teti Library. *Collection:* Books: 17,000 (physical), 144,463 (digital/electronic); Serial titles: 80 (physical), 7,800 (digital/electronic); Databases: 30. Weekly public service hours: 63.

Computer facilities: 100 computers available on campus for general student use. A campuswide network can be accessed from student residence rooms and from off campus. Online class registration is available.
Website: http://www.nhia.edu/

General Application Contact: Graduate Admissions, 603-836 2122, E-mail: gradadmissions@nhia.edu.

GRADUATE UNITS

Graduate Programs Students: 60 full-time (39 women), 12 part-time (all women); includes 2 minority (both Hispanic/Latino). Average age 44. 50 applicants, 58% accepted, 13 enrolled. *Faculty:* 31 part-time/adjunct (14 women). *Financial support:* In 2015–16, 57 students received support, including 8 teaching assistantships (averaging $1,000 per year); scholarships/grants and unspecified assistantships also available. Support available to part-time students. Financial award application deadline: 6/1; financial award applicants required to submit FAFSA. *Degree program information:* Part-time programs available. Part-time. Offers art education (MA); creative writing (MFA); photography (MFA); teaching visual arts (MAT); visual arts (MFA); writing for stage and screen (MFA). *Application deadline:* For fall admission, 5/1 priority date for domestic students; for spring admission, 11/1 priority date for domestic students. Applications are processed on a rolling basis. *Application fee:* $50. Electronic applications accepted. *Application Contact:* Erin Sweeney, Graduate Admissions, 603-836 2122, E-mail: gradadmissions@nhia.edu. *Interim Dean of Graduate Studies*, Lucinda Bliss, 603-836 2522, E-mail: lucindabliss@nhia.edu.

NEW JERSEY CITY UNIVERSITY, Jersey City, NJ 07305-1597

General Information State-supported, coed, comprehensive institution. *Enrollment:* 8,237 graduate, professional, and undergraduate students; 406 full-time matriculated graduate/professional students (286 women), 1,514 part-time matriculated graduate/professional students (1,113 women). *Enrollment by degree level:* 1,367 master's, 88 doctoral, 18 other advanced degrees. *Graduate faculty:* 94 full-time (56 women), 68 part-time/adjunct (35 women). Tuition, state resident: part-time $566.55 per credit. Tuition, nonresident: part-time $998.15 per credit. *Required fees:* $108 per credit. Part-time tuition and fees vary according to class time, degree level, campus/location and program. *Graduate housing:* On-campus housing not available. *Student services:* Campus employment opportunities, campus safety program, career counseling, child daycare facilities, free psychological counseling, international student services, services for students with disabilities. *Library:* Congressman Frank J. Guarini Library. *Collection:* Books: 300,000 (physical), 150,000 (digital/electronic); Serial titles: 150 (physical), 32,000 (digital/electronic); Databases: 152. Weekly public service hours: 82.

Computer facilities: Computer purchase and lease plans are available. 844 computers available on campus for general student use. A campuswide network can be accessed from student residence rooms and from off campus. Online class registration is available.
Website: http://www.njcu.edu/

General Application Contact: Jose Balda, Director of Admissions, 201-200-3234, E-mail: jbalda@njcu.edu.

GRADUATE UNITS

College of Professional Studies *Financial support:* Career-related internships or fieldwork and unspecified assistantships available. *Degree program information:* Part-time and evening/weekend programs available. Part-time, evening/weekend. Offers civil security leadership (D Sc); community health education (MS); criminal justice (MS); health administration (MS); national security studies (MS, Certificate); school health education (MS). *Application deadline:* For fall admission, 8/1 priority date for domestic students; for spring admission, 12/1 for domestic students. Applications are processed on a rolling basis. *Application fee:* $0.

Debra Cannon Partridge Wolfe College of Education *Financial support:* Fellowships, research assistantships, career-related internships or fieldwork, and unspecified assistantships available. *Degree program information:* Part-time and evening/weekend programs available. Part-time, evening/weekend. Offers bilingual/bicultural education (MA); counselor education (MA); early childhood education (MAT); education (MA, MAT, Ed D); educational administration and supervision (MA); educational technology (MA); educational technology leadership (Ed D); elementary education (MAT); English as a second language (MA); secondary education (MAT); special education (MA); urban education (MA); urban education world language (MA). *Application deadline:* For fall admission, 8/1 for domestic students; for spring admission, 12/1 for domestic students. *Application fee:* $0.

Department of Business Administration *Financial support:* Career-related internships or fieldwork and unspecified assistantships available. *Degree program information:* Part-time and evening/weekend programs available. Part-time, evening/weekend. Offers accounting (MS); finance (MBA, MS, Graduate Certificate); organizational management and leadership (MBA). *Application deadline:* For fall admission, 8/1 priority date for domestic students; for spring admission, 12/1 for domestic students. Applications are processed on a rolling basis.

Graduate Studies and Continuing Education *Financial support:* Fellowships, research assistantships, career-related internships or fieldwork, and unspecified assistantships available. *Degree program information:* Part-time and evening/weekend programs available. Part-time, evening/weekend, online learning. *Application deadline:* For fall admission, 8/1 priority date for domestic students; for spring admission, 12/1 for domestic students. Applications are processed on a rolling basis. *Application fee:* $55.

William J. Maxwell College of Arts and Sciences *Financial support:* Career-related internships or fieldwork and unspecified assistantships available. *Degree program information:* Part-time and evening/weekend programs available. Part-time, evening/weekend. Offers art (MFA); art education (MA); arts and sciences (MA, MFA, MM); mathematics education (MA); music education (MA); performance (MM); studio art (MFA). *Application deadline:* For fall admission, 8/1 priority date for domestic students; for spring admission, 12/1 for domestic students. Applications are processed on a rolling basis. *Application fee:* $0.

NEW JERSEY INSTITUTE OF TECHNOLOGY, Newark, NJ 07102

General Information State-supported, coed, university. CGS member. *Enrollment:* 11,325 graduate, professional, and undergraduate students; 2,038 full-time matriculated graduate/professional students (579 women), 1,074 part-time matriculated graduate/professional students (265 women). *Enrollment by degree level:* 2,694 master's, 413 doctoral, 5 other advanced degrees. *Graduate faculty:* 410 full-time (82 women), 391 part-time/adjunct (90 women). Tuition, state resident: full-time $18,108; part-time $1006 per credit. Tuition, nonresident: full-time $25,992; part-time $1444 per credit. *Required fees:* $2808; $156 per credit. *Graduate housing:* Room and/or apartments available on a first-come, first-served basis to single students; on-campus housing not available to married students. Typical cost: $13,296 (including board). Housing application deadline: 3/31. *Student services:* Campus employment opportunities, campus safety program, career counseling, child daycare facilities, exercise/wellness program, free psychological counseling, international student services, low-cost health insurance, services for students with disabilities, teacher training, writing training. *Library:* Van Houten Library plus 1 other. *Collection:* Books: 170,618 (physical), 27,759 (digital/electronic); Serial titles: 59 (physical), 33,674 (digital/electronic); Databases: 33. Weekly public service hours: 105; students can reserve study rooms.

Computer facilities: Computer purchase and lease plans are available. 1,938 computers available on campus for general student use. A campuswide network can be accessed from student residence rooms and from off campus. Online class registration is available.
Website: http://www.njit.edu/

General Application Contact: Stephen Eck, Director of Admissions, 973-596-3300, Fax: 973-596-3461, E-mail: admissions@njit.edu.

GRADUATE UNITS

College of Architecture Students: 45 full-time (17 women), 11 part-time (4 women); includes 17 minority (2 Black or African American, non-Hispanic/Latino; 3 Asian, non-Hispanic/Latino; 11 Hispanic/Latino; 1 Two or more races, non-Hispanic/Latino), 16 international. Average age 31. 124 applicants, 48% accepted, 22 enrolled. *Faculty:* 32 full-time (9 women), 44 part-time/adjunct (17 women). *Financial support:* In 2015–16, 28 research assistantships with tuition reimbursements (averaging $6,792 per year) were awarded; fellowships with tuition reimbursements, teaching assistantships with tuition reimbursements, career-related internships or fieldwork, Federal Work-Study, institutionally sponsored loans, scholarships/grants, and unspecified assistantships also available. Financial award application deadline: 1/15. In 2015, 23 master's awarded. *Degree program information:* Part-time and evening/weekend programs available. Part-time, evening/weekend. Offers architecture (M Arch, MS Arch); infrastructure planning (MIP); urban systems (PhD). *Application deadline:* For fall admission, 6/1 priority date for domestic students, 5/1 priority date for international students; for spring admission, 11/15 priority date for domestic and international students. Applications are processed on a rolling basis. *Application fee:* $75. Electronic applications accepted. *Application*

Contact: Stephen Eck, Director of Admissions, 973-596-3300, Fax: 973-596-3461, E-mail: admissions@njit.edu. *Dean*, Urs P. Gauchat, 973-596-3080, E-mail: urs.p.gauchat@njit.edu.

College of Science and Liberal Arts Students: 212 full-time (82 women), 94 part-time (37 women); includes 72 minority (22 Black or African American, non-Hispanic/Latino; 25 Asian, non-Hispanic/Latino; 19 Hispanic/Latino; 6 Two or more races, non-Hispanic/Latino), 164 international. Average age 29. 519 applicants, 62% accepted, 104 enrolled. *Faculty:* 153 full-time (35 women), 100 part-time/adjunct (40 women). *Financial support:* In 2015–16, 56 research assistantships with full tuition reimbursements (averaging $17,711 per year), 52 teaching assistantships with full tuition reimbursements (averaging $17,914 per year) were awarded; fellowships with full tuition reimbursements also available. Financial award application deadline: 1/15. In 2015, 98 master's, 21 doctorates, 3 other advanced degrees awarded. *Degree program information:* Part-time and evening/weekend programs available. Part-time, evening/weekend. Offers applied mathematics (MS); applied physics (M Sc, PhD); applied statistics (MS, Certificate); biology (MS, PhD); biostatistics (MS); chemistry (MS, PhD); computational biology (MS); environmental science (MS, PhD); history (MA, MAT); materials science and engineering (MS, PhD); mathematical and computational finance (MS); mathematics science (PhD); pharmaceutical chemistry (MS); practice of technical communications (Certificate); professional and technical communications (MS). *Application deadline:* For fall admission, 6/1 priority date for domestic students, 5/1 priority date for international students; for spring admission, 11/15 priority date for domestic and international students. Applications are processed on a rolling basis. *Application fee:* $75. Electronic applications accepted. *Application Contact:* Stephen Eck, Director of Admissions, 973-596-3300, Fax: 973-596-3461, E-mail: admissions@njit.edu. *Dean*, Dr. Kevin Belfield, 973-596-3676, Fax: 973-565-0586, E-mail: kevin.d.belfield@njit.edu.

Newark College of Engineering Students: 946 full-time (226 women), 580 part-time (122 women); includes 397 minority (93 Black or African American, non-Hispanic/Latino; 136 Asian, non-Hispanic/Latino; 145 Hispanic/Latino; 23 Two or more races, non-Hispanic/Latino), 808 international. Average age 28. 3,111 applicants, 62% accepted, 591 enrolled. *Faculty:* 139 full-time (22 women), 152 part-time/adjunct (18 women). *Financial support:* In 2015–16, fellowships with partial tuition reimbursements (averaging $3,900 per year), 68 research assistantships with partial tuition reimbursements (averaging $18,120 per year), 68 teaching assistantships with partial tuition reimbursements (averaging $13,325 per year) were awarded. Financial award application deadline: 1/15. In 2015, 570 master's, 31 doctorates awarded. *Degree program information:* Part-time and evening/weekend programs available. Part-time, evening/weekend. Offers biomedical engineering (MS, PhD); chemical engineering (MS, PhD); computer engineering (MS, PhD); electrical engineering (MS, PhD); engineering management (MS); environmental engineering (PhD); healthcare systems management (MS); industrial engineering (MS, PhD); Internet engineering (MS); manufacturing engineering (MS); mechanical engineering (MS, PhD); occupational safety and health engineering (MS); pharmaceutical bioprocessing (MS); pharmaceutical engineering (MS); pharmaceutical systems management (MS); power and energy systems (MS); telecommunications (MS); transportation (MS, PhD). *Application deadline:* For fall admission, 6/1 priority date for domestic students, 5/1 priority date for international students; for spring admission, 11/15 priority date for domestic and international students. Applications are processed on a rolling basis. *Application fee:* $75. Electronic applications accepted. *Application Contact:* Stephen Eck, Director of Admissions, 973-596-3300, Fax: 973-596-3461, E-mail: admissions@njit.edu. *Dean*, Dr. Moshe Kam, 973-596-5534, E-mail: moshe.kam@njit.edu.

School of Management Students: 85 full-time (27 women), 147 part-time (47 women); includes 105 minority (26 Black or African American, non-Hispanic/Latino; 32 Asian, non-Hispanic/Latino; 40 Hispanic/Latino; 7 Two or more races, non-Hispanic/Latino), 56 international. Average age 32. 384 applicants, 61% accepted, 103 enrolled. *Faculty:* 26 full-time (8 women), 27 part-time/adjunct (3 women). *Financial support:* In 2015–16, 3 teaching assistantships with partial tuition reimbursements (averaging $10,080 per year) were awarded; fellowships with tuition reimbursements, research assistantships with tuition reimbursements, career-related internships or fieldwork, Federal Work-Study, institutionally sponsored loans, and unspecified assistantships also available. Financial award application deadline: 1/15. In 2015, 96 master's, 14 other advanced degrees awarded. *Degree program information:* Part-time and evening/weekend programs available. Part-time, evening/weekend. Offers business administration (MBA); finance for managers (Certificate); international business (MS); management (MS); management essentials (Certificate); management of technology (Certificate). *Application deadline:* For fall admission, 6/1 priority date for domestic students, 5/1 priority date for international students; for spring admission, 11/15 priority date for domestic and international students. Applications are processed on a rolling basis. *Application fee:* $75. Electronic applications accepted. *Application Contact:* Stephen Eck, Director of Admissions, 973-596-3300, Fax: 973-596-3461, E-mail: admissions@njit.edu. *Interim Dean*, Dr. Reggie Caudill, 973-596-5856, Fax: 973-596-3074, E-mail: reggie.j.caudill@njit.edu.

Ying Wu College of Computing Sciences Students: 750 full-time (227 women), 242 part-time (55 women); includes 154 minority (29 Black or African American, non-Hispanic/Latino; 68 Asian, non-Hispanic/Latino; 46 Hispanic/Latino; 11 Two or more races, non-Hispanic/Latino), 723 international. Average age 27. 2,549 applicants, 56% accepted, 440 enrolled. *Faculty:* 55 full-time (7 women), 43 part-time/adjunct (4 women). *Financial support:* In 2015–16, 3 fellowships with partial tuition reimbursements (averaging $3,600 per year), 33 research assistantships with partial tuition reimbursements (averaging $17,359 per year), 19 teaching assistantships with partial tuition reimbursements (averaging $11,225 per year) were awarded; career-related internships or fieldwork, Federal Work-Study, institutionally sponsored loans, and unspecified assistantships also available. Financial award application deadline: 1/15. In 2015, 312 master's, 13 doctorates, 14 other advanced degrees awarded. *Degree program information:* Part-time and evening/weekend programs available. Part-time, evening/weekend. Offers big data management and mining (Certificate); business and information systems (Certificate); computer science (MS, PhD); data mining (Certificate); information security (Certificate); information systems (MS, PhD); information technology administration and security (MS); IT administration (Certificate); network security and information assurance (Certificate); software engineering analysis/design (Certificate); Web systems development (Certificate). *Application deadline:* For fall admission, 6/1 priority date for domestic students, 5/1 priority date for international students; for spring admission, 11/15 priority date for domestic and international students. Applications are processed on a rolling basis. *Application fee:* $75. Electronic applications accepted. *Application Contact:* Kathryn Kelly, Director of Admissions, 973-596-3300, Fax: 973-596-3461, E-mail: admissions@njit.edu. *Dean*, Dr. Marek Rusinkiewicz, 973-542-3383, Fax: 973-596-5777, E-mail: marek.rusinkiewicz@njit.edu.

NEWMAN THEOLOGICAL COLLEGE, Edmonton, AB T6V 1H3, Canada

General Information Independent-religious, coed, graduate-only institution. *Enrollment:* 30 full-time matriculated graduate/professional students (5 women), 96 part-time matriculated graduate/professional students (70 women). *Enrollment by degree level:* 116 master's, 10 other advanced degrees. *Graduate faculty:* 12 full-time (2 women), 24 part-time/adjunct (8 women). *Tuition, area resident:* Full-time $6390 Canadian dollars; part-time $639 Canadian dollars per credit. *Required fees:* $160 Canadian dollars; $70 Canadian dollars per unit. $35 Canadian dollars per semester. One-time fee: $45 Canadian dollars. Tuition and fees vary according to course level and campus/location. *Graduate housing:* On-campus housing not available. *Student services:* Campus employment opportunities, career counseling, free psychological counseling, services for students with disabilities. *Library:* Sopchyshyn Family Library. *Collection:* Books: 69,405 (physical); Serial titles: 7,859 (physical). Students can reserve study rooms.

Computer facilities: 6 computers available on campus for general student use. Website: http://www.newman.edu/

General Application Contact: Maria Saulnier, Registrar, 780-392-2451, Fax: 780-462-4013, E-mail: registrar@newman.edu.

GRADUATE UNITS

Religious Education Programs ***Faculty:*** 6 part-time/adjunct. *Financial support:* Tuition bursaries available. Support available to part-time students. Financial award application deadline: 5/31. *Degree program information:* Part-time programs available. Part-time, online learning. Offers Catholic school administration (Graduate Certificate); religious education (MRE). *Application deadline:* For fall admission, 8/4 priority date for domestic students; for winter admission, 1/2 priority date for domestic students; for spring admission, 5/6 priority date for domestic students. Applications are processed on a rolling basis. *Application fee:* $45 ($250 for international students). *Application Contact:* Maria Saulnier, Registrar, 780-392-2451, Fax: 780-462-4013, E-mail: registrar@newman.edu. *Director*, Sandra Talarico, 780-392-2450 Ext. 2214, Fax: 780-462-4013, E-mail: sandra.talarico@newman.edu.

Theology Programs ***Faculty:*** 2 part-time/adjunct. *Financial support:* Tuition bursaries available. Support available to part-time students. Financial award application deadline: 5/31. *Degree program information:* Part-time programs available. Part-time. Offers theology (M Div, M Th, MTS). *Application deadline:* For fall admission, 8/4 priority date for domestic students; for winter admission, 1/2 priority date for domestic students; for spring admission, 5/6 priority date for domestic students. Applications are processed on a rolling basis. *Application fee:* $45 ($250 for international students). *Application Contact:* Maria Saulnier, Registrar, 780-392-2451, Fax: 780-462-4013, E-mail: registrar@newman.edu. *Academic Dean and President*, Dr. Jason West, 780-392-2450 Ext. 5222, Fax: 780-462-4013, E-mail: jason.west@newman.edu.

NEWMAN UNIVERSITY, Wichita, KS 67213-2097

General Information Independent-religious, coed, comprehensive institution. *Graduate housing:* Rooms and/or apartments available on a first-come, first-served basis to single and married students. Housing application deadline: 8/1.

GRADUATE UNITS

Graduate Theology Program ***Degree program information:*** Part-time programs available. Part-time, online learning. Offers theological studies (MTS); theology (MA).

Master of Science in Education Program ***Degree program information:*** Part-time and evening/weekend programs available. Part-time, evening/weekend, online learning. Offers building leadership (MS Ed); curriculum and instruction (MS Ed); organizational leadership (MS Ed). Electronic applications accepted.

MBA Program ***Degree program information:*** Part-time programs available. Part-time. Offers finance (MBA); international business (MBA); leadership (MBA); management (MBA); management information technology (MBA). Electronic applications accepted.

School of Nursing and Allied Health Offers nurse anesthesia (MS). Electronic applications accepted.

School of Social Work Online learning. Offers social work (MSW).

NEW MEXICO HIGHLANDS UNIVERSITY, Las Vegas, NM 87701

General Information State-supported, coed, comprehensive institution. CGS member. *Enrollment:* 3,563 graduate, professional, and undergraduate students; 597 full-time matriculated graduate/professional students (429 women), 713 part-time matriculated graduate/professional students (489 women). *Enrollment by degree level:* 1,310 master's. *Graduate faculty:* 96 full-time (43 women), 52 part-time/adjunct (38 women). *Graduate housing:* Rooms and/or apartments guaranteed to single and married students. *Student services:* Career counseling, child daycare facilities, exercise/wellness program, free psychological counseling, international student services, low-cost health insurance, services for students with disabilities, teacher training, writing training. *Library:* Thomas C. Donnelly Library. *Research affiliation:* Spectra Gases, Inc. (chemistry), Los Alamos National Laboratory (chemistry), Sigma Aldrich (chemistry).

Computer facilities: A campuswide network can be accessed from student residence rooms and from off campus. Online class registration is available. Website: http://www.nmhu.edu/

General Application Contact: Diane Trujillo, Administrative Assistant, Graduate Studies, 505-454-3266, Fax: 505-426-2117, E-mail: dtrujillo@nmhu.edu.

GRADUATE UNITS

Graduate Studies ***Degree program information:*** Part-time programs available. Part-time.

College of Arts and Sciences Degree program information: Part-time programs available. Part-time. Offers arts and sciences (MA, MS); chemistry (MS); English (MA); human performance and sport (MA); media arts and computer science (MS); natural science (MS); psychology (MS); public affairs (MA); Southwest studies (MA). Electronic applications accepted.

School of Business, Media and Technology Offers business administration (MBA); media arts and computer science (MA); media arts and technology (MA).

School of Education Degree program information: Part-time programs available. Part-time. Offers curriculum and instruction (MA); educational leadership (MA); professional counseling (MA); special education (MA).

School of Social Work Degree program information: Part-time programs available. Part-time. Offers bilingual/bicultural clinical practice (MSW); clinical practice (MSW).

NEW MEXICO INSTITUTE OF MINING AND TECHNOLOGY, Socorro, NM 87801

General Information State-supported, coed, university. *Enrollment:* 2,150 graduate, professional, and undergraduate students; 247 full-time matriculated graduate/professional students (74 women), 146 part-time matriculated graduate/professional students (67 women). *Enrollment by degree level:* 291 master's, 89 doctoral, 2 other advanced degrees. *Graduate faculty:* 120 full-time (24 women), 30 part-time/adjunct (9 women). Tuition, state resident: full-time $5811; part-time $322.81 per credit. Tuition, nonresident: full-time $19,220; part-time $1067.79 per credit. *Required fees:* $1030. Tuition and fees vary according to course load. *Graduate housing:* Rooms and/or apartments available on a first-come, first-served basis to single and married students. Typical cost: $5590 per year for single students; $6750 per year for married students. Room charges vary according to board plan and housing facility selected. Housing application deadline: 6/1. *Student services:* Campus employment opportunities, campus safety program, career counseling, child daycare facilities, free psychological counseling, grant writing training, international student services, low-cost health insurance, multicultural affairs office, services for students with disabilities. *Library:* The Skeen Library. *Research affiliation:* National Center for Atmospheric Research (atmosphere research), National Radio Astronomy Observatory (astronomy), Joint Center for Materials Research (materials engineering, metallurgy), Gas Technology Institute (natural gas recovery), Optical Surface Technologies LLC (custom optical components).

Computer facilities: 225 computers available on campus for general student use. A campuswide network can be accessed from student residence rooms and from off campus. Online class registration is available. Website: http://www.nmt.edu/

General Application Contact: Dr. Lorie Liebrock, Dean of Graduate Studies, 575-835-5513, Fax: 575-835-5476, E-mail: graduate@nmt.edu.

GRADUATE UNITS

Center for Graduate Studies Offers applied and industrial mathematics (PhD); astrophysics (PhD); atmospheric physics (PhD); biology (MS); chemistry (MS, PhD); computer science (MS, PhD); electrical engineering (MS); environmental engineering (MS); explosives engineering (MS); fluid and thermal sciences (MS); geobiology (PhD); geochemistry (MS, PhD); geology (MS, PhD); geophysics (MS, PhD); geotechnical engineering (MS); hydrology (MS, PhD); industrial mathematics (MS); instrumentation (MS); materials engineering (MS, PhD); mathematical physics (PhD); mathematics (MS); mechatronics systems engineering (MS); mining engineering (MS); operations research and statistics (MS); petroleum engineering (MS, PhD); physics (MS); science teaching (MST); solid mechanics (MS); STEM education (MEM). Electronic applications accepted.

NEW MEXICO STATE UNIVERSITY, Las Cruces, NM 88003-8001

General Information State-supported, coed, university. CGS member. *Enrollment:* 15,490 graduate, professional, and undergraduate students; 1,572 full-time matriculated graduate/professional students (808 women), 1,331 part-time matriculated graduate/professional students (827 women). *Enrollment by degree level:* 2,036 master's, 839 doctoral, 28 other advanced degrees. *Graduate faculty:* 533 full-time (218 women), 44 part-time/adjunct (22 women). Tuition, state resident: full-time $4086. Tuition, nonresident: full-time $14,254. *Required fees:* $853; $284.40. Tuition and fees vary according to course load. *Graduate housing:* Rooms and/or apartments available on a first-come, first-served basis to single and married students. Typical cost: $3484 per year ($4353 including board) for single students; $662 per year ($662 including board) for married students. Room and board charges vary according to board plan and housing facility selected. Housing application deadline: 7/1. *Student services:* Campus employment opportunities, campus safety program, career counseling, child daycare facilities, exercise/wellness program, free psychological counseling, grant writing training, international student services, low-cost health insurance, multicultural affairs office, services for students with disabilities, teacher training, writing training. *Library:* New Mexico State University Library - Zuhl plus 1 other. *Collection:* Books: 1.5 million (physical), 724 (digital/electronic); Serial titles: 474 (physical), 1,055 (digital/electronic); Databases: 434. Weekly public service hours: 112; students can reserve study rooms. *Research affiliation:* Sandia National Laboratories (energy research, computation), General Electric Company (GE) (water resources research), United States Army Research Laboratories (information sciences), U.S. Air Force Research Lab (space weather, high energy research), Sapphire Energy (biofuel research), Los Alamos National Laboratory (energy research, environmental sciences, information sciences).

Computer facilities: Computer purchase and lease plans are available. 371 computers available on campus for general student use. A campuswide network can be accessed from student residence rooms and from off campus. Online class registration, antivirus software; student portal online with file share/storage space, student employee clock-in, payments system, hardware rentals, short-term tablet checkout, software discounts are available.
Website: http://www.nmsu.edu/

General Application Contact: Dr. Loui Reyes, Dean, 575-646-5745, Fax: 575-646-7758, E-mail: gradinfo@nmsu.edu.

GRADUATE UNITS

College of Agricultural, Consumer and Environmental Sciences Students: 134 full-time (91 women), 45 part-time (22 women); includes 41 minority (1 Black or African American, non-Hispanic/Latino; 2 American Indian or Alaska Native, non-Hispanic/Latino; 1 Asian, non-Hispanic/Latino; 35 Hispanic/Latino; 2 Two or more races, non-Hispanic/Latino), 39 international. Average age 29. 100 applicants, 57% accepted, 46 enrolled. *Faculty:* 72 full-time (23 women), 2 part-time/adjunct (1 woman). *Financial support:* In 2015–16, 140 students received support, including 4 fellowships (averaging $4,088 per year), 49 research assistantships (averaging $19,179 per year), 50 teaching assistantships (averaging $16,131 per year); career-related internships or fieldwork, Federal Work-Study, scholarships/grants, traineeships, health care benefits, and unspecified assistantships also available. Support available to part-time students. Financial award application deadline: 3/1. In 2015, 52 master's, 7 doctorates awarded. *Degree program information:* Part-time and evening/weekend programs available. Part-time, evening/weekend. Offers agribusiness (MBA); agricultural and extension education (MA); agricultural, consumer and environmental sciences (M Ag, MA, MBA, MS, DED, PhD); animal science (MS, PhD); economic development (DED); entomology, plant pathology and weed science (MS); family and child science (MS); family and consumer science education (MS); fish, wildlife and conservation ecology (MS); food science and technology (MS); horticulture (MS); human nutrition and dietetic science (MS); marriage and family therapy (MS); plant and environmental sciences (MS, PhD); water science management (MS). *Application deadline:* For fall admission, 7/1 priority date for domestic students; for spring admission, 11/1 for domestic students. Applications are processed on a rolling basis. *Application fee:* $40 ($50 for international students). Electronic applications accepted. *Application Contact:* Dr. James Libbin, Associate Dean/Director of Academic Program, 575-646-3210, Fax: 575-646-5975, E-mail: jlibbin@nmsu.edu. *Dean,* Dr. Lowell Catlett, 575-646-1806, Fax: 575-646-5975, E-mail: agdean@nmsu.edu.

College of Arts and Sciences Students: 531 full-time (238 women), 286 part-time (162 women); includes 237 minority (14 Black or African American, non-Hispanic/Latino; 7 American Indian or Alaska Native, non-Hispanic/Latino; 15 Asian, non-Hispanic/Latino; 184 Hispanic/Latino; 1 Native Hawaiian or other Pacific Islander, non-Hispanic/Latino; 16 Two or more races, non-Hispanic/Latino), 203 international. Average age 32. 811 applicants, 43% accepted, 194 enrolled. *Faculty:* 236 full-time (90 women), 15 part-time/adjunct (9 women). *Financial support:* In 2015–16, 527 students received support, including 37 fellowships (averaging $3,911 per year), 77 research assistantships (averaging $18,034 per year), 310 teaching assistantships (averaging $15,201 per year); career-related internships or fieldwork, Federal Work-Study, scholarships/grants, traineeships, health care benefits, and unspecified assistantships also available. Support available to part-time students. Financial award application deadline: 3/1. In 2015, 210 master's, 39 doctorates, 14 other advanced degrees awarded. *Degree program information:* Part-time programs available. Part-time, online learning. Offers anthropology (MA); applied geography (MAG); art history (MA); arts and sciences (MA, MAG, MCJ, MFA, MM, MPA, MS, PhD, Graduate Certificate); astronomy (MS, PhD); bioinformatics (MS); biology (MS, PhD); biotechnology (MS); chemistry (MS, PhD); communication studies (MA); computer science (MS, PhD); conducting (MM); creative writing (MA, MFA); criminal justice (MCJ); cultural resource management (Graduate Certificate); engineering psychology (PhD); English studies for teachers (MA); geological sciences (MS); government (MA); history (MA); literature (MA); mathematical sciences (MS, PhD); museum studies (Graduate Certificate); music education (MM); performance (MM); public administration (MPA); public history (MA); rhetoric and professional communication (MA, PhD); sociology (MA); space physics (MS); Spanish (MA); studio art (MFA). *Application fee:* $40 ($50 for international students). Electronic applications accepted. *Application Contact:* Graduate Admissions, 575-646-3121, E-mail: admissions@nmsu.edu. *Interim Dean,* Dr. Enrico Pontelli, 575-646-3500, Fax: 575-646-6096, E-mail: epontell@nmsu.edu.

College of Business Students: 142 full-time (65 women), 131 part-time (66 women); includes 106 minority (8 Black or African American, non-Hispanic/Latino; 4 American Indian or Alaska Native, non-Hispanic/Latino; 5 Asian, non-Hispanic/Latino; 86 Hispanic/Latino; 3 Two or more races, non-Hispanic/Latino), 54 international. Average age 31. 256 applicants, 49% accepted, 59 enrolled. *Faculty:* 59 full-time (18 women), 1 (woman) part-time/adjunct. *Financial support:* In 2015–16, 124 students received support, including 5 fellowships (averaging $4,088 per year), 1 research assistantship (averaging $8,482 per year), 62 teaching assistantships (averaging $15,921 per year); career-related internships or fieldwork, Federal Work-Study, scholarships/grants, traineeships, health care benefits, and unspecified assistantships also available. Support available to part-time students. Financial award application deadline: 3/1. In 2015, 104 master's, 8 doctorates, 15 other advanced degrees awarded. *Degree program information:* Part-time programs available. Part-time. Offers accountancy (MACCT); agribusiness (MBA); applied statistics (MS); business (MA, MACCT, MBA, MS, DED, PhD, Graduate Certificate); economic development (DED); economics (MA); finance (MBA, Graduate Certificate); information systems (MBA); management (PhD); marketing (PhD); public utility regulation and economics (Graduate Certificate). *Application deadline:* For fall admission, 7/1 priority date for domestic students; for spring admission, 11/1 for domestic students. Applications are processed on a rolling basis. *Application fee:* $40 ($50 for international students). Electronic applications accepted. *Application Contact:* Graduate Admissions, 575-646-3121, E-mail: admissions@nmsu.edu. *Dean,* Dr. James Hoffman, 575-646-2821, Fax: 575-646-6155, E-mail: jhoffman@nmsu.edu.

College of Education Students: 281 full-time (208 women), 469 part-time (359 women); includes 424 minority (27 Black or African American, non-Hispanic/Latino; 11 American Indian or Alaska Native, non-Hispanic/Latino; 19 Asian, non-Hispanic/Latino; 354 Hispanic/Latino; 1 Native Hawaiian or other Pacific Islander, non-Hispanic/Latino; 12 Two or more races, non-Hispanic/Latino), 38 international. Average age 36. 452 applicants, 47% accepted, 169 enrolled. *Faculty:* 66 full-time (51 women), 12 part-time/adjunct (7 women). *Financial support:* In 2015–16, 250 students received support, including 6 fellowships (averaging $4,088 per year), 20 research assistantships (averaging $12,908 per year), 47 teaching assistantships (averaging $12,105 per year); career-related internships or fieldwork, Federal Work-Study, scholarships/grants, traineeships, health care benefits, and unspecified assistantships also available. Support available to part-time students. Financial award application deadline: 3/1. In 2015, 215 master's, 35 doctorates, 14 other advanced degrees awarded. *Degree program information:* Part-time and evening/weekend programs available. Part-time, evening/weekend, blended/hybrid learning. Offers autism spectrum disorders (MA); bilingual education (MA); bilingual/multicultural special education (Ed D, PhD); communication disorders (MA); counseling (MA); counseling psychology (PhD); curriculum and instruction (Ed D); deaf and hard of hearing (MA, Ed S); early childhood education (MA); education (MA, MAT, Ed D, PhD, Ed S, Graduate Certificate); educational administration (MA); educational diagnostics (Ed S); educational leadership (Ed D, PhD); educational learning technologies (MA); online teaching and learning (Graduate Certificate); school psychology (Ed S); special education (MA, Ed D, PhD, Ed S); speech-language pathology (MA); teaching (MAT); teaching English to speakers of other languages (MA). *Application deadline:* Applications are processed on a rolling basis. *Application fee:* $40 ($50 for international students). Electronic applications accepted. *Application Contact:* Dr. David Rutledge, Graduate Education Advising, 575-646-5411, Fax: 575-646-6032, E-mail: rutledge@nmsu.edu. *Dean,* Dr. Donald Pope Davis, 575-646-5858, Fax: 575-646-6032, E-mail: dpd@nmsu.edu.

College of Engineering Students: 234 full-time (54 women), 200 part-time (46 women); includes 109 minority (12 Black or African American, non-Hispanic/Latino; 3 American Indian or Alaska Native, non-Hispanic/Latino; 6 Asian, non-Hispanic/Latino; 80 Hispanic/Latino; 8 Two or more races, non-Hispanic/Latino), 198 international. Average age 30. 362 applicants, 50% accepted, 87 enrolled. *Faculty:* 62 full-time (10 women), 2 part-time/adjunct (0 women). *Financial support:* In 2015–16, 240 students received support, including 9 fellowships (averaging $4,217 per year), 74 research assistantships (averaging $15,540 per year), 99 teaching assistantships (averaging $13,186 per year); career-related internships or fieldwork, Federal Work-Study, scholarships/grants, traineeships, health care benefits, and unspecified assistantships also available. Support available to part-time students. Financial award application deadline: 3/1. In 2015, 116 master's, 24 doctorates, 6 other advanced degrees awarded. *Degree program information:* Part-time programs available. Part-time. Offers aerospace engineering (MSAE); chemical and materials engineering (MS Ch E, PhD); civil and geological engineering (MSCE, PhD); engineering (MS Ch E, MS Env E, MSAE, MSCE, MSEE, MSIE, MSME, PhD, Graduate Certificate); environmental engineering (MS Env E); industrial engineering (MSIE, PhD); mechanical engineering (MSME, PhD); systems engineering (Graduate Certificate). *Application deadline:* For fall admission, 7/1 priority date for domestic students; for spring admission, 11/1 for domestic students. Applications are processed on a rolling basis. *Application fee:* $40 ($50 for international students). Electronic applications accepted. *Application Contact:* Graduate Admissions, 575-646-3121, E-mail: admissions@nmsu.edu. *Interim Dean,* Dr. Steven Stochaj, 575-646-7234, Fax: 575-646-3549, E-mail: engrdean@nmsu.edu.

Klipsch School of Electrical and Computer Engineering Students: 81 full-time (12 women), 54 part-time (9 women); includes 29 minority (2 Black or African American, non-Hispanic/Latino; 1 American Indian or Alaska Native, non-Hispanic/Latino; 25 Hispanic/Latino; 1 Two or more races, non-Hispanic/Latino), 74 international. Average age 29. 116 applicants, 51% accepted, 24 enrolled. *Faculty:* 17 full-time (1 woman), 1 part-time/adjunct (0 women). *Financial support:* In 2015–16, 77 students received support, including 1 fellowship (averaging $4,088 per year), 26 research assistantships (averaging $17,191 per year), 29 teaching assistantships (averaging $12,644 per year); career-related internships or fieldwork, Federal Work-Study, scholarships/grants, traineeships, health care benefits, and unspecified assistantships also available. Support available to part-time students. Financial award application deadline: 3/1. In 2015, 31 master's, 5 doctorates, 2 other advanced degrees awarded. *Degree program information:* Part-time and evening/weekend programs available. Part-time, evening/weekend, 100% online. Offers electrical and computer engineering (MSEE, PhD, Graduate Certificate). *Application deadline:* For fall admission, 3/1 priority date for domestic and international students; for spring admission, 8/1 priority date for domestic and international students. Applications are processed on a rolling basis. *Application fee:* $40 ($50 for international students). Electronic applications accepted. *Application Contact:* 575-646-3115, Fax: 575-646-1435, E-mail: eceoffice@nmsu.edu. *Department Head*, Dr. Satishkuma Ranade, 575-646-3115, Fax: 575-646-1435, E-mail: sranade@nmsu.edu.

College of Health and Social Services Students: 187 full-time (154 women), 164 part-time (134 women); includes 191 minority (24 Black or African American, non-Hispanic/Latino; 9 American Indian or Alaska Native, non-Hispanic/Latino; 7 Asian, non-Hispanic/Latino; 147 Hispanic/Latino; 4 Two or more races, non-Hispanic/Latino), 13 international. Average age 36. 215 applicants, 72% accepted, 94 enrolled. *Faculty:* 37 full-time (28 women), 8 part-time/adjunct (5 women). *Financial support:* In 2015–16, 90 students received support, including 1 research assistantship (averaging $12,724 per year), 20 teaching assistantships (averaging $9,634 per year); career-related internships or fieldwork, Federal Work-Study, scholarships/grants, traineeships, health care benefits, and unspecified assistantships also available. Support available to part-time students. Financial award application deadline: 3/1. In 2015, 86 master's, 11 doctorates, 3 other advanced degrees awarded. *Degree program information:* Part-time and evening/weekend programs available. Part-time, evening/weekend, online learning. Offers health and social services (MPH, MSN, MSW, DNP, PhD, Graduate Certificate); public health (MPH, Graduate Certificate). *Application deadline:* For fall admission, 7/1 priority date for domestic students. Applications are processed on a rolling basis. *Application fee:* $40 ($50 for international students). Electronic applications accepted. *Application Contact:* Graduate Admissions, 575-646-3121, E-mail: admissions@nmsu.edu. *Interim Dean*, Dr. Donna Wagner, 575-646-3526, Fax: 575-646-6166, E-mail: dlwagner@nmsu.edu.

School of Nursing Students: 24 full-time (18 women), 90 part-time (80 women); includes 49 minority (10 Black or African American, non-Hispanic/Latino; 1 American Indian or Alaska Native, non-Hispanic/Latino; 4 Asian, non-Hispanic/Latino; 32 Hispanic/Latino; 2 Two or more races, non-Hispanic/Latino), 1 international. Average age 43. 40 applicants, 58% accepted, 17 enrolled. *Faculty:* 16 full-time (15 women). *Financial support:* In 2015–16, 23 students received support, including 1 teaching assistantship (averaging $9,473 per year); career-related internships or fieldwork, Federal Work-Study, scholarships/grants, traineeships, health care benefits, and unspecified assistantships also available. Support available to part-time students. Financial award application deadline: 3/1. In 2015, 6 master's, 11 doctorates awarded. Blended/hybrid learning. Offers adult/geriatric nursing (DNP); family nurse practitioner (DNP); family/psychiatric mental health nursing (DNP); nursing administration (MSN); nursing science (PhD); public/community health nursing (DNP). *Application deadline:* For fall admission, 1/15 for domestic students; for spring admission, 1/15 priority date for domestic students; for summer admission, 1/15 for domestic students. *Application fee:* $40 ($50 for international students). Electronic applications accepted. *Application Contact:* Dr. Teresa Keller, Director of Graduate Studies, 575-646-4370, Fax: 575-646-2167, E-mail: tkeller@nmsu.edu. *Department Head*, Dr. Kathleen Huttlinger, 575-646-3812, Fax: 575-646-2167, E-mail: khuttlin@nmsu.edu.

School of Social Work Students: 130 full-time (110 women), 20 part-time (17 women); includes 108 minority (8 Black or African American, non-Hispanic/Latino; 5 American Indian or Alaska Native, non-Hispanic/Latino; 1 Asian, non-Hispanic/Latino; 92 Hispanic/Latino; 2 Two or more races, non-Hispanic/Latino), 1 international. Average age 32. 113 applicants, 78% accepted, 71 enrolled. *Faculty:* 11 full-time (7 women), 5 part-time/adjunct (4 women). *Financial support:* In 2015–16, 51 students received support, including 1 research assistantship (averaging $12,724 per year), 10 teaching assistantships (averaging $9,306 per year); career-related internships or fieldwork, Federal Work-Study, scholarships/grants, traineeships, health care benefits, and unspecified assistantships also available. Support available to part-time students. Financial award application deadline: 3/1. In 2015, 56 master's awarded. *Degree program information:* Part-time programs available. Part-time. Offers social work (MSW). *Application deadline:* For fall admission, 1/16 priority date for domestic students, 2/16 priority date for international students. Applications are processed on a rolling basis. *Application fee:* $40 ($50 for international students). Electronic applications accepted. *Application Contact:* Dr. Maria Gurrola, Coordinator, MSW Program in Las Cruces, 575-646-4830, Fax: 575-646-4116, E-mail: gurrola@nmsu.edu. *Director/Associate Dean*, Dr. Tina Hancock, 575-646-2143, Fax: 575-646-4116, E-mail: thancock@nmsu.edu.

Graduate School Students: 36 full-time (16 women), 30 part-time (16 women); includes 17 minority (3 Black or African American, non-Hispanic/Latino; 14 Hispanic/Latino), 22 international. Average age 38. 36 applicants, 42% accepted, 10 enrolled. *Faculty:* 3 full-time (0 women). *Financial support:* In 2015–16, 33 students received support, including 1 fellowship (averaging $4,088 per year), 15 research assistantships (averaging $18,684 per year), 8 teaching assistantships (averaging $15,379 per year); career-related internships or fieldwork, Federal Work-Study, scholarships/grants, traineeships, health care benefits, and unspecified assistantships also available. Support available to part-time students. In 2015, 11 master's, 7 doctorates awarded. *Degree program information:* Part-time and evening/weekend programs available. Part-time, evening/weekend, online learning. Offers interdisciplinary studies (MA, MS, PhD); molecular biology (MS, PhD); water science management (MS, PhD). *Application fee:* $40 ($50 for international students). Electronic applications accepted. *Application Contact:* Graduate Admissions, 575-646-3121, E-mail: admissions@nmsu.edu. *Dean*, Dr. Loui Reyes, 575-646-5746, Fax: 575-646-7758, E-mail: gradinfo@nmsu.edu.

NEW ORLEANS BAPTIST THEOLOGICAL SEMINARY, New Orleans, LA 70126-4858

General Information Independent-religious, coed, primarily men, comprehensive institution. *Graduate housing:* Rooms and/or apartments available to single and married students.

GRADUATE UNITS

Graduate and Professional Programs *Degree program information:* Evening/weekend programs available. Evening/weekend. Offers theology (M Div, MA, MACE, MAMFC, MMCM, D Min, DEM, DMA, PhD).

Division of Biblical Studies Offers biblical studies (M Div, MA, PhD).

Division of Christian Education Ministries *Degree program information:* Evening/weekend programs available. Evening/weekend, online learning. Offers Christian education (M Div, MACE, D Min, DEM, PhD).

Division of Church Music Ministries Online learning. Offers church music ministries (M Div, MMCM, DMA).

Division of Pastoral Ministries Online learning. Offers pastoral ministries (M Div, MAMFC, D Min, PhD).

Division of Theological and Historical Studies Online learning. Offers theological and historical studies (M Div, MA, D Min, PhD).

NEW SAINT ANDREWS COLLEGE, Moscow, ID 83843

General Information Independent-religious, coed, comprehensive institution. *Graduate housing:* On-campus housing not available.

GRADUATE UNITS

Graduate School *Degree program information:* Part-time programs available. Part-time. Offers classical Christian studies (Graduate Certificate); theology and letters (MA). Electronic applications accepted.

THE NEW SCHOOL, New York, NY 10011

General Information Independent, coed, university. *Enrollment by degree level:* 2,756 master's, 495 doctoral, 102 other advanced degrees. *Graduate faculty:* 215 full-time (101 women), 416 part-time/adjunct (175 women). *Tuition, area resident:* Full-time $40,974; part-time $1654 per credit. *Required fees:* $138 per semester. Part-time tuition and fees vary according to course load and program. *Graduate housing:* Room and/or apartments available on a first-come, first-served basis to single students; on-campus housing not available to married students. Typical cost: $20,550 per year ($23,820 including board). Room and board charges vary according to board plan, campus/location and housing facility selected. Housing application deadline: 7/1. *Student services:* Campus employment opportunities, campus safety program, career counseling, exercise/wellness program, free psychological counseling, international student services, low-cost health insurance, multicultural affairs office, services for students with disabilities, teacher training, writing training. *Research affiliation:* The Goldman Sachs Group, Inc., Siemens, Raytheon Corporation, National Geospatial-Intelligence Agency, Environmental Systems Research Institute, Dow Jones & Company, Inc.
Website: http://www.newschool.edu/

General Application Contact: Heather Fomin, Senior Director of Admissions, 212-229-5150, E-mail: admission@newschool.edu.

GRADUATE UNITS

College of Performing Arts Students: 208 full-time (125 women), 1 part-time (0 women); includes 32 minority (7 Black or African American, non-Hispanic/Latino; 11 Asian, non-Hispanic/Latino; 11 Hispanic/Latino; 3 Two or more races, non-Hispanic/Latino), 99 international. Average age 25. 741 applicants, 49% accepted, 95 enrolled. *Faculty:* 12 full-time (8 women), 115 part-time/adjunct (41 women). *Financial support:* Fellowships, teaching assistantships, career-related internships or fieldwork, Federal Work-Study, scholarships/grants, and unspecified assistantships available. Support available to part-time students. Financial award application deadline: 3/1; financial award applicants required to submit FAFSA. In 2015, 58 master's, 33 other advanced degrees awarded. Offers collaborative piano (MM, Professional Diploma); composition (MM, Professional Diploma); drama (MFA); guitar (MM); harpsichord (MM); orchestral conducting (MM); orchestral instruments (MM, Professional Diploma); piano (MM, Professional Diploma); theory (MM); voice (MM, Professional Diploma). *Application deadline:* For fall admission, 12/1 priority date for domestic and international students; for spring admission, 11/1 priority date for domestic and international students. *Application fee:* $50. Electronic applications accepted. *Application Contact:* Georgia Schmitt, Director of Admissions, 212-580-0210 Ext. 4805, E-mail: copaadmissions@newschool.edu. *Executive Dean, College of Performing Arts*, Richard Kessler, 212-580-0210 Ext. 4800, E-mail: copadeans@newschool.edu.

School of Drama Students: 56 full-time (29 women); includes 13 minority (4 Black or African American, non-Hispanic/Latino; 1 Asian, non-Hispanic/Latino; 7 Hispanic/Latino; 1 Two or more races, non-Hispanic/Latino), 6 international. Average age 27. 183 applicants, 19% accepted, 20 enrolled. *Faculty:* 37 part-time/adjunct (18 women). *Financial support:* Fellowships, teaching assistantships, career-related internships or fieldwork, Federal Work-Study, scholarships/grants, and unspecified assistantships available. Support available to part-time students. Financial award application deadline: 3/1; financial award applicants required to submit FAFSA. In 2015, 26 master's awarded. Offers acting (MFA); directing (MFA); playwriting (MFA). *Application deadline:* For fall admission, 1/10 priority date for domestic and international students. *Application fee:* $50. Electronic applications accepted. *Application Contact:* Georgia Schmitt, Director of Admissions, 212-580-0210 Ext. 4805, E-mail: copaadmissions@newschool.edu. *Dean, School of Drama*, Pippin Parker, 212-229-5859 Ext. 2636, E-mail: dramamfa@newschool.edu.

The New School for Social Research Students: 610 full-time (291 women), 224 part-time (127 women); includes 139 minority (22 Black or African American, non-Hispanic/Latino; 1 American Indian or Alaska Native, non-Hispanic/Latino; 26 Asian, non-Hispanic/Latino; 64 Hispanic/Latino; 26 Two or more races, non-Hispanic/Latino), 273 international. Average age 32. 810 applicants, 75% accepted, 171 enrolled. *Faculty:* 74 full-time (31 women), 13 part-time/adjunct (2 women). *Financial support:* Fellowships, research assistantships, teaching assistantships, career-related internships or fieldwork, Federal Work-Study, scholarships/grants, and tuition waivers (full and partial) available. Support available to part-time students. Financial award application deadline: 3/1; financial award applicants required to submit FAFSA. In 2015, 200 master's, 73 doctorates awarded. *Degree program information:* Part-time and evening/weekend programs available. Part-time, evening/weekend. Offers anthropology (M Phil, MA, PhD); clinical psychology (PhD); cognitive, social and developmental psychology (PhD); economics (M Phil, MA, MS, PhD); general psychology (MA); global political economy and finance (MA); historical studies (PhD); liberal studies (MA); philosophy (M Phil, MA); politics (M Phil, MA, PhD); psychoanalysis (PhD); social research (M Phil, MA, MS, PhD); sociology (M Phil, MA). *Application deadline:* For fall admission, 8/1 for domestic students, 6/1 priority date for international students; for spring admission, 10/15 for domestic and international students. Applications are processed on a rolling basis. *Application fee:* $50. Electronic applications accepted. *Application Contact:* Dana Messinger, Director of Admissions, 212-229-5150, Fax: 212-627-2695, E-mail: socialresearchadmit@newschool.edu. *Dean and Professor of Economics*, Dr. William Milberg, 212-229-5777, E-mail: milbergw@newschool.edu.

Parsons Paris Students: 25 full-time (21 women); includes 5 minority (1 Black or African American, non-Hispanic/Latino; 2 Asian, non-Hispanic/Latino; 1 Hispanic/Latino; 1 Two or more races, non-Hispanic/Latino), 13 international. Average age 26. 36 applicants, 78% accepted, 16 enrolled. *Faculty:* 5 full-time (2 women), 24 part-time/adjunct (15 women). *Financial support:* Application deadline: 3/1; applicants required to submit FAFSA. In 2015, 3 master's awarded. Offers art and design (MA, MFA); design and technology (MFA); fashion studies (MA); history of design and curatorial studies (MA). *Application deadline:* For fall admission, 1/1 for domestic and international students. Applications are processed on a rolling basis. *Application fee:* $50. Electronic applications accepted. *Application Contact:* Mike Fakih, Director of Admissions, Parsons Paris, 33 176 21 76 67, E-mail: thinkparsonsparis@newschool.edu. *Professor*, Dean Susan Taylor-Leduc, 33-176217661, E-mail: leducs@newschool.edu.

Parsons School of Design Students: 853 full-time (613 women), 69 part-time (45 women); includes 158 minority (39 Black or African American, non-Hispanic/Latino; 53 Asian, non-Hispanic/Latino; 52 Hispanic/Latino; 2 Native Hawaiian or other Pacific Islander, non-Hispanic/Latino; 12 Two or more races, non-Hispanic/Latino), 490 international. Average age 27. 1,853 applicants, 54% accepted, 455 enrolled. *Faculty:* 82 full-time (38 women), 144 part-time/adjunct (68 women). *Financial support:* Research assistantships, teaching assistantships, career-related internships or fieldwork, Federal Work-Study, scholarships/grants, unspecified assistantships, and travel funding; tuition waivers for students who are also New School employees available. Support available to part-time students. Financial award application deadline: 3/1; financial award applicants required to submit FAFSA. In 2015, 349 master's awarded. Offers architecture (M Arch); design (M Arch, MA, MFA, MS); design and technology (MFA); design and urban ecologies (MS); design studies (MFA); fashion design and society (MFA); fashion studies (MA); fine arts (MFA); history of design and curatorial studies (MA); industrial design (MFA); interior design (MFA); lighting design (MFA); photography (MFA); theories of urban practice (MA); transdisciplinary design (MFA). *Application deadline:* For fall admission, 1/1 for domestic and international students. Applications are processed on a rolling basis. *Application fee:* $50. Electronic applications accepted. *Application Contact:* Courtney Malenius, Director of Graduate Admission, 212-229-5150, E-mail: thinkparsonsgrad@newschool.edu. *Executive Dean*, Joel Towers, 212-229-8950, E-mail: parsonsdean@newschool.edu.

Schools of Public Engagement Students: 814 full-time (570 women), 493 part-time (336 women); includes 465 minority (192 Black or African American, non-Hispanic/Latino; 2 American Indian or Alaska Native, non-Hispanic/Latino; 55 Asian, non-Hispanic/Latino; 172 Hispanic/Latino; 44 Two or more races, non-Hispanic/Latino), 259 international. Average age 30. 1,302 applicants, 84% accepted, 457 enrolled. *Faculty:* 53 full-time (25 women), 111 part-time/adjunct (49 women). *Financial support:* Fellowships, research assistantships, teaching assistantships, career-related internships or fieldwork, Federal Work-Study, scholarships/grants, and unspecified assistantships available. Support available to part-time students. Financial award application deadline: 3/1; financial award applicants required to submit FAFSA. In 2015, 545 master's, 4 doctorates, 51 other advanced degrees awarded. *Degree program information:* Part-time and evening/weekend programs available. Part-time, evening/weekend, online learning. Offers creative writing (MFA); documentary media studies (Graduate Certificate); environmental policy and sustainability management (MS); international affairs (MA, MS); leadership and change (Graduate Certificate); media management (MS, Graduate Certificate); media studies (MA); nonprofit management (MS); organizational change management (MS, Graduate Certificate); public and urban policy (PhD); public engagement (MA, MFA, MS, PhD, Certificate, Graduate Certificate); sustainability strategies (Certificate); teaching English to speakers of other languages (MA); urban policy analysis and management (MS). *Application deadline:* Applications are processed on a rolling basis. *Application fee:* $50. Electronic applications accepted. *Application Contact:* Heather Fomin, Senior Director of Admissions, 212-229-5150 Ext. 3230, E-mail: admission@newschool.edu. *Executive Dean*, Mary Watson, 212-229-5615 Ext. 5613, E-mail: watsonm@newschool.edu.

NEWSCHOOL OF ARCHITECTURE AND DESIGN, San Diego, CA 92101-6634

General Information Proprietary, coed, primarily men, comprehensive institution. *Research affiliation:* Academy of Neuroscience for Architecture (neuroscience and architecture).

GRADUATE UNITS

Program in Architecture ***Degree program information:*** Part-time programs available. Part-time, online learning. Offers architecture (M Arch, MS).

Program in Construction Management ***Degree program information:*** Part-time programs available. Part-time, online learning. Offers construction management (MCM). Electronic applications accepted.

NEW YORK ACADEMY OF ART, New York, NY 10013-2911

General Information Independent, coed, graduate-only institution. *Graduate housing:* On-campus housing not available.

GRADUATE UNITS

Master of Fine Arts Program Offers drawing (MFA); painting (MFA); sculpture (MFA).

NEW YORK CHIROPRACTIC COLLEGE, Seneca Falls, NY 13148-0800

General Information Independent, coed, graduate-only institution. *Graduate housing:* Rooms and/or apartments available on a first-come, first-served basis to single and married students. *Research affiliation:* Foot Levelers, Inc. (orthotics research), Atrium Innovations (nutrition), Nimmo Education Foundation (muscle physiology).

GRADUATE UNITS

Doctor of Chiropractic Program Offers chiropractic (DC). Electronic applications accepted.

Finger Lakes School of Acupuncture and Oriental Medicine Offers acupuncture (MS); acupuncture and Oriental medicine (MS). Electronic applications accepted.

Program in Applied Clinical Nutrition ***Degree program information:*** Part-time and evening/weekend programs available. Part-time, evening/weekend. Offers applied clinical nutrition (MS). Electronic applications accepted.

Program in Clinical Anatomy Offers clinical anatomy (MS). Electronic applications accepted.

Program in Human Anatomy and Physiology Instruction Online learning. Offers human anatomy and physiology (MS).

NEW YORK COLLEGE OF HEALTH PROFESSIONS, Syosset, NY 11791-4413

General Information Independent, coed, comprehensive institution. *Graduate housing:* On-campus housing not available. *Research affiliation:* North Shore Hospital (acupuncture).

GRADUATE UNITS

Graduate School of Oriental Medicine ***Degree program information:*** Part-time programs available. Part-time. Offers acupuncture (MS); Oriental medicine (MS).

NEW YORK COLLEGE OF PODIATRIC MEDICINE, New York, NY 10035

General Information Independent, coed, graduate-only institution. *Graduate housing:* Rooms and/or apartments available on a first-come, first-served basis to single and married students. Housing application deadline: 8/15. *Research affiliation:* Cyberlogics (ultrasound use), Novartis Pharmaceuticals (fungal diseases of nail), Prescription Dispensing Laboratories (topical verapamil), Anodyne Corporation (light energy applications).

GRADUATE UNITS

Professional Program Offers podiatric medicine (DPM).

NEW YORK COLLEGE OF TRADITIONAL CHINESE MEDICINE, Mineola, NY 11501

General Information Independent, coed, graduate-only institution.

GRADUATE UNITS

Graduate Programs

NEW YORK FILM ACADEMY, Burbank, CA 91505

General Information Independent, coed, comprehensive institution.
Website: http://www.nyfa.com/

GRADUATE UNITS

Program in Filmmaking-Los Angeles Offers acting for film (MFA); cinematography (MFA); documentary film (MFA); film and media production (MA); filmmaking (MFA); game design (MFA); photography (MFA); producing (MA, MFA); screenwriting (MA, MFA).

Program in Filmmaking–South Beach, Florida Offers acting for film (MFA); cinematography (MFA); documentary film (MFA); film and media production (MA); filmmaking (MFA); game design (MFA); photography (MFA); producing (MA, MFA); screenwriting (MA, MFA).

NEW YORK INSTITUTE OF TECHNOLOGY, Old Westbury, NY 11568-8000

General Information Independent, coed, university. *Enrollment:* 8,048 graduate, professional, and undergraduate students; 3,085 full-time matriculated graduate/professional students (1,431 women), 904 part-time matriculated graduate/professional students (439 women). *Enrollment by degree level:* 2,608 master's, 1,340 doctoral, 41 other advanced degrees. *Graduate faculty:* 177 full-time (66 women), 210 part-time/adjunct (81 women). *Tuition, area resident:* Full-time $20,790; part-time $1155 per credit. *Required fees:* $95; $75 per credit. Full-time tuition and fees vary according to degree level, campus/location and program. Part-time tuition and fees vary according to course load and campus/location. *Graduate housing:* Room and/or apartments available on a first-come, first-served basis to single students; on-campus housing not available to married students. Typical cost: $8450 per year ($13,090 including board). Room and board charges vary according to board plan, campus/location and housing facility selected. *Student services:* Campus employment opportunities, campus safety program, career counseling, exercise/wellness program, free psychological counseling, international student services, low-cost health insurance, services for students with disabilities, writing training. *Library:* George and Gertrude Wisser Memorial Library plus 3 others. *Collection:* Books: 177,496 (physical), 64,280 (digital/electronic); Serial titles: 424 (physical), 80,477 (digital/electronic); Databases: 200. Weekly public service hours: 78; students can reserve study rooms.

Computer facilities: 1,250 computers available on campus for general student use. A campuswide network can be accessed from student residence rooms and from off campus. Online class registration is available.
Website: http://www.nyit.edu/

General Application Contact: Alice Dolitsky, Director, Graduate Admissions, 516-686-7520, Fax: 516-686-1116, E-mail: nyitgrad@nyit.edu.

GRADUATE UNITS

College of Arts and Sciences Students: 140 full-time (91 women), 51 part-time (28 women); includes 20 minority (11 Black or African American, non-Hispanic/Latino; 9 Hispanic/Latino), 124 international. Average age 27. 218 applicants, 66% accepted, 72 enrolled. *Faculty:* 13 full-time (6 women), 20 part-time/adjunct (8 women). *Financial support:* Research assistantships with partial tuition reimbursements, career-related internships or fieldwork, scholarships/grants, health care benefits, tuition waivers (partial), and unspecified assistantships available. Support available to part-time students. Financial award application deadline: 3/1; financial award applicants required to submit FAFSA. In 2015, 83 master's awarded. *Degree program information:* Part-time and evening/weekend programs available. Part-time, evening/weekend. Offers arts and entertainment leadership (Advanced Certificate); arts and sciences (MA, MFA, Advanced Certificate); communication arts (MA); computer graphics (MFA); leadership in the arts and entertainment industries (MA). *Application deadline:* For fall admission, 6/1 for domestic students, 7/1 for international students; for spring admission, 12/1 for domestic and international students. Applications are processed on a rolling basis. *Application fee:* $50. Electronic applications accepted. *Application Contact:* Alice Dolitsky, Director, Graduate Admissions, 516-686-1316, Fax: 516-686-1116, E-mail: nyitgrad@nyit.edu. *Dean*, Dr. Jim Simon, 516-686-7665, E-mail: james.simon@nyit.edu.

College of Osteopathic Medicine Students: 1,227 full-time (598 women), 3 part-time (1 woman); includes 538 minority (39 Black or African American, non-Hispanic/Latino; 1 American Indian or Alaska Native, non-Hispanic/Latino; 466 Asian, non-Hispanic/Latino; 27 Hispanic/Latino; 1 Native Hawaiian or other Pacific Islander, non-Hispanic/Latino; 4 Two or more races, non-Hispanic/Latino). Average age 27. 6,515 applicants, 7% accepted, 272 enrolled. *Faculty:* 69 full-time (25 women), 24 part-time/adjunct (10 women). *Financial support:* Fellowships with partial tuition reimbursements and tuition waivers (full and partial) available. Financial award application deadline: 4/1; financial award applicants required to submit FAFSA. In 2015, 15 master's, 269 doctorates awarded. Offers medical/healthcare simulation (MS); osteopathic medicine (DO). *Application deadline:* For fall admission, 2/1 for domestic students. Applications are processed on a rolling basis. *Application fee:* $80. Electronic applications accepted. *Application Contact:* Edward Dettling, Acting Director of Admissions, 516-686-3747, Fax:

516-686-3831, E-mail: comadm@nyit.edu. *Dean*, Dr. Wolfgang Gilliar, 516-686-3722, Fax: 516-686-3830, E-mail: wgilliar@nyit.edu.

School of Architecture and Design Students: 21 full-time (15 women), 1 part-time (0 women); includes 1 minority (Asian, non-Hispanic/Latino), 21 international. Average age 26. 65 applicants, 38% accepted, 15 enrolled. *Faculty:* 1 full-time (0 women), 8 part-time/adjunct (1 woman). *Financial support:* Research assistantships with partial tuition reimbursements, career-related internships or fieldwork, scholarships/grants, health care benefits, tuition waivers (full and partial), and unspecified assistantships available. Support available to part-time students. Financial award application deadline: 3/1; financial award applicants required to submit FAFSA. In 2015, 6 master's awarded. *Degree program information:* Part-time programs available. Part-time. Offers architecture, urban and regional design (MS). *Application deadline:* For fall admission, 3/1 for domestic and international students. Applications are processed on a rolling basis. *Application fee:* $50. Electronic applications accepted. *Application Contact:* Alice Dolitsky, Director, Graduate Admissions, 516-686-7520, Fax: 516-686-1116, E-mail: nyitgrad@nyit.edu. *Dean*, Judith DiMaio, 516-686-7594, Fax: 516-686-7921, E-mail: arch@nyit.edu.

School of Education Students: 40 full-time (32 women), 226 part-time (166 women); includes 88 minority (38 Black or African American, non-Hispanic/Latino; 2 American Indian or Alaska Native, non-Hispanic/Latino; 18 Asian, non-Hispanic/Latino; 25 Hispanic/Latino; 5 Two or more races, non-Hispanic/Latino), 2 international. Average age 32. 216 applicants, 63% accepted, 102 enrolled. *Faculty:* 10 full-time (6 women), 38 part-time/adjunct (24 women). *Financial support:* Research assistantships with partial tuition reimbursements, career-related internships or fieldwork, scholarships/grants, health care benefits, tuition waivers (full and partial), and unspecified assistantships available. Support available to part-time students. Financial award application deadline: 3/1; financial award applicants required to submit FAFSA. In 2015, 77 master's, 2 other advanced degrees awarded. *Degree program information:* Part-time and evening/weekend programs available. Part-time, evening/weekend, 100% online, blended/hybrid learning. Offers adolescence education: mathematics (MS); adolescence education: science (MS); childhood education (MS); early childhood (MS); education (MS, Advanced Certificate, Advanced Diploma); emerging technologies for trainers (Advanced Certificate); instructional design for global e-learning (Advanced Certificate); instructional technology (MS); school counseling (MS); school leadership and technology (Advanced Diploma); STEM education (Advanced Certificate); teaching 21st century skills (Advanced Certificate); virtual education (Advanced Certificate). *Application deadline:* For fall admission, 7/1 for international students; for spring admission, 12/1 for international students. Applications are processed on a rolling basis. *Application fee:* $50. Electronic applications accepted. *Application Contact:* Alice Dolitsky, Director, Graduate Admissions, 516-686-7520, Fax: 516-686-1116, E-mail: nyitgrad@nyit.edu. *Interim Dean, School of Education*, Dr. Jess Boronico, 516-686-7541, E-mail: soeinfo@nyit.edu.

School of Engineering and Computing Sciences Students: 997 full-time (291 women), 402 part-time (105 women); includes 100 minority (35 Black or African American, non-Hispanic/Latino; 35 Asian, non-Hispanic/Latino; 24 Hispanic/Latino; 1 Native Hawaiian or other Pacific Islander, non-Hispanic/Latino; 5 Two or more races, non-Hispanic/Latino), 1,213 international. Average age 25. 4,673 applicants, 57% accepted, 539 enrolled. *Faculty:* 26 full-time (5 women), 38 part-time/adjunct (2 women). *Financial support:* Research assistantships with partial tuition reimbursements, career-related internships or fieldwork, scholarships/grants, health care benefits, tuition waivers (full and partial), and unspecified assistantships available. Support available to part-time students. Financial award application deadline: 3/1; financial award applicants required to submit FAFSA. In 2015, 346 master's, 3 other advanced degrees awarded. *Degree program information:* Part-time and evening/weekend programs available. Part-time, evening/weekend, 100% online, blended/hybrid learning. Offers computer science (MS); electrical and computer engineering (MS); energy management (MS); energy technology (Advanced Certificate); engineering and computing sciences (MS, Advanced Certificate); environmental management (Advanced Certificate); environmental technology and sustainability (MS); facilities management (Advanced Certificate); information, network, and computer security (MS); infrastructure security management (Advanced Certificate). *Application deadline:* For fall admission, 7/1 for domestic students, 6/1 for international students; for spring admission, 12/1 for domestic students, 11/1 for international students. Applications are processed on a rolling basis. *Application fee:* $50. Electronic applications accepted. *Application Contact:* Alice Dolitsky, Director, Graduate Admissions, 516-686-7520, Fax: 516-686-1116, E-mail: nyitgrad@nyit.edu. *Dean*, Dr. Nada Anid, 516-686-7931, Fax: 516-625-7933, E-mail: nanid@nyit.edu.

School of Health Professions Students: 333 full-time (245 women), 66 part-time (49 women); includes 127 minority (22 Black or African American, non-Hispanic/Latino; 67 Asian, non-Hispanic/Latino; 32 Hispanic/Latino; 1 Native Hawaiian or other Pacific Islander, non-Hispanic/Latino; 5 Two or more races, non-Hispanic/Latino), 3 international. Average age 26. 2,979 applicants, 8% accepted, 138 enrolled. *Faculty:* 21 full-time (15 women), 40 part-time/adjunct (25 women). *Financial support:* Research assistantships with partial tuition reimbursements, career-related internships or fieldwork, scholarships/grants, health care benefits, tuition waivers (full and partial), and unspecified assistantships available. Support available to part-time students. Financial award application deadline: 3/1; financial award applicants required to submit FAFSA. In 2015, 104 master's, 31 doctorates awarded. *Degree program information:* Part-time and evening/weekend programs available. Part-time, evening/weekend, 100% online. Offers clinical nutrition (MS); health professions (MS, DPT); occupational therapy (MS); physical therapy (DPT); physician assistant studies (MS). *Application deadline:* For fall admission, 10/1 for domestic and international students. Applications are processed on a rolling basis. *Application fee:* $50. Electronic applications accepted. *Application Contact:* Alice Dolitsky, Director, Graduate Admissions, 516-686-7520, Fax: 516-686-1116, E-mail: nyitgrad@nyit.edu. *Dean*, Dr. Patricia Chute, 516-686-3939, Fax: 516-686-3854, E-mail: pchute@nyit.edu.

School of Management Students: 327 full-time (159 women), 154 part-time (89 women); includes 53 minority (15 Black or African American, non-Hispanic/Latino; 26 Asian, non-Hispanic/Latino; 8 Hispanic/Latino; 2 Native Hawaiian or other Pacific Islander, non-Hispanic/Latino; 2 Two or more races, non-Hispanic/Latino), 376 international. Average age 26. 864 applicants, 59% accepted, 224 enrolled. *Faculty:* 36 full-time (8 women), 40 part-time/adjunct (9 women). *Financial support:* Research assistantships with partial tuition reimbursements, career-related internships or fieldwork, scholarships/grants, health care benefits, tuition waivers (full and partial), and unspecified assistantships available. Support available to part-time students. Financial award application deadline: 3/1; financial award applicants required to submit FAFSA. In 2015, 168 master's, 4 other advanced degrees awarded. *Degree program information:* Part-time and evening/weekend programs available. Part-time, evening/weekend. Offers executive business administration (MBA); human resource management (Advanced Certificate); human resource management and labor relations (MS); management (MBA); professional accounting (MBA). *Application deadline:* For fall admission, 7/1 for international students; for spring admission, 12/1 for international students. Applications are processed on a rolling basis. *Application fee:* $50. Electronic applications accepted. *Application Contact:* Alice Dolitsky, Director, Graduate Admissions, 516-686-7520, Fax: 516-686-1116, E-mail: nyitgrad@nyit.edu. *Dean*, Dr. Jess Boronico, 516-686-7838, Fax: 516-686-7430, E-mail: jboronic@nyit.edu.

NEW YORK LAW SCHOOL, New York, NY 10013

General Information Independent, coed, graduate-only institution. *Enrollment by degree level:* 38 master's, 893 doctoral. *Graduate faculty:* 61 full-time (27 women), 59 part-time/adjunct (16 women). *Tuition, area resident:* Full-time $47,600; part-time $36,680 per year. *Required fees:* $1640; $1200 per unit. Tuition and fees vary according to course load and degree level. *Graduate housing:* Room and/or apartments available on a first-come, first-served basis to single students; on-campus housing not available to married students. Typical cost: $20,700 per year. Room charges vary according to housing facility selected. Housing application deadline: 7/1. *Student services:* Campus employment opportunities, campus safety program, career counseling, exercise/wellness program, free psychological counseling, international student services, low-cost health insurance, multicultural affairs office, services for students with disabilities, writing training. *Library:* Mendik Library. *Collection:* Books: 316,632 (physical), 246,854 (digital/electronic); Serial titles: 5,461 (physical); Databases: 134. Weekly public service hours: 98.

Computer facilities: 64 computers available on campus for general student use. A campuswide network can be accessed from student residence rooms and from off campus. Online class registration is available.
Website: http://www.nyls.edu/

General Application Contact: Mae Estrada, Associate Dean for Enrollment Management, Financial Aid and Diversity Initiatives, 212-431-2888, Fax: 212-966-1522, E-mail: admissions@nyls.edu.

GRADUATE UNITS

Graduate Programs Students: 608 full-time (334 women), 323 part-time (169 women); includes 315 minority (78 Black or African American, non-Hispanic/Latino; 54 Asian, non-Hispanic/Latino; 153 Hispanic/Latino; 1 Native Hawaiian or other Pacific Islander, non-Hispanic/Latino; 29 Two or more races, non-Hispanic/Latino), 30 international. Average age 28. 2,828 applicants, 54% accepted, 316 enrolled. *Faculty:* 61 full-time (27 women), 59 part-time/adjunct (16 women). *Financial support:* In 2015–16, 730 students received support, including 121 fellowships (averaging $2,990 per year), 61 research assistantships (averaging $4,720 per year), 15 teaching assistantships (averaging $4,753 per year); career-related internships or fieldwork, Federal Work-Study, and scholarships/grants also available. Support available to part-time students. Financial award application deadline: 7/1; financial award applicants required to submit FAFSA. In 2015, 32 master's, 352 doctorates awarded. *Degree program information:* Part-time and evening/weekend programs available. Part-time, evening/weekend. Offers law (JD); taxation (LL M). JD/MBA offered jointly with Baruch College of the City University of New York; JD/MA in forensic psychology offered jointly with John Jay College of Criminal Justice of the City University of New York. *Application deadline:* For fall admission, 7/1 priority date for domestic and international students; for winter admission, 11/15 priority date for domestic and international students. Applications are processed on a rolling basis. *Application fee:* $0. Electronic applications accepted. *Application Contact:* Mae Estrada, Associate Dean for Enrollment Management, Financial Aid and Diversity Initiatives, 212-431-2888, Fax: 212-966-1522, E-mail: admissions@nyls.edu. *Dean and President*, Anthony W. Crowell, 212-431-2840, Fax: 212-219-3752, E-mail: acrowell@nyls.edu.

NEW YORK MEDICAL COLLEGE, Valhalla, NY 10595-1691

General Information Independent, coed, graduate-only institution. CGS member. *Enrollment by degree level:* 416 master's, 995 doctoral, 15 other advanced degrees. *Graduate faculty:* 1,399 full-time (576 women), 1,958 part-time/adjunct (738 women). *Tuition, area resident:* Full-time $44,355; part-time $1025 per credit. *Required fees:* $500; $95 per year. One-time fee: $140 part-time. Tuition and fees vary according to course load and program. *Graduate housing:* Rooms and/or apartments available on a first-come, first-served basis to single and married students. Typical cost: $10,800 per year for single students; $17,320 per year for married students. Room charges vary according to housing facility selected. Housing application deadline: 7/15. *Student services:* Campus employment opportunities, campus safety program, career counseling, exercise/wellness program, free psychological counseling, international student services, low-cost health insurance, multicultural affairs office, services for students with disabilities, teacher training, writing training. *Library:* Health Sciences Library plus 1 other. *Collection:* Books: 44,401 (physical), 146,161 (digital/electronic); Serial titles: 9 (physical), 16,663 (digital/electronic); Databases: 151. Weekly public service hours: 88; study areas open 24 hours, 5–7 days a week; students can reserve study rooms. *Research affiliation:* Weill Cornell Medical Center (cardiovascular disease), Duke University (neonatology), Tufts University (infectious diseases), Yale University (pediatric cardiology), Columbia University College of Physicians and Surgeons (neurosciences), Seattle Children's Hospital (pediatric pulmonary disease).

Computer facilities: 60 computers available on campus for general student use. A campuswide network can be accessed from student residence rooms.
Website: http://www.nymc.edu/

General Application Contact: Pamela Suett, Director of Recruitment, School of Health Sciences and Practice, 914-594-4510, Fax: 914-594-4292, E-mail: shsp_admissions@nymc.edu.

GRADUATE UNITS

Graduate School of Basic Medical Sciences ***Degree program information:*** Part-time and evening/weekend programs available. Part-time, evening/weekend. Offers basic medical sciences (MS, PhD); biochemistry and molecular biology (PhD); cell biology and anatomy (PhD); microbiology and immunology (MS); pathology (MS, PhD); pharmacology (PhD); physiology (MS). Electronic applications accepted.

School of Health Sciences and Practice Offers behavioral sciences and health promotion (MPH, Graduate Certificate); biostatistics (MS); emergency preparedness (Graduate Certificate); environmental health science (MPH); epidemiology (MPH); global health (Graduate Certificate); health education (Graduate Certificate); health policy and management (MPH, Dr PH, Graduate Certificate); health sciences and practice (MPH, MS, DPT, Dr PH, Graduate Certificate); industrial hygiene (Graduate Certificate); physical therapy (DPT); public health (Graduate Certificate); speech-language pathology (MS).

School of Medicine Students: 823 full-time (392 women); includes 349 minority (67 Black or African American, non-Hispanic/Latino; 173 Asian, non-Hispanic/Latino; 92 Hispanic/Latino; 17 Two or more races, non-Hispanic/Latino), 11 international. Average age 25. 13,235 applicants, 4% accepted, 202 enrolled. *Faculty:* 982 full-time (375 women), 1,269 part-time/adjunct (416 women). *Financial support:* In 2015–16, 417 students received support. Research assistantships, Federal Work-Study, institutionally sponsored loans, and scholarships/grants available. Financial award application deadline: 4/30; financial award applicants required to submit FAFSA. In 2015, 204 doctorates awarded. Offers medicine (MD). *Application deadline:* For fall admission, 1/31 for domestic and international students. Applications are processed on a rolling basis. *Application fee:* $120. Electronic applications accepted. *Application Contact:* Fern Juster, MD, Associate Dean of Admissions, 914-594-4507, Fax: 914-594-4613, E-mail: mdadmit@nymc.edu. *Senior Associate Dean for Medical Education*, Jennifer Koestler, MD, 914-594-4500, E-mail: jennifer_koestler@nymc.edu.

NEW YORK SCHOOL OF INTERIOR DESIGN, New York, NY 10021-5110

General Information Independent, coed, primarily women, comprehensive institution. *Enrollment:* 538 graduate, professional, and undergraduate students; 154 full-time matriculated graduate/professional students (129 women), 3 part-time matriculated graduate/professional students (2 women). *Enrollment by degree level:* 157 master's. *Graduate faculty:* 33 part-time/adjunct (15 women). *Tuition, area resident:* Full-time $31,400. *Required fees:* $750. *Graduate housing:* Room and/or apartments available on a first-come, first-served basis to single students; on-campus housing not available to married students. Typical cost: $15,910 per year. Housing application deadline: 5/1. *Student services:* Campus employment opportunities, career counseling, free psychological counseling, international student services, low-cost health insurance. *Research affiliation:* Metropolitan New York Library Council-Research Consortium.

Computer facilities: 135 computers available on campus for general student use. A campuswide network can be accessed from student residence rooms and from off campus. Online class registration is available.
Website: http://www.nysid.edu/

General Application Contact: Russell Kaplan, Admissions Administrator, 212-472-1500 Ext. 205, Fax: 212-472-1867, E-mail: rkaplan@nysid.edu.

GRADUATE UNITS

Program in Healthcare Interior Design Average age 31. *Financial support:* Applicants required to submit FAFSA. Offers healthcare interior design (MPS). *Application deadline:* For fall admission, 2/1 priority date for domestic and international students. *Application fee:* $60 ($100 for international students). Electronic applications accepted. *Application Contact:* Celeste Collins, Associate Director of Admissions, 212-472-1500 Ext. 206, Fax: 212-472-1867, E-mail: ccollins@nysid.edu. *Department Head*, Victor Dadras, 212-472-1500, Fax: 212-288-6577, E-mail: vdadras@nysid.edu.

Program in Interior Design (Post-Professional Level) Students: 21 full-time (14 women). Average age 27. 63 applicants, 43% accepted, 21 enrolled. *Faculty:* 1 (woman) full-time, 6 part-time/adjunct (1 woman). *Financial support:* Career-related internships or fieldwork, Federal Work-Study, institutionally sponsored loans, scholarships/grants, and unspecified assistantships available. Financial award application deadline: 8/1; financial award applicants required to submit FAFSA. Offers interior design (MFA). *Application deadline:* For fall admission, 2/1 priority date for domestic and international students. *Application fee:* $60 ($100 for international students). Electronic applications accepted. *Application Contact:* Celeste Collins, Associate Director of Admissions, 212-472-1500 Ext. 206, Fax: 212-472-1867, E-mail: ccollins@nysid.edu. *Director of MFA Programs*, Barbara Lowenthal, 212-472-1500 Ext. 467, Fax: 212-288-6577, E-mail: blowenthal@nysid.edu.

Program in Interior Design (Professional-Level) Students: 103 full-time (86 women), 1 (woman) part-time; includes 36 minority (4 Black or African American, non-Hispanic/Latino; 26 Asian, non-Hispanic/Latino; 5 Hispanic/Latino; 1 Two or more races, non-Hispanic/Latino), 7 international. Average age 28. 157 applicants, 33% accepted, 48 enrolled. *Faculty:* 4 full-time (1 woman), 26 part-time/adjunct (15 women). *Financial support:* Career-related internships or fieldwork, Federal Work-Study, institutionally sponsored loans, scholarships/grants, and unspecified assistantships available. Financial award application deadline: 8/1; financial award applicants required to submit FAFSA. Offers interior design (MFA). *Application deadline:* For fall admission, 2/1 for domestic and international students. *Application fee:* $60 ($100 for international students). Electronic applications accepted. *Application Contact:* Celeste Collins, Associate Director of Admissions, 212-472-1500 Ext. 206, Fax: 212-472-1867, E-mail: ccollins@nysid.edu. *Director of MFA Programs*, Barbara Lowenthal, 212-472-1500, Fax: 212-288-6577, E-mail: blowenthal@nysid.edu.

Program in Interior Lighting Design Students: 8 full-time (5 women); includes 1 minority (Hispanic/Latino). Average age 38. 25 applicants, 44% accepted, 8 enrolled. *Faculty:* 1 full-time (0 women), 5 part-time/adjunct (3 women). *Financial support:* Application deadline: 8/1; applicants required to submit FAFSA. Offers interior lighting design (MPS). *Application deadline:* For fall admission, 2/1 for domestic and international students. *Application fee:* $60 ($100 for international students). Electronic applications accepted. *Application Contact:* Celeste Collins, Associate Director of Admissions, 212-472-1500 Ext. 206, Fax: 212-472-1867, E-mail: ccollins@nysid.edu. *Director of MPS Programs*, John Katimaris, 212-472-1500, E-mail: john@johnkatimaris.com.

Program in Sustainable Interior Environments Students: 10 full-time (8 women); includes 5 minority (3 Asian, non-Hispanic/Latino; 2 Hispanic/Latino). Average age 27. 22 applicants, 50% accepted, 8 enrolled. *Faculty:* 1 full-time (0 women), 5 part-time/adjunct (2 women). *Financial support:* Federal Work-Study available. Financial award applicants required to submit FAFSA. In 2015, 9 master's awarded. Offers sustainable interior environments (MPS). *Application deadline:* For fall admission, 2/1 priority date for domestic and international students. Applications are processed on a rolling basis. *Application fee:* $60 ($100 for international students). Electronic applications accepted. *Application Contact:* Celeste Collins, Director of Admissions, 212-472-1500 Ext. 206, Fax: 212-472-1867, E-mail: ccollins@nysid.edu. *Director of MPS Programs*, Ethan Lu, 212-472-1500, Fax: 212-472-3500, E-mail: elu@nysid.edu.

NEW YORK STUDIO SCHOOL OF DRAWING, PAINTING AND SCULPTURE, New York, NY 10011

General Information Independent, coed, comprehensive institution.

GRADUATE UNITS

Certificate Program Offers studio art (Certificate).

MFA Program Offers painting (MFA); sculpture (MFA).

NEW YORK THEOLOGICAL SEMINARY, New York, NY 10115

General Information Independent-religious, coed, graduate-only institution. *Graduate housing:* On-campus housing not available. *Research affiliation:* Bellevue Hospital Center, Goldwater Memorial Hospital, Institutes of Religion and Health, Lutheran Medical Center, Postgraduate Center for Mental Health.

GRADUATE UNITS

Graduate and Professional Programs *Degree program information:* Part-time programs available. Part-time. Offers theology (M Div, MPS, MSW, D Min). MSW offered jointly with Fordham University.

NEW YORK UNIVERSITY, New York, NY 10012-1019

General Information Independent, coed, university. CGS member. *Graduate housing:* Room and/or apartments available on a first-come, first-served basis to single students; on-campus housing not available to married students. Housing application deadline: 5/1. *Research affiliation:* Center for the Study of Complex Malaria in India, National Institutes of Health (biology), Materials Research Science and Engineering Centers: Semantophoretic Assemblies, NSF (chemistry), Training in Systems and Integrative Neuroscience, National Institutes of Health (neural science), Research Network on Opening Governance, MacArthur Foundation (technology management and innovation), Assessment of Learning Outcomes and Social Effects in Community-Based Education in Afghanistan (human development and social change), Data Science Environments Program, Gordon and Betty Moore Foundation (data science).

GRADUATE UNITS

College of Dentistry Offers biomaterials science (MS); clinical research (MS); dentistry (MS, DDS, Advanced Certificate); endodontics (Advanced Certificate); oral and maxillofacial surgery (Advanced Certificate); orthodontics (Advanced Certificate); pediatric dentistry (Advanced Certificate); periodontics (Advanced Certificate); prosthodontics (Advanced Certificate). Electronic applications accepted.

College of Global Public Health *Degree program information:* Part-time programs available. Part-time, online learning. Offers biological basis of public health (PhD); community and international health (MPH); global health leadership (MPH); health systems and health services research (PhD); population and community health (PhD); public health nutrition (MPH); social and behavioral sciences (MPH); socio-behavioral health (PhD). Electronic applications accepted.

Gallatin School of Individualized Study *Degree program information:* Part-time and evening/weekend programs available. Part-time, evening/weekend. Offers individualized study (MA). Electronic applications accepted.

Graduate School of Arts and Science *Degree program information:* Part-time and evening/weekend programs available. Part-time, evening/weekend. Offers African diaspora (PhD); African history (PhD); Africana studies (MA); American studies (MA, PhD); anthropology (MA, PhD); anthropology and French studies (PhD); applied economic analysis (Advanced Certificate); archival management (Advanced Certificate); arts and science (MA, MFA, MS, PhD, Advanced Certificate); Atlantic history (PhD); bioethics (MA); biology (PhD); biomedical journalism (MS); cancer and molecular biology (PhD); chemistry (MS, PhD); classics (MA, PhD); cognition and perception (PhD); community psychology (PhD); comparative literature (MA, PhD); composition and theory (MA, PhD); computational biology (PhD); computers in biological research (MS); creative writing (MA, MFA); cultural reporting and criticism (MA); data science (MS); developmental genetics (PhD); early music performance (Advanced Certificate); East Asian studies (MA, PhD); economics (MA, PhD); English and American literature (MA, PhD); environmental health sciences (MS, PhD); ethnomusicology (MA, PhD); French studies and sociology (PhD); French studies/history (PhD); French studies/journalism (MA); general biology (MS); general psychology (MA); German studies and critical thought (MA, PhD); Hebrew and Judaic studies (MA, PhD); Hebrew and Judaic studies/history (PhD); Hebrew and Judaic studies/museum studies (MA); historical and sustainable architecture (MA); history (MA, PhD); humanities and social thought (MA); immunology and microbiology (PhD); industrial/organizational psychology (MA); Irish and Irish American studies (MA); Italian (MA, PhD); Italian studies (MA); journalism (MA); Latin American and Caribbean studies/journalism (MA); linguistics (MA, PhD); Middle Eastern history (MA); Middle Eastern studies/history (PhD); molecular genetics (PhD); museum studies (MA, Advanced Certificate); Near Eastern studies/journalism (MA); neurobiology (PhD); oral biology (MS); philosophy (MA, PhD); physics (MS, PhD); plant biology (PhD); poetics and theory (Advanced Certificate); political campaign management (MA); politics (MA, PhD); Portuguese (MA, PhD); psychotherapy and psychoanalysis (Advanced Certificate); public history (Advanced Certificate); recombinant DNA technology (MS); religion (Advanced Certificate); religious studies (MA); Russian literature (MA); science and environmental reporting (Advanced Certificate); Slavic literature (MA); social theory (Advanced Certificate); social/personality psychology (PhD); sociology (MA, PhD); Spanish (PhD); Spanish and Latin American literatures and cultures (MA); Spanish language and translation (MA); world history (MA). Electronic applications accepted.

Center for European Studies Offers European studies (MA). Electronic applications accepted.

Center for French Civilization and Culture ***Degree program information:*** Part-time and evening/weekend programs available. Part-time, evening/weekend. Offers French (PhD); French civilization (PhD); French civilization and culture (MA, PhD, Advanced Certificate); French language and civilization (MA); French literature (MA); French studies (MA, PhD, Advanced Certificate); French studies and anthropology (PhD); French studies and history (PhD); French studies and journalism (MA); French studies and sociology (PhD); Romance languages and literatures (MA).

Center for Latin American and Caribbean Studies ***Degree program information:*** Part-time programs available. Part-time. Offers Latin American and Caribbean studies (MA).

Center for Neural Science Offers neural science (PhD).

Courant Institute of Mathematical Sciences ***Degree program information:*** Part-time and evening/weekend programs available. Part-time, evening/weekend. Offers atmosphere ocean science and mathematics (PhD); computer science (MS, PhD); information systems (MS); mathematics (MS, PhD); mathematics and statistics/operations research (MS); mathematics in finance (MS); scientific computing (MS).

Hagop Kevorkian Center for Near Eastern Studies ***Degree program information:*** Part-time and evening/weekend programs available. Part-time, evening/weekend. Offers Middle Eastern and Islamic studies (MA, PhD); Middle Eastern and Islamic studies/history (PhD); Near Eastern studies (MA); Near Eastern studies/journalism (MA); Near Eastern studies/museum studies (MA).

Institute for Law and Society Offers law and society (MA, PhD).

Institute for the Study of the Ancient World Offers study of the ancient world (PhD). Electronic applications accepted.

Institute of Fine Arts ***Degree program information:*** Part-time programs available. Part-time. Offers architectural studies (PhD); art history and archaeology (MA, PhD); classical art and archaeology (PhD); curatorial studies (PhD); East and South Asian art (PhD); Near Eastern art and archaeology (PhD).

Leonard N. Stern School of Business *Degree program information:* Part-time and evening/weekend programs available. Part-time, evening/weekend. Offers accounting

(MBA, PhD); business (MBA, PhD); economics (MBA, PhD); entertainment, media and technology (MBA); finance (MBA, PhD); general marketing (MBA); information systems (MBA, PhD); management organizations (MBA); marketing (PhD); operations management (MBA, PhD); organization theory (PhD); organizational behavior (PhD); product management (MBA); statistics (MBA, PhD); strategy (PhD). Electronic applications accepted.

Polytechnic School of Engineering Offers applied physics (MS, PhD); bioinformatics (MS); biomedical engineering (MS, PhD); biotechnology (MS); biotechnology and entrepreneurship (MS); chemical engineering (MS, PhD); chemistry (MS); civil engineering (MS, PhD); computer engineering (MS, Certificate); computer science (MS, PhD); construction management (MS); cyber security (Graduate Certificate); electrical engineering (MS, PhD); electronic business management (Advanced Certificate); engineering (MS, PhD, Advanced Certificate, Certificate, Graduate Certificate); entrepreneurship (Advanced Certificate); environmental engineering (MS); environmental science (MS); financial engineering (MS, Advanced Certificate); financial technology management (Advanced Certificate); human resources management (Advanced Certificate); industrial engineering (MS); information management (Advanced Certificate); integrated digital media (MS, Graduate Certificate); management (MS); management of technology (MS); manufacturing engineering (MS); materials chemistry (PhD); mathematics (MS, PhD); mechanical engineering (MS, PhD); organizational behavior (MS); project management (Advanced Certificate); risk management (Advanced Certificate); software engineering (Graduate Certificate); systems engineering (MS); technology management (MBA, PhD, Advanced Certificate); telecommunications management (Advanced Certificate); transportation management (MS); transportation planning and engineering (MS, PhD); urban systems engineering and management (MS). Electronic applications accepted.

Robert F. Wagner Graduate School of Public Service ***Degree program information:*** Part-time programs available. Part-time. Offers global public policy and management (EMPA); health finance (MPA); health policy analysis (MPA); health services management (MPA); international health (MPA); public administration (PhD); public and nonprofit management and policy (MPA, Advanced Certificate); public service (EMPA, MPA, MUP, PhD, Advanced Certificate); urban planning (MUP). Electronic applications accepted.

Rory Meyers College of Nursing Students: 53 full-time (33 women), 650 part-time (566 women); includes 261 minority (73 Black or African American, non-Hispanic/Latino; 3 American Indian or Alaska Native, non-Hispanic/Latino; 126 Asian, non-Hispanic/Latino; 43 Hispanic/Latino; 3 Native Hawaiian or other Pacific Islander, non-Hispanic/Latino; 13 Two or more races, non-Hispanic/Latino), 29 international. Average age 37. 473 applicants, 66% accepted, 161 enrolled. *Faculty:* 58 full-time (56 women), 76 part-time/adjunct (65 women). *Financial support:* In 2015–16, 126 students received support, including 8 research assistantships with full tuition reimbursements available (averaging $26,330 per year); career-related internships or fieldwork, Federal Work-Study, and scholarships/grants also available. Support available to part-time students. Financial award application deadline: 3/1; financial award applicants required to submit FAFSA. In 2015, 198 master's, 19 doctorates, 5 other advanced degrees awarded. *Degree program information:* Part-time programs available. Part-time. Offers adult-gerontology acute care nurse practitioner (MS, Advanced Certificate); adult-gerontology primary care nurse practitioner (MS, Advanced Certificate); family nurse practitioner (MS, Advanced Certificate); gerontology nurse practitioner (Advanced Certificate); nurse-midwifery (MS, Advanced Certificate); nursing (MS, DNP, PhD, Advanced Certificate); nursing administration (MS, Advanced Certificate); nursing education (MS, Advanced Certificate); nursing informatics (MS, Advanced Certificate); pediatrics nurse practitioner (MS, Advanced Certificate); psychiatric-mental health nurse practitioner (MS, Advanced Certificate); research and theory development in nursing science (PhD). *Application deadline:* For fall admission, 6/15 for domestic and international students; for spring admission, 12/1 for domestic and international students; for summer admission, 3/1 for domestic and international students. *Application fee:* $80. Electronic applications accepted. *Application Contact:* Samantha Jaser, Assistant Director, Graduate Student Affairs and Admissions, 212-992-7653, Fax: 212-995-4302, E-mail: saj283@nyu.edu. *Senior Associate Dean for Academic Programs,* Dr. James Pace, 212-992-7343, E-mail: james.pace@nyu.edu.

School of Continuing and Professional Studies ***Degree program information:*** Part-time and evening/weekend programs available. Part-time, evening/weekend, online learning. Electronic applications accepted.

Center for Foreign Languages, Translation and Interpretation Degree program information: Part-time and evening/weekend programs available. Part-time, evening/weekend. Offers translation (MS). Electronic applications accepted.

Center for Global Affairs Degree program information: Part-time and evening/weekend programs available. Part-time, evening/weekend. Offers global affairs (MS); global energy (Advanced Certificate); peacebuilding (Advanced Certificate); transnational security (Advanced Certificate). Electronic applications accepted.

Center for Publishing Degree program information: Part-time and evening/weekend programs available. Part-time, evening/weekend. Offers digital and print media (MS). Electronic applications accepted.

Division of Humanities, Arts, and Writing Degree program information: Part-time and evening/weekend programs available. Part-time, evening/weekend, online learning. Offers professional writing (MS). Electronic applications accepted.

Division of Programs in Business Degree program information: Part-time and evening/weekend programs available. Part-time, evening/weekend, online learning. Offers benefits and compensation (Advanced Certificate); brand management (MS); core business competencies (Advanced Certificate); corporate and organizational communication (MS); database technologies (MS); digital marketing (MS); enterprise risk management (MS, Advanced Certificate); graphic communications management and technology (MA); human resource management (Advanced Certificate); human resource management and development (MS); information technologies (Advanced Certificate); integrated marketing (MS); interactive motion graphics and visual effects (MS); leadership and human capital management (MS, Advanced Certificate); management and systems (MS, Advanced Certificate); marketing analytics (MS); marketing and public relations (MS); organizational and executive coaching (Advanced Certificate); public relations management (MS); strategy and leadership (MS, Advanced Certificate); systems management (MS). Electronic applications accepted.

The George Heyman Jr. Center for Philanthropy and Fundraising Degree program information: Part-time and evening/weekend programs available. Part-time, evening/weekend. Offers fundraising and grantmaking (MS). Electronic applications accepted.

Schack Institute of Real Estate Degree program information: Part-time and evening/weekend programs available. Part-time, evening/weekend. Offers construction management (MS, Advanced Certificate); finance and investment (MS); global real estate (MS); real estate (MS, Advanced Certificate); real estate development (MS); real estate management (MS); sustainable development (MS); the business of development (MS). Electronic applications accepted.

Tisch Center for Hospitality and Tourism Degree program information: Part-time and evening/weekend programs available. Part-time, evening/weekend. Offers brand strategy (MS); hospitality industry studies (MS, Advanced Certificate); hotel finance (MS); lodging operations (MS); revenue management (MS); tourism management (MS, Advanced Certificate). Electronic applications accepted.

Tisch Institute for Sports Management, Media, and Business Degree program information: Part-time and evening/weekend programs available. Part-time, evening/weekend. Offers global sports media (MS); professional and collegiate sports operations (MS); sports business (Advanced Certificate); sports law (MS); sports marketing and sales (MS). Electronic applications accepted.

School of Law ***Degree program information:*** Part-time programs available. Part-time, online learning. Offers law (LL M, JD, JSD); law and business (Advanced Certificate); taxation (MSL, Advanced Certificate). Electronic applications accepted.

School of Medicine Offers medicine (MS, MD, PhD).

Sackler Institute of Graduate Biomedical Sciences Offers biomedical imaging (PhD); biomedical informatics (PhD); cellular and molecular biology (PhD); computational biology (PhD); developmental genetics (PhD); genome integrity (PhD); immunology (PhD); immunology and inflammation (PhD); microbiology (PhD); molecular biophysics (PhD); molecular oncology (PhD); molecular oncology and tumor immunology (PhD); molecular pharmacology (PhD); neuroscience and physiology (PhD); pathobiology and translational medicine (PhD); stem cell biology (PhD). Electronic applications accepted.

Silver School of Social Work ***Degree program information:*** Part-time and evening/weekend programs available. Part-time, evening/weekend. Offers social work (MSW, PhD). Electronic applications accepted.

Steinhardt School of Culture, Education, and Human Development ***Degree program information:*** Part-time programs available. Part-time. Offers advanced occupational therapy (MA); applied statistics for social science research (MS); art education (MA); art therapy (MA); art, education, and community practice (MA); bilingual education (MA, PhD, Advanced Certificate); business and workplace education (MA, Advanced Certificate); business education (MA, Advanced Certificate); childhood (MA); childhood education (MA); clinical nutrition (MS); clinically rich integrated science (MA); clinically-based English education, grades 7-12 (MA); communication sciences and disorders (MS, PhD); costume studies (MA); counseling (MA, PhD, Advanced Certificate); counseling and guidance (MA, Advanced Certificate); counseling for mental health and wellness (MA); counseling psychology (PhD); culture, education, and human development (MA, MFA, MM, MPH, MS, DPS, DPT, Ed D, PhD, Advanced Certificate, Post Master's Certificate, Postbaccalaureate Certificate); dance education (MA, Advanced Certificate); developmental psychology (PhD); digital media design for learning (MA, Advanced Certificate); drama therapy (MA); early childhood (MA); early childhood and childhood education (MA); early childhood education (MA); early childhood education/early childhood special education (MA); education and Jewish studies (MA, PhD); education policy (MA); educational and developmental psychology (MA, PhD); educational communication and technology (MA, MS, PhD, Advanced Certificate); educational leadership (MA, Ed D, PhD, Advanced Certificate); educational leadership, politics and advocacy (MA); educational theatre (MA, Ed D, PhD); educational theatre and English 7-12 (MA); educational theatre and social studies 7-12 (MA); educational theatre in colleges and communities (MA, Ed D, PhD); educational theatre, all grades (MA); English education (MA, PhD, Advanced Certificate); English education, grades 7-12 (MA); environmental conservation education (MA); food studies (MA, PhD); foreign language education (MA); games for learning (MS); higher and postsecondary education (PhD); higher education (MA, Ed D, PhD); higher education administration (Ed D); higher education and student affairs (MA); history of education (MA, PhD); human development and social intervention (MA); instrumental performance (MM); international education (MA, PhD, Advanced Certificate); LGBT health, education, and social services (Advanced Certificate); literacy education (MA); mathematics education (MA); media, culture and communication (MA, PhD); multilingual/multicultural studies (MA, PhD, Advanced Certificate); music business (MA); music education (MA); music performance and composition (MM, PhD, Advanced Certificate); music technology (MA, MM, PhD); music theatre (MM); music theory and composition (MM); music therapy (MA); nutrition and dietetics (MS, PhD); occupational therapy (MS, DPS); orthopedic physical therapy (Advanced Certificate); performing arts administration (MA); physical therapy (MA, DPT, PhD); piano performance (MM); psychology and social intervention (PhD); rehabilitation sciences (PhD); research in occupational therapy (PhD); school building leader (MA); school district leader (Advanced Certificate); social and cultural studies of education (MA); social studies education (MA); sociology of education (MA, PhD); special education (MA); studio art (MA, MFA, Advanced Certificate); teachers of art, all grades (MA); teaching and learning (Ed D, PhD); teaching art/social studies 7-12 (MA); teaching dance in the professions (MA); teaching dance, all grades (MA, Advanced Certificate); teaching English to speakers of other languages (MA, PhD); teaching foreign languages, 7-12 (MA); teaching French as a foreign language (MA); teaching social studies 7-12 (MA); teaching Spanish as a foreign language (MA); visual arts administration (MA); visual culture (MA); vocal pedagogy (Advanced Certificate); vocal performance (MM); workplace learning (Advanced Certificate). Electronic applications accepted.

Tisch School of the Arts Offers acting (MFA); arts (MA, MFA, MPS, PhD); arts politics (MA); dance (MFA); design for stage and film (MFA); dramatic writing (MFA); interactive telecommunications (MPS); moving image archiving and preservation (MA); musical theatre writing (MFA); performance studies (MA, PhD). Electronic applications accepted.

Game Center Offers game design (MFA).

Kanbar Institute of Film and Television Offers film and television (MFA). Electronic applications accepted.

NIAGARA UNIVERSITY, Niagara University, NY 14109

General Information Independent-religious, coed, comprehensive institution. *Enrollment:* 4,128 graduate, professional, and undergraduate students; 507 full-time matriculated graduate/professional students (320 women), 363 part-time matriculated graduate/professional students (266 women). *Enrollment by degree level:* 747 master's, 57 doctoral, 66 other advanced degrees. *Graduate faculty:* 58 full-time, 52 part-time/adjunct. Tuition and fees vary according to course load and program. *Graduate housing:* Room and/or apartments available to single students; on-campus housing not available to married students. Typical cost: $12,300 (including board). Room and board charges vary according to housing facility selected. Housing application deadline: 8/1. *Student services:* Campus employment opportunities, campus safety program, career counseling, exercise/wellness program, free psychological counseling, international student services, low-cost health insurance, multicultural affairs office, services for students with disabilities. *Library:* Our Lady of Angels Library plus 1 other. *Collection:* Books: 171,911 (physical), 322,812 (digital/electronic); Serial titles: 160 (physical), 31,384 (digital/electronic); Databases: 85. Weekly public service hours: 106; study areas open 24 hours, 5–7 days a week; students can reserve study rooms. *Research affiliation:* Roswell Park Memorial Institute.

Computer facilities: 81 computers available on campus for general student use. A campuswide network can be accessed from student residence rooms. Online class registration is available.
Website: http://www.niagara.edu/

General Application Contact: Evan Pierce, Associate Director for Academic Affairs, Graduate Studies, 716-286-8327, Fax: 716-286-8710, E-mail: epierce@niagara.edu.

GRADUATE UNITS

Graduate Division of Arts and Sciences Students: 34 full-time (15 women), 19 part-time (9 women); includes 10 minority (4 Black or African American, non-Hispanic/Latino; 5 Hispanic/Latino; 1 Two or more races, non-Hispanic/Latino), 17 international. Average age 30. *Faculty:* 5 full-time (all women). *Financial support:* Research assistantships with tuition reimbursements, teaching assistantships with tuition reimbursements, career-related internships or fieldwork, Federal Work-Study, scholarships/grants, and unspecified assistantships available. Support available to part-time students. Financial award application deadline: 4/15; financial award applicants required to submit FAFSA. In 2015, 24 master's awarded. *Degree program information:* Part-time and evening/weekend programs available. Part-time, evening/weekend. Offers criminal justice (MS); criminal justice administration (MS); interdisciplinary studies (MA). *Application deadline:* For fall admission, 8/1 for domestic students. Applications are processed on a rolling basis. *Application fee:* $30. *Application Contact:* Evan Pierce, Associate Dean for Graduate Recruitment, 716-286-8769, Fax: 716-286-8170. *Dean*, Dr. Timothy Ireland, 716-286-8060, Fax: 716-286-8061, E-mail: toi@niagara.edu.

Graduate Division of Business Administration Students: 183 full-time (79 women), 63 part-time (37 women); includes 22 minority (6 Black or African American, non-Hispanic/Latino; 1 American Indian or Alaska Native, non-Hispanic/Latino; 8 Asian, non-Hispanic/Latino; 4 Hispanic/Latino; 3 Two or more races, non-Hispanic/Latino), 83 international. Average age 27. *Faculty:* 25 full-time (7 women). *Financial support:* Fellowships, research assistantships, career-related internships or fieldwork, and Federal Work-Study available. Support available to part-time students. Financial award application deadline: 4/15; financial award applicants required to submit FAFSA. In 2015, 106 master's awarded. *Degree program information:* Part-time and evening/weekend programs available. Part-time, evening/weekend. Offers accounting (MBA); business administration (MBA); finance (MBA, MS); financial planning (MBA); healthcare administration (MBA, MHA); human resources (MBA); international management (MBA); professional accountancy (MBA); strategic management (MBA); strategic marketing management (MBA); strategic wealth management (MBA). *Application deadline:* For fall admission, 8/1 for domestic students; for spring admission, 11/1 for domestic students. Applications are processed on a rolling basis. *Application fee:* $30. Electronic applications accepted. *Application Contact:* Evan Pierce, Associate Director for Graduate Recruitment, 716-286-8769, Fax: 716-286-8170, E-mail: epierce@niagara.edu. *MBA Director/Chair of the Marketing Department*, Dr. Paul Richardson, 716-286-8169, Fax: 716-286-8206, E-mail: psr@niagara.edu.

Graduate Division of Education Students: 245 full-time (201 women), 259 part-time (208 women); includes 49 minority (23 Black or African American, non-Hispanic/Latino; 1 American Indian or Alaska Native, non-Hispanic/Latino; 2 Asian, non-Hispanic/Latino; 15 Hispanic/Latino; 1 Native Hawaiian or other Pacific Islander, non-Hispanic/Latino; 7 Two or more races, non-Hispanic/Latino), 75 international. Average age 29. *Faculty:* 30 full-time (16 women), 19 part-time/adjunct (0 women). *Financial support:* Research assistantships with tuition reimbursements, teaching assistantships with tuition reimbursements, career-related internships or fieldwork, Federal Work-Study, scholarships/grants, and unspecified assistantships available. Financial award application deadline: 4/15; financial award applicants required to submit FAFSA. In 2015, 161 master's, 5 doctorates, 45 other advanced degrees awarded. *Degree program information:* Part-time and evening/weekend programs available. Part-time, evening/weekend. Offers early childhood and childhood education (MS Ed, Certificate); educational leadership (MS Ed, PhD, Certificate); foundations of teaching (MS Ed); foundations of teaching math, science, and technology education (MA); leadership and policy (PhD); literacy instruction (MS Ed); mental health counseling (MS, Certificate); middle and adolescence education (MS Ed, Certificate); school administration/supervision (MS Ed); school building leader (MS Ed, Certificate); school business administration (MS Ed); school counseling (MS Ed, Certificate); school district business leader (Certificate); school district leader (MS Ed, Certificate); school psychology (MS, Certificate); special education (grades 1-12) (MS Ed, Certificate); teacher education (MS Ed, Certificate); teaching English to speakers of other languages (MS Ed, Certificate). *Application deadline:* For fall admission, 8/1 for domestic students. Applications are processed on a rolling basis. *Application fee:* $30. *Application Contact:* Evan Pierce, Associate Director for Graduate Recruitment, 716-286-8769, Fax: 716-286-8170, E-mail: epierce@niagara.edu. *Interim Dean*, Dr. Chandra Foote, 716-286-8549, Fax: 716-286-8561, E-mail: cjf@niagara.edu.

NICHOLLS STATE UNIVERSITY, Thibodaux, LA 70310

General Information State-supported, coed, comprehensive institution. *Graduate housing:* Rooms and/or apartments available on a first-come, first-served basis to single and married students. Housing application deadline: 4/15.

GRADUATE UNITS

Graduate Studies ***Financial support:*** Research assistantships with full tuition reimbursements, teaching assistantships with full tuition reimbursements, and unspecified assistantships available. Support available to part-time students. *Degree program information:* Part-time and evening/weekend programs available. Part-time, evening/weekend, online learning. *Application deadline:* For fall admission, 8/1 priority date for domestic students, 7/1 priority date for international students; for spring admission, 12/1 priority date for domestic students, 11/1 priority date for international students. Applications are processed on a rolling basis. *Application fee:* $20 ($30 for international students).

College of Arts and Sciences Degree program information: Part-time and evening/weekend programs available. Part-time, evening/weekend. Offers arts and sciences (MS); marine and environmental biology (MS). Electronic applications accepted.

College of Business Administration Financial support: Research assistantships with full tuition reimbursements and unspecified assistantships available. Financial award application deadline: 6/1. *Degree program information:* Part-time and evening/weekend programs available. Part-time, evening/weekend. Offers business administration (MBA). *Application deadline:* For fall admission, 8/1 priority date for domestic students, 7/1 priority date for international students; for spring admission, 12/1 priority date for domestic students, 11/1 priority date for international students. Applications are processed on a rolling basis. *Application fee:* $20 ($30 for international students). Electronic applications accepted.

College of Education Financial support: Research assistantships with full tuition reimbursements and teaching assistantships with full tuition reimbursements available. Financial award application deadline: 6/17. *Degree program information:* Part-time and evening/weekend programs available. Part-time, evening/weekend. Offers clinical mental health counseling (MA); curriculum and instruction (M Ed); education (M Ed, MA, MAT, SSP); educational leadership (M Ed); elementary education (MAT); human performance education (MAT); middle school education (MAT); school counseling (M Ed); school psychology (SSP); secondary education (MAT). *Application deadline:* For fall admission, 8/1 priority date for domestic students, 7/1 for international students; for spring admission, 12/1 priority date for domestic students, 11/1 for international students. Applications are processed on a rolling basis. *Application fee:* $20 ($30 for international students). Electronic applications accepted.

College of Nursing and Allied Health Offers family nurse practitioner (MSN); nurse executive (MSN); nursing education (MSN); psychiatric/mental health nurse practitioner (MSN).

NICHOLS COLLEGE, Dudley, MA 01571-5000

General Information Independent, coed, comprehensive institution. *Graduate housing:* On-campus housing not available.

GRADUATE UNITS

Graduate and Professional Studies ***Degree program information:*** Part-time and evening/weekend programs available. Part-time, evening/weekend, online learning. Offers business administration (MBA); organizational leadership (MSOL). Electronic applications accepted.

NIPISSING UNIVERSITY, North Bay, ON P1B 8L7, Canada

General Information Province-supported, coed, comprehensive institution. *Graduate housing:* Room and/or apartments available to single students; on-campus housing not available to married students. Housing application deadline: 6/13. *Research affiliation:* Canada Space Agency (CSA) and MacDonald, Dettwiler and Associates Ltd. (MDA–RADARSAT-2) (remote sensing), Education Quality and Accountability Office (EQAO) (assessing educational quality), Ontario Association of Deans of Education (OADE) (assessing pre-service practicum processes), Tembec (forestry restoration), Metals in the Human Environment Research Network (MITHE-RN) (assessing environmental pollutants on aquatic ecosystems).

GRADUATE UNITS

Faculty of Education ***Degree program information:*** Part-time and evening/weekend programs available. Part-time, evening/weekend. Offers education (M Ed, Certificate).

NORFOLK STATE UNIVERSITY, Norfolk, VA 23504

General Information State-supported, coed, comprehensive institution. CGS member. *Graduate housing:* Room and/or apartments available to single students; on-campus housing not available to married students. Housing application deadline: 3/1. *Research affiliation:* Department of Energy/NASA (fundamental and applied research studies), NASA-Langley Research Center (NASA interests, aerospace applications, lidar application), National Science Foundation (fundamental and applied research studies), Department of Education (Title III projects, No Child Left Behind Initiative), University of Virginia's Integrative Graduate Education and Research Traineeship (IGERT) (science and engineering interactions with matter), Applied Research Center (technology transfer).

GRADUATE UNITS

School of Graduate Studies ***Degree program information:*** Part-time programs available. Part-time. Electronic applications accepted.

School of Education Degree program information: Part-time programs available. Part-time. Offers early childhood education (MAT); education (MA, MAT); pre-elementary education (MA); principal preparation (MA); secondary education (MAT); severe disabilities (MA); teaching (MA); urban education/administration (MA).

School of Liberal Arts Degree program information: Part-time programs available. Part-time. Offers community/clinical psychology (MA); criminal justice (MA); liberal arts (MA, MFA, MM, Psy D); media and communication (MA); music (MM); music education (MM); performance (MM); psychology (Psy D); theory and composition (MM); urban affairs (MA); visual studies (MA, MFA).

School of Science and Technology Offers computer science (MS); electronics engineering (MS); materials science (MS); optical engineering (MS); science and technology (MS).

School of Social Work Degree program information: Part-time programs available. Part-time. Offers social work (MSW, PhD).

NORTH AMERICAN UNIVERSITY, Houston, TX 77038

General Information Independent, coed, comprehensive institution.

GRADUATE UNITS

Program in Educational Leadership Offers educational leadership (M Ed).

NORTH CAROLINA AGRICULTURAL AND TECHNICAL STATE UNIVERSITY, Greensboro, NC 27411

General Information State-supported, coed, university. CGS member. *Graduate housing:* Room and/or apartments available on a first-come, first-served basis to single students; on-campus housing not available to married students. Housing application deadline: 5/8. *Research affiliation:* North Carolina Biotechnology Research Center (biotechnology), Boeing Company (aerospace engineering), Northrop Grumman Corporation (high performance computing), Research Triangle Institute (environmental protection, advanced technology), Rockwell, Inc. (avionics technology, communications technology), Honeywell (industrial automation control).

GRADUATE UNITS

School of Graduate Studies ***Degree program information:*** Part-time and evening/weekend programs available. Part-time, evening/weekend. Electronic applications accepted.

College of Arts and Sciences Degree program information: Part-time and evening/weekend programs available. Part-time, evening/weekend. Offers applied mathematics (MS); arts and sciences (MA, MAT, MS, MSW); biology (MS); biology education (MAT); chemistry (MS, PhD); computational sciences (MS); English (MA); English and African-American literature (MA); English education (MAT, MS); physics (MS); sociology and social work (MSW).

College of Engineering Degree program information: Part-time programs available. Part-time. Offers bioengineering (MS); biological engineering (MS); chemical engineering (MS); civil engineering (MSCE); computer science (MSCS); electrical engineering (MSEE, PhD); engineering (MS, MSCE, MSCS, MSE, MSEE, MSIE, MSME, PhD); industrial engineering (MSIE, PhD); mechanical engineering (MSME, PhD).

School of Agriculture and Environmental Sciences Degree program information: Part-time and evening/weekend programs available. Part-time, evening/weekend. Offers agricultural economics (MS); agricultural education (MS); agriculture and environmental sciences (MAT, MS); animal health science (MS); child development early education and family studies (MAT); family and consumer sciences (MAT); food and nutrition (MS); plant, soil and environmental science (MS).

School of Business and Economics Offers accounting (MBA); business education (MAT); human resources management (MBA); supply chain systems (MBA).

School of Education Degree program information: Part-time and evening/weekend programs available. Part-time, evening/weekend. Offers adult education (MS); counseling (MS); education (MA Ed, MAT, MS); elementary education (MA Ed); instructional technology (MS); physical education (MAT, MS); reading education (MA Ed); school administration (MS); teaching (MAT).

School of Technology Degree program information: Part-time and evening/weekend programs available. Part-time, evening/weekend. Offers construction management (MSTM); electronics and computer technology (MSIT, MSTM); environmental and occupational safety (MSTM); graphic communication systems (MSTM); information technology (MSIT, MSTM); manufacturing (MSTM); occupational safety and health (MSTM); technology (MAT, MSIT, MSTM); technology education (MAT).

NORTH CAROLINA CENTRAL UNIVERSITY, Durham, NC 27707-3129

General Information State-supported, coed, comprehensive institution. CGS member. *Graduate housing:* Room and/or apartments available on a first-come, first-served basis to single students; on-campus housing not available to married students. Housing application deadline: 7/1.

GRADUATE UNITS

College of Behavioral and Social Sciences Offers athletic administration (MS); behavioral and social sciences (MA, MPA, MS); criminal justice (MS); physical education (MS); psychology (MA); public administration (MPA); recreation administration (MS); therapeutic recreation (MS).

College of Liberal Arts ***Financial support:*** Fellowships, research assistantships, teaching assistantships, career-related internships or fieldwork, Federal Work-Study, institutionally sponsored loans, and scholarships/grants available. Support available to part-time students. Financial award application deadline: 5/1. *Degree program information:* Part-time and evening/weekend programs available. Part-time, evening/weekend. Offers English (MA); history (MA); jazz studies (MM); liberal arts (MA, MM). *Application deadline:* For fall admission, 8/1 for domestic students. *Application fee:* $30.

College of Science and Technology Offers applied mathematics (MS); biology (MS); chemistry (MS); earth sciences (MS); mathematics education (MS); physics (MS); pure mathematics (MS); science and technology (MS).

School of Business ***Financial support:*** Teaching assistantships, Federal Work-Study, institutionally sponsored loans, and unspecified assistantships available. Support available to part-time students. Financial award application deadline: 5/1; financial award applicants required to submit FAFSA. *Degree program information:* Part-time and evening/weekend programs available. Part-time, evening/weekend. Offers business (MBA). *Application deadline:* For fall admission, 8/1 for domestic students. *Application fee:* $30.

School of Education ***Financial support:*** Fellowships, research assistantships, teaching assistantships, career-related internships or fieldwork, Federal Work-Study, institutionally sponsored loans, and scholarships/grants available. Support available to part-time students. Financial award application deadline: 5/1. *Degree program information:* Part-time and evening/weekend programs available. Part-time, evening/weekend. Offers career counseling (MA); communication disorders (M Ed); education (M Ed, MA, MSA); educational technology (MA); instructional technology (M Ed); school administration (MSA); school counseling (MA); special education (M Ed). *Application deadline:* For fall admission, 8/1 for domestic students. *Application fee:* $30.

School of Law ***Financial support:*** Career-related internships or fieldwork, Federal Work-Study, and institutionally sponsored loans available. Support available to part-time students. Financial award application deadline: 5/1; financial award applicants required to submit FAFSA. *Degree program information:* Part-time and evening/weekend programs available. Part-time, evening/weekend. Offers law (JD). *Application deadline:* For fall admission, 4/15 for domestic students. *Application fee:* $30.

School of Library and Information Sciences ***Financial support:*** Fellowships, research assistantships, career-related internships or fieldwork, institutionally sponsored loans, scholarships/grants, and unspecified assistantships available. Support available to part-time students. Financial award application deadline: 5/1; financial award applicants required to submit FAFSA. *Degree program information:* Part-time and evening/weekend programs available. Part-time, evening/weekend. Offers library and information sciences (MIS, MLS). *Application deadline:* For fall admission, 8/1 for domestic students. *Application fee:* $30.

NORTH CAROLINA STATE UNIVERSITY, Raleigh, NC 27695

General Information State-supported, coed, university. CGS member. *Graduate housing:* Rooms and/or apartments available on a first-come, first-served basis to single and married students. *Research affiliation:* Triangle Universities Nuclear Laboratory, Research Triangle Institute, Highlands Biological Station, National Humanities Center, Microelectronics Center of North Carolina, North Carolina–Japan Center.

GRADUATE UNITS

College of Veterinary Medicine ***Degree program information:*** Part-time programs available. Part-time. Offers cell biology (MS, PhD); infectious disease (MS, PhD); pathology (MS, PhD); pharmacology (MS, PhD); population medicine (MS, PhD); specialized veterinary medicine (MSpVM); veterinary medicine (MS, MSpVM, MVPH, DVM, PhD); veterinary public health (MVPH). Electronic applications accepted.

Graduate School ***Degree program information:*** Part-time and evening/weekend programs available. Part-time, evening/weekend, online learning. Electronic applications accepted.

College of Agriculture and Life Sciences Degree program information: Part-time programs available. Part-time. Offers agricultural and extension education (Ed D); agricultural and resource economics (MS); agricultural education (MAE, MS, Certificate); agriculture and life sciences (M Tox, MAE, MB, MBAE, MFG, MFM, MFS, MG, MMB, MN, MP, MS, MZS, Ed D, PhD, Certificate); animal and poultry science (PhD); animal science (MS); biochemistry (PhD); bioinformatics (MB, PhD); biological and agricultural engineering (MBAE, MS, PhD, Certificate); crop science (MS, PhD); entomology (MS, PhD); environmental and molecular toxicology (M Tox, MS, PhD); extension education (MS); financial mathematics (MFM); food science (MFS, MS, PhD); functional genomics (MFG, MS, PhD); genetics (MG, MS, PhD); genomic sciences (MS, PhD); horticultural science (MS, PhD, Certificate); immunology (MS, PhD); microbial biotechnology (MMB); microbiology (MMB, MS, PhD); nutrition (MN, MS, PhD); physiology (MP, MS, PhD); plant biology (MS, PhD); plant pathology (MS, PhD); poultry science (MS); soil science (MS, PhD); zoology (MS, MZS, PhD). Electronic applications accepted.

College of Design Degree program information: Part-time programs available. Part-time. Offers architecture (M Arch); art and design (MAD); design (M Arch, MAD, MGD, MID, MLA, PhD); graphic design (MGD); industrial design (MID); landscape architecture (MLA). Electronic applications accepted.

College of Education Degree program information: Part-time programs available. Part-time. Offers adult and community college education (M Ed, MS, Ed D); agency counseling (M Ed, MS); business and marketing education (M Ed, MS); counselor education (M Ed, MS, PhD); curriculum and instruction (M Ed, MS, PhD); education (M Ed, MS, MS Ed, MSA, Ed D, PhD, Certificate); educational administration and supervision (Ed D); educational research and policy analysis (PhD); elementary education (M Ed); higher education administration (M Ed, MS, Ed D); human resource development (MS); instructional technology (M Ed, MS); mathematics education (M Ed, MS, PhD); middle grades education (M Ed, MS); school administration (MSA); science education (M Ed, MS, PhD); secondary English education (M Ed, MS Ed); social studies education (M Ed); special education (M Ed, MS); technology education (M Ed, MS, Ed D); training and development (M Ed, Ed D, Certificate). Electronic applications accepted.

College of Engineering Degree program information: Part-time programs available. Part-time. Offers aerospace engineering (MS, PhD); biomedical engineering (MS, PhD); chemical engineering (M Ch E, MS, PhD); civil engineering (MCE, MS, PhD); computer engineering (MS, PhD); computer networking (MS); computer science (MC Sc, MS, PhD); electrical engineering (MS, PhD); engineering (M Ch E, M Eng, MC Sc, MCE, MIE, MIMS, MMSE, MNE, MOR, MS, PhD); industrial engineering (MIE, MS, PhD); integrated manufacturing systems engineering (MIMS); materials science and engineering (MMSE, MS, PhD); mechanical engineering (MS, PhD); nuclear engineering (MNE, MS, PhD); operations research (MOR, MS, PhD). Electronic applications accepted.

College of Humanities and Social Sciences Degree program information: Part-time and evening/weekend programs available. Part-time, evening/weekend. Offers anthropology (MA); bioarchaeology (MA); communication (MS); communication, rhetoric, and digital media (PhD); creative writing (MFA); cultural anthropology (MA); developmental psychology (PhD); English (MA); environmental anthropology (MA); ergonomics and experimental psychology (PhD); French language and literature (MA); history (MA); humanities and social sciences (M Soc, MA, MFA, MIS, MPA, MS, MSW, PhD, Certificate); industrial/organizational psychology (PhD); international studies (MIS); liberal studies (MA); nonprofit management (Certificate); psychology in the public interest (PhD); public administration (MPA, PhD); public history (MA); school psychology (PhD); social work (MSW); sociology (M Soc, MS, PhD); Spanish language and literature (MA); technical communication (MS). Electronic applications accepted.

College of Natural Resources Degree program information: Part-time programs available. Part-time. Offers fisheries and wildlife sciences (MFWS, MS, PhD); forestry and environmental resources (MF, MS, PhD); natural resource management (MPRTM, MS); natural resources (MF, MFWS, MNR, MPRTM, MS, MWPS, PhD); park and recreation management (MPRTM, MS); parks, recreation and tourism management (PhD); recreational sport management (MPRTM, MS); spatial information science (MPRTM, MS); tourism policy and development (MPRTM, MS); wood and paper science (MS, MWPS, PhD). Electronic applications accepted.

College of Physical and Mathematical Sciences Degree program information: Part-time programs available. Part-time. Offers applied mathematics (MS, PhD); biomathematics (M Biomath, MS, PhD); chemistry (MS, PhD); marine, earth, and atmospheric sciences (MS, PhD); mathematics (MS, PhD); meteorology (MS, PhD); oceanography (MS, PhD); physical and mathematical sciences (M Biomath, M Stat, MS, PhD); physics (MS, PhD); statistics (M Stat, MS, PhD). Electronic applications accepted.

College of Textiles Degree program information: Part-time and evening/weekend programs available. Part-time, evening/weekend, online learning. Offers fiber and polymer science (PhD); textile and apparel technology and management (MS, MT); textile chemistry (MS); textile engineering (MS); textile technology management (PhD); textiles (MS, MT, PhD). Electronic applications accepted.

Institute for Advanced Analytics Offers analytics (MS). Electronic applications accepted.

Poole College of Management Degree program information: Part-time programs available. Part-time. Offers accounting (MAC); biosciences management (MBA); economics (M Econ, MA, PhD); entrepreneurship and technology commercialization (MBA); financial management (MBA); innovation management (MBA); management (M Econ, MA, MAC, MBA, MS, PhD); marketing management (MBA); services management (MBA); supply chain management (MBA). Electronic applications accepted.

NORTH CENTRAL COLLEGE, Naperville, IL 60566-7063

General Information Independent-religious, coed, comprehensive institution. CGS member. *Enrollment:* 2,962 graduate, professional, and undergraduate students; 85 full-time matriculated graduate/professional students (45 women), 144 part-time matriculated graduate/professional students (81 women). *Enrollment by degree level:* 229 master's. *Graduate faculty:* 26 full-time (10 women), 25 part-time/adjunct (9 women). *Tuition, area resident:* Full-time $19,800; part-time $825 per credit hour. *Graduate housing:* Room and/or apartments available on a first-come, first-served basis to single students; on-campus housing not available to married students. Typical cost: $6999 per year ($10,089 including board). *Student services:* Campus employment opportunities, campus safety program, career counseling, free psychological counseling, international student services, multicultural affairs office, services for students with disabilities, teacher training, writing training. *Library:* Oesterle Library. *Collection:* Books: 127,514 (physical), 51,983 (digital/electronic); Databases: 129.

Computer facilities: 360 computers available on campus for general student use. A campuswide network can be accessed from student residence rooms and from off campus. Online class registration, software packages are available.
Website: http://www.northcentralcollege.edu/

General Application Contact: Wendy Kulpinski, Director of Graduate Admission, 630-637-5808, Fax: 630-637-5819, E-mail: wekulpinski@noctrl.edu.

GRADUATE UNITS

Graduate Programs Students: 85 full-time (45 women), 144 part-time (81 women); includes 38 minority (9 Black or African American, non-Hispanic/Latino; 4 Asian, non-Hispanic/Latino; 23 Hispanic/Latino; 2 Two or more races, non-Hispanic/Latino), 8 international. Average age 30. 223 applicants, 61% accepted, 78 enrolled. *Faculty:* 26 full-time (10 women), 25 part-time/adjunct (9 women). *Financial support:* Unspecified assistantships available. Support available to part-time students. Financial award applicants required to submit FAFSA. In 2015, 101 master's awarded. *Degree program information:* Part-time and evening/weekend programs available. Part-time, evening/weekend. Offers business administration (MBA, MIBA); change management (MBA); culture and society (MALS); curriculum and instruction (MA Ed); ethics and public service (MALS); finance (MBA); higher education leadership (MLD); human resource management (MBA); international business administration (MIBA); leadership and administration (MA Ed); management (MBA); marketing (MBA); professional leadership (MLD); social entrepreneurship (MLD); sports leadership (MLD); Web and Internet applications (MS); writing, editing, and publishing (MALS). *Application deadline:* For fall admission, 8/15 for domestic students, 7/15 for international students; for winter admission, 12/1 for domestic students, 11/1 for international students; for spring admission, 2/1 for domestic students, 12/1 for international students. Applications are processed on a rolling basis. *Application fee:* $25. Electronic applications accepted. *Application Contact:* Wendy Kulpinski, Director of Graduate and Professional Studies Admission, 630-637-5808, Fax: 630-637-5819, E-mail: wekulpinski@noctrl.edu. *Dean of Graduate and Professional Studies*, Dr. Pamela Monaco, 630-637-5384, Fax: 630-637-5844, E-mail: pjmonaco@noctrl.edu.

NORTHCENTRAL UNIVERSITY, Scottsdale, AZ 85255

General Information Proprietary, coed, upper-level institution. CGS member. *Enrollment:* 11,029 graduate, professional, and undergraduate students; 5,279 full-time matriculated graduate/professional students (3,209 women), 5,582 part-time matriculated graduate/professional students (3,878 women). *Enrollment by degree level:* 3,510 master's, 6,921 doctoral, 430 other advanced degrees. *Graduate faculty:* 87 full-time (56 women), 361 part-time/adjunct (187 women). *Tuition, area resident:* Full-time $16,821; part-time $935 per credit hour. One-time fee: $350. *Student services:* Career counseling, services for students with disabilities. *Library:* Northcentral University Library (Virtual). *Research affiliation:* Coalition for Research to Practice (mental health services; aligning academic training with workforce demands).

Computer facilities: Online class registration is available.
Website: http://www.ncu.edu/

General Application Contact: Enrollment Advisor, Enrollment Advisor, 866-776-0331, Fax: 928-541-7817, E-mail: admissions@ncu.edu.

GRADUATE UNITS

Graduate Studies Students: 5,279 full-time (3,209 women), 5,582 part-time (3,878 women); includes 3,754 minority (2,446 Black or African American, non-Hispanic/Latino; 74 American Indian or Alaska Native, non-Hispanic/Latino; 228 Asian, non-Hispanic/Latino; 615 Hispanic/Latino; 46 Native Hawaiian or other Pacific Islander, non-Hispanic/Latino; 345 Two or more races, non-Hispanic/Latino). Average age 46. *Faculty:* 87 full-time (56 women), 361 part-time/adjunct (187 women). *Financial support:* Scholarships/grants available. In 2015, 799 master's, 399 doctorates, 230 other advanced degrees awarded. *Degree program information:* Part-time and evening/weekend programs available. Part-time, evening/weekend, online only, 100% online. Offers business (MBA, DBA, PhD, Postbaccalaureate Certificate); education (M Ed, Ed D, PhD, Ed S, Post-Master's Certificate, Postbaccalaureate Certificate); marriage and family therapy (MA, PhD, Post-Master's Certificate, Postbaccalaureate Certificate); psychology (MA, PhD, Post-Master's Certificate, Postbaccalaureate Certificate). *Application deadline:* Applications are processed on a rolling basis. *Application fee:* $0. Electronic applications accepted. *Application Contact:* Ken Boutelle, Vice President, Enrollment Services, 888-628-4979, E-mail: enrollmentservices@ncu.edu. *Acting Provost*, Dr. David Harpool, 888-327-2877 Ext. 8181, E-mail: provost@ncu.edu.

NORTH DAKOTA STATE UNIVERSITY, Fargo, ND 58102

General Information State-supported, coed, university. CGS member. *Enrollment:* 14,516 graduate, professional, and undergraduate students; 672 full-time matriculated graduate/professional students (328 women), 1,466 part-time matriculated graduate/professional students (720 women). *Enrollment by degree level:* 1,186 master's, 731 doctoral, 10 other advanced degrees. *Graduate faculty:* 441 full-time (151 women), 35 part-time/adjunct (12 women). *Graduate housing:* Rooms and/or apartments available on a first-come, first-served basis to single and married students. *Student services:* Campus employment opportunities, career counseling, child daycare facilities, exercise/wellness program, free psychological counseling, international student services, low-cost health insurance, multicultural affairs office, services for students with disabilities. *Library:* North Dakota State University Library plus 4 others. Students can reserve study rooms. *Research affiliation:* U.S. Department of Agriculture (USDA)-Metabolism and Radiation Laboratory.

Computer facilities: Computer purchase and lease plans are available. 601 computers available on campus for general student use. A campuswide network can be accessed from student residence rooms. Online class registration, online course content (e.g., learning management system, lecture capture video recordings) are available.
Website: http://www.ndsu.edu/

General Application Contact: Elizabeth Worth, Student Recruitment Coordinator, 701-231-8476, Fax: 701-231-6524, E-mail: elizabeth.worth@ndsu.edu.

GRADUATE UNITS

College of Graduate and Interdisciplinary Studies Students: 672 full-time (328 women), 1,466 part-time (720 women); includes 151 minority (35 Black or African American, non-Hispanic/Latino; 19 American Indian or Alaska Native, non-Hispanic/Latino; 45 Asian, non-Hispanic/Latino; 30 Hispanic/Latino; 2 Native Hawaiian or other Pacific Islander, non-Hispanic/Latino; 20 Two or more races, non-Hispanic/Latino), 629 international. Average age 31. 1,836 applicants, 49% accepted, 675 enrolled. *Faculty:* 445 full-time (151 women), 34 part-time/adjunct (11 women). *Financial support:* Fellowships with full tuition reimbursements, research assistantships with full tuition reimbursements, teaching assistantships with full tuition reimbursements, career-related internships or fieldwork, Federal Work-Study, institutionally sponsored loans, scholarships/grants, traineeships, tuition waivers (full and partial), and unspecified assistantships available. Support available to part-time students. Financial award applicants required to submit FAFSA. In 2015, 435 master's, 123 doctorates, 85 other advanced degrees awarded. *Degree program information:* Part-time and evening/weekend programs available. Part-time, evening/weekend, 100% online, blended/hybrid learning. Offers cellular and molecular biology (PhD); college teaching (Certificate); environmental and conservation sciences (MS, PhD); food protection (Certificate); food safety (MS, PhD); genomics and bioinformatics (MS, PhD); managerial logistics (MML); materials and nanotechnology (MS, PhD); science, technology, engineering, and mathematics education (PhD); transportation and logistics (PhD); transportation and urban systems (MS). *Application fee:* $35. Electronic applications accepted. *Application Contact:* Elizabeth Worth, Student Recruitment Coordinator, 701-231-8476, Fax: 701-231-6524, E-mail: elizabeth.worth@ndsu.edu. *Dean*, Dr. Claudia Tomany, 701-231-7033, Fax: 701-231-6524.

College of Agriculture, Food Systems, and Natural Resources Financial support: Fellowships with full tuition reimbursements, research assistantships with full tuition reimbursements, teaching assistantships with full tuition reimbursements, career-related internships or fieldwork, Federal Work-Study, and institutionally sponsored loans available. Support available to part-time students. *Degree program information:* Part-time programs available. Part-time. Offers agribusiness and applied economics (MS); agriculture, food systems, and natural resources (MS, PhD); animal sciences (MS, PhD); cereal science (MS, PhD); entomology (MS, PhD); horticulture (MS); international agribusiness (MS); microbiology (MS); molecular pathogenesis (PhD); natural resources management (MS, PhD); plant pathology (MS, PhD); plant sciences (MS, PhD); soil sciences (MS, PhD). *Application deadline:* Applications are processed on a rolling basis. *Application fee:* $35. Electronic applications accepted. *Application Contact:* Elizabeth Worth, Marketing, Recruitment, and Public Relations Coordinator, 701-231-8476, Fax: 701-231-6524, E-mail: elizabeth.worth@ndsu.edu. *Dean*, Dr. Kenneth F. Grafton, 701-231-6693, Fax: 701-231-8520, E-mail: k.grafton@ndsu.edu.

College of Arts, Humanities and Social Sciences Faculty: 27 full-time, 3 part-time/adjunct. *Financial support:* Fellowships with full tuition reimbursements, research assistantships with full tuition reimbursements, teaching assistantships with full tuition reimbursements, career-related internships or fieldwork, Federal Work-Study, institutionally sponsored loans, scholarships/grants, and tuition waivers (full) available. Support available to part-time students. *Degree program information:* Part-time and evening/weekend programs available. Part-time, evening/weekend. Offers anthropology (MA, MS); architecture (M Arch); arts, humanities and social sciences (M Arch, M Ed, MA, MM, MS, DMA, PhD); communication (PhD); community development (MA, MS); composition (MA); conducting (MM, DMA); criminal justice (PhD); criminal justice administration (MS); history (MA, MS, PhD); literature (MA); mass communication (MA, MS); music education (MM); performance (MM, DMA); rhetoric, writing and culture (PhD); social science (MA, MS); sociology (MS); speech communication (MA, MS). *Application deadline:* Applications are processed on a rolling basis. *Application fee:* $35. Electronic applications accepted. *Application Contact:* Elizabeth Worth, Marketing, Recruitment, and Public Relations Coordinator, 701-231-8476, Fax: 701-231-6524, E-mail: elizabeth.worth@ndsu.edu. *Dean*, Dr. Kent Sandstrom, 701-231-8338, Fax: 701-231-1047, E-mail: kent.sandstrom@ndsu.edu.

College of Business Financial support: Research assistantships, teaching assistantships, institutionally sponsored loans, and tuition waivers (partial) available. Support available to part-time students. Financial award application deadline: 5/15; financial award applicants required to submit FAFSA. *Degree program information:* Part-time and evening/weekend programs available. Part-time, evening/weekend. Offers accountancy (M Acc); business administration (MBA). *Application deadline:* For fall admission, 7/1 priority date for domestic students, 5/1 priority date for international students; for spring admission, 11/15 for domestic students, 8/1 priority date for international students. Applications are processed on a rolling basis. *Application fee:* $35. Electronic applications accepted. *Application Contact:* Dr. Scott Beaulier, Dean, 701-231-8978, E-mail: scott.beaulier@ndsu.edu. *Dean*, Dr. Scott Beaulier, 701-231-8978, E-mail: scott.beaulier@ndsu.edu.

College of Engineering Financial support: Fellowships with full tuition reimbursements, research assistantships with full tuition reimbursements, teaching assistantships with full tuition reimbursements, career-related internships or fieldwork, Federal Work-Study, institutionally sponsored loans, scholarships/grants, and tuition waivers (full) available. Support available to part-time students. Financial award application deadline: 4/15. *Degree program information:* Part-time programs available. Part-time. Offers civil and environmental engineering (PhD); civil engineering (MS, PhD); construction management (MCM, MS, Graduate Certificate); electrical and computer engineering (ME, MS, PhD); engineering (MCM, ME, MS, PhD, Graduate Certificate); environmental and conservation science (PhD); environmental engineering (MS); industrial and manufacturing engineering (PhD); industrial engineering and management (MS); manufacturing engineering (MS); materials and nanotechnology (PhD); mechanical engineering (MS, PhD); natural resource management (PhD); science, technology, engineering, mathematics education (STEM) (PhD); transportation and logistics (PhD). *Application deadline:* For fall admission, 4/1 priority date for domestic students, 5/1 priority date for international students; for spring admission, 10/1 priority date for domestic students, 8/1 priority date for international students. Applications are processed on a rolling basis. *Application fee:* $35. Electronic applications accepted. *Application Contact:* Dr. Gary R. Smith, Dean, 701-231-7494, Fax: 701-231-8957, E-mail: gary.smith@ndsu.edu. *Dean*, Dr. Gary R. Smith, 701-231-7494, Fax: 701-231-8957, E-mail: gary.smith@ndsu.edu.

College of Health Professions Financial support: Research assistantships with full tuition reimbursements, career-related internships or fieldwork, Federal Work-Study, institutionally sponsored loans, and scholarships/grants available. Financial award application deadline: 4/1. *Degree program information:* Part-time programs available. Part-time. Offers health professions (MPH, MS, DNP, PhD, Pharm D); nursing (MS, DNP); pharmacy (MS, PhD, Pharm D). *Application deadline:* Applications are processed on a rolling basis. *Application fee:* $35. Electronic applications accepted. *Application Contact:* Dr. Charles D. Peterson, Dean, 701-231-5383, Fax: 701-231-7606. *Dean*, Dr. Charles D. Peterson, 701-231-5383, Fax: 701-231-7606.

College of Human Development and Education Financial support: Fellowships, research assistantships, teaching assistantships, career-related internships or fieldwork, Federal Work-Study, institutionally sponsored loans, and tuition waivers (full) available. Support available to part-time students. *Degree program information:* Part-time and evening/weekend programs available. Part-time, evening/weekend, online learning. Offers agricultural education (M Ed, MS); athletic training (MAT, MS); clinical mental health counseling (M Ed, MS); counselor education (M Ed, MS, PhD); counselor education and supervision (PhD); couple and family therapy (PhD); curriculum and instruction (M Ed, MS); developmental science (PhD); dietetics (MS); education (PhD); educational leadership (M Ed, MS, Ed S); exercise science and nutrition (PhD); exercise/nutrition science (MS); family and consumer sciences education (M Ed, MS); family financial planning (MS, Certificate); gerontology (MS, Certificate); health promotion (MPH); history education (M Ed, MS); human development and education (M Ed, MAT, MPH, MS, Ed D, PhD, Certificate, Ed S);

institutional analysis (Ed D); leadership in physical education and sport (MS); mathematics education (M Ed, MS); merchandising (MS, Certificate); music education (M Ed, MS); occupational and adult education (Ed D); school counseling (M Ed, MS); science education (M Ed, MS); youth development (MS). *Application deadline:* Applications are processed on a rolling basis. *Application fee:* $35. Electronic applications accepted. *Application Contact:* Elizabeth Worth, Marketing, Recruitment, and Public Relations Coordinator, 701-231-8476, Fax: 701-231-6524, E-mail: elizabeth.worth@ndsu.edu. *Dean*, Dr. Margaret Fitzgerald, 701-231-8211, Fax: 701-231-7174, E-mail: margaret.fitzgerald@ndsu.edu.

College of Science and Mathematics Financial support: Fellowships with full tuition reimbursements, research assistantships with full tuition reimbursements, teaching assistantships with full tuition reimbursements, career-related internships or fieldwork, Federal Work-Study, institutionally sponsored loans, scholarships/grants, traineeships, tuition waivers (full and partial), and unspecified assistantships available. Support available to part-time students. Financial award applicants required to submit FAFSA. *Degree program information:* Part-time programs available. Part-time. Offers applied mathematics (MS, PhD); biochemistry (MS, PhD); biology (MS); botany (MS, PhD); cellular and molecular biology (PhD); chemistry (MS, PhD); clinical psychology (MS); coatings and polymeric materials (MS, PhD); computer science (MS, PhD); genomics (PhD); health and social psychology (PhD); mathematics (MS, PhD); physics (MS, PhD); psychological clinical science (PhD); psychology (MS); science and mathematics (MS, PhD, Certificate); software engineering (MS, MSE, PhD, Certificate); sports statistics (PhD); statistics (MS, PhD, Certificate); visual and cognitive neuroscience (PhD); zoology (MS, PhD). *Application deadline:* Applications are processed on a rolling basis. *Application fee:* $35. Electronic applications accepted. *Application Contact:* Elizabeth Worth, Marketing, Recruitment, and Public Relations Coordinator, 701-231-8476, Fax: 701-231-6524, E-mail: elizabeth.worth@ndsu.edu. *Dean*, Dr. Scott A. Wood, 701-231-7411, E-mail: scott.wood@ndsu.edu.

NORTHEASTERN ILLINOIS UNIVERSITY, Chicago, IL 60625-4699

General Information State-supported, coed, comprehensive institution. CGS member. *Graduate housing:* On-campus housing not available. *Research affiliation:* Advocate Health Care Network (health care cost containment), Lutheran General Hospital (clinical cardiology), Advocate Medical Group (health care outcomes research).

GRADUATE UNITS

College of Graduate Studies and Research ***Degree program information:*** Part-time and evening/weekend programs available. Part-time, evening/weekend. Electronic applications accepted.

College of Arts and Sciences Degree program information: Part-time and evening/weekend programs available. Part-time, evening/weekend. Offers applied mathematics (MS); arts and sciences (MA, MS); biology (MS); chemistry (MS); communication, media and theatre (MA); composition/writing (MA); computer science (MS); geography and environmental studies (MA); gerontology (MA); history (MA); Latin American literatures and cultures (MA); linguistics (MA); literature (MA); mathematics (MS); music (MA); pedagogical content knowledge for teaching elementary and middle school mathematics (MS); political science (MA); secondary education mathematics (MS); teaching English as a second/foreign language (MA); TESL (MA). Electronic applications accepted.

College of Business and Management Degree program information: Part-time and evening/weekend programs available. Part-time, evening/weekend. Offers accounting (MSA); business administration (MBA); finance (MBA); management (MBA); marketing (MBA). Electronic applications accepted.

College of Education Degree program information: Part-time and evening/weekend programs available. Part-time, evening/weekend. Offers bicultural/bilingual education (MAT); bilingual/bicultural education (MAT, MSI); community counseling (MA); early childhood education (MAT); education (MA, MAT, MS, MSI); educational administration and supervision (MA); educational leadership (MA); exercise science (MS); family counseling (MA); gifted education (MA); human resource development (MA); inner city studies (MA); language arts - elementary education (MAT, MSI); language arts - secondary education (MAT, MSI); learning behavior specialist (MA, MS); literacy education (MA); rehabilitation counseling (MA); school counseling (MA). Electronic applications accepted.

NORTHEASTERN SEMINARY AT ROBERTS WESLEYAN COLLEGE, Rochester, NY 14624

General Information Independent-religious, coed, graduate-only institution. *Graduate housing:* On-campus housing not available.

GRADUATE UNITS

Graduate and Professional Programs ***Degree program information:*** Evening/weekend programs available. Evening/weekend. Offers ministry (D Min); theological studies (MA); theology (M Div). M Div/MSW offered jointly with Roberts Wesleyan College. Electronic applications accepted.

NORTHEASTERN STATE UNIVERSITY, Tahlequah, OK 74464-2399

General Information State-supported, coed, comprehensive institution. *Enrollment:* 8,276 graduate, professional, and undergraduate students; 477 full-time matriculated graduate/professional students (339 women), 755 part-time matriculated graduate/professional students (559 women). *Enrollment by degree level:* 1,119 master's, 113 doctoral. *Graduate faculty:* 128 full-time (69 women), 15 part-time/adjunct (10 women). Tuition, state resident: part-time $189.60 per credit hour. Tuition, nonresident: part-time $462.60 per credit hour. *Required fees:* $37.40 per credit hour. *Graduate housing:* Rooms and/or apartments available on a first-come, first-served basis to single and married students. Typical cost: $2782 per year ($6490 including board) for single students. Room and board charges vary according to board plan and housing facility selected. Housing application deadline: 6/1. *Student services:* Campus employment opportunities, campus safety program, career counseling, exercise/wellness program, free psychological counseling, international student services, low-cost health insurance, multicultural affairs office, services for students with disabilities, teacher training. *Library:* John Vaughn Library. *Collection:* Books: 440,635 (physical), 113,231 (digital/electronic); Serial titles: 5,144 (physical), 50,929 (digital/electronic); Databases: 77. Weekly public service hours: 93; students can reserve study rooms.

Computer facilities: Computer purchase and lease plans are available. 1,160 computers available on campus for general student use. A campuswide network can be accessed from student residence rooms and from off campus. Online class registration is available.
Website: http://www.nsuok.edu/

General Application Contact: Dr. Donna Trout, Graduate Program Coordinator, 918-449-6123, Fax: 918-449-6120, E-mail: troutdk@nsuok.edu.

GRADUATE UNITS

College of Business and Technology Students: 43 full-time (17 women), 145 part-time (68 women); includes 73 minority (10 Black or African American, non-Hispanic/Latino; 28 American Indian or Alaska Native, non-Hispanic/Latino; 7 Asian, non-Hispanic/Latino; 11 Hispanic/Latino; 17 Two or more races, non-Hispanic/Latino), 18 international. Average age 34. *Faculty:* 16 full-time (5 women). *Financial support:* Teaching assistantships and Federal Work-Study available. Financial award application deadline: 3/1. In 2015, 61 master's awarded. *Degree program information:* Part-time and evening/weekend programs available. Part-time, evening/weekend. Offers accounting and financial analysis (MS); business administration (MBA, PMBA); business and technology (MBA, MEHS, MS, PMBA); environmental, health, and safety management (MEHS). *Application deadline:* For fall admission, 6/1 priority date for domestic students. Applications are processed on a rolling basis. *Application fee:* $0 ($25 for international students). *Application Contact:* Margie Railey, Administrative Assistant, 918-456-5511 Ext. 2093, Fax: 918-458-2061, E-mail: railey@nsouk.edu. *Dean*, Dr. Roger Collier, 918-444-2900, E-mail: colliere@nsuok.edu.

College of Education Students: 167 full-time (133 women), 429 part-time (352 women); includes 226 minority (26 Black or African American, non-Hispanic/Latino; 112 American Indian or Alaska Native, non-Hispanic/Latino; 5 Asian, non-Hispanic/Latino; 14 Hispanic/Latino; 69 Two or more races, non-Hispanic/Latino), 5 international. Average age 36. *Faculty:* 42 full-time (28 women), 5 part-time/adjunct (4 women). *Financial support:* Teaching assistantships, career-related internships or fieldwork, and Federal Work-Study available. Financial award application deadline: 3/1. In 2015, 168 master's awarded. *Degree program information:* Part-time and evening/weekend programs available. Part-time, evening/weekend. Offers counseling psychology (MS); early childhood education (M Ed); education (M Ed, MS, MS Ed); health and kinesiology (MS); higher education leadership (MS); library media and information technology (MS); reading (M Ed); school administration (M Ed); school counseling (M Ed); special education - autism spectrum disorder (M Ed); substance abuse counseling (MS); teaching (M Ed). *Application deadline:* For fall admission, 6/1 priority date for domestic students. Applications are processed on a rolling basis. *Application fee:* $25. Electronic applications accepted. *Application Contact:* Margie Railey, Administrative Assistant, 918-456-5511 Ext. 2093, Fax: 918-458-2061, E-mail: railey@nsouk.edu. *Dean of the College of Education*, Dr. Deborah Landry, 918-444-3700, E-mail: landryd@nsuok.edu.

College of Liberal Arts Students: 34 full-time (22 women), 66 part-time (43 women); includes 37 minority (10 Black or African American, non-Hispanic/Latino; 11 American Indian or Alaska Native, non-Hispanic/Latino; 4 Hispanic/Latino; 12 Two or more races, non-Hispanic/Latino). Average age 34. *Faculty:* 16 full-time (5 women), 1 (woman) part-time/adjunct. *Financial support:* Teaching assistantships and Federal Work-Study available. Financial award application deadline: 3/1. In 2015, 30 master's awarded. *Degree program information:* Part-time and evening/weekend programs available. Part-time, evening/weekend. Offers American studies (MA); communication (MA); criminal justice (MS); English (MA); liberal arts (MA, MS). *Application deadline:* For fall admission, 6/1 priority date for domestic students. Applications are processed on a rolling basis. *Application fee:* $25. Electronic applications accepted. *Application Contact:* Zoe Storer, Administrative Assistant, 918-444-3532, E-mail: storerz@nsuok.edu. *Dean of Liberal Arts Administration*, Dr. Phillip Bridgmon, 918-444-3618, Fax: 918-458-2348, E-mail: bridgmon@nsuok.edu.

College of Optometry Students: 113 full-time (64 women); includes 33 minority (2 Black or African American, non-Hispanic/Latino; 16 American Indian or Alaska Native, non-Hispanic/Latino; 5 Asian, non-Hispanic/Latino; 6 Hispanic/Latino; 4 Two or more races, non-Hispanic/Latino). Average age 25. *Faculty:* 32 full-time (13 women), 17 part-time/adjunct (7 women). *Financial support:* Federal Work-Study, institutionally sponsored loans, scholarships/grants, tuition waivers (partial), and residencies available. Financial award application deadline: 5/1; financial award applicants required to submit FAFSA. In 2015, 28 doctorates awarded. Offers optometry (OD). Applicants must be a resident of Oklahoma, Arkansas, Kansas, Colorado, New Mexico, Missouri, Texas, or Nebraska. *Application deadline:* For fall admission, 2/1 for domestic students. Applications are processed on a rolling basis. *Application fee:* $45. Electronic applications accepted. *Application Contact:* Sandy Medearis, Director of Optometry Student Affairs, 918-444-4006, Fax: 918-458-2104, E-mail: medearis@nsuok.edu. *Dean of Oklahoma College of Optometry*, Dr. Douglas Penisten, 918-444-4025, E-mail: penisten@nsuok.edu.

College of Science and Health Professions Students: 120 full-time (103 women), 97 part-time (82 women); includes 70 minority (2 Black or African American, non-Hispanic/Latino; 28 American Indian or Alaska Native, non-Hispanic/Latino; 4 Asian, non-Hispanic/Latino; 8 Hispanic/Latino; 1 Native Hawaiian or other Pacific Islander, non-Hispanic/Latino; 27 Two or more races, non-Hispanic/Latino), 3 international. Average age 32. *Faculty:* 35 full-time (25 women), 5 part-time/adjunct (all women). In 2015, 60 master's awarded. Offers mathematics education (M Ed); natural sciences (MS); nursing education (MSN); occupational therapy (MS); science and health professions (M Ed, MS, MSN); science education (M Ed); speech-language pathology (MS). *Application fee:* $25. *Application Contact:* Linda Brown, Secretary, 918-444-3801, E-mail: brownl@nsuok.edu. *Dean*, Dr. Pamela Hathorn, 918-444-3800, E-mail: hathorn@nsuok.edu.

NORTHEASTERN UNIVERSITY, Boston, MA 02115-5096

General Information Independent, coed, university. CGS member. *Enrollment:* 24,944 graduate, professional, and undergraduate students; 6,855 full-time matriculated graduate/professional students (3,238 women), 6,855 part-time matriculated graduate/professional students (3,896 women). *Enrollment by degree level:* 9,908 master's, 3,480 doctoral, 412 other advanced degrees. *Graduate faculty:* 1,346 full-time (563 women), 595 part-time/adjunct (306 women). Tuition and fees vary according to course load and program. *Student services:* Campus employment opportunities, campus safety program, career counseling, child daycare facilities, exercise/wellness program, free psychological counseling, grant writing training, international student services, low-cost health insurance, multicultural affairs office, services for students with disabilities, teacher training. *Library:* Snell Library plus 3 others. *Research affiliation:* Jobs for America's Graduates (labor studies), Cytyc Corporation (medical technology), BBN Technologies (information technology), Analog Devices, Inc. (electronics), General Electric Company (GE) (engineering).

Computer facilities: Computer purchase and lease plans are available. A campuswide network can be accessed from student residence rooms and from off campus. Online class registration is available.
Website: http://www.northeastern.edu/

GRADUATE UNITS

Bouvé College of Health Sciences Students: 1,416 full-time (1,049 women), 310 part-time (248 women). *Faculty:* 194 full-time (120 women), 169 part-time/adjunct (136 women). *Financial support:* Applicants required to submit FAFSA. In 2015, 374 master's, 313 doctorates, 37 other advanced degrees awarded. *Degree program information:* Part-time and evening/weekend programs available. Part-time, evening/weekend, online learning. Offers applied behavior analysis (MS, CAGS); audiology (Au D); biomedical nanotechnology (MS); college student development and counseling (MS, CAGS); counseling psychology (MS, PhD, CAGS); exercise science (MS); health informatics (MS); medicinal chemistry (MS); nurse anesthesia (DNP, CAGS); nursing (MS, PhD, CAGS); nursing practice (DNP); personal health informatics (PhD); pharmaceutical sciences (MS, PhD); pharmacology (MS); pharmacy (Pharm D); physical therapy (Postbaccalaureate Certificate); physician assistant (MS); population health (PhD); school psychology (MS, PhD, CAGS); speech-language pathology (MS); urban health (MPH). *Application fee:* $75. Electronic applications accepted. *Application Contact:* Molly Schnabel, Senior Director of Graduate Affairs, 617-373-2708, Fax: 617-373-4701, E-mail: bouvegrad@neu.edu. *Professor and Interim Dean*, John R. Reynolds, 617-373-3323, Fax: 617-373-3030.

College of Arts, Media and Design Students: 185 full-time (112 women), 7 part-time (all women). *Faculty:* 142 full-time (50 women), 91 part-time/adjunct (40 women). *Financial support:* Applicants required to submit FAFSA. In 2015, 71 master's awarded. Offers architecture (M Arch); game science and design (MS); information design and visualization (MFA); interdisciplinary arts (MFA); journalism (MA); music industry leadership (MS); studio art (MFA); sustainable building systems (MS); sustainable urban environments (M Des). *Application fee:* $75. Electronic applications accepted. *Application Contact:* Jane Amidon, Associate Dean for Graduate Programs and Research, E-mail: gscamd@neu.edu. *Dean*, Dr. Elizabeth Hudson.

College of Computer and Information Science Students: 913 full-time (263 women), 44 part-time (15 women). *Faculty:* 68 full-time (21 women), 29 part-time/adjunct (8 women). *Financial support:* Research assistantships, teaching assistantships, scholarships/grants, health care benefits, and unspecified assistantships available. Financial award applicants required to submit FAFSA. In 2015, 274 master's, 12 doctorates awarded. *Degree program information:* Part-time and evening/weekend programs available. Part-time, evening/weekend. Offers computer science (MS, PhD); game science and design (MS); health informatics (MS); information assurance (MS, PhD); network science (PhD); personal health informatics (PhD). *Application fee:* $75. Electronic applications accepted. *Application Contact:* Dr. Rajmohan Rajaraman, Professor/Associate Dean/Director of the Graduate School, 617-373-8493, E-mail: gradschool@ccs.neu.edu. *Professor and Dean*, Dr. Carla Brodley.

College of Engineering Students: 2,454 full-time (784 women), 187 part-time (37 women). *Faculty:* 190 full-time (51 women), 50 part-time/adjunct (9 women). *Financial support:* Fellowships, research assistantships, teaching assistantships, career-related internships or fieldwork, scholarships/grants, health care benefits, tuition waivers, and unspecified assistantships available. Support available to part-time students. Financial award applicants required to submit FAFSA. In 2015, 668 master's, 53 doctorates awarded. *Degree program information:* Part-time programs available. Part-time, online learning. Offers bioengineering (MS, PhD); chemical engineering (MS, PhD); civil engineering (MS, PhD); computer engineering (PhD); computer systems engineering (MS); electrical and computer engineering (MS); electrical and computer engineering leadership (MS); electrical engineering (PhD); energy systems (MS); engineering leadership (Certificate); engineering management (MS, Certificate); industrial engineering (MS, PhD); information assurance (PhD); information systems (MS); interdisciplinary engineering (PhD); mechanical engineering (MS, PhD); operations research (MS); telecommunication systems management (MS). *Application fee:* $75. Electronic applications accepted. *Application Contact:* Jeffery Hengel, Director of Graduate Admissions, 617-373-2711, E-mail: j.hengel@neu.edu. *Associate Dean, Graduate Education*, Dr. Sara Wadia-Fascetti, 617-373-2711.

College of Professional Studies Students: 4,930 part-time (3,046 women). *Faculty:* 72 full-time (44 women), 865 part-time/adjunct (380 women). *Financial support:* Applicants required to submit FAFSA. In 2015, 1,310 master's awarded. *Degree program information:* Part-time and evening/weekend programs available. Part-time, evening/weekend, 100% online, blended/hybrid learning. Offers applied nutrition (MS); college athletics administration (MSL); commerce and economic development (MS); corporate and organizational communication (MS); criminal justice (MS); digital media (MPS); elearning and instructional design (M Ed); elementary education (MAT); geographic information technology (MPS); global studies and international relations (MS); higher education administration (M Ed); homeland security (MA); human services (MS); informatics (MPS); leadership (MS); learning analytics (M Ed); learning and instruction (M Ed); nonprofit management (MS); professional sports administration (MSL); project management (MS); regulatory affairs for drugs, biologics, and medical devices (MS); respiratory care leadership (MS); special education (M Ed); technical communication (MS). *Application deadline:* Applications are processed on a rolling basis. *Application fee:* $0. Electronic applications accepted. *Dean/Vice President for Professional Education*, Dr. John LaBrie.

College of Science Students: 517 full-time (252 women), 80 part-time (39 women). *Faculty:* 216 full-time (70 women), 62 part-time/adjunct (20 women). *Financial support:* Fellowships with tuition reimbursements, research assistantships with tuition reimbursements, teaching assistantships with tuition reimbursements, career-related internships or fieldwork, scholarships/grants, health care benefits, tuition waivers (full and partial), and unspecified assistantships available. Support available to part-time students. Financial award applicants required to submit FAFSA. In 2015, 94 master's, 46 doctorates awarded. *Degree program information:* Part-time programs available. Part-time. Offers applied mathematics (MS); bioinformatics (MS); biology (PhD); biotechnology (MS); chemistry (MS, PhD); ecology, evolution, and marine biology (PhD); marine biology (MS); mathematics (MS, PhD); network science (PhD); operations research (MSOR); physics (MS, PhD); psychology (PhD). *Application deadline:* Applications are processed on a rolling basis. *Application fee:* $75. Electronic applications accepted. *Application Contact:* Graduate Student Services, 617-373-4275, E-mail: gradcos@neu.edu. *Interim Dean*, Dr. Jonathan Tilly.

College of Social Sciences and Humanities Students: 467 full-time (274 women), 92 part-time (56 women). *Faculty:* 227 full-time (107 women), 55 part-time/adjunct (29 women). *Financial support:* Teaching assistantships, career-related internships or fieldwork, scholarships/grants, health care benefits, tuition waivers (full and partial), and unspecified assistantships available. Support available to part-time students. Financial award applicants required to submit FAFSA. In 2015, 160 master's, 32 doctorates awarded. Online learning. Offers criminology and criminal justice (MSCJ); criminology and justice policy (PhD); economics (MA, PhD); English (MA, PhD); international affairs (MA); law and public policy (PhD); political science (MA, PhD); public administration (MPA); public history (MA); public policy (MPP); security and resilience studies (MS); sociology (MA, PhD); urban and regional policy (MS); urban informatics (MS); world history (MA, PhD). *Application fee:* $75. Electronic applications accepted. *Application Contact:* Amber Crowe, Administrative Coordinator, 617-373-5990, Fax: 617-373-7281, E-mail: gradcssh@neu.edu. *Dean*, Dr. Uta Poiger, 617-373-5173.

D'Amore-McKim School of Business Students: 437 full-time (203 women), 1,342 part-time (544 women). *Faculty:* 188 full-time (71 women), 47 part-time/adjunct (11 women). *Financial support:* Scholarships/grants available. Financial award applicants required to submit FAFSA. In 2015, 795 master's awarded. *Degree program information:* Part-time and evening/weekend programs available. Part-time, evening/weekend, online learning. Offers accounting (MS); business administration (EMBA, MBA); finance (MS); innovation (MS); international business (MS); international management (MS); taxation (MS); technological entrepreneurship (MS). *Application fee:* $75. Electronic applications accepted. *Application Contact:* Evelyn Tate, Director, Graduate Recruitment and Admissions, 617-373-3258, Fax: 617-373-8564, E-mail: e.tate@neu.edu. *Associate Dean, Graduate Business Programs*, Kate Klepper, 617-373-5417, Fax: 617-373-8564, E-mail: k.klepper@neu.edu.

School of Education ***Degree program information:*** Part-time and evening/weekend programs available. Part-time, evening/weekend. Offers curriculum, teaching, learning, and leadership (Ed D); elearning and instructional design (M Ed); elementary licensure (MAT); higher education administration (M Ed, Ed D); learning analytics (M Ed); learning and instruction (M Ed); organizational leadership studies (Ed D); secondary licensure (MAT); special education (M Ed). *Application Contact:* College of Professional Studies Office of Admissions, 877-668-7727, E-mail: cpsadmissions@neu.edu.

School of Law Students: 520 full-time (329 women). *Faculty:* 48 full-time (29 women), 19 part-time/adjunct (9 women). *Financial support:* Scholarships/grants available. Financial award applicants required to submit FAFSA. In 2015, 34 master's, 171 doctorates awarded. Online learning. Offers health policy and law (LL M); human rights (LL M); international business law (LL M); law (LL M, MLS, JD); law and economic development (LL M). JD/MPH offered jointly with Tufts University; JD/MSA/MBA with Graduate School of Professional Accounting; JD/MS with Program in Law and Public Policy; JD/MELP with Vermont Law School; and JD/MA with Brandeis University. *Application deadline:* Applications are processed on a rolling basis. *Application fee:* $75. Electronic applications accepted. *Application Contact:* Information Contact, 617-373-2395, Fax: 617-373-8865, E-mail: lawadmissions@neu.edu. *Dean*, Jeremy R. Paul, 617-373-3307, Fax: 617-373-8793, E-mail: j.paul@neu.edu.

NORTHEAST OHIO MEDICAL UNIVERSITY, Rootstown, OH 44272-0095

General Information State-supported, coed, graduate-only institution. *Enrollment by degree level:* 921 doctoral, 1 other advanced degree. *Graduate faculty:* 513 full-time (192 women), 2,199 part-time/adjunct (748 women). Tuition, state resident: part-time $565 per credit hour. Tuition, nonresident: part-time $576 per credit hour. Full-time tuition and fees vary according to program and student level. *Graduate housing:* Rooms and/or apartments guaranteed to single and married students. *Student services:* Campus employment opportunities, campus safety program, career counseling, free psychological counseling, low-cost health insurance, multicultural affairs office, services for students with disabilities. *Library:* Oliver Ocasek Regional Medical Information Center. *Collection:* Books: 3,694 (physical), 3,000 (digital/electronic); Serial titles: 2 (physical), 60 (digital/electronic); Databases: 115. Weekly public service hours: 74; study areas open 24 hours, 5–7 days a week. *Research affiliation:* Austen BioInnovation Institute in Akron (pharmacology, drug delivery, biotechnology, community health), American Heart Association (physiology, biochemistry), National Science Foundation (anatomy), National Institutes of Health (anatomy, biochemistry, immunology, neurobiology, microbiology), Summa Health Systems (orthopedics, anatomy), Margaret Clark Morgan Foundation (schizophrenia, mental illness).

Computer facilities: 50 computers available on campus for general student use. A campuswide network can be accessed from student residence rooms and from off campus. Online class registration is available.
Website: http://www.neomed.edu/

General Application Contact: Heidi Terry, Director, Admissions and Student Services, 330-325-6270, E-mail: admission@neomed.edu.

GRADUATE UNITS

College of Graduate Studies Students: 15 full-time (7 women), 26 part-time (11 women); includes 7 minority (5 Asian, non-Hispanic/Latino; 2 Hispanic/Latino). Average age 27. *Faculty:* 15 part-time/adjunct (6 women). *Financial support:* In 2015–16, 18 students received support. In 2015, 9 master's, 1 doctorate awarded. *Degree program information:* Part-time programs available. Part-time. Offers bioethics (Certificate); health-system pharmacy administration (MS); integrated pharmaceutical medicine (MS, PhD); public health (MS). *Application deadline:* For fall admission, 9/1 priority date for domestic students; for winter admission, 1/5 priority date for domestic students. Applications are processed on a rolling basis. Electronic applications accepted. *Application Contact:* Heidi Terry, Executive Director, Enrollment Services, 330-325-6479, E-mail: hterry@neoucom.edu. *Dean*, Dr. Walter E. Horton, Jr..

College of Medicine Students: 596 full-time (280 women); includes 238 minority (13 Black or African American, non-Hispanic/Latino; 1 American Indian or Alaska Native, non-Hispanic/Latino; 196 Asian, non-Hispanic/Latino; 12 Hispanic/Latino; 1 Native Hawaiian or other Pacific Islander, non-Hispanic/Latino; 15 Two or more races, non-Hispanic/Latino). Average age 24. 3,105 applicants, 8% accepted, 160 enrolled. *Faculty:* 462 full-time (172 women), 1,724 part-time/adjunct (484 women). *Financial support:* In 2015–16, 599 students received support. Institutionally sponsored loans and scholarships/grants available. Financial award application deadline: 4/15; financial award applicants required to submit FAFSA. In 2015, 128 doctorates awarded. Offers medicine (MD). *Application deadline:* For fall admission, 8/1 priority date for domestic students; for winter admission, 10/1 for domestic students. Applications are processed on a rolling basis. *Application fee:* $40. Electronic applications accepted. *Application Contact:* Heidi Terry, Executive Director, Enrollment Services, 330-325-6479, E-mail: hterry@neoucom.edu. *Dean*, Dr. Jeffrey L. Susman, 330-325-6254.

College of Pharmacy Students: 299 full-time (173 women); includes 51 minority (14 Black or African American, non-Hispanic/Latino; 28 Asian, non-Hispanic/Latino; 5 Hispanic/Latino; 4 Two or more races, non-Hispanic/Latino). Average age 26. 315 applicants, 46% accepted, 75 enrolled. *Faculty:* 51 full-time (20 women), 463 part-time/adjunct (258 women). *Financial support:* In 2015–16, 300 students received support. Scholarships/grants available. Financial award application deadline: 4/15; financial award applicants required to submit FAFSA. In 2015, 61 doctorates awarded. Offers pharmacy (Pharm D). *Application deadline:* For fall admission, 9/1 priority date for domestic students; for winter admission, 1/5 for domestic students. Applications are processed on a rolling basis. *Application fee:* $50. Electronic applications accepted. *Application Contact:* Heidi Terry, Executive Director, Enrollment Services, 330-325-6479, E-mail: hterry@neoucom.edu. *Dean*, Dr. Charles Taylor, 330-325-6461, Fax: 330-325-5930.

NORTHERN ARIZONA UNIVERSITY, Flagstaff, AZ 86011

General Information State-supported, coed, university. CGS member. *Enrollment:* 29,031 graduate, professional, and undergraduate students; 1,863 full-time matriculated graduate/professional students (1,206 women), 2,048 part-time matriculated graduate/professional students (1,415 women). *Graduate faculty:* 973 full-time (494 women), 616 part-time/adjunct (232 women). *Tuition, area resident:* Full-time $8710.

Tuition, nonresident: full-time $20,350. *Required fees:* $896. *Graduate housing:* Rooms and/or apartments available on a first-come, first-served basis to single and married students. Typical cost: $5140 per year for single students. *Student services:* Campus employment opportunities, campus safety program, career counseling, child daycare facilities, exercise/wellness program, free psychological counseling, grant writing training, international student services, low-cost health insurance, multicultural affairs office, services for students with disabilities, teacher training, writing training. *Library:* Cline Library. *Collection:* Books: 460,817 (physical), 192,956 (digital/electronic); Serial titles: 81,140 (physical). Weekly public service hours: 117; students can reserve study rooms. *Research affiliation:* W.L. Gore and Associates, Inc., Museum of Northern Arizona, Lowell Observatory, Rocky Mountain Forest and Range Experiment Station, U.S. Naval Observatory, U.S. Geological Survey (USGS).

Computer facilities: Computer purchase and lease plans are available. A campuswide network can be accessed from student residence rooms and from off campus. Online class registration is available.
Website: http://www.nau.edu/

General Application Contact: Graduate Admissions, 928-523-4348, Fax: 928-523-8950, E-mail: graduate@nau.edu.

GRADUATE UNITS

Graduate College Students: 1,863 full-time (1,206 women), 2,048 part-time (1,415 women); includes 1,043 minority (99 Black or African American, non-Hispanic/Latino; 173 American Indian or Alaska Native, non-Hispanic/Latino; 69 Asian, non-Hispanic/Latino; 564 Hispanic/Latino; 4 Native Hawaiian or other Pacific Islander, non-Hispanic/Latino; 134 Two or more races, non-Hispanic/Latino), 96 international. Average age 34. 4,284 applicants, 38% accepted, 1067 enrolled. *Faculty:* 973 full-time (494 women), 616 part-time/adjunct (232 women). *Financial support:* In 2015–16, 47 fellowships, 81 research assistantships with full tuition reimbursements (averaging $13,000 per year), 386 teaching assistantships with full tuition reimbursements (averaging $10,000 per year) were awarded; career-related internships or fieldwork, Federal Work-Study, institutionally sponsored loans, scholarships/grants, traineeships, health care benefits, tuition waivers (full and partial), and unspecified assistantships also available. Support available to part-time students. Financial award applicants required to submit FAFSA. In 2015, 1,196 master's, 52 doctorates, 177 other advanced degrees awarded. *Degree program information:* Part-time programs available. Part-time, 100% online, blended/hybrid learning. *Application deadline:* For fall admission, 3/1 for international students; for spring admission, 10/1 for international students. Applications are processed on a rolling basis. *Application fee:* $65. Electronic applications accepted. *Application Contact:* Tiuna Sutton, Coordinator, 928-523-4348, Fax: 928-523-8950, E-mail: graduate@nau.edu. *Dean,* Dr. Maribeth Watwood, 928-523-9322, Fax: 928-523-8950, E-mail: maribeth.watwood@nau.edu.

College of Arts and Letters Financial support: Fellowships, research assistantships, teaching assistantships, Federal Work-Study, scholarships/grants, health care benefits, tuition waivers (full and partial), and unspecified assistantships available. Financial award applicants required to submit FAFSA. *Degree program information:* Part-time programs available. Part-time. Offers applied linguistics (PhD); arts and letters (MA, MAT, MFA, MM, PhD, Certificate); choral conducting (MM); composition (MM); creative writing (MFA); English (MA); history (MA); instrumental conducting (MM); instrumental performance (MM); musicology (MM); performance (Certificate); piano accompanying and chamber music (MM); professional writing (Certificate); Spanish (MAT); Spanish education (MAT); Suzuki violin/viola (MM); teaching English as a second language (MA, Certificate); theory (MM); vocal performance (MM). *Application deadline:* Applications are processed on a rolling basis. *Application fee:* $65. Electronic applications accepted. *Dean,* Dr. Michael Vincent, 928-523-8632, E-mail: michael.vincent@nau.edu.

College of Education Financial support: Research assistantships with full tuition reimbursements, teaching assistantships with full tuition reimbursements, career-related internships or fieldwork, Federal Work-Study, scholarships/grants, health care benefits, tuition waivers (full and partial), and unspecified assistantships available. Financial award applicants required to submit FAFSA. *Degree program information:* Part-time and evening/weekend programs available. Part-time, evening/weekend, online learning. Offers autism spectrum disorders (Certificate); bilingual/multicultural education (M Ed); career and technical education (M Ed, Certificate); community college teaching and learning (Certificate); community college/higher education (M Ed); counseling (MA); culturally and linguistically diverse special education (Certificate); curriculum and instruction (Ed D); early childhood education (M Ed); early childhood special education (M Ed); education (M Ed, MA, Ed D, PhD, Certificate, Ed S); educational foundations (M Ed); educational leadership (M Ed, Ed D); educational psychology (PhD); educational technology (M Ed, Certificate); elementary education (M Ed); English as a second language (Certificate); human relations (M Ed); mild/moderate disabilities (M Ed); positive behavior support (Certificate); principal (Certificate); principal K-12 (M Ed); school counseling (M Ed); school leadership K-12 (M Ed); school psychology (Ed S); secondary education (M Ed); special education (M Ed); student affairs (M Ed); superintendent (Certificate). *Application deadline:* Applications are processed on a rolling basis. *Application fee:* $65. Electronic applications accepted. *Dean,* Ramona Mellott, 928-523-6534, Fax: 928-523-8700, E-mail: ramona.mellott@nau.edu.

College of Engineering, Forestry, and Natural Sciences Financial support: Fellowships, research assistantships, and teaching assistantships available. Financial award applicants required to submit FAFSA. Offers applied physics (MS); applied statistics (Certificate); astronomy (PhD); biological sciences (MS, PhD); chemistry (MS); civil engineering (M Eng, MSE); climate science and solutions (MS); computer science (MSE); earth sciences and environmental sustainability (PhD); electrical and computer engineering (M Eng, MSE); engineering (M Eng, MSE); engineering, forestry, and natural sciences (M Eng, MAST, MAT, MF, MS, MSE, MSF, PhD, Certificate); environmental engineering (M Eng, MSE); environmental sciences and policy (MS); forest science (PhD); forestry (MF, MSF); geology (MS); mathematics (MS); mathematics education (MS); mechanical engineering (M Eng, MSE); science teaching (MAST, Certificate); statistics (MS); teaching science (MAT). *Application fee:* $65. *Dean,* Paul W. Jagodzinski, 928-523-2701, Fax: 928-523-2300, E-mail: paul.jagodzinski@nau.edu.

College of Health and Human Services Financial support: Research assistantships and tuition waivers (full and partial) available. Financial award applicants required to submit FAFSA. *Degree program information:* Part-time programs available. Part-time. Offers clinical speech-language pathology (MS); family nurse practitioner (MSN, Certificate); health and human services (MPAS, MS, MSN, DNP, DPT, Certificate); nurse generalist (MSN); nursing practice (DNP); physical therapy (DPT); physician assistant (MPAS). *Application fee:* $65. *Executive Dean,* Leslie Schulz, 928-523-4331, E-mail: leslie.schulz@nau.edu.

College of Social and Behavioral Sciences Financial support: Fellowships with full tuition reimbursements, research assistantships with full tuition reimbursements, and teaching assistantships with full tuition reimbursements available. Financial award applicants required to submit FAFSA. *Degree program information:* Part-time programs available. Part-time. Offers applied criminology (MS); applied geospatial sciences (MS); applied sociology (MA); archaeology (MA); assistive technology (Certificate); clinical health psychology (MA); communication (MA); community planning (Certificate); disability policy and practice (Certificate); ethnic studies (Graduate Certificate); general psychology (MA); geographic information systems (Certificate); linguistic anthropology (MA); political science (MA, PhD); public administration (MPA); public management (Certificate); social and behavioral sciences (MA, MPA, MS, PhD, Certificate, Graduate Certificate); sociocultural anthropology (MA); sustainable communities (MA); teaching psychology (MA); women's and gender studies (Graduate Certificate). *Application deadline:* Applications are processed on a rolling basis. *Application fee:* $65. Electronic applications accepted. *Dean,* Dr. Karen Pugliesi, 928-523-2672, Fax: 928-523-7185, E-mail: karen.pugliesi@nau.edu.

NAU-Yuma Financial support: Applicants required to submit FAFSA. Offers administration (M Adm). *Application deadline:* Applications are processed on a rolling basis. *Application fee:* $65. Electronic applications accepted. *Associate Vice President/Campus Executive Officer,* Dr. Larry Gould, 928-317-6475, E-mail: larry.gould@nau.edu.

The W. A. Franke College of Business Financial support: Research assistantships, Federal Work-Study, institutionally sponsored loans, scholarships/grants, health care benefits, tuition waivers (partial), and unspecified assistantships available. Support available to part-time students. Financial award applicants required to submit FAFSA. *Degree program information:* Part-time programs available. Part-time. Offers business (MBA). *Application deadline:* For fall admission, 5/15 priority date for domestic students, 3/1 priority date for international students. Applications are processed on a rolling basis. *Application fee:* $65. Electronic applications accepted. *Application Contact:* Michelle Brown, Assistant to the Dean, 928-523-7345, Fax: 928-523-6559, E-mail: michelle.brown@nau.edu. *Dean,* Craig Van Slyke, 928-523-5633, Fax: 928-523-7331, E-mail: craig.vanslyke@nau.edu.

NORTHERN ILLINOIS UNIVERSITY, De Kalb, IL 60115-2854

General Information State-supported, coed, university. CGS member. *Enrollment:* 20,130 graduate, professional, and undergraduate students; 2,278 full-time matriculated graduate/professional students (1,067 women), 2,160 part-time matriculated graduate/professional students (1,198 women). *Enrollment by degree level:* 3,190 master's, 1,226 doctoral, 22 other advanced degrees. *Graduate faculty:* 672 full-time (248 women), 66 part-time/adjunct (17 women). *Graduate housing:* Rooms and/or apartments available on a first-come, first-served basis to single and married students. *Student services:* Campus employment opportunities, campus safety program, career counseling, child daycare facilities, exercise/wellness program, free psychological counseling, grant writing training, international student services, low-cost health insurance, services for students with disabilities, teacher training, writing training. *Library:* Founders Memorial Library plus 4 others. *Collection:* Books: 1.8 million (physical), 471,409 (digital/electronic); Serial titles: 600 (physical), 76,936 (digital/electronic); Databases: 318. Students can reserve study rooms. *Research affiliation:* Field Museum of Natural History, Burpee Museum of Natural History, Argonne National Laboratory, Fermi National Accelerator Laboratory.

Computer facilities: 1,500 computers available on campus for general student use. A campuswide network can be accessed from student residence rooms and from off campus. Online class registration is available.
Website: http://www.niu.edu/

General Application Contact: Dr. Bradley G. Bond, Dean, Graduate School, 815-753-0395, Fax: 815-753-6366, E-mail: gradsch@niu.edu.

GRADUATE UNITS

College of Law Students: 211 full-time (102 women), 42 part-time (19 women); includes 64 minority (18 Black or African American, non-Hispanic/Latino; 2 American Indian or Alaska Native, non-Hispanic/Latino; 13 Asian, non-Hispanic/Latino; 27 Hispanic/Latino; 2 Native Hawaiian or other Pacific Islander, non-Hispanic/Latino; 2 Two or more races, non-Hispanic/Latino). Average age 29. 560 applicants, 64% accepted, 84 enrolled. *Faculty:* 22 full-time (11 women). *Financial support:* In 2015–16, 6 teaching assistantships were awarded; research assistantships, career-related internships or fieldwork, Federal Work-Study, tuition waivers (full and partial), and unspecified assistantships also available. Support available to part-time students. Financial award application deadline: 3/1; financial award applicants required to submit FAFSA. In 2015, 100 doctorates awarded. *Degree program information:* Part-time programs available. Part-time. Offers law (JD). *Application deadline:* For fall admission, 4/1 priority date for domestic and international students. Applications are processed on a rolling basis. Electronic applications accepted. *Application Contact:* Sarah Scarpelli, Director of Admissions and Financial Aid, 815-753-8535, Fax: 815-753-5680, E-mail: lawadm@niu.edu. *Dean,* Mark Cordes, 815-753-1380, Fax: 815-753-8552, E-mail: mcordes@niu.edu.

Graduate School Students: 2,067 full-time (965 women), 2,118 part-time (1,179 women); includes 783 minority (252 Black or African American, non-Hispanic/Latino; 1 American Indian or Alaska Native, non-Hispanic/Latino; 207 Asian, non-Hispanic/Latino; 237 Hispanic/Latino; 1 Native Hawaiian or other Pacific Islander, non-Hispanic/Latino; 85 Two or more races, non-Hispanic/Latino), 881 international. Average age 32. 4,254 applicants, 50% accepted, 946 enrolled. *Faculty:* 672 full-time (248 women), 66 part-time/adjunct (17 women). *Financial support:* In 2015–16, 368 research assistantships with full tuition reimbursements, 779 teaching assistantships with full tuition reimbursements were awarded; fellowships with full tuition reimbursements, career-related internships or fieldwork, Federal Work-Study, scholarships/grants, tuition waivers (full), and staff assistantships also available. Support available to part-time students. Financial award applicants required to submit FAFSA. In 2015, 1,434 master's, 153 doctorates, 17 other advanced degrees awarded. *Degree program information:* Part-time and evening/weekend programs available. Part-time, evening/weekend, online learning. *Application deadline:* For fall admission, 8/1 for domestic students, 5/1 for international students; for spring admission, 12/1 for domestic students, 10/1 for international students. Applications are processed on a rolling basis. *Application fee:* $40. Electronic applications accepted. *Application Contact:* Graduate School Information, 815-753-0395, E-mail: gradsch@niu.edu. *Dean,* Dr. Bradley G. Bond, 815-753-9403, Fax: 815-753-6366, E-mail: bbond@niu.edu.

College of Business Students: 415 full-time (144 women), 500 part-time (175 women); includes 225 minority (50 Black or African American, non-Hispanic/Latino; 107 Asian, non-Hispanic/Latino; 50 Hispanic/Latino; 1 Native Hawaiian or other Pacific Islander, non-Hispanic/Latino; 17 Two or more races, non-Hispanic/Latino), 225 international. Average age 31. 796 applicants, 65% accepted, 427 enrolled. *Faculty:* 53 full-time (17 women), 3 part-time/adjunct (0 women). *Financial support:* In 2015–16, 4 research assistantships with full tuition reimbursements were awarded; fellowships with full tuition reimbursements, teaching assistantships with full tuition reimbursements, career-related internships or fieldwork, Federal Work-Study, scholarships/grants, tuition waivers (full), and unspecified assistantships also available. Support available to part-time students. Financial award applicants required to submit FAFSA. In 2015, 451 master's awarded. *Degree program information:* Part-time and evening/weekend programs available. Part-time, evening/weekend. Offers accountancy (MAS, MST); business (MAS, MBA, MST); business administration (MBA). *Application deadline:* For fall admission, 6/1 for domestic students, 5/1 for international students; for spring admission, 11/1 for domestic students, 10/1 for international students. Applications are processed on a rolling basis. *Application fee:* $40. Electronic applications accepted. *Application Contact:* Office of Graduate Studies in Business, 815-753-6301. *Dean*, Dr. Denise Schoenbachler, 815-753-6225, Fax: 815-753-5305, E-mail: denises@niu.edu.

College of Education Students: 341 full-time (216 women), 836 part-time (587 women); includes 276 minority (136 Black or African American, non-Hispanic/Latino; 1 American Indian or Alaska Native, non-Hispanic/Latino; 29 Asian, non-Hispanic/Latino; 85 Hispanic/Latino; 25 Two or more races, non-Hispanic/Latino), 66 international. Average age 35. 472 applicants, 65% accepted, 184 enrolled. *Faculty:* 110 full-time (66 women), 5 part-time/adjunct (3 women). *Financial support:* In 2015–16, 1 research assistantship with full tuition reimbursement was awarded; fellowships with full tuition reimbursements, teaching assistantships with full tuition reimbursements, career-related internships or fieldwork, Federal Work-Study, scholarships/grants, tuition waivers (full), and staff assistantships also available. Support available to part-time students. Financial award applicants required to submit FAFSA. In 2015, 344 master's, 57 doctorates, 14 other advanced degrees awarded. *Degree program information:* Part-time and evening/weekend programs available. Part-time, evening/weekend, online learning. Offers adult and higher education (MS Ed, Ed D); counseling (MS Ed, Ed D); curriculum and instruction (MS Ed, Ed D); early childhood education (MS Ed); education (MS, MS Ed, Ed D, Ed S); educational administration (MS Ed, Ed D, Ed S); educational psychology (MS Ed, Ed D); educational research and evaluation (MS); elementary education (MS Ed); foundations of education (MS Ed); instructional technology (MS Ed, Ed D); literacy education (MS Ed); physical education (MS Ed); school business management (MS Ed); special education (MS Ed); sport management (MS). *Application deadline:* For fall admission, 6/1 for domestic students, 5/1 for international students; for spring admission, 11/1 for domestic students, 10/1 for international students. Applications are processed on a rolling basis. *Application fee:* $40. Electronic applications accepted. *Application Contact:* Graduate School Office, 815-753-0395, E-mail: gradsch@niu.edu. *Dean*, Laurie Elish-Piper, 815-753-1949, Fax: 851-753-2100.

College of Engineering and Engineering Technology Students: 183 full-time (24 women), 129 part-time (22 women); includes 38 minority (10 Black or African American, non-Hispanic/Latino; 10 Asian, non-Hispanic/Latino; 13 Hispanic/Latino; 5 Two or more races, non-Hispanic/Latino), 204 international. Average age 26. 625 applicants, 50% accepted, 117 enrolled. *Faculty:* 36 full-time (2 women), 2 part-time/adjunct (0 women). *Financial support:* In 2015–16, 6 research assistantships with full tuition reimbursements, 9 teaching assistantships with full tuition reimbursements were awarded; fellowships with full tuition reimbursements, career-related internships or fieldwork, Federal Work-Study, scholarships/grants, tuition waivers (full), and unspecified assistantships also available. Support available to part-time students. Financial award applicants required to submit FAFSA. In 2015, 121 master's awarded. *Degree program information:* Part-time and evening/weekend programs available. Part-time, evening/weekend. Offers electrical engineering (MS); engineering and engineering technology (MS); industrial engineering (MS); industrial management (MS); mechanical engineering (MS). *Application deadline:* For fall admission, 6/1 for domestic students, 5/1 for international students; for spring admission, 11/1 for domestic students, 10/1 for international students. Applications are processed on a rolling basis. *Application fee:* $40. Electronic applications accepted. *Application Contact:* Graduate School Office, 815-753-0395, E-mail: gradsch@niu.edu. *Dean*, Dr. Promod Vohra, 815-753-1281, Fax: 815-753-1310, E-mail: pvohra@niu.edu.

College of Health and Human Sciences Students: 271 full-time (206 women), 233 part-time (208 women); includes 97 minority (22 Black or African American, non-Hispanic/Latino; 29 Asian, non-Hispanic/Latino; 27 Hispanic/Latino; 19 Two or more races, non-Hispanic/Latino), 8 international. Average age 30. 511 applicants, 34% accepted, 95 enrolled. *Faculty:* 46 full-time (37 women), 5 part-time/adjunct (3 women). *Financial support:* In 2015–16, 3 research assistantships with full tuition reimbursements were awarded; fellowships with full tuition reimbursements, teaching assistantships with full tuition reimbursements, career-related internships or fieldwork, Federal Work-Study, scholarships/grants, tuition waivers (full), and staff assistantships also available. Support available to part-time students. Financial award applicants required to submit FAFSA. In 2015, 159 master's, 44 doctorates awarded. *Degree program information:* Part-time and evening/weekend programs available. Part-time, evening/weekend. Offers allied health and communicative disorders (MA, MPT, Au D, DPT, TDPT); applied family and child studies (MS); communicative disorders (MA, Au D); health and human sciences (MA, MPH, MPT, MS, Au D, DPT, TDPT); nursing (MS); nutrition and dietetics (MS); physical therapy (MPT, DPT, TDPT); public health (MPH). *Application deadline:* For fall admission, 6/1 for domestic students, 5/1 for international students; for spring admission, 11/1 for domestic students, 10/1 for international students. Applications are processed on a rolling basis. *Application fee:* $40. Electronic applications accepted. *Application Contact:* Graduate School Office, 815-753-0395, E-mail: gradsch@niu.edu. *Interim Dean*, Dr. Derryl Block, 815-753-6157.

College of Liberal Arts and Sciences Students: 741 full-time (316 women), 366 part-time (157 women); includes 122 minority (29 Black or African American, non-Hispanic/Latino; 28 Asian, non-Hispanic/Latino; 52 Hispanic/Latino; 13 Two or more races, non-Hispanic/Latino), 345 international. Average age 29. 1,686 applicants, 44% accepted, 258 enrolled. *Faculty:* 342 full-time (99 women), 36 part-time/adjunct (7 women). *Financial support:* Fellowships with full tuition reimbursements, research assistantships with full tuition reimbursements, teaching assistantships with full tuition reimbursements, career-related internships or fieldwork, Federal Work-Study, scholarships/grants, tuition waivers (full), and unspecified assistantships available. Support available to part-time students. Financial award applicants required to submit FAFSA. In 2015, 348 master's, 59 doctorates awarded. *Degree program information:* Part-time and evening/weekend programs available. Part-time, evening/weekend. Offers anthropology (MA); biological sciences (MS, PhD); chemistry (MS, PhD); communication studies (MA); computer science (MS); economics (MA, PhD); English (MA, PhD); French (MA); geography (MS, PhD); geology (MS, PhD); history (MA, PhD); liberal arts and sciences (MA, MPA, MS, PhD); mathematical sciences (PhD); mathematics (MS); philosophy (MA); physics (MS, PhD); political science (MA, PhD); psychology (MA, PhD); public administration (MPA); sociology (MA); Spanish (MA); statistics (MS). *Application deadline:* For fall admission, 6/1 for domestic students, 5/1 for international students; for spring admission, 11/1 for domestic students, 10/1 for international students. Applications are processed on a rolling basis. *Application fee:* $40. Electronic applications accepted. *Application Contact:* Graduate School Office, 815-753-0395, E-mail: gradsch@niu.edu. *Acting Dean*, Dr. Christopher McCord, 815-753-1061, Fax: 815-753-7950, E-mail: mccord@niu.edu.

College of Visual and Performing Arts Students: 116 full-time (59 women), 54 part-time (30 women); includes 25 minority (5 Black or African American, non-Hispanic/Latino; 4 Asian, non-Hispanic/Latino; 10 Hispanic/Latino; 6 Two or more races, non-Hispanic/Latino), 33 international. Average age 29. 164 applicants, 57% accepted, 45 enrolled. *Faculty:* 85 full-time (27 women), 15 part-time/adjunct (4 women). *Financial support:* Fellowships with full tuition reimbursements, research assistantships with full tuition reimbursements, teaching assistantships with full tuition reimbursements, career-related internships or fieldwork, Federal Work-Study, scholarships/grants, tuition waivers (full), and staff assistantships available. Support available to part-time students. Financial award applicants required to submit FAFSA. In 2015, 54 master's, 4 other advanced degrees awarded. *Degree program information:* Part-time and evening/weekend programs available. Part-time, evening/weekend. Offers art (MA, MFA, MS); music (MM, Performer's Certificate); theatre and dance (MFA); visual and performing arts (MA, MFA, MM, MS, Performer's Certificate). *Application deadline:* For fall admission, 5/1 for international students; for spring admission, 10/1 for international students. Applications are processed on a rolling basis. *Application fee:* $40. Electronic applications accepted. *Application Contact:* Graduate School Office, 815-753-0395, E-mail: gradsch@niu.edu. *Interim Dean*, Dr. Paul Bauer, 815-753-1138, Fax: 815-753-8372, E-mail: paulbauer@niu.edu.

NORTHERN KENTUCKY UNIVERSITY, Highland Heights, KY 41099

General Information State-supported, coed, comprehensive institution. CGS member. *Graduate housing:* Room and/or apartments available on a first-come, first-served basis to single students; on-campus housing not available to married students. Housing application deadline: 5/1.

GRADUATE UNITS

Chase College of Law ***Degree program information:*** Part-time and evening/weekend programs available. Part-time, evening/weekend. Offers law (JD). Electronic applications accepted.

Office of Graduate Programs ***Degree program information:*** Part-time and evening/weekend programs available. Part-time, evening/weekend, online learning. Electronic applications accepted.

College of Arts and Sciences Degree program information: Part-time and evening/weekend programs available. Part-time, evening/weekend, online learning. Offers arts and sciences (MA, MPA, MS, Certificate); composition and rhetoric (Certificate); creative writing (Certificate); cultural studies and discourses (Certificate); English (MA); industrial psychology (Certificate); industrial-organizational psychology (MS); integrative studies (MA); non-profit management (Certificate); occupational health psychology (Certificate); organizational psychology (Certificate); professional writing (Certificate); public administration (MPA); public history (MA). Electronic applications accepted.

College of Business Degree program information: Part-time and evening/weekend programs available. Part-time, evening/weekend. Offers accountancy (M Acc); advanced taxation (Certificate); business (M Acc, MBA, MS, Certificate); business administration (MBA, Certificate); executive leadership and organizational change (MS). Electronic applications accepted.

College of Education and Human Services Degree program information: Part-time and evening/weekend programs available. Part-time, evening/weekend. Offers clinical mental health counseling (MS); education (MA, Certificate); education and human services (MA, MAT, MS, MSW, Ed D, Certificate, Ed S); educational leadership (Ed D, Ed S); school counseling (MA); social work (MSW); special education (Certificate); teaching (MAT). Electronic applications accepted.

College of Informatics Degree program information: Part-time and evening/weekend programs available. Part-time, evening/weekend. Offers business informatics (MS, Certificate); communication (MA); communication teaching (Certificate); computer information technology (MSCIT); computer science (MSCS); corporate information security (Certificate); documentary studies (Certificate); enterprise resource planning (Certificate); geographic information systems (Certificate); health informatics (MS, Certificate); informatics (MA, MS, MSCIT, MSCS, Certificate); public relations (Certificate); relationships (Certificate); secure software engineering (Certificate). Electronic applications accepted.

School of Nursing and Health Professions Degree program information: Part-time and evening/weekend programs available. Part-time, evening/weekend, online learning. Offers health science (MS); nursing (MSHS, MSN, DNP, Certificate, Post-Master's Certificate); nursing and health professions (MS, MSHS, MSN, DNP, Certificate, Post-Master's Certificate). Electronic applications accepted.

NORTHERN MICHIGAN UNIVERSITY, Marquette, MI 49855-5301

General Information State-supported, coed, comprehensive institution. CGS member. *Graduate housing:* Rooms and/or apartments available on a first-come, first-served basis to single and married students. Housing application deadline: 6/30.

GRADUATE UNITS

Office of Graduate Education and Research ***Degree program information:*** Part-time and evening/weekend programs available. Part-time, evening/weekend, online learning. Electronic applications accepted.

College of Arts and Sciences Degree program information: Part-time programs available. Part-time, online learning. Offers applied behavior analysis (MS); arts and sciences (MA, MFA, MS, Graduate Certificate); biochemistry (MS); biology (MS); creative writing (MFA); literature (MA); pedagogy (MA); performance improvement (Graduate Certificate); psychology (MS); teaching English to speakers of other languages (Graduate Certificate); theater (MA); training and performance improvement (MS); writing (MA). Electronic applications accepted.

College of Business Degree program information: Part-time programs available. Part-time. Offers business (MBA). Electronic applications accepted.

College of Health Sciences and Professional Studies Degree program information: Part-time programs available. Part-time. Offers administration and supervision (MAE); clinical molecular genetics (MS); elementary education (MAE); exercise science (MS); health sciences and professional studies (MA, MA Ed, MAE, MPA, MS, MSN, DNP); higher education in student affairs (MA); instruction (MAE); learning disabilities

(MAE); nursing (MSN, DNP); public administration (MPA); reading education (MAE); science education (MS); secondary education (MAE).

NORTHERN SEMINARY, Lombard, IL 60148-5698

General Information Independent-religious, coed, primarily men, graduate-only institution. *Enrollment by degree level:* 117 master's, 88 doctoral. *Graduate faculty:* 6 full-time (1 woman), 33 part-time/adjunct (8 women). *Tuition, area resident:* Full-time $18,000; part-time $9000 per semester. *Required fees:* $360; $360 per unit. $120 per quarter. Tuition and fees vary according to degree level. *Graduate housing:* Rooms and/or apartments available on a first-come, first-served basis to single and married students. Typical cost: $6705 per year for single students; $6705 per year for married students. Room charges vary according to housing facility selected. Housing application deadline: 8/30. *Student services:* Campus employment opportunities, low-cost health insurance. *Library:* Brimsom Grow Library. *Collection:* Books: 53,200 (physical). Weekly public service hours: 30; students can reserve study rooms.

Computer facilities: 8 computers available on campus for general student use. A campuswide network can be accessed. Online class registration, X are available.
Website: http://www.seminary.edu/

General Application Contact: Isaac Ampil, Director of Admissions, 630-620-2175, Fax: 630-620-2190, E-mail: admissions@seminary.edu.

GRADUATE UNITS

Graduate and Professional Programs Students: 126 full-time (34 women), 80 part-time (32 women); includes 89 minority (73 Black or African American, non-Hispanic/Latino; 6 Asian, non-Hispanic/Latino; 8 Hispanic/Latino; 2 Two or more races, non-Hispanic/Latino), 3 international. Average age 44. *Faculty:* 6 full-time (1 woman), 33 part-time/adjunct (8 women). *Financial support:* Scholarships/grants available. Support available to part-time students. Financial award application deadline: 9/1; financial award applicants required to submit FAFSA. *Degree program information:* Part-time and evening/weekend programs available. Part-time, evening/weekend. Offers Biblical studies (M Div); Christian community development (D Min); Christian ministry (MACM); contextual theology (D Min); New Testament (MANT); New Testament context (D Min); theology (M Div); theology and mission (MA); worship (MAW). *Application deadline:* For fall admission, 8/25 for domestic students, 2/1 for international students; for winter admission, 12/10 for domestic students, 2/1 for international students; for spring admission, 3/15 for domestic students, 2/1 for international students. Applications are processed on a rolling basis. *Application fee:* $35. Electronic applications accepted. *Application Contact:* Isaac Ampil, Director of Admissions, 630-620-2175, Fax: 630-620-2190, E-mail: admissions@seminary.edu. *President*, Dr. William Shiell, 630-620-2101, Fax: 630-620-2190.

NORTHERN STATE UNIVERSITY, Aberdeen, SD 57401-7198

General Information State-supported, coed, comprehensive institution. *Graduate housing:* Room and/or apartments available on a first-come, first-served basis to single students; on-campus housing not available to married students. Housing application deadline: 8/1. *Research affiliation:* AASCU–Grants Resource Center.

GRADUATE UNITS

MME Program in Music Education ***Degree program information:*** Part-time programs available. Part-time, online learning. Offers music education (MME). Electronic applications accepted.

MS Ed Program in Counseling ***Degree program information:*** Part-time programs available. Part-time, online learning. Offers clinical mental health counseling (MS Ed); school counseling (MS Ed). Electronic applications accepted.

MS Ed Program in Educational Studies ***Degree program information:*** Part-time programs available. Part-time, online learning. Offers educational studies (MS Ed). Electronic applications accepted.

MS Ed Program in Instructional Design in E-learning ***Degree program information:*** Part-time programs available. Part-time, online learning. Offers instructional design in e-learning (MS Ed). Electronic applications accepted.

MS Ed Program in Leadership and Administration ***Degree program information:*** Part-time and evening/weekend programs available. Part-time, evening/weekend, online learning. Offers leadership and administration (MS Ed). Electronic applications accepted.

MS Ed Program in Sport Performance and Leadership ***Degree program information:*** Part-time programs available. Part-time. Offers sport performance and leadership (MS Ed). Electronic applications accepted.

MS Ed Program in Teaching and Learning ***Degree program information:*** Part-time and evening/weekend programs available. Part-time, evening/weekend, online learning. Offers teaching and learning (MS Ed). Electronic applications accepted.

MS Program in Banking and Financial Services ***Degree program information:*** Part-time programs available. Part-time, online learning. Offers banking and financial services (MS). Electronic applications accepted.

MS Program in Training and Development in E-learning ***Degree program information:*** Part-time programs available. Part-time, online learning. Offers training and development in e-learning (MS). Electronic applications accepted.

NORTH GREENVILLE UNIVERSITY, Tigerville, SC 29688-1892

General Information Independent-religious, coed, comprehensive institution. *Graduate housing:* Room and/or apartments available on a first-come, first-served basis to single students; on-campus housing not available to married students. Housing application deadline: 8/1.

GRADUATE UNITS

T. Walter Brashier Graduate School ***Degree program information:*** Part-time and evening/weekend programs available. Part-time, evening/weekend, online learning. Offers Christian ministry (MCM, D Min); education (M Ed, MAT); financial planning (MBA); human resources (MBA). Electronic applications accepted.

NORTH PARK THEOLOGICAL SEMINARY, Chicago, IL 60625-4895

General Information Independent-religious, coed, graduate-only institution. *Graduate housing:* Rooms and/or apartments available to single and married students. Housing application deadline: 9/1. *Research affiliation:* Northside Chicago Theological Institute, Covenant Archives and Historical Society, American Theological Library Association.

GRADUATE UNITS

Graduate and Professional Programs ***Degree program information:*** Part-time programs available. Part-time. Offers adult ministry (Certificate); camping and retreat ministry (Certificate); children and family ministry (Certificate); Christian formation (MA); Christian ministry (MACM); faith and health (Certificate); intercultural studies (Certificate); justice ministry (Certificate); leadership and administration (Certificate); preaching (D Min); spiritual direction (Certificate); theological studies (MATS); theology (M Div); youth ministry (Certificate).

NORTH PARK UNIVERSITY, Chicago, IL 60625-4895

General Information Independent-religious, coed, comprehensive institution. *Graduate housing:* Rooms and/or apartments available to single and married students.

GRADUATE UNITS

School of Business and Nonprofit Management ***Degree program information:*** Part-time and evening/weekend programs available. Part-time, evening/weekend, online learning. Offers business and nonprofit management (MBA, MHEA, MHRM, MM, MNA).

School of Education Offers education (MA).

School of Music Offers vocal performance (MM).

School of Nursing ***Degree program information:*** Part-time and evening/weekend programs available. Part-time, evening/weekend. Offers advanced practice nursing (MS); leadership and management (MS).

NORTHWEST CHRISTIAN UNIVERSITY, Eugene, OR 97401-3745

General Information Independent-religious, coed, comprehensive institution. *Enrollment:* 740 graduate, professional, and undergraduate students; 182 full-time matriculated graduate/professional students (129 women), 25 part-time matriculated graduate/professional students (14 women). *Enrollment by degree level:* 207 master's. *Graduate faculty:* 13 full-time (5 women), 15 part-time/adjunct (10 women). *Tuition, area resident:* Full-time $7500; part-time $3750 per semester. *Required fees:* $85 per semester. Tuition and fees vary according to course load and program. *Graduate housing:* On-campus housing not available. *Student services:* Campus employment opportunities, career counseling, free psychological counseling, services for students with disabilities, teacher training, writing training. *Library:* Edward P. Kellenberger Library. *Collection:* Books: 66,982 (physical), 14 (digital/electronic); Serial titles: 155 (physical), 487,355 (digital/electronic); Databases: 89. Weekly public service hours: 70.

Computer facilities: 16 computers available on campus for general student use. A campuswide network can be accessed from student residence rooms and from off campus. Online class registration is available.
Website: http://www.nwcu.edu/

General Application Contact: Heath Alexander, Recruiter, 541-684-7348, E-mail: halexander@nwcu.edu.

GRADUATE UNITS

School of Business and Management Students: 51 full-time (29 women), 9 part-time (4 women); includes 11 minority (2 Black or African American, non-Hispanic/Latino; 1 American Indian or Alaska Native, non-Hispanic/Latino; 1 Asian, non-Hispanic/Latino; 5 Hispanic/Latino; 1 Native Hawaiian or other Pacific Islander, non-Hispanic/Latino; 1 Two or more races, non-Hispanic/Latino). Average age 36. *Faculty:* 3 full-time (0 women), 3 part-time/adjunct (1 woman). In 2015, 14 master's awarded. *Degree program information:* Part-time and evening/weekend programs available. Part-time, evening/weekend, online only, 100% online. Offers accounting (MBA); management (MBA). *Application deadline:* For fall admission, 3/15 for domestic students. Applications are processed on a rolling basis. Electronic applications accepted. *Assistant Dean*, Dr. Peter Diffenderfer, 541-684-7441, Fax: 541-684-7336, E-mail: pdiffenderfer@nwcu.edu.

School of Education and Counseling Students: 67 full-time (47 women), 78 part-time (62 women); includes 24 minority (3 Black or African American, non-Hispanic/Latino; 3 American Indian or Alaska Native, non-Hispanic/Latino; 3 Asian, non-Hispanic/Latino; 8 Hispanic/Latino; 7 Two or more races, non-Hispanic/Latino). Average age 36. *Faculty:* 9 full-time (5 women), 12 part-time/adjunct (9 women). In 2015, 55 master's awarded. *Degree program information:* Part-time and evening/weekend programs available. Part-time, evening/weekend, 100% online, blended/hybrid learning. Offers clinical mental health counseling (MA); curriculum and instructional technology (M Ed); elementary teaching (MAT); English for speakers of other languages (ESOL) (MAT); school counseling (MA); secondary teaching (MAT). *Application deadline:* For fall admission, 3/15 for domestic students. Applications are processed on a rolling basis. Electronic applications accepted. *Dean, Education and Counseling*, Gene James, 541-684-7261, Fax: 541-684-7310, E-mail: gjames@nwcu.edu.

NORTHWESTERN COLLEGE, Orange City, IA 51041-1996

General Information Independent-religious, coed, comprehensive institution.

GRADUATE UNITS

Program in Education Online learning. Offers early childhood (M Ed); master teacher (M Ed); teacher leadership (M Ed, Graduate Certificate).

NORTHWESTERN HEALTH SCIENCES UNIVERSITY, Bloomington, MN 55431-1599

General Information Independent, coed, graduate-only institution. *Graduate housing:* On-campus housing not available. *Research affiliation:* University of Minnesota, Center for Spirituality and Healing (education research), University of Western States (clinical research), University of Pittsburgh (education research).

GRADUATE UNITS

College of Acupuncture and Oriental Medicine Offers acupuncture (M Ac); Oriental medicine (MOM). Electronic applications accepted.

College of Chiropractic Offers chiropractic (DC). Electronic applications accepted.

NORTHWESTERN OKLAHOMA STATE UNIVERSITY, Alva, OK 73717-2799

General Information State-supported, coed, comprehensive institution. *Graduate housing:* Room and/or apartments available to single students; on-campus housing not available to married students.

GRADUATE UNITS

Program in American Studies ***Degree program information:*** Part-time programs available. Part-time. Offers American studies (MA).

School of Professional Studies ***Degree program information:*** Part-time programs available. Part-time. Offers adult education management and administration (M Ed); counseling psychology (MCP); curriculum and instruction (M Ed); educational leadership (M Ed); elementary education (M Ed); reading specialist (M Ed); school counseling (M Ed); secondary education (M Ed).

NORTHWESTERN POLYTECHNIC UNIVERSITY, Fremont, CA 94539-7482

General Information Independent, coed, comprehensive institution. *Graduate housing:* Room and/or apartments available on a first-come, first-served basis to single students; on-campus housing not available to married students. Housing application deadline: 7/15.

GRADUATE UNITS

School of Business and Information Technology *Degree program information:* Part-time and evening/weekend programs available. Part-time, evening/weekend. Offers business and information technology (MBA, DBA).

School of Engineering *Degree program information:* Part-time and evening/weekend programs available. Part-time, evening/weekend. Offers computer engineering (DCE); computer science (MS); computer systems engineering (MS); electrical engineering (MS).

NORTHWESTERN STATE UNIVERSITY OF LOUISIANA, Natchitoches, LA 71497

General Information State-supported, coed, comprehensive institution. CGS member. *Graduate housing:* Room and/or apartments available on a first-come, first-served basis to single students; on-campus housing not available to married students. Housing application deadline: 3/1. *Research affiliation:* NASA (Strategic Defense Initiative), Central State Hospital, Federal Records and Archives Services.

GRADUATE UNITS

Graduate Studies and Research *Degree program information:* Part-time and evening/weekend programs available. Part-time, evening/weekend, online learning. Offers clinical psychology (MS); English (MA); health and human performance (MS); homeland security (MS). Electronic applications accepted.

College of Education and Human Development Offers adult and continuing education (MA); counseling (Ed S); curriculum and instruction (M Ed); early childhood education and teaching (M Ed, MAT); education and human development (M Ed, MA, MAT, Ed S); educational leadership (M Ed, Ed S); educational technology (Ed S); educational technology leadership (M Ed); elementary education (MAT); elementary teaching (Ed S); middle school education (MAT); reading (Ed S); school counseling (MA); secondary education (MAT); secondary teaching (Ed S); special education (Ed S); student affairs in higher education (MA). Electronic applications accepted.

College of Nursing and School of Allied Health Degree program information: Part-time programs available. Part-time. Offers nursing and allied health (MS, MSN); radiologic sciences (MS). Electronic applications accepted.

School of Creative and Performing Arts Offers art (MA); fine and graphic arts (MA); music (MM). Electronic applications accepted.

NORTHWESTERN UNIVERSITY, Evanston, IL 60208

General Information Independent, coed, university. CGS member. *Graduate housing:* Rooms and/or apartments available on a first-come, first-served basis to single students and available to married students. Housing application deadline: 9/1. *Research affiliation:* Dow Chemical Company (materials science and engineering), E.I. du Pont de Nemours and Company (physics), Exxon Chemical Company (chemical engineering), Ford Motor Company (mechanical engineering), Medtronics, Inc. (cardiology), Amoco Oil Company (materials science and engineering).

GRADUATE UNITS

Feinberg School of Medicine Offers biostatistics (PhD); clinical investigation (MSCI); epidemiology (PhD); health and biomedical informatics (PhD); health services and outcomes research (PhD); healthcare quality and patient safety (PhD); medicine (MS, MSCI, DPT, MD, PhD); neuroscience (PhD); physical therapy (DPT); public health (MPH); translational outcomes in science (PhD). Electronic applications accepted.

The Graduate School *Degree program information:* Part-time and evening/weekend programs available. Part-time, evening/weekend. Offers biochemistry (PhD); bioengineering and biotechnology (PhD); biotechnology (PhD); cell and molecular biology (PhD); clinical investigation (MSCI, Certificate); clinical psychology (PhD); developmental and systems biology (PhD); gender and sexuality studies (Graduate Certificate); genetic counseling (MS); marital and family therapy (MS); nanotechnology (PhD); neurobiology (PhD); neuroscience (PhD); structural biology and biophysics (PhD). Electronic applications accepted.

Center for International and Comparative Studies Offers international and comparative studies (Certificate).

Judd A. and Marjorie Weinberg College of Arts and Sciences Degree program information: Part-time and evening/weekend programs available. Part-time, evening/weekend. Offers African American studies (PhD); African studies (Graduate Certificate); ancient philosophy (PhD); anthropology (PhD); applied physics (PhD); art history (PhD); arts and sciences (MA, MFA, MS, PhD, Graduate Certificate); brain, behavior and cognition (PhD); chemistry (PhD); clinical psychology (PhD); cognitive psychology (PhD); comparative literary studies (PhD); earth and planetary sciences (PhD); economics (PhD); English (MA, PhD); French/Francophone studies (PhD); German literature and critical thought (PhD); history (PhD); Italian studies (Graduate Certificate); linguistics (PhD); mathematics (PhD); neurobiology and physiology (MS); personality psychology (PhD); philosophy (PhD); physics and astronomy (PhD); plant biology and conservation (MA, PhD); political science (PhD); religious studies (PhD); Slavic languages and literature (PhD); social psychology (PhD); sociology (PhD); Spanish and Portuguese (PhD); statistics (MS, PhD); visual arts (MFA).

Kellogg School of Management Degree program information: Part-time and evening/weekend programs available. Part-time, evening/weekend. Offers accounting information and management (MBA, PhD); analytical finance (MBA); business administration (MBA); decision sciences (MBA); entrepreneurship and innovation (MBA); finance (PhD); health enterprise management (MBA); human resources management (MBA); international business (MBA); management (MBA, MS, PhD); management and organizations (MBA, PhD); management and organizations and sociology (PhD); management and strategy (PhD); management studies (MS); managerial analytics (MBA); managerial economics (MBA); managerial economics and decision sciences (PhD); managerial economics and strategy (PhD); marketing (MBA, PhD); marketing management (MBA); media management (MBA); operations management (MBA, PhD); real estate (MBA); social enterprise at Kellogg (MBA). PhD admissions and degree offered through The Graduate School. Electronic applications accepted.

School of Communication Degree program information: Part-time programs available. Part-time. Offers audiology (Au D); communication (MA, MFA, MS, MSC, Au D, PhD); communication sciences and disorders (PhD); communication studies (PhD); directing (MFA); documentary media (MFA); leadership for creative enterprises (MS); managerial communication (MSC); media, technology and society (PhD); performance studies (MA, PhD); screen cultures (MA, PhD); speech, language, and learning (MS); stage design (MFA); technology and social behavior (PhD); theatre and drama (PhD); writing for the screen and stage (MFA). MA, MFA, and PhD admissions and degrees offered through The Graduate School; MSC admissions and degrees offered through the School of Communication.

School of Education and Social Policy Degree program information: Part-time and evening/weekend programs available. Part-time, evening/weekend. Offers education (MS); elementary teaching (MS); human development and social policy (PhD); learning and organizational change (MS); learning sciences (MA, PhD); secondary teaching (MS); teacher leadership (MS). MA and PhD admissions and degrees offered through The Graduate School. Electronic applications accepted.

Henry and Leigh Bienen School of Music Offers brass performance (MM, DMA); composition (DMA); conducting (MM, DMA); jazz studies (MM); music education (MME, PhD); music theory (MM); music theory and cognition (PhD); musicology (MM, PhD); percussion performance (MM, DMA); performance (MM); piano pedagogy (MME); piano performance (MM, DMA); piano performance and collaborative arts (MM, DMA); piano performance and pedagogy (MM, DMA); string performance (MM, DMA); theory (MM); voice and opera performance (MM, DMA); woodwind performance (MM, DMA). PhD admissions and degree offered through The Graduate School. Electronic applications accepted.

McCormick School of Engineering and Applied Science *Degree program information:* Part-time and evening/weekend programs available. Part-time, evening/weekend. Offers analytics (MS); biomedical engineering (MS, PhD); biotechnology (MS); chemical engineering (MS, PhD); computer engineering (MS, PhD); computer science (MS, PhD); design innovation (MBA, MS); electrical engineering (MS, PhD); engineering and applied science (MBA, MEM, MIT, MME, MMM, MPD, MS, PhD, Certificate); engineering management (MEM); engineering sciences and applied mathematics (MS, PhD); environmental engineering and science (MS, PhD); geotechnical engineering (MS, PhD); industrial engineering and management science (MS, PhD); information technology (MS); integrated computational materials engineering (Certificate); materials science and engineering (MS, PhD); mechanical engineering (MS, PhD); mechanics of materials and solids (MS, PhD); product design and development management (MS); project management (MS); robotics (MS); structural engineering and materials (MS, PhD); theoretical and applied mechanics (MS, PhD); transportation systems analysis and planning (MS, PhD). MS and PhD admissions and degrees offered through The Graduate School. Electronic applications accepted.

Segal Design Institute Offers engineering design and innovation (MS).

Medill School of Journalism, Media, and Integrated Marketing Communications Offers brand strategy (MSIMC); content marketing (MSIMC); direct and interactive marketing (MSIMC); integrated marketing communications (MSIMC); interactive publishing (MSJ); magazine writing/editing (MSJ); marketing analytics (MSIMC); reporting (MSJ); strategic communications (MSIMC); video/broadcast (MSJ). Electronic applications accepted.

Pritzker School of Law Offers international human rights (LL M); law (JD); law and business (LL M); science law (MSL); tax (LL M in Tax). Executive LL M programs offered in Madrid (Spain), Seoul (South Korea), and Tel Aviv (Israel). Electronic applications accepted.

School of Professional Studies Offers American literature (MA); American studies (MA); analytics and business intelligence (MS); British literature (MA); clinical research (MS); comparative and world literature (MA); computer-based data mining (MS); creative writing (MA, MFA); database and Internet technologies (MS); global health (MS); global policy (MA); health services policy (MA); healthcare compliance (MS); history (MA); information systems (MS); information systems management (MS); information systems security (MS); marketing analytics (MS); medical informatics (MS); predictive modeling (MS); public administration (MA); public policy (MA); quality systems (MS); religious and ethical studies (MA); risk analytics (MS); software project management and development (MS); sports administration (MA); Web analytics (MS).

NORTHWEST MISSOURI STATE UNIVERSITY, Maryville, MO 64468-6001

General Information State-supported, coed, comprehensive institution. *Enrollment:* 6,593 graduate, professional, and undergraduate students; 446 full-time matriculated graduate/professional students (156 women), 529 part-time matriculated graduate/professional students (307 women). *Enrollment by degree level:* 918 master's, 20 doctoral, 37 other advanced degrees. *Graduate faculty:* 314. Tuition, state resident: part-time $359 per credit hour. Tuition, nonresident: part-time $612 per credit hour. *Required fees:* $106 per credit hour. *Graduate housing:* Rooms and/or apartments available on a first-come, first-served basis to single and married students. Housing application deadline: 6/1. *Student services:* Campus employment opportunities, campus safety program, career counseling, free psychological counseling, international student services, low-cost health insurance, multicultural affairs office, services for students with disabilities, writing training. *Library:* Owens Library. *Collection:* Books: 243,085 (physical). Students can reserve study rooms.

Computer facilities: Computer purchase and lease plans are available. 6,465 computers available on campus for general student use. A campuswide network can be accessed from student residence rooms and from off campus. Online class registration, online courses with library and databases are available.
Website: http://www.nwmissouri.edu/

General Application Contact: Dr. Gregory Haddock, Dean of Graduate School, 660-562-1145, Fax: 660-562-1096, E-mail: gradsch@nwmissouri.edu.

GRADUATE UNITS

Graduate School Students: 446 full-time (156 women), 529 part-time (307 women). *Financial support:* Research assistantships with full tuition reimbursements, teaching assistantships with full tuition reimbursements, career-related internships or fieldwork, Federal Work-Study, institutionally sponsored loans, scholarships/grants, and administrative assistantships, tutorial assistantships available. Financial award application deadline: 4/1; financial award applicants required to submit FAFSA. *Degree program information:* Part-time and evening/weekend programs available. Part-time, evening/weekend. *Application deadline:* For fall admission, 7/1 for domestic and international students; for spring admission, 11/15 for domestic and international students. Applications are processed on a rolling basis. *Application fee:* $0 ($50 for international students). Electronic applications accepted. *Application Contact:* Terry Immel, Executive Secretary, 660-562-1145, Fax: 660-562-1096, E-mail: gradsch@nwmissouri.edu. *Dean,* Dr. Gregory Haddock, 660-562-1145, Fax: 660-562-1096, E-mail: gradsch@nwmissouri.edu.

College of Arts and Sciences Students: 326 full-time (100 women), 217 part-time (89 women). *Financial support:* Research assistantships with full tuition reimbursements, teaching assistantships with full tuition reimbursements, and administrative assistantships, tutorial assistantships available. Financial award application deadline: 4/1; financial award applicants required to submit FAFSA. *Degree program information:* Part-time programs available. Part-time. Offers applied computer science (MS); arts and sciences (MA, MME, MS, MS Ed, Certificate); biology (MS); English (MA); English education (MS Ed); English: English pedagogy (MA); geographic information systems (MS, Certificate); history (MA); instructional technology (MS); mathematics (MS); music education (MME); teaching history (MS Ed); teaching mathematics (MS Ed); teaching: science (MS Ed). *Application deadline:* For fall admission, 7/1 for domestic and international students; for spring admission, 11/15 for domestic and international students. Applications are processed on a rolling basis. *Application fee:* $0 ($50 for international students). Electronic applications accepted. *Dean*, Dr. Michael Steiner, 660-562-1197.

College of Education and Human Services Students: 69 full-time (36 women), 215 part-time (157 women). *Financial support:* Research assistantships with full tuition reimbursements, teaching assistantships with full tuition reimbursements, and unspecified assistantships available. Financial award application deadline: 4/1; financial award applicants required to submit FAFSA. *Degree program information:* Part-time programs available. Part-time. Offers applied health and sport sciences (MS); education and human services (MS, MS Ed, Ed S); educational leadership (MS Ed, Ed S); educational leadership: elementary (MS Ed); educational leadership: K-12 (MS Ed); educational leadership: secondary (MS Ed); elementary school principalship (Ed S); guidance and counseling (MS Ed); health and physical education (MS Ed); reading (MS Ed); recreation (MS); secondary school principalship (Ed S); special education (MS Ed); sport and exercise psychology (MS); superintendency (Ed S); teaching: early childhood education (MS Ed); teaching: elementary (self-contained) (MS Ed); teaching: English language learners (MS Ed); teaching: middle school (MS Ed). *Application deadline:* For fall admission, 7/1 for domestic and international students; for spring admission, 11/15 for domestic and international students. Applications are processed on a rolling basis. *Application fee:* $0 ($50 for international students). Electronic applications accepted. *Dean*, Dr. Joyce Piveral, 660-562-1778.

Melvin and Valorie Booth College of Business and Professional Studies Students: 50 full-time (19 women), 67 part-time (41 women). *Financial support:* Research assistantships with full tuition reimbursements, teaching assistantships with full tuition reimbursements, career-related internships or fieldwork, and administrative assistantships, tutorial assistantships available. Financial award application deadline: 4/1; financial award applicants required to submit FAFSA. *Degree program information:* Part-time programs available. Part-time. Offers agricultural economics (MBA); agriculture (MS); business administration (MBA); business and professional studies (MBA, MS, MS Ed, Certificate); information technology management (MBA); teaching agriculture (MS Ed). *Application deadline:* For fall admission, 7/1 for domestic and international students; for spring admission, 11/15 for domestic and international students. Applications are processed on a rolling basis. *Application fee:* $0 ($50 for international students). Electronic applications accepted. *Dean of Graduate School*, Dr. Gregory Haddock, 660-562-1145, Fax: 660-562-1096, E-mail: gradsch@nwmissouri.edu.

NORTHWEST NAZARENE UNIVERSITY, Nampa, ID 83686-5897

General Information Independent-religious, coed, comprehensive institution. *Enrollment:* 2,229 graduate, professional, and undergraduate students; 551 full-time matriculated graduate/professional students (352 women), 161 part-time matriculated graduate/professional students (92 women). *Enrollment by degree level:* 712 master's, 39 doctoral. *Graduate faculty:* 20 full-time (13 women), 117 part-time/adjunct (57 women). *Graduate housing:* On-campus housing not available. *Student services:* Career counseling, free psychological counseling, multicultural affairs office, teacher training. *Library:* John E. Riley Library.

Computer facilities: Computer purchase and lease plans are available. A campuswide network can be accessed from student residence rooms. Online class registration is available.
Website: http://www.nnu.edu/

General Application Contact: Dr. Paula Kellerer, Dean, College of Adult and Graduate Studies, 208-467-8729, Fax: 208-467-8252, E-mail: pkellerer@nnu.edu.

GRADUATE UNITS

Graduate Studies ***Degree program information:*** Part-time and evening/weekend programs available. Part-time, evening/weekend, online learning. Offers addiction studies (MSW); business administration (MBA); clinical counseling (MS); clinical mental health practice (MSW); curriculum and instruction (M Ed); educational leadership (M Ed, Ed D, PhD, Ed S); healthcare (MBA); management, community planning and social administration (MSW); marriage and family counseling (MS); medical social work (MSW); missional leadership (M Div, MA); nursing (MSN); pastoral ministry (MA); school counseling (MS); spiritual formation (M Div, MA); youth, children, and family ministry (M Div, MA). Electronic applications accepted.

NORTHWEST UNIVERSITY, Kirkland, WA 98033

General Information Independent-religious, coed, comprehensive institution. *Graduate housing:* Rooms and/or apartments available on a first-come, first-served basis to single and married students.

GRADUATE UNITS

College of Business ***Degree program information:*** Part-time and evening/weekend programs available. Part-time, evening/weekend. Offers business administration (MBA); international business (MBA); project management (MBA); social entrepreneurship (MBA). Electronic applications accepted.

College of Ministry ***Degree program information:*** Part-time and evening/weekend programs available. Part-time, evening/weekend, online learning. Offers ministry (MIM); missional leadership (MA); theology and culture (MA). Electronic applications accepted.

College of Social and Behavioral Sciences ***Degree program information:*** Evening/weekend programs available. Evening/weekend. Offers counseling psychology (MA, Psy D); international community development (MA).

School of Education ***Degree program information:*** Part-time and evening/weekend programs available. Part-time, evening/weekend. Offers education (M Ed); teaching (MIT). Electronic applications accepted.

NORTHWOOD UNIVERSITY, MICHIGAN CAMPUS, Midland, MI 48640-2398

General Information Independent, coed, comprehensive institution. *Graduate housing:* Room and/or apartments available on a first-come, first-served basis to single students. Housing application deadline: 8/30. *Research affiliation:* Motor & Equipment Manufacturers Association (automotive engineering), Specialized Equipment Manufacturers Association (automotive engineering), Automotive Aftermarket Industry Association (automotive engineering), Automotive Warehouse Distributors Association (automotive engineering).

GRADUATE UNITS

DeVos Graduate School ***Degree program information:*** Part-time and evening/weekend programs available. Part-time, evening/weekend, online learning. Offers management (MBA, MSOL). MBA also offered on Florida and Texas campuses; MSOL offered online only. Electronic applications accepted.

NORWICH UNIVERSITY, Northfield, VT 05663

General Information Independent, coed, comprehensive institution. *Enrollment:* 996 full-time matriculated graduate/professional students (325 women). *Enrollment by degree level:* 996 master's. *Graduate faculty:* 5 full-time (1 woman), 126 part-time/adjunct (32 women). *Student services:* Services for students with disabilities. *Library:* Kreitzberg Library.

Computer facilities: A campuswide network can be accessed from student residence rooms and from off campus.
Website: http://www.norwich.edu/

General Application Contact: Admissions Advisor, 800-460-5597, Fax: 802-485-2533, E-mail: masters@online.norwich.edu.

GRADUATE UNITS

College of Graduate and Continuing Studies Students: 996 full-time (325 women); includes 152 minority (80 Black or African American, non-Hispanic/Latino; 4 American Indian or Alaska Native, non-Hispanic/Latino; 20 Asian, non-Hispanic/Latino; 20 Hispanic/Latino; 1 Native Hawaiian or other Pacific Islander, non-Hispanic/Latino; 27 Two or more races, non-Hispanic/Latino), 20 international. Average age 37. 576 applicants, 91% accepted, 383 enrolled. *Faculty:* 5 full-time (1 woman), 126 part-time/adjunct (32 women). *Financial support:* In 2015–16, 546 students received support. Scholarships/grants available. Financial award application deadline: 8/5; financial award applicants required to submit FAFSA. In 2015, 578 master's awarded. *Degree program information:* Evening/weekend programs available. Evening/weekend, mostly all online with a week-long residency requirement. Offers construction management (MBA); construction management engineering (MCE); criminal justice and public safety (MPA); diplomacy (MA); environmental/water resources engineering (MCE); finance (MBA); fiscal management (MPA); geotechnical engineering (MCE); history (MA); information security and assurance (MS); international development and influence (MPA); leadership (MS); military history (MA); municipal governance (MPA); nonprofit management (MPA); nursing administration (MSN); nursing education (MSN); organizational leadership (MBA); policy analysis and analytics (MPA); project management (MBA); public administration leadership and crisis management (MPA); public works and sustainability (MPA); structural engineering (MCE); supply chain management and logistics (MBA). *Application deadline:* For fall admission, 8/15 for domestic and international students; for winter admission, 11/14 for domestic and international students; for spring admission, 2/13 for domestic and international students; for summer admission, 5/15 for domestic and international students. Applications are processed on a rolling basis. Electronic applications accepted. *Application Contact:* Admissions Office, 800-460-5597, E-mail: masters@online.norwich.edu. *Vice President and Dean*, Dr. William H. Clements, 802-485-2567, Fax: 802-485-2533, E-mail: bclements@norwich.edu.

NOTRE DAME COLLEGE, South Euclid, OH 44121-4293

General Information Independent-religious, coed, comprehensive institution. *Graduate housing:* On-campus housing not available.

GRADUATE UNITS

Graduate Programs ***Degree program information:*** Part-time and evening/weekend programs available. Part-time, evening/weekend. Offers mild/moderate needs (M Ed); reading (M Ed); security policy studies (MA, Graduate Certificate); technology (M Ed).

NOTRE DAME DE NAMUR UNIVERSITY, Belmont, CA 94002-1908

General Information Independent-religious, coed, comprehensive institution. *Graduate housing:* Room and/or apartments available on a first-come, first-served basis to single students; on-campus housing not available to married students. Housing application deadline: 6/1.

GRADUATE UNITS

Division of Academic Affairs ***Financial support:*** Career-related internships or fieldwork, scholarships/grants, and unspecified assistantships available. Support available to part-time students. Financial award applicants required to submit FAFSA. *Degree program information:* Part-time and evening/weekend programs available. Part-time, evening/weekend, online learning. *Application deadline:* For fall admission, 8/1 priority date for domestic students; for spring admission, 12/1 priority date for domestic students. Applications are processed on a rolling basis. *Application fee:* $60. Electronic applications accepted.

College of Arts and Sciences ***Financial support:*** Unspecified assistantships available. Support available to part-time students. Financial award applicants required to submit FAFSA. *Degree program information:* Part-time programs available. Part-time, online learning. Offers art therapy (MA); arts and sciences (MA, MFA, MS); clinical psychology (MS); clinical psychology: marital and family therapy (MS); English (MA); musical performance (MFA, Certificate). *Application deadline:* For fall admission, 8/1 for domestic students; for spring admission, 12/1 for domestic students. Applications are processed on a rolling basis. *Application fee:* $60. Electronic applications accepted.

School of Business and Management ***Financial support:*** Scholarships/grants available. Support available to part-time students. Financial award applicants required to submit FAFSA. *Degree program information:* Part-time programs available. Part-time, online learning. Offers business administration (MBA); business and management (MBA, MPA, MSM); entrepreneurship (MBA); finance (MBA); human resource management (MBA, MPA); marketing (MBA); media and promotion (MBA); public administration (MPA); public affairs administration (MPA); social enterprise (MPA); systems management (MSM); technology and operations management (MBA). *Application deadline:* For fall admission, 8/1 for domestic students; for spring admission, 12/1 for domestic students. Applications are processed on a rolling basis. *Application fee:* $60. Electronic applications accepted.

School of Education and Leadership ***Financial support:*** Career-related internships or fieldwork available. Support available to part-time students. Financial award applicants required to submit FAFSA. *Degree program information:* Part-time and evening/weekend programs available. Part-time, evening/weekend. Offers curriculum and instruction (MA); education and leadership (MA, Ed D); school administration (MA); special education (MA). *Application deadline:* For fall admission, 8/1 for domestic students; for spring admission, 12/1 for domestic students. Applications are processed on a rolling basis. *Application fee:* $60. Electronic applications accepted.

NOTRE DAME OF MARYLAND UNIVERSITY, Baltimore, MD 21210-2476

General Information Independent-religious, coed, primarily women, comprehensive institution. *Graduate housing:* On-campus housing not available.

GRADUATE UNITS

Graduate Studies *Degree program information:* Part-time and evening/weekend programs available. Part-time, evening/weekend. Offers contemporary communication (MA); instructional leadership for changing populations (PhD); leadership in teaching (MA); liberal studies (MA); management (MA); nonprofit management (MA); teaching (MA); teaching English to speakers of other languages (MA). Electronic applications accepted.

NOTRE DAME SEMINARY, New Orleans, LA 70118-4391

General Information Independent-religious, coed, primarily men, graduate-only institution. *Graduate housing:* Room and/or apartments guaranteed to single students; on-campus housing not available to married students. Housing application deadline: 7/31.

GRADUATE UNITS

Graduate School of Theology *Degree program information:* Part-time programs available. Part-time. Offers theology (M Div, MA).

NOVA SOUTHEASTERN UNIVERSITY, Fort Lauderdale, FL 33314-7796

General Information Independent, coed, university. *Enrollment:* 23,236 graduate, professional, and undergraduate students; 9,892 full-time matriculated graduate/professional students (6,617 women), 8,703 part-time matriculated graduate/professional students (6,279 women). *Enrollment by degree level:* 9,197 master's, 8,602 doctoral, 745 other advanced degrees. *Graduate housing:* Rooms and/or apartments guaranteed to single and married students. *Student services:* Campus employment opportunities, campus safety program, career counseling, exercise/wellness program, free psychological counseling, international student services, low-cost health insurance, services for students with disabilities, teacher training. *Library:* Alvin Sherman Library, Research, and Information Technology Center plus 4 others. Study areas open 24 hours, 5–7 days a week; students can reserve study rooms.

Computer facilities: 3,000 computers available on campus for general student use. A campuswide network can be accessed from student residence rooms and from off campus. Online class registration is available.
Website: http://www.nova.edu/

General Application Contact: Information Contact, 800-541-6682, E-mail: nsuinfo@nsu.nova.edu.

GRADUATE UNITS

Abraham S. Fischler College of Education Students: 2,336 full-time (1,843 women), 2,770 part-time (2,281 women); includes 3,202 minority (1,682 Black or African American, non-Hispanic/Latino; 15 American Indian or Alaska Native, non-Hispanic/Latino; 63 Asian, non-Hispanic/Latino; 1,344 Hispanic/Latino; 5 Native Hawaiian or other Pacific Islander, non-Hispanic/Latino; 93 Two or more races, non-Hispanic/Latino), 38 international. Average age 41. 1,753 applicants, 47% accepted, 581 enrolled. *Faculty:* 94 full-time (58 women), 204 part-time/adjunct (145 women). *Financial support:* In 2015–16, 67 students received support. Career-related internships or fieldwork and Federal Work-Study available. Support available to part-time students. Financial award application deadline: 4/15; financial award applicants required to submit FAFSA. In 2015, 861 master's, 388 doctorates, 138 other advanced degrees awarded. *Degree program information:* Part-time and evening/weekend programs available. Part-time, evening/weekend, 100% online, blended/hybrid learning. Offers education (MS, Ed D, PhD, Ed S); instructional technology and distance education (MS); teaching and learning (MA). *Application deadline:* Applications are processed on a rolling basis. *Application fee:* $50. Electronic applications accepted. *Application Contact:* Adriana Garay, Executive Director for Marketing, Recruitment and Admissions, 800-986-3223 Ext. 8500, E-mail: fserecruit@nova.edu. *Dean,* Dr. Lynne Shrum, 954-262-8731, Fax: 954-262-3894, E-mail: lshrum@nova.edu.

College of Arts, Humanities, and Social Sciences Students: 551 full-time (411 women), 690 part-time (557 women); includes 708 minority (429 Black or African American, non-Hispanic/Latino; 1 American Indian or Alaska Native, non-Hispanic/Latino; 26 Asian, non-Hispanic/Latino; 223 Hispanic/Latino; 1 Native Hawaiian or other Pacific Islander, non-Hispanic/Latino; 28 Two or more races, non-Hispanic/Latino), 57 international. Average age 37. *Faculty:* 29 full-time (18 women), 27 part-time/adjunct (21 women). *Financial support:* In 2015–16, 170 students received support. Teaching assistantships, career-related internships or fieldwork, Federal Work-Study, scholarships/grants, and unspecified assistantships available. Financial award application deadline: 4/1; financial award applicants required to submit CSS PROFILE. In 2015, 246 master's, 83 doctorates, 29 other advanced degrees awarded. *Degree program information:* Part-time and evening/weekend programs available. Part-time, evening/weekend, online learning. Offers advanced conflict resolution practice (Graduate Certificate); college student affairs (MS); conflict analysis and resolution (MS, PhD); cross-disciplinary studies (MA); family studies (Graduate Certificate); family systems health care (Graduate Certificate); family therapy (MS, PhD); marriage and family therapy (DMFT); peace studies (Graduate Certificate); qualitative research (Graduate Certificate); solution focused coaching (Graduate Certificate). *Application deadline:* For fall admission, 5/17 priority date for domestic and international students; for winter admission, 12/1 priority date for domestic and international students; for spring admission, 4/1 priority date for domestic and international students. Applications are processed on a rolling basis. *Application fee:* $50. Electronic applications accepted. *Application Contact:* Marcia Arango, Student Recruitment Coordinator, 954-262-3006, Fax: 954-262-3968, E-mail: marango@nsu.nova.edu. *Dean,* Dr. Honggang Yang, 954-262-3016, Fax: 954-262-3968, E-mail: yangh@nova.edu.

College of Dental Medicine Students: 597 full-time (308 women), 5 part-time (0 women); includes 275 minority (9 Black or African American, non-Hispanic/Latino; 120 Asian, non-Hispanic/Latino; 130 Hispanic/Latino; 16 Two or more races, non-Hispanic/Latino), 86 international. Average age 28. 2,274 applicants, 11% accepted, 124 enrolled. *Faculty:* 106 full-time (38 women), 163 part-time/adjunct (31 women). *Financial support:* In 2015–16, 54 students received support. Application deadline: 4/15; applicants required to submit FAFSA. In 2015, 15 master's, 129 doctorates awarded. Offers dental medicine (DMD); dentistry (MS). *Application deadline:* For fall admission, 12/31 for domestic students, 1/1 for international students. Applications are processed on a rolling basis. *Application fee:* $50. Electronic applications accepted. *Application Contact:* Su-Ann Zarrett, Associate Director of HPD Admissions, 954-262-1108, Fax: 954-262-2282, E-mail: zarrett@nsu.nova.edu. *Dean,* Dr. Linda C. Niessen, 954-262-7334, Fax: 954-262-3293, E-mail: lniessen@nova.edu.

College of Engineering and Computing Students: 115 full-time (37 women), 717 part-time (201 women); includes 381 minority (152 Black or African American, non-Hispanic/Latino; 4 American Indian or Alaska Native, non-Hispanic/Latino; 66 Asian, non-Hispanic/Latino; 142 Hispanic/Latino; 17 Two or more races, non-Hispanic/Latino), 142 international. Average age 40. 390 applicants, 74% accepted. *Faculty:* 20 full-time (6 women), 24 part-time/adjunct (3 women). *Financial support:* In 2015–16, 61 students received support. Application deadline: 4/15; applicants required to submit FAFSA. In 2015, 164 master's, 53 doctorates awarded. *Degree program information:* Part-time and evening/weekend programs available. Part-time, evening/weekend, online learning. Offers computer science (MS, PhD); information assurance (PhD); information security (MS); information systems (PhD); information technology (MS); management information systems (MS); software engineering (MS). *Application deadline:* Applications are processed on a rolling basis. *Application fee:* $50. Electronic applications accepted. *Application Contact:* Nancy Ruidiaz, Director, Admissions, 954-262-2026, Fax: 954-262-2752, E-mail: azoulayn@nova.edu. *Interim Dean,* Dr. Amon B. Seagull, 954-262-2000, Fax: 954-262-2752, E-mail: amons@nova.edu.

College of Health Care Sciences Students: 1,590 full-time (1,179 women), 969 part-time (819 women); includes 831 minority (234 Black or African American, non-Hispanic/Latino; 8 American Indian or Alaska Native, non-Hispanic/Latino; 151 Asian, non-Hispanic/Latino; 378 Hispanic/Latino; 1 Native Hawaiian or other Pacific Islander, non-Hispanic/Latino; 59 Two or more races, non-Hispanic/Latino), 18 international. Average age 30. 8,133 applicants, 14% accepted, 728 enrolled. *Faculty:* 109 full-time (64 women), 100 part-time/adjunct (65 women). *Financial support:* In 2015–16, 151 students received support, including 4 research assistantships (averaging $3,500 per year); institutionally sponsored loans and unspecified assistantships also available. Financial award application deadline: 4/15; financial award applicants required to submit FAFSA. In 2015, 556 master's, 105 doctorates awarded. Online learning. Offers anesthesiologist assistant (MSA); audiology (Au D); health science (MH Sc, DHSc, PhD); occupational therapy (MOT, Dr OT, PhD); physical therapy (DPT, TDPT); physician assistant (MMS). *Application deadline:* For winter admission, 4/15 for domestic students; for summer admission, 12/15 for domestic and international students. Applications are processed on a rolling basis. *Application fee:* $50. Electronic applications accepted. *Application Contact:* Joey Jankie, Admissions Counselor, 954-262-7249, E-mail: joey@nova.edu. *Dean,* Dr. Stanley Wilson, 954-262-1203, E-mail: swilson@nova.edu.

College of Medical Sciences Students: 44 full-time (19 women); includes 20 minority (4 Black or African American, non-Hispanic/Latino; 4 Asian, non-Hispanic/Latino; 10 Hispanic/Latino; 2 Two or more races, non-Hispanic/Latino). Average age 25. *Financial support:* Application deadline: 4/15; applicants required to submit FAFSA. In 2015, 4 master's awarded. Offers biomedical sciences (MBS). *Application deadline:* For fall admission, 4/15 for domestic students. Applications are processed on a rolling basis. *Application fee:* $50. *Application Contact:* Lori B. Dribin, PhD, Assistant Dean for Student Affairs, 954-262-1341, Fax: 954-262-1802, E-mail: lorib@nova.edu. *Dean,* Dr. Harold E. Laubach, 954-262-1303, Fax: 954-262-1802, E-mail: harold@nova.edu.

College of Nursing Students: 1 (woman) full-time, 506 part-time (461 women); includes 329 minority (163 Black or African American, non-Hispanic/Latino; 34 Asian, non-Hispanic/Latino; 122 Hispanic/Latino; 1 Native Hawaiian or other Pacific Islander, non-Hispanic/Latino; 9 Two or more races, non-Hispanic/Latino), 2 international. Average age 39. *Faculty:* 23 full-time (22 women), 40 part-time/adjunct (35 women). *Financial support:* In 2015–16, 41 students received support. Traineeships available. Financial award application deadline: 4/15; financial award applicants required to submit FAFSA. In 2015, 91 master's, 15 doctorates awarded. *Degree program information:* Part-time and evening/weekend programs available. Part-time, evening/weekend, 100% online, blended/hybrid learning, online PhD program with annual one-week summer institute that is delivered face-to-face on the main campus. Offers advanced practice registered nurse (APRN) (MSN); nursing (PhD); nursing (MSN); nursing practice (DNP). *Application deadline:* For fall admission, 3/1 priority date for domestic students, 3/1 for international students; for winter admission, 11/1 for domestic and international students. Applications are processed on a rolling basis. *Application fee:* $50. Electronic applications accepted. *Dean,* Dr. Marcella Rutherford, 954-262-1963, E-mail: rmarcell@nova.edu.

College of Optometry Students: 446 full-time (304 women), 2 part-time (both women); includes 186 minority (31 Black or African American, non-Hispanic/Latino; 76 Asian, non-Hispanic/Latino; 67 Hispanic/Latino; 12 Two or more races, non-Hispanic/Latino), 52 international. Average age 26. *Financial support:* In 2015–16, 52 students received support. Federal Work-Study, institutionally sponsored loans, and scholarships/grants available. Support available to part-time students. Financial award application deadline: 4/15; financial award applicants required to submit FAFSA. In 2015, 2 master's, 95 doctorates awarded. Online learning. Offers optometry (MS, OD). *Application deadline:* For fall admission, 4/1 for domestic and international students. Applications are processed on a rolling basis. *Application fee:* $50. Electronic applications accepted. *Application Contact:* Juan Saavedra, Admissions Counselor, 954-262-1132, Fax: 954-262-2282, E-mail: jsaavedra@nova.edu. *Dean,* Dr. David Loshin, 954-262-1404, Fax: 954-262-1818.

College of Osteopathic Medicine Students: 1,027 full-time (436 women), 189 part-time (124 women); includes 560 minority (92 Black or African American, non-Hispanic/Latino; 260 Asian, non-Hispanic/Latino; 174 Hispanic/Latino; 1 Native Hawaiian or other Pacific Islander, non-Hispanic/Latino; 33 Two or more races, non-Hispanic/Latino), 45 international. Average age 28. 4,012 applicants, 12% accepted, 246 enrolled. *Faculty:* 107 full-time (55 women), 1,235 part-time/adjunct (297 women). *Financial support:* In 2015–16, 39 students received support, including 24 fellowships (averaging $45,593 per year); research assistantships, teaching assistantships, Federal Work-Study, and scholarships/grants also available. Financial award application deadline: 6/1; financial award applicants required to submit FAFSA. In 2015, 75 master's, 237 doctorates, 4 other advanced degrees awarded. Offers biomedical informatics (MS, Graduate Certificate); disaster and emergency preparedness (MS); osteopathic medicine (DO); public health (MPH). *Application deadline:* For fall admission, 1/15 for domestic students. Applications are processed on a rolling basis. *Application fee:* $50. Electronic applications accepted. *Application Contact:* Monica Sanchez, Admissions Counselor, College of Osteopathic Medicine, 954-262-1110, Fax: 954-262-2282, E-mail: mh1156@nova.edu. *Dean,* Elaine M. Wallace, DO, 954-262-1407, E-mail: ewallace@nova.edu.

College of Pharmacy Students: 971 full-time (655 women), 25 part-time (12 women); includes 705 minority (57 Black or African American, non-Hispanic/Latino; 177 Asian, non-Hispanic/Latino; 451 Hispanic/Latino; 1 Native Hawaiian or other Pacific Islander, non-Hispanic/Latino; 19 Two or more races, non-Hispanic/Latino), 96 international. Average age 27. 1,024 applicants, 41% accepted, 255 enrolled. *Faculty:* 67 full-time (31 women), 3 part-time/adjunct (1 woman). *Financial support:* In 2015–16, 131 students received support, including 11 teaching assistantships with full tuition reimbursements available (averaging $18,000 per year); career-related internships or fieldwork, Federal Work-Study, institutionally sponsored loans, and scholarships/grants also available. Financial award application deadline: 4/15; financial award applicants required to submit FAFSA. In 2015, 226 doctorates awarded. Offers drug development (pharmaceutics) (PhD); molecular medicine and pharmacogenomics (PhD); pharmacy (Pharm D); social and administrative pharmacy (PhD). *Application deadline:* For fall admission, 3/15 for domestic students, 2/1 for international students. Applications are processed on a rolling basis. *Application fee:* $50. Electronic applications accepted. *Application Contact:* Jeffrey Jurkas, Coordinator of Admissions and Recruitment, 954-262-1240, Fax: 954-262-2282, E-mail: nsupharmacyinfo@nova.edu. *Dean*, Dr. Lisa Deziel, 954-262-1304, Fax: 954-262-2278, E-mail: copdean@nova.edu.

College of Psychology Students: 881 full-time (753 women), 900 part-time (763 women); includes 892 minority (289 Black or African American, non-Hispanic/Latino; 2 American Indian or Alaska Native, non-Hispanic/Latino; 44 Asian, non-Hispanic/Latino; 510 Hispanic/Latino; 2 Native Hawaiian or other Pacific Islander, non-Hispanic/Latino; 45 Two or more races, non-Hispanic/Latino), 93 international. Average age 31. 1,186 applicants, 51% accepted, 398 enrolled. *Faculty:* 50 full-time (19 women), 119 part-time/adjunct (69 women). *Financial support:* In 2015–16, 215 students received support, including 15 research assistantships, 68 teaching assistantships (averaging $4,800 per year); career-related internships or fieldwork, Federal Work-Study, institutionally sponsored loans, scholarships/grants, and unspecified assistantships also available. Support available to part-time students. Financial award application deadline: 4/15; financial award applicants required to submit FAFSA. In 2015, 510 master's, 110 doctorates awarded. Online learning. Offers clinical psychology (PhD, Psy D); counseling (MS); general psychology (MS); mental health counseling (MS); school counseling (MS). *Application deadline:* Applications are processed on a rolling basis. *Application fee:* $50. Electronic applications accepted. *Application Contact:* Carlos Perez, Enrollment Management, 954-262-5790, Fax: 954-262-3893, E-mail: cpsinfo@cps.nova.edu. *Dean*, Dr. Karen Grosby, 954-262-5701, Fax: 954-262-3859, E-mail: grosby@nova.edu.

Halmos College of Natural Sciences and Oceanography Students: 100 full-time (57 women), 114 part-time (76 women); includes 32 minority (6 Black or African American, non-Hispanic/Latino; 1 American Indian or Alaska Native, non-Hispanic/Latino; 6 Asian, non-Hispanic/Latino; 10 Hispanic/Latino; 9 Two or more races, non-Hispanic/Latino), 5 international. Average age 30. 85 applicants, 60% accepted, 39 enrolled. *Faculty:* 17 full-time (3 women), 22 part-time/adjunct (11 women). *Financial support:* In 2015–16, 157 students received support, including 14 fellowships with tuition reimbursements available (averaging $25,000 per year), 42 research assistantships with tuition reimbursements available (averaging $19,000 per year); teaching assistantships, career-related internships or fieldwork, Federal Work-Study, scholarships/grants, health care benefits, tuition waivers (full and partial), and unspecified assistantships also available. Support available to part-time students. Financial award application deadline: 4/15; financial award applicants required to submit FAFSA. In 2015, 47 master's, 2 doctorates, 9 other advanced degrees awarded. *Degree program information:* Part-time and evening/weekend programs available. Part-time, evening/weekend, 100% online, blended/hybrid learning. Offers biological sciences (MS); coastal studies (Certificate); coastal zone management (MS); marine and coastal climate change (Certificate); marine and coastal studies (MA); marine biology (MS); marine biology and oceanography (PhD); marine environmental sciences (MS). *Application deadline:* Applications are processed on a rolling basis. *Application fee:* $50. Electronic applications accepted. *Application Contact:* Dr. Bernhard Riegl, Chair, Department of Marine and Environmental Sciences, 954-262-3600, Fax: 954-262-4020, E-mail: rieglb@nova.edu. *Dean*, Dr. Richard Dodge, 954-262-3600, Fax: 954-262-4020, E-mail: dodge@nsu.nova.edu.

H. Wayne Huizenga College of Business and Entrepreneurship Students: 902 full-time (532 women), 1,966 part-time (1,238 women); includes 1,967 minority (870 Black or African American, non-Hispanic/Latino; 3 American Indian or Alaska Native, non-Hispanic/Latino; 102 Asian, non-Hispanic/Latino; 936 Hispanic/Latino; 2 Native Hawaiian or other Pacific Islander, non-Hispanic/Latino; 54 Two or more races, non-Hispanic/Latino), 230 international. Average age 34. 1,080 applicants, 66% accepted, 532 enrolled. *Faculty:* 51 full-time (21 women), 92 part-time/adjunct (30 women). *Financial support:* In 2015–16, 325 students received support. Federal Work-Study and scholarships/grants available. Support available to part-time students. Financial award application deadline: 4/15; financial award applicants required to submit FAFSA. In 2015, 900 master's awarded. *Degree program information:* Part-time and evening/weekend programs available. Part-time, evening/weekend, 100% online, blended/hybrid learning. Offers accounting (M Acc); business intelligence/analytics (MBA); entrepreneurship (MBA); finance (MBA); human resource management (MBA); international business (MBA); management (MBA); marketing (MBA); process improvement (MBA); public administration (MPA); real estate development (MS); sport revenue generation (MBA); supply chain management (MBA); taxation (M Tax). *Application deadline:* For fall admission, 8/5 priority date for domestic students, 7/29 priority date for international students; for winter admission, 12/16 priority date for domestic students, 12/9 priority date for international students; for summer admission, 4/15 priority date for domestic and international students. Applications are processed on a rolling basis. *Application fee:* $50. Electronic applications accepted. *Application Contact:* Zeida Rodriguez, Associate Director of Enrollment Services, 954-262-5163, Fax: 954-262-3822, E-mail: zeida@nova.edu. *Dean*, Dr. J. Preston Jones, 954-262-5127, E-mail: prestonj@nova.edu.

Shepard Broad College of Law Students: 563 full-time (297 women), 350 part-time (242 women); includes 435 minority (141 Black or African American, non-Hispanic/Latino; 3 American Indian or Alaska Native, non-Hispanic/Latino; 23 Asian, non-Hispanic/Latino; 253 Hispanic/Latino; 3 Native Hawaiian or other Pacific Islander, non-Hispanic/Latino; 12 Two or more races, non-Hispanic/Latino), 31 international. Average age 29. 1,440 applicants, 57% accepted, 322 enrolled. *Faculty:* 51 full-time (24 women), 33 part-time/adjunct (12 women). *Financial support:* In 2015–16, 261 students received support, including 12 fellowships (averaging $1,917 per year); Federal Work-Study, scholarships/grants, tuition waivers (partial), and unspecified assistantships also available. Support available to part-time students. Financial award application deadline: 4/15; financial award applicants required to submit FAFSA. In 2015, 34 master's, 288 doctorates awarded. *Degree program information:* Part-time and evening/weekend programs available. Part-time, evening/weekend, 100% online, blended/hybrid learning. Offers education law (MS); employment law (MS); health law (MS); law (JD); law and policy (MS). JD/MURP offered jointly with Florida Atlantic University. *Application deadline:* For fall admission, 5/1 priority date for domestic and international students; for winter admission, 12/19 for domestic and international students; for spring admission, 3/31 for domestic and international students; for summer admission, 6/20 for domestic and international students. Applications are processed on a rolling basis. *Application fee:* $53. Electronic applications accepted. *Application Contact:* William Perez, Assistant Dean of Admissions, 954-262-6121, Fax: 954-262-3844, E-mail: wperez1@nova.edu. *Dean*, Jon M. Garon, 954-262-6100, Fax: 954-262-2862, E-mail: garon@nova.edu.

NSCAD UNIVERSITY, Halifax, NS B3J 3J6, Canada

General Information Province-supported, coed, comprehensive institution. *Graduate housing:* On-campus housing not available.

GRADUATE UNITS

Program in Fine Arts Offers craft (MFA); design (M Des); fine and media arts (MFA).

NYACK COLLEGE, Nyack, NY 10960

General Information Independent-religious, coed, comprehensive institution. *Enrollment:* 2,664 graduate, professional, and undergraduate students; 487 full-time matriculated graduate/professional students (247 women), 632 part-time matriculated graduate/professional students (379 women). *Enrollment by degree level:* 1,017 master's, 102 doctoral. *Graduate faculty:* 24 full-time (8 women), 56 part-time/adjunct (24 women). Tuition and fees vary according to program. *Graduate housing:* Rooms and/or apartments available on a first-come, first-served basis to single and married students. Housing application deadline: 9/1. *Student services:* Campus employment opportunities, career counseling, free psychological counseling, international student services, low-cost health insurance, services for students with disabilities, writing training. *Library:* Bailey Library plus 3 others.

Computer facilities: A campuswide network can be accessed. Online class registration is available.
Website: http://www.nyack.edu/

General Application Contact: 800-541-6891, Fax: 845-348-3912, E-mail: admissions.grad@nyack.edu.

GRADUATE UNITS

Alliance Graduate School of Counseling Students: 61 full-time (51 women), 166 part-time (146 women); includes 168 minority (83 Black or African American, non-Hispanic/Latino; 40 Asian, non-Hispanic/Latino; 42 Hispanic/Latino; 3 Two or more races, non-Hispanic/Latino), 7 international. Average age 38. *Financial support:* Career-related internships or fieldwork and scholarships/grants available. Financial award applicants required to submit FAFSA. In 2015, 66 master's awarded. *Degree program information:* Part-time and evening/weekend programs available. Part-time, evening/weekend. Offers marriage and family therapy (MA); mental health counseling (MA). *Application deadline:* For fall admission, 8/1 for domestic students, 2/15 for international students; for spring admission, 12/15 for domestic students, 7/15 for international students. Applications are processed on a rolling basis. *Application fee:* $30. Electronic applications accepted. *Application Contact:* 800-541-6891, Fax: 845-348-3912, E-mail: admissions.grad@nyack.edu. *Director*, Dr. Carol Robles, 845-770-5730, Fax: 845-348-3923.

Alliance Theological Seminary Students: 309 full-time (122 women), 397 part-time (180 women); includes 548 minority (207 Black or African American, non-Hispanic/Latino; 139 Asian, non-Hispanic/Latino; 197 Hispanic/Latino; 5 Two or more races, non-Hispanic/Latino), 43 international. Average age 42. *Financial support:* Career-related internships or fieldwork, Federal Work-Study, and scholarships/grants available. Financial award applicants required to submit FAFSA. In 2015, 129 master's, 10 doctorates awarded. *Degree program information:* Part-time and evening/weekend programs available. Part-time, evening/weekend, 100% online. Offers Biblical literature (MA); Christian ministry (MPS); intercultural studies (MA); ministry (D Min); theology and missions (M Div); urban ministry (MPS). *Application deadline:* Applications are processed on a rolling basis. *Application fee:* $30. Electronic applications accepted. *Application Contact:* Julian Williams, ATS Associate Director of Admissions, 800-541-6891, Fax: 845-348-3912, E-mail: admissions.ats@nyack.edu. *Dean*, Dr. Ronald Walborn, 845-770-5715, Fax: 845-358-1663.

College of Bible and Christian Ministry Students: 2 full-time (0 women), 10 part-time (3 women); includes 6 minority (1 Black or African American, non-Hispanic/Latino; 4 Hispanic/Latino; 1 Two or more races, non-Hispanic/Latino), 1 international. Average age 32. *Financial support:* Applicants required to submit FAFSA. *Degree program information:* Part-time and evening/weekend programs available. Part-time, evening/weekend, blended/hybrid learning. Offers ancient Judaism and Christian origins (MA). *Application deadline:* Applications are processed on a rolling basis. *Application fee:* $30. Electronic applications accepted. *Application Contact:* 800-541-6891, Fax: 845-348-3912, E-mail: admissions.grad@nyack.edu. *Director*, Dr. Steven Notley, 646-378-6148, E-mail: steven.notley@nyack.edu.

School of Business and Leadership Students: 70 full-time (38 women), 22 part-time (15 women); includes 65 minority (46 Black or African American, non-Hispanic/Latino; 2 Asian, non-Hispanic/Latino; 17 Hispanic/Latino), 8 international. Average age 38. *Financial support:* Applicants required to submit FAFSA. In 2015, 61 master's awarded. *Degree program information:* Part-time and evening/weekend programs available. Part-time, evening/weekend, 100% online. Offers business administration (MBA); organizational leadership (MS). *Application deadline:* Applications are processed on a rolling basis. *Application fee:* $50. Electronic applications accepted. *Application Contact:* Lisa Ray, Admissions Associate, 800-541-6891, Fax: 845-348-3912, E-mail: admissions.grad@nyack.edu. *Dean*, Dr. Anita Underwood, 845-675-4511, Fax: 845-353-5812.

School of Education Students: 30 full-time (25 women), 23 part-time (21 women); includes 31 minority (8 Black or African American, non-Hispanic/Latino; 3 Asian, non-Hispanic/Latino; 19 Hispanic/Latino; 1 Two or more races, non-Hispanic/Latino), 3 international. Average age 34. *Financial support:* Scholarships/grants available. Financial award applicants required to submit FAFSA. In 2015, 13 master's awarded. *Degree program information:* Part-time programs available. Part-time, 100% online. Offers childhood education (MS); childhood special education (MS); TESOL (MAT, MS). *Application deadline:* Applications are processed on a rolling basis. *Application fee:* $30. Electronic applications accepted. *Application Contact:* Darla Her, Admissions Associate, 800-541-6891, Fax: 845-348-3912, E-mail: admissions.grad@nyack.edu. *Dean*, Dr. JoAnn Looney, 845-675-4538, Fax: 845-358-0874.

School of Social Work Students: 15 full-time (11 women), 14 part-time (all women); includes 22 minority (13 Black or African American, non-Hispanic/Latino; 1 American Indian or Alaska Native, non-Hispanic/Latino; 1 Asian, non-Hispanic/Latino; 7 Hispanic/Latino), 1 international. Average age 35. *Financial support:* Institutionally sponsored loans available. Financial award applicants required to submit FAFSA. *Degree program information:* Part-time and evening/weekend programs available. Part-time, evening/weekend. Offers clinical social work (MSW). *Application deadline:* Applications are processed on a rolling basis. *Application fee:* $45. Electronic applications accepted. *Application Contact:* DeLissa Dixon, Admissions Associate, 646-378-6105, E-mail: admissions.grad@nyack.edu. *Associate Dean*, Dr. Kwi Yun, 646-378-6170, E-mail: kwi.yun@nyack.edu.

OAKLAND CITY UNIVERSITY, Oakland City, IN 47660-1099

General Information Independent-religious, coed, comprehensive institution. *Graduate housing:* Rooms and/or apartments guaranteed to single students and available on a first-come, first-served basis to married students. Housing application deadline: 7/1.

GRADUATE UNITS

Chapman Seminary ***Degree program information:*** Part-time programs available. Part-time. Offers religious studies (M Div, D Min).

School of Adult and Extended Learning ***Degree program information:*** Part-time and evening/weekend programs available. Part-time, evening/weekend. Offers adult and extended learning (MBA).

School of Education Offers educational leadership (Ed D); teaching (MA).

OAKLAND UNIVERSITY, Rochester, MI 48309-4401

General Information State-supported, coed, university. CGS member. *Enrollment:* 20,261 graduate, professional, and undergraduate students; 1,688 full-time matriculated graduate/professional students (968 women), 1,688 part-time matriculated graduate/professional students (933 women). *Enrollment by degree level:* 2,530 master's, 951 doctoral, 247 other advanced degrees. *Graduate faculty:* 305 full-time (131 women), 97 part-time/adjunct (46 women). *Tuition, area resident:* Part-time $655 per credit. Tuition and fees vary according to program. *Graduate housing:* Rooms and/or apartments available on a first-come, first-served basis to single and married students. Housing application deadline: 9/1. *Student services:* Campus employment opportunities, campus safety program, career counseling, child daycare facilities, exercise/wellness program, free psychological counseling, international student services, low-cost health insurance, multicultural affairs office, services for students with disabilities. *Library:* Kresge Library plus 1 other. *Collection:* Books: 579,176 (physical), 344,635 (digital/electronic); Serial titles: 395 (physical), 26,313 (digital/electronic); Databases: 289. Weekly public service hours: 168; study areas open 24 hours, 5–7 days a week; students can reserve study rooms. *Research affiliation:* Beaumont Hospital Corporation (eye research, nursing), Henry Ford Health Systems (medical physics).

Computer facilities: A campuswide network can be accessed from student residence rooms and from off campus. Online class registration is available.
Website: http://www.oakland.edu/

General Application Contact: Katherine Z. Rowley, Associate Director of Graduate Study and Lifelong Learning, 248-370-3167, Fax: 248-370-4114, E-mail: kzrowley@oakland.edu.

GRADUATE UNITS

Graduate Study and Lifelong Learning Students: 1,688 full-time (968 women), 1,688 part-time (933 women); includes 564 minority (226 Black or African American, non-Hispanic/Latino; 17 American Indian or Alaska Native, non-Hispanic/Latino; 220 Asian, non-Hispanic/Latino; 67 Hispanic/Latino; 34 Two or more races, non-Hispanic/Latino), 394 international. Average age 31. 3,327 applicants, 32% accepted, 970 enrolled. *Faculty:* 305 full-time (131 women), 97 part-time/adjunct (46 women). *Financial support:* Fellowships, research assistantships, teaching assistantships, career-related internships or fieldwork, Federal Work-Study, institutionally sponsored loans, and tuition waivers (full) available. Financial award application deadline: 3/1; financial award applicants required to submit FAFSA. In 2015, 792 master's, 143 doctorates, 63 other advanced degrees awarded. *Degree program information:* Part-time and evening/weekend programs available. Part-time, evening/weekend. *Application deadline:* For fall admission, 5/1 for international students; for winter admission, 9/1 for international students. Applications are processed on a rolling basis. *Application fee:* $0. Electronic applications accepted. *Application Contact:* Kathryn Rowley, 248-370-4058, Fax: 248-370-4114, E-mail: kzrowley@oakland.edu. *Dean of Graduate Education,* Claudia Petrescu, 248-370-3169, Fax: 248-370-4114, E-mail: cpetrescu@oakland.edu.

College of Arts and Sciences Students: 220 full-time (124 women), 151 part-time (88 women); includes 56 minority (29 Black or African American, non-Hispanic/Latino; 1 American Indian or Alaska Native, non-Hispanic/Latino; 14 Asian, non-Hispanic/Latino; 9 Hispanic/Latino; 3 Two or more races, non-Hispanic/Latino), 41 international. Average age 30. 520 applicants, 31% accepted, 103 enrolled. *Faculty:* 100 full-time (34 women), 14 part-time/adjunct (7 women). *Financial support:* Fellowships, research assistantships, teaching assistantships, career-related internships or fieldwork, Federal Work-Study, institutionally sponsored loans, and tuition waivers (full) available. Financial award application deadline: 3/1; financial award applicants required to submit FAFSA. In 2015, 114 master's, 11 doctorates, 7 other advanced degrees awarded. *Degree program information:* Part-time and evening/weekend programs available. Part-time, evening/weekend. Offers applied mathematical sciences (PhD); applied statistics (MS); arts and sciences (MA, MM, MPA, MS, PhD, Certificate, Graduate Certificate, PMC); biology (MA, MS); biomedical sciences (Graduate Certificate); biomedical sciences: biological communication (PhD); biomedical sciences: health and environmental chemistry (PhD); chemistry (MS); English (MA); history (MA); industrial applied mathematics (MS); liberal studies (MA); linguistics (MA); local government management (Graduate Certificate); mathematical statistics (MS); mathematics (MA); medical physics (PhD); music (MM); music education (PhD); non-profit and organizational management (PMC); physics (MS); public administration (MPA); statistical methods (Certificate); teaching English as a second language (Certificate). *Application deadline:* Applications are processed on a rolling basis. *Application fee:* $0. Electronic applications accepted. *Dean,* Kevin J. Corcoran, 248-370-2140, Fax: 248-370-4280, E-mail: corcoran@oakland.edu.

School of Business Administration Students: 140 full-time (60 women), 325 part-time (112 women); includes 49 minority (19 Black or African American, non-Hispanic/Latino; 3 American Indian or Alaska Native, non-Hispanic/Latino; 16 Asian, non-Hispanic/Latino; 11 Hispanic/Latino), 61 international. Average age 31. 294 applicants, 48% accepted, 142 enrolled. *Faculty:* 33 full-time (9 women), 11 part-time/adjunct (2 women). *Financial support:* Career-related internships or fieldwork, Federal Work-Study, institutionally sponsored loans, and tuition waivers (full) available. Financial award application deadline: 3/1; financial award applicants required to submit FAFSA. In 2015, 137 master's, 4 other advanced degrees awarded. *Degree program information:* Part-time and evening/weekend programs available. Part-time, evening/weekend. Offers accounting (M Acc, Certificate); business administration (EMBA, M Acc, MBA, MS, Certificate); economics (MBA, Certificate); entrepreneurship (Certificate); finance (Certificate); general management (Certificate); human resource management (Certificate); information technology management (MS); international business (Certificate); management and marketing (EMBA); management information systems (Certificate); marketing (Certificate); production and operations management (Certificate). *Application deadline:* For fall admission, 8/15 priority date for domestic students, 5/1 priority date for international students; for winter admission, 12/1 priority date for domestic students, 9/1 priority date for international students; for spring admission, 4/15 priority date for domestic students. Applications are processed on a rolling basis. Electronic applications accepted. *Dean,* Dr. Michael A. Mazzeo, 248-370-2957, Fax: 248-370-4974.

School of Education and Human Services Students: 329 full-time (265 women), 732 part-time (584 women); includes 58 minority (18 Black or African American, non-Hispanic/Latino; 7 American Indian or Alaska Native, non-Hispanic/Latino; 16 Asian, non-Hispanic/Latino; 6 Hispanic/Latino; 11 Two or more races, non-Hispanic/Latino), 30 international. Average age 34. 723 applicants, 54% accepted, 298 enrolled. *Faculty:* 50 full-time (29 women), 52 part-time/adjunct (34 women). *Financial support:* Career-related internships or fieldwork, Federal Work-Study, institutionally sponsored loans, and tuition waivers (full) available. Financial award application deadline: 3/1; financial award applicants required to submit FAFSA. In 2015, 293 master's, 21 doctorates, 35 other advanced degrees awarded. *Degree program information:* Part-time and evening/weekend programs available. Part-time, evening/weekend. Offers advanced microcomputer applications (Graduate Certificate); applied behavior analysis (Graduate Certificate); autism spectrum disorder (Graduate Certificate); counseling (MA, PhD, Certificate); digital literacies and learning (Graduate Certificate); early childhood education (M Ed, PhD, Ed S); early education and intervention (Ed S); education and human services (M Ed, MA, MAT, PhD, Certificate, Ed S, Graduate Certificate, PMC); educational leadership (M Ed, PhD); educational studies (M Ed); elementary education (MAT); emotional impairment (Graduate Certificate); higher education (Certificate); microcomputer applications (Graduate Certificate); reading and language arts (MAT); reading education (PhD); reading, language arts and literature (PMC); school administration (Ed S); secondary education (MAT); special education (M Ed, Graduate Certificate); specific learning disabilities (Graduate Certificate); teaching and learning (Graduate Certificate). *Application deadline:* Applications are processed on a rolling basis. *Application fee:* $0. Electronic applications accepted. *Dean,* Dr. Jopn Margerum-Leys, 248-370-3045, Fax: 248-370-4202, E-mail: jmargerumleys@oakland.edu.

School of Engineering and Computer Science Students: 262 full-time (79 women), 350 part-time (52 women); includes 62 minority (18 Black or African American, non-Hispanic/Latino; 3 American Indian or Alaska Native, non-Hispanic/Latino; 35 Asian, non-Hispanic/Latino; 6 Hispanic/Latino), 223 international. Average age 30. 648 applicants, 31% accepted, 152 enrolled. *Faculty:* 53 full-time (11 women), 14 part-time/adjunct (1 woman). *Financial support:* Federal Work-Study, institutionally sponsored loans, and tuition waivers (full) available. Financial award application deadline: 3/1; financial award applicants required to submit FAFSA. In 2015, 140 master's, 14 doctorates awarded. *Degree program information:* Part-time and evening/weekend programs available. Part-time, evening/weekend. Offers computer science (MS); computer science and informatics (PhD); electrical and computer engineering (MS, PhD); embedded systems (MS); engineering and computer science (MS, PhD, Graduate Certificate); engineering management (MS); industrial and systems engineering (MS); mechanical engineering (MS, PhD); mechatronics (MS); productivity improvement (Graduate Certificate); software engineering and information technology (MS); systems engineering (PhD). *Application deadline:* For fall admission, 8/1 priority date for domestic students, 5/1 priority date for international students; for winter admission, 12/1 priority date for domestic students, 9/1 priority date for international students; for spring admission, 4/1 priority date for domestic students. Applications are processed on a rolling basis. *Application fee:* $0. Electronic applications accepted. *Dean/Professor,* Dr. Louay M. Chamra, 248-370-2217, E-mail: chamra@oakland.edu.

School of Health Sciences Students: 195 full-time (145 women), 59 part-time (35 women); includes 22 minority (9 Black or African American, non-Hispanic/Latino; 1 American Indian or Alaska Native, non-Hispanic/Latino; 6 Asian, non-Hispanic/Latino; 6 Two or more races, non-Hispanic/Latino), 17 international. Average age 26. 742 applicants, 13% accepted, 77 enrolled. *Faculty:* 21 full-time (13 women), 5 part-time/adjunct (2 women). *Financial support:* Fellowships, Federal Work-Study, institutionally sponsored loans, and tuition waivers (full) available. Financial award application deadline: 3/1; financial award applicants required to submit FAFSA. In 2015, 33 master's, 41 doctorates, 15 other advanced degrees awarded. Offers clinical exercise science (Dr Sc PT); complementary medicine and wellness (Dr Sc PT); corporate worksite wellness (Dr Sc PT); exercise science (MS, Dr Sc PT, Graduate Certificate); health sciences (MS, DPT, Dr Sc PT, TDPT, Graduate Certificate); neurological rehabilitation (Dr Sc PT, TDPT); orthopedic manual physical therapy (Dr Sc PT, TDPT, Graduate Certificate); orthopedic physical therapy (Graduate Certificate); orthopedics (Dr Sc PT, TDPT); pediatric rehabilitation (Dr Sc PT, TDPT); physical therapy (DPT); safety management (MS); teaching and learning for rehabilitation professionals (Dr Sc PT, TDPT). *Application deadline:* For fall admission, 10/15 for domestic and international students. Applications are processed on a rolling basis. *Application fee:* $0. Electronic applications accepted. *Interim Dean/Associate Professor,* Dr. Richard J. Rozek, 248-370-3562, Fax: 248-364-3562, E-mail: rozek@oakland.edu.

School of Nursing Students: 150 full-time (123 women), 71 part-time (62 women); includes 144 minority (16 Black or African American, non-Hispanic/Latino; 2 American Indian or Alaska Native, non-Hispanic/Latino; 99 Asian, non-Hispanic/Latino; 14 Hispanic/Latino; 13 Two or more races, non-Hispanic/Latino), 19 international. Average age 34. 400 applicants, 22% accepted, 73 enrolled. *Faculty:* 17 full-time (all women), 5 part-time/adjunct (2 women). *Financial support:* Federal Work-Study, institutionally sponsored loans, and tuition waivers (full) available. Financial award application deadline: 3/1; financial award applicants required to submit FAFSA. In 2015, 75 master's, 9 doctorates, 2 other advanced degrees awarded. *Degree program information:* Part-time and evening/weekend programs available. Part-time, evening/weekend. Offers adult gerontological nurse practitioner (MSN, PMC); family nurse practitioner (MSN, PMC); nurse anesthesia (MSN, PMC); nursing (MSN, DNP, PMC); nursing practice (DNP). *Application fee:* $0. Electronic applications accepted. *Interim Dean/Associate Professor,* Dr. Gary Moore, 248-364-8787, E-mail: moore@oakland.edu.

OAKWOOD UNIVERSITY, Huntsville, AL 35896

General Information Independent-religious, coed, comprehensive institution. *Enrollment:* 15 full-time matriculated graduate/professional students (4 women), 1 part-time matriculated graduate/professional student. *Enrollment by degree level:* 16 master's. *Graduate faculty:* 7 part-time/adjunct (0 women). *Tuition, area resident:* Full-time $9666; part-time $537 per credit hour. *Required fees:* $394 per semester. *Graduate housing:* On-campus housing not available. *Library:* Eva B. Dykes Library.

Computer facilities: 350 computers available on campus for general student use. A campuswide network can be accessed from student residence rooms and from off campus. Online class registration is available.
Website: http://www.oakwood.edu/

General Application Contact: Malcolm Taylor, Director, Enrollment Management, 256-726-7356, Fax: 256-726-7154, E-mail: admission@oakwood.edu.

GRADUATE UNITS

Program in Pastoral Studies Students: 15 full-time (4 women), 1 part-time (0 women). *Faculty:* 7 part-time/adjunct (0 women). Offers pastoral studies (MA). *Application fee:* $100. *Application Contact:* Malcolm Taylor, Director, Enrollment Management, 256-726-7356, Fax: 256-726-7154, E-mail: admission@oakwood.edu. *Dean, Department of Religion and Theology,* Dr. Dedrick Blue, 256-726-7365, Fax: 256-726-7366, E-mail: dblue@oakwood.edu.

OBERLIN COLLEGE, Oberlin, OH 44074

General Information Independent, coed, comprehensive institution. *Enrollment:* 2,929 graduate, professional, and undergraduate students; 16 full-time matriculated graduate/professional students (5 women). *Enrollment by degree level:* 16 master's. *Graduate housing:* Room and/or apartments available on a first-come, first-served basis to single students; on-campus housing not available to married students. Housing application deadline: 6/15. *Student services:* Campus employment opportunities, campus safety program, career counseling, exercise/wellness program, free psychological counseling, international student services, multicultural affairs office, services for students with disabilities, writing training. *Library:* Mudd Center Library plus 3 others. *Collection:* Books: 1.5 million (physical); Serial titles: 177,089 (physical). Students can reserve study rooms.

Computer facilities: Computer purchase and lease plans are available. 340 computers available on campus for general student use. A campuswide network can be accessed from student residence rooms and from off campus. Online class registration is available.
Website: http://www.oberlin.edu/

General Application Contact: Michael Manderen, Director of Conservatory Admissions, 440-775-8413, Fax: 440-775-6972, E-mail: conservatory.admissions@oberlin.edu.

GRADUATE UNITS

Conservatory of Music Students: 16 full-time (5 women). 123 applicants, 14% accepted, 11 enrolled. *Financial support:* Career-related internships or fieldwork, Federal Work-Study, and scholarships/grants available. Financial award application deadline: 2/15; financial award applicants required to submit CSS PROFILE or FAFSA. Offers contemporary chamber music (MM); historical performance (MM); music education (MMT); performance (AD); piano technology (AD). *Application deadline:* For fall admission, 12/1 for domestic and international students. *Application fee:* $100. Electronic applications accepted. *Application Contact:* Michael Manderen, Director of Conservatory Admissions, 440-775-8413, Fax: 440-775-6972, E-mail: conservatory.admissions@oberlin.edu. *Dean*, Andrea Kalyn, 440-775-8200.

OBLATE SCHOOL OF THEOLOGY, San Antonio, TX 78216-6693

General Information Independent-religious, coed, graduate-only institution.

GRADUATE UNITS

Graduate and Professional Programs ***Degree program information:*** Part-time programs available. Part-time, online learning. Offers African-American pastoral leadership (D Min); divinity (M Div); pastoral leadership (D Min); pastoral ministry (MAP Min); pastoral studies (Certificate); spiritual formation in the local community (D Min); spirituality (MA Sp, PhD); spirituality and ministry (D Min); theology (MA Th); U.S. Hispanic/Latino ministry (D Min).

OCCIDENTAL COLLEGE, Los Angeles, CA 90041-3314

General Information Independent, coed, comprehensive institution. *Graduate housing:* On-campus housing not available.

GRADUATE UNITS

Graduate Studies ***Degree program information:*** Part-time programs available. Part-time. Offers biology (MA); elementary education (MAT); secondary education (MAT).

OGLALA LAKOTA COLLEGE, Kyle, SD 57752-0490

General Information State and locally supported, coed, comprehensive institution. *Graduate housing:* On-campus housing not available.

GRADUATE UNITS

Graduate Studies ***Degree program information:*** Part-time and evening/weekend programs available. Part-time, evening/weekend. Offers educational administration (MA); Lakota leadership and management (MA).

OHIO DOMINICAN UNIVERSITY, Columbus, OH 43219-2099

General Information Independent-religious, coed, comprehensive institution. *Enrollment:* 2,534 graduate, professional, and undergraduate students; 474 full-time matriculated graduate/professional students (290 women), 98 part-time matriculated graduate/professional students (59 women). *Enrollment by degree level:* 571 master's, 1 other advanced degree. *Graduate faculty:* 44 full-time (19 women), 52 part-time/adjunct (12 women). *Tuition, area resident:* Full-time $6960; part-time $580 per credit hour. *Required fees:* $450; $450 per unit. Tuition and fees vary according to program. *Graduate housing:* Room and/or apartments available on a first-come, first-served basis to single students; on-campus housing not available to married students. *Student services:* Campus employment opportunities, campus safety program, career counseling, exercise/wellness program, free psychological counseling, international student services, multicultural affairs office, services for students with disabilities, writing training. *Library:* Spangler Library. *Collection:* Books: 88,676 (physical), 97,381 (digital/electronic); Serial titles: 684 (physical), 20,072 (digital/electronic); Databases: 196. Students can reserve study rooms.

Computer facilities: 350 computers available on campus for general student use. A campuswide network can be accessed from student residence rooms and from off campus. Online class registration is available.
Website: http://www.ohiodominican.edu/

General Application Contact: John W. Naughton, Director for Graduate Admissions, 614-251-4721, Fax: 614-251-6654, E-mail: grad@ohiodominican.edu.

GRADUATE UNITS

Graduate Programs Students: 474 full-time (290 women), 98 part-time (59 women); includes 121 minority (78 Black or African American, non-Hispanic/Latino; 1 American Indian or Alaska Native, non-Hispanic/Latino; 19 Asian, non-Hispanic/Latino; 12 Hispanic/Latino; 2 Native Hawaiian or other Pacific Islander, non-Hispanic/Latino; 9 Two or more races, non-Hispanic/Latino), 5 international. Average age 31. 765 applicants, 30% accepted, 181 enrolled. *Faculty:* 44 full-time (19 women), 52 part-time/adjunct (12 women). *Financial support:* Applicants required to submit FAFSA. *Degree program information:* Part-time and evening/weekend programs available. Part-time, evening/weekend, 100% online, blended/hybrid learning. *Application deadline:* For fall admission, 8/15 for domestic students, 6/10 for international students; for spring admission, 1/4 for domestic students, 11/2 for international students; for summer admission, 5/30 for domestic students. Applications are processed on a rolling basis. *Application fee:* $25. Electronic applications accepted. *Application Contact:* John W. Naughton, Director for Graduate Admissions, 614-251-4721, Fax: 614-251-6654, E-mail: grad@ohiodominican.edu. *Associate Vice President for Academic Affairs*, Dr. Linda Wolf, 614-251-4715, Fax: 614-253-3656, E-mail: wolfl2@ohiodominican.edu.

Division of Arts and Letters Students: 20 full-time (17 women), 25 part-time (11 women); includes 3 minority (all Black or African American, non-Hispanic/Latino). Average age 40. 11 applicants, 100% accepted, 9 enrolled. *Financial support:* Applicants required to submit FAFSA. *Degree program information:* Part-time and evening/weekend programs available. Part-time, evening/weekend, 100% online. Offers English (MA); liberal studies (MA); theology (MA). *Application deadline:* For fall admission, 8/15 for domestic students, 6/10 for international students; for spring admission, 1/4 for domestic students, 11/2 for international students; for summer admission, 5/30 for domestic students. Applications are processed on a rolling basis. *Application fee:* $25. Electronic applications accepted. *Application Contact:* John W. Naughton, Director for Graduate Admissions, 614-251-4721, Fax: 614-251-6654, E-mail: grad@ohiodominican.edu. *Chair, Division of Arts and Letters*, Dr. Bruce Gartner, 614-251-4604, Fax: 614-253-3656, E-mail: gartnerb@ohiodominican.edu.

Division of Business Students: 220 full-time (106 women), 52 part-time (29 women); includes 101 minority (69 Black or African American, non-Hispanic/Latino; 1 American Indian or Alaska Native, non-Hispanic/Latino; 14 Asian, non-Hispanic/Latino; 9 Hispanic/Latino; 2 Native Hawaiian or other Pacific Islander, non-Hispanic/Latino; 6 Two or more races, non-Hispanic/Latino), 4 international. Average age 32. 72 applicants, 92% accepted, 58 enrolled. *Financial support:* Applicants required to submit FAFSA. *Degree program information:* Part-time and evening/weekend programs available. Part-time, evening/weekend, 100% online, blended/hybrid learning. Offers accounting (MBA); business administration (MBA); finance (MBA); healthcare administration (MS); leadership (MBA); public administration (MBA); sport management (MS). *Application deadline:* For fall admission, 8/15 for domestic students, 6/10 for international students; for spring admission, 1/4 for domestic students, 11/2 for international students; for summer admission, 5/30 for domestic students. Applications are processed on a rolling basis. *Application fee:* $25. Electronic applications accepted. *Application Contact:* John W. Naughton, Director for Graduate Admissions, 614-251-4615, Fax: 614-251-6654, E-mail: grad@ohiodominican.edu. *Director of Graduate Business Programs*, Dr. Anna Parkman, 614-251-4569, E-mail: parkmana@ohiodominican.edu.

Division of Education Students: 78 full-time (60 women), 21 part-time (19 women); includes 8 minority (2 Black or African American, non-Hispanic/Latino; 2 Asian, non-Hispanic/Latino; 2 Hispanic/Latino; 2 Two or more races, non-Hispanic/Latino), 1 international. Average age 34. 80 applicants, 95% accepted, 65 enrolled. *Financial support:* Tuition waivers and tuition discount for Diocesan teachers available. Financial award applicants required to submit FAFSA. *Degree program information:* Part-time and evening/weekend programs available. Part-time, evening/weekend, 100% online, blended/hybrid learning. Offers curriculum and instruction (M Ed); educational leadership (M Ed); teaching English to speakers of other languages (MA). *Application deadline:* For fall admission, 8/15 for domestic students, 6/10 for international students; for spring admission, 1/4 for domestic students, 11/2 for international students; for summer admission, 5/30 for domestic students. Applications are processed on a rolling basis. *Application fee:* $25. Electronic applications accepted. *Application Contact:* John W. Naughton, Director for Graduate Admissions, 614-251-4721, Fax: 614-251-6654, E-mail: grad@ohiodominican.edu. *Associate Professor/Chair of Education Division*, Dr. JoAnn Hohenbrink, 614-251-4759, E-mail: hohenbrj@ohiodominican.edu.

Division of Math, Computer and Natural Science Students: 151 full-time (106 women); includes 7 minority (2 Black or African American, non-Hispanic/Latino; 3 Asian, non-Hispanic/Latino; 1 Hispanic/Latino; 1 Two or more races, non-Hispanic/Latino). Average age 25. 602 applicants, 13% accepted, 49 enrolled. *Financial support:* Applicants required to submit FAFSA. Offers physician assistant studies (MS). *Application deadline:* For fall admission, 11/1 for domestic and international students. Applications are processed on a rolling basis. Electronic applications accepted. *Application Contact:* John W. Naughton, Director for Graduate Admissions, 614-251-4721, Fax: 614-251-6654, E-mail: grad@ohiodominican.edu. *Program Director*, Prof. Shonna Riedlinger, 614-251-8988, E-mail: riedlins@ohiodominican.edu.

OHIO NORTHERN UNIVERSITY, Ada, OH 45810-1599

General Information Independent-religious, coed, comprehensive institution. *Enrollment:* 3,238 graduate, professional, and undergraduate students; 973 full-time matriculated graduate/professional students (614 women), 6 part-time matriculated graduate/professional students (5 women). *Enrollment by degree level:* 31 master's, 948 doctoral. *Graduate faculty:* 42 full-time (22 women), 7 part-time/adjunct (2 women). *Graduate housing:* Room and/or apartments available on a first-come, first-served basis to single students; on-campus housing not available to married students. *Student services:* Campus employment opportunities, campus safety program, career counseling, child daycare facilities, exercise/wellness program, free psychological counseling, international student services, multicultural affairs office, services for students with disabilities. *Library:* Heterick Memorial Library plus 1 other. Students can reserve study rooms.

Computer facilities: A campuswide network can be accessed from student residence rooms and from off campus. Online class registration is available.
Website: http://www.onu.edu/

General Application Contact: Deborah Miller, Director of Admissions, 419-772-2464, E-mail: d-miller@onu.edu.

GRADUATE UNITS

Claude W. Pettit College of Law Students: 204 full-time (102 women), 3 part-time (all women); includes 40 minority (20 Black or African American, non-Hispanic/Latino; 5 American Indian or Alaska Native, non-Hispanic/Latino; 4 Asian, non-Hispanic/Latino; 9 Hispanic/Latino; 1 Native Hawaiian or other Pacific Islander, non-Hispanic/Latino; 1 Two or more races, non-Hispanic/Latino), 11 international. Average age 26. 460 applicants, 49% accepted, 69 enrolled. *Faculty:* 17 full-time (10 women), 6 part-time/adjunct (2 women). *Financial support:* Career-related internships or fieldwork, Federal Work-Study, institutionally sponsored loans, and scholarships/grants available. Financial award applicants required to submit FAFSA. In 2015, 19 master's, 94 doctorates awarded. Offers law (LL M, JD). *Application deadline:* Applications are processed on a rolling basis. Electronic applications accepted. *Application Contact:* Rachel Frey, Director of Law Admissions, 419-772-2213, Fax: 419-772-2758, E-mail: r-frey@onu.edu. *Dean*, Dr. Richard Bales, 419-772-3051, Fax: 419-772-3051, E-mail: r-bales@onu.edu.

Raabe College of Pharmacy Students: 750 full-time (500 women), 1 (woman) part-time; includes 69 minority (14 Black or African American, non-Hispanic/Latino; 26 Asian, non-Hispanic/Latino; 8 Hispanic/Latino; 21 Two or more races, non-Hispanic/Latino), 26 international. Average age 22. 656 applicants, 45% accepted, 176 enrolled. *Faculty:* 26 full-time (12 women), 3 part-time/adjunct (2 women). *Financial support:* Federal Work-Study, institutionally sponsored loans, and scholarships/grants available. Financial award applicants required to submit FAFSA. In 2015, 164 doctorates awarded. Offers pharmacy (Pharm D). Students enter the program as undergraduates. *Application Contact:* Dr. Kelly Shields, Assistant Dean of Student Services, 419-772-2752, Fax: 419-

772-2752, E-mail: k-shields@onu.edu. *Interim Dean*, Dr. Tom Kier, 419-772-2282, Fax: 419-772-2282, E-mail: t-kier@onu.edu.

THE OHIO STATE UNIVERSITY, Columbus, OH 43210

General Information State-supported, coed, university. CGS member. *Graduate housing:* Rooms and/or apartments available on a first-come, first-served basis to single and married students. *Research affiliation:* Transportation Research Center, Midwest Universities Consortium for International Activities, Children's Hospital (pediatrics), Ohio Learning Network (education).

GRADUATE UNITS

College of Dentistry Students: 520 full-time (219 women), 5 part-time (4 women); includes 95 minority (12 Black or African American, non-Hispanic/Latino; 2 American Indian or Alaska Native, non-Hispanic/Latino; 49 Asian, non-Hispanic/Latino; 18 Hispanic/Latino; 14 Two or more races, non-Hispanic/Latino), 28 international. Average age 26. *Faculty:* 77. *Financial support:* Fellowships with tuition reimbursements, research assistantships with tuition reimbursements, teaching assistantships with tuition reimbursements, Federal Work-Study, institutionally sponsored loans, and health care benefits available. Financial award application deadline: 2/15. In 2015, 31 master's, 112 doctorates awarded. Offers dental anesthesiology (MS); dental hygiene (MDH); dentistry (DDS); endodontics (MS); oral and maxillofacial pathology (MS); oral and maxillofacial surgery (MS); oral biology (PhD); orthodontics (MS); pediatric dentistry (MS); periodontology (MS); prosthodontics (MS). *Application deadline:* For fall admission, 10/1 for domestic and international students; for summer admission, 4/11 for domestic students, 3/10 for international students. Applications are processed on a rolling basis. Electronic applications accepted. *Dean*, Dr. Patrick M. Lloyd, 614-292-9755, E-mail: lloyd.256@osu.edu.

College of Medicine Offers medicine (MOT, MS, DPT, MD, PhD). Electronic applications accepted.

School of Biomedical Science Offers biomedical science (PhD); biomedical sciences (PhD). Electronic applications accepted.

School of Health and Rehabilitation Sciences Students: 337 full-time (260 women), 13 part-time (10 women); includes 27 minority (2 Black or African American, non-Hispanic/Latino; 1 American Indian or Alaska Native, non-Hispanic/Latino; 8 Asian, non-Hispanic/Latino; 10 Hispanic/Latino; 6 Two or more races, non-Hispanic/Latino), 3 international. Average age 25. *Faculty:* 42. *Financial support:* Fellowships with tuition reimbursements, research assistantships with full tuition reimbursements, teaching assistantships with full tuition reimbursements, traineeships, unspecified assistantships, and administrative assistantships available. Financial award application deadline: 3/1. In 2015, 68 master's, 60 doctorates awarded. *Degree program information:* Part-time programs available. Part-time. Offers allied health (MS); anatomy (MS, PhD); health and rehabilitation sciences (MOT, MS, DPT, PhD); occupational therapy (MOT); physical therapy (DPT). *Application deadline:* Applications are processed on a rolling basis. *Application fee:* $60 ($70 for international students). Electronic applications accepted. *Application Contact:* Graduate and Professional Admissions, 614-292-9444, Fax: 614-292-3895, E-mail: gpadmissions@osu.edu. *Director*, Dr. Deborah S. Larsen, 614-292-5645, Fax: 614-292-0210, E-mail: larsen.64@osu.edu.

College of Optometry Students: 263 full-time (181 women); includes 33 minority (4 Black or African American, non-Hispanic/Latino; 19 Asian, non-Hispanic/Latino; 5 Hispanic/Latino; 5 Two or more races, non-Hispanic/Latino), 2 international. Average age 25. *Faculty:* 34. *Financial support:* Research assistantships with full tuition reimbursements, teaching assistantships with full tuition reimbursements, institutionally sponsored loans, and scholarships/grants available. Financial award application deadline: 2/15; financial award applicants required to submit FAFSA. In 2015, 9 master's, 66 doctorates awarded. Offers optometry (OD); vision science (MS, PhD). *Application deadline:* For fall admission, 3/31 for domestic and international students; for spring admission, 12/1 for domestic students, 11/1 for international students. Applications are processed on a rolling basis. *Application fee:* $60 ($70 for international students). Electronic applications accepted. *Application Contact:* Office of Student Affairs, College of Optometry, 614-292-2647, Fax: 614-292-7493, E-mail: admissions@optometry.osu.edu. *Dean*, Dr. Karla Zadnik, 614-292-6603, E-mail: zadnik.4@osu.edu.

College of Pharmacy Students: 574 full-time (315 women); includes 142 minority (26 Black or African American, non-Hispanic/Latino; 1 American Indian or Alaska Native, non-Hispanic/Latino; 93 Asian, non-Hispanic/Latino; 17 Hispanic/Latino; 1 Native Hawaiian or other Pacific Islander, non-Hispanic/Latino; 4 Two or more races, non-Hispanic/Latino), 53 international. Average age 25. *Faculty:* 50. *Financial support:* Fellowships with full tuition reimbursements, research assistantships with full tuition reimbursements, teaching assistantships with full tuition reimbursements, career-related internships or fieldwork, Federal Work-Study, institutionally sponsored loans, scholarships/grants, and traineeships available. In 2015, 17 master's, 132 doctorates awarded. Offers pharmacy (MS, PhD, Pharm D). *Application deadline:* For fall admission, 12/15 for domestic and international students. *Application fee:* $60 ($70 for international students). Electronic applications accepted. *Application Contact:* Dr. Henry J. Mann, Dean and Professor, 614-292-5711, Fax: 614-292-2588, E-mail: mann.414@osu.edu. *Dean and Professor*, Dr. Henry J. Mann, 614-292-5711, Fax: 614-292-2588, E-mail: mann.414@osu.edu.

College of Public Health Students: 268 full-time (189 women), 67 part-time (49 women); includes 73 minority (22 Black or African American, non-Hispanic/Latino; 1 American Indian or Alaska Native, non-Hispanic/Latino; 29 Asian, non-Hispanic/Latino; 12 Hispanic/Latino; 9 Two or more races, non-Hispanic/Latino), 11 international. Average age 28. *Faculty:* 44. *Financial support:* Fellowships with tuition reimbursements and research assistantships with tuition reimbursements available. In 2015, 114 master's, 7 doctorates awarded. *Degree program information:* Part-time programs available. Part-time. Offers public health (MHA, MPH, MS, PhD). *Application deadline:* For fall admission, 12/1 priority date for domestic students, 11/1 priority date for international students. Applications are processed on a rolling basis. *Application fee:* $60 ($70 for international students). Electronic applications accepted. *Application Contact:* Dr. William J. Martin, II, Dean and Professor, 614-292-8350, E-mail: martin.3047@osu.edu. *Dean and Professor*, Dr. William J. Martin, II, 614-292-8350, E-mail: martin.3047@osu.edu.

College of Veterinary Medicine Students: 723 full-time (585 women), 14 part-time (9 women); includes 87 minority (7 Black or African American, non-Hispanic/Latino; 2 American Indian or Alaska Native, non-Hispanic/Latino; 24 Asian, non-Hispanic/Latino; 39 Hispanic/Latino; 15 Two or more races, non-Hispanic/Latino), 33 international. Average age 26. *Faculty:* 105. In 2015, 26 master's, 166 doctorates awarded. Offers comparative and veterinary medicine (MS, PhD); veterinary medicine (MS, DVM, PhD). *Application deadline:* For fall admission, 9/15 for domestic and international students. Applications are processed on a rolling basis. *Application fee:* $60 ($70 for international students). Electronic applications accepted. *Application Contact:* Graduate and Professional Admissions, 614-292-9444, Fax: 614-292-3895, E-mail: gpadmissions@osu.edu. *Dean/Chair/Professor*, Dr. Rustin M. Moore, 614-688-8749, Fax: 614-292-3544, E-mail: moore.66@osu.edu.

Graduate School ***Degree program information:*** Part-time and evening/weekend programs available. Part-time, evening/weekend. Offers biostatistics (PhD). Electronic applications accepted.

Center for Applied Plant Sciences Students: 9 full-time (7 women), 1 (woman) part-time. Average age 26. *Financial support:* Fellowships with tuition reimbursements and research assistantships with tuition reimbursements available. Offers applied plant sciences (PhD). *Application deadline:* For fall admission, 11/15 priority date for domestic and international students. Applications are processed on a rolling basis. *Application fee:* $60 ($70 for international students). Electronic applications accepted. *Application Contact:* Graduate and Professional Admissions, 614-292-9444, Fax: 614-292-3895, E-mail: gpadmissions@osu.edu. *Director*, Dr. Erich Grotewold, 614-292-2483, E-mail: grotewold.1@osu.edu.

Center for Latin American Studies ***Financial support:*** Fellowships with tuition reimbursements available. In 2015, 1 master's awarded. Offers Latin American studies (MA). *Application deadline:* For fall admission, 12/13 priority date for domestic students, 11/30 priority date for international students; for spring admission, 12/12 for domestic students, 11/10 for international students; for summer admission, 4/10 for domestic students, 3/13 for international students. Applications are processed on a rolling basis. *Application fee:* $60 ($70 for international students). Electronic applications accepted. *Application Contact:* Graduate and Professional Admissions, 614-292-9444, Fax: 614-292-3895, E-mail: gpadmissions@osu.edu. *Director*, Dr. Abril Trigo, 614-292-8695, E-mail: trigo.1@osu.edu.

Center for Slavic and East European Studies Students: 14 full-time (5 women), 1 part-time. Average age 26. *Financial support:* Fellowships, Federal Work-Study, and institutionally sponsored loans available. Support available to part-time students. In 2015, 5 master's awarded. Offers Slavic and East European studies (MA). *Application deadline:* For fall admission, 12/13 priority date for domestic students, 11/30 priority date for international students; for spring admission, 11/10 for domestic and international students; for summer admission, 3/13 for domestic and international students. Applications are processed on a rolling basis. *Application fee:* $60 ($70 for international students). Electronic applications accepted. *Application Contact:* Graduate and Professional Admissions, 614-292-9444, Fax: 614-292-3895, E-mail: gpadmissions@osu.edu. *Director*, Dr. Yana Hashamova, E-mail: hashamova.1@osu.edu.

College of Arts and Sciences ***Degree program information:*** Part-time programs available. Part-time. Offers acting (MFA); African-American and African studies (MA, PhD); ancient Greek and Latin (MA, PhD); anthropology (MA, PhD); art (MFA); art education (MA); arts administration, education and policy (PhD); arts and humanities (MA, MFA, MM, DMA, PhD); arts and sciences (M Mus, MA, MFA, MMS, MS, DMA, PhD); arts policy and administration (MA); astronomy (MS, PhD); atmospheric sciences (MS, PhD); audiology (Au D); behavioral neuroscience (PhD); biochemistry (PhD); biophysics (MS, PhD); biostatistics (PhD); cell and developmental biology (MS, PhD); chemical physics (MS, PhD); chemistry (MS, PhD); Chinese (MA, PhD); choreography (MFA); clinical psychology (PhD); cognitive psychology (PhD); communication (MA, PhD); comparative studies (MA, PhD); computational sciences (MMS); dance (MFA, PhD); dance and technology (MFA); dance studies (PhD); design (MA, MFA); design research and development (MFA); developmental psychology (PhD); digital animation and interactive media (MFA); earth sciences (MS, PhD); economics (MA, PhD); English (MA, MFA, PhD); evolution, ecology, and organismal biology (MS, PhD); French (MA, PhD); genetics (MS, PhD); geodetic science (MS, PhD); geography (MA, PhD); geological sciences (MS, PhD); Germanic languages and literatures (MA, PhD); Greek studies (MA); hearing science (PhD); history (MA, PhD); history of art (MA, PhD); history, theory and literature (MFA); intellectual and developmental disabilities psychology (PhD); Italian (MA); Italian studies (PhD); Japanese (MA, PhD); Latin studies (MA, PhD); lighting and production (MFA); linguistics (MA, PhD); mathematical biosciences (MMS); mathematics (PhD); mathematics for educators (MMS); microbiology (MS, PhD); modern Greek (MA, PhD); molecular biology (MS, PhD); molecular, cellular and developmental biology (MS, PhD); movement analysis, Laban studies, notation and dance documentation (MFA); music (MA, MM, DMA, PhD); natural and mathematical sciences (M Appl Stat, MMS, MS, PhD); Near Eastern languages and cultures (MA, PhD); neuroscience (PhD); performance (MFA); philosophy (MA, PhD); physics (MS, PhD); political science (PhD); quantitative psychology (PhD); Slavic linguistics (MA, PhD); Slavic literature, film, and cultural studies (MA, PhD); social and behavioral sciences (MA, MS, Au D, PhD); social psychology (PhD); sociology (PhD); Spanish and Portuguese (MA, PhD); speech-language pathology (MA); speech-language science (PhD); statistics (M Appl Stat, MS, PhD); theatre (PhD); theatre studies (MA); women's, gender and sexuality studies (MA, PhD). Electronic applications accepted.

College of Education and Human Ecology Students: 752 full-time (529 women), 218 part-time (152 women); includes 149 minority (71 Black or African American, non-Hispanic/Latino; 3 American Indian or Alaska Native, non-Hispanic/Latino; 21 Asian, non-Hispanic/Latino; 39 Hispanic/Latino; 15 Two or more races, non-Hispanic/Latino), 202 international. Average age 31. *Faculty:* 140. *Financial support:* Fellowships with tuition reimbursements, research assistantships with tuition reimbursements, teaching assistantships with tuition reimbursements, career-related internships or fieldwork, Federal Work-Study, institutionally sponsored loans, scholarships/grants, traineeships, health care benefits, and unspecified assistantships available. Support available to part-time students. In 2015, 348 master's, 76 doctorates, 7 other advanced degrees awarded. Offers consumer sciences (MS, PhD); education and human ecology (M Ed, MA, MS, PhD, Ed S); educational studies (M Ed, MA, PhD, Ed S); human development and family science (PhD); human nutrition (MS, PhD); kinesiology (MA, PhD); teaching and learning (M Ed, MA, PhD, Ed S). *Application deadline:* Applications are processed on a rolling basis. *Application fee:* $60 ($70 for international students). Electronic applications accepted. *Application Contact:* Graduate and Professional Admissions, 614-292-9444, Fax: 614-292-3895, E-mail: gpadmissions@osu.edu. *Dean*, Dr. Cheryl Achterberg, 614-292-2461, Fax: 614-292-8052, E-mail: achterberg.1@osu.edu.

College of Engineering Students: 1,782 full-time (409 women), 143 part-time (30 women); includes 145 minority (33 Black or African American, non-Hispanic/Latino; 3 American Indian or Alaska Native, non-Hispanic/Latino; 56 Asian, non-Hispanic/Latino; 36 Hispanic/Latino; 17 Two or more races, non-Hispanic/Latino), 1,131 international. Average age 26. *Faculty:* 325. *Financial support:* Fellowships with tuition reimbursements, research assistantships with tuition reimbursements, teaching assistantships with tuition reimbursements, career-related internships or fieldwork, Federal Work-Study, institutionally sponsored loans, and unspecified assistantships available. Support available to part-time students. In 2015, 495 master's, 167 doctorates awarded. *Degree program information:* Part-time and evening/weekend programs available. Part-time, evening/weekend. Offers aerospace engineering (MS,

PhD); architecture (M Arch); biomedical engineering (MS, PhD); chemical engineering (MS, PhD); city and regional planning (MCRP, PhD); civil engineering (MS, PhD); computer science and engineering (MS, PhD); electrical and computer engineering (MS, PhD); electrical engineering (MS, PhD); engineering (M Arch, M Land Arch, MCRP, MS, PhD); industrial and systems engineering (MS, PhD); landscape architecture (M Land Arch); materials science and engineering (MS, PhD); mechanical engineering (MS, PhD); nuclear engineering (MS, PhD); welding engineering (MS, PhD). *Application deadline:* For fall admission, 11/30 priority date for domestic and international students. Applications are processed on a rolling basis. *Application fee:* $60 ($70 for international students). Electronic applications accepted. *Application Contact:* Graduate and Professional Admissions, 614-292-9444, Fax: 614-292-3895, E-mail: gpadmissions@osu.edu. *Dean,* Dr. David B. Williams, 614-292-2836, Fax: 614-292-9615, E-mail: williams.4219@osu.edu.

College of Food, Agricultural, and Environmental Sciences Students: 483 full-time (268 women), 61 part-time (37 women); includes 58 minority (13 Black or African American, non-Hispanic/Latino; 1 American Indian or Alaska Native, non-Hispanic/Latino; 15 Asian, non-Hispanic/Latino; 20 Hispanic/Latino; 9 Two or more races, non-Hispanic/Latino), 186 international. Average age 28. *Faculty:* 308. *Financial support:* Fellowships with tuition reimbursements, research assistantships with tuition reimbursements, teaching assistantships with tuition reimbursements, career-related internships or fieldwork, Federal Work-Study, institutionally sponsored loans, and unspecified assistantships available. Support available to part-time students. In 2015, 135 master's, 56 doctorates awarded. *Degree program information:* Part-time programs available. Part-time. Offers agricultural and extension education (M Ed, MS, PhD); agricultural, environmental, and development economics (MS, PhD); animal sciences (MAS, MS, PhD); ecological restoration (MS, PhD); ecosystem science (MS, PhD); entomology (MPHM, MS, PhD); environment and natural resources (MENR); environmental science (MS, PhD); environmental social sciences (MS, PhD); fisheries and wildlife science (MS, PhD); food science and technology (MS, PhD); food, agricultural, and biological engineering (MS, PhD); food, agricultural, and environmental sciences (M Ed, MAS, MENR, MPHM, MS, PhD); forest science (MS, PhD); horticulture and crop science (MS, PhD); plant pathology (MPHM, MS, PhD); rural sociology (MS, PhD); soil science (MS, PhD). *Application deadline:* Applications are processed on a rolling basis. *Application fee:* $60 ($70 for international students). Electronic applications accepted. *Application Contact:* Graduate and Professional Admissions, 614-292-9444, Fax: 614-292-3895, E-mail: gpadmissions@osu.edu. *Interim Vice President and Dean,* Dr. Lonnie King, 614-292-3676, E-mail: king.1518@osu.edu.

College of Nursing Students: 496 full-time (413 women), 218 part-time (200 women); includes 108 minority (42 Black or African American, non-Hispanic/Latino; 32 Asian, non-Hispanic/Latino; 20 Hispanic/Latino; 14 Two or more races, non-Hispanic/Latino), 5 international. Average age 33. *Faculty:* 43. *Financial support:* Fellowships, research assistantships, teaching assistantships, Federal Work-Study, institutionally sponsored loans, and unspecified assistantships available. Support available to part-time students. In 2015, 164 master's, 28 doctorates awarded. *Degree program information:* Part-time programs available. Part-time. Offers nursing (MS, DNP, PhD). *Application deadline:* For fall admission, 12/13 priority date for domestic students, 11/30 priority date for international students; for summer admission, 10/12 for domestic and international students. Applications are processed on a rolling basis. *Application fee:* $60 ($70 for international students). Electronic applications accepted. *Application Contact:* Graduate and Professional Admissions, 614-292-9444, Fax: 614-292-3895, E-mail: gpadmissions@osu.edu. *Dean,* Dr. Bernadette M. Melnyk, 614-292-4844, Fax: 614-292-4535, E-mail: melnyk.15@osu.edu.

College of Social Work Students: 391 full-time (341 women), 62 part-time (53 women); includes 82 minority (54 Black or African American, non-Hispanic/Latino; 6 Asian, non-Hispanic/Latino; 11 Hispanic/Latino; 11 Two or more races, non-Hispanic/Latino), 16 international. Average age 29. *Faculty:* 28. *Financial support:* Fellowships, research assistantships, teaching assistantships, Federal Work-Study, institutionally sponsored loans, and unspecified assistantships available. Support available to part-time students. In 2015, 246 master's, 3 doctorates awarded. *Degree program information:* Part-time programs available. Part-time. Offers social work (MSW, PhD). *Application deadline:* For fall admission, 12/13 priority date for domestic students, 11/30 priority date for international students; for summer admission, 4/1 for domestic students, 3/1 for international students. Applications are processed on a rolling basis. *Application fee:* $60 ($70 for international students). Electronic applications accepted. *Application Contact:* Graduate and Professional Admissions, 614-292-6031, Fax: 614-292-3656, E-mail: gpadmissions@osu.edu. *Dean,* Dr. Tom Gregoire, 614-292-9426, E-mail: gregoire.5@osu.edu.

East Asian Studies Center Students: 11 full-time (5 women); includes 1 minority (Two or more races, non-Hispanic/Latino), 2 international. Average age 27. In 2015, 2 master's awarded. Offers East Asian studies (MA). *Application deadline:* For fall admission, 12/13 priority date for domestic students, 11/30 priority date for international students; for spring admission, 12/1 for domestic students, 11/1 for international students; for summer admission, 4/10 for domestic students, 3/13 for international students. Applications are processed on a rolling basis. *Application fee:* $60 ($70 for international students). Electronic applications accepted. *Application Contact:* Graduate and Professional Admissions, 614-292-9444, Fax: 614-292-3895, E-mail: gpadmissions@osu.edu. *Associate Professor,* Dr. Etsuyo Yuasa, 614-292-5816, E-mail: yuasa.1@osu.edu.

John Glenn College of Public Affairs Students: 118 full-time (64 women), 48 part-time (36 women); includes 28 minority (13 Black or African American, non-Hispanic/Latino; 6 Asian, non-Hispanic/Latino; 5 Hispanic/Latino; 1 Native Hawaiian or other Pacific Islander, non-Hispanic/Latino; 3 Two or more races, non-Hispanic/Latino), 12 international. Average age 31. *Faculty:* 19. *Financial support:* Fellowships, research assistantships, teaching assistantships, Federal Work-Study, institutionally sponsored loans, and unspecified assistantships available. Support available to part-time students. In 2015, 83 master's, 2 doctorates awarded. *Degree program information:* Part-time programs available. Part-time. Offers public administration (MA, MPA); public policy and management (PhD). *Application deadline:* For fall admission, 12/1 priority date for domestic students, 11/30 priority date for international students; for spring admission, 11/15 for domestic and international students; for summer admission, 4/1 for domestic and international students. Applications are processed on a rolling basis. *Application fee:* $60 ($70 for international students). Electronic applications accepted. *Application Contact:* Graduate and Professional Admissions, 614-292-6031, Fax: 614-292-3656, E-mail: gpadmissions@osu.edu. *Dean,* Dr. Trevor Brown, 614-292-4533, Fax: 614-292-4868, E-mail: brown.2296@osu.edu.

Max M. Fisher College of Business Students: 717 full-time (326 women), 300 part-time (100 women); includes 161 minority (50 Black or African American, non-Hispanic/Latino; 2 American Indian or Alaska Native, non-Hispanic/Latino; 64 Asian, non-Hispanic/Latino; 30 Hispanic/Latino; 2 Native Hawaiian or other Pacific Islander, non-Hispanic/Latino; 13 Two or more races, non-Hispanic/Latino), 314 international. Average age 29. *Faculty:* 96. *Financial support:* Fellowships, research assistantships, teaching assistantships, career-related internships or fieldwork, Federal Work-Study, institutionally sponsored loans, and unspecified assistantships available. Support available to part-time students. In 2015, 506 master's, 8 doctorates awarded. *Degree program information:* Part-time and evening/weekend programs available. Part-time, evening/weekend. Offers accounting (M Acc); accounting and management information systems (M Acc, PhD); business (M Acc, MA, MBA, MBLE, MBOE, MF, MHRM, PhD); business administration (MA, MBA, PhD); business logistics engineering (MBLE); business operational excellence (MBOE); finance (MF); human resource management (MHRM, PhD); labor and human resources (PhD). *Application deadline:* Applications are processed on a rolling basis. *Application fee:* $60 ($70 for international students). Electronic applications accepted. *Application Contact:* Graduate and Professional Admissions, 614-292-9444, Fax: 614-292-3656, E-mail: gpadmissions@osu.edu. *Dean/Chair,* Dr. Anil K. Makhija, 614-292-2666, E-mail: makhija.1@osu.edu.

Moritz College of Law Offers law (LL M, MSL, JD). Electronic applications accepted.

THE OHIO STATE UNIVERSITY AT LIMA, Lima, OH 45804

General Information State-supported, coed, comprehensive institution. *Enrollment:* 1,010 graduate, professional, and undergraduate students; 7 matriculated graduate/professional students (5 women). *Enrollment by degree level:* 7 master's. *Graduate faculty:* 36. *Graduate housing:* On-campus housing not available. *Student services:* Campus safety program, career counseling, child daycare facilities, exercise/wellness program, free psychological counseling, grant writing training, international student services, low-cost health insurance, multicultural affairs office, services for students with disabilities, teacher training, writing training. *Library:* Lima Campus Library plus 1 other.

Computer facilities: Computer purchase and lease plans are available. A campuswide network can be accessed. Online class registration is available.
Website: http://lima.osu.edu/

General Application Contact: Graduate and Professional Admissions, 614-292-9444, Fax: 614-292-3895, E-mail: gpadmissions@osu.edu.

GRADUATE UNITS

Graduate Programs Students: 7 (5 women). Average age 31. *Faculty:* 36. *Financial support:* Application deadline: 2/15. *Degree program information:* Part-time programs available. Part-time. Offers social work (MSW). *Application deadline:* For fall admission, 4/1 for domestic students, 3/1 for international students; for spring admission, 10/15 for domestic and international students; for summer admission, 4/10 for domestic students, 3/1 for international students. Applications are processed on a rolling basis. *Application fee:* $60 ($70 for international students). Electronic applications accepted. *Application Contact:* Graduate and Professional Admissions, 614-292-9444, Fax: 614-292-3895, E-mail: gpadmissions@osu.edu. *Dean and Director,* Dr. Charlene Gilbert, 419-995-8481, E-mail: gilbert.583@osu.edu.

THE OHIO STATE UNIVERSITY AT MARION, Marion, OH 43302-5695

General Information State-supported, coed, comprehensive institution. *Enrollment:* 1,085 graduate, professional, and undergraduate students. *Graduate faculty:* 36. *Graduate housing:* On-campus housing not available. *Student services:* Campus employment opportunities, campus safety program, career counseling, child daycare facilities, exercise/wellness program, free psychological counseling, grant writing training, international student services, low-cost health insurance, multicultural affairs office, services for students with disabilities, teacher training, writing training. *Library:* Marion Campus Library plus 1 other.

Computer facilities: Computer purchase and lease plans are available. A campuswide network can be accessed. Online class registration is available.
Website: http://osumarion.osu.edu/

General Application Contact: Graduate and Professional Admissions, 614-292-9444, Fax: 614-292-3985, E-mail: gpadmissions@osu.edu.

GRADUATE UNITS

Graduate Programs ***Faculty:*** 36. *Financial support:* Application deadline: 2/15; applicants required to submit FAFSA. *Degree program information:* Part-time programs available. Part-time. Offers education (MA). *Application deadline:* Applications are processed on a rolling basis. *Application fee:* $60 ($70 for international students). Electronic applications accepted. *Application Contact:* Graduate and Professional Admissions, 614-292-9444, Fax: 614-292-3895, E-mail: gpadmissions@osu.edu. *Dean/Director,* Dr. Gregory S. Rose, 740-725-6218, E-mail: rose.9@osu.edu.

THE OHIO STATE UNIVERSITY–MANSFIELD CAMPUS, Mansfield, OH 44906-1599

General Information State-supported, coed, comprehensive institution. *Enrollment:* 1,199 graduate, professional, and undergraduate students; 9 matriculated graduate/professional students (all women). *Enrollment by degree level:* 9 master's. *Graduate faculty:* 40. *Graduate housing:* On-campus housing not available. *Student services:* Campus employment opportunities, campus safety program, career counseling, child daycare facilities, exercise/wellness program, free psychological counseling, grant writing training, international student services, low-cost health insurance, multicultural affairs office, services for students with disabilities, teacher training, writing training. *Library:* Bromfield Library plus 1 other.

Computer facilities: Computer purchase and lease plans are available. A campuswide network can be accessed. Online class registration is available.
Website: http://www.mansfield.osu.edu/

General Application Contact: Graduate and Professional Admissions, 614-292-9444, Fax: 614-292-3895, E-mail: gpadmissions@osu.edu.

GRADUATE UNITS

Graduate Programs Students: 9 (all women). Average age 32. *Faculty:* 40. *Financial support:* Teaching assistantships with full tuition reimbursements, Federal Work-Study, and scholarships/grants available. Support available to part-time students. Financial award application deadline: 2/15; financial award applicants required to submit FAFSA. *Degree program information:* Part-time programs available. Part-time. Offers education (MA); social work (MSW). *Application deadline:* For fall admission, 4/1 for domestic students, 3/1 for international students; for spring admission, 10/15 for domestic and international students. Applications are processed on a rolling basis. *Application fee:* $60 ($70 for international students). Electronic applications accepted. *Application Contact:* Graduate and Professional Admissions, 614-292-9444, Fax: 614-292-3895, E-mail: gpadmissions@osu.edu. *Dean and Director,* Dr. Stephen M. Gavazzi, 419-755-4221, Fax: 419-755-4241, E-mail: gavazzi.1@osu.edu.

THE OHIO STATE UNIVERSITY–NEWARK CAMPUS, Newark, OH 43055-1797

General Information State-supported, coed, comprehensive institution. *Enrollment:* 2,476 graduate, professional, and undergraduate students; 13 matriculated graduate/professional students (11 women). *Enrollment by degree level:* 13 master's. *Graduate faculty:* 52. *Graduate housing:* Rooms and/or apartments available on a first-come, first-served basis to single and married students. *Student services:* Campus safety program, career counseling, child daycare facilities, exercise/wellness program, free psychological counseling, grant writing training, international student services, low-cost health insurance, multicultural affairs office, services for students with disabilities, teacher training, writing training. *Library:* Newark Campus Library plus 1 other.

Computer facilities: Computer purchase and lease plans are available. A campuswide network can be accessed from student residence rooms. Online class registration is available.
Website: http://www.newark.osu.edu/

General Application Contact: Graduate and Professional Admissions, 614-292-9444, Fax: 614-292-3985, E-mail: gpadmissions@osu.edu.

GRADUATE UNITS

Graduate Programs Students: 13 (11 women); includes 2 minority (1 Black or African American, non-Hispanic/Latino; 1 Two or more races, non-Hispanic/Latino). Average age 31. *Faculty:* 52. *Financial support:* Application deadline: 2/15. *Degree program information:* Part-time programs available. Part-time. Offers education - teaching and learning (MA); social work (MSW). *Application deadline:* For fall admission, 3/1 for domestic and international students. Applications are processed on a rolling basis. *Application fee:* $60 ($70 for international students). Electronic applications accepted. *Application Contact:* Graduate and Professional Admissions, 614-292-9444, Fax: 614-292-3985, E-mail: gpadmissions@osu.edu. *Dean/Director,* Dr. William L. MacDonald, 740-366-9333 Ext. 330, E-mail: macdonald.24@osu.edu.

OHIO UNIVERSITY, Athens, OH 45701-2979

General Information State-supported, coed, university. CGS member. *Graduate housing:* Rooms and/or apartments available on a first-come, first-served basis to single and married students. Housing application deadline: 5/1.

GRADUATE UNITS

Graduate College ***Degree program information:*** Part-time and evening/weekend programs available. Part-time, evening/weekend, online learning. Electronic applications accepted.

Center for International Studies Degree program information: Part-time programs available. Part-time. Offers African studies (MA); Asian studies (MA); communications and development studies (MA); development studies (MA); international studies (MA); Latin American studies (MA). Electronic applications accepted.

College of Arts and Sciences Degree program information: Part-time and evening/weekend programs available. Part-time, evening/weekend. Offers applied economics (MA); applied linguistics (MA); arts and sciences (MA, MFE, MS, MSS, PhD); astronomy (MS, PhD); biological sciences (MS, PhD); cell biology and physiology (MS, PhD); chemistry and biochemistry (MS, PhD); clinical psychology (MS, PhD); ecology and evolutionary biology (MS, PhD); English language and literature (MA, PhD); environmental and plant biology (MS, PhD); environmental geochemistry (MS); environmental geology (MS); environmental/hydrology (MS); exercise physiology and muscle biology (MS, PhD); experimental psychology (MA, PhD); financial economics (MFE); French (MA); geography (MA, MS); geology (MS); geology education (MS); geomorphology/surficial processes (MS); geophysics (MS); history (MA, PhD); hydrogeology (MS); mathematics (MS, PhD); microbiology (MS, PhD); molecular and cellular biology (MS, PhD); neuroscience (MS, PhD); organizational psychology (MA, PhD); philosophy (MA); physics (MS, PhD); political science (MA); sedimentology (MS); social sciences (MSS); sociology (MA); Spanish (MA); structure/tectonics (MS). Electronic applications accepted.

College of Business Degree program information: Part-time and evening/weekend programs available. Part-time, evening/weekend, online learning. Offers athletic administration (MS); business (MBA, MS, MSA); executive management (MBA); finance (MBA); healthcare (MBA); sports administration (MSA). Electronic applications accepted.

College of Fine Arts Degree program information: Part-time and evening/weekend programs available. Part-time, evening/weekend, online learning. Offers accompanying (MM); art history (MA); ceramics (MFA); composition (MM); conducting (MM); film (MFA); film studies (MA); fine arts (MA, MFA, MM, PhD, Certificate); graphic design (MFA); history/literature (MM); interdisciplinary arts (PhD); music education (MM); music therapy (MM); painting (MFA); performance (MM, Certificate); performance/pedagogy (MM); photography (MFA); printmaking (MFA); sculpture (MFA); theater (MA, MFA); theory (MM). Electronic applications accepted.

College of Health Sciences and Professions Degree program information: Part-time and evening/weekend programs available. Part-time, evening/weekend, online learning. Offers acute care nurse practitioner (MSN); acute care nurse practitioner and family nurse practitioner (MSN); acute care nurse practitioner and nurse administrator (MSN); acute care nurse practitioner and nurse educator (MSN); athletic training (MS); clinical audiology (Au D); communication sciences and disorders (MA, Au D, PhD); early child development and family life (MS); family nurse practitioner (MSN); family studies (MS); food and nutrition (MS); health administration (MHA); health sciences and professions (MA, MHA, MPH, MS, MSN, MSW, Au D, DPT, PhD); hearing science (PhD); human and consumer sciences (MS); nurse administrator (MSN); nurse administrator and family nurse practitioner (MSN); nurse educator (MSN); nurse educator and family nurse practitioner (MSN); nurse educator and nurse administrator (MSN); physical therapy (DPT); physiology of exercise (MS); public health (MPH); social work (MSW); speech language pathology (MA); speech language science (PhD). Electronic applications accepted.

Gladys W. and David H. Patton College of Education and Human Services Degree program information: Part-time and evening/weekend programs available. Part-time, evening/weekend. Offers adolescent to young adult education (M Ed); apparel, textiles, and merchandising (MS); coaching education (MS); college student personnel (M Ed); community/agency counseling (M Ed); computer education and technology (M Ed); counselor education (PhD); cultural studies (M Ed); curriculum and instruction (M Ed, PhD); early childhood/special education (M Ed); education and human services (M Ed, MS, MSA, Ed D, PhD); educational administration (M Ed, Ed D); educational research and evaluation (M Ed, PhD); higher education (PhD); instructional technology (PhD); intervention specialist/mild-moderate needs (M Ed); intervention specialist/moderate-intensive needs (M Ed); mathematics education (PhD); middle childhood education (M Ed); reading education (M Ed); recreation studies (MS); rehabilitation counseling (M Ed); school counseling (M Ed); social studies education (PhD). Electronic applications accepted.

Russ College of Engineering and Technology Degree program information: Part-time programs available. Part-time. Offers biomedical engineering (MS); chemical engineering (MS, PhD); civil engineering (PhD); computer science (MS); construction engineering and management (MS); electrical engineering (MS); electrical engineering and computer science (PhD); engineering and technology (M Eng Mgt, MS, PhD); environmental (MS); geotechnical and geoenvironmental (MS); industrial and systems engineering (M Eng Mgt, MS); industrial engineering (PhD); mechanical engineering (MS, PhD); mechanics (MS); structures (MS); transportation (MS); water resources (MS). Electronic applications accepted.

Scripps College of Communication Degree program information: Part-time programs available. Part-time. Offers communication (MA, MCTP, MS, PhD); health communication (PhD); information and telecommunication systems (MCTP); journalism (MS, PhD); mass communication (PhD); media arts and studies (MA); organizational communication (MA); relating and organizing (PhD); rhetoric and public culture (PhD); visual communication (MA). Electronic applications accepted.

Voinovich School of Leadership and Public Affairs Offers environmental studies (MS); public administration (MPA). Electronic applications accepted.

Heritage College of Osteopathic Medicine Students: 716 full-time (333 women); includes 166 minority (62 Black or African American, non-Hispanic/Latino; 3 American Indian or Alaska Native, non-Hispanic/Latino; 61 Asian, non-Hispanic/Latino; 30 Hispanic/Latino; 10 Two or more races, non-Hispanic/Latino). Average age 26. 5,088 applicants, 7% accepted, 240 enrolled. *Faculty:* 98 full-time (45 women), 35 part-time/adjunct (15 women). *Financial support:* In 2015–16, 187 students received support, including 17 fellowships with full tuition reimbursements available (averaging $13,236 per year); Federal Work-Study, institutionally sponsored loans, scholarships/grants, and tuition waivers (partial) also available. Financial award applicants required to submit FAFSA. In 2015, 125 doctorates awarded. Offers osteopathic medicine (DO). Applicants must be U.S. residents to apply. *Application deadline:* For fall admission, 2/1 for domestic students. Applications are processed on a rolling basis. *Application fee:* $60. Electronic applications accepted. *Application Contact:* Jill Harman, Director of Admissions, 740-593-2147, Fax: 740-593-2256, E-mail: harmanj@ohio.edu. *Executive Dean,* Dr. Kenneth Johnson, 740-593-9350, Fax: 740-593-0761, E-mail: wilcox@ohio.edu.

OHIO VALLEY UNIVERSITY, Vienna, WV 26105-8000

General Information Independent-religious, coed, comprehensive institution.

GRADUATE UNITS

School of Graduate Education Online learning. Offers curriculum and instruction (M Ed).

OHR HAMEIR THEOLOGICAL SEMINARY, Cortlandt Manor, NY 10567

General Information Independent-religious, men only, comprehensive institution.

GRADUATE UNITS

Graduate Programs

OKLAHOMA BAPTIST UNIVERSITY, Shawnee, OK 74804

General Information Independent-religious, coed, comprehensive institution. *Graduate housing:* Rooms and/or apartments available on a first-come, first-served basis to single and married students. Housing application deadline: 4/15.

GRADUATE UNITS

Program in Business Administration Online learning. Offers business administration (MBA); energy management (MBA).

Program in Marriage and Family Therapy ***Degree program information:*** Part-time and evening/weekend programs available. Part-time, evening/weekend. Offers marriage and family therapy (MS). Electronic applications accepted.

Program in Nursing Offers global nursing (MSN); nursing education (MSN).

OKLAHOMA CHRISTIAN UNIVERSITY, Oklahoma City, OK 73136-1100

General Information Independent-religious, coed, comprehensive institution. *Enrollment:* 2,581 graduate, professional, and undergraduate students; 315 full-time matriculated graduate/professional students (96 women), 267 part-time matriculated graduate/professional students (90 women). *Enrollment by degree level:* 582 master's. *Graduate faculty:* 28 full-time (5 women), 26 part-time/adjunct (2 women). *Tuition, area resident:* Full-time $4995; part-time $3300 per semester hour. Tuition and fees vary according to program. *Graduate housing:* Rooms and/or apartments available on a first-come, first-served basis to single and married students. Typical cost: $3870 per year ($7030 including board) for single students; $3870 per year ($7030 including board) for married students. Room and board charges vary according to board plan and housing facility selected. Housing application deadline: 8/31. *Student services:* Campus employment opportunities, campus safety program, exercise/wellness program, free psychological counseling, international student services, writing training. *Library:* Tom and Ada Beam Library plus 1 other. *Collection:* Books: 131,852 (physical), 65,127 (digital/electronic); Serial titles: 83 (physical), 41,832 (digital/electronic); Databases: 63. Weekly public service hours: 83; students can reserve study rooms.

Computer facilities: 101 computers available on campus for general student use. A campuswide network can be accessed from student residence rooms and from off campus. Online class registration is available.
Website: http://www.oc.edu/

General Application Contact: Angie Ricketts, Admissions Counselor, 405-425-5587, E-mail: angie.ricketts@oc.edu.

GRADUATE UNITS

Graduate School of Business Students: 150 full-time (100 women), 137 part-time (95 women). 374 applicants, 213 enrolled. *Faculty:* 24 full-time (17 women), 4 part-time/adjunct (1 woman). In 2015, 188 master's awarded. *Degree program information:* Part-time programs available. Part-time, 100% online. Offers accounting (M Acc, MBA); financial services (MBA); general business (MBA); health services management (MBA); human resources (MBA); international business (MBA); leadership and organizational development (MBA); marketing (MBA); project management (MBA). *Application fee:* $25. Electronic applications accepted. *Application Contact:* Angie Ricketts, Graduate School Admissions Counselor, 405-425-5587, E-mail: angie.ricketts@oc.edu. *Chair,* Dr. Ken Johnson, 405-425-5567, E-mail: ken.johnson@oc.edu.

Graduate School of Engineering and Computer Science Students: 198 full-time (139 women), 42 part-time (26 women). 296 applicants, 174 enrolled. *Faculty:* 10 full-time (2 women), 8 part-time/adjunct (1 woman). In 2015, 67 master's awarded. *Degree program* *information:* Part-time programs available. Part-time. Offers electrical and computer engineering (MSE); engineering management (MSE); mechanical engineering (MSE); software engineering (MSCS, MSE). *Application deadline:* Applications are processed on a rolling basis. *Application fee:* $25. Electronic applications accepted. *Application Contact:* Angie Ricketts, Admissions Counselor, 405-425-5587, E-mail: angie.ricketts@oc.edu. *Director for Graduate School Engineering*, Mary Ann Brown, 405-425-5579.

Graduate School of Theology Students: 49 full-time (1 woman), 7 part-time (all women). 42 applicants, 22 enrolled. *Faculty:* 7 full-time (0 women). *Financial support:* Career-related internships or fieldwork, Federal Work-Study, scholarships/grants, and tuition waivers (partial) available. Support available to part-time students. Financial award application deadline: 3/1. In 2015, 8 master's awarded. *Degree program information:* Part-time programs available. Part-time, online learning. Offers Biblical studies (MACM); family ministry (M Div); ministry (M Div); scripture (MTS); theology (MTS); youth ministry (M Div). *Application deadline:* For fall admission, 8/15 priority date for domestic and international students; for spring admission, 1/3 priority date for domestic and international students. Applications are processed on a rolling basis. *Application fee:* $25. Electronic applications accepted. *Application Contact:* Josh Bailey, Admissions Counselor, 405-425-5389, Fax: 405-425-5076, E-mail: josh.bailey@oc.edu. *Dean*, Dr. Charles Rix, 405-425-5379, E-mail: charles.rix@oc.edu.

OKLAHOMA CITY UNIVERSITY, Oklahoma City, OK 73106-1402

General Information Independent-religious, coed, comprehensive institution. *Enrollment:* 2,987 graduate, professional, and undergraduate students; 846 full-time matriculated graduate/professional students (449 women), 316 part-time matriculated graduate/professional students (163 women). *Enrollment by degree level:* 583 master's, 579 doctoral. *Graduate faculty:* 98 full-time (41 women), 72 part-time/adjunct (32 women). *Tuition, area resident:* Part-time $590 per credit hour. One-time fee: $250 full-time. Tuition and fees vary according to degree level and program. *Graduate housing:* Rooms and/or apartments available on a first-come, first-served basis to single and married students. Typical cost: $4100 per year ($8624 including board) for single students; $4100 per year ($8624 including board) for married students. Room and board charges vary according to board plan and housing facility selected. Housing application deadline: 6/15. *Student services:* Campus employment opportunities, campus safety program, career counseling, exercise/wellness program, free psychological counseling, international student services, low-cost health insurance, multicultural affairs office, services for students with disabilities, teacher training, writing training. *Library:* Dulaney Browne Library plus 1 other. *Collection:* Books: 326,514 (physical), 240,741 (digital/electronic); Serial titles: 581 (physical), 3,060 (digital/electronic); Databases: 142. Weekly public service hours: 99; students can reserve study rooms.

Computer facilities: Computer purchase and lease plans are available. 368 computers available on campus for general student use. A campuswide network can be accessed from student residence rooms and from off campus. Online class registration is available.
Website: http://www.okcu.edu/

General Application Contact: Michael Harrington, Director of Graduate Admissions, 800-633-7242, Fax: 405-208-5916, E-mail: gadmissions@okcu.edu.

GRADUATE UNITS

Kramer School of Nursing Students: 125 full-time (107 women), 30 part-time (29 women); includes 46 minority (13 Black or African American, non-Hispanic/Latino; 11 American Indian or Alaska Native, non-Hispanic/Latino; 10 Asian, non-Hispanic/Latino; 5 Hispanic/Latino; 7 Two or more races, non-Hispanic/Latino), 19 international. Average age 38. 54 applicants, 78% accepted, 31 enrolled. *Faculty:* 11 full-time (all women), 6 part-time/adjunct (5 women). *Financial support:* In 2015–16, 89 students received support. Federal Work-Study, institutionally sponsored loans, scholarships/grants, and tuition waivers (full and partial) available. Support available to part-time students. Financial award application deadline: 3/1; financial award applicants required to submit FAFSA. In 2015, 17 master's, 7 doctorates awarded. *Degree program information:* Part-time and evening/weekend programs available. Part-time, evening/weekend, online learning. Offers clinical nurse leader (MSN); nursing (DNP, PhD); nursing education (MSN). *Application deadline:* Applications are processed on a rolling basis. *Application fee:* $50. Electronic applications accepted. *Application Contact:* Michael Harrington, Director of Graduate Admissions, 800-633-7242, Fax: 405-208-5916, E-mail: gadmissions@okcu.edu. *Dean, Kramer School of Nursing*, Dr. Lois Salmeron, 405-208-5900, Fax: 405-208-5914, E-mail: lsalmeron@okcu.edu.

Meinders School of Business Students: 162 full-time (51 women), 208 part-time (81 women); includes 68 minority (11 Black or African American, non-Hispanic/Latino; 8 American Indian or Alaska Native, non-Hispanic/Latino; 11 Asian, non-Hispanic/Latino; 23 Hispanic/Latino; 15 Two or more races, non-Hispanic/Latino), 113 international. Average age 30. 961 applicants, 46% accepted, 124 enrolled. *Faculty:* 18 full-time (6 women), 11 part-time/adjunct (3 women). *Financial support:* In 2015–16, 277 students received support. Career-related internships or fieldwork, Federal Work-Study, institutionally sponsored loans, scholarships/grants, and tuition waivers (full and partial) available. Support available to part-time students. Financial award application deadline: 6/1; financial award applicants required to submit FAFSA. In 2015, 154 master's awarded. *Degree program information:* Part-time and evening/weekend programs available. Part-time, evening/weekend, 100% online. Offers business (MBA, MSA); computer science (MS); energy legal studies (MS); energy management (MS). *Application deadline:* Applications are processed on a rolling basis. *Application fee:* $50. Electronic applications accepted. *Application Contact:* Michael Harrington, Director of Graduate Admission, 800-633-7242, Fax: 405-208-5916, E-mail: gadmissions@okcu.edu. *Dean*, Dr. Steve Agee, 405-208-5275, Fax: 405-208-5008, E-mail: sagee@okcu.edu.

Petree College of Arts and Sciences Students: 88 full-time (67 women), 48 part-time (37 women); includes 32 minority (14 Black or African American, non-Hispanic/Latino; 2 American Indian or Alaska Native, non-Hispanic/Latino; 4 Asian, non-Hispanic/Latino; 5 Hispanic/Latino; 7 Two or more races, non-Hispanic/Latino), 35 international. Average age 34. 119 applicants, 66% accepted, 53 enrolled. *Faculty:* 20 full-time (9 women), 14 part-time/adjunct (8 women). *Financial support:* In 2015–16, 20 students received support. Federal Work-Study, institutionally sponsored loans, scholarships/grants, and tuition waivers (full and partial) available. Support available to part-time students. Financial award application deadline: 6/1; financial award applicants required to submit FAFSA. In 2015, 100 master's awarded. *Degree program information:* Part-time and evening/weekend programs available. Part-time, evening/weekend. Offers applied behavioral studies (M Ed); applied sociology: nonprofit leadership (MA); creative writing (MFA); criminology (MS); early childhood education (M Ed); elementary education (M Ed); general studies (MLA); leadership/management (MLA); moving image arts (MFA); professional counseling (M Ed); teaching (MA); teaching English to speakers of other languages (MA). *Application deadline:* Applications are processed on a rolling basis. *Application fee:* $50. Electronic applications accepted. *Application Contact:* Michael Harrington, Director of Graduate Admissions, 800-633-7242, Fax: 405-208-5356, E-mail: gadmissions@okcu.edu. *Interim Dean*, Dr. Amy Cataldi, 405-208-5446, Fax: 405-208-5447, E-mail: acataldi@okcu.edu.

School of Law Students: 419 full-time (202 women), 27 part-time (14 women); includes 142 minority (28 Black or African American, non-Hispanic/Latino; 24 American Indian or Alaska Native, non-Hispanic/Latino; 16 Asian, non-Hispanic/Latino; 34 Hispanic/Latino; 1 Native Hawaiian or other Pacific Islander, non-Hispanic/Latino; 39 Two or more races, non-Hispanic/Latino), 4 international. Average age 28. 555 applicants, 72% accepted, 159 enrolled. *Faculty:* 22 full-time (8 women), 33 part-time/adjunct (12 women). *Financial support:* In 2015–16, 337 students received support. Career-related internships or fieldwork, Federal Work-Study, institutionally sponsored loans, scholarships/grants, and tuition waivers (full and partial) available. Support available to part-time students. Financial award application deadline: 2/1; financial award applicants required to submit FAFSA. In 2015, 133 doctorates awarded. *Degree program information:* Part-time and evening/weekend programs available. Part-time, evening/weekend. Offers law (LL M, JD). *Application deadline:* For fall admission, 8/1 for domestic and international students. *Application fee:* $50. Electronic applications accepted. *Application Contact:* Dr. Laurie W. Jones, Associate Dean of Admissions, Law School, 405-208-5354, Fax: 405-208-5814, E-mail: ljones@okcu.edu. *Dean*, Dr. Valerie K. Couch, 405-208-5440, Fax: 405-208-6041, E-mail: vcouch@okcu.edu.

Wanda L. Bass School of Music Students: 52 full-time (22 women), 3 part-time (2 women); includes 12 minority (6 Black or African American, non-Hispanic/Latino; 1 American Indian or Alaska Native, non-Hispanic/Latino; 2 Hispanic/Latino; 3 Two or more races, non-Hispanic/Latino), 12 international. Average age 25. 94 applicants, 55% accepted, 22 enrolled. *Faculty:* 23 full-time (6 women), 12 part-time/adjunct (6 women). *Financial support:* In 2015–16, 55 students received support. Career-related internships or fieldwork, Federal Work-Study, institutionally sponsored loans, scholarships/grants, and tuition waivers (full and partial) available. Support available to part-time students. Financial award application deadline: 6/1; financial award applicants required to submit FAFSA. In 2015, 22 master's awarded. *Degree program information:* Part-time programs available. Part-time. Offers composition (MM); conducting (MM); musical theatre (MM); opera performance (MM); performance (MM); vocal coaching (MM). *Application deadline:* Applications are processed on a rolling basis. *Application fee:* $50. Electronic applications accepted. *Application Contact:* Michael Harrington, Director of Graduate Admission, 800-633-7242, Fax: 405-208-5916, E-mail: gadmissions@okcu.edu. *Dean*, Mark Parker, 405-208-5474, Fax: 405-208-5971, E-mail: mparker@okcu.edu.

OKLAHOMA STATE UNIVERSITY, Stillwater, OK 74078

General Information State-supported, coed, university. CGS member. *Enrollment:* 25,806 graduate, professional, and undergraduate students; 1,862 full-time matriculated graduate/professional students (951 women), 2,731 part-time matriculated graduate/professional students (1,146 women). *Enrollment by degree level:* 2,685 master's, 1,846 doctoral, 62 other advanced degrees. *Graduate faculty:* 1,221 full-time (438 women), 209 part-time/adjunct (115 women). Tuition, state resident: full-time $3528; part-time $196 per credit hour. Tuition, nonresident: full-time $14,144; part-time $785.75 per credit hour. *Required fees:* $1895; $105.25 per credit hour. Tuition and fees vary according to campus/location. *Graduate housing:* Rooms and/or apartments available on a first-come, first-served basis to single and married students. Typical cost: $4590 per year ($8190 including board) for single students; $10,200 per year for married students. Room and board charges vary according to board plan and housing facility selected. *Student services:* Campus employment opportunities, campus safety program, career counseling, exercise/wellness program, free psychological counseling, grant writing training, international student services, low-cost health insurance, multicultural affairs office, services for students with disabilities, teacher training, writing training. *Library:* Edmon Low Library plus 3 others. Weekly public service hours: 146; study areas open 24 hours, 5–7 days a week; students can reserve study rooms. *Research affiliation:* Allens, Inc. (horticulture and landscape architecture), General Motors (industrial engineering and management), Simons Foundation (mathematics), Mid-America Athletic Trainers Association (applied health and educational psychology), California Strawberry Commission. (nutritional sciences), LiteCure, LLC (veterinary clinical sciences).

Computer facilities: Computer purchase and lease plans are available. A campuswide network can be accessed from student residence rooms and from off campus. Online class registration is available.
Website: http://www.okstate.edu/

General Application Contact: Dr. Sheryl Tucker, Dean, 405-744-6368, Fax: 405-744-0355, E-mail: gradi@okstate.edu.

GRADUATE UNITS

Center for Veterinary Health Sciences Online learning. Offers veterinary biomedical sciences (MS, PhD); veterinary health sciences (MS, DVM, PhD); veterinary medicine (DVM).

College of Agricultural Science and Natural Resources Students: 136 full-time (63 women), 351 part-time (170 women); includes 64 minority (3 Black or African American, non-Hispanic/Latino; 14 American Indian or Alaska Native, non-Hispanic/Latino; 3 Asian, non-Hispanic/Latino; 14 Hispanic/Latino; 30 Two or more races, non-Hispanic/Latino), 149 international. Average age 29. 265 applicants, 57% accepted, 95 enrolled. *Faculty:* 220 full-time (51 women), 8 part-time/adjunct (0 women). *Financial support:* In 2015–16, 246 research assistantships (averaging $17,794 per year), 51 teaching assistantships (averaging $15,582 per year) were awarded; fellowships, career-related internships or fieldwork, Federal Work-Study, scholarships/grants, health care benefits, tuition waivers (partial), and unspecified assistantships also available. Support available to part-time students. Financial award application deadline: 3/1; financial award applicants required to submit FAFSA. In 2015, 114 master's, 36 doctorates awarded. Online learning. Offers agricultural economics (M Ag, MS, PhD); agricultural education, communications and leadership (M Ag, MS, PhD); agricultural science and natural resources (M Ag, MS, PhD); animal sciences (M Ag, MS); biochemistry and molecular biology (MS, PhD); biosystems engineering (MS, PhD); crop science (PhD); entomology (PhD); entomology and plant pathology (MS); environmental and natural resources (MS, PhD); environmental science (PhD); food science (MS, PhD); horticulture (M Ag, MS); natural resource ecology and management (M Ag, MS, PhD); plant and soil sciences (MS); plant pathology (PhD); plant science (PhD); soil science (M Ag, PhD). *Application deadline:* For fall admission, 3/1 priority date for domestic and international students; for spring admission, 8/1 priority date for domestic and international students. Applications are processed on a rolling basis. *Application fee:* $40 ($75 for international students). Electronic applications accepted. *Vice President/Dean*, Dr. Thomas Coon, 405-744-5395, E-mail: thomas.coon@okstate.edu.

College of Arts and Sciences Students: 311 full-time (171 women), 619 part-time (247 women); includes 140 minority (22 Black or African American, non-Hispanic/Latino; 19 American Indian or Alaska Native, non-Hispanic/Latino; 14 Asian, non-Hispanic/Latino; 30 Hispanic/Latino; 1 Native Hawaiian or other Pacific Islander, non-Hispanic/Latino; 54 Two or more races, non-Hispanic/Latino), 253 international. Average age 30. 1,458 applicants, 29% accepted, 228 enrolled. *Faculty:* 467 full-time (169 women), 46 part-time/adjunct (30 women). *Financial support:* In 2015–16, 107 research assistantships (averaging $19,034 per year), 543 teaching assistantships (averaging $17,840 per year) were awarded; career-related internships or fieldwork, Federal Work-Study, scholarships/grants, health care benefits, tuition waivers (partial), and unspecified assistantships also available. Support available to part-time students. Financial award application deadline: 3/1; financial award applicants required to submit FAFSA. In 2015, 208 master's, 66 doctorates awarded. Offers applied mathematics (MS, PhD); arts and sciences (MA, MFA, MM, MS, PhD); botany (MS); chemistry (MS, PhD); clinical psychology (PhD); communication sciences and disorders (MS); computer science (MS, PhD); creative writing (MFA); English (MA, PhD); environmental science (MS, PhD); fire and emergency management administration (MS, PhD); general psychology (MS); geography (MS, PhD); history (MA, PhD); integrative biology (MS, PhD); lifespan development psychology (PhD); mathematics education (MS, PhD); microbiology and molecular genetics (MS, PhD); pedagogy and performance (MM); philosophy (MA); photonics (MS, PhD); physics (MS, PhD); plant science (PhD); political science (MA); pure mathematics (MS, PhD); sociology (MS, PhD); statistics (MS, PhD); theatre (MA). *Application deadline:* For fall admission, 3/1 priority date for domestic and international students; for spring admission, 8/1 priority date for domestic and international students. Applications are processed on a rolling basis. *Application fee:* $40 ($75 for international students). Electronic applications accepted. *Dean*, Dr. Bret Danilowicz, 405-744-5663, Fax: 405-744-1797, E-mail: bret.danilowicz@okstate.edu.

School of Geology Students: 38 full-time (11 women), 52 part-time (16 women); includes 15 minority (2 Black or African American, non-Hispanic/Latino; 3 American Indian or Alaska Native, non-Hispanic/Latino; 1 Asian, non-Hispanic/Latino; 2 Hispanic/Latino; 7 Two or more races, non-Hispanic/Latino), 19 international. Average age 30. 119 applicants, 25% accepted, 20 enrolled. *Faculty:* 18 full-time (4 women). *Financial support:* In 2015–16, 27 research assistantships (averaging $15,707 per year), 34 teaching assistantships (averaging $10,211 per year) were awarded; career-related internships or fieldwork, Federal Work-Study, scholarships/grants, health care benefits, tuition waivers (partial), and unspecified assistantships also available. Support available to part-time students. Financial award application deadline: 3/1; financial award applicants required to submit FAFSA. In 2015, 23 master's awarded. Offers geology (MS, PhD). *Application deadline:* For fall admission, 3/1 priority date for international students; for spring admission, 8/1 priority date for international students. Applications are processed on a rolling basis. *Application fee:* $40 ($75 for international students). Electronic applications accepted. *Department Head*, Dr. Estella Atekwana, 405-744-6358, Fax: 405-744-7841, E-mail: estella.atekwana@okstate.edu.

School of Media and Strategic Communications Students: 11 full-time (6 women), 19 part-time (13 women); includes 8 minority (5 Black or African American, non-Hispanic/Latino; 1 Hispanic/Latino; 2 Two or more races, non-Hispanic/Latino), 1 international. Average age 28. 17 applicants, 82% accepted, 11 enrolled. *Faculty:* 21 full-time (8 women), 4 part-time/adjunct (0 women). *Financial support:* In 2015–16, 1 research assistantship (averaging $19,200 per year), 6 teaching assistantships (averaging $19,200 per year) were awarded; career-related internships or fieldwork, Federal Work-Study, scholarships/grants, health care benefits, tuition waivers (partial), and unspecified assistantships also available. Support available to part-time students. Financial award application deadline: 3/1; financial award applicants required to submit FAFSA. In 2015, 6 master's awarded. Offers mass communication (MS). *Application deadline:* For fall admission, 3/1 priority date for international students; for spring admission, 8/1 priority date for international students. Applications are processed on a rolling basis. *Application fee:* $40 ($75 for international students). Electronic applications accepted. *Interim Director*, Dr. Craig Freem, 405-744-7676, Fax: 405-744-7104, E-mail: freemanc@okstate.edu.

College of Education Students: 293 full-time (187 women), 550 part-time (359 women); includes 203 minority (54 Black or African American, non-Hispanic/Latino; 39 American Indian or Alaska Native, non-Hispanic/Latino; 8 Asian, non-Hispanic/Latino; 51 Hispanic/Latino; 51 Two or more races, non-Hispanic/Latino), 26 international. Average age 35. 329 applicants, 57% accepted, 142 enrolled. *Faculty:* 92 full-time (60 women), 74 part-time/adjunct (49 women). *Financial support:* In 2015–16, 57 research assistantships (averaging $11,763 per year), 91 teaching assistantships (averaging $9,828 per year) were awarded; career-related internships or fieldwork, Federal Work-Study, scholarships/grants, health care benefits, tuition waivers (partial), and unspecified assistantships also available. Support available to part-time students. Financial award application deadline: 3/1; financial award applicants required to submit FAFSA. In 2015, 160 master's, 59 doctorates awarded. *Degree program information:* Part-time programs available. Part-time, online learning. Offers education (MS, Ed D, PhD, Ed S). *Application deadline:* For fall admission, 3/1 priority date for domestic and international students; for spring admission, 8/1 priority date for domestic and international students. Applications are processed on a rolling basis. *Application fee:* $40 ($75 for international students). Electronic applications accepted. *Interim Dean*, Dr. Robert Davis, 405-744-6350, Fax: 405-744-6350, E-mail: robert.davis@okstate.edu.

School of Applied Health and Educational Psychology Students: 189 full-time (126 women), 162 part-time (97 women); includes 94 minority (18 Black or African American, non-Hispanic/Latino; 16 American Indian or Alaska Native, non-Hispanic/Latino; 3 Asian, non-Hispanic/Latino; 29 Hispanic/Latino; 28 Two or more races, non-Hispanic/Latino), 10 international. Average age 31. 184 applicants, 43% accepted, 65 enrolled. *Faculty:* 38 full-time (22 women), 11 part-time/adjunct (8 women). *Financial support:* In 2015–16, 29 research assistantships (averaging $11,712 per year), 72 teaching assistantships (averaging $9,941 per year) were awarded; career-related internships or fieldwork, Federal Work-Study, scholarships/grants, health care benefits, tuition waivers (partial), and unspecified assistantships also available. Support available to part-time students. Financial award application deadline: 3/1; financial award applicants required to submit FAFSA. In 2015, 72 master's, 21 doctorates awarded. *Degree program information:* Part-time programs available. Part-time. Offers applied behavioral studies (Ed D); applied health and educational psychology (MS, PhD, Ed S). *Application deadline:* For fall admission, 3/1 priority date for international students; for spring admission, 8/1 priority date for international students. Applications are processed on a rolling basis. *Application fee:* $40 ($75 for international students). Electronic applications accepted. *Head*, Dr. Aric Warren, 405-744-6040, Fax: 405-744-6779, E-mail: aric.warren@okstate.edu.

School of Educational Studies Students: 60 full-time (29 women), 197 part-time (112 women); includes 63 minority (22 Black or African American, non-Hispanic/Latino; 14 American Indian or Alaska Native, non-Hispanic/Latino; 3 Asian, non-Hispanic/Latino; 15 Hispanic/Latino; 9 Two or more races, non-Hispanic/Latino), 10 international. Average age 38. 88 applicants, 77% accepted, 55 enrolled. *Faculty:* 26 full-time (12 women), 29 part-time/adjunct (10 women). *Financial support:* In 2015–16, 23 research assistantships (averaging $11,649 per year), 12 teaching assistantships (averaging $9,145 per year) were awarded; career-related internships or fieldwork, Federal Work-Study, scholarships/grants, health care benefits, tuition waivers (partial), and unspecified assistantships also available. Support available to part-time students. Financial award application deadline: 3/1; financial award applicants required to submit FAFSA. In 2015, 27 master's, 30 doctorates awarded. *Degree program information:* Part-time programs available. Part-time. Offers higher education (Ed D). *Application deadline:* For fall admission, 3/1 priority date for international students; for spring admission, 8/1 priority date for international students. Applications are processed on a rolling basis. *Application fee:* $40 ($75 for international students). Electronic applications accepted. *Head*, Dr. Jesse Mendez, 405-744-9447, Fax: 405-744-7758, E-mail: jesse.perez.mendez@okstate.edu.

School of Teaching and Curriculum Leadership Students: 44 full-time (32 women), 191 part-time (150 women); includes 46 minority (14 Black or African American, non-Hispanic/Latino; 9 American Indian or Alaska Native, non-Hispanic/Latino; 2 Asian, non-Hispanic/Latino; 7 Hispanic/Latino; 14 Two or more races, non-Hispanic/Latino), 6 international. Average age 38. 56 applicants, 71% accepted, 22 enrolled. *Faculty:* 27 full-time (26 women), 34 part-time/adjunct (31 women). *Financial support:* In 2015–16, 5 research assistantships (averaging $12,582 per year), 7 teaching assistantships (averaging $9,836 per year) were awarded; career-related internships or fieldwork, Federal Work-Study, scholarships/grants, health care benefits, tuition waivers (partial), and unspecified assistantships also available. Support available to part-time students. Financial award application deadline: 3/1; financial award applicants required to submit FAFSA. In 2015, 61 master's, 6 doctorates awarded. *Degree program information:* Part-time programs available. Part-time. Offers teaching and curriculum leadership (MS, PhD). *Application deadline:* For fall admission, 3/1 priority date for international students; for spring admission, 8/1 priority date for international students. Applications are processed on a rolling basis. *Application fee:* $40 ($75 for international students). Electronic applications accepted. *Interim Department Head*, Dr. Jennifer Sanders, 405-744-9214, Fax: 405-744-6290, E-mail: jenn.sanders10@okstate.edu.

College of Engineering, Architecture and Technology Students: 241 full-time (53 women), 376 part-time (68 women); includes 69 minority (9 Black or African American, non-Hispanic/Latino; 6 American Indian or Alaska Native, non-Hispanic/Latino; 10 Asian, non-Hispanic/Latino; 16 Hispanic/Latino; 1 Native Hawaiian or other Pacific Islander, non-Hispanic/Latino; 27 Two or more races, non-Hispanic/Latino), 357 international. Average age 28. 1,307 applicants, 30% accepted, 168 enrolled. *Faculty:* 121 full-time (12 women), 10 part-time/adjunct (1 woman). *Financial support:* In 2015–16, 151 research assistantships (averaging $17,923 per year), 131 teaching assistantships (averaging $15,632 per year) were awarded; career-related internships or fieldwork, Federal Work-Study, scholarships/grants, health care benefits, tuition waivers (partial), and unspecified assistantships also available. Support available to part-time students. Financial award application deadline: 3/1; financial award applicants required to submit FAFSA. In 2015, 268 master's, 52 doctorates awarded. Online learning. Offers engineering, architecture and technology (MS, PhD). *Application deadline:* For fall admission, 3/1 priority date for domestic and international students; for spring admission, 8/1 priority date for domestic and international students. Applications are processed on a rolling basis. *Application fee:* $40 ($75 for international students). Electronic applications accepted. *Dean*, Dr. Paul Tikalsky, 405-744-5140, E-mail: paul.tikalsky@okstate.edu.

School of Chemical Engineering Students: 13 full-time (4 women), 30 part-time (10 women); includes 4 minority (1 Black or African American, non-Hispanic/Latino; 1 American Indian or Alaska Native, non-Hispanic/Latino; 1 Asian, non-Hispanic/Latino; 1 Hispanic/Latino), 28 international. Average age 28. 72 applicants, 15% accepted, 8 enrolled. *Faculty:* 17 full-time (3 women). *Financial support:* In 2015–16, 25 research assistantships (averaging $23,348 per year), 11 teaching assistantships (averaging $20,673 per year) were awarded; career-related internships or fieldwork, Federal Work-Study, scholarships/grants, health care benefits, tuition waivers (partial), and unspecified assistantships also available. Support available to part-time students. Financial award application deadline: 3/1; financial award applicants required to submit FAFSA. In 2015, 9 master's, 9 doctorates awarded. Offers chemical engineering (MS, PhD). *Application deadline:* For fall admission, 3/1 priority date for international students; for spring admission, 8/1 priority date for international students. Applications are processed on a rolling basis. *Application fee:* $40 ($75 for international students). Electronic applications accepted. *Head*, Dr. Rob Whiteley, 405-744-5280, Fax: 405-744-6338, E-mail: rob.whiteley@okstate.edu.

School of Civil and Environmental Engineering Students: 41 full-time (9 women), 37 part-time (6 women); includes 5 minority (1 Black or African American, non-Hispanic/Latino; 1 American Indian or Alaska Native, non-Hispanic/Latino; 1 Hispanic/Latino; 2 Two or more races, non-Hispanic/Latino), 58 international. Average age 28. 125 applicants, 42% accepted, 21 enrolled. *Faculty:* 18 full-time (1 woman), 2 part-time/adjunct (0 women). *Financial support:* In 2015–16, 30 research assistantships (averaging $18,624 per year), 13 teaching assistantships (averaging $16,076 per year) were awarded; career-related internships or fieldwork, Federal Work-Study, scholarships/grants, health care benefits, tuition waivers (partial), and unspecified assistantships also available. Support available to part-time students. Financial award application deadline: 3/1; financial award applicants required to submit FAFSA. In 2015, 28 master's, 10 doctorates awarded. Offers civil engineering (MS, PhD); environmental engineering (MS). *Application deadline:* For fall admission, 3/1 priority date for international students; for spring admission, 8/1 priority date for international students. Applications are processed on a rolling basis. *Application fee:* $40 ($75 for international students). Electronic applications accepted. *Department Head*, Dr. John Veenstra, 405-744-5190, Fax: 405-744-7554, E-mail: jveenst@okstate.edu.

School of Electrical and Computer Engineering Students: 78 full-time (25 women), 71 part-time (16 women); includes 13 minority (1 American Indian or Alaska Native, non-Hispanic/Latino; 3 Asian, non-Hispanic/Latino; 4 Hispanic/Latino; 5 Two or more races, non-Hispanic/Latino), 110 international. Average age 27. 447 applicants, 27% accepted, 36 enrolled. *Faculty:* 24 full-time (1 woman), 1 part-time/adjunct (0 women). *Financial support:* In 2015–16, 27 research assistantships (averaging $16,104 per year), 23 teaching assistantships (averaging $13,870 per year) were awarded; career-related internships or fieldwork, Federal Work-Study, scholarships/grants, health care benefits, tuition waivers (partial), and unspecified assistantships also available. Support available to part-time students. Financial award application deadline: 3/1; financial award applicants required to submit FAFSA. In 2015, 101 master's, 17 doctorates awarded. Online learning. Offers electrical and computer engineering (MS, PhD). *Application deadline:* For fall admission, 3/1 priority date for international students; for spring admission, 8/1 priority date for international students. Applications are processed on a rolling basis. *Application fee:* $40 ($75 for international students). Electronic applications accepted. *Department Head*, Dr. Jeffrey Young, 405-744-5151, Fax: 405-744-9198, E-mail: jl.young@okstate.edu.

School of Industrial Engineering and Management Students: 75 full-time (9 women), 130 part-time (19 women); includes 27 minority (5 Black or African American, non-Hispanic/Latino; 2 American Indian or Alaska Native, non-Hispanic/Latino; 4 Asian, non-Hispanic/Latino; 8 Hispanic/Latino; 1 Native Hawaiian or other Pacific Islander, non-Hispanic/Latino; 7 Two or more races, non-Hispanic/Latino), 94 international. Average age 30. 358 applicants, 36% accepted, 64 enrolled. *Faculty:* 15 full-time (3 women), 1 part-time/adjunct (0 women). *Financial support:* In 2015–16, 17 research assistantships (averaging $17,859 per year), 22 teaching assistantships (averaging $18,390 per year) were awarded; career-related internships or fieldwork, Federal Work-Study, scholarships/grants, health care benefits, tuition waivers (partial), and unspecified assistantships also available. Support available to part-time students. Financial award application deadline: 3/1; financial award applicants required to submit FAFSA. In 2015, 93 master's, 4 doctorates awarded. Online learning. Offers industrial engineering and management (MS, PhD). *Application deadline:* For fall admission, 3/1 priority date for international students; for spring admission, 8/1 priority date for international students. Applications are processed on a rolling basis. *Application fee:* $40 ($75 for international students). Electronic applications accepted. *Application Contact:* Dr. Manjunath Kamath, Director of Graduate Program, 405-744-6055, Fax: 405-744-4654, E-mail: m.kamath@okstate.edu. *Head,* Dr. Sunderesh Heragu, 405-744-6055, Fax: 405-744-4654, E-mail: sunderesh.heragu@okstate.edu.

School of Mechanical and Aerospace Engineering Students: 30 full-time (5 women), 96 part-time (14 women); includes 17 minority (2 Black or African American, non-Hispanic/Latino; 1 American Indian or Alaska Native, non-Hispanic/Latino; 2 Asian, non-Hispanic/Latino; 1 Hispanic/Latino; 11 Two or more races, non-Hispanic/Latino), 60 international. Average age 27. 277 applicants, 23% accepted, 32 enrolled. *Faculty:* 28 full-time (0 women), 6 part-time/adjunct (1 woman). *Financial support:* In 2015–16, 51 research assistantships (averaging $15,716 per year), 62 teaching assistantships (averaging $14,319 per year) were awarded; career-related internships or fieldwork, Federal Work-Study, scholarships/grants, health care benefits, tuition waivers (partial), and unspecified assistantships also available. Support available to part-time students. Financial award application deadline: 3/1; financial award applicants required to submit FAFSA. In 2015, 35 master's, 12 doctorates awarded. Online learning. Offers mechanical and aerospace engineering (MS, PhD); mechanical engineering (MS, PhD). *Application deadline:* For fall admission, 3/1 priority date for international students; for spring admission, 8/1 priority date for international students. Applications are processed on a rolling basis. *Application fee:* $40 ($75 for international students). Electronic applications accepted. *Application Contact:* Dr. Charlotte Fore, Manager of Graduate Studies and Research Development, 405-744-5900, Fax: 405-744-7873, E-mail: charlotte.fore@okstate.edu. *Department Head,* Dr. Daniel E. Fisher, 405-744-5900, Fax: 405-744-7873, E-mail: maehead@okstate.edu.

College of Human Sciences Students: 93 full-time (73 women), 128 part-time (96 women); includes 43 minority (16 Black or African American, non-Hispanic/Latino; 5 American Indian or Alaska Native, non-Hispanic/Latino; 5 Asian, non-Hispanic/Latino; 6 Hispanic/Latino; 11 Two or more races, non-Hispanic/Latino), 57 international. Average age 31. 162 applicants, 55% accepted, 58 enrolled. *Faculty:* 87 full-time (59 women), 21 part-time/adjunct (14 women). *Financial support:* In 2015–16, 80 research assistantships (averaging $12,722 per year), 55 teaching assistantships (averaging $12,268 per year) were awarded; career-related internships or fieldwork, Federal Work-Study, scholarships/grants, health care benefits, tuition waivers (partial), and unspecified assistantships also available. Support available to part-time students. Financial award application deadline: 3/1; financial award applicants required to submit FAFSA. In 2015, 54 master's, 12 doctorates awarded. Online learning. Offers design, housing and merchandising (MS, PhD); human development and family science (MS, PhD); human sciences (MS, PhD); marriage and family therapy (MS); nutritional sciences (MS, PhD). *Application deadline:* For fall admission, 3/1 priority date for domestic and international students; for spring admission, 8/1 priority date for domestic and international students. Applications are processed on a rolling basis. *Application fee:* $40 ($75 for international students). Electronic applications accepted. *Dean,* Dr. Stephan M. Wilson, 405-744-9805, Fax: 405-744-7113, E-mail: stephan.m.wilson@okstate.edu.

School of Hotel and Restaurant Administration Students: 11 full-time (7 women), 32 part-time (23 women); includes 5 minority (2 Black or African American, non-Hispanic/Latino; 3 Hispanic/Latino), 34 international. Average age 33. 38 applicants, 55% accepted, 12 enrolled. *Faculty:* 17 full-time (7 women), 5 part-time/adjunct (0 women). *Financial support:* In 2015–16, 11 research assistantships (averaging $15,132 per year), 16 teaching assistantships (averaging $15,770 per year) were awarded; career-related internships or fieldwork, Federal Work-Study, scholarships/grants, health care benefits, tuition waivers (partial), and unspecified assistantships also available. Support available to part-time students. Financial award application deadline: 3/1; financial award applicants required to submit FAFSA. In 2015, 3 master's, 4 doctorates awarded. Offers hotel and restaurant administration (MS, PhD). *Application deadline:* For fall admission, 3/1 priority date for international students; for spring admission, 8/1 priority date for international students. Applications are processed on a rolling basis. *Application fee:* $40 ($75 for international students). Electronic applications accepted. *Application Contact:* Dr. Li Miao, Graduate Coordinator, 405-744-1277, Fax: 405-744-6299, E-mail: lm@okstate.edu. *Director,* Dr. Ben Goh, 405-744-7651, Fax: 405-744-6299, E-mail: ben.goh@okstate.edu.

Graduate College Students: 59 full-time (26 women), 130 part-time (65 women); includes 38 minority (3 Black or African American, non-Hispanic/Latino; 7 American Indian or Alaska Native, non-Hispanic/Latino; 9 Asian, non-Hispanic/Latino; 9 Hispanic/Latino; 10 Two or more races, non-Hispanic/Latino), 53 international. Average age 31. 358 applicants, 87% accepted, 70 enrolled. *Faculty:* 4 full-time (2 women), 3 part-time/adjunct (0 women). *Financial support:* In 2015–16, 10 research assistantships (averaging $15,876 per year) were awarded; career-related internships or fieldwork, Federal Work-Study, scholarships/grants, health care benefits, tuition waivers (partial), and unspecified assistantships also available. Support available to part-time students. Financial award application deadline: 3/1; financial award applicants required to submit FAFSA. In 2015, 45 master's, 9 doctorates awarded. Offers aerospace security (Graduate Certificate); bioenergy and sustainable technology (Graduate Certificate); business data mining (Graduate Certificate); business sustainability (Graduate Certificate); environmental science (MS); international studies (MS); non-profit management (Graduate Certificate); teaching English to speakers of other languages (Graduate Certificate); telecommunications management (MS). Programs are interdisciplinary. *Application deadline:* For fall admission, 3/1 priority date for domestic and international students; for spring admission, 8/1 priority date for domestic and international students. Applications are processed on a rolling basis. *Application fee:* $40 ($75 for international students). Electronic applications accepted. *Application Contact:* Dr. Susan Mathew, Assistant Director of Graduate Admissions, 405-744-6368, Fax: 405-744-0355, E-mail: gradi@okstate.edu. *Dean,* Dr. Sheryl Tucker, 405-744-6368, Fax: 405-744-0355, E-mail: gradi@okstate.edu.

Spears School of Business Students: 392 full-time (113 women), 542 part-time (123 women); includes 125 minority (23 Black or African American, non-Hispanic/Latino; 9 American Indian or Alaska Native, non-Hispanic/Latino; 20 Asian, non-Hispanic/Latino; 40 Hispanic/Latino; 2 Native Hawaiian or other Pacific Islander, non-Hispanic/Latino; 31 Two or more races, non-Hispanic/Latino), 276 international. Average age 29. 1,306 applicants, 31% accepted, 275 enrolled. *Faculty:* 138 full-time (35 women), 30 part-time/adjunct (11 women). *Financial support:* In 2015–16, 69 research assistantships (averaging $19,278 per year), 97 teaching assistantships (averaging $16,055 per year) were awarded; career-related internships or fieldwork, Federal Work-Study, scholarships/grants, health care benefits, tuition waivers (partial), and unspecified assistantships also available. Support available to part-time students. Financial award application deadline: 3/1; financial award applicants required to submit FAFSA. In 2015, 429 master's, 29 doctorates awarded. *Degree program information:* Part-time programs available. Part-time, online learning. Offers business (MBA, MS, PhD); business administration (PhD); economics and legal studies in business (MS, PhD); entrepreneurship (MBA, MS, PhD); finance (MS, PhD); management (MBA, MS, PhD); management information systems (MS); management science and information systems (PhD); marketing (MBA); telecommunications management (MS). *Application deadline:* For fall admission, 3/1 priority date for domestic and international students; for spring admission, 8/1 priority date for domestic and international students. Applications are processed on a rolling basis. *Application fee:* $40 ($75 for international students). Electronic applications accepted. *Dean,* Dr. Ken Eastman, 405-744-5064, Fax: 405-744-8956, E-mail: ken.eastman@okstate.edu.

School of Accounting Students: 54 full-time (28 women), 18 part-time (13 women); includes 4 minority (1 Hispanic/Latino; 3 Two or more races, non-Hispanic/Latino), 7 international. Average age 24. 64 applicants, 23% accepted, 13 enrolled. *Faculty:* 15 full-time (7 women), 5 part-time/adjunct (3 women). *Financial support:* In 2015–16, 6 research assistantships (averaging $22,681 per year), 17 teaching assistantships (averaging $12,022 per year) were awarded; career-related internships or fieldwork, Federal Work-Study, scholarships/grants, health care benefits, tuition waivers (partial), and unspecified assistantships also available. Support available to part-time students. Financial award application deadline: 3/1; financial award applicants required to submit FAFSA. In 2015, 52 master's, 4 doctorates awarded. *Degree program information:* Part-time programs available. Part-time. Offers accounting (MS, PhD). *Application deadline:* For fall admission, 3/1 priority date for international students; for spring admission, 8/1 priority date for international students. Applications are processed on a rolling basis. *Application fee:* $40 ($75 for international students). Electronic applications accepted. *Application Contact:* Dr. Alyssa Vowell, Graduate Coordinator, 405-744-6635, Fax: 405-744-1680, E-mail: alyssa.vowell@okstate.edu. *Department Head,* Dr. Robert Cornell, 405-744-6377, Fax: 405-744-1680, E-mail: robert.cornell@okstate.edu.

OKLAHOMA STATE UNIVERSITY CENTER FOR HEALTH SCIENCES, Tulsa, OK 74107-1898

General Information State-supported, coed, graduate-only institution. *Enrollment by degree level:* 187 master's, 449 doctoral. *Graduate faculty:* 105 full-time (23 women), 830 part-time/adjunct (204 women). *Graduate housing:* On-campus housing not available. *Student services:* Campus employment opportunities, campus safety program, career counseling, exercise/wellness program, free psychological counseling, low-cost health insurance, services for students with disabilities. *Library:* Oklahoma State University Center for Health Sciences Medical Library. *Collection:* Books: 42,831 (physical), 1,985 (digital/electronic); Serial titles: 483 (physical), 14,658 (digital/electronic); Databases: 72. Weekly public service hours: 105; students can reserve study rooms. *Research affiliation:* Viropharma, Inc. (pharmaceutical sciences), Ingenex (pharmaceutical sciences), The Procter & Gamble Company (pharmaceutical sciences), Glaxo-Smith Kline (pharmaceutical sciences), Sun River, Inc. (cognitive rehabilitation), Merck & Company, Inc. (pharmaceutical sciences).

Computer facilities: 56 computers available on campus for general student use. A campuswide network can be accessed from off campus. Online class registration is available.
Website: http://www.healthsciences.okstate.edu/

General Application Contact: Lindsey Kirkpatrick, Assistant Director of Admissions and Recruitment, 800-677-1972, Fax: 918-561-8243.

GRADUATE UNITS

College of Osteopathic Medicine Students: 441 full-time (194 women); includes 137 minority (20 Black or African American, non-Hispanic/Latino; 20 American Indian or Alaska Native, non-Hispanic/Latino; 43 Asian, non-Hispanic/Latino; 22 Hispanic/Latino; 32 Two or more races, non-Hispanic/Latino). Average age 27. 2,278 applicants, 5% accepted, 97 enrolled. *Faculty:* 102 full-time (23 women), 813 part-time/adjunct (196 women). *Financial support:* In 2015–16, 189 students received support. Federal Work-Study, institutionally sponsored loans, scholarships/grants, and tuition waivers available. Financial award application deadline: 4/1; financial award applicants required to submit FAFSA. In 2015, 87 doctorates awarded. Offers osteopathic medicine (DO). *Application deadline:* For fall admission, 2/1 for domestic students. Applications are processed on a rolling basis. *Application fee:* $65. Electronic applications accepted. *Application Contact:* Maghin Abernathy, Director of Admissions, 800-677-1972, Fax: 918-561-8243, E-mail: maghin.abernathy@okstate.edu. *Provost and Dean, Center for Health Sciences,* Dr. Kayse M. Shrum, 918-561-8201, Fax: 918-561-8413, E-mail: amy.green@okstate.edu.

Graduate Program in Forensic Sciences Students: 10 full-time (7 women), 51 part-time (13 women); includes 6 minority (2 American Indian or Alaska Native, non-Hispanic/Latino; 2 Hispanic/Latino; 1 Native Hawaiian or other Pacific Islander, non-Hispanic/Latino; 1 Two or more races, non-Hispanic/Latino). Average age 31. 63 applicants, 89% accepted, 49 enrolled. *Faculty:* 3 full-time (0 women), 15 part-time/adjunct (5 women). *Financial support:* In 2015–16, 16 students received support, including 8 research assistantships (averaging $12,000 per year); career-related internships or fieldwork, Federal Work-Study, health care benefits, tuition waivers (partial), and unspecified assistantships also available. Financial award application deadline: 4/1; financial award applicants required to submit FAFSA. In 2015, 6 master's awarded. *Degree program information:* Part-time and evening/weekend programs available. Part-time, evening/weekend, 100% online, blended/hybrid learning. Offers forensic sciences (MS). *Application deadline:* For fall admission, 3/1 priority date for domestic students, 3/1 for international students; for spring admission, 10/1 priority date for domestic students, 10/1 for international students; for summer admission, 7/1 priority date for domestic students, 7/1 for international students. Applications are processed on a rolling basis. *Application fee:* $50 ($75 for international students). Electronic applications accepted. *Application Contact:* Cathy Newsome, Coordinator, 918-561-1108, Fax: 918-561-8414, E-mail: cathy.newsome@okstate.edu. *Director,* Dr. Robert W. Allen, 918-561-1292, Fax: 918-561-8794, E-mail: robert.w.allen@okstate.edu.

Program in Biomedical Sciences Students: 44 full-time (18 women); includes 11 minority (2 Black or African American, non-Hispanic/Latino; 3 American Indian or Alaska Native, non-Hispanic/Latino; 4 Asian, non-Hispanic/Latino; 1 Hispanic/Latino; 1 Two or more races, non-Hispanic/Latino), 5 international. Average age 26. 33 applicants, 61% accepted, 15 enrolled. *Faculty:* 38 full-time (8 women), 1 part-time/adjunct (0 women). *Financial support:* In 2015–16, 14 students received support, including 12 research assistantships with full tuition reimbursements available (averaging $21,180 per year), 2 teaching assistantships with full tuition reimbursements available (averaging $21,180 per year); Federal Work-Study, health care benefits, and tuition waivers (full) also available. Financial award application deadline: 4/1; financial award applicants required to submit FAFSA. In 2015, 6 master's, 2 doctorates awarded. Offers biomedical sciences (MS, PhD). *Application deadline:* For fall admission, 1/15 for domestic and international students. *Application fee:* $50 ($75 for international students). Electronic applications accepted. *Application Contact:* Patrick Anderson, Coordinator of Graduate Admissions, 800-677-1972, Fax: 918-561-8243, E-mail: patrick.anderson@okstate.edu. *Director,* Dr. Randall L. Davis, 918-561-8408, Fax: 918-561-8276.

Program in Health Care Administration Students: 108 full-time (74 women), 194 part-time (124 women); includes 76 minority (22 Black or African American, non-Hispanic/Latino; 26 American Indian or Alaska Native, non-Hispanic/Latino; 8 Asian, non-Hispanic/Latino; 8 Hispanic/Latino; 1 Native Hawaiian or other Pacific Islander, non-Hispanic/Latino; 11 Two or more races, non-Hispanic/Latino), 10 international. Average age 32. 64 applicants, 97% accepted, 57 enrolled. *Faculty:* 1 full-time (0 women), 5 part-time/adjunct (2 women). *Financial support:* In 2015–16, 1 teaching assistantship with full tuition reimbursement (averaging $18,000 per year) was awarded. Financial award applicants required to submit FAFSA. In 2015, 38 master's awarded. *Degree program information:* Part-time and evening/weekend programs available. Part-time, evening/weekend, 100% online. Offers health care administration (MS). *Application deadline:* For fall admission, 7/1 for domestic students; for spring admission, 12/1 for domestic students. *Application fee:* $50 ($75 for international students). *Application Contact:* Patrick Anderson, Coordinator of Graduate Admissions, 918-561-1228, Fax: 918-561-8243, E-mail: patrick.anderson@okstate.edu. *Director,* Dr. James D. Hess, 918-561-1105, Fax: 918-561-1416, E-mail: jim.hess@okstate.edu.

OKLAHOMA WESLEYAN UNIVERSITY, Bartlesville, OK 74006-6299

General Information Independent-religious, coed, comprehensive institution.

GRADUATE UNITS

Professional Studies Division

OLD DOMINION UNIVERSITY, Norfolk, VA 23529

General Information State-supported, coed, university. CGS member. *Enrollment:* 24,672 graduate, professional, and undergraduate students; 1,531 full-time matriculated graduate/professional students (956 women), 2,118 part-time matriculated graduate/professional students (1,141 women). *Enrollment by degree level:* 2,331 master's, 1,226 doctoral, 92 other advanced degrees. *Graduate faculty:* 697 full-time (257 women), 87 part-time/adjunct (44 women). Tuition, state resident: full-time $11,136; part-time $464 per credit hour. Tuition, nonresident: full-time $27,840; part-time $1160 per credit hour. *Required fees:* $64 per semester. Tuition and fees vary according to campus/location, program and reciprocity agreements. *Graduate housing:* Room and/or apartments available on a first-come, first-served basis to single students; on-campus housing not available to married students. Typical cost: $5860 per year ($10,404 including board). Room and board charges vary according to board plan and housing facility selected. Housing application deadline: 5/1. *Student services:* Campus employment opportunities, campus safety program, career counseling, exercise/wellness program, free psychological counseling, grant writing training, international student services, low-cost health insurance, multicultural affairs office, services for students with disabilities, teacher training. *Library:* Patricia W. and Douglas Perry Library plus 3 others. *Collection:* Books: 813,758 (physical), 1.3 million (digital/electronic); Serial titles: 11,819 (physical), 45,462 (digital/electronic); Databases: 228. Weekly public service hours: 146; study areas open 24 hours, 5–7 days a week; students can reserve study rooms. *Research affiliation:* Commonwealth Center for Advanced Manufacturing (advanced engineering and manufacturing), Joint Staff J7 (modeling and simulation for training), Thomas Jefferson National Accelerator Facility (high energy physics and laser processing), National Institute of Aerospace (aerodynamic testing and evaluation), Eastern Virginia Medical School (medicine), Virginia Institute of Marine Science (marine science).

Computer facilities: 2,005 computers available on campus for general student use. A campuswide network can be accessed from student residence rooms and from off campus. Online class registration, online courses are available.
Website: http://www.odu.edu/

General Application Contact: William Heffelfinger, Director of Graduate Admissions, 757-683-5554, Fax: 757-683-3255, E-mail: gradadmit@odu.edu.

GRADUATE UNITS

College of Arts and Letters Students: 157 full-time (94 women), 215 part-time (139 women); includes 79 minority (40 Black or African American, non-Hispanic/Latino; 3 Asian, non-Hispanic/Latino; 13 Hispanic/Latino; 2 Native Hawaiian or other Pacific Islander, non-Hispanic/Latino; 21 Two or more races, non-Hispanic/Latino), 22 international. Average age 34. 276 applicants, 66% accepted, 117 enrolled. *Faculty:* 135 full-time (61 women), 11 part-time/adjunct (4 women). *Financial support:* In 2015–16, 214 students received support, including 4 fellowships with tuition reimbursements available (averaging $15,000 per year), 16 research assistantships with tuition reimbursements available (averaging $10,000 per year), 58 teaching assistantships with tuition reimbursements available (averaging $10,000 per year); career-related internships or fieldwork, institutionally sponsored loans, scholarships/grants, and unspecified assistantships also available. Support available to part-time students. Financial award application deadline: 2/15; financial award applicants required to submit CSS PROFILE or FAFSA. In 2015, 87 master's, 28 doctorates awarded. *Degree program information:* Part-time and evening/weekend programs available. Part-time, evening/weekend, online learning. Offers applied linguistics (MA); applied sociology (MA); arts and letters (MA, MFA, MME, PhD); conflict and cooperation (MA, PhD); creative writing (MFA); criminology and criminal justice (PhD); English (MA, PhD); history (MA); humanities (MA); interdependence and transnationalism (MA, PhD); international cultural studies (MA, PhD); international political economy and development (MA, PhD); lifespan and digital communication (MA); modeling and simulation (MA, PhD); music education (MME); U.S. foreign policy and international relations (MA, PhD). *Application deadline:* For fall admission, 6/1 priority date for domestic students, 2/15 for international students; for spring admission, 11/1 priority date for domestic students, 10/1 for international students. *Application fee:* $50. Electronic applications accepted. *Application Contact:* Dr. David C. Earnest, Associate Dean, 757-683-6077, Fax: 757-683-5746, E-mail: dearnest@odu.edu. *Dean,* Dr. Charles E. Wilson, Jr., 757-683-3925, Fax: 757-683-5746, E-mail: cwilson@odu.edu.

College of Health Sciences Students: 295 full-time (223 women), 118 part-time (102 women); includes 80 minority (40 Black or African American, non-Hispanic/Latino; 1 American Indian or Alaska Native, non-Hispanic/Latino; 13 Asian, non-Hispanic/Latino; 10 Hispanic/Latino; 16 Two or more races, non-Hispanic/Latino), 15 international. Average age 33. 1,047 applicants, 25% accepted, 202 enrolled. *Faculty:* 64 full-time (42 women), 3 part-time/adjunct. *Financial support:* In 2015–16, 37 students received support, including 7 fellowships with full tuition reimbursements available (averaging $15,000 per year), 12 research assistantships with partial tuition reimbursements available (averaging $15,000 per year), 9 teaching assistantships with partial tuition reimbursements available (averaging $13,000 per year); career-related internships or fieldwork, institutionally sponsored loans, scholarships/grants, health care benefits, tuition waivers (full and partial), and unspecified assistantships also available. Support available to part-time students. Financial award application deadline: 2/15; financial award applicants required to submit FAFSA. In 2015, 108 master's, 78 doctorates awarded. *Degree program information:* Part-time and evening/weekend programs available. Part-time, evening/weekend, 100% online, blended/hybrid learning. Offers advanced practice (DNP); athletic training (MSAT); health sciences (MS, MSAT, MSN, DNP, DPT, PhD); health services research (PhD); nurse executive (DNP). *Application deadline:* Applications are processed on a rolling basis. *Application fee:* $50. Electronic applications accepted. *Application Contact:* William Heffelfinger, Director of Graduate Admissions, 757-683-5554, Fax: 757-683-3255, E-mail: gradadmit@odu.edu. *Dean,* Dr. Shelley Mishoe, 757-683-4960, Fax: 757-683-5674, E-mail: smishoe@odu.edu.

School of Community and Environmental Health Students: 9 full-time (6 women), 15 part-time (8 women); includes 9 minority (7 Black or African American, non-Hispanic/Latino; 1 Hispanic/Latino; 1 Two or more races, non-Hispanic/Latino). Average age 29. 12 applicants, 83% accepted, 8 enrolled. *Faculty:* 5 full-time (2 women), 4 part-time/adjunct (2 women). *Financial support:* In 2015–16, 3 research assistantships with tuition reimbursements (averaging $14,000 per year), 2 teaching assistantships with partial tuition reimbursements (averaging $10,000 per year) were awarded; career-related internships or fieldwork, institutionally sponsored loans, scholarships/grants, and tuition waivers (partial) also available. Financial award applicants required to submit FAFSA. In 2015, 6 master's awarded. *Degree program information:* Part-time and evening/weekend programs available. Part-time, evening/weekend, online learning. Offers community and environmental health (MS). *Application deadline:* For fall admission, 8/1 priority date for domestic students, 7/1 priority date for international students; for winter admission, 11/1 priority date for domestic students, 10/1 priority date for international students; for spring admission, 4/1 priority date for domestic students, 3/1 priority date for international students. Applications are processed on a rolling basis. *Application fee:* $50. Electronic applications accepted. *Application Contact:* William Heffelfinger, Director of Graduate Admissions, 757-683-5554, Fax: 757-683-3255, E-mail: gradadmit@odu.edu. *Graduate Program Director,* Dr. Anna Jeng, 757-683-4594, Fax: 757-683-4410, E-mail: hjeng@odu.edu.

School of Dental Hygiene Students: 9 full-time (all women), 16 part-time (all women); includes 5 minority (4 Black or African American, non-Hispanic/Latino; 1 Hispanic/Latino), 2 international. Average age 34. 12 applicants, 25% accepted, 2 enrolled. *Faculty:* 10 full-time (9 women). *Financial support:* In 2015–16, 4 students received support, including 4 teaching assistantships with partial tuition reimbursements available (averaging $10,000 per year); scholarships/grants and health care benefits also available. Support available to part-time students. Financial award application deadline: 2/15; financial award applicants required to submit CSS PROFILE or FAFSA. In 2015, 3 master's awarded. *Degree program information:* Part-time and evening/weekend programs available. Part-time, evening/weekend, blended/hybrid learning. Offers dental hygiene (MS). *Application deadline:* For fall admission, 7/1 for domestic students, 4/15 for international students; for spring admission, 12/1 for domestic students, 10/1 for international students; for summer admission, 3/1 for domestic students, 2/1 for international students. Applications are processed on a rolling basis. *Application fee:* $50. Electronic applications accepted. *Application Contact:* William Heffelfinger, Director of Graduate Admissions, 757-683-5554, Fax: 757-683-3255, E-mail: gradadmit@odu.edu. *Assistant Dean/Graduate Program Director,* Deborah B. Bauman, 757-683-6079, Fax: 757-683-4753, E-mail: dbauman@odu.edu.

School of Nursing Students: 116 full-time (105 women), 72 part-time (61 women); includes 34 minority (18 Black or African American, non-Hispanic/Latino; 1 American Indian or Alaska Native, non-Hispanic/Latino; 5 Asian, non-Hispanic/Latino; 2 Hispanic/Latino; 8 Two or more races, non-Hispanic/Latino), 7 international. Average age 39. 199 applicants, 42% accepted, 74 enrolled. *Faculty:* 6 full-time (5 women), 17 part-time/adjunct (15 women). *Financial support:* In 2015–16, 18 students received support, including 2 research assistantships with partial tuition reimbursements available (averaging $10,000 per year), 1 teaching assistantship (averaging $2,500 per year); career-related internships or fieldwork, scholarships/grants, traineeships, and tuition waivers (partial) also available. Support available to part-time students. Financial award application deadline: 2/15; financial award applicants required to submit FAFSA. In 2015, 67 master's, 27 doctorates awarded. *Degree program information:* Part-time programs available. Part-time, 100% online, blended/hybrid learning. Offers adult gerontology clinical nurse specialist/educator role (MSN); adult-gerontology clinical nurse specialist/educator (MSN); advanced practice nursing (DNP); family nurse practitioner (MSN); neonatal nurse practitioner (MSN); nurse anesthesia (MSN); nurse educator (MSN); nurse executive (MSN); nurse midwifery (MSN); pediatric nurse practitioner (MSN). *Application deadline:* For fall admission, 3/1 for domestic students, 4/15 for international students; for spring admission, 9/15 for domestic students. *Application fee:* $50. Electronic applications accepted. *Application Contact:* Sue Parker, Coordinator, Graduate Student Services, 757-683-4298, Fax: 757-683-5253, E-mail: sparker@odu.edu. *Chair,* Dr. Karen Karlowicz, 757-683-5262, Fax: 757-683-5253, E-mail: nursgpd@odu.edu.

School of Physical Therapy and Athletic Training Students: 130 full-time (81 women); includes 22 minority (7 Black or African American, non-Hispanic/Latino; 5 Asian, non-Hispanic/Latino; 4 Hispanic/Latino; 6 Two or more races, non-Hispanic/Latino), 1 international. Average age 25. 584 applicants, 14% accepted, 44 enrolled. *Faculty:* 13 full-time (8 women), 5 part-time/adjunct (3 women). *Financial support:* In 2015–16, 6 students received support, including 1 fellowship (averaging $15,000 per year), 4 teaching assistantships with partial tuition reimbursements available (averaging $7,500 per year); career-related internships or fieldwork, scholarships/grants, and unspecified assistantships also available. Financial award applicants required to submit FAFSA. In 2015, 47 doctorates awarded. Offers athletic training (MSAT); physical therapy (DPT). *Application deadline:* For fall admission, 11/1 for domestic and international students. *Application fee:* $50. Electronic applications accepted. *Application Contact:* William Heffelfinger, Director of Graduate Admissions, 757-683-5554, Fax: 757-683-3255,

E-mail: gradadmit@odu.edu. *Graduate Program Director,* Dr. George Maihafer, 757-683-4519, Fax: 757-683-4410, E-mail: ptgpd@odu.edu.

College of Sciences Students: 268 full-time (118 women), 192 part-time (87 women); includes 57 minority (20 Black or African American, non-Hispanic/Latino; 17 Asian, non-Hispanic/Latino; 13 Hispanic/Latino; 7 Two or more races, non-Hispanic/Latino), 157 international. Average age 29. *Faculty:* 143 full-time (31 women), 33 part-time/adjunct (7 women). *Financial support:* In 2015–16, 3 fellowships (averaging $5,000 per year), 158 research assistantships with tuition reimbursements (averaging $18,000 per year), 101 teaching assistantships with tuition reimbursements (averaging $16,000 per year) were awarded; career-related internships or fieldwork, scholarships/grants, and tuition waivers (partial) also available. Support available to part-time students. Financial award application deadline: 2/15; financial award applicants required to submit FAFSA. In 2015, 94 master's, 39 doctorates awarded. *Degree program information:* Part-time and evening/weekend programs available. Part-time, evening/weekend. Offers analytical (MS, PhD); applied experimental psychology (PhD); applied mathematics (MS, PhD); biochemistry (MS, PhD); biology (MS); biomedical sciences (PhD); clinical psychology (PhD); computer science (MS, PhD); ecological sciences (PhD); environmental (MS, PhD); human factors psychology (PhD); industrial/organizational psychology (PhD); inorganic (MS, PhD); ocean and earth sciences (MS); oceanography (PhD); organic (MS, PhD); physical (MS, PhD); physics (MS, PhD); psychology (MS, PhD); sciences (MS, PhD). *Application fee:* $50. Electronic applications accepted. *Application Contact:* William Heffelfinger, Director of Graduate Admissions, 757-683-5554, Fax: 757-683-3255, E-mail: gradadmit@odu.edu. *Dean,* Dr. Chris Platsoucas, 757-683-3274, Fax: 757-683-3034, E-mail: cplatsoucas@odu.edu.

Darden College of Education Students: 515 full-time (412 women), 755 part-time (560 women); includes 332 minority (218 Black or African American, non-Hispanic/Latino; 3 American Indian or Alaska Native, non-Hispanic/Latino; 19 Asian, non-Hispanic/Latino; 59 Hispanic/Latino; 1 Native Hawaiian or other Pacific Islander, non-Hispanic/Latino; 32 Two or more races, non-Hispanic/Latino), 22 international. Average age 33. 1,125 applicants, 72% accepted. *Faculty:* 94 full-time (55 women), 62 part-time/adjunct (40 women). *Financial support:* In 2015–16, 141 students received support, including 4 fellowships with tuition reimbursements available (averaging $15,000 per year), 60 research assistantships with tuition reimbursements available (averaging $15,000 per year), 72 teaching assistantships with tuition reimbursements available (averaging $15,000 per year); career-related internships or fieldwork, Federal Work-Study, institutionally sponsored loans, scholarships/grants, tuition waivers (partial), and unspecified assistantships also available. Support available to part-time students. Financial award application deadline: 2/15; financial award applicants required to submit CSS PROFILE or FAFSA. In 2015, 435 master's, 62 doctorates, 40 other advanced degrees awarded. *Degree program information:* Part-time and evening/weekend programs available. Part-time, evening/weekend, online learning. Offers adapted curriculum K-12 (MS Ed); advanced practice (Ed S); chemistry (MS Ed); clinical mental health counseling (MS Ed); college counseling (MS Ed); community college leadership (PhD); community college teaching (MS); counselor education (PhD); curriculum and instruction (MS Ed, PhD); early childhood education (MS Ed, PhD); early childhood special education (MS Ed); education (PhD); educational leadership (MS Ed); educational leadership and administration (MS Ed, PhD, Ed S); English (MS Ed); exercise and wellness (MS Ed); general curriculum K-12 (MS Ed); higher education (MS Ed, PhD, Ed S); human movement science (PhD); human resources training (PhD); instructional design and technology (PhD); instructional technology (MS Ed); library science (MS Ed); literacy leadership (PhD); physical education (MS Ed); reading specialist (MS Ed); school counseling (MS Ed); secondary education (MS Ed); special education (PhD); speech-language pathology (MS Ed); sport management (MS Ed); technology education (PhD). *Application deadline:* For fall admission, 6/1 priority date for domestic and international students; for spring admission, 11/1 priority date for domestic and international students. Applications are processed on a rolling basis. *Application fee:* $50. Electronic applications accepted. *Application Contact:* Nechell Bonds, Director of Admissions, 757-683-3685, Fax: 757-683-3255, E-mail: gradadmit@odu.edu. *Dean,* Dr. Jane S. Bray, 757-683-3938, Fax: 757-683-5083, E-mail: jsbray@odu.edu.

Frank Batten College of Engineering and Technology Students: 167 full-time (42 women), 544 part-time (111 women); includes 156 minority (62 Black or African American, non-Hispanic/Latino; 1 American Indian or Alaska Native, non-Hispanic/Latino; 41 Asian, non-Hispanic/Latino; 33 Hispanic/Latino; 2 Native Hawaiian or other Pacific Islander, non-Hispanic/Latino; 17 Two or more races, non-Hispanic/Latino), 180 international. Average age 32. 558 applicants, 63% accepted, 144 enrolled. *Faculty:* 93 full-time (12 women), 32 part-time/adjunct (5 women). *Financial support:* In 2015–16, 168 students received support, including 8 fellowships with tuition reimbursements available (averaging $15,000 per year), 92 research assistantships with tuition reimbursements available (averaging $15,000 per year), 68 teaching assistantships with tuition reimbursements available (averaging $15,000 per year); career-related internships or fieldwork, Federal Work-Study, institutionally sponsored loans, scholarships/grants, and unspecified assistantships also available. Support available to part-time students. Financial award applicants required to submit FAFSA. In 2015, 247 master's, 31 doctorates awarded. *Degree program information:* Part-time and evening/weekend programs available. Part-time, evening/weekend, 100% online, blended/hybrid learning. Offers aerospace engineering (ME, MS, D Eng, PhD); biomedical engineering (ME, MS, PhD); civil engineering (ME, MS); civil engineering/environmental engineering (D Eng, PhD); electrical and computer engineering (ME, MS, PhD); engineering and technology (ME, MEM, MS, D Eng, PhD); engineering management (MEM, MS, PhD); engineering management and systems engineering (D Eng); environmental engineering (ME, MS); mechanical engineering (ME, MS, D Eng, PhD); modeling and simulation (ME, MS, D Eng, PhD); systems engineering (ME). *Application deadline:* For fall admission, 6/1 for domestic students, 2/15 priority date for international students; for spring admission, 11/1 for domestic students, 10/1 for international students. Applications are processed on a rolling basis. *Application fee:* $50. Electronic applications accepted. *Application Contact:* Dr. Linda Vahala, Associate Dean, 757-683-3789, Fax: 757-683-4898, E-mail: lvahala@odu.edu. *Dean,* Dr. Oktay Baysal, 757-683-3789, Fax: 757-683-4898, E-mail: obaysal@odu.edu.

Strome College of Business Students: 129 full-time (67 women), 294 part-time (142 women); includes 117 minority (73 Black or African American, non-Hispanic/Latino; 11 Asian, non-Hispanic/Latino; 15 Hispanic/Latino; 1 Native Hawaiian or other Pacific Islander, non-Hispanic/Latino; 17 Two or more races, non-Hispanic/Latino), 84 international. Average age 33. 438 applicants, 49% accepted, 156 enrolled. *Faculty:* 83 full-time (19 women), 9 part-time/adjunct (3 women). *Financial support:* In 2015–16, 94 students received support, including 3 fellowships with partial tuition reimbursements available (averaging $1,500 per year), 154 research assistantships with tuition reimbursements available (averaging $6,400 per year), 8 teaching assistantships with tuition reimbursements available (averaging $15,000 per year); career-related internships or fieldwork, Federal Work-Study, scholarships/grants, tuition waivers (partial), and unspecified assistantships also available. Financial award application deadline: 2/15; financial award applicants required to submit FAFSA. In 2015, 110 master's, 16 doctorates awarded. *Degree program information:* Part-time and evening/weekend programs available. Part-time, evening/weekend, online learning. Offers accounting (MS); business (MA, MBA, MPA, MS, PMBA, PhD); business administration (MBA, PMBA, PhD); economics (MA); finance (PhD); information technology (PhD); marketing (PhD); multi sector public service (MPA); public administration (MPA); public administration and urban policy (PhD); strategic management (PhD). *Application deadline:* For fall admission, 6/1 priority date for domestic and international students; for winter admission, 11/1 priority date for domestic and international students. Applications are processed on a rolling basis. *Application fee:* $50. Electronic applications accepted. *Application Contact:* Dr. Ali Ardalan, Associate Dean, 757-683-3520, Fax: 757-683-4076, E-mail: aardalan@odu.edu. *Dean,* Dr. Vinod Agarwal, 757-683-3526, Fax: 757-683-4076, E-mail: vagarwal@odu.edu.

OLIVET COLLEGE, Olivet, MI 49076-9701

General Information Independent-religious, coed, comprehensive institution. *Enrollment:* 44 full-time matriculated graduate/professional students (30 women). *Enrollment by degree level:* 44 master's. *Graduate faculty:* 3 full-time (2 women), 6 part-time/adjunct (5 women). *Student services:* Career counseling, free psychological counseling, international student services, multicultural affairs office, teacher training, writing training. *Library:* Burrage Library.

Computer facilities: 118 computers available on campus for general student use. A campuswide network can be accessed from student residence rooms and from off campus. Online class registration is available.
Website: http://www.olivetcollege.edu/

General Application Contact: Diane Joy Joslin-Gould, Director, 269-749-7113, Fax: 269-749-6620, E-mail: djoslingould@olivetcollege.edu.

GRADUATE UNITS

Program in Insurance Online learning. Offers insurance (MBA). *Application deadline:* For fall admission, 9/15 for domestic students. Applications are processed on a rolling basis. *Application fee:* $0. Electronic applications accepted. *Director,* Kelly M. Parker, 269-749-7633, E-mail: kmparker@olivetcollege.edu.

OLIVET NAZARENE UNIVERSITY, Bourbonnais, IL 60914

General Information Independent-religious, coed, comprehensive institution. *Graduate housing:* Room and/or apartments available to single students; on-campus housing not available to married students. Housing application deadline: 8/15.

GRADUATE UNITS

Graduate School ***Degree program information:*** Part-time and evening/weekend programs available. Part-time, evening/weekend. Offers business administration (MBA); practical ministries (MPM).

Division of Education Degree program information: Evening/weekend programs available. Evening/weekend. Offers curriculum and instruction (MAE); elementary education (MAT); library information specialist (MAE); reading specialist (MAE); school leadership (MAE); secondary education (MAT).

Division of Religion Degree program information: Part-time programs available. Part-time. Offers biblical literature (MA); religion (MA); theology (MA).

Program in Organizational Leadership Offers organizational leadership (MOL).

OPEN UNIVERSITY, Milton Keynes MK7 6AA, United Kingdom

General Information Public, coed, comprehensive institution.

GRADUATE UNITS

Graduate Programs

ORAL ROBERTS UNIVERSITY, Tulsa, OK 74171

General Information Independent-religious, coed, comprehensive institution. *Graduate housing:* Room and/or apartments available on a first-come, first-served basis to single students; on-campus housing not available to married students.

GRADUATE UNITS

School of Business ***Degree program information:*** Part-time programs available. Part-time, online learning. Offers accounting (MBA); entrepreneurship (MBA); finance (MBA); international business (MBA); management (MBA); marketing (MBA); non-profit management (MBA); not for profit management (MNM). Electronic applications accepted.

School of Education ***Degree program information:*** Part-time programs available. Part-time, online learning. Offers Christian school administration (K-12) (MA Ed, Ed D); Christian school curriculum development (MA Ed); college and higher education administration (Ed D); public school administration (K-12) (MA Ed, Ed D); public school teaching (MA Ed).

School of Theology and Missions ***Degree program information:*** Part-time programs available. Part-time, online learning. Offers biblical literature (MA); Christian counseling (MA); divinity (M Div); missions (MA); practical theology (MA); theological/historical studies (MA); theology (D Min). Electronic applications accepted.

OREGON COLLEGE OF ART & CRAFT, Portland, OR 97225

General Information Independent, coed, comprehensive institution.

GRADUATE UNITS

MFA Program Offers craft (MFA).

OREGON COLLEGE OF ORIENTAL MEDICINE, Portland, OR 97216

General Information Independent, coed, graduate-only institution. *Graduate housing:* On-campus housing not available.

GRADUATE UNITS

Graduate Program in Acupuncture and Oriental Medicine ***Degree program information:*** Part-time programs available. Part-time. Offers acupuncture and Oriental medicine (M Ac OM, MAcOM, DAOM).

OREGON HEALTH & SCIENCE UNIVERSITY, Portland, OR 97239-3098

General Information State-related, coed, upper-level institution. *Graduate housing:* On-campus housing not available. *Research affiliation:* Oregon Regional Primate Research Center.

GRADUATE UNITS

School of Dentistry Offers biomaterials and biomechanics (MS); dentistry (MS, DMD, Certificate); endodontics (Certificate); oral and maxillofacial surgery (Certificate); oral molecular biology (MS); orthodontics (MS, Certificate); pediatric dentistry (Certificate); periodontology (MS, Certificate); restorative dentistry (MS). Electronic applications accepted.

School of Medicine Students: 937 full-time (514 women), 459 part-time (257 women); includes 322 minority (31 Black or African American, non-Hispanic/Latino; 9 American Indian or Alaska Native, non-Hispanic/Latino; 169 Asian, non-Hispanic/Latino; 68 Hispanic/Latino; 3 Native Hawaiian or other Pacific Islander, non-Hispanic/Latino; 42 Two or more races, non-Hispanic/Latino), 52 international. Average age 33. 7,917 applicants, 8% accepted, 474 enrolled. *Faculty:* 2,708. *Financial support:* Fellowships, research assistantships, teaching assistantships, career-related internships or fieldwork, Federal Work-Study, institutionally sponsored loans, scholarships/grants, health care benefits, and full tuition and stipends (for PhD students) available. Support available to part-time students. Financial award application deadline: 3/1; financial award applicants required to submit FAFSA. In 2015, 176 master's, 164 doctorates, 80 other advanced degrees awarded. *Degree program information:* Part-time programs available. Part-time. Offers medicine (MBA, MBST, MCR, MPAS, MPH, MS, MSCNU, MD, PhD, Certificate, Graduate Certificate). *Application deadline:* Applications are processed on a rolling basis. Electronic applications accepted. *Application Contact:* Registrar's Office, 503-494-7800. *Dean*, Dr. Mark Richardson, 503-494-8220, Fax: 503-494-3400.

Graduate Programs in Medicine Students: 317 full-time (186 women), 459 part-time (257 women); includes 182 minority (19 Black or African American, non-Hispanic/Latino; 4 American Indian or Alaska Native, non-Hispanic/Latino; 95 Asian, non-Hispanic/Latino; 43 Hispanic/Latino; 2 Native Hawaiian or other Pacific Islander, non-Hispanic/Latino; 19 Two or more races, non-Hispanic/Latino), 51 international. Average age 33. 2,451 applicants, 17% accepted, 26 enrolled. *Faculty:* 333 full-time (124 women), 605 part-time/adjunct (187 women). *Financial support:* Fellowships, research assistantships, teaching assistantships, scholarships/grants, health care benefits, and full tuition and stipends (for PhD students) available. *Degree program information:* Part-time programs available. Part-time. Offers behavioral neuroscience (PhD); biochemistry and molecular biology (PhD); biomedical engineering (PhD); cancer biology (PhD); cell and developmental biology (PhD); clinical informatics (MS, PhD, Certificate); clinical research (MCR, Certificate); computer science and engineering (MS, PhD); dietetics (Certificate); electrical engineering (MS, PhD); environmental science and engineering (MS, PhD); health information management (Certificate); healthcare management (MBA, MS, Certificate); human nutrition (MS); medicine (MBA, MCR, MPAS, MS, MSCNU, PhD, Certificate); molecular and cellular biosciences (PhD); molecular and medical genetics (PhD); molecular microbiology and immunology (PhD); neuroscience (PhD); physician assistant studies (MPAS); physiology and pharmacology (PhD). *Application deadline:* Applications are processed on a rolling basis. *Application fee:* $70. Electronic applications accepted. *Application Contact:* Lorie Gookin, Admissions Coordinator, 503-494-6222, E-mail: somgrad@ohsu.edu. *Associate Dean for Graduate Studies*, Dr. Allison Fryer, 503-494-6222, E-mail: somgrad@ohsu.edu.

School of Nursing ***Degree program information:*** Part-time programs available. Part-time. Offers adult-gerontology acute care nurse practitioner (MN, DNP, PMC); family nurse practitioner (MN, MS, DNP, Post Master's Certificate); health systems and organizational leadership (MN, PMC); mental health nursing (MN, MS, Post Master's Certificate); nurse anesthesia (MN, MS); nurse midwifery (MN, DNP, Post Master's Certificate); nursing (MN, MPH, MS, DNP, PhD, Post Master's Certificate); nursing education (MN, MS, Post Master's Certificate); pediatric nurse practitioner (MN, DNP, PMC). Electronic applications accepted.

OREGON INSTITUTE OF TECHNOLOGY, Klamath Falls, OR 97601-8801

General Information State-supported, coed, comprehensive institution. *Graduate housing:* Room and/or apartments available on a first-come, first-served basis to single students; on-campus housing not available to married students. Housing application deadline: 3/1.

GRADUATE UNITS

Program in Manufacturing Engineering Technology ***Degree program information:*** Part-time programs available. Part-time, online learning. Offers manufacturing engineering technology (MS). Electronic applications accepted.

OREGON STATE UNIVERSITY, Corvallis, OR 97331

General Information State-supported, coed, university. CGS member. *Enrollment:* 29,576 graduate, professional, and undergraduate students; 3,507 full-time matriculated graduate/professional students (1,636 women), 678 part-time matriculated graduate/professional students (364 women). *Enrollment by degree level:* 2,051 master's, 2,134 doctoral. *Graduate faculty:* 969 full-time (329 women), 168 part-time/adjunct (72 women). Tuition, state resident: full-time $12,150; part-time $450 per credit. Tuition, nonresident: full-time $20,952; part-time $776 per credit. *Required fees:* $1572; $1443 per unit. One-time fee: $350. Tuition and fees vary according to course load, campus/location and program. *Graduate housing:* Rooms and/or apartments guaranteed to single students and available on a first-come, first-served basis to married students. Typical cost: $10,383 per year ($13,155 including board) for single students. Room and board charges vary according to board plan and housing facility selected. Housing application deadline: 5/1. *Student services:* Campus employment opportunities, campus safety program, career counseling, child daycare facilities, exercise/wellness program, free psychological counseling, grant writing training, international student services, low-cost health insurance, multicultural affairs office, services for students with disabilities, teacher training, writing training. *Library:* Valley Library plus 2 others. *Collection:* Books: 1.8 million (physical), 90,372 (digital/electronic); Databases: 196. Study areas open 24 hours, 5–7 days a week; students can reserve study rooms. *Research affiliation:* W.M. Keck Foundation (science, engineering), David and Lucille Packard Foundation (science, environmental science), William and Flora Hewlett Foundation (science, engineering), George and Betty Moore Foundation (medical research, science education), Comer Science and Educational Foundation (science).

Computer facilities: Computer purchase and lease plans are available. 2,179 computers available on campus for general student use. A campuswide network can be accessed from student residence rooms and from off campus. Online class registration is available.
Website: http://www.oregonstate.edu/

General Application Contact: Graduate School, 541-737-4881, Fax: 541-737-3313, E-mail: graduate.admissions@oregonstate.edu.

GRADUATE UNITS

College of Agricultural Sciences Students: 336 full-time (186 women), 25 part-time (11 women); includes 39 minority (3 Black or African American, non-Hispanic/Latino; 1 American Indian or Alaska Native, non-Hispanic/Latino; 2 Asian, non-Hispanic/Latino; 19 Hispanic/Latino; 14 Two or more races, non-Hispanic/Latino), 79 international. Average age 30. 492 applicants, 22% accepted, 75 enrolled. *Faculty:* 160 full-time (45 women), 26 part-time/adjunct (9 women). *Financial support:* Fellowships, research assistantships, teaching assistantships, career-related internships or fieldwork, Federal Work-Study, and institutionally sponsored loans available. Support available to part-time students. Financial award application deadline: 2/1. In 2015, 99 master's, 25 doctorates awarded. *Degree program information:* Part-time programs available. Part-time. Offers agricultural education (M Ag, MS); agricultural sciences (M Ag, MA, MAIS, MS, PSM, PhD); animal sciences (M Ag, MS, PhD); applied economics (MA, MS, PhD); botany and plant pathology (M Ag, MA, MS, PhD); crop science (M Ag, MS, PhD); fisheries and wildlife administration (PSM); fisheries science (MAIS, MS, PhD); food science and technology (MS, PhD); horticulture (M Ag, MS, PhD); rangeland ecology and management (M Ag, MS, PhD); soil science (M Ag, MS, PhD); toxicology (M Ag, MS, PhD); wildlife science (M Ag, MS, PhD). *Application fee:* $75 ($85 for international students). *Dean*, Dr. Dan Arp, 541-737-2331.

College of Business Students: 188 full-time (91 women), 77 part-time (32 women); includes 31 minority (1 Black or African American, non-Hispanic/Latino; 1 American Indian or Alaska Native, non-Hispanic/Latino; 15 Asian, non-Hispanic/Latino; 6 Hispanic/Latino; 2 Native Hawaiian or other Pacific Islander, non-Hispanic/Latino; 6 Two or more races, non-Hispanic/Latino), 150 international. Average age 30. *Faculty:* 51 full-time (21 women), 3 part-time/adjunct (1 woman). *Financial support:* Fellowships, teaching assistantships, career-related internships or fieldwork, Federal Work-Study, and institutionally sponsored loans available. In 2015, 88 master's, 4 doctorates awarded. *Degree program information:* Part-time programs available. Part-time, blended/hybrid learning. Offers accounting (MBA, PhD); apparel design (MA, MS); business (MA, MBA, MS, PhD); business analytics (MBA); clean technology (MBA); commercialization (MBA); cultural and historic aspects of the near environment (MA, MS, PhD); executive leadership (MBA); global operations (MBA); human behavior in the near environment (MA, MS, PhD); innovation/commercialization (PhD); interior design (MA, MS); marketing (MBA); merchandising management (MA, MS, PhD); research thesis (MBA); textiles (MA, MS, PhD); wealth management (MBA). *Application fee:* $75 ($85 for international students). *Application Contact:* Dr. Jim Coakley, Associate Dean for Academic Programs, 541-737-5510, E-mail: jim.coakley@bus.oregonstate.edu. *Dean*, Dr. Mitzi Montoya.

College of Earth, Ocean, and Atmospheric Sciences Students: 135 full-time (75 women), 16 part-time (6 women); includes 16 minority (1 Black or African American, non-Hispanic/Latino; 2 Asian, non-Hispanic/Latino; 9 Hispanic/Latino; 4 Two or more races, non-Hispanic/Latino), 26 international. Average age 29. *Faculty:* 67 full-time (18 women), 7 part-time/adjunct (3 women). *Financial support:* Fellowships, research assistantships, teaching assistantships, career-related internships or fieldwork, Federal Work-Study, and institutionally sponsored loans available. Support available to part-time students. Financial award application deadline: 1/5. In 2015, 26 master's, 15 doctorates awarded. *Degree program information:* Part-time programs available. Part-time. Offers atmospheric sciences (MA, MS, PhD); earth, ocean, and atmospheric sciences (MA, MS, PhD); geographic information science (MA, MS, PhD); geological oceanography (MA, MS, PhD); geophysics (MA, MS, PhD); marine resource management (MA, MS); ocean ecology and biogeochemistry (MS, PhD); physical geography (MA, MS, PhD); physical oceanography (MA, MS, PhD); resource geography (MA, MS, PhD); solid earth processes and history (MA, MS, PhD); surface earth processes and history (MA, MS, PhD). *Application deadline:* For fall admission, 1/5 for domestic students. *Application fee:* $75 ($85 for international students). *Application Contact:* Cori Hall, Head Advisor, 541-737-3715, E-mail: cori.hall@oregonstate.edu. *Interim Dean and Professor*, Dr. Roy Haggerty.

College of Education Students: 185 full-time (125 women), 235 part-time (173 women); includes 89 minority (15 Black or African American, non-Hispanic/Latino; 5 American Indian or Alaska Native, non-Hispanic/Latino; 20 Asian, non-Hispanic/Latino; 30 Hispanic/Latino; 2 Native Hawaiian or other Pacific Islander, non-Hispanic/Latino; 17 Two or more races, non-Hispanic/Latino), 4 international. Average age 35. *Faculty:* 44 full-time (26 women), 33 part-time/adjunct (20 women). *Financial support:* Fellowships, research assistantships, teaching assistantships, career-related internships or fieldwork, Federal Work-Study, and institutionally sponsored loans available. Support available to part-time students. Financial award application deadline: 2/1. In 2015, 119 master's, 30 doctorates awarded. *Degree program information:* Part-time programs available. Part-time, 100% online, blended/hybrid learning. Offers adult and higher education (Ed M); collegiate education (PhD); counseling (M Coun, MS, PhD); education (Ed M, M Coun, MAT, MS, Ed D, PhD); elementary education (MAT); free-choice learning (PhD); mathematics education (MS, PhD); music education (MAT); school-based education (PhD); teaching: advanced mathematics education (MAT); teaching: integrated science education (MAT); teaching: language arts education (MAT). *Application fee:* $75 ($85 for international students). *Dean*, Dr. Larry Flick.

College of Engineering Students: 1,006 full-time (203 women), 152 part-time (45 women); includes 82 minority (5 Black or African American, non-Hispanic/Latino; 30 Asian, non-Hispanic/Latino; 26 Hispanic/Latino; 21 Two or more races, non-Hispanic/Latino), 657 international. Average age 28. *Faculty:* 177 full-time (27 women), 9 part-time/adjunct (3 women). *Financial support:* Fellowships with full tuition reimbursements, research assistantships with full tuition reimbursements, teaching assistantships with full tuition reimbursements, and instructorships available. In 2015, 233 master's, 62 doctorates awarded. *Degree program information:* Part-time programs available. Part-time, 100% online. Offers advanced manufacturing (M Eng, MS, PhD); algorithms and cryptography (M Eng, MS, PhD); analog and mixed signal (M Eng, MS, PhD); application of nuclear techniques (M Eng, MS, PhD); arms control technology (M Eng, MS, PhD); artificial intelligence and machine learning (M Eng, MS, PhD); artificial intelligence, machine learning and data science (M Eng, MS, PhD); assistive robots (M Eng, MS, PhD); autonomous robots (M Eng, MS, PhD); bio-based products and fuels (M Eng, MS, PhD); biological systems analysis (M Eng, MS, PhD); bioprocessing (M Eng, MS, PhD); bioremediation (PhD); chemical engineering (MS, PhD); chemistry (MS, PhD); civil engineering (M Eng, MS, PhD); coastal and ocean engineering (M Eng, MS, PhD); communications and signal processing (M Eng, MS, PhD); computer graphics, visualization, and vision (M Eng, MS, PhD); computer systems (M Eng, MS, PhD); computer systems and networking (M Eng, MS, PhD); construction engineering management (M Eng, MS, PhD); design (M Eng, MS, PhD); ecosystems analysis and modeling (M Eng, MS, PhD); electrical and computer engineering (MS, PhD); energy systems (M Eng, MS, PhD); engineering (M Eng, MHP, MMP, MS, PhD); engineering education (M Eng, MS, PhD); engineering management (M Eng, MS, PhD); environmental fluid mechanics (M Eng, MS, PhD); environmental microbiology (M Eng, MS, PhD); environmental modeling (M Eng, MS, PhD); forest products (MS, PhD); geomatics (M Eng, MS, PhD); geotechnical engineering (M Eng, MS, PhD); human systems engineering (M Eng, MS, PhD); human-computer interaction (M Eng, MS, PhD); human-robot interaction (M Eng, MS, PhD); information systems engineering (M Eng, MS, PhD); infrastructure materials (M Eng, MS, PhD); legged locomotion (M Eng, MS, PhD); manipulation (M Eng, MS); manufacturing systems engineering (M Eng, MS, PhD); materials and devices (M Eng, MS, PhD); materials mechanics (M Eng, MS, PhD); mathematics (MS, PhD); mechanical engineering (MS, PhD); medical health physics (MMP, MS, PhD); mobile robots (M Eng, MS, PhD); multi-robot coordination (M Eng, MS, PhD); multiphase phenomena (M Eng, MS, PhD); nuclear engineering (MS, PhD); nuclear instrumentation and applications (M Eng, MS, PhD); nuclear medicine (M Eng, MS, PhD); nuclear power generation (M Eng, MS, PhD); nuclear reactor engineering (M Eng, MS, PhD); nuclear systems design and modeling (M Eng, MS, PhD); nuclear waste management (M Eng, MS, PhD); numerical methods for reactor analysis (M Eng); physics (MS, PhD); programming languages (M Eng, MS, PhD); radiation health physics (MHP, MS, PhD); radio frequencies/microwaves/optoelectronics (M Eng, MS, PhD); renewable energy (M Eng, MS, PhD); robotics (M Eng, MS, PhD); software engineering (M Eng, MS, PhD); structural engineering (M Eng, MS, PhD); subsurface flow and transport (M Eng, MS, PhD); therapeutic radiologic physics (MMP, MS, PhD); thermal fluid sciences (M Eng, MS, PhD); transportation engineering (M Eng); water and wastewater treatment (M Eng, MS, PhD); water quality (M Eng, MS, PhD); water resources (M Eng, MS, PhD). *Application fee:* $75 ($85 for international students). *Application Contact:* Dr. Christine Kelly, Associate Dean, Academic and Student Affairs, E-mail: christine.kelly@oregonstate.edu. *Dean,* Scott Ashford.

College of Forestry Students: 139 full-time (55 women), 61 part-time (30 women); includes 50 minority (1 Black or African American, non-Hispanic/Latino; 2 American Indian or Alaska Native, non-Hispanic/Latino; 4 Asian, non-Hispanic/Latino; 37 Hispanic/Latino; 6 Two or more races, non-Hispanic/Latino), 37 international. Average age 33. *Faculty:* 56 full-time (14 women), 10 part-time/adjunct (2 women). *Financial support:* Fellowships, research assistantships, teaching assistantships, career-related internships or fieldwork, Federal Work-Study, institutionally sponsored loans, and unspecified assistantships available. Support available to part-time students. In 2015, 45 master's, 11 doctorates awarded. *Degree program information:* Part-time programs available. Part-time, 100% online. Offers biodeterioration and materials protection (MS, PhD); chemistry and chemical processing (MS, PhD); engineering for sustainable forestry (MF, MS, PhD); fisheries management (MNR); forest biology (MF); forest biometrics and geomatics (MF, MS, PhD); forest operations planning and management (MF, MS, PhD); forest policy analysis and economics (MF, MS, PhD); forest products business and marketing (MS, PhD); forest watershed management (MF, MS, PhD); forest, wildlife and landscape ecology (MF, MS, PhD); forestry (MF, MNR, MS, PhD); genetics and physiology (MF, MS, PhD); geographic information science (MNR); integrated social and ecological systems (MF, MS, PhD); physics and moisture relations (MS, PhD); process modeling and analysis (MS, PhD); renewable materials sciences and engineered composites (MS, PhD); restoration and sustainable management (MF, MS, PhD); science of conservation (MF, MS, PhD); silviculture (MF); silviculture, fire, and forest health (MF, MS, PhD); social science, policy, and natural resources (MF, MS, PhD); soil-plant-atmosphere continuum (MF, MS, PhD); sustainable natural resources (MNR); sustainable recreation and tourism (MF, MS); water conflict management and transformation (MNR); wood anatomy and quality (MS, PhD); wood engineering and mechanics (MS, PhD). *Application fee:* $75 ($85 for international students). *Dean,* Dr. Thomas Maness.

College of Liberal Arts Students: 234 full-time (162 women), 27 part-time (14 women); includes 45 minority (4 Black or African American, non-Hispanic/Latino; 1 American Indian or Alaska Native, non-Hispanic/Latino; 3 Asian, non-Hispanic/Latino; 26 Hispanic/Latino; 1 Native Hawaiian or other Pacific Islander, non-Hispanic/Latino; 10 Two or more races, non-Hispanic/Latino), 36 international. Average age 31. 75 applicants, 113% accepted. *Faculty:* 120 full-time (64 women), 15 part-time/adjunct (10 women). *Financial support:* Fellowships, research assistantships, teaching assistantships, career-related internships or fieldwork, Federal Work-Study, and institutionally sponsored loans available. Support available to part-time students. Financial award application deadline: 2/1. In 2015, 95 master's, 4 doctorates awarded. *Degree program information:* Part-time programs available. Part-time. Offers applied anthropology (MA, PhD); applied cognition (MS, PhD); art and morality (MA); bioethics (MA); college and university characteristics and environments (MS); contemporary Hispanic studies (MA); development of the physical, biological, and environmental sciences (MA, MS, PhD); energy policy (MPP, PhD); engineering psychology (MS, PhD); environmental action (MA); environmental ethics (MA); environmental imagination (MA); environmental policy (MPP, PhD); environmental thinking (MA); fiction (MFA); health psychology (MS, PhD); history of science and medicine (MA, MS, PhD); history, development, and current issues in higher education (MS); intellectual and social history of science in Europe and the U.S. (MA, MS, PhD); international policy (MPP, PhD); law, crime, and policy (MPP, PhD); leadership and management of administrative departments (MS); liberal arts (MA, MFA, MPP, MS, PhD); literature and culture (MA); nonfiction writing (MFA); poetry (MFA); program oversight (MS); rhetoric, writing and culture (MA); rural policy (MPP, PhD); science and technology policy (MPP, PhD); social policy (MPP, PhD); student development theory and application (MS); women, gender, and sexuality studies (MA, PhD). *Application fee:* $60. *Dean,* Dr. Larry Rodgers.

College of Pharmacy Students: 371 full-time (199 women), 14 part-time (11 women); includes 175 minority (6 Black or African American, non-Hispanic/Latino; 1 American Indian or Alaska Native, non-Hispanic/Latino; 131 Asian, non-Hispanic/Latino; 16 Hispanic/Latino; 1 Native Hawaiian or other Pacific Islander, non-Hispanic/Latino; 20 Two or more races, non-Hispanic/Latino), 24 international. Average age 27. *Faculty:* 30 full-time (15 women). *Financial support:* Career-related internships or fieldwork available. In 2015, 87 doctorates awarded. *Degree program information:* Part-time programs available. Part-time. Offers medicinal chemistry (MS, PhD); natural products chemistry (MS, PhD); pharmaceutics (MS, PhD); pharmacoeconomics (MS, PhD); pharmacokinetics (MS, PhD); pharmacology (MS, PhD); pharmacy (MS, PhD, Pharm D); toxicology (MS, PhD). *Application fee:* $60. *Application Contact:* Angela Austin Haney, Director of Student Services/Head Advisor, 541-737-5784, E-mail: angela.austinhaney@oregonstate.edu. *Dean,* Dr. Mark Zabriskie.

College of Public Health and Human Sciences Students: 189 full-time (137 women), 26 part-time (18 women); includes 58 minority (5 Black or African American, non-Hispanic/Latino; 3 American Indian or Alaska Native, non-Hispanic/Latino; 14 Asian, non-Hispanic/Latino; 23 Hispanic/Latino; 1 Native Hawaiian or other Pacific Islander, non-Hispanic/Latino; 12 Two or more races, non-Hispanic/Latino), 27 international. Average age 31. *Faculty:* 61 full-time (38 women), 9 part-time/adjunct (5 women). *Financial support:* Institutionally sponsored loans available. In 2015, 78 master's, 16 doctorates awarded. Offers athletic training (MATRN); biophysical kinesiology (MS, PhD); biostatistics (MPH); environmental and occupational health and safety (MPH, PhD); epidemiology (MPH, PhD); health management and policy (MPH); health policy (PhD); health promotion and health behavior (MPH, PhD); human development and family studies (MS, PhD); international health (MPH); nutrition (MS, PhD); psychosocial kinesiology (MS, PhD); public health and human sciences (MATRN, MPH, MS, PhD). *Application Contact:* Dr. S. Marie Harvey, Associate Dean for Research and Graduate Studies, 541-737-3825, Fax: 541-737-4230, E-mail: marie.harvey@oregonstate.edu. *Dean and Professor,* Dr. Tammy Bray.

College of Science Students: 396 full-time (149 women), 14 part-time (3 women); includes 57 minority (4 Black or African American, non-Hispanic/Latino; 1 American Indian or Alaska Native, non-Hispanic/Latino; 25 Asian, non-Hispanic/Latino; 12 Hispanic/Latino; 1 Native Hawaiian or other Pacific Islander, non-Hispanic/Latino; 14 Two or more races, non-Hispanic/Latino), 109 international. Average age 28. *Faculty:* 128 full-time (44 women), 12 part-time/adjunct (4 women). In 2015, 45 master's, 34 doctorates awarded. *Degree program information:* Part-time programs available. Part-time. Offers actuarial science (MA, MS, PhD); algebra (MA, MS, PhD); analysis (MA, MS, PhD); analytical chemistry (MA, MS, PhD); applied mathematics (MA, MS, PhD); atomic physics (MA, MS, PhD); behavioral ecology (MA, MS, PhD); behavioral endocrinology (MA, MS, PhD); biochemistry (MA, MS, PhD); biophysics (MA, MS, PhD); cell biology (MA, MS, PhD); chemical ecology (MA, MS, PhD); computational mathematics (MA, MS, PhD); computational physics (MA, MS, PhD); conservation biology (MA, MS, PhD); developmental biology (MA, MS, PhD); differential equations (MA, MS, PhD); environmental microbiology (MA, MS, PhD); financial mathematics (MA, MS, PhD); food microbiology (MA, MS, PhD); genomics (MA, MS, PhD); geometry (MA, MS, PhD); immunology (MA, MS, PhD); inorganic chemistry (MA, MS, PhD); materials chemistry (MA, MS, PhD); mathematics education (MA); microbial ecology (MA, MS, PhD); microbial evolution (MA, MS, PhD); nuclear chemistry (MA, MS, PhD); nuclear physics (MA, MS, PhD); optical physics (MA, MS, PhD); organic chemistry (MA, MS, PhD); parasitology (MA, MS, PhD); particle physics (MA, MS, PhD); pathogenic microbiology (MA, MS, PhD); physical chemistry (MA, MS, PhD); physics education (MA, MS, PhD); relativity (MA, MS, PhD); science (MA, MS, PhD); solid state physics (MA, MS, PhD); statistics (MA, MS, PhD); virology (MA). *Application fee:* $75 ($85 for international students). *Dean,* Dr. Sastry Pantula.

College of Veterinary Medicine Students: 227 full-time (191 women), 3 part-time (all women); includes 26 minority (1 American Indian or Alaska Native, non-Hispanic/Latino; 8 Asian, non-Hispanic/Latino; 11 Hispanic/Latino; 6 Two or more races, non-Hispanic/Latino), 3 international. Average age 27. *Faculty:* 41 full-time (18 women), 3 part-time/adjunct (2 women). *Financial support:* Fellowships and research assistantships available. In 2015, 57 doctorates awarded. Offers veterinary medicine (DVM). DVM admissions open only to residents of Oregon and other states participating in the Western Interstate Commission for Higher Education. *Application deadline:* For fall admission, 9/15 for domestic students. *Application Contact:* Admissions, 541-737-2098, E-mail: cvmproginfo@oregonstate.edu. *Dean,* Dr. Susan J. Tornquist.

Interdisciplinary/Institutional Programs Students: 154 full-time (86 women), 36 part-time (19 women); includes 36 minority (3 Black or African American, non-Hispanic/Latino; 3 American Indian or Alaska Native, non-Hispanic/Latino; 9 Asian, non-Hispanic/Latino; 15 Hispanic/Latino; 1 Native Hawaiian or other Pacific Islander, non-Hispanic/Latino; 5 Two or more races, non-Hispanic/Latino), 28 international. Average age 31. In 2015, 40 master's, 10 doctorates awarded. *Degree program information:* Part-time programs available. Part-time. Offers biogeochemistry (MS, PhD); bioinformatics (PhD); biomedical sciences (MS, PhD); biotechnology (PhD); cell biology (PhD); clinical sciences (MS, PhD); developmental biology (PhD); ecology (MS, PhD); environmental education (MS, PhD); environmental sciences (PSM); genome biology (PhD); groundwater engineering (MS, PhD); interdisciplinary studies (MAIS); molecular biology (PhD); molecular pathogenesis (PhD); molecular virology (PhD); natural resources (MS, PhD); plant molecular biology (PhD); quantitative analysis (MS, PhD); social science (MS, PhD); structural biology (PhD); surface water engineering (MS, PhD); water resources (MS, PhD); water resources policy and management (MS); water resources science (MS, PhD); watershed engineering (MS, PhD). *Application fee:* $75 ($85 for international students). *Dean,* Dr. Brenda McComb.

OREGON STATE UNIVERSITY–CASCADES, Bend, OR 97701

General Information State-supported, coed, comprehensive institution.

GRADUATE UNITS

Program in Counseling Offers community counseling (MS); school counseling (MS).

Program in Education Offers education (MAT).

OTIS COLLEGE OF ART AND DESIGN, Los Angeles, CA 90045-9785

General Information Independent, coed, comprehensive institution. *Graduate housing:* On-campus housing not available.

GRADUATE UNITS

Program in Fine Arts Offers new genres (MFA); painting (MFA); photography (MFA); sculpture (MFA). Electronic applications accepted.

Program in Graphic Design Offers graphic design (MFA). Electronic applications accepted.

Program in Public Practice Offers public practice (MFA). Electronic applications accepted.

Program in Writing Offers writing (MFA). Electronic applications accepted.

OTTAWA UNIVERSITY, Ottawa, KS 66067-3399

General Information Independent-religious, coed, comprehensive institution. *Graduate housing:* On-campus housing not available.

GRADUATE UNITS

Graduate Studies-Arizona *Degree program information:* Part-time and evening/weekend programs available. Part-time, evening/weekend, online learning. Offers business administration (MBA); Christian counseling (MA); community college counseling (MA); curriculum and instruction (MA); early childhood (MA); education intervention (MA); education leadership (MA); education technology (MA); expressive arts therapy (MA); finance (MBA); human resources (MA, MBA); leadership (MBA); marketing (MBA); marriage and family therapy (MA); Montessori early childhood education (MA); Montessori elementary education (MA); professional development (MA); school guidance counseling (MA); special education - cross categorical (MA); treatment of trauma, abuse and deprivation (MA). Electronic applications accepted.

Graduate Studies-International Online learning. Offers business administration (MBA). Electronic applications accepted.

Graduate Studies-Kansas City *Degree program information:* Part-time and evening/weekend programs available. Part-time, evening/weekend, online learning. Offers business administration (MBA); human resources (MA). Electronic applications accepted.

Graduate Studies-Wisconsin *Degree program information:* Part-time and evening/weekend programs available. Part-time, evening/weekend, online learning. Offers business administration (MBA). Electronic applications accepted.

OTTERBEIN UNIVERSITY, Westerville, OH 43081

General Information Independent-religious, coed, comprehensive institution. CGS member. *Graduate housing:* On-campus housing not available.

GRADUATE UNITS

Department of Business, Accounting and Economics ***Degree program information:*** Part-time and evening/weekend programs available. Part-time, evening/weekend. Offers business, accounting and economics (MBA).

Department of Education Offers education (MAE, MAT).

Department of Nursing ***Degree program information:*** Part-time and evening/weekend programs available. Part-time, evening/weekend, online learning. Offers advanced practice nurse educator (Certificate); clinical nurse leader (MSN); family nurse practitioner (MSN, Certificate); nurse anesthesia (MSN, Certificate); nursing (DNP); nursing service administration (MSN).

OUR LADY OF THE LAKE COLLEGE, Baton Rouge, LA 70808

General Information Independent-religious, coed, comprehensive institution. *Graduate housing:* On-campus housing not available.

GRADUATE UNITS

School of Arts, Sciences and Health Professions Offers health administration (MHA); physician assistant studies (MMS).

School of Nursing Offers administration (MS); education (MS); nurse anesthesia (MS); nursing (MS).

OUR LADY OF THE LAKE UNIVERSITY OF SAN ANTONIO, San Antonio, TX 78207-4689

General Information Independent-religious, coed, comprehensive institution. *Enrollment:* 3,334 graduate, professional, and undergraduate students; 1,657 full-time matriculated graduate/professional students (1,302 women), 116 part-time matriculated graduate/professional students (88 women). *Enrollment by degree level:* 1,447 master's, 325 doctoral, 1 other advanced degree. *Graduate faculty:* 53 full-time (39 women), 95 part-time/adjunct (55 women). *Tuition, area resident:* Full-time $14,796; part-time $822 per credit hour. *Required fees:* $232 per semester. Tuition and fees vary according to course load, degree level, campus/location and program. *Graduate housing:* Room and/or apartments available on a first-come, first-served basis to single students; on-campus housing not available to married students. Typical cost: $4200 per year ($7556 including board). Room and board charges vary according to housing facility selected. Housing application deadline: 7/15. *Student services:* Campus employment opportunities, campus safety program, career counseling, exercise/wellness program, free psychological counseling, international student services, low-cost health insurance, services for students with disabilities, teacher training. *Library:* The Sueltenfuss Library. *Collection:* Books: 71,610 (physical), 51,161 (digital/electronic); Serial titles: 416 (physical), 60,823 (digital/electronic); Databases: 53. Weekly public service hours: 95; study areas open 24 hours, 5–7 days a week. *Research affiliation:* Texas Higher Education Coordinating Board: Teacher Quality (education), Texas Regional Collaborative (education).

Computer facilities: 230 computers available on campus for general student use. A campuswide network can be accessed from student residence rooms and from off campus. Online class registration is available.
Website: http://www.ollusa.edu/

General Application Contact: Graduate Admissions Office, 210-431-3995, Fax: 210-431-3945, E-mail: gradadm@ollusa.edu.

GRADUATE UNITS

College of Arts and Sciences Students: 12 full-time (9 women), 4 part-time (3 women); includes 12 minority (1 Black or African American, non-Hispanic/Latino; 11 Hispanic/Latino). Average age 34. 7 applicants, 86% accepted, 3 enrolled. *Faculty:* 5 full-time (3 women), 1 (woman) part-time/adjunct. *Financial support:* In 2015–16, 6 students received support. Federal Work-Study, scholarships/grants, unspecified assistantships, and tuition discounts available. Support available to part-time students. Financial award application deadline: 5/1; financial award applicants required to submit FAFSA. In 2015, 3 master's awarded. *Degree program information:* Part-time and evening/weekend programs available. Part-time, evening/weekend. Offers arts and sciences (MA); literature, creative writing, and social justice (MA). *Application deadline:* For fall admission, 4/15 for domestic and international students; for spring admission, 11/15 for domestic and international students; for summer admission, 2/15 for domestic and international students. *Application fee:* $40 ($50 for international students). Electronic applications accepted. *Application Contact:* Graduate Admission, 210-431-3995, Fax: 210-431-3945, E-mail: gradadm@lake.ollusa.edu. *Dean for the College of Arts and Science*, Dr. Michael Laney, 210-431-4170, E-mail: mjlaney@lake.ollusa.edu.

School of Business and Leadership Students: 634 full-time (392 women), 56 part-time (33 women); includes 507 minority (81 Black or African American, non-Hispanic/Latino; 1 American Indian or Alaska Native, non-Hispanic/Latino; 11 Asian, non-Hispanic/Latino; 406 Hispanic/Latino; 2 Native Hawaiian or other Pacific Islander, non-Hispanic/Latino; 6 Two or more races, non-Hispanic/Latino), 2 international. Average age 39. 253 applicants, 84% accepted, 153 enrolled. *Faculty:* 16 full-time (9 women), 37 part-time/adjunct (12 women). *Financial support:* In 2015–16, 103 students received support. Federal Work-Study, scholarships/grants, unspecified assistantships, and tuition discounts available. Support available to part-time students. Financial award application deadline: 5/1; financial award applicants required to submit FAFSA. In 2015, 150 master's, 18 doctorates awarded. *Degree program information:* Part-time and evening/weekend programs available. Part-time, evening/weekend, 100% online, blended/hybrid learning. Offers accounting (MS); finance (MBA); healthcare management (MBA); information systems and security (MS); leadership studies (PhD); management (MBA); nonprofit management (MS); organizational leadership (MS). *Application fee:* $40 ($50 for international students). Electronic applications accepted. *Application Contact:* Graduate Admission, 210-431-3995, Fax: 210-431-3945, E-mail: gradadm@ollusa.edu. *Dean for the School of Business and Leadership*, Dr. Dwayne Banks, 210-434-6711 Ext. 5561, E-mail: sbdean@ollusa.edu.

School of Professional Studies Students: 1,010 full-time (900 women), 80 part-time (72 women); includes 659 minority (242 Black or African American, non-Hispanic/Latino; 5 American Indian or Alaska Native, non-Hispanic/Latino; 8 Asian, non-Hispanic/Latino; 394 Hispanic/Latino; 2 Native Hawaiian or other Pacific Islander, non-Hispanic/Latino; 8 Two or more races, non-Hispanic/Latino), 1 international. Average age 34. 688 applicants, 63% accepted, 279 enrolled. *Faculty:* 34 full-time (28 women), 58 part-time/adjunct (42 women). *Financial support:* In 2015–16, 100 students received support, including 14 research assistantships (averaging $2,250 per year), 5 teaching assistantships (averaging $2,250 per year); Federal Work-Study, scholarships/grants, unspecified assistantships, and tuition discounts also available. Support available to part-time students. Financial award application deadline: 5/1; financial award applicants required to submit FAFSA. In 2015, 241 master's, 7 doctorates awarded. *Degree program information:* Part-time and evening/weekend programs available. Part-time, evening/weekend, 100% online, blended/hybrid learning. Offers communication and learning disorders (MA); community health (MA); counseling psychology (Psy D); curriculum and instruction (M Ed); family, couple, and individual psychotherapy (MS); integrated science teaching (M Ed); psychology (MS); school counseling (M Ed); school psychology (MS); social work (MSW); sociology (MA). *Application deadline:* For fall admission, 4/15 for domestic and international students; for spring admission, 11/15 for domestic and international students; for summer admission, 2/15 for domestic and international students. *Application fee:* $40 ($50 for international students). Electronic applications accepted. *Application Contact:* Graduate Admission, 210-431-3995 Ext. 2314, Fax: 210-431-3945, E-mail: gradadm@lake.ollusa.edu. *Dean*, Dr. Marcheta Evans, 210-431-4140, E-mail: sps@ollusa.edu.

Worden School of Social Service Students: 761 full-time (674 women), 34 part-time (32 women); includes 459 minority (218 Black or African American, non-Hispanic/Latino; 5 American Indian or Alaska Native, non-Hispanic/Latino; 5 Asian, non-Hispanic/Latino; 222 Hispanic/Latino; 2 Native Hawaiian or other Pacific Islander, non-Hispanic/Latino; 7 Two or more races, non-Hispanic/Latino). Average age 35. 299 applicants, 95% accepted, 149 enrolled. *Faculty:* 9 full-time (all women), 45 part-time/adjunct (34 women). *Financial support:* In 2015–16, 16 students received support, including 6 research assistantships (averaging $2,250 per year), 1 teaching assistantship (averaging $2,250 per year); Federal Work-Study, scholarships/grants, unspecified assistantships, and tuition discounts also available. Support available to part-time students. Financial award application deadline: 5/1; financial award applicants required to submit FAFSA. In 2015, 126 master's awarded. *Degree program information:* Part-time and evening/weekend programs available. Part-time, evening/weekend, 100% online, blended/hybrid learning. Offers social work (MSW). *Application deadline:* For fall admission, 7/15 for domestic and international students; for spring admission, 11/15 for domestic and international students; for summer admission, 4/15 for domestic and international students. Applications are processed on a rolling basis. *Application fee:* $40 ($50 for international students). Electronic applications accepted. *Application Contact:* Office of Graduate Admissions, 210-431-3995, Fax: 210-431-3945, E-mail: gradadm@lake.ollusa.edu. *Program Director*, Rebecca Gomez, 210-434-6711 Ext. 5578, E-mail: rjgomez@ollusa.edu.

OXFORD GRADUATE SCHOOL, Dayton, TN 37321-6736

General Information Independent-religious, coed, graduate-only institution. *Graduate housing:* Rooms and/or apartments guaranteed to single students and available to married students.

GRADUATE UNITS

Graduate Programs Offers family life education (M Litt); organizational leadership (M Litt); sociological integration of religion and society (D Phil).

PACE UNIVERSITY, New York, NY 10038

General Information Independent, coed, university. *Enrollment:* 8,724 graduate, professional, and undergraduate students; 2,141 full-time matriculated graduate/professional students (1,248 women), 1,924 part-time matriculated graduate/professional students (1,216 women). *Enrollment by degree level:* 3,147 master's, 885 doctoral, 33 other advanced degrees. *Tuition, area resident:* Part-time $1195 per credit. *Required fees:* $260 per semester. Tuition and fees vary according to degree level, campus/location and program. *Graduate housing:* Room and/or apartments available on a first-come, first-served basis to single students; on-campus housing not available to married students. *Student services:* Campus employment opportunities, career counseling, free psychological counseling, grant writing training, international student services, low-cost health insurance, multicultural affairs office, services for students with disabilities, teacher training, writing training. *Library:* Henry Birnbaum Library. *Collection:* Books: 406,016 (physical), 34,307 (digital/electronic); Serial titles: 75 (physical), 143,640 (digital/electronic); Databases: 208. Weekly public service hours: 93; students can reserve study rooms.

Computer facilities: 164 computers available on campus for general student use. A campuswide network can be accessed from student residence rooms and from off campus. Online class registration, administrative functions - pay tuition, view student records, update personal information, view financial aid and complete health insurance waiver are available.
Website: http://www.pace.edu/nyc

General Application Contact: Susan Ford-Goldschein, Director of Graduate Admissions, 212-346-1531, Fax: 212-346-1585, E-mail: graduateadmission@pace.edu.

GRADUATE UNITS

College of Health Professions Students: 153 full-time (119 women), 460 part-time (417 women); includes 256 minority (104 Black or African American, non-Hispanic/Latino; 10 American Indian or Alaska Native, non-Hispanic/Latino; 84 Asian, non-Hispanic/Latino; 42 Hispanic/Latino; 16 Two or more races, non-Hispanic/Latino), 2 international. Average age 33. 1,277 applicants, 28% accepted, 202 enrolled. *Faculty:* 22 full-time (20 women), 31 part-time/adjunct (27 women). *Financial support:* Teaching assistantships, scholarships/grants, and unspecified assistantships available. Financial award application deadline: 2/15; financial award applicants required to submit FAFSA. In 2015, 248 master's, 20 doctorates awarded. *Degree program information:* Part-time programs available. Part-time, 100% online, blended/hybrid learning. Offers health professions (MS, DNP, Advanced Certificate); physician assistant studies (MS). *Application deadline:* For fall admission, 3/1 for domestic students; for spring admission, 12/1 for domestic students. *Application fee:* $70. Electronic applications accepted. *Application Contact:* Susan Ford-Goldschein, Dean of Graduate Admissions, 212-346-1531, Fax: 212-346-1585, E-mail: graduateadmission@pace.edu. *Dean, College of Health Professions*, Dr. Harriet R. Feldman, 914-773-3341, Fax: 914-773-3341, E-mail: hfeldman@pace.edu.

Lienhard School of Nursing Students: 3 full-time (all women), 415 part-time (385 women); includes 196 minority (97 Black or African American, non-Hispanic/Latino; 2 American Indian or Alaska Native, non-Hispanic/Latino; 57 Asian, non-Hispanic/Latino; 33 Hispanic/Latino; 7 Two or more races, non-Hispanic/Latino), 2 international. Average age 34. 291 applicants, 69% accepted, 129 enrolled. *Faculty:* 11 full-time (10 women), 31 part-time/adjunct (27 women). *Financial support:* Research assistantships, teaching assistantships, career-related internships or fieldwork, Federal Work-Study, tuition waivers (partial), and unspecified assistantships available. Support available to part-time students. Financial award application deadline: 2/15; financial award applicants required to submit FAFSA. In 2015, 129 master's, 20 doctorates, 7 other advanced degrees awarded. *Degree program information:* Part-time and evening/weekend programs available. Part-time, evening/weekend, blended/hybrid learning. Offers family nurse practitioner (MS); nurse education (Advanced Certificate); nursing education (MS); nursing leadership (Advanced Certificate); nursing practice (DNP). *Application deadline:* For fall admission, 3/1 for domestic and international students. Applications are processed on a rolling basis. *Application fee:* $70. Electronic applications accepted. *Application Contact:* Susan Ford-Goldschein, Director of Graduate Admissions, 212-346-1531,

Fax: 212-346-1585, E-mail: graduateadmission@pace.edu. *Dean, College of Health Professions*, Dr. Harriet R. Feldman, 914-773-3341, E-mail: hfeldman@pace.edu.

Dyson College of Arts and Sciences Students: 450 full-time (337 women), 274 part-time (196 women); includes 270 minority (109 Black or African American, non-Hispanic/Latino; 1 American Indian or Alaska Native, non-Hispanic/Latino; 37 Asian, non-Hispanic/Latino; 99 Hispanic/Latino; 1 Native Hawaiian or other Pacific Islander, non-Hispanic/Latino; 23 Two or more races, non-Hispanic/Latino), 85 international. Average age 28. 725 applicants, 63% accepted, 226 enrolled. *Financial support:* In 2015–16, 34 research assistantships with partial tuition reimbursements (averaging $2,918 per year) were awarded; teaching assistantships, career-related internships or fieldwork, Federal Work-Study, scholarships/grants, and tuition waivers (partial) also available. Support available to part-time students. Financial award application deadline: 2/15; financial award applicants required to submit FAFSA. In 2015, 268 master's, 23 doctorates, 4 other advanced degrees awarded. *Degree program information:* Part-time and evening/weekend programs available. Part-time, evening/weekend, 100% online, blended/hybrid learning. Offers acting (MFA); arts and sciences (MA, MFA, MPA, MS, MS Ed, PhD, Psy D, Certificate); biochemistry and molecular biology (MS); book publishing (Certificate); business side of publishing (Certificate); digital publishing (Certificate); directing (MFA); environmental science (MS); forensic science (MS); government management (MPA); grief and loss (MPA); health care administration (MPA); magazine publishing (Certificate); management for public safety and homeland security (MA); management for public safety and homeland security professionals (MA); media and communication arts (MA); mental health counseling (MS, PhD); not-for-profit management (MPA); playwriting (MFA); psychology (MA); publishing (MS); school psychology (MS Ed); school-clinical child psychology (MS Ed, Psy D); substance abuse (MS). *Application deadline:* For fall admission, 8/1 for domestic students, 6/1 for international students; for spring admission, 12/1 for domestic students, 10/1 for international students. Applications are processed on a rolling basis. *Application fee:* $70. Electronic applications accepted. *Application Contact:* Susan Ford-Goldschein, Director of Admissions, 212-346-1531, Fax: 212-346-1585, E-mail: graduateadmission@pace.edu. *Dean*, Dr. Nira Herrmann, 212-346-1517, Fax: 212-346-1725, E-mail: nherrmann@pace.edu.

Lubin School of Business Students: 554 full-time (298 women), 430 part-time (199 women); includes 233 minority (62 Black or African American, non-Hispanic/Latino; 110 Asian, non-Hispanic/Latino; 48 Hispanic/Latino; 13 Two or more races, non-Hispanic/Latino), 468 international. Average age 29. 1,148 applicants, 64% accepted, 300 enrolled. *Financial support:* Research assistantships, career-related internships or fieldwork, Federal Work-Study, and tuition waivers (full and partial) available. Support available to part-time students. Financial award application deadline: 2/15; financial award applicants required to submit FAFSA. In 2015, 471 master's, 10 doctorates awarded. *Degree program information:* Part-time and evening/weekend programs available. Part-time, evening/weekend, blended/hybrid learning. Offers business (MBA, MS, DPS, APC); business economics (APC); e-business (APC); entrepreneurship (MBA); executive management (MBA); finance (DPS); financial management (MBA, APC); human resource management (MBA, MS); information systems (MBA); international business (MBA, APC); international economics (APC); investment management (MBA, MS, APC); management (DPS); marketing (DPS, APC); marketing management (MBA); public accounting (MBA, MS, APC); social media and mobile marketing (MS); strategic management (MBA); taxation (MBA, MS). *Application deadline:* For fall admission, 8/1 priority date for domestic students, 6/1 for international students; for spring admission, 12/1 priority date for domestic students, 10/1 for international students; for summer admission, 5/1 priority date for domestic students, 3/1 for international students. Applications are processed on a rolling basis. *Application fee:* $70. Electronic applications accepted. *Application Contact:* Susan Ford-Goldschein, Director of Graduate Admissions, 212-346-1531, Fax: 212-346-1585, E-mail: graduateadmission@pace.edu. *Dean, Lubin School of Business*, Neil S. Braun, 212-618-6600, Fax: 212-618-6603, E-mail: nbraun@pace.edu.

Pace Law School *Degree program information:* Part-time programs available. Part-time. Offers comparative legal studies (LL M); environmental law (LL M, SJD); law (JD). JD/MA offered jointly with Sarah Lawrence College; JD/MEM offered jointly with Yale University School of Forestry and Environmental Studies. Electronic applications accepted.

School of Education Students: 112 full-time (95 women), 432 part-time (306 women); includes 179 minority (89 Black or African American, non-Hispanic/Latino; 1 American Indian or Alaska Native, non-Hispanic/Latino; 24 Asian, non-Hispanic/Latino; 55 Hispanic/Latino; 10 Two or more races, non-Hispanic/Latino), 9 international. Average age 30. 181 applicants, 78% accepted, 72 enrolled. *Faculty:* 19 full-time (13 women), 86 part-time/adjunct (49 women). *Financial support:* In 2015–16, 17 students received support, including 17 research assistantships with partial tuition reimbursements available (averaging $6,020 per year); career-related internships or fieldwork and Federal Work-Study also available. Financial award application deadline: 2/15; financial award applicants required to submit FAFSA. In 2015, 261 master's, 11 other advanced degrees awarded. *Degree program information:* Part-time and evening/weekend programs available. Part-time, evening/weekend. Offers adolescent education (MST); childhood education (MST); early childhood development, learning and intervention (MST); educational technology studies (MS); inclusive adolescent education (MST); integrated instruction for educational technology (Certificate); integrated instruction for literacy and technology (Certificate); literacy (MS Ed); special education (MS Ed). *Application deadline:* For fall admission, 8/1 priority date for domestic students, 6/1 for international students; for spring admission, 12/1 priority date for domestic students, 10/1 for international students. Applications are processed on a rolling basis. *Application fee:* $70. Electronic applications accepted. *Application Contact:* Susan Ford-Goldschein, Director of Graduate Admissions, 212-346-1531, Fax: 212-346-1585, E-mail: graduateadmission@pace.edu. *Dean, School of Education*, Dr. Xiao-Lei Wang, 914-773-3876, E-mail: xwang@pace.edu.

Seidenberg School of Computer Science and Information Systems Students: 341 full-time (103 women), 297 part-time (79 women); includes 189 minority (72 Black or African American, non-Hispanic/Latino; 4 American Indian or Alaska Native, non-Hispanic/Latino; 60 Asian, non-Hispanic/Latino; 49 Hispanic/Latino; 4 Two or more races, non-Hispanic/Latino), 269 international. Average age 32. 599 applicants, 89% accepted, 248 enrolled. *Faculty:* 26 full-time (7 women), 7 part-time/adjunct (2 women). *Financial support:* In 2015–16, 45 students received support. Research assistantships, career-related internships or fieldwork, scholarships/grants, and unspecified assistantships available. Support available to part-time students. Financial award application deadline: 2/15; financial award applicants required to submit FAFSA. In 2015, 130 master's, 12 doctorates, 13 other advanced degrees awarded. *Degree program information:* Part-time and evening/weekend programs available. Part-time, evening/weekend, online only, 100% online, blended/hybrid learning. Offers computer science (MS); computing science (DPS); information systems (MS); Internet technology (MS); security and information assurance (Certificate); software development and engineering (MS, Certificate); telecommunications (Certificate); telecommunications systems and networks (MS). *Application deadline:* For fall admission, 8/1 priority date for domestic students, 6/1 for international students; for spring admission, 12/1 for domestic students, 10/1 for international students. Applications are processed on a rolling basis. *Application fee:* $70. Electronic applications accepted. *Application Contact:* Susan Ford-Goldschein, Director of Graduate Admissions, 914-422-4283, Fax: 212-346-1585, E-mail: graduateadmission@pace.edu. *Dean, Seidenberg School of Computer Science and Information Systems*, Dr. Jonathan Hill, 212-346-1864, E-mail: jhill@pace.edu.

PACIFICA GRADUATE INSTITUTE, Carpinteria, CA 93013

General Information Proprietary, coed, graduate-only institution. *Graduate housing:* Rooms and/or apartments guaranteed to single and married students. Housing application deadline: 8/15. *Research affiliation:* Elton B. Stevens Company (EBSCO) (journal management), American Psychological Association (psychology), North California Consortium of Psychology Libraries (psychology).

GRADUATE UNITS

Graduate Programs Offers clinical psychology (PhD); counseling psychology (MA); depth psychology (MA, PhD); mythological studies (MA, PhD).

PACIFIC COLLEGE OF ORIENTAL MEDICINE, San Diego, CA 92108

General Information Proprietary, coed, graduate-only institution. *Graduate housing:* On-campus housing not available. *Research affiliation:* National Institutes of Health (complimentary and alternative medicine).

GRADUATE UNITS

Graduate Program ***Degree program information:*** Part-time and evening/weekend programs available. Part-time, evening/weekend. Offers Oriental medicine (MSTOM, DAOM).

PACIFIC COLLEGE OF ORIENTAL MEDICINE–CHICAGO, Chicago, IL 60601

General Information Proprietary, coed, graduate-only institution. *Graduate housing:* On-campus housing not available. *Research affiliation:* Children's Memorial Hospital of Chicago (pediatric research).

GRADUATE UNITS

Graduate Program ***Degree program information:*** Part-time and evening/weekend programs available. Part-time, evening/weekend. Offers oriental medicine (MTOM).

PACIFIC COLLEGE OF ORIENTAL MEDICINE-NEW YORK, New York, NY 10010

General Information Proprietary, coed, graduate-only institution. *Graduate housing:* On-campus housing not available.

GRADUATE UNITS

Graduate Program ***Degree program information:*** Part-time and evening/weekend programs available. Part-time, evening/weekend. Offers Oriental medicine (MSTOM).

PACIFIC LUTHERAN UNIVERSITY, Tacoma, WA 98447

General Information Independent-religious, coed, comprehensive institution. *Enrollment:* 3,275 graduate, professional, and undergraduate students; 186 full-time matriculated graduate/professional students (123 women), 124 part-time matriculated graduate/professional students (81 women). *Enrollment by degree level:* 295 master's, 15 doctoral. *Graduate faculty:* 38 full-time (19 women), 32 part-time/adjunct (13 women). *Tuition, area resident:* Part-time $940 per credit. Tuition and fees vary according to program. *Graduate housing:* Rooms and/or apartments available on a first-come, first-served basis to single and married students. Typical cost: $4870 per year ($10,330 including board) for single students; $7240 per year ($12,170 including board) for married students. Room and board charges vary according to board plan and housing facility selected. Housing application deadline: 5/1. *Student services:* Campus employment opportunities, campus safety program, career counseling, exercise/wellness program, free psychological counseling, grant writing training, international student services, low-cost health insurance, multicultural affairs office, services for students with disabilities, teacher training, writing training. *Library:* Robert A. L. Mortvedt Library.

Computer facilities: 735 computers available on campus for general student use. A campuswide network can be accessed from student residence rooms and from off campus. Online class registration is available. Website: http://www.plu.edu/

General Application Contact: Marie Boisvert, Director of Graduate Admissions, 253-535-8570, Fax: 253-536-5136, E-mail: gradadmission@plu.edu.

GRADUATE UNITS

Division of Humanities Students: 43 part-time (33 women); includes 3 minority (1 Asian, non-Hispanic/Latino; 2 Hispanic/Latino). Average age 44. 31 applicants, 71% accepted, 13 enrolled. *Faculty:* 2 full-time (1 woman). *Financial support:* In 2015–16, 25 students received support, including 6 fellowships (averaging $1,667 per year); scholarships/grants, health care benefits, and unspecified assistantships also available. Support available to part-time students. Financial award application deadline: 3/1; financial award applicants required to submit FAFSA. In 2015, 19 master's awarded. *Degree program information:* Part-time programs available. Part-time, blended/hybrid learning. Offers creative writing (MFA). *Application deadline:* For fall admission, 11/30 for domestic and international students; for summer admission, 2/15 for domestic and international students. Applications are processed on a rolling basis. *Application fee:* $55. Electronic applications accepted. *Application Contact:* Rick Barot, Director of MFA in Creative Writing Program, 253-535-7318, E-mail: mfa@plu.edu. *Dean*, Dr. James Albrecht, 253-535-7698, Fax: 253-535-7321, E-mail: albrecjm@plu.edu.

Division of Social Sciences Students: 40 full-time (35 women), 12 part-time (10 women); includes 15 minority (5 Black or African American, non-Hispanic/Latino; 1 American Indian or Alaska Native, non-Hispanic/Latino; 3 Asian, non-Hispanic/Latino; 4 Hispanic/Latino; 2 Two or more races, non-Hispanic/Latino), 2 international. Average age 30. 71 applicants, 48% accepted, 23 enrolled. *Faculty:* 6 full-time (3 women), 10 part-time/adjunct (7 women). *Financial support:* In 2015–16, 54 students received support, including 13 fellowships (averaging $2,044 per year); career-related internships or fieldwork, Federal Work-Study, scholarships/grants, health care benefits, and unspecified assistantships also available. Support available to part-time students. Financial award application deadline: 3/1; financial award applicants required to submit FAFSA. In 2015, 14 master's awarded. Offers marriage and family therapy (MA). *Application deadline:* For fall admission, 1/31 priority date for domestic and international students. *Application fee:* $55. Electronic applications accepted. *Application Contact:* Marie Boisvert, Director of Graduate Admission, 253-535-8570, Fax: 253-536-5136, E-mail: admissions@plu.edu. *Associate Professor and Program Director*, Dr. David Ward, 253-535-7196.

School of Business Students: 24 full-time (10 women), 19 part-time (6 women); includes 6 minority (1 Black or African American, non-Hispanic/Latino; 3 Hispanic/Latino; 2 Two or more races, non-Hispanic/Latino), 5 international. Average age 33. 41 applicants, 71% accepted, 20 enrolled. *Faculty:* 9 full-time (3 women), 4 part-time/adjunct (2 women). *Financial support:* In 2015–16, 18 students received support, including 8 fellowships (averaging $3,575 per year); career-related internships or fieldwork, Federal Work-Study, scholarships/grants, health care benefits, and unspecified assistantships also available. Support available to part-time students. Financial award application deadline: 3/1. In 2015, 28 master's awarded. *Degree program information:* Part-time and evening/weekend programs available. Part-time, evening/weekend. Offers accounting (MSA); business (MBA, MS, MSA, MSF); business administration (MBA); finance (MSF). *Application deadline:* Applications are processed on a rolling basis. *Application fee:* $40. Electronic applications accepted. *Application Contact:* Juanita Reed, Director, MBA Program, 253-535-7252, Fax: 253-535-8723, E-mail: plumba@plu.edu. *Dean, School of Business,* Dr. Nancy Albers-Miller, 253-535-7251, Fax: 253-535-8723, E-mail: plumba@plu.edu.

School of Education and Kinesiology Students: 33 full-time (22 women), 28 part-time (17 women); includes 9 minority (5 Asian, non-Hispanic/Latino; 3 Hispanic/Latino; 1 Native Hawaiian or other Pacific Islander, non-Hispanic/Latino). Average age 33. 134 applicants, 60% accepted, 55 enrolled. *Faculty:* 11 full-time (5 women), 10 part-time/adjunct (3 women). *Financial support:* In 2015–16, 66 students received support, including 10 fellowships (averaging $3,000 per year); Federal Work-Study, scholarships/grants, health care benefits, and unspecified assistantships also available. Support available to part-time students. Financial award application deadline: 3/1; financial award applicants required to submit FAFSA. In 2015, 59 master's awarded. *Degree program information:* Part-time and evening/weekend programs available. Part-time, evening/weekend. Offers education and kinesiology (MAE); initial teaching certification (MAE). *Application deadline:* For fall admission, 11/20 priority date for domestic and international students; for winter admission, 1/15 priority date for domestic and international students; for spring admission, 3/7 priority date for domestic and international students. Applications are processed on a rolling basis. *Application fee:* $55. Electronic applications accepted. *Application Contact:* Marie Boisvert, Director of Graduate Admission, 253-535-8570, Fax: 253-536-5136, E-mail: gradadmission@plu.edu. *Dean,* Dr. Frank Kline, 253-535-7272, E-mail: klinefm@plu.edu.

School of Nursing Students: 49 full-time (39 women), 15 part-time (13 women); includes 20 minority (3 Black or African American, non-Hispanic/Latino; 2 American Indian or Alaska Native, non-Hispanic/Latino; 6 Asian, non-Hispanic/Latino; 5 Hispanic/Latino; 4 Two or more races, non-Hispanic/Latino), 1 international. Average age 34. 124 applicants, 35% accepted, 31 enrolled. *Faculty:* 6 full-time (5 women), 7 part-time/adjunct (all women). *Financial support:* In 2015–16, 60 students received support, including 14 fellowships (averaging $643 per year); Federal Work-Study, scholarships/grants, and health care benefits also available. Financial award application deadline: 3/1; financial award applicants required to submit FAFSA. In 2015, 23 master's awarded. Offers entry level nursing (MSN); nursing (MSN, DNP). *Application deadline:* For fall admission, 11/15 priority date for domestic and international students. Applications are processed on a rolling basis. *Application fee:* $55. Electronic applications accepted. *Application Contact:* Marie Boisvert, Director, Graduate Admission, 253-535-8570, Fax: 253-536-5136, E-mail: gradadmission@plu.edu. *Associate Dean of Graduate Nursing Programs/Associate Professor of Nursing,* Dr. Teri Woo, 253-535-7686, Fax: 253-535-7590, E-mail: gradnurs@plu.edu.

PACIFIC NORTHWEST COLLEGE OF ART, Portland, OR 97209

General Information Independent, coed, comprehensive institution.

GRADUATE UNITS

Program in Applied Craft and Design Offers applied craft and design (MFA). Program offered in collaboration with Oregon College of Art & Craft.

Program in Collaborative Design Offers collaborative design (MFA).

Program in Critical Theory and Creative Research Offers critical theory and creative research (MA).

Program in Visual Studies Offers visual studies (MFA).

PACIFIC OAKS COLLEGE, Pasadena, CA 91103

General Information Independent, coed, primarily women, upper-level institution. *Graduate housing:* Room and/or apartments available to single students; on-campus housing not available to married students.

GRADUATE UNITS

Graduate School *Degree program information:* Part-time and evening/weekend programs available. Part-time, evening/weekend, online learning. Offers early childhood education (MA); human development (MA); marriage, family and child counseling (MA); preliminary education specialist (MA); preliminary multiple subject (MA).

PACIFIC RIM CHRISTIAN UNIVERSITY, Honolulu, HI 96819

General Information Independent-religious, coed, comprehensive institution.

GRADUATE UNITS

Program in Christian Ministry Offers Christian ministry (MA).

PACIFIC SCHOOL OF RELIGION, Berkeley, CA 94709-1323

General Information Independent, coed, graduate-only institution. *Graduate housing:* Rooms and/or apartments guaranteed to single and married students. Housing application deadline: 4/1. *Research affiliation:* Center for Women and Religion (women's studies), Center for Ethics and Social Policy (business ethics), Disciples Seminary Foundation (theology), Swedenborgean House of Studies (theology), Bay Area Faith and Health Consortium (public health).

GRADUATE UNITS

Graduate and Professional Programs *Degree program information:* Part-time programs available. Part-time. Offers religion (M Div, MA, MTS, D Min, PhD, Th D, CAPS, CMS, CSS, CTS). MA, PhD, Th D offered jointly with Graduate Theological Union; D Min with Church Divinity School of the Pacific. Electronic applications accepted.

PACIFIC STATES UNIVERSITY, Los Angeles, CA 90010

General Information Independent, coed, comprehensive institution. *Graduate housing:* Room and/or apartments available on a first-come, first-served basis to single students; on-campus housing not available to married students.

GRADUATE UNITS

College of Business *Degree program information:* Part-time and evening/weekend programs available. Part-time, evening/weekend, online learning. Offers accounting (MBA); finance (MBA); international business (MBA, DBA); management of information technology (MBA); real estate management (MBA).

College of Computer Science and Information Systems *Degree program information:* Part-time and evening/weekend programs available. Part-time, evening/weekend. Offers computer science (MS); information systems (MS).

PACIFIC UNION COLLEGE, Angwin, CA 94508-9707

General Information Independent-religious, coed, comprehensive institution.

GRADUATE UNITS

Education Department *Degree program information:* Part-time programs available. Part-time. Offers education (M Ed); elementary teaching (MAT); secondary teaching (MAT).

PACIFIC UNIVERSITY, Forest Grove, OR 97116-1797

General Information Independent, coed, comprehensive institution. *Graduate housing:* On-campus housing not available. *Research affiliation:* NEI/PEDIG–JAEB Center of Health Research (amblyopia treatment), BSK (student thesis projects), CIBA Vision (contact lenses), Cooper Vision (contact lenses), The Ohio State University/Vistakon-Johnson & Johnson (adolescent and child vision care).

GRADUATE UNITS

College of Business Offers business administration (MBA); finance (MSF).

College of Education *Degree program information:* Part-time and evening/weekend programs available. Part-time, evening/weekend. Offers early childhood education (MAT); education (MAE); elementary education (MAT); ESOL (MAT); high school education (MAT); middle school education (MAT); special education (MAT); speech-language pathology (MS); STEM education (MAT); talented and gifted (M Ed); visual function in learning (M Ed). Electronic applications accepted.

College of Optometry Offers optometry (OD); vision science (MS, PhD). Electronic applications accepted.

Healthcare Administration Program Offers healthcare administration (MHA).

Program in Social Work Offers social work (MSW).

Program in Writing *Degree program information:* Part-time programs available. Part-time. Offers writing (MFA).

School of Audiology Offers audiology (Au D).

School of Occupational Therapy Offers occupational therapy (OTD). Electronic applications accepted.

School of Pharmacy Offers pharmacy (Pharm D). Electronic applications accepted.

School of Physical Therapy Offers athletic training (MSAT); physical therapy (DPT). Electronic applications accepted.

School of Physician Assistant Studies Offers physician assistant studies (MS).

School of Professional Psychology *Degree program information:* Part-time programs available. Part-time. Offers applied psychological science (MA, MS); clinical psychology (PhD, Psy D). Electronic applications accepted.

PALM BEACH ATLANTIC UNIVERSITY, West Palm Beach, FL 33416-4708

General Information Independent-religious, coed, comprehensive institution. *Enrollment:* 3,918 graduate, professional, and undergraduate students; 790 full-time matriculated graduate/professional students (512 women), 89 part-time matriculated graduate/professional students (62 women). *Enrollment by degree level:* 522 master's, 357 doctoral. *Graduate faculty:* 35 full-time (20 women), 53 part-time/adjunct (20 women). *Tuition, area resident:* Part-time $525 per credit hour. *Graduate housing:* On-campus housing not available. *Student services:* Campus employment opportunities, campus safety program, career counseling, exercise/wellness program, services for students with disabilities, writing training. *Library:* Warren Library plus 1 other. *Collection:* Books: 135,395 (physical), 152,861 (digital/electronic); Databases: 92. Weekly public service hours: 98; students can reserve study rooms.

Computer facilities: 350 computers available on campus for general student use. A campuswide network can be accessed from student residence rooms and from off campus. Online class registration is available.
Website: http://www.pba.edu/

General Application Contact: Joe Sharp, Dean of Admissions, 888-468-6722, E-mail: grad@pba.edu.

GRADUATE UNITS

Gregory School of Pharmacy Students: 293 full-time (168 women), 21 part-time (13 women); includes 178 minority (45 Black or African American, non-Hispanic/Latino; 2 American Indian or Alaska Native, non-Hispanic/Latino; 47 Asian, non-Hispanic/Latino; 69 Hispanic/Latino; 2 Native Hawaiian or other Pacific Islander, non-Hispanic/Latino; 13 Two or more races, non-Hispanic/Latino), 8 international. Average age 26. 552 applicants, 30% accepted, 76 enrolled. *Faculty:* 25 full-time (17 women), 6 part-time/adjunct (3 women). *Financial support:* In 2015–16, 49 students received support. Scholarships/grants and employee education grants available. Financial award application deadline: 5/1; financial award applicants required to submit FAFSA. In 2015, 67 doctorates awarded. Offers pharmacy (Pharm D). *Application deadline:* For fall admission, 3/1 priority date for domestic and international students. Applications are processed on a rolling basis. *Application fee:* $150. Electronic applications accepted. *Application Contact:* Lucas Whittaker, Director of Pharmacy Admissions, 561-803-2751, E-mail: lucas_whittaker@pba.edu. *Interim Dean,* Dr. Scott Mohrland, 561-803-2701, E-mail: scott_mohrland@pba.edu.

MacArthur School of Leadership Students: 69 full-time (37 women), 12 part-time (8 women); includes 52 minority (33 Black or African American, non-Hispanic/Latino; 2 Asian, non-Hispanic/Latino; 14 Hispanic/Latino; 3 Two or more races, non-Hispanic/Latino), 5 international. Average age 39. 50 applicants, 96% accepted, 39 enrolled. *Faculty:* 1 full-time (0 women), 7 part-time/adjunct (0 women). *Financial support:* In 2015–16, 20 students received support. Scholarships/grants and employee education grants available. Financial award application deadline: 5/1; financial award applicants required to submit FAFSA. In 2015, 36 master's awarded. *Degree program information:* Part-time and evening/weekend programs available. Part-time, evening/weekend, blended/hybrid learning. Offers leadership (MS). *Application deadline:* Applications are processed on a rolling basis. *Application fee:* $50. Electronic applications accepted. *Application Contact:* Graduate Admissions, 888-468-6722, E-mail: grad@pba.edu. *Dean,* Dr. Craig Domeck, 561-803-2318, E-mail: craig_domeck@pba.edu.

Rinker School of Business Students: 80 full-time (35 women), 19 part-time (11 women); includes 43 minority (15 Black or African American, non-Hispanic/Latino; 8 Asian, non-Hispanic/Latino; 17 Hispanic/Latino; 2 Native Hawaiian or other Pacific Islander, non-Hispanic/Latino; 1 Two or more races, non-Hispanic/Latino), 19 international. Average age 31. 32 applicants, 91% accepted, 29 enrolled. *Faculty:* 9 full-time (1 woman). *Financial support:* In 2015–16, 13 students received support. Scholarships/grants and employee education grants available. Financial award application deadline: 5/1; financial award applicants required to submit FAFSA. In 2015, 40 master's awarded. *Degree program information:* Part-time and evening/weekend programs available. Part-time, evening/weekend. Offers business (MBA). *Application deadline:* Applications are processed on a rolling basis. *Application fee:* $50. Electronic applications accepted. *Application Contact:* Graduate Admissions, 888-468-6722, Fax: 561-803-2115, E-mail: grad@pba.edu. *MBA Program Director,* Dr. David Smith, 561-803-2473, E-mail: david_smith@pba.edu.

School of Education and Behavioral Studies Students: 267 full-time (228 women), 29 part-time (25 women); includes 157 minority (66 Black or African American, non-Hispanic/Latino; 4 Asian, non-Hispanic/Latino; 73 Hispanic/Latino; 1 Native Hawaiian or other Pacific Islander, non-Hispanic/Latino; 13 Two or more races, non-Hispanic/Latino), 6 international. Average age 34. 88 applicants, 93% accepted, 70 enrolled. *Faculty:* 9 full-time (3 women), 14 part-time/adjunct (10 women). *Financial support:* In 2015–16, 11 students received support. Career-related internships or fieldwork, scholarships/grants, and employee education grants available. Financial award application deadline: 5/1; financial award applicants required to submit FAFSA. In 2015, 105 master's awarded. *Degree program information:* Part-time and evening/weekend programs available. Part-time, evening/weekend. Offers counseling psychology (MS). *Application deadline:* Applications are processed on a rolling basis. *Application fee:* $50. Electronic applications accepted. *Application Contact:* Graduate Admissions, 888-468-6722, E-mail: grad@pba.edu. *Program Director,* Dr. Gene Sale, 561-803-2352.

School of Ministry Students: 34 full-time (4 women), 4 part-time (0 women); includes 8 minority (2 Black or African American, non-Hispanic/Latino; 1 Asian, non-Hispanic/Latino; 5 Hispanic/Latino), 2 international. Average age 28. 18 applicants, 100% accepted, 16 enrolled. *Faculty:* 11 part-time/adjunct (1 woman). *Financial support:* In 2015–16, 25 students received support. Scholarships/grants, unspecified assistantships, and employee education grants available. Financial award application deadline: 5/1; financial award applicants required to submit FAFSA. In 2015, 2 master's awarded. *Degree program information:* Part-time programs available. Part-time. Offers ministry (M Div). *Application deadline:* Applications are processed on a rolling basis. *Application fee:* $50. Electronic applications accepted. *Application Contact:* Graduate Admissions, 888-468-6722, E-mail: grad@pba.edu. *Dean,* Dr. Randy Richards, 561-803-2295.

School of Nursing Students: 43 full-time (37 women), 1 (woman) part-time; includes 22 minority (11 Black or African American, non-Hispanic/Latino; 2 Asian, non-Hispanic/Latino; 8 Hispanic/Latino; 1 Two or more races, non-Hispanic/Latino). Average age 32. 34 applicants, 100% accepted, 24 enrolled. *Faculty:* 5 part-time/adjunct (4 women). *Financial support:* In 2015–16, 13 students received support. Scholarships/grants and employee education grants available. Financial award application deadline: 5/1; financial award applicants required to submit FAFSA. *Degree program information:* Part-time programs available. Part-time. Offers family nurse practitioner (DNP); health systems leadership (MSN). *Application deadline:* Applications are processed on a rolling basis. *Application fee:* $50. Electronic applications accepted. *Application Contact:* Graduate Admissions, 888-468-6722, E-mail: grad@pba.edu. *Dean,* Joanne Masella, 561-803-2827.

PALMER COLLEGE OF CHIROPRACTIC, Davenport, IA 52803-5287

General Information Independent, coed, comprehensive institution. *Enrollment:* 2,225 full-time matriculated graduate/professional students (797 women), 18 part-time matriculated graduate/professional students (5 women). *Enrollment by degree level:* 14 master's, 2,229 doctoral. *Graduate faculty:* 149 full-time (57 women), 35 part-time/adjunct (15 women). *Student services:* Campus employment opportunities, campus safety program, career counseling, child daycare facilities, exercise/wellness program, free psychological counseling, international student services, low-cost health insurance, services for students with disabilities. *Library:* David D. Palmer Health Sciences Library.

Computer facilities: 94 computers available on campus for general student use. A campuswide network can be accessed.
Website: http://www.palmer.edu/

General Application Contact: Karen Eden, Director of Admissions, 563-884-5656, Fax: 563-884-5414, E-mail: pcadmit@palmer.edu.

GRADUATE UNITS

Division of Graduate Studies Students: 7 full-time (2 women), 1 (woman) part-time; includes 1 minority (Black or African American, non-Hispanic/Latino). 3 applicants, 100% accepted, 3 enrolled. *Faculty:* 8 full-time (3 women), 3 part-time/adjunct (2 women). *Financial support:* In 2015–16, 7 students received support, including 7 research assistantships with full tuition reimbursements available (averaging $30,000 per year), teaching assistantships with tuition reimbursements available (averaging $6,269 per year); tuition waivers (full) and unspecified assistantships also available. Financial award application deadline: 8/1; financial award applicants required to submit FAFSA. In 2015, 5 master's awarded. Offers clinical research (MS). *Application deadline:* For fall admission, 8/1 for domestic and international students; for spring admission, 5/28 for domestic students. Applications are processed on a rolling basis. *Application fee:* $50. Electronic applications accepted. *Application Contact:* Lori Byrd, Program Coordinator, 563-884-5198, Fax: 563-884-5227, E-mail: lori.byrd@plamer.edu. *Interim Vice President for Academic Affairs,* Dr. Dan Weinert, 563-884-5761, Fax: 563-884-5624, E-mail: weinert_d@palmer.edu.

Professional Program ***Financial support:*** Career-related internships or fieldwork, Federal Work-Study, and scholarships/grants available. Support available to part-time students. Financial award application deadline: 4/1; financial award applicants required to submit FAFSA. *Degree program information:* Part-time programs available. Part-time. Offers chiropractic (DC). *Application deadline:* Applications are processed on a rolling basis. *Application fee:* $50. Electronic applications accepted. *Application Contact:* Karen Eden, Senior Director of Admissions, 563-884-5656, Fax: 563-884-5414, E-mail: pcadmit@palmer.edu. *Chancellor,* Dr. Dennis Marchiori, 563-884-5466, Fax: 563-884-5624, E-mail: marchiori_d@palmer.edu.

Professional Program–Florida Campus ***Financial support:*** Career-related internships or fieldwork, Federal Work-Study, and scholarships/grants available. Support available to part-time students. Financial award application deadline: 4/1; financial award applicants required to submit FAFSA. *Degree program information:* Part-time programs available. Part-time. Offers chiropractic (DC). *Application fee:* $50. *Application Contact:* Admissions Representative, 866-585-9677, Fax: 386-763-2620, E-mail: pcaf_admiss@palmer.edu. *Chancellor,* Dr. Dennis Marchiori, 563-884-5511, Fax: 563-884-5409, E-mail: marchiori_d@palmer.edu.

Professional Program–West Campus ***Financial support:*** Career-related internships or fieldwork, Federal Work-Study, and scholarships/grants available. Support available to part-time students. Financial award application deadline: 4/1; financial award applicants required to submit FAFSA. *Degree program information:* Part-time programs available. Part-time. Offers chiropractic (DC). *Application deadline:* Applications are processed on a rolling basis. *Application fee:* $50. Electronic applications accepted. *Application Contact:* Julie Behn, Campus Enrollment Director, 408-944-6121, Fax: 408-944-6032, E-mail: julie.behn@palmer.edu.

PALO ALTO UNIVERSITY, Palo Alto, CA 94304

General Information Independent, coed, upper-level institution.

GRADUATE UNITS

MA in Counseling Program ***Degree program information:*** Part-time programs available. Part-time, online learning. Offers counseling (MA). Electronic applications accepted.

MS in Psychology (PhD Prep) Program ***Degree program information:*** Part-time programs available. Part-time, online learning. Offers psychology (MS). Electronic applications accepted.

PGSP-Stanford Psy D Consortium Program Offers psychology (Psy D). Program offered jointly with Stanford University. Electronic applications accepted.

PhD in Clinical Psychology Program Offers clinical psychology (PhD). Electronic applications accepted.

PARIS COLLEGE OF ART, 75010 Paris, France

General Information Independent, coed, comprehensive institution. *International tuition:* 27,200 euros full-time. *Tuition, area resident:* Full-time 13,600 euros.

Computer facilities: A campuswide network can be accessed.
Website: http://www.paris.edu/

GRADUATE UNITS

Graduate Programs Offers accessories design (MA); fashion design: new materials and technologies (MA); fashion film and photography (MA); interior design (MA); transdisciplinary new media (MA, MFA).

PARKER UNIVERSITY, Dallas, TX 75229-5668

General Information Independent, coed, graduate-only institution. *Graduate housing:* On-campus housing not available.

GRADUATE UNITS

Doctor of Chiropractic Program ***Degree program information:*** Part-time programs available. Part-time. Offers chiropractic (DC). Electronic applications accepted.

PARK UNIVERSITY, Parkville, MO 64152-3795

General Information Independent, coed, comprehensive institution. CGS member.

GRADUATE UNITS

School of Graduate and Professional Studies ***Degree program information:*** Part-time and evening/weekend programs available. Part-time, evening/weekend, online learning. Offers adult education (M Ed); business and government leadership (Graduate Certificate); business, government, and global society (MPA); communication and leadership (MA); creative and life writing (Graduate Certificate); disaster and emergency management (MPA, Graduate Certificate); educational leadership (M Ed); finance (MBA, Graduate Certificate); general business (MBA); global business (Graduate Certificate); healthcare administration (MHA); healthcare services management and leadership (Graduate Certificate); international business (MBA); language and literacy (M Ed); leadership of international healthcare organizations (Graduate Certificate); management information systems (MBA, Graduate Certificate); music performance (ADP, Graduate Certificate); nonprofit and community services management (MPA); nonprofit leadership (Graduate Certificate); performance (MM); public management (MPA); social work (MSW); teacher leadership (M Ed). Electronic applications accepted.

PAYNE THEOLOGICAL SEMINARY, Wilberforce, OH 45384-3474

General Information Independent-religious, coed, graduate-only institution. *Graduate housing:* Rooms and/or apartments available on a first-come, first-served basis to single and married students. Housing application deadline: 8/15.

GRADUATE UNITS

Program in Theology ***Degree program information:*** Part-time and evening/weekend programs available. Part-time, evening/weekend, online learning. Offers theology (M Div).

PEIRCE COLLEGE, Philadelphia, PA 19102-4699

General Information Independent, coed, primarily women, comprehensive institution.

GRADUATE UNITS

Program in Organizational Leadership and Management Offers organizational leadership and management (MS).

PENN STATE ERIE, THE BEHREND COLLEGE, Erie, PA 16563-0001

General Information State-related, coed, comprehensive institution. *Graduate housing:* Room and/or apartments available on a first-come, first-served basis to single students; on-campus housing not available to married students. *Student services:* Campus employment opportunities, campus safety program, career counseling, child daycare facilities, exercise/wellness program, free psychological counseling, grant writing training, international student services, low-cost health insurance, multicultural affairs office, services for students with disabilities. *Library:* John M. Lilley Library.

Computer facilities: Computer purchase and lease plans are available. A campuswide network can be accessed from student residence rooms and from off campus. Online class registration is available.
Website: http://www.pserie.psu.edu/

General Application Contact: Ann M. Burbules, Assistant Director of Graduate Admissions, 814-898-7255, Fax: 814-898-6053, E-mail: amb29@psu.edu.

GRADUATE UNITS

Graduate School Students: 31 full-time (11 women), 121 part-time (32 women); includes 7 minority (2 Black or African American, non-Hispanic/Latino; 2 Asian, non-Hispanic/Latino; 2 Hispanic/Latino; 1 Two or more races, non-Hispanic/Latino), 1 international. Average age 31. 59 applicants, 90% accepted, 34 enrolled. *Financial support:* Federal Work-Study available. Financial award application deadline: 3/1; financial award applicants required to submit FAFSA. In 2015, 48 master's awarded. *Degree program information:* Part-time programs available. Part-time. Offers accounting (MPAC); business administration (MBA); project management (MPM); quality and manufacturing management (MMM). *Application deadline:* Applications are processed on a rolling basis. *Application fee:* $65. Electronic applications accepted. *Application Contact:* Ann M. Burbules, Assistant Director, Graduate Admissions, 866-374-3378, Fax: 814-898-6053, E-mail: psbehrendmba@psu.edu. *Chancellor,* Dr. Donald L. Birx, 814-898-6160, Fax: 814-898-6461.

PENN STATE GREAT VALLEY, Malvern, PA 19355-1488

General Information State-related, coed, graduate-only institution. *Enrollment by degree level:* 420 master's. *Graduate housing:* On-campus housing not available. *Student services:* Campus employment opportunities, campus safety program, career counseling, grant writing training, international student services, low-cost health insurance, multicultural affairs office, services for students with disabilities. *Library:* Great Valley Library.

Computer facilities: Online class registration is available.
Website: http://www.gv.psu.edu/

General Application Contact: JoAnn Kelly, Director of Admissions, 610-648-3315, Fax: 610-725-5296, E-mail: gvadmiss@psu.edu.

GRADUATE UNITS

Graduate Studies Students: 92 full-time (41 women), 337 part-time (104 women); includes 80 minority (16 Black or African American, non-Hispanic/Latino; 38 Asian, non-Hispanic/Latino; 18 Hispanic/Latino; 1 Native Hawaiian or other Pacific Islander, non-Hispanic/Latino; 7 Two or more races, non-Hispanic/Latino), 63 international. Average age 32. 320 applicants, 67% accepted, 87 enrolled. *Financial support:* Fellowships, research assistantships, teaching assistantships, Federal Work-Study, scholarships/grants, health care benefits, and unspecified assistantships available. Support available to part-time students. Financial award application deadline: 3/1; financial award applicants required to submit FAFSA. In 2015, 172 master's awarded. *Degree program information:* Part-time and evening/weekend programs available. Part-time, evening/weekend. *Application deadline:* Applications are processed on a rolling basis. *Application fee:* $65. Electronic applications accepted. *Application Contact:* JoAnn Kelly, Director of Admissions, 610-648-3315, Fax: 610-725-5296, E-mail: gvadmiss@psu.edu. *Chancellor*, Dr. Craig S. Edelbrock, 610-648-3202, Fax: 610-889-1334.

Engineering Division Offers engineering management (MEM); software engineering (MSE); systems engineering (M Eng, Certificate). *Application Contact:* JoAnn Kelly, Director of Admissions, 610-648-3315, Fax: 610-725-5296, E-mail: jek2@psu.edu. *Chancellor*, Dr. Craig S. Edelbrock, 610-648-3202 Ext. 610, Fax: 610-889-1334.

Management Division Offers business administration (MBA); cyber security (Certificate); data analytics (Certificate); finance (M Fin, Certificate); health sector management (Certificate); human resource management (Certificate); information science (MSIS); leadership development (MLD); sustainable management practices (Certificate). *Application Contact:* JoAnn Kelly, Director of Admissions, 610-648-3315, Fax: 610-725-5296, E-mail: jek2@psu.edu. *Chancellor*, Dr. Craig S. Edelbrock, 610-648-3202, Fax: 610-889-1334.

PENN STATE HARRISBURG, Middletown, PA 17057-4898

General Information State-related, coed, comprehensive institution. *Enrollment:* 4,678 graduate, professional, and undergraduate students; 229 full-time matriculated graduate/professional students (136 women), 583 part-time matriculated graduate/professional students (360 women). *Enrollment by degree level:* 723 master's. *Graduate housing:* Room and/or apartments available on a first-come, first-served basis to single students; on-campus housing not available to married students. *Student services:* Campus employment opportunities, campus safety program, career counseling, child daycare facilities, exercise/wellness program, free psychological counseling, grant writing training, international student services, low-cost health insurance, multicultural affairs office, services for students with disabilities, teacher training, writing training. *Library:* Penn State Harrisburg Library.

Computer facilities: Computer purchase and lease plans are available. A campuswide network can be accessed from student residence rooms and from off campus. Online class registration is available.
Website: http://www.hbg.psu.edu/

General Application Contact: Robert W. Coffman, Jr., Director of Enrollment Management, Recruitment and Admissions, 717-948-6250, Fax: 717-948-6325, E-mail: hbgadmit@psu.edu.

GRADUATE UNITS

Graduate School Students: 229 full-time (136 women), 583 part-time (360 women); includes 112 minority (42 Black or African American, non-Hispanic/Latino; 2 American Indian or Alaska Native, non-Hispanic/Latino; 35 Asian, non-Hispanic/Latino; 26 Hispanic/Latino; 7 Two or more races, non-Hispanic/Latino), 107 international. Average age 32. 794 applicants, 57% accepted, 176 enrolled. *Financial support:* Fellowships, research assistantships, teaching assistantships, career-related internships or fieldwork, Federal Work-Study, and unspecified assistantships available. Support available to part-time students. Financial award application deadline: 3/1; financial award applicants required to submit FAFSA. In 2015, 277 master's, 7 doctorates awarded. *Degree program information:* Part-time and evening/weekend programs available. Part-time, evening/weekend. *Application deadline:* Applications are processed on a rolling basis. *Application fee:* $65. Electronic applications accepted. *Application Contact:* Robert W. Coffman, Jr., Director of Enrollment Management, Recruitment and Admissions, 717-948-6250, Fax: 717-948-6325, E-mail: hbgadmit@psu.edu. *Chancellor*, Dr. Mukund S. Kulkarni, 717-948-6105, Fax: 717-948-6452.

School of Behavioral Sciences and Education Degree program information: Part-time and evening/weekend programs available. Part-time, evening/weekend. Offers adult education (M Ed, D Ed); adult education in the health and medical professions (Certificate); applied behavior analysis (MA); applied clinical psychology (MA); applied psychological research (MA); clinical psychology (Certificate); community psychology and social change (MA); English as a second language (ESL) program specialist and leadership (Certificate); folklore and ethnography (Certificate); health psychology (Certificate); literacy education (M Ed); literacy leadership (Certificate); teaching and curriculum (M Ed); training and development (M Ed, Certificate). *Application Contact:* Robert W. Coffman, Jr., Director of Enrollment Management, Recruitment and Admissions, 717-948-6250, Fax: 717-948-6325, E-mail: hbgadmit@psu.edu. *Chancellor*, Dr. Mukund S. Kulkarni, 717-948-6105, Fax: 717-948-6452.

School of Business Administration Degree program information: Part-time and evening/weekend programs available. Part-time, evening/weekend. Offers accounting (MPA); business administration (MBA); information systems (MS). *Application Contact:* Robert W. Coffman, Jr., Director of Enrollment Management, Admissions, 717-948-6250, Fax: 717-948-6325, E-mail: hbgadmit@psu.edu. *Chancellor*, Dr. Mukund S. Kulkarni, 717-948-6105, Fax: 717-948-6452.

School of Humanities Degree program information: Evening/weekend programs available. Evening/weekend. Offers American studies (MA, PhD); communications (MA); heritage and museum practice (Certificate); humanities (MA); writing instruction specialist (Certificate). *Application Contact:* Robert W. Coffman, Jr., Director of Enrollment Management, Admissions, 717-948-6250, Fax: 717-948-6325, E-mail: hbgadmit@psu.edu. *Chancellor*, Dr. Mukund S. Kulkarni, 717-948-6105, Fax: 717-948-6452.

School of Public Affairs Offers criminal justice (MA); health administration (MHA); homeland security (MPS, Certificate); long term care (Certificate); non-profit administration (Certificate); public administration (MPA, PhD); public budgeting and financial management (Certificate); public sector human resource management (Certificate). *Application Contact:* Robert W. Coffman, Jr., Director of Enrollment Management, Admissions, 717-948-6250, Fax: 717-948-6325, E-mail: hbgadmit@psu.edu. *Chancellor*, Dr. Mukund S. Kulkarni, 717-948-6105, Fax: 717-948-6452.

School of Science, Engineering and Technology Degree program information: Part-time and evening/weekend programs available. Part-time, evening/weekend. Offers computer science (MS); electrical engineering (M Eng, MS); engineering management (MPS); engineering science (M Eng); environmental engineering (M Eng); environmental pollution control (MEPC, MS); structural engineering (Certificate). *Application Contact:* Robert W. Coffman, Jr., Director of Enrollment Management, Admissions, 717-948-6250, Fax: 717-948-6325, E-mail: hbgadmit@psu.edu. *Chancellor*, Dr. Mukund S. Kulkarni, 717-948-6105, Fax: 717-948-6452.

PENN STATE HERSHEY MEDICAL CENTER, Hershey, PA 17033-2360

General Information State-related, coed, graduate-only institution. *Graduate faculty:* 209 full-time (47 women), 7 part-time/adjunct (3 women). *Graduate housing:* Rooms and/or apartments available on a first-come, first-served basis to single and married students. *Student services:* Campus safety program, career counseling, child daycare facilities, exercise/wellness program, free psychological counseling, grant writing training, international student services, low-cost health insurance, multicultural affairs office, services for students with disabilities, teacher training, writing training. *Library:* George T. Harrell Health Sciences Library.

Computer facilities: Online class registration is available.
Website: http://www.hmc.psu.edu/college/

General Application Contact: Dr. Michael F. Verderame, Associate Dean of Graduate Studies, 717-531-8892, Fax: 717-531-0786, E-mail: grad-hmc@psu.edu.

GRADUATE UNITS

College of Medicine *Financial support:* In 2015–16, 99 students received support, including research assistantships with full tuition reimbursements available (averaging $22,260 per year); fellowships with full tuition reimbursements available, career-related internships or fieldwork, scholarships/grants, health care benefits, and unspecified assistantships also available. Offers medicine (MPAS, MPH, MS, Dr PH, MD, PhD). *Application deadline:* Applications are processed on a rolling basis. *Application fee:* $65. Electronic applications accepted. *Application Contact:* Dr. Sheila L. Vrana, Interim Vice Dean for Research and Graduate Studies, 717-531-7199, Fax: 717-531-0786, E-mail: grad-hmc@psu.edu. *Dean*, Dr. A. Craig Hillemeier, 717-531-8323, Fax: 717-531-0786, E-mail: grad-hmc@psu.edu.

Graduate School Programs in the Biomedical Sciences Financial support: In 2015–16, 3 fellowships with full tuition reimbursements (averaging $27,250 per year), 30 research assistantships with full tuition reimbursements (averaging $26,196 per year) were awarded; career-related internships or fieldwork, scholarships/grants, health care benefits, tuition waivers (full), and unspecified assistantships also available. Offers anatomy (MS, PhD); biochemistry and molecular genetics (MS, PhD); biomedical sciences (MS, PhD); biostatistics (PhD); cell and developmental biology (PhD); immunology and infectious disease (PhD); laboratory animal medicine (MS); life sciences (MS, PhD); molecular and evolutionary genetics (PhD); molecular medicine (PhD); molecular toxicology (PhD); neurobiology (PhD); neuroscience (MS, PhD); public health (MPH, Dr PH); public health sciences (MS); translational therapeutics (MS, PhD); virology and immunology (MS, PhD). *Application deadline:* Applications are processed on a rolling basis. *Application fee:* $65. Electronic applications accepted. *Application Contact:* Kristin E. Smith, Director of Graduate Admissions, 717-531-1045, Fax: 717-531-0786, E-mail: kec17@psu.edu. *Associate Dean of Graduate Studies*, Dr. Charles Lang, 717-531-8892, Fax: 717-531-0786, E-mail: grad-hmc@psu.edu.

PENN STATE UNIVERSITY - DICKINSON LAW, University Park, PA 16802-1017

General Information State-related, coed, graduate-only institution. *Enrollment by degree level:* 1 master's, 157 doctoral. *Graduate faculty:* 26 full-time (15 women), 18 part-time/adjunct (6 women). Tuition, state resident: full-time $44,400. Tuition, nonresident: full-time $44,400. *Required fees:* $678. *Student services:* Campus employment opportunities, campus safety program, career counseling, exercise/wellness program, free psychological counseling, international student services, low-cost health insurance, services for students with disabilities. *Library:* H. Laddie Montague Jr. Law Library.

Computer facilities: 20 computers available on campus for general student use. A campuswide network can be accessed. Online class registration is available.
Website: http://law.psu.edu/

General Application Contact: Rebekah A. Saidman-Krauss, Assistant Dean of Admissions and Financial Aid, 717-240-5207, E-mail: ras1075@psu.edu.

GRADUATE UNITS

Graduate and Professional Programs Students: 158 full-time (76 women); includes 33 minority (10 Black or African American, non-Hispanic/Latino; 8 Asian, non-Hispanic/Latino; 7 Hispanic/Latino; 8 Two or more races, non-Hispanic/Latino), 6 international. Average age 27. 967 applicants, 38% accepted, 64 enrolled. *Faculty:* 26 full-time (15 women), 18 part-time/adjunct (6 women). *Financial support:* In 2015–16, 156 students received support. Research assistantships, Federal Work-Study, and scholarships/grants available. Financial award application deadline: 4/15; financial award applicants required to submit FAFSA. In 2015, 57 doctorates awarded. Offers law (LL M, JD). *Application deadline:* Applications are processed on a rolling basis. *Application fee:* $69. Electronic applications accepted. *Application Contact:* Rebekah A. Saidman-Krauss, Assistant Dean of Admissions and Financial Aid, 717-240-5207, E-mail: ras1075@psu.edu. *Interim Dean*, Gary S. Gildin, 717-240-5238, Fax: 717-240-5213, E-mail: gsg2@psu.edu.

PENN STATE UNIVERSITY PARK, University Park, PA 16802

General Information State-related, coed, university. CGS member. *Enrollment:* 47,307 graduate, professional, and undergraduate students; 5,890 full-time matriculated graduate/professional students (2,612 women), 675 part-time matriculated graduate/professional students (364 women). *Enrollment by degree level:* 1,928 master's, 4,637 doctoral. *Graduate housing:* Rooms and/or apartments available on a first-come, first-served basis to single and married students. *Student services:* Campus employment opportunities, campus safety program, career counseling, child daycare facilities, exercise/wellness program, free psychological counseling, grant writing training, international student services, low-cost health insurance, multicultural affairs office, services for students with disabilities, teacher training, writing training. *Library:* Pattee and Paterno Library plus 14 others. *Collection:* Books: 5 million (physical), 387,000 (digital/electronic); Serial titles: 59,012 (physical), 110,000 (digital/electronic); Databases: 749. Weekly public service hours: 148; study areas open 24 hours, 5–7 days a week; students can reserve study rooms.

Computer facilities: Computer purchase and lease plans are available. 6,200 computers available on campus for general student use. A campuswide network can be accessed from student residence rooms and from off campus. Online class registration is available.
Website: http://www.psu.edu/

General Application Contact: Lori Stania, Director, Graduate Student Services, 814-865-1795, Fax: 814-863-4627, E-mail: l-gswww@lists.psu.edu.

GRADUATE UNITS

Graduate School Students: 5,450 full-time (2,425 women), 656 part-time (356 women); includes 728 minority (174 Black or African American, non-Hispanic/Latino; 4 American Indian or Alaska Native, non-Hispanic/Latino; 212 Asian, non-Hispanic/Latino; 258 Hispanic/Latino; 3 Native Hawaiian or other Pacific Islander, non-Hispanic/Latino; 77 Two or more races, non-Hispanic/Latino), 2,575 international. Average age 29. 15,274 applicants, 24% accepted, 1406 enrolled. *Financial support:* Fellowships, research assistantships, teaching assistantships, career-related internships or fieldwork, Federal Work-Study, scholarships/grants, traineeships, health care benefits, and unspecified assistantships available. Support available to part-time students. Financial award application deadline: 3/1; financial award applicants required to submit FAFSA. In 2015, 1,275 master's, 673 doctorates awarded. *Degree program information:* Part-time and evening/weekend programs available. Part-time, evening/weekend, online learning. *Application deadline:* Applications are processed on a rolling basis. *Application fee:* $65. Electronic applications accepted. *Application Contact:* Lori Stania, Director, Graduate Student Services, 814-865-1795, Fax: 814-863-4627, E-mail: l-gswww@lists.psu.edu. *Vice Provost for Graduate Education/Dean, Graduate School*, Dr. Regina Vasilatos-Younken, 814-865-2516, Fax: 814-863-4627.

College of Agricultural Sciences Students: 398 full-time (241 women), 21 part-time (10 women). Average age 29. 576 applicants, 18% accepted, 69 enrolled. *Financial support:* Fellowships, research assistantships, teaching assistantships, career-related internships or fieldwork, Federal Work-Study, scholarships/grants, traineeships, health care benefits, and unspecified assistantships available. Support available to part-time students. Financial award application deadline: 3/1; financial award applicants required to submit FAFSA. *Degree program information:* Part-time and evening/weekend programs available. Part-time, evening/weekend, online learning. Offers agricultural and biological engineering (MS, PhD); agricultural and extension education (M Ed, MS, PhD, Certificate); agricultural sciences (M Ed, MPS, MS, PhD, Certificate); agricultural, environmental and regional economics (MS, PhD); agronomy (MS, PhD); animal science (MPS, MS, PhD); applied youth, family and community education (M Ed); biorenewable systems (MS, PhD); community and economic development (MPS); entomology (MS, PhD); food science (MS); forest resources (MS, PhD); horticulture (MS, PhD); pathobiology (MS, PhD); plant pathology (MS, PhD); rural sociology (MS, PhD); soil science (MS, PhD); turfgrass management (MPS); wildlife and fisheries science (MS, PhD). *Application deadline:* Applications are processed on a rolling basis. *Application fee:* $65. Electronic applications accepted. *Application Contact:* Lori Stania, Director, Graduate Student Services, 814-865-1795, Fax: 814-863-4627, E-mail: l-gswww@lists.psu.edu. *Dean*, Dr. Richard T. Roush, 814-865-2541, Fax: 814-865-3103.

College of Arts and Architecture Students: 249 full-time (165 women), 19 part-time (11 women). Average age 29. 533 applicants, 35% accepted, 67 enrolled. *Financial support:* Fellowships, research assistantships, teaching assistantships, career-related internships or fieldwork, Federal Work-Study, scholarships/grants, traineeships, health care benefits, and unspecified assistantships available. Support available to part-time students. Financial award application deadline: 3/1; financial award applicants required to submit FAFSA. *Degree program information:* Part-time and evening/weekend programs available. Part-time, evening/weekend, online learning. Offers architecture (M Arch, MS, PhD); art (MFA); art education (MPS, MS, PhD, Certificate); art history (MA, PhD); arts and architecture (M Arch, M Mus, MA, MFA, MLA, MME, MPS, MS, DMA, PhD, Certificate); composition theory (M Mus); conducting (M Mus); geodesign (MPS); landscape architecture (MLA, MS); music (MA); music education (MME, PhD, Certificate); pedagogy and performance (M Mus); performance (M Mus); piano performance (DMA); theatre (MFA). *Application deadline:* Applications are processed on a rolling basis. *Application fee:* $65. Electronic applications accepted. *Application Contact:* Lori Stania, Director, Graduate Student Services, 814-865-1795, Fax: 814-863-4627, E-mail: l-gswww@lists.psu.edu. *Dean*, Dr. Barbara O. Korner, 814-865-2592, Fax: 814-865-2018.

College of Communications Students: 52 full-time (35 women), 6 part-time (4 women). Average age 30. 148 applicants, 26% accepted, 13 enrolled. *Financial support:* Fellowships, research assistantships, teaching assistantships, career-related internships or fieldwork, Federal Work-Study, scholarships/grants, traineeships, health care benefits, and unspecified assistantships available. Support available to part-time students. Financial award application deadline: 3/1; financial award applicants required to submit FAFSA. *Degree program information:* Part-time and evening/weekend programs available. Part-time, evening/weekend, online learning. Offers communications (MA, PhD); mass communications (PhD); media studies (MA). *Application deadline:* Applications are processed on a rolling basis. *Application fee:* $65. Electronic applications accepted. *Application Contact:* Lori Stania, Director, Graduate Student Services, 814-865-1795, Fax: 814-863-4627, E-mail: l-gswww@lists.psu.edu. *Dean*, Dr. Marie C. Hardin, 814-863-1484, Fax: 814-863-8044.

College of Earth and Mineral Sciences Students: 385 full-time (139 women), 26 part-time (9 women). Average age 28. 741 applicants, 18% accepted, 64 enrolled. *Financial support:* Fellowships, research assistantships, teaching assistantships, career-related internships or fieldwork, Federal Work-Study, scholarships/grants, traineeships, health care benefits, and unspecified assistantships available. Support available to part-time students. Financial award application deadline: 3/1; financial award applicants required to submit FAFSA. *Degree program information:* Part-time and evening/weekend programs available. Part-time, evening/weekend, online learning. Offers earth and mineral engineering (MS, PhD); earth and mineral sciences (M Ed, MGIS, MS, PhD); earth sciences (M Ed); geographic information systems (MGIS); geography (MS, PhD); geosciences (MS, PhD); meteorology (MS, PhD). *Application deadline:* Applications are processed on a rolling basis. *Application fee:* $65. Electronic applications accepted. *Application Contact:* Lori Stania, Director, Graduate Student Services, 814-865-1795, Fax: 814-863-4627, E-mail: l-gswww@lists.psu.edu. *Dean*, Dr. William E. Easterling, III, 814-865-7482, Fax: 814-863-7708.

College of Education Students: 536 full-time (378 women), 244 part-time (151 women). Average age 33. 650 applicants, 49% accepted, 145 enrolled. *Financial support:* Fellowships, research assistantships, teaching assistantships, career-related internships or fieldwork, Federal Work-Study, scholarships/grants, traineeships, health care benefits, and unspecified assistantships available. Support available to part-time students. Financial award application deadline: 3/1; financial award applicants required to submit FAFSA. *Degree program information:* Part-time and evening/weekend programs available. Part-time, evening/weekend, online learning. Offers adult education (M Ed, D Ed, PhD, Certificate); counselor education (M Ed, D Ed, PhD, Certificate); curriculum and instruction (M Ed, MS, PhD, Certificate); education (M Ed, MA, MPS, MS, D Ed, PhD, Certificate); educational leadership (M Ed, D Ed, PhD, Certificate); educational psychology (MS, PhD, Certificate); educational theory and policy (MA, PhD); higher education (M Ed, MS, D Ed, PhD); learning, design, and technology (M Ed, MS, PhD, Certificate); organization development and change (MPS); school psychology (M Ed, MS, PhD, Certificate); special education (M Ed, MS, PhD, Certificate); workforce education and development (M Ed, MS, PhD). *Application deadline:* Applications are processed on a rolling basis. *Application fee:* $65. Electronic applications accepted. *Application Contact:* Lori Stania, Director, Graduate Student Services, 814-865-1795, Fax: 814-863-4627, E-mail: l-gswww@lists.psu.edu. *Dean*, Dr. David H. Monk, 814-865-2523, Fax: 814-865-0555.

College of Engineering Students: 1,311 full-time (295 women), 92 part-time (15 women). Average age 26. 4,799 applicants, 24% accepted, 357 enrolled. *Financial support:* Fellowships, research assistantships, teaching assistantships, career-related internships or fieldwork, Federal Work-Study, scholarships/grants, traineeships, health care benefits, and unspecified assistantships available. Support available to part-time students. Financial award application deadline: 3/1; financial award applicants required to submit FAFSA. *Degree program information:* Part-time and evening/weekend programs available. Part-time, evening/weekend, online learning. Offers aerospace engineering (M Eng, MS, PhD); architectural engineering (M Eng, MAE, MS, PhD); chemical engineering (MS, PhD); civil engineering (M Eng, MS, PhD); computer science and engineering (M Eng, MS, PhD); electrical engineering (M Eng, MS, PhD); engineering (M Eng, MAE, MS, PhD); engineering design (M Eng, MS); engineering mechanics (M Eng); engineering science (M Eng); engineering science and mechanics (MS, PhD); environmental engineering (M Eng, MS, PhD); industrial engineering (MS, PhD); mechanical engineering (MS, PhD); nuclear engineering (M Eng, MS, PhD). *Application deadline:* Applications are processed on a rolling basis. *Application fee:* $65. Electronic applications accepted. *Application Contact:* Lori Stania, Director, Graduate Student Services, 814-865-1795, Fax: 814-863-4627, E-mail: l-gswww@lists.psu.edu. *Dean*, Dr. Amr S. Elnashai, 814-865-7537, Fax: 814-863-4749.

College of Health and Human Development Students: 324 full-time (222 women), 19 part-time (11 women). Average age 28. 644 applicants, 29% accepted, 93 enrolled. *Financial support:* Fellowships, research assistantships, teaching assistantships, career-related internships or fieldwork, Federal Work-Study, scholarships/grants, traineeships, health care benefits, and unspecified assistantships available. Support available to part-time students. Financial award application deadline: 3/1; financial award applicants required to submit FAFSA. *Degree program information:* Part-time and evening/weekend programs available. Part-time, evening/weekend, online learning. Offers biobehavioral health (MS, PhD); communication sciences and disorders (MS, PhD, Certificate); health and human development (MHA, MS, PhD, Certificate); health policy and administration (MHA, MS, PhD); hotel, restaurant, and institutional management (MS, PhD); human development and family studies (MS, PhD); kinesiology (MS, PhD, Certificate); nutritional science (MS, PhD); recreation, park and tourism management (MS, PhD). *Application deadline:* Applications are processed on a rolling basis. *Application fee:* $65. Electronic applications accepted. *Application Contact:* Lori Stania, Director, Graduate Student Services, 814-865-1795, Fax: 814-863-4627, E-mail: l-gswww@lists.psu.edu. *Dean*, Dr. Ann C. Crouter, 814-865-1420, Fax: 814-865-3282.

College of Information Sciences and Technology Students: 111 full-time (35 women), 12 part-time (3 women). Average age 28. 149 applicants, 42% accepted, 28 enrolled. *Financial support:* Fellowships, research assistantships, teaching assistantships, career-related internships or fieldwork, Federal Work-Study, institutionally sponsored loans, scholarships/grants, traineeships, health care benefits, and unspecified assistantships available. Support available to part-time students. Financial award application deadline: 3/1; financial award applicants required to submit FAFSA. *Degree program information:* Part-time and evening/weekend programs available. Part-time, evening/weekend, online learning. Offers information sciences and technology (MPS, MS, PhD). *Application deadline:* For fall admission, 12/15 for domestic and international students. Applications are processed on a rolling basis. *Application fee:* $65. Electronic applications accepted. *Application Contact:* Lori Stania, Director, Graduate Student Services, 814-865-1795, Fax: 814-863-4627, E-mail: l-gswww@lists.psu.edu. *Dean*, Dr. Andrew L. Sears, 814-865-3528, Fax: 814-865-7485.

College of Nursing Students: 69 full-time (57 women), 50 part-time (45 women). Average age 32. 69 applicants, 55% accepted, 34 enrolled. *Financial support:* Fellowships, research assistantships, teaching assistantships, career-related internships or fieldwork, Federal Work-Study, scholarships/grants, traineeships, health care benefits, and unspecified assistantships available. Support available to part-time students. Financial award application deadline: 3/1; financial award applicants required to submit FAFSA. *Degree program information:* Part-time and evening/weekend programs available. Part-time, evening/weekend, online learning. Offers nursing (MS, MSN, DNP, PhD). *Application deadline:* Applications are processed on a rolling basis. *Application fee:* $65. Electronic applications accepted. *Application Contact:* Lori Stania, Director, Graduate Student Services, 814-865-1795, Fax: 814-863-4627, E-mail: l-gswww@lists.psu.edu. *Dean*, Dr. Paula F. Milone-Nuzzo, 814-863-0245, Fax: 814-865-3779.

College of the Liberal Arts Students: 749 full-time (398 women), 42 part-time (27 women). Average age 28. 2,672 applicants, 18% accepted, 159 enrolled. *Financial support:* Fellowships, research assistantships, teaching assistantships, career-related internships or fieldwork, Federal Work-Study, scholarships/grants, traineeships, health care benefits, and unspecified assistantships available. Support available to part-time students. Financial award application deadline: 3/1; financial award applicants required to submit FAFSA. *Degree program information:* Part-time and evening/weekend programs available. Part-time, evening/weekend, online learning. Offers anthropology (MA, PhD); applied linguistics (PhD); communication arts and sciences (MA, PhD); comparative literature (MA, PhD); criminology (MA, PhD); economics (MA, PhD); English (MA, MFA, PhD); French (MA, PhD); German (MA, PhD); history (MA, PhD); human resources and employment relations (MPS, MS); labor and global workers' rights (MPS); liberal arts (MA, MFA, MPS, MS, PhD); philosophy (MA, PhD); political science (MA, PhD); psychology (MS, PhD); psychology of leadership at work (MPS); Russian and comparative literature (MA);

sociology (MA, PhD); Spanish (MA, PhD); teaching English as a second language (MA). *Application deadline:* Applications are processed on a rolling basis. *Application fee:* $65. Electronic applications accepted. *Application Contact:* Lori Stania, Director, Graduate Student Services, 814-865-1795, Fax: 814-863-4627, E-mail: l-gswww@lists.psu.edu. *Dean*, Dr. Susan Welch, 814-865-7691, Fax: 814-863-2085.

Eberly College of Science Students: 712 full-time (257 women), 33 part-time (14 women). Average age 26. 1,746 applicants, 16% accepted, 105 enrolled. *Financial support:* Fellowships, research assistantships, teaching assistantships, career-related internships or fieldwork, Federal Work-Study, scholarships/grants, traineeships, health care benefits, and unspecified assistantships available. Support available to part-time students. Financial award application deadline: 3/1; financial award applicants required to submit FAFSA. *Degree program information:* Part-time programs available. Part-time, online learning. Offers applied statistics (MAS); astronomy and astrophysics (MS, PhD); biochemistry, microbiology, and molecular biology (MS, PhD); biology (MS, PhD); biotechnology (MBIOT); chemistry (MS, PhD); mathematics (M Ed, MA, D Ed, PhD); physics (M Ed, MS, PhD); science (M Ed, MA, MAS, MBIOT, MS, D Ed, PhD); statistics (MA, MS, PhD). *Application deadline:* Applications are processed on a rolling basis. *Application fee:* $65. Electronic applications accepted. *Application Contact:* Lori Stania, Director, Graduate Student Services, 814-865-1795, Fax: 814-863-4627, E-mail: l-gswww@lists.psu.edu. *Dean*, Dr. Douglas R. Cavener, 814-865-9591, Fax: 814-865-3634.

Intercollege Graduate Programs Students: 167 full-time (60 women), 4 part-time (1 woman). Average age 25. 1,122 applicants, 15% accepted, 79 enrolled. *Financial support:* Fellowships, research assistantships, teaching assistantships, career-related internships or fieldwork, Federal Work-Study, scholarships/grants, traineeships, health care benefits, and unspecified assistantships available. Support available to part-time students. Financial award application deadline: 3/1; financial award applicants required to submit FAFSA. *Degree program information:* Part-time and evening/weekend programs available. Part-time, evening/weekend, online learning. Offers acoustics (M Eng, MS, PhD); bioengineering (MS, PhD); ecology (MS, PhD); environmental pollution control (MEPC, MS); materials science and engineering (MS, PhD); molecular, cellular, and integrative biosciences (MS, PhD); physiology (MS, PhD); plant biology (MS, PhD); renewable energy and sustainability systems (MPS). *Application deadline:* Applications are processed on a rolling basis. *Application fee:* $65. Electronic applications accepted. *Application Contact:* Lori Stania, Director, Graduate Student Services, 814-865-1795, Fax: 814-863-4627, E-mail: l-gswww@lists.psu.edu. *Vice Provost for Graduate Education and Dean of the Graduate School*, Dr. Regina Vasilatos-Younken, 814-865-2516, Fax: 814-863-4627.

The Mary Jean and Frank P. Smeal College of Business Students: 294 full-time (92 women), 1 part-time (0 women). Average age 29. 1,204 applicants, 24% accepted, 139 enrolled. *Financial support:* Fellowships, research assistantships, teaching assistantships, career-related internships or fieldwork, Federal Work-Study, scholarships/grants, traineeships, health care benefits, and unspecified assistantships available. Support available to part-time students. Financial award application deadline: 3/1; financial award applicants required to submit FAFSA. *Degree program information:* Part-time and evening/weekend programs available. Part-time, evening/weekend, online learning. Offers accounting (M Acc); business administration (MBA, MS, PhD); supply chain management (MPS). *Application deadline:* Applications are processed on a rolling basis. *Application fee:* $65. Electronic applications accepted. *Application Contact:* Lori Stania, Director, Graduate Student Services, 814-865-1795, Fax: 814-863-4627, E-mail: l-gswww@lists.psu.edu. *Dean*, Dr. Charles H. Whiteman, 814-863-0448, Fax: 814-865-7064.

School of International Affairs Students: 87 full-time (48 women), 2 part-time (0 women). Average age 24. 221 applicants, 84% accepted, 54 enrolled. *Financial support:* Fellowships, research assistantships, teaching assistantships, career-related internships or fieldwork, Federal Work-Study, scholarships/grants, traineeships, health care benefits, and unspecified assistantships available. Support available to part-time students. Financial award application deadline: 3/1; financial award applicants required to submit FAFSA. *Degree program information:* Part-time and evening/weekend programs available. Part-time, evening/weekend, online learning. Offers international affairs (MIA). *Application deadline:* Applications are processed on a rolling basis. *Application fee:* $65. Electronic applications accepted. *Application Contact:* Lori Stania, Director, Graduate Student Services, 814-865-1795, Fax: 814-863-4627, E-mail: l-gswww@lists.psu.edu. *Interim Director*, James W. Houck, 814-863-1521, Fax: 814-863-7274.

Penn State Law Students: 460 full-time (195 women). 2,061 applicants, 45% accepted, 170 enrolled. *Faculty:* 43 full-time (18 women), 11 part-time/adjunct (7 women). Offers law (LL M, JD, SJD). *Application deadline:* For fall admission, 3/31 for domestic students. Applications are processed on a rolling basis. *Application fee:* $60. Electronic applications accepted. *Application Contact:* Amanda DiPolvere, Assistant Dean, Admissions and Financial Aid, 800-840-1122, E-mail: admissions@pennstatelaw.psu.edu. *Interim Dean*, James W. Houck, 814-863-1521.

PENNSYLVANIA ACADEMY OF THE FINE ARTS, Philadelphia, PA 19102

General Information Independent, coed, comprehensive institution. *Graduate housing:* On-campus housing not available.

GRADUATE UNITS

Division of Graduate Studies Offers drawing (MFA, Postbaccalaureate Certificate); painting (MFA, Postbaccalaureate Certificate); printmaking (MFA, Postbaccalaureate Certificate); sculpture (MFA, Postbaccalaureate Certificate). MFA program also available in a low-residency format. Electronic applications accepted.

PENNSYLVANIA COLLEGE OF HEALTH SCIENCES, Lancaster, PA 17602

General Information Independent, coed, primarily women, comprehensive institution.

GRADUATE UNITS

Graduate Programs Offers administration (MSN); education (MSHS, MSN); healthcare administration (MHA).

PENTECOSTAL THEOLOGICAL SEMINARY, Cleveland, TN 37320-3330

General Information Independent-religious, coed, graduate-only institution. *Graduate housing:* Rooms and/or apartments available to single and married students.

GRADUATE UNITS

Graduate and Professional Programs ***Degree program information:*** Part-time programs available. Part-time. Offers biblical studies (MTS); church ministries (MA); counseling (MA); discipleship and Christian formation (MA); ministry (D Min); Pentecostal theology (MTS); theology (M Div).

PEPPERDINE UNIVERSITY, Malibu, CA 90263

General Information Independent-religious, coed, university. *Enrollment:* 7,632 graduate, professional, and undergraduate students; 2,310 full-time matriculated graduate/professional students (1,321 women), 1,758 part-time matriculated graduate/professional students (1,043 women). *Enrollment by degree level:* 2,841 master's, 1,227 doctoral. *Graduate faculty:* 172 full-time (60 women), 227 part-time/adjunct (127 women). *Graduate housing:* Rooms and/or apartments available on a first-come, first-served basis to single and married students. *Student services:* Campus employment opportunities, campus safety program, career counseling, exercise/wellness program, free psychological counseling, international student services, low-cost health insurance, multicultural affairs office, services for students with disabilities, teacher training. *Library:* Payson Library plus 6 others. *Collection:* Books: 365,165 (physical), 339,374 (digital/electronic); Serial titles: 529 (physical), 53,284 (digital/electronic); Databases: 148. Weekly public service hours: 112; students can reserve study rooms.

Computer facilities: Computer purchase and lease plans are available. 218 computers available on campus for general student use. A campuswide network can be accessed from student residence rooms and from off campus. Online class registration is available. Website: http://www.pepperdine.edu/

General Application Contact: Kristy Collins, Dean of Admission and Enrollment Management, Seaver College, 310-506-4392, Fax: 310-506-4861, E-mail: admission-seaver@pepperdine.edu.

GRADUATE UNITS

Graduate School of Education and Psychology Students: 710 full-time (556 women), 813 part-time (610 women); includes 624 minority (198 Black or African American, non-Hispanic/Latino; 10 American Indian or Alaska Native, non-Hispanic/Latino; 121 Asian, non-Hispanic/Latino; 246 Hispanic/Latino; 9 Native Hawaiian or other Pacific Islander, non-Hispanic/Latino; 40 Two or more races, non-Hispanic/Latino), 67 international. 821 applicants, 83% accepted, 384 enrolled. *Faculty:* 43 full-time (24 women), 142 part-time/adjunct (102 women). *Financial support:* Research assistantships, teaching assistantships, career-related internships or fieldwork, Federal Work-Study, institutionally sponsored loans, scholarships/grants, and unspecified assistantships available. Support available to part-time students. Financial award applicants required to submit FAFSA. In 2015, 405 master's, 103 doctorates awarded. *Degree program information:* Part-time and evening/weekend programs available. Part-time, evening/weekend, online learning. Offers education and psychology (MA, MS, Ed D, Psy D). *Application deadline:* Applications are processed on a rolling basis. *Application fee:* $55. *Application Contact:* Barbara Moore, Director, Recruitment and Admissions, 310-568-5744, E-mail: barbara.moore@pepperdine.edu. *Dean*, Dr. Helen Williams, 310-568-5615, E-mail: helen.williams@pepperdine.edu.

Division of Education Students: 272 full-time (187 women), 386 part-time (265 women); includes 276 minority (124 Black or African American, non-Hispanic/Latino; 6 American Indian or Alaska Native, non-Hispanic/Latino; 52 Asian, non-Hispanic/Latino; 72 Hispanic/Latino; 5 Native Hawaiian or other Pacific Islander, non-Hispanic/Latino; 17 Two or more races, non-Hispanic/Latino), 36 international. Average age 39. 333 applicants, 94% accepted, 175 enrolled. *Faculty:* 16 full-time (8 women), 2 part-time/adjunct (both women). *Financial support:* Research assistantships, teaching assistantships, career-related internships or fieldwork, institutionally sponsored loans, and scholarships/grants available. Support available to part-time students. Financial award application deadline: 7/1; financial award applicants required to submit FAFSA. In 2015, 143 master's, 84 doctorates awarded. *Degree program information:* Part-time and evening/weekend programs available. Part-time, evening/weekend, online learning. Offers administration and preliminary administrative services (MS); education (MA); educational leadership, administration, and policy (Ed D); learning technologies (MA, Ed D); organization change (Ed D); organizational leadership (Ed D); social entrepreneurship and change (MA); teaching (MA); teaching: TESOL (MA). *Application deadline:* Applications are processed on a rolling basis. *Application fee:* $55. *Application Contact:* Melissa Mansfield, Admissions Manager, Education Division, 310-568-5786, E-mail: jennifer.agatep@pepperdine.edu. *Associate Dean, Education Division*, Dr. Martine Jago, 310-568-2828, E-mail: martine.jago@pepperdine.edu.

Division of Psychology Students: 438 full-time (369 women), 427 part-time (345 women); includes 348 minority (74 Black or African American, non-Hispanic/Latino; 4 American Indian or Alaska Native, non-Hispanic/Latino; 69 Asian, non-Hispanic/Latino; 174 Hispanic/Latino; 4 Native Hawaiian or other Pacific Islander, non-Hispanic/Latino; 23 Two or more races, non-Hispanic/Latino), 31 international. Average age 31. 488 applicants, 76% accepted, 209 enrolled. *Faculty:* 27 full-time (16 women), 19 part-time/adjunct (10 women). *Financial support:* Research assistantships, teaching assistantships, career-related internships or fieldwork, and scholarships/grants available. Support available to part-time students. Financial award application deadline: 7/1; financial award applicants required to submit FAFSA. In 2015, 262 master's, 19 doctorates awarded. *Degree program information:* Part-time and evening/weekend programs available. Part-time, evening/weekend. Offers behavioral psychology (MS); clinical psychology (Psy D); clinical psychology (MA); clinical psychology with Latinos (MA); psychology (MA). *Application deadline:* For fall admission, 2/1 for domestic students. Applications are processed on a rolling basis. *Application fee:* $55. *Application Contact:* Deanna Lazaro Schwartz, Admissions Manager, Psychology, 310-568-5777, E-mail: deanna.lazaro@pepperdine.edu. *Associate Dean, Psychology Division*, Dr. Robert A. deMayo, 310-568-5747, E-mail: robert.demayo@pepperdine.edu.

Graziadio School of Business and Management Students: 884 full-time (393 women), 768 part-time (337 women); includes 414 minority (122 Black or African American, non-Hispanic/Latino; 3 American Indian or Alaska Native, non-Hispanic/Latino; 160 Asian, non-Hispanic/Latino; 126 Hispanic/Latino; 1 Native Hawaiian or other Pacific Islander, non-Hispanic/Latino; 2 Two or more races, non-Hispanic/Latino), 360 international. Average age 31. 2,120 applicants, 61% accepted, 448 enrolled. *Faculty:* 86 full-time (22 women), 35 part-time/adjunct (13 women). *Financial support:* Career-related internships or fieldwork, institutionally sponsored loans, scholarships/grants, and unspecified assistantships available. Support available to part-time students. Financial award applicants required to submit FAFSA. In 2015, 659 master's awarded. *Degree program information:* Part-time programs available. Part-time. Offers accounting (MS); applied analytics (MS); applied finance (MS); business administration (MBA); business and management (MBA, MS); global business (MS); human resources (MS); management and leadership (MS); organization development (MS). *Application fee:* $75. Electronic applications accepted. *Application Contact:* Morag Knapp, Assistant Director of Admission, Graziadio School of Business and Management, 310-568-5527, E-mail: morag.knapp@pepperdine.edu. *Interim Dean*, Dr. David M. Smith, 310-568-5689, Fax: 310-568-5500, E-mail: david.smith@pepperdine.edu.

School of Law Students: 637 full-time (331 women), 60 part-time (32 women); includes 208 minority (31 Black or African American, non-Hispanic/Latino; 3 American Indian or Alaska Native, non-Hispanic/Latino; 66 Asian, non-Hispanic/Latino; 76 Hispanic/Latino; 32 Two or more races, non-Hispanic/Latino), 46 international. Average age 27. 2,735 applicants, 52% accepted, 249 enrolled. *Faculty:* 38 full-time (12 women), 43 part-time/adjunct (12 women). *Financial support:* Fellowships, research assistantships, teaching assistantships, career-related internships or fieldwork, Federal Work-Study, institutionally sponsored loans, and scholarships/grants available. Support available to part-time students. Financial award application deadline: 4/1; financial award applicants required to submit FAFSA. In 2015, 60 master's, 198 doctorates awarded. Offers dispute resolution (MDR); law (LL M, MDR, JD). *Application deadline:* For fall admission, 3/1 for domestic and international students. Applications are processed on a rolling basis. *Application fee:* $60. Electronic applications accepted. *Application Contact:* Shannon Phillips, Director of Admissions and Records, 310-506-4631, Fax: 310-506-4266, E-mail: shannon.phillips@pepperdine.edu. *Dean, School of Law,* Dr. Deanell Tacha, 310-506-4621, E-mail: deanell.tacha@pepperdine.edu.

School of Public Policy Students: 61 full-time (29 women), 9 part-time (3 women); includes 24 minority (12 Black or African American, non-Hispanic/Latino; 2 American Indian or Alaska Native, non-Hispanic/Latino; 4 Asian, non-Hispanic/Latino; 4 Hispanic/Latino; 1 Native Hawaiian or other Pacific Islander, non-Hispanic/Latino; 1 Two or more races, non-Hispanic/Latino), 13 international. Average age 26. 158 applicants, 67% accepted, 34 enrolled. *Faculty:* 5 full-time (2 women), 7 part-time/adjunct (0 women). *Financial support:* Institutionally sponsored loans and scholarships/grants available. Financial award application deadline: 5/1; financial award applicants required to submit FAFSA. In 2015, 47 master's awarded. Offers American politics (MPP); economics (MPP); international relations (MPP); state and local policy (MPP). *Application deadline:* For fall admission, 6/15 for domestic students. Applications are processed on a rolling basis. *Application fee:* $50. Electronic applications accepted. *Application Contact:* Melinda E. Van Hemert, Assistant Dean for Student Services and Financial Aid, 310-506-7492, Fax: 310-506-7494, E-mail: melinda.vanhemert@pepperdine.edu. *Dean, School of Public Policy,* Dr. Pete Peterson, 310-506-7490, Fax: 310-506-7494, E-mail: pete.n.peterson@pepperdine.edu.

Seaver College Students: 18 full-time (12 women), 108 part-time (61 women); includes 30 minority (9 Black or African American, non-Hispanic/Latino; 10 Asian, non-Hispanic/Latino; 10 Hispanic/Latino; 1 Two or more races, non-Hispanic/Latino), 4 international. Average age 30. 157 applicants, 50% accepted, 50 enrolled. *Financial support:* Fellowships, research assistantships, teaching assistantships, career-related internships or fieldwork, Federal Work-Study, institutionally sponsored loans, scholarships/grants, and tuition waivers (partial) available. Support available to part-time students. Financial award application deadline: 2/15; financial award applicants required to submit FAFSA. In 2015, 24 master's awarded. *Degree program information:* Part-time and evening/weekend programs available. Part-time, evening/weekend. Offers business (MS); communication (MA, MFA); humanities (MA, MFA); religion (M Div, MA, MS). *Application deadline:* For fall admission, 2/1 priority date for domestic students. Applications are processed on a rolling basis. *Application fee:* $55. *Application Contact:* Joy Brown, Admission Counselor, 310-506-4392, E-mail: joy.brown@pepperdine.edu. *Assistant Dean, Special Academic and Graduate Programs for Seaver College,* Dr. Dana Dudley, 310-506-6047, Fax: 310-506-4816, E-mail: dana.dudley@pepperdine.edu.

Division of Business Students: 2 full-time (both women), 29 part-time (17 women); includes 7 minority (3 Black or African American, non-Hispanic/Latino; 2 Asian, non-Hispanic/Latino; 1 Hispanic/Latino; 1 Two or more races, non-Hispanic/Latino). Average age 22. Offers accounting (MS). *Application deadline:* For fall admission, 2/1 priority date for domestic students. *Application fee:* $55. Electronic applications accepted. *Chair/Professor of English,* Dr. Maire Mullins, 310-506-4894, E-mail: maire.mullins@pepperdine.edu.

Division of Communication Students: 3 full-time (2 women), 27 part-time (20 women); includes 6 minority (2 Asian, non-Hispanic/Latino; 2 Hispanic/Latino; 1 Native Hawaiian or other Pacific Islander, non-Hispanic/Latino; 1 Two or more races, non-Hispanic/Latino), 2 international. *Financial support:* Research assistantships, teaching assistantships, career-related internships or fieldwork, and scholarships/grants available. Support available to part-time students. Financial award applicants required to submit FAFSA. In 2015, 5 master's awarded. *Degree program information:* Part-time programs available. Part-time. Offers cinematic media production (MFA); strategic communication (MA). *Application deadline:* For fall admission, 2/1 priority date for domestic students, 2/1 for international students. Applications are processed on a rolling basis. *Application fee:* $65. Electronic applications accepted. *Application Contact:* Michael Truschke, Dean of Admission and Enrollment Management, 310-506-6165, Fax: 310-506-4861, E-mail: admission-seaver@pepperdine.edu. *Chair/Professor of Journalism,* Dr. Kenneth E. Waters, 310-506-4245, E-mail: ken.waters@pepperdine.edu.

Division of Humanities Students: 3 full-time (all women), 57 part-time (33 women); includes 14 minority (4 Black or African American, non-Hispanic/Latino; 5 Asian, non-Hispanic/Latino; 4 Hispanic/Latino; 1 Two or more races, non-Hispanic/Latino). Average age 31. *Financial support:* Applicants required to submit FAFSA. In 2015, 14 master's awarded. *Degree program information:* Part-time programs available. Part-time. Offers American studies (MA); writing for screen and television (MFA). *Application deadline:* For fall admission, 2/1 priority date for domestic students. Applications are processed on a rolling basis. *Application fee:* $65. *Chair/Professor of English,* Dr. Michael G. Ditmore, 310-506-4182, Fax: 310-506-7307, E-mail: michael.ditmore@pepperdine.edu.

Division of Religion Students: 1 (woman) full-time, 10 part-time (3 women); includes 1 minority (Hispanic/Latino). Average age 32. *Financial support:* Applicants required to submit FAFSA. In 2015, 2 master's awarded. *Degree program information:* Part-time and evening/weekend programs available. Part-time, evening/weekend. Offers ministry (MS); religion (M Div, MA). *Application deadline:* For fall admission, 2/1 priority date for domestic students. Applications are processed on a rolling basis. *Application fee:* $65. Electronic applications accepted. *Chair/Professor,* Dr. Timothy Willis, 310-506-4352, Fax: 310-506-7271, E-mail: timothy.willis@pepperdine.edu.

PERU STATE COLLEGE, Peru, NE 68421

General Information State-supported, coed, comprehensive institution. *Graduate housing:* Rooms and/or apartments available to single and married students.

GRADUATE UNITS

Graduate Programs ***Degree program information:*** Part-time programs available. Part-time, online learning. Offers curriculum and instruction (MS Ed); organizational management (MS).

PFEIFFER UNIVERSITY, Misenheimer, NC 28109-0960

General Information Independent-religious, coed, comprehensive institution. *Graduate housing:* On-campus housing not available.

GRADUATE UNITS

Program in Business Administration ***Degree program information:*** Part-time and evening/weekend programs available. Part-time, evening/weekend, online learning. Offers business administration (MBA).

Program in Elementary Education Offers elementary education (MAT, MS).

Program in Health Administration Offers health administration (MHA).

Program in Leadership and Organizational Change Offers leadership and organizational change (MS).

Program in Practical Theology ***Degree program information:*** Part-time and evening/weekend programs available. Part-time, evening/weekend. Offers practical theology (MA).

PHILADELPHIA COLLEGE OF OSTEOPATHIC MEDICINE, Philadelphia, PA 19131-1694

General Information Independent, coed, graduate-only institution. *Graduate housing:* On-campus housing not available. *Research affiliation:* Intracell (biotechnology inflammation), Proteapex (biotechnology), Novartis Pharmaceuticals (drug development), Theramunex (biotechnology inflammation), Lankenau Institute for Medical Research (cell biology), Cleveland Museum Natural History (developmental biology).

GRADUATE UNITS

Graduate and Professional Programs Offers applied behavior analysis (Certificate); biomedical sciences (MS); clinical health psychology (Post-Doctoral Certificate); clinical neuropsychology (Post-Doctoral Certificate); clinical psychology (Psy D); forensic medicine (MS); health sciences (MS); mental health counseling (MS); organizational development and leadership (MS); osteopathic medicine (DO); psychology (Certificate); school psychology (MS, Psy D, Ed S).

PHILADELPHIA UNIVERSITY, Philadelphia, PA 19144

General Information Independent, coed, comprehensive institution. *Graduate housing:* On-campus housing not available.

GRADUATE UNITS

College of Architecture and the Built Environment Offers architecture (M Arch); architecture and the built environment (MS); construction management (MS); geodesign (MS); high performance building (MS); interior architecture (MS); sustainable design (MS).

College of Science, Health and the Liberal Arts ***Degree program information:*** Part-time and evening/weekend programs available. Part-time, evening/weekend, online learning. Offers community and trauma counseling (MS); disaster medicine and management (MS); midwifery (MS); nurse midwifery (Postbaccalaureate Certificate); occupational therapy (MS, OTD); physician assistant studies (MS); science, health and the liberal arts (MS, Postbaccalaureate Certificate). Electronic applications accepted.

School of Business Administration ***Degree program information:*** Part-time and evening/weekend programs available. Part-time, evening/weekend, online learning. Offers business administration (MBA, MS); general business (MBA); global fashion enterprise (MS); innovation (MBA); management (MBA); marketing (MBA); strategic design (MBA); strategic design business administration (MBA); taxation (MS). Electronic applications accepted.

School of Engineering and Textiles ***Degree program information:*** Part-time programs available. Part-time. Offers engineering and textiles (MS, PhD); industrial design (MS); interactive design and media (MS); modeling, simulation and data analytics (MS); surface imaging (MS); textile design (MS); textile engineering (MS); textile engineering and sciences (PhD). Electronic applications accepted.

PHILLIPS GRADUATE INSTITUTE, Encino, CA 91316-1509

General Information Independent, coed, graduate-only institution. *Graduate housing:* On-campus housing not available.

GRADUATE UNITS

Program in Organizational Management and Consulting ***Degree program information:*** Evening/weekend programs available. Evening/weekend. Offers organizational management and consulting (Psy D). Electronic applications accepted.

Programs in Marriage and Family Therapy and School Counseling ***Degree program information:*** Evening/weekend programs available. Evening/weekend. Offers art therapy (MA); marriage and family therapy (MA); school counseling (MA). Electronic applications accepted.

PHILLIPS THEOLOGICAL SEMINARY, Tulsa, OK 74116

General Information Independent-religious, coed, graduate-only institution. *Graduate housing:* On-campus housing not available.

GRADUATE UNITS

Programs in Theology ***Degree program information:*** Part-time programs available. Part-time, online learning. Offers administration of church agencies (M Div); campus ministry (M Div); church-related social work (M Div); college and seminary teaching (M Div); global mission work (M Div); institutional chaplaincy (M Div); ministerial vocations in Christian education (M Div); ministry (D Min); ministry and culture (MAMC); ministry of music (M Div); parish ministry (D Min); pastoral care and counseling (M Div); pastoral counseling (D Min); pastoral ministry (M Div); practices of ministry (D Min); theological studies (MTS).

PHOENIX SEMINARY, Phoenix, AZ 85018

General Information Independent-religious, coed, graduate-only institution.

GRADUATE UNITS

Graduate Programs ***Degree program information:*** Part-time and evening/weekend programs available. Part-time, evening/weekend. Offers Biblical and theological studies (Graduate Diploma); Biblical communication (M Div); Biblical leadership (MA); Christian counseling (Graduate Diploma); counseling and family (M Div); leadership development (M Div); ministry (D Min); professional counseling (MA).

PIEDMONT COLLEGE, Demorest, GA 30535

General Information Independent-religious, coed, comprehensive institution. *Enrollment:* 2,264 graduate, professional, and undergraduate students; 330 full-time matriculated graduate/professional students (242 women), 650 part-time matriculated graduate/professional students (532 women). *Enrollment by degree level:* 519 master's, 88 doctoral, 373 other advanced degrees. *Tuition, area resident:* Full-time $8478. *Graduate housing:* Room and/or apartments available to single students; on-campus housing not available to married students. Typical cost: $6048 per year ($9400 including board). Housing application deadline: 4/1. *Student services:* Campus employment opportunities, campus safety program, career counseling, exercise/wellness program, services for students with disabilities, teacher training, writing training. *Library:* Arrendale

Library plus 2 others. *Collection:* Books: 99,693 (physical), 180,346 (digital/electronic); Serial titles: 24,272 (digital/electronic).

Computer facilities: 150 computers available on campus for general student use. A campuswide network can be accessed from student residence rooms and from off campus. Online class registration is available.
Website: http://www.piedmont.edu/

General Application Contact: Kathleen Anderson, Director of Graduate Enrollment Management, 706-778-8500 Ext. 1181, Fax: 706-776-0150, E-mail: kanderson@piedmont.edu.

GRADUATE UNITS

School of Business Students: 38 full-time (23 women), 29 part-time (18 women); includes 8 minority (7 Black or African American, non-Hispanic/Latino; 1 American Indian or Alaska Native, non-Hispanic/Latino). Average age 30. 46 applicants, 50% accepted, 19 enrolled. *Financial support:* Federal Work-Study and unspecified assistantships available. Financial award applicants required to submit FAFSA. In 2015, 41 master's awarded. *Degree program information:* Part-time and evening/weekend programs available. Part-time, evening/weekend. Offers business (MBA). *Application deadline:* For fall admission, 7/15 for domestic students; for spring admission, 12/1 for domestic students. Applications are processed on a rolling basis. Electronic applications accepted. *Application Contact:* Kathleen Anderson, Director of Graduate Enrollment Management, 706-778-8500 Ext. 1181, Fax: 706-778-0150, E-mail: kanderson@piedmont.edu. *Dean*, Dr. John Misner, 706-778-3000 Ext. 1349, Fax: 706-778-0701, E-mail: jmisner@piedmont.edu.

School of Education Students: 290 full-time (217 women), 614 part-time (508 women); includes 131 minority (97 Black or African American, non-Hispanic/Latino; 4 American Indian or Alaska Native, non-Hispanic/Latino; 5 Asian, non-Hispanic/Latino; 11 Hispanic/Latino; 6 Native Hawaiian or other Pacific Islander, non-Hispanic/Latino; 8 Two or more races, non-Hispanic/Latino), 6 international. Average age 37. 257 applicants, 64% accepted, 160 enrolled. *Financial support:* Career-related internships or fieldwork, Federal Work-Study, and unspecified assistantships available. Support available to part-time students. Financial award applicants required to submit FAFSA. In 2015, 288 master's, 243 other advanced degrees awarded. *Degree program information:* Part-time and evening/weekend programs available. Part-time, evening/weekend. Offers art education (MAT); curriculum and instruction (Ed S); early childhood education (MA, MAT); instructional technology (MAT); middle grades education (MA, MAT); music education (MAT); secondary education (MA, MAT); special education (MA, MAT). *Application deadline:* For fall admission, 7/15 for domestic students; for spring admission, 12/1 for domestic students. Applications are processed on a rolling basis. Electronic applications accepted. *Application Contact:* Kathleen Anderson, Director of Graduate Enrollment Management, 706-778-8500 Ext. 1181, Fax: 706-778-0150, E-mail: kanderson@piedmont.edu. *Dean*, Dr. Don Gnecco, 706-778-3000 Ext. 1201, Fax: 706-776-9608, E-mail: dgnecco@piedmont.edu.

PIEDMONT INTERNATIONAL UNIVERSITY, Winston-Salem, NC 27101-5197

General Information Independent-religious, coed, comprehensive institution. *Enrollment:* 13 full-time matriculated graduate/professional students (1 woman), 71 part-time matriculated graduate/professional students (6 women). *Enrollment by degree level:* 74 master's, 10 doctoral. *Graduate faculty:* 4 full-time (0 women), 10 part-time/adjunct (0 women). *Tuition, area resident:* Part-time $295 per credit. *Required fees:* $180 per semester. Tuition and fees vary according to course load. *Graduate housing:* Rooms and/or apartments available on a first-come, first-served basis to single and married students. Housing application deadline: 5/1. *Student services:* Campus employment opportunities, campus safety program, career counseling, writing training. *Library:* George Manuel Memorial Library.

Computer facilities: 20 computers available on campus for general student use. A campuswide network can be accessed from student residence rooms and from off campus. Online class registration is available.
Website: http://www.piedmontu.edu/

General Application Contact: Angela D. Hoover, Director of Graduate Admissions, 336-714-7927, Fax: 336-725-5522, E-mail: hoovera@piedmontu.edu.

GRADUATE UNITS

Graduate School Students: 28 full-time (6 women), 136 part-time (44 women); includes 28 minority (17 Black or African American, non-Hispanic/Latino; 2 Asian, non-Hispanic/Latino; 8 Hispanic/Latino; 1 Two or more races, non-Hispanic/Latino), 4 international. Average age 40. 12 applicants, 100% accepted. *Faculty:* 5 full-time (0 women), 8 part-time/adjunct (1 woman). *Financial support:* Career-related internships or fieldwork, Federal Work-Study, and scholarships/grants available. Support available to part-time students. Financial award applicants required to submit FAFSA. In 2015, 23 master's awarded. *Degree program information:* Part-time programs available. Part-time, online learning. Offers Biblical studies (PhD); curriculum and instruction (M Ed); divinity (M Div); educational leadership (M Ed); leadership (MA, PhD); ministry (MA Min, D Min); non-language track (MABS); PhD preparation track (MABS). *Application deadline:* For fall admission, 8/15 priority date for domestic students; for spring admission, 1/1 for domestic students. Applications are processed on a rolling basis. *Application fee:* $30. Electronic applications accepted. *Application Contact:* Angela Hoover, Director of Graduate Admissions, 336-714-7927, Fax: 336-725-5522, E-mail: hoovera@piedmontu.edu. *Dean*, Dr. Larry Tyler, 336-714-7989, Fax: 336-714-2715, E-mail: tylerl@piedmontu.edu.

Temple Baptist Seminary ***Degree program information:*** Part-time and evening/weekend programs available. Part-time, evening/weekend, online learning. Offers theology (M Div, D Min). *Application Contact:* M. Chris Dunn, Graduate Admissions Representative, 336-714-7016, E-mail: dunnm@piedmontu.edu. *Vice President*, Dr. Barkev S. Trachian, 336-714-7910, Fax: 336-714-2795, E-mail: trachianb@piedmontu.edu.

PINCHOT UNIVERSITY, Seattle, WA 98104

General Information Independent, coed, graduate-only institution.

GRADUATE UNITS

MBA Programs Offers business administration (MBA).

Organization Systems Renewal Program Offers organizational leadership (MA).

PITTSBURGH THEOLOGICAL SEMINARY, Pittsburgh, PA 15206-2596

General Information Independent-religious, coed, graduate-only institution. *Enrollment by degree level:* 134 master's, 115 doctoral. *Graduate faculty:* 16 full-time (5 women), 6 part-time/adjunct (2 women). *Tuition, area resident:* Full-time $11,520; part-time $358 per credit. *Required fees:* $300; $300 per year. $100. One-time fee: $125. *Graduate housing:* Rooms and/or apartments available on a first-come, first-served basis to single and married students. Typical cost: $5175 per year for single students; $6244 per year for married students. Housing application deadline: 6/1. *Student services:* Campus employment opportunities, campus safety program, career counseling, exercise/wellness program, free psychological counseling, international student services, low-cost health insurance, services for students with disabilities, writing training. *Library:* Clifford E. Barbour Library. *Collection:* Books: 304,623 (physical), 71 (digital/electronic); Serial titles: 779 (physical), 156 (digital/electronic); Databases: 23. Weekly public service hours: 67.

Computer facilities: 15 computers available on campus for general student use. A campuswide network can be accessed from student residence rooms and from off campus. Online class registration is available.
Website: http://www.pts.edu/

General Application Contact: Rev. Anthony Rivera, Associate Director of Recruiting and Admissions, 412-924-1450, Fax: 412-924-1383, E-mail: arivera@pts.edu.

GRADUATE UNITS

Graduate and Professional Programs Students: 203 full-time (67 women), 46 part-time (23 women); includes 60 minority (48 Black or African American, non-Hispanic/Latino; 3 Asian, non-Hispanic/Latino; 4 Hispanic/Latino; 1 Native Hawaiian or other Pacific Islander, non-Hispanic/Latino; 4 Two or more races, non-Hispanic/Latino), 14 international. Average age 35. 57 applicants, 93% accepted, 44 enrolled. *Faculty:* 16 full-time (5 women), 6 part-time/adjunct (2 women). *Financial support:* In 2015–16, 104 students received support. Career-related internships or fieldwork, scholarships/grants, and institutional work-study available. Financial award application deadline: 5/1; financial award applicants required to submit FAFSA. In 2015, 29 master's, 8 doctorates awarded. *Degree program information:* Part-time and evening/weekend programs available. Part-time, evening/weekend. Offers divinity (M Div); ministry (D Min); theological studies (MA); theology (Th M); theology and ministry (MA); theology/biblical studies (MA). M Div/MSW offered jointly with University of Pittsburgh; JD/M Div with Duquesne University; M Div/MS with Carnegie Mellon University. *Application deadline:* For fall admission, 6/30 priority date for domestic students, 12/1 for international students; for winter admission, 10/15 priority date for domestic students; for spring admission, 1/15 priority date for domestic students. Applications are processed on a rolling basis. *Application fee:* $50. Electronic applications accepted. *Application Contact:* Dr. James Downey, Vice President for Enrollment and Institutional Effectiveness, 412-924-1450, Fax: 412-924-1750, E-mail: jdowney@pts.edu. *Dean of Faculty and Vice President for Academic Affairs*, Dr. Heathear H. Vacek, 412-924-1374, Fax: 412-924-1774, E-mail: hvacek@pts.edu.

PITTSBURG STATE UNIVERSITY, Pittsburg, KS 66762

General Information State-supported, coed, comprehensive institution. CGS member. *Enrollment:* 7,244 graduate, professional, and undergraduate students; 228 full-time matriculated graduate/professional students, 407 part-time matriculated graduate/professional students. *Enrollment by degree level:* 1,012 master's, 30 other advanced degrees. *Graduate faculty:* 126 full-time (40 women), 35 part-time/adjunct (14 women). Tuition, state resident: part-time $305 per credit hour. Tuition and fees vary according to course load, degree level and campus/location. *Graduate housing:* Rooms and/or apartments available on a first-come, first-served basis to single and married students. Typical cost: $7372 (including board) for single students; $7372 (including board) for married students. Housing application deadline: 8/15. *Student services:* Campus employment opportunities, campus safety program, career counseling, exercise/wellness program, free psychological counseling, international student services, low-cost health insurance, multicultural affairs office, services for students with disabilities, teacher training, writing training. *Library:* Leonard H. Axe Library plus 2 others. *Research affiliation:* Cargill, Inc. (vegetable oil).

Computer facilities: A campuswide network can be accessed from student residence rooms and from off campus. Online class registration is available.
Website: http://www.pittstate.edu/

General Application Contact: Lisa Allen, Assistant Director, 620-235-4218, Fax: 620-235-4219, E-mail: lallen@pittstate.edu.

GRADUATE UNITS

Graduate School Students: 387 full-time (223 women), 764 part-time (518 women); includes 130 minority (30 Black or African American, non-Hispanic/Latino; 25 American Indian or Alaska Native, non-Hispanic/Latino; 6 Asian, non-Hispanic/Latino; 31 Hispanic/Latino; 38 Two or more races, non-Hispanic/Latino), 165 international. 836 applicants, 83% accepted, 362 enrolled. *Faculty:* 223 full-time (74 women), 129 part-time/adjunct (68 women). *Financial support:* In 2015–16, 6 research assistantships with partial tuition reimbursements (averaging $5,000 per year), 104 teaching assistantships with full tuition reimbursements (averaging $5,500 per year) were awarded; career-related internships or fieldwork, Federal Work-Study, and unspecified assistantships also available. Financial award application deadline: 2/1; financial award applicants required to submit FAFSA. In 2015, 512 master's, 13 other advanced degrees awarded. *Degree program information:* Part-time and evening/weekend programs available. Part-time, evening/weekend, 100% online, blended/hybrid learning. *Application deadline:* For fall admission, 6/1 for international students; for spring admission, 10/15 for international students; for summer admission, 4/1 for international students. Applications are processed on a rolling basis. *Application fee:* $35 ($60 for international students). Electronic applications accepted. *Application Contact:* Lisa Allen, Assistant Director, 620-235-4223, Fax: 620-235-4219, E-mail: lallen@pittstate.edu. *Dean of Graduate and Continuing Studies*, Dr. Pawan Kahol, 620-235-4222, Fax: 620-235-4219, E-mail: pkahol@pittstate.edu.

College of Arts and Sciences Students: 191 (116 women); includes 31 minority (5 Black or African American, non-Hispanic/Latino; 6 American Indian or Alaska Native, non-Hispanic/Latino; 1 Asian, non-Hispanic/Latino; 6 Hispanic/Latino; 13 Two or more races, non-Hispanic/Latino), 33 international. *Financial support:* In 2015–16, 6 research assistantships with partial tuition reimbursements (averaging $5,000 per year), 48 teaching assistantships with full tuition reimbursements (averaging $5,500 per year) were awarded; career-related internships or fieldwork, Federal Work-Study, and unspecified assistantships also available. Financial award application deadline: 2/1; financial award applicants required to submit FAFSA. In 2015, 88 master's awarded. *Degree program information:* Part-time programs available. Part-time, 100% online, blended/hybrid learning. Offers arts and sciences (MA, MM, MS, MSN); biology (MS); chemistry (MS); communication (MA); conducting (MM); education (MM); English (MA); history (MA); mathematics (MS); nursing (MSN); performance (MM); physics (MS); polymer chemistry (MS). *Application deadline:* For fall admission, 6/1 for international students; for spring admission, 10/15 for international students; for summer admission, 4/1 for international students. Applications are processed on a rolling basis. *Application fee:* $35 ($60 for international students). Electronic applications accepted. *Application Contact:* Lisa Allen, Assistant Director, 620-235-

4223, Fax: 620-235-4219, E-mail: lallen@pittstate.edu. *Interim Dean*, Dr. Mary Carol Pomatto, 620-235-4432, E-mail: mpomatto@pittstate.edu.

College of Education Students: 550 (409 women); includes 61 minority (17 Black or African American, non-Hispanic/Latino; 12 American Indian or Alaska Native, non-Hispanic/Latino; 2 Asian, non-Hispanic/Latino; 16 Hispanic/Latino; 14 Two or more races, non-Hispanic/Latino), 8 international. *Financial support:* In 2015–16, 25 teaching assistantships with full tuition reimbursements (averaging $5,500 per year) were awarded; career-related internships or fieldwork, Federal Work-Study, and unspecified assistantships also available. Financial award application deadline: 2/1; financial award applicants required to submit FAFSA. In 2015, 266 master's, 13 other advanced degrees awarded. *Degree program information:* Part-time programs available. Part-time, 100% online, blended/hybrid learning. Offers advanced studies in leadership (Ed S); counselor education (MS); education (MS, Ed S); educational leadership (MS); educational technology (MS); general school administration (Ed S); health, human performance, and recreation (MS); psychology (MS); school counseling (MS); school psychology (Ed S); special education (MS). *Application deadline:* For fall admission, 6/1 for international students; for spring admission, 10/15 for international students; for summer admission, 4/1 for international students. Applications are processed on a rolling basis. *Application fee:* $35 ($60 for international students). Electronic applications accepted. *Application Contact:* Lisa Allen, Assistant Director, 620-235-4223, Fax: 620-235-4219, E-mail: lallen@pittstate.edu. *Dean*, Dr. Howard Smith, 620-235-4518, Fax: 620-235-4520, E-mail: hwsmith@pittstate.edu.

College of Technology Students: 230 (88 women); includes 24 minority (6 Black or African American, non-Hispanic/Latino; 5 American Indian or Alaska Native, non-Hispanic/Latino; 3 Asian, non-Hispanic/Latino; 4 Hispanic/Latino; 6 Two or more races, non-Hispanic/Latino), 96 international. *Financial support:* In 2015–16, 14 teaching assistantships with full tuition reimbursements (averaging $5,500 per year) were awarded; career-related internships or fieldwork, Federal Work-Study, and unspecified assistantships also available. Financial award application deadline: 2/1; financial award applicants required to submit FAFSA. In 2015, 104 master's, 2 other advanced degrees awarded. *Degree program information:* Part-time programs available. Part-time, 100% online, blended/hybrid learning. Offers career and technical education (MS); construction engineering technology (MET); electrical engineering technology (MET); general engineering technology (MET); human resource development (MS); manufacturing engineering technology (MET); mechanical engineering technology (MET); plastics engineering technology (MET); technology (MS); workforce development and education (Ed S). *Application deadline:* For fall admission, 6/1 for international students; for spring admission, 10/15 for international students; for summer admission, 4/1 for international students. Applications are processed on a rolling basis. *Application fee:* $35 ($60 for international students). Electronic applications accepted. *Application Contact:* Lisa Allen, Assistant Director, 620-235-4223, Fax: 620-235-4219, E-mail: lallen@pittstate.edu. *Dean*, Dr. Bruce Dallman, 620-235-4365.

Kelce College of Business Students: 62 (30 women); includes 7 minority (1 Black or African American, non-Hispanic/Latino; 2 American Indian or Alaska Native, non-Hispanic/Latino; 1 Hispanic/Latino; 3 Two or more races, non-Hispanic/Latino), 19 international. *Financial support:* In 2015–16, 15 teaching assistantships with full tuition reimbursements (averaging $5,500 per year) were awarded; research assistantships, career-related internships or fieldwork, Federal Work-Study, and unspecified assistantships also available. Financial award application deadline: 2/1; financial award applicants required to submit FAFSA. In 2015, 55 master's awarded. Offers accounting (MBA); business (MBA); general administration (MBA); international business (MBA). *Application deadline:* For fall admission, 6/1 for international students; for spring admission, 10/15 for international students; for summer admission, 4/1 for international students. Applications are processed on a rolling basis. *Application fee:* $35 ($60 for international students). Electronic applications accepted. *Application Contact:* Lisa Allen, Assistant Director, 620-235-4218, Fax: 620-235-4219, E-mail: lallen@pittstate.edu. *Dean*, Dr. Paul Grimes, 620-235-4590, Fax: 620-235-4578, E-mail: pgrimes@pittstate.edu.

PLYMOUTH STATE UNIVERSITY, Plymouth, NH 03264-1595

General Information State-supported, coed, comprehensive institution. *Graduate housing:* Rooms and/or apartments available on a first-come, first-served basis to single students and guaranteed to married students. Housing application deadline: 5/1. *Research affiliation:* Hubbard Brook Experimental Forest (science), New Hampshire Department of Environmental Services (science), White Mountain National Forest (science), National Oceanic and Atmospheric Administration (NOAA) (science).

GRADUATE UNITS

College of Graduate Studies *Degree program information:* Part-time and evening/weekend programs available. Part-time, evening/weekend, online learning.

Graduate Studies in Business *Degree program information:* Part-time and evening/weekend programs available. Part-time, evening/weekend, online learning. Offers general management (MBA).

Graduate Studies in Education *Degree program information:* Part-time and evening/weekend programs available. Part-time, evening/weekend, online learning. Offers applied meteorology (MS); art education (MAT); athletic training (MS); biology (MS); clinical mental health counseling (MS, CAGS); counseling (M Ed); curriculum and instruction (M Ed); education (CAGS); educational leadership (M Ed, CAGS); elementary education (M Ed); English education (M Ed); environmental science and policy (MS); health education (M Ed); heritage studies (M Ed); higher education (Ed D); human relations (M Ed); integrated arts (M Ed); language education (M Ed); learning, leadership and community (Ed D); library media (M Ed); mathematics education (M Ed); music education (M Ed); physical education (M Ed); reading and writing (M Ed); school counseling (M Ed); school psychology (M Ed, CAGS); science (MS); science education (MAT, MS); secondary education (M Ed); social studies education (M Ed); special education (M Ed); teaching (MAT).

Program in Historic Preservation Offers historic preservation (MA).

Program in Personal and Organizational Wellness Offers personal and organizational wellness (MA).

POINT LOMA NAZARENE UNIVERSITY, San Diego, CA 92106-2899

General Information Independent-religious, coed, comprehensive institution. *Enrollment:* 3,663 graduate, professional, and undergraduate students; 290 full-time matriculated graduate/professional students (202 women), 570 part-time matriculated graduate/professional students (418 women). *Enrollment by degree level:* 860 master's, 1 other advanced degree. *Graduate housing:* On-campus housing not available. *Student services:* Campus employment opportunities, campus safety program, career counseling, free psychological counseling, international student services, low-cost health insurance, services for students with disabilities, teacher training. *Library:* Ryan Library.

Computer facilities: 346 computers available on campus for general student use. A campuswide network can be accessed from student residence rooms and from off campus. Online class registration is available.
Website: http://www.pointloma.edu/

General Application Contact: Laura Leinweber, Director, Graduate Admissions, 866-692-4723, E-mail: gradinfo@pointloma.edu.

GRADUATE UNITS

Department of Biology Students: 19 part-time (16 women); includes 6 minority (1 Black or African American, non-Hispanic/Latino; 2 Asian, non-Hispanic/Latino; 2 Hispanic/Latino; 1 Two or more races, non-Hispanic/Latino). Average age 33. 5 applicants, 100% accepted, 3 enrolled. *Faculty:* 4 full-time (2 women). *Financial support:* Available to part-time students. Applicants required to submit FAFSA. In 2015, 7 master's awarded. *Degree program information:* Part-time programs available. Part-time. Offers biology (MA, MS). *Application deadline:* For fall admission, 7/26 priority date for domestic students; for spring admission, 11/29 priority date for domestic students; for summer admission, 5/23 priority date for domestic students. *Application fee:* $50. *Application Contact:* Laura Leinweber, Graduate Enrollment Counselor, 866-692-4723, E-mail: lauraleinweber@pointloma.edu. *Director of Master's Program in Biology*, Dr. Dianne Anderson, 619-849-2705, E-mail: dianneanderson@pointloma.edu.

Department of Kinesiology Students: 32 full-time (14 women), 2 part-time (1 woman); includes 15 minority (1 Asian, non-Hispanic/Latino; 12 Hispanic/Latino; 2 Two or more races, non-Hispanic/Latino), 1 international. Average age 25. 80 applicants, 81% accepted, 34 enrolled. *Faculty:* 1 full-time, 6 part-time/adjunct (2 women). *Financial support:* Teaching assistantships, scholarships/grants, and unspecified assistantships available. *Degree program information:* Part-time programs available. Part-time, online learning. Offers sport performance (MS). *Application fee:* $50. *Application Contact:* Claire Buckley, Director, Graduate Admissions, 619-563-2846, E-mail: clairebuckley@pointloma.edu. *Chair*, Jeff Sullivan, 619-849-2629, E-mail: jeffsullivan@pointloma.edu.

Fermanian School of Business Students: 28 full-time (11 women), 44 part-time (21 women); includes 28 minority (4 Black or African American, non-Hispanic/Latino; 3 Asian, non-Hispanic/Latino; 17 Hispanic/Latino; 4 Two or more races, non-Hispanic/Latino), 3 international. Average age 30. 41 applicants, 95% accepted, 27 enrolled. *Faculty:* 6 full-time, 5 part-time/adjunct (1 woman). *Financial support:* Applicants required to submit FAFSA. In 2015, 67 master's awarded. *Degree program information:* Part-time and evening/weekend programs available. Part-time, evening/weekend. Offers general business (MBA); healthcare management (MBA); innovation and entrepreneurship (MBA); organizational leadership (MBA); project management (MBA). *Application deadline:* For fall admission, 7/26 priority date for domestic students; for spring admission, 11/29 priority date for domestic students; for summer admission, 4/2 priority date for domestic students. Applications are processed on a rolling basis. *Application fee:* $50. Electronic applications accepted. *Application Contact:* Claire Buckley, Director of Graduate Admission, 619-563-2846, E-mail: clairebuckley@pointloma.edu. *Dean of Graduate Business Education*, Dan Bothe, 619-849-2394, E-mail: danbothe@pointloma.edu.

Program in Organizational Leadership Students: 35 part-time (25 women); includes 13 minority (3 Black or African American, non-Hispanic/Latino; 1 Asian, non-Hispanic/Latino; 7 Hispanic/Latino; 2 Two or more races, non-Hispanic/Latino), 1 international. Average age 33. 14 applicants, 86% accepted, 11 enrolled. *Faculty:* 7 part-time/adjunct (2 women). Online learning. Offers organizational leadership (MA). *Application deadline:* For fall admission, 8/8 priority date for domestic students. *Application Contact:* Claire Buckley, Director, Graduate Admissions, 619-563-2846, E-mail: clairebuckley@pointloma.edu.

School of Education Students: 224 full-time (174 women), 348 part-time (267 women); includes 249 minority (20 Black or African American, non-Hispanic/Latino; 2 American Indian or Alaska Native, non-Hispanic/Latino; 17 Asian, non-Hispanic/Latino; 186 Hispanic/Latino; 4 Native Hawaiian or other Pacific Islander, non-Hispanic/Latino; 20 Two or more races, non-Hispanic/Latino), 2 international. Average age 32. 194 applicants, 91% accepted, 145 enrolled. *Faculty:* 10 full-time (8 women), 76 part-time/adjunct (59 women). *Financial support:* Career-related internships or fieldwork and scholarships/grants available. Support available to part-time students. Financial award application deadline: 4/10; financial award applicants required to submit FAFSA. In 2015, 109 master's awarded. *Degree program information:* Part-time and evening/weekend programs available. Part-time, evening/weekend. Offers counseling and guidance (MA); education (MA, MAT); education specialist mild to moderate (MAT); education specialist moderate to severe (MAT); educational leadership (MA); multiple subject (MAT); single subject (MAT); special education (MA); teaching and learning (MA). *Application deadline:* For fall admission, 8/4 priority date for domestic students; for spring admission, 12/8 priority date for domestic students; for summer admission, 4/13 priority date for domestic students. Applications are processed on a rolling basis. *Application fee:* $50. Electronic applications accepted. *Application Contact:* Claire Buckley, Director of Graduate Admission, 619-563-2846, E-mail: clairebuckley@pointloma.edu. *Dean*, Dr. Deborah Erickson, 619-849-2332, Fax: 619-849-2579, E-mail: deberickson@pointloma.edu.

School of Ministry Students: 15 part-time (3 women); includes 2 minority (1 Black or African American, non-Hispanic/Latino; 1 American Indian or Alaska Native, non-Hispanic/Latino). Average age 36. 7 applicants, 71% accepted, 2 enrolled. *Faculty:* 5 full-time (1 woman). *Financial support:* In 2015–16, 6 students received support. Scholarships/grants available. Financial award application deadline: 6/5; financial award applicants required to submit FAFSA. In 2015, 9 master's awarded. *Degree program information:* Part-time programs available. Part-time, online only, nine-week quads with eight weeks of online coursework and a one-week intensive. Offers ministry (M Min). *Application deadline:* For fall admission, 8/30 priority date for domestic students; for spring admission, 4/4 priority date for domestic students; for summer admission, 6/20 priority date for domestic students. Applications are processed on a rolling basis. *Application fee:* $0. Electronic applications accepted. *Application Contact:* Claire Buckley, Director of Graduate Admissions, 619-563-2846, E-mail: clairebuckley@pointloma.edu. *Dean*, Mark Maddix, 619-849-2234, E-mail: markmaddix@pointloma.edu.

School of Nursing Students: 1 (woman) full-time, 74 part-time (61 women); includes 35 minority (4 Black or African American, non-Hispanic/Latino; 15 Asian, non-Hispanic/Latino; 10 Hispanic/Latino; 3 Native Hawaiian or other Pacific Islander, non-Hispanic/Latino; 3 Two or more races, non-Hispanic/Latino), 2 international. Average age 38. 34 applicants, 88% accepted, 18 enrolled. *Faculty:* 6 full-time (5 women), 2 part-time/adjunct (both women). *Financial support:* Applicants required to submit FAFSA. In 2015, 40 master's awarded. *Degree program information:* Part-time programs available. Part-time. Offers adult/gerontology nursing (MSN); family/individual health (MSN); general nursing (MSN); nursing (Post-MSN Certificate); pediatric nursing (MSN);

psychiatric mental health (MSN). *Application deadline:* For fall admission, 7/5 priority date for domestic students; for spring admission, 11/1 priority date for domestic students; for summer admission, 3/22 priority date for domestic students. Applications are processed on a rolling basis. *Application fee:* $50. *Application Contact:* Claire Buckley, Director of Graduate Admissions, 619-563-2846, E-mail: clairebuckley@pointloma.edu. *Dean of the School of Nursing,* Dr. Barb Taylor, 619-849-2766, E-mail: bataylor@pointloma.edu.

POINT PARK UNIVERSITY, Pittsburgh, PA 15222-1984

General Information Independent, coed, comprehensive institution. CGS member. *Graduate housing:* Room and/or apartments available on a first-come, first-served basis to single students; on-campus housing not available to married students. Housing application deadline: 7/31.

GRADUATE UNITS

Conservatory of Performing Arts Offers theatre arts-acting (MFA). Electronic applications accepted.

School of Arts and Sciences ***Degree program information:*** Part-time and evening/weekend programs available. Part-time, evening/weekend. Offers arts and sciences (M Ed, MA, MS); clinical-community psychology (MA); criminal justice administration (MS); curriculum and instruction (MA); educational administration (MA); engineering management (MS); environmental studies (MS); special education (M Ed); teaching and leadership (M Ed). Electronic applications accepted.

School of Business ***Degree program information:*** Part-time and evening/weekend programs available. Part-time, evening/weekend. Offers business (MBA); organizational leadership (MA). Electronic applications accepted.

School of Communication ***Degree program information:*** Part-time and evening/weekend programs available. Part-time, evening/weekend. Offers communication (MA). Electronic applications accepted.

POLYTECHNIC UNIVERSITY OF PUERTO RICO, Hato Rey, PR 00919

General Information Independent, coed, comprehensive institution. CGS member. *Graduate housing:* On-campus housing not available. *Research affiliation:* University of Missouri (engineering, mathematics and science), University of Puerto Rico, Mayaguez Campus (electrical engineering), Virginia Polytechnic Institute and State University (mechanical and electrical engineering), Naval Research Laboratories (mechanical and electrical engineering), Department of Energy Laboratories (electrical engineering).

GRADUATE UNITS

Graduate School ***Degree program information:*** Part-time and evening/weekend programs available. Part-time, evening/weekend.

POLYTECHNIC UNIVERSITY OF PUERTO RICO, MIAMI CAMPUS, Miami, FL 33166

General Information Independent, coed, comprehensive institution.

GRADUATE UNITS

Graduate School ***Degree program information:*** Part-time and evening/weekend programs available. Part-time, evening/weekend, online learning. Electronic applications accepted.

POLYTECHNIC UNIVERSITY OF PUERTO RICO, ORLANDO CAMPUS, Orlando, FL 32825

General Information Independent, coed, comprehensive institution. *Graduate housing:* On-campus housing not available.

GRADUATE UNITS

Graduate School ***Degree program information:*** Part-time and evening/weekend programs available. Part-time, evening/weekend, online learning. Electronic applications accepted.

PONCE HEALTH SCIENCES UNIVERSITY, Ponce, PR 00732-7004

General Information Independent, coed, graduate-only institution. *Research affiliation:* The University of Texas at San Antonio (health disparities, proteomics, bioinformatics), H.L. Moffitt Cancer Center (cancer biology, oncology), Oregon Health and Science University (neurosciences, cancer, inflammation), University of Puerto Rico, Mayaguez Campus (cancer biology, molecular genetics), University of Puerto Rico, Medical Sciences Campus (translational research), University of Maryland–Institute of Human Virology (HIV/AIDS research).

GRADUATE UNITS

Professional Program Offers medicine (MD).

Program in Biomedical Sciences Offers biomedical sciences (PhD).

Program in Clinical Psychology Offers clinical psychology (PhD, Psy D).

Program in Public Health Offers epidemiology (Dr PH); public health (MPH).

PONTIFICAL CATHOLIC UNIVERSITY OF PUERTO RICO, Ponce, PR 00717-0777

General Information Independent-religious, coed, university. *Graduate housing:* Room and/or apartments available to single students; on-campus housing not available to married students. Housing application deadline: 7/15.

GRADUATE UNITS

College of Arts and Humanities ***Degree program information:*** Part-time and evening/weekend programs available. Part-time, evening/weekend. Offers arts and humanities (MA, Professional Certificate); grammar and writing (Professional Certificate); Hispanic studies (MA); history (MA); painting and drawing (MA); theology and philosophy (M Div).

College of Business Administration ***Degree program information:*** Part-time and evening/weekend programs available. Part-time, evening/weekend. Offers accounting (MBA); business administration (MBA, DBA, PhD, Professional Certificate); finance (MBA); general business (MBA, Professional Certificate); human resources (MBA, Professional Certificate); international business (MBA); management (MBA); management and accounting (Professional Certificate); management information systems (MBA, Professional Certificate); maritime logistics and transportation (Professional Certificate); marketing (MBA); office administration (MBA, MS).

College of Education ***Degree program information:*** Part-time and evening/weekend programs available. Part-time, evening/weekend. Offers business teacher education (M Ed, PhD); counselor education (M Ed); curriculum and instruction (M Ed, PhD); education (M Ed, MA Ed, MRE, PhD); education-general (M Ed, MA Ed); educational leadership and administration (PhD); educational psychology (M Ed); English as a second language (M Ed).

College of Graduate Studies in Behavioral Science and Community Affairs ***Degree program information:*** Part-time and evening/weekend programs available. Part-time, evening/weekend. Offers clinical psychology (PhD, Psy D); clinical social work (MSW); criminology (MA); industrial psychology (PhD); psychology (PhD); public administration (MSS); rehabilitation counseling (MA).

College of Sciences ***Degree program information:*** Part-time and evening/weekend programs available. Part-time, evening/weekend. Offers chemistry (MS); environmental sciences (MS); medical-surgical nursing (MSN); mental health and psychiatric nursing (MSN); sciences (MS, Certificate).

School of Medical Technology Offers medical technology (Certificate).

School of Law ***Degree program information:*** Part-time and evening/weekend programs available. Part-time, evening/weekend. Offers law (JD).

PONTIFICAL COLLEGE JOSEPHINUM, Columbus, OH 43235

General Information Independent-religious, men only, comprehensive institution. *Graduate housing:* Room and/or apartments guaranteed to single students; on-campus housing not available to married students. Housing application deadline: 8/15.

GRADUATE UNITS

School of Theology ***Degree program information:*** Part-time programs available. Part-time. Offers theology (M Div, MA). All students are sponsored/selected by their diocese.

POPE ST. JOHN XXIII NATIONAL SEMINARY, Weston, MA 02493-2618

General Information Independent-religious, men only, graduate-only institution. *Graduate housing:* Room and/or apartments available to single students; on-campus housing not available to married students. Housing application deadline: 8/1.

GRADUATE UNITS

Graduate Program Offers theology (M Div).

PORTLAND STATE UNIVERSITY, Portland, OR 97207-0751

General Information State-supported, coed, university. CGS member. *Enrollment:* 27,488 graduate, professional, and undergraduate students; 2,714 full-time matriculated graduate/professional students (1,593 women), 2,284 part-time matriculated graduate/professional students (1,373 women). *Enrollment by degree level:* 3,871 master's, 661 doctoral, 466 other advanced degrees. *Graduate faculty:* 848 full-time (398 women), 651 part-time/adjunct (321 women). Tuition, state resident: full-time $10,040. Tuition, nonresident: full-time $14,063. *Graduate housing:* Rooms and/or apartments available on a first-come, first-served basis to single and married students. Housing application deadline: 8/30. *Student services:* Campus employment opportunities, campus safety program, career counseling, child daycare facilities, exercise/wellness program, free psychological counseling, international student services, low-cost health insurance, multicultural affairs office, services for students with disabilities, teacher training, writing training. *Library:* Branford P. Millar Library plus 1 other. Students can reserve study rooms. *Research affiliation:* City of Portland (civil engineering, urban planning), Bonneville Power Administration (civil and mechanical engineering, geology, urban studies), Battelle Pacific Northwest Laboratories (computer science, geographic information systems, mechanical engineering, science education), Intel Corporation (electronic cooling, engineering), Tri-County Metropolitan Transportation District of Oregon, Tektronix (electrical engineering).

Computer facilities: A campuswide network can be accessed from student residence rooms and from off campus. Online class registration is available.
Website: http://www.pdx.edu/

General Application Contact: 503-725-3511, Fax: 503-725-5525, E-mail: admissions@pdx.edu.

GRADUATE UNITS

Graduate Studies Students: 2,714 full-time (1,593 women), 2,284 part-time (1,373 women); includes 945 minority (116 Black or African American, non-Hispanic/Latino; 62 American Indian or Alaska Native, non-Hispanic/Latino; 225 Asian, non-Hispanic/Latino; 358 Hispanic/Latino; 11 Native Hawaiian or other Pacific Islander, non-Hispanic/Latino; 173 Two or more races, non-Hispanic/Latino), 643 international. Average age 34. 6,204 applicants, 52% accepted, 2113 enrolled. *Faculty:* 848 full-time (398 women), 651 part-time/adjunct (321 women). *Financial support:* In 2015–16, 268 research assistantships with tuition reimbursements (averaging $7,520 per year), 472 teaching assistantships with tuition reimbursements (averaging $7,112 per year) were awarded; fellowships, career-related internships or fieldwork, Federal Work-Study, scholarships/grants, tuition waivers (partial), and unspecified assistantships also available. Support available to part-time students. Financial award application deadline: 3/1; financial award applicants required to submit FAFSA. In 2015, 1,678 master's, 77 doctorates awarded. *Degree program information:* Part-time and evening/weekend programs available. Part-time, evening/weekend, online learning. *Application deadline:* For fall admission, 6/1 for domestic students, 3/1 for international students; for winter admission, 10/1 for domestic students, 7/1 for international students; for spring admission, 2/1 for domestic students, 11/1 for international students. Applications are processed on a rolling basis. *Application fee:* $50. *Application Contact:* Kelly Doherty, Director of Graduate Admissions, 503-725-5391, Fax: 503-725-3416, E-mail: dohertyk@pdx.edu. *Associate Vice Provost,* Dr. Margaret Everett, 503-725-5258, Fax: 503-725-3416, E-mail: everettm@pdx.edu.

College of Liberal Arts and Sciences Students: 733 full-time (441 women), 370 part-time (202 women); includes 198 minority (26 Black or African American, non-Hispanic/Latino; 13 American Indian or Alaska Native, non-Hispanic/Latino; 57 Asian, non-Hispanic/Latino; 63 Hispanic/Latino; 2 Native Hawaiian or other Pacific Islander, non-Hispanic/Latino; 37 Two or more races, non-Hispanic/Latino), 145 international. Average age 32. 1,472 applicants, 47% accepted, 435 enrolled. *Faculty:* 362 full-time (154 women), 184 part-time/adjunct (98 women). *Financial support:* In 2015–16, 46 research assistantships with tuition reimbursements (averaging $9,106 per year), 287 teaching assistantships with tuition reimbursements (averaging $8,191 per year) were awarded; career-related internships or fieldwork, Federal Work-Study, scholarships/grants, and tuition waivers (partial) also available. Support available to part-time students. Financial award application deadline: 3/1; financial award applicants required to submit FAFSA. In 2015, 304 master's, 30 doctorates awarded. *Degree program information:* Part-time and evening/weekend programs available. Part-time, evening/weekend. Offers anthropology (MA); applied economics (MA, MS); biology (MA, MS, PhD); chemistry (MA, MS, PhD); computational intelligence (Certificate); computer modeling and simulation (Certificate); conflict resolution (MA, MS); English (MA, MFA); environmental management (MEM); environmental sciences and resources (PhD); environmental sciences/biology (PhD); environmental sciences/chemistry (PhD); environmental sciences/civil engineering (PhD); environmental sciences/geography (PhD); environmental sciences/geology (PhD); environmental sciences/physics (PhD); environmental studies (MS); French (MA);

general arts and letters education (MAT, MST); general economics (MA, MS); general science education (MAT, MST); general social science education (MAT, MST); general speech communication (MA, MS, Certificate); geography (MA, MAT, MS, MST, PhD); geology (MA, MS); German (MA); history (MA); Japanese (MA); liberal arts and sciences (MA, MAT, MEM, MFA, MS, MST, MST, PhD, Certificate); mathematical sciences (PhD); mathematics education (PhD); physics (MA, MS, PhD); psychology (MA, MS, PhD); science/environmental science (MST); science/geology (MAT, MST); sociology (MA, MS, PhD); Spanish (MA); speech-language pathology (MA, MS); statistics (MS); systems science (MS); systems science/anthropology (PhD); systems science/business administration (PhD); systems science/civil engineering (PhD); systems science/economics (PhD); systems science/engineering management (PhD); systems science/general (PhD); systems science/mathematical sciences (PhD); systems science/mechanical engineering (PhD); systems science/psychology (PhD); systems science/sociology (PhD); teaching English to speakers of other languages (MA); world literature and language (MA). *Application deadline:* Applications are processed on a rolling basis. *Application fee:* $50. *Application Contact:* 503-725-3511, Fax: 503-725-5525. *Dean*, Dr. Karen Marrongelle, 503-725-3514, Fax: 503-725-3693.

College of the Arts Students: 101 full-time (57 women), 19 part-time (10 women); includes 19 minority (5 Black or African American, non-Hispanic/Latino; 2 Asian, non-Hispanic/Latino; 8 Hispanic/Latino; 4 Two or more races, non-Hispanic/Latino), 6 international. Average age 31. 225 applicants, 43% accepted, 60 enrolled. *Faculty:* 69 full-time (33 women), 147 part-time/adjunct (62 women). *Financial support:* In 2015–16, 4 research assistantships with partial tuition reimbursements (averaging $4,685 per year), 28 teaching assistantships with partial tuition reimbursements (averaging $4,144 per year) were awarded; career-related internships or fieldwork, Federal Work-Study, scholarships/grants, tuition waivers (partial), and unspecified assistantships also available. Support available to part-time students. Financial award application deadline: 3/1; financial award applicants required to submit FAFSA. In 2015, 46 master's awarded. *Degree program information:* Part-time programs available. Part-time. Offers architecture (M Arch); conducting (MMC); drawing (MFA); mixed media (MFA); music education (MAT, MST); painting (MFA); performance (MMP); printmaking (MFA); sculpture (MFA); the arts (M Arch, MA, MAT, MFA, MMC, MMP, MS, MST); theater (MA, MS). *Application deadline:* For fall admission, 3/1 for domestic and international students. Applications are processed on a rolling basis. *Application fee:* $50. *Application Contact:* Abel De la Cruz, Student Advisor, 503-725-3105, Fax: 503-725-5525, E-mail: the-arts@pdx.edu. *Dean*, William Bucker, 503-725-3105, Fax: 503-725-3351.

College of Urban and Public Affairs Students: 300 full-time (186 women), 213 part-time (151 women); includes 102 minority (11 Black or African American, non-Hispanic/Latino; 8 American Indian or Alaska Native, non-Hispanic/Latino; 14 Asian, non-Hispanic/Latino; 48 Hispanic/Latino; 21 Two or more races, non-Hispanic/Latino), 37 international. Average age 33. 564 applicants, 51% accepted, 179 enrolled. *Faculty:* 89 full-time (44 women), 54 part-time/adjunct (19 women). *Financial support:* In 2015–16, 83 research assistantships with tuition reimbursements (averaging $5,800 per year), 13 teaching assistantships with full tuition reimbursements (averaging $9,118 per year) were awarded; fellowships, career-related internships or fieldwork, Federal Work-Study, scholarships/grants, tuition waivers (partial), and unspecified assistantships also available. Support available to part-time students. Financial award application deadline: 3/1; financial award applicants required to submit FAFSA. In 2015, 173 master's, 10 doctorates awarded. *Degree program information:* Part-time and evening/weekend programs available. Part-time, evening/weekend. Offers aging (Certificate); community health (PhD); criminology and criminal justice (MS, PhD); government (MA, MAT, MPA, MS, MST, PhD); health administration (MPA, MPH); health education (MA, MS); health promotion (MPH); health studies (MPA, MPH); political science (MA, MAT, MS, MST, PhD); public administration (MPA); public affairs and policy (PhD); urban and public affairs (MA, MAT, MPA, MPH, MS, MST, MURP, MUS, PhD, Certificate); urban and regional planning (MURP); urban studies (MUS, PhD); urban studies and planning (MURP, MUS, PhD). *Application fee:* $50. *Dean*, Dr. Stephen Percy, 503-725-5143, Fax: 503-725-5199, E-mail: spercy@pdx.edu.

Maseeh College of Engineering and Computer Science Students: 439 full-time (114 women), 312 part-time (87 women); includes 88 minority (12 Black or African American, non-Hispanic/Latino; 1 American Indian or Alaska Native, non-Hispanic/Latino; 42 Asian, non-Hispanic/Latino; 20 Hispanic/Latino; 2 Native Hawaiian or other Pacific Islander, non-Hispanic/Latino; 11 Two or more races, non-Hispanic/Latino), 405 international. Average age 31. 1,080 applicants, 44% accepted, 247 enrolled. *Faculty:* 99 full-time (16 women), 34 part-time/adjunct (3 women). *Financial support:* In 2015–16, 64 research assistantships with tuition reimbursements (averaging $7,175 per year), 68 teaching assistantships with tuition reimbursements (averaging $3,834 per year) were awarded; career-related internships or fieldwork, Federal Work-Study, scholarships/grants, and unspecified assistantships also available. Support available to part-time students. Financial award application deadline: 3/1; financial award applicants required to submit FAFSA. In 2015, 274 master's, 14 doctorates awarded. *Degree program information:* Part-time and evening/weekend programs available. Part-time, evening/weekend. Offers civil and environmental engineering (M Eng, MS, PhD); civil and environmental engineering management (M Eng); computer science (MS, PhD); electrical and computer engineering (M Eng, MS, PhD); engineering and computer science (M Eng, ME, MS, MSE, PhD, Certificate); engineering and technology management (M Eng); engineering management (MS); environmental sciences and resources (PhD); manufacturing engineering (ME); manufacturing management (M Eng); mechanical engineering (M Eng, MS, PhD); software engineering (MSE); systems science (PhD); systems science/engineering management (PhD). *Application deadline:* For fall admission, 4/1 for domestic students, 3/1 for international students; for winter admission, 9/1 for domestic and international students; for spring admission, 2/1 for domestic and international students. *Application fee:* $50. *Application Contact:* Yeruwelle de Rouen, Outreach and Recruitment Manager, 503-725-5030, Fax: 503-725-2825, E-mail: derouen@pdx.edu. *Dean*, Dr. Renjeng Su, 503-725-8393, Fax: 503-725-2825, E-mail: renjengs@pdx.edu.

School of Business Administration Students: 199 full-time (87 women), 208 part-time (75 women); includes 82 minority (9 Black or African American, non-Hispanic/Latino; 4 American Indian or Alaska Native, non-Hispanic/Latino; 41 Asian, non-Hispanic/Latino; 19 Hispanic/Latino; 9 Two or more races, non-Hispanic/Latino), 85 international. Average age 33. 609 applicants, 61% accepted, 235 enrolled. *Faculty:* 59 full-time (30 women), 64 part-time/adjunct (23 women). *Financial support:* In 2015–16, 17 research assistantships with partial tuition reimbursements (averaging $7,170 per year) were awarded; career-related internships or fieldwork, Federal Work-Study, scholarships/grants, tuition waivers (partial), and unspecified assistantships also available. Support available to part-time students. Financial award application deadline: 3/1; financial award applicants required to submit FAFSA. In 2015, 181 master's awarded. *Degree program information:* Part-time and evening/weekend programs available. Part-time, evening/weekend. Offers business administration (MBA, MIM, MRED, MS, MSFA, PhD); financial analysis (MSFA); global supply chain management (MS); international management (MIM); real estate development (MRED). *Application deadline:* For fall admission, 4/1 for domestic students, 3/1 for international students. *Application fee:* $50. Electronic applications accepted. *Application Contact:* Pam Mitchell, Administrator, 503-725-3730, Fax: 503-725-5850, E-mail: pamm@sba.pdx.edu. *Dean*, Dr. Daniel Connolly, 503-725-3714, Fax: 503-725-5850.

School of Education Students: 484 full-time (358 women), 691 part-time (523 women); includes 252 minority (24 Black or African American, non-Hispanic/Latino; 15 American Indian or Alaska Native, non-Hispanic/Latino; 50 Asian, non-Hispanic/Latino; 117 Hispanic/Latino; 7 Native Hawaiian or other Pacific Islander, non-Hispanic/Latino; 39 Two or more races, non-Hispanic/Latino), 28 international. Average age 36. 658 applicants, 60% accepted, 356 enrolled. *Faculty:* 61 full-time (39 women), 105 part-time/adjunct (75 women). *Financial support:* In 2015–16, 12 research assistantships with tuition reimbursements (averaging $6,860 per year), 3 teaching assistantships with tuition reimbursements (averaging $5,916 per year) were awarded; career-related internships or fieldwork, Federal Work-Study, institutionally sponsored loans, scholarships/grants, and unspecified assistantships also available. Support available to part-time students. Financial award application deadline: 3/1; financial award applicants required to submit FAFSA. In 2015, 482 master's, 12 doctorates awarded. *Degree program information:* Part-time and evening/weekend programs available. Part-time, evening/weekend. Offers education (M Ed, MA, MAT, MS, MST, Ed D). *Application deadline:* For fall admission, 4/1 for domestic and international students; for winter admission, 9/1 for domestic and international students; for spring admission, 11/1 for domestic and international students. *Application fee:* $50. Electronic applications accepted. *Application Contact:* Information Contact, 503-725-4619, Fax: 503-725-5599, E-mail: gseinfo@pdx.edu. *Dean*, Dr. Randy Hitz, 503-725-4697, Fax: 503-725-5399, E-mail: hitz@pdx.edu.

School of Social Work Students: 384 full-time (306 women), 205 part-time (170 women); includes 164 minority (30 Black or African American, non-Hispanic/Latino; 18 American Indian or Alaska Native, non-Hispanic/Latino; 17 Asian, non-Hispanic/Latino; 61 Hispanic/Latino; 38 Two or more races, non-Hispanic/Latino), 3 international. Average age 35. 768 applicants, 39% accepted, 232 enrolled. *Faculty:* 35 full-time (26 women), 25 part-time/adjunct (18 women). *Financial support:* In 2015–16, 7 research assistantships with tuition reimbursements (averaging $13,574 per year), 5 teaching assistantships with tuition reimbursements (averaging $11,401 per year) were awarded; career-related internships or fieldwork, Federal Work-Study, scholarships/grants, tuition waivers (partial), and unspecified assistantships also available. Support available to part-time students. Financial award application deadline: 3/1; financial award applicants required to submit FAFSA. In 2015, 224 master's, 5 doctorates awarded. *Degree program information:* Part-time programs available. Part-time. Offers social work (MSW); social work and social research (PhD). *Application deadline:* For fall admission, 2/1 for domestic and international students. *Application fee:* $50. *Application Contact:* Prof. Sarah Bradley, Director of MSW Program, 503-725-8028, Fax: 503-725-5545, E-mail: bradles@pdx.edu. *Dean*, Dr. Laura B. Nissen, 503-725-3997, Fax: 503-725-5545, E-mail: nissen@pdx.edu.

POST UNIVERSITY, Waterbury, CT 06723-2540

General Information Independent, coed, comprehensive institution.

GRADUATE UNITS

Program in Business Administration Online learning. Offers accounting (MSA); business administration (MBA); corporate innovation (MBA); entrepreneurship (MBA); finance (MBA); healthcare (MBA); leadership (MBA); marketing (MBA); project management (MBA).

Program in Education Online learning. Offers education (M Ed); higher education administration (M Ed); instructional design and technology (M Ed); online teaching (M Ed); teaching and learning (M Ed); TESOL (teaching English to speakers of other languages) (M Ed).

Program in Human Services ***Degree program information:*** Part-time and evening/weekend programs available. Part-time, evening/weekend, online learning. Offers human services (MS); human services/alcohol and drug counseling (MS); human services/clinical counseling (MS); human services/non-profit management (MS).

Program in Public Administration Online learning. Offers public administration (MPA).

PRAIRIE VIEW A&M UNIVERSITY, Prairie View, TX 77446-0519

General Information State-supported, coed, university. *Enrollment:* 8,268 graduate, professional, and undergraduate students; 541 full-time matriculated graduate/professional students (350 women), 804 part-time matriculated graduate/professional students (571 women). *Enrollment by degree level:* 1,161 master's, 148 doctoral, 36 other advanced degrees. *Graduate faculty:* 115 full-time (46 women), 31 part-time/adjunct (24 women). Tuition, state resident: full-time $4243; part-time $237.29 per credit hour. Tuition, nonresident: full-time $11,798; part-time $657 per credit hour. *Required fees:* $2762; $172.10 per credit hour. *Graduate housing:* Rooms and/or apartments available on a first-come, first-served basis to single and married students. Typical cost: $8419 (including board) for single students. Housing application deadline: 4/16. *Student services:* Campus employment opportunities, campus safety program, career counseling, exercise/wellness program, free psychological counseling, grant writing training, international student services, low-cost health insurance, multicultural affairs office, services for students with disabilities, teacher training, writing training. *Library:* John B. Coleman Library plus 3 others. *Collection:* Books: 342,665 (physical), 16,526 (digital/electronic); Serial titles: 232 (physical); Databases: 81. Weekly public service hours: 97; students can reserve study rooms. *Research affiliation:* U.S. Department of Education (DOE) (engineering), U.S. Department of Energy (engineering and sciences), Science and Engineering Alliance, NASA (space radiation on material systems and devices), Lawrence Livermore National Laboratory (engineering and sciences), Sandia National Laboratories (engineering and chemistry).

Computer facilities: 341 computers available on campus for general student use. A campuswide network can be accessed from student residence rooms and from off campus. Online class registration is available.
Website: http://www.pvamu.edu/

General Application Contact: Pauline Walker, Office of Graduate Admissions, 936-261-3521, Fax: 936-261-3529, E-mail: gradadmissions@pvamu.edu.

GRADUATE UNITS

College of Agriculture and Human Sciences Students: 51 full-time (43 women), 26 part-time (23 women); includes 71 minority (65 Black or African American, non-Hispanic/Latino; 2 Asian, non-Hispanic/Latino; 4 Hispanic/Latino), 2 international.

Average age 32. 52 applicants, 63% accepted, 26 enrolled. *Faculty:* 4 full-time (2 women). *Financial support:* In 2015–16, 12 students received support, including 12 research assistantships (averaging $14,400 per year); career-related internships or fieldwork, Federal Work-Study, institutionally sponsored loans, scholarships/grants, tuition waivers (full and partial), and unspecified assistantships also available. Support available to part-time students. Financial award application deadline: 4/1; financial award applicants required to submit FAFSA. In 2015, 25 master's awarded. *Degree program information:* Part-time and evening/weekend programs available. Part-time, evening/weekend. Offers interdisciplinary human sciences (MS). *Application deadline:* For fall admission, 7/1 priority date for domestic students, 6/1 priority date for international students; for spring admission, 11/1 priority date for domestic students, 10/1 priority date for international students; for summer admission, 3/1 priority date for domestic students, 2/1 priority date for international students. Applications are processed on a rolling basis. *Application fee:* $50. Electronic applications accepted. *Application Contact:* Pauline Walker, Administrative Assistant II, 936-261-3521, Fax: 936-261-3529, E-mail: gradadmissions@pvamu.edu. *Interim Dean and Director of Land-Grant Programs,* Dr. James Palmer, 936-261-2214, E-mail: jmpalmer@pvamu.edu.

College of Arts and Sciences Students: 13 full-time (10 women), 5 part-time (3 women); includes 14 minority (12 Black or African American, non-Hispanic/Latino; 1 Asian, non-Hispanic/Latino; 1 Hispanic/Latino), 3 international. Average age 29. 22 applicants, 50% accepted, 6 enrolled. *Faculty:* 9 full-time (3 women). *Financial support:* Fellowships, research assistantships, teaching assistantships, career-related internships or fieldwork, Federal Work-Study, institutionally sponsored loans, and tuition waivers (full and partial) available. Support available to part-time students. Financial award application deadline: 4/1; financial award applicants required to submit FAFSA. In 2015, 8 master's awarded. *Degree program information:* Part-time and evening/weekend programs available. Part-time, evening/weekend. Offers arts and sciences (MA, MS); chemistry (MS). *Application deadline:* For fall admission, 7/1 priority date for domestic students, 6/1 priority date for international students; for spring admission, 11/15 priority date for domestic students, 10/1 priority date for international students; for summer admission, 3/1 priority date for domestic students, 2/1 priority date for international students. Applications are processed on a rolling basis. *Application fee:* $50. Electronic applications accepted. *Application Contact:* Pauline Walker, Administrative Assistant II, Research and Graduate Studies, 936-261-3521, Fax: 936-261-3529, E-mail: gradadmissions@pvamu.edu. *Dean,* Dr. Danny R. Kelley, 936-261-3180, Fax: 936-261-3188, E-mail: drkelley@pvamu.edu.

Division of Social Work, Behavioral and Political Sciences Students: 3 full-time (all women), 2 part-time (1 woman); all minorities (all Black or African American, non-Hispanic/Latino). Average age 33. 8 applicants, 25% accepted, 1 enrolled. *Faculty:* 4 full-time (1 woman). *Financial support:* Federal Work-Study, institutionally sponsored loans, and scholarships/grants available. Financial award application deadline: 4/1; financial award applicants required to submit FAFSA. In 2015, 8 master's awarded. *Degree program information:* Part-time and evening/weekend programs available. Part-time, evening/weekend. Offers sociology (MA). *Application deadline:* For fall admission, 7/1 priority date for domestic students, 6/1 priority date for international students; for spring admission, 11/1 priority date for domestic students, 10/1 priority date for international students; for summer admission, 3/1 priority date for domestic students, 2/1 priority date for international students. Applications are processed on a rolling basis. *Application fee:* $50. Electronic applications accepted. *Application Contact:* Pauline Walker, Administrative Assistant II, Research and Graduate Studies, 936-261-3521, Fax: 936-261-3529, E-mail: gradadmissions@pvamu.edu. *Division Head,* Dr. Walle Engedayehu, 936-261-3200, Fax: 936-261-3229, E-mail: waengedayehu@pvamu.edu.

College of Business Students: 79 full-time (44 women), 170 part-time (97 women); includes 218 minority (195 Black or African American, non-Hispanic/Latino; 11 Asian, non-Hispanic/Latino; 12 Hispanic/Latino), 12 international. Average age 31. 196 applicants, 61% accepted, 91 enrolled. *Faculty:* 18 full-time (3 women). *Financial support:* Career-related internships or fieldwork, Federal Work-Study, institutionally sponsored loans, and tuition waivers (partial) available. Support available to part-time students. Financial award application deadline: 4/1; financial award applicants required to submit FAFSA. In 2015, 77 master's awarded. *Degree program information:* Part-time and evening/weekend programs available. Part-time, evening/weekend. Offers accounting (MS); general business administration (MBA). *Application deadline:* For fall admission, 7/1 for domestic students, 6/1 priority date for international students; for spring admission, 11/1 for domestic students, 10/1 priority date for international students; for summer admission, 3/1 for domestic students, 2/1 for international students. Applications are processed on a rolling basis. *Application fee:* $50. Electronic applications accepted. *Application Contact:* Kimberly Gordon, Interim Director, Graduate Programs in Business, 936-261-9217, Fax: 936-261-9232, E-mail: cob@pvamu.edu. *Dean,* Dr. Munir Quddus, 936-261-9200, Fax: 936-261-9241, E-mail: cob@pvamu.edu.

College of Education Students: 126 full-time (96 women), 387 part-time (300 women); includes 480 minority (449 Black or African American, non-Hispanic/Latino; 3 American Indian or Alaska Native, non-Hispanic/Latino; 1 Asian, non-Hispanic/Latino; 25 Hispanic/Latino; 2 Two or more races, non-Hispanic/Latino), 6 international. Average age 35. 425 applicants, 55% accepted, 166 enrolled. *Faculty:* 27 full-time (13 women), 11 part-time/adjunct (10 women). *Financial support:* Career-related internships or fieldwork, institutionally sponsored loans, scholarships/grants, and unspecified assistantships available. Support available to part-time students. Financial award application deadline: 4/1; financial award applicants required to submit FAFSA. In 2015, 152 master's, 15 doctorates awarded. *Degree program information:* Part-time and evening/weekend programs available. Part-time, evening/weekend, online learning. Offers counseling (MA, MS Ed); curriculum and instruction (M Ed, MA Ed, MS Ed); education (M Ed, MA, MA Ed, MS, MS Ed, PhD); educational administration (M Ed, MS Ed); educational leadership (PhD); health education (M Ed, MS); physical education (M Ed, MS); special education (M Ed, MS Ed). *Application deadline:* For fall admission, 7/1 priority date for domestic students, 6/1 priority date for international students; for spring admission, 11/1 priority date for domestic students, 10/1 priority date for international students; for summer admission, 4/1 priority date for domestic students, 3/1 priority date for international students. Applications are processed on a rolling basis. *Application fee:* $50. Electronic applications accepted. *Application Contact:* Pauline Walker, Administrative Assistant II, Research and Graduate Studies, 936-261-3521, Fax: 936-261-3529, E-mail: gradadmissions@pvamu.edu. *Dean,* Dr. Phyllis Metcalf-Turner, 936-261-3600, Fax: 936-261-3621, E-mail: pmmetcalf@pvamu.edu.

College of Engineering Students: 126 full-time (46 women), 47 part-time (12 women); includes 71 minority (56 Black or African American, non-Hispanic/Latino; 12 Asian, non-Hispanic/Latino; 3 Hispanic/Latino), 82 international. Average age 30. 194 applicants, 46% accepted, 78 enrolled. *Faculty:* 29 full-time (6 women), 1 (woman) part-time/adjunct. *Financial support:* Research assistantships, teaching assistantships, career-related internships or fieldwork, institutionally sponsored loans, scholarships/grants, health care benefits, tuition waivers (partial), and unspecified assistantships available. Financial award application deadline: 3/1; financial award applicants required to submit FAFSA. In 2015, 45 master's, 6 doctorates awarded. *Degree program information:* Part-time and evening/weekend programs available. Part-time, evening/weekend. Offers computer information systems (MSCIS); computer science (MSCS); electrical engineering (MSEE, PhDEE); engineering (MS Engr). *Application deadline:* For fall admission, 7/1 priority date for domestic students, 6/1 priority date for international students; for spring admission, 11/1 priority date for domestic students, 10/1 priority date for international students; for summer admission, 3/1 priority date for domestic students, 2/1 priority date for international students. Applications are processed on a rolling basis. *Application fee:* $50. Electronic applications accepted. *Application Contact:* Pauline Walker, Administrative Assistant II, Research and Graduate Studies, 936-261-3521, Fax: 936-261-3529, E-mail: gradadmissions@pvamu.edu. *Dean,* Dr. Kendall T. Harris, 936-261-9900, Fax: 936-261-9868, E-mail: tharris@pvamu.edu.

College of Juvenile Justice and Psychology Students: 35 full-time (31 women), 37 part-time (27 women); includes 62 minority (59 Black or African American, non-Hispanic/Latino; 2 Hispanic/Latino; 1 Two or more races, non-Hispanic/Latino), 7 international. Average age 30. 124 applicants, 37% accepted, 41 enrolled. *Faculty:* 7 full-time (4 women), 7 part-time/adjunct (3 women). *Financial support:* In 2015–16, 14 students received support, including 14 research assistantships (averaging $24,000 per year); career-related internships or fieldwork, Federal Work-Study, institutionally sponsored loans, tuition waivers (full and partial), and unspecified assistantships also available. Support available to part-time students. Financial award application deadline: 3/1; financial award applicants required to submit FAFSA. In 2015, 27 master's, 4 doctorates awarded. *Degree program information:* Part-time and evening/weekend programs available. Part-time, evening/weekend. Offers clinical adolescent psychology (PhD); juvenile forensic psychology (MSJFP); juvenile justice (MSJJ, PhD). *Application deadline:* For fall admission, 7/1 priority date for domestic students, 6/1 priority date for international students; for spring admission, 11/1 priority date for domestic students, 10/1 priority date for international students; for summer admission, 3/1 priority date for domestic students, 2/1 priority date for international students. Applications are processed on a rolling basis. *Application fee:* $50. Electronic applications accepted. *Application Contact:* Pauline Walker, Executive Secretary, Graduate Program, 936-261-3521, Fax: 936-261-3529, E-mail: gradadmissions@pvamu.edu. *Dean,* Dr. Tamara L. Brown, 936-261-5206, Fax: 936-261-5253, E-mail: tlbrown@pvamu.edu.

College of Nursing Students: 65 full-time (58 women), 78 part-time (71 women); includes 128 minority (94 Black or African American, non-Hispanic/Latino; 24 Asian, non-Hispanic/Latino; 9 Hispanic/Latino; 1 Two or more races, non-Hispanic/Latino), 5 international. Average age 35. 84 applicants, 44% accepted, 25 enrolled. *Faculty:* 11 full-time (all women), 7 part-time/adjunct (6 women). *Financial support:* Career-related internships or fieldwork, Federal Work-Study, institutionally sponsored loans, scholarships/grants, and traineeships available. Support available to part-time students. Financial award application deadline: 4/1; financial award applicants required to submit FAFSA. In 2015, 63 master's awarded. *Degree program information:* Part-time and evening/weekend programs available. Part-time, evening/weekend. Offers family nurse practitioner (MSN); nursing administration (MSN); nursing education (MSN). *Application deadline:* For fall admission, 7/1 priority date for domestic students, 6/1 priority date for international students; for spring admission, 11/1 priority date for domestic students, 10/1 priority date for international students; for summer admission, 3/1 priority date for domestic students, 2/1 priority date for international students. Applications are processed on a rolling basis. *Application fee:* $50. Electronic applications accepted. *Application Contact:* Dr. Forest Smith, Director of Student Services and Admissions, 713-797-7031, Fax: 713-797-7012, E-mail: fdsmith@pvamu.edu. *Dean,* Dr. Betty N. Adams, 713-797-7009, Fax: 713-797-7013, E-mail: bnadams@pvamu.edu.

School of Architecture Students: 42 full-time (19 women), 22 part-time (9 women); includes 59 minority (48 Black or African American, non-Hispanic/Latino; 11 Hispanic/Latino), 3 international. Average age 30. 63 applicants, 65% accepted, 35 enrolled. *Faculty:* 4 full-time (0 women), 4 part-time/adjunct (3 women). *Financial support:* In 2015–16, 3 students received support. Career-related internships or fieldwork, Federal Work-Study, institutionally sponsored loans, scholarships/grants, tuition waivers (full and partial), and unspecified assistantships available. Support available to part-time students. Financial award application deadline: 4/1; financial award applicants required to submit FAFSA. In 2015, 32 master's awarded. *Degree program information:* Part-time and evening/weekend programs available. Part-time, evening/weekend. Offers architecture (M Arch); community development (MCD). *Application deadline:* For fall admission, 7/1 priority date for domestic students, 6/1 priority date for international students; for spring admission, 11/1 priority date for domestic students, 10/1 priority date for international students; for summer admission, 3/1 priority date for domestic students, 2/1 priority date for international students. Applications are processed on a rolling basis. *Application fee:* $50. Electronic applications accepted. *Application Contact:* Pauline Walker, Administrative Assistant II, Research and Graduate Studies, 936-261-3521, Fax: 936-261-3529, E-mail: gradadmissions@pvamu.edu. *Dean,* Dr. Ikhlas Sabouni, 936-261-9800, Fax: 936-261-9826, E-mail: isabouni@pvamu.edu.

PRATT INSTITUTE, Brooklyn, NY 11205-3899

General Information Independent, coed, comprehensive institution. *Enrollment:* 4,617 graduate, professional, and undergraduate students; 1,261 full-time matriculated graduate/professional students (909 women), 113 part-time matriculated graduate/professional students (91 women). *Enrollment by degree level:* 1,370 master's, 4 other advanced degrees. *Tuition, area resident:* Full-time $28,638. *Required fees:* $1932. *Graduate housing:* Room and/or apartments available on a first-come, first-served basis to single students; on-campus housing not available to married students. Typical cost: $17,646 per year ($21,712 including board). Room and board charges vary according to board plan and housing facility selected. Housing application deadline: 5/1. *Student services:* Campus employment opportunities, campus safety program, career counseling, exercise/wellness program, free psychological counseling, grant writing training, international student services, low-cost health insurance, multicultural affairs office, services for students with disabilities, teacher training, writing training. *Library:* Pratt Institute Library. *Research affiliation:* The Procter & Gamble Company (product design), General Motors (transportation), Ford Motor Company (transportation).

Computer facilities: A campuswide network can be accessed from student residence rooms and from off campus. Online class registration is available.
Website: http://www.pratt.edu/

General Application Contact: Young Hah, Director of Graduate Admissions, 718-636-3683, Fax: 718-636-3670, E-mail: yhah@pratt.edu.

GRADUATE UNITS

School of Architecture Students: 326 full-time (172 women), 11 part-time (7 women); includes 82 minority (22 Black or African American, non-Hispanic/Latino; 24 Asian, non-Hispanic/Latino; 34 Hispanic/Latino; 2 Two or more races, non-Hispanic/Latino), 91 international. Average age 28. 747 applicants, 77% accepted, 117 enrolled. *Faculty:* 10 full-time (4 women), 99 part-time/adjunct (31 women). *Financial support:* Career-related internships or fieldwork, Federal Work-Study, institutionally sponsored loans, scholarships/grants, health care benefits, and unspecified assistantships available. Support available to part-time students. Financial award application deadline: 2/1; financial award applicants required to submit FAFSA. In 2015, 136 master's awarded. Offers architecture (M Arch, MS, MS Arch, MSCRP); architecture (first-professional) (M Arch); architecture (post-professional) (MS Arch); architecture and urban design (MS); city and regional planning (MSCRP); facilities management (MS); historic preservation (MS); sustainable environmental systems (MS); urban place making and management (MS). *Application deadline:* For fall admission, 1/5 for domestic and international students; for spring admission, 10/1 for domestic and international students. *Application fee:* $50 ($90 for international students). Electronic applications accepted. *Application Contact:* Young Hah, Director of Graduate Admissions, 718-636-3683, Fax: 718-399-4242, E-mail: yhah@pratt.edu. *Dean*, Thomas Hanrahan, 718-399-4304, Fax: 718-399-4315, E-mail: hanrahan@pratt.edu.

School of Art Students: 364 full-time (293 women), 9 part-time (8 women); includes 87 minority (28 Black or African American, non-Hispanic/Latino; 1 American Indian or Alaska Native, non-Hispanic/Latino; 26 Asian, non-Hispanic/Latino; 26 Hispanic/Latino; 6 Two or more races, non-Hispanic/Latino), 153 international. Average age 27. 875 applicants, 50% accepted, 140 enrolled. *Faculty:* 22 full-time (13 women), 141 part-time/adjunct (68 women). *Financial support:* Career-related internships or fieldwork, Federal Work-Study, institutionally sponsored loans, scholarships/grants, health care benefits, and unspecified assistantships available. Support available to part-time students. Financial award application deadline: 2/1; financial award applicants required to submit FAFSA. In 2015, 135 master's awarded. *Degree program information:* Part-time programs available. Part-time. Offers art (MFA, MPS, MS, Adv C); art and design education (MS, Adv C); art therapy and creativity development (MPS); arts and cultural management (MPS); dance/movement therapy (MS); design management (MPS); digital arts (MFA); integrated practices (MFA); painting and drawing (MFA); photography (MFA); printmaking (MFA); sculpture (MFA). *Application deadline:* For fall admission, 1/5 for domestic and international students; for spring admission, 10/1 for domestic and international students. *Application fee:* $50 ($90 for international students). Electronic applications accepted. *Application Contact:* Young Hah, Director of Graduate Admissions, 718-636-3683, Fax: 718-399-4242, E-mail: yhah@pratt.edu. *Dean*, Gerry Snyder, 718-636-3619, E-mail: gsnyder@pratt.edu.

School of Design Students: 389 full-time (296 women), 10 part-time (8 women); includes 60 minority (9 Black or African American, non-Hispanic/Latino; 32 Asian, non-Hispanic/Latino; 15 Hispanic/Latino; 1 Native Hawaiian or other Pacific Islander, non-Hispanic/Latino; 3 Two or more races, non-Hispanic/Latino), 222 international. Average age 26. 882 applicants, 51% accepted, 151 enrolled. *Faculty:* 12 full-time (5 women), 136 part-time/adjunct (56 women). *Financial support:* Career-related internships or fieldwork, Federal Work-Study, institutionally sponsored loans, scholarships/grants, and unspecified assistantships available. Support available to part-time students. Financial award application deadline: 2/1; financial award applicants required to submit FAFSA. In 2015, 142 master's awarded. *Degree program information:* Part-time programs available. Part-time. Offers communications design (MFA); design (MFA, MID, MS); industrial design (MID); interior design (MFA); package design (MS). *Application deadline:* For fall admission, 1/5 for domestic and international students; for spring admission, 10/1 for domestic and international students. *Application fee:* $50 ($90 for international students). Electronic applications accepted. *Application Contact:* Young Hah, Director of Graduate Admissions, 718-636-3683, Fax: 718-636-3670, E-mail: yhah@pratt.edu. *Dean, School of Design*, Anita Cooney, 718-687-5744, Fax: 718-636-3410, E-mail: acooney@pratt.edu.

School of Information Students: 75 full-time (59 women), 70 part-time (60 women); includes 42 minority (12 Black or African American, non-Hispanic/Latino; 11 Asian, non-Hispanic/Latino; 15 Hispanic/Latino; 4 Two or more races, non-Hispanic/Latino), 1 international. Average age 32. 133 applicants, 92% accepted, 46 enrolled. *Faculty:* 9 full-time (4 women), 26 part-time/adjunct (13 women). *Financial support:* Career-related internships or fieldwork, Federal Work-Study, institutionally sponsored loans, scholarships/grants, health care benefits, and unspecified assistantships available. Support available to part-time students. Financial award application deadline: 2/1; financial award applicants required to submit FAFSA. In 2015, 91 master's, 2 other advanced degrees awarded. *Degree program information:* Part-time programs available. Part-time. Offers archives (Adv C); conservation and digital curation (Adv C); data analytics and visualization (MS); digital humanities (Adv C); information experience design (MS); library and information science (MS, Adv C); library and information science: library media specialist (MS); library media specialist (Adv C); museum libraries (Adv C); museums and digital culture (MS); user experience (Adv C). *Application deadline:* For fall admission, 1/5 for domestic and international students; for spring admission, 10/1 for domestic and international students. Applications are processed on a rolling basis. *Application fee:* $50 ($90 for international students). Electronic applications accepted. *Application Contact:* Young Hah, Director of Graduate Admissions, 718-636-3683, Fax: 718-399-4242, E-mail: yhah@pratt.edu. *Dean*, Dr. Tula Giannini, 212-647-7682, Fax: 212-367-2492, E-mail: giannini@pratt.edu.

School of Liberal Arts and Sciences Students: 78 full-time (63 women), 8 part-time (7 women); includes 27 minority (11 Black or African American, non-Hispanic/Latino; 3 Asian, non-Hispanic/Latino; 10 Hispanic/Latino; 3 Two or more races, non-Hispanic/Latino), 13 international. Average age 27. 172 applicants, 69% accepted, 35 enrolled. *Financial support:* Career-related internships or fieldwork, Federal Work-Study, institutionally sponsored loans, scholarships/grants, health care benefits, and unspecified assistantships available. Support available to part-time students. Financial award application deadline: 2/1; financial award applicants required to submit FAFSA. In 2015, 22 master's awarded. Offers history of art and design (MS); liberal arts and sciences (MA, MFA, MS); media studies (MA); performance and performance studies (MFA); writing (MFA). *Application deadline:* For fall admission, 1/5 for domestic and international students; for spring admission, 10/1 for domestic and international students. *Application fee:* $50 ($90 for international students). Electronic applications accepted. *Application Contact:* Young Hah, Director of Graduate Admissions, 718-636-3683, Fax: 718-399-4242, E-mail: yhah@pratt.edu. *Dean*, Andrew W. Barnes, 718-636-3570, Fax: 718-399-4586, E-mail: awbarnes@pratt.edu.

PRESCOTT COLLEGE, Prescott, AZ 86301

General Information Independent, coed, comprehensive institution. *Graduate housing:* On-campus housing not available. *Research affiliation:* Packard Foundation (Kino Bay research), Marshall Foundation (youth and wilderness), U.S. Department of Agriculture (USDA) (agro-ecology), National Park Service (forest health).

GRADUATE UNITS

Graduate Programs ***Degree program information:*** Part-time programs available. Part-time, online learning. Offers adventure education (MA); adventure-based environmental education (MA); adventure-based psychotherapy (MA); counseling psychology (MA); early childhood education (MA); early childhood special education (MA); ecopsychology (MA); ecotherapy (MA); education (MA); elementary education (MA); environmental education leadership and administration (MA); environmental studies (MA); equine-assisted learning (MA); equine-assisted mental health (MA); expressive arts therapy (MA); humanities (MA); school guidance counseling (MA); secondary education (MA); social justice and human rights (MA); somatic psychology (MA); special education: learning disabilities (MA); special education: mental retardation (MA); special education: serious emotional disabilities (MA); student-directed concentrations (MA); student-directed independent study (MA); sustainability education (PhD). Electronic applications accepted.

PRESIDIO GRADUATE SCHOOL, San Francisco, CA 94129

General Information Independent, coed, graduate-only institution.

GRADUATE UNITS

Graduate Programs in Sustainable Management Offers sustainable management (MBA, MPA, Certificate). MBA/JD offered in conjunction with the University of California, Hastings College of the Law.

PRINCETON THEOLOGICAL SEMINARY, Princeton, NJ 08542-0803

General Information Independent-religious, coed, graduate-only institution. *Graduate housing:* Rooms and/or apartments available on a first-come, first-served basis to single and married students. *Research affiliation:* Center of Theological Inquiry.

GRADUATE UNITS

Graduate and Professional Programs ***Degree program information:*** Part-time programs available. Part-time. Offers theology (M Div, MA, Th M, D Min, PhD). Electronic applications accepted.

PRINCETON UNIVERSITY, Princeton, NJ 08544-1019

General Information Independent, coed, university. CGS member. *Graduate housing:* Rooms and/or apartments available to single and married students. Housing application deadline: 4/15. *Research affiliation:* Institute for Advanced Study (physics and mathematics), Brookhaven National Laboratory (experimental physics), Textile Research Institute (polymer research), National Oceanic and Atmospheric Administration (NOAA)–GFD Laboratory (weather prediction).

GRADUATE UNITS

Graduate School Offers anthropology (PhD); applied and computational mathematics (PhD); astronomy (PhD); atmospheric and oceanic sciences (PhD); chemistry (PhD); classical and hellenic studies (PhD); classical art and archaeology (PhD); classical philosophy (PhD); comparative literature (PhD); composition (PhD); demography (PhD, Certificate); East Asian art and archaeology (PhD); East Asian studies (PhD); ecology and evolutionary biology (PhD); economics (PhD); economics and demography (PhD); English (PhD); French language and literature (PhD); geosciences (PhD); German (PhD); history (PhD); history (the ancient world) (PhD); history of science (PhD); industrial chemistry (MS); literature and philology (PhD); mathematics (PhD); molecular biology (PhD); musicology (PhD); Near Eastern studies (MA, PhD); neuroscience (PhD); ocean sciences and marine biology (PhD); philosophy (PhD); philosophy of science (PhD); physics (PhD); plasma physics (PhD); political philosophy (PhD); politics (PhD); psychology (PhD); public affairs and demography (PhD); religion (PhD); Russian and Slavic linguistics (PhD); Russian literature (PhD); sociology (PhD); sociology and demography (PhD); Spanish and Portuguese languages and cultures (PhD). Electronic applications accepted.

Bendheim Center for Finance Offers finance (M Fin). Electronic applications accepted.

School of Architecture Offers architecture (M Arch, PhD). Electronic applications accepted.

School of Engineering and Applied Science Offers chemical engineering (M Eng, MSE, PhD); civil and environmental engineering (M Eng, MSE, PhD); computer science (MSE, PhD); electrical engineering (M Eng, PhD); engineering and applied science (M Eng, MSE, PhD); mechanical and aerospace engineering (M Eng, MSE, PhD); operations research and financial engineering (M Eng, MSE, PhD). Electronic applications accepted.

Woodrow Wilson School of Public and International Affairs Offers public affairs (MPA, PhD); public policy (MPP). JD/MPA offered jointly with Columbia University, New York University, Stanford University. Electronic applications accepted.

Princeton Institute for the Science and Technology of Materials (PRISM) Offers materials (PhD).

Princeton Neuroscience Institute Offers neuroscience (PhD). Electronic applications accepted.

PROVIDENCE COLLEGE, Providence, RI 02918

General Information Independent-religious, coed, comprehensive institution. *Enrollment:* 4,735 graduate, professional, and undergraduate students; 212 full-time matriculated graduate/professional students (103 women), 217 part-time matriculated graduate/professional students (125 women). *Enrollment by degree level:* 429 master's. *Graduate faculty:* 39 full-time (14 women), 41 part-time/adjunct (20 women). *Graduate housing:* On-campus housing not available. *Student services:* Campus employment opportunities, campus safety program, career counseling, exercise/wellness program, international student services, low-cost health insurance, multicultural affairs office, services for students with disabilities, teacher training, writing training. *Library:* Phillips Memorial Library. *Collection:* Books: 389,000 (physical), 1.3 million (digital/electronic); Serial titles: 565 (physical), 52,000 (digital/electronic); Databases: 120. Weekly public service hours: 116; students can reserve study rooms.

Computer facilities: Computer purchase and lease plans are available. 376 computers available on campus for general student use. A campuswide network can be accessed from student residence rooms and from off campus. Online class registration is available.
Website: http://www.providence.edu/

General Application Contact: Rev. Mark D. Nowel, Dean of Undergraduate and Graduate Studies, 401-865-2649, Fax: 401-865-1496, E-mail: mnowel@providence.edu.

GRADUATE UNITS

Department of History ***Financial support:*** Career-related internships or fieldwork, institutionally sponsored loans, and unspecified assistantships available. Support available to part-time students. Financial award application deadline: 8/1; financial award applicants required to submit FAFSA. *Degree program information:* Part-time and evening/weekend programs available. Part-time, evening/weekend. Offers American history (MA); modern European history (MA). *Application deadline:* For fall admission, 8/1 priority date for domestic and international students; for spring admission, 12/31 priority date for domestic students, 12/1 priority date for international students. Applications are processed on a rolling basis. *Application fee:* $55.

Department of Religious Studies ***Financial support:*** Career-related internships or fieldwork and unspecified assistantships available. Support available to part-time students. Financial award application deadline: 8/1; financial award applicants required to submit FAFSA. *Degree program information:* Part-time and evening/weekend programs available. Part-time, evening/weekend. Offers Biblical studies (MA); theology (MA, MTS). *Application deadline:* For fall admission, 8/1 priority date for domestic and international students; for spring admission, 12/1 priority date for domestic and international students. Applications are processed on a rolling basis. *Application fee:* $55.

Program in Counseling ***Financial support:*** Career-related internships or fieldwork, institutionally sponsored loans, and unspecified assistantships available. Support available to part-time students. Financial award application deadline: 8/1; financial award applicants required to submit FAFSA. *Degree program information:* Part-time and evening/weekend programs available. Part-time, evening/weekend. Offers counseling (M Ed). *Application deadline:* For fall admission, 8/1 priority date for domestic and international students; for spring admission, 12/1 priority date for domestic and international students. Applications are processed on a rolling basis. *Application fee:* $55.

Program in Literacy ***Financial support:*** Career-related internships or fieldwork, institutionally sponsored loans, and unspecified assistantships available. Support available to part-time students. Financial award application deadline: 8/1; financial award applicants required to submit FAFSA. *Degree program information:* Part-time and evening/weekend programs available. Part-time, evening/weekend. Offers literacy (M Ed). *Application deadline:* For fall admission, 8/1 priority date for domestic and international students; for spring admission, 12/1 priority date for domestic and international students. Applications are processed on a rolling basis. *Application fee:* $55.

Program in Special Education ***Financial support:*** Career-related internships or fieldwork and unspecified assistantships available. Support available to part-time students. Financial award application deadline: 8/1; financial award applicants required to submit FAFSA. *Degree program information:* Part-time and evening/weekend programs available. Part-time, evening/weekend. Offers special education (M Ed). *Application deadline:* For fall admission, 8/1 priority date for domestic and international students; for spring admission, 12/1 priority date for domestic and international students. Applications are processed on a rolling basis. *Application fee:* $55.

Program in Teaching Mathematics ***Financial support:*** Institutionally sponsored loans and unspecified assistantships available. Support available to part-time students. Financial award application deadline: 8/1; financial award applicants required to submit FAFSA. *Degree program information:* Part-time and evening/weekend programs available. Part-time, evening/weekend. Offers teaching mathematics (MA). *Application deadline:* For fall admission, 8/1 priority date for domestic and international students; for spring admission, 12/1 priority date for domestic and international students. Applications are processed on a rolling basis. *Application fee:* $55.

Program in Urban Teaching ***Financial support:*** Career-related internships or fieldwork, institutionally sponsored loans, and unspecified assistantships available. Support available to part-time students. Financial award application deadline: 8/1; financial award applicants required to submit FAFSA. *Degree program information:* Part-time and evening/weekend programs available. Part-time, evening/weekend. Offers urban teaching (M Ed). *Application deadline:* For fall admission, 8/1 for domestic and international students; for spring admission, 12/1 for domestic and international students. Applications are processed on a rolling basis. *Application fee:* $55.

Programs in Administration ***Financial support:*** Career-related internships or fieldwork, institutionally sponsored loans, and unspecified assistantships available. Support available to part-time students. Financial award application deadline: 8/1; financial award applicants required to submit FAFSA. *Degree program information:* Part-time and evening/weekend programs available. Part-time, evening/weekend. Offers elementary administration (M Ed); secondary administration (M Ed). *Application deadline:* For fall admission, 8/1 priority date for domestic and international students; for spring admission, 12/1 priority date for domestic and international students. Applications are processed on a rolling basis. *Application fee:* $55.

Providence Alliance for Catholic Teachers (PACT) Program Average age 23. *Financial support:* Application deadline: 8/1; applicants required to submit FAFSA. Offers secondary education (M Ed). *Application deadline:* For fall admission, 2/14 priority date for domestic students, 3/1 priority date for international students. Applications are processed on a rolling basis. *Application fee:* $55.

School of Business ***Financial support:*** Federal Work-Study, institutionally sponsored loans, and unspecified assistantships available. Support available to part-time students. Financial award application deadline: 8/1; financial award applicants required to submit FAFSA. *Degree program information:* Part-time and evening/weekend programs available. Part-time, evening/weekend. Offers accounting (MBA); finance (MBA); international business (MBA); management (MBA); marketing (MBA); not-for-profit organizations (MBA). *Application deadline:* For fall admission, 7/15 priority date for domestic and international students; for spring admission, 11/15 priority date for domestic and international students; for summer admission, 4/15 priority date for domestic students. Applications are processed on a rolling basis. *Application fee:* $55.

PROVIDENCE UNIVERSITY COLLEGE & THEOLOGICAL SEMINARY, Otterburne, MB R0A 1G0, Canada

General Information Independent-religious, coed, comprehensive institution. *Graduate housing:* Rooms and/or apartments guaranteed to single students and available on a first-come, first-served basis to married students. Housing application deadline: 8/15.

GRADUATE UNITS

Theological Seminary ***Degree program information:*** Part-time programs available. Part-time. Offers children's ministry (Certificate); Christian studies (MA, Certificate); counseling (MA); cross-cultural discipleship (Certificate); divinity (M Div); educational studies (MA); global studies (MA); lay counseling (Diploma); ministry (D Min); teaching English to speakers of other languages (Certificate); theological studies (MA); training teacher of English to speakers of other languages (Certificate); youth ministry (Certificate).

PURCHASE COLLEGE, STATE UNIVERSITY OF NEW YORK, Purchase, NY 10577-1400

General Information State-supported, coed, comprehensive institution. *Enrollment:* 4,207 graduate, professional, and undergraduate students; 86 full-time matriculated graduate/professional students (43 women), 6 part-time matriculated graduate/professional students (3 women). *Enrollment by degree level:* 92 master's. Tuition, state resident: full-time $10,870; part-time $453 per credit. Tuition, nonresident: full-time $22,210; part-time $925 per credit. *Graduate housing:* Rooms and/or apartments available on a first-come, first-served basis to single and married students. *Student services:* Campus employment opportunities, campus safety program, career counseling, child daycare facilities, exercise/wellness program, free psychological counseling, international student services, low-cost health insurance, services for students with disabilities. *Library:* Purchase College Library.

Computer facilities: 600 computers available on campus for general student use. A campuswide network can be accessed from student residence rooms and from off campus. Online class registration is available.
Website: http://www.purchase.edu/

General Application Contact: Sabrina Johnston, Admissions Counselor, 914-251-6479, Fax: 914-251-6314, E-mail: admissn@purchase.edu.

GRADUATE UNITS

Conservatory of Music Offers composition (MM); instrumental performance (MM); jazz studies (MM); studio composition (MM); voice and opera studies (MM). Electronic applications accepted.

Conservatory of Theatre Arts Offers theatre design/technology (MFA). Electronic applications accepted.

School of Art and Design Offers art and design (MFA). Electronic applications accepted.

School of Humanities Offers art history (MA). Electronic applications accepted.

PURDUE UNIVERSITY, West Lafayette, IN 47907

General Information State-supported, coed, university. CGS member. *Graduate housing:* Rooms and/or apartments available on a first-come, first-served basis to single and married students. Housing application deadline: 3/1.

GRADUATE UNITS

College of Engineering ***Degree program information:*** Part-time programs available. Part-time, online learning. Offers agricultural and biological engineering (MS, MSABE, MSE, PhD); biomedical engineering (MSBME, PhD); engineering (MS, MSAAE, MSABE, MSBME, MSCE, MSChE, MSE, MSECE, MSIE, MSME, MSMSE, MSNE, PhD, Certificate); engineering professional education (MS, MSE). Electronic applications accepted.

Division of Environmental and Ecological Engineering Offers environmental and ecological engineering (MS, PhD).

School of Aeronautics and Astronautics Engineering Degree program information: Part-time programs available. Part-time, online learning. Offers aeronautics and astronautics engineering (MS, MSAAE, MSE, PhD). Electronic applications accepted.

School of Chemical Engineering Offers chemical engineering (MSChE, PhD). Electronic applications accepted.

School of Civil Engineering Degree program information: Part-time programs available. Part-time. Offers civil engineering (MS, MSCE, MSE, PhD). Electronic applications accepted.

School of Electrical and Computer Engineering Degree program information: Part-time programs available. Part-time, online learning. Offers electrical and computer engineering (MS, MSE, MSECE, PhD). MS and PhD degree programs in biomedical engineering offered jointly with School of Mechanical Engineering and School of Chemical Engineering. Electronic applications accepted.

School of Engineering Education Offers engineering education (PhD). Electronic applications accepted.

School of Industrial Engineering Degree program information: Part-time programs available. Part-time, online learning. Offers industrial engineering (MS, MSIE, PhD). Electronic applications accepted.

School of Materials Engineering Degree program information: Part-time programs available. Part-time. Offers materials engineering (MSMSE, PhD). Electronic applications accepted.

School of Mechanical Engineering Degree program information: Part-time programs available. Part-time, online learning. Offers mechanical engineering (MS, MSE, MSME, PhD, Certificate). MS and PhD degree programs in biomedical engineering offered jointly with School of Electrical and Computer Engineering and School of Chemical Engineering. Electronic applications accepted.

School of Nuclear Engineering Degree program information: Part-time programs available. Part-time. Offers nuclear engineering (MS, MSNE, PhD). Electronic applications accepted.

College of Pharmacy and Pharmacal Sciences ***Degree program information:*** Part-time programs available. Part-time. Offers biophysical and computational chemistry (PhD); cancer research (PhD); clinical pharmacy (MS, PhD); immunology and infectious disease (PhD); industrial and physical pharmacy (MS, PhD, Certificate); medicinal biochemistry and molecular biology (PhD); medicinal chemistry and chemical biology (PhD); medicinal chemistry and molecular pharmacology (MS, PhD); molecular pharmacology (PhD); neuropharmacology, neurodegeneration, and neurotoxicity (PhD); pharmaceutics (PhD); pharmacy administration (MS, PhD); pharmacy and pharmacal sciences (MS, PhD, Pharm D, Certificate); pharmacy practice (MS, PhD); regulatory quality compliance (MS, Certificate); systems biology and functional genomics (PhD). Electronic applications accepted.

Graduate School ***Degree program information:*** Part-time and evening/weekend programs available. Part-time, evening/weekend, online learning. Offers biomedical sciences (PhD); biomolecular structure and biophysics (PhD); biotechnology (PhD); chemical biology (PhD); chromatin and regulation of gene expression (PhD); ecological sciences and engineering (MS, PhD); food science (MS, PhD); information security (MS); integrative neuroscience (PhD); integrative plant sciences (PhD); membrane biology (PhD); microbiology (PhD); molecular evolutionary and cancer biology (PhD); molecular evolutionary genetics (PhD); molecular virology (PhD); philosophy and literature (PhD). MD/PhD offered jointly with Indiana University–Purdue University Indianapolis. Electronic applications accepted.

College of Agriculture Degree program information: Part-time programs available. Part-time. Offers agricultural economics (MS, PhD); agriculture (EMBA, M Agr, MA, MS, MSF, PhD); agronomy (MS, PhD); animal sciences (MS, PhD); biochemistry (MS, PhD); botany and plant pathology (MS, PhD); entomology (MS, PhD); fisheries and aquatic sciences (MS, MSF, PhD); food and agricultural business (EMBA); food science (MS, PhD); forest biology (MS, MSF, PhD); horticulture (M Agr, MS, PhD); natural resource social science (MS, PhD); natural resources social science (MSF); quantitative ecology (MS, MSF, PhD); wildlife science (MS, MSF, PhD); wood products and wood products manufacturing (MS, MSF, PhD); youth development and agricultural education (MA, PhD). Electronic applications accepted.

College of Education Degree program information: Part-time and evening/weekend programs available. Part-time, evening/weekend. Offers administration (MS Ed, PhD, Ed S); agricultural and extension education (PhD, Ed S); agriculture and extension education (MS, MS Ed); art education (PhD); counseling and development (MS Ed, PhD); curriculum studies (MS Ed, PhD, Ed S); education (MS, MS Ed, PhD, Ed S); education of the gifted (MS Ed); educational psychology (MS Ed, PhD); educational technology (MS Ed, PhD, Ed S); elementary education (MS Ed); family and consumer sciences education (MS Ed, PhD, Ed S); foreign language education (MS Ed, PhD, Ed S); foundations of education (MS Ed, PhD); higher education administration (MS Ed, PhD); industrial technology (PhD, Ed S); language arts (MS Ed, PhD, Ed S); literacy (MS Ed, PhD, Ed S); mathematics/science education (MS, MS Ed, PhD, Ed S); social studies (MS Ed, PhD); social studies education (Ed S); special education (MS Ed, PhD); vocational/industrial education (MS Ed, PhD, Ed S); vocational/technical education (MS Ed, PhD, Ed S). Electronic applications accepted.

College of Health and Human Sciences Degree program information: Part-time programs available. Part-time. Offers animal health (MS, PhD); athletic training education administration (MS, PhD); audiology clinic (MS, Au D, PhD); behavioral neuroscience (PhD); biochemical and molecular nutrition (MS, PhD); biomechanics (MS, PhD); clinical psychology (PhD); cognitive psychology (PhD); consumer behavior (MS, PhD); developmental studies (MS, PhD); exercise physiology (MS, PhD); family and consumer economics (MS, PhD); family studies (MS, PhD); growth and development (MS, PhD); health and human sciences (MS, Au D, PhD); health education (MS, PhD); health physics (MS, PhD); history/philosophy of sport (MS, PhD); hospitality and tourism management (MS, PhD); human and clinical nutrition (MS, PhD); industrial/organizational psychology (PhD); linguistics (MS, PhD); marriage and family therapy (MS, PhD); mathematical and computational cognitive science (PhD); medical physics (MS, PhD); motor control and development (MS, PhD); occupational and environmental health science (MS, PhD); physical education pedagogy (PhD); physical education teacher education (MS); public health and education (MS, PhD); radiation biology (PhD); recreation and sport management (MS, PhD); speech and hearing science (MS, PhD); speech-language pathology (MS, PhD); sport and exercise psychology (MS, PhD); toxicology (PhD). Electronic applications accepted.

College of Liberal Arts Degree program information: Part-time and evening/weekend programs available. Part-time, evening/weekend. Offers American studies (MA, PhD); anthropology (MS, PhD); art and design (MA); communication (MA, MS, PhD); comparative literature (MA, PhD); creative writing (MFA); French (MA, MAT, PhD); German (MA, MAT, PhD); history (MA, PhD); Japanese pedagogy (MA); liberal arts (MA, MAT, MFA, MS, Au D, PhD); linguistics (MS, PhD); literature (MA, PhD); philosophy (MA, PhD); political science (MA, PhD); sociology (MS, PhD); Spanish (MA, MAT, PhD); theatre (MA, MFA). Electronic applications accepted.

College of Science Degree program information: Part-time programs available. Part-time. Offers analytical chemistry (MS, PhD); applied statistics (MS); biochemistry (MS, PhD); biophysics (PhD); cell and developmental biology (PhD); chemical education (MS, PhD); computational finance (MS); computational science and engineering (MS); computer sciences (MS, PhD); earth and atmospheric sciences (MS, PhD); ecology, evolutionary and population biology (MS, PhD); genetics (MS, PhD); inorganic chemistry (MS, PhD); mathematics (MS, PhD); microbiology (MS, PhD); molecular biology (PhD); neurobiology (MS, PhD); organic chemistry (MS, PhD); physical chemistry (MS, PhD); physics (MS, PhD); plant physiology (PhD); science (MS, PhD, Certificate); statistics (PhD). Electronic applications accepted.

College of Technology Online learning. Offers aviation and aerospace management (MS); building construction management (MS); computer and information technology (MS); computer graphics technology (MS, PhD); leadership (MS, PhD); organizational leadership (MS); technology (MS, PhD); technology innovation (MS). Electronic applications accepted.

Krannert School of Management Offers business administration (EMBA, MBA); economics (PhD); finance (MSF); global executive business administration (MBA); human resource management (MSHRM); industrial administration (MSIA); management (EMBA, MBA, MSF, MSHRM, MSIA, PhD); organizational behavior and human resource management (PhD). Electronic applications accepted.

School of Veterinary Medicine ***Degree program information:*** Part-time and evening/weekend programs available. Part-time, evening/weekend. Offers anatomy (MS, PhD); basic medical sciences (MS, PhD); comparative epidemiology and public health (MS); comparative epidemiology and public heath (PhD); comparative microbiology and immunology (MS, PhD); comparative pathobiology (MS, PhD); interdisciplinary studies (PhD); lab animal medicine (MS); pharmacology (MS, PhD); physiology (MS, PhD); veterinary anatomic pathology (MS); veterinary clinical pathology (MS); veterinary clinical sciences (MS, PhD); veterinary medicine (MS, DVM, PhD).

PURDUE UNIVERSITY NORTHWEST, Hammond, IN 46323-2094

General Information State-supported, coed, comprehensive institution. *Graduate housing:* Room and/or apartments available on a first-come, first-served basis to single students; on-campus housing not available to married students.

GRADUATE UNITS

Graduate Studies Office ***Degree program information:*** Part-time and evening/weekend programs available. Part-time, evening/weekend, online learning. Electronic applications accepted.

School of Education Offers counseling (MS Ed); educational administration (MS Ed); human services (MS Ed); instructional technology (MS Ed); mental health counseling (MS Ed); school counseling (MS Ed); special education (MS Ed).

School of Engineering, Mathematics, and Science Degree program information: Part-time and evening/weekend programs available. Part-time, evening/weekend, online learning. Offers biology (MS); biology teaching (MS); biotechnology (MS); computer engineering (MSE); computer science (MS); electrical engineering (MSE); engineering (MS); engineering, mathematics, and science (MAT, MS, MSE); mathematics (MAT, MS); mechanical engineering (MSE). Electronic applications accepted.

School of Liberal Arts and Social Sciences Degree program information: Part-time programs available. Part-time. Offers child development and family studies (MS); communication (MA); English (MA); history (MA); liberal arts and social sciences (MA, MS); marriage and family therapy (MS).

School of Management Degree program information: Part-time and evening/weekend programs available. Part-time, evening/weekend. Offers accountancy (M Acc); business administration (MBA); business administration for executives (EMBA). Electronic applications accepted.

School of Nursing Degree program information: Part-time programs available. Part-time, online learning. Offers adult health clinical nurse specialist (MS); critical care clinical nurse specialist (MS); family nurse practitioner (MS); nurse executive (MS). Electronic applications accepted.

School of Technology Offers technology (MS).

PURDUE UNIVERSITY NORTHWEST, Westville, IN 46391-9542

General Information State-supported, coed, comprehensive institution. *Graduate housing:* On-campus housing not available.

GRADUATE UNITS

Program in Education ***Degree program information:*** Part-time and evening/weekend programs available. Part-time, evening/weekend. Offers elementary education (MS Ed). Electronic applications accepted.

QUEENS COLLEGE OF THE CITY UNIVERSITY OF NEW YORK, Flushing, NY 11367-1597

General Information State and locally supported, coed, comprehensive institution. CGS member. *Enrollment:* 19,520 graduate, professional, and undergraduate students; 436 full-time matriculated graduate/professional students (308 women), 2,778 part-time matriculated graduate/professional students (1,938 women). *Enrollment by degree level:* 2,634 master's, 580 other advanced degrees. *Graduate faculty:* 612 full-time (283 women), 922 part-time/adjunct (470 women). Tuition, state resident: full-time $5065; part-time $425 per credit. Tuition, nonresident: part-time $780 per credit. *Required fees:* $522. Part-time tuition and fees vary according to course load and program. *Graduate housing:* Room and/or apartments available on a first-come, first-served basis to single students; on-campus housing not available to married students. *Student services:* Campus employment opportunities, career counseling, child daycare facilities, free psychological counseling, international student services, low-cost health insurance, services for students with disabilities, teacher training, writing training. *Library:* The Benjamin S. Rosenthal Library plus 1 other. *Collection:* Books: 897,791 (physical), 465,482 (digital/electronic); Serial titles: 294 (physical), 109,489 (digital/electronic); Databases: 272. Weekly public service hours: 90; students can reserve study rooms. *Research affiliation:* Hudson River Foundation (earth and environmental sciences), Consortium for Ocean Leadership (earth and environmental sciences), Institute for New Economic Thinking (economics), Social Explorer (sociology), Wildlife Conservation Society (biology), IBM (computer science).

Computer facilities: 2,445 computers available on campus for general student use. A campuswide network can be accessed from student residence rooms and from off campus. Online class registration is available.
Website: http://www.qc.cuny.edu/

General Application Contact: Richard Alvarez, Vice President for Enrollment and Student Retention, 718-997-5929, Fax: 718-997-5193, E-mail: graduate_admissions@qc.cuny.edu.

GRADUATE UNITS

Arts and Humanities Division Students: 104 full-time (69 women), 479 part-time (312 women); includes 191 minority (33 Black or African American, non-Hispanic/Latino; 70 Asian, non-Hispanic/Latino; 88 Hispanic/Latino), 66 international. Average age 32. 795 applicants, 40% accepted, 203 enrolled. *Faculty:* 157 full-time (77 women), 260 part-time/adjunct (152 women). *Financial support:* Career-related internships or fieldwork available. Financial award application deadline: 4/1; financial award applicants required to submit FAFSA. In 2015, 119 master's, 12 other advanced degrees awarded. *Degree program information:* Part-time programs available. Part-time. Offers applied linguistics (MA); art history (MA); art studio (MFA); arts and humanities (MA, MFA, MS Ed, AC, Advanced Diploma); creative writing and literary translation (MFA); French (MA); Italian (MA); literature (MA); Spanish (MA); speech-language pathology (MA); teaching English to speakers of other languages (MS Ed). *Application deadline:* For fall admission, 4/1 for domestic students; for spring admission, 11/1 for domestic students. Applications are processed on a rolling basis. *Application fee:* $125. Electronic applications accepted. *Dean*, Dr. William McClure, 718-997-5790, E-mail: william.mcclure@qc.cuny.edu.

Aaron Copland School of Music Students: 35 full-time (10 women), 169 part-time (80 women); includes 59 minority (11 Black or African American, non-Hispanic/Latino; 30 Asian, non-Hispanic/Latino; 18 Hispanic/Latino), 52 international. Average age 29. 214 applicants, 57% accepted, 74 enrolled. *Faculty:* 28 full-time (7 women), 64 part-time/adjunct (26 women). *Financial support:* Career-related internships or fieldwork, Federal Work-Study, institutionally sponsored loans, and tuition waivers (partial) available. Support available to part-time students. Financial award application deadline: 4/1; financial award applicants required to submit FAFSA. In 2015, 31 master's, 12 other advanced degrees awarded. *Degree program information:* Part-time programs available. Part-time. Offers chamber music (Advanced Diploma); classical performance (MM); jazz studies (MM); music (MA); music (preK-12) (MS Ed); music and production (AC); performance (AC, Advanced Diploma). *Application deadline:* For fall admission, 4/1 for domestic students; for spring admission, 11/1 for domestic students. Applications are processed on a rolling basis. *Application fee:* $125. Electronic applications accepted. *Chair/Director*, Dr. Edward Smaldone, 718-997-3800, E-mail: edward.smaldone@qc.cuny.edu.

Division of Education Students: 212 full-time (180 women), 1,241 part-time (1,018 women); includes 573 minority (127 Black or African American, non-Hispanic/Latino; 4 American Indian or Alaska Native, non-Hispanic/Latino; 184 Asian, non-Hispanic/Latino; 258 Hispanic/Latino), 28 international. Average age 30. 1,069 applicants, 68% accepted, 540 enrolled. *Faculty:* 70 full-time (49 women), 118 part-time/adjunct (77 women). *Financial support:* Career-related internships or fieldwork available. Financial award application deadline: 4/1; financial award applicants required to submit FAFSA. In 2015, 425 master's, 130 other advanced degrees awarded. *Degree program information:* Part-time and evening/weekend programs available. Part-time, evening/weekend. Offers adolescent biology (MAT); art (MS Ed); bilingual education (MS Ed); biology (MS Ed, AC); chemistry (MS Ed, AC); childhood education (MAT); childhood education and special education (MAT); childhood education-bilingual education (MAT, AC); counselor education (MS Ed); early childhood education (MAT); earth sciences (MS Ed, AC); education (MA, MAT, MS Ed, AC); elementary education (MS Ed); English (MS Ed, AC); French (MS Ed, AC); Italian (MS Ed, AC); literacy education (MS Ed); mathematics (MS Ed, AC); music (MS Ed, AC); physics (MS Ed, AC); school building leader (AC); school district leader (AC); school psychology (MS Ed); social studies (MS Ed, AC); Spanish (MS Ed, AC); special education (MS Ed, AC). *Application deadline:* For fall admission, 4/1 for domestic students; for spring admission, 11/1 for domestic students. Applications are processed on a rolling basis. *Application fee:* $125. Electronic applications accepted. *Dean*, Dr. Craig Michaels, 718-997-5220, E-mail: craig.michaels@qc.cuny.edu.

Division of Social Sciences Students: 61 full-time (34 women), 605 part-time (340 women); includes 335 minority (103 Black or African American, non-Hispanic/Latino; 1 American Indian or Alaska Native, non-Hispanic/Latino; 149 Asian, non-Hispanic/Latino; 82 Hispanic/Latino), 48 international. Average age 33. 441 applicants, 60% accepted,

219 enrolled. *Faculty:* 145 full-time (62 women), 189 part-time/adjunct (64 women). *Financial support:* Career-related internships or fieldwork available. Financial award application deadline: 4/1; financial award applicants required to submit FAFSA. In 2015, 207 master's awarded. *Degree program information:* Part-time and evening/weekend programs available. Part-time, evening/weekend. Offers accounting (MS); data analytics and applied social research (MA); history (MA); liberal studies (MA); library and information studies (MLS, AC); sociology (MA); urban affairs (MA); urban studies (MA). *Application deadline:* For fall admission, 4/1 for domestic students; for spring admission, 11/1 for domestic students. Applications are processed on a rolling basis. *Application fee:* $125. Electronic applications accepted. *Dean*, Dr. Michael Wolfe, 718-997-5211, E-mail: michael.wolfe@qc.cuny.edu.

Graduate School of Library and Information Studies Students: 17 full-time (14 women), 153 part-time (104 women); includes 56 minority (19 Black or African American, non-Hispanic/Latino; 14 Asian, non-Hispanic/Latino; 23 Hispanic/Latino), 3 international. Average age 38. 113 applicants, 63% accepted, 64 enrolled. *Faculty:* 11 full-time (7 women), 13 part-time/adjunct (10 women). *Financial support:* Career-related internships or fieldwork and unspecified assistantships available. Financial award application deadline: 4/1; financial award applicants required to submit FAFSA. In 2015, 62 master's awarded. *Degree program information:* Part-time and evening/weekend programs available. Part-time, evening/weekend. Offers archives, records management and preservation (AC); children's and young adult services in the public library (AC); library media specialist (MLS, AC); library science (MLS, AC); library science and history (MLS). *Application deadline:* For fall admission, 4/1 for domestic students; for spring admission, 11/1 for domestic students. Applications are processed on a rolling basis. *Application fee:* $125. Electronic applications accepted. *Director/Chair*, Dr. Roberta Brody, 718-997-3790, E-mail: roberta.brody@qc.cuny.edu.

Mathematics and Natural Sciences Division Students: 59 full-time (25 women), 452 part-time (267 women); includes 172 minority (60 Black or African American, non-Hispanic/Latino; 1 American Indian or Alaska Native, non-Hispanic/Latino; 58 Asian, non-Hispanic/Latino; 53 Hispanic/Latino), 84 international. Average age 29. 454 applicants, 60% accepted, 183 enrolled. *Faculty:* 157 full-time (55 women), 271 part-time/adjunct (131 women). *Financial support:* Career-related internships or fieldwork available. Financial award application deadline: 4/1; financial award applicants required to submit FAFSA. In 2015, 83 master's, 7 other advanced degrees awarded. *Degree program information:* Part-time programs available. Part-time. Offers applied behavior analysis (MA, AC); behavioral neuroscience (MA); biology (MA); chemistry (MA); computer science (MA); exercise science specialist (MS); family and consumer science (K-12) (AC); family and consumer science/teacher (K-12) (MS Ed); mathematics (MA); mathematics and natural sciences (MA, MAT, MS, MS Ed, AC); nutrition and exercise science (MS); nutrition specialist (MS); physical education (K-12) (AC); physical education/teaching curriculum (pre K-12) (MS Ed); physics (MA); psychology (MA). *Application deadline:* For fall admission, 4/1 for domestic students; for spring admission, 11/1 for domestic students. Applications are processed on a rolling basis. *Application fee:* $125. Electronic applications accepted. *Dean*, Dr. Martin Klotz, 718-997-4105, E-mail: martin.klotz@qc.cuny.edu.

School of Earth and Environmental Sciences Students: 14 part-time (6 women); includes 2 minority (1 Black or African American, non-Hispanic/Latino; 1 Hispanic/Latino), 2 international. Average age 27. 11 applicants, 55% accepted, 3 enrolled. *Faculty:* 17 full-time (3 women), 9 part-time/adjunct (2 women). *Financial support:* Career-related internships or fieldwork and unspecified assistantships available. Financial award application deadline: 4/1; financial award applicants required to submit FAFSA. In 2015, 6 master's awarded. *Degree program information:* Part-time and evening/weekend programs available. Part-time, evening/weekend. Offers applied environmental geoscience (MS); geological and environmental science (MA). *Application deadline:* For fall admission, 4/1 for domestic students; for spring admission, 11/1 for domestic students. Applications are processed on a rolling basis. *Application fee:* $125. Electronic applications accepted. *Chairperson*, Dr. George Hendrey, 718-997-3300, E-mail: george.hendrey@qc.cuny.edu.

QUEEN'S UNIVERSITY AT KINGSTON, Kingston, ON K7L 3N6, Canada

General Information Province-supported, coed, university. CGS member. *Graduate housing:* Rooms and/or apartments available to single students and available on a first-come, first-served basis to married students. Housing application deadline: 6/15.

GRADUATE UNITS

Faculty of Law ***Degree program information:*** Part-time programs available. Part-time. Offers law (LL M, JD).

Queens School of Business Offers business (M Sc, MBA, PhD); consulting and project management (MBA); finance (MBA); innovation and entrepreneurship (MBA); marketing (MBA).

Queen's School of Religion ***Degree program information:*** Part-time programs available. Part-time. Offers religion (M Div, MTS, Certificate).

School of Graduate Studies ***Degree program information:*** Part-time programs available. Part-time.

Faculty of Applied Science Degree program information: Part-time programs available. Part-time. Offers applied science (M Eng, M Sc, M Sc Eng, PhD); chemical engineering (M Sc, PhD); civil engineering (M Eng, M Sc Eng, PhD); electrical and computer engineering (M Eng, M Sc, M Sc Eng, PhD); mechanical and materials engineering (M Eng, M Sc, M Sc Eng, PhD); mining engineering (M Eng, M Sc, M Sc Eng, PhD). Electronic applications accepted.

Faculty of Arts and Sciences Degree program information: Part-time programs available. Part-time. Offers arts and sciences (M Sc, M Sc Eng, MA, PhD); biology (M Sc, PhD); brain behavior and cognitive science (MA, PhD); Canadian politics (PhD); chemistry (M Sc, PhD); classics, Greek, Latin (MA); clinical psychology (MA, PhD); communication and Information technology (MA, PhD); comparative politics (PhD); computing (M Sc, PhD); developmental psychology (MA, PhD); English language and literature (MA, PhD); feminist sociology (MA, PhD); French studies (MA, PhD); gender and politics (PhD); geography (M Sc, MA, PhD); geological sciences and geological engineering (M Sc, M Sc Eng, PhD); German (MA, PhD); international relations (PhD); mathematics (M Sc, M Sc Eng, PhD); philosophy (MA, PhD); physics (M Sc, M Sc Eng, PhD); political theory (PhD); religious studies (MA); social personality psychology (MA, PhD); socio-legal studies (MA, PhD); sociological theory (MA, PhD); Spanish language and literature (MA); statistics (M Sc, M Sc Eng, PhD). Electronic applications accepted.

Faculty of Education Degree program information: Part-time programs available. Part-time. Offers education (M Ed, PhD).

Faculty of Health Sciences Degree program information: Part-time programs available. Part-time. Offers biochemistry (M Sc, PhD); biology of reproduction (M Sc, PhD); cancer (M Sc, PhD); cardiovascular pathophysiology (M Sc, PhD); cell and molecular biology (M Sc, PhD); drug metabolism (M Sc, PhD); endocrinology (M Sc, PhD); epidemiology (PhD); epidemiology and population health (M Sc); health and chronic illness (M Sc); health sciences (M Sc, M Sc OT, M Sc PT, MPH, PhD, Certificate); health services (M Sc); microbiology and immunology (M Sc, PhD); motor control (M Sc, PhD); neural regeneration (M Sc, PhD); neurophysiology (M Sc, PhD); nurse scientist (PhD); occupational therapy (M Sc OT); pathology and molecular medicine (M Sc, PhD); pharmacology and toxicology (M Sc, PhD); physical therapy (M Sc PT); physiology (M Sc, PhD); policy research and clinical epidemiology (M Sc); primary health care nurse practitioner (Certificate); public health (MPH); rehabilitation science (M Sc, PhD); women's and children's health (M Sc). Electronic applications accepted.

School of Industrial Relations Degree program information: Part-time programs available. Part-time. Offers industrial relations (MIR).

School of Kinesiology and Health Studies Degree program information: Part-time programs available. Part-time. Offers applied exercise science (PhD); biomechanics/ergonomics (M Sc); exercise physiology (M Sc); social psychology of sport and exercise rehabilitation (MA); sociology of sport (MA). Electronic applications accepted.

School of Policy Studies Degree program information: Part-time programs available. Part-time. Offers policy studies (MIR, MPA).

School of Urban and Regional Planning Degree program information: Part-time programs available. Part-time. Offers urban and regional planning (M Pl).

School of Medicine Offers medicine (MD). Electronic applications accepted.

QUEENS UNIVERSITY OF CHARLOTTE, Charlotte, NC 28274-0002

General Information Independent-religious, coed, comprehensive institution. *Graduate housing:* On-campus housing not available.

GRADUATE UNITS

College of Arts and Sciences ***Degree program information:*** Part-time programs available. Part-time, online learning. Offers creative writing (MFA); interior design (MA). Electronic applications accepted.

Knight School of Communication ***Degree program information:*** Part-time and evening/weekend programs available. Part-time, evening/weekend, online learning. Offers organizational and strategic communication (MA).

McColl School of Business ***Degree program information:*** Part-time and evening/weekend programs available. Part-time, evening/weekend, online learning. Offers business administration (EMBA, MBA, PMBA); organization development (MSOD). Electronic applications accepted.

Presbyterian School of Nursing Offers clinical nurse leader (MSN); nurse educator (MSN); nursing administrator (MSN). Electronic applications accepted.

Wayland H. Cato, Jr. School of Education ***Degree program information:*** Part-time and evening/weekend programs available. Part-time, evening/weekend, online learning. Offers educational leadership (MA); K-6 (MAT); literacy K-12 (M Ed).

QUINCY UNIVERSITY, Quincy, IL 62301-2699

General Information Independent-religious, coed, comprehensive institution. *Enrollment:* 1,293 graduate, professional, and undergraduate students; 19 full-time matriculated graduate/professional students (10 women), 108 part-time matriculated graduate/professional students (37 women). *Enrollment by degree level:* 127 master's. *Graduate faculty:* 11 full-time (6 women), 10 part-time/adjunct (7 women). *Tuition, area resident:* Full-time $3600; part-time $1200 per credit. Tuition and fees vary according to program. *Graduate housing:* Room and/or apartments available to single students; on-campus housing not available to married students. *Student services:* Campus employment opportunities, campus safety program, career counseling, exercise/wellness program, free psychological counseling, international student services, low-cost health insurance, multicultural affairs office, services for students with disabilities, teacher training, writing training. *Library:* Brenner Library.

Computer facilities: 221 computers available on campus for general student use. A campuswide network can be accessed from student residence rooms and from off campus. Online class registration is available.
Website: http://www.quincy.edu/

General Application Contact: Office of Admissions, 217-228-5210, Fax: 217-228-5479, E-mail: admissions@quincy.edu.

GRADUATE UNITS

Master of Arts in Communication Program Students: 10 full-time (4 women), 6 part-time (2 women); includes 2 minority (1 Black or African American, non-Hispanic/Latino; 1 Asian, non-Hispanic/Latino). *Financial support:* Applicants required to submit FAFSA. *Degree program information:* Part-time and evening/weekend programs available. Part-time, evening/weekend, online learning. Offers communication (MA). *Application deadline:* Applications are processed on a rolling basis. *Application fee:* $25. Electronic applications accepted. *Application Contact:* Office of Admissions, 217-228-5210, Fax: 217-228-5479, E-mail: admissions@quincy.edu. *Assistant Professor, Communication*, Christine Tracy, 217-228-5432 Ext. 3105, E-mail: tracych@quincy.edu.

Master of Science in Education Counseling Program Students: 1 (woman) full-time, 35 part-time (29 women); includes 3 minority (all Black or African American, non-Hispanic/Latino). *Faculty:* 2 full-time (1 woman). *Financial support:* Applicants required to submit FAFSA. In 2015, 5 master's awarded. *Degree program information:* Part-time and evening/weekend programs available. Part-time, evening/weekend. Offers college personnel (MS Ed); counseling (MS Ed); school counseling (MS Ed). *Application deadline:* Applications are processed on a rolling basis. *Application fee:* $25. Electronic applications accepted. *Application Contact:* Office of Admissions, 217-228-5210, Fax: 217-228-5479, E-mail: admissions@quincy.edu. *Director*, Dr. Kenneth Oliver, 217-228-5432 Ext. 3113, E-mail: oliveke@quincy.edu.

Master of Science in Education Programs Students: 5 full-time (4 women), 40 part-time (28 women); includes 7 minority (6 Black or African American, non-Hispanic/Latino; 1 Asian, non-Hispanic/Latino). *Faculty:* 7 full-time (4 women), 8 part-time/adjunct (5 women). *Financial support:* Applicants required to submit FAFSA. In 2015, 62 master's awarded. *Degree program information:* Part-time and evening/weekend programs available. Part-time, evening/weekend, online learning. Offers curriculum and instruction (MS Ed); leadership (MS Ed); reading education (MS Ed); special education (MS Ed); teacher leader (MS Ed). *Application deadline:* Applications are processed on a rolling basis. *Application fee:* $25. Electronic applications accepted. *Application Contact:* Office of Admissions, 217-228-5210, Fax: 217-228-5479, E-mail: admissions@quincy.edu. *Director*, Dr. Bruce Alan Spitzer, 217-228-5432 Ext. 3106, E-mail: spitzbr@quincy.edu.

MBA Program Students: 3 full-time (0 women), 27 part-time (12 women); includes 1 minority (American Indian or Alaska Native, non-Hispanic/Latino), 1 international. *Faculty:* 5 full-time (3 women). *Financial support:* Applicants required to submit FAFSA.

In 2015, 18 master's awarded. *Degree program information:* Part-time and evening/weekend programs available. Part-time, evening/weekend, online learning. Offers business administration (MBA). *Application deadline:* Applications are processed on a rolling basis. *Application fee:* $25. Electronic applications accepted. *Application Contact:* Office of Admissions, 217-228-5210, Fax: 217-228-5479, E-mail: admissions@quincy.edu. *Director*, Dr. Cynthia Haliemun, 217-228-5432 Ext. 3067, E-mail: haliecy@quincy.edu.

QUINNIPIAC UNIVERSITY, Hamden, CT 06518-1940

General Information Independent, coed, comprehensive institution. *Enrollment:* 9,654 graduate, professional, and undergraduate students; 650 full-time matriculated graduate/professional students (415 women), 1,010 part-time matriculated graduate/professional students (663 women). *Enrollment by degree level:* 1,327 master's, 275 doctoral, 58 other advanced degrees. *Graduate faculty:* 157 full-time (100 women), 310 part-time/adjunct (161 women). Tuition and fees vary according to course load and program. *Graduate housing:* Rooms and/or apartments available on a first-come, first-served basis to single and married students. *Student services:* Campus employment opportunities, campus safety program, career counseling, exercise/wellness program, free psychological counseling, international student services, low-cost health insurance, multicultural affairs office, services for students with disabilities. *Library:* Arnold Bernhard Library plus 3 others. Weekly public service hours: 60; study areas open 24 hours, 5–7 days a week; students can reserve study rooms.

Computer facilities: Computer purchase and lease plans are available. 600 computers available on campus for general student use. A campuswide network can be accessed from student residence rooms and from off campus. Online class registration, e-commerce 'Q' card for local merchants, food service, dorm card access are available. Website: http://www.quinnipiac.edu/

General Application Contact: Graduate Admissions, 800-462-1944, Fax: 203-582-3443, E-mail: graduate@quinnipiac.edu.

GRADUATE UNITS

College of Arts and Sciences Students: 14 full-time (4 women), 20 part-time (14 women); includes 6 minority (2 Black or African American, non-Hispanic/Latino; 2 Asian, non-Hispanic/Latino; 2 Hispanic/Latino), 7 international. 49 applicants, 45% accepted, 12 enrolled. *Faculty:* 6 full-time (4 women), 3 part-time/adjunct (0 women). *Financial support:* Career-related internships or fieldwork, Federal Work-Study, scholarships/grants, and unspecified assistantships available. Support available to part-time students. Financial award application deadline: 6/1; financial award applicants required to submit FAFSA. In 2015, 10 master's awarded. *Degree program information:* Part-time and evening/weekend programs available. Part-time, evening/weekend. Offers arts and sciences (MS); molecular and cell biology (MS). *Application deadline:* For fall admission, 7/30 priority date for domestic students, 4/30 for international students; for spring admission, 12/15 priority date for domestic students, 9/15 for international students. Applications are processed on a rolling basis. *Application fee:* $45. Electronic applications accepted. *Application Contact:* The Office of Graduate Admissions, 800-462-1944, Fax: 203-582-3443, E-mail: graduate@quinnipiac.edu.

Frank H. Netter MD School of Medicine Students: 247 full-time (105 women); includes 92 minority (10 Black or African American, non-Hispanic/Latino; 69 Asian, non-Hispanic/Latino; 13 Hispanic/Latino). Average age 26. 5,303 applicants, 5% accepted, 94 enrolled. *Faculty:* 30 full-time (9 women), 6 part-time/adjunct (3 women). *Financial support:* In 2015–16, 89 students received support. Scholarships/grants available. Financial award application deadline: 3/28; financial award applicants required to submit FAFSA. Offers anesthesiologist assistant (MMS); medicine (MMS, MD). *Application deadline:* For fall admission, 12/31 for domestic students. Applications are processed on a rolling basis. Electronic applications accepted. *Application Contact:* Michael Cole, Director of Admissions for Operations, 203-582-7766, E-mail: medicine@quinnipiac.edu. *Dean*, Dr. Bruce Koeppen, 203-582-5301.

School of Business and Engineering Students: 145 full-time (63 women), 530 part-time (288 women); includes 123 minority (40 Black or African American, non-Hispanic/Latino; 1 American Indian or Alaska Native, non-Hispanic/Latino; 23 Asian, non-Hispanic/Latino; 50 Hispanic/Latino; 9 Two or more races, non-Hispanic/Latino), 20 international. 383 applicants, 84% accepted, 267 enrolled. *Faculty:* 44 full-time (15 women), 17 part-time/adjunct (6 women). *Financial support:* Career-related internships or fieldwork, Federal Work-Study, scholarships/grants, and unspecified assistantships available. Support available to part-time students. Financial award application deadline: 6/1; financial award applicants required to submit FAFSA. In 2015, 253 master's awarded. *Degree program information:* Part-time and evening/weekend programs available. Part-time, evening/weekend, 100% online, blended/hybrid learning. Offers business and engineering (MBA, MS); chartered financial analyst (MBA); health care management (MBA); organizational leadership (MS); supply chain management (MBA). *Application deadline:* For fall admission, 7/30 priority date for domestic students, 4/30 priority date for international students; for spring admission, 12/15 priority date for domestic students, 9/15 priority date for international students. Applications are processed on a rolling basis. *Application fee:* $45. Electronic applications accepted. *Application Contact:* Office of Graduate Admissions, 800-462-1944, Fax: 203-582-3443, E-mail: graduate@quinnipiac.edu.

School of Communications Students: 61 full-time (31 women), 82 part-time (51 women); includes 38 minority (20 Black or African American, non-Hispanic/Latino; 1 American Indian or Alaska Native, non-Hispanic/Latino; 2 Asian, non-Hispanic/Latino; 13 Hispanic/Latino; 2 Two or more races, non-Hispanic/Latino), 4 international. 118 applicants, 91% accepted, 75 enrolled. *Faculty:* 15 full-time (10 women), 30 part-time/adjunct (11 women). *Financial support:* Career-related internships or fieldwork, Federal Work-Study, scholarships/grants, and unspecified assistantships available. Support available to part-time students. Financial award application deadline: 6/1; financial award applicants required to submit FAFSA. In 2015, 80 master's awarded. *Degree program information:* Part-time and evening/weekend programs available. Part-time, evening/weekend, online learning. Offers communications (MS); interactive media (MS); journalism (MS); production (MS); public relations (MS); social media (MS); sports journalism (MS). *Application deadline:* For fall admission, 7/30 priority date for domestic students, 4/30 priority date for international students; for spring admission, 12/15 priority date for domestic students, 9/15 priority date for international students. Applications are processed on a rolling basis. *Application fee:* $45. Electronic applications accepted. *Program Director*, Phillip Simon.

School of Education Students: 87 full-time (64 women), 136 part-time (106 women); includes 19 minority (6 Black or African American, non-Hispanic/Latino; 2 Asian, non-Hispanic/Latino; 9 Hispanic/Latino; 2 Two or more races, non-Hispanic/Latino). 168 applicants, 92% accepted, 139 enrolled. *Faculty:* 15 full-time (14 women), 51 part-time/adjunct (28 women). *Financial support:* Career-related internships or fieldwork, Federal Work-Study, and unspecified assistantships available. Support available to part-time students. Financial award application deadline: 6/1; financial award applicants required to submit FAFSA. In 2015, 95 master's, 22 other advanced degrees awarded. *Degree program information:* Part-time and evening/weekend programs available. Part-time, evening/weekend, online learning. Offers biology (MAT); education (MAT, MS, Diploma); educational leadership (Diploma); elementary education (MAT); English (MAT); history/social studies (MAT); instructional design (MS); mathematics (MAT); Spanish (MAT); teacher leadership (MS). *Application deadline:* Applications are processed on a rolling basis. *Application fee:* $45. Electronic applications accepted.

School of Health Sciences Students: 271 full-time (189 women), 91 part-time (68 women); includes 67 minority (27 Black or African American, non-Hispanic/Latino; 1 American Indian or Alaska Native, non-Hispanic/Latino; 17 Asian, non-Hispanic/Latino; 22 Hispanic/Latino), 16 international. 1,688 applicants, 15% accepted, 174 enrolled. *Faculty:* 64 full-time (45 women), 95 part-time/adjunct (56 women). *Financial support:* Federal Work-Study, scholarships/grants, and unspecified assistantships available. Support available to part-time students. Financial award applicants required to submit FAFSA. In 2015, 131 master's awarded. Offers cardiovascular perfusion (MHS); health sciences (MHS, MHS, MSW); medical laboratory sciences (MHS); pathologists' assistant (MHS); physician assistant (MHS); radiologist assistant (MHS); social work (MSW). *Application deadline:* Applications are processed on a rolling basis. *Application fee:* $45. Electronic applications accepted. *Application Contact:* Office of Graduate Admissions, 800-462-1944, Fax: 203-582-3443, E-mail: graduate@quinnipiac.edu.

School of Law Students: 208 full-time (110 women), 59 part-time (32 women); includes 41 minority (20 Black or African American, non-Hispanic/Latino; 4 American Indian or Alaska Native, non-Hispanic/Latino; 6 Asian, non-Hispanic/Latino; 11 Hispanic/Latino). Average age 26. 614 applicants, 63% accepted, 93 enrolled. *Faculty:* 20 full-time (7 women), 27 part-time/adjunct (7 women). *Financial support:* In 2015–16, 220 students received support, including 27 fellowships (averaging $1,250 per year), 45 research assistantships (averaging $2,200 per year); career-related internships or fieldwork, Federal Work-Study, and scholarships/grants also available. Support available to part-time students. Financial award application deadline: 4/15; financial award applicants required to submit FAFSA. In 2015, 113 doctorates awarded. *Degree program information:* Part-time and evening/weekend programs available. Part-time, evening/weekend. Offers law (LL M, JD). *Application deadline:* For fall admission, 3/1 priority date for domestic and international students. Applications are processed on a rolling basis. *Application fee:* $65. Electronic applications accepted. *Application Contact:* Edwin Wilkes, Associate Vice-President/Dean of Law School Admissions, 203-582-3400, Fax: 203-582-3339, E-mail: law@quinnipiac.edu. *Dean*, Jennifer Brown, 203-582-3200, Fax: 203-582-3209, E-mail: law@quinnipiac.edu.

School of Nursing Students: 72 full-time (64 women), 151 part-time (136 women); includes 45 minority (19 Black or African American, non-Hispanic/Latino; 15 Asian, non-Hispanic/Latino; 10 Hispanic/Latino; 1 Two or more races, non-Hispanic/Latino), 1 international. 182 applicants, 65% accepted, 86 enrolled. *Faculty:* 19 full-time (18 women), 13 part-time/adjunct (9 women). *Financial support:* Federal Work-Study, scholarships/grants, and unspecified assistantships available. Support available to part-time students. Financial award application deadline: 6/1; financial award applicants required to submit FAFSA. In 2015, 16 doctorates awarded. *Degree program information:* Part-time programs available. Part-time. Offers adult nurse practitioner (MSN, DNP); care of populations (DNP); family nurse practitioner (MSN, DNP); nurse anesthesia (DNP); nursing (MSN, DNP); nursing leadership (DNP). *Application deadline:* Applications are processed on a rolling basis. *Application fee:* $45. Electronic applications accepted.

See Display on next page and Close-Up on page 895.

RABBI ISAAC ELCHANAN THEOLOGICAL SEMINARY, New York, NY 10033-2807

General Information Independent-religious, men only, graduate-only institution. *Graduate housing:* Rooms and/or apartments guaranteed to single students and available on a first-come, first-served basis to married students. Housing application deadline: 6/1.

GRADUATE UNITS

Graduate Program Offers theology (Certificate of Advanced Ordination, Certificate of Ordination).

RABBINICAL ACADEMY MESIVTA RABBI CHAIM BERLIN, Brooklyn, NY 11230-4715

General Information Independent-religious, men only, comprehensive institution. *Graduate housing:* Room and/or apartments available to single students; on-campus housing not available to married students. Housing application deadline: 9/30.

GRADUATE UNITS

Graduate Program Offers Talmudic law and rabbinics (Advanced Talmudic Degree, Second Talmudic Degree).

RABBINICAL COLLEGE BETH SHRAGA, Monsey, NY 10952-3035

General Information Independent-religious, men only, comprehensive institution.

GRADUATE UNITS

Graduate Programs Offers theology.

RABBINICAL COLLEGE BOBOVER YESHIVA B'NEI ZION, Brooklyn, NY 11219

General Information Independent-religious, men only, comprehensive institution. *Graduate housing:* Room and/or apartments available to single students; on-campus housing not available to married students.

GRADUATE UNITS

Graduate Programs Offers theology.

RABBINICAL COLLEGE CH'SAN SOFER, Brooklyn, NY 11204

General Information Independent-religious, men only, comprehensive institution.

GRADUATE UNITS

Graduate Programs Offers theology.

RABBINICAL COLLEGE OF LONG ISLAND, Long Beach, NY 11561-3305

General Information Independent-religious, men only, comprehensive institution.

GRADUATE UNITS

Graduate Programs Offers theology.

RABBINICAL SEMINARY OF AMERICA, Flushing, NY 11367

General Information Independent-religious, men only, comprehensive institution. *Graduate housing:* Room and/or apartments available to single students; on-campus housing not available to married students. Housing application deadline: 6/15.

GRADUATE UNITS

Graduate Programs School offers a master's and first professional degree.

RADFORD UNIVERSITY, Radford, VA 24142

General Information State-supported, coed, comprehensive institution. CGS member. *Enrollment:* 9,743 graduate, professional, and undergraduate students; 530 full-time matriculated graduate/professional students (418 women), 315 part-time matriculated graduate/professional students (232 women). *Enrollment by degree level:* 683 master's, 127 doctoral, 35 other advanced degrees. *Graduate faculty:* 150 full-time (90 women), 38 part-time/adjunct (27 women). Tuition, state resident: full-time $7640; part-time $318 per credit hour. Tuition, nonresident: full-time $16,394; part-time $683 per credit hour. *Required fees:* $3021; $127 per credit hour. Tuition and fees vary according to course load and program. *Graduate housing:* On-campus housing not available. *Student services:* Campus employment opportunities, campus safety program, career counseling, exercise/wellness program, free psychological counseling, grant writing training, international student services, low-cost health insurance, multicultural affairs office, services for students with disabilities, teacher training, writing training. *Library:* McConnell Library. *Collection:* Books: 354,642 (physical), 379,388 (digital/electronic); Databases: 388. Students can reserve study rooms. *Research affiliation:* U.S. Department of Health and Human Services (nursing, psychology), Virginia Department of Social Services (social work), Virginia Department of Education (teacher education and leadership), Verizon Foundation (communication sciences and disorders), National Science Foundation (communication sciences and disorders, nursing, criminal justice, psychology, mathematics, biology, computer science), U.S. Department of Education (DOE) (teacher education and leadership).

Computer facilities: Computer purchase and lease plans are available. 810 computers available on campus for general student use. A campuswide network can be accessed from student residence rooms and from off campus. Online class registration, online financial aid status and student accounts payable are available.
Website: http://www.radford.edu/

General Application Contact: Rebecca Conner, Director of Graduate Enrollment, 540-831-6296, Fax: 540-831-6061, E-mail: gradcollege@radford.edu.

GRADUATE UNITS

College of Graduate and Professional Studies Students: 530 full-time (418 women), 315 part-time (232 women); includes 115 minority (57 Black or African American, non-Hispanic/Latino; 3 American Indian or Alaska Native, non-Hispanic/Latino; 14 Asian, non-Hispanic/Latino; 26 Hispanic/Latino; 1 Native Hawaiian or other Pacific Islander, non-Hispanic/Latino; 14 Two or more races, non-Hispanic/Latino), 12 international. Average age 29. 1,264 applicants, 46% accepted, 346 enrolled. *Faculty:* 150 full-time (90 women), 38 part-time/adjunct (27 women). *Financial support:* In 2015–16, 312 students received support, including 14 fellowships (averaging $13,800 per year), 166 research assistantships with partial tuition reimbursements available (averaging $5,873 per year), 64 teaching assistantships with partial tuition reimbursements available (averaging $10,344 per year); career-related internships or fieldwork, institutionally sponsored loans, traineeships, health care benefits, and unspecified assistantships also available. Financial award application deadline: 3/1; financial award applicants required to submit FAFSA. In 2015, 384 master's, 34 doctorates, 18 other advanced degrees awarded. *Degree program information:* Part-time and evening/weekend programs available. Part-time, evening/weekend, 100% online, blended/hybrid learning. *Application deadline:* Applications are processed on a rolling basis. *Application fee:* $50. Electronic applications accepted. *Application Contact:* Rebecca Conner, Director, Graduate Enrollment, 540-831-6296, Fax: 540-831-6061, E-mail: gradcollege@radford.edu. *Dean*, Dr. Dennis Grady, 540-831-5724, Fax: 540-831-6061, E-mail: gradcollege@radford.edu.

College of Business and Economics Students: 13 full-time (3 women), 28 part-time (9 women); includes 2 minority (1 Asian, non-Hispanic/Latino; 1 Hispanic/Latino), 7 international. Average age 32. 34 applicants, 79% accepted, 13 enrolled. *Faculty:* 7 full-time (2 women). *Financial support:* In 2015–16, 8 students received support, including 4 research assistantships (averaging $9,000 per year), 3 teaching assistantships with partial tuition reimbursements available (averaging $10,000 per year); career-related internships or fieldwork, Federal Work-Study, institutionally sponsored loans, scholarships/grants, and unspecified assistantships also available. Financial award application deadline: 3/1; financial award applicants required to submit FAFSA. In 2015, 26 master's awarded. *Degree program information:* Part-time and evening/weekend programs available. Part-time, evening/weekend, online learning. Offers business administration (MBA); business and economics (MBA). *Application deadline:* For fall admission, 2/15 priority date for domestic students, 12/1 for international students; for spring admission, 7/1 for international students. Applications are processed on a rolling basis. *Application fee:* $50. Electronic applications accepted. *Application Contact:* Rebecca Conner, Director, Graduate Enrollment, 540-831-6296, Fax: 540-831-6061, E-mail: gradcollege@radford.edu. *Director, MBA Program*, Stacey Turmel, 540-831-6905, Fax: 540-831-6103, E-mail: rumba@radford.edu.

College of Education and Human Development Students: 121 full-time (103 women), 173 part-time (137 women); includes 32 minority (18 Black or African American, non-Hispanic/Latino; 3 Asian, non-Hispanic/Latino; 9 Hispanic/Latino; 2 Two or more races, non-Hispanic/Latino), 2 international. Average age 31. 162 applicants, 91% accepted, 115 enrolled. *Faculty:* 31 full-time (20 women), 9 part-time/adjunct (6 women). *Financial support:* In 2015–16, 51 students received support, including 33 research assistantships (averaging $7,588 per year), 3 teaching assistantships with partial tuition reimbursements available (averaging $11,000 per year); career-related internships or fieldwork, Federal Work-Study, institutionally sponsored loans, scholarships/grants, and unspecified assistantships also available. Financial award application deadline: 3/1; financial award applicants required to submit FAFSA. In 2015, 179 master's, 6 other advanced degrees awarded. *Degree program information:* Part-time and evening/weekend programs available. Part-time, evening/weekend. Offers adapted curriculum (MS); autism studies (Certificate); clinical mental health counseling (MS); curriculum and instruction (MS); early childhood education (MS); early childhood special education (MS); education (MS); education and human development (MS, Certificate); educational leadership (MS, Certificate); educational technology (MS); general curriculum (MS); hearing impairment (MS); literacy education (MS); math education content area studies (MS); school counseling (MS); special education (MS, Certificate); visual impairment (MS). *Application deadline:* For fall admission, 2/15 priority date for domestic students, 12/1 for international students; for spring admission, 7/1 for international students. Applications are processed on a rolling basis. *Application fee:* $50. Electronic applications accepted. *Application*

Contact: Rebecca Conner, Director, Graduate Enrollment, 540-831-6296, Fax: 540-831-6061, E-mail: gradcollege@radford.edu. *Dean*, Dr. Kenna Colley, 540-831-6374, Fax: 540-831-5440, E-mail: cehd@radford.edu.

College of Humanities and Behavioral Sciences Students: 113 full-time (83 women), 14 part-time (11 women); includes 16 minority (8 Black or African American, non-Hispanic/Latino; 2 Asian, non-Hispanic/Latino; 1 Hispanic/Latino; 1 Native Hawaiian or other Pacific Islander, non-Hispanic/Latino; 4 Two or more races, non-Hispanic/Latino). Average age 25. 213 applicants, 53% accepted, 60 enrolled. *Faculty:* 47 full-time (27 women), 3 part-time/adjunct (1 woman). *Financial support:* In 2015–16, 101 students received support, including 10 fellowships (averaging $13,800 per year), 41 research assistantships with tuition reimbursements available (averaging $6,458 per year), 44 teaching assistantships with partial tuition reimbursements available (averaging $10,341 per year); career-related internships or fieldwork, Federal Work-Study, institutionally sponsored loans, scholarships/grants, and unspecified assistantships also available. Financial award application deadline: 3/1; financial award applicants required to submit FAFSA. In 2015, 66 master's, 3 doctorates, 12 other advanced degrees awarded. *Degree program information:* Part-time and evening/weekend programs available. Part-time, evening/weekend. Offers clinical psychology (MA, MS); corporate and professional communication (MS); counseling psychology (Psy D); criminal justice (MA, MS); English (MA, MS); experimental psychology (MA); humanities and behavioral sciences (MA, MS, Psy D, Certificate, Ed S); industrial/organizational psychology (MA, MS); psychology (MA, MS); school psychology (Ed S). *Application deadline:* For fall admission, 2/15 priority date for domestic students, 12/1 for international students; for spring admission, 7/1 for international students. Applications are processed on a rolling basis. *Application fee:* $50. Electronic applications accepted. *Application Contact:* Rebecca Conner, Director, Graduate Enrollment, 540-831-6296, Fax: 540-831-6061, E-mail: gradcollege@radford.edu. *Dean*, Dr. Katherine Hawkins, 540-831-5149, Fax: 540-831-5970, E-mail: chbs@radford.edu.

College of Visual and Performing Arts Students: 32 full-time (22 women), 15 part-time (8 women); includes 10 minority (2 Black or African American, non-Hispanic/Latino; 2 American Indian or Alaska Native, non-Hispanic/Latino; 2 Asian, non-Hispanic/Latino; 3 Hispanic/Latino; 1 Two or more races, non-Hispanic/Latino), 2 international. Average age 31. 42 applicants, 71% accepted, 19 enrolled. *Faculty:* 22 full-time (9 women), 7 part-time/adjunct (3 women). *Financial support:* In 2015–16, 23 students received support, including 11 research assistantships (averaging $7,750 per year), 10 teaching assistantships with partial tuition reimbursements available (averaging $10,300 per year); career-related internships or fieldwork, Federal Work-Study, institutionally sponsored loans, scholarships/grants, and unspecified assistantships also available. Financial award application deadline: 3/1; financial award applicants required to submit FAFSA. In 2015, 16 master's awarded. *Degree program information:* Part-time programs available. Part-time. Offers design thinking (MFA); music (MA); music education (MS); music therapy (MS); studio art (MFA); visual and performing arts (MA, MFA, MS). *Application deadline:* For fall admission, 2/15 priority date for domestic students, 12/1 for international students; for spring admission, 7/1 for international students. Applications are processed on a rolling basis. *Application fee:* $50. Electronic applications accepted. *Application Contact:* Rebecca Conner, Director, Graduate Enrollment, 540-831-6296, Fax: 540-831-6061, E-mail: gradcollege@radford.edu. *Dean*, Dr. Margaret Devaney, 540-831-5265, Fax: 540-831-6313, E-mail: cvpa411@radford.edu.

Waldron College of Health and Human Services Students: 251 full-time (207 women), 85 part-time (67 women); includes 55 minority (29 Black or African American, non-Hispanic/Latino; 1 American Indian or Alaska Native, non-Hispanic/Latino; 6 Asian, non-Hispanic/Latino; 12 Hispanic/Latino; 7 Two or more races, non-Hispanic/Latino), 1 international. Average age 27. 813 applicants, 33% accepted, 139 enrolled. *Faculty:* 41 full-time (32 women), 19 part-time/adjunct (17 women). *Financial support:* In 2015–16, 129 students received support, including 77 research assistantships (averaging $4,396 per year), 4 teaching assistantships with partial tuition reimbursements available (averaging $10,250 per year); career-related internships or fieldwork, Federal Work-Study, institutionally sponsored loans, scholarships/grants, and unspecified assistantships also available. Financial award application deadline: 3/1; financial award applicants required to submit FAFSA. In 2015, 97 master's, 31 doctorates awarded. *Degree program information:* Part-time and evening/weekend programs available. Part-time, evening/weekend, online learning. Offers health and human services (MA, MOT, MS, MSW, DNP, DPT); nursing practice (DNP); occupational therapy (MOT); physical therapy (DPT); social work (MSW); speech-language pathology (MA, MS). *Application deadline:* For fall admission, 2/15 priority date for domestic students, 12/1 for international students; for spring admission, 7/1 for international students. Applications are processed on a rolling basis. *Application fee:* $50. Electronic applications accepted. *Application Contact:* Rebecca Conner, Director, Graduate Enrollment, 540-831-6296, Fax: 540-831-6061, E-mail: gradcollege@radford.edu. *Dean*, Dr. Kenneth Cox, 540-831-7600, Fax: 540-831-7744.

RAMAPO COLLEGE OF NEW JERSEY, Mahwah, NJ 07430-1680

General Information State-supported, coed, comprehensive institution. *Enrollment:* 6,026 graduate, professional, and undergraduate students; 49 full-time matriculated graduate/professional students (35 women), 316 part-time matriculated graduate/professional students (225 women). *Enrollment by degree level:* 365 master's. *Graduate faculty:* 27 full-time (18 women), 26 part-time/adjunct (11 women). Tuition, state resident: part-time $597.05 per credit. Tuition, nonresident: part-time $597.05 per credit. *Required fees:* $129.45 per credit. *Graduate housing:* On-campus housing not available. *Student services:* Career counseling, services for students with disabilities. *Library:* George T. Potter Library. *Research affiliation:* The Valley Hospital (nursing), New Jersey Association of State Colleges and Universities (veterans' issues), New Jersey Meadowlands Commission (environment).

Computer facilities: A campuswide network can be accessed from student residence rooms and from off campus. Online class registration is available.
Website: http://www.ramapo.edu/

General Application Contact: Anthony Dovi, Associate Director of Admissions, Adult Learners and Graduate Programs, 201-684-7305, Fax: 201-684-7964, E-mail: adovi@ramapo.edu.

GRADUATE UNITS

Master of Arts in Educational Leadership Program Students: 20 full-time (10 women), 25 part-time (15 women); includes 8 minority (1 Black or African American, non-Hispanic/Latino; 2 Asian, non-Hispanic/Latino; 5 Hispanic/Latino). Average age 34. 45 applicants, 64% accepted, 23 enrolled. *Faculty:* 5 full-time, 3 part-time/adjunct. *Financial support:* Career-related internships or fieldwork available. Financial award application deadline: 3/1; financial award applicants required to submit FAFSA. In 2015, 30 master's awarded. *Degree program information:* Part-time programs available. Part-time. Offers educational leadership (MA). *Application deadline:* For fall admission, 5/1 for domestic and international students; for spring admission, 12/1 for domestic and international students. Applications are processed on a rolling basis. *Application fee:* $60. Electronic applications accepted. *Application Contact:* M. Joyce Wilson, Secretarial Assistant, 201-684-7721, Fax: 201-684-6699, E-mail: jwilson@ramapo.edu. *Associate Professor, Educational Leadership*, Dr. Brian P. Chinni, 201-684-7613, E-mail: bchinni@ramapo.edu.

Master of Arts in Liberal Studies Program Students: 8 part-time (4 women). Average age 50. 1 applicant. *Faculty:* 6 full-time (4 women), 1 part-time/adjunct (0 women). *Financial support:* Career-related internships or fieldwork available. Financial award application deadline: 3/1; financial award applicants required to submit FAFSA. In 2015, 4 master's awarded. *Degree program information:* Part-time programs available. Part-time. Offers liberal studies (MA). *Application deadline:* For fall admission, 5/1 for domestic and international students; for spring admission, 12/1 for domestic and international students. Applications are processed on a rolling basis. *Application fee:* $60. Electronic applications accepted. *Application Contact:* Anthony Dovi, Associate Director of Admissions, Adult Learners, and Graduate Programs, 201-684-7305, Fax: 201-684-7964, E-mail: adovi@ramapo.edu. *Director*, Dr. Anthony T. Padovano, 201-684-7430, Fax: 201-684-7973, E-mail: apadovan@ramapo.edu.

Master of Arts in Special Education Program Students: 44 part-time (37 women); includes 3 minority (all Hispanic/Latino). Average age 29. 29 applicants, 83% accepted, 21 enrolled. *Faculty:* 2 full-time (both women), 2 part-time/adjunct (both women). *Financial support:* Career-related internships or fieldwork available. Financial award application deadline: 3/1; financial award applicants required to submit FAFSA. *Degree program information:* Part-time programs available. Part-time. Offers special education (MA). *Application deadline:* For fall admission, 5/1 for domestic and international students; for spring admission, 12/1 for domestic and international students. Applications are processed on a rolling basis. *Application fee:* $60. Electronic applications accepted. *Application Contact:* M. Joyce Wilson, Secretarial Assistant, 201-684-7721, Fax: 201-684-6699, E-mail: jwilson@ramapo.edu. *Director*, Dr. Julie Norflus-Good, 201-684-7246, E-mail: jgood@ramapo.edu.

Master of Arts in Sustainability Studies Program Students: 1 (woman) full-time, 18 part-time (14 women); includes 4 minority (all Hispanic/Latino), 1 international. Average age 35. 17 applicants, 100% accepted, 10 enrolled. *Faculty:* 5 full-time (1 woman). *Financial support:* Career-related internships or fieldwork available. Financial award application deadline: 3/1; financial award applicants required to submit FAFSA. *Degree program information:* Part-time programs available. Part-time. Offers sustainability studies (MA). *Application deadline:* For fall admission, 5/1 for domestic and international students; for spring admission, 12/1 for domestic and international students. Applications are processed on a rolling basis. *Application fee:* $60. Electronic applications accepted. *Application Contact:* Anthony Dovi, Assistant Director of Admissions, Adult Learners and Graduate Programs, 201-684-7305, Fax: 201-684-7964, E-mail: adovi@ramapo.edu. *Director/Associate Professor, Environmental Studies*, Dr. Ashwani Vasishth, 201-684-6616, E-mail: vasishth@ramapo.edu.

Master of Business Administration Program Students: 62 part-time (28 women); includes 19 minority (6 Black or African American, non-Hispanic/Latino; 1 American Indian or Alaska Native, non-Hispanic/Latino; 4 Asian, non-Hispanic/Latino; 7 Hispanic/Latino; 1 Two or more races, non-Hispanic/Latino), 2 international. Average age 32. 100 applicants, 56% accepted, 34 enrolled. *Faculty:* 4 full-time (all women). *Financial support:* In 2015–16, 3 students received support. Career-related internships or fieldwork and scholarships/grants available. Financial award application deadline: 5/1; financial award applicants required to submit FAFSA. In 2015, 25 master's awarded. *Degree program information:* Part-time and evening/weekend programs available. Part-time-only, evening/weekend. Offers leadership (MBA). *Application deadline:* For fall admission, 5/1 for domestic and international students. Applications are processed on a rolling basis. *Application fee:* $60. Electronic applications accepted. *Application Contact:* Timothy Landers, Assistant Dean/Director of the MBA Program, 201-684-7771, E-mail: tlanders@ramapo.edu. *Dean of the Anisfield School of Business*, Dr. Lewis M. Chakrin, 201-684-7377, E-mail: lchakrin@ramapo.edu.

Master of Science in Educational Technology Program Students: 1 (woman) full-time, 94 part-time (70 women); includes 12 minority (2 Black or African American, non-Hispanic/Latino; 1 American Indian or Alaska Native, non-Hispanic/Latino; 2 Asian, non-Hispanic/Latino; 7 Hispanic/Latino), 1 international. Average age 34. 59 applicants, 88% accepted, 35 enrolled. *Faculty:* 13 part-time/adjunct (5 women). *Financial support:* Career-related internships or fieldwork available. Financial award application deadline: 3/1; financial award applicants required to submit FAFSA. In 2015, 43 master's awarded. *Degree program information:* Part-time and evening/weekend programs available. Part-time, evening/weekend. Offers educational technology (MS). *Application deadline:* For fall admission, 5/1 for domestic and international students; for spring admission, 12/1 for domestic and international students. Applications are processed on a rolling basis. *Application fee:* $60. Electronic applications accepted. *Application Contact:* M. Joyce Wilson, Administrative Assistant, 201-684-7721, Fax: 201-684-6699, E-mail: jwilson@ramapo.edu. *Director of the Master in Educational Technology Program*, Dr. Richard Russo, 201-684-7899, Fax: 201-684-6699, E-mail: rrusso@ramapo.edu.

Master of Science in Nursing Program Students: 1 full-time (0 women), 49 part-time (43 women); includes 16 minority (4 Black or African American, non-Hispanic/Latino; 8 Asian, non-Hispanic/Latino; 3 Hispanic/Latino; 1 Two or more races, non-Hispanic/Latino). Average age 35. 36 applicants, 81% accepted, 25 enrolled. *Faculty:* 3 full-time (all women), 1 part-time/adjunct (0 women). *Financial support:* Career-related internships or fieldwork available. Financial award application deadline: 3/1; financial award applicants required to submit FAFSA. In 2015, 6 master's awarded. *Degree program information:* Part-time programs available. Part-time. Offers nursing education (MSN). *Application deadline:* For fall admission, 5/1 for domestic and international students; for spring admission, 12/1 for domestic and international students. Applications are processed on a rolling basis. *Application fee:* $60. Electronic applications accepted. *Application Contact:* Anthony Dovi, Associate Director of Admissions, Adult Learners and Graduate Programs, 201-684-7305, Fax: 201-684-7964, E-mail: adovi@ramapo.edu. *Assistant Dean in Charge of Nursing Programs/Professor*, Dr. Kathleen M. Burke, 201-684-7737, Fax: 201-684-7954, E-mail: kmburke@ramapo.edu.

Master of Social Work Program Students: 26 full-time (23 women), 12 part-time (all women); includes 12 minority (7 Black or African American, non-Hispanic/Latino; 5 Hispanic/Latino). Average age 32. 112 applicants, 53% accepted, 37 enrolled. *Faculty:* 4 full-time (all women), 4 part-time/adjunct (all women). *Financial support:* Career-related internships or fieldwork available. Financial award application deadline: 3/1; financial award applicants required to submit FAFSA. *Degree program information:* Part-time programs available. Part-time. Offers social work (MSW). *Application deadline:* For fall admission, 3/1 for domestic and international students. Applications are processed on a rolling basis. *Application fee:* $60. Electronic applications accepted. *Application Contact:* Dr. Ann Marie Moreno, Assistant Dean/Director of MSW Program, 201-684-7191, E-mail: amoreno@ramapo.edu. *Assistant Dean, Director of MSW Program*, Dr. Ann Marie Moreno, 201-684-7191, E-mail: amoreno@ramapo.edu.

RANDOLPH COLLEGE, Lynchburg, VA 24503

General Information Independent-religious, coed, comprehensive institution.

GRADUATE UNITS

Programs in Education Offers curriculum and instruction (MAT); special education-learning disabilities (M Ed, MAT).

RECONSTRUCTIONIST RABBINICAL COLLEGE, Wyncote, PA 19095-1898

General Information Independent-religious, coed, graduate-only institution. *Enrollment by degree level:* 45 master's. *Graduate faculty:* 6 full-time (4 women), 26 part-time/adjunct (16 women). *Tuition, area resident:* Full-time $23,000. *Graduate housing:* On-campus housing not available. *Student services:* Campus employment opportunities, career counseling, international student services, low-cost health insurance, services for students with disabilities. *Library:* Mordecai M. Kaplan Library.

Computer facilities: 20 computers available on campus for general student use.
Website: http://www.rrc.edu/

General Application Contact: Rabbi Amber Powers, Vice President for Student Development, 215-576-0800 Ext. 145, Fax: 215-576-6143, E-mail: apowers@rrc.edu.

GRADUATE UNITS

Graduate Programs Students: 45 full-time (25 women). *Faculty:* 6 full-time (4 women), 26 part-time/adjunct (16 women). *Financial support:* Fellowships with full tuition reimbursements, research assistantships with partial tuition reimbursements, teaching assistantships, career-related internships or fieldwork, institutionally sponsored loans, and scholarships/grants available. Financial award application deadline: 4/15. *Degree program information:* Part-time programs available. Part-time. Offers Jewish studies (MAJS); rabbinics (MAHL, DHL); women's studies (Certificate). Certificate offered jointly with Temple University. *Application deadline:* Applications are processed on a rolling basis. *Application fee:* $50. *Application Contact:* Rabbi Amber Powers, Vice President for Student Development, 215-576-0800 Ext. 145, Fax: 215-576-6143, E-mail: apowers@rrc.edu. *President*, Rabbi Deborah Waxman, PhD, 215-576-0800 Ext. 129, Fax: 215-576-6143.

REED COLLEGE, Portland, OR 97202-8199

General Information Independent, coed, comprehensive institution. *Graduate housing:* On-campus housing not available.

GRADUATE UNITS

Graduate Program in Liberal Studies ***Degree program information:*** Part-time and evening/weekend programs available. Part-time, evening/weekend. Offers liberal studies (MALS). Electronic applications accepted.

REFORMED EPISCOPAL SEMINARY, Blue Bell, PA 19422

General Information Independent-religious, coed, graduate-only institution. *Graduate housing:* Room and/or apartments available on a first-come, first-served basis to single students; on-campus housing not available to married students.

GRADUATE UNITS

Graduate Program Offers theology (M Div).

REFORMED PRESBYTERIAN THEOLOGICAL SEMINARY, Pittsburgh, PA 15208-2594

General Information Independent-religious, coed, primarily men, graduate-only institution. *Graduate housing:* Rooms and/or apartments available on a first-come, first-served basis to single and married students.

GRADUATE UNITS

Graduate and Professional Programs ***Degree program information:*** Part-time and evening/weekend programs available. Part-time, evening/weekend. Offers theology (M Div, MTS, D Min). Electronic applications accepted.

REFORMED THEOLOGICAL SEMINARY–ATLANTA CAMPUS, Marietta, GA 30067

General Information Independent-religious, coed, primarily men, graduate-only institution.

GRADUATE UNITS

Graduate Programs Offers theology (M Div, MABS, MAR, D Min, Certificate).

REFORMED THEOLOGICAL SEMINARY–CHARLOTTE CAMPUS, Charlotte, NC 28226-6318

General Information Independent-religious, coed, primarily men, graduate-only institution. *Graduate housing:* On-campus housing not available.

GRADUATE UNITS

Graduate and Professional Programs ***Degree program information:*** Part-time programs available. Part-time. Offers biblical studies (MA); ministry (D Min); pastoral ministry (M Div); theological studies (MA). Electronic applications accepted.

REFORMED THEOLOGICAL SEMINARY–HOUSTON CAMPUS, Houston, TX 77024

General Information Independent-religious, coed, primarily men, graduate-only institution. *Graduate housing:* On-campus housing not available.

GRADUATE UNITS

Graduate Program Offers Biblical studies (MA). Electronic applications accepted.

REFORMED THEOLOGICAL SEMINARY–JACKSON CAMPUS, Jackson, MS 39209-3099

General Information Independent-religious, coed, primarily men, graduate-only institution. *Graduate housing:* Rooms and/or apartments available on a first-come, first-served basis to single and married students.

GRADUATE UNITS

Graduate and Professional Programs Offers Bible, theology, and missions (Certificate); Biblical exegesis (M Div); biblical studies (MA); Christian education (MA); counseling (M Div); marriage and family therapy (MA); ministry (D Min); missions (M Div, MA, D Min); theological studies (MA).

REFORMED THEOLOGICAL SEMINARY–ORLANDO CAMPUS, Oviedo, FL 32765-7197

General Information Independent-religious, coed, primarily men, graduate-only institution. *Enrollment by degree level:* 258 master's, 44 doctoral, 2 other advanced degrees. *Graduate faculty:* 11 full-time (0 women), 11 part-time/adjunct (2 women). *Tuition, area resident:* Full-time $16,625. *Required fees:* $160. Tuition and fees vary according to course load. *Graduate housing:* Rooms and/or apartments available on a first-come, first-served basis to single and married students. *Student services:* Campus employment opportunities, career counseling, free psychological counseling, international student services, writing training. *Library:* RTS Library. *Collection:* Books: 85,943 (physical), 73,000 (digital/electronic); Serial titles: 90 (physical). Weekly public service hours: 69.

Computer facilities: 6 computers available on campus for general student use. A campuswide network can be accessed. Online class registration is available.
Website: http://www.rts.edu/

General Application Contact: David S. Veldkamp, Director of Admissions, 800-752-4382, Fax: 407-366-9425, E-mail: applications.orlando@rts.edu.

GRADUATE UNITS

Graduate Program Students: 304. *Faculty:* 11 full-time (0 women), 11 part-time/adjunct (2 women). *Degree program information:* Part-time programs available. Part-time, online learning. Offers Bible (Certificate); biblical studies (MA); counseling (MA); missions (Certificate); reformed expository preaching (D Min); reformed theology and ministry (D Min); theological studies (MA); theology (M Div, Certificate). *Application deadline:* Applications are processed on a rolling basis. *Application fee:* $75. Electronic applications accepted. *Application Contact:* David S. Veldkamp, Director of Admissions, 800-752-4382, Fax: 407-366-9425, E-mail: applications.orlando@rts.edu. *President*, Dr. Don Sweeting, 407-278-4406, Fax: 407-366-9425.

REFORMED THEOLOGICAL SEMINARY–WASHINGTON D.C., McLean, VA 22102

General Information Independent-religious, coed, primarily men, graduate-only institution. *Graduate housing:* On-campus housing not available.

GRADUATE UNITS

Graduate and Professional Programs ***Degree program information:*** Part-time and evening/weekend programs available. Part-time, evening/weekend. Offers Bible (M Div); practical theology (M Div); religion (MA); theology (M Div). Electronic applications accepted.

REGENT COLLEGE, Vancouver, BC V6T 2E4, Canada

General Information Independent-religious, coed, graduate-only institution. *Graduate housing:* On-campus housing not available.

GRADUATE UNITS

Program in Theology ***Degree program information:*** Part-time programs available. Part-time. Offers theology (M Div, MATS, Th M, Dip CS). Electronic applications accepted.

REGENT'S UNIVERSITY LONDON, London NW1 4NS, United Kingdom

General Information Independent, coed, comprehensive institution.

GRADUATE UNITS

Webster Graduate School ***Degree program information:*** Part-time programs available. Part-time. Offers business (MBA); finance (MS); human resources (MA); information technology management (MA); international business (MA); international non-governmental organizations (MA); international relations (MA); management and leadership (MA); marketing (MA).

REGENT UNIVERSITY, Virginia Beach, VA 23464-9800

General Information Independent-religious, coed, comprehensive institution. *Enrollment:* 7,429 graduate, professional, and undergraduate students; 984 full-time matriculated graduate/professional students (620 women), 3,182 part-time matriculated graduate/professional students (1,962 women). *Enrollment by degree level:* 2,719 master's, 1,332 doctoral, 115 other advanced degrees. *Graduate faculty:* 121 full-time (41 women), 295 part-time/adjunct (114 women). *Tuition, area resident:* Full-time $17,376; part-time $724 per credit. *Required fees:* $750; $250 per semester. $250 per semester. Tuition and fees vary according to course load, degree level and program. *Graduate housing:* Rooms and/or apartments available on a first-come, first-served basis to single and married students. Typical cost: $8885 per year ($11,405 including board) for single students; $11,925 per year ($14,445 including board) for married students. Room and board charges vary according to board plan and housing facility selected. Housing application deadline: 5/1. *Student services:* Campus employment opportunities, campus safety program, career counseling, free psychological counseling, international student services, low-cost health insurance, services for students with disabilities, teacher training, writing training. *Library:* Regent University Library plus 1 other. *Collection:* Books: 322,124 (physical), 460,170 (digital/electronic); Serial titles: 308 (physical), 353,033 (digital/electronic); Databases: 219. Weekly public service hours: 102; students can reserve study rooms.

Computer facilities: 70 computers available on campus for general student use. A campuswide network can be accessed from student residence rooms and from off campus. Online class registration is available.
Website: http://www.regent.edu/

General Application Contact: Heidi Cece, Executive Director of University Admissions, 800-373-5504, Fax: 757-352-4381, E-mail: admissions@regent.edu.

GRADUATE UNITS

Graduate School Students: 984 full-time (620 women), 3,182 part-time (1,962 women); includes 1,752 minority (1,386 Black or African American, non-Hispanic/Latino; 21 American Indian or Alaska Native, non-Hispanic/Latino; 85 Asian, non-Hispanic/Latino; 201 Hispanic/Latino; 3 Native Hawaiian or other Pacific Islander, non-Hispanic/Latino; 56 Two or more races, non-Hispanic/Latino), 137 international. Average age 39. 4,597 applicants, 50% accepted, 1513 enrolled. *Faculty:* 121 full-time (41 women), 295 part-time/adjunct (114 women). *Financial support:* Fellowships with tuition reimbursements, research assistantships with tuition reimbursements, teaching assistantships with tuition reimbursements, career-related internships or fieldwork, scholarships/grants, health care benefits, tuition waivers (full and partial), and unspecified assistantships available. Support available to part-time students. Financial award application deadline: 9/1; financial award applicants required to submit FAFSA. In 2015, 668 master's, 271 doctorates awarded. *Degree program information:* Part-time and evening/weekend programs available. Part-time, evening/weekend, 100% online, blended/hybrid learning. *Application deadline:* Applications are processed on a rolling basis. *Application fee:* $50. Electronic applications accepted. *Application Contact:* Heidi Cece, Executive Director of University Admissions, 800-373-5504, Fax: 757-352-4381, E-mail: admissions@regent.edu. *Executive Vice President for Academic Affairs*, Dr. Gerson Moreno-Riano, 757-352-4320, Fax: 757-352-4448, E-mail: gmorenoriano@regent.edu.

Robertson School of Government Students: 40 full-time (17 women), 78 part-time (43 women); includes 46 minority (36 Black or African American, non-Hispanic/Latino; 7

Hispanic/Latino; 3 Two or more races, non-Hispanic/Latino), 3 international. Average age 33. 166 applicants, 50% accepted, 57 enrolled. *Faculty:* 9 full-time (1 woman), 11 part-time/adjunct (3 women). *Financial support:* Career-related internships or fieldwork, scholarships/grants, health care benefits, tuition waivers (full and partial), and unspecified assistantships available. Support available to part-time students. Financial award application deadline: 9/1; financial award applicants required to submit FAFSA. In 2015, 48 master's awarded. *Degree program information:* Part-time and evening/weekend programs available. Part-time, evening/weekend, 100% online, blended/hybrid learning. Offers government (MA); public administration (MPA). *Application deadline:* For fall admission, 5/1 priority date for domestic students; for spring admission, 11/1 priority date for domestic students. Applications are processed on a rolling basis. *Application fee:* $50. Electronic applications accepted. *Application Contact:* Heidi Cece, Executive Director of University Admissions, 800-373-5504, Fax: 757-352-4381, E-mail: admissions@regent.edu. *Dean*, Dr. Eric Patterson, 757-352-4616, Fax: 757-352-4735, E-mail: epatterson@regent.edu.

School of Business and Leadership Students: 79 full-time (46 women), 786 part-time (385 women); includes 389 minority (322 Black or African American, non-Hispanic/Latino; 4 American Indian or Alaska Native, non-Hispanic/Latino; 21 Asian, non-Hispanic/Latino; 33 Hispanic/Latino; 1 Native Hawaiian or other Pacific Islander, non-Hispanic/Latino; 8 Two or more races, non-Hispanic/Latino), 70 international. Average age 41. 767 applicants, 53% accepted, 268 enrolled. *Faculty:* 8 full-time (2 women), 16 part-time/adjunct (4 women). *Financial support:* Career-related internships or fieldwork, scholarships/grants, health care benefits, tuition waivers (full and partial), and unspecified assistantships available. Support available to part-time students. Financial award application deadline: 9/1; financial award applicants required to submit FAFSA. In 2015, 107 master's, 65 doctorates awarded. *Degree program information:* Part-time and evening/weekend programs available. Part-time, evening/weekend, 100% online, blended/hybrid learning. Offers business administration (MBA); leadership (Certificate); organizational leadership (MA, PhD); strategic leadership (DSL). *Application deadline:* For fall admission, 5/1 priority date for domestic students; for spring admission, 10/1 priority date for domestic students. Applications are processed on a rolling basis. *Application fee:* $50. Electronic applications accepted. *Application Contact:* Heidi Cece, Executive Director of University Admissions, 800-373-5504, Fax: 757-352-4381, E-mail: admissions@regent.edu. *Dean*, Dr. Doris Gomez, 757-352-4686, Fax: 757-352-4634, E-mail: dorigom@regent.edu.

School of Communication and the Arts Students: 85 full-time (49 women), 277 part-time (179 women); includes 131 minority (95 Black or African American, non-Hispanic/Latino; 4 American Indian or Alaska Native, non-Hispanic/Latino; 7 Asian, non-Hispanic/Latino; 21 Hispanic/Latino; 1 Native Hawaiian or other Pacific Islander, non-Hispanic/Latino; 3 Two or more races, non-Hispanic/Latino), 9 international. Average age 36. 270 applicants, 59% accepted, 111 enrolled. *Faculty:* 17 full-time (2 women), 40 part-time/adjunct (13 women). *Financial support:* Fellowships with tuition reimbursements, career-related internships or fieldwork, scholarships/grants, health care benefits, tuition waivers (full and partial), and unspecified assistantships available. Support available to part-time students. Financial award application deadline: 9/1; financial award applicants required to submit FAFSA. In 2015, 69 master's, 16 doctorates awarded. *Degree program information:* Part-time programs available. Part-time, 100% online, blended/hybrid learning. Offers acting (MFA); communication (MA, PhD); directing for cinema/television (MFA); film and TV (MA); journalism (MA); producing for cinema/television (MFA); script and screenwriting (MFA); theatre (MA). *Application deadline:* For fall admission, 3/1 priority date for domestic students; for spring admission, 10/1 priority date for domestic students. Applications are processed on a rolling basis. *Application fee:* $50. Electronic applications accepted. *Application Contact:* Heidi Cece, Executive Director of University Admissions, 800-373-5504, Fax: 757-352-4381, E-mail: admissions@regent.edu. *Dean*, Dr. Mitch Land, 757-352-4916, Fax: 757-352-4291, E-mail: mland@regent.edu.

School of Divinity Students: 120 full-time (51 women), 669 part-time (272 women); includes 387 minority (319 Black or African American, non-Hispanic/Latino; 7 American Indian or Alaska Native, non-Hispanic/Latino; 23 Asian, non-Hispanic/Latino; 32 Hispanic/Latino; 6 Two or more races, non-Hispanic/Latino), 26 international. Average age 43. 747 applicants, 46% accepted, 248 enrolled. *Faculty:* 18 full-time (3 women), 40 part-time/adjunct (2 women). *Financial support:* Fellowships with tuition reimbursements, career-related internships or fieldwork, scholarships/grants, health care benefits, tuition waivers (full and partial), and unspecified assistantships available. Support available to part-time students. Financial award application deadline: 9/1; financial award applicants required to submit FAFSA. In 2015, 106 master's, 12 doctorates awarded. *Degree program information:* Part-time and evening/weekend programs available. Part-time, evening/weekend, 100% online, blended/hybrid learning. Offers divinity (M Div); leadership and renewal (D Min); practical theology (MA); theological studies (MTS, PhD). *Application deadline:* For fall admission, 5/1 priority date for domestic students. Applications are processed on a rolling basis. *Application fee:* $50. Electronic applications accepted. *Application Contact:* Heidi Cece, Executive Director of University Admissions, 800-373-5504, Fax: 757-352-4381, E-mail: admissions@regent.edu. *Dean*, Dr. Cornelius Bekker, 757-352-4401, Fax: 757-352-4597, E-mail: clbekker@regent.edu.

School of Education Students: 71 full-time (56 women), 962 part-time (768 women); includes 419 minority (338 Black or African American, non-Hispanic/Latino; 3 American Indian or Alaska Native, non-Hispanic/Latino; 15 Asian, non-Hispanic/Latino; 51 Hispanic/Latino; 12 Two or more races, non-Hispanic/Latino), 7 international. Average age 40. 922 applicants, 62% accepted, 445 enrolled. *Faculty:* 21 full-time (11 women), 69 part-time/adjunct (41 women). *Financial support:* Fellowships, career-related internships or fieldwork, scholarships/grants, health care benefits, tuition waivers (full and partial), and unspecified assistantships available. Support available to part-time students. Financial award application deadline: 4/1; financial award applicants required to submit FAFSA. In 2015, 219 master's, 16 doctorates awarded. *Degree program information:* Part-time and evening/weekend programs available. Part-time, evening/weekend, 100% online, blended/hybrid learning. Offers adult education (Ed D, PhD, Ed S); advanced education leadership (Ed S); advanced educational leadership (Ed D, PhD); career switcher (M Ed); character education (Ed D, PhD, Ed S); Christian education leadership (Ed D, Ed S); Christian school administration (M Ed); curriculum and instruction (M Ed); educational leadership (M Ed); educational psychology (Ed D, PhD, Ed S); educational technology and online learning (Ed D, PhD, Ed S); elementary education (M Ed); exceptional education executive leadership (Ed D, Ed S); higher education (Ed D, PhD, Ed S); higher education leadership and management (Ed D, Ed S); individualized degree plan (M Ed); K-12 school leadership (Ed D, PhD, Ed S); leadership in mathematics education (M Ed, Ed S); reading specialist (M Ed); special education (M Ed, Ed D, PhD, Ed S); student affairs (M Ed); TESOL (M Ed). *Application deadline:* For fall admission, 4/1 priority date for domestic students; for spring admission, 10/15 priority date for domestic students. Applications are processed on a rolling basis. *Application fee:* $50. Electronic applications accepted. *Application Contact:* Heidi Cece, Executive Director of University Admissions, 800-373-5504, Fax: 757-352-4381, E-mail: admissions@regent.edu. *Dean*, Dr. Donald Finn, 757-352-4278, Fax: 757-352-4318, E-mail: dfinn@regent.edu.

School of Law Students: 321 full-time (190 women), 107 part-time (75 women); includes 177 minority (119 Black or African American, non-Hispanic/Latino; 1 American Indian or Alaska Native, non-Hispanic/Latino; 7 Asian, non-Hispanic/Latino; 33 Hispanic/Latino; 1 Native Hawaiian or other Pacific Islander, non-Hispanic/Latino; 16 Two or more races, non-Hispanic/Latino), 6 international. Average age 32. 765 applicants, 57% accepted, 185 enrolled. *Faculty:* 19 full-time (6 women), 78 part-time/adjunct (25 women). *Financial support:* Career-related internships or fieldwork, scholarships/grants, health care benefits, tuition waivers (full and partial), and unspecified assistantships available. Support available to part-time students. Financial award application deadline: 2/1; financial award applicants required to submit FAFSA. In 2015, 15 master's, 120 doctorates awarded. *Degree program information:* Part-time programs available. Part-time, 100% online, blended/hybrid learning. Offers American legal studies (LL M); human rights (LL M); law (MA, JD). *Application deadline:* For fall admission, 3/1 for domestic students. Applications are processed on a rolling basis. *Application fee:* $50. Electronic applications accepted. *Application Contact:* Katie Kerley, Director of Law Admissions, 877-267-5072, Fax: 757-352-4139, E-mail: lawschool@regent.edu. *Dean*, Michael Hernandez, 757-352-4040, Fax: 757-352-4595, E-mail: michher@regent.edu.

School of Psychology and Counseling Students: 268 full-time (211 women), 303 part-time (240 women); includes 203 minority (157 Black or African American, non-Hispanic/Latino; 2 American Indian or Alaska Native, non-Hispanic/Latino; 12 Asian, non-Hispanic/Latino; 24 Hispanic/Latino; 8 Two or more races, non-Hispanic/Latino), 16 international. Average age 35. 960 applicants, 33% accepted, 199 enrolled. *Faculty:* 29 full-time (16 women), 41 part-time/adjunct (26 women). *Financial support:* Research assistantships with tuition reimbursements, teaching assistantships with tuition reimbursements, career-related internships or fieldwork, scholarships/grants, health care benefits, tuition waivers (full and partial), and unspecified assistantships available. Support available to part-time students. Financial award application deadline: 9/1; financial award applicants required to submit FAFSA. In 2015, 104 master's, 42 doctorates awarded. *Degree program information:* Part-time and evening/weekend programs available. Part-time, evening/weekend, 100% online, blended/hybrid learning. Offers clinical psychology (Psy D); counseling (MA); counseling studies (CAGS); counselor education and supervision (PhD); general psychology (MS); human services counseling (MA). PhD program offered online only. *Application deadline:* For fall admission, 4/1 priority date for domestic students; for spring admission, 11/1 priority date for domestic students. Applications are processed on a rolling basis. *Application fee:* $50. Electronic applications accepted. *Application Contact:* Heidi Cece, Executive Director of University Admissions, 800-373-5504, Fax: 757-352-4381, E-mail: admissions@regent.edu. *Dean*, Dr. William Hathaway, 757-352-4294, Fax: 757-352-4282, E-mail: willhat@regent.edu.

REGIS COLLEGE, Toronto, ON M5S 2Z5, Canada

General Information Independent-religious, coed, graduate-only institution. *Graduate housing:* Room and/or apartments available on a first-come, first-served basis to single students; on-campus housing not available to married students. *Research affiliation:* Lonergan Research Institute (theology/philosophy), Lupina Foundation (research and innovation related to health/society issues).

GRADUATE UNITS

Graduate and Professional Programs Offers eastern Christian studies (Certificate); Ignatian spirituality (Diploma); ministry (D Min); ministry and spirituality (MAMS); philosophical studies (Diploma); retreat direction (Certificate); sacred theology (STM, STD, STB, STL); spiritual direction (Diploma); theological studies (MTS, Diploma); theology (M Div, MA, Th M, PhD, Th D).

REGIS COLLEGE, Weston, MA 02493

General Information Independent-religious, coed, comprehensive institution. *Enrollment:* 1,954 graduate, professional, and undergraduate students; 250 full-time matriculated graduate/professional students, 900 part-time matriculated graduate/professional students. *Graduate housing:* Room and/or apartments available on a first-come, first-served basis to single students; on-campus housing not available to married students. *Student services:* Campus employment opportunities, campus safety program, career counseling, exercise/wellness program, international student services, low-cost health insurance, multicultural affairs office, services for students with disabilities, teacher training, writing training. *Library:* Regis College Library. *Collection:* Books: 108,313 (physical), 421,975 (digital/electronic); Serial titles: 126 (physical), 153 (digital/electronic); Databases: 58. Weekly public service hours: 108. *Research affiliation:* Beth Israel Deaconess Medical Center (nursing), Caritas Norwood Hospital (nursing), Boston Medical Center (nursing), Lahey Clinic Medical Center (nursing).

Computer facilities: 196 computers available on campus for general student use. A campuswide network can be accessed from student residence rooms and from off campus. Online class registration, online bills, financial aid award letters and check-in requirements are available.
Website: http://www.regiscollege.edu/

General Application Contact: Shelagh Tomaino, Director of Graduate Admission, 781-768-7330, Fax: 781-768-7071, E-mail: graduatedepartment@regiscollege.edu.

GRADUATE UNITS

Department of Education ***Financial support:*** Fellowships with full tuition reimbursements, Federal Work-Study, and scholarships/grants available. Financial award applicants required to submit FAFSA. *Degree program information:* Part-time and evening/weekend programs available. Part-time, evening/weekend. Offers elementary teacher (MAT); higher education leadership (Ed D); reading (MAT); special education (MAT). *Application deadline:* Applications are processed on a rolling basis. *Application fee:* $60. Electronic applications accepted. *Application Contact:* Shelagh Tomaino, Associate Director, Graduate Admission, 781-768-7188, Fax: 781-768-7071, E-mail: shelagh.tomaino@regiscollege.edu. *Program Director*, Dr. Leona McCaughey-Oreszak, 781-768-7421, Fax: 781-768-7159, E-mail: leona.mccaughey-oreszak@regiscollege.edu.

Program in Heritage Studies for a Global Society *Degree program information:* Part-time programs available. Part-time. Offers biocultural diversity (MA); cultural heritage in literature (MA); cultural heritage in teaching (MA); cultural heritage in the workplace (MA); public heritage (MA). *Application deadline:* Applications are processed on a rolling basis. *Application Contact:* Shelagh Tomaino, Associate Director, Graduate

Admission, 781-768-7188, Fax: 781-768-7071, E-mail: shelagh.tomaino@regiscollege.edu. *Director*, Kathryn Edney, 781-768-7196.

Program in Organizational and Professional Communication ***Financial support:*** Scholarships/grants available. Financial award applicants required to submit FAFSA. *Degree program information:* Part-time and evening/weekend programs available. Part-time, evening/weekend. Offers organizational and professional communication (MS). *Application deadline:* Applications are processed on a rolling basis. *Application fee:* $50. *Application Contact:* Shelagh Tomaino, Associate Director, Graduate Admission, 781-768-7188, Fax: 781-768-7071, E-mail: shelagh.tomaino@regiscollege.edu. *Director*, Colleen Malachowski, 781-768-7373, Fax: 781-768-7159, E-mail: colleen.malachowski@regiscollege.edu.

Program in Professional Writing for New Media Offers professional writing for new media (Certificate). *Application Contact:* Christine Petherick, Administrative Coordinator, Planning and Enrollment, 866-438-7330, Fax: 781-768-7071, E-mail: christine.petherick@regiscollege.edu.

Program in Regulatory and Clinical Research Management ***Financial support:*** Career-related internships or fieldwork and scholarships/grants available. Financial award applicants required to submit FAFSA. *Degree program information:* Part-time and evening/weekend programs available. Part-time, evening/weekend. Offers regulatory and clinical research management (MS). *Application deadline:* Applications are processed on a rolling basis. *Application fee:* $50. *Application Contact:* Shelagh Tomaino, Associate Director, Graduate Admission, 781-768-7188, Fax: 781-768-7071, E-mail: shelagh.tomaino@regiscollege.edu. *Director*, Joni Beshansky, 781-768-7008, E-mail: jodi.beshansky@regiscollege.edu.

School of Nursing and Health Sciences ***Financial support:*** Research assistantships, Federal Work-Study, scholarships/grants, traineeships, and unspecified assistantships available. Support available to part-time students. Financial award applicants required to submit FAFSA. *Degree program information:* Part-time and evening/weekend programs available. Part-time, evening/weekend. Offers applied behavior analysis (MS); biomedical sciences (MS); counseling psychology (MA); health administration (MS); molecular imaging and therapeutics (MS); nurse practitioner (Certificate); nursing (MS, DNP); nursing education (Certificate); occupational therapy (MS). *Application deadline:* Applications are processed on a rolling basis. *Application fee:* $50. Electronic applications accepted. *Application Contact:* Shelagh Tomaino, Associate Director, Graduate Admission, 781-768-7188, Fax: 781-768-7071, E-mail: shelagh.tomaino@regiscollege.edu.

REGIS UNIVERSITY, Denver, CO 80221-1099

General Information Independent-religious, coed, comprehensive institution. *Enrollment:* 8,725 graduate, professional, and undergraduate students; 2,448 full-time matriculated graduate/professional students (1,594 women), 1,206 part-time matriculated graduate/professional students (783 women). *Enrollment by degree level:* 3,093 master's, 561 doctoral. *Graduate faculty:* 124 full-time (68 women), 362 part-time/adjunct (218 women). *Graduate housing:* Room and/or apartments available on a first-come, first-served basis to single students; on-campus housing not available to married students. Housing application deadline: 5/1. *Student services:* Campus employment opportunities, campus safety program, career counseling, exercise/wellness program, grant writing training, international student services, services for students with disabilities, writing training. *Library:* Dayton Memorial Library. *Collection:* Books: 393,000 (physical), 118,000 (digital/electronic); Databases: 248. Weekly public service hours: 101; students can reserve study rooms. *Research affiliation:* Commission for Accelerated Programs, Learning Anytime Anywhere Partnership (Internet-based technology), Transparency by Design (online programs, best practices).

Computer facilities: Computer purchase and lease plans are available. 600 computers available on campus for general student use. A campuswide network can be accessed from student residence rooms and from off campus. Online class registration is available.
Website: http://www.regis.edu/

General Application Contact: Cate Clark, Director of Admissions, 303-458-4900, Fax: 303-964-5534, E-mail: regisadm@regis.edu.

GRADUATE UNITS

College of Business and Economics Students: 555 full-time (325 women), 395 part-time (229 women); includes 270 minority (63 Black or African American, non-Hispanic/Latino; 5 American Indian or Alaska Native, non-Hispanic/Latino; 47 Asian, non-Hispanic/Latino; 132 Hispanic/Latino; 23 Two or more races, non-Hispanic/Latino), 22 international. Average age 36. 504 applicants, 73% accepted, 135 enrolled. *Faculty:* 24 full-time (6 women), 69 part-time/adjunct (32 women). *Financial support:* Scholarships/grants available. Financial award application deadline: 4/15; financial award applicants required to submit FAFSA. In 2015, 358 degrees awarded. *Degree program information:* Part-time and evening/weekend programs available. Part-time, evening/weekend, 100% online, blended/hybrid learning. Offers accounting (MS); enterprise resource leadership and planning (MSOL); executive leadership (Certificate); finance and accounting (MBA); human resource management and leadership (MSOL); management (MBA); marketing (MBA); nonprofit leadership (Post-Graduate Certificate); nonprofit management (MNM); nonprofit organizational capacity building (Certificate); operations management (MBA); organizational leadership and management (MSOL); project leadership and management (MSOL); strategic business management (Certificate); strategic human resource integration (Certificate); strategic management (MBA). Programs offered at Colorado Springs Campus, Northwest Denver Campus, Southeast Denver Campus, Fort Collins Campus, Broomfield Campus, Henderson (Nevada) Campus, and Summerlin (Nevada) Campus. *Application deadline:* For fall admission, 8/15 priority date for domestic students, 8/13 for international students; for winter admission, 10/10 priority date for domestic students, 9/8 for international students; for spring admission, 1/10 priority date for domestic students, 11/17 for international students; for summer admission, 5/1 priority date for domestic students. Applications are processed on a rolling basis. *Application fee:* $75. Electronic applications accepted. *Application Contact:* Cate Clark, Director of Admissions, 303-458-4900, Fax: 303-964-5534, E-mail: ruadmissions@regis.edu. *Academic Dean*, Dr. Timothy Keane.

College of Computer and Information Sciences Students: 272 full-time (80 women), 210 part-time (58 women); includes 164 minority (53 Black or African American, non-Hispanic/Latino; 4 American Indian or Alaska Native, non-Hispanic/Latino; 42 Asian, non-Hispanic/Latino; 50 Hispanic/Latino; 1 Native Hawaiian or other Pacific Islander, non-Hispanic/Latino; 14 Two or more races, non-Hispanic/Latino), 32 international. Average age 38. 335 applicants, 82% accepted, 153 enrolled. *Faculty:* 14 full-time (3 women), 17 part-time/adjunct (8 women). *Financial support:* Scholarships/grants available. Financial award application deadline: 4/15; financial award applicants required to submit FAFSA. In 2015, 200 master's awarded. *Degree program information:* Part-time and evening/weekend programs available. Part-time, evening/weekend, 100% online, blended/hybrid learning. Offers agile technologies (Certificate); cybersecurity (Certificate); data science (M Sc); database administration with Oracle (Certificate); database development (Certificate); database technologies (M Sc); enterprise Java software development (Certificate); enterprise resource planning (Certificate); executive information technology (Certificate); health care informatics (Certificate); information assurance (M Sc); information assurance policy management (Certificate); information technology management (M Sc); mobile software development (Certificate); software engineering (M Sc, Certificate); software engineering and database technology (M Sc); storage area networks (Certificate); systems engineering (M Sc, Certificate). *Application deadline:* For fall admission, 8/15 priority date for domestic students, 7/13 for international students; for winter admission, 10/10 priority date for domestic students, 9/8 for international students; for spring admission, 1/10 priority date for domestic students, 11/17 for international students; for summer admission, 5/1 priority date for domestic students. Applications are processed on a rolling basis. *Application fee:* $75. Electronic applications accepted. *Application Contact:* Cate Clark, Director of Admissions, 303-458-4900, Fax: 303-964-5534, E-mail: ruadmissions@regis.edu. *Academic Dean*, Shari Plantz-Masters.

College of Contemporary Liberal Studies Students: 481 full-time (380 women), 316 part-time (249 women); includes 194 minority (56 Black or African American, non-Hispanic/Latino; 5 American Indian or Alaska Native, non-Hispanic/Latino; 10 Asian, non-Hispanic/Latino; 97 Hispanic/Latino; 3 Native Hawaiian or other Pacific Islander, non-Hispanic/Latino; 23 Two or more races, non-Hispanic/Latino), 9 international. Average age 37. 343 applicants, 83% accepted, 219 enrolled. *Faculty:* 44 full-time (29 women), 137 part-time/adjunct (79 women). *Financial support:* Scholarships/grants available. Financial award application deadline: 4/15; financial award applicants required to submit FAFSA. In 2015, 446 master's awarded. *Degree program information:* Part-time and evening/weekend programs available. Part-time, evening/weekend, 100% online, blended/hybrid learning. Offers creative writing (MFA); criminology (M Sc); curriculum, instruction and assessment (M Ed); elementary education (M Ed); professional studies (M Ed, MA, Certificate, Post-Graduate Certificate); reading (M Ed); secondary education (M Ed); special education (M Ed); teacher/educational leadership (M Ed); teaching the linguistically diverse (M Ed). *Application deadline:* For fall admission, 8/15 priority date for domestic students, 7/13 for international students; for winter admission, 10/10 priority date for domestic students, 9/8 for international students; for spring admission, 1/10 priority date for domestic students, 11/17 for international students; for summer admission, 5/1 priority date for domestic students. Applications are processed on a rolling basis. *Application fee:* $75. Electronic applications accepted. *Application Contact:* Cate Clark, Director of Admissions, 303-458-4900, Fax: 303-964-5534, E-mail: ruadmissions@regis.edu. *Academic Dean*, Dr. Elisa Robyn.

Regis College Students: 60 full-time (38 women), 11 part-time (8 women); includes 13 minority (4 Asian, non-Hispanic/Latino; 7 Hispanic/Latino; 2 Two or more races, non-Hispanic/Latino), 2 international. Average age 27. 390 applicants, 71% accepted, 45 enrolled. *Faculty:* 2 full-time (1 woman), 22 part-time/adjunct (12 women). *Financial support:* Federal Work-Study and scholarships/grants available. Financial award application deadline: 4/15; financial award applicants required to submit FAFSA. In 2015, 29 master's awarded. *Degree program information:* Part-time programs available. Part-time. Offers biomedical sciences (MS); development practice (MA); environmental biology (MS). *Application deadline:* For fall admission, 5/15 priority date for domestic students, 4/1 priority date for international students; for spring admission, 12/15 priority date for domestic students. Applications are processed on a rolling basis. *Application fee:* $75. Electronic applications accepted. *Application Contact:* Sarah Engel, Director of Admissions, 303-458-4900, Fax: 303-964-5534, E-mail: ruadmissions@regis.edu. *Academic Dean*, Dr. Thomas Bowie.

Rueckert-Hartman College for Health Professions Students: 1,080 full-time (771 women), 274 part-time (239 women); includes 388 minority (59 Black or African American, non-Hispanic/Latino; 6 American Indian or Alaska Native, non-Hispanic/Latino; 109 Asian, non-Hispanic/Latino; 163 Hispanic/Latino; 1 Native Hawaiian or other Pacific Islander, non-Hispanic/Latino; 50 Two or more races, non-Hispanic/Latino), 7 international. Average age 34. 2,188 applicants, 31% accepted, 303 enrolled. *Faculty:* 40 full-time (29 women), 116 part-time/adjunct (86 women). *Financial support:* In 2015–16, 102 students received support. Federal Work-Study and scholarships/grants available. Financial award application deadline: 4/15; financial award applicants required to submit FAFSA. In 2015, 329 master's, 160 doctorates awarded. *Degree program information:* Part-time and evening/weekend programs available. Part-time, evening/weekend, 100% online, blended/hybrid learning. Offers addictions counseling (Post-Graduate Certificate); advanced practice nurse specialization (DNP); counseling (MA); counseling children and adolescents (Post-Graduate Certificate); counseling military families (Post-Graduate Certificate); depth psychotherapy (Post-Graduate Certificate); family nurse practitioner (MSN); health care business management (Certificate); health care quality and patient safety (Certificate); health industry leadership (MBA); health professions (Postbaccalaureate Certificate); health services administration (MS); marriage and family therapy (MA); neonatal nurse practitioner (MSN); nursing education or leadership (MSN); orthopedic manual physical therapy fellowship (Certificate); pharmacy (Pharm D); physical therapy (DPT). *Application deadline:* For fall admission, 8/15 priority date for domestic students; for spring admission, 1/10 priority date for domestic students; for summer admission, 5/1 priority date for domestic students. Applications are processed on a rolling basis. *Application fee:* $75. Electronic applications accepted. *Application Contact:* Cate Clark, Director of Admissions, 303-458-4900, Fax: 303-964-5534, E-mail: ruadmissions@regis.edu. *Academic Dean*, Dr. Janet Houser.

REINHARDT UNIVERSITY, Waleska, GA 30183-2981

General Information Independent-religious, coed, comprehensive institution. *Graduate housing:* Room and/or apartments available on a first-come, first-served basis to single students; on-campus housing not available to married students.

GRADUATE UNITS

Program in Early Childhood Education ***Degree program information:*** Part-time and evening/weekend programs available. Part-time, evening/weekend, online learning. Offers early childhood education (M Ed, MAT). Electronic applications accepted.

Program in Music ***Degree program information:*** Part-time and evening/weekend programs available. Part-time, evening/weekend, online learning. Offers conducting (MM); music education (MM); piano pedagogy (MM).

Reinhardt Advantage MBA Program ***Degree program information:*** Part-time and evening/weekend programs available. Part-time, evening/weekend. Offers business administration (MBA). Program offered at North Fulton Center in Alpharetta, GA and at The Chambers at City Center in Woodstock, GA. Electronic applications accepted.

RELAY GRADUATE SCHOOL OF EDUCATION, New York, NY 10011

General Information Independent, coed, graduate-only institution.

GRADUATE UNITS

Graduate Programs Online learning. Offers education (MAT). Program also offered at Chicago, Delaware, Houston, Memphis, New Orleans, and Newark campuses.

RENSSELAER AT HARTFORD, Hartford, CT 06120-2991

General Information Independent, coed, graduate-only institution. *Graduate housing:* On-campus housing not available.

GRADUATE UNITS

Department of Computer and Information Science *Degree program information:* Part-time and evening/weekend programs available. Part-time, evening/weekend. Offers computer science (MS); information technology (MS). Electronic applications accepted.

Department of Engineering *Degree program information:* Part-time and evening/weekend programs available. Part-time, evening/weekend. Offers computer and systems engineering (ME); electrical engineering (ME, MS); engineering (ME, MS); engineering science (MS); mechanical engineering (ME, MS). Electronic applications accepted.

Lally School of Management and Technology *Degree program information:* Part-time and evening/weekend programs available. Part-time, evening/weekend, online learning. Offers management and technology (MBA, MS). Electronic applications accepted.

RENSSELAER POLYTECHNIC INSTITUTE, Troy, NY 12180-3590

General Information Independent, coed, university. CGS member. *Enrollment:* 7,113 graduate, professional, and undergraduate students; 2,515 full-time matriculated graduate/professional students (775 women), 489 part-time matriculated graduate/professional students (137 women). *Enrollment by degree level:* 839 master's, 2,165 doctoral. *Graduate faculty:* 2,247 full-time (506 women), 302 part-time/adjunct (77 women). *Graduate housing:* Rooms and/or apartments available on a first-come, first-served basis to single and married students. *Student services:* Campus employment opportunities, campus safety program, career counseling, exercise/wellness program, free psychological counseling, grant writing training, international student services, low-cost health insurance, multicultural affairs office, services for students with disabilities, teacher training, writing training. *Library:* Folsom Library plus 2 others. *Research affiliation:* Skidmore, Owings & Merrill (SOM) (built environment (solar concentrators, phytoremediation, integrated hybrid flow control, parametric design)), Disney (synthetic characters), General Electric Company (GE) (renewable energy, power electronic, and imaging research), IBM (high performance computing, advanced modeling and simulation research), Boeing (flow control, computational fluid dynamics), Mount Sinai School of Medicine (biomedical and clinical research (healthcare analytics, orthopedic-musculoskeletal research, imaging, brain-machine interfaces)).

Computer facilities: Computer purchase and lease plans are available. A campuswide network can be accessed from student residence rooms and from off campus. Online class registration, billing, downloadable software, Web pages are available.
Website: http://www.rpi.edu/

General Application Contact: Jarron Decker, Acting Director of Graduate Admissions, 518-276-3062, Fax: 518-276-4072, E-mail: gradadmissions@rpi.edu.

GRADUATE UNITS

Graduate School Students: 1,064 full-time (322 women), 226 part-time (65 women); includes 142 minority (27 Black or African American, non-Hispanic/Latino; 63 Asian, non-Hispanic/Latino; 34 Hispanic/Latino; 18 Two or more races, non-Hispanic/Latino), 548 international. Average age 28. 3,591 applicants, 29% accepted, 417 enrolled. *Faculty:* 970 full-time (217 women), 137 part-time/adjunct (35 women). *Financial support:* Fellowships with full tuition reimbursements, research assistantships with full tuition reimbursements, teaching assistantships with full tuition reimbursements, career-related internships or fieldwork, scholarships/grants, health care benefits, and tuition waivers (partial) available. Financial award application deadline: 1/1. In 2015, 257 master's, 157 doctorates awarded. *Degree program information:* Part-time and evening/weekend programs available. Part-time, evening/weekend. *Application deadline:* For fall admission, 1/1 priority date for domestic and international students; for spring admission, 8/15 priority date for domestic and international students. Applications are processed on a rolling basis. *Application fee:* $75. Electronic applications accepted. *Application Contact:* Graduate Admissions, 518-276-6216, E-mail: gradadmissions@rpi.edu.

Lally School of Management Students: 114 full-time (51 women), 64 part-time (31 women); includes 12 minority (4 Black or African American, non-Hispanic/Latino; 6 Asian, non-Hispanic/Latino; 2 Two or more races, non-Hispanic/Latino), 123 international. Average age 31. 760 applicants, 34% accepted, 91 enrolled. *Faculty:* 151 full-time (30 women), 29 part-time/adjunct (11 women). *Financial support:* Scholarships/grants available. Financial award application deadline: 1/1; financial award applicants required to submit FAFSA. In 2015, 104 master's, 10 doctorates awarded. *Degree program information:* Part-time and evening/weekend programs available. Part-time, evening/weekend. Offers business analytics (MS); management (MBA, MS, PhD); quantitative finance and risk analytics (MS); supply chain management (MS); technology commercialization and entrepreneurship (MS). *Application deadline:* For fall admission, 1/1 priority date for domestic and international students; for spring admission, 8/15 priority date for domestic and international students. Applications are processed on a rolling basis. *Application fee:* $75. Electronic applications accepted. *Application Contact:* Office of Graduate Admissions, 518-276-6216, E-mail: gradadmissions@rpi.edu. *Associate Dean, Lally School of Management*, Dr. Gina O'Connor, 518-276-6842, E-mail: oconng@rpi.edu.

School of Architecture Students: 106 full-time (38 women), 6 part-time (0 women); includes 21 minority (12 Asian, non-Hispanic/Latino; 4 Hispanic/Latino; 5 Two or more races, non-Hispanic/Latino), 20 international. *Faculty:* 91 full-time (19 women), 32 part-time/adjunct (8 women). *Financial support:* In 2015–16, research assistantships (averaging $21,500 per year), teaching assistantships (averaging $21,500 per year) were awarded; fellowships and scholarships/grants also available. Financial award application deadline: 1/1. Offers architectural acoustics (PhD); architectural sciences (MS, PhD); architecture (M Arch I); built ecologies (MS, PhD); geofutures (M Arch II); lighting (MS, PhD). *Application deadline:* For fall admission, 1/1 priority date for domestic and international students; for spring admission, 8/15 for domestic and international students; for summer admission, 1/1 for domestic and international students. Applications are processed on a rolling basis. *Application fee:* $75. Electronic applications accepted. *Application Contact:* Office of Graduate Admissions, 518-276-2716, E-mail: gradadmissions@rpi.edu. *Graduate Program Director*, Chris Perry, 518-276-4785, E-mail: perryc3@rpi.edu.

School of Engineering Students: 449 full-time (113 women), 125 part-time (30 women); includes 59 minority (7 Black or African American, non-Hispanic/Latino; 33 Asian, non-Hispanic/Latino; 12 Hispanic/Latino; 7 Two or more races, non-Hispanic/Latino), 260 international. Average age 27. 1,617 applicants, 24% accepted, 166 enrolled. *Faculty:* 372 full-time (66 women), 39 part-time/adjunct (8 women). *Financial support:* In 2015–16, 364 students received support, including research assistantships (averaging $18,500 per year), teaching assistantships (averaging $18,500 per year); fellowships also available. Financial award application deadline: 1/1. In 2015, 106 master's, 78 doctorates awarded. *Degree program information:* Part-time programs available. Part-time. Offers aeronautical engineering (M Eng, MS, D Eng, PhD); biomedical engineering (MS, D Eng, PhD); chemical engineering (M Eng, MS, D Eng, PhD); civil engineering (M Eng, MS, D Eng, PhD); computer and systems engineering (M Eng, MS, D Eng, PhD); decision sciences and engineering systems (PhD); electrical engineering (M Eng, MS, D Eng, PhD); engineering (M Eng, MS, D Eng, PhD); engineering physics (MS, PhD); environmental engineering (M Eng, MS, D Eng, PhD); industrial and management engineering (M Eng, MS); materials science and engineering (M Eng, MS, D Eng, PhD); mechanical engineering (M Eng, MS, D Eng, PhD); nuclear engineering (M Eng, MS, D Eng, PhD); systems engineering and technology management (M Eng); transportation engineering (M Eng, MS, D Eng, PhD). *Application deadline:* For fall admission, 1/1 priority date for domestic and international students; for spring admission, 8/15 priority date for domestic and international students. Applications are processed on a rolling basis. *Application fee:* $75. Electronic applications accepted. *Application Contact:* Office of Graduate Admissions, 518-276-6216, E-mail: gradadmissions@rpi.edu. *Associate Dean, School of Engineering*, Dr. Tarek Abdoun, 518-276-6544, E-mail: abdout@rpi.edu.

School of Humanities, Arts, and Social Sciences Students: 61 full-time (30 women), 8 part-time (2 women); includes 11 minority (3 Black or African American, non-Hispanic/Latino; 2 Asian, non-Hispanic/Latino; 5 Hispanic/Latino; 1 Two or more races, non-Hispanic/Latino), 6 international. Average age 32. 188 applicants, 29% accepted, 20 enrolled. *Faculty:* 81 full-time (32 women), 4 part-time/adjunct (1 woman). *Financial support:* In 2015–16, 66 students received support, including research assistantships (averaging $18,500 per year), teaching assistantships (averaging $18,500 per year); fellowships and scholarships/grants also available. Financial award application deadline: 1/1. In 2015, 15 master's, 9 doctorates awarded. *Degree program information:* Part-time and evening/weekend programs available. Part-time, evening/weekend, online learning. Offers cognitive science (PhD); communication and rhetoric (MS, PhD); electronic arts (MFA, PhD); human-computer interaction (MS); humanities, arts, and social sciences (MFA, MS, PhD); science and technology studies (MS, PhD). *Application deadline:* For fall admission, 1/1 priority date for domestic students, 1/15 priority date for international students; for spring admission, 8/15 priority date for domestic and international students. Applications are processed on a rolling basis. *Application fee:* $75. Electronic applications accepted. *Application Contact:* Office of Graduate Admissions, 518-276-6216, E-mail: gradadmissions@rpi.edu. *Associate Dean for Research and Graduate Studies*, Dr. Nancy Campbell, 518-276-6065, E-mail: campbn2@rpi.edu.

School of Science Students: 334 full-time (90 women), 23 part-time (2 women); includes 42 minority (13 Black or African American, non-Hispanic/Latino; 10 Asian, non-Hispanic/Latino; 13 Hispanic/Latino; 6 Two or more races, non-Hispanic/Latino), 139 international. Average age 28. 887 applicants, 32% accepted, 113 enrolled. *Faculty:* 275 full-time (70 women), 33 part-time/adjunct (7 women). *Financial support:* In 2015–16, 289 students received support, including research assistantships (averaging $18,500 per year), teaching assistantships (averaging $18,500 per year); fellowships also available. Financial award application deadline: 1/1. In 2015, 77 master's, 40 doctorates awarded. Offers applied mathematics (MS); biochemistry and biophysics (MS, PhD); biology (MS, PhD); chemistry (MS, PhD); computer science (MS, PhD); geology (MS, PhD); information technology and Web science (MS); mathematics (MS, PhD); multi-disciplinary science (MS, PhD); physics, applied physics and astronomy (MS, PhD); science (MS, PhD). *Application deadline:* For fall admission, 1/1 priority date for domestic and international students; for spring admission, 8/15 priority date for domestic and international students. Applications are processed on a rolling basis. *Application fee:* $75. Electronic applications accepted. *Application Contact:* Office of Graduate Admissions, 518-276-6216, E-mail: gradadmissions@rpi.edu. *Associate Dean, School of Science*, Dr. Wilfredo Colon, 518-276-2515, E-mail: colonw@rpi.edu.

RESEARCH COLLEGE OF NURSING, Kansas City, MO 64132

General Information Independent, coed, primarily women, comprehensive institution. *Enrollment:* 474 graduate, professional, and undergraduate students; 4 full-time matriculated graduate/professional students (2 women), 148 part-time matriculated graduate/professional students (132 women). *Enrollment by degree level:* 152 master's. *Graduate faculty:* 9 full-time (all women), 5 part-time/adjunct (2 women). *Graduate housing:* Rooms and/or apartments available on a first-come, first-served basis to single and married students. *Student services:* Campus safety program, child daycare facilities. *Library:* Greenlease Library.

Computer facilities: 125 computers available on campus for general student use. A campuswide network can be accessed from student residence rooms and from off campus. Online class registration is available.
Website: http://www.researchcollege.edu/

General Application Contact: Leslie Burry, Director of Transfer and Graduate Recruitment, 816-995-2820, Fax: 816-995-2813, E-mail: leslie.burry@researchcollege.edu.

GRADUATE UNITS

Nursing Program Students: 4 full-time (2 women), 148 part-time (132 women); includes 15 minority (9 Black or African American, non-Hispanic/Latino; 1 American Indian or Alaska Native, non-Hispanic/Latino; 3 Asian, non-Hispanic/Latino; 1 Native Hawaiian or other Pacific Islander, non-Hispanic/Latino; 1 Two or more races, non-Hispanic/Latino). *Faculty:* 9 full-time (all women), 5 part-time/adjunct (2 women). *Financial support:* Applicants required to submit FAFSA. In 2015, 34 master's awarded. *Degree program information:* Part-time programs available. Part-time, 100% online. Offers adult-gerontological nurse practitioner (MSN); executive practice and healthcare leadership (MSN); family nurse practitioner (MSN); nursing (MSN). *Application deadline:* Applications are processed on a rolling basis. *Application fee:* $65. Electronic applications accepted. *Application Contact:* Leslie Burry, Director of Transfer and Graduate Recruitment, 816-995-2820, Fax: 816-995-2813, E-mail: leslie.burry@researchcollege.edu. *President and Dean*, Dr. Nancy O. DeBasio, 816-995-2815, Fax: 816-995-2817, E-mail: nancy.debasio@researchcollege.edu.

RESURRECTION UNIVERSITY, Chicago, IL 60622

General Information Independent, coed, upper-level institution.

GRADUATE UNITS

Nursing Program Offers nursing (MSN).

RHODE ISLAND COLLEGE, Providence, RI 02908-1991

General Information State-supported, coed, comprehensive institution. *Enrollment:* 8,512 graduate, professional, and undergraduate students; 188 full-time matriculated graduate/professional students (150 women), 515 part-time matriculated graduate/professional students (409 women). *Enrollment by degree level:* 612 master's, 49 doctoral, 42 other advanced degrees. *Graduate faculty:* 102 full-time (59 women), 80 part-time/adjunct (60 women). Tuition, state resident: full-time $8928; part-time $372 per credit. Tuition, nonresident: full-time $17,376; part-time $724 per credit. *Required fees:* $604; $22 per credit. One-time fee: $74. *Graduate housing:* On-campus housing not available. *Student services:* Campus employment opportunities, career counseling, free psychological counseling, international student services, low-cost health insurance, multicultural affairs office, services for students with disabilities. *Library:* Adams Library. *Collection:* Books: 583,807 (physical), 153,307 (digital/electronic); Serial titles: 1,514 (physical), 55,052 (digital/electronic); Databases: 153. Weekly public service hours: 79.

Computer facilities: Computer purchase and lease plans are available. 220 computers available on campus for general student use. A campuswide network can be accessed from student residence rooms and from off campus. Online class registration is available.
Website: http://www.ric.edu/

General Application Contact: Dr. Leslie Schuster, Interim Dean of Graduate Studies, 401-456-9723, E-mail: graduatestudies@ric.edu.

GRADUATE UNITS

School of Graduate Studies Students: 188 full-time (150 women), 515 part-time (409 women); includes 91 minority (26 Black or African American, non-Hispanic/Latino; 2 American Indian or Alaska Native, non-Hispanic/Latino; 16 Asian, non-Hispanic/Latino; 42 Hispanic/Latino; 3 Native Hawaiian or other Pacific Islander, non-Hispanic/Latino; 2 Two or more races, non-Hispanic/Latino), 3 international. Average age 33. *Faculty:* 102 full-time (59 women), 80 part-time/adjunct (60 women). *Financial support:* In 2015–16, 27 teaching assistantships with full tuition reimbursements (averaging $2,301 per year) were awarded; career-related internships or fieldwork, Federal Work-Study, traineeships, health care benefits, tuition waivers (partial), and unspecified assistantships also available. Support available to part-time students. Financial award application deadline: 5/15; financial award applicants required to submit FAFSA. In 2015, 240 master's, 4 doctorates, 39 other advanced degrees awarded. *Degree program information:* Part-time and evening/weekend programs available. Part-time, evening/weekend. *Application deadline:* For fall admission, 3/1 priority date for domestic students; for spring admission, 11/1 for domestic students. Applications are processed on a rolling basis. *Application fee:* $50. Electronic applications accepted. *Application Contact:* Graduate Studies, 401-456-8700. *Interim Dean of Graduate Studies*, Dr. Leslie Schuster, 401-456-9723, E-mail: graduatestudies@ric.edu.

Faculty of Arts and Sciences Students: 12 full-time (5 women), 29 part-time (13 women); includes 2 minority (1 Hispanic/Latino; 1 Native Hawaiian or other Pacific Islander, non-Hispanic/Latino). Average age 30. *Faculty:* 54 full-time (23 women), 12 part-time/adjunct (7 women). *Financial support:* In 2015–16, 15 teaching assistantships with full tuition reimbursements (averaging $2,542 per year) were awarded; research assistantships with tuition reimbursements, career-related internships or fieldwork, Federal Work-Study, scholarships/grants, health care benefits, and unspecified assistantships also available. Support available to part-time students. Financial award application deadline: 5/15; financial award applicants required to submit FAFSA. In 2015, 23 master's awarded. *Degree program information:* Part-time and evening/weekend programs available. Part-time, evening/weekend. Offers art education (MA, MAT); arts and sciences (MA, MAT, MM Ed, MPA, CGS); biology (MA); creative writing (MA, CGS); English (MA); health psychology (CGS); history (MA); literature (CGS); mathematics (MA); mathematics content specialist (CGS); media studies (MA); modern biological sciences (CGS); music education (MAT, MM Ed); psychology (MA); public administration (MPA). *Application deadline:* For fall admission, 3/1 for domestic students; for spring admission, 11/1 for domestic students. Applications are processed on a rolling basis. *Application fee:* $50. Electronic applications accepted. *Application Contact:* Graduate Studies, 401-456-8700. *Dean*, Dr. Earl Simson, 401-456-8107, E-mail: esimson@ric.edu.

Feinstein School of Education and Human Development Students: 68 full-time (62 women), 290 part-time (235 women); includes 39 minority (8 Black or African American, non-Hispanic/Latino; 9 Asian, non-Hispanic/Latino; 19 Hispanic/Latino; 2 Native Hawaiian or other Pacific Islander, non-Hispanic/Latino; 1 Two or more races, non-Hispanic/Latino), 1 international. Average age 34. *Faculty:* 31 full-time (22 women), 38 part-time/adjunct (28 women). *Financial support:* In 2015–16, 4 teaching assistantships with full tuition reimbursements (averaging $2,625 per year) were awarded; career-related internships or fieldwork, Federal Work-Study, scholarships/grants, health care benefits, and unspecified assistantships also available. Support available to part-time students. Financial award application deadline: 5/15; financial award applicants required to submit FAFSA. In 2015, 121 master's, 4 doctorates, 39 other advanced degrees awarded. *Degree program information:* Part-time and evening/weekend programs available. Part-time, evening/weekend. Offers advanced counseling (CGS); advanced studies in teaching and learning (M Ed); agency counseling (MA); autism education (CGS); clinical mental health counseling (MS); co-occurring disorders (MA, CGS); early childhood education (M Ed); education (PhD); education and human development (M Ed, MA, MAT, MS, PhD, CAGS, CGS); educational leadership (M Ed); elementary education (M Ed, MAT); English (MAT); French (MAT); health education (M Ed); history (MAT); math (MAT); mental health counseling (CAGS); physical education (CGS); reading (M Ed); school counseling (MA); school psychology (CAGS); secondary education (MAT); severe intellectual disabilities (CGS); Spanish (MAT); special education (M Ed); teacher leadership (CGS); teaching English as a second language (M Ed). *Application deadline:* For fall admission, 3/1 for domestic students; for spring admission, 11/1 for domestic students. Applications are processed on a rolling basis. *Application fee:* $50. Electronic applications accepted. *Application Contact:* Graduate Studies, 401-456-8700. *Dean*, Dr. Donald Halquist, 401-456-8110, E-mail: dhalquist@ric.edu.

School of Management Students: 4 full-time (1 woman), 13 part-time (5 women); includes 6 minority (3 Asian, non-Hispanic/Latino; 3 Hispanic/Latino). Average age 31. *Faculty:* 1 (woman) full-time, 2 part-time/adjunct (1 woman). *Financial support:* Federal Work-Study, scholarships/grants, health care benefits, and unspecified assistantships available. Support available to part-time students. Financial award application deadline: 5/15; financial award applicants required to submit FAFSA. In 2015, 15 master's awarded. *Degree program information:* Part-time and evening/weekend programs available. Part-time, evening/weekend. Offers accounting (MP Ac); financial planning (CGS); management (MP Ac, CGS). *Application deadline:* For fall admission, 3/1 for domestic students. Applications are processed on a rolling basis. *Application fee:* $50. Electronic applications accepted. *Application Contact:* Graduate Studies, 401-456-8700. *Interim Dean*, Dr. Jeanne Haser-Lafond, 401-456-8009, E-mail: jhaser@ric.edu.

School of Nursing Students: 11 full-time (6 women), 78 part-time (68 women); includes 11 minority (3 Black or African American, non-Hispanic/Latino; 4 Asian, non-Hispanic/Latino; 3 Hispanic/Latino; 1 Two or more races, non-Hispanic/Latino), 2 international. Average age 36. *Faculty:* 7 full-time (all women), 13 part-time/adjunct (all women). *Financial support:* In 2015–16, 5 teaching assistantships with full tuition reimbursements (averaging $1,800 per year) were awarded; Federal Work-Study, scholarships/grants, health care benefits, and unspecified assistantships also available. Support available to part-time students. Financial award application deadline: 5/15; financial award applicants required to submit FAFSA. In 2015, 13 master's awarded. *Degree program information:* Part-time programs available. Part-time. Offers nursing (MSN). *Application deadline:* For fall admission, 2/15 for domestic students. Applications are processed on a rolling basis. *Application fee:* $50. Electronic applications accepted. *Application Contact:* Graduate Studies, 401-456-8700. *Dean*, Dr. Jane Williams, 401-456-8013, Fax: 401-456-9608, E-mail: jwilliams@ric.edu.

School of Social Work Students: 93 full-time (76 women), 105 part-time (88 women); includes 33 minority (15 Black or African American, non-Hispanic/Latino; 2 American Indian or Alaska Native, non-Hispanic/Latino; 16 Hispanic/Latino). Average age 31. *Faculty:* 9 full-time (6 women), 15 part-time/adjunct (11 women). *Financial support:* Career-related internships or fieldwork, Federal Work-Study, scholarships/grants, health care benefits, and unspecified assistantships available. Support available to part-time students. Financial award application deadline: 5/15; financial award applicants required to submit FAFSA. In 2015, 68 master's awarded. *Degree program information:* Part-time programs available. Part-time. Offers social work (MSW). *Application deadline:* For fall admission, 2/1 for domestic students. Applications are processed on a rolling basis. *Application fee:* $50. Electronic applications accepted. *Application Contact:* Graduate Studies, 401-456-8700. *Dean*, Dr. Sue Pearlmutter, 401-456-8042, E-mail: spearlmutter@ric.edu.

RHODE ISLAND SCHOOL OF DESIGN, Providence, RI 02903-2784

General Information Independent, coed, comprehensive institution. *Enrollment:* 2,481 graduate, professional, and undergraduate students; 467 full-time matriculated graduate/professional students (317 women). *Enrollment by degree level:* 467 master's. *Graduate faculty:* 79 full-time (29 women), 166 part-time/adjunct (75 women). *Tuition, area resident:* Full-time $45,530. *Required fees:* $310. *Graduate housing:* Rooms and/or apartments available on a first-come, first-served basis to single and married students. Typical cost: $7950 per year for single students; $9950 per year for married students. Room charges vary according to board plan and housing facility selected. *Student services:* Campus employment opportunities, campus safety program, career counseling, exercise/wellness program, free psychological counseling, grant writing training, international student services, low-cost health insurance, multicultural affairs office, services for students with disabilities, teacher training, writing training. *Library:* Fleet Library. *Collection:* Books: 157,011 (physical), 143,200 (digital/electronic); Serial titles: 330 (physical), 1,200 (digital/electronic); Databases: 30. Weekly public service hours: 88; students can reserve study rooms.

Computer facilities: Computer purchase and lease plans are available. 65 computers available on campus for general student use. A campuswide network can be accessed from student residence rooms and from off campus. Online class registration is available.
Website: http://www.risd.edu/

General Application Contact: Molly Pettengil, Graduate Admissions Officer, 401-454-6312, Fax: 401-454-6309, E-mail: admissions@risd.edu.

GRADUATE UNITS

Division of Architecture and Design Students: 322 full-time (218 women); includes 38 minority (3 Black or African American, non-Hispanic/Latino; 18 Asian, non-Hispanic/Latino; 12 Hispanic/Latino; 5 Two or more races, non-Hispanic/Latino), 192 international. Average age 26. 1,128 applicants, 36% accepted, 156 enrolled. *Faculty:* 66 full-time (23 women), 130 part-time/adjunct (27 women). *Financial support:* Fellowships, research assistantships, teaching assistantships, Federal Work-Study, scholarships/grants, and unspecified assistantships available. Financial award application deadline: 2/15; financial award applicants required to submit FAFSA. In 2015, 111 master's awarded. Offers architecture (M Arch); architecture and design (M Arch, M Des, MA, MFA, MID, MLA); furniture design (MFA); graphic design (MFA); industrial design (MID); interior architecture (MA); interior studies (adaptive reuse/narrative environments) (M Des); landscape architecture (MLA). *Application deadline:* For fall admission, 2/1 for domestic and international students. *Application fee:* $60. *Application Contact:* Molly Pettengil, Graduate Admissions Officer, 401-454-6312, Fax: 401-454-6309, E-mail: mpetteng@risd.edu. *Dean,* Nancy Skolos, 401-454-6280, Fax: 401-454-6718, E-mail: nskolos@risd.edu.

Division of Fine Arts Students: 99 full-time (63 women); includes 15 minority (2 Black or African American, non-Hispanic/Latino; 5 Asian, non-Hispanic/Latino; 7 Hispanic/Latino; 1 Two or more races, non-Hispanic/Latino), 35 international. Average age 27. 606 applicants, 14% accepted, 49 enrolled. *Faculty:* 31 full-time (13 women), 55 part-time/adjunct (35 women). *Financial support:* Fellowships, research assistantships, teaching assistantships, Federal Work-Study, scholarships/grants, and unspecified assistantships available. Financial award application deadline: 2/15; financial award applicants required to submit FAFSA. In 2015, 46 master's awarded. Offers ceramics (MFA); glass (MFA); jewelry and metalsmithing (MFA); painting (MFA); photography (MFA); printmaking (MFA); sculpture (MFA); textiles (MFA). *Application deadline:* For fall admission, 2/1 for domestic and international students. *Application fee:* $60. Electronic applications accepted. *Application Contact:* Molly Pettengil, Assistant Director for Graduate Recruitment, 401-454-6312, Fax: 401-454-6309, E-mail: mpetteng@risd.edu. *Dean*, Sheri Wills, 401-454-6183, Fax: 401-454-6198, E-mail: swills@risd.edu.

Graduate Studies Students: 46 full-time (36 women); includes 7 minority (5 Asian, non-Hispanic/Latino; 2 Hispanic/Latino), 17 international. Average age 28. 177 applicants, 38% accepted, 31 enrolled. *Faculty:* 12 full-time (5 women), 27 part-time/adjunct (15 women). *Financial support:* Fellowships, research assistantships, teaching assistantships, Federal Work-Study, scholarships/grants, and unspecified assistantships available. Financial award application deadline: 2/15; financial award applicants required to submit FAFSA. In 2015, 24 master's awarded. Offers art education (MA, MAT); digital media (MFA). *Application deadline:* For fall admission, 2/1 for domestic and international students. *Application fee:* $60. Electronic applications accepted. *Application Contact:* Molly Pettengil, Assistant Director for Graduate Recruitment, 401-454-6312, Fax: 401-454-6309, E-mail: mpetteng@risd.edu.

RHODES COLLEGE, Memphis, TN 38112-1690

General Information Independent, coed, comprehensive institution. *Graduate housing:* Room and/or apartments available on a first-come, first-served basis to single students; on-campus housing not available to married students. Housing application deadline: 3/1.

GRADUATE UNITS

Department of Commerce and Business ***Degree program information:*** Part-time programs available. Part-time. Offers accounting (MS).

RICE UNIVERSITY, Houston, TX 77251-1892

General Information Independent, coed, university. CGS member. *Graduate housing:* Rooms and/or apartments available on a first-come, first-served basis to single and married students. Housing application deadline: 7/15. *Research affiliation:* Fermi National Accelerator Laboratory, Los Alamos National Laboratory, Brookhaven National Laboratory, Arecibo Observatory, Houston Area Research Center.

GRADUATE UNITS

Graduate Programs ***Degree program information:*** Part-time programs available. Part-time. Offers education (MAT). Electronic applications accepted.

George R. Brown School of Engineering Degree program information: Part-time programs available. Part-time. Offers bioengineering (MS, PhD); bioinformatics (PhD); biostatistics (PhD); chemical and biomolecular engineering (MS, PhD); chemical engineering (M Ch E); circuits, controls, and communication systems (MS, PhD); civil engineering (MCE, MS, PhD); computational and applied mathematics (MA, MCAM, PhD); computational finance (PhD); computational science and engineering (PhD); computer science (MCS, MS, PhD); computer science and engineering (MS, PhD); electrical engineering (MEE); engineering (M Ch E, M Stat, MA, MBE, MCAM, MCE, MCS, MEE, MEE, MES, MME, MMS, MS, PhD); environmental engineering (MEE, MES, MS, PhD); environmental science (MEE, MES, MS, PhD); general statistics (PhD); lasers, microwaves, and solid-state electronics (MS, PhD); materials science (MMS, MS, PhD); mechanical engineering (MME, MS, PhD); statistics (M Stat, MA). MD/PhD offered jointly with Baylor College of Medicine, The University of Texas Health Science Center at Houston. Electronic applications accepted.

Jesse H. Jones Graduate School of Management Degree program information: Evening/weekend programs available. Evening/weekend. Offers business administration (EMBA, MBA, PMBA). Electronic applications accepted.

School of Architecture Offers architecture (M Arch, D Arch); urban design (M Arch). Electronic applications accepted.

School of Humanities Offers African religions (PhD); African-American religions (PhD); art history (PhD); contemplative studies (PhD); English (MA, PhD); ghosticism, esotericism, mysticism (PhD); history (MA, PhD); humanities (MA, PhD); Islam (PhD); Jewish thought and philosophy (PhD); linguistics (MA, PhD); modern Christianity in thought and popular culture (PhD); philosophy (MA, PhD); psychology of religion (PhD); the Bible and beyond (PhD).

School of Social Sciences Offers archaeology (MA, PhD); cognitive sciences (MA, PhD); economics (PhD); energy economics (MEECON); industrial-organizational/social psychology (MA, PhD); political science (PhD); psychology (MA, PhD); social sciences (MA, MEECON, PhD); social-cultural anthropology (MA, PhD); sociology (PhD).

Shepherd School of Music Offers composition (MM, DMA); conducting (MM); musicology (MM); performance (MM, DMA); theory (MM).

Susanne M. Glasscock School of Continuing Studies Degree program information: Part-time and evening/weekend programs available. Part-time, evening/weekend. Offers liberal studies (MLS).

Wiess School of Natural Sciences Degree program information: Part-time programs available. Part-time. Offers biochemistry and cell biology (MA, PhD); chemistry (MA); earth science (MS, PhD); ecology and evolutionary biology (MA, MS, PhD); inorganic chemistry (PhD); mathematics (PhD); nanoscale physics (MS); natural sciences (MA, MS, MST, PhD); organic chemistry (PhD); physical chemistry (PhD); physics and astronomy (PhD); science teaching (MST). Electronic applications accepted.

Wiess School–Professional Science Master's Programs Offers bioscience research and health policy (MS); environmental analysis and decision making (MS); geophysics (MS); nanoscale physics (MS); professional science (MS).

Rice Quantum Institute Offers quantum physics (MS, PhD). Electronic applications accepted.

RICHMOND, THE AMERICAN INTERNATIONAL UNIVERSITY IN LONDON, Richmond, Surrey TW10 6JP, United Kingdom

General Information Independent, coed, comprehensive institution. *Graduate housing:* Room and/or apartments available on a first-come, first-served basis to single students; on-campus housing not available to married students. Housing application deadline: 8/1.

GRADUATE UNITS

MA in Art History Program ***Degree program information:*** Part-time programs available. Part-time. Offers art history (MA). Electronic applications accepted.

MA in International Relations Program ***Degree program information:*** Part-time programs available. Part-time. Offers international relations (MA). Electronic applications accepted.

RICHMONT GRADUATE UNIVERSITY, Atlanta, GA 30339

General Information Independent-religious, coed, graduate-only institution. *Enrollment by degree level:* 274 master's. *Graduate faculty:* 20 full-time (10 women), 42 part-time/adjunct (14 women). *Tuition, area resident:* Part-time $615 per credit hour. *Required fees:* $200 per semester. One-time fee: $250. *Student services:* Campus employment opportunities, campus safety program, career counseling, free psychological counseling, services for students with disabilities, writing training. *Library:* Richmont Graduate University Library plus 1 other. *Collection:* Books: 37,000 (physical), 15,000 (digital/electronic); Databases: 8.

Computer facilities: 14 computers available on campus for general student use. A campuswide network can be accessed from off campus. Online class registration is available.
Website: http://www.richmont.edu/

General Application Contact: Admissions, 888-924-6774, Fax: 866-363-4323, E-mail: admissions@richmont.edu.

GRADUATE UNITS

School of Counseling ***Financial support:*** Career-related internships or fieldwork, scholarships/grants, and unspecified assistantships available. Financial award application deadline: 5/1. In 2015, 61 master's awarded. *Degree program information:* Part-time and evening/weekend programs available. Part-time, evening/weekend. Offers clinical mental health counseling (MA); marriage and family therapy (MA). *Application deadline:* Applications are processed on a rolling basis. *Application fee:* $50. Electronic applications accepted. *Application Contact:* Admissions, 888-924-6774, Fax: 866-363-4323, E-mail: admissions@richmont.edu. *Dean of the School of Counseling,* Dr. Stephen P. Bradshaw, E-mail: sbradshaw@richmont.edu.

School of Ministry Students: 29 full-time (9 women), 16 part-time (10 women). Average age 38. *Financial support:* Scholarships/grants, tuition waivers (partial), and unspecified assistantships available. Financial award application deadline: 5/1; financial award applicants required to submit FAFSA. In 2015, 16 master's awarded. *Degree program information:* Part-time and evening/weekend programs available. Part-time, evening/weekend, 100% online, blended/hybrid learning. Offers ministry (MA); spiritual direction (Graduate Certificate); spiritual formation and direction (MA). *Application deadline:* For fall admission, 5/1 priority date for domestic students. Applications are processed on a rolling basis. *Application fee:* $50. Electronic applications accepted. *Application Contact:* Scottie Blackburn, Admissions Counselor, 404-835-6118, Fax: 404-239-9460, E-mail: sblackburn@richmont.edu. *Dean of the School of Ministry,* Dr. Micheal Steward, 404-835-6129, Fax: 404-239-9460, E-mail: msteward@richmont.edu.

RIDER UNIVERSITY, Lawrenceville, NJ 08648-3001

General Information Independent, coed, comprehensive institution.

GRADUATE UNITS

College of Business Administration ***Degree program information:*** Part-time and evening/weekend programs available. Part-time, evening/weekend. Offers accountancy (M Acc); business administration (EMBA, M Acc, MBA). Electronic applications accepted.

College of Liberal Arts, Education, and Sciences ***Degree program information:*** Part-time and evening/weekend programs available. Part-time, evening/weekend. Offers applied psychology (MA); business communication (MA). Electronic applications accepted.

Department of Graduate Education, Leadership and Counseling ***Degree program information:*** Part-time and evening/weekend programs available. Part-time, evening/weekend. Offers alternative route in special education (Certificate); business education (Certificate); counseling services (MA, Certificate, Ed S); curriculum, instruction and supervision (MA, Certificate); director of school counseling (Certificate); educational administration (MA, Certificate); elementary education (Certificate); English as a second language (Certificate); English education (Certificate); mathematics education (Certificate); organizational leadership (MA); preschool to grade 3 (Certificate); principal (Certificate); reading specialist (Certificate); reading/language arts (MA, Certificate); school administrator (Certificate); school counseling services (Certificate); school psychology (Certificate, Ed S); science education (Certificate); social studies education (Certificate); special education (MA, Certificate); supervisor (Certificate); teacher certification (Certificate); teacher of students with disabilities (Certificate); teacher of the handicapped (Certificate); teaching (MA); world languages (Certificate). Electronic applications accepted.

Westminster Choir College Offers choral conducting (MM); composition (MM); music (MAT, MM, MME, MVP); music education (MAT, MM, MME); organ performance (MM); piano accompanying and coaching (MM); piano pedagogy and performance (MM); piano performance (MM); sacred music (MM); vocal pedagogy and performance (MM); vocal training (MVP). Electronic applications accepted.

RIVIER UNIVERSITY, Nashua, NH 03060

General Information Independent-religious, coed, comprehensive institution. *Graduate housing:* On-campus housing not available.

GRADUATE UNITS

School of Graduate Studies ***Degree program information:*** Part-time programs available. Part-time. Offers business administration (MBA); clinical psychology (MS); computer information systems (MS); computer science (MS); curriculum and instruction (M Ed); early childhood education (M Ed); educational administration (M Ed); educational studies (M Ed); elementary education (M Ed); elementary education and general special education (M Ed); emotional and behavioral disorders (M Ed); English (MAT); experimental psychology (MS); general social education (M Ed); leadership and learning (Ed D, CAGS); learning disabilities (M Ed); learning disabilities and reading (M Ed); mathematics (MAT); mental health counseling (MA); reading (M Ed); school counseling (M Ed); social studies education (MAT); Spanish (MAT); writing and literature (MA). Electronic applications accepted.

Division of Nursing Degree program information: Part-time and evening/weekend programs available. Part-time, evening/weekend. Offers adult psychiatric/mental health practitioner (MS); family nurse practitioner (MS); nursing education (MS). Electronic applications accepted.

THE ROBERT E. WEBBER INSTITUTE FOR WORSHIP STUDIES, Orange Park, FL 32073

General Information Independent-religious, coed, graduate-only institution.

GRADUATE UNITS

Doctor of Worship Studies Program Offers worship studies (DWS).

Master of Worship Studies Program Offers worship studies (MWS).

ROBERT MORRIS UNIVERSITY, Moon Township, PA 15108-1189

General Information Independent, coed, university. *Enrollment:* 5,377 graduate, professional, and undergraduate students; 880 part-time matriculated graduate/professional students (490 women). *Enrollment by degree level:* 645 master's, 235 doctoral. *Graduate faculty:* 90 full-time (44 women), 16 part-time/adjunct (10 women). *Tuition, area resident:* Part-time $900 per credit. Part-time tuition and fees vary according to degree level and program. *Graduate housing:* On-campus housing not available. *Student services:* Campus employment opportunities, campus safety program, career counseling, exercise/wellness program, international student services, multicultural affairs office, services for students with disabilities. *Library:* Robert Morris University Library. *Collection:* Books: 96,055 (physical), 161,645 (digital/electronic); Serial titles: 244 (physical), 146 (digital/electronic); Databases: 72. Weekly public service hours: 91; study areas open 24 hours, 5–7 days a week.

Computer facilities: Computer purchase and lease plans are available. 300 computers available on campus for general student use. A campuswide network can be accessed from student residence rooms and from off campus. Online class registration, online payment are available.
Website: http://www.rmu.edu/

General Application Contact: Kellie L. Laurenzi, Associate Vice President, 412-397-5200, Fax: 412-397-2425, E-mail: graduateadmissions@rmu.edu.

GRADUATE UNITS

Graduate Studies Students: 880 part-time (490 women); includes 100 minority (56 Black or African American, non-Hispanic/Latino; 11 Asian, non-Hispanic/Latino; 3 Hispanic/Latino; 30 Two or more races, non-Hispanic/Latino), 71 international. Average age 34. 658 applicants, 45% accepted, 215 enrolled. *Faculty:* 90 full-time (44 women), 16 part-time/adjunct (10 women). *Financial support:* Research assistantships with partial tuition reimbursements, Federal Work-Study, institutionally sponsored loans, and unspecified assistantships available. Support available to part-time students. Financial award application deadline: 5/1; financial award applicants required to submit FAFSA. In 2015, 358 master's, 71 doctorates awarded. *Degree program information:* Part-time and evening/weekend programs available. Part-time, evening/weekend, online learning. *Application deadline:* For fall admission, 7/1 priority date for domestic and international students; for spring admission, 11/1 priority date for domestic and international students. Applications are processed on a rolling basis. *Application fee:* $35. Electronic applications accepted. *Application Contact:* Kellie L. Laurenzi, Associate Vice President, 412-397-5200, Fax: 412-397-5915, E-mail: laurenzi@rmu.edu. *Provost and Senior Vice President,* David L. Jamison, 412-397-6225, Fax: 412-397-3851, E-mail: jamison@rmu.edu.

School of Business Students: 195 part-time (82 women); includes 11 minority (4 Black or African American, non-Hispanic/Latino; 3 Asian, non-Hispanic/Latino; 4 Two or more races, non-Hispanic/Latino), 5 international. Average age 30. 144 applicants, 38% accepted, 44 enrolled. *Faculty:* 26 full-time (10 women), 3 part-time/adjunct (all women). *Financial support:* Research assistantships with partial tuition reimbursements, Federal Work-Study, institutionally sponsored loans, and unspecified assistantships available. Support available to part-time students. Financial award application deadline: 5/1; financial award applicants required to submit FAFSA. In 2015, 103 master's awarded. *Degree program information:* Part-time and evening/weekend programs available. Part-time, evening/weekend, online learning. Offers business administration (MBA); human resource management (MS); taxation (MS). *Application deadline:* For fall admission, 7/1 priority date for domestic and international students; for spring admission, 11/1 priority date for domestic and international students. Applications are processed on a rolling basis. *Application fee:* $35. Electronic applications accepted. *Application Contact:* Dr. Manmohan D. Chaubey, Director, Graduate Programs, 412-397-3537, E-mail: graduateadmissions@rmu.edu. *Acting Dean,* Dr. Lois D. Bryan, 412-397-6339, Fax: 412-397-2585, E-mail: bryan@rmu.edu.

School of Communications and Information Systems Students: 273 part-time (111 women); includes 45 minority (25 Black or African American, non-Hispanic/Latino; 6 Asian, non-Hispanic/Latino; 1 Hispanic/Latino; 13 Two or more races, non-Hispanic/Latino), 56 international. Average age 34. 253 applicants, 43% accepted, 65 enrolled. *Faculty:* 26 full-time (12 women), 4 part-time/adjunct (0 women). *Financial support:* Research assistantships with partial tuition reimbursements, institutionally sponsored loans, and unspecified assistantships available. Support available to part-time students. Financial award application deadline: 5/1. In 2015, 163 master's, 18 doctorates awarded. *Degree program information:* Part-time and evening/weekend programs available. Part-time, evening/weekend, online learning. Offers communication and information systems (MS); cyber security (MS); data analytics (MS); information security and assurance (MS); information systems and communications (D Sc); information systems management (MS); information technology project management (MS); Internet information systems (MS); organizational leadership (MS). *Application deadline:* For fall admission, 7/1 priority date for domestic and international students; for spring admission, 11/1 priority date for domestic and international students. Applications are processed on a rolling basis. *Application fee:* $35. Electronic applications accepted. *Application Contact:* Kellie L. Laurenzi, Associate Vice President, 412-397-5200, Fax: 412-397-5915, E-mail: graduateadmissions@rmu.edu. *Dean,* Ann Marie M. Le Blanc, 412-397-6433, Fax: 412-397-6469, E-mail: leblanc@rmu.edu.

School of Education and Social Sciences Students: 156 part-time (104 women); includes 14 minority (7 Black or African American, non-Hispanic/Latino; 7 Two or more races, non-Hispanic/Latino), 1 international. Average age 34. 63 applicants, 54% accepted, 24 enrolled. *Faculty:* 17 full-time (9 women), 3 part-time/adjunct (1 woman). In 2015, 49 master's, 26 doctorates awarded. *Degree program information:* Part-time and evening/weekend programs available. Part-time, evening/weekend, online learning. Offers business education (MS); counseling psychology (MS); education (Postbaccalaureate Certificate); higher education (MS); instructional leadership (MS); instructional management and leadership (PhD); special education (MS). *Application deadline:* For fall admission, 7/1 priority date for domestic and international students; for spring admission, 11/1 priority date for domestic and international students. Applications are processed on a rolling basis. *Application fee:* $35. Electronic applications accepted. *Dean,* Dr. Mary Ann Rafoth, 412-397-6020, Fax: 412-397-6044, E-mail: rafoth@rmu.edu.

School of Engineering, Mathematics and Science Students: 33 part-time (6 women); includes 4 minority (2 Black or African American, non-Hispanic/Latino; 1 Asian, non-Hispanic/Latino; 1 Hispanic/Latino), 8 international. Average age 31. 47 applicants, 21% accepted, 6 enrolled. *Faculty:* 6 full-time (1 woman). *Financial support:* Federal Work-Study, institutionally sponsored loans, and unspecified assistantships available. Financial award application deadline: 5/1; financial award applicants required to submit FAFSA. In 2015, 34 master's awarded. *Degree program information:* Part-time and evening/weekend programs available. Part-time, evening/weekend. Offers engineering management (MS). *Application deadline:* For fall admission, 7/1 priority date for domestic and international students; for spring admission, 11/1 priority date for domestic and international students. Applications are processed on a rolling basis. *Application fee:* $35. Electronic applications accepted. *Dean,* Dr. Maria V. Kalevitch, 412-397-4020, Fax: 412-397-2472, E-mail: kalevitch@rmu.edu.

School of Nursing and Health Sciences Students: 222 part-time (186 women); includes 26 minority (18 Black or African American, non-Hispanic/Latino; 1 Asian, non-Hispanic/Latino; 1 Hispanic/Latino; 6 Two or more races, non-Hispanic/Latino), 1 international. Average age 37. 151 applicants, 59% accepted, 76 enrolled. *Faculty:* 15 full-time (12 women), 6 part-time/adjunct (all women). *Financial support:* Federal Work-Study, institutionally sponsored loans, and unspecified assistantships available. Financial award application deadline: 5/1; financial award applicants required to submit FAFSA. In 2015, 10 master's, 30 doctorates awarded. *Degree program information:* Part-time and evening/weekend programs available. Part-time, evening/weekend. Offers nursing and health sciences (MSN, DNP). *Application deadline:* For fall admission, 7/1 priority date for domestic and international students; for spring admission, 11/1 priority date for domestic and international students. Applications are processed on a rolling basis. *Application fee:* $35. Electronic applications accepted. *Dean,* Dr. Valerie M. Howard, 412-397-6801, Fax: 412-397-3277, E-mail: howardv@rmu.edu.

ROBERT MORRIS UNIVERSITY ILLINOIS, Chicago, IL 60605

General Information Independent, coed, comprehensive institution. *Enrollment:* 3,056 graduate, professional, and undergraduate students; 237 full-time matriculated graduate/professional students (122 women), 180 part-time matriculated graduate/professional students (109 women). *Enrollment by degree level:* 417 master's. *Graduate faculty:* 5 full-time (2 women), 27 part-time/adjunct (8 women). *Student services:* Campus employment opportunities, career counseling, exercise/wellness program, free psychological counseling, international student services, services for students with disabilities, writing training. *Library:* Information Technology Library. *Collection:* Books: 161,574 (physical), 41,676 (digital/electronic); Serial titles: 4 (physical); Databases: 43. Weekly public service hours: 74; students can reserve study rooms.

Computer facilities: 1,360 computers available on campus for general student use. A campuswide network can be accessed from student residence rooms. Online class registration, online credentials, online payments, online student accounts, online degree audit are available.
Website: http://www.robertmorris.edu/

General Application Contact: Danielle Naffziger, Vice President of Marketing and Graduate Enrollment, 312-935-4532, Fax: 312-935-6020, E-mail: dnaffziger@robertmorris.edu.

GRADUATE UNITS

Morris Graduate School of Management Students: 208 full-time (113 women), 141 part-time (76 women); includes 206 minority (113 Black or African American, non-Hispanic/Latino; 1 American Indian or Alaska Native, non-Hispanic/Latino; 15 Asian, non-Hispanic/Latino; 70 Hispanic/Latino; 1 Native Hawaiian or other Pacific Islander, non-Hispanic/Latino; 6 Two or more races, non-Hispanic/Latino), 22 international. Average age 33. 206 applicants, 58% accepted, 99 enrolled. *Faculty:* 9 full-time (4 women), 28 part-time/adjunct (10 women). *Financial support:* In 2015–16, 434 students received support. Federal Work-Study, scholarships/grants, and unspecified assistantships available. Support available to part-time students. Financial award applicants required to submit FAFSA. In 2015, 249 master's awarded. *Degree program information:* Part-time and evening/weekend programs available. Part-time, evening/weekend. Offers accounting (MBA); accounting/finance (MBA); business analytics (MIS); design and media (MM); educational technology (MM); health care administration (MM); higher education administration (MM); human resource management (MBA); information security (MIS); information systems (MBA, MIS); law enforcement administration (MM); management (MBA); management/finance (MBA); management/human resource management (MBA); mobile computing (MIS); sports administration (MM). *Application deadline:* Applications are processed on a rolling basis. *Application fee:* $20 ($100 for international students). Electronic applications accepted. *Application Contact:* Danielle Naffziger, Vice President of Marketing and Graduate Enrollment, 312-935-4532, Fax: 312-935-6020, E-mail: dnaffziger@robertmorris.edu. *Dean,* Kayed Akkawi, 312-935-6050, Fax: 312-935-6020, E-mail: kakkawi@robertmorris.edu.

ROBERTS WESLEYAN COLLEGE, Rochester, NY 14624-1997

General Information Independent-religious, coed, comprehensive institution. *Enrollment:* 1,712 graduate, professional, and undergraduate students; 316 full-time matriculated graduate/professional students (255 women), 72 part-time matriculated graduate/professional students (63 women). *Enrollment by degree level:* 388 master's. *Graduate faculty:* 35 full-time (22 women), 47 part-time/adjunct (27 women). *Graduate housing:* Rooms and/or apartments available on a first-come, first-served basis to single and married students. *Student services:* Campus employment opportunities, campus safety program, career counseling, exercise/wellness program, international student services, multicultural affairs office, services for students with disabilities. *Library:* B. Thomas Golisano Library. *Collection:* Books: 144,185 (physical), 8,954 (digital/electronic); Databases: 106. Study areas open 24 hours, 5–7 days a week; students can reserve study rooms.

Computer facilities: 140 computers available on campus for general student use. A campuswide network can be accessed from student residence rooms and from off campus. Online class registration is available.
Website: http://www.roberts.edu/

General Application Contact: Office of Admissions, 800-777-4792, E-mail: age-admissions@roberts.edu.

GRADUATE UNITS

Department of Nursing Students: 66 full-time (64 women); includes 9 minority (6 Black or African American, non-Hispanic/Latino; 1 American Indian or Alaska Native, non-Hispanic/Latino; 2 Hispanic/Latino), 9 international. Average age 35. 53 applicants, 83% accepted, 41 enrolled. *Faculty:* 6 full-time (all women), 5 part-time/adjunct (3 women). *Financial support:* In 2015–16, 49 students received support. Scholarships/grants available. Financial award applicants required to submit FAFSA. In 2015, 2 master's awarded. *Degree program information:* Evening/weekend programs available. Evening/weekend, online learning. Offers nursing education (MSN); nursing leadership and administration (MSN). *Application deadline:* Applications are processed on a rolling basis. *Application fee:* $0. Electronic applications accepted. *Application Contact:* Brenda Mutton, Admissions Coordinator, 585-594-6686, E-mail: mutton_brenda@roberts.edu. *Chairperson/Director of Graduate Program,* Dr. Cheryl B. Crotser, 585-594-6668, E-mail: crotser_cheryl@roberts.edu.

Department of Social Work ***Financial support:*** Fellowships, career-related internships or fieldwork, scholarships/grants, and tuition waivers (partial) available. Financial award applicants required to submit FAFSA. Offers child and family practice (MSW); mental health practice (MSW). *Application deadline:* For fall admission, 4/1 priority date for domestic students. Applications are processed on a rolling basis. *Application fee:* $35. *Application Contact:* Beverly Keim, Assistant Director of Graduate Admissions, 585-594-6232, E-mail: keimb@roberts.edu. *Dean,* Dr. David Skiff, 585-594-6578, E-mail: skiffd@roberts.edu.

Graduate Business Programs ***Financial support:*** Applicants required to submit FAFSA. *Degree program information:* Evening/weekend programs available. Evening/weekend. Offers strategic leadership (MS); strategic marketing (MS). *Application deadline:* Applications are processed on a rolling basis. *Application fee:* $35. *Application Contact:* Office of Admissions, 800-777-4RWC, E-mail: admissions@roberts.edu. *Dean,* Dr. Steven Bovee, 585-594-6763, Fax: 716-594-6316, E-mail: bovees@roberts.edu.

Graduate Teacher Education Programs ***Financial support:*** Career-related internships or fieldwork available. Financial award application deadline: 9/1; financial award applicants required to submit FAFSA. *Degree program information:* Part-time and evening/weekend programs available. Part-time, evening/weekend. Offers adolescence and special education (M Ed); childhood and special education (M Ed); literacy education (M Ed); special education (M Ed). *Application deadline:* For fall admission, 6/1 for domestic and international students; for spring admission, 11/1 for domestic and international students; for summer admission, 3/1 for domestic and international students. Applications are processed on a rolling basis. Electronic applications accepted. *Application Contact:* Paul Ziegler, Director of Marketing and Recruitment, 585-594-6146, Fax: 585-594-6108, E-mail: ziegler_paul@roberts.edu. *Director,* Dr. Diana Abbott, 585-594-6936, E-mail: abbott_diana@roberts.edu.

Health Administration Programs Students: 73 full-time (60 women). Average age 34. *Faculty:* 2 full-time (0 women), 4 part-time/adjunct (all women). *Financial support:* Applicants required to submit FAFSA. In 2015, 23 master's awarded. *Degree program information:* Evening/weekend programs available. Evening/weekend, online learning. Offers health administration (MS); healthcare informatics administration (MS). *Application deadline:* Applications are processed on a rolling basis. *Application fee:* $35. *Application Contact:* Cheryl Johnson, Program Coordinator, 585-594-6452, Fax: 585-594-6940, E-mail: johnson_cheryl@roberts.edu. *Chair,* Joe McCarthy, 585-594-6990, Fax: 585-594-6940, E-mail: mccarthyj@roberts.edu.

ROCHESTER COLLEGE, Rochester Hills, MI 48307-2764

General Information Independent-religious, coed, comprehensive institution.

GRADUATE UNITS

Center for Missional Leadership Offers missional leadership (MRE).

ROCHESTER INSTITUTE OF TECHNOLOGY, Rochester, NY 14623-5603

General Information Independent, coed, comprehensive institution. CGS member. *Enrollment:* 16,640 graduate, professional, and undergraduate students; 2,188 full-time matriculated graduate/professional students (745 women), 905 part-time matriculated graduate/professional students (310 women). *Enrollment by degree level:* 2,859 master's, 210 doctoral, 24 other advanced degrees. *Tuition, area resident:* Full-time $41,084; part-time $1742 per credit hour. *Required fees:* $274. Tuition and fees vary according to course load and program. *Graduate housing:* Rooms and/or apartments available on a first-come, first-served basis to single and married students. Typical cost: $7162 per year ($12,274 including board) for single students; $7162 per year ($12,274 including board) for married students. Room and board charges vary according to board plan, campus/location and housing facility selected. *Student services:* Campus employment opportunities, campus safety program, career counseling, child daycare facilities, exercise/wellness program, free psychological counseling, grant writing training, international student services, low-cost health insurance, multicultural affairs office, services for students with disabilities, teacher training, writing training. *Library:* Wallace Memorial Library. *Collection:* Books: 429,176 (physical), 240,712 (digital/electronic); Serial titles: 58,293 (digital/electronic); Databases: 113. Weekly public service hours: 147; study areas open 24 hours, 5–7 days a week; students can reserve study rooms. *Research affiliation:* Ortho Clinical Diagnostics (simulation and mathematical modeling), Hewlett Packard (printing and packaging research and testing), Delphi (fuel cell technology), Toyota Corporation (systems engineering, supply chain, manufacturing), Corning Inc. (thin-film transistor (TFT) fabrication, device modeling, and performance), Library of Congress (image permanence, storage, and sustainable preservation).

Computer facilities: Computer purchase and lease plans are available. 2,500 computers available on campus for general student use. A campuswide network can be accessed from student residence rooms and from off campus. Online class registration, student account information are available.
Website: http://www.rit.edu/

General Application Contact: Diane Ellison, Associate Vice President, Graduate Enrollment Services, 585-475-2229, Fax: 585-475-7164, E-mail: gradinfo@rit.edu.

GRADUATE UNITS

Graduate Enrollment Services Students: 2,188 full-time (745 women), 905 part-time (310 women); includes 217 minority (59 Black or African American, non-Hispanic/Latino; 5 American Indian or Alaska Native, non-Hispanic/Latino; 63 Asian, non-Hispanic/Latino; 63 Hispanic/Latino; 27 Two or more races, non-Hispanic/Latino), 1,840 international. Average age 27. 6,659 applicants, 41% accepted, 962 enrolled. *Financial support:* In 2015–16, 1,686 students received support. Research assistantships, teaching assistantships, career-related internships or fieldwork, scholarships/grants, health care benefits, and unspecified assistantships available. Support available to part-time students. Financial award applicants required to submit FAFSA. In 2015, 782 master's, 25 doctorates, 47 other advanced degrees awarded. *Degree program information:* Part-time and evening/weekend programs available. Part-time, evening/weekend, online learning. *Application deadline:* Applications are processed on a rolling basis. *Application fee:* $60. Electronic applications accepted. *Associate Vice President,* Diane Ellison, 585-475-2229, Fax: 585-475-7164, E-mail: gradinfo@rit.edu.

College of Applied Science and Technology Students: 224 full-time (61 women), 147 part-time (61 women); includes 33 minority (14 Black or African American, non-Hispanic/Latino; 9 Asian, non-Hispanic/Latino; 6 Hispanic/Latino; 4 Two or more races, non-Hispanic/Latino), 234 international. Average age 28. 584 applicants, 61% accepted, 120 enrolled. *Financial support:* In 2015–16, 261 students received support. Research assistantships with partial tuition reimbursements available, teaching assistantships with partial tuition reimbursements available, career-related internships or fieldwork, scholarships/grants, and unspecified assistantships available. Support available to part-time students. Financial award applicants required to submit FAFSA. In 2015, 107 master's, 1 other advanced degree awarded. *Degree program information:* Part-time and evening/weekend programs available. Part-time, evening/weekend, 100% online, blended/hybrid learning. Offers applied science and technology (MS, Advanced Certificate); engineering technology (MS); environmental, health and safety management (MS); facility management (MS); hospitality and tourism management (MS); human resources development (MS); international hospitality and service innovation (MS, Advanced Certificate); manufacturing and mechanical systems integration (MS); organizational learning (Advanced Certificate); packaging science (MS); service leadership and innovation (MS); telecommunications engineering technology (MS); training, design and assessment (Advanced Certificate). *Application deadline:* Applications are processed on a rolling basis. *Application fee:* $60. Electronic applications accepted. *Application Contact:* Diane Ellison, Associate Vice President, Graduate Enrollment Services, 585-475-2229, Fax: 585-475-7164, E-mail: gradinfo@rit.edu. *Dean,* Dr. H. Fred Walker, 585-475-6439, E-mail: hfwast@rit.edu.

College of Health Sciences and Technology Students: 20 full-time (15 women), 15 part-time (9 women); includes 5 minority (4 Black or African American, non-Hispanic/Latino; 1 Asian, non-Hispanic/Latino), 1 international. Average age 31. 41 applicants, 41% accepted, 8 enrolled. *Financial support:* In 2015–16, 16 students received support. Research assistantships with partial tuition reimbursements available, teaching assistantships with partial tuition reimbursements available, career-related internships or fieldwork, scholarships/grants, and unspecified assistantships available. Support available to part-time students. Financial award applicants required to submit FAFSA. In 2015, 9 master's awarded. *Degree program information:* Part-time and evening/weekend programs available. Part-time, evening/weekend, 100% online. Offers health care finance (Advanced Certificate); health sciences and technology (MFA, MS, Advanced Certificate); health systems administration (MS, Advanced Certificate); medical illustration (MFA). *Application deadline:* Applications are processed on a rolling basis. *Application fee:* $60. Electronic applications accepted. *Application Contact:* Diane Ellison, Associate Vice President, Graduate Enrollment Services, 585-475-2229, Fax: 585-475-7164, E-mail: gradinfo@rit.edu. *Vice President and Dean, Institute and College of Health Sciences and Technology,* Dr. Daniel Ornt, 585-475-4017, Fax: 585-475-4330, E-mail: daniel.ornt@rit.edu.

College of Imaging Arts and Sciences Students: 190 full-time (118 women), 80 part-time (45 women); includes 21 minority (3 Black or African American, non-Hispanic/Latino; 8 Asian, non-Hispanic/Latino; 6 Hispanic/Latino; 4 Two or more races, non-Hispanic/Latino), 169 international. Average age 27. 729 applicants, 36% accepted, 92 enrolled. *Financial support:* In 2015–16, 163 students received support. Teaching assistantships with partial tuition reimbursements available, career-related internships or fieldwork, scholarships/grants, and unspecified assistantships available. Support available to part-time students. Financial award applicants required to submit FAFSA. In 2015, 90 master's awarded. *Degree program information:* Part-time programs available. Part-time, 100% online. Offers ceramics (MFA); film and animation (MFA); fine arts studio (MFA, Advanced Certificate); furniture design (MFA); glass (MFA); imaging arts and sciences (MFA, MS, MST, Advanced Certificate); imaging arts, photography and related media (MFA); industrial design (MFA); metals and jewelry design (MFA); non-toxic printmaking (Advanced Certificate); print media (MS); user experience design and development (Advanced Certificate); visual arts-all grades (MST); visual communication design (MFA). *Application deadline:* For fall admission, 2/15 priority date for domestic and international students. Applications are processed on a rolling basis. *Application fee:* $60. Electronic applications accepted. *Application Contact:* Diane Ellison, Associate Vice President, Graduate Enrollment Services, 585-475-2229, Fax: 585-475-7164, E-mail: gradinfo@rit.edu. *Dean,* Dr. Lorraine Justice, 585-475-2733, E-mail: glg8801@rit.edu.

College of Liberal Arts Students: 56 full-time (39 women), 28 part-time (15 women); includes 13 minority (6 Black or African American, non-Hispanic/Latino; 1 American Indian or Alaska Native, non-Hispanic/Latino; 1 Asian, non-Hispanic/Latino; 5 Hispanic/Latino), 20 international. Average age 27. 118 applicants, 44% accepted, 32 enrolled. *Financial support:* In 2015–16, 49 students received support. Research assistantships with partial tuition reimbursements available, teaching assistantships with partial tuition reimbursements available, career-related internships or fieldwork, scholarships/grants, and unspecified assistantships available. Support available to part-time students. Financial award applicants required to submit FAFSA. In 2015, 32 master's, 13 other advanced degrees awarded. *Degree program information:* Part-time programs available. Part-time, 100% online. Offers communication and digital media (Advanced Certificate); communication and media technologies (MS); criminal justice (MS); engineering psychology (Advanced Certificate); experimental psychology (MS); liberal arts (MS, Advanced Certificate); public policy (MS); school psychology (MS, Advanced Certificate); science, technology and public policy (MS). *Application deadline:* For fall admission, 2/15 priority date for domestic and international students; for spring admission, 12/15 priority date for domestic and international students. Applications are processed on a rolling basis. *Application fee:* $60. Electronic applications accepted. *Application Contact:* Diane Ellison, Associate Vice President, Graduate Enrollment Services, 585-475-2229, Fax: 585-475-7164, E-mail: gradinfo@rit.edu. *Dean,* Dr. James Winebrake, 585-475-2929, Fax: 585-475-7120, E-mail: libarts@rit.edu.

College of Science Students: 189 full-time (71 women), 122 part-time (46 women); includes 33 minority (6 Black or African American, non-Hispanic/Latino; 11 Asian, non-Hispanic/Latino; 8 Hispanic/Latino; 8 Two or more races, non-Hispanic/Latino), 124 international. Average age 28. 367 applicants, 40% accepted, 73 enrolled. *Financial support:* In 2015–16, 149 students received support. Research assistantships with tuition reimbursements available, teaching assistantships with tuition reimbursements available, career-related internships or fieldwork, institutionally sponsored loans, scholarships/grants, unspecified assistantships, and health care benefits (for PhD program only) available. Support available to part-time students. Financial award applicants required to submit FAFSA. In 2015, 49 master's, 9 doctorates, 2 other advanced degrees awarded. *Degree program information:* Part-time and evening/weekend programs available. Part-time, evening/weekend, 100% online. Offers applied and computational mathematics (MS); applied statistics (MS, Advanced Certificate); astrophysical science and technology (MS, PhD); bioinformatics (MS); chemistry (MS); color science (MS, PhD); environmental science (MS); imaging science (MS, PhD); life sciences (MS); materials science and engineering (MS); physics and astronomy (MS, PhD); science (MS, PhD, Advanced Certificate). *Application deadline:* For fall admission, 2/15 priority date for domestic and international students; for spring admission, 12/15 priority date for domestic and international students. Applications are processed on a rolling basis. *Application fee:* $60. Electronic applications accepted. *Application Contact:* Diane Ellison, Associate Vice President, Graduate Enrollment Services, 585-475-2229, Fax: 585-475-7164, E-mail: gradinfo@rit.edu. *Dean,* Dr. Sophia Maggelakis, 585-475-5221, Fax: 585-475-2398, E-mail: science@rit.edu.

Golisano College of Computing and Information Sciences Students: 704 full-time (185 women), 149 part-time (28 women); includes 30 minority (6 Black or African American, non-Hispanic/Latino; 1 American Indian or Alaska Native, non-Hispanic/Latino; 12 Asian, non-Hispanic/Latino; 8 Hispanic/Latino; 3 Two or more races, non-Hispanic/Latino), 717 international. Average age 25. 2,165 applicants, 40% accepted, 262 enrolled. *Financial support:* In 2015–16, 729 students received support. Research assistantships with tuition reimbursements available, teaching assistantships with tuition reimbursements available, career-related internships or fieldwork, scholarships/grants, unspecified assistantships, and health care benefits (for PhD program only) available. Support available to part-time students. Financial award applicants required to submit FAFSA. In 2015, 190 master's, 7 doctorates, 20 other advanced degrees awarded. *Degree program information:* Part-time and evening/weekend programs available. Part-time, evening/weekend, 100% online. Offers big data analytics (Advanced Certificate); computer science (MS, Advanced Certificate); computing and information sciences (MS, PhD, Advanced Certificate); computing security (MS); game design and development (MS); human computer interaction (MS); information assurance (Advanced Certificate); information sciences and technologies (MS); medical informatics (MS); networking and systems administration (MS); networking, planning and design (Advanced Certificate); software engineering (MS); Web development (Advanced Certificate). *Application* *deadline:* For fall admission, 2/15 priority date for domestic and international students; for spring admission, 12/15 priority date for domestic and international students. Applications are processed on a rolling basis. *Application fee:* $60. Electronic applications accepted. *Application Contact:* Diane Ellison, Associate Vice President, Graduate Enrollment Services, 585-475-2229, Fax: 585-475-7164, E-mail: gradinfo@rit.edu. *Interim Dean,* Dr. Anne Haake, 585-475-7203, Fax: 585-475-4775, E-mail: gccis-email@rit.edu.

Golisano Institute for Sustainability Students: 82 full-time (40 women), 11 part-time (3 women); includes 6 minority (1 Black or African American, non-Hispanic/Latino; 1 Asian, non-Hispanic/Latino; 2 Hispanic/Latino; 2 Two or more races, non-Hispanic/Latino), 47 international. Average age 28. 141 applicants, 55% accepted, 24 enrolled. *Financial support:* In 2015–16, 79 students received support. Research assistantships with tuition reimbursements available, teaching assistantships with tuition reimbursements available, career-related internships or fieldwork, scholarships/grants, unspecified assistantships, and health care benefits (for PhD program only) available. Support available to part-time students. Financial award applicants required to submit FAFSA. In 2015, 10 master's, 1 doctorate awarded. *Degree program information:* Part-time programs available. Part-time. Offers architecture (M Arch); sustainability (PhD); sustainable systems (MS). *Application deadline:* For fall admission, 2/15 priority date for domestic and international students; for spring admission, 12/15 priority date for domestic and international students. Applications are processed on a rolling basis. *Application fee:* $60. Electronic applications accepted. *Application Contact:* Diane Ellison, Associate Vice President, Graduate Enrollment Services, 585-475-2229, Fax: 585-475-7164, E-mail: gradinfo@rit.edu. *Associate Provost and Director,* Dr. Nabil Nasr, 585-475-5101, E-mail: info@sustainability.rit.edu.

Kate Gleason College of Engineering Students: 447 full-time (75 women), 199 part-time (32 women); includes 39 minority (10 Black or African American, non-Hispanic/Latino; 12 Asian, non-Hispanic/Latino; 17 Hispanic/Latino), 393 international. Average age 26. 1,805 applicants, 34% accepted, 171 enrolled. *Financial support:* In 2015–16, 442 students received support. Fellowships with tuition reimbursements available, research assistantships with tuition reimbursements available, teaching assistantships with tuition reimbursements available, career-related internships or fieldwork, scholarships/grants, tuition waivers (full and partial), unspecified assistantships, and health care benefits (for PhD program only) available. Support available to part-time students. Financial award applicants required to submit FAFSA. In 2015, 153 master's, 8 doctorates awarded. *Degree program information:* Part-time and evening/weekend programs available. Part-time, evening/weekend, 100% online. Offers computer engineering (MS); electrical and microelectronic engineering (ME, MS); electrical engineering (MS); engineering (ME, MS, PhD, Advanced Certificate); engineering management (ME); industrial and systems engineering (ME, MS); Lean Six Sigma (Advanced Certificate); manufacturing leadership (MS); mechanical engineering (ME, MS); microelectronic engineering (MS); microelectronic manufacturing engineering (ME); microsystems engineering (PhD); product development (MS); statistical quality (Advanced Certificate); sustainable engineering (ME, MS). *Application deadline:* For fall admission, 2/15 priority date for domestic and international students. Applications are processed on a rolling basis. *Application fee:* $60. Electronic applications accepted. *Application Contact:* Diane Ellison, Associate Vice President, Graduate Enrollment Services, 585-475-2229, Fax: 585-475-7164, E-mail: gradinfo@rit.edu. *Dean,* Dr. Doreen Edwards, 585-475-2145, Fax: 585-475-6879, E-mail: coe@rit.edu.

National Technical Institute for the Deaf Students: 34 full-time (29 women), 2 part-time (1 woman); includes 4 minority (1 American Indian or Alaska Native, non-Hispanic/Latino; 2 Hispanic/Latino; 1 Two or more races, non-Hispanic/Latino), 3 international. Average age 30. 33 applicants, 52% accepted, 15 enrolled. *Financial support:* In 2015–16, 31 students received support. Fellowships with partial tuition reimbursements available, research assistantships with partial tuition reimbursements available, career-related internships or fieldwork, scholarships/grants, and unspecified assistantships available. Support available to part-time students. Financial award applicants required to submit FAFSA. In 2015, 18 master's awarded. *Degree program information:* Part-time and evening/weekend programs available. Part-time, evening/weekend, blended/hybrid learning. Offers deaf studies (MS); health care interpretation (MS); secondary education for the deaf and hard of hearing (MS). *Application deadline:* For fall admission, 2/15 priority date for domestic and international students. Applications are processed on a rolling basis. *Application fee:* $60. Electronic applications accepted. *Application Contact:* Diane Ellison, Assistant Vice President, Graduate Enrollment Services, 585-475-2229, Fax: 585-475-7164, E-mail: gradinfo@rit.edu. *President,* Dr. Gerard J. Buckley, 585-475-6317, Fax: 585-475-5978, E-mail: gbuckley@ntid.rit.edu.

Saunders College of Business Students: 180 full-time (76 women), 103 part-time (42 women); includes 17 minority (1 Black or African American, non-Hispanic/Latino; 1 American Indian or Alaska Native, non-Hispanic/Latino; 5 Asian, non-Hispanic/Latino; 7 Hispanic/Latino; 3 Two or more races, non-Hispanic/Latino), 92 international. Average age 30. 620 applicants, 52% accepted, 148 enrolled. *Financial support:* In 2015–16, 133 students received support. Research assistantships with partial tuition reimbursements available, teaching assistantships with partial tuition reimbursements available, career-related internships or fieldwork, Federal Work-Study, scholarships/grants, and unspecified assistantships available. Support available to part-time students. Financial award applicants required to submit FAFSA. In 2015, 101 master's awarded. *Degree program information:* Part-time and evening/weekend programs available. Part-time, evening/weekend, 100% online, blended/hybrid learning. Offers accounting (MBA, MS); business (Exec MBA, MBA, MS); business administration (MBA); computational finance (MS); entrepreneurship and innovative ventures (MS); executive business administration (Exec MBA); finance (MS); management (MS); marketing (MBA). *Application deadline:* Applications are processed on a rolling basis. *Application fee:* $60. Electronic applications accepted. *Application Contact:* Diane Ellison, Associate Vice President, Graduate Enrollment Services, 585-475-2229, Fax: 585-475-7164, E-mail: gradinfo@rit.edu. *Dean,* Dr. Jacqueline Mozrall, 585-475-6025, E-mail: gradbus@saunders.rit.edu.

School of Individualized Study Students: 31 full-time (12 women), 49 part-time (28 women); includes 10 minority (7 Black or African American, non-Hispanic/Latino; 1 American Indian or Alaska Native, non-Hispanic/Latino; 2 Hispanic/Latino), 37 international. Average age 32. 56 applicants, 41% accepted, 17 enrolled. *Financial support:* In 2015–16, 12 students received support. Career-related internships or fieldwork, scholarships/grants, and unspecified assistantships available. Support available to part-time students. Financial award applicants required to submit FAFSA. In 2015, 23 master's, 11 other advanced degrees awarded. *Degree program information:* Part-time and evening/weekend programs available. Part-time, evening/weekend, 100% online, blended/hybrid learning. Offers individualized studies (MS, Advanced Certificate); professional studies (MS); project management (Advanced Certificate). *Application deadline:* Applications are processed on a rolling basis. *Application fee:* $60. Electronic applications accepted. *Application Contact:* Diane Ellison, Associate Vice President, Graduate Enrollment Services, 585-475-2229, Fax: 585-475-7164, E-mail: gradinfo@rit.edu. *Executive Director,* Dr. James Hall, 585-475-2295, Fax: 585-475-6292, E-mail: sois@rit.edu.

THE ROCKEFELLER UNIVERSITY, New York, NY 10021-6399

General Information Independent, coed, graduate-only institution. CGS member. *Enrollment by degree level:* 15 master's, 194 doctoral. *Graduate faculty:* 73 full-time (10 women). *Graduate housing:* Rooms and/or apartments guaranteed to single and married students. Housing application deadline: 6/1. *Student services:* Campus safety program, career counseling, child daycare facilities, exercise/wellness program, free psychological counseling, grant writing training, low-cost health insurance, teacher training. *Library:* Rita and Frits Markus Library. *Collection:* Books: 108,225 (digital/electronic). Weekly public service hours: 40; study areas open 24 hours, 5–7 days a week.

Computer facilities: 32 computers available on campus for general student use. A campuswide network can be accessed from student residence rooms and from off campus. Online class registration is available.
Website: http://www.rockefeller.edu/

General Application Contact: Kristen Cullen, Graduate Admissions Administrator/Registrar, 212-327-8086, Fax: 212-327-8505, E-mail: phd@rockefeller.edu.

GRADUATE UNITS

Graduate Program in Biomedical Sciences Students: 209 full-time (84 women); includes 38 minority (3 Black or African American, non-Hispanic/Latino; 18 Asian, non-Hispanic/Latino; 17 Hispanic/Latino), 78 international. Average age 25. 755 applicants, 10% accepted, 22 enrolled. *Faculty:* 72 full-time (11 women). *Financial support:* In 2015–16, 209 students received support. Fellowships with full tuition reimbursements available, institutionally sponsored loans, scholarships/grants, traineeships, and health care benefits available. In 2015, 9 master's, 28 doctorates awarded. Offers biomedical sciences (MS, PhD). *Application deadline:* For fall and winter admission, 12/1 for domestic and international students. *Application fee:* $50. Electronic applications accepted. *Application Contact:* Kristen Cullen, Graduate Admissions Administrator/Registrar, 212-327-8086, Fax: 212-327-8505, E-mail: phd@rockefeller.edu. *Dean of Graduate and Postgraduate Studies/Vice President,* Dr. Sidney Strickland, 212-327-8086, Fax: 212-327-8505, E-mail: phd@rockefeller.edu.

ROCKFORD UNIVERSITY, Rockford, IL 61108-2393

General Information Independent, coed, comprehensive institution. *Graduate housing:* Room and/or apartments available on a first-come, first-served basis to single students; on-campus housing not available to married students.

GRADUATE UNITS

Graduate Studies ***Degree program information:*** Part-time and evening/weekend programs available. Part-time, evening/weekend. Offers business administration (MBA); early childhood education (MAT); elementary education (MAT); instructional strategies (MAT); reading (MAT); secondary education (MAT); special education (MAT). Electronic applications accepted.

ROCKHURST UNIVERSITY, Kansas City, MO 64110-2561

General Information Independent-religious, coed, comprehensive institution. *Enrollment:* 2,825 graduate, professional, and undergraduate students; 403 full-time matriculated graduate/professional students (276 women), 345 part-time matriculated graduate/professional students (149 women). *Enrollment by degree level:* 579 master's, 140 doctoral, 29 other advanced degrees. *Graduate faculty:* 50 full-time (34 women), 38 part-time/adjunct (29 women). *Graduate housing:* Room and/or apartments available on a first-come, first-served basis to single students; on-campus housing not available to married students. *Student services:* Campus employment opportunities, campus safety program, career counseling, free psychological counseling, international student services, services for students with disabilities, teacher training. *Library:* Greenlease Library. *Collection:* Books: 182,393 (physical), 153,518 (digital/electronic); Serial titles: 23 (physical), 71,330 (digital/electronic); Databases: 116. Weekly public service hours: 85.

Computer facilities: 270 computers available on campus for general student use. A campuswide network can be accessed from student residence rooms. Online class registration, campus portal and mobile application are available.
Website: http://www.rockhurst.edu/

General Application Contact: Cheryl Hooper, Director of Graduate Recruitment, 816-501-4097, Fax: 816-501-4241, E-mail: graduate.admission@rockhurst.edu.

GRADUATE UNITS

College of Health and Human Services Students: 281 full-time (231 women), 77 part-time (58 women); includes 32 minority (10 Black or African American, non-Hispanic/Latino; 1 American Indian or Alaska Native, non-Hispanic/Latino; 5 Asian, non-Hispanic/Latino; 11 Hispanic/Latino; 5 Two or more races, non-Hispanic/Latino), 1 international. 819 applicants, 57% accepted, 148 enrolled. *Faculty:* 31 full-time (30 women), 20 part-time/adjunct (18 women). *Financial support:* Applicants required to submit FAFSA. In 2015, 124 master's, 48 doctorates awarded. *Degree program information:* Part-time and evening/weekend programs available. Part-time, evening/weekend. Offers communication sciences and disorders (MS); education (M Ed); health and human services (M Ed, MOT, MS, DPT); occupational therapy (MOT); physical therapy (DPT). *Application deadline:* Applications are processed on a rolling basis. *Application fee:* $25. Electronic applications accepted. *Application Contact:* Cheryl Hooper, Director of Graduate Admission, 816-501-4097, Fax: 816-501-4241, E-mail: cheryl.hooper@rockhurst.edu. *Interim Dean,* Dr. Michael Clump, 816-501-4767, E-mail: michael.clump@rockhurst.edu.

Helzberg School of Management Students: 122 full-time (45 women), 268 part-time (91 women); includes 61 minority (23 Black or African American, non-Hispanic/Latino; 1 American Indian or Alaska Native, non-Hispanic/Latino; 27 Asian, non-Hispanic/Latino; 9 Hispanic/Latino; 1 Two or more races, non-Hispanic/Latino), 7 international. 288 applicants, 74% accepted, 119 enrolled. *Faculty:* 19 full-time (4 women), 18 part-time/adjunct (11 women). *Financial support:* Career-related internships or fieldwork available. Support available to part-time students. Financial award application deadline: 4/1; financial award applicants required to submit FAFSA. In 2015, 115 master's, 16 other advanced degrees awarded. *Degree program information:* Part-time and evening/weekend programs available. Part-time, evening/weekend. Offers accounting (MBA); business intelligence (MBA, Certificate); data science (MBA, Certificate); entrepreneurship (MBA); finance (MBA); fundraising leadership (MBA, Certificate); healthcare management (MBA, Certificate); human capital (Certificate); international business (Certificate); management (MBA, Certificate); nonprofit administration

(Certificate); organizational development (Certificate); science leadership (Certificate). *Application deadline:* For fall admission, 7/25 priority date for domestic students; for spring admission, 12/15 priority date for domestic students. Applications are processed on a rolling basis. *Application fee:* $25. Electronic applications accepted. *Application Contact:* Matthew Honeycutt, Director of MBA Advising, 816-501-4823, E-mail: matthew.honeycutt@rockhurst.edu. *Dean*, Cheryl McConnell, 816-501-4201, Fax: 816-501-4650, E-mail: cheryl.mcconnell@rockhurst.edu.

ROCKY MOUNTAIN COLLEGE, Billings, MT 59102-1796

General Information Independent-religious, coed, comprehensive institution. *Enrollment:* 1,035 graduate, professional, and undergraduate students; 96 full-time matriculated graduate/professional students (57 women), 1 (woman) part-time matriculated graduate/professional student. *Enrollment by degree level:* 97 master's. *Graduate faculty:* 8 full-time (4 women), 6 part-time/adjunct (2 women). *Graduate housing:* Rooms and/or apartments available on a first-come, first-served basis to single and married students. Typical cost: $3692 per year ($8004 including board) for single students; $4804 per year ($9116 including board) for married students. Room and board charges vary according to board plan and housing facility selected. *Student services:* Campus employment opportunities, campus safety program, career counseling, free psychological counseling, international student services, services for students with disabilities, teacher training. *Library:* Paul M. Adams Memorial Library. *Collection:* Books: 54,453 (physical), 4,108 (digital/electronic); Serial titles: 384 (physical), 33,265 (digital/electronic); Databases: 64. Weekly public service hours: 88.

Computer facilities: 113 computers available on campus for general student use. A campuswide network can be accessed from student residence rooms and from off campus. Online class registration is available.
Website: http://www.rocky.edu/

General Application Contact: Austin Mapston, Dean of Enrollment Services, 406-657-1026, Fax: 406-657-1189, E-mail: admissions@rocky.edu.

GRADUATE UNITS

Program in Accountancy Students: 1 (woman) part-time. Average age 26. *Faculty:* 2 full-time (0 women). *Financial support:* Applicants required to submit FAFSA. In 2015, 8 master's awarded. *Degree program information:* Part-time programs available. Part-time. Offers accountancy (M Acc). *Application deadline:* Applications are processed on a rolling basis. *Application fee:* $35 ($40 for international students). Electronic applications accepted. *Application Contact:* Austin Mapston, Dean of Enrollment Services, 406-657-1026, Fax: 406-657-1189, E-mail: admissions@rocky.edu. *Professor of Business Administration and Economics*, Anthony Piltz, 406-657-1069, E-mail: piltza@rocky.edu.

Program in Educational Leadership Students: 23 full-time (10 women); includes 1 minority (American Indian or Alaska Native, non-Hispanic/Latino). Average age 36. *Faculty:* 2 full-time (both women), 3 part-time/adjunct (1 woman). *Financial support:* Applicants required to submit FAFSA. In 2015, 23 master's awarded. Offers educational leadership (M Ed). *Application deadline:* Applications are processed on a rolling basis. *Application fee:* $35 ($40 for international students). Electronic applications accepted. *Director of Educational Leadership and Distance Education*, Dr. Stevie Schmitz, 406-657-1134, E-mail: schmitzs@rocky.edu.

Program in Physician Assistant Studies Students: 73 full-time (47 women); includes 12 minority (1 Black or African American, non-Hispanic/Latino; 6 Hispanic/Latino; 5 Two or more races, non-Hispanic/Latino). Average age 29. *Faculty:* 4 full-time (2 women), 3 part-time/adjunct (1 woman). *Financial support:* Applicants required to submit FAFSA. In 2015, 31 master's awarded. Offers physician assistant studies (MPAS). *Application deadline:* Applications are processed on a rolling basis. *Application fee:* $35. Electronic applications accepted. *Application Contact:* Calley Thompson, PA Admissions Counselor, 406-657-1198, E-mail: calley.thompson@rocky.edu. *Program Director*, Heather Heggem, 406-657-1190, E-mail: heather.heggem@rocky.edu.

ROCKY MOUNTAIN COLLEGE OF ART + DESIGN, Lakewood, CO 80214

General Information Proprietary, coed, comprehensive institution.

GRADUATE UNITS

Program in Education, Leadership + Emerging Technologies Online learning. Offers education, leadership and emerging technologies (MA).

ROCKY MOUNTAIN UNIVERSITY OF HEALTH PROFESSIONS, Provo, UT 84606

General Information Proprietary, coed, graduate-only institution. *Research affiliation:* Aegis Corporation.

GRADUATE UNITS

Doctor of Nursing Practice Program Offers nursing practice (DNP).

Doctor of Science Program in Clinical Electrophysiology Online learning. Offers clinical electrophysiology (D Sc).

Program in Occupational Therapy Online learning. Offers occupational therapy (OTD). Electronic applications accepted.

Program in Physician Assistant Studies Offers physician assistant studies (MPAS).

Program in Speech-Language Pathology Offers speech-language pathology (Clin Sc D).

Programs in Physical Therapy Offers physical therapy (DPT, TDPT).

ROCKY VISTA UNIVERSITY, Parker, CO 80134

General Information Proprietary, coed, graduate-only institution.

GRADUATE UNITS

College of Osteopathic Medicine Offers osteopathic medicine (DO).

ROGER WILLIAMS UNIVERSITY, Bristol, RI 02809

General Information Independent, coed, comprehensive institution. *Enrollment:* 4,808 graduate, professional, and undergraduate students; 185 full-time matriculated graduate/professional students (94 women), 61 part-time matriculated graduate/professional students (28 women). *Enrollment by degree level:* 245 master's, 1 other advanced degree. *Graduate faculty:* 28 full-time (10 women), 17 part-time/adjunct (4 women). *Graduate housing:* Room and/or apartments available on a first-come, first-served basis to single students; on-campus housing not available to married students. Housing application deadline: 5/1. *Student services:* Campus employment opportunities, campus safety program, career counseling, exercise/wellness program, free psychological counseling, international student services, low-cost health insurance, multicultural affairs office, services for students with disabilities, teacher training, writing training. *Library:* Roger Williams University Library plus 1 other. *Collection:* Books: 234,065 (physical), 533,150 (digital/electronic); Databases: 168.

Computer facilities: 540 computers available on campus for general student use. A campuswide network can be accessed from student residence rooms and from off campus. Online class registration is available.
Website: http://www.rwu.edu/

General Application Contact: Marcus Hanscom, Graduate Admission Director, 401-254-3345, Fax: 401-254-3557, E-mail: mhanscom@rwu.edu.

GRADUATE UNITS

Feinstein College of Arts and Sciences Students: 34 full-time (27 women); includes 3 minority (1 Asian, non-Hispanic/Latino; 2 Hispanic/Latino). Average age 25. 73 applicants, 75% accepted, 18 enrolled. *Faculty:* 9 full-time (4 women). *Financial support:* In 2015–16, 9 students received support. Federal Work-Study and scholarships/grants available. Financial award application deadline: 6/15; financial award applicants required to submit FAFSA. In 2015, 16 master's awarded. *Degree program information:* Part-time and evening/weekend programs available. Part-time, evening/weekend, online learning. Offers clinical psychology (MA); forensic psychology (MA). *Application deadline:* For fall admission, 3/15 priority date for domestic students. *Application fee:* $50. Electronic applications accepted. *Application Contact:* Lori Vales, Director of Graduate Admissions, 401-254-3345, Fax: 401-254-3557, E-mail: gradadmit@rwu.edu. *Dean*, Robert Eisinger, 401-254-3149, E-mail: reisinger@rwu.edu.

School of Architecture, Art and Historic Preservation Students: 93 full-time (33 women), 2 part-time (0 women); includes 14 minority (2 Black or African American, non-Hispanic/Latino; 1 Asian, non-Hispanic/Latino; 8 Hispanic/Latino; 3 Two or more races, non-Hispanic/Latino), 5 international. Average age 25. 74 applicants, 92% accepted, 42 enrolled. *Faculty:* 9 full-time (1 woman), 8 part-time/adjunct (1 woman). *Financial support:* In 2015–16, 84 students received support. Federal Work-Study and scholarships/grants available. Financial award application deadline: 6/15; financial award applicants required to submit FAFSA. In 2015, 47 master's awarded. Offers architecture (M Arch); art and architectural history (MA); historical preservation (MS). *Application deadline:* For fall admission, 4/1 priority date for domestic students. *Application fee:* $50. Electronic applications accepted. *Application Contact:* Marcus Hanscom, Director of Graduate Admissions, 401-254-6200, Fax: 401-254-3345, E-mail: gradadmit@rwu.edu. *Dean*, Stephen White, 401-254-3607, E-mail: swhite@rwu.edu.

School of Education Students: 4 full-time (all women), 10 part-time (all women). Average age 34. 4 applicants, 100% accepted, 4 enrolled. *Faculty:* 3 full-time (2 women), 4 part-time/adjunct (3 women). *Financial support:* Application deadline: 6/15; applicants required to submit FAFSA. In 2015, 19 master's awarded. *Degree program information:* Part-time and evening/weekend programs available. Part-time, evening/weekend. Offers education (MA, MAT). *Application deadline:* Applications are processed on a rolling basis. *Application fee:* $50. Electronic applications accepted. *Application Contact:* Marcus Hanscom, Graduate Admission Coordinator, 401-254-3345, Fax: 401-254-3557, E-mail: gradadmit@rwu.edu. *Dean of School of Education*, Kelly Donnell, 401-254-5743, Fax: 401-254-3710, E-mail: rmccormack@rwu.edu.

School of Justice Studies Students: 54 full-time (30 women), 49 part-time (18 women); includes 18 minority (9 Black or African American, non-Hispanic/Latino; 3 Asian, non-Hispanic/Latino; 5 Hispanic/Latino; 1 Native Hawaiian or other Pacific Islander, non-Hispanic/Latino), 3 international. Average age 37. 58 applicants, 95% accepted, 30 enrolled. *Faculty:* 7 full-time (3 women), 5 part-time/adjunct (0 women). *Financial support:* Application deadline: 6/15; applicants required to submit FAFSA. In 2015, 29 master's awarded. *Degree program information:* Part-time and evening/weekend programs available. Part-time, evening/weekend, online learning. Offers criminal justice (MS); cybersecurity (MS); leadership (MS); public administration (MPA). *Application deadline:* Applications are processed on a rolling basis. *Application fee:* $50. Electronic applications accepted. *Application Contact:* Lori Vales, Graduate Admissions Coordinator, 401-254-6200, Fax: 401-254-3557, E-mail: gradadmit@rwu.edu. *Dean*, Dr. Stephanie Manzi, 401-254-3021, Fax: 401-254-3431, E-mail: smanzi@rwu.edu.

School of Law Students: 370 full-time (189 women); includes 85 minority (28 Black or African American, non-Hispanic/Latino; 1 American Indian or Alaska Native, non-Hispanic/Latino; 7 Asian, non-Hispanic/Latino; 38 Hispanic/Latino; 11 Two or more races, non-Hispanic/Latino), 1 international. Average age 26. 952 applicants, 80% accepted, 147 enrolled. *Faculty:* 24 full-time (14 women), 52 part-time/adjunct (20 women). *Financial support:* In 2015–16, 243 students received support, including 13 fellowships (averaging $498 per year), 38 research assistantships (averaging $911 per year); career-related internships or fieldwork and Federal Work-Study also available. Support available to part-time students. Financial award application deadline: 3/31; financial award applicants required to submit FAFSA. In 2015, 129 doctorates awarded. *Degree program information:* Part-time programs available. Part-time. Offers law (MSL, JD). JD/MMA and JD/MLRHR offered jointly with University of Rhode Island; JD/MSCJ with School of Justice Studies. *Application deadline:* For fall admission, 4/1 priority date for domestic and international students. Applications are processed on a rolling basis. *Application fee:* $60. Electronic applications accepted. *Application Contact:* Michael W. Donnelly-Boylen, Assistant Dean of Admissions, 800-633-2727, Fax: 401-254-4516, E-mail: mdonnelly-boylen@rwu.edu. *Dean*, Michael Yelnosky, 401-254-4500, Fax: 401-254-3525, E-mail: myelnosky@rwu.edu.

ROLLINS COLLEGE, Winter Park, FL 32789-4499

General Information Independent, coed, comprehensive institution. *Enrollment:* 2,521 graduate, professional, and undergraduate students; 289 full-time matriculated graduate/professional students (164 women), 296 part-time matriculated graduate/professional students (166 women). *Enrollment by degree level:* 548 master's, 37 doctoral. *Graduate faculty:* 43 full-time (15 women), 26 part-time/adjunct (13 women). *Graduate housing:* Room and/or apartments available on a first-come, first-served basis to single students; on-campus housing not available to married students. *Student services:* Campus employment opportunities, campus safety program, career counseling, exercise/wellness program, free psychological counseling, international student services, low-cost health insurance, multicultural affairs office, services for students with disabilities, writing training. *Library:* Olin Library. *Collection:* Books: 208,757 (physical), 50,995 (digital/electronic); Serial titles: 2,374 (physical), 151,077 (digital/electronic); Databases: 93. Study areas open 24 hours, 5–7 days a week; students can reserve study rooms.

Computer facilities: 307 computers available on campus for general student use. A campuswide network can be accessed from student residence rooms and from off campus. Online class registration is available.
Website: http://www.rollins.edu/

General Application Contact: Information Contact, 407-646-2000.

GRADUATE UNITS

Crummer Graduate School of Business Students: 194 full-time (87 women), 149 part-time (59 women); includes 92 minority (23 Black or African American, non-Hispanic/Latino; 17 Asian, non-Hispanic/Latino; 49 Hispanic/Latino; 3 Two or more races, non-Hispanic/Latino), 35 international. Average age 30. 320 applicants, 53%

accepted, 129 enrolled. *Faculty:* 21 full-time (2 women), 10 part-time/adjunct (1 woman). *Financial support:* In 2015–16, 130 students received support. Federal Work-Study and scholarships/grants available. Support available to part-time students. Financial award applicants required to submit FAFSA. In 2015, 142 master's awarded. *Degree program information:* Part-time and evening/weekend programs available. Part-time, evening/weekend, online learning. Offers business administration (EDBA); entrepreneurship (MBA); finance (MBA); international business (MBA); management (MBA); marketing (MBA); operations and technology management (MBA). *Application deadline:* Applications are processed on a rolling basis. *Application fee:* $50. Electronic applications accepted. *Application Contact:* Maralyn E. Graham, Admissions Coordinator, 407-646-2405, Fax: 407-646-1550, E-mail: mbaadmissions@rollins.edu. *Dean*, Tom McEvoy, 407-646-2249, Fax: 407-646-1550, E-mail: tmcevoy@rollins.edu.

Hamilton Holt School Students: 91 full-time (75 women), 139 part-time (103 women); includes 69 minority (22 Black or African American, non-Hispanic/Latino; 3 American Indian or Alaska Native, non-Hispanic/Latino; 7 Asian, non-Hispanic/Latino; 34 Hispanic/Latino; 3 Two or more races, non-Hispanic/Latino), 8 international. Average age 34. 142 applicants, 77% accepted, 98 enrolled. *Faculty:* 14 full-time (6 women), 12 part-time/adjunct (8 women). *Financial support:* In 2015–16, 51 students received support. Federal Work-Study, scholarships/grants, and unspecified assistantships available. Support available to part-time students. Financial award applicants required to submit FAFSA. In 2015, 68 master's awarded. *Degree program information:* Part-time and evening/weekend programs available. Part-time, evening/weekend. Offers applied behavior analysis and clinical science (MA); clinical mental health counseling (MA); elementary education (M Ed, MAT); health services administration (MHSA); human resources (MHR); liberal studies (MLS). *Application fee:* $50. *Application Contact:* Graduate Program Admission, 407-646-2232, Fax: 407-646-1551. *Dean*, Dr. David Richard, 407-646-2292, Fax: 407-646-1551, E-mail: dcrichard@rollins.edu.

ROOSEVELT UNIVERSITY, Chicago, IL 60605

General Information Independent, coed, comprehensive institution. CGS member. *Graduate housing:* Room and/or apartments available on a first-come, first-served basis to single students; on-campus housing not available to married students. Housing application deadline: 7/1.

GRADUATE UNITS

Graduate Division ***Degree program information:*** Part-time and evening/weekend programs available. Part-time, evening/weekend. Electronic applications accepted.

Chicago College of Performing Arts Degree program information: Part-time and evening/weekend programs available. Part-time, evening/weekend. Offers directing and dramaturgy (MFA); music (MM); musical theatre (MFA); performing arts (MA, MFA, MM, Diploma); piano pedagogy (Diploma); theatre (MA, MFA); theatre-directing (MA); theatre-performance (MFA).

College of Arts and Sciences Degree program information: Part-time and evening/weekend programs available. Part-time, evening/weekend. Offers anthropology (MA); applied economics (MA); arts and sciences (MA, MFA, MPA, MS, MSC, MSIMC, MSJ, MST, PhD, Psy D, Certificate); biotechnology and chemical science (MS); clinical professional psychology (MA); clinical psychology (MA, Psy D); computer science (MSC); creative writing (MFA); economics (MA); English (MA); history (MA); industrial/organizational psychology (MA, PhD); integrated marketing communications (MSIMC); journalism (MSJ); mathematical sciences (MS); mathematics (MS); political science (MA); public administration (MPA); sociology (MA); Spanish (MA); telecommunications (MST); women's and gender studies (MA, Certificate).

College of Education Degree program information: Part-time and evening/weekend programs available. Part-time, evening/weekend. Offers counseling and human services (MA); early childhood education (MA); education (MA, Ed D); educational leadership (MA, Ed D); elementary education (MA); reading teacher education (MA); secondary education (MA); special education (MA); teacher leadership (MA).

College of Pharmacy Offers pharmacy (Pharm D).

College of Professional Studies Degree program information: Part-time and evening/weekend programs available. Part-time, evening/weekend. Offers hospitality management (MS); training and development (MA).

Walter E. Heller College of Business Administration Degree program information: Part-time and evening/weekend programs available. Part-time, evening/weekend. Offers accounting (MSA); business administration (MBA, MS, MSA, MSHRM, MSIB, MSIS, Certificate); commercial real estate development (Certificate); human resource management (MSHRM); information systems (MSIS); international business (MSIB); real estate (MBA, MS).

ROSALIND FRANKLIN UNIVERSITY OF MEDICINE AND SCIENCE, North Chicago, IL 60064-3095

General Information Independent, coed, graduate-only institution. CGS member. *Graduate housing:* Rooms and/or apartments available on a first-come, first-served basis to single and married students. Housing application deadline: 3/13. *Research affiliation:* Argonne National Laboratory (medical physics), Veterans Administration Hospital (pulmonary medicine).

GRADUATE UNITS

Chicago Medical School Offers medicine (MD).

College of Health Professions ***Degree program information:*** Part-time programs available. Part-time, online learning. Offers biomedical sciences (MS); clinical nutrition (MS); clinical psychology (MS, PhD); health professions (MS, D Sc, DNAP, DPT, PhD, TDPT, Certificate); health professions education (MS); health promotion and wellness (MS); healthcare administration and management (MS, Certificate); interprofessional studies (D Sc, PhD); nurse anesthesia (DNAP); nutrition education (MS); pathologists' assistant (MS); physical therapy (MS, DPT, TDPT); physician assistant (MS).

College of Pharmacy Offers pharmacy (Pharm D).

Dr. William M. Scholl College of Podiatric Medicine Offers podiatric medicine (DPM).

School of Graduate and Postdoctoral Studies - Interdisciplinary Graduate Program in Biomedical Sciences Offers biochemistry and molecular biology (PhD); cell biology and anatomy (PhD); cellular and molecular pharmacology (MS, PhD); microbiology and immunology (PhD); neuroscience (PhD); physiology and biophysics (MS, PhD). Electronic applications accepted.

ROSE-HULMAN INSTITUTE OF TECHNOLOGY, Terre Haute, IN 47803-3999

General Information Independent, coed, primarily men, comprehensive institution. *Enrollment:* 2,356 graduate, professional, and undergraduate students; 51 full-time matriculated graduate/professional students (12 women), 34 part-time matriculated graduate/professional students (6 women). *Enrollment by degree level:* 85 master's. *Graduate faculty:* 116 full-time (21 women), 6 part-time/adjunct (2 women). *Tuition, area resident:* Full-time $43,122. *Graduate housing:* On-campus housing not available. *Student services:* Campus employment opportunities, career counseling, exercise/wellness program, free psychological counseling, international student services, low-cost health insurance, services for students with disabilities. *Library:* John A. Logan Library. *Collection:* Books: 42,383 (physical), 238,322 (digital/electronic); Serial titles: 70 (physical), 10,372 (digital/electronic); Databases: 31. Weekly public service hours: 101.

Computer facilities: Computer purchase and lease plans are available. 45 computers available on campus for general student use. A campuswide network can be accessed from student residence rooms and from off campus. Online class registration is available. Website: http://www.rose-hulman.edu/

General Application Contact: Dr. Azad Siahmakoun, Associate Dean of the Faculty, 812-877-8400, Fax: 812-877-8061, E-mail: siahmako@rose-hulman.edu.

GRADUATE UNITS

Faculty of Engineering and Applied Sciences Students: 51 full-time (12 women), 34 part-time (6 women); includes 7 minority (1 Black or African American, non-Hispanic/Latino; 1 American Indian or Alaska Native, non-Hispanic/Latino; 3 Asian, non-Hispanic/Latino; 2 Two or more races, non-Hispanic/Latino), 39 international. Average age 25. 114 applicants, 74% accepted, 31 enrolled. *Faculty:* 116 full-time (21 women), 6 part-time/adjunct (2 women). *Financial support:* In 2015–16, 73 students received support. Fellowships with tuition reimbursements available, research assistantships with tuition reimbursements available, institutionally sponsored loans, scholarships/grants, and tuition waivers (full and partial) available. In 2015, 60 master's awarded. *Degree program information:* Part-time and evening/weekend programs available. Part-time, evening/weekend. Offers biology and biomedical engineering (MS); chemical engineering (M Eng, MS); civil engineering (MS); electrical and computer engineering (M Eng); electrical engineering (MS); engineering and applied sciences (M Eng, MS); engineering management (M Eng, MS); environmental engineering (MS); mechanical engineering (M Eng, MS); optical engineering (MS); software engineering (MS); systems engineering and management (MS). *Application deadline:* For fall admission, 2/1 priority date for domestic students. Applications are processed on a rolling basis. *Application fee:* $0. Electronic applications accepted. *Application Contact:* Dr. Azad Siahmakoun, Associate Dean of the Faculty, 812-877-8400, Fax: 812-877-8061, E-mail: siahmako@rose-hulman.edu.

ROSEMAN UNIVERSITY OF HEALTH SCIENCES, Henderson, NV 89014

General Information Private, coed, graduate-only institution. *Enrollment by degree level:* 44 master's, 1,091 doctoral. *Graduate faculty:* 99 full-time (34 women), 79 part-time/adjunct (15 women). *Graduate housing:* On-campus housing not available. *Student services:* Campus employment opportunities, campus safety program, free psychological counseling, international student services, low-cost health insurance, services for students with disabilities. *Library:* Roseman University Library plus 1 other.

Computer facilities: 28 computers available on campus for general student use. Website: http://www.roseman.edu/

General Application Contact: Dr. Okeleke Nzeogwu, Director, MBA Program, 702-968-1659, E-mail: onzeogwu@roseman.edu.

GRADUATE UNITS

College of Dental Medicine - Henderson Campus Students: 30 full-time (11 women); includes 14 minority (13 Asian, non-Hispanic/Latino; 1 Two or more races, non-Hispanic/Latino). Average age 30. 125 applicants, 13% accepted, 10 enrolled. *Faculty:* 5 full-time (2 women), 9 part-time/adjunct (1 woman). *Financial support:* In 2015–16, 1 student received support. Scholarships/grants, health care benefits, and stipends available. Financial award application deadline: 5/1; financial award applicants required to submit FAFSA. In 2015, 11 other advanced degrees awarded. Offers business administration (MBA); dental medicine (Post-Doctoral Certificate). *Application deadline:* For fall admission, 9/15 for domestic students. Applications are processed on a rolling basis. *Application fee:* $50. *Application Contact:* Rochelle Sharp, Administrative Assistant to the Dean, 702-968-1682, E-mail: rsharp@roseman.edu. *Dean*, Dr. Jaleh Pourhamidi, 702-968-1652, Fax: 702-968-5277, E-mail: jpourhamidi@roseman.edu.

College of Dental Medicine - South Jordan, Utah Campus Students: 320 full-time (114 women); includes 103 minority (1 American Indian or Alaska Native, non-Hispanic/Latino; 87 Asian, non-Hispanic/Latino; 10 Hispanic/Latino; 5 Two or more races, non-Hispanic/Latino), 7 international. Average age 28. 1,785 applicants, 10% accepted, 82 enrolled. *Faculty:* 38 full-time (5 women), 37 part-time/adjunct (2 women). *Financial support:* In 2015–16, 13 students received support. Federal Work-Study and scholarships/grants available. Financial award application deadline: 5/1; financial award applicants required to submit FAFSA. In 2015, 64 doctorates awarded. Offers dental medicine (DMD). *Application deadline:* For fall admission, 12/1 for domestic and international students. Applications are processed on a rolling basis. *Application fee:* $75. Electronic applications accepted. *Application Contact:* Alicia Spittle, Admissions Coordinator, 801-878-1405, E-mail: aspittle@roseman.edu. *Dean, College of Dental Medicine*, Dr. Frank W. Licari, 801-878-1400, E-mail: flicari@roseman.edu.

College of Pharmacy Students: 741 full-time (404 women); includes 407 minority (38 Black or African American, non-Hispanic/Latino; 2 American Indian or Alaska Native, non-Hispanic/Latino; 284 Asian, non-Hispanic/Latino; 37 Hispanic/Latino; 10 Native Hawaiian or other Pacific Islander, non-Hispanic/Latino; 36 Two or more races, non-Hispanic/Latino), 8 international. Average age 28. 658 applicants, 60% accepted, 252 enrolled. *Faculty:* 49 full-time (23 women), 12 part-time/adjunct (5 women). *Financial support:* In 2015–16, 34 students received support. Federal Work-Study and scholarships/grants available. Financial award application deadline: 5/1; financial award applicants required to submit FAFSA. In 2015, 260 doctorates awarded. Offers pharmacy (Pharm D). *Application deadline:* For fall admission, 2/1 for domestic and international students. Applications are processed on a rolling basis. *Application fee:* $60. *Application Contact:* Dr. Helen Park, Director of Admissions and Student Affairs, 702-968-5248, Fax: 702-968-1644, E-mail: hpark@roseman.edu. *Dean*, Dr. Scott Stolte, 702-968-5944, Fax: 702-990-4435, E-mail: sstolte@roseman.edu.

MBA Program Students: 4 full-time (3 women), 40 part-time (25 women); includes 17 minority (8 Black or African American, non-Hispanic/Latino; 7 Asian, non-Hispanic/Latino; 2 Hispanic/Latino), 1 international. Average age 39. 18 applicants, 100% accepted, 18 enrolled. *Faculty:* 5 full-time (2 women), 21 part-time/adjunct (7 women). *Financial support:* In 2015–16, 3 students received support. Scholarships/grants available. Support available to part-time students. Financial award application deadline: 5/1; financial award applicants required to submit FAFSA. In 2015, 12 master's awarded. *Degree program information:* Part-time and evening/weekend programs available. Part-time, evening/weekend. Offers business administration (MBA). *Application deadline:* Applications are processed on a rolling basis. *Application fee:* $100. *Program Director*, Dr. Okeleke Nzeogwu, 702-968-1659, Fax: 702-968-1685, E-mail: onzeogwu@roseman.edu.

ROSEMONT COLLEGE, Rosemont, PA 19010-1699

General Information Independent-religious, coed, comprehensive institution. *Graduate housing:* Room and/or apartments available on a first-come, first-served basis to single students; on-campus housing not available to married students. Housing application deadline: 8/1.

GRADUATE UNITS

Schools of Graduate and Professional Studies ***Degree program information:*** Part-time and evening/weekend programs available. Part-time, evening/weekend, online learning. Offers business administration (MBA); creative writing (MFA); elementary certification (MA); human services (MA); leadership (MS); management (MS); PreK-4 (MA); publishing (MA); school counseling (MA). Electronic applications accepted.

ROWAN UNIVERSITY, Glassboro, NJ 08028-1701

General Information State-supported, coed, comprehensive institution. CGS member. *Enrollment:* 16,155 graduate, professional, and undergraduate students; 1,347 full-time matriculated graduate/professional students (714 women), 1,638 part-time matriculated graduate/professional students (1,143 women). *Enrollment by degree level:* 1,433 master's, 1,131 doctoral, 402 other advanced degrees. *Graduate faculty:* 228 full-time (110 women), 206 part-time/adjunct (109 women). *International tuition:* $8710 full-time. *Tuition, area resident:* Full-time $8710; part-time $871 per credit. Tuition, state resident: full-time $8710; part-time $871 per credit. Tuition, nonresident: full-time $8710; part-time $871 per credit. *Required fees:* $1510; $151 per credit. *Graduate housing:* Room and/or apartments available on a first-come, first-served basis to single students; on-campus housing not available to married students. Housing application deadline: 5/1. *Student services:* Campus employment opportunities, campus safety program, career counseling, child daycare facilities, exercise/wellness program, free psychological counseling, international student services, low-cost health insurance, multicultural affairs office, services for students with disabilities, teacher training, writing training. *Library:* Keith and Shirley Campbell Library plus 4 others. *Collection:* Databases: 12. Students can reserve study rooms.

Computer facilities: 900 computers available on campus for general student use. A campuswide network can be accessed from student residence rooms and from off campus. Online class registration, online library are available.
Website: http://www.rowan.edu/

General Application Contact: Jeffrey Fields, College of Graduate and Continuing Education, 856-256-4747, E-mail: cgce@rowan.edu.

GRADUATE UNITS

Graduate School ***Degree program information:*** Part-time and evening/weekend programs available. Part-time, evening/weekend. Electronic applications accepted.

College of Communication and Creative Arts Degree program information: Part-time and evening/weekend programs available. Part-time, evening/weekend. Offers communication and creative arts (MA, CGS); editing and publishing (CGS); integrated marketing communication and new media (CGS); public relations/advertising (MA); writing (MA); writing, composition, and rhetoric (CGS). Electronic applications accepted.

College of Education Degree program information: Part-time and evening/weekend programs available. Part-time, evening/weekend. Offers autism spectrum disorders (CGS); bilingual/bicultural education (CGS); counseling in educational settings (MA); education (M Ed, MA, MST, Ed D, CAGS, CGS, Ed S, Postbaccalaureate Certificate); educational leadership (Ed D, CAGS); educational technology (CGS); elementary education (MST); ESL education (CGS); higher education administration (MA); learning disabilities (MA, CGS); music education (MA); principal preparation (CAGS); reading education (MA, CGS); reading/writing literacy (CGS); school administration (MA); school and public librarianship (MA); school nursing (Postbaccalaureate Certificate); school psychology (MA, Ed S); science teaching (MST); secondary education (MST); special education (MA, CGS); subject matter education (MST); supervisor (CAGS); teacher leadership (M Ed); teacher of reading (Postbaccalaureate Certificate); teacher of students with disabilities (Postbaccalaureate Certificate); teaching and learning (CGS); teaching STEM (MA); theatre education (MST). Electronic applications accepted.

College of Engineering Degree program information: Part-time and evening/weekend programs available. Part-time, evening/weekend. Offers chemical engineering (MS); civil engineering (MEM, MS); electrical engineering (MS); engineering (MEM, MS, MSE); mechanical engineering (MS). Electronic applications accepted.

College of Humanities and Social Sciences Offers criminal justice (MA); history (MA, CGS); humanities and social sciences (MA, CGS).

College of Performing Arts Degree program information: Part-time and evening/weekend programs available. Part-time, evening/weekend. Offers performance (MM); performing arts (MA, MM, MST); theatre arts administration (MA). Electronic applications accepted.

College of Science and Mathematics Degree program information: Part-time and evening/weekend programs available. Part-time, evening/weekend. Offers applied behavioral analysis (MA, CAGS); bioinformatics (MS); biological science (MS); clinical mental health counseling (MA, CAGS); computer science (MS); mathematics (MA, CGS); middle grades math education (CGS); networks (CGS); nursing (MS); pharmaceutical sciences (MS); psychology (MA, CAGS); science and mathematics (MA, MS, CAGS, CGS). Electronic applications accepted.

Rohrer College of Business Degree program information: Part-time and evening/weekend programs available. Part-time, evening/weekend. Offers business (MBA, CAGS, CGS); business administration (MBA). Electronic applications accepted.

School of Biomedical Science and Health Professions Degree program information: Part-time and evening/weekend programs available. Part-time, evening/weekend, online learning. Offers health and exercise science (MA); wellness and lifestyle management (MA). Electronic applications accepted.

School of Osteopathic Medicine Offers osteopathic medicine (DO). Electronic applications accepted.

ROYAL MILITARY COLLEGE OF CANADA, Kingston, ON K7K 7B4, Canada

General Information Federally supported, coed, university.

GRADUATE UNITS

Division of Graduate Studies and Research ***Degree program information:*** Part-time programs available. Part-time, online learning. Electronic applications accepted.

Continuing Studies Offers business administration (MBA); defense management and policy (MA); history (PhD); war studies (MA). Electronic applications accepted.

Engineering Division Offers chemical and materials (M Eng); chemical and materials science (M Sc, PhD); chemistry (M Eng); civil engineering (M Eng, MA Sc, PhD); computer engineering (M Eng, PhD); electrical engineering (M Eng, PhD); engineering (M Eng, M Sc, MA Sc, PhD); environmental (PhD); environmental engineering (M Eng, PhD); environmental science (M Sc, PhD); mechanical engineering (M Eng, MA Sc, PhD); nuclear (PhD); nuclear engineering (M Eng, MA Sc, PhD); nuclear science (M Sc, PhD); software engineering (M Eng, PhD). Electronic applications accepted.

Science Division Offers chemical engineering (M Eng, MA Sc, PhD); chemistry (M Sc, PhD); computer science (M Sc); mathematics (M Sc); physics (M Sc); science (M Eng, M Sc, MA Sc, PhD). Electronic applications accepted.

ROYAL ROADS UNIVERSITY, Victoria, BC V9B 5Y2, Canada

General Information Province-supported, coed, upper-level institution. *Graduate housing:* Room and/or apartments available on a first-come, first-served basis to single students; on-campus housing not available to married students.

GRADUATE UNITS

Graduate Studies Online learning. Offers conflict analysis (G Dip); conflict analysis and management (MA); destination development (Graduate Certificate); disaster and emergency management (MA); environment and management (M Sc, MA); environmental education and communication (MA, G Dip, Graduate Certificate); executive coaching (Graduate Certificate); health systems leadership (Graduate Certificate); human security and peacebuilding (MA); international hotel management (MA); project management (Graduate Certificate); public relations management (Graduate Certificate); strategic human resources management (Graduate Certificate); sustainable tourism (Graduate Certificate); tourism leadership (Graduate Certificate); tourism management (MA). Electronic applications accepted.

Faculty of Management Online learning. Offers digital technologies management (MBA); executive management (MBA); human resources management (MBA). Electronic applications accepted.

RUSH UNIVERSITY, Chicago, IL 60612-3832

General Information Independent, coed, upper-level institution. CGS member. *Graduate housing:* Rooms and/or apartments available on a first-come, first-served basis to single and married students.

GRADUATE UNITS

College of Health Sciences ***Financial support:*** Career-related internships or fieldwork, Federal Work-Study, institutionally sponsored loans, and scholarships/grants available. Support available to part-time students. Financial award application deadline: 4/1; financial award applicants required to submit FAFSA. *Degree program information:* Part-time and evening/weekend programs available. Part-time, evening/weekend. Offers audiology (Au D); clinical laboratory management (MS); clinical nutrition (MS); health sciences (MS, Au D, PhD); health systems management (MS, PhD); medical laboratory science (MS); occupational therapy (MS); perfusion technology (MS); physician assistant studies (MS); respiratory care (MS); speech-language pathology (MS). Electronic applications accepted. *Application Contact:* 312-942-7120, E-mail: chs_admissions@rush.edu.

College of Nursing Students: 368 full-time (314 women), 722 part-time (664 women); includes 252 minority (83 Black or African American, non-Hispanic/Latino; 4 American Indian or Alaska Native, non-Hispanic/Latino; 77 Asian, non-Hispanic/Latino; 86 Hispanic/Latino; 2 Native Hawaiian or other Pacific Islander, non-Hispanic/Latino). Average age 31. *Faculty:* 43 full-time (40 women), 52 part-time/adjunct (49 women). *Financial support:* Research assistantships, teaching assistantships, Federal Work-Study, scholarships/grants, traineeships, and health care benefits available. Support available to part-time students. Financial award application deadline: 3/1; financial award applicants required to submit FAFSA. In 2015, 249 master's, 68 doctorates awarded. *Degree program information:* Part-time programs available. Part-time, online learning. Offers adult gerontology acute care clinical nurse specialist (DNP); adult gerontology acute care nurse practitioner (DNP); adult gerontology primary care clinical nurse specialist (DNP); adult gerontology primary care nurse practitioner (DNP); advanced public health nursing (DNP); clinical nurse leader (MSN); family nurse practitioner (DNP); leadership to enhance population health outcomes (DNP); neonatal clinical nurse specialist (DNP); neonatal nurse practitioner (DNP, Post-Graduate Certificate); nurse anesthesia (DNP); nursing (MSN, DNP, PhD, Post-Graduate Certificate); nursing science (PhD); pediatric acute care nurse practitioner (DNP, Post-Graduate Certificate); pediatric clinical nurse specialist (DNP); pediatric primary care nurse practitioner (DNP); pediatric primary nurse practitioner (Post-Graduate Certificate); psychiatric mental health nurse practitioner (DNP); systems leadership (DNP). *Application deadline:* For fall admission, 1/2 for domestic students; for winter admission, 10/15 for domestic students; for spring admission, 8/3 for domestic students; for summer admission, 12/1 for domestic students. Applications are processed on a rolling basis. *Application fee:* $100. Electronic applications accepted. *Application Contact:* Jennifer Thorndyke, Admissions Specialist for the College of Nursing, 312-563-7526, E-mail: jennifer_thorndyke@rush.edu. *Dean,* Dr. Marquis Foreman, 312-942-7117, Fax: 312-942-3043, E-mail: marquis_d_foreman@rush.edu.

Graduate College ***Degree program information:*** Part-time programs available. Part-time. Offers physiology (PhD). Electronic applications accepted.

Division of Anatomy and Cell Biology Offers anatomy and cell biology (MS, PhD). Electronic applications accepted.

Division of Biochemistry Offers biochemistry (MS, PhD). Electronic applications accepted.

Division of Immunology and Microbiology Offers immunology (MS, PhD); microbiology (PhD); virology (MS, PhD).

Division of Medical Physics Offers medical physics (MS, PhD). Electronic applications accepted.

Division of Neuroscience Offers neuroscience (MS, PhD). Electronic applications accepted.

Division of Pharmacology Offers clinical research (MS); pharmacology (MS, PhD).

Rush Medical College Students: 509 full-time (261 women); includes 198 minority (29 Black or African American, non-Hispanic/Latino; 4 American Indian or Alaska Native, non-Hispanic/Latino; 118 Asian, non-Hispanic/Latino; 44 Hispanic/Latino; 3 Native Hawaiian or other Pacific Islander, non-Hispanic/Latino). Average age 26. 6,982 applicants, 4% accepted, 128 enrolled. *Faculty:* 659 full-time (307 women), 173 part-time/adjunct (74 women). *Financial support:* In 2015–16, 314 students received support. Federal Work-Study, institutionally sponsored loans, and scholarships/grants available. Financial award application deadline: 3/1; financial award applicants required to submit FAFSA. In 2015, 132 doctorates awarded. Offers medicine (MD). *Application deadline:* For fall admission, 11/1 for domestic students. Applications are processed on a rolling basis. *Application fee:* $100. Electronic applications accepted. *Application*

Contact: Jill M. Volk, Director of Admissions and Recruitment, 312-942-6915, Fax: 312-942-6840, E-mail: rmc_admissions@rush.edu. *Assistant Dean, Admissions and Recruitment,* Dr. Cynthia E. Boyd, 312-942-6915, Fax: 312-942-6840, E-mail: rmc_admissions@rush.edu.

RUTGERS UNIVERSITY–CAMDEN, Camden, NJ 08102-1401

General Information State-supported, coed, university. *Graduate housing:* Rooms and/or apartments available to single and married students.

GRADUATE UNITS

Graduate School of Arts and Sciences ***Degree program information:*** Part-time and evening/weekend programs available. Part-time, evening/weekend. Offers American and public history (MA); biology (MS); chemistry (MS); childhood studies (MA, PhD); computational and integrative biology (MS, PhD); computer science (MS); creative writing (MFA); criminal justice (MA); education policy and leadership (MPA); English (MA); industrial mathematics (MBS); industrial/applied mathematics (MS); international public service and development (MPA); liberal studies (MALS); mathematical computer science (MS); physical therapy (DPT); psychology (MA); public management (MPA); pure mathematics (MS); teaching in mathematical sciences (MS). Electronic applications accepted.

School of Business ***Degree program information:*** Part-time and evening/weekend programs available. Part-time, evening/weekend. Offers business (MBA). Electronic applications accepted.

School of Law ***Degree program information:*** Part-time and evening/weekend programs available. Part-time, evening/weekend. Offers law (JD). JD/MCRP, JD/MA, JD/MPA, JD/MSW, JD/MS offered jointly with Rutgers, The State University of New Jersey, New Brunswick; JD/MPA, JD/MD, JD/DO with University of Medicine and Dentistry of New Jersey. Electronic applications accepted.

School of Public Health ***Degree program information:*** Part-time and evening/weekend programs available. Part-time, evening/weekend. Offers general public health (Certificate); health systems and policy (MPH). Electronic applications accepted.

RUTGERS UNIVERSITY–NEWARK, Newark, NJ 07102

General Information State-supported, coed, university. CGS member. *Graduate housing:* Room and/or apartments available to single students; on-campus housing not available to married students. Housing application deadline: 5/15.

GRADUATE UNITS

Graduate School ***Degree program information:*** Part-time and evening/weekend programs available. Part-time, evening/weekend. Offers accounting (PhD); accounting information systems (PhD); American political system (MA); American studies (MA, PhD); analytical chemistry (MS, PhD); applied physics (MS, PhD); biochemistry (MS, PhD); biology (MS, PhD); cognitive neuroscience (PhD); cognitive science (PhD); computational biology (MS); computer information systems (PhD); creative writing (MFA); economics (MA); English (MA); environmental geology (MS); environmental science (MS, PhD); finance (PhD); health care administration (MPA); history (MA, MAT); human resources administration (MPA); information technology (PhD); inorganic chemistry (MS, PhD); international business (PhD); international relations (MA); jazz history and research (MA); management science (PhD); marketing (PhD); mathematical sciences (PhD); organic chemistry (MS, PhD); organization management (PhD); perception (PhD); physical chemistry (MS, PhD); psychobiology (PhD); public administration (PhD); public management (MPA); public policy analysis (MPA); social cognition (PhD); urban systems (PhD); urban systems and issues (MPA). Electronic applications accepted.

Division of Global Affairs ***Degree program information:*** Part-time and evening/weekend programs available. Part-time, evening/weekend. Offers global affairs (MS, PhD). Electronic applications accepted.

Graduate School of Biomedical Sciences ***Degree program information:*** Part-time and evening/weekend programs available. Part-time, evening/weekend. Offers biochemistry and molecular biology (MS, PhD); biodefense (Certificate); biomedical engineering (PhD); biomedical sciences (interdisciplinary) (PhD); biomedical sciences (multidisciplinary) (PhD); cell biology and molecular medicine (PhD); cellular biology, neuroscience and physiology (PhD); infection, immunity and inflammation (PhD); integrative neuroscience (PhD); microbiology and molecular genetics (PhD); molecular biology, genetics and cancer (PhD); molecular pathology and immunology (PhD); neuroscience (Certificate); pharmacological sciences (Certificate); pharmacology and physiology (PhD); stem cell (Certificate). PhD in biomedical engineering offered jointly with New Jersey Institute of Technology. Electronic applications accepted.

School of Criminal Justice Offers criminal justice (MA, PhD). Electronic applications accepted.

New Jersey Medical School Offers medicine (MD). Electronic applications accepted.

Rutgers Business School–Newark and New Brunswick ***Degree program information:*** Part-time and evening/weekend programs available. Part-time, evening/weekend. Offers accountancy (M Accy); accounting (PhD); accounting information systems (PhD); business (MBA, MFA, MHSM, MIT, MRE); business administration (MBA); business of fashion (MBA); economics (PhD); finance (PhD); financial analysis (MFA); healthcare services management (MHSM); individualized study (PhD); information technology (PhD); international business (PhD); management science (PhD); marketing science (PhD); organizational management (PhD); pharmaceutical management (MBA); professional accounting (MBA); quantitative finance (MQF); real estate and logistics (MRE); science, technology and management (PhD); supply chain management (PhD). Electronic applications accepted.

Rutgers School of Dental Medicine Offers dental science (MS); dentistry (DMD); endodontics (Certificate); oral medicine (Certificate); orthodontics (Certificate); pediatric dentistry (Certificate); periodontics (Certificate); prosthodontics (Certificate). DMD/MPH offered jointly with New Jersey Institute of Technology, Rutgers, The State University of New Jersey, Camden. Electronic applications accepted.

Rutgers School of Nursing ***Degree program information:*** Part-time programs available. Part-time. Offers adult health (MSN); adult occupational health (MSN); advanced practice nursing (MSN, Post Master's Certificate); family nurse practitioner (MSN); nurse anesthesia (MSN); nursing (MSN); nursing informatics (MSN); urban health (PhD); women's health practitioner (MSN). Electronic applications accepted.

School of Health Related Professions ***Degree program information:*** Part-time programs available. Part-time. Offers biomedical informatics (MS, PhD); clinical laboratory sciences (MS); clinical nutrition (MS, DCN); community counseling (MS); dietetic internship (Certificate); health care informatics (Certificate); health care management (MS); health related professions (MS, DCN, DPT, PhD, Certificate); health sciences (MS, PhD); nutrition (PhD); physical therapy (DPT); physician assistant (MS); psychiatric rehabilitation (MS, PhD); radiologist assistant (MS); rehabilitation counseling (MS). Electronic applications accepted.

School of Law ***Degree program information:*** Part-time and evening/weekend programs available. Part-time, evening/weekend. Offers law (JD). JD/MCRP, JD/PhD offered jointly with Rutgers, The State University of New Jersey, New Brunswick.

School of Public Health ***Degree program information:*** Part-time and evening/weekend programs available. Part-time, evening/weekend. Offers clinical epidemiology (Certificate); dental public health (MPH); general public health (Certificate); public policy and oral health services administration (Certificate); quantitative methods (MPH); urban health (MPH). Electronic applications accepted.

RUTGERS UNIVERSITY–NEW BRUNSWICK, Piscataway, NJ 08854-8097

General Information State-supported, coed, university. CGS member. *Graduate housing:* Rooms and/or apartments available to single and married students.

GRADUATE UNITS

Edward J. Bloustein School of Planning and Public Policy ***Degree program information:*** Part-time and evening/weekend programs available. Part-time, evening/weekend, online learning. Offers planning and public policy (MCRP, MCRS, MPAP, MPH, MPP, Dr PH, PhD); public policy (MPAP, MPP); urban planning and policy development (MCRP, MCRS). Electronic applications accepted.

Ernest Mario School of Pharmacy Offers medicinal chemistry (MS, PhD); pharmaceutical science (MS, PhD); pharmacy (Pharm D). Electronic applications accepted.

Graduate School-New Brunswick ***Degree program information:*** Part-time and evening/weekend programs available. Part-time, evening/weekend, online learning. Offers African-American history (PhD); air pollution and resources (MS, PhD); American politics (PhD); anthropology (MA, PhD); applied mathematics (MS, PhD); applied statistics (MS); aquatic biology (MS, PhD); aquatic chemistry (MS, PhD); art history (MA, PhD); astronomy (MS, PhD); atmospheric science (MS, PhD); behavioral neuroscience (PhD); bilingualism and second language acquisition (MA, PhD); biochemistry (PhD); biological chemistry (MS, PhD); biophysics (PhD); biostatistics (MS); cell and developmental biology (MS, PhD); chemical and biochemical engineering (MS, PhD); chemistry and physics of aerosol and hydrosol systems (MS, PhD); civil and environmental engineering (MS, PhD); classics (MA, MAT, PhD); clinical psychology (PhD); cognitive psychology (PhD); communications and solid-state electronics (MS, PhD); comparative literature (MA, PhD); comparative politics (PhD); computational biology and molecular biophysics (PhD); computer engineering (MS, PhD); computer science (MS, PhD); condensed matter physics (MS, PhD); control systems (MS, PhD); cultural heritage and preservation studies (MA); curatorial studies (Certificate); data mining (MS); design and control (MS, PhD); digital signal processing (MS, PhD); early American history (PhD); early modern European history (PhD); east Asian history (PhD); East Asian languages and cultures (MA); ecology and evolution (MS, PhD); economics (MA, PhD); elementary particle physics (MS, PhD); endocrinology and animal biosciences (MS, PhD); entomology (MS, PhD); environmental chemistry (MS, PhD); environmental microbiology (MS, PhD); environmental toxicology (MS, PhD); exposure assessment (PhD); fate and effects of pollutants (MS, PhD); fluid mechanics (MS, PhD); food and business economics (MS); food science (M Phil, MS, PhD); French (MA, PhD); French studies (MAT); geography (MA, MS, PhD); geological sciences (MS, PhD); German (MAT, PhD); German literature (MA, PhD); global and comparative history (PhD); historic preservation (Certificate); history (PhD); history of diplomacy and foreign relations (PhD); history of technology, environment and health (PhD); history of the Atlantic cultures and African diaspora (PhD); horticulture and plant technology (MS, PhD); industrial and systems engineering (MS, PhD); industrial-occupational toxicology (MS, PhD); information technology (MS); inorganic chemistry (MS, PhD); interdisciplinary classical studies and ancient history (MA, PhD); interdisciplinary health psychology (PhD); intermediate energy nuclear physics (MS); international relations (PhD); Italian (MA, PhD); Italian literature and literary criticism (MA); Jewish studies (MA, Certificate); language, literature and culture (MAT); Latin American history (PhD); linguistics (PhD); literatures in English (PhD); manufacturing systems engineering (MS); materials science and engineering (MS, PhD); mathematics (MS, PhD); mechanics (MS, PhD); medieval history (PhD); microbiology and molecular genetics (MS, PhD); modern European history (PhD); molecular and cellular biology (MS, PhD); nineteenth and twentieth century American history (PhD); nuclear physics (MS, PhD); nutritional sciences (MS, PhD); nutritional toxicology (MS, PhD); oceanography (MS, PhD); operations research (PhD); organic chemistry (MS, PhD); organismal and population biology (MS, PhD); pharmaceutical toxicology (MS, PhD); philosophy (PhD); physical chemistry (MS, PhD); physics (MST); plant pathology (MS, PhD); political theory (PhD); pollution prevention and control (MS, PhD); public law (PhD); quality and productivity management (MS); quality and reliability engineering (MS); religious studies (MA, Graduate Certificate); social psychology (PhD); sociology (MA, PhD); solid mechanics (MS, PhD); Spanish (MA, MAT, PhD); Spanish literature (MA, PhD); statistics (MS, PhD); surface science (PhD); theoretical physics (MS, PhD); thermal sciences (MS, PhD); translation (MA); United Nations and global policy studies (MA); water and wastewater treatment (MS, PhD); water resources (MS, PhD); women and politics (PhD); women's and gender history (PhD); women's and gender studies (MA, PhD).

Graduate School of Applied and Professional Psychology Offers applied and professional psychology (Psy M, Psy D); clinical psychology (Psy M, Psy D); school psychology (Psy M, Psy D). Electronic applications accepted.

Graduate School of Biomedical Sciences Offers biochemistry (MS, PhD); biochemistry and molecular biology (MS, PhD); biomedical engineering (MS, PhD); biomedical science (MS); biomedical sciences (MBS, MS, PhD); cellular and molecular pharmacology (MS, PhD); clinical and translational science (MS); environmental sciences/exposure assessment (PhD); exposure science and assessment (PhD); microbiology and molecular genetics (MS, PhD); molecular genetics, microbiology and immunology (MS, PhD); neuroscience (MS, PhD); physiology and integrative biology (MS, PhD); toxicology (PhD). Electronic applications accepted.

Graduate School of Education ***Degree program information:*** Part-time and evening/weekend programs available. Part-time, evening/weekend. Offers college student affairs (Ed M); early childhood/elementary education (Ed M, Ed D); education (Ed M, Ed D, PhD); educational administration and supervision (Ed M, Ed D); educational policy (PhD); educational psychology (PhD); educational statistics, measurement and evaluation (Ed M); English as a second language education (Ed M); English education (Ed M); language education (Ed M, Ed D); learning, cognition and development (Ed M); literacy education (Ed M, Ed D, PhD); mathematics education (Ed M, Ed D, PhD); reading education (Ed M); school counseling and counseling psychology (Ed M); science education (Ed M, Ed D); social and philosophical foundations of education (Ed M, Ed D); social studies education (Ed M, Ed D); special education (Ed M, Ed D). Electronic applications accepted.

Mason Gross School of the Arts ***Degree program information:*** Part-time programs available. Part-time. Offers acting (MFA); arts (MFA, MM, DMA, AD); collaborative piano (MM, DMA); conducting: choral (MM, DMA); conducting: instrumental (MM, DMA);

conducting: orchestral (MM, DMA); design (MFA); directing (MFA); drawing (MFA); jazz studies (MM); music (DMA, AD); music education (MM, DMA); music performance (MM); painting (MFA); playwriting (MFA); sculpture (MFA); stage management (MFA); visual arts (MFA).

Robert Wood Johnson Medical School Offers medicine (MD). Electronic applications accepted.

School of Communication, Information and Library Studies ***Degree program information:*** Part-time programs available. Part-time, online learning. Offers communication and information studies (MCIS); communication, information and library studies (MCIS, MLS, PhD); communication, library and information science and media studies (PhD); library and information science (MLS). Electronic applications accepted.

School of Management and Labor Relations ***Degree program information:*** Part-time and evening/weekend programs available. Part-time, evening/weekend. Offers human resource management (MHRM); industrial relations and human resources (PhD); labor and employment relations (MLER). Electronic applications accepted.

School of Public Health ***Degree program information:*** Part-time and evening/weekend programs available. Part-time, evening/weekend. Offers biostatistics (MPH, MS, Dr PH, PhD); clinical epidemiology (Certificate); environmental and occupational health (MPH, Dr PH, PhD, Certificate); epidemiology (MPH, Dr PH, PhD); general public health (Certificate); health education and behavioral science (MPH, Dr PH, PhD); health systems and policy (MPH, PhD); public health (MPH, MS, Dr PH, PhD, Certificate); public health preparedness (Certificate). Electronic applications accepted.

School of Social Work ***Degree program information:*** Part-time programs available. Part-time. Offers social work (MSW, PhD). Electronic applications accepted.

RYERSON UNIVERSITY, Toronto, ON M5B 2K3, Canada

General Information Province-supported, coed, comprehensive institution. CGS member.

GRADUATE UNITS

School of Graduate Studies Offers photographic preservation and collections management (MA).

SACRED HEART MAJOR SEMINARY, Detroit, MI 48206-1799

General Information Independent-religious, coed, comprehensive institution. *Graduate housing:* Room and/or apartments guaranteed to single students; on-campus housing not available to married students. Housing application deadline: 8/1.

GRADUATE UNITS

School of Theology ***Degree program information:*** Part-time and evening/weekend programs available. Part-time, evening/weekend. Offers pastoral studies (MAPS); theology (M Div, MA).

SACRED HEART SCHOOL OF THEOLOGY, Hales Corners, WI 53130-0429

General Information Independent-religious, coed, primarily men, graduate-only institution. *Graduate housing:* Room and/or apartments guaranteed to single students; on-campus housing not available to married students.

GRADUATE UNITS

Graduate and Professional Programs ***Degree program information:*** Part-time programs available. Part-time. Offers priestly formation (Certificate); theology (M Div, MA).

SACRED HEART UNIVERSITY, Fairfield, CT 06825

General Information Independent-religious, coed, comprehensive institution. *Enrollment:* 8,235 graduate, professional, and undergraduate students; 1,066 full-time matriculated graduate/professional students (723 women), 1,891 part-time matriculated graduate/professional students (1,445 women). *Enrollment by degree level:* 2,199 master's, 252 doctoral, 506 other advanced degrees. *Graduate faculty:* 136 full-time (78 women), 140 part-time/adjunct (84 women). *Tuition, area resident:* Part-time $654 per credit hour. *Student services:* Campus employment opportunities, campus safety program, career counseling, exercise/wellness program, free psychological counseling, international student services, low-cost health insurance, multicultural affairs office, services for students with disabilities, teacher training, writing training. *Library:* Ryan Matura Library plus 1 other. *Collection:* Books: 125,041 (physical), 121,464 (digital/electronic); Serial titles: 1,249 (physical); Databases: 122. Students can reserve study rooms.

Computer facilities: 424 computers available on campus for general student use. A campuswide network can be accessed from student residence rooms and from off campus. Online class registration is available.
Website: http://www.sacredheart.edu/

General Application Contact: William Sweeney, Director of Graduate Admissions Operations, 203-365-4727, E-mail: gradstudies@sacredheart.edu.

GRADUATE UNITS

Graduate Programs Students: 1,066 full-time (723 women), 1,891 part-time (1,445 women); includes 456 minority (177 Black or African American, non-Hispanic/Latino; 5 American Indian or Alaska Native, non-Hispanic/Latino; 72 Asian, non-Hispanic/Latino; 162 Hispanic/Latino; 5 Native Hawaiian or other Pacific Islander, non-Hispanic/Latino; 35 Two or more races, non-Hispanic/Latino), 389 international. Average age 32. 3,436 applicants, 55% accepted, 935 enrolled. *Faculty:* 136 full-time (78 women), 140 part-time/adjunct (84 women). *Financial support:* Unspecified assistantships available. Financial award applicants required to submit FAFSA. In 2015, 765 master's, 80 doctorates, 87 other advanced degrees awarded. *Degree program information:* Part-time and evening/weekend programs available. Part-time, evening/weekend, online learning. *Application deadline:* Applications are processed on a rolling basis. *Application fee:* $75. Electronic applications accepted. *Application Contact:* William Sweeney, Director of Graduate Admissions Operations, 203-365-4827, E-mail: sweeneyw@sacredheart.edu. *Acting Provost and Vice President for Academic Affairs*, Rupendra Paliwal, 203-371-7851, E-mail: paliwalr@sacredheart.edu.

College of Arts and Sciences Students: 375 full-time (181 women), 313 part-time (175 women); includes 96 minority (46 Black or African American, non-Hispanic/Latino; 5 Asian, non-Hispanic/Latino; 35 Hispanic/Latino; 1 Native Hawaiian or other Pacific Islander, non-Hispanic/Latino; 9 Two or more races, non-Hispanic/Latino), 353 international. Average age 27. 1,256 applicants, 72% accepted, 261 enrolled. *Faculty:* 41 full-time (21 women), 25 part-time/adjunct (6 women). *Financial support:* Unspecified assistantships available. Financial award applicants required to submit FAFSA. In 2015, 220 master's awarded. *Degree program information:* Part-time and evening/weekend programs available. Part-time, evening/weekend, online learning. Offers applied psychology (MS); arts and sciences (MA, MA Comm, MAT, MS, Graduate Certificate); chemistry (MS); children, health, and media (MA); computer game design and development (Graduate Certificate); computer science and information technology (MS); computer science gaming (MS); corporate communication and public relations (MA Comm); criminal justice (MA); cybersecurity (MS); data analytics (Graduate Certificate); database design (Graduate Certificate); digital multimedia journalism (MA Comm); digital multimedia production (MA Comm); environmental systems analysis and management (MS); film and television (MA); information technology (Graduate Certificate); information technology and network security (Graduate Certificate); interactive multimedia (Graduate Certificate); media and social justice (MA); social work (MSW); sports communication and media (MA); Web development (Graduate Certificate). *Application deadline:* Applications are processed on a rolling basis. *Application fee:* $75. Electronic applications accepted. *Application Contact:* William Sweeney, Director of Graduate Admissions Operations, 203-365-4827, E-mail: gradstudies@sacredheart.edu. *Dean of College of Arts and Sciences*, Robin Cautin, 203-396-8020, E-mail: cautinr@sacredheart.edu.

College of Health Professions Students: 369 full-time (299 women), 740 part-time (673 women); includes 177 minority (74 Black or African American, non-Hispanic/Latino; 2 American Indian or Alaska Native, non-Hispanic/Latino; 40 Asian, non-Hispanic/Latino; 45 Hispanic/Latino; 1 Native Hawaiian or other Pacific Islander, non-Hispanic/Latino; 15 Two or more races, non-Hispanic/Latino), 1 international. Average age 34. 1,504 applicants, 26% accepted, 231 enrolled. *Faculty:* 44 full-time (35 women), 65 part-time/adjunct (52 women). *Financial support:* Research assistantships and unspecified assistantships available. Financial award applicants required to submit FAFSA. In 2015, 201 master's, 74 doctorates awarded. *Degree program information:* Part-time and evening/weekend programs available. Part-time, evening/weekend, online learning. Offers exercise science and nutrition (MS); health professions (MS, MSN, MSOT, DNP, DPT, Graduate Certificate); healthcare informatics (MS); occupational therapy (MSOT); physical therapy (DPT, Graduate Certificate); speech-language pathology (MS). *Application deadline:* Applications are processed on a rolling basis. *Application fee:* $60. Electronic applications accepted. *Application Contact:* Kathy Dilks, Executive Director of Graduate Admissions, 203-396-8259, Fax: 203-365-4732, E-mail: gradstudies@sacredheart.edu. *Dean*, Dr. Patricia Walker, 203-396-8024, Fax: 203-396-8075, E-mail: walkerp@sacredheart.edu.

College of Nursing Students: 19 full-time (18 women), 777 part-time (711 women); includes 144 minority (56 Black or African American, non-Hispanic/Latino; 2 American Indian or Alaska Native, non-Hispanic/Latino; 33 Asian, non-Hispanic/Latino; 41 Hispanic/Latino; 2 Native Hawaiian or other Pacific Islander, non-Hispanic/Latino; 10 Two or more races, non-Hispanic/Latino). Average age 38. 116 applicants, 53% accepted, 50 enrolled. *Faculty:* 17 full-time (all women), 21 part-time/adjunct (18 women). *Financial support:* Unspecified assistantships available. Financial award applicants required to submit FAFSA. In 2015, 192 master's, 13 doctorates awarded. *Degree program information:* Part-time and evening/weekend programs available. Part-time, evening/weekend, online learning. Offers clinical nurse leader (MSN); clinical practice (DNP); family nurse practitioner (MSN, Graduate Certificate); leadership (DNP); nurse educator (MSN); nursing management and executive leadership (MSN); patient care services (MSN). *Application deadline:* For fall admission, 2/15 for domestic and international students. Applications are processed on a rolling basis. *Application fee:* $75. Electronic applications accepted. *Application Contact:* William Sweeney, Director of Graduate Admissions Operations, 203-365-4716, Fax: 203-365-4732, E-mail: gradstudies@sacredheart.edu. *Dean of Nursing*, Mary Alice Donius, 203-365-4508, E-mail: doniusm@sacredheart.edu.

Isabelle Farrington College of Education Students: 194 full-time (160 women), 533 part-time (409 women); includes 90 minority (35 Black or African American, non-Hispanic/Latino; 2 American Indian or Alaska Native, non-Hispanic/Latino; 7 Asian, non-Hispanic/Latino; 36 Hispanic/Latino; 1 Native Hawaiian or other Pacific Islander, non-Hispanic/Latino; 9 Two or more races, non-Hispanic/Latino), 1 international. Average age 35. 309 applicants, 98% accepted, 263 enrolled. *Faculty:* 19 full-time (9 women), 29 part-time/adjunct (14 women). *Financial support:* Teaching assistantships with partial tuition reimbursements and unspecified assistantships available. Financial award applicants required to submit FAFSA. In 2015, 211 master's, 87 other advanced degrees awarded. *Degree program information:* Part-time and evening/weekend programs available. Part-time, evening/weekend. Offers administration (CAS); advanced educational studies for teachers (CAS); education (MAT, CAS, Graduate Certificate); educational technology (Graduate Certificate); literacy (CAS); teaching (MAT); TESOL (MAT). *Application deadline:* Applications are processed on a rolling basis. *Application fee:* $75. Electronic applications accepted. *Application Contact:* William Sweeney, Director of Graduate Admissions, 203-365-4827, E-mail: sweeneyw@sacredheart.edu. *Dean*, Dr. Jim Carl, 203-396-8454, Fax: 203-365-7513, E-mail: carlj@sacredheart.edu.

Jack Welch College of Business Students: 100 full-time (47 women), 230 part-time (122 women); includes 84 minority (29 Black or African American, non-Hispanic/Latino; 17 Asian, non-Hispanic/Latino; 35 Hispanic/Latino; 3 Two or more races, non-Hispanic/Latino), 21 international. Average age 31. 268 applicants, 94% accepted, 169 enrolled. *Faculty:* 28 full-time (9 women), 13 part-time/adjunct (5 women). *Financial support:* Unspecified assistantships available. Financial award applicants required to submit FAFSA. In 2015, 79 master's awarded. *Degree program information:* Part-time and evening/weekend programs available. Part-time, evening/weekend. Offers accounting (MBA, MS, Graduate Certificate); administration (MBA); business (MBA, MS, DBA, Graduate Certificate); core business skills (Graduate Certificate); corporate finance (Graduate Certificate); digital marketing (MS); finance (DBA); finance and investment management (MS); global investments (Graduate Certificate); human resource management (MS, Graduate Certificate); leadership (Graduate Certificate); marketing (Graduate Certificate). *Application deadline:* Applications are processed on a rolling basis. *Application fee:* $75. Electronic applications accepted. *Application Contact:* William Sweeney, Director of Graduate Admissions, 203-365-4827, E-mail: sweeneyw@sacredheart.edu. *Dean*, Dr. John Chalykoff, 203-396-8084, Fax: 203-365-7538, E-mail: chalykoffj@sacredheart.edu.

SAGE GRADUATE SCHOOL, Troy, NY 12180-4115

General Information Independent, coed, graduate-only institution. *Enrollment by degree level:* 924 master's, 235 doctoral, 57 other advanced degrees. *Graduate faculty:* 49 full-time (41 women), 111 part-time/adjunct (83 women). *Tuition, area resident:* Full-time $12,240; part-time $680 per credit hour. Tuition and fees vary according to degree level and program. *Graduate housing:* Room and/or apartments available on a first-come, first-served basis to single students; on-campus housing not available to married students. Housing application deadline: 5/1. *Student services:* Career counseling, low-cost health insurance. *Library:* James Wheelock Clark Library plus 1 other. Weekly public service hours: 65; students can reserve study rooms. *Research affiliation:* Rensselaer Polytechnic Institute (education), St. Peter's Hospital (health care services), University at Albany, State University of New York (public health), Albany Medical

College (health care services), University at Albany, State University of New York (health and the environment), National Center for Adaptive Neurotechnologies (NCAN).

Computer facilities: 437 computers available on campus for general student use. A campuswide network can be accessed from student residence rooms and from off campus. Online class registration is available.
Website: http://www.sage.edu/

General Application Contact: Wendy D. Diefendorf, Director of Graduate and Adult Admission, 518-244-2443, Fax: 518-244-6880, E-mail: sgsadm@sage.edu.

GRADUATE UNITS

Esteves School of Education Students: 125 full-time (107 women), 276 part-time (221 women); includes 108 minority (37 Black or African American, non-Hispanic/Latino; 13 Asian, non-Hispanic/Latino; 42 Hispanic/Latino; 2 Native Hawaiian or other Pacific Islander, non-Hispanic/Latino; 14 Two or more races, non-Hispanic/Latino), 1 international. Average age 33. 521 applicants, 44% accepted, 140 enrolled. *Faculty:* 15 full-time (11 women), 39 part-time/adjunct (28 women). *Financial support:* Fellowships, research assistantships, Federal Work-Study, scholarships/grants, tuition waivers (partial), and unspecified assistantships available. Support available to part-time students. Financial award application deadline: 3/1; financial award applicants required to submit FAFSA. In 2015, 128 master's, 13 doctorates, 5 other advanced degrees awarded. *Degree program information:* Part-time and evening/weekend programs available. Part-time, evening/weekend. Offers applied behavior analysis and autism (MS, Post Master's Certificate); childhood education/literacy (MS); childhood special education (MS Ed); education (MS, MS Ed, Ed D, Post Master's Certificate); educational leadership (Ed D); literacy (MS Ed); literacy/childhood special education (MS Ed); school counseling (MS, Post Master's Certificate); school health education (MS); special education (MS Ed). *Application deadline:* Applications are processed on a rolling basis. *Application fee:* $40. Electronic applications accepted. *Application Contact:* Wendy D. Diefendorf, Director of Graduate and Adult Admission, 518-244-2443, Fax: 518-244-6880, E-mail: diefew@sage.edu. *Interim Dean, Esteves School of Education*, Dr. John Pelizza, 518-244-2051, Fax: 518-244-2334, E-mail: pelizj@sage.edu.

School of Health Sciences Students: 340 full-time (289 women), 327 part-time (299 women); includes 96 minority (38 Black or African American, non-Hispanic/Latino; 3 American Indian or Alaska Native, non-Hispanic/Latino; 22 Asian, non-Hispanic/Latino; 15 Hispanic/Latino; 18 Two or more races, non-Hispanic/Latino), 4 international. Average age 31. 998 applicants, 30% accepted, 198 enrolled. *Faculty:* 31 full-time (28 women), 60 part-time/adjunct (51 women). *Financial support:* Fellowships, research assistantships, Federal Work-Study, scholarships/grants, and unspecified assistantships available. Support available to part-time students. Financial award application deadline: 3/1; financial award applicants required to submit FAFSA. In 2015, 97 master's, 46 doctorates, 44 other advanced degrees awarded. *Degree program information:* Part-time and evening/weekend programs available. Part-time, evening/weekend. Offers adult gerontology acute care (Post Master's Certificate); adult gerontology nurse practitioner (MS, Certificate); applied nutrition (MS); community psychology (MA); counseling and community psychology (MA); dietetic internship (Certificate); education and leadership (DNS); family nurse practitioner (MS, Post Master's Certificate); family psychiatric mental health (Post Master's Certificate); forensic mental health (Certificate); gerontological nurse practitioner (Post Master's Certificate); health sciences (MA, MS, DNS, DPT, Certificate, Post Master's Certificate, Postbaccalaureate Certificate); nurse administrator/executive (Post Master's Certificate); nutrition (Certificate); occupational therapy (MS); physical therapy (DPT); psychiatric mental health nurse clinical nurse specialist (MS); psychiatric mental health nurse practitioner (MS, Post Master's Certificate). *Application deadline:* Applications are processed on a rolling basis. *Application fee:* $40. Electronic applications accepted. *Application Contact:* Wendy D. Diefendorf, Director of Graduate and Adult Admission, 518-244-2443, Fax: 518-244-6880, E-mail: diefew@sage.edu. *Dean, School of Health Sciences*, Dr. Theresa Hand, 518-244-2264, Fax: 518-244-4571, E-mail: handt@sage.edu.

School of Management Students: 39 full-time (27 women), 109 part-time (70 women); includes 33 minority (19 Black or African American, non-Hispanic/Latino; 10 Asian, non-Hispanic/Latino; 4 Hispanic/Latino), 8 international. Average age 33. 162 applicants, 40% accepted, 43 enrolled. *Faculty:* 3 full-time (2 women), 11 part-time/adjunct (4 women). *Financial support:* Fellowships, research assistantships, Federal Work-Study, scholarships/grants, and unspecified assistantships available. Support available to part-time students. Financial award application deadline: 3/1; financial award applicants required to submit FAFSA. In 2015, 42 master's awarded. *Degree program information:* Part-time and evening/weekend programs available. Part-time, evening/weekend, 100% online. Offers business strategy (MBA); finance (MBA); gerontology (MS); human resources (MBA); management (MBA, MS); marketing (MBA); organization management (MS). *Application deadline:* Applications are processed on a rolling basis. *Application fee:* $40. Electronic applications accepted. *Application Contact:* Wendy D. Diefendorf, Director of Graduate and Adult Admission, 518-244-2443, Fax: 518-244-6880, E-mail: diefew@sage.edu. *Dean, School of Management*, Dr. Kimberly Fredericks, 518-292-1782, Fax: 518-292-1964, E-mail: fredek1@sage.edu.

SAGINAW VALLEY STATE UNIVERSITY, University Center, MI 48710

General Information State-supported, coed, comprehensive institution. *Enrollment:* 9,766 graduate, professional, and undergraduate students; 270 full-time matriculated graduate/professional students (191 women), 575 part-time matriculated graduate/professional students (426 women). *Enrollment by degree level:* 786 master's, 41 doctoral, 18 other advanced degrees. *Graduate faculty:* 52 full-time (30 women), 34 part-time/adjunct (20 women). Tuition, state resident: full-time $9515; part-time $514 per credit hour. Tuition, nonresident: full-time $17,899; part-time $980 per credit hour. *Required fees:* $263; $14.60 per credit hour. Tuition and fees vary according to degree level. *Graduate housing:* Room and/or apartments available on a first-come, first-served basis to single students; on-campus housing not available to married students. *Student services:* Campus employment opportunities, career counseling, exercise/wellness program, free psychological counseling, international student services, multicultural affairs office, services for students with disabilities, writing training. *Library:* Zahnow Library. *Collection:* Books: 217,900 (physical), 107,479 (digital/electronic); Serial titles: 127 (physical), 50,291 (digital/electronic); Databases: 63. Weekly public service hours: 95.

Computer facilities: Computer purchase and lease plans are available. 424 computers available on campus for general student use. A campuswide network can be accessed from student residence rooms and from off campus. Online class registration is available. Website: http://www.svsu.edu/

General Application Contact: Jenna Briggs, Director, Graduate and International Admissions, 989-964-6096, Fax: 989-964-2788, E-mail: gradadm@svsu.edu.

GRADUATE UNITS

College of Arts and Behavioral Sciences Students: 43 full-time (26 women), 31 part-time (21 women); includes 17 minority (12 Black or African American, non-Hispanic/Latino; 2 Asian, non-Hispanic/Latino; 2 Hispanic/Latino; 1 Two or more races, non-Hispanic/Latino), 18 international. Average age 28. 60 applicants, 60% accepted, 25 enrolled. *Faculty:* 8 full-time (3 women), 5 part-time/adjunct (1 woman). *Financial support:* Federal Work-Study and scholarships/grants available. Support available to part-time students. Financial award applicants required to submit FAFSA. In 2015, 40 master's awarded. *Degree program information:* Part-time and evening/weekend programs available. Part-time, evening/weekend. Offers administrative science (MA); arts and behavioral sciences (MA); communication and media administration (MA). *Application deadline:* For fall admission, 7/15 for international students; for winter admission, 11/15 for international students; for spring admission, 4/15 for international students. Applications are processed on a rolling basis. *Application fee:* $30 ($90 for international students). Electronic applications accepted. *Application Contact:* Jenna Briggs, Director, Graduate and International Admissions, 989-964-6096, Fax: 989-964-2788, E-mail: gradadm@svsu.edu. *Dean*, Dr. Joni Boye-Beaman, 989-964-4062, Fax: 989-964-7232, E-mail: jbb@svsu.edu.

College of Business and Management Students: 47 full-time (13 women), 50 part-time (22 women); includes 6 minority (5 Black or African American, non-Hispanic/Latino; 1 Two or more races, non-Hispanic/Latino), 51 international. Average age 29. 220 applicants, 30% accepted, 27 enrolled. *Faculty:* 13 full-time (4 women), 2 part-time/adjunct (0 women). *Financial support:* Federal Work-Study and scholarships/grants available. Support available to part-time students. Financial award application deadline: 4/1; financial award applicants required to submit FAFSA. In 2015, 42 master's awarded. *Degree program information:* Part-time and evening/weekend programs available. Part-time, evening/weekend. Offers business administration (MBA); business and management (MBA). *Application deadline:* For fall admission, 7/15 for international students; for winter admission, 11/15 for international students; for spring admission, 4/15 for international students. Applications are processed on a rolling basis. *Application fee:* $30 ($90 for international students). Electronic applications accepted. *Application Contact:* Jenna Briggs, Director, Graduate and International Admissions, 989-964-6096, Fax: 989-964-2788, E-mail: gradadm@svsu.edu. *MBA Program Coordinator*, Dr. Mark McCartney, 989-964-4064.

College of Education Students: 21 full-time (19 women), 302 part-time (238 women); includes 25 minority (14 Black or African American, non-Hispanic/Latino; 3 Asian, non-Hispanic/Latino; 5 Hispanic/Latino; 3 Two or more races, non-Hispanic/Latino), 6 international. Average age 34. 111 applicants, 90% accepted, 72 enrolled. *Faculty:* 14 full-time (9 women), 20 part-time/adjunct (15 women). *Financial support:* Federal Work-Study and scholarships/grants available. Support available to part-time students. Financial award applicants required to submit FAFSA. In 2015, 172 master's, 22 other advanced degrees awarded. *Degree program information:* Part-time and evening/weekend programs available. Part-time, evening/weekend, online learning. Offers chief business officers (M Ed); e-learning (MA); early childhood education (MAT); education (M Ed, MA, MAT, Ed S); education leadership (Ed S); educational administration and supervision (M Ed); educational leadership (M Ed); elementary classroom teaching (MAT); elementary school (MAT); instructional technology (MA); K-12 literacy specialist (MAT); middle school (MAT); middle school classroom teaching (MAT); principalship (M Ed); reading education (MAT); secondary classroom teaching (MAT); secondary school (MAT); special education (MAT); superintendency (M Ed); teaching Chinese as a foreign language (MAT). *Application deadline:* For fall admission, 7/15 for international students; for winter admission, 11/15 for international students; for spring admission, 4/15 for international students. Applications are processed on a rolling basis. *Application fee:* $30 ($90 for international students). Electronic applications accepted. *Application Contact:* Jenna Briggs, Director, Graduate and International Admissions, 989-964-6096, Fax: 989-964-2788, E-mail: gradadm@svsu.edu. *Dean*, Dr. Craig C. Douglas, 989-964-4057, Fax: 989-964-4563, E-mail: coeconnect@svsu.edu.

College of Health and Human Services Students: 155 full-time (133 women), 189 part-time (143 women); includes 27 minority (10 Black or African American, non-Hispanic/Latino; 1 American Indian or Alaska Native, non-Hispanic/Latino; 2 Asian, non-Hispanic/Latino; 7 Hispanic/Latino; 7 Two or more races, non-Hispanic/Latino), 17 international. Average age 28. 141 applicants, 60% accepted, 62 enrolled. *Faculty:* 18 full-time (15 women), 5 part-time/adjunct (4 women). *Financial support:* Federal Work-Study and scholarships/grants available. Support available to part-time students. Financial award application deadline: 4/1; financial award applicants required to submit FAFSA. In 2015, 102 master's awarded. *Degree program information:* Part-time and evening/weekend programs available. Part-time, evening/weekend. Offers clinical nurse specialist (MSN); health and human services (MS, MSN, MSOT, DNP); health leadership (MS); health system nurse specialist (MSN); nurse practitioner (MSN, DNP); nursing (MSN); occupational therapy (MSOT). *Application deadline:* For fall admission, 7/15 for international students; for winter admission, 11/15 for international students; for spring admission, 4/15 for international students. Applications are processed on a rolling basis. *Application fee:* $30 ($90 for international students). Electronic applications accepted. *Application Contact:* Jenna Briggs, Director, Graduate and International Admissions, 989-964-6096, Fax: 989-964-2788, E-mail: gradadm@svsu.edu. *Dean*, Dr. Judith Ruland, 989-964-4145, Fax: 989-964-4024, E-mail: jruland@svsu.edu.

College of Science, Engineering, and Technology Students: 4 full-time (0 women), 3 part-time (2 women); includes 1 minority (Black or African American, non-Hispanic/Latino), 4 international. Average age 27. 69 applicants, 13% accepted, 4 enrolled. *Faculty:* 1 full-time (0 women), 2 part-time/adjunct (0 women). *Financial support:* Federal Work-Study and scholarships/grants available. Support available to part-time students. Financial award application deadline: 4/1; financial award applicants required to submit FAFSA. In 2015, 5 master's awarded. *Degree program information:* Part-time and evening/weekend programs available. Part-time, evening/weekend. Offers energy and materials (MS). *Application deadline:* For fall admission, 7/15 for international students; for winter admission, 11/15 for international students; for spring admission, 4/15 for international students. Applications are processed on a rolling basis. *Application fee:* $30 ($90 for international students). Electronic applications accepted. *Application Contact:* Jenna Briggs, Director, Graduate and International Admissions, 989-964-6096, Fax: 989-964-2788, E-mail: gradadm@svsu.edu. *Program Coordinator*, Dr. Robert Tuttle, 989-964-4144, Fax: 989-964-2717.

ST. AMBROSE UNIVERSITY, Davenport, IA 52803-2898

General Information Independent-religious, coed, comprehensive institution. CGS member. *Graduate housing:* Room and/or apartments available on a first-come, first-served basis to single students; on-campus housing not available to married students. Housing application deadline: 3/1.

GRADUATE UNITS

College of Arts and Sciences ***Degree program information:*** Part-time and evening/weekend programs available. Part-time, evening/weekend. Offers arts and sciences (MCJ, MP Th, MSITM); criminal justice (MCJ); information technology management (MSITM); juvenile justice education (MCJ); pastoral theology (MP Th). Electronic applications accepted.

College of Business ***Degree program information:*** Part-time and evening/weekend programs available. Part-time, evening/weekend. Offers accounting (MAC); business (MAC, MBA, MOL, DBA); business administration (DBA); health care (MBA); human resources (MBA); organizational leadership (MOL). Electronic applications accepted.

College of Education and Health Sciences ***Degree program information:*** Part-time and evening/weekend programs available. Part-time, evening/weekend, online learning. Offers education and health sciences (M Ed, MEA, MOT, MSLP, MSN, MSW, DPT); educational administration (MEA); nursing (MSN); occupational therapy (MOT); physical therapy (DPT); social work (MSW); special education (M Ed); speech-language pathology (MSLP); teaching (M Ed). Electronic applications accepted.

ST. ANDREW'S COLLEGE, Saskatoon, SK S7N 0W3, Canada

General Information Independent-religious, coed, graduate-only institution.

GRADUATE UNITS

Graduate Programs in Theology Offers theology (M Div, MTS, STM, D Min, Diploma).

ST. ANDREW'S COLLEGE IN WINNIPEG, Winnipeg, MB R3T 2M7, Canada

General Information Independent-religious, coed, primarily men, graduate-only institution. *Graduate housing:* Rooms and/or apartments available to single and married students. Housing application deadline: 7/31.

GRADUATE UNITS

Graduate Programs Offers theology (M Div).

SAINT ANTHONY COLLEGE OF NURSING, Rockford, IL 61108-2468

General Information Independent-religious, coed, primarily women, upper-level institution.

GRADUATE UNITS

Graduate Program ***Degree program information:*** Part-time programs available. Part-time. Offers nursing (MSN).

ST. AUGUSTINE'S SEMINARY OF TORONTO, Scarborough, ON M1M 1M3, Canada

General Information Independent-religious, coed, primarily men, graduate-only institution. *Graduate housing:* On-campus housing not available.

GRADUATE UNITS

Graduate and Professional Programs ***Degree program information:*** Part-time and evening/weekend programs available. Part-time, evening/weekend. Offers divinity (M Div); lay ministry (Diploma); religious education (MRE); theological studies (MTS, Diploma).

ST. BERNARD'S SCHOOL OF THEOLOGY AND MINISTRY, Rochester, NY 14618

General Information Independent-religious, coed, graduate-only institution. *Enrollment by degree level:* 96 master's, 5 other advanced degrees. *Graduate faculty:* 4 full-time (3 women), 4 part-time/adjunct (1 woman). *Tuition, area resident:* Full-time $10,644; part-time $3548 per year. *Required fees:* $40 per semester. *Graduate housing:* On-campus housing not available. *Student services:* Services for students with disabilities, writing training. *Library:* Rush Rhees Library at University of Rochester plus 1 other. *Research affiliation:* Colgate Rochester Crozer Divinity School.

Computer facilities: 3 computers available on campus for general student use. A campuswide network can be accessed. Online class registration is available.
Website: http://www.stbernards.edu/

General Application Contact: Jonathan C Schott, Director of Recruitment, Admissions, Financial Aid and Alumni, 585-271-3657 Ext. 289, Fax: 585-271-2045, E-mail: admissions@stbernards.edu.

GRADUATE UNITS

Graduate and Professional Programs Students: 1 (woman) full-time, 102 part-time (59 women); includes 6 minority (1 Black or African American, non-Hispanic/Latino; 3 Asian, non-Hispanic/Latino; 2 Hispanic/Latino). *Faculty:* 4 full-time (3 women), 4 part-time/adjunct (1 woman). *Financial support:* In 2015–16, 30 students received support. Fellowships, research assistantships, teaching assistantships, career-related internships or fieldwork, scholarships/grants, and tuition waivers (partial) available. Support available to part-time students. Financial award application deadline: 4/15; financial award applicants required to submit FAFSA. *Degree program information:* Part-time and evening/weekend programs available. Part-time, evening/weekend. Offers pastoral studies (MA, Certificate); theological studies (MA); theology (M Div). *Application deadline:* Applications are processed on a rolling basis. *Application fee:* $75. *Application Contact:* Jonathan C. Schott, Director of Recruitment, Admissions, Financial Aid and Alumni, 585-271-3657 Ext. 289, Fax: 585-271-2045, E-mail: admissions@stbernards.edu. *President,* Rev. George Heyman, 585-271-3657 Ext. 292, Fax: 585-271-2045, E-mail: gheyman@stbernards.edu.

ST. BONAVENTURE UNIVERSITY, St. Bonaventure, NY 14778-2284

General Information Independent-religious, coed, comprehensive institution. CGS member. *Enrollment:* 2,011 graduate, professional, and undergraduate students; 187 full-time matriculated graduate/professional students (122 women), 127 part-time matriculated graduate/professional students (87 women). *Enrollment by degree level:* 299 master's, 15 other advanced degrees. *Graduate faculty:* 30 full-time (13 women), 27 part-time/adjunct (17 women). *Tuition, area resident:* Part-time $711 per credit. One-time fee: $100. *Graduate housing:* Room and/or apartments available on a first-come, first-served basis to single students; on-campus housing not available to married students. Typical cost: $5888 per year. Room charges vary according to board plan. Housing application deadline: 3/19. *Student services:* Campus employment opportunities, career counseling, free psychological counseling, international student services, low-cost health insurance, multicultural affairs office, services for students with disabilities, teacher training. *Library:* Friedsam Memorial Library. *Collection:* Books: 451,753 (physical), 17,777 (digital/electronic); Serial titles: 253 (physical), 30,682 (digital/electronic); Databases: 63. Weekly public service hours: 109; students can reserve study rooms.

Computer facilities: 300 computers available on campus for general student use. A campuswide network can be accessed from student residence rooms and from off campus. Online class registration is available.
Website: http://www.sbu.edu/

General Application Contact: Bruce Campbell, Director of Graduate Admissions, 716-375-2429, Fax: 716-375-4015, E-mail: gradsch@sbu.edu.

GRADUATE UNITS

School of Graduate Studies Students: 187 full-time (122 women), 127 part-time (87 women); includes 34 minority (12 Black or African American, non-Hispanic/Latino; 2 American Indian or Alaska Native, non-Hispanic/Latino; 5 Asian, non-Hispanic/Latino; 9 Hispanic/Latino; 6 Two or more races, non-Hispanic/Latino), 4 international. Average age 29. 164 applicants, 98% accepted, 98 enrolled. *Faculty:* 30 full-time (13 women), 27 part-time/adjunct (17 women). *Financial support:* In 2015–16, 14 fellowships with partial tuition reimbursements (averaging $3,500 per year) were awarded; career-related internships or fieldwork, Federal Work-Study, scholarships/grants, health care benefits, and unspecified assistantships also available. Support available to part-time students. Financial award application deadline: 4/15; financial award applicants required to submit FAFSA. In 2015, 212 master's, 20 other advanced degrees awarded. *Degree program information:* Part-time and evening/weekend programs available. Part-time, evening/weekend. Offers English (MA). *Application deadline:* For fall admission, 3/15 priority date for domestic students, 2/1 priority date for international students; for spring admission, 10/15 priority date for domestic students, 7/1 priority date for international students. Applications are processed on a rolling basis. *Application fee:* $0. Electronic applications accepted. *Application Contact:* Bruce Campbell, Director of Graduate Admissions, 716-375-2429, Fax: 716-375-4015, E-mail: gradsch@sbu.edu. *Provost and Vice President for Academic Affairs,* Dr. Joseph E. Zimmer, 716-375-2121, Fax: 716-375-7834, E-mail: jezimmer@sbu.edu.

Russell J. Jandoli School of Journalism and Mass Communication Students: 42 full-time (26 women), 34 part-time (21 women); includes 12 minority (6 Black or African American, non-Hispanic/Latino; 4 Hispanic/Latino; 2 Two or more races, non-Hispanic/Latino), 3 international. Average age 30. 45 applicants, 91% accepted, 31 enrolled. *Faculty:* 5 full-time (3 women), 8 part-time/adjunct (5 women). *Financial support:* Federal Work-Study, scholarships/grants, health care benefits, tuition waivers (partial), and unspecified assistantships available. Support available to part-time students. Financial award application deadline: 4/15; financial award applicants required to submit FAFSA. In 2015, 30 master's awarded. *Degree program information:* Part-time and evening/weekend programs available. Part-time, evening/weekend, online learning. Offers integrated marketing communications (MA); journalism and mass communication (MA); strategic leadership (MA). *Application deadline:* For fall admission, 6/15 priority date for domestic students, 2/1 priority date for international students; for spring admission, 10/15 priority date for domestic students, 7/1 priority date for international students. Applications are processed on a rolling basis. *Application fee:* $0. Electronic applications accepted. *Application Contact:* Bruce Campbell, Director of Graduate Admissions, 716-375-2429, Fax: 716-375-4015, E-mail: gradsch@sbu.edu. *Dean,* Dr. Pauline Hoffmann, 716-375-2578, Fax: 716-375-2588, E-mail: hoffmann@sbu.edu.

School of Business Students: 49 full-time (24 women), 34 part-time (19 women); includes 12 minority (3 Black or African American, non-Hispanic/Latino; 2 American Indian or Alaska Native, non-Hispanic/Latino; 3 Asian, non-Hispanic/Latino; 3 Hispanic/Latino; 1 Two or more races, non-Hispanic/Latino), 1 international. Average age 29. 45 applicants, 100% accepted, 29 enrolled. *Faculty:* 11 full-time (2 women), 4 part-time/adjunct (all women). *Financial support:* Career-related internships or fieldwork, Federal Work-Study, scholarships/grants, health care benefits, and unspecified assistantships available. Support available to part-time students. Financial award application deadline: 4/15; financial award applicants required to submit FAFSA. In 2015, 48 master's awarded. *Degree program information:* Part-time and evening/weekend programs available. Part-time, evening/weekend, online learning. Offers general business (MBA). *Application deadline:* For fall admission, 6/15 priority date for domestic students, 2/1 priority date for international students; for spring admission, 11/1 priority date for domestic students, 7/1 priority date for international students. Applications are processed on a rolling basis. *Application fee:* $0. Electronic applications accepted. *Application Contact:* Bruce Campbell, Director of Graduate Admissions, 716-375-2429, Fax: 716-375-4015, E-mail: gradsch@sbu.edu. *Dean,* Dr. Carol Fischer, 716-375-2092, Fax: 716-372-2191, E-mail: bmac@sbu.edu.

School of Education Students: 87 full-time (69 women), 57 part-time (45 women); includes 8 minority (3 Black or African American, non-Hispanic/Latino; 2 Hispanic/Latino; 3 Two or more races, non-Hispanic/Latino). Average age 29. 60 applicants, 100% accepted, 31 enrolled. *Faculty:* 14 full-time (7 women), 15 part-time/adjunct (12 women). *Financial support:* Career-related internships or fieldwork, Federal Work-Study, scholarships/grants, health care benefits, tuition waivers (partial), and unspecified assistantships available. Support available to part-time students. Financial award application deadline: 4/15; financial award applicants required to submit FAFSA. In 2015, 81 master's, 20 Adv Cs awarded. *Degree program information:* Part-time and evening/weekend programs available. Part-time, evening/weekend. Offers adolescence education (MS Ed); adolescent literacy 5-12 (MS Ed); childhood literacy B-6 (MS Ed); community mental health counseling (MS Ed); education (MS Ed, Adv C); educational leadership (MS Ed); gifted education (MS Ed, Adv C); gifted education and students with disabilities (MS Ed); rehabilitation counseling (MS Ed); school building leader (Adv C); school counseling (MS Ed); school counselor (Adv C); school district leader (Adv C). *Application deadline:* For fall admission, 6/15 priority date for domestic students, 2/1 priority date for international students; for spring admission, 11/15 priority date for domestic students, 7/1 priority date for international students. Applications are processed on a rolling basis. *Application fee:* $0. Electronic applications accepted. *Application Contact:* Bruce Campbell, Director of Graduate Admissions, 716-375-2429, Fax: 716-375-4015, E-mail: gradsch@sbu.edu. *Dean,* Dr. Nancy Casey, 716-375-2394, Fax: 716-375-2360, E-mail: jezimmer@sbu.edu.

School of Franciscan Studies Students: 1 (woman) part-time; minority (Asian, non-Hispanic/Latino). Average age 44. *Financial support:* Federal Work-Study, scholarships/grants, health care benefits, and unspecified assistantships available. Support available to part-time students. Financial award application deadline: 4/15; financial award applicants required to submit FAFSA. In 2015, 3 master's awarded. *Degree program information:* Part-time programs available. Part-time. Offers Franciscan studies (MA). *Application deadline:* For fall admission, 3/15 priority date for domestic students, 2/1 priority date for international students. Applications are processed on a rolling basis. *Application fee:* $0. Electronic applications accepted. *Application Contact:* Bruce Campbell, Director of Graduate Admissions, 716-375-2429, Fax: 716-375-4015, E-mail: gradsch@sbu.edu. *Dean,* Fr. David Couturier, OFM, 716-375-2160, E-mail: dcouturi@sbu.edu.

ST. CATHERINE UNIVERSITY, St. Paul, MN 55105

General Information Independent-religious, Undergraduate: women only; graduate: coed, comprehensive institution. CGS member. *Enrollment:* 4,961 graduate, professional, and undergraduate students; 675 full-time matriculated graduate/professional students (589 women), 966 part-time matriculated graduate/professional students (872 women). *Enrollment by degree level:* 1,319 master's, 166 doctoral, 156 other advanced degrees. *Graduate faculty:* 70 full-time (59 women), 57 part-time/adjunct (44 women). Tuition and fees vary according to program. *Graduate housing:* Rooms and/or apartments available on a first-come, first-served basis to single and married students. Housing application deadline: 5/1. *Student services:* Campus employment opportunities, campus safety program, career counseling, child daycare facilities, exercise/wellness program, free psychological counseling, international student services, low-cost health insurance, multicultural affairs office, services for students with disabilities. *Library:* St. Catherine Library.

Computer facilities: Computer purchase and lease plans are available. A campuswide network can be accessed from student residence rooms and from off campus. Online class registration, transcript are available.
Website: http://www.stkate.edu/

General Application Contact: Sylvia Alexander-Sedey, Senior Admissions Counselor, 651-690-6933, Fax: 651-690-6064, E-mail: graduate_study@stkate.edu.

GRADUATE UNITS

Graduate Programs ***Degree program information:*** Part-time and evening/weekend programs available. Part-time, evening/weekend, online learning. Offers adult gerontological nurse practitioner (MS); catechetical ministry (Certificate); education - initial licensure (MA); education - Montessori education (MA); education–curriculum and instruction (MA); healthcare (MBA); holistic health studies (MA); integrated marketing communications (MBA); library and information science (MLIS); management (MBA); neonatal nurse practitioner (MS); nurse educator (MS); nursing (DNP); nursing: entry-level (MS); occupational therapy (MA, OTD); organizational leadership (MA); pastoral ministry (Certificate); pediatric nurse practitioner (MS); physical therapy (DPT); physician assistant studies (MPAS); social work (MSW, DSW); spiritual direction (Certificate); theology (MA).

SAINT CHARLES BORROMEO SEMINARY, OVERBROOK, Wynnewood, PA 19096

General Information Independent-religious, coed, primarily men, comprehensive institution. *Graduate housing:* Room and/or apartments guaranteed to single students; on-campus housing not available to married students. Housing application deadline: 7/15.

GRADUATE UNITS

Graduate and Professional Programs ***Degree program information:*** Part-time and evening/weekend programs available. Part-time, evening/weekend. Offers Catholic studies (MA).

Division of Theology Offers theology (M Div, MA).

ST. CLOUD STATE UNIVERSITY, St. Cloud, MN 56301-4498

General Information State-supported, coed, comprehensive institution. CGS member. *Graduate housing:* Room and/or apartments available on a first-come, first-served basis to single students; on-campus housing not available to married students. Housing application deadline: 4/15.

GRADUATE UNITS

School of Graduate Studies ***Degree program information:*** Part-time and evening/weekend programs available. Part-time, evening/weekend, online learning. Electronic applications accepted.

College of Liberal Arts Offers conducting and literature (MM); English (MA, MS); history (MA, MS); industrial-organizational psychology (MS); liberal arts (MA, MM, MS); mass communications (MS); music education (MM); piano pedagogy (MM); teaching English as a second language (MA).

College of Science and Engineering Offers applied statistics (MS); biology (MA, MS); computer science (MS); electrical engineering (MS); engineering management (MEM); environmental and technological studies (MS); information assurance (MS); mathematics (MS); mechanical engineering (MS); regulatory affairs and services (MS); science and engineering (MA, MEM, MS). Electronic applications accepted.

College of Social Sciences Degree program information: Part-time programs available. Part-time. Offers applied economics (MS); criminal justice (MS); criminal justice administration (MS); cultural resource management archeology (MS); geography and planning (MS); public and nonprofit institutions (MS); public safety executive leadership (MS); social sciences (MA, MS, MSW). Electronic applications accepted.

Herberger Business School Degree program information: Part-time and evening/weekend programs available. Part-time, evening/weekend. Offers business (MBA, MS); business administration (MBA); information assurance (MS). Electronic applications accepted.

School of Education Degree program information: Part-time and evening/weekend programs available. Part-time, evening/weekend, online learning. Offers child and family studies (MS); college counseling and student development (MS); curriculum and instruction (MS); developmental/cognitive disabilities (MS); education (MS, Ed D); emotional/behavioral disorders (MS); gifted and talented (MS); higher education administration (MS, Ed D); information media (MS); learning disabilities (MS); rehabilitation counseling (MS); school counseling (MS); social responsibility (MS); special education (MS).

School of Health and Human Services Offers applied behavior analysis (MS); communication sciences and disorders (MS); community counseling (MS); educational administration and leadership (MS); educational leadership and community psychology (Spt); exercise science (MS); gerontology (MS); health and human services (MS, MSW, Spt); marriage and family therapy (MS); social work (MSW); sports management (MS).

ST. EDWARD'S UNIVERSITY, Austin, TX 78704

General Information Independent-religious, coed, comprehensive institution. *Enrollment:* 4,620 graduate, professional, and undergraduate students; 179 full-time matriculated graduate/professional students (134 women), 362 part-time matriculated graduate/professional students (228 women). *Enrollment by degree level:* 541 master's. *Tuition, area resident:* Full-time $23,778; part-time $1321 per credit hour. *Required fees:* $50 per trimester. Full-time tuition and fees vary according to course load and program. *Graduate housing:* On-campus housing not available. *Student services:* Campus employment opportunities, campus safety program, career counseling, exercise/wellness program, free psychological counseling, international student services, low-cost health insurance, services for students with disabilities, writing training. *Library:* Munday Library. *Collection:* Books: 76,800 (physical), 341,000 (digital/electronic); Serial titles: 72 (physical), 160,000 (digital/electronic); Databases: 160. Weekly public service hours: 103; students can reserve study rooms.

Computer facilities: 967 computers available on campus for general student use. A campuswide network can be accessed from student residence rooms and from off campus. Online class registration, online library, ability to change address and biographical data, look at transcripts, pull up statements of account, grades, online progress reports and degree audit, campus job postings, student timesheets, financial aid information are available.
Website: http://www.stedwards.edu/

General Application Contact: David Bralower, Director of Graduate Admission, 512-233-1424, Fax: 512-464-8877, E-mail: davidcb@stedwards.edu.

GRADUATE UNITS

Bill Munday School of Business Students: 40 full-time (20 women), 178 part-time (82 women); includes 85 minority (18 Black or African American, non-Hispanic/Latino; 7 Asian, non-Hispanic/Latino; 55 Hispanic/Latino; 1 Native Hawaiian or other Pacific Islander, non-Hispanic/Latino; 4 Two or more races, non-Hispanic/Latino), 16 international. Average age 32. 217 applicants, 65% accepted, 77 enrolled. In 2015, 97 master's awarded. *Degree program information:* Part-time and evening/weekend programs available. Part-time, evening/weekend. Offers accounting (M Ac, MBA); business (Certificate); business administration (MBA); digital management (MBA); finance (Certificate); leadership and change (MS). *Application deadline:* For fall admission, 6/1 priority date for domestic and international students; for spring admission, 10/1 priority date for domestic and international students; for summer admission, 3/1 priority date for domestic and international students. Applications are processed on a rolling basis. *Application fee:* $50. Electronic applications accepted. *Application Contact:* Mike Leveriza, Graduate Recruiter, 512-448-8745, Fax: 512-464-8877, E-mail: mleveriz@stedwards.edu. *Dean*, Dr. Nancy Schreiber, 512-428-1287, Fax: 512-428-1217, E-mail: nschreib@stedwards.edu.

New College Students: 101 full-time (86 women), 184 part-time (146 women); includes 96 minority (18 Black or African American, non-Hispanic/Latino; 1 American Indian or Alaska Native, non-Hispanic/Latino; 9 Asian, non-Hispanic/Latino; 62 Hispanic/Latino; 6 Two or more races, non-Hispanic/Latino), 2 international. Average age 33. 201 applicants, 59% accepted, 65 enrolled. In 2015, 122 master's awarded. *Degree program information:* Part-time and evening/weekend programs available. Part-time, evening/weekend. Offers college student development (MA); counseling (MA); global issues (MLA); humanities (MLA); liberal arts (Certificate); social justice (MLA); social sciences (MLA). *Application deadline:* For fall admission, 6/1 priority date for domestic and international students; for spring admission, 10/1 priority date for domestic and international students; for summer admission, 3/1 priority date for domestic and international students. Applications are processed on a rolling basis. *Application fee:* $50. Electronic applications accepted. *Application Contact:* Jane Hamann, Graduate Admission Counselor, 512-326-7333, Fax: 512-464-8877, E-mail: jhamann1@stedwards.edu. *Dean*, Dr. Ramsey Fowler, 512-448-8736, Fax: 512-448-8492, E-mail: ramseyf@stedwards.edu.

School of Behavioral and Social Sciences Students: 38 full-time (28 women); includes 8 minority (1 Asian, non-Hispanic/Latino; 7 Hispanic/Latino), 1 international. Average age 26. 67 applicants, 58% accepted, 21 enrolled. In 2015, 15 master's awarded. Offers environmental management and sustainability (PSM). *Application deadline:* For fall admission, 2/15 priority date for domestic and international students. Applications are processed on a rolling basis. *Application fee:* $50. Electronic applications accepted. *Application Contact:* Jane Hamann, Graduate Admission Counselor, 512-326-7333, Fax: 512-464-8877, E-mail: jhamann1@stedwards.edu. *Program Director*, Dr. Peter Beck, 512-428-1249, Fax: 512-233-1664, E-mail: peterab@stedwards.edu.

ST. FRANCIS COLLEGE, Brooklyn Heights, NY 11201-4398

General Information Independent-religious, coed, comprehensive institution.

GRADUATE UNITS

Program in Professional Accountancy Offers professional accountancy (MS).

SAINT FRANCIS MEDICAL CENTER COLLEGE OF NURSING, Peoria, IL 61603-3783

General Information Independent-religious, coed, primarily women, upper-level institution. *Enrollment:* 678 graduate, professional, and undergraduate students; 10 full-time matriculated graduate/professional students (9 women), 267 part-time matriculated graduate/professional students (244 women). *Enrollment by degree level:* 243 master's, 25 doctoral, 9 other advanced degrees. *Graduate faculty:* 10 full-time (all women), 5 part-time/adjunct (all women). *Graduate housing:* Room and/or apartments available on a first-come, first-served basis to single students; on-campus housing not available to married students. Housing application deadline: 3/15. *Student services:* Campus safety program, exercise/wellness program, free psychological counseling, multicultural affairs office. *Library:* Sister Mary Ludgera Pieperbeck Learning and Resource Center plus 1 other. *Collection:* Books: 2,461 (physical); Serial titles: 18 (physical); Databases: 3. Students can reserve study rooms.

Computer facilities: 62 computers available on campus for general student use. A campuswide network can be accessed from student residence rooms and from off campus. Online class registration is available.
Website: http://www.sfmccon.edu/

General Application Contact: Dr. Janice F. Boundy, Associate Dean, 309-655-2230, Fax: 309-624-8973, E-mail: jan.f.boundy@osfhealthcare.org.

GRADUATE UNITS

Graduate Programs Students: 13 full-time (12 women), 257 part-time (228 women); includes 23 minority (14 Black or African American, non-Hispanic/Latino; 3 Asian, non-Hispanic/Latino; 4 Hispanic/Latino; 2 Two or more races, non-Hispanic/Latino). Average age 37. 86 applicants, 86% accepted, 44 enrolled. *Faculty:* 14 full-time (all women), 5 part-time/adjunct (all women). *Financial support:* In 2015–16, 18 students received support. Scholarships/grants and tuition waivers (partial) available. Support available to part-time students. Financial award application deadline: 6/15; financial award applicants required to submit FAFSA. In 2015, 61 master's, 6 doctorates awarded. *Degree program information:* Part-time programs available. Part-time, 100% online, blended/hybrid learning. Offers adult gerontology (MSN); clinical nurse leader (MSN); family nurse practitioner (MSN); family psychiatric mental health nurse practitioner (MSN); neonatal nurse practitioner (MSN); nurse clinician (Post-Graduate Certificate); nurse educator (MSN, Post-Graduate Certificate); nursing (DNP); nursing management leadership (MSN). *Application deadline:* For fall admission, 6/1 priority date for domestic and international students; for spring admission, 11/15 priority date for domestic and international students. Applications are processed on a rolling basis. *Application fee:* $50. *Application Contact:* Dr. Kim A. Mitchell, Dean, Graduate Program, 309-655-2201, Fax: 309-624-8973, E-mail: kim.a.mitchell@osfhealthcare.org. *President of the College*, Dr. Patti A. Stockert, 309-655-4124, Fax: 309-624-8973, E-mail: patricia.a.stockert@osfhealthcare.org.

SAINT FRANCIS UNIVERSITY, Loretto, PA 15940-0600

General Information Independent-religious, coed, comprehensive institution. *Graduate housing:* On-campus housing not available. *Student services:* Campus employment opportunities, campus safety program, career counseling, exercise/wellness program, free psychological counseling, low-cost health insurance, multicultural affairs office, services for students with disabilities, writing training. *Library:* Saint Francis University Library. *Collection:* Books: 76,787 (physical), 153,616 (digital/electronic); Databases: 74.

Computer facilities: Computer purchase and lease plans are available. 75 computers available on campus for general student use. A campuswide network can be accessed from student residence rooms and from off campus. Online class registration is available. Website: http://www.francis.edu/

General Application Contact: Dr. Peter Raymond Skoner, Associate Provost, 814-472-3085, Fax: 814-472-3365, E-mail: pskoner@francis.edu.

GRADUATE UNITS

Department of Occupational Therapy Offers occupational therapy (MOT). *Application Contact:* Dr. Peter Raymond Skoner, Associate Vice President for Academic Affairs, 814-472-3085, Fax: 814-472-3365, E-mail: pskoner@francis.edu.

Department of Physical Therapy *Financial support:* Teaching assistantships with partial tuition reimbursements and unspecified assistantships available. Offers physical therapy (DPT). *Application deadline:* For winter admission, 1/15 for domestic and international students. *Application fee:* $30. Electronic applications accepted. *Application Contact:* Dr. Peter Raymond Skoner, Associate Provost, 814-472-3085, Fax: 814-472-3365, E-mail: pskoner@francis.edu. *Chair/Associate Professor,* Dr. Ivan J. Mulligan, 814-472-3123, Fax: 814-472-3140, E-mail: imulligan@francis.edu.

Department of Physician Assistant Sciences *Financial support:* Applicants required to submit FAFSA. Offers physician assistant sciences (MPAS). *Application deadline:* For fall admission, 10/1 for domestic and international students. Applications are processed on a rolling basis. *Application fee:* $175. Electronic applications accepted.

Graduate Education Program *Financial support:* Applicants required to submit FAFSA. *Degree program information:* Part-time programs available. Part-time, 100% online, blended/hybrid learning. Offers education (M Ed); leadership (M Ed); reading (M Ed). *Application deadline:* Applications are processed on a rolling basis. *Application fee:* $30. *Application Contact:* Sherri L. Toth, Coordinator, 814-472-3058, Fax: 814-472-3864, E-mail: stoth@francis.edu. *Director,* Dr. Janette D. Kelly, 814-472-3068, Fax: 814-472-3864, E-mail: jkelly@francis.edu.

Health Science Program *Financial support:* Available to part-time students. Applicants required to submit FAFSA. *Degree program information:* Part-time and evening/weekend programs available. Part-time, evening/weekend, online learning. Offers health science (MHS). *Application deadline:* For fall admission, 7/19 for domestic and international students; for spring admission, 11/15 for domestic and international students; for summer admission, 3/22 for domestic and international students. Applications are processed on a rolling basis. *Application fee:* $50. Electronic applications accepted. *Application Contact:* Jean A. Kline, Administrative Assistant, 814-472-3357, Fax: 814-472-3066, E-mail: jkline@francis.edu.

Medical Science Program *Financial support:* Available to part-time students. Applicants required to submit FAFSA. *Degree program information:* Part-time and evening/weekend programs available. Part-time, evening/weekend, online learning. Offers medical science (MMS). *Application deadline:* For fall admission, 6/15 for domestic students; for spring admission, 11/15 for domestic students; for summer admission, 3/15 for domestic students. Applications are processed on a rolling basis. *Application fee:* $0. Electronic applications accepted. *Application Contact:* Jean A. Kline, Administrative Assistant, 814-472-3357, Fax: 814-472-3066, E-mail: jkline@francis.edu.

School of Business *Financial support:* Fellowships with partial tuition reimbursements, career-related internships or fieldwork, and unspecified assistantships available. Financial award application deadline: 8/15. *Degree program information:* Part-time and evening/weekend programs available. Part-time, evening/weekend. Offers business administration (MBA); human resource management (MHRM). *Application deadline:* For fall admission, 8/15 priority date for domestic and international students; for spring admission, 12/1 priority date for domestic students, 12/1 for international students. Applications are processed on a rolling basis. *Application fee:* $30. *Application Contact:* Nicole Marie Bauman, Coordinator, Graduate Business Programs, 814-472-3026, Fax: 814-472-3369, E-mail: nbauman@francis.edu. *Director, Graduate Business Programs,* Dr. Randy L. Frye, 814-472-3041, Fax: 814-472-3174, E-mail: rfrye@francis.edu.

ST. FRANCIS XAVIER UNIVERSITY, Antigonish, NS B2G 2W5, Canada

General Information Independent-religious, coed, comprehensive institution. *Graduate housing:* Room and/or apartments available on a first-come, first-served basis to single students; on-campus housing not available to married students. Housing application deadline: 7/1.

GRADUATE UNITS

Graduate Studies *Degree program information:* Part-time programs available. Part-time, online learning. Offers adult education (M Ad Ed); biology (M Sc); Celtic studies (MA); chemistry (M Sc); computer science (M Sc); curriculum and instruction (M Ed); earth sciences (M Sc); educational administration and leadership (M Ed); physics (M Sc).

ST. JOHN FISHER COLLEGE, Rochester, NY 14618-3597

General Information Independent-religious, coed, comprehensive institution. *Enrollment:* 3,823 graduate, professional, and undergraduate students; 644 full-time matriculated graduate/professional students (406 women), 361 part-time matriculated graduate/professional students (270 women). *Enrollment by degree level:* 495 master's, 510 doctoral. *Graduate faculty:* 78 full-time (48 women), 28 part-time/adjunct (19 women). *Tuition, area resident:* Part-time $860 per credit hour. *Required fees:* $10 per credit hour. Tuition and fees vary according to degree level and program. *Graduate housing:* On-campus housing not available. *Student services:* Campus employment opportunities, campus safety program, career counseling, child daycare facilities, exercise/wellness program, free psychological counseling, international student services, low-cost health insurance, multicultural affairs office, services for students with disabilities, teacher training, writing training. *Library:* Charles J. Lavery Library plus 1 other. *Collection:* Books: 162,694 (physical), 137,162 (digital/electronic); Databases: 197. Students can reserve study rooms.

Computer facilities: 550 computers available on campus for general student use. A campuswide network can be accessed from student residence rooms and from off campus. Online class registration is available.
Website: http://www.sjfc.edu/

General Application Contact: Rebecca Norman, Associate Director of Transfer and Graduate Admissions, 585-385-8064, Fax: 585-385-8344, E-mail: rnorman@sjfc.edu.

GRADUATE UNITS

Ralph C. Wilson Jr. School of Education Students: 178 full-time (121 women), 105 part-time (80 women); includes 84 minority (59 Black or African American, non-Hispanic/Latino; 2 American Indian or Alaska Native, non-Hispanic/Latino; 3 Asian, non-Hispanic/Latino; 15 Hispanic/Latino; 2 Native Hawaiian or other Pacific Islander, non-Hispanic/Latino; 3 Two or more races, non-Hispanic/Latino). Average age 37. 201 applicants, 79% accepted, 114 enrolled. *Faculty:* 17 full-time (13 women), 15 part-time/adjunct (10 women). *Financial support:* Scholarships/grants available. Financial award applicants required to submit FAFSA. In 2015, 88 master's, 36 doctorates awarded. *Degree program information:* Part-time and evening/weekend programs available. Part-time, evening/weekend. Offers adolescence education: English with special education (MS Ed); adolescence education: French with special education (MS Ed); adolescence education: social studies with special education (MS Ed); adolescence education: Spanish with special education (MS Ed); childhood education (MS); childhood education/special education (Certificate); education (MS, MS Ed, Ed D, Certificate); educational leadership (MS Ed); executive leadership (Ed D); literacy birth to grade 6 (MS); literacy grades 5 to 12 (MS). *Application deadline:* Applications are processed on a rolling basis. *Application fee:* $30. Electronic applications accepted. *Application Contact:* Rebecca Norman, Associate Director of Transfer and Graduate Admissions, 585-385-8064, E-mail: rnorman@sjfc.edu. *Interim Dean,* Dr. Michael Wischnowski, 585-385-7361, E-mail: mwischnowski@sjfc.edu.

School of Business Students: 64 full-time (25 women), 74 part-time (38 women); includes 14 minority (3 Black or African American, non-Hispanic/Latino; 4 Asian, non-Hispanic/Latino; 6 Hispanic/Latino; 1 Two or more races, non-Hispanic/Latino), 3 international. Average age 27. 108 applicants, 80% accepted, 58 enrolled. *Faculty:* 13 full-time (3 women), 5 part-time/adjunct (1 woman). *Financial support:* Scholarships/grants available. Financial award applicants required to submit FAFSA. In 2015, 72 master's awarded. *Degree program information:* Part-time and evening/weekend programs available. Part-time, evening/weekend. Offers business (MBA); business administration (MBA). *Application deadline:* Applications are processed on a rolling basis. *Application fee:* $30. Electronic applications accepted. *Application Contact:* Rebecca Norman, Associate Director of Transfer and Graduate Admissions, 585-385-8064, E-mail: rnorman@sjfc.edu. *Interim Dean,* Dr. Raymond Shady, 585-385-8098, E-mail: rshady@sjfc.edu.

Wegmans School of Nursing Students: 69 full-time (59 women), 164 part-time (149 women); includes 42 minority (22 Black or African American, non-Hispanic/Latino; 6 Asian, non-Hispanic/Latino; 12 Hispanic/Latino; 2 Two or more races, non-Hispanic/Latino), 2 international. Average age 31. 146 applicants, 57% accepted, 67 enrolled. *Faculty:* 17 full-time (13 women), 8 part-time/adjunct (6 women). *Financial support:* Scholarships/grants available. Financial award applicants required to submit FAFSA. In 2015, 47 master's, 4 doctorates awarded. *Degree program information:* Part-time and evening/weekend programs available. Part-time, evening/weekend. Offers advanced practice nursing (MS); clinical nurse specialist (Certificate); family nurse practitioner (Certificate); mental health counseling (MS); nursing (MS, DNP, Certificate); nursing practice (DNP). *Application deadline:* Applications are processed on a rolling basis. Electronic applications accepted. *Application Contact:* Rebecca Norman, Associate Director of Transfer and Graduate Admissions, 585-385-8064, E-mail: rnorman@sjfc.edu. *Dean,* Dr. Diane Cooney-Miner, 585-385-8241, Fax: 585-385-8466, E-mail: dcooney-miner@sjfc.edu.

Wegmans School of Pharmacy Students: 331 full-time (197 women), 2 part-time (0 women); includes 64 minority (14 Black or African American, non-Hispanic/Latino; 2 American Indian or Alaska Native, non-Hispanic/Latino; 34 Asian, non-Hispanic/Latino; 9 Hispanic/Latino; 5 Two or more races, non-Hispanic/Latino), 7 international. Average age 25. 571 applicants, 25% accepted, 87 enrolled. *Faculty:* 32 full-time (20 women), 1 (woman) part-time/adjunct. *Financial support:* Scholarships/grants available. Financial award applicants required to submit FAFSA. In 2015, 69 doctorates awarded. Offers pharmacy (Pharm D). *Application deadline:* For fall admission, 3/1 for domestic students. Applications are processed on a rolling basis. Electronic applications accepted. *Application Contact:* Rebecca Norman, Associate Director of Transfer and Graduate Admissions, 585-385-8064, E-mail: rnorman@sjfc.edu. *Interim Dean,* Dr. Christine Birnie, 585-385-7202, E-mail: cbirnie@sjfc.edu.

ST. JOHN'S COLLEGE, Annapolis, MD 21401

General Information Independent, coed, comprehensive institution. *Graduate housing:* On-campus housing not available.

GRADUATE UNITS

Graduate Institute *Degree program information:* Evening/weekend programs available. Evening/weekend. Offers liberal arts (MALA). Electronic applications accepted.

ST. JOHN'S COLLEGE, Santa Fe, NM 87505

General Information Independent, coed, comprehensive institution. *Graduate housing:* Rooms and/or apartments available on a first-come, first-served basis to single and married students. Housing application deadline: 4/1.

GRADUATE UNITS

Graduate Institute in Liberal Education *Degree program information:* Evening/weekend programs available. Evening/weekend. Offers Eastern classics (MA); liberal arts (MA); liberal education (MA).

ST. JOHN'S SEMINARY, Camarillo, CA 93012-2598

General Information Independent-religious, coed, primarily men, graduate-only institution. *Graduate housing:* Room and/or apartments guaranteed to single students; on-campus housing not available to married students.

GRADUATE UNITS

Graduate and Professional Programs *Degree program information:* Part-time programs available. Part-time. Offers divinity (M Div); pastoral ministry (MAPM); theology (MA). Electronic applications accepted.

SAINT JOHN'S SEMINARY, Brighton, MA 02135

General Information Independent-religious, coed, graduate-only institution. *Graduate housing:* Room and/or apartments available to single students; on-campus housing not available to married students. Housing application deadline: 8/1.

GRADUATE UNITS

Graduate Programs Offers theology (M Div, MA Th, MAM).

SAINT JOHN'S UNIVERSITY, Collegeville, MN 56321

General Information Independent-religious, Undergraduate: men only; graduate: coed, comprehensive institution. *Graduate housing:* Rooms and/or apartments available on a first-come, first-served basis to single and married students. *Research affiliation:* Hill Monastic Manuscript Library (monastic studies, liturgy, spirituality), Center for Ecumenical and Cultural Research, Arca Artium (visual and book arts).

GRADUATE UNITS

Saint John's School of Theology and Seminary ***Degree program information:*** Part-time programs available. Part-time, online learning. Offers divinity (M Div); liturgical music (MA); liturgical studies (MA); pastoral ministry (MA); theology (MA). Electronic applications accepted.

ST. JOHN'S UNIVERSITY, Queens, NY 11439

General Information Independent-religious, coed, university. CGS member. *Graduate housing:* Room and/or apartments available on a first-come, first-served basis to single students; on-campus housing not available to married students. *Research affiliation:* Thinkmap, Inc. (education and technology), Hoffman LaRoche Inc. (pharmaceutical research), RAND Corporation, Jewish Board of Family and Children's Services (mental health and social services), Merck & Company, Inc. (pharmaceutical research), ABITEC (specialty chemicals).

GRADUATE UNITS

College of Pharmacy and Health Sciences ***Degree program information:*** Part-time and evening/weekend programs available. Part-time, evening/weekend, online learning. Offers pharmaceutical sciences (MPH, MS, PhD); pharmacy administration (MS); pharmacy and health sciences (MPH, MS, PhD); public health (MPH); toxicology (MS). Electronic applications accepted.

College of Professional Studies ***Degree program information:*** Part-time and evening/weekend programs available. Part-time, evening/weekend, online learning. Offers computer science, mathematics and science (MS); criminal justice leadership (MPS); international communications (MS); sport management (MPS). Electronic applications accepted.

Institute for Biotechnology Offers biological/pharmaceutical biotechnology (MS). Electronic applications accepted.

The Peter J. Tobin College of Business ***Degree program information:*** Part-time and evening/weekend programs available. Part-time, evening/weekend, online learning. Offers accounting (MBA, MS); business (MBA, MS); business analytics (MBA); controllership (MBA); finance (MBA, MS); international business (MBA); investment management (MS); management (MBA); marketing (MBA); taxation (MBA, MS). Electronic applications accepted.

School of Risk Management, Insurance and Actuarial Science Online learning. Offers enterprise risk management (MS); management of risk (MS); risk management (MBA). Electronic applications accepted.

St. John's College of Liberal Arts and Sciences ***Degree program information:*** Part-time and evening/weekend programs available. Part-time, evening/weekend, online learning. Offers art and design (MA); biological sciences (MS, PhD); chemistry (MS); clinical psychology (MA, PhD); clinical psychology-child (PhD); clinical psychology-general (PhD); communication sciences and disorders (MA, Au D); criminology and justice (MA); English (MA, DA); general experimental psychology (MA); global development and social justice (MA); government and politics (MA, Adv C); history (MA); international law and diplomacy (Adv C); liberal arts and sciences (MA, MLS, MS, Au D, DA, PhD, Psy D, Adv C); liberal studies (MA); modern world history (DA); public administration (Adv C); public history (MA); school psychology (MS, Psy D); sociology (MA); Spanish (MA); theology (MA). Electronic applications accepted.

Division of Library and Information Science ***Degree program information:*** Part-time and evening/weekend programs available. Part-time, evening/weekend, online learning. Offers library and information science (MS, Adv C). Electronic applications accepted.

Institute of Asian Studies ***Degree program information:*** Part-time and evening/weekend programs available. Part-time, evening/weekend. Offers Asian studies (Adv C); Chinese studies (MA, Adv C); East Asian culture studies (Adv C); East Asian studies (MA). Electronic applications accepted.

The School of Education ***Degree program information:*** Part-time and evening/weekend programs available. Part-time, evening/weekend, online learning. Offers adolescent education (MS Ed, Certificate); childhood education (MS Ed); clinical mental health counseling (MS Ed, Adv C); early childhood education (MS Ed); education (MS Ed, Ed D, PhD, Adv C, Certificate); literacy (MS Ed, PhD, Adv C); middle school education (Certificate); school counseling (MS Ed, Adv C); school counseling with bilingual extension (MS Ed); teaching children with disabilities in childhood education (MS Ed, Adv C); teaching English to speakers of other languages and bilingual education (MS Ed, Adv C); teaching literacy (Adv C); teaching literacy 5-12 (MS Ed); teaching literacy B-12 (MS Ed); teaching literacy B-6 (MS Ed); teaching literacy B-6 and children with disabilities (MS Ed). Electronic applications accepted.

Division of Administrative and Instructional Leadership ***Degree program information:*** Part-time and evening/weekend programs available. Part-time, evening/weekend, online learning. Offers administration and supervision (Ed D); educational administration and supervision (Ed D); gifted education (Certificate); instructional leadership (Ed D, Adv C); school building leadership (MS Ed, Adv C); school building leadership/school district leadership (Adv C); school district leadership (Adv C). Electronic applications accepted.

School of Law ***Degree program information:*** Part-time and evening/weekend programs available. Part-time, evening/weekend. Offers bankruptcy (LL M); international and comparative sports law (LL M); law (LL M, JD); transnational legal practice (LL M); U.S. legal studies (LL M). Electronic applications accepted.

SAINT JOSEPH'S COLLEGE, Rensselaer, IN 47978

General Information Independent-religious, coed, comprehensive institution. *Graduate housing:* Rooms and/or apartments available on a first-come, first-served basis to single students and available to married students. Housing application deadline: 6/20.

GRADUATE UNITS

Rensselaer Program of Church Music and Liturgy ***Degree program information:*** Part-time programs available. Part-time. Offers church music and liturgy (MA); pastoral liturgy and music (Diploma). Offered during summer only.

ST. JOSEPH'S COLLEGE, LONG ISLAND CAMPUS, Patchogue, NY 11772-2399

General Information Independent, coed, comprehensive institution. *Enrollment:* 3,537 graduate, professional, and undergraduate students; 87 full-time matriculated graduate/professional students (50 women), 562 part-time matriculated graduate/professional students (438 women). *Enrollment by degree level:* 649 master's. *Graduate faculty:* 1 full-time (0 women), 26 part-time/adjunct (13 women). *Tuition, area resident:* Full-time $14,850; part-time $825 per credit. *Required fees:* $440. *Graduate housing:* On-campus housing not available. *Student services:* Campus employment opportunities, campus safety program, career counseling, exercise/wellness program, free psychological counseling, low-cost health insurance, multicultural affairs office, services for students with disabilities, teacher training, writing training. *Library:* Callahan Library plus 1 other. *Collection:* Books: 96,681 (physical), 119,855 (digital/electronic); Serial titles: 224 (physical), 102,167 (digital/electronic); Databases: 173. Weekly public service hours: 80; students can reserve study rooms.

Computer facilities: 265 computers available on campus for general student use. A campuswide network can be accessed. Online class registration, Library Databases, Learning Management System, Course Evaluations, Print Management, Virtual Application Labs, Office 365, Student Suggestion Box are available.
Website: http://www.sjcny.edu/

General Application Contact: Jodi A. Duffy, Director of Graduate and Professional Studies Admissions, 631-687-4525, E-mail: jduffy@sjcny.edu.

GRADUATE UNITS

Program in Nursing Students: 18 part-time (17 women); includes 6 minority (2 Black or African American, non-Hispanic/Latino; 2 Asian, non-Hispanic/Latino; 2 Hispanic/Latino). Average age 44. 10 applicants, 90% accepted, 8 enrolled. *Faculty:* 1 (woman) part-time/adjunct. In 2015, 3 master's awarded. Offers nursing (MS). *Associate Chair/Director,* Florence Jerdan, 631-687-5180, E-mail: fjerdan@sjcny.edu.

Programs in Business Management and Administration Students: 10 full-time (0 women), 63 part-time (40 women); includes 21 minority (10 Black or African American, non-Hispanic/Latino; 3 Asian, non-Hispanic/Latino; 8 Hispanic/Latino). Average age 36. 44 applicants, 82% accepted, 28 enrolled. *Faculty:* 11 part-time/adjunct (3 women). In 2015, 14 master's awarded. Offers accounting (MBA); business administration (MBA); business management and administration (EMBA, MBA). *Professor and Chair,* Eileen White Jahn, 631-687-1296, E-mail: ejahn@sjcny.edu.

Field of Executive Business Administration Students: 10 full-time (0 women), 63 part-time (40 women); includes 21 minority (10 Black or African American, non-Hispanic/Latino; 3 Asian, non-Hispanic/Latino; 8 Hispanic/Latino). Average age 36. 44 applicants, 82% accepted, 28 enrolled. *Faculty:* 11 part-time/adjunct (3 women). In 2015, 14 master's awarded. Offers executive business administration (EMBA). *Application deadline:* Applications are processed on a rolling basis. *Application fee:* $25. Electronic applications accepted. *Application Contact:* Jodi A. Duffy, Senior Associate Director of Graduate Admissions, 631-687-4501, E-mail: jduffy@sjcny.edu. *Director and Assistant Professor,* Charles Pendola, 631-687-1297, E-mail: cpendola@sjcny.edu.

Programs in Education Students: 17 full-time (15 women), 281 part-time (245 women); includes 16 minority (2 Black or African American, non-Hispanic/Latino; 2 Asian, non-Hispanic/Latino; 9 Hispanic/Latino; 3 Two or more races, non-Hispanic/Latino). Average age 25. 181 applicants, 81% accepted, 112 enrolled. *Faculty:* 11 part-time/adjunct (3 women). In 2015, 134 master's awarded. Offers education (MA); mathematics education (MA). *Application Contact:* Jodi A. Duffy, Senior Associate Director of Graduate Admissions, 631-687-4525, E-mail: jduffy@sjcny.edu. *Assistant Professor and Associate Chair,* Victoria Hong, 631-687-2646, E-mail: vhong@sjcny.edu.

Field in Special Education Students: 14 full-time (12 women), 130 part-time (104 women); includes 10 minority (1 Black or African American, non-Hispanic/Latino; 1 Asian, non-Hispanic/Latino; 5 Hispanic/Latino; 3 Two or more races, non-Hispanic/Latino). Average age 25. 78 applicants, 82% accepted, 45 enrolled. *Faculty:* 1 full-time (0 women), 9 part-time/adjunct (5 women). In 2015, 72 master's awarded. Offers special education (MA). *Associate Professor/Department Chair,* Sr. Nancy Gilchriest, 631-687-1472, E-mail: ngilchriest@sjcny.edu.

Field of Infant/Toddler Early Childhood Special Education Students: 1 (woman) full-time, 32 part-time (all women); includes 2 minority (both Hispanic/Latino). Average age 26. 40 applicants, 78% accepted, 24 enrolled. *Faculty:* 2 part-time/adjunct (both women). *Financial support:* Applicants required to submit FAFSA. In 2015, 11 master's awarded. *Degree program information:* Part-time and evening/weekend programs available. Part-time, evening/weekend. Offers infant/toddler early childhood special education (MA). *Application deadline:* For fall admission, 8/1 for domestic students, 5/1 for international students. Applications are processed on a rolling basis. *Application fee:* $25. Electronic applications accepted. *Application Contact:* Jodi A. Duffy, Senior Associate Director of Graduate Admissions, 631-687-4525, E-mail: jduffy@sjcny.edu. *Assistant Professor and Chair,* Sr. Mary Ann Cashin, 631-687-1235, E-mail: mcashin@sjcny.edu.

Field of Literacy and Cognition Students: 2 full-time (both women), 119 part-time (109 women); includes 4 minority (1 Black or African American, non-Hispanic/Latino; 1 Asian, non-Hispanic/Latino; 2 Hispanic/Latino). Average age 25. 63 applicants, 81% accepted, 43 enrolled. *Faculty:* 2 part-time/adjunct (both women). In 2015, 51 master's awarded. Offers literacy and cognition (MA). *Application deadline:* Applications are processed on a rolling basis. Electronic applications accepted. *Application Contact:* Jodi A. Duffy, Senior Associate Director of Graduate Admissions, 631-687-4525, E-mail: jduffy@sjcny.edu. *Assistant Professor and Chair,* Sr. Mary Ann Cashin, 631-687-1235, E-mail: mcashin@sjcny.edu.

Programs in Health Care Administration Students: 4 full-time (3 women), 22 part-time (16 women); includes 6 minority (2 Black or African American, non-Hispanic/Latino; 1 Asian, non-Hispanic/Latino; 2 Hispanic/Latino; 1 Two or more races, non-Hispanic/Latino). Average age 38. 7 applicants, 100% accepted, 6 enrolled. *Faculty:* 11 part-time/adjunct (3 women). In 2015, 2 master's awarded. Offers health care administration (MBA); health care management (MBA); health care management - health information systems (MBA). *Application Contact:* Jodi A. Duffy, Senior Associate Director of Graduate Admissions, 631-687-4525, E-mail: jduffy@sjcny.edu. *Director and Assistant Professor,* Charles Pendola, 631-687-1297, E-mail: cpendola@sjcny.edu.

Programs in Management Students: 16 full-time (11 women), 108 part-time (83 women); includes 38 minority (19 Black or African American, non-Hispanic/Latino; 3 Asian, non-Hispanic/Latino; 16 Hispanic/Latino). Average age 37. 75 applicants, 72% accepted, 45 enrolled. *Faculty:* 12 part-time/adjunct (3 women). In 2015, 32 master's awarded. Offers health care management (MS); human resources management (MS); human services leadership (MS); organizational management (MS). *Application deadline:* Applications are processed on a rolling basis. *Application fee:* $25. Electronic applications accepted. *Application Contact:* Jodi A. Duffy, Senior Associate Director of Graduate Admissions, E-mail: tsaladino@stony.edu. *Director and Assistant Professor,* Charles Pendola, 631-687-1297, E-mail: cpendola@sjcny.edu.

ST. JOSEPH'S COLLEGE, NEW YORK, Brooklyn, NY 11205-3688

General Information Independent, coed, comprehensive institution. *Enrollment:* 1,212 graduate, professional, and undergraduate students; 41 full-time matriculated graduate/professional students (25 women), 181 part-time matriculated graduate/professional students (150 women). *Enrollment by degree level:* 222 master's. *Graduate faculty:* 3 full-time (2 women), 10 part-time/adjunct (6 women). *Tuition, area resident:* Full-time $14,850; part-time $825 per credit. *Required fees:* $440. *Graduate housing:* On-campus housing not available. *Student services:* Campus employment opportunities, campus safety program, career counseling, exercise/wellness program, free psychological counseling, low-cost health insurance, services for students with disabilities, teacher training, writing training. *Library:* McEntegart Hall Library plus 1 other. *Collection:* Books: 79,020 (physical), 119,855 (digital/electronic); Serial titles: 35 (physical), 102,167 (digital/electronic); Databases: 173. Weekly public service hours: 74; students can reserve study rooms.

Computer facilities: 238 computers available on campus for general student use. A campuswide network can be accessed from off campus. Online class registration, Library Databases, Learning Management System, Course Evaluations, Print Management, Virtual Application Labs, Office 365, Student Suggestion Box are available.
Website: http://www.sjcny.edu/

General Application Contact: Roberto Figueroa, Director, Graduate and Adult Admissions, 718-940-5828, E-mail: rfigueroa@sjcny.edu.

GRADUATE UNITS

Program in Creative Writing Students: 24 full-time (16 women); includes 3 minority (2 Black or African American, non-Hispanic/Latino; 1 Hispanic/Latino). Average age 39. 26 applicants, 92% accepted, 13 enrolled. *Faculty:* 1 full-time (0 women), 1 part-time/adjunct (0 women). In 2015, 16 master's awarded. Offers creative writing (MFA). *Associate Professor/Chair,* Ted Hamm, 718-940-5307, E-mail: thamm@sjcny.edu.

Program in Nursing Students: 33 part-time (30 women); includes 30 minority (27 Black or African American, non-Hispanic/Latino; 1 Hispanic/Latino; 2 Two or more races, non-Hispanic/Latino). Average age 44. 13 applicants, 85% accepted, 10 enrolled. *Faculty:* 1 (woman) part-time/adjunct. In 2015, 7 master's awarded. Offers nursing (MS). *Associate Professor/Director,* Florence Jerdan, 718-940-9892, E-mail: fjerdan@sjcny.edu.

Programs in Business Management and Administration Students: 5 full-time (3 women), 29 part-time (21 women); includes 30 minority (16 Black or African American, non-Hispanic/Latino; 4 Asian, non-Hispanic/Latino; 9 Hispanic/Latino; 1 Two or more races, non-Hispanic/Latino). Average age 42. 20 applicants, 65% accepted, 12 enrolled. *Faculty:* 2 full-time (both women), 6 part-time/adjunct (3 women). In 2015, 15 master's awarded. Offers accounting (MBA); business administration (MBA); executive business administration (EMBA); management (MS). *Associate Professor/Associate Chair,* Stanley Fox, 718-940-5787, E-mail: sfox@sjcny.edu.

Field of Executive Business Administration Students: 5 full-time (3 women), 28 part-time (20 women); includes 29 minority (15 Black or African American, non-Hispanic/Latino; 4 Asian, non-Hispanic/Latino; 9 Hispanic/Latino; 1 Two or more races, non-Hispanic/Latino). Average age 42. 20 applicants, 65% accepted, 12 enrolled. *Faculty:* 2 full-time (both women), 6 part-time/adjunct (3 women). In 2015, 15 master's awarded. Offers executive business administration (EMBA). *Co-Director of Graduate Management Studies/Assistant Professor,* Sharon Didier, 718-940-5790, E-mail: sdidier@sjcny.edu.

Programs in Education Students: 47 part-time (45 women); includes 9 minority (all Hispanic/Latino). Average age 23. 26 applicants, 88% accepted, 19 enrolled. *Faculty:* 2 part-time/adjunct (both women). In 2015, 11 master's awarded. Offers literacy and cognition (MA); special education (MA). *Professor/Associate Chair,* Sr. Margaret Buckley, 718-940-5860, E-mail: mbuckley@sjcny.edu.

Field of Literacy and Cognition Students: 17 part-time (all women); includes 6 minority (all Hispanic/Latino). Average age 23. 12 applicants, 92% accepted, 8 enrolled. *Faculty:* 2 part-time/adjunct (both women). In 2015, 11 master's awarded. Offers literacy and cognition (MA). *Professor/Associate Chair/Director of the Special Education Program,* Susan Straut-Collard, 718-940-5689, E-mail: sstrautcollard@sjcny.edu.

Field of Special Education Students: 30 part-time (28 women); includes 3 minority (all Hispanic/Latino). Average age 23. 14 applicants, 86% accepted, 11 enrolled. *Faculty:* 2 part-time/adjunct (both women). Offers severe and multiple disabilities (MA). *Professor/Associate Chair,* Sr. Margaret Buckley, 718-940-5860, E-mail: mbuckley@sjcny.edu.

Programs in Health Care Administration Students: 4 full-time (2 women), 15 part-time (10 women); includes 16 minority (13 Black or African American, non-Hispanic/Latino; 2 Asian, non-Hispanic/Latino; 1 Hispanic/Latino). Average age 35. *Faculty:* 2 full-time (both women), 6 part-time/adjunct (3 women). In 2015, 7 master's awarded. Offers health care management (MBA); health care management - health information systems (MBA). *Application Contact:* John Fitzgerald, Associate Director, Admissions, 718-940-5810, Fax: 718-636-8303, E-mail: jfitzgerald3@sjcny.edu. *Associate Professor and Chair,* Lauren Pete, 718-940-5890, E-mail: lpete@sjcny.edu.

Field in Health Care Management - Health Information Systems Students: 4 full-time (2 women), 13 part-time (8 women); includes 15 minority (12 Black or African American, non-Hispanic/Latino; 2 Asian, non-Hispanic/Latino; 1 Hispanic/Latino). Average age 35. *Faculty:* 2 full-time (both women), 6 part-time/adjunct (3 women). In 2015, 4 master's awarded. Offers health care management - health information systems (MBA). *Application Contact:* John Fitzgerald, Associate Director, Admissions, 718-940-5810, Fax: 718-636-8303, E-mail: jfitzgerald3@sjcny.edu. *Chair,* Lauren Pete, 718-940-5890, E-mail: lpete@sjcny.edu.

Programs in Management Offers human resources management (MS); management (MBA, MS); organizational management (MS). *Application Contact:* John Fitzgerald, Associate Director, Admissions, 718-940-5810, Fax: 718-636-8303, E-mail: jfitzgerald3@sjcny.edu.

Field in Health Care Management Students: 1 (woman) full-time, 17 part-time (13 women); includes 13 minority (7 Black or African American, non-Hispanic/Latino; 1 Asian, non-Hispanic/Latino; 5 Hispanic/Latino). Average age 38. 21 applicants, 48% accepted, 8 enrolled. *Faculty:* 2 full-time (both women), 6 part-time/adjunct (3 women). In 2015, 14 master's awarded. Offers health care management (MBA, MS). *Associate Professor/Chair,* Lauren Pete, 718-940-5890, E-mail: lpete@sjcny.edu.

Field in Human Services Management and Leadership Students: 10 part-time (8 women); includes 9 minority (5 Black or African American, non-Hispanic/Latino; 4 Hispanic/Latino). Average age 42. 7 applicants, 86% accepted, 5 enrolled. *Faculty:* 2 full-time (both women), 6 part-time/adjunct (3 women). In 2015, 6 master's awarded. Offers human services management and leadership (MS). *Associate Professor/Associate Chair,* Candis Best, 718-940-5849, E-mail: cbest@sjcny.edu.

SAINT JOSEPH'S COLLEGE OF MAINE, Standish, ME 04084

General Information Independent-religious, coed, comprehensive institution. *Graduate housing:* On-campus housing not available.

GRADUATE UNITS

Master of Accountancy Program ***Degree program information:*** Part-time programs available. Part-time, online learning. Offers accountancy (M Acc). Electronic applications accepted.

Master of Arts in Pastoral Theology Program ***Degree program information:*** Part-time programs available. Part-time, online learning. Offers pastoral theology (MA).

Master of Business Administration in Leadership Program ***Degree program information:*** Part-time programs available. Part-time, online learning. Offers leadership (MBA).

Master of Health Administration Program ***Degree program information:*** Part-time programs available. Part-time, online learning. Offers health administration (MHA). Degree program is external; available only by correspondence and online. Electronic applications accepted.

Master of Science in Education Program ***Degree program information:*** Part-time programs available. Part-time, online learning. Offers adult education and training (MS Ed); Catholic school leadership (MS Ed); health care educator (MS Ed); school educator (MS Ed). Program available by correspondence. Electronic applications accepted.

Master of Science in Nursing Program ***Degree program information:*** Part-time programs available. Part-time, online learning. Offers administration (MSN); education (MSN); family nurse practitioner (MSN); nursing administration and leadership (Certificate); nursing and health care education (Certificate). Electronic applications accepted.

ST. JOSEPH'S SEMINARY, Yonkers, NY 10704

General Information Independent-religious, coed, graduate-only institution. *Graduate housing:* Room and/or apartments guaranteed to single students; on-campus housing not available to married students.

GRADUATE UNITS

Graduate and Professional Programs Offers Catholic philosophical studies (MA); divinity (M Div); pastoral studies (MAPS); theology (MA).

SAINT JOSEPH'S UNIVERSITY, Philadelphia, PA 19131-1395

General Information Independent-religious, coed, comprehensive institution. *Graduate housing:* On-campus housing not available.

GRADUATE UNITS

College of Arts and Sciences ***Degree program information:*** Part-time and evening/weekend programs available. Part-time, evening/weekend, online learning. Offers administration/police executive (MS); adult learning and training (MS); arts and sciences (MA, MS, Ed D, Certificate, Post-Master's Certificate); behavior analysis (MS, Post-Master's Certificate); biology (MA, MS); computer science (MS); criminal justice (MS); criminology (MS); curriculum supervisor (Certificate); educational leadership (MS, Ed D); elementary education (MS, Certificate); elementary/middle school education (Certificate); environmental protection and safety management (MS); federal law (MS); gerontological services (MS); health administration (MS); health education (MS); healthcare ethics (MS); homeland security (MS); instructional technology (MS, Certificate); intelligence and crime (MS); long-term care administration (MS); mathematics and computer science (Post-Master's Certificate); nurse anesthesia (MS); organization dynamics and leadership (MS); organizational psychology and development (MS); principal (Certificate); probation, parole, and corrections (MS); professional education (MS); psychology (MS); public safety management (MS); reading specialist (MS, Certificate); reading supervisor (Certificate); school nurse certification (MS); secondary education (MS, Certificate); special education (MS, Certificate); superintendent's letter of eligibility (Certificate); supervisor of special education (Certificate); writing studies (MA). Electronic applications accepted.

Erivan K. Haub School of Business ***Degree program information:*** Part-time and evening/weekend programs available. Part-time, evening/weekend, online learning. Offers accounting (MBA, Postbaccalaureate Certificate); business (MBA, MS, Post Master's Certificate, Postbaccalaureate Certificate); business intelligence (MBA); executive business administration (MBA); executive pharmaceutical marketing (Post Master's Certificate); finance (MBA); financial services (MS); food marketing (MBA, MS); general business (MBA); health and medical services administration (MBA); international business (MBA); international marketing (MS); managing human capital (MBA); marketing (MBA); pharmaceutical marketing (MBA). Electronic applications accepted.

ST. LAWRENCE UNIVERSITY, Canton, NY 13617-1455

General Information Independent, coed, comprehensive institution. *Graduate housing:* Room and/or apartments available on a first-come, first-served basis to single students; on-campus housing not available to married students. Housing application deadline: 4/1.

GRADUATE UNITS

Department of Education ***Degree program information:*** Part-time and evening/weekend programs available. Part-time, evening/weekend. Offers combined school building leadership/school district leadership (CAS); counseling and human development (M Ed, MS, CAS); educational leadership (M Ed, CAS); general studies in education (M Ed); mental health counseling (MS); school building leadership (M Ed); school counseling (M Ed, CAS); school district leadership (CAS).

SAINT LEO UNIVERSITY, Saint Leo, FL 33574-6665

General Information Independent-religious, coed, comprehensive institution. *Enrollment:* 6,138 graduate, professional, and undergraduate students; 206 full-time matriculated graduate/professional students (168 women), 3,562 part-time matriculated graduate/professional students (2,125 women). *Enrollment by degree level:* 3,657 master's, 72 doctoral, 39 other advanced degrees. *Graduate faculty:* 86 full-time (32 women), 138 part-time/adjunct (61 women). *Tuition, area resident:* Full-time $12,510; part-time $695 per semester hour. Tuition and fees vary according to degree level, campus/location and program. *Graduate housing:* Room and/or apartments available on a first-come, first-served basis to single students; on-campus housing not available to married students. *Student services:* Campus employment opportunities, career counseling, exercise/wellness program, free psychological counseling, international student services, low-cost health insurance, multicultural affairs office, services for students with disabilities, teacher training, writing training. *Library:* Cannon Memorial Library plus 1 other. *Collection:* Books: 119,833 (physical), 458,286 (digital/electronic); Serial titles: 265 (physical), 179,570 (digital/electronic); Databases: 148. Weekly public service hours: 119. *Research affiliation:* American Jewish Committee (religion).

Computer facilities: Computer purchase and lease plans are available. 150 computers available on campus for general student use. A campuswide network can be accessed from student residence rooms and from off campus. Online class registration, campus

residents are issued a laptop for their personal use are available.
Website: http://www.saintleo.edu/

General Application Contact: Jennifer Shelley, Senior Associate Director of Graduate Admissions, 800-707-8846, Fax: 352-588-7873, E-mail: grad.admissions@saintleo.edu.

GRADUATE UNITS

Graduate Business Studies Students: 1,887 full-time (1,024 women), 7 part-time (3 women); includes 821 minority (603 Black or African American, non-Hispanic/Latino; 5 American Indian or Alaska Native, non-Hispanic/Latino; 35 Asian, non-Hispanic/Latino; 156 Hispanic/Latino; 2 Native Hawaiian or other Pacific Islander, non-Hispanic/Latino; 20 Two or more races, non-Hispanic/Latino), 35 international. Average age 38. *Faculty:* 49 full-time (12 women), 63 part-time/adjunct (24 women). *Financial support:* In 2015–16, 116 students received support. Career-related internships or fieldwork, scholarships/grants, and health care benefits available. Financial award application deadline: 3/1; financial award applicants required to submit FAFSA. In 2015, 782 master's awarded. *Degree program information:* Part-time and evening/weekend programs available. Part-time, evening/weekend, online learning. Offers accounting (M Acc, MBA); cybersecurity (MS); health care management (MBA); human resource management (MBA); information security management (MBA); marketing (MBA); marketing research and social media analytics (MBA); project management (MBA); sport business (MBA). *Application deadline:* For fall admission, 7/1 priority date for domestic and international students; for spring admission, 11/12 priority date for domestic students, 11/1 for international students. Applications are processed on a rolling basis. *Application fee:* $80. Electronic applications accepted. *Application Contact:* Jennifer Shelley, Senior Associate Director of Graduate Admissions, 800-707-8846, Fax: 352-588-7873, E-mail: grad.admissions@saintleo.edu. *Assistant Dean, Graduate Studies in Business*, Dr. Lorrie McGovern, 352-588-7390, Fax: 352-588-8912, E-mail: mbaslu@saintleo.edu.

Graduate Studies in Education Students: 472 part-time (365 women); includes 96 minority (52 Black or African American, non-Hispanic/Latino; 2 Asian, non-Hispanic/Latino; 36 Hispanic/Latino; 6 Two or more races, non-Hispanic/Latino), 2 international. Average age 36. *Faculty:* 11 full-time (10 women), 18 part-time/adjunct (14 women). *Financial support:* In 2015–16, 17 students received support. Career-related internships or fieldwork, scholarships/grants, and health care benefits available. Financial award application deadline: 3/1; financial award applicants required to submit FAFSA. In 2015, 269 master's awarded. *Degree program information:* Part-time and evening/weekend programs available. Part-time, evening/weekend, online learning. Offers educational leadership (M Ed); exceptional student education (M Ed); instructional design (MS); instructional leadership (M Ed); reading (M Ed). *Application deadline:* For fall admission, 7/1 priority date for domestic students, 7/1 for international students; for winter admission, 7/1 for international students; for spring admission, 11/1 priority date for domestic students. Applications are processed on a rolling basis. *Application fee:* $80. Electronic applications accepted. *Application Contact:* Jennifer Shelley, Senior Associate Director of Graduate Admissions, 800-707-8846, Fax: 352-588-7873, E-mail: grad.admissions@saintleo.edu. *Director of Graduate Studies in Education*, Dr. Fern Aefsky, 352-588-8309, Fax: 352-588-8861, E-mail: kara.winkler@saintleo.edu.

Graduate Studies in Human Services Students: 11 full-time (all women); all minorities (all Black or African American, non-Hispanic/Latino). Average age 38. *Faculty:* 1 (woman) full-time, 1 (woman) part-time/adjunct. *Financial support:* Career-related internships or fieldwork, scholarships/grants, and health care benefits available. Financial award applicants required to submit FAFSA. *Degree program information:* Part-time and evening/weekend programs available. Part-time, evening/weekend. Offers human services (MS). *Application deadline:* For fall admission, 7/1 for domestic and international students; for spring admission, 11/1 for domestic and international students. *Application fee:* $80. *Application Contact:* Stephanie Stinski, Assistant Director, Saint Leo University Savannah Center, 912-352-8331 Ext. 3023, Fax: 912-353-9337, E-mail: stephanie.stinski@saintleo.edu. *Department Chair, Human Services*, Dr. Susan Kinsella, 912-352-8331 Ext. 3022, Fax: 912-353-9337, E-mail: susan.kinsella@saintleo.edu.

Graduate Studies in Public Safety Administration Students: 6 full-time (4 women), 765 part-time (481 women); includes 408 minority (326 Black or African American, non-Hispanic/Latino; 6 American Indian or Alaska Native, non-Hispanic/Latino; 5 Asian, non-Hispanic/Latino; 59 Hispanic/Latino; 12 Two or more races, non-Hispanic/Latino), 1 international. Average age 37. *Faculty:* 8 full-time (3 women), 30 part-time/adjunct (7 women). *Financial support:* In 2015–16, 14 students received support. Scholarships/grants and health care benefits available. Financial award application deadline: 3/1; financial award applicants required to submit FAFSA. In 2015, 184 master's awarded. *Degree program information:* Part-time and evening/weekend programs available. Part-time, evening/weekend, 100% online, blended/hybrid learning. Offers criminal justice (MS); critical incident management (MS). *Application deadline:* For fall admission, 7/1 priority date for domestic and international students; for spring admission, 11/1 priority date for domestic and international students. Applications are processed on a rolling basis. *Application fee:* $80. Electronic applications accepted. *Application Contact:* Jennifer Shelley, Senior Associate Director of Graduate Admissions, 800-707-8846, Fax: 352-588-7873, E-mail: grad.admissions@saintleo.edu. *Director of Department of Public Safety Administration*, Dr. Robert Diemer, 352-588-8974, Fax: 352-588-8289, E-mail: robert.diemer@saintleo.edu.

Graduate Studies in Social Work Students: 175 full-time (153 women), 65 part-time (53 women); includes 91 minority (60 Black or African American, non-Hispanic/Latino; 2 American Indian or Alaska Native, non-Hispanic/Latino; 3 Asian, non-Hispanic/Latino; 21 Hispanic/Latino; 5 Two or more races, non-Hispanic/Latino). Average age 37. 250 applicants, 70% accepted, 108 enrolled. *Faculty:* 8 full-time (6 women), 21 part-time/adjunct (18 women). *Financial support:* In 2015–16, 2 students received support. Career-related internships or fieldwork and health care benefits available. Financial award application deadline: 3/1. In 2015, 51 master's awarded. Online only, blended/hybrid learning. Offers advanced clinical practice (MSW). *Application deadline:* For fall admission, 6/1 for domestic and international students. *Application fee:* $80. Electronic applications accepted. *Application Contact:* Jennifer Shelley, Senior Associate Director of Graduate Admissions, 800-707-8846, Fax: 352-588-7873, E-mail: grad.admissions@saintleo.edu. *Director of Graduate Studies in Social Work*, Dr. Cindy Lee, 352-588-8869, Fax: 352-588-8289, E-mail: cindy.lee@saintleo.edu.

Graduate Studies in Theology Students: 269 full-time (79 women); includes 51 minority (39 Black or African American, non-Hispanic/Latino; 1 Asian, non-Hispanic/Latino; 9 Hispanic/Latino; 2 Two or more races, non-Hispanic/Latino), 1 international. Average age 50. *Faculty:* 12 full-time (1 woman), 4 part-time/adjunct (2 women). *Financial support:* In 2015–16, 3 students received support. Scholarships/grants and health care benefits available. Financial award application deadline: 3/1; financial award applicants required to submit FAFSA. In 2015, 27 master's awarded. *Degree program information:* Part-time and evening/weekend programs available. Part-time, evening/weekend, 100% online, blended/hybrid learning. Offers theology (MA). *Application deadline:* For fall admission, 7/1 priority date for domestic and international students; for spring admission, 11/1 priority date for domestic and international students. Applications are processed on a rolling basis. *Application fee:* $80. Electronic applications accepted. *Application Contact:* Jennifer Shelley, Senior Associate Director of Graduate Admission, 800-707-8846, Fax: 352-588-7873, E-mail: grad.admissions@saintleo.edu. *Director, Graduate Theology*, Dr. Randall Woodard, 352-588-8239, Fax: 352-588-8404, E-mail: randall.woodard@saintleo.edu.

ST. LOUIS COLLEGE OF PHARMACY, St. Louis, MO 63110-1088

General Information Independent, coed, comprehensive institution. *Enrollment:* 1,389 graduate, professional, and undergraduate students; 937 full-time matriculated graduate/professional students (558 women), 16 part-time matriculated graduate/professional students (7 women). *Enrollment by degree level:* 953 doctoral. *Graduate faculty:* 91 full-time (54 women), 56 part-time/adjunct (28 women). *Tuition, area resident:* Full-time $30,976; part-time $1033 per credit hour. *Required fees:* $498; $498 per unit. *Graduate housing:* Room and/or apartments available on a first-come, first-served basis to single students; on-campus housing not available to married students. Typical cost: $9762 (including board). Room and board charges vary according to board plan. Housing application deadline: 6/1. *Student services:* Campus employment opportunities, campus safety program, career counseling, exercise/wellness program, free psychological counseling, international student services, low-cost health insurance, multicultural affairs office, services for students with disabilities, writing training. *Library:* O. J. Cloughly Alumni Library. *Collection:* Books: 56,675 (physical), 175,165 (digital/electronic); Serial titles: 63 (physical), 217 (digital/electronic); Databases: 64. Weekly public service hours: 101; study areas open 24 hours, 5–7 days a week; students can reserve study rooms. *Research affiliation:* Express Scripts (pharmacy).

Computer facilities: 1,390 computers available on campus for general student use. A campuswide network can be accessed from student residence rooms and from off campus. Online class registration is available.
Website: http://www.stlcop.edu/

General Application Contact: Chase Davis, Director of Admissions, 314-446-8140, Fax: 314-446-8309, E-mail: chase.davis@stlcop.edu.

GRADUATE UNITS

Professional Program Students: 937 full-time (558 women), 16 part-time (7 women); includes 277 minority (46 Black or African American, non-Hispanic/Latino; 5 American Indian or Alaska Native, non-Hispanic/Latino; 202 Asian, non-Hispanic/Latino; 8 Hispanic/Latino; 2 Native Hawaiian or other Pacific Islander, non-Hispanic/Latino; 14 Two or more races, non-Hispanic/Latino), 24 international. Average age 22. 204 applicants, 12% accepted, 10 enrolled. *Faculty:* 78 full-time (46 women), 25 part-time/adjunct (18 women). *Financial support:* In 2015–16, 547 students received support. Federal Work-Study and scholarships/grants available. Financial award application deadline: 12/1; financial award applicants required to submit FAFSA. In 2015, 204 doctorates awarded. Offers pharmacy (Pharm D). *Application fee:* $55. Electronic applications accepted. *Application Contact:* Chase Davis, Director of Admissions, 314-446-8140, Fax: 314-446-8309, E-mail: chase.davis@stlcop.edu. *Dean of Pharmacy*, Dr. Bruce Canaday.

SAINT LOUIS UNIVERSITY, St. Louis, MO 63103

General Information Independent-religious, coed, university. CGS member. *Graduate housing:* Rooms and/or apartments available to single and married students. Housing application deadline: 5/1. *Research affiliation:* AT&T Foundation (communication), National Center for Atmospheric Research (earth and atmospheric sciences), Argonne National Laboratory (energy, physics, chemistry, mathematics and computer science), Small Business Administration (business, administration and entrepreneurship), Monsanto Chemical Corporation (chemistry), Missouri Botanical Garden (biology, plant science).

GRADUATE UNITS

Graduate Education ***Degree program information:*** Part-time and evening/weekend programs available. Part-time, evening/weekend, online learning. Offers anatomy (MS-R, PhD); biochemistry and molecular biology (PhD); biomedical sciences (MS-R, PhD); molecular microbiology and immunology (PhD); pathology (PhD); pharmacological and physiological science (PhD). Electronic applications accepted.

Center for Advanced Dental Education Offers endodontics (MSD); orthodontics (MSD); periodontics (MSD). Electronic applications accepted.

Center for Health Care Ethics Offers clinical health care ethics (Certificate); health care ethics (PhD). Electronic applications accepted.

College of Arts and Sciences Degree program information: Part-time and evening/weekend programs available. Part-time, evening/weekend. Offers American studies (MA, MA-R, PhD); arts and sciences (M Pr Met, MA, MA-R, MS, MS-R, PhD); biology (MS, MS-R, PhD); chemistry (MS, MS-R, PhD); clinical psychology (MS-R, PhD); communication (MA, MA-R); communication sciences and disorders (MA, MA-R); English (MA, MA-R, PhD); experimental psychology (MS-R, PhD); French (MA); geophysics (PhD); geoscience (MS); historical theology (MA, PhD); history (MA, MA-R, PhD); industrial-organizational psychology (PhD); mathematics (MA, MA-R, PhD); meteorology (M Pr Met, MS-R, PhD); philosophy (MA, MA-R, PhD); political science (MA); psychology (PhD); Spanish (MA); theology (MA). Electronic applications accepted.

College of Education and Public Service Degree program information: Part-time programs available. Part-time. Offers Catholic school leadership (MA); counseling and family therapy (PhD); curriculum and instruction (MA, Ed D, PhD); education and public service (MA, MA-R, MAPA, MAT, MAUA, MSW, MUPRED, Ed D, PhD, Certificate, Ed S); educational administration (MA, Ed D, PhD, Ed S); educational foundations (MA, Ed D, PhD); geographic information systems (Certificate); higher education (MA, Ed D, PhD); human development counseling (MA); marriage and family therapy (Certificate); organizational development (Certificate); public administration (MAPA); public policy analysis (PhD); school counseling (MA, MA-R); social work (MSW); special education (MA); student personnel administration (MA); teaching (MAT); urban affairs (MAUA); urban planning and real estate development (MUPRED). Electronic applications accepted.

Doisy College of Health Sciences Degree program information: Part-time programs available. Part-time. Offers athletic training (MAT); health sciences (MAT, MMS, MOT, MS, MSN, DNP, DPT, PhD, Certificate); medical dietetics (MS); nursing (MSN, DNP, PhD, Certificate); nutrition and physical performance (MS); occupational science and occupational therapy (MOT); physical therapy (DPT); physician assistant education (MMS).

John Cook School of Business Degree program information: Part-time and evening/weekend programs available. Part-time, evening/weekend. Offers accounting (M Acct, MBA); business (EMIB, M Acct, MBA, MSF, PhD); business administration

(MBA); executive international business (EMIB); finance (MBA, MSF); international business (MBA). Electronic applications accepted.

Parks College of Engineering, Aviation, and Technology Degree program information: Part-time programs available. Part-time, online learning. Offers biomedical engineering (MS, MS-R, PhD); engineering, aviation, and technology (MS, MS-R, PhD).

School of Medicine Offers medicine (MD). Electronic applications accepted.

School of Public Health Degree program information: Part-time programs available. Part-time. Offers biosecurity (Certificate); community health (MPH, MS, MSPH); health administration (MHA); health management and policy (MHA, MPH, PhD); health policy (MPH); public health (PhD); public health studies (PhD).

School of Law *Degree program information:* Part-time and evening/weekend programs available. Part-time, evening/weekend. Offers law (LL M, JD). Electronic applications accepted.

SAINT LOUIS UNIVERSITY–MADRID CAMPUS, 28003 Madrid, Spain

General Information Independent-religious, coed, comprehensive institution. *Graduate housing:* Room and/or apartments guaranteed to single students. *Research affiliation:* Universidad Autonoma de Madrid (English philology), Pontificia Universidade Catolica do Rio de Janeiro, Sogang University, Korea.

GRADUATE UNITS

Graduate Programs *Degree program information:* Part-time programs available. Part-time. Offers English (MA); Spanish (MA).

SAINT MARTIN'S UNIVERSITY, Lacey, WA 98503

General Information Independent-religious, coed, comprehensive institution. *Enrollment:* 1,689 graduate, professional, and undergraduate students; 241 full-time matriculated graduate/professional students (148 women), 85 part-time matriculated graduate/professional students (58 women). *Enrollment by degree level:* 307 master's, 19 other advanced degrees. *Graduate faculty:* 21 full-time (10 women), 35 part-time/adjunct (19 women). *Tuition, area resident:* Full-time $13,140; part-time $1095 per credit hour. *Graduate housing:* Room and/or apartments available on a first-come, first-served basis to single students; on-campus housing not available to married students. Typical cost: $16,030 (including board). Room and board charges vary according to board plan and housing facility selected. Housing application deadline: 3/15. *Student services:* Campus employment opportunities, campus safety program, career counseling, exercise/wellness program, free psychological counseling, international student services, low-cost health insurance, multicultural affairs office, services for students with disabilities, writing training. *Library:* O'Grady Library. *Collection:* Books: 89,682 (physical), 142,447 (digital/electronic); Serial titles: 90 (physical), 14,849 (digital/electronic); Databases: 104. Weekly public service hours: 88; students can reserve study rooms.

Computer facilities: 80 computers available on campus for general student use. A campuswide network can be accessed from student residence rooms. Online class registration is available.
Website: http://www.stmartin.edu/

General Application Contact: Casey Caronna, Administrative Assistant, 360-412-6142, E-mail: ccaronna@stmartin.edu.

GRADUATE UNITS

Office of Graduate Studies Students: 241 full-time (148 women), 85 part-time (58 women); includes 90 minority (28 Black or African American, non-Hispanic/Latino; 2 American Indian or Alaska Native, non-Hispanic/Latino; 8 Asian, non-Hispanic/Latino; 28 Hispanic/Latino; 5 Native Hawaiian or other Pacific Islander, non-Hispanic/Latino; 19 Two or more races, non-Hispanic/Latino), 24 international. Average age 33. 195 applicants, 56% accepted, 86 enrolled. *Faculty:* 21 full-time (10 women), 35 part-time/adjunct (19 women). *Financial support:* Career-related internships or fieldwork, institutionally sponsored loans, and scholarships/grants available. Support available to part-time students. Financial award application deadline: 3/1; financial award applicants required to submit FAFSA. In 2015, 131 master's awarded. *Degree program information:* Part-time and evening/weekend programs available. Part-time, evening/weekend. Offers civil engineering (MCE); counseling psychology (MAC); engineering management (M Eng Mgt); mechanical engineering (MME). *Application deadline:* For fall admission, 4/1 priority date for domestic and international students; for spring admission, 11/1 for domestic students, 11/1 priority date for international students. Applications are processed on a rolling basis. *Application fee:* $50. Electronic applications accepted. *Application Contact:* Casey Caronna, Administrative Assistant, 360-412-6142, E-mail: ccaronna@stmartin.edu.

College of Education Students: 67 full-time (43 women), 23 part-time (17 women); includes 21 minority (6 Black or African American, non-Hispanic/Latino; 1 Asian, non-Hispanic/Latino; 9 Hispanic/Latino; 1 Native Hawaiian or other Pacific Islander, non-Hispanic/Latino; 4 Two or more races, non-Hispanic/Latino). Average age 32. 32 applicants, 22% accepted, 5 enrolled. *Faculty:* 10 full-time (8 women), 16 part-time/adjunct (11 women). *Financial support:* Career-related internships or fieldwork, Federal Work-Study, institutionally sponsored loans, and unspecified assistantships available. Support available to part-time students. Financial award application deadline: 3/1; financial award applicants required to submit FAFSA. In 2015, 12 master's awarded. *Degree program information:* Part-time and evening/weekend programs available. Part-time, evening/weekend. Offers administration (M Ed); English as a second language (M Ed); guidance and counseling (M Ed); reading (M Ed); special education (M Ed); teaching (MIT). *Application deadline:* For fall admission, 4/1 priority date for domestic and international students; for spring admission, 11/1 priority date for domestic and international students. Applications are processed on a rolling basis. *Application fee:* $50. Electronic applications accepted. *Application Contact:* Casey Caronna, Administrative Assistant, 360-412-6142, E-mail: ccaronna@stmartin.edu. *Associate Dean, College of Education and Counseling Psychology,* Dr. Steve Siera, 360-438-4509, Fax: 360-438-4486, E-mail: ssiera@stmartin.edu.

School of Business Students: 58 full-time (27 women), 21 part-time (8 women); includes 25 minority (10 Black or African American, non-Hispanic/Latino; 1 American Indian or Alaska Native, non-Hispanic/Latino; 4 Asian, non-Hispanic/Latino; 6 Hispanic/Latino; 1 Native Hawaiian or other Pacific Islander, non-Hispanic/Latino; 3 Two or more races, non-Hispanic/Latino), 15 international. Average age 31. 77 applicants, 64% accepted, 41 enrolled. *Faculty:* 2 full-time (1 woman), 10 part-time/adjunct (3 women). *Financial support:* Career-related internships or fieldwork and scholarships/grants available. Support available to part-time students. Financial award application deadline: 3/1; financial award applicants required to submit FAFSA. In 2015, 21 master's awarded. *Degree program information:* Part-time and evening/weekend programs available. Part-time, evening/weekend. Offers business (MBA). *Application deadline:* For fall admission, 7/1 priority date for domestic and international students; for spring admission, 12/1 for domestic students, 12/1 priority date for international students. Applications are processed on a rolling basis. *Application fee:* $50. Electronic applications accepted. *Application Contact:* Casey Caronna, Administrative Assistant, 360-412-6142, E-mail: ccaronna@stmartin.edu. *Director, MBA Program,* Dr. Donald Conant, 360-556-7359, E-mail: dconant@stmartin.edu.

SAINT MARY-OF-THE-WOODS COLLEGE, Saint Mary of the Woods, IN 47876

General Information Independent-religious, coed, primarily women, comprehensive institution. *Graduate housing:* Rooms and/or apartments guaranteed to single students and available to married students.

GRADUATE UNITS

Program in Art Therapy *Degree program information:* Part-time and evening/weekend programs available. Part-time, evening/weekend, online learning. Offers art therapy (MA, Post-Master's Certificate). Electronic applications accepted.

Program in Leadership Development Offers leadership development (MLD).

Program in Music Therapy *Degree program information:* Part-time programs available. Part-time, online learning. Offers music therapy (MA). Electronic applications accepted.

Program in Pastoral Theology *Degree program information:* Part-time and evening/weekend programs available. Part-time, evening/weekend, online learning. Offers pastoral theology (MA); youth ministry (Graduate Certificate).

SAINT MARY'S COLLEGE, Notre Dame, IN 46556

General Information Independent-religious, women only, comprehensive institution. *Enrollment:* 1,657 graduate, professional, and undergraduate students; 29 full-time matriculated graduate/professional students (26 women), 9 part-time matriculated graduate/professional students (8 women). *Enrollment by degree level:* 30 master's, 8 doctoral. *Graduate faculty:* 19 full-time (17 women), 2 part-time/adjunct (1 woman). *Tuition, area resident:* Part-time $750 per credit hour. *Required fees:* $400 per unit. Tuition and fees vary according to program. *Graduate housing:* Room and/or apartments available on a first-come, first-served basis to single students; on-campus housing not available to married students. Typical cost: $7180 per year ($11,500 including board). Room and board charges vary according to board plan, campus/location and housing facility selected. Housing application deadline: 5/1. *Student services:* Campus employment opportunities, campus safety program, career counseling, child daycare facilities, exercise/wellness program, international student services, multicultural affairs office, services for students with disabilities, writing training. *Library:* Cushwa-Leighton Library. *Collection:* Books: 241,996 (physical), 8,398 (digital/electronic); Serial titles: 28,880 (digital/electronic); Databases: 82. Weekly public service hours: 54; study areas open 24 hours, 5–7 days a week; students can reserve study rooms.

Computer facilities: Computer purchase and lease plans are available. 291 computers available on campus for general student use. A campuswide network can be accessed from student residence rooms and from off campus. Online class registration is available.
Website: http://www.saintmarys.edu/

General Application Contact: Melissa Fruscione, Associate Director of Admission, Graduate Programs, 574-284-5098, E-mail: mfruscione@saintmarys.edu.

GRADUATE UNITS

Graduate Programs Students: 29 full-time (26 women), 9 part-time (8 women). *Faculty:* 20 full-time (18 women), 2 part-time/adjunct (1 woman). Offers data science (MS); nursing (DNP); speech language pathology (MS). *Application Contact:* Melissa Fruscione, Associate Director of Graduate Admissions, 574-284-5098, E-mail: graduateadmission@saintmarys.edu.

SAINT MARY'S COLLEGE OF CALIFORNIA, Moraga, CA 94575

General Information Independent-religious, coed, upper-level institution. CGS member. *Enrollment:* 572 full-time matriculated graduate/professional students (330 women), 531 part-time matriculated graduate/professional students (399 women). *Enrollment by degree level:* 1,036 master's, 67 doctoral. *Graduate faculty:* 198 full-time (105 women), 255 part-time/adjunct (170 women). *Tuition, area resident:* Full-time $35,472. *Required fees:* $55; $55 per unit. Tuition and fees vary according to course load and program. *Graduate housing:* Room and/or apartments available on a first-come, first-served basis to single students; on-campus housing not available to married students. Typical cost: $7830 per year ($14,490 including board). Room and board charges vary according to board plan and housing facility selected. Housing application deadline: 6/1. *Student services:* Campus employment opportunities, campus safety program, career counseling, exercise/wellness program, free psychological counseling, international student services, low-cost health insurance, multicultural affairs office, services for students with disabilities, teacher training. *Library:* St. Albert Hall Library.

Computer facilities: 244 computers available on campus for general student use. A campuswide network can be accessed from student residence rooms and from off campus. Online class registration, student accounts are available.
Website: http://www.stmarys-ca.edu/

General Application Contact: Hernan Bucheli, Vice Provost for Enrollment, 925-631-4277, Fax: 925-376-8339, E-mail: hmb5@stmarys-ca.edu.

GRADUATE UNITS

Kalmanovitz School of Education *Financial support:* Career-related internships or fieldwork and tuition waivers (partial) available. Support available to part-time students. Financial award application deadline: 2/15; financial award applicants required to submit FAFSA. *Degree program information:* Part-time and evening/weekend programs available. Part-time, evening/weekend. Offers career counseling (MA); coaching and facilitation (MA); college student services (Credential); education (M Ed, MA, MA Ed, Ed D, Credential); educational administration (MA); educational leadership (Ed D); general counseling (MA); marriage and family therapy (MA); organizational leadership and change (MA); peacebuilding and conflict transformation (MA); preliminary administrative services (Credential); pupil personnel services (Credential); reading and language arts (MA); school counseling (MA); school psychology (MA); social justice (MA); special education (M Ed); supervision and leadership (MA); teaching (MA Ed); teaching leadership (MA). *Application deadline:* Applications are processed on a rolling basis. *Application fee:* $50. *Application Contact:* Jane Joyce, Coordinator, Recruitment and Admissions, 925-631-4700, Fax: 925-376-8379, E-mail: soereq@stmarys-ca.edu. *Dean,* Christopher Sindt, 925-631-4309, Fax: 925-376-8379.

School of Economics and Business Administration *Financial support:* Career-related internships or fieldwork available. Support available to part-time students. Financial award applicants required to submit FAFSA. *Degree program information:*

Part-time and evening/weekend programs available. Part-time, evening/weekend. Offers executive business administration (MBA); financial analysis and investment management (MS); professional business administration (MBA). *Application deadline:* Applications are processed on a rolling basis. *Application fee:* $50. *Application Contact:* Bob Peterson, Director of Admissions, 925-631-4505, Fax: 925-376-6521, E-mail: bpeterso@stmarys-ca.edu. *Dean*, Dr. Zhan Li, 925-631-4514, Fax: 925-376-6521.

School of Liberal Arts ***Financial support:*** Fellowships, teaching assistantships, career-related internships or fieldwork, institutionally sponsored loans, and tuition waivers (partial) available. Support available to part-time students. Financial award applicants required to submit FAFSA. *Degree program information:* Part-time programs available. Part-time. Offers creative writing (MFA); dance: creative practice (MFA); dance: design and production (MFA); fitness management (MA); liberal arts (MA, MFA); sport management (MA); sport studies (MA). *Application Contact:* Michael Beseda, Vice Provost for Enrollment, 925-631-4277, Fax: 925-376-8339, E-mail: mbeseda@stmarys-ca.edu. *Dean*, Sheila Hassell Hughes, 925-631-4145, Fax: 925-631-4490, E-mail: soladean@stmarys-ca.edu.

ST. MARY'S COLLEGE OF MARYLAND, St. Mary's City, MD 20686-3001

General Information State-supported, coed, comprehensive institution. *Graduate housing:* Room and/or apartments available on a first-come, first-served basis to single students; on-campus housing not available to married students. Housing application deadline: 5/1.

GRADUATE UNITS

Department of Educational Studies Offers educational studies (MAT). Electronic applications accepted.

SAINT MARY SEMINARY AND GRADUATE SCHOOL OF THEOLOGY, Wickliffe, OH 44092-2527

General Information Independent-religious, coed, primarily men, graduate-only institution. *Graduate housing:* Room and/or apartments available to single students; on-campus housing not available to married students.

GRADUATE UNITS

Graduate and Professional Programs ***Degree program information:*** Part-time programs available. Part-time. Offers theology (M Div, MA, D Min).

ST. MARY'S SEMINARY AND UNIVERSITY, Baltimore, MD 21210-1994

General Information Independent-religious, coed, primarily men, graduate-only institution. *Graduate housing:* Room and/or apartments guaranteed to single students; on-campus housing not available to married students. Housing application deadline: 8/15.

GRADUATE UNITS

Ecumenical Institute of Theology ***Degree program information:*** Part-time and evening/weekend programs available. Part-time, evening/weekend. Offers church ministries (MA); theology (MA Th, Certificate).

School of Theology ***Degree program information:*** Part-time programs available. Part-time. Offers theology (M Div, MA Th, STD, STB, STL).

SAINT MARY'S UNIVERSITY, Halifax, NS B3H 3C3, Canada

General Information Province-supported, coed, comprehensive institution. *Graduate housing:* Rooms and/or apartments available on a first-come, first-served basis to single students and available to married students.

GRADUATE UNITS

Faculty of Arts ***Degree program information:*** Part-time and evening/weekend programs available. Part-time, evening/weekend. Offers arts (MA, Certificate, Graduate Diploma); Atlantic Canada studies (MA, Certificate); criminology (MA); history (MA); international development studies (MA, Graduate Diploma); philosophy (MA); theology and religious studies (MA); women and gender studies (MA).

Faculty of Commerce ***Degree program information:*** Part-time and evening/weekend programs available. Part-time, evening/weekend. Offers commerce (MBA, MF, PhD).

Faculty of Science ***Degree program information:*** Part-time programs available. Part-time. Offers applied psychology (M Sc, PhD); applied science (M Sc); astronomy (M Sc, PhD); science (M Sc, PhD).

ST. MARY'S UNIVERSITY, San Antonio, TX 78228-8507

General Information Independent-religious, coed, comprehensive institution. *Enrollment:* 3,625 graduate, professional, and undergraduate students; 943 full-time matriculated graduate/professional students (456 women), 373 part-time matriculated graduate/professional students (187 women). *Enrollment by degree level:* 451 master's, 855 doctoral, 10 other advanced degrees. *Graduate faculty:* 54 full-time (22 women), 52 part-time/adjunct (14 women). *Tuition, area resident:* Full-time $15,600; part-time $830 per credit hour. *Required fees:* $148 per semester. *Graduate housing:* Room and/or apartments available on a first-come, first-served basis to single students; on-campus housing not available to married students. Typical cost: $2764 per year. Room charges vary according to board plan. Housing application deadline: 5/1. *Student services:* Campus employment opportunities, career counseling, exercise/wellness program, free psychological counseling, international student services, low-cost health insurance, services for students with disabilities. *Library:* Louis J. Blume Library plus 1 other. *Collection:* Books: 195,486 (physical), 84,385 (digital/electronic); Serial titles: 498 (physical), 32,005 (digital/electronic); Databases: 137. Weekly public service hours: 100. *Research affiliation:* Southeast Research Consortium (behavioral science, biomedical engineering, social science).

Computer facilities: Computer purchase and lease plans are available. 200 computers available on campus for general student use. A campuswide network can be accessed from student residence rooms and from off campus. Online class registration is available.
Website: http://www.stmarytx.edu/

General Application Contact: Kim Thornton, Director, Graduate and Adult Enrollment Services, 210-436-3101, E-mail: akthornton@stmarytx.edu.

GRADUATE UNITS

Graduate Studies Students: 159 full-time (113 women), 220 part-time (138 women); includes 172 minority (20 Black or African American, non-Hispanic/Latino; 2 American Indian or Alaska Native, non-Hispanic/Latino; 16 Asian, non-Hispanic/Latino; 134 Hispanic/Latino), 47 international. Average age 33. 327 applicants, 47% accepted, 88 enrolled. *Faculty:* 54 full-time (22 women), 52 part-time/adjunct (14 women). *Financial support:* Fellowships, research assistantships, career-related internships or fieldwork, Federal Work-Study, institutionally sponsored loans, scholarships/grants, health care benefits, tuition waivers, and unspecified assistantships available. Financial award application deadline: 3/31; financial award applicants required to submit FAFSA. In 2015, 118 master's, 14 doctorates, 8 other advanced degrees awarded. *Degree program information:* Part-time and evening/weekend programs available. Part-time, evening/weekend, 100% online. Offers Catholic school leadership (MA); clinical mental health counseling (MA); communication studies (MA); conflict transformation (Certificate); counselor education and supervision (PhD); education (MA); educational leadership (MA); English literature and language (MA); industrial/organizational psychology (MA, MS); international conflict resolution (MA); international development (MA); international relations (MA); marriage and family therapy (MA, PhD); public administration (MPA); public communication, public policy and public leadership (Certificate); security policy (MA); theology (MA). *Application deadline:* For fall admission, 7/1 for domestic students; for spring admission, 11/15 for domestic students; for summer admission, 4/1 for domestic students. Applications are processed on a rolling basis. Electronic applications accepted. *Application Contact:* Kim Thornton, Director, Graduate and Adult Enrollment Services, 210-436-3101, E-mail: kthornton@stmarytx.edu. *Interim Dean of Graduate Studies*, Dr. Megan Mustain, 210-436-3554, E-mail: mmustain@stmarytx.edu.

Greehey School of Business Students: 49 full-time (15 women), 3 part-time (1 woman); includes 16 minority (2 Black or African American, non-Hispanic/Latino; 1 American Indian or Alaska Native, non-Hispanic/Latino; 1 Asian, non-Hispanic/Latino; 12 Hispanic/Latino), 4 international. Average age 27. 65 applicants, 60% accepted, 23 enrolled. *Financial support:* Research assistantships, institutionally sponsored loans, scholarships/grants, and unspecified assistantships available. Financial award application deadline: 3/31; financial award applicants required to submit FAFSA. In 2015, 22 master's awarded. *Degree program information:* Part-time and evening/weekend programs available. Part-time, evening/weekend. Offers business administration (MBA). *Application deadline:* For fall admission, 7/1 for domestic students; for spring admission, 11/15 for domestic students; for summer admission, 4/1 for domestic students. *Application fee:* $0. Electronic applications accepted. *Application Contact:* Jeremy Grace, Director, Master of Business Administration Programs, 210-431-2027, E-mail: jmgrace@stmarytx.edu. *Director, Master of Business Administration Programs*, Jeremy Grace, 210-431-2027, E-mail: jmgrace@stmarytx.edu.

School of Law Students: 722 full-time (328 women), 109 part-time (44 women); includes 390 minority (36 Black or African American, non-Hispanic/Latino; 9 American Indian or Alaska Native, non-Hispanic/Latino; 20 Asian, non-Hispanic/Latino; 325 Hispanic/Latino), 32 international. Average age 29. *Financial support:* Application deadline: 2/15; applicants required to submit FAFSA. In 2015, 26 master's, 216 doctorates awarded. Offers American legal studies (LL M); international and comparative law (LL M); international criminal law (LL M); law (LL M, MJ, JD). *Application deadline:* For fall admission, 3/1 for domestic students. *Dean*, Stephen Sheppard, 210-436-3684, E-mail: sheppard@stmarytx.edu.

School of Science, Engineering and Technology Students: 52 full-time (17 women), 41 part-time (4 women); includes 19 minority (1 Black or African American, non-Hispanic/Latino; 1 Asian, non-Hispanic/Latino; 17 Hispanic/Latino), 59 international. Average age 30. 246 applicants, 26% accepted, 16 enrolled. *Financial support:* Application deadline: 3/31; applicants required to submit FAFSA. In 2015, 79 master's awarded. *Degree program information:* Part-time and evening/weekend programs available. Part-time, evening/weekend, blended/hybrid learning. Offers computer engineering (MS); computer information systems (MS); computer science (MS); cybersecurity (MS); electrical engineering (MS); engineering systems management (MS); industrial engineering (MS); science, engineering and technology (MS, Certificate); software engineering (MS, Certificate). *Application deadline:* For fall admission, 7/1 for domestic students; for spring admission, 11/15 for domestic students; for summer admission, 4/1 for domestic students. Applications are processed on a rolling basis. Electronic applications accepted. *Application Contact:* Dr. Winston F. Erevelles, Dean, 210-436-3996, E-mail: werevelles@stmarytx.edu. *Dean*, Dr. Winston F. Erevelles, 210-436-3996, E-mail: werevelles@stmarytx.edu.

SAINT MARY'S UNIVERSITY OF MINNESOTA, Winona, MN 55987-1399

General Information Independent-religious, coed, comprehensive institution. *Enrollment:* 5,931 graduate, professional, and undergraduate students; 2,532 full-time matriculated graduate/professional students (1,739 women), 1,308 part-time matriculated graduate/professional students (899 women). *Enrollment by degree level:* 3,225 master's, 305 doctoral, 310 other advanced degrees. *Graduate faculty:* 12 full-time (7 women), 332 part-time/adjunct (187 women). Tuition and fees vary according to degree level and program. *Student services:* Campus safety program, services for students with disabilities, teacher training, writing training. *Library:* Fitzgerald Library plus 1 other. *Collection:* Books: 210,639 (physical), 10,144 (digital/electronic); Serial titles: 169 (physical), 82,154 (digital/electronic); Databases: 77. Weekly public service hours: 97; students can reserve study rooms.

Computer facilities: 200 computers available on campus for general student use. A campuswide network can be accessed from student residence rooms and from off campus. Online class registration is available.
Website: http://www.smumn.edu/

General Application Contact: James Callinan, Director of Admission for Graduate and Professional Programs, 612-728-5158, Fax: 612-728-5121, E-mail: jcallina@smumn.edu.

GRADUATE UNITS

Schools of Graduate and Professional Programs Students: 2,532 full-time (1,739 women), 1,308 part-time (899 women); includes 509 minority (277 Black or African American, non-Hispanic/Latino; 13 American Indian or Alaska Native, non-Hispanic/Latino; 105 Asian, non-Hispanic/Latino; 83 Hispanic/Latino; 3 Native Hawaiian or other Pacific Islander, non-Hispanic/Latino; 28 Two or more races, non-Hispanic/Latino), 114 international. Average age 35. *Faculty:* 12 full-time (7 women), 332 part-time/adjunct (187 women). *Financial support:* Applicants required to submit FAFSA. In 2015, 919 master's, 13 doctorates, 245 other advanced degrees awarded. *Degree program information:* Part-time and evening/weekend programs available. Part-time, evening/weekend, 100% online, blended/hybrid learning. *Application deadline:* Applications are processed on a rolling basis. Electronic applications accepted. *Application Contact:* James Callinan, Director of Admissions for Graduate and Professional Programs, 612-728-5158, Fax: 612-728-5121, E-mail: jcallina@smumn.edu. *Vice President*, Br. Robert Smith, 612-728-5201, Fax: 612-728-5169, E-mail: rsmith@smumn.edu.

Graduate School of Business and Technology Students: 757 full-time (444 women), 318 part-time (182 women); includes 212 minority (128 Black or African American, non-Hispanic/Latino; 2 American Indian or Alaska Native, non-Hispanic/Latino; 46

Asian, non-Hispanic/Latino; 26 Hispanic/Latino; 1 Native Hawaiian or other Pacific Islander, non-Hispanic/Latino; 9 Two or more races, non-Hispanic/Latino), 83 international. Average age 36. *Degree program information:* Part-time and evening/weekend programs available. Part-time, evening/weekend, 100% online, blended/hybrid learning. Offers accountancy (MS); arts and cultural management (MA); business administration (MBA, DBA); business and technology (MA, MBA, MS, DBA, Certificate); geographic information science (MS, Certificate); human development (MA); human resource management (MA); information technology management (MS); international business (MA); international development (MA); management (MA); organizational leadership (MA); philanthropy and development (MA); project management (MS, Certificate); public safety administration (MA). *Application deadline:* Applications are processed on a rolling basis. Electronic applications accepted. *Application Contact:* James Callinan, Director of Admissions for Graduate and Professional Programs, 612-728-5158, Fax: 612-728-5121, E-mail: jcallina@smumn.edu. *Dean*, Dr. Thomas Marpe, 612-457-6967, E-mail: tmarpe@smumn.edu.

Graduate School of Education Students: 1,034 full-time (734 women), 681 part-time (475 women); includes 136 minority (61 Black or African American, non-Hispanic/Latino; 5 American Indian or Alaska Native, non-Hispanic/Latino; 24 Asian, non-Hispanic/Latino; 34 Hispanic/Latino; 2 Native Hawaiian or other Pacific Islander, non-Hispanic/Latino; 10 Two or more races, non-Hispanic/Latino), 21 international. Average age 35. *Degree program information:* Part-time and evening/weekend programs available. Part-time, evening/weekend, 100% online, blended/hybrid learning. Offers behavioral disorders (Certificate); culturally responsive teaching (Certificate); education (M Ed, MA, Ed D, Certificate, Ed S); educational administration (Certificate, Ed S); educational leadership (MA, Ed D); gifted and talented instruction (Certificate); instruction (MA, Certificate); K-12 reading teacher (Certificate); LaSallian leadership (MA); LaSallian studies (MA); learning design and technology (M Ed); learning disabilities (Certificate); literacy education (MA); special education (MA); teaching and learning (M Ed). *Application deadline:* Applications are processed on a rolling basis. Electronic applications accepted. *Application Contact:* James Callinan, Director of Admissions for Graduate and Professional Programs, 612-728-5185, Fax: 612-728-5121, E-mail: jcallina@smumn.edu. *Dean*, Dr. Rebecca Hopkins, 507-457-6620, E-mail: rhopkins@smumn.edu.

Graduate School of Health and Human Services Students: 741 full-time (561 women), 309 part-time (242 women); includes 723 minority (88 Black or African American, non-Hispanic/Latino; 6 American Indian or Alaska Native, non-Hispanic/Latino; 35 Asian, non-Hispanic/Latino; 23 Hispanic/Latino; 562 Native Hawaiian or other Pacific Islander, non-Hispanic/Latino; 9 Two or more races, non-Hispanic/Latino), 10 international. Average age 33. *Degree program information:* Part-time and evening/weekend programs available. Part-time, evening/weekend, 100% online, blended/hybrid learning. Offers addiction studies (Certificate); counseling and psychological services (MA); counseling psychology (Psy D); health and human services (MA, MS, Psy D, Certificate); health and human services administration (MA); marriage and family therapy (MA, Certificate); nurse anesthesia (MS). *Application deadline:* Applications are processed on a rolling basis. Electronic applications accepted. *Application Contact:* James Callinan, Director of Admissions for Graduate and Professional Programs, 612-728-5185, Fax: 612-728-5121, E-mail: jcallina@smumn.edu. *Dean*, Dr. Todd Reinhart, 507-457-1758, E-mail: treinhar@smumn.edu.

SAINT MEINRAD SCHOOL OF THEOLOGY, Saint Meinrad, IN 47577

General Information Independent-religious, coed, primarily men, graduate-only institution. *Enrollment by degree level:* 184 master's. *Graduate faculty:* 22 full-time (2 women), 5 part-time/adjunct (1 woman). *Tuition, area resident:* Full-time $22,800; part-time $410 per credit hour. *Required fees:* $2900; $29 per course. *Graduate housing:* On-campus housing not available. *Student services:* Campus employment opportunities, campus safety program, exercise/wellness program, free psychological counseling, low-cost health insurance, writing training. *Library:* Archabbey Library. Students can reserve study rooms.

Computer facilities: 30 computers available on campus for general student use. A campuswide network can be accessed from student residence rooms and from off campus.
Website: http://www.saintmeinrad.edu/

General Application Contact: Rev. Luke Waugh, OSB, Director of Enrollment, 812-357-6422, Fax: 812-357-6462, E-mail: apply@saintmeinrad.edu.

GRADUATE UNITS

Master of Arts (Catholic Philosophical Studies) Program Students: 16 full-time (0 women); includes 3 minority (1 Black or African American, non-Hispanic/Latino; 2 Hispanic/Latino), 3 international. Average age 32. *Faculty:* 21 full-time (2 women), 6 part-time/adjunct (0 women). *Financial support:* Applicants required to submit FAFSA. In 2015, 12 master's awarded. Offers Catholic philosophical studies (MA). *Application deadline:* For fall admission, 7/31 for domestic and international students; for winter admission, 11/15 for domestic and international students. Applications are processed on a rolling basis. Electronic applications accepted. *Application Contact:* Fr. Luke Waugh, OSB, Director of Enrollment, 812-357-6422, Fax: 812-357-6462, E-mail: lwaugh@saintmeinrad.edu. *Academic Dean*, Dr. Robert Alvis, 812-357-6543, Fax: 812-357-6816, E-mail: ralvis@saintmeinrad.edu.

Master of Arts (Pastoral Theology) Program Students: 28 part-time (18 women). Average age 50. *Faculty:* 22 full-time (2 women), 5 part-time/adjunct (1 woman). *Financial support:* Federal Work-Study, institutionally sponsored loans, and scholarships/grants available. Support available to part-time students. Financial award application deadline: 7/31; financial award applicants required to submit FAFSA. *Degree program information:* Part-time and evening/weekend programs available. Part-time, evening/weekend. Offers pastoral theology (MA). *Application deadline:* For fall admission, 7/31 for domestic and international students; for winter admission, 11/15 for domestic and international students. Applications are processed on a rolling basis. *Application fee:* $30. Electronic applications accepted. *Application Contact:* Fr. Luke Waugh, OSB, Director of Enrollment, 812-357-6422, Fax: 812-357-6462, E-mail: apply@saintmeinrad.edu. *Academic Dean*, Dr. Robert Alvis, 812-357-6543.

Master of Arts (Theology) Program Students: 3 full-time (1 woman), 25 part-time (10 women). Average age 45. *Faculty:* 22 full-time (2 women), 5 part-time/adjunct (1 woman). *Financial support:* Federal Work-Study, institutionally sponsored loans, and scholarships/grants available. Support available to part-time students. Financial award application deadline: 7/31; financial award applicants required to submit FAFSA. *Degree program information:* Part-time and evening/weekend programs available. Part-time, evening/weekend. Offers theology (MA). *Application deadline:* For fall admission, 7/31 for domestic and international students; for winter admission, 11/15 for domestic and international students. Applications are processed on a rolling basis. *Application fee:* $30. Electronic applications accepted. *Application Contact:* Fr. Luke Waugh, OSB, Director of Enrollment, 812-357-6422, Fax: 812-357-6462, E-mail: apply@saintmeinrad.edu. *Director of Graduate Theology Programs*, Sr. Jeana Visel, OSB, 812-357-6678, Fax: 812-357-6816.

Master of Divinity Program Students: 103 full-time (0 women). *Faculty:* 22 full-time (2 women), 5 part-time/adjunct (1 woman). *Financial support:* Federal Work-Study, institutionally sponsored loans, and scholarships/grants available. Support available to part-time students. Financial award application deadline: 7/31; financial award applicants required to submit FAFSA. Offers divinity (M Div). *Application deadline:* For fall admission, 7/31 for domestic and international students; for winter admission, 11/15 for domestic and international students. Applications are processed on a rolling basis. *Application fee:* $0. Electronic applications accepted. *Application Contact:* Fr. Luke Waugh, OSB, Director of Enrollment, 812-357-6422, Fax: 812-357-6462, E-mail: apply@saintmeinrad.edu. *Academic Dean*, Dr. Robert Alvis, 812-357-6543, Fax: 812-357-6816, E-mail: ralvis@saintmeinrad.edu.

SAINT MICHAEL'S COLLEGE, Colchester, VT 05439

General Information Independent-religious, coed, comprehensive institution. *Enrollment:* 2,367 graduate, professional, and undergraduate students; 47 full-time matriculated graduate/professional students (37 women), 121 part-time matriculated graduate/professional students (96 women). *Enrollment by degree level:* 168 master's. *Tuition, area resident:* Full-time $10,620; part-time $590 per credit. Part-time tuition and fees vary according to course load and program. *Graduate housing:* Rooms and/or apartments available on a first-come, first-served basis to single and married students. Housing application deadline: 5/1. *Student services:* Campus employment opportunities, campus safety program, career counseling, international student services, multicultural affairs office. *Library:* Durick Library. *Collection:* Books: 228,866 (physical), 218,339 (digital/electronic); Serial titles: 1,760 (physical), 120,012 (digital/electronic); Databases: 160. Weekly public service hours: 102.

Computer facilities: Computer purchase and lease plans are available. 79 computers available on campus for general student use. A campuswide network can be accessed from student residence rooms and from off campus. Online class registration is available.
Website: http://www.smcvt.edu/

General Application Contact: Lindsay A. Damici, Marketing Communications Manager, 802-654-2556, Fax: 802-654-2732.

GRADUATE UNITS

Graduate Programs ***Financial support:*** Fellowships, research assistantships, teaching assistantships with full tuition reimbursements, career-related internships or fieldwork, Federal Work-Study, institutionally sponsored loans, scholarships/grants, tuition waivers (partial), and unspecified assistantships available. Financial award applicants required to submit FAFSA. *Degree program information:* Part-time and evening/weekend programs available. Part-time, evening/weekend. Offers arts in education (M Ed, CAGS); clinical psychology (MA); curriculum (M Ed, CAGS); literacy (M Ed, CAGS); school leadership (M Ed, CAGS); special education (M Ed, CAGS); teaching English to speakers of other languages (MATESOL, Certificate). *Application deadline:* Applications are processed on a rolling basis. *Application fee:* $50. Electronic applications accepted. *Application Contact:* Lindsay A. Damici, Marketing Communications Manager, 802-654-2556, Fax: 802-654-2732.

ST. NORBERT COLLEGE, De Pere, WI 54115-2099

General Information Independent-religious, coed, comprehensive institution. *Enrollment:* 2,180 graduate, professional, and undergraduate students; 99 part-time matriculated graduate/professional students (54 women). *Enrollment by degree level:* 99 master's. *Graduate faculty:* 4 full-time (0 women), 10 part-time/adjunct (3 women). *Tuition, area resident:* Part-time $675 per credit. *Graduate housing:* On-campus housing not available. *Student services:* Campus safety program, career counseling, child daycare facilities, exercise/wellness program, free psychological counseling, international student services, multicultural affairs office, services for students with disabilities, teacher training, writing training. *Library:* Miriam B. and James J. Mulva Library plus 1 other. *Collection:* Books: 244,394 (physical), 89,468 (digital/electronic); Serial titles: 97,261 (physical), 97,415 (digital/electronic). Weekly public service hours: 116; students can reserve study rooms.

Computer facilities: Computer purchase and lease plans are available. 214 computers available on campus for general student use. A campuswide network can be accessed from student residence rooms and from off campus. Online class registration is available.
Website: http://www.snc.edu/

General Application Contact: Brenda Busch, Associate Director of Graduate Recruitment, 920-403-3942, Fax: 920-403-4072, E-mail: brenda.busch@snc.edu.

GRADUATE UNITS

Master of Arts in Liberal Studies Program Students: 14 part-time (9 women); includes 3 minority (1 American Indian or Alaska Native, non-Hispanic/Latino; 2 Hispanic/Latino). Average age 42. 2 applicants, 100% accepted, 2 enrolled. *Faculty:* 2 part-time/adjunct (1 woman). In 2015, 3 master's awarded. *Degree program information:* Part-time and evening/weekend programs available. Part-time-only, evening/weekend. Offers liberal studies (MA). *Application deadline:* Applications are processed on a rolling basis. *Application fee:* $50. Electronic applications accepted. *Application Contact:* Dinah Grassel, Program Coordinator, 920-403-3957, Fax: 920-403-4086, E-mail: dinah.grassel@snc.edu. *Director*, Dr. Howard Ebert, 920-403-3956, Fax: 920-403-4086, E-mail: howard.ebert@snc.edu.

Master of Theological Studies Program Students: 54 part-time (35 women); includes 9 minority (8 Hispanic/Latino; 1 Two or more races, non-Hispanic/Latino). Average age 51. 6 applicants, 100% accepted, 6 enrolled. *Faculty:* 6 part-time/adjunct (2 women). *Financial support:* In 2015–16, 20 students received support. Scholarships/grants available. Support available to part-time students. In 2015, 6 master's awarded. *Degree program information:* Part-time and evening/weekend programs available. Part-time-only, evening/weekend. Offers theological studies (MTS). *Application deadline:* Applications are processed on a rolling basis. *Application fee:* $50. Electronic applications accepted. *Application Contact:* Dinah Grassel, Program Coordinator, 920-403-3957, Fax: 920-403-4086, E-mail: dinah.grassel@snc.edu. *Director*, Dr. Howard Ebert, 920-403-3956, Fax: 920-403-4086, E-mail: howard.ebert@snc.edu.

Program in Business Administration Students: 31 part-time (10 women); includes 2 minority (1 American Indian or Alaska Native, non-Hispanic/Latino; 1 Two or more races, non-Hispanic/Latino). Average age 33. 35 applicants, 94% accepted, 31 enrolled. *Faculty:* 4 full-time (0 women), 2 part-time/adjunct (0 women). *Financial support:* Federal Work-Study available. Financial award application deadline: 3/1; financial award applicants required to submit FAFSA. *Degree program information:* Part-time programs available. Part-time. Offers business (MBA); health care (MBA); supply chain and manufacturing (MBA). *Application deadline:* For fall admission, 8/5 for domestic students; for spring admission, 3/7 for domestic students. Applications are processed on a rolling basis. *Application fee:* $50. Electronic applications accepted. *Application Contact:* Brenda Busch, Associate Director of Graduate Recruitment, 920-403-3942, Fax: 920-403-4072, E-mail: brenda.busch@snc.edu. *Executive Assistant*, Lisa Gray, 920-403-3449, E-mail: lisa.gray@snc.edu.

ST. PATRICK'S SEMINARY & UNIVERSITY, Menlo Park, CA 94025-3596

General Information Independent-religious, coed, primarily men, graduate-only institution. *Graduate housing:* Room and/or apartments guaranteed to single students; on-campus housing not available to married students. Housing application deadline: 8/15.

GRADUATE UNITS

School of Theology ***Degree program information:*** Part-time programs available. Part-time. Offers theology (M Div, MA, STB). STB offered jointly with St. Mary's Seminary and University.

SAINT PAUL SCHOOL OF THEOLOGY, Overland Park, KS 66211

General Information Independent-religious, coed, graduate-only institution. *Graduate housing:* Rooms and/or apartments available to single and married students. Housing application deadline: 5/31.

GRADUATE UNITS

Graduate and Professional Programs ***Degree program information:*** Part-time programs available. Part-time. Offers theology (M Div, MA, MTS, D Min).

SAINT PAUL UNIVERSITY, Ottawa, ON K1S 1C4, Canada

General Information Province-supported, coed, university. *Graduate housing:* Room and/or apartments available to single students; on-campus housing not available to married students.

GRADUATE UNITS

Faculty of Canon Law ***Degree program information:*** Part-time programs available. Part-time. Offers canon law (MCL, JCD, PhD, Graduate Certificate, JCL); canonical practice (Graduate Certificate); ecclesiastical administration (Graduate Certificate).

Faculty of Human Sciences Offers conflict studies (MA); counseling and spirituality (MA); individual and/or marital/couple counseling (MA Past St); individual or marital/couple counseling (MA); mission and interreligious studies (MA); pastoral care in health care services (MA Past St); spiritual care (MA). Programs offered in French and English.

Faculty of Theology Offers theology (MA Th, MP Th, MRE, D Min, D Th, PhD, L Th).

ST. PETER'S SEMINARY, London, ON N6A 3Y1, Canada

General Information Independent-religious, coed, primarily men, graduate-only institution.

GRADUATE UNITS

Department of Theology Offers theology (M Div, MTS).

SAINT PETER'S UNIVERSITY, Jersey City, NJ 07306-5997

General Information Independent-religious, coed, comprehensive institution. *Graduate housing:* On-campus housing not available.

GRADUATE UNITS

Graduate Business Programs ***Degree program information:*** Part-time and evening/weekend programs available. Part-time, evening/weekend. Offers accountancy (MS); business (MBA, MS); business analytics (MS); finance (MBA); health care administration (MBA); human resource management (MBA); international business (MBA); management (MBA); management information systems (MBA); marketing (MBA); risk management (MBA). Electronic applications accepted.

Graduate Programs in Education ***Degree program information:*** Part-time and evening/weekend programs available. Part-time, evening/weekend. Offers 6-8 middle school education (MA Ed, Certificate); director of school counseling services (Certificate); educational leadership (MA Ed, Ed D); higher education (Ed D); K-12 secondary education (MA Ed, Certificate); K-5 elementary education (MA Ed, Certificate); literacy (MA Ed); middle school mathematics (Certificate); professional/associate counselor (Certificate); reading (MA Ed); school business administrator (Certificate); school counseling (MA, Certificate); special education (MA Ed, Certificate); teaching (MA Ed, Certificate). Electronic applications accepted.

Program in Criminal Justice Administration ***Degree program information:*** Part-time and evening/weekend programs available. Part-time, evening/weekend. Offers federal law enforcement administration (MA); police administration (MA). Electronic applications accepted.

Program in Public Administration Offers public administration (MPA).

School of Nursing ***Degree program information:*** Part-time and evening/weekend programs available. Part-time, evening/weekend. Offers adult nurse practitioner (MSN, Certificate); advanced practice (DNP); case management (MSN, DNP); nursing (MSN, DNP, Certificate). Electronic applications accepted.

SAINTS CYRIL AND METHODIUS SEMINARY, Orchard Lake, MI 48324

General Information Independent-religious, coed, graduate-only institution. *Graduate housing:* Room and/or apartments guaranteed to single students; on-campus housing not available to married students. Housing application deadline: 7/1.

GRADUATE UNITS

Graduate and Professional Programs ***Degree program information:*** Part-time programs available. Part-time. Offers pastoral ministry (MAPM); religious education (MARE); theology (M Div, MA).

ST. STEPHEN'S COLLEGE, Edmonton, AB T6G 2J6, Canada

General Information Independent-religious, coed, graduate-only institution. *Graduate housing:* On-campus housing not available.

GRADUATE UNITS

Programs in Theology ***Degree program information:*** Part-time and evening/weekend programs available. Part-time, evening/weekend, online learning. Offers ministry (D Min); pastoral counseling (MA); social transformation ministry (MA); spirituality and liturgy (MA); theological studies (MTS); theology (M Th). Electronic applications accepted.

ST. THOMAS AQUINAS COLLEGE, Sparkill, NY 10976

General Information Independent, coed, comprehensive institution. *Graduate housing:* On-campus housing not available. *Research affiliation:* Lederle Laboratories (science education), Lamont Doherty Laboratories (science education).

GRADUATE UNITS

Division of Business Administration ***Degree program information:*** Part-time and evening/weekend programs available. Part-time, evening/weekend. Offers business administration (MBA); finance (MBA); management (MBA); marketing (MBA). Electronic applications accepted.

Division of Teacher Education ***Degree program information:*** Part-time and evening/weekend programs available. Part-time, evening/weekend. Offers adolescence education (MST); childhood and special education (MST); childhood education (MST); educational leadership (MS Ed); reading (MS Ed, PMC); special education (MS Ed, PMC); teaching (MS Ed). Electronic applications accepted.

ST. THOMAS UNIVERSITY, Miami Gardens, FL 33054-6459

General Information Independent-religious, coed, comprehensive institution. *Graduate housing:* Room and/or apartments available on a first-come, first-served basis to single students; on-campus housing not available to married students. Housing application deadline: 7/1.

GRADUATE UNITS

Biscayne College Offers guidance and counseling (MS, Post-Master's Certificate); marriage and family therapy (MS, Post-Master's Certificate); mental health counseling (MS).

School of Business Offers accounting (MBA); business (M Acc, MBA, MIB, MS, MSM, Certificate); business administration (M Acc, MBA, Certificate); general management (MSM, Certificate); health management (MBA, MSM, Certificate); human resource management (MBA, MSM, Certificate); international business (MBA, MIB, MSM, Certificate); justice administration (MSM, Certificate); management accounting (MSM, Certificate); public management (MSM, Certificate); sports administration (MS).

School of Law Online learning. Offers international human rights (LL M); international taxation (LL M); law (JD). Electronic applications accepted.

School of Leadership Studies ***Degree program information:*** Part-time and evening/weekend programs available. Part-time, evening/weekend. Offers art management (MA); electronic media (MA); executive management (MPS); Hispanic media (MA, Certificate); leadership studies (MA, MPS, MS, Ed D, Certificate).

Institute for Education ***Degree program information:*** Part-time and evening/weekend programs available. Part-time, evening/weekend. Offers earth/space science (Certificate); educational administration (MS, Certificate); educational leadership (Ed D); elementary education (MS); ESOL (Certificate); gifted education (Certificate); instructional technology (MS, Certificate); professional/studies (Certificate); reading (MS, Certificate); special education (MS). Electronic applications accepted.

School of Theology and Ministry Offers theology and ministry (MA, PhD, Certificate).

Institute for Pastoral Ministries ***Degree program information:*** Part-time and evening/weekend programs available. Part-time, evening/weekend. Offers pastoral ministries (MA, Certificate); practical theology (PhD). Electronic applications accepted.

ST. TIKHON'S ORTHODOX THEOLOGICAL SEMINARY, South Canaan, PA 18459

General Information Independent-religious, men only, graduate-only institution. *Enrollment by degree level:* 22 master's. *Graduate faculty:* 8 full-time (1 woman), 6 part-time/adjunct (0 women). *Tuition, area resident:* Full-time $3360; part-time $1260 per year. *Required fees:* $720; $720 per unit. One-time fee: $215. *Graduate housing:* Room and/or apartments guaranteed to single students; on-campus housing not available to married students. Typical cost: $3600 (including board). *Student services:* Career counseling. *Library:* St. Tikhon's Seminary Library. *Collection:* Books: 41,000 (physical); Serial titles: 700 (physical); Databases: 4. Weekly public service hours: 6; study areas open 24 hours, 5–7 days a week.

Computer facilities: 10 computers available on campus for general student use. A campuswide network can be accessed from student residence rooms.
Website: http://www.stots.edu/

General Application Contact: Steven Voytovich, Dean and Director of Admissions, 570-561-1818 Ext. 101, E-mail: steven.voytovich@stots.edu.

GRADUATE UNITS

Divinity Program Students: 20 full-time (1 woman), 2 part-time (0 women); includes 1 minority (Black or African American, non-Hispanic/Latino), 3 international. Average age 30. 6 applicants, 100% accepted, 6 enrolled. *Faculty:* 8 full-time (1 woman), 6 part-time/adjunct (0 women). *Financial support:* Scholarships/grants and tuition waivers (full and partial) available. In 2015, 15 master's awarded. *Degree program information:* Part-time programs available. Part-time. Offers divinity (M Div). *Application deadline:* For fall admission, 7/30 for domestic students, 6/30 for international students. Applications are processed on a rolling basis. *Application fee:* $15. *Dean/Director of Admissions*, Steven Voytovich, 570-561-1818 Ext. 101, Fax: 570-937-4139, E-mail: steven.voytovich@stots.edu.

SAINT VINCENT COLLEGE, Latrobe, PA 15650-2690

General Information Independent-religious, coed, comprehensive institution. *Graduate housing:* Room and/or apartments available on a first-come, first-served basis to single students; on-campus housing not available to married students.

GRADUATE UNITS

Program in Business Offers business (MS).

Program in Education ***Degree program information:*** Part-time and evening/weekend programs available. Part-time, evening/weekend. Offers curriculum and instruction (MS); instructional design and technology (MS); school administration and supervision (MS); special education (MS).

Program in Health Science Offers nurse anesthesia (MS).

ST. VINCENT DE PAUL REGIONAL SEMINARY, Boynton Beach, FL 33436-4899

General Information Independent-religious, coed, primarily men, graduate-only institution. *Graduate housing:* Room and/or apartments guaranteed to single students; on-campus housing not available to married students.

GRADUATE UNITS

Graduate and Professional Programs ***Degree program information:*** Part-time programs available. Part-time. Offers theology (M Div, MA Th).

SAINT VINCENT SEMINARY, Latrobe, PA 15650-2690

General Information Independent-religious, coed, primarily men, graduate-only institution. *Enrollment by degree level:* 49 master's. *Graduate faculty:* 5 full-time (1 woman), 19 part-time/adjunct (2 women). *Tuition, area resident:* Full-time $25,308; part-time $840 per credit. *Graduate housing:* Room and/or apartments guaranteed to single students; on-campus housing not available to married students. Typical cost: $6154 per year ($12,510 including board). Housing application deadline: 8/15. *Student services:* Campus safety program, exercise/wellness program, free psychological counseling, international student services, services for students with disabilities, writing training. *Library:* Latimer Family Library. *Collection:* Books: 387,292 (physical), 3 (digital/electronic); Serial titles: 269 (physical); Databases: 27. Weekly public service hours: 84.

Computer facilities: 68 computers available on campus for general student use. A campuswide network can be accessed from student residence rooms and from off campus. Online class registration is available.
Website: http://www.saintvincentseminary.edu/

General Application Contact: Rev. Patrick T. Cronauer, OSB, Academic Dean, 724-805-2324, Fax: 724-805-2880, E-mail: patrick.cronauer@stvincent.edu.

GRADUATE UNITS

School of Theology Students: 46 full-time (0 women), 3 part-time (0 women); includes 6 minority (1 American Indian or Alaska Native, non-Hispanic/Latino; 4 Asian, non-Hispanic/Latino; 1 Two or more races, non-Hispanic/Latino), 8 international. Average age 37. 13 applicants, 100% accepted, 13 enrolled. *Faculty:* 5 full-time (1 woman), 19 part-time/adjunct (2 women). *Financial support:* In 2015–16, 49 students received support. Scholarships/grants available. Support available to part-time students. Financial award application deadline: 8/15. In 2015, 9 master's awarded. *Degree program information:* Part-time and evening/weekend programs available. Part-time, evening/weekend. Offers ecclesial ministry (MA); ministry (M Div); monastic studies (MA); sacred scripture (MA); systematic theology (MA). *Application deadline:* For fall admission, 8/15 priority date for domestic students, 8/15 for international students. Applications are processed on a rolling basis. *Application fee:* $34. *Application Contact:* Rev. Patrick T. Cronauer, OSB, Academic Dean, 724-805-2324, Fax: 724-805-2880, E-mail: patrick.cronauer@stvincent.edu. *President/Rector,* Very Rev. Edward M. Mazich, OSB, 724-805-2845, Fax: 724-532-5052, E-mail: edward.mazich@stvincent.edu.

ST. VLADIMIR'S ORTHODOX THEOLOGICAL SEMINARY, Crestwood, NY 10707-1699

General Information Independent-religious, coed, primarily men, graduate-only institution. *Graduate housing:* Rooms and/or apartments available on a first-come, first-served basis to single and married students. Housing application deadline: 5/1.

GRADUATE UNITS

Graduate School of Theology ***Degree program information:*** Part-time programs available. Part-time. Offers general theological studies (MA); liturgical music (MA); religious education (MA); theology (M Div, M Th, D Min). MA in general theological studies, M Div offered jointly with St. Nersess Seminary.

SAINT XAVIER UNIVERSITY, Chicago, IL 60655-3105

General Information Independent-religious, coed, comprehensive institution. CGS member. *Graduate housing:* Room and/or apartments available on a first-come, first-served basis to single students; on-campus housing not available to married students. Housing application deadline: 8/15. *Research affiliation:* Alexian Brothers Hospital, Holy Cross Hospital, Little Company of Mary Hospital, Mercy Center for Health Care Services.

GRADUATE UNITS

Graduate Studies ***Degree program information:*** Part-time and evening/weekend programs available. Part-time, evening/weekend. Electronic applications accepted.

College of Arts and Sciences Degree program information: Part-time and evening/weekend programs available. Part-time, evening/weekend. Offers arts and sciences (MA, MACS, MS); computer science (MACS); speech-language pathology (MS).

Graham School of Management Degree program information: Part-time and evening/weekend programs available. Part-time, evening/weekend. Offers employee health benefits (Certificate); finance (MBA); financial fraud examination and management (MBA, Certificate); financial planning (MBA, Certificate); generalist/individualized (MBA); health administration (MBA); managed care (Certificate); management (MBA); marketing (MBA); project management (MBA, Certificate). Electronic applications accepted.

School of Education Degree program information: Part-time and evening/weekend programs available. Part-time, evening/weekend. Offers counseling (MA); curriculum and instruction (MA); early childhood education (MA); educational administration (MA); elementary education (MA); individualized studies (MA); music education (MA); reading (MA); secondary education (MA); Spanish education (MA); special education (MA); teaching and leadership (MA).

School of Nursing Degree program information: Part-time and evening/weekend programs available. Part-time, evening/weekend. Offers nursing (MSN, Certificate).

SALEM COLLEGE, Winston-Salem, NC 27101

General Information Independent-religious, coed, primarily women, comprehensive institution. *Graduate housing:* On-campus housing not available.

GRADUATE UNITS

Department of Education ***Degree program information:*** Part-time and evening/weekend programs available. Part-time, evening/weekend, online learning. Offers art education (MAT); elementary education (M Ed, MAT); language and literacy (M Ed); middle school education (MAT); school counseling (M Ed); second language studies (MAT); secondary education (MAT); special education (M Ed, MAT).

SALEM INTERNATIONAL UNIVERSITY, Salem, WV 26426-0500

General Information Independent, coed, comprehensive institution. *Graduate housing:* Rooms and/or apartments available on a first-come, first-served basis to single students and available to married students.

GRADUATE UNITS

School of Business ***Degree program information:*** Part-time programs available. Part-time, online learning. Offers information security (MBA); international business (MBA). Electronic applications accepted.

School of Education ***Degree program information:*** Part-time and evening/weekend programs available. Part-time, evening/weekend, online learning. Offers curriculum and instruction (M Ed); educational leadership (M Ed). Electronic applications accepted.

SALEM STATE UNIVERSITY, Salem, MA 01970-5353

General Information State-supported, coed, comprehensive institution. CGS member. *Graduate housing:* On-campus housing not available.

GRADUATE UNITS

School of Graduate Studies ***Degree program information:*** Part-time and evening/weekend programs available. Part-time, evening/weekend. Offers adult-gerontology primary care nursing (MSN); advanced professional studies in counseling (Graduate Certificate); art (MAT); business administration (MBA); chemistry (MAT); counseling and psychological services (MS, Graduate Certificate); criminal justice (MS); early childhood education (M Ed); education (CAGS); elementary education (M Ed); English (MA, MAT); geo-information science (MS); higher education in student affairs (M Ed); history (MA, MAT); humanities (M Ed); library media studies (M Ed); math/science (MAT); mathematics (MAT, MS); middle school general science (MAT); middle school math (MAT); nursing administration (MSN); nursing education (MSN); occupational therapy (MS); physical education (M Ed); reading (M Ed); school counseling (M Ed); secondary education (M Ed); social work (MSW); Spanish (MAT); special education (M Ed); teaching English as a second language (MAT).

★ SALISBURY UNIVERSITY, Salisbury, MD 21801-6837

General Information State-supported, coed, comprehensive institution. CGS member. *Enrollment:* 8,671 graduate, professional, and undergraduate students; 403 full-time matriculated graduate/professional students (307 women), 351 part-time matriculated graduate/professional students (254 women). *Enrollment by degree level:* 705 master's, 49 doctoral. *Graduate faculty:* 86 full-time (49 women), 37 part-time/adjunct (27 women). *Graduate housing:* On-campus housing not available. *Student services:* Campus employment opportunities, campus safety program, career counseling, exercise/wellness program, free psychological counseling, international student services, multicultural affairs office, services for students with disabilities, teacher training, writing training. *Library:* Blackwell Library plus 1 other. *Collection:* Books: 216,500 (physical), 220 (digital/electronic); Serial titles: 862 (physical), 146 (digital/electronic); Databases: 102. Weekly public service hours: 111; students can reserve study rooms. *Research affiliation:* Maryland Higher Education Commission (Maryland off-shore wind industry supply chain/workforce development research), Maryland Department of Public Safety and Correctional Services (scenario analysis research), Boards of Education for 16 Maryland Counties (economic impact analysis/decision support dashboards), Eastern Shore of Maryland Education Consortium (resource allocation research), City of Salisbury (market and feasibility analysis), Maryland's Small Business Development Center Network (disaster preparedness and contingency planning research).

Computer facilities: 500 computers available on campus for general student use. A campuswide network can be accessed from student residence rooms and from off campus. Online class registration, University accounts, student Web hosting are available.
Website: http://www.salisbury.edu/

General Application Contact: Lacie Doyle, Graduate Enrollment Management Specialist, 410-548-3546, Fax: 410-677-0052, E-mail: lhdoyle@salisbury.edu.

GRADUATE UNITS

Department of Biological Sciences Students: 8 full-time (2 women), 1 (woman) part-time. Average age 25. 10 applicants, 60% accepted, 5 enrolled. *Faculty:* 7 full-time (4 women). *Financial support:* In 2015–16, 1 research assistantship with full tuition reimbursement (averaging $14,000 per year) was awarded; career-related internships or fieldwork, institutionally sponsored loans, scholarships/grants, and unspecified assistantships also available. Support available to part-time students. Financial award application deadline: 3/1; financial award applicants required to submit FAFSA. In 2015, 4 master's awarded. *Degree program information:* Part-time programs available. Part-time. Offers applied biology (MS). *Application deadline:* For fall admission, 3/1 priority date for domestic and international students; for spring admission, 10/1 priority date for domestic and international students. *Application fee:* $65. Electronic applications accepted. *Application Contact:* Valerie Butler, Administrative Assistant, 410-543-6490, Fax: 410-543-6433, E-mail: vwbutler@salisbury.edu. *Graduate Program Director, Applied Biology,* Dr. Dana Price, 410-543-6498, Fax: 410-543-6433, E-mail: dlprice@salisbury.edu.

Department of Conflict Analysis and Dispute Resolution Students: 27 full-time (15 women), 9 part-time (5 women); includes 12 minority (8 Black or African American, non-Hispanic/Latino; 3 Hispanic/Latino; 1 Two or more races, non-Hispanic/Latino), 3 international. Average age 27. 25 applicants, 100% accepted, 20 enrolled. *Faculty:* 5 full-time (0 women). *Financial support:* In 2015–16, 7 research assistantships with full tuition reimbursements (averaging $8,000 per year) were awarded; career-related internships or fieldwork, institutionally sponsored loans, scholarships/grants, and unspecified assistantships also available. Support available to part-time students. Financial award application deadline: 3/1; financial award applicants required to submit FAFSA. In 2015, 19 master's awarded. *Degree program information:* Part-time programs available. Part-time. Offers conflict analysis and dispute resolution (MA). *Application deadline:* For fall admission, 4/14 priority date for domestic and international students. Applications are processed on a rolling basis. *Application fee:* $65. Electronic applications accepted. *Application Contact:* Dr. Jacques Koko, Graduate Program Director, Conflict Analysis and Dispute Resolution, 410-677-0135, E-mail: jlkoko@salisbury.edu. *Chair, Conflict Analysis and Dispute Resolution,* Dr. Ignaciyas Soosaipillai, 410-543-6435, E-mail: iksoosaipillai@salisbury.edu.

Department of English Students: 16 full-time (10 women), 23 part-time (18 women); includes 3 minority (2 Black or African American, non-Hispanic/Latino; 1 Two or more races, non-Hispanic/Latino), 7 international. Average age 32. 17 applicants, 100% accepted, 14 enrolled. *Faculty:* 12 full-time (7 women). *Financial support:* In 2015–16, 1 research assistantship with full tuition reimbursement (averaging $10,000 per year), 12 teaching assistantships with full tuition reimbursements (averaging $9,498 per year) were awarded; career-related internships or fieldwork, institutionally sponsored loans, tuition waivers, and unspecified assistantships also available. Support available to part-time students. Financial award application deadline: 3/1; financial award applicants required to submit FAFSA. In 2015, 25 master's awarded. *Degree program information:* Part-time programs available. Part-time. Offers creative writing (MA); English (MA); film (MA); literature (MA); secondary education (MA); TESOL (MA); writing and rhetoric (MA). *Application deadline:* For fall admission, 3/15 for domestic and international students; for spring admission, 10/1 for domestic and international students. Applications are processed on a rolling basis. *Application fee:* $65. Electronic applications accepted. *Graduate Program Director, English,* Dr. Christopher Vilmar, 410-677-6511, E-mail: csvilmar@salisbury.edu.

Department of Health and Sport Sciences ***Financial support:*** Career-related internships or fieldwork, institutionally sponsored loans, scholarships/grants, and unspecified assistantships available. Support available to part-time students. Financial award application deadline: 3/1; financial award applicants required to submit FAFSA. Offers athletic training (MSAT). *Application fee:* $65. *Graduate Program Director, Athletic Training*, Dr. Jenny Toonstra, 410-677-5493, E-mail: jltoonstra@salisbury.edu.

Department of Health Sciences Students: 36 full-time (17 women), 18 part-time (8 women); includes 4 minority (2 Black or African American, non-Hispanic/Latino; 1 Asian, non-Hispanic/Latino; 1 Hispanic/Latino), 1 international. Average age 25. 21 applicants, 100% accepted, 19 enrolled. *Faculty:* 4 full-time (0 women), 1 part-time/adjunct (0 women). *Financial support:* In 2015–16, 5 research assistantships with full tuition reimbursements (averaging $8,500 per year) were awarded; career-related internships or fieldwork, institutionally sponsored loans, scholarships/grants, and unspecified assistantships also available. Support available to part-time students. Financial award application deadline: 3/1; financial award applicants required to submit FAFSA. In 2015, 18 master's awarded. *Degree program information:* Part-time programs available. Part-time. Offers applied health physiology (MS). *Application deadline:* For fall admission, 7/1 for domestic and international students; for spring admission, 12/1 for domestic and international students; for summer admission, 5/1 for domestic and international students. Applications are processed on a rolling basis. *Application fee:* $65. Electronic applications accepted. *Application Contact:* Dr. Thomas Pellinger, Faculty, Applied Health Physiology, 410-677-0144, Fax: 410-548-9185, E-mail: tkpellinger@salisbury.edu. *Graduate Program Director, Applied Health Physiology*, Dr. Randy Insley, 410-677-0145, Fax: 410-548-9185, E-mail: rcinsley@salisbury.edu.

Department of History Students: 6 full-time (1 woman), 10 part-time (3 women); includes 1 minority (Black or African American, non-Hispanic/Latino). Average age 26. 8 applicants, 88% accepted, 5 enrolled. *Faculty:* 8 full-time (1 woman). *Financial support:* In 2015–16, 3 research assistantships with full tuition reimbursements (averaging $8,000 per year) were awarded; institutionally sponsored loans and scholarships/grants also available. Support available to part-time students. Financial award application deadline: 3/1; financial award applicants required to submit FAFSA. In 2015, 6 master's awarded. *Degree program information:* Part-time and evening/weekend programs available. Part-time, evening/weekend. Offers history (MA). *Application deadline:* For fall admission, 5/15 priority date for domestic and international students; for spring admission, 10/1 priority date for domestic and international students. Applications are processed on a rolling basis. *Application fee:* $65. Electronic applications accepted. *Graduate Program Director, History*, Dr. Richard Bowler, 410-677-3251, E-mail: cxcarayon@salisbury.edu.

Department of Mathematics Education Students: 2 full-time (both women), 10 part-time (6 women); includes 2 minority (1 Black or African American, non-Hispanic/Latino; 1 American Indian or Alaska Native, non-Hispanic/Latino). Average age 27. 6 applicants, 100% accepted, 6 enrolled. *Faculty:* 2 full-time (both women). *Financial support:* Career-related internships or fieldwork, institutionally sponsored loans, scholarships/grants, and unspecified assistantships available. Support available to part-time students. Financial award application deadline: 3/1; financial award applicants required to submit FAFSA. In 2015, 4 master's awarded. *Degree program information:* Part-time programs available. Part-time. Offers high school (MSME); mathematics (MSME); middle school (MSME). *Application deadline:* For fall admission, 5/15 priority date for domestic and international students; for spring admission, 10/1 priority date for domestic and international students. Applications are processed on a rolling basis. *Application fee:* $65. Electronic applications accepted. *Application Contact:* Dr. Jennifer Bergner, Graduate Program Director, Mathematics Education, 410-677-5429, E-mail: jabergner@salisbury.edu.

Department of Social Work Students: 209 full-time (193 women), 99 part-time (87 women); includes 63 minority (35 Black or African American, non-Hispanic/Latino; 2 American Indian or Alaska Native, non-Hispanic/Latino; 2 Asian, non-Hispanic/Latino; 14 Hispanic/Latino; 10 Two or more races, non-Hispanic/Latino), 1 international. Average age 32. 228 applicants, 73% accepted, 146 enrolled. *Faculty:* 18 full-time (17 women), 21 part-time/adjunct (17 women). *Financial support:* In 2015–16, 3 teaching assistantships with full tuition reimbursements (averaging $4,000 per year) were awarded; career-related internships or fieldwork, institutionally sponsored loans, scholarships/grants, and unspecified assistantships also available. Support available to part-time students. Financial award application deadline: 3/1; financial award applicants required to submit FAFSA. In 2015, 71 master's awarded. *Degree program information:* Part-time and evening/weekend programs available. Part-time, evening/weekend, online learning. Offers social work (MSW). *Application deadline:* For fall admission, 2/1 for domestic and international students. *Application fee:* $65. Electronic applications accepted. *Graduate Program Director, Social Work*, Karen McCabe, 410-543-6307, E-mail: klmccabe@salisbury.edu.

DNP in Nursing Program Students: 22 full-time (20 women), 1 (woman) part-time; includes 9 minority (7 Black or African American, non-Hispanic/Latino; 1 Hispanic/Latino; 1 Two or more races, non-Hispanic/Latino). Average age 35. 16 applicants, 56% accepted, 6 enrolled. *Faculty:* 7 full-time (5 women). *Financial support:* In 2015–16, 18 students received support. Career-related internships or fieldwork, institutionally sponsored loans, scholarships/grants, and unspecified assistantships available. Support available to part-time students. Financial award application deadline: 3/1; financial award applicants required to submit FAFSA. In 2015, 8 doctorates awarded. *Degree program information:* Part-time programs available. Part-time. Offers family nurse practitioner (DNP); nursing (DNP); nursing leadership (DNP). *Application deadline:* For fall admission, 5/15 priority date for domestic students, 3/15 priority date for international students. Applications are processed on a rolling basis. *Application fee:* $65. Electronic applications accepted. *Application Contact:* Carmel Boger, Administrative Assistant, 410-543-6420, Fax: 410-548-3313, E-mail: ciboger@salisbury.edu. *Graduate Program Director, Nursing (DNP)*, Dr. Lisa Seldomridge, 410-543-6344, Fax: 410-548-3313, E-mail: laseldomridge@salisbury.edu.

MS in Nursing Program Students: 6 part-time (5 women); includes 1 minority (Black or African American, non-Hispanic/Latino). Average age 33. 1 applicant. *Faculty:* 5 full-time (3 women). *Financial support:* In 2015–16, 18 students received support, including 1 research assistantship with full tuition reimbursement available (averaging $8,000 per year); career-related internships or fieldwork, institutionally sponsored loans, scholarships/grants, and unspecified assistantships also available. Support available to part-time students. Financial award application deadline: 3/1; financial award applicants required to submit FAFSA. In 2015, 6 master's awarded. *Degree program information:* Part-time programs available. Part-time. Offers clinical nurse educator (MS); health care leadership (MS); nursing (MS). *Application deadline:* For fall admission, 5/15 priority date for domestic and international students. Applications are processed on a rolling basis. *Application fee:* $65. Electronic applications accepted. *Application Contact:* Carmel Boger, Administrative Assistant, 410-543-6420, Fax: 410-548-3313, E-mail: ciboger@salisbury.edu. *Graduate Program Director, Nursing*, Dr. Lisa Seldomridge, 410-543-6344, Fax: 410-548-3313, E-mail: laseldomridge@salisbury.edu.

Perdue School of Business Students: 34 full-time (18 women), 18 part-time (6 women); includes 5 minority (1 Black or African American, non-Hispanic/Latino; 1 Asian, non-Hispanic/Latino; 1 Hispanic/Latino; 2 Two or more races, non-Hispanic/Latino), 5 international. Average age 26. 47 applicants, 98% accepted, 40 enrolled. *Faculty:* 4 full-time (2 women), 1 part-time/adjunct (0 women). *Financial support:* In 2015–16, 5 research assistantships with full tuition reimbursements (averaging $8,000 per year) were awarded; career-related internships or fieldwork, institutionally sponsored loans, scholarships/grants, and unspecified assistantships also available. Support available to part-time students. Financial award application deadline: 3/1; financial award applicants required to submit FAFSA. In 2015, 30 master's awarded. *Degree program information:* Part-time and evening/weekend programs available. Part-time, evening/weekend, 100% online. Offers business (MBA). *Application deadline:* For fall admission, 3/1 priority date for domestic and international students. Applications are processed on a rolling basis. *Application fee:* $65. Electronic applications accepted. *Graduate Program Director, Business Administration*, Yvonne Downie Hanley, 410-548-3983, E-mail: yxdownie@salisbury.edu.

Program in Contemporary Curriculum Theory and Instruction: Literacy Students: 15 full-time (13 women), 11 part-time (7 women); includes 1 minority (Two or more races, non-Hispanic/Latino), 1 international. Average age 36. 13 applicants, 85% accepted, 11 enrolled. *Faculty:* 3 full-time (all women). *Financial support:* Fellowships available. Financial award application deadline: 3/1; financial award applicants required to submit FAFSA. *Degree program information:* Part-time programs available. Part-time. Offers contemporary curriculum theory and instruction: literacy (Ed D). *Application deadline:* For fall admission, 3/31 priority date for domestic and international students. Applications are processed on a rolling basis. *Application fee:* $65. Electronic applications accepted. *Graduate Program Director, Contemporary Curriculum Theory and Instruction: Literacy (Ed D)*, Dr. Judith Franzak, 410-677-0238, E-mail: jkfranzak@salisbury.edu.

Program in Curriculum and Instruction Students: 16 full-time (8 women), 73 part-time (60 women); includes 7 minority (4 Black or African American, non-Hispanic/Latino; 2 Hispanic/Latino; 1 Two or more races, non-Hispanic/Latino), 1 international. Average age 28. 20 applicants, 100% accepted, 19 enrolled. *Faculty:* 8 full-time (5 women), 9 part-time/adjunct (7 women). *Financial support:* In 2015–16, 4 research assistantships with full tuition reimbursements (averaging $8,000 per year) were awarded; career-related internships or fieldwork, institutionally sponsored loans, scholarships/grants, and unspecified assistantships also available. Support available to part-time students. Financial award application deadline: 3/1; financial award applicants required to submit FAFSA. In 2015, 38 master's awarded. *Degree program information:* Part-time and evening/weekend programs available. Part-time, evening/weekend. Offers curriculum and instruction (M Ed). *Application deadline:* For fall admission, 3/1 priority date for domestic and international students; for spring admission, 10/1 priority date for domestic and international students; for summer admission, 10/1 priority date for domestic and international students. Applications are processed on a rolling basis. *Application fee:* $65. Electronic applications accepted. *Director, Master of Education Programs*, Dr. Gwen Beegle, 410-543-6393, E-mail: gpbeegle@salisbury.edu.

Program in Educational Leadership Students: 37 part-time (22 women); includes 5 minority (2 Black or African American, non-Hispanic/Latino; 2 Hispanic/Latino; 1 Two or more races, non-Hispanic/Latino). Average age 32. 5 applicants, 100% accepted, 5 enrolled. *Faculty:* 2 full-time (0 women), 4 part-time/adjunct (1 woman). *Financial support:* Career-related internships or fieldwork, institutionally sponsored loans, and unspecified assistantships available. Support available to part-time students. Financial award application deadline: 3/1; financial award applicants required to submit FAFSA. In 2015, 14 master's awarded. *Degree program information:* Part-time and evening/weekend programs available. Part-time, evening/weekend. Offers educational leadership (M Ed). *Application deadline:* For fall admission, 3/1 priority date for domestic and international students; for spring admission, 10/1 priority date for domestic and international students; for summer admission, 10/1 priority date for domestic and international students. Applications are processed on a rolling basis. *Application fee:* $65. Electronic applications accepted. *Graduate Program Director, Educational Leadership*, Dr. Douglas DeWitt, 410-543-6286, Fax: 410-677-0249, E-mail: dmdewitt@salisbury.edu.

Program in Geographic Information Systems Management Students: 5 full-time (2 women), 11 part-time (3 women); includes 1 minority (Hispanic/Latino), 2 international. Average age 35. 6 applicants, 100% accepted, 5 enrolled. *Faculty:* 3 full-time (0 women). *Financial support:* In 2015–16, 3 research assistantships with full tuition reimbursements (averaging $9,000 per year) were awarded; institutionally sponsored loans and unspecified assistantships also available. Support available to part-time students. Financial award application deadline: 3/1; financial award applicants required to submit FAFSA. In 2015, 9 master's awarded. *Degree program information:* Part-time programs available. Part-time, 100% online. Offers geographic information systems management (MS). *Application deadline:* For fall admission, 7/1 priority date for domestic and international students; for spring admission, 10/1 priority date for domestic and international students; for summer admission, 10/1 priority date for domestic and international students. Applications are processed on a rolling basis. *Application fee:* $65. Electronic applications accepted. *Application Contact:* Jennifer Gordy, Program Management Specialist, 410-543-6460, Fax: 410-548-4506, E-mail: jlgordy@salisbury.edu. *Director*, Dr. Michael Scott, 410-543-6456, Fax: 410-548-4506, E-mail: msscott@salisbury.edu.

Program in Reading Specialist Students: 1 (woman) full-time, 22 part-time (20 women); includes 2 minority (both Black or African American, non-Hispanic/Latino). Average age 28. 6 applicants, 100% accepted, 6 enrolled. *Faculty:* 3 full-time (all women). *Financial support:* In 2015–16, 2 research assistantships with full tuition reimbursements (averaging $8,000 per year) were awarded; career-related internships or fieldwork, institutionally sponsored loans, scholarships/grants, and unspecified assistantships also available. Support available to part-time students. Financial award application deadline: 3/1; financial award applicants required to submit FAFSA. In 2015, 4 master's awarded. *Degree program information:* Part-time and evening/weekend programs available. Part-time, evening/weekend. Offers reading specialist (M Ed). *Application deadline:* For fall admission, 3/1 priority date for domestic and international students; for spring admission, 10/1 priority date for domestic and international students; for summer admission, 10/1 priority date for domestic and international students. Applications are processed on a rolling basis. *Application fee:* $65. Electronic applications accepted. *Application Contact:* Dr. Patricia Richards, Graduate Program Director, Reading Specialist, 410-543-6379, E-mail: porichards@salisbury.edu. *Director, Master of Education Programs*, Dr. Gwen Beegle, 410-543-6393, E-mail: gpbeegle@salisbury.edu.

Program in Teaching Students: 6 full-time (5 women), 2 part-time (both women); includes 1 minority (Black or African American, non-Hispanic/Latino). Average age 28. *Faculty:* 2 full-time (1 woman), 2 part-time/adjunct (both women). *Financial support:* In 2015–16, 6 students received support, including 1 research assistantship with full tuition reimbursement available (averaging $10,000 per year); career-related internships or fieldwork, institutionally sponsored loans, scholarships/grants, and unspecified assistantships also available. Support available to part-time students. Financial award application deadline: 3/1; financial award applicants required to submit FAFSA. In 2015,

14 master's awarded. Offers secondary education (MAT). *Application deadline:* For winter admission, 12/15 for domestic and international students. *Application fee:* $65. Electronic applications accepted. *Graduate Program Director, Teaching (MAT)*, Dr. Regina Royer, 410-548-3949, E-mail: rdroyer@salisbury.edu.

See Display below and Close-Up on page 897.

SALUS UNIVERSITY, Elkins Park, PA 19027-1598

General Information Independent, coed, graduate-only institution. *Graduate housing:* On-campus housing not available. *Research affiliation:* Dynamis Pharmaceuticals (diabetes research), DakDak (photobiology).

GRADUATE UNITS

College of Education and Rehabilitation ***Degree program information:*** Part-time programs available. Part-time, online learning. Offers education of children and youth with visual and multiple impairments (M Ed, Certificate); low vision rehabilitation (MS, Certificate); orientation and mobility therapy (MS, Certificate); vision rehabilitation therapy (MS, Certificate).

College of Health Sciences Offers physician assistant (MMS); public health (MPH). Electronic applications accepted.

College of Optometry Offers optometry (OD). Electronic applications accepted.

George S. Osborne College of Audiology Offers audiology (Au D). Electronic applications accepted.

SALVE REGINA UNIVERSITY, Newport, RI 02840-4192

General Information Independent-religious, coed, comprehensive institution. *Graduate housing:* On-campus housing not available.

GRADUATE UNITS

Holistic Graduate Programs ***Degree program information:*** Part-time and evening/weekend programs available. Part-time, evening/weekend. Offers expressive and creative arts (CAGS, CGS); holistic counseling (MA); holistic leadership (MA, CAGS, CGS); holistic leadership and change management (CAGS); holistic studies (CGS); substance abuse and treatment (CAGS); substance abuse foundations in holistic studies (CGS). Electronic applications accepted.

Program in Administration of Justice and Homeland Security ***Degree program information:*** Part-time and evening/weekend programs available. Part-time, evening/weekend, online learning. Offers administration of justice and homeland security (MS); cybersecurity and intelligence (CGS); digital forensics (CGS); leadership in justice (CGS). Electronic applications accepted.

Program in Business Administration ***Degree program information:*** Part-time and evening/weekend programs available. Part-time, evening/weekend, online learning. Offers cybersecurity issues in business (MBA); entrepreneurial enterprise (MBA); health care administration and management (MBA); social ventures (MBA). Electronic applications accepted.

Program in Healthcare Administration and Management ***Degree program information:*** Part-time and evening/weekend programs available. Part-time, evening/weekend, online learning. Offers healthcare administration and management (MS, CGS). Electronic applications accepted.

Program in Humanities ***Degree program information:*** Part-time and evening/weekend programs available. Part-time, evening/weekend, online learning. Offers humanitarian assistance (MA); humanities (PhD); public humanities (MA); religion, peace and justice (MA). Electronic applications accepted.

Program in International Relations ***Degree program information:*** Part-time and evening/weekend programs available. Part-time, evening/weekend, online learning. Offers international relations (MA, Certificate). Electronic applications accepted.

Program in Management ***Degree program information:*** Part-time and evening/weekend programs available. Part-time, evening/weekend, online learning. Offers innovation and strategic management (MS); nonprofit management (CGS). Electronic applications accepted.

Program in Nursing ***Degree program information:*** Part-time and evening/weekend programs available. Part-time, evening/weekend. Offers nursing (DNP). Electronic applications accepted.

Program in Rehabilitation Counseling ***Degree program information:*** Part-time and evening/weekend programs available. Part-time, evening/weekend. Offers mental health (CAGS); rehabilitation counseling (MA); substance abuse (CGS). Electronic applications accepted.

SAMFORD UNIVERSITY, Birmingham, AL 35229

General Information Independent-religious, coed, university. *Enrollment:* 5,206 graduate, professional, and undergraduate students; 1,797 full-time matriculated graduate/professional students (1,044 women), 183 part-time matriculated graduate/professional students (122 women). *Enrollment by degree level:* 757 master's, 1,195 doctoral, 28 other advanced degrees. *Graduate faculty:* 149 full-time (76 women), 59 part-time/adjunct (24 women). *Tuition, area resident:* Full-time $18,673; part-time $766 per credit hour. *Required fees:* $550. Tuition and fees vary according to course load, degree level and student level. *Graduate housing:* Room and/or apartments available on a first-come, first-served basis to single students; on-campus housing not available to married students. Typical cost: $2826 per year ($4615 including board). Housing application deadline: 5/1. *Student services:* Campus employment opportunities, campus safety program, career counseling, exercise/wellness program, free psychological counseling, grant writing training, international student services, low-cost health insurance, services for students with disabilities, teacher training, writing training. *Library:* University Library plus 4 others. *Collection:* Books: 625,811 (physical), 175,176 (digital/electronic); Serial titles: 2,129 (physical), 98,188 (digital/electronic); Databases: 250. Weekly public service hours: 94; students can reserve study rooms. *Research affiliation:* Cystic Fibrosis Foundation (Bethesda, MD) (drug discovery research), UAB School of Public Health (UAB Lister Hill Center for Health Policy) (health economics, health policy, public health), University of Alabama at Birmingham (pharmacy and medicine), Beacon Center of Tennessee (applied microeconomics, economic history), Institute for Faith (work and economics), Clinical Research Institute, Wallace Memorial Baptist Hospital.

Computer facilities: 330 computers available on campus for general student use. A campuswide network can be accessed from student residence rooms and from off campus. Online class registration, free online storage and tech support are available. Website: http://www.samford.edu/

General Application Contact: Brian L. Kennedy, Director of Recruitment, 205-726-4176, Fax: 205-726-2171, E-mail: blkenned@samford.edu.

GRADUATE UNITS

Beeson School of Divinity Students: 156 full-time (30 women), 10 part-time (4 women); includes 23 minority (16 Black or African American, non-Hispanic/Latino; 1 American Indian or Alaska Native, non-Hispanic/Latino; 3 Asian, non-Hispanic/Latino; 2 Hispanic/Latino; 1 Two or more races, non-Hispanic/Latino), 4 international. Average age 29. 64 applicants, 94% accepted, 38 enrolled. *Faculty:* 14 full-time (2 women), 6 part-time/adjunct (1 woman). *Financial support:* In 2015–16, 134 students received support. Federal Work-Study, institutionally sponsored loans, scholarships/grants, and tuition waivers (full and partial) available. Financial award application deadline: 2/15; financial award applicants required to submit FAFSA. In 2015, 36 master's, 4 doctorates awarded. *Degree program information:* Part-time programs available. Part-time. Offers divinity (M Div, MATS, D Min). *Application deadline:* For fall admission, 2/15 for domestic and international students; for spring admission, 10/1 for domestic and international students. *Application fee:* $35. Electronic applications accepted. *Application Contact:* Sherri S Brown, Director of Admission, 205-726-2066, Fax: 205-726-4120, E-mail: sbrown5@samford.edu. *Dean*, Dr. Timothy George, 205-726-2632, E-mail: tfgeorge@samford.edu.

Brock School of Business Students: 73 full-time (30 women), 15 part-time (5 women); includes 13 minority (7 Black or African American, non-Hispanic/Latino; 2 Asian, non-Hispanic/Latino; 4 Hispanic/Latino), 10 international. Average age 28. 100 applicants, 47% accepted, 32 enrolled. *Faculty:* 13 full-time (2 women), 4 part-time/adjunct (0 women). *Financial support:* In 2015–16, 36 students received support. Career-related internships or fieldwork, institutionally sponsored loans, scholarships/grants, and tuition waivers (partial) available. Support available to part-time students. Financial award application deadline: 3/1; financial award applicants required to submit FAFSA. In 2015, 73 master's awarded. *Degree program information:* Part-time and evening/weekend programs available. Part-time-only, evening/weekend, 100% online, blended/hybrid learning. Offers entrepreneurship (MBA); finance (MBA); marketing (MBA). *Application deadline:* For fall admission, 7/1 for domestic students, 6/1 for international students; for spring admission, 12/1 for domestic students, 11/1 for international students; for summer admission, 4/1 for domestic students. Applications are processed on a rolling basis. *Application fee:* $35. Electronic applications accepted. *Application Contact:* Elizabeth Gambrell, Assistant Director of Academic Programs, 205-726-2040, Fax: 205-726-2540, E-mail: eagambre@samford.edu. *Assistant Dean*, Dr. Barbara Cartledge, 205-726-2935, Fax: 205-726-2540, E-mail: bhcartle@samford.edu.

Cumberland School of Law Students: 458 full-time (216 women), 8 part-time (5 women); includes 64 minority (31 Black or African American, non-Hispanic/Latino; 2 American Indian or Alaska Native, non-Hispanic/Latino; 8 Asian, non-Hispanic/Latino; 18 Hispanic/Latino; 5 Two or more races, non-Hispanic/Latino), 1 international. Average age 26. 659 applicants, 65% accepted, 185 enrolled. *Faculty:* 20 full-time (6 women), 21 part-time/adjunct (6 women). *Financial support:* In 2015–16, 301 students received support. Career-related internships or fieldwork, Federal Work-Study, institutionally sponsored loans, and scholarships/grants available. Financial award application deadline: 3/1; financial award applicants required to submit FAFSA. In 2015, 139 doctorates awarded. Offers law (MCL, JD). JD/MPH, JD/MPA offered jointly with The University of Alabama at Birmingham. *Application deadline:* For fall admission, 2/28 priority date for domestic and international students. Applications are processed on a rolling basis. *Application fee:* $50. Electronic applications accepted. *Application Contact:* Ken England, Director of Admissions and Administration, 205-726-2887, Fax: 205-726-4457, E-mail: law.admissions@samford.edu. *Dean*, Henry C. Strickland, 205-726-2704, Fax: 205-726-4457, E-mail: hcstrick@samford.edu.

Howard College of Arts and Sciences Students: 21 full-time (7 women), 2 part-time; includes 4 minority (all Black or African American, non-Hispanic/Latino), 14 international. Average age 25. 20 applicants, 80% accepted, 8 enrolled. *Faculty:* 8 full-time (2 women), 4 part-time/adjunct (0 women). *Financial support:* In 2015–16, 1 student received support. Application deadline: 3/1; applicants required to submit FAFSA. In 2015, 33 master's awarded. *Degree program information:* Part-time and evening/weekend programs available. Part-time, evening/weekend. Offers energy management and policy (MSEM). *Application deadline:* For fall admission, 8/1 for domestic and international students; for winter admission, 12/1 for domestic and international students; for spring admission, 12/1 for domestic and international students; for summer admission, 5/1 for domestic and international students. Applications are processed on a rolling basis. *Application fee:* $35. *Application Contact:* Dr. Ronald N. Hunsinger, Professor/Chair, Biological and Environmental Sciences, 205-726-2944, Fax: 205-726-2479, E-mail: rnhunsin@samford.edu.

Ida V. Moffett School of Nursing Students: 300 full-time (228 women), 40 part-time (36 women); includes 65 minority (28 Black or African American, non-Hispanic/Latino; 4 American Indian or Alaska Native, non-Hispanic/Latino; 8 Asian, non-Hispanic/Latino; 13 Hispanic/Latino; 12 Two or more races, non-Hispanic/Latino). Average age 35. 69 applicants, 77% accepted, 52 enrolled. *Faculty:* 19 full-time (all women), 5 part-time/adjunct (1 woman). *Financial support:* In 2015–16, 56 students received support. Institutionally sponsored loans, scholarships/grants, and traineeships available. Financial award application deadline: 3/1; financial award applicants required to submit FAFSA. In 2015, 98 master's, 16 doctorates awarded. *Degree program information:* Part-time programs available. Part-time, blended/hybrid learning. Offers administration (DNP); advanced practice (DNP); family nurse practitioner (MSN); health systems management and leadership (MSN); nurse anesthesia (MSN); nurse educator (MSN). *Application deadline:* For fall admission, 6/1 for domestic and international students; for spring admission, 9/1 for domestic and international students. *Application fee:* $65. Electronic applications accepted. *Application Contact:* Allyson Maddox, Director of Graduate Student Services, Ida V. Moffett School of Nursing, 205-726-2047, Fax: 205-726-4179, E-mail: amaddox@samford.edu. *Vice Provost, College of Health Sciences/Dean/Professor*, Dr. Nena F. Sanders, 205-726-2612, Fax: 205-726-4179, E-mail: nfsander@samford.edu.

McWhorter School of Pharmacy Students: 495 full-time (308 women), 7 part-time (2 women); includes 95 minority (47 Black or African American, non-Hispanic/Latino; 1 American Indian or Alaska Native, non-Hispanic/Latino; 36 Asian, non-Hispanic/Latino; 5 Hispanic/Latino; 6 Two or more races, non-Hispanic/Latino), 9 international. Average age 25. 451 applicants, 42% accepted, 146 enrolled. *Faculty:* 40 full-time (23 women), 2 part-time/adjunct (1 woman). *Financial support:* In 2015–16, 187 students received support. Research assistantships, teaching assistantships, Federal Work-Study, institutionally sponsored loans, and scholarships/grants available. Financial award application deadline: 3/1; financial award applicants required to submit FAFSA. In 2015, 119 doctorates awarded. Offers pharmacy (Pharm D). *Application deadline:* For spring admission, 3/1 for domestic and international students. Applications are processed on a rolling basis. *Application fee:* $25. Electronic applications accepted. *Application Contact:* Jon M. Parker, Assistant Director of Pharmacy Admissions, 205-726-4242, Fax: 205-726-4141, E-mail: jmparker@samford.edu. *Dean/Professor*, Dr. Michael A. Crouch, 205-726-2820, Fax: 205-726-2759, E-mail: macrouch@samford.edu.

Orlean Bullard Beeson School of Education Students: 194 full-time (146 women), 98 part-time (69 women); includes 61 minority (54 Black or African American, non-Hispanic/Latino; 4 American Indian or Alaska Native, non-Hispanic/Latino; 1 Asian, non-Hispanic/Latino; 2 Hispanic/Latino), 1 international. Average age 36. 113 applicants, 96% accepted, 80 enrolled. *Faculty:* 20 full-time (14 women), 41 part-time/adjunct (32 women). *Financial support:* In 2015–16, 229 students received support. Scholarships/grants available. Financial award application deadline: 3/1; financial award applicants required to submit FAFSA. In 2015, 60 master's, 19 doctorates, 3 Certificates awarded. *Degree program information:* Part-time and evening/weekend programs available. Part-time, evening/weekend, blended/hybrid learning. Offers early childhood/elementary education (MS Ed); educational leadership (MS Ed, Ed D); elementary education (MS Ed); gifted education (MS Ed, Certificate); instructional design and technology (MS Ed); instructional leadership (MS Ed, Certificate, Ed S); K-12 collaborative special education (MS Ed); secondary education (MS Ed); teacher leader (Ed S). *Application deadline:* For fall admission, 7/15 for domestic students, 7/1 for international students; for spring admission, 11/15 for domestic and international students; for summer admission, 4/15 for domestic and international students. *Application fee:* $35. Electronic applications accepted. *Application Contact:* Brooke Karr, Graduate Admissions Coordinator, 205-729-2783, Fax: 205-726-4233, E-mail: kbgilrea@samford.edu. *Dean*, Dr. Jean Box, 205-726-2565, Fax: 205-726-4233, E-mail: jabox@samford.edu.

School of Health Professions Students: 53 full-time (38 women); includes 1 minority (Two or more races, non-Hispanic/Latino). Average age 24. 117 applicants, 73% accepted, 55 enrolled. *Faculty:* 11 full-time (8 women). *Financial support:* In 2015–16, 7 students received support. Application deadline: 3/1; applicants required to submit FAFSA. *Degree program information:* Evening/weekend programs available. Evening/weekend, online learning. Offers athletic training (MAT); physical therapy (DPT); speech language pathology (MS). *Application deadline:* For fall admission, 6/1 for domestic students; for spring admission, 10/1 for domestic students. *Application fee:* $120. Electronic applications accepted. *Application Contact:* Dr. Marian Carter, Assistant Dean of Enrollment Management and Student Services, 205-726-2611, Fax: 205-726-2666, E-mail: mwcarter@samford.edu. *Dean, School of Health Professions*, Dr. Alan P. Jung, 205-726-2716, Fax: 205-726-2666, E-mail: apjung@samford.edu.

School of Public Health Students: 36 full-time (35 women), 1 (woman) part-time; includes 9 minority (1 American Indian or Alaska Native, non-Hispanic/Latino; 8 Asian, non-Hispanic/Latino). Average age 27. 19 applicants, 89% accepted, 15 enrolled. *Faculty:* 10 full-time (8 women), 1 part-time/adjunct (0 women). *Financial support:* In 2015–16, 15 students received support. Scholarships/grants available. Financial award application deadline: 3/1; financial award applicants required to submit FAFSA. *Degree program information:* Part-time and evening/weekend programs available. Part-time, evening/weekend, 100% online. Offers clinical social work (MSW); global community development (MSW); public health (MPH). *Application deadline:* For fall admission, 6/1 for domestic and international students; for spring admission, 10/1 for domestic and international students. *Application fee:* $75. Electronic applications accepted. *Application Contact:* Dr. Marian Carter, Assistant Dean of Enrollment Management and Student Services, 205-726-2611, Fax: 205-726-2666, E-mail: mwcarter@samford.edu. *Dean, School of Public Health*, Dr. Keith Elder.

School of the Arts Students: 11 full-time (6 women), 2 part-time (0 women); includes 2 minority (both Black or African American, non-Hispanic/Latino). Average age 27. 9 applicants, 100% accepted, 5 enrolled. *Faculty:* 17 full-time (5 women), 4 part-time/adjunct (2 women). *Financial support:* In 2015–16, 7 students received support. Federal Work-Study, scholarships/grants, and unspecified assistantships available. Financial award application deadline: 3/1; financial award applicants required to submit FAFSA. In 2015, 8 master's awarded. *Degree program information:* Part-time programs available. Part-time. Offers church music (MM); music education (MME); piano performance and pedagogy (MM); vocal performance (MM). MME program offered in traditional, fifth year non-traditional, and national board cohort formats. *Application deadline:* For fall admission, 11/15 priority date for domestic and international students; for spring admission, 4/15 priority date for domestic and international students; for summer admission, 8/1 for domestic and international students. Applications are processed on a rolling basis. *Application fee:* $35. Electronic applications accepted. *Application Contact:* Dr. Demondrae Thurman, Professor of Music/Director of Graduate Studies, 205-726-2389, Fax: 205-726-2165, E-mail: dthurman@samford.edu. *Dean*, Dr. Joseph Hopkin, 205-726-2778, Fax: 205-726-2615, E-mail: jhopkins@samford.edu.

SAM HOUSTON STATE UNIVERSITY, Huntsville, TX 77341

General Information State-supported, coed, university. CGS member. *Graduate housing:* Room and/or apartments available on a first-come, first-served basis to single students; on-campus housing not available to married students. Housing application deadline: 8/20. *Research affiliation:* Texas Criminal Justice Division, Texas Department of Corrections, Research Division.

GRADUATE UNITS

College of Business Administration ***Degree program information:*** Part-time and evening/weekend programs available. Part-time, evening/weekend, online learning. Offers accounting (MS); banking and financial institutions (EMBA); business administration (EMBA, MBA, MS); project management (MS). Electronic applications accepted.

College of Criminal Justice ***Degree program information:*** Part-time and evening/weekend programs available. Part-time, evening/weekend, online learning. Offers criminal justice (MS, PhD); criminal justice and criminology (MA); criminal justice leadership and management (MS); forensic science (MS); homeland security studies (MS); victim services management (MS). Electronic applications accepted.

College of Education ***Degree program information:*** Part-time and evening/weekend programs available. Part-time, evening/weekend, online learning. Offers administration (M Ed); counseling (M Ed, MA, PhD); curriculum and instruction (M Ed); developmental education administration (Ed D); education (M Ed, MA, MLS, Ed D, PhD); educational leadership (Ed D); higher education administration (MA); instructional leadership (M Ed, MA); international literacy (M Ed); library science (MLS); reading (M Ed); special education (M Ed, MA). Electronic applications accepted.

College of Fine Arts and Mass Communication ***Degree program information:*** Part-time programs available. Part-time. Offers dance (MFA); digital media (MA); fine arts and mass communication (MA, MFA, MM). Electronic applications accepted.

School of Music ***Degree program information:*** Part-time programs available. Part-time. Offers music (MM). Electronic applications accepted.

College of Health Sciences ***Degree program information:*** Part-time programs available. Part-time. Offers dietetics (MS); family and consumer sciences (MS); health (MA); health sciences (MA, MS); sport and human performance (MA); sport management (MA). Electronic applications accepted.

College of Humanities and Social Sciences ***Degree program information:*** Part-time programs available. Part-time, online learning. Offers communication studies (MA); creative writing, editing, and publishing (MFA); English (MA); history (MA); humanities and social sciences (MA, MFA, MPA, PhD, SSP); political science (MA); psychology (MA, PhD, SSP); public administration (MPA); sociology (MA); Spanish (MA). Electronic applications accepted.

College of Sciences ***Degree program information:*** Part-time and evening/weekend programs available. Part-time, evening/weekend. Offers agriculture (MS); applied geographic information science (MS); biological sciences (MA, MS); chemistry (MS); computing and information science (MS); digital forensics (MS); geographic information science (Certificate); information assurance and security (MS); mathematics (MA, MS); sciences (MA, MS, PhD, Certificate); statistics (MS). Electronic applications accepted.

SAMUEL MERRITT UNIVERSITY, Oakland, CA 94609-3108

General Information Independent, coed, primarily women, upper-level institution. *Enrollment:* 1,603 graduate, professional, and undergraduate students; 972 full-time matriculated graduate/professional students (680 women), 65 part-time matriculated graduate/professional students (50 women). *Enrollment by degree level:* 704 master's, 326 doctoral, 7 other advanced degrees. *Graduate faculty:* 93 full-time (64 women), 99 part-time/adjunct (73 women). *Tuition, area resident:* Part-time $1251 per unit. *Required fees:* $50 per unit. One-time fee: $300. *Graduate housing:* On-campus housing not available. *Student services:* Campus employment opportunities, campus safety program, career counseling, free psychological counseling, low-cost health insurance, services for students with disabilities. *Library:* John A. Graziano Memorial Library plus 2 others. *Collection:* Books: 12,036 (physical), 137 (digital/electronic); Serial titles: 16,894 (physical); Databases: 34. Weekly public service hours: 10; students can reserve study rooms. *Research affiliation:* Summit Medical Center (nursing).

Computer facilities: 152 computers available on campus for general student use. A campuswide network can be accessed. Online class registration is available. Website: http://www.samuelmerritt.edu/

General Application Contact: Timothy Cranford, Dean of Admissions, 510-869-1550, Fax: 510-869-6525, E-mail: admission@samuelmerritt.edu.

GRADUATE UNITS

Department of Occupational Therapy Students: 116 full-time (98 women); includes 50 minority (4 Black or African American, non-Hispanic/Latino; 22 Asian, non-Hispanic/Latino; 16 Hispanic/Latino; 8 Two or more races, non-Hispanic/Latino). Average age 29. 249 applicants, 21% accepted, 38 enrolled. *Faculty:* 9 full-time (7 women), 11 part-time/adjunct (9 women). *Financial support:* In 2015–16, 15 students received support. Career-related internships or fieldwork, Federal Work-Study, and scholarships/grants available. Support available to part-time students. Financial award application deadline: 3/2; financial award applicants required to submit FAFSA. In 2015, 37 master's awarded. Offers occupational therapy (MOT). *Application deadline:* For fall admission, 10/1 priority date for domestic students. *Application fee:* $50. Electronic applications accepted. *Application Contact:* Timothy Cranford, Dean of Admission, 510-869-1550, Fax: 510-869-6525, E-mail: admission@samuelmerritt.edu. *Chair,* Kate Hayner, 510-869-4780, E-mail: khayner@samuelmerritt.edu.

Department of Physical Therapy Students: 104 full-time (60 women), 4 part-time (3 women); includes 54 minority (1 Black or African American, non-Hispanic/Latino; 28 Asian, non-Hispanic/Latino; 20 Hispanic/Latino; 1 Native Hawaiian or other Pacific Islander, non-Hispanic/Latino; 4 Two or more races, non-Hispanic/Latino). Average age 28. 585 applicants, 16% accepted, 34 enrolled. *Faculty:* 11 full-time (9 women), 22 part-time/adjunct (14 women). *Financial support:* In 2015–16, 17 students received support. Career-related internships or fieldwork, Federal Work-Study, and scholarships/grants available. Financial award application deadline: 3/2; financial award applicants required to submit FAFSA. Offers physical therapy (DPT). *Application deadline:* For fall admission, 10/1 priority date for domestic students. *Application fee:* $50. Electronic applications accepted. *Application Contact:* Timothy Cranford, Dean of Admissions, 510-869-1550, Fax: 510-869-6525, E-mail: admission@samuelmerritt.edu. *Co-Chair,* Dr. Nicole Christensen, 510-869-6567, Fax: 510-869-6282, E-mail: nchristensen@samuelmerritt.edu.

Department of Physician Assistant Studies Students: 128 full-time (93 women), 2 part-time (both women); includes 65 minority (4 Black or African American, non-Hispanic/Latino; 24 Asian, non-Hispanic/Latino; 27 Hispanic/Latino; 2 Native Hawaiian or other Pacific Islander, non-Hispanic/Latino; 8 Two or more races, non-Hispanic/Latino). Average age 32. 2,065 applicants, 3% accepted, 44 enrolled. *Faculty:* 8 full-time (5 women), 9 part-time/adjunct (4 women). *Financial support:* Federal Work-Study, institutionally sponsored loans, and scholarships/grants available. Financial award application deadline: 3/2; financial award applicants required to submit FAFSA. In 2015, 39 master's awarded. Offers physician assistant studies (MPA). *Application deadline:* For fall admission, 10/1 priority date for domestic students. *Application fee:* $50. Electronic applications accepted. *Application Contact:* Timothy Cranford, Dean of Admission, 510-869-1550, Fax: 510-869-6525, E-mail: admission@samuelmerritt.edu.

School of Nursing Students: 437 full-time (350 women), 59 part-time (45 women); includes 327 minority (29 Black or African American, non-Hispanic/Latino; 3 American Indian or Alaska Native, non-Hispanic/Latino; 163 Asian, non-Hispanic/Latino; 95 Hispanic/Latino; 9 Native Hawaiian or other Pacific Islander, non-Hispanic/Latino; 28 Two or more races, non-Hispanic/Latino). Average age 33. 392 applicants, 43% accepted, 126 enrolled. *Faculty:* 47 full-time (40 women), 50 part-time/adjunct (43 women). *Financial support:* In 2015–16, 34 students received support. Career-related internships or fieldwork, Federal Work-Study, scholarships/grants, and traineeships available. Support available to part-time students. Financial award application deadline: 3/2; financial award applicants required to submit FAFSA. In 2015, 31 master's awarded. *Degree program information:* Part-time and evening/weekend programs available. Part-time, evening/weekend, 100% online, blended/hybrid learning. Offers case management (MSN); family nurse practitioner (MSN, Certificate); nurse anesthetist (MSN, Certificate); nursing (DNP). *Application deadline:* For fall admission, 1/1 priority date for domestic students; for spring admission, 7/1 for domestic students; for summer admission, 1/1 for domestic students. Applications are processed on a rolling basis. *Application fee:* $50. Electronic applications accepted. *Application Contact:* Timothy Cranford, Dean of Admission, 510-869-6576, Fax: 510-869-6525, E-mail: admission@samuelmerritt.edu. *Graduate Coordinator,* Dr. Audrey Berman, 510-869-6733, Fax: 510-869-6525.

SAN DIEGO STATE UNIVERSITY, San Diego, CA 92182

General Information State-supported, coed, university. CGS member. *Graduate housing:* Room and/or apartments available on a first-come, first-served basis to single students; on-campus housing not available to married students. Housing application deadline: 5/1. *Research affiliation:* Robert Wood Johnson Foundation (public health), General Atomics (technical student services), William and Flora Hewlett Foundation (teacher education), American Heart Association (biology), Children's Hospital and Research Center (children's health), Qualcomm (wireless and telecommunications).

GRADUATE UNITS

Graduate and Research Affairs ***Degree program information:*** Part-time and evening/weekend programs available. Part-time, evening/weekend. Offers interdisciplinary studies (MA, MS). Electronic applications accepted.

College of Arts and Letters ***Degree program information:*** Part-time and evening/weekend programs available. Part-time, evening/weekend. Offers anthropology (MA); applied linguistics and English as a second language (CAL); arts and letters (MA, MFA, PhD, CAL); Asian studies (MA); computational linguistics (MA); creative writing (MFA); economics (MA); English (MA); English as a second language/applied linguistics (MA); European studies (MA); general linguistics (MA); geography (MA, PhD); history (MA); Latin American studies (MA); lesbian, gay, bisexual and transgender studies (Graduate Certificate); liberal arts and sciences (MA); philosophy (MA); political science (MA); rhetoric and writing studies (MA); sociology (MA); Spanish (MA); women's studies (MA). Electronic applications accepted.

College of Business Administration ***Degree program information:*** Part-time and evening/weekend programs available. Part-time, evening/weekend. Offers accountancy (MS); business administration (MBA, MS); entrepreneurship (MS); finance (MS); human resources management (MS); information systems (MS); management science (MS); marketing (MS); sports business management (MBA). Electronic applications accepted.

College of Education ***Degree program information:*** Part-time and evening/weekend programs available. Part-time, evening/weekend. Offers child development (MS); counseling and school psychology (MS); education (MA, MS, Ed D, PhD); educational leadership (MA); educational leadership in post-secondary education (MA); educational technology (MA); educational technology and teaching and learning (Ed D); elementary curriculum and instruction (MA); multi-cultural emphasis (PhD); policy studies in language and cross cultural education (MA); reading education (MA); rehabilitation counseling (MS); secondary curriculum and instruction (MA); special education (MA). Electronic applications accepted.

College of Engineering ***Degree program information:*** Part-time and evening/weekend programs available. Part-time, evening/weekend. Offers aerospace engineering (MS); civil engineering (MS); electrical engineering (MS); engineering (MS, PhD); engineering mechanics (MS); engineering sciences and applied mechanics (PhD); flight dynamics (MS); fluid dynamics (MS); manufacture and design (MS); mechanical engineering (MS). Electronic applications accepted.

College of Health and Human Services ***Degree program information:*** Part-time and evening/weekend programs available. Part-time, evening/weekend. Offers audiology (Au D); biometry (MPH); communicative disorders (MA); environmental health (MPH); epidemiology (MPH, PhD); exercise physiology (MS); gerontology (MS); global emergency preparedness and response (MS); global health (PhD); health and human services (MA, MPH, MS, MSW, Au D, DPT, PhD); health behavior (PhD); health promotion (MPH); health services administration (MPH); kinesiology (MA); language and communicative disorders (PhD); nursing (MS); nutritional sciences (MS); physical therapy (DPT); social work (MSW); toxicology (MS). Electronic applications accepted.

College of Professional Studies and Fine Arts ***Degree program information:*** Part-time programs available. Part-time. Offers advertising and public relations (MA); art history (MA); city planning (MCP); composition (acoustic and electronic) (MM); conducting (MM); criminal justice administration (MPA); criminal justice and criminology (MS); critical-cultural studies (MA); ethnomusicology (MA); interaction studies (MA); intercultural and international studies (MA); jazz studies (MM); musicology (MA); new media studies (MA); news and information studies (MA); performance (MM); piano pedagogy (MA); professional studies and fine arts (MA, MCP, MFA, MM, MPA, MS); public administration (MPA); studio arts (MA, MFA); telecommunications and media management (MA); television, film, and new media production (MA); theatre arts (MA, MFA); theory (MA).

College of Sciences ***Degree program information:*** Part-time programs available. Part-time. Offers applied mathematics (MS); astronomy (MS); biology (MA, MS); cell and molecular biology (PhD); chemistry and biochemistry (MA, MS, PhD); clinical psychology (MS, PhD); computational science (MS, PhD); computer science (MS); ecology (MS, PhD); geological sciences (MS); industrial and organizational psychology (MS); mathematics (MA); mathematics and science education (PhD); microbiology (MS); molecular biology (MA, MS); physics (MA, MS); program evaluation (MS); psychology (MA); radiological physics (MS); regulatory affairs (MS); sciences (MA, MS, PhD); statistics (MS). Electronic applications accepted.

SANFORD BURNHAM PREBYS MEDICAL DISCOVERY INSTITUTE, La Jolla, CA 92037

General Information Independent, coed, graduate-only institution.

GRADUATE UNITS

Graduate School of Biomedical Sciences Offers biomedical sciences (PhD).

SAN FRANCISCO ART INSTITUTE, San Francisco, CA 94133

General Information Independent, coed, comprehensive institution. *Enrollment:* 599 graduate, professional, and undergraduate students; 170 full-time matriculated graduate/professional students (108 women), 17 part-time matriculated graduate/professional students (11 women). *Enrollment by degree level:* 177 master's, 10 other advanced degrees. *Graduate faculty:* 19 full-time (9 women), 36 part-time/adjunct (18 women). *Tuition, area resident:* Full-time $42,334; part-time $1859 per credit. *Required fees:* $870; $870 per unit. *Graduate housing:* Room and/or apartments available on a first-come, first-served basis to single students; on-campus housing not available to married students. Typical cost: $11,500 (including board). Housing application deadline: 6/1. *Student services:* Campus employment opportunities, campus safety program, career counseling, free psychological counseling, grant writing training, international student services, low-cost health insurance, services for students with disabilities, writing training. *Library:* Anne Bremer Memorial Library plus 1 other. *Collection:* Books: 31,831 (physical); Serial titles: 126 (physical), 791 (digital/electronic); Databases: 6. Weekly public service hours: 59. *Research affiliation:* San Francisco Museum of Modern Art (art history, museum studies, contemporary art), Headlands Center for the Arts (multidisciplinary art exhibition), Kadist Art Foundation (contemporary art exhibition), Yerba Buena Center for the Arts (art exhibits), Tremaine Foundation (education; art, environment, and learning disabilities), Prelinger Library (library).

Computer facilities: 150 computers available on campus for general student use. A campuswide network can be accessed. Online class registration is available. Website: http://www.sfai.edu/

General Application Contact: Nicole Crescenzi, Director of Graduate Admissions, 415-351-3517, Fax: 415-749-4592, E-mail: ncrescenzi@sfai.edu.

GRADUATE UNITS

Master of Arts Programs Students: 11 full-time (all women); includes 2 minority (1 Hispanic/Latino; 1 Two or more races, non-Hispanic/Latino), 3 international. Average age 26. 52 applicants, 62% accepted, 8 enrolled. *Faculty:* 3 full-time (all women), 25 part-time/adjunct (13 women). *Financial support:* In 2015–16, fellowships (averaging $30,000 per year), teaching assistantships (averaging $2,750 per year) were awarded; career-related internships or fieldwork, Federal Work-Study, scholarships/grants, and unspecified assistantships also available. Support available to part-time students. Financial award application deadline: 3/1; financial award applicants required to submit FAFSA. In 2015, 7 master's awarded. Offers exhibition and museum studies (MA); history and theory of contemporary art (MA). *Application deadline:* For fall admission, 1/15 priority date for domestic and international students. Applications are processed on a rolling basis. *Application fee:* $85. Electronic applications accepted. *Application Contact:* Jana Rumberger, Associate Director of Recruitment, 415-351-3507, Fax: 415-749-4592, E-mail: jrumberger@sfai.edu. *Chair, Master of Arts Department,* Claire Daigle, 415-351-3573 Ext. 1004, Fax: 415-641-1205, E-mail: cdaigle@sfai.edu.

Master of Fine Arts Programs Students: 152 full-time (91 women), 17 part-time (11 women); includes 34 minority (1 Black or African American, non-Hispanic/Latino; 9 Asian, non-Hispanic/Latino; 13 Hispanic/Latino; 11 Two or more races, non-Hispanic/Latino), 64 international. Average age 30. 399 applicants, 57% accepted, 78 enrolled. *Faculty:* 19 full-time (9 women), 36 part-time/adjunct (18 women). *Financial support:* In 2015–16, fellowships (averaging $30,000 per year), teaching assistantships (averaging $2,750 per year) were awarded; career-related internships or fieldwork, Federal Work-Study, scholarships/grants, and unspecified assistantships also available. Support available to part-time students. Financial award application deadline: 3/1; financial award applicants required to submit FAFSA. In 2015, 95 master's, 16 other advanced degrees awarded. *Degree program information:* Part-time programs available. Part-time. Offers studio art (MFA, Certificate). *Application deadline:* For fall admission, 1/15 priority date for domestic and international students; for spring admission, 11/15 priority date for domestic and international students. Applications are processed on a rolling basis. *Application fee:* $85. Electronic applications accepted. *Application Contact:* Nicole Crescenzi, Director of Graduate Admissions, 415-351-3517, Fax: 415-749-4592, E-mail: ncrescenzi@sfai.edu. *Chair, Master of Fine Arts Department,* Maria Elena Gonzalez, 415-351-3574, Fax: 415-641-1205, E-mail: megonzalez@sfai.edu.

SAN FRANCISCO CONSERVATORY OF MUSIC, San Francisco, CA 94102

General Information Independent, coed, comprehensive institution. *Enrollment:* 379 graduate, professional, and undergraduate students; 218 full-time matriculated graduate/professional students (125 women), 3 part-time matriculated graduate/professional students (1 woman). *Enrollment by degree level:* 184 master's, 37 other advanced degrees. *Graduate faculty:* 28 full-time (8 women), 96 part-time/adjunct (30 women). *Tuition, area resident:* Full-time $41,200; part-time $1816 per credit. *Required fees:* $1010; $1010 per unit. Tuition and fees vary according to course load. *Graduate housing:* Rooms and/or apartments available on a first-come, first-served basis to single and married students. Typical cost: $13,700 per year ($20,200 including board) for single students; $23,800 per year ($36,800 including board) for married students. Room and board charges vary according to board plan and housing facility selected. Housing application deadline: 5/31. *Student services:* Campus employment opportunities, campus safety program, career counseling, free psychological counseling, grant writing training, low-cost health insurance, services for students with disabilities, teacher training, writing training. *Library:* San Francisco Conservatory of Music Library. *Collection:* Books: 19,059 (physical), 2,971 (digital/electronic); Serial titles: 70 (physical), 374 (digital/electronic); Databases: 13. Weekly public service hours: 72.

Computer facilities: 13 computers available on campus for general student use. A campuswide network can be accessed. Online class registration is available.
Website: http://www.sfcm.edu/

General Application Contact: Melissa Cocco-Mitten, Director of Admissions, 415-503-6231, Fax: 415-503-6299, E-mail: admit@sfcm.edu.

GRADUATE UNITS

Graduate Division Students: 218 full-time (125 women), 3 part-time (1 woman); includes 44 minority (2 Black or African American, non-Hispanic/Latino; 3 American Indian or Alaska Native, non-Hispanic/Latino; 19 Asian, non-Hispanic/Latino; 7 Hispanic/Latino; 1 Native Hawaiian or other Pacific Islander, non-Hispanic/Latino; 12 Two or more races, non-Hispanic/Latino), 74 international. Average age 25. 678 applicants, 38% accepted, 114 enrolled. *Faculty:* 28 full-time (8 women), 96 part-time/adjunct (30 women). *Financial support:* In 2015–16, 222 students received support. Federal Work-Study, scholarships/grants, and unspecified assistantships available. Financial award application deadline: 2/15; financial award applicants required to submit FAFSA. In 2015, 79 master's awarded. Offers brass (MM); chamber music (MM); collaborative piano (MM); composition (MM); conducting (MM); guitar (MM); percussion (MM); piano and organ (MM); strings (MM); voice (MM); woodwinds (MM). *Application deadline:* For fall admission, 12/1 for domestic and international students; for spring admission, 10/1 for domestic and international students. *Application fee:* $110. Electronic applications accepted. *Application Contact:* Melissa Cocco-Mitten, Director of Admission, 415-503-6207, Fax: 415-503-6299, E-mail: admit@sfcm.edu. *Provost and Dean,* Kate Sheeran, 415-503-6251, Fax: 415-503-6205, E-mail: cibert@sfcm.edu.

SAN FRANCISCO STATE UNIVERSITY, San Francisco, CA 94132-1722

General Information State-supported, coed, university. *Enrollment:* 30,256 graduate, professional, and undergraduate students; 2,040 full-time matriculated graduate/professional students (1,297 women), 1,267 part-time matriculated graduate/professional students (781 women). Tuition, state resident: full-time $6738. Tuition, nonresident: full-time $15,666. *Required fees:* $1004. *Graduate housing:* Room and/or apartments available on a first-come, first-served basis to single students; on-campus housing not available to married students. *Student services:* Campus employment opportunities, campus safety program, career counseling, child daycare facilities, exercise/wellness program, free psychological counseling, international student services, low-cost health insurance, multicultural affairs office, services for students with disabilities, teacher training. *Library:* J. Paul Leonard Library. Study areas open 24 hours, 5–7 days a week; students can reserve study rooms.

Computer facilities: Computer purchase and lease plans are available. 2,500 computers available on campus for general student use. A campuswide network can be accessed from student residence rooms and from off campus. Online class registration is available.
Website: http://www.sfsu.edu/

General Application Contact: Noah Price, Director of Graduate Admissions, 415-338-2234, Fax: 415-405-0340, E-mail: nprice@sfsu.edu.

GRADUATE UNITS

Division of Graduate Studies ***Financial support:*** Fellowships, research assistantships, teaching assistantships, career-related internships or fieldwork, Federal Work-Study, institutionally sponsored loans, tuition waivers (partial), and unspecified assistantships available. Support available to part-time students. Financial award application deadline: 3/1; financial award applicants required to submit FAFSA. *Degree program information:* Part-time and evening/weekend programs available. Part-time, evening/weekend. *Application fee:* $55. *Application Contact:* Noah Price, Director, Graduate Admissions, 415-405-3506, Fax: 415-405-0340, E-mail: nprice@sfsu.edu. *Dean,* Dr. Ann Hallum, 415-338-2231, Fax: 415-405-0340, E-mail: glider@sfsu.edu.

College of Business Offers accounting (MSA); business (EMBA, MA, MBA, MSA); decision sciences/operations research (MBA); economics (MA); ethics and compliance (MBA); finance (MBA); global business and innovation (MBA); healthcare administration (MBA); hospitality and tourism management (MBA); information systems (MBA); leadership (MBA); marketing (MBA); nonprofit and social enterprise leadership (MBA); sustainable business (MBA). *Application Contact:* Manuel Maranan, Director of Admissions, Recruitment and External Relations, 415-817-4323, Fax: 415-817-4340, E-mail: mmaranan@sfsu.edu. *Dean,* Linda Oubre, 415-338-3650, Fax: 415-338-6237, E-mail: loubre@sfsu.edu.

College of Education Offers adult education (MA); autism spectrum (AC); communicative disorders (MS); early childhood education (MA); early childhood special education (AC); education (MA, MS, Ed D, PhD, AC, Certificate, Credential); educational administration (MA, Credential); educational leadership (Ed D); elementary education (MA); equity and social justice (MA); guide dog mobility (AC); instructional technologies (MA); language and literacy education (MA, Certificate, Credential); mathematics education (MA); orientation and mobility (MA, Credential); reading (Certificate); reading and language arts (Credential); secondary education (MA, Credential); special education (MA, PhD); special interest (MA). *Application Contact:* Victoria Narkewicz, Executive Assistant, 415-338-2687, Fax: 415-338-7019, E-mail: toria@sfsu.edu. *Dean,* Dr. Judith Munter, 415-338-2687, Fax: 415-338-7019, E-mail: jhmunter@sfsu.edu.

College of Ethnic Studies ***Degree program information:*** Part-time programs available. Part-time. Offers Asian American studies (MA); ethnic studies (MA). *Application Contact:* Dr. Amy Sueyoshi, Associate Dean, 415-338-1693, Fax: 415-338-1739, E-mail: ethnicst@sfsu.edu. *Dean,* Dr. Kenneth Monteiro, 415-338-1693, Fax: 415-338-1739, E-mail: ethnicst@sfsu.edu.

College of Health and Social Sciences ***Financial support:*** Fellowships, research assistantships, teaching assistantships, career-related internships or fieldwork, Federal Work-Study, institutionally sponsored loans, and unspecified assistantships available. *Degree program information:* Part-time programs available. Part-time. Offers adult acute care (MS); clinical nurse specialist (MS); clinical rehabilitation and mental health counseling (MS); community/public health nursing (MS); consumer and family studies/dietetics (MA); counseling (MS); criminal justice administration (MPA); environmental administration and policy (MPA); family nurse practitioner (MS, Certificate); gerontology (MA); health and social sciences (MA, MPA, MPH, MS, MSC, MSW, DPT, Dr Sc PT, Certificate, Credential); health education (MPH); human sexuality studies (MA); kinesiology (MS); marriage, family, and child counseling (MSC); nonprofit administration (MPA); nursing administration (MS); pediatrics (MS); physical therapy (DPT, Dr Sc PT); public management (MPA); public policy (MPA); recreation, parks, and tourism (MS); school counseling (Credential); social work (MSW); urban administration (MPA); women's health (MS). *Application Contact:* Christina Alcantara, Assistant to the Dean, 415-338-3327, Fax: 415-338-0586, E-mail: cba@sfsu.edu. *Interim Dean,* Dr. Alvin Alvarez, 415-338-3326, Fax: 415-338-0586, E-mail: aalvarez@sfsu.edu.

College of Liberal and Creative Arts ***Financial support:*** Teaching assistantships, career-related internships or fieldwork, and Federal Work-Study available. *Degree program information:* Part-time and evening/weekend programs available. Part-time, evening/weekend. Offers archaeology (MA); art (MFA); art history (MA); biological/physical anthropology (MA); broadcast and electronic communication arts (MA); chamber music (MM); Chinese (MA); cinema (MA, MFA); classical performance (MM); classics (MA); communication studies (MA); comparative literature (MA); composition (MA, Certificate); conducting (MM); creative writing (MA, MFA); drama (MA); French (MA); German (MA); history (MA); humanities and liberal studies (MA); immigrant literacies (Certificate); industrial arts (MA); international relations (MA); Italian (MA); Japanese (MA); liberal and creative arts (MA, MFA, MM, Certificate); linguistics (MA); literature (MA); museum studies (MA); music education (MA); music history (MA); philosophy (MA); political science (MA); social/cultural anthropology (MA); Spanish (MA); teaching English to speakers of other languages (MA); teaching post-secondary reading (Certificate); theatre arts (MFA); visual anthropology (MA); women and gender studies (MA). *Application Contact:* Florence Tu, Executive Assistant to the Dean, 415-338-7692, Fax: 415-338-6159, E-mail: ftu@sfsu.edu. *Dean,* Dr. Daniel Bernardi, 415-338-1471, Fax: 415-338-6159, E-mail: bernardi@sfsu.edu.

College of Science and Engineering ***Degree program information:*** Part-time programs available. Part-time. Offers astronomy (MS); biochemistry (MS); biotechnology (PSM); cell and molecular biology (MS); chemistry and biochemistry (MS); clinical psychology (MS); computing and business (MS); computing for life sciences (MS); developmental psychology (MA); ecology, evolution, and conservation biology (MS); embedded electrical and computer systems (MS); energy systems (MS); geographic information science (MS); geography and environment (MA); geosciences (MS); industrial/organizational psychology (MS); marine biology (MS); marine science (MS); mathematics (MA); microbiology (MS); mind, brain, and behavior (MA); physics and astronomy (MS); physiology and behavioral biology (MS); resource management and environmental planning (MA); school psychology (MS, Credential); science (PSM); science and engineering (MA, MS, PSM, Credential); social psychology (MA); software engineering (MS); stem cell science (PSM); structural/earthquake engineering (MS). *Application deadline:* Applications are processed on a rolling basis. Electronic applications accepted. *Application Contact:* Nadia Chan, Executive Assistant to the Dean, 415-338-1571, Fax: 415-338-6136, E-mail: nadiach@sfsu.edu. *Dean,* Dr. Keith Bowman, 415-338-1571, Fax: 415-338-6136, E-mail: kjbowman@sfsu.edu.

SAN FRANCISCO THEOLOGICAL SEMINARY, San Anselmo, CA 94960-2997

General Information Independent-religious, coed, graduate-only institution. *Graduate housing:* Rooms and/or apartments available on a first-come, first-served basis to single and married students. Housing application deadline: 5/1.

GRADUATE UNITS

Graduate and Professional Programs ***Degree program information:*** Part-time programs available. Part-time. Offers theology (M Div, MA, MATS, D Min, PhD, Th D). MA, Th D, PhD, M Div/MA offered jointly with Graduate Theological Union.

SAN JOAQUIN COLLEGE OF LAW, Clovis, CA 93612-1312

General Information Independent, coed, graduate-only institution. *Graduate housing:* On-campus housing not available.

GRADUATE UNITS

Law Program ***Degree program information:*** Part-time and evening/weekend programs available. Part-time, evening/weekend. Offers law (JD).

SAN JOSE STATE UNIVERSITY, San Jose, CA 95192-0001

General Information State-supported, coed, comprehensive institution. CGS member. *Enrollment:* 32,773 graduate, professional, and undergraduate students; 3,589 full-time matriculated graduate/professional students (2,200 women), 3,418 part-time matriculated graduate/professional students (2,038 women). *Enrollment by degree level:* 7,007 master's. *Graduate housing:* Room and/or apartments available on a first-come, first-served basis to single students; on-campus housing not available to married students. *Student services:* Campus employment opportunities, campus safety program, career counseling, child daycare facilities, free psychological counseling, international student services, low-cost health insurance, multicultural affairs office, services for students with disabilities. *Library:* Dr. Martin Luther King Jr. Library plus 1 other. *Research affiliation:* Moss Landing Marine Laboratories.

Computer facilities: Computer purchase and lease plans are available. A campuswide network can be accessed from student residence rooms and from off campus. Online class registration is available.
Website: http://www.sjsu.edu/

General Application Contact: Deanna Gonzalez, Associate Director, Undergraduate and Graduate Admissions, 408-924-2013, Fax: 408-924-2050, E-mail: deanna.gonzales@sjsu.edu.

GRADUATE UNITS

Graduate Studies and Research Students: 3,589 full-time (2,200 women), 3,417 part-time (2,037 women); includes 2,259 minority (174 Black or African American, non-Hispanic/Latino; 22 American Indian or Alaska Native, non-Hispanic/Latino; 1,254 Asian, non-Hispanic/Latino; 809 Hispanic/Latino), 1,590 international. Average age 32. 6,686 applicants, 44% accepted, 1976 enrolled. *Financial support:* Fellowships, research assistantships, teaching assistantships, career-related internships or fieldwork, Federal Work-Study, institutionally sponsored loans, scholarships/grants, and tuition waivers (partial) available. Support available to part-time students. Financial award applicants required to submit FAFSA. In 2015, 2,768 master's awarded. *Degree program information:* Part-time and evening/weekend programs available. Part-time, evening/weekend, online learning. *Application deadline:* For fall admission, 6/29 for domestic students; for spring admission, 11/30 for domestic students. Applications are processed on a rolling basis. *Application fee:* $55. Electronic applications accepted. *Application Contact:* 408-924-2480, Fax: 408-924-2477. *Associate Vice President,* Dr. Pam Stacks, 408-924-2427, Fax: 408-924-2612.

Charles W. Davidson College of Engineering Students: 978 full-time (275 women), 985 part-time (327 women); includes 426 minority (24 Black or African American, non-Hispanic/Latino; 3 American Indian or Alaska Native, non-Hispanic/Latino; 362 Asian, non-Hispanic/Latino; 37 Hispanic/Latino), 1,287 international. Average age 28. 1,925 applicants, 55% accepted, 527 enrolled. *Financial support:* Teaching assistantships, career-related internships or fieldwork, Federal Work-Study, and institutionally sponsored loans available. Support available to part-time students. Financial award applicants required to submit FAFSA. In 2015, 945 master's awarded. *Degree program information:* Part-time programs available. Part-time. Offers engineering (MS). *Application deadline:* For fall admission, 6/29 for domestic students; for spring admission, 11/30 for domestic students. Applications are processed on a rolling basis. *Application fee:* $59. Electronic applications accepted. *Application Contact:* 408-924-2480, Fax: 408-924-2477. *Dean,* Dr. Belle Wei, 408-924-3800, Fax: 408-924-3818.

College of Applied Sciences and Arts Students: 219 full-time (155 women), 140 part-time (103 women); includes 472 minority (38 Black or African American, non-Hispanic/Latino; 2 American Indian or Alaska Native, non-Hispanic/Latino; 190 Asian, non-Hispanic/Latino; 238 Hispanic/Latino; 4 Native Hawaiian or other Pacific Islander, non-Hispanic/Latino), 28 international. Average age 31. 1,404 applicants, 37% accepted, 360 enrolled. *Financial support:* Career-related internships or fieldwork, Federal Work-Study, institutionally sponsored loans, and scholarships/grants available. Support available to part-time students. Financial award application deadline: 6/15; financial award applicants required to submit FAFSA. In 2015, 850 master's awarded. *Degree program information:* Part-time and evening/weekend programs available. Part-time, evening/weekend. Offers big data (Certificate); California library media teacher services (Credential); collaborative response to family violence (Certificate); justice studies (MS); kinesiology (MA); library and information science (MLIS, Certificate); mass communication (MA); nutritional science (MS); occupational therapy (MS); public health (MPH); pupil personnel services (Credential); recreation (MS); social work (MSW); Spanish language counseling (Certificate); strategic management of digital assets and services (Certificate). *Application deadline:* For fall admission, 6/29 for domestic students; for spring admission, 11/30 for domestic students. Applications are processed on a rolling basis. *Application fee:* $55. Electronic applications accepted. *Application Contact:* 408-924-2480, Fax: 408-924-2477. *Dean,* Dr. Mary Schutten, 408-924-2900, Fax: 408-924-2901, E-mail: mary.schutten@sjsu.edu.

College of Humanities and the Arts Students: 65 full-time (38 women), 29 part-time (20 women); includes 85 minority (5 Black or African American, non-Hispanic/Latino; 34 Asian, non-Hispanic/Latino; 46 Hispanic/Latino), 28 international. Average age 32. 298 applicants, 53% accepted, 93 enrolled. *Financial support:* Applicants required to submit FAFSA. In 2015, 98 master's awarded. Offers art (MA, MFA); computational linguistics (Certificate); English (MA, MFA); French (MA); humanities and arts (Certificate); linguistics (MA); music (MA); philosophy (MA); professional and technical communication (Certificate); Spanish (MA); teaching English to speakers of other languages (MA); TESOL (Certificate); theatre arts (MA). *Application deadline:* For fall admission, 6/29 for domestic students; for spring admission, 11/30 for domestic students. Applications are processed on a rolling basis. *Application fee:* $55. Electronic applications accepted. *Application Contact:* 408-924-2480, Fax: 408-924-2477. *Dean,* Lisa Vollendorf, 408-924-4300, Fax: 408-924-4365, E-mail: lisa.vollendorf@sjsu.edu.

College of Science Students: 118 full-time (68 women), 52 part-time (25 women); includes 125 minority (5 Black or African American, non-Hispanic/Latino; 97 Asian, non-Hispanic/Latino; 23 Hispanic/Latino), 121 international. Average age 27. 1,236 applicants, 21% accepted, 171 enrolled. *Financial support:* Teaching assistantships, career-related internships or fieldwork, Federal Work-Study, and institutionally sponsored loans available. Support available to part-time students. Financial award applicants required to submit FAFSA. In 2015, 168 master's awarded. *Degree program information:* Part-time and evening/weekend programs available. Part-time, evening/weekend. Offers biological sciences (MA, MS); biotechnology (MBT); chemistry (MA, MS); computer science (MS); cybersecurity (Certificate); cybersecurity: core technologies (Certificate); geology (MS); marine science (MS); mathematics (MA, MS); meteorology (MS); physics (MS); science education (MA); statistics (MS); Unix system administration (Certificate). *Application deadline:* For fall admission, 6/29 for domestic students; for spring admission, 11/30 for domestic students. Applications are processed on a rolling basis. *Application fee:* $55. Electronic applications accepted. *Application Contact:* 408-924-2480, Fax: 408-924-2477. *Dean,* J. Michael Parrish, 408-924-4800, Fax: 408-924-4815.

College of Social Sciences Students: 108 full-time (74 women), 51 part-time (28 women); includes 188 minority (16 Black or African American, non-Hispanic/Latino; 1 American Indian or Alaska Native, non-Hispanic/Latino; 56 Asian, non-Hispanic/Latino; 112 Hispanic/Latino; 3 Native Hawaiian or other Pacific Islander, non-Hispanic/Latino), 60 international. Average age 29. 517 applicants, 54% accepted, 158 enrolled. *Financial support:* Teaching assistantships, career-related internships or fieldwork, Federal Work-Study, institutionally sponsored loans, scholarships/grants, and tuition waivers (partial) available. Support available to part-time students. Financial award applicants required to submit FAFSA. In 2015, 144 master's awarded. *Degree program information:* Part-time and evening/weekend programs available. Part-time, evening/weekend. Offers applications of technology in planning (Certificate); applied anthropology (MA); communication studies (MS); community design and development (Certificate); economics (MA); environmental planning (Certificate); geographic information science (Certificate); geography (MA); global citizenship (Certificate); history (MA); Mexican American studies (MA); psychology (MA, MS); public administration (MA); real estate development (Certificate); social sciences (MPA, MS); sociology (MA); transportation and land use planning (Certificate). *Application deadline:* For fall admission, 6/29 for domestic students; for spring admission, 11/30 for domestic students. Applications are processed on a rolling basis. *Application fee:* $55. Electronic applications accepted. *Application Contact:* 408-924-2480, Fax: 408-924-2477. *Dean,* Walt Jacobs, 408-924-5306, Fax: 408-924-5303.

Connie L. Lurie College of Education Students: 146 full-time (117 women), 28 part-time (25 women); includes 253 minority (18 Black or African American, non-Hispanic/Latino; 80 Asian, non-Hispanic/Latino; 155 Hispanic/Latino), 22 international. Average age 29. 579 applicants, 39% accepted, 175 enrolled. *Financial support:* Career-related internships or fieldwork available. Financial award applicants required to submit FAFSA. In 2015, 218 master's awarded. *Degree program information:* Evening/weekend programs available. Evening/weekend. Offers child and adolescent development (MA); common core mathematics (K-8) (Certificate, Credential); education (MA, Credential); educational leadership (MA, Ed D, Credential); elementary education (MA); K-12 school counseling (Credential); K-12 school counseling internship (Credential); school child welfare attendance (Credential); single subject (Credential). *Application deadline:* For fall admission, 6/29 for domestic students; for spring admission, 11/30 for domestic students. Applications are processed on a rolling basis. *Application fee:* $55. Electronic applications accepted. *Application Contact:* 408-924-2480, Fax: 408-924-2477. *Dean,* Elaine Chin, 408-924-3600, Fax: 408-924-3713.

Lucas Graduate School of Business Students: 69 full-time (40 women), 16 part-time (10 women); includes 58 minority (1 Black or African American, non-Hispanic/Latino; 37 Asian, non-Hispanic/Latino; 14 Hispanic/Latino; 6 Native Hawaiian or other Pacific Islander, non-Hispanic/Latino), 40 international. Average age 26. 403 applicants, 34% accepted, 85 enrolled. *Financial support:* Applicants required to submit FAFSA. In 2015, 179 master's awarded. *Degree program information:* Part-time and evening/weekend programs available. Part-time, evening/weekend, online learning. Offers accountancy (MS); business administration (MBA); taxation (MS); transportation management (MS). *Application deadline:* For fall admission, 6/29 for domestic students; for spring admission, 11/30 for domestic students. Applications are processed on a rolling basis. *Application fee:* $55. Electronic applications accepted. *Application Contact:* 408-924-2480, Fax: 408-924-2477. *Interim Dean,* Dr. Marlene Turner, 408-924-3420, Fax: 408-924-3426.

SAN JUAN BAUTISTA SCHOOL OF MEDICINE, Caguas, PR 00726-4968

General Information Independent, coed, graduate-only institution. *Graduate housing:* On-campus housing not available. *Student services:* Campus employment opportunities, campus safety program, career counseling, exercise/wellness program, free psychological counseling, grant writing training, international student services, low-cost health insurance, multicultural affairs office, services for students with disabilities, writing training. *Library:* SJB Digital Library plus 1 other. *Research affiliation:* Universidad Central del Caribe (molecular biology), Fundacion de Investigacion de Puerto Rico (clinical and translational research), University of Puerto Rico, Medical Sciences Campus (molecular biology, microbiology, neurosciences, pediatrics, public health), Ponce School of Medicine and Health Sciences (virology, immunology), Veteran Affairs (clinical research).

Computer facilities: 50 computers available on campus for general student use.
Website: https://www.sanjuanbautista.edu/

General Application Contact: Jaymi Sanchez, Admissions, 787-743-3038 Ext. 236, Fax: 787-746-3093, E-mail: jsanchez@sanjuanbautista.edu.

GRADUATE UNITS

Graduate and Professional Programs ***Financial support:*** Applicants required to submit FAFSA. *Application deadline:* For fall admission, 12/15 priority date for domestic students. Applications are processed on a rolling basis. *Application fee:* $100. *Application Contact:* Jaymi Sanchez, Admissions Officer, 787-743-3038 Ext. 236, Fax: 787-746-3093, E-mail: jsanchez@sanjuanbautista.edu. *President/Dean,* Dr. Yocasta Brugal, 787-743-3038, Fax: 787-746-3093, E-mail: xbrugal@sanjuanbautista.edu.

SANTA CLARA UNIVERSITY, Santa Clara, CA 95053

General Information Independent-religious, coed, university. *Enrollment:* 8,680 graduate, professional, and undergraduate students; 1,986 full-time matriculated graduate/professional students (1,012 women), 1,233 part-time matriculated graduate/professional students (598 women). *Enrollment by degree level:* 2,368 master's, 706 doctoral, 145 other advanced degrees. *Graduate faculty:* 264 full-time (105 women), 52 part-time/adjunct (19 women). Tuition and fees vary according to course load, degree level and program. *Graduate housing:* Rooms and/or apartments available on a first-come, first-served basis to single and married students. Housing application deadline: 6/1. *Student services:* Campus employment opportunities, campus safety program, career counseling, child daycare facilities, exercise/wellness program, free psychological counseling, international student services, low-cost health insurance, multicultural affairs office, services for students with disabilities, teacher training, writing training. *Library:* University Library plus 1 other. Students can reserve study rooms.

Computer facilities: Computer purchase and lease plans are available. 824 computers available on campus for general student use. A campuswide network can be accessed from student residence rooms and from off campus. Online class registration is available.
Website: http://www.scu.edu/

GRADUATE UNITS

College of Arts and Sciences Students: 9 full-time (6 women), 53 part-time (33 women); includes 33 minority (7 Asian, non-Hispanic/Latino; 24 Hispanic/Latino; 2 Two or more races, non-Hispanic/Latino), 4 international. Average age 44. 13 applicants, 92% accepted, 8 enrolled. *Faculty:* 1 full-time (0 women), 6 part-time/adjunct (2 women). *Financial support:* In 2015–16, 87 students received support. Fellowships, research assistantships, teaching assistantships, career-related internships or fieldwork, Federal Work-Study, scholarships/grants, traineeships, health care benefits, tuition waivers, and unspecified assistantships available. Support available to part-time students. Financial award applicants required to submit FAFSA. In 2015, 12 master's awarded. *Degree program information:* Part-time and evening/weekend programs available. Part-time, evening/weekend. Offers pastoral ministries (MA). *Application deadline:* For fall admission, 7/1 for domestic students; for winter admission, 10/1 for domestic students; for spring admission, 2/14 for domestic students. Applications are processed on a rolling basis. *Application fee:* $50. Electronic applications accepted. *Application Contact:* Saralynn Ferrara, Senior Administrative Assistant, 408-554-4831, E-mail: sferrara@scu.edu. *Director, Graduate Program in Pastoral Ministries*, Gary Macy, 408-554-2357, E-mail: gmacy@scu.edu.

Jesuit School of Theology Students: 135 full-time (34 women), 11 part-time (7 women); includes 72 minority (26 Black or African American, non-Hispanic/Latino; 1 American Indian or Alaska Native, non-Hispanic/Latino; 28 Asian, non-Hispanic/Latino; 14 Hispanic/Latino; 1 Native Hawaiian or other Pacific Islander, non-Hispanic/Latino; 2 Two or more races, non-Hispanic/Latino). Average age 36. *Faculty:* 17 full-time (5 women). *Financial support:* Scholarships/grants and unspecified assistantships available. Financial award application deadline: 3/1; financial award applicants required to submit FAFSA. In 2015, 50 master's, 6 doctorates awarded. *Degree program information:* Part-time and evening/weekend programs available. Part-time, evening/weekend, 100% online. Offers Biblical languages (MABL); Biblical studies (MTS); Christian spirituality (MTS); church history (MTS); cultural and historical studies of Catholicism (MTS); ethics and social theory/religion and society (MTS); history of art and religion (MTS); liturgical studies (MTS); pastoral ministry (M Div); systematic and philosophical theology (MTS); theology (MA, MTS, Th M, STD, STB, STL). *Application deadline:* For fall admission, 3/1 priority date for domestic students; for spring admission, 10/1 priority date for domestic students. Applications are processed on a rolling basis. *Application fee:* $50. Electronic applications accepted. *Application Contact:* Barbara Godoy, Assistant Dean of Enrollment Management, 510-549-5016, E-mail: bgodoy@jstb.edu. *Associate Academic Dean*, Alison Benders, 510-549-5055, E-mail: abenders@jstb.edu.

Leavey School of Business Students: 418 full-time (214 women), 407 part-time (160 women); includes 220 minority (8 Black or African American, non-Hispanic/Latino; 167 Asian, non-Hispanic/Latino; 32 Hispanic/Latino; 3 Native Hawaiian or other Pacific Islander, non-Hispanic/Latino; 10 Two or more races, non-Hispanic/Latino), 338 international. Average age 30. 506 applicants, 68% accepted, 219 enrolled. *Faculty:* 93 full-time (24 women), 34 part-time/adjunct (12 women). *Financial support:* In 2015–16, 277 students received support. Fellowships, research assistantships, teaching assistantships, career-related internships or fieldwork, Federal Work-Study, scholarships/grants, traineeships, health care benefits, tuition waivers, and unspecified assistantships available. Support available to part-time students. Financial award applicants required to submit FAFSA. In 2015, 342 master's awarded. *Degree program information:* Part-time and evening/weekend programs available. Part-time, evening/weekend. Offers business administration (MBA); business analytics (MS); finance (MS); information systems (MS); supply chain management and analytics (MS). *Application deadline:* Applications are processed on a rolling basis. *Application fee:* $100 ($150 for international students). Electronic applications accepted. *Application Contact:* Taryn Upchurch, Director, Graduate Admissions and Financial Aid, 408-554-4539. *Dean*, Caryn Beck-Dudley.

School of Education and Counseling Psychology Students: 262 full-time (215 women), 340 part-time (264 women); includes 257 minority (19 Black or African American, non-Hispanic/Latino; 1 American Indian or Alaska Native, non-Hispanic/Latino; 74 Asian, non-Hispanic/Latino; 138 Hispanic/Latino; 25 Two or more races, non-Hispanic/Latino), 38 international. Average age 31. 235 applicants, 67% accepted, 100 enrolled. *Faculty:* 31 full-time (21 women), 9 part-time/adjunct (2 women). *Financial support:* In 2015–16, 218 students received support. Fellowships, research assistantships, teaching assistantships, career-related internships or fieldwork, Federal Work-Study, scholarships/grants, traineeships, health care benefits, and tuition waivers available. Support available to part-time students. Financial award applicants required to submit FAFSA. In 2015, 238 master's, 25 other advanced degrees awarded. *Degree program information:* Part-time and evening/weekend programs available. Part-time, evening/weekend. Offers alternative and correctional education (Certificate); counseling (MA); counseling psychology (MA); educational leadership (MA); interdisciplinary education (MA); teacher education (MAT). *Application deadline:* Applications are processed on a rolling basis. *Application fee:* $50. Electronic applications accepted. *Application Contact:* Atika Raza, Admissions and Financial Aid Director, 408-551-7884, E-mail: araza@scu.edu. *Dean*, Dr. Carol Ann Glittens, 408-554-4723, Fax: 408-554-4367.

School of Engineering Students: 544 full-time (237 women), 364 part-time (103 women); includes 215 minority (7 Black or African American, non-Hispanic/Latino; 149 Asian, non-Hispanic/Latino; 42 Hispanic/Latino; 1 Native Hawaiian or other Pacific Islander, non-Hispanic/Latino; 16 Two or more races, non-Hispanic/Latino), 529 international. Average age 28. 1,335 applicants, 38% accepted, 243 enrolled. *Faculty:* 63 full-time (24 women), 6 part-time/adjunct (4 women). *Financial support:* In 2015–16, 89 students received support. Fellowships, research assistantships, teaching assistantships, career-related internships or fieldwork, Federal Work-Study, scholarships/grants, traineeships, health care benefits, tuition waivers, and unspecified assistantships available. Support available to part-time students. Financial award applicants required to submit FAFSA. In 2015, 343 master's, 2 doctorates awarded. *Degree program information:* Part-time and evening/weekend programs available. Part-time, evening/weekend. Offers applied mathematics (MS); bioengineering (MS); civil engineering (MS); computer science and engineering (MS, PhD); electrical engineering (MS, PhD); engineering (Engineer); engineering management and leadership (MS); mechanical engineering (MS, PhD); software engineering (MS); sustainable energy (MS); thermofluids (Certificate). *Application deadline:* For fall admission, 4/1 for domestic and international students; for winter admission, 9/9 for domestic students, 9/2 for international students; for spring admission, 2/17 for domestic students, 12/9 for international students. *Application fee:* $60. Electronic applications accepted. *Application Contact:* Stacey Tinker, Director of Admissions and Marketing, 408-554-4748, Fax: 408-554-4323, E-mail: stinker@scu.edu. *Associate Dean for Graduate Studies*, Dr. Alex Zecevic, 408-554-2394, E-mail: azecevic@scu.edu.

School of Law Students: 618 full-time (306 women), 58 part-time (31 women); includes 277 minority (21 Black or African American, non-Hispanic/Latino; 1 American Indian or Alaska Native, non-Hispanic/Latino; 128 Asian, non-Hispanic/Latino; 93 Hispanic/Latino; 1 Native Hawaiian or other Pacific Islander, non-Hispanic/Latino; 33 Two or more races, non-Hispanic/Latino), 47 international. Average age 27. 2,411 applicants, 61% accepted, 283 enrolled. *Faculty:* 60 full-time (31 women), 3 part-time/adjunct (1 woman). *Financial support:* In 2015–16, 457 students received support. Fellowships, research assistantships, teaching assistantships, career-related internships or fieldwork, Federal Work-Study, scholarships/grants, traineeships, health care benefits, tuition waivers, and unspecified assistantships available. Support available to part-time students. Financial award application deadline: 2/1; financial award applicants required to submit FAFSA. In 2015, 45 master's, 218 doctorates awarded. *Degree program information:* Part-time and evening/weekend programs available. Part-time, evening/weekend. Offers high tech law (Certificate); intellectual property (LL M); international and comparative law (LL M); international law (Certificate); law (JD); privacy law (Certificate); public interest and social justice law (Certificate); United States law (LL M). LL M in United States law track only open to non-U.S. attorneys. *Application deadline:* Applications are processed on a rolling basis. *Application fee:* $75. Electronic applications accepted. *Application Contact:* Nanette Cannon, Director of Admissions, 408-551-1846, E-mail: ncannon@scu.edu. *Dean*, Lisa Kloppenberg, 408-554-4362.

SARAH LAWRENCE COLLEGE, Bronxville, NY 10708-5999

General Information Independent, coed, comprehensive institution. CGS member. *Graduate housing:* On-campus housing not available. *Research affiliation:* Westchester/New York Medical College, New York Hospital–Cornell Medical Center, Albert Einstein College of Medicine, New York University Medical Center, Columbia University Medical Center.

GRADUATE UNITS

Graduate Studies ***Degree program information:*** Part-time programs available. Part-time. Offers art of teaching (MS Ed); child development (MA); creative non-fiction (MFA); dance (MFA); dance/movement therapy (MS); fiction (MFA); health advocacy (MA); human genetics (MS); poetry (MFA); theater (MFA); women's history (MA). Electronic applications accepted.

SAVANNAH COLLEGE OF ART AND DESIGN, Savannah, GA 31402-3146

General Information Independent, coed, comprehensive institution. CGS member. *Enrollment:* 12,455 graduate, professional, and undergraduate students; 1,576 full-time matriculated graduate/professional students (986 women), 694 part-time matriculated graduate/professional students (449 women). *Enrollment by degree level:* 2,269 master's, 1 other advanced degree. *Graduate faculty:* 526 full-time (214 women), 169 part-time/adjunct (91 women). *Tuition, area resident:* Full-time $35,325. Tuition and fees vary according to course load. *Graduate housing:* Room and/or apartments available on a first-come, first-served basis to single students; on-campus housing not available to married students. Typical cost: $8889 per year ($14,019 including board). Room and board charges vary according to board plan, campus/location and housing facility selected. Housing application deadline: 4/1. *Student services:* Campus employment opportunities, campus safety program, career counseling, exercise/wellness program, free psychological counseling, international student services, multicultural affairs office, services for students with disabilities, writing training. *Library:* Jen Library plus 4 others. *Collection:* Books: 265,565 (physical), 91,046 (digital/electronic); Serial titles: 913 (physical), 45,322 (digital/electronic); Databases: 87. Weekly public service hours: 117; students can reserve study rooms.

Computer facilities: Computer purchase and lease plans are available. 3,571 computers available on campus for general student use. A campuswide network can be accessed from student residence rooms and from off campus. Online class registration is available.
Website: http://www.scad.edu/

General Application Contact: Jenny Jaquillard, Executive Director of Admissions, Recruitment and Events, 912-525-5100, Fax: 912-525-5985, E-mail: admission@scad.edu.

GRADUATE UNITS

Graduate School ***Degree program information:*** Part-time programs available. Part-time, online learning. Offers accessory design (MA, MFA); advertising (MA, MFA); animation (MA, MFA); architectural history (MA, MFA); architecture (M Arch); art and design (M Arch, MA, MFA, MUD, Graduate Certificate); art history (MA); arts administration (MA); cinema studies (MA); design for sustainability (MA); design management (MA, MFA); dramatic writing (MFA); fashion (MA, MFA); fibers (MA, MFA); film and television (MA, MFA); furniture design (MA, MFA); graphic design (MA, MFA); historic preservation (MA, MFA, Graduate Certificate); illustration (MA, MFA); industrial design (MA, MFA); interactive design and game development (MA, MFA, Graduate Certificate); interior design (MA, MFA); jewelry (MA, MFA); luxury and fashion management (MA, MFA); motion media design (MA, MFA); painting (MA, MFA); performing arts (MFA); photography (MA, MFA); printmaking (MFA); production design (MA, MFA); sculpture (MA, MFA); sequential art (MA, MFA); sound design (MA, MFA); themed entertainment design (MFA); urban design and development (MUD); visual effects (MA, MFA); writing (MFA). Electronic applications accepted.

SAVANNAH STATE UNIVERSITY, Savannah, GA 31404

General Information State-supported, coed, comprehensive institution. CGS member. *Graduate housing:* Room and/or apartments available on a first-come, first-served basis to single students; on-campus housing not available to married students. Housing application deadline: 5/1. *Research affiliation:* Office of Naval Research (ONR) (marine science), Living Marine Resources Cooperative Science Center (LMRCSC) (marine science), National Institute of Mental Health (NIMH) (social work), U.S. Department of Homeland Security (urban studies and planning), Skidaway Institute of Oceanography (marine science), University of Georgia Marine Education Center & Aquarium (marine science).

GRADUATE UNITS

Master of Business Administration Program *Degree program information:* Part-time and evening/weekend programs available. Part-time, evening/weekend. Offers business administration (MBA). Electronic applications accepted.

Master of Public Administration Program *Degree program information:* Part-time programs available. Part-time. Offers city management (MPA); human resources (MPA). Electronic applications accepted.

Master of Science in Marine Sciences Program *Degree program information:* Part-time programs available. Part-time. Offers applied marine science (MSMS); marine science research (MSMS); professional advancement (MSMS). Electronic applications accepted.

Master of Science in Urban Studies and Planning Program *Degree program information:* Part-time programs available. Part-time. Offers urban studies and planning (MSUS). Electronic applications accepted.

Master of Social Work Program Offers social work (MSW).

SAYBROOK UNIVERSITY, San Francisco, CA 94111-1920

General Information Independent, coed, graduate-only institution. *Research affiliation:* Rollo May Center for Humanistic Studies.

GRADUATE UNITS

LIOS MA Residential Programs Offers leadership and organization development (MA); psychology counseling (MA).

School of Clinical Psychology Offers clinical psychology (MA). Program offered jointly with Bastyr University.

School of Mind-Body Medicine Offers mind-body medicine (MS, PhD, Certificate). Electronic applications accepted.

School of Organizational Leadership and Transformation Offers organizational leadership and transformation (MA). Program offered jointly with Bastyr University.

School of Psychology and Interdisciplinary Inquiry Online learning. Offers human science (MA, PhD); organizational systems (MA, PhD); psychology (MA, PhD). Electronic applications accepted.

SCHILLER INTERNATIONAL UNIVERSITY, 69115 Heidelberg, Germany

General Information Independent, coed, comprehensive institution. *Graduate housing:* Room and/or apartments available on a first-come, first-served basis to single students; on-campus housing not available to married students.

GRADUATE UNITS

MBA Programs, Heidelberg, Germany *Degree program information:* Part-time and evening/weekend programs available. Part-time, evening/weekend. Offers international business (MBA, MIM); management of information technology (MBA).

SCHILLER INTERNATIONAL UNIVERSITY, F-75015 Paris, France

General Information Independent, coed, comprehensive institution. *Graduate housing:* On-campus housing not available.

GRADUATE UNITS

MBA Program Paris, France *Degree program information:* Part-time and evening/weekend programs available. Part-time, evening/weekend, online learning. Offers international business (MBA). Bilingual French/English MBA available for native French speakers.

Program in International Relations and Diplomacy *Degree program information:* Part-time and evening/weekend programs available. Part-time, evening/weekend. Offers international relations and diplomacy (MA).

SCHILLER INTERNATIONAL UNIVERSITY, 28002 Madrid, Spain

General Information Independent, coed, comprehensive institution. *Graduate housing:* On-campus housing not available.

GRADUATE UNITS

MBA Program, Madrid, Spain *Degree program information:* Part-time programs available. Part-time. Offers international business (MBA).

SCHILLER INTERNATIONAL UNIVERSITY, Largo, FL 33771

General Information Independent, coed, comprehensive institution. *Graduate housing:* Room and/or apartments available on a first-come, first-served basis to single students; on-campus housing not available to married students. Housing application deadline: 8/1.

GRADUATE UNITS

MBA Programs, Florida *Degree program information:* Part-time and evening/weekend programs available. Part-time, evening/weekend, online learning. Offers financial planning (MBA); information technology (MBA); international business (MBA); international hotel and tourism management (MBA).

SCHOOL OF ADVANCED AIR AND SPACE STUDIES, Maxwell AFB, AL 36112-6424

General Information Federally supported, coed, primarily men, graduate-only institution.

GRADUATE UNITS

Program in Airpower Art and Science Offers airpower art and science (MA). Available to active duty military officers only.

SCHOOL OF THE ART INSTITUTE OF CHICAGO, Chicago, IL 60603-3103

General Information Independent, coed, comprehensive institution. *Graduate housing:* Room and/or apartments available on a first-come, first-served basis to single students; on-campus housing not available to married students. Housing application deadline: 3/21.

GRADUATE UNITS

Graduate Division *Degree program information:* Part-time programs available. Part-time. Offers architecture (M Arc); art and technology studies (MFA); art education and art teaching (MAAE, MAT); art therapy (MAAT); arts administration (MAAAP); ceramics (MFA); design for emerging technologies (MFA); designed objects (M Des); fashion, body, and garment (M Des, Certificate); fiber and material studies (MFA); film, video, and new media (MFA); historic preservation (MSHP); interior architecture (M Arc); modern art history, theory, and criticism (MA); new arts journalism (MA); painting and drawing (MFA); performance (MFA); photography (MFA); printmaking (MFA); sculpture (MFA); sound (MFA); visual and critical studies (MA); visual communication (MFA); writing (MFA, Certificate).

SCHOOL OF THE MUSEUM OF FINE ARTS, BOSTON, Boston, MA 02115

General Information Independent, coed, comprehensive institution. *Enrollment:* 499 graduate, professional, and undergraduate students; 148 full-time matriculated graduate/professional students (111 women), 2 part-time matriculated graduate/professional students (1 woman). *Enrollment by degree level:* 130 master's, 20 other advanced degrees. *Graduate faculty:* 40 full-time (27 women), 49 part-time/adjunct (35 women). *Tuition, area resident:* Full-time $42,404; part-time $4840 per course. *Required fees:* $3256. *Graduate housing:* Room and/or apartments available on a first-come, first-served basis to single students; on-campus housing not available to married students. Typical cost: $10,950 per year. Housing application deadline: 5/1. *Student services:* Campus employment opportunities, campus safety program, career counseling, free psychological counseling, international student services, low-cost health insurance, teacher training, writing training. *Library:* W. Van Alan Clark, Jr. Library plus 1 other.

Computer facilities: Computer purchase and lease plans are available. 177 computers available on campus for general student use. A campuswide network can be accessed. Online class registration is available.
Website: http://www.smfa.edu/

General Application Contact: Admissions Counselor, 617-369-3626, Fax: 617-369-4264, E-mail: admissions@smfa.edu.

GRADUATE UNITS

Graduate Programs Students: 129 full-time (94 women), 2 part-time (1 woman); includes 20 minority (3 Black or African American, non-Hispanic/Latino; 8 Asian, non-Hispanic/Latino; 7 Hispanic/Latino; 2 Two or more races, non-Hispanic/Latino), 29 international. Average age 29. 206 applicants, 69% accepted, 66 enrolled. *Faculty:* 37 full-time (21 women), 30 part-time/adjunct (17 women). *Financial support:* In 2015–16, 105 students received support, including 14 fellowships (averaging $8,000 per year), 30 teaching assistantships (averaging $1,500 per year); career-related internships or fieldwork, Federal Work-Study, scholarships/grants, tuition waivers (partial), and unspecified assistantships also available. Support available to part-time students. Financial award application deadline: 2/15; financial award applicants required to submit FAFSA. In 2015, 60 master's, 27 other advanced degrees awarded. Offers art education (MAT); studio art (MFA, Postbaccalaureate Certificate). *Application deadline:* For fall admission, 2/1 priority date for domestic and international students. Applications are processed on a rolling basis. *Application fee:* $65. Electronic applications accepted. *Application Contact:* Admissions Representative, 617-369-3626, Fax: 617-369-4264, E-mail: admissions@smfa.edu. *Associate Dean of Graduate Programs*, Lisa Bynoe, 617-369-3870, E-mail: lbynoe@smfa.edu.

SCHOOL OF VISUAL ARTS, New York, NY 10010-3994

General Information Proprietary, coed, comprehensive institution. *Graduate housing:* Room and/or apartments available on a first-come, first-served basis to single students; on-campus housing not available to married students.

GRADUATE UNITS

Graduate Programs Offers art education (MAT); art practice (MFA); art therapy (MPS); art writing (MFA); branding (MPS); computer art (MFA); critical theory and the arts (MA); curatorial practice (MA); design (MFA); design for social innovation (MFA); design research, writing and criticism (MA); digital photography (MPS); directing (MPS); fashion photography (MPS); fine arts (MFA); illustration as visual essay (MFA); interaction design (MFA); photography, video and related media (MFA); products of design (MFA); social documentary film (MFA); visual narrative (MFA). Electronic applications accepted.

SCHREINER UNIVERSITY, Kerrville, TX 78028-5697

General Information Independent-religious, coed, comprehensive institution. *Graduate housing:* Room and/or apartments available on a first-come, first-served basis to single students; on-campus housing not available to married students.

GRADUATE UNITS

Department of Education *Degree program information:* Part-time and evening/weekend programs available. Part-time, evening/weekend, online learning. Offers education (M Ed); principal (Certificate). Electronic applications accepted.

MBA Program *Degree program information:* Part-time programs available. Part-time, online learning. Offers ethical leadership (MBA). Electronic applications accepted.

THE SCRIPPS RESEARCH INSTITUTE, La Jolla, CA 92037

General Information Independent, coed, graduate-only institution. *Graduate housing:* On-campus housing not available.

GRADUATE UNITS

Kellogg School of Science and Technology Offers chemical and biological sciences (PhD). Electronic applications accepted.

SEABURY-WESTERN THEOLOGICAL SEMINARY, Evanston, IL 60201-2976

General Information Independent-religious, coed, graduate-only institution. *Graduate housing:* Rooms and/or apartments available to single students and available on a first-come, first-served basis to married students. Housing application deadline: 5/30.

GRADUATE UNITS

School of Theology *Degree program information:* Part-time programs available. Part-time. Offers advanced theological studies (Certificate); church music and liturgy (MTS); congregational development (D Min); preaching (D Min); theological studies (MA); theology (M Div, L Th). D Min in congregational development offered in summer only; D Min in preaching offered jointly with Chicago Theological Seminary, Lutheran School of Theology at Chicago, McCormick Theological Seminary, and Northern Baptist Theological Seminary.

SEATTLE INSTITUTE OF ORIENTAL MEDICINE, Seattle, WA 98115

General Information Proprietary, coed, primarily women, graduate-only institution. *Graduate housing:* On-campus housing not available.

GRADUATE UNITS

Graduate Program Offers Oriental medicine (M Ac OM).

SEATTLE PACIFIC UNIVERSITY, Seattle, WA 98119-1997

General Information Independent-religious, coed, comprehensive institution. *Enrollment:* 4,175 graduate, professional, and undergraduate students; 707 full-time matriculated graduate/professional students (533 women), 214 part-time matriculated graduate/professional students (139 women). *Enrollment by degree level:* 741 master's, 180 doctoral. *Graduate housing:* Rooms and/or apartments available on a first-come, first-served basis to single and married students. Housing application deadline: 8/1.

Student services: Campus employment opportunities, campus safety program, career counseling, exercise/wellness program, free psychological counseling, international student services, low-cost health insurance, multicultural affairs office, services for students with disabilities, teacher training, writing training. *Library:* University Library. *Research affiliation:* Washington Research Center/Gates Foundation (education effectiveness), Fred Hutchinson Cancer Research Center (cancer and tumors), Battelle Research Center (business marketing).

Computer facilities: 150 computers available on campus for general student use. A campuswide network can be accessed from student residence rooms and from off campus. Online class registration is available.
Website: http://www.spu.edu/

General Application Contact: 206-281-2091, E-mail: gradadmissions@spu.edu.

GRADUATE UNITS

Doctoral Program in Education Students: 25 full-time (16 women), 25 part-time (16 women); includes 7 minority (1 Black or African American, non-Hispanic/Latino; 1 American Indian or Alaska Native, non-Hispanic/Latino; 3 Asian, non-Hispanic/Latino; 1 Hispanic/Latino; 1 Two or more races, non-Hispanic/Latino), 3 international. Average age 41. 11 applicants, 27% accepted, 3 enrolled. *Financial support:* Career-related internships or fieldwork available. Financial award applicants required to submit FAFSA. In 2015, 4 doctorates awarded. Offers education (Ed D, PhD). *Application deadline:* For fall admission, 8/15 for domestic students; for winter admission, 11/15 for domestic students; for spring admission, 2/15 for domestic students; for summer admission, 5/15 for domestic students. Applications are processed on a rolling basis. *Application fee:* $50. *Director of Doctoral Programs*, Andrew Lumpe, 206-281-2369, E-mail: lumpea@spu.edu.

Educational Leadership Programs Students: 46 full-time (37 women), 42 part-time (23 women); includes 10 minority (2 Black or African American, non-Hispanic/Latino; 3 American Indian or Alaska Native, non-Hispanic/Latino; 4 Hispanic/Latino; 1 Two or more races, non-Hispanic/Latino), 3 international. Average age 39. 38 applicants, 76% accepted, 19 enrolled. *Financial support:* Career-related internships or fieldwork available. Financial award applicants required to submit FAFSA. In 2015, 9 master's awarded. *Degree program information:* Part-time and evening/weekend programs available. Part-time, evening/weekend. Offers educational leadership (M Ed, Ed D); principal (Certificate); program administrator (Certificate); superintendent (Certificate). *Application deadline:* For fall admission, 8/15 priority date for domestic students; for winter admission, 11/15 for domestic students; for spring admission, 2/15 priority date for domestic students; for summer admission, 5/15 for domestic students. Applications are processed on a rolling basis. *Application fee:* $50. Electronic applications accepted. *Application Contact:* The Graduate Center, 206-281-2091. *Chair,* Dr. William Prenevost, 206-281-2370, Fax: 206-281-2756, E-mail: prenew@spu.edu.

Industrial Organizational Psychology Program Students: 66 full-time (47 women), 13 part-time (6 women); includes 12 minority (2 Black or African American, non-Hispanic/Latino; 5 Asian, non-Hispanic/Latino; 5 Two or more races, non-Hispanic/Latino), 2 international. Average age 27. 88 applicants, 35% accepted, 31 enrolled. *Financial support:* Applicants required to submit FAFSA. In 2015, 33 master's, 3 doctorates awarded. Offers industrial organizational psychology (MA, PhD). *Application deadline:* For fall admission, 12/15 for domestic and international students. *Application fee:* $50. Electronic applications accepted. *Application Contact:* The Graduate Center, 206-281-2091. *Chair,* Dr. Robert B. McKenna, 206-281-2629, E-mail: rmckenna@spu.edu.

MA in Teaching English to Speakers of Other Languages Program Students: 18 full-time (16 women), 1 (woman) part-time; includes 3 minority (1 American Indian or Alaska Native, non-Hispanic/Latino; 2 Hispanic/Latino), 6 international. Average age 32. 16 applicants, 31% accepted, 5 enrolled. *Financial support:* Career-related internships or fieldwork available. Financial award applicants required to submit FAFSA. In 2015, 5 master's awarded. *Degree program information:* Part-time programs available. Part-time. Offers K-12 (MA); teaching English to speakers of other languages (MA). *Application deadline:* For fall admission, 8/1 priority date for domestic students; for winter admission, 12/1 for domestic students; for spring admission, 3/1 for domestic students; for summer admission, 5/1 for domestic students. Applications are processed on a rolling basis. *Application fee:* $50. Electronic applications accepted. *Application Contact:* 206-281-2091. *Program Director,* Dr. Kathryn Bartholomew, 206-281-3533, Fax: 206-281-2500, E-mail: kbarthol@spu.edu.

Master of Arts in Management Program Students: 23 full-time (14 women); includes 2 minority (both Asian, non-Hispanic/Latino), 1 international. Average age 26. 6 applicants, 33% accepted, 2 enrolled. Offers faith and business (MA); human resources (MA); social and sustainable management (MA). *Application deadline:* For fall admission, 6/15 for domestic students. *Application fee:* $50.

Master of Arts in Teaching Program Students: 103 full-time (80 women), 17 part-time (16 women); includes 12 minority (2 Black or African American, non-Hispanic/Latino; 2 American Indian or Alaska Native, non-Hispanic/Latino; 2 Asian, non-Hispanic/Latino; 5 Hispanic/Latino; 1 Two or more races, non-Hispanic/Latino), 1 international. Average age 31. 49 applicants, 45% accepted, 22 enrolled. *Financial support:* Scholarships/grants available. Financial award applicants required to submit FAFSA. In 2015, 85 master's awarded. *Degree program information:* Part-time and evening/weekend programs available. Part-time, evening/weekend. Offers teaching (MAT). *Application deadline:* For fall admission, 3/15 for domestic students. *Application fee:* $50. Electronic applications accepted. *Application Contact:* The Graduate Center, 206-281-2091.

Master of Arts in Theology Program Students: 20 full-time (9 women), 11 part-time (2 women); includes 9 minority (5 Black or African American, non-Hispanic/Latino; 1 Asian, non-Hispanic/Latino; 3 Two or more races, non-Hispanic/Latino), 2 international. Average age 33. 16 applicants, 81% accepted, 13 enrolled. *Financial support:* Application deadline: 4/1; applicants required to submit FAFSA. In 2015, 2 master's awarded. Offers Asian American ministry (MA); business and applied theology (MA); Christian leadership (MA); Christian scripture (MA); Christian studies (Graduate Certificate); reconciliation and intercultural studies (MA); theology (MA). *Application deadline:* For fall admission, 7/1 for domestic students, 6/15 for international students. Applications are processed on a rolling basis. *Application fee:* $50. Electronic applications accepted. *Dean,* Dr. Doug Strong, 206-281-2473, E-mail: dstrong@spu.edu.

Master of Business Administration Program Students: 37 full-time (17 women), 12 part-time (6 women); includes 13 minority (3 Black or African American, non-Hispanic/Latino; 7 Asian, non-Hispanic/Latino; 2 Hispanic/Latino; 1 Two or more races, non-Hispanic/Latino), 8 international. Average age 30. 34 applicants, 21% accepted, 7 enrolled. *Financial support:* Scholarships/grants available. Financial award applicants required to submit FAFSA. In 2015, 37 master's awarded. *Degree program information:* Part-time programs available. Part-time. Offers business administration (MBA); social and sustainable enterprise (MBA). *Application deadline:* For fall admission, 8/1 for domestic and international students; for winter admission, 11/1 for domestic and international students; for spring admission, 2/1 for domestic and international students. Applications are processed on a rolling basis. *Application fee:* $50. Electronic applications accepted. *Application Contact:* 206-281-2091. *Associate Dean for Graduate Studies,* Gary Karns, 206-281-2948, Fax: 206-281-2733.

The Master of Divinity Program Students: 36 full-time (19 women), 6 part-time (2 women); includes 10 minority (4 Black or African American, non-Hispanic/Latino; 4 Asian, non-Hispanic/Latino; 2 Two or more races, non-Hispanic/Latino). Average age 33. 25 applicants, 52% accepted, 13 enrolled. *Financial support:* Scholarships/grants available. Financial award applicants required to submit FAFSA. In 2015, 8 master's awarded. Offers divinity (M Div). *Application deadline:* For fall admission, 7/1 for domestic students. *Application fee:* $50. *Dean,* Dr. Doug Strong, 206-281-2473, E-mail: dstrong@spu.edu.

Master of Education in Literacy Program Students: 7 full-time (all women), 5 part-time (4 women). Average age 35. 5 applicants, 80% accepted, 4 enrolled. *Financial support:* Scholarships/grants available. Financial award applicants required to submit FAFSA. In 2015, 5 master's awarded. *Degree program information:* Part-time programs available. Part-time. Offers literacy (M Ed). *Application deadline:* For fall admission, 8/15 for domestic students; for winter admission, 11/15 for domestic students; for spring admission, 2/15 for domestic students; for summer admission, 5/15 for domestic students. Applications are processed on a rolling basis. *Application fee:* $50. Electronic applications accepted. *Application Contact:* The Graduate Center, 206-281-2091. *Chair,* Dr. Scott F. Beers, 206-281-2707, E-mail: sbeers@spu.edu.

Master of Education in School Counseling Program Students: 48 full-time (44 women), 3 part-time (all women); includes 7 minority (2 Asian, non-Hispanic/Latino; 2 Hispanic/Latino; 1 Native Hawaiian or other Pacific Islander, non-Hispanic/Latino; 2 Two or more races, non-Hispanic/Latino). Average age 30. 49 applicants, 27% accepted, 13 enrolled. *Financial support:* Scholarships/grants available. Financial award applicants required to submit FAFSA. In 2015, 18 master's awarded. *Degree program information:* Part-time programs available. Part-time. Offers school counseling (M Ed, Certificate). *Application deadline:* For fall admission, 4/1 priority date for domestic students. *Application fee:* $50. Electronic applications accepted. *Application Contact:* 206-281-2091. *Chair,* Dr. June Hyun, 206-281-2671, Fax: 206-281-2756, E-mail: jhyun@spu.edu.

Master of Education in Teacher Leadership Program Students: 25 full-time (21 women), 2 part-time (1 woman). Average age 35. 14 applicants, 64% accepted, 9 enrolled. *Financial support:* Applicants required to submit FAFSA. In 2015, 23 master's awarded. *Degree program information:* Part-time and evening/weekend programs available. Part-time, evening/weekend. Offers reading/language arts education (M Ed). *Application deadline:* For fall admission, 8/15 priority date for domestic students, 7/1 for international students; for winter admission, 11/15 for domestic students; for spring admission, 2/15 for domestic students, 3/1 for international students; for summer admission, 5/15 for domestic students. Applications are processed on a rolling basis. *Application fee:* $50. Electronic applications accepted. *Application Contact:* The Graduate Center, 206-281-2091. *Chair,* Robin Henrikson, 360-461-4422, E-mail: henrir@spu.edu.

Master of Fine Arts in Creative Writing Program Students: 22 full-time (13 women); includes 1 minority (Hispanic/Latino). Average age 38. *Financial support:* Applicants required to submit FAFSA. In 2015, 11 master's awarded. *Degree program information:* Part-time programs available. Part-time. Offers creative writing (MFA). *Application deadline:* For winter admission, 11/15 for domestic students; for summer admission, 5/15 for domestic students. *Application fee:* $50. Electronic applications accepted. *Application Contact:* The Graduate Center, 206-281-2091. *Director,* Dr. Gregory Wolfe, 206-281-2109, E-mail: gwolfe@spu.edu.

Master of Science in Information Systems Management Program Students: 27 full-time (21 women), 6 part-time (0 women); includes 3 minority (all Asian, non-Hispanic/Latino), 22 international. Average age 30. 25 applicants, 40% accepted, 10 enrolled. *Financial support:* Applicants required to submit FAFSA. In 2015, 14 master's awarded. *Degree program information:* Part-time programs available. Part-time. Offers information systems management (MS). *Application deadline:* For fall admission, 8/1 for domestic students, 6/1 for international students; for winter admission, 11/1 for domestic and international students; for spring admission, 2/1 for domestic students, 12/1 for international students; for summer admission, 5/1 for domestic students. Applications are processed on a rolling basis. *Application fee:* $50. Electronic applications accepted. *Application Contact:* 206-281-2091. *Associate Dean for Graduate Studies,* Gary Karns, 206-281-2948, Fax: 206-281-2733.

MS in Marriage and Family Therapy Program Students: 64 full-time (54 women), 12 part-time (9 women); includes 7 minority (2 American Indian or Alaska Native, non-Hispanic/Latino; 2 Asian, non-Hispanic/Latino; 2 Hispanic/Latino; 1 Two or more races, non-Hispanic/Latino), 2 international. Average age 28. 99 applicants, 45% accepted, 45 enrolled. *Financial support:* Fellowships and Federal Work-Study available. Financial award applicants required to submit FAFSA. In 2015, 29 master's awarded. *Degree program information:* Part-time programs available. Part-time. Offers marriage and family therapy (MS); medical family therapy (Certificate). *Application deadline:* For fall admission, 1/23 for domestic students, 2/1 for international students. Applications are processed on a rolling basis. *Application fee:* $50. Electronic applications accepted. *Chair,* Dr. Scott Edwards, 206-281-2681, E-mail: sedwards@spu.edu.

MS in Nursing Program Students: 39 full-time (36 women), 30 part-time (25 women); includes 14 minority (3 Black or African American, non-Hispanic/Latino; 7 Asian, non-Hispanic/Latino; 3 Hispanic/Latino; 1 Two or more races, non-Hispanic/Latino), 1 international. Average age 38. 60 applicants, 48% accepted, 29 enrolled. *Financial support:* Fellowships and scholarships/grants available. Financial award applicants required to submit FAFSA. In 2015, 23 master's awarded. *Degree program information:* Part-time programs available. Part-time. Offers administration (MSN); adult/gerontology nurse practitioner (MSN); clinical nurse specialist (MSN); family nurse practitioner (MSN, Certificate); informatics (MSN); nurse educator (MSN). *Application deadline:* For fall admission, 1/15 priority date for domestic students; for spring admission, 1/15 for domestic students. Applications are processed on a rolling basis. *Application fee:* $50. Electronic applications accepted. *Associate Dean,* Dr. Christine Hoyle, 206-281-2469, E-mail: hoylec@spu.edu.

PhD in Clinical Psychology Program Students: 53 full-time (45 women), 20 part-time (19 women); includes 10 minority (3 Black or African American, non-Hispanic/Latino; 3 Asian, non-Hispanic/Latino; 2 Hispanic/Latino; 2 Two or more races, non-Hispanic/Latino), 2 international. Average age 27. 147 applicants, 9% accepted, 13 enrolled. *Financial support:* Fellowships and scholarships/grants available. Financial award applicants required to submit FAFSA. In 2015, 10 doctorates awarded. Offers clinical psychology (PhD). *Application deadline:* For fall admission, 12/15 for domestic and international students. Electronic applications accepted. *Application Contact:* 206-281-2091. *Chair,* Dr. David G. Stewart, 206-281-2660, E-mail: davidste@spu.edu.

PhD in Counselor Education Program Students: 5 full-time (3 women), 5 part-time (3 women); includes 3 minority (1 Black or African American, non-Hispanic/Latino; 1 Asian, non-Hispanic/Latino; 1 Two or more races, non-Hispanic/Latino). Average age 36. 4 applicants. In 2015, 1 doctorate awarded. Offers counselor education (PhD). *Application deadline:* For fall admission, 8/15 for domestic students; for winter admission, 11/15 for domestic students; for spring admission, 2/15 for domestic students; for summer admission, 5/15 for domestic students. *Application fee:* $50. *Director,* Andrew Lumpe, 206-281-2369, E-mail: lumpea@spu.edu.

Program in Digital Education Leadership Students: 10 full-time (9 women), 4 part-time (3 women). Average age 36. 11 applicants, 91% accepted, 10 enrolled. Offers digital education leadership (M Ed). *Application deadline:* For fall admission, 9/8 for domestic students. *Application Contact:* Graduate Center, 206-281-2091. *Dean,* Rick Eigenbrood, 206-281-2710, E-mail: eigend@spu.edu.

Program in Teaching Mathematics and Science Students: 25 full-time (19 women); includes 1 minority (Asian, non-Hispanic/Latino). Average age 31. In 2015, 20 master's awarded. Offers teaching mathematics and science (MTMS). *Application deadline:* For fall admission, 8/15 for domestic students; for winter admission, 11/15 for domestic students; for spring admission, 2/15 for domestic students; for summer admission, 5/15 for domestic students. *Graduate Teacher Education Chair,* David W. Dento, 206-281-2504, E-mail: dentod@spu.edu.

THE SEATTLE SCHOOL OF THEOLOGY AND PSYCHOLOGY, Seattle, WA 98121

General Information Independent-religious, coed, graduate-only institution.

GRADUATE UNITS

Graduate Programs ***Degree program information:*** Part-time programs available. Part-time.

SEATTLE UNIVERSITY, Seattle, WA 98122-1090

General Information Independent-religious, coed, comprehensive institution. *Enrollment:* 7,273 graduate, professional, and undergraduate students; 1,355 full-time matriculated graduate/professional students (862 women), 1,398 part-time matriculated graduate/professional students (823 women). *Graduate faculty:* 149 full-time (77 women), 75 part-time/adjunct (51 women). *Graduate housing:* Room and/or apartments available on a first-come, first-served basis to single students; on-campus housing not available to married students. *Student services:* Campus employment opportunities, campus safety program, career counseling, exercise/wellness program, free psychological counseling, international student services, low-cost health insurance, multicultural affairs office, services for students with disabilities, teacher training, writing training. *Library:* Lemieux Library & McGoldrick Learning Commons plus 1 other. *Research affiliation:* Swedish Medical Centers (nursing).

Computer facilities: Computer purchase and lease plans are available. 467 computers available on campus for general student use. A campuswide network can be accessed from student residence rooms and from off campus. Online class registration is available.
Website: http://www.seattleu.edu/

General Application Contact: Janet Shandley, Director of Graduate Admissions, 206-296-5900, Fax: 206-298-5656, E-mail: grad_admissions@seattleu.edu.

GRADUATE UNITS

Albers School of Business and Economics Students: 272 full-time (147 women), 319 part-time (135 women); includes 138 minority (15 Black or African American, non-Hispanic/Latino; 2 American Indian or Alaska Native, non-Hispanic/Latino; 82 Asian, non-Hispanic/Latino; 23 Hispanic/Latino; 4 Native Hawaiian or other Pacific Islander, non-Hispanic/Latino; 12 Two or more races, non-Hispanic/Latino), 134 international. Average age 30. 453 applicants, 67% accepted, 200 enrolled. *Faculty:* 47 full-time (17 women), 16 part-time/adjunct (6 women). *Financial support:* In 2015–16, 182 students received support. Fellowships with partial tuition reimbursements available, research assistantships, career-related internships or fieldwork, Federal Work-Study, scholarships/grants, and unspecified assistantships available. Support available to part-time students. Financial award application deadline: 6/1; financial award applicants required to submit FAFSA. In 2015, 251 master's, 248 other advanced degrees awarded. *Degree program information:* Part-time and evening/weekend programs available. Part-time, evening/weekend. Offers accounting (MPAC); business administration (MBA, Certificate); business analytics (MSBA, Certificate); business and economics (EMBA, MBA, MPAC, MSBA, MSF, Certificate); finance (MSF, Certificate). *Application deadline:* For fall admission, 8/20 priority date for domestic students, 4/1 priority date for international students; for winter admission, 11/20 priority date for domestic students, 9/1 priority date for international students; for spring admission, 2/20 priority date for domestic students, 12/1 priority date for international students; for summer admission, 5/20 priority date for domestic students, 1/1 priority date for international students. Applications are processed on a rolling basis. *Application fee:* $55. Electronic applications accepted. *Application Contact:* Jeff Millard, Assistant Dean of Graduate Programs, 206-296-5700, E-mail: albersgrad@seattleu.edu. *Dean,* Dr. Joseph M. Phillips, Jr., 206-296-5700, Fax: 206-296-5795, E-mail: phillipsj@seattleu.edu.

Center for Leadership Formation Students: 58 full-time (31 women); includes 13 minority (2 Black or African American, non-Hispanic/Latino; 6 Asian, non-Hispanic/Latino; 3 Hispanic/Latino; 1 Native Hawaiian or other Pacific Islander, non-Hispanic/Latino; 1 Two or more races, non-Hispanic/Latino). Average age 40. 55 applicants, 89% accepted, 44 enrolled. *Faculty:* 18 full-time (9 women), 6 part-time/adjunct (2 women). *Financial support:* In 2015–16, 15 students received support. Scholarships/grants available. Financial award applicants required to submit FAFSA. In 2015, 16 master's, 14 other advanced degrees awarded. *Degree program information:* Evening/weekend programs available. Evening/weekend. Offers leadership (EMBA, Certificate). *Application deadline:* Applications are processed on a rolling basis. *Application fee:* $55. Electronic applications accepted. *Application Contact:* Sommer Harrison, Manager, Graduate Programs Outreach, 206-296-2529, E-mail: emba@seattleu.edu. *Associate Dean of Executive Education,* Dr. Marilyn Gist, 206-296-5413, E-mail: gistm@seattleu.edu.

College of Arts and Sciences ***Degree program information:*** Part-time and evening/weekend programs available. Part-time, evening/weekend. Offers arts and sciences (MA Psych, MACJ, MFA, MNPL, MPA, MSAL, Certificate); arts leadership (MFA); crime analysis (Certificate); criminal justice (MACJ); existential and phenomenological therapeutic psychology (MA Psych). Electronic applications accepted.

Center for the Study of Sport and Exercise Degree program information: Part-time and evening/weekend programs available. Part-time, evening/weekend. Offers sport and exercise (MSAL). Electronic applications accepted.

Institute of Public Service Degree program information: Part-time and evening/weekend programs available. Part-time, evening/weekend. Offers public service (MNPL, MPA). Electronic applications accepted.

College of Education ***Degree program information:*** Part-time and evening/weekend programs available. Part-time, evening/weekend. Offers adult education and training (M Ed, MA, Certificate); counseling and school psychology (MA, Certificate, Ed S); education (M Ed, MA, MIT, Ed D, Certificate, Ed S, Post-Master's Certificate); educational administration (M Ed, MA, Certificate, Ed S); educational leadership (Ed D); literacy (M Ed, Post-Master's Certificate); special education (M Ed, MA, Certificate); student development administration (M Ed, MA); teacher education (MIT); teaching English to speakers of other languages (M Ed, MA, Certificate). Electronic applications accepted.

College of Nursing ***Degree program information:*** Part-time and evening/weekend programs available. Part-time, evening/weekend. Offers adult/gerontological nurse practitioner (MSN); advanced community public health (MSN); advanced community public health nursing (MSN); family nurse practitioner (MSN); family psychiatric mental health nurse practitioner (MSN); nurse midwifery (MSN); nursing (MSN, DNP); psychiatric mental health nurse practitioner (MSN).

College of Science and Engineering ***Degree program information:*** Part-time and evening/weekend programs available. Part-time, evening/weekend. Offers computer science (MSCS); science and engineering (MSCS, MSE); software engineering (MSE).

School of Law Students: 628 full-time (325 women), 163 part-time (78 women); includes 258 minority (24 Black or African American, non-Hispanic/Latino; 6 American Indian or Alaska Native, non-Hispanic/Latino; 102 Asian, non-Hispanic/Latino; 69 Hispanic/Latino; 5 Native Hawaiian or other Pacific Islander, non-Hispanic/Latino; 52 Two or more races, non-Hispanic/Latino), 7 international. Average age 27. 1,550 applicants, 58% accepted, 203 enrolled. *Faculty:* 47 full-time (25 women), 48 part-time/adjunct (16 women). *Financial support:* In 2015–16, 500 students received support. Career-related internships or fieldwork, Federal Work-Study, and scholarships/grants available. Support available to part-time students. Financial award application deadline: 2/15; financial award applicants required to submit FAFSA. In 2015, 320 doctorates awarded. *Degree program information:* Part-time programs available. Part-time. Offers law (JD). *Application deadline:* For fall admission, 3/1 priority date for domestic and international students. Applications are processed on a rolling basis. *Application fee:* $60. Electronic applications accepted. *Application Contact:* Gerald Heppler, Interim Director of Admission, 206-398-4205, Fax: 206-398-4058, E-mail: hepplerg@seattleu.edu. *Dean,* Annette E. Clark, 206-398-4300, Fax: 206-398-4310, E-mail: annclark@seattleu.edu.

School of Theology and Ministry ***Degree program information:*** Part-time programs available. Part-time, online learning. Offers divinity (M Div); pastoral counseling (MAPC); pastoral studies (MAPS); theology and ministry (M Div, MAPC, MAPS, MATL, MATS, Certificate); transformational leadership (MATL); transforming spirituality (MATS, Certificate). Electronic applications accepted.

SELMA UNIVERSITY, Selma, AL 36701-5299

General Information Independent-religious, coed, comprehensive institution.

GRADUATE UNITS

Graduate Programs Offers Bible and Christian education (MA); Bible and pastoral ministry (MA).

SEMINARY OF THE IMMACULATE CONCEPTION, Huntington, NY 11743-1696

General Information Independent-religious, coed, graduate-only institution. *Graduate housing:* Room and/or apartments guaranteed to single students; on-campus housing not available to married students. Housing application deadline: 8/30.

GRADUATE UNITS

School of Theology ***Degree program information:*** Part-time and evening/weekend programs available. Part-time, evening/weekend. Offers pastoral studies (MA); theology (M Div, MA, D Min, Certificate).

SEMINARY OF THE SOUTHWEST, Austin, TX 78768-2247

General Information Independent-religious, coed, graduate-only institution. *Enrollment by degree level:* 90 master's, 5 other advanced degrees. *Graduate faculty:* 10 full-time (4 women), 11 part-time/adjunct (3 women). *Tuition, area resident:* Full-time $13,810; part-time $575 per credit hour. *Required fees:* $95; $55 per credit hour. $225 per semester. Tuition and fees vary according to class time. *Graduate housing:* Rooms and/or apartments available on a first-come, first-served basis to single and married students. Typical cost: $5220 per year for single students; $14,400 per year for married students. Room charges vary according to housing facility selected. Housing application deadline: 8/1. *Student services:* Exercise/wellness program, writing training. *Library:* Booher Library. *Collection:* Books: 154,085 (physical), 28,854 (digital/electronic); Serial titles: 390 (physical), 54 (digital/electronic); Databases: 67. Weekly public service hours: 90; students can reserve study rooms.

Computer facilities: 8 computers available on campus for general student use. A campuswide network can be accessed. Online class registration is available.
Website: http://www.ssw.edu/

General Application Contact: Beth Jordan, Enrollment Manager, 512-472-4133 Ext. 357, Fax: 512-472-3098, E-mail: beth.jordan@ssw.edu.

GRADUATE UNITS

Graduate and Professional Programs Students: 46 full-time (19 women), 52 part-time (41 women); includes 18 minority (6 Black or African American, non-Hispanic/Latino; 1 American Indian or Alaska Native, non-Hispanic/Latino; 6 Hispanic/Latino; 5 Two or more races, non-Hispanic/Latino). Average age 49. 48 applicants, 65% accepted, 26 enrolled. *Faculty:* 10 full-time (3 women), 9 part-time/adjunct (4 women). *Financial support:* In 2015–16, 30 students received support. Career-related internships or fieldwork and scholarships/grants available. Support available to part-time students. Financial award application deadline: 6/15. In 2015, 31 master's, 1 other advanced degree awarded. *Degree program information:* Part-time and evening/weekend programs available. Part-time, evening/weekend. Offers theology (M Div, MAC, MAR, MCPC, MSF, Advanced Diploma). *Application deadline:* For fall admission, 6/30 priority date for domestic and international students; for spring admission, 12/1 priority date for domestic and international students. Applications are processed on a rolling basis. *Application fee:* $50. *Application Contact:* Jennielle Strother, Vice President of Enrollment Management, 512-472-4133 Ext. 375, Fax: 512-472-3098, E-mail: jennielle.strother@ssw.edu. *Dean and President,* Rev. Dr. Cynthia Briggs Kittredge, 512-472-4133 Ext. 332, Fax: 512-472-3098, E-mail: cynthia.kittredge@ssw.edu.

SETON HALL UNIVERSITY, South Orange, NJ 07079-2697

General Information Independent-religious, coed, university. CGS member. *Graduate housing:* On-campus housing not available.

GRADUATE UNITS

College of Arts and Sciences *Degree program information:* Part-time and evening/weekend programs available. Part-time, evening/weekend, online learning. Offers analytical chemistry (MS, PhD); arts and sciences (MA, MPA, MS, PhD, Graduate Certificate); Asian studies (MA); biochemistry (MS, PhD); biology (MS); biology/business administration (MS); chemistry (MS); corporate and professional communication (MA); experimental psychology (MS); history (MA); inorganic chemistry (MS, PhD); Jewish-Christian studies (MA); literature (MA); microbiology (MS); molecular bioscience (PhD); molecular bioscience/neuroscience (PhD); museum professions (MA); nonprofit organization management (Graduate Certificate); organic chemistry (MS, PhD); physical chemistry (MS, PhD); public administration (MPA); strategic communication (MA); strategic communication and leadership (MA). Electronic applications accepted.

College of Education and Human Services *Degree program information:* Part-time and evening/weekend programs available. Part-time, evening/weekend. Offers college student personnel administration (MA); counseling psychology (MA, PhD); education and human services (MA, MS, Ed D, Exec Ed D, PhD, Ed S, Professional Diploma); education research, assessment and program evaluation (PhD); higher education administration (Ed D, PhD); human resource training and development (MA); individualized (MA); instructional design (MA); K–12 administration and supervision (Ed D, Exec Ed D, Ed S); K–12 leadership, management and policy (Ed D, Exec Ed D, Ed S); marriage and family therapy (MA, MS, Ed S, Professional Diploma); psychological studies (MA); school and community psychology (MA); school counseling (MA); school library media specialist (MA); special education (MA); sports and exercise psychology (MA). Electronic applications accepted.

College of Nursing *Degree program information:* Part-time programs available. Part-time, online learning. Offers advanced practice in primary health care (MSN, DNP); entry into practice (MSN); health systems administration (MSN, DNP); nursing (PhD); nursing case management (MSN); nursing education (MA); school nurse (MSN). Electronic applications accepted.

Immaculate Conception Seminary School of Theology *Degree program information:* Part-time and evening/weekend programs available. Part-time, evening/weekend. Offers Christian spirituality (Certificate); great spiritual books (Certificate); pastoral ministry (M Div, MA, Certificate); scripture studies (Certificate); Seminary's Theological Education for Parish Services (STEPS) (Certificate); theology (MA). Electronic applications accepted.

School of Diplomacy and International Relations Students: 110. Average age 26. *Faculty:* 17 full-time, 10 part-time/adjunct. *Financial support:* In 2015–16, fellowships with partial tuition reimbursements (averaging $6,810 per year), research assistantships with partial tuition reimbursements (averaging $13,620 per year) were awarded; career-related internships or fieldwork, scholarships/grants, and unspecified assistantships also available. *Degree program information:* Part-time and evening/weekend programs available. Part-time, evening/weekend, 100% online, blended/hybrid learning. Offers diplomacy and international relations (MA); global health management (Graduate Certificate); post-conflict state reconstruction and sustainability (Graduate Certificate); United Nations studies (Graduate Certificate). *Application deadline:* For fall admission, 3/31 priority date for domestic students; for spring admission, 10/30 priority date for domestic students. Applications are processed on a rolling basis. *Application fee:* $75. Electronic applications accepted. *Application Contact:* Daniel Kristo, Director of Graduate Admissions, 973-275-2142, Fax: 973-275-2519, E-mail: daniel.kristo@shu.edu.

School of Health and Medical Sciences *Degree program information:* Part-time and evening/weekend programs available. Part-time, evening/weekend. Offers athletic training (MS); health and medical sciences (MS, DPT, PhD); health sciences (PhD); occupational therapy (MS); physician assistant (MS); professional physical therapy (DPT); speech-language pathology (MS). Electronic applications accepted.

School of Law *Degree program information:* Part-time and evening/weekend programs available. Part-time, evening/weekend. Offers health law (LL M, JD); intellectual property (LL M, JD); law (MSJ). MD/JD, MD/MSJ offered jointly with University of Medicine and Dentistry of New Jersey. Electronic applications accepted.

Stillman School of Business Students: 89 full-time (35 women), 228 part-time (82 women); includes 126 minority (30 Black or African American, non-Hispanic/Latino; 1 American Indian or Alaska Native, non-Hispanic/Latino; 72 Asian, non-Hispanic/Latino; 23 Hispanic/Latino). Average age 31. 289 applicants, 58% accepted, 95 enrolled. *Faculty:* 26 full-time (5 women), 19 part-time/adjunct (1 woman). *Financial support:* In 2015–16, 25 students received support, including 25 research assistantships with full tuition reimbursements available (averaging $24,687 per year); career-related internships or fieldwork, scholarships/grants, and unspecified assistantships also available. Financial award application deadline: 6/30; financial award applicants required to submit FAFSA. In 2015, 150 master's awarded. *Degree program information:* Part-time and evening/weekend programs available. Part-time, evening/weekend. Offers accounting (MBA, MS, Certificate); business (MBA, MS, Certificate); CPA (Certificate); entrepreneurship (Certificate); finance (MBA, Certificate); information technology management (MBA); international business (MBA); management (MBA); marketing (MBA); professional accounting (MS); sport management (MBA); supply chain management (MBA, Certificate); taxation (Certificate). *Application deadline:* For fall admission, 5/31 priority date for domestic students, 3/31 priority date for international students; for spring admission, 10/31 priority date for domestic students, 9/30 priority date for international students; for summer admission, 4/30 priority date for domestic students, 3/31 priority date for international students. Applications are processed on a rolling basis. *Application fee:* $75. Electronic applications accepted. *Application Contact:* Catherine Bianchi, Director of Graduate Admissions, 973-761-9262, Fax: 973-761-9208, E-mail: catherine.bianchi@shu.edu. *Dean,* Dr. Joyce Strawser, 973-761-9013, Fax: 973-275-2465, E-mail: joyce.strawser@shu.edu.

SETON HILL UNIVERSITY, Greensburg, PA 15601

General Information Independent-religious, coed, comprehensive institution. *Tuition, area resident:* Part-time $704 per credit. Part-time tuition and fees vary according to program. *Graduate housing:* Room and/or apartments available on a first-come, first-served basis to single students; on-campus housing not available to married students. Housing application deadline: 7/1. *Student services:* Campus employment opportunities, career counseling, exercise/wellness program, international student services, multicultural affairs office, services for students with disabilities, teacher training, writing training. *Library:* Reeves Memorial Library. *Collection:* Books: 72,274 (physical), 127,160 (digital/electronic); Serial titles: 2,919 (physical); Databases: 37. Students can reserve study rooms.

Computer facilities: Computer purchase and lease plans are available. 66 computers available on campus for general student use. A campuswide network can be accessed from student residence rooms and from off campus. Online class registration is available.
Website: http://www.setonhill.edu/

General Application Contact: Lisa Glessner, Director of Graduate and Adult Studies, 724-838-4208, Fax: 724-830-1891, E-mail: gadmit@setonhill.edu.

GRADUATE UNITS

Program in Art Therapy *Financial support:* Federal Work-Study, scholarships/grants, and tuition discounts available. Financial award application deadline: 8/15; financial award applicants required to submit FAFSA. *Degree program information:* Part-time programs available. Part-time. Offers art therapy (MA). *Application deadline:* For fall admission, 7/1 for domestic and international students; for spring admission, 11/30 for domestic and international students. Applications are processed on a rolling basis. *Application fee:* $0. Electronic applications accepted.

Program in Business Administration *Financial support:* Federal Work-Study, scholarships/grants, and tuition discounts available. Financial award application deadline: 8/15; financial award applicants required to submit FAFSA. *Degree program information:* Part-time and evening/weekend programs available. Part-time, evening/weekend. Offers accounting (MBA); entrepreneurship (MBA, Certificate); management (MBA). *Application deadline:* Applications are processed on a rolling basis. *Application fee:* $0. Electronic applications accepted. *Application Contact:* Lisa Glessner. *Director,* Dr. Douglas Nelson, 724-830-4738, E-mail: dnelson@setonhill.edu.

Program in Elementary Education/Middle Level Education *Financial support:* Scholarships/grants and tuition discounts available. Financial award application deadline: 8/15; financial award applicants required to submit FAFSA. *Degree program information:* Part-time and evening/weekend programs available. Part-time, evening/weekend, online learning. Offers elementary education/middle level education (MA, Certificate). *Application deadline:* Applications are processed on a rolling basis. *Application fee:* $0. Electronic applications accepted.

Program in Genocide and Holocaust Studies *Financial support:* Scholarships/grants available. Financial award application deadline: 8/15; financial award applicants required to submit FAFSA. *Degree program information:* Part-time and evening/weekend programs available. Part-time, evening/weekend, online learning. Offers genocide and Holocaust studies (Certificate). *Application deadline:* Applications are processed on a rolling basis. *Application fee:* $0. Electronic applications accepted.

Program in Marriage and Family Therapy *Financial support:* Federal Work-Study, scholarships/grants, tuition waivers (partial), and unspecified assistantships available. Support available to part-time students. Financial award application deadline: 8/15; financial award applicants required to submit FAFSA. *Degree program information:* Part-time and evening/weekend programs available. Part-time, evening/weekend. Offers marriage and family therapy (MA). *Application deadline:* For fall admission, 8/15 priority date for domestic students; for spring admission, 12/15 for domestic students. Applications are processed on a rolling basis. *Application fee:* $35. Electronic applications accepted. *Application Contact:* Lisa Glessner, Program Counselor, 724-830-4209, E-mail: lglessner@setonhill.edu.

Program in Orthodontics *Financial support:* Application deadline: 5/15; applicants required to submit FAFSA. Offers orthodontics (MS, Certificate). *Application deadline:* For fall admission, 9/15 priority date for domestic students, 9/15 for international students.

Program in Physician Assistant *Financial support:* Application deadline: 8/15; applicants required to submit FAFSA. Offers physician assistant (MS). *Application deadline:* For spring admission, 1/15 priority date for domestic students. Electronic applications accepted. *Application Contact:* Lisa Glessner.

Program in Special Education *Financial support:* Scholarships/grants and tuition discounts available. Financial award application deadline: 8/15; financial award applicants required to submit FAFSA. *Degree program information:* Part-time and evening/weekend programs available. Part-time, evening/weekend, online learning. Offers special education (MA). *Application deadline:* Applications are processed on a rolling basis. *Application fee:* $0. Electronic applications accepted.

Program in Writing Popular Fiction *Financial support:* Scholarships/grants and tuition discounts available. Financial award application deadline: 8/15; financial award applicants required to submit FAFSA. *Degree program information:* Part-time programs available. Part-time. Offers writing popular fiction (MFA, Certificate). *Application deadline:* For spring admission, 4/5 for domestic students. *Application fee:* $35. *Application Contact:* Ellen Monnich, Assistant Director, Graduate and Adult Studies, 724-838-4221, E-mail: monnich@setonhill.edu. *Director,* Dr. Nicole Peeler, 724-552-2967, E-mail: peeler@setonhill.edu.

SEWANEE: THE UNIVERSITY OF THE SOUTH, Sewanee, TN 37383-1000

General Information Independent-religious, coed, comprehensive institution. *Enrollment:* 1,797 graduate, professional, and undergraduate students. *Graduate housing:* Rooms and/or apartments available on a first-come, first-served basis to single and married students. *Student services:* Campus employment opportunities, campus safety program, career counseling, child daycare facilities, free psychological counseling, international student services, multicultural affairs office, writing training. *Library:* Jessie Ball duPont Library. *Collection:* Books: 784,306 (physical), 622,710 (digital/electronic); Serial titles: 4,508 (physical), 10,570 (digital/electronic); Databases: 342. Weekly public service hours: 107; study areas open 24 hours, 5–7 days a week; students can reserve study rooms.

Computer facilities: 267 computers available on campus for general student use. A campuswide network can be accessed from student residence rooms and from off campus. Online class registration is available.
Website: http://www.sewanee.edu/

GRADUATE UNITS

School of Theology Students: 74 full-time (28 women), 4 part-time (2 women); includes 5 minority (2 Black or African American, non-Hispanic/Latino; 1 American Indian or Alaska Native, non-Hispanic/Latino; 2 Two or more races, non-Hispanic/Latino), 5 international. Average age 39. *Faculty:* 18. *Financial support:* Institutionally sponsored loans and scholarships/grants available. Support available to part-time students. Financial award application deadline: 5/2. In 2015, 26 master's, 6 doctorates awarded. *Degree program information:* Part-time programs available. Part-time. Offers theology (M Div, MA, STM, D Min). *Application deadline:* Applications are processed on a rolling basis. *Application fee:* $0. *Application Contact:* Rev. Annwn H. Myers, Associate Dean for Recruiting and Admission, 931-598-1373, E-mail: amyers@sewanee.edu. *Dean,* Very Rev. Dr. J. Neil Alexander, 931-598-1288, Fax: 931-598-1412, E-mail: deansot@sewanee.edu.

Sewanee School of Letters Students: 55 part-time (30 women); includes 4 minority (1 Black or African American, non-Hispanic/Latino; 1 Hispanic/Latino; 2 Two or more races, non-Hispanic/Latino). Average age 42. *Faculty:* 9. *Financial support:* Application deadline: 3/1; applicants required to submit FAFSA. In 2015, 9 master's awarded. *Degree program information:* Part-time programs available. Part-time. Offers American and English literature (MA); creative writing (MFA). *Application deadline:* Applications are processed on a rolling basis. *Application fee:* $40. Electronic applications accepted. *Application Contact:* April R. Alvarez, Coordinator, 931-598-1636, Fax: 931-598-3303. *Director,* Dr. John M. Grammer, 931-598-1483, Fax: 931-598-3303, E-mail: jgrammer@sewanee.edu.

SHASTA BIBLE COLLEGE, Redding, CA 96002

General Information Independent-religious, coed, comprehensive institution. *Graduate housing:* Rooms and/or apartments available on a first-come, first-served basis to single and married students.

GRADUATE UNITS

Program in Biblical Counseling ***Degree program information:*** Part-time programs available. Part-time. Offers biblical counseling and Christian family life education (MA).

Program in Christian Ministry ***Degree program information:*** Part-time programs available. Part-time, online learning. Offers Christian ministry (MA).

Program in School and Church Administration ***Degree program information:*** Part-time and evening/weekend programs available. Part-time, evening/weekend. Offers school and church administration (MS).

SHAWNEE STATE UNIVERSITY, Portsmouth, OH 45662-4344

General Information State-supported, coed, comprehensive institution.

GRADUATE UNITS

Program in Curriculum and Instruction Offers curriculum and instruction (M Ed).

Program in Occupational Therapy Offers occupational therapy (MOT).

SHAW UNIVERSITY, Raleigh, NC 27601-2399

General Information Independent-religious, coed, comprehensive institution. *Graduate housing:* Room and/or apartments available on a first-come, first-served basis to single students; on-campus housing not available to married students. *Research affiliation:* The Louisville Institute (grants for book writing and theological research), Wabash Center (philosophy of religious education), The Society of Biblical Literature (biblical studies), The American Academy of Religion (theology, ethics, Church history, contemporary issues), Society for the Study of Black Religion (African American churches), The Association of Theological Schools (theological research grants).

GRADUATE UNITS

Department of Education ***Degree program information:*** Part-time and evening/weekend programs available. Part-time, evening/weekend. Offers curriculum and instruction (MS). Electronic applications accepted.

Divinity School ***Degree program information:*** Part-time and evening/weekend programs available. Part-time, evening/weekend. Offers divinity (M Div, MACE). Electronic applications accepted.

SHENANDOAH UNIVERSITY, Winchester, VA 22601-5195

General Information Independent-religious, coed, comprehensive institution. *Enrollment:* 3,820 graduate, professional, and undergraduate students; 934 full-time matriculated graduate/professional students (662 women), 753 part-time matriculated graduate/professional students (525 women). *Enrollment by degree level:* 650 master's, 936 doctoral, 101 other advanced degrees. *Graduate faculty:* 151 full-time (84 women), 66 part-time/adjunct (47 women). *Tuition, area resident:* Full-time $19,920; part-time $830 per credit. *Required fees:* $620; $460 per term. Tuition and fees vary according to course load and program. *Graduate housing:* Rooms and/or apartments available on a first-come, first-served basis to single and married students. Typical cost: $9920 (including board) for single students. Room and board charges vary according to board plan. Housing application deadline: 6/1. *Student services:* Campus employment opportunities, campus safety program, career counseling, child daycare facilities, exercise/wellness program, free psychological counseling, international student services, low-cost health insurance, multicultural affairs office, services for students with disabilities, writing training. *Library:* Alson H. Smith, Jr. Library plus 1 other. *Collection:* Books: 136,000 (physical), 215,000 (digital/electronic); Serial titles: 700 (physical), 85,000 (digital/electronic); Databases: 119. Weekly public service hours: 96.

Computer facilities: Computer purchase and lease plans are available. 32 computers available on campus for general student use. A campuswide network can be accessed from student residence rooms and from off campus. Online class registration, online student account information are available.
Website: http://www.su.edu/

General Application Contact: Andrew Woodall, Dean of Admissions, 540-665-4581, Fax: 540-665-4627, E-mail: admit@su.edu.

GRADUATE UNITS

Bernard J. Dunn School of Pharmacy Students: 403 full-time (266 women), 162 part-time (107 women); includes 264 minority (88 Black or African American, non-Hispanic/Latino; 2 American Indian or Alaska Native, non-Hispanic/Latino; 147 Asian, non-Hispanic/Latino; 21 Hispanic/Latino; 6 Two or more races, non-Hispanic/Latino), 25 international. Average age 31. 481 applicants, 51% accepted, 136 enrolled. *Faculty:* 39 full-time (26 women), 11 part-time/adjunct (6 women). *Financial support:* In 2015–16, 11 students received support. Career-related internships or fieldwork, scholarships/grants, and unspecified assistantships available. Support available to part-time students. Financial award application deadline: 3/15; financial award applicants required to submit FAFSA. In 2015, 122 doctorates awarded. *Degree program information:* Part-time and evening/weekend programs available. Part-time, evening/weekend, online learning. Offers pharmacy (Pharm D). *Application deadline:* For fall admission, 3/1 for domestic and international students. *Application fee:* $30. Electronic applications accepted. *Application Contact:* Andrew Woodall, Executive Director of Recruitment and Admissions, 540-665-4581, Fax: 540-665-4627, E-mail: admit@su.edu. *Dean,* Alan McKay, PhD, 540-665-1282, Fax: 540-665-1283, E-mail: amckay@su.edu.

College of Arts and Sciences Students: 10 full-time (9 women), 11 part-time (all women); includes 1 minority (Black or African American, non-Hispanic/Latino). Average age 30. 20 applicants, 95% accepted, 12 enrolled. *Faculty:* 1 full-time (0 women), 3 part-time/adjunct (2 women). *Financial support:* Career-related internships or fieldwork, scholarships/grants, and unspecified assistantships available. Financial award application deadline: 3/15; financial award applicants required to submit FAFSA. In 2015, 8 master's awarded. *Degree program information:* Part-time and evening/weekend programs available. Part-time, evening/weekend. Offers applied behavior analysis (MS). *Application deadline:* For fall admission, 7/15 for domestic and international students. *Application fee:* $30. Electronic applications accepted. *Application Contact:* Andrew Woodall, Executive Director of Recruitment and Admissions, 540-665-4581, Fax: 540-665-4627, E-mail: admit@su.edu. *Dean,* Jeff W. Coker, PhD, 540-665-4587, Fax: 540-665-4644, E-mail: jcoker2@su.edu.

Eleanor Wade Custer School of Nursing Students: 33 full-time (31 women), 62 part-time (57 women); includes 21 minority (17 Black or African American, non-Hispanic/Latino; 3 Asian, non-Hispanic/Latino; 1 Hispanic/Latino). Average age 36. 55 applicants, 87% accepted, 39 enrolled. *Faculty:* 10 full-time (all women), 7 part-time/adjunct (4 women). *Financial support:* In 2015–16, 13 students received support, including 3 fellowships (averaging $1,000 per year); scholarships/grants and unspecified assistantships also available. Financial award application deadline: 3/15; financial award applicants required to submit FAFSA. In 2015, 32 master's, 3 doctorates, 19 other advanced degrees awarded. Offers family nurse practitioner (MSN, DNP, Post-Graduate Certificate); health informatics (Certificate); health systems leadership (DNP); nurse midwifery (MSN, Post-Graduate Certificate); nursing education (Post-Graduate Certificate); psychiatric mental health nurse practitioner (MSN, DNP, Post-Graduate Certificate). *Application deadline:* For fall admission, 1/15 priority date for domestic and international students; for spring admission, 11/1 for domestic and international students; for summer admission, 3/15 for domestic and international students. *Application fee:* $30. Electronic applications accepted. *Application Contact:* Andrew Woodall, Executive Director of Recruitment and Admissions, 540-665-4581, Fax: 540-665-4627, E-mail: admit@su.edu. *Dean,* Kathryn Ganske, PhD, RN, 540-678-4374, Fax: 540-665-5519, E-mail: kganske@su.edu.

Harry F. Byrd, Jr. School of Business Students: 33 full-time (12 women), 42 part-time (25 women); includes 21 minority (10 Black or African American, non-Hispanic/Latino; 2 American Indian or Alaska Native, non-Hispanic/Latino; 5 Asian, non-Hispanic/Latino; 3 Hispanic/Latino; 1 Native Hawaiian or other Pacific Islander, non-Hispanic/Latino), 16 international. Average age 31. 113 applicants, 46% accepted, 24 enrolled. *Faculty:* 18 full-time (6 women), 2 part-time/adjunct (0 women). *Financial support:* In 2015–16, 24 students received support. Scholarships/grants and unspecified assistantships available. Financial award application deadline: 3/15; financial award applicants required to submit FAFSA. In 2015, 41 master's, 2 other advanced degrees awarded. *Degree program information:* Part-time and evening/weekend programs available. Part-time, evening/weekend. Offers business (MBA); healthcare management (Certificate). *Application deadline:* For fall admission, 5/1 for domestic and international students; for spring admission, 11/1 for domestic and international students; for summer admission, 3/1 for domestic and international students. *Application fee:* $30. Electronic applications accepted. *Application Contact:* Andrew Woodall, Executive Director of Recruitment and Admissions, 540-665-4581, Fax: 540-665-4627, E-mail: admit@su.edu. *Dean,* Miles K. Davis, PhD, 540-665-4572, Fax: 540-665-5437, E-mail: mdavi3@su.edu.

School of Education and Human Development Students: 18 full-time (14 women), 266 part-time (190 women); includes 40 minority (23 Black or African American, non-Hispanic/Latino; 6 Asian, non-Hispanic/Latino; 9 Hispanic/Latino; 2 Two or more races, non-Hispanic/Latino), 4 international. Average age 37. 121 applicants, 94% accepted, 83 enrolled. *Faculty:* 12 full-time (10 women), 26 part-time/adjunct (20 women). *Financial support:* In 2015–16, 5 students received support, including 1 teaching assistantship (averaging $9,000 per year); Federal Work-Study, scholarships/grants, and unspecified assistantships also available. Financial award application deadline: 3/15; financial award applicants required to submit FAFSA. In 2015, 115 master's, 7 doctorates, 41 other advanced degrees awarded. *Degree program information:* Part-time and evening/weekend programs available. Part-time, evening/weekend. Offers administrative leadership (D Ed); educational administration (MSE); elementary school teacher education (Certificate); health and physical education (Certificate); individual focus (MSE); middle school teacher education (Certificate); organizational leadership (MS, D Prof); secondary school teacher education (Certificate); special education (MSE); teaching (MSE). *Application deadline:* For fall admission, 7/16 priority date for domestic students, 7/15 priority date for international students; for spring admission, 10/15 priority date for domestic and international students; for summer admission, 2/15 priority date for domestic and international students. *Application fee:* $30. Electronic applications accepted. *Application Contact:* Andrew Woodall, Executive Director of Recruitment and Admissions, 540-665-4581, Fax: 540-665-4627, E-mail: admit@su.edu. *Director,* Dennis William Kellison, PhD, 540-535-7324, Fax: 540-665-4726, E-mail: dkelliso@su.edu.

School of Health Professions Students: 353 full-time (283 women), 115 part-time (92 women); includes 68 minority (11 Black or African American, non-Hispanic/Latino; 2 American Indian or Alaska Native, non-Hispanic/Latino; 33 Asian, non-Hispanic/Latino; 21 Hispanic/Latino; 1 Native Hawaiian or other Pacific Islander, non-Hispanic/Latino), 7 international. Average age 28. 1,574 applicants, 21% accepted, 122 enrolled. *Faculty:* 29 full-time (23 women), 14 part-time/adjunct (10 women). *Financial support:* In 2015–16, 48 students received support. Career-related internships or fieldwork, scholarships/grants, and unspecified assistantships available. Support available to part-time students. Financial award application deadline: 3/15; financial award applicants required to submit FAFSA. In 2015, 75 master's, 85 doctorates awarded. Online learning. Offers health professions (MS, DPT, Certificate). *Application deadline:* For fall admission, 7/31 for domestic and international students; for summer admission, 5/1 for domestic and international students. *Application fee:* $30. Electronic applications accepted. *Application Contact:* Andrew Woodall, Executive Director of Recruitment and Admissions, 540-665-4581, Fax: 540-665-4627, E-mail: admit@su.edu.

Division of Athletic Training Students: 34 full-time (19 women), 7 part-time (5 women); includes 10 minority (5 Black or African American, non-Hispanic/Latino; 1 Asian, non-Hispanic/Latino; 2 Hispanic/Latino; 1 Native Hawaiian or other Pacific Islander, non-Hispanic/Latino; 1 Two or more races, non-Hispanic/Latino). Average age 25. 37 applicants, 78% accepted, 22 enrolled. *Faculty:* 5 full-time (4 women), 5 part-time/adjunct (4 women). *Financial support:* In 2015–16, 4 students received support. Scholarships/grants available. Support available to part-time students. Financial award application deadline: 3/15; financial award applicants required to submit FAFSA. In 2015, 18 master's, 5 other advanced degrees awarded. Offers athletic training (MS); performing arts medicine (Certificate). *Application deadline:* For summer admission, 4/1 for domestic and international students. *Application fee:* $30. Electronic applications accepted. *Application Contact:* Andrew Woodall, Executive Director of Recruitment and Admissions, 540-665-4581, Fax: 540-665-4627, E-mail: admit@su.edu. *Director,* Rose A. Schmieg, PhD, 540-545-7385, Fax: 540-545-7387, E-mail: rschmieg@su.edu.

Division of Occupational Therapy Students: 91 full-time (83 women), 27 part-time (24 women); includes 17 minority (6 Black or African American, non-Hispanic/Latino; 4 Asian, non-Hispanic/Latino; 6 Hispanic/Latino; 1 Two or more races, non-Hispanic/Latino). Average age 27. 169 applicants, 59% accepted, 48 enrolled. *Faculty:* 6 full-time (all women), 6 part-time/adjunct (all women). *Financial support:* In 2015–16, 11 students received support. Scholarships/grants and unspecified assistantships available. Financial award application deadline: 3/15; financial award applicants required to submit FAFSA. In 2015, 27 master's awarded. Offers occupational therapy (MS). *Application deadline:* For fall admission, 10/15 for domestic and international students. *Application fee:* $140. Electronic applications accepted. *Application Contact:* Linda Burrows, OT Admissions Coordinator, 540-665-5559, Fax: 540-665-5530, E-mail: lburrows@su.edu. *Interim Division Director,* Cathy F. Shanholtz, PhD, 540-678-4313, Fax: 540-665-5564, E-mail: cshanhol2@su.edu.

Division of Physical Therapy Students: 143 full-time (105 women), 87 part-time (55 women); includes 46 minority (4 Black or African American, non-Hispanic/Latino; 1 American Indian or Alaska Native, non-Hispanic/Latino; 28 Asian, non-Hispanic/Latino; 9 Hispanic/Latino; 4 Two or more races, non-Hispanic/Latino), 11 international. Average age 30. 525 applicants, 26% accepted, 95 enrolled. *Faculty:* 12 full-time (8 women), 2 part-time/adjunct (1 woman). *Financial support:* In 2015–16, 13 students received support. Career-related internships or fieldwork, scholarships/grants, and unspecified assistantships available. Financial award application deadline: 3/15; financial award applicants required to submit FAFSA. In 2015, 90 doctorates awarded. Minimal on-campus study. Offers physical therapy (DPT). *Application deadline:* For fall admission, 10/1 for domestic and international students; for summer admission, 4/1 for domestic and international students. *Application fee:* $30. Electronic applications accepted. *Application Contact:* Andrew Woodall, Executive Director of Recruitment and Admissions, 540-665-4581, Fax: 540-665-4627, E-mail: admit@su.edu. *Director,* Dr. Karen Abraham, 540-665-5520, Fax: 540-545-7387, E-mail: kabraham@su.edu.

Division of Physician Assistant Studies Students: 116 full-time (96 women), 2 part-time (1 woman); includes 16 minority (2 Black or African American, non-Hispanic/Latino; 8 Asian, non-Hispanic/Latino; 5 Hispanic/Latino; 1 Two or more races, non-Hispanic/Latino), 1 international. Average age 27. 827 applicants, 7% accepted, 42 enrolled. *Faculty:* 7 full-time (6 women), 7 part-time/adjunct (4 women). *Financial support:* In 2015–16, 8 students received support. Scholarships/grants and unspecified assistantships available. Financial award application deadline: 3/15; financial award applicants required to submit FAFSA. In 2015, 40 master's awarded. Offers physician assistant (MS). *Application deadline:* For summer admission, 1/15 for domestic and international students. *Application fee:* $175. Electronic applications accepted. *Application Contact:* Cathy Carr, Admissions Coordinator, 540-545-7381, Fax: 540-542-6210, E-mail: pa@su.edu. *Director and Associate Professor,* Dr. Rachel A. Carlson, 540-542-6208, Fax: 540-542.6210, E-mail: rcarlso2@su.edu.

Shenandoah Conservatory Students: 53 full-time (27 women), 87 part-time (50 women); includes 26 minority (7 Black or African American, non-Hispanic/Latino; 1 American Indian or Alaska Native, non-Hispanic/Latino; 4 Asian, non-Hispanic/Latino; 12 Hispanic/Latino; 2 Two or more races, non-Hispanic/Latino), 17 international. Average age 32. 129 applicants, 76% accepted, 46 enrolled. *Faculty:* 37 full-time (10 women), 14 part-time/adjunct (6 women). *Financial support:* In 2015–16, 34 students received support, including 12 teaching assistantships with tuition reimbursements available (averaging $9,000 per year); scholarships/grants and unspecified assistantships also available. Financial award application deadline: 3/15; financial award applicants required to submit FAFSA. In 2015, 28 master's, 7 doctorates, 8 other advanced degrees awarded. *Degree program information:* Part-time programs available. Part-time. Offers church music (MM, Certificate); collaborative piano (MM); composition (MM); music (Artist Diploma); music education (MME); music therapy (MMT); music therapy certification eligibility (Certificate); pedagogy (MM, DMA); performance (MM, DMA); performing arts leadership and management (MS). *Application deadline:* For fall admission, 1/15 for domestic and international students; for summer admission, 4/15 for domestic and international students. *Application fee:* $30. Electronic applications accepted. *Application Contact:* Andrew Woodall, Executive Director of Recruitment and Advancement, 540-665-4581, Fax: 540-665-4627, E-mail: admit@su.edu. *Dean,* Dr. Michael J. Stepniak, 540-665-4600, Fax: 540-665-5402, E-mail: mstepnia@su.edu.

SHEPHERDS THEOLOGICAL SEMINARY, Cary, NC 27518

General Information Independent-religious, coed, graduate-only institution.

GRADUATE UNITS

Graduate Programs Offers church ministry (MA); New Testament (M Div); Old Testament (M Div); theology (M Div).

SHEPHERD UNIVERSITY, Los Angeles, CA 90065

General Information Independent-religious, coed, comprehensive institution.

GRADUATE UNITS

Cornel School of Contemporary Music Offers contemporary music (MM). Electronic applications accepted.

Hollywood CG School of Digital Arts Offers game art and design (MSIT); visual effects and animation (MSIT).

School of Theology Offers theology (M Div, D Min).

SHEPHERD UNIVERSITY, Shepherdstown, WV 25443

General Information State-supported, coed, comprehensive institution.

GRADUATE UNITS

Program in Curriculum and Instruction Offers curriculum and instruction (MA).

SHERMAN COLLEGE OF CHIROPRACTIC, Spartanburg, SC 29304-1452

General Information Independent, coed, graduate-only institution. *Enrollment by degree level:* 391 doctoral. *Graduate faculty:* 25 full-time (14 women), 15 part-time/adjunct (8 women). *Tuition, area resident:* Full-time $31,064; part-time $7766 per quarter. *Graduate housing:* Room and/or apartments available to single students. Typical cost: $10,000 per year ($13,600 including board). *Student services:* Campus employment opportunities, campus safety program, free psychological counseling, international student services, services for students with disabilities. *Library:* Tom and Mae Bahan Library. *Research affiliation:* American Public Health Service (chiropractic research), Upper Cervical Research Foundation (chiropractic).

Computer facilities: 44 computers available on campus for general student use. A campuswide network can be accessed. Online class registration is available.
Website: http://www.sherman.edu/

General Application Contact: Kristy Shepherd, Senior Director of Enrollment Services, 864-578-8770 Ext. 221, Fax: 864-599-4860, E-mail: kshepherd@sherman.edu.

GRADUATE UNITS

Professional Program *Financial support:* Career-related internships or fieldwork, Federal Work-Study, institutionally sponsored loans, and scholarships/grants available. Support available to part-time students. Financial award applicants required to submit FAFSA. Offers chiropractic (DC). *Application deadline:* For fall admission, 8/22 for domestic students, 4/3 for international students; for spring admission, 2/15 for domestic students; for summer admission, 5/30 for domestic students, 1/25 for international students. Applications are processed on a rolling basis. *Application fee:* $50. Electronic applications accepted. *Application Contact:* Dr. Robert Irwin, Provost, 864-578-8770 Ext. 223, Fax: 864-599-4860, E-mail: admissions@sherman.edu.

SHILOH UNIVERSITY, Kalona, IA 52247

General Information Independent, coed, comprehensive institution. *Enrollment:* 37 graduate, professional, and undergraduate students; 1 full-time matriculated graduate/professional student, 26 part-time matriculated graduate/professional students (5 women). *Enrollment by degree level:* 22 master's, 5 other advanced degrees. *Graduate faculty:* 3 full-time (0 women), 9 part-time/adjunct (1 woman). *Tuition, area resident:* Full-time $3000; part-time $167 per credit hour. Tuition and fees vary according to degree level. *Student services:* Writing training.
Website: http://www.shilohuniversity.edu/

General Application Contact: Andrew Thompson, Admissions Coordinator, 319-656-2447, Fax: 319-656-2448, E-mail: andy.thompson@shilohuniversity.edu.

GRADUATE UNITS

Graduate Programs Students: 1 full-time (0 women), 26 part-time (5 women); includes 3 minority (1 Black or African American, non-Hispanic/Latino; 1 Hispanic/Latino; 1 Native Hawaiian or other Pacific Islander, non-Hispanic/Latino), 2 international. Average age 47. 7 applicants, 71% accepted, 5 enrolled. *Faculty:* 3 full-time (0 women), 9 part-time/adjunct (1 woman). In 2015, 1 master's awarded. *Degree program information:* Part-time and evening/weekend programs available. Part-time, evening/weekend, 100% online. Offers biblical and pastoral studies (MA); Christian ministries (M Div); leadership of church and spiritual formation (D Min); theological studies (MA). *Application deadline:* For fall admission, 7/5 priority date for domestic and international students; for spring admission, 11/8 priority date for domestic and international students; for summer admission, 3/6 priority date for domestic and international students. Applications are processed on a rolling basis. *Application fee:* $0. Electronic applications accepted. *Application Contact:* Andrew Thompson, Admissions Coordinator, 319-656-2447, Fax: 319-656-2448, E-mail: admissions@shilohuniversity.edu. *Vice President of Academics,* Dr. Wesley Pinkham, 319-656-2447, Fax: 319-656-2448, E-mail: wess.pinkham@shilohuniversity.edu.

SHIPPENSBURG UNIVERSITY OF PENNSYLVANIA, Shippensburg, PA 17257-2299

General Information State-supported, coed, comprehensive institution. CGS member. *Enrollment:* 7,058 graduate, professional, and undergraduate students; 363 full-time matriculated graduate/professional students (242 women), 575 part-time matriculated graduate/professional students (320 women). *Enrollment by degree level:* 926 master's, 10 doctoral, 2 other advanced degrees. *Graduate faculty:* 141 full-time (53 women), 27 part-time/adjunct (17 women). Tuition, state resident: part-time $470 per credit. Tuition, nonresident: part-time $705 per credit. *Required fees:* $137 per credit. *Graduate housing:* On-campus housing not available. *Student services:* Campus employment opportunities, campus safety program, career counseling, child daycare facilities, exercise/wellness program, free psychological counseling, grant writing training, international student services, low-cost health insurance, multicultural affairs office, services for students with disabilities, teacher training, writing training. *Library:* Ezra Lehman Memorial Library plus 1 other. *Collection:* Books: 356,623 (physical), 54,429 (digital/electronic); Serial titles: 41 (physical), 1,092 (digital/electronic); Databases: 91. Weekly public service hours: 97.

Computer facilities: 1,100 computers available on campus for general student use. A campuswide network can be accessed from student residence rooms and from off campus. Online class registration, personal Web pages are available.
Website: http://www.ship.edu/

General Application Contact: Jeremy R. Goshorn, Assistant Dean of Graduate Admissions, 717-477-1231, Fax: 717-477-4016, E-mail: jrgoshorn@ship.edu.

GRADUATE UNITS

School of Graduate Studies Students: 363 full-time (242 women), 575 part-time (320 women); includes 121 minority (65 Black or African American, non-Hispanic/Latino; 1 American Indian or Alaska Native, non-Hispanic/Latino; 13 Asian, non-Hispanic/Latino; 22 Hispanic/Latino; 1 Native Hawaiian or other Pacific Islander, non-Hispanic/Latino; 19 Two or more races, non-Hispanic/Latino), 67 international. Average age 30. 1,022 applicants, 59% accepted, 379 enrolled. *Faculty:* 141 full-time (53 women), 27 part-time/adjunct (17 women). *Financial support:* In 2015–16, 142 students received support. Research assistantships, career-related internships or fieldwork, scholarships/grants, unspecified assistantships, and resident hall director and student payroll positions available. Support available to part-time students. Financial award application deadline: 3/1; financial award applicants required to submit FAFSA. In 2015, 341 master's awarded. *Degree program information:* Part-time and evening/weekend programs available. Part-time, evening/weekend, 100% online, blended/hybrid learning. *Application deadline:* For fall admission, 4/30 for international students; for spring admission, 9/30 for international students. Applications are processed on a rolling basis. *Application fee:* $45. Electronic applications accepted. *Application Contact:* Jeremy R. Goshorn, Assistant Dean of Graduate Admissions, 717-477-1231, Fax: 717-477-4016, E-mail: jrgoshorn@ship.edu. *Dean/Associate Provost,* Dr. Tracy Schoolcraft, 717-477-1148, Fax: 717-477-4038, E-mail: tascho@ship.edu.

College of Arts and Sciences Students: 118 full-time (65 women), 130 part-time (62 women); includes 37 minority (21 Black or African American, non-Hispanic/Latino; 1 American Indian or Alaska Native, non-Hispanic/Latino; 1 Asian, non-Hispanic/Latino; 7 Hispanic/Latino; 7 Two or more races, non-Hispanic/Latino), 35 international. Average age 28. 316 applicants, 64% accepted, 111 enrolled. *Faculty:* 71 full-time (24 women), 3 part-time/adjunct (2 women). *Financial support:* In 2015–16, 58 students received support, including 75 research assistantships (averaging $5,000 per year); career-related internships or fieldwork, scholarships/grants, unspecified assistantships, and resident hall director and student payroll positions also available. Support available to part-time students. Financial award application deadline: 3/1; financial award applicants required to submit FAFSA. In 2015, 103 master's awarded. *Degree program information:* Part-time and evening/weekend programs available. Part-time, evening/weekend. Offers applied history (MA); arts and sciences (MA, MPA, MS); biology (MS); communication studies (MS); computer science (MS); geoenvironmental studies (MS); organizational development and leadership (MS); psychological science (MS); public administration (MPA). *Application deadline:* For fall admission, 4/30 for international students; for spring admission, 9/30 for international students. Applications are processed on a rolling basis. *Application fee:* $45. Electronic applications accepted. *Application Contact:* Jeremy R. Goshorn, Assistant Dean of Graduate Admissions, 717-477-1231, Fax: 717-477-4016, E-mail: jrgoshorn@ship.edu. *Dean,* Dr. James H. Mike, 717-477-1151, Fax: 717-477-4026, E-mail: jhmike@ship.edu.

College of Education and Human Services Students: 204 full-time (162 women), 239 part-time (177 women); includes 59 minority (33 Black or African American, non-Hispanic/Latino; 3 Asian, non-Hispanic/Latino; 12 Hispanic/Latino; 1 Native Hawaiian or other Pacific Islander, non-Hispanic/Latino; 10 Two or more races, non-Hispanic/Latino), 12 international. Average age 29. 473 applicants, 57% accepted,

186 enrolled. *Faculty:* 48 full-time (24 women), 19 part-time/adjunct (13 women). *Financial support:* In 2015–16, 70 students received support. Research assistantships, career-related internships or fieldwork, scholarships/grants, unspecified assistantships, and resident hall director and student payroll positions available. Support available to part-time students. Financial award application deadline: 3/1; financial award applicants required to submit FAFSA. In 2015, 138 master's awarded. *Degree program information:* Part-time and evening/weekend programs available. Part-time, evening/weekend. Offers administration of justice (MS); clinical mental health (MS); college counseling (MS); college student personnel (MS); couple and family counseling (Certificate); curriculum and instruction (M Ed); education and human services (M Ed, MAT, MS, MSW, Ed D, Certificate); educational leadership (Ed D); reading (M Ed); school administration principal K-12 (M Ed); school counseling (M Ed); social work (MSW); special education (M Ed); STEM education (MAT). *Application deadline:* For fall admission, 4/30 for international students; for spring admission, 9/30 for international students. Applications are processed on a rolling basis. *Application fee:* $45. Electronic applications accepted. *Application Contact:* Jeremy R. Goshorn, Assistant Dean of Graduate Admissions, 717-477-1231, Fax: 717-477-4016, E-mail: jrgoshorn@ship.edu. *Dean of the College of Education and Human Services*, Dr. James R. Johnson, 717-477-1373, Fax: 717-477-4012, E-mail: jrjohnson@ship.edu.

John L. Grove College of Business Students: 41 full-time (15 women), 206 part-time (81 women); includes 25 minority (11 Black or African American, non-Hispanic/Latino; 9 Asian, non-Hispanic/Latino; 3 Hispanic/Latino; 2 Two or more races, non-Hispanic/Latino), 20 international. Average age 32. 233 applicants, 55% accepted, 82 enrolled. *Faculty:* 22 full-time (5 women), 5 part-time/adjunct (2 women). *Financial support:* In 2015–16, 14 students received support. Research assistantships, career-related internships or fieldwork, scholarships/grants, unspecified assistantships, and resident hall director and student payroll positions available. Support available to part-time students. Financial award application deadline: 3/1; financial award applicants required to submit FAFSA. In 2015, 100 master's awarded. *Degree program information:* Part-time and evening/weekend programs available. Part-time, evening/weekend, 100% online. Offers advanced studies in business (Certificate); advanced supply chain and logistics management (Certificate); business administration (MBA); management information systems (Certificate). *Application deadline:* For fall admission, 4/30 for international students; for spring admission, 9/30 for international students. Applications are processed on a rolling basis. *Application fee:* $45. Electronic applications accepted. *Application Contact:* Jeremy R. Goshorn, Associate Dean of Graduate Admissions, 717-477-1231, Fax: 717-477-4016, E-mail: jrgoshorn@ship.edu. *Dean of the College of Business*, Dr. John G. Kooti, 717-477-1435, Fax: 717-477-4003, E-mail: jgkooti@ship.edu.

SHORTER UNIVERSITY, Rome, GA 30165

General Information Independent-religious, coed, comprehensive institution. *Enrollment:* 1,472 graduate, professional, and undergraduate students; 44 full-time matriculated graduate/professional students (26 women), 61 part-time matriculated graduate/professional students (45 women). *Enrollment by degree level:* 105 master's. *Graduate faculty:* 9 full-time (3 women), 25 part-time/adjunct (9 women). *Graduate housing:* Room and/or apartments available on a first-come, first-served basis to single students; on-campus housing not available to married students. Housing application deadline: 3/30. *Student services:* Career counseling. *Library:* Livingston Library. *Collection:* Books: 124,378 (physical), 321,000 (digital/electronic); Databases: 186. Students can reserve study rooms.

Computer facilities: 100 computers available on campus for general student use. A campuswide network can be accessed from student residence rooms. Online class registration is available.
Website: http://www.shorter.edu/

General Application Contact: Patrick McElhaney, Director of Admissions, 800-868-6980, E-mail: pmcelhaney@shorter.edu.

GRADUATE UNITS

Professional Studies Students: 44 full-time (26 women), 61 part-time (45 women); includes 62 minority (57 Black or African American, non-Hispanic/Latino; 2 Hispanic/Latino; 3 Two or more races, non-Hispanic/Latino), 7 international. Average age 39. *Faculty:* 9 full-time (3 women), 25 part-time/adjunct (9 women). *Financial support:* Institutionally sponsored loans and scholarships/grants available. Financial award applicants required to submit FAFSA. In 2015, 177 master's awarded. *Degree program information:* Evening/weekend programs available. Evening/weekend. Offers accountancy (MAC); business administration (MBA); management (MM). *Application deadline:* Applications are processed on a rolling basis. *Application fee:* $50. Electronic applications accepted. *Application Contact:* Irene Barassa, Admissions Specialist, 678-260-3531, E-mail: ibarassa@shorter.edu. *Dean of Students*, Jacqueline Avant, 678-260-3538, E-mail: javant@shorter.edu.

SH'OR YOSHUV RABBINICAL COLLEGE, Lawrence, NY 11559-1714

General Information Independent-religious, men only, comprehensive institution.

GRADUATE UNITS

Graduate Programs

SIENA HEIGHTS UNIVERSITY, Adrian, MI 49221-1796

General Information Independent-religious, coed, comprehensive institution. *Graduate housing:* Rooms and/or apartments available on a first-come, first-served basis to single and married students. Housing application deadline: 5/1.

GRADUATE UNITS

Graduate College ***Degree program information:*** Part-time and evening/weekend programs available. Part-time, evening/weekend. Offers clinical mental health counseling (MA); educational leadership (Specialist); leadership (MA); teacher education (MA). Electronic applications accepted.

SIERRA NEVADA COLLEGE, Incline Village, NV 89451

General Information Independent, coed, comprehensive institution. *Graduate housing:* On-campus housing not available.

GRADUATE UNITS

Teacher Education Program ***Degree program information:*** Part-time and evening/weekend programs available. Part-time, evening/weekend, online learning. Offers advanced teaching and leadership (M Ed); elementary education (MAT); secondary education (MAT). Electronic applications accepted.

SILICON VALLEY UNIVERSITY, San Jose, CA 95131

General Information Proprietary, coed, comprehensive institution.

GRADUATE UNITS

Graduate Programs

SILVER LAKE COLLEGE OF THE HOLY FAMILY, Manitowoc, WI 54220-9319

General Information Independent-religious, coed, comprehensive institution. *Graduate housing:* Room and/or apartments guaranteed to single students; on-campus housing not available to married students. Housing application deadline: 6/1.

GRADUATE UNITS

Division of Graduate Studies ***Degree program information:*** Part-time and evening/weekend programs available. Part-time, evening/weekend, online learning. Offers administrative leadership (MA Ed); management and organizational development (MS); music education-Kodaly emphasis (MM); special education (MASE); teacher leadership (MA Ed). Electronic applications accepted.

SIMMONS COLLEGE, Boston, MA 02115

General Information Independent, Undergraduate: women only; graduate: coed, university. CGS member. *Enrollment:* 5,660 graduate, professional, and undergraduate students; 1,288 full-time matriculated graduate/professional students (1,149 women), 2,491 part-time matriculated graduate/professional students (2,160 women). *Enrollment by degree level:* 3,426 master's, 211 doctoral, 142 other advanced degrees. *Graduate faculty:* 116 full-time (87 women), 330 part-time/adjunct (278 women). *Graduate housing:* Room and/or apartments available on a first-come, first-served basis to single students; on-campus housing not available to married students. *Student services:* Campus employment opportunities, campus safety program, career counseling, exercise/wellness program, free psychological counseling, grant writing training, international student services, low-cost health insurance, multicultural affairs office, services for students with disabilities, writing training. *Library:* Beatley Library. *Collection:* Books: 222,898 (physical); Databases: 94. Weekly public service hours: 105; students can reserve study rooms. *Research affiliation:* Carnegie Corporation of New York (gender equality in higher education in Sub-Saharan African universities), Harvard Medical School (women in academic medicine), Institute for Quantitative Social Science, Harvard University (usability), Boston Children's Hospital (scholarly communication), University College London (cultural heritage and informatics), Oxfam America (gender mainstreaming).

Computer facilities: Computer purchase and lease plans are available. 350 computers available on campus for general student use. A campuswide network can be accessed from student residence rooms and from off campus. Online class registration is available.
Website: http://www.simmons.edu/

General Application Contact: Kristen Haack, Assistant Vice President, Enrollment Management and Graduate Admission, 617-521-2917, Fax: 617-521-3058, E-mail: kristen.haack@simmons.edu.

GRADUATE UNITS

College of Arts and Sciences Students: 5 full-time (all women), 43 part-time (36 women); includes 8 minority (4 Black or African American, non-Hispanic/Latino; 2 Hispanic/Latino; 2 Two or more races, non-Hispanic/Latino), 1 international. Average age 27. 50 applicants, 84% accepted, 19 enrolled. *Faculty:* 20 full-time (13 women), 1 part-time/adjunct (0 women). *Financial support:* In 2015–16, 8 teaching assistantships with partial tuition reimbursements (averaging $4,000 per year) were awarded; scholarships/grants also available. Financial award applicants required to submit FAFSA. In 2015, 22 master's, 1 other advanced degree awarded. *Degree program information:* Part-time programs available. Part-time. Offers behavior analysis (MS, PhD, Ed S); elementary, middle or high school teacher (MAT); general and special education (MAT); public policy (MPP); special education (MS Ed, Ed S); teaching English as a second language (MA, CAGS). *Application deadline:* For fall admission, 8/1 for domestic and international students; for spring admission, 12/15 for domestic and international students; for summer admission, 5/1 for domestic and international students. Applications are processed on a rolling basis. *Application fee:* $35. Electronic applications accepted. *Application Contact:* Patricia Flaherty, Director, Graduate Studies Admission, 617-521-3902, Fax: 617-521-3058, E-mail: gsa@simmons.edu. *Dean*, Dr. Renee White, 617-521-2079.

School of Library and Information Science Students: 312 full-time (268 women), 509 part-time (400 women); includes 111 minority (22 Black or African American, non-Hispanic/Latino; 14 Asian, non-Hispanic/Latino; 43 Hispanic/Latino; 1 Native Hawaiian or other Pacific Islander, non-Hispanic/Latino; 31 Two or more races, non-Hispanic/Latino), 19 international. Average age 30. 536 applicants, 90% accepted, 274 enrolled. *Faculty:* 24 full-time (19 women), 25 part-time/adjunct (17 women). *Financial support:* In 2015–16, 12 research assistantships (averaging $4,000 per year) were awarded; scholarships/grants, tuition waivers, and unspecified assistantships also available. Financial award application deadline: 2/1; financial award applicants required to submit FAFSA. In 2015, 281 master's, 3 doctorates, 14 other advanced degrees awarded. *Degree program information:* Part-time and evening/weekend programs available. Part-time, evening/weekend, 100% online, blended/hybrid learning. Offers children's literature (MA); library and information science (MS, PhD, Certificate); writing for children (MFA). *Application deadline:* For fall admission, 3/1 for domestic and international students; for spring admission, 9/1 for domestic and international students; for summer admission, 2/1 for domestic and international students. Applications are processed on a rolling basis. *Application fee:* $65. Electronic applications accepted. *Application Contact:* Sarah Petrakos, Assistant Dean for Admission and Recruitment, 617-521-2868, Fax: 617-521-3192, E-mail: gslisadm@simmons.edu. *Dean*, Dr. Eileen G. Abels, 617-521-2869.

School of Management Students: 66 full-time (59 women), 144 part-time (133 women); includes 55 minority (26 Black or African American, non-Hispanic/Latino; 11 Asian, non-Hispanic/Latino; 16 Hispanic/Latino; 2 Two or more races, non-Hispanic/Latino), 18 international. Average age 32. 105 applicants, 88% accepted, 49 enrolled. *Faculty:* 17 full-time (12 women), 9 part-time/adjunct (8 women). *Financial support:* Scholarships/grants and unspecified assistantships available. Financial award applicants required to submit FAFSA. In 2015, 86 master's awarded. *Degree program information:* Part-time and evening/weekend programs available. Part-time, evening/weekend. Offers business administration (MBA); health care (MBA); management (MS). *Application deadline:* Applications are processed on a rolling basis. *Application fee:* $75. Electronic applications accepted. *Application Contact:* Melissa Terrio, Director of Graduate Admissions, 617-521-3840, Fax: 617-521-3880, E-mail: somadm@simmons.edu. *Dean*, Cathy Minehan, 617-521-2846.

School of Nursing and Health Sciences Students: 333 full-time (305 women), 889 part-time (813 women); includes 250 minority (88 Black or African American, non-Hispanic/Latino; 3 American Indian or Alaska Native, non-Hispanic/Latino; 65 Asian, non-Hispanic/Latino; 67 Hispanic/Latino; 2 Native Hawaiian or other Pacific Islander, non-Hispanic/Latino; 25 Two or more races, non-Hispanic/Latino), 9 international. Average age 33. 846 applicants, 66% accepted, 441 enrolled. *Faculty:* 21 full-time (17 women), 171 part-time/adjunct (157 women). *Financial support:* In 2015–16, 12 research assistantships (averaging $6,000 per year) were awarded; scholarships/grants and unspecified assistantships also available. In 2015, 70 master's, 45 doctorates awarded. *Degree program information:* Part-time programs available. Part-time, blended/hybrid learning. Offers didactic dietetics (Certificate); dietetic internship (Certificate); health education profession (PhD); health professions education (CAGS); nursing (MS); nursing practice (DNP); nutrition and health promotion (MS); physical therapy (DPT); sports nutrition (Certificate). *Application deadline:* For fall admission, 6/1 for international students. *Application fee:* $50. Electronic applications accepted. *Application Contact:* Brett DiMarzo, Director of Graduate Admission, 617-521-2651, Fax: 617-521-3137, E-mail: brett.dimarzo@simmons.edu. *Dean*, Dr. Judy Beal, 617-521-2139.

School of Social Work Students: 572 full-time (512 women), 906 part-time (778 women); includes 310 minority (143 Black or African American, non-Hispanic/Latino; 3 American Indian or Alaska Native, non-Hispanic/Latino; 44 Asian, non-Hispanic/Latino; 93 Hispanic/Latino; 2 Native Hawaiian or other Pacific Islander, non-Hispanic/Latino; 25 Two or more races, non-Hispanic/Latino), 22 international. Average age 30. 958 applicants, 81% accepted, 490 enrolled. *Faculty:* 34 full-time (26 women), 124 part-time/adjunct (96 women). *Financial support:* In 2015–16, 11 research assistantships (averaging $4,000 per year), 6 teaching assistantships (averaging $4,000 per year) were awarded; scholarships/grants also available. In 2015, 159 master's, 2 doctorates awarded. *Degree program information:* Part-time programs available. Part-time, 100% online. Offers social work (MSW, PhD). *Application deadline:* Applications are processed on a rolling basis. *Application fee:* $45. Electronic applications accepted. *Application Contact:* Carlos D. Frontado, Director of Admissions, 617-521-3920, Fax: 617-521-3980, E-mail: ssw@simmons.edu. *Dean*, Dr. Cheryl Parks, 617-521-3293, E-mail: cheryl.parks@simmons.edu.

SIMON FRASER UNIVERSITY, Burnaby, BC V5A 1S6, Canada

General Information Province-supported, coed, university. CGS member. *Graduate housing:* Rooms and/or apartments available on a first-come, first-served basis to single and married students. Housing application deadline: 12/1. *Research affiliation:* BC Cancer Agency (health sciences, biomedical sciences, physiology, kinesiology), TRIUMF (physics), Ballard Power Systems (mechatronics), Bamfield Marine Research Station (marine biology, ecology, archaeology).

GRADUATE UNITS

Office of Graduate Studies ***Degree program information:*** Part-time and evening/weekend programs available. Part-time, evening/weekend, online learning. Electronic applications accepted.

Faculty of Applied Sciences Offers applied sciences (M Eng, M Sc, MA Sc, PhD, Graduate Certificate); computing science (M Sc, PhD); engineering science (M Eng, MA Sc, PhD); mechatronic systems engineering (MA Sc, PhD). Electronic applications accepted.

Faculty of Arts and Social Sciences Degree program information: Part-time and evening/weekend programs available. Part-time, evening/weekend. Offers anthropology (MA, PhD); applied legal studies (MA); arts and social sciences (M Pub, M Sc, M Urb, MA, MALS, MPP, PhD, Graduate Certificate, Graduate Diploma); criminology (MA, PhD); economics (MA, PhD); English (MA, PhD); French (MA); gender, sexuality and women's studies (MA, PhD); gerontology (MA, PhD); history (MA, PhD); humanities (MA); international studies (MA); Latin American studies (MA, Graduate Certificate); liberal studies (MALS); linguistics (MA, PhD); philosophy (MA, PhD); political science (MA, PhD); psychology (MA, PhD); public policy (MPP); publishing (M Pub); sociology (MA, PhD); teachers of English (MA); urban studies (M Urb, Graduate Diploma). Electronic applications accepted.

Faculty of Business Administration Online learning. Offers business administration (EMBA, PhD, Graduate Diploma); finance (M Sc); management of technology (MBA); management of technology/biotechnology (MBA).

Faculty of Education Offers arts education (M Ed, MA, Ed D, PhD); counseling psychology (M Ed, MA); curriculum and instruction (M Ed); curriculum and instruction foundations (M Ed, MA); curriculum theory and implementation (PhD); education (M Ed, M Sc, MA, Ed D, PhD, Graduate Diploma); educational leadership (M Ed, MA, Ed D); educational practice (M Ed); educational psychology (M Ed, MA, PhD); educational technology and learning design (M Ed, MA, PhD); languages, cultures, and literacies (PhD); mathematics education (PhD); philosophy of education (PhD); secondary mathematics education (M Ed, M Sc); teaching English as a second/foreign language (M Ed). Electronic applications accepted.

Faculty of Environment Offers archaeology (MA, PhD); environment (M Sc, MA, MRM, PhD, Graduate Diploma); geography (M Sc, MA, PhD); quantitative methods in fisheries management (Graduate Diploma); resource and environmental management (MRM, PhD); resource and environmental planning (MRM).

Faculty of Health Sciences Offers global health (Graduate Diploma); health sciences (M Sc, PhD); public health (MPH). Electronic applications accepted.

Faculty of Science Offers actuarial science (M Sc); applied and computational mathematics (M Sc, PhD); bioinformatics (Graduate Diploma); biological sciences (M Sc, PhD); biomedical physiology and kinesiology (M Sc, PhD); chemistry (M Sc, PhD); earth sciences (M Sc, PhD); environmental toxicology (MET); mathematics (M Sc, PhD); molecular biology and biochemistry (M Sc, PhD); operations research (M Sc, PhD); pest management (MPM); physics (M Sc, PhD); science (M Sc, MET, MPM, PhD, Graduate Diploma); statistics (M Sc, PhD). Electronic applications accepted.

School for the Contemporary Arts Offers contemporary arts (MA, MFA). Electronic applications accepted.

School of Communication Offers communication (MA, PhD). MA/MA program in global communication offered jointly with the Communication University of China. Electronic applications accepted.

School of Interactive Arts and Technology Offers interactive arts and technology (M Sc, MA, PhD). Electronic applications accepted.

SIMPSON COLLEGE, Indianola, IA 50125-1297

General Information Independent-religious, coed, comprehensive institution.

GRADUATE UNITS

Department of Education Offers secondary education (MAT).

Department of Social Sciences ***Degree program information:*** Evening/weekend programs available. Evening/weekend. Offers criminal justice (MACJ).

SIMPSON UNIVERSITY, Redding, CA 96003-8606

General Information Independent-religious, coed, comprehensive institution. *Enrollment:* 1,162 graduate, professional, and undergraduate students; 84 full-time matriculated graduate/professional students (55 women), 115 part-time matriculated graduate/professional students (74 women). *Enrollment by degree level:* 112 master's, 87 other advanced degrees. *Graduate faculty:* 42 part-time/adjunct (14 women). Tuition and fees vary according to program. *Graduate housing:* On-campus housing not available. *Student services:* Campus employment opportunities, campus safety program, career counseling, international student services, services for students with disabilities, teacher training. *Library:* Start-Kilgour Memorial Library. Students can reserve study rooms.

Computer facilities: 50 computers available on campus for general student use. A campuswide network can be accessed from student residence rooms. Online class registration is available.
Website: http://www.simpsonu.edu/

General Application Contact: Stacy Burgess, Director of Admissions for Adult and Graduate Studies, 530-226-4961, Fax: 530-226-4861, E-mail: sburgess@simpsonu.edu.

GRADUATE UNITS

A.W. Tozer Theological Seminary Students: 6 full-time (2 women), 27 part-time (9 women); includes 5 minority (1 Black or African American, non-Hispanic/Latino; 2 Asian, non-Hispanic/Latino; 1 Hispanic/Latino; 1 Two or more races, non-Hispanic/Latino), 2 international. Average age 37. *Faculty:* 21 part-time/adjunct (2 women). *Financial support:* Scholarships/grants available. Support available to part-time students. Financial award application deadline: 7/1; financial award applicants required to submit FAFSA. In 2015, 12 master's awarded. *Degree program information:* Part-time and evening/weekend programs available. Part-time, evening/weekend, 100% online, blended/hybrid learning. Offers ministry leadership (MA). *Application deadline:* For fall admission, 8/1 for domestic and international students; for spring admission, 12/1 for domestic and international students; for summer admission, 4/1 for domestic and international students. Applications are processed on a rolling basis. *Application fee:* $35. Electronic applications accepted. *Application Contact:* Stacy Burgess, Director of Admissions for Adult and Graduate Studies, 530-226-4961, Fax: 530-226-4861, E-mail: admissions@simpsonu.edu. *Dean*, Dr. Patrick Blewett, 530-226-4144, Fax: 530-226-4871, E-mail: pblewett@simpsonu.edu.

School of Education Students: 39 full-time (25 women), 81 part-time (59 women); includes 19 minority (2 Black or African American, non-Hispanic/Latino; 1 American Indian or Alaska Native, non-Hispanic/Latino; 2 Asian, non-Hispanic/Latino; 9 Hispanic/Latino; 5 Two or more races, non-Hispanic/Latino), 2 international. Average age 32. *Faculty:* 4 full-time (1 woman), 39 part-time/adjunct (24 women). *Financial support:* Scholarships/grants available. Financial award applicants required to submit FAFSA. In 2015, 19 master's awarded. *Degree program information:* Part-time and evening/weekend programs available. Part-time, evening/weekend. Offers education (MA); education and preliminary administrative services credential (MA); education and preliminary teaching credential (MA); teaching (MA). *Application deadline:* Applications are processed on a rolling basis. *Application fee:* $35. Electronic applications accepted. *Application Contact:* Stacy Burgess, Director of Admissions for Adult and Graduate Studies, 530-226-4961, E-mail: sburgess@simpsonu.edu. *Dean of Education*, Dr. Glee Brooks, 530-226-4188, Fax: 530-226-4872, E-mail: gbrooks@simpsonu.edu.

School of Graduate Studies Students: 39 full-time (28 women), 7 part-time (6 women); includes 15 minority (1 Black or African American, non-Hispanic/Latino; 3 Asian, non-Hispanic/Latino; 8 Hispanic/Latino; 3 Two or more races, non-Hispanic/Latino), 1 international. Average age 35. *Faculty:* 21 part-time/adjunct (12 women). *Financial support:* Applicants required to submit FAFSA. In 2015, 21 master's awarded. *Degree program information:* Evening/weekend programs available. Evening/weekend, blended/hybrid learning. Offers counseling psychology (MA); organizational leadership (MA). *Application deadline:* For fall admission, 3/1 for domestic and international students; for spring admission, 11/1 for domestic and international students. *Application fee:* $35. Electronic applications accepted. *Application Contact:* Stacy Burgess, Director of Admissions for Adult and Graduate Studies, 530-226-4961, E-mail: sburgess@simpsonu.edu. *Dean*, Adeline Jackson, 530-226-4788, E-mail: ajackson@simpsonu.edu.

SINTE GLESKA UNIVERSITY, Mission, SD 57555

General Information Independent, coed, comprehensive institution. *Graduate housing:* Rooms and/or apartments available on a first-come, first-served basis to single and married students.

GRADUATE UNITS

Graduate Education Program ***Degree program information:*** Part-time and evening/weekend programs available. Part-time, evening/weekend. Offers elementary education (M Ed).

SIOUX FALLS SEMINARY, Sioux Falls, SD 57105-1599

General Information Independent-religious, coed, graduate-only institution. *Graduate housing:* On-campus housing not available.

GRADUATE UNITS

Graduate and Professional Programs ***Degree program information:*** Part-time programs available. Part-time. Offers Bible and theology (MA); Christian leadership (MA); counseling (MA); marriage and family therapy (MA, Certificate); ministry (D Min); pastoral care and counseling (M Div); theological studies (Certificate).

SIT GRADUATE INSTITUTE, Brattleboro, VT 05302-0676

General Information Independent, coed, graduate-only institution. *Graduate housing:* Rooms and/or apartments available on a first-come, first-served basis to single and married students. Housing application deadline: 7/1.

GRADUATE UNITS

Graduate Programs ***Degree program information:*** Part-time programs available. Part-time, online learning. Offers conflict transformation (MA); intercultural service, leadership, and management (MA); international education (MA); sustainable development (MA); TESOL (MAT). Electronic applications accepted.

SITTING BULL COLLEGE, Fort Yates, ND 58538-9701

General Information Independent, coed, comprehensive institution.

GRADUATE UNITS

Program in Environmental Science Offers environmental science (MS).

SLIPPERY ROCK UNIVERSITY OF PENNSYLVANIA, Slippery Rock, PA 16057-1383

General Information State-supported, coed, comprehensive institution. *Enrollment:* 8,628 graduate, professional, and undergraduate students; 368 full-time matriculated graduate/professional students (264 women), 579 part-time matriculated graduate/professional students (437 women). *Enrollment by degree level:* 781 master's, 166 doctoral. *Graduate faculty:* 64 full-time (39 women), 2 part-time/adjunct (1 woman). Tuition, state resident: full-time $8460; part-time $470 per credit. Tuition, nonresident: full-time $12,690; part-time $705 per credit. *Required fees:* $2878; $160 per credit. Tuition and fees vary according to degree level and program. *Graduate housing:* Room and/or apartments available on a first-come, first-served basis to single students; on-campus housing not available to married students. Typical cost: $6620 per year ($10,022 including board). Room and board charges vary according to board plan and housing facility selected. *Student services:* Campus employment opportunities, campus safety program, career counseling, child daycare facilities, exercise/wellness program, free psychological counseling, international student services, multicultural affairs office, services for students with disabilities, writing training. *Library:* Bailey Library. *Collection:* Books: 322,966 (physical), 252,327 (digital/electronic); Serial titles: 243 (physical), 84,124 (digital/electronic); Databases: 126. Weekly public service hours: 87; students can reserve study rooms.

Computer facilities: Computer purchase and lease plans are available. 1,339 computers available on campus for general student use. A campuswide network can be accessed from student residence rooms and from off campus. Online class registration is available.
Website: http://www.sru.edu/

General Application Contact: Brandi Weber-Mortimer, Director of Graduate Admissions, 724-738-2051, Fax: 724-738-2146, E-mail: graduate.admissions@sru.edu.

GRADUATE UNITS

Graduate Studies (Recruitment) Students: 368 full-time (264 women), 579 part-time (437 women); includes 56 minority (26 Black or African American, non-Hispanic/Latino; 2 American Indian or Alaska Native, non-Hispanic/Latino; 6 Asian, non-Hispanic/Latino; 13 Hispanic/Latino; 2 Native Hawaiian or other Pacific Islander, non-Hispanic/Latino; 7 Two or more races, non-Hispanic/Latino), 5 international. Average age 28. 1,157 applicants, 61% accepted, 391 enrolled. *Faculty:* 64 full-time (39 women), 2 part-time/adjunct (1 woman). *Financial support:* In 2015–16, 167 students received support. Career-related internships or fieldwork, Federal Work-Study, institutionally sponsored loans, scholarships/grants, tuition waivers (partial), and unspecified assistantships available. Support available to part-time students. Financial award application deadline: 5/1; financial award applicants required to submit FAFSA. In 2015, 291 master's, 48 doctorates awarded. *Degree program information:* Part-time and evening/weekend programs available. Part-time, evening/weekend, online only, 100% online. *Application deadline:* For fall admission, 3/1 priority date for domestic students, 5/1 priority date for international students; for spring admission, 10/1 priority date for domestic students, 9/1 priority date for international students. Applications are processed on a rolling basis. *Application fee:* $25 ($30 for international students). Electronic applications accepted. *Director of Graduate Admissions*, Brandi Weber-Mortimer, 724-738-4340, Fax: 724-738-2146, E-mail: graduate.admissions@sru.edu.

College of Business Students: 18 full-time (11 women), 8 part-time (3 women); includes 3 minority (1 Black or African American, non-Hispanic/Latino; 1 American Indian or Alaska Native, non-Hispanic/Latino; 1 Asian, non-Hispanic/Latino), 1 international. Average age 28. 94 applicants, 27% accepted, 16 enrolled. *Faculty:* 6 full-time (4 women), 1 part-time/adjunct (0 women). *Financial support:* In 2015–16, 6 students received support. Career-related internships or fieldwork, Federal Work-Study, institutionally sponsored loans, scholarships/grants, tuition waivers (partial), and unspecified assistantships available. Support available to part-time students. Financial award application deadline: 5/1; financial award applicants required to submit FAFSA. In 2015, 14 master's awarded. *Degree program information:* Part-time and evening/weekend programs available. Part-time, evening/weekend. Offers accounting/finance (MBA); business (MBA); general (MBA); marketing/management (MBA). *Application deadline:* For fall admission, 3/1 priority date for domestic students, 5/1 priority date for international students; for spring admission, 10/1 priority date for domestic students, 9/1 priority date for international students. Applications are processed on a rolling basis. *Application fee:* $25 ($30 for international students). Electronic applications accepted. *Application Contact:* Brandi Weber-Mortimer, Director of Graduate Admissions, 724-738-2051, Fax: 724-738-2146, E-mail: graduate.admissions@sru.edu. *Dean*, Dr. Lawrence Shao, 724-738-2687, Fax: 724-738-4767, E-mail: lawrence.shao@sru.edu.

College of Education Students: 188 full-time (142 women), 409 part-time (333 women); includes 26 minority (13 Black or African American, non-Hispanic/Latino; 1 Asian, non-Hispanic/Latino; 7 Hispanic/Latino; 1 Native Hawaiian or other Pacific Islander, non-Hispanic/Latino; 4 Two or more races, non-Hispanic/Latino), 3 international. Average age 29. 540 applicants, 80% accepted, 264 enrolled. *Faculty:* 33 full-time (19 women). *Financial support:* In 2015–16, 87 students received support. Career-related internships or fieldwork, Federal Work-Study, institutionally sponsored loans, scholarships/grants, tuition waivers (partial), and unspecified assistantships available. Support available to part-time students. Financial award application deadline: 5/1; financial award applicants required to submit FAFSA. In 2015, 210 master's awarded. *Degree program information:* Part-time and evening/weekend programs available. Part-time, evening/weekend, 100% online. Offers adapted physical activity (MS); autism (M Ed); clinical mental health counseling (MA); education (M Ed, MA, MS, Ed D); educational leadership (M Ed); elementary education (M Ed); master teacher (M Ed); secondary education (M Ed); special education (Ed D); student affairs (MA); student affairs in higher education (MA); supervision (M Ed); technology for online instruction (M Ed). *Application deadline:* For fall admission, 3/1 priority date for domestic students, 5/1 priority date for international students; for spring admission, 10/1 priority date for domestic students, 9/1 priority date for international students. Applications are processed on a rolling basis. *Application fee:* $25 ($30 for international students). Electronic applications accepted. *Application Contact:* Brandi Weber-Mortimer, Director of Graduate Admissions, 724-738-2051, Fax: 724-738-2146, E-mail: graduate.admissions@sru.edu. *Dean*, Dr. A. Keith Dils, 724-738-2007, Fax: 724-738-2880, E-mail: keith.dils@sru.edu.

College of Health, Environment, and Science Students: 150 full-time (102 women), 108 part-time (69 women); includes 17 minority (7 Black or African American, non-Hispanic/Latino; 1 American Indian or Alaska Native, non-Hispanic/Latino; 3 Asian, non-Hispanic/Latino; 3 Hispanic/Latino; 1 Native Hawaiian or other Pacific Islander, non-Hispanic/Latino; 2 Two or more races, non-Hispanic/Latino), 1 international. Average age 27. 427 applicants, 42% accepted, 258 enrolled. *Faculty:* 14 full-time (10 women), 1 (woman) part-time/adjunct. *Financial support:* In 2015–16, 66 students received support. Career-related internships or fieldwork, Federal Work-Study, institutionally sponsored loans, scholarships/grants, tuition waivers (partial), and unspecified assistantships available. Support available to part-time students. Financial award application deadline: 5/1; financial award applicants required to submit FAFSA. In 2015, 48 master's, 48 doctorates awarded. *Degree program information:* Part-time and evening/weekend programs available. Part-time, evening/weekend, 100% online. Offers environmental education (M Ed); health, environment, and science (M Ed, MS, DPT); park and resource management (MS); physical therapy (DPT). *Application deadline:* For fall admission, 3/1 priority date for domestic students, 5/1 priority date for international students; for spring admission, 10/1 priority date for domestic students, 9/1 priority date for international students. Applications are processed on a rolling basis. *Application fee:* $25 ($30 for international students). Electronic applications accepted. *Application Contact:* Brandi Weber-Mortimer, Director of Graduate Admissions, 724-738-2051, Fax: 724-738-2146, E-mail: graduate.admissions@sru.edu. *Interim Dean*, Dr. Jerry Chmielewski, 724-738-2489, Fax: 724-738-2881, E-mail: jerry.chmielewski@sru.edu.

College of Liberal Arts Students: 12 full-time (9 women), 54 part-time (32 women); includes 10 minority (5 Black or African American, non-Hispanic/Latino; 1 Asian, non-Hispanic/Latino; 3 Hispanic/Latino; 1 Two or more races, non-Hispanic/Latino). Average age 31. 79 applicants, 68% accepted, 35 enrolled. *Faculty:* 11 full-time (6 women). *Financial support:* In 2015–16, 8 students received support. Career-related internships or fieldwork, Federal Work-Study, institutionally sponsored loans, scholarships/grants, tuition waivers (partial), and unspecified assistantships available. Support available to part-time students. Financial award application deadline: 5/1; financial award applicants required to submit FAFSA. In 2015, 19 master's awarded. *Degree program information:* Part-time and evening/weekend programs available. Part-time, evening/weekend, online only, 100% online. Offers criminal justice (MA); English (MA); history (MA); liberal arts (MA). *Application deadline:* For fall admission, 3/1 priority date for domestic students, 5/1 priority date for international students; for spring admission, 10/1 priority date for domestic students, 9/1 priority date for international students. Applications are processed on a rolling basis. *Application fee:* $25 ($30 for international students). Electronic applications accepted. *Application Contact:* Brandi Weber-Mortimer, Director of Graduate Admissions, 724-738-2051, Fax: 724-738-2146, E-mail: graduate.admissions@sru.edu. *Dean*, Dr. Eva Tsuquiashi-Daddesio, 724-738-2400, Fax: 724-738-2146, E-mail: eva.tsuquiashi@sru.edu.

SMITH COLLEGE, Northampton, MA 01063

General Information Independent, Undergraduate: women only; graduate: coed, comprehensive institution. *Enrollment:* 2,874 graduate, professional, and undergraduate students; 309 full-time matriculated graduate/professional students (262 women), 87 part-time matriculated graduate/professional students (70 women). *Enrollment by degree level:* 310 master's, 64 doctoral, 22 other advanced degrees. *Graduate faculty:* 270 full-time (149 women), 24 part-time/adjunct (13 women). *Tuition, area resident:* Full-time $34,560; part-time $1440 per credit. Tuition and fees vary according to course load and program. *Graduate housing:* Room and/or apartments available on a first-come, first-served basis to single students; on-campus housing not available to married students. Typical cost: $7740 per year ($15,470 including board). Housing application deadline: 5/1. *Student services:* Campus employment opportunities, campus safety program, career counseling, child daycare facilities, exercise/wellness program, international student services, low-cost health insurance, multicultural affairs office, services for students with disabilities, teacher training, writing training. *Library:* Neilson Library.

Computer facilities: Computer purchase and lease plans are available. A campuswide network can be accessed from student residence rooms and from off campus. Online class registration is available.
Website: http://www.smith.edu/

General Application Contact: Danielle Ramdath, Director of Graduate Programs, 413-585-3050, Fax: 413-585-3054, E-mail: dramdath@smith.edu.

GRADUATE UNITS

Graduate and Special Programs Students: 65 full-time (59 women), 15 part-time (14 women); includes 8 minority (2 Black or African American, non-Hispanic/Latino; 3 Asian, non-Hispanic/Latino; 3 Hispanic/Latino), 5 international. Average age 27. 156 applicants, 42% accepted, 52 enrolled. *Faculty:* 270 full-time (149 women), 24 part-time/adjunct (13 women). *Financial support:* In 2015–16, 78 students received support, including 7 fellowships with full tuition reimbursements available, 7 research assistantships with full tuition reimbursements available (averaging $13,710 per year), 19 teaching assistantships with full tuition reimbursements available (averaging $13,710 per year); scholarships/grants also available. Support available to part-time students. Financial award application deadline: 1/15; financial award applicants required to submit CSS PROFILE or FAFSA. In 2015, 41 master's, 8 other advanced degrees awarded. *Degree program information:* Part-time programs available. Part-time. Offers biological sciences (MAT, MS); dance (MFA); elementary education (MAT); exercise and sport studies (MS); middle school education (MAT); physics (MAT); secondary education (MAT); theatre (MFA); women in mathematics (Postbaccalaureate Certificate). *Application deadline:* For fall admission, 4/1 for domestic students, 1/15 for international students; for spring admission, 12/1 for domestic students. *Application fee:* $60. *Application Contact:* Ruth Morgan, Program Assistant, 413-585-3050, Fax: 413-585-3054, E-mail: gradstdy@smith.edu. *Director*, Danielle Ramdath, 413-585-3050, Fax: 413-585-3054, E-mail: dramdath@smith.edu.

School for Social Work Students: 234 full-time (197 women), 68 part-time (54 women); includes 80 minority (17 Black or African American, non-Hispanic/Latino; 2 American Indian or Alaska Native, non-Hispanic/Latino; 15 Asian, non-Hispanic/Latino; 30 Hispanic/Latino; 1 Native Hawaiian or other Pacific Islander, non-Hispanic/Latino; 15 Two or more races, non-Hispanic/Latino), 11 international. Average age 32. 441 applicants, 55% accepted, 113 enrolled. *Faculty:* 18 full-time (14 women), 103 part-time/adjunct (79 women). *Financial support:* In 2015–16, 235 students received support. Career-related internships or fieldwork and scholarships/grants available. Financial award application deadline: 3/1; financial award applicants required to submit FAFSA. In 2015, 122 master's, 8 doctorates awarded. Offers social work (MSW, PhD). *Application deadline:* For fall admission, 2/21 for domestic students, 2/1 for international students. Applications are processed on a rolling basis. *Application fee:* $60. *Application Contact:* Irene Rodriguez Martin, Associate Dean, Graduate Enrollment and Student Services, 413-585-7960, Fax: 413-585-7994, E-mail: imartin@smith.edu. *Dean/Professor*, Dr. Marianne Yoshioka, 413-585-7977, E-mail: myoshioka@smith.edu.

SOFIA UNIVERSITY, Palo Alto, CA 94303

General Information Independent, coed, graduate-only institution. *Graduate housing:* On-campus housing not available.

GRADUATE UNITS

Hybrid: Face-to-Face/Online Programs Online learning. Offers transpersonal psychology (MA, PhD). Electronic applications accepted.

Residential Programs ***Degree program information:*** Part-time and evening/weekend programs available. Part-time, evening/weekend. Offers clinical psychology (Psy D); computer science (MS); counseling psychology (MA); transpersonal psychology (MA, PhD). Electronic applications accepted.

SOKA UNIVERSITY OF AMERICA, Aliso Viejo, CA 92656

General Information Independent, coed, comprehensive institution. *Graduate housing:* Room and/or apartments available to single students; on-campus housing not available to married students.

GRADUATE UNITS

Graduate School of Education ***Degree program information:*** Evening/weekend programs available. Evening/weekend. Offers education (MA).

SONOMA STATE UNIVERSITY, Rohnert Park, CA 94928-3609

General Information State-supported, coed, comprehensive institution. *Graduate housing:* Room and/or apartments available on a first-come, first-served basis to single students; on-campus housing not available to married students. Housing application deadline: 1/1. *Research affiliation:* Kenwood Vineyards (science), Bimimetica Shantee CA (bioacoustics, metabolic flux modeling), Gallo Family Vineyards (science), Natural Industries, Inc. (Sudden Oak Death research), Clean Filtration Technologies (environmental microbiology fund).

GRADUATE UNITS

Department of English ***Degree program information:*** Part-time and evening/weekend programs available. Part-time, evening/weekend. Offers American literature (MA); creative writing (MA); English literature (MA); world literature (MA).

Institute of Interdisciplinary Studies/Special Major ***Degree program information:*** Part-time programs available. Part-time. Offers interdisciplinary studies (MA, MS).

School of Business and Economics ***Degree program information:*** Part-time and evening/weekend programs available. Part-time, evening/weekend. Offers business administration (MBA); executive business administration (MBA); wine business (MBA).

School of Education ***Degree program information:*** Part-time and evening/weekend programs available. Part-time, evening/weekend. Offers curriculum, teaching, and learning (MA); early childhood education (MA); education (Ed D); educational administration (MA); multiple subject (Credential); reading and literacy (MA); single subject (Credential); special education (MA, Credential).

School of Science and Technology ***Degree program information:*** Part-time programs available. Part-time. Offers adapted physical education (MA); biochemistry (MA); ecology (MS); environmental biology (MS); evolutionary biology (MS); family nurse practitioner (MSN); functional morphology (MS); interdisciplinary (MA); interdisciplinary pre-occupational therapy (MA); lifetime physical activity (MA); molecular and cell biology (MS); organismal biology (MS); physical education (MA); pre-physical therapy (MA); science and technology (MA, MS, MSN).

School of Social Sciences ***Degree program information:*** Part-time and evening/weekend programs available. Part-time, evening/weekend. Offers administration of nonprofit agencies (Certificate); counseling (MA); cultural resources management (MA); history (MA); licensed professional clinical counseling (MA); marriage, family, and child counseling (MA); public administration (MPA); pupil personnel services (MA); social sciences (MA, MPA, Certificate).

SOTHEBY'S INSTITUTE OF ART–LONDON, WC1B 3EE London, United Kingdom

General Information Private, coed, graduate-only institution. *Enrollment by degree level:* 181 master's. *Graduate faculty:* 43 full-time (27 women). *International tuition:* 28,800 British pounds full-time. *Tuition, area resident:* Full-time 24,900 British pounds. Tuition and fees vary according to class time, program and student level. *Student services:* Campus safety program, career counseling, international student services, writing training. *Library:* Sotheby's Institute of Art library plus 1 other. *Collection:* Books: 20,000 (physical). *Research affiliation:* University of Manchester.

Computer facilities: A campuswide network can be accessed. Online class registration is available.
Website: http://www.sothebysinstitute.com/london/index.html

General Application Contact: Melba Remice, Director, Global Admissions, 212-517-2834, E-mail: admissions@sothebysinstitute.com.

GRADUATE UNITS

Graduate Programs Students: 181 full-time (159 women). *Faculty:* 43 full-time (27 women). Offers art business (MA); contemporary art (MA); fine and decorative art and design (MA); modern and contemporary Asian art (MA). *Application Contact:* Melba Remice, Director, Global Admissions, 212-517-2834, E-mail: admissions@sothebysinstitute.com.

SOTHEBY'S INSTITUTE OF ART–NEW YORK, New York, NY 10021

General Information Proprietary, coed, graduate-only institution. *Enrollment by degree level:* 127 master's. *Graduate faculty:* 24 full-time (11 women). *Tuition, area resident:* Full-time $68,900. *Required fees:* $17,000. Tuition and fees vary according to program. *Graduate housing:* On-campus housing not available. *Student services:* Campus employment opportunities, campus safety program, career counseling, international student services, services for students with disabilities, writing training. *Library:* Sotheby's Institute of Art Library plus 1 other. *Collection:* Books: 10,000 (physical), 250 (digital/electronic).

Computer facilities: A campuswide network can be accessed. Online class registration is available.
Website: http://www.sothebysinstitute.com/newyork/index.html

General Application Contact: Melba Remice, Director of Global Admissions, 212-517-2834, E-mail: admissions@sothebysinstitute.com.

GRADUATE UNITS

Graduate Programs Students: 127 full-time (111 women). *Faculty:* 24 full-time (11 women). Offers art business (MA); contemporary art (MA); fine and decorative art and design (MA). *Application fee:* $100. Electronic applications accepted. *Application Contact:* Melba Remice, Director of Global Admissions, 212-517-2834, E-mail: admissions@sothebysinstitute.com.

SOUTH BAYLO UNIVERSITY, Anaheim, CA 92801-1701

General Information Independent, coed, graduate-only institution. *Graduate housing:* On-campus housing not available. *Research affiliation:* University of California Irvine College of Medicine (complimentary and alternative medicine), National Nutritional Foods Association (herbs and nutritional supplements), Henan College of Traditional Chinese Medicine (herbology and acupuncture), Kaiser Permanente (patient care: acupuncture and Oriental medicine), University of Illinois at Chicago (testing of herbal formulations).

GRADUATE UNITS

Program in Oriental Medicine and Acupuncture ***Degree program information:*** Evening/weekend programs available. Evening/weekend. Offers Oriental medicine and acupuncture (MS). Electronic applications accepted.

SOUTH CAROLINA STATE UNIVERSITY, Orangeburg, SC 29117-0001

General Information State-supported, coed, comprehensive institution. *Enrollment:* 3,054 graduate, professional, and undergraduate students; 199 full-time matriculated graduate/professional students (149 women), 201 part-time matriculated graduate/professional students (150 women). *Enrollment by degree level:* 314 master's, 55 doctoral, 31 other advanced degrees. *Graduate faculty:* 46 full-time (25 women), 15 part-time/adjunct (8 women). Tuition, state resident: full-time $8906; part-time $495 per credit hour. Tuition, nonresident: full-time $18,674; part-time $1037 per credit hour. *Required fees:* $2497; $66 per credit hour. *Graduate housing:* Room and/or apartments available on a first-come, first-served basis to single students; on-campus housing not available to married students. Typical cost: $8000 per year. *Student services:* Campus employment opportunities, career counseling, exercise/wellness program, free psychological counseling, international student services, low-cost health insurance, multicultural affairs office, services for students with disabilities, teacher training, writing training. *Library:* Miller F. Whittaker Library. *Collection:* Books: 313,029 (physical), 195,578 (digital/electronic); Serial titles: 46 (physical), 35 (digital/electronic); Databases: 114. Weekly public service hours: 85.

Computer facilities: 400 computers available on campus for general student use. A campuswide network can be accessed from student residence rooms and from off campus. Online class registration is available.
Website: http://www.scsu.edu/

General Application Contact: Dr. Frederick Evans, Dean, College of Graduate and Professional Studies, 803-536-7097, Fax: 803-536-8812, E-mail: fevans6@scsu.edu.

GRADUATE UNITS

College of Graduate and Professional Studies Students: 199 full-time (149 women), 201 part-time (150 women); includes 358 minority (354 Black or African American, non-Hispanic/Latino; 2 Asian, non-Hispanic/Latino; 2 Hispanic/Latino), 2 international. Average age 32. 173 applicants, 77% accepted, 108 enrolled. *Faculty:* 46 full-time (25 women), 15 part-time/adjunct (8 women). *Financial support:* Fellowships, career-related internships or fieldwork, Federal Work-Study, institutionally sponsored loans, scholarships/grants, and unspecified assistantships available. Financial award application deadline: 6/1. In 2015, 101 master's, 30 doctorates, 14 other advanced degrees awarded. *Degree program information:* Part-time and evening/weekend programs available. Part-time, evening/weekend. Offers agribusiness (MBA); counselor education (M Ed); early childhood education (MAT); education (M Ed); educational leadership and administration (Ed D, Ed S); elementary education (M Ed, MAT); English (MAT); entrepreneurship (MBA); general science/biology (MAT); individual and family development (MS); mathematics (MAT); nutritional sciences (MS); rehabilitation counseling (MA); secondary education (M Ed); special education (M Ed); speech pathology and audiology (MA); transportation (MS). *Application deadline:* For fall admission, 6/15 for domestic and international students; for spring admission, 11/1 for domestic and international students. Applications are processed on a rolling basis. *Application fee:* $25. Electronic applications accepted. *Application Contact:* Curtis Foskey, Coordinator of Graduate Admission, 803-536-8419, Fax: 803-536-8812, E-mail: cfoskey@scsu.edu. *Dean, College of Graduate and Professional Studies,* Dr. Frederick Evans, 803-536-7097, Fax: 803-536-8812, E-mail: fevans6@scsu.edu.

SOUTH COLLEGE, Knoxville, TN 37917

General Information Proprietary, coed, primarily women, comprehensive institution.

GRADUATE UNITS

Program in Physician Assistant Studies Offers physician assistant studies (MHS).

SOUTH DAKOTA SCHOOL OF MINES AND TECHNOLOGY, Rapid City, SD 57701-3995

General Information State-supported, coed, university. *Enrollment:* 2,843 graduate, professional, and undergraduate students; 208 full-time matriculated graduate/professional students (54 women), 119 part-time matriculated graduate/professional students (28 women). *Enrollment by degree level:* 224 master's, 94 doctoral, 9 other advanced degrees. *Graduate faculty:* 151 full-time (38 women), 27 part-time/adjunct (11 women). *Graduate housing:* Room and/or apartments available on a first-come, first-served basis to single students; on-campus housing not available to married students. *Student services:* Campus safety program, career counseling, exercise/wellness program, free psychological counseling, international student services, low-cost health insurance, multicultural affairs office, services for students with disabilities. *Library:* Devereaux Library plus 1 other. *Research affiliation:* Raven Industries (composite and thin films), Black Hills Power (NDA-Lightning (experimental and data collection)), CalxAqua (filtration media), RESPEC, Inc. (mining and waste storage), HFWebster (cold spray applications), Nanofiber Sperations (cutting edge separation media composed of functionalized nanofibers).

Computer facilities: Computer purchase and lease plans are available. 105 computers available on campus for general student use. A campuswide network can be accessed from student residence rooms and from off campus. Online class registration is available.
Website: http://www.sdsmt.edu/

General Application Contact: Dr. Douglas P. Wells, Dean of Graduate Education, 605-394-1763, Fax: 605-394-1767, E-mail: graduate_admissions@sdsmt.edu.

GRADUATE UNITS

Graduate Division ***Financial support:*** Fellowships, research assistantships with tuition reimbursements, teaching assistantships with tuition reimbursements, Federal Work-Study, and institutionally sponsored loans available. Support available to part-time students. Financial award application deadline: 5/15. *Degree program information:* Part-time programs available. Part-time. Offers atmospheric and environmental sciences (MS, PhD); biomedical engineering (MS, PhD); chemical and biological engineering (PhD); chemical engineering (MS); civil and environmental engineering (MS, PhD); computational sciences and robotics (MS); construction engineering management (MS); electrical engineering (MS); engineering management (MS); geology and geological engineering (MS, PhD); materials engineering and science (MS, PhD); mechanical engineering (MS, PhD); mining engineering (MS); nanoscience and nanoengineering (PhD); paleontology (MS); physics (MS, PhD). *Application deadline:* For fall admission, 7/15 priority date for domestic students, 4/1 for international students; for spring admission, 11/1 for domestic students, 9/1 for international students. Applications are processed on a rolling basis. *Application fee:* $35. Electronic applications accepted.

College of Engineering Financial support: Fellowships, research assistantships with partial tuition reimbursements, teaching assistantships with partial tuition reimbursements, Federal Work-Study, and institutionally sponsored loans available. Support available to part-time students. Financial award application deadline: 5/15. *Degree program information:* Part-time programs available. Part-time, online learning. Offers engineering (MS, PhD). *Application deadline:* For fall admission, 7/1 priority date for domestic students, 4/1 for international students; for spring admission, 11/1 for domestic students, 9/1 for international students. Applications are processed on a rolling basis. *Application fee:* $35. Electronic applications accepted.

College of Science and Letters Financial support: Fellowships, research assistantships with tuition reimbursements, and teaching assistantships with partial tuition reimbursements available. Financial award application deadline: 5/15. *Degree program information:* Part-time programs available. Part-time. Offers science and letters (MS, PhD). *Application deadline:* For fall admission, 7/5 priority date for domestic students, 4/1 for international students; for spring admission, 10/1 priority date for domestic students, 9/1 for international students. *Application fee:* $35.

SOUTH DAKOTA STATE UNIVERSITY, Brookings, SD 57007

General Information State-supported, coed, university. CGS member. *Graduate housing:* Rooms and/or apartments available to single and married students.

GRADUATE UNITS

Graduate School ***Degree program information:*** Part-time and evening/weekend programs available. Part-time, evening/weekend, online learning.

College of Agriculture and Biological Sciences Degree program information: Part-time programs available. Part-time. Offers agricultural and biosystems engineering (MS, PhD); agriculture and biological sciences (MS, PhD); agronomy (PhD); animal science (MS, PhD); animal sciences (MS, PhD); biological sciences (MS, PhD); economics (MS); plant science (MS); sociology (MS, PhD); wildlife and fisheries sciences (MS, PhD).

College of Arts and Science Degree program information: Part-time programs available. Part-time. Offers arts and science (MA, MS, PhD); chemistry (MS, PhD); communication studies and journalism (MS); English (MA); geography (MS).

College of Education and Human Sciences Offers agricultural education (MS); athletic training (MS); counseling and human resource development (M Ed, MS); curriculum and instruction (M Ed); dietetics (MS); education and human sciences (M Ed, MFCS, MS, PhD); educational administration (M Ed); family financial planning (MS); human sciences (MS); merchandising (MS); nutrition and exercise sciences (MS, PhD); sport and recreation studies (MS).

College of Engineering Degree program information: Part-time programs available. Part-time. Offers agricultural, biosystems and mechanical engineering (PhD); biological sciences (MS, PhD); computational science and statistics (PhD); electrical engineering (PhD); engineering (MS); geospatial science and engineering (PhD); industrial management (MS); mathematics (MS); statistics (MS).

College of Nursing Degree program information: Part-time and evening/weekend programs available. Part-time, evening/weekend, online learning. Offers nursing (MS, PhD).

College of Pharmacy Offers biological science (MS); pharmaceutical sciences (PhD); pharmacy (MS, PhD, Pharm D).

SOUTHEASTERN BAPTIST THEOLOGICAL SEMINARY, Wake Forest, NC 27588-1889

General Information Independent-religious, coed, comprehensive institution. *Graduate housing:* Rooms and/or apartments available on a first-come, first-served basis to single and married students.

GRADUATE UNITS

Graduate and Professional Programs Offers advanced biblical studies (M Div); Christian education (M Div, MACE); Christian ethics (PhD); Christian ministry (M Div); Christian planting (M Div); church music (MACM); counseling (MACO); evangelism (PhD); language (M Div); ministry (D Min); New Testament (PhD); Old Testament (PhD); philosophy (PhD); theology (Th M, PhD); women's studies (M Div).

SOUTHEASTERN LOUISIANA UNIVERSITY, Hammond, LA 70402

General Information State-supported, coed, comprehensive institution. *Enrollment:* 14,594 graduate, professional, and undergraduate students; 369 full-time matriculated graduate/professional students (248 women), 658 part-time matriculated graduate/professional students (529 women). *Enrollment by degree level:* 823 master's, 108 doctoral. *Graduate faculty:* 150 full-time (72 women), 20 part-time/adjunct (12 women). *Tuition, area resident:* Full-time $5551; part-time $436 per credit hour. Tuition, nonresident: full-time $18,115; part-time $1129 per credit hour. *Required fees:* $1559. *Graduate housing:* Room and/or apartments available on a first-come, first-served basis to single students; on-campus housing not available to married students. Typical cost: $5450 per year ($7840 including board). Room and board charges vary according to board plan and housing facility selected. Housing application deadline: 6/15. *Student services:* Campus employment opportunities, campus safety program, career counseling, exercise/wellness program, free psychological counseling, international student services, low-cost health insurance, multicultural affairs office, services for students with disabilities, teacher training, writing training. *Library:* Linus A. Sims Memorial Library plus 1 other. *Collection:* Books: 1.5 million (physical), 142,728 (digital/electronic); Serial titles: 1,176 (physical), 391 (digital/electronic). *Research affiliation:* Lake Ponchartrain Basin Foundation (water quality and wetland ecology), Bradken Manufacturing (steel), Petroleum Research Fund (chemistry), Gaylord Chemical Company (chemical manufacturing), Ochsner Medical Center (medicine).

Computer facilities: 1,031 computers available on campus for general student use. A campuswide network can be accessed from student residence rooms and from off campus. Online class registration, campus Webmail, student newspaper, transcripts, bookstore are available.
Website: http://www.selu.edu/

General Application Contact: Amanda Harper, Graduate Admissions Analyst, 985-549-5620, Fax: 985-549-5882, E-mail: admissions@southeastern.edu.

GRADUATE UNITS

College of Arts, Humanities and Social Sciences Students: 89 full-time (54 women), 101 part-time (55 women); includes 37 minority (11 Black or African American, non-Hispanic/Latino; 5 Asian, non-Hispanic/Latino; 15 Hispanic/Latino; 6 Two or more races, non-Hispanic/Latino), 10 international. Average age 28. 103 applicants, 65% accepted, 42 enrolled. *Faculty:* 55 full-time (20 women), 10 part-time/adjunct (3 women). *Financial support:* In 2015–16, 28 research assistantships (averaging $9,255 per year), 21 teaching assistantships (averaging $8,450 per year) were awarded; career-related internships or fieldwork, Federal Work-Study, and institutionally sponsored loans also available. Support available to part-time students. Financial award application deadline: 5/1; financial award applicants required to submit FAFSA. In 2015, 21 master's awarded. *Degree program information:* Part-time programs available. Part-time. Offers arts, humanities and social sciences (M Mus, MA, MS); creative writing (MA); history (MA); language and theory (MA); music (M Mus); organizational communication (MA); professional writing (MA); psychology (MA); sociology and criminal justice (MS). *Application deadline:* For fall admission, 7/15 priority date for domestic students, 6/1 priority date for international students; for spring admission, 12/1 priority date for domestic students, 10/1 priority date for international students. Applications are processed on a rolling basis. *Application fee:* $20 ($30 for international students). Electronic applications accepted. *Application Contact:* Amanda Harper, Graduate Admissions Analyst, 985-549-5620, Fax: 985-549-5632, E-mail: admissions@selu.edu. *Dean*, Dr. Karen Fontenot, 985-549-2101, Fax: 985-549-5014, E-mail: kfontenot@selu.edu.

College of Business Students: 59 full-time (27 women), 13 part-time (7 women); includes 20 minority (8 Black or African American, non-Hispanic/Latino; 7 Asian, non-Hispanic/Latino; 4 Hispanic/Latino; 1 Two or more races, non-Hispanic/Latino), 7 international. Average age 29. 70 applicants, 51% accepted, 21 enrolled. *Faculty:* 12 full-time (1 woman). *Financial support:* Research assistantships, career-related internships or fieldwork, Federal Work-Study, institutionally sponsored loans, and scholarships/grants available. Support available to part-time students. Financial award application deadline: 5/1; financial award applicants required to submit FAFSA. In 2015, 15 master's awarded. Offers business (MBA). *Application deadline:* For fall admission, 7/15 priority date for domestic students, 6/1 priority date for international students; for spring admission, 12/1 priority date for domestic students, 10/1 priority date for international students. Applications are processed on a rolling basis. *Application fee:* $20 ($30 for international students). Electronic applications accepted. *Application Contact:* Amanda Harper, Graduate Admissions Analyst, 985-549-5620, Fax: 985-549-5882, E-mail: admissions@selu.edu. *Interim Dean*, Dr. Antoinette Phillips, 985-549-2258, Fax: 985-549-5038, E-mail: business@selu.edu.

College of Education Students: 163 full-time (131 women), 199 part-time (182 women); includes 86 minority (49 Black or African American, non-Hispanic/Latino; 1 American Indian or Alaska Native, non-Hispanic/Latino; 5 Asian, non-Hispanic/Latino; 19 Hispanic/Latino; 1 Native Hawaiian or other Pacific Islander, non-Hispanic/Latino; 11 Two or more races, non-Hispanic/Latino), 3 international. Average age 31. 180 applicants, 61% accepted, 54 enrolled. *Faculty:* 26 full-time (17 women), 1 part-time/adjunct (0 women). *Financial support:* In 2015–16, 5 research assistantships (averaging $9,440 per year), 4 teaching assistantships (averaging $8,425 per year) were awarded; career-related internships or fieldwork, Federal Work-Study, institutionally sponsored loans, scholarships/grants, and unspecified assistantships also available. Support available to part-time students. Financial award application deadline: 5/1; financial award applicants required to submit FAFSA. In 2015, 40 master's, 14 doctorates awarded. *Degree program information:* Part-time programs available. Part-time. Offers curriculum and instruction (M Ed); education (M Ed, MAT, Ed D); educational leadership (M Ed, Ed D); elementary education (MAT); special education (M Ed); special education: early interventionist (MAT). *Application deadline:* For fall admission, 7/15 priority date for domestic students, 6/1 priority date for international students; for spring admission, 12/1 priority date for domestic students, 10/1 priority date for international students. Applications are processed on a rolling basis. *Application fee:* $20 ($30 for international students). Electronic applications accepted. *Application Contact:* Amanda Harper, Graduate Admissions Analyst, 985-549-5620, Fax: 985-549-5632, E-mail: admissions@selu.edu. *Interim Dean*, Dr. Shirley Jacob, 985-549-2217, Fax: 985-549-2070, E-mail: sjacob@selu.edu.

College of Nursing and Health Sciences Students: 137 full-time (115 women), 218 part-time (190 women); includes 79 minority (47 Black or African American, non-Hispanic/Latino; 6 Asian, non-Hispanic/Latino; 17 Hispanic/Latino; 9 Two or more races, non-Hispanic/Latino), 1 international. Average age 31. 271 applicants, 68% accepted, 40 enrolled. *Faculty:* 39 full-time (32 women), 6 part-time/adjunct (5 women). *Financial support:* In 2015–16, 71 research assistantships (averaging $7,113 per year), 3 teaching assistantships (averaging $9,366 per year) were awarded; career-related internships or fieldwork, Federal Work-Study, institutionally sponsored loans, scholarships/grants, and unspecified assistantships also available. Support available to part-time students. Financial award application deadline: 5/1; financial award applicants required to submit FAFSA. In 2015, 48 master's, 8 doctorates awarded. *Degree program information:* Part-time programs available. Part-time. Offers communication sciences and disorders (MS); counselor education (M Ed); health and kinesiology (MA); nursing and health sciences (M Ed, MA, MS, MSN, DNP). *Application deadline:* For fall admission, 7/15 priority date for domestic students, 6/1 priority date for international students; for spring admission, 12/1 priority date for domestic students, 10/1 priority date for international students. Applications are processed on a rolling basis. *Application fee:* $20 ($30 for international students). Electronic applications accepted. *Application Contact:* Amanda Harper, Graduate Admissions Analyst, 985-549-5620, Fax: 985-549-5632, E-mail: admissions@selu.edu. *Dean*, Dr. Ann Carruth, 985-549-3772, Fax: 985-549-5179, E-mail: acarruth@selu.edu.

College of Science and Technology Students: 32 full-time (15 women), 11 part-time (7 women); includes 16 minority (5 Black or African American, non-Hispanic/Latino; 7 Asian, non-Hispanic/Latino; 4 Hispanic/Latino), 10 international. Average age 32. 45 applicants, 42% accepted, 16 enrolled. *Faculty:* 31 full-time (8 women), 1 part-time/adjunct (0 women). *Financial support:* In 2015–16, 18 students received support, including 4 research assistantships (averaging $9,550 per year), 10 teaching assistantships (averaging $10,100 per year); fellowships, career-related internships or fieldwork, Federal Work-Study, institutionally sponsored loans, and unspecified assistantships also available. Support available to part-time students. Financial award application deadline: 5/1; financial award applicants required to submit FAFSA. In 2015, 6 master's awarded. *Degree program information:* Part-time programs available. Part-time. Offers biology (MS); integrated science and technology (MS); science and technology (MS). *Application deadline:* For fall admission, 7/15 priority date for domestic students, 6/1 priority date for international students; for spring admission, 12/1 priority date for domestic students, 10/1 priority date for international students. Applications are processed on a rolling basis. *Application fee:* $20 ($30 for international students). Electronic applications accepted. *Application Contact:* Amanda Harper, Graduate Admissions Analyst, 985-549-5620, Fax: 985-549-5632, E-mail: admissions@selu.edu. *Dean*, Dr. Daniel McCarthy, 985-549-2055, Fax: 985-549-3396, E-mail: dmccarthy@selu.edu.

SOUTHEASTERN OKLAHOMA STATE UNIVERSITY, Durant, OK 74701-0609

General Information State-supported, coed, comprehensive institution. *Graduate housing:* Rooms and/or apartments available on a first-come, first-served basis to single and married students. Housing application deadline: 6/15. *Research affiliation:* U.S.

Department of the Interior (biological sciences), U.S. Department of Agriculture (USDA) (biological sciences), National Science Foundation (chemistry, computer science, physical sciences), U.S. Fish and Wildlife Service (biological sciences), National Institutes of Health (biological sciences, chemistry, computer science, physical sciences).

GRADUATE UNITS

Department of Aviation Science ***Degree program information:*** Part-time and evening/weekend programs available. Part-time, evening/weekend. Offers aerospace administration and logistics (MS). Electronic applications accepted.

School of Arts and Sciences ***Degree program information:*** Part-time and evening/weekend programs available. Part-time, evening/weekend. Offers biology (MT); computer information systems (MT); occupational safety and health (MT). Electronic applications accepted.

School of Behavioral Sciences ***Degree program information:*** Part-time and evening/weekend programs available. Part-time, evening/weekend. Offers clinical mental health counseling (MS). Electronic applications accepted.

School of Business ***Degree program information:*** Part-time and evening/weekend programs available. Part-time, evening/weekend. Offers business (MBA). Electronic applications accepted.

School of Education ***Degree program information:*** Part-time and evening/weekend programs available. Part-time, evening/weekend. Offers math specialist (M Ed); reading specialist (M Ed); school administration (M Ed); school counseling (M Ed). Electronic applications accepted.

SOUTHEASTERN UNIVERSITY, Lakeland, FL 33801-6099

General Information Independent-religious, coed, comprehensive institution.

GRADUATE UNITS

College of Business and Legal Studies ***Degree program information:*** Evening/weekend programs available. Evening/weekend, online learning. Offers business administration (MBA). Electronic applications accepted.

College of Christian Ministries and Religion ***Degree program information:*** Evening/weekend programs available. Evening/weekend, online learning. Offers ministerial leadership (MA).

College of Education Offers educational leadership (M Ed); elementary education (M Ed); teaching and learning (M Ed).

Department of Behavioral and Social Sciences ***Degree program information:*** Evening/weekend programs available. Evening/weekend. Offers human services (MA); professional counseling (MS); school counseling (MS).

SOUTHEAST MISSOURI STATE UNIVERSITY, Cape Girardeau, MO 63701-4799

General Information State-supported, coed, comprehensive institution. CGS member. *Enrollment:* 11,987 graduate, professional, and undergraduate students; 487 full-time matriculated graduate/professional students (279 women), 779 part-time matriculated graduate/professional students (501 women). *Enrollment by degree level:* 1,156 master's, 19 doctoral, 91 other advanced degrees. *Graduate faculty:* 224 full-time (106 women), 35 part-time/adjunct (17 women). Tuition, state resident: part-time $260.80 per credit hour. Tuition, nonresident: part-time $486.80 per credit hour. *Required fees:* $33.70 per credit hour. *Graduate housing:* Room and/or apartments available on a first-come, first-served basis to single students; on-campus housing not available to married students. Housing application deadline: 12/1. *Student services:* Campus employment opportunities, campus safety program, career counseling, child daycare facilities, exercise/wellness program, free psychological counseling, international student services, multicultural affairs office, services for students with disabilities, teacher training, writing training. *Library:* Kent Library. *Collection:* Books: 479,454 (physical), 145 (digital/electronic); Serial titles: 14,888 (physical), 4 (digital/electronic); Databases: 123. Weekly public service hours: 93.

Computer facilities: 1,241 computers available on campus for general student use. A campuswide network can be accessed from student residence rooms. Online class registration is available.
Website: http://www.semo.edu/

General Application Contact: Dr. Charles D. McAllister, Dean, School of Graduate Studies, 573-651-2062, Fax: 573-651-2001, E-mail: graduateschool@semo.edu.

GRADUATE UNITS

School of Graduate Studies Students: 492 full-time (284 women), 912 part-time (612 women); includes 87 minority (53 Black or African American, non-Hispanic/Latino; 2 American Indian or Alaska Native, non-Hispanic/Latino; 13 Asian, non-Hispanic/Latino; 16 Hispanic/Latino; 3 Two or more races, non-Hispanic/Latino), 334 international. Average age 31. 924 applicants, 69% accepted, 523 enrolled. *Faculty:* 218 full-time (101 women), 34 part-time/adjunct (14 women). *Financial support:* In 2015–16, 426 students received support, including 9 research assistantships with full tuition reimbursements available (averaging $8,467 per year), 108 teaching assistantships with full tuition reimbursements available (averaging $8,467 per year); career-related internships or fieldwork, Federal Work-Study, scholarships/grants, traineeships, tuition waivers (full), and unspecified assistantships also available. Financial award application deadline: 6/30; financial award applicants required to submit FAFSA. In 2015, 363 master's, 42 other advanced degrees awarded. *Degree program information:* Part-time and evening/weekend programs available. Part-time, evening/weekend, online learning. Offers biology (MNS); career counseling (MA); chemistry (MNS); communication disorders (MA); counseling (MA, Ed S); counseling education (Ed S); criminal justice (MS); educational administration (MA, Ed D, Ed S); educational leadership (Ed D); elementary administration (MA); elementary education (MA); English (MA); environmental science (MS); exceptional child education (MA); heritage education (Certificate); higher education administration (MA); historic preservation (Certificate); history (MA); human environmental studies (MA); mathematics (MNS); mental health counseling (MA); nursing (MSN); nutrition and exercise science (MS); public administration (MPA); public history (MA); school counseling (MA); secondary administration (MA); secondary education (MA); teacher leadership (MA, Ed S); teaching English to speakers of other languages (MA); technology management (MS). *Application deadline:* For fall admission, 8/1 for domestic students, 6/1 for international students; for spring admission, 11/21 for domestic students, 10/1 for international students; for summer admission, 5/15 for domestic students. Applications are processed on a rolling basis. *Application fee:* $30 ($40 for international students). Electronic applications accepted. *Application Contact:* Alisa Aleen McFerron, Assistant Director of Admissions for Operations, 573-651-5937, E-mail: amcferron@semo.edu. *Dean, School of Graduate Studies,* Dr. Charles D. McAllister, 573-651-2062, Fax: 573-651-2001, E-mail: graduateschool@semo.edu.

Harrison College of Business Students: 68 full-time (40 women), 132 part-time (46 women); includes 21 minority (9 Black or African American, non-Hispanic/Latino; 9 Asian, non-Hispanic/Latino; 2 Hispanic/Latino; 1 Two or more races, non-Hispanic/Latino), 60 international. Average age 30. *Faculty:* 27 full-time (7 women), 1 (woman) part-time/adjunct. *Financial support:* In 2015–16, 60 students received support. Career-related internships or fieldwork, Federal Work-Study, scholarships/grants, traineeships, tuition waivers (full), and unspecified assistantships available. Financial award application deadline: 6/30; financial award applicants required to submit FAFSA. In 2015, 57 master's awarded. *Degree program information:* Part-time and evening/weekend programs available. Part-time, evening/weekend, online learning. Offers accounting (MBA); entrepreneurship (MBA); environmental management (MBA); financial management (MBA); general management (MBA); health administration (MBA); industrial management (MBA); international business (MBA); organizational management (MS); sport management (MBA). *Application deadline:* For fall admission, 8/1 for domestic students, 6/1 for international students; for spring admission, 11/21 for domestic students, 10/1 for international students; for summer admission, 5/15 for domestic students. Applications are processed on a rolling basis. *Application fee:* $30 ($40 for international students). Electronic applications accepted. *Application Contact:* Gail Amick, Admissions Specialist, 573-651-2590, Fax: 573-651-5936, E-mail: gamick@semo.edu. *Director, Graduate Business Studies,* Dr. Kenneth A. Heischmidt, 573-651-2912, Fax: 573-651-5032, E-mail: kheischmidt@semo.edu.

SOUTHERN ADVENTIST UNIVERSITY, Collegedale, TN 37315-0370

General Information Independent-religious, coed, comprehensive institution. *Graduate housing:* Rooms and/or apartments available on a first-come, first-served basis to single and married students. Housing application deadline: 7/1.

GRADUATE UNITS

School of Business and Management ***Degree program information:*** Part-time and evening/weekend programs available. Part-time, evening/weekend, online learning. Offers accounting (MBA); church administration (MSA); church and nonprofit leadership (MBA); financial management (MFM); healthcare administration (MBA); management (MBA); marketing management (MBA); outdoor education (MSA). Electronic applications accepted.

School of Education and Psychology ***Degree program information:*** Part-time and evening/weekend programs available. Part-time, evening/weekend. Offers clinical mental health counseling (MS); inclusive education (MS Ed); instructional leadership (MS Ed); literacy education (MS Ed); outdoor teacher education (MS Ed); school counseling (MS). Electronic applications accepted.

School of Nursing ***Degree program information:*** Part-time programs available. Part-time. Offers acute care nurse practitioner (MSN); adult nurse practitioner (MSN); family nurse practitioner (MSN); nurse educator (MSN). Electronic applications accepted.

School of Religion ***Degree program information:*** Part-time programs available. Part-time. Offers Biblical and theological studies (MA); church leadership and management (M Min); church ministry and homiletics (M Min); evangelism and world mission (M Min); religious studies (MA).

School of Social Work Online learning. Offers social work (MSW).

SOUTHERN ARKANSAS UNIVERSITY–MAGNOLIA, Magnolia, AR 71753

General Information State-supported, coed, comprehensive institution. *Enrollment:* 4,095 graduate, professional, and undergraduate students; 336 full-time matriculated graduate/professional students (69 women), 636 part-time matriculated graduate/professional students (292 women). *Enrollment by degree level:* 972 master's. *Graduate faculty:* 33 full-time (17 women), 25 part-time/adjunct (11 women). Tuition, state resident: part-time $217 per credit hour. Tuition, nonresident: part-time $403 per credit hour. *Required fees:* $769 per semester. Tuition and fees vary according to course load and program. *Graduate housing:* Rooms and/or apartments available on a first-come, first-served basis to single and married students. Typical cost: $2980 per year ($5668 including board) for single students; $5727 per year ($7071 including board) for married students. Room and board charges vary according to board plan and housing facility selected. Housing application deadline: 6/1. *Student services:* Campus employment opportunities, campus safety program, career counseling, exercise/wellness program, free psychological counseling, international student services, low-cost health insurance, multicultural affairs office, services for students with disabilities, writing training. *Library:* Magale Library. *Collection:* Books: 176,437 (physical), 7,779 (digital/electronic); Serial titles: 314 (physical), 69 (digital/electronic); Databases: 155. Weekly public service hours: 87.

Computer facilities: 199 computers available on campus for general student use. A campuswide network can be accessed from student residence rooms and from off campus. Online class registration is available.
Website: http://www.saumag.edu/

General Application Contact: Shrijana Malakar, Admissions, School of Graduate Studies, 870-235-4150, Fax: 870-235-5227, E-mail: smalakar@saumag.edu.

GRADUATE UNITS

School of Graduate Studies Students: 336 full-time (69 women), 636 part-time (292 women); includes 124 minority (109 Black or African American, non-Hispanic/Latino; 6 American Indian or Alaska Native, non-Hispanic/Latino; 5 Asian, non-Hispanic/Latino; 1 Hispanic/Latino; 3 Two or more races, non-Hispanic/Latino), 554 international. Average age 28. 531 applicants, 88% accepted, 345 enrolled. *Faculty:* 33 full-time (17 women), 25 part-time/adjunct (11 women). *Financial support:* Career-related internships or fieldwork, Federal Work-Study, scholarships/grants, tuition waivers (full), and unspecified assistantships available. Financial award applicants required to submit FAFSA. In 2015, 155 master's awarded. *Degree program information:* Part-time programs available. Part-time, 100% online, blended/hybrid learning. Offers agriculture (MS); business administration (MBA); computer and information sciences (MS); elementary or secondary education (M Ed); higher, adult and lifelong education (M Ed); kinesiology (M Ed); library media and information specialist (M Ed); mental health and clinical counseling (MS); public administration (MPA); school counseling K-12 (M Ed); student affairs and college counseling (M Ed); teaching (MAT). *Application deadline:* For fall admission, 7/20 for domestic students, 7/5 for international students; for spring admission, 12/1 for domestic students, 11/15 for international students; for summer admission, 6/1 for domestic students, 5/1 for international students. Applications are processed on a rolling basis. *Application fee:* $25 ($50 for international students). Electronic applications accepted. *Application Contact:* Shrijana Malakar, Admissions Specialist, 870-235-4150, Fax: 870-235-5227, E-mail: smalakar@saumag.edu. *Dean, School of Graduate Studies,* Dr. Kim Bloss, 870-235-4150, Fax: 870-235-5227, E-mail: kkbloss@saumag.edu.

THE SOUTHERN BAPTIST THEOLOGICAL SEMINARY, Louisville, KY 40280-0004

General Information Independent-religious, coed, comprehensive institution. *Graduate housing:* Rooms and/or apartments available on a first-come, first-served basis to single and married students.

GRADUATE UNITS

Billy Graham School of Missions, Evangelism and Ministry ***Degree program information:*** Part-time and evening/weekend programs available. Part-time, evening/weekend, online learning. Offers ministry (D Min); missiology (MA, D Miss); missions and evangelism (M Div, Th M, PhD); theological studies (MA).

School of Theology ***Degree program information:*** Part-time and evening/weekend programs available. Part-time, evening/weekend, online learning. Offers applied theology (D Min); biblical and theological studies (M Div); biblical counseling (M Div, MA, D Min); biblical spirituality (D Min); Christian ministry (M Div); expository preaching (D Min); pastoral studies (M Div); theological studies (MA); theology (Th M, PhD); worldview and apologetics (M Div).

SOUTHERN CALIFORNIA INSTITUTE OF ARCHITECTURE, Los Angeles, CA 90013

General Information Independent, coed, comprehensive institution. *Graduate housing:* On-campus housing not available.

GRADUATE UNITS

Graduate Program in Architecture Offers architecture (M Arch). Electronic applications accepted.

SOUTHERN CALIFORNIA SEMINARY, El Cajon, CA 92019

General Information Independent-religious, coed, comprehensive institution. *Graduate housing:* Rooms and/or apartments available on a first-come, first-served basis to single and married students.

GRADUATE UNITS

Graduate and Professional Programs ***Degree program information:*** Part-time and evening/weekend programs available. Part-time, evening/weekend, online learning. Offers Biblical studies (MABS); counseling psychology (MACP); marriage and family therapy (MAMFT); psychology (Psy D); religious studies (MRS); theology (M Div). Electronic applications accepted.

SOUTHERN CALIFORNIA UNIVERSITY OF HEALTH SCIENCES, Whittier, CA 90609-1166

General Information Independent, coed, graduate-only institution. *Graduate housing:* On-campus housing not available. *Research affiliation:* Samueli Institute (alternative health care), Anton B. Burg Foundation (alternative health care).

GRADUATE UNITS

College of Eastern Medicine ***Degree program information:*** Part-time and evening/weekend programs available. Part-time, evening/weekend. Offers Eastern medicine (MAOM, DAOM). Electronic applications accepted.

Los Angeles College of Chiropractic Offers chiropractic (DC). Electronic applications accepted.

SOUTHERN COLLEGE OF OPTOMETRY, Memphis, TN 38104-2222

General Information Independent, coed, graduate-only institution. *Graduate housing:* On-campus housing not available.

GRADUATE UNITS

Professional Program Offers optometry (OD).

SOUTHERN CONNECTICUT STATE UNIVERSITY, New Haven, CT 06515-1355

General Information State-supported, coed, comprehensive institution. CGS member. *Enrollment:* 10,473 graduate, professional, and undergraduate students; 818 full-time matriculated graduate/professional students (610 women), 1,549 part-time matriculated graduate/professional students (1,079 women). *Enrollment by degree level:* 1,944 master's, 84 doctoral, 339 other advanced degrees. *Graduate faculty:* 204 full-time (113 women), 72 part-time/adjunct (38 women). Tuition, state resident: full-time $4968; part-time $494 per credit hour. Tuition, nonresident: full-time $16,078; part-time $509 per credit hour. *Required fees:* $4632; $55 per semester. Tuition and fees vary according to program. *Graduate housing:* Room and/or apartments available on a first-come, first-served basis to single students; on-campus housing not available to married students. Typical cost: $6402 per year ($11,614 including board). Room and board charges vary according to board plan and housing facility selected. *Student services:* Campus employment opportunities, campus safety program, career counseling, exercise/wellness program, free psychological counseling, international student services, low-cost health insurance, multicultural affairs office, services for students with disabilities, teacher training, writing training. *Library:* Hilton C. Buley Library.

Computer facilities: 800 computers available on campus for general student use. A campuswide network can be accessed from student residence rooms and from off campus. Online class registration is available.
Website: http://www.southernct.edu/

General Application Contact: Lisa Galvin, Director of Graduate Admissions, 203-392-5250, Fax: 203-392-5235, E-mail: gradinfo@southernct.edu.

GRADUATE UNITS

School of Graduate Studies Students: 818 full-time (610 women), 1,549 part-time (1,079 women); includes 457 minority (233 Black or African American, non-Hispanic/Latino; 1 American Indian or Alaska Native, non-Hispanic/Latino; 50 Asian, non-Hispanic/Latino; 141 Hispanic/Latino; 1 Native Hawaiian or other Pacific Islander, non-Hispanic/Latino; 31 Two or more races, non-Hispanic/Latino), 24 international. Average age 33. 2,471 applicants, 29% accepted, 579 enrolled. *Faculty:* 185 full-time (95 women), 96 part-time/adjunct (58 women). *Financial support:* Fellowships, research assistantships, teaching assistantships, career-related internships or fieldwork, Federal Work-Study, scholarships/grants, and unspecified assistantships available. Support available to part-time students. Financial award application deadline: 4/15; financial award applicants required to submit FAFSA. In 2015, 779 master's, 9 doctorates, 112 other advanced degrees awarded. *Degree program information:* Part-time and evening/weekend programs available. Part-time, evening/weekend, online learning. *Application deadline:* Applications are processed on a rolling basis. *Application fee:* $50. Electronic applications accepted. *Application Contact:* Lisa Galvin, Director of Graduate Admissions, 203-392-5240, Fax: 203-392-5235, E-mail: galvinl1@southernct.edu. *Dean*, Dr. Gregory Paveza, 203-392-5240, Fax: 203-392-5235, E-mail: pavezag1@southernct.edu.

School of Arts and Sciences Students: 111 full-time (55 women), 256 part-time (156 women); includes 86 minority (33 Black or African American, non-Hispanic/Latino; 8 Asian, non-Hispanic/Latino; 31 Hispanic/Latino; 14 Two or more races, non-Hispanic/Latino), 6 international. Average age 32. 418 applicants, 37% accepted, 128 enrolled. *Faculty:* 71 full-time (37 women), 9 part-time/adjunct (2 women). *Financial support:* Teaching assistantships and career-related internships or fieldwork available. In 2015, 134 master's awarded. Offers art education (MS); arts and sciences (MA, MFA, MS, Diploma); biology (MS); chemistry (MS); computer science (MS); English (MA, MS); environmental education (MS); history (MA, MS); mathematics (MS); multicultural-bilingual education/teaching English to speakers of other languages (MS); political science (MS); psychology (MA); romance languages (MA); science education (MS, Diploma); sociology (MS); women's studies (MA). *Application deadline:* Applications are processed on a rolling basis. *Application fee:* $50. Electronic applications accepted. *Application Contact:* Lisa Galvin, Director of Graduate Admissions, 203-392-5240, Fax: 203-392-5235, E-mail: galvinl1@southernct.edu. *Dean*, Steven Breese, 203-392-5468, Fax: 203-392-6807, E-mail: breese@southernct.edu.

School of Business Students: 81 full-time (43 women), 89 part-time (43 women); includes 62 minority (32 Black or African American, non-Hispanic/Latino; 11 Asian, non-Hispanic/Latino; 15 Hispanic/Latino; 4 Two or more races, non-Hispanic/Latino), 5 international. Average age 31. 211 applicants, 30% accepted, 52 enrolled. *Faculty:* 15 full-time (1 woman), 9 part-time/adjunct (3 women). *Financial support:* Career-related internships or fieldwork, scholarships/grants, and unspecified assistantships available. Financial award application deadline: 4/15; financial award applicants required to submit FAFSA. In 2015, 40 master's awarded. *Degree program information:* Part-time and evening/weekend programs available. Part-time, evening/weekend. Offers business (MBA); business administration (MBA). *Application deadline:* For fall admission, 7/1 priority date for domestic students. Applications are processed on a rolling basis. *Application fee:* $50. Electronic applications accepted. *Application Contact:* Lisa Galvin, Director of Graduate Admissions, 203-392-5240, Fax: 203-392-5235, E-mail: galvinl1@southernct.edu. *Dean*, Dr. Samuel Andoh, 203-392-5616, Fax: 203-392-5674, E-mail: andohs1@southernct.edu.

School of Education Students: 211 full-time (172 women), 514 part-time (395 women); includes 92 minority (50 Black or African American, non-Hispanic/Latino; 1 American Indian or Alaska Native, non-Hispanic/Latino; 9 Asian, non-Hispanic/Latino; 29 Hispanic/Latino; 3 Two or more races, non-Hispanic/Latino), 5 international. Average age 33. 781 applicants, 28% accepted, 184 enrolled. *Faculty:* 43 full-time (27 women), 21 part-time/adjunct (10 women). *Financial support:* Career-related internships or fieldwork, scholarships/grants, and unspecified assistantships available. Financial award application deadline: 4/15; financial award applicants required to submit FAFSA. In 2015, 274 master's, 12 doctorates, 203 other advanced degrees awarded. *Degree program information:* Part-time programs available. Part-time. Offers classroom teacher specialist (Diploma); community counseling (MS); counseling (Diploma); education (MLS, MS, MS Ed, Ed D, Diploma); educational coach (Diploma); educational leadership (Ed D, Diploma); elementary education (MS); information studies (Diploma); library science (MLS); reading (MS, Diploma); research, statistics, and measurement (MS); school counseling (MS); school psychology (MS, Diploma); special education (MS Ed). *Application fee:* $50. Electronic applications accepted. *Application Contact:* Lisa Galvin, Director of Graduate Admissions, 203-392-5240, Fax: 203-392-5235, E-mail: galvinl1@southernct.edu. *Dean*, Dr. Stephen Hegedus, 203-392-5900, E-mail: hegeduss1@southernct.edu.

School of Health and Human Services Students: 331 full-time (273 women), 224 part-time (176 women); includes 109 minority (56 Black or African American, non-Hispanic/Latino; 11 Asian, non-Hispanic/Latino; 35 Hispanic/Latino; 7 Two or more races, non-Hispanic/Latino), 6 international. Average age 30. 951 applicants, 23% accepted, 174 enrolled. *Faculty:* 58 full-time (39 women), 24 part-time/adjunct (16 women). *Financial support:* Career-related internships or fieldwork, scholarships/grants, and unspecified assistantships available. Financial award application deadline: 4/15; financial award applicants required to submit FAFSA. In 2015, 188 master's awarded. *Degree program information:* Part-time and evening/weekend programs available. Part-time, evening/weekend. Offers family nurse practitioner (MSN); health and human services (MPH, MS, MSN, MSW); human performance (MS); nursing education (MSN); physical education (MS); public health (MPH); recreation and leisure studies (MS); school health education (MS); social work (MSW); speech pathology (MS); sport psychology (MS). *Application fee:* $50. Electronic applications accepted. *Application Contact:* Lisa Galvin, Director of Graduate Admissions, 203-392-5240, Fax: 203-392-5235, E-mail: galvinl1@southernct.edu. *Dean*, Dr. Sandra Bulmer, 203-392-7015, Fax: 203-302-8067, E-mail: bulmers1@southernct.edu.

SOUTHERN EVANGELICAL SEMINARY, Matthews, NC 28105

General Information Independent-religious, coed, primarily men, graduate-only institution. *Graduate housing:* On-campus housing not available.

GRADUATE UNITS

Graduate Programs ***Degree program information:*** Part-time and evening/weekend programs available. Part-time, evening/weekend, online learning. Offers apologetics (MA, D Min, Certificate); Christian education (MA); church ministry (MA, Certificate); divinity (Certificate); Islamic studies (MA, Certificate); Jewish studies (MA); philosophy (MA); philosophy of religion (PhD); religion (MA); theology (M Div); youth ministry (MA).

SOUTHERN ILLINOIS UNIVERSITY CARBONDALE, Carbondale, IL 62901-4701

General Information State-supported, coed, university. CGS member. *Enrollment:* 17,292 graduate, professional, and undergraduate students; 2,535 full-time matriculated graduate/professional students (1,212 women), 1,305 part-time matriculated graduate/professional students (647 women). *Graduate faculty:* 803 full-time (209 women), 26 part-time/adjunct (15 women). *Graduate housing:* Rooms and/or apartments available on a first-come, first-served basis to single and married students. *Student services:* Campus employment opportunities, campus safety program, career counseling, child daycare facilities, exercise/wellness program, free psychological counseling, grant writing training, international student services, low-cost health insurance, services for students with disabilities, teacher training. *Library:* Morris Library plus 1 other. *Collection:* Books: 3.1 million (physical), 285,320 (digital/electronic); Serial titles: 38,291 (physical); Databases: 170. Weekly public service hours: 100; students can reserve study rooms. *Research affiliation:* Argonne National Laboratory, NASA-Ames Research Center.

Computer facilities: Computer purchase and lease plans are available. 1,900 computers available on campus for general student use. A campuswide network can be accessed from student residence rooms and from off campus. Online class registration is available.
Website: http://www.siuc.edu/

General Application Contact: Susan Babbit, Admissions Supervisor, 618-453-4557, Fax: 618-453-4562, E-mail: susan@siu.edu.

GRADUATE UNITS

Graduate School Students: 1,855 full-time (982 women), 1,477 part-time (720 women); includes 401 minority (266 Black or African American, non-Hispanic/Latino; 16 American Indian or Alaska Native, non-Hispanic/Latino; 77 Asian, non-Hispanic/Latino; 42 Hispanic/Latino), 912 international. 3,254 applicants, 38% accepted, 1189 enrolled. *Faculty:* 780 full-time (198 women), 14 part-time/adjunct (9 women). *Financial support:* Fellowships with full tuition reimbursements, research assistantships with full tuition reimbursements, teaching assistantships with full tuition reimbursements, career-related internships or fieldwork, Federal Work-Study, institutionally sponsored loans, tuition waivers (full), and dissertation research awards, clinical assistantships available. Support available to part-time students. Financial award application deadline: 4/18. In 2015, 1,094 master's, 184 doctorates awarded. *Degree program information:* Part-time programs available. Part-time. Offers molecular, cellular and systemic physiology (MS, PhD); molecular, cellular, and systemic physiology (PhD); pharmacology (MS, PhD); physician assistant studies (MSPA). *Application deadline:* Applications are processed on a rolling basis. *Application fee:* $65. *Application Contact:* Susan Babbitt, Admissions Supervisor, 618-453-4557, E-mail: susan@siu.edu. *Dean,* Dr. Yueh-Ting Lee, 618-453-4527, E-mail: leey@siu.edu.

College of Agriculture Students: 67 full-time (32 women), 38 part-time (12 women); includes 5 minority (4 Black or African American, non-Hispanic/Latino; 1 Hispanic/Latino), 15 international. 66 applicants, 45% accepted, 27 enrolled. *Faculty:* 41 full-time (8 women). *Financial support:* In 2015–16, 35 students received support. Fellowships, research assistantships, teaching assistantships, career-related internships or fieldwork, Federal Work-Study, institutionally sponsored loans, and tuition waivers (full) available. Support available to part-time students. In 2015, 29 master's awarded. *Degree program information:* Part-time programs available. Part-time. Offers agribusiness economics (MS); agriculture (MS); animal science (MS); food and nutrition (MS); forestry (MS); plant, soil, and general agriculture (MS). *Application deadline:* Applications are processed on a rolling basis. *Application fee:* $50. *Application Contact:* Associate Dean of the Graduate School, 618-536-7791. *Dean,* Mickey A. Latour, 618-453-2469.

College of Applied Science Students: 126 full-time (43 women), 33 part-time (7 women); includes 10 minority (6 Black or African American, non-Hispanic/Latino; 4 Asian, non-Hispanic/Latino), 56 international. 171 applicants, 44% accepted, 75 enrolled. *Faculty:* 12 full-time (8 women). *Financial support:* In 2015–16, 20 students received support, including 6 research assistantships with full tuition reimbursements available, 14 teaching assistantships with full tuition reimbursements available; fellowships with full tuition reimbursements available and unspecified assistantships also available. In 2015, 33 master's awarded. Offers applied science (M Arch, MS); architecture (M Arch); fire service and homeland security (MS); medical dosimetry (MS). *Application fee:* $65. Electronic applications accepted. *Application Contact:* Chad Waters, Administrative Aide, 618-453-7020, E-mail: cwaters@siu.edu. *Dean,* Dr. Scott Collins, 618-453-8800, E-mail: scollins@siu.edu.

College of Business and Administration Students: 81 full-time (37 women), 121 part-time (47 women); includes 18 minority (12 Black or African American, non-Hispanic/Latino; 6 Asian, non-Hispanic/Latino), 85 international. Average age 26. 124 applicants, 43% accepted, 49 enrolled. *Faculty:* 41 full-time (7 women), 6 part-time/adjunct (2 women). *Financial support:* In 2015–16, 38 students received support, including 7 research assistantships with full tuition reimbursements available, 31 teaching assistantships with full tuition reimbursements available; fellowships, Federal Work-Study, institutionally sponsored loans, and tuition waivers (full) also available. Support available to part-time students. In 2015, 128 master's, 5 doctorates awarded. *Degree program information:* Part-time programs available. Part-time. Offers accountancy (M Acc, PhD); business administration (MBA, PhD); business and administration (M Acc, MBA, PhD). *Application deadline:* For fall admission, 6/15 priority date for domestic students. Applications are processed on a rolling basis. *Application fee:* $65. Electronic applications accepted. *Application Contact:* Jeffery Reece, Administrative Aide, 618-453-3030, Fax: 618-453-7961, E-mail: jreece@siu.edu. *Acting Dean,* Dr. Jason Greene, 618-453-7960, E-mail: jgreene@business.siu.edu.

College of Education and Human Services Students: 256 full-time (163 women), 265 part-time (179 women); includes 114 minority (87 Black or African American, non-Hispanic/Latino; 11 Asian, non-Hispanic/Latino; 16 Hispanic/Latino), 150 international. Average age 34. 527 applicants, 40% accepted, 211 enrolled. *Faculty:* 175 full-time (74 women), 25 part-time/adjunct (6 women). *Financial support:* In 2015–16, 283 students received support, including 3 fellowships, 113 research assistantships with full tuition reimbursements available, 164 teaching assistantships with full tuition reimbursements available; career-related internships or fieldwork, Federal Work-Study, institutionally sponsored loans, traineeships, tuition waivers (full), and unspecified assistantships also available. Support available to part-time students. In 2015, 336 master's, 40 doctorates awarded. *Degree program information:* Part-time programs available. Part-time. Offers behavior analysis and therapy (MS); communication disorders and sciences (MS); community health education (MPH); curriculum and instruction (MS Ed, PhD); education (MS Ed); education administration (MS Ed, PhD); education and human services (MPH, MS, MS Ed, MSW, PhD); educational administration (MS Ed, PhD); educational psychology (MS Ed, PhD); health education (MS Ed, PhD); higher education (MS Ed); kinesiology (MS Ed); recreation (MS Ed); social work (MSW); special education (MS Ed, PhD); workforce education and development (MS Ed, PhD). *Application deadline:* Applications are processed on a rolling basis. *Application fee:* $65. Electronic applications accepted. *Application Contact:* Supervisor, Admissions, 618-453-2415. *Interim Dean,* Dr. Lyle J. White, 618-453-2415, E-mail: coehsdean@siu.edu.

College of Engineering Students: 262 full-time (44 women), 200 part-time (31 women); includes 19 minority (8 Black or African American, non-Hispanic/Latino; 1 American Indian or Alaska Native, non-Hispanic/Latino; 5 Asian, non-Hispanic/Latino; 5 Hispanic/Latino), 338 international. 558 applicants, 31% accepted, 166 enrolled. *Faculty:* 55 full-time (3 women), 3 part-time/adjunct (0 women). *Financial support:* In 2015–16, 154 students received support, including 4 fellowships with full tuition reimbursements available, 38 research assistantships with full tuition reimbursements available, 108 teaching assistantships with full tuition reimbursements available; Federal Work-Study, institutionally sponsored loans, and tuition waivers (full) also available. Support available to part-time students. In 2015, 187 master's, 24 doctorates awarded. Offers biomedical engineering (ME, MS); civil and environmental engineering (ME); civil engineering (MS); electrical and computer engineering (MS, PhD); engineering (ME, MS, PhD); engineering science (PhD); engineering sciences (PhD); mechanical engineering (MS); mining engineering (MS); quality engineering and management (MS). *Application deadline:* Applications are processed on a rolling basis. *Application fee:* $65. *Application Contact:* Toni Baker, Office Administrator, 618-453-7980, E-mail: toni@engr.siu.edu. *Dean,* Dr. John J. Warwick, 618-453-4321, E-mail: warwick@siu.edu.

College of Liberal Arts Students: 445 full-time (227 women), 344 part-time (167 women); includes 65 minority (35 Black or African American, non-Hispanic/Latino; 1 American Indian or Alaska Native, non-Hispanic/Latino; 15 Asian, non-Hispanic/Latino; 12 Hispanic/Latino; 2 Native Hawaiian or other Pacific Islander, non-Hispanic/Latino), 349 international. 806 applicants, 34% accepted, 259 enrolled. *Faculty:* 254 full-time (87 women), 8 part-time/adjunct (3 women). *Financial support:* In 2015–16, 510 students received support, including 16 fellowships, 111 research assistantships, 370 teaching assistantships; career-related internships or fieldwork, Federal Work-Study, institutionally sponsored loans, scholarships/grants, and tuition waivers (full) also available. Support available to part-time students. In 2015, 211 master's, 70 doctorates awarded. *Degree program information:* Part-time programs available. Part-time. Offers anthropology (MA, PhD); applied linguistics (MA); clinical psychology (PhD); communication studies (MA, MS, PhD); composition (MA, PhD); counseling psychology (PhD); creative writing (MFA); criminology and criminal justice (MA, PhD); drawing (MFA); economics (MA, MS, PhD); experimental psychology (MA, MS); fiber/weaving (MFA); foreign languages and literatures (MA); geography (MS, PhD); glass (MFA); history (MA, PhD); liberal arts (MA, MFA, MM, MPA, MS, PhD); metalsmithing/blacksmithing (MFA); music (MM); painting (MFA); philosophy (MA, PhD); political science (MA, PhD); public administration (MPA); sociology (MA, PhD); speech/theater (PhD); teaching English to speakers of other languages (MA); theater (MFA). *Application deadline:* Applications are processed on a rolling basis. *Application fee:* $65. *Application Contact:* Amanda Hine, Assistant, 618-453-2466, E-mail: ahine@siu.edu. *Dean,* Dr. Meera Komarraju, 618-453-2466, E-mail: cola.dean@siu.edu.

College of Mass Communication and Media Arts Students: 52 full-time (26 women), 27 part-time (15 women); includes 9 minority (8 Black or African American, non-Hispanic/Latino; 1 Asian, non-Hispanic/Latino), 33 international. Average age 28. 57 applicants, 35% accepted, 6 enrolled. *Faculty:* 35 full-time (9 women), 2 part-time/adjunct (0 women). *Financial support:* In 2015–16, 51 students received support, including 2 fellowships with full tuition reimbursements available, 5 research assistantships with full tuition reimbursements available, 37 teaching assistantships with full tuition reimbursements available; career-related internships or fieldwork, Federal Work-Study, institutionally sponsored loans, and tuition waivers (full) also available. Support available to part-time students. In 2015, 24 master's, 6 doctorates awarded. *Degree program information:* Part-time programs available. Part-time. Offers mass communication and media arts (MA, MFA, MS, PhD); media theory and research (MA); professional media and media management studies (MS). *Application deadline:* For fall admission, 2/1 for domestic students. Applications are processed on a rolling basis. *Application fee:* $65. *Application Contact:* Cathy Lilley, Office Manager, 618-453-3785, E-mail: mcmagrad@siu.edu. *Interim Dean,* Dr. Dafna Lemish, 618-453-7708, E-mail: dafnalemish@siu.edu.

College of Science Students: 273 full-time (119 women), 210 part-time (75 women); includes 32 minority (10 Black or African American, non-Hispanic/Latino; 16 Asian, non-Hispanic/Latino; 6 Hispanic/Latino), 313 international. 625 applicants, 37% accepted, 61 enrolled. *Faculty:* 137 full-time (8 women), 2 part-time/adjunct (0 women). *Financial support:* In 2015–16, 294 students received support, including 4 fellowships, 111 research assistantships, 176 teaching assistantships; career-related internships or fieldwork, Federal Work-Study, institutionally sponsored loans, scholarships/grants, and tuition waivers (full) also available. Support available to part-time students. In 2015, 164 master's, 32 doctorates awarded. *Degree program information:* Part-time programs available. Part-time. Offers biological sciences (MS); chemistry and biochemistry (MS, PhD); computer science (MS, PhD); environmental resources and policy (PhD); geology (MS); geosciences (PhD); mathematics (MA, MS, PhD); molecular biology, microbiology, and biochemistry (MS, PhD); physics (MS, PhD); plant biology (MS, PhD); science (MA, MS, PhD); zoology (MS, PhD). *Application deadline:* Applications are processed on a rolling basis. *Application fee:* $65. *Application Contact:* Donna Bennett, Office Manager, 618-536-6666, E-mail: donnab@siu.edu. *Dean,* Dr. Laurie Achenbach, 618-536-6666, E-mail: laurie@cos.siu.edu.

School of Law Students: 8 full-time (6 women), 2 part-time (1 woman); includes 3 minority (all Black or African American, non-Hispanic/Latino). Average age 27. 14 applicants, 57% accepted, 5 enrolled. *Faculty:* 23 full-time (11 women), 12 part-time/adjunct (6 women). *Financial support:* Career-related internships or fieldwork, Federal Work-Study, institutionally sponsored loans, scholarships/grants, and health care benefits available. Support available to part-time students. Financial award application deadline: 4/1; financial award applicants required to submit FAFSA. In 2015, 7 master's awarded. *Degree program information:* Part-time programs available. Part-time. Offers general law (LL M, MLS); health law and policy (LL M, MLS); law (JD); legal studies (MLS). *Application deadline:* For fall admission, 3/1 for domestic and international students. Applications are processed on a rolling basis. *Application fee:* $65. Electronic applications accepted. *Application Contact:* Lisa David, Admissions Coordinator, 618-453-8767, Fax: 618-453-8769, E-mail: ldavid@law.siu.edu. *Assistant Dean,* Michael Ruiz, 618-453-8763, Fax: 618-453-8769, E-mail: mikeruiz@siu.edu.

SOUTHERN ILLINOIS UNIVERSITY EDWARDSVILLE, Edwardsville, IL 62026-0001

General Information State-supported, coed, comprehensive institution. CGS member. *Enrollment:* 14,265 graduate, professional, and undergraduate students; 719 full-time matriculated graduate/professional students (419 women), 1,239 part-time matriculated graduate/professional students (773 women). *Graduate faculty:* 394. Tuition, state resident: full-time $5026; part-time $837 per course. Tuition, nonresident: full-time $12,566; part-time $2094 per course. *Required fees:* $1682; $474 per course. Tuition and fees vary according to course load, campus/location and program. *Graduate housing:* Rooms and/or apartments available on a first-come, first-served basis to single and married students. Typical cost: $4420 per year for single students; $4440 per year for married students. Housing application deadline: 5/1. *Student services:* Campus employment opportunities, campus safety program, career counseling, exercise/wellness program, free psychological counseling, grant writing training, international student services, low-cost health insurance, multicultural affairs office, services for students with disabilities, teacher training, writing training. *Library:* Lovejoy Library. *Collection:* Books: 2.5 million (physical), 51,070 (digital/electronic); Serial titles: 328 (physical), 34,724 (digital/electronic). Students can reserve study rooms. *Research affiliation:* Long Island Veterinary Clinic (electrical engineering), SSM DePaul Health Center (nursing), Nurturenergy (mechanical engineering), Tulsa Dental Products (dental medicine), Mallinckrodt (pharmacy), Schlumberger (mechanical engineering).

Computer facilities: Computer purchase and lease plans are available. 767 computers available on campus for general student use. A campuswide network can be accessed from student residence rooms and from off campus. Online class registration, online job finder are available.
Website: http://www.siue.edu/

General Application Contact: Bob Skorczewski, Coordinator of International and Graduate Recruitment, 618-650-3705, Fax: 618-650-3618, E-mail: graduateadmissions@siue.edu.

GRADUATE UNITS

Graduate School Students: 719 full-time (419 women), 1,239 part-time (773 women); includes 336 minority (181 Black or African American, non-Hispanic/Latino; 1 American Indian or Alaska Native, non-Hispanic/Latino; 58 Asian, non-Hispanic/Latino; 46 Hispanic/Latino; 2 Native Hawaiian or other Pacific Islander, non-Hispanic/Latino; 48 Two or more races, non-Hispanic/Latino), 273 international. 1,869 applicants, 60% accepted, 798 enrolled. *Faculty:* 394. *Financial support:* In 2015–16, 481 students received support, including 22 fellowships with full tuition reimbursements available (averaging $8,370 per year), 118 research assistantships with full tuition reimbursements available, 250 teaching assistantships with full tuition reimbursements available; career-related internships or fieldwork, Federal Work-Study, institutionally sponsored loans, scholarships/grants, traineeships, tuition waivers (full), and unspecified assistantships also available. Support available to part-time students. Financial award application deadline: 3/1; financial award applicants required to submit FAFSA. *Degree program information:* Part-time and evening/weekend programs available. Part-time, evening/weekend, blended/hybrid learning. Offers cultural heritage and resources management (MA, MS); diversity training (MA, MS); healthcare informatics (MS); organizational design thinking (MS); sustainability (MS). *Application deadline:* For fall admission, 7/22 for domestic students, 7/15 for international students; for spring admission, 12/9 for domestic students, 11/15 for international students; for summer admission, 4/29 for domestic students, 4/15 for international students. Applications are processed on a rolling basis. *Application fee:* $30. Electronic applications accepted. *Application Contact:* Bob Skorczewski, Coordinator of International and Graduate Recruitment, 618-650-3705, Fax: 618-650-3618, E-mail: graduateadmissions@siue.edu. *Associate Provost for Research/Dean of the Graduate School*, Dr. Jerry Weinberg, 618-650-3010, Fax: 618-650-3523, E-mail: graduateschool@siue.edu.

College of Arts and Sciences Students: 272 full-time (175 women), 367 part-time (243 women); includes 122 minority (79 Black or African American, non-Hispanic/Latino; 11 Asian, non-Hispanic/Latino; 13 Hispanic/Latino; 2 Native Hawaiian or other Pacific Islander, non-Hispanic/Latino; 17 Two or more races, non-Hispanic/Latino), 59 international. *Faculty:* 219. *Financial support:* In 2015–16, 232 students received support. Fellowships with full tuition reimbursements available, research assistantships with full tuition reimbursements available, teaching assistantships with full tuition reimbursements available, career-related internships or fieldwork, Federal Work-Study, institutionally sponsored loans, scholarships/grants, traineeships, and unspecified assistantships available. Support available to part-time students. Financial award application deadline: 3/1; financial award applicants required to submit FAFSA. *Degree program information:* Part-time and evening/weekend programs available. Part-time, evening/weekend, online learning. Offers art studio (MFA); art therapy counseling (MA); arts and sciences (MA, MFA, MM, MPA, MS, MSW, PSM, Postbaccalaureate Certificate); biology (MA, MS); chemistry (MS); computational and applied mathematics (MS); corporate and organizational communication (MA); creative writing (MA); environmental science management (PSM); environmental sciences (MS); geography (MS); health communication (MA); history (MA); interpersonal communication (MA); literature (MA, Postbaccalaureate Certificate); mass communications (MS); media literacy (Postbaccalaureate Certificate); museum studies (Postbaccalaureate Certificate); music (MM); music education (MM); music performance (MM); piano pedagogy (Postbaccalaureate Certificate); postsecondary mathematics education (MS); public administration (MPA); public relations (MA); pure mathematics (MS); school social work (MSW); social work (MSW); sociology (MA); statistics and operations research (MS); teaching English as a second language (MA, Postbaccalaureate Certificate); teaching of writing (MA, Postbaccalaureate Certificate); vocal pedagogy (Postbaccalaureate Certificate). *Application deadline:* For fall admission, 7/22 for domestic students, 7/15 for international students; for spring admission, 12/9 for domestic students, 11/15 for international students; for summer admission, 4/29 for domestic students, 4/15 for international students. Applications are processed on a rolling basis. *Application fee:* $30. Electronic applications accepted. *Application Contact:* Bob Skorczewski, Coordinator of International and Graduate Recruitment, 618-650-3705, Fax: 618-650-3618, E-mail: graduateadmissions@siue.edu. *Dean*, Dr. Greg Budzban, 618-650-5047, E-mail: college_arts_sciences@siue.edu.

School of Business Students: 112 full-time (49 women), 85 part-time (48 women); includes 26 minority (8 Black or African American, non-Hispanic/Latino; 11 Asian, non-Hispanic/Latino; 4 Hispanic/Latino; 3 Two or more races, non-Hispanic/Latino), 30 international. 190 applicants, 72% accepted. *Financial support:* In 2015–16, 3 fellowships with full tuition reimbursements, 26 research assistantships with full tuition reimbursements, 11 teaching assistantships with full tuition reimbursements were awarded; institutionally sponsored loans, scholarships/grants, and unspecified assistantships also available. Financial award application deadline: 3/1; financial award applicants required to submit FAFSA. In 2015, 112 master's awarded. *Degree program information:* Part-time and evening/weekend programs available. Part-time, evening/weekend. Offers accountancy (MSA); business (MA, MBA, MMR, MS, MSA); business analytics (MBA); computer management and information systems (MS); economics and finance (MA, MS); management information systems (MBA); marketing research (MMR); project management (MBA); taxation (MSA). *Application deadline:* For fall admission, 7/24 for domestic students, 7/15 for international students; for spring admission, 12/11 for domestic students, 11/15 for international students; for summer admission, 4/29 for domestic students, 4/15 for international students. Applications are processed on a rolling basis. *Application fee:* $30. Electronic applications accepted. *Application Contact:* Bob Skorczewski, Coordinator of International and Graduate Recruitment, 618-650-3705, Fax: 618-650-3618, E-mail: gradadmissions@siue.edu. *Interim Dean*, Dr. John Navin, 618-650-3822, E-mail: jnavin@siue.edu.

School of Education, Health, and Human Behavior Students: 157 full-time (123 women), 389 part-time (265 women); includes 105 minority (72 Black or African American, non-Hispanic/Latino; 1 American Indian or Alaska Native, non-Hispanic/Latino; 5 Asian, non-Hispanic/Latino; 12 Hispanic/Latino; 15 Two or more races, non-Hispanic/Latino), 12 international. 626 applicants, 51% accepted. *Faculty:* 66. *Financial support:* In 2015–16, 81 students received support, including 5 fellowships with full tuition reimbursements available, 21 research assistantships with full tuition reimbursements available, 41 teaching assistantships with full tuition reimbursements available; institutionally sponsored loans, scholarships/grants, and unspecified assistantships also available. Financial award application deadline: 3/1; financial award applicants required to submit FAFSA. In 2015, 168 master's, 6 doctorates, 35 other advanced degrees awarded. *Degree program information:* Part-time and evening/weekend programs available. Part-time, evening/weekend. Offers clinical child and school psychology (MS); clinical psychology (MA); college student personnel administration (MS Ed); curriculum and instruction (MS Ed); education, health, and human behavior (MA, MS, MS Ed, Ed D, Ed S, Post-Master's Certificate, Postbaccalaureate Certificate, SD); educational administration (MS Ed, Ed S); educational leadership (MS Ed, Ed D, Ed S, Postbaccalaureate Certificate); exercise and sport psychology (MS); exercise physiology (MS); industrial-organizational psychology (MA); instructional technology (MS Ed); learning, culture, and society (MS Ed); literacy education (MS Ed); literacy specialist (Post-Master's Certificate); physical education and coaching pedagogy (MS Ed); school psychology (SD); special education (MS Ed, Post-Master's Certificate); speech-language pathology (MS); Web-based learning (Postbaccalaureate Certificate). *Application deadline:* For fall admission, 7/24 for domestic students, 7/15 for international students; for spring admission, 12/11 for domestic students, 11/15 for international students; for summer admission, 4/29 for domestic students, 4/15 for international students. Applications are processed on a rolling basis. *Application fee:* $30. Electronic applications accepted. *Application Contact:* Bob Skorczewski, Coordinator of International and Graduate Recruitment, 618-650-3705, Fax: 618-650-3618, E-mail: gradadmissions@siue.edu. *Dean*, Dr. Curt Lox, 618-650-3350, E-mail: clox@siue.edu.

School of Engineering Students: 116 full-time (27 women), 171 part-time (68 women); includes 14 minority (3 Black or African American, non-Hispanic/Latino; 8 Asian, non-Hispanic/Latino; 1 Hispanic/Latino; 2 Two or more races, non-Hispanic/Latino), 157 international. 441 applicants, 41% accepted. *Financial support:* In 2015–16, 4 fellowships with full tuition reimbursements, 35 research assistantships with full tuition reimbursements, 51 teaching assistantships with full tuition reimbursements were awarded; institutionally sponsored loans, scholarships/grants, and unspecified assistantships also available. Financial award application deadline: 3/1; financial award applicants required to submit FAFSA. In 2015, 89 master's awarded. *Degree program information:* Part-time and evening/weekend programs available. Part-time, evening/weekend. Offers computer science (MS); electrical engineering (MS); engineering (MS); environmental engineering (MS); geotechnical engineering (MS); industrial engineering (MS); mechanical engineering (MS); structural engineering (MS); transportation engineering (MS). *Application deadline:* For fall admission, 7/24 for domestic students, 7/15 for international students; for spring admission, 12/11 for domestic students, 11/15 for international students; for summer admission, 4/29 for domestic students, 4/15 for international students. Applications are processed on a rolling basis. *Application fee:* $30. Electronic applications accepted. *Application Contact:* Bob Skorczewski, Coordinator of International and Graduate Recruitment, 618-650-3705, Fax: 618-650-3618, E-mail: gradadmissions@siue.edu. *Dean*, Dr. Hasan Sevim, 618-650-2541, E-mail: hsevim@siue.edu.

School of Nursing Students: 76 full-time (50 women), 180 part-time (165 women); includes 29 minority (12 Black or African American, non-Hispanic/Latino; 7 Asian, non-Hispanic/Latino; 6 Hispanic/Latino; 4 Two or more races, non-Hispanic/Latino). 87 applicants, 86% accepted. *Financial support:* In 2015–16, 5 teaching assistantships with full tuition reimbursements were awarded; fellowships with full tuition reimbursements, research assistantships with full tuition reimbursements, institutionally sponsored loans, scholarships/grants, and unspecified assistantships also available. Financial award application deadline: 3/1; financial award applicants required to submit FAFSA. In 2015, 136 master's, 5 doctorates, 1 other advanced degree awarded. *Degree program information:* Part-time and evening/weekend programs available. Part-time, evening/weekend. Offers family nurse practitioner (MS, Post-Master's Certificate); health care and nursing administration (MS, Post-Master's Certificate); nurse anesthesia (DNP); nurse educator (MS, Post-Master's Certificate); nursing (MS, DNP, Post-Master's Certificate). *Application deadline:* For fall admission, 3/1 for domestic and international students; for summer admission, 6/1 for domestic and international students. *Application fee:* $30. Electronic applications accepted. *Application Contact:* Bob Skorczewski, Coordinator of International and Graduate Recruitment, 618-650-3705, Fax: 618-650-3854, E-mail: gradadmissions@siue.edu. *Interim Dean*, Dr. Laura Bernaix, 618-650-3956, Fax: 618-650-3854, E-mail: lbernai@siue.edu.

School of Dental Medicine 547 applicants, 15% accepted. *Faculty:* 15 full-time (5 women). *Financial support:* Application deadline: 3/1; applicants required to submit FAFSA. In 2015, 45 doctorates awarded. Offers dental medicine (DMD). *Application deadline:* For fall admission, 6/1 priority date for domestic and international students. Electronic applications accepted. *Dean*, Dr. Bruce Rotter, 618-474-7000, Fax: 618-474-7249, E-mail: sdmapps@siue.edu.

School of Pharmacy 220 applicants, 46% accepted. *Faculty:* 40 full-time (23 women). *Financial support:* Career-related internships or fieldwork, Federal Work-Study, institutionally sponsored loans, scholarships/grants, and traineeships available. Support available to part-time students. Financial award application deadline: 3/1; financial award applicants required to submit FAFSA. In 2015, 76 doctorates awarded. Offers pharmacy education (Pharm D); pharmacy pediatrics (Pharm D). *Application deadline:* For fall admission, 2/1 for domestic and international students. *Application fee:* $40. Electronic applications accepted. *Application Contact:* Connie Stamper-Carr, Director of Student Affairs, 618-650-5150, Fax: 618-650-5152, E-mail: pharmacy@siue.edu. *Dean*, Dr. Gireesh V. Gupchup, 618-650-5150, Fax: 618-650-5152, E-mail: pharmacy@siue.edu.

SOUTHERN METHODIST UNIVERSITY, Dallas, TX 75275

General Information Independent-religious, coed, university. CGS member. *Graduate housing:* Rooms and/or apartments available on a first-come, first-served basis to single and married students. Housing application deadline: 5/31.

GRADUATE UNITS

Annette Caldwell Simmons School of Education and Human Development ***Degree program information:*** Part-time and evening/weekend programs available. Part-time, evening/weekend. Offers bilingual/ESL education (MBE); counseling (MS); dispute resolution (MA); education (M Ed, PhD); education and human development (M Ed, MA, MBE, MLS, MS, PhD, Certificate); gifted education (MBE); liberal studies (MLS); reading and writing (M Ed); special education (M Ed); sport management (MS).

Bobby B. Lyle School of Engineering ***Degree program information:*** Part-time and evening/weekend programs available. Part-time, evening/weekend, online learning. Offers air pollution control and atmospheric sciences (PhD); applied science (MS); civil engineering (MS); computer engineering (MS, PhD); computer science (MS, PhD); datacenter systems engineering (MS); electrical engineering (MSEE, PhD); engineering (MA, MS, MS Cp E, MSEE, MSEM, MSIEM, MSME, DE, PhD); engineering management (MSEM, DE); environmental engineering (MS); environmental science (MS); information engineering and management (MSIEM); manufacturing systems management (MS); mechanical engineering (MSME, PhD); operations research (MS, PhD); packaging of electronic and optical devices (MS); security engineering (MS); software engineering (MS, DE); structural engineering (PhD); sustainability and development (MA); systems engineering (MS, PhD); telecommunications (MS); water and wastewater engineering (PhD).

Cox School of Business *Degree program information:* Part-time and evening/weekend programs available. Part-time, evening/weekend. Offers accounting (MSA); business (Exec MBA); business administration (EMBA, MBA); entrepreneurship (MS); finance (MBA, MSF); financial statement analysis (PMBA); general business (MBA); information technology and operations management (MBA); management (MSM); marketing (MBA); real estate (MBA); strategy (MBA); strategy and entrepreneurship (MBA). Electronic applications accepted.

Dedman College of Humanities and Sciences *Degree program information:* Part-time and evening/weekend programs available. Part-time, evening/weekend. Offers anthropology (PhD); applied economics (MA); applied economics and predictive analytics (MS); applied geophysics (MS); chemistry (MS, PhD); classical/medieval history (MA); clinical psychology (PhD); computational and applied mathematics (MS, PhD); earth sciences (MS, PhD); economics (PhD); English (MA, PhD); European history (MA); Hebrew Bible/Old Testament (PhD); history (PhD); history of the Christian tradition (PhD); humanities and sciences (MA, MS, PhD); Ibero-American history (MA); law and economics (MA); materials science and engineering (MS, PhD); medical anthropology (MA); medieval studies (MA); molecular and cellular biology (MA, MS, PhD); New Testament (PhD); physics (MS, PhD); religion and culture (PhD); religious ethics (PhD); religious studies (MA); statistical science (MS, PhD); systematics theology (PhD); United States history (MA). Electronic applications accepted.

Dedman School of Law *Degree program information:* Part-time and evening/weekend programs available. Part-time, evening/weekend. Offers law (JD, SJD); law (for foreign law school graduates) (LL M); law (general) (LL M); taxation (LL M). Electronic applications accepted.

Meadows School of the Arts *Degree program information:* Evening/weekend programs available. Evening/weekend. Offers arts (MA, MFA, MM, MM, MSM, PhD, Diploma). Electronic applications accepted.

Division of Art Offers studio art (MFA).

Division of Art History Degree program information: Part-time and evening/weekend programs available. Part-time, evening/weekend. Offers art history (MA); rhetorics of art, space and culture (PhD).

Division of Arts Management and Arts Entrepreneurship Offers international arts management (MM). MM offered jointly with Bocconi University Graduate School of Management in Milan and HEC Montreal. Electronic applications accepted.

Division of Music Degree program information: Part-time programs available. Part-time. Offers composition (MM); conducting (MM); music education (MM); music history and literature (MM); performance (MM); piano performance and pedagogy (MM); theory pedagogy (MM). Electronic applications accepted.

Division of Theatre Offers acting (MFA); design (MFA). Electronic applications accepted.

Temerlin Advertising Institute Offers advertising (MA). Electronic applications accepted.

Perkins School of Theology *Degree program information:* Part-time programs available. Part-time. Offers theology (CMM, M Div, MSM, MTS, D Min).

SOUTHERN NAZARENE UNIVERSITY, Bethany, OK 73008

General Information Independent-religious, coed, comprehensive institution. *Graduate housing:* Rooms and/or apartments available on a first-come, first-served basis to single and married students. Housing application deadline: 8/1.

GRADUATE UNITS

College of Professional and Graduate Studies *Degree program information:* Part-time and evening/weekend programs available. Part-time, evening/weekend. Offers counseling psychology (MA, MSCP); marital and family therapy (MA). Electronic applications accepted.

School of Business Degree program information: Part-time and evening/weekend programs available. Part-time, evening/weekend, online learning. Offers business administration (MBA); health care management (MBA); management (MS Mgt). Electronic applications accepted.

School of Kinesiology Offers sports management and administration (MA).

School of Nursing Degree program information: Part-time and evening/weekend programs available. Part-time, evening/weekend. Offers nursing education (MS); nursing leadership (MS).

SOUTHERN NEW HAMPSHIRE UNIVERSITY, Manchester, NH 03106-1045

General Information Independent, coed, university. *Graduate housing:* Room and/or apartments available on a first-come, first-served basis to single students; on-campus housing not available to married students.

GRADUATE UNITS

School of Arts and Sciences *Degree program information:* Part-time and evening/weekend programs available. Part-time, evening/weekend. Offers community mental health (Graduate Certificate); community mental health and mental health counseling (MS); fiction and nonfiction (MFA); teaching English as a foreign language (MS). Electronic applications accepted.

School of Business *Degree program information:* Part-time and evening/weekend programs available. Part-time, evening/weekend, online learning. Offers accounting (MBA, MS, Graduate Certificate); accounting finance (MS); accounting/auditing (MS); accounting/forensic accounting (MS); accounting/taxation (MS); athletic administration (MBA, Graduate Certificate); business administration (IMBA, MBA, Certificate, Graduate Certificate); corporate social responsibility (MBA); entrepreneurship (MBA); finance (MBA, MS, Graduate Certificate); finance/corporate finance (MS); finance/investments and securities (MS); forensic accounting (MBA); healthcare informatics (MBA); healthcare management (MBA); human resource management (Graduate Certificate); information technology (MS, Graduate Certificate); information technology management (MBA); international business (Graduate Certificate); international business and information technology (Graduate Certificate); international finance (Graduate Certificate); international sport management (Graduate Certificate); justice studies (MBA); leadership of nonprofit organizations (Graduate Certificate); marketing (MBA, MS, Graduate Certificate); operations and project management (MS); operations and supply chain management (MBA, Graduate Certificate); organizational leadership (MS); project management (MBA, Graduate Certificate); Six Sigma (MBA); Six Sigma quality (Graduate Certificate); social media marketing (MBA); sport management (MBA, MS, Graduate Certificate); sustainability and environmental compliance (MBA); workplace conflict management (MBA). Electronic applications accepted.

School of Education *Degree program information:* Part-time and evening/weekend programs available. Part-time, evening/weekend, online learning. Offers business education (M Ed); child development (M Ed); curriculum and instruction (M Ed); education (M Ed); educational leadership (M Ed, Ed D); educational studies (M Ed); elementary education (M Ed); English (MAT); English for speakers of other languages (M Ed); reading and writing specialist (M Ed); school business administration (Certificate); secondary education (M Ed); special education (M Ed); technology integration specialist (M Ed). Electronic applications accepted.

SOUTHERN OREGON UNIVERSITY, Ashland, OR 97520

General Information State-supported, coed, comprehensive institution. *Enrollment:* 6,052 graduate, professional, and undergraduate students; 253 full-time matriculated graduate/professional students (167 women), 414 part-time matriculated graduate/professional students (291 women). *Enrollment by degree level:* 667 master's. *Graduate faculty:* 212 full-time (92 women), 104 part-time/adjunct (67 women). *Graduate housing:* Rooms and/or apartments available on a first-come, first-served basis to single and married students. Housing application deadline: 8/1. *Student services:* Campus employment opportunities, campus safety program, career counseling, child daycare facilities, exercise/wellness program, free psychological counseling, international student services, low-cost health insurance, multicultural affairs office, services for students with disabilities, teacher training, writing training. *Library:* Lenn and Dixie Hannon Library. *Collection:* Books: 340,015 (physical), 135,298 (digital/electronic); Databases: 80. Students can reserve study rooms. *Research affiliation:* U.S. Forest Service (biology, ecology studies), U.S. Fish and Wildlife Service (forensics), Oregon Shakespeare Festival (theatre arts), Crater Lake National Park (scientific studies), Bureau of Land Management (ecological studies), Bear Creek Corporation (environmental studies).

Computer facilities: Computer purchase and lease plans are available. 750 computers available on campus for general student use. A campuswide network can be accessed from student residence rooms and from off campus. Online class registration, online account information including bill payment, online employee records for student workers are available.
Website: http://www.sou.edu/

General Application Contact: Kelly Moutsatson, Director of Admissions, 541-552-6411, Fax: 541-552-8403, E-mail: admissions@sou.edu.

GRADUATE UNITS

Graduate Studies Students: 253 full-time (167 women), 414 part-time (291 women); includes 51 minority (1 Black or African American, non-Hispanic/Latino; 10 American Indian or Alaska Native, non-Hispanic/Latino; 8 Asian, non-Hispanic/Latino; 23 Hispanic/Latino; 9 Two or more races, non-Hispanic/Latino), 18 international. Average age 35. 391 applicants, 73% accepted, 227 enrolled. *Faculty:* 212 full-time (92 women), 104 part-time/adjunct (67 women). *Financial support:* In 2015–16, 14 students received support, including 14 research assistantships with partial tuition reimbursements available; career-related internships or fieldwork, Federal Work-Study, institutionally sponsored loans, scholarships/grants, and unspecified assistantships also available. Support available to part-time students. In 2015, 274 master's awarded. *Degree program information:* Part-time and evening/weekend programs available. Part-time, evening/weekend, online learning. Offers applied computer science (PSM); applied mathematics (PSM); environmental education (MS); French language teaching (MA); interdisciplinary studies (MIS); performance (MM); psychology (MHC); Spanish language teaching (MA). *Application deadline:* For fall admission, 7/31 priority date for domestic and international students; for winter admission, 11/15 priority date for domestic and international students; for spring admission, 1/7 priority date for domestic and international students. Applications are processed on a rolling basis. *Application fee:* $50. Electronic applications accepted. *Application Contact:* Kelly Moutsatson, Director of Admissions, 541-552-6411, Fax: 541-552-8403, E-mail: admissions@sou.edu. *Dean of Graduate Studies,* Dr. Jody Waters, 541-552-6121, E-mail: watersj@sou.edu.

Ashland Center for Theatre Studies Degree program information: Part-time programs available. Part-time. Offers theatre studies (MTS). Electronic applications accepted.

School of Business Degree program information: Part-time and evening/weekend programs available. Part-time, evening/weekend, online learning. Offers accounting (Postbaccalaureate Certificate); business administration (MBA); international management (MIM). Electronic applications accepted.

School of Education Online learning. Offers elementary education (MA Ed, MS Ed); secondary education (MA Ed, MS Ed); teaching (MAT). Electronic applications accepted.

SOUTHERN UNIVERSITY AND AGRICULTURAL AND MECHANICAL COLLEGE, Baton Rouge, LA 70813

General Information State-supported, coed, university. CGS member. *Graduate housing:* Room and/or apartments available on a first-come, first-served basis to single students; on-campus housing not available to married students. Housing application deadline: 6/30. *Research affiliation:* NASA (mechanical engineering), Michigan State University (language screening of African-Americans), University of Georgia (substance abuse prevention), The University of Alabama (diabetes), NASA (drinking water remote sensing), Livingston Observatory (gravitational waves, cosmic gravity waves, black waves).

GRADUATE UNITS

College of Business Offers business (MBA).

Graduate School *Degree program information:* Part-time programs available. Part-time. Offers science/mathematics education (PhD); special education (M Ed, PhD).

College of Agricultural, Family and Consumer Sciences Offers urban forestry (MS).

College of Arts and Humanities Offers arts and humanities (MA); mass communication (MA); social sciences (MA).

College of Education Offers administration and supervision (M Ed); counselor education (MA); education (M Ed, MA, MS, PhD); educational leadership (M Ed); elementary education (M Ed); media (M Ed); mental health counseling (MA); secondary education (M Ed); therapeutic recreation (MS).

College of Engineering Offers engineering (ME).

College of Sciences Degree program information: Part-time programs available. Part-time. Offers analytical chemistry (MS); biochemistry (MS); biology (MS); environmental sciences (MS); information systems (MS); inorganic chemistry (MS); mathematics (MS); micro/minicomputer architecture (MS); operating systems (MS); organic chemistry (MS); physical chemistry (MS); physics (MS); rehabilitation counseling (MS); sciences (MA, MS).

Nelson Mandela School of Public Policy and Urban Affairs Offers criminal justice (MS); public administration (MPA); public policy (PhD); public policy and urban affairs (MA, MPA, MS, PhD); social sciences (MA).

School of Nursing *Degree program information:* Part-time programs available. Part-time. Offers educator/administrator (PhD); family health nursing (MSN); family nurse practitioner (Post Master's Certificate); geriatric nurse practitioner/gerontology (PhD).

Southern University Law Center *Degree program information:* Part-time and evening/weekend programs available. Part-time, evening/weekend. Offers law (JD). Electronic applications accepted.

SOUTHERN UNIVERSITY AT NEW ORLEANS, New Orleans, LA 70126-1009

General Information State-supported, coed, primarily women, comprehensive institution. *Graduate housing:* Room and/or apartments available on a first-come, first-served basis to single students; on-campus housing not available to married students.

GRADUATE UNITS

School of Graduate Studies *Degree program information:* Part-time and evening/weekend programs available. Part-time, evening/weekend. Offers criminal justice (MA); management information systems (MS); museum studies (MA); social work (MSW).

SOUTHERN UTAH UNIVERSITY, Cedar City, UT 84720-2498

General Information State-supported, coed, comprehensive institution. *Enrollment:* 8,881 graduate, professional, and undergraduate students; 197 full-time matriculated graduate/professional students (99 women), 649 part-time matriculated graduate/professional students (408 women). *Enrollment by degree level:* 846 master's. *Graduate faculty:* 40 full-time (9 women), 31 part-time/adjunct (10 women). Tuition and fees vary according to program. *Graduate housing:* Room and/or apartments available on a first-come, first-served basis to single students; on-campus housing not available to married students. Typical cost: $3167 per year ($7067 including board). Room and board charges vary according to board plan and housing facility selected. *Student services:* Campus employment opportunities, campus safety program, career counseling, exercise/wellness program, free psychological counseling, international student services, low-cost health insurance, multicultural affairs office, services for students with disabilities, teacher training. *Library:* Gerald R Sherratt Library. *Collection:* Books: 236,516 (physical), 176,187 (digital/electronic); Databases: 218. Students can reserve study rooms.

Computer facilities: A campuswide network can be accessed from student residence rooms and from off campus. Online class registration is available.
Website: http://www.suu.edu/

General Application Contact: Jay Sorensen, Graduate Recruitment Coordinator, 435-865-8189, Fax: 435-865-8223, E-mail: jaysorensen1@suu.edu.

GRADUATE UNITS

Master of Accountancy/MBA Dual Degree Program 6 applicants, 83% accepted. *Financial support:* Unspecified assistantships available. *Degree program information:* Part-time programs available. Part-time, 100% online. *Application deadline:* For fall admission, 3/1 for domestic and international students; for spring admission, 10/1 for domestic and international students; for summer admission, 3/1 for domestic and international students. Applications are processed on a rolling basis. *Application fee:* $60 ($65 for international students). Electronic applications accepted. *Application Contact:* Paula Alger, Advisor/Curriculum Coordinator, 435-865-8157, Fax: 435-586-5493, E-mail: alger@suu.edu.

Program in Accounting Students: 38 full-time (10 women), 37 part-time (13 women); includes 3 minority (1 Asian, non-Hispanic/Latino; 2 Hispanic/Latino). Average age 28. 49 applicants, 78% accepted, 28 enrolled. *Financial support:* Unspecified assistantships available. In 2015, 53 master's awarded. *Degree program information:* Part-time programs available. Part-time, online learning. Offers accounting (M Acc). *Application deadline:* For fall admission, 3/1 for domestic and international students; for spring admission, 10/1 for domestic and international students; for summer admission, 3/1 for domestic and international students. Applications are processed on a rolling basis. *Application fee:* $60 ($65 for international students). Electronic applications accepted. *Application Contact:* Paula Alger, Advisor/Curriculum Coordinator, 435-865-8157, Fax: 435-586-5493, E-mail: alger@suu.edu. *Chair, Accounting Department,* Dr. David Christensen, 435-865-8058, Fax: 435-586-5493, E-mail: christensen@suu.edu.

Program in Arts Administration Students: 10 full-time (8 women), 23 part-time (21 women); includes 2 minority (1 Asian, non-Hispanic/Latino; 1 Hispanic/Latino), 1 international. Average age 34. 30 applicants, 70% accepted, 21 enrolled. *Financial support:* Tuition waivers and unspecified assistantships available. In 2015, 4 master's awarded. *Degree program information:* Part-time programs available. Part-time. Offers arts administration (MA, MFA). *Application deadline:* For fall admission, 2/15 for domestic and international students. Applications are processed on a rolling basis. *Application fee:* $60 ($65 for international students). Electronic applications accepted. *Program Director/Assistant Professor,* Rachel Bishop, 435-586-7873, Fax: 435-865-8657, E-mail: bishopr@suu.edu.

Program in Business Administration Students: 19 full-time (5 women), 27 part-time (7 women); includes 2 minority (1 Black or African American, non-Hispanic/Latino; 1 Hispanic/Latino), 1 international. Average age 32. 49 applicants, 59% accepted, 28 enrolled. *Financial support:* Unspecified assistantships available. In 2015, 19 master's awarded. *Degree program information:* Part-time programs available. Part-time, 100% online. Offers business administration (MBA). *Application deadline:* For fall admission, 3/1 for domestic and international students; for spring admission, 10/1 for domestic and international students; for summer admission, 3/1 for domestic students, 2/1 for international students. Applications are processed on a rolling basis. *Application fee:* $60 ($65 for international students). Electronic applications accepted. *Application Contact:* Paula Alger, Advisor/Curriculum Coordinator, 435-865-8157, Fax: 435-586-5493, E-mail: alger@suu.edu. *Department Chair/MBA Program Director,* Dr. Kim Craft, 435-586-5414, Fax: 435-586-5493, E-mail: craft@suu.edu.

Program in Communication Students: 21 full-time (9 women), 35 part-time (23 women); includes 9 minority (1 Black or African American, non-Hispanic/Latino; 1 American Indian or Alaska Native, non-Hispanic/Latino; 1 Asian, non-Hispanic/Latino; 5 Hispanic/Latino; 1 Native Hawaiian or other Pacific Islander, non-Hispanic/Latino), 1 international. Average age 30. 27 applicants, 85% accepted, 17 enrolled. *Financial support:* Teaching assistantships with tuition reimbursements and unspecified assistantships available. Financial award application deadline: 3/15. In 2015, 19 master's awarded. *Degree program information:* Part-time and evening/weekend programs available. Part-time, evening/weekend, 100% online. Offers communication (MA). *Application deadline:* For fall admission, 6/15 for domestic and international students; for spring admission, 10/15 for domestic and international students. Applications are processed on a rolling basis. *Application fee:* $60 ($65 for international students). Electronic applications accepted. *Application Contact:* Dr. Matthew Barton, Graduate Coordinator, 435-586-7970, Fax: 435-865-8352, E-mail: bartonm@suu.edu. *Department Chair,* Dr. Arthur Challis, 435-586-7994, Fax: 435-865-8352, E-mail: challis@suu.edu.

Program in Education Students: 11 full-time (7 women), 411 part-time (297 women); includes 18 minority (3 American Indian or Alaska Native, non-Hispanic/Latino; 5 Asian, non-Hispanic/Latino; 8 Hispanic/Latino; 2 Native Hawaiian or other Pacific Islander, non-Hispanic/Latino). Average age 38. 105 applicants, 93% accepted, 79 enrolled. *Financial support:* Tuition waivers (partial) available. In 2015, 147 master's awarded. *Degree program information:* Part-time programs available. Part-time, online only, 100% online. Offers education (M Ed, Certificate). *Application deadline:* For fall admission, 7/15 for domestic and international students; for spring admission, 11/15 for domestic and international students; for summer admission, 4/15 for domestic and international students. Applications are processed on a rolling basis. *Application fee:* $60 ($65 for international students). Electronic applications accepted. *Application Contact:* Tamara Lovell, Program Specialist, 435-865-8759, Fax: 435-865-8485, E-mail: tamaralovell@suu.edu. *Chair,* Dr. Bart Reynolds, 435-865-8125, Fax: 435-865-8485, E-mail: reynolds@suu.edu.

Program in Public Administration Students: 39 full-time (18 women), 58 part-time (24 women); includes 11 minority (1 Black or African American, non-Hispanic/Latino; 1 American Indian or Alaska Native, non-Hispanic/Latino; 3 Asian, non-Hispanic/Latino; 5 Hispanic/Latino; 1 Native Hawaiian or other Pacific Islander, non-Hispanic/Latino), 3 international. Average age 33. 52 applicants, 75% accepted, 34 enrolled. *Financial support:* Tuition waivers (full and partial) and unspecified assistantships available. Financial award application deadline: 5/31. In 2015, 30 master's awarded. *Degree program information:* Part-time and evening/weekend programs available. Part-time, evening/weekend, online learning. Offers public administration (MPA). *Application deadline:* For fall admission, 7/15 for domestic and international students; for spring admission, 11/15 for domestic and international students; for summer admission, 4/15 for domestic and international students. Applications are processed on a rolling basis. *Application fee:* $60 ($65 for international students). Electronic applications accepted. *MPA Program Director,* Dr. Ravi Roy, 435-865-8153, Fax: 435-586-1925, E-mail: royr@suu.edu.

Program in Sports Conditioning Students: 10 full-time (4 women), 36 part-time (6 women); includes 6 minority (4 Black or African American, non-Hispanic/Latino; 2 Hispanic/Latino). Average age 29. 23 applicants, 74% accepted, 16 enrolled. In 2015, 12 master's awarded. *Degree program information:* Part-time programs available. Part-time, online only, 100% online. Offers sports conditioning (MS). *Application deadline:* For fall admission, 7/15 for domestic and international students; for spring admission, 10/15 for domestic and international students; for summer admission, 2/15 for domestic and international students. Applications are processed on a rolling basis. *Application fee:* $60 ($65 for international students). Electronic applications accepted. *Application Contact:* Stephanie Smith, 435-586-1558, Fax: 435-865-8057, E-mail: stephanie-smith@leavitt.com. *Interim Department Chair,* Dr. Camille Thomas, 435-586-7815, Fax: 435-865-8057, E-mail: camillethomas1@suu.edu.

SOUTHERN WESLEYAN UNIVERSITY, Central, SC 29630-1020

General Information Independent-religious, coed, comprehensive institution. *Graduate housing:* On-campus housing not available.

GRADUATE UNITS

Program in Business Administration *Degree program information:* Evening/weekend programs available. Evening/weekend. Offers business administration (MBA).

Program in Christian Ministries *Degree program information:* Part-time and evening/weekend programs available. Part-time, evening/weekend. Offers Christian ministries (M Min).

Program in Education *Degree program information:* Evening/weekend programs available. Evening/weekend. Offers education (M Ed). Program also offered at Greenville, S. C. site.

Program in Management *Degree program information:* Evening/weekend programs available. Evening/weekend. Offers management (MSM).

SOUTH FLORIDA BIBLE COLLEGE AND THEOLOGICAL SEMINARY, Deerfield Beach, FL 33441

General Information Proprietary, coed, comprehensive institution.

GRADUATE UNITS

Graduate Programs Offers biblical studies (MA); theology (M Div).

SOUTH UNIVERSITY, Montgomery, AL 36116-1120

General Information Proprietary, coed, comprehensive institution.

GRADUATE UNITS

Program in Business Administration Offers business administration (MBA).

Program in Clinical Mental Health Counseling Offers clinical mental health counseling (MA).

Program in Criminal Justice Offers criminal justice (MS).

Program in Healthcare Administration Offers healthcare administration (MBA).

Program in Information Systems and Technology Offers information systems and technology (MS).

Program in Nursing Offers nursing (MSN).

Program in Public Administration Offers public administration (MPA).

SOUTH UNIVERSITY, Royal Palm Beach, FL 33411

General Information Proprietary, coed, comprehensive institution.

GRADUATE UNITS

Program in Business Administration Offers business administration (MBA); healthcare administration (MBA).

Program in Clinical Mental Health Counseling Offers clinical mental health counseling (MA).

Program in Criminal Justice Offers criminal justice (MS).

Program in Information Systems and Technology Offers information systems and technology (MS).

Program in Nursing Offers family nurse practitioner (MS).

Program in Occupational Therapy Offers occupational therapy (OTD).

Program in Public Administration Offers public administration (MPA).

SOUTH UNIVERSITY, Tampa, FL 33614

General Information Proprietary, coed, comprehensive institution.

GRADUATE UNITS

Program in Business Administration Offers business administration (MBA).

Program in Criminal Justice Offers criminal justice (MS).

Program in Healthcare Administration Offers healthcare administration (MBA).

Program in Information Systems and Technology Offers information systems and technology (MS).

Program in Nursing Offers adult health nurse practitioner (MS); family nurse practitioner (MS); nurse educator (MS).

Program in Physician Assistant Studies Offers physician assistant studies (MS).

SOUTH UNIVERSITY, Savannah, GA 31406

General Information Proprietary, coed, comprehensive institution.

GRADUATE UNITS

Graduate Programs

College of Arts and Sciences Offers arts and sciences (MA, MS); clinical mental health counseling (MA); criminal justice (MS).

College of Business Offers corrections (MBA); entrepreneurship and small business (MBA); healthcare administration (MBA); hospitality management (MBA); leadership (MS); public administration (MPA); sustainability (MBA).

College of Health Professions Offers anesthesiologist assistant (MM Sc); health professions (MM Sc, MS); physician assistant studies (MS).

College of Nursing Offers nurse educator (MS).

Doctor of Ministry Program Offers ministry (D Min).

School of Pharmacy

SOUTH UNIVERSITY, Novi, MI 48377

General Information Proprietary, coed, comprehensive institution.

GRADUATE UNITS

Program in Business Administration Offers business administration (MBA).

Program in Clinical Mental Health Counseling Offers clinical mental health counseling (MA).

Program in Leadership Offers leadership (MS).

Program in Ministry Offers ministry (D Min).

Program in Nursing Offers nursing (MSN).

SOUTH UNIVERSITY, High Point, NC 27265

General Information Proprietary, coed, comprehensive institution.

GRADUATE UNITS

Program in Business Administration Offers business administration (MBA).

Program in Clinical Mental Health Counseling Offers clinical mental health counseling (MA).

SOUTH UNIVERSITY, Cleveland, OH 44128

General Information Proprietary, coed, comprehensive institution.

GRADUATE UNITS

Program in Business Administration Offers business administration (MBA).

Program in Clinical Mental Health Counseling Offers clinical mental health counseling (MA).

SOUTH UNIVERSITY, Columbia, SC 29203

General Information Proprietary, coed, comprehensive institution.

GRADUATE UNITS

Program in Business Administration Offers business administration (MBA).

Program in Clinical Mental Health Counseling Offers clinical mental health counseling (MA).

Program in Criminal Justice Offers criminal justice (MS).

Program in Healthcare Administration Offers healthcare administration (MBA).

Program in Leadership Offers leadership (MS).

Program in Nursing Offers nursing (MSN).

Program in Pharmacy Offers pharmacy (Pharm D).

SOUTH UNIVERSITY, Round Rock, TX 78681

General Information Proprietary, coed, comprehensive institution.

GRADUATE UNITS

Program in Business Administration Offers business administration (MBA).

Program in Clinical Mental Health Counseling Offers clinical mental health counseling (MA).

Program in Information Systems and Technology Offers information systems and technology (MS).

SOUTH UNIVERSITY, Glen Allen, VA 23060

General Information Proprietary, coed, comprehensive institution.

GRADUATE UNITS

Program in Business Administration Offers business administration (MBA).

Program in Clinical Mental Health Counseling Offers clinical mental health counseling (MA).

Program in Nursing Offers nursing (MSN).

SOUTH UNIVERSITY, Virginia Beach, VA 23452

General Information Proprietary, coed, comprehensive institution.

GRADUATE UNITS

Program in Business Administration Offers business administration (MBA).

Program in Clinical Mental Health Counseling Offers clinical mental health counseling (MA).

Program in Information Systems and Technology Offers information systems and technology (MS).

Program in Leadership Offers leadership (MS).

Program in Nursing Offers family nurse practitioner (MSN).

SOUTHWEST ACUPUNCTURE COLLEGE, Santa Fe, NM 87505

General Information Private, coed, primarily women, graduate-only institution. *Graduate housing:* On-campus housing not available.

GRADUATE UNITS

Program in Oriental Medicine, Boulder Campus ***Degree program information:*** Part-time programs available. Part-time. Offers Oriental medicine (MS).

Program in Oriental Medicine, Santa Fe Campus ***Degree program information:*** Part-time programs available. Part-time. Offers Oriental medicine (MS). Electronic applications accepted.

SOUTHWEST BAPTIST UNIVERSITY, Bolivar, MO 65613-2597

General Information Independent-religious, coed, comprehensive institution. *Graduate housing:* Room and/or apartments available on a first-come, first-served basis to single students; on-campus housing not available to married students.

GRADUATE UNITS

Program in Business ***Degree program information:*** Part-time programs available. Part-time, online learning. Offers business administration (MBA); health administration (MBA).

Program in Education ***Degree program information:*** Part-time programs available. Part-time. Offers education (MS); educational administration (MS, Ed S).

Program in Physical Therapy Offers physical therapy (DPT).

SOUTHWEST COLLEGE OF NATUROPATHIC MEDICINE AND HEALTH SCIENCES, Tempe, AZ 85282

General Information Independent, coed, graduate-only institution. *Enrollment by degree level:* 385 doctoral. *Graduate faculty:* 21 full-time (10 women), 59 part-time/adjunct (41 women). *Tuition, area resident:* Full-time $32,651; part-time $317 per credit. *Required fees:* $1740. One-time fee: $935 full-time. Tuition and fees vary according to course load, program and student level. *Graduate housing:* On-campus housing not available. *Student services:* Campus employment opportunities, career counseling. *Library:* SCNM Library. *Collection:* Books: 5,000 (physical), 186 (digital/electronic); Serial titles: 80 (physical), 250 (digital/electronic); Databases: 20. Weekly public service hours: 45; students can reserve study rooms. *Research affiliation:* Arizona State University, Biodesign Institute (immune modulation, virology), Aviratek, LLC (antimicrobial botanicals), Arizona State University, Biodesign Institute (genomics, herbal medicine).

Computer facilities: 16 computers available on campus for general student use. A campuswide network can be accessed from student residence rooms and from off campus. Online class registration is available.
Website: http://www.scnm.edu/

General Application Contact: Eve Adams, Director of Admissions, 480-858-9100 Ext. 213, Fax: 480-222-9413, E-mail: e.adams@scnm.edu.

GRADUATE UNITS

Program in Naturopathic Medicine Students: 367 full-time (271 women), 18 part-time (16 women); includes 136 minority (37 Black or African American, non-Hispanic/Latino; 3 American Indian or Alaska Native, non-Hispanic/Latino; 32 Asian, non-Hispanic/Latino; 45 Hispanic/Latino; 2 Native Hawaiian or other Pacific Islander, non-Hispanic/Latino; 17 Two or more races, non-Hispanic/Latino), 29 international. Average age 30. 179 applicants, 72% accepted, 83 enrolled. *Faculty:* 21 full-time (10 women), 59 part-time/adjunct (41 women). *Financial support:* In 2015–16, 169 students received support. Federal Work-Study and scholarships/grants available. Financial award application deadline: 5/1; financial award applicants required to submit FAFSA. In 2015, 96 doctorates awarded. Offers naturopathic medicine (ND). *Application deadline:* For fall admission, 3/1 priority date for domestic and international students; for spring admission, 12/1 priority date for domestic and international students. Applications are processed on a rolling basis. *Application fee:* $115. Electronic applications accepted. *Application Contact:* Eve Adams, Director of Admissions, 480-858-9100 Ext. 213, Fax: 480-222-9413, E-mail: e.adams@scnm.edu. *Chief Academic Officer,* Dr. Margot Gregory, 480-858-9100 Ext. 207, E-mail: m.gregory@scnm.edu.

SOUTHWESTERN ADVENTIST UNIVERSITY, Keene, TX 76059

General Information Independent-religious, coed, comprehensive institution. *Graduate housing:* Rooms and/or apartments available on a first-come, first-served basis to single and married students. Housing application deadline: 8/31.

GRADUATE UNITS

Business Administration Department ***Degree program information:*** Part-time and evening/weekend programs available. Part-time, evening/weekend. Offers accounting (MBA); finance (MBA); management/leadership (MBA).

Education Department ***Degree program information:*** Part-time and evening/weekend programs available. Part-time, evening/weekend. Offers curriculum and instruction with reading emphasis (M Ed); educational leadership (M Ed).

SOUTHWESTERN ASSEMBLIES OF GOD UNIVERSITY, Waxahachie, TX 75165-5735

General Information Independent-religious, coed, comprehensive institution. *Graduate housing:* Room and/or apartments guaranteed to single students.

GRADUATE UNITS

Thomas F. Harrison School of Graduate Studies ***Degree program information:*** Part-time and evening/weekend programs available. Part-time, evening/weekend, online learning. Offers Bible and theology (MS); Biblical studies (M Div); Christian school administration (MS); counseling (M Div); counseling psychology (clinical) (MCP); cross cultural missions (M Div); curriculum development (MS); early education administration (M Ed); history (MA); human services counseling (MS); middle and secondary education (M Ed); practical theology (M Div); theological studies (M Div). Electronic applications accepted.

SOUTHWESTERN BAPTIST THEOLOGICAL SEMINARY, Fort Worth, TX 76122-0000

General Information Independent-religious, coed, primarily men, graduate-only institution. *Graduate housing:* Rooms and/or apartments available on a first-come, first-served basis to single and married students. *Research affiliation:* Campus Crusade for Christ/Jesus Film Project (evangelical missions), DAWN: Discipling A Whole Nation (evangelical missions).

GRADUATE UNITS

Jack D. Terry School of Church and Family Ministries ***Degree program information:*** Part-time and evening/weekend programs available. Part-time, evening/weekend. Offers church and family ministries (MA, MACE, MACSE, DEM, PhD). Electronic applications accepted.

Roy Fish School of Evangelism and Missions Offers cross-cultural missions (MTS); evangelism (M Div); evangelism and missions (D Min); international church planting (M Div); Islamic studies (M Div, MA Islamic); missiology (MA Miss); missions (M Div); North American church planting (M Div); North American evangelism and international missions (D Min); theology (Th M); world Christian studies (PhD).

School of Church Music ***Degree program information:*** Part-time programs available. Part-time. Offers church music (MACM, MAWSHP, MM, DMA, PhD). Electronic applications accepted.

School of Preaching Offers preaching (Th M, D Min, PhD, Certificate).

School of Theology ***Degree program information:*** Part-time and evening/weekend programs available. Part-time, evening/weekend. Offers ministry (D Min); theology (PhD). Electronic applications accepted.

SOUTHWESTERN CHRISTIAN UNIVERSITY, Bethany, OK 73008-0340

General Information Independent-religious, coed, comprehensive institution.

GRADUATE UNITS

Program in Ministry ***Degree program information:*** Part-time programs available. Part-time. Offers church planting (M Min); church revitalization and renewal (M Min); intercultural studies (M Min); leadership (M Min); life coaching (M Min); pastoral ministries (M Min); work place ministries (M Min). Electronic applications accepted.

SOUTHWESTERN COLLEGE, Winfield, KS 67156-2499

General Information Independent-religious, coed, comprehensive institution. *Enrollment:* 1,471 graduate, professional, and undergraduate students; 63 full-time matriculated graduate/professional students (44 women), 217 part-time matriculated graduate/professional students (113 women). *Enrollment by degree level:* 221 master's, 58 doctoral, 1 other advanced degree. *Graduate faculty:* 12 full-time (8 women), 55 part-time/adjunct (25 women). *Tuition, area resident:* Full-time $8316; part-time $462 per credit hour. *Required fees:* $150; $75 per semester. $30 per term. Tuition and fees vary according to degree level, campus/location and program. *Graduate housing:* Rooms and/or apartments available on a first-come, first-served basis to single and married students. Typical cost: $3200 per year ($6900 including board) for single students. Room and board charges vary according to board plan, campus/location and housing facility selected. *Student services:* Campus employment opportunities, campus safety program, career counseling, exercise/wellness program, free psychological counseling, international student services, services for students with disabilities, teacher training, writing training. *Library:* Harold and Mary Ellen Deets Library plus 1 other. *Collection:* Books: 62,000 (physical), 380,000 (digital/electronic); Serial titles: 81 (physical), 81 (digital/electronic); Databases: 101. Weekly public service hours: 81; students can reserve study rooms.

Computer facilities: Computer purchase and lease plans are available. 50 computers available on campus for general student use. A campuswide network can be accessed from student residence rooms and from off campus. Online class registration is available.
Website: http://www.sckans.edu/

General Application Contact: Dean Clark, Vice President for Enrollment Management, 620-229-6364, Fax: 620-229-6344, E-mail: dean.clark@sckans.edu.

GRADUATE UNITS

Education Programs Students: 53 full-time (40 women), 112 part-time (79 women); includes 16 minority (7 Black or African American, non-Hispanic/Latino; 2 Asian, non-Hispanic/Latino; 6 Hispanic/Latino; 1 Two or more races, non-Hispanic/Latino), 50 international. Average age 37. 61 applicants, 85% accepted, 31 enrolled. *Faculty:* 10 full-time (7 women), 26 part-time/adjunct (16 women). *Financial support:* In 2015–16, 4 students received support. Scholarships/grants available. Financial award applicants required to submit FAFSA. In 2015, 72 master's, 7 doctorates awarded. *Degree program information:* Part-time and evening/weekend programs available. Part-time, evening/weekend, online learning. Offers curriculum and instruction (M Ed); early childhood education (M Ed); educational leadership (Ed D); special education (M Ed); teaching (MA). *Application deadline:* Applications are processed on a rolling basis. *Application fee:* $40. Electronic applications accepted. *Application Contact:* Dennis Russell, Director of Admissions and Student Success, 888-684-5335, Fax: 888-684-5218, E-mail: dennis.russell@sckans.edu. *Dean of Education*, Dr. Cameron Carlson, 800-846-1543 Ext. 6115, Fax: 620-229-6341, E-mail: cameron.carlson@sckans.edu.

Fifth-Year Graduate Programs Students: 10 full-time (4 women), 15 part-time (5 women); includes 4 minority (2 American Indian or Alaska Native, non-Hispanic/Latino; 2 Hispanic/Latino), 7 international. Average age 25. 40 applicants, 100% accepted, 18 enrolled. *Faculty:* 2 full-time (1 woman), 4 part-time/adjunct (1 woman). *Financial support:* In 2015–16, 11 students received support, including 1 fellowship (averaging $11,394 per year); scholarships/grants also available. Financial award applicants required to submit FAFSA. In 2015, 10 master's awarded. *Degree program information:* Part-time programs available. Part-time. Offers management (MBA). *Application deadline:* For fall admission, 8/29 for domestic students; for spring admission, 1/17 for domestic students. Applications are processed on a rolling basis. *Application fee:* $25. Electronic applications accepted. *Application Contact:* Dean Clark, Vice President for Enrollment Management, 800-846-1543 Ext. 6364, Fax: 620-229-6344, E-mail: dean.clark@sckans.edu. *Professor of Business/Business Division Chair*, Dr. Kurt Keiser, 620-229-6361, E-mail: kurt.keiser@sckans.edu.

Professional Studies Programs Students: 90 part-time (29 women); includes 21 minority (9 Black or African American, non-Hispanic/Latino; 3 American Indian or Alaska Native, non-Hispanic/Latino; 1 Asian, non-Hispanic/Latino; 4 Hispanic/Latino; 4 Two or more races, non-Hispanic/Latino). Average age 38. 79 applicants, 89% accepted, 20 enrolled. *Faculty:* 1 (woman) full-time, 28 part-time/adjunct (9 women). *Financial support:* In 2015–16, 7 students received support. Applicants required to submit FAFSA. In 2015, 61 master's awarded. *Degree program information:* Part-time and evening/weekend programs available. Part-time, evening/weekend, online only, 100% online. Offers business administration (MBA); leadership (MS); management (MS); security administration (MS); specialized ministries (MA); theological studies (MA). *Application deadline:* Applications are processed on a rolling basis. *Application fee:* $40. Electronic applications accepted. *Application Contact:* Dennis Russell, Director of Admissions and Student Success, 888-684-5335, Fax: 316-688-5218, E-mail: enrollment@sckans.edu. *Vice President for Enrollment Management*, Susan Backofen, 888-684-5335 Ext. 214, Fax: 316-688-5218, E-mail: susan.backofen@sckans.edu.

SOUTHWESTERN COLLEGE, Santa Fe, NM 87502-4788

General Information Independent, coed, primarily women, graduate-only institution. *Graduate housing:* On-campus housing not available.

GRADUATE UNITS

Program in Art Therapy/Counseling ***Degree program information:*** Part-time and evening/weekend programs available. Part-time, evening/weekend. Offers art therapy/counseling (MA).

Program in Counseling ***Degree program information:*** Part-time and evening/weekend programs available. Part-time, evening/weekend. Offers counseling (MA).

Program in Grief, Loss and Trauma Counseling ***Degree program information:*** Part-time and evening/weekend programs available. Part-time, evening/weekend, online learning. Offers grief, loss and trauma counseling (MA, Certificate).

Program in Integral Somatic Psychology Offers integral somatic psychology (Certificate).

Program in Psychodrama and Action Methods Offers psychodrama and action methods (Certificate).

Program in Transformational Ecopsychology Offers transformational ecopsychology (Certificate).

SOUTHWESTERN LAW SCHOOL, Los Angeles, CA 90010

General Information Independent, coed, graduate-only institution. *Enrollment by degree level:* 977 doctoral. *Graduate faculty:* 62 full-time (30 women), 36 part-time/adjunct (10 women). *Tuition, area resident:* Full-time $48,080; part-time $32,060 per year. *Required fees:* $200; $200 per year. *Graduate housing:* Rooms and/or apartments available on a first-come, first-served basis to single and married students. *Student services:* Campus employment opportunities, campus safety program, career counseling, exercise/wellness program, free psychological counseling, international student services, low-cost health insurance, multicultural affairs office, services for students with disabilities, writing training. *Library:* Leigh H. Taylor Law Library. Weekly public service hours: 108; students can reserve study rooms.

Computer facilities: 107 computers available on campus for general student use. A campuswide network can be accessed from student residence rooms. Online class registration is available.
Website: http://www.swlaw.edu/

General Application Contact: Lisa Gear, Assistant Dean of Admissions, 213-738-6834, Fax: 213-383-1688, E-mail: admissions@swlaw.edu.

GRADUATE UNITS

Graduate and Professional Programs Students: 659 full-time (393 women), 318 part-time (173 women); includes 336 minority (50 Black or African American, non-Hispanic/Latino; 7 American Indian or Alaska Native, non-Hispanic/Latino; 158 Asian, non-Hispanic/Latino; 121 Hispanic/Latino), 7 international. Average age 27. *Faculty:* 62 full-time (30 women), 36 part-time/adjunct (10 women). *Financial support:* Research assistantships, career-related internships or fieldwork, Federal Work-Study, institutionally sponsored loans, scholarships/grants, and tuition waivers (full and partial) available. Support available to part-time students. Financial award application deadline: 4/1; financial award applicants required to submit FAFSA. *Degree program information:* Part-time and evening/weekend programs available. Part-time, evening/weekend, online learning. Offers entertainment and media law (LL M); individualized studies (LL M); law (JD). *Application deadline:* For fall admission, 4/1 priority date for domestic and international students. Applications are processed on a rolling basis. *Application fee:* $60. Electronic applications accepted. *Application Contact:* Lisa Gear, Assistant Dean of Admissions, 213-738-6834, Fax: 213-383-1688, E-mail: admissions@swlaw.edu. *Dean*, Susan Westerberg Prager, 213-738-6710, Fax: 213-383-1688.

SOUTHWESTERN OKLAHOMA STATE UNIVERSITY, Weatherford, OK 73096-3098

General Information State-supported, coed, comprehensive institution. *Graduate housing:* Rooms and/or apartments available on a first-come, first-served basis to single and married students. Housing application deadline: 8/19. *Research affiliation:* Gulf Coast Research Laboratory.

GRADUATE UNITS

College of Arts and Sciences ***Degree program information:*** Part-time programs available. Part-time. Offers art education (M Ed); arts and sciences (M Ed, MM); English (M Ed); mathematics (M Ed); music education (MM); natural sciences (M Ed); performance (MM); social sciences (M Ed).

College of Pharmacy Offers pharmacy (Pharm D).

College of Professional and Graduate Studies ***Degree program information:*** Part-time and evening/weekend programs available. Part-time, evening/weekend, online learning.

School of Behavioral Sciences and Education ***Degree program information:*** Part-time and evening/weekend programs available. Part-time, evening/weekend, online learning. Offers community counseling (M Ed); early childhood education (M Ed); educational administration (M Ed); elementary education (M Ed); health sciences and microbiology (M Ed); kinesiology (M Ed); parks and recreation management (M Ed); school counseling (M Ed); school psychology (MS); school psychometry (M Ed); secondary education (M Ed); special education (M Ed).

School of Business and Technology ***Degree program information:*** Part-time and evening/weekend programs available. Part-time, evening/weekend, online learning. Offers business and technology (MBA). MBA distance learning degree program offered to Oklahoma residents only.

SOUTHWEST MINNESOTA STATE UNIVERSITY, Marshall, MN 56258

General Information State-supported, coed, comprehensive institution. *Graduate housing:* Room and/or apartments available to single students; on-campus housing not available to married students.

GRADUATE UNITS

Department of Business and Public Affairs ***Degree program information:*** Part-time and evening/weekend programs available. Part-time, evening/weekend, online learning. Offers leadership (MBA); management (MBA); marketing (MBA). Electronic applications accepted.

Department of Education ***Degree program information:*** Part-time and evening/weekend programs available. Part-time, evening/weekend, online learning. Offers ESL (MS); math (MS); reading (MS); special education (MS); teaching, learning and leadership (MS).

SOUTHWEST UNIVERSITY, Kenner, LA 70062

General Information Proprietary, coed, comprehensive institution.

GRADUATE UNITS

MBA Program Offers business administration (MBA); management (MBA); organizational management (MBA).

Program in Criminal Justice Offers criminal justice (MS).

Program in Management Offers management (MA).

Program in Organizational Management Offers organizational management (MA).

SOUTHWEST UNIVERSITY OF VISUAL ARTS, Tucson, AZ 85716-2505

General Information Proprietary, coed, comprehensive institution.

GRADUATE UNITS

MFA Programs Offers motion arts (MFA); painting and drawing (MFA); photography (MFA).

SPALDING UNIVERSITY, Louisville, KY 40203-2188

General Information Independent-religious, coed, comprehensive institution. CGS member. *Enrollment:* 2,202 graduate, professional, and undergraduate students; 715 full-time matriculated graduate/professional students (583 women), 300 part-time matriculated graduate/professional students (239 women). *Enrollment by degree level:* 807 master's, 208 doctoral. *Graduate faculty:* 61 full-time (42 women), 86 part-time/adjunct (55 women). *Graduate housing:* Room and/or apartments available on a first-come, first-served basis to single students; on-campus housing not available to married students. Typical cost: $6100 per year ($8900 including board). Room and board charges vary according to board plan and housing facility selected. Housing application deadline: 6/25. *Student services:* Campus employment opportunities, campus safety program, career counseling, exercise/wellness program, free psychological counseling, international student services, services for students with disabilities, teacher training, writing training. *Library:* Spalding Library plus 1 other. *Collection:* Books: 101,266 (physical), 575 (digital/electronic); Serial titles: 102 (physical), 100,000 (digital/electronic); Databases: 58. Students can reserve study rooms.

Computer facilities: 236 computers available on campus for general student use. A campuswide network can be accessed from student residence rooms and from off campus. Online class registration is available.
Website: http://www.spalding.edu/

General Application Contact: Admissions Office, 502-585-7111, Fax: 502-992-2418, E-mail: admissions@spalding.edu.

GRADUATE UNITS

Graduate Studies Students: 715 full-time (583 women), 300 part-time (239 women); includes 228 minority (171 Black or African American, non-Hispanic/Latino; 4 American Indian or Alaska Native, non-Hispanic/Latino; 12 Asian, non-Hispanic/Latino; 14 Hispanic/Latino; 5 Native Hawaiian or other Pacific Islander, non-Hispanic/Latino; 22 Two or more races, non-Hispanic/Latino), 4 international. Average age 35. 567 applicants, 53% accepted, 251 enrolled. *Faculty:* 57 full-time (39 women), 55 part-time/adjunct (39 women). *Financial support:* In 2015–16, 70 research assistantships (averaging $6,029 per year) were awarded; career-related internships or fieldwork, Federal Work-Study, scholarships/grants, traineeships, and unspecified assistantships also available. Support available to part-time students. Financial award applicants required to submit FAFSA. In 2015, 306 master's, 29 doctorates awarded. *Degree program information:* Part-time and evening/weekend programs available. Part-time, evening/weekend. *Application deadline:* Applications are processed on a rolling basis. *Application fee:* $30. *Application Contact:* Admissions Office, 502-585-7111, E-mail: admissions@spalding.edu. *Provost*, Dr. Randy Strickland, 502-873-4405, E-mail: rstrickland@spalding.edu.

College of Education Students: 114 full-time (91 women), 64 part-time (47 women); includes 75 minority (65 Black or African American, non-Hispanic/Latino; 5 Hispanic/Latino; 5 Two or more races, non-Hispanic/Latino). Average age 39. 156 applicants, 78% accepted, 118 enrolled. *Faculty:* 12 full-time (9 women), 22 part-time/adjunct (18 women). *Financial support:* Scholarships/grants, traineeships, and unspecified assistantships available. Financial award applicants required to submit FAFSA. In 2015, 50 master's, 13 doctorates awarded. *Degree program information:* Part-time and evening/weekend programs available. Part-time, evening/weekend. Offers art teacher education (MAT); business teacher education (MAT); education (M Ed, MA, MAT, Ed D); elementary school education (MAT); executive scholar-practitioner (Ed D); foreign language (MAT); high school education (MAT); middle school education (MAT); secondary education (MAT); special education (learning and behavioral disorders) (MAT); student guidance counselor (MA); teacher leader (M Ed). *Application fee:* $30. *Application Contact:* Valerie Anderson, Administrative Assistant, 502-873-4260, E-mail: vanderson@spalding.edu. *Dean*, Dr. Beverly Keepers, 502-873-4268, E-mail: bkeepers@spalding.edu.

College of Social Sciences and Humanities Students: 153 full-time (113 women), 55 part-time (33 women); includes 38 minority (28 Black or African American, non-Hispanic/Latino; 2 American Indian or Alaska Native, non-Hispanic/Latino; 3 Asian, non-Hispanic/Latino; 5 Two or more races, non-Hispanic/Latino), 2 international. Average age 29. 76 applicants, 71% accepted, 54 enrolled. *Faculty:* 13 full-time (10 women), 12 part-time/adjunct (3 women). *Financial support:* Career-related internships or fieldwork, Federal Work-Study, scholarships/grants, and unspecified assistantships available. Financial award applicants required to submit FAFSA. In 2015, 59 master's awarded. *Degree program information:* Part-time and evening/weekend programs available. Part-time, evening/weekend, online learning. Offers business and communication (MS); social sciences and humanities (MFA, MS); writing (MFA). *Application fee:* $30. *Application Contact:* Gloria Johansen, Administrative Assistant, 502-873-4254, E-mail: gjohansen@spalding.edu. *Associate Dean*, Dr. Melissa Chastain, 502-873-4251, E-mail: mchastain@spalding.edu.

Kosair College of Health and Natural Sciences Students: 422 full-time (357 women), 128 part-time (110 women); includes 91 minority (59 Black or African American, non-Hispanic/Latino; 1 American Indian or Alaska Native, non-Hispanic/Latino; 8 Asian, non-Hispanic/Latino; 8 Hispanic/Latino; 3 Native Hawaiian or other Pacific Islander, non-Hispanic/Latino; 12 Two or more races, non-Hispanic/Latino), 2 international. Average age 31. 331 applicants, 37% accepted, 76 enrolled. *Faculty:* 44 full-time (29 women), 4 part-time/adjunct (3 women). *Financial support:* Career-related internships or fieldwork, scholarships/grants, traineeships, and unspecified assistantships available. Support available to part-time students. Financial award applicants required to submit FAFSA. In 2015, 161 master's, 14 doctorates awarded. *Degree program information:* Part-time and evening/weekend programs available. Part-time, evening/weekend. Offers adult nurse practitioner (MSN, PMC); applied behavior analysis (MS); athletic training (MS); clinical psychology (MA, Psy D); family nurse practitioner (MSN, PMC); health and natural sciences (MA, MS, MSN, MSW, DNP, Psy D, PMC); leadership in nursing and healthcare (MSN); occupational therapy (MS); pediatric nurse practitioner (MSN, PMC); social work (MSW). *Application deadline:* For winter admission, 2/1 for domestic students. *Application fee:* $30. *Application Contact:* Cynthia James, Administrative Assistant, 502-873-4290, E-mail: cjames@spalding.edu. *Dean*, Dr. Joanne Berryman, 502-873-4281, E-mail: jberryman@spalding.edu.

SPERTUS INSTITUTE FOR JEWISH LEARNING AND LEADERSHIP, Chicago, IL 60605-1901

General Information Independent, coed, graduate-only institution. *Enrollment by degree level:* 258 master's, 32 doctoral. *Graduate faculty:* 4 full-time (1 woman), 49 part-time/adjunct (16 women). *Graduate housing:* On-campus housing not available. *Library:* Asher Library.

Computer facilities: 10 computers available on campus for general student use.
Website: http://www.spertus.edu/

General Application Contact: Tal Rosen, Director, Center for Jewish Leadership, 312-322-1711, E-mail: trosen@spertus.edu.

GRADUATE UNITS

Program in Jewish Studies Students: 93 part-time. *Faculty:* 1 part-time/adjunct. *Financial support:* Scholarships/grants available. Support available to part-time students. Financial award applicants required to submit FAFSA. *Degree program information:* Part-time and evening/weekend programs available. Part-time, evening/weekend, online learning. Offers Jewish studies (MAJPS, MAJS, DJS, DSJS). *Application deadline:* Applications are processed on a rolling basis. *Application fee:* $50. *Application Contact:* Susan Greenwald, Assistant Director of Recruitment and Alumni Affairs, 312-322-1707, Fax: 312-994-5360, E-mail: nwhiteside@spertus.edu. *Provost and Vice President*, Dr. Dean Phillip Bell, 312-322-1791, Fax: 312-994-5360, E-mail: dbell@spertus.edu.

SPRING ARBOR UNIVERSITY, Spring Arbor, MI 49283-9799

General Information Independent-religious, coed, comprehensive institution. *Graduate housing:* Rooms and/or apartments available on a first-come, first-served basis to single and married students. Housing application deadline: 5/1.

GRADUATE UNITS

Gainey School of Business ***Degree program information:*** Part-time and evening/weekend programs available. Part-time, evening/weekend, online learning. Offers business (MBA).

School of Arts and Sciences ***Degree program information:*** Part-time programs available. Part-time, online learning. Offers communication (MA); spiritual formation and leadership (MA).

School of Education ***Degree program information:*** Part-time and evening/weekend programs available. Part-time, evening/weekend, online learning. Offers education (MAE); reading (MAR); special education (MSE). Electronic applications accepted.

School of Human Services ***Degree program information:*** Part-time and evening/weekend programs available. Part-time, evening/weekend, online learning. Offers counseling (MAC); family studies (MAFS); nursing (MSN). Electronic applications accepted.

SPRINGFIELD COLLEGE, Springfield, MA 01109-3797

General Information Independent, coed, comprehensive institution. *Graduate housing:* Rooms and/or apartments available on a first-come, first-served basis to single and married students. Housing application deadline: 5/1.

GRADUATE UNITS

Graduate Programs ***Degree program information:*** Part-time and evening/weekend programs available. Part-time, evening/weekend. Offers adapted physical education (MS); advanced-level coaching (M Ed); alcohol and substance abuse services (M Ed); art therapy (M Ed, MS, CAGS); athletic administration (MS); athletic counseling (MS, CAGS); athletic training (MS); business administration (MBA); clinical mental health counseling (M Ed, CAGS); counseling psychology (Psy D); educational studies (M Ed); exercise physiology (MS); health promotion and disease prevention (MS); human services (MS); industrial and organizational psychology (M Ed, CAGS); occupational therapy (MS); physical therapy (DPT); physician assistant (MS); psychiatric rehabilitation and substance abuse counseling (M Ed); recreation management (M Ed); school guidance counseling (M Ed, CAGS); secondary education (M Ed); special education (M Ed); sport and exercise psychology (MS); sport management (M Ed, MS); student personnel administration in higher education (M Ed). Electronic applications accepted.

School of Social Work ***Degree program information:*** Part-time and evening/weekend programs available. Part-time, evening/weekend. Offers advanced practice with children and adolescents (Post-Master's Certificate); social work (MSW). Electronic applications accepted.

See Display on next page and Close-Up on page 899.

SPRING HILL COLLEGE, Mobile, AL 36608-1791

General Information Independent-religious, coed, comprehensive institution. *Enrollment:* 1,496 graduate, professional, and undergraduate students; 6 full-time matriculated graduate/professional students (1 woman), 120 part-time matriculated graduate/professional students (68 women). *Enrollment by degree level:* 98 master's, 28 other advanced degrees. *Graduate faculty:* 17 full-time (7 women), 9 part-time/adjunct (4 women). *Tuition, area resident:* Full-time $8200; part-time $490 per credit hour. Tuition and fees vary according to program. *Graduate housing:* On-campus housing not available. *Student services:* Campus safety program, career counseling, exercise/wellness program, writing training. *Library:* Marnie and John Burke Memorial Library plus 1 other.

Computer facilities: A campuswide network can be accessed from student residence rooms and from off campus. Online class registration is available.
Website: http://www.shc.edu/

General Application Contact: Robert Stewart, Vice President of Enrollment, 251-380-3030, Fax: 251-460-2186, E-mail: rstewart@shc.edu.

GRADUATE UNITS

Graduate Programs Students: 6 full-time (1 woman), 120 part-time (68 women); includes 26 minority (18 Black or African American, non-Hispanic/Latino; 2 American Indian or Alaska Native, non-Hispanic/Latino; 3 Asian, non-Hispanic/Latino; 3 Hispanic/Latino), 3 international. Average age 40. *Faculty:* 17 full-time (7 women), 9 part-time/adjunct (4 women). *Financial support:* Applicants required to submit FAFSA. In 2015, 47 master's, 3 other advanced degrees awarded. *Degree program information:* Part-time and evening/weekend programs available. Part-time, evening/weekend. Offers business administration (MBA); clinical nurse leader (MSN, Post-Master's Certificate); early childhood education (MAT, MS Ed); educational theory (MS Ed); elementary education (MAT, MS Ed); faith companioning (Postbaccalaureate Certificate); fine arts (MLA); history and social science (MLA); leadership and ethics (MLA, Postbaccalaureate Certificate); literature (MLA); pastoral ministry (Postbaccalaureate Certificate); pastoral studies (MPS); secondary education (MAT, MS Ed); spiritual direction (Postbaccalaureate Certificate); studio art (Postbaccalaureate Certificate); theological studies (MTS); theology (MA). *Application deadline:* For fall admission, 8/1 priority date for domestic and international students; for spring admission, 12/1 priority date for domestic and international students. Applications are processed on a rolling basis. *Application fee:* $25 ($35 for international students). Electronic applications accepted. *Vice President of Enrollment*, Robert Stewart, 251-380-3030, Fax: 251-460-2186, E-mail: rstewart@shc.edu.

STANFORD UNIVERSITY, Stanford, CA 94305-9991

General Information Independent, coed, university. CGS member. *Enrollment:* 16,770 graduate, professional, and undergraduate students; 8,741 full-time matriculated graduate/professional students (3,398 women), 455 part-time matriculated graduate/professional students (152 women). *Enrollment by degree level:* 3,453 master's, 5,743 doctoral. *Graduate faculty:* 2,153 full-time (603 women). *Tuition, area resident:* Full-time $45,729. *Required fees:* $591. *Graduate housing:* Rooms and/or apartments guaranteed to single and married students. Typical cost: $13,915 per year for single students; $23,437 per year for married students. Room charges vary according to housing facility selected. Housing application deadline: 5/5. *Student services:* Campus employment opportunities, campus safety program, career counseling, child daycare facilities, exercise/wellness program, free psychological counseling, international student services, low-cost health insurance, multicultural affairs office, services for students with disabilities, teacher training. *Library:* Green Library plus 20 others. *Collection:* Books: 9.3 million (physical), 1.5 million (digital/electronic); Serial titles: 77,000 (physical). Study areas open 24 hours, 5–7 days a week; students can reserve study rooms.

Computer facilities: Computer purchase and lease plans are available. 1,000 computers available on campus for general student use. A campuswide network can be accessed from student residence rooms and from off campus. Online class registration, Stanford houses one of the most extensive computing environments of any university worldwide are available.
Website: http://www.stanford.edu/

General Application Contact: Graduate Admissions, 866-432-7472, Fax: 650-723-8371, E-mail: gradadmissions@stanford.edu.

GRADUATE UNITS

Graduate School of Business Offers business (MBA, PhD). Electronic applications accepted.

Graduate School of Education Offers curriculum and teacher education (MA); education (MA, MAE, PhD); elementary education (MAE); international comparative education (MA, PhD); learning, design, and technology (MA); policy, organization, and leadership studies (MA); secondary education (MAE). Electronic applications accepted.

Law School Offers corporate governance and practice (LL M); environmental law and policy (LL M); international economic law, business and policy (LL M); international legal studies (JSM); law (JD, JSD); law, science and technology (LL M); legal studies (MLS). Electronic applications accepted.

School of Earth, Energy and Environmental Sciences Offers earth system science (MS, PhD); earth, energy and environmental sciences (MS, PhD, Eng); energy resources engineering (MS, PhD, Eng); geological sciences (MS, PhD, Eng); geophysics (MS, PhD); petroleum engineering (MS, PhD). Electronic applications accepted.

School of Engineering Offers aeronautics and astronautics (MS, PhD, Eng); atmosphere and energy (MS, PhD); biomechanical engineering (MS); chemical engineering (MS, PhD); computer science (MS, PhD); construction (MS); electrical engineering (MS, PhD); engineering (MS, PhD, Engr); environmental engineering and science (MS, PhD, Eng); environmental fluid mechanics and hydrology (PhD); geomechanics (MS); management science and engineering (MS, PhD); materials science and engineering (MS, PhD, Engr); mechanical engineering (MS, PhD, Engr); product design (MS); structural engineering (MS). Electronic applications accepted.

Institute for Computational and Mathematical Engineering Offers computational and mathematical engineering (MS, PhD). Electronic applications accepted.

School of Humanities and Sciences Offers anthropology (MA); applied and engineering physics (MS); applied physics (PhD); archaeology (PhD); art history (PhD); art practice (MFA); biology (MS, PhD); biophysics (PhD); chemistry (PhD); Chinese (MA, PhD); classics (MA, PhD); communication (MA); communication theory and research (PhD); comparative literature (PhD); composition (DMA); computer-based music theory and acoustics (PhD); culture and society (PhD); data science (MS); design (MFA); documentary film and video (MFA); ecology and environment (PhD); economics (PhD); English (MA, PhD); financial mathematics (MS); French (MA, PhD); French and Italian (PhD); German studies (MA, PhD); history (MA, PhD); humanities and sciences (MA, MFA, MS, DMA, PhD); Italian (MA, PhD); Japanese (MA, PhD); linguistics (MA, PhD); mathematics (PhD); modern thought and literature (PhD); music, science, and technology (MA); musicology (PhD); philosophy (MA, PhD); physics (PhD); political science (MA, PhD); psychology (PhD); religious studies (PhD); Slavic languages and literatures (PhD); sociology (PhD); Spanish (MA, PhD); statistics (PhD); theater and performance studies (PhD). Electronic applications accepted.

Center for East Asian Studies Offers East Asian studies (MA). Electronic applications accepted.

Center for Russian, East European and Eurasian Studies Offers Russian, East European and Eurasian studies (MA). Electronic applications accepted.

School of Medicine Offers bioengineering (MS, PhD); medicine (MS, MD, PhD). Electronic applications accepted.

Graduate Programs in Medicine Offers biochemistry (PhD); biostatistics (PhD); chemical and systems biology (PhD); developmental biology (MS, PhD); epidemiology and clinical research (MS, PhD); genetics (PhD); health policy (MS, PhD); medicine (MS, PhD); microbiology and immunology (PhD); molecular and cellular physiology (PhD); structural biology (PhD). Electronic applications accepted.

Stanford Center for Biomedical Informatics Research Offers biomedical informatics research (MS, PhD). Electronic applications accepted.

STARR KING SCHOOL FOR THE MINISTRY, Berkeley, CA 94709-1209

General Information Independent-religious, coed, graduate-only institution. *Graduate housing:* On-campus housing not available.

GRADUATE UNITS

Professional Program Offers theology (M Div).

STATE UNIVERSITY OF NEW YORK AT FREDONIA, Fredonia, NY 14063-1136

General Information State-supported, coed, comprehensive institution. *Enrollment:* 4,845 graduate, professional, and undergraduate students; 153 full-time matriculated graduate/professional students (124 women), 105 part-time matriculated graduate/professional students (70 women). *Enrollment by degree level:* 219 master's, 29 other advanced degrees. *Graduate faculty:* 53 full-time (31 women), 13 part-time/adjunct (9 women). Tuition, state resident: full-time $10,870; part-time $453 per credit. Tuition, nonresident: full-time $22,210; part-time $925 per credit. *Required fees:* $1604; $66.70 per credit. *Graduate housing:* Room and/or apartments available on a first-come, first-served basis to single students; on-campus housing not available to married students. Typical cost: $8900 per year. Room charges vary according to board plan and housing facility selected. Housing application deadline: 8/24. *Student services:* Campus employment opportunities, campus safety program, career counseling, child daycare facilities, exercise/wellness program, free psychological counseling, grant writing training, international student services, low-cost health insurance, multicultural affairs office, services for students with disabilities, teacher training, writing training.

Library: Daniel A. Reed Library. *Collection:* Books: 18 million (physical); Serial titles: 48,000 (physical). Students can reserve study rooms.

Computer facilities: Computer purchase and lease plans are available. 500 computers available on campus for general student use. A campuswide network can be accessed from student residence rooms and from off campus. Online class registration is available.
Website: http://www.fredonia.edu/

General Application Contact: Wendy S. Dunst, Interim Graduate Recruitment and Admissions Associate, 716-673-3808, Fax: 716-673-3712,
E-mail: wendy.dunst@fredonia.edu.

GRADUATE UNITS

College of Education ***Degree program information:*** Part-time programs available. Part-time. Offers literacy education (MS Ed); TESOL (MS Ed). Electronic applications accepted.

College of Liberal Arts and Sciences ***Degree program information:*** Part-time and evening/weekend programs available. Part-time, evening/weekend. Offers biology (MS); interdisciplinary studies (MS); speech pathology (MS). Electronic applications accepted.

School of Music ***Degree program information:*** Part-time programs available. Part-time. Offers music education (MM). Electronic applications accepted.

STATE UNIVERSITY OF NEW YORK AT NEW PALTZ, New Paltz, NY 12561

General Information State-supported, coed, comprehensive institution. *Enrollment:* 7,752 graduate, professional, and undergraduate students; 452 full-time matriculated graduate/professional students (275 women), 343 part-time matriculated graduate/professional students (240 women). *Enrollment by degree level:* 795 master's. *Graduate faculty:* 122 full-time (68 women), 57 part-time/adjunct (37 women). *Graduate housing:* On-campus housing not available. *Student services:* Campus employment opportunities, campus safety program, career counseling, child daycare facilities, free psychological counseling, international student services, low-cost health insurance, services for students with disabilities, teacher training. *Library:* Sojourner Truth Library. *Collection:* Books: 403,918 (physical), 125,596 (digital/electronic); Serial titles: 253 (physical), 280 (digital/electronic); Databases: 117. Weekly public service hours: 120; students can reserve study rooms.

Computer facilities: 800 computers available on campus for general student use. A campuswide network can be accessed from student residence rooms and from off campus. Online class registration is available.
Website: http://www.newpaltz.edu/

General Application Contact: Vika Shock, Director of Graduate Admissions, 845-257-3285, Fax: 845-257-3284, E-mail: gradschool@newpaltz.edu.

GRADUATE UNITS

Graduate School Students: 452 full-time (275 women), 343 part-time (240 women); includes 135 minority (21 Black or African American, non-Hispanic/Latino; 2 American Indian or Alaska Native, non-Hispanic/Latino; 20 Asian, non-Hispanic/Latino; 80 Hispanic/Latino; 1 Native Hawaiian or other Pacific Islander, non-Hispanic/Latino; 11 Two or more races, non-Hispanic/Latino), 146 international. Average age 28. 1,099 applicants, 50% accepted, 304 enrolled. *Faculty:* 122 full-time (68 women), 57 part-time/adjunct (37 women). *Financial support:* Career-related internships or fieldwork, Federal Work-Study, institutionally sponsored loans, scholarships/grants, traineeships, health care benefits, tuition waivers (full and partial), and unspecified assistantships available. Support available to part-time students. Financial award application deadline: 8/1; financial award applicants required to submit FAFSA. In 2015, 416 master's, 27 other advanced degrees awarded. *Degree program information:* Part-time and evening/weekend programs available. Part-time, evening/weekend. *Application deadline:* For fall admission, 5/15 for domestic and international students; for spring admission, 11/15 for domestic and international students. *Application fee:* $50. Electronic applications accepted. *Application Contact:* Vika Shock, Director of Graduate Admissions, 845-257-3285, Fax: 845-257-3284, E-mail: gradschool@newpaltz.edu. *Associate Provost for Academic Affairs/Dean*, Dr. Laurel M. Garrick Duhaney, 845-257-3947.

School of Business Students: 61 full-time (28 women), 15 part-time (9 women); includes 25 minority (4 Black or African American, non-Hispanic/Latino; 5 Asian, non-Hispanic/Latino; 14 Hispanic/Latino; 2 Two or more races, non-Hispanic/Latino), 11 international. Average age 26. 60 applicants, 68% accepted, 28 enrolled. *Faculty:* 15 full-time (6 women), 2 part-time/adjunct (1 woman). *Financial support:* In 2015–16, 6 research assistantships with partial tuition reimbursements (averaging $5,000 per year), 1 teaching assistantship with partial tuition reimbursement (averaging $5,000 per year) were awarded; scholarships/grants, traineeships, and unspecified assistantships also available. Financial award application deadline: 8/1. In 2015, 43 master's awarded. *Degree program information:* Part-time and evening/weekend programs available. Part-time, evening/weekend. Offers business administration (MBA); public accountancy (MBA). *Application deadline:* Applications are processed on a rolling basis. *Application fee:* $50. Electronic applications accepted. *Application Contact:* Aaron Hines, Director of MBA Program, 845-257-2968, E-mail: mba@newpaltz.edu. *Dean*, Dr. Kristin Backhaus, 845-257-2930, E-mail: mba@newpaltz.edu.

School of Education Students: 133 full-time (105 women), 240 part-time (178 women); includes 70 minority (11 Black or African American, non-Hispanic/Latino; 2 American Indian or Alaska Native, non-Hispanic/Latino; 4 Asian, non-Hispanic/Latino; 47 Hispanic/Latino; 1 Native Hawaiian or other Pacific Islander, non-Hispanic/Latino; 5 Two or more races, non-Hispanic/Latino), 1 international. Average age 30. 209 applicants, 83% accepted, 135 enrolled. *Faculty:* 29 full-time (21 women), 29 part-time/adjunct (24 women). *Financial support:* Scholarships/grants available. Financial award application deadline: 8/1. In 2015, 227 master's, 27 other advanced degrees awarded. *Degree program information:* Part-time and evening/weekend programs available. Part-time, evening/weekend. Offers adolescence education: biology (MAT, MS Ed); adolescence education: chemistry (MAT, MS Ed); adolescence education: earth science (MAT, MS Ed); adolescence education: English (MAT, MS Ed); adolescence education: French (MAT, MS Ed); adolescence education: social studies (MAT, MS Ed); adolescence education: Spanish (MAT, MS Ed); adolescence special education (7-12) (MS Ed); adolescence special education and literacy (MS Ed); childhood education 1-6 (MS Ed, MST); childhood special education (1-6) (MS Ed); childhood special education and literacy (MS Ed); early childhood special education (B-2) (MS Ed); education (MAT, MPS, MS Ed, MST, AC, CAS); educational leadership (MS Ed); humanistic/multicultural education (MPS, AC); literacy education 5-12 (MS Ed); literacy education and childhood special education (MS Ed); literacy education B-6 (MS Ed); multicultural education (AC); school building leader (CAS); school district business leader (CAS); school district leader (CAS); second language education (MS Ed, AC); special education (MS Ed); teaching English language learners (AC). *Application deadline:* For fall admission, 3/1 for domestic and international students; for spring admission, 10/1 for domestic and international students. *Application fee:* $50. Electronic applications accepted. *Application Contact:* Vika Shock, Director of Graduate Admissions, 845-257-3285, Fax: 845-257-3284, E-mail: gradschool@newpaltz.edu. *Dean*, Dr. Michael Rosenberg, 845-257-2800, E-mail: schoolofed@newpaltz.edu.

School of Fine and Performing Arts Students: 48 full-time (35 women), 21 part-time (15 women); includes 10 minority (2 Black or African American, non-Hispanic/Latino; 3 Asian, non-Hispanic/Latino; 5 Hispanic/Latino), 13 international. Average age 30. 81 applicants, 58% accepted, 29 enrolled. *Faculty:* 25 full-time (17 women), 8 part-time/adjunct (5 women). *Financial support:* Application deadline: 8/1. In 2015, 26 master's awarded. *Degree program information:* Part-time and evening/weekend programs available. Part-time, evening/weekend. Offers ceramics (MFA); fine and performing arts (MFA, MS, MS Ed); metal (MFA); music therapy (MS); painting/drawing (MFA); printmaking (MFA); sculpture (MFA); visual arts education (MS Ed). *Application deadline:* For fall admission, 2/15 priority date for domestic students, 2/15 for international students. Applications are processed on a rolling basis. *Application fee:* $50. Electronic applications accepted. *Application Contact:* Vika Shock, Director of Graduate Admissions, 845-257-3285, Fax: 845-257-3284, E-mail: gradschool@newpaltz.edu. *Dean*, Prof. Jeni Mokren, 845-257-3860, E-mail: mokrenj@newpaltz.edu.

School of Liberal Arts and Sciences Students: 91 full-time (75 women), 53 part-time (34 women); includes 25 minority (3 Black or African American, non-Hispanic/Latino; 5 Asian, non-Hispanic/Latino; 13 Hispanic/Latino; 4 Two or more races, non-Hispanic/Latino), 3 international. Average age 27. 297 applicants, 30% accepted, 58 enrolled. *Faculty:* 34 full-time (22 women), 7 part-time/adjunct (6 women). *Financial support:* In 2015–16, 2 research assistantships with partial tuition reimbursements (averaging $5,000 per year), 27 teaching assistantships with partial tuition reimbursements (averaging $5,000 per year) were awarded. Financial award application deadline: 8/1. In 2015, 68 master's awarded. *Degree program information:* Part-time and evening/weekend programs available. Part-time, evening/weekend. Offers communication disorders (MS); English (MA); liberal arts and sciences (MA, MS, AC); mental health counseling (MS, AC); psychology (MA); school counseling (MS). *Application deadline:* For fall admission, 2/1 for domestic and international students; for spring admission, 11/15 for domestic and international students. Applications are processed on a rolling basis. *Application fee:* $50. Electronic applications accepted. *Application Contact:* Vika Shock, Director of Graduate Admissions, 845-257-3285, E-mail: gradschool@newpaltz.edu. *Dean*, Dr. Laura Barrett, 845-257-3520, E-mail: barrett@newpaltz.edu.

School of Science and Engineering Students: 119 full-time (32 women), 14 part-time (4 women); includes 5 minority (1 Black or African American, non-Hispanic/Latino; 3 Asian, non-Hispanic/Latino; 1 Hispanic/Latino), 118 international. Average age 24. 450 applicants, 44% accepted, 54 enrolled. *Faculty:* 19 full-time (2 women), 11 part-time/adjunct (1 woman). *Financial support:* In 2015–16, 11 fellowships, 5 teaching assistantships with partial tuition reimbursements (averaging $5,000 per year) were awarded. Financial award application deadline: 8/1. In 2015, 52 master's awarded. *Degree program information:* Part-time and evening/weekend programs available. Part-time, evening/weekend. Offers computer science (MS); electrical engineering (MS); science and engineering (MS). *Application deadline:* For fall admission, 5/15 for domestic and international students; for spring admission, 11/15 for domestic and international students. Applications are processed on a rolling basis. *Application fee:* $50. Electronic applications accepted. *Application Contact:* Vika Shock, Director of Graduate Admission, 845-257-3285, E-mail: gradschool@newpaltz.edu. *Dean*, Dr. Daniel Freedman, 845-257-3728, E-mail: freedmad@newpaltz.edu.

STATE UNIVERSITY OF NEW YORK AT OSWEGO, Oswego, NY 13126

General Information State-supported, coed, comprehensive institution. CGS member. *Graduate housing:* Room and/or apartments available on a first-come, first-served basis to single students; on-campus housing not available to married students. Housing application deadline: 4/1. *Research affiliation:* Intel Corporation (research and education), IBM (research and education), Alcan (research and education), MACTEC (research and education), IBM (research and education), Entergy (research and education).

GRADUATE UNITS

Graduate Studies ***Degree program information:*** Part-time programs available. Part-time. Offers art (MA); graphic design and digital media (MA).

College of Liberal Arts and Sciences Degree program information: Part-time programs available. Part-time. Offers chemistry (MS); English (MA); history (MA); human computer interaction (MA); liberal arts and sciences (MA, MS).

School of Business Degree program information: Part-time and evening/weekend programs available. Part-time, evening/weekend. Offers business (MBA).

School of Education Degree program information: Part-time programs available. Part-time. Offers adolescence education (MST); agriculture (MS Ed); art education (MAT); business and marketing (MS Ed); childhood education (MST); curriculum and instruction (MS Ed); education (MAT, MS, MS Ed, MST, CAS); educational administration (CAS); family and consumer sciences (MS Ed); health careers (MS Ed); literacy education (MS Ed); mental health counseling (MS); school building leadership (CAS); special education (MS Ed); technical education (MS Ed); technology (MS Ed); trade education (MS Ed).

STATE UNIVERSITY OF NEW YORK AT PLATTSBURGH, Plattsburgh, NY 12901-2681

General Information State-supported, coed, comprehensive institution. *Graduate housing:* Room and/or apartments available on a first-come, first-served basis to single students; on-campus housing not available to married students. Housing application deadline: 5/1. *Research affiliation:* New York State Sea Grant (environmental science), Miner Agricultural Research Institute (environmental science).

GRADUATE UNITS

Division of Education, Health, and Human Services ***Degree program information:*** Part-time programs available. Part-time. Offers adolescence education (MST); biology 7-12 (MST); birth to grade 2 (MS Ed); birth to grade 6 (MS Ed); birth-grade 6 (MS Ed); chemistry 7-12 (MST); childhood education (grades 1-6) (MST); clinical mental health counseling (MS, Advanced Certificate); early childhood birth-grade 6 (Advanced Certificate); earth science 7-12 (MST); education, health, and human services (MA, MS, MS Ed, MST, Advanced Certificate, CAS); educational leadership (CAS); English 7-12 (MST); French 7-12 (MST); grades 1 to 6 (MS Ed); grades 5-12 (MS Ed); grades 7 to 12 (MS Ed); mathematics 7-12 (MST); physics 7-12 (MST); school counselor (MS Ed,

CAS); social studies 7-12 (MST); Spanish 7-12 (MST); speech-language pathology (MA); student affairs counseling (MS); teacher education: teaching and learning (MS Ed).

School of Arts and Sciences ***Degree program information:*** Part-time programs available. Part-time. Offers arts and sciences (MA, MS, PSM, CAS); natural science (MS, PSM); school psychology (MA, CAS).

STATE UNIVERSITY OF NEW YORK COLLEGE AT CORTLAND, Cortland, NY 13045

General Information State-supported, coed, comprehensive institution. *Enrollment:* 6,926 graduate, professional, and undergraduate students; 242 full-time matriculated graduate/professional students, 401 part-time matriculated graduate/professional students. *Graduate faculty:* 58 full-time. *Graduate housing:* Room and/or apartments available on a first-come, first-served basis to single students; on-campus housing not available to married students. Typical cost: $7740 per year. *Student services:* Campus employment opportunities, campus safety program, career counseling, child daycare facilities, exercise/wellness program, free psychological counseling, international student services, low-cost health insurance, multicultural affairs office, services for students with disabilities, teacher training, writing training. *Library:* Memorial Library.

Computer facilities: A campuswide network can be accessed from student residence rooms and from off campus.
Website: http://www.cortland.edu/

GRADUATE UNITS

Graduate Studies ***Financial support:*** Fellowships, career-related internships or fieldwork, Federal Work-Study, scholarships/grants, tuition waivers (partial), and unspecified assistantships available. Support available to part-time students. Financial award applicants required to submit CSS PROFILE or FAFSA. *Degree program information:* Part-time and evening/weekend programs available. Part-time, evening/weekend. *Application deadline:* For fall admission, 7/1 for domestic students, 4/1 for international students; for spring admission, 12/1 for domestic students, 7/1 for international students. Applications are processed on a rolling basis. *Application fee:* $65. Electronic applications accepted. *Application Contact:* Doug Langhans, Graduate and International Admissions Coordinator, 607-753-4800, Fax: 607-753-5988, E-mail: graduate.admissions@cortland.edu.

School of Arts and Sciences Financial support: Career-related internships or fieldwork, Federal Work-Study, tuition waivers (partial), and unspecified assistantships available. Support available to part-time students. Financial award applicants required to submit CSS PROFILE or FAFSA. *Degree program information:* Part-time and evening/weekend programs available. Part-time, evening/weekend. Offers arts and sciences (MA, MAT, MS Ed); biology (MAT); chemistry (MAT); English (MA); history (MA); mathematics (MAT); mathematics and physics (MS Ed); physics (MAT, MS Ed); second language education (MS Ed). *Application deadline:* For fall admission, 7/1 for domestic and international students; for spring admission, 12/1 for domestic and international students. Applications are processed on a rolling basis. *Application fee:* $65. *Application Contact:* R. Bruce Mattingly, Dean, 607-753-4312. *Dean,* R. Bruce Mattingly, 607-753-4312.

School of Education Financial support: Career-related internships or fieldwork, Federal Work-Study, tuition waivers (partial), and unspecified assistantships available. Support available to part-time students. *Degree program information:* Part-time and evening/weekend programs available. Part-time, evening/weekend. Offers childhood education (MST); education (MS Ed, MST, CAS); literacy education (MS Ed); school building leader (CAS); school building leader and school district leader (CAS); school district business leader (CAS); school district leader (CAS); teaching students with disabilities (MS Ed). *Application deadline:* For fall admission, 7/1 for domestic and international students; for spring admission, 12/1 for domestic and international students. *Application fee:* $65. *Application Contact:* Andrea Lachance, Dean, 607-753-5430, Fax: 607-753-5432, E-mail: andrea.lachance@cortland.edu. *Dean,* Andrea Lachance, 607-753-5430, Fax: 607-753-5432, E-mail: andrea.lachance@cortland.edu.

School of Professional Studies Financial support: Fellowships, career-related internships or fieldwork, Federal Work-Study, tuition waivers (partial), and alumni assistantships available. Support available to part-time students. Financial award applicants required to submit CSS PROFILE or FAFSA. *Degree program information:* Part-time and evening/weekend programs available. Part-time, evening/weekend. Offers adapted physical education (MS Ed); coaching pedagogy (MS Ed); community health (MS); health education (MST); international sport management (MS); outdoor education (MS, MS Ed); physical education leadership (MS Ed); recreation management (MS, MS Ed); sport management (MS); therapeutic recreation (MS, MS Ed). *Application deadline:* For fall admission, 7/1 for domestic and international students; for spring admission, 12/1 for domestic and international students. Applications are processed on a rolling basis. *Application fee:* $65. *Application Contact:* Graduate Admissions Office, 607-753-4800, Fax: 607-753-5988, E-mail: graduate.admissions@cortland.edu. *Dean,* Dr. John Cottone, 607-753-2701.

STATE UNIVERSITY OF NEW YORK COLLEGE AT GENESEO, Geneseo, NY 14454-1401

General Information State-supported, coed, comprehensive institution. *Enrollment:* 5,699 graduate, professional, and undergraduate students; 50 full-time matriculated graduate/professional students (39 women), 60 part-time matriculated graduate/professional students (51 women). *Enrollment by degree level:* 110 master's. *Graduate faculty:* 16 full-time (8 women), 2 part-time/adjunct (both women). Tuition, state resident: full-time $10,870; part-time $453 per credit. Tuition, nonresident: full-time $22,210; part-time $925 per credit. *Required fees:* $815; $67.50 per credit. $33.75. One-time fee: $408 full-time; $34 part-time. *Graduate housing:* Room and/or apartments available on a first-come, first-served basis to single students; on-campus housing not available to married students. Typical cost: $8480 per year ($12,950 including board). Housing application deadline: 5/1. *Student services:* Campus employment opportunities, campus safety program, career counseling, exercise/wellness program, free psychological counseling, grant writing training, international student services, low-cost health insurance, multicultural affairs office, services for students with disabilities, teacher training. *Library:* Milne Library plus 1 other. *Collection:* Books: 343,506 (physical), 48,043 (digital/electronic); Serial titles: 1,420 (physical), 218,467 (digital/electronic); Databases: 411. Weekly public service hours: 109; students can reserve study rooms. *Research affiliation:* Mt. Hope Family Center (psychology), Center for Nanomaterials and Nanoelectronics (chemistry), Greater Rochester Summer Learning Association (education), Great Lakes Research Consortium (biology), University of Rochester Laboratory for Laser Energetics (nuclear physics), Genesee Valley Health Partnership (health).

Computer facilities: 361 computers available on campus for general student use. A campuswide network can be accessed from student residence rooms and from off campus. Online class registration is available.
Website: http://www.geneseo.edu/

General Application Contact: Michael R. George, Graduate Enrollment Coordinator, 585-245-5148, Fax: 585-245-5550, E-mail: georgem@geneseo.edu.

GRADUATE UNITS

Graduate Studies Students: 50 full-time (39 women), 60 part-time (51 women); includes 7 minority (2 Black or African American, non-Hispanic/Latino; 2 Asian, non-Hispanic/Latino; 2 Hispanic/Latino; 1 Two or more races, non-Hispanic/Latino), 1 international. Average age 25. 52 applicants, 98% accepted, 37 enrolled. *Faculty:* 16 full-time (8 women), 2 part-time/adjunct (both women). *Financial support:* In 2015–16, 9 students received support, including 9 research assistantships with full tuition reimbursements available (averaging $10,274 per year); career-related internships or fieldwork, scholarships/grants, health care benefits, tuition waivers (full), and unspecified assistantships also available. Support available to part-time students. Financial award application deadline: 4/1; financial award applicants required to submit FAFSA. In 2015, 72 master's awarded. *Degree program information:* Part-time and evening/weekend programs available. Part-time, evening/weekend. *Application deadline:* For fall admission, 3/1 for domestic students; for spring admission, 10/1 for domestic students. *Application fee:* $50. *Application Contact:* Michael R. George, Graduate Enrollment Coordinator, 585-245-5148, E-mail: georgem@geneseo.edu. *Dean of Curriculum and Academic Services,* Dr. Savitri V. Iyer, 585-245-5541, Fax: 585-245-5032, E-mail: iyer@geneseo.edu.

School of Business Students: 15 full-time (5 women), 1 international. Average age 23. 20 applicants, 100% accepted, 15 enrolled. *Faculty:* 5 full-time (2 women). *Financial support:* Research assistantships with full tuition reimbursements available. Financial award application deadline: 4/1; financial award applicants required to submit FAFSA. In 2015, 5 master's awarded. Offers accounting (MS). *Application deadline:* For fall admission, 2/1 priority date for domestic students; for spring admission, 9/1 for domestic students. *Application fee:* $50. *Application Contact:* Michael R. George, Graduate Enrollment Coordinator, 585-245-5148, Fax: 585-245-5550, E-mail: georgem@geneseo.edu. *Dean of the School of Business,* Dr. Denise Rotondo, 585-245-5367, Fax: 585-245-5467, E-mail: rotondo@geneseo.edu.

School of Education Students: 35 full-time (34 women), 60 part-time (51 women); includes 7 minority (2 Black or African American, non-Hispanic/Latino; 2 Asian, non-Hispanic/Latino; 2 Hispanic/Latino; 1 Two or more races, non-Hispanic/Latino). Average age 25. 32 applicants, 97% accepted, 22 enrolled. *Faculty:* 7 full-time (4 women), 2 part-time/adjunct (both women). *Financial support:* In 2015–16, 9 students received support, including 9 research assistantships with full tuition reimbursements available (averaging $10,274 per year); scholarships/grants, health care benefits, tuition waivers (full), and unspecified assistantships also available. Support available to part-time students. Financial award application deadline: 4/1; financial award applicants required to submit FAFSA. In 2015, 67 master's awarded. *Degree program information:* Part-time and evening/weekend programs available. Part-time, evening/weekend. Offers adolescence education (MS Ed); childhood multicultural education (1-6) (MS Ed); early childhood education (MS Ed); literacy (MS Ed). *Application deadline:* For fall admission, 3/1 priority date for domestic students; for spring admission, 10/1 for domestic students. *Application fee:* $50. *Application Contact:* Michael R. George, Graduate Enrollment Coordinator, 585-245-5148, Fax: 585-245-5550, E-mail: georgem@geneseo.edu. *Dean of School of Education,* Dr. Anjoo Sikka, 585-245-5151, Fax: 585-245-5220, E-mail: sikka@geneseo.edu.

STATE UNIVERSITY OF NEW YORK COLLEGE AT OLD WESTBURY, Old Westbury, NY 11568-0210

General Information State-supported, coed, comprehensive institution. *Enrollment:* 4,353 graduate, professional, and undergraduate students; 134 full-time matriculated graduate/professional students (81 women), 94 part-time matriculated graduate/professional students (45 women). *Enrollment by degree level:* 217 master's, 11 other advanced degrees. *Graduate faculty:* 30 full-time (12 women), 11 part-time/adjunct (4 women). Tuition, state resident: full-time $10,870; part-time $453 per credit. Tuition, nonresident: full-time $22,210; part-time $925 per credit. *Required fees:* $23.85 per credit. $76 per semester. Tuition and fees vary according to course load. *Graduate housing:* Room and/or apartments available on a first-come, first-served basis to single students; on-campus housing not available to married students. Typical cost: $7000 per year ($10,390 including board). Room and board charges vary according to board plan. *Student services:* Campus safety program, career counseling, child daycare facilities, exercise/wellness program, free psychological counseling, international student services, services for students with disabilities, teacher training, writing training. *Library:* SUNY College at Old Westbury Library plus 1 other. *Collection:* Databases: 138. Weekly public service hours: 99.

Computer facilities: 480 computers available on campus for general student use. A campuswide network can be accessed from student residence rooms and from off campus. Online class registration, financial aid, billing information are available.
Website: http://www.oldwestbury.edu/

General Application Contact: Philip D'Angelo, Graduate Admissions Office, 516-876-3073, E-mail: enroll@oldwestbury.edu.

GRADUATE UNITS

Program in Liberal Studies Students: 5 full-time (1 woman), 4 part-time (3 women); includes 4 minority (1 Black or African American, non-Hispanic/Latino; 1 Asian, non-Hispanic/Latino; 2 Hispanic/Latino). Average age 38. 11 applicants, 91% accepted, 9 enrolled. *Faculty:* 2 full-time (both women). Offers liberal studies (MA). *Application deadline:* Applications are processed on a rolling basis. *Application fee:* $50. Electronic applications accepted. *Application Contact:* Philip D'Angelo, Graduate Admissions Office, 516-876-3073, E-mail: enroll@oldwestbury.edu. *Associate Professor, American Studies,* Dr. Amanda Frisken, 516-876-4853, E-mail: friskena@oldwestbury.edu.

Program in Mental Health Counseling Students: 31 full-time (27 women); includes 12 minority (5 Black or African American, non-Hispanic/Latino; 7 Hispanic/Latino), 1 international. Average age 30. 23 applicants, 87% accepted, 16 enrolled. *Faculty:* 3 full-time (0 women), 2 part-time/adjunct (both women). In 2015, 14 master's awarded. Offers mental health counseling (MS). *Application Contact:* Philip D'Angelo, Graduate Admissions Office, 516-876-3073, E-mail: enroll@oldwestbury.edu.

School of Business Students: 54 full-time (21 women), 52 part-time (23 women); includes 26 minority (4 Black or African American, non-Hispanic/Latino; 9 Asian, non-Hispanic/Latino; 13 Hispanic/Latino), 2 international. Average age 30. 40 applicants, 93% accepted, 28 enrolled. *Faculty:* 10 full-time (2 women), 1 part-time/adjunct (0 women). In 2015, 49 master's awarded. *Degree program information:* Part-time and evening/weekend programs available. Part-time, evening/weekend. Offers accounting (MS); taxation (MS). *Application deadline:* For fall admission, 6/15 priority date for domestic students; for spring admission, 11/15 priority date for domestic students. Applications are processed on a rolling basis. *Application fee:* $50. Electronic applications accepted. *Application Contact:* Philip D'Angelo, Graduate Admissions Office, 516-876-3073, E-mail: enroll@oldwestbury.edu. *Director of Graduate Business Programs*, Rita Buttermilch, 516-876-3900, E-mail: buttermilchr@oldwestbury.edu.

School of Education Students: 41 full-time (30 women), 24 part-time (15 women); includes 24 minority (3 Black or African American, non-Hispanic/Latino; 2 Asian, non-Hispanic/Latino; 18 Hispanic/Latino; 1 Two or more races, non-Hispanic/Latino), 1 international. Average age 29. 29 applicants, 83% accepted, 20 enrolled. *Faculty:* 17 full-time (9 women), 5 part-time/adjunct (2 women). In 2015, 21 master's awarded. *Degree program information:* Part-time and evening/weekend programs available. Part-time, evening/weekend. Offers biology (MAT, MS); chemistry (MAT, MS); English language arts (MAT, MS); math (MAT, MS); social studies (MAT, MS); Spanish (MAT, MS). *Application fee:* $50. *Application Contact:* Philip D'Angelo, Graduate Admissions Office, 516-876-3073, E-mail: enroll@oldwestbury.edu. *Dean, School of Education*, Dr. Nancy Brown, 516-876-3275, E-mail: brownn@oldwestbury.edu.

STATE UNIVERSITY OF NEW YORK COLLEGE AT ONEONTA, Oneonta, NY 13820-4015

General Information State-supported, coed, comprehensive institution. *Graduate housing:* Room and/or apartments available on a first-come, first-served basis to single students; on-campus housing not available to married students. Housing application deadline: 5/1. *Research affiliation:* New York State Historical Association (history, museum studies).

GRADUATE UNITS

Graduate Education ***Degree program information:*** Part-time and evening/weekend programs available. Part-time, evening/weekend, online learning. Offers biology (MA); earth sciences (MA); history museum studies (MA); nutrition and dietetics (MS).

Division of Education Degree program information: Part-time and evening/weekend programs available. Part-time, evening/weekend. Offers adolescence education (MS Ed); childhood education (MS Ed); educational psychology and counseling (MS Ed, CAS); educational technology specialist (MS Ed); elementary education and reading (MS Ed); literacy education (MS Ed); school counselor K-12 (MS Ed, CAS); secondary education (MS Ed); special education (MS Ed).

STATE UNIVERSITY OF NEW YORK COLLEGE AT POTSDAM, Potsdam, NY 13676

General Information State-supported, coed, comprehensive institution. *Graduate housing:* Room and/or apartments available on a first-come, first-served basis to single students; on-campus housing not available to married students.

GRADUATE UNITS

Crane School of Music ***Degree program information:*** Part-time programs available. Part-time. Offers music education (MM); music performance (MM). Electronic applications accepted.

School of Arts and Sciences ***Degree program information:*** Part-time and evening/weekend programs available. Part-time, evening/weekend. Offers arts and sciences (MA); English and communication (MA); mathematics (MA). Electronic applications accepted.

School of Education and Professional Studies Online learning. Offers adolescence (grades 7-12) (MS Ed); childhood (grades 1-6) (MS Ed); childhood education (MST); community health (MS); curriculum and instruction (MS Ed); early childhood (birth-grade 2) (MS Ed); education and professional studies (MS Ed, MST); educational technology specialist (MS Ed); English education (MST); literacy educator (MS Ed); literacy specialist (MS Ed); mathematics education (MST); organizational performance, leadership and technology (MS Ed); science education (MST); social studies education (MST). Electronic applications accepted.

STATE UNIVERSITY OF NEW YORK COLLEGE OF ENVIRONMENTAL SCIENCE AND FORESTRY, Syracuse, NY 13210-2779

General Information State-supported, coed, university. CGS member. *Enrollment:* 2,384 graduate, professional, and undergraduate students; 362 full-time matriculated graduate/professional students (188 women), 98 part-time matriculated graduate/professional students (46 women). *Enrollment by degree level:* 273 master's, 187 doctoral. *Graduate faculty:* 121 full-time (34 women), 42 part-time/adjunct (15 women). Tuition, state resident: full-time $10,870; part-time $453 per credit. Tuition, nonresident: full-time $22,210; part-time $925 per credit. *Required fees:* $1075; $89.22 per credit. *Graduate housing:* On-campus housing not available. *Student services:* Campus employment opportunities, campus safety program, career counseling, exercise/wellness program, free psychological counseling, grant writing training, international student services, low-cost health insurance, multicultural affairs office, writing training. *Library:* F. Franklin Moon Library plus 1 other. *Research affiliation:* U.S. Department of Agriculture (USDA) (forest and natural resources management), NASA (remote sensing and GIS), New York State Department of Agriculture & Markets (green infrastructure and food systems), New York State Department of Environmental Conservation (environmental conservation and wildlife management), Honeywell (brownfields remediation), Department of Commerce (Great Lakes water).

Computer facilities: Computer purchase and lease plans are available. 350 computers available on campus for general student use. A campuswide network can be accessed from student residence rooms and from off campus. Online class registration is available.
Website: http://www.esf.edu/

General Application Contact: Scott Shannon, Dean, Instruction and Graduate Studies, 315-470-6599, Fax: 315-470-6978, E-mail: esfgrad@esf.edu.

GRADUATE UNITS

Department of Chemistry Students: 33 full-time (13 women), 5 part-time (2 women); includes 2 minority (1 Black or African American, non-Hispanic/Latino; 1 Asian, non-Hispanic/Latino), 10 international. 55 applicants, 67% accepted, 12 enrolled. *Faculty:* 17 full-time (2 women), 1 part-time/adjunct (0 women). *Financial support:* In 2015–16, 40 students received support, including 5 fellowships with full tuition reimbursements available (averaging $4,000 per year), 19 research assistantships with full tuition reimbursements available (averaging $20,000 per year), 44 teaching assistantships with full tuition reimbursements available (averaging $21,300 per year); Federal Work-Study, institutionally sponsored loans, scholarships/grants, health care benefits, unspecified assistantships, and departmental tuition assistance also available. Financial award application deadline: 6/30; financial award applicants required to submit FAFSA. In 2015, 4 master's, 7 doctorates awarded. Offers biochemistry (MPS, MS, PhD); environmental chemistry (MPS, MS, PhD); organic chemistry of natural products (MPS, MS, PhD); polymer chemistry (MPS, MS, PhD). *Application deadline:* For fall admission, 2/1 priority date for domestic and international students; for spring admission, 11/1 priority date for domestic and international students. Applications are processed on a rolling basis. *Application fee:* $60. Electronic applications accepted. *Application Contact:* Scott Shannon, Associate Provost for Instruction/Dean of the Graduate School, 315-470-6599, Fax: 315-470-6978, E-mail: sshannon@esf.edu. *Chair*, Prof. Ivan Gitsov, 315-470-6851, Fax: 315-470-6856, E-mail: igivanov@syr.edu.

Department of Environmental and Forest Biology Students: 81 full-time (47 women), 57 part-time (24 women); includes 9 minority (1 Black or African American, non-Hispanic/Latino; 2 American Indian or Alaska Native, non-Hispanic/Latino; 1 Asian, non-Hispanic/Latino; 3 Hispanic/Latino; 2 Two or more races, non-Hispanic/Latino), 15 international. Average age 28. 47 applicants, 49% accepted, 15 enrolled. *Faculty:* 29 full-time (9 women), 4 part-time/adjunct (3 women). *Financial support:* In 2015–16, 4 fellowships with tuition reimbursements, 36 research assistantships with tuition reimbursements, 39 teaching assistantships with tuition reimbursements (averaging $11,490 per year) were awarded; Federal Work-Study, institutionally sponsored loans, scholarships/grants, health care benefits, and unspecified assistantships also available. Financial award application deadline: 6/30. In 2015, 15 master's, 7 doctorates awarded. Offers applied ecology (MPS); chemical ecology (MPS, MS, PhD); conservation biology (MPS, MS, PhD); ecology (MPS, MS, PhD); entomology (MPS, MS, PhD); environmental interpretation (MPS, MS, PhD); environmental physiology (MPS, MS, PhD); fish and wildlife biology and management (MPS, MS, PhD); forest pathology and mycology (MPS, MS, PhD); plant biotechnology (MPS); plant science and biotechnology (MPS, MS, PhD). *Application deadline:* For fall admission, 2/1 priority date for domestic and international students; for spring admission, 11/1 priority date for domestic and international students. Applications are processed on a rolling basis. *Application fee:* $60. *Application Contact:* Dr. Danilo D. Fernando, Director, Graduate Program/Associate Professor, 315-470-6746, Fax: 315-470-6934, E-mail: dfernando@esf.edu. *Chair*, Dr. Donald J. Leopold, 315-470-6760, Fax: 315-470-6934, E-mail: djleopold@esf.edu.

Department of Environmental Resources Engineering Students: 28 full-time (12 women), 10 part-time (6 women); includes 4 minority (1 Black or African American, non-Hispanic/Latino; 2 Asian, non-Hispanic/Latino; 1 Hispanic/Latino), 17 international. Average age 25. 40 applicants, 60% accepted, 5 enrolled. *Faculty:* 8 full-time (1 woman), 9 part-time/adjunct (3 women). *Financial support:* In 2015–16, 22 students received support, including 8 research assistantships with tuition reimbursements available (averaging $14,000 per year), 14 teaching assistantships with tuition reimbursements available; fellowships with tuition reimbursements available, Federal Work-Study, institutionally sponsored loans, scholarships/grants, health care benefits, and unspecified assistantships also available. Financial award application deadline: 6/30; financial award applicants required to submit FAFSA. In 2015, 15 master's, 5 doctorates awarded. *Degree program information:* Part-time programs available. Part-time. Offers ecological engineering (MPS, MS, PhD); environmental management (MPS); environmental resources engineering (MPS, MS, PhD); geospatial information science and engineering (MPS, MS, PhD); water resources engineering (MPS, MS, PhD). *Application deadline:* For fall admission, 1/15 priority date for domestic and international students; for spring admission, 11/1 priority date for domestic and international students. Applications are processed on a rolling basis. *Application fee:* $60. *Application Contact:* Scott Shannon, Dean of the Graduate School, 315-470-6599, Fax: 315-470-6978, E-mail: esfgrad@esf.edu. *Chair*, Dr. Theodore Endreny, 315-470-6565, Fax: 315-470-6958, E-mail: te@esf.edu.

Department of Environmental Studies Students: 16 full-time (11 women), 2 part-time (both women), 3 international. 9 applicants, 89% accepted, 2 enrolled. *Faculty:* 10 full-time (7 women), 7 part-time/adjunct (5 women). Offers environmental studies (MPS, MS). *Application fee:* $60. *Application Contact:* Scott Shannon, Associate Provost for Instruction/Dean of the Graduate School, 315-470-6599, Fax: 315-470-6978, E-mail: sshannon@esf.edu. *Chair*, Bennette Whitmore, 315-470-6636, E-mail: bwhitmor@esf.edu.

Department of Forest and Natural Resources Management Students: 40 full-time (24 women), 5 part-time (0 women); includes 6 minority (2 American Indian or Alaska Native, non-Hispanic/Latino; 1 Asian, non-Hispanic/Latino; 2 Hispanic/Latino; 1 Two or more races, non-Hispanic/Latino), 10 international. 41 applicants, 68% accepted, 16 enrolled. *Faculty:* 34 full-time (9 women), 7 part-time/adjunct (0 women). *Financial support:* Fellowships with tuition reimbursements, research assistantships with tuition reimbursements, teaching assistantships with tuition reimbursements, career-related internships or fieldwork, Federal Work-Study, institutionally sponsored loans, scholarships/grants, health care benefits, and unspecified assistantships available. Financial award application deadline: 6/30; financial award applicants required to submit FAFSA. Offers ecology and ecosystems (MPS, MS, PhD); economics, governance and human dimensions (MPS, MS, PhD); forest and natural resources management (MPS, MS, PhD); monitoring, analysis and modeling (MPS, MS, PhD). *Application deadline:* For fall admission, 2/1 priority date for domestic and international students; for spring admission, 11/1 priority date for domestic and international students. Applications are processed on a rolling basis. *Application fee:* $60. *Application Contact:* Scott Shannon, Dean, Instruction and Graduate Studies, 315-470-6599, Fax: 315-470-6978, E-mail: esfgrad@esf.edu. *Chair*, Dr. David Newman, 315-470-6534, Fax: 315-470-6535.

Department of Landscape Architecture Students: 32 full-time (16 women), 2 part-time (both women); includes 2 minority (1 Asian, non-Hispanic/Latino; 1 Hispanic/Latino), 7 international. 60 applicants, 58% accepted, 10 enrolled. *Faculty:* 11 full-time (4 women), 9 part-time/adjunct (3 women). *Financial support:* Fellowships with tuition reimbursements, research assistantships with tuition reimbursements, teaching assistantships with tuition reimbursements, career-related internships or fieldwork, and Federal Work-Study available. Support available to part-time students. Financial award application deadline: 6/30; financial award applicants required to submit FAFSA. Offers community design and planning (MLA, MS); cultural landscape studies and conservation (MLA, MS); landscape and urban ecology (MLA, MS). *Application deadline:* For fall admission, 2/1 priority date for domestic and international students; for spring admission, 11/1 priority date for domestic and international students. Applications are processed on a rolling basis. *Application fee:* $60. *Application Contact:* Scott Shannon, Associate Provost for Instruction/Dean of the Graduate School, 315-470-6599, Fax: 315-470-6978, E-mail: esfgrad@esf.edu. *Chair*, Dr. Douglas Johnston, 315-470-6544, Fax: 315-470-6540, E-mail: dmjohnst@esf.edu.

Department of Paper and Bioprocess Engineering Students: 31 full-time (14 women), 5 part-time (1 woman); includes 3 minority (1 Black or African American, non-Hispanic/Latino; 1 Asian, non-Hispanic/Latino; 1 Hispanic/Latino), 20 international. Average age 25. 21 applicants, 90% accepted, 11 enrolled. *Faculty:* 13 full-time (2 women), 4 part-time/adjunct (0 women). *Financial support:* In 2015–16, 17 students received support, including 11 research assistantships with full tuition reimbursements available (averaging $14,000 per year), 9 teaching assistantships with full tuition reimbursements available (averaging $12,000 per year); fellowships with full tuition reimbursements available, career-related internships or fieldwork, Federal Work-Study, institutionally sponsored loans, scholarships/grants, health care benefits, and unspecified assistantships also available. Support available to part-time students. Financial award application deadline: 6/30; financial award applicants required to submit FAFSA. In 2015, 2 master's, 3 doctorates, 4 other advanced degrees awarded. Offers biomaterials engineering (MS, PhD); bioprocess engineering (MPS, MS, PhD); bioprocessing (Advanced Certificate); paper science and engineering (MPS, MS, PhD); sustainable engineering management (MPS). *Application deadline:* For fall admission, 2/1 priority date for domestic and international students; for spring admission, 11/1 priority date for domestic and international students. Applications are processed on a rolling basis. *Application fee:* $60. *Application Contact:* Scott Shannon, Associate Provost and Dean, Instruction and Graduate Studies, 315-470-6599, Fax: 315-470-6978, E-mail: esfgrad@esf.edu. *Chair*, Dr. Gary M. Scott, 315-470-6501, Fax: 315-470-6945, E-mail: gscott@esf.edu.

Department of Sustainable Construction Management and Engineering Students: 7 full-time (3 women), 4 part-time (2 women); includes 1 minority (Hispanic/Latino), 4 international. 12 applicants, 42% accepted, 2 enrolled. *Financial support:* Fellowships with full tuition reimbursements, research assistantships with full tuition reimbursements, teaching assistantships with full tuition reimbursements, career-related internships or fieldwork, Federal Work-Study, institutionally sponsored loans, scholarships/grants, health care benefits, and unspecified assistantships available. Financial award application deadline: 6/30; financial award applicants required to submit FAFSA. Offers construction management (MPS, MS, PhD); sustainable construction (MPS, MS, PhD); wood science (MPS, MS, PhD). *Application deadline:* For fall admission, 2/1 priority date for domestic and international students; for spring admission, 11/1 priority date for domestic and international students. Applications are processed on a rolling basis. *Application fee:* $60. *Application Contact:* Dr. Dudley J. Raynal, Dean, Instruction and Graduate Studies, 315-470-6599, Fax: 315-470-6879, E-mail: esfgrad@esf.edu. *Chair*, Dr. Susan E. Anagnost, 315-470-6880, Fax: 315-470-6879, E-mail: seanagno@esf.edu.

Program in Environmental Science Students: 56 full-time (33 women), 17 part-time (10 women); includes 6 minority (2 Asian, non-Hispanic/Latino; 3 Hispanic/Latino; 1 Two or more races, non-Hispanic/Latino), 34 international. 85 applicants, 44% accepted, 13 enrolled. *Faculty:* 1 full-time (0 women), 1 (woman) part-time/adjunct. *Financial support:* Fellowships with tuition reimbursements, research assistantships with tuition reimbursements, teaching assistantships with tuition reimbursements, career-related internships or fieldwork, Federal Work-Study, institutionally sponsored loans, scholarships/grants, health care benefits, and unspecified assistantships available. Support available to part-time students. Financial award application deadline: 6/30; financial award applicants required to submit FAFSA. *Degree program information:* Part-time programs available. Part-time. Offers biophysical and ecological economics (MPS); coupled natural and human systems (MPS); ecosystem restoration (MPS); environmental and community land planning (MPS, MS); environmental and natural resources policy (PhD); environmental communication and participatory processes (PhD); environmental monitoring and modeling (MPS); environmental policy and democratic processes (MPS, MS); water and wetland resource studies (MPS, MS). *Application deadline:* For fall admission, 2/1 priority date for domestic and international students; for spring admission, 11/1 priority date for domestic and international students. Applications are processed on a rolling basis. *Application fee:* $60. *Application Contact:* Dr. Dudley J. Raynal, Dean, Instruction and Graduate Studies, 315-470-6599, Fax: 315-470-6978, E-mail: esfgrad@esf.edu. *Coordinator*, Dr. Ruth Yanai, 315-470-6955, Fax: 315-470-6700, E-mail: rdyanai@esf.edu.

STATE UNIVERSITY OF NEW YORK COLLEGE OF OPTOMETRY, New York, NY 10036

General Information State-supported, coed, graduate-only institution. *Graduate housing:* On-campus housing not available. *Research affiliation:* Schnurmacher Institute for Vision Research (vision science).

GRADUATE UNITS

Graduate Programs ***Degree program information:*** Part-time programs available. Part-time. Offers vision science (PhD).

Professional Program Offers optometry (OD). Electronic applications accepted.

STATE UNIVERSITY OF NEW YORK COLLEGE OF TECHNOLOGY AT DELHI, Delhi, NY 13753

General Information State-supported, coed, comprehensive institution.

GRADUATE UNITS

Program in Nursing Education Offers nursing education (MS).

STATE UNIVERSITY OF NEW YORK DOWNSTATE MEDICAL CENTER, Brooklyn, NY 11203-2098

General Information State-supported, coed, upper-level institution. *Graduate housing:* Rooms and/or apartments available on a first-come, first-served basis to single and married students. Housing application deadline: 5/29. *Research affiliation:* Brooklyn Veterans Administration Medical Center, Polytechnic Institute of New York University (biomedical engineering).

GRADUATE UNITS

College of Medicine Offers medicine (MPH, MD); urban and immigrant health (MPH).

College of Nursing ***Degree program information:*** Part-time and evening/weekend programs available. Part-time, evening/weekend. Offers clinical nurse specialist (MS, Post Master's Certificate); nurse anesthesia (MS); nurse midwifery (MS, Post Master's Certificate); nurse practitioner (MS, Post Master's Certificate); nursing (MS).

School of Graduate Studies Offers bioimaging and neuroengineering (PhD); biomedical engineering (MS); molecular and cellular biology (PhD); neural and behavioral science (PhD).

STATE UNIVERSITY OF NEW YORK EMPIRE STATE COLLEGE, Saratoga Springs, NY 12866-4391

General Information State-supported, coed, comprehensive institution. *Graduate housing:* On-campus housing not available.

GRADUATE UNITS

School for Graduate Studies ***Degree program information:*** Part-time and evening/weekend programs available. Part-time, evening/weekend, online learning. Offers adult learning (MA); community and economic development (MA); global leadership (MBA); labor and policy studies (MA); learning and emerging technologies (MA); liberal studies (MA); management (MBA); nursing education (MSN); social policy (MA); teaching (MAT); teaching and learning (M Ed). Electronic applications accepted.

STATE UNIVERSITY OF NEW YORK MARITIME COLLEGE, Throggs Neck, NY 10465-4198

General Information State-supported, coed, comprehensive institution. *Graduate housing:* Room and/or apartments available to single students; on-campus housing not available to married students. *Research affiliation:* Port Authority of New York and New Jersey (transportation), Transportation Infrastructure Research Consortium, Transportation Research Board (maritime transportation).

GRADUATE UNITS

Program in International Transportation Management ***Degree program information:*** Part-time and evening/weekend programs available. Part-time, evening/weekend. Offers international transportation management (MS).

STATE UNIVERSITY OF NEW YORK POLYTECHNIC INSTITUTE, Utica, NY 13504-3050

General Information State-supported, coed, comprehensive institution. *Graduate housing:* Room and/or apartments available on a first-come, first-served basis to single students; on-campus housing not available to married students. Housing application deadline: 6/15. *Research affiliation:* Assured Information Security, Inc. (cyber security), Masconic Research Laboratory (heart research), New West Technologies (mechanical engineering), Air Force Research Lab (computer science/systems and signal processing).

GRADUATE UNITS

Colleges of Nanoscale Science and Engineering Offers nanoscale engineering (MS, PhD); nanoscale science (MS, PhD).

Program in Accountancy ***Degree program information:*** Part-time programs available. Part-time, online learning. Offers accountancy (MS). Electronic applications accepted.

Program in Business Administration in Technology Management ***Degree program information:*** Part-time programs available. Part-time, online learning. Offers accounting and finance (MBA); business management (MBA); health services management (MBA); human resource management (MBA); marketing management (MBA). Electronic applications accepted.

Program in Computer and Information Science ***Degree program information:*** Part-time and evening/weekend programs available. Part-time, evening/weekend. Offers computer and information science (MS). Electronic applications accepted.

Program in Family Nurse Practitioner ***Degree program information:*** Part-time programs available. Part-time, online learning. Offers family nurse practitioner (MS, CAS). Electronic applications accepted.

Program in Information Design and Technology ***Degree program information:*** Part-time programs available. Part-time, online learning. Offers information design and technology (MS). Electronic applications accepted.

Program in Network and Computer Security ***Degree program information:*** Part-time programs available. Part-time. Offers network and computer security (MS). Electronic applications accepted.

Program in Nursing Education ***Degree program information:*** Part-time programs available. Part-time, online learning. Offers nursing education (MS, CAS). Electronic applications accepted.

Program in Telecommunications ***Degree program information:*** Part-time and evening/weekend programs available. Part-time, evening/weekend. Offers telecommunications (MS). Electronic applications accepted.

STATE UNIVERSITY OF NEW YORK UPSTATE MEDICAL UNIVERSITY, Syracuse, NY 13210-2334

General Information State-supported, coed, upper-level institution. CGS member. *Graduate housing:* Rooms and/or apartments available on a first-come, first-served basis to single and married students. Housing application deadline: 8/1.

GRADUATE UNITS

College of Graduate Studies Offers anatomy (MS, PhD); biochemistry (MS); biochemistry and molecular biology (PhD); microbiology (MS); microbiology and immunology (PhD); neuroscience (PhD); pharmacology (PhD); physiology (MS, PhD). Electronic applications accepted.

College of Medicine Offers medicine (MD). Electronic applications accepted.

College of Nursing ***Degree program information:*** Part-time programs available. Part-time, online learning. Offers nurse practitioner (Post Master's Certificate); nursing (MS). Electronic applications accepted.

Department of Physical Therapy ***Degree program information:*** Part-time and evening/weekend programs available. Part-time, evening/weekend, online learning. Offers physical therapy (DPT). Electronic applications accepted.

Program in Medical Technology Offers medical technology (MS).

STEPHEN F. AUSTIN STATE UNIVERSITY, Nacogdoches, TX 75962

General Information State-supported, coed, comprehensive institution. *Graduate housing:* Rooms and/or apartments available on a first-come, first-served basis to single students and available to married students. Housing application deadline: 6/1. *Research affiliation:* University Health Center at Tyler (biotechnology, environmental science).

GRADUATE UNITS

Graduate School ***Degree program information:*** Part-time and evening/weekend programs available. Part-time, evening/weekend, online learning. Electronic applications accepted.

College of Applied Arts and Science Degree program information: Part-time programs available. Part-time. Offers applied arts and science (MA, MIS, MSW); communication (MA); interdisciplinary studies (MIS); mass communication (MA); social work (MSW).

College of Business Degree program information: Part-time and evening/weekend programs available. Part-time, evening/weekend. Offers business (MBA, MPAC, MS); computer science (MS); management and marketing (MBA); professional accountancy (MPAC).

College of Education Degree program information: Part-time and evening/weekend programs available. Part-time, evening/weekend. Offers athletic training (MS); counseling (MA); early childhood education (M Ed); education (M Ed, MA, MS, Ed D); educational leadership (Ed D); elementary education (M Ed); human sciences (MS); kinesiology (M Ed); school psychology (MA); secondary education (M Ed); special education (M Ed); speech pathology (MS).

College of Fine Arts Degree program information: Part-time programs available. Part-time. Offers art (MA); design (MFA); drawing (MFA); fine arts (MA, MFA, MM); music (MA, MM); painting (MFA); sculpture (MFA).

College of Forestry and Agriculture Offers agriculture (MS); forestry (MF, MS, PhD); forestry and agriculture (MF, MS, PhD).

College of Liberal Arts Degree program information: Part-time and evening/weekend programs available. Part-time, evening/weekend. Offers English (MA); history (MA); liberal arts (MA, MPA); psychology (MA); public administration (MPA).

College of Sciences and Mathematics Degree program information: Part-time programs available. Part-time. Offers biology (MS); biotechnology (MS); chemistry (MS); environmental science (MS); geology (MS, MSNS); mathematics (MS); mathematics education (MS); physics (MS); sciences and mathematics (MS, MSNS); statistics (MS).

STEPHENS COLLEGE, Columbia, MO 65215-0002

General Information Independent, Undergraduate: women only; graduate: coed, comprehensive institution. *Enrollment by degree level:* 178 master's, 7 other advanced degrees. *Graduate faculty:* 6 full-time (5 women), 19 part-time/adjunct (10 women). *Tuition, area resident:* Part-time $396 per credit hour. *Required fees:* $45 per credit hour. *Graduate housing:* On-campus housing not available. *Student services:* Campus employment opportunities, teacher training. *Library:* Hugh Stephens Library.

Computer facilities: 130 computers available on campus for general student use. A campuswide network can be accessed from student residence rooms and from off campus. Online class registration is available.
Website: http://www.stephens.edu/

General Application Contact: Lindsey Boudinot, Director of Graduate, Online and Certificate Programs, 800-388-7579, E-mail: online@stephens.edu.

GRADUATE UNITS

Division of Graduate and Continuing Studies ***Degree program information:*** Part-time and evening/weekend programs available. Part-time, evening/weekend, online learning. Offers business (MSL); counseling (M Ed, PGC); curriculum and instruction (M Ed); health information administration (Postbaccalaureate Certificate). Electronic applications accepted.

STETSON UNIVERSITY, DeLand, FL 32723

General Information Independent, coed, comprehensive institution. *Enrollment:* 4,330 graduate, professional, and undergraduate students; 969 full-time matriculated graduate/professional students (520 women), 298 part-time matriculated graduate/professional students (153 women). *Enrollment by degree level:* 402 master's, 865 doctoral. *Graduate faculty:* 80 full-time (44 women), 69 part-time/adjunct (27 women). *Graduate housing:* Rooms and/or apartments available to single and married students. *Student services:* Campus employment opportunities, campus safety program, career counseling, free psychological counseling, international student services, multicultural affairs office, services for students with disabilities, teacher training. *Library:* DuPont-Ball Library plus 1 other. *Collection:* Books: 454,022 (physical), 1.6 million (digital/electronic); Serial titles: 311 (physical), 114,491 (digital/electronic); Databases: 130. Weekly public service hours: 99; students can reserve study rooms.

Computer facilities: 500 computers available on campus for general student use. A campuswide network can be accessed from student residence rooms and from off campus. Online class registration is available.
Website: http://www.stetson.edu/

General Application Contact: Jamie Vanderlip, Assistant Director for Transfer and Graduate Admissions, 386-822-7100, Fax: 386-822-7112, E-mail: gradadmissions@stetson.edu.

GRADUATE UNITS

College of Arts and Sciences Students: 142 full-time (120 women), 15 part-time (11 women); includes 37 minority (8 Black or African American, non-Hispanic/Latino; 1 American Indian or Alaska Native, non-Hispanic/Latino; 2 Asian, non-Hispanic/Latino; 24 Hispanic/Latino; 2 Two or more races, non-Hispanic/Latino), 1 international. Average age 31. 126 applicants, 71% accepted, 62 enrolled. *Faculty:* 10 full-time (8 women), 4 part-time/adjunct (3 women). *Financial support:* In 2015–16, 84 students received support. Career-related internships or fieldwork, Federal Work-Study, scholarships/grants, tuition waivers (partial), and unspecified assistantships available. Support available to part-time students. In 2015, 75 master's awarded. *Degree program information:* Part-time and evening/weekend programs available. Part-time, evening/weekend. Offers arts and sciences (M Ed, MS, Ed S). *Application deadline:* For fall admission, 8/1 priority date for domestic students; for spring admission, 1/1 priority date for domestic students; for summer admission, 5/1 priority date for domestic students. Applications are processed on a rolling basis. *Application fee:* $50. Electronic applications accepted. *Application Contact:* Jamie Vanderlip, Associate Director of Admissions, 386-822-7100, Fax: 386-822-7112, E-mail: jlvander@stetson.edu. *Dean,* Dr. Karen Ryan, 386-822-7515.

Division of Education Students: 142 full-time (120 women), 15 part-time (11 women); includes 37 minority (8 Black or African American, non-Hispanic/Latino; 1 American Indian or Alaska Native, non-Hispanic/Latino; 2 Asian, non-Hispanic/Latino; 24 Hispanic/Latino; 2 Two or more races, non-Hispanic/Latino), 1 international. Average age 31. 126 applicants, 71% accepted, 62 enrolled. *Faculty:* 10 full-time (8 women), 4 part-time/adjunct (3 women). *Financial support:* In 2015–16, 84 students received support. Career-related internships or fieldwork, Federal Work-Study, institutionally sponsored loans, scholarships/grants, tuition waivers (partial), and unspecified assistantships available. Support available to part-time students. In 2015, 69 master's awarded. *Degree program information:* Part-time and evening/weekend programs available. Part-time, evening/weekend. Offers curriculum and instruction (Ed S); education (M Ed, MS, Ed S); educational leadership (M Ed); elementary education - educating for social justice (M Ed); marriage, couple and family counseling (MS); school counseling (MS). *Application deadline:* For fall admission, 8/1 priority date for domestic students; for spring admission, 1/1 priority date for domestic students; for summer admission, 5/1 priority date for domestic students. Applications are processed on a rolling basis. *Application fee:* $50. Electronic applications accepted. *Application Contact:* Jamie Vanderlip, Associate Director of Graduate Admissions, 386-822-7100, Fax: 386-822-7112, E-mail: jlvander@stetson.edu. *Dean,* Dr. Karen Ryan, 386-822-7515.

College of Law Students: 783 full-time (403 women), 123 part-time (64 women); includes 224 minority (49 Black or African American, non-Hispanic/Latino; 2 American Indian or Alaska Native, non-Hispanic/Latino; 23 Asian, non-Hispanic/Latino; 128 Hispanic/Latino; 22 Two or more races, non-Hispanic/Latino), 20 international. Average age 28. 2,274 applicants, 51% accepted, 249 enrolled. *Faculty:* 49 full-time (26 women), 66 part-time/adjunct (26 women). *Financial support:* In 2015–16, 510 students received support, including 61 fellowships (averaging $726 per year), 86 research assistantships (averaging $911 per year), 42 teaching assistantships (averaging $933 per year); Federal Work-Study, scholarships/grants, and health care benefits also available. Support available to part-time students. Financial award application deadline: 8/15; financial award applicants required to submit FAFSA. In 2015, 28 master's, 281 doctorates awarded. *Degree program information:* Part-time and evening/weekend programs available. Part-time, evening/weekend, 100% online. Offers advocacy (LL M); elder law (LL M); international law (LL M); law (JD). *Application deadline:* For fall admission, 5/15 for domestic and international students. Applications are processed on a rolling basis. *Application fee:* $55. Electronic applications accepted. *Application Contact:* Laura Zuppo, Assistant Dean of Admissions and Financial Planning, 727-562-7802, Fax: 727-343-0136, E-mail: lawadmit@law.stetson.edu. *Dean/Professor of Law,* Christopher M. Pietruszkiewicz, 727-562-7809, Fax: 727-562-6428, E-mail: cmp@law.stetson.edu.

School of Business Administration Students: 107 full-time (43 women), 52 part-time (30 women); includes 49 minority (12 Black or African American, non-Hispanic/Latino; 7 Asian, non-Hispanic/Latino; 15 Hispanic/Latino; 15 Two or more races, non-Hispanic/Latino), 14 international. Average age 31. 155 applicants, 73% accepted, 71 enrolled. *Faculty:* 17 full-time (5 women), 3 part-time/adjunct (1 woman). *Financial support:* In 2015–16, 33 students received support. Career-related internships or fieldwork, Federal Work-Study, institutionally sponsored loans, tuition waivers, and unspecified assistantships available. Support available to part-time students. Financial award application deadline: 3/15. In 2015, 85 master's awarded. *Degree program information:* Part-time and evening/weekend programs available. Part-time, evening/weekend. Offers accounting (M Acc); business administration (M Acc, MBA). *Application deadline:* For fall admission, 8/1 for domestic students; for spring admission, 1/1 for domestic students; for summer admission, 5/1 for domestic students. Applications are processed on a rolling basis. *Application fee:* $50. Electronic applications accepted. *Application Contact:* Jamie Vanderlip, Associate Director of Admissions, 386-822-7100, Fax: 386-822-7112, E-mail: jlvander@stetson.edu. *Dean, School of Business Administration,* Dr. Neal P. Mero, 386-822-7405.

STEVENS-HENAGER COLLEGE, Salt Lake City, UT 84123

General Information Independent, coed, comprehensive institution.

★ STEVENS INSTITUTE OF TECHNOLOGY, Hoboken, NJ 07030

General Information Independent, coed, university. CGS member. *Enrollment:* 6,359 graduate, professional, and undergraduate students; 2,129 full-time matriculated graduate/professional students (638 women), 1,102 part-time matriculated graduate/professional students (284 women). *Enrollment by degree level:* 2,799 master's, 343 doctoral, 89 other advanced degrees. *Graduate faculty:* 291 full-time (65 women), 149 part-time/adjunct (30 women). *Tuition, area resident:* Full-time $32,200; part-time $1450 per credit. *Required fees:* $1150; $550 per unit. $275 per semester. *Graduate housing:* Room and/or apartments available on a first-come, first-served basis to single students; on-campus housing not available to married students. Typical cost: $13,500 (including board). Room and board charges vary according to board plan, campus/location and housing facility selected. *Student services:* Campus employment opportunities, campus safety program, career counseling, exercise/wellness program, free psychological counseling, grant writing training, international student services, low-cost health insurance, multicultural affairs office, services for students with disabilities, teacher training, writing training. *Library:* Samuel Williams Library plus 1 other. *Research affiliation:* Department of Homeland Security (secure maritime systems), Department of Defense (systems engineering), National Science Foundation (nanotechnology and multi-scale systems), AT&T (intelligent networked systems), National Science Foundation (secure systems and information assurance).

Computer facilities: 500 computers available on campus for general student use. A campuswide network can be accessed from student residence rooms and from off campus. Online class registration, online account information, debit dining program, laundry status are available.
Website: http://www.stevens.edu/

General Application Contact: Shobi Sividasan, Dean of Graduate Admissions, 888-783-8367, Fax: 888-555-1306, E-mail: graduate@stevens.edu.

GRADUATE UNITS

Graduate School Students: 2,129 full-time (638 women), 1,102 part-time (284 women); includes 310 minority (60 Black or African American, non-Hispanic/Latino; 4 American Indian or Alaska Native, non-Hispanic/Latino; 196 Asian, non-Hispanic/Latino; 38 Hispanic/Latino; 12 Two or more races, non-Hispanic/Latino), 1,863 international. Average age 28. 5,623 applicants, 58% accepted, 1086 enrolled. *Faculty:* 291 full-time (65 women), 149 part-time/adjunct (30 women). *Financial support:* Fellowships, research assistantships, teaching assistantships, career-related internships or fieldwork, Federal Work-Study, scholarships/grants, and unspecified assistantships available. Financial award application deadline: 2/15; financial award applicants required to submit FAFSA. In 2015, 1,401 master's, 60 doctorates, 523 other advanced degrees awarded. *Degree program information:* Part-time and evening/weekend programs available. Part-time, evening/weekend, online learning. *Application deadline:* For fall admission, 6/1 for domestic students, 4/15 for international students; for spring admission, 11/30 for domestic students, 11/1 for international students. Applications are processed on a rolling basis. *Application fee:* $60. Electronic applications accepted. *Application Contact:* Shobi Sivadasan, Dean of Graduate Admissions and Enrollment Management, 201-216-5319, Fax: 888-511-1306, E-mail: shobi.sivadasan@stevens.edu.

Charles V. Schaefer Jr. School of Engineering Students: 1,364 full-time (381 women), 320 part-time (75 women); includes 118 minority (19 Black or African American, non-Hispanic/Latino; 78 Asian, non-Hispanic/Latino; 12 Hispanic/Latino; 9 Two or more races, non-Hispanic/Latino), 1,186 international. Average age 26. 3,473 applicants, 57% accepted, 612 enrolled. *Faculty:* 179 full-time (35 women), 82 part-time/adjunct (8 women). *Financial support:* Fellowships, research assistantships, teaching assistantships, career-related internships or fieldwork, Federal Work-Study, scholarships/grants, and unspecified assistantships available. Financial award application deadline: 2/15; financial award applicants required to submit FAFSA. In 2015, 324 master's, 15 doctorates, 227 other advanced degrees awarded. *Degree program information:* Part-time and evening/weekend programs available. Part-time, evening/weekend, online learning. Offers additive manufacturing (Certificate); advanced manufacturing (Certificate); air pollution technology (Certificate); analytical chemistry (Certificate); applied coastal oceanography (Certificate); applied mathematics (MS); applied optics (Certificate); applied statistics (Certificate); armament engineering (M Eng); atmosphere and environmental science and engineering (Certificate); atmospheric and environmental science and engineering (Certificate); autonomous robotics (Certificate); bioinformatics (Certificate); biomedical chemistry (Certificate); biomedical engineering (M Eng, PhD, Certificate);

chemical biology (MS, PhD, Certificate); chemical engineering (M Eng, PhD, Engr); chemical physiology (Certificate); chemistry (MS, PhD); civil engineering (M Eng, PhD, Certificate, Engr); computational fluid mechanics and heat transfer (Certificate); computer and electrical engineering (M Eng); computer engineering (M Eng, PhD, Certificate); computer graphics (Certificate); computer science (MS, PhD, Certificate); computer systems (M Eng, Certificate); construction management (MS, Certificate); cybersecurity (MS); data communications and networks (M Eng); database management systems (Certificate); design and production management (Certificate); digital systems design (M Eng); distributed systems (Certificate); electrical engineering (M Eng, PhD, Certificate); elements of computer science (Certificate); engineered software systems (M Eng); engineering (M Eng, MS, PhD, Certificate, Engr); enterprise and cloud computing (MS); enterprise computing (Certificate); enterprise security and information assurance (Certificate); environmental engineering (M Eng, PhD, Certificate); environmental hydrology (Certificate); environmental processes (M Eng); geotechnical/geoenvironmental engineering (M Eng, Engr); health informatics (Certificate); hydraulics (Certificate); hydrologic modeling (M Eng); image processing and multimedia (M Eng); information system security (M Eng); information systems (M Eng); inland and coastal environmental hydrodynamics (M Eng); integrated product development (M Eng); manufacturing technologies (M Eng); maritime systems (MS); materials science and engineering (M Eng, PhD); mathematics (MS, PhD); mechanical engineering (M Eng, PhD, Eng); media and broadcast engineering (MS); medical devices (Certificate); microdevices and microsystems (Certificate); microelectronics (Certificate); microelectronics and photonics (M Eng, MS, PhD); modeling of environmental systems (M Eng); multi-hazard engineering (Certificate); multimedia experience and management (Certificate); nanotechnology (PhD); networked information systems (MS, Certificate); networks and systems administration (Certificate); nuclear power engineering (Certificate); ocean engineering (M Eng, PhD); ordnance engineering (Certificate); pharmaceutical manufacturing (M Eng, MS, Certificate); photonics (Certificate); physics (M Eng, MS, PhD); polymer chemistry (Certificate); power generation (Certificate); product architecture and engineering (M Eng); robotics and control (Certificate); service oriented computing (Certificate); ship hydrodynamics (Certificate); soil and groundwater pollution control (M Eng); stochastic systems (Certificate); stochastic systems and optimization (MS); stormwater management (M Eng); structural analysis and design (Certificate); structural engineering (M Eng, Certificate, Engr); surface water hydrology (Certificate); systems reliability and design (M Eng); transportation engineering (M Eng); vibration and noise control (Certificate); water resources engineering (M Eng, Certificate). *Application deadline:* For fall admission, 6/1 for domestic students, 4/15 for international students; for spring admission, 11/30 for domestic students, 11/1 for international students. Applications are processed on a rolling basis. *Application fee:* $60. Electronic applications accepted. *Application Contact:* Graduate Admissions, 888-783-8367, Fax: 888-555-1306, E-mail: graduate@stevens.edu. *Interim Dean*, Dr. Keith G. Sheppard, 201-216-5263.

College of Arts and Letters Students: 4 full-time (1 woman), 1 (woman) part-time, 1 international. Average age 27. 7 applicants, 14% accepted, 1 enrolled. *Faculty:* 34 full-time (14 women), 6 part-time/adjunct (5 women). *Financial support:* Fellowships, research assistantships, teaching assistantships, career-related internships or fieldwork, Federal Work-Study, scholarships/grants, and unspecified assistantships available. Financial award application deadline: 2/15; financial award applicants required to submit FAFSA. In 2015, 4 master's awarded. *Degree program information:* Part-time and evening/weekend programs available. Part-time, evening/weekend. Offers arts and letters (MA, Graduate Certificate); policy and innovation (MA, Graduate Certificate). *Application deadline:* For fall admission, 6/1 for domestic students, 4/15 for international students; for spring admission, 11/30 for domestic students, 11/1 for international students. Applications are processed on a rolling basis. *Application fee:* $60. Electronic applications accepted. *Application Contact:* Graduate Admission, 888-783-8367, Fax: 888-511-1306, E-mail: graduate@stevens.edu. *Dean*, Dr. Kelland Thomas.

School of Business Students: 442 full-time (173 women), 464 part-time (151 women); includes 137 minority (30 Black or African American, non-Hispanic/Latino; 4 American Indian or Alaska Native, non-Hispanic/Latino; 87 Asian, non-Hispanic/Latino; 13 Hispanic/Latino; 3 Two or more races, non-Hispanic/Latino), 421 international. Average age 31. 1,432 applicants, 58% accepted, 284 enrolled. *Faculty:* 42 full-time (7 women), 26 part-time/adjunct (8 women). *Financial support:* Fellowships, research assistantships, teaching assistantships, career-related internships or fieldwork, Federal Work-Study, scholarships/grants, and unspecified assistantships available. Financial award application deadline: 2/15; financial award applicants required to submit FAFSA. In 2015, 337 master's, 4 doctorates, 61 other advanced degrees awarded. *Degree program information:* Part-time and evening/weekend programs available. Part-time, evening/weekend, online learning. Offers business (EMBA, EMTM, MBA, MS, PhD, Certificate); business administration (EMBA); business intelligence and analytics (MBA); computer science (MS); e-commerce (MS); engineering management (MBA); enterprise systems (MS); entrepreneurial information technology (MS); finance (MBA); general management (MS); global innovation management (MS); human resource management (MS); information architecture (MS); information management (MS, PhD, Certificate); information security (MS); information systems (MBA); information technology in financial services industry (MS); information technology in the pharmaceutical industry (MS); information technology outsourcing management (MS); innovation and entrepreneurship (MBA); management of wireless networks (MS); marketing (MBA); online security, technology and business (MS); pharmaceutical management (MBA); professional communications (Certificate); project management (MBA, MS, Certificate); software engineering (MS); technical management (MS); technology commercialization (MS); technology management (EMBA, MBA, MS, PhD); technology management for experienced professionals (MS, Certificate); telecommunications (MS); telecommunications management (MBA, PhD, Certificate). *Application deadline:* For fall admission, 6/1 for domestic students, 4/15 for international students; for spring admission, 11/30 for domestic students, 11/1 for international students. Applications are processed on a rolling basis. *Application fee:* $60. Electronic applications accepted. *Application Contact:* Graduate Admissions, 888-793-8367, Fax: 888-511-1306, E-mail: graduate@stevens.edu. *Dean*, Dr. Gregory Prastacos, 201-216-8366, E-mail: gprastac@stevens.edu.

School of Systems and Enterprises Students: 320 full-time (84 women), 317 part-time (59 women); includes 55 minority (11 Black or African American, non-Hispanic/Latino; 31 Asian, non-Hispanic/Latino; 13 Hispanic/Latino), 255 international. Average age 31. 703 applicants, 67% accepted, 189 enrolled. *Faculty:* 34 full-time (8 women), 26 part-time/adjunct (3 women). *Financial support:* Fellowships, research assistantships, teaching assistantships, career-related internships or fieldwork, Federal Work-Study, scholarships/grants, and unspecified assistantships available. Financial award application deadline: 2/15; financial award applicants required to submit FAFSA. In 2015, 287 master's, 10 doctorates, 208 other advanced degrees awarded. *Degree program information:* Part-time and evening/weekend programs available. Part-time, evening/weekend. Offers engineering management (M Eng, PhD, Certificate); enterprise systems (Certificate); financial engineering (MS, PhD, Certificate); socio-technical systems (MS, PhD); software engineering (MS, Certificate); space systems engineering (M Eng, Certificate); systems and enterprises (M Eng, MS, PhD, Certificate); systems and supportability engineering (Certificate); systems design and operational effectiveness (Certificate); systems engineering (M Eng, PhD); systems engineering and architecting (Certificate); systems engineering management (Certificate); systems engineering of embedded/cyber-physical systems (Certificate); systems engineering security (Certificate). *Application deadline:* For fall admission, 6/1 for domestic students, 4/15 for international students; for spring admission, 11/30 for domestic students, 11/1 for international students. Applications are processed on a rolling basis. *Application fee:* $60. Electronic applications accepted. *Application Contact:* Graduate Admissions, 888-783-8367, Fax: 888-511-1306, E-mail: graduate@stevens.edu. *Dean*, Dr. Dinesh Verma, 201-216-8645, Fax: 201-216-5541, E-mail: dinesh.verma@stevens.edu.

See Display on next page and Close-Up on page 901.

STEVENSON UNIVERSITY, Stevenson, MD 21153

General Information Independent, coed, comprehensive institution. *Enrollment:* 4,185 graduate, professional, and undergraduate students; 77 full-time matriculated graduate/professional students (47 women), 507 part-time matriculated graduate/professional students (389 women). *Enrollment by degree level:* 584 master's. *Graduate faculty:* 10 full-time (8 women), 50 part-time/adjunct (21 women). *Tuition, area resident:* Full-time $12,060; part-time $670 per credit. *Required fees:* $125 per semester. Tuition and fees vary according to program. *Graduate housing:* On-campus housing not available. *Student services:* Campus employment opportunities, campus safety program, career counseling, exercise/wellness program, multicultural affairs office, services for students with disabilities. *Library:* Stevenson University Learning Resource Center-Greenspring Campus plus 1 other. *Collection:* Books: 84,739 (physical), 308,920 (digital/electronic); Serial titles: 286 (physical), 28,752 (digital/electronic); Databases: 79. Students can reserve study rooms.

Computer facilities: Computer purchase and lease plans are available. 300 computers available on campus for general student use. A campuswide network can be accessed from student residence rooms and from off campus. Online class registration is available.
Website: http://www.stevenson.edu/

General Application Contact: Angela Reynolds, Director, Recruitment and Admissions, 443-352-4414, Fax: 443-352-4440, E-mail: amreynolds@stevenson.edu.

GRADUATE UNITS

Master of Arts in Teaching Program Students: 15 part-time (11 women); includes 3 minority (1 Black or African American, non-Hispanic/Latino; 2 Asian, non-Hispanic/Latino). Average age 27. 11 applicants, 82% accepted, 5 enrolled. *Faculty:* 3 part-time/adjunct (all women). *Financial support:* Applicants required to submit FAFSA. *Degree program information:* Part-time programs available. Part-time, blended/hybrid learning. Offers secondary biology (MAT); secondary chemistry (MAT); secondary mathematics (MAT). *Application deadline:* Applications are processed on a rolling basis. Electronic applications accepted. *Application Contact:* Amanda Courter, Senior Enrollment Counselor, 443-352-4243, Fax: 443-352-4440, E-mail: acourter@stevenson.edu. *Associate Dean of Teacher Education*, Anne P. Davis.

Program in Business and Technology Management Students: 29 full-time (16 women), 105 part-time (56 women); includes 60 minority (49 Black or African American, non-Hispanic/Latino; 1 American Indian or Alaska Native, non-Hispanic/Latino; 9 Asian, non-Hispanic/Latino; 1 Hispanic/Latino). Average age 31. 64 applicants, 77% accepted, 25 enrolled. *Faculty:* 1 full-time (0 women), 12 part-time/adjunct (3 women). *Financial support:* Applicants required to submit FAFSA. In 2015, 41 master's awarded. *Degree program information:* Part-time programs available. Part-time, online only, 100% online. Offers advanced information technology (MS); emerging technology (MS); innovative leadership (MS). *Application deadline:* Applications are processed on a rolling basis. *Application fee:* $0. Electronic applications accepted. *Application Contact:* Tonia Cristino, Assistant Director, Recruitment and Admissions, 443-352-4058, Fax: 443-394-0538, E-mail: tcristino@stevenson.edu. *Coordinator*, Steven Engorn, 443-352-4220, Fax: 443-394-0538, E-mail: sengorn@stevenson.edu.

Program in Communication Studies Students: 14 part-time (9 women); includes 3 minority (1 Black or African American, non-Hispanic/Latino; 2 Hispanic/Latino). Average age 25. 37 applicants, 70% accepted, 14 enrolled. *Faculty:* 2 part-time/adjunct (1 woman). *Financial support:* Applicants required to submit FAFSA. *Degree program information:* Part-time programs available. Part-time, online only, 100% online, blended/hybrid learning. Offers communication studies (MS). *Application deadline:* Applications are processed on a rolling basis. Electronic applications accepted. *Application Contact:* Amanda Courter, Senior Enrollment Counselor, 443-352-4243, Fax: 443-352-4440, E-mail: acourter@stevenson.edu.

Program in Cyber Forensics Students: 5 full-time (1 woman), 33 part-time (15 women); includes 9 minority (all Black or African American, non-Hispanic/Latino). Average age 35. 11 applicants, 73% accepted, 6 enrolled. *Faculty:* 6 part-time/adjunct (0 women). *Financial support:* Applicants required to submit FAFSA. In 2015, 7 master's awarded. *Degree program information:* Part-time programs available. Part-time, blended/hybrid learning. Offers cyber forensics (MS). *Application deadline:* Applications are processed on a rolling basis. Electronic applications accepted. *Application Contact:* William Wellein, Enrollment Counselor, 443-352-5843, Fax: 443-394-0538, E-mail: wwellein@stevenson.edu. *Program Coordinator*, Michael Robinson, Fax: 443-394-0538, E-mail: mrobinson4614@stevenson.edu.

Program in Forensic Science Students: 20 full-time (14 women), 23 part-time (18 women); includes 19 minority (18 Black or African American, non-Hispanic/Latino; 1 Hispanic/Latino). Average age 27. 28 applicants, 71% accepted, 16 enrolled. *Faculty:* 4 full-time (3 women), 5 part-time/adjunct (2 women). *Financial support:* Applicants required to submit FAFSA. In 2015, 23 master's awarded. *Degree program information:* Part-time programs available. Part-time. Offers biology (MS); chemistry (MS); crime scene investigation (MS). Program offered in partnership with Maryland State Police Forensic Sciences Division. *Application deadline:* Applications are processed on a rolling basis. *Application fee:* $0. Electronic applications accepted. *Application Contact:* William Wellein, Enrollment Counselor, 443-352-5843, Fax: 443-394-0538, E-mail: wwellein@stevenson.edu. *Coordinator*, John Tobin, PhD, 443-352-4142, Fax: 443-394-0538, E-mail: jtobin@stevenson.edu.

Program in Forensic Studies Students: 17 full-time (11 women), 114 part-time (90 women); includes 54 minority (51 Black or African American, non-Hispanic/Latino; 1 American Indian or Alaska Native, non-Hispanic/Latino; 2 Asian, non-Hispanic/Latino). Average age 30. 79 applicants, 75% accepted, 35 enrolled. *Faculty:* 3 full-time (all women), 14 part-time/adjunct (1 woman). *Financial support:* Applicants required to submit FAFSA. In 2015, 52 master's awarded. *Degree program information:* Part-time programs available. Part-time, blended/hybrid learning. Offers computer forensics (MS); criminalistics (MS); forensic accounting (MS); forensic legal professional (MS); interdisciplinary track (MS); investigations (MS). *Application deadline:* Applications are processed on a rolling basis. *Application fee:* $0. Electronic applications accepted. *Application Contact:* William Wellein, Enrollment Counselor, 443-352-5843, Fax: 443-394-0538, E-mail: wwellein@stevenson.edu. *Associate Dean*, Thomas Coogan, JD, 443-352-4075, Fax: 443-394-0538, E-mail: tcoogan@stevenson.edu.

Program in Healthcare Management Students: 6 full-time (5 women), 25 part-time (21 women); includes 15 minority (9 Black or African American, non-Hispanic/Latino; 5 Asian, non-Hispanic/Latino; 1 Hispanic/Latino). Average age 32. 28 applicants, 32% accepted, 5 enrolled. *Faculty:* 2 full-time (both women), 7 part-time/adjunct (5 women). *Financial support:* Applicants required to submit FAFSA. In 2015, 2 master's awarded. *Degree program information:* Part-time programs available. Part-time, online only, 100% online. Offers project management (MS); quality management and patient safety (MS). *Application deadline:* Applications are processed on a rolling basis. Electronic applications accepted. *Application Contact:* Amanda Courter, Enrollment Counselor, 443-352-4243, Fax: 443-394-0538, E-mail: acourter@stevenson.edu. *Coordinator*, Sharon Buchbinder, PhD, 443-394-9290, Fax: 443-394-0538, E-mail: sbuchbinder@stevenson.edu.

Program in Nursing Students: 178 part-time (169 women); includes 67 minority (53 Black or African American, non-Hispanic/Latino; 12 Asian, non-Hispanic/Latino; 2 Hispanic/Latino). Average age 40. 83 applicants, 75% accepted, 44 enrolled. *Faculty:* 4 full-time (all women), 7 part-time/adjunct (all women). *Financial support:* Applicants required to submit FAFSA. In 2015, 37 master's awarded. *Degree program information:* Part-time programs available. Part-time, blended/hybrid learning. Offers nursing education (MS); nursing leadership/management (MS); population-based care coordination (MS). *Application deadline:* Applications are processed on a rolling basis. *Application fee:* $0. Electronic applications accepted. *Application Contact:* Amanda Courter, Enrollment Counselor, 443-352-4243, Fax: 443-394-0538, E-mail: acourter@stevenson.edu. *Associate Dean*, Judith Feustle, PhD, 443-352-4292, Fax: 443-394-0538, E-mail: jfeustle@stevenson.edu.

STOCKTON UNIVERSITY, Galloway, NJ 08205-9441

General Information State-supported, coed, comprehensive institution. CGS member. *Enrollment:* 8,674 graduate, professional, and undergraduate students; 336 full-time matriculated graduate/professional students (273 women), 480 part-time matriculated graduate/professional students (360 women). *Enrollment by degree level:* 724 master's, 92 doctoral. *Graduate faculty:* 64 full-time (43 women), 29 part-time/adjunct (13 women). Tuition, state resident: full-time $13,968; part-time $582 per credit. Tuition, nonresident: full-time $21,502; part-time $895 per credit. *Required fees:* $4200; $175 per credit. $90. Tuition and fees vary according to degree level. *Graduate housing:* Room and/or apartments available on a first-come, first-served basis to single students; on-campus housing not available to married students. Typical cost: $7756 per year ($11,707 including board). Room and board charges vary according to board plan and housing facility selected. Housing application deadline: 4/1. *Student services:* Campus employment opportunities, campus safety program, career counseling, child daycare facilities, exercise/wellness program, free psychological counseling, grant writing training, international student services, low-cost health insurance, services for students with disabilities, teacher training, writing training. *Library:* Richard E. Bjork Library. *Collection:* Books: 228,380 (physical), 135,000 (digital/electronic); Serial titles: 127 (physical), 73,336 (digital/electronic). Weekly public service hours: 95. *Research affiliation:* Association of State Colleges (civic engagement), Jewish Foundation (Holocaust studies), Wetlands Institute (marine biology), Aviation Research and Technology Park (aviation research), Nature Conservancy of New Jersey (environmental studies).

Computer facilities: 1,198 computers available on campus for general student use. A campuswide network can be accessed from student residence rooms and from off campus. Online class registration is available.
Website: http://www.stockton.edu/

General Application Contact: Tara Williams, Assistant Director of Graduate Enrollment Management, 609-626-3640, E-mail: gradschool@stockton.edu.

GRADUATE UNITS

Office of Graduate Studies Students: 336 full-time (273 women), 480 part-time (360 women); includes 145 minority (37 Black or African American, non-Hispanic/Latino; 30 Asian, non-Hispanic/Latino; 60 Hispanic/Latino; 18 Two or more races, non-Hispanic/Latino), 4 international. Average age 32. 1,202 applicants, 36% accepted, 303 enrolled. *Faculty:* 70 full-time (46 women), 39 part-time/adjunct (25 women). *Financial support:* Fellowships, research assistantships, career-related internships or fieldwork, Federal Work-Study, scholarships/grants, and unspecified assistantships available. Support available to part-time students. Financial award application deadline: 3/1; financial award applicants required to submit FAFSA. In 2015, 217 master's, 32 doctorates awarded. *Degree program information:* Part-time programs available. Part-time. Offers American studies (MA, Certificate); business administration (MBA); communication disorders (MS); computational science (MS); criminal justice (MA); education (MA); environmental science (PSM); Holocaust and genocide studies (MA); instructional technology (MA); nursing (MSN); occupational therapy (MSOT); organizational leadership (Ed D); physical therapy (DPT); social work (MSW). *Application deadline:* For fall admission, 7/1 for domestic and international students. Applications are processed on a rolling basis. *Application fee:* $50. Electronic applications accepted. *Application Contact:* Tara Williams, Assistant Director of Graduate Enrollment, 609-626-3640, Fax: 609-626-6050, E-mail: gradschool@stockton.edu. *Director of Graduate Enrollment Management*, AmyBeth Glass, 609-652-4298, E-mail: graduatestudies@stockton.edu.

STONY BROOK UNIVERSITY, STATE UNIVERSITY OF NEW YORK, Stony Brook, NY 11794

General Information State-supported, coed, university. CGS member. *Enrollment:* 25,272 graduate, professional, and undergraduate students; 5,260 full-time matriculated graduate/professional students (2,548 women), 2,589 part-time matriculated graduate/professional students (1,822 women). *Enrollment by degree level:* 4,056 master's, 3,271 doctoral, 522 other advanced degrees. *Graduate faculty:* 1,660 full-time (625 women), 721 part-time/adjunct (370 women). Tuition, state resident: full-time $10,870; part-time $453 per credit hour. Tuition, nonresident: full-time $22,210; part-time $925 per credit hour. *Graduate housing:* Rooms and/or apartments available to single and married students. Housing application deadline: 5/15. *Student services:* Campus employment opportunities, campus safety program, career counseling, child daycare facilities, exercise/wellness program, free psychological counseling, grant writing training, international student services, multicultural affairs office, services for students with disabilities, teacher training, writing training. *Library:* Frank Melville, Jr. Memorial

Library plus 7 others. *Collection:* Books: 1.9 million (physical), 347,302 (digital/electronic); Serial titles: 1,327 (physical), 107,277 (digital/electronic); Databases: 653. Weekly public service hours: 92. *Research affiliation:* Veterans Affairs Medical Center, Nassau University Medical Center, Winthrop University Hospital, Cold Spring Harbor Laboratory, Brookhaven National Laboratory.

Computer facilities: Computer purchase and lease plans are available. 1,746 computers available on campus for general student use. A campuswide network can be accessed from student residence rooms and from off campus. Online class registration is available.
Website: http://www.stonybrook.edu/

General Application Contact: Melissa Jordan, Assistant Dean for Records and Admission, 631-632-9712, Fax: 631-632-7243, E-mail: gradadmissions@stonybrook.edu.

GRADUATE UNITS

Graduate School Students: 3,453 full-time (1,441 women), 689 part-time (318 women); includes 587 minority (98 Black or African American, non-Hispanic/Latino; 6 American Indian or Alaska Native, non-Hispanic/Latino; 259 Asian, non-Hispanic/Latino; 178 Hispanic/Latino; 2 Native Hawaiian or other Pacific Islander, non-Hispanic/Latino; 44 Two or more races, non-Hispanic/Latino), 2,018 international. 9,635 applicants, 33% accepted, 1107 enrolled. *Faculty:* 916 full-time (302 women), 357 part-time/adjunct (178 women). *Financial support:* In 2015–16, 118 fellowships, 641 research assistantships, 807 teaching assistantships were awarded; career-related internships or fieldwork, Federal Work-Study, institutionally sponsored loans, scholarships/grants, traineeships, health care benefits, tuition waivers (full), and unspecified assistantships also available. In 2015, 1,088 master's, 347 doctorates, 26 other advanced degrees awarded. *Degree program information:* Part-time and evening/weekend programs available. Part-time, evening/weekend. *Application deadline:* For fall admission, 1/15 for domestic and international students; for spring admission, 10/1 for domestic and international students. *Application fee:* $100. *Application Contact:* Melissa Jordan, Assistant Dean for Records and Admission, 631-632-9712, Fax: 631-632-7243, E-mail: gradadmissions@stonybrook.edu. *Dean*, Dr. Charles Taber, 631-632-7035, Fax: 631-632-7243, E-mail: lori.carron@stonybrook.edu.

College of Arts and Sciences Students: 1,605 full-time (777 women), 202 part-time (130 women); includes 288 minority (46 Black or African American, non-Hispanic/Latino; 3 American Indian or Alaska Native, non-Hispanic/Latino; 90 Asian, non-Hispanic/Latino; 117 Hispanic/Latino; 1 Native Hawaiian or other Pacific Islander, non-Hispanic/Latino; 31 Two or more races, non-Hispanic/Latino), 693 international. 3,696 applicants, 28% accepted, 397 enrolled. *Faculty:* 540 full-time (201 women), 166 part-time/adjunct (92 women). *Financial support:* In 2015–16, 60 fellowships, 332 research assistantships, 347 teaching assistantships were awarded; career-related internships or fieldwork, Federal Work-Study, scholarships/grants, traineeships, health care benefits, and unspecified assistantships also available. In 2015, 269 master's, 228 doctorates, 16 other advanced degrees awarded. *Degree program information:* Part-time and evening/weekend programs available. Part-time, evening/weekend. Offers Africana studies (MA, Certificate); anthropological sciences (PhD); anthropology (MA); applied ecology (MA); art history and criticism (MA, PhD); arts and sciences (MA, MAPP, MAT, MFA, MM, MS, DMA, PhD, Advanced Certificate, Certificate, Graduate Certificate); astronomy (PhD); biochemistry and cell biology (MS); biochemistry and molecular biology (PhD); biochemistry and structural biology (PhD); biological sciences (MA); chemistry (MS, PhD); clinical psychology (PhD); cognitive/experimental psychology (PhD); comparative literature (MA, PhD); cultural studies (PhD, Certificate); dramaturgy (MFA); earth science (MAT); ecology and evolution (PhD); economics (MA, PhD); English (MA, PhD); English education (MAT); French (MA); genetics (PhD); geosciences (MS, PhD); Hispanic languages and literature (MA, PhD); history (MA, PhD); immunology and pathology (PhD); integrative neuroscience (PhD); Italian (MA); linguistics (MA, PhD); mathematics (MA, MAT, PhD); modern research instrumentation (MS); molecular and cellular biology (MA, PhD); music history/theory (MA, PhD); music performance (MM, DMA); neuroscience (MS, PhD); philosophy (MA, PhD, Advanced Certificate); physics (MA, MAT, MS, PhD); physics education (MAT); political science (MA, PhD); psychology (MA); public policy (MAPP); public policy and urban development (MA); Romance languages (MA); social and health psychology (PhD); sociology (MA, PhD); STEM education (PhD); studio art (MFA); teaching English to speakers of other languages (MA); teaching writing (Graduate Certificate); theatre arts (MA); women's studies (Certificate). *Application deadline:* For fall admission, 1/15 for domestic students; for spring admission, 10/1 for domestic students. *Application fee:* $100. *Application Contact:* Melissa Jordan, Assistant Dean for Records and Admission, 631-632-9712, Fax: 631-632-7243, E-mail: melissa.jordan@stonybrook.edu. *Dean*, Dr. Sacha Kopp, 631-632-6999, Fax: 631-632-6900, E-mail: sacha.kopp@stonybrook.edu.

College of Business Students: 190 full-time (101 women), 124 part-time (50 women); includes 73 minority (10 Black or African American, non-Hispanic/Latino; 1 American Indian or Alaska Native, non-Hispanic/Latino; 41 Asian, non-Hispanic/Latino; 16 Hispanic/Latino; 1 Native Hawaiian or other Pacific Islander, non-Hispanic/Latino; 4 Two or more races, non-Hispanic/Latino), 75 international. Average age 29. 262 applicants, 68% accepted, 81 enrolled. *Faculty:* 37 full-time (11 women), 18 part-time/adjunct (5 women). *Financial support:* In 2015–16, 1 teaching assistantship was awarded; research assistantships also available. In 2015, 133 master's awarded. Offers accounting (MBA); business (MBA, MS, Certificate); business administration (MBA); finance (MS); health care management (MBA); innovation, human resources, management, or operations management (MBA); marketing (MBA). *Application deadline:* For fall admission, 6/15 for domestic students, 3/15 for international students; for spring admission, 11/15 for domestic students, 10/15 for international students. *Application fee:* $100. *Application Contact:* Erica Robey, Graduate Coordinator, 631-632-7171, Fax: 631-632-8181, E-mail: oss@stonybrook.edu. *Dean*, Dr. Manuel London, 631-632-7171, Fax: 631-632-8181, E-mail: manuel.london@stonybrook.edu.

College of Engineering and Applied Sciences Students: 1,283 full-time (355 women), 251 part-time (61 women); includes 132 minority (17 Black or African American, non-Hispanic/Latino; 92 Asian, non-Hispanic/Latino; 20 Hispanic/Latino; 3 Two or more races, non-Hispanic/Latino), 1,179 international. Average age 26. 5,193 applicants, 32% accepted, 475 enrolled. *Faculty:* 183 full-time (40 women), 36 part-time/adjunct (8 women). *Financial support:* In 2015–16, 19 fellowships, 236 research assistantships, 150 teaching assistantships were awarded; career-related internships or fieldwork also available. In 2015, 584 master's, 90 doctorates awarded. *Degree program information:* Part-time and evening/weekend programs available. Part-time, evening/weekend. Offers applied mathematics and statistics (MS, PhD, Advanced Certificate); biomedical engineering (MS, PhD, Certificate); civil engineering (MS, PhD, Graduate Certificate); computer engineering (MS, PhD); computer science (MS, PhD); educational technology (MS); electrical engineering (MS, PhD); energy and environmental systems (MS, Advanced Certificate); engineering and applied sciences (MS, PhD, Advanced Certificate, Certificate, Graduate Certificate); global operations management (MS); information systems (Certificate); information systems engineering (MS); materials science and engineering (MS, PhD); mechanical engineering (MS, PhD); medical physics (MS, PhD); software engineering (Certificate); technology, policy, and innovation (PhD). *Application deadline:* For fall admission, 1/15 for domestic students; for spring admission, 10/1 for domestic students. *Application fee:* $100. *Application Contact:* Melissa Jordan, Assistant Dean for Records and Admission, 631-632-9712, Fax: 631-632-7243, E-mail: gradadmissions@stonybrook.edu. *Dean*, Dr. Fotis Sotiropoulos, 631-632-8380, Fax: 631-632-8205, E-mail: fotis.sotiropoulos@stonybrook.edu.

School of Marine and Atmospheric Sciences Students: 130 full-time (77 women), 7 part-time (all women); includes 19 minority (2 Black or African American, non-Hispanic/Latino; 1 American Indian or Alaska Native, non-Hispanic/Latino; 6 Asian, non-Hispanic/Latino; 8 Hispanic/Latino; 2 Two or more races, non-Hispanic/Latino), 42 international. Average age 27. 154 applicants, 38% accepted, 32 enrolled. *Faculty:* 45 full-time (11 women), 4 part-time/adjunct (2 women). *Financial support:* In 2015–16, 11 fellowships, 60 research assistantships, 28 teaching assistantships were awarded; career-related internships or fieldwork and tuition waivers (full) also available. In 2015, 28 master's, 16 doctorates awarded. Offers atmospheric sciences (MS, PhD); geospatial sciences (Graduate Certificate); marine and atmospheric sciences (MA, MS, PhD, Graduate Certificate); marine conservation and policy (MA); marine sciences (MS, PhD). *Application deadline:* For fall admission, 1/15 for domestic students; for spring admission, 10/1 for domestic students. *Application fee:* $100. *Application Contact:* Carol Dovi, Coordinator, 631-632-8681, Fax: 631-632-8200. *Interim Dean*, Dr. Larry Swanson, 631-632-8700, Fax: 631-632-8820, E-mail: larry.swanson@stonybrook.edu.

School of Journalism Students: 7 full-time (5 women), 5 part-time (4 women); includes 2 minority (1 Hispanic/Latino; 1 Two or more races, non-Hispanic/Latino), 1 international. Average age 29. *Faculty:* 10 full-time (3 women), 29 part-time/adjunct (9 women). *Financial support:* In 2015–16, 1 teaching assistantship was awarded. In 2015, 3 master's awarded. Offers health communication (Certificate); journalism (MS). *Application deadline:* For fall admission, 4/30 for domestic students; for spring admission, 10/1 for domestic students. *Application fee:* $100. *Application Contact:* Maureen Robinson, Coordinator, 631-632-1073, E-mail: maureen.robinson@stonybrook.edu. *Dean*, Prof. Howard Schneider, 631-632-7403, E-mail: howard.schneider@stonybrook.edu.

School of Professional Development Students: 181 full-time (115 women), 905 part-time (621 women); includes 191 minority (62 Black or African American, non-Hispanic/Latino; 28 Asian, non-Hispanic/Latino; 95 Hispanic/Latino; 6 Two or more races, non-Hispanic/Latino), 6 international. Average age 33. 286 applicants, 87% accepted, 155 enrolled. *Faculty:* 88 part-time/adjunct (36 women). *Financial support:* Fellowships, research assistantships, teaching assistantships, and career-related internships or fieldwork available. Support available to part-time students. In 2015, 319 master's, 246 other advanced degrees awarded. *Degree program information:* Part-time and evening/weekend programs available. Part-time, evening/weekend, online learning. Offers biology (MAT); chemistry (MAT); coaching (Graduate Certificate); earth science (MAT); educational computing (Graduate Certificate); educational leadership (Advanced Certificate); English (MAT); environmental management (MPS, Graduate Certificate); French (MAT); German (MAT); higher education administration (MA, Certificate); human resource management (MS, Graduate Certificate); industrial management (Graduate Certificate); information systems management (Graduate Certificate); Italian (MAT); liberal studies (MA); mathematics (MAT); operations research (Graduate Certificate); physics (MAT); school district business leadership (Advanced Certificate); social studies (MAT); Spanish (MAT). *Application deadline:* For fall admission, 1/15 for domestic students; for spring admission, 10/1 for domestic students. Applications are processed on a rolling basis. *Application fee:* $100. *Application Contact:* Melissa Jordan, Assistant Dean, 631-632-7751, E-mail: melissa.jordan@stonybrook.edu. *Interim Dean*, Dr. Ken Lindblom, 631-632-7993, Fax: 631-632-9046, E-mail: kenneth.lindblom@stonybrook.edu.

Stony Brook Medicine Students: 1,802 full-time (1,085 women), 1,014 part-time (893 women); includes 951 minority (261 Black or African American, non-Hispanic/Latino; 5 American Indian or Alaska Native, non-Hispanic/Latino; 436 Asian, non-Hispanic/Latino; 219 Hispanic/Latino; 30 Two or more races, non-Hispanic/Latino), 64 international. 10,895 applicants, 17% accepted, 1119 enrolled. *Financial support:* In 2015–16, 24 fellowships, 33 research assistantships, 1 teaching assistantship were awarded. In 2015, 518 master's, 266 doctorates, 72 other advanced degrees awarded. Offers biomedical informatics (MS, PhD). *Application deadline:* For fall admission, 1/15 for domestic students; for spring admission, 10/1 for domestic students. *Application fee:* $100. *Application Contact:* Melissa Jordan, Assistant Dean for Records and Admission, 631-632-9712, Fax: 631-632-7243, E-mail: gradadmissions@stonybrook.edu. *Chief Executive Officer*, Dr. Reuven L. Pasternak, 631-444-2701.

School of Dental Medicine Students: 194 full-time (103 women); includes 49 minority (3 Black or African American, non-Hispanic/Latino; 35 Asian, non-Hispanic/Latino; 10 Hispanic/Latino; 1 Two or more races, non-Hispanic/Latino), 3 international. 1,428 applicants, 9% accepted, 53 enrolled. *Faculty:* 33 full-time (17 women), 70 part-time/adjunct (20 women). *Financial support:* Fellowships, research assistantships, teaching assistantships, and Federal Work-Study available. In 2015, 39 doctorates, 15 other advanced degrees awarded. Offers dental medicine (DDS); endodontics (Certificate); oral biology and pathology (MS, PhD); orthodontics (Certificate); periodontics (Certificate). *Application deadline:* For fall admission, 1/15 for domestic students; for spring admission, 10/1 for domestic students. *Application fee:* $100. *Application Contact:* Patricia Berry, Acting Director of Admissions, 631-632-3745, Fax: 631-632-7130, E-mail: patricia.berry@stonybrook.edu. *Dean*, Dr. Mary R. Truhlar, 631-632-8950, Fax: 631-632-7130, E-mail: mary.truhlar@stonybrookmedicine.edu.

School of Health Technology and Management Students: 488 full-time (301 women), 99 part-time (82 women); includes 167 minority (34 Black or African American, non-Hispanic/Latino; 3 American Indian or Alaska Native, non-Hispanic/Latino; 84 Asian, non-Hispanic/Latino; 41 Hispanic/Latino; 5 Two or more races, non-Hispanic/Latino), 12 international. Average age 28. 2,646 applicants, 14% accepted, 260 enrolled. *Faculty:* 67 full-time (41 women), 64 part-time/adjunct (45 women). *Financial support:* Fellowships, research assistantships, teaching assistantships, career-related internships or fieldwork, Federal Work-Study, and institutionally sponsored loans available. Financial award application deadline: 3/15. In 2015, 104 master's, 71 doctorates, 34 other advanced degrees awarded. Offers health care management (Advanced Certificate); health care policy and management (MS); occupational therapy (MS); physical therapy (DPT); physician assistant (MS). *Application deadline:* For fall admission, 1/15 for domestic students; for spring admission, 10/1 for domestic students. *Application fee:* $100. *Application Contact:* Dr. Richard W. Johnson, Associate Dean for Graduate Studies, 631-444-3251, Fax: 631-444-7621, E-mail:

richard.johnson@stonybrook.edu. *Dean,* Dr. Craig A. Lehmann, 631-444-2252, Fax: 631-444-7621, E-mail: craig.lehmann@stonybrook.edu.

School of Medicine Students: 695 full-time (329 women), 88 part-time (75 women); includes 308 minority (46 Black or African American, non-Hispanic/Latino; 199 Asian, non-Hispanic/Latino; 53 Hispanic/Latino; 10 Two or more races, non-Hispanic/Latino), 41 international. 5,697 applicants, 11% accepted, 248 enrolled. *Faculty:* 580 full-time (222 women), 72 part-time/adjunct (42 women). *Financial support:* In 2015–16, 24 fellowships, 33 research assistantships, 8 teaching assistantships were awarded; career-related internships or fieldwork, Federal Work-Study, and tuition waivers (full) also available. In 2015, 62 master's, 132 doctorates, 8 other advanced degrees awarded. Offers anatomical sciences (PhD); community health (MPH); evaluation sciences (MPH); family violence (MPH); health communication (Certificate); health economics (MPH); medicine (MPH, MS, MD, PhD, Advanced Certificate, Certificate); molecular and cellular pharmacology (PhD); molecular genetics and microbiology (PhD); nutrition (MS, Advanced Certificate); physiology and biophysics (PhD); population health (MPH); population health and clinical outcomes research (PhD); substance abuse (MPH). *Application deadline:* For fall admission, 1/15 for domestic students; for spring admission, 10/1 for domestic students. *Application fee:* $100. *Application Contact:* Dr. Jack Fuhrer, Associate Dean of Admissions, 631-444-2113, Fax: 631-444-6032, E-mail: somadmissions@stonybrook.edu. *Dean and Senior Vice President of Health Sciences,* Dr. Kenneth Kaushansky, 631-444-2113, Fax: 631-444-6032, E-mail: kenneth.kaushansky@stonybrook.edu.

School of Nursing Students: 52 full-time (49 women), 811 part-time (724 women); includes 302 minority (125 Black or African American, non-Hispanic/Latino; 2 American Indian or Alaska Native, non-Hispanic/Latino; 105 Asian, non-Hispanic/Latino; 62 Hispanic/Latino; 8 Two or more races, non-Hispanic/Latino), 6 international. Average age 37. 708 applicants, 63% accepted, 367 enrolled. *Faculty:* 37 full-time (34 women), 43 part-time/adjunct (37 women). *Financial support:* Fellowships, research assistantships, teaching assistantships, career-related internships or fieldwork, Federal Work-Study, institutionally sponsored loans, and traineeships available. Financial award application deadline: 3/15. In 2015, 143 master's, 20 doctorates, 15 other advanced degrees awarded. Blended/hybrid learning. Offers adult health nurse practitioner (Certificate); adult health/primary care nursing (MS, DNP); child health nurse practitioner (Certificate); child health nursing (MS, DNP); family nurse practitioner (MS, DNP, Certificate); mental health/psychiatric nursing (MS, DNP, Certificate); neonatal nurse practitioner (Certificate); neonatal nursing (MS, DNP); nurse midwifery (MS, DNP, Certificate); nursing (MS, DNP, Certificate); nursing education (MS, Certificate); nursing leadership (MS, Certificate); nursing practice (DNP); perinatal women's health nursing (MS, DNP, Certificate). *Application deadline:* For fall admission, 12/3 for domestic students. *Application fee:* $100. *Application Contact:* Karen Allard, Admissions Coordinator, 631-444-6628, Fax: 631-444-3136, E-mail: karen.allard@stonybrook.edu. *Dean,* Dr. Lee Anne Xippolitos, 631-444-3200, Fax: 631-444-6628, E-mail: lee.xippolitos@stonybrook.edu.

School of Social Welfare Students: 373 full-time (303 women), 16 part-time (12 women); includes 125 minority (53 Black or African American, non-Hispanic/Latino; 13 Asian, non-Hispanic/Latino; 53 Hispanic/Latino; 6 Two or more races, non-Hispanic/Latino), 2 international. Average age 29. 416 applicants, 74% accepted, 191 enrolled. *Faculty:* 12 full-time (7 women), 42 part-time/adjunct (25 women). *Financial support:* Fellowships, research assistantships, teaching assistantships, career-related internships or fieldwork, Federal Work-Study, and institutionally sponsored loans available. Financial award applicants required to submit FAFSA. In 2015, 209 master's, 4 doctorates awarded. *Degree program information:* Part-time programs available. Part-time. Offers social welfare (PhD); social work (MSW). *Application deadline:* For fall admission, 1/15 for domestic students; for spring admission, 10/1 for domestic students. *Application fee:* $100. *Application Contact:* Jennifer Davidson, Program Coordinator, 631-444-8361, Fax: 631-444-7565, E-mail: jennifer.davidson@stonybrook.edu. *Dean and Assistant Vice President for Social Determinants of Health,* Dr. Jacqueline B. Mondros, 631-444-2139, Fax: 631-444-7565, E-mail: jacqueline.mondros@stonybrook.edu.

Stony Brook Southampton Students: 61 full-time (33 women), 73 part-time (50 women); includes 16 minority (4 Black or African American, non-Hispanic/Latino; 1 American Indian or Alaska Native, non-Hispanic/Latino; 4 Asian, non-Hispanic/Latino; 5 Hispanic/Latino; 2 Two or more races, non-Hispanic/Latino), 7 international. Average age 36. 107 applicants, 75% accepted, 46 enrolled. *Faculty:* 4 full-time (2 women), 33 part-time/adjunct (18 women). *Financial support:* In 2015–16, 8 teaching assistantships were awarded. In 2015, 30 master's awarded. Offers fiction (MFA); film (MFA); poetry (MFA); scientific writing (MFA); scriptwriting (MFA). *Application deadline:* For fall admission, 1/15 for domestic students; for spring admission, 10/1 for domestic students. *Application fee:* $100. *Application Contact:* Adrienne Unger, Coordinator, 631-632-5030, E-mail: adrienne.unger@stonybrook.edu. *Director,* Dr. Robert Reeves, 631-632-5028, Fax: 631-632-2576, E-mail: robert.reeves@stonybrook.edu.

STRATFORD UNIVERSITY, Baltimore, MD 21202-3230

General Information Proprietary, coed, comprehensive institution.

GRADUATE UNITS

Program in International Hospitality Management ***Degree program information:*** Part-time and evening/weekend programs available. Part-time, evening/weekend, online learning. Offers international hospitality management (MS).

STRATFORD UNIVERSITY, Falls Church, VA 22043

General Information Proprietary, coed, comprehensive institution. *Enrollment:* 1,241 graduate, professional, and undergraduate students; 703 full-time matriculated graduate/professional students (226 women), 189 part-time matriculated graduate/professional students (101 women). *Enrollment by degree level:* 892 master's. *Tuition, area resident:* Full-time $4455; part-time $2227.50 per course. One-time fee: $100. *Graduate housing:* On-campus housing not available. *Student services:* Campus employment opportunities, career counseling, exercise/wellness program, international student services, multicultural affairs office, services for students with disabilities, writing training. *Library:* Learning Resource Center.

Computer facilities: 104 computers available on campus for general student use. A campuswide network can be accessed. Online class registration is available.
Website: http://www.stratford.edu/

General Application Contact: Admissions, 800-444-0804, E-mail: fcadmissions@stratford.edu.

GRADUATE UNITS

School of Graduate Studies Students: 703 full-time (226 women), 189 part-time (101 women); includes 681 minority (172 Black or African American, non-Hispanic/Latino; 38 American Indian or Alaska Native, non-Hispanic/Latino; 445 Asian, non-Hispanic/Latino; 16 Hispanic/Latino; 8 Native Hawaiian or other Pacific Islander, non-Hispanic/Latino; 2 Two or more races, non-Hispanic/Latino). Average age 30. *Financial support:* Federal Work-Study and scholarships/grants available. Financial award applicants required to submit FAFSA. *Degree program information:* Part-time and evening/weekend programs available. Part-time, evening/weekend, 100% online, blended/hybrid learning. Offers business administration (IMBA, MBA); cyber security (MS); cyber security leadership and policy (MS); digital forensics (MS); entrepreneurship (IMBA); finance (IMBA); global leadership (IMBA); healthcare administration (MS); information systems (MS); information technology (DIT); information technology and e-commerce (IMBA); international hospitality management (MS); marketing (IMBA); networking and telecommunications (MS); software engineering (MS). *Application deadline:* Applications are processed on a rolling basis. *Application fee:* $50. Electronic applications accepted. *Application Contact:* Admissions, 800-444-0804, E-mail: fcadmissions@stratford.edu. *President,* Dr. Richard R. Shurtz, 703-539-6890, Fax: 703-539-6960.

STRAYER UNIVERSITY, Washington, DC 20005-2603

General Information Proprietary, coed, comprehensive institution. *Graduate housing:* On-campus housing not available.

GRADUATE UNITS

Graduate Studies ***Degree program information:*** Part-time and evening/weekend programs available. Part-time, evening/weekend, online learning. Offers accounting (MS); acquisition (MBA); business administration (MBA); communications technology (MS); educational management (M Ed); finance (MBA); health services administration (MHSA); hospitality and tourism management (MBA); human resource management (MBA); information systems (MS); management (MBA); management information systems (MS); marketing (MBA); professional accounting (MS); public administration (MPA); supply chain management (MBA); technology in education (M Ed). Programs also offered at campus locations in Birmingham, AL; Chamblee, GA; Cobb County, GA; Morrow, GA; White Marsh, MD; Charleston, SC; Columbia, SC; Greensboro, NC; Greenville, SC; Lexington, KY; Louisville, KY; Nashville, TN; North Raleigh, NC; Washington, DC. Electronic applications accepted.

SUFFOLK UNIVERSITY, Boston, MA 02108-2770

General Information Independent, coed, comprehensive institution. *Enrollment:* 8,046 graduate, professional, and undergraduate students; 1,195 full-time matriculated graduate/professional students (718 women), 1,255 part-time matriculated graduate/professional students (710 women). *Enrollment by degree level:* 1,172 master's, 1,263 doctoral, 15 other advanced degrees. *Tuition, area resident:* Full-time $41,440; part-time $1383 per credit hour. *Required fees:* $52; $52 per unit. Part-time tuition and fees vary according to course load and program. *Graduate housing:* On-campus housing not available. *Student services:* Campus employment opportunities, campus safety program, career counseling, exercise/wellness program, free psychological counseling, grant writing training, international student services, low-cost health insurance, multicultural affairs office, services for students with disabilities, teacher training, writing training. *Library:* Mildred Sawyer Library plus 3 others. *Collection:* Books: 153,430 (physical), 167,498 (digital/electronic); Serial titles: 308 (physical), 24,000 (digital/electronic); Databases: 188. Weekly public service hours: 16; students can reserve study rooms.

Computer facilities: Computer purchase and lease plans are available. 403 computers available on campus for general student use. A campuswide network can be accessed from student residence rooms and from off campus. Online class registration is available.
Website: http://www.suffolk.edu/

General Application Contact: Cory Meyers, Director of Graduate Admissions, 617-573-8302, Fax: 617-305-1733, E-mail: grad.admission@suffolk.edu.

GRADUATE UNITS

College of Arts and Sciences Students: 170 full-time (139 women), 160 part-time (130 women); includes 56 minority (17 Black or African American, non-Hispanic/Latino; 9 Asian, non-Hispanic/Latino; 25 Hispanic/Latino; 5 Two or more races, non-Hispanic/Latino), 56 international. Average age 28. 707 applicants, 51% accepted, 132 enrolled. *Faculty:* 54 full-time (25 women), 39 part-time/adjunct (21 women). *Financial support:* In 2015–16, 199 students received support, including 196 fellowships (averaging $8,910 per year); career-related internships or fieldwork, Federal Work-Study, institutionally sponsored loans, scholarships/grants, and unspecified assistantships also available. Support available to part-time students. Financial award application deadline: 4/1; financial award applicants required to submit FAFSA. In 2015, 173 master's, 16 doctorates, 3 other advanced degrees awarded. *Degree program information:* Part-time and evening/weekend programs available. Part-time, evening/weekend. Offers administration of higher education (M Ed, CAGS); arts and sciences (M Ed, MA, MAC, MS, MSCJS, MSPS, PhD, CAGS, Certificate, Graduate Certificate); clinical psychology (PhD); college admission counseling (Certificate); communication studies (MAC); ethics and public policy (MS); integrated marketing communication (MAC); international relations (MSPS); mental health counseling (MS, CAGS); political science (MSPS); professional politics (MSPS, CAGS); public relations and advertising (MAC); school counseling (MS, CAGS); sociology (MSCJS). *Application deadline:* For fall admission, 6/15 priority date for domestic students, 6/15 for international students; for spring admission, 11/1 priority date for domestic students, 11/1 for international students. Applications are processed on a rolling basis. *Application fee:* $50. Electronic applications accepted. *Application Contact:* Mara Marzocchi, Associate Director of Graduate Admissions, 617-573-8302, Fax: 617-305-1733, E-mail: grad.admission@suffolk.edu. *Dean,* Maria Toyoda, 617-573-8265, Fax: 617-573-8513, E-mail: mtoyada@suffolk.edu.

Law School Students: 728 full-time (414 women), 466 part-time (249 women); includes 276 minority (87 Black or African American, non-Hispanic/Latino; 3 American Indian or Alaska Native, non-Hispanic/Latino; 63 Asian, non-Hispanic/Latino; 112 Hispanic/Latino; 11 Two or more races, non-Hispanic/Latino), 47 international. Average age 27. 1,834 applicants, 70% accepted, 334 enrolled. *Faculty:* 69 full-time (35 women), 43 part-time/adjunct (15 women). *Financial support:* In 2015–16, 531 students received support, including 2 fellowships (averaging $10,905 per year); career-related internships or fieldwork, Federal Work-Study, institutionally sponsored loans, and scholarships/grants also available. Support available to part-time students. Financial award application deadline: 3/1; financial award applicants required to submit FAFSA. In 2015, 465 doctorates awarded. *Degree program information:* Part-time and evening/weekend programs available. Part-time, evening/weekend. Offers business law and financial services (JD); civil litigation (JD); global law and technology (LL M); health and biomedical law (JD); intellectual property law (JD); international law (JD). *Application deadline:* For fall admission, 3/1 for domestic and international students. Applications are processed on a rolling basis. *Application fee:* $60. Electronic applications accepted. *Application Contact:* Mathew Gavin, Assistant Dean for Admissions and Financial Aid, 617-573-8144, Fax: 617-994-6838, E-mail: ilawadm@suffolk.edu. *Dean,* Andrew Perlman, 617-573-8144, Fax: 617-994-6838, E-mail: lawadmin@suffolk.edu.

New England School of Art and Design Students: 56 full-time (47 women), 41 part-time (36 women); includes 10 minority (2 Black or African American, non-Hispanic/Latino; 5 Asian, non-Hispanic/Latino; 3 Hispanic/Latino), 38 international. Average age 28. 111 applicants. *Faculty:* 14 full-time (8 women), 25 part-time/adjunct (13 women). *Financial support:* In 2015–16, 65 students received support, including 64 fellowships (averaging $6,459 per year). Financial award application deadline: 4/1; financial award applicants required to submit FAFSA. In 2015, 41 degrees awarded. *Degree program information:* Part-time and evening/weekend programs available. Part-time, evening/weekend. Offers graphic design (MA); interior architecture (MA). *Application deadline:* For fall admission, 6/15 priority date for domestic students, 6/15 for international students; for spring admission, 11/1 priority date for domestic students, 11/1 for international students. Applications are processed on a rolling basis. *Application fee:* $50. Electronic applications accepted. *Application Contact:* Mara Marzocchi, Associate Director of Graduate Admissions, 617-573-8302, Fax: 617-305-1733, E-mail: grad.admission@suffolk.edu. *Department Chair,* Audrey Goldstein, 617-997-4290, E-mail: agoldstein@suffolk.edu.

Sawyer Business School Students: 297 full-time (165 women), 629 part-time (331 women); includes 197 minority (81 Black or African American, non-Hispanic/Latino; 1 American Indian or Alaska Native, non-Hispanic/Latino; 47 Asian, non-Hispanic/Latino; 59 Hispanic/Latino; 9 Two or more races, non-Hispanic/Latino), 150 international. Average age 31. 995 applicants, 68% accepted, 295 enrolled. *Faculty:* 56 full-time (20 women), 28 part-time/adjunct (10 women). *Financial support:* In 2015–16, 439 students received support, including 417 fellowships (averaging $10,357 per year); career-related internships or fieldwork, Federal Work-Study, and institutionally sponsored loans also available. Support available to part-time students. Financial award application deadline: 4/1; financial award applicants required to submit FAFSA. In 2015, 402 master's, 4 other advanced degrees awarded. *Degree program information:* Part-time and evening/weekend programs available. Part-time, evening/weekend, online learning. Offers accounting (MBA, MSA, Graduate Certificate); business (EMBA, GMBA, MBA, MBAH, MHA, MPA, MSA, MSF, MSFSB, MST, APC, CASPA, CPASF, Graduate Certificate); business administration (APC); entrepreneurship (MBA); executive business administration (EMBA); finance (MBA); global business administration (GMBA); health administration (MBAH, MHA); international business (MBA); marketing (MBA); nonprofit management (MBA, MPA); organizational behavior (MBA); public administration (CASPA); state and local government (MPA); strategic management (MBA); supply chain management (MBA); taxation (MBA, MST). *Application deadline:* For fall admission, 6/15 priority date for domestic students, 6/15 for international students; for spring admission, 11/1 for domestic and international students. Applications are processed on a rolling basis. *Application fee:* $50. Electronic applications accepted. *Application Contact:* Mara Marzocchi, Associate Director of Graduate Admissions, 617-573-8302, Fax: 617-305-1733, E-mail: grad.admission@suffolk.edu. *Dean,* William J. O'Neill, JD, 617-573-2665, Fax: 617-573-8704, E-mail: woneill@suffolk.edu.

SULLIVAN UNIVERSITY, Louisville, KY 40205

General Information Proprietary, coed, comprehensive institution. *Graduate housing:* On-campus housing not available.

GRADUATE UNITS

School of Business ***Degree program information:*** Part-time programs available. Part-time, online learning. Offers business (EMBA, MBA, MPM, MSCM, MSCS, MSHRL, MSM, MSMIT, PhD, Pharm D).

SUL ROSS STATE UNIVERSITY, Alpine, TX 79832

General Information State-supported, coed, comprehensive institution. *Enrollment:* 1,973 graduate, professional, and undergraduate students; 150 full-time matriculated graduate/professional students (79 women), 683 part-time matriculated graduate/professional students (425 women). *Enrollment by degree level:* 833 master's. *Graduate faculty:* 58 full-time (15 women), 8 part-time/adjunct (3 women). *Graduate housing:* Rooms and/or apartments available on a first-come, first-served basis to single and married students. Typical cost: $2391 per year ($1445 including board) for single students; $1445 per year ($2391 including board) for married students. Room and board charges vary according to board plan and housing facility selected. *Student services:* Campus employment opportunities, campus safety program, career counseling, exercise/wellness program, free psychological counseling, teacher training, writing training. *Library:* Bryan Wildenthal Memorial Library. *Research affiliation:* Chihuahuan Desert Research Institute (biology, geology), Big Bend National Park (biology, geology).

Computer facilities: A campuswide network can be accessed from student residence rooms and from off campus.
Website: http://www.sulross.edu/

General Application Contact: Pamela Pipes, Director of Records and Registration, 432-837-8050, Fax: 432-837-8431, E-mail: ppipes@sulross.edu.

GRADUATE UNITS

College of Arts and Sciences ***Financial support:*** Research assistantships, teaching assistantships, career-related internships or fieldwork, Federal Work-Study, and institutionally sponsored loans available. Support available to part-time students. Financial award application deadline: 5/1; financial award applicants required to submit FAFSA. *Degree program information:* Part-time and evening/weekend programs available. Part-time, evening/weekend. Offers art history (MA); arts and sciences (MA, MS); biology (MS); English (MA); general psychology (MA); geology (MS); history (MA); political science (MA); psychology (MA); studio art (MA). *Application deadline:* Applications are processed on a rolling basis. *Application fee:* $0 ($50 for international students). *Application Contact:* Carol Greer, Administrative Secretary, 432-837-8368, Fax: 432-837-8382, E-mail: cgreer@sulross.edu. *Dean,* Dr. Jay Downing, 432-837-8368, Fax: 432-837-8382, E-mail: jdowning@sulross.edu.

College of Professional Studies ***Financial support:*** Teaching assistantships, career-related internships or fieldwork, Federal Work-Study, and institutionally sponsored loans available. Support available to part-time students. Financial award application deadline: 5/1; financial award applicants required to submit FAFSA. *Degree program information:* Part-time and evening/weekend programs available. Part-time, evening/weekend. Offers business administration (EMBA, MBA); counseling (M Ed); criminal justice (MS); educational diagnostics (M Ed, Certificate); homeland security (MS); master reading teacher (Certificate); physical education (M Ed); reading specialist (M Ed, Certificate); school administration (M Ed); Texas reading specialist (M Ed). Two-year Executive MBA program in cooperation with La Universidad de Chihuahua, Mexico (UACH). *Application fee:* $0 ($50 for international students). *Application Contact:* Joyce Robinson, Administrative Secretary, 432-837-8134, Fax: 432-837-8133, E-mail: joycer@sulross.edu. *Dean,* Melanie A. Croy, 432-837-8134, Fax: 432-837-8133, E-mail: mcroy@sulross.edu.

Division of Agricultural and Natural Resource Science Students: 17 full-time (9 women), 12 part-time (10 women); includes 8 minority (1 Black or African American, non-Hispanic/Latino; 1 American Indian or Alaska Native, non-Hispanic/Latino; 6 Hispanic/Latino). *Financial support:* Research assistantships, teaching assistantships, career-related internships or fieldwork, Federal Work-Study, and institutionally sponsored loans available. Support available to part-time students. Financial award application deadline: 5/1; financial award applicants required to submit FAFSA. *Degree program information:* Part-time programs available. Part-time. Offers agricultural and natural resource science (M Ag, MS); animal science (M Ag, MS); range and wildlife management (M Ag, MS). *Application deadline:* Applications are processed on a rolling basis. *Application fee:* $0 ($50 for international students). *Application Contact:* Saskia van Hecke, Administrative Secretary, 432-837-8201, Fax: 432-837-8409, E-mail: saskia.van-hecke@sulross.edu. *Dean,* Dr. Robert Kinucan, 432-837-8201, Fax: 432-837-8406, E-mail: kinucan@sulross.edu.

Rio Grande College of Sul Ross State University ***Degree program information:*** Part-time and evening/weekend programs available. Part-time, evening/weekend, online learning. Offers business administration (MBA); teacher education (M Ed).

SUM BIBLE COLLEGE & THEOLOGICAL SEMINARY, Oakland, CA 94603

General Information Independent-religious, coed, comprehensive institution.

GRADUATE UNITS

Graduate Programs Offers biblical studies (MA); Christian leadership (MA); theology (M Div).

SUMMIT UNIVERSITY, Clarks Summit, PA 18411-1297

General Information Independent-religious, coed, comprehensive institution. *Graduate housing:* Room and/or apartments available on a first-come, first-served basis to single students; on-campus housing not available to married students.

GRADUATE UNITS

Baptist Bible Seminary ***Degree program information:*** Part-time and evening/weekend programs available. Part-time, evening/weekend, online learning. Offers Biblical apologetics (MA); church education (M Div, M Min); church planting (M Div, M Min); global ministry (M Div, M Min); leadership in communication (D Min); leadership in counseling and spiritual development (D Min); leadership in global ministry (D Min); leadership in pastoral ministry (D Min); leadership in theological studies (D Min); military chaplaincy (M Div); ministry (PhD); organizational leadership (M Min); outreach pastor (M Div, M Min); pastoral counseling (M Div, M Min); pastoral leadership (M Div, M Min); theology (Th M); worship ministries leadership (M Div, M Min); youth pastor (M Div, M Min). Electronic applications accepted.

Graduate Studies ***Degree program information:*** Part-time and evening/weekend programs available. Part-time, evening/weekend, online learning. Offers Bible (MA); counseling (MA, MS); curriculum and instruction (M Ed); educational administration (M Ed); intercultural studies (MA); literature (MA); missions (MA); organizational leadership (MA); reading specialist (M Ed); secondary English/communications (M Ed); social entrepreneurship (MA); worldview studies (MA). MA in missions program available only for Association of Baptists for World Evangelism missionary personnel.

SWEDISH INSTITUTE, COLLEGE OF HEALTH SCIENCES, New York, NY 10001-6700

General Information Proprietary, coed, comprehensive institution. *Graduate housing:* On-campus housing not available.

GRADUATE UNITS

Graduate Program ***Degree program information:*** Part-time and evening/weekend programs available. Part-time, evening/weekend.

SWEET BRIAR COLLEGE, Sweet Briar, VA 24595

General Information Independent, women only, comprehensive institution. *Graduate housing:* Room and/or apartments available on a first-come, first-served basis to single students; on-campus housing not available to married students.

GRADUATE UNITS

Department of Education ***Degree program information:*** Part-time programs available. Part-time. Offers education (M Ed, MAT). Electronic applications accepted.

SYRACUSE UNIVERSITY, Syracuse, NY 13244

General Information Independent, coed, university. CGS member. *Enrollment:* 21,789 graduate, professional, and undergraduate students; 4,752 full-time matriculated graduate/professional students (2,358 women), 1,638 part-time matriculated graduate/professional students (796 women). *Enrollment by degree level:* 4,354 master's, 1,849 doctoral, 187 other advanced degrees. *Graduate faculty:* 1,092 full-time (424 women), 559 part-time/adjunct (265 women). *Tuition, area resident:* Full-time $25,974; part-time $1443 per credit hour. *Required fees:* $802; $50 per course. Tuition and fees vary according to course load and program. *Graduate housing:* On-campus housing not available. *Student services:* Campus employment opportunities, campus safety program, career counseling, child daycare facilities, exercise/wellness program, free psychological counseling, grant writing training, international student services, low-cost health insurance, multicultural affairs office, services for students with disabilities, teacher training, writing training. *Library:* E. S. Bird Library plus 3 others. *Collection:* Books: 3.9 million (physical), 356,185 (digital/electronic); Serial titles: 35,260 (physical), 144,811 (digital/electronic); Databases: 1,189. Weekly public service hours: 146; study areas open 24 hours, 5–7 days a week; students can reserve study rooms. *Research affiliation:* South Side Innovation Center (business incubator and entrepreneurship development), IBM Green Data Center (advanced infrastructure and smarter computing technologies), Institute for Manufacturing Enterprises (promoting learning in manufacturing enterprises through teaching, application, integration, discovery, and service), Syracuse Research Corporation (defense, environmental and intelligence systems), Center of Excellence (environmental and energy systems innovation), Say Yes to Education, Inc. (academic support and funding to high school students).

Computer facilities: Computer purchase and lease plans are available. 3,500 computers available on campus for general student use. A campuswide network can be accessed from student residence rooms and from off campus. Online class registration, library, web conferencing, learning management system (Blackboard), blogging service, personal Websites, "View My Advising Report" digital asset management system, office software, online video training are available.
Website: http://www.syr.edu/

General Application Contact: 315-443-4492, Fax: 315-443-3423, E-mail: grad@syr.edu.

GRADUATE UNITS

College of Arts and Sciences Students: 718 full-time (416 women), 64 part-time (42 women); includes 134 minority (31 Black or African American, non-Hispanic/Latino; 2 American Indian or Alaska Native, non-Hispanic/Latino; 28 Asian, non-Hispanic/Latino; 51 Hispanic/Latino; 2 Native Hawaiian or other Pacific Islander, non-Hispanic/Latino; 20 Two or more races, non-Hispanic/Latino), 181 international. Average age 27. 2,492 applicants, 22% accepted, 247 enrolled. *Faculty:* 332 full-time (126 women), 135 part-time/adjunct (84 women). *Financial support:* Fellowships with full tuition reimbursements, research assistantships with tuition reimbursements, teaching assistantships with tuition reimbursements, career-related internships or fieldwork, Federal Work-Study, scholarships/grants, health care benefits, tuition waivers, and unspecified assistantships available. Support available to part-time students. Financial award application deadline: 1/1. In 2015, 156 master's, 67 doctorates, 45 other advanced degrees awarded. *Degree program information:* Part-time programs available. Part-time. Offers applied statistics (MS); art history (MA); arts and sciences (MA, MFA, MS, Au D, PhD, CAS); arts leadership (MA, CAS); audiology (Au D, PhD); biology (MS, PhD); chemistry (MS, PhD); clinical psychology (PhD); college science teaching (PhD); composition and cultural rhetoric (PhD); computational linguistics (MS); creative writing (MFA); earth sciences (MA, MS, PhD); English (MA, PhD); experimental psychology (PhD); firearm and tool mark examination (CAS); forensic science (MS); French and Francophone studies (MA); language teaching (TESOL/TLOTE) (CAS); linguistic studies (MA); mathematics (MS, PhD); mathematics education (MS, PhD); medicolegal death investigation (CAS); Pan-African studies (MA); philosophy (MA, PhD); physics (MS, PhD); religion (MA, PhD); school psychology (PhD); social psychology (PhD); Spanish literature and culture (MA); speech-language pathology (MS); structural biology, biochemistry, and biophysics (PhD). *Application deadline:* For fall admission, 1/1 priority date for domestic and international students. Applications are processed on a rolling basis. *Application fee:* $75. Electronic applications accepted. *Application Contact:* Cassidy Perrault, Administrative Specialist, 315-443-2875, E-mail: clperrea@syr.edu. *Dean*, Dr. Karin Ruhlandt, 315-443-4070, E-mail: kruhland@syr.edu.

College of Engineering and Computer Science Students: 973 full-time (242 women), 174 part-time (30 women); includes 55 minority (18 Black or African American, non-Hispanic/Latino; 1 American Indian or Alaska Native, non-Hispanic/Latino; 24 Asian, non-Hispanic/Latino; 7 Hispanic/Latino; 1 Native Hawaiian or other Pacific Islander, non-Hispanic/Latino; 4 Two or more races, non-Hispanic/Latino), 931 international. Average age 25. 3,549 applicants, 34% accepted, 372 enrolled. *Faculty:* 91 full-time (19 women), 23 part-time/adjunct (2 women). *Financial support:* Fellowships with full tuition reimbursements, research assistantships with tuition reimbursements, teaching assistantships with tuition reimbursements, scholarships/grants, and tuition waivers (partial) available. Financial award application deadline: 1/1; financial award applicants required to submit FAFSA. In 2015, 392 master's, 31 doctorates, 1 other advanced degree awarded. *Degree program information:* Part-time and evening/weekend programs available. Part-time, evening/weekend. Offers bioengineering (MS, PhD); chemical engineering (MS, PhD); civil engineering (MS, PhD); computer and information science and engineering (PhD); computer engineering (MS); computer science (MS); cybersecurity (MS, CAS); electrical and computer engineering (PhD); electrical engineering (MS); energy systems engineering (MS); engineering and computer science (MS, PhD, CAS); engineering management (MS); environmental engineering (MS); environmental engineering science (MS); environmental health (CAS); mechanical and aerospace engineering (MS, PhD); microwave engineering (CAS); sustainable enterprise (CAS). *Application deadline:* For fall admission, 7/1 priority date for domestic students, 6/1 priority date for international students; for spring admission, 11/15 priority date for domestic students, 10/15 priority date for international students. Applications are processed on a rolling basis. *Application fee:* $75. Electronic applications accepted. *Application Contact:* Kathleen Joyce, Assistant Dean, 314-443-2219, E-mail: topgrads@syr.edu. *Dean, College of Engineering and Computer Science*, Dr. Teresa Dahlberg, 315-443-2545, E-mail: dahlberg@syr.edu.

College of Law Students: 544 full-time (230 women), 3 part-time (2 women); includes 108 minority (28 Black or African American, non-Hispanic/Latino; 1 American Indian or Alaska Native, non-Hispanic/Latino; 20 Asian, non-Hispanic/Latino; 45 Hispanic/Latino; 14 Two or more races, non-Hispanic/Latino), 57 international. Average age 25. 1,909 applicants, 54% accepted, 236 enrolled. *Faculty:* 44 full-time (16 women), 21 part-time/adjunct (8 women). *Financial support:* In 2015–16, 487 students received support. Fellowships, research assistantships, career-related internships or fieldwork, Federal Work-Study, institutionally sponsored loans, scholarships/grants, and tuition waivers (partial) available. Support available to part-time students. Financial award application deadline: 2/15. In 2015, 191 doctorates awarded. *Degree program information:* Part-time programs available. Part-time. Offers law (JD). *Application deadline:* For fall admission, 4/1 priority date for domestic and international students. Applications are processed on a rolling basis. *Application fee:* $70. Electronic applications accepted. *Application Contact:* Nikki Laubenstein, Director of Admissions, 315-443-1962, Fax: 315-443-9568, E-mail: admissions@law.syr.edu. *Interim Dean*, William Banks, 315-443-3678, E-mail: wcbanks@law.syr.edu.

College of Visual and Performing Arts Students: 178 full-time (105 women), 12 part-time (7 women); includes 24 minority (4 Black or African American, non-Hispanic/Latino; 3 Asian, non-Hispanic/Latino; 9 Hispanic/Latino; 8 Two or more races, non-Hispanic/Latino), 67 international. Average age 26. 547 applicants, 36% accepted, 93 enrolled. *Faculty:* 129 full-time (52 women), 127 part-time/adjunct (53 women). *Financial support:* Fellowships with full tuition reimbursements, teaching assistantships with tuition reimbursements, institutionally sponsored loans, and unspecified assistantships available. Financial award application deadline: 1/1; financial award applicants required to submit FAFSA. In 2015, 52 master's awarded. Offers art photography (MFA); art video (MFA); audio arts (MA); communication and rhetorical studies (MA); composition (MM); conducting (MM); film (MFA); illustration (MFA); museum studies (MA); music and performance (MM); studio art (MFA); studio arts (MFA); visual and performing arts (M Mu, M Mus, MA, MFA, MM, MS); voice pedagogy (MM). *Application deadline:* For fall admission, 2/1 priority date for domestic and international students; for spring admission, 3/1 priority date for domestic students. *Application fee:* $75. Electronic applications accepted. *Application Contact:* Therese West, Information Contact, 315-443-0137, E-mail: admissg@syr.edu. *Dean, College of Visual and Performing Arts*, Dr. Ann Clarke, 315-443-8070, E-mail: anclarke@syr.edu.

David B. Falk College of Sport and Human Dynamics Students: 244 full-time (199 women), 112 part-time (89 women); includes 61 minority (34 Black or African American, non-Hispanic/Latino; 2 American Indian or Alaska Native, non-Hispanic/Latino; 5 Asian, non-Hispanic/Latino; 11 Hispanic/Latino; 1 Native Hawaiian or other Pacific Islander, non-Hispanic/Latino; 8 Two or more races, non-Hispanic/Latino), 40 international. Average age 30. 492 applicants, 74% accepted, 174 enrolled. *Faculty:* 69 full-time (41 women), 20 part-time/adjunct (15 women). *Financial support:* Fellowships with full tuition reimbursements, research assistantships with tuition reimbursements, teaching assistantships with tuition reimbursements, and tuition waivers available. Financial award application deadline: 1/1; financial award applicants required to submit FAFSA. In 2015, 130 master's, 4 doctorates, 31 other advanced degrees awarded. *Degree program information:* Part-time and evening/weekend programs available. Part-time, evening/weekend. Offers addiction studies (MA, CAS); child and family studies (MA, MS, PhD); food studies (MS); global health (MS); marriage and family therapy (MA, PhD); nutrition science (MA, MS); social work (MSW); social work and marriage and family therapysport and human dynamics (MA, MS, MSW, PhD, CAS); sport venue and event management (MS); trauma-informed practice (CAS). *Application deadline:* For fall admission, 3/15 priority date for domestic and international students; for spring admission, 11/15 priority date for domestic students, 11/15 for international students; for summer admission, 3/15 priority date for domestic students, 3/15 for international students. *Application fee:* $75. Electronic applications accepted. *Application Contact:* Felicia Otero, Director of College Admissions, 315-443-5555, Fax: 315-443-2562, E-mail: falk@syr.edu. *Dean*, Dr. Diane Lyden Murphy, 315-443-5582, Fax: 315-443-2562.

Martin J. Whitman School of Management Students: 367 full-time (182 women), 531 part-time (171 women); includes 191 minority (70 Black or African American, non-Hispanic/Latino; 4 American Indian or Alaska Native, non-Hispanic/Latino; 43 Asian, non-Hispanic/Latino; 62 Hispanic/Latino; 2 Native Hawaiian or other Pacific Islander, non-Hispanic/Latino; 10 Two or more races, non-Hispanic/Latino), 290 international. Average age 30. 1,650 applicants, 53% accepted, 343 enrolled. *Faculty:* 76 full-time (25 women), 31 part-time/adjunct (14 women). *Financial support:* In 2015–16, 45 students received support. Fellowships with full tuition reimbursements available, research assistantships with tuition reimbursements available, teaching assistantships with tuition reimbursements available, career-related internships or fieldwork, and scholarships/grants available. In 2015, 260 master's, 3 doctorates awarded. *Degree program information:* Part-time programs available. Part-time, online learning. Offers accounting (MBA, PhD); business analytics (MBA, MS); entrepreneurship (MS); finance (MBA, MS, PhD); management (MBA, MS, MS Acct, PhD); management information systems (PhD); marketing management (MBA); real estate (MBA); supply chain management (MBA, MS, PhD). *Application deadline:* For fall admission, 2/15 for domestic and international students. Applications are processed on a rolling basis. *Application fee:* $75. Electronic applications accepted. *Application Contact:* Shri Ramakrishnan, Assistant Director, Graduate Recruitment, 315-443-3497, E-mail: sramak01@syr.edu. *Associate Dean for Master's Programs*, Don Harter, 315-443-3502, E-mail: dharter@syr.edu.

Maxwell School of Citizenship and Public Affairs Students: 548 full-time (287 women), 91 part-time (57 women); includes 84 minority (23 Black or African American, non-Hispanic/Latino; 4 American Indian or Alaska Native, non-Hispanic/Latino; 23 Asian, non-Hispanic/Latino; 27 Hispanic/Latino; 7 Two or more races, non-Hispanic/Latino), 225 international. Average age 31. 1,458 applicants, 52% accepted, 328 enrolled. *Faculty:* 151 full-time (61 women), 33 part-time/adjunct (11 women). *Financial support:* Fellowships with full tuition reimbursements, research assistantships with tuition reimbursements, and teaching assistantships with tuition reimbursements available. Financial award application deadline: 1/1. In 2015, 244 master's, 34 doctorates, 117 other advanced degrees awarded. *Degree program information:* Part-time programs available. Part-time, online learning. Offers anthropology (MA, PhD); citizenship and public affairs (EMIR, EMPA, MA, MPA, MPH, MS Sc, PhD, CAS); conflict resolution (CAS); economics (MA, PhD); economics and international relationsgeography (MA, PhD); health services management and policy (CAS); history (MA, PhD); international relations (EMIR, MA); leadership of international and non-governmental organizations (CAS); political science (MA, PhD); public administration (EMPA, MPA, PhD); public administration and international relationspublic diplomacypublic health (MPH); public infrastructure management and leadership (CAS); social sciences (MA, PhD); sociology (MA, PhD). *Application deadline:* For fall admission, 2/1 priority date for domestic and international students. Applications are processed on a rolling basis. *Application fee:* $75. Electronic applications accepted. *Application Contact:* Christine Omolino, Director, Admission and Financial Aid, 315-443-4000, E-mail: comolino@maxwell.syr.edu. *Dean*, Dr. James Steinberg, 315-443-4000, E-mail: jbstein@syr.edu.

School of Architecture Students: 109 full-time (39 women), 1 (woman) part-time; includes 16 minority (5 Black or African American, non-Hispanic/Latino; 5 Asian, non-Hispanic/Latino; 5 Hispanic/Latino; 1 Two or more races, non-Hispanic/Latino), 66 international. Average age 26. 249 applicants, 40% accepted, 27 enrolled. *Faculty:* 40 full-time (14 women), 9 part-time/adjunct (1 woman). *Financial support:* Fellowships with full tuition reimbursements, research assistantships with tuition reimbursements, and teaching assistantships with tuition reimbursements available. Financial award application deadline: 1/1. In 2015, 28 master's awarded. Offers architecture (M Arch). *Application deadline:* For fall admission, 2/1 priority date for domestic and international students. *Application fee:* $75. Electronic applications accepted. *Application Contact:* Vittoria Buccina, Director, Graduate and Undergraduate Recruitment, 315-443-5074, E-mail: vabuccin@syr.edu. *Graduate Director*, Jean Francois Bedard, 315-443-1041, Fax: 315-443-5082.

School of Education Students: 347 full-time (249 women), 258 part-time (172 women); includes 125 minority (59 Black or African American, non-Hispanic/Latino; 4 American Indian or Alaska Native, non-Hispanic/Latino; 14 Asian, non-Hispanic/Latino; 33 Hispanic/Latino; 2 Native Hawaiian or other Pacific Islander, non-Hispanic/Latino; 13 Two or more races, non-Hispanic/Latino), 70 international. Average age 32. 560 applicants, 64% accepted, 183 enrolled. *Faculty:* 49 full-time (28 women), 50 part-time/adjunct (35 women). *Financial support:* Fellowships with full tuition reimbursements, research assistantships with tuition reimbursements, teaching assistantships with tuition reimbursements, career-related internships or fieldwork, institutionally sponsored loans, scholarships/grants, health care benefits, tuition waivers (partial), and unspecified assistantships available. Financial award application deadline: 1/15; financial award applicants required to submit FAFSA. In 2015, 173 master's, 10 doctorates, 26 other advanced degrees awarded. *Degree program information:* Part-time programs available. Part-time. Offers art education (MS); biology (MS, PhD); chemistry (MS, PhD); clinical mental health counseling (MS); counseling and counselor education (PhD); cultural foundations of education (MS, PhD, CAS); disability studies (CAS); early childhood special education (MS); earth science (MS, PhD); education (M Mus, MM, MS, Ed D, PhD, CAS); educational leadership (MS, Ed D, CAS); educational technology (CAS); English education preparation (grades 7-12) (MS); exercise science (MS); higher education (MS, PhD); inclusive special education (grades 1-6) (MS); inclusive special education (grades 7-12) (MS); inclusive special education: severe/multiple disabilities (MS); instructional design foundation (CAS); instructional design, development, and evaluation (MS, PhD, CAS); instructional technology (MS); literacy education (PhD); literacy education (birth - grade 12) (MS); mathematics education (MS, PhD); music education (MM, MS); physics (MS, PhD); school counseling (MS, CAS); school district business leadership (CAS); social studies education preparation (grades 7-12) (MS); special education (PhD); student affairs counseling (MS); teaching and curriculum (MS, PhD); teaching English language learners (preK- 12) (MS). *Application deadline:* Applications are processed on a rolling basis. *Application fee:* $75. Electronic applications accepted. *Application Contact:* Speranza Migliore, Graduate Recruiter, School of Education, 315-443-2505, E-mail: gradrcrt@syr.edu. *Dean*, Dr. Joanna Masingila, 315-443-4751, E-mail: jomasing@syr.edu.

School of Information Studies Students: 461 full-time (224 women), 257 part-time (127 women); includes 102 minority (46 Black or African American, non-Hispanic/Latino; 1 American Indian or Alaska Native, non-Hispanic/Latino; 30 Asian, non-Hispanic/Latino; 18 Hispanic/Latino; 7 Two or more races, non-Hispanic/Latino), 350 international. Average age 29. 1,817 applicants, 38% accepted, 312 enrolled. *Faculty:* 42 full-time (15 women), 30 part-time/adjunct (7 women). *Financial support:* Fellowships with full tuition reimbursements, research assistantships with tuition reimbursements, teaching assistantships with tuition reimbursements, and scholarships/grants available. Financial award application deadline: 1/1. In 2015, 263 master's, 9 doctorates, 135 other advanced degrees awarded. *Degree program information:* Part-time and evening/weekend programs available. Part-time, evening/weekend, online learning. Offers cultural heritage preservation (CAS); data science (CAS); e-government management and leadership (CAS); information management (MS); information science and technology (PhD); information security management (CAS); information studies (MS, PhD, CAS); information systems and telecommunications management (CAS); library and information science (MS); library and information science: school media (MS); school media (CAS); telecommunications and network management (MS). *Application deadline:* For fall admission, 1/1 priority date for domestic students, 2/1 priority date for international students; for spring admission, 10/15 priority date for domestic and international students. Applications are processed on a rolling basis. *Application fee:* $75. Electronic applications accepted. *Application Contact:* Susan Corieri, Director of Enrollment Management, 315-443-2575, E-mail: ist@syr.edu. *Interim Dean,* Dr. Jeffrey Stanton, 315-443-2736, E-mail: jmstanto@syr.edu.

S. I. Newhouse School of Public Communications Students: 253 full-time (177 women), 131 part-time (95 women); includes 104 minority (55 Black or African American, non-Hispanic/Latino; 3 American Indian or Alaska Native, non-Hispanic/Latino; 13 Asian, non-Hispanic/Latino; 27 Hispanic/Latino; 6 Two or more races, non-Hispanic/Latino), 106 international. Average age 28. 821 applicants, 62% accepted, 244 enrolled. *Faculty:* 72 full-time (28 women), 45 part-time/adjunct (23 women). *Financial support:* Fellowships with full tuition reimbursements, research assistantships with partial tuition reimbursements, scholarships/grants, and instructional associate positions with partial tuition reimbursements available. Financial award application deadline: 2/1. In 2015, 203 master's, 4 doctorates awarded. Online learning. Offers advertising (MA); arts journalism (MA); broadcast and digital journalism (MS); communications management (MS); computational journalism (MS); documentary film and history (MA); magazine, newspaper, and online journalism (MA); mass communications (PhD); media studies (MA); new media management (MS); photography (MS); public communications (MA, MS, PhD); public diplomacypublic relations (MS); television, radio, and film (MA). *Application deadline:* For fall admission, 1/15 priority date for domestic and international students; for summer admission, 1/15 priority date for domestic and international students. *Application fee:* $45. Electronic applications accepted. *Application Contact:* Martha Coria, Graduate Records Office, 315-443-4039, Fax: 315-443-1834, E-mail: pcgrad@syr.edu. *Dean,* Lorraine Branham, 315-443-3372, E-mail: lbranham@syr.edu.

TABOR COLLEGE, Hillsboro, KS 67063

General Information Independent-religious, coed, comprehensive institution.

GRADUATE UNITS

Graduate Program Offers accounting (MBA). Program offered at the Wichita campus only.

TAFT UNIVERSITY SYSTEM, Denver, CO 80246

General Information Proprietary, coed, graduate-only institution.

GRADUATE UNITS

The Boyer Graduate School of Education Offers education (M Ed).

Taft Law School Offers American jurisprudence (LL M); law (JD); taxation (LL M).

W. Edwards Deming School of Business Offers taxation (MS).

TALMUDICAL ACADEMY OF NEW JERSEY, Adelphia, NJ 07710

General Information Independent-religious, men only, comprehensive institution.

GRADUATE UNITS

Graduate Program

TALMUDIC UNIVERSITY, Miami Beach, FL 33140

General Information Independent-religious, men only, comprehensive institution. *Graduate housing:* Rooms and/or apartments available on a first-come, first-served basis to single and married students.

GRADUATE UNITS

Program in Talmudic Law Offers Talmudic law (MRE).

TARLETON STATE UNIVERSITY, Stephenville, TX 76402

General Information State-supported, coed, comprehensive institution. *Enrollment:* 12,333 graduate, professional, and undergraduate students; 370 full-time matriculated graduate/professional students (211 women), 1,213 part-time matriculated graduate/professional students (745 women). *Enrollment by degree level:* 1,462 master's, 121 doctoral. *Graduate faculty:* 101 full-time (43 women), 41 part-time/adjunct (18 women). Tuition, state resident: part-time $204 per credit hour. Tuition, nonresident: part-time $594 per credit hour. *Required fees:* $1994 per unit. *Graduate housing:* Rooms and/or apartments available on a first-come, first-served basis to single and married students. Typical cost: $3380 per year ($7132 including board) for single students. Room and board charges vary according to board plan and housing facility selected. Housing application deadline: 8/1. *Student services:* Campus employment opportunities, campus safety program, career counseling, child daycare facilities, exercise/wellness program, free psychological counseling, grant writing training, international student services, low-cost health insurance, multicultural affairs office, services for students with disabilities, teacher training, writing training. *Library:* Dick Smith Library plus 1 other.

Computer facilities: 1,200 computers available on campus for general student use. A campuswide network can be accessed from student residence rooms and from off campus. Online class registration is available.
Website: http://www.tarleton.edu/

General Application Contact: Jillian Bam, Graduate Admissions Coordinator, 254-968-9104, Fax: 254-968-9670, E-mail: bam@tarleton.edu.

GRADUATE UNITS

College of Graduate Studies Students: 419 full-time (228 women), 1,316 part-time (786 women); includes 444 minority (218 Black or African American, non-Hispanic/Latino; 7 American Indian or Alaska Native, non-Hispanic/Latino; 23 Asian, non-Hispanic/Latino; 196 Hispanic/Latino), 61 international. Average age 36. *Faculty:* 211 full-time (89 women), 31 part-time/adjunct (13 women). *Financial support:* Research assistantships, teaching assistantships, career-related internships or fieldwork, Federal Work-Study, institutionally sponsored loans, scholarships/grants, and tuition waivers (partial) available. Support available to part-time students. Financial award application deadline: 5/1; financial award applicants required to submit FAFSA. *Degree program information:* Part-time and evening/weekend programs available. Part-time, evening/weekend, online learning. *Application deadline:* For fall admission, 8/15 priority date for domestic students; for spring admission, 1/7 for domestic students. *Application fee:* $45 ($130 for international students). Electronic applications accepted. *Application Contact:* Jillian Bam, Graduate Admissions Coordinator, 254-968-9104, Fax: 254-968-9670, E-mail: bam@tarleton.edu. *Dean,* Dr. Barry Lambert, 254-968-9463, Fax: 254-968-9670, E-mail: blambert@tarleton.edu.

College of Agricultural and Environmental Sciences Students: 65 full-time (41 women), 46 part-time (34 women); includes 11 minority (2 Black or African American, non-Hispanic/Latino; 1 American Indian or Alaska Native, non-Hispanic/Latino; 5 Hispanic/Latino; 3 Two or more races, non-Hispanic/Latino). Average age 27. 45 applicants, 82% accepted, 29 enrolled. *Faculty:* 17 full-time (4 women), 6 part-time/adjunct (1 woman). *Financial support:* Research assistantships, teaching assistantships, career-related internships or fieldwork, Federal Work-Study, and institutionally sponsored loans available. Support available to part-time students. Financial award application deadline: 5/1; financial award applicants required to submit FAFSA. In 2015, 35 master's awarded. *Degree program information:* Part-time and evening/weekend programs available. Part-time, evening/weekend, online learning. Offers agricultural and consumer resources (MS); agricultural and environmental sciences (MS); agricultural and natural resource sciences (MS). *Application deadline:* For fall admission, 8/15 priority date for domestic students; for spring admission, 1/7 for domestic students. Applications are processed on a rolling basis. *Application fee:* $30 ($130 for international students). Electronic applications accepted. *Application Contact:* Information Contact, 254-968-9104, Fax: 254-968-9670, E-mail: gradoffice@tarleton.edu. *Dean,* Dr. Don Cawthon, 254-968-9277, Fax: 254-968-9655, E-mail: cawthon@tarleton.edu.

College of Business Administration Students: 79 full-time (42 women), 415 part-time (213 women); includes 120 minority (54 Black or African American, non-Hispanic/Latino; 1 American Indian or Alaska Native, non-Hispanic/Latino; 12 Asian, non-Hispanic/Latino; 49 Hispanic/Latino; 4 Two or more races, non-Hispanic/Latino), 6 international. Average age 33. 232 applicants, 78% accepted, 159 enrolled. *Faculty:* 24 full-time (4 women), 2 part-time/adjunct (0 women). *Financial support:* Research assistantships, teaching assistantships, career-related internships or fieldwork, Federal Work-Study, and institutionally sponsored loans available. Support available to part-time students. Financial award application deadline: 5/1; financial award applicants required to submit FAFSA. In 2015, 137 master's awarded. *Degree program information:* Part-time and evening/weekend programs available. Part-time, evening/weekend, online learning. Offers accounting (M Acc); business administration (M Acc, MBA, MS); human resources management (MS); information systems (MS). *Application deadline:* For fall admission, 8/15 priority date for domestic students; for spring admission, 1/7 for domestic students. Applications are processed on a rolling basis. *Application fee:* $30 ($130 for international students). Electronic applications accepted. *Application Contact:* Information Contact, 254-968-9104, Fax: 254-968-9670, E-mail: gradoffice@tarleton.edu. *Dean,* Dr. Adolfo Benavides, 254-968-9496, Fax: 254-968-9496, E-mail: benavides@tarleton.edu.

College of Education Students: 141 full-time (98 women), 478 part-time (353 women); includes 171 minority (76 Black or African American, non-Hispanic/Latino; 5 American Indian or Alaska Native, non-Hispanic/Latino; 4 Asian, non-Hispanic/Latino; 69 Hispanic/Latino; 17 Two or more races, non-Hispanic/Latino), 1 international. Average age 36. 171 applicants, 86% accepted, 119 enrolled. *Faculty:* 43 full-time (24 women), 9 part-time/adjunct (5 women). *Financial support:* Research assistantships, teaching assistantships with partial tuition reimbursements, career-related internships or fieldwork, Federal Work-Study, institutionally sponsored loans, and tuition waivers (partial) available. Support available to part-time students. Financial award application deadline: 5/1; financial award applicants required to submit FAFSA. In 2015, 190 master's, 11 doctorates awarded. *Degree program information:* Part-time and evening/weekend programs available. Part-time, evening/weekend, online learning. Offers applied psychology (MS); education (M Ed, MS, Ed D, Certificate); educational administration (M Ed); educational diagnostician (M Ed); educational leadership (Ed D, Certificate); elementary education (M Ed); instructional design and technology (M Ed); instructional leadership (M Ed); kinesiology (MS); professional reading specialist (M Ed); secondary education (M Ed); special education (M Ed); technology applications (M Ed); technology director (M Ed). *Application deadline:* For fall admission, 8/15 priority date for domestic students; for spring admission, 1/7 for domestic students. Applications are processed on a rolling basis. *Application fee:* $30 ($130 for international students). Electronic applications accepted. *Application Contact:* Information Contact, 254-968-9104, Fax: 254-968-9670, E-mail: gradoffice@tarleton.edu. *Dean,* Dr. Jill Burk, 254-968-9089, Fax: 254-968-9525, E-mail: burk@tarleton.edu.

College of Liberal and Fine Arts Students: 54 full-time (17 women), 171 part-time (84 women); includes 80 minority (40 Black or African American, non-Hispanic/Latino; 2 Asian, non-Hispanic/Latino; 34 Hispanic/Latino; 4 Two or more races, non-Hispanic/Latino), 24 international. Average age 35. 72 applicants, 83% accepted, 55 enrolled. *Faculty:* 63 full-time (29 women), 8 part-time/adjunct (5 women). *Financial support:* Research assistantships and teaching assistantships available. Financial award application deadline: 5/1; financial award applicants required to submit FAFSA. In 2015, 48 master's awarded. *Degree program information:* Part-time and evening/weekend programs available. Part-time, evening/weekend. Offers communication studies (MA); criminal justice (MCJ); English (MA); history (MA); liberal and fine arts (MA, MCJ, MM, MPA); music education (MM); public administration (MPA). *Application deadline:* For fall admission, 8/15 priority date for domestic students; for spring admission, 1/7 for domestic students. Applications are processed on a rolling basis. *Application fee:* $30 ($130 for international students). Electronic applications accepted. *Application Contact:* Information Contact, 254-968-9104, Fax: 254-968-9670, E-mail: gradoffice@tarleton.edu. *Interim Dean,* Kelli Styron, 254-968-9141, Fax: 254-968-9784, E-mail: styron@tarleton.edu.

College of Science and Technology Students: 80 full-time (30 women), 206 part-time (102 women); includes 90 minority (46 Black or African American, non-Hispanic/Latino; 5 Asian, non-Hispanic/Latino; 39 Hispanic/Latino), 30 international. Average age 32. 38 applicants, 89% accepted, 25 enrolled. *Faculty:* 64 full-time (28 women), 6 part-time/adjunct (2 women). *Financial support:* Research assistantships, teaching assistantships, career-related internships or fieldwork, Federal Work-Study, and tuition waivers (partial) available. Support available to part-time students. Financial award application deadline: 5/1; financial award applicants required to submit FAFSA. In 2015, 22 master's awarded. *Degree program information:* Part-time and evening/weekend programs available. Part-time, evening/weekend, online learning. Offers biology (MS); environmental science (MS); mathematics (MS);

medical laboratory sciences (MS); nursing administration (MSN); nursing education (MSN); quality and engineering management (MS); science and technology (MA, MS, MSN, MSW); social work (MSW). *Application deadline:* For fall admission, 8/15 priority date for domestic students; for spring admission, 1/7 for domestic students. Applications are processed on a rolling basis. *Application fee:* $30 ($130 for international students). Electronic applications accepted. *Application Contact:* Information Contact, 254-968-9104, Fax: 254-968-9670, E-mail: gradoffice@tarleton.edu. *Dean*, Dr. James Pierce, 254-968-9781, Fax: 254-968-0549, E-mail: jrpierce@tarleton.edu.

TAYLOR COLLEGE AND SEMINARY, Edmonton, AB T6J 4T3, Canada

General Information Independent-religious, coed, comprehensive institution. *Graduate housing:* Room and/or apartments available on a first-come, first-served basis to single students; on-campus housing not available to married students. Housing application deadline: 8/1.

GRADUATE UNITS

Graduate and Professional Programs ***Degree program information:*** Part-time programs available. Part-time, online learning. Offers Christian studies (Diploma); intercultural studies (MA, Diploma); theology (M Div, MTS).

TAYLOR UNIVERSITY, Upland, IN 46989-1001

General Information Independent-religious, coed, comprehensive institution. *Graduate housing:* On-campus housing not available.

GRADUATE UNITS

Master of Arts in Higher Education and Student Development Program ***Degree program information:*** Part-time programs available. Part-time. Offers higher education and student development (MA).

Master of Business Administration Program ***Degree program information:*** Part-time programs available. Part-time. Offers emerging business strategies (MBA); global leadership (MBA).

TEACHERS COLLEGE, COLUMBIA UNIVERSITY, New York, NY 10027-6696

General Information Independent, coed, graduate-only institution. *Enrollment by degree level:* 3,576 master's, 1,343 doctoral. *Graduate faculty:* 170. *Tuition, area resident:* Part-time $1454 per credit. *Required fees:* $428 per semester. One-time fee: $475 full-time. Full-time tuition and fees vary according to course load. *Graduate housing:* Rooms and/or apartments available on a first-come, first-served basis to single and married students. Housing application deadline: 12/1. *Student services:* Campus employment opportunities, campus safety program, career counseling, exercise/wellness program, free psychological counseling, grant writing training, international student services, low-cost health insurance, multicultural affairs office, services for students with disabilities, teacher training, writing training. *Library:* Gottesman Libraries. *Collection:* Books: 845,365 (physical), 191,963 (digital/electronic); Serial titles: 47,206 (digital/electronic); Databases: 228. Weekly public service hours: 100; students can reserve study rooms.

Computer facilities: 418 computers available on campus for general student use. A campuswide network can be accessed from student residence rooms. Online class registration is available.
Website: http://www.tc.columbia.edu/

General Application Contact: David Estrella, Director of Admissions, 212-678-3305, E-mail: dpe2103@tc.columbia.edu.

GRADUATE UNITS

Department of Arts and Humanities Students: 296 full-time (232 women), 603 part-time (429 women); includes 389 minority (53 Black or African American, non-Hispanic/Latino; 1 American Indian or Alaska Native, non-Hispanic/Latino; 224 Asian, non-Hispanic/Latino; 85 Hispanic/Latino; 26 Two or more races, non-Hispanic/Latino), 67 international. *Financial support:* Fellowships, research assistantships, teaching assistantships, career-related internships or fieldwork, Federal Work-Study, institutionally sponsored loans, tuition waivers (full and partial), and unspecified assistantships available. Support available to part-time students. *Degree program information:* Part-time and evening/weekend programs available. Part-time, evening/weekend. Offers applied linguistics (MA, Ed D); art and art education (Ed M, MA, Ed D, Ed DCT); arts administration (MA); bilingual and bicultural education (MA); global competence (Certificate); history and education (Ed D, PhD); music and music education (Ed DCT); philosophy and education (MA, Ed D, PhD); social studies education (Ed M, PhD); teaching English to speakers of other languages (Ed M); teaching of English and English education (Ed M, MA, Ed D, PhD); teaching of social studies (MA); TESOL (MA, Ed D). *Application Contact:* David Estrella, Director of Admissions, 212-678-3305, Fax: 212-678-4171, E-mail: estrella@tc.columbia.edu. *Department Chair*, Prof. William Gaudelli, 212-678-3150, E-mail: wg74@columbia.edu.

Department of Biobehavioral Sciences Students: 121 full-time (103 women), 218 part-time (171 women); includes 157 minority (30 Black or African American, non-Hispanic/Latino; 58 Asian, non-Hispanic/Latino; 63 Hispanic/Latino; 6 Two or more races, non-Hispanic/Latino), 6 international. *Financial support:* Fellowships, teaching assistantships, career-related internships or fieldwork, Federal Work-Study, institutionally sponsored loans, traineeships, and tuition waivers (full and partial) available. Support available to part-time students. *Degree program information:* Part-time and evening/weekend programs available. Part-time, evening/weekend. Offers applied exercise physiology (Ed M, MA, Ed D); communication sciences and disorders (MS, Ed D, PhD); kinesiology (PhD); motor learning and control (Ed M, MA); motor learning/movement science (Ed D); neuroscience and education (MS); physical education (MA, Ed D). *Application Contact:* David Estrella, Director of Admissions, E-mail: estrella@tc.columbia.edu. *Chair*, Prof. Carol Garber, E-mail: garber@tc.columbia.edu.

Department of Counseling and Clinical Psychology Students: 282 full-time (235 women), 368 part-time (284 women); includes 280 minority (53 Black or African American, non-Hispanic/Latino; 2 American Indian or Alaska Native, non-Hispanic/Latino; 126 Asian, non-Hispanic/Latino; 78 Hispanic/Latino; 21 Two or more races, non-Hispanic/Latino), 32 international. *Degree program information:* Part-time programs available. Part-time. Offers clinical psychology (PhD); counseling psychology (Ed M, Ed D, PhD); mental health counseling (ME); psychological counseling (ME, ND); psychology in education (MA, ND); school counselor (ME). *Application Contact:* David Estrella, Director of Admission, 212-678-3305, E-mail: estrella@tc.columbia.edu. *Head*, Prof. Marie Miville, 212-678-3343, Fax: 212-678-3275, E-mail: miville@tc.columbia.edu.

Department of Curriculum and Teaching Students: 153 full-time (136 women), 352 part-time (327 women); includes 226 minority (45 Black or African American, non-Hispanic/Latino; 2 American Indian or Alaska Native, non-Hispanic/Latino; 106 Asian, non-Hispanic/Latino; 54 Hispanic/Latino; 19 Two or more races, non-Hispanic/Latino), 13 international. *Degree program information:* Part-time and evening/weekend programs available. Part-time, evening/weekend. Offers curriculum and teaching (Ed M, MA, Ed D); curriculum and teaching: elementary education (MA); curriculum and teaching: secondary education (MA); early childhood education (MA, Ed D); early childhood education: special education (MA); elementary education-gifted extension (MA); elementary inclusive education (MA); gifted education (MA); literacy specialist (MA); secondary inclusive education (MA); special inclusive elementary education (MA). *Application Contact:* David Estrella, Director of Admission, 212-678-3305, Fax: 212-678-4171, E-mail: estrella@tc.columbia.edu. *Chair*, Prof. Nancy Lesko, E-mail: lesko@tc.columbia.edu.

Department of Education Policy and Social Analysis Students: 104 full-time (80 women), 156 part-time (112 women); includes 151 minority (34 Black or African American, non-Hispanic/Latino; 1 American Indian or Alaska Native, non-Hispanic/Latino; 75 Asian, non-Hispanic/Latino; 35 Hispanic/Latino; 6 Two or more races, non-Hispanic/Latino), 23 international. Offers economics and education (Ed M, MA, PhD); education policy (Ed M, MA, Ed D, PhD); politics and education (Ed M, MA, Ed D, PhD); sociology and education (Ed M, MA, Ed D, PhD). *Application Contact:* David Estrella, Director of Admissions, 212-678-3305, E-mail: estrella@tc.columbia.edu. *Chair*, Dr. Jeffrey Henig, 212-678-8313, Fax: 212-678-3589, E-mail: henig@tc.columbia.edu.

Department of Health and Behavior Studies Students: 186 full-time (168 women), 362 part-time (319 women); includes 199 minority (50 Black or African American, non-Hispanic/Latino; 1 American Indian or Alaska Native, non-Hispanic/Latino; 73 Asian, non-Hispanic/Latino; 59 Hispanic/Latino; 1 Native Hawaiian or other Pacific Islander, non-Hispanic/Latino; 15 Two or more races, non-Hispanic/Latino), 13 international. *Degree program information:* Part-time and evening/weekend programs available. Part-time, evening/weekend. Offers applied behavior analysis (MA, PhD); applied educational psychology: school psychology (Ed M, PhD); behavioral nutrition (PhD); community health education (MS); community nutrition education (Ed M); education of deaf and hard of hearing (MA, PhD); health education (MA, Ed D); hearing impairment (Ed D); intellectual disability/autism (MA, Ed D, PhD); nursing education (Advanced Certificate); nutrition and education (MS); nutrition and exercise physiology (MS); nutrition and public health (MS); nutrition education (Ed D); physical disabilities (Ed D); reading specialist (MA); severe or multiple disabilities (MA); special education (Ed M, MA, Ed D); teaching of sign language (MA). *Application Contact:* David Estrella, Director of Admission, 212-678-3305, E-mail: estrella@tc.columbia.edu. *Chair*, Prof. Stephen T. Peverly, 212-678-3964, Fax: 212-678-8259, E-mail: stp4@columbia.edu.

Department of Human Development Students: 140 full-time (97 women), 167 part-time (125 women); includes 170 minority (18 Black or African American, non-Hispanic/Latino; 123 Asian, non-Hispanic/Latino; 22 Hispanic/Latino; 7 Two or more races, non-Hispanic/Latino), 51 international. *Degree program information:* Part-time programs available. Part-time. Offers applied statistics (MS); cognitive studies in education (MA, Ed D, PhD); developmental psychology (MA, Ed D, PhD); educational psychology-human cognition and learning (Ed M, MA, Ed D, PhD); learning analytics (MS); measurement and evaluation (ME, Ed D, PhD); measurement, evaluation, and statistics (MA, MS, Ed D, PhD). *Application Contact:* David Estrella, Director of Admission, 212-678-3305, E-mail: estrella@tc.columbia.edu. *Chair*, Prof. Matthew S. Johnson, 212-678-3882, Fax: 212-678-3837, E-mail: johnson@tc.columbia.edu.

Department of International and Transcultural Studies Students: 78 full-time (59 women), 200 part-time (166 women); includes 145 minority (22 Black or African American, non-Hispanic/Latino; 1 American Indian or Alaska Native, non-Hispanic/Latino; 74 Asian, non-Hispanic/Latino; 35 Hispanic/Latino; 13 Two or more races, non-Hispanic/Latino), 21 international. *Degree program information:* Part-time programs available. Part-time. Offers anthropology and education (MA, Ed D, PhD); applied anthropology (PhD); comparative and international education (MA, Ed D, PhD); international educational development (Ed M, MA, Ed D, PhD). *Application Contact:* David Estrella, Director of Admission, 212-678-3305, E-mail: estrella@tc.columbia.edu. *Chair*, Prof. Herve Varenne, E-mail: varenne@tc.columbia.edu.

Department of Mathematics, Science and Technology Students: 134 full-time (89 women), 285 part-time (168 women); includes 219 minority (49 Black or African American, non-Hispanic/Latino; 124 Asian, non-Hispanic/Latino; 31 Hispanic/Latino; 15 Two or more races, non-Hispanic/Latino), 29 international. *Degree program information:* Part-time and evening/weekend programs available. Part-time, evening/weekend. Offers biology 7-12 (MA); chemistry 7-12 (MA); communication and education (MA); communications (Ed M); communications and education (Ed D); computing in education (MA); computing in education-online (MA); earth science 7-12 (MA); instructional technology and media (Ed M, MA, Ed D); mathematics education (Ed M, MA, Ed D, Ed DCT, PhD); physics 7-12 (MA); science and dental education (MA); science education (Ed M, MS, Ed DCT, PhD); supervisor/teacher of science education (MA); technology specialist (MA). *Application Contact:* David Estrella, Director of Admission, E-mail: estrella@tc.columbia.edu. *Chair*, Dr. O. Roger Anderson, 212-678-3405, Fax: 212-678-8129, E-mail: ora@ldeo.columbia.edu.

Department of Organization and Leadership Students: 285 full-time (173 women), 491 part-time (344 women); includes 333 minority (119 Black or African American, non-Hispanic/Latino; 1 American Indian or Alaska Native, non-Hispanic/Latino; 102 Asian, non-Hispanic/Latino; 97 Hispanic/Latino; 14 Two or more races, non-Hispanic/Latino), 36 international. *Degree program information:* Part-time and evening/weekend programs available. Part-time, evening/weekend. Offers adult education guided intensive study (Ed D); adult learning and leadership (Ed M, MA, ME, Ed D); educational leadership (Ed D); higher and postsecondary education (MA, ME, Ed D); leadership, policy and politics (Ed D); nurse education (MA); nurse executive (MA, Ed D); private school leadership (Ed M, MA, ME); public school building leadership (Ed M, MA, ME); social and organizational psychology (MA); urban education leaders (Ed D). *Application Contact:* David Estrella, Director of Admission, E-mail: estrella@tc.columbia.edu. *Chair*, Prof. Anna Neumann, 212-678-3272, Fax: 212-678-3036, E-mail: neumann@tc.columbia.edu.

Interdisciplinary Programs Students: 7 full-time (4 women), 21 part-time (13 women); includes 15 minority (6 Black or African American, non-Hispanic/Latino; 1 American Indian or Alaska Native, non-Hispanic/Latino; 7 Asian, non-Hispanic/Latino; 1 Two or more races, non-Hispanic/Latino), 1 international. *Degree program information:* Part-time programs available. Part-time. Offers interdisciplinary studies (Ed M, MA, ME, Ed D). *Application Contact:* David Estrella, Director of Admissions, E-mail: estrella@tc.columbia.edu.

TÉLÉ-UNIVERSITÉ, Québec, QC G1K 9H5, Canada

General Information Province-supported, coed, comprehensive institution. *Graduate housing:* On-campus housing not available.

GRADUATE UNITS

Graduate Programs *Degree program information:* Part-time programs available. Part-time. Offers computer science (PhD); corporate finance (MS); distance learning (MS).

TELSHE YESHIVA–CHICAGO, Chicago, IL 60625-5598

General Information Independent-religious, men only, comprehensive institution.

GRADUATE UNITS

Graduate Program

★ TEMPLE UNIVERSITY, Philadelphia, PA 19122-6096

General Information State-related, coed, university. CGS member. *Enrollment:* 38,027 graduate, professional, and undergraduate students; 4,336 full-time matriculated graduate/professional students (2,526 women), 1,539 part-time matriculated graduate/professional students (1,056 women). *Enrollment by degree level:* 2,143 master's, 3,254 doctoral, 131 other advanced degrees. *Graduate faculty:* 1,002 full-time (448 women), 568 part-time/adjunct (311 women). *Graduate housing:* Rooms and/or apartments available on a first-come, first-served basis to single and married students. Housing application deadline: 5/1. *Student services:* Campus employment opportunities, campus safety program, career counseling, exercise/wellness program, free psychological counseling, grant writing training, international student services, low-cost health insurance, multicultural affairs office, services for students with disabilities, teacher training, writing training. *Library:* Paley Library plus 6 others. *Collection:* Books: 3.5 million (physical), 944,928 (digital/electronic); Serial titles: 1,080 (physical), 234,296 (digital/electronic); Databases: 1,939. Weekly public service hours: 68; students can reserve study rooms.

Computer facilities: Computer purchase and lease plans are available. 8,282 computers available on campus for general student use. A campuswide network can be accessed from student residence rooms and from off campus. Online class registration, student accounts, Web hosting are available.
Website: http://www.temple.edu/

General Application Contact: Coordinator of Outreach, 215-204-1380, Fax: 215-204-8781, E-mail: grad@temple.edu.

GRADUATE UNITS

Beasley School of Law Students: 534 full-time (264 women), 150 part-time (64 women); includes 181 minority (65 Black or African American, non-Hispanic/Latino; 2 American Indian or Alaska Native, non-Hispanic/Latino; 59 Asian, non-Hispanic/Latino; 49 Hispanic/Latino; 6 Two or more races, non-Hispanic/Latino), 7 international. Average age 26. 1,956 applicants, 43% accepted, 217 enrolled. *Faculty:* 71 full-time (35 women), 100 part-time/adjunct (33 women). *Financial support:* In 2015–16, 457 students received support, including research assistantships (averaging $5,500 per year), teaching assistantships (averaging $5,500 per year); fellowships, Federal Work-Study, scholarships/grants, tuition waivers (full and partial), and unspecified assistantships also available. Support available to part-time students. Financial award application deadline: 3/1; financial award applicants required to submit FAFSA. In 2015, 254 doctorates awarded. *Degree program information:* Part-time and evening/weekend programs available. Part-time, evening/weekend. Offers law (JD); legal education (SJD); taxation (LL M); transnational law (LL M); trial advocacy (LL M). *Application deadline:* For fall admission, 3/1 for domestic and international students. Applications are processed on a rolling basis. *Application fee:* $60. Electronic applications accepted. *Application Contact:* Johanne L. Johnston, Assistant Dean for Admissions and Financial Aid, 800-560-1428, Fax: 215-204-9319, E-mail: lawadmis@temple.edu. *Dean,* JoAnne A. Epps, 215-204-7863, Fax: 215-204-1185, E-mail: law@temple.edu.

Center for the Performing and Cinematic Arts Students: 284 full-time (172 women), 38 part-time (22 women); includes 53 minority (16 Black or African American, non-Hispanic/Latino; 16 Asian, non-Hispanic/Latino; 13 Hispanic/Latino; 8 Two or more races, non-Hispanic/Latino), 83 international. 544 applicants, 47% accepted, 119 enrolled. *Faculty:* 89 full-time (39 women), 77 part-time/adjunct (43 women). *Financial support:* Fellowships, research assistantships, teaching assistantships, Federal Work-Study, scholarships/grants, health care benefits, and unspecified assistantships available. In 2015, 98 master's, 10 doctorates awarded. Offers performing and cinematic arts (Ed M, M Arch, MA, MFA, MM, MMT, DMA, PhD). *Application fee:* $60. Electronic applications accepted. *Application Contact:* Tara Schumacher, Coordinator, Graduate School, 215-204-6575, Fax: 215-204-8781, E-mail: tara.schumacher@temple.edu. *Dean and Vice Provost for the Arts,* Dr. Robert Stroker, 215-777-9196, E-mail: robert.stroker@temple.edu.

Boyer College of Music and Dance Students: 217 full-time (140 women), 41 part-time (23 women); includes 38 minority (8 Black or African American, non-Hispanic/Latino; 18 Asian, non-Hispanic/Latino; 7 Hispanic/Latino; 5 Two or more races, non-Hispanic/Latino), 66 international. 395 applicants, 56% accepted, 91 enrolled. *Faculty:* 46 full-time (21 women), 43 part-time/adjunct (21 women). *Financial support:* Fellowships with tuition reimbursements, research assistantships with tuition reimbursements, teaching assistantships with tuition reimbursements, career-related internships or fieldwork, Federal Work-Study, scholarships/grants, health care benefits, and unspecified assistantships available. Financial award application deadline: 3/1; financial award applicants required to submit FAFSA. In 2015, 64 master's, 11 doctorates awarded. *Degree program information:* Part-time programs available. Part-time, online learning. Offers choral conducting (MM); collaborative piano/chamber music (MM); collaborative piano/opera coaching (MM); composition (MM, PhD); dance (MA, MFA, PhD); instrumental conducting (MM); music and dance (MA, MFA, MM, MMT, DMA, PhD); music education (MM, PhD); music history (MM); music performance (MM, DMA); music studies (PhD); music theory (MM, PhD); music therapy (MMT, PhD); musicology (MM, PhD); opera (MM); piano pedagogy (MM); string pedagogy (MM). *Application deadline:* For fall admission, 12/15 for international students; for spring admission, 8/1 for international students. Applications are processed on a rolling basis. *Application fee:* $60. Electronic applications accepted. *Application Contact:* James Short, Director of Undergraduate and Graduate Admissions, 215-204-8598, Fax: 215-204-4957, E-mail: jshort@temple.edu. *Dean,* Dr. Robert Stroker, 215-204-8301, Fax: 215-204-4957, E-mail: rstroker@temple.edu.

Division of Theater, Film and Media Arts Students: 55 full-time (33 women), 8 part-time (3 women); includes 11 minority (3 Black or African American, non-Hispanic/Latino; 4 Hispanic/Latino; 4 Two or more races, non-Hispanic/Latino), 13 international. 48 applicants, 38% accepted, 14 enrolled. *Faculty:* 30 full-time (8 women), 34 part-time/adjunct (18 women). *Financial support:* Application deadline: 3/1; applicants required to submit FAFSA. In 2015, 14 master's awarded. Offers acting (MFA); design (MFA); directing (MFA); film and media arts (MA, MFA); musical theater collaboration (MFA); musical theater studies (MA); playwriting (MFA); theater, film and media arts (MA, MFA). *Application fee:* $60. Electronic applications accepted. *Application Contact:* Leah Dempsey, Assistant Director for Administration, E-mail: leahdempsey@temple.edu. *Dean and Vice Provost for the Arts,* Dr. Robert Stroker, 215-777-9196, E-mail: robert.stroker@temple.edu.

College of Education Students: 340 full-time (248 women), 501 part-time (330 women); includes 218 minority (132 Black or African American, non-Hispanic/Latino; 2 American Indian or Alaska Native, non-Hispanic/Latino; 29 Asian, non-Hispanic/Latino; 36 Hispanic/Latino; 19 Two or more races, non-Hispanic/Latino), 24 international. 709 applicants, 61% accepted, 244 enrolled. *Faculty:* 68 full-time (38 women), 83 part-time/adjunct (55 women). *Financial support:* Research assistantships with full tuition reimbursements, teaching assistantships with full tuition reimbursements, career-related internships or fieldwork, Federal Work-Study, scholarships/grants, health care benefits, and unspecified assistantships available. Financial award application deadline: 1/15; financial award applicants required to submit FAFSA. In 2015, 229 master's, 41 doctorates, 50 other advanced degrees awarded. *Degree program information:* Part-time and evening/weekend programs available. Part-time, evening/weekend. Offers adult and organizational development (Ed M); career and technical education (Ed M); counseling psychology (Ed M, PhD); education (Ed M, MS Ed, Ed D, PhD, Ed S); educational leadership (Ed M); educational leadership and policy studies (Ed M, Ed D); educational psychology (Ed M); middle grades education (Ed M); school psychology (Ed M, PhD, Ed S); secondary education (Ed M); special education (Ed M); teaching English to speakers of other languages (MS Ed); urban education (Ed M). *Application deadline:* For fall admission, 4/1 for domestic students, 1/1 for international students; for spring admission, 10/1 for domestic students, 7/3 for international students. Applications are processed on a rolling basis. *Application fee:* $60. Electronic applications accepted. *Application Contact:* Linda Pryor, Enrollment Management, 215-204-5634, E-mail: educate@temple.edu. *Dean,* Dr. Gregory Anderson, 215-204-8017, Fax: 215-204-5622, E-mail: coedean@temple.edu.

College of Engineering Students: 142 full-time (43 women), 63 part-time (13 women); includes 27 minority (9 Black or African American, non-Hispanic/Latino; 12 Asian, non-Hispanic/Latino; 5 Hispanic/Latino; 1 Two or more races, non-Hispanic/Latino), 95 international. 326 applicants, 60% accepted, 55 enrolled. *Faculty:* 63 full-time (13 women), 19 part-time/adjunct (4 women). *Financial support:* In 2015–16, 23 students received support. Fellowships with full tuition reimbursements available, research assistantships with full tuition reimbursements available, teaching assistantships with full tuition reimbursements available, Federal Work-Study, institutionally sponsored loans, scholarships/grants, health care benefits, and unspecified assistantships available. Financial award application deadline: 3/1; financial award applicants required to submit FAFSA. In 2015, 31 master's, 11 doctorates awarded. *Degree program information:* Part-time and evening/weekend programs available. Part-time, evening/weekend. Offers bioengineering (MS, PhD); civil engineering (MSCE); electrical engineering (MSEE); engineering (MS, MS Env E, MSCE, MSEE, MSME, PhD, Certificate, Graduate Certificate); engineering management (MS, Certificate); environmental engineering (MS Env E); mechanical engineering (MSME); storm water management (Graduate Certificate). *Application deadline:* For fall admission, 3/1 priority date for domestic and international students; for spring admission, 11/1 priority date for domestic students, 8/1 priority date for international students. Applications are processed on a rolling basis. *Application fee:* $60. Electronic applications accepted. *Application Contact:* Leslie Levin, Assistant Director, Recruitment and Marketing, 215-204-7800, Fax: 215-204-6936, E-mail: gradengr@temple.edu. *Dean,* Dr. Keya Sadeghipour, 215-204-5285.

College of Liberal Arts Students: 624 full-time (285 women), 71 part-time (35 women); includes 153 minority (62 Black or African American, non-Hispanic/Latino; 1 American Indian or Alaska Native, non-Hispanic/Latino; 31 Asian, non-Hispanic/Latino; 43 Hispanic/Latino; 1 Native Hawaiian or other Pacific Islander, non-Hispanic/Latino; 15 Two or more races, non-Hispanic/Latino), 70 international. 1,195 applicants, 30% accepted, 133 enrolled. *Faculty:* 302 full-time (128 women), 115 part-time/adjunct (61 women). *Financial support:* Fellowships, research assistantships, teaching assistantships, career-related internships or fieldwork, Federal Work-Study, institutionally sponsored loans, scholarships/grants, and tuition waivers (full and partial) available. Support available to part-time students. Financial award application deadline: 1/15; financial award applicants required to submit FAFSA. In 2015, 84 master's, 65 doctorates, 3 other advanced degrees awarded. *Degree program information:* Part-time programs available. Part-time. Offers African American studies (MA, PhD); anthropology (PhD); creative writing (MFA); criminal justice (MA, PhD); economics (MA, PhD); English (MA, PhD); geographic information systems (PSM, Graduate Certificate); geography and urban studies (MA, PhD); history (MA, PhD); liberal arts (MA, MFA, MS, PSM, PhD, Graduate Certificate); philosophy (MA, PhD); political science (MA, PhD); psychology (MA, MS, PhD); religion (MA, PhD); sociology (MA, PhD); Spanish (MA, PhD). *Application deadline:* For fall admission, 12/15 for international students; for spring admission, 8/1 for international students. *Application fee:* $60. Electronic applications accepted. *Application Contact:* Dr. Shawn Schurr, Vice Dean, 215-204-7743, E-mail: schurr@temple.edu. *Dean,* Dr. William Stull, 215-204-8880, Fax: 215-204-5022, E-mail: william.stull@temple.edu.

College of Public Health Students: 736 full-time (595 women), 485 part-time (384 women); includes 371 minority (199 Black or African American, non-Hispanic/Latino; 1 American Indian or Alaska Native, non-Hispanic/Latino; 60 Asian, non-Hispanic/Latino; 83 Hispanic/Latino; 3 Native Hawaiian or other Pacific Islander, non-Hispanic/Latino; 25 Two or more races, non-Hispanic/Latino), 21 international. 1,307 applicants, 44% accepted, 237 enrolled. *Faculty:* 130 full-time (86 women), 48 part-time/adjunct (34 women). *Financial support:* Fellowships, research assistantships, teaching assistantships with full tuition reimbursements, career-related internships or fieldwork, Federal Work-Study, institutionally sponsored loans, traineeships, and tuition waivers (partial) available. Support available to part-time students. Financial award application deadline: 1/15. In 2015, 365 master's, 109 doctorates awarded. *Degree program information:* Part-time and evening/weekend programs available. Part-time, evening/weekend, online learning. Offers adult-gerontology primary care (DNP); athletic training (MSAT, DAT); communication sciences and disorders (PhD); epidemiology (MS, PhD); family-individual across the lifespan (DNP); health informatics (MS); kinesiology (MS, PhD); nursing (DNP); occupational therapy (MOT, DOT); physical therapy (DPT, TDPT); public health (MA, MOT, MPH, MS, MSAT, MSW, DAT, DNP, DOT, DPT, PhD, TDPT); social and behavioral science (MPH, PhD); speech-language-hearing (MA); therapeutic recreation (MS). *Application fee:* $60. *Dean,* Dr. Laura Siminoff, 215-707-4802, Fax: 215-707-7819.

School of Social Work Students: 320 full-time (265 women), 186 part-time (156 women); includes 199 minority (136 Black or African American, non-Hispanic/Latino; 1 American Indian or Alaska Native, non-Hispanic/Latino; 7 Asian, non-Hispanic/Latino; 47 Hispanic/Latino; 1 Native Hawaiian or other Pacific Islander, non-Hispanic/Latino; 7 Two or more races, non-Hispanic/Latino), 3 international. 399 applicants, 66% accepted, 109 enrolled. *Faculty:* 31 full-time (20 women), 20 part-time/adjunct (16 women). *Financial support:* Research assistantships with tuition reimbursements, career-related internships or fieldwork, Federal Work-Study, scholarships/grants, traineeships, tuition waivers (partial), unspecified assistantships, and field assistantships available. Support available to part-time students. Financial award application deadline: 1/1. In 2015, 219 master's awarded. *Degree program information:* Part-time and evening/weekend programs available. Part-time, evening/weekend. Offers social work (MSW). *Application deadline:* For fall admission, 3/15 priority date for domestic students, 2/15 for international students; for spring admission, 11/1 priority date for domestic students, 10/15 for international students; for summer admission, 3/15 for domestic students, 2/15 for international students. Applications are processed on a rolling basis. *Application fee:* $60. Electronic applications accepted. *Application Contact:* Cheryl A. Hyde, Associate Professor/MSW Program Director, 215-204-7112, E-mail: chyde@temple.edu. *Interim Chair/Associate Professor*, Bernie Newman, 215-204-1205, Fax: 215-204-9606, E-mail: bernie.newman@temple.edu.

College of Science and Technology Students: 366 full-time (128 women), 46 part-time (19 women); includes 57 minority (11 Black or African American, non-Hispanic/Latino; 33 Asian, non-Hispanic/Latino; 9 Hispanic/Latino; 4 Two or more races, non-Hispanic/Latino), 187 international. 459 applicants, 53% accepted, 118 enrolled. *Faculty:* 169 full-time (41 women), 9 part-time/adjunct (3 women). *Financial support:* Fellowships, research assistantships, teaching assistantships, career-related internships or fieldwork, Federal Work-Study, institutionally sponsored loans, scholarships/grants, tuition waivers (full and partial), and laboratory assistantships available. Financial award application deadline: 1/15; financial award applicants required to submit FAFSA. In 2015, 50 master's, 32 doctorates awarded. *Degree program information:* Part-time and evening/weekend programs available. Part-time, evening/weekend. Offers applied mathematics (MA); biology (MS, PMS, PhD); biotechnology (MS); chemistry (MA, PhD); computer and information science (PhD); computer science (MS); earth and environmental sciences (MS, PhD); information science and technology (MS); mathematics (PhD); physics (MA, PhD); pure mathematics (MA); science and technology (MA, MS, PMS, PhD). *Application deadline:* For fall admission, 1/5 for domestic students, 12/15 for international students; for spring admission, 9/15 for domestic students, 8/1 for international students. Applications are processed on a rolling basis. *Application fee:* $60. Electronic applications accepted. *Application Contact:* Tara Schumacher, Coordinator of Outreach, 215-204-1380, Fax: 215-204-8781, E-mail: tara.schumacher@temple.edu. *Dean*, Dr. Michael Klein, 215-204-2888, Fax: 215-204-1255, E-mail: cstdean@temple.edu.

Fox School of Business ***Degree program information:*** Part-time and evening/weekend programs available. Part-time, evening/weekend, online learning. Offers accountancy (MS); accounting (MBA, PhD); actuarial science (MS); business (EMBA, IMBA, MBA, MHM, MS, PhD); business management (MBA); entrepreneurship (PhD); finance (MS, PhD); financial engineering (MS); financial management (MBA); healthcare and life sciences innovation (MBA); human resource management (MBA, MS); innovation management and entrepreneurship (MS); international business (IMBA, PhD); IT management (MBA); management information systems (PhD); marketing (MS, PhD); marketing management (MBA); pharmaceutical management (MBA); risk management and insurance (PhD); statistics (MS, PhD); strategic management (EMBA, MBA, PhD); tourism and sport (PhD). Electronic applications accepted.

Kornberg School of Dentistry Offers advanced education in general dentistry (Certificate); dentistry (MS, DMD, Certificate); endodontology (Certificate); oral biology (MS); orthodontics (Certificate); periodontology (Certificate). Electronic applications accepted.

School of Media and Communication Students: 86 full-time (64 women), 41 part-time (29 women); includes 18 minority (8 Black or African American, non-Hispanic/Latino; 4 Asian, non-Hispanic/Latino; 4 Hispanic/Latino; 2 Two or more races, non-Hispanic/Latino), 35 international. 187 applicants, 48% accepted, 39 enrolled. *Faculty:* 73 full-time (35 women), 91 part-time/adjunct (46 women). *Financial support:* Fellowships, teaching assistantships with partial tuition reimbursements, career-related internships or fieldwork, Federal Work-Study, institutionally sponsored loans, tuition waivers (full and partial), and unspecified assistantships available. Financial award application deadline: 1/15; financial award applicants required to submit FAFSA. In 2015, 26 master's, 3 doctorates awarded. *Degree program information:* Part-time and evening/weekend programs available. Part-time, evening/weekend. Offers communication management (MS); journalism (MJ); media and communication (MA, MJ, MS, PhD); media studies and production (MA). *Application deadline:* For fall admission, 12/15 for international students. *Application fee:* $60. Electronic applications accepted. *Application Contact:* Nicole McKenna, Director, Office of Research and Graduate Studies, 215-204-1497, Fax: 215-204-0310, E-mail: nmckenna@temple.edu. *Dean*, David Boardman, 215-204-4822, Fax: 215-204-4811, E-mail: dboardman@temple.edu.

School of Medicine Students: 1,025 full-time (488 women), 19 part-time (14 women); includes 354 minority (47 Black or African American, non-Hispanic/Latino; 188 Asian, non-Hispanic/Latino; 87 Hispanic/Latino; 2 Native Hawaiian or other Pacific Islander, non-Hispanic/Latino; 30 Two or more races, non-Hispanic/Latino), 36 international. 170 applicants, 27% accepted, 32 enrolled. *Faculty:* 29 full-time (13 women), 1 (woman) part-time/adjunct. *Financial support:* In 2015–16, 70 fellowships with full tuition reimbursements (averaging $26,500 per year), 41 research assistantships with full tuition reimbursements (averaging $26,500 per year) were awarded; scholarships/grants and health care benefits also available. Financial award application deadline: 2/15; financial award applicants required to submit FAFSA. In 2015, 18 master's, 227 doctorates awarded. Offers biomedical sciences (MS); medicine (MS, MD, PhD). *Application deadline:* For fall admission, 2/15 for domestic and international students. *Application fee:* $60. Electronic applications accepted. *Application Contact:* Tracy Burton, Office of Admissions, 215-707-2423, E-mail: tusmgrad@temple.edu. *Associate Dean*, Dr. Scott K. Shore, 215-707-2423, Fax: 215-707-5072, E-mail: sks@temple.edu.

School of Pharmacy Students: 648 full-time (350 women), 272 part-time (190 women); includes 273 minority (40 Black or African American, non-Hispanic/Latino; 1 American Indian or Alaska Native, non-Hispanic/Latino; 168 Asian, non-Hispanic/Latino; 19 Hispanic/Latino; 45 Two or more races, non-Hispanic/Latino), 159 international. 128 applicants, 54% accepted, 55 enrolled. *Faculty:* 38 full-time (18 women), 36 part-time/adjunct (16 women). *Financial support:* Fellowships with tuition reimbursements, research assistantships with tuition reimbursements, teaching assistantships with tuition reimbursements, career-related internships or fieldwork, Federal Work-Study, and institutionally sponsored loans available. Financial award application deadline: 1/15; financial award applicants required to submit FAFSA. In 2015, 91 master's, 137 doctorates awarded. *Degree program information:* Part-time and evening/weekend programs available. Part-time, evening/weekend, online learning. Offers medicinal chemistry (MS, PhD); pharmaceutics (MS, PhD); pharmacodynamics (MS, PhD); pharmacy (MS, PhD, Pharm D); quality assurance/regulatory affairs (MS). *Application deadline:* For fall admission, 2/1 priority date for domestic and international students. *Application fee:* $60. Electronic applications accepted. *Application Contact:* E-mail: phscgrad@temple.edu. *Dean*, Dr. Peter H. Doukas, 215-707-4990, Fax: 215-707-5620, E-mail: pdoukas@temple.edu.

School of Podiatric Medicine Offers podiatric medicine (DPM). DPM/PhD offered jointly with Drexel University, University of Pennsylvania.

School of Tourism and Hospitality Management Students: 58 full-time (31 women), 29 part-time (13 women); includes 24 minority (16 Black or African American, non-Hispanic/Latino; 6 Hispanic/Latino; 2 Two or more races, non-Hispanic/Latino), 19 international. 107 applicants, 60% accepted, 32 enrolled. *Faculty:* 29 full-time (8 women), 13 part-time/adjunct (5 women). *Financial support:* In 2015–16, 2 fellowships with full tuition reimbursements (averaging $25,000 per year), 10 research assistantships with full tuition reimbursements (averaging $23,000 per year), 4 teaching assistantships with full tuition reimbursements (averaging $23,000 per year) were awarded. Financial award application deadline: 3/1; financial award applicants required to submit FAFSA. In 2015, 30 master's awarded. *Degree program information:* Part-time and evening/weekend programs available. Part-time, evening/weekend. Offers sport business (MS); tourism and hospitality management (MTHM); tourism and sport (PhD). *Application deadline:* For fall admission, 3/1 priority date for domestic students, 1/15 priority date for international students; for spring admission, 8/15 priority date for domestic students, 6/30 priority date for international students. Applications are processed on a rolling basis. *Application fee:* $60. Electronic applications accepted. *Application Contact:* James Alton, Manager of Graduate Student Services, 215-204-7140, Fax: 215-204-8705, E-mail: jim.alton@temple.edu. *Associate Dean*, Dr. Moshe H. Porat, 215-204-8701, Fax: 215-204-8705, E-mail: moshe.porat@temple.edu.

Tyler School of Art Students: 139 full-time (98 women), 12 part-time (9 women); includes 26 minority (6 Black or African American, non-Hispanic/Latino; 7 Asian, non-Hispanic/Latino; 10 Hispanic/Latino; 3 Two or more races, non-Hispanic/Latino), 15 international. 466 applicants, 27% accepted, 55 enrolled. *Faculty:* 66 full-time (36 women), 93 part-time/adjunct (46 women). *Financial support:* Fellowships with full tuition reimbursements, research assistantships with full tuition reimbursements, teaching assistantships with full tuition reimbursements, career-related internships or fieldwork, Federal Work-Study, and institutionally sponsored loans available. Support available to part-time students. Financial award application deadline: 1/15; financial award applicants required to submit FAFSA. In 2015, 43 master's, 3 doctorates awarded. *Degree program information:* Part-time and evening/weekend programs available. Part-time, evening/weekend. Offers architecture (M Arch); art (Ed M, M Arch, MA, MFA, ML Arch, MS, PhD, Graduate Certificate); art education (Ed M); art history (MA, PhD); ceramics/glass (MFA); city and regional planning (MS); fibers and material studies (MFA); graphic and interactive design (MFA); landscape architecture (ML Arch); metals/jewelry/CAD-CAM (MFA); painting (MFA); photography (MFA); printmaking (MFA); sculpture (MFA); sustainable community planning (Graduate Certificate); transportation planning (Graduate Certificate). *Application deadline:* Applications are processed on a rolling basis. *Application fee:* $60. Electronic applications accepted. *Application Contact:* Nicole Hall, Director of Admissions, 215-777-9090, E-mail: tylerart@temple.edu. *Dean and Vice Provost for the Arts*, Dr. Robert Stroker, 215-777-9000, E-mail: tyler@temple.edu.

See Display on next page and Close-Up on page 903.

TENNESSEE STATE UNIVERSITY, Nashville, TN 37209-1561

General Information State-supported, coed, comprehensive institution. CGS member. *Graduate housing:* Rooms and/or apartments available on a first-come, first-served basis to single and married students. Housing application deadline: 8/1. *Student services:* Campus employment opportunities, campus safety program, career counseling, child daycare facilities, exercise/wellness program, free psychological counseling, international student services, low-cost health insurance, services for students with disabilities, teacher training, writing training. *Library:* Martha M. Brown/Lois H. Daniel Library plus 1 other.

Computer facilities: 1,025 computers available on campus for general student use. A campuswide network can be accessed from student residence rooms and from off campus. Online class registration is available.
Website: http://www.tnstate.edu/

General Application Contact: Julie Roberts, Director of Graduate School Admissions, 615-963-5968, Fax: 615-963-5963, E-mail: gradschool@tnstate.edu.

GRADUATE UNITS

The School of Graduate Studies and Research ***Financial support:*** Fellowships, research assistantships, teaching assistantships, career-related internships or fieldwork, institutionally sponsored loans, scholarships/grants, traineeships, and unspecified assistantships available. Support available to part-time students. Financial award applicants required to submit FAFSA. *Application deadline:* For fall admission, 7/1 for domestic students; for spring admission, 11/1 for domestic students. *Application fee:* $25.

College of Agriculture, Human and Natural Sciences Financial support: Research assistantships, teaching assistantships, Federal Work-Study, and unspecified assistantships available. *Degree program information:* Part-time and evening/weekend programs available. Part-time, evening/weekend. Offers agricultural sciences (MS); biological sciences (MS, PhD); biotechnology (PhD); chemistry (MS). *Application deadline:* For fall admission, 4/1 priority date for domestic students. *Application fee:* $25. *Application Contact:* Deborah Chisom, Director of Graduate Admissions, 615-963-5962, Fax: 615-963-5963, E-mail: dchiscom@tnstate.edu. *Dean*, Dr. Chandra Reddy, 615-963-5438, Fax: 615-963-5888.

College of Business Financial support: Research assistantships and teaching assistantships available. *Degree program information:* Part-time and evening/weekend programs available. Part-time, evening/weekend, online learning. Offers business (MBA). *Application deadline:* For fall admission, 4/1 priority date for domestic and international students. Applications are processed on a rolling basis. *Application fee:* $25. Electronic applications accepted. *Application Contact:* Anis Mnif, Director, 615-963-7295, Fax: 615-963-7139, E-mail: amnif@tnstate.edu. *Dean*, Dr. Millicent Lownes-Jackson, 615-963-7127, Fax: 615-963-7139, E-mail: mlownes@tnstate.edu.

College of Education Financial support: Fellowships, research assistantships, teaching assistantships, career-related internships or fieldwork, and institutionally sponsored loans available. Support available to part-time students. Financial award application deadline: 5/1; financial award applicants required to submit FAFSA. *Degree program information:* Part-time and evening/weekend programs available. Part-time, evening/weekend. Offers counseling psychology (MS); curriculum and instruction (M Ed, Ed D); education (M Ed, MA Ed, MS, Ed D, PhD, Ed S); elementary education (M Ed); special education (M Ed). *Application deadline:* Applications are processed on a rolling basis. *Application fee:* $25. *Application Contact:* Deborah Chisom, Director of Graduate Admissions, 615-963-5962, Fax: 615-963-5963, E-mail: dchiscom@tnstate.edu. *Dean*, Dr. Kimberly King-Jupiter, 615-963-5446, E-mail: kkingjup@tnstate.edu.

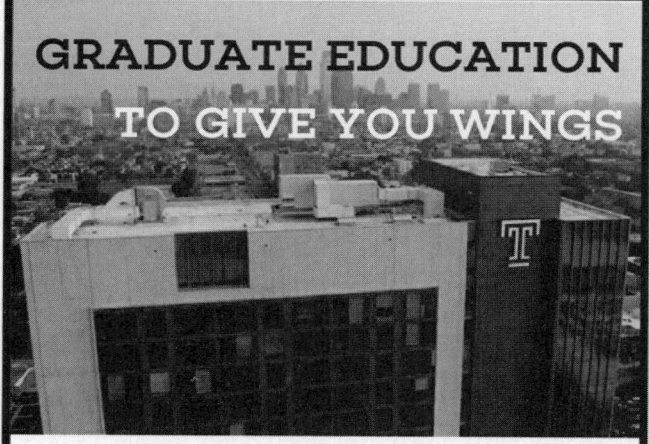

College of Engineering Financial support: Research assistantships and teaching assistantships available. *Degree program information:* Part-time and evening/weekend programs available. Part-time, evening/weekend. Offers biomedical engineering (ME); civil engineering (ME); computer and information systems engineering (MS, PhD); electrical engineering (ME); environmental engineering (ME); manufacturing engineering (ME); mathematical sciences (MS); mechanical engineering (ME). *Application deadline:* For fall admission, 4/1 priority date for domestic students. *Application fee:* $25. *Application Contact:* Deborah Chisom, Director of Graduate Admissions, 615-963-5962, Fax: 615-963-5963, E-mail: dchiscom@tnstate.edu. *Dean*, Dr. S. Keith Hargrove, 615-963-5409, Fax: 615-963-5397, E-mail: skhargrove@tnstate.edu.

College of Health Sciences Financial support: Fellowships, research assistantships, teaching assistantships, and scholarships/grants available. Financial award application deadline: 3/15. *Degree program information:* Part-time and evening/weekend programs available. Part-time, evening/weekend. Offers exercise science (MA Ed); family nurse practitioner (MSN, Certificate); health sciences (MA Ed, MOT, MPH, MS, MSN, DPT, Certificate); holistic nurse practitioner (MSN); holistic nursing (Certificate); nursing education (MSN, Certificate); occupational therapy (MOT); physical therapy (DPT); public health (MPH); speech and hearing science (MS); sports administration (MA Ed). *Application deadline:* For fall admission, 4/1 for domestic students. Applications are processed on a rolling basis. *Application fee:* $25. Electronic applications accepted.

College of Liberal Arts Financial support: Fellowships, research assistantships, teaching assistantships, and unspecified assistantships available. Support available to part-time students. Financial award application deadline: 4/1. *Degree program information:* Part-time and evening/weekend programs available. Part-time, evening/weekend. Offers criminal justice (MCJ); liberal arts (MCJ). *Application deadline:* For fall admission, 4/1 priority date for domestic and international students. Applications are processed on a rolling basis. *Application fee:* $25. Electronic applications accepted.

College of Public Service Financial support: Research assistantships and teaching assistantships available. Support available to part-time students. *Degree program information:* Part-time and evening/weekend programs available. Part-time, evening/weekend. Offers human resource management (MPS); public administration (MPA, PhD); social work (MSW); strategic leadership (MPS); training and development (MPS). *Application deadline:* For fall admission, 3/1 priority date for domestic students. *Application fee:* $25.

TENNESSEE TECHNOLOGICAL UNIVERSITY, Cookeville, TN 38505

General Information State-supported, coed, university. CGS member. *Enrollment:* 352 full-time matriculated graduate/professional students (178 women), 731 part-time matriculated graduate/professional students (385 women). *Enrollment by degree level:* 867 master's, 144 doctoral, 72 other advanced degrees. *Graduate faculty:* 341 full-time (62 women). Tuition, state resident: full-time $8961; part-time $6132 per credit hour. Tuition, nonresident: full-time $23,121; part-time $14,608 per credit hour. *Graduate housing:* Rooms and/or apartments available on a first-come, first-served basis to single and married students. Housing application deadline: 6/1. *Student services:* Campus employment opportunities, campus safety program, career counseling, child daycare facilities, exercise/wellness program, free psychological counseling, international student services, low-cost health insurance, multicultural affairs office, services for students with disabilities, teacher training. *Library:* Angelo and Jennette Volpe Library and Media Center. *Research affiliation:* Center for Excellence in Teacher Evaluation, Appalachian Center for Crafts, Center of Excellence in Water Resources, Center of Excellence in Manufacturing Resources, Center of Excellence in Energy Systems Research.

Computer facilities: 227 computers available on campus for general student use. A campuswide network can be accessed from student residence rooms. Online class registration, 590 additional computers are available for student use in individual departmental labs are available.
Website: http://www.tntech.edu/

General Application Contact: Shelia K. Kendrick, Coordinator of Graduate Studies, 931-372-3808, Fax: 931-372-3497, E-mail: skendrick@tntech.edu.

GRADUATE UNITS

College of Graduate Studies Students: 352 full-time (178 women), 731 part-time (385 women); includes 77 minority (38 Black or African American, non-Hispanic/Latino; 2 American Indian or Alaska Native, non-Hispanic/Latino; 9 Asian, non-Hispanic/Latino; 12 Hispanic/Latino; 1 Native Hawaiian or other Pacific Islander, non-Hispanic/Latino; 15 Two or more races, non-Hispanic/Latino), 144 international. Average age 27. 1,293 applicants, 46% accepted, 314 enrolled. *Faculty:* 341 full-time (62 women). *Financial support:* In 2015–16, 50 fellowships (averaging $8,000 per year), 152 research assistantships (averaging $6,973 per year), 103 teaching assistantships (averaging $6,213 per year) were awarded; career-related internships or fieldwork and Federal Work-Study also available. Support available to part-time students. Financial award application deadline: 4/1. In 2015, 310 master's, 19 doctorates, 31 other advanced degrees awarded. *Degree program information:* Part-time and evening/weekend programs available. Part-time, evening/weekend, online learning. *Application deadline:* For fall admission, 7/1 for domestic students, 5/1 for international students; for spring admission, 12/1 for domestic students, 10/1 for international students; for summer admission, 5/1 for domestic students, 2/1 for international students. Applications are processed on a rolling basis. *Application fee:* $35 ($40 for international students). Electronic applications accepted. *Application Contact:* Shelia K. Kendrick, Coordinator of Graduate Studies, 931-372-3808, Fax: 931-372-3497, E-mail: skendrick@tntech.edu. *Senior Associate Provost and Dean of Graduate Studies*, Dr. Mark A. Stephens, 931-372-3233, Fax: 931-372-3497, E-mail: mstephens@tntech.edu.

College of Arts and Sciences Students: 30 full-time (17 women), 38 part-time (18 women); includes 6 minority (2 Black or African American, non-Hispanic/Latino; 2 Hispanic/Latino; 2 Two or more races, non-Hispanic/Latino), 9 international. Average age 27. 65 applicants, 40% accepted, 15 enrolled. *Faculty:* 78 full-time (15 women). *Financial support:* In 2015–16, 30 research assistantships (averaging $7,600 per year), 36 teaching assistantships (averaging $6,630 per year) were awarded; fellowships and career-related internships or fieldwork also available. Support available to part-time students. Financial award application deadline: 4/1. In 2015, 24 master's awarded. *Degree program information:* Part-time programs available. Part-time. Offers arts and sciences (MA, MS); chemistry (MS); English (MA); fish, game, and wildlife management (MS); mathematics (MS). *Application deadline:* For fall admission, 8/1 for domestic students, 5/1 for international students; for spring admission, 12/1 for domestic students, 10/1 for international students; for summer admission, 5/1 for domestic students, 2/1 for international students. Applications are processed on a rolling basis. *Application fee:* $35 ($40 for international students).

Electronic applications accepted. *Application Contact:* Shelia K. Kendrick, Coordinator of Graduate Studies, 931-372-3808, Fax: 931-372-3497, E-mail: skendrick@tntech.edu. *Dean*, Dr. Paul Semmes, 931-372-3118, Fax: 931-372-6142, E-mail: psemmes@tntech.edu.

College of Business Students: 47 full-time (18 women), 165 part-time (61 women); includes 13 minority (5 Black or African American, non-Hispanic/Latino; 3 Asian, non-Hispanic/Latino; 2 Hispanic/Latino; 3 Two or more races, non-Hispanic/Latino), 9 international. Average age 25. 228 applicants, 54% accepted, 81 enrolled. *Faculty:* 28 full-time (5 women). *Financial support:* In 2015–16, 5 fellowships (averaging $10,000 per year), 18 research assistantships (averaging $4,000 per year), teaching assistantships (averaging $4,000 per year) were awarded. Support available to part-time students. Financial award application deadline: 4/1. In 2015, 63 master's awarded. *Degree program information:* Part-time and evening/weekend programs available. Part-time, evening/weekend, online learning. Offers accounting (MBA); finance (MBA); human resource management (MBA); international business (MBA); management information systems (MBA). *Application deadline:* For fall admission, 8/1 for domestic students, 5/1 for international students; for spring admission, 12/1 for domestic students, 10/1 for international students; for summer admission, 5/1 for domestic students, 2/1 for international students. Applications are processed on a rolling basis. *Application fee:* $35 ($40 for international students). Electronic applications accepted. *Application Contact:* Shelia K. Kendrick, Coordinator of Graduate Studies, 931-372-3808, Fax: 931-372-3497, E-mail: skendrick@tntech.edu. *Interim Director,* Kate Nicewicz, 931-372-3600, Fax: 931-372-6249, E-mail: knicewicz@tntech.edu.

College of Education Students: 145 full-time (99 women), 249 part-time (177 women); includes 36 minority (20 Black or African American, non-Hispanic/Latino; 2 American Indian or Alaska Native, non-Hispanic/Latino; 1 Asian, non-Hispanic/Latino; 6 Hispanic/Latino; 7 Two or more races, non-Hispanic/Latino), 8 international. Average age 27. 227 applicants, 68% accepted, 110 enrolled. *Faculty:* 58 full-time (16 women). *Financial support:* In 2015–16, 42 fellowships (averaging $8,000 per year), 33 research assistantships (averaging $4,000 per year), 26 teaching assistantships (averaging $4,000 per year) were awarded; career-related internships or fieldwork also available. Support available to part-time students. Financial award application deadline: 4/1. In 2015, 136 master's, 5 doctorates, 31 other advanced degrees awarded. *Degree program information:* Part-time and evening/weekend programs available. Part-time, evening/weekend. Offers adapted physical education (MA); advanced studies in teaching and learning (M Ed); agency counseling (Ed S); applied behavior analysis (PhD); case management and supervision (MA); curriculum (MA, Ed S); early childhood education (MA, Ed S); education (M Ed, MA, PhD, Ed S); educational psychology (MA, Ed S); educational technology (MA, Ed S); elementary education (MA, Ed S); elementary/middle school physical education (MA); exceptional learning (PhD); instructional leadership (MA, Ed S); library science (MA, Ed S); lifetime wellness (MA); literacy (PhD); mental health counseling (MA); music (MA); program planning and evaluation (PhD); reading (MA, Ed S); school counseling (MA, Ed S); school psychology (MA, Ed S); secondary education (MA, Ed S); special education (MA, Ed S); sport management (MA); STEM education (MA, Ed S). *Application deadline:* For fall admission, 8/1 for domestic students, 5/1 for international students; for spring admission, 12/1 for domestic students, 10/1 for international students; for summer admission, 5/1 for domestic students, 2/1 for international students. Applications are processed on a rolling basis. *Application fee:* $35 ($40 for international students). Electronic applications accepted. *Application Contact:* Shelia K. Kendrick, Coordinator of Graduate Studies, 931-372-3808, Fax: 931-372-3497, E-mail: skendrick@tntech.edu. *Dean*, Dr. Jennifer Shank, 931-372-3124, Fax: 931-372-6319, E-mail: jshank@tntech.edu.

College of Engineering Students: 94 full-time (21 women), 124 part-time (19 women); includes 10 minority (2 Black or African American, non-Hispanic/Latino; 4 Asian, non-Hispanic/Latino; 1 Hispanic/Latino; 1 Native Hawaiian or other Pacific Islander, non-Hispanic/Latino; 2 Two or more races, non-Hispanic/Latino), 111 international. Average age 28. 684 applicants, 35% accepted, 66 enrolled. *Faculty:* 76 full-time (2 women). *Financial support:* In 2015–16, 3 fellowships (averaging $8,000 per year), 71 research assistantships (averaging $9,293 per year), 41 teaching assistantships (averaging $7,223 per year) were awarded; career-related internships or fieldwork also available. Support available to part-time students. Financial award application deadline: 4/1. In 2015, 30 master's, 9 doctorates awarded. *Degree program information:* Part-time programs available. Part-time. Offers chemical engineering (MS); civil and environmental engineering (MS); computer software and scientific applications (MS); electrical and computer engineering (MS); engineering (MS, PhD); Internet-based computing (MS); mechanical engineering (MS). *Application deadline:* For fall admission, 8/1 for domestic students, 5/1 for international students; for spring admission, 12/1 for domestic students, 10/1 for international students. Applications are processed on a rolling basis. *Application fee:* $35 ($40 for international students). Electronic applications accepted. *Application Contact:* Shelia K. Kendrick, Coordinator of Graduate Studies, 931-372-3808, Fax: 931-372-3497, E-mail: skendrick@tntech.edu. *Dean*, Dr. Joseph Rencis, 931-372-3172, Fax: 931-372-6172, E-mail: jjrencis@tntech.edu.

School of Environmental Studies Students: 8 full-time (1 woman), 17 part-time (5 women), 7 international. 18 applicants, 50% accepted, 5 enrolled. *Financial support:* In 2015–16, 5 research assistantships (averaging $10,000 per year), 3 teaching assistantships (averaging $10,000 per year) were awarded. Financial award application deadline: 4/1. In 2015, 5 doctorates awarded. *Degree program information:* Part-time programs available. Part-time. Offers biology (PhD); chemistry (PhD); enviromental informatics (PSM); environmental studies (PSM, PhD). *Application deadline:* For fall admission, 8/1 for domestic students, 5/1 for international students; for spring admission, 2/1 for domestic students, 1/1 for international students; for summer admission, 5/1 for domestic students, 2/1 for international students. Applications are processed on a rolling basis. *Application fee:* $35 ($40 for international students). Electronic applications accepted. *Application Contact:* Shelia K. Kendrick, Coordinator of Graduate Studies, 931-372-3808, Fax: 931-372-3497, E-mail: skendrick@tntech.edu. *Interim Director*, Dr. Hayden Mattingly, 931-372-6246, E-mail: hmattingly@tntech.edu.

School of Professional Studies Students: 7 full-time (2 women), 43 part-time (25 women); includes 7 minority (all Black or African American, non-Hispanic/Latino). 29 applicants, 79% accepted, 22 enrolled. *Financial support:* Application deadline: 4/1. In 2015, 10 master's awarded. *Degree program information:* Part-time and evening/weekend programs available. Part-time, evening/weekend, online learning. Offers human resources leadership (MPS); strategic leadership (MPS); training and development (MPS). *Application deadline:* For fall admission, 8/1 for domestic students, 5/1 for international students; for spring admission, 12/1 for domestic students, 10/1 for international students; for summer admission, 5/1 for domestic students, 2/1 for international students. Applications are processed on a rolling basis. *Application fee:* $35 ($40 for international students). Electronic applications accepted. *Application Contact:* Shelia K. Kendrick, Coordinator of Graduate Studies, 931-372-3808, Fax: 931-372-3497, E-mail: skendrick@tntech.edu. *Interim Director, School of Professional Studies*, Dr. Joseph Roberts, 931-372-6223, E-mail: jmroberts@tntech.edu.

Whitson-Hester School of Nursing Students: 21 full-time (20 women), 95 part-time (80 women); includes 5 minority (2 Black or African American, non-Hispanic/Latino; 1 Asian, non-Hispanic/Latino; 1 Hispanic/Latino; 1 Two or more races, non-Hispanic/Latino). 42 applicants, 57% accepted, 15 enrolled. *Financial support:* Application deadline: 4/1. In 2015, 47 master's awarded. *Degree program information:* Part-time and evening/weekend programs available. Part-time, evening/weekend, online learning. Offers family nurse practitioner (MSN); informatics (MSN); nursing administration (MSN); nursing education (MSN). *Application deadline:* For fall admission, 8/1 for domestic students, 5/1 for international students; for spring admission, 12/1 for domestic students, 10/1 for international students; for summer admission, 5/1 for domestic students, 2/1 for international students. Applications are processed on a rolling basis. *Application fee:* $35 ($40 for international students). Electronic applications accepted. *Application Contact:* Shelia K. Kendrick, Coordinator of Graduate Studies, 931-372-3808, Fax: 931-372-3497, E-mail: skendrick@tntech.edu. *Dean*, Dr. Huey-Ming Tzeng, 931-372-3547, Fax: 931-372-6244, E-mail: htzeng@tntech.edu.

TENNESSEE WESLEYAN COLLEGE, Athens, TN 37303

General Information Independent-religious, coed, comprehensive institution.

GRADUATE UNITS

Department of Education ***Degree program information:*** Evening/weekend programs available. Evening/weekend. Offers curriculum leadership (MS).

TEXAS A&M INTERNATIONAL UNIVERSITY, Laredo, TX 78041-1900

General Information State-supported, coed, comprehensive institution. CGS member. *Graduate housing:* Rooms and/or apartments available on a first-come, first-served basis to single and married students.

GRADUATE UNITS

Office of Graduate Studies and Research ***Degree program information:*** Part-time programs available. Part-time.

A.R. Sanchez School of Business Degree program information: Part-time and evening/weekend programs available. Part-time, evening/weekend. Offers accounting (MP Acc); business (MBA, MP Acc, MSIS, PhD); information systems (MSIS); international banking and finance (MBA); international business management (MBA, PhD).

College of Arts and Sciences Degree program information: Part-time programs available. Part-time, online learning. Offers arts and sciences (MA, MACP, MPA, MS, PhD); biology (MS); counseling psychology (MACP); criminal justice (MS); English (MA); Hispanic studies (PhD); history and political thought (MA); language, literature and translation (MA); mathematics (MS); political science (MA); psychology (MS); public administration (MPA).

College of Education Degree program information: Part-time and evening/weekend programs available. Part-time, evening/weekend. Offers curriculum and pedagogy (MS); education (MS, MS Ed); educational administration (MS Ed); generic special education (MS Ed); school counseling (MS).

College of Nursing and Health Sciences Offers family nurse practitioner (MSN).

TEXAS A&M UNIVERSITY, College Station, TX 77843

General Information State-supported, coed, university. CGS member. *Enrollment:* 63,429 graduate, professional, and undergraduate students; 11,899 full-time matriculated graduate/professional students (5,054 women), 2,697 part-time matriculated graduate/professional students (1,309 women). *Enrollment by degree level:* 6,723 master's, 7,781 doctoral, 92 other advanced degrees. *Graduate faculty:* 2,620. Tuition, state resident: full-time $5598; part-time $2799 per semester hour. Tuition, nonresident: full-time $15,125; part-time $7563 per semester hour. *Required fees:* $2869; $1435 per semester hour. $718 per semester. Tuition and fees vary according to course load and program. *Graduate housing:* Rooms and/or apartments available on a first-come, first-served basis to single and married students. Typical cost: $10,388 (including board) for single students; $10,388 (including board) for married students. Room and board charges vary according to housing facility selected. *Student services:* Campus employment opportunities, campus safety program, career counseling, child daycare facilities, exercise/wellness program, free psychological counseling, grant writing training, international student services, low-cost health insurance, multicultural affairs office, services for students with disabilities, teacher training, writing training. *Library:* Sterling C. Evans Library plus 6 others. *Collection:* Books: 5.4 million (physical), 1.6 million (digital/electronic); Serial titles: 7,706 (physical), 114,132 (digital/electronic); Databases: 2,281. Weekly public service hours: 144; study areas open 24 hours, 5–7 days a week; students can reserve study rooms. *Research affiliation:* U.S. Department of Agriculture (USDA) (agriculture), National Science Foundation (geosciences), Joint Oceanographic Institutions, Inc. (geosciences), Texas Department of Transportation (transportation).

Computer facilities: 2,282 computers available on campus for general student use. A campuswide network can be accessed from student residence rooms and from off campus. Online class registration is available.
Website: http://www.tamu.edu/

General Application Contact: Graduate Admissions, 979-458-0427, E-mail: admissions@tamu.edu.

GRADUATE UNITS

Baylor College of Dentistry Students: 495 full-time (245 women), 36 part-time (11 women); includes 267 minority (61 Black or African American, non-Hispanic/Latino; 2 American Indian or Alaska Native, non-Hispanic/Latino; 111 Asian, non-Hispanic/Latino; 89 Hispanic/Latino; 1 Native Hawaiian or other Pacific Islander, non-Hispanic/Latino; 3 Two or more races, non-Hispanic/Latino), 20 international. Average age 31. 109 applicants, 100% accepted, 140 enrolled. *Faculty:* 286. *Financial support:* In 2015–16, 268 students received support, including 31 research assistantships with tuition reimbursements available (averaging $4,414 per year), 35 teaching assistantships with tuition reimbursements available (averaging $28,751 per year); career-related internships or fieldwork, institutionally sponsored loans, scholarships/grants, traineeships, health care benefits, tuition waivers (full and partial), and unspecified assistantships also available. Support available to part-time students. Financial award applicants required to submit FAFSA. In 2015, 22 master's, 3 doctorates, 106 other advanced degrees awarded. Offers dentistry (MS, DDS, PhD, Certificate). *Application fee:* $35. Electronic applications accepted. *Application Contact:* Dr. Jack L. Long, Associate Dean for Student Affairs, 214-828-8232, Fax: 214-874-4572, E-mail: jlong@

bcd.tamhsc.edu. *Dean*, Dr. Lawrence E. Wolinsky, 214-828-8300, E-mail: wolinsky@bcd.tamhsc.edu.

Bush School of Government and Public Service Students: 315 full-time (151 women), 9 part-time (1 woman); includes 75 minority (20 Black or African American, non-Hispanic/Latino; 7 Asian, non-Hispanic/Latino; 37 Hispanic/Latino; 2 Native Hawaiian or other Pacific Islander, non-Hispanic/Latino; 9 Two or more races, non-Hispanic/Latino), 44 international. Average age 28. 294 applicants, 77% accepted, 147 enrolled. *Faculty:* 59. *Financial support:* In 2015–16, 363 students received support, including 14 fellowships with tuition reimbursements available (averaging $17,987 per year), 55 research assistantships with tuition reimbursements available (averaging $5,904 per year); career-related internships or fieldwork, institutionally sponsored loans, scholarships/grants, traineeships, health care benefits, tuition waivers (full and partial), and unspecified assistantships also available. Support available to part-time students. Financial award application deadline: 3/15; financial award applicants required to submit FAFSA. In 2015, 143 master's awarded. Offers homeland security (Certificate); international affairs (MIA, Certificate); national security affairs (Certificate); non-profit management (Certificate); public service and administration (MPSA). *Application deadline:* For fall admission, 1/15 for domestic and international students. *Application fee:* $50 ($90 for international students). Electronic applications accepted. *Application Contact:* Kathryn Meyer, Director of Recruitment and Admissions, 979-458-4767, Fax: 979-845-4155, E-mail: bushschooladmissions@tamu.edu. *Dean*, Dr. Ryan Crocker, 979-862-8007, E-mail: rcrocker@tamu.edu.

College of Agriculture and Life Sciences Students: 1,030 full-time (539 women), 331 part-time (165 women); includes 232 minority (36 Black or African American, non-Hispanic/Latino; 3 American Indian or Alaska Native, non-Hispanic/Latino; 33 Asian, non-Hispanic/Latino; 145 Hispanic/Latino; 15 Two or more races, non-Hispanic/Latino), 426 international. Average age 30. 763 applicants, 52% accepted, 289 enrolled. *Faculty:* 292. *Financial support:* In 2015–16, 1,042 students received support, including 159 fellowships with tuition reimbursements available (averaging $11,771 per year), 398 research assistantships with tuition reimbursements available (averaging $6,966 per year), 262 teaching assistantships with tuition reimbursements available (averaging $6,226 per year); career-related internships or fieldwork, institutionally sponsored loans, scholarships/grants, traineeships, health care benefits, tuition waivers (full and partial), and unspecified assistantships also available. Support available to part-time students. Financial award application deadline: 3/15; financial award applicants required to submit FAFSA. In 2015, 197 master's, 106 doctorates awarded. *Degree program information:* Part-time programs available. Part-time, blended/hybrid learning. Offers agricultural development (M Agr); agricultural economics (M Agr, MS, PhD); agricultural education (Ed D); agricultural leadership, education and communication (M Ed, MS, Ed D, PhD); agricultural systems management (MS); agriculture and life sciences (M Agr, M Ed, M Engr, MEIM, MRRD, MS, MWSc, Ed D, PhD); agronomy (MS, PhD); animal breeding (MS, PhD); animal science (M Agr, MS, PhD); biochemistry (MS, PhD); biological and agricultural engineering (M Engr, MS, PhD); ecosystem science and management (M Agr, MS, PhD); entomology (MS, PhD); equine industry management (MEIM); food science and technology (M Agr); forestry (MS, PhD); horticulture (M Agr, MS, PhD); nutrition (MS, PhD); physiology of reproduction (MS, PhD); plant pathology (MS, PhD); poultry science (M Agr, MS, PhD); rangeland ecology and management (M Agr, MS, PhD); recreation and resources development (MRRD); recreation, park, and tourism sciences (MS, PhD); soil science (MS, PhD); wildlife and fisheries sciences (MS, PhD); wildlife science (MWSc). *Application deadline:* For fall admission, 7/21 priority date for domestic students, 6/1 priority date for international students; for spring admission, 12/1 priority date for domestic students, 10/1 priority date for international students. Applications are processed on a rolling basis. *Application fee:* $50 ($90 for international students). Electronic applications accepted. *Application Contact:* Graduate Admissions, 979-845-1044, E-mail: graduate-admissions@tamu.edu. *Vice Chancellor and Dean for Agriculture and Life Sciences*, Dr. Mark A. Hussey, 979-845-4747, Fax: 979-845-9938, E-mail: mhussey@tamu.edu.

College of Architecture Students: 435 full-time (199 women), 65 part-time (22 women); includes 61 minority (11 Black or African American, non-Hispanic/Latino; 14 Asian, non-Hispanic/Latino; 34 Hispanic/Latino; 2 Two or more races, non-Hispanic/Latino), 284 international. Average age 28. 589 applicants, 58% accepted, 148 enrolled. *Faculty:* 86. *Financial support:* In 2015–16, 356 students received support, including 11 fellowships with tuition reimbursements available (averaging $10,204 per year), 91 research assistantships with tuition reimbursements available (averaging $4,310 per year), 84 teaching assistantships with tuition reimbursements available (averaging $4,130 per year); career-related internships or fieldwork, institutionally sponsored loans, scholarships/grants, traineeships, health care benefits, tuition waivers (full and partial), and unspecified assistantships also available. Support available to part-time students. Financial award application deadline: 3/15; financial award applicants required to submit FAFSA. In 2015, 131 master's, 27 doctorates awarded. Offers architecture (M Arch, MFA, MLA, MLPD, MS, MUP, PhD, Certificate); construction management (MS); health systems and design (Certificate); land and property development (MLPD); landscape architecture (MLA); urban and regional planning (MUP); urban and regional science (PhD); visualization (MFA, MS). *Application deadline:* For fall admission, 1/15 priority date for domestic and international students. Applications are processed on a rolling basis. *Application fee:* $50 ($90 for international students). Electronic applications accepted. *Application Contact:* Graduate Admissions, 979-458-0427, E-mail: admissions@tamu.edu. *Dean*, Dr. Jorge Vanegas, 979-845-1223, Fax: 979-845-4491, E-mail: jvanegas@tamu.edu.

College of Education and Human Development Students: 678 full-time (472 women), 881 part-time (627 women); includes 517 minority (165 Black or African American, non-Hispanic/Latino; 4 American Indian or Alaska Native, non-Hispanic/Latino; 52 Asian, non-Hispanic/Latino; 260 Hispanic/Latino; 3 Native Hawaiian or other Pacific Islander, non-Hispanic/Latino; 33 Two or more races, non-Hispanic/Latino), 173 international. Average age 33. 669 applicants, 68% accepted, 321 enrolled. *Faculty:* 161. *Financial support:* In 2015–16, 683 students received support, including 24 fellowships with tuition reimbursements available (averaging $13,358 per year), 199 research assistantships with tuition reimbursements available (averaging $6,144 per year), 138 teaching assistantships with tuition reimbursements available (averaging $5,965 per year); career-related internships or fieldwork, institutionally sponsored loans, scholarships/grants, traineeships, health care benefits, tuition waivers (full and partial), and unspecified assistantships also available. Support available to part-time students. Financial award application deadline: 3/15; financial award applicants required to submit FAFSA. In 2015, 369 master's, 101 doctorates awarded. *Degree program information:* Part-time and evening/weekend programs available. Part-time, evening/weekend, blended/hybrid learning. Offers athletic training (MS); bilingual education (M Ed, MS); counseling psychology (PhD); curriculum and instruction (M Ed, MS, Ed D, PhD); education and human development (M Ed, MS, Ed D, PhD); educational administration (M Ed, MS, Ed D, PhD); educational human resource development (MS, PhD); educational psychology (M Ed, MS, PhD); educational technology (M Ed); health education (M Ed, MS, Ed D, PhD); kinesiology (MS, PhD); school psychology (PhD); special education (M Ed, MS); sports management (MS). *Application deadline:* Applications are processed on a rolling basis. *Application fee:* $50 ($90 for international students). Electronic applications accepted. *Application Contact:* Dr. George Cunningham, Professor and Associate Dean for Academic Affairs, 979-845-5311, E-mail: gbcunningham@tamu.edu. *Professor and Dean*, Dr. Joyce Alexander, 979-862-6649, E-mail: joycemalexander@tamu.edu.

College of Engineering Students: 2,969 full-time (608 women), 593 part-time (130 women); includes 442 minority (70 Black or African American, non-Hispanic/Latino; 7 American Indian or Alaska Native, non-Hispanic/Latino; 139 Asian, non-Hispanic/Latino; 190 Hispanic/Latino; 3 Native Hawaiian or other Pacific Islander, non-Hispanic/Latino; 33 Two or more races, non-Hispanic/Latino), 2,282 international. Average age 29. 9,794 applicants, 21% accepted, 946 enrolled. *Faculty:* 432. *Financial support:* In 2015–16, 2,484 students received support, including 207 fellowships with tuition reimbursements available (averaging $13,290 per year), 1,168 research assistantships with tuition reimbursements available (averaging $6,919 per year), 387 teaching assistantships with tuition reimbursements available (averaging $6,310 per year); career-related internships or fieldwork, institutionally sponsored loans, scholarships/grants, traineeships, health care benefits, tuition waivers (full and partial), and unspecified assistantships also available. Support available to part-time students. Financial award applicants required to submit FAFSA. In 2015, 764 master's, 213 doctorates awarded. *Degree program information:* Part-time programs available. Part-time, online learning. Offers aerospace engineering (M Eng, MS, PhD); biomedical engineering (M Eng, MS, D Eng, PhD); chemical engineering (M Eng, MS, PhD); civil engineering (M Eng, MS, PhD); computer engineering (M Eng, MS, PhD); computer science (MCS, MS, PhD); electrical engineering (M Eng, MS, PhD); engineering (M Eng, MCS, MID, MS, D Eng, PhD); health physics (MS); industrial distribution (MID); industrial engineering (M Eng, MS, PhD); materials science and engineering (M Eng, MS, PhD); mechanical engineering (M Eng, MS, PhD); nuclear engineering (M Eng, MS, PhD); ocean engineering (M Eng, MS, PhD); petroleum engineering (M Eng, MS, PhD). *Application fee:* $50 ($90 for international students). Electronic applications accepted. *Application Contact:* Dr. John C. Criscione, Assistant Dean for Graduate Programs, 979-845-5428, E-mail: jccriscione@tamu.edu. *Dean and Vice Chancellor*, Dr. M. Katherine Banks, 979-845-1306, E-mail: k-banks@tamu.edu.

College of Geosciences Students: 286 full-time (110 women), 65 part-time (30 women); includes 41 minority (6 Black or African American, non-Hispanic/Latino; 1 American Indian or Alaska Native, non-Hispanic/Latino; 10 Asian, non-Hispanic/Latino; 21 Hispanic/Latino; 3 Two or more races, non-Hispanic/Latino), 128 international. Average age 28. 526 applicants, 23% accepted, 86 enrolled. *Faculty:* 90. *Financial support:* In 2015–16, 300 students received support, including 47 fellowships with tuition reimbursements available (averaging $11,040 per year), 100 research assistantships with tuition reimbursements available (averaging $7,861 per year), 99 teaching assistantships with tuition reimbursements available (averaging $6,998 per year); career-related internships or fieldwork, institutionally sponsored loans, traineeships, health care benefits, tuition waivers (full and partial), and unspecified assistantships also available. Support available to part-time students. Financial award application deadline: 3/15; financial award applicants required to submit FAFSA. In 2015, 53 master's, 25 doctorates awarded. *Degree program information:* Part-time programs available. Part-time. Offers atmospheric science (MS, PhD); geography (MS, PhD); geology (MS, PhD); geophysics (MS, PhD); geosciences (MGsc, MS, PhD); oceanography (MS, PhD). *Application deadline:* For fall admission, 3/1 priority date for domestic students; for spring admission, 12/1 for domestic students. Applications are processed on a rolling basis. *Application fee:* $50 ($90 for international students). Electronic applications accepted. *Application Contact:* Dr. Eric A. Riggs, Associate Professor and Associate Dean, 979-845-3651, E-mail: emriggs@geos.tamu.edu. *Dean*, Dr. Kate C. Miller, 979-845-3651, E-mail: dean@geosciences.tamu.edu.

College of Liberal Arts Students: 688 full-time (359 women), 149 part-time (81 women); includes 162 minority (33 Black or African American, non-Hispanic/Latino; 2 American Indian or Alaska Native, non-Hispanic/Latino; 16 Asian, non-Hispanic/Latino; 104 Hispanic/Latino; 7 Two or more races, non-Hispanic/Latino), 303 international. Average age 31. 1,160 applicants, 31% accepted, 212 enrolled. *Faculty:* 221. *Financial support:* In 2015–16, 578 students received support, including 94 fellowships with tuition reimbursements available (averaging $18,520 per year), 130 research assistantships with tuition reimbursements available (averaging $6,184 per year), 329 teaching assistantships with tuition reimbursements available (averaging $6,191 per year); career-related internships or fieldwork, institutionally sponsored loans, scholarships/grants, traineeships, health care benefits, tuition waivers (full and partial), unspecified assistantships, and assistant lecturer positions also available. Support available to part-time students. Financial award application deadline: 3/15; financial award applicants required to submit FAFSA. In 2015, 128 master's, 99 doctorates awarded. *Degree program information:* Part-time programs available. Part-time. Offers anthropology (MA, PhD); clinical psychology (PhD); communication (MA, PhD); economics (MS, PhD); English (MA, PhD); Hispanic studies (MA, PhD); history (MA, PhD); industrial/organizational psychology (PhD); liberal arts (MA, MS, PhD); modern languages (MA); performance studies (MA); philosophy (MA, PhD); political science (MA, PhD); psychology (MS); sociology (MS, PhD). *Application fee:* $50 ($90 for international students). Electronic applications accepted. *Application Contact:* Dr. Patricia A. Hurley, Associate Dean for Faculty and Graduate Programs, 979-845-8541, Fax: 979-845-5164, E-mail: pat-hurley@tamu.edu. *Dean*, Dr. Pamela R. Matthews, 979-862-6797, Fax: 979-845-5164, E-mail: p-matthews@tamu.edu.

College of Medicine Students: 897 full-time (426 women), 19 part-time (17 women); includes 413 minority (31 Black or African American, non-Hispanic/Latino; 4 American Indian or Alaska Native, non-Hispanic/Latino; 266 Asian, non-Hispanic/Latino; 103 Hispanic/Latino; 2 Native Hawaiian or other Pacific Islander, non-Hispanic/Latino; 7 Two or more races, non-Hispanic/Latino), 57 international. Average age 27. 258 applicants, 100% accepted, 220 enrolled. *Faculty:* 113. *Financial support:* In 2015–16, 436 students received support, including 1 fellowship with tuition reimbursement available (averaging $1,000 per year), 108 research assistantships with tuition reimbursements available (averaging $8,949 per year), 1 teaching assistantship with tuition reimbursement available (averaging $8,167 per year); career-related internships or fieldwork, institutionally sponsored loans, scholarships/grants, traineeships, health care benefits, tuition waivers (full and partial), and unspecified assistantships also available. Support available to part-time students. Financial award applicants required to submit FAFSA. In 2015, 4 master's, 19 doctorates awarded. Offers education for healthcare professionals (MS); medical sciences (PhD); medicine (MD). *Application deadline:* For fall admission, 10/1 for domestic and international students. *Application fee:* $200. Electronic applications accepted. *Application Contact:* Filomeno G. Maldonado, Associate Dean of Admissions, 979-436-0231, Fax: 979-436-0097, E-mail: fgmaldonado@medicine.tamhsc.edu. *Interim Senior Vice President and Chief Operating*

Officer, Dr. Paul E. Ogden, MD, 979-436-0202, Fax: 979-436-0092, E-mail: ogden@medicine.tamhsc.edu.

College of Nursing Students: 10 full-time (8 women), 27 part-time (23 women); includes 4 minority (2 Black or African American, non-Hispanic/Latino; 1 Asian, non-Hispanic/Latino; 1 Hispanic/Latino). Average age 35. 30 applicants, 100% accepted, 30 enrolled. *Faculty:* 47. *Financial support:* In 2015–16, 4 students received support. Career-related internships or fieldwork, institutionally sponsored loans, scholarships/grants, traineeships, health care benefits, tuition waivers (full and partial), and unspecified assistantships available. Support available to part-time students. Financial award applicants required to submit FAFSA. Offers family nurse practitioner (MSN); nursing education (MSN). *Application Contact:* Jennifer Frank, Program Coordinator for Recruitment and Admission, 979-436-0110, E-mail: conadmissions@tamhsc.edu. *Founding Dean*, Dr. Sharon A. Wilkerson, 979-436-0111, Fax: 979-436-0098, E-mail: wilkerson@tamhsc.edu.

College of Science Students: 884 full-time (253 women), 353 part-time (110 women); includes 191 minority (21 Black or African American, non-Hispanic/Latino; 3 American Indian or Alaska Native, non-Hispanic/Latino; 72 Asian, non-Hispanic/Latino; 74 Hispanic/Latino; 21 Two or more races, non-Hispanic/Latino), 509 international. Average age 29. 1,008 applicants, 50% accepted, 240 enrolled. *Faculty:* 262. *Financial support:* In 2015–16, 772 students received support, including 112 fellowships with tuition reimbursements available (averaging $12,266 per year), 314 research assistantships with tuition reimbursements available (averaging $8,045 per year), 341 teaching assistantships with tuition reimbursements available (averaging $7,774 per year); career-related internships or fieldwork, institutionally sponsored loans, scholarships/grants, traineeships, health care benefits, tuition waivers (full and partial), and unspecified assistantships also available. Support available to part-time students. Financial award applicants required to submit FAFSA. In 2015, 102 master's, 122 doctorates awarded. *Degree program information:* Part-time programs available. Part-time. Offers analytics (MS); applied physics (PhD); biology (MS, PhD); chemistry (MS, PhD); mathematics (MS, PhD); microbiology (MS, PhD); physics (MS, PhD); science (MS, PhD); statistics (MS, PhD). *Application fee:* $50 ($90 for international students). *Application Contact:* Mark Zoran, Associate Dean for Graduate Studies, 979-458-8001, Fax: 979-845-6077, E-mail: zoran@science.tamu.edu. *Dean*, Dr. Meigan Aronson, 979-845-8817, Fax: 979-845-6077, E-mail: maronson@science.tamu.edu.

College of Veterinary Medicine and Biomedical Sciences Students: 791 full-time (584 women), 50 part-time (34 women); includes 170 minority (21 Black or African American, non-Hispanic/Latino; 1 American Indian or Alaska Native, non-Hispanic/Latino; 43 Asian, non-Hispanic/Latino; 89 Hispanic/Latino; 1 Native Hawaiian or other Pacific Islander, non-Hispanic/Latino; 15 Two or more races, non-Hispanic/Latino), 60 international. Average age 29. 241 applicants, 89% accepted, 206 enrolled. *Faculty:* 134. *Financial support:* In 2015–16, 763 students received support, including 24 fellowships with tuition reimbursements available (averaging $11,758 per year), 106 research assistantships with tuition reimbursements available (averaging $7,379 per year), 25 teaching assistantships with tuition reimbursements available (averaging $6,754 per year); career-related internships or fieldwork, institutionally sponsored loans, scholarships/grants, traineeships, health care benefits, tuition waivers (full and partial), unspecified assistantships, and clinical associateships also available. Support available to part-time students. Financial award application deadline: 3/15; financial award applicants required to submit FAFSA. In 2015, 63 master's, 13 doctorates awarded. *Degree program information:* Part-time programs available. Part-time. Offers veterinary medicine and biomedical sciences (MS, DVM, PhD). *Application deadline:* For fall admission, 10/1 for domestic and international students. *Application fee:* $50 ($90 for international students). *Application Contact:* Graduate Admissions, 979-845-1044, E-mail: admissions@tamu.edu. *Dean*, Dr. Eleanor M. Green, 979-845-5053, Fax: 979-845-5088, E-mail: emgreen@tamu.edu.

Irma Lerma Rangel College of Pharmacy Students: 406 full-time (215 women), 1 (woman) part-time; includes 312 minority (24 Black or African American, non-Hispanic/Latino; 1 American Indian or Alaska Native, non-Hispanic/Latino; 141 Asian, non-Hispanic/Latino; 136 Hispanic/Latino; 1 Native Hawaiian or other Pacific Islander, non-Hispanic/Latino; 9 Two or more races, non-Hispanic/Latino), 1 international. Average age 26. 126 applicants, 100% accepted, 118 enrolled. *Faculty:* 46. *Financial support:* In 2015–16, 189 students received support. Career-related internships or fieldwork, institutionally sponsored loans, scholarships/grants, traineeships, health care benefits, tuition waivers (full and partial), and unspecified assistantships available. Support available to part-time students. Financial award applicants required to submit FAFSA. Offers pharmacy (Pharm D). *Application deadline:* For fall admission, 11/3 for domestic students. *Application fee:* $100. Electronic applications accepted. *Application Contact:* Maria de Leon, Director of Admission, 361-221-0642, E-mail: mdeleon@tamhsc.edu. *Dean*, Dr. Indra K. Reddy, 361-593-4273, Fax: 361-593-4929, E-mail: ireddy@pharmacy.tamhsc.edu.

Mays Business School Students: 1,126 full-time (415 women), 42 part-time (15 women); includes 192 minority (19 Black or African American, non-Hispanic/Latino; 67 Asian, non-Hispanic/Latino; 95 Hispanic/Latino; 1 Native Hawaiian or other Pacific Islander, non-Hispanic/Latino; 10 Two or more races, non-Hispanic/Latino), 350 international. Average age 27. 2,137 applicants, 31% accepted, 387 enrolled. *Faculty:* 93. *Financial support:* In 2015–16, 761 students received support, including 27 fellowships with tuition reimbursements available (averaging $9,591 per year), 126 research assistantships with tuition reimbursements available (averaging $5,436 per year), 98 teaching assistantships with tuition reimbursements available (averaging $3,147 per year); career-related internships or fieldwork, institutionally sponsored loans, scholarships/grants, traineeships, health care benefits, tuition waivers, and unspecified assistantships also available. Support available to part-time students. Financial award application deadline: 3/15; financial award applicants required to submit FAFSA. In 2015, 619 master's awarded. Offers accounting (MS); business (MBA, MRE, MS); finance (MS); land economics and real estate (MRE); management (MS); management information systems (MS); marketing (MS). *Application deadline:* Applications are processed on a rolling basis. *Application fee:* $50 ($90 for international students). Electronic applications accepted. *Application Contact:* Director, MBA Program, 979-845-4714, Fax: 979-862-2393, E-mail: msprogram@mays.tamu.edu. *Dean*, Dr. Eli Jones, 979-845-4711, Fax: 979-845-6639, E-mail: elijones@tamu.edu.

School of Law Students: 576 full-time (281 women), 5 part-time (1 woman); includes 148 minority (38 Black or African American, non-Hispanic/Latino; 3 American Indian or Alaska Native, non-Hispanic/Latino; 15 Asian, non-Hispanic/Latino; 80 Hispanic/Latino; 12 Two or more races, non-Hispanic/Latino), 4 international. Average age 29. 373 applicants, 100% accepted, 139 enrolled. *Faculty:* 73. *Financial support:* In 2015–16, 296 students received support, including 1 fellowship with tuition reimbursement available (averaging $5,000 per year); career-related internships or fieldwork, institutionally sponsored loans, scholarships/grants, traineeships, health care benefits, and tuition waivers (full and partial) also available. Support available to part-time students. Financial award applicants required to submit FAFSA. In 2015, 227 doctorates awarded. Offers law (JD). *Application deadline:* For fall admission, 7/8 for domestic students. Applications are processed on a rolling basis. *Application fee:* $55. *Application Contact:* Law School Admissions, 817-212-4040, E-mail: law-admissions@law.tamu.edu. *Dean*, Dr. Andrew P. Morriss, 817-212-4139, Fax: 817-212-4139, E-mail: amorriss@law.tamu.edu.

School of Public Health Students: 313 full-time (189 women), 71 part-time (41 women); includes 169 minority (40 Black or African American, non-Hispanic/Latino; 38 Asian, non-Hispanic/Latino; 88 Hispanic/Latino; 3 Two or more races, non-Hispanic/Latino), 88 international. Average age 30. 138 applicants, 100% accepted, 126 enrolled. *Faculty:* 68. *Financial support:* In 2015–16, 186 students received support, including 2 fellowships with tuition reimbursements available (averaging $17,190 per year), 55 research assistantships with tuition reimbursements available (averaging $5,728 per year), 14 teaching assistantships with tuition reimbursements available (averaging $5,836 per year); career-related internships or fieldwork, institutionally sponsored loans, scholarships/grants, traineeships, health care benefits, tuition waivers (full and partial), and unspecified assistantships also available. Support available to part-time students. Financial award applicants required to submit FAFSA. In 2015, 139 master's, 5 doctorates awarded. *Degree program information:* Part-time programs available. Part-time, blended/hybrid learning. Offers health administration (MHA); health policy and management (MPH); health promotion and community health sciences (MPH); health services research (PhD). *Application deadline:* For fall admission, 8/27 for domestic students; for spring admission, 1/14 for domestic students. *Application fee:* $120. Electronic applications accepted. *Application Contact:* Erin E. Schneider, Associate Director of Admissions and Recruitment, 979-436-9380, E-mail: eschneider@sph.tamhsc.edu. *Dean*, Dr. Jay Maddock, 979-436-9322, Fax: 979-458-1878, E-mail: maddock@tamhsc.edu.

TEXAS A&M UNIVERSITY AT GALVESTON, Galveston, TX 77553-1675

General Information State-supported, coed, comprehensive institution. CGS member. *Enrollment:* 119 full-time matriculated graduate/professional students (52 women), 40 part-time matriculated graduate/professional students (18 women). *Enrollment by degree level:* 117 master's, 42 doctoral. *Graduate faculty:* 40 full-time (10 women). Tuition, state resident: full-time $5804; part-time $2902 per semester. Tuition, nonresident: full-time $12,950; part-time $6475 per semester. Tuition and fees vary according to course load and program. *Graduate housing:* Room and/or apartments available on a first-come, first-served basis to single students; on-campus housing not available to married students. Typical cost: $11,728 (including board). Room and board charges vary according to board plan and housing facility selected. *Student services:* Campus employment opportunities, campus safety program, career counseling, exercise/wellness program, free psychological counseling, international student services, low-cost health insurance, multicultural affairs office, services for students with disabilities, writing training. *Library:* Jack K. Williams Library.

Computer facilities: 150 computers available on campus for general student use. A campuswide network can be accessed from student residence rooms and from off campus. Online class registration, degree plan progress, billing statement are available. Website: http://www.tamug.edu/

General Application Contact: Nicole Kinslow, Director of Graduate Studies, 409-740-4937, Fax: 409-740-4754, E-mail: kinslown@tamug.edu.

GRADUATE UNITS

Department of Marine Biology Students: 45 full-time (31 women), 9 part-time (4 women); includes 5 minority (1 Black or African American, non-Hispanic/Latino; 1 Asian, non-Hispanic/Latino; 2 Hispanic/Latino; 1 Two or more races, non-Hispanic/Latino), 9 international. Average age 29. 42 applicants, 55% accepted, 16 enrolled. *Faculty:* 18 full-time (5 women). *Financial support:* In 2015–16, 44 students received support, including 15 research assistantships (averaging $7,603 per year), 25 teaching assistantships (averaging $7,045 per year); scholarships/grants, health care benefits, and unspecified assistantships also available. Financial award application deadline: 3/1; financial award applicants required to submit FAFSA. In 2015, 3 master's, 3 doctorates awarded. Offers marine biology (MS, PhD). *Application deadline:* For fall admission, 5/15 for domestic students, 5/1 for international students; for spring admission, 10/15 for domestic students, 10/1 for international students. *Application fee:* $50. Electronic applications accepted. *Application Contact:* Nicole Kinslow, Director of Graduate Studies, 409-740-4937, Fax: 409-740-4754, E-mail: kinslown@tamug.edu. *Professor/Chair of Marine Biology Interdisciplinary Program*, Dr. John Schwarz, 409-740-4428, E-mail: schwarzj@tamug.edu.

Department of Marine Sciences Students: 21 full-time (12 women), 10 part-time (6 women); includes 3 minority (1 Asian, non-Hispanic/Latino; 2 Two or more races, non-Hispanic/Latino), 4 international. Average age 27. 17 applicants, 88% accepted, 12 enrolled. *Faculty:* 15 full-time (3 women). *Financial support:* In 2015–16, 22 students received support, including 2 research assistantships (averaging $5,690 per year), 11 teaching assistantships (averaging $7,275 per year); scholarships/grants, health care benefits, and unspecified assistantships also available. Financial award application deadline: 3/31; financial award applicants required to submit FAFSA. In 2015, 15 master's awarded. *Degree program information:* Part-time programs available. Part-time. Offers marine resources management (MMRM). *Application deadline:* For fall admission, 6/15 for domestic students, 6/1 for international students; for spring admission, 10/15 for domestic students, 10/1 for international students. *Application fee:* $50 ($90 for international students). Electronic applications accepted. *Application Contact:* Dr. Wesley Highfield, Assistant Professor/Graduate Advisor, 409-740-4518, Fax: 409-740-4429, E-mail: schlemme@tamug.edu. *Department Head*, Dr. Kyeong Park, 409-740-4710.

Department of Maritime Administration Students: 48 full-time (8 women), 8 part-time (2 women); includes 9 minority (3 Black or African American, non-Hispanic/Latino; 2 Asian, non-Hispanic/Latino; 3 Hispanic/Latino; 1 Two or more races, non-Hispanic/Latino), 4 international. Average age 28. 21 applicants, 95% accepted, 17 enrolled. *Faculty:* 7 full-time (2 women). *Financial support:* In 2015–16, 28 students received support, including 2 research assistantships (averaging $5,651 per year), 10 teaching assistantships (averaging $6,970 per year); scholarships/grants and unspecified assistantships also available. Financial award application deadline: 3/15; financial award applicants required to submit FAFSA. In 2015, 16 master's awarded. *Degree program information:* Part-time and evening/weekend programs available. Part-time, evening/weekend. Offers maritime administration and logistics (MMAL). *Application deadline:* For fall admission, 6/15 for domestic students, 6/1 for international students; for spring admission, 10/15 for domestic students, 10/1 for international students. *Application fee:* $50 ($90 for international students). Electronic applications accepted. *Application Contact:* Nicole Kinslow, Director of Graduate Studies, 409-740-4937, Fax: 409-740-4754, E-mail: kinslown@tamug.edu. *Professor/Chair of Maritime Administration*, Dr. Joan P. Mileski, 409-740-4978, E-mail: mileskij@tamug.edu.

TEXAS A&M UNIVERSITY–CENTRAL TEXAS, Killeen, TX 76549

General Information State-supported, coed, upper-level institution. CGS member.

GRADUATE UNITS

Graduate Studies and Research

TEXAS A&M UNIVERSITY–COMMERCE, Commerce, TX 75429-3011

General Information State-supported, coed, university. CGS member. *Enrollment:* 12,302 graduate, professional, and undergraduate students; 1,521 full-time matriculated graduate/professional students (806 women), 3,139 part-time matriculated graduate/professional students (1,982 women). *Enrollment by degree level:* 3,882 master's, 612 doctoral, 166 other advanced degrees. *Graduate faculty:* 224 full-time (96 women), 73 part-time/adjunct (34 women). Tuition, state resident: full-time $3630. Tuition, nonresident: full-time $10,650. *Required fees:* $1870. Tuition and fees vary according to course load, degree level and program. *Graduate housing:* Rooms and/or apartments available on a first-come, first-served basis to single and married students. Typical cost: $8106 (including board) for single students. Room and board charges vary according to board plan and housing facility selected. *Library:* Gee Library.

Computer facilities: A campuswide network can be accessed from student residence rooms and from off campus. Online class registration is available.
Website: http://www.tamuc.edu/

General Application Contact: Vicky Turner, Doctoral Degree and Special Programs Coordinator, 903-886-5167, E-mail: vicky.turner@tamuc.edu.

GRADUATE UNITS

College of Business Students: 422 full-time (204 women), 1,077 part-time (526 women); includes 614 minority (289 Black or African American, non-Hispanic/Latino; 6 American Indian or Alaska Native, non-Hispanic/Latino; 115 Asian, non-Hispanic/Latino; 162 Hispanic/Latino; 2 Native Hawaiian or other Pacific Islander, non-Hispanic/Latino; 40 Two or more races, non-Hispanic/Latino), 138 international. Average age 34. 1,110 applicants, 64% accepted, 493 enrolled. *Faculty:* 133 full-time (59 women), 23 part-time/adjunct (3 women). *Financial support:* In 2015–16, 20 research assistantships with partial tuition reimbursements (averaging $8,000 per year) were awarded; Federal Work-Study, institutionally sponsored loans, scholarships/grants, health care benefits, and unspecified assistantships also available. Financial award application deadline: 5/1; financial award applicants required to submit FAFSA. In 2015, 601 master's awarded. *Degree program information:* Part-time and evening/weekend programs available. Part-time, evening/weekend, online learning. Offers accounting (MSA); business administration (MBA); business analytics (MS); finance (MSF); management (MS); marketing (MS). *Application deadline:* Applications are processed on a rolling basis. *Application fee:* $50. Electronic applications accepted. *Application Contact:* Vicky Turner, Doctoral Degree and Special Programs Coordinator, 903-886-5167, E-mail: vicky.turner@tamuc.edu. *Interim Dean of College of Business*, John Humphreys, 903-886-5191, Fax: 903-886-5650, E-mail: john.humphreys@tamuc.edu.

College of Education and Human Services Students: 431 full-time (345 women), 1,455 part-time (1,136 women); includes 745 minority (431 Black or African American, non-Hispanic/Latino; 6 American Indian or Alaska Native, non-Hispanic/Latino; 28 Asian, non-Hispanic/Latino; 223 Hispanic/Latino; 57 Two or more races, non-Hispanic/Latino), 17 international. Average age 39. 1,070 applicants, 54% accepted, 452 enrolled. *Faculty:* 265 full-time (151 women), 56 part-time/adjunct (40 women). *Financial support:* In 2015–16, 39 research assistantships with partial tuition reimbursements (averaging $9,000 per year), 17 teaching assistantships with partial tuition reimbursements (averaging $9,000 per year) were awarded; career-related internships or fieldwork, Federal Work-Study, institutionally sponsored loans, scholarships/grants, health care benefits, and unspecified assistantships also available. Financial award application deadline: 5/1; financial award applicants required to submit FAFSA. In 2015, 537 master's, 48 doctorates, 5 other advanced degrees awarded. *Degree program information:* Part-time programs available. Part-time. Offers education and human services (M Ed, MA, MS, MSW, Ed D, PhD, SSP). *Application deadline:* Applications are processed on a rolling basis. *Application fee:* $50. Electronic applications accepted. *Application Contact:* Vicky Turner, Doctoral Degree and Special Programs Coordinator, 903-886-5167, E-mail: vicky.turner@tamuc.edu. *Dean*, Dr. Timothy Letzring, 903-886-5181, Fax: 903-886-5905, E-mail: tim.letzring@tamuc.edu.

College of Humanities, Social Sciences and Arts Students: 121 full-time (79 women), 374 part-time (223 women); includes 160 minority (72 Black or African American, non-Hispanic/Latino; 6 Asian, non-Hispanic/Latino; 61 Hispanic/Latino; 21 Two or more races, non-Hispanic/Latino), 21 international. Average age 38. 333 applicants, 56% accepted, 149 enrolled. *Faculty:* 102 full-time (47 women), 19 part-time/adjunct (5 women). *Financial support:* In 2015–16, 9 research assistantships with partial tuition reimbursements (averaging $9,000 per year), 68 teaching assistantships with partial tuition reimbursements (averaging $9,000 per year) were awarded; Federal Work-Study, institutionally sponsored loans, scholarships/grants, health care benefits, and unspecified assistantships also available. Financial award application deadline: 5/1; financial award applicants required to submit FAFSA. In 2015, 90 master's, 7 doctorates awarded. *Degree program information:* Part-time programs available. Part-time. Offers humanities, social sciences and arts (MA, MFA, MM, MS, PhD). *Application deadline:* Applications are processed on a rolling basis. *Application fee:* $50. Electronic applications accepted. *Application Contact:* Vicky Turner, Doctoral Degree and Special Programs Coordinator, 903-886-5167, E-mail: vicky.turner@tamuc.edu. *Dean*, Dr. Salvatore Attardo, 903-886-5166, Fax: 903-886-5774, E-mail: salvatore.attardo@tamuc.edu.

College of Science and Engineering Students: 543 full-time (176 women), 203 part-time (79 women); includes 58 minority (22 Black or African American, non-Hispanic/Latino; 11 Asian, non-Hispanic/Latino; 17 Hispanic/Latino; 8 Two or more races, non-Hispanic/Latino), 568 international. Average age 27. 1,103 applicants, 53% accepted, 282 enrolled. *Faculty:* 108 full-time (6 women), 26 part-time/adjunct (0 women). *Financial support:* In 2015–16, 11 research assistantships with partial tuition reimbursements (averaging $8,000 per year), 41 teaching assistantships with partial tuition reimbursements (averaging $8,000 per year) were awarded; health care benefits and unspecified assistantships also available. Financial award applicants required to submit FAFSA. In 2015, 198 master's awarded. *Degree program information:* Part-time programs available. Part-time. Offers science and engineering (MS, Certificate). *Application deadline:* Applications are processed on a rolling basis. *Application fee:* $50. Electronic applications accepted. *Application Contact:* Vicky Turner, Doctoral Degree and Special Programs Coordinator, 903-886-5167, E-mail: vicky.turner@tamuc.edu. *Dean*, Dr. Brent L. Donham, 903-886-5390, Fax: 903-886-5199.

School of Agriculture Students: 4 full-time (2 women), 30 part-time (18 women); includes 9 minority (1 Black or African American, non-Hispanic/Latino; 1 Asian, non-Hispanic/Latino; 5 Hispanic/Latino; 2 Two or more races, non-Hispanic/Latino), 3 international. Average age 29. 22 applicants, 50% accepted, 9 enrolled. *Faculty:* 9 full-time (1 woman). *Financial support:* In 2015–16, 6 research assistantships with partial tuition reimbursements (averaging $8,000 per year), 6 teaching assistantships with partial tuition reimbursements (averaging $8,000 per year) were awarded; Federal Work-Study, institutionally sponsored loans, scholarships/grants, health care benefits, and unspecified assistantships also available. Financial award application deadline: 5/1; financial award applicants required to submit FAFSA. In 2015, 13 master's awarded. *Degree program information:* Part-time programs available. Part-time. Offers agriculture (MS). *Application deadline:* Applications are processed on a rolling basis. *Application fee:* $50. Electronic applications accepted. *Application Contact:* Vicky Turner, Doctoral Degree and Special Programs Coordinator, 903-886-5167, E-mail: vicky.turner@tamuc.edu. *Interim Director*, Dr. Derald Harp, 903-886-5351, Fax: 903-886-5990, E-mail: derald.harp@tamuc.edu.

TEXAS A&M UNIVERSITY–CORPUS CHRISTI, Corpus Christi, TX 78412-5503

General Information State-supported, coed, university. CGS member. *Enrollment:* 11,661 graduate, professional, and undergraduate students; 641 full-time matriculated graduate/professional students (373 women), 1,204 part-time matriculated graduate/professional students (857 women). *Enrollment by degree level:* 1,612 master's, 194 doctoral, 39 other advanced degrees. *Graduate faculty:* 215 full-time (78 women), 51 part-time/adjunct (32 women). *Graduate housing:* Room and/or apartments available on a first-come, first-served basis to single students; on-campus housing not available to married students. Housing application deadline: 5/1. *Student services:* Campus employment opportunities, campus safety program, career counseling, exercise/wellness program, free psychological counseling, grant writing training, international student services, low-cost health insurance, multicultural affairs office, services for students with disabilities, teacher training, writing training. *Library:* Mary and Jeff Bell Library. *Collection:* Books: 376,758 (physical), 8,287 (digital/electronic); Serial titles: 15,316 (physical), 128,035 (digital/electronic); Databases: 260. Weekly public service hours: 105; students can reserve study rooms.

Computer facilities: 1,236 computers available on campus for general student use. A campuswide network can be accessed from student residence rooms and from off campus. Online class registration is available.
Website: http://www.tamucc.edu/

General Application Contact: Graduate Admissions Coordinator, 361-825-2177, Fax: 361-825-2755, E-mail: gradweb@tamucc.edu.

GRADUATE UNITS

College of Graduate Studies Students: 585 full-time (355 women), 1,249 part-time (866 women); includes 777 minority (81 Black or African American, non-Hispanic/Latino; 7 American Indian or Alaska Native, non-Hispanic/Latino; 71 Asian, non-Hispanic/Latino; 593 Hispanic/Latino; 3 Native Hawaiian or other Pacific Islander, non-Hispanic/Latino; 22 Two or more races, non-Hispanic/Latino), 257 international. Average age 33. 1,599 applicants, 43% accepted, 557 enrolled. *Financial support:* Research assistantships, teaching assistantships, career-related internships or fieldwork, institutionally sponsored loans, scholarships/grants, health care benefits, and unspecified assistantships available. Support available to part-time students. Financial award application deadline: 3/15; financial award applicants required to submit FAFSA. In 2015, 523 master's, 31 doctorates awarded. *Degree program information:* Part-time and evening/weekend programs available. Part-time, evening/weekend, 100% online, blended/hybrid learning. *Application deadline:* For fall admission, 7/15 priority date for domestic students, 5/1 priority date for international students; for spring admission, 11/15 priority date for domestic students, 9/1 priority date for international students. Applications are processed on a rolling basis. *Application fee:* $50 ($70 for international students). Electronic applications accepted. *Application Contact:* Sandra Kureska, Director, Graduate Studies, 361-825-3883, Fax: 361-825-2755, E-mail: gradweb@tamucc.edu. *Dean, College of Graduate Studies*, Dr. JoAnn Canales, 361-825-3847, Fax: 361-825-2755, E-mail: joann.canales@tamucc.edu.

College of Business Students: 141 full-time (80 women), 378 part-time (173 women); includes 191 minority (27 Black or African American, non-Hispanic/Latino; 1 American Indian or Alaska Native, non-Hispanic/Latino; 28 Asian, non-Hispanic/Latino; 131 Hispanic/Latino; 4 Two or more races, non-Hispanic/Latino), 119 international. Average age 32. 414 applicants, 53% accepted, 168 enrolled. *Financial support:* Research assistantships, teaching assistantships, career-related internships or fieldwork, Federal Work-Study, institutionally sponsored loans, scholarships/grants, health care benefits, and unspecified assistantships available. Support available to part-time students. Financial award application deadline: 3/15; financial award applicants required to submit FAFSA. In 2015, 136 master's awarded. *Degree program information:* Part-time and evening/weekend programs available. Part-time, evening/weekend, online learning. Offers accounting (M Acc); health care administration (MBA); international business (MBA). *Application deadline:* For fall admission, 7/15 priority date for domestic students, 5/1 priority date for international students; for spring admission, 11/15 priority date for domestic students, 9/1 priority date for international students; for summer admission, 4/15 priority date for domestic students, 2/1 priority date for international students. Applications are processed on a rolling basis. *Application fee:* $50 ($70 for international students). Electronic applications accepted. *Application Contact:* Sharon Polansky, Director, Master's Program, 361-825-3448, Fax: 361-825-2755, E-mail: gradweb@tamucc.edu. *Dean*, Dr. John Gamble, 361-825-6045, Fax: 361-825-2725, E-mail: john.gamble@tamucc.edu.

College of Education Students: 163 full-time (122 women), 221 part-time (170 women); includes 250 minority (26 Black or African American, non-Hispanic/Latino; 2 American Indian or Alaska Native, non-Hispanic/Latino; 6 Asian, non-Hispanic/Latino; 209 Hispanic/Latino; 7 Two or more races, non-Hispanic/Latino), 27 international. Average age 35. 255 applicants, 55% accepted, 113 enrolled. *Financial support:* Research assistantships, teaching assistantships, career-related internships or fieldwork, Federal Work-Study, institutionally sponsored loans, scholarships/grants, health care benefits, and unspecified assistantships available. Support available to part-time students. Financial award application deadline: 3/15; financial award applicants required to submit FAFSA. In 2015, 134 master's, 26 doctorates awarded. *Degree program information:* Part-time and evening/weekend programs available. Part-time, evening/weekend, online learning. Offers counseling (MS); counselor education (PhD); curriculum and instruction (MS, PhD); early childhood education (MS); educational administration (MS); educational leadership (Ed D); elementary education (MS); instructional design and educational technology (MS); kinesiology (MS); reading (MS); secondary education (MS); special education (MS). *Application deadline:* For fall admission, 7/15 priority date for domestic students, 5/1 priority date for international students; for spring admission, 11/15 priority date for domestic students, 9/1 priority date for international students. Applications are processed on a rolling basis. *Application fee:* $50 ($70 for international students). Electronic applications accepted. *Application Contact:* Graduate Admissions Coordinator, 361-

825-2177, Fax: 361-825-2755, E-mail: gradweb@tamucc.edu. *Dean*, Dr. Arthur Hernandez, 361-825-2660, E-mail: art.hernandez@tamucc.edu.

College of Liberal Arts Students: 77 full-time (50 women), 98 part-time (64 women); includes 92 minority (6 Black or African American, non-Hispanic/Latino; 1 American Indian or Alaska Native, non-Hispanic/Latino; 3 Asian, non-Hispanic/Latino; 79 Hispanic/Latino; 3 Two or more races, non-Hispanic/Latino), 12 international. Average age 32. 158 applicants, 47% accepted, 64 enrolled. *Financial support:* Research assistantships, teaching assistantships, career-related internships or fieldwork, Federal Work-Study, institutionally sponsored loans, scholarships/grants, health care benefits, and unspecified assistantships available. Support available to part-time students. Financial award application deadline: 3/15; financial award applicants required to submit FAFSA. In 2015, 52 master's awarded. *Degree program information:* Part-time and evening/weekend programs available. Part-time, evening/weekend. Offers communication (MA); English (MA); history (MA); psychology (MA); public administration (MPA); studio art (MA, MFA). *Application deadline:* For fall admission, 7/15 for domestic students, 5/1 for international students; for spring admission, 11/15 priority date for domestic students, 9/1 priority date for international students. Applications are processed on a rolling basis. *Application fee:* $50 ($70 for international students). Electronic applications accepted. *Application Contact:* Graduate Admissions Coordinator, 361-825-2177, Fax: 361-825-2755, E-mail: gradweb@tamucc.edu. *Interim Dean*, Dr. Mark Hartlaub, 361-825-2659, Fax: 361-825-5844, E-mail: mark.hartlaub@tamucc.edu.

College of Nursing and Health Sciences Students: 12 full-time (11 women), 375 part-time (322 women); includes 200 minority (20 Black or African American, non-Hispanic/Latino; 1 American Indian or Alaska Native, non-Hispanic/Latino; 27 Asian, non-Hispanic/Latino; 142 Hispanic/Latino; 3 Native Hawaiian or other Pacific Islander, non-Hispanic/Latino; 7 Two or more races, non-Hispanic/Latino), 1 international. Average age 38. 337 applicants, 42% accepted, 128 enrolled. *Financial support:* Research assistantships, teaching assistantships, career-related internships or fieldwork, Federal Work-Study, institutionally sponsored loans, scholarships/grants, health care benefits, and unspecified assistantships available. Support available to part-time students. Financial award application deadline: 3/15; financial award applicants required to submit FAFSA. In 2015, 102 master's awarded. *Degree program information:* Part-time and evening/weekend programs available. Part-time, evening/weekend, online only, 100% online. Offers family nurse practitioner (MSN); leadership in nursing systems (MSN); nurse educator (MSN). *Application deadline:* For fall admission, 4/15 priority date for domestic and international students; for spring admission, 1/7 for domestic and international students; for summer admission, 5/27 for domestic and international students. Applications are processed on a rolling basis. *Application fee:* $50 ($70 for international students). Electronic applications accepted. *Application Contact:* Graduate Admissions Coordinator, 361-825-2177, Fax: 361-825-2755, E-mail: gradweb@tamucc.edu. *Dean*, Dr. Mary Jane Hamilton, 361-825-2469, E-mail: mary.hamilton@tamucc.edu.

College of Science and Engineering Students: 192 full-time (92 women), 77 part-time (37 women); includes 44 minority (2 Black or African American, non-Hispanic/Latino; 2 American Indian or Alaska Native, non-Hispanic/Latino; 7 Asian, non-Hispanic/Latino; 32 Hispanic/Latino; 1 Two or more races, non-Hispanic/Latino), 98 international. Average age 28. 435 applicants, 38% accepted, 84 enrolled. *Financial support:* Research assistantships, teaching assistantships, career-related internships or fieldwork, Federal Work-Study, institutionally sponsored loans, scholarships/grants, health care benefits, and unspecified assistantships available. Support available to part-time students. Financial award application deadline: 3/15; financial award applicants required to submit FAFSA. In 2015, 99 master's, 5 doctorates awarded. *Degree program information:* Part-time and evening/weekend programs available. Part-time, evening/weekend. Offers biology (MS); coastal and marine system science (MS, PhD); computer science (MS); environmental science (MS); fisheries and mariculture (MS); geospatial computing science (PhD); geospatial surveying engineering (MS); mathematics (MS). *Application deadline:* For fall admission, 7/15 priority date for domestic students, 5/1 priority date for international students; for spring admission, 11/15 priority date for domestic students, 9/1 priority date for international students. Applications are processed on a rolling basis. *Application fee:* $50 ($70 for international students). Electronic applications accepted. *Application Contact:* Graduate Admissions Coordinator, 361-825-2177, Fax: 361-825-2755, E-mail: gradweb@tamucc.edu. *Dean*, Dr. Frank Pezold, 361-825-2349, E-mail: frank.pezold@tamucc.edu.

TEXAS A&M UNIVERSITY–KINGSVILLE, Kingsville, TX 78363

General Information State-supported, coed, university. *Enrollment:* 9,207 graduate, professional, and undergraduate students; 1,750 full-time matriculated graduate/professional students (500 women), 849 part-time matriculated graduate/professional students (379 women). *Enrollment by degree level:* 2,378 master's, 181 doctoral, 40 other advanced degrees. *Graduate faculty:* 128 full-time (41 women), 51 part-time/adjunct (20 women). *Graduate housing:* Room and/or apartments available on a first-come, first-served basis to single students; on-campus housing not available to married students. Typical cost: $8407 (including board). Housing application deadline: 8/1. *Student services:* Campus employment opportunities, campus safety program, career counseling, child daycare facilities, exercise/wellness program, free psychological counseling, international student services, services for students with disabilities, teacher training, writing training. *Library:* James C. Jernigan Library. *Collection:* Books: 655,779 (physical), 207,818 (digital/electronic); Serial titles: 467 (physical), 40,228 (digital/electronic); Databases: 142. Weekly public service hours: 100; students can reserve study rooms. *Research affiliation:* American Chemical Society (chemistry: the use of terminally-functionalized atactic-polypropylene oligomers as supports for catalysis), Texas Citrus Producers Board (agriculture: citrus center grapefruit research), Exxon Mobile (summer internships for students), East Wildlife Foundation (agriculture: bird populations, deer research), The Brown Foundation (agriculture: invasive grass research), Wildlife Pharmaceuticals, Inc. (agriculture: deer).

Computer facilities: 400 computers available on campus for general student use. A campuswide network can be accessed. Online class registration is available.
Website: http://www.tamuk.edu/

General Application Contact: Dr. Mohamed Abdelrahman, Dean, College of Graduate Studies, 361-593-2808, Fax: 361-593-3412, E-mail: mohamed.abdelrahman@tamuk.edu.

GRADUATE UNITS

College of Graduate Studies ***Degree program information:*** Part-time programs available. Part-time, online learning. Electronic applications accepted.

College of Arts and Sciences Students: 140 full-time (86 women), 74 part-time (42 women); includes 134 minority (14 Black or African American, non-Hispanic/Latino; 2 American Indian or Alaska Native, non-Hispanic/Latino; 1 Asian, non-Hispanic/Latino; 114 Hispanic/Latino; 1 Native Hawaiian or other Pacific Islander, non-Hispanic/Latino; 2 Two or more races, non-Hispanic/Latino), 52 international. Average age 27. 197 applicants, 53% accepted, 66 enrolled. *Faculty:* 42 full-time (14 women), 18 part-time/adjunct (6 women). In 2015, 83 master's awarded. Offers arts and sciences (MA, MM, MS); biology (MS); chemistry (MS); communication sciences and disorders (MS); criminology (MS); cultural studies (MA); English (MA, MS); mathematics (MS); music (MM); music education (MM); psychology (MA, MS); sociology (MA, MS); Spanish (MA); statistical analytics, computing and modeling (MS). *Application fee:* $35 ($50 for international students). Electronic applications accepted. *Dean of Arts and Sciences*, Dolores Guerrero, 361-593-2761, E-mail: dolores.guerrero@tamuk.edu.

College of Business Administration Students: 57 full-time (24 women), 32 part-time (10 women); includes 59 minority (10 Black or African American, non-Hispanic/Latino; 9 Asian, non-Hispanic/Latino; 38 Hispanic/Latino; 2 Two or more races, non-Hispanic/Latino). Average age 32. 51 applicants, 96% accepted, 37 enrolled. *Faculty:* 15 full-time (8 women), 1 part-time/adjunct (0 women). *Financial support:* Career-related internships or fieldwork, Federal Work-Study, institutionally sponsored loans, scholarships/grants, health care benefits, tuition waivers (full and partial), and unspecified assistantships available. Support available to part-time students. In 2015, 27 master's awarded. Online only, 100% online, blended/hybrid learning. Offers business administration (MBA). *Application deadline:* Applications are processed on a rolling basis. *Application fee:* $35 ($50 for international students). Electronic applications accepted. *Application Contact:* Dr. Natalya Delcoure, Dean, College of Business Administration, 361-593-3801, E-mail: natalya.delcoure@tamuk.edu. *Dean, College of Business Administration*, Dr. Natalya Delcoure, 361-593-3801, E-mail: natalya.delcoure@tamuk.edu.

College of Education and Human Performance Students: 142 full-time (105 women), 299 part-time (207 women); includes 327 minority (16 Black or African American, non-Hispanic/Latino; 1 American Indian or Alaska Native, non-Hispanic/Latino; 2 Asian, non-Hispanic/Latino; 307 Hispanic/Latino; 1 Two or more races, non-Hispanic/Latino), 32 international. Average age 35. 149 applicants, 89% accepted, 94 enrolled. *Faculty:* 19 full-time (11 women), 23 part-time/adjunct (12 women). *Financial support:* Research assistantships, teaching assistantships, career-related internships or fieldwork, Federal Work-Study, institutionally sponsored loans, scholarships/grants, health care benefits, tuition waivers (partial), and unspecified assistantships available. Support available to part-time students. In 2015, 102 master's, 20 doctorates awarded. 100% online, blended/hybrid learning. Offers adult education (M Ed); bilingual education (M Ed, Ed D); counseling and guidance (MA, MS); early childhood education (M Ed); education and human performance (M Ed, MA, MS, Ed D, Certificate); educational administration (MA, MS); educational leadership (Ed D); health and kinesiology (MA, MS); instructional technology (MS); reading specialization (MS); special education (M Ed). *Application deadline:* Applications are processed on a rolling basis. *Application fee:* $35 ($50 for international students). Electronic applications accepted. *Application Contact:* Alberto Ruiz, Dean, College of Education & Human Performance, 361-593-2802, E-mail: alberto.ruiz@tamuk.edu. *Dean, College of Education & Human Performance*, Alberto Ruiz, 361-593-2802, E-mail: alberto.ruiz@tamuk.edu.

Dick and Mary Lewis Kleberg College of Agriculture, Natural Resources and Human Sciences Offers agribusiness (MS); agricultural science (MS); agriculture, natural resources and human sciences (MS, PhD); animal science (MS); horticulture (PhD); human sciences (MS); plant and soil science (MS); ranch management (MS); range and wildlife management (MS); wildlife science (PhD). Electronic applications accepted.

Frank H. Dotterweich College of Engineering Offers chemical engineering (ME, MS); civil engineering (ME, MS); computer science (MS); electrical engineering (ME, MS); engineering (ME, MS, PhD); environmental engineering (ME, MS, PhD); industrial engineering (ME, MS); industrial management (MS); mechanical engineering (ME, MS); natural gas engineering (ME, MS); sustainable energy systems engineering (PhD). Electronic applications accepted.

TEXAS A&M UNIVERSITY–SAN ANTONIO, San Antonio, TX 78224

General Information State-supported, coed, comprehensive institution.

GRADUATE UNITS

Department of Curriculum and Kinesiology ***Degree program information:*** Part-time and evening/weekend programs available. Part-time, evening/weekend. Offers bilingual education (MA); early childhood education (M Ed); kinesiology (MS); reading (MS); special education (M Ed). Electronic applications accepted.

Department of Leadership and Counseling ***Degree program information:*** Part-time and evening/weekend programs available. Part-time, evening/weekend. Offers counseling and guidance (MA); educational leadership (MA). Electronic applications accepted.

School of Arts and Sciences ***Degree program information:*** Part-time and evening/weekend programs available. Part-time, evening/weekend. Offers English (MA). Electronic applications accepted.

School of Business ***Degree program information:*** Part-time and evening/weekend programs available. Part-time, evening/weekend. Offers business administration (MBA); enterprise resource planning systems (MBA); finance (MBA); healthcare management (MBA); human resources management (MBA); information assurance and security (MBA); international business (MBA); professional accounting (MPA); project management (MBA); supply chain management (MBA). Electronic applications accepted.

TEXAS A&M UNIVERSITY–TEXARKANA, Texarkana, TX 75505-5518

General Information State-supported, coed, upper-level institution. *Graduate housing:* On-campus housing not available.

GRADUATE UNITS

Graduate Studies and Research ***Degree program information:*** Part-time and evening/weekend programs available. Part-time, evening/weekend. Electronic applications accepted.

College of Business Degree program information: Part-time and evening/weekend programs available. Part-time, evening/weekend. Offers accounting (MSA); business administration (MBA, MS). Electronic applications accepted.

College of Education and Liberal Arts Degree program information: Part-time and evening/weekend programs available. Part-time, evening/weekend. Offers adult education (MS); curriculum and instruction (M Ed); education (MS); educational administration (M Ed); English (MA); instructional technology (MS); interdisciplinary studies (MA, MS); special education (MS). Electronic applications accepted.

College of Health and Behavioral Sciences Degree program information: Part-time and evening/weekend programs available. Part-time, evening/weekend. Offers counseling psychology (MS). Electronic applications accepted.

TEXAS CHIROPRACTIC COLLEGE, Pasadena, TX 77505-1699

General Information Independent, coed, graduate-only institution. *Graduate housing:* On-campus housing not available.

GRADUATE UNITS

Professional Program Offers chiropractic (DC).

TEXAS CHRISTIAN UNIVERSITY, Fort Worth, TX 76129-0002

General Information Independent-religious, coed, university. CGS member. *Enrollment:* 10,323 graduate, professional, and undergraduate students; 1,259 full-time matriculated graduate/professional students (695 women), 150 part-time matriculated graduate/professional students (106 women). *Enrollment by degree level:* 927 master's, 479 doctoral, 3 other advanced degrees. *Graduate faculty:* 368 full-time (150 women), 63 part-time/adjunct (22 women). *Tuition, area resident:* Full-time $26,640; part-time $1480 per credit hour. *Required fees:* $48; $48 per unit. Tuition and fees vary according to program. *Graduate housing:* Rooms and/or apartments available on a first-come, first-served basis to single and married students. Housing application deadline: 5/1. *Student services:* Campus employment opportunities, campus safety program, career counseling, exercise/wellness program, free psychological counseling, international student services, low-cost health insurance, multicultural affairs office, services for students with disabilities, teacher training, writing training. *Library:* Mary Couts Burnett Library. *Collection:* Books: 1.4 million (physical), 557,097 (digital/electronic); Serial titles: 1,212 (physical), 107,696 (digital/electronic); Databases: 406. Weekly public service hours: 139; study areas open 24 hours, 5–7 days a week; students can reserve study rooms. *Research affiliation:* Lockheed Martin Corporation (business), Botanical Research Institute of Texas, Inc. (biology, environmental science, ranch management), The University of Texas Southwestern Medical School (health sciences), NextEra (environmental science, wind energy), University of North Texas Health Science Center at Fort Worth (physics, biology), Bell Helicopter (engineering).

Computer facilities: 1,400 computers available on campus for general student use. A campuswide network can be accessed from student residence rooms and from off campus. Online class registration is available.
Website: http://www.tcu.edu/

General Application Contact: Anita Unger, Admissions, TCU Graduate Studies Office, 817-257-7515, Fax: 817-257-7484, E-mail: frogmail@tcu.edu.

GRADUATE UNITS

AddRan College of Liberal Arts Students: 130 full-time (74 women), 1 part-time (0 women); includes 29 minority (7 Black or African American, non-Hispanic/Latino; 1 Asian, non-Hispanic/Latino; 18 Hispanic/Latino; 3 Two or more races, non-Hispanic/Latino), 1 international. Average age 31. 93 applicants, 62% accepted, 33 enrolled. *Faculty:* 56 full-time (21 women), 5 part-time/adjunct (3 women). In 2015, 6 master's, 8 doctorates awarded. Offers criminal justice and criminology (MS); English (MA, PhD); Latin America (MA, PhD); liberal arts (MA, MS, PhD); rhetoric and composition (PhD); United States (MA, PhD). *Application deadline:* Applications are processed on a rolling basis. *Application fee:* $60. Electronic applications accepted. *Application Contact:* Admissions, TCU Graduate Studies Office, 817-257-7515, Fax: 817-257-7484, E-mail: frogmail@tcu.edu. *Associate Dean*, Dr. Don M. Coerver, 817-257-6290, Fax: 817-257-7709, E-mail: d.coerver@tcu.edu.

Bob Schieffer College of Communication Students: 24 full-time (18 women), 9 part-time (6 women); includes 6 minority (1 Black or African American, non-Hispanic/Latino; 1 Asian, non-Hispanic/Latino; 2 Hispanic/Latino; 2 Two or more races, non-Hispanic/Latino), 2 international. Average age 26. 34 applicants, 56% accepted, 15 enrolled. *Faculty:* 23 full-time (12 women), 1 part-time/adjunct (0 women). *Financial support:* In 2015–16, 20 students received support, including 18 teaching assistantships with full tuition reimbursements available (averaging $10,000 per year); research assistantships, health care benefits, tuition waivers (full and partial), and unspecified assistantships also available. Financial award application deadline: 2/15. In 2015, 12 master's awarded. *Degree program information:* Part-time programs available. Part-time. Offers communication studies (MS); strategic communication (MS). *Application deadline:* For fall admission, 2/15 for domestic and international students; for spring admission, 10/15 for domestic and international students. *Application fee:* $60. Electronic applications accepted. *Application Contact:* Alicia Craff, Academic Advisor, 817-257-5917, Fax: 817-257-5921, E-mail: a.e.craff@tcu.edu. *Associate Dean*, Dr. Daxton Stewart, 817-257-5911, Fax: 817-257-5921, E-mail: d.stewart@tcu.edu.

School of Strategic Communication Students: 16 full-time (10 women), 2 part-time (1 woman); includes 5 minority (1 Black or African American, non-Hispanic/Latino; 1 Asian, non-Hispanic/Latino; 1 Hispanic/Latino; 2 Two or more races, non-Hispanic/Latino), 2 international. Average age 26. 20 applicants, 65% accepted, 9 enrolled. *Faculty:* 7 full-time (6 women). *Financial support:* In 2015–16, 11 students received support, including 9 teaching assistantships (averaging $9,000 per year); tuition waivers (full) also available. Financial award application deadline: 2/15; financial award applicants required to submit FAFSA. In 2015, 6 master's awarded. *Degree program information:* Part-time programs available. Part-time. Offers strategic communication (MS). *Application deadline:* For fall admission, 6/1 for domestic and international students; for spring admission, 10/15 for domestic and international students. Applications are processed on a rolling basis. *Application fee:* $60. Electronic applications accepted. *Application Contact:* Dr. Julie O'Neil, Graduate Director, 817-257-6966, Fax: 817-257-7322, E-mail: j.oneil@tcu.edu. *Director*, Dr. Jacque Lambiase, 817-257-6552, Fax: 817-257-7322, E-mail: j.lambiase@tcu.edu.

College of Education Students: 168 full-time (134 women), 30 part-time (22 women); includes 69 minority (23 Black or African American, non-Hispanic/Latino; 2 American Indian or Alaska Native, non-Hispanic/Latino; 6 Asian, non-Hispanic/Latino; 33 Hispanic/Latino; 5 Two or more races, non-Hispanic/Latino), 7 international. Average age 32. 124 applicants, 68% accepted, 67 enrolled. *Faculty:* 29 full-time (21 women), 8 part-time/adjunct (5 women). *Financial support:* In 2015–16, 152 students received support, including 6 research assistantships with full tuition reimbursements available, 36 teaching assistantships with full tuition reimbursements available; career-related internships or fieldwork, scholarships/grants, and unspecified assistantships also available. Support available to part-time students. Financial award application deadline: 2/1; financial award applicants required to submit FAFSA. In 2015, 66 master's, 8 doctorates awarded. *Degree program information:* Part-time and evening/weekend programs available. Part-time, evening/weekend. Offers counseling (M Ed); curriculum and instruction (M Ed); education (M Ed, Ed D, PhD, Certificate); educational leadership (M Ed, Ed D); special education (M Ed). *Application deadline:* For fall admission, 2/1 for domestic and international students; for spring admission, 11/16 for domestic and international students; for summer admission, 2/1 for domestic and international students. *Application fee:* $60. Electronic applications accepted. *Application Contact:* Lori Kimball, Administrative Program Specialist, 817-257-7661, E-mail: l.kimball@tcu.edu. *Associate Dean*, Dr. Jan Lacina, 817-257-6786, E-mail: j.lacina@tcu.edu.

College of Fine Arts Students: 68 full-time (37 women), 7 part-time (6 women); includes 13 minority (2 Asian, non-Hispanic/Latino; 10 Hispanic/Latino; 1 Two or more races, non-Hispanic/Latino), 17 international. Average age 28. 115 applicants, 43% accepted, 34 enrolled. *Faculty:* 55 full-time (17 women), 12 part-time/adjunct (5 women). *Financial support:* In 2015–16, 66 students received support, including 88 teaching assistantships with full tuition reimbursements available (averaging $34,120 per year); career-related internships or fieldwork, scholarships/grants, tuition waivers (full and partial), and unspecified assistantships also available. Financial award application deadline: 4/15. In 2015, 26 master's, 2 doctorates awarded. Offers fine arts (M Mus, MA, MFA, MM Ed, DMA, Artist Diploma). *Application deadline:* For fall admission, 2/1 for domestic and international students; for spring admission, 10/1 for domestic and international students. Applications are processed on a rolling basis. *Application fee:* $60. Electronic applications accepted. *Application Contact:* Donna Smolik, TCU College of Fine Arts Graduate Office, 817-257-7603, Fax: 817-257-5672, E-mail: cfagradinfo@tcu.edu. *Associate Dean, College of Fine Arts*, Dr. H. Joseph Butler, 817-257-7603, Fax: 817-257-5672, E-mail: cfagradinfo@tcu.edu.

School of Art Students: 16 full-time (15 women), 1 (woman) part-time; includes 4 minority (all Hispanic/Latino), 1 international. Average age 31. 35 applicants, 40% accepted, 9 enrolled. *Faculty:* 12 full-time (6 women), 1 (woman) part-time/adjunct. *Financial support:* In 2015–16, 18 students received support, including 17 teaching assistantships (averaging $10,000 per year); institutionally sponsored loans, scholarships/grants, tuition waivers (full), and unspecified assistantships also available. Financial award application deadline: 4/15. In 2015, 10 master's awarded. Offers art history (MA); studio art (MFA). *Application deadline:* For fall admission, 2/1 for domestic and international students. *Application fee:* $60. Electronic applications accepted. *Application Contact:* Donna Smolik, TCU College of Fine Arts Graduate Office, 817-257-7603, Fax: 817-257-5672, E-mail: cfagradinfo@tcu.edu. *Director*, Dr. Sally Packard, 817-257-7643, E-mail: s.packard@tcu.edu.

School of Music Students: 50 full-time (21 women), 6 part-time (5 women); includes 9 minority (2 Asian, non-Hispanic/Latino; 6 Hispanic/Latino; 1 Two or more races, non-Hispanic/Latino), 16 international. Average age 27. 77 applicants, 47% accepted, 25 enrolled. *Faculty:* 38 full-time (7 women), 11 part-time/adjunct (4 women). *Financial support:* In 2015–16, 52 research assistantships with full tuition reimbursements (averaging $6,000 per year) were awarded; career-related internships or fieldwork, institutionally sponsored loans, scholarships/grants, tuition waivers, and unspecified assistantships also available. Financial award application deadline: 12/1; financial award applicants required to submit CSS PROFILE or FAFSA. In 2015, 16 master's, 2 doctorates awarded. Offers composition (DMA); conducting (M Mus, DMA); music (M Mus, MM Ed, DMA); music education (MM Ed); music theory (M Mus); musicology (M Mus); percussion (Artist Diploma); performance (M Mus, DMA); piano pedagogy (M Mus, DMA); voice pedagogy (M Mus); winds (Artist Diploma). *Application deadline:* For fall admission, 12/1 for domestic and international students; for spring admission, 9/1 for domestic and international students. *Application fee:* $60. Electronic applications accepted. *Application Contact:* Dr. Joseph Butler, Associate Dean, College of Fine Arts, 817-257-6629, E-mail: j.butler@tcu.edu. *Director*, Dr. Richard C. Gipson, 817-257-7602.

College of Science and Engineering Students: 122 full-time (59 women), 7 part-time (0 women); includes 22 minority (1 Black or African American, non-Hispanic/Latino; 5 Asian, non-Hispanic/Latino; 12 Hispanic/Latino; 4 Two or more races, non-Hispanic/Latino), 27 international. Average age 27. 169 applicants, 33% accepted, 40 enrolled. *Faculty:* 87 full-time (25 women), 3 part-time/adjunct (1 woman). *Financial support:* Tuition waivers and unspecified assistantships available. Financial award application deadline: 2/1. In 2015, 33 master's, 13 doctorates awarded. *Degree program information:* Part-time programs available. Part-time. Offers applied mathematics (MS); biology (MA, MS); chemistry and biochemistry (MA, MS, PhD); developmental trauma (MS); experimental psychology (MS, PhD); mathematics (MAT, PhD); physics (MA, MS, PhD); pure mathematics (MS); science and engineering (MA, MAT, MEM, MS, PhD). *Application deadline:* For fall admission, 2/1 for domestic and international students; for spring admission, 9/1 for domestic and international students. *Application fee:* $60. Electronic applications accepted. *Associate Dean for Administration and Graduate Programs*, Dr. Magnus Rittby, 817-257-7729, Fax: 817-257-7736, E-mail: m.rittby@tcu.edu.

School of Geology, Energy and the Environment Students: 32 full-time (10 women), 3 part-time (0 women); includes 5 minority (1 Black or African American, non-Hispanic/Latino; 2 Asian, non-Hispanic/Latino; 2 Hispanic/Latino), 3 international. Average age 27. 56 applicants, 25% accepted, 10 enrolled. *Faculty:* 13 full-time (4 women), 1 part-time/adjunct (0 women). *Financial support:* In 2015–16, 15 teaching assistantships with full tuition reimbursements (averaging $16,000 per year) were awarded; unspecified assistantships also available. Financial award application deadline: 2/1. In 2015, 15 master's awarded. *Degree program information:* Part-time programs available. Part-time. Offers environmental science (MA, MEM, MS); geology (MS). *Application deadline:* For fall admission, 2/1 for domestic and international students; for spring admission, 9/1 for domestic and international students. *Application fee:* $60. Electronic applications accepted. *Graduate Advisor*, Dr. Helge Alsleben, 817-257-7270, Fax: 817-257-7789, E-mail: h.alsleben@tcu.edu.

Harris College of Nursing and Health Sciences Students: 321 full-time (232 women), 50 part-time (47 women); includes 90 minority (13 Black or African American, non-Hispanic/Latino; 4 American Indian or Alaska Native, non-Hispanic/Latino; 28 Asian, non-Hispanic/Latino; 34 Hispanic/Latino; 1 Native Hawaiian or other Pacific Islander, non-Hispanic/Latino; 10 Two or more races, non-Hispanic/Latino), 2 international. Average age 32. 597 applicants, 31% accepted, 148 enrolled. *Faculty:* 53 full-time (38 women), 6 part-time/adjunct (3 women). *Financial support:* Applicants required to submit FAFSA. In 2015, 81 master's, 58 doctorates awarded. Online learning. Offers advanced generalist (MSW); advanced practice registered nurse (DNP); clinical nurse leader (MSN, Certificate); clinical nurse specialist (MSN); kinesiology (MS); nursing administration (DNP); nursing and health sciences (MHS, MS, MSN, MSW, DNP, DNP-A, Certificate); nursing education (MSN). *Application fee:* $60. Electronic applications accepted. *Dean*, Dr. Susan Weeks, 817-257-6749, E-mail: s.weeks@tcu.edu.

Davies School of Communication Sciences and Disorders Students: 39 full-time (36 women); includes 12 minority (1 Black or African American, non-Hispanic/Latino; 10 Hispanic/Latino; 1 Two or more races, non-Hispanic/Latino). Average age 23. 285 applicants, 7% accepted, 20 enrolled. *Faculty:* 7 full-time (6 women). *Financial support:* In 2015–16, 40 students received support, including 40 research assistantships (averaging $35,000 per year); tuition waivers (partial) and unspecified assistantships also available. Financial award application deadline: 1/15; financial award applicants required to submit FAFSA. In 2015, 20 master's awarded. Offers speech-language pathology (MS). *Application deadline:* For fall admission, 1/15 for domestic and international students. *Application fee:* $60. Electronic applications accepted. *Application Contact:* Janet Smith, Administrative Assistant, 817-257-7620, E-mail: janet.smith@tcu.edu. *Director*, Dr. Christopher Watts, 817-257-7620, E-mail: c.watts@tcu.edu.

School of Nurse Anesthesia Students: 168 full-time (104 women); includes 33 minority (2 Black or African American, non-Hispanic/Latino; 2 American Indian or Alaska Native, non-Hispanic/Latino; 13 Asian, non-Hispanic/Latino; 12 Hispanic/Latino; 4 Two or more races, non-Hispanic/Latino). Average age 30. 194 applicants, 40% accepted, 63 enrolled. *Faculty:* 11 full-time (5 women). *Financial support:* Applicants required to submit FAFSA. In 2015, 34 doctorates awarded. Offers nurse anesthesia (DNP-A). *Application deadline:* For fall and spring admission, 7/1 for domestic and international students. Applications are processed on a rolling basis. *Application fee:* $60. Electronic applications accepted. *Application Contact:* Renee Gist, Administrative Assistant, 817-257-7887, Fax: 817-257-5472, E-mail: r.gist@tcu.edu. *Director*, Dr. Kay K. Sanders, 817-257-7887, Fax: 817-257-5472, E-mail: k.sanders@tcu.edu.

Master of Liberal Arts Program Students: 63 full-time (31 women), 30 part-time (23 women); includes 22 minority (8 Black or African American, non-Hispanic/Latino; 1 Asian, non-Hispanic/Latino; 11 Hispanic/Latino; 1 Native Hawaiian or other Pacific Islander, non-Hispanic/Latino; 1 Two or more races, non-Hispanic/Latino). Average age 33. 66 applicants, 94% accepted, 42 enrolled. *Faculty:* 11 part-time/adjunct (1 woman). *Financial support:* In 2015–16, 50 students received support. Scholarships/grants, unspecified assistantships, and employee tuition benefits available. Financial award applicants required to submit FAFSA. In 2015, 33 master's awarded. *Degree program information:* Part-time and evening/weekend programs available. Part-time, evening/weekend, 100% online. Offers liberal arts (MLA). *Application deadline:* For fall admission, 8/15 for domestic students, 6/1 for international students; for spring admission, 1/15 for domestic students, 11/1 for international students. Applications are processed on a rolling basis. *Application fee:* $60. Electronic applications accepted. *Application Contact:* Anita Unger, Graduate Program Coordinator, 817-257-7515, Fax: 817-257-7484, E-mail: a.unger@tcu.edu. *Associate Provost/Dean of University Programs*, Dr. Bonnie Melhart, 817-257-7104, Fax: 817-257-7484, E-mail: b.melhart@tcu.edu.

Neeley School of Business Students: 358 full-time (108 women), 22 part-time (7 women); includes 49 minority (10 Black or African American, non-Hispanic/Latino; 4 American Indian or Alaska Native, non-Hispanic/Latino; 10 Asian, non-Hispanic/Latino; 23 Hispanic/Latino; 2 Native Hawaiian or other Pacific Islander, non-Hispanic/Latino), 30 international. Average age 30. 317 applicants, 98% accepted, 220 enrolled. *Faculty:* 59 full-time (16 women), 16 part-time/adjunct (4 women). *Financial support:* Career-related internships or fieldwork, scholarships/grants, and unspecified assistantships available. Financial award application deadline: 4/1; financial award applicants required to submit FAFSA. In 2015, 190 master's awarded. *Degree program information:* Part-time and evening/weekend programs available. Part-time, evening/weekend. Offers accounting (MBA); audit (M Ac); business (M Ac, MBA); business administration (MBA); finance (MBA); marketing (MBA); supply and value chain management (MBA); taxation (M Ac); valuation and reporting (M Ac). *Application deadline:* For fall admission, 3/1 for domestic and international students; for winter admission, 1/15 for domestic and international students; for spring admission, 11/1 for domestic and international students; for summer admission, 1/15 for domestic and international students. Applications are processed on a rolling basis. *Application fee:* $100. Electronic applications accepted. *Application Contact:* Graduate Programs Admissions Office, 817-257-7531, E-mail: mbainfo@tcu.edu. *Dean*, Dr. Homer Erekson, 817-257-7511, E-mail: neeleynews@tcu.edu.

TEXAS HEALTH AND SCIENCE UNIVERSITY, Austin, TX 78704

General Information Private, coed, graduate-only institution. *Enrollment by degree level:* 102 master's, 9 doctoral. *Graduate faculty:* 8 full-time (3 women), 7 part-time/adjunct (5 women). *Tuition, area resident:* Full-time $10,260; part-time $7560 per trimester. *Required fees:* $1600; $1200 per trimester. $600 per trimester. One-time fee: $388. Tuition and fees vary according to course load, degree level and program. *Graduate housing:* On-campus housing not available. *Student services:* Campus employment opportunities, campus safety program, career counseling, exercise/wellness program, international student services, multicultural affairs office, services for students with disabilities. *Library:* General Shu-Ping Tsao Library. *Collection:* Books: 5,272 (physical); Serial titles: 47 (physical). Weekly public service hours: 40.

Computer facilities: 7 computers available on campus for general student use. A campuswide network can be accessed. Online class registration is available.
Website: http://www.thsu.edu/

General Application Contact: Caleb Li, Admissions Coordinator, 512-444-8082, Fax: 512-444-6345, E-mail: admissions@thsu.edu.

GRADUATE UNITS

Graduate Programs Students: 102 full-time (64 women), 9 part-time (8 women); includes 43 minority (1 Black or African American, non-Hispanic/Latino; 1 American Indian or Alaska Native, non-Hispanic/Latino; 35 Asian, non-Hispanic/Latino; 6 Hispanic/Latino). Average age 34. *Faculty:* 8 full-time (3 women), 7 part-time/adjunct (5 women). *Financial support:* Teaching assistantships with partial tuition reimbursements, career-related internships or fieldwork, Federal Work-Study, institutionally sponsored loans, scholarships/grants, and tuition waivers (partial) available. Financial award applicants required to submit FAFSA. Offers acupuncture and Oriental medicine (MS, DAOM); business administration (MBA); healthcare management (MBA). *Application deadline:* For fall admission, 8/25 priority date for domestic and international students; for spring admission, 12/22 priority date for domestic and international students. Applications are processed on a rolling basis. *Application fee:* $75 ($300 for international students). Electronic applications accepted. *Application Contact:* Caleb Li, Admissions Coordinator, 512-444-8082, Fax: 512-444-6345, E-mail: admissions@thsu.edu. *Vice President of Academic Affairs*, Dr. David G. Vequist, IV, 512-444-8082.

TEXAS LUTHERAN UNIVERSITY, Seguin, TX 78155-5999

General Information Independent-religious, coed, comprehensive institution.

GRADUATE UNITS

Program in Accounting Offers accounting (M Acy).

TEXAS SOUTHERN UNIVERSITY, Houston, TX 77004-4584

General Information State-supported, coed, university. CGS member. *Graduate housing:* Room and/or apartments available on a first-come, first-served basis to single students; on-campus housing not available to married students. Housing application deadline: 7/15. *Research affiliation:* Environmental Research & Technology Transfer Center (chemistry and environmental toxicology), Institute for International and Immigration Law; Center on Legal Pedagogy (law), Innovative Transportation Research Institute (transportation planning and management), NASA University Research Biotechnology & Environmental Health (biology), Economic Development Center; JP Chase Center for Financial Education (business), Gerald B. Smith Center for Entrepreneurship & Executive Development (business, urban planning and environmental policy).

GRADUATE UNITS

College of Education ***Degree program information:*** Part-time and evening/weekend programs available. Part-time, evening/weekend. Offers bilingual education (M Ed); counseling (M Ed); counselor education (Ed D); curriculum and instruction (Ed D); education (M Ed, MS, Ed D); educational administration (M Ed, Ed D); health education (MS); human performance (MS); secondary education (M Ed). Electronic applications accepted.

College of Liberal Arts and Behavioral Sciences ***Degree program information:*** Part-time and evening/weekend programs available. Part-time, evening/weekend. Offers English (MA); fine arts (MA); history (MA); human services and consumer sciences (MS); liberal arts and behavioral sciences (MA, MS); music (MA); psychology (MA); sociology (MA). Electronic applications accepted.

College of Pharmacy and Health Sciences Online learning. Offers health care administration (MS); pharmaceutical sciences (MS, PhD); pharmacy and health sciences (MS, PhD, Pharm D); pharmacy practice (Pharm D). Electronic applications accepted.

Jesse H. Jones School of Business ***Degree program information:*** Part-time and evening/weekend programs available. Part-time, evening/weekend. Offers business (MBA, MS); business administration (MBA); management information systems (MS). Electronic applications accepted.

School of Public Affairs ***Degree program information:*** Part-time programs available. Part-time. Offers administration of justice (MS, PhD); public administration (MPA); public affairs (MPA, MS, PhD); urban planning and environmental policy (MS, PhD). Electronic applications accepted.

School of Science and Technology ***Degree program information:*** Part-time and evening/weekend programs available. Part-time, evening/weekend. Offers biology (MS); chemistry (MS); computer science (MS); environmental toxicology (MS, PhD); industrial technology (MS); mathematics (MS); science and technology (MS, PhD); transportation, planning and management (MS). Electronic applications accepted.

Tavis Smiley School of Communication ***Degree program information:*** Part-time programs available. Part-time. Offers communication (MA). Electronic applications accepted.

Thurgood Marshall School of Law Offers law (JD). Electronic applications accepted.

TEXAS STATE UNIVERSITY, San Marcos, TX 78666

General Information State-supported, coed, university. CGS member. *Enrollment:* 37,979 graduate, professional, and undergraduate students; 2,301 full-time matriculated graduate/professional students (1,447 women), 1,627 part-time matriculated graduate/professional students (1,029 women). *Enrollment by degree level:* 3,460 master's, 468 doctoral. *Graduate faculty:* 732 full-time (331 women), 133 part-time/adjunct (75 women). Tuition, state resident: full-time $7400; part-time $617 per credit hour. Tuition, nonresident: full-time $16,760; part-time $1397 per credit hour. *Required fees:* $1996; $676 per semester. Full-time tuition and fees vary according to course load. *Graduate housing:* Room and/or apartments available on a first-come, first-served basis to single students; on-campus housing not available to married students. Typical cost: $9500 per year ($12,110 including board). Room and board charges vary according to board plan and housing facility selected. Housing application deadline: 7/1. *Student services:* Campus employment opportunities, campus safety program, career counseling, exercise/wellness program, free psychological counseling, international student services, low-cost health insurance, multicultural affairs office, services for students with disabilities, teacher training, writing training. *Library:* Alkek Library plus 1 other. *Collection:* Books: 1.5 million (physical), 625,065 (digital/electronic); Databases: 487. Students can reserve study rooms. *Research affiliation:* Omega Optics, Inc. (engineering), Quantum Materials Corporation (material physics), McGraw Hill (curriculum development), Benchmark Ecological Service, Inc. (environmental protection), Edwards Aquifer Authority (conservation), Nanohmics (nanotechnology).

Computer facilities: Computer purchase and lease plans are available. 3,233 computers available on campus for general student use. A campuswide network can be accessed from student residence rooms and from off campus. Online class registration is available.
Website: http://www.txstate.edu/

General Application Contact: Dr. Andrea Golato, Dean of Graduate School, 512-245-2581, Fax: 512-245-8365, E-mail: gradcollege@txstate.edu.

GRADUATE UNITS

The Graduate College Students: 2,301 full-time (1,447 women), 1,627 part-time (1,029 women); includes 1,332 minority (277 Black or African American, non-Hispanic/Latino; 13 American Indian or Alaska Native, non-Hispanic/Latino; 114 Asian, non-Hispanic/Latino; 867 Hispanic/Latino; 61 Two or more races, non-Hispanic/Latino), 358 international. Average age 31. 3,672 applicants, 50% accepted, 1104 enrolled. *Faculty:* 732 full-time (331 women), 133 part-time/adjunct (75 women). *Financial support:* In 2015–16, 2,086 students received support, including 190 research assistantships (averaging $15,868 per year), 876 teaching assistantships (averaging $13,733 per year); fellowships, career-related internships or fieldwork, Federal Work-Study, institutionally sponsored loans, scholarships/grants, unspecified assistantships, and laboratory instructorships, stipends also available. Support available to part-time students. Financial award application deadline: 4/1; financial award applicants required to submit FAFSA. In 2015, 1,314 master's, 52 doctorates, 38 other advanced degrees awarded. *Degree program information:* Part-time and evening/weekend programs available. Part-time, evening/weekend, blended/hybrid learning. *Application deadline:* For fall admission, 6/15 for domestic students, 6/1 for international students; for spring admission, 10/15 for domestic students, 10/1 for international students. Applications are processed on a rolling basis. *Application fee:* $40 ($90 for international students). Electronic applications accepted. *Dean*, Dr. Andrea Golato, 512-245-2581, Fax: 512-245-8365, E-mail: gradcollege@txstate.edu.

College of Applied Arts Students: 275 full-time (220 women), 238 part-time (174 women); includes 199 minority (55 Black or African American, non-Hispanic/Latino; 1 American Indian or Alaska Native, non-Hispanic/Latino; 7 Asian, non-Hispanic/Latino; 125 Hispanic/Latino; 11 Two or more races, non-Hispanic/Latino), 18 international. Average age 31. 459 applicants, 54% accepted, 135 enrolled. *Faculty:* 73 full-time (37 women), 16 part-time/adjunct (14 women). *Financial support:* In 2015–16, 274 students received support, including 37 research assistantships (averaging $14,434 per year), 44 teaching assistantships (averaging $15,103 per year); career-related internships or fieldwork, Federal Work-Study, and institutionally sponsored loans also available. Support available to part-time students. Financial award application deadline: 4/1; financial award applicants required to submit FAFSA. In 2015, 233 master's, 5 doctorates awarded. *Degree program information:* Part-time and evening/weekend programs available. Part-time, evening/weekend, blended/hybrid learning. Offers agricultural education (M Ed); applied arts (M Ed, MAIS, MS, MSCJ, MSIS, MSW, PhD); criminal justice (MSCJ, PhD); family and child studies (MS);

human nutrition (MS); management of technical education (M Ed); merchandising and consumer studies (MS); occupational education (MAIS, MSIS); social work (MSW). *Application deadline:* For fall admission, 6/15 priority date for domestic students, 6/1 for international students; for spring admission, 10/15 priority date for domestic students, 10/1 for international students. Applications are processed on a rolling basis. *Application fee:* $40 ($90 for international students). Electronic applications accepted. *Application Contact:* Dr. Andrea Golato, Dean of Graduate School, 512-245-2581, Fax: 512-245-8365, E-mail: gradcollege@txstate.edu. *Dean*, Dr. T. Jaime Chahin, 512-245-3333, Fax: 512-245-3338, E-mail: tc03@txstate.edu.

College of Education Students: 529 full-time (385 women), 608 part-time (455 women); includes 440 minority (87 Black or African American, non-Hispanic/Latino; 5 American Indian or Alaska Native, non-Hispanic/Latino; 27 Asian, non-Hispanic/Latino; 304 Hispanic/Latino; 17 Two or more races, non-Hispanic/Latino), 26 international. Average age 32. 788 applicants, 63% accepted, 286 enrolled. *Faculty:* 114 full-time (69 women), 59 part-time/adjunct (39 women). *Financial support:* In 2015–16, 580 students received support, including 41 research assistantships (averaging $19,366 per year), 174 teaching assistantships (averaging $12,557 per year); fellowships, career-related internships or fieldwork, Federal Work-Study, and institutionally sponsored loans also available. Support available to part-time students. Financial award application deadline: 4/1; financial award applicants required to submit FAFSA. In 2015, 388 master's, 26 doctorates awarded. *Degree program information:* Part-time and evening/weekend programs available. Part-time, evening/weekend. Offers adult, professional and community education (MA, PhD); athletic training (MS); community counseling (MA); developmental education (MA, Ed D, PhD); education (M Ed, MA, MS, MSRLS, Ed D, PhD, SSP); educational leadership and school improvement (MA, PhD); educational technology (M Ed); elementary education (M Ed, MA); elementary education - bilingual/bicultural (M Ed, MA); health education (M Ed); instructional leadership (MA); marital, couple and family counseling (MA); physical education (M Ed); professional counseling (MA); reading education (M Ed); recreation and leisure services (MSRLS); recreation management (MSRLS); school counseling (MA); school psychology (SSP); secondary education (M Ed, MA); special education (M Ed); student affairs in higher education (M Ed); therapeutic recreation (MSRLS). *Application deadline:* For fall admission, 2/1 priority date for domestic students, 2/1 for international students; for spring admission, 10/1 priority date for domestic students, 10/1 for international students. Applications are processed on a rolling basis. *Application fee:* $40 ($90 for international students). Electronic applications accepted. *Application Contact:* Dr. Andrea Golato, Dean of Graduate School, 512-245-2581, Fax: 512-245-8365, E-mail: gradcollege@txstate.edu. *Dean*, Dr. Stan Carpenter, 512-245-2150, Fax: 512-245-3158, E-mail: sc33@txstate.edu.

College of Fine Arts and Communication Students: 163 full-time (82 women), 59 part-time (31 women); includes 77 minority (10 Black or African American, non-Hispanic/Latino; 1 American Indian or Alaska Native, non-Hispanic/Latino; 1 Asian, non-Hispanic/Latino; 61 Hispanic/Latino; 4 Two or more races, non-Hispanic/Latino), 22 international. Average age 29. 183 applicants, 61% accepted, 76 enrolled. *Faculty:* 93 full-time (44 women), 16 part-time/adjunct (6 women). *Financial support:* In 2015–16, 161 students received support, including 1 research assistantship (averaging $12,158 per year), 112 teaching assistantships (averaging $10,690 per year); career-related internships or fieldwork, Federal Work-Study, institutionally sponsored loans, scholarships/grants, and unspecified assistantships also available. Support available to part-time students. Financial award application deadline: 3/1; financial award applicants required to submit FAFSA. In 2015, 69 master's awarded. *Degree program information:* Part-time and evening/weekend programs available. Part-time, evening/weekend. Offers communication design (MFA); communication studies (MA); directing (MFA); fine arts and communication (MA, MFA, MM); mass communication (MA); music (MM); music education (MM); playwriting (MA); theatre history, dramatic criticism and dramaturgy (MA). *Application deadline:* For fall admission, 6/15 priority date for domestic students, 6/1 for international students; for spring admission, 10/15 priority date for domestic students, 10/1 for international students. Applications are processed on a rolling basis. *Application fee:* $40 ($90 for international students). Electronic applications accepted. *Application Contact:* Dr. Andrea Golato, Dean of Graduate School, 512-245-2581, Fax: 512-245-8365, E-mail: gradcollege@txstate.edu. *Dean of the College of Fine Arts and Communication*, Dr. John Fleming, 512-245-2308, Fax: 512-245-8386, E-mail: jf18@txstate.edu.

College of Health Professions Students: 311 full-time (233 women), 24 part-time (19 women); includes 136 minority (35 Black or African American, non-Hispanic/Latino; 2 American Indian or Alaska Native, non-Hispanic/Latino; 17 Asian, non-Hispanic/Latino; 76 Hispanic/Latino; 6 Two or more races, non-Hispanic/Latino), 17 international. Average age 28. 663 applicants, 24% accepted, 106 enrolled. *Faculty:* 50 full-time (35 women), 18 part-time/adjunct (10 women). *Financial support:* In 2015–16, 184 students received support, including 3 research assistantships (averaging $10,928 per year), 45 teaching assistantships (averaging $8,461 per year); fellowships, career-related internships or fieldwork, Federal Work-Study, institutionally sponsored loans, scholarships/grants, unspecified assistantships, and stipends also available. Support available to part-time students. Financial award application deadline: 3/1; financial award applicants required to submit FAFSA. In 2015, 85 master's awarded. *Degree program information:* Part-time and evening/weekend programs available. Part-time, evening/weekend. Offers communication disorders (MA, MSCD); family nurse practitioner (MS); health information management (MHIHIM); health professions (MA, MHA, MHIHIM, MS, MSCD, DPT); healthcare administration (MHA); physical therapy (DPT). *Application deadline:* For fall admission, 2/1 priority date for domestic and international students; for spring admission, 10/1 for domestic and international students. Applications are processed on a rolling basis. *Application fee:* $40 ($90 for international students). Electronic applications accepted. *Application Contact:* Dr. Andrea Golato, Dean of Graduate School, 512-245-2581, Fax: 512-245-8365, E-mail: gradcollege@txstate.edu. *Dean*, Dr. Ruth Welborn, 512-245-3300, Fax: 512-245-3791, E-mail: mw01@txstate.edu.

College of Liberal Arts Students: 463 full-time (271 women), 337 part-time (190 women); includes 269 minority (51 Black or African American, non-Hispanic/Latino; 1 American Indian or Alaska Native, non-Hispanic/Latino; 14 Asian, non-Hispanic/Latino; 191 Hispanic/Latino; 12 Two or more races, non-Hispanic/Latino), 34 international. Average age 31. 773 applicants, 53% accepted, 240 enrolled. *Faculty:* 208 full-time (86 women), 9 part-time/adjunct (4 women). *Financial support:* In 2015–16, 489 students received support, including 27 research assistantships (averaging $14,885 per year), 252 teaching assistantships (averaging $13,710 per year); fellowships, career-related internships or fieldwork, Federal Work-Study, institutionally sponsored loans, scholarships/grants, and unspecified assistantships also available. Support available to part-time students. Financial award application deadline: 3/1; financial award applicants required to submit FAFSA. In 2015, 249 master's, 8 doctorates awarded. *Degree program information:* Part-time and evening/weekend programs available. Part-time, evening/weekend. Offers anthropology (MA); applied philosophy and ethics (MA); applied sociology (MS); creative writing (MFA); dementia and aging studies (MS); geographic education (PhD); geographic information science (PhD); geography (MAG, MS, PhD); history (M Ed, MA); human resources in public administration (MPA); international relations (MPA); international studies (MA); legal and judicial administration (MPA); legal studies (MA); liberal arts (M Ed, MA, MAG, MAIS, MFA, MPA, MS, MSIS, PhD); literature (MA); political science (MA); psychological research (MA); public finance administration (MPA); rhetoric and composition (MA); sociology (MA); Spanish (MA); sustainability (MAIS, MSIS); technical communication (MA); urban and environmental planning (MPA). *Application deadline:* For fall admission, 6/15 priority date for domestic students, 6/1 for international students; for spring admission, 10/15 priority date for domestic students, 10/1 for international students. Applications are processed on a rolling basis. *Application fee:* $40 ($90 for international students). Electronic applications accepted. *Application Contact:* Dr. Andrea Golato, Dean of Graduate School, 512-245-2581, Fax: 512-245-8365, E-mail: gradcollege@txstate.edu. *Dean*, Dr. Michael Hennessy, 512-245-2317, Fax: 512-245-8291, E-mail: liberalarts@txstate.edu.

College of Science and Engineering Students: 361 full-time (162 women), 160 part-time (65 women); includes 94 minority (19 Black or African American, non-Hispanic/Latino; 2 American Indian or Alaska Native, non-Hispanic/Latino; 19 Asian, non-Hispanic/Latino; 49 Hispanic/Latino; 5 Two or more races, non-Hispanic/Latino), 215 international. Average age 29. 496 applicants, 53% accepted, 150 enrolled. *Faculty:* 142 full-time (39 women), 6 part-time/adjunct (0 women). *Financial support:* In 2015–16, 183 students received support, including 77 research assistantships (averaging $15,508 per year), 214 teaching assistantships (averaging $17,380 per year); career-related internships or fieldwork, Federal Work-Study, institutionally sponsored loans, scholarships/grants, health care benefits, unspecified assistantships, and laboratory instructorships also available. Support available to part-time students. Financial award application deadline: 3/1; financial award applicants required to submit FAFSA. In 2015, 140 master's, 13 doctorates awarded. *Degree program information:* Part-time and evening/weekend programs available. Part-time, evening/weekend. Offers applied mathematics (MS); aquatic resources (MS, PhD); biochemistry (MS); biology (MA, MS); chemistry (MA, MS); computer science (MA, MS); electrical engineering (MS); industrial engineering (MS); manufacturing engineering (MS); material physics (MS); materials science, engineering, and commercialization (PhD); mathematics (M Ed, MS); mathematics education (PhD); middle school mathematics teaching (M Ed); physics (MS); population and conservation biology (MS); science and engineering (M Ed, MA, MS, MSIS, PhD); software engineering (MS); technology management (MS); wildlife ecology (MS). *Application deadline:* For fall admission, 6/15 for domestic students, 6/1 for international students; for spring admission, 10/15 for domestic students, 10/1 for international students. Applications are processed on a rolling basis. *Application fee:* $40 ($90 for international students). Electronic applications accepted. *Application Contact:* Dr. Andrea Golato, Dean of Graduate School, 512-245-2581, Fax: 512-245-8365, E-mail: gradcollege@txstate.edu. *Interim Dean*, Dr. Robert Habingreither, 512-245-2119, Fax: 512-245-8095, E-mail: rh03@txstate.edu.

Emmett and Miriam McCoy College of Business Administration Students: 199 full-time (94 women), 201 part-time (95 women); includes 117 minority (20 Black or African American, non-Hispanic/Latino; 1 American Indian or Alaska Native, non-Hispanic/Latino; 29 Asian, non-Hispanic/Latino; 61 Hispanic/Latino; 6 Two or more races, non-Hispanic/Latino), 26 international. Average age 30. 292 applicants, 55% accepted, 111 enrolled. *Faculty:* 52 full-time (21 women), 8 part-time/adjunct (1 woman). *Financial support:* In 2015–16, 190 students received support, including 4 research assistantships (averaging $11,429 per year), 35 teaching assistantships (averaging $12,237 per year); Federal Work-Study, institutionally sponsored loans, scholarships/grants, health care benefits, and unspecified assistantships also available. Support available to part-time students. Financial award application deadline: 3/1; financial award applicants required to submit FAFSA. In 2015, 150 master's awarded. *Degree program information:* Part-time programs available. Part-time. Offers accounting (M Acy); accounting and information technology (MS); business administration (M Acy, MBA, MS); human resource management (MS). *Application deadline:* For fall admission, 6/1 for domestic and international students; for spring admission, 10/1 for domestic and international students. Applications are processed on a rolling basis. *Application fee:* $40 ($90 for international students). Electronic applications accepted. *Application Contact:* Dr. Andrea Golato, Dean of Graduate School, 512-245-2581, Fax: 512-245-8365, E-mail: gradcollege@txstate.edu. *Dean of the College of Business Administration*, Dr. Denise Smart, 512-245-2311, Fax: 512-245-8375, E-mail: ds37@txstate.edu.

TEXAS TECH UNIVERSITY, Lubbock, TX 79409

General Information State-supported, coed, university. CGS member. *Enrollment:* 35,859 graduate, professional, and undergraduate students; 4,202 full-time matriculated graduate/professional students (2,001 women), 2,103 part-time matriculated graduate/professional students (1,149 women). *Enrollment by degree level:* 3,337 master's, 2,968 doctoral. *Graduate faculty:* 1,326 full-time (499 women), 201 part-time/adjunct (111 women). Tuition, state resident: full-time $6477; part-time $269.89 per credit hour. Tuition, nonresident: full-time $15,837; part-time $659.89 per credit hour. *Required fees:* $2751; $36.50 per credit hour. $937.50 per semester. Tuition and fees vary according to course level. *Graduate housing:* Room and/or apartments available on a first-come, first-served basis to single students; on-campus housing not available to married students. Typical cost: $4510 per year ($7955 including board). Room and board charges vary according to board plan and housing facility selected. Housing application deadline: 5/1. *Student services:* Campus employment opportunities, campus safety program, career counseling, exercise/wellness program, free psychological counseling, grant writing training, international student services, low-cost health insurance, multicultural affairs office, services for students with disabilities, teacher training, writing training. *Library:* Texas Tech Library plus 3 others. *Collection:* Books: 2.8 million (physical), 152,941 (digital/electronic); Serial titles: 3,340 (physical), 155,013 (digital/electronic); Databases: 382. Weekly public service hours: 146; study areas open 24 hours, 5–7 days a week; students can reserve study rooms. *Research affiliation:* National Cattlemen's Beef Association (development and production of beef), U.S. Department of Agriculture (USDA) (food safety; development and production in agriculture), U.S. Department of Energy (research and development in wind energy), U.S. Department of Energy (research and development in wind energy), U.S. Department of Defense/U.S. Army (pulsed power and nanotechnology for defense applications), Bayer Crop Science (cotton genetics and production).

Computer facilities: Computer purchase and lease plans are available. 2,084 computers available on campus for general student use. A campuswide network can be accessed from student residence rooms and from off campus. Online class registration,

online degree plans, accounts, transcripts, schedules, financial aid, course and instructor evaluations are available.
Website: http://www.ttu.edu/

General Application Contact: Shelby Cearley, Director of Graduate and International Admissions, 806-742-2787, Fax: 806-742-4038, E-mail: graduate.admissions@ttu.edu.

GRADUATE UNITS

Graduate School Students: 3,636 full-time (1,738 women), 2,097 part-time (1,147 women); includes 1,149 minority (244 Black or African American, non-Hispanic/Latino; 17 American Indian or Alaska Native, non-Hispanic/Latino; 94 Asian, non-Hispanic/Latino; 688 Hispanic/Latino; 5 Native Hawaiian or other Pacific Islander, non-Hispanic/Latino; 101 Two or more races, non-Hispanic/Latino), 1,623 international. Average age 31. 6,584 applicants, 39% accepted, 1543 enrolled. *Faculty:* 1,289 full-time (488 women), 199 part-time/adjunct (111 women). *Financial support:* In 2015–16, 3,755 students received support, including 3,659 fellowships (averaging $3,210 per year), 1,117 research assistantships (averaging $12,057 per year), 1,649 teaching assistantships (averaging $13,052 per year); career-related internships or fieldwork, Federal Work-Study, scholarships/grants, traineeships, health care benefits, and unspecified assistantships also available. Support available to part-time students. Financial award application deadline: 4/15; financial award applicants required to submit FAFSA. In 2015, 1,429 master's, 332 doctorates awarded. *Degree program information:* Part-time and evening/weekend programs available. Part-time, evening/weekend, online learning. Offers arid land studies (MS); biotechnology (MS); heritage management (MS); interdisciplinary studies (MA, MS); museum science (MA); wind science and engineering (PhD). *Application deadline:* For fall admission, 6/1 priority date for domestic students, 1/15 for international students; for spring admission, 9/1 priority date for domestic students, 6/15 for international students. Applications are processed on a rolling basis. *Application fee:* $60. Electronic applications accepted. *Application Contact:* Shannon Samson, Coordinator of Graduate School Recruitment, 806-834-5201, Fax: 806-742-1746, E-mail: gradschool@ttu.edu. *Vice Provost for Graduate and Postdoctoral Affairs/Dean of the Graduate School*, Dr. Mark Sheridan, 806-834-5537, Fax: 806-742-1746, E-mail: mark.sheridan@ttu.edu.

College of Agricultural Sciences and Natural Resources Students: 274 full-time (135 women), 116 part-time (51 women); includes 39 minority (6 Black or African American, non-Hispanic/Latino; 1 Asian, non-Hispanic/Latino; 26 Hispanic/Latino; 6 Two or more races, non-Hispanic/Latino), 105 international. Average age 29. 260 applicants, 53% accepted, 95 enrolled. *Faculty:* 98 full-time (30 women), 18 part-time/adjunct (4 women). *Financial support:* In 2015–16, 341 students received support, including 273 fellowships (averaging $3,021 per year), 241 research assistantships (averaging $12,172 per year), 57 teaching assistantships (averaging $6,700 per year); health care benefits and unspecified assistantships also available. Financial award application deadline: 12/1; financial award applicants required to submit FAFSA. In 2015, 88 master's, 31 doctorates awarded. 100% online, blended/hybrid learning. Offers agribusiness (MAB); agricultural and applied economics (MS, PhD); agricultural communications (MS); agricultural communications and education (PhD); agricultural education (MS, Ed D); agricultural sciences and natural resources (MAB, MLA, MS, Ed D, PhD); animal science (MS, PhD); food science (MS); horticulture science (MS); landscape architecture (MLA); plant and soil science (MS, PhD); wildlife, aquatic, and wildlands science and management (MS, PhD). *Application deadline:* For fall admission, 6/1 priority date for domestic students, 1/15 priority date for international students; for spring admission, 9/1 priority date for domestic students, 6/15 priority date for international students. Applications are processed on a rolling basis. *Application fee:* $60. Electronic applications accepted. *Application Contact:* Dr. Michael Ballou, Associate Dean for Research, 806-834-6513, Fax: 806-742-2836, E-mail: michael.ballou@ttu.edu. *Professor/Dean*, Dr. Michael L. Galyean, 806-742-2808, Fax: 806-742-2836, E-mail: michael.galyean@ttu.edu.

College of Architecture Students: 86 full-time (23 women), 26 part-time (2 women); includes 50 minority (1 Black or African American, non-Hispanic/Latino; 44 Hispanic/Latino; 1 Native Hawaiian or other Pacific Islander, non-Hispanic/Latino; 4 Two or more races, non-Hispanic/Latino), 19 international. Average age 25. 92 applicants, 65% accepted, 37 enrolled. *Faculty:* 43 full-time (12 women), 6 part-time/adjunct (1 woman). *Financial support:* In 2015–16, 72 students received support, including 73 fellowships (averaging $5,193 per year), 2 research assistantships (averaging $7,800 per year); teaching assistantships, career-related internships or fieldwork, Federal Work-Study, institutionally sponsored loans, scholarships/grants, traineeships, health care benefits, and unspecified assistantships also available. Support available to part-time students. Financial award application deadline: 3/1; financial award applicants required to submit FAFSA. In 2015, 71 master's, 1 doctorate awarded. *Degree program information:* Part-time programs available. Part-time. Offers architecture (M Arch, MS); land use planning, management, and design (PhD). *Application deadline:* For fall admission, 6/1 priority date for domestic students, 1/15 priority date for international students; for spring admission, 9/1 priority date for domestic students, 6/15 priority date for international students. Applications are processed on a rolling basis. *Application fee:* $60. Electronic applications accepted. *Application Contact:* Jeff Rammage, Graduate Advisor, 806-742-3169 Ext. 247, Fax: 806-742-1400, E-mail: jeffrey.rammage@ttu.edu. *Dean*, Prof. Andrew Vernooy, 806-742-3136, Fax: 806-742-1400, E-mail: andrew.vernooy@ttu.edu.

College of Arts and Sciences Students: 1,072 full-time (532 women), 224 part-time (124 women); includes 216 minority (40 Black or African American, non-Hispanic/Latino; 5 American Indian or Alaska Native, non-Hispanic/Latino; 24 Asian, non-Hispanic/Latino; 124 Hispanic/Latino; 1 Native Hawaiian or other Pacific Islander, non-Hispanic/Latino; 22 Two or more races, non-Hispanic/Latino), 416 international. Average age 29. 1,460 applicants, 36% accepted, 333 enrolled. *Faculty:* 483 full-time (177 women), 46 part-time/adjunct (21 women). *Financial support:* In 2015–16, 1,126 students received support, including 873 fellowships (averaging $2,580 per year), 325 research assistantships (averaging $8,826 per year), 881 teaching assistantships (averaging $13,404 per year); career-related internships or fieldwork, Federal Work-Study, institutionally sponsored loans, scholarships/grants, traineeships, health care benefits, and unspecified assistantships also available. Support available to part-time students. Financial award application deadline: 4/15; financial award applicants required to submit FAFSA. In 2015, 256 master's, 91 doctorates awarded. *Degree program information:* Part-time and evening/weekend programs available. Part-time, evening/weekend. Offers anthropology (MA); applied linguistics (MA); applied physics (MS); arts and sciences (MA, MPA, MS, MSW, PSM, PhD); atmospheric science (MS); biology (MS, PhD); chemical biology (MS); chemistry (MS, PhD); classics (MA); clinical psychology (PhD); counseling psychology (MA, PhD); economics (MA, PhD); English (MA, PhD); environmental sustainability and natural resources management (PSM); environmental toxicology (MS, PhD); forensic sciences (MS); general experimental psychology (MA, PhD); geography (MS); geosciences (MS, PhD); German (MA); history (MA, PhD); kinesiology (MS); languages and cultures (MA); mathematics (MA, MS, PhD); microbiology (MS); philosophy (MA); physics (MS, PhD); political science (MA, PhD); psychology (MA); public administration (MPA); Romance languages (MA); social work (MSW); sociology (MA); Spanish (PhD); sport management (MS); statistics (MS); technical communication (MA); technical communication and rhetoric (PhD); zoology (MS, PhD). *Application deadline:* For fall admission, 6/1 priority date for domestic students, 1/15 priority date for international students; for spring admission, 9/1 priority date for domestic students, 6/15 priority date for international students. Applications are processed on a rolling basis. *Application fee:* $60. Electronic applications accepted. *Application Contact:* Dr. Jorge Iber, Associate Dean, 806-742-3833, Fax: 806-742-3893, E-mail: jorge.iber@ttu.edu. *Dean*, Dr. W. Brent Lindquist, 806-742-3831, Fax: 806-742-3893, E-mail: brent.lindquist@ttu.edu.

College of Education Students: 338 full-time (260 women), 772 part-time (574 women); includes 348 minority (101 Black or African American, non-Hispanic/Latino; 6 American Indian or Alaska Native, non-Hispanic/Latino; 9 Asian, non-Hispanic/Latino; 209 Hispanic/Latino; 23 Two or more races, non-Hispanic/Latino), 85 international. Average age 36. 636 applicants, 59% accepted, 299 enrolled. *Faculty:* 100 full-time (66 women), 46 part-time/adjunct (40 women). *Financial support:* In 2015–16, 656 students received support, including 630 fellowships (averaging $3,111 per year), 111 research assistantships (averaging $11,265 per year), 3 teaching assistantships (averaging $4,200 per year); career-related internships or fieldwork, Federal Work-Study, institutionally sponsored loans, scholarships/grants, traineeships, health care benefits, and unspecified assistantships also available. Support available to part-time students. Financial award application deadline: 2/15; financial award applicants required to submit FAFSA. In 2015, 183 master's, 69 doctorates awarded. *Degree program information:* Part-time and evening/weekend programs available. Part-time, evening/weekend. Offers bilingual education (M Ed); counselor education (M Ed, PhD); curriculum and instruction (M Ed, PhD); distance education (M Ed); education (M Ed, MS, Ed D, PhD); educational leadership (M Ed, Ed D, PhD); educational psychology (M Ed, PhD); elementary education (M Ed); higher education (M Ed, Ed D); higher education research (PhD); instructional technology (M Ed, Ed D); language/literacy education (M Ed); multidisciplinary science (MS); secondary education (M Ed); special education (M Ed, Ed D, PhD). *Application deadline:* For fall admission, 6/1 priority date for domestic students, 1/15 priority date for international students; for spring admission, 9/1 priority date for domestic students, 6/15 priority date for international students. Applications are processed on a rolling basis. *Application fee:* $60. Electronic applications accepted. *Application Contact:* Kellie Dreyer, Coordinator, 806-834-3977, Fax: 806-742-2179, E-mail: kellie.dreyer@ttu.edu. *Dean*, Dr. Scott Ridley, 806-834-1431, Fax: 806-742-2179, E-mail: scott.ridley@ttu.edu.

College of Human Sciences Students: 299 full-time (188 women), 144 part-time (100 women); includes 76 minority (16 Black or African American, non-Hispanic/Latino; 6 Asian, non-Hispanic/Latino; 43 Hispanic/Latino; 11 Two or more races, non-Hispanic/Latino), 122 international. Average age 31. 304 applicants, 57% accepted, 113 enrolled. *Faculty:* 100 full-time (68 women), 24 part-time/adjunct (18 women). *Financial support:* In 2015–16, 346 students received support, including 327 fellowships (averaging $4,693 per year), 82 research assistantships (averaging $10,057 per year), 147 teaching assistantships (averaging $11,973 per year); institutionally sponsored loans, scholarships/grants, and unspecified assistantships also available. Financial award application deadline: 2/1; financial award applicants required to submit FAFSA. In 2015, 69 master's, 34 doctorates awarded. *Degree program information:* Part-time programs available. Part-time, online learning. Offers environmental design (MS); family and consumer sciences education (MS, PhD); gerontology (MS); hospitality administration (PhD); hospitality and retail management (MS); human development and family studies (MS, PhD); human sciences (MS, PhD); interior and environmental design (PhD); marriage and family therapy (MS, PhD); nutritional sciences (MS, PhD); personal financial planning (MS, PhD). *Application deadline:* For fall admission, 6/1 priority date for domestic students, 1/15 priority date for international students; for spring admission, 9/1 priority date for domestic students, 6/15 priority date for international students. Applications are processed on a rolling basis. *Application fee:* $60. Electronic applications accepted. *Application Contact:* Prof. Mitzi Lauderdale, Associate Dean for Students, 806-834-0529, Fax: 806-742-1849, E-mail: mitzi.lauderdale@ttu.edu. *Dean*, Dr. Linda C. Hoover, 806-742-3031, Fax: 806-742-1849, E-mail: linda.hoover@ttu.edu.

College of Media and Communication Students: 87 full-time (54 women), 73 part-time (48 women); includes 34 minority (5 Black or African American, non-Hispanic/Latino; 25 Hispanic/Latino; 1 Native Hawaiian or other Pacific Islander, non-Hispanic/Latino; 3 Two or more races, non-Hispanic/Latino), 16 international. Average age 27. 139 applicants, 67% accepted, 67 enrolled. *Faculty:* 54 full-time (22 women), 8 part-time/adjunct (6 women). *Financial support:* In 2015–16, 111 students received support, including 75 fellowships (averaging $4,480 per year), 40 research assistantships (averaging $7,606 per year), 78 teaching assistantships (averaging $8,064 per year); career-related internships or fieldwork, scholarships/grants, and unspecified assistantships also available. Support available to part-time students. Financial award application deadline: 4/15; financial award applicants required to submit FAFSA. In 2015, 57 master's, 9 doctorates awarded. *Degree program information:* Part-time and evening/weekend programs available. Part-time, evening/weekend, 100% online. Offers communication studies (MA); mass communications (MA); media and communications (PhD). *Application deadline:* For fall admission, 6/1 priority date for domestic students, 1/15 priority date for international students; for spring admission, 9/1 priority date for domestic students, 6/15 priority date for international students. Applications are processed on a rolling basis. *Application fee:* $60. Electronic applications accepted. *Application Contact:* Shannon Samson, Coordinator of Graduate School Recruitment, 806-834-5201, Fax: 806-742-1746, E-mail: gradschool@ttu.edu. *Graduate Director*, Dr. Coy Callison, 806-834-5344, E-mail: coy.callison@ttu.edu.

College of Visual and Performing Arts Students: 229 full-time (127 women), 105 part-time (64 women); includes 57 minority (11 Black or African American, non-Hispanic/Latino; 2 Asian, non-Hispanic/Latino; 35 Hispanic/Latino; 9 Two or more races, non-Hispanic/Latino), 57 international. Average age 32. 240 applicants, 54% accepted, 78 enrolled. *Faculty:* 115 full-time (48 women), 12 part-time/adjunct (8 women). *Financial support:* In 2015–16, 308 students received support, including 286 fellowships (averaging $3,052 per year), 10 research assistantships (averaging $10,208 per year), 190 teaching assistantships (averaging $7,969 per year); Federal Work-Study, institutionally sponsored loans, scholarships/grants, health care benefits, tuition waivers (partial), and unspecified assistantships also available. Financial award application deadline: 2/1; financial award applicants required to submit FAFSA. In 2015, 62 master's, 19 doctorates awarded. *Degree program information:* Part-time programs available. Part-time. Offers art (MFA); art education (MAE); art history (MA);

fine arts (PhD); music (MM, DMA); music education (MM Ed); theatre arts (MA, MFA); visual and performing arts (MA, MAE, MFA, MM, MM Ed, DMA, PhD). *Application deadline:* For fall admission, 6/1 priority date for domestic students, 1/15 priority date for international students; for spring admission, 9/1 priority date for domestic students, 6/15 priority date for international students. Applications are processed on a rolling basis. *Application fee:* $60. Electronic applications accepted. *Application Contact:* Shannon Samson, Coordinator of Graduate School Recruitment, 806-834-5201, Fax: 806-742-1746, E-mail: gradschool@ttu.edu. *Interim Dean*, Prof. Andrew Martin, 806-834-3748, Fax: 806-742-0695, E-mail: andrew.martin@ttu.edu.

Edward E. Whitacre Jr. College of Engineering Students: 712 full-time (172 women), 180 part-time (31 women); includes 86 minority (16 Black or African American, non-Hispanic/Latino; 1 American Indian or Alaska Native, non-Hispanic/Latino; 22 Asian, non-Hispanic/Latino; 42 Hispanic/Latino; 5 Two or more races, non-Hispanic/Latino), 608 international. Average age 28. 2,202 applicants, 25% accepted, 194 enrolled. *Faculty:* 156 full-time (25 women), 17 part-time/adjunct (2 women). *Financial support:* In 2015–16, 648 students received support, including 581 fellowships (averaging $2,540 per year), 272 research assistantships (averaging $17,514 per year), 225 teaching assistantships (averaging $18,464 per year). Financial award application deadline: 4/15; financial award applicants required to submit FAFSA. In 2015, 207 master's, 59 doctorates awarded. *Degree program information:* Part-time and evening/weekend programs available. Part-time, evening/weekend, online learning. Offers bioengineering (MS); chemical engineering (MS Ch E, PhD); civil engineering (MSCE, PhD); computer science (MS, PhD); electrical engineering (MSEE, PhD); engineering (M Engr, MENVEGR, MS, MS Ch E, MSCE, MSEE, MSIE, MSME, MSPE, MSSEM, PhD); environmental engineering (MENVEGR); industrial engineering (MSIE, PhD); mechanical engineering (MSME, PhD); petroleum engineering (MSPE, PhD); software engineering (MS); systems and engineering management (MSSEM, PhD). *Application deadline:* For fall admission, 6/1 priority date for domestic students, 1/15 priority date for international students; for spring admission, 9/1 priority date for domestic students, 6/15 priority date for international students. Applications are processed on a rolling basis. *Application fee:* $60. Electronic applications accepted. *Application Contact:* Dr. Stephen Ekwaro-Osire, Associate Dean of Research and Graduate Programs, Edward E. Whitacre Jr. College of Engineering, 806-742-3451, Fax: 806-742-3493, E-mail: stephen.ekwaro-osire@ttu.edu. *Dean, Edward E. Whitacre Jr. College of Engineering*, Dr. Albert Sacco, Jr., 806-742-3451, Fax: 806-742-3493, E-mail: al.sacco-jr@ttu.edu.

Rawls College of Business Administration Students: 931 full-time (350 women); includes 226 minority (36 Black or African American, non-Hispanic/Latino; 3 American Indian or Alaska Native, non-Hispanic/Latino; 35 Asian, non-Hispanic/Latino; 132 Hispanic/Latino; 1 Native Hawaiian or other Pacific Islander, non-Hispanic/Latino; 19 Two or more races, non-Hispanic/Latino), 172 international. Average age 29. 1,041 applicants, 38% accepted, 283 enrolled. *Faculty:* 67 full-time (8 women). *Financial support:* In 2015–16, 157 students received support, including 25 research assistantships (averaging $22,725 per year), 27 teaching assistantships (averaging $22,725 per year); fellowships, career-related internships or fieldwork, Federal Work-Study, scholarships/grants, health care benefits, and unspecified assistantships also available. Financial award applicants required to submit FAFSA. In 2015, 363 master's, 13 doctorates awarded. *Degree program information:* Evening/weekend programs available. Evening/weekend. Offers accounting (MSA, PhD); business statistics (MS, PhD); data science (MS); finance (MS, PhD); general business (MBA); healthcare management (MS); information systems and operations management (PhD); management (PhD); marketing (PhD); STEM (MBA). *Application deadline:* For fall admission, 7/1 priority date for domestic students, 1/15 for international students; for spring admission, 12/1 priority date for domestic students, 6/15 for international students; for summer admission, 5/1 for domestic students. Applications are processed on a rolling basis. *Application fee:* $60. Electronic applications accepted. *Application Contact:* Chathry Keaton, Applications Manager, Graduate and Professional Programs, 806-742-3184, Fax: 806-742-3958, E-mail: rawlsgrad@ttu.edu. *Dean*, Dr. Paul Goebel, 806-742-3188, Fax: 806-742-1092, E-mail: paul.goebel@ttu.edu.

School of Law Students: 566 full-time (263 women), 6 part-time (2 women); includes 147 minority (12 Black or African American, non-Hispanic/Latino; 1 American Indian or Alaska Native, non-Hispanic/Latino; 19 Asian, non-Hispanic/Latino; 71 Hispanic/Latino; 2 Native Hawaiian or other Pacific Islander, non-Hispanic/Latino; 42 Two or more races, non-Hispanic/Latino), 18 international. Average age 26. 1,222 applicants, 55% accepted, 182 enrolled. *Faculty:* 37 full-time (11 women), 2 part-time/adjunct (0 women). *Financial support:* In 2015–16, 87 students received support. Research assistantships, teaching assistantships, Federal Work-Study, scholarships/grants, tuition waivers, and tutorships available. Financial award application deadline: 5/1; financial award applicants required to submit FAFSA. In 2015, 8 master's awarded. Offers law (JD); United States legal studies (LL M). *Application deadline:* For fall admission, 3/1 priority date for domestic and international students. Applications are processed on a rolling basis. *Application fee:* $50. Electronic applications accepted. *Application Contact:* Stephen M. Perez, Associate Dean for Admissions and Financial Aid, 806-834-5024, E-mail: admissions.law@ttu.edu. *Dean/Professor of Law*, Darby Dickerson, 806-834-5421, Fax: 806-742-4014, E-mail: darby.dickerson@ttu.edu.

TEXAS TECH UNIVERSITY HEALTH SCIENCES CENTER, Lubbock, TX 79430

General Information State-supported, coed, graduate-only institution. *Graduate housing:* On-campus housing not available.

GRADUATE UNITS

Graduate School of Biomedical Sciences Offers biomedical sciences (MS, PhD); biotechnology (MS); pharmaceutical sciences (MS, PhD). Electronic applications accepted.

School of Health Professions Students: 689 full-time (520 women), 347 part-time (203 women); includes 374 minority (56 Black or African American, non-Hispanic/Latino; 5 American Indian or Alaska Native, non-Hispanic/Latino; 94 Asian, non-Hispanic/Latino; 194 Hispanic/Latino; 4 Native Hawaiian or other Pacific Islander, non-Hispanic/Latino; 21 Two or more races, non-Hispanic/Latino), 1 international. Average age 30. 2,201 applicants, 22% accepted, 480 enrolled. *Faculty:* 69 full-time (38 women), 4 part-time/adjunct (3 women). *Financial support:* Research assistantships, teaching assistantships, career-related internships or fieldwork, institutionally sponsored loans, scholarships/grants, and unspecified assistantships available. Financial award application deadline: 9/1; financial award applicants required to submit FAFSA. In 2015, 255 master's, 101 doctorates awarded. Online learning. Offers athletic training (MAT); clinical practice management (MS); health professions (MAT, MOT, MPAS, MRC, MS, Au D, DPT, PhD, Sc D, TDPT); molecular pathology (MS); occupational therapy (MOT); physical therapy (DPT, Sc D, TDPT); physician assistant studies (MPAS); rehabilitation counseling (MRC); rehabilitation sciences (PhD); speech, language and hearing sciences (MS, Au D, PhD). *Application deadline:* Applications are processed on a rolling basis. *Application fee:* $40. Electronic applications accepted. *Application Contact:* Lindsay Johnson, Associate Dean for Admissions and Student Affairs, 806-743-3220, Fax: 806-743-2994, E-mail: lindsay.johnson@ttuhsc.edu. *Associate Dean for Admissions and Student Affairs*, Lindsay R. Johnson, 806-743-3220, Fax: 806-743-2994, E-mail: lindsay.johnson@ttuhsc.edu.

School of Medicine Offers medicine (MD). Open only to residents of Texas, eastern New Mexico, and southwestern Oklahoma; MD/PhD offered jointly with Texas Tech University; JD/MD with School of Law. Electronic applications accepted.

School of Nursing ***Degree program information:*** Part-time programs available. Part-time, online learning. Offers acute care nurse practitioner (MSN, Certificate); administration (MSN); advanced practice (DNP); education (MSN); executive leadership (DNP); family nurse practitioner (MSN, Certificate); geriatric nurse practitioner (MSN, Certificate); pediatric nurse practitioner (MSN, Certificate).

TEXAS WESLEYAN UNIVERSITY, Fort Worth, TX 76105-1536

General Information Independent-religious, coed, comprehensive institution. *Enrollment:* 2,647 graduate, professional, and undergraduate students; 456 full-time matriculated graduate/professional students (245 women), 212 part-time matriculated graduate/professional students (183 women). *Enrollment by degree level:* 555 master's, 112 doctoral, 1 other advanced degree. *Graduate faculty:* 10 full-time (7 women), 46 part-time/adjunct (23 women). *Graduate housing:* Room and/or apartments available on a first-come, first-served basis to single students; on-campus housing not available to married students. Typical cost: $5072 per year ($8651 including board). Housing application deadline: 8/12. *Student services:* Campus employment opportunities, campus safety program, career counseling, exercise/wellness program, free psychological counseling, international student services, low-cost health insurance, multicultural affairs office, services for students with disabilities, teacher training, writing training. *Library:* Eunice and James L. West Library plus 1 other. *Collection:* Books: 118,901 (physical), 140,706 (digital/electronic); Serial titles: 1,499 (physical), 114,869 (digital/electronic); Databases: 85. Weekly public service hours: 75.

Computer facilities: 605 computers available on campus for general student use. A campuswide network can be accessed from student residence rooms and from off campus. Online class registration is available.
Website: http://www.txwes.edu/

General Application Contact: Beth Hargrove, Director of Graduate Admissions, 817-531-4930, Fax: 817-531-4261, E-mail: bhargrove@txwes.edu.

GRADUATE UNITS

Graduate Programs Students: 456 full-time (245 women), 212 part-time (183 women); includes 235 minority (81 Black or African American, non-Hispanic/Latino; 5 American Indian or Alaska Native, non-Hispanic/Latino; 33 Asian, non-Hispanic/Latino; 99 Hispanic/Latino; 17 Two or more races, non-Hispanic/Latino), 40 international. Average age 33. 766 applicants, 32% accepted, 206 enrolled. *Faculty:* 35 full-time (15 women), 15 part-time/adjunct (9 women). *Financial support:* In 2015–16, 8 students received support. Fellowships with tuition reimbursements available, career-related internships or fieldwork, Federal Work-Study, institutionally sponsored loans, scholarships/grants, and tuition waivers (full and partial) available. Support available to part-time students. Financial award application deadline: 3/15; financial award applicants required to submit FAFSA. In 2015, 192 master's, 28 doctorates awarded. *Degree program information:* Part-time and evening/weekend programs available. Part-time, evening/weekend, 100% online. Offers business administration (MBA); education (M Ed, Ed D); marriage and family therapy (MSMFT, PhD); nurse anesthesia (MHS, MSNA, DNAP); professional counseling (MA); school counseling (MS). *Application deadline:* Applications are processed on a rolling basis. *Application fee:* $58. Electronic applications accepted. *Application Contact:* Beth Hargrove, Director of Graduate Admissions, 817-531-4498, E-mail: bhargrove@txwes.edu. *Provost*, Dr. Allen Henderson, 817-531-4405, Fax: 817-531-4499, E-mail: ahenderson@txwes.edu.

TEXAS WOMAN'S UNIVERSITY, Denton, TX 76201

General Information State-supported, coed, primarily women, university. CGS member. *Enrollment:* 15,286 graduate, professional, and undergraduate students; 1,936 full-time matriculated graduate/professional students (1,699 women), 3,270 part-time matriculated graduate/professional students (2,886 women). *Enrollment by degree level:* 3,887 master's, 1,095 doctoral, 111 other advanced degrees. *Graduate faculty:* 335 full-time (240 women), 143 part-time/adjunct (111 women). *International tuition:* $11,465 full-time. Tuition, state resident: full-time $4380; part-time $243 per credit hour. Tuition, nonresident: full-time $11,400; part-time $633 per credit hour. *Required fees:* $1778; $99 per credit hour. $283 per semester. One-time fee: $50. Tuition and fees vary according to course load and program. *Graduate housing:* Rooms and/or apartments available on a first-come, first-served basis to single and married students. Typical cost: $3700 per year ($7443 including board) for single students; $3700 per year ($7443 including board) for married students. Room and board charges vary according to board plan and housing facility selected. Housing application deadline: 2/18. *Student services:* Campus employment opportunities, campus safety program, career counseling, exercise/wellness program, free psychological counseling, grant writing training, international student services, low-cost health insurance, multicultural affairs office, services for students with disabilities, teacher training, writing training. *Library:* Blagg-Huey Library. *Collection:* Books: 597,142 (physical), 214,621 (digital/electronic); Databases: 219. Weekly public service hours: 116; students can reserve study rooms.

Computer facilities: 1,000 computers available on campus for general student use. A campuswide network can be accessed from student residence rooms and from off campus. Online class registration is available.
Website: http://www.twu.edu/

General Application Contact: Dr. Samuel Wheeler, Assistant Director of Admissions, 940-898-3188, Fax: 940-898-3081, E-mail: wheelersr@twu.edu.

GRADUATE UNITS

Graduate School Students: 1,936 full-time (1,699 women), 3,270 part-time (2,886 women); includes 2,312 minority (917 Black or African American, non-Hispanic/Latino; 23 American Indian or Alaska Native, non-Hispanic/Latino; 515 Asian, non-Hispanic/Latino; 711 Hispanic/Latino; 8 Native Hawaiian or other Pacific Islander, non-Hispanic/Latino; 138 Two or more races, non-Hispanic/Latino), 198 international. Average age 34. 3,288 applicants, 50% accepted, 1220 enrolled. *Faculty:* 335 full-time (240 women), 143 part-time/adjunct (111 women). *Financial support:* In 2015–16, 1,797 students received support, including 299 research assistantships (averaging $12,044 per year), 100 teaching assistantships (averaging $12,044 per year); career-related internships or fieldwork, Federal Work-Study, institutionally sponsored loans, scholarships/grants, traineeships, health care benefits, tuition waivers (partial), and unspecified assistantships also available. Support available to part-time students. Financial award application deadline: 3/1; financial award applicants required to submit FAFSA. In 2015, 1,583 master's, 204 doctorates awarded. *Degree program information:*

Part-time and evening/weekend programs available. Part-time, evening/weekend, 100% online, blended/hybrid learning. *Application deadline:* For fall admission, 7/1 priority date for domestic students, 3/1 for international students; for spring admission, 12/1 priority date for domestic students, 7/1 for international students. Applications are processed on a rolling basis. *Application fee:* $50 ($75 for international students). Electronic applications accepted. *Application Contact:* Dr. Samuel Wheeler, Assistant Director of Admissions, 940-898-3188, Fax: 940-898-3081, E-mail: wheelersr@twu.edu. *Dean of Graduate School*, Dr. Larry LeFlore, 940-898-3415, Fax: 940-898-3412, E-mail: gradschool@twu.edu.

College of Arts and Sciences Students: 624 full-time (520 women), 815 part-time (670 women); includes 774 minority (387 Black or African American, non-Hispanic/Latino; 6 American Indian or Alaska Native, non-Hispanic/Latino; 131 Asian, non-Hispanic/Latino; 203 Hispanic/Latino; 3 Native Hawaiian or other Pacific Islander, non-Hispanic/Latino; 44 Two or more races, non-Hispanic/Latino), 93 international. Average age 34. 783 applicants, 64% accepted, 374 enrolled. *Faculty:* 115 full-time (65 women), 23 part-time/adjunct (10 women). *Financial support:* In 2015–16, 529 students received support, including 173 research assistantships (averaging $12,208 per year), 75 teaching assistantships (averaging $12,208 per year); career-related internships or fieldwork, Federal Work-Study, institutionally sponsored loans, scholarships/grants, traineeships, health care benefits, and unspecified assistantships also available. Support available to part-time students. Financial award application deadline: 3/1; financial award applicants required to submit FAFSA. In 2015, 703 master's, 20 doctorates awarded. *Degree program information:* Part-time and evening/weekend programs available. Part-time, evening/weekend, online learning. Offers art (MA, MFA); arts (MA, MFA, PhD); arts and sciences (MA, MFA, MS, PhD, SSP); biology (MS); chemistry (MS); counseling psychology (MA, PhD); dance (MA, MFA, PhD); drama (MA); English (MA); government (MA); history (MA); informatics (MS); instrumental pedagogy (MA); instrumental performance (MA); mathematics (MS); mathematics teaching (MS); molecular biology (PhD); multicultural women's and gender studies (MA, PhD); music (MA); music education (MA); music therapy (MA); piano performance (MA); rhetoric (PhD); school psychology (PhD, SSP); sociology (MA, PhD); vocal pedagogy (MA); vocal performance (MA). *Application deadline:* For fall admission, 7/1 priority date for domestic students, 3/1 for international students; for spring admission, 12/1 priority date for domestic students, 7/1 for international students. Applications are processed on a rolling basis. *Application fee:* $50 ($75 for international students). Electronic applications accepted. *Application Contact:* Dr. Samuel Wheeler, Assistant Director of Admissions, 940-898-3188, Fax: 940-898-3081, E-mail: wheelersr@twu.edu. *Dean*, Dr. Abigail Tilton, 940-898-3326, Fax: 940-898-3366, E-mail: cas@twu.edu.

College of Health Sciences Students: 1,030 full-time (912 women), 499 part-time (410 women); includes 523 minority (127 Black or African American, non-Hispanic/Latino; 4 American Indian or Alaska Native, non-Hispanic/Latino; 139 Asian, non-Hispanic/Latino; 219 Hispanic/Latino; 34 Two or more races, non-Hispanic/Latino), 53 international. Average age 34. 1,629 applicants, 28% accepted, 332 enrolled. *Faculty:* 96 full-time (72 women), 28 part-time/adjunct (24 women). *Financial support:* In 2015–16, 747 students received support, including 59 research assistantships (averaging $11,499 per year), 15 teaching assistantships (averaging $11,499 per year); career-related internships or fieldwork, Federal Work-Study, institutionally sponsored loans, scholarships/grants, traineeships, health care benefits, and unspecified assistantships also available. Support available to part-time students. Financial award application deadline: 3/1; financial award applicants required to submit FAFSA. In 2015, 407 master's, 115 doctorates awarded. *Degree program information:* Part-time and evening/weekend programs available. Part-time, evening/weekend, online learning. Offers adapted physical education (MS, PhD); biomechanics (MS, PhD); coaching (MS); deaf education (MS); exercise and sports nutrition (MS); exercise physiology (MS, PhD); food science (MS); health care administration (MHA); health sciences (MA, MHA, MOT, MS, DPT, OTD, PhD); health studies (MS, PhD); nutrition (MS, PhD); occupational therapy (MOT, OTD, PhD); physical therapy (DPT, PhD); speech-language pathology (MS); sport management (MS, PhD). *Application deadline:* For fall admission, 7/1 priority date for domestic students, 3/1 for international students; for spring admission, 12/1 priority date for domestic students, 7/1 for international students. Applications are processed on a rolling basis. *Application fee:* $50 ($75 for international students). Electronic applications accepted. *Application Contact:* Dr. Samuel Wheeler, Assistant Director of Admissions, 940-898-3188, Fax: 940-898-3081, E-mail: wheelersr@twu.edu. *Interim Dean*, Ron Hovis, 940-898-2852, Fax: 940-898-2853, E-mail: rhovis@twu.edu.

College of Nursing Students: 39 full-time (37 women), 958 part-time (888 women); includes 566 minority (226 Black or African American, non-Hispanic/Latino; 8 American Indian or Alaska Native, non-Hispanic/Latino; 221 Asian, non-Hispanic/Latino; 88 Hispanic/Latino; 3 Native Hawaiian or other Pacific Islander, non-Hispanic/Latino; 20 Two or more races, non-Hispanic/Latino), 37 international. Average age 36. 430 applicants, 65% accepted, 193 enrolled. *Faculty:* 55 full-time (51 women), 42 part-time/adjunct (35 women). *Financial support:* In 2015–16, 149 students received support, including 10 research assistantships (averaging $5,600 per year), 1 teaching assistantship (averaging $5,600 per year); career-related internships or fieldwork, Federal Work-Study, institutionally sponsored loans, scholarships/grants, traineeships, health care benefits, and unspecified assistantships also available. Support available to part-time students. Financial award application deadline: 3/1; financial award applicants required to submit FAFSA. In 2015, 248 master's, 10 doctorates awarded. *Degree program information:* Part-time programs available. Part-time, online learning. Offers acute care nurse practitioner (MS); adult health clinical nurse specialist (MS); adult health nurse practitioner (MS); child health clinical nurse specialist (MS); clinical nurse leader (MS); family nurse practitioner (MS); health systems management (MS); nursing education (MS); nursing practice (DNP); nursing science (PhD); pediatric nurse practitioner (MS); women's health clinical nurse specialist (MS); women's health nurse practitioner (MS). *Application deadline:* For fall admission, 5/1 priority date for domestic students, 3/1 for international students; for spring admission, 9/15 priority date for domestic students, 7/1 for international students. Applications are processed on a rolling basis. *Application fee:* $50 ($75 for international students). Electronic applications accepted. *Application Contact:* Dr. Samuel Wheeler, Assistant Director of Admissions, 940-898-3188, Fax: 940-898-3081, E-mail: wheelersr@twu.edu. *Dean*, Dr. Anita G. Hufft, 940-898-2401, Fax: 940-898-2437, E-mail: nursing@twu.edu.

College of Professional Education Students: 238 full-time (225 women), 890 part-time (825 women); includes 441 minority (187 Black or African American, non-Hispanic/Latino; 5 American Indian or Alaska Native, non-Hispanic/Latino; 23 Asian, non-Hispanic/Latino; 195 Hispanic/Latino; 31 Two or more races, non-Hispanic/Latino), 17 international. Average age 36. 429 applicants, 61% accepted, 206 enrolled. *Faculty:* 62 full-time (48 women), 50 part-time/adjunct (41 women). *Financial support:* In 2015–16, 332 students received support, including 40 research assistantships (averaging $12,164 per year), 8 teaching assistantships (averaging $12,164 per year); career-related internships or fieldwork, Federal Work-Study, institutionally sponsored loans, scholarships/grants, traineeships, health care benefits, and unspecified assistantships also available. Support available to part-time students. Financial award application deadline: 3/1; financial award applicants required to submit FAFSA. In 2015, 367 master's, 17 doctorates awarded. *Degree program information:* Part-time and evening/weekend programs available. Part-time, evening/weekend. Offers child development (MS); counseling and development (MS); early childhood development and education (PhD); early childhood education (M Ed); educational administration (M Ed, MA); family studies (MS, PhD); family therapy (MS, PhD); library science (MA, MLS); professional education (M Ed, MA, MAT, MLS, MS, PhD); reading education (M Ed, MA, PhD); special education (M Ed, MA, PhD); teaching (MAT); teaching, learning, and curriculum (M Ed, MA). *Application deadline:* For fall admission, 7/1 priority date for domestic students, 3/1 for international students; for spring admission, 12/1 priority date for domestic students, 7/1 for international students. Applications are processed on a rolling basis. *Application fee:* $50 ($75 for international students). Electronic applications accepted. *Application Contact:* Dr. Samuel Wheeler, Assistant Director of Admissions, 940-898-3188, Fax: 940-898-3081, E-mail: wheelersr@twu.edu. *Interim Dean*, Dr. Jerry Whitworth, 940-898-2202, Fax: 940-898-2209, E-mail: cope@twu.edu.

School of Management Financial support: Research assistantships, career-related internships or fieldwork, Federal Work-Study, institutionally sponsored loans, scholarships/grants, traineeships, health care benefits, and unspecified assistantships available. Support available to part-time students. Financial award application deadline: 3/1; financial award applicants required to submit FAFSA. *Degree program information:* Part-time programs available. Part-time. Offers accounting (MBA); business administration (MBA); health systems management (MHSM). *Application deadline:* For fall admission, 8/1 priority date for domestic students, 3/1 for international students; for spring admission, 12/1 priority date for domestic students, 7/1 for international students. Applications are processed on a rolling basis. *Application fee:* $50 ($75 for international students). Electronic applications accepted. *Application Contact:* Dr. Samuel Wheeler, Assistant Director of Admissions, 940-898-3188, Fax: 940-898-3081, E-mail: wheelersr@twu.edu. *Director*, Dr. Margaret A. Young, 940-898-2105, Fax: 940-898-2120, E-mail: myoung13@twu.edu.

THEOLOGICAL UNIVERSITY OF THE CARIBBEAN, St. Just, PR 00978-0901

General Information Independent-religious, coed, comprehensive institution.

GRADUATE UNITS

Graduate Programs Offers childhood and adolescent education (MA); counseling and pastoral care (MA); ministry (D Min); missions (MA).

THOMAS COLLEGE, Waterville, ME 04901-5097

General Information Independent, coed, comprehensive institution. *Graduate housing:* On-campus housing not available.

GRADUATE UNITS

Graduate School *Degree program information:* Part-time and evening/weekend programs available. Part-time, evening/weekend. Offers business (MBA); computer technology education (MS); education (MS); human resource management (MBA). Electronic applications accepted.

THOMAS EDISON STATE UNIVERSITY, Trenton, NJ 08608-1176

General Information State-supported, coed, comprehensive institution. *Graduate housing:* On-campus housing not available.

GRADUATE UNITS

Heavin School of Arts and Sciences *Degree program information:* Part-time programs available. Part-time, online learning. Offers arts and sciences (MAEL, MALS, Graduate Certificate); educational leadership (MAEL); homeland security (Graduate Certificate); liberal studies (MALS); online learning and teaching (Graduate Certificate). Electronic applications accepted.

John S. Watson School of Public Service and Continuing Studies *Degree program information:* Part-time programs available. Part-time, online learning. Offers public service leadership (MPSL). Electronic applications accepted.

School of Applied Science and Technology *Degree program information:* Part-time programs available. Part-time, online learning. Offers applied science and technology (Graduate Certificate); clinical trials management (Graduate Certificate). Electronic applications accepted.

School of Business and Management *Degree program information:* Part-time programs available. Part-time, online learning. Offers business and management (MSHRM, MSM, Graduate Certificate); human resources management (MSHRM, Graduate Certificate); management (MSM); organizational leadership (Graduate Certificate). Electronic applications accepted.

W. Cary Edwards School of Nursing *Degree program information:* Part-time programs available. Part-time, online learning. Offers nurse educator (Post-Master's Certificate); nursing (MSN, DNP, Post-Master's Certificate). Electronic applications accepted.

THOMAS JEFFERSON SCHOOL OF LAW, San Diego, CA 92110-2905

General Information Independent, coed, graduate-only institution. *Graduate housing:* Rooms and/or apartments available on a first-come, first-served basis to single and married students. Housing application deadline: 5/1.

GRADUATE UNITS

Graduate and Professional Programs *Degree program information:* Part-time and evening/weekend programs available. Part-time, evening/weekend. Offers law (JD). JD/MBA offered in partnership with San Diego State University. Electronic applications accepted.

THOMAS JEFFERSON UNIVERSITY, Philadelphia, PA 19107

General Information Independent, coed, university. CGS member. *Graduate housing:* Rooms and/or apartments available to single and married students. *Research affiliation:* Christiana Care Health Services (biomedical research), Lankenau Institute for Medical Research (biomedical research), A.I. du Pont for Children Nemours (biomedical research), University of Delaware (biomedical research).

GRADUATE UNITS

Jefferson College of Biomedical Sciences Students: 124 full-time (69 women), 78 part-time (42 women); includes 42 minority (10 Black or African American, non-Hispanic/Latino; 22 Asian, non-Hispanic/Latino; 10 Hispanic/Latino), 27 international. 277 applicants, 38% accepted, 77 enrolled. *Faculty:* 190 full-time (53 women), 37 part-time/adjunct (15 women). *Financial support:* Fellowships, Federal Work-Study, institutionally sponsored loans, scholarships/grants, and traineeships available. Support available to part-time students. Financial award application deadline: 5/1; financial award applicants required to submit FAFSA. In 2015, 36 master's, 18 doctorates, 3 other advanced degrees awarded. *Degree program information:* Part-time and evening/weekend programs available. Part-time, evening/weekend. Offers biochemistry and molecular pharmacology (PhD); biomedical sciences (MS, PhD, Certificate); cell and developmental biology (MS, PhD); clinical research (MS); clinical research and trials: implementation (Certificate); clinical research: operations (Certificate); forensic toxicology (MS); genetics, genomics and cancer biology (PhD); human clinical investigation: theory (Certificate); immunology and microbial pathogenesis (PhD); infectious disease control (Certificate); microbiology (MS); neuroscience (PhD); patient-centered research (Certificate); pharmacology (MS). *Application deadline:* Applications are processed on a rolling basis. *Application fee:* $50. Electronic applications accepted. *Application Contact:* Marc E. Stearns, Director of Admissions, 215-503-0155, Fax: 215-503-3433, E-mail: jgsbs-info@jefferson.edu. *Dean*, Dr. Gerald B. Grunwald, 215-503-4191, Fax: 215-503-6690, E-mail: gerald.grunwald@jefferson.edu.

Jefferson College of Nursing Students: 65 full-time (49 women), 401 part-time (360 women); includes 75 minority (38 Black or African American, non-Hispanic/Latino; 27 Asian, non-Hispanic/Latino; 10 Hispanic/Latino), 2 international. Average age 33. 325 applicants, 65% accepted, 139 enrolled. *Faculty:* 39 full-time (38 women). *Financial support:* In 2015–16, 337 students received support. Federal Work-Study, institutionally sponsored loans, and scholarships/grants available. Support available to part-time students. Financial award application deadline: 4/1; financial award applicants required to submit FAFSA. In 2015, 194 master's, 10 doctorates awarded. *Degree program information:* Part-time programs available. Part-time, online learning. Offers nursing (MS, DNP). *Application deadline:* For fall admission, 4/1 priority date for domestic and international students; for spring admission, 9/1 priority date for domestic and international students; for summer admission, 1/2 priority date for domestic and international students. Applications are processed on a rolling basis. Electronic applications accepted. *Application Contact:* Tina Heuges, Associate Director of Admissions, 215-503-1754, Fax: 215-503-7241, E-mail: tina.heuges@jefferson.edu. *Associate Dean, Graduate Programs*, Dr. Ksenia Zukowsky, 215-503-9426, E-mail: ksenia.zukowsky@jefferson.edu.

Jefferson School of Health Professions Students: 472 full-time (371 women), 55 part-time (51 women); includes 36 minority (29 Black or African American, non-Hispanic/Latino; 4 Asian, non-Hispanic/Latino; 3 Hispanic/Latino). Average age 28. 3,751 applicants, 10% accepted, 236 enrolled. *Financial support:* In 2015–16, 406 students received support. Federal Work-Study, institutionally sponsored loans, scholarships/grants, and unspecified assistantships available. Support available to part-time students. Financial award application deadline: 4/1; financial award applicants required to submit FAFSA. In 2015, 154 master's, 57 doctorates awarded. Offers bioscience technologies (MS); couple and family therapy (MFT); health professions (MFT, MS, DPT, OTD, Certificate); healthcare education (Certificate); occupational therapy (MS, OTD); physical therapy (DPT); physician assistant studies (MS); radiologic and imaging sciences (MS). *Application deadline:* Applications are processed on a rolling basis. Electronic applications accepted. *Application Contact:* Donald Sharples, Director of Graduate Admissions, 215-503-1044, E-mail: donald.sharples@jefferson.edu. *Dean*, Dr. Janice Burke, 215-955-6000.

Jefferson School of Pharmacy Students: 267 full-time (162 women), 10 part-time (4 women); includes 27 minority (13 Black or African American, non-Hispanic/Latino; 1 American Indian or Alaska Native, non-Hispanic/Latino; 8 Asian, non-Hispanic/Latino; 5 Hispanic/Latino). Average age 26. 617 applicants, 29% accepted, 85 enrolled. *Financial support:* In 2015–16, 161 students received support. Federal Work-Study, institutionally sponsored loans, and scholarships/grants available. Financial award application deadline: 4/1; financial award applicants required to submit FAFSA. In 2015, 89 doctorates awarded. Offers pharmacy (Pharm D). *Application deadline:* For fall admission, 3/1 for domestic and international students. Applications are processed on a rolling basis. *Application fee:* $25. Electronic applications accepted. *Application Contact:* Niki M. Kelley, Associate Director of Admissions, 215-503-1041, E-mail: niki.kelley@jefferson.edu. *Dean*, Dr. Rebecca S. Finley, 215-955-6300.

Jefferson School of Population Health ***Degree program information:*** Part-time and evening/weekend programs available. Part-time, evening/weekend, online learning. Offers applied health economics and outcomes research (MS, PhD, Certificate); behavioral health science (PhD); health policy (MS, PhD, Certificate); healthcare quality and safety (MS, PhD, Certificate); population health (Certificate); public health (MPH, Certificate). Electronic applications accepted.

Sidney Kimmel Medical College Students: 1,056 full-time (526 women); includes 323 minority (20 Black or African American, non-Hispanic/Latino; 4 American Indian or Alaska Native, non-Hispanic/Latino; 218 Asian, non-Hispanic/Latino; 81 Hispanic/Latino), 40 international. Average age 23. 10,504 applicants, 4% accepted, 267 enrolled. *Faculty:* 1,165 full-time (417 women), 75 part-time/adjunct (39 women). *Financial support:* In 2015–16, 445 students received support. Federal Work-Study, institutionally sponsored loans, and scholarships/grants available. Financial award application deadline: 3/1; financial award applicants required to submit FAFSA. In 2015, 281 doctorates awarded. Offers medicine (MD). *Application deadline:* For fall admission, 11/15 for domestic and international students. Applications are processed on a rolling basis. *Application fee:* $80. Electronic applications accepted. *Application Contact:* Dr. Clara Callahan, Dean for Students and Admissions, 215-955-4077, Fax: 215-955-5151, E-mail: clara.callahan@jefferson.edu. *Dean*, Dr. Mark Tykowcinski, 215-955-6980, Fax: 215-923-6939, E-mail: mark.tykowcinski@jefferson.edu.

THOMAS MORE COLLEGE, Crestview Hills, KY 41017-3495

General Information Independent-religious, coed, comprehensive institution. *Enrollment:* 1,909 graduate, professional, and undergraduate students; 157 full-time matriculated graduate/professional students (60 women), 21 part-time matriculated graduate/professional students (15 women). *Enrollment by degree level:* 178 master's. *Graduate faculty:* 15 full-time (7 women), 3 part-time/adjunct (2 women). *Tuition, area resident:* Part-time $505 per credit hour. *Required fees:* $100 per course. Tuition and fees vary according to course load and program. *Graduate housing:* On-campus housing not available. *Student services:* Campus employment opportunities, career counseling, exercise/wellness program, free psychological counseling, international student services, multicultural affairs office, services for students with disabilities, teacher training. *Library:* Thomas More College Library plus 1 other. *Collection:* Books: 87,667 (physical), 3,056 (digital/electronic); Serial titles: 329 (physical); Databases: 65. Weekly public service hours: 76.

Computer facilities: 96 computers available on campus for general student use. A campuswide network can be accessed from student residence rooms and from off campus. Online class registration is available.
Website: http://www.thomasmore.edu/

General Application Contact: Judy Bautista, Director of Adult and Professional Education, 859-341-4554, Fax: 859-344-3589, E-mail: judy.bautista@thomasmore.edu.

GRADUATE UNITS

Program in Business Administration Students: 151 full-time (59 women); includes 14 minority (10 Black or African American, non-Hispanic/Latino; 1 American Indian or Alaska Native, non-Hispanic/Latino; 3 Hispanic/Latino), 3 international. Average age 33. 78 applicants, 88% accepted, 48 enrolled. *Faculty:* 11 full-time (3 women), 2 part-time/adjunct (both women). *Financial support:* In 2015–16, 24 students received support. Scholarships/grants available. Financial award application deadline: 3/15; financial award applicants required to submit FAFSA. In 2015, 38 master's awarded. *Degree program information:* Evening/weekend programs available. Evening/weekend, 100% online. Offers business administration (MBA). *Application deadline:* Applications are processed on a rolling basis. *Application fee:* $0. Electronic applications accepted. *Application Contact:* Judy Bautista, Enrollment Manager, 859-341-4554, Fax: 859-578-3589, E-mail: judy.bautista@thomasmore.edu. *Chair of Business Administration*, Dr. Anne Busse, 859-344-3612, Fax: 859-344-3345, E-mail: bussea@thomasmore.edu.

Program in Teacher Leader Students: 9 part-time (7 women); includes 1 minority (Black or African American, non-Hispanic/Latino). Average age 32. *Faculty:* 2 full-time (both women). *Financial support:* In 2015–16, 4 students received support. Institutionally sponsored loans and scholarships/grants available. Financial award application deadline: 3/15; financial award applicants required to submit FAFSA. *Degree program information:* Part-time and evening/weekend programs available. Part-time, evening/weekend. Offers teacher leader (M Ed). *Application deadline:* Applications are processed on a rolling basis. Electronic applications accepted. *Application Contact:* Judy Bautista, Director of Adult and Professional Education, 859-341-4554, Fax: 859-344-3589, E-mail: judy.bautista@thomasmore.edu. *Director*, Dr. Kim Haverkos, 859-344-3359, E-mail: haverkk@thomasmore.edu.

Program in Teaching Students: 6 full-time (1 woman), 12 part-time (8 women). Average age 34. 12 applicants, 100% accepted, 8 enrolled. *Faculty:* 3 full-time (all women), 1 part-time/adjunct (0 women). *Financial support:* In 2015–16, 4 students received support. Federal Work-Study, institutionally sponsored loans, and scholarships/grants available. Financial award application deadline: 3/15; financial award applicants required to submit FAFSA. In 2015, 10 master's awarded. *Degree program information:* Part-time programs available. Part-time. Offers teaching (MAT). *Application deadline:* For fall admission, 5/1 for domestic students. Applications are processed on a rolling basis. *Application fee:* $0. Electronic applications accepted. *Director*, Joyce Fortney Hamberg, PhD, 859-344-3338, Fax: 859-344-3345, E-mail: hamberj@thomasmore.edu.

THOMAS UNIVERSITY, Thomasville, GA 31792-7499

General Information Independent, coed, comprehensive institution. *Graduate housing:* Room and/or apartments available on a first-come, first-served basis to single students; on-campus housing not available to married students. Housing application deadline: 8/1.

GRADUATE UNITS

Department of Business Administration ***Degree program information:*** Part-time programs available. Part-time. Offers business administration (MBA). Electronic applications accepted.

Department of Education ***Degree program information:*** Part-time programs available. Part-time. Offers education (M Ed). Electronic applications accepted.

Department of Human Services ***Degree program information:*** Part-time programs available. Part-time. Offers community counseling (MSCC); rehabilitation counseling (MRC). Electronic applications accepted.

Department of Nursing ***Degree program information:*** Part-time programs available. Part-time. Offers nursing (MSN). Electronic applications accepted.

THOMPSON RIVERS UNIVERSITY, Kamloops, BC V2C 0C8, Canada

General Information Province-supported, coed, comprehensive institution. CGS member.

GRADUATE UNITS

Program in Business Administration ***Degree program information:*** Part-time programs available. Part-time. Offers business administration (MBA).

Program in Education ***Degree program information:*** Part-time programs available. Part-time. Offers education (M Ed).

Program in Environmental Science Offers environmental science (MS).

Program in Social Work Offers social work (MSW).

TIFFIN UNIVERSITY, Tiffin, OH 44883-2161

General Information Independent, coed, comprehensive institution. *Enrollment:* 3,511 graduate, professional, and undergraduate students; 123 full-time matriculated graduate/professional students (92 women), 929 part-time matriculated graduate/professional students (521 women). *Enrollment by degree level:* 1,048 master's, 4 other advanced degrees. *Graduate faculty:* 85 full-time (40 women), 64 part-time/adjunct (25 women). *Tuition, area resident:* Full-time $21,000. Tuition and fees vary according to program. *Graduate housing:* Room and/or apartments available on a first-come, first-served basis to single students; on-campus housing not available to married students. Typical cost: $9900 (including board). Room and board charges vary according to board plan, campus/location and housing facility selected. Housing application deadline: 8/1. *Student services:* Campus employment opportunities, campus safety program, career counseling, exercise/wellness program, free psychological counseling, international student services, low-cost health insurance, multicultural affairs office, services for students with disabilities. *Library:* Pfeiffer Library plus 1 other. *Collection:* Books: 40,849 (physical), 125,971 (digital/electronic); Serial titles: 120 (physical), 25,420 (digital/electronic); Databases: 187. Weekly public service hours: 73.

Computer facilities: Computer purchase and lease plans are available. 280 computers available on campus for general student use. A campuswide network can be accessed from student residence rooms and from off campus. Online class registration is available.
Website: http://www.tiffin.edu/

General Application Contact: Nikki Hintze, Director of Graduate Admissions and Student Services, 800-968-6446 Ext. 3445, Fax: 419-443-5002, E-mail: hintzenm@tiffin.edu.

GRADUATE UNITS

Program in Business Administration Students: 10 full-time (4 women), 497 part-time (240 women); includes 91 minority (67 Black or African American, non-Hispanic/Latino;

1 American Indian or Alaska Native, non-Hispanic/Latino; 5 Asian, non-Hispanic/Latino; 15 Hispanic/Latino; 3 Two or more races, non-Hispanic/Latino), 102 international. Average age 31. 214 applicants, 86% accepted, 146 enrolled. *Financial support:* Unspecified assistantships available. Support available to part-time students. Financial award application deadline: 7/31; financial award applicants required to submit FAFSA. *Degree program information:* Part-time and evening/weekend programs available. Part-time, evening/weekend, online learning. Offers finance (MBA); general management (MBA); healthcare administration (MBA); human resource management (MBA); international business (MBA); leadership (MBA); marketing (MBA); non-profit management (MBA); sports management (MBA). *Application deadline:* For fall admission, 8/15 for domestic students, 8/1 for international students; for spring admission, 1/9 for domestic students, 12/1 for international students. Applications are processed on a rolling basis. *Application fee:* $50. Electronic applications accepted. *Application Contact:* Nikki Hintze, Director of Graduate and Distance Education Academic Advising, 800-968-6446 Ext. 3596, Fax: 419-443-5002, E-mail: hintzenm@tiffin.edu. *Dean of Graduate Studies*, Dr. Bonnie Tiell, 419-448-3261, Fax: 419-443-5002, E-mail: btiell@tiffin.edu.

Program in Criminal Justice Students: 82 full-time (60 women), 192 part-time (110 women); includes 86 minority (71 Black or African American, non-Hispanic/Latino; 11 Hispanic/Latino; 1 Native Hawaiian or other Pacific Islander, non-Hispanic/Latino; 3 Two or more races, non-Hispanic/Latino), 5 international. Average age 31. 178 applicants, 76% accepted, 68 enrolled. *Financial support:* Available to part-time students. Application deadline: 7/31; applicants required to submit FAFSA. *Degree program information:* Part-time and evening/weekend programs available. Part-time, evening/weekend, 100% online, blended/hybrid learning. Offers criminal justice (MS). *Application deadline:* For fall admission, 9/3 for domestic students, 8/1 for international students; for spring admission, 1/9 priority date for domestic students, 12/1 for international students. Applications are processed on a rolling basis. *Application fee:* $50. Electronic applications accepted. *Application Contact:* Nikki Hintze, Director of Graduate and Distance Education Academic Advising, 800-968-6446 Ext. 3596, Fax: 419-443-5002, E-mail: hintzenm@tiffin.edu. *Dean of Criminal Justice and Security Studies*, Dr. Robert James Orr, III, 419-448-3319, Fax: 419-443-5002, E-mail: orrrj@tiffin.edu.

Program in Education Students: 99 part-time (75 women); includes 26 minority (20 Black or African American, non-Hispanic/Latino; 1 Asian, non-Hispanic/Latino; 4 Hispanic/Latino; 1 Two or more races, non-Hispanic/Latino). Average age 32. 31 applicants, 90% accepted, 24 enrolled. *Financial support:* Unspecified assistantships available. *Degree program information:* Part-time and evening/weekend programs available. Part-time, evening/weekend, online only, 100% online, blended/hybrid learning. Offers educational technology management (M Ed); higher education administration (M Ed). *Application deadline:* Applications are processed on a rolling basis. Electronic applications accepted. *Application Contact:* Nikki Hintze, Director of Graduate Admissions and Student Services, 800-968-6446 Ext. 3445, Fax: 419-443-5002, E-mail: hintzenm@tiffin.edu.

Program in Humanities Students: 17 full-time (15 women), 116 part-time (75 women); includes 25 minority (15 Black or African American, non-Hispanic/Latino; 2 Asian, non-Hispanic/Latino; 6 Hispanic/Latino; 2 Two or more races, non-Hispanic/Latino). Average age 36. 84 applicants, 80% accepted, 43 enrolled. *Financial support:* Unspecified assistantships available. Financial award applicants required to submit FAFSA. *Degree program information:* Part-time and evening/weekend programs available. Part-time, evening/weekend, online only, 100% online, blended/hybrid learning. Offers art and visual media (MH); communication (MH); creative writing (MH); English (MH); film studies (MH); humanities (MH); individualized studies (MH). *Application deadline:* For fall admission, 9/1 for domestic students; for spring admission, 1/9 for domestic students. Applications are processed on a rolling basis. *Application fee:* $50. Electronic applications accepted. *Application Contact:* Nikki Hintze, Director of Graduate and Distance Education Academic Advising, 800-968-6446 Ext. 3596, Fax: 419-443-5002, E-mail: hintzenm@tiffin.edu. *Program Chair*, Dr. Jason Slone, 419-448-3015, Fax: 419-443-5002, E-mail: burtonav@tiffin.edu.

Program in Psychology Students: 13 full-time (12 women), 21 part-time (17 women); includes 10 minority (8 Black or African American, non-Hispanic/Latino; 2 Hispanic/Latino). Average age 30. 34 applicants, 82% accepted, 20 enrolled. *Degree program information:* Part-time and evening/weekend programs available. Part-time, evening/weekend, online only, 100% online. Offers psychology (MS). *Application deadline:* Applications are processed on a rolling basis. Electronic applications accepted. *Application Contact:* Nikki Hintze, Director of Graduate Admissions and Student Services, 800-968-6446 Ext. 3445, Fax: 419-443-5002, E-mail: hintzenm@tiffin.edu.

TORONTO SCHOOL OF THEOLOGY, Toronto, ON M5S 2C3, Canada

General Information Independent-religious, coed, graduate-only institution. *Graduate faculty:* 26 full-time (all women), 76 part-time/adjunct (all women). *Library:* University of Toronto Libraries plus 7 others.
Website: http://www.tst.edu/

General Application Contact: David Wagschal, GCTS Administrator, 416-978-4050, Fax: 416-978-7821, E-mail: inquiries@tst.edu.

GRADUATE UNITS

Graduate Programs Students: 538 full-time (164 women), 515 part-time (267 women). *Faculty:* 100 full-time (26 women), 271 part-time/adjunct (76 women). *Financial support:* Career-related internships or fieldwork available. Online learning. Offers theology (M Div, MA, MAMS, MPS, MRE, MSM, MTS, Th M, D Min, PhD, Th D). *Application deadline:* For fall admission, 1/15 priority date for domestic and international students. Applications are processed on a rolling basis. *Application fee:* $120 Canadian dollars. Electronic applications accepted. *Application Contact:* David Wagschal, Administrator, Graduate Centre for Theological Studies, 416-978-4050, Fax: 416-978-7821, E-mail: inquiries@tst.edu. *Director*, Dr. Alan L. Hayes, 416-978-7822, Fax: 416-978-7821, E-mail: alan.hayes@utoronto.ca.

TOURO COLLEGE, New York, NY 10010

General Information Independent, coed, comprehensive institution. *Enrollment:* 12,021 graduate, professional, and undergraduate students; 1,760 full-time matriculated graduate/professional students (1,296 women), 2,271 part-time matriculated graduate/professional students (1,831 women). *Enrollment by degree level:* 3,989 master's, 42 doctoral. *Graduate faculty:* 94 full-time, 157 part-time/adjunct. *Student services:* Career counseling, free psychological counseling, low-cost health insurance. *Library:* Touro College Library plus 14 others.

Computer facilities: A campuswide network can be accessed from off campus. Online class registration is available.
Website: http://www.touro.edu/

General Application Contact: Dr. Benjamin Enoma, Director, Graduate Admissions.

GRADUATE UNITS

Graduate School of Education Students: 656 full-time (557 women), 1,934 part-time (1,614 women); includes 719 minority (305 Black or African American, non-Hispanic/Latino; 5 American Indian or Alaska Native, non-Hispanic/Latino; 129 Asian, non-Hispanic/Latino; 255 Hispanic/Latino; 3 Native Hawaiian or other Pacific Islander, non-Hispanic/Latino; 22 Two or more races, non-Hispanic/Latino), 28 international. 1,422 applicants, 50% accepted, 675 enrolled. *Faculty:* 75 full-time, 131 part-time/adjunct. *Financial support:* Federal Work-Study available. Financial award applicants required to submit FAFSA. In 2015, 6 master's awarded. *Degree program information:* Part-time and evening/weekend programs available. Part-time, evening/weekend, online learning. Offers education and special education (MS); education biology (MS); instructional technology (MS); mathematics education (MS); school leadership (MS); teaching English to speakers of other languages (MS); teaching literacy (MS). *Application deadline:* For fall admission, 8/26 for domestic students, 7/15 for international students; for spring admission, 12/31 for domestic students, 12/15 for international students. Applications are processed on a rolling basis. *Application fee:* $50. *Application Contact:* Natalie Arroyo, Admissions, 212-463-0400. *Dean*, Dr. Arnold Spinner, 212-463-0400 Ext. 5561, Fax: 212-462-4889, E-mail: aspinner@touro.edu.

Graduate School of Jewish Studies Students: 4 full-time (2 women), 29 part-time (14 women). *Faculty:* 4 full-time, 20 part-time/adjunct. *Financial support:* Tuition waivers (full and partial) available. Support available to part-time students. *Degree program information:* Part-time programs available. Part-time. Offers Jewish studies (MA). *Application fee:* $50. *Dean*, Dr. Michael Shmidman, 212-213-2230.

Graduate School of Social Work Students: 252 full-time (218 women), 48 part-time (40 women); includes 158 minority (93 Black or African American, non-Hispanic/Latino; 1 American Indian or Alaska Native, non-Hispanic/Latino; 7 Asian, non-Hispanic/Latino; 53 Hispanic/Latino; 4 Two or more races, non-Hispanic/Latino), 1 international. Offers social work (MSW). *Application Contact:* Tina Atherall, Director of Recruitment, Admissions and Enrollment Management, 212-463-0400 Ext. 5630, Fax: 212-627-3693, E-mail: bradley.karasik@touro.edu. *Dean*, Dr. Steven Huberman, 212-463-0400 Ext. 5269, E-mail: msw@touro.edu.

Graduate School of Technology Students: 100 full-time (44 women), 129 part-time (70 women); includes 133 minority (35 Black or African American, non-Hispanic/Latino; 2 American Indian or Alaska Native, non-Hispanic/Latino; 78 Asian, non-Hispanic/Latino; 16 Hispanic/Latino; 2 Two or more races, non-Hispanic/Latino), 5 international. Offers information systems (MS); instructional technology (MS); Web and multimedia design (MA). *Dean of the Graduate School of Technology*, Dr. Isaac Herskowitz, 202-463-0400 Ext. 5231, E-mail: issac.herskowitz@touro.edu.

Jacob D. Fuchsberg Law Center Students: 519 full-time (290 women), 30 part-time (14 women); includes 211 minority (62 Black or African American, non-Hispanic/Latino; 4 American Indian or Alaska Native, non-Hispanic/Latino; 49 Asian, non-Hispanic/Latino; 96 Hispanic/Latino), 8 international. *Financial support:* Fellowships, career-related internships or fieldwork, and Federal Work-Study available. Support available to part-time students. Financial award application deadline: 5/1. *Degree program information:* Part-time and evening/weekend programs available. Part-time, evening/weekend. Offers general law (LL M); law (JD); U.S. legal studies (LL M). JD/MBA offered with Long Island University-LIU Post or Dowling College; JD/MPA offered with Long Island University-LIU Post; JD/MSW offered with Stony Brook University, State University of New York. *Application deadline:* Applications are processed on a rolling basis. *Application fee:* $60. *Application Contact:* Office of Admissions, 631-761-7010, E-mail: admissions@tourolaw.edu. *Dean*, Patricia E. Salkin, 631-761-7100.

School of Health Sciences Students: 1,057 full-time (772 women), 121 part-time (88 women); includes 243 minority (59 Black or African American, non-Hispanic/Latino; 1 American Indian or Alaska Native, non-Hispanic/Latino; 102 Asian, non-Hispanic/Latino; 58 Hispanic/Latino; 1 Native Hawaiian or other Pacific Islander, non-Hispanic/Latino; 22 Two or more races, non-Hispanic/Latino), 102 international. *Faculty:* 20 full-time, 94 part-time/adjunct. *Financial support:* Fellowships available. Offers industrial-organizational psychology (MS); mental health counseling (MS); occupational therapy (MS); physical therapy (DPT); physician assistant (MS); school psychology (MS); speech-language pathology (MS). *Application Contact:* Brian J. Diele, Director of Student Administrative Services, 631-665-1600 Ext. 6311, E-mail: brian.diele@touro.edu. *Dean, School of Health Sciences*, Dr. Louis Primavera, 516-673-3200, E-mail: louis.primavera@touro.edu.

TOURO UNIVERSITY CALIFORNIA, Vallejo, CA 94592

General Information Independent, coed, graduate-only institution. *Graduate housing:* On-campus housing not available. *Research affiliation:* University of California San Francisco (cancer, HIV/AIDS), National Health Institute (cardiac arrest in teens), Genetech (cancer), National Institutes of Health (diabetes).

GRADUATE UNITS

Graduate Programs ***Degree program information:*** Part-time and evening/weekend programs available. Part-time, evening/weekend. Offers education (MA); medical health sciences (MS); osteopathic medicine (DO); pharmacy (Pharm D); public health (MPH). Electronic applications accepted.

TOWSON UNIVERSITY, Towson, MD 21252-0001

General Information State-supported, coed, university. CGS member. *Enrollment:* 22,284 graduate, professional, and undergraduate students; 1,076 full-time matriculated graduate/professional students (759 women), 2,085 part-time matriculated graduate/professional students (1,503 women). *Enrollment by degree level:* 2,716 master's, 170 doctoral, 275 other advanced degrees. *Graduate faculty:* 306 full-time (167 women), 118 part-time/adjunct (67 women). Tuition, state resident: full-time $7440; part-time $372 per unit. Tuition, nonresident: full-time $15,400; part-time $770 per unit. *Required fees:* $2360; $118 per year. $354 per term. *Graduate housing:* On-campus housing not available. *Student services:* Campus employment opportunities, campus safety program, career counseling, child daycare facilities, exercise/wellness program, free psychological counseling, international student services, low-cost health insurance, multicultural affairs office, services for students with disabilities, teacher training, writing training. *Library:* Cook Library. *Collection:* Books: 400,331 (physical), 254,992 (digital/electronic); Serial titles: 668 (physical), 39,152 (digital/electronic); Databases: 198. Weekly public service hours: 109. *Research affiliation:* Exelon Generation Company (biology), Prometheus Computing (computer science), KCI Technologies (computer science), Intelligent Fusion (computer science), Plant Sensory Systems (computer science), RTR Technologies (computer science).

Computer facilities: 2,500 computers available on campus for general student use. A campuswide network can be accessed from student residence rooms and from off campus. Online class registration is available.
Website: http://www.towson.edu/

General Application Contact: University Admissions, 410-704-2113, Fax: 410-704-3030, E-mail: grads@towson.edu.

GRADUATE UNITS

Arts Integration Institute Students: 38 part-time (all women). Offers arts integration (Postbaccalaureate Certificate). Program offered jointly with The Johns Hopkins University, University of Maryland, College Park and University of Maryland, Baltimore County. *Application deadline:* Applications are processed on a rolling basis. *Application fee:* $45. Electronic applications accepted. *Application Contact:* Alicia Arkell-Kleis, University Admissions, 410-704-2113, Fax: 410-704-3030, E-mail: grads@towson.edu. *Program Director,* Prof. Susan Rotkovitz, 410-704-3658, E-mail: srotkovitz@towson.edu.

Baltimore Hebrew Institute Students: 3 full-time (all women), 17 part-time (8 women); includes 4 minority (all Black or African American, non-Hispanic/Latino). Offers Jewish communal service (MAJCS, Postbaccalaureate Certificate); Jewish education (MAJE, Postbaccalaureate Certificate); Jewish studies (MAJS). *Application deadline:* Applications are processed on a rolling basis. *Application fee:* $45. Electronic applications accepted. *Application Contact:* Alicia Arkell-Kleis, University Admissions, 410-704-2113, Fax: 410-704-3030, E-mail: grads@towson.edu. *Director,* Dr. Hana Bor, 410-704-4719, E-mail: hbor@towson.edu.

Program in Accounting and Business Advisory Services Students: 22 full-time (7 women), 17 part-time (9 women); includes 10 minority (5 Black or African American, non-Hispanic/Latino; 4 Asian, non-Hispanic/Latino; 1 Two or more races, non-Hispanic/Latino), 9 international. *Degree program information:* Part-time and evening/weekend programs available. Part-time, evening/weekend. Offers accounting and business advisory services (MS). Program offered jointly with University of Baltimore. *Application deadline:* Applications are processed on a rolling basis. *Application fee:* $45. Electronic applications accepted. *Application Contact:* Alicia Arkell-Kleis, University Admissions, 410-704-2113, Fax: 410-704-3030, E-mail: grads@towson.edu. *Graduate Program Director,* Dr. Martin Freedman, 410-704-4143, E-mail: mfreedman@towson.edu.

Program in Action Research for School Improvement Students: 1 (woman) part-time. Offers action research for school improvement (Postbaccalaureate Certificate). *Application deadline:* Applications are processed on a rolling basis. *Application fee:* $45. Electronic applications accepted. *Application Contact:* Alicia Arkell-Kleis, University Admissions, 410-704-2113, Fax: 410-704-3030, E-mail: grads@towson.edu. *Director,* Dr. Marilyn L. Nicholas, 410-704-2987, E-mail: mnicholas@towson.edu.

Program in Applied and Industrial Mathematics Students: 9 full-time (4 women), 16 part-time (6 women); includes 5 minority (4 Black or African American, non-Hispanic/Latino; 1 Two or more races, non-Hispanic/Latino), 3 international. *Financial support:* Application deadline: 4/1; applicants required to submit FAFSA. *Degree program information:* Part-time and evening/weekend programs available. Part-time, evening/weekend. Offers applied and industrial mathematics (MS). *Application deadline:* Applications are processed on a rolling basis. *Application fee:* $45. Electronic applications accepted. *Application Contact:* Alicia Arkell-Kleis, University Admissions, 410-704-2113, Fax: 410-704-3030, E-mail: grads@towson.edu. *Graduate Program Director,* Dr. Moustapha Pemy, 410-704-3585, E-mail: mpemy@towson.edu.

Program in Applied Gerontology Students: 3 full-time (2 women), 7 part-time (6 women); includes 3 minority (2 Black or African American, non-Hispanic/Latino; 1 Hispanic/Latino). *Financial support:* Application deadline: 4/1. Offers applied gerontology (MS, Postbaccalaureate Certificate). *Application deadline:* Applications are processed on a rolling basis. *Application fee:* $45. Electronic applications accepted. *Application Contact:* Alicia Arkell-Kleis, University Admissions, 410-704-2113, Fax: 410-704-3030, E-mail: grads@towson.edu. *Graduate Program Director,* Dr. Mary Carter, 410-704-4643, E-mail: mcarter@towson.edu.

Program in Applied Information Technology Students: 124 full-time (49 women), 174 part-time (49 women); includes 100 minority (66 Black or African American, non-Hispanic/Latino; 20 Asian, non-Hispanic/Latino; 8 Hispanic/Latino; 6 Two or more races, non-Hispanic/Latino), 77 international. Offers applied information technology (MS, D Sc); database management systems (Postbaccalaureate Certificate); information security and assurance (Postbaccalaureate Certificate); information systems management (Postbaccalaureate Certificate); Internet applications development (Postbaccalaureate Certificate); networking technologies (Postbaccalaureate Certificate); software engineering (Postbaccalaureate Certificate). *Application deadline:* Applications are processed on a rolling basis. *Application fee:* $45. Electronic applications accepted. *Application Contact:* Alicia Arkell-Kleis, University Admissions, 410-704-2113, Fax: 410-704-3030, E-mail: grads@towson.edu. *Graduate Program Director,* Dr. Suranjan Chakraborty, 410-704-4769, E-mail: schakraborty@towson.edu.

Program in Applied Physics Students: 6 full-time (1 woman), 1 part-time (0 women); includes 3 minority (2 Black or African American, non-Hispanic/Latino; 1 Two or more races, non-Hispanic/Latino). Offers applied physics (MS). *Application deadline:* Applications are processed on a rolling basis. *Application fee:* $45. Electronic applications accepted. *Application Contact:* Alicia Arkell-Kleis, University Admissions, 410-704-2113, Fax: 410-704-3030, E-mail: grads@towson.edu. *Graduate Program Director,* Dr. Raj Kolagani, 410-704-3134, E-mail: rkolagani@towson.edu.

Program in Art Education Students: 1 full-time (0 women), 25 part-time (20 women); includes 3 minority (2 Black or African American, non-Hispanic/Latino; 1 Asian, non-Hispanic/Latino). *Financial support:* Application deadline: 4/1. *Degree program information:* Part-time and evening/weekend programs available. Part-time, evening/weekend. Offers art education (M Ed). *Application deadline:* Applications are processed on a rolling basis. *Application fee:* $45. Electronic applications accepted. *Application Contact:* Alicia Arkell-Kleis, University Admissions, 410-704-2113, Fax: 410-704-3030, E-mail: grads@towson.edu. *Graduate Program Director,* Dr. Ray Martens, 410-704-3819, E-mail: rmartens@towson.edu.

Program in Audiology Students: 50 full-time (45 women); includes 7 minority (3 Black or African American, non-Hispanic/Latino; 1 Asian, non-Hispanic/Latino; 2 Hispanic/Latino; 1 Two or more races, non-Hispanic/Latino), 1 international. *Financial support:* Application deadline: 4/1. Offers audiology (Au D). *Application deadline:* For fall admission, 2/1 for domestic students. *Application fee:* $45. Electronic applications accepted. *Application Contact:* Alicia Arkell-Kleis, University Admissions, 410-704-2113, Fax: 410-704-3030, E-mail: grads@towson.edu. *Graduate Program Director,* Dr. Jennifer Smart, 410-704-3105, E-mail: audiology@towson.edu.

Program in Autism Studies Students: 9 full-time (all women), 48 part-time (42 women); includes 7 minority (6 Black or African American, non-Hispanic/Latino; 1 Hispanic/Latino), 1 international. Offers autism studies (Postbaccalaureate Certificate). *Application deadline:* Applications are processed on a rolling basis. *Application fee:* $45. Electronic applications accepted. *Application Contact:* Alicia Arkell-Kleis, University Admissions, 410-704-2113, Fax: 410-704-3030, E-mail: grads@towson.edu. *Graduate Program Director,* Dr. Connie Anderson, 410-704-4640, E-mail: connieanderson@towson.edu.

Program in Biology Students: 20 full-time (11 women), 24 part-time (12 women); includes 11 minority (7 Black or African American, non-Hispanic/Latino; 3 Asian, non-Hispanic/Latino; 1 Two or more races, non-Hispanic/Latino), 2 international. *Financial support:* Application deadline: 4/1. *Degree program information:* Part-time and evening/weekend programs available. Part-time, evening/weekend. Offers biology (MS). *Application fee:* $45. Electronic applications accepted. *Application Contact:* Alicia Arkell-Kleis, University Admissions, 410-704-2113, Fax: 410-704-3030, E-mail: grads@towson.edu. *Graduate Program Co-Director,* Dr. John Lapolla, 410-704-3121, E-mail: jlapolla@towson.edu.

Program in Child Life, Administration and Family Collaboration Students: 15 full-time (all women), 12 part-time (all women); includes 2 minority (1 Black or African American, non-Hispanic/Latino; 1 Asian, non-Hispanic/Latino). Offers child life, administration and family collaboration (MS). *Application fee:* $45. Electronic applications accepted. *Application Contact:* Alicia Arkell-Kleis, University Admissions, 410-704-2113, Fax: 410-704-3030, E-mail: grads@towson.edu. *Graduate Program Director,* Prof. Lisa Martinelli Beasley, 410-704-3766, E-mail: lmartinelli@towson.edu.

Program in Clinical Psychology Students: 98 full-time (74 women), 15 part-time (9 women); includes 28 minority (13 Black or African American, non-Hispanic/Latino; 4 Asian, non-Hispanic/Latino; 7 Hispanic/Latino; 4 Two or more races, non-Hispanic/Latino), 1 international. *Financial support:* Application deadline: 4/1. *Degree program information:* Part-time and evening/weekend programs available. Part-time, evening/weekend. Offers clinical psychology (MA). *Application deadline:* For fall admission, 2/1 for domestic and international students. *Application fee:* $45. Electronic applications accepted. *Application Contact:* Alicia Arkell-Kleis, University Admissions, 410-704-2113, Fax: 410-704-3030, E-mail: grads@towson.edu. *Graduate Program Director,* Dr. Elizabeth Katz, 410-704-3221, E-mail: clinincalpsyc@towson.edu.

Program in Clinician-Administrator Transition Students: 17 full-time (all women), 20 part-time (19 women); includes 7 minority (6 Black or African American, non-Hispanic/Latino; 1 Asian, non-Hispanic/Latino), 1 international. *Financial support:* Application deadline: 4/1. Offers clinician-administrator transition (MS, Postbaccalaureate Certificate). *Application deadline:* Applications are processed on a rolling basis. *Application fee:* $45. Electronic applications accepted. *Application Contact:* Alicia Arkell-Kleis, University Admissions, 410-704-2113, Fax: 410-704-3030, E-mail: grads@towson.edu. *Graduate Program Director,* Dr. Kathleen Ogle, 410-704-4049, E-mail: mweinstein@towson.edu.

Program in Communications Management Students: 5 full-time (3 women), 18 part-time (15 women); includes 6 minority (all Black or African American, non-Hispanic/Latino). *Financial support:* Application deadline: 4/1. Offers communications management (MS). *Application deadline:* For fall admission, 1/15 for domestic students. *Application fee:* $45. Electronic applications accepted. *Application Contact:* Alicia Arkell-Kleis, University Admissions, 410-704-2113, Fax: 410-704-3030, E-mail: grads@towson.edu. *Graduate Program Director,* Dr. Beth Haller, 410-704-2442, E-mail: bhaller@towson.edu.

Program in Computer Science Students: 71 full-time (19 women), 79 part-time (20 women); includes 33 minority (13 Black or African American, non-Hispanic/Latino; 15 Asian, non-Hispanic/Latino; 3 Hispanic/Latino; 2 Two or more races, non-Hispanic/Latino), 44 international. *Financial support:* Application deadline: 4/1. *Degree program information:* Part-time and evening/weekend programs available. Part-time, evening/weekend. Offers computer science (MS). *Application deadline:* Applications are processed on a rolling basis. *Application fee:* $45. Electronic applications accepted. *Application Contact:* Alicia Arkell-Kleis, University Admissions, 410-704-2113, Fax: 410-704-3030, E-mail: grads@towson.edu. *Graduate Program Director,* Dr. Yanggon Kim, 410-704-3782, E-mail: ykim@towson.edu.

Program in Counseling Psychology Students: 4 part-time (all women); includes 1 minority (Hispanic/Latino). *Financial support:* Application deadline: 4/1. *Degree program information:* Part-time and evening/weekend programs available. Part-time, evening/weekend. Offers counseling psychology (CAS). *Application deadline:* Applications are processed on a rolling basis. *Application fee:* $45. Electronic applications accepted. *Application Contact:* Alicia Arkell-Kleis, University Admissions, 410-704-2113, Fax: 410-704-3030, E-mail: grads@towson.edu. *Graduate Program Director,* Dr. Christa Schmidt, 410-704-3063, E-mail: ckschmidt@townson.edu.

Program in Early Childhood Education Students: 3 full-time (all women), 111 part-time (110 women); includes 16 minority (7 Black or African American, non-Hispanic/Latino; 4 Asian, non-Hispanic/Latino; 4 Hispanic/Latino; 1 Two or more races, non-Hispanic/Latino), 1 international. *Financial support:* Application deadline: 4/1. *Degree program information:* Part-time and evening/weekend programs available. Part-time, evening/weekend. Offers early childhood education (M Ed, CAS). *Application deadline:* Applications are processed on a rolling basis. *Application fee:* $45. Electronic applications accepted. *Application Contact:* Alicia Arkell-Kleis, University Admissions, 410-704-2113, Fax: 410-704-3030, E-mail: grads@towson.edu. *Graduate Program Director,* Dr. Janese Daniels, 410-704-4832, E-mail: ecedgrad@towson.edu.

Program in e-Business and Technology Management Students: 5 full-time (1 woman), 33 part-time (14 women); includes 8 minority (4 Black or African American, non-Hispanic/Latino; 2 Asian, non-Hispanic/Latino; 1 Hispanic/Latino; 1 Two or more races, non-Hispanic/Latino), 3 international. Offers project, program and portfolio management (Postbaccalaureate Certificate); supply chain management (MS, Postbaccalaureate Certificate). *Application deadline:* Applications are processed on a rolling basis. *Application fee:* $45. Electronic applications accepted. *Application Contact:* Jennifer Bethke, University Admissions, 410-704-2113, Fax: 410-704-3030, E-mail: grads@towson.edu. *Director,* Dr. Chaodong Hang, 410-704-4658, E-mail: chan@towson.edu.

Program in Elementary Education ***Degree program information:*** Part-time and evening/weekend programs available. Part-time, evening/weekend. Offers elementary education (M Ed). Electronic applications accepted.

Program in Environmental Science Students: 8 full-time (6 women), 21 part-time (12 women); includes 3 minority (2 Black or African American, non-Hispanic/Latino; 1 Two or more races, non-Hispanic/Latino). *Financial support:* Application deadline: 4/1. *Degree program information:* Part-time and evening/weekend programs available. Part-time, evening/weekend. Offers environmental science (MS, Postbaccalaureate Certificate). *Application deadline:* Applications are processed on a rolling basis. *Application fee:* $45. Electronic applications accepted. *Application Contact:* Alicia Arkell-Kleis, University Admissions, 410-704-2113, Fax: 410-704-3030, E-mail: grads@towson.edu. *Graduate Program Director,* Dr. David Ownby, 410-704-2946, E-mail: downby@towson.edu.

Program in Family-Professional Collaboration Students: 15 full-time (all women), 13 part-time (all women); includes 3 minority (2 Black or African American, non-Hispanic/Latino; 1 Asian, non-Hispanic/Latino). Offers family-professional collaboration (Postbaccalaureate Certificate). *Application deadline:* Applications are processed on a rolling basis. *Application fee:* $45. Electronic applications accepted. *Application Contact:* Alicia Arkell-Kleis, University Admissions, 410-704-2113, Fax: 410-704-3030, E-mail: grads@towson.edu. *Graduate Program Director,* Dr. Karen Eskow, 410-704-5851, E-mail: keskow@towson.edu.

Program in Forensic Science Students: 34 full-time (25 women), 15 part-time (14 women); includes 13 minority (8 Black or African American, non-Hispanic/Latino; 1 Asian, non-Hispanic/Latino; 1 Hispanic/Latino; 3 Two or more races, non-Hispanic/Latino), 2 international. Offers forensic science (MS). *Application deadline:* Applications are processed on a rolling basis. *Application fee:* $45. Electronic applications accepted. *Application Contact:* Alicia Arkell-Kleis, University Admissions, 410-704-2113, Fax: 410-704-3030, E-mail: grads@towson.edu. *Graduate Program Director*, Mark Profili, 410-704-2668, E-mail: mprofili@towson.edu.

Program in Geography and Environmental Planning Students: 13 full-time (5 women), 11 part-time (5 women); includes 3 minority (2 Black or African American, non-Hispanic/Latino; 1 Two or more races, non-Hispanic/Latino), 1 international. *Financial support:* Application deadline: 4/1. *Degree program information:* Part-time and evening/weekend programs available. Part-time, evening/weekend. Offers geography and environmental planning (MA). *Application deadline:* Applications are processed on a rolling basis. *Application fee:* $45. Electronic applications accepted. *Application Contact:* Alicia Arkell-Kleis, University Admissions, 410-704-2113, Fax: 410-704-3030, E-mail: grads@towson.edu. *Graduate Program Director*, Dr. Charles Schmitz, 410-704-2966, E-mail: cschmitz@towson.edu.

Program in Health Science Students: 10 full-time (8 women), 65 part-time (50 women); includes 33 minority (27 Black or African American, non-Hispanic/Latino; 3 Asian, non-Hispanic/Latino; 2 Hispanic/Latino; 1 Two or more races, non-Hispanic/Latino), 2 international. *Financial support:* Application deadline: 4/1. *Degree program information:* Part-time and evening/weekend programs available. Part-time, evening/weekend. Offers health science (MS). *Application deadline:* Applications are processed on a rolling basis. *Application fee:* $45. Electronic applications accepted. *Application Contact:* Alicia Arkell-Kleis, University Admissions, 410-704-2113, Fax: 410-704-3030, E-mail: grads@towson.edu. *Graduate Program Director*, Dr. Susan Radius, 410-704-4216, E-mail: sradius@towson.edu.

Program in Humanities Students: 2 full-time (1 woman), 16 part-time (7 women); includes 3 minority (1 Black or African American, non-Hispanic/Latino; 2 Two or more races, non-Hispanic/Latino). *Financial support:* Application deadline: 4/1. *Degree program information:* Part-time and evening/weekend programs available. Part-time, evening/weekend. Offers humanities (MA). *Application deadline:* Applications are processed on a rolling basis. *Application fee:* $45. Electronic applications accepted. *Application Contact:* Alicia Arkell-Kleis, University Admissions, 410-704-2113, Fax: 410-704-3030, E-mail: grads@towson.edu. *Graduate Program Director*, Dr. Lana Portolano, 410-704-3770, E-mail: mportolano@towson.edu.

Program in Human Resource Development Students: 15 full-time (13 women), 215 part-time (179 women); includes 54 minority (32 Black or African American, non-Hispanic/Latino; 4 Asian, non-Hispanic/Latino; 10 Hispanic/Latino; 8 Two or more races, non-Hispanic/Latino), 3 international. *Financial support:* Application deadline: 4/1. *Degree program information:* Part-time and evening/weekend programs available. Part-time, evening/weekend. Offers human resource development (MS). *Application deadline:* Applications are processed on a rolling basis. *Application fee:* $45. Electronic applications accepted. *Application Contact:* Alicia Arkell-Kleis, University Admissions, 410-704-2113, Fax: 410-704-3030, E-mail: grads@towson.edu. *Graduate Program Director*, Dr. Alan Clardy, 410-704-3069, E-mail: aclardy@towson.edu.

Program in Instructional Technology Students: 19 full-time (17 women), 177 part-time (148 women); includes 26 minority (17 Black or African American, non-Hispanic/Latino; 4 Hispanic/Latino; 2 Native Hawaiian or other Pacific Islander, non-Hispanic/Latino; 3 Two or more races, non-Hispanic/Latino), 7 international. *Financial support:* Application deadline: 4/1. *Degree program information:* Part-time and evening/weekend programs available. Part-time, evening/weekend. Offers instructional design and training (MS); instructional technology (Ed D). *Application deadline:* For fall admission, 8/1 for domestic students, 7/15 for international students. *Application fee:* $45. Electronic applications accepted. *Application Contact:* Alicia Arkell-Kleis, University Admissions, 410-704-2113, Fax: 410-704-3030, E-mail: grads@towson.edu. *Graduate Program Director*, Dr. Liyan Song, 410-704-5751, E-mail: lsong@towson.edu.

Program in Integrated Homeland Security Management Students: 9 full-time (6 women), 29 part-time (13 women); includes 16 minority (14 Black or African American, non-Hispanic/Latino; 1 Hispanic/Latino; 1 Two or more races, non-Hispanic/Latino). *Financial support:* Application deadline: 4/1. *Degree program information:* Part-time and evening/weekend programs available. Part-time, evening/weekend. Offers integrated homeland security management (MS); security assessment and management (Postbaccalaureate Certificate). *Application deadline:* Applications are processed on a rolling basis. *Application fee:* $45. Electronic applications accepted. *Application Contact:* Alicia Arkell-Kleis, University Admissions, 410-704-2113, Fax: 410-704-3030, E-mail: grads@towson.edu. *Graduate Program Director*, Dr. Joseph Clark, 410-704-4490, E-mail: jrclark@towson.edu.

Program in Integrated STEM Instructional Leadership Students: 1 (woman) part-time. Offers integrated STEM instructional leadership (Postbaccalaureate Certificate). Electronic applications accepted. *Application Contact:* University Admissions, 410-704-2113, Fax: 410-704-3030, E-mail: grads@towson.edu. *Director*, Pam Lottero-Perdue, 410-704-4598, E-mail: plotteroperdue@towson.edu.

Program in Interactive Media Design Students: 17 part-time (14 women); includes 9 minority (5 Black or African American, non-Hispanic/Latino; 1 Asian, non-Hispanic/Latino; 1 Hispanic/Latino; 2 Two or more races, non-Hispanic/Latino). Online learning. Offers interactive media design (Postbaccalaureate Certificate). *Application deadline:* Applications are processed on a rolling basis. *Application fee:* $45. Electronic applications accepted. *Application Contact:* Alicia Arkell-Kleis, University Admissions, 410-704-2113, Fax: 410-704-3030, E-mail: grads@towson.edu. *Graduate Program Director*, Prof. Bridget Sullivan, 410-704-2802, E-mail: bsullivan@towson.edu.

Program in Interdisciplinary Arts Infusion Students: 11 part-time (10 women); includes 5 minority (4 Black or African American, non-Hispanic/Latino; 1 Hispanic/Latino). Offers interdisciplinary arts infusion (MA). *Application deadline:* For fall admission, 4/22 priority date for domestic students. *Application Contact:* University Admissions, 410-704-2113, Fax: 410-704-3030, E-mail: grads@towson.edu.

Program in Kinesiology Students: 24 part-time (12 women); includes 1 minority (Black or African American, non-Hispanic/Latino). Offers kinesiology (MS). *Application deadline:* Applications are processed on a rolling basis. *Application fee:* $45. Electronic applications accepted. *Application Contact:* Alicia Arkell-Kleis, University Admissions, 410-704-2113, Fax: 410-704-3030, E-mail: grads@towson.edu. *Graduate Program Director*, Dr. Alex Vigo-Valentine, 410-704-3172, E-mail: avigo@towson.edu.

Program in Marketing Intelligence Students: 4 full-time (2 women), 6 part-time (3 women); includes 2 minority (1 Black or African American, non-Hispanic/Latino; 1 Two or more races, non-Hispanic/Latino), 4 international. Offers marketing intelligence (MS). *Application Contact:* University Admissions, 410-704-2113, Fax: 410-704-3030, E-mail: grads@towson.edu. *Director*, Dr. Philippe Duverger, 410-704-3538, E-mail: pduverger@towson.edu.

Program in Mathematics Education Students: 1 (woman) full-time, 38 part-time (27 women); includes 10 minority (4 Black or African American, non-Hispanic/Latino; 2 Asian, non-Hispanic/Latino; 1 Hispanic/Latino; 3 Two or more races, non-Hispanic/Latino). *Financial support:* Application deadline: 4/1. *Degree program information:* Part-time and evening/weekend programs available. Part-time, evening/weekend. Offers mathematics education (MS). *Application deadline:* Applications are processed on a rolling basis. *Application fee:* $45. Electronic applications accepted. *Application Contact:* Alicia Arkell-Kleis, University Admissions, 410-704-2113, Fax: 410-704-3030, E-mail: grads@towson.edu. *Graduate Program Director*, Dr. Maureen Yarnevich, 410-704-2988, E-mail: myarnevich@towson.edu.

Program in Music Education Students: 5 full-time (4 women), 22 part-time (13 women); includes 3 minority (1 Asian, non-Hispanic/Latino; 2 Hispanic/Latino). *Financial support:* Application deadline: 4/1. *Degree program information:* Part-time and evening/weekend programs available. Part-time, evening/weekend. Offers music education (MS, Postbaccalaureate Certificate). *Application deadline:* Applications are processed on a rolling basis. *Application fee:* $45. Electronic applications accepted. *Application Contact:* Alicia Arkell-Kleis, University Admissions, 410-704-2113, Fax: 410-704-3030, E-mail: grads@towson.edu. *Graduate Program Director*, Dr. Melissa McCabe, 410-704-2765, E-mail: mmccabe@towson.edu.

Program in Music Performance and Composition Students: 3 full-time (1 woman), 10 part-time (4 women); includes 2 minority (1 Black or African American, non-Hispanic/Latino; 1 Two or more races, non-Hispanic/Latino), 1 international. *Financial support:* Application deadline: 4/1. *Degree program information:* Part-time and evening/weekend programs available. Part-time, evening/weekend. Offers music performance and composition (MM). *Application deadline:* Applications are processed on a rolling basis. *Application fee:* $45. Electronic applications accepted. *Application Contact:* Alicia Arkell-Kleis, University Admissions, 410-704-2113, Fax: 410-704-3030, E-mail: grads@towson.edu. *Graduate Program Director*, Prof. Terry Ewell, 410-704-2824, E-mail: tewell@towson.edu.

Program in Nursing Students: 12 full-time (10 women), 45 part-time (43 women); includes 19 minority (15 Black or African American, non-Hispanic/Latino; 2 Asian, non-Hispanic/Latino; 1 Hispanic/Latino; 1 Two or more races, non-Hispanic/Latino), 3 international. *Financial support:* Application deadline: 4/1. *Degree program information:* Part-time programs available. Part-time. Offers nursing (MS); nursing education (Postbaccalaureate Certificate). *Application deadline:* Applications are processed on a rolling basis. *Application fee:* $45. Electronic applications accepted. *Application Contact:* Alicia Arkell-Kleis, University Admissions, 410-704-2113, Fax: 410-704-3030, E-mail: grads@towson.edu. *Graduate Program Director*, Dr. Nikki Austin, 410-704-4389, E-mail: nursinggradprogram@towson.edu.

Program in Occupational Science Students: 4 full-time (3 women), 8 part-time (6 women); includes 4 minority (2 Black or African American, non-Hispanic/Latino; 1 Asian, non-Hispanic/Latino; 1 Two or more races, non-Hispanic/Latino), 1 international. *Financial support:* Application deadline: 4/1. *Degree program information:* Part-time and evening/weekend programs available. Part-time, evening/weekend. Offers occupational science (Sc D). *Application deadline:* For fall admission, 8/15 for domestic and international students; for winter admission, 11/15 for domestic and international students; for spring admission, 1/15 for domestic and international students. Applications are processed on a rolling basis. *Application fee:* $45. Electronic applications accepted. *Application Contact:* Alicia Arkell-Kleis, University Admissions, 410-704-2113, Fax: 410-704-3030, E-mail: grads@towson.edu. *Graduate Program Director*, Dr. Beth Merryman, 410-704-3499, E-mail: bmerryman@towson.edu.

Program in Occupational Therapy Students: 152 full-time (145 women), 1 (woman) part-time; includes 17 minority (5 Black or African American, non-Hispanic/Latino; 5 Asian, non-Hispanic/Latino; 5 Hispanic/Latino; 2 Two or more races, non-Hispanic/Latino). *Financial support:* Application deadline: 4/1. Offers occupational therapy (MS). *Application deadline:* For spring admission, 8/1 for domestic students. Applications are processed on a rolling basis. *Application fee:* $45. Electronic applications accepted. *Application Contact:* Lynne Murphy, University Admissions, 410-704-2113, Fax: 410-704-3030, E-mail: grads@towson.edu. *Graduate Program Director*, Dr. Sonia Lawson, 410-704-2313, E-mail: slawson@towson.edu.

Program in Organizational Change Students: 4 full-time (all women), 110 part-time (94 women); includes 30 minority (26 Black or African American, non-Hispanic/Latino; 1 Asian, non-Hispanic/Latino; 2 Hispanic/Latino; 1 Two or more races, non-Hispanic/Latino). Offers organizational change (CAS). *Application deadline:* Applications are processed on a rolling basis. *Application fee:* $45. Electronic applications accepted. *Application Contact:* Alicia Arkell-Kleis, University Admissions, 410-704-2113, Fax: 410-704-3030, E-mail: grads@towson.edu. *Graduate Program Director*, Dr. Jessica Shiller, 410-704-5383, E-mail: jshiller@towson.edu.

Program in Physician Assistant Studies Students: 63 full-time (53 women); includes 10 minority (4 Black or African American, non-Hispanic/Latino; 3 Asian, non-Hispanic/Latino; 2 Hispanic/Latino; 1 Two or more races, non-Hispanic/Latino), 1 international. *Financial support:* Application deadline: 4/1. Offers physician assistant studies (MS). *Application deadline:* Applications are processed on a rolling basis. *Application fee:* $45. Electronic applications accepted. *Application Contact:* Alicia Arkell-Kleis, University Admissions, 410-704-2113, Fax: 410-704-3030, E-mail: grads@towson.edu. *Graduate Program Director*, Prof. Jack Goble, 443-840-1159, E-mail: jgoblejr@ccbmd.edu.

Program in Professional Studies Students: 8 full-time (6 women), 18 part-time (14 women); includes 6 minority (4 Black or African American, non-Hispanic/Latino; 2 Asian, non-Hispanic/Latino), 1 international. *Financial support:* Application deadline: 4/1. *Degree program information:* Part-time and evening/weekend programs available. Part-time, evening/weekend. Offers art history (MA); individualized plan (MA). *Application deadline:* Applications are processed on a rolling basis. *Application fee:* $45. Electronic applications accepted. *Application Contact:* Alicia Arkell-Kleis, University Admissions, 410-704-2113, Fax: 410-704-3030, E-mail: grads@towson.edu. *Graduate Program Director*, Dr. James Smith, 410-704-4620, E-mail: jmsmith@towson.edu.

Program in Professional Writing Students: 21 full-time (12 women), 40 part-time (34 women); includes 13 minority (7 Black or African American, non-Hispanic/Latino; 1 Asian, non-Hispanic/Latino; 2 Hispanic/Latino; 3 Two or more races, non-Hispanic/Latino). *Financial support:* Application deadline: 4/1. *Degree program information:* Part-time and evening/weekend programs available. Part-time, evening/weekend. Offers professional writing (MS). *Application deadline:* For fall admission, 3/1 for domestic students; for spring admission, 10/1 for domestic students. Applications are processed on a rolling basis. *Application fee:* $45. Electronic applications accepted. *Application Contact:* Alicia Arkell-Kleis, University Admissions, 410-704-2113, Fax: 410-704-3030, E-mail: grads@towson.edu. *Graduate Program Director*, Prof. Goeffrey Becker, 410-704-5196, E-mail: gbecker@towson.edu.

Program in Reading Students: 5 full-time (4 women), 173 part-time (163 women); includes 13 minority (6 Black or African American, non-Hispanic/Latino; 1 American Indian or Alaska Native, non-Hispanic/Latino; 3 Hispanic/Latino; 3 Two or more races, non-Hispanic/Latino). *Financial support:* Application deadline: 4/1. *Degree program information:* Part-time and evening/weekend programs available. Part-time, evening/weekend. Offers reading (M Ed); reading education (CAS). *Application deadline:* Applications are processed on a rolling basis. *Application fee:* $45. Electronic applications accepted. *Application Contact:* Dr. Steve Mogge, University Admissions, 410-704-2113, Fax: 410-704-3030, E-mail: grads@towson.edu. *Graduate Program Director*, Dr. Gilda Martinez-Alba, 410-704-2480, E-mail: gmartinez@towson.edu.

Program in School Psychology Students: 16 full-time (14 women), 12 part-time (9 women); includes 7 minority (2 Black or African American, non-Hispanic/Latino; 2 Asian, non-Hispanic/Latino; 2 Hispanic/Latino; 1 Two or more races, non-Hispanic/Latino). *Financial support:* Application deadline: 4/1. *Degree program information:* Part-time and evening/weekend programs available. Part-time, evening/weekend. Offers school psychology (CAS). *Application deadline:* For fall admission, 1/15 for domestic students. *Application fee:* $45. Electronic applications accepted. *Application Contact:* Alicia Arkell-Kleis, University Admissions, 410-704-2113, Fax: 410-704-3030, E-mail: grads@towson.edu. *Graduate Program Director*, Dr. Susan Bartels, 410-704-3070, E-mail: sbartels@towson.edu.

Program in Secondary Education Students: 2 part-time (both women). *Financial support:* Application deadline: 4/1. *Degree program information:* Part-time and evening/weekend programs available. Part-time, evening/weekend. Offers secondary education (M Ed). *Application deadline:* Applications are processed on a rolling basis. *Application fee:* $45. Electronic applications accepted. *Application Contact:* Alicia Arkell-Kleis, University Admissions, 410-704-2113, Fax: 410-704-3030, E-mail: grads@towson.edu. *Graduate Program Director*, Dr. Todd Kenreich, 410-704-4956, E-mail: scedmed@towson.edu.

Program in Social Science Students: 5 full-time (2 women), 15 part-time (9 women); includes 7 minority (4 Black or African American, non-Hispanic/Latino; 1 Hispanic/Latino; 2 Two or more races, non-Hispanic/Latino). *Financial support:* Application deadline: 4/1. *Degree program information:* Part-time and evening/weekend programs available. Part-time, evening/weekend. Offers social science (MS). *Application deadline:* For fall admission, 10/15 for domestic and international students; for spring admission, 4/15 for domestic and international students. Applications are processed on a rolling basis. *Application fee:* $45. Electronic applications accepted. *Application Contact:* Alicia Arkell-Kleis, University Admissions, 410-704-2113, Fax: 410-704-3030, E-mail: grads@towson.edu. *Graduate Program Director*, Dr. Michael Korzi, 410-704-5219, E-mail: mkorzi@towson.edu.

Program in Special Education Students: 4 full-time (all women), 144 part-time (134 women); includes 16 minority (7 Black or African American, non-Hispanic/Latino; 3 Asian, non-Hispanic/Latino; 5 Hispanic/Latino; 1 Two or more races, non-Hispanic/Latino). *Degree program information:* Part-time and evening/weekend programs available. Part-time, evening/weekend. Offers special education (M Ed). *Application deadline:* For fall admission, 2/15 for domestic and international students; for spring admission, 10/15 for domestic and international students. Applications are processed on a rolling basis. *Application fee:* $45. Electronic applications accepted. *Application Contact:* Alicia Arkell-Kleis, University Admissions, 410-704-2113, Fax: 410-704-3030, E-mail: grads@towson.edu. *Graduate Program Director*, Dr. Andrea Parrish, 410-704-3835, E-mail: aparrish@towson.edu.

Program in Speech-Language Pathology Students: 91 full-time (all women), 1 (woman) part-time; includes 4 minority (2 Black or African American, non-Hispanic/Latino; 2 Two or more races, non-Hispanic/Latino). *Financial support:* Application deadline: 4/1. Offers speech-language pathology (MS). *Application deadline:* For fall admission, 1/15 for domestic students. Applications are processed on a rolling basis. *Application fee:* $45. Electronic applications accepted. *Application Contact:* Alicia Arkell-Kleis, University Admissions, 410-704-2113, Fax: 410-704-3030, E-mail: grads@towson.edu. *Graduate Program Director*, Dr. Karen Fallon, 410-704-2437, E-mail: slpgrad@towson.edu.

Program in Studio Arts Students: 12 full-time (8 women), 6 part-time (2 women); includes 3 minority (1 Asian, non-Hispanic/Latino; 1 Hispanic/Latino; 1 Two or more races, non-Hispanic/Latino), 1 international. *Financial support:* Application deadline: 4/1. Offers studio arts (MFA). *Application deadline:* For fall admission, 2/1 for domestic students; for spring admission, 11/1 for domestic students. *Application fee:* $45. Electronic applications accepted. *Application Contact:* Alicia Arkell-Kleis, University Admissions, 410-704-2113, Fax: 410-704-3030, E-mail: grads@towson.edu. *Graduate Program Director*, Prof. Tonia Matthews, 410-704-2803, E-mail: tmatthews@towson.edu.

Program in Teaching Students: 95 full-time (62 women), 65 part-time (48 women); includes 24 minority (12 Black or African American, non-Hispanic/Latino; 5 Asian, non-Hispanic/Latino; 5 Hispanic/Latino; 2 Two or more races, non-Hispanic/Latino), 3 international. *Financial support:* Application deadline: 4/1. Offers teaching (MAT). *Application deadline:* For fall admission, 6/15 for domestic and international students; for spring admission, 10/15 for domestic and international students. Applications are processed on a rolling basis. *Application fee:* $45. Electronic applications accepted. *Application Contact:* Judith Reber, University Admissions, 410-704-2113, Fax: 410-704-3030, E-mail: grads@towson.edu. *Graduate Program Director*, Judith Reber, 410-704-5388, E-mail: jreber@towson.edu.

Program in Theatre Students: 6 full-time (3 women); includes 1 minority (Two or more races, non-Hispanic/Latino). *Financial support:* Application deadline: 4/1. Offers theatre (MFA). *Application deadline:* For fall admission, 3/1 for domestic students. *Application fee:* $45. Electronic applications accepted. *Application Contact:* Alicia Arkell-Kleis, University Admissions, 410-704-2113, Fax: 410-704-3030, E-mail: grads@towson.edu. *Graduate Program Director*, Prof. Naoko Maeshiba, 410-704-2791, E-mail: nmaeshiba@towson.edu.

Program in Women's Studies Students: 6 full-time (5 women), 4 part-time (all women); includes 4 minority (2 Black or African American, non-Hispanic/Latino; 1 Asian, non-Hispanic/Latino; 1 Hispanic/Latino), 1 international. *Financial support:* Application deadline: 4/1. Offers women's studies (MS, Postbaccalaureate Certificate). *Application deadline:* Applications are processed on a rolling basis. *Application fee:* $45. Electronic applications accepted. *Application Contact:* Alicia Arkell-Kleis, University Admissions, 410-704-2113, Fax: 410-704-3030, E-mail: grads@towson.edu. *Graduate Program Director*, Dr. Kate Wilkinson, 410-704-5744, E-mail: kwilkinson@towson.edu.

TOYOTA TECHNOLOGICAL INSTITUTE AT CHICAGO, Chicago, IL 60637

General Information Proprietary, coed, graduate-only institution.

GRADUATE UNITS

Program in Computer Science Offers computer science (PhD).

TRENT UNIVERSITY, Peterborough, ON K9J 7B8, Canada

General Information Province-supported, coed, university. *Graduate housing:* Room and/or apartments available to single students; on-campus housing not available to married students. Housing application deadline: 7/10. *Research affiliation:* Watershed Science Centre (watershed studies), Ontario Power Generation, Inc. (acid rain deposition), Enbridge Consumers Gas (ozone depletion), Forensics Laboratory (DNA testing).

GRADUATE UNITS

Graduate Studies ***Degree program information:*** Part-time programs available. Part-time. Offers anthropology (MA); applications of modeling in the natural and social sciences (MA); biology (M Sc, PhD); chemistry (M Sc); computer studies (M Sc); cultural studies (PhD); environmental and resource studies (M Sc, PhD); geography (M Sc, PhD); indigenous studies (PhD); materials science (M Sc); physics (M Sc).

The Frost Centre for Canadian Studies and Indigenous Studies Degree program information: Part-time programs available. Part-time. Offers Canadian studies (PhD); Canadian studies and indigenous studies (MA).

TREVECCA NAZARENE UNIVERSITY, Nashville, TN 37210-2877

General Information Independent-religious, coed, comprehensive institution. *Enrollment:* 2,640 graduate, professional, and undergraduate students; 590 full-time matriculated graduate/professional students (431 women), 211 part-time matriculated graduate/professional students (143 women). *Enrollment by degree level:* 624 master's, 169 doctoral, 8 other advanced degrees. *Graduate faculty:* 32 full-time (11 women), 44 part-time/adjunct (21 women). *Tuition, area resident:* Full-time $10,012. Tuition and fees vary according to degree level and program. *Graduate housing:* Rooms and/or apartments available to single and married students. Housing application deadline: 6/15. *Student services:* Services for students with disabilities, teacher training. *Library:* Waggoner Library. *Collection:* Books: 82,769 (physical), 174,810 (digital/electronic); Serial titles: 432 (physical), 115,695 (digital/electronic); Databases: 62. Weekly public service hours: 95.

Computer facilities: 200 computers available on campus for general student use. A campuswide network can be accessed from student residence rooms and from off campus. Online class registration is available.
Website: http://www.trevecca.edu/

General Application Contact: School of Graduate and Continuing Studies, 844-TNU-GRAD, E-mail: sgcsadmissions@trevecca.edu.

GRADUATE UNITS

Graduate Business Programs Students: 111 full-time (71 women), 7 part-time (4 women); includes 58 minority (52 Black or African American, non-Hispanic/Latino; 2 Asian, non-Hispanic/Latino; 4 Hispanic/Latino), 2 international. Average age 32. *Faculty:* 9 full-time (0 women), 9 part-time/adjunct (3 women). *Financial support:* Applicants required to submit FAFSA. In 2015, 67 master's awarded. *Degree program information:* Evening/weekend programs available. Evening/weekend, online learning. Offers business administration (MBA); information technology (MS); management (MSM). *Application deadline:* Applications are processed on a rolling basis. *Application fee:* $0. Electronic applications accepted. *Application Contact:* 615-248-1529, E-mail: sgcsadmissions@trevecca.edu. *Director of Graduate and Professional Programs for School of Business*, Dr. Rick Mann, 615-248-1529, E-mail: management@trevecca.edu.

Graduate Counseling Program Students: 136 full-time (105 women), 43 part-time (32 women); includes 31 minority (25 Black or African American, non-Hispanic/Latino; 2 Hispanic/Latino; 4 Two or more races, non-Hispanic/Latino). Average age 34. *Faculty:* 7 full-time (1 woman), 9 part-time/adjunct (6 women). *Financial support:* Applicants required to submit FAFSA. In 2015, 59 master's, 6 doctorates awarded. *Degree program information:* Part-time and evening/weekend programs available. Part-time, evening/weekend. Offers clinical counseling: teaching and supervision (PhD); clinical mental health counseling (MA); marriage and family counseling/therapy (MMFC/T). *Application deadline:* Applications are processed on a rolling basis. *Application fee:* $0. Electronic applications accepted. *Application Contact:* 615-248-1384, Fax: 615-248-1662, E-mail: admissions_gradcouns@trevecca.edu. *Director*, Dr. Peter Wilson, 615-248-1384, Fax: 615-248-1662, E-mail: admissions_gradcouns@trevecca.edu.

Graduate Education Program Students: 115 full-time (97 women), 17 part-time (16 women); includes 33 minority (29 Black or African American, non-Hispanic/Latino; 1 Asian, non-Hispanic/Latino; 1 Native Hawaiian or other Pacific Islander, non-Hispanic/Latino; 2 Two or more races, non-Hispanic/Latino). Average age 35. *Faculty:* 6 full-time (5 women), 13 part-time/adjunct (8 women). *Financial support:* Applicants required to submit FAFSA. In 2015, 80 master's awarded. *Degree program information:* Part-time and evening/weekend programs available. Part-time, evening/weekend, online learning. Offers curriculum, assessment, and instruction K-12 (M Ed); educational leadership (M Ed); English second language (M Ed); library and information science (MLI Sc); special education: visual impairments (M Ed); teaching (MAT); turnaround school leadership (Ed S). *Application deadline:* Applications are processed on a rolling basis. Electronic applications accepted. *Application Contact:* 844-TNU-GRAD, E-mail: sgcsadmissions@trevecca.edu. *Dean, School of Education/Director of Graduate Education Programs*, Dr. Suzie Harris, 615-248-1201, Fax: 615-248-1597, E-mail: admissions_ged@trevecca.edu.

Graduate Leadership Programs Students: 108 full-time (78 women), 128 part-time (85 women); includes 122 minority (116 Black or African American, non-Hispanic/Latino; 4 Hispanic/Latino; 2 Two or more races, non-Hispanic/Latino). Average age 40. *Faculty:* 2 full-time (1 woman), 12 part-time/adjunct (3 women). *Financial support:* Applicants required to submit FAFSA. In 2015, 53 master's, 43 doctorates awarded. Online learning. Offers leadership and professional practice (Ed D); organizational leadership (MOL). *Application deadline:* Applications are processed on a rolling basis. *Application fee:* $0. Electronic applications accepted. *Application Contact:* 844-TNU-GRAD, E-mail: sgcsadmissions@trevecca.edu. *Director of Master of Organizational Leadership*, Dr. Tom Middendorf, 615-248-1529, E-mail: sgcsadmissions@trevecca.edu.

Graduate Physician Assistant Program Students: 97 full-time (75 women). Average age 25. *Faculty:* 4 full-time (all women), 1 (woman) part-time/adjunct. *Financial support:* Applicants required to submit FAFSA. In 2015, 44 master's awarded. Offers physician assistant (MS). *Application deadline:* For fall admission, 11/1 for domestic students. *Application Contact:* 615-248-1225, E-mail: admissions_pa@trevecca.edu. *Director*, Dr. Bret Reeves, 615-248-1225, E-mail: admissions_pa@trevecca.edu.

Graduate Religion Programs Students: 23 full-time (5 women), 16 part-time (6 women); includes 12 minority (8 Black or African American, non-Hispanic/Latino; 1 Asian, non-Hispanic/Latino; 2 Hispanic/Latino; 1 Two or more races, non-Hispanic/Latino), 1 international. Average age 43. *Faculty:* 4 full-time (0 women). *Financial support:* Applicants required to submit FAFSA. In 2015, 6 master's awarded. *Degree program information:* Part-time programs available. Part-time, online learning. Offers biblical and theological studies (MA); Christian ministry (MA). *Application deadline:* Applications are processed on a rolling basis. *Application fee:* $0. Electronic applications accepted. *Application Contact:* 844-TNU-GRAD, E-mail: sgcsadmissions@trevecca.edu. *Dean, School of Theology and Christian Ministry/Director, Graduate Religion Program*, Dr. Tim Green, 615-248-1378, Fax: 615-248-7417.

TRIDENT UNIVERSITY INTERNATIONAL, Cypress, CA 90630

General Information Independent, coed, university.

GRADUATE UNITS

College of Business Administration ***Degree program information:*** Part-time and evening/weekend programs available. Part-time, evening/weekend, online learning. Offers business administration (MBA, PhD); conflict and negotiation management (MBA); criminal justice administration (MBA); entrepreneurship (MBA); finance (MBA); general management (MBA); government accounting (MBA); human resource management (MBA); information security and digital assurance management (MBA); information technology management (MBA); international business (MBA); logistics management (MBA); marketing (MBA); project management (MBA); public management (MBA); quality management (MBA); strategic leadership (MBA). Electronic applications accepted.

College of Education ***Degree program information:*** Part-time and evening/weekend programs available. Part-time, evening/weekend, online learning. Offers adult education (MA Ed); aviation education (MA Ed); children's literacy development (MA Ed); e-learning (MA Ed); e-learning leadership (MA Ed, PhD); early childhood education (MA Ed); education (MA Ed, PhD); educational leadership (MA Ed); enrollment management (MA Ed); higher education (MA Ed); higher education leadership (PhD); K-12 leadership (PhD); teaching and instruction (MA Ed); training and development (MA Ed). Electronic applications accepted.

College of Health Sciences ***Degree program information:*** Part-time and evening/weekend programs available. Part-time, evening/weekend, online learning. Offers clinical research administration (MS, Certificate); emergency and disaster management (MS, Certificate); environmental health science (Certificate); health care administration (PhD); health care management (MS); health education (MS, Certificate); health informatics (Certificate); health sciences (MS, PhD, Certificate); international health (MS); international health: educator or researcher option (PhD); international health: practitioner option (PhD); law and expert witness studies (MS, Certificate); public health (MS); quality assurance (Certificate). Electronic applications accepted.

College of Information Systems ***Degree program information:*** Part-time and evening/weekend programs available. Part-time, evening/weekend, online learning. Offers business intelligence (Certificate); information technology management (MS). Electronic applications accepted.

TRINE UNIVERSITY, Angola, IN 46703-1764

General Information Independent, coed, comprehensive institution. *Graduate housing:* Room and/or apartments available on a first-come, first-served basis to single students; on-campus housing not available to married students. Housing application deadline: 3/1.

GRADUATE UNITS

Allen School of Engineering and Technology ***Degree program information:*** Part-time and evening/weekend programs available. Part-time, evening/weekend. Offers civil engineering (ME); engineering management (MS).

Program in Criminal Justice ***Degree program information:*** Part-time and evening/weekend programs available. Part-time, evening/weekend. Offers emergency management (MS); forensic psychology (MS); law (MS); public administration (MS).

TRINITY BAPTIST COLLEGE, Jacksonville, FL 32221

General Information Independent-religious, coed, comprehensive institution. *Graduate housing:* On-campus housing not available.

GRADUATE UNITS

Graduate Programs Online learning. Offers educational leadership (M Ed); special education (M Ed).

TRINITY CHRISTIAN COLLEGE, Palos Heights, IL 60463-0929

General Information Independent-religious, coed, comprehensive institution.

GRADUATE UNITS

Program in Counseling Psychology ***Degree program information:*** Evening/weekend programs available. Evening/weekend, online learning. Offers counseling psychology (MA).

Program in Special Education ***Degree program information:*** Evening/weekend programs available. Evening/weekend. Offers special education (MA). Electronic applications accepted.

TRINITY COLLEGE, Toronto, ON M5S 1H8, Canada

General Information Independent-religious, coed, graduate-only institution. *Graduate housing:* Room and/or apartments available on a first-come, first-served basis to single students; on-campus housing not available to married students. Housing application deadline: 7/15.

GRADUATE UNITS

Faculty of Divinity ***Degree program information:*** Part-time programs available. Part-time. Offers ministry (Diploma); ministry for church musicians (Diploma); theology (M Div, MA, MTS, Th M, D Min, PhD, Th D, Diploma, L Th).

TRINITY COLLEGE, Hartford, CT 06106-3100

General Information Independent, coed, comprehensive institution. *Enrollment:* 2,397 graduate, professional, and undergraduate students; 159 part-time matriculated graduate/professional students (83 women). *Enrollment by degree level:* 159 master's. *Graduate faculty:* 15 part-time/adjunct (4 women). *Tuition, area resident:* Part-time $2415 per credit. *Required fees:* $50 per term. One-time fee: $75 part-time. Part-time tuition and fees vary according to course load. *Graduate housing:* On-campus housing not available. *Student services:* Campus safety program, career counseling, exercise/wellness program, free psychological counseling, multicultural affairs office, services for students with disabilities, writing training. *Library:* Trinity College Library plus 1 other.

Computer facilities: 249 computers available on campus for general student use. A campuswide network can be accessed from student residence rooms and from off campus. Online class registration, Web pages are available.
Website: http://www.trincoll.edu/

General Application Contact: Anique Thompson, Administrative Assistant, Graduate Studies, 860-297-2151, Fax: 860-297-2521, E-mail: anique.thompson@trincoll.edu.

GRADUATE UNITS

Graduate Programs ***Faculty:*** 2 part-time/adjunct. *Financial support:* Fellowships with partial tuition reimbursements, scholarships/grants, and tuition waivers (full) available. Support available to part-time students. Financial award application deadline: 4/1; financial award applicants required to submit FAFSA. *Degree program information:* Part-time and evening/weekend programs available. Part-time, evening/weekend. Offers American culture studies (MA); literary studies (MA); museums and communities (MA); public policy studies (MA); writing, rhetoric, and media arts (MA). *Application deadline:* For fall admission, 5/1 for domestic students; for spring admission, 11/15 for domestic students. *Application fee:* $75. Electronic applications accepted. *Application Contact:* Anique Thompson, Administrative Assistant, Graduate Studies, 860-297-2151, Fax: 860-297-5179, E-mail: anique.thompson@trincoll.edu. *Dean of Graduate Studies*, Dr. William R. Barnett, 860-297-2527, Fax: 860-297-5179, E-mail: william.barnett@trincoll.edu.

TRINITY INTERNATIONAL UNIVERSITY, Deerfield, IL 60015-1284

General Information Independent-religious, coed, university. *Graduate housing:* Rooms and/or apartments available on a first-come, first-served basis to single and married students.

GRADUATE UNITS

Trinity Evangelical Divinity School ***Degree program information:*** Part-time programs available. Part-time, online learning. Offers Biblical and Near Eastern archaeology and languages (MA); Christian studies (MA, Certificate); Christian thought (MA); church history (MA, Th M); congregational ministry: pastor-teacher (M Div); congregational ministry: team ministry (M Div); counseling ministries (MA); counseling psychology (MA); cross-cultural ministry (M Div); educational studies (PhD); evangelism (MA); history of Christianity in America (MA); intercultural studies (MA, PhD); leadership and ministry management (D Min); military chaplaincy (D Min); ministry (MA); mission and evangelism (Th M); missions and evangelism (D Min); New Testament (MA, Th M); Old Testament (Th M); Old Testament and Semitic languages (MA); pastoral care (M Div); pastoral care and counseling (D Min); pastoral counseling and psychology (Th M); pastoral theology (Th M); philosophy of religion (MA); preaching (D Min); religion (MA); research ministry (M Div); systematic theology (Th M); theological studies (PhD); urban ministry (MA). Electronic applications accepted.

Trinity Graduate School ***Degree program information:*** Part-time and evening/weekend programs available. Part-time, evening/weekend, online learning. Offers bioethics (MA); communication and culture (MA); counseling psychology (MA); instructional leadership (M Ed); teaching (MA). Electronic applications accepted.

Trinity Law School ***Degree program information:*** Part-time and evening/weekend programs available. Part-time, evening/weekend. Offers law (JD).

TRINITY INTERNATIONAL UNIVERSITY FLORIDA, Davie, FL 33324

General Information Independent-religious, coed, graduate-only institution. *Graduate housing:* On-campus housing not available.

GRADUATE UNITS

Divinity School Offers Christian studies (MA, Certificate).

Graduate School Offers counseling psychology (MA).

TRINITY LUTHERAN SEMINARY, Columbus, OH 43209-2334

General Information Independent-religious, coed, graduate-only institution. *Graduate housing:* Rooms and/or apartments available on a first-come, first-served basis to single and married students. Housing application deadline: 5/15.

GRADUATE UNITS

Graduate and Professional Programs ***Degree program information:*** Part-time programs available. Part-time. Offers African American studies (MTS); Biblical studies (MTS, STM); Christian education (MA); Christian spirituality (STM); church in the world (MTS); church music (MA); divinity (M Div); general theological studies (MTS); mission and evangelism (STM); pastoral leadership and practice (STM); youth and family ministry (MA). Electronic applications accepted.

TRINITY SCHOOL FOR MINISTRY, Ambridge, PA 15003-2397

General Information Independent-religious, coed, graduate-only institution. *Graduate housing:* On-campus housing not available.

GRADUATE UNITS

Graduate Programs ***Degree program information:*** Part-time programs available. Part-time. Offers Anglican studies (Diploma); basic Christian studies (Diploma); divinity (M Div); ministry (D Min); mission and evangelism (MAME, Diploma); religion (MAR); youth ministry (Diploma).

TRINITY UNIVERSITY, San Antonio, TX 78212-7200

General Information Independent-religious, coed, comprehensive institution. *Enrollment:* 2,479 graduate, professional, and undergraduate students; 158 full-time matriculated graduate/professional students (106 women), 48 part-time matriculated graduate/professional students (29 women). *Enrollment by degree level:* 206 master's. *Graduate housing:* On-campus housing not available. *Student services:* Campus employment opportunities, campus safety program, career counseling, exercise/wellness program, free psychological counseling, international student services, services for students with disabilities, teacher training, writing training. *Library:* Elizabeth Huth Coates Library plus 1 other.

Computer facilities: Computer purchase and lease plans are available. 500 computers available on campus for general student use. A campuswide network can be accessed from student residence rooms and from off campus. Online class registration is available.
Website: http://www.trinity.edu/

General Application Contact: Office of the Registrar, 210-999-7201, Fax: 210-999-7202, E-mail: roffice@trinity.edu.

GRADUATE UNITS

Department of Education Students: 81 full-time (64 women), 7 part-time (all women); includes 39 minority (9 Black or African American, non-Hispanic/Latino; 2 Asian, non-Hispanic/Latino; 26 Hispanic/Latino; 2 Two or more races, non-Hispanic/Latino), 2 international. Average age 27. *Faculty:* 9 full-time (all women), 14 part-time/adjunct (10 women). *Financial support:* Application deadline: 5/1; applicants required to submit FAFSA. In 2015, 59 master's awarded. *Degree program information:* Part-time and evening/weekend programs available. Part-time, evening/weekend. Offers school leadership (M Ed); school psychology (MA); teaching (MAT). *Application Contact:* Office of the Registrar, 210-999-7201, Fax: 210-999-7202, E-mail: roffice@trinity.edu. *Chair*, Dr. Shari Albright, 210-999-7506, Fax: 210-999-7592, E-mail: salbrig1@trinity.edu.

Department of Health Care Administration Students: 51 full-time (26 women), 40 part-time (21 women); includes 31 minority (4 Black or African American, non-Hispanic/Latino; 1 American Indian or Alaska Native, non-Hispanic/Latino; 7 Asian, non-Hispanic/Latino; 18 Hispanic/Latino; 1 Two or more races, non-Hispanic/Latino). Average age 28. *Faculty:* 6 full-time (1 woman), 6 part-time/adjunct (0 women). *Financial support:* Fellowships, institutionally sponsored loans, scholarships/grants, and unspecified assistantships available. Support available to part-time students. Financial award application deadline: 5/1; financial award applicants required to submit FAFSA. In 2015, 29 master's awarded. *Degree program information:* Part-time programs available.

Part-time, online learning. Offers health care administration (MS). *Application deadline:* Applications are processed on a rolling basis. *Application fee:* $50. Electronic applications accepted. *Professor and Department Chair,* Dr. Ed Schumacher, 210-999-8107, E-mail: hca@trinity.edu.

School of Business Students: 26 full-time (16 women), 1 (woman) part-time; includes 9 minority (1 Asian, non-Hispanic/Latino; 8 Hispanic/Latino), 4 international. Average age 23. *Faculty:* 5 full-time (3 women), 4 part-time/adjunct (0 women). *Financial support:* Institutionally sponsored loans and scholarships/grants available. Financial award application deadline: 5/1; financial award applicants required to submit FAFSA. In 2015, 21 master's awarded. Offers accounting (MS). *Application deadline:* For fall admission, 2/1 for domestic and international students. Electronic applications accepted. *Application Contact:* Dr. Julie Persellin, Director of the Accounting Program, 210-999-7230, E-mail: jpersell@trinity.edu. *Chair, Department of Accounting,* Dr. Michael Wilkins, 210-999-7347, E-mail: mwilkin2@trinity.edu.

TRINITY WASHINGTON UNIVERSITY, Washington, DC 20017-1094

General Information Independent-religious, women only, comprehensive institution. *Graduate housing:* Room and/or apartments available on a first-come, first-served basis to single students; on-campus housing not available to married students.

GRADUATE UNITS

School of Business and Graduate Studies ***Degree program information:*** Part-time and evening/weekend programs available. Part-time, evening/weekend. Offers business administration (MBA); communication (MA); international security studies (MA); organizational management (MSA).

School of Education ***Degree program information:*** Part-time and evening/weekend programs available. Part-time, evening/weekend. Offers clinical mental health counseling (MA); early childhood education (MAT); educating for change (M Ed); educational administration (MSA); elementary education (MAT); reading (M Ed); school counseling (MA); secondary education (MAT); special education (MAT).

TRINITY WESTERN UNIVERSITY, Langley, BC V2Y 1Y1, Canada

General Information Independent-religious, coed, comprehensive institution. *Graduate housing:* On-campus housing not available.

GRADUATE UNITS

ACTS Seminaries ***Degree program information:*** Part-time programs available. Part-time. Offers Christian studies (MA); cross cultural ministry (MA); theology (M Div, M Th, MAMFT, MLE, MTS, D Min).

School of Graduate Studies Offers biblical studies (MA); business (MA, Certificate); Christian ministry (MA); counseling psychology (MA); education (MA, Certificate); general humanities (MAIH); healthcare (MA, Certificate); international business (MBA); linguistics (MA); management of the growing enterprise (MBA); non-profit (MA, Certificate); non-profit and charitable organization management (MBA); specialized (MAIH); teaching English to speakers of other languages (TESOL) (MA).

School of Nursing Offers nursing (MSN).

TRI-STATE BIBLE COLLEGE, South Point, OH 45680-8402

General Information Independent-religious, coed, comprehensive institution.

GRADUATE UNITS

Graduate Program Offers Biblical studies (MA). Electronic applications accepted.

TRI-STATE COLLEGE OF ACUPUNCTURE, New York, NY 10011

General Information Independent, coed, graduate-only institution. *Enrollment by degree level:* 112 master's. *Graduate faculty:* 5 full-time (2 women), 32 part-time/adjunct (24 women). *Tuition, area resident:* Full-time $23,600; part-time $11,800 per semester. *Required fees:* $395; $395 per year. *Graduate housing:* On-campus housing not available. *Student services:* Campus safety program, career counseling, low-cost health insurance, teacher training.

Computer facilities: 5 computers available on campus for general student use. Website: http://www.tsca.edu/

General Application Contact: Sandra Turner, Admissions Office, 212-242-2255, Fax: 212-242-2920, E-mail: sandra.turner@tsca.edu.

GRADUATE UNITS

Graduate Programs Students: 95 full-time (65 women), 17 part-time (11 women); includes 16 minority (1 Black or African American, non-Hispanic/Latino; 13 Asian, non-Hispanic/Latino; 2 Hispanic/Latino). *Faculty:* 5 full-time (2 women), 32 part-time/adjunct (24 women). *Financial support:* Application deadline: 7/15; applicants required to submit FAFSA. *Degree program information:* Evening/weekend programs available. Evening/weekend. Offers acupuncture (MS); Chinese herbology (Certificate); Oriental medicine (MS). *Application deadline:* For fall admission, 6/15 priority date for domestic students. Applications are processed on a rolling basis. *Application fee:* $50. *Application Contact:* Sandra Turner, Admissions Office, 212-242-2255, Fax: 212-242-2920, E-mail: sandra.turner@tsca.edu.

TROY UNIVERSITY, Troy, AL 36082

General Information State-supported, coed, comprehensive institution. *Enrollment:* 18,430 graduate, professional, and undergraduate students; 954 full-time matriculated graduate/professional students (682 women), 1,729 part-time matriculated graduate/professional students (1,295 women). *Graduate faculty:* 143 full-time (43 women), 176 part-time/adjunct (40 women). Tuition, state resident: full-time $7146; part-time $397 per credit hour. Tuition, nonresident: full-time $14,292; part-time $794 per credit hour. *Required fees:* $802. Tuition and fees vary according to campus/location and program. *Graduate housing:* Rooms and/or apartments available on a first-come, first-served basis to single students and available to married students. Typical cost: $5815 (including board) for single students. Housing application deadline: 7/31. *Student services:* Campus employment opportunities, campus safety program, career counseling, child daycare facilities, exercise/wellness program, free psychological counseling, grant writing training, international student services, low-cost health insurance, services for students with disabilities, teacher training, writing training. *Library:* Lurleen B. Wallace Library (Troy Campus) plus 2 others. *Research affiliation:* Systemics Research Fund (protozoan symbionts), Birmingham Audubon Society (Alabama flora and fauna).

Computer facilities: 1,435 computers available on campus for general student use. A campuswide network can be accessed from student residence rooms and from off campus. Online class registration is available.
Website: http://www.troy.edu/

General Application Contact: Brenda K. Campbell, Director of Graduate Admissions, 334-670-3178, Fax: 334-670-3733, E-mail: bcamp@troy.edu.

GRADUATE UNITS

Graduate School Students: 1,145 full-time (773 women), 2,040 part-time (1,302 women); includes 1,909 minority (1,445 Black or African American, non-Hispanic/Latino; 36 American Indian or Alaska Native, non-Hispanic/Latino; 74 Asian, non-Hispanic/Latino; 135 Hispanic/Latino; 219 Two or more races, non-Hispanic/Latino). Average age 31. 2,007 applicants, 82% accepted, 694 enrolled. *Faculty:* 143 full-time (43 women), 176 part-time/adjunct (40 women). *Financial support:* Fellowships, career-related internships or fieldwork, and scholarships/grants available. Support available to part-time students. Financial award application deadline: 5/1; financial award applicants required to submit FAFSA. In 2015, 1,133 master's, 13 doctorates, 20 other advanced degrees awarded. *Degree program information:* Part-time and evening/weekend programs available. Part-time, evening/weekend, 100% online, blended/hybrid learning. *Application deadline:* Applications are processed on a rolling basis. *Application fee:* $50. Electronic applications accepted. *Application Contact:* Jessica A. Kimbro, Director of Graduate Admissions, 334-670-3178, E-mail: jacord@troy.edu. *Associate Provost/Dean,* Dr. Dianne Barron, 334-670-3189, Fax: 334-670-3912, E-mail: dlbarron@troy.edu.

College of Arts and Sciences Students: 256 full-time (112 women), 694 part-time (372 women); includes 558 minority (332 Black or African American, non-Hispanic/Latino; 19 American Indian or Alaska Native, non-Hispanic/Latino; 23 Asian, non-Hispanic/Latino; 27 Hispanic/Latino; 157 Two or more races, non-Hispanic/Latino). Average age 30. 788 applicants, 70% accepted, 150 enrolled. *Faculty:* 67 full-time (22 women), 23 part-time/adjunct (7 women). *Financial support:* Fellowships, career-related internships or fieldwork, and scholarships/grants available. Support available to part-time students. Financial award applicants required to submit FAFSA. In 2015, 311 master's awarded. *Degree program information:* Part-time and evening/weekend programs available. Part-time, evening/weekend. Offers American history (MA); arts and sciences (MA, MPA, MS, MS Sc, Certificate); biological science (MS); biomedical sciences (MS, Certificate); computer science (MS); criminal justice (MS); environmental policy (MS); environmental science (MS); European history (MA); government contracting (MPA); health care administration (MPA); justice administration (MPA); national security affairs (MPA); nonprofit management (MPA); public human resources management (MPA); public management (MPA); regional affairs (MS); social science (MS Sc). *Application deadline:* Applications are processed on a rolling basis. *Application fee:* $50. Electronic applications accepted. *Application Contact:* Jessica A. Kimbro, Director of Graduate Admissions, 334-670-3178, E-mail: jacord@troy.edu. *Dean,* Dr. James Rinehart, 334-670-5646, Fax: 334-670-3547, E-mail: rinehart@troy.edu.

College of Business Students: 151 full-time (78 women), 605 part-time (397 women); includes 393 minority (314 Black or African American, non-Hispanic/Latino; 5 American Indian or Alaska Native, non-Hispanic/Latino; 38 Asian, non-Hispanic/Latino; 19 Hispanic/Latino; 1 Native Hawaiian or other Pacific Islander, non-Hispanic/Latino; 16 Two or more races, non-Hispanic/Latino). Average age 33. 493 applicants, 85% accepted, 204 enrolled. *Faculty:* 42 full-time (12 women), 5 part-time/adjunct (1 woman). *Financial support:* In 2015–16, 5 research assistantships were awarded; career-related internships or fieldwork and scholarships/grants also available. Support available to part-time students. Financial award applicants required to submit FAFSA. In 2015, 349 master's awarded. *Degree program information:* Part-time and evening/weekend programs available. Part-time, evening/weekend, 100% online, blended/hybrid learning. Offers accountancy (M Acc); accounting (EMBA, MBA); applied management (MSM); business (EMBA, M Acc, MA, MBA, MBAi, MS, MSM, MTX, Certificate); criminal justice (EMBA); economics (MA); finance (MBA); general management (EMBA, MBA); healthcare management (EMBA, MSM); human resources management (MS); information systems (EMBA, MBA, MSM); international economic development (MBA); international hospitality management (MSM); international management (MSM); leadership and organizational effectiveness (MSM); public management (MS, MSM); taxation (MTX, Certificate). *Application deadline:* Applications are processed on a rolling basis. *Application fee:* $50. Electronic applications accepted. *Application Contact:* Jessica A. Kimbro, Director of Graduate Admissions, 334-670-3178, Fax: 334-670-3733, E-mail: bcamp@troy.edu. *Dean,* Dr. Judson Edwards, 334-670-3989, Fax: 334-670-3708, E-mail: jcedwards@troy.edu.

College of Communication and Fine Arts Students: 35 full-time (30 women), 68 part-time (48 women); includes 57 minority (48 Black or African American, non-Hispanic/Latino; 3 American Indian or Alaska Native, non-Hispanic/Latino; 4 Hispanic/Latino; 2 Two or more races, non-Hispanic/Latino). Average age 29. 41 applicants, 98% accepted, 30 enrolled. *Faculty:* 6 full-time (3 women). *Financial support:* Fellowships, career-related internships or fieldwork, and scholarships/grants available. Support available to part-time students. Financial award applicants required to submit FAFSA. In 2015, 42 master's awarded. *Degree program information:* Part-time and evening/weekend programs available. Part-time, evening/weekend. Offers strategic communication (MS). *Application deadline:* For fall admission, 6/1 for international students; for spring admission, 10/15 for international students. Applications are processed on a rolling basis. *Application fee:* $50. Electronic applications accepted. *Application Contact:* Jessica A. Kimbro, Director of Graduate Admissions, 334-670-3178, E-mail: jacord@troy.edu. *Dean,* Dr. Larry Blocher, 334-670-3869, Fax: 334-670-3547, E-mail: lblocher@troy.edu.

College of Education Students: 443 full-time (348 women), 753 part-time (632 women); includes 680 minority (572 Black or African American, non-Hispanic/Latino; 7 American Indian or Alaska Native, non-Hispanic/Latino; 7 Asian, non-Hispanic/Latino; 67 Hispanic/Latino; 27 Two or more races, non-Hispanic/Latino). Average age 34. 409 applicants, 93% accepted, 192 enrolled. *Faculty:* 91 full-time (36 women), 38 part-time/adjunct (22 women). *Financial support:* Fellowships, career-related internships or fieldwork, and scholarships/grants available. Support available to part-time students. Financial award applicants required to submit FAFSA. In 2015, 354 master's, 5 other advanced degrees awarded. *Degree program information:* Part-time and evening/weekend programs available. Part-time, evening/weekend. Offers adult education (MS); agency counseling (Ed S); art education (MS); biology (MS); clinical mental health (MS); community counseling (MS, Ed S); computer science (MS); corrections counseling (MS); early childhood education (MS, Ed S); education (MS, MS Ed, Ed S); educational administration/leadership (MS, Ed S); elementary education (Ed S); gifted education (MS); history (MS); instrumental (MS); K-6 elementary education (MS); language arts (MS); mathematics (MS); physical education (MS); postsecondary education (MS Ed); reading specialist (MS); rehabilitation counseling (MS); school counseling (MS, Ed S); school psychology (MS, Ed S); school psychometry (MS); second language instruction (MS); social science (MS); social service counseling (MS); student affairs counseling (MS); substance abuse counseling (MS); vocal/choral (MS). *Application deadline:* For fall admission, 6/1 for international students; for spring admission, 10/15 for international students. Applications are processed on a rolling basis. *Application fee:* $50. Electronic applications accepted. *Application Contact:* Jessica A. Kimbro, Director of Graduate

Admissions, 334-670-3178, E-mail: jacord@troy.edu. *Dean*, Dr. Kathryn Hildebrand, 334-670-3365, Fax: 334-670-3474, E-mail: khildebrand@troy.edu.

College of Health and Human Services Students: 260 full-time (205 women), 278 part-time (211 women); includes 222 minority (179 Black or African American, non-Hispanic/Latino; 2 American Indian or Alaska Native, non-Hispanic/Latino; 6 Asian, non-Hispanic/Latino; 18 Hispanic/Latino; 17 Two or more races, non-Hispanic/Latino). Average age 31. 276 applicants, 91% accepted, 118 enrolled. *Faculty:* 40 full-time (26 women), 16 part-time/adjunct (14 women). *Financial support:* Tuition waivers and unspecified assistantships available. Support available to part-time students. Financial award application deadline: 4/5; financial award applicants required to submit FAFSA. In 2015, 77 master's, 13 doctorates, 15 other advanced degrees awarded. *Degree program information:* Part-time and evening/weekend programs available. Part-time, evening/weekend. Offers adult health (MSN); clinical nurse specialist adult health (DNP); clinical nurse specialist maternal infant (DNP); family nurse practitioner (MSN, DNP, PMC); health and human services (MS, MS Sc, MSN, MSW, DNP, PMC); informatics specialist (MSN); maternal infant (MSN); social work (MSW); sport and fitness management (MS). *Application deadline:* Applications are processed on a rolling basis. *Application fee:* $50. Electronic applications accepted. *Application Contact:* Jessica A. Kimbro, Director of Graduate Admissions, 334-670-3178, E-mail: jacord@troy.edu. *Associate Dean*, Dr. John Miller, 334-670-3712, Fax: 334-670-3743, E-mail: johnm@troy.edu.

TRUMAN STATE UNIVERSITY, Kirksville, MO 63501-4221

General Information State-supported, coed, comprehensive institution. CGS member. *Enrollment:* 6,208 graduate, professional, and undergraduate students; 245 full-time matriculated graduate/professional students (180 women), 28 part-time matriculated graduate/professional students (22 women). *Enrollment by degree level:* 266 master's, 7 other advanced degrees. Tuition, state resident: full-time $6870; part-time $343.50 per credit hour. Tuition, nonresident: full-time $11,790; part-time $589.50 per credit hour. Tuition and fees vary according to course load and program. *Graduate housing:* Rooms and/or apartments available on a first-come, first-served basis to single and married students. Typical cost: $8480 (including board) for single students; $8480 (including board) for married students. Room and board charges vary according to board plan and campus/location. Housing application deadline: 5/1. *Student services:* Campus employment opportunities, campus safety program, career counseling, grant writing training, international student services, low-cost health insurance, multicultural affairs office, services for students with disabilities, writing training. *Library:* Pickler Memorial Library. *Collection:* Books: 507,509 (physical), 307,057 (digital/electronic); Serial titles: 639 (physical), 2,382 (digital/electronic); Databases: 104. Students can reserve study rooms. *Research affiliation:* Gulf Coast Research Laboratory (marine science), Kirksville College of Osteopathic Medicine (biology).

Computer facilities: 1,099 computers available on campus for general student use. A campuswide network can be accessed from student residence rooms and from off campus. Online class registration is available.
Website: http://www.truman.edu/

General Application Contact: Stephanie Rudolph, Graduate Office Administrative Assistant, 660-785-4109, Fax: 660-785-7460, E-mail: gradinfo@truman.edu.

GRADUATE UNITS

Graduate School Students: 226 full-time (158 women), 21 part-time (9 women); includes 4 minority (all Asian, non-Hispanic/Latino). Average age 23. 129 applicants, 82% accepted, 106 enrolled. *Faculty:* 94 full-time (39 women). *Financial support:* Fellowships, research assistantships with tuition reimbursements, teaching assistantships with tuition reimbursements, career-related internships or fieldwork, Federal Work-Study, institutionally sponsored loans, scholarships/grants, and unspecified assistantships available. Financial award application deadline: 5/1; financial award applicants required to submit FAFSA. In 2015, 137 master's awarded. *Application deadline:* For fall admission, 6/1 priority date for domestic and international students; for spring admission, 11/1 priority date for domestic and international students. Applications are processed on a rolling basis. *Application fee:* $40 ($0 for international students). Electronic applications accepted. *Application Contact:* Stephanie Rudolph, Graduate Office Administrative Assistant, 660-785-4109, E-mail: gradinfo@truman.edu. *Dean of Graduate Studies*, Dr. Maria Di Stefano, 660-785-4109, Fax: 660-785-7460, E-mail: mdistefa@truman.edu.

School of Arts and Letters Students: 31 full-time (14 women). Average age 23. 24 applicants, 96% accepted, 17 enrolled. *Faculty:* 44 full-time (19 women). *Financial support:* In 2015–16, research assistantships with tuition reimbursements (averaging $8,000 per year), teaching assistantships with tuition reimbursements (averaging $8,000 per year) were awarded; career-related internships or fieldwork and Federal Work-Study also available. Financial award application deadline: 5/1; financial award applicants required to submit FAFSA. In 2015, 10 master's awarded. Offers arts and letters (MA, MS); biology (MS); English (MA); music (MA). *Application deadline:* For fall admission, 6/1 priority date for domestic and international students; for spring admission, 11/1 priority date for domestic students, 11/1 for international students. Applications are processed on a rolling basis. *Application fee:* $0. Electronic applications accepted. *Application Contact:* Stephanie Rudolph, Graduate Office Administrative Assistant, 660-785-4109, Fax: 660-785-7460, E-mail: gradinfo@truman.edu. *Dean*, Dr. Priscilla Riggle, 660-785-7777, Fax: 660-785-7109.

School of Business Financial support: Research assistantships with tuition reimbursements, teaching assistantships with tuition reimbursements, career-related internships or fieldwork, and Federal Work-Study available. Financial award application deadline: 5/1; financial award applicants required to submit FAFSA. Offers accounting (M Ac); business (M Ac). *Application deadline:* For fall admission, 6/1 for domestic and international students; for spring admission, 11/1 for domestic and international students; for summer admission, 4/1 for domestic and international students. Applications are processed on a rolling basis. *Application fee:* $40. Electronic applications accepted. *Application Contact:* Stephanie Rudolph, Graduate Office Secretary, 660-785-4109, Fax: 660-785-7460, E-mail: sdunn@truman.edu. *Dean*, Dr. Renee Wachter, 660-785-4346, Fax: 660-785-7471, E-mail: rwachter@truman.edu.

School of Health Sciences and Education Financial support: Fellowships, career-related internships or fieldwork, and Federal Work-Study available. Financial award application deadline: 5/1; financial award applicants required to submit FAFSA. Offers communication disorders (MA); education (MAE); health sciences and education (MA, MAE). *Application deadline:* For fall admission, 6/15 priority date for domestic and international students; for spring admission, 11/1 for domestic students, 11/1 priority date for international students. Applications are processed on a rolling basis. *Application fee:* $40. Electronic applications accepted. *Application Contact:* Stephanie Rudolph, Graduate Office Secretary, 660-785-4109, Fax: 660-785-7460, E-mail: sdunn@truman.edu. *Dean*, Dr. Sam Minner, 660-785-4383, Fax: 660-785-4393, E-mail: minner@truman.edu.

School of Science and Mathematics Offers athletic training (MAT). *Application Contact:* Stephanie Rudolph, Graduate Office Secretary, 660-785-4109, Fax: 660-785-7460, E-mail: sdunn@truman.edu. *Dean of Graduate Studies*, Dr. Maria Di Stefano, 660-785-4109, Fax: 660-785-7460, E-mail: mdistefa@truman.edu.

TUFTS UNIVERSITY, Medford, MA 02155

General Information Independent, coed, university. CGS member. *Enrollment:* 11,137 graduate, professional, and undergraduate students; 4,947 full-time matriculated graduate/professional students (2,916 women), 703 part-time matriculated graduate/professional students (439 women). *Enrollment by degree level:* 2,427 master's, 2,921 doctoral, 302 other advanced degrees. *Graduate faculty:* 1,009 full-time (439 women), 502 part-time/adjunct (231 women). *Tuition, area resident:* Full-time $48,412; part-time $1210 per credit hour. *Required fees:* $806. Full-time tuition and fees vary according to degree level, program and student level. Part-time tuition and fees vary according to course load. *Graduate housing:* Room and/or apartments available on a first-come, first-served basis to single students; on-campus housing not available to married students. Housing application deadline: 4/15. *Student services:* Campus employment opportunities, campus safety program, career counseling, child daycare facilities, exercise/wellness program, free psychological counseling, international student services, low-cost health insurance, multicultural affairs office, services for students with disabilities, teacher training, writing training. *Library:* Tisch Library plus 3 others. *Collection:* Books: 996,087 (physical), 432,887 (digital/electronic); Serial titles: 610 (physical); Databases: 83,216. Weekly public service hours: 110; students can reserve study rooms. *Research affiliation:* Maine Medical Center (medicine), The Stockholm Environmental Institute (environmental science and policy), Caritas St. Elizabeth's Medical Center (medicine), Tufts-New England Medical Center (medicine), Lahey Clinic Medical Center (medicine), Baystate Medical Center (medicine).

Computer facilities: Computer purchase and lease plans are available. 1,039 computers available on campus for general student use. A campuswide network can be accessed from student residence rooms and from off campus. Online class registration, Cloud storage for all students, staff, and faculty are available.
Website: http://www.tufts.edu/

General Application Contact: Information Contact, 617-628-5000.

GRADUATE UNITS

Cummings School of Veterinary Medicine Offers animals and public policy (MS); biomedical sciences (PhD); conservation medicine (MS); veterinary medicine (DVM). Electronic applications accepted.

The Fletcher School of Law and Diplomacy Online learning. Offers law and diplomacy (LL M, MA, MALD, MIB, PhD). Electronic applications accepted.

The Gerald J. and Dorothy R. Friedman School of Nutrition Science and Policy ***Degree program information:*** Part-time programs available. Part-time. Offers agriculture, food and environment (MS, PhD); biochemical and molecular nutrition (PhD); dietetic internship (MS); food policy and applied nutrition (MS, PhD); humanitarian assistance (MAHA); nutrition (MS, PhD); nutrition communication (MS); nutritional epidemiology (MS, PhD). Electronic applications accepted.

Graduate School of Arts and Sciences ***Degree program information:*** Part-time programs available. Part-time. Offers analytical chemistry (MS, PhD); art education (MAT); art history (MA); art history and museum studies (MA); arts and sciences (MA, MAT, MFA, MPP, MS, OTD, PhD, Certificate, Ed S); astrophysics (MS, PhD); bioengineering (Certificate); biology (MS, PhD); bioorganic chemistry (MS, PhD); biotechnology (Certificate); biotechnology engineering (Certificate); chemical physics (PhD); child study and human development (MA, PhD); classical archaeology (MA); classics (MA); classics with teaching licensure (MA); cognitive science (PhD); community development (MA); community environmental studies (Certificate); computer science (Certificate); computer science minor (Certificate); drama (MA); dramatic literature and criticism (PhD); early childhood education (MAT); economics (MS); education (MA, MAT, MS, PhD); educational studies (MA); elementary education (MAT); English (MA, PhD); environmental chemistry (MS, PhD); environmental management (Certificate); environmental policy (MA); epidemiology (Certificate); ethnomusicology (MA); French (MA); German (MA); German with teaching licensure (MA); health and human welfare (MA); history (MA, PhD); history and museum studies (MA); housing policy (MA); human-computer interaction (Certificate); inorganic chemistry (MS, PhD); interdisciplinary studies (PhD); international environment/development policy (MA); management of community organizations (Certificate); manufacturing engineering (Certificate); mathematics (MS, PhD); microwave and wireless engineering (Certificate); middle and secondary education (MA, MAT); museum education (MA); museum studies (Certificate); music history and literature (MA); music theory and composition (MA); occupational therapy (Certificate); organic chemistry (MS, PhD); philosophy (MA); physical chemistry (MS, PhD); physics (MS, PhD); physics education (PhD); program evaluation (Certificate); psychology (MS, PhD); public policy (MPP); school psychology (MA, Ed S); secondary education (MA); soft materials robotics (PhD); STEM education (MS, PhD); studio art (MFA); theater history (PhD). Electronic applications accepted.

Sackler School of Graduate Biomedical Sciences Students: 228 full-time (140 women), 3 part-time (1 woman); includes 55 minority (10 Black or African American, non-Hispanic/Latino; 29 Asian, non-Hispanic/Latino; 8 Hispanic/Latino; 8 Two or more races, non-Hispanic/Latino), 41 international. Average age 33. 623 applicants, 14% accepted, 46 enrolled. *Faculty:* 200 full-time (60 women). *Financial support:* In 2015–16, 175 research assistantships with full tuition reimbursements (averaging $32,000 per year) were awarded; traineeships and health care benefits also available. Financial award application deadline: 12/15. In 2015, 7 master's, 28 doctorates, 4 other advanced degrees awarded. Offers biomedical sciences (MS, PhD, Certificate); cancer biology (PhD); clinical and translational science (MS, PhD, Certificate); developmental and regenerative biology (PhD); genetics (PhD); immunology (PhD); mammalian genetics at jax (PhD); medically-oriented research in graduate education (PhD); molecular and cellular medicine (PhD); molecular microbiology (PhD); neuroscience (PhD); pharmacology and drug development (MS); pharmacology and experimental therapeutics (PhD); structural and chemical biology (PhD). *Application deadline:* For fall admission, 12/15 priority date for domestic and international students. *Application fee:* $70. Electronic applications accepted. *Application Contact:* Dr. Elizabeth Storrs, Registrar/Director of Enrollment Services, 617-636-6767, Fax: 617-636-0375, E-mail: sackler-school@tufts.edu. *Dean*, Dr. Naomi Rosenberg, 617-636-6767, Fax: 617-636-0375, E-mail: naomi.rosenberg@tufts.edu.

School of Dental Medicine Offers dental medicine (MS, DMD, Certificate); dentistry (Certificate). DMD/MPH offered with School of Medicine.

School of Engineering ***Degree program information:*** Part-time programs available. Part-time. Offers bioengineering (ME, MS); bioinformatics (MS); biomedical engineering (PhD); biotechnology engineering (PhD); chemical and biological engineering (ME, MS, PhD); civil engineering (ME, MS, PhD); cognitive science (PhD); computer science (MS,

PhD); electrical engineering (MS, PhD); engineering (ME, MS, MSEM, PhD); environmental engineering (ME, MS, PhD); human factors (MS); mechanical engineering (ME, MS, PhD). Electronic applications accepted.

The Gordon Institute Degree program information: Part-time programs available. Part-time. Offers engineering management (MSEM); innovation and management (MS). Electronic applications accepted.

School of Medicine Offers biomedical sciences (MS); health communication (MS, Certificate); medicine (MPH, MS, Dr PH, MD, Certificate); pain research, education and policy (MS, Certificate); physician assistant (MS); public health (MPH, Dr PH). *Application Contact:* General Informational Contact, 617-636-7000. *Dean*, Dr. Harris Berman, 617-636-6565.

See Display below and Close-Up on page 905.

TULANE UNIVERSITY, New Orleans, LA 70118-5669

General Information Independent, coed, university. CGS member. *Enrollment:* 13,449 graduate, professional, and undergraduate students; 4,385 full-time matriculated graduate/professional students (2,369 women), 725 part-time matriculated graduate/professional students (367 women). *Enrollment by degree level:* 3,034 master's, 1,978 doctoral, 98 other advanced degrees. *Graduate faculty:* 63 full-time (31 women), 38 part-time/adjunct (22 women). *Tuition, area resident:* Full-time $47,658; part-time $2648 per credit hour. *Required fees:* $1980; $44.50 per credit hour. $550 per term. Tuition and fees vary according to course load, degree level and program. *Graduate housing:* Rooms and/or apartments available on a first-come, first-served basis to single and married students. Typical cost: $9660 per year for single students; $19,200 per year for married students. Room charges vary according to board plan, campus/location and housing facility selected. *Student services:* Campus employment opportunities, campus safety program, career counseling, child daycare facilities, exercise/wellness program, free psychological counseling, grant writing training, international student services, low-cost health insurance, multicultural affairs office, services for students with disabilities, teacher training, writing training. *Library:* Howard Tilton Memorial Library plus 8 others. *Collection:* Books: 4.5 million (physical); Serial titles: 137,773 (physical). *Research affiliation:* Genentech (clinical research in antiviral treatment and pulmonary disease), AbbVie (clinical research in the areas of infectious disease and cancer), New Orleans BioInnovation Center (NOBIC) (business consulting and start-up support, including educational events), Louisiana Cancer Research Consortium (research in treatment and prevention of cancer), American Heart Association (clinical research in cardiovascular diseases), New Orleans BioInnovation Center (development and commercialization of new technologies).

Computer facilities: 556 computers available on campus for general student use. A campuswide network can be accessed from student residence rooms and from off campus. Online class registration is available.
Website: http://www.tulane.edu/

General Application Contact: Ashley Robison, Senior Program Coordinator, 504-247-1213, Fax: 504-865-6723, E-mail: ogps@tulane.edu.

GRADUATE UNITS

A. B. Freeman School of Business Students: 576 full-time (297 women), 329 part-time (155 women); includes 102 minority (40 Black or African American, non-Hispanic/Latino; 1 American Indian or Alaska Native, non-Hispanic/Latino; 24 Asian, non-Hispanic/Latino; 35 Hispanic/Latino; 2 Two or more races, non-Hispanic/Latino), 540 international. Average age 27. 1,681 applicants, 82% accepted, 613 enrolled. *Faculty:* 59 full-time (17 women), 43 part-time/adjunct (7 women). *Financial support:* In 2015–16, 153 students received support. Fellowships with tuition reimbursements available, research assistantships, teaching assistantships, career-related internships or fieldwork, Federal Work-Study, tuition waivers (full and partial), and unspecified assistantships available. Support available to part-time students. Financial award application deadline: 4/15; financial award applicants required to submit FAFSA. In 2015, 620 master's, 6 doctorates awarded. *Degree program information:* Part-time and evening/weekend programs available. Part-time, evening/weekend. Offers accounting (M Acct); analytics (MBA); banking and financial services (M Fin); energy (M Fin, MBA); entrepreneurship (MBA); finance (MBA, PhD); international business (MBA); international management (MBA); strategic management and leadership (MBA). *Application deadline:* For fall admission, 11/1 priority date for domestic and international students; for winter admission, 1/6 for domestic and international students; for spring admission, 3/1 priority date for domestic and international students; for summer admission, 5/5 for domestic students. Applications are processed on a rolling basis. *Application fee:* $125. Electronic applications accepted. *Application Contact:* Melissa Booth, Director of Graduate Admissions and Financial Aid, 800-223-5402, E-mail: freeman.admissions@tulane.edu. *Dean*, Ira Solomon, PhD, 504-865-5407, Fax: 504-865-5491, E-mail: businessdean@tulane.edu.

Program in Liberal Arts *Degree program information:* Part-time programs available. Part-time. Offers liberal arts (MLA).

School of Architecture *Financial support:* Fellowships, Federal Work-Study, and scholarships/grants available. Support available to part-time students. Financial award application deadline: 2/1; financial award applicants required to submit FAFSA. *Degree program information:* Part-time programs available. Part-time. Offers architecture (M Arch, M Arch II, MPS, MSRED). *Application deadline:* For fall admission, 2/15 for domestic and international students. *Application fee:* $35.

School of Law *Financial support:* Fellowships, career-related internships or fieldwork, Federal Work-Study, institutionally sponsored loans, scholarships/grants, and tuition waivers (full and partial) available. Financial award application deadline: 2/15; financial award applicants required to submit FAFSA. Offers American business law (LL M); international development (MS, PhD); law (JD, SJD). *Application deadline:* For fall admission, 3/15 priority date for domestic and international students. Applications are processed on a rolling basis. *Application fee:* $60. Electronic applications accepted.

The Payson Center for International Development Degree program information: Part-time programs available. Part-time. Offers international development (MS, PhD); law and development (LL M). Electronic applications accepted.

School of Liberal Arts *Financial support:* Fellowships with full tuition reimbursements, research assistantships with full tuition reimbursements, teaching assistantships with full tuition reimbursements, career-related internships or fieldwork, Federal Work-Study, institutionally sponsored loans, scholarships/grants, traineeships, tuition waivers, and unspecified assistantships available. Financial award application deadline: 2/1; financial award applicants required to submit FAFSA. *Degree program information:* Part-time programs available. Part-time. Offers anthropology (PhD); classical studies (MA); design and technical production (MFA); economics (MA, PhD); English (MA); French (MA, PhD); history (MA, PhD); history of art (MA); liberal arts (MA, MFA, PhD); music (MA, MFA); philosophy (MA, PhD); political science (PhD); Portuguese (MA); sociology (MA); Spanish and Portuguese (PhD); studio art (MFA).

Application deadline: For fall admission, 2/1 for domestic and international students. *Application fee:* $45. Electronic applications accepted.

Roger Thayer Stone Center for Latin American Studies Financial support: Fellowships, teaching assistantships, career-related internships or fieldwork, Federal Work-Study, and institutionally sponsored loans available. Financial award application deadline: 2/1. Offers Latin American studies (MA, PhD). *Application deadline:* For fall admission, 2/1 for domestic and international students. *Application fee:* $45. Electronic applications accepted.

School of Medicine *Financial support:* Fellowships, research assistantships, teaching assistantships, career-related internships or fieldwork, Federal Work-Study, institutionally sponsored loans, and scholarships/grants available. Financial award application deadline: 2/1. Offers medicine (MS, MD, PhD). *Application deadline:* For winter admission, 1/15 for domestic and international students. *Application fee:* $95.

Graduate Programs in Biomedical Sciences Financial support: Fellowships, research assistantships, teaching assistantships, career-related internships or fieldwork, Federal Work-Study, institutionally sponsored loans, scholarships/grants, traineeships, tuition waivers (full), and unspecified assistantships available. Financial award application deadline: 2/1; financial award applicants required to submit FAFSA. Offers biochemistry and molecular biology (MS); biomedical sciences (MS, PhD); human genetics (MS); microbiology and immunology (MS); molecular and cellular biology (PhD); neuroscience (MS, PhD); pharmacology (MS); physiology (MS); structural and cellular biology (MS, PhD). *Application deadline:* For fall admission, 2/1 for domestic and international students. *Application fee:* $61.

School of Public Health and Tropical Medicine *Financial support:* Fellowships, research assistantships, teaching assistantships, Federal Work-Study, scholarships/grants, and traineeships available. Support available to part-time students. Financial award application deadline: 4/15; financial award applicants required to submit FAFSA. *Degree program information:* Part-time and evening/weekend programs available. Part-time, evening/weekend, online learning. Offers biostatistics and bioinformatics (MS, MSPH, PhD); clinical tropical medicine and travelers health (Diploma); community health sciences (MPH); epidemiology (MPH, MS, Dr PH, PhD); global community health and behavioral sciences (Dr PH, PhD); global environmental health sciences (MPH, MSPH, PhD); global health management and policy (MHA, MPH, PhD, Sc D); parasitology (PhD); public health (MSPH); public health and tropical medicine (MPHTM). MS and PhD offered through the Graduate School. *Application deadline:* For fall admission, 4/15 priority date for domestic and international students; for winter admission, 10/15 priority date for domestic and international students. Applications are processed on a rolling basis. *Application fee:* $40. Electronic applications accepted.

School of Science and Engineering *Financial support:* Fellowships with full tuition reimbursements, research assistantships with full tuition reimbursements, teaching assistantships with full tuition reimbursements, career-related internships or fieldwork, Federal Work-Study, institutionally sponsored loans, scholarships/grants, health care benefits, tuition waivers (full and partial), and unspecified assistantships available. Support available to part-time students. Financial award application deadline: 12/1. *Degree program information:* Part-time programs available. Part-time. Offers biomedical engineering (MS, PhD); cell and molecular biology (MS, PhD); chemical and biomolecular engineering (MS, PhD); chemistry (MS, PhD); ecology and evolutionary biology (MS, PhD); interdisciplinary studies (PhD); mathematics (MS, PhD); neuroscience (MS, PhD); physics (PhD); psychology (MS, PhD); science and engineering (MS, PhD). MS and PhD offered through the Graduate School. *Application deadline:* For fall admission, 12/1 priority date for domestic and international students; for spring admission, 5/1 priority date for domestic and international students. Applications are processed on a rolling basis. *Application fee:* $0. Electronic applications accepted.

School of Social Work *Financial support:* Fellowships and Federal Work-Study available. Financial award applicants required to submit FAFSA. *Degree program information:* Part-time programs available. Part-time. Offers city, culture and community (PhD); disaster resilience leadership (MS); social work (MSW, DSW). *Application deadline:* For fall admission, 3/31 priority date for domestic students. Applications are processed on a rolling basis. *Application fee:* $25. Electronic applications accepted.

TUSCULUM COLLEGE, Greeneville, TN 37743-9997

General Information Independent-religious, coed, comprehensive institution. *Enrollment:* 1,809 graduate, professional, and undergraduate students; 109 full-time matriculated graduate/professional students (65 women), 81 part-time matriculated graduate/professional students (50 women). *Enrollment by degree level:* 190 master's. *Graduate faculty:* 13 full-time (6 women), 9 part-time/adjunct (4 women). *Tuition, area resident:* Full-time $7497; part-time $357 per credit hour. *Graduate housing:* On-campus housing not available. *Student services:* Career counseling, child daycare facilities. *Library:* Thomas J. Garland Library plus 2 others. *Collection:* Books: 47,855 (physical), 432,852 (digital/electronic); Databases: 152. Students can reserve study rooms.

Computer facilities: 200 computers available on campus for general student use. A campuswide network can be accessed from student residence rooms and from off campus. Online class registration is available.
Website: http://www.tusculum.edu/

General Application Contact: Lindsey Seal, Director of Enrollment, 423-636-7300 Ext. 5906, E-mail: lseal@tusculum.edu.

GRADUATE UNITS

Graduate School Students: 109 full-time (65 women), 81 part-time (50 women); includes 19 minority (11 Black or African American, non-Hispanic/Latino; 3 American Indian or Alaska Native, non-Hispanic/Latino; 4 Hispanic/Latino; 1 Two or more races, non-Hispanic/Latino). Average age 33. 107 applicants, 82% accepted, 71 enrolled. *Faculty:* 13 full-time (6 women), 9 part-time/adjunct (4 women). *Financial support:* In 2015–16, 32 students received support. In 2015, 118 master's awarded. *Degree program information:* Evening/weekend programs available. Evening/weekend. Offers adult education (MA Ed); business administration (MBA); K–12 (MA Ed); teaching (MAT). *Application deadline:* Applications are processed on a rolling basis. *Application fee:* $0. *Application Contact:* Lindsey Seal, Director of Enrollment, 423-636-7300 Ext. 5906, E-mail: lseal@tusculum.edu. *Vice President of Academic Affairs,* Dr. Ron May, 423-636-7300 Ext. 5305, Fax: 423-638-7166, E-mail: rmay@tusculum.edu.

TUSKEGEE UNIVERSITY, Tuskegee, AL 36088

General Information Independent, coed, comprehensive institution. *Graduate housing:* Rooms and/or apartments available to single students and available on a first-come, first-served basis to married students. Housing application deadline: 5/1. *Research affiliation:* Boeing (engineering), Chevron (engineering), 3M (engineering), Department of Education (agriculture), Department of Defense (agriculture).

GRADUATE UNITS

Graduate Programs *Degree program information:* Part-time programs available. Part-time. Offers integrative biosciences (PhD).

Andrew F. Brimmer College of Business and Information Science Offers information systems and security management (MS).

College of Agriculture, Environment and Nutrition Sciences Offers agricultural and resource economics (MS); agriculture, environment and nutrition sciences (MS); animal and poultry breeding (MS); animal and poultry nutrition (MS); animal and poultry physiology (MS); animal and poultry sciences (MS); environmental sciences (MS); food and nutritional sciences (MS); plant and soil sciences (MS).

College of Arts and Sciences Offers arts and sciences (MS); biology (MS); chemistry (MS).

College of Engineering Offers electrical engineering (MSEE); engineering (MSEE, MSME, PhD); materials science and engineering (PhD); mechanical engineering (MSME).

College of Veterinary Medicine, Nursing and Allied Health Offers occupational therapy (MS); veterinary medicine (MS, DVM); veterinary medicine, nursing and allied health (MS, DVM).

TYNDALE UNIVERSITY COLLEGE & SEMINARY, Toronto, ON M2M 4B3, Canada

General Information Independent-religious, coed, comprehensive institution. *Graduate housing:* Room and/or apartments available on a first-come, first-served basis to single students; on-campus housing not available to married students.

GRADUATE UNITS

Graduate Programs *Degree program information:* Part-time programs available. Part-time, online learning. Offers Biblical studies (M Div); Christian foundations (MTS); Christian studies (Diploma); counseling (M Div); educational ministry (M Div); missions (M Div, Diploma); pastoral and Chinese ministry (M Div); pastoral ministry (M Div); Pentecostal studies (MTS); spiritual formation (M Div, Diploma); theological studies (M Div); theology (Th M); worship and liturgy (M Div, MTS); youth and family ministry (M Div). Electronic applications accepted.

UNIFICATION THEOLOGICAL SEMINARY, Barrytown, NY 12507

General Information Independent-religious, coed, primarily men, graduate-only institution. *Enrollment by degree level:* 51 master's, 31 doctoral. *Graduate faculty:* 3 full-time (1 woman), 12 part-time/adjunct (2 women). *Tuition, area resident:* Full-time $11,040; part-time $460 per credit. *Required fees:* $320; $250 per unit. $125 per semester. Tuition and fees vary according to degree level. *Graduate housing:* Rooms and/or apartments available on a first-come, first-served basis to single and married students. Typical cost: $5400 per year for single students; $9600 per year for married students. Room charges vary according to housing facility selected. *Student services:* Campus employment opportunities, career counseling, free psychological counseling, international student services, writing training. *Library:* Seminary Library plus 1 other. *Collection:* Books: 58,445 (physical), 210,000 (digital/electronic); Serial titles: 8 (physical), 4 (digital/electronic); Databases: 4. Weekly public service hours: 48.

Computer facilities: 16 computers available on campus for general student use. A campuswide network can be accessed from student residence rooms. Online class registration is available.
Website: http://www.uts.edu/

General Application Contact: Henry Christopher, Director of Admissions, 845-752-3000 Ext. 244, Fax: 845-752-3014, E-mail: h.christopher@uts.edu.

GRADUATE UNITS

Graduate Program, Main Campus Students: 29 full-time (6 women), 10 part-time (4 women); includes 21 minority (15 Black or African American, non-Hispanic/Latino; 4 Asian, non-Hispanic/Latino; 1 Hispanic/Latino; 1 Two or more races, non-Hispanic/Latino), 12 international. Average age 58. *Faculty:* 2 full-time (1 woman), 4 part-time/adjunct (0 women). *Financial support:* In 2015–16, 14 students received support. Scholarships/grants and on-campus employment available. Financial award application deadline: 6/15; financial award applicants required to submit FAFSA. In 2015, 14 master's, 4 doctorates awarded. *Degree program information:* Part-time and evening/weekend programs available. Part-time, evening/weekend. Offers divinity (M Div); ministry (D Min); religious education (MRE); religious studies (MA). *Application deadline:* For fall admission, 3/15 priority date for domestic students; for spring admission, 9/15 priority date for domestic students. Applications are processed on a rolling basis. *Application fee:* $30. Electronic applications accepted. *Application Contact:* Henry Christopher, Director of Admissions, 845-752-3000 Ext. 244, Fax: 845-752-3014, E-mail: h.christopher@uts.edu. *Vice-President for Academic Affairs,* Dr. Kathy Winings, 845-752-3000 Ext. 228, Fax: 845-752-3014, E-mail: academics@uts.edu.

Graduate Program, Maryland Satellite Center Offers theology (M Div, MA, MRE). *Application Contact:* Henry Christopher, Director of Admissions and Financial Aid, 212-563-6647 Ext. 105, E-mail: admissions@uts.edu. *Director,* John Paul James, 240-384-7860.

New York Extension Center Students: 24 full-time (9 women), 17 part-time (9 women); includes 18 minority (11 Black or African American, non-Hispanic/Latino; 5 Asian, non-Hispanic/Latino; 1 Hispanic/Latino; 1 Two or more races, non-Hispanic/Latino), 18 international. Average age 43. *Faculty:* 3 full-time (1 woman), 8 part-time/adjunct (1 woman). *Financial support:* In 2015–16, 41 students received support. Career-related internships or fieldwork, scholarships/grants, tuition waivers (partial), and on-campus employment (for international students) available. Support available to part-time students. Financial award application deadline: 6/15; financial award applicants required to submit FAFSA. *Degree program information:* Part-time and evening/weekend programs available. Part-time, evening/weekend. Offers divinity (M Div); religious education (MRE); religious studies (MA). *Application deadline:* For fall admission, 8/15 priority date for domestic students; for spring admission, 1/15 priority date for domestic students. Applications are processed on a rolling basis. *Application fee:* $30. Electronic applications accepted. *Application Contact:* Joy Theriot, Recruiter, 212-563-6647 Ext. 110, Fax: 212-563-6431, E-mail: j.theriot@uts.edu. *Vice-President for Academic Affairs,* Dr. Kathy Winings, 212-563-6647 Ext. 101, Fax: 212-563-6431, E-mail: academics@uts.edu.

UNIFORMED SERVICES UNIVERSITY OF THE HEALTH SCIENCES, Bethesda, MD 20814-4799

General Information Federally supported, coed, graduate-only institution. *Enrollment by degree level:* 44 master's, 780 doctoral. *Graduate faculty:* 372 full-time (119 women), 4,044 part-time/adjunct (908 women). *Graduate housing:* On-campus housing not available. *Student services:* Campus safety program, career counseling, exercise/wellness program, free psychological counseling, grant writing training, low-cost health insurance, multicultural affairs office, writing training. *Library:* James A. Zimble Learning Resource Center. Study areas open 24 hours, 5–7 days a week; students can reserve study rooms. *Research affiliation:* National Library of Medicine, National Institutes of Health, Walter Reed Army Institute of Research, Armed Forces Institute of Pathology, U.S. Armed Forces Radiobiology Research Institute.

Computer facilities: 100 computers available on campus for general student use. A campuswide network can be accessed. Online class registration is available.
Website: http://www.usuhs.edu/

General Application Contact: Tina Finley, Program Administrative Specialist, 301-295-3913, Fax: 301-295-6772, E-mail: netina.finley@usuhs.edu.

GRADUATE UNITS

Daniel K. Inouye Graduate School of Nursing Students: 51 full-time (29 women); includes 17 minority (8 Black or African American, non-Hispanic/Latino; 4 Asian, non-Hispanic/Latino; 4 Hispanic/Latino; 1 Two or more races, non-Hispanic/Latino). Average age 34. 75 applicants, 68% accepted, 51 enrolled. *Faculty:* 38 full-time (22 women), 2 part-time/adjunct (1 woman). In 2015, 4 master's, 24 doctorates awarded. Offers adult-gerontology clinical nurse specialist (MSN, DNP); family nurse practitioner (DNP); nurse anesthesia (DNP); nursing science (PhD); psychiatric mental health nurse practitioner (DNP); women's health nurse practitioner (DNP). MSN and DNP programs available to military officers only; PhD to military and DoD students only. *Application deadline:* For fall admission, 7/1 for domestic students; for winter admission, 2/15 for domestic students. *Application fee:* $0. Electronic applications accepted. *Application Contact:* Terry Lynn Malavakis, Recording Secretary for Admissions Committee/Registrar/Program Analyst, 301-295-1055, Fax: 301-295-1707, E-mail: terry.malavakis@usuhs.edu. *Associate Dean for Academic Affairs,* Dr. Diane C. Seibert, 301-295-1080, Fax: 301-295-1707, E-mail: diane.seibert@usuhs.edu.

F. Edward Hebert School of Medicine Offers medicine (MPH, MS, MSPH, MTMH, Dr PH, MD, PhD).

Graduate Programs in the Biomedical Sciences and Public Health Students: 240 full-time (133 women); includes 40 minority (15 Black or African American, non-Hispanic/Latino; 13 Asian, non-Hispanic/Latino; 12 Hispanic/Latino), 30 international. Average age 25. 598 applicants, 17% accepted, 77 enrolled. *Faculty:* 372 full-time (119 women), 4,044 part-time/adjunct (908 women). *Financial support:* In 2015–16, 50 fellowships (averaging $43,000 per year) were awarded; research assistantships, career-related internships or fieldwork, scholarships/grants, health care benefits, and tuition waivers (full) also available. In 2015, 19 master's, 50 doctorates awarded. Offers clinical psychology (PhD); emerging infectious diseases (PhD); environmental health sciences (PhD); healthcare administration and policy (MS); medical and clinical psychology (PhD); medical psychology (PhD); medical zoology (PhD); medicine (MS, PhD); molecular and cell biology (MS, PhD); neuroscience (PhD); preventive medicine and biometrics (MPH, MS, MSPH, MTMH, Dr PH, PhD); public health (MPH, MSPH, Dr PH); tropical medicine and hygiene (MTMH). *Application deadline:* For fall admission, 12/15 priority date for domestic students. Applications are processed on a rolling basis. *Application fee:* $0. Electronic applications accepted. *Application Contact:* Tina Finley, Administrative Officer, 301-295-3642, Fax: 301-295-6772, E-mail: netina.finley@usuhs.edu. *Associate Dean,* Dr. Gregory Mueller, 301-295-3507, E-mail: gregory.mueller@usuhs.edu.

UNION COLLEGE, Barbourville, KY 40906-1499

General Information Independent-religious, coed, comprehensive institution. *Graduate housing:* Rooms and/or apartments available to single and married students.

GRADUATE UNITS

Graduate Programs ***Degree program information:*** Part-time and evening/weekend programs available. Part-time, evening/weekend. Offers clinical psychology (MA); counseling psychology (MA); elementary education (MA); health (MA Ed); health and physical education (MA); middle grades (MA); music education (MA); principalship (MA); reading specialist (MA); school psychology (MA); secondary education (MA); special education (MA).

UNION COLLEGE, Lincoln, NE 68506-4300

General Information Independent-religious, coed, comprehensive institution. *Graduate housing:* Rooms and/or apartments available on a first-come, first-served basis to single and married students.

GRADUATE UNITS

Physician Assistant Program Offers physician assistant (MPAS). Electronic applications accepted.

UNION INSTITUTE & UNIVERSITY, Cincinnati, OH 45206-1925

General Information Independent, coed, university. *Enrollment:* 1,391 graduate, professional, and undergraduate students; 313 full-time matriculated graduate/professional students (228 women), 134 part-time matriculated graduate/professional students (101 women). *Enrollment by degree level:* 172 master's, 179 doctoral, 11 other advanced degrees. *Graduate faculty:* 26 full-time (14 women), 31 part-time/adjunct (20 women). Tuition and fees vary according to degree level and program. *Student services:* Career counseling, international student services, services for students with disabilities, writing training. *Library:* Union Institute & University Library plus 1 other. *Collection:* Books: 266,339 (digital/electronic); Serial titles: 27,641 (digital/electronic); Databases: 159. Weekly public service hours: 50.

Computer facilities: Computer purchase and lease plans are available. 65 computers available on campus for general student use. A campuswide network can be accessed from off campus. Online class registration, CampusWeb-online access to basic information and grades are available.
Website: http://www.myunion.edu/

General Application Contact: Admissions Office, 513-861-6400, E-mail: admissions@myunion.edu.

GRADUATE UNITS

Individualized Master of Arts Program Students: 9 full-time (7 women), 70 part-time (56 women); includes 33 minority (22 Black or African American, non-Hispanic/Latino; 1 American Indian or Alaska Native, non-Hispanic/Latino; 6 Hispanic/Latino; 4 Two or more races, non-Hispanic/Latino). Average age 40. *Faculty:* 2 full-time (both women), 9 part-time/adjunct (7 women). *Financial support:* Career-related internships or fieldwork and tuition waivers available. Financial award applicants required to submit FAFSA. In 2015, 45 master's awarded. *Degree program information:* Part-time programs available. Part-time, online only, 100% online. Offers creativity studies (MA); health and wellness (MA); history and culture (MA); leadership, public policy, and social issues (MA); literature and writing (MA). *Application deadline:* For spring admission, 3/13 for domestic students. Applications are processed on a rolling basis. *Application fee:* $50. Electronic applications accepted. *Application Contact:* Director of Admissions, 800-861-6400.

Master of Arts Program in Clinical Mental Health Counseling Students: 34 full-time (29 women), 29 part-time (20 women); includes 11 minority (7 Black or African American, non-Hispanic/Latino; 1 Asian, non-Hispanic/Latino; 2 Hispanic/Latino; 1 Two or more races, non-Hispanic/Latino). Average age 40. *Faculty:* 4 full-time (2 women), 6 part-time/adjunct (4 women). *Financial support:* Federal Work-Study available. Financial award applicants required to submit FAFSA. In 2015, 12 master's awarded. Online only, blended/hybrid learning. Offers clinical mental health counseling (MA). *Application deadline:* Applications are processed on a rolling basis. *Application fee:* $50. Electronic applications accepted. *Application Contact:* Director of Admissions, 888-828-8575. *Dean,* Dr. Bill Lax, 802-254-0152, E-mail: bill.lax@myunion.edu.

Master of Science Program in Organizational Leadership Students: 49 full-time (21 women), 5 part-time (2 women); includes 33 minority (18 Black or African American, non-Hispanic/Latino; 2 American Indian or Alaska Native, non-Hispanic/Latino; 1 Asian, non-Hispanic/Latino; 7 Hispanic/Latino; 2 Native Hawaiian or other Pacific Islander, non-Hispanic/Latino; 3 Two or more races, non-Hispanic/Latino). Average age 40. *Faculty:* 6 part-time/adjunct (2 women). *Financial support:* Federal Work-Study available. In 2015, 14 master's awarded. *Degree program information:* Part-time programs available. Part-time, online only, 100% online. Offers organizational leadership (MA). *Application deadline:* Applications are processed on a rolling basis. *Application fee:* $50. Electronic applications accepted. *Application Contact:* Admissions Office, 513-861-6400, E-mail: admissions@myunion.edu.

PhD Program in Interdisciplinary Studies Students: 122 full-time (76 women), 19 part-time (14 women); includes 76 minority (58 Black or African American, non-Hispanic/Latino; 4 American Indian or Alaska Native, non-Hispanic/Latino; 2 Asian, non-Hispanic/Latino; 8 Hispanic/Latino; 3 Native Hawaiian or other Pacific Islander, non-Hispanic/Latino; 1 Two or more races, non-Hispanic/Latino). Average age 46. *Faculty:* 9 full-time (5 women), 16 part-time/adjunct (7 women). *Financial support:* Federal Work-Study and scholarships/grants available. Financial award application deadline: 5/1; financial award applicants required to submit FAFSA. In 2015, 22 doctorates awarded. *Degree program information:* Part-time programs available. Part-time, online only, blended/hybrid learning. Offers education studies (PhD); ethical and creative leadership (PhD); humanities and culture (PhD); public policy and social change (PhD). Program requires participation in brief on-campus residencies twice each year (January and July). *Application deadline:* Applications are processed on a rolling basis. *Application fee:* $50. Electronic applications accepted. *Application Contact:* Admissions Counselor, 800-486-3116. *Dean,* Dr. Arlene Sacks, 513-861-6400, E-mail: arlene.sacks@myunion.edu.

UNION PRESBYTERIAN SEMINARY, Richmond, VA 23227-4597

General Information Independent-religious, coed, graduate-only institution. *Graduate housing:* Rooms and/or apartments available on a first-come, first-served basis to single and married students. Housing application deadline: 6/30.

GRADUATE UNITS

Graduate and Professional Programs ***Degree program information:*** Part-time and evening/weekend programs available. Part-time, evening/weekend, online learning. Electronic applications accepted.

UNION THEOLOGICAL SEMINARY IN THE CITY OF NEW YORK, New York, NY 10027-5710

General Information Independent-religious, coed, graduate-only institution. *Graduate housing:* Rooms and/or apartments available on a first-come, first-served basis to single and married students. Housing application deadline: 5/15.

GRADUATE UNITS

Graduate and Professional Programs ***Degree program information:*** Part-time programs available. Part-time. Offers theology (M Div, MA, STM, Ed D, PhD). Ed D offered jointly with Teachers College, Columbia University; M Div/MSSW with Columbia University.

UNION UNIVERSITY, Jackson, TN 38305-3697

General Information Independent-religious, coed, comprehensive institution. *Graduate housing:* Rooms and/or apartments available on a first-come, first-served basis to single and married students.

GRADUATE UNITS

Institute for International and Intercultural Studies ***Degree program information:*** Part-time and evening/weekend programs available. Part-time, evening/weekend. Offers international and intercultural studies (MAIS). Electronic applications accepted.

McAfee School of Business Administration ***Degree program information:*** Evening/weekend programs available. Evening/weekend, online learning. Offers accountancy (M Acc). Program also available at Germantown campus. Electronic applications accepted.

School of Education ***Degree program information:*** Part-time and evening/weekend programs available. Part-time, evening/weekend, online learning. Offers education (M Ed, MA Ed); education administration generalist (Ed S); educational leadership (Ed D); educational supervision (Ed S); higher education (Ed D). M Ed also available at Germantown campus. Electronic applications accepted.

School of Nursing Offers executive leadership (DNP); nurse anesthesia (DNP); nurse practitioner (DNP); nursing education (MSN, PMC). Electronic applications accepted.

School of Social Work Offers social work (MSW).

School of Theology and Missions ***Degree program information:*** Part-time and evening/weekend programs available. Part-time, evening/weekend, online learning. Offers Christian studies (MCS); expository preaching (D Min). Electronic applications accepted.

UNITED STATES ARMY COMMAND AND GENERAL STAFF COLLEGE, Fort Leavenworth, KS 66027-2301

General Information Federally supported, coed, primarily men, graduate-only institution. *Graduate housing:* Rooms and/or apartments available to single and married students.

GRADUATE UNITS

Graduate Program Offers military art and science (MMAS). Only career military officers are selected to attend United States Army Command and General Staff College; Graduate Program is voluntary for first-year students, but mandatory for second-year students.

UNITED STATES INTERNATIONAL UNIVERSITY–AFRICA, Nairobi 00800, Kenya

General Information Independent, coed, comprehensive institution. *Graduate housing:* Room and/or apartments available on a first-come, first-served basis to single students; on-campus housing not available to married students. Housing application deadline: 7/31.

GRADUATE UNITS

School of Arts and Sciences *Degree program information:* Part-time and evening/weekend programs available. Part-time, evening/weekend. Offers counseling psychology (MA); international relations (MA).

School of Business Administration *Degree program information:* Part-time and evening/weekend programs available. Part-time, evening/weekend. Offers business administration (GEMBA); entrepreneurship (MBA); finance (MBA); human resource management (MBA); information technology management (MBA); integrated studies (MBA); international business administration (MBA); management and organizational development (MS); marketing (MBA); organizational development (EMS); strategic management (MBA).

UNITED STATES MERCHANT MARINE ACADEMY, Kings Point, NY 11024-1699

General Information Federally supported, coed, comprehensive institution.

GRADUATE UNITS

Graduate Program Offers marine engineering (MS).

UNITED STATES SPORTS ACADEMY, Daphne, AL 36526-7055

General Information Independent, coed, upper-level institution. *Graduate housing:* On-campus housing not available.

GRADUATE UNITS

Graduate Programs *Degree program information:* Part-time programs available. Part-time, online learning. Offers sport management (MSS, Ed D); sport studies (MSS); sports coaching (MSS); sports fitness and health (MSS); sports medicine (MSS). Electronic applications accepted.

UNITED STATES UNIVERSITY, Chula Vista, CA 91911

General Information Proprietary, coed, comprehensive institution.

GRADUATE UNITS

Family Nurse Practitioner Program Offers family nurse practitioner (MSN).

UNITED TALMUDICAL SEMINARY, Brooklyn, NY 11211

General Information Independent-religious, men only, comprehensive institution.

GRADUATE UNITS

Graduate Programs

UNITED THEOLOGICAL SEMINARY, Dayton, OH 45426

General Information Independent-religious, coed, graduate-only institution.

GRADUATE UNITS

Graduate and Professional Programs *Degree program information:* Part-time and evening/weekend programs available. Part-time, evening/weekend, online learning. Offers theology (M Div, MA, MATS, D Min). Electronic applications accepted.

UNITED THEOLOGICAL SEMINARY OF THE TWIN CITIES, New Brighton, MN 55112-2598

General Information Independent-religious, coed, graduate-only institution. *Graduate housing:* Rooms and/or apartments available on a first-come, first-served basis to single and married students.

GRADUATE UNITS

Graduate Programs *Degree program information:* Part-time and evening/weekend programs available. Part-time, evening/weekend. Offers advanced theological studies (Diploma); justice and peace studies (M Div, MA); leadership toward racial justice (M Div, MA, Certificate); Methodist studies (M Div, MA, Certificate); ministry (D Min); ministry renewal and professional development (Certificate); pastoral care and counseling (M Div, MA, MARL); religion and theology (MA); theological and religious studies (Certificate); theology and the arts (M Div, MA); urban ministry (M Div, MA, MARL); women's studies: religion, theology and ministry (M Div, MA).

UNITY COLLEGE, Unity, ME 04988

General Information Independent, coed, comprehensive institution.

GRADUATE UNITS

Program in Professional Science Online learning. Offers sustainability science (MS); sustainable natural resource management (MS).

UNIVERSIDAD ADVENTISTA DE LAS ANTILLAS, Mayagüez, PR 00681-0118

General Information Independent-religious, coed, comprehensive institution. *Graduate housing:* Rooms and/or apartments available on a first-come, first-served basis to single and married students.

GRADUATE UNITS

EGECED Department Offers curriculum and instruction (M Ed); medical surgical nursing (MN); school administration and supervision (M Ed). Electronic applications accepted.

UNIVERSIDAD CENTRAL DEL CARIBE, Bayamón, PR 00960-6032

General Information Independent, coed, comprehensive institution. *Graduate housing:* On-campus housing not available.

GRADUATE UNITS

Program in Substance Abuse Counseling Offers substance abuse counseling (MHS).

School of Medicine Offers anatomy and cell biology (MA, MS); biochemistry (MS); biomedical sciences (MA); cellular and molecular biology (PhD); medicine (MA, MS, MD, PhD); microbiology and immunology (MA, MS); pharmacology (MS); physiology (MS).

UNIVERSIDAD DE LAS AMERICAS, A.C., 06700 Mexico City, Mexico

General Information Independent, coed, comprehensive institution.

GRADUATE UNITS

Program in Business Administration Offers finance (MBA); marketing research (MBA); production and quality (MBA).

Program in Education Offers education (M Ed).

Program in International Organizations and Institutions Offers international organizations and institutions (MA).

Program in Psychology Offers family therapy (MA).

UNIVERSIDAD DE LAS AMÉRICAS PUEBLA, Puebla CP 72810, Mexico

General Information Independent, coed, university. CGS member. *Graduate housing:* On-campus housing not available. *Research affiliation:* Empacadora San Marcos S. A. de C. U. (food service), Volkswagen de Mexico S. A. de C. U. (mechanical engineering), Institute Mexicano del Tecnologa del agua (electronic engineering), Frugosa S. A. de C. U. (chemical engineering).

GRADUATE UNITS

Division of Graduate Studies *Degree program information:* Part-time and evening/weekend programs available. Part-time, evening/weekend.

School of Business and Economics Degree program information: Part-time and evening/weekend programs available. Part-time, evening/weekend. Offers business administration (MBA); finance (M Adm).

School of Engineering Degree program information: Part-time and evening/weekend programs available. Part-time, evening/weekend. Offers chemical engineering (MS); computer science (PhD); construction management (M Adm); electronic engineering (MS); engineering (M Adm, MS, PhD); food sciences (MS); food technology (MS); industrial engineering (MS); manufacturing administration (MS); production management (M Adm).

School of Humanities Degree program information: Part-time and evening/weekend programs available. Part-time, evening/weekend. Offers humanities (MA); information design (MA); linguistics (MA); literature (MA).

School of Sciences Degree program information: Part-time and evening/weekend programs available. Part-time, evening/weekend. Offers biotechnology (MS); clinical analysis (biomedicine) (MS); sciences (MS).

School of Social Sciences Degree program information: Part-time and evening/weekend programs available. Part-time, evening/weekend. Offers American studies (MA); anthropology (MA); archaeology (MA); economics (MA); education (MA); finance (M Adm); psychology (MA); social sciences (M Adm, MA).

UNIVERSIDAD DEL ESTE, Carolina, PR 00984

General Information Independent, coed, comprehensive institution.

GRADUATE UNITS

Graduate School Offers accounting (MBA); adult education (M Ed); agribusiness (MBA); criminal justice and criminology (MA); curriculum and instruction - early education (M Ed); curriculum and instruction - elementary (M Ed); curriculum and instruction - English (M Ed); curriculum and instruction - Spanish (M Ed); human resources (MBA); information security management (MBA); information technology and Web business development (MBA); management (MBA); public policy (MPA); social work (MA); special education (M Ed); strategic leadership (MBA).

UNIVERSIDAD DEL TURABO, Gurabo, PR 00778-3030

General Information Independent, coed, university. CGS member. *Graduate housing:* On-campus housing not available.

GRADUATE UNITS

Graduate Programs *Degree program information:* Part-time and evening/weekend programs available. Part-time, evening/weekend, online learning. Offers administration of school libraries (M Ed, Certificate); athletic training (MPHE); coaching (MPHE); curriculum and instruction and appropriate environment (D Ed); curriculum and teaching (M Ed); educational administration (M Ed); educational leadership (D Ed); environmental analysis (MSE); environmental management (MSE); environmental science (D Sc); guidance counseling (M Ed); library service and information technology (M Ed); special education (M Ed); teaching at primary level (M Ed); teaching English as a second language (M Ed); teaching of fine arts (M Ed); wellness (MPHE).

School in Business Administration Degree program information: Part-time and evening/weekend programs available. Part-time, evening/weekend. Offers accounting (MBA); business administration (MBA, DBA); human resources (MBA); logistics and materials management (MBA); management (MBA, DBA); management of information systems (DBA); marketing (MBA); project management (MBA); quality management (MBA).

School of Engineering Offers engineering (MS); telecommunication and network administration (MS).

School of Health Sciences Offers family nurse practitioner (MSN); family nurse practitioner - adult nursing (MSN, Certificate); health sciences (MS, MSN, ND); naturopathy (ND); speech and language pathology (MS).

School of Social Sciences and Humanities Offers arts administration (MPA); conflict and mediation studies (MPA); counseling psychology (M Psych, Psy D, Certificate); criminal justice studies (MPA); forensic science (MPA); human services administration (MPA); social sciences and humanities (M Psych, MPA, Psy D, Certificate).

UNIVERSIDAD DE MONTERREY, 66238 San Pedro Garza Garcia, NL, Mexico

General Information Independent-religious, coed, comprehensive institution.

GRADUATE UNITS

Graduate Programs

UNIVERSIDAD METROPOLITANA, San Juan, PR 00928-1150

General Information Independent, coed, comprehensive institution. CGS member. *Graduate housing:* On-campus housing not available. *Research affiliation:* Berkeley National Laboratories (bioremediation), University Corporation for Atmospheric Research (computer science, atmospheric science), University of Colorado Boulder (computer science, biology), University of Puerto Rico (physics, chemistry), University of Utah (computational chemistry), Howard University (computational chemistry).

GRADUATE UNITS

School of Business Administration *Degree program information:* Part-time and evening/weekend programs available. Part-time, evening/weekend. Offers accounting (MBA); finance (MBA); human resources management (MBA); international business (MBA); management (MBA); management information systems (MBA); marketing (MBA). Electronic applications accepted.

School of Education *Degree program information:* Part-time and evening/weekend programs available. Part-time, evening/weekend. Offers administration and supervision (M Ed); curriculum and teaching (M Ed); education (M Ed, Ed D); educational administration and supervision (M Ed); managing recreation and sports services (M Ed); pedagogy (PhD); pre-school centers administration (M Ed); special education (M Ed); teaching of adult physical education (M Ed); teaching of elementary physical education (M Ed); teaching of physical education (M Ed); teaching of secondary physical education (M Ed). Electronic applications accepted.

School of Environmental Affairs ***Degree program information:*** Part-time programs available. Part-time. Offers environmental management (MSEM); environmental planning (MP); environmental studies (MAES). Electronic applications accepted.

School of Health Sciences Offers case management (Certificate); health sciences (MSN, Certificate); nursing (MSN); oncology nursing (Certificate).

School of Social Sciences, Humanities and Communications Offers counseling psychology (MA).

UNIVERSITÉ DE MONCTON, Moncton, NB E1A 3E9, Canada

General Information Province-supported, coed, comprehensive institution. *Graduate housing:* Rooms and/or apartments available on a first-come, first-served basis to single and married students.

GRADUATE UNITS

Faculty of Administration ***Degree program information:*** Part-time and evening/weekend programs available. Part-time, evening/weekend, online learning. Offers administration (MBA). Electronic applications accepted.

Faculty of Arts and Social Sciences ***Degree program information:*** Part-time programs available. Part-time. Offers arts and social sciences (MA, MPA, MSW, PhD); economics (MA); French studies (MA, PhD); history (MA); public administration (MPA). Electronic applications accepted.

School of Social Work Offers social work (MSW).

Faculty of Education ***Degree program information:*** Part-time programs available. Part-time. Offers education (M Ed, MA Ed).

Graduate Studies in Education Degree program information: Part-time programs available. Part-time. Offers educational psychology (M Ed, MA Ed); guidance (M Ed, MA Ed); school administration (M Ed, MA Ed); teaching (M Ed, MA Ed).

Faculty of Engineering Offers civil engineering (M Sc A); electrical engineering (M Sc A); industrial engineering (M Sc A); mechanical engineering (M Sc A).

Faculty of Sciences ***Degree program information:*** Part-time programs available. Part-time. Offers biochemistry (M Sc); biology (M Sc); chemistry (M Sc); information technology (M Sc, Certificate, Diploma); mathematics (M Sc); physics and astronomy (M Sc); sciences (M Sc, Certificate, Diploma). Electronic applications accepted.

School of Food Science, Nutrition and Family Studies ***Degree program information:*** Part-time programs available. Part-time. Offers foods/nutrition (M Sc). Electronic applications accepted.

UNIVERSITÉ DE MONTRÉAL, Montréal, QC H3C 3J7, Canada

General Information Province-supported, coed, university. *Graduate housing:* Room and/or apartments available on a first-come, first-served basis to single students; on-campus housing not available to married students. Housing application deadline: 2/1. *Research affiliation:* Centre Hospitalier Universitaire Mere-Enfant de l'Hopital Sainte-Justine, Centre de Recherche de L'Hopital Sacre-Coeur, Institut de Recherches Cliniques de Montreal, Institut de Cardiologie de Montreal, Institut Universitaire de geriatric de Montreal.

GRADUATE UNITS

Department of Kinesiology Offers kinesiology (M Sc, DESS); physical activity (M Sc, PhD). Electronic applications accepted.

Faculty of Arts and Sciences ***Degree program information:*** Part-time programs available. Part-time. Offers anthropology (M Sc, PhD); applied human sciences (PhD); art history (MA, PhD); arts and sciences (M Sc, MA, MIS, PhD, DESS); biological sciences (M Sc, PhD); chemistry (M Sc, PhD); classical studies (MA); communication (PhD); communication sciences (M Sc); comparative literature (MA); computer systems (M Sc, PhD); demography (M Sc, PhD); economics (M Sc, PhD); electronic commerce (M Sc); English studies (MA, PhD); environment and durable development (DESS); film studies (MA, PhD); French literature (MA, PhD); geography (M Sc, PhD, DESS); German literature (PhD); German studies (MA); Hispanic literature (PhD); Hispanic studies (MA); history (MA, PhD); international studies (M Sc, DESS); linguistics (MA, PhD); literature (PhD); mathematical and computational finance (M Sc, DESS); mathematics (M Sc, PhD); museology (MA); philosophy (MA, PhD); physics (M Sc, PhD); political science (M Sc, PhD); psychology (M Sc, PhD); societies, public policies and health (DESS); sociology (M Sc, PhD); statistics (M Sc, PhD); translation (MA, PhD, DESS). Electronic applications accepted.

School of Criminology Offers criminology (M Sc, PhD). Electronic applications accepted.

School of Industrial Relations Degree program information: Part-time programs available. Part-time. Offers industrial relations (M Sc, PhD, DESS). Electronic applications accepted.

School of Library and Information Sciences Offers information sciences (MIS, PhD). Electronic applications accepted.

School of Psychoeducation Degree program information: Part-time programs available. Part-time. Offers psychoeducation (M Sc, PhD). Electronic applications accepted.

School of Social Service Degree program information: Part-time programs available. Part-time. Offers social administration (DESS); social work (M Sc, PhD). M Sc and PhD offered jointly with McGill University. Electronic applications accepted.

Faculty of Dental Medicine Offers dental medicine (M Sc, Certificate); multidisciplinary residency (Certificate); oral and dental sciences (M Sc); orthodontics (M Sc); pediatric dentistry (M Sc); prosthodontics rehabilitation (M Sc); stomatology residency (Certificate). Electronic applications accepted.

Faculty of Education ***Degree program information:*** Part-time and evening/weekend programs available. Part-time, evening/weekend. Offers administration and foundations of education (M Ed, MA, PhD, DESS); didactics (M Ed, MA, PhD, DESS); education (M Ed, MA, PhD, DESS); psychopedagogy and andragogy (M Ed, MA, PhD, DESS). Electronic applications accepted.

Faculty of Environmental Design and Planning Offers environmental design and planning (M Sc A, PhD); environmental planning and design projects (DESS); game design (DESS); urban management for developing countries (DESS); urban planning (M Urb). DESS programs offered jointly with HEC Montreal and École Polytechnique de Montréal. Electronic applications accepted.

Faculty of Law ***Degree program information:*** Part-time programs available. Part-time. Offers business law (DESS); common law (North America) (JD); international law (DESS); law (LL M, LL D, DDN, DESS, LL B); tax law (LL M). Electronic applications accepted.

Faculty of Medicine Offers biochemistry (M Sc, PhD, DEPD); bioethics (MA, DESS); bioinformatics (M Sc, PhD); biomedical sciences (M Sc, PhD); clinical biochemistry (DEPD); community health (M Sc, DESS); echography transoesophagian perioperatoryenvironment, health and disaster management (DESS); environmental and occupational health (M Sc); genetic counseling (DESS); health administration (M Sc, DESS); health sciencesinsurance medicine and expertise (English) (DESS); insurance medicine and expertise in health sciences (DESS); medical genetics (DESS); medicine (M Sc, M Sc A, MA, PMS, DES, MD, PhD, DEPD, DESS); microbiology and immunology (M Sc, PhD); mobility and posture (DESS); molecular biology (M Sc, PhD); neurological sciences (M Sc, PhD); nutrition (M Sc, PhD, DESS); occupational therapy (DESS); pathology and cellular biology (M Sc, PhD); pharmacology (M Sc, PhD); physiology (M Sc, PhD); public health (PhD); toxicology and risk analysis (DESS). Electronic applications accepted.

Institute of Biomedical Engineering Offers biomedical engineering (M Sc A, PhD, DESS). M Sc A and PhD programs offered jointly with École Polytechnique de Montréal. Electronic applications accepted.

School of Speech Therapy and Audiology Offers audiology (PMS); speech therapy (PMS, DESS). Electronic applications accepted.

Faculty of Music Offers composition (M Mus, D Mus); interpretation (M Mus, D Mus, DESS); music (MA, PhD); orchestral repertoire (DESS). Electronic applications accepted.

Faculty of Nursing ***Degree program information:*** Part-time programs available. Part-time. Offers nursing (M Sc, PhD, Certificate, DESS). PhD offered jointly with McGill University. Electronic applications accepted.

Faculty of Pharmacy ***Degree program information:*** Part-time programs available. Part-time. Offers drugs development (DESS); pharmaceutical care (DESS); pharmaceutical practice (M Sc); pharmaceutical sciences (M Sc, PhD); pharmacist-supervisor teacher (DESS). Electronic applications accepted.

Faculty of Theology and Sciences of Religions Offers health, spirituality and bioethics (DESS); practical theology (MA, PhD); religious sciences (MA, PhD); theology (MA, D Th, PhD, L Th); theology-Biblical studies (PhD). Electronic applications accepted.

Faculty of Veterinary Medicine Offers veterinary medicine (M Sc, DES, PhD); veterinary sciences (M Sc, PhD); virology and immunology (PhD). Electronic applications accepted.

School of Optometry ***Degree program information:*** Part-time programs available. Part-time. Offers optometry (M Sc, OD, DESS); vision sciences (M Sc); visual impairment intervention-orientation and mobility (DESS); visual impairment intervention-readaptation (DESS). Electronic applications accepted.

UNIVERSITÉ DE SAINT-BONIFACE, Saint-Boniface, MB R2H 0H7, Canada

General Information Independent-religious, coed, comprehensive institution.

GRADUATE UNITS

Department of Education Offers education (M Ed).

Program in Canadian Studies Offers Canadian studies (MA).

UNIVERSITÉ DE SHERBROOKE, Sherbrooke, QC J1K 2R1, Canada

General Information Independent, coed, university. *Graduate housing:* Room and/or apartments available to single students; on-campus housing not available to married students. Housing application deadline: 6/1. *Research affiliation:* Societe de Microelectronique Industrielle.

GRADUATE UNITS

Faculty of Administration ***Degree program information:*** Part-time and evening/weekend programs available. Part-time, evening/weekend. Offers accounting (M Sc); administration (EMBA, M Adm, M Sc, M Tax, MBA, DBA, PhD, Diploma); business administration (EMBA, MBA, DBA); e-commerce (M Sc); economic development (PhD); economics (M Sc); executive business administration (EMBA); finance (M Sc); general management (MBA); governance, audit and security of information technology (M Adm); international business (M Sc); management and governance of cooperatives and mutuals (M Adm); management information systems (M Sc); marketing (M Sc); marketing communications (M Adm); organizational change and intervention (M Sc); public management (M Adm); taxation (M Tax, Diploma).

Faculty of Education ***Degree program information:*** Part-time and evening/weekend programs available. Part-time, evening/weekend. Offers education (M Ed, MA, Diploma); elementary education (M Ed, Diploma); postsecondary education training (M Ed, Diploma); school administration (M Ed); sciences of education (MA); special education (M Ed, Diploma).

Faculty of Engineering ***Degree program information:*** Part-time programs available. Part-time. Offers chemical engineering (M Sc A, PhD); civil engineering (M Sc A, PhD); electrical engineering (M Sc A, PhD); engineering (M Eng, M Env, M Sc A, PhD, Diploma); engineering management (M Eng, Diploma); environment (M Env); mechanical engineering (M Sc A, PhD). Electronic applications accepted.

Faculty of Law ***Degree program information:*** Part-time and evening/weekend programs available. Part-time, evening/weekend. Offers alternative dispute resolution (LL M, Diploma); business law (Diploma); common law (JD); criminal and penal law (Diploma); health law (LL M, Diploma); international law (LL M); law (LL D); legal management (Diploma); notarial law (Diploma); transnational law (Diploma). Electronic applications accepted.

Faculty of Letters and Human Sciences ***Degree program information:*** Part-time programs available. Part-time. Offers comparative Canadian literature (MA, PhD); economics (MA); French literature (MA, PhD); geography and remote sensing (M Sc, PhD); gerontology (MA); history (MA); letters and human sciences (M Psych, M Sc, MA, MSS, PhD, Diploma); linguistics (MA); philosophy (MA); social service (MSS); theatre (MA).

Institute of Management and Development of Cooperatives Offers management and development of cooperatives (MA, Diploma).

Faculty of Medicine and Health Sciences ***Degree program information:*** Part-time programs available. Part-time. Offers medicine (MD); medicine and health sciences (M Sc, MD, PhD). Electronic applications accepted.

Graduate Programs in Medicine Degree program information: Part-time programs available. Part-time. Offers biochemistry (M Sc, PhD); cell biology (M Sc, PhD); clinical sciences (M Sc, PhD); immunology (M Sc, PhD); medicine (M Sc, PhD); microbiology (M Sc, PhD); pharmacology (M Sc, PhD); physiology and biophysics (M Sc, PhD); radiobiology (M Sc, PhD). Electronic applications accepted.

Faculty of Physical Education and Sports ***Degree program information:*** Part-time programs available. Part-time. Offers kinanthropology (M Sc); physical activity (Diploma); physical education (M Sc, Diploma).

Faculty of Sciences Offers biology (M Sc, PhD, Diploma); chemistry (M Sc, PhD, Diploma); informatics (M Sc, PhD); mathematics (M Sc, PhD); physics (M Sc, PhD); sciences (M Sc, PhD, Diploma).

Centre de Formation en Technologies de L'information Offers information technologies (M Sc, Diploma). Electronic applications accepted.

Centre Universitaire de Formation en Environnement Online learning. Offers environment (M Sc, Diploma). Electronic applications accepted.

Faculty of Theology and Religious Studies ***Degree program information:*** Part-time and evening/weekend programs available. Part-time, evening/weekend, online learning. Offers applied ethics (Diploma); human science of religions (MA); intercultural training (Diploma); philosophy (MA, PhD); spiritual anthropology (Diploma); theology (MA, PhD, Diploma).

UNIVERSITÉ DU QUÉBEC À CHICOUTIMI, Chicoutimi, QC G7H 2B1, Canada

General Information Province-supported, coed, university. CGS member. *Graduate housing:* Room and/or apartments available to single students; on-campus housing not available to married students.

GRADUATE UNITS

Graduate Programs ***Degree program information:*** Part-time programs available. Part-time. Offers didactics of French-mother tongue (Diploma); earth sciences (M Sc A); education (M Ed, MA, PhD); engineering (M Sc A, PhD); ethics (Diploma); fine arts (MA); genetics (M Sc); linguistics (MA); literary studies (MA); mineral resources (PhD); project management (M Sc); regional studies (MA); renewable resources (M Sc); small and medium-sized organization management (M Sc); theology (pastoral studies) (MA, PhD).

UNIVERSITÉ DU QUÉBEC À MONTRÉAL, Montréal, QC H3C 3P8, Canada

General Information Province-supported, coed, university. CGS member. *Graduate housing:* Room and/or apartments available to single students; on-campus housing not available to married students. *Research affiliation:* Labopharm, Inc. (pharmacology), Hydro-Quebec (environmental sciences), Bell (computer sciences), Microcreatif (computer sciences), University Corporation for Atmospheric Research.

GRADUATE UNITS

Graduate Programs ***Degree program information:*** Part-time programs available. Part-time. Offers accounting (M Sc, MPA, Diploma); actuarial sciences (Diploma); art history (PhD); art studies (MA); atmospheric sciences (M Sc); biology (M Sc, PhD); business administration (PhD); business administration (research) (MBA); chemistry (M Sc, PhD); communications (MA, PhD); dance (MA); death (Diploma); Earth and atmospheric sciences (PhD); Earth science (M Sc); earth sciences (M Sc); economics (M Sc, PhD); education (M Ed, MA, PhD); education of the environmental sciences (Diploma); environmental sciences (M Sc, PhD, Certificate); ergonomics in occupational health and safety (Diploma); finance (Diploma); fine arts (MA); geographical information systems (Diploma); geography (M Sc); history (MA, PhD); human movement studies (M Sc); linguistics (MA, PhD); literary studies (MA, PhD); management consultant (Diploma); management information systems (M Sc, M Sc A); mathematics (M Sc, PhD); meteorology (PhD, Diploma); mineral resources (PhD); museology (MA); non-renewable resources (DESS); philosophy (MA, PhD); political science (MA, PhD); project management (MGP, Diploma); psychology (D Ps, PhD); religious sciences (MA, PhD); semiology (PhD); sexology (MA); social and labor law (Certificate); social intervention (MA); sociology (MA, PhD); study and practices of the arts (PhD); urban analysis and management (MA); urban studies (MA, PhD).

UNIVERSITÉ DU QUÉBEC À RIMOUSKI, Rimouski, QC G5L 3A1, Canada

General Information Province-supported, coed, comprehensive institution. CGS member. *Graduate housing:* Rooms and/or apartments available on a first-come, first-served basis to single and married students. *Research affiliation:* Institut des Sciences de la Mer de Rimouski (ISMER) (marine sciences), CRDT (territory development), Centre d'Etudes Nordiques (Nordicity), Quebec Ocean (oceans), Centre Recherche en Forestene (forestry).

GRADUATE UNITS

Graduate Programs ***Degree program information:*** Part-time programs available. Part-time. Offers biology (PhD); business administration (MBA); education (M Ed, MA, PhD, Diploma); engineering (M Sc A); ethics (MA, Diploma); literary studies (MA, PhD); management of marine resources (M Sc, Diploma); management of people in working situation (M Sc, Diploma); nursing studies (M Sc, Diploma); oceanography (M Sc, PhD); project management (M Sc, Diploma); psychosocial studies (MA); regional development (MA, PhD, Diploma); wildlife resources management (M Sc, Diploma).

UNIVERSITÉ DU QUÉBEC À TROIS-RIVIÈRES, Trois-Rivières, QC G9A 5H7, Canada

General Information Province-supported, coed, university. CGS member. *Graduate housing:* Room and/or apartments available to single students; on-campus housing not available to married students. Housing application deadline: 2/1.

GRADUATE UNITS

Graduate Programs ***Degree program information:*** Part-time programs available. Part-time. Offers accounting science (MBA); biophysics and cellular biology (M Sc, PhD); business administration (MBA, DBA); chemistry (M Sc); chiropractic (DC); education (M Ed, PhD); educational administration (DESS); electrical engineering (M Sc A, PhD); environmental sciences (M Sc, PhD); finance (DESS); industrial engineering (M Sc, DESS); labor relations (DESS); leisure, culture and tourism sciences (MA, DESS); literary studies (MA); mathematics and computer science (M Sc); matter and energy (MS, PhD); nursing sciences (M Sc, DESS); philosophy (MA, PhD); physical education (M Sc); psychoeducation (M Ed, PhD); psychology (PhD, Certificate); social communication (MA, DESS).

UNIVERSITÉ DU QUÉBEC, ÉCOLE DE TECHNOLOGIE SUPÉRIEURE, Montréal, QC H3C 1K3, Canada

General Information Province-supported, coed, primarily men, comprehensive institution. CGS member. *Graduate housing:* Rooms and/or apartments available on a first-come, first-served basis to single and married students.

GRADUATE UNITS

Graduate Programs Online learning. Offers engineering (M Eng, PhD, Diploma).

UNIVERSITÉ DU QUÉBEC, ÉCOLE NATIONALE D'ADMINISTRATION PUBLIQUE, Quebec, QC G1K 9E5, Canada

General Information Province-supported, coed, graduate-only institution. CGS member. *Graduate housing:* On-campus housing not available.

GRADUATE UNITS

Graduate Program in Public Administration ***Degree program information:*** Part-time programs available. Part-time. Offers international administration (MAP, Diploma); public administration (MAGU, MAP, PhD, Diploma); urban analysis and management (MAGU).

UNIVERSITÉ DU QUÉBEC EN ABITIBI-TÉMISCAMINGUE, Rouyn-Noranda, QC J9X 5E4, Canada

General Information Province-supported, coed, comprehensive institution. CGS member. *Graduate housing:* Room and/or apartments available on a first-come, first-served basis to single students; on-campus housing not available to married students. Housing application deadline: 3/1.

GRADUATE UNITS

Graduate Programs ***Degree program information:*** Part-time programs available. Part-time. Offers biology (MS); business administration (MBA); education (M Ed, MA, PhD, DESS); engineering (ME); environmental sciences (PhD); mineral engineering (ME); mining engineering (DESS); organization management (M Sc); project management (M Sc, DESS); social work (MSW); sustainable forest ecosystem management (MS).

UNIVERSITÉ DU QUÉBEC EN OUTAOUAIS, Gatineau, QC J8X 3X7, Canada

General Information Province-supported, coed, university. CGS member. *Graduate housing:* Rooms and/or apartments available on a first-come, first-served basis to single and married students.

GRADUATE UNITS

Graduate Programs ***Degree program information:*** Part-time and evening/weekend programs available. Part-time, evening/weekend. Offers accounting (MA, DESS, Diploma); computer science (M Sc, PhD, DESS); education (M Ed, MA, PhD, DESS, Diploma); executive certified management accounting (MA, MBA, DESS); financial services (MBA, DESS, Diploma); industrial relations (M Sc, MA, PhD, Diploma); nursing (M Sc, DESS, Diploma); project management (M Sc, MA, DESS, Diploma); psychoeducation (M Ed, MA); regional development (MA); second and foreign language teaching (Diploma); social work (MA). Electronic applications accepted.

UNIVERSITÉ DU QUÉBEC, INSTITUT NATIONAL DE LA RECHERCHE SCIENTIFIQUE, Québec, QC G1K 9A9, Canada

General Information Province-supported, coed, graduate-only institution. CGS member. *Graduate housing:* On-campus housing not available. *Research affiliation:* Axis Photonique, Tecosol Inc., Bio-K Plus International Inc.

GRADUATE UNITS

Graduate Programs ***Degree program information:*** Part-time programs available. Part-time. Electronic applications accepted.

Research Center–Energy Materials Telecommunications Degree program information: Part-time programs available. Part-time. Offers energy and materials science (M Sc, PhD); telecommunications (M Sc, PhD). Electronic applications accepted.

Research Center–INRS–Institut Armand-Frappier Degree program information: Part-time programs available. Part-time. Offers applied microbiology (M Sc); biology (PhD); experimental health sciences (M Sc); virology and immunology (M Sc, PhD). Electronic applications accepted.

Research Center–Urbanization Culture Society Degree program information: Part-time programs available. Part-time. Offers demography (M Sc, PhD); research practices and public action (MA, DESS); urban studies (M Sc, PhD). Electronic applications accepted.

Research Center–Water Earth Environment Degree program information: Part-time programs available. Part-time. Offers earth sciences (M Sc, PhD); earth sciences - environmental technologies (M Sc); water sciences (M Sc, PhD). Electronic applications accepted.

UNIVERSITÉ LAVAL, Québec, QC G1K 7P4, Canada

General Information Independent, coed, university. *Graduate housing:* Room and/or apartments available on a first-come, first-served basis to single students; on-campus housing not available to married students. *Research affiliation:* Centre Hospitalier Universitaire de Quebec (biomedical research), Institut National d'optique (optics and photonics), Centre de Developpement de la Geomatique (applied geomatics), Institut Maurice-Lamontagne (oceanography), Forintek Canada (forestry and wood processing), Societe des pades de Sciences Naturelles du Quebec (biology).

GRADUATE UNITS

Faculty of Administrative Sciences ***Degree program information:*** Part-time programs available. Part-time, online learning. Offers accounting (MBA); administrative sciences (M Sc, MBA, PhD, Diploma); administrative studies (M Sc, PhD); agri-food management (MBA); electronic business (MBA, Diploma); factory management and logistics (MBA); finance (MBA); financial engineering (M Sc); firm management (MBA); geomatic management (MBA); information technology management (MBA); international management (MBA); management (MBA); management accounting (MBA, Diploma); marketing (MBA); modeling and organizational decision (MBA); occupational health and safety management (MBA); organizations management and development (Diploma); pharmacy management (MBA); public accountancy (MBA, Diploma); social and environmental responsibility (MBA); technological entrepreneurship (Diploma). Electronic applications accepted.

Faculty of Agricultural and Food Sciences ***Degree program information:*** Part-time programs available. Part-time. Offers agri-food engineering (M Sc); agricultural and food sciences (M Sc, PhD, Diploma); agricultural economics (M Sc); agricultural microbiology (M Sc); agro-food microbiology (PhD); animal sciences (M Sc, PhD); consumer sciences (Diploma); environmental technology (M Sc); food sciences and technology (M Sc, PhD); integrated rural development (Diploma); nutrition (M Sc, PhD); plant biology (M Sc, PhD); soils and environment science (M Sc, PhD). Electronic applications accepted.

Faculty of Architecture, Planning and Visual Arts Offers architecture, planning and visual arts (M Arch, M Sc, MA, MATDR, PhD); planning and regional development (MATDR, PhD). Electronic applications accepted.

School of Architecture Degree program information: Part-time programs available. Part-time. Offers architecture (M Arch, M Sc). Electronic applications accepted.

School of Visual Arts Offers graphic design and multimedia (MA); visual arts (MA). Electronic applications accepted.

Faculty of Dentistry Offers buccal and maxillofacial surgery (DESS); dentistry (M Sc, DMD, DESS); gerodontology (DESS); multidisciplinary dentistry (DESS); periodontics (DESS). Electronic applications accepted.

Faculty of Education ***Degree program information:*** Part-time programs available. Part-time. Offers didactics (MA, PhD); education (MA, PhD, Diploma); educational administration and evaluation (MA, PhD); educational pedagogy (Diploma); educational practice (Diploma); educational psychology (MA, PhD); orientation sciences (MA, PhD); pedagogy management and development (Diploma); school adaptation (Diploma); teaching technology (MA, PhD). Electronic applications accepted.

Faculty of Forestry, Geography and Geomatics Offers agroforestry (M Sc); forestry sciences (M Sc, PhD); forestry, geography and geomatics (M Sc, M Sc Geogr, PhD); geographical sciences (M Sc Geogr, PhD); geography (M Sc Geogr, PhD); geomatics sciences (M Sc, PhD); wood sciences (M Sc, PhD). Electronic applications accepted.

Faculty of Law ***Degree program information:*** Part-time programs available. Part-time. Offers environment, sustainable development and food safety (LL M); international and transnational law (LL M, Diploma); law (LL M, LL D, Diploma); law of business (LL M, Diploma); notarial law (Diploma). Electronic applications accepted.

Faculty of Letters ***Degree program information:*** Part-time programs available. Part-time. Offers ancient civilization (MA, PhD); archaeology (MA, PhD); art history (MA, PhD); English literatures (MA, PhD); ethnology of French-speaking people in North America (MA, PhD); history (MA, PhD, Diploma); international journalism (Diploma); letters (MA, PhD, Diploma); linguistics (MA, PhD); literary studies (MA, PhD); literature and arts of the screen and stage (PhD); literature and arts of the screen and stage (MA); museology (Diploma); public communication (MA, PhD); public relations (Diploma); Spanish literature (MA, PhD); terminology and translation (MA, Diploma). Electronic applications accepted.

Faculty of Medicine ***Degree program information:*** Part-time programs available. Part-time. Offers accident prevention and occupational health and safety management (Diploma); anatomy–pathology (DESS); anesthesiology (DESS); cardiology (DESS); care of older people (Diploma); cellular and molecular biology (M Sc, PhD); clinical research (DESS); community health (M Sc, PhD); dermatology (DESS); diagnostic radiology (DESS); emergency medicine (Diploma); epidemiology (M Sc, PhD); experimental medicine (M Sc, PhD); family medicine (DESS); general surgery (DESS); geriatrics (DESS); hematology (DESS); internal medicine (DESS); kinesiology (M Sc, PhD); maternal and fetal medicine (Diploma); medical biochemistry (DESS); medical microbiology and infectious diseases (DESS); medical oncology (DESS); medicine (M Sc, MD, PhD, DESS, Diploma); microbiology-immunology (M Sc, PhD); nephrology (DESS); neurobiology (M Sc, PhD); neurology (DESS); neurosurgery (DESS); obstetrics and gynecology (DESS); ophthalmology (DESS); orthopedic surgery (DESS); oto-rhino-laryngology (DESS); palliative medicine (Diploma); pediatrics (DESS); physiology-endocrinology (M Sc, PhD); plastic surgery (DESS); psychiatry (DESS); pulmonary medicine (DESS); radiology–oncology (DESS); speech therapy (M Sc); thoracic surgery (DESS); urology (DESS). Electronic applications accepted.

Faculty of Music Offers composition (M Mus); instrumental didactics (M Mus); interpretation (M Mus); music (M Mus, PhD); music education (M Mus, PhD); musicology (M Mus, PhD). Electronic applications accepted.

Faculty of Nursing Offers nursing (M Sc, PhD, DESS, Diploma). Electronic applications accepted.

Faculty of Pharmacy ***Degree program information:*** Part-time programs available. Part-time. Offers community pharmacy (DESS); hospital pharmacy (M Sc); pharmacy (M Sc, PhD, DESS). Electronic applications accepted.

Faculty of Philosophy Offers philosophy (MA, PhD). Electronic applications accepted.

Faculty of Sciences and Engineering ***Degree program information:*** Part-time programs available. Part-time. Offers aerospace engineering (M Sc); biochemistry (M Sc, PhD); biology (M Sc, PhD); chemical engineering (M Sc, PhD); chemistry (M Sc, PhD); civil engineering (M Sc, PhD); computer science (M Sc, PhD); earth sciences (M Sc, PhD); electrical engineering (M Sc, PhD); environmental technologies (M Sc); environmental technology (M Sc); geology (M Sc, PhD); industrial engineering (Diploma); mathematics (M Sc, PhD); mechanical engineering (M Sc, PhD); metallurgical engineering (M Sc, PhD); microbiology (M Sc, PhD); mining engineering (M Sc, PhD); oceanography (PhD); physics (M Sc, PhD); sciences and engineering (M Sc, PhD, Diploma); software engineering (Diploma); statistics (M Sc); urban infrastructure engineering (Diploma). Electronic applications accepted.

Faculty of Social Sciences ***Degree program information:*** Part-time programs available. Part-time. Offers anthropology (MA, PhD); economics (MA, PhD); feminist studies (Diploma); industrial relations (MA, PhD); policy analysis (MA); political science (MA, PhD); social sciences (M Serv Soc, MA, PhD, Psy D, Diploma); sociology (MA, PhD). Electronic applications accepted.

School of Psychology Offers clinical psychology (PhD); community psychology (PhD); psychology (PhD, Psy D). Electronic applications accepted.

School of Social Work Offers social work (M Serv Soc, PhD). Electronic applications accepted.

Faculty of Theology and Religious Sciences Offers applied ethics (DESS); human sciences of religion (MA, PhD); practical theology (D Th P); theology (MA, PhD); theology and religious sciences (MA, D Th P, PhD, DESS). Electronic applications accepted.

Québec Institute for Advanced International Studies Offers advanced international studies (MA, PhD); international relations (MA, PhD). Electronic applications accepted.

UNIVERSITÉ SAINTE-ANNE, Church Point, NS B0W 1M0, Canada

General Information Province-supported, coed, comprehensive institution.

GRADUATE UNITS

Program in Education ***Degree program information:*** Part-time programs available. Part-time. Offers education (M Ed).

UNIVERSITY AT ALBANY, STATE UNIVERSITY OF NEW YORK, Albany, NY 12222-0001

General Information State-supported, coed, university. CGS member. *Graduate housing:* Rooms and/or apartments available on a first-come, first-served basis to single and married students. Housing application deadline: 9/1. *Research affiliation:* Wadsworth Laboratories, New York State Department of Health (biomedical sciences, epidemiology, environmental health), Naval Research Laboratories (organizational structures (public administration)), General Electric Corporate Research and Development Center (nanoscale science and engineering), IBM–Watson Research Laboratories (artificial intelligence, computer science), Whiteface Mountain Observatory (earth and atmospheric sciences), Woods Hole Oceanographic Institution.

GRADUATE UNITS

College of Arts and Sciences ***Degree program information:*** Part-time and evening/weekend programs available. Part-time, evening/weekend. Offers African studies (MA); Afro-American studies (MA); anthropology (MA, PhD); art (MA, MFA); arts and sciences (MA, MALS, MFA, MRP, MS, PhD, Certificate); atmospheric science (MS, PhD); behavioral neuroscience (PhD); biodiversity, conservation, and policy (MS); chemistry (MS, PhD); clinical psychology (PhD); cognitive psychology (PhD); communication (MA); demography (Certificate); ecology and evolutionary biology (PhD); economic forcasting (MA); economics (MA, PhD); English (MA, PhD); forensic biology (MS); geography (MA); history (MA, PhD); industrial/organizational psychology (MA, PhD); Latin American, Caribbean, and U.S. Latino studies (MA, PhD, Certificate); liberal studies (MALS); mathematics (MA, PhD); molecular, cellular, developmental, and neural biology (PhD); philosophy (MA, PhD); physics (MS, PhD); public history (Certificate); regional planning (MRP); social-personality psychology (PhD); sociology (MA, PhD); sociology and communication (PhD); Spanish (MA, PhD); urban policy (Certificate); women's, gender and sexuality studies (MA).

College of Computing and Information ***Degree program information:*** Part-time programs available. Part-time. Offers computer science (MS, PhD); information science (MS, PhD); information studies (MS, CAS); library and information science (CAS). Electronic applications accepted.

Nelson A. Rockefeller College of Public Affairs and Policy ***Degree program information:*** Part-time programs available. Part-time. Offers financial management and public economics (MPA); financial market regulation (MPA); health policy (MPA); healthcare management (MPA); homeland security (MPA); human resources management (MPA); information strategy and management (MPA); local government management (MPA); nonprofit management (MPA); nonprofit management and leadership (Certificate); organizational behavior and theory (MPA, PhD); planning and policy analysis (CAS); policy analytic methods (MPA); political science (MA, PhD); politics and administration (PhD); public affairs and policy (MA, MPA, PhD, CAS, Certificate); public finance (PhD); public management (PhD); public policy (PhD); public sector management (Certificate); women and public policy (Certificate). Electronic applications accepted.

School of Business ***Degree program information:*** Part-time and evening/weekend programs available. Part-time, evening/weekend. Offers accounting (MS); business (MBA, MS); business administration (MBA); cyber security (MBA); entrepreneurship (MBA); finance (MBA); forensic accounting (MS); human resource information systems (MBA); information technology management (MBA); marketing (MBA); professional accounting (MS); tax practice (MS); taxation (MS). Electronic applications accepted.

School of Criminal Justice ***Degree program information:*** Part-time programs available. Part-time. Offers criminal justice (MA, PhD). Electronic applications accepted.

School of Education ***Degree program information:*** Part-time and evening/weekend programs available. Part-time, evening/weekend. Offers counseling psychology (MS, PhD); curriculum and instruction (PhD, CAS); curriculum development and instructional technology (MS); education (MS, PhD, Psy D, CAS); educational administration and policy studies (MS, PhD, CAS); educational psychology (PhD); educational psychology and methodology (MS); educational research (CAS); general education studies (MS); literacy teaching and learning (MS, PhD, CAS); mental health counseling (MS); school psychology (Psy D, CAS); special education (MS, PhD). Electronic applications accepted.

School of Public Health Offers environmental and occupational health (MS, PhD); environmental chemistry (MS, PhD); epidemiology and biostatistics (MS, PhD); health policy, management, and behavior (MPH, MS, Dr PH, PhD); immunobiology and infectious diseases (MS, PhD); immunology and infectious diseases (MS, PhD); neuroscience (MS, PhD); public health (MPH, MS, Dr PH, PhD, Certificate); structural and cell biology (MS, PhD); toxicology (MS, PhD). Electronic applications accepted.

School of Social Welfare ***Degree program information:*** Part-time and evening/weekend programs available. Part-time, evening/weekend. Offers social welfare (MSW, PhD). Electronic applications accepted.

UNIVERSITY AT BUFFALO, THE STATE UNIVERSITY OF NEW YORK, Buffalo, NY 14260

General Information State-supported, coed, university. CGS member. *Graduate housing:* Rooms and/or apartments available on a first-come, first-served basis to single students and available to married students. Housing application deadline: 5/1. *Research affiliation:* Hauptman-Woodward Medical Research Institute, Roswell Park Cancer Institute, Veterans Administration Medical Center, Calspan–University of Buffalo Research Center, Roswell Park Cancer Institute.

GRADUATE UNITS

Graduate School Students: 7,526 full-time (3,647 women), 2,009 part-time (1,124 women); includes 1,138 minority (337 Black or African American, non-Hispanic/Latino; 36 American Indian or Alaska Native, non-Hispanic/Latino; 621 Asian, non-Hispanic/Latino; 74 Hispanic/Latino; 70 Two or more races, non-Hispanic/Latino), 3,037 international. 23,214 applicants, 34% accepted, 3374 enrolled. *Faculty:* 1,622 full-time (573 women), 215 part-time/adjunct (76 women). *Financial support:* In 2015–16, 2,451 students received support. Fellowships with tuition reimbursements available, research assistantships with tuition reimbursements available, teaching assistantships with tuition reimbursements available, career-related internships or fieldwork, Federal Work-Study, institutionally sponsored loans, scholarships/grants, traineeships, tuition waivers (full and partial), unspecified assistantships, and stipends available. Support available to part-time students. Financial award applicants required to submit FAFSA. In 2015, 3,077 master's, 589 doctorates, 95 other advanced degrees awarded. *Degree program information:* Part-time and evening/weekend programs available. Part-time, evening/weekend, online learning. *Application deadline:* Applications are processed on a rolling basis. *Application fee:* $75. Electronic applications accepted. *Application Contact:* Lisa C. Coia, Assistant Director, 716-645-3482, Fax: 716-645-6998, E-mail: grad@buffalo.edu. *Vice Provost for Graduate Education/Dean of the Graduate School,* Dr. Graham Hammill, 716-645-2939, Fax: 716-645-6142, E-mail: grad@buffalo.edu.

College of Arts and Sciences Degree program information: Part-time programs available. Part-time. Offers American studies (MA, PhD); anthropology (MA, PhD); art (MFA); art history (MA); arts and sciences (MA, MAH, MFA, MM, MS, Au D, PhD, Advanced Certificate, Certificate); arts management (MA); audiology (Au D); biological sciences (MA, MS, PhD); Canadian studies (Advanced Certificate); Caribbean and Latina/o American studies (MA); chemistry (MA, PhD); classics (MA, PhD); communication (MA, PhD); communicative disorders and sciences (MA, PhD); comparative literature (MA, PhD); computational science (Advanced Certificate); contemporary performance (Advanced Certificate); earth systems science (MA, MS); economic geography and business geographics (MS); economics (MA, MS, PhD); English (MA, PhD); environmental modeling and analysis (MA); evolution, ecology and behavior (MS, PhD, Certificate); film and media study (MAH); financial economics (Certificate); French (MA, PhD); geographic information science (MA, MS); geography (MA, PhD); geology (MA, MS, PhD); GIS and environmental analysis (Certificate); global gender studies (MA, PhD); health geography (MS); health services (Certificate); historical musicology and music theory (PhD); history (MA, PhD); information and Internet economics (Certificate); interdisciplinary computational linguistics (MS); international economics (Certificate); international trade (MA); law and regulation (Certificate); linguistics (MA, PhD); mathematics (MA, PhD); media arts production (MFA); media study (PhD); medicinal chemistry (MS, PhD); music composition (MA, PhD); music history (MA); music performance (MM); music theory (MA); new media design (Certificate); philosophy (MA, PhD); physics (MS, PhD); political science (MA, PhD); psychology (MA, PhD); public history (MA); social media (MAH); sociology (MA, PhD); Spanish (MA, PhD); studio art (MFA); theatre and performance (MA, PhD); transportation and business geographics (MA); urban and regional analysis (MA); urban and regional economics (Certificate); visual studies (MA). Electronic applications accepted.

Graduate Programs in Cancer Research and Biomedical Sciences at Roswell Park Cancer Institute Students: 115 full-time (63 women); includes 12 minority (5 Black or African American, non-Hispanic/Latino; 2 Asian, non-Hispanic/Latino; 4 Hispanic/Latino; 1 Native Hawaiian or other Pacific Islander, non-Hispanic/Latino), 31 international. 166 applicants, 33% accepted, 28 enrolled. *Faculty:* 126 full-time (36 women). *Financial support:* In 2015–16, 94 students received support, including 94 research assistantships with full tuition reimbursements available (averaging $25,000 per year); scholarships/grants, health care benefits, and unspecified assistantships also available. Financial award application deadline: 1/5. In 2015, 25 master's, 12 doctorates awarded. Offers cancer pathology and prevention (PhD); cellular and molecular biology (PhD); immunology (PhD); interdisciplinary natural sciences (MS); molecular and cellular biophysics and biochemistry (PhD); molecular pharmacology and cancer therapeutics (PhD). *Application deadline:* For fall admission, 1/5 priority date for domestic and international students. *Application fee:* $75. Electronic applications accepted. *Application Contact:* Dr. Norman J. Karin, Associate Dean, 716-845-2339, Fax: 716-845-8178, E-mail: norman.karin@roswellpark.edu. *Associate Dean*, Dr. Norman J. Karin, 716-845-2339, Fax: 716-845-8178, E-mail: norman.karin@roswellpark.edu.

Graduate School of Education Students: 511 full-time (385 women), 711 part-time (521 women); includes 133 minority (80 Black or African American, non-Hispanic/Latino; 10 American Indian or Alaska Native, non-Hispanic/Latino; 35 Asian, non-Hispanic/Latino; 8 Hispanic/Latino), 110 international. Average age 32. 892 applicants, 72% accepted, 401 enrolled. *Faculty:* 71 full-time (26 women), 148 part-time/adjunct (108 women). *Financial support:* In 2015–16, 87 fellowships (averaging $7,185 per year), 128 research assistantships with tuition reimbursements (averaging $10,645 per year) were awarded; teaching assistantships, Federal Work-Study, institutionally sponsored loans, scholarships/grants, tuition waivers (full and partial), and unspecified assistantships also available. Support available to part-time students. Financial award applicants required to submit FAFSA. In 2015, 355 master's, 44 doctorates, 70 other advanced degrees awarded. *Degree program information:* Part-time programs available. Part-time, 100% online. Offers applied statistical analysis (Advanced Certificate); biology education (Ed M, Certificate); chemistry education (Ed M, Certificate); childhood education (Ed M); childhood education with bilingual extension (Ed M); counseling/school psychology (PhD); counselor education (PhD); curriculum, instruction and the science of learning (PhD); early childhood education (Ed M); early childhood education with bilingual extension (Ed M); earth science education (Ed M, Certificate); economics and education policy analysis (MA); education (Ed M, MA, MS, Ed D, PhD, Advanced Certificate, Certificate); education and technology (Ed M); education studies (Ed M); educational administration (Ed M, Ed D, PhD); educational culture, policy and society (PhD); educational psychology (MA, PhD); educational technology and new literacies (Certificate); educational technology and new literacies (Advanced Certificate); elementary education (Ed D); English education (Ed M, Certificate); English for speakers of other languages (Ed M); foreign and second language education (PhD); French education (Ed M, Certificate); German education (Ed M, Certificate); gifted education (Certificate); higher education administration (Ed M, PhD); information and library science (MS); Latin education (Ed M, Certificate); library and information studies (Certificate); literacy specialist (Ed M); literacy teaching and learning (Certificate); mathematics education (Ed M, Certificate); mental health counseling (MS, Certificate); music education (Ed M, Certificate); music learning theory (Advanced Certificate); physics education (Ed M, Certificate); rehabilitation counseling (MS, Advanced Certificate); school building leadership (Certificate); school business and human resource administration (Certificate); school counseling (Ed M, Certificate); school district business leadership (Certificate); school district leadership (Certificate); school librarianship (MS); science and the public (Ed M); social studies education (Ed M, Certificate); Spanish education (Ed M, Certificate); special education (PhD); teaching English to speakers of other languages (Ed M). *Application deadline:* Applications are processed on a rolling basis. *Application fee:* $50. Electronic applications accepted. *Application Contact:* Dr. Radhika Suresh, Assistant Dean for Enrollment Management, 716-645-2110, Fax: 716-645-7937, E-mail: gse-info@buffalo.edu. *Dean*, Dr. Jaekyung Lee, 716-645-6640, Fax: 716-645-2479, E-mail: gse-info@buffalo.edu.

Law School Students: 507 full-time (255 women), 5 part-time (2 women); includes 86 minority (19 Black or African American, non-Hispanic/Latino; 21 Asian, non-Hispanic/Latino; 30 Hispanic/Latino; 16 Two or more races, non-Hispanic/Latino), 28 international. Average age 26. 1,119 applicants, 54% accepted, 160 enrolled. *Faculty:* 49 full-time (22 women), 95 part-time/adjunct (35 women). *Financial support:* Career-related internships or fieldwork, Federal Work-Study, institutionally sponsored loans, scholarships/grants, tuition waivers (partial), and unspecified assistantships available. Financial award application deadline: 3/1; financial award applicants required to submit FAFSA. In 2015, 189 doctorates awarded. Offers criminal law (LL M); general law (LL M); law (JD). *Application deadline:* For fall admission, 3/1 priority date for domestic and international students. Applications are processed on a rolling basis. *Application fee:* $85. Electronic applications accepted. *Application Contact:* Lillie V. Wiley-Upshaw, Vice Dean for Admissions and Student Life, 716-645-2907, Fax: 716-645-6676, E-mail: law-admissions@buffalo.edu. *Interim Dean*, James A. Gardner, 716-645-2052, Fax: 716-645-2064, E-mail: jgard@buffalo.edu.

School of Architecture and Planning Degree program information: Part-time programs available. Part-time. Offers architecture (M Arch); architecture and planning (M Arch, MS Arch, MUP, PhD, Certificate); ecological practices (MS Arch); historic preservation (Certificate); historic preservation and urban design (MS Arch); inclusive design (MS Arch); real estate development (MS Arch); situated technology (MS Arch); urban and regional planning (PhD). Electronic applications accepted.

School of Dental Medicine Offers biomaterials (MS); dental medicine (MS, DDS, PhD, Certificate); oral biology (PhD); oral sciences (MS); orthodontics (MS, Certificate). Electronic applications accepted.

School of Engineering and Applied Sciences Degree program information: Part-time and evening/weekend programs available. Part-time, evening/weekend, online learning. Offers aerospace engineering (MS, PhD); biomedical engineering (MS, PhD); chemical and biological engineering (ME, MS, PhD); civil engineering (ME, MS, PhD); computer science and engineering (MS, PhD); electrical engineering (ME, MS, PhD); engineering and applied sciences (ME, MS, PhD, Certificate); engineering science (MS); industrial and systems engineering (ME, MS, PhD); information assurance (Certificate); mechanical engineering (MS, PhD). Electronic applications accepted.

School of Management Students: 442 full-time (182 women), 200 part-time (73 women); includes 68 minority (16 Black or African American, non-Hispanic/Latino; 1 American Indian or Alaska Native, non-Hispanic/Latino; 47 Asian, non-Hispanic/Latino; 3 Hispanic/Latino; 1 Two or more races, non-Hispanic/Latino), 221 international. Average age 30. 2,317 applicants, 45% accepted, 485 enrolled. *Faculty:* 82 full-time (24 women), 38 part-time/adjunct (7 women). *Financial support:* In 2015–16, 161 students received support. Fellowships, research assistantships with tuition reimbursements available, teaching assistantships with partial tuition reimbursements available, career-related internships or fieldwork, Federal Work-Study, institutionally sponsored loans, scholarships/grants, health care benefits, and unspecified assistantships available. Financial award application deadline: 2/15. In 2015, 471 master's, 11 doctorates awarded. *Degree program information:* Part-time and evening/weekend programs available. Part-time, evening/weekend. Offers accounting (MS); business administration (PMBA); finance (MS); management (EMBA, MBA, PhD); management information systems (MS); supply chains and operations management (MS). *Application deadline:* For fall admission, 10/15 priority date for domestic and international students; for winter admission, 2/1 priority date for domestic and international students; for spring admission, 4/15 for domestic students; for summer admission, 5/15 for domestic students. *Application fee:* $100. Electronic applications accepted. *Application Contact:* Meghan Felser, Associate Director of Admissions and Recruiting, 716-645-3204, Fax: 716-645-2341, E-mail: mpwood@buffalo.edu. *Assistant Dean and Director of Graduate Programs*, Erin K. O'Brien, 716-645-3204, Fax: 716-645-2341, E-mail: ekobrien@buffalo.edu.

School of Medicine and Biomedical Sciences Students: 788 full-time (367 women); includes 252 minority (27 Black or African American, non-Hispanic/Latino; 3 American Indian or Alaska Native, non-Hispanic/Latino; 128 Asian, non-Hispanic/Latino; 63 Hispanic/Latino; 31 Two or more races, non-Hispanic/Latino), 64 international. 4,937 applicants, 9% accepted, 196 enrolled. *Faculty:* 456 full-time (136 women), 310 part-time/adjunct (177 women). *Financial support:* In 2015–16, 142 students received support, including 112 fellowships with full tuition reimbursements available (averaging $13,083 per year), 85 research assistantships with full tuition reimbursements available (averaging $24,843 per year), 8 teaching assistantships with full tuition reimbursements available (averaging $19,967 per year); career-related internships or fieldwork, Federal Work-Study, institutionally sponsored loans, scholarships/grants, traineeships, health care benefits, and unspecified assistantships also available. Financial award application deadline: 2/1; financial award applicants required to submit FAFSA. In 2015, 33 master's, 160 doctorates awarded. Offers anatomical sciences (MA, PhD); biochemistry (MA, PhD); biomedical sciences (PhD); biophysics (MS, PhD); biotechnology (MS); genetics, genomics and bioinformatics (MS, PhD); medicine (MD); medicine and biomedical sciences (MA, MS, MD, PhD); microbiology and immunology (MA, PhD); neuroscience (MS, PhD); pathology (MA, PhD); pharmacology (MS, PhD); physiology (MA, PhD); structural biology (MS, PhD). *Application deadline:* For fall admission, 2/1 for domestic and international students. Applications are processed on a rolling basis. *Application fee:* $0. Electronic applications accepted. *Application Contact:* Elizabeth A. White, Administrative Director, 716-829-3399, Fax: 716-829-2437, E-mail: bethw@buffalo.edu. *Dean*, Dr. Michael E. Cain, 716-829-3955, Fax: 716-829-3395, E-mail: mcain@buffalo.edu.

School of Nursing Students: 61 full-time (37 women), 137 part-time (114 women); includes 35 minority (17 Black or African American, non-Hispanic/Latino; 1 American Indian or Alaska Native, non-Hispanic/Latino; 17 Asian, non-Hispanic/Latino), 7 international. Average age 32. 193 applicants, 49% accepted, 75 enrolled. *Financial support:* In 2015–16, 80 students received support, including 2 fellowships with tuition reimbursements available (averaging $17,000 per year), 4 research assistantships with tuition reimbursements available (averaging $10,600 per year), 7 teaching assistantships with tuition reimbursements available (averaging $10,600 per year); scholarships/grants, traineeships, health care benefits, and unspecified assistantships also available. Financial award application deadline: 2/1; financial award applicants required to submit FAFSA. In 2015, 6 master's, 37 doctorates awarded. *Degree program information:* Part-time programs available. Part-time, 100% online. Offers adult gerontology nurse practitioner (DNP); family nurse practitioner (DNP); health care systems and leadership (MS); nurse anesthetist (DNP); nursing (PhD); nursing education (Certificate); psychiatric/mental health nurse practitioner (DNP). *Application deadline:* For fall admission, 7/1 for domestic students, 2/1 for international students; for spring admission, 12/1 for domestic students, 10/1 for international students; for summer admission, 2/1 for domestic students. Applications are processed on a rolling basis. *Application fee:* $75. Electronic applications accepted. *Application Contact:* Jennifer H. VanLaeken, Director of Graduate Student Services, 716-829-3311, Fax: 716-829-2067, E-mail: jhv2@buffalo.edu. *Dean and Professor*, Dr. Marsha L. Lewis, 716-829-2533, Fax: 716-829-2566, E-mail: ubnursingdean@buffalo.edu.

School of Pharmacy and Pharmaceutical Sciences Students: 567 full-time (326 women), 9 part-time (4 women); includes 216 minority (22 Black or African American, non-Hispanic/Latino; 1 American Indian or Alaska Native, non-Hispanic/Latino; 185 Asian, non-Hispanic/Latino; 8 Hispanic/Latino), 46 international. Average age 24. 894 applicants, 27% accepted, 158 enrolled. *Faculty:* 40 full-time (13 women), 11 part-time/adjunct (3 women). *Financial support:* In 2015–16, 358 students received support, including 3 fellowships (averaging $50,903 per year), 45 research assistantships with full tuition reimbursements available (averaging $23,994 per year); scholarships/grants also available. Financial award application deadline: 3/1; financial award applicants required to submit FAFSA. In 2015, 9 master's, 140 doctorates awarded. Offers pharmaceutical sciences (MS, PhD); pharmacy (Pharm D); pharmacy and pharmaceutical sciences (MS, PhD, Pharm D). *Application deadline:* For fall admission, 2/1 priority date for domestic and international students. Applications are processed on a rolling basis. *Application fee:* $50. Electronic applications accepted. *Application Contact:* Dr. Jennifer M. Hess, Associate Dean, 716-645-2825 Ext. 1, Fax: 716-829-6568, E-mail: prepharm@buffalo.edu. *Dean*, Dr. James M. O'Donnell, 716-645-2823, Fax: 716-829-6568.

School of Public Health and Health Professions Students: 470 full-time (301 women), 50 part-time (32 women); includes 57 minority (13 Black or African American, non-Hispanic/Latino; 43 Asian, non-Hispanic/Latino; 1 Hispanic/Latino), 88 international. Average age 26. 775 applicants, 54% accepted, 253 enrolled. *Faculty:* 60 full-time (27 women), 12 part-time/adjunct (5 women). *Financial support:* In 2015–16, 47 students received support, including 8 fellowships with full tuition reimbursements available (averaging $2,500 per year), 15 research assistantships with full tuition reimbursements available (averaging $15,000 per year), 16 teaching assistantships with full tuition reimbursements available (averaging $8,500 per year); career-related internships or fieldwork, Federal Work-Study, institutionally sponsored loans, scholarships/grants, tuition waivers (full and partial), and unspecified assistantships also available. Financial award application deadline: 3/15; financial award applicants required to submit FAFSA. In 2015, 1,126 master's, 49 doctorates, 20 other advanced degrees awarded. *Degree program information:* Part-time programs available. Part-time. Offers assistive and rehabilitation technology (Certificate); biostatistics (MA, MPH, PhD); community health and health behavior (MPH, PhD); epidemiology (MS, PhD); exercise science (MS, PhD); nutrition (MS, Advanced Certificate); occupational therapy (MS); physical therapy (DPT); public health (MPH); public health and health professions (MA, MPH, MS, DPT, PhD, Advanced Certificate, Certificate); rehabilitation science (PhD). *Application deadline:* For fall admission, 2/1 priority date for domestic and international students. *Application fee:* $50. Electronic applications accepted. *Dean*, Dr. Lynn Kozlowski, 716-829-6951, Fax: 716-829-6040, E-mail: lk22@buffalo.edu.

School of Social Work Students: 286 full-time (251 women), 202 part-time (164 women); includes 86 minority (50 Black or African American, non-Hispanic/Latino; 7 Asian, non-Hispanic/Latino; 19 Hispanic/Latino; 10 Two or more races, non-Hispanic/Latino), 27 international. Average age 29. 469 applicants, 81% accepted, 281 enrolled. *Faculty:* 30 full-time (23 women), 47 part-time/adjunct (37 women). *Financial support:* In 2015–16, 6 fellowships with full tuition reimbursements (averaging $12,400 per year), 3 research assistantships with full tuition reimbursements (averaging $15,000 per year), 6 teaching assistantships with full tuition reimbursements (averaging $5,000 per year) were awarded; Federal Work-Study, scholarships/grants, health care benefits, tuition waivers (full and partial), unspecified assistantships, and instructorships and research grants (for PhD students) also available. Financial award application deadline: 4/30; financial award applicants required to submit FAFSA. In 2015, 195 master's, 3 doctorates awarded. *Degree program information:* Part-time programs available. Part-time, 100% online, blended/hybrid learning. Offers social welfare (PhD); social work (MSW). *Application deadline:* For fall admission, 3/1 priority date for domestic and international students; for spring admission, 9/15 for domestic and international students; for summer admission, 2/1 for domestic and international students. *Application fee:* $75. Electronic applications accepted. *Application Contact:* Maria Carey, Admissions Processor, 716-645-3381, Fax: 716-645-3456, E-mail: sw-info@buffalo.edu. *Dean*, Dr. Nancy J. Smyth, 716-645-3381, Fax: 716-645-3883, E-mail: sw-dean@buffalo.edu.

UNIVERSITY OF ADVANCING TECHNOLOGY, Tempe, AZ 85283-1042

General Information Proprietary, coed, primarily men, comprehensive institution. *Graduate housing:* Room and/or apartments available on a first-come, first-served basis to single students; on-campus housing not available to married students.

GRADUATE UNITS

Master of Science Program in Technology Offers advancing computer science (MS); emerging technologies (MS); game production and management (MS); information assurance (MS); technology leadership (MS). Electronic applications accepted.

THE UNIVERSITY OF AKRON, Akron, OH 44325

General Information State-supported, coed, university. CGS member. *Enrollment:* 23,046 graduate, professional, and undergraduate students; 2,516 full-time matriculated graduate/professional students (1,204 women), 1,564 part-time matriculated graduate/professional students (999 women). *Enrollment by degree level:* 2,679 master's, 1,325 doctoral, 76 other advanced degrees. *Graduate faculty:* 449 full-time (158 women), 436 part-time/adjunct (246 women). Tuition, state resident: full-time $7958; part-time $442 per credit hour. Tuition, nonresident: full-time $13,464; part-time $748 per credit hour. *Required fees:* $1404. *Graduate housing:* Room and/or apartments available on a first-come, first-served basis to single students; on-campus housing not available to married students. Typical cost: $7020 per year ($10,968 including board). Housing application deadline: 3/1. *Student services:* Campus employment opportunities, campus safety program, career counseling, exercise/wellness program, free psychological counseling, international student services, low-cost health insurance, multicultural affairs office, services for students with disabilities. *Library:* Bierce Library plus 2 others. *Collection:* Books: 1.6 million (physical), 392,371 (digital/electronic); Serial titles: 43,420 (physical), 61,175 (digital/electronic); Databases: 381. Study areas open 24 hours, 5–7 days a week; students can reserve study rooms.

Computer facilities: Computer purchase and lease plans are available. 3,150 computers available on campus for general student use. A campuswide network can be accessed from student residence rooms and from off campus. Online class registration, library laptops for student checkout are available.
Website: http://www.uakron.edu/

General Application Contact: Lauri Thorpe, Associate Dean, Enrollment, 330-972-6367, Fax: 330-972-6475, E-mail: lauri@uakron.edu.

GRADUATE UNITS

Graduate School Students: 2,225 full-time (1,081 women), 1,408 part-time (928 women); includes 424 minority (233 Black or African American, non-Hispanic/Latino; 5 American Indian or Alaska Native, non-Hispanic/Latino; 72 Asian, non-Hispanic/Latino; 65 Hispanic/Latino; 1 Native Hawaiian or other Pacific Islander, non-Hispanic/Latino; 48 Two or more races, non-Hispanic/Latino), 946 international. Average age 30. 3,577 applicants, 56% accepted, 985 enrolled. *Faculty:* 450 full-time (158 women), 436 part-time/adjunct (246 women). *Financial support:* In 2015–16, 38 fellowships with full tuition reimbursements, 500 research assistantships with full tuition reimbursements, 758 teaching assistantships with full tuition reimbursements were awarded; unspecified assistantships and administrative assistantships also available. In 2015, 1,155 master's, 126 doctorates awarded. *Degree program information:* Part-time and evening/weekend programs available. Part-time, evening/weekend. *Application deadline:* For fall admission, 12/1 priority date for domestic and international students. Applications are processed on a rolling basis. *Application fee:* $45 ($70 for international students). Electronic applications accepted. *Application Contact:* Charles Beneke, Associate Dean, Academics, 330-972-2565, Fax: 330-972-6475, E-mail: beneke@uakron.edu. *Executive Dean*, Dr. Chand Midha, 330-972-7664, Fax: 330-972-6475, E-mail: cmidha@uakron.edu.

Buchtel College of Arts and Sciences Students: 542 full-time (252 women), 202 part-time (132 women); includes 120 minority (51 Black or African American, non-Hispanic/Latino; 1 American Indian or Alaska Native, non-Hispanic/Latino; 30 Asian, non-Hispanic/Latino; 25 Hispanic/Latino; 13 Two or more races, non-Hispanic/Latino), 145 international. Average age 29. 860 applicants, 47% accepted, 234 enrolled. *Faculty:* 232 full-time (81 women), 116 part-time/adjunct (49 women). *Financial support:* In 2015–16, 1 fellowship with full tuition reimbursement, 58 research assistantships with full tuition reimbursements, 370 teaching assistantships with full tuition reimbursements were awarded; career-related internships or fieldwork, Federal Work-Study, institutionally sponsored loans, scholarships/grants, and unspecified assistantships also available. Support available to part-time students. In 2015, 274 master's, 27 doctorates awarded. *Degree program information:* Part-time and evening/weekend programs available. Part-time, evening/weekend. Offers accompanying (MM); adult development and aging (PhD); applied mathematics (MS); applied politics (MAP); arts administration (MA); arts and sciences (MA, MAP, MFA, MM, MPA, MS, PhD); biology (MS); chemistry (MS, PhD); child and family development (MA); clothing, textiles and interiors (MA); communication (MA); composition (MA, MM); computer science (MS); counseling psychology (MA, PhD); creative writing (MFA); earth science (MS); economics (MA); engineering geology (MS); environmental geology (MS); geology (MS); geophysics (MS); history (MA, PhD); industrial/organizational psychology (MA, PhD); integrated bioscience (PhD); literature (MA); mathematics (MS); music education (MM); music technology (MM); performance (MM); physics (MS); political science (MA); psychology (MA); public administration (MPA); sociology (MA, PhD); Spanish (MA); statistics (MS); theatre arts (MA); theory (MM). *Application deadline:* For fall admission, 1/15 for domestic and international students. Applications are processed on a rolling basis. *Application fee:* $45 ($70 for international students). Electronic applications accepted. *Interim Dean*, Dr. John Green, 330-972-5182, E-mail: green@uakron.edu.

College of Business Administration Students: 286 full-time (133 women), 213 part-time (67 women); includes 44 minority (18 Black or African American, non-Hispanic/Latino; 15 Asian, non-Hispanic/Latino; 5 Hispanic/Latino; 6 Two or more races, non-Hispanic/Latino), 162 international. 400 applicants, 65% accepted, 183 enrolled. *Faculty:* 48 full-time (9 women), 37 part-time/adjunct (9 women). *Financial support:* In 2015–16, 112 teaching assistantships with full tuition reimbursements were awarded; Federal Work-Study also available. In 2015, 153 master's awarded. *Degree program information:* Part-time and evening/weekend programs available. Part-time, evening/weekend. Offers accounting information systems (MS); business administration (MBA, MS, MSA, MSM, MT); finance (MBA); global technological innovation (MBA); healthcare management (MBA); information systems management (MSM); international business (MBA); management (MBA, MSM); professional accountancy (MS); strategic marketing (MBA); supply chain management (MBA); taxation (MT); technological innovation (MSM). *Application deadline:* For fall admission, 7/15 for domestic and international students; for spring admission, 11/15 for domestic and international students; for summer admission, 4/15 for domestic students, 3/15 for international students. *Application fee:* $45 ($70 for international students). Electronic applications accepted. *Application Contact:* Dr. William Hauser, Director of Graduate Business Programs, 330-972-7043, Fax: 330-972-6588, E-mail: whauser@uakron.edu. *Interim Dean*, Dr. Ravi Krovi, 330-972-7442, E-mail: cbadean@uakron.edu.

College of Education Students: 132 full-time (82 women), 263 part-time (195 women); includes 68 minority (47 Black or African American, non-Hispanic/Latino; 1 American Indian or Alaska Native, non-Hispanic/Latino; 6 Asian, non-Hispanic/Latino; 6 Hispanic/Latino; 8 Two or more races, non-Hispanic/Latino), 31 international. 230 applicants, 74% accepted, 125 enrolled. *Faculty:* 28 full-time (21 women), 77 part-time/adjunct (52 women). *Financial support:* In 2015–16, 5 research assistantships with full tuition reimbursements, 23 teaching assistantships with full tuition reimbursements were awarded; unspecified assistantships also available. In 2015, 194 master's awarded. *Degree program information:* Part-time programs available. Part-time. Offers assessment and evaluation (MA, Certificate); curriculum and instruction (MS); education (MA, MS); elementary education - literacy (MA); higher education administration (MA, MS); instructional technology (MA); principalship (MA, MS); special education (MA). *Application deadline:* Applications are processed on a rolling basis. *Application fee:* $45 ($70 for international students). Electronic applications accepted. *Application Contact:* Kelly Chaff, College Program Specialist, 330-972-7028, E-mail: klchaff@uakron.edu. *Interim Dean*, Dr. Susan Clark, 330-972-7780, E-mail: sclark1@uakron.edu.

College of Engineering Students: 356 full-time (83 women), 83 part-time (12 women); includes 19 minority (1 Black or African American, non-Hispanic/Latino; 8 Asian, non-Hispanic/Latino; 6 Hispanic/Latino; 1 Native Hawaiian or other Pacific Islander, non-Hispanic/Latino; 3 Two or more races, non-Hispanic/Latino), 308 international. 509 applicants, 52% accepted, 112 enrolled. *Faculty:* 92 full-time (14 women), 27 part-time/adjunct (1 woman). *Financial support:* In 2015–16, 1 fellowship with full tuition reimbursement, 163 research assistantships with full tuition reimbursements, 134 teaching assistantships with full tuition reimbursements were awarded; career-related internships or fieldwork and Federal Work-Study also available. In 2015, 63 master's, 44 doctorates awarded. *Degree program information:* Part-time and evening/weekend programs available. Part-time, evening/weekend. Offers biomedical engineering (MS); chemical engineering (MS); civil engineering (MS); electrical engineering (MS); engineering (PhD); mechanical engineering (MS). *Application deadline:* Applications are processed on a rolling basis. *Application fee:* $45 ($70 for international students). Electronic applications accepted. *Application Contact:* Dr. Craig Menzemer, Associate Dean, 330-972-5536, E-mail: ccmenze@uakron.edu. *Interim Dean*, Dr. Mario Garzia, 330-972-7709, E-mail: mgarzia@uakron.edu.

College of Health Professions Students: 530 full-time (403 women), 500 part-time (390 women); includes 162 minority (89 Black or African American, non-Hispanic/Latino; 2 American Indian or Alaska Native, non-Hispanic/Latino; 21 Asian, non-Hispanic/Latino; 24 Hispanic/Latino; 26 Two or more races, non-Hispanic/Latino), 17 international. 883 applicants, 40% accepted, 298 enrolled. *Faculty:* 46 full-time (29 women), 176 part-time/adjunct (135 women). *Financial support:* In 2015–16, 32 fellowships with tuition reimbursements, 45 research assistantships with tuition reimbursements, 118 teaching assistantships with tuition reimbursements were awarded; unspecified assistantships also available. In 2015, 351 master's, 16 doctorates awarded. Offers audiology (Au D); child life (MA); classroom guidance for teachers (MA, MS); clinical mental health counseling (MA, MS); counseling psychology (PhD); counselor education and supervision (PhD); exercise physiology/adult fitness (MA, MS); health professions (MA, MPH, MS, MSN, MSW, Au D, DNP, PhD); marriage and family therapy (MA, MS); nursing (MSN, PhD); nursing practice (DNP); public health (MPH); school counseling (MA, MS); social work (MSW); speech-language pathology (MA); sports science/coaching (MA); sports science/coaching education (MS). *Application deadline:* For fall admission, 1/1 for domestic and international students. Applications are processed on a rolling basis. *Application fee:* $45 ($70 for international students). Electronic applications accepted. *Dean*, Dr. David Gordon, 330-972-7552, E-mail: dgordon1@uakron.edu.

College of Polymer Science and Polymer Engineering Students: 338 full-time (107 women), 22 part-time (8 women); includes 17 minority (6 Black or African American, non-Hispanic/Latino; 1 American Indian or Alaska Native, non-Hispanic/Latino; 7 Asian, non-Hispanic/Latino; 2 Hispanic/Latino; 1 Two or more races, non-Hispanic/Latino), 285 international. 329 applicants, 38% accepted, 102 enrolled. *Faculty:* 33 full-time (4 women), 3 part-time/adjunct (0 women). *Financial support:* In

2015–16, 4 fellowships with full tuition reimbursements, 229 research assistantships with full tuition reimbursements, 1 teaching assistantship with full tuition reimbursement were awarded. In 2015, 61 master's, 31 doctorates awarded. *Degree program information:* Part-time and evening/weekend programs available. Part-time, evening/weekend. Offers polymer engineering (MS, PhD); polymer science (MS, PhD). *Application deadline:* For fall admission, 12/1 priority date for domestic and international students. *Application fee:* $45 ($70 for international students). Electronic applications accepted. *Application Contact:* Dr. Mark Foster, Associate Dean, 330-972-5904, E-mail: mdf1@uakron.edu. *Dean*, Dr. Eric Amis, 330-972-7500, E-mail: amis@uakron.edu.

School of Law Students: 295 full-time (114 women), 133 part-time (64 women); includes 60 minority (23 Black or African American, non-Hispanic/Latino; 14 Asian, non-Hispanic/Latino; 16 Hispanic/Latino; 7 Two or more races, non-Hispanic/Latino), 2 international. Average age 31. 738 applicants, 65% accepted, 147 enrolled. *Faculty:* 38 full-time (16 women), 16 part-time/adjunct (2 women). *Financial support:* In 2015–16, 264 students received support. Career-related internships or fieldwork, scholarships/grants, and tuition waivers (full and partial) available. Support available to part-time students. Financial award applicants required to submit FAFSA. In 2015, 8 master's, 142 doctorates awarded. *Degree program information:* Part-time and evening/weekend programs available. Part-time, evening/weekend. Offers intellectual property law (LL M); law (JD). *Application deadline:* For fall admission, 3/1 priority date for domestic and international students. Applications are processed on a rolling basis. *Application fee:* $45 ($70 for international students). Electronic applications accepted. *Application Contact:* Lauri S. File, Assistant Dean of Admission and Financial Aid, 330-972-7331, Fax: 330-258-2343, E-mail: lfile@uakron.edu. *Dean*, Martin H. Belsky, 330-972-6359, Fax: 330-258-2343, E-mail: belsky@uakron.edu.

THE UNIVERSITY OF ALABAMA, Tuscaloosa, AL 35487

General Information State-supported, coed, university. CGS member. *Enrollment:* 37,098 graduate, professional, and undergraduate students; 3,251 full-time matriculated graduate/professional students (1,778 women), 1,699 part-time matriculated graduate/professional students (1,113 women). *Enrollment by degree level:* 2,884 master's, 1,978 doctoral, 88 other advanced degrees. *Graduate faculty:* 939 full-time (363 women), 55 part-time/adjunct (21 women). Tuition, state resident: full-time $10,170. Tuition, nonresident: full-time $25,950. *Graduate housing:* On-campus housing not available. *Student services:* Campus employment opportunities, campus safety program, career counseling, child daycare facilities, exercise/wellness program, free psychological counseling, grant writing training, international student services, low-cost health insurance, multicultural affairs office, services for students with disabilities, teacher training, writing training. *Library:* Amelia Gayle Gorgas Library plus 8 others. *Collection:* Books: 3.3 million (physical), 1.4 million (digital/electronic); Serial titles: 712 (physical), 84,127 (digital/electronic); Databases: 940. Weekly public service hours: 146; study areas open 24 hours, 5–7 days a week; students can reserve study rooms. *Research affiliation:* Mercedes-Benz (automotive engineering), Georgia Pacific LLC (safety technology), PCORI (health disparities), TDK Corp. (materials science), Lockheed Martin Corporation (business analytics), Dynetics, Inc. (aerospace engineering).

Computer facilities: 2,500 computers available on campus for general student use. A campuswide network can be accessed from student residence rooms and from off campus. Online class registration is available.
Website: http://www.ua.edu/

General Application Contact: Patrick D. Fuller, Senior Graduate Admissions Counselor, 205-348-5923, Fax: 205-348-0400, E-mail: patrick.d.fuller@ua.edu.

GRADUATE UNITS

Graduate School Students: 3,251 full-time (1,778 women), 1,699 part-time (1,113 women); includes 981 minority (619 Black or African American, non-Hispanic/Latino; 21 American Indian or Alaska Native, non-Hispanic/Latino; 78 Asian, non-Hispanic/Latino; 177 Hispanic/Latino; 6 Native Hawaiian or other Pacific Islander, non-Hispanic/Latino; 80 Two or more races, non-Hispanic/Latino), 511 international. Average age 31. 6,887 applicants, 39% accepted, 1666 enrolled. *Faculty:* 899 full-time (347 women), 21 part-time/adjunct (14 women). *Financial support:* In 2015–16, 1,102 students received support, including 251 fellowships with tuition reimbursements available (averaging $13,000 per year), 656 research assistantships with tuition reimbursements available (averaging $14,041 per year), 900 teaching assistantships with tuition reimbursements available (averaging $14,991 per year); career-related internships or fieldwork, Federal Work-Study, institutionally sponsored loans, scholarships/grants, traineeships, health care benefits, tuition waivers (full and partial), and unspecified assistantships also available. Support available to part-time students. Financial award application deadline: 2/15; financial award applicants required to submit FAFSA. In 2015, 1,581 master's, 443 doctorates, 39 other advanced degrees awarded. *Degree program information:* Part-time and evening/weekend programs available. Part-time, evening/weekend, online learning. *Application deadline:* For fall admission, 7/1 priority date for domestic students, 3/15 for international students; for spring admission, 11/1 priority date for domestic students, 7/1 for international students. Applications are processed on a rolling basis. *Application fee:* $50 ($60 for international students). Electronic applications accepted. *Application Contact:* Lesley Campbell, Director of Graduate Recruitment, 205-348-0051, Fax: 205-348-0400, E-mail: lesley.campbell@ua.edu. *Dean*, Dr. David A. Francko, 205-348-8280, Fax: 205-348-0400, E-mail: dfrancko@ua.edu.

Capstone College of Nursing Students: 124 full-time (100 women), 209 part-time (181 women); includes 112 minority (76 Black or African American, non-Hispanic/Latino; 1 American Indian or Alaska Native, non-Hispanic/Latino; 9 Asian, non-Hispanic/Latino; 22 Hispanic/Latino; 1 Native Hawaiian or other Pacific Islander, non-Hispanic/Latino; 3 Two or more races, non-Hispanic/Latino), 2 international. Average age 43. 303 applicants, 57% accepted, 128 enrolled. *Faculty:* 23 full-time (20 women), 1 part-time/adjunct (0 women). *Financial support:* In 2015–16, 2 fellowships with full tuition reimbursements (averaging $15,000 per year) were awarded; scholarships/grants also available. Financial award application deadline: 7/1; financial award applicants required to submit FAFSA. In 2015, 42 master's, 54 doctorates awarded. *Degree program information:* Part-time programs available. Part-time, online learning. Offers nursing (MSN, DNP, Ed D). *Application deadline:* For fall admission, 6/1 priority date for domestic students; for winter admission, 11/1 for domestic students; for spring admission, 4/1 priority date for domestic students. Applications are processed on a rolling basis. *Application fee:* $50 ($60 for international students). Electronic applications accepted. *Application Contact:* Dr. Marsha H. Adams, Senior Associate Dean, 205-348-1044, Fax: 205-348-5559, E-mail: madams@ua.edu. *Dean*, Dr. Suzanne Prevost, 205-348-1040, Fax: 205-348-5559, E-mail: sprevost@ua.edu.

College of Arts and Sciences Students: 939 full-time (499 women), 111 part-time (63 women); includes 155 minority (76 Black or African American, non-Hispanic/Latino; 3 American Indian or Alaska Native, non-Hispanic/Latino; 14 Asian, non-Hispanic/Latino; 46 Hispanic/Latino; 16 Two or more races, non-Hispanic/Latino), 178 international. Average age 28. 1,830 applicants, 27% accepted, 275 enrolled. *Faculty:* 399 full-time (150 women), 7 part-time/adjunct (5 women). *Financial support:* In 2015–16, 555 students received support. Fellowships with full tuition reimbursements available, research assistantships with full tuition reimbursements available, teaching assistantships with full tuition reimbursements available, career-related internships or fieldwork, Federal Work-Study, institutionally sponsored loans, scholarships/grants, tuition waivers (full and partial), and unspecified assistantships available. Support available to part-time students. Financial award applicants required to submit FAFSA. In 2015, 235 master's, 84 doctorates awarded. *Degree program information:* Part-time programs available. Part-time, online learning. Offers acting (MFA); American studies (MA); anthropology (MA, PhD); applied mathematics (PhD); arranging (MM); art history (MA); arts and sciences (MA, MATESOL, MFA, MM, MPA, MS, DMA, PhD); biological sciences (MS, PhD); chemistry (MS, PhD); choral conducting (MM, DMA); church music (MM); clinical psychology (PhD); composition (MM, DMA); composition and rhetoric (PhD); costume design (MFA); creative writing (MFA); criminal justice (MS); directing (MFA); earth system science (MS); experimental psychology (PhD); French (MA, PhD); French and Spanish (PhD); geographic information science (MS); geological sciences (MS, PhD); German (MA); history (MA, PhD); literature (MA, PhD); mathematics (MA, PhD); music education (MA, PhD); musicology (MM); performance (MM, DMA); physics (MS, PhD); planning (MS); political science (MA, PhD); public administration (MPA); pure mathematics (PhD); rhetoric and composition (MA); Romance languages (MA, PhD); scene design/technical production (MFA); Spanish (MA, PhD); speech language pathology (MS); stage management (MFA); studio art (MA, MFA); teaching English as a second language (MATESOL); theatre (MFA); theatre management/administration (MFA); theory (MM); wind conducting (MM, DMA); women's studies (MA). *Application fee:* $50 ($60 for international students). Electronic applications accepted. *Application Contact:* Patrick D. Fuller, Senior Graduate Admissions Counselor, 205-348-5923, Fax: 205-348-0400, E-mail: patrick.d.fuller@ua.edu. *Dean*, Dr. Robert F. Olin, 205-348-7007, Fax: 205-348-0272, E-mail: olin@as.ua.edu.

College of Communication and Information Sciences Students: 152 full-time (99 women), 164 part-time (130 women); includes 46 minority (24 Black or African American, non-Hispanic/Latino; 1 American Indian or Alaska Native, non-Hispanic/Latino; 5 Asian, non-Hispanic/Latino; 9 Hispanic/Latino; 7 Two or more races, non-Hispanic/Latino), 29 international. Average age 32. 256 applicants, 66% accepted, 102 enrolled. *Faculty:* 61 full-time (26 women), 1 (woman) part-time/adjunct. *Financial support:* In 2015–16, 78 students received support, including 3 fellowships with tuition reimbursements available (averaging $15,000 per year), 34 research assistantships with tuition reimbursements available (averaging $13,045 per year), 38 teaching assistantships with tuition reimbursements available (averaging $13,045 per year); institutionally sponsored loans, health care benefits, and unspecified assistantships also available. Financial award application deadline: 2/15. In 2015, 129 master's, 11 doctorates awarded. Offers advertising and public relations (MA); book arts (MFA); communication and information sciences (MA, MFA, MLIS, PhD); communication studies (MA); journalism (MA); library and information studies (MLIS, PhD); telecommunication and film (MA). *Application deadline:* For fall admission, 2/15 priority date for domestic and international students; for winter admission, 11/1 priority date for international students; for spring admission, 11/1 priority date for domestic students. Applications are processed on a rolling basis. *Application fee:* $50 ($60 for international students). Electronic applications accepted. *Application Contact:* Diane Shaddix, Information Contact, 205-348-8593, Fax: 205-348-6774, E-mail: dshaddix@bama.ua.edu. *Associate Dean for Graduate Studies*, Dr. Jennings Bryant, 205-348-8593, Fax: 205-348-6774.

College of Education Students: 358 full-time (242 women), 559 part-time (397 women); includes 215 minority (158 Black or African American, non-Hispanic/Latino; 6 American Indian or Alaska Native, non-Hispanic/Latino; 13 Asian, non-Hispanic/Latino; 21 Hispanic/Latino; 2 Native Hawaiian or other Pacific Islander, non-Hispanic/Latino; 15 Two or more races, non-Hispanic/Latino), 32 international. Average age 37. 439 applicants, 67% accepted, 213 enrolled. *Faculty:* 106 full-time (53 women), 3 part-time/adjunct (all women). *Financial support:* In 2015–16, 42 research assistantships with tuition reimbursements were awarded; teaching assistantships with tuition reimbursements, career-related internships or fieldwork, Federal Work-Study, institutionally sponsored loans, scholarships/grants, and unspecified assistantships also available. Financial award applicants required to submit FAFSA. In 2015, 186 master's, 78 doctorates, 39 other advanced degrees awarded. *Degree program information:* Part-time programs available. Part-time, online learning. Offers alternative sport pedagogy (MA); choral music education (MA); collaborative special education (M Ed, Ed S); early intervention (M Ed, Ed S); education (M Ed, MA, Ed D, PhD, Ed S); educational administration (Ed D, PhD); educational leadership (MA, Ed S); educational studies in psychology, research methodology and counseling (MA, Ed D, PhD, Ed S); elementary education (MA, Ed D, PhD, Ed S); exercise science (PhD); gifted and talented education (M Ed, Ed S); higher education administration (MA, Ed D, PhD); instructional leadership (Ed D, PhD); instrumental music education (MA); multiple abilities (M Ed); music education (Ed D, PhD, Ed S); secondary education (MA, Ed D, PhD, Ed S); special education (Ed D, PhD). *Application deadline:* For fall admission, 7/1 for domestic and international students; for spring admission, 11/15 for domestic students, 11/17 for international students. Applications are processed on a rolling basis. *Application fee:* $50 ($60 for international students). *Application Contact:* Dr. Kathy S. Wetzel, Assistant Dean for Student Services, 205-348-1154, Fax: 205-348-0080, E-mail: kwetzel@bamaed.ua.edu. *Dean*, Dr. James E. McLean, 205-348-6052.

College of Engineering Students: 230 full-time (52 women), 41 part-time (3 women); includes 20 minority (7 Black or African American, non-Hispanic/Latino; 5 Asian, non-Hispanic/Latino; 5 Hispanic/Latino; 3 Two or more races, non-Hispanic/Latino), 134 international. Average age 28. 362 applicants, 34% accepted, 58 enrolled. *Faculty:* 119 full-time (16 women), 1 part-time/adjunct (0 women). *Financial support:* In 2015–16, 188 students received support, including 23 fellowships with full tuition reimbursements available (averaging $16,022 per year), 85 research assistantships with full tuition reimbursements available (averaging $16,022 per year), 73 teaching assistantships with full tuition reimbursements available (averaging $16,022 per year); career-related internships or fieldwork, Federal Work-Study, and institutionally sponsored loans also available. Financial award application deadline: 2/15. In 2015, 61 master's, 31 doctorates awarded. *Degree program information:* Part-time programs available. Part-time, online learning. Offers aerospace engineering (MSAEM); chemical and biological engineering (MS Ch E, PhD); civil engineering (MSCE, PhD); computer science (MS, PhD); electrical engineering (MS, PhD); engineering (MS, MS Ch E, MS Met E, MSAEM, MSCE, PhD); engineering science and mechanics (PhD); environmental engineering (MS); materials science (PhD); mechanical engineering (MS, PhD); metallurgical and materials engineering (MS Met E, PhD). *Application deadline:* For fall admission, 7/1 for domestic students, 4/15 for international students; for spring admission, 11/15 for domestic students, 9/1 for international students. Applications are processed on a rolling basis. *Application fee:* $50 ($60 for international students). Electronic applications accepted. *Application Contact:* Dr. David A. Francko, Dean, 205-348-8280, Fax: 205-348-0400, E-mail: dfrancko@ua.edu. *Dean*, Dr. Charles Karr, 205-348-6405, Fax: 205-348-8573.

College of Human Environmental Sciences Students: 191 full-time (139 women), 345 part-time (250 women); includes 139 minority (94 Black or African American, non-Hispanic/Latino; 3 American Indian or Alaska Native, non-Hispanic/Latino; 5 Asian, non-Hispanic/Latino; 24 Hispanic/Latino; 2 Native Hawaiian or other Pacific Islander, non-Hispanic/Latino; 11 Two or more races, non-Hispanic/Latino), 6 international. Average age 33. 330 applicants, 75% accepted, 203 enrolled. *Faculty:* 49 full-time (37 women), 5 part-time/adjunct (4 women). *Financial support:* In 2015–16, 2 research assistantships with full tuition reimbursements (averaging $9,000 per year) were awarded; fellowships with tuition reimbursements, teaching assistantships with full tuition reimbursements, career-related internships or fieldwork, Federal Work-Study, institutionally sponsored loans, and scholarships/grants also available. In 2015, 236 master's, 4 doctorates awarded. *Degree program information:* Part-time and evening/weekend programs available. Part-time, evening/weekend, online learning. Offers apparel and textiles (MSHES); consumer sciences (MS); health education and promotion (PhD); health studies (MA); human development and family studies (MSHES); human environmental sciences (MA, MS, MSHES, PhD); human nutrition and hospitality management (MSHES); interactive technology (MS); marriage and family therapy (MSHES); parent and family life education (MSHES); quality management (MS); restaurant and meeting management (MS); rural community health (MS); sport management (MS). *Application deadline:* For fall admission, 7/6 for domestic students. Applications are processed on a rolling basis. *Application fee:* $50 ($60 for international students). Electronic applications accepted. *Application Contact:* Patrick D. Fuller, Admissions Officer, 205-348-5923, Fax: 205-348-0400, E-mail: patrick.d.fuller@ua.edu. *Dean*, Dr. Milla D. Boschung, 205-348-6250, Fax: 205-348-1786, E-mail: mboschun@ches.ua.edu.

Manderson Graduate School of Business Students: 492 full-time (196 women), 117 part-time (34 women); includes 76 minority (33 Black or African American, non-Hispanic/Latino; 2 American Indian or Alaska Native, non-Hispanic/Latino; 9 Asian, non-Hispanic/Latino; 15 Hispanic/Latino; 1 Native Hawaiian or other Pacific Islander, non-Hispanic/Latino; 16 Two or more races, non-Hispanic/Latino), 89 international. Average age 28. 1,040 applicants, 52% accepted, 303 enrolled. *Faculty:* 109 full-time (22 women), 2 part-time/adjunct (0 women). *Financial support:* In 2015–16, 64 research assistantships with tuition reimbursements (averaging $14,500 per year), 69 teaching assistantships with tuition reimbursements (averaging $16,500 per year) were awarded; fellowships with tuition reimbursements, career-related internships or fieldwork, Federal Work-Study, institutionally sponsored loans, and scholarships/grants also available. Support available to part-time students. In 2015, 388 master's, 27 doctorates awarded. *Degree program information:* Part-time and evening/weekend programs available. Part-time, evening/weekend, online learning. Offers accounting (M Acc, PhD); applied statistics (MS, PhD); business (EMBA, M Acc, MA, MBA, MS, MTA, PhD); economics (MA, PhD); finance (MS, PhD); general commerce and business (EMBA, MBA); management (MA, MS, PhD); marketing (MS, PhD); operations management (MS, PhD); tax accounting (MTA). *Application deadline:* For winter admission, 1/2 priority date for domestic students, 1/1 priority date for international students; for spring admission, 4/15 for domestic and international students. Applications are processed on a rolling basis. *Application fee:* $50 ($60 for international students). Electronic applications accepted. *Application Contact:* Blake Bedsole, Coordinator of Graduate Recruiting and Admissions, 205-348-9122, Fax: 205-348-4504, E-mail: bbedsole@cba.ua.edu. *Associate Dean*, Dr. J. Brian Gray, 205-348-8912, Fax: 205-348-4504, E-mail: bgray@cba.ua.edu.

School of Social Work Students: 301 full-time (266 women), 39 part-time (35 women); includes 113 minority (94 Black or African American, non-Hispanic/Latino; 1 American Indian or Alaska Native, non-Hispanic/Latino; 2 Asian, non-Hispanic/Latino; 9 Hispanic/Latino; 7 Two or more races, non-Hispanic/Latino), 7 international. Average age 31. 626 applicants, 32% accepted, 140 enrolled. *Faculty:* 26 full-time (18 women), 1 (woman) part-time/adjunct. *Financial support:* In 2015–16, 113 students received support, including 6 research assistantships with full tuition reimbursements available (averaging $12,744 per year), 5 teaching assistantships with full tuition reimbursements available (averaging $12,744 per year); career-related internships or fieldwork, scholarships/grants, traineeships, health care benefits, and unspecified assistantships also available. Financial award application deadline: 2/1; financial award applicants required to submit FAFSA. In 2015, 218 master's, 2 doctorates awarded. Online learning. Offers social work (MSW, PhD). *Application deadline:* For fall admission, 2/1 priority date for domestic and international students; for spring admission, 9/1 priority date for domestic and international students; for summer admission, 9/1 priority date for domestic students, 2/1 priority date for international students. Applications are processed on a rolling basis. *Application fee:* $50 ($60 for international students). Electronic applications accepted. *Application Contact:* Casey Barnes, Admissions Coordinator, 205-348-8413, Fax: 205-348-9419, E-mail: cbarnes@sw.ua.edu. *Dean*, Dr. Lucinda L. Roff, 205-348-3924, Fax: 205-348-9419, E-mail: lroff@sw.ua.edu.

Interdisciplinary Programs Students: 6 full-time (3 women), 8 part-time (6 women); includes 5 minority (all Black or African American, non-Hispanic/Latino). Average age 42. 1 applicant, 100% accepted, 1 enrolled. In 2015, 4 doctorates awarded. *Degree program information:* Part-time and evening/weekend programs available. Part-time, evening/weekend. Offers interdisciplinary studies (PhD). *Application deadline:* For fall admission, 5/1 for international students; for winter admission, 9/15 for international students. Applications are processed on a rolling basis. Electronic applications accepted. *Application Contact:* Patrick D. Fuller, Senior Graduate Admissions Counselor, 205-348-5923, Fax: 205-348-0400, E-mail: patrick.d.fuller@ua.edu. *Assistant Dean of the Graduate School*, Dr. Andrew Mark Goodliffe, 205-348-8283, Fax: 205-348-0400, E-mail: amg@ua.edu.

School of Law Students: 440 full-time (191 women), 95 part-time (33 women); includes 102 minority (57 Black or African American, non-Hispanic/Latino; 4 American Indian or Alaska Native, non-Hispanic/Latino; 17 Asian, non-Hispanic/Latino; 20 Hispanic/Latino; 4 Two or more races, non-Hispanic/Latino), 9 international. Average age 27. 1,583 applicants, 27% accepted, 210 enrolled. *Faculty:* 40 full-time (16 women), 34 part-time/adjunct (7 women). *Financial support:* Applicants required to submit FAFSA. In 2015, 71 master's, 145 doctorates awarded. Offers business transactions (LL M); comparative law (LL M, JSD); law (JD, JSD); taxation (LL M in Tax). *Application deadline:* Applications are processed on a rolling basis. *Application fee:* $40. Electronic applications accepted. *Application Contact:* Martha Griffith, Assistant Director for Admissions, 205-348-7945, Fax: 205-348-3917, E-mail: mgriffith@law.ua.edu. *Associate Dean for Academic Affairs*, Claude R. Arrington, 205-348-6557, Fax: 205-348-3077, E-mail: carrington@law.ua.edu.

THE UNIVERSITY OF ALABAMA AT BIRMINGHAM, Birmingham, AL 35294

General Information State-supported, coed, university. CGS member. *Enrollment:* 18,542 graduate, professional, and undergraduate students; 3,840 full-time matriculated graduate/professional students (2,314 women), 2,917 part-time matriculated graduate/professional students (1,995 women). *Enrollment by degree level:* 4,139 master's, 2,420 doctoral, 198 other advanced degrees. *Graduate faculty:* 1,791 full-time (649 women), 142 part-time/adjunct (60 women). Tuition, state resident: full-time $7340. Tuition, nonresident: full-time $16,628. Full-time tuition and fees vary according to course load and program. *Graduate housing:* Room and/or apartments available on a first-come, first-served basis to single students; on-campus housing not available to married students. Typical cost: $5900 per year. Room charges vary according to board plan. Housing application deadline: 5/1. *Student services:* Campus employment opportunities, campus safety program, career counseling, exercise/wellness program, free psychological counseling, grant writing training, international student services, low-cost health insurance, multicultural affairs office, services for students with disabilities, teacher training, writing training. *Library:* Mervyn Sterne Library plus 2 others. *Collection:* Books: 1.3 million (physical). Students can reserve study rooms. *Research affiliation:* Southern Research Institute (cancer therapeutics, biodefense).

Computer facilities: A campuswide network can be accessed from student residence rooms and from off campus. Online class registration, transcript requests are available. Website: http://www.uab.edu/

General Application Contact: Holly Hebard, Director of Graduate School Operations, 205-934-8227, Fax: 205-934-8413, E-mail: gradschool@uab.edu.

GRADUATE UNITS

Collat School of Business ***Degree program information:*** Part-time programs available. Part-time, online learning. Offers accounting (M Acct); business (M Acct, MBA, MS); business administration (MBA); management information systems (MS). MD/MBA program offered in partnership with the School of Medicine. Electronic applications accepted.

College of Arts and Sciences ***Degree program information:*** Part-time and evening/weekend programs available. Part-time, evening/weekend, online learning. Offers anthropology (MA); applied mathematics (PhD); art history (MA); arts and sciences (MA, MPA, MS, MSCJ, MSFS, PhD); behavioral neuroscience (PhD); biology (MS, PhD); chemistry (MS, PhD); communication management (MA); computer and information sciences (MS, PhD); computer forensics and security management (MS); creative writing (MA); criminal justice (MSCJ); forensic science (MSFS); history (MA); lifespan developmental psychology (PhD); literature (MA); mathematics (MS); medical sociology (PhD); medical/clinical psychology (PhD); physics (MS, PhD); psychology (MA); public management and planning (MPA); rhetoric and composition (MA). Electronic applications accepted.

Graduate Programs in Joint Health Sciences Students: 332 full-time (162 women); includes 130 minority (35 Black or African American, non-Hispanic/Latino; 2 American Indian or Alaska Native, non-Hispanic/Latino; 62 Asian, non-Hispanic/Latino; 23 Hispanic/Latino; 8 Two or more races, non-Hispanic/Latino), 52 international. Average age 26. *Financial support:* In 2015–16, fellowships with full tuition reimbursements (averaging $29,000 per year) were awarded. In 2015, 81 doctorates awarded. Offers basic medical sciences (MSBMS); biochemistry, structural and stem cell biology (PhD); cancer biology (PhD); cell, molecular, and developmental biology (PhD); genetics, genomics and bioinformatics (PhD); health sciences (MSBMS, PhD); microbiology (PhD); neurobiology (PhD); pathobiology and molecular medicine (PhD); pharmacology and toxicology (PhD). *Application deadline:* For fall admission, 12/1 priority date for domestic students, 1/15 for international students. Applications are processed on a rolling basis. *Application fee:* $0 ($60 for international students). Electronic applications accepted. *Application Contact:* Holly Hebard, Director of Student and Academic Services, 205-996-5696, E-mail: hghebard@uab.edu. *Associate Dean for Graduate Biomedical Sciences*, Dr. David A. Schneider, 205-934-2845.

School of Dentistry Offers dentistry (MS, DMD).

School of Education ***Degree program information:*** Part-time and evening/weekend programs available. Part-time, evening/weekend, online learning. Offers arts education (MA Ed); community health and human services (MA Ed); counseling (MA); curriculum education (Ed S); early childhood education (MA Ed, PhD); education (MA, MA Ed, Ed D, PhD, Ed S); educational leadership (MA Ed, Ed D, Ed S); elementary education (MA Ed); English as a second language (MA Ed, Ed S); health education and promotion (PhD); high school education (MA Ed); reading (MA Ed); special education (MA Ed). Electronic applications accepted.

School of Engineering ***Degree program information:*** Part-time and evening/weekend programs available. Part-time, evening/weekend, online learning. Offers advanced safety engineering and management (M Eng); biomedical engineering (MSBME, PhD); civil engineering (MSCE, PhD); computational engineering (PhD); computer engineering (PhD); construction engineering management (M Eng); electrical engineering (MSEE); engineering (M Eng, MS Mt E, MSBME, MSCE, MSEE, MSME, PhD); environmental health and safety engineering (PhD); information engineering management (M Eng); materials engineering (MS Mt E, PhD); mechanical engineering (MSME); research/design (MSME); technology/engineering management (MSME). Electronic applications accepted.

School of Health Professions ***Degree program information:*** Part-time programs available. Part-time, online learning. Offers administration/health services (D Sc, PhD); biotechnology (MS); clinical laboratory science (MS); genetic counseling (MS); health administration (MSHA); health informatics (MSHI); health professions (MS, MSHA, MSHI, MSPAS, D Sc, DPT, PhD, Certificate); low vision rehabilitation (Certificate); nutrition sciences (MS, PhD); occupational therapy (MS); physical therapy (DPT); physician assistant studies (MSPAS); rehabilitation science (PhD). Electronic applications accepted.

School of Medicine Students: 780 full-time (346 women); includes 177 minority (33 Black or African American, non-Hispanic/Latino; 6 American Indian or Alaska Native, non-Hispanic/Latino; 71 Asian, non-Hispanic/Latino; 3 Hispanic/Latino; 64 Two or more races, non-Hispanic/Latino). Average age 25. 3,768 applicants, 7% accepted, 186 enrolled. *Financial support:* In 2015–16, 233 students received support. Career-related internships or fieldwork and scholarships/grants available. Financial award application deadline: 5/1; financial award applicants required to submit FAFSA. In 2015, 181 doctorates awarded. Offers medicine (MD). *Application deadline:* For fall admission, 11/1 for domestic students. *Application fee:* $80. Electronic applications accepted. *Application Contact:* 205-934-2433, Fax: 205-934-8740, E-mail: medschool@uab.edu. *Senior Vice President/Dean, School of Medicine*, Dr. Selwyn M. Vickers, 205-934-1111, Fax: 205-934-0333.

School of Nursing ***Degree program information:*** Part-time programs available. Part-time. Offers nurse anesthesia (MSN); nursing (MSN, DNP, PhD). Electronic applications accepted.

School of Optometry Offers optometry (MS, OD, PhD); sensory impairment (PhD); vision science (MS, PhD). Electronic applications accepted.

School of Public Health ***Degree program information:*** Part-time programs available. Part-time. Offers applied epidemiology and pharmacoepidemiology (MSPH); biostatistics (MPH, MS, MSPH, PhD); clinical and translational science (MSPH); environmental health (MPH); environmental health and toxicology (MSPH); environmental health sciences research (PhD); epidemiology (MPH); general theory and practice (MPH); health behavior (MPH); health care organization (MPH); health education and promotion (PhD); health policy quantitative policy analysis (MPH); industrial hygiene (MPH, MSPH, PhD); maternal and child health policy (Dr PH); maternal and child health policy and leadership (MPH); occupational health and safety (MPH); outcomes research (MSPH, Dr PH); public health (MPH, MS, MSPH, Dr PH, PhD); public health management (Dr PH); public health preparedness management (MPH). Electronic applications accepted.

THE UNIVERSITY OF ALABAMA IN HUNTSVILLE, Huntsville, AL 35899

General Information State-supported, coed, university. CGS member. *Enrollment:* 7,866 graduate, professional, and undergraduate students; 703 full-time matriculated graduate/professional students (296 women), 1,077 part-time matriculated graduate/professional students (512 women). *Enrollment by degree level:* 1,346 master's, 400 doctoral, 34 other advanced degrees. *Graduate faculty:* 264 full-time (82 women), 56 part-time/adjunct (21 women). *International tuition:* $21,402 full-time. *Tuition, area resident:* Full-time $9548; part-time $547 per credit hour. Tuition, state resident: full-time $9548; part-time $547 per credit hour. Tuition, nonresident: full-time $21,402; part-time $1224 per credit hour. *Graduate housing:* Rooms and/or apartments available on a first-come, first-served basis to single and married students. Housing application deadline: 6/1. *Student services:* Campus employment opportunities, campus safety program, career counseling, child daycare facilities, exercise/wellness program, free psychological counseling, grant writing training, international student services, low-cost health insurance, multicultural affairs office, services for students with disabilities, teacher training, writing training. *Library:* Louis Salmon Library. *Collection:* Books: 400,000 (physical), 69,504 (digital/electronic); Serial titles: 1,411 (physical), 233 (digital/electronic); Databases: 129. *Research affiliation:* Oak Ridge, Lawrence Livermore and Savannah River National Labs - Y12National Security Complex (neutron science, energy technologies, high-performance computing, systems biology, materials science at the nanoscale, national security), Cummings Research Park/Boeing/ADTRAN/SAIC/Teledyne Brown Engineering/Lockheed Martin/Dynetics, Inc. (computer science, aerospace engineering, information systems, space systems, defense systems, informatics), National Oceanic and Atmospheric Administration (NOAA) (climate modeling, weather and air quality research, oceans, satellites), Hudson Alpha Institute for Biotechnology (medical research, biotechnology, genomic research, molecular biology), Department of Defense/U.S. Army Aviation and Missile Command (missile research, development and engineering and manufacturing technology), NASA/Marshall Space Flight Center/Goddard Space Flight Center (space science, earth science, information technology, materials science, optical science).

Computer facilities: 1,227 computers available on campus for general student use. A campuswide network can be accessed from student residence rooms and from off campus. Online class registration is available.
Website: http://www.uah.edu/

General Application Contact: Kim Gray, Admissions Coordinator, Graduate Studies, 256-824-6198, Fax: 256-824-6002, E-mail: deangrad@uah.edu.

GRADUATE UNITS

School of Graduate Studies Students: 703 full-time (296 women), 1,077 part-time (512 women); includes 277 minority (153 Black or African American, non-Hispanic/Latino; 16 American Indian or Alaska Native, non-Hispanic/Latino; 53 Asian, non-Hispanic/Latino; 38 Hispanic/Latino; 17 Two or more races, non-Hispanic/Latino), 267 international. Average age 33. 1,485 applicants, 74% accepted, 601 enrolled. *Faculty:* 264 full-time (82 women), 56 part-time/adjunct (21 women). *Financial support:* In 2015–16, 4 fellowships with full tuition reimbursements (averaging $13,113 per year), 153 research assistantships with tuition reimbursements (averaging $12,999 per year), 168 teaching assistantships with tuition reimbursements (averaging $10,019 per year) were awarded; career-related internships or fieldwork, Federal Work-Study, institutionally sponsored loans, scholarships/grants, traineeships, health care benefits, tuition waivers (full and partial), and unspecified assistantships also available. Support available to part-time students. Financial award application deadline: 4/1; financial award applicants required to submit FAFSA. In 2015, 424 master's, 46 doctorates awarded. *Degree program information:* Part-time and evening/weekend programs available. Part-time, evening/weekend, 100% online, blended/hybrid learning. *Application deadline:* For fall admission, 7/16 priority date for domestic students, 4/1 priority date for international students; for spring admission, 11/30 priority date for domestic students, 9/1 priority date for international students. Applications are processed on a rolling basis. *Application fee:* $50. Electronic applications accepted. *Application Contact:* Kim Gray, Graduate Studies Admissions Coordinator, 256-824-6002, Fax: 256-824-6405, E-mail: deangrad@uah.edu. *Dean of Graduate Studies*, Dr. David Berkowitz, 256-824-6002, Fax: 256-824-6405, E-mail: deangrad@uah.edu.

College of Arts, Humanities, and Social Sciences Financial support: Research assistantships with tuition reimbursements, teaching assistantships with full tuition reimbursements, career-related internships or fieldwork, Federal Work-Study, institutionally sponsored loans, scholarships/grants, health care benefits, tuition waivers (full and partial), and unspecified assistantships available. Support available to part-time students. Financial award application deadline: 4/1; financial award applicants required to submit FAFSA. *Degree program information:* Part-time and evening/weekend programs available. Part-time, evening/weekend. Offers arts, humanities and social sciences (MA, Certificate); education (MA); English (MA); history (MA); industrial/organizational psychology (MA); psychology (MA); public affairs (MA); technical writing (Certificate); TESOL (Certificate). *Application deadline:* For fall admission, 7/15 priority date for domestic students, 4/1 priority date for international students; for spring admission, 11/30 priority date for domestic students, 9/1 priority date for international students. Applications are processed on a rolling basis. *Application fee:* $50. Electronic applications accepted. *Application Contact:* Kim Gray, Graduate Studies Admissions Coordinator, 256-824-6002, Fax: 256-824-6405, E-mail: deangrad@uah.edu. *Dean*, Dr. Mitch Berbrier, 256-824-6200, Fax: 256-824-6949, E-mail: dean-ahs@uah.edu.

College of Business Administration Financial support: Research assistantships with tuition reimbursements, teaching assistantships with tuition reimbursements, career-related internships or fieldwork, Federal Work-Study, institutionally sponsored loans, scholarships/grants, health care benefits, tuition waivers (full and partial), and unspecified assistantships available. Support available to part-time students. Financial award application deadline: 4/1; financial award applicants required to submit FAFSA. *Degree program information:* Part-time and evening/weekend programs available. Part-time, evening/weekend. Offers accounting (M Acc); business administration (M Acc, MBA, MS, MSIS, MSM, MSMS, Certificate); business analytics (MSMS); cybersecurity (MS, Certificate); enterprise resource planning (Certificate); federal contracting and procurement management (Certificate); human resource management (MSM); information systems (MSIS); management (MBA); supply chain and logistics management (MS); supply chain management (Certificate); technology and innovation management (Certificate). *Application deadline:* For fall admission, 7/15 priority date for domestic students, 4/1 priority date for international students; for spring admission, 11/30 priority date for domestic students, 9/1 priority date for international students. Applications are processed on a rolling basis. *Application fee:* $50. Electronic applications accepted. *Application Contact:* Jennifer Pettitt, Director of Advising, 256-824-6681, Fax: 256-824-7571, E-mail: jennifer.pettitt@uah.edu. *Dean*, Jason Greene, 256-824-4424, Fax: 256-824-7571, E-mail: jason.greene@uah.edu.

College of Engineering Financial support: Fellowships with full tuition reimbursements, research assistantships with tuition reimbursements, teaching assistantships with tuition reimbursements, career-related internships or fieldwork, Federal Work-Study, institutionally sponsored loans, scholarships/grants, health care benefits, tuition waivers, and unspecified assistantships available. Support available to part-time students. Financial award application deadline: 4/1; financial award applicants required to submit FAFSA. *Degree program information:* Part-time and evening/weekend programs available. Part-time, evening/weekend, online learning. Offers aerospace systems engineering (MS, PhD); biotechnology science and engineering (PhD); chemical and materials engineering (MSE); civil and environmental engineering (PhD); civil engineering (MSE); computer engineering (MSE, PhD); electrical engineering (MSE, PhD); engineering (MS, MSE, MSOR, MSSE, PhD); engineering management (MSE, PhD); industrial engineering (MSE, PhD); materials science (PhD); mechanical engineering (PhD); operations research (MSOR); optical science and engineering (PhD); software engineering (MSSE); systems engineering (MSE, PhD). *Application deadline:* For fall admission, 7/15 priority date for domestic students, 4/1 priority date for international students; for spring admission, 11/30 priority date for domestic students, 9/1 priority date for international students. Applications are processed on a rolling basis. *Application fee:* $50. Electronic applications accepted. *Application Contact:* Kim Gray, Graduate Studies Admissions Coordinator, 256-824-6002, Fax: 256-824-6405, E-mail: deangrad@uah.edu. *Dean*, Dr. Shankar Mahalingam, 256-824-6474, Fax: 256-824-6843, E-mail: coedean@uah.edu.

College of Nursing Financial support: Teaching assistantships with full tuition reimbursements, career-related internships or fieldwork, Federal Work-Study, institutionally sponsored loans, scholarships/grants, traineeships, health care benefits, and unspecified assistantships available. Support available to part-time students. Financial award application deadline: 4/1; financial award applicants required to submit FAFSA. *Degree program information:* Part-time and evening/weekend programs available. Part-time, evening/weekend, online learning. Offers family nurse practitioner (Certificate); nursing (MSN, DNP); nursing education (Certificate). DNP offered jointly with The University of Alabama at Birmingham. *Application deadline:* For fall admission, 7/15 for domestic students, 4/1 for international students; for spring admission, 11/30 for domestic students, 9/1 for international students. Applications are processed on a rolling basis. *Application fee:* $50. Electronic applications accepted. *Application Contact:* Charles Davis, Director of Graduate Admission and Advisement, 256-824-6669, Fax: 256-824-6026, E-mail: charles.davis@uah.edu. *Dean*, Dr. Marsha Adams, 256-824-6345, Fax: 256-824-6026, E-mail: marsha.adams@uah.edu.

College of Science Financial support: Fellowships with full tuition reimbursements, research assistantships with tuition reimbursements, teaching assistantships with tuition reimbursements, career-related internships or fieldwork, Federal Work-Study, institutionally sponsored loans, scholarships/grants, health care benefits, tuition waivers (full and partial), and unspecified assistantships available. Support available to part-time students. Financial award application deadline: 4/1; financial award applicants required to submit FAFSA. *Degree program information:* Part-time and evening/weekend programs available. Part-time, evening/weekend. Offers applied mathematics (PhD); atmospheric science (MS, PhD); biology (MS); biotechnology science and engineering (PhD); chemistry (MS); computer science (MS, PhD); cybersecurity (MS); education (MA, MS); materials science (MS, PhD); mathematics (MA, MS); modeling and simulation (MS, PhD, Certificate); optics and photonics technology (MS); physics (MS, PhD); science (MA, MS, MSSE, PhD, Certificate); software engineering (MSSE, Certificate). *Application deadline:* For fall admission, 7/15 priority date for domestic students, 4/1 priority date for international students; for spring admission, 11/30 priority date for domestic students, 9/1 priority date for international students. Applications are processed on a rolling basis. *Application fee:* $50. Electronic applications accepted. *Application Contact:* Kim Gray, Graduate Studies Admissions Coordinator, 256-824-6002, Fax: 256-824-6405, E-mail: deangrad@uah.edu. *Dean*, Dr. Sundar Christopher, 256-824-6605, Fax: 256-824-6819, E-mail: cosdean@uah.edu.

UNIVERSITY OF ALASKA ANCHORAGE, Anchorage, AK 99508

General Information State-supported, coed, comprehensive institution. CGS member. *Graduate housing:* Rooms and/or apartments available on a first-come, first-served basis to single and married students. Housing application deadline: 7/1. *Research affiliation:* Conoco Phillips (energy), Habitat for Humanity (project management), BP Alaska (energy), Municipality of Anchorage (government), Providence Hospital (health care).

GRADUATE UNITS

College of Arts and Sciences ***Degree program information:*** Part-time programs available. Part-time. Offers anthropology (MA); arts and sciences (MA, MFA, MS, PhD); biological sciences (MS); clinical psychology (MS); clinical-community psychology with rural-indigenous emphasis (PhD); creative writing and literary arts (MFA); English (MA); interdisciplinary studies (MA, MS).

College of Business and Public Policy ***Degree program information:*** Part-time and evening/weekend programs available. Part-time, evening/weekend. Offers business administration (MBA); business and public policy (MBA, MPA, MS, Certificate); global supply chain management (MS); public administration (MPA); supply chain management (Certificate).

College of Education ***Degree program information:*** Part-time programs available. Part-time. Offers counseling and guidance (M Ed); early childhood special education (M Ed); education (M Ed, Certificate); educational leadership (M Ed); master teacher

(M Ed); principal licensure (Certificate); special education (M Ed, Certificate); superintendent (Certificate); teaching (MAT).

College of Health ***Degree program information:*** Part-time and evening/weekend programs available. Part-time, evening/weekend. Offers health (MPH, MS, MSW, Certificate); public health practice (MPH).

School of Nursing Degree program information: Part-time and evening/weekend programs available. Part-time, evening/weekend. Offers nursing (MS).

School of Social Work Degree program information: Part-time and evening/weekend programs available. Part-time, evening/weekend, online learning. Offers clinical social work practice (Certificate); social work (MSW); social work management (Certificate). Electronic applications accepted.

School of Engineering ***Degree program information:*** Part-time and evening/weekend programs available. Part-time, evening/weekend. Offers applied environmental science and technology (M AEST, MS); arctic engineering (MS); civil engineering (MCE, MS); coastal, ocean, and port engineering (Certificate); engineering (M AEST, MCE, MS, Certificate); engineering management (MS); project management (MS); science management (MS).

UNIVERSITY OF ALASKA FAIRBANKS, Fairbanks, AK 99775-7520

General Information State-supported, coed, university. CGS member. *Enrollment:* 517 full-time matriculated graduate/professional students (260 women), 519 part-time matriculated graduate/professional students (314 women). *Enrollment by degree level:* 660 master's, 329 doctoral, 47 other advanced degrees. *Graduate faculty:* 312 full-time (124 women), 6 part-time/adjunct (3 women). Tuition, state resident: full-time $7614; part-time $423 per credit. Tuition, nonresident: full-time $15,552; part-time $864 per credit. *Required fees:* $38 per credit. $187 per semester. Tuition and fees vary according to course level, course load, program and reciprocity agreements. *Graduate housing:* Rooms and/or apartments available on a first-come, first-served basis to single and married students. Typical cost: $4564 per year ($8884 including board) for single students; $8865 per year ($13,185 including board) for married students. Room and board charges vary according to board plan, campus/location and housing facility selected. Housing application deadline: 8/1. *Student services:* Campus employment opportunities, campus safety program, career counseling, exercise/wellness program, free psychological counseling, grant writing training, international student services, low-cost health insurance, multicultural affairs office, services for students with disabilities, teacher training, writing training. *Library:* Rasmuson Library plus 2 others. *Research affiliation:* Institute of Northern Forestry, Alaska Cooperative Fishery and Wildlife Research Unit.

Computer facilities: 125 computers available on campus for general student use. A campuswide network can be accessed from student residence rooms and from off campus. Online class registration, university portal, campus wireless access are available.
Website: http://www.uaf.edu/

General Application Contact: Mary Kreta, Director of Admissions, 907-474-7500, E-mail: admissions@uaf.edu.

GRADUATE UNITS

College of Engineering and Mines Students: 70 full-time (15 women), 52 part-time (10 women); includes 15 minority (2 Black or African American, non-Hispanic/Latino; 4 American Indian or Alaska Native, non-Hispanic/Latino; 1 Asian, non-Hispanic/Latino; 4 Hispanic/Latino; 4 Two or more races, non-Hispanic/Latino), 42 international. Average age 31. 119 applicants, 36% accepted, 30 enrolled. *Faculty:* 50 full-time (8 women). *Financial support:* In 2015–16, 29 research assistantships with full tuition reimbursements (averaging $11,124 per year), 36 teaching assistantships with full tuition reimbursements (averaging $6,567 per year) were awarded; fellowships with full tuition reimbursements, career-related internships or fieldwork, Federal Work-Study, scholarships/grants, health care benefits, and unspecified assistantships also available. Support available to part-time students. Financial award application deadline: 7/1; financial award applicants required to submit FAFSA. In 2015, 30 master's, 5 doctorates awarded. *Degree program information:* Part-time programs available. Part-time. Offers arctic engineering (MS); civil engineering (MCE, MS); computer science (MS); design and construction management (Graduate Certificate); electrical engineering (MEE, MS); engineering (PhD); engineering and mines (MCE, MEE, MS, PhD, Graduate Certificate); engineering and science management (MS); environmental engineering (MS, PhD); environmental quality science (MS); geological engineering (MS); mechanical engineering (MS); mineral preparation engineering (MS); mining engineering (MS); petroleum engineering (MS); science management (MS). *Application deadline:* For fall admission, 6/1 for domestic students, 3/1 for international students; for spring admission, 10/15 for domestic students, 9/1 for international students. Applications are processed on a rolling basis. *Application fee:* $60. Electronic applications accepted. *Application Contact:* Mary Kreta, Director of Admissions, 907-474-7500, Fax: 907-474-7097, E-mail: admissions@uaf.edu. *Dean*, Dr. Douglas J. Goering, 907-474-7730, Fax: 907-474-6994, E-mail: fycem@uaf.edu.

College of Liberal Arts Students: 85 full-time (53 women), 130 part-time (91 women); includes 44 minority (4 Black or African American, non-Hispanic/Latino; 15 American Indian or Alaska Native, non-Hispanic/Latino; 5 Asian, non-Hispanic/Latino; 7 Hispanic/Latino; 3 Native Hawaiian or other Pacific Islander, non-Hispanic/Latino; 10 Two or more races, non-Hispanic/Latino), 19 international. Average age 36. 160 applicants, 44% accepted, 48 enrolled. *Faculty:* 58 full-time (26 women). *Financial support:* In 2015–16, 7 research assistantships with tuition reimbursements (averaging $11,000 per year), 70 teaching assistantships with tuition reimbursements (averaging $10,412 per year) were awarded; fellowships with tuition reimbursements, career-related internships or fieldwork, Federal Work-Study, scholarships/grants, health care benefits, and unspecified assistantships also available. Support available to part-time students. Financial award application deadline: 7/1; financial award applicants required to submit FAFSA. In 2015, 37 master's, 3 doctorates awarded. *Degree program information:* Part-time programs available. Part-time, online learning. Offers anthropology (MA, PhD); applied linguistics (MA); arctic policy (MA); art (MFA); ceramics (MFA); clinical-community psychology (PhD); computer art (MFA); creative writing (MFA); cross-cultural studies (MA); drawing (MFA); environmental politics and policy (MA); justice (MA); liberal arts (MA, MFA, MM, PhD); literature (MA); music (MM); Northern history (MA); painting (MFA); photography (MFA); printmaking (MFA); professional communication (MA); sculpture (MFA). *Application deadline:* For fall admission, 6/1 for domestic students, 3/1 for international students; for spring admission, 10/15 for domestic students, 9/1 for international students. Applications are processed on a rolling basis. *Application fee:* $60. Electronic applications accepted. *Application Contact:* Mary Kreta, Director of Admissions, 907-474-7500, Fax: 907-474-7097, E-mail: admissions@uaf.edu. *Dean*, Todd Sherman, 907-474-7231, Fax: 907-474-5817, E-mail: uaf-cla@uaf.edu.

College of Natural Sciences and Mathematics Students: 187 full-time (80 women), 58 part-time (31 women); includes 19 minority (3 American Indian or Alaska Native, non-Hispanic/Latino; 6 Asian, non-Hispanic/Latino; 4 Hispanic/Latino; 6 Two or more races, non-Hispanic/Latino), 46 international. Average age 30. 253 applicants, 23% accepted, 50 enrolled. *Faculty:* 82 full-time (32 women), 1 part-time/adjunct (0 women). *Financial support:* In 2015–16, 87 research assistantships with full tuition reimbursements (averaging $16,267 per year), 65 teaching assistantships with full tuition reimbursements (averaging $14,469 per year) were awarded; fellowships with full tuition reimbursements, career-related internships or fieldwork, Federal Work-Study, scholarships/grants, health care benefits, and unspecified assistantships also available. Support available to part-time students. Financial award application deadline: 7/1; financial award applicants required to submit FAFSA. In 2015, 28 master's, 21 doctorates awarded. *Degree program information:* Part-time programs available. Part-time. Offers atmospheric science (MS, PhD); biochemistry and neuroscience (PhD); biology and wildlife (MS, PhD, Graduate Certificate); chemistry (MA, MS); computational physics (MS); environmental chemistry (PhD); geology (MS, PhD); geophysics (MS, PhD); mathematics (PhD); natural sciences and mathematics (MA, MS, PhD, Graduate Certificate); physics (MS, PhD); space physics (MS); statistics (MS, Graduate Certificate). *Application deadline:* For fall admission, 6/1 for domestic students, 3/1 for international students; for spring admission, 10/15 for domestic students, 9/1 for international students. Applications are processed on a rolling basis. *Application fee:* $60. Electronic applications accepted. *Application Contact:* Mary Kreta, Director of Admissions, 907-474-7500, Fax: 907-474-7097, E-mail: admissions@uaf.edu. *Dean*, Dr. Paul Layer, 907-474-7608, Fax: 907-474-5101, E-mail: fycnsm@uaf.edu.

College of Rural and Community Development Students: 3 full-time (1 woman), 20 part-time (17 women); includes 9 minority (7 American Indian or Alaska Native, non-Hispanic/Latino; 2 Two or more races, non-Hispanic/Latino), 1 international. Average age 39. 6 applicants, 50% accepted, 3 enrolled. *Faculty:* 8 full-time (7 women). *Financial support:* In 2015–16, 1 research assistantship with full tuition reimbursement (averaging $6,294 per year), 1 teaching assistantship with full tuition reimbursement (averaging $11,955 per year) were awarded; fellowships with full tuition reimbursements, Federal Work-Study, scholarships/grants, and health care benefits also available. Support available to part-time students. Financial award application deadline: 2/15; financial award applicants required to submit FAFSA. In 2015, 3 master's awarded. *Degree program information:* Part-time programs available. Part-time, online learning. Offers rural and community development (MA); rural development (MA). *Application deadline:* For fall admission, 6/1 for domestic students, 3/1 for international students; for spring admission, 10/15 for domestic students, 9/1 for international students. Applications are processed on a rolling basis. *Application fee:* $60. Electronic applications accepted. *Application Contact:* Mary Kreta, Director of Admissions, 907-474-7500, Fax: 907-474-7097, E-mail: admissions@uaf.edu. *Vice Chancellor for the College of Rural and Community Development*, Evon Peter, 907-474-7143, Fax: 907-474-5824, E-mail: uaf-crcd-vice-chancellor@alaska.edu.

Graduate School for Interdisciplinary Studies Students: 8 full-time (all women), 17 part-time (13 women); includes 11 minority (8 American Indian or Alaska Native, non-Hispanic/Latino; 1 Hispanic/Latino; 2 Two or more races, non-Hispanic/Latino). Average age 50. 25 applicants, 4% accepted, 1 enrolled. *Faculty:* 7 full-time (all women). *Financial support:* Fellowships with full tuition reimbursements, research assistantships with full tuition reimbursements, teaching assistantships with full tuition reimbursements, career-related internships or fieldwork, Federal Work-Study, scholarships/grants, health care benefits, and unspecified assistantships available. Support available to part-time students. Financial award application deadline: 2/15; financial award applicants required to submit FAFSA. In 2015, 1 master's, 3 doctorates awarded. *Degree program information:* Part-time programs available. Part-time. Offers indigenous studies (PhD); interdisciplinary studies (MA, MS, PhD). *Application deadline:* For fall admission, 3/1 for domestic and international students; for spring admission, 10/1 for domestic students, 9/1 for international students. Applications are processed on a rolling basis. *Application fee:* $60. Electronic applications accepted. *Application Contact:* Mary Kreta, Director of Admissions, 907-474-7500, Fax: 907-474-7097, E-mail: admissions@uaf.edu. *Dean*, John Eichelberger, 907-474-7716, Fax: 907-474-1984, E-mail: fyinds@uaf.edu.

School of Education Students: 44 full-time (26 women), 111 part-time (85 women); includes 21 minority (7 American Indian or Alaska Native, non-Hispanic/Latino; 1 Asian, non-Hispanic/Latino; 7 Hispanic/Latino; 1 Native Hawaiian or other Pacific Islander, non-Hispanic/Latino; 5 Two or more races, non-Hispanic/Latino), 1 international. Average age 36. 54 applicants, 61% accepted, 29 enrolled. *Faculty:* 20 full-time (12 women), 1 (woman) part-time/adjunct. *Financial support:* In 2015–16, 4 teaching assistantships with full tuition reimbursements (averaging $8,351 per year) were awarded; fellowships with full tuition reimbursements, research assistantships with full tuition reimbursements, career-related internships or fieldwork, Federal Work-Study, scholarships/grants, health care benefits, and unspecified assistantships also available. Support available to part-time students. Financial award application deadline: 6/1; financial award applicants required to submit FAFSA. In 2015, 47 master's, 41 other advanced degrees awarded. Online learning. Offers community counseling (M Ed); education (M Ed, Graduate Certificate); elementary education (M Ed); secondary education (M Ed); special education (M Ed). *Application deadline:* For fall admission, 2/15 for domestic and international students; for spring admission, 10/1 for domestic students, 8/1 for international students. *Application fee:* $60. Electronic applications accepted. *Application Contact:* Mary Kreta, Director of Admissions, 907-474-7500, Fax: 907-474-7097, E-mail: admissions@uaf.edu. *Interim Dean*, Steve Atwater, 907-474-7341, Fax: 907-474-5451, E-mail: uaf-soe-school@alaska.edu.

School of Fisheries and Ocean Sciences Students: 68 full-time (46 women), 50 part-time (29 women); includes 12 minority (4 Asian, non-Hispanic/Latino; 7 Hispanic/Latino; 1 Two or more races, non-Hispanic/Latino), 9 international. Average age 31. 62 applicants, 29% accepted, 18 enrolled. *Faculty:* 55 full-time (24 women), 2 part-time/adjunct (0 women). *Financial support:* In 2015–16, 49 research assistantships with full tuition reimbursements (averaging $12,326 per year), 11 teaching assistantships with full tuition reimbursements (averaging $10,645 per year) were awarded; fellowships with full tuition reimbursements, career-related internships or fieldwork, Federal Work-Study, scholarships/grants, health care benefits, and unspecified assistantships also available. Support available to part-time students. Financial award application deadline: 2/15; financial award applicants required to submit FAFSA. In 2015, 23 master's, 7 doctorates awarded. *Degree program information:* Part-time programs available. Part-time. Offers fisheries (MS, PhD); fisheries and ocean sciences (MS, PhD); marine biology (MS, PhD); oceanography (MS, PhD). *Application deadline:* For fall admission, 5/1 for domestic students, 4/1 for international students; for spring admission, 9/15 for domestic students, 8/15 for international students. Applications are processed on a rolling basis. *Application fee:* $60. Electronic applications accepted. *Application Contact:* Mary Kreta, Director of Admissions, 907-474-7500, Fax: 907-474-7097, E-mail: admissions@alaska.edu. *Dean*, Michael Castellini, 907-474-7824, Fax: 907-474-7204, E-mail: info@sfos.uaf.edu.

School of Management Students: 29 full-time (14 women), 56 part-time (23 women); includes 15 minority (3 Black or African American, non-Hispanic/Latino; 6 American

Indian or Alaska Native, non-Hispanic/Latino; 2 Asian, non-Hispanic/Latino; 2 Hispanic/Latino; 2 Two or more races, non-Hispanic/Latino), 3 international. Average age 31. 73 applicants, 62% accepted, 33 enrolled. *Faculty:* 17 full-time (4 women). *Financial support:* In 2015–16, 1 research assistantship with full tuition reimbursement (averaging $3,315 per year), 14 teaching assistantships with full tuition reimbursements (averaging $13,594 per year) were awarded; fellowships with full tuition reimbursements, career-related internships or fieldwork, Federal Work-Study, scholarships/grants, health care benefits, and unspecified assistantships also available. Support available to part-time students. Financial award application deadline: 7/1; financial award applicants required to submit FAFSA. In 2015, 33 master's awarded. *Degree program information:* Part-time programs available. Part-time, online learning. Offers capital markets (MBA); general management (MBA); management (MBA, MS, MSDM); resource and applied economics (MS); security and disaster management (MSDM). *Application deadline:* For fall admission, 3/1 priority date for domestic students, 2/15 for international students; for spring admission, 9/1 priority date for domestic students, 9/1 for international students. Applications are processed on a rolling basis. *Application fee:* $60. Electronic applications accepted. *Application Contact:* Mary Kreta, Director of Admissions, 907-474-7500, Fax: 907-474-7097, E-mail: admissions@uaf.edu. *Dean*, Dr. Mark Herrmann, 907-474-7461, Fax: 907-474-5219, E-mail: uaf-som@alaska.edu.

School of Natural Resources and Extension Students: 23 full-time (17 women), 25 part-time (15 women); includes 2 minority (1 Hispanic/Latino; 1 Two or more races, non-Hispanic/Latino), 3 international. Average age 36. 21 applicants, 38% accepted, 7 enrolled. *Faculty:* 16 full-time (4 women), 2 part-time/adjunct (both women). *Financial support:* In 2015–16, 11 research assistantships with full tuition reimbursements (averaging $10,656 per year), 4 teaching assistantships with full tuition reimbursements (averaging $8,551 per year) were awarded; fellowships with full tuition reimbursements, career-related internships or fieldwork, Federal Work-Study, scholarships/grants, health care benefits, and unspecified assistantships also available. Support available to part-time students. Financial award application deadline: 2/15; financial award applicants required to submit FAFSA. In 2015, 7 master's, 1 doctorate awarded. *Degree program information:* Part-time programs available. Part-time. Offers natural resources and sustainability (PhD); natural resources management (MS). *Application deadline:* For fall admission, 6/1 for domestic students, 3/1 for international students; for spring admission, 10/15 for domestic students, 9/1 for international students. Applications are processed on a rolling basis. *Application fee:* $60. Electronic applications accepted. *Application Contact:* Mary Kreta, Director of Admissions, 907-474-7500, Fax: 907-474-7097, E-mail: admissions@uaf.edu. *Interim Dean*, Stephen Sparrow, 907-474-9450, Fax: 907-474-6268, E-mail: fysnras@uaf.edu.

UNIVERSITY OF ALASKA SOUTHEAST, Juneau, AK 99801

General Information State-supported, coed, comprehensive institution. *Graduate housing:* Rooms and/or apartments available on a first-come, first-served basis to single and married students. Housing application deadline: 5/1. *Research affiliation:* National Park Service (environmental resources, cultural studies), North Pacific Research Board (marine biology, oceanography), U.S. Department of Education (DOE) (teaching, early childhood education), Natural Science Foundation (marine biology), U.S. Department of Agriculture (USDA) (forest service), Alaska Department of Education (teaching).

GRADUATE UNITS

Graduate Programs ***Degree program information:*** Part-time and evening/weekend programs available. Part-time, evening/weekend, online learning. Offers business administration (MBA); early childhood education (M Ed, MAT); educational technology (M Ed); elementary education (MAT); public administration (MPA); reading (M Ed); secondary education (MAT). Electronic applications accepted.

UNIVERSITY OF ALBERTA, Edmonton, AB T6G 2E1, Canada

General Information Province-supported, coed, university. CGS member. *Graduate housing:* Rooms and/or apartments available on a first-come, first-served basis to single and married students.

GRADUATE UNITS

Faculty of Extension Offers communications and technology (MA).

Faculty of Graduate Studies and Research ***Degree program information:*** Part-time and evening/weekend programs available. Part-time, evening/weekend. Offers accounting (PhD); adult education (M Ed, Ed D, PhD); agricultural economics (M Ag, M Sc, PhD); agricultural, food and nutritional science (M Ag, M Eng, M Sc, PhD); agroforestry (M Ag, M Sc, MF); ancient history (PhD); anthropology (MA, PhD); applied linguistics (Germanic, Romance, Slavic) (MA); applied mathematics (M Sc, PhD); applied music (M Mus); astrophysics (M Sc, PhD); biostatistics (M Sc); business administration (Exec MBA, MBA); chemical engineering (M Eng, M Sc, PhD); chemistry (M Sc, PhD); Chinese literature (MA); choral conducting (M Mus); classical archaeology (MA, PhD); classical literature (PhD); classics (MA); communications (M Eng, M Sc, PhD); communications and technology (MACT); composition (M Mus); computer engineering (M Eng, M Sc, PhD); computing science (M Sc, PhD); condensed matter (M Sc, PhD); conservation biology (M Sc, PhD); construction engineering and management (M Eng, M Sc, PhD); counseling psychology (M Ed, PhD); criminal justice (MA); demography (MA, PhD); design (MFA); directing (MFA); drama (MA); drawing (MFA); earth and atmospheric sciences (M Sc, MA, PhD); East Asian interdisciplinary studies (MA); economics (MA, PhD); economics and finance (MA); educational administration and leadership (M Ed, Ed D, PhD, Postgraduate Diploma); educational psychology (M Ed, PhD); electromagnetics (M Eng, M Sc, PhD); elementary education (M Ed, Ed D, PhD); engineering management (M Eng); English (MA, PhD); environmental and natural resource economics (PhD); environmental biology and ecology (M Sc, PhD); environmental engineering (M Eng, M Sc, PhD); environmental science (M Sc, PhD); experimental linguistics (M Sc, PhD); family ecology and practice (M Sc, PhD); finance (PhD); First Nations education (M Ed, Ed D, PhD); forest biology and management (M Sc, PhD); forest economics (M Ag, M Sc, PhD); French language, literatures and linguistics (PhD); French language, literatures, and linguistics (MA); geoenvironmental engineering (M Eng, M Sc, PhD); geophysics (M Sc, PhD); geotechnical engineering (M Eng, M Sc, PhD); Germanic languages, literatures and linguistics (PhD); Germanic languages, literatures, and linguistics (MA); history (MA, PhD); history of art, design, and visual culture (MA); human resources/industrial relations (PhD); industrial design (M Des); instructional technology (M Ed); international business (MBA); Italian studies (MA); Japanese literature (MA); land reclamation and remediation (M Sc, PhD); leisure and sport management (MBA); management science (PhD); marketing (PhD); materials engineering (M Eng, M Sc, PhD); mathematical finance (M Sc, PhD); mathematical physics (M Sc, PhD); mathematics (M Sc, PhD); mechanical engineering (M Eng, M Sc, PhD); medical physics (M Sc, PhD); microbiology and biotechnology (M Sc, PhD); mining engineering (M Eng, M Sc, PhD); molecular biology and genetics (M Sc, PhD); music (PhD); nanotechnology and microdevices (M Eng, M Sc, PhD); natural resources and energy (MBA); occupational therapy (M Sc, PhD); organ and choral conductors (D Mus); organizational analysis (PhD); painting (MFA); petroleum engineering (M Eng, M Sc, PhD); pharmacology (M Sc, PhD); pharmacy and pharmaceutical sciences (M Sc, PhD); philosophy (MA, PhD); physical education (M Sc); physical therapy (M Sc, PhD); physiology and cell biology (M Sc, PhD); piano (D Mus); plant biology (M Sc, PhD); political science (MA, PhD); power/power electronics (M Eng, M Sc, PhD); printmaking (MFA); process control (M Eng, M Sc, PhD); protected areas and wildlands management (M Sc, PhD); psychology (M Sc, MA, PhD); recreation and physical education (MA, PhD); rural sociology (M Ag, M Sc); school counseling (M Ed); school psychology (M Ed, PhD); sculpture (MFA); secondary education (M Ed, Ed D, PhD); Slavic languages and literatures (Russian, Ukrainian) (MA, PhD); Slavic linguistics (Russian, Ukrainian) (MA, PhD); sociology (MA, PhD); soil science (M Ag, M Sc, PhD); Spanish and Latin American studies (MA, PhD); special education (M Ed, PhD); special education-deafness studies (M Ed); speech pathology and audiology (PhD); speech-language pathology (M Sc); statistics (M Sc, PhD, Postgraduate Diploma); structural engineering (M Eng, M Sc, PhD); subatomic physics (M Sc, PhD); systematics and evolution (M Sc, PhD); systems (M Eng, M Sc, PhD); teaching English as a second language (M Ed); technology commercialization (MBA); textiles and clothing (M Sc, MA, PhD); theoretical, cultural and international studies in education (M Ed, Ed D, PhD); Ukrainian folklore (MA, PhD); visual communication design (M Des); water and land resources (M Ag, M Sc, PhD); water resources (M Eng, M Sc, PhD); welding (M Eng); wildlife ecology and management (M Sc, PhD). Electronic applications accepted.

Facultè Saint Jean Degree program information: Part-time and evening/weekend programs available. Part-time, evening/weekend, online learning. Offers education (M Ed).

Faculty of Nursing Degree program information: Part-time programs available. Part-time. Offers nursing (MN, PhD).

Faculty of Rehabilitation Medicine Offers rehabilitation medicine (PhD). Electronic applications accepted.

School of Library and Information Studies Offers library and information studies (MLIS). Electronic applications accepted.

Faculty of Law ***Degree program information:*** Part-time programs available. Part-time. Offers law (LL M, PhD). Electronic applications accepted.

Faculty of Medicine and Dentistry Offers dental hygiene (Diploma); dentistry (DDS); medicine and dentistry (M Sc, DDS, MD, PhD, Diploma); orthodontics (M Sc, PhD); TMD/orofacial pain (M Sc). Electronic applications accepted.

Graduate Programs in Medicine Degree program information: Part-time programs available. Part-time. Offers biochemistry (M Sc, PhD); biomedical engineering (M Sc); cell and molecular biology (M Sc, PhD); medical genetics (M Sc, PhD); medical microbiology and immunology (M Sc, PhD); medical sciences (M Sc, PhD); medicine (M Sc, MD, PhD); neuroscience (M Sc, PhD); obstetrics and gynecology (MD); oncology (M Sc, PhD); ophthalmology (M Sc, PhD); pediatrics (M Sc, PhD); physiology (M Sc, PhD); psychiatry (M Sc, PhD); radiology and diagnostic imaging (M Sc); surgery (M Sc, PhD).

School of Public Health Offers clinical epidemiology (M Sc, MPH); environmental and occupational health (MPH); environmental health sciences (M Sc); epidemiology (M Sc); global health (M Sc, MPH); health policy and management (MPH); health policy research (M Sc); health technology assessment (MPH); occupational health (M Sc); population health (M Sc); public health (M Sc, MPH, PhD, Postgraduate Diploma); public health leadership (MPH); public health sciences (PhD); quantitative methods (MPH).

Centre for Health Promotion Studies Degree program information: Part-time programs available. Part-time, online learning. Offers health promotion (M Sc, Postgraduate Diploma).

UNIVERSITY OF ANTELOPE VALLEY, Lancaster, CA 93534

General Information Proprietary, coed, comprehensive institution.

GRADUATE UNITS

Program in Business Management Offers business management (MS).

Program in Criminal Justice Offers criminal justice (MS).

THE UNIVERSITY OF ARIZONA, Tucson, AZ 85721

General Information State-supported, coed, university. CGS member. *Graduate housing:* Rooms and/or apartments available on a first-come, first-served basis to single students and available to married students. Housing application deadline: 5/1. *Research affiliation:* Smithsonian Astrophysical Observatory (astronomy), Research Corporation (astronomy), National Center for Atmospheric Research (atmospheric physics), Kitt Peak National Observatory (astronomy), Argonne National Laboratory (physics).

GRADUATE UNITS

College of Agriculture and Life Sciences ***Financial support:*** In 2015–16, 108 research assistantships with tuition reimbursements (averaging $16,433 per year), 49 teaching assistantships with tuition reimbursements (averaging $16,636 per year) were awarded; fellowships with tuition reimbursements, career-related internships or fieldwork, Federal Work-Study, institutionally sponsored loans, scholarships/grants, traineeships, health care benefits, tuition waivers (full and partial), and unspecified assistantships also available. *Degree program information:* Part-time programs available. Part-time. Offers agricultural and biosystems engineering (MS, PhD); agricultural and resource economics (MS); agricultural education (MAE, MS, Graduate Certificate); agriculture and life sciences (MAE, MHE Ed, MS, PhD, Graduate Certificate); animal sciences (MS, PhD); arid lands resource sciences (PhD); nutritional sciences (MS, PhD); soil, water and environmental science (MS, PhD, Graduate Certificate). *Application deadline:* For fall admission, 1/1 for domestic students, 12/1 for international students. Applications are processed on a rolling basis. *Application fee:* $75. Electronic applications accepted. *Application Contact:* 520-621-3612, Fax: 520-621-7196. *Dean*, Dr. Shane Burgess, 520-621-7621, Fax: 520-621-7196, E-mail: dean@cals.arizona.edu.

School of Animal and Comparative Biomedical Sciences Financial support: Research assistantships, teaching assistantships, health care benefits, and unspecified assistantships available. Financial award application deadline: 3/22. Offers animal and comparative biomedical sciences (MS, PhD). *Application deadline:* For fall admission, 2/28 for domestic students, 12/1 for international students. *Application fee:* $75. Electronic applications accepted. *Application Contact:* Kathryn Johansen, Administrative Assistant, 520-621-4507, E-mail: millerk@email.arizona.edu. *Head*, Andre-Denis Wright, 520-621-0868, E-mail: adwright@email.arizona.edu.

School of Family and Consumer Sciences Financial support: Fellowships, research assistantships, teaching assistantships, career-related internships or fieldwork, Federal Work-Study, institutionally sponsored loans, scholarships/grants, health care benefits, tuition waivers (full), and unspecified assistantships available. Financial award application deadline: 3/1. *Degree program information:* Part-time programs available. Part-time. Offers family and consumer sciences (PhD). *Application* *deadline:* Applications are processed on a rolling basis. *Application fee:* $75. Electronic applications accepted. *Application Contact:* 520-621-1075. *Director*, Dr. Jana Hawley, E-mail: hawleyj@email.arizona.edu.

School of Natural Resources and the Environment Financial support: Fellowships, research assistantships, teaching assistantships, career-related internships or fieldwork, scholarships/grants, health care benefits, tuition waivers (full and partial), and unspecified assistantships available. Offers ecology and management of rangelands (MS, PhD); natural resources (MS, PhD); water, society, and policy (MS); watershed management (MS, PhD). *Application deadline:* For fall admission, 6/1 for domestic students, 12/1 for international students; for spring admission, 10/1 for domestic students, 6/1 for international students. *Application fee:* $75. Electronic applications accepted. *Application Contact:* 520-621-7255. *Director*, Dr. Stuart Marsh, E-mail: smarsh@email.arizona.edu.

School of Plant Sciences Financial support: Research assistantships, teaching assistantships, career-related internships or fieldwork, Federal Work-Study, scholarships/grants, health care benefits, tuition waivers (partial), and unspecified assistantships available. *Degree program information:* Part-time programs available. Part-time. Offers plant pathology (MS, PhD); plant sciences (MS, PhD). *Application deadline:* For fall admission, 12/1 for domestic and international students; for spring admission, 6/1 for domestic and international students. Applications are processed on a rolling basis. *Application fee:* $75. Electronic applications accepted. *Application Contact:* 520-621-1945. *Director*, Dr. Karen Schumaker, E-mail: schumake@ag.arizona.edu.

College of Architecture, Planning, and Landscape Architecture *Financial support:* Research assistantships, teaching assistantships, career-related internships or fieldwork, Federal Work-Study, scholarships/grants, health care benefits, tuition waivers (full and partial), and unspecified assistantships available. *Degree program information:* Part-time programs available. Part-time. Offers architecture, planning, and landscape architecture (M Ar, M Arch, ML Arch, MRED, MS, PhD, Graduate Certificate); planning (MS). *Application deadline:* For fall admission, 2/1 for domestic students, 1/1 for international students. Applications are processed on a rolling basis. *Application fee:* $75. Electronic applications accepted. *Application Contact:* 520-621-6751, E-mail: capla@email.arizona.edu. *Dean*, Janice A. Cervelli, E-mail: jcervell@email.arizona.edu.

College of Architecture, Planning and Landscape Architecture Financial support: Research assistantships, teaching assistantships, career-related internships or fieldwork, scholarships/grants, health care benefits, tuition waivers (full), and unspecified assistantships available. Financial award application deadline: 1/31. Offers architecture, planning and landscape architecture (M Ar, ML Arch, MRED, MS, PhD, Graduate Certificate). *Application deadline:* For fall admission, 1/15 for domestic and international students. *Application fee:* $75. Electronic applications accepted. *Application Contact:* Christopher J. Brazil, Program Coordinator, 520-621-9819, Fax: 520-626-6448, E-mail: cjb1@email.arizona.edu. *Dean*, Janice A. Cervelli, 520-621-6751, Fax: 520-626-6448, E-mail: capla@email.arizona.edu.

School of Architecture Financial support: Research assistantships, teaching assistantships, health care benefits, and unspecified assistantships available. Offers architecture (M Arch, MS). *Application deadline:* For fall admission, 2/1 for domestic students, 12/1 for international students; for spring admission, 2/1 for domestic and international students. *Application fee:* $75. Electronic applications accepted. *Director*, Robert Miller, E-mail: millerr@u.arizona.edu.

College of Education *Financial support:* Research assistantships, teaching assistantships, career-related internships or fieldwork, Federal Work-Study, institutionally sponsored loans, scholarships/grants, health care benefits, tuition waivers (full and partial), and unspecified assistantships available. Support available to part-time students. Financial award application deadline: 3/1. *Degree program information:* Part-time programs available. Part-time, online learning. Offers counseling and mental health (MA); cross-categorical special education (MA); deaf and hard of hearing (MA); education (M Ed, MA, MS, Ed D, PhD, Certificate, Ed S); educational leadership (M Ed, Ed D, Ed S); educational psychology (MA, PhD); educational research methodology (Certificate); family studies and human development (M Ed); higher education (MA, PhD); language, reading and culture (MA, Ed D, PhD, Ed S); learning disabilities (MA); motivating learning environments (Certificate); reading instruction (Graduate Certificate); rehabilitation counseling (MA, PhD); school counseling (MA); school psychology (PhD, Ed S); severe and multiple disabilities (MA); special education (MA, PhD); teaching and teacher education (M Ed, MA, PhD); visual impairment (MA). *Application deadline:* For fall admission, 2/1 priority date for domestic and international students; for spring admission, 10/1 priority date for domestic students, 9/1 priority date for international students. Applications are processed on a rolling basis. *Application fee:* $75. Electronic applications accepted. *Application Contact:* Dr. Ronald Marx, Dean, E-mail: ronmarx@email.arizona.edu. *Dean*, Dr. Ronald Marx, E-mail: ronmarx@email.arizona.edu.

College of Engineering *Financial support:* Research assistantships, teaching assistantships, institutionally sponsored loans, scholarships/grants, health care benefits, and unspecified assistantships available. *Degree program information:* Part-time programs available. Part-time, online learning. Offers aerospace engineering (MS, PhD); chemical engineering (MS, PhD); civil engineering and engineering mechanics (MS, PhD); electrical and computer engineering (MS, PhD); engineering (ME, MS, PhD, Certificate); engineering management (Graduate Certificate); environmental engineering (MS, PhD); industrial engineering (MS); materials science and engineering (MS, PhD); mechanical engineering (MS, PhD); mining and geological engineering (MS, PhD); mining engineering (Certificate); systems and industrial engineering (MS, PhD); systems engineering (MS, PhD, Graduate Certificate). *Application fee:* $75. Electronic applications accepted. *Application Contact:* Dr. Jeff Goldberg, Dean, 520-621-6594, Fax: 520-621-2232, E-mail: twp@engr.arizona.edu. *Dean*, Dr. Jeff Goldberg, 520-621-6594, Fax: 520-621-2232, E-mail: twp@engr.arizona.edu.

College of Fine Arts *Faculty:* 147. *Financial support:* Research assistantships, teaching assistantships, career-related internships or fieldwork, Federal Work-Study, institutionally sponsored loans, scholarships/grants, health care benefits, tuition waivers (full and partial), and unspecified assistantships available. Support available to part-time students. *Degree program information:* Part-time programs available. Part-time. Offers fine arts (MA, MFA, MM, PhD, Graduate Certificate). *Application fee:* $75. Electronic applications accepted. *Application Contact:* 520-621-1302, Fax: 520-621-1307, E-mail: finearts@email.arizona.edu.

School of Art Financial support: Research assistantships, teaching assistantships, career-related internships or fieldwork, Federal Work-Study, institutionally sponsored loans, scholarships/grants, health care benefits, tuition waivers (full and partial), and unspecified assistantships available. Support available to part-time students. Financial award application deadline: 4/1. *Degree program information:* Part-time programs available. Part-time. Offers art (MA, MFA, PhD); art education (MA); art history (MA); art history and education (PhD); history and theory of art (PhD). *Application deadline:* For fall admission, 2/1 for domestic and international students. Applications are processed on a rolling basis. *Application fee:* $75. Electronic applications accepted. *Application Contact:* 520-621-7570. *Interim Director*, Colin Blakely, E-mail: cblakely@email.arizona.edu.

School of Dance Financial support: Teaching assistantships available. Offers dance (MFA). *Application fee:* $75. Electronic applications accepted. *Application Contact:* General Information Contact, 520-621-4698. *Director*, Jory Hancock, E-mail: jory@email.arizona.edu.

School of Music Financial support: Research assistantships, teaching assistantships, career-related internships or fieldwork, institutionally sponsored loans, scholarships/grants, health care benefits, tuition waivers (full), and unspecified assistantships available. Support available to part-time students. Financial award application deadline: 2/15; financial award applicants required to submit FAFSA. *Degree program information:* Part-time programs available. Part-time. Offers composition (MM, DMA); conducting (MM, DMA); ethnomusicology (MM); music (MM, PhD); music education (MM, PhD); music theory (MM, PhD); musical arts (DMA); musicology (MM); performance (MM, DMA). *Application deadline:* For fall admission, 6/1 for domestic students, 12/1 for international students; for spring admission, 10/1 for domestic students, 6/1 for international students. Applications are processed on a rolling basis. *Application fee:* $75. Electronic applications accepted. *Application Contact:* 520-621-1655. *Director*, Ed Reid, E-mail: ereid@email.arizona.edu.

School of Theatre, Film and Television Financial support: Research assistantships, teaching assistantships, career-related internships or fieldwork, Federal Work-Study, institutionally sponsored loans, scholarships/grants, health care benefits, tuition waivers (full), and unspecified assistantships available. Financial award application deadline: 3/1; financial award applicants required to submit FAFSA. Offers theatre, film and television (MFA). *Application deadline:* For fall admission, 2/15 for domestic students, 12/1 for international students. Applications are processed on a rolling basis. *Application fee:* $75. Electronic applications accepted. *Application Contact:* 520-621-7008. *Director*, Bruce Brockman, E-mail: brockma5@email.arizona.edu.

College of Humanities *Financial support:* Research assistantships, teaching assistantships, career-related internships or fieldwork, Federal Work-Study, institutionally sponsored loans, scholarships/grants, health care benefits, tuition waivers (full and partial), and unspecified assistantships available. Support available to part-time students. *Degree program information:* Part-time programs available. Part-time. Offers classics (MA); creative writing (MFA); East Asian studies (MA, PhD); English (MA, PhD); English language/linguistics (MA, PhD); ESL (MA); French and Italian (MA); German (MA); humanities (MA, MFA, PhD); rhetoric, composition and the teaching of English (MA, PhD); Russian (MA); Spanish (MA, PhD); teaching English as a second language (Graduate Certificate); transcultural German (PhD). *Application deadline:* Applications are processed on a rolling basis. *Application fee:* $75. Electronic applications accepted. *Application Contact:* Dr. Mary Wildner-Bassett, Dean. *Dean*, Dr. Mary Wildner-Bassett.

College of Medicine *Financial support:* Fellowships, research assistantships, teaching assistantships, career-related internships or fieldwork, Federal Work-Study, institutionally sponsored loans, scholarships/grants, traineeships, tuition waivers (full and partial), and unspecified assistantships available. Support available to part-time students. *Degree program information:* Part-time programs available. Part-time. Offers cellular and molecular medicine (MS, PhD); immunobiology (PhD); medical sciences (MS, PhD); medicine (MS, MD, PhD, Graduate Certificate). MD program open only to state residents. *Application Contact:* Dr. Stuart Flynn, Dean. *Dean*, Dr. Stuart Flynn.

College of Nursing *Financial support:* Research assistantships, teaching assistantships, career-related internships or fieldwork, institutionally sponsored loans, scholarships/grants, traineeships, health care benefits, tuition waivers (full), and unspecified assistantships available. Financial award application deadline: 6/1. *Degree program information:* Part-time programs available. Part-time, online learning. Offers health care informatics (Certificate); nurse practitioner (MS); nursing (DNP, PhD). *Application deadline:* For fall admission, 1/15 for domestic and international students. Applications are processed on a rolling basis. *Application fee:* $75. Electronic applications accepted. *Application Contact:* Dr. Joan Shaver, Dean, 520-626-7124, Fax: 520-626-6424, E-mail: cmurdaugh@nursing.arizona.edu. *Dean*, Dr. Joan Shaver, 520-626-7124, Fax: 520-626-6424, E-mail: cmurdaugh@nursing.arizona.edu.

College of Optical Sciences *Financial support:* Fellowships, research assistantships, teaching assistantships, and scholarships/grants available. Financial award application deadline: 1/1. *Degree program information:* Part-time programs available. Part-time. Offers optical sciences (MS, PhD, Graduate Certificate). *Application deadline:* For fall admission, 1/1 for domestic students, 12/1 for international students. Applications are processed on a rolling basis. *Application fee:* $75. Electronic applications accepted. *Application Contact:* Dr. Thomas L. Koch, Dean, 520-621-6997, Fax: 520-621-9613, E-mail: tlkoch@email.arizona.edu. *Dean*, Dr. Thomas L. Koch, 520-621-6997, Fax: 520-621-9613, E-mail: tlkoch@email.arizona.edu.

College of Pharmacy *Financial support:* Research assistantships, teaching assistantships, career-related internships or fieldwork, Federal Work-Study, institutionally sponsored loans, scholarships/grants, health care benefits, tuition waivers (full and partial), and unspecified assistantships available. Support available to part-time students. Offers medical pharmacology (MS, PhD); medicinal and natural products chemistry (MS, PhD); perfusion science (MS); pharmaceutical economics (MS, PhD); pharmaceutics and pharmacokinetics (MS, PhD); pharmacy (MS, PhD, Pharm D). *Application deadline:* For fall admission, 1/1 for domestic and international students. *Application fee:* $75. *Application Contact:* 520-626-1427, Fax: 520-621-4063. *Interim Dean*, Dr. John E. Murphy, 520-626-1657.

College of Science *Financial support:* Research assistantships, teaching assistantships, career-related internships or fieldwork, Federal Work-Study, institutionally sponsored loans, scholarships/grants, health care benefits, tuition waivers (full and partial), and unspecified assistantships available. Support available to part-time students. *Degree program information:* Part-time programs available. Part-time. Offers applied biosciences (PSM); astronomy (PhD); atmospheric sciences (MS, PhD); biochemistry (PhD); computer science (MS, PhD); ecology and evolutionary biology (MS, PhD); geosciences (MS, PSM, PhD); hydrology (PhD); mathematics (MA, MS, PhD); medical physics (PSM); molecular and cellular biology (MS, PhD); physics (PhD); planetary sciences (MS, PhD); psychology (MA, PhD); science (MS, PSM, PhD, Certificate, Graduate Certificate); secondary mathematics education (MA); speech, language, and hearing sciences (MS, PhD, Certificate). *Application fee:* $75. Electronic applications accepted. *Application Contact:* Dr. Joaquin Ruiz, Dean, 520-621-4090, Fax: 520-621-8389, E-mail: jruiz@email.arizona.edu. *Dean*, Dr. Joaquin Ruiz, 520-621-4090, Fax: 520-621-8389, E-mail: jruiz@email.arizona.edu.

College of Social and Behavioral Sciences *Financial support:* Research assistantships, teaching assistantships, career-related internships or fieldwork, Federal Work-Study, institutionally sponsored loans, scholarships/grants, health care benefits, tuition waivers (full and partial), and unspecified assistantships available. Support available to part-time students. *Degree program information:* Part-time and evening/weekend programs available. Part-time, evening/weekend. Offers communication (MA, PhD); gender and women's studies (MA, PhD, Certificate); history (MA, PhD, Graduate Certificate); human language technology (MS); linguistics and anthropology (PhD); Native American linguistics (MA); philosophy (MA, PhD); political science (MA, PhD); public administration (MPA); public administration and policy (PhD); social and behavioral sciences (MA, MPA, MS, PhD, Certificate, Graduate Certificate); sociology (MA, PhD). *Application fee:* $75. Electronic applications accepted. *Dean,* Dr. John Paul Jones, 520-621-1112, Fax: 520-621-9424, E-mail: jpjones@email.arizona.edu.

Center for Latin American Studies Financial support: Research assistantships, teaching assistantships, career-related internships or fieldwork, Federal Work-Study, institutionally sponsored loans, scholarships/grants, health care benefits, tuition waivers (full and partial), and unspecified assistantships available. *Degree program information:* Part-time programs available. Part-time. Offers Latin American studies (MA). *Application deadline:* For fall admission, 2/1 for domestic students, 12/1 for international students. *Application fee:* $75. Electronic applications accepted. *Application Contact:* 520-626-7242. *Director,* Dr. Linda Green, 520-626-7242, Fax: 520-626-7248, E-mail: lbgreen@email.arizona.edu.

School of Anthropology Financial support: Research assistantships, teaching assistantships, career-related internships or fieldwork, Federal Work-Study, institutionally sponsored loans, scholarships/grants, health care benefits, tuition waivers (full and partial), and unspecified assistantships available. *Degree program information:* Part-time programs available. Part-time. Offers anthropology (MA, MS, PhD, Graduate Certificate). *Application deadline:* For fall admission, 3/1 for domestic and international students. Applications are processed on a rolling basis. *Application fee:* $75. Electronic applications accepted. *Application Contact:* Scott Ellegood, Academic Advisor, 520-626-1767, Fax: 520-621-2088, E-mail: ellegood@email.arizona.edu. *Director,* Dr. Diane Austin, 520-621-2585, Fax: 520-621-2088, E-mail: daustin@email.arizona.edu.

School of Geography and Development Financial support: Research assistantships, teaching assistantships, career-related internships or fieldwork, scholarships/grants, health care benefits, and unspecified assistantships available. Financial award application deadline: 2/1. *Degree program information:* Part-time programs available. Part-time. Offers geographic information systems technology (MA); geography (PhD). *Application deadline:* For fall admission, 1/15 for domestic and international students. *Application fee:* $75. Electronic applications accepted. *Application Contact:* Elizabeth Cordova, Information Contact, 520-621-7486, Fax: 520-621-2889, E-mail: elizabec@email.arizona.edu. *Interim Director,* Dr. Connie Woodhouse, 520-621-7062, Fax: 520-621-2889.

School of Information Resources and Library Science Financial support: Teaching assistantships, career-related internships or fieldwork, Federal Work-Study, institutionally sponsored loans, scholarships/grants, health care benefits, tuition waivers (full and partial), and unspecified assistantships available. Financial award application deadline: 3/1. *Degree program information:* Part-time programs available. Part-time. Offers information resources and library science (MA, PhD). *Application deadline:* For spring admission, 9/1 for domestic and international students. Applications are processed on a rolling basis. *Application fee:* $75. Electronic applications accepted. *Application Contact:* Geraldine Fragoso, Program Manager, 520-621-3565, Fax: 520-621-3279, E-mail: gfragoso@email.arizona.edu. *Director,* Dr. Brian Heidorn, 520-621-3565, Fax: 520-621-3279, E-mail: heidorn@email.arizona.edu.

School of Journalism Financial support: Fellowships, scholarships/grants, and tuition waivers (full and partial) available. Financial award applicants required to submit FAFSA. *Degree program information:* Part-time programs available. Part-time. Offers international journalism studies (MA); professional journalism (MA). *Application deadline:* For fall admission, 2/15 for domestic students; for spring admission, 10/1 for domestic students. Applications are processed on a rolling basis. *Application fee:* $75. Electronic applications accepted. *Application Contact:* Mary Mueller, Graduate Adviser, 520-621-7556, Fax: 520-621-7557, E-mail: journal@email.arizona.edu. *Director,* Dr. David Cuillier, 520-626-9694, E-mail: bcfortna@email.arizona.edu.

School of Middle Eastern and North African Studies Financial support: Research assistantships, teaching assistantships, Federal Work-Study, institutionally sponsored loans, health care benefits, tuition waivers (full), and unspecified assistantships available. Support available to part-time students. *Degree program information:* Part-time and evening/weekend programs available. Part-time, evening/weekend. Offers Middle Eastern and North African studies (MA, PhD, Graduate Certificate). *Application deadline:* For fall admission, 1/15 for domestic students, 12/1 for international students; for spring admission, 10/1 for domestic students, 6/1 for international students. Applications are processed on a rolling basis. *Application fee:* $75. Electronic applications accepted. *Director,* Dr. Benjamin Fortna, 520-621-8013, E-mail: bcfortna@email.arizona.edu.

Eller College of Management *Financial support:* Research assistantships, teaching assistantships, career-related internships or fieldwork, Federal Work-Study, scholarships/grants, health care benefits, tuition waivers (partial), and unspecified assistantships available. Financial award application deadline: 3/15. *Degree program information:* Evening/weekend programs available. Evening/weekend. Offers accounting (M Ac, MS); business administration (MBA); economics (MA, PhD); finance (MS); management (M Ac, MA, MBA, MS, PhD, Graduate Certificate); management and organization (MS, PhD); management information systems (MS, Graduate Certificate); marketing (MBA, MS, PhD). *Application deadline:* Applications are processed on a rolling basis. *Application fee:* $75. Electronic applications accepted. *Application Contact:* Information Contact, 520-621-2165, Fax: 520-621-8105, E-mail: mbaadmissions@eller.arizona.edu. *Dean,* Dr. Jeff Schatzberg, 520-621-2165, Fax: 520-621-8105.

Graduate Interdisciplinary Programs *Financial support:* Research assistantships, teaching assistantships, career-related internships or fieldwork, Federal Work-Study, institutionally sponsored loans, scholarships/grants, health care benefits, tuition waivers (full and partial), and unspecified assistantships available. Support available to part-time students. *Degree program information:* Part-time programs available. Part-time. Offers American Indian studies (MA, PhD); applied mathematics (MS, PMS, PhD); biomedical engineering (MS, PhD); cancer biology (PhD); entomology (MA); entomology and insect science (MS, PhD); genetics (MS, PhD); mathematical sciences (PMS); neuroscience (PhD); physiological sciences (MS, PhD); second language acquisition and teaching (PhD); statistics (MS, PhD). *Application deadline:* For fall admission, 2/1 for domestic students, 1/15 for international students. *Application fee:* $75. *Application Contact:* 520-621-8368, E-mail: gidp@email.arizona.edu. *Dean,* Dr. Andrew Carnie, 520-621-3512, Fax: 520-621-4101, E-mail: gradadm@grad.arizona.edu.

James E. Rogers College of Law Offers indigenous peoples law and policy (LL M); international trade and business law (LL M); law (JD). Electronic applications accepted.

Mel and Enid Zuckerman College of Public Health *Financial support:* Research assistantships, teaching assistantships, health care benefits, and unspecified assistantships available. Offers biostatistics (MS, PhD); epidemiology (MS, PhD); public health (MPH, MS, MSPH, Dr PH, PhD, Graduate Certificate). *Application deadline:* For fall admission, 1/1 for domestic and international students. Applications are processed on a rolling basis. *Application fee:* $75. Electronic applications accepted. *Application Contact:* Stephanie Springer, Special Assistant to the Dean, 520-626-2112, E-mail: coph-admit@email.arizona.edu. *Dean,* Dr. Iman Hakim, 520-626-7083, E-mail: ihakim@email.arizona.edu.

UNIVERSITY OF ARKANSAS, Fayetteville, AR 72701-1201

General Information State-supported, coed, university. CGS member. *Enrollment:* 26,754 graduate, professional, and undergraduate students; 1,437 full-time matriculated graduate/professional students (729 women), 2,493 part-time matriculated graduate/professional students (1,105 women). *Graduate housing:* Room and/or apartments available on a first-come, first-served basis to single students; on-campus housing not available to married students. *Student services:* Campus employment opportunities, campus safety program, career counseling, exercise/wellness program, free psychological counseling, international student services, low-cost health insurance, multicultural affairs office, services for students with disabilities, teacher training, writing training. *Library:* David W. Mullins Library plus 5 others. *Collection:* Books: 1.9 million (physical), 540,879 (digital/electronic); Serial titles: 6,611 (physical), 58,358 (digital/electronic); Databases: 314. Weekly public service hours: 109; students can reserve study rooms. *Research affiliation:* Southern Regional Education Board, Southeastern Universities Research Association, Southern Regional Education Board Uncommon Facilities Program, Oak Ridge Associated Universities, Science Coalition, National Minority Graduate Feeder Project.

Computer facilities: Computer purchase and lease plans are available. 675 computers available on campus for general student use. A campuswide network can be accessed from student residence rooms and from off campus. Online class registration is available.
Website: http://www.uark.edu/

General Application Contact: The Graduate School, 479-575-4401, Fax: 479-575-5908, E-mail: gradinfo@uark.edu.

GRADUATE UNITS

Graduate School Students: 1,437 full-time (729 women), 2,493 part-time (1,105 women); includes 646 minority (245 Black or African American, non-Hispanic/Latino; 55 American Indian or Alaska Native, non-Hispanic/Latino; 86 Asian, non-Hispanic/Latino; 176 Hispanic/Latino; 1 Native Hawaiian or other Pacific Islander, non-Hispanic/Latino; 83 Two or more races, non-Hispanic/Latino), 708 international. *Financial support:* In 2015–16, 761 research assistantships, 484 teaching assistantships with full tuition reimbursements were awarded; fellowships with tuition reimbursements, career-related internships or fieldwork, Federal Work-Study, institutionally sponsored loans, scholarships/grants, traineeships, and unspecified assistantships also available. Support available to part-time students. Financial award application deadline: 4/1; financial award applicants required to submit FAFSA. In 2015, 1,114 master's, 162 doctorates awarded. *Degree program information:* Part-time programs available. Part-time, online learning. Offers cell and molecular biology (MS, PhD); comparative literature and cultural studies (MA, PhD); environmental dynamics (PhD); microelectronics and photonics (MS, PhD); public policy (PhD); space and planetary sciences (MS, PhD). *Application deadline:* Applications are processed on a rolling basis. *Application fee:* $40 ($50 for international students). Electronic applications accepted. *Application Contact:* Graduate Admissions, 479-575-6246, Fax: 479-575-5908, E-mail: gradinfo@uark.edu. *Dean,* Dr. Kim L. Needy, 479-575-4401, Fax: 479-575-5908, E-mail: gradinfo@uark.edu.

College of Education and Health Professions Students: 437 full-time (337 women), 591 part-time (394 women); includes 176 minority (96 Black or African American, non-Hispanic/Latino; 25 American Indian or Alaska Native, non-Hispanic/Latino; 8 Asian, non-Hispanic/Latino; 30 Hispanic/Latino; 17 Two or more races, non-Hispanic/Latino), 47 international. *Financial support:* In 2015–16, 110 research assistantships, 15 teaching assistantships were awarded; fellowships with tuition reimbursements, career-related internships or fieldwork, and Federal Work-Study also available. Support available to part-time students. Financial award application deadline: 4/1; financial award applicants required to submit FAFSA. In 2015, 347 master's, 56 doctorates awarded. Offers adult and lifelong learning (M Ed, Ed D); athletic training (MAT); childhood education (MAT); communication disorders (MS); community health promotion (MS, PhD); counseling (MS, PhD, Ed S); curriculum and instruction (M Ed, PhD, Ed S); education and health professions (M Ed, MAT, MAT, MS, MSN, Ed D, PhD, Ed S); education policy (PhD); educational leadership (M Ed, Ed D, Ed S); educational statistics and research methods (MS, PhD); educational technology (M Ed); health science (MS, PhD); higher education (M Ed, Ed D, Ed S); human resource and workforce development education (M Ed, Ed D); kinesiology (MS, PhD); middle-level education (MAT); nursing (MSN); physical education (M Ed, MAT); recreation and sports management (M Ed, Ed D); rehabilitation (MS, PhD); secondary education (M Ed, MAT, Ed S); special education (M Ed, MAT); vocational education (MAT). *Application deadline:* For fall admission, 4/1 for international students; for spring admission, 10/1 for international students. Applications are processed on a rolling basis. *Application fee:* $40 ($50 for international students). Electronic applications accepted. *Application Contact:* Graduate Admissions, 479-575-6246, Fax: 479-575-5908, E-mail: gradinfo@uark.edu. *Dean,* Dr. Thomas E. Smith, 479-575-3208, Fax: 479-575-3119, E-mail: tecsmith@uark.edu.

College of Engineering Students: 166 full-time (47 women), 585 part-time (119 women); includes 115 minority (48 Black or African American, non-Hispanic/Latino; 5 American Indian or Alaska Native, non-Hispanic/Latino; 16 Asian, non-Hispanic/Latino; 29 Hispanic/Latino; 1 Native Hawaiian or other Pacific Islander, non-Hispanic/Latino; 16 Two or more races, non-Hispanic/Latino), 178 international. *Financial support:* In 2015–16, 198 research assistantships, 21 teaching assistantships were awarded; fellowships with tuition reimbursements, career-related internships or fieldwork, and Federal Work-Study also available. Support available to part-time students. Financial award application deadline: 4/1; financial award applicants required to submit FAFSA. In 2015, 330 master's, 17 doctorates awarded. Offers biological and agricultural engineering (MSE, PhD); biological engineering (MSBE); biomedical engineering (MSBME); chemical engineering (MS Ch E, MSE, PhD); civil engineering (MSCE, MSE, PhD); computer engineering (MS Cmp E, MSE, PhD); computer science (MS, PhD); electrical engineering (MSEE, PhD); engineering (MS, MS Cmp E, MS Ch E, MS En E, MS Tc E, MSBE, MSBME, MSCE, MSE, MSEE, MSIE, MSME, MSOR, MSTE, PhD); environmental engineering (MS En E, MSE); industrial engineering (MSE, MSIE, PhD); mechanical engineering (MSE, MSME, PhD); operations management (MS); operations research (MSE, MSOR); telecommunications engineering (MS Tc E); transportation engineering (MSE, MSTE). *Application deadline:* For fall admission, 4/1 for international students; for spring admission, 10/1 for international students. Applications are processed on a rolling basis. *Application fee:* $40 ($50 for international students). Electronic applications accepted. *Application Contact:* Dr. Terry Martin, Associate Dean for Academic Affairs, 479-575-3052, E-mail: tmartin@uark.edu. *Dean*, Dr. John English, 479-575-4153, Fax: 479-575-4346.

Dale Bumpers College of Agricultural, Food and Life Sciences Students: 103 full-time (55 women), 207 part-time (98 women); includes 28 minority (9 Black or African American, non-Hispanic/Latino; 5 Asian, non-Hispanic/Latino; 9 Hispanic/Latino; 5 Two or more races, non-Hispanic/Latino), 88 international. 164 applicants, 59% accepted. *Financial support:* In 2015–16, 167 research assistantships, 7 teaching assistantships were awarded; fellowships with tuition reimbursements, career-related internships or fieldwork, Federal Work-Study, scholarships/grants, and unspecified assistantships also available. Support available to part-time students. Financial award application deadline: 4/1; financial award applicants required to submit FAFSA. In 2015, 82 master's, 13 doctorates awarded. Offers agricultural and extension education (MS); agricultural economics (MS); agricultural, food and life sciences (MS, PhD); agronomy (MS, PhD); animal science (MS, PhD); entomology (MS, PhD); food safety (MS); food science (MS, PhD); horticulture (MS); human environmental sciences (MS); plant pathology (MS); plant science (PhD); poultry science (MS, PhD). *Application deadline:* For fall admission, 4/1 for international students; for spring admission, 10/1 for international students. Applications are processed on a rolling basis. *Application fee:* $40 ($50 for international students). Electronic applications accepted. *Application Contact:* Graduate Admissions, 479-575-6246, Fax: 479-575-5908, E-mail: gradinfo@uark.edu. *Dean*, Dr. Michael E. Vayda, 479-575-2034, Fax: 479-575-7273, E-mail: mvayda@uark.edu.

J. William Fulbright College of Arts and Sciences Students: 367 full-time (194 women), 484 part-time (219 women); includes 95 minority (19 Black or African American, non-Hispanic/Latino; 12 American Indian or Alaska Native, non-Hispanic/Latino; 11 Asian, non-Hispanic/Latino; 35 Hispanic/Latino; 1 Native Hawaiian or other Pacific Islander, non-Hispanic/Latino; 17 Two or more races, non-Hispanic/Latino), 137 international. *Financial support:* In 2015–16, 143 research assistantships, 373 teaching assistantships with full tuition reimbursements were awarded; fellowships, career-related internships or fieldwork, Federal Work-Study, institutionally sponsored loans, and traineeships also available. Support available to part-time students. Financial award application deadline: 4/1; financial award applicants required to submit FAFSA. In 2015, 194 master's, 39 doctorates awarded. Offers anthropology (MA, PhD); applied physics (MS); art (MFA); arts and sciences (MA, MFA, MM, MPA, MS, MSW, PhD); biological sciences (MA, MS, PhD); chemistry (MS, PhD); communication (MA); creative writing (MFA); English (MA, PhD); French (MA); geography (MA); geology (MS); German (MA); history (MA, PhD); journalism (MA); mathematics (MS, PhD); music (MM); philosophy (MA, PhD); physics (MS, PhD); physics education (MA); political science (MA, MPA); psychology (MA, PhD); public administration (MPA); secondary mathematics (MA); social work (MSW); sociology (MA); Spanish (MA); statistics (MS); theatre (MA, MFA). *Application deadline:* For fall admission, 4/1 for international students; for spring admission, 10/1 for international students. Applications are processed on a rolling basis. *Application fee:* $40 ($50 for international students). Electronic applications accepted. *Application Contact:* Dr. Yvette Murphy-Erby, Associate Dean, 479-575-3711, E-mail: ymurphy@uark.edu. *Dean*, Dr. Todd Shields, 479-575-4801, Fax: 479-575-2642, E-mail: tshield@uark.edu.

Sam M. Walton College of Business Administration Students: 172 full-time (63 women), 215 part-time (67 women); includes 80 minority (21 Black or African American, non-Hispanic/Latino; 2 American Indian or Alaska Native, non-Hispanic/Latino; 20 Asian, non-Hispanic/Latino; 27 Hispanic/Latino; 10 Two or more races, non-Hispanic/Latino), 67 international. *Financial support:* In 2015–16, 64 research assistantships, 17 teaching assistantships were awarded; fellowships, career-related internships or fieldwork, and Federal Work-Study also available. Support available to part-time students. Financial award application deadline: 4/1; financial award applicants required to submit FAFSA. In 2015, 143 master's, 10 doctorates awarded. Offers accounting (M Acc); business administration (M Acc, MA, MBA, MIS, PhD); economics (MA, PhD); information systems (MIS). *Application fee:* $40 ($50 for international students). *Application Contact:* Rebel Smith, Assistant Director of Marketing and Recruiting, 479-575-6123, E-mail: gsb@walton.uark.edu. *Dean*, Dr. Matt Waller, 479-575-5949, E-mail: mwaller@walton.uark.edu.

School of Law Students: 410 full-time (163 women); includes 74 minority (26 Black or African American, non-Hispanic/Latino; 6 American Indian or Alaska Native, non-Hispanic/Latino; 9 Asian, non-Hispanic/Latino; 24 Hispanic/Latino; 1 Native Hawaiian or other Pacific Islander, non-Hispanic/Latino; 8 Two or more races, non-Hispanic/Latino), 3 international. *Financial support:* In 2015–16, fellowships with full tuition reimbursements (averaging $6,000 per year), 8 research assistantships (averaging $2,500 per year) were awarded; teaching assistantships, career-related internships or fieldwork, Federal Work-Study, and scholarships/grants also available. Support available to part-time students. Financial award application deadline: 4/1; financial award applicants required to submit FAFSA. In 2015, 131 doctorates awarded. Offers agricultural law (LL M); law (JD). *Application deadline:* For fall admission, 4/1 for domestic students. Applications are processed on a rolling basis. *Application fee:* $0. *Application Contact:* James K. Miller, Associate Dean for Students, 479-575-3102, E-mail: jkmiller@uark.edu. *Dean*, Stacy L. Leeds, 479-575-5601, Fax: 479-575-3320, E-mail: sleeds@uark.edu.

UNIVERSITY OF ARKANSAS AT LITTLE ROCK, Little Rock, AR 72204-1099

General Information State-supported, coed, university. CGS member. *Enrollment:* 1,086 full-time matriculated graduate/professional students (604 women), 1,230 part-time matriculated graduate/professional students (777 women). *Enrollment by degree level:* 1,397 master's, 337 doctoral, 582 other advanced degrees. *Graduate faculty:* 318 full-time (136 women). Tuition, state resident: part-time $300 per credit hour. Tuition, nonresident: part-time $690 per credit hour. *Required fees:* $100 per credit hour. One-time fee: $40 full-time. *Graduate housing:* Room and/or apartments available on a first-come, first-served basis to single students; on-campus housing not available to married students. Typical cost: $5708 (including board). Housing application deadline: 9/1. *Student services:* Campus employment opportunities, campus safety program, career counseling, exercise/wellness program, free psychological counseling, international student services, low-cost health insurance, multicultural affairs office, services for students with disabilities, teacher training, writing training. *Library:* Ottenheimer Library.

Computer facilities: A campuswide network can be accessed from student residence rooms and from off campus. Online class registration is available.
Website: http://www.ualr.edu/

General Application Contact: Dana J. Steele, Assistant Dean of the Graduate School, 501-569-3206, Fax: 501-569-3039, E-mail: djsteele@ualr.edu.

GRADUATE UNITS

Graduate School Students: 1,059 full-time (609 women), 1,202 part-time (762 women); includes 589 minority (402 Black or African American, non-Hispanic/Latino; 15 American Indian or Alaska Native, non-Hispanic/Latino; 40 Asian, non-Hispanic/Latino; 77 Hispanic/Latino; 55 Two or more races, non-Hispanic/Latino), 250 international. Average age 33. 2,781 applicants, 48% accepted, 751 enrolled. *Faculty:* 349 full-time (138 women). *Financial support:* In 2015–16, 228 students received support, including 4 fellowships with partial tuition reimbursements available, 128 research assistantships with full tuition reimbursements available (averaging $6,500 per year), 100 teaching assistantships with full tuition reimbursements available (averaging $6,500 per year); career-related internships or fieldwork, Federal Work-Study, institutionally sponsored loans, scholarships/grants, traineeships, and unspecified assistantships also available. Support available to part-time students. Financial award application deadline: 3/1; financial award applicants required to submit FAFSA. In 2015, 552 master's, 188 doctorates, 57 other advanced degrees awarded. *Degree program information:* Part-time and evening/weekend programs available. Part-time, evening/weekend, online learning. *Application deadline:* For fall admission, 8/1 for domestic and international students; for spring admission, 12/15 for domestic and international students; for summer admission, 5/1 for domestic and international students. Applications are processed on a rolling basis. *Application fee:* $40. Electronic applications accepted. *Assistant Dean of the Graduate School*, Dana J. Steele, 501-569-3206, Fax: 501-569-3039, E-mail: djsteele@ualr.edu.

Clinton School of Public Service Offers public service (MPS, Graduate Certificate).

College of Arts, Letters, and Sciences Degree program information: Part-time and evening/weekend programs available. Part-time, evening/weekend. Offers applied statistics (Graduate Certificate); art education (MA); art history (MA); arts, letters, and sciences (MA, MS, Graduate Certificate); biology (MS); chemistry (MA, MS); mathematical sciences (MS); philosophy and interdisciplinary studies (MA); public history (MA); second languages (MA); studio art (MA).

College of Business Degree program information: Part-time and evening/weekend programs available. Part-time, evening/weekend. Offers business administration (MBA); business information systems (MS, Graduate Certificate); management (Graduate Certificate).

College of Education and Health Professions Degree program information: Part-time and evening/weekend programs available. Part-time, evening/weekend. Offers administration (MA); adult education (M Ed); clinical social work (MSW); college student affairs (MA); counselor education (M Ed); curriculum and instruction (M Ed); education and health professions (M Ed, MA, MS, MSW, Ed D, Ed S, Graduate Certificate); educational administration and supervision (M Ed, Ed D, Ed S); exercise science (MS); gerontology (Graduate Certificate); gifted and talented education (M Ed, Graduate Certificate); health education and promotion (MS); health professions teaching and learning (MA); higher education (MA, Ed D); learning systems technology education (M Ed); management and community practice (MSW); middle childhood education (M Ed); reading education (M Ed, PhD, Ed S); rehabilitation counseling (MA, Graduate Certificate); rehabilitation for the blind: orientation and mobility (MA); secondary education (M Ed); social work (MSW, Graduate Certificate); special education (M Ed); sport management (MS); two-year college teaching (MA).

College of Social Sciences and Communication Degree program information: Part-time and evening/weekend programs available. Part-time, evening/weekend. Offers applied communication studies (MA); applied psychology (MAP); conflict mediation (Graduate Certificate); criminal justice (MA, MS, PhD); mass communication (MA); nonprofit management (Graduate Certificate); professional and technical writing (MA); public administration (MPA); social sciences and communication (MA, MAP, MPA, MS, PhD, Graduate Certificate).

George W. Donaghey College of Engineering and Information Technology Degree program information: Part-time and evening/weekend programs available. Part-time, evening/weekend. Offers applied science (MS, PhD); bioinformatics (MS, PhD); computer science (MS, PhD); construction management (MS); engineering and information technology (MS, PhD, Graduate Certificate); geospatial technology (Graduate Certificate); information quality (MS, PhD, Graduate Certificate); systems engineering (MS, PhD, Graduate Certificate); technology innovation (Graduate Certificate).

William H. Bowen School of Law ***Degree program information:*** Part-time and evening/weekend programs available. Part-time, evening/weekend. Offers law (JD). Electronic applications accepted.

UNIVERSITY OF ARKANSAS AT MONTICELLO, Monticello, AR 71656

General Information State-supported, coed, comprehensive institution. *Graduate housing:* Rooms and/or apartments guaranteed to single students and available on a first-come, first-served basis to married students. Housing application deadline: 8/15.

GRADUATE UNITS

School of Education ***Degree program information:*** Part-time and evening/weekend programs available. Part-time, evening/weekend, online learning. Offers education (M Ed, MAT); educational leadership (M Ed). Electronic applications accepted.

School of Forest Resources ***Degree program information:*** Part-time programs available. Part-time. Offers forest resources (MS). Electronic applications accepted.

UNIVERSITY OF ARKANSAS AT PINE BLUFF, Pine Bluff, AR 71601-2799

General Information State-supported, coed, comprehensive institution. *Graduate housing:* Rooms and/or apartments available to single and married students. Housing application deadline: 8/1.

GRADUATE UNITS

School of Agriculture, Fisheries and Human Sciences Offers aquaculture and fisheries (MS).

School of Arts and Sciences Offers addiction studies (MS).

School of Education ***Degree program information:*** Part-time and evening/weekend programs available. Part-time, evening/weekend. Offers early childhood education (M Ed); secondary education (M Ed); teaching (MAT).

UNIVERSITY OF ARKANSAS FOR MEDICAL SCIENCES, Little Rock, AR 72205-7199

General Information State-supported, coed, university. *Graduate housing:* Rooms and/or apartments available on a first-come, first-served basis to single and married students. Housing application deadline: 7/15. *Research affiliation:* National Center for

Toxicological Research, Veterans Administration Hospital, Oak Ridge Associated Universities, Arkansas Children's Hospital.

GRADUATE UNITS

College of Health Professions ***Degree program information:*** Part-time programs available. Part-time, online learning. Offers audiology (Au D); communication sciences and disorders (MS, PhD); genetic counseling (MS); nuclear medicine advanced associate (MIS); physician assistant studies (MPAS); radiologist assistant (MIS). PhD offered through consortium with University of Arkansas at Little Rock and University of Central Arkansas. Electronic applications accepted.

College of Medicine Offers medicine (MD). Electronic applications accepted.

College of Nursing ***Degree program information:*** Part-time programs available. Part-time. Offers nursing (PhD).

College of Pharmacy Offers pharmacy (MS, Pharm D). Electronic applications accepted.

College of Public Health ***Degree program information:*** Part-time programs available. Part-time. Offers biostatistics (MPH); environmental and occupational health (MPH, Certificate); epidemiology (MPH, PhD); health behavior and health education (MPH); health policy and management (MPH); health promotion and prevention research (PhD); health services administration (MHSA); health systems research (PhD); public health (Certificate); public health leadership (Dr PH). Electronic applications accepted.

Graduate School ***Degree program information:*** Part-time programs available. Part-time. Offers biochemistry and molecular biology (MS, PhD); bioinformatics (MS, PhD); cellular physiology and molecular biophysics (MS, PhD); clinical nutrition (MS); interdisciplinary biomedical sciences (MS, PhD, Certificate); interdisciplinary toxicology (MS); microbiology and immunology (PhD); neurobiology and developmental sciences (PhD); pharmacology (PhD). Bioinformatics programs hosted jointly with the University of Arkansas at Little Rock. Electronic applications accepted.

UNIVERSITY OF BALTIMORE, Baltimore, MD 21201-5779

General Information State-supported, coed, comprehensive institution. *Graduate housing:* On-campus housing not available.

GRADUATE UNITS

Graduate School ***Degree program information:*** Part-time and evening/weekend programs available. Part-time, evening/weekend, online learning. Electronic applications accepted.

College of Public Affairs Offers criminal justice (MS); health systems management (MS); human services administration (MS); negotiations and conflict management (MS); public administration (MPA, DPA); public affairs (MPA, MS, DPA).

Merrick School of Business Degree program information: Part-time and evening/weekend programs available. Part-time, evening/weekend, online learning. Offers accounting and business advisory services (MS); accounting fundamentals (Graduate Certificate); business (MBA, MS, Graduate Certificate); business/finance (MS); forensic accounting (Graduate Certificate); global leadership (MS); innovation management and technology commercialization (MS); taxation (MS). Electronic applications accepted.

Yale Gordon College of Arts and Sciences Degree program information: Part-time and evening/weekend programs available. Part-time, evening/weekend. Offers arts and sciences (MA, MFA, MS, DS); counseling psychology (MS); creative writing and publishing arts (MFA); information and interaction design (DS); integrated design (MFA); interaction design and information architecture (MS); legal and ethical studies (MA); publications design (MA). Electronic applications accepted.

Joint University of Baltimore/Towson University (UB/Towson) MBA Program ***Degree program information:*** Part-time and evening/weekend programs available. Part-time, evening/weekend, online learning. Offers business administration (MBA). MBA/MSN, MBA/Pharm D offered jointly with University of Maryland, Baltimore.

School of Law Students: 515 full-time (268 women), 338 part-time (166 women); includes 251 minority (138 Black or African American, non-Hispanic/Latino; 42 Asian, non-Hispanic/Latino; 49 Hispanic/Latino; 22 Two or more races, non-Hispanic/Latino), 15 international. Average age 27. 1,180 applicants, 52% accepted, 200 enrolled. *Faculty:* 59 full-time (27 women), 76 part-time/adjunct (24 women). *Financial support:* In 2015–16, 368 students received support. Research assistantships, teaching assistantships, career-related internships or fieldwork, Federal Work-Study, and scholarships/grants available. Support available to part-time students. Financial award application deadline: 4/1; financial award applicants required to submit FAFSA. In 2015, 268 doctorates awarded. *Degree program information:* Part-time and evening/weekend programs available. Part-time, evening/weekend. Offers law (JD); law of the United States (LL M); taxation (LL M). JD/MS offered jointly with Division of Criminology, Criminal Justice, and Social Policy; JD/PhD with University of Maryland, Baltimore. *Application deadline:* For fall admission, 7/15 for domestic students, 4/1 priority date for international students. Applications are processed on a rolling basis. *Application fee:* $60. Electronic applications accepted. *Application Contact:* Jeffrey L. Zavrotny, Assistant Dean for Admissions, 410-837-5809, Fax: 410-837-4188, E-mail: jzavrotny@ubalt.edu. *Dean,* Ronald Weich, 410-837-4458.

UNIVERSITY OF BRIDGEPORT, Bridgeport, CT 06604

General Information Independent, coed, comprehensive institution. CGS member. *Graduate housing:* Rooms and/or apartments guaranteed to single students and available on a first-come, first-served basis to married students. Housing application deadline: 8/15. *Research affiliation:* Connecticut Medicine Research Consortia, Marine Biology Station, Burndy Library.

GRADUATE UNITS

Acupuncture Institute ***Degree program information:*** Part-time programs available. Part-time. Offers acupuncture (MS). *Application deadline:* For fall admission, 8/1 priority date for domestic students, 8/1 for international students; for spring admission, 12/1 priority date for domestic students, 12/1 for international students. Applications are processed on a rolling basis. *Application fee:* $50. Electronic applications accepted.

College of Chiropractic ***Financial support:*** Federal Work-Study and institutionally sponsored loans available. Support available to part-time students. Financial award application deadline: 6/1; financial award applicants required to submit FAFSA. Offers chiropractic (DC). *Application deadline:* For fall admission, 4/1 priority date for domestic and international students; for spring admission, 11/1 priority date for domestic and international students. Applications are processed on a rolling basis. *Application fee:* $75. Electronic applications accepted.

College of Naturopathic Medicine ***Financial support:*** Federal Work-Study, institutionally sponsored loans, and scholarships/grants available. Financial award application deadline: 4/1; financial award applicants required to submit FAFSA. Offers naturopathic medicine (ND). *Application deadline:* For fall admission, 8/1 priority date for domestic and international students; for spring admission, 12/1 for domestic students, 2/1 priority date for international students. Applications are processed on a rolling basis. *Application fee:* $75. Electronic applications accepted.

College of Public and International Affairs ***Financial support:*** Applicants required to submit FAFSA. *Degree program information:* Part-time and evening/weekend programs available. Part-time, evening/weekend. Offers East Asian and Pacific Rim studies (MA); global development and peace (MA); global media and communication studies (MA). *Application deadline:* For fall admission, 8/1 priority date for domestic and international students; for spring admission, 12/1 priority date for domestic and international students. *Application fee:* $50.

Fones School of Dental Hygiene ***Financial support:*** Applicants required to submit FAFSA. *Degree program information:* Part-time and evening/weekend programs available. Part-time, evening/weekend, online learning. Offers dental hygiene (MS). *Application deadline:* For fall admission, 8/1 priority date for domestic and international students; for spring admission, 12/1 priority date for domestic and international students. *Application fee:* $50.

Nutrition Institute ***Financial support:*** Available to part-time students. Application deadline: 6/1; applicants required to submit FAFSA. *Degree program information:* Part-time and evening/weekend programs available. Part-time, evening/weekend, online learning. Offers human nutrition (MS). *Application deadline:* For fall admission, 8/1 priority date for domestic and international students; for spring admission, 12/1 priority date for domestic and international students. Applications are processed on a rolling basis. *Application fee:* $50. Electronic applications accepted.

Physician Assistant Institute Offers physician assistant (MS). *Application deadline:* For fall admission, 8/1 for domestic and international students; for spring admission, 12/1 priority date for domestic and international students. Applications are processed on a rolling basis. *Application fee:* $50.

School of Arts and Sciences ***Financial support:*** Fellowships, research assistantships, teaching assistantships, career-related internships or fieldwork, Federal Work-Study, scholarships/grants, and unspecified assistantships available. Support available to part-time students. Financial award application deadline: 6/1; financial award applicants required to submit FAFSA. *Degree program information:* Part-time and evening/weekend programs available. Part-time, evening/weekend. Offers arts and sciences (MS); clinical mental health counseling (MS); college student personnel (MS); community counseling (MS); human resource development (MS); human service (MS). *Application deadline:* For fall admission, 8/1 priority date for domestic and international students; for spring admission, 12/1 priority date for domestic and international students. Applications are processed on a rolling basis. *Application fee:* $50. Electronic applications accepted.

School of Business ***Financial support:*** Fellowships, research assistantships, teaching assistantships, career-related internships or fieldwork, Federal Work-Study, institutionally sponsored loans, and tuition waivers (partial) available. Support available to part-time students. Financial award application deadline: 6/1; financial award applicants required to submit FAFSA. *Degree program information:* Part-time and evening/weekend programs available. Part-time, evening/weekend. Offers accounting (MBA); finance (MBA); general business (MBA); global financial services (MBA); human resource management (MBA); information systems and knowledge management (MBA); international business (MBA); management (MBA); marketing (MBA); operations management (MBA); small business and entrepreneurship (MBA); specialized business (MBA). *Application deadline:* For fall admission, 8/1 priority date for domestic and international students; for spring admission, 12/1 priority date for domestic and international students. Applications are processed on a rolling basis. *Application fee:* $50. Electronic applications accepted.

School of Education ***Financial support:*** Fellowships, research assistantships, teaching assistantships, career-related internships or fieldwork, Federal Work-Study, and institutionally sponsored loans available. Support available to part-time students. Financial award application deadline: 6/1; financial award applicants required to submit FAFSA. *Degree program information:* Part-time and evening/weekend programs available. Part-time, evening/weekend. Offers education (MS, Ed D, Diploma); educational management (Ed D, Diploma); elementary education (MS, Diploma); intermediate administrator or supervisor (Diploma); leadership (Ed D); middle school education (MS); music education (MS); remedial reading and language arts (Diploma); secondary education (MS, Diploma). *Application deadline:* For fall admission, 8/1 priority date for domestic and international students; for spring admission, 12/1 priority date for domestic and international students. Applications are processed on a rolling basis. *Application fee:* $50. Electronic applications accepted.

School of Engineering ***Financial support:*** Fellowships, research assistantships, teaching assistantships, career-related internships or fieldwork, Federal Work-Study, institutionally sponsored loans, and tuition waivers (partial) available. Support available to part-time students. Financial award application deadline: 6/1; financial award applicants required to submit FAFSA. *Degree program information:* Part-time and evening/weekend programs available. Part-time, evening/weekend, online learning. Offers biomedical engineering (MS); computer engineering (MS); computer science (MS); computer science and engineering (PhD); electrical engineering (MS); engineering (MS, PhD); mechanical engineering (MS); technology management (MS, PhD). *Application deadline:* For fall admission, 8/1 priority date for domestic and international students; for spring admission, 12/1 priority date for domestic and international students. Applications are processed on a rolling basis. *Application fee:* $50. Electronic applications accepted.

Shintaro Akatsu School of Design ***Financial support:*** Application deadline: 8/1; applicants required to submit FAFSA. *Degree program information:* Part-time and evening/weekend programs available. Part-time, evening/weekend. Offers design management (MPS). *Application deadline:* For fall admission, 8/1 priority date for domestic and international students; for spring admission, 12/1 priority date for domestic and international students. Applications are processed on a rolling basis. *Application fee:* $50. Electronic applications accepted.

THE UNIVERSITY OF BRITISH COLUMBIA, Vancouver, BC V6T 1Z1, Canada

General Information Province-supported, coed, university. CGS member. *Graduate housing:* Rooms and/or apartments available on a first-come, first-served basis to single and married students. Housing application deadline: 3/1. *Research affiliation:* Pulp and Paper Research Institute of Canada (pulp and paper research), Pacific Environment Institute, Pacific Biological Station (fisheries and oceanography), British Columbia Research (chemical and biological science technology), Forintek Canada (forest technology), National Research Council of Canada Institute of Machinery Research (machinery research).

GRADUATE UNITS

Faculty of Applied Science ***Degree program information:*** Part-time programs available. Part-time. Offers applied science (M Arch, M Eng, M Sc, MA Sc, MASA,

MASLA, MLA, MSN, MSS, PhD); chemical engineering (M Eng, M Sc, MA Sc, PhD); civil engineering (M Eng, MA Sc, PhD); electrical and computer engineering (M Eng, MA Sc, PhD); materials and metallurgy (M Sc, PhD); mechanical engineering (M Eng, MA Sc, PhD); metals and materials engineering (MA Sc, PhD); mining engineering (M Eng, MA Sc, PhD); nursing (MSN, PhD); software systems (MSS). Electronic applications accepted.

School of Architecture and Landscape Architecture Offers architecture (M Arch, MASA); landscape architecture (MASLA, MLA). Electronic applications accepted.

Faculty of Arts Offers ancient culture, religion, and ethnicity (MA); anthropology (MA, PhD); art history (MA, PhD, Diploma); arts (M Mus, M Sc, MA, MAS, MFA, MJ, MLIS, MSW, DMA, PhD, CAS, Diploma); Asian studies (MA, PhD); behavioral neuroscience (MA, PhD); classical and near eastern archaeology (MA); classics (MA, PhD); clinical psychology (MA, PhD); cognitive science (MA, PhD); creative writing (MFA); creative writing and film production (MFA); creative writing and theatre (MFA); critical and curatorial studies (MA); developmental psychology (MA, PhD); economics (MA, PhD); English (MA, PhD); film (MA, MFA, Diploma); film production (MFA, Diploma); film studies (MA); French (MA, PhD); geography (M Sc, MA, PhD); Germanic studies (MA, PhD); health psychology (MA, PhD); Hispanic studies (MA, PhD); history (MA, PhD); linguistics (MA, PhD); philosophy (MA, PhD); political science (MA, PhD); quantitative methods (MA, PhD); religious studies (MA, PhD); social/personality psychology (MA, PhD); sociology (MA, PhD); theatre (MA, MFA, PhD); theatre design (MFA); theatre directing (MFA); visual art (MFA). Electronic applications accepted.

Institute for Gender, Race, Sexuality, and Social Justice Offers gender, race, sexuality, and social justice (MA, PhD).

School of Journalism Offers journalism (MJ). Electronic applications accepted.

School of Library, Archival and Information Studies Degree program information: Part-time programs available. Part-time. Offers archival studies (MAS); children's literature (MA); library and information studies (MLIS); library, archival and information studies (PhD). Electronic applications accepted.

School of Music Degree program information: Part-time programs available. Part-time. Offers music (M Mus, MA, DMA, PhD). Electronic applications accepted.

School of Social Work Offers social work (MSW, PhD). Electronic applications accepted.

Faculty of Dentistry *Degree program information:* Part-time programs available. Part-time. Offers dental science (M Sc, PhD); dentistry (M Sc, DMD, PhD, Certificate, Diploma); periodontics (Diploma). Electronic applications accepted.

Faculty of Education *Degree program information:* Part-time and evening/weekend programs available. Part-time, evening/weekend, online learning. Offers adult education (M Ed, MA); adult learning and global change (M Ed); art education (M Ed, MA); business education (MA); counseling psychology (M Ed, MA, PhD); curriculum studies (M Ed, MA, PhD); development, learning and culture (PhD); education (M Ed, M Sc, MA, MET, MHK, Ed D, PhD, Diploma); educational administration (M Ed, MA); educational leadership and policy (Ed D); educational studies (PhD); guidance studies (Diploma); higher education (M Ed, MA); home economics education (M Ed, MA); human development, learning and culture (M Ed, MA); library education (M Ed); literacy education (M Ed, MA, PhD); math education (M Ed, MA); measurement and evaluation and research methodology (M Ed); measurement, evaluation and research methodology (MA); measurement, evaluation, and research methodology (PhD); modern language education (M Ed, MA, PhD); music education (M Ed, MA); physical education (M Ed, MA); school psychology (M Ed, MA, PhD); science education (M Ed, MA); social studies education (M Ed, MA); society, culture and politics in education (M Ed, MA); special education (M Ed, MA, PhD, Diploma); teaching English as a second language (M Ed, MA, PhD); technology studies education (M Ed, MA). Electronic applications accepted.

Centre for Cross-Faculty Inquiry in Education Degree program information: Part-time and evening/weekend programs available. Part-time, evening/weekend. Offers curriculum and instruction (M Ed, MA, PhD); early childhood education (M Ed, MA). Electronic applications accepted.

School of Human Kinetics Degree program information: Part-time programs available. Part-time. Offers human kinetics (M Sc, MA, MHK, PhD). Electronic applications accepted.

Faculty of Forestry Offers forestry (M Sc, MA Sc, MF, MSFM, PhD). Electronic applications accepted.

Faculty of Land and Food Systems *Degree program information:* Part-time programs available. Part-time. Offers agricultural economics (M Sc); applied animal biology (M Sc, PhD); food and resource economics (MFRE); food science (M Sc, MFS, PhD); human nutrition (M Sc, PhD); land and food systems (M Sc, MFRE, MFS, MLWS, PhD); land and water systems (MLWS); plant science (M Sc, PhD); soil science (M Sc, PhD). Electronic applications accepted.

Faculty of Law *Degree program information:* Part-time programs available. Part-time. Offers law (LL M, LL M CL, PhD). Electronic applications accepted.

Faculty of Medicine *Degree program information:* Part-time programs available. Part-time. Offers anesthesiology, pharmacology and therapeutics (M Sc, PhD); biochemistry and molecular biology (M Sc, PhD); cellular and physiological sciences (M Sc, PhD); experimental medicine (M Sc, PhD); experimental pathology (M Sc, PhD); genetic counselling (M Sc); medical genetics (M Sc, PhD); medicine (M Sc, MH Sc, MHA, MOT, MPH, MPT, MRSc, MD, PhD); occupational science and occupational therapy (MOT); reproductive and developmental sciences (M Sc, PhD); surgery (M Sc). Open only to Canadian residents.

School of Audiology and Speech Sciences Offers audiology and speech sciences (M Sc, PhD). Electronic applications accepted.

School of Population and Public Health Online learning. Offers health administration (MHA); health care and epidemiology (MH Sc, PhD); public health (MPH). Electronic applications accepted.

School of Rehabilitation Sciences Offers rehabilitation sciences (M Sc, MOT, MPT, MRSc, PhD). Electronic applications accepted.

Faculty of Pharmaceutical Sciences Offers pharmaceutical sciences (M Sc, PhD, Pharm D). Electronic applications accepted.

Faculty of Science *Degree program information:* Part-time programs available. Part-time. Offers astronomy (M Sc, PhD); atmospheric science (M Sc, PhD); botany (M Sc, PhD); chemistry (M Sc, PhD); computer science (M Sc, PhD); geological engineering (M Eng, MA Sc, PhD); geological sciences (M Sc, PhD); geophysics (M Sc, MA Sc, PhD); mathematics (M Sc, MA, PhD); microbiology and immunology (M Sc, PhD); oceanography (M Sc, PhD); physics (M Sc, PhD); science (M Eng, M Sc, MA, MA Sc, PhD); statistics (M Sc, PhD); zoology (M Sc, PhD). Electronic applications accepted.

Genetics Graduate Program Offers genetics (M Sc, PhD).

Institute of Applied Mathematics Offers applied mathematics (M Sc, PhD).

Institute of Asian Research Offers Asian research (MAAPPS). Electronic applications accepted.

Program in Resource Management and Environmental Studies Offers resource management and environmental studies (M Sc, MA, PhD). Electronic applications accepted.

Sauder School of Business *Degree program information:* Part-time and evening/weekend programs available. Part-time, evening/weekend. Offers accounting (PhD); business (IMBA, M Sc, MBA, MM, PhD); finance (PhD); management information systems (PhD); management science (PhD); marketing (PhD); operations research (MM); organizational behavior (PhD); strategy and business economics (PhD); transportation and logistics (PhD); urban land economics (PhD). Electronic applications accepted.

School of Community and Regional Planning Offers community and regional planning (M Sc P, MAP, PhD). Electronic applications accepted.

School of Environmental Health *Degree program information:* Part-time programs available. Part-time. Offers environmental health (M Sc, PhD). Electronic applications accepted.

UNIVERSITY OF CALGARY, Calgary, AB T2N 1N4, Canada

General Information Province-supported, coed, university. CGS member. *Graduate housing:* Rooms and/or apartments available on a first-come, first-served basis to single and married students. Housing application deadline: 3/31. *Research affiliation:* Alta Telecommunications Research Centre, Alberta Sulphur Research, Calgary Society for Students with Learning Difficulties, Canadian Institute of Resources Law, Canadian Music Centre, Canadian Energy Research Institute.

GRADUATE UNITS

Cumming School of Medicine *Degree program information:* Part-time programs available. Part-time. Offers biochemistry and molecular biology (M Sc, PhD); biomedical technology (MBT); cancer biology (M Sc, PhD); cardiovascular and respiratory sciences (M Sc, PhD); community health sciences (M Sc, PhD); critical care medicine (M Sc, PhD); gastrointestinal sciences (M Sc, PhD); joint injury and arthritis (M Sc, PhD); medicine (M Sc, MBT, MCM, MD, PhD); microbiology, immunology and infectious diseases (M Sc, PhD); molecular and medical genetics (M Sc, PhD); mountain medicine and high altitude physiology (M Sc, PhD); neuroscience (M Sc, PhD); pathologists' assistant (M Sc, PhD). Electronic applications accepted.

Faculty of Graduate Studies *Degree program information:* Part-time and evening/weekend programs available. Part-time, evening/weekend, online learning. Offers interdisciplinary research (M Sc, MA, PhD); resources and the environment (M Sc, MA, PhD).

Centre for Military and Strategic Studies Degree program information: Part-time programs available. Part-time. Offers military and strategic studies (MSS, PhD). PhD offered in special cases only.

Faculty of Arts Degree program information: Part-time and evening/weekend programs available. Part-time, evening/weekend. Offers anthropology (MA, PhD); archaeology (MA); art (MA, MFA); arts (MA, PhD); clinical psychology (M Sc, PhD); communication and culture (MA, MCS, PhD); design and technical theatre (MFA); directing (MFA); economics (MA, PhD); English (MA, PhD); French (MA, PhD); geography (M Sc, MA, MGIS, PhD); German (MA); Greek and Roman studies (MA, PhD); history (MA, PhD); linguistics (MA, PhD); music (M Mus, MA, PhD); philosophy (MA, PhD); playwriting (MFA); political science (MA, PhD); psychology (M Sc, PhD); religious studies (MA, PhD); sociology (MA, PhD); Spanish (MA, PhD); theatre studies (MFA). Electronic applications accepted.

Faculty of Environmental Design Offers architecture (M Arch); environmental design (M Env Des, PhD); planning (M Plan).

Faculty of Kinesiology Offers kinesiology (M Kin, M Sc, PhD). Electronic applications accepted.

Faculty of Nursing Degree program information: Part-time programs available. Part-time. Offers nursing (MN, PhD, PMD). Electronic applications accepted.

Faculty of Science Degree program information: Part-time programs available. Part-time. Offers analytical chemistry (M Sc, PhD); applied chemistry (M Sc, PhD); biological sciences (M Sc, PhD); computer science (M Sc, PhD); geology (M Sc, PhD); geophysics (M Sc, PhD); hydrology (M Sc, PhD); inorganic chemistry (M Sc, PhD); mathematics and statistics (M Sc, PhD); organic chemistry (M Sc, PhD); physical chemistry (M Sc, PhD); physics and astronomy (M Sc, PhD); polymer chemistry (M Sc, PhD); science (M Sc, PhD); software engineering (M Sc); theoretical chemistry (M Sc, PhD).

Faculty of Social Work Offers social work (MSW, PhD, Postgraduate Diploma). Electronic applications accepted.

Haskayne School of Business Degree program information: Part-time and evening/weekend programs available. Part-time, evening/weekend. Offers business (EMBA, MBA, PhD); business administration (EMBA, MBA); management (MBA, PhD).

Schulich School of Engineering Degree program information: Part-time and evening/weekend programs available. Part-time, evening/weekend. Offers avalanche mechanics (M Sc, PhD); biomedical engineering (M Sc, PhD); chemical engineering (M Eng, M Sc, PhD); civil engineering (M Eng, M Sc, PhD); electrical and computer engineering (M Eng, M Sc, PhD); energy and environment engineering (M Eng, M Sc, PhD); energy and environmental systems (M Eng, M Sc, PhD); engineering (M Eng, M Sc, MPM, PhD); environmental engineering (M Eng, M Sc, PhD); geomatics engineering (M Eng, M Sc, PhD); geotechnical engineering (M Eng, M Sc, PhD); materials science (M Eng, M Sc, PhD); mechanical and manufacturing engineering (M Eng, M Sc, PhD); petroleum engineering (M Eng, M Sc, PhD); project management (M Eng, M Sc, PhD); reservoir characterization (M Eng, M Sc); structures and solid mechanics (M Eng, M Sc, PhD); transportation engineering (M Eng, M Sc, PhD); water resources (M Eng, M Sc, PhD). Electronic applications accepted.

Werklund School of Education Degree program information: Part-time and evening/weekend programs available. Part-time, evening/weekend, online learning. Offers adult learning (M Ed, MA, Ed D, PhD); counseling psychology (M Sc, MC, PhD); curriculum and learning (M Ed, MA, Ed D, PhD); education (M Ed, M Sc, MA, MC, Ed D, PhD); educational leadership (M Ed, MA, Ed D, PhD); languages and diversity (M Ed, MA, Ed D, PhD); learning sciences (M Ed, MA, Ed D, PhD); school and applied child psychology (M Ed, M Sc, PhD). Electronic applications accepted.

Faculty of Law Offers law (LL M, JD, Postbaccalaureate Certificate); natural resources, energy and environmental law (LL M, Postbaccalaureate Certificate).

UNIVERSITY OF CALIFORNIA, BERKELEY, Berkeley, CA 94720-1500

General Information State-supported, coed, university. CGS member. *Graduate housing:* Rooms and/or apartments available to single and married students.

GRADUATE UNITS

Graduate Division ***Degree program information:*** Part-time and evening/weekend programs available. Part-time, evening/weekend. Offers Asian studies (PhD); bioengineering (PhD); comparative biochemistry (PhD); East Asian studies (MA); energy and resources (MA, MS, PhD); international and area studies (MA, PhD); Latin American studies (MA); neuroscience (PhD); Northeast Asian studies (MA); South Asian studies (MA); Southeast Asian studies (MA); vision science (MS, PhD).

College of Chemistry Offers chemical engineering (MS, PhD); chemistry (MS, PhD).

College of Engineering Offers applied science and technology (PhD); computer science (MS, PhD); electrical engineering (MS, PhD); engineering (M Eng, MS, D Eng, PhD); engineering and project management (M Eng, MS, D Eng, PhD); engineering science (M Eng, MS, PhD); environmental engineering (M Eng, MS, D Eng, PhD); geoengineering (M Eng, MS, D Eng, PhD); industrial engineering and operations research (M Eng, MS, D Eng, PhD); mechanical engineering (M Eng, MS, D Eng, PhD); nuclear engineering (M Eng, MS, D Eng, PhD); structural engineering, mechanics and materials (M Eng, MS, D Eng, PhD); transportation engineering (M Eng, MS, D Eng, PhD).

College of Environmental Design Offers architecture (M Arch); building science (MS, PhD); building structures, construction and materials (MS, PhD); city and regional planning (MCP, PhD); design (MA); design theories, methods, and practices (MS, PhD); environmental design (M Arch, MA, MCP, MLA, MS, MUD, PhD); environmental design in developing countries (MS, PhD); history of architecture and urbanism (MS, PhD); landscape architecture (MLA); landscape architecture and environmental planning (PhD); social and cultural processes in architecture and urbanism (MS, PhD); urban design (MUD).

College of Letters and Science Offers African American studies (PhD); ancient history and Mediterranean archaeology (MA, PhD); anthropology (MA, PhD); applied mathematics (PhD); art practice (MFA); astrophysics (PhD); biophysics (PhD); Buddhist studies (PhD); Chinese language (PhD); classical archaeology (MA, PhD); classics (MA, PhD); comparative literature (PhD); composition (PhD); Czech (PhD); demography (PhD); economics (PhD); endocrinology (MA, PhD); English (PhD); ethnic studies (PhD); ethnomusicology (PhD); folklore (MA); French (PhD); geography (PhD); geology (MA, MS, PhD); geophysics (MA, MS, PhD); German (PhD); Greek (MA); Hindi (MA, PhD); Hispanic languages and literature (PhD); history (PhD); history of art (PhD); Indonesian (MA, PhD); integrative biology (PhD); Italian (PhD); Italian studies (PhD); Japanese language (PhD); Jewish studies (PhD); Latin (MA); letters and science (MA, MFA, MS, PhD); linguistics (PhD); logic and the methodology of science (PhD); mathematics (MA, PhD); medical anthropology (PhD); molecular and cell biology (PhD); musicology (PhD); Near Eastern religions (PhD); Near Eastern studies (MA, PhD); performance studies (PhD); philosophy (PhD); physics (PhD); Polish (PhD); political science (PhD); psychology (PhD); rhetoric (PhD); Russian (PhD); Sanskrit (MA, PhD); Scandinavian languages and literatures (PhD); Serbo-Croatian (PhD); sociology (PhD); sociology and demography (MA, PhD); Spanish (PhD); statistics (MA, PhD); Tamil (MA, PhD). Electronic applications accepted.

College of Natural Resources Offers agricultural and resource economics (PhD); environmental science, policy, and management (MS, PhD); forestry (MF); microbiology (PhD); molecular and biochemical nutrition (PhD); molecular toxicology (PhD); natural resources (MF, MS, PhD); plant biology (PhD); range management (MS).

Graduate School of Journalism Offers journalism (MJ).

Graduate School of Public Policy Offers public policy (MPP, PhD).

Haas School of Business Students: 648 full-time (257 women), 932 part-time (253 women); includes 457 minority (18 Black or African American, non-Hispanic/Latino; 1 American Indian or Alaska Native, non-Hispanic/Latino; 373 Asian, non-Hispanic/Latino; 37 Hispanic/Latino; 1 Native Hawaiian or other Pacific Islander, non-Hispanic/Latino; 27 Two or more races, non-Hispanic/Latino), 253 international. *Faculty:* 84 full-time (20 women), 149 part-time/adjunct (35 women). *Financial support:* Application deadline: 3/1. *Degree program information:* Part-time and evening/weekend programs available. Part-time, evening/weekend. Offers accounting (PhD); business (EMBA, MBA, MFE, PhD); business administration (EMBA, MBA, PhD); business and public policy (PhD); finance (PhD); financial engineering (MFE); management of organizations (PhD); marketing (PhD); real estate (PhD). *Dean,* Richard K. Lyons, 510-643-2027, Fax: 510-642-9128, E-mail: lyons@haas.berkeley.edu.

School of Education Offers development in mathematics and science (MA); education (MA, PhD); education in mathematics, science, and technology (MA, PhD); human development and education (MA, PhD); science and mathematics education (PhD); special education (PhD).

School of Information Offers information (MIMS, PhD).

School of Public Health Offers biostatistics (MA, PhD); environmental health sciences (MPH, MS, Dr PH, PhD); epidemiology (MS, PhD); health policy (PhD); infectious diseases (MPH, PhD); infectious diseases and immunity (PhD); public health (MA, MPH, MS, Dr PH, PhD).

School of Social Welfare Offers social welfare (MSW, PhD).

School of Law Offers jurisprudence and social policy (PhD); law (LL M, JD, JSD).

School of Optometry Offers optometry (OD, Certificate). Electronic applications accepted.

UC Berkeley Extension ***Degree program information:*** Part-time and evening/weekend programs available. Part-time, evening/weekend, online learning. Offers accounting (Certificate); alcohol and drug abuse studies (Certificate); business administration (Certificate); clinical research conduct and management (Certificate); college admissions and career planning (Certificate); construction management (Certificate); finance (Certificate); global business management (Certificate); human resource management (Certificate); HVAC (Certificate); information systems and management (Postbaccalaureate Certificate); integrated circuit design and techniques (online) (Certificate); interior design and interior architecture (Certificate); landscape architecture (Certificate); leadership in sustainability and environmental management (Professional Certificate); management (Certificate); marketing (Certificate); project management (Certificate); solar energy and green building (Professional Certificate); sustainable design (Professional Certificate); teaching English as a second language (Certificate); UNIX/LINUX system administration (Certificate); visual arts (Postbaccalaureate Certificate); writing (Postbaccalaureate Certificate).

UNIVERSITY OF CALIFORNIA, DAVIS, Davis, CA 95616

General Information State-supported, coed, university. CGS member. *Graduate housing:* Rooms and/or apartments available to single and married students. Housing application deadline: 4/1.

GRADUATE UNITS

College of Engineering ***Degree program information:*** Part-time programs available. Part-time. Offers aeronautical engineering (M Engr, MS, D Engr, PhD, Certificate); applied science (MS, PhD); biological systems engineering (M Engr, MS, D Engr, PhD); biomedical engineering (MS, PhD); chemical engineering (MS, PhD); civil and environmental engineering (M Engr, MS, D Engr, PhD, Certificate); computer science (MS, PhD); electrical and computer engineering (MS, PhD); engineering (M Engr, MS, D Engr, PhD, Certificate); materials science and engineering (MS, PhD); mechanical engineering (M Engr, MS, D Engr, PhD, Certificate); transportation, technology and policy (MS, PhD). Electronic applications accepted.

Graduate School of Management Students: 134 full-time (53 women), 424 part-time (166 women); includes 200 minority (9 Black or African American, non-Hispanic/Latino; 120 Asian, non-Hispanic/Latino; 45 Hispanic/Latino; 4 Native Hawaiian or other Pacific Islander, non-Hispanic/Latino; 22 Two or more races, non-Hispanic/Latino), 74 international. Average age 29. 1,048 applicants, 27% accepted, 209 enrolled. *Faculty:* 31 full-time (11 women), 39 part-time/adjunct (9 women). *Financial support:* In 2015–16, 102 students received support. Fellowships, teaching assistantships with partial tuition reimbursements available, career-related internships or fieldwork, institutionally sponsored loans, scholarships/grants, health care benefits, tuition waivers (partial), and unspecified assistantships available. Financial award application deadline: 3/1; financial award applicants required to submit FAFSA. In 2015, 233 master's awarded. *Degree program information:* Part-time and evening/weekend programs available. Part-time, evening/weekend. Offers business administration (MBA); management (MBA, MP Ac); professional accountancy (MP Ac). *Application deadline:* For fall admission, 11/4 priority date for domestic and international students. *Application fee:* $125. Electronic applications accepted. *Application Contact:* Kathy Gleed, Senior Director of Admissions, 530-752-7658, Fax: 530-754-9355, E-mail: admissions@gsm.ucdavis.edu. *Senior Assistant Dean of Student Affairs,* James Stevens, 530-752-7658, Fax: 530-754-9355, E-mail: admissions@gsm.ucdavis.edu.

Graduate Studies Offers acting (MFA); agricultural and environmental chemistry (MS, PhD); agricultural and resource economics (MS, PhD); animal behavior (PhD); animal biology (MAM, MS, PhD); anthropology (MA, PhD); applied linguistics (MA, PhD); applied mathematics (MS, PhD); art (MFA); art history (MA); atmospheric sciences (MS, PhD); avian sciences (MS); biochemistry and molecular biology (MS, PhD); biophysics (MS, PhD); biostatistics (MS, PhD); cell and developmental biology (MS, PhD); chemistry (MS, PhD); child development (MS); clinical research (MAS); communication (MA); community development (MS); comparative literature (PhD); comparative pathology (MS, PhD); composition (MA, PhD); conducting (MA, PhD); creative writing (MA); cultural studies (MA, PhD); dramatic art (PhD); ecology (MS, PhD); economics (MA, PhD); education (MA, Ed D); English (MA, PhD); entomology (MS, PhD); epidemiology (MS, PhD); exercise science (MS); food science (MS, PhD); forensic science (MS); French (PhD); genetics (MS, PhD); geography (MA, PhD); geology (MS, PhD); German (MA, PhD); health informatics (MS); history (MA, PhD); horticulture and agronomy (MS); human development (PhD); hydrologic sciences (MS, PhD); immunology (MS, PhD); instructional studies (PhD); integrated pest management (MS); international agricultural development (MS); linguistics (MA); mathematics (MA, MAT, PhD); microbiology (MS, PhD); molecular, cellular and integrative physiology (MS, PhD); musicology (MA, PhD); Native American studies (MA, PhD); neuroscience (PhD); nutrition (MS, PhD); pharmacology/toxicology (MS, PhD); philosophy (MA, PhD); physics (MS, PhD); plant biology (MS, PhD); plant pathology (MS, PhD); political science (MA, PhD); population biology (PhD); psychological studies (PhD); psychology (PhD); sociocultural studies (PhD); sociology (MA, PhD); soils and biogeochemistry (MS, PhD); Spanish (MA, PhD); statistics (MS, PhD); textile arts and costume design (MFA); textiles (MS); viticulture and enology (MS, PhD). Electronic applications accepted.

School of Law Students: 494 full-time (264 women); includes 186 minority (6 Black or African American, non-Hispanic/Latino; 88 Asian, non-Hispanic/Latino; 58 Hispanic/Latino; 1 Native Hawaiian or other Pacific Islander, non-Hispanic/Latino; 33 Two or more races, non-Hispanic/Latino), 27 international. Average age 24. 2,996 applicants, 31% accepted, 180 enrolled. *Faculty:* 43 full-time (18 women), 21 part-time/adjunct (7 women). *Financial support:* In 2015–16, 359 students received support, including 6 research assistantships with partial tuition reimbursements available, 38 teaching assistantships with partial tuition reimbursements available; Federal Work-Study, institutionally sponsored loans, scholarships/grants, and health care benefits also available. Financial award application deadline: 3/2; financial award applicants required to submit FAFSA. In 2015, 186 doctorates awarded. Offers law (LL M, JD). *Application deadline:* For fall admission, 3/15 priority date for domestic students, 3/15 for international students. Applications are processed on a rolling basis. *Application fee:* $0. Electronic applications accepted. *Application Contact:* Kristen Mercado, JD, Director, Admissions, 530-752-6477, Fax: 530-754-8371, E-mail: admissions@law.ucdavis.edu. *Dean,* Kevin R. Johnson, 530-752-0243, Fax: 530-752-7279, E-mail: krjohnson@ucdavis.edu.

School of Medicine Offers medicine (MD). Electronic applications accepted.

School of Veterinary Medicine Offers preventive veterinary medicine (MPVM); veterinary medicine (MPVM, DVM, Certificate).

UNIVERSITY OF CALIFORNIA, HASTINGS COLLEGE OF THE LAW, San Francisco, CA 94102-4978

General Information State-supported, coed, graduate-only institution. *Graduate housing:* Rooms and/or apartments available on a first-come, first-served basis to single and married students.

GRADUATE UNITS

Graduate Programs Offers law (LL M, MSL, JD). Electronic applications accepted.

UNIVERSITY OF CALIFORNIA, IRVINE, Irvine, CA 92697

General Information State-supported, coed, university. CGS member. *Graduate housing:* Rooms and/or apartments available on a first-come, first-served basis to single and married students. *Student services:* Campus employment opportunities, campus safety program, career counseling, child daycare facilities, exercise/wellness program, free psychological counseling, grant writing training, international student services, low-cost health insurance, multicultural affairs office, services for students with disabilities, teacher training, writing training. *Library:* Langson Library plus 4 others. *Collection:* Books: 2.2 million (physical), 1.1 million (digital/electronic); Serial titles: 4,801 (physical), 149,915 (digital/electronic); Databases: 1,241. Study areas open 24 hours, 5–7 days a week; students can reserve study rooms.

Computer facilities: 1,500 computers available on campus for general student use. A campuswide network can be accessed from student residence rooms and from off campus. Online class registration is available.
Website: http://www.uci.edu/

General Application Contact: Sheree McPeak, Student Affairs Officer, Graduate Division, 949-824-4611, Fax: 949-824-9096, E-mail: ymcpeak@uci.edu.

GRADUATE UNITS

Claire Trevor School of the Arts Students: 138 full-time (82 women), 6 part-time (3 women); includes 50 minority (6 Black or African American, non-Hispanic/Latino; 11 Asian, non-Hispanic/Latino; 20 Hispanic/Latino; 13 Two or more races, non-Hispanic/Latino), 9 international. Average age 29. 397 applicants, 16% accepted, 46 enrolled. *Financial support:* Fellowships, teaching assistantships, institutionally sponsored loans, traineeships, health care benefits, and unspecified assistantships available. Financial award application deadline: 3/1; financial award applicants required to submit FAFSA. In 2015, 44 master's, 2 doctorates awarded. Offers accompanying (MFA); acting (MFA); art (MFA); arts (MFA, PhD); choral conducting (MFA); composition and technology (MFA); dance (MFA); design and stage management (MFA); directing (MFA); drama (MFA); drama and theatre (PhD); guitar/lute performance (MFA); instrumental performance (MFA); jazz instrumental/composition (MFA); piano performance (MFA); vocal performance (MFA). *Application deadline:* For fall admission, 1/15 for domestic and international students. Applications are processed on a rolling basis. *Application fee:* $90 ($110 for international students). Electronic applications accepted. *Application Contact:* Prof. Vincent Olivieri, Associate Dean, 949-824-5684, Fax: 949-824-2450, E-mail: olivieri@uci.edu. *Interim Dean*, Dr. Stephen Barker, 949-824-8792, Fax: 949-824-2450, E-mail: barker@uci.edu.

Donald Bren School of Information and Computer Sciences Students: 429 full-time (117 women), 37 part-time (8 women); includes 44 minority (1 Black or African American, non-Hispanic/Latino; 31 Asian, non-Hispanic/Latino; 6 Hispanic/Latino; 6 Two or more races, non-Hispanic/Latino), 339 international. Average age 27. 3,626 applicants, 12% accepted, 171 enrolled. *Financial support:* Fellowships, research assistantships with full tuition reimbursements, teaching assistantships, institutionally sponsored loans, traineeships, health care benefits, and unspecified assistantships available. Financial award applicants required to submit FAFSA. In 2015, 123 master's, 40 doctorates awarded. Offers computer science (MS, PhD); informatics (MS, PhD); information and computer science (MS, PhD); networked systems (MS, PhD); statistics (MS, PhD). *Application deadline:* For fall admission, 12/15 for domestic and international students. *Application fee:* $90 ($110 for international students). Electronic applications accepted. *Application Contact:* Kris Bolcer, Director of Student Affairs, 949-824-5156, Fax: 949-824-4163, E-mail: kbolcer@uci.edu. *Dean*, Prof. Hal S. Stern, 949-824-7405, Fax: 949-824-3976, E-mail: sternh@uci.edu.

Francisco J. Ayala School of Biological Sciences Students: 290 full-time (151 women), 2 part-time (1 woman); includes 114 minority (5 Black or African American, non-Hispanic/Latino; 1 American Indian or Alaska Native, non-Hispanic/Latino; 57 Asian, non-Hispanic/Latino; 38 Hispanic/Latino; 1 Native Hawaiian or other Pacific Islander, non-Hispanic/Latino; 12 Two or more races, non-Hispanic/Latino), 36 international. Average age 27. 837 applicants, 19% accepted, 82 enrolled. *Financial support:* Fellowships with full tuition reimbursements, research assistantships with full tuition reimbursements, teaching assistantships with full tuition reimbursements, career-related internships or fieldwork, institutionally sponsored loans, scholarships/grants, traineeships, health care benefits, and unspecified assistantships available. Financial award application deadline: 3/1; financial award applicants required to submit FAFSA. In 2015, 34 master's, 36 doctorates awarded. Offers biological science (MS); biological sciences (MS, PhD); biological sciences and educational media design (MS); biotechnology (MS); biotechnology management (MS); interdisciplinary cellular and molecular biosciences (PhD); mathematical, computational and systems biology (PhD); neuroscience (PhD). *Application deadline:* For fall admission, 12/15 for domestic and international students. Applications are processed on a rolling basis. *Application fee:* $90 ($110 for international students). Electronic applications accepted. *Application Contact:* Prof. R. Michael Mulligan, Associate Dean, 949-824-8433, Fax: 949-824-4709, E-mail: rmmullig@uci.edu. *Dean*, Prof. Frank Laferla, 949-824-5315, Fax: 949-824-3035, E-mail: laferla@uci.edu.

Henry Samueli School of Engineering Students: 909 full-time (292 women), 96 part-time (25 women); includes 175 minority (7 Black or African American, non-Hispanic/Latino; 1 American Indian or Alaska Native, non-Hispanic/Latino; 113 Asian, non-Hispanic/Latino; 39 Hispanic/Latino; 15 Two or more races, non-Hispanic/Latino), 623 international. Average age 26. 4,725 applicants, 20% accepted, 336 enrolled. *Financial support:* Fellowships with tuition reimbursements, research assistantships with full tuition reimbursements, teaching assistantships with tuition reimbursements, institutionally sponsored loans, traineeships, health care benefits, and unspecified assistantships available. Financial award application deadline: 3/1; financial award applicants required to submit FAFSA. In 2015, 313 master's, 87 doctorates awarded. *Degree program information:* Part-time programs available. Part-time. Offers biomedical engineering (MS, PhD); chemical and biochemical engineering (MS, PhD); civil and environmental engineering (MS, PhD); electrical engineering and computer science (MS, PhD); engineering (MS, PhD); engineering management (MS); materials science and engineering (MS, PhD); mechanical and aerospace engineering (MS, PhD); networked systems (MS, PhD). *Application deadline:* For fall admission, 1/15 priority date for domestic students, 1/15 for international students. Applications are processed on a rolling basis. *Application fee:* $90 ($110 for international students). Electronic applications accepted. *Application Contact:* Jean Bennett, Director of Graduate Student Affairs, 949-824-6475, Fax: 949-824-8200, E-mail: jean.bennett@uci.edu. *Dean*, Gregory N. Washington, 949-824-4333, Fax: 949-824-8200, E-mail: engineering@uci.edu.

Institute of Transportation Studies Students: 14 full-time (6 women); includes 3 minority (all Asian, non-Hispanic/Latino), 10 international. Average age 29. 32 applicants, 53% accepted, 6 enrolled. *Financial support:* Fellowships, research assistantships with full tuition reimbursements, teaching assistantships, institutionally sponsored loans, traineeships, health care benefits, and unspecified assistantships available. Financial award application deadline: 3/1. In 2015, 2 master's, 3 doctorates awarded. Offers transportation studies (MA, PhD). *Application deadline:* For fall admission, 1/15 for domestic and international students. *Application fee:* $90 ($110 for international students). *Application Contact:* Anne Marie DeFeo, Administrative Manager, 949-824-6564, E-mail: amdefeo@uci.edu. *Director*, Jean-Daniel Saphores, 949-824-4214, Fax: 949-824-8385, E-mail: sritchie@uci.edu.

The Paul Merage School of Business Students: 526 full-time (202 women), 288 part-time (111 women); includes 312 minority (13 Black or African American, non-Hispanic/Latino; 29 American Indian or Alaska Native, non-Hispanic/Latino; 256 Asian, non-Hispanic/Latino; 11 Hispanic/Latino; 3 Native Hawaiian or other Pacific Islander, non-Hispanic/Latino), 239 international. Average age 33. 2,079 applicants, 29% accepted, 336 enrolled. *Financial support:* Career-related internships or fieldwork, Federal Work-Study, institutionally sponsored loans, scholarships/grants, traineeships, health care benefits, and unspecified assistantships available. Support available to part-time students. Financial award application deadline: 3/1; financial award applicants required to submit FAFSA. In 2015, 392 master's, 6 doctorates awarded. *Degree program information:* Part-time and evening/weekend programs available. Part-time, evening/weekend. Offers business (EMBA, MBA, MPA, PhD); business administration (EMBA, MBA); health care administration (MBA); management (PhD); professional accountancy (MPA). *Application deadline:* For fall admission, 1/2 priority date for domestic and international students. Applications are processed on a rolling basis. *Application fee:* $90 ($110 for international students). Electronic applications accepted. *Dean*, Eric Spangenberg, 949-824-8470, E-mail: ers@uci.edu.

Programs in Health Sciences Students: 79 full-time (63 women), 25 part-time (21 women); includes 54 minority (3 Black or African American, non-Hispanic/Latino; 28 Asian, non-Hispanic/Latino; 15 Hispanic/Latino; 8 Two or more races, non-Hispanic/Latino), 11 international. Average age 29. 377 applicants, 42% accepted, 56 enrolled. In 2015, 30 master's awarded. Offers health sciences (MPH, MSN, PhD); medicinal chemistry and pharmacology (PhD); nursing science (MSN); public health (MPH, PhD). *Application fee:* $80 ($100 for international students). *Application Contact:* Sheree McPeak, Graduate Division, 949-824-4611, Fax: 949-824-9096, E-mail: ogsfront@uci.edu.

School of Education Students: 274 full-time (211 women); includes 138 minority (2 Black or African American, non-Hispanic/Latino; 76 Asian, non-Hispanic/Latino; 45 Hispanic/Latino; 1 Native Hawaiian or other Pacific Islander, non-Hispanic/Latino; 14 Two or more races, non-Hispanic/Latino), 16 international. Average age 27. 601 applicants, 59% accepted, 216 enrolled. *Financial support:* Fellowships, research assistantships with full tuition reimbursements, institutionally sponsored loans, traineeships, health care benefits, and unspecified assistantships available. Financial award application deadline: 3/1; financial award applicants required to submit FAFSA. In 2015, 152 master's, 9 doctorates awarded. *Degree program information:* Part-time and evening/weekend programs available. Part-time, evening/weekend. Offers educational administration (Ed D); educational administration and leadership (Ed D); elementary and secondary education (MAT). *Application deadline:* For fall admission, 1/2 priority date for domestic students, 1/2 for international students. *Application fee:* $90 ($110 for international students). Electronic applications accepted. *Application Contact:* Denise Earley, Assistant Director of Student Affairs, 949-824-4022, E-mail: denise.earley@uci.edu. *Interim Dean*, Mark Warschauer, 949-824-2526, Fax: 949-824-9103, E-mail: markw@uci.edu.

School of Humanities Students: 277 full-time (145 women), 4 part-time (3 women); includes 95 minority (8 Black or African American, non-Hispanic/Latino; 21 Asian, non-Hispanic/Latino; 39 Hispanic/Latino; 27 Two or more races, non-Hispanic/Latino), 24 international. Average age 32. 1,045 applicants, 10% accepted, 52 enrolled. *Financial support:* Fellowships with tuition reimbursements, research assistantships with full tuition reimbursements, teaching assistantships with tuition reimbursements, institutionally sponsored loans, traineeships, health care benefits, and unspecified assistantships available. Financial award application deadline: 3/1; financial award applicants required to submit FAFSA. In 2015, 66 master's, 45 doctorates awarded. Offers Chinese (MA, PhD); classics (MA, PhD); comparative literature (MA, PhD); creative writing (MFA); culture and theory (PhD); East Asian languages and literatures (MA, PhD); English (MA, PhD); English and American literature (PhD); French (MA, PhD); German (MA, PhD); history (MA, PhD); humanities (MA, MAT, MFA, PhD); Japanese (MA, PhD); philosophy (MA, PhD); Spanish (MA, MAT, PhD); visual studies (MA, PhD); writing (MFA). *Application deadline:* For fall admission, 1/15 for domestic and international students. Applications are processed on a rolling basis. *Application fee:* $90 ($110 for international students). Electronic applications accepted. *Application Contact:* Amy Fujitani, Director of Graduate Student Affairs, 949-824-4303, Fax: 949-824-1360, E-mail: amy.fujitani@uci.edu. *Dean*, Georges Abbeele, 949-824-5133, E-mail: gvandena@uci.edu.

School of Law Offers law (JD). *Application deadline:* For fall admission, 3/1 for domestic students. *Application fee:* $0. Electronic applications accepted. *Dean*, Erwin Chemerinsky, 949-824-7722, E-mail: echemerinsky@law.uci.edu.

School of Medicine Students: 581 full-time (299 women), 44 part-time (23 women); includes 115 minority (8 Black or African American, non-Hispanic/Latino; 3 American Indian or Alaska Native, non-Hispanic/Latino; 61 Asian, non-Hispanic/Latino; 40 Hispanic/Latino; 3 Two or more races, non-Hispanic/Latino), 25 international. Average age 29. 255 applicants, 21% accepted, 29 enrolled. *Financial support:* Fellowships, research assistantships with full tuition reimbursements, teaching assistantships, career-related internships or fieldwork, institutionally sponsored loans, traineeships, health care benefits, and unspecified assistantships available. Financial award application deadline: 3/1; financial award applicants required to submit FAFSA. In 2015, 21 master's, 20 doctorates awarded. Offers biological sciences (MS, PhD); biomedical and translational science (MS); environmental health sciences (MS); environmental toxicology (PhD); epidemiology (MS, PhD); experimental pathology (PhD); exposure sciences and risk assessment (PhD); genetic counseling (MS); medicine (MS, MD, PhD); pharmacological sciences (PhD). *Application deadline:* For fall admission, 1/15 for domestic and international students. *Application fee:* $90 ($110 for international students). Electronic applications accepted. *Application Contact:* Leora Fellus, Graduate Studies Director, 949-824-1028, E-mail: lfellus@uci.edu. *Interim Dean*, Dr. Michael Stamos, 949-824-6262, Fax: 949-824-6377, E-mail: mstamos@uci.edu.

School of Physical Sciences Students: 510 full-time (138 women), 10 part-time (2 women); includes 129 minority (3 Black or African American, non-Hispanic/Latino; 2 American Indian or Alaska Native, non-Hispanic/Latino; 71 Asian, non-Hispanic/Latino; 31 Hispanic/Latino; 1 Native Hawaiian or other Pacific Islander, non-Hispanic/Latino; 21 Two or more races, non-Hispanic/Latino), 108 international. Average age 27. 1,025 applicants, 27% accepted, 84 enrolled. *Financial support:* Fellowships, research assistantships with full tuition reimbursements, teaching assistantships, career-related internships or fieldwork, institutionally sponsored loans, traineeships, health care benefits, and unspecified assistantships available. Financial award application deadline: 3/1; financial award applicants required to submit FAFSA. In 2015, 67 master's, 71 doctorates awarded. Offers chemical and materials physics (MS, PhD); chemistry (MS, PhD); earth system science (MS, PhD); mathematics (MS, PhD); physical sciences (MS, PhD); physics (MS, PhD). *Application deadline:* For fall admission, 1/15 priority date for domestic and international students. Applications are processed on a rolling basis. *Application fee:* $90 ($110 for international students). Electronic applications accepted. *Application Contact:* Prof. Roger McWilliams, Associate Dean, 949-824-6228, Fax: 949-824-2174, E-mail: mcw@uci.edu. *Dean*, Kenneth C. Janda, 949-824-6022, Fax: 949-824-2261, E-mail: kcjanda@uci.edu.

School of Social Ecology Students: 285 full-time (180 women), 51 part-time (26 women); includes 140 minority (14 Black or African American, non-Hispanic/Latino; 2 American Indian or Alaska Native, non-Hispanic/Latino; 43 Asian, non-Hispanic/Latino; 62 Hispanic/Latino; 19 Two or more races, non-Hispanic/Latino), 41 international. Average age 29. 618 applicants, 37% accepted, 116 enrolled. *Financial support:* Fellowships, research assistantships with full tuition reimbursements, teaching assistantships, institutionally sponsored loans, traineeships, health care benefits, and unspecified assistantships available. Financial award application deadline: 3/1; financial award applicants required to submit FAFSA. In 2015, 97 master's, 17 doctorates awarded. Offers criminology, law and society (MAS, PhD); environmental analysis and design (PhD); epidemiology and public health (PhD); planning, policy and design (PhD); psychology and social behavior (PhD); social ecology (PhD); urban and regional planning (MURP). *Application deadline:* For fall admission, 1/15 priority date for domestic students, 1/15 for international students. Applications are processed on a rolling basis. *Application fee:* $90 ($110 for international students). Electronic applications accepted. *Application Contact:* Jennifer Craig, Director of Graduate Student Services, 949-824-5918, E-mail: craigj@uci.edu. *Dean,* Nancy Guerra, 949-824-6094, Fax: 949-824-1845, E-mail: nguerra1@uci.edu.

School of Social Sciences Students: 391 full-time (174 women), 2 part-time (1 woman); includes 113 minority (7 Black or African American, non-Hispanic/Latino; 2 American Indian or Alaska Native, non-Hispanic/Latino; 39 Asian, non-Hispanic/Latino; 47 Hispanic/Latino; 18 Two or more races, non-Hispanic/Latino), 46 international. Average age 28. 754 applicants, 25% accepted, 92 enrolled. *Financial support:* Fellowships, research assistantships with full tuition reimbursements, teaching assistantships, institutionally sponsored loans, traineeships, health care benefits, and unspecified assistantships available. Financial award application deadline: 3/1; financial award applicants required to submit FAFSA. In 2015, 64 master's, 54 doctorates awarded. Offers anthropology (MA, PhD); demographic and social analysis (MA); economics (MA, PhD); philosophy (PhD); political psychology (PhD); political sciences (PhD); psychology (PhD); public choice (MA, PhD); social networks (PhD); social science (PhD); social sciences (MA, PhD); sociology and social relations (PhD); transportation economics (MA, PhD). *Application deadline:* For fall admission, 1/15 priority date for domestic students, 1/15 for international students. Applications are processed on a rolling basis. *Application fee:* $90 ($110 for international students). Electronic applications accepted. *Application Contact:* John Sommerhauser, Graduate Affairs Director, 949-824-4074, E-mail: saberi@uci.edu. *Dean,* Bill Maurer, 949-824-6802, E-mail: wmmaurer@uci.edu.

Institute for Mathematical Behavioral Sciences Students: 9 full-time (2 women); includes 3 minority (1 Asian, non-Hispanic/Latino; 1 Hispanic/Latino; 1 Two or more races, non-Hispanic/Latino), 2 international. Average age 32. 10 applicants, 40% accepted, 3 enrolled. *Financial support:* Fellowships, research assistantships with full tuition reimbursements, teaching assistantships, institutionally sponsored loans, traineeships, health care benefits, and unspecified assistantships available. Financial award application deadline: 3/1; financial award applicants required to submit FAFSA. In 2015, 2 master's, 1 doctorate awarded. Offers games, decisions, and dynamical systems (PhD); mathematical behavioral sciences (MA). *Application deadline:* For fall admission, 1/15 priority date for domestic students, 1/15 for international students. Applications are processed on a rolling basis. *Application fee:* $90 ($110 for international students). Electronic applications accepted. *Application Contact:* John Sommerhauser, Director of Graduate Affairs, 949-824-4074, E-mail: john.sommerhauser@uci.edu. *Graduate Program Director,* Louis Narens, 949-824-5360, E-mail: lnarens@uci.edu.

UNIVERSITY OF CALIFORNIA, LOS ANGELES, Los Angeles, CA 90095

General Information State-supported, coed, university. CGS member. *Graduate housing:* Rooms and/or apartments available on a first-come, first-served basis to single and married students.

GRADUATE UNITS

David Geffen School of Medicine Offers biological chemistry (MS, PhD); biomathematics (MS, PhD); biomedical physics (MS, PhD); cellular and molecular pathology (MS, PhD); clinical research (MS); experimental pathology (MS, PhD); human genetics (MS, PhD); medicine (MS, MD, PhD); microbiology, immunology and molecular genetics (MS, PhD); molecular and medical pharmacology (MS, PhD); neurobiology (MS, PhD); neuroscience (PhD); physiology (PhD). Electronic applications accepted.

Graduate Division Electronic applications accepted.

College of Letters and Science Offers Afro-American studies (MA); American Indian studies (MA); anthropology (MA, PhD); applied linguistics (PhD); applied linguistics and teaching English as a second language (MA); archaeology (MA, PhD); art history (MA, PhD); Asian languages and cultures (MA, PhD); Asian-American studies (MA); astronomy (MAT, MS, PhD); atmospheric and oceanic sciences (MS, PhD); biochemistry and molecular biology (MS, PhD); bioinformatics (MS, PhD); biological chemistry (PhD); cellular and molecular pathology (PhD); chemistry (MS, PhD); classics (MA, PhD); comparative literature (MA, PhD); conservation of archaeological and ethnographic materials (MA); ecology and evolutionary biology (MA, PhD); economics (MA, PhD); English (MA, PhD); French and Francophone studies (MA, PhD); gender studies (MA, PhD); geochemistry (MS, PhD); geography (MA, PhD); geology (MS, PhD); geophysics and space physics (MS, PhD); Germanic languages (MA, PhD); Greek (MA); Hispanic languages and literature (PhD); history (MA, PhD); human genetics (PhD); Indo-European studies (PhD); Italian (MA, PhD); Latin (MA); letters and science (MA, MAT, MS, PhD, Certificate); linguistics (MA, PhD); mathematics (MA, MAT, PhD); microbiology, immunology, and molecular genetics (PhD); molecular biology (PhD); molecular toxicology (PhD); molecular, cell and developmental biology (MA, PhD); molecular, cellular and integrative physiology (PhD); musicology (MA, PhD); Near Eastern languages and cultures (MA, PhD); neurobiology (PhD); oral biology (PhD); philosophy (MA, PhD); physics (MS, PhD); physiological science (MS); physiology (PhD); political science (MA, PhD); Portuguese (MA); psychology (MA, PhD); Scandinavian (MA); Slavic languages and literatures (MA, PhD); sociology (MA, PhD); Spanish (MA); statistics (MS, PhD); teaching English as a second language (Certificate). Electronic applications accepted.

Graduate School of Education and Information Studies ***Degree program information:*** Part-time and evening/weekend programs available. Part-time, evening/weekend. Offers archival studies (MLIS); education (M Ed, MA, Ed D, PhD); education and information studies (M Ed, MA, MLIS, Ed D, PhD, Certificate); educational leadership (Ed D); informatics (MLIS); information studies (PhD); library and information science (Certificate); library studies (MLIS); moving image archive studies (MA); rare books, print and visual culture (MLIS); special education (PhD). Electronic applications accepted.

Henry Samueli School of Engineering and Applied Science Students: 2,064 full-time (471 women); includes 503 minority (18 Black or African American, non-Hispanic/Latino; 3 American Indian or Alaska Native, non-Hispanic/Latino; 340 Asian, non-Hispanic/Latino; 106 Hispanic/Latino; 36 Two or more races, non-Hispanic/Latino), 1,131 international. 6,541 applicants, 28% accepted, 805 enrolled. *Faculty:* 164 full-time (23 women), 24 part-time/adjunct (1 woman). *Financial support:* In 2015–16, 617 fellowships, 1,502 research assistantships, 664 teaching assistantships were awarded; career-related internships or fieldwork, Federal Work-Study, institutionally sponsored loans, and tuition waivers (full and partial) also available. Financial award application deadline: 3/2; financial award applicants required to submit FAFSA. In 2015, 557 master's, 159 doctorates awarded. *Degree program information:* Evening/weekend programs available. Evening/weekend, 100% online. Offers aerospace engineering (MS, PhD); bioengineering (MS, PhD); chemical and biomolecular engineering (MS, PhD); civil and environmental engineering (MS, PhD); computer science (MS, PhD); electrical engineering (MS, PhD); engineering (MS); engineering and applied science (MS, PhD); manufacturing engineering (MS); materials science and engineering (MS, PhD); mechanical engineering (MS, PhD). *Application deadline:* For fall admission, 12/1 for domestic and international students. *Application fee:* $90 ($110 for international students). Electronic applications accepted. *Application Contact:* Jan LaBuda, Director, Office of Academic and Student Affairs, 310-825-2514, Fax: 310-825-2473, E-mail: jan@seas.ucla.edu. *Associate Dean, Academic and Student Affairs,* Dr. Richard D. Wesel, 310-825-2942, E-mail: wesel@ee.ucla.edu.

Institute of the Environment and Sustainability Offers environmental science and engineering (D Env).

International Institute Offers African studies (MA); East Asian studies (MA); Islamic studies (MA, PhD); Latin American studies (MA). Electronic applications accepted.

School of Nursing Offers nursing (MSN, PhD). Electronic applications accepted.

School of Public Affairs Offers public affairs (MA, MPP, MSW, PhD); public policy (MPP); social welfare (MSW, PhD); urban planning (MA, PhD). Electronic applications accepted.

School of Public Health Offers biostatistics (MPH, MS, Dr PH, PhD); environmental health sciences (MS, PhD); environmental science and engineering (D Env); epidemiology (MPH, MS, Dr PH, PhD); health services (MPH, MS, Dr PH, PhD); molecular toxicology (PhD); public health (MPH, MS, D Env, Dr PH, PhD). Electronic applications accepted.

School of the Arts and Architecture Offers architecture and urban design (M Arch, MA, PhD); art (MFA); arts and architecture (M Arch, MA, MFA, MM, DMA, PhD); composition (MA, PhD); culture and performance (MA, PhD); dance (MFA); design media arts (MFA); ethnomusicology (MA, PhD); performance (MM, DMA). Electronic applications accepted.

School of Theater, Film and Television Offers animation (MFA); cinema and media studies (MA, PhD); cinematography (MFA); film and television (MA, MFA, PhD); moving image archive studies (MA); production (MFA); screenwriting (MFA); theater (MA, MFA); theater and performance studies (PhD); theater, film and television (MA, MFA, PhD). Electronic applications accepted.

UCLA Anderson School of Management Students: 859 full-time (265 women), 1,192 part-time (345 women); includes 698 minority (43 Black or African American, non-Hispanic/Latino; 486 Asian, non-Hispanic/Latino; 70 Hispanic/Latino; 3 Native Hawaiian or other Pacific Islander, non-Hispanic/Latino; 96 Two or more races, non-Hispanic/Latino), 453 international. Average age 31. 5,868 applicants, 25% accepted, 900 enrolled. *Faculty:* 83 full-time (19 women), 98 part-time/adjunct (19 women). *Financial support:* In 2015–16, 648 students received support, including 470 fellowships (averaging $28,901 per year), 1 research assistantship (averaging $2,619 per year), 236 teaching assistantships with partial tuition reimbursements available (averaging $5,771 per year); career-related internships or fieldwork, institutionally sponsored loans, and scholarships/grants also available. Support available to part-time students. In 2015, 807 master's, 9 doctorates awarded. *Degree program information:* Part-time and evening/weekend programs available. Part-time, evening/weekend. Offers accounting (PhD); Asia Pacific (EMBA); business administration (EMBA, MBA); decisions, operations and technology management (PhD); finance (PhD); financial engineering (MFE); global economics and management (PhD); management and organizations (PhD); marketing (PhD); strategy and policy (PhD). *Application deadline:* For fall admission, 10/6 priority date for domestic and international students; for winter admission, 1/5 for domestic and international students; for spring admission, 4/12 for domestic and international students. Applications are processed on a rolling basis. *Application fee:* $200. Electronic applications accepted. *Application Contact:* Alex Lawrence, Assistant Dean, MBA Admissions and Financial Aid, 310-825-6944, Fax: 310-825-8582, E-mail: mba.admissions@anderson.ucla.edu. *Dean/Chair in Management,* Dr. Judy D. Olian, 310-825-7982, Fax: 310-206-2073, E-mail: judy.olian@anderson.ucla.edu.

School of Dentistry Offers dentistry (MS, DDS, PhD, Certificate); oral biology (MS, PhD). Electronic applications accepted.

School of Law Offers law (LL M, JD, SJD). Electronic applications accepted.

UNIVERSITY OF CALIFORNIA, MERCED, Merced, CA 95343

General Information State-supported, coed, university. CGS member. *Enrollment:* 6,685 graduate, professional, and undergraduate students; 447 full-time matriculated graduate/professional students (191 women), 1 part-time matriculated graduate/professional student. *Enrollment by degree level:* 42 master's, 406 doctoral. *Graduate faculty:* 202 full-time (77 women). Tuition, state resident: full-time $11,220; part-time $5610 per semester. Tuition, nonresident: full-time $26,322; part-time $13,161 per semester. *Required fees:* $1657; $1657 per year. *Graduate housing:* On-campus housing not available. *Student services:* Campus employment opportunities, campus safety program, career counseling, child daycare facilities, exercise/wellness program, free psychological counseling, grant writing training, international student services, low-cost health insurance, multicultural affairs office, services for students with disabilities, teacher training, writing training. *Library:* Kolligian Library. Students can reserve study rooms. *Research affiliation:* Genentech (genomics), American Heart Association (physiology, cell biology), Southern California Research Initiative for Solar Energy (solar energy), Jet Propulsion Laboratory (environmental monitoring via drone fleet), Yosemite and Sequoia National Parks (environmental systems, hydrology), Silicon Mechanics (computational science).

Computer facilities: 230 computers available on campus for general student use. A campuswide network can be accessed from student residence rooms and from off campus. Online class registration, student calendar, 10Gb online cloud storage, free office software are available.
Website: http://www.ucmerced.edu/

General Application Contact: Tsu Ya, Director of Admissions and Academic Services, 209-228-4521, Fax: 209-228-6906, E-mail: tya@ucmerced.edu.

GRADUATE UNITS

Graduate Division Students: 447 full-time (191 women), 1 part-time (0 women); includes 156 minority (9 Black or African American, non-Hispanic/Latino; 1 American Indian or Alaska Native, non-Hispanic/Latino; 57 Asian, non-Hispanic/Latino; 68 Hispanic/Latino; 3 Native Hawaiian or other Pacific Islander, non-Hispanic/Latino; 18 Two or more races, non-Hispanic/Latino), 122 international. Average age 29. 609 applicants, 48% accepted, 138 enrolled. *Faculty:* 202 full-time (77 women). *Financial support:* In 2015–16, 430 students received support, including 31 fellowships with full tuition reimbursements available (averaging $24,260 per year), 92 research assistantships with full tuition reimbursements available (averaging $18,842 per year), 304 teaching assistantships with full tuition reimbursements available (averaging $18,538 per year); scholarships/grants, traineeships, and health care benefits also available. Financial award application deadline: 1/15. In 2015, 33 master's, 30 doctorates awarded. *Application deadline:* For fall admission, 1/15 for domestic and international students. *Application fee:* $90 ($110 for international students). Electronic applications accepted. *Application Contact:* Tsu Ya, Director of Admissions and Academic Services, 209-228-4521, Fax: 209-228-6906, E-mail: tya@ucmerced.edu. *Dean,* Dr. Marjorie S. Zatz, 209-228-2408, E-mail: mzatz@ucmerced.edu.

School of Engineering Students: 143 full-time (40 women); includes 29 minority (2 Black or African American, non-Hispanic/Latino; 13 Asian, non-Hispanic/Latino; 10 Hispanic/Latino; 1 Native Hawaiian or other Pacific Islander, non-Hispanic/Latino; 3 Two or more races, non-Hispanic/Latino), 76 international. Average age 28. 235 applicants, 42% accepted, 47 enrolled. *Faculty:* 42 full-time (7 women). *Financial support:* In 2015–16, 135 students received support, including 12 fellowships with full tuition reimbursements available (averaging $24,231 per year), 32 research assistantships with full tuition reimbursements available (averaging $18,842 per year), 56 teaching assistantships with full tuition reimbursements available (averaging $18,538 per year); scholarships/grants, traineeships, and health care benefits also available. Financial award application deadline: 1/15. In 2015, 16 master's, 13 doctorates awarded. Offers biological engineering and small scale technologies (MS, PhD); electrical engineering and computer science (MS, PhD); environmental systems (MS, PhD); mechanical engineering (MS); mechanical engineering and applied mechanics (PhD). *Application deadline:* For fall admission, 1/15 priority date for domestic and international students. Applications are processed on a rolling basis. *Application fee:* $90 ($110 for international students). Electronic applications accepted. *Application Contact:* Tsu Ya, Director of Admissions and Academic Services, 209-228-4521, Fax: 209-228-6906, E-mail: tya@ucmerced.edu. *Dean,* Dr. Mark Matsumoto, Fax: 209-228-4047, E-mail: mmatsumoto@ucmerced.edu.

School of Natural Sciences Students: 156 full-time (64 women); includes 58 minority (3 Black or African American, non-Hispanic/Latino; 23 Asian, non-Hispanic/Latino; 22 Hispanic/Latino; 1 Native Hawaiian or other Pacific Islander, non-Hispanic/Latino; 9 Two or more races, non-Hispanic/Latino), 37 international. Average age 27. 199 applicants, 57% accepted, 45 enrolled. *Faculty:* 63 full-time (25 women). *Financial support:* In 2015–16, 151 students received support, including 12 fellowships with full tuition reimbursements available (averaging $23,614 per year), 37 research assistantships with full tuition reimbursements available (averaging $18,842 per year), 127 teaching assistantships with full tuition reimbursements available (averaging $18,538 per year); scholarships/grants, traineeships, and health care benefits also available. Financial award application deadline: 1/15. In 2015, 12 master's, 11 doctorates awarded. Offers applied mathematics (MS, PhD); chemistry and chemical biology (MS, PhD); physics (MS, PhD); quantitative and systems biology (MS, PhD). *Application deadline:* For fall admission, 1/15 for domestic and international students. *Application fee:* $90 ($110 for international students). Electronic applications accepted. *Application Contact:* Tsu Ya, Director of Graduate Admissions and Academic Services, 209-228-4521, Fax: 209-228-6906, E-mail: tya@ucmerced.edu. *Dean,* Dr. Juan C. Meza, 209-228-4487, Fax: 209-228-4060, E-mail: jcmeza@ucmerced.edu.

School of Social Sciences, Humanities and Arts Students: 148 full-time (87 women), 1 part-time (0 women); includes 60 minority (4 Black or African American, non-Hispanic/Latino; 1 American Indian or Alaska Native, non-Hispanic/Latino; 12 Asian, non-Hispanic/Latino; 36 Hispanic/Latino; 1 Native Hawaiian or other Pacific Islander, non-Hispanic/Latino; 6 Two or more races, non-Hispanic/Latino), 19 international. Average age 31. 175 applicants, 47% accepted, 46 enrolled. *Faculty:* 97 full-time (45 women). *Financial support:* In 2015–16, 144 students received support, including 7 fellowships with full tuition reimbursements available (averaging $25,417 per year), 12 research assistantships with full tuition reimbursements available (averaging $18,842 per year), 121 teaching assistantships with full tuition reimbursements available (averaging $18,538 per year); scholarships/grants, traineeships, and health care benefits also available. Financial award application deadline: 1/15. In 2015, 5 master's, 6 doctorates awarded. Offers cognitive and information sciences (PhD); interdisciplinary humanities (MA, PhD); psychological sciences (MA, PhD); social sciences (MA, PhD); sociology (MA, PhD). *Application deadline:* For fall admission, 1/15 for domestic and international students. *Application fee:* $90 ($110 for international students). Electronic applications accepted. *Application Contact:* Tsu Ya, Director of Admissions and Academic Services, 209-228-4521, Fax: 209-228-6906, E-mail: tya@ucmerced.edu. *Dean,* Dr. Jill Robbins, E-mail: jillrobbins@ucmerced.edu.

UNIVERSITY OF CALIFORNIA, RIVERSIDE, Riverside, CA 92521-0102

General Information State-supported, coed, university. CGS member. *Enrollment by degree level:* 909 master's, 2,008 doctoral, 181 other advanced degrees. *Graduate faculty:* 689 full-time (221 women). *International tuition:* $31,767.50 full-time. *Tuition, area resident:* Full-time $16,665.50; part-time $11,055.54. Tuition, state resident: full-time $16,665.50; part-time $11,055.54. Tuition, nonresident: full-time $31,768. *Required fees:* $16,665.50; $11,055.54 per quarter. $3685.18 per quarter. Tuition and fees vary according to program. *Graduate housing:* Rooms and/or apartments available on a first-come, first-served basis to single and married students. Housing application deadline: 6/1. *Student services:* Campus safety program, career counseling, child daycare facilities, exercise/wellness program, free psychological counseling, international student services, low-cost health insurance, multicultural affairs office, services for students with disabilities, teacher training, writing training. *Library:* Tomas Rivera Library plus 4 others. *Research affiliation:* Los Alamos National Laboratory (botany and plant sciences, chemistry, earth sciences, physics), Brookhaven National Laboratory (chemistry, physics), U.S. Salinity Laboratory (environmental sciences, biochemistry), J. Paul Getty Museum (art history), Lawrence Livermore National Laboratory (archaeology), Fermi National Accelerator Laboratory (physics).

Computer facilities: Computer purchase and lease plans are available. 556 computers available on campus for general student use. A campuswide network can be accessed from student residence rooms and from off campus. Online class registration, online viewing of financial information are available.
Website: http://www.ucr.edu/

GRADUATE UNITS

Graduate Division ***Degree program information:*** Part-time and evening/weekend programs available. Part-time, evening/weekend. Offers anthropology (MA, MS, PhD); archival management (MA); art history (MA, PhD); biochemistry and molecular biology (MS, PhD); bioengineering (MS, PhD); biomedical sciences (PhD); cell, molecular, and developmental biology (MS, PhD); chemical and environmental engineering (MS, PhD); chemistry (MS, PhD); classics (PhD); comparative literature (MA, PhD); composition (PhD); computer engineering (MS); computer science (MS, PhD); creative writing and writing for the performing arts (MFA); cultural politics and production (PhD); economics (MA, PhD); electrical engineering (MS, PhD); English (MA, PhD); entomology (MS, PhD); environmental sciences (MS, PhD); environmental toxicology (MS, PhD); ethnomusicology (MA); evolution, ecology and organismal biology (MS, PhD); experimental choreography (MFA); genomics and bioinformatics (PhD); geological sciences (MS, PhD); history (PhD); materials science and engineering (MS); mathematics (MS, PhD); mechanical engineering (MS, PhD); microbiology (MS, PhD); neuroscience (PhD); philosophy (MA, PhD); physics (MS, PhD); plant biology (MS, PhD); plant pathology (MS, PhD); political science (MA, PhD); psychology (PhD); religious studies (MA, PhD); sociology (MA, PhD); Southeast Asian studies (MA); Spanish (MA, PhD); statistics (MS); visual arts (MFA). Electronic applications accepted.

The A. Gary Anderson Graduate School of Management Financial support: Fellowships with partial tuition reimbursements, research assistantships with full tuition reimbursements, teaching assistantships with partial tuition reimbursements, career-related internships or fieldwork, institutionally sponsored loans, scholarships/grants, and tuition waivers (full) available. Financial award application deadline: 5/1; financial award applicants required to submit FAFSA. *Degree program information:* Part-time and evening/weekend programs available. Part-time, evening/weekend. Offers business administration (MBA, PhD). *Application deadline:* For fall admission, 9/1 for domestic students, 5/1 for international students; for winter admission, 12/1 for domestic students, 9/1 for international students; for spring admission, 3/1 for domestic students, 10/1 for international students. Applications are processed on a rolling basis. *Application fee:* $100 ($125 for international students). Electronic applications accepted.

Graduate School of Education Financial support: Fellowships with full tuition reimbursements, research assistantships with full tuition reimbursements, teaching assistantships with full tuition reimbursements, career-related internships or fieldwork, Federal Work-Study, institutionally sponsored loans, scholarships/grants, and unspecified assistantships available. Financial award application deadline: 1/5. Offers autism (M Ed); diversity and equity (M Ed); education specialist (Credential); education, society, and culture (MA, PhD); educational psychology (MA, PhD); general education (M Ed); higher education administration and policy (M Ed, PhD); multiple subject (Credential); reading (M Ed); school psychology (PhD); single subject (Credential); special education (M Ed, MA, PhD); TESOL (M Ed). *Application deadline:* For fall admission, 9/1 for domestic students, 5/1 for international students; for winter admission, 11/15 for domestic students, 7/1 for international students; for spring admission, 3/1 for domestic students, 10/1 for international students. Applications are processed on a rolling basis. *Application fee:* $80 ($100 for international students). Electronic applications accepted.

UNIVERSITY OF CALIFORNIA, SAN DIEGO, La Jolla, CA 92093

General Information State-supported, coed, university. CGS member. *Enrollment:* 5,058 full-time matriculated graduate/professional students (1,847 women), 652 part-time matriculated graduate/professional students (278 women). *Enrollment by degree level:* 2,390 master's, 3,320 doctoral. Tuition, state resident: full-time $11,220. Tuition, nonresident: full-time $26,322. *Required fees:* $1800. *Graduate housing:* Rooms and/or apartments available on a first-come, first-served basis to single and married students. *Student services:* Campus employment opportunities, campus safety program, career counseling, child daycare facilities, exercise/wellness program, free psychological counseling, grant writing training, international student services, low-cost health insurance, multicultural affairs office, services for students with disabilities, teacher training, writing training. *Library:* Geisel Library. *Research affiliation:* Sanford Burnham Institute, NOAA Fisheries, Veterans Administration Medical Center, Scripps Research Institute, La Jolla Institute for Allergy and Immunology, Salk Institute for Biological Studies.

Computer facilities: A campuswide network can be accessed from student residence rooms and from off campus. Online class registration is available.
Website: http://www.ucsd.edu/

General Application Contact: Graduate Admissions Office, 858-534-3554, E-mail: gradadmissions@ucsd.edu.

GRADUATE UNITS

Graduate Division Students: 5,058 full-time (1,847 women), 652 part-time (278 women); includes 1,446 minority (127 Black or African American, non-Hispanic/Latino; 40 American Indian or Alaska Native, non-Hispanic/Latino; 843 Asian, non-Hispanic/Latino; 428 Hispanic/Latino; 8 Native Hawaiian or other Pacific Islander, non-Hispanic/Latino), 2,143 international. 19,285 applicants, 24% accepted, 1957 enrolled. *Financial support:* Fellowships with tuition reimbursements, research assistantships with tuition reimbursements, teaching assistantships with partial tuition reimbursements, career-related internships or fieldwork, institutionally sponsored loans, scholarships/grants, traineeships, health care benefits, and unspecified assistantships available. Support available to part-time students. Financial award applicants required to submit FAFSA. In 2015, 1,158 master's, 512 doctorates awarded. Offers acting (MFA); aerospace engineering (MS, PhD); anthropology (PhD); applied mathematics (MA); applied mechanics (MS, PhD); applied ocean science (MS, PhD); applied physics (MS, PhD); architecture-based enterprise systems engineering (MAS); art history, theory and criticism (PhD); bioengineering (M Eng, MS, PhD); biomedical informatics (PhD); biophysics (PhD); chemical engineering (MS, PhD); chemistry (MS, PhD); climate science and policy (MAS); clinical psychology (PhD); cognitive science (PhD); communication (PhD); communication - science studies (PhD); communication theory and systems (MS, PhD); computational science (PhD); computational science, mathematics and engineering (MS); computer engineering (MS, PhD); computer science (MS, PhD); computer science and engineering (MAS); contemporary dance and performance (MFA); contemporary music performance (DMA); design (MFA); directing (MFA); drama and theatre (PhD); earth sciences (MS, PhD); economics (PhD); education (M Ed); educational leadership (Ed D); electronic circuits and systems (MS, PhD); engineering physics (MS, PhD); engineering sciences (PhD); epidemiology (PhD); ethnic studies (PhD); geophysics (PhD); global health (PhD); health behavior (PhD); health policy and law (MAS); history (MA, PhD); history - science studies (PhD); intelligent systems, robotics and control (MS, PhD); interdisciplinary cognitive science (PhD); Judaic studies (MA); language and communicative disorders (PhD); Latin American studies (MA); linguistics (PhD); literature (PhD); marine biodiversity and conservation (MAS); marine biology (MS, PhD); materials science and engineering (MS, PhD); mathematics (MA, PhD); mathematics and science education (PhD); mechanical engineering (MS, PhD); medical device engineering (MAS); medical devices and systems (MS, PhD); multi-scale biology (PhD); music (MA, PhD); nanoengineering (MS, PhD); nanoscale devices and systems (MS, PhD); oceanography (MS, PhD); philosophy (PhD); philosophy - science studies (PhD); photonics (MS, PhD); physics (MS, PhD); playwriting (MFA); political science (PhD); political science and international affairs

(PhD); psychology (PhD); signal and image processing (MS, PhD); sociology (PhD); sociology - science studies (PhD); stage management (MFA); statistics (MS, PhD); structural engineering (MS, PhD); structural health monitoring, prognosis, and validated simulations (MS); teaching and learning (MA, Ed D); visual arts (MFA); wireless embedded systems (MAS); writing (MFA). *Application fee:* $90 ($110 for international students). Electronic applications accepted. *Application Contact:* Graduate Admissions, 858-534-3554, E-mail: gradadmissions@ucsd.edu. *Dean*, Dr. Kim Barrett, 858-534-6655, E-mail: graduatedean@ucsd.edu.

Division of Biological Sciences Students: 287 full-time (160 women), 5 part-time (2 women); includes 117 minority (5 Black or African American, non-Hispanic/Latino; 82 Asian, non-Hispanic/Latino; 29 Hispanic/Latino; 1 Native Hawaiian or other Pacific Islander, non-Hispanic/Latino), 81 international. 679 applicants, 25% accepted, 99 enrolled. *Financial support:* Fellowships, research assistantships, teaching assistantships, scholarships/grants, traineeships, and unspecified assistantships available. Financial award applicants required to submit FAFSA. In 2015, 24 doctorates awarded. Offers anthropogeny (PhD); bioinformatics (PhD); biology (PhD); interdisciplinary environmental research (PhD); multi-scale biology (PhD); quantitative biology (PhD). PhD in biology offered jointly with San Diego State University. *Application deadline:* For fall admission, 12/1 for domestic students. *Application fee:* $105 ($125 for international students). Electronic applications accepted. *Application Contact:* Brandon Keith, Graduate Admissions Coordinator, 858-534-8983, E-mail: biogradprog@ucsd.edu. *Graduate Director*, Dr. Jens Lykke-Andersen, 858-534-2580, E-mail: jlykkeandersen@ucsd.edu.

Rady School of Management Students: 307 full-time (115 women), 51 part-time (12 women); includes 82 minority (8 Black or African American, non-Hispanic/Latino; 58 Asian, non-Hispanic/Latino; 16 Hispanic/Latino), 171 international. 1,640 applicants, 25% accepted, 204 enrolled. *Faculty:* 28 full-time (5 women), 5 part-time/adjunct (1 woman). *Financial support:* Fellowships, teaching assistantships, and scholarships/grants available. Financial award applicants required to submit FAFSA. In 2015, 103 master's, 1 doctorate awarded. *Degree program information:* Part-time and evening/weekend programs available. Part-time, evening/weekend. Offers business administration (MBA); finance (MF); management (PhD). *Application deadline:* Applications are processed on a rolling basis. *Application fee:* $200. Electronic applications accepted. *Application Contact:* Jay Bryant, Director of Graduate Recruitment and Admissions, 858-534-0864, E-mail: radygradadmissions@ucsd.edu. *Dean*, Robert Sullivan, 858-822-0830, E-mail: rssullivan@ucsd.edu.

School of Global Policy and Strategy Degree program information: Part-time programs available. Part-time. Offers international affairs (MAS, MIA); political science and international affairs (PhD); public policy (MPP). Electronic applications accepted.

School of Medicine Students: 505 full-time (247 women). Offers anthropogony (PhD); audiology (Au D); bioinformatics (PhD); biomedical science (PhD); biostatistics (PhD); clinical research (MAS); leadership of healthcare organizations (MAS); medicine (MAS, Au D, MD, PhD); multi-scale biology (PhD); neurosciences (PhD). *Application fee:* $90. *Application Contact:* 858-534-3880, E-mail: somadmissions@ucsd.edu. *Associate Dean for Admissions*, Dr. Carolyn J. Kelly, MD.

School of Pharmacy and Pharmaceutical Sciences Students: 249 full-time (171 women). *Faculty:* 33. Offers pharmacy and pharmaceutical sciences (Pharm D). *Application deadline:* For fall admission, 11/2 for domestic students. *Application fee:* $90. *Application Contact:* 858-822-4900, Fax: 858-822-5591, E-mail: sppsadmissions@ucsd.edu. *Dean*, Dr. James McKerrow.

UNIVERSITY OF CALIFORNIA, SAN FRANCISCO, San Francisco, CA 94143

General Information State-supported, coed, graduate-only institution. CGS member. *Graduate housing:* Rooms and/or apartments available to single and married students.

GRADUATE UNITS

Graduate Division *Degree program information:* Part-time programs available. Part-time. Offers biochemistry and molecular biology (PhD); bioengineering (PhD); biomedical imaging (MS); biomedical sciences (PhD); cell biology (PhD); developmental biology (PhD); genetics (PhD); history of health sciences (MA, PhD); medical anthropology (PhD); neuroscience (PhD); oral and craniofacial sciences (MS, PhD); physical therapy (DPT, DPTSc).

School of Nursing Offers nursing (MS, PhD); sociology (PhD).

School of Dentistry Offers dentistry (DDS).

School of Medicine Students: 647 full-time (330 women); includes 354 minority (47 Black or African American, non-Hispanic/Latino; 2 American Indian or Alaska Native, non-Hispanic/Latino; 156 Asian, non-Hispanic/Latino; 94 Hispanic/Latino; 9 Native Hawaiian or other Pacific Islander, non-Hispanic/Latino; 46 Two or more races, non-Hispanic/Latino). Average age 24. 7,453 applicants, 4% accepted, 149 enrolled. *Faculty:* 2,035 full-time (871 women), 368 part-time/adjunct (195 women). *Financial support:* In 2015–16, 517 students received support. Federal Work-Study, institutionally sponsored loans, scholarships/grants, and tuition waivers (partial) available. Financial award application deadline: 2/1; financial award applicants required to submit FAFSA. In 2015, 163 doctorates awarded. Offers medicine (MD, PhD). *Application deadline:* For fall admission, 10/15 for domestic students. Applications are processed on a rolling basis. *Application fee:* $80 ($100 for international students). Electronic applications accepted. *Application Contact:* Hallen Chung, Director of Admissions, 415-476-8090, Fax: 415-476-5490, E-mail: hallen.chung@ucsf.edu. *Dean*, Dr. Talmadge E. King, Jr., 415-476-2342, Fax: 415-476-0689.

School of Pharmacy Offers bioinformatics (PhD); biophysics (PhD); chemistry and chemical biology (PhD); pharmaceutical sciences and pharmacogenomics (PhD); pharmacy (MS, PhD, Pharm D). Electronic applications accepted.

UNIVERSITY OF CALIFORNIA, SANTA BARBARA, Santa Barbara, CA 93106-2014

General Information State-supported, coed, university. CGS member. *Enrollment:* 23,497 graduate, professional, and undergraduate students; 2,890 full-time matriculated graduate/professional students (1,285 women). *Enrollment by degree level:* 590 master's, 2,295 doctoral, 5 other advanced degrees. *Graduate faculty:* 982 full-time (304 women), 251 part-time/adjunct (100 women). *Graduate housing:* Rooms and/or apartments guaranteed to single students and available on a first-come, first-served basis to married students. Housing application deadline: 6/1. *Student services:* Campus employment opportunities, campus safety program, career counseling, child daycare facilities, exercise/wellness program, free psychological counseling, grant writing training, international student services, low-cost health insurance, multicultural affairs office, services for students with disabilities, teacher training, writing training. *Library:* Davidson Library plus 1 other. *Collection:* Books: 4.2 million (physical), 705,118 (digital/electronic). Study areas open 24 hours, 5–7 days a week; students can reserve study rooms. *Research affiliation:* California NanoSystems Institute, The Institute for Social, Behavioral and Economic Research, National Center for Ecological Analysis and Synthesis, The Institute for Collaborative Biotechnologies, Institute for Polymers and Organic Solids, Mitsubishi Chemical Center for Advanced Materials.

Computer facilities: 700 computers available on campus for general student use. A campuswide network can be accessed from student residence rooms and from off campus. Online class registration is available.
Website: http://www.ucsb.edu/

General Application Contact: Dr. Walter Boggan, Assistant Director, Graduate Admissions, 805-893-2322, Fax: 805-893-8259, E-mail: gradadmissions@graddiv.ucsb.edu.

GRADUATE UNITS

Graduate Division Students: 2,890 full-time (1,283 women); includes 577 minority (46 Black or African American, non-Hispanic/Latino; 23 American Indian or Alaska Native, non-Hispanic/Latino; 239 Asian, non-Hispanic/Latino; 233 Hispanic/Latino; 36 Native Hawaiian or other Pacific Islander, non-Hispanic/Latino), 704 international. Average age 29. 9,087 applicants, 20% accepted, 781 enrolled. *Faculty:* 982 full-time (304 women), 251 part-time/adjunct (100 women). *Financial support:* In 2015–16, 2,199 students received support, including 1,370 fellowships with tuition reimbursements available (averaging $11,841 per year), 811 research assistantships with tuition reimbursements available (averaging $12,489 per year), 1,593 teaching assistantships with tuition reimbursements available (averaging $11,460 per year); career-related internships or fieldwork, Federal Work-Study, institutionally sponsored loans, scholarships/grants, traineeships, health care benefits, tuition waivers (full and partial), and unspecified assistantships also available. Support available to part-time students. Financial award applicants required to submit FAFSA. In 2015, 505 master's, 360 doctorates, 58 other advanced degrees awarded. *Application fee:* $80 ($100 for international students). Electronic applications accepted. *Application Contact:* Dr. Haley Orton, Assistant Director, Graduate Admissions, 805-893-2277, Fax: 805-893-8259, E-mail: gradadmissions@graddiv.ucsb.edu. *Dean*, Prof. Carol Genetti, 805-893-2013, Fax: 805-893-8259, E-mail: graddeans@graddiv.ucsb.edu.

College of Engineering Students: 705 full-time (150 women); includes 93 minority (6 Black or African American, non-Hispanic/Latino; 3 American Indian or Alaska Native, non-Hispanic/Latino; 57 Asian, non-Hispanic/Latino; 21 Hispanic/Latino; 6 Native Hawaiian or other Pacific Islander, non-Hispanic/Latino), 335 international. Average age 27. 3,853 applicants, 16% accepted, 201 enrolled. *Faculty:* 137 full-time (19 women), 22 part-time/adjunct (0 women). *Financial support:* In 2015–16, 487 students received support, including 188 fellowships with tuition reimbursements available (averaging $20,023 per year), 505 research assistantships with tuition reimbursements available (averaging $23,804 per year), 256 teaching assistantships with partial tuition reimbursements available (averaging $15,879 per year); career-related internships or fieldwork, Federal Work-Study, institutionally sponsored loans, scholarships/grants, traineeships, health care benefits, tuition waivers (full and partial), and unspecified assistantships also available. Financial award applicants required to submit FAFSA. In 2015, 127 master's, 85 doctorates awarded. Offers bioengineering (PhD); chemical engineering (MS, PhD); communications, control and signal processing (MS, PhD); computer engineering (MS, PhD); computer science (PhD); electronics and photonics (MS, PhD); engineering (MS, MTM, PhD); materials (MS, PhD); mechanical engineering (MS); technology management (MTM). *Application fee:* $90 ($110 for international students). Electronic applications accepted. *Application Contact:* 805-893-3207, E-mail: engrdean@engineering.ucsb.edu. *Dean*, Dr. Rod C. Alferness, 805-893-3141, E-mail: alferness@engineering.ucsb.edu.

College of Letters and Sciences Students: 1,647 full-time (752 women); includes 346 minority (24 Black or African American, non-Hispanic/Latino; 16 American Indian or Alaska Native, non-Hispanic/Latino; 143 Asian, non-Hispanic/Latino; 142 Hispanic/Latino; 21 Native Hawaiian or other Pacific Islander, non-Hispanic/Latino), 309 international. Average age 29. 4,418 applicants, 21% accepted, 371 enrolled. *Faculty:* 782 full-time (261 women), 220 part-time/adjunct (95 women). *Financial support:* In 2015–16, 1,395 students received support, including 727 fellowships with tuition reimbursements available (averaging $12,839 per year), 348 research assistantships with tuition reimbursements available (averaging $11,736 per year), 1,309 teaching assistantships with partial tuition reimbursements available (averaging $12,664 per year); career-related internships or fieldwork, Federal Work-Study, institutionally sponsored loans, scholarships/grants, traineeships, health care benefits, tuition waivers (full and partial), and unspecified assistantships also available. Support available to part-time students. Financial award applicants required to submit FAFSA. In 2015, 243 master's, 238 doctorates awarded. Offers ancient history (PhD); ancient Mediterranean studies (PhD); applied linguistics (PhD); applied mathematics (MA); art (MFA); art history (PhD); astrophysics (PhD); biochemistry and molecular biology (PhD); bioengineering (PhD); brass (MM); chemistry (MA, MS, PhD); classics (MA, PhD); cognitive science (PhD); communication (PhD); comparative literature (PhD); composition (MA, PhD); conducting (MM, DMA); dynamical neuroscience (PhD); earth science (MS, PhD); East Asian languages and cultural studies (MA); East Asian literatures (PhD); ecology, evolution, and marine biology (MA, PhD); economics (MA); English (PhD); ethnomusicology (MA, PhD); European medieval studies (PhD); feminist studies (MA, PhD); film and media studies (PhD); financial mathematics and statistics (PhD); French (PhD); geography (MA, PhD); global culture, ideology, and religion (MA, PhD); global government, human rights, and civil society (MA, PhD); global studies (PhD); Hispanic languages and literatures (PhD); Hispanic linguistics (MA); humanities and fine arts (MA, MFA, MM, MS, DMA, PhD); interdisciplinary emphasis: Black studies (PhD); interdisciplinary emphasis: environment and society (PhD); interdisciplinary emphasis: feminist studies (PhD); interdisciplinary emphasis: global studies (PhD); interdisciplinary emphasis: language, interaction and social organization (PhD); interdisciplinary emphasis: quantitative methods in the social sciences (PhD); interdisciplinary emphasis: technology and society (PhD); keyboard (MM, DMA); language, interaction and social organization (PhD); Latin American and Iberian studies (MA); letters and sciences (MA, MFA, MM, MS, DMA, PhD); linguistics (PhD); literature and theory (MA); Luso-Brazilian literature (MA); marine science (MS, PhD); mathematical economics (PhD); mathematics (MA, PhD); mathematics, life, and physical sciences (MA, MS, PhD); media arts and technology (MS, PhD); molecular, cellular, and developmental biology (MA, PhD); musicology (MA, PhD); philosophy (PhD); physics (PhD); piano accompanying (MM); political economy, sustainable development, and the environment (MA, PhD); political science (PhD); psychology (PhD); public finance (PhD); public historical studies (PhD); quantitative methods in the social sciences (PhD); religious studies (MA, PhD); social sciences (MA, PhD); society and technology (PhD); sociocultural anthropology (PhD); sociology (PhD); Spanish or Spanish-American literature (MA); statistics (MA); statistics and applied probability (PhD); strings (MM, DMA); technology and society (PhD); theater studies (MA, PhD); theory (MA, PhD); translation studies (PhD); transportation (PhD); voice (MM, DMA);

women's studies (PhD); woodwinds (MM). *Application fee:* $90 ($110 for international students). Electronic applications accepted. *Application Contact:* Graduate Admissions Coordinator, 805-893-2104, Fax: 805-893-8259, E-mail: gradadmissions@graddiv.ucsb.edu. *Executive Dean*, Dr. David Marshall, 805-893-4327, E-mail: dmarshall@ltsc.ucsb.edu.

Donald Bren School of Environmental Science and Management Students: 213 full-time (129 women); includes 33 minority (3 Black or African American, non-Hispanic/Latino; 1 American Indian or Alaska Native, non-Hispanic/Latino; 11 Asian, non-Hispanic/Latino; 16 Hispanic/Latino; 2 Native Hawaiian or other Pacific Islander, non-Hispanic/Latino), 32 international. Average age 27. 404 applicants, 51% accepted, 85 enrolled. *Faculty:* 22 full-time (3 women), 5 part-time/adjunct (1 woman). *Financial support:* In 2015–16, 63 students received support, including 23 fellowships with tuition reimbursements available, 3 research assistantships with tuition reimbursements available, 33 teaching assistantships with tuition reimbursements available; career-related internships or fieldwork and tuition waivers (full and partial) also available. Financial award application deadline: 12/15; financial award applicants required to submit FAFSA. In 2015, 70 master's, 7 doctorates awarded. Offers economics and environmental science (PhD); environmental science and management (MESM, PhD); technology and society (PhD). *Application deadline:* For fall admission, 12/15 priority date for domestic and international students. *Application fee:* $90 ($110 for international students). Electronic applications accepted. *Application Contact:* Kristen Robinson, Director of Admissions and Outreach, 805-893-4886, Fax: 805-893-7612, E-mail: admissions@bren.ucsb.edu. *Dean*, Dr. Steven Gaines, 805-893-7363, Fax: 805-893-7611, E-mail: gaines@bren.ucsb.edu.

Gevirtz Graduate School of Education Students: 325 full-time (252 women); includes 105 minority (13 Black or African American, non-Hispanic/Latino; 3 American Indian or Alaska Native, non-Hispanic/Latino; 28 Asian, non-Hispanic/Latino; 54 Hispanic/Latino; 7 Native Hawaiian or other Pacific Islander, non-Hispanic/Latino), 28 international. Average age 34. 412 applicants, 19% accepted, 124 enrolled. *Faculty:* 44 full-time (26 women), 1 part-time/adjunct (0 women). *Financial support:* In 2015–16, 240 students received support, including 373 fellowships with partial tuition reimbursements available (averaging $6,320 per year), 66 research assistantships with tuition reimbursements available (averaging $4,112 per year), 120 teaching assistantships with partial tuition reimbursements available (averaging $3,457 per year); career-related internships or fieldwork also available. Financial award applicants required to submit FAFSA. In 2015, 65 master's, 30 doctorates, 50 other advanced degrees awarded. Offers counseling, clinical and school psychology (MA, PhD, Credential); education (MA, PhD); teacher education (M Ed, Credential). *Application deadline:* Applications are processed on a rolling basis. *Application fee:* $90 ($110 for international students). Electronic applications accepted. *Application Contact:* Martiza Fuljencio, Student Affairs Officer, 805-893-2137, Fax: 805-893-2588, E-mail: maritza@education.ucsb.edu. *Student and Academic Affairs Manager*, Amy Meredith, 805-893-2137, Fax: 805-893-2588, E-mail: amyh@education.ucsb.edu.

UNIVERSITY OF CALIFORNIA, SANTA CRUZ, Santa Cruz, CA 95064

General Information State-supported, coed, university. CGS member. *Graduate housing:* Rooms and/or apartments available on a first-come, first-served basis to single and married students. Housing application deadline: 5/20. *Research affiliation:* Center for Biomimetic MicroElectronic Systems (science and engineering), Center for Information Technology Research in the Interest of Society (science and engineering), Institute for Regenerative Medicine (science and engineering), Center for Adaptive Optics (science and engineering), Center for Biomolecular Science and Engineering (science and engineering), Institute for Quantitative Biology (science and engineering).

GRADUATE UNITS

Division of Graduate Studies Electronic applications accepted.

Division of Humanities Offers history (MA, PhD); history of consciousness (PhD); humanities (MA, PhD); linguistics (MA, PhD); literature (MA, PhD); philosophy (MA, PhD). Electronic applications accepted.

Division of Physical and Biological Sciences Offers astronomy and astrophysics (PhD); chemistry and biochemistry (MS, PhD); earth and planetary sciences (MS, PhD); ecology and evolutionary biology (MA, PhD); environmental toxicology (MS, PhD); mathematics (MA, PhD); molecular, cellular, and developmental biology (MA, PhD); ocean sciences (MS, PhD); physical and biological sciences (MA, MS, PhD, Certificate); physics (MS, PhD); science communication (Certificate). Electronic applications accepted.

Division of Social Sciences Offers applied economics and finance (MS); cultural anthropology (PhD); education (MA, PhD); environmental studies (PhD); international economics (PhD); politics (PhD); psychology (PhD); social documentation (MA); social sciences (MA, MS, PhD); sociology (PhD). Electronic applications accepted.

Division of the Arts Offers arts (MA, MFA, DMA, PhD, Certificate); digital arts and new media (MFA); ethnomusicology (MA); film and digital media (PhD); music (PhD); music composition (MA, DMA); music composition (DMA); performance practice (MA); theater arts (Certificate); visual studies (PhD). Electronic applications accepted.

Jack Baskin School of Engineering Offers bioinformatics (MS, PhD); computer engineering (MS, PhD); computer science (MS, PhD); electrical engineering (MS, PhD); engineering (MS, PhD); network engineering (MS); statistics and applied mathematics (MS, PhD); technology and information management (MS, PhD). Electronic applications accepted.

UNIVERSITY OF CENTRAL ARKANSAS, Conway, AR 72035-0001

General Information State-supported, coed, university. CGS member. *Graduate housing:* Rooms and/or apartments available on a first-come, first-served basis to single and married students. Housing application deadline: 7/1. *Research affiliation:* 3M Corporation, State Farm Foundation (insurance), Arkansas Game and Fish Commission, Acxiom (math, computers), Arkansas Educational Television Network.

GRADUATE UNITS

Graduate School ***Degree program information:*** Part-time and evening/weekend programs available. Part-time, evening/weekend, online learning. Offers leadership studies (PhD).

College of Business Administration Degree program information: Part-time and evening/weekend programs available. Part-time, evening/weekend. Offers accounting (M Acc); business administration (M Acc, MBA).

College of Education Degree program information: Part-time and evening/weekend programs available. Part-time, evening/weekend, online learning. Offers collaborative instructional specialist (ages 0-8) (MSE); collaborative instructional specialist (grades 4-12) (MSE); college student personnel (MS); district-level administration (PMC); education (MAT, MS, MSE, Ed S, Graduate Certificate, PMC); educational leadership - district level (Ed S); gifted and talented education (Graduate Certificate); instructional facilitator (Graduate Certificate); instructional technology (MS); library media and information technology (MS); reading education (MSE); school counseling (MS); school leadership (MS); school-based leadership adult education program administration (PMC); school-based leadership building administration (PMC); school-based leadership curriculum administration (PMC); school-based leadership gifted and talented program administration (PMC); school-based leadership special education program administration (PMC); special education (MSE, Graduate Certificate); special education instructional specialist grades 4-12 (Graduate Certificate); special education instructional specialist P-4 (Graduate Certificate); teaching (MAT); teaching and learning (MSE). Electronic applications accepted.

College of Fine Arts and Communication Degree program information: Part-time programs available. Part-time. Offers choral conducting (MM); creative writing (MFA); digital filmmaking (MFA); fine arts and communication (MFA, MM, PC); instrumental conducting (MM); music (PC); music education (MM); music theory (MM); performance (MM). Electronic applications accepted.

College of Health and Behavioral Sciences Degree program information: Part-time and evening/weekend programs available. Part-time, evening/weekend, online learning. Offers adult nurse practitioner (PMC); clinical nurse leader (PMC); clinical nurse specialist (MSN); communication sciences and disorders (PhD); community counseling (MS); counseling psychology (MS); family and consumer sciences (MS); family nurse practitioner (PMC); health and behavioral sciences (MS, MSN, DPT, PhD, PMC); health education (MS); kinesiology (MS); nurse educator (PMC); nurse practitioner (MSN); occupational therapy (MS); physical therapy (DPT, PhD); school psychology (MS, PhD, PMC); speech-language pathology (MS). Electronic applications accepted.

College of Liberal Arts Degree program information: Part-time programs available. Part-time. Offers community and economic development (MS); English (MA); foreign languages (MA); geographic and information systems (MGIS, Graduate Certificate); geographic information systems (MGIS, Certificate); history (MA); liberal arts (MA, MGIS, MS, Certificate, Graduate Certificate). Electronic applications accepted.

College of Natural Sciences and Math Degree program information: Part-time programs available. Part-time. Offers applied computing (MS); applied mathematics (MS); biological science (MS); math education (MA); natural sciences and math (MA, MS). Electronic applications accepted.

UNIVERSITY OF CENTRAL FLORIDA, Orlando, FL 32816

General Information State-supported, coed, university. CGS member. *Enrollment:* 63,002 graduate, professional, and undergraduate students; 3,863 full-time matriculated graduate/professional students (2,094 women), 3,730 part-time matriculated graduate/professional students (2,309 women). *Graduate faculty:* 1,412 full-time (580 women), 601 part-time/adjunct (317 women). Tuition, state resident: part-time $288.16 per credit hour. Tuition, nonresident: part-time $1071.31 per credit hour. *Graduate housing:* Room and/or apartments available on a first-come, first-served basis to single students; on-campus housing not available to married students. Housing application deadline: 3/1. *Student services:* Campus employment opportunities, campus safety program, career counseling, child daycare facilities, exercise/wellness program, free psychological counseling, grant writing training, international student services, low-cost health insurance, multicultural affairs office, services for students with disabilities, teacher training, writing training. *Library:* University Library plus 1 other. *Collection:* Books: 1.5 million (physical), 149,176 (digital/electronic); Serial titles: 1,079 (physical), 52,337 (digital/electronic); Databases: 481. Weekly public service hours: 106; students can reserve study rooms.

Computer facilities: Computer purchase and lease plans are available. 4,260 computers available on campus for general student use. A campuswide network can be accessed from student residence rooms and from off campus. Online class registration is available.
Website: http://www.ucf.edu/

General Application Contact: Director, Admissions and Student Services, 407-882-0065, Fax: 407-823-6442, E-mail: gradadmissions@ucf.edu.

GRADUATE UNITS

College of Arts and Humanities Students: 265 full-time (140 women), 253 part-time (136 women); includes 120 minority (20 Black or African American, non-Hispanic/Latino; 1 American Indian or Alaska Native, non-Hispanic/Latino; 12 Asian, non-Hispanic/Latino; 79 Hispanic/Latino; 8 Two or more races, non-Hispanic/Latino), 28 international. Average age 31. 452 applicants, 60% accepted, 174 enrolled. *Faculty:* 289 full-time (136 women), 86 part-time/adjunct (39 women). *Financial support:* In 2015–16, 105 students received support, including 45 fellowships with partial tuition reimbursements available (averaging $4,700 per year), 6 research assistantships with partial tuition reimbursements available (averaging $6,700 per year), 85 teaching assistantships with partial tuition reimbursements available (averaging $7,800 per year); career-related internships or fieldwork, Federal Work-Study, institutionally sponsored loans, scholarships/grants, tuition waivers (partial), and unspecified assistantships also available. Financial award application deadline: 3/1; financial award applicants required to submit FAFSA. In 2015, 147 master's, 7 doctorates, 44 other advanced degrees awarded. *Degree program information:* Part-time and evening/weekend programs available. Part-time, evening/weekend. Offers arts and humanities (MA, MFA, MS, PhD, Certificate); creative writing (MFA); English (MA, Certificate); ESOL endorsement K-12 (Certificate); history (MA); Spanish (MA); teaching English as a foreign language (Certificate); teaching English to speakers of other languages (MA, Certificate); texts and technology (PhD). *Application fee:* $30. Electronic applications accepted. *Application Contact:* Director, Admissions and Student Services, 407-823-2766, Fax: 407-823-6442, E-mail: gradadmissions@ucf.edu. *Dean*, Dr. Jose Fernandez, 407-823-2573, E-mail: jose.fernandez@ucf.edu.

Florida Interactive Entertainment Academy Students: 55 full-time (15 women), 63 part-time (16 women); includes 29 minority (4 Black or African American, non-Hispanic/Latino; 4 Asian, non-Hispanic/Latino; 20 Hispanic/Latino; 1 Two or more races, non-Hispanic/Latino), 13 international. Average age 26. 129 applicants, 62% accepted, 55 enrolled. *Faculty:* 10 full-time (0 women). In 2015, 54 master's awarded. Offers interactive entertainment (MS). *Application Contact:* Director, Admissions and Student Services, 407-823-2766, Fax: 407-823-6442, E-mail: gradadmissions@ucf.edu. *Executive Director*, Ben Noel, 407-235-3612, Fax: 407-317-7094, E-mail: bnoel@fiea.ucf.edu.

School of Performing Arts Students: 27 full-time (17 women), 28 part-time (20 women); includes 10 minority (1 Black or African American, non-Hispanic/Latino; 6 Hispanic/Latino; 3 Two or more races, non-Hispanic/Latino), 1 international. Average age 33. 33 applicants, 58% accepted, 16 enrolled. *Faculty:* 51 full-time (19 women), 14 part-time/adjunct (8 women). *Financial support:* In 2015–16, 21 students received support, including 7 fellowships with partial tuition reimbursements available (averaging $6,300 per year), 18 teaching assistantships with partial tuition reimbursements available (averaging $7,300 per year); career-related internships or fieldwork, Federal Work-Study, institutionally sponsored loans, tuition waivers (partial), and unspecified assistantships also available. Financial award application deadline: 3/1; financial award applicants required to submit FAFSA. In 2015, 15 master's awarded. *Degree program information:* Part-time and evening/weekend programs available. Part-time, evening/weekend. Offers music (MA); theatre (MA, MFA). *Application deadline:* For fall admission, 7/15 for domestic students; for spring admission, 12/1 for domestic students. *Application fee:* $30. Electronic applications accepted. *Application Contact:* Director, Admissions and Student Services, 407-823-2766, Fax: 407-823-6442, E-mail: gradadmissions@ucf.edu. *Chair,* Jeffrey Moore, 407-823-2879, Fax: 407-823-3378, E-mail: jeffrey.moore@ucf.edu.

School of Visual Arts and Design Students: 22 full-time (13 women), 7 part-time (1 woman); includes 6 minority (2 Black or African American, non-Hispanic/Latino; 2 Asian, non-Hispanic/Latino; 2 Hispanic/Latino), 3 international. Average age 29. 32 applicants, 41% accepted, 8 enrolled. *Faculty:* 51 full-time (20 women), 20 part-time/adjunct (4 women). *Financial support:* In 2015–16, 17 students received support, including 8 fellowships with partial tuition reimbursements available (averaging $8,300 per year), 12 teaching assistantships with partial tuition reimbursements available (averaging $6,400 per year); scholarships/grants and unspecified assistantships also available. In 2015, 10 master's awarded. Offers digital media (MA); emerging media (MFA). *Application fee:* $30. Electronic applications accepted. *Application Contact:* Director, Admissions and Student Services, 407-823-2766, Fax: 407-823-6442, E-mail: gradadmissions@ucf.edu. *Director,* Byron Clercx, 407-823-3145, E-mail: byron.clercx@ucf.edu.

College of Business Administration Students: 267 full-time (115 women), 621 part-time (309 women); includes 307 minority (66 Black or African American, non-Hispanic/Latino; 2 American Indian or Alaska Native, non-Hispanic/Latino; 62 Asian, non-Hispanic/Latino; 159 Hispanic/Latino; 1 Native Hawaiian or other Pacific Islander, non-Hispanic/Latino; 17 Two or more races, non-Hispanic/Latino), 29 international. Average age 30. 776 applicants, 63% accepted, 415 enrolled. *Faculty:* 123 full-time (33 women), 14 part-time/adjunct (5 women). *Financial support:* In 2015–16, 115 students received support, including 35 fellowships with partial tuition reimbursements available (averaging $4,100 per year), 40 research assistantships with partial tuition reimbursements available (averaging $5,500 per year), 65 teaching assistantships with partial tuition reimbursements available (averaging $10,300 per year); career-related internships or fieldwork, Federal Work-Study, institutionally sponsored loans, tuition waivers (partial), and unspecified assistantships also available. Financial award application deadline: 3/1; financial award applicants required to submit FAFSA. In 2015, 290 master's, 6 doctorates, 10 other advanced degrees awarded. *Degree program information:* Part-time and evening/weekend programs available. Part-time, evening/weekend. Offers business administration (MBA, MSA, MSBM, MSM, MSRE, MST, PhD, Graduate Certificate); entrepreneurship (Graduate Certificate); management (MSM); sport business management (MSBM); technology ventures (Graduate Certificate). *Application deadline:* For spring admission, 11/1 priority date for domestic students. *Application fee:* $30. Electronic applications accepted. *Application Contact:* Director, Graduate Admissions, 407-823-2776, Fax: 407-823-6442, E-mail: gradadmissions@ucf.edu. *Dean,* Dr. Paul Jarley, 407-823-2183, E-mail: pjarley@bus.ucf.edu.

Dr. P. Phillips School of Real Estate Students: 1 full-time (0 women), 23 part-time (10 women); includes 13 minority (2 Black or African American, non-Hispanic/Latino; 4 Asian, non-Hispanic/Latino; 7 Hispanic/Latino). Average age 36. 37 applicants, 76% accepted, 25 enrolled. *Financial support:* In 2015–16, 1 student received support. In 2015, 18 master's awarded. *Degree program information:* Part-time programs available. Part-time. Offers real estate (MSRE). *Application Contact:* Director, Graduate Admissions, 407-823-2776, Fax: 407-823-6442, E-mail: gradadmissions@ucf.edu. *Chair and Director,* Dr. Ajai Singh, 407-823-5756, Fax: 407-823-6676, E-mail: aks@ucf.edu.

Kenneth G. Dixon School of Accounting Students: 101 full-time (45 women), 84 part-time (43 women); includes 59 minority (4 Black or African American, non-Hispanic/Latino; 22 Asian, non-Hispanic/Latino; 28 Hispanic/Latino; 5 Two or more races, non-Hispanic/Latino), 5 international. Average age 27. 136 applicants, 59% accepted, 57 enrolled. *Faculty:* 23 full-time (10 women), 1 (woman) part-time/adjunct. *Financial support:* In 2015–16, 21 students received support, including 1 fellowship with partial tuition reimbursement available (averaging $5,000 per year), 1 research assistantship with partial tuition reimbursement available (averaging $9,300 per year), 20 teaching assistantships with partial tuition reimbursements available (averaging $6,700 per year); career-related internships or fieldwork, Federal Work-Study, institutionally sponsored loans, tuition waivers (partial), and unspecified assistantships also available. Financial award application deadline: 3/1; financial award applicants required to submit FAFSA. In 2015, 70 master's awarded. *Degree program information:* Part-time and evening/weekend programs available. Part-time, evening/weekend. Offers accounting (MSA, MST); taxation (MST). *Application deadline:* For fall admission, 6/15 priority date for domestic students; for spring admission, 11/1 priority date for domestic students. Electronic applications accepted. *Application Contact:* Director, Graduate Admissions, 407-823-2776, Fax: 407-823-6442, E-mail: gradadmissions@ucf.edu. *Director,* Dr. Greg Trompeter, 407-823-2876, Fax: 407-823-3881, E-mail: gregory.trompeter@ucf.edu.

College of Education and Human Performance Students: 692 full-time (520 women), 1,055 part-time (830 women); includes 538 minority (220 Black or African American, non-Hispanic/Latino; 2 American Indian or Alaska Native, non-Hispanic/Latino; 44 Asian, non-Hispanic/Latino; 240 Hispanic/Latino; 32 Two or more races, non-Hispanic/Latino), 39 international. Average age 32. 1,225 applicants, 59% accepted, 477 enrolled. *Faculty:* 126 full-time (80 women), 126 part-time/adjunct (83 women). *Financial support:* In 2015–16, 160 students received support, including 66 fellowships with partial tuition reimbursements available (averaging $5,200 per year), 99 research assistantships with partial tuition reimbursements available (averaging $5,800 per year), 72 teaching assistantships with partial tuition reimbursements available (averaging $6,100 per year); career-related internships or fieldwork, Federal Work-Study, institutionally sponsored loans, tuition waivers (partial), and unspecified assistantships also available. Financial award application deadline: 3/1; financial award applicants required to submit FAFSA. In 2015, 524 master's, 77 doctorates, 127 other advanced degrees awarded. *Degree program information:* Part-time and evening/weekend programs available. Part-time, evening/weekend. Offers applied exercise physiology (MS); autism spectrum disorders (Certificate); career and technical education (MA); career counseling (Certificate); communication sciences and disorders (PhD); community college education (Certificate); counselor education (M Ed, MA, Certificate, Ed S); e-learning professional development (Certificate); early childhood education (PhD); education (Ed D); education and human performance (M Ed, MA, MAT, MS, Ed D, PhD, Certificate, Ed S); educational leadership (MA, Ed D, Ed S); elementary education (PhD); exceptional education (PhD); exceptional student education (M Ed, MA, Certificate); exceptional student education K-12 (MA); exercise physiology (PhD); higher education (PhD); instructional design and technology (MA, Certificate); instructional design for simulations (Certificate); instructional technology (PhD); instructional/educational technology (Certificate); marriage, couple, and family therapy (MA, Certificate); mathematics education (PhD); methodology, measurement and analysis (PhD); play therapy (Certificate); pre-kindergarten disabilities (Certificate); reading education (PhD); school psychology (Ed S); science education (PhD); severe or profound disabilities (Certificate); social science education (PhD); special education (Certificate); sport and exercise science (MS); TESOL (PhD). *Application fee:* $30. Electronic applications accepted. *Application Contact:* Director, Admissions and Student Services, 407-823-2766, Fax: 407-823-6442, E-mail: gradadmissions@ucf.edu. *Dean,* Dr. Pamela S. Carroll, 407-823-5529, E-mail: pamela.carroll@ucf.edu.

School of Teaching, Learning, and Leadership Students: 87 full-time (71 women), 380 part-time (313 women); includes 142 minority (58 Black or African American, non-Hispanic/Latino; 1 American Indian or Alaska Native, non-Hispanic/Latino; 14 Asian, non-Hispanic/Latino; 59 Hispanic/Latino; 10 Two or more races, non-Hispanic/Latino), 5 international. Average age 32. 242 applicants, 74% accepted, 127 enrolled. *Faculty:* 74 full-time (54 women), 62 part-time/adjunct (46 women). *Financial support:* In 2015–16, 1 student received support, including 1 research assistantship with partial tuition reimbursement available (averaging $7,100 per year); career-related internships or fieldwork, Federal Work-Study, institutionally sponsored loans, tuition waivers (partial), and unspecified assistantships also available. Financial award application deadline: 3/1; financial award applicants required to submit FAFSA. In 2015, 209 master's, 33 other advanced degrees awarded. *Degree program information:* Part-time and evening/weekend programs available. Part-time, evening/weekend. Offers applied learning and instruction (MA); art education (M Ed, MAT); educational and instructional technology (MA); educational leadership (Ed S); elementary education (M Ed, MA); English language (MAT); English language arts education (M Ed); K-8 mathematics and science education (M Ed, Certificate); mathematics education (MAT); middle school mathematics (MAT); reading education (M Ed); science education (M Ed, MAT); social science education (M Ed, MAT); teacher education (MAT); teacher leadership (M Ed); teaching excellence (Certificate). *Application deadline:* For fall admission, 7/15 for domestic students; for spring admission, 12/15 for domestic students. *Application fee:* $30. Electronic applications accepted. *Application Contact:* Director, Admissions and Student Services, 407-823-2766, Fax: 407-823-6442, E-mail: gradadmissions@ucf.edu. *Co-Director,* Dr. Michael Hynes, 407-823-6076, E-mail: michael.hynes@ucf.edu.

College of Engineering and Computer Science Students: 841 full-time (173 women), 496 part-time (109 women); includes 275 minority (39 Black or African American, non-Hispanic/Latino; 70 Asian, non-Hispanic/Latino; 142 Hispanic/Latino; 24 Two or more races, non-Hispanic/Latino), 590 international. Average age 30. 1,502 applicants, 61% accepted, 384 enrolled. *Faculty:* 158 full-time (23 women), 37 part-time/adjunct (0 women). *Financial support:* In 2015–16, 424 students received support, including 104 fellowships with partial tuition reimbursements available (averaging $4,900 per year), 273 research assistantships with partial tuition reimbursements available (averaging $10,000 per year), 178 teaching assistantships with partial tuition reimbursements available (averaging $9,700 per year); career-related internships or fieldwork, Federal Work-Study, institutionally sponsored loans, tuition waivers (partial), and unspecified assistantships also available. Financial award application deadline: 3/1; financial award applicants required to submit FAFSA. In 2015, 329 master's, 77 doctorates, 39 other advanced degrees awarded. *Degree program information:* Part-time and evening/weekend programs available. Part-time, evening/weekend. Offers aerospace engineering (MSAE); civil engineering (MS, MSCE, PhD, Certificate); computer engineering (MS Cp E, PhD); computer science (MS, PhD); construction engineering (Certificate); digital forensics (MS); electrical engineering (MSEE, PhD, Certificate); electronic circuits (Certificate); engineering and computer science (MS, MS Cp E, MS Env E, MSAE, MSCE, MSEE, MSIE, MSME, MSMSE, PhD, Certificate); environmental engineering (MS, MS Env E, PhD); industrial engineering and management systems (MSIE, PhD, Certificate); materials science and engineering (MSMSE, PhD); mechanical engineering (MSME, PhD). *Application deadline:* For fall admission, 7/15 for domestic students; for spring admission, 12/1 for domestic students. *Application fee:* $30. Electronic applications accepted. *Application Contact:* Director, Admissions and Student Services, 407-823-2766, Fax: 407-823-6442, E-mail: gradadmissions@ucf.edu. *Dean,* Dr. Michael Georgiopoulos, 407-823-2156, E-mail: michaelg@ucf.edu.

College of Graduate Studies Students: 67 full-time (21 women), 79 part-time (23 women); includes 41 minority (7 Black or African American, non-Hispanic/Latino; 5 Asian, non-Hispanic/Latino; 25 Hispanic/Latino; 1 Native Hawaiian or other Pacific Islander, non-Hispanic/Latino; 3 Two or more races, non-Hispanic/Latino), 16 international. Average age 34. 97 applicants, 68% accepted, 43 enrolled. *Financial support:* In 2015–16, 30 students received support, including 11 fellowships with partial tuition reimbursements available (averaging $3,600 per year), 28 research assistantships with partial tuition reimbursements available (averaging $12,500 per year), 2 teaching assistantships with partial tuition reimbursements available (averaging $16,300 per year). In 2015, 31 master's, 10 doctorates, 22 other advanced degrees awarded. Offers gender studies (Certificate); interdisciplinary studies (MS); modeling and simulation (MS, PhD, Certificate); nanotechnology (MS, PSM). *Application Contact:* Director, Admissions and Student Services, 407-823-2766, Fax: 407-823-6442, E-mail: gradadmissions@ucf.edu. *Interim Vice Provost and Dean,* Dr. Mubarak Shah, 407-823-6432, Fax: 407-823-6442, E-mail: mubarak.shah@mail.ucf.edu.

College of Health and Public Affairs Students: 828 full-time (652 women), 742 part-time (538 women); includes 646 minority (298 Black or African American, non-Hispanic/Latino; 2 American Indian or Alaska Native, non-Hispanic/Latino; 71 Asian, non-Hispanic/Latino; 236 Hispanic/Latino; 39 Two or more races, non-Hispanic/Latino), 26 international. Average age 30. 1,333 applicants, 58% accepted, 490 enrolled. *Faculty:* 150 full-time (83 women), 130 part-time/adjunct (71 women). *Financial support:* In 2015–16, 67 students received support, including 28 fellowships with partial tuition reimbursements available (averaging $6,000 per year), 17 research assistantships with partial tuition reimbursements available (averaging $7,500 per year), 33 teaching assistantships with partial tuition reimbursements available (averaging $7,100 per year); career-related internships or fieldwork, Federal Work-Study, institutionally sponsored loans, traineeships, tuition waivers (partial), and unspecified assistantships also available. Financial award application deadline: 3/1; financial award applicants required to submit FAFSA. In 2015, 590 master's, 59 doctorates, 88 other advanced degrees awarded. *Degree program information:* Part-time and evening/weekend programs available. Part-time, evening/weekend. Offers communication sciences and disorders (MA); corrections leadership (Certificate); criminal justice (MS, PhD); health and public affairs (MA, MNM, MPA, MRA, MS, MSW, DPT, PhD, Certificate); health care informatics (MS); health information administration (Certificate); health services administration (MS); juvenile justice leadership (Certificate); medical speech-language pathology

(Certificate); physical therapy (DPT); police leadership (Certificate); public affairs (PhD); research administration (MRA, Certificate). Electronic applications accepted. *Application Contact:* Director, Admissions and Student Services, 407-823-2766, Fax: 407-823-6442, E-mail: gradadmissions@ucf.edu. *Dean,* Dr. Michael Frumkin, 407-823-0171, E-mail: michael.frumkin@ucf.edu.

School of Public Administration Students: 100 full-time (74 women), 287 part-time (216 women); includes 160 minority (91 Black or African American, non-Hispanic/Latino; 8 Asian, non-Hispanic/Latino; 55 Hispanic/Latino; 6 Two or more races, non-Hispanic/Latino), 4 international. Average age 32. 253 applicants, 79% accepted, 145 enrolled. *Faculty:* 18 full-time (9 women), 19 part-time/adjunct (9 women). *Financial support:* In 2015–16, 4 students received support, including 2 fellowships with partial tuition reimbursements available (averaging $5,500 per year), 1 research assistantship with partial tuition reimbursement available (averaging $8,400 per year), 1 teaching assistantship (averaging $6,700 per year); career-related internships or fieldwork, Federal Work-Study, institutionally sponsored loans, tuition waivers (partial), and unspecified assistantships also available. Financial award application deadline: 3/1; financial award applicants required to submit FAFSA. In 2015, 95 master's, 27 other advanced degrees awarded. *Degree program information:* Part-time and evening/weekend programs available. Part-time, evening/weekend. Offers emergency management and homeland security (Certificate); fundraising (Certificate); non-profit management (MNM, Certificate); urban and regional planning (MS). *Application deadline:* For fall admission, 7/1 for domestic students; for spring admission, 12/1 for domestic students. *Application fee:* $30. Electronic applications accepted. *Application Contact:* Director, Admissions and Student Services, 407-823-2766, Fax: 407-823-6442, E-mail: gradadmissions@ucf.edu. *Director,* Dr. Naim Kapucu, 407-823-3693, Fax: 407-823-5651, E-mail: naim.kapucu@ucf.edu.

School of Social Work Students: 202 full-time (178 women), 66 part-time (58 women); includes 142 minority (64 Black or African American, non-Hispanic/Latino; 2 Asian, non-Hispanic/Latino; 65 Hispanic/Latino; 11 Two or more races, non-Hispanic/Latino). Average age 29. 203 applicants, 66% accepted, 89 enrolled. *Faculty:* 21 full-time (18 women), 17 part-time/adjunct (12 women). *Financial support:* In 2015–16, 2 students received support, including 1 fellowship with partial tuition reimbursement available (averaging $5,000 per year), 1 research assistantship with partial tuition reimbursement available (averaging $6,200 per year); career-related internships or fieldwork, Federal Work-Study, institutionally sponsored loans, and unspecified assistantships also available. Financial award application deadline: 3/1; financial award applicants required to submit FAFSA. In 2015, 171 master's, 24 other advanced degrees awarded. *Degree program information:* Part-time and evening/weekend programs available. Part-time, evening/weekend. Offers military social work (Certificate); social work (MSW). *Application deadline:* For fall admission, 3/1 for domestic students. *Application fee:* $30. Electronic applications accepted. *Application Contact:* Director, Admissions and Student Services, 407-823-2766, Fax: 407-823-6442, E-mail: gradadmissions@ucf.edu. *Director,* Dr. Bonnie Yegidis, 407-823-2114, E-mail: bonnie.yegidis@ucf.edu.

College of Medicine ***Financial support:*** Fellowships, research assistantships, and teaching assistantships available. Offers medicine (MS, MD, PhD). *Application Contact:* Director, Admissions and Registration, 407-823-2766, Fax: 407-823-6442, E-mail: gradadmissions@ucf.edu. *Vice President for Medical Affairs/Dean,* Dr. Deborah C. German, 407-266-1000, E-mail: deborah.german@ucf.edu.

Burnett School of Biomedical Sciences Students: 80 full-time (44 women), 6 part-time (4 women); includes 23 minority (8 Black or African American, non-Hispanic/Latino; 10 Asian, non-Hispanic/Latino; 4 Hispanic/Latino; 1 Two or more races, non-Hispanic/Latino), 19 international. Average age 27. 118 applicants, 47% accepted, 30 enrolled. *Faculty:* 13 full-time (4 women), 1 (woman) part-time/adjunct. *Financial support:* In 2015–16, 55 students received support, including 16 fellowships with partial tuition reimbursements available (averaging $3,500 per year), 48 research assistantships with partial tuition reimbursements available (averaging $8,000 per year), 44 teaching assistantships with partial tuition reimbursements available (averaging $6,500 per year). In 2015, 19 master's, 8 doctorates awarded. Offers biomedical sciences (MS, PhD); biotechnology (MS). Electronic applications accepted. *Application Contact:* Director, Admissions and Student Services, 407-823-2766, Fax: 407-823-6442, E-mail: gradadmissions@ucf.edu. *Director,* Dr. Griffith Parks, 407-226-1000, E-mail: griffith.parks@ucf.edu.

College of Nursing Students: 55 full-time (50 women), 245 part-time (219 women); includes 82 minority (31 Black or African American, non-Hispanic/Latino; 2 American Indian or Alaska Native, non-Hispanic/Latino; 12 Asian, non-Hispanic/Latino; 35 Hispanic/Latino; 1 Native Hawaiian or other Pacific Islander, non-Hispanic/Latino; 1 Two or more races, non-Hispanic/Latino), 1 international. Average age 38. 169 applicants, 60% accepted, 76 enrolled. *Faculty:* 47 full-time (41 women), 74 part-time/adjunct (72 women). *Financial support:* In 2015–16, 27 students received support, including 26 fellowships with partial tuition reimbursements available (averaging $9,010 per year), 1 research assistantship with partial tuition reimbursement available (averaging $14,400 per year), 1 teaching assistantship with partial tuition reimbursement available (averaging $12,100 per year); career-related internships or fieldwork, Federal Work-Study, institutionally sponsored loans, traineeships, and unspecified assistantships also available. Financial award application deadline: 3/1; financial award applicants required to submit FAFSA. In 2015, 90 master's, 16 doctorates, 3 other advanced degrees awarded. *Degree program information:* Part-time and evening/weekend programs available. Part-time, evening/weekend. Offers nursing (MSN, DNP, PhD, Post-Master's Certificate). *Application deadline:* For fall admission, 2/15 for domestic students; for spring admission, 9/15 for domestic students. *Application fee:* $30. Electronic applications accepted. *Application Contact:* Director, Admissions and Student Services, 407-823-2766, Fax: 407-823-6442, E-mail: gradadmissions@ucf.edu. *Dean,* Dr. Mary Lou Sole, 407-823-5496, Fax: 407-823-5675, E-mail: mary.sole@ucf.edu.

College of Optics and Photonics Students: 106 full-time (19 women), 10 part-time (1 woman); includes 8 minority (1 Asian, non-Hispanic/Latino; 6 Hispanic/Latino; 1 Two or more races, non-Hispanic/Latino), 71 international. Average age 26. 186 applicants, 32% accepted, 29 enrolled. *Faculty:* 40 full-time (6 women), 17 part-time/adjunct (1 woman). *Financial support:* In 2015–16, 74 students received support, including 20 fellowships with partial tuition reimbursements available (averaging $7,800 per year), 74 research assistantships with partial tuition reimbursements available (averaging $12,400 per year), 5 teaching assistantships with partial tuition reimbursements available (averaging $8,000 per year); career-related internships or fieldwork, Federal Work-Study, institutionally sponsored loans, tuition waivers (partial), and unspecified assistantships also available. Financial award application deadline: 3/1; financial award applicants required to submit FAFSA. In 2015, 16 master's, 22 doctorates awarded. *Degree program information:* Part-time and evening/weekend programs available. Part-time, evening/weekend. Offers optics and photonics (MS, PhD). *Application deadline:* For fall admission, 2/1 priority date for domestic students; for spring admission, 12/1 for domestic students. *Application fee:* $30. Electronic applications accepted. *Application Contact:* Director, Admissions and Student Services, 407-823-2766, Fax: 407-823-6442, E-mail: gradadmissions@ucf.edu. *Dean and Director,* Dr. Bahaa E. Saleh, 407-823-6817, E-mail: besaleh@creol.ucf.edu.

College of Sciences Students: 629 full-time (326 women), 182 part-time (102 women); includes 184 minority (37 Black or African American, non-Hispanic/Latino; 1 American Indian or Alaska Native, non-Hispanic/Latino; 44 Asian, non-Hispanic/Latino; 85 Hispanic/Latino; 1 Native Hawaiian or other Pacific Islander, non-Hispanic/Latino; 16 Two or more races, non-Hispanic/Latino), 127 international. Average age 29. 1,132 applicants, 38% accepted, 226 enrolled. *Faculty:* 317 full-time (108 women), 58 part-time/adjunct (23 women). *Financial support:* In 2015–16, 450 students received support, including 125 fellowships with partial tuition reimbursements available (averaging $5,300 per year), 131 research assistantships with partial tuition reimbursements available (averaging $10,100 per year), 333 teaching assistantships with partial tuition reimbursements available (averaging $10,400 per year). In 2015, 187 master's, 68 doctorates, 29 other advanced degrees awarded. Offers anthropology (MA); applied experimental and human factors psychology (PhD); applied sociology (MA); chemistry (MS, PhD); clinical psychology (MA, MS, PhD); computer forensics (Certificate); conservation biology (MS, PhD, Certificate); industrial/organizational psychology (MS, PhD); intelligence and national security (Certificate); mathematical science (MS, PhD, Certificate); Maya studies (Certificate); physics (MS, PhD); political science (MA); SAS data mining (Certificate); sciences (MA, MS, PhD, Certificate); security studies (PhD); sociology (PhD); statistical computing (MS). *Application Contact:* Director, Admissions and Student Services, 407-823-2766, Fax: 407-823-6442, E-mail: gradadmissions@ucf.edu. *Dean,* Dr. Michael Johnson, 407-823-1911, E-mail: michael.johnson@ucf.edu.

Nicholson School of Communication Students: 32 full-time (21 women), 29 part-time (24 women); includes 19 minority (8 Black or African American, non-Hispanic/Latino; 3 Asian, non-Hispanic/Latino; 8 Hispanic/Latino), 10 international. Average age 27. 47 applicants, 79% accepted, 16 enrolled. *Faculty:* 41 full-time (18 women), 20 part-time/adjunct (11 women). *Financial support:* In 2015–16, 18 students received support, including 2 fellowships with partial tuition reimbursements available (averaging $4,000 per year), 3 research assistantships with partial tuition reimbursements available (averaging $5,950 per year), 15 teaching assistantships with partial tuition reimbursements available (averaging $7,400 per year); career-related internships or fieldwork, Federal Work-Study, institutionally sponsored loans, tuition waivers (partial), and unspecified assistantships also available. Financial award application deadline: 3/1; financial award applicants required to submit FAFSA. In 2015, 27 master's, 9 other advanced degrees awarded. *Degree program information:* Part-time and evening/weekend programs available. Part-time, evening/weekend. Offers communication (MA); corporate communication (Certificate). *Application deadline:* For fall admission, 7/15 for domestic students; for spring admission, 12/7 for domestic students. *Application fee:* $30. Electronic applications accepted. *Application Contact:* Director, Admissions and Student Services, 407-823-2766, Fax: 407-823-6442, E-mail: gradadmissions@ucf.edu.

Rosen College of Hospitality Management Students: 48 full-time (34 women), 70 part-time (50 women); includes 20 minority (5 Black or African American, non-Hispanic/Latino; 3 Asian, non-Hispanic/Latino; 9 Hispanic/Latino; 3 Two or more races, non-Hispanic/Latino), 15 international. Average age 30. 169 applicants, 57% accepted, 69 enrolled. *Faculty:* 51 full-time (20 women), 28 part-time/adjunct (11 women). *Financial support:* In 2015–16, 18 students received support, including 5 fellowships with partial tuition reimbursements available (averaging $2,200 per year), 17 teaching assistantships with partial tuition reimbursements available (averaging $10,200 per year); research assistantships also available. In 2015, 36 master's, 10 other advanced degrees awarded. Offers destination marketing and management (Certificate); event management (Certificate); hospitality and tourism management (MS); hospitality management (PhD). *Application deadline:* For fall admission, 2/1 for domestic students. *Application fee:* $30. Electronic applications accepted. *Application Contact:* Director, Admissions and Student Services, 407-823-2766, Fax: 407-823-6442, E-mail: gradadmissions@ucf.edu. *Dean,* Dr. Abraham C. Pizam, 407-903-8010, E-mail: abraham.pizam@ucf.edu.

UNIVERSITY OF CENTRAL MISSOURI, Warrensburg, MO 64093

General Information State-supported, coed, comprehensive institution. CGS member. *Enrollment:* 14,395 graduate, professional, and undergraduate students; 2,161 full-time matriculated graduate/professional students (723 women), 2,077 part-time matriculated graduate/professional students (1,061 women). *Enrollment by degree level:* 4,047 master's, 23 doctoral, 168 other advanced degrees. *Graduate faculty:* 336 full-time (145 women), 39 part-time/adjunct (25 women). Tuition, state resident: full-time $6683; part-time $278.45 per credit hour. Tuition, nonresident: full-time $13,366; part-time $556.90 per credit hour. *Required fees:* $701; $29.20 per credit hour. Tuition and fees vary according to degree level and campus/location. *Graduate housing:* Rooms and/or apartments available on a first-come, first-served basis to single and married students. Typical cost: $6417 per year for single students; $6327 per year for married students. Room charges vary according to board plan and housing facility selected. Housing application deadline: 8/1. *Student services:* Campus employment opportunities, campus safety program, career counseling, child daycare facilities, exercise/wellness program, free psychological counseling, grant writing training, international student services, low-cost health insurance, multicultural affairs office, services for students with disabilities, teacher training, writing training. *Library:* James C. Kirkpatrick Library. Students can reserve study rooms.

Computer facilities: 6,395 computers available on campus for general student use. A campuswide network can be accessed from student residence rooms and from off campus. Online class registration is available.
Website: http://www.ucmo.edu/

General Application Contact: Brittany Lawrence, Graduate Student Services Coordinator, 660-543-8423, E-mail: gradinfo@ucmo.edu.

GRADUATE UNITS

The Graduate School Students: 2,161 full-time (723 women), 2,077 part-time (1,061 women); includes 188 minority (93 Black or African American, non-Hispanic/Latino; 4 American Indian or Alaska Native, non-Hispanic/Latino; 15 Asian, non-Hispanic/Latino; 32 Hispanic/Latino; 1 Native Hawaiian or other Pacific Islander, non-Hispanic/Latino; 43 Two or more races, non-Hispanic/Latino), 2,514 international. Average age 28. 3,454 applicants, 68% accepted, 1632 enrolled. *Faculty:* 336 full-time (145 women), 39 part-time/adjunct (25 women). *Financial support:* In 2015–16, 97 students received support, including 146 research assistantships with partial tuition reimbursements available (averaging $7,500 per year), 73 teaching assistantships with partial tuition reimbursements available (averaging $7,500 per year); career-related internships or fieldwork, Federal Work-Study, scholarships/grants, and administrative and laboratory assistantships also available. Support available to part-time students. Financial award application deadline: 3/1; financial award applicants required to submit FAFSA. In 2015,

1,530 master's, 53 other advanced degrees awarded. *Degree program information:* Part-time programs available. Part-time, 100% online, blended/hybrid learning. Offers accountancy (MA); accounting (MBA); applied mathematics (MS); aviation safety (MA); biology (MS); business administration (MBA); career and technical education leadership (MS); college student personnel administration (MS); communication (MA); computer science (MS); counseling (MS); criminal justice (MS); educational leadership (Ed D); educational technology (MS); elementary and early childhood education (MSE); English (MA); environmental studies (MA); finance (MBA); history (MA); human services/educational technology (Ed S); human services/learning resources (Ed S); human services/professional counseling (Ed S); industrial hygiene (MS); industrial management (MS); information systems (MBA); information technology (MS); kinesiology (MS); library science and information services (MS); literacy education (MSE); marketing (MBA); mathematics (MS); music (MA); occupational safety management (MS); psychology (MS); rural family nursing (MS); school administration (MSE); social gerontology (MS); sociology (MA); special education (MSE); speech language pathology (MS); superintendency (Ed S); teaching (MAT); teaching English as a second language (MA); technology (MS); technology management (PhD); theatre (MA). *Application deadline:* For fall admission, 6/1 priority date for domestic and international students; for spring admission, 10/1 priority date for domestic and international students; for summer admission, 4/1 priority date for domestic and international students. Applications are processed on a rolling basis. *Application fee:* $30 ($75 for international students). Electronic applications accepted. *Application Contact:* Brittany Lawrence, Graduate Student Services Coordinator, 660-543-4621, Fax: 660-543-4778, E-mail: gradinfo@ucmo.edu. *Director of Graduate School and International Admissions*, Tina Church-Hockett, 660-543-4621, Fax: 660-543-4778, E-mail: church@ucmo.edu.

UNIVERSITY OF CENTRAL OKLAHOMA, Edmond, OK 73034-5209

General Information State-supported, coed, comprehensive institution. CGS member. *Graduate housing:* Rooms and/or apartments available on a first-come, first-served basis to single and married students. Housing application deadline: 7/1. *Research affiliation:* National Science Foundation, U.S. Department of Education (DOE), U.S. Department of Veteran Affairs, Oklahoma Department of Human Services, Oklahoma Idea Network of Biomedical Research Excellence, Oklahoma Small Business Administration.

GRADUATE UNITS

The Jackson College of Graduate Studies ***Degree program information:*** Part-time and evening/weekend programs available. Part-time, evening/weekend. Electronic applications accepted.

College of Business Degree program information: Part-time programs available. Part-time. Offers accounting (MBA); management (MBA). Electronic applications accepted.

College of Education and Professional Studies Degree program information: Part-time programs available. Part-time. Offers adult and higher education (M Ed); athletic training (MS); bilingual education/teaching English as a second language (M Ed); counseling psychology (MA); early childhood education (M Ed); education and professional studies (M Ed, MA, MS); educational leadership (M Ed); elementary education (M Ed); experimental psychology (MA); family and child studies (MS); forensic psychology (MA); general psychology (MA); library media education (M Ed); nutrition-food management (MS); reading (M Ed); school counseling (M Ed); school psychology (MA); secondary education (M Ed); special education (M Ed); speech-language pathology (MS); wellness management (MS). Electronic applications accepted.

College of Fine Arts and Design Degree program information: Part-time and evening/weekend programs available. Part-time, evening/weekend, online learning. Offers design (MFA); fine arts and design (MFA, MM); jazz (MM); music (MM). Electronic applications accepted.

College of Liberal Arts Degree program information: Part-time programs available. Part-time. Offers creative writing (MA, MFA); crime and intelligence analysis (MA); criminal justice management and administration (MA); gerontology (MA); history (MA); international affairs (MA); liberal arts (MA, MFA, MPA); museum studies (MA); political science (MA); public administration (MPA); sociology (MA); traditional studies (MA). Electronic applications accepted.

College of Mathematics and Science Degree program information: Part-time programs available. Part-time. Offers applied mathematical sciences (MS); biology (MS); biomedical engineering (MS); electrical engineering (MS); mathematics and science (MS); mechanical systems (MS); nursing (MS); physics (MS). Electronic applications accepted.

Forensic Science Institute Offers biology/chemistry (MS); forensic science (MS). Electronic applications accepted.

UNIVERSITY OF CHARLESTON, Charleston, WV 25304-1099

General Information Independent, coed, comprehensive institution. *Enrollment:* 2,327 graduate, professional, and undergraduate students; 581 full-time matriculated graduate/professional students (272 women), 19 part-time matriculated graduate/professional students (9 women). *Enrollment by degree level:* 221 master's, 379 doctoral. *Graduate faculty:* 42 full-time (30 women), 14 part-time/adjunct (3 women). *Tuition, area resident:* Full-time $20,602; part-time $425 per credit. *Required fees:* $200. *Graduate housing:* Rooms and/or apartments available on a first-come, first-served basis to single and married students. *Student services:* Campus employment opportunities, campus safety program, career counseling, free psychological counseling, international student services, low-cost health insurance, services for students with disabilities. *Library:* Schoenbaum Library plus 1 other. *Research affiliation:* Walmart (pharmacy).

Computer facilities: 200 computers available on campus for general student use. A campuswide network can be accessed from student residence rooms and from off campus. Online class registration is available.
Website: http://www.ucwv.edu/

General Application Contact: Sandy Dolin, Application Coordinator, 800-357-4752, Fax: 304-357-4750, E-mail: admissions@ucwv.edu.

GRADUATE UNITS

Doctor of Executive Leadership Program Students: 71 full-time (24 women), 12 part-time (7 women); includes 15 minority (10 Black or African American, non-Hispanic/Latino; 2 American Indian or Alaska Native, non-Hispanic/Latino; 2 Asian, non-Hispanic/Latino; 1 Hispanic/Latino). Average age 45. Offers leadership (DEL). *Application deadline:* Applications are processed on a rolling basis. Electronic applications accepted. *Application Contact:* David Cooper, Applications Coordinator, E-mail: davidcooper@ucwv.edu. *Program Director*, Dr. Ruth Wylie, E-mail: ruthwylie@ucwv.edu.

Master of Business Administration Program Students: 67 full-time (28 women); includes 4 minority (all Black or African American, non-Hispanic/Latino), 4 international. Average age 33. *Financial support:* Scholarships/grants and unspecified assistantships available. Financial award application deadline: 3/1; financial award applicants required to submit FAFSA. *Degree program information:* Part-time and evening/weekend programs available. Part-time, evening/weekend. Offers business administration (MBA). *Application deadline:* Applications are processed on a rolling basis. *Application fee:* $50. Electronic applications accepted. *Application Contact:* Bobby Redd, Admissions Representative, 304-860-5621, E-mail: bobbyredd@ucwv.edu. *Program Director*, Rick Ferris, 304-720-6680, E-mail: mba@ucwv.edu.

Master of Forensic Accounting Program Students: 9 full-time (6 women); includes 2 minority (both Black or African American, non-Hispanic/Latino). Average age 36. *Financial support:* Applicants required to submit FAFSA. *Degree program information:* Part-time programs available. Part-time, online learning. Offers forensic accounting (EMFA). *Application deadline:* Applications are processed on a rolling basis. *Application fee:* $50. Electronic applications accepted. *Application Contact:* Bobby Redd, Admissions Representative, 304-860-5621, E-mail: bobbyredd@ucwv.edu. *Program Director*, Christina Chard, 304-352-0033, E-mail: christinachard@ucwv.edu.

Master of Science in Strategic Leadership Program Students: 96 full-time (26 women), 2 part-time; includes 6 minority (5 Black or African American, non-Hispanic/Latino; 1 Two or more races, non-Hispanic/Latino), 3 international. Average age 37. Offers strategic leadership (MS). *Application Contact:* David Cooper, Admissions Representative, 304-352-0013, E-mail: davidcooper@ucwv.edu. *Associate Dean of Leadership*, Dr. John Barnette, 304-720-6688, E-mail: johnbarnette@ucwv.edu.

Physician Assistant Program Students: 47 full-time (36 women); includes 3 minority (all Asian, non-Hispanic/Latino), 1 international. Average age 27. *Financial support:* Career-related internships or fieldwork available. Offers physician assistant (MPAS). *Application deadline:* Applications are processed on a rolling basis. Electronic applications accepted. *Application Contact:* Pam Carden, Admissions Coordinator, 304-357-4968, E-mail: pamcarden@ucwv.edu. *Program Director*, Jennifer Pack, 304-357-4790, E-mail: jenniferpack@ucwv.edu.

School of Pharmacy Students: 291 full-time (152 women), 5 part-time (2 women); includes 96 minority (41 Black or African American, non-Hispanic/Latino; 2 American Indian or Alaska Native, non-Hispanic/Latino; 39 Asian, non-Hispanic/Latino; 9 Hispanic/Latino; 1 Native Hawaiian or other Pacific Islander, non-Hispanic/Latino; 4 Two or more races, non-Hispanic/Latino), 9 international. Average age 26. *Financial support:* Career-related internships or fieldwork and scholarships/grants available. Financial award application deadline: 3/1; financial award applicants required to submit FAFSA. Offers pharmacy (Pharm D). *Application deadline:* For fall admission, 2/1 for domestic and international students. Applications are processed on a rolling basis. Electronic applications accepted. *Application Contact:* Jamie Bero, Director of Recruitment and Admissions, 304-357-4889, E-mail: staciegeise@ucwv.edu. *Dean*, Dr. Michelle Easton, 304-357-4889, Fax: 304-357-4868, E-mail: michelleeaston@ucwv.edu.

UNIVERSITY OF CHICAGO, Chicago, IL 60637-1513

General Information Independent, coed, university. CGS member. *Enrollment:* 12,962 graduate, professional, and undergraduate students; 6,858 full-time matriculated graduate/professional students (2,925 women), 2,077 part-time matriculated graduate/professional students (509 women). *Enrollment by degree level:* 5,841 master's, 3,094 doctoral. *Graduate faculty:* 2,215 full-time (752 women), 519 part-time/adjunct (187 women). *Graduate housing:* Rooms and/or apartments available on a first-come, first-served basis to single and married students. *Student services:* Campus employment opportunities, campus safety program, career counseling, exercise/wellness program, free psychological counseling, grant writing training, international student services, low-cost health insurance, multicultural affairs office, services for students with disabilities, teacher training, writing training. *Library:* Joseph Regenstein Library plus 5 others. *Collection:* Books: 9.6 million (physical), 1.4 million (digital/electronic); Databases: 1,337. *Research affiliation:* National Opinion Research Center (social science), Fermilab (high-energy physics), Argonne National Laboratory (energy, materials), Marine Biological Laboratory (molecular biology), Fermilab (high-energy physics), Argonne National Laboratory (energy, materials).

Computer facilities: Computer purchase and lease plans are available. 300 computers available on campus for general student use. A campuswide network can be accessed from student residence rooms and from off campus. Online class registration is available.
Website: http://www.uchicago.edu/

General Application Contact: Elysse Longiotti, Program Coordinator, Graduate Enrollment and Initiatives, 773-702-3760, Fax: 773-702-4199, E-mail: gradadmissions@uchicago.edu.

GRADUATE UNITS

Booth School of Business Students: 1,416 full-time (510 women), 1,627 part-time (395 women). *Faculty:* 158 full-time (22 women), 16 part-time/adjunct (3 women). *Financial support:* Fellowships and scholarships/grants available. Financial award applicants required to submit FAFSA. In 2015, 1,349 master's, 25 doctorates awarded. *Degree program information:* Part-time and evening/weekend programs available. Part-time, evening/weekend. Offers accounting (MBA); analytic finance (MBA); analytic management (MBA); business (MBA, PhD, Certificate); business administration (MBA, Certificate); econometrics and statistics (MBA); economics (MBA); entrepreneurship (MBA); executive business administration (MBA); finance (MBA); general management (MBA); health administration and policy (Certificate); international business (MBA); managerial and organizational behavior (MBA); marketing management (MBA); operations management (MBA); strategic management (MBA). Electronic applications accepted. *Application Contact:* Admissions, 773-702-7369, E-mail: admissions@chicagobooth.edu. *Dean*, Dr. Sunil Kumar, 773-702-1680, E-mail: sunil.kumar@chicagobooth.edu.

Divinity School Students: 305 full-time (119 women), 11 part-time (5 women); includes 41 minority (17 Black or African American, non-Hispanic/Latino; 16 Asian, non-Hispanic/Latino; 4 Hispanic/Latino; 4 Two or more races, non-Hispanic/Latino), 44 international. 381 applicants, 51% accepted, 93 enrolled. *Faculty:* 30 full-time (7 women), 3 part-time/adjunct (0 women). *Financial support:* In 2015–16, 305 students received support, including 21 fellowships with tuition reimbursements available (averaging $24,000 per year); career-related internships or fieldwork, Federal Work-Study, institutionally sponsored loans, scholarships/grants, health care benefits, and tuition waivers (full and partial) also available. Support available to part-time students. Financial award application deadline: 12/15; financial award applicants required to submit FAFSA. In 2015, 59 master's, 12 doctorates awarded. *Degree program information:* Part-time programs available. Part-time. Offers anthropology and sociology of religions (PhD); Bible (PhD); divinity (AM, AMRS, M Div, MA, PhD); history of Christianity (PhD); history of Judaism (PhD); history of religions (PhD); Islamic studies

(PhD); ministry (M Div); philosophy of religions (PhD); religion (MA, PhD); religion, literature, and visual culture (PhD); religions in America (PhD); religious ethics (PhD); religious studies (MA); theology (PhD). *Application deadline:* For fall admission, 12/15 for domestic and international students. *Application fee:* $75. Electronic applications accepted. *Application Contact:* John W. Howell, Coordinator for Recruiting and Admissions, 773-702-8249, Fax: 773-834-4581, E-mail: divinityadmissions@uchicago.edu. *Dean/Associate Professor of Religion and Literature*, Dr. Richard A. Rosengarten, 773-702-8200.

Division of the Biological Sciences Students: 415 full-time (187 women), 24 part-time (13 women); includes 99 minority (17 Black or African American, non-Hispanic/Latino; 44 Asian, non-Hispanic/Latino; 32 Hispanic/Latino; 1 Native Hawaiian or other Pacific Islander, non-Hispanic/Latino; 5 Two or more races, non-Hispanic/Latino), 77 international. 1,161 applicants, 21% accepted, 99 enrolled. *Faculty:* 195 full-time (59 women), 7 part-time/adjunct. *Financial support:* Fellowships, research assistantships with full tuition reimbursements, institutionally sponsored loans, scholarships/grants, traineeships, and health care benefits available. Financial award applicants required to submit FAFSA. In 2015, 29 master's, 65 doctorates awarded. Offers biochemistry and molecular biophysics (PhD); biological sciences (MS, PhD); cancer biology (PhD); cell and molecular biology (PhD); computational neuroscience (PhD); development, regeneration, and stem cell biology (PhD); ecology and evolution (PhD); evolutionary biology (PhD); genetics, genomics and systems biology (PhD); human genetics (PhD); immunology (PhD); integrative biology (PhD); interdisciplinary scientist training (PhD); medical physics (PhD); microbiology (PhD); molecular metabolism and nutrition (PhD); neurobiology (PhD); public health sciences (MS, PhD). *Application deadline:* For fall admission, 12/1 for domestic and international students. *Application fee:* $90. Electronic applications accepted. *Application Contact:* E-mail: bsd.ogpa@lists.uchicago.edu. *Dean and Executive Vice President for Medical Affairs*, Kenneth Polonsky, MD.

Division of the Humanities Students: 793 full-time (389 women), 8 part-time (4 women); includes 110 minority (20 Black or African American, non-Hispanic/Latino; 4 American Indian or Alaska Native, non-Hispanic/Latino; 28 Asian, non-Hispanic/Latino; 40 Hispanic/Latino; 18 Two or more races, non-Hispanic/Latino), 205 international. 2,122 applicants, 14% accepted, 420 enrolled. *Faculty:* 243 full-time (101 women), 47 part-time/adjunct (19 women). *Financial support:* Fellowships, teaching assistantships, career-related internships or fieldwork, Federal Work-Study, institutionally sponsored loans, scholarships/grants, health care benefits, and tuition waivers (full and partial) available. Financial award application deadline: 12/15; financial award applicants required to submit FAFSA. In 2015, 145 master's, 66 doctorates awarded. Offers ancient Greek and Roman philosophy (PhD); ancient Mediterranean world (PhD); ancient philosophy (PhD); anthropology and linguistics (PhD); art history (PhD); cinema and media studies (PhD); classical languages and literatures (PhD); classics (MA); comparative literature (MA); creative writing (MA); digital humanities (MA); East Asian languages and civilizations (PhD); English language and literature (PhD); French (PhD); Germanic languages and literatures (PhD); Germanic studies (MA); humanities (MA, MFA, PhD); Italian (PhD); linguistics (MA, PhD); music (PhD); Near Eastern languages and civilizations (PhD); philosophy (MA, PhD); Renaissance and early modern studies (PhD); Romance languages and literatures (MA); South Asian languages and civilizations (MA, PhD); Spanish (PhD); transformations in the classical tradition (PhD); visual arts (MFA). *Application deadline:* For fall admission, 12/15 for domestic and international students. *Application fee:* $90. Electronic applications accepted. *Application Contact:* Michael Beetley, Assistant Dean of Students, 773-702-1552, Fax: 773-834-9148, E-mail: humanitiesadmissions@uchicago.edu. *Dean of Students*, Martina Munsters.

Division of the Physical Sciences Offers applied mathematics (PhD); astronomy and astrophysics (PhD); atmospheric sciences (PhD); biophysical science (PhD); chemistry (PhD); computer science (MS, PhD); cosmochemistry (PhD); earth sciences (PhD); financial mathematics (MS); mathematics (PhD); paleobiology (PhD); physical sciences (MS, PhD); physics (PhD); planetary and space sciences (PhD); statistics (MS, PhD). Electronic applications accepted.

Division of the Social Sciences Students: 1,140 full-time (505 women), 2 part-time (1 woman); includes 221 minority (58 Black or African American, non-Hispanic/Latino; 10 American Indian or Alaska Native, non-Hispanic/Latino; 47 Asian, non-Hispanic/Latino; 66 Hispanic/Latino; 40 Two or more races, non-Hispanic/Latino), 395 international. 2,843 applicants, 38% accepted, 315 enrolled. *Faculty:* 190 full-time (63 women), 14 part-time/adjunct (1 woman). *Financial support:* In 2015–16, 275 students received support, including 99 fellowships with full tuition reimbursements available (averaging $23,000 per year); career-related internships or fieldwork, Federal Work-Study, institutionally sponsored loans, scholarships/grants, and health care benefits also available. Financial award application deadline: 12/15. In 2015, 321 master's, 119 doctorates awarded. Offers anthropology (PhD); comparative human development (PhD); computational social science (MA); conceptual and historical studies of science (PhD); economics (PhD); history (PhD); international relations (MA); political science (PhD); psychology (PhD); social sciences (MA, PhD); social thought (PhD); sociology (PhD). *Application deadline:* For fall admission, 12/15 for domestic and international students. *Application fee:* $90. Electronic applications accepted. *Application Contact:* Office of the Dean of Students, 773-702-8415, E-mail: admissions@ssd.uchicago.edu. *Dean*, Prof. David Nirenberg.

Center for Latin American Studies Students: 6 full-time (4 women); includes 1 minority (Hispanic/Latino). Average age 25. 16 applicants, 50% accepted, 3 enrolled. *Financial support:* In 2015–16, 6 students received support. Federal Work-Study, institutionally sponsored loans, and scholarships/grants available. Financial award application deadline: 1/5. In 2015, 3 master's awarded. Offers Latin American studies (MA). *Application deadline:* For fall admission, 1/5 priority date for domestic and international students. *Application fee:* $90. Electronic applications accepted. *Application Contact:* Office of the Dean of Students, 773-702-8415, E-mail: admissions@ssd.uchicago.edu. *Director*, Prof. Brodwyn Fischer, Fax: 773-702-8420, E-mail: clas@uchicago.edu.

Center for Middle Eastern Studies Offers Middle Eastern studies (MA). Electronic applications accepted.

Graham School of Continuing Liberal and Professional Studies ***Degree program information:*** Part-time and evening/weekend programs available. Part-time, evening/weekend. Offers analytics (M Sc); liberal arts (MLA); threat and response management (M Sc); urban teacher education (MAT). Electronic applications accepted.

Harris School of Public Policy Offers computational analysis and public policy (MS); environmental science and policy (MS); public policy (AM, MPP, MS, PhD); public policy studies (AM); research methods (AM). Electronic applications accepted.

Institute for Molecular Engineering Offers molecular engineering (PhD). Electronic applications accepted.

The Law School Students: 617 full-time (272 women); includes 182 minority (32 Black or African American, non-Hispanic/Latino; 69 Asian, non-Hispanic/Latino; 66 Hispanic/Latino; 15 Two or more races, non-Hispanic/Latino), 33 international. Average age 24. 4,111 applicants, 22% accepted, 183 enrolled. *Faculty:* 74 full-time (26 women), 50 part-time/adjunct (17 women). *Financial support:* In 2015–16, 468 students received support. Career-related internships or fieldwork, institutionally sponsored loans, and scholarships/grants available. Financial award application deadline: 3/1; financial award applicants required to submit FAFSA. In 2015, 72 master's, 199 doctorates awarded. Offers law (LL M, MCL, DCL, JD, JSD). *Application deadline:* For fall admission, 3/1 priority date for domestic students. Applications are processed on a rolling basis. *Application fee:* $75. Electronic applications accepted. *Application Contact:* Ann K. Perry, Associate Dean of Admissions and Financial Aid, 773-834-4425, Fax: 773-834-0942, E-mail: admissions@law.uchicago.edu. *Dean*, Thomas J. Miles, 773-702-9494, Fax: 773-834-4409.

Pritzker School of Medicine Offers medicine (MD). Electronic applications accepted.

School of Social Service Administration ***Degree program information:*** Part-time and evening/weekend programs available. Part-time, evening/weekend. Offers social service administration (AM, MA, PhD). AM/M Div offered jointly with the Divinity School, MBA/AM offered jointly with Booth School of Business, MPP/AM offered jointly with Harris School of Public Policy. Electronic applications accepted.

UNIVERSITY OF CINCINNATI, Cincinnati, OH 45221

General Information State-supported, coed, university. CGS member. *Graduate housing:* Rooms and/or apartments available on a first-come, first-served basis to single and married students. Housing application deadline: 7/1.

GRADUATE UNITS

College of Law Students: 295 full-time (134 women), 1 (woman) part-time; includes 46 minority (25 Black or African American, non-Hispanic/Latino; 9 Asian, non-Hispanic/Latino; 10 Hispanic/Latino; 2 Two or more races, non-Hispanic/Latino), 19 international. Average age 25. 852 applicants, 57% accepted, 119 enrolled. *Faculty:* 37 full-time (20 women), 28 part-time/adjunct (7 women). *Financial support:* In 2015–16, 235 students received support, including 16 fellowships (averaging $3,500 per year); research assistantships, career-related internships or fieldwork, Federal Work-Study, scholarships/grants, tuition waivers (full and partial), and unspecified assistantships also available. Financial award application deadline: 3/15; financial award applicants required to submit FAFSA. In 2015, 109 doctorates awarded. Offers law (JD). *Application deadline:* For fall admission, 3/15 priority date for domestic and international students. Applications are processed on a rolling basis. *Application fee:* $35. Electronic applications accepted. *Application Contact:* Al Watson, Senior Assistant Dean and Director of Admissions, 513-556-0077, Fax: 513-556-2391, E-mail: alfred.watson@uc.edu. *Dean*, Jennifer S. Bard, 513-556-0121, Fax: 513-556-2391, E-mail: jennifer.bard@uc.edu.

Graduate School ***Degree program information:*** Part-time and evening/weekend programs available. Part-time, evening/weekend, online learning. Offers neuroscience (PhD). Electronic applications accepted.

Carl H. Lindner College of Business Students: 505 full-time (215 women), 604 part-time (248 women); includes 120 minority (49 Black or African American, non-Hispanic/Latino; 1 American Indian or Alaska Native, non-Hispanic/Latino; 40 Asian, non-Hispanic/Latino; 20 Hispanic/Latino; 1 Native Hawaiian or other Pacific Islander, non-Hispanic/Latino; 9 Two or more races, non-Hispanic/Latino), 422 international. Average age 29. 1,870 applicants, 46% accepted, 471 enrolled. *Faculty:* 93 full-time (27 women), 36 part-time/adjunct (6 women). *Financial support:* In 2015–16, 242 students received support, including 25 research assistantships with tuition reimbursements available (averaging $23,250 per year), 25 teaching assistantships with tuition reimbursements available (averaging $3,000 per year); scholarships/grants, tuition waivers (full and partial), and unspecified assistantships also available. Financial award application deadline: 3/15; financial award applicants required to submit FAFSA. In 2015, 481 master's, 6 doctorates awarded. *Degree program information:* Part-time and evening/weekend programs available. Part-time, evening/weekend, 100% online, blended/hybrid learning. Offers accounting (MS, PhD); applied economics (MA); business (MA, MBA, MS, PhD); business administration (MBA); business analytics (MS); economics (PhD); finance (MS, PhD); information systems (MS, PhD); management (PhD); marketing (MS, PhD); operations and business analytics (PhD); taxation (MS). *Application deadline:* For fall admission, 3/15 priority date for domestic students, 3/15 for international students. Applications are processed on a rolling basis. *Application fee:* $65 ($70 for international students). Electronic applications accepted. *Application Contact:* Dona Clary, Director, Graduate Programs, 513-556-3546, Fax: 513-558-7006, E-mail: dona.clary@uc.edu. *Dean*, Dr. David Szymanski, 513-556-7001, Fax: 513-556-4891, E-mail: david.szymanski@uc.edu.

College-Conservatory of Music Offers arts administration (MA); choral conducting (MM, DMA); composition (MM, DMA); directing (MFA); keyboard studies (MM, DMA, AD); music (MA, MFA, MM, DMA, PhD, AD); music education (MM); music history (MM); music theory (MM, PhD); musicology (PhD); orchestral conducting (MM, DMA); performance (MM, DMA, AD); theater design and production (MFA); voice and opera (MM, DMA); wind conducting (MM, DMA). Electronic applications accepted.

College of Allied Health Sciences Degree program information: Part-time programs available. Part-time. Offers allied health sciences (MA, MS, MSW, Au D, DPT, PhD); communication sciences and disorders (MA, Au D, PhD); medical genetics (MS); nutritional sciences (MS); rehabilitation sciences (DPT); social work (MSW).

College of Design, Architecture, Art, and Planning Degree program information: Part-time programs available. Part-time. Offers architecture (M Arch); art history (MA); community planning (MCP); design, architecture, art, and planning (M Arch, M Des, MA, MCP, MFA, PhD); fashion design (M Des); fine arts (MFA); graphic design (M Des); industrial design (M Des); interaction design (M Des); product development (M Des); regional development planning (PhD); visual arts education (MA). Electronic applications accepted.

College of Education, Criminal Justice, and Human Services Degree program information: Part-time programs available. Part-time, online learning. Offers community health (MS); counseling (Ed D); counselor education (CAGS); criminal justice (MS, PhD); curriculum and instruction (M Ed, Ed D); deaf studies (Certificate); early childhood education (M Ed); education (M Ed, Ed D, PhD, Ed S); education, criminal justice, and human services (M Ed, MA, MS, Ed D, PhD, CAGS, Certificate, Ed S); educational leadership (M Ed, Ed S); educational studies (M Ed, PhD); health education (MS, PhD); health promotion and education (M Ed); human services (M Ed, MA, MS, Ed D, PhD, CAGS, Ed S); mental health (MA); middle childhood education (M Ed); postsecondary literacy instruction (Certificate); reading/literacy (M Ed, Ed D); school counseling (M Ed); school psychology (PhD, Ed S); secondary education (M Ed); special education (M Ed, Ed D); teaching English as a second language (Ed D, Certificate); teaching science (MS); urban educational leadership (Ed D). Electronic applications accepted.

College of Engineering and Applied Science Degree program information: Part-time and evening/weekend programs available. Part-time, evening/weekend. Offers aerospace engineering and engineering mechanics (MS, PhD); biomechanics (PhD); chemical engineering (MS, PhD); civil engineering (MS, PhD); computer engineering (MS); computer science (MS); computer science and engineering (PhD); electrical engineering (MS, PhD); engineering and applied science (MS, PhD); environmental engineering (MS, PhD); environmental sciences (MS, PhD); industrial engineering (PhD); materials science and engineering (MS, PhD); mechanical engineering (MS, PhD); medical imaging (PhD); nuclear engineering (PhD); tissue engineering (PhD).

College of Medicine Offers biomedical informatics (PhD, Graduate Certificate); biomedical research (MS); biomedical sciences (MS, PhD, Graduate Certificate); cancer and cell biology (PhD); cell biophysics (PhD); environmental and industrial hygiene (MS, PhD); environmental and occupational medicine (MS); environmental genetics and molecular toxicology (MS, PhD); epidemiology and biostatistics (MS, PhD); immunobiology (PhD); immunology (MS, PhD); medical physics (MS); medicine (MS, MD, PhD, Graduate Certificate); molecular and developmental biology (PhD); molecular genetics, biochemistry and microbiology (MS, PhD); occupational safety and ergonomics (MS, PhD); pathology (PhD); pharmacology (PhD); physiology (PhD). Electronic applications accepted.

College of Nursing Degree program information: Part-time programs available. Part-time, online learning. Offers clinical nurse specialist (MSN); nurse anesthesia (MSN); nurse midwifery (MSN); nurse practitioner (MSN); nursing (PhD). Electronic applications accepted.

McMicken College of Arts and Sciences Degree program information: Part-time and evening/weekend programs available. Part-time, evening/weekend. Offers analytical chemistry (MS, PhD); anthropology (MA); applied mathematics (MS, PhD); arts and sciences (MA, MALER, MAT, MS, PhD, Certificate); biochemistry (MS, PhD); biological sciences (MS, PhD); classics (MA, PhD); clinical psychology (PhD); communication (MA); English and comparative literature (MA, MAT, PhD); experimental psychology (PhD); French (MA, PhD); geography (MA, PhD); geology (MS, PhD); German studies (MA, PhD); history (MA, PhD); inorganic chemistry (MS, PhD); interdisciplinary studies (PhD); labor and employment relations (MALER); mathematics education (MAT); organic chemistry (MS, PhD); organizational leadership (MALER); philosophy (MA, PhD); physical chemistry (MS, PhD); physics (MS, PhD); political science (MA, PhD); polymer chemistry (MS, PhD); pure mathematics (MS, PhD); Romance languages and literatures (PhD); sensors (PhD); sociology (MA, PhD); Spanish (MA, PhD); statistics (MS, PhD); women's, gender, and sexuality studies (MA, Certificate).

James L. Winkle College of Pharmacy *Degree program information:* Part-time programs available. Part-time. Offers pharmacy (MS, PhD, Pharm D).

Division of Pharmaceutical Sciences Offers pharmaceutical sciences (MS, PhD).

Division of Pharmacy Practice Offers pharmacy practice (Pharm D).

UNIVERSITY OF COLORADO BOULDER, Boulder, CO 80309

General Information State-supported, coed, university. CGS member. *Enrollment:* 32,775 graduate, professional, and undergraduate students; 4,769 full-time matriculated graduate/professional students (1,988 women), 873 part-time matriculated graduate/professional students (347 women). *Graduate faculty:* 1,128 full-time (364 women). *Graduate housing:* Rooms and/or apartments available to single and married students. *Student services:* Campus employment opportunities, campus safety program, career counseling, child daycare facilities, free psychological counseling, international student services, low-cost health insurance. *Library:* Norlin Library plus 5 others. *Collection:* Books: 7.1 million (physical), 584,830 (digital/electronic); Databases: 228. Students can reserve study rooms. *Research affiliation:* National Institute of Standards and Technology (NIST), National Oceanic and Atmospheric Administration (NOAA), U.S. West Advanced Technologies, NASA, National Center for Atmospheric Research.

Computer facilities: Computer purchase and lease plans are available. 1,804 computers available on campus for general student use. A campuswide network can be accessed from student residence rooms and from off campus. Online class registration, training, tutorials, workshops, seminars, standard and academic software, student government voting are available.
Website: http://www.colorado.edu/

GRADUATE UNITS

Graduate School Students: 3,796 full-time (1,576 women), 850 part-time (341 women); includes 612 minority (49 Black or African American, non-Hispanic/Latino; 13 American Indian or Alaska Native, non-Hispanic/Latino; 145 Asian, non-Hispanic/Latino; 295 Hispanic/Latino; 2 Native Hawaiian or other Pacific Islander, non-Hispanic/Latino; 108 Two or more races, non-Hispanic/Latino), 1,005 international. Average age 29. 10,409 applicants, 30% accepted, 1219 enrolled. *Faculty:* 1,035 full-time (339 women). *Financial support:* In 2015–16, 7,651 students received support, including 867 fellowships (averaging $3,911 per year), 1,205 research assistantships with tuition reimbursements available (averaging $33,779 per year), 1,512 teaching assistantships with tuition reimbursements available (averaging $31,542 per year); institutionally sponsored loans, scholarships/grants, health care benefits, and unspecified assistantships also available. Financial award applicants required to submit FAFSA. In 2015, 935 master's, 419 doctorates awarded. Offers museum and field studies (MS). *Application fee:* $50 ($70 for international students). Electronic applications accepted. *Application Contact:* E-mail: gradinfo@colorado.edu.

College of Arts and Sciences Students: 1,899 full-time (936 women), 189 part-time (64 women); includes 258 minority (16 Black or African American, non-Hispanic/Latino; 5 American Indian or Alaska Native, non-Hispanic/Latino; 54 Asian, non-Hispanic/Latino; 128 Hispanic/Latino; 1 Native Hawaiian or other Pacific Islander, non-Hispanic/Latino; 54 Two or more races, non-Hispanic/Latino), 271 international. Average age 28. 5,792 applicants, 21% accepted, 460 enrolled. *Faculty:* 700 full-time (250 women). *Financial support:* In 2015–16, 4,307 students received support, including 461 fellowships (averaging $3,952 per year), 562 research assistantships with tuition reimbursements available (averaging $33,408 per year), 1,092 teaching assistantships with tuition reimbursements available (averaging $32,889 per year); institutionally sponsored loans, scholarships/grants, health care benefits, and unspecified assistantships also available. Financial award applicants required to submit FAFSA. In 2015, 319 master's, 262 doctorates awarded. Offers animal behavior (MA); anthropology (MA, PhD); applied mathematics (MS, PhD); art history (MA); arts and sciences (MA, MFA, MS, Au D, PhD); astrophysics (MS, PhD); atmospheric and oceanic sciences (MS, PhD); audiology (Au D, PhD); biochemistry (PhD); biology (MA, PhD); cellular structure and function (MA, PhD); ceramics (MFA); chemical physics (PhD); chemistry (MS); Chinese (MA, PhD); classics (MA, PhD); clinical research and practice in audiology (PhD); comparative literature (MA, PhD); dance (MFA); developmental biology (MA, PhD); drawing (MFA); economics (MA, PhD); environmental biology (MA, PhD); environmental studies (MS, PhD); ethnic studies (PhD); evolutionary biology (MA, PhD); French (MA, PhD); geography (MA, PhD); geology (MS, PhD); geophysics (PhD); German (MA); Hispanic linguistics (MA); history (MA, PhD); integrative physiology (MS, PhD); international affairs (MA); Japanese (MA, PhD); linguistics (MA, PhD); liquid crystal science and technology (PhD); literature (MA, PhD); mathematical physics (PhD); mathematics (MA, MS, PhD); medical physics (PhD); medieval and early modern Hispanic literatures (PhD); molecular biology (MA, PhD); neurobiology (MA); optical sciences and engineering (PhD); painting (MFA); peninsular and Latin American literature (MA, PhD); philosophy (MA, PhD); photography and media arts (MFA); physics (MS, PhD); planetary science (MS, PhD); political science (MA, PhD); population biology (MA); population genetics (PhD); printmaking (MFA); psychology and neuroscience (MA, PhD); public policy (MA); religious studies (MA); sculpture (MFA); sociology (PhD); speech, language and hearing sciences (MA, PhD); speech-language pathology (MA, PhD); theatre (MA, PhD). *Application fee:* $50 ($70 for international students). Electronic applications accepted.

College of Engineering and Applied Science Students: 1,454 full-time (372 women), 426 part-time (94 women); includes 211 minority (18 Black or African American, non-Hispanic/Latino; 6 American Indian or Alaska Native, non-Hispanic/Latino; 73 Asian, non-Hispanic/Latino; 74 Hispanic/Latino; 40 Two or more races, non-Hispanic/Latino), 702 international. Average age 28. 3,627 applicants, 41% accepted, 589 enrolled. *Faculty:* 202 full-time (35 women). *Financial support:* In 2015–16, 2,333 students received support, including 207 fellowships (averaging $4,605 per year), 527 research assistantships with tuition reimbursements available (averaging $35,346 per year), 202 teaching assistantships with tuition reimbursements available (averaging $32,532 per year); institutionally sponsored loans, scholarships/grants, health care benefits, and unspecified assistantships also available. Financial award applicants required to submit FAFSA. In 2015, 390 master's, 110 doctorates awarded. Offers aerospace engineering sciences (MS, PhD); building systems engineering (MS, PhD); chemical and biological engineering (ME, MS, PhD); computer science (ME, MS, PhD); construction engineering management (MS, PhD); electrical, computer and energy engineering (ME, MS, PhD); engineering and applied science (ME, MS, PhD); environmental engineering (MS, PhD); geotechnical engineering and geomechanics (MS, PhD); hydrology, water resources and environmental fluid mechanics (MS, PhD); information and communication technology for development (MS); mechanical engineering (ME, MS, PhD); operations and logistics (ME); quality and process (ME); research and development (ME); structural engineering and structural mechanics (MS, PhD); technology, media, and society (PhD); telecommunications (MS). *Application fee:* $50 ($70 for international students). Electronic applications accepted.

College of Media, Communication and Information Students: 106 full-time (69 women), 5 part-time (all women); includes 11 minority (1 Black or African American, non-Hispanic/Latino; 2 Asian, non-Hispanic/Latino; 8 Hispanic/Latino), 9 international. Average age 30. 180 applicants, 41% accepted, 44 enrolled. *Faculty:* 35 full-time (15 women). *Financial support:* In 2015–16, 244 students received support, including 10 fellowships (averaging $2,292 per year), 38 research assistantships with tuition reimbursements available (averaging $25,690 per year), 73 teaching assistantships with tuition reimbursements available (averaging $31,096 per year); institutionally sponsored loans, scholarships/grants, health care benefits, and unspecified assistantships also available. Financial award application deadline: 3/1; financial award applicants required to submit FAFSA. In 2015, 22 master's, 5 doctorates awarded. Offers communication (MA, PhD); critical media practices (MFA); interdisciplinary documentary media practices (MFA); intermedia art, writing and performance (PhD); journalism (MA, PhD); mass communication research (MA); media research and practice (PhD); media studies (PhD); newsgathering (MA). *Application deadline:* For fall admission, 2/1 for domestic students, 12/1 for international students. Applications are processed on a rolling basis. *Application fee:* $50 ($70 for international students). Electronic applications accepted. *Application Contact:* E-mail: cmcigrad@colorado.edu.

College of Music Students: 172 full-time (86 women), 38 part-time (20 women); includes 28 minority (3 Black or African American, non-Hispanic/Latino; 8 Asian, non-Hispanic/Latino; 11 Hispanic/Latino; 6 Two or more races, non-Hispanic/Latino), 18 international. Average age 30. 467 applicants, 35% accepted, 62 enrolled. *Faculty:* 63 full-time (20 women). *Financial support:* In 2015–16, 377 students received support, including 129 fellowships (averaging $2,739 per year), 1 research assistantship with tuition reimbursement available (averaging $6,680 per year), 103 teaching assistantships with tuition reimbursements available (averaging $20,648 per year); institutionally sponsored loans, scholarships/grants, health care benefits, and unspecified assistantships also available. Financial award application deadline: 3/1; financial award applicants required to submit FAFSA. In 2015, 54 master's, 24 doctorates awarded. Offers composition (M Mus, D Mus A); conducting (M Mus); instrumental conducting and literature (D Mus A); literature and performance of choral music (D Mus A); music education (M Mus Ed, PhD); music theory (M Mus); musicology (PhD); performance (M Mus, D Mus A); performance and pedagogy (M Mus, D Mus A). *Application deadline:* For fall admission, 12/1 for domestic and international students; for spring admission, 10/1 for domestic and international students. Applications are processed on a rolling basis. *Application fee:* $50 ($70 for international students). Electronic applications accepted. *Application Contact:* E-mail: gradmusc@colorado.edu.

School of Education Students: 154 full-time (103 women), 189 part-time (155 women); includes 101 minority (11 Black or African American, non-Hispanic/Latino; 2 American Indian or Alaska Native, non-Hispanic/Latino; 8 Asian, non-Hispanic/Latino; 72 Hispanic/Latino; 1 Native Hawaiian or other Pacific Islander, non-Hispanic/Latino; 7 Two or more races, non-Hispanic/Latino), 5 international. Average age 34. 290 applicants, 40% accepted, 57 enrolled. *Faculty:* 35 full-time (19 women). *Financial support:* In 2015–16, 357 students received support, including 56 fellowships (averaging $3,746 per year), 74 research assistantships with tuition reimbursements available (averaging $30,448 per year), 32 teaching assistantships with tuition reimbursements available (averaging $18,107 per year); institutionally sponsored loans, scholarships/grants, health care benefits, and unspecified assistantships also available. Financial award applicants required to submit FAFSA. In 2015, 142 master's, 18 doctorates awarded. Offers curriculum and instruction (MA, PhD); education (MA, PhD); educational and psychological studies (MA, PhD); educational equity and cultural diversity (MA, PhD); educational foundations, policy and practice (MA, PhD); educational foundations, policy, and practice (MA, PhD); multicultural education (MA); research and evaluation methodology (PhD). *Application deadline:* For fall admission, 2/1 for domestic students, 12/1 for international students; for spring admission, 9/1 for domestic and international students. *Application fee:* $50 ($70 for international students). Electronic applications accepted.

Leeds School of Business Students: 419 full-time (152 women), 13 part-time (2 women); includes 45 minority (5 Black or African American, non-Hispanic/Latino; 1 American Indian or Alaska Native, non-Hispanic/Latino; 17 Asian, non-Hispanic/Latino;

10 Hispanic/Latino; 12 Two or more races, non-Hispanic/Latino), 71 international. Average age 28. 487 applicants, 47% accepted, 107 enrolled. *Faculty:* 52 full-time (9 women). *Financial support:* In 2015–16, 340 students received support, including 208 fellowships (averaging $4,551 per year), 21 research assistantships with tuition reimbursements available (averaging $44,839 per year), 11 teaching assistantships with tuition reimbursements available (averaging $46,158 per year); institutionally sponsored loans, scholarships/grants, health care benefits, and unspecified assistantships also available. Financial award applicants required to submit FAFSA. In 2015, 210 master's, 10 doctorates awarded. Offers business (MBA, MS, PhD). *Application deadline:* For fall admission, 3/1 for domestic and international students. Applications are processed on a rolling basis. *Application fee:* $50 ($70 for international students). Electronic applications accepted.

Division of Business Administration Students: 161 full-time (68 women), 5 part-time (1 woman); includes 24 minority (1 Black or African American, non-Hispanic/Latino; 12 Asian, non-Hispanic/Latino; 3 Hispanic/Latino; 8 Two or more races, non-Hispanic/Latino), 36 international. Average age 26. 225 applicants, 18% accepted, 26 enrolled. *Financial support:* In 2015–16, 142 students received support, including 55 fellowships (averaging $3,484 per year), 21 research assistantships with tuition reimbursements available (averaging $44,839 per year), 11 teaching assistantships with tuition reimbursements available (averaging $46,158 per year); institutionally sponsored loans, scholarships/grants, health care benefits, and unspecified assistantships also available. Financial award applicants required to submit FAFSA. In 2015, 101 master's, 10 doctorates awarded. Offers accounting (MS, PhD); finance (PhD); information systems (PhD); marketing (PhD); operations (PhD); strategic, organizational, and entrepreneurial studies (PhD). *Application deadline:* For fall admission, 3/31 for domestic students, 3/1 for international students; for spring admission, 10/31 for domestic and international students. *Application fee:* $50 ($70 for international students). Electronic applications accepted. *Application Contact:* E-mail: leedsms@colorado.edu.

Division of MBA Students: 258 full-time (84 women), 8 part-time (1 woman); includes 21 minority (4 Black or African American, non-Hispanic/Latino; 1 American Indian or Alaska Native, non-Hispanic/Latino; 5 Asian, non-Hispanic/Latino; 7 Hispanic/Latino; 4 Two or more races, non-Hispanic/Latino), 35 international. Average age 30. 262 applicants, 72% accepted, 81 enrolled. *Financial support:* In 2015–16, 198 students received support, including 153 fellowships (averaging $4,935 per year); institutionally sponsored loans, scholarships/grants, health care benefits, and unspecified assistantships also available. Financial award applicants required to submit FAFSA. In 2015, 111 master's awarded. Offers business administration (MBA). *Application deadline:* Applications are processed on a rolling basis. *Application fee:* $50 ($70 for international students). Electronic applications accepted. *Application Contact:* E-mail: leedsmba@colorado.edu.

School of Law Students: 554 full-time (260 women), 10 part-time (4 women); includes 106 minority (15 Black or African American, non-Hispanic/Latino; 9 American Indian or Alaska Native, non-Hispanic/Latino; 22 Asian, non-Hispanic/Latino; 54 Hispanic/Latino; 1 Native Hawaiian or other Pacific Islander, non-Hispanic/Latino; 5 Two or more races, non-Hispanic/Latino), 6 international. Average age 27. 1,095 applicants, 100% accepted, 215 enrolled. *Faculty:* 41 full-time (16 women). *Financial support:* In 2015–16, 1,013 students received support, including 737 fellowships (averaging $8,646 per year), 15 teaching assistantships with tuition reimbursements available (averaging $1,907 per year); institutionally sponsored loans, scholarships/grants, health care benefits, and unspecified assistantships also available. Financial award applicants required to submit FAFSA. In 2015, 160 doctorates awarded. Offers law (JD). *Application deadline:* For fall admission, 2/15 for domestic students. Applications are processed on a rolling basis. *Application fee:* $50 ($70 for international students). Electronic applications accepted. *Application Contact:* E-mail: lawadmin@colorado.edu.

UNIVERSITY OF COLORADO COLORADO SPRINGS, Colorado Springs, CO 80918

General Information State-supported, coed, university. CGS member. *Enrollment:* 11,696 graduate, professional, and undergraduate students; 394 full-time matriculated graduate/professional students (231 women), 1,167 part-time matriculated graduate/professional students (613 women). *Enrollment by degree level:* 1,319 master's, 215 doctoral, 27 other advanced degrees. *Graduate faculty:* 441 full-time (231 women), 313 part-time/adjunct (169 women). Tuition, state resident: full-time $9914. Tuition, nonresident: full-time $19,330. Tuition and fees vary according to course load, degree level, program and reciprocity agreements. *Graduate housing:* Room and/or apartments available on a first-come, first-served basis to single students; on-campus housing not available to married students. Typical cost: $8300 per year ($9500 including board). Room and board charges vary according to board plan and housing facility selected. *Student services:* Campus employment opportunities, campus safety program, career counseling, child daycare facilities, exercise/wellness program, free psychological counseling, grant writing training, international student services, low-cost health insurance, multicultural affairs office, services for students with disabilities, teacher training, writing training. *Library:* Kraemer Family Library. *Collection:* Books: 439,248 (physical), 32,499 (digital/electronic); Databases: 178. Students can reserve study rooms. *Research affiliation:* 100Kin10 (education), The Coleman Institute for Cognitive Disabilities (age-related cognitive decline), Western Regional Radon Training Center (radon mitigation), Northrop Grumman Corporation (engineering), National Geographic Society Education Foundation (geography and environmental studies).

Computer facilities: Computer purchase and lease plans are available. 959 computers available on campus for general student use. A campuswide network can be accessed from student residence rooms and from off campus. Online class registration, student portal, learning management system are available.
Website: http://www.uccs.edu/

General Application Contact: KrisAnn McBroom, Graduate School Administrator, 719-255-3417, Fax: 719-255-3045, E-mail: gradinfo@uccs.edu.

GRADUATE UNITS

College of Business Students: 51 full-time (17 women), 211 part-time (92 women); includes 45 minority (9 Black or African American, non-Hispanic/Latino; 10 Asian, non-Hispanic/Latino; 15 Hispanic/Latino; 1 Native Hawaiian or other Pacific Islander, non-Hispanic/Latino; 10 Two or more races, non-Hispanic/Latino), 11 international. Average age 34. 103 applicants, 71% accepted, 46 enrolled. *Faculty:* 42 full-time (16 women), 30 part-time/adjunct (9 women). *Financial support:* In 2015–16, 29 students received support. Career-related internships or fieldwork, Federal Work-Study, and scholarships/grants available. Support available to part-time students. Financial award application deadline: 3/1; financial award applicants required to submit FAFSA. In 2015, 117 master's awarded. *Degree program information:* Part-time and evening/weekend programs available. Part-time, evening/weekend, 100% online, blended/hybrid learning. Offers business (MBA). *Application deadline:* For fall admission, 6/1 for domestic and international students; for spring admission, 11/1 for domestic and international students; for summer admission, 4/1 for domestic and international students. Applications are processed on a rolling basis. *Application fee:* $60 ($100 for international students). Electronic applications accepted. *Application Contact:* Whitney Porter, Assistant Director of Graduate Programs, 719-255-3408, E-mail: cobgrad@uccs.edu. *Dean,* Dr. Venkateshwar Reddy, 719-255-3113, Fax: 719-255-3100, E-mail: vreddy@uccs.edu.

College of Education Students: 164 full-time (108 women), 261 part-time (185 women); includes 80 minority (21 Black or African American, non-Hispanic/Latino; 12 Asian, non-Hispanic/Latino; 38 Hispanic/Latino; 2 Native Hawaiian or other Pacific Islander, non-Hispanic/Latino; 7 Two or more races, non-Hispanic/Latino), 16 international. Average age 35. 217 applicants, 84% accepted, 131 enrolled. *Faculty:* 30 full-time (20 women), 31 part-time/adjunct (21 women). *Financial support:* In 2015–16, 86 students received support. Career-related internships or fieldwork, Federal Work-Study, scholarships/grants, and unspecified assistantships available. Support available to part-time students. Financial award application deadline: 3/1; financial award applicants required to submit FAFSA. In 2015, 184 master's, 4 doctorates awarded. *Degree program information:* Part-time and evening/weekend programs available. Part-time, evening/weekend, 100% online, blended/hybrid learning. Offers counseling and human services (MA); curriculum and instruction (MA); educational leadership (MA, PhD); special education (MA). *Application deadline:* For fall admission, 2/1 priority date for domestic students, 2/1 for international students; for spring admission, 10/15 for domestic students, 10/1 for international students. Applications are processed on a rolling basis. *Application fee:* $60 ($100 for international students). Electronic applications accepted. *Application Contact:* The College of Education Student Resource Office, 719-255-4996, E-mail: education@uccs.edu. *Dean,* Dr. Valerie Martin Conley, 719-255-4133, E-mail: vmconley@uccs.edu.

College of Engineering and Applied Science Students: 34 full-time (10 women), 252 part-time (49 women); includes 43 minority (6 Black or African American, non-Hispanic/Latino; 1 American Indian or Alaska Native, non-Hispanic/Latino; 10 Asian, non-Hispanic/Latino; 22 Hispanic/Latino; 4 Two or more races, non-Hispanic/Latino), 108 international. Average age 33. 261 applicants, 67% accepted, 67 enrolled. *Faculty:* 42 full-time (7 women), 26 part-time/adjunct (5 women). *Financial support:* In 2015–16, 31 students received support. Career-related internships or fieldwork, Federal Work-Study, and scholarships/grants available. Support available to part-time students. Financial award application deadline: 3/1; financial award applicants required to submit FAFSA. In 2015, 60 master's, 11 doctorates awarded. *Degree program information:* Part-time and evening/weekend programs available. Part-time, evening/weekend. Offers computer science (MS); electrical engineering (MS); energy engineering (ME); engineering and applied science (ME, MS, PhD); engineering management (ME); information assurance (ME); mechanical engineering (MS); software engineering (ME); space operations (ME); systems engineering (ME). *Application deadline:* For fall admission, 6/1 for domestic students, 4/1 for international students; for spring admission, 11/1 for domestic students, 10/1 for international students. Applications are processed on a rolling basis. *Application fee:* $60 ($100 for international students). *Application Contact:* Dawn House, Office of Student Support, 719-255-3246, E-mail: dhouse@uccs.edu. *Dean,* Dr. Ramaswami Dandapani, 719-255-3543, Fax: 719-255-3542, E-mail: rdan@cas.uccs.edu.

College of Letters, Arts and Sciences Students: 56 full-time (40 women), 197 part-time (106 women); includes 42 minority (4 Black or African American, non-Hispanic/Latino; 2 American Indian or Alaska Native, non-Hispanic/Latino; 7 Asian, non-Hispanic/Latino; 25 Hispanic/Latino; 4 Two or more races, non-Hispanic/Latino), 11 international. Average age 32. 360 applicants, 33% accepted, 73 enrolled. *Faculty:* 246 full-time (131 women), 131 part-time/adjunct (75 women). *Financial support:* In 2015–16, 117 students received support. Career-related internships or fieldwork, Federal Work-Study, scholarships/grants, and unspecified assistantships available. Support available to part-time students. Financial award application deadline: 3/1; financial award applicants required to submit FAFSA. In 2015, 82 master's, 4 doctorates awarded. *Degree program information:* Part-time and evening/weekend programs available. Part-time, evening/weekend, blended/hybrid learning. Offers applied mathematics (MS); communication (MA); geography and environmental studies (MA); history (MA); interdisciplinary sciences (M Sc); letters, arts and sciences (M Sc, MA, MS, PhD); mathematics (PhD); physics (PhD); psychology (MA, PhD); sociology (MA). *Application deadline:* Applications are processed on a rolling basis. *Application fee:* $60 ($100 for international students). Electronic applications accepted. *Application Contact:* Sarah Elsey, Graduate Recruitment and Retention Specialist, 719-255-3072, E-mail: gradinfo@uccs.edu. *Dean of the Graduate School,* Dr. Kelli Klebe, 719-255-3779, Fax: 719-255-3045, E-mail: kklebe@uccs.edu.

Helen and Arthur E. Johnson Beth-El College of Nursing and Health Sciences Students: 65 full-time (43 women), 137 part-time (129 women); includes 34 minority (5 Black or African American, non-Hispanic/Latino; 6 Asian, non-Hispanic/Latino; 19 Hispanic/Latino; 4 Two or more races, non-Hispanic/Latino), 1 international. Average age 34. 113 applicants, 55% accepted, 31 enrolled. *Faculty:* 10 full-time (9 women), 8 part-time/adjunct (6 women). *Financial support:* In 2015–16, 58 students received support. Career-related internships or fieldwork, Federal Work-Study, and scholarships/grants available. Support available to part-time students. Financial award application deadline: 3/1; financial award applicants required to submit FAFSA. In 2015, 39 master's, 7 doctorates awarded. *Degree program information:* Part-time programs available. Part-time, 100% online, blended/hybrid learning. Offers nursing practice (DNP); primary care nurse practitioner (MSN). *Application deadline:* For fall admission, 3/15 priority date for domestic students, 3/15 for international students; for spring admission, 8/15 for domestic and international students. Applications are processed on a rolling basis. *Application fee:* $60 ($100 for international students). Electronic applications accepted. *Application Contact:* Diane Busch, Program Assistant II, 719-255-4424, Fax: 719-255-4416, E-mail: dbusch@uccs.edu. *Graduate Department Chairperson,* Dr. Amy Silva-Smith, 719-255-4490, Fax: 719-255-4416, E-mail: asilvasm@uccs.edu.

School of Public Affairs Students: 24 full-time (11 women), 107 part-time (57 women); includes 36 minority (11 Black or African American, non-Hispanic/Latino; 3 Asian, non-Hispanic/Latino; 17 Hispanic/Latino; 5 Two or more races, non-Hispanic/Latino), 3 international. Average age 35. 38 applicants, 89% accepted, 25 enrolled. *Faculty:* 15 full-time (5 women), 11 part-time/adjunct (3 women). *Financial support:* In 2015–16, 25 students received support. Career-related internships or fieldwork and scholarships/grants available. Support available to part-time students. Financial award application deadline: 3/1; financial award applicants required to submit FAFSA. In 2015, 30 master's awarded. *Degree program information:* Part-time and evening/weekend programs available. Part-time, evening/weekend, 100% online, blended/hybrid learning. Offers criminal justice (MCJ); public administration (MPA). *Application deadline:* Applications are processed on a rolling basis. *Application fee:* $60 ($100 for international students). Electronic applications accepted. *Application Contact:* Crista Hill, Outreach Student Services Specialist, 719-255-4993, Fax: 719-255-4183, E-mail: chill12@uccs.edu. *Dean,* Dr. George Reed, 719-255-4109, E-mail: george.reed@uccs.edu.

UNIVERSITY OF COLORADO DENVER, Denver, CO 80217-3364

General Information State-supported, coed, university. CGS member. *Enrollment:* 23,670 graduate, professional, and undergraduate students; 6,748 full-time matriculated graduate/professional students (3,949 women), 1,668 part-time matriculated graduate/professional students (1,046 women). *Enrollment by degree level:* 5,369 master's, 2,964 doctoral, 83 other advanced degrees. *Graduate faculty:* 3,462 full-time (1,849 women), 877 part-time/adjunct (459 women). *Graduate housing:* Room and/or apartments available on a first-come, first-served basis to single students; on-campus housing not available to married students. *Student services:* Campus employment opportunities, campus safety program, career counseling, child daycare facilities, exercise/wellness program, free psychological counseling, international student services, low-cost health insurance, services for students with disabilities, teacher training, writing training. *Library:* Auraria Library plus 1 other. *Research affiliation:* The Children's Hospital (pediatrics), National Jewish Health (pediatrics, immunology, respiratory disease), Denver Health (trauma, primary care, under-served populations).

Computer facilities: 750 computers available on campus for general student use. A campuswide network can be accessed from student residence rooms and from off campus. Online class registration is available.
Website: http://www.ucdenver.edu/

General Application Contact: Graduate School Admissions, 303-556-2704, E-mail: admissions@ucdenver.edu.

GRADUATE UNITS

Business School Students: 1,026 full-time (395 women), 275 part-time (104 women); includes 201 minority (28 Black or African American, non-Hispanic/Latino; 3 American Indian or Alaska Native, non-Hispanic/Latino; 79 Asian, non-Hispanic/Latino; 75 Hispanic/Latino; 16 Two or more races, non-Hispanic/Latino), 164 international. Average age 31. 820 applicants, 67% accepted, 329 enrolled. *Faculty:* 61 full-time (19 women), 40 part-time/adjunct (11 women). *Financial support:* In 2015–16, 371 students received support. Fellowships, research assistantships, teaching assistantships, Federal Work-Study, institutionally sponsored loans, scholarships/grants, and traineeships available. Financial award application deadline: 4/1; financial award applicants required to submit FAFSA. In 2015, 528 master's, 3 doctorates awarded. *Degree program information:* Part-time and evening/weekend programs available. Part-time, evening/weekend, online learning. Offers accounting and information systems audit and control (MS); accounting and information systems audit control (MS); auditing and forensic accounting (MS); bioinnovation and entrepreneurship (MBA); brand management and marketing communication (MS); business (MBA, MS, MSIB, PhD); business intelligence (MBA); business intelligence systems (MS); business strategy (MBA, MS); business to business marketing (MBA); business to consumer marketing (MBA); change and innovation (MS); change management (MBA); computer science and information systems (PhD); controllership and financial leadership (MS); corporate financial management (MBA); decision sciences (MS); digital health entrepreneurship (MS); economics (MS); enterprise risk management (MS); enterprise technology management (MBA, MS); entrepreneurship (MBA); entrepreneurship and innovation (MS); finance (MS); financial analysis and management (MS); financial and commodities risk management (MS); geographic information systems (MS); global energy management (MS); global management (MS); global marketing (MS); health administration (MS); health information technology (MS); high-tech and entrepreneurial marketing (MS); human resources management (MBA); international business (MBA); investment management (MBA); leadership (MS); managing for sustainability (MBA, MS); managing human resources (MS); marketing for sustainability (MS); marketing research (MS); risk management and insurance (MS); sports and entertainment management (MBA, MS); sports and entertainment marketing (MS); taxation (MS); technology innovation and entrepreneurship (MS); Web and mobile computing (MS). *Application deadline:* For fall admission, 4/15 priority date for domestic students, 3/15 priority date for international students; for spring admission, 10/15 priority date for domestic students, 9/15 priority date for international students; for summer admission, 2/15 priority date for domestic students, 1/15 priority date for international students. Applications are processed on a rolling basis. *Application fee:* $50 ($75 for international students). Electronic applications accepted. *Application Contact:* 303-315-8200, E-mail: bschool.admissions@ucdenver.edu. *Interim Dean*, Dr. Gary Kochenberger, 303-315-8000, E-mail: gary.kochenberger@ucdenver.edu.

College of Architecture and Planning Students: 354 full-time (164 women), 24 part-time (11 women); includes 63 minority (5 Black or African American, non-Hispanic/Latino; 1 American Indian or Alaska Native, non-Hispanic/Latino; 8 Asian, non-Hispanic/Latino; 37 Hispanic/Latino; 12 Two or more races, non-Hispanic/Latino), 41 international. Average age 29. 468 applicants, 43% accepted, 133 enrolled. *Faculty:* 28 full-time (9 women), 29 part-time/adjunct (10 women). *Financial support:* In 2015–16, 276 students received support. Fellowships with tuition reimbursements available, research assistantships, teaching assistantships, Federal Work-Study, institutionally sponsored loans, scholarships/grants, and traineeships available. Financial award application deadline: 4/1; financial award applicants required to submit FAFSA. In 2015, 162 master's, 4 doctorates awarded. *Degree program information:* Part-time programs available. Part-time. Offers architecture (M Arch); architecture and planning (M Arch, MLA, MS, MUD, MURP, PhD); economic and community development planning (MURP); historic preservation (MS); history of architecture, landscape and urbanism (PhD); land use and environmental planning (MURP); landscape architecture (MLA); sustainable and healthy environments (PhD); urban design (MUD); urban place making (MURP). *Application deadline:* For fall admission, 2/1 for domestic students, 1/1 for international students; for spring admission, 10/1 for domestic students. Applications are processed on a rolling basis. *Application fee:* $50 ($75 for international students). Electronic applications accepted. *Application Contact:* Rachael Kuroiwa, Manager of Admissions and Outreach, 303-315-2325, E-mail: rachael.kuroiwa@ucdenver.edu. *Dean*, Dr. Mark Gelernter, 303-315-1000, E-mail: mark.gelernter@ucdenver.edu.

College of Arts and Media Students: 19 full-time (6 women), 10 part-time (1 woman); includes 8 minority (3 Asian, non-Hispanic/Latino; 4 Hispanic/Latino; 1 Two or more races, non-Hispanic/Latino), 2 international. Average age 31. 21 applicants, 71% accepted, 14 enrolled. *Faculty:* 31 full-time (10 women), 3 part-time/adjunct (0 women). *Financial support:* In 2015–16, 1 student received support. Federal Work-Study, institutionally sponsored loans, scholarships/grants, traineeships, and unspecified assistantships available. Financial award application deadline: 4/1; financial award applicants required to submit FAFSA. In 2015, 5 master's awarded. *Degree program information:* Part-time and evening/weekend programs available. Part-time, evening/weekend. Offers recording arts (MS). *Application deadline:* For fall admission, 4/1 for domestic students, 3/1 for international students. *Application fee:* $50 ($75 for international students). Electronic applications accepted. *Application Contact:* Lisa Funderburg, Program Assistant, 303-352-3833, E-mail: lisa.funderburg@ucdenver.edu. *Recording Arts Area Head*, Pete Buchwald, E-mail: peter.buchwald@ucdenver.edu.

College of Engineering and Applied Science Students: 365 full-time (105 women), 143 part-time (34 women); includes 74 minority (13 Black or African American, non-Hispanic/Latino; 1 American Indian or Alaska Native, non-Hispanic/Latino; 21 Asian, non-Hispanic/Latino; 28 Hispanic/Latino; 1 Native Hawaiian or other Pacific Islander, non-Hispanic/Latino; 10 Two or more races, non-Hispanic/Latino), 233 international. Average age 29. 761 applicants, 45% accepted, 130 enrolled. *Faculty:* 71 full-time (18 women), 20 part-time/adjunct (4 women). *Financial support:* In 2015–16, 169 students received support. Fellowships, research assistantships, teaching assistantships, Federal Work-Study, institutionally sponsored loans, scholarships/grants, and traineeships available. Financial award application deadline: 4/1; financial award applicants required to submit FAFSA. In 2015, 134 master's, 9 doctorates awarded. *Degree program information:* Part-time and evening/weekend programs available. Part-time, evening/weekend. Offers civil engineering (M Eng, EASPh D); civil engineering systems (PhD); computer science (MS); computer science and engineering (EASPh D); computer science and information systems (PhD); device design and entrepreneurship (MS, PhD); electrical engineering (M Eng); engineering and applied science (M Eng, MS, EASPh D, PhD); environmental and sustainability engineering (MS, PhD); geographic information systems (MS); geotechnical engineering (MS, PhD); hydrology and hydraulics (MS, PhD); mechanical engineering (M Eng, MS); mechanics (MS); research (MS, PhD); structural engineering (MS, PhD); thermal sciences (MS); translational bioengineering (MS, PhD); transportation engineering (MS, PhD). *Application fee:* $50 ($75 for international students). Electronic applications accepted. *Application Contact:* Graduate School Admissions, 303-556-2704, E-mail: admissions@ucdenver.edu. *Dean*, Dr. Mark Ingber, 303-556-2870, Fax: 303-556-2511, E-mail: marc.ingber@ucdenver.edu.

College of Liberal Arts and Sciences Students: 409 full-time (232 women), 201 part-time (115 women); includes 139 minority (22 Black or African American, non-Hispanic/Latino; 8 American Indian or Alaska Native, non-Hispanic/Latino; 18 Asian, non-Hispanic/Latino; 70 Hispanic/Latino; 21 Two or more races, non-Hispanic/Latino), 34 international. Average age 32. 607 applicants, 51% accepted, 150 enrolled. *Faculty:* 204 full-time (81 women), 30 part-time/adjunct (13 women). *Financial support:* In 2015–16, 215 students received support. Fellowships, research assistantships, teaching assistantships, Federal Work-Study, institutionally sponsored loans, scholarships/grants, and traineeships available. Financial award application deadline: 4/1; financial award applicants required to submit FAFSA. In 2015, 134 master's, 9 doctorates awarded. *Degree program information:* Part-time and evening/weekend programs available. Part-time, evening/weekend. Offers animal behavior (MS); applied linguistics (MA); applied mathematics (MS, PhD); applied science (MIS); archaeological studies (MA); biological anthropology (MA); biology (MS); cell and developmental biology (MS); chemistry (MS); clinical health (PhD); communication (MA); community health science (MSS); computer science (MIS); ecology (MS); economics (MA); environmental sciences (MS); European history (MA); evolutionary biology (MS); genetics (MS); global history (MA); health and behavioral sciences (PhD); humanities (MH); integrative and systems biology (PhD); international studies (MSS); liberal arts and sciences (MA, MH, MIS, MS, MSS, PhD); literature (MA); mathematics (MIS); medical anthropology (MA); microbiology (MS); molecular biology (MS); neurobiology (MS); philosophy and theory (MH); plant systematics (MS); political science (MA); psychology (MA); public history (MA); rhetoric and teaching of writing (MA); social justice (MSS); society and the environment (MSS); sociology (MA); Spanish (MA); sustainable development and political ecology (MA); U.S. history (MA); visual studies (MH); women's and gender studies (MSS). *Application fee:* $50 ($75 for international students). Electronic applications accepted. *Application Contact:* College of Liberal Arts and Sciences, 303-556-2555, E-mail: clas@ucdenver.edu. *Dean*, Pamela Jansma, 303-556-2557, E-mail: pamela.jansma@ucdenver.edu.

College of Nursing Students: 367 full-time (332 women), 141 part-time (118 women); includes 79 minority (16 Black or African American, non-Hispanic/Latino; 2 American Indian or Alaska Native, non-Hispanic/Latino; 8 Asian, non-Hispanic/Latino; 37 Hispanic/Latino; 16 Two or more races, non-Hispanic/Latino), 6 international. Average age 36. 321 applicants, 53% accepted, 145 enrolled. *Faculty:* 109 full-time (100 women), 55 part-time/adjunct (50 women). *Financial support:* In 2015–16, 148 students received support. Fellowships, research assistantships, teaching assistantships, Federal Work-Study, institutionally sponsored loans, scholarships/grants, traineeships, and unspecified assistantships available. Support available to part-time students. Financial award application deadline: 4/1; financial award applicants required to submit FAFSA. In 2015, 151 master's, 36 doctorates awarded. *Degree program information:* Part-time and evening/weekend programs available. Part-time, evening/weekend, online learning. Offers adult clinical nurse specialist (MS); adult nurse practitioner (MS); family nurse practitioner (MS); family psychiatric mental health nurse practitioner (MS); health care informatics (MS); nurse-midwifery (MS); nursing (DNP, PhD); nursing leadership and health care systems (MS); pediatric nurse practitioner (MS); special studies (MS); women's health (MS). *Application deadline:* For fall admission, 2/15 for domestic students, 1/15 for international students; for spring admission, 7/1 for domestic students, 6/1 for international students. *Application fee:* $50 ($75 for international students). Electronic applications accepted. *Application Contact:* Judy Campbell, Graduate Programs Coordinator, 303-724-8503, E-mail: judy.campbell@ucdenver.edu. *Dean*, Dr. Sarah Thompson, 303-724-1679, E-mail: sarah.a.thompson@ucdenver.edu.

Colorado School of Public Health Students: 444 full-time (342 women), 103 part-time (85 women); includes 131 minority (13 Black or African American, non-Hispanic/Latino; 4 American Indian or Alaska Native, non-Hispanic/Latino; 45 Asian, non-Hispanic/Latino; 51 Hispanic/Latino; 1 Native Hawaiian or other Pacific Islander, non-Hispanic/Latino; 17 Two or more races, non-Hispanic/Latino), 18 international. Average age 30. 924 applicants, 24% accepted, 186 enrolled. *Faculty:* 90 full-time (65 women), 24 part-time/adjunct (17 women). *Financial support:* In 2015–16, 357 students received support. Fellowships, research assistantships, teaching assistantships, Federal Work-Study, institutionally sponsored loans, scholarships/grants, traineeships, and unspecified assistantships available. Financial award application deadline: 4/1. In 2015, 151 master's, 3 doctorates awarded. *Degree program information:* Part-time programs available. Part-time. Offers biostatistics and informatics (MS, PhD); community and behavioral health (MPH, Dr PH); environmental and occupational health (MPH); epidemiology (MS, PhD); health services research (PhD); health systems, management and policy (MPH); public health (MPH, MS, Dr PH, PhD). *Application deadline:* For fall admission, 1/15 for domestic and international students. *Application fee:* $50 ($75 for international students). Electronic applications accepted. *Application Contact:* Office of Student Affairs, 303-724-4613, Fax: 303-724-4620, E-mail: admissions.csph@ucdenver.edu. *Dean*, Dr. David Goff, 303-724-7304, E-mail: david.goff@ucdenver.edu.

School of Dental Medicine Students: 449 full-time (212 women); includes 123 minority (7 Black or African American, non-Hispanic/Latino; 2 American Indian or Alaska Native, non-Hispanic/Latino; 61 Asian, non-Hispanic/Latino; 42 Hispanic/Latino; 11 Two or more races, non-Hispanic/Latino), 15 international. Average age 27. *Faculty:* 89 full-time (34 women), 48 part-time/adjunct (14 women). *Financial support:* In 2015–16, 159 students received support. Fellowships, research assistantships, teaching assistantships, Federal Work-Study, institutionally sponsored loans, scholarships/grants, and traineeships available. Financial award application deadline: 4/1; financial award applicants required to submit FAFSA. In 2015, 25 master's, 116 doctorates awarded. Offers dental surgery (DDS); orthodontics (MS); periodontics (MS). *Application deadline:* For fall admission, 12/31 for domestic students, 12/15 for international students. *Application fee:* $50 ($75 for international students). Electronic applications accepted. *Application Contact:* Graduate Student Admissions, 303-724-7122, Fax: 303-724-7109, E-mail: ddsadmissioninquiries@ucdenver.edu. *Dean,* Dr. Denise K. Kassebaum, 303-724-7100, Fax: 303-724-7109, E-mail: denise.kassebaum@ucdenver.edu.

School of Education and Human Development Students: 953 full-time (756 women), 415 part-time (337 women); includes 233 minority (40 Black or African American, non-Hispanic/Latino; 1 American Indian or Alaska Native, non-Hispanic/Latino; 29 Asian, non-Hispanic/Latino; 128 Hispanic/Latino; 35 Two or more races, non-Hispanic/Latino), 16 international. Average age 33. 576 applicants, 71% accepted, 307 enrolled. *Faculty:* 65 full-time (43 women), 100 part-time/adjunct (74 women). *Financial support:* In 2015–16, 581 students received support. Fellowships, research assistantships, teaching assistantships, Federal Work-Study, institutionally sponsored loans, scholarships/grants, and traineeships available. Financial award application deadline: 4/1; financial award applicants required to submit FAFSA. In 2015, 388 master's, 13 doctorates, 18 other advanced degrees awarded. *Degree program information:* Part-time and evening/weekend programs available. Part-time, evening/weekend, online learning. Offers administrative leadership and policy studies (MA, Ed S); counseling (MA); e-learning design and implementation (MA); early childhood education (MA); education and human development (MA, MS Ed, Ed D, PhD, Ed S); educational psychology (MA); educational studies and research (PhD); elementary linguistically diverse education (MA); elementary math and science education (MA); elementary math education (MA); elementary reading and writing (MA); elementary science education (MA); executive leadership (Ed D); instructional design and adult learning (MA); instructional leadership (Ed D); K-12 teaching (MA); mathematics education (MS Ed); school counseling (MA); school psychology (Ed S); secondary English education (MA); secondary linguistically diverse education (MA); secondary math education (MA); secondary reading and writing (MA); secondary science education (MA); special education (MA). *Application fee:* $50 ($75 for international students). Electronic applications accepted. *Application Contact:* Student Services Center, 303-315-6300, Fax: 303-315-6311, E-mail: education@ucdenver.edu. *Dean,* Rebecca Kantor, 303-315-6343, E-mail: rebecca.kantor@ucdenver.edu.

School of Medicine Students: 1,407 full-time (815 women), 44 part-time (28 women); includes 252 minority (26 Black or African American, non-Hispanic/Latino; 5 American Indian or Alaska Native, non-Hispanic/Latino; 98 Asian, non-Hispanic/Latino; 95 Hispanic/Latino; 1 Native Hawaiian or other Pacific Islander, non-Hispanic/Latino; 27 Two or more races, non-Hispanic/Latino), 20 international. Average age 27. *Faculty:* 2,862 full-time (1,609 women), 550 part-time/adjunct (305 women). *Financial support:* In 2015–16, 1,446 students received support. Fellowships, research assistantships, teaching assistantships, career-related internships or fieldwork, Federal Work-Study, institutionally sponsored loans, scholarships/grants, traineeships, and unspecified assistantships available. Financial award application deadline: 3/15; financial award applicants required to submit FAFSA. In 2015, 81 master's, 255 doctorates awarded. Offers anesthesiology (MS); biochemistry (PhD); biochemistry and molecular genetics (PhD); bioinformatics (PhD); biomedical sciences (MS, PhD); biomolecular structure (PhD); biophysics and genetics (MS, PhD); cancer biology (PhD); cell biology, stem cells, and developmental biology (PhD); child health associate (MPAS); clinical investigation (PhD); clinical sciences (MS); computational bioscience (PhD); health information technology (PhD); health services research (PhD); human medical genetics and genomics (PhD); immunology (PhD); medicine (MPAS, MS, DPT, MD, PhD); microbiology (PhD); microbiology and immunology (PhD); modern human anatomy (MS); molecular biology (PhD); neuroscience (PhD); pharmacology (PhD); physical therapy (DPT); physiology (PhD); rehabilitation science (PhD). *Application fee:* $50 ($75 for international students). Electronic applications accepted. *Application Contact:* W. Vidal Dickerson, Director of Student Life, Admissions, 303-724-6407, E-mail: somadmin@ucdenver.edu. *Dean,* Dr. John Reilly, Jr., 303-724-0882, E-mail: john.reillyjr@ucdenver.edu.

School of Pharmacy Students: 669 full-time (404 women), 146 part-time (99 women); includes 311 minority (50 Black or African American, non-Hispanic/Latino; 5 American Indian or Alaska Native, non-Hispanic/Latino; 188 Asian, non-Hispanic/Latino; 61 Hispanic/Latino; 1 Native Hawaiian or other Pacific Islander, non-Hispanic/Latino; 6 Two or more races, non-Hispanic/Latino), 43 international. Average age 27. 259 applicants, 70% accepted, 162 enrolled. *Faculty:* 120 full-time (54 women), 24 part-time/adjunct (15 women). *Financial support:* In 2015–16, 490 students received support. Fellowships, research assistantships, teaching assistantships, Federal Work-Study, institutionally sponsored loans, scholarships/grants, traineeships, and unspecified assistantships available. Financial award application deadline: 3/15; financial award applicants required to submit FAFSA. In 2015, 195 doctorates awarded. Online learning. Offers clinical pharmaceutical sciences (PhD); pharmaceutical biotechnology (PhD); pharmaceutical outcomes research (PhD); pharmacy (PhD, Pharm D); toxicology (PhD). *Application deadline:* For fall admission, 12/1 for domestic students, 11/1 for international students. *Application fee:* $150. Electronic applications accepted. *Application Contact:* Jackie Milowski, Department of Pharmaceutical Sciences Administrative Assistant, 303-724-7263, E-mail: jackie.milowski@ucdenver.edu. *Dean,* Dr. Ralph Altiere, 303-724-2631, E-mail: ralph.altiere@ucdenver.edu.

School of Public Affairs Students: 286 full-time (186 women), 166 part-time (114 women); includes 80 minority (10 Black or African American, non-Hispanic/Latino; 6 American Indian or Alaska Native, non-Hispanic/Latino; 10 Asian, non-Hispanic/Latino; 50 Hispanic/Latino; 2 Native Hawaiian or other Pacific Islander, non-Hispanic/Latino; 2 Two or more races, non-Hispanic/Latino), 18 international. Average age 33. 251 applicants, 71% accepted, 91 enrolled. *Faculty:* 23 full-time (12 women), 19 part-time/adjunct (6 women). *Financial support:* In 2015–16, 104 students received support, including 3 fellowships with full tuition reimbursements available (averaging $15,000 per year); research assistantships, teaching assistantships, Federal Work-Study, institutionally sponsored loans, scholarships/grants, traineeships, and unspecified assistantships also available. Support available to part-time students. Financial award application deadline: 4/1; financial award applicants required to submit FAFSA. In 2015, 133 master's, 8 doctorates awarded. *Degree program information:* Part-time and evening/weekend programs available. Part-time, evening/weekend, online learning. Offers criminal justice (MCJ); public administration (MPA); public affairs (PhD). *Application deadline:* For fall admission, 2/1 priority date for domestic students, 1/15 priority date for international students; for spring admission, 10/15 priority date for domestic students. *Application fee:* $50 ($75 for international students). Electronic applications accepted. *Application Contact:* Antoinette Sandoval, Student Service Specialist, 303-315-2487, Fax: 303-315-2229, E-mail: antoinette.sandoval@ucdenver.edu. *Dean,* Paul Teske, 303-315-2805, Fax: 303-315-2229, E-mail: paul.teske@ucdenver.edu.

UNIVERSITY OF CONNECTICUT, Storrs, CT 06269

General Information State-supported, coed, university. CGS member. *Graduate housing:* Rooms and/or apartments available on a first-come, first-served basis to single and married students. Housing application deadline: 4/1. *Research affiliation:* U.S. Navy–Submarine Medical Research Laboratory, Haskins Laboratories.

GRADUATE UNITS

Graduate School ***Financial support:*** Fellowships, research assistantships with full tuition reimbursements, teaching assistantships with full tuition reimbursements, career-related internships or fieldwork, and Federal Work-Study available. Financial award application deadline: 2/1; financial award applicants required to submit FAFSA. *Degree program information:* Part-time and evening/weekend programs available. Part-time, evening/weekend, online learning. *Application deadline:* For fall admission, 2/1 priority date for domestic and international students; for spring admission, 11/1 for domestic students, 10/1 for international students. Applications are processed on a rolling basis. *Application fee:* $55. Electronic applications accepted.

College of Agriculture, Health and Natural Resources Financial support: Fellowships, research assistantships with full tuition reimbursements, teaching assistantships with full tuition reimbursements, Federal Work-Study, scholarships/grants, health care benefits, and unspecified assistantships available. Financial award application deadline: 2/1; financial award applicants required to submit FAFSA. Offers agricultural and resource economics (MS, PhD); agriculture, health and natural resources (MS, PhD); animal science (MS, PhD); exercise science (MS, PhD); natural resources management and engineering (MS, PhD); nutritional sciences (MS, PhD); pathobiology (MS, PhD); physical therapy (DPT); plant and soil sciences (MS, PhD); sport management (MS). *Application deadline:* For fall admission, 2/1 priority date for domestic and international students; for spring admission, 11/1 for domestic students, 10/1 for international students. Applications are processed on a rolling basis. *Application fee:* $55. Electronic applications accepted.

College of Liberal Arts and Sciences Financial support: Fellowships, research assistantships with full tuition reimbursements, teaching assistantships with full tuition reimbursements, career-related internships or fieldwork, Federal Work-Study, scholarships/grants, health care benefits, and unspecified assistantships available. Financial award application deadline: 2/1; financial award applicants required to submit FAFSA. Offers anthropology (MA, PhD); applied financial mathematics (MS); applied genomics (MS); audiology (Au D, PhD); behavioral neuroscience (PhD); biopsychology (PhD); botany (MS, PhD); chemistry (MS, PhD); clinical psychology (MA, PhD); cognition and instruction (PhD); communication processes (MA); comparative physiology (MS, PhD); culture, health and human development (Graduate Certificate); developmental psychology (MA, PhD); ecological psychology (PhD); economics (MA, PhD); English (MA, PhD); European studies (MA); experimental psychology (PhD); general psychology (MA, PhD); geography (PhD); geological sciences (MS, PhD); history (MA, PhD); human development and family studies (MA, PhD); industrial/organizational psychology (PhD); international studies (MA); Italian history and culture (MA); Judaic studies (MA); language and cognition (PhD); Latino and Latin American studies (MA); liberal arts and sciences (MA, MPA, MS, Au D, PhD, Certificate, Graduate Certificate); linguistics (MA, PhD); medieval studies (MA, PhD); neuroscience (PhD); philosophy (MA, PhD); physics (MS, PhD); political science (MA, PhD); public administration (MPA); quantitative research methods (Graduate Certificate); social psychology (MA, PhD); sociology (MA, PhD); speech-language pathology (MA, Au D, PhD); statistics (MS, PhD); survey research (MA). *Application deadline:* For fall admission, 2/1 priority date for domestic and international students; for spring admission, 11/1 for domestic students, 10/1 for international students. Applications are processed on a rolling basis. *Application fee:* $55. Electronic applications accepted.

eCampus Online learning. Offers continuing studies (MS, Certificate); human resource management (MS); occupational safety and health management (Certificate).

Neag School of Education Average age 32. *Financial support:* Fellowships, research assistantships with full tuition reimbursements, teaching assistantships with full tuition reimbursements, Federal Work-Study, scholarships/grants, health care benefits, and unspecified assistantships available. Financial award application deadline: 2/1; financial award applicants required to submit FAFSA. Offers adult learning (MA, PhD); agriculture (MA); agriculture education (PhD); bilingual and bicultural education (MA, PhD); cognition and instruction (MA, PhD); cognition science (MA, PhD); counseling psychology (PhD); education (MA, PhD); educational administration (MA); elementary education (MA, PhD); English education (MA, PhD); gifted and talented education (Graduate Certificate); higher education and student affairs (MA); history and social sciences education (MA, PhD); mathematics education (MA, PhD); music education (MA); reading education (MA, PhD); school counseling (MA); science education (MA, PhD); secondary education (MA, PhD); world languages education (MA, PhD). *Application deadline:* For fall admission, 2/1 priority date for domestic and international students; for spring admission, 11/1 for domestic students, 10/1 for international students. Applications are processed on a rolling basis. *Application fee:* $55. Electronic applications accepted.

School of Business Financial support: Fellowships, research assistantships with full tuition reimbursements, teaching assistantships with full tuition reimbursements, career-related internships or fieldwork, Federal Work-Study, scholarships/grants, health care benefits, and unspecified assistantships available. Financial award application deadline: 2/1; financial award applicants required to submit FAFSA. Offers accounting (MS); business administration (MBA, PhD); finance (PhD); health care management and insurance studies (MBA); management (PhD); management consulting (MBA); marketing (PhD); marketing intelligence (MBA). *Application deadline:* For fall admission, 2/1 priority date for domestic and international students; for spring admission, 11/1 for domestic students, 10/1 for international students. Applications are processed on a rolling basis. Electronic applications accepted.

School of Engineering Financial support: Fellowships, research assistantships with full tuition reimbursements, teaching assistantships with full tuition reimbursements, career-related internships or fieldwork, Federal Work-Study, scholarships/grants, health care benefits, and unspecified assistantships available. Financial award application deadline: 2/1; financial award applicants required to submit FAFSA. Offers biomedical engineering (MS, PhD); chemical engineering (MS, PhD); civil engineering (MS, PhD); computer science (MS, PhD); electrical engineering (MS, PhD); engineering (M Eng, MS, PhD); environmental engineering (MS, PhD); materials science and engineering (MS, PhD); mechanical engineering (MS, PhD); metallurgy and materials engineering (M Eng). *Application deadline:* For fall admission, 2/1 priority date for domestic and international students; for spring admission, 11/1 for domestic students, 10/1 for international students. Applications are processed on a rolling basis. *Application fee:* $55. Electronic applications accepted.

School of Fine Arts Financial support: Fellowships, research assistantships with full tuition reimbursements, teaching assistantships with full tuition reimbursements, Federal Work-Study, scholarships/grants, health care benefits, and unspecified assistantships available. Financial award application deadline: 2/1; financial award applicants required to submit FAFSA. Offers acting (MA, MFA); conducting (M Mus, DMA); design (MA, MFA); fine arts (M Mus, MA, MFA, DMA, PhD); historical musicology (MA); music theory (MA); music theory and history (PhD); performance (M Mus, DMA); puppetry (MA, MFA); technical direction (MA, MFA). *Application deadline:* For fall admission, 2/1 priority date for domestic and international students; for spring admission, 11/1 for domestic students, 10/1 for international students. Applications are processed on a rolling basis. *Application fee:* $55. Electronic applications accepted.

School of Nursing Financial support: Fellowships, research assistantships with full tuition reimbursements, teaching assistantships with full tuition reimbursements, Federal Work-Study, scholarships/grants, health care benefits, and unspecified assistantships available. Financial award application deadline: 2/1; financial award applicants required to submit FAFSA. Offers nursing (MS, DNP, PhD, Post-Master's Certificate). *Application deadline:* For fall admission, 5/1 for domestic and international students; for spring admission, 11/1 for domestic students, 10/1 for international students. Applications are processed on a rolling basis. *Application fee:* $55. Electronic applications accepted.

School of Pharmacy Financial support: Fellowships, research assistantships with full tuition reimbursements, teaching assistantships with full tuition reimbursements, career-related internships or fieldwork, Federal Work-Study, scholarships/grants, traineeships, health care benefits, and unspecified assistantships available. Financial award application deadline: 2/1; financial award applicants required to submit FAFSA. Offers medicinal chemistry (MS, PhD); pharmaceutics (MS, PhD); pharmacology (MS, PhD); pharmacology and toxicology (MS, PhD); pharmacy (MS, PhD, Pharm D); toxicology (MS, PhD). *Application deadline:* For fall admission, 2/1 priority date for domestic and international students; for spring admission, 11/1 for domestic students, 10/1 for international students. Applications are processed on a rolling basis. *Application fee:* $55. Electronic applications accepted.

School of Social Work Financial support: Research assistantships with full tuition reimbursements, teaching assistantships with full tuition reimbursements, Federal Work-Study, health care benefits, and unspecified assistantships available. Financial award application deadline: 2/1; financial award applicants required to submit FAFSA. Offers social work (MSW, PhD). *Application deadline:* For fall admission, 2/1 priority date for domestic and international students; for spring admission, 11/1 for domestic students, 10/1 for international students. Applications are processed on a rolling basis. *Application fee:* $55. Electronic applications accepted.

Institute of Materials Science Offers materials science (MS, PhD); polymer science and engineering (MS, PhD).

School of Law ***Degree program information:*** Part-time programs available. Part-time. Offers law (JD). Electronic applications accepted.

UNIVERSITY OF CONNECTICUT HEALTH CENTER, Farmington, CT 06030

General Information State-supported, coed, graduate-only institution. *Graduate housing:* On-campus housing not available.

GRADUATE UNITS

Graduate School ***Degree program information:*** Part-time and evening/weekend programs available. Part-time, evening/weekend. Offers biomedical sciences (PhD); biomedical sciences - integrated (PhD); cell analysis and modeling (PhD); cell biology (PhD); clinical and translational research (MS); genetics and developmental biology (PhD); immunology (PhD); molecular biology and biochemistry (PhD); neuroscience (PhD); public health (MPH); skeletal biology and regeneration (PhD).

School of Dental Medicine Offers dental medicine (MDS, DMD, Certificate); dental science (MDS). Electronic applications accepted.

School of Medicine Offers medicine (MD). Electronic applications accepted.

UNIVERSITY OF DALLAS, Irving, TX 75062-4736

General Information Independent-religious, coed, university. *Graduate housing:* Room and/or apartments available on a first-come, first-served basis to single students; on-campus housing not available to married students. Housing application deadline: 6/1.

GRADUATE UNITS

Braniff Graduate School of Liberal Arts ***Degree program information:*** Part-time programs available. Part-time. Offers American studies (MAS); art (MA, MFA); classics (MA, MC); English (MA); humanities (M Hum, MA); liberal arts (M Hum, M Pol, M Psych, M Th, MA, MAS, MC, MCSL, MEL, MFA, MPM, MRE, MTS, PhD); philosophy (MA); politics (M Pol, MA); psychology (M Psych, MA); theology (M Th, MA).

Institute of Philosophic Studies Offers literature (PhD); philosophy (PhD); politics (PhD).

Institute for Religious and Pastoral Studies ***Degree program information:*** Part-time and evening/weekend programs available. Part-time, evening/weekend, online learning. Offers religious and pastoral studies (MCSL, MPM, MRE, MTS).

Satish and Yasmin Gupta College of Business ***Degree program information:*** Part-time and evening/weekend programs available. Part-time, evening/weekend, online learning. Offers accounting (MBA, MS); business administration (DBA); business analytics (MS); business management (MBA); corporate finance (MBA); cybersecurity (MS); finance (MS); financial services (MBA); global business (MBA, MS); health services management (MBA); human resource management (MBA); information and technology managemeny (MS); information assurance (MBA); information technology (MBA); information technology service management (MBA); marketing management (MBA); organization development (MBA); project management (MBA); sports and entertainment management (MBA); strategic leadership (MBA); supply chain management (MBA). Electronic applications accepted.

UNIVERSITY OF DAYTON, Dayton, OH 45469

General Information Independent-religious, coed, university. CGS member. *Graduate housing:* Room and/or apartments available on a first-come, first-served basis to single students; on-campus housing not available to married students. *Research affiliation:* American Chemical Council (geological studies), Battelle Memorial Institute (fuels research), Dayton Area Graduate Studies Institute (materials testing), Kern Family Foundation (curriculum development), Kettering Health Network (engineering and design), Good Will Easter Seals (Alzheimer's disease and dementia research).

GRADUATE UNITS

Department of Biology Students: 18 full-time (11 women), 1 part-time (0 women); includes 2 minority (both Asian, non-Hispanic/Latino), 8 international. Average age 26. 63 applicants, 8% accepted, 5 enrolled. *Faculty:* 16 full-time (6 women). *Financial support:* In 2015–16, 3 research assistantships with full tuition reimbursements (averaging $18,760 per year), 15 teaching assistantships with full tuition reimbursements (averaging $18,760 per year) were awarded; institutionally sponsored loans, health care benefits, and unspecified assistantships also available. Financial award applicants required to submit FAFSA. In 2015, 3 master's, 5 doctorates awarded. Offers biology (MS, PhD). *Application deadline:* For fall admission, 1/31 priority date for domestic and international students. Applications are processed on a rolling basis. *Application fee:* $0 ($50 for international students). Electronic applications accepted. *Application Contact:* Dr. Amit Singh, Director, Biology Graduate Programs, 937-229-2894, Fax: 937-229-2021, E-mail: asingh1@udayton.edu. *Chair,* Dr. Mark G. Nielsen, 937-229-2521, Fax: 937-229-2021, E-mail: mnielsen1@udayton.edu.

Department of Chemical Engineering Students: 28 full-time (9 women), 4 part-time (1 woman), 26 international. Average age 25. 91 applicants, 54% accepted, 16 enrolled. *Faculty:* 9 full-time (2 women), 5 part-time/adjunct (1 woman). *Financial support:* In 2015–16, 1 research assistantship with full tuition reimbursement (averaging $18,000 per year) was awarded; teaching assistantships, institutionally sponsored loans, and health care benefits also available. Financial award application deadline: 3/1; financial award applicants required to submit FAFSA. In 2015, 33 master's awarded. *Degree program information:* Part-time and evening/weekend programs available. Part-time, evening/weekend. Offers bioengineering (MS); chemical engineering (MS Ch E). *Application deadline:* Applications are processed on a rolling basis. *Application fee:* $0 ($50 for international students). Electronic applications accepted. *Application Contact:* Dr. Kevin Myers, Graduate Program Director, 937-229-2627, E-mail: kmyers1@udayton.edu. *Chair,* Dr. Charles Browning, 937-229-2627, E-mail: cbrowning1@udayton.edu.

Department of Chemistry Students: 3 full-time (2 women); includes 1 minority (Asian, non-Hispanic/Latino). Average age 35. 52 applicants, 8% accepted, 4 enrolled. *Faculty:* 5 full-time (0 women). *Financial support:* In 2015–16, 3 students received support, including 5 teaching assistantships with full tuition reimbursements available (averaging $12,876 per year); institutionally sponsored loans and health care benefits also available. Financial award application deadline: 5/1; financial award applicants required to submit FAFSA. In 2015, 1 master's awarded. Offers chemistry (MS). *Application deadline:* For fall admission, 5/1 priority date for domestic and international students; for winter admission, 7/1 priority date for international students; for spring admission, 11/1 priority date for international students. Applications are processed on a rolling basis. *Application fee:* $0 ($50 for international students). Electronic applications accepted. *Application Contact:* Dr. Kevin Church, Graduate Program Director, 937-229-2659, E-mail: kchurch1@udayton.edu. *Chair,* Dr. David Johnson, 937-229-2631, E-mail: djohnson1@udayton.edu.

Department of Civil and Environmental Engineering and Engineering Mechanics Students: 32 full-time (5 women), 11 part-time (2 women); includes 1 minority (Hispanic/Latino), 33 international. Average age 27. 70 applicants, 39% accepted, 4 enrolled. *Faculty:* 9 full-time (2 women), 3 part-time/adjunct (1 woman). *Financial support:* In 2015–16, 3 students received support, including 1 research assistantship with partial tuition reimbursement available (averaging $13,156 per year); institutionally sponsored loans, scholarships/grants, and department-funded awards (averaging $2448 per year) also available. Financial award application deadline: 3/1; financial award applicants required to submit FAFSA. In 2015, 14 master's awarded. *Degree program information:* Part-time and evening/weekend programs available. Part-time, evening/weekend. Offers engineering mechanics (MSEM); environmental engineering (MSCE); geotechnical engineering (MSCE); structural engineering (MSCE); transportation engineering (MSCE); water resources engineering (MSCE). *Application deadline:* For fall admission, 8/1 priority date for domestic students, 5/1 priority date for international students; for spring admission, 11/1 priority date for international students. Applications are processed on a rolling basis. *Application fee:* $0 ($50 for international students). Electronic applications accepted. *Application Contact:* 937-229-4462, E-mail: graduateadmission@udayton.edu. *Chair,* Dr. Donald V. Chase, 937-229-3847, Fax: 937-229-3491, E-mail: dchase1@udayton.edu.

Department of Communication Students: 15 full-time (14 women), 4 part-time (3 women); includes 1 minority (Hispanic/Latino), 9 international. Average age 27. 81 applicants, 32% accepted, 10 enrolled. *Faculty:* 11 full-time (5 women). *Financial support:* In 2015–16, 7 students received support, including 1 research assistantship with full tuition reimbursement available (averaging $10,914 per year), 8 teaching assistantships with full tuition reimbursements available (averaging $10,914 per year); institutionally sponsored loans, health care benefits, and unspecified assistantships also available. Financial award application deadline: 3/1; financial award applicants required to submit FAFSA. In 2015, 22 master's awarded. *Degree program information:* Part-time and evening/weekend programs available. Part-time, evening/weekend. Offers communication (MA); interdisciplinary communication (MA). *Application deadline:* For fall admission, 3/1 priority date for domestic and international students. Applications are processed on a rolling basis. *Application fee:* $0 ($50 for international students). Electronic applications accepted. *Application Contact:* Dr. JeeHee Han, Graduate Program Director, 937-229-2486, E-mail: jhan01@udayton.edu. *Chair,* Dr. Jon A. Hess, 937-229-2028, E-mail: jhess1@udayton.edu.

Department of Computer Science Students: 92 full-time (32 women), 13 part-time (3 women); includes 2 minority (1 Asian, non-Hispanic/Latino; 1 Hispanic/Latino), 97 international. Average age 24. 203 applicants, 42% accepted, 13 enrolled. *Faculty:* 9 full-time (1 woman), 2 part-time/adjunct (0 women). *Financial support:* In 2015–16, 5 students received support, including 9 teaching assistantships with full tuition reimbursements available (averaging $11,322 per year); institutionally sponsored loans, health care benefits, and unspecified assistantships also available. Financial award application deadline: 3/1; financial award applicants required to submit FAFSA. In 2015, 16 master's awarded. *Degree program information:* Part-time programs available. Part-time. Offers computer science (MCS). *Application deadline:* Applications are processed on a rolling basis. *Application fee:* $0 ($50 for international students). Electronic applications accepted. *Application Contact:* 937-229-4462, E-mail: graduateadmission@udayton.edu. *Chair,* Dr. Mehdi Zargham, 937-229-3831, E-mail: mzargham1@udayton.edu.

Department of Counselor Education and Human Services Students: 202 full-time (155 women), 102 part-time (86 women); includes 60 minority (43 Black or African American, non-Hispanic/Latino; 2 Asian, non-Hispanic/Latino; 10 Hispanic/Latino; 5 Two or more races, non-Hispanic/Latino), 10 international. Average age 31. 295 applicants, 47% accepted, 103 enrolled. *Faculty:* 10 full-time (6 women), 24 part-time/adjunct (15 women). *Financial support:* In 2015–16, 10 research assistantships with full tuition reimbursements (averaging $8,720 per year) were awarded; career-related internships or fieldwork, institutionally sponsored loans, health care benefits, and unspecified assistantships also available. Financial award application deadline: 3/1; financial award applicants required to submit FAFSA. In 2015, 115 master's, 9 Ed Ss awarded. *Degree program information:* Part-time and evening/weekend programs available. Part-time, evening/weekend. Offers clinical mental health counseling (MS Ed); college student personnel (MS Ed); higher education administration (MS Ed); human services (MS Ed); school counseling (MS Ed); school psychology (MS Ed, Ed S). *Application deadline:* For fall admission, 3/10 priority date for domestic and international students; for spring admission, 9/10 priority date for domestic and international students; for summer admission, 12/1 priority date for domestic and international students. *Application fee:* $0 ($50 for international students). Electronic applications accepted. *Application Contact:* Kathleen Brown, Administrative Assistant, 937-229-3644, Fax: 937-229-1055, E-mail: kbrown1@udayton.edu. *Chairperson,* Dr. Molly Schaller, 937-229-3644, Fax: 937-229-1055, E-mail: mschaller1@udayton.edu.

Department of Electrical and Computer Engineering Students: 167 full-time (33 women), 36 part-time (7 women); includes 8 minority (2 Black or African American, non-Hispanic/Latino; 5 Asian, non-Hispanic/Latino; 1 Two or more races, non-Hispanic/Latino), 150 international. Average age 28. 495 applicants, 40% accepted, 66 enrolled. *Faculty:* 17 full-time (0 women), 16 part-time/adjunct (2 women). *Financial support:* In 2015–16, 24 research assistantships with full tuition reimbursements (averaging $12,500 per year), 25 teaching assistantships with full tuition reimbursements (averaging $10,000 per year) were awarded; fellowships, institutionally sponsored loans, health care benefits, and unspecified assistantships also available. Financial award application deadline: 3/1; financial award applicants required to submit FAFSA. In 2015, 88 master's, 8 doctorates awarded. *Degree program information:* Part-time programs available. Part-time. Offers computer engineering (MS); electrical engineering (MSEE, PhD). *Application deadline:* For fall admission, 8/1 for domestic students, 5/1 priority date for international students; for spring admission, 11/1 priority date for international students. Applications are processed on a rolling basis. *Application fee:* $0 ($50 for international students). Electronic applications accepted. *Application Contact:* E-mail: graduateadmission@udayton.edu. *Chair,* Dr. Guru Subramanyam, 937-229-3188, Fax: 937-229-4529, E-mail: gsubramanyam1@udayton.edu.

Department of Engineering Management and Systems Students: 61 full-time (12 women), 37 part-time (9 women); includes 5 minority (2 Black or African American, non-Hispanic/Latino; 1 Asian, non-Hispanic/Latino; 2 Hispanic/Latino), 38 international. Average age 30. 186 applicants, 55% accepted, 35 enrolled. *Faculty:* 4 full-time (1 woman), 9 part-time/adjunct (1 woman). *Financial support:* Application deadline: 3/1; applicants required to submit FAFSA. In 2015, 27 master's awarded. *Degree program information:* Part-time and evening/weekend programs available. Part-time, evening/weekend, blended/hybrid learning. Offers engineering management (MSEM); management science (MSMS). *Application deadline:* Applications are processed on a rolling basis. *Application fee:* $0. Electronic applications accepted. *Application Contact:* 937-229-4462, E-mail: graduateadmission@udayton.edu. *Chair,* Dr. Edward Mykytka, 937-229-2238, E-mail: emykytkal1@udayton.edu.

Department of English Students: 22 full-time (17 women), 3 part-time (all women), 11 international. Average age 30. 44 applicants, 48% accepted, 6 enrolled. *Faculty:* 25 full-time (14 women). *Financial support:* In 2015–16, 9 teaching assistantships with full tuition reimbursements (averaging $10,800 per year) were awarded; institutionally sponsored loans and health care benefits also available. Financial award application deadline: 12/15; financial award applicants required to submit FAFSA. In 2015, 8 master's awarded. *Degree program information:* Part-time and evening/weekend programs available. Part-time, evening/weekend, 100% online. Offers literature (MA); teaching (MA); writing (MA). *Application deadline:* For fall admission, 6/15 priority date for domestic and international students; for spring admission, 12/15 priority date for domestic and international students. Applications are processed on a rolling basis. *Application fee:* $0 ($50 for international students). Electronic applications accepted. *Application Contact:* Dr. Tereza Szeghi, Director of Graduate Studies, 937-229-3443, E-mail: tszeghi1@udayton.edu. *Chair,* Dr. Andrew Slade, 937-229-3434, Fax: 937-229-3563, E-mail: aslade1@udayton.edu.

Department of Health and Sport Science Students: 16 full-time (10 women), 4 part-time (1 woman); includes 2 minority (1 Black or African American, non-Hispanic/Latino; 1 Asian, non-Hispanic/Latino), 2 international. Average age 24. 150 applicants, 45% accepted, 38 enrolled. *Faculty:* 7 full-time (3 women). *Financial support:* In 2015–16, 3 research assistantships with full tuition reimbursements (averaging $10,289 per year), 3 teaching assistantships with full tuition reimbursements (averaging $10,289 per year) were awarded; career-related internships or fieldwork, institutionally sponsored loans, health care benefits, and unspecified assistantships also available. Financial award application deadline: 3/1; financial award applicants required to submit FAFSA. In 2015, 5 master's awarded. Offers exercise science (MS Ed). *Application deadline:* For fall admission, 2/15 priority date for domestic students, 5/1 priority date for international students; for winter admission, 7/1 for international students; for spring admission, 11/1 priority date for international students. Applications are processed on a rolling basis. *Application fee:* $0 ($50 for international students). Electronic applications accepted. *Application Contact:* Laura Greger, Administrative Assistant, 937-229-4225, E-mail: lgreger1@udayton.edu. *Chair,* Dr. Lloyd Laubach, 937-229-4240, Fax: 937-229-4244, E-mail: llaubach1@udayton.edu.

Department of Materials Engineering Students: 54 full-time (12 women), 12 part-time (4 women); includes 8 minority (3 Black or African American, non-Hispanic/Latino; 3 Asian, non-Hispanic/Latino; 2 Hispanic/Latino), 23 international. Average age 31. 115 applicants, 48% accepted, 18 enrolled. *Faculty:* 2 full-time (0 women), 9 part-time/adjunct (0 women). *Financial support:* In 2015–16, 2 research assistantships with full tuition reimbursements (averaging $12,412 per year) were awarded; institutionally sponsored loans, health care benefits, and unspecified assistantships also available. Support available to part-time students. Financial award application deadline: 3/1; financial award applicants required to submit FAFSA. In 2015, 33 master's, 6 doctorates awarded. *Degree program information:* Part-time and evening/weekend programs available. Part-time, evening/weekend. Offers materials engineering (MS Mat E, DE, PhD). *Application deadline:* For fall admission, 8/1 priority date for domestic students, 5/1 priority date for international students; for winter admission, 7/1 for international students; for spring admission, 11/1 priority date for international students. Applications are processed on a rolling basis. *Application fee:* $0 ($50 for international students). Electronic applications accepted. *Chair/Interim Graduate Program Director,* Dr. Charles Browning, 937-229-2679, E-mail: cbrowning1@udayton.edu.

Department of Mathematics Students: 31 full-time (13 women), 5 part-time (2 women); includes 3 minority (2 Black or African American, non-Hispanic/Latino; 1 Hispanic/Latino), 27 international. Average age 26. 121 applicants, 29% accepted, 10 enrolled. *Faculty:* 19 full-time (7 women). *Financial support:* In 2015–16, 6 students received support, including 6 teaching assistantships with full tuition reimbursements available (averaging $14,750 per year); institutionally sponsored loans and health care benefits also available. Financial award application deadline: 3/1; financial award applicants required to submit FAFSA. In 2015, 26 master's awarded. *Degree program information:* Part-time programs available. Part-time. Offers applied mathematics (MAS); financial mathematics (MFM); mathematics education (MME). *Application deadline:* Applications are processed on a rolling basis. *Application fee:* $0 ($50 for international students). Electronic applications accepted. *Application Contact:* Dr. Paul W. Eloe, Graduate Program Director/Professor, 937-229-2016, E-mail: peloe1@udayton.edu. *Chair,* Dr. Joe D. Mashburn, 937-229-2511, Fax: 937-229-2566, E-mail: jmashburn1@udayton.edu.

Department of Mechanical and Aerospace Engineering Students: 158 full-time (33 women), 38 part-time (5 women); includes 6 minority (2 Black or African American, non-Hispanic/Latino; 1 Asian, non-Hispanic/Latino; 2 Hispanic/Latino; 1 Two or more races, non-Hispanic/Latino), 128 international. Average age 27. 340 applicants, 44% accepted, 58 enrolled. *Faculty:* 15 full-time (3 women), 10 part-time/adjunct (1 woman). *Financial support:* In 2015–16, 3 fellowships with full tuition reimbursements (averaging $25,000 per year), 21 research assistantships with full tuition reimbursements (averaging $13,000 per year), 8 teaching assistantships with full tuition reimbursements (averaging $8,000 per year) were awarded; institutionally sponsored loans, health care benefits, and tuition waivers also available. Support available to part-time students. Financial award application deadline: 3/1; financial award applicants required to submit FAFSA. In 2015, 66 master's awarded. *Degree program information:* Part-time programs available. Part-time, online learning. Offers aerospace engineering (MSAE, DE, PhD); mechanical engineering (MSME, DE, PhD); renewable and clean energy (MS). *Application deadline:* Applications are processed on a rolling basis. *Application fee:* $0 ($50 for international students). Electronic applications accepted. *Application Contact:* Dr. Vinod Jain, Graduate Program Director, 937-229-2992, Fax: 937-229-4766, E-mail: vjain1@udayton.edu. *Chair,* Dr. Kelly Kissock, 937-229-2999, Fax: 937-229-4766, E-mail: jkissock1@udayton.edu.

Department of Physical Therapy Students: 111 full-time (65 women); includes 8 minority (2 Black or African American, non-Hispanic/Latino; 1 Asian, non-Hispanic/Latino; 2 Hispanic/Latino; 3 Two or more races, non-Hispanic/Latino). Average age 24. 209 applicants, 28% accepted, 36 enrolled. *Faculty:* 9 full-time (4 women), 23 part-time/adjunct (18 women). *Financial support:* In 2015–16, 7 research assistantships with partial tuition reimbursements (averaging $10,900 per year) were awarded; institutionally sponsored loans and health care benefits also available. Financial award application deadline: 3/1; financial award applicants required to submit FAFSA. In 2015, 38 doctorates awarded. Offers physical therapy (DPT). *Application deadline:* For fall admission, 10/1 priority date for domestic students, 9/1 priority date for international students. Electronic applications accepted. *Application Contact:* Trista Cathcart, Admissions Coordinator, 937-229-5611, Fax: 937-229-5601, E-mail: tcathcart1@udayton.edu. *Chair/Associate Professor,* Dr. Philip A. Anloague, 937-229-5600, Fax: 937-229-5601, E-mail: panalogue1@udayton.edu.

Department of Physician Assistant Education Students: 65 full-time (47 women); includes 9 minority (1 Black or African American, non-Hispanic/Latino; 3 Asian, non-Hispanic/Latino; 4 Hispanic/Latino; 1 Two or more races, non-Hispanic/Latino). Average age 27. 611 applicants, 17% accepted, 30 enrolled. *Faculty:* 6 full-time (all women), 1 (woman) part-time/adjunct. *Financial support:* Career-related internships or fieldwork and institutionally sponsored loans available. Financial award application deadline: 3/1; financial award applicants required to submit FAFSA. Offers physician assistant education (MPAP). *Application deadline:* For fall admission, 12/1 priority date for domestic and international students. *Application fee:* $175. Electronic applications accepted. *Application Contact:* Amy Kidwell, 937-229-2900, E-mail: akidwell1@udayton.edu. *Founding Chair/Director,* Susan Wulff, 937-229-3377, E-mail: swulff1@udayton.edu.

Department of Religious Studies Students: 48 full-time (17 women), 8 part-time (4 women); includes 6 minority (1 Black or African American, non-Hispanic/Latino; 3 Asian, non-Hispanic/Latino; 2 Hispanic/Latino), 1 international. Average age 33. 82 applicants, 52% accepted, 18 enrolled. *Faculty:* 19 full-time (7 women), 6 part-time/adjunct (2 women). *Financial support:* In 2015–16, 36 students received support, including 4 fellowships with full tuition reimbursements available (averaging $17,600 per year), 7 research assistantships with full tuition reimbursements available (averaging $10,413 per year), 16 teaching assistantships with full tuition reimbursements available (averaging $17,600 per year); institutionally sponsored loans, scholarships/grants, health care benefits, and unspecified assistantships also available. Support available to part-time students. Financial award application deadline: 2/2; financial award applicants required to submit FAFSA. In 2015, 15 master's, 5 doctorates awarded. *Degree program information:* Part-time programs available. Part-time. Offers pastoral ministry (MA); theological studies (MA); theology (PhD). *Application deadline:* For fall admission, 2/2 priority date for domestic and international students. Applications are processed on a rolling basis. *Application fee:* $0 ($50 for international students). Electronic applications accepted. *Application Contact:* Amy Doorley, Graduate Program Coordinator, 937-229-4321, Fax: 937-229-4330, E-mail: adoorley1@udayton.edu. *Chair,* Dr. Daniel Thompson, 937-229-4321, Fax: 937-229-4330.

Department of Teacher Education Students: 91 full-time (84 women), 126 part-time (106 women); includes 14 minority (8 Black or African American, non-Hispanic/Latino; 2 Asian, non-Hispanic/Latino; 3 Hispanic/Latino; 1 Two or more races, non-Hispanic/Latino), 33 international. Average age 32. 140 applicants, 54% accepted, 39 enrolled. *Faculty:* 26 full-time (19 women), 59 part-time/adjunct (52 women). *Financial support:* In 2015–16, 6 research assistantships with full tuition reimbursements (averaging $8,900 per year), 2 teaching assistantships with full tuition reimbursements (averaging $8,900 per year) were awarded; career-related internships or fieldwork, institutionally sponsored loans, health care benefits, and unspecified assistantships also available. Financial award application deadline: 3/1; financial award applicants required to submit FAFSA. In 2015, 69 master's awarded. *Degree program information:* Part-time and evening/weekend programs available. Part-time, evening/weekend, online learning. Offers early childhood leadership and advocacy (MS Ed); interdisciplinary education studies (MS Ed); leadership in educational systems (MS Ed); literacy (MS Ed); mathematics education (MS Ed); music education (MS Ed); teacher as leader (MS Ed); teacher education (MS Ed); technology-enhanced learning (MS Ed); trans-disciplinary early childhood education (MS Ed). *Application deadline:* Applications are processed on a rolling basis. *Application fee:* $0 ($50 for international students). Electronic applications accepted. *Application Contact:* Gina Seiter, Graduate Program Advisor, 937-229-3103, E-mail: gseiter1@udayton.edu. *Chair,* Dr. Connie L. Bowman, 937-229-3305, E-mail: cbowman1@udayton.edu.

Doctoral Program in Educational Leadership Students: 54 full-time (26 women); includes 6 minority (5 Black or African American, non-Hispanic/Latino; 1 Hispanic/Latino), 3 international. Average age 41. 21 applicants, 24% accepted, 4 enrolled. *Faculty:* 7 full-time (3 women). *Financial support:* In 2015–16, 4 research assistantships with partial tuition reimbursements (averaging $11,120 per year) were awarded; institutionally sponsored loans, health care benefits, and unspecified assistantships also available. Financial award application deadline: 3/1; financial award applicants required to submit FAFSA. In 2015, 6 doctorates awarded. *Degree program information:* Part-time and evening/weekend programs available. Part-time, evening/weekend. Offers educational leadership (PhD); higher education administration (PhD); preK-12 school administration (PhD). *Application deadline:* For fall admission, 5/1 priority date for domestic and international students; for winter admission, 7/1 for international students; for spring admission, 11/1 priority date for domestic and international students. Applications are processed on a rolling basis. *Application fee:* $0 ($50 for international students). Electronic applications accepted. *Application Contact:* Nancy Crouchley, Administrative Assistant, 937-229-4003, Fax: 937-229-4729, E-mail: ncrouchley1@udayton.edu. *Interim Director*, Dr. Charles J. Russo, 937-229-3722, Fax: 937-229-4824, E-mail: crusso1@udayton.edu.

Educational Leadership Program ***Degree program information:*** Part-time and evening/weekend programs available. Part-time, evening/weekend, online learning. Offers educational leadership (MS Ed, Ed S). Electronic applications accepted.

Program in Clinical Psychology Students: 13 full-time (9 women), 2 part-time (1 woman). Average age 26. 91 applicants, 11% accepted, 9 enrolled. *Faculty:* 28 full-time (18 women). *Financial support:* In 2015–16, 11 research assistantships with full tuition reimbursements (averaging $11,342 per year) were awarded; institutionally sponsored loans, traineeships, and health care benefits also available. Financial award application deadline: 3/1; financial award applicants required to submit FAFSA. In 2015, 7 master's awarded. Offers clinical psychology (MA). *Application deadline:* For fall admission, 2/15 priority date for domestic and international students. *Application fee:* $0 ($50 for international students). Electronic applications accepted. *Application Contact:* 937-229-4462, E-mail: graduateadmission@udayton.edu. *Director*, Dr. Catherine L. Zois, 937-229-2164, Fax: 937-229-3900, E-mail: czois1@udayton.edu.

Program in Electro-Optics Students: 43 full-time (7 women), 9 part-time (4 women); includes 3 minority (2 Black or African American, non-Hispanic/Latino; 1 Asian, non-Hispanic/Latino), 29 international. Average age 29. 99 applicants, 42% accepted, 18 enrolled. *Faculty:* 4 full-time (0 women), 4 part-time/adjunct (0 women). *Financial support:* In 2015–16, 17 research assistantships with full tuition reimbursements (averaging $21,000 per year), 7 teaching assistantships with full tuition reimbursements (averaging $21,000 per year) were awarded; institutionally sponsored loans, health care benefits, and unspecified assistantships also available. Financial award applicants required to submit FAFSA. In 2015, 14 master's, 4 doctorates awarded. *Degree program information:* Part-time programs available. Part-time. Offers electro-optics (MSEO, PhD). *Application deadline:* Applications are processed on a rolling basis. *Application fee:* $0 ($50 for international students). Electronic applications accepted. *Application Contact:* 937-229-4462, E-mail: graduateadmission@udayton.edu. *Director*, Dr. Partha P. Banerjee, 937-229-2797, Fax: 937-229-2099, E-mail: pbanerjee1@udayton.edu.

Program in General Psychology Students: 5 full-time (all women), 1 (woman) part-time; includes 3 minority (2 Black or African American, non-Hispanic/Latino; 1 Hispanic/Latino). Average age 24. 34 applicants, 12% accepted, 3 enrolled. *Faculty:* 12 full-time (5 women). *Financial support:* In 2015–16, 5 students received support, including 5 research assistantships with full tuition reimbursements available (averaging $11,342 per year); institutionally sponsored loans, traineeships, and health care benefits also available. Financial award application deadline: 3/1; financial award applicants required to submit FAFSA. In 2015, 4 master's awarded. Offers general psychology (MA). *Application deadline:* For fall admission, 3/1 priority date for domestic and international students. *Application fee:* $0 ($50 for international students). Electronic applications accepted. *Application Contact:* 937-229-4462, E-mail: graduateadmission@udayton.edu. *Graduate Program Director*, Dr. R. Matthew Montoya, 937-229-2656, Fax: 937-229-3900, E-mail: mmontoya1@udayton.edu.

Program in Public Administration Students: 14 full-time (10 women), 6 part-time (3 women); includes 2 minority (1 Black or African American, non-Hispanic/Latino; 1 Hispanic/Latino), 1 international. Average age 31. 63 applicants, 52% accepted, 20 enrolled. *Faculty:* 6 full-time (2 women), 6 part-time/adjunct (2 women). *Financial support:* In 2015–16, 3 research assistantships with full tuition reimbursements (averaging $11,587 per year) were awarded; institutionally sponsored loans, health care benefits, and unspecified assistantships also available. Financial award application deadline: 3/1; financial award applicants required to submit FAFSA. In 2015, 7 master's awarded. *Degree program information:* Part-time and evening/weekend programs available. Part-time, evening/weekend. Offers public administration (MPA). *Application deadline:* Applications are processed on a rolling basis. *Application fee:* $0 ($50 for international students). Electronic applications accepted. *Application Contact:* 937-229-4462, E-mail: graduateadmission@udayton.edu. *Graduate Program Director*, Dr. Michelle Pautz, 937-229-3651, Fax: 937-229-1400, E-mail: mpautz1@udayton.edu.

School of Business Administration Students: 94 full-time (35 women), 85 part-time (38 women); includes 14 minority (5 Black or African American, non-Hispanic/Latino; 4 Asian, non-Hispanic/Latino; 5 Hispanic/Latino), 26 international. Average age 30. 437 applicants, 44% accepted, 53 enrolled. *Faculty:* 24 full-time (9 women), 5 part-time/adjunct (1 woman). *Financial support:* In 2015–16, 10 research assistantships with partial tuition reimbursements (averaging $8,535 per year) were awarded; institutionally sponsored loans, health care benefits, and unspecified assistantships also available. Financial award application deadline: 3/1; financial award applicants required to submit FAFSA. In 2015, 93 master's awarded. *Degree program information:* Part-time and evening/weekend programs available. Part-time, evening/weekend. Offers accounting (MBA); cyber security (MBA); finance (MBA); marketing (MBA). *Application deadline:* For fall admission, 5/1 priority date for international students; for spring admission, 7/1 priority date for international students; for summer admission, 11/1 priority date for international students. Applications are processed on a rolling basis. *Application fee:* $0 ($50 for international students). Electronic applications accepted. *Application Contact:* Mandy Schrank, MBA Program Manager, 937-229-3733, Fax: 937-229-3882, E-mail: mschrank2@udayton.edu. *Director, MBA Program*, John M. Gentner, 937-229-3733, Fax: 937-229-3882, E-mail: jgentner1@udayton.edu.

School of Law Students: 253 full-time (115 women), 14 part-time (5 women); includes 41 minority (24 Black or African American, non-Hispanic/Latino; 5 Asian, non-Hispanic/Latino; 12 Hispanic/Latino), 19 international. Average age 27. 1,044 applicants, 70% accepted, 115 enrolled. *Faculty:* 9 full-time (5 women), 4 part-time/adjunct (1 woman). *Financial support:* In 2015–16, 1 teaching assistantship (averaging $2,500 per year) was awarded; institutionally sponsored loans and scholarships/grants also available. Financial award applicants required to submit FAFSA. In 2015, 8 master's, 96 doctorates awarded. *Degree program information:* Part-time programs available. Part-time. Offers law (LL M, MSL, JD). *Application deadline:* Applications are processed on a rolling basis. *Application fee:* $0. Electronic applications accepted. *Application Contact:* Claire Schrader, Assistant Dean/Executive Director of Enrollment Management and Marketing, 937-229-3555, Fax: 937-229-4194, E-mail: lawinfo@udayton.edu. *Dean*, Paul McGreal, 937-229-3795, Fax: 937-229-2469.

UNIVERSITY OF DELAWARE, Newark, DE 19716

General Information State-related, coed, university. CGS member. *Graduate housing:* Rooms and/or apartments available to single and married students. Housing application deadline: 3/15. *Research affiliation:* Hagley Museum, Winterthur Museum, Longwood Gardens, Bartol Research Foundation.

GRADUATE UNITS

Alfred Lerner College of Business and Economics ***Degree program information:*** Part-time and evening/weekend programs available. Part-time, evening/weekend. Offers accounting (MS); business administration (MBA); business and economics (MA, MBA, MS, PhD); economic education (PhD); economics (MA, MS, PhD); economics for entrepreneurship and educators (MA); finance (MS); financial service analytics (PhD); hospitality information management (MS); information systems and technology management (MS). Electronic applications accepted.

Center for Energy and Environmental Policy Offers energy and environmental policy (MA, MEEP, PhD); urban affairs and public policy (PhD). Electronic applications accepted.

College of Agriculture and Natural Resources ***Degree program information:*** Part-time programs available. Part-time. Offers agricultural and resource economics (MS); agricultural education (MA); agriculture and natural resources (MA, MS, PhD); animal sciences (MS, PhD); bioresources engineering (MS); entomology and applied ecology (MS, PhD); food sciences (MS); operations research (MS); plant and soil sciences (MS, PhD); public horticulture (MS); statistics (MS). Electronic applications accepted.

College of Arts and Sciences ***Degree program information:*** Part-time and evening/weekend programs available. Part-time, evening/weekend. Offers acting (MFA); American material culture (MA); applied mathematics (MS, PhD); art (MA, MFA); art conservation (MS); art history (MA, PhD); arts and sciences (MA, MALS, MFA, MM, MS, DPT, PhD); behavioral neuroscience (PhD); biochemistry (MA, MS, PhD); biomechanics and movement science (MS, PhD); biotechnology (MS); cancer biology (MS, PhD); cell and extracellular matrix biology (MS, PhD); cell and systems physiology (MS, PhD); chemistry (MA, MS, PhD); clinical psychology (PhD); cognitive psychology (PhD); communication (MA); composition (MM); criminology (MA, PhD); developmental biology (MS, PhD); ecology and evolution (MS, PhD); English and American literature (MA, PhD); fashion and apparel studies (MS); foreign languages and literatures (MA); foreign languages pedagogy (MA); history (MA, PhD); history of technology and industrialization (MA, PhD); liberal studies (MALS); linguistics (PhD); linguistics and cognitive science (MA); mathematics (MS, PhD); microbiology (MS, PhD); molecular biology and genetics (MS, PhD); music education (MM); performance (MM); physics and astronomy (MS, PhD); political science and international relations (MA, PhD); preservation studies (PhD); social psychology (PhD); sociology (MA, PhD); stage management (MFA); technical Chinese translation (MA); technical production (MFA). Electronic applications accepted.

School of Public Policy and Administration ***Degree program information:*** Part-time and evening/weekend programs available. Part-time, evening/weekend. Offers disaster science and management (MS, PhD); governance planning and management (PhD); historic preservation (MA); public administration (MPA); public policy and administration (MA, MPA, PhD); social and urban policy (PhD); technology, environment and society (PhD); urban affairs and public policy (MA). Electronic applications accepted.

College of Earth, Ocean, and Environment Offers geography (MA, MS, PhD); geological sciences (MA, PhD); geology (MS, PhD); marine science and policy (MMP, MS, PhD); ocean engineering (MS, PhD). Electronic applications accepted.

School of Marine Science and Policy Offers marine policy (MMP); marine studies (MS, PhD); oceanography (PhD).

College of Education and Human Development ***Degree program information:*** Part-time and evening/weekend programs available. Part-time, evening/weekend. Offers education and human development (M Ed, MA, MEEP, MI, MPA, MS, Ed D, PhD, Ed S); human development and family studies (MS, PhD). Electronic applications accepted.

School of Education ***Degree program information:*** Part-time and evening/weekend programs available. Part-time, evening/weekend. Offers education (PhD); educational leadership (Ed D); higher education (M Ed); instruction (MI); reading (M Ed); school leadership (M Ed); school psychology (MA, Ed S); teaching English as a second language (TESL) (MA). Electronic applications accepted.

College of Engineering ***Degree program information:*** Part-time and evening/weekend programs available. Part-time, evening/weekend, online learning. Offers chemical engineering (M Ch E, PhD); computer and information sciences (MS, PhD); electrical and computer engineering (MSECE, PhD); engineering (M Ch E, MAS, MCE, MEM, MMSE, MS, MSECE, MSME, PhD); environmental engineering (MAS, MCE, PhD); geotechnical engineering (MAS, MCE, PhD); materials science and engineering (MMSE, PhD); mechanical engineering (MEM, MSME, PhD); ocean engineering (MAS, MCE, PhD); structural engineering (MAS, MCE, PhD); transportation engineering (MAS, MCE, PhD); water resource engineering (MAS, MCE, PhD). Electronic applications accepted.

College of Health Sciences ***Degree program information:*** Part-time and evening/weekend programs available. Part-time, evening/weekend, online learning. Offers adult nurse practitioner (MSN, PMC); cardiopulmonary clinical nurse specialist (MSN, PMC); cardiopulmonary clinical nurse specialist/adult nurse practitioner (MSN, PMC); family nurse practitioner (MSN, PMC); gerontology clinical nurse specialist (MSN, PMC); gerontology clinical nurse specialist geriatric nurse practitioner (PMC); gerontology clinical nurse specialist/geriatric nurse practitioner (MSN); health promotion (MS); health sciences (MS, MSN, DPT, PMC); health services administration (MSN, PMC); human nutrition (MS); kinesiology and applied physiology (MS, PhD); nursing of children clinical nurse specialist (MSN, PMC); nursing of children clinical nurse specialist/pediatric nurse practitioner (MSN, PMC); oncology/immune deficiency clinical nurse specialist (MSN, PMC); oncology/immune deficiency clinical nurse specialist/adult nurse practitioner (MSN, PMC); perinatal/women's health clinical nurse specialist (MSN, PMC); perinatal/women's health clinical nurse specialist/women's health nurse practitioner (MSN, PMC); physical therapy (DPT); psychiatric nursing clinical nurse specialist (MSN, PMC). Electronic applications accepted.

UNIVERSITY OF DENVER, Denver, CO 80208

General Information Independent, coed, university. CGS member. *Enrollment:* 11,797 graduate, professional, and undergraduate students; 3,178 full-time matriculated graduate/professional students (1,992 women), 2,694 part-time matriculated graduate/professional students (1,484 women). *Enrollment by degree level:* 3,984 master's, 1,577 doctoral, 387 other advanced degrees. *Graduate faculty:* 701 full-time (309 women), 585 part-time/adjunct (307 women). *Graduate housing:* Rooms and/or apartments available on a first-come, first-served basis to single and married students. Housing application deadline: 5/1. *Student services:* Campus employment opportunities, campus safety program, career counseling, exercise/wellness program, free psychological counseling, international student services, low-cost health insurance, multicultural affairs office, services for students with disabilities, teacher training, writing training. *Library:* Anderson Academic Commons plus 1 other. *Collection:* Books: 1.4 million (physical), 1.9 million (digital/electronic); Serial titles: 340,218 (physical), 116,793 (digital/electronic); Databases: 1,782. Weekly public service hours: 145; study areas open 24 hours, 5–7 days a week; students can reserve study rooms. *Research affiliation:* National Center for Atmospheric Research (infrared measurements).

Computer facilities: Computer purchase and lease plans are available. 150 computers available on campus for general student use. A campuswide network can be accessed from student residence rooms and from off campus. Online class registration is available.
Website: http://www.du.edu/

General Application Contact: Office of Graduate Studies, 303-871-2831, E-mail: gradinfo@du.edu.

GRADUATE UNITS

Daniel Felix Ritchie School of Engineering and Computer Science Students: 18 full-time (5 women), 139 part-time (31 women); includes 13 minority (1 Black or African American, non-Hispanic/Latino; 3 Asian, non-Hispanic/Latino; 8 Hispanic/Latino; 1 Two or more races, non-Hispanic/Latino), 83 international. Average age 29. 231 applicants, 63% accepted, 41 enrolled. *Faculty:* 36 full-time (4 women), 8 part-time/adjunct (4 women). *Financial support:* In 2015–16, 67 students received support, including 21 research assistantships with tuition reimbursements available (averaging $13,636 per year), 29 teaching assistantships with tuition reimbursements available (averaging $14,176 per year); Federal Work-Study, institutionally sponsored loans, scholarships/grants, health care benefits, and unspecified assistantships also available. Support available to part-time students. Financial award application deadline: 2/15; financial award applicants required to submit FAFSA. In 2015, 60 master's, 10 doctorates awarded. Offers bioengineering (MS); computer engineering (MS); computer science (MS, PhD); electrical and computer engineering (PhD); electrical engineering (MS); engineering (MS, PhD); engineering and computer science (MS, PhD); engineering-management (MS); materials science (MS, PhD); mechanical engineering (MS, PhD); mechatronic systems engineering (MS, PhD). *Application deadline:* Applications are processed on a rolling basis. *Application fee:* $65. Electronic applications accepted. *Application Contact:* Information Contact, 303-871-3787, E-mail: ritchieschool@du.edu. *Dean*, JB Holston, 303-871-3733, Fax: 303-871-2716, E-mail: jb.holston@du.edu.

Daniels College of Business Students: 417 full-time (166 women), 352 part-time (163 women); includes 109 minority (25 Black or African American, non-Hispanic/Latino; 3 American Indian or Alaska Native, non-Hispanic/Latino; 28 Asian, non-Hispanic/Latino; 41 Hispanic/Latino; 12 Two or more races, non-Hispanic/Latino), 199 international. Average age 30. 1,287 applicants, 62% accepted, 300 enrolled. *Faculty:* 111 full-time (38 women), 61 part-time/adjunct (15 women). *Financial support:* In 2015–16, 503 students received support, including 95 teaching assistantships with tuition reimbursements available (averaging $1,835 per year); career-related internships or fieldwork, Federal Work-Study, institutionally sponsored loans, scholarships/grants, and unspecified assistantships also available. Support available to part-time students. Financial award application deadline: 2/15; financial award applicants required to submit FAFSA. In 2015, 591 master's awarded. *Degree program information:* Part-time and evening/weekend programs available. Part-time, evening/weekend. Offers business (M Acc, MBA, MS); business administration (MBA); business analytics (MBA, MS); general business administration (MBA); management (MS); marketing (MBA, MS). *Application deadline:* For fall admission, 11/15 priority date for domestic students, 11/14 priority date for international students; for spring admission, 1/1 priority date for domestic and international students. Applications are processed on a rolling basis. *Application fee:* $100. Electronic applications accepted. *Application Contact:* Information Contact, 303-871-3416, Fax: 303-871-4466, E-mail: daniels@du.edu. *Dean*, Dr. Brent Chrite, 303-871-4324, Fax: 303-871-2156, E-mail: brent.chrite@du.edu.

Franklin L. Burns School of Real Estate and Construction Management Students: 10 full-time (3 women), 68 part-time (22 women); includes 12 minority (4 Black or African American, non-Hispanic/Latino; 1 American Indian or Alaska Native, non-Hispanic/Latino; 1 Asian, non-Hispanic/Latino; 5 Hispanic/Latino; 1 Two or more races, non-Hispanic/Latino), 6 international. Average age 36. 58 applicants, 83% accepted, 32 enrolled. *Faculty:* 9 full-time (1 woman), 2 part-time/adjunct (0 women). *Financial support:* In 2015–16, 39 students received support, including 5 teaching assistantships with tuition reimbursements available (averaging $1,937 per year); career-related internships or fieldwork, Federal Work-Study, institutionally sponsored loans, scholarships/grants, and unspecified assistantships also available. Support available to part-time students. Financial award application deadline: 2/15; financial award applicants required to submit FAFSA. In 2015, 40 master's awarded. *Degree program information:* Part-time and evening/weekend programs available. Part-time, evening/weekend. Offers real estate and the built environment (MBA, MS). *Application deadline:* For fall admission, 11/15 priority date for domestic and international students; for spring admission, 10/1 priority date for domestic and international students. Applications are processed on a rolling basis. *Application fee:* $100. Electronic applications accepted. *Associate Professor and Director*, Dr. Barbara Jackson, 303-871-3470, Fax: 303-871-2971, E-mail: barbara.jackson@du.edu.

Reiman School of Finance Students: 49 full-time (20 women), 30 part-time (10 women); includes 4 minority (1 Black or African American, non-Hispanic/Latino; 1 Asian, non-Hispanic/Latino; 1 Hispanic/Latino; 1 Two or more races, non-Hispanic/Latino), 55 international. Average age 25. 382 applicants, 52% accepted, 26 enrolled. *Faculty:* 18 full-time (4 women), 5 part-time/adjunct (1 woman). *Financial support:* In 2015–16, 45 students received support, including 3 teaching assistantships with tuition reimbursements available (averaging $1,239 per year); career-related internships or fieldwork, Federal Work-Study, institutionally sponsored loans, scholarships/grants, and unspecified assistantships also available. Support available to part-time students. Financial award application deadline: 2/15; financial award applicants required to submit FAFSA. In 2015, 75 master's awarded. *Degree program information:* Part-time and evening/weekend programs available. Part-time, evening/weekend. Offers applied quantitative finance (MS); finance (MBA). *Application deadline:* For fall admission, 11/15 priority date for domestic and international students; for spring admission, 10/1 priority date for domestic and international students. Applications are processed on a rolling basis. *Application fee:* $100. Electronic applications accepted. *Associate Professor and Director, Reiman School of Finance*, Dr. Thomajean (Tommi) Johnsen, 303-871-2282, Fax: 303-871-4580, E-mail: thomajean.johnsen@du.edu.

School of Accountancy Students: 47 full-time (30 women), 51 part-time (38 women); includes 9 minority (5 Asian, non-Hispanic/Latino; 4 Hispanic/Latino), 61 international. Average age 25. 312 applicants, 60% accepted, 47 enrolled. *Faculty:* 17 full-time (7 women), 6 part-time/adjunct (1 woman). *Financial support:* In 2015–16, 68 students received support, including 13 teaching assistantships with tuition reimbursements available (averaging $1,891 per year); career-related internships or fieldwork, Federal Work-Study, institutionally sponsored loans, scholarships/grants, and unspecified assistantships also available. Support available to part-time students. Financial award application deadline: 2/15; financial award applicants required to submit FAFSA. In 2015, 127 master's awarded. *Degree program information:* Part-time and evening/weekend programs available. Part-time, evening/weekend. Offers accounting (M Acc, MBA). *Application deadline:* For fall admission, 11/15 priority date for domestic and international students; for spring admission, 10/1 priority date for domestic and international students. Applications are processed on a rolling basis. *Application fee:* $100. Electronic applications accepted. *Professor/Director, School of Accountancy*, Dr. Sharon Lassar, 303-871-2032, Fax: 303-871-2016, E-mail: slassar@du.edu.

Division of Arts, Humanities and Social Sciences Students: 154 full-time (100 women), 173 part-time (109 women); includes 62 minority (6 Black or African American, non-Hispanic/Latino; 2 American Indian or Alaska Native, non-Hispanic/Latino; 11 Asian, non-Hispanic/Latino; 32 Hispanic/Latino; 11 Two or more races, non-Hispanic/Latino), 34 international. Average age 27. 899 applicants, 37% accepted, 143 enrolled. *Faculty:* 236 full-time (113 women), 7 part-time/adjunct (4 women). *Financial support:* In 2015–16, 282 students received support, including 13 research assistantships with tuition reimbursements available (averaging $15,064 per year), 135 teaching assistantships with tuition reimbursements available (averaging $11,399 per year); career-related internships or fieldwork, Federal Work-Study, institutionally sponsored loans, scholarships/grants, and unspecified assistantships also available. Support available to part-time students. Financial award application deadline: 2/15; financial award applicants required to submit FAFSA. In 2015, 110 master's, 18 doctorates, 4 other advanced degrees awarded. *Degree program information:* Part-time programs available. Part-time. Offers affect/social psychology (PhD); archaeology (MA); arts, humanities and social sciences (MA, MFA, MM, MPP, MS, PhD, Certificate); clinical child psychology (PhD); cognitive psychology (PhD); creative writing (PhD); critical theory and religion (MA); cultural anthropology (MA); culture and communication (MA, PhD); developmental psychology (PhD); economics (MA); emergent digital practices (MA, MFA); international and intercultural communication (MA); interpersonal and family communication (MA, PhD); literary studies (MA, PhD); lived religions (MA); media and globalization (MA); museum and heritage studies (MA); philosophy of religion (MA); religion and international studies (MA); rhetoric and communication ethics (MA, PhD); rhetoric and theory (PhD); sacred texts (MA); strategic communication (MA). *Application deadline:* Applications are processed on a rolling basis. *Application fee:* $65. Electronic applications accepted. *Application Contact:* Information Contact, 360-871-4449, Fax: 303-871-4436, E-mail: ahss@du.edu. *Dean*, Dr. Danny McIntosh, 303-871-4449, Fax: 303-871-4436, E-mail: daniel.mcintosh@du.edu.

Institute for Public Policy Studies Students: 19 full-time (6 women), 6 part-time (1 woman); includes 2 minority (1 Black or African American, non-Hispanic/Latino; 1 Two or more races, non-Hispanic/Latino). Average age 26. 25 applicants, 88% accepted, 10 enrolled. *Faculty:* 4 full-time (0 women). *Financial support:* In 2015–16, 20 students received support, including 5 teaching assistantships with tuition reimbursements available (averaging $2,083 per year); Federal Work-Study, scholarships/grants, and unspecified assistantships also available. Financial award application deadline: 2/15; financial award applicants required to submit FAFSA. In 2015, 11 master's awarded. Offers public policy studies (MPP). *Application deadline:* For fall admission, 7/1 priority date for domestic and international students; for winter admission, 11/15 priority date for domestic and international students. Applications are processed on a rolling basis. *Application fee:* $65. Electronic applications accepted. *Application Contact:* Erin Dietrich, Manager, Admissions and Communications, 303-871-3252, Fax: 303-871-3066, E-mail: erin.dietrich@du.edu. *Co-Director*, Richard Caldwell, 303-871-2468, Fax: 303-871-3066, E-mail: richard.caldwell@du.edu.

Lamont School of Music Students: 29 full-time (11 women), 64 part-time (36 women); includes 17 minority (1 Black or African American, non-Hispanic/Latino; 1 American Indian or Alaska Native, non-Hispanic/Latino; 5 Asian, non-Hispanic/Latino; 8 Hispanic/Latino; 2 Two or more races, non-Hispanic/Latino), 12 international. Average age 26. 126 applicants, 90% accepted, 55 enrolled. *Faculty:* 31 full-time (9 women), 34 part-time/adjunct (15 women). *Financial support:* In 2015–16, 82 students received support, including 34 teaching assistantships with tuition reimbursements available (averaging $6,841 per year); career-related internships or fieldwork, Federal Work-Study, institutionally sponsored loans, scholarships/grants, tuition waivers, and unspecified assistantships also available. Support available to part-time students. Financial award application deadline: 2/15; financial award applicants required to submit FAFSA. In 2015, 21 master's, 4 other advanced degrees awarded. *Degree program information:* Part-time programs available. Part-time. Offers composition (MM); composition - jazz emphasis (MM); conducting (MM, Certificate); jazz studies (Certificate); music theory (MA); musicology (MA); orchestral studies (Certificate); pedagogy (MM); performance (MM, Certificate); performance - jazz emphasis (MM); Suzuki teaching (Certificate). *Application deadline:* For fall admission, 1/15 priority date for domestic and international students. Applications are processed on a rolling basis. *Application fee:* $65. Electronic applications accepted. *Application Contact:* Stephen Campbell, Director of Admission, 303-871-6973, Fax: 303-871-3118, E-mail: stephen.l.campbell@du.edu. *Professor and Director*, Nancy Cochran, 303-871-6986, Fax: 303-871-3118, E-mail: nancy.cochran@du.edu.

School of Art and Art History Students: 7 full-time (6 women), 14 part-time (all women); includes 4 minority (1 Black or African American, non-Hispanic/Latino; 3 Hispanic/Latino). Average age 24. 16 applicants, 88% accepted, 7 enrolled. *Faculty:* 15 full-time (10 women), 12 part-time/adjunct (9 women). *Financial support:* In 2015–16, 18 students received support, including 1 research assistantship with tuition reimbursement available (averaging $2,500 per year), 8 teaching assistantships with tuition reimbursements available (averaging $7,506 per year); career-related internships or fieldwork, Federal Work-Study, institutionally sponsored loans, scholarships/grants, and unspecified assistantships also available. Support available to part-time students. Financial award application deadline: 2/15; financial award applicants required to submit FAFSA. In 2015, 6 master's awarded. *Degree program information:* Part-time programs available. Part-time. Offers art history (MA); museum studies (MA). *Application deadline:* For fall admission, 1/31 priority date for domestic and international students. Applications are processed on a rolling basis. *Application fee:* $65. Electronic applications accepted. *Application Contact:* Dr. Annabeth Headrick, Associate Professor and Graduate Art History Advisor, 303-871-3574, Fax: 303-871-4112, E-mail: annabeth.headrick@du.edu. *Associate Professor and Director*, Catherine Chauvin, 303-871-2367, Fax: 303-871-4112, E-mail: catherine.chauvin@du.edu.

Division of Natural Sciences and Mathematics Students: 22 full-time (11 women), 129 part-time (61 women); includes 24 minority (4 Black or African American, non-Hispanic/Latino; 1 American Indian or Alaska Native, non-Hispanic/Latino; 1 Asian, non-Hispanic/Latino; 16 Hispanic/Latino; 2 Two or more races, non-Hispanic/Latino), 28 international. Average age 29. 261 applicants, 54% accepted, 61 enrolled. *Faculty:* 82 full-time (23 women), 22 part-time/adjunct (8 women). *Financial support:* In 2015–16, 138 students received support, including 22 research assistantships with tuition reimbursements available (averaging $16,932 per year), 70 teaching assistantships with tuition reimbursements available (averaging $17,702 per year); career-related internships or fieldwork, institutionally sponsored loans, scholarships/grants, and unspecified assistantships also available. Support available to part-time students. Financial award application deadline: 2/15; financial award applicants required to submit FAFSA. In 2015, 34 master's, 7 doctorates awarded. *Degree program information:* Part-time and evening/weekend programs available. Part-time, evening/weekend. Offers biology, ecology and evolution (MS, PhD); biomedical sciences (PSM); cell and molecular biology (MS, PhD); chemistry (MA, MS, PhD); geographic information science (MS); geography (MA, PhD); mathematics (MA, MS, PhD); natural sciences and mathematics (MA, MS, PSM, PhD); physics (MS, PhD). *Application deadline:* Applications are processed on a rolling basis. *Application fee:* $65. Electronic applications accepted. *Application Contact:* Kirsten Norwood, Executive Assistant to the Dean, 303-871-2693, Fax: 303-871-3223, E-mail: kirsten.norwood@du.edu. *Dean,* Dr. Andrei Kutateladze, 303-871-2995, Fax: 303-871-3223, E-mail: andrei.kutateladze@du.edu.

DU/Iliff Joint PhD Program in the Study of Religion Students: 33 full-time (15 women), 24 part-time (7 women); includes 11 minority (4 Black or African American, non-Hispanic/Latino; 1 Asian, non-Hispanic/Latino; 6 Hispanic/Latino). Average age 40. 24 applicants, 29% accepted, 3 enrolled. *Financial support:* In 2015–16, 29 students received support, including 14 teaching assistantships with tuition reimbursements available (averaging $2,619 per year); scholarships/grants and unspecified assistantships also available. In 2015, 10 doctorates awarded. *Degree program information:* Part-time programs available. Part-time. Offers the study of religion (PhD). Program jointly offered with Iliff School of Theology. *Application deadline:* For fall admission, 1/5 priority date for domestic and international students. Applications are processed on a rolling basis. *Application fee:* $65. Electronic applications accepted. *Application Contact:* Information Contact, 303-765-3117, E-mail: jointphd@iliff.edu. *Director,* Dr. Greg Robbins, 303-871-2751.

Graduate School of Professional Psychology Students: 216 full-time (169 women), 55 part-time (37 women); includes 55 minority (7 Black or African American, non-Hispanic/Latino; 1 American Indian or Alaska Native, non-Hispanic/Latino; 9 Asian, non-Hispanic/Latino; 26 Hispanic/Latino; 12 Two or more races, non-Hispanic/Latino), 14 international. Average age 26. 701 applicants, 33% accepted, 128 enrolled. *Faculty:* 17 full-time (9 women), 27 part-time/adjunct (15 women). *Financial support:* In 2015–16, 102 students received support, including 29 teaching assistantships with tuition reimbursements available (averaging $2,738 per year); career-related internships or fieldwork, Federal Work-Study, institutionally sponsored loans, scholarships/grants, unspecified assistantships, and clinical assistantships also available. Support available to part-time students. Financial award application deadline: 2/15; financial award applicants required to submit FAFSA. In 2015, 89 master's, 30 doctorates awarded. Offers clinical psychology (Psy D); forensic psychology (MA); international disaster psychology (MA); sport and performance psychology (MA); sport coaching (MA). *Application fee:* $65. Electronic applications accepted. *Application Contact:* Admissions Counselor, 303-871-3736, Fax: 303-871-4220, E-mail: gsppinfo@du.edu. *Dean,* Dr. Shelly Smith-Acuna, 303-871-3880, Fax: 303-871-4220, E-mail: shelly.smith-acuna@du.edu.

Graduate School of Social Work Students: 490 full-time (429 women), 14 part-time (13 women); includes 105 minority (11 Black or African American, non-Hispanic/Latino; 8 American Indian or Alaska Native, non-Hispanic/Latino; 5 Asian, non-Hispanic/Latino; 63 Hispanic/Latino; 1 Native Hawaiian or other Pacific Islander, non-Hispanic/Latino; 17 Two or more races, non-Hispanic/Latino), 2 international. Average age 28. 855 applicants, 77% accepted, 285 enrolled. *Faculty:* 39 full-time (29 women), 105 part-time/adjunct (90 women). *Financial support:* In 2015–16, 456 students received support, including 12 teaching assistantships with tuition reimbursements available (averaging $13,706 per year); Federal Work-Study, scholarships/grants, and unspecified assistantships also available. Support available to part-time students. Financial award application deadline: 2/15; financial award applicants required to submit FAFSA. In 2015, 284 master's, 5 doctorates, 88 other advanced degrees awarded. *Degree program information:* Part-time and evening/weekend programs available. Part-time, evening/weekend. Offers animal-assisted social work (Certificate); couples and family therapy (Certificate); social work (MSW, PhD); social work with Latinos/as (Certificate). *Application deadline:* For fall admission, 8/1 priority date for domestic and international students. Applications are processed on a rolling basis. *Application fee:* $65. Electronic applications accepted. *Application Contact:* Colin Schneider, Director of Enrollment Management, 303-871-3634, Fax: 303-871-2845, E-mail: gssw-admission@du.edu. *Dean,* Dr. Amanda Moore McBride, 303-871-2203, Fax: 303-871-2845.

Josef Korbel School of International Studies Students: 406 full-time (238 women), 26 part-time (13 women); includes 82 minority (11 Black or African American, non-Hispanic/Latino; 14 Asian, non-Hispanic/Latino; 46 Hispanic/Latino; 11 Two or more races, non-Hispanic/Latino), 42 international. Average age 27. 724 applicants, 89% accepted, 185 enrolled. *Faculty:* 42 full-time (15 women), 20 part-time/adjunct (7 women). *Financial support:* In 2015–16, 275 students received support, including 2 research assistantships with tuition reimbursements available (averaging $7,250 per year), 4 teaching assistantships with tuition reimbursements available (averaging $1,488 per year); career-related internships or fieldwork, Federal Work-Study, institutionally sponsored loans, scholarships/grants, and unspecified assistantships also available. Support available to part-time students. Financial award application deadline: 2/15; financial award applicants required to submit FAFSA. In 2015, 203 master's, 2 doctorates, 38 other advanced degrees awarded. *Degree program information:* Part-time programs available. Part-time. Offers conflict resolution (MA); global business and corporate social responsibility (Certificate); global finance, trade and economic integration (MA); global health affairs (Certificate); homeland security (Certificate); humanitarian assistance (Certificate); international administration (MA); international development (MA); international human rights (MA); international security (MA); international studies (MA, PhD); religion and international affairs (Certificate). *Application deadline:* For fall admission, 1/15 priority date for domestic and international students; for winter admission, 11/1 for domestic and international students. Applications are processed on a rolling basis. *Application fee:* $65. Electronic applications accepted. *Application Contact:* Brad Miller, Director of Graduate Admissions, 303-871-2989, Fax: 303-871-2124, E-mail: brad.miller@du.edu. *Dean,* Christopher R. Hill, 303-871-2359, Fax: 303-871-2456, E-mail: christopher.r.hill@du.edu.

Morgridge College of Education Students: 497 full-time (386 women), 359 part-time (263 women); includes 202 minority (52 Black or African American, non-Hispanic/Latino; 8 American Indian or Alaska Native, non-Hispanic/Latino; 23 Asian, non-Hispanic/Latino; 100 Hispanic/Latino; 2 Native Hawaiian or other Pacific Islander, non-Hispanic/Latino; 17 Two or more races, non-Hispanic/Latino), 35 international. Average age 32. 1,061 applicants, 66% accepted, 414 enrolled. *Faculty:* 43 full-time (31 women), 57 part-time/adjunct (37 women). *Financial support:* In 2015–16, 682 students received support, including 40 research assistantships with tuition reimbursements available (averaging $11,231 per year), 66 teaching assistantships with tuition reimbursements available (averaging $4,258 per year); career-related internships or fieldwork, Federal Work-Study, institutionally sponsored loans, scholarships/grants, and unspecified assistantships also available. Support available to part-time students. Financial award application deadline: 2/15; financial award applicants required to submit FAFSA. In 2015, 344 master's, 30 doctorates, 187 other advanced degrees awarded. *Degree program information:* Part-time and evening/weekend programs available. Part-time, evening/weekend, online learning. Offers child, family and school psychology (MA, PhD, Ed S); counseling psychology (MA, PhD); curriculum and instruction (MA, Ed D, PhD); curriculum instruction and teaching (Certificate); early childhood special education (MA, Certificate); educational leadership and policy studies (MA, Ed D, PhD, Certificate); higher education (Ed D, PhD); library and information science (MLIS); research methods and statistics (MA, PhD). *Application deadline:* Applications are processed on a rolling basis. *Application fee:* $65. Electronic applications accepted. *Application Contact:* Jodi Dye, Director of Admissions, 303-871-2510, Fax: 303-871-4456, E-mail: jodi.dye@du.edu. *Dean,* Dr. Karen Riley, 303-871-3665, Fax: 303-871-4456, E-mail: karen.riley@du.edu.

Sturm College of Law Students: 1,796 full-time (908 women), 358 part-time (210 women); includes 374 minority (46 Black or African American, non-Hispanic/Latino; 8 American Indian or Alaska Native, non-Hispanic/Latino; 62 Asian, non-Hispanic/Latino; 188 Hispanic/Latino; 2 Native Hawaiian or other Pacific Islander, non-Hispanic/Latino; 68 Two or more races, non-Hispanic/Latino), 92 international. Average age 28. 1,762 applicants, 63% accepted, 330 enrolled. *Faculty:* 158 full-time (82 women), 158 part-time/adjunct (48 women). *Financial support:* In 2015–16, 521 students received support, including 8 teaching assistantships with tuition reimbursements available (averaging $6,966 per year); career-related internships or fieldwork, Federal Work-Study, institutionally sponsored loans, scholarships/grants, unspecified assistantships, and tutorships also available. Support available to part-time students. Financial award application deadline: 2/15; financial award applicants required to submit FAFSA. In 2015, 122 master's, 275 doctorates, 90 Certificates awarded. *Degree program information:* Part-time and evening/weekend programs available. Part-time, evening/weekend. Offers environmental and natural resources law and policy (LL M, MLS); law (LL M, MLS, MRLS, MSLA, MT, JD, Certificate); legal administration (MSLA, Certificate); natural resources law and policy (Certificate); tax (LL M, MT). *Application deadline:* Applications are processed on a rolling basis. Electronic applications accepted. *Application Contact:* Yvonne Cherena-Pacheco, Associate Director of Admissions, 303-871-6192, Fax: 303-871-6992, E-mail: admissions@law.du.edu. *Dean,* Dr. Bruce Smith, 303-871-6103, Fax: 303-871-6992.

University College Students: 69 full-time (36 women), 1,277 part-time (707 women); includes 273 minority (97 Black or African American, non-Hispanic/Latino; 6 American Indian or Alaska Native, non-Hispanic/Latino; 26 Asian, non-Hispanic/Latino; 108 Hispanic/Latino; 2 Native Hawaiian or other Pacific Islander, non-Hispanic/Latino; 34 Two or more races, non-Hispanic/Latino), 115 international. Average age 34. 686 applicants, 93% accepted, 430 enrolled. *Faculty:* 11 full-time (6 women), 132 part-time/adjunct (53 women). *Financial support:* In 2015–16, 6 students received support. Applicants required to submit FAFSA. In 2015, 413 master's, 162 other advanced degrees awarded. *Degree program information:* Part-time and evening/weekend programs available. Part-time, evening/weekend, online learning. Offers arts and culture (Certificate); communication management (Certificate); geographic information systems (MS, Certificate); global affairs (MLS, Certificate); organizational and professional communication (MPS); strategic human resources (Certificate). *Application deadline:* For fall admission, 6/21 priority date for domestic students, 5/1 priority date for international students; for winter admission, 9/14 priority date for domestic students, 9/19 priority date for international students; for spring admission, 1/11 for domestic students, 12/12 for international students; for summer admission, 3/29 priority date for domestic students, 3/6 priority date for international students. Applications are processed on a rolling basis. *Application fee:* $75. Electronic applications accepted. *Application Contact:* Information Contact, 303-871-2291, E-mail: ucoladm@du.edu. *Dean,* Dr. Michael McGuire, 303-871-3518, Fax: 303-871-3303, E-mail: mmcguire@du.edu.

UNIVERSITY OF DETROIT MERCY, Detroit, MI 48221

General Information Independent-religious, coed, university. *Enrollment:* 4,920 graduate, professional, and undergraduate students; 1,580 full-time matriculated graduate/professional students (789 women), 668 part-time matriculated graduate/professional students (410 women). *Enrollment by degree level:* 1,008 master's, 1,172 doctoral, 68 other advanced degrees. *Graduate faculty:* 121 full-time (54 women), 54 part-time/adjunct (20 women). *Tuition, area resident:* Full-time $26,802; part-time $1489 per credit. Tuition and fees vary according to course load and program. *Graduate housing:* Room and/or apartments available on a first-come, first-served basis to single students; on-campus housing not available to married students. Typical cost: $12,980 (including board). Room and board charges vary according to board plan and housing facility selected. *Student services:* Campus employment opportunities, campus safety program, career counseling, free psychological counseling, international student services, low-cost health insurance, services for students with disabilities, teacher training, writing training. *Library:* McNichols Campus Library. *Collection:* Books: 468,257 (physical), 175,312 (digital/electronic); Serial titles: 107,735 (digital/electronic); Databases: 84. Weekly public service hours: 80.

Computer facilities: 157 computers available on campus for general student use. A campuswide network can be accessed from student residence rooms. Online class registration is available.
Website: http://www.udmercy.edu/

General Application Contact: Deborah Stieffel, Vice President for Enrollment Management and Student Affairs, 313-993-1245, Fax: 313-993-3326, E-mail: admissions@udmercy.edu.

GRADUATE UNITS

College of Business Administration ***Financial support:*** Research assistantships, career-related internships or fieldwork, Federal Work-Study, and unspecified assistantships available. Support available to part-time students. Financial award application deadline: 8/1; financial award applicants required to submit FAFSA. In 2015, 53 master's, 7 other advanced degrees awarded. *Degree program information:* Part-time and evening/weekend programs available. Part-time, evening/weekend, 100% online, blended/hybrid learning. Offers business administration (MBA); business fundamentals (Certificate); business turnaround management (Certificate); ethical leadership and change management (Certificate); finance (Certificate); forensic accounting (Certificate). *Application deadline:* For fall admission, 8/1 priority date for domestic students. Applications are processed on a rolling basis. *Application fee:* $30 ($50 for international students). Electronic applications accepted. *Application Contact:* Carrol Parris, Student Services Coordinator, 313-993-1203, Fax: 313-993-1673, E-mail:

parriscl@udmercy.edu. *Dean*, Dr. Joseph Eisenhauer, 313-993-1204, Fax: 313-993-1052, E-mail: joseph.eisenhauer@udmercy.edu.

College of Engineering and Science Students: 102 full-time (20 women), 80 part-time (14 women); includes 19 minority (8 Black or African American, non-Hispanic/Latino; 9 Asian, non-Hispanic/Latino; 2 Hispanic/Latino), 112 international. Average age 30. 300 applicants, 45% accepted, 35 enrolled. *Faculty:* 54 full-time (16 women), 32 part-time/adjunct (8 women). *Financial support:* Fellowships, teaching assistantships, career-related internships or fieldwork, and Federal Work-Study available. Financial award application deadline: 8/1; financial award applicants required to submit FAFSA. In 2015, 60 master's awarded. *Degree program information:* Part-time and evening/weekend programs available. Part-time, evening/weekend. Offers chemistry (MS); civil and environmental engineering (DE); electrical and computer engineering (ME); electrical engineering (DE); engineering management (M Eng Mgt); environmental engineering (MEE); mechanical engineering (MME, DE); product development (MS); software engineering (MSSE); teaching of mathematics (MATM). *Application deadline:* For fall admission, 8/1 priority date for domestic students. Applications are processed on a rolling basis. *Application fee:* $30 ($50 for international students). Electronic applications accepted. *Application Contact:* Matt Fortescu, Graduate Studies Coordinator, 313-993-3378, Fax: 313-993-1187, E-mail: fortesme@udmercy.edu. *Dean*, Gary Kuleck, 313-993-1216, Fax: 313-993-1187, E-mail: kuleckga@udmercy.edu.

College of Health Professions ***Financial support:*** Institutionally sponsored loans and tuition waivers (partial) available. Support available to part-time students. Financial award applicants required to submit FAFSA. Offers clinical nurse leader (MSN); family nurse practitioner (MSN); health services administration (MHSA); health systems management (MSN); nurse anesthesia (MS); nursing (DNP); nursing education (MSN, Certificate); nursing leadership and financial management (Certificate); outcomes performance management (Certificate); physician assistant (MS). *Application fee:* $30 ($50 for international students). *Dean*, Dr. Christine M. Pacini, RN, 313-993-6055, Fax: 313-993-6175.

College of Liberal Arts and Education ***Financial support:*** Fellowships, career-related internships or fieldwork, and Federal Work-Study available. *Degree program information:* Part-time and evening/weekend programs available. Part-time, evening/weekend. Offers addiction counseling (MA); addiction studies (Certificate); clinical mental health counseling (MA); clinical psychology (MA, PhD); computer and information systems (MS); criminal justice (MA); curriculum and instruction (MA); economics (MA); educational administration (MA); financial economics (MA); industrial/organizational psychology (MA); information assurance (MS); intelligence analysis (MA); liberal studies (MALS); religious studies (MA); school counseling (MA, Certificate); school psychology (Spec); security administration (MS); special education: emotionally impaired/behaviorally disordered (MA); special education: learning disabilities (MA). *Application deadline:* For fall admission, 8/1 priority date for domestic students. Applications are processed on a rolling basis. *Application fee:* $30 ($50 for international students). *Dean*, Dr. Mark Denham, 313-993-3250, Fax: 313-993-1266, E-mail: liberalarts@udmercy.edu.

School of Architecture Offers architecture (M Arch); community development (MA). *Application deadline:* Applications are processed on a rolling basis. *Application fee:* $30 ($50 for international students). *Dean*, Will Wittig, 313-993-1532, Fax: 313-993-1512, E-mail: architecture@udmercy.edu.

School of Dentistry ***Financial support:*** Career-related internships or fieldwork, Federal Work-Study, and stipends available. Financial award application deadline: 4/15. Offers dentistry (MS, DDS, Certificate). *Application fee:* $50. *Dean*, Dr. Mert N. Aksu, 313-494-6621.

School of Law ***Financial support:*** Career-related internships or fieldwork, Federal Work-Study, and institutionally sponsored loans available. Support available to part-time students. *Degree program information:* Part-time programs available. Part-time. Offers law (JD). *Application deadline:* For fall admission, 4/15 for domestic students. *Application fee:* $50. *Dean*, Phyllis L. Crocker, 313-596-0210.

UNIVERSITY OF DUBUQUE, Dubuque, IA 52001-5099

General Information Independent-religious, coed, comprehensive institution. *Graduate housing:* Rooms and/or apartments available on a first-come, first-served basis to single students and available to married students.

GRADUATE UNITS

Program in Business Administration ***Degree program information:*** Part-time and evening/weekend programs available. Part-time, evening/weekend. Offers business administration (MBA). Electronic applications accepted.

Program in Communication ***Degree program information:*** Part-time and evening/weekend programs available. Part-time, evening/weekend. Offers information technologies communication (MAC); leadership and management (MAC); strategic and corporate communication (MAC). Electronic applications accepted.

University of Dubuque Theological Seminary Online learning. Offers theology (M Div, MAMC, D Min).

UNIVERSITY OF EVANSVILLE, Evansville, IN 47722

General Information Independent-religious, coed, comprehensive institution. *Research affiliation:* Council of Independent Colleges (higher education administration), The New American Colleges and Universities (higher education administration), Independent Colleges of Indiana (higher education administration), Military Family Research Institute (higher education administration).

GRADUATE UNITS

Center for Adult Education ***Degree program information:*** Part-time and evening/weekend programs available. Part-time, evening/weekend. Offers public service administration (MS).

College of Education and Health Sciences Offers education and health sciences (MS, DPT); physical therapy (DPT).

School of Public Health ***Degree program information:*** Part-time and evening/weekend programs available. Part-time, evening/weekend. Offers health services administration (MS).

THE UNIVERSITY OF FINDLAY, Findlay, OH 45840-3653

General Information Independent-religious, coed, comprehensive institution. *Graduate housing:* Room and/or apartments available on a first-come, first-served basis to single students; on-campus housing not available to married students. *Research affiliation:* The Ohio State University Research Foundation (biology), Rollin M. Gerstacker Foundation (environmental research), Department of Agriculture (wildlife research), Department of Education (bilingual teaching research), Department of Education (technology innovation), Department of Health and Human Services (terrorism preparedness).

GRADUATE UNITS

Office of Graduate Admissions ***Degree program information:*** Part-time and evening/weekend programs available. Part-time, evening/weekend, online learning. Offers athletic training (MAT); business (MBA); education (MA Ed); environmental, safety and health management (MSEM); health informatics (MS); occupational therapy (MOT); pharmacy (Pharm D); physical therapy (DPT); physician assistant (MPA); rhetoric and writing (MA); teaching English to speakers of other languages (TESOL) and bilingual education (MA). Electronic applications accepted.

UNIVERSITY OF FLORIDA, Gainesville, FL 32611

General Information State-supported, coed, university. CGS member. *Graduate housing:* Rooms and/or apartments available on a first-come, first-served basis to single and married students. *Research affiliation:* Los Alamos National Laboratory (high magnetic field research), National Center for Automated Information Research (law and business data), Oracle Corporation (database management), IBM (information infrastructure), Association of Universities for Research in Astronomy (Gemini multinational telescope).

GRADUATE UNITS

College of Dentistry Offers dentistry (MS, DMD, PhD, Certificate); endodontics (MS, Certificate); foreign trained dentistry (Certificate); oral biology (PhD); orthodontics (MS, Certificate); periodontology (MS, Certificate); prosthodontics (MS, Certificate).

College of Medicine Offers biochemistry and molecular biology (PhD); biomedical sciences (MS, PhD); clinical investigation (MS); epidemiology (MS); genetics (PhD); immunology and microbiology (PhD); medicine (MPAS, MPH, MS, MD, PhD); molecular cell biology (PhD); molecular genetics and microbiology (MS); neuroscience (PhD); physician assistant (MPAS); physiology and pharmacology (PhD); public health (MPH). Electronic applications accepted.

College of Veterinary Medicine ***Degree program information:*** Part-time programs available. Part-time. Offers forensic toxicology (Certificate); veterinary medical sciences (MS, PhD); veterinary medicine (MS, DVM, PhD, Certificate).

Graduate School ***Degree program information:*** Part-time and evening/weekend programs available. Part-time, evening/weekend, online learning. Electronic applications accepted.

College of Agricultural and Life Sciences Students: 951 full-time (499 women), 370 part-time (213 women); includes 160 minority (35 Black or African American, non-Hispanic/Latino; 7 American Indian or Alaska Native, non-Hispanic/Latino; 29 Asian, non-Hispanic/Latino; 89 Hispanic/Latino), 433 international. Average age 31. 921 applicants, 36% accepted, 255 enrolled. *Faculty:* 346 full-time (93 women), 12 part-time/adjunct (4 women). *Financial support:* Career-related internships or fieldwork, Federal Work-Study, institutionally sponsored loans, and unspecified assistantships available. Support available to part-time students. Financial award application deadline: 2/1; financial award applicants required to submit FAFSA. In 2015, 208 master's, 129 doctorates awarded. *Degree program information:* Part-time programs available. Part-time. Offers agribusiness (MS); agricultural and life sciences (MAB, MFAS, MFRC, MS, DPM, PhD, Certificate); agricultural education and communication (MS, PhD); agroecology (MS); agronomy (MS, PhD); animal molecular and cellular biology (MS, PhD); animal sciences (MS, PhD); community studies (MS); environmental education and communications (Certificate); environmental horticulture (MS, PhD); family and youth development (MS); family, youth and community sciences (MS); fisheries and aquatic sciences (MFAS, MS, PhD); food and resource economics (MAB, MS, PhD); food science (PhD); food science and human nutrition (MS); forest resources and conservation (MFRC, MS, PhD); geographic information systems (MS); horticultural sciences (MS, PhD); hydrologic sciences (MS, PhD); microbiology and cell science (MS, PhD); nonprofit organization development (MS); nutritional sciences (MS, PhD); plant medicine (DPM); plant molecular and cellular biology (MS, PhD); plant pathology (MS, PhD); soil and water science (MS, PhD); toxicology (MS, PhD); tropical conservation and development (MAB, MS, DPM, PhD); wildlife ecology and conservation (MS, PhD). *Application deadline:* Applications are processed on a rolling basis. *Application fee:* $30. Electronic applications accepted. *Application Contact:* Office of Admissions, 352-392-1365, E-mail: webrequests@admissions.ufl.edu. *Dean*, Dr. Teresa Balser, 352-392-1961, E-mail: tcbalser@ufl.edu.

College of Design, Construction and Planning Students: 350 full-time (139 women), 140 part-time (72 women); includes 86 minority (15 Black or African American, non-Hispanic/Latino; 2 American Indian or Alaska Native, non-Hispanic/Latino; 15 Asian, non-Hispanic/Latino; 54 Hispanic/Latino), 147 international. Average age 31. 468 applicants, 56% accepted, 91 enrolled. *Faculty:* 54 full-time (17 women), 4 part-time/adjunct (1 woman). *Financial support:* Career-related internships or fieldwork, Federal Work-Study, and unspecified assistantships available. Support available to part-time students. Financial award applicants required to submit FAFSA. In 2015, 121 master's, 15 doctorates awarded. *Degree program information:* Part-time programs available. Part-time, online learning. Offers architecture (M Arch, MSAS); construction management (MSCM, PhD); design, construction and planning (M Arch, MAURP, MFES, MICM, MID, MLA, MSAS, MSCM, MURP, PhD); fire and emergency services (MFES); geographic information systems (MAURP, MLA, PhD); historic preservation (M Arch, MAURP, MID, MLA, MSAS, MSCM, PhD); interior design (MID, PhD); international construction (MICM); landscape architecture (MLA, PhD); sustainable architecture (M Arch, MSAS); sustainable construction (MSCM); sustainable design (M Arch, MAURP, MID, MLA, MSAS, MSCM); tropical conservation and development (MAURP); urban and regional planning (MAURP, MURP, PhD); wetland sciences (MAURP, MLA). *Application deadline:* Applications are processed on a rolling basis. *Application fee:* $30. Electronic applications accepted. *Application Contact:* Office of Admissions, 352-392-1365, E-mail: webrequests@admissions.ufl.edu. *Dean*, Christopher Silver, PhD, 352-392-4836, Fax: 352-392-7266, E-mail: silver2@ufl.edu.

College of Education Students: 654 full-time (543 women), 491 part-time (375 women); includes 289 minority (115 Black or African American, non-Hispanic/Latino; 8 American Indian or Alaska Native, non-Hispanic/Latino; 33 Asian, non-Hispanic/Latino; 133 Hispanic/Latino), 115 international. Average age 31. 654 applicants, 53% accepted, 181 enrolled. *Faculty:* 72 full-time (49 women). *Financial support:* Career-related internships or fieldwork, Federal Work-Study, and unspecified assistantships available. Support available to part-time students. Financial award applicants required to submit FAFSA. In 2015, 348 master's, 71 doctorates, 67 other advanced degrees awarded. *Degree program information:* Part-time and evening/weekend programs available. Part-time, evening/weekend, online learning. Offers counseling and counselor education (Ed D, PhD); curriculum and instruction (M Ed, MAE, Ed D, PhD, Ed S); early childhood education (M Ed, MAE); education (M Ed, MAE, Ed D, PhD, Ed S); educational leadership (M Ed, MAE, Ed D, PhD, Ed S); elementary education (M Ed, MAE); English education (M Ed, MAE); higher education administration (Ed D, PhD); marriage and family counseling (M Ed, MAE, Ed D, PhD, Ed S); mathematics education (M Ed, MAE); mental health counseling (M Ed, MAE, Ed D, PhD, Ed S); reading education (M Ed, MAE); research and evaluation methodology (M Ed, MAE, Ed D, PhD); school counseling and guidance (M Ed, MAE, Ed D, PhD, Ed S); school psychology (M Ed, MAE, Ed D, PhD, Ed S); science education (M Ed, MAE); social studies education (M Ed, MAE); special education (M Ed, MAE, Ed D, PhD, Ed S); student personnel in higher education (M Ed, MAE). *Application deadline:* For fall admission, 5/15 for domestic students, 12/1 for international students; for spring admission, 9/15 for domestic students, 3/1 for international students. Applications are processed on a rolling basis. *Application fee:* $30. Electronic applications accepted. *Application Contact:* Office of Admissions, 352-392-1365, E-mail: webrequests@admissions.ufl.edu. *Dean and Professor,* Glenn E. Good, PhD, 352-273-4135, E-mail: ggood@ufl.edu.

College of Engineering Degree program information: Part-time programs available. Part-time, online learning. Offers aerospace engineering (ME, MS, PhD); agricultural and biological engineering (ME, MS, PhD); biological systems modeling (Certificate); biomedical engineering (ME, MS, PhD, Certificate); chemical engineering (ME, MS, PhD, Engr); civil engineering (ME, MS, PhD); clinical and translational science (PhD); coastal and oceanographic engineering (ME, MS, PhD); computer engineering (ME, MS, PhD); computer science (MS); digital arts and sciences (MS); electrical and computer engineering (ME, MS, PhD); engineering (ME, MS, PhD, Certificate, Engr); environmental engineering sciences (ME, MS, PhD, Engr); geographic information systems (ME, MS, PhD); hydrologic sciences (ME, MS, PhD); imaging science and technology (PhD); industrial and systems engineering (ME, MS, PhD, Engr); material science and engineering (MS); materials science and engineering (ME, PhD); mechanical engineering (ME, MS, PhD); medical physics (MS, PhD); nuclear engineering (ME, PhD); nuclear engineering (MS); nuclear engineering sciences (ME, MS, PhD); quantitative finance (PhD); structural engineering (ME, MS); wetland sciences (ME, MS, PhD). Electronic applications accepted.

College of Health and Human Performance Students: 244 full-time (133 women), 58 part-time (25 women); includes 48 minority (19 Black or African American, non-Hispanic/Latino; 1 American Indian or Alaska Native, non-Hispanic/Latino; 11 Asian, non-Hispanic/Latino; 17 Hispanic/Latino), 52 international. Average age 27. 360 applicants, 52% accepted, 102 enrolled. *Faculty:* 40 full-time (12 women), 7 part-time/adjunct (4 women). *Financial support:* Career-related internships or fieldwork, Federal Work-Study, institutionally sponsored loans, and unspecified assistantships available. Support available to part-time students. Financial award application deadline: 2/1; financial award applicants required to submit FAFSA. In 2015, 67 master's, 22 doctorates awarded. *Degree program information:* Part-time programs available. Part-time. Offers applied physiology and kinesiology (MS); athletic training/sports medicine (MS); bio behavioral science (MS); clinical exercise physiology (MS); exercise physiology (MS); health and human performance (PhD); health communication (Graduate Certificate); health education and behavior (MS); human performance (MS); recreation, parks and tourism (MS); sport management (MS). *Application deadline:* For fall admission, 3/1 priority date for domestic students, 2/1 for international students; for spring admission, 9/15 for domestic students, 7/1 for international students. Applications are processed on a rolling basis. *Application fee:* $30. Electronic applications accepted. *Application Contact:* Office of Admissions, 352-392-1365, E-mail: webrequests@admissions.ufl.edu. *Dean/Professor,* Dr. Michael Reid, 352-294-1600, E-mail: michael.reid@ufl.edu.

College of Journalism and Communications Students: 130 full-time (92 women), 160 part-time (117 women); includes 77 minority (29 Black or African American, non-Hispanic/Latino; 8 Asian, non-Hispanic/Latino; 40 Hispanic/Latino), 72 international. Average age 31. 410 applicants, 39% accepted, 86 enrolled. *Faculty:* 33 full-time (17 women), 3 part-time/adjunct (2 women). *Financial support:* Career-related internships or fieldwork, Federal Work-Study, institutionally sponsored loans, and unspecified assistantships available. Support available to part-time students. Financial award application deadline: 3/15; financial award applicants required to submit FAFSA. In 2015, 102 master's, 12 doctorates awarded. *Degree program information:* Part-time programs available. Part-time, online learning. Offers advertising (M Adv); international/intercultural communication (MAMC); journalism (MAMC); mass communication (MAMC, PhD); public relations (MAMC); science/health communication (MAMC); telecommunication (MAMC). *Application deadline:* For fall admission, 4/1 for domestic students, 1/30 for international students; for spring admission, 4/15 for domestic students, 7/15 for international students. Applications are processed on a rolling basis. *Application fee:* $30. Electronic applications accepted. *Application Contact:* Debbie M. Treise, PhD, Senior Associate Dean, Division of Graduate Studies and Research, 352-392-6557, E-mail: dtreise@jou.ufl.edu. *Dean,* Diane McFarlin, 352-392-0466, Fax: 352-392-1794, E-mail: dmcfarlin@ufl.edu.

College of Liberal Arts and Sciences Students: 1,025 full-time (105 women), 849 part-time (108 women); includes 265 minority (73 Black or African American, non-Hispanic/Latino; 7 American Indian or Alaska Native, non-Hispanic/Latino; 70 Asian, non-Hispanic/Latino; 115 Hispanic/Latino), 754 international. Average age 29. 4,643 applicants, 21% accepted, 388 enrolled. *Faculty:* 486 full-time (135 women), 66 part-time/adjunct (30 women). *Financial support:* Career-related internships or fieldwork, Federal Work-Study, institutionally sponsored loans, and unspecified assistantships available. Support available to part-time students. Financial award applicants required to submit FAFSA. In 2015, 226 master's, 230 doctorates awarded. *Degree program information:* Part-time programs available. Part-time. Offers anthropology (MA, MAT, PhD); applications of geographic technologies (MA, MS); astronomy (MS, MST, PhD); botany (MS, MST, PhD); chemistry (MS, MST, PhD); classical studies (MA, PhD); clinical and translational science (PhD); counseling psychology (PhD); creative writing (MFA); criminology, law, and society (MA, PhD); educational policy (PhD); English (MA, PhD); French and Francophone studies (MA, PhD); gender and development (Graduate Certificate); geographic information systems (MA, MS, PhD); geography (MA, MS, PhD); geology (MS, MST, PhD); German (MA, PhD); historic preservation (MA, PhD); history (MA, PhD); hydrologic sciences (MS, PhD); imaging science and technology (PhD); international development policy and administration (MA, Certificate); international relations (MA, MAT); Jewish studies (MA); Latin (MA, MAT, ML); Latin American studies (MA, Certificate); liberal arts and sciences (M Ag, M Stat, MA, MAT, MDP, MFA, ML, MS, MS Stat, MST, MWS, PhD, Certificate, Graduate Certificate); linguistics (MA, PhD); mathematics (MAT, MS, MST, PhD); philosophy (MA, PhD); physics (MS, MST, PhD); political campaigning (MA, Certificate); political science (MA, PhD); psychology (MA, MS, PhD); public affairs (MA, Certificate); quantitative finance (PhD); religion (MA, PhD); sociology (MA, PhD); Spanish (MA, MAT, PhD); statistics (M Stat, MS Stat, PhD); sustainable development practice (MDP); teaching English as a second language (Certificate); tropical conservation and development (MA, MS, MST, PhD); wetland sciences (MA, MS, MST, PhD); women's and gender studies (MA, PhD); women's studies (MA, Graduate Certificate); zoology (MS, MST, PhD). *Application deadline:* Applications are processed on a rolling basis. *Application fee:* $30. Electronic applications accepted. *Application Contact:* Dr. Albert R. Matheny, III, Associate Dean for Student Affairs, 352-392-1521, Fax: 351-392-3584, E-mail: matheny@polisci.ufl.edu. *Dean,* Dr. Paul D'Anieri, 352-392-0780, Fax: 352-392-3584, E-mail: danieri@clas.ufl.edu.

College of Nursing Students: 58 full-time (33 women), 31 part-time (27 women); includes 16 minority (6 Black or African American, non-Hispanic/Latino; 6 Asian, non-Hispanic/Latino; 4 Hispanic/Latino), 5 international. Average age 38. 44 applicants, 20% accepted, 8 enrolled. *Faculty:* 13 full-time (11 women), 5 part-time/adjunct (3 women). *Financial support:* In 2015–16, 6 fellowships, 2 research assistantships were awarded; career-related internships or fieldwork and Federal Work-Study also available. Support available to part-time students. Financial award applicants required to submit FAFSA. In 2015, 63 master's, 6 doctorates awarded. *Degree program information:* Part-time programs available. Part-time. Offers clinical and translational science (PhD); clinical nursing (DNP); nursing (MSN); nursing sciences (PhD). *Application deadline:* For fall admission, 3/15 priority date for domestic students, 3/15 for international students. Applications are processed on a rolling basis. *Application fee:* $30. Electronic applications accepted. *Application Contact:* Bridgette Hart-Sams, Coordinator, Student Academic Services, 352-273-6331, Fax: 352-273-6440, E-mail: bhart@ufl.edu. *Dean, College of Nursing,* Anna M. McDaniel, PhD, 352-273-6324, Fax: 352-273-6505, E-mail: annammcdaniel@ufl.edu.

College of Pharmacy Students: 153 full-time (94 women), 471 part-time (318 women); includes 148 minority (68 Black or African American, non-Hispanic/Latino; 6 American Indian or Alaska Native, non-Hispanic/Latino; 34 Asian, non-Hispanic/Latino; 40 Hispanic/Latino), 92 international. Average age 34. 411 applicants, 46% accepted, 167 enrolled. *Faculty:* 44 full-time (14 women), 22 part-time/adjunct (6 women). *Financial support:* Federal Work-Study, institutionally sponsored loans, tuition waivers (full), and unspecified assistantships available. Support available to part-time students. Financial award application deadline: 4/15; financial award applicants required to submit FAFSA. In 2015, 201 master's, 8 doctorates awarded. *Degree program information:* Part-time and evening/weekend programs available. Part-time, evening/weekend, online learning. Offers clinical and translational sciences (PhD); clinical pharmaceutical sciences (PhD); clinical pharmacy (MSP); clinical toxicology (MSP, Certificate); drug chemistry (Certificate); environmental forensics (Certificate); forensic death investigation (Certificate); forensic DNA and serology (MSP, Certificate); forensic drug chemistry (MSP); forensic science (MSP); forensic toxicology (Certificate); medicinal chemistry (MSP, PhD); pharmaceutical chemistry (MSP); pharmaceutical outcomes and policy (MSP, PhD); pharmaceutical sciences (MSP, PhD); pharmacodynamics (MSP, PhD); pharmacy (MSP, PhD). *Application deadline:* For fall admission, 5/1 for domestic and international students; for winter admission, 8/1 for domestic and international students; for spring admission, 2/1 for domestic and international students. Applications are processed on a rolling basis. *Application fee:* $30. Electronic applications accepted. *Dean/Professor,* Julie A. Johnson, Pharm D, 352-273-6007, E-mail: johnson@cop.ufl.edu.

College of Public Health and Health Professions Students: 644 full-time (493 women), 142 part-time (106 women); includes 180 minority (62 Black or African American, non-Hispanic/Latino; 3 American Indian or Alaska Native, non-Hispanic/Latino; 50 Asian, non-Hispanic/Latino; 65 Hispanic/Latino), 121 international. Average age 29. 1,615 applicants, 26% accepted, 196 enrolled. *Faculty:* 91 full-time (48 women), 78 part-time/adjunct (46 women). *Financial support:* Career-related internships or fieldwork, Federal Work-Study, institutionally sponsored loans, and unspecified assistantships available. Support available to part-time students. Financial award applicants required to submit FAFSA. In 2015, 186 master's, 89 doctorates, 52 other advanced degrees awarded. *Degree program information:* Part-time programs available. Part-time. Offers audiology (Au D); biostatistics (MS, PhD); clinical and translational science (PhD); communication sciences and disorders (MA, PhD); environmental health (MPH, PhD); epidemiology (MPH, MS, PhD); health administration (MHA); health management and policy (MPH); health services research (PhD); occupational therapy (MHS, MOT); one health (MHS, PhD); physical therapy (DPT); psychology (MS); public health (MPH, PhD, Certificate); public health and health professions (MA, MHA, MHS, MHS, MOT, MPH, MS, Au D, DPT, PhD, Certificate); public health practice (MPH); rehabilitation science (PhD); social and behavioral sciences (MPH). *Application deadline:* Applications are processed on a rolling basis. *Application fee:* $30. Electronic applications accepted. *Application Contact:* Office of Admissions, 352-392-1365, E-mail: webrequests@admissions.ufl.edu. *Dean,* Dr. Michael G. Perri, 352-273-6214, Fax: 352-273-6199, E-mail: mperri@phhp.ufl.edu.

College of The Arts Students: 200 full-time (107 women), 216 part-time (133 women); includes 95 minority (37 Black or African American, non-Hispanic/Latino; 8 American Indian or Alaska Native, non-Hispanic/Latino; 11 Asian, non-Hispanic/Latino; 39 Hispanic/Latino), 30 international. Average age 29. 119 applicants, 21% accepted, 17 enrolled. *Faculty:* 74 full-time (26 women), 9 part-time/adjunct (4 women). *Financial support:* Career-related internships or fieldwork, Federal Work-Study, institutionally sponsored loans, and unspecified assistantships available. Support available to part-time students. Financial award applicants required to submit FAFSA. In 2015, 14 master's awarded. Online learning. Offers art (MA); art education (MA); art history (MA, PhD); arts (MA, MFA, MM, PhD, Graduate Certificate); choral conducting (MM); composition (MM, PhD); electronic music (MM); ethnomusicology (MM); instrumental conducting (MM); museology (MA); music (MM, PhD); music education (MM, PhD); music history and literature (MM, PhD); music theory (MM); performance (MM); sacred music (MM); theatre (MFA). *Application deadline:* For spring admission, 11/1 for domestic and international students. Applications are processed on a rolling basis. *Application fee:* $30. Electronic applications accepted. *Application Contact:* Michelle Threadgill, College Graduate Advising Assistant, 352-846-3425, Fax: 352-846-3446, E-mail: graduate@arts.ufl.edu. *Dean,* Lucinda Lavelli, 352-392-0207, Fax: 352-392-3802, E-mail: llavelli@arts.ufl.edu.

School of Natural Resources and Environment Students: 93 full-time (57 women), 12 part-time (8 women); includes 11 minority (3 Black or African American, non-Hispanic/Latino; 1 American Indian or Alaska Native, non-Hispanic/Latino; 2 Asian, non-Hispanic/Latino; 5 Hispanic/Latino), 32 international. Average age 32. 42 applicants, 62% accepted, 24 enrolled. *Faculty:* 265. *Financial support:* Applicants required to submit FAFSA. In 2015, 9 master's, 13 doctorates awarded. Offers interdisciplinary ecology (MS, PhD). *Application deadline:* For fall admission, 2/1 priority date for domestic students, 2/1 for international students. Applications are processed on a rolling basis. *Application fee:* $30. Electronic applications accepted. *Application Contact:* Office of Graduate Admissions, 352-392-1365, E-mail: webrequests@admissions.ufl.edu. *Director,* Dr. Thomas K. Frazer, 352-392-9230, Fax: 352-392-9748, E-mail: frazer@ufl.edu.

Warrington College of Business Administration Students: 1,166 full-time (441 women), 653 part-time (215 women). Average age 32. 853 applicants, 41% accepted, 269 enrolled. *Financial support:* Career-related internships or fieldwork, Federal Work-Study, institutionally sponsored loans, and unspecified assistantships available.

Support available to part-time students. Financial award applicants required to submit FAFSA. *Degree program information:* Part-time and evening/weekend programs available. Part-time, evening/weekend, online learning. Offers accounting (M Acc, PhD); business administration (M Acc, MA, MBA, MS, PhD, Certificate); competitive strategy (MBA); economics (MA, PhD); entrepreneurship (MS); finance (MBA, MS, PhD); financial services (Certificate); global management (MBA); Graham-Buffett security analysis (MBA); health care risk management (MS); human resource management (MBA); information systems and operations management (MBA, PhD); insurance (PhD); international business (MA); international studies (MBA); management (MBA, MS, PhD); marketing (MA, MS, PhD); quantitative finance (PhD); real estate (MBA, MS); real estate and urban analysis (PhD); supply chain management (Certificate). *Application deadline:* Applications are processed on a rolling basis. *Application fee:* $30. Electronic applications accepted.

Levin College of Law Offers comparative law (LL M); environmental and land use law (LL M); international taxation (LL M); law (JD); taxation (LL M, SJD). Electronic applications accepted.

UNIVERSITY OF FORT LAUDERDALE, Lauderhill, FL 33313

General Information Independent-religious, coed, comprehensive institution.

GRADUATE UNITS

Graduate Program Offers ministry (MS).

UNIVERSITY OF GEORGIA, Athens, GA 30602

General Information State-supported, coed, comprehensive institution. CGS member. *Graduate housing:* Rooms and/or apartments available on a first-come, first-served basis to single and married students. *Research affiliation:* Skidaway Institute of Oceanography, Southeast Water Laboratory, Russell Research Laboratory, Organization for Tropical Studies.

GRADUATE UNITS

Biomedical and Health Sciences Institute Offers neuroscience (PhD).

College of Agricultural and Environmental Sciences Offers agricultural and environmental sciences (MA Ext, MADS, MAE, MAL, MFT, MPPPM, MS, PhD); agricultural economics (MAE, MS, PhD); agricultural engineering (MS); agricultural leadership, education, and communication (MA Ext, MAL); animal and dairy science (PhD); animal and dairy sciences (MADS); animal nutrition (PhD); animal science (MS); biological and agricultural engineering (PhD); biological engineering (MS); crop and soil sciences (MS, PhD); dairy science (MS); entomology (MS, PhD); environmental economics (MS); food science (MS, PhD); food technology (MFT); horticulture (MS, PhD); plant pathology (MS, PhD); plant protection and pest management (MPPPM); poultry science (MS, PhD). Electronic applications accepted.

Institute of Plant Breeding, Genetics and Genomics Offers plant breeding, genetics and genomics (MS, PhD).

College of Education Offers adult education (M Ed, Ed D, PhD, Ed S); art education (MA Ed, Ed D, PhD, Ed S); college student affairs administration (M Ed, PhD); communication science and disorders (M Ed, MA, PhD, Ed S); counseling and student personnel (PhD); counseling psychology (PhD); early childhood education (M Ed, MAT, PhD, Ed S); education (M Ed, MA, MA Ed, MAT, MM Ed, MS, Ed D, PhD, Ed S); education of the gifted (Ed D); educational administration and policy (M Ed, PhD, Ed S); educational leadership (Ed D); educational psychology (M Ed, MA, Ed D, PhD, Ed S); elementary education (PhD); English education (M Ed, Ed S); higher education (PhD); human resource and organizational design (M Ed); instructional technology (M Ed, PhD, Ed S); kinesiology (MS, PhD); language and literacy education (PhD); learning, design, and technology (M Ed, PhD, Ed S); mathematics education (M Ed, Ed D, PhD, Ed S); middle school education (M Ed, PhD, Ed S); music education (MM Ed, Ed D, Ed S); professional counseling (M Ed); professional school counseling (Ed S); reading education (M Ed, Ed D, Ed S); recreation and leisure studies (M Ed, MA, PhD); science education (M Ed, Ed D, PhD, Ed S); social studies education (M Ed, Ed D, PhD, Ed S); special education (M Ed, Ed D, PhD, Ed S); teaching additional languages (M Ed, Ed S); workforce education (M Ed, MAT, Ed D, PhD, Ed S). Electronic applications accepted.

College of Environment and Design Offers environmental planning and design (MEPD); historic preservation (MHP); landscape architecture (MLA).

College of Family and Consumer Sciences Offers child and family development (MS, PhD); early childhood education (MAT); family and consumer sciences (MAT, MFCS, MS, PhD); foods and nutrition (MFCS, MS, PhD); historical/cultural aspects of dress and textiles (MS); housing and consumer economics (MS, PhD); interior environments (MS); merchandising/international trade (MS); textile analysis (PhD); textile chemical processes (PhD); textile products and standards (PhD); textile science (MS). Electronic applications accepted.

College of Pharmacy Offers clinical and experimental therapeutics (PhD); pharmaceutical and biomedical sciences (PhD); pharmacy (MS, PhD, Pharm D, Certificate); pharmacy care administration (PhD). Electronic applications accepted.

College of Public Health Offers environmental health science (MPH, MSEH); health policy and management (MPH); health promotion and behavior (MPH, PhD); public health (MPH, MSEH, Dr PH, PhD, Certificate).

Institute of Gerontology Offers gerontology (Certificate).

College of Veterinary Medicine Offers food animal medicine (MFAM); infectious diseases (MS, PhD); large animal medicine (MS); pathology (MS, PhD); pharmacology (MS, PhD); physiology (MS, PhD); population health (MAM); small animal medicine and surgery (MS); veterinary anatomy (MS); veterinary medicine (MAM, MFAM, MS, DVM, PhD). Electronic applications accepted.

Faculty of Engineering Offers engineering (MS).

Franklin College of Arts and Sciences Offers analytical chemistry (MS, PhD); anthropology (MA, PhD); applied mathematical science (MAMS); archaeological resource management (MS); arts and sciences (MA, MAMS, MAT, MFA, MM, MS, DMA, PhD, Certificate); biochemistry and molecular biology (MS, PhD); cellular biology (MS, PhD); classical languages (MA); comparative literature (MA, PhD); computer science (MS, PhD); creative writing (MFA, PhD); English (MA, MAT, PhD); French (MA); genetics (MS, PhD); geography (MA, MS, PhD); geology (MS, PhD); German (MA); Greek (MA); history (MA, PhD); inorganic chemistry (MS, PhD); interpersonal and health communication (MA, PhD); Latin (MA); linguistics (MA, PhD); marine sciences (MS, PhD); mathematics (MA, PhD); microbiology (MS, PhD); organic chemistry (MS, PhD); philosophy (MA, PhD); physical chemistry (MS, PhD); physics (MS, PhD); plant biology (MS, PhD); psychology (MS, PhD); religion (MA); rhetorical studies (MA, PhD); Romance languages (MA, PhD); sociology (MA, PhD); Spanish (MA); statistics (MS, PhD); theatre (MFA, PhD). Electronic applications accepted.

Artificial Intelligence Center Offers artificial intelligence (MS). Electronic applications accepted.

Hugh Hodgson School of Music Offers music (MA, MM, DMA, PhD). Electronic applications accepted.

Institute for Women's Studies Offers women's studies (Certificate).

Lamar Dodd School of Art Offers art (MFA, PhD); art history (MA). Electronic applications accepted.

Grady School of Journalism and Mass Communication Offers journalism and mass communication (MA); mass communication (PhD). Electronic applications accepted.

Institute of Bioinformatics Offers bioinformatics (MS, PhD, Graduate Certificate).

School of Ecology Offers conservation ecology and sustainable development (MS); ecology (MS, PhD). Electronic applications accepted.

School of Forestry and Natural Resources Offers forestry and natural resources (MFR, MS, PhD). Electronic applications accepted.

School of Law Offers law (LL M, JD). Electronic applications accepted.

School of Public and International Affairs Offers international affairs (MA, MIP, PhD); political science (MA, PhD); public administration (MPA, PhD); public and international affairs (MA, MIP, MPA, PhD). Electronic applications accepted.

School of Social Work ***Degree program information:*** Part-time and evening/weekend programs available. Part-time, evening/weekend. Offers social work (MA, MSW, PhD, Certificate). Electronic applications accepted.

Terry College of Business Offers business (M Acc, MA, MBA, MIT, MMR, PhD); business administration (MA, MBA, PhD); economics (MA, PhD); Internet technology (MIT); management information systems (PhD). Electronic applications accepted.

J.M. Tull School of Accounting Offers accounting (M Acc). Electronic applications accepted.

UNIVERSITY OF GREAT FALLS, Great Falls, MT 59405

General Information Independent-religious, coed, comprehensive institution. *Graduate housing:* On-campus housing not available.

GRADUATE UNITS

Graduate Studies ***Degree program information:*** Part-time programs available. Part-time, online learning. Offers counseling (MSC); criminal justice (MSM); education (M Ed); human development (MSM); management (MSM); secondary teaching (MAT). Electronic applications accepted.

UNIVERSITY OF GUAM, Mangilao, GU 96923

General Information Territory-supported, coed, comprehensive institution. *Graduate housing:* Room and/or apartments available on a first-come, first-served basis to single students; on-campus housing not available to married students. Housing application deadline: 5/1. *Research affiliation:* Bernice Pauahi Bishop Museum (science, cultural preservation), Pilar Project, Inc. (salvage of artifacts, archaeology), Cancer Research Center of Hawaii (cancer research).

GRADUATE UNITS

Office of Graduate Studies ***Degree program information:*** Part-time programs available. Part-time.

College of Liberal Arts and Social Sciences Degree program information: Part-time programs available. Part-time. Offers ceramics (MA); English (MA); graphics (MA); liberal arts and social sciences (MA); Micronesian studies (MA); painting (MA).

College of Natural and Applied Sciences Offers environmental science (MS); natural and applied sciences (MS, MSW); social work (MSW); tropical marine biology (MS).

School of Business and Public Administration Degree program information: Part-time programs available. Part-time. Offers business administration (PMBA); business and public administration (MPA, PMBA); public administration (MPA).

School of Education Degree program information: Part-time programs available. Part-time. Offers administration and supervision (M Ed); counseling (MA); education (M Ed, MA); language and literacy (M Ed); secondary education (M Ed); special education (M Ed); teaching English to speakers of other languages (M Ed).

UNIVERSITY OF GUELPH, Guelph, ON N1G 2W1, Canada

General Information Province-supported, coed, university. *Graduate housing:* Rooms and/or apartments available to single and married students. Housing application deadline: 5/28.

GRADUATE UNITS

Graduate Studies ***Degree program information:*** Part-time and evening/weekend programs available. Part-time, evening/weekend, online learning. Offers biophysics (M Sc, PhD). Electronic applications accepted.

Collaborative International Development Studies Degree program information: Part-time programs available. Part-time. Offers international development studies (M Eng, M Sc, MA, MBA, PhD).

College of Arts Degree program information: Part-time programs available. Part-time. Offers arts (MA, MFA, PhD); drama (MA); English (MA); European studies (MA); French studies (MA); history (MA, PhD); literary studies/theatre studies in English (PhD); philosophy (MA, PhD); studio art (MFA).

College of Biological Science Degree program information: Part-time programs available. Part-time. Offers biochemistry (M Sc, PhD); biological science (M Sc, PhD); biophysics (M Sc, PhD); botany (M Sc, PhD); microbiology (M Sc, PhD); molecular biology and genetics (M Sc, PhD); nutritional sciences (M Sc, PhD); zoology (M Sc, PhD). Electronic applications accepted.

College of Management and Economics Offers economics (MA, PhD); food and agribusiness management (MBA); hospitality and tourism management (MBA); leadership (MA); management and economics (M Sc, MA, MBA, PhD); marketing and consumer studies (M Sc).

College of Physical and Engineering Science Degree program information: Part-time programs available. Part-time. Offers applied computer science (M Sc); applied mathematics (PhD); applied statistics (PhD); biological engineering (M Eng, M Sc, MA Sc, PhD); chemistry and biochemistry (M Sc, PhD); computer science (PhD); engineering systems and computing (M Eng, M Sc, MA Sc, PhD); environmental engineering (M Eng, M Sc, MA Sc, PhD); mathematics and statistics (M Sc); physical and engineering science (M Eng, M Sc, MA Sc, PhD); physics (M Sc, PhD); water resources engineering (M Eng, M Sc, MA Sc, PhD).

College of Social and Applied Human Sciences Degree program information: Part-time programs available. Part-time. Offers anthropology (MA); applied nutrition (MAN); applied social psychology (MA, PhD); clinical psychology: applied development emphasis (PhD); clinical psychology: applied developmental emphasis (MA); comparative politics (MA); crime and criminal justice policy (MA); criminology and criminal justice policy (MA); family relations and human development (M Sc, PhD); geography (M Sc, MA, PhD); industrial/organizational psychology (MA, PhD); international development (MA); neuroscience and applied cognitive science (MA,

PhD); political science (MA); public policy and public administration (MA); social and applied human sciences (M Sc, MA, MAN, PhD); sociology (MA, PhD); the Americas (Canada emphasis) (MA).

Ontario Agricultural College ***Degree program information:*** Part-time programs available. Part-time, online learning. Offers agricultural economics (M Sc, PhD); agriculture (M Sc, MLA, PhD, Diploma); animal and poultry science (M Sc, PhD); aquaculture (M Sc); atmospheric science (M Sc, PhD); capacity development and extension (M Sc); entomology (M Sc, PhD); environmental and agricultural earth sciences (M Sc, PhD); environmental microbiology and biotechnology (M Sc, PhD); environmental toxicology (M Sc, PhD); food safety and quality assurance (M Sc); food science (M Sc, PhD); international rural planning and development (M Sc); land resources management (M Sc, PhD); landscape architecture (MLA); plant agriculture (M Sc, PhD); plant and forest systems (M Sc, PhD); plant pathology (M Sc, PhD); rural planning and development (M Sc); rural planning and development in Canada (M Sc); rural studies (PhD); soil science (M Sc, PhD).

Ontario Veterinary College Offers toxicology (M Sc, PhD); veterinary medicine (M Sc, DV Sc, PhD, Diploma).

Graduate Programs in Veterinary Sciences Offers anatomic pathology (DV Sc, Diploma); anesthesiology (M Sc, DV Sc); cardiology (DV Sc, Diploma); clinical pathology (Diploma); clinical studies (Diploma); comparative pathology (M Sc, PhD); dermatology (M Sc); diagnostic imaging (M Sc, DV Sc); emergency/critical care (M Sc, DV Sc, Diploma); epidemiology (M Sc, DV Sc, PhD); health management (DV Sc); immunology (M Sc, PhD); laboratory animal science (DV Sc); medicine (M Sc, DV Sc); morphology (M Sc, PhD); neurology (M Sc, DV Sc); neuroscience (M Sc, DV Sc, PhD); ophthalmology (M Sc, DV Sc); pathology (M Sc, PhD, Diploma); pharmacology (M Sc, DV Sc, PhD); physiology (M Sc, DV Sc, PhD); population medicine and health management (M Sc); surgery (M Sc, DV Sc); swine health management (M Sc); theriogenology (M Sc, DV Sc); toxicology (M Sc, DV Sc, PhD); veterinary infectious diseases (M Sc, PhD); veterinary sciences (M Sc, DV Sc, PhD, Diploma); zoo animal/wildlife medicine (DV Sc).

UNIVERSITY OF HARTFORD, West Hartford, CT 06117-1599

General Information Independent, coed, comprehensive institution. CGS member. *Graduate housing:* On-campus housing not available.

GRADUATE UNITS

Barney School of Business ***Degree program information:*** Part-time and evening/weekend programs available. Part-time, evening/weekend. Offers business (MBA, MSAT, Certificate); business administration (MBA); professional accounting (Certificate); taxation (MSAT). Electronic applications accepted.

College of Arts and Sciences ***Degree program information:*** Part-time and evening/weekend programs available. Part-time, evening/weekend. Offers arts and sciences (MA, MS, Psy D); biology (MS); clinical practices (MA, Psy D); communication (MA); general experimental psychology (MA); neuroscience (MS); organizational behavior (MS); psychology (MA); school psychology (MS). Electronic applications accepted.

College of Education, Nursing, and Health Professions ***Degree program information:*** Part-time and evening/weekend programs available. Part-time, evening/weekend. Offers administration and supervision (CAGS); community/public health nursing (MSN); counseling (M Ed, MS, Sixth Year Certificate); early childhood education (M Ed); education, nursing, and health professions (M Ed, MS, MSN, MSPT, DPT, Ed D, CAGS, Sixth Year Certificate); educational leadership (Ed D, CAGS); educational technology (M Ed); elementary education (M Ed); nursing education (MSN); nursing management (MSN); physical therapy (MSPT, DPT). Electronic applications accepted.

College of Engineering, Technology and Architecture ***Degree program information:*** Part-time and evening/weekend programs available. Part-time, evening/weekend. Offers architecture (M Arch); engineering (M Eng); engineering, technology and architecture (M Arch, M Eng). Electronic applications accepted.

Hartford Art School ***Degree program information:*** Part-time programs available. Part-time. Offers art (MFA). Electronic applications accepted.

The Hartt School ***Degree program information:*** Part-time programs available. Part-time. Offers choral conducting (MM Ed); composition (MM, DMA, Artist Diploma, Diploma); conducting (MM, DMA, Artist Diploma, Diploma); early childhood education (MM Ed); instrumental conducting (MM Ed); Kodály (MM Ed); music (CAGS); music education (DMA, PhD); music history (MM); music theory (MM); pedagogy (MM Ed); performance (MM, MM Ed, DMA, Artist Diploma, Diploma); research (MM Ed); technology (MM Ed). Electronic applications accepted.

UNIVERSITY OF HAWAII AT HILO, Hilo, HI 96720-4091

General Information State-supported, coed, comprehensive institution. *Graduate housing:* Rooms and/or apartments available on a first-come, first-served basis to single and married students.

GRADUATE UNITS

Program in Clinical Psychopharmacology Offers clinical psychopharmacology (MS). Electronic applications accepted.

Program in Counseling Psychology Offers counseling psychology (MA).

Program in Education ***Degree program information:*** Part-time and evening/weekend programs available. Part-time, evening/weekend. Offers education (M Ed). Electronic applications accepted.

Program in Hawaiian and Indigenous Language and Culture Revitalization Offers Hawaiian and indigenous language and culture revitalization (PhD). Electronic applications accepted.

Program in Hawaiian Language and Literature Offers Hawaiian language and literature (MA). Electronic applications accepted.

Program in Indigenous Language and Culture Education Offers indigenous language and culture education (MA). Electronic applications accepted.

Program in Nursing Practice Offers nursing practice (DNP). Electronic applications accepted.

Program in Pharmaceutical Sciences Offers pharmaceutical sciences (PhD). Electronic applications accepted.

Program in Pharmacy Offers pharmacy (Pharm D). Electronic applications accepted.

Program in Teaching Offers teaching (MA). Electronic applications accepted.

Program in Tropical Conservation Biology and Environmental Science Offers tropical conservation biology and environmental science (MS). Electronic applications accepted.

UNIVERSITY OF HAWAII AT MANOA, Honolulu, HI 96822

General Information State-supported, coed, university. CGS member. *Enrollment:* 18,865 graduate, professional, and undergraduate students; 2,911 full-time matriculated graduate/professional students (1,722 women), 1,371 part-time matriculated graduate/professional students (885 women). *Enrollment by degree level:* 2,192 master's, 1,633 doctoral, 457 other advanced degrees. *Graduate faculty:* 1,343 full-time (479 women), 211 part-time/adjunct (58 women). *Graduate housing:* Rooms and/or apartments available to single and married students. Housing application deadline: 5/1. *Student services:* Campus employment opportunities, campus safety program, career counseling, child daycare facilities, exercise/wellness program, free psychological counseling, international student services, low-cost health insurance, multicultural affairs office, services for students with disabilities, teacher training, writing training. *Library:* Hamilton Library plus 6 others. *Collection:* Books: 3.2 million (physical), 146,716 (digital/electronic); Serial titles: 21,624 (physical), 55,895 (digital/electronic); Databases: 302. Weekly public service hours: 84; study areas open 24 hours, 5–7 days a week; students can reserve study rooms. *Research affiliation:* Bernice Pauahi Bishop Museum (anthropology, zoology), Hawaiian Volcano Observatory (geology, geophysics), Honolulu Academy of Arts, East-West Center (communication, geography, economics), U.S. Geological Survey (USGS), Hawaii Agriculture Research Center.

Computer facilities: Computer purchase and lease plans are available. 172 computers available on campus for general student use. A campuswide network can be accessed from student residence rooms and from off campus. Online class registration is available.
Website: http://manoa.hawaii.edu/

General Application Contact: Jarren Miki, Director of Graduate Admissions, 808-956-8544, Fax: 808-956-4261, E-mail: admissions@grad.hawaii.edu.

GRADUATE UNITS

Graduate Division ***Degree program information:*** Part-time programs available. Part-time. Offers communication and information sciences (PhD); international cultural studies (Graduate Certificate). Electronic applications accepted.

College of Arts and Humanities Students: 127 full-time, 50 part-time. Average age 33. 218 applicants, 56% accepted, 70 enrolled. *Financial support:* In 2015–16, 67 students received support, including 97 fellowships, 8 research assistantships, 66 teaching assistantships; career-related internships or fieldwork, Federal Work-Study, institutionally sponsored loans, scholarships/grants, and tuition waivers (full and partial) also available. Support available to part-time students. Financial award applicants required to submit FAFSA. In 2015, 46 master's, 4 doctorates awarded. *Degree program information:* Part-time programs available. Part-time. Offers American studies (MA, PhD); art history (MA); arts and humanities (M Mus, MA, MFA, PhD, Graduate Certificate); communicology (MA); dance (MA, MFA); historic preservation (Graduate Certificate); history (MA, PhD); museum studies (Graduate Certificate); music (M Mus, MA, PhD); philosophy (MA, PhD); religion (MA); theatre (MA, MFA, PhD); visual arts (MFA). *Application fee:* $100. *Application Contact:* Graduate Division, 808-956-8544. *Dean,* Thomas Bingham, 808-956-6460.

College of Education Students: 348 full-time, 392 part-time. Average age 38. 536 applicants, 65% accepted, 291 enrolled. *Financial support:* In 2015–16, 24 students received support, including 122 fellowships, 84 research assistantships, 9 teaching assistantships; career-related internships or fieldwork, Federal Work-Study, institutionally sponsored loans, and tuition waivers (full and partial) also available. Support available to part-time students. In 2015, 312 master's, 13 doctorates, 3 other advanced degrees awarded. *Degree program information:* Part-time and evening/weekend programs available. Part-time, evening/weekend. Offers curriculum and instruction (PhD); curriculum studies (M Ed); disability and diversity studies (Graduate Certificate); early childhood education (M Ed); education (M Ed, M Ed T, MS, Ed D, PhD, Graduate Certificate); educational administration (M Ed); educational foundations (M Ed); educational policy studies (PhD); educational psychology (PhD); educational technology (M Ed); exceptionalities (PhD); kinesiology (MS, PhD); learning design and technology (PhD); professional practice (Ed D); special education (M Ed); teaching (M Ed T). *Application fee:* $100. *Application Contact:* Graduate Division, 808-956-8544. *Dean,* Christine Sorensen, 808-956-7703.

College of Engineering Students: 35 full-time, 34 part-time. Average age 29. 96 applicants, 52% accepted, 36 enrolled. *Faculty:* 75 full-time (3 women). *Financial support:* In 2015–16, 30 fellowships, 103 research assistantships, 21 teaching assistantships were awarded; career-related internships or fieldwork, Federal Work-Study, and tuition waivers (full and partial) also available. Financial award applicants required to submit FAFSA. In 2015, 35 master's, 10 doctorates awarded. *Degree program information:* Part-time programs available. Part-time. Offers civil and environmental engineering (MS, PhD); electrical engineering (MS, PhD); engineering (MS, PhD); mechanical engineering (MS, PhD). *Application deadline:* Applications are processed on a rolling basis. *Application fee:* $100. *Application Contact:* Graduate Division, 808-956-8544. *Dean,* Peter E. Crouch, 808-956-7727, Fax: 808-956-2291.

College of Languages, Linguistics and Literature Average age 34. 288 applicants, 46% accepted, 82 enrolled. *Financial support:* In 2015–16, 100 fellowships, 15 research assistantships, 135 teaching assistantships were awarded; career-related internships or fieldwork, Federal Work-Study, institutionally sponsored loans, and tuition waivers (full and partial) also available. Support available to part-time students. Financial award applicants required to submit FAFSA. In 2015, 100 master's, 22 doctorates, 1 other advanced degree awarded. *Degree program information:* Part-time programs available. Part-time. Offers Chinese (MA, PhD); English (MA, PhD); English as a second language (MA, Graduate Certificate); French (MA); Japanese (MA, PhD); Korean (MA, PhD); languages, linguistics and literature (MA, PhD, Graduate Certificate); linguistics (MA, PhD); second language acquisition (PhD); Spanish (MA). *Application fee:* $100. *Application Contact:* Graduate Division, 808-956-8544. *Dean,* Robert Bley-Vroman, 808-956-8516, Fax: 808-956-9879.

College of Natural Sciences Students: 11 full-time, 34 part-time. Average age 32. 297 applicants, 34% accepted, 58 enrolled. *Faculty:* 230 full-time (45 women), 17 part-time/adjunct (2 women). *Financial support:* In 2015–16, 41 students received support, including 59 fellowships, 134 research assistantships, 108 teaching assistantships; institutionally sponsored loans and tuition waivers (full and partial) also available. Support available to part-time students. In 2015, 48 master's, 35 doctorates awarded. *Degree program information:* Part-time programs available. Part-time. Offers advanced library and information science (Graduate Certificate); astronomy (MS, PhD); botany (MS, PhD); chemistry (MS, PhD); computer science (MS, PhD); library and information science (MLI Sc, Graduate Certificate); mathematics (MA, PhD); microbiology (MS, PhD); natural sciences (MA, MLI Sc, MS, PhD, Graduate Certificate); physics (MS, PhD); zoology (MS, PhD). *Application fee:* $100. *Application Contact:* Graduate Division, 808-956-8544. *Dean,* William Ditto, 808-956-6451, E-mail: wditto@hawaii.edu.

College of Social Sciences Average age 33. 503 applicants, 40% accepted, 127 enrolled. *Faculty:* 239 full-time (82 women), 61 part-time/adjunct (19 women). *Financial support:* In 2015–16, 2 students received support, including 142 fellowships, 117 research assistantships, 79 teaching assistantships; career-related internships or fieldwork, Federal Work-Study, institutionally sponsored loans, and tuition waivers (full and partial) also available. Support available to part-time students. Financial award applicants required to submit FAFSA. In 2015, 115 master's, 40 doctorates, 16 other advanced degrees awarded. *Degree program information:* Part-time and evening/weekend programs available. Part-time, evening/weekend. Offers advanced women's studies (Graduate Certificate); anthropology (MA, PhD); clinical psychology (PhD); communication (MA); community and cultural psychology (PhD); community and culture (MA); community planning (MURP); conflict resolution (Graduate Certificate); disaster management and humanitarian assistance (Graduate Certificate); disaster preparedness and emergency management (Graduate Certificate); economics (MA, PhD); environmental planning and sustainability (MURP); geography (MA, PhD); international development planning (MURP); land use, transportation and infrastructure planning (MURP); ocean policy (Graduate Certificate); planning studies (Graduate Certificate); political science (MA, PhD); psychology (MA, PhD, Graduate Certificate); public administration (MPA, Graduate Certificate); public policy (Graduate Certificate); social sciences (MA, MPA, MURP, PhD, Graduate Certificate); sociology (MA, PhD); telecommunication and information resource management (Graduate Certificate); urban and regional planning (PhD, Graduate Certificate). *Application fee:* $100. *Application Contact:* Graduate Division, 808-956-8544. *Dean*, Richard Dubanoski, 808-956-6570, Fax: 808-956-2340, E-mail: dickd@hawaii.edu.

College of Tropical Agriculture and Human Resources Students: 99 full-time, 28 part-time. Average age 34. 137 applicants, 60% accepted, 44 enrolled. *Financial support:* In 2015–16, 12 students received support, including 37 fellowships, 129 research assistantships, 16 teaching assistantships; career-related internships or fieldwork, Federal Work-Study, institutionally sponsored loans, tuition waivers (full and partial), and unspecified assistantships also available. In 2015, 30 master's, 10 doctorates awarded. *Degree program information:* Part-time programs available. Part-time. Offers animal sciences (MS); bioengineering (MS); entomology (MS, PhD); food science (MS); molecular bioscience and bioengineering (MS); molecular biosciences and bioengineering (PhD); natural resources and environmental management (MS, PhD); nutrition (PhD); nutritional sciences (MS, PhD); tropical agriculture and human resources (MS, PhD); tropical plant and soil sciences (MS, PhD); tropical plant pathology (MS, PhD). *Application fee:* $100. *Application Contact:* Graduate Division, 808-956-8544. *Interim Dean*, Sylvia Yuen, 808-956-8234, Fax: 808-956-9105, E-mail: syuen@hawaii.edu.

Hawai'inuakea School of Hawaiian Knowledge Students: 25 full-time, 11 part-time. Average age 34. 20 applicants, 80% accepted, 13 enrolled. *Faculty:* 20 full-time (11 women). *Financial support:* In 2015–16, 19 fellowships, 9 research assistantships, 8 teaching assistantships were awarded. In 2015, 7 master's awarded. *Degree program information:* Part-time programs available. Part-time. Offers Hawaiian (MA); Hawaiian studies (MA). *Application deadline:* For fall admission, 3/1 for domestic and international students. *Application fee:* $100. *Application Contact:* Graduate Division, 808-956-8544. *Dean*, Maenette Ah Nee-Benham, 808-956-0980, Fax: 808-956-0411, E-mail: mbenham@hawaii.edu.

School of Nursing and Dental Hygiene Students: 167 full-time (145 women), 118 part-time (104 women); includes 128 minority (3 Black or African American, non-Hispanic/Latino; 1 American Indian or Alaska Native, non-Hispanic/Latino; 57 Asian, non-Hispanic/Latino; 14 Hispanic/Latino; 4 Native Hawaiian or other Pacific Islander, non-Hispanic/Latino; 49 Two or more races, non-Hispanic/Latino), 2 international. Average age 41. 253 applicants, 42% accepted, 88 enrolled. *Faculty:* 32 full-time (27 women), 22 part-time/adjunct (11 women). *Financial support:* In 2015–16, 78 fellowships (averaging $1,277 per year), 3 research assistantships (averaging $16,824 per year), 2 teaching assistantships (averaging $14,382 per year) were awarded. In 2015, 20 master's, 8 doctorates awarded. *Degree program information:* Part-time programs available. Part-time, online learning. Offers clinical nurse specialist (MS); nurse practitioner (MS); nursing (PhD, Graduate Certificate); nursing administration (MS). *Application deadline:* For fall admission, 2/1 for domestic and international students. *Application fee:* $100. *Application Contact:* Maureen Shannon, Graduate Chair, 808-956-5201, Fax: 808-956-3257, E-mail: maureens@hawaii.edu. *Dean*, Mary Boland, 808-956-8522, Fax: 808-956-3257, E-mail: mgboland@hawaii.edu.

School of Ocean and Earth Science and Technology Students: 75 full-time, 8 part-time. Average age 31. 269 applicants, 22% accepted, 39 enrolled. *Faculty:* 170 full-time (30 women), 23 part-time/adjunct (3 women). *Financial support:* In 2015–16, 25 students received support, including 18 fellowships, 140 research assistantships, 17 teaching assistantships; career-related internships or fieldwork, Federal Work-Study, institutionally sponsored loans, and tuition waivers (full and partial) also available. Financial award applicants required to submit FAFSA. In 2015, 25 master's, 19 doctorates awarded. *Degree program information:* Part-time programs available. Part-time. Offers high-pressure geophysics and geochemistry (MS, PhD); hydrogeology and engineering geology (MS, PhD); marine biology (MS, PhD); marine geology and geophysics (MS, PhD); meteorology (MS, PhD); ocean and earth science and technology (MS, PhD); ocean and resources engineering (MS, PhD); oceanography (MS, PhD); planetary geosciences and remote sensing (MS, PhD); seismology and solid-earth geophysics (MS, PhD); volcanology, petrology, and geochemistry (MS, PhD). *Application fee:* $100. *Application Contact:* Graduate Division, 808-956-8544. *Dean*, Brian Taylor, 808-956-6182, E-mail: taylorb@hawaii.edu.

School of Pacific and Asian Studies Average age 34. 111 applicants, 59% accepted, 38 enrolled. *Faculty:* 132 full-time (50 women), 1 part-time/adjunct (0 women). *Financial support:* In 2015–16, 26 fellowships, 2 research assistantships, 12 teaching assistantships were awarded; career-related internships or fieldwork, Federal Work-Study, and tuition waivers (full) also available. In 2015, 28 master's awarded. *Degree program information:* Part-time programs available. Part-time. Offers Asian studies (MA, Graduate Certificate); Chinese studies (Graduate Certificate); Japanese studies (Graduate Certificate); Korean studies (Graduate Certificate); Pacific and Asian studies (MA, Graduate Certificate); Pacific Island studies (MA, Graduate Certificate); Philippine studies (Graduate Certificate); Southeast Asian studies (Graduate Certificate). *Application fee:* $100. *Application Contact:* Graduate Division, 808-956-8544. *Dean*, Edward J. Shultz, 808-956-8818, E-mail: shultz@hawaii.edu.

School of Social Work Students: 197 full-time (150 women), 20 part-time (15 women); includes 38 minority (3 Black or African American, non-Hispanic/Latino; 2 Asian, non-Hispanic/Latino; 30 Hispanic/Latino; 2 Native Hawaiian or other Pacific Islander, non-Hispanic/Latino; 1 Two or more races, non-Hispanic/Latino), 4 international. Average age 35. 145 applicants, 78% accepted, 82 enrolled. *Faculty:* 27 full-time (19 women). *Financial support:* In 2015–16, 23 fellowships with tuition reimbursements (averaging $2,966 per year), 9 research assistantships with tuition reimbursements (averaging $16,793 per year), 1 teaching assistantship (averaging $14,382 per year) were awarded; career-related internships or fieldwork, Federal Work-Study, institutionally sponsored loans, and tuition waivers (full) also available. Support available to part-time students. Financial award application deadline: 2/1; financial award applicants required to submit FAFSA. In 2015, 108 master's awarded. *Degree program information:* Part-time programs available. Part-time. Offers social welfare (PhD); social work (MSW). *Application deadline:* For fall admission, 1/15 for domestic and international students. Applications are processed on a rolling basis. *Application fee:* $100. *Application Contact:* Crystal Mills, Graduate Chair, 808-956-3832, Fax: 808-956-5964, E-mail: millsc@hawaii.edu. *Dean*, Jon Matsuoka, 808-956-6300, E-mail: jmatsuok@hawaii.edu.

School of Travel Industry Management Students: 13 full-time (11 women), 1 part-time; includes 2 minority (1 Asian, non-Hispanic/Latino; 1 Hispanic/Latino), 11 international. Average age 31. 17 applicants, 53% accepted, 4 enrolled. *Faculty:* 8 full-time (3 women). *Financial support:* In 2015–16, 1 fellowship with partial tuition reimbursement (averaging $6,000 per year) was awarded; career-related internships or fieldwork, scholarships/grants, tuition waivers (full and partial), and unspecified assistantships also available. Financial award application deadline: 3/1. In 2015, 2 master's awarded. *Degree program information:* Part-time programs available. Part-time. Offers travel industry management (MS). *Application deadline:* For fall admission, 3/1 for domestic and international students. Applications are processed on a rolling basis. *Application fee:* $100. Electronic applications accepted. *Application Contact:* Dexter J. L. Choy, Graduate Chair, 808-956-9840, Fax: 808-956-5378, E-mail: djlchoy@hawaii.edu.

Shadier College of Business Students: 101 full-time, 66 part-time. Average age 33. *Financial support:* In 2015–16, 32 students received support, including 113 fellowships, 36 research assistantships, 1 teaching assistantship; career-related internships or fieldwork, Federal Work-Study, and tuition waivers (full) also available. Support available to part-time students. In 2015, 260 master's, 4 doctorates awarded. *Degree program information:* Part-time and evening/weekend programs available. Part-time, evening/weekend. Offers accounting (M Acc); accounting law (M Acc); Asian business studies (MBA); Asian finance (PhD); business (EMBA, M Acc, MBA, MHRM, MS, PhD, Graduate Certificate); Chinese business studies (MBA); decision sciences (MBA); entrepreneurship (MBA, Graduate Certificate); executive business administration (EMBA); finance (MBA); finance and banking (MBA); global information technology management (PhD); human resources management (MHRM); information management (MBA); information systems (M Acc); information technology (MBA); international accounting (PhD); international business (MBA); international marketing (PhD); international organization and strategy (PhD); Japanese business studies (MBA); marketing (MBA); organizational behavior (MBA); organizational management (MBA); real estate (MBA); student-designed track (MBA); taxation (M Acc); Vietnam focused business administration (EMBA). *Application fee:* $100. *Application Contact:* Graduate Division, 808-956-8544. *Dean*, V. Vance Roley, 808-956-8377.

John A. Burns School of Medicine Students: 28 (162 women). 315 applicants, 39% accepted, 77 enrolled. *Financial support:* In 2015–16, 62 fellowships, 70 research assistantships, 2 teaching assistantships were awarded; career-related internships or fieldwork, Federal Work-Study, institutionally sponsored loans, and tuition waivers (full and partial) also available. Support available to part-time students. Financial award applicants required to submit FAFSA. In 2015, 23 master's, 10 doctorates, 1 other advanced degree awarded. *Degree program information:* Part-time programs available. Part-time. Offers cell and molecular biology (MS, PhD); communication sciences and disorders (MS); developmental and reproductive biology (MS, PhD); epidemiology (PhD); global health and population studies (Graduate Certificate); medicine (MPH, MS, Dr PH, MD, PhD, Graduate Certificate); public health (MPH, MS, Dr PH). *Application fee:* $100. *Application Contact:* Jarren Uyehara-Fujii, Director of Graduate Admissions, 808-956-8544, Fax: 808-956-4261, E-mail: admissions@grad.hawaii.edu. *Dean*, Dr. Jerris R. Hedges, 808-692-0881.

Graduate Programs in Biomedical Sciences Students: 9 full-time (7 women), 6 part-time (5 women); includes 7 minority (2 Black or African American, non-Hispanic/Latino; 2 Asian, non-Hispanic/Latino; 1 Native Hawaiian or other Pacific Islander, non-Hispanic/Latino; 2 Two or more races, non-Hispanic/Latino), 3 international. Average age 42. 1 applicant, 100% accepted, 1 enrolled. *Faculty:* 17 full-time (10 women), 1 part-time/adjunct (0 women). *Financial support:* In 2015–16, 1 fellowship (averaging $18,126 per year), 1 research assistantship (averaging $23,022 per year) were awarded; career-related internships or fieldwork, Federal Work-Study, institutionally sponsored loans, and tuition waivers (full and partial) also available. Support available to part-time students. In 2015, 1 master's, 3 doctorates awarded. *Degree program information:* Part-time programs available. Part-time. Offers biomedical sciences (MS, PhD); tropical medicine (MS, PhD). *Application deadline:* For fall admission, 6/1 for domestic and international students. *Application fee:* $100. *Application Contact:* Rosanne Harrigan, Graduate Chairperson, 808-692-0904, Fax: 808-692-1247, E-mail: harrigan@hawaii.edu. *Dean*, Dr. Jerris R. Hedges, 808-692-0881.

School of Architecture Students: 60 full-time (29 women), 9 part-time (7 women); includes 51 minority (1 American Indian or Alaska Native, non-Hispanic/Latino; 28 Asian, non-Hispanic/Latino; 5 Hispanic/Latino; 4 Native Hawaiian or other Pacific Islander, non-Hispanic/Latino; 13 Two or more races, non-Hispanic/Latino), 8 international. Average age 33. 28 applicants, 43% accepted, 9 enrolled. *Faculty:* 10 full-time (3 women). *Financial support:* In 2015–16, 31 students received support, including 11 fellowships (averaging $3,020 per year), 2 research assistantships with full tuition reimbursements available (averaging $17,496 per year); teaching assistantships with full tuition reimbursements available, institutionally sponsored loans, scholarships/grants, and unspecified assistantships also available. Financial award applicants required to submit FAFSA. *Degree program information:* Part-time programs available. Part-time. Offers architecture (D Arch). *Application deadline:* For fall admission, 5/1 for domestic and international students; for spring admission, 9/1 for domestic students, 8/1 for international students. *Application fee:* $100. *Application Contact:* Spencer Leineweber, Graduate Field Chairperson, 808-956-7228, Fax: 808-956-7778, E-mail: aspencer@hawaii.edu.

William S. Richardson School of Law Offers law (LL M, JD, Graduate Certificate).

UNIVERSITY OF HOLY CROSS, New Orleans, LA 70131-7399

General Information Independent-religious, coed, comprehensive institution. *Graduate housing:* On-campus housing not available.

GRADUATE UNITS

Program in Education and Counseling ***Degree program information:*** Part-time and evening/weekend programs available. Part-time, evening/weekend. Offers administration and supervision (M Ed); curriculum and instruction (M Ed); marriage and family counseling (MA); school counseling (M Ed, MA).

UNIVERSITY OF HOUSTON, Houston, TX 77204

General Information State-supported, coed, university. CGS member. *Graduate housing:* Rooms and/or apartments available on a first-come, first-served basis to single and married students. *Research affiliation:* Keck Consortium.

GRADUATE UNITS

Bauer College of Business ***Degree program information:*** Part-time and evening/weekend programs available. Part-time, evening/weekend. Offers accountancy (MS Accy); accountancy and taxation (PhD); business (MBA, MS, MS Accy, PhD); decision and information sciences (PhD); finance (MS); management (PhD); marketing (PhD). Electronic applications accepted.

College of Architecture Offers architecture (MS); architecture studies (MA); space architecture (MS). Electronic applications accepted.

College of Education ***Degree program information:*** Part-time programs available. Part-time. Offers administration and supervision (M Ed, Ed D); administration and supervision - higher education (M Ed); counseling (M Ed); counseling psychology (PhD); curriculum and instruction (M Ed, Ed D); education (M Ed, Ed D, PhD); educational psychology (M Ed); higher education (M Ed); historical, social, and cultural foundations of education (M Ed); professional leadership (Ed D); school psychology (PhD); school psychology and individual differences (PhD); special education (M Ed). Electronic applications accepted.

College of Liberal Arts and Social Sciences ***Degree program information:*** Part-time programs available. Part-time, online learning. Offers anthropology (MA); applied economics (MA); applied English linguistics (MA); clinical psychology (PhD); communication sciences and disorders (MA); creative writing (MFA); creative writing and literature (MA, PhD); developmental psychology (PhD); economics (MA, PhD); English (MA, PhD); exercise science (MS); history (MA, PhD); human nutrition (MS); human space exploration sciences (MS); industrial/organizational psychology (PhD); kinesiology (PhD); liberal arts and social sciences (M Ed, MA, MFA, MM, MS, DMA, PhD); philosophy (MA); physical education (M Ed); political science (MA, PhD); psychology (MA); public administration (MA); social psychology (PhD); sociology (MA); Spanish (MA, PhD); world cultures and literatures (MA). Electronic applications accepted.

Jack J. Valenti School of Communication Degree program information: Part-time programs available. Part-time. Offers health communication (MA); mass communication studies (MA); public relations studies (MA); speech communication (MA). Electronic applications accepted.

Moores School of Music Degree program information: Part-time programs available. Part-time. Offers accompanying and chamber music (MM); applied music (MM); composition (MM); music education (DMA); music theory (MM); performance (DMA). Electronic applications accepted.

School of Art Offers art history (MA); interdisciplinary practice and emerging forms (MFA); painting (MFA); studio art (MFA). Electronic applications accepted.

School of Theatre and Dance Degree program information: Part-time programs available. Part-time. Offers theatre (MA, MFA). Electronic applications accepted.

College of Natural Sciences and Mathematics ***Degree program information:*** Part-time programs available. Part-time, online learning. Offers applied mathematics (MS); atmospheric science (PhD); biochemistry (MA, PhD); biology (MA); chemistry (MA, PhD); computer science (MA, PhD); geology (MA, PhD); geophysics (PhD); mathematics (MA, PhD); natural sciences and mathematics (MA, MS, PhD); physics (MA, PhD). Electronic applications accepted.

College of Optometry ***Degree program information:*** Part-time programs available. Part-time. Offers optometry (MS, OD, PhD); physiological optics (MS, PhD). Electronic applications accepted.

College of Pharmacy ***Degree program information:*** Part-time programs available. Part-time. Offers pharmaceutics (MSPHR, PhD); pharmacology (MSPHR, PhD); pharmacy (Pharm D); pharmacy administration (MSPHR, PhD). Electronic applications accepted.

College of Technology ***Degree program information:*** Part-time programs available. Part-time. Offers construction management (MS); engineering technology (MS); future studies in commerce (MS); human resources development (MS); information security (MS); network communications (M Tech); supply chain and logistics technology (MS); technology (M Tech, MS); technology project management (MS). Electronic applications accepted.

Conrad N. Hilton College of Hotel and Restaurant Management ***Degree program information:*** Part-time programs available. Part-time. Offers hospitality management (MS). Electronic applications accepted.

Cullen College of Engineering ***Degree program information:*** Part-time programs available. Part-time. Offers biomedical engineering (PhD); chemical engineering (MCHE, PhD); civil engineering (MCE, PhD); electrical engineering (MEE, MSEE, PhD); engineering (M Pet E, MCE, MCHE, MEE, MIE, MME, MSEE, MSME, PhD); industrial engineering (MIE, PhD); mechanical engineering (MME, MSME, PhD); petroleum engineering (M Pet E).

Graduate College of Social Work ***Degree program information:*** Part-time programs available. Part-time. Offers social work (MSW, PhD).

Law Center ***Degree program information:*** Part-time and evening/weekend programs available. Part-time, evening/weekend. Offers energy, environment, and natural resources (LL M); health law (LL M); intellectual property and information law (LL M); international law (LL M); law (LL M, JD); tax law (LL M). Electronic applications accepted.

School of Nursing Offers family nurse practitioner (MSN); nursing administration (MSN); nursing education (MSN). Electronic applications accepted.

UNIVERSITY OF HOUSTON–CLEAR LAKE, Houston, TX 77058-1002

General Information State-supported, coed, comprehensive institution. CGS member. *Graduate housing:* Rooms and/or apartments available on a first-come, first-served basis to single students and available to married students. *Research affiliation:* Baylor College of Medicine (life sciences), NASA–Johnson Space Center (computer science, computer engineering), Schlumberger (ergonomic software).

GRADUATE UNITS

School of Business ***Degree program information:*** Part-time and evening/weekend programs available. Part-time, evening/weekend. Offers accounting (MS); business (MA, MBA, MHA, MS); business administration (MBA); environmental management (MS); finance (MS); healthcare administration (MHA); human resource management (MA); management information systems (MS); professional accounting (MS). Electronic applications accepted.

School of Education ***Degree program information:*** Part-time and evening/weekend programs available. Part-time, evening/weekend. Offers counseling (MS); curriculum and instruction (MS); early childhood education (MS); education (MS, Ed D); educational leadership (Ed D); educational management (MS); instructional technology (MS); multicultural studies (MS); reading (MS); school library and information science (MS). Electronic applications accepted.

School of Human Sciences and Humanities ***Degree program information:*** Part-time and evening/weekend programs available. Part-time, evening/weekend. Offers behavioral sciences (MA); clinical psychology (MA); criminology (MA); cross cultural studies (MA); family therapy (MA); fitness and human performance (MA); history (MA); human sciences and humanities (MA); humanities (MA); literature (MA); school psychology (MA).

School of Science and Computer Engineering ***Degree program information:*** Part-time and evening/weekend programs available. Part-time, evening/weekend. Offers biological sciences (MS); biotechnology (MS); chemistry (MS); computer engineering (MS); computer information systems (MS); computer science (MS); environmental science (MS); mathematical sciences (MS); physics (MS); science and computer engineering (MS); software engineering (MS); statistics (MS); system engineering (MS).

UNIVERSITY OF HOUSTON–DOWNTOWN, Houston, TX 77002

General Information State-supported, coed, comprehensive institution. *Enrollment:* 14,262 graduate, professional, and undergraduate students; 67 full-time matriculated graduate/professional students (46 women), 542 part-time matriculated graduate/professional students (309 women). *Enrollment by degree level:* 609 master's. *Graduate faculty:* 45 full-time (19 women), 7 part-time/adjunct (4 women). *Graduate housing:* On-campus housing not available. *Student services:* Campus employment opportunities, campus safety program, career counseling, exercise/wellness program, free psychological counseling, international student services, low-cost health insurance, services for students with disabilities, teacher training. *Library:* W. I. Dykes Library.

Computer facilities: A campuswide network can be accessed. Online class registration is available.
Website: http://www.uhd.edu/

General Application Contact: Ceshia Love, Director of Graduate and International Admissions, 713-221-8093, Fax: 713-221-8658, E-mail: gradadmissions@uhd.edu.

GRADUATE UNITS

College of Business Students: 9 full-time (7 women), 783 part-time (409 women); includes 591 minority (290 Black or African American, non-Hispanic/Latino; 2 American Indian or Alaska Native, non-Hispanic/Latino; 71 Asian, non-Hispanic/Latino; 214 Hispanic/Latino; 1 Native Hawaiian or other Pacific Islander, non-Hispanic/Latino; 13 Two or more races, non-Hispanic/Latino), 30 international. Average age 33. 583 applicants, 91% accepted, 409 enrolled. *Faculty:* 40 full-time (17 women), 2 part-time/adjunct (0 women). *Financial support:* Application deadline: 4/1; applicants required to submit FAFSA. In 2015, 42 master's awarded. *Degree program information:* Part-time and evening/weekend programs available. Part-time, evening/weekend. Offers business (MBA, MSM); finance (MBA); human resource management (MBA); investment management (MBA); leadership (MBA); sales management and business development (MBA); security management for executives (MSM); supply chain management (MBA). *Application deadline:* For fall admission, 7/15 for domestic and international students. *Application fee:* $35 ($60 for international students). Electronic applications accepted. *Application Contact:* Ceshia Love, Director of Graduate and International Admissions, 713-221-8093, Fax: 713-223-7408, E-mail: gradadmissions@uhd.edu. *Dean, College of Business,* Dr. D. Michael Fields, 713-221-8179, Fax: 713-221-8675, E-mail: fieldsd@uhd.edu.

College of Humanities and Social Sciences Students: 26 full-time (20 women), 83 part-time (63 women); includes 66 minority (44 Black or African American, non-Hispanic/Latino; 3 Asian, non-Hispanic/Latino; 17 Hispanic/Latino; 2 Two or more races, non-Hispanic/Latino), 1 international. Average age 38. 70 applicants, 97% accepted, 57 enrolled. *Faculty:* 10 full-time (4 women), 5 part-time/adjunct (3 women). *Financial support:* Application deadline: 4/1; applicants required to submit FAFSA. In 2015, 19 master's awarded. *Degree program information:* Part-time and evening/weekend programs available. Part-time, evening/weekend, 100% online. Offers humanities and social sciences (MA, MS); non-profit management (MA); rhetoric and composition (MA); technical communication (MS). *Application fee:* $35 ($60 for international students). Electronic applications accepted. *Application Contact:* Ceshia Love, Director of Graduate and International Admissions, 713-221-8093, Fax: 713-223-7408, E-mail: gradadmissions@uhd.edu. *Dean,* Dr. DoVeanna Fulton, 713-221-8009, Fax: 713-223-7465, E-mail: fultond@uhd.edu.

College of Public Service Students: 14 full-time (5 women), 89 part-time (62 women); includes 74 minority (35 Black or African American, non-Hispanic/Latino; 7 Asian, non-Hispanic/Latino; 31 Hispanic/Latino; 1 Two or more races, non-Hispanic/Latino). Average age 35. 66 applicants, 70% accepted, 31 enrolled. *Faculty:* 15 full-time (8 women), 4 part-time/adjunct (3 women). *Financial support:* Federal Work-Study and scholarships/grants available. Financial award application deadline: 4/1; financial award applicants required to submit FAFSA. In 2015, 29 master's awarded. *Degree program information:* Part-time and evening/weekend programs available. Part-time, evening/weekend, 100% online. Offers criminal justice (MS); curriculum and instruction (MAT); urban education (MAT). *Application fee:* $35 ($60 for international students). Electronic applications accepted. *Application Contact:* Ceshia Love, Director of Graduate and International Admissions, 713-221-8093, Fax: 713-223-7408, E-mail: gradadmissions@uhd.edu. *Interim Dean,* Dr. Leigh Van Horn, 713-221-8991, Fax: 713-226-5274, E-mail: vanhornl@uhd.edu.

College of Sciences and Technology Students: 4 full-time (2 women), 9 part-time (6 women); includes 7 minority (2 Black or African American, non-Hispanic/Latino; 1 Asian, non-Hispanic/Latino; 4 Hispanic/Latino), 3 international. Average age 33. 19 applicants, 79% accepted, 12 enrolled. *Faculty:* 3 full-time (1 woman), 1 part-time/adjunct (0 women). *Financial support:* Applicants required to submit FAFSA. *Degree program information:* Part-time and evening/weekend programs available. Part-time, evening/weekend. Offers data analytics (MS). *Application deadline:* For fall admission, 7/15 for domestic students. *Application fee:* $35 ($60 for international students). Electronic applications accepted. *Application Contact:* Ceshia Love, Director of Graduate and International Admissions, 713-221-8093, Fax: 713-221-8658, E-mail: gradadmissions@uhd.edu. *Dean,* Dr. J. Akif Uzman, 713-221-8019, E-mail: st_dean@uhd.edu.

UNIVERSITY OF HOUSTON–VICTORIA, Victoria, TX 77901-4450

General Information State-supported, coed, upper-level institution. *Graduate housing:* On-campus housing not available.

GRADUATE UNITS

School of Arts and Sciences ***Degree program information:*** Part-time and evening/weekend programs available. Part-time, evening/weekend, online learning. Offers arts and sciences (MA, MAIS, MFA, MS); biological sciences (MS); biomedical sciences (MS); computer information systems (MS); computer science (MS); counseling psychology (MA); creative writing (MFA); forensic psychology (MA); forensic science (MS); interdisciplinary studies (MAIS); publishing (MS); school psychology (MA). Electronic applications accepted.

School of Business Administration ***Degree program information:*** Part-time and evening/weekend programs available. Part-time, evening/weekend, online learning. Offers accounting (MBA); economic development and entrepreneurship (MS); finance (GMBA, MBA); general business (MBA); international business (MBA); management (GMBA, MBA); marketing (MBA). Electronic applications accepted.

School of Education, Health Professions and Human Development ***Degree program information:*** Part-time and evening/weekend programs available. Part-time, evening/weekend, online learning. Offers administration and supervision (M Ed); adult and higher education (M Ed); counselor education (M Ed); curriculum and instruction (M Ed); educational technology (M Ed); special education (M Ed). Electronic applications accepted.

UNIVERSITY OF IDAHO, Moscow, ID 83844-2282

General Information State-supported, coed, university. CGS member. *Enrollment:* 11,372 graduate, professional, and undergraduate students; 1,238 full-time matriculated graduate/professional students (539 women), 832 part-time matriculated graduate/professional students (357 women). *Enrollment by degree level:* 1,223 master's, 1,493 doctoral, 65 other advanced degrees. *Graduate faculty:* 423 full-time (143 women), 40 part-time/adjunct (16 women). Tuition, state resident: full-time $6205; part-time $399 per credit hour. Tuition, nonresident: full-time $20,209; part-time $1177 per credit hour. *Required fees:* $2017; $58 per credit hour. Full-time tuition and fees vary according to course load and reciprocity agreements. *Graduate housing:* Rooms and/or apartments available on a first-come, first-served basis to single and married students. Typical cost: $8328 (including board) for single students. Room and board charges vary according to board plan and housing facility selected. *Student services:* Campus employment opportunities, campus safety program, career counseling, exercise/wellness program, free psychological counseling, grant writing training, international student services, low-cost health insurance, multicultural affairs office, services for students with disabilities, writing training. *Library:* University of Idaho Library plus 1 other. *Collection:* Books: 1.4 million (physical), 540,212 (digital/electronic); Serial titles: 26,448 (physical), 47,228 (digital/electronic). *Research affiliation:* Idaho Water Resources Research Institute (water resources), Idaho Geological Survey, Snake River Conservation Research Center (soil and water problems), Battelle Pacific Northwest Laboratories (biological sciences, homeland security), Idaho Nuclear Environmental Engineering Laboratory (energy research), Inland Northwest Research Alliance (INRA) (science and technology).

Computer facilities: Computer purchase and lease plans are available. 510 computers available on campus for general student use. A campuswide network can be accessed from student residence rooms and from off campus. Online class registration is available.
Website: http://www.uidaho.edu/

General Application Contact: Sean Scoggin, Graduate Recruitment Coordinator, 208-885-4723, Fax: 208-885-4406, E-mail: graduateadmissions@uidaho.edu.

GRADUATE UNITS

College of Graduate Studies Students: 1,238 full-time (539 women), 832 part-time (357 women); includes 260 minority (32 Black or African American, non-Hispanic/Latino; 31 American Indian or Alaska Native, non-Hispanic/Latino; 36 Asian, non-Hispanic/Latino; 112 Hispanic/Latino; 49 Two or more races, non-Hispanic/Latino), 223 international. Average age 33. 2,180 applicants, 35% accepted, 472 enrolled. *Faculty:* 423 full-time (143 women), 40 part-time/adjunct (16 women). *Financial support:* Fellowships, research assistantships, teaching assistantships, career-related internships or fieldwork, Federal Work-Study, institutionally sponsored loans, scholarships/grants, and tuition waivers (full and partial) available. Support available to part-time students. Financial award applicants required to submit FAFSA. In 2015, 516 master's, 95 doctorates, 131 other advanced degrees awarded. Online learning. Offers interdisciplinary studies (MA, MS). *Application deadline:* For fall admission, 8/1 for domestic students; for spring admission, 12/15 for domestic students. Applications are processed on a rolling basis. *Application fee:* $60 ($70 for international students). Electronic applications accepted. *Application Contact:* Rance Larsen, Director of Graduate Admissions, E-mail: graduateadmissions@uidaho.edu. *Dean of the College of Graduate Studies*, Dr. Jerry McMurtry, 208-885-6243, Fax: 208-885-6198, E-mail: uigrad@uidaho.edu.

College of Agricultural and Life Sciences Students: 93 full-time (50 women), 51 part-time (28 women). Average age 31. *Faculty:* 71 full-time (24 women). *Financial support:* Research assistantships, teaching assistantships, career-related internships or fieldwork, and Federal Work-Study available. Support available to part-time students. Financial award application deadline: 2/15; financial award applicants required to submit FAFSA. In 2015, 24 master's, 4 doctorates awarded. Offers agricultural and life sciences (MS, PhD); agricultural economics (MS); agricultural education (MS); animal physiology (PhD); animal science (MS); applied economics (MS); engineering and science (PhD); engineering and science (MS); entomology (MS, PhD); family and consumer sciences (MS); food science (MS, PhD); law, management and policy (MS, PhD); plant science (MS, PhD); science and management (MS, PhD); soil and land resources (MS, PhD). *Application deadline:* For fall admission, 8/1 for domestic students; for spring admission, 12/15 for domestic students. Applications are processed on a rolling basis. *Application fee:* $60 ($70 for international students). Electronic applications accepted. *Application Contact:* Sean Scoggin, Graduate Recruitment Coordinator, 208-885-4723, Fax: 208-885-6198, E-mail: gadms@uidaho.edu. *Dean*, Dr. Michael Parrella, 208-885-6681, E-mail: ag@uidaho.edu.

College of Art and Architecture Students: 81 full-time (32 women), 8 part-time (0 women). Average age 31. *Faculty:* 16 full-time (5 women). *Financial support:* Applicants required to submit FAFSA. In 2015, 53 master's awarded. Offers architecture (M Arch); art (MFA); bioregional planning and community design (MS); integrated architecture and design (MS); landscape architecture (MLA); teaching art (MAT). *Application deadline:* For fall admission, 8/1 for domestic students; for spring admission, 12/15 for domestic students. Applications are processed on a rolling basis. *Application fee:* $60. Electronic applications accepted. *Application Contact:* Sean Scoggin, Graduate Recruitment Coordinator, 208-885-4001, Fax: 208-885-4406, E-mail: graduateadmissions@uidaho.edu. *Dean*, Dr. Mark Hoversten, 208-885-4409, E-mail: caa@uidaho.edu.

College of Business and Economics Students: 57 full-time (19 women), 7 part-time (4 women). Average age 32. *Faculty:* 14 full-time (6 women). *Financial support:* Research assistantships, teaching assistantships, Federal Work-Study, and scholarships/grants available. Support available to part-time students. Financial award applicants required to submit FAFSA. In 2015, 31 master's awarded. Offers accountancy (M Acct); business and economics (M Acct, MBA); general management (MBA). *Application deadline:* For fall admission, 8/1 for domestic students; for spring admission, 12/15 for domestic students. Applications are processed on a rolling basis. *Application fee:* $60. Electronic applications accepted. *Application Contact:* Sean Scoggin, Graduate Recruitment Coordinator, 208-885-4001, Fax: 208-885-4406, E-mail: graduateadmissions@uidaho.edu. *Dean*, Dr. Mario Reyes, 208-885-6478, E-mail: cbe@uidaho.edu.

College of Education Students: 156 full-time (103 women), 280 part-time (163 women). Average age 39. *Faculty:* 56 full-time (31 women). *Financial support:* Teaching assistantships and Federal Work-Study available. Support available to part-time students. Financial award applicants required to submit FAFSA. In 2015, 153 master's, 26 doctorates, 30 other advanced degrees awarded. Offers adult/organizational learning and leadership (MS, Ed S); athletic training (MSAT, DAT); career and technology education (M Ed); curriculum and instruction (M Ed, Ed S); education (Ed D); educational leadership (M Ed, Ed S); movement and leisure sciences (MS); physical education (M Ed); rehabilitation counseling and human services (M Ed, MS); school counseling (M Ed, MS); special education (M Ed). *Application deadline:* For fall admission, 8/1 for domestic students; for spring admission, 12/15 for domestic students. Applications are processed on a rolling basis. *Application fee:* $60. Electronic applications accepted. *Application Contact:* Sean Scoggin, Graduate Recruitment Coordinator, 208-885-4001, Fax: 208-885-4406, E-mail: graduateadmissions@uidaho.edu. *Dean*, Dr. Corinne Mantle-Bromley, 208-885-6772, E-mail: coe@uidaho.edu.

College of Engineering Students: 110 full-time (10 women), 231 part-time (36 women). Average age 35. *Faculty:* 57 full-time, 6 part-time/adjunct. *Financial support:* Fellowships, research assistantships, teaching assistantships, career-related internships or fieldwork, and Federal Work-Study available. Support available to part-time students. Financial award applicants required to submit FAFSA. In 2015, 90 master's, 18 doctorates awarded. Offers biological engineering (M Engr, MS, PhD); chemical engineering (M Engr, MS, PhD); civil engineering (M Engr, MS, PhD); computer engineering (M Engr, MS); computer science (MS, PhD); electrical engineering (M Engr, MS, PhD); engineering (M Engr, MS, PhD); engineering management (M Engr); geological engineering (MS); materials science and engineering (MS, PhD); mechanical engineering (M Engr, MS, PhD); metallurgical engineering (MS); nuclear engineering (M Engr, MS, PhD); technology management (MS). *Application deadline:* For fall admission, 8/1 for domestic students; for spring admission, 12/15 for domestic students. Applications are processed on a rolling basis. *Application fee:* $60. Electronic applications accepted. *Application Contact:* Sean Scoggin, Graduate Recruitment Coordinator, 208-885-4001, Fax: 208-885-4406, E-mail: graduateadmissions@uidaho.edu. *Dean*, Dr. Larry Stauffer, 208-885-6470, E-mail: deanengr@uidaho.edu.

College of Letters, Arts and Social Sciences Students: 142 full-time (69 women), 61 part-time (36 women). Average age 32. *Faculty:* 80 full-time (29 women). *Financial support:* Fellowships, research assistantships, teaching assistantships, and Federal Work-Study available. Support available to part-time students. Financial award applicants required to submit FAFSA. In 2015, 65 master's awarded. Offers anthropology (MA); creative writing (MFA); English (MA, MAT); history (MA, PhD); letters, arts and social sciences (M Mus, MA, MAT, MFA, MPA, MS, PhD); music (M Mus, MA); philosophy (MA); political science (MA, PhD); psychology (MS); public administration (MPA); teaching English as a second language (MA); theatre arts (MFA). *Application deadline:* For fall admission, 8/1 for domestic students; for spring admission, 12/15 for domestic students. Applications are processed on a rolling basis. *Application fee:* $60. Electronic applications accepted. *Application Contact:* Sean Scoggin, Graduate Recruitment Coordinator, 208-885-4001, Fax: 208-885-4406, E-mail: graduateadmissions@uidaho.edu. *Acting Dean*, Dr. Andrew Kersten, 208-885-6426, E-mail: class@uidaho.edu.

College of Natural Resources Students: 148 full-time (82 women), 146 part-time (68 women). Average age 36. *Faculty:* 61 full-time (17 women). *Financial support:* Fellowships, research assistantships, teaching assistantships, and Federal Work-Study available. Support available to part-time students. Financial award applicants required to submit FAFSA. In 2015, 62 master's, 29 doctorates awarded. Offers environmental science (MS, PhD); natural resources (MNR, MS, PSM, PhD). *Application deadline:* For fall admission, 8/1 for domestic students; for spring admission, 12/15 for domestic students. Applications are processed on a rolling basis. *Application fee:* $60. Electronic applications accepted. *Application Contact:* Sean Scoggin, Graduate Recruitment Coordinator, 208-885-4723, Fax: 208-885-4406, E-mail: graduateadmissions@uidaho.edu. *Dean*, Dr. Kurt Scott Pregitzer, 208-885-8981, Fax: 208-885-5534, E-mail: cnr@uidaho.edu.

College of Science Students: 150 full-time (57 women), 44 part-time (19 women). Average age 32. *Faculty:* 72 full-time (17 women). *Financial support:* Applicants required to submit FAFSA. In 2015, 32 master's, 15 doctorates awarded. Offers bioinformatics and computational biology (MS, PhD); biology (MS, PhD); chemistry (MS, PhD); geography (MS, PhD); geology (MS, PhD); hydrology (MS); mathematics (MAT, MS, PhD); microbiology, molecular biology and biochemistry (PhD); neuroscience (MS, PhD); physics (MS, PhD); science (MAT, MS, PhD); statistical science (MS). *Application deadline:* Applications are processed on a rolling basis. *Application fee:* $60. Electronic applications accepted. *Application Contact:* Sean Scoggin, Graduate Recruitment Coordinator, 208-885-4001, Fax: 208-885-4406, E-mail: graduateadmissions@uidaho.edu. *Dean*, Dr. Paul Joyce, 208-885-6195, E-mail: science@uidaho.edu.

College of Law Students: 331 full-time, 9 part-time. Average age 29. *Faculty:* 30 full-time, 10 part-time/adjunct. *Financial support:* Career-related internships or fieldwork, Federal Work-Study, and institutionally sponsored loans available. Financial award applicants required to submit FAFSA. Offers business law and entrepreneurship (JD); law (JD); litigation and alternative dispute resolution (JD); Native American law (JD); natural resources and environmental law (JD). *Application deadline:* For fall admission, 2/15 for domestic students. Applications are processed on a rolling basis. *Application fee:* $50 ($60 for international students). Electronic applications accepted. *Application Contact:* Carole Wells, Director of Admissions, 208-885-2300, Fax: 208-885-2252, E-mail: lawadmit@uidaho.edu. *Dean*, Mark Adams, 208-885-4977, E-mail: uilaw@uidaho.edu.

UNIVERSITY OF ILLINOIS AT CHICAGO, Chicago, IL 60607-7128

General Information State-supported, coed, university. CGS member. *Enrollment:* 29,048 graduate, professional, and undergraduate students; 8,116 full-time matriculated graduate/professional students (4,350 women), 3,357 part-time matriculated graduate/professional students (2,199 women). *Enrollment by degree level:* 5,075 master's, 5,472 doctoral, 74 other advanced degrees. *Graduate faculty:* 2,166 full-time (1,008 women), 1,165 part-time/adjunct (497 women). Tuition, state resident: full-time $11,480; part-time $3826 per credit. Tuition, nonresident: full-time $23,720; part-time $7906 per credit. *Required fees:* $1333 per semester. Part-time tuition and fees vary according to course load and program. *Graduate housing:* Room and/or apartments available on a first-come, first-served basis to single students; on-campus housing not available to married students. Typical cost: $7808 per year ($10,871 including board). Room and board charges vary according to board plan. Housing application deadline: 3/1. *Student services:* Campus employment opportunities, campus safety program, career counseling, child daycare facilities, exercise/wellness program, free psychological counseling, international student services, low-cost health insurance, multicultural affairs office, services for students with disabilities, teacher training, writing training. *Library:* Richard J. Daley Library plus 2 others. *Collection:* Books: 2.3 million (physical), 487,836 (digital/electronic); Serial titles: 61,000 (digital/electronic); Databases: 1,000. Weekly public service hours: 132; study areas open 24 hours, 5–7 days a week; students can reserve study rooms. *Research affiliation:* Chicago Manufacturing Technology Extension Center (manufacturing research and development, industrial research), Eastern Cooperative Oncology Group (clinical cancer research), Argonne National Laboratory (battery performance), National Surgical Adjuvant Breast and Bowel Project (prevention of breast cancer).

Computer facilities: Computer purchase and lease plans are available. 1,052 computers available on campus for general student use. A campuswide network can be accessed from student residence rooms and from off campus. Online class registration is available.
Website: http://www.uic.edu/

General Application Contact: Jackie Perry, Graduate College Receptionist, 312-413-2550, Fax: 312-413-0185, E-mail: gradcoll@uic.edu.

GRADUATE UNITS

College of Applied Health Sciences Students: 488 full-time (371 women), 578 part-time (409 women); includes 343 minority (112 Black or African American, non-Hispanic/Latino; 132 Asian, non-Hispanic/Latino; 69 Hispanic/Latino; 2 Native Hawaiian or other Pacific Islander, non-Hispanic/Latino; 28 Two or more races, non-Hispanic/Latino), 57 international. Average age 34. 2,328 applicants, 39% accepted, 425 enrolled. *Faculty:* 95 full-time (58 women), 84 part-time/adjunct (54 women). *Financial support:* In 2015–16, 2 fellowships with full tuition reimbursements were awarded; research assistantships with full tuition reimbursements, teaching assistantships with full tuition reimbursements, career-related internships or fieldwork, Federal Work-Study, institutionally sponsored loans, traineeships, tuition waivers (full and partial), and unspecified assistantships also available. Financial award application deadline: 3/1; financial award applicants required to submit FAFSA. In 2015, 198 master's, 66 doctorates, 40 other advanced degrees awarded. *Degree program information:* Part-time programs available. Part-time. Offers applied health sciences (MS, DPT, OTD, PhD, CAS, Certificate); biomedical visualization (MS); disability and human development (MS); health informatics (MS, CAS); health information management (Certificate); kinesiology (MS, PhD); nutrition (MS, PhD); occupational therapy (MS, OTD); physical therapy (MS, DPT). *Application deadline:* For fall admission, 3/15 for domestic students, 2/15 for international students; for spring admission, 11/1 for domestic students. Applications are processed on a rolling basis. *Application fee:* $60. Electronic applications accepted. *Application Contact:* Receptionist, 312-413-2550, E-mail: gradcoll@uic.edu. *Dean*, Prof. Bo Fernhall, 312-996-6695, Fax: 312-413-0086, E-mail: fernhall@uic.edu.

College of Architecture, Design and the Arts Students: 137 full-time (82 women), 23 part-time (17 women); includes 43 minority (5 Black or African American, non-Hispanic/Latino; 1 American Indian or Alaska Native, non-Hispanic/Latino; 14 Asian, non-Hispanic/Latino; 18 Hispanic/Latino; 5 Two or more races, non-Hispanic/Latino), 24 international. Average age 29. 400 applicants, 43% accepted, 60 enrolled. *Faculty:* 82 full-time (40 women), 63 part-time/adjunct (19 women). *Financial support:* Fellowships with full tuition reimbursements, research assistantships with full tuition reimbursements, teaching assistantships with full tuition reimbursements, career-related internships or fieldwork, Federal Work-Study, institutionally sponsored loans, scholarships/grants, traineeships, tuition waivers (full), and unspecified assistantships available. Support available to part-time students. Financial award application deadline: 3/1. In 2015, 69 master's, 2 doctorates awarded. *Degree program information:* Part-time and evening/weekend programs available. Part-time, evening/weekend. Offers architecture, design and the arts (M Arch, M Des, MA, MFA, MS, MS Arch, PhD). *Application deadline:* For fall admission, 2/1 for domestic and international students. Applications are processed on a rolling basis. *Application fee:* $60. Electronic applications accepted. *Application Contact:* Receptionist, 312-413-2550, E-mail: gradcoll@uic.edu. *Dean*, Prof. Steve Everett, 312-996-2006, E-mail: steve3@uic.edu.

School of Architecture Students: 46 full-time (17 women), 1 (woman) part-time; includes 16 minority (1 Black or African American, non-Hispanic/Latino; 7 Asian, non-Hispanic/Latino; 5 Hispanic/Latino; 3 Two or more races, non-Hispanic/Latino), 1 international. Average age 26. *Faculty:* 18 full-time (6 women), 16 part-time/adjunct (8 women). *Financial support:* Fellowships with full tuition reimbursements, research assistantships with full tuition reimbursements, teaching assistantships with full tuition reimbursements, institutionally sponsored loans, scholarships/grants, traineeships, and tuition waivers (full) available. Financial award application deadline: 1/15; financial award applicants required to submit FAFSA. Offers architecture (M Arch, MA, MS, MS Arch). *Application deadline:* For fall admission, 1/15 priority date for domestic and international students. Applications are processed on a rolling basis. *Application fee:* $60. Electronic applications accepted. *Application Contact:* Stephanie Niebuhr, Graduate Academic Advisor, 312-996-3335. *Director*, Dr. Robert Somol, 312-996-3335, E-mail: somol@uic.edu.

School of Art and Art History Students: 73 full-time (52 women), 21 part-time (15 women); includes 24 minority (4 Black or African American, non-Hispanic/Latino; 1 American Indian or Alaska Native, non-Hispanic/Latino; 6 Asian, non-Hispanic/Latino; 11 Hispanic/Latino; 2 Two or more races, non-Hispanic/Latino), 12 international. Average age 30. *Faculty:* 24 full-time (15 women), 7 part-time/adjunct (1 woman). *Financial support:* Fellowships with full tuition reimbursements, research assistantships with full tuition reimbursements, teaching assistantships with full tuition reimbursements, career-related internships or fieldwork, Federal Work-Study, scholarships/grants, traineeships, tuition waivers (full), and unspecified assistantships available. Support available to part-time students. Financial award application deadline: 3/1; financial award applicants required to submit FAFSA. *Degree program information:* Part-time and evening/weekend programs available. Part-time, evening/weekend. Offers art history (MA); electronic visualization (MFA); museum and exhibition studies (MA); new media arts (MFA). *Application deadline:* For fall admission, 1/1 priority date for domestic and international students; for spring admission, 10/1 for domestic students, 7/15 for international students. *Application fee:* $60. Electronic applications accepted. *Application Contact:* Receptionist, 312-413-2550, E-mail: gradcoll@uic.edu. *Director*, Prof. Lisa Yun Lee, 312-413-5358, E-mail: lisalee@uic.edu.

School of Design Students: 18 full-time (13 women), 1 (woman) part-time; includes 3 minority (1 Asian, non-Hispanic/Latino; 2 Hispanic/Latino), 11 international. Average age 27. *Faculty:* 20 full-time (10 women), 15 part-time/adjunct (4 women). *Financial support:* Fellowships with full tuition reimbursements, research assistantships with full tuition reimbursements, teaching assistantships with full tuition reimbursements, career-related internships or fieldwork, Federal Work-Study, traineeships, tuition waivers (full), and unspecified assistantships available. Financial award application deadline: 2/1; financial award applicants required to submit FAFSA. Offers graphic design (M Des); industrial design (M Des). *Application deadline:* For fall admission, 12/15 priority date for domestic and international students. Applications are processed on a rolling basis. *Application fee:* $40 ($50 for international students). Electronic applications accepted. *Application Contact:* Bonnie Osborne, Graduate Secretary, 312-996-3337. *Director*, Marcia Lausen, 312-996-5699, E-mail: mlausen@uic.edu.

College of Dentistry Students: 391 full-time (201 women), 13 part-time (10 women); includes 191 minority (25 Black or African American, non-Hispanic/Latino; 117 Asian, non-Hispanic/Latino; 44 Hispanic/Latino; 1 Native Hawaiian or other Pacific Islander, non-Hispanic/Latino; 4 Two or more races, non-Hispanic/Latino), 13 international. Average age 28. 408 applicants, 21% accepted, 58 enrolled. *Faculty:* 95 full-time (35 women), 95 part-time/adjunct (38 women). *Financial support:* Fellowships, research assistantships, teaching assistantships, Federal Work-Study, scholarships/grants, traineeships, and unspecified assistantships available. In 2015, 20 master's, 108 doctorates awarded. Offers dentistry (MS, DDS, DMD, PhD); oral sciences (MS, PhD). *Application deadline:* For fall admission, 12/1 for domestic and international students. Applications are processed on a rolling basis. *Application fee:* $85. Electronic applications accepted. *Application Contact:* Jackie Perry, Graduate College Receptionist, 312-413-2550, Fax: 312-413-0185, E-mail: gradcoll@uic.edu. *Dean*, Dr. Clark Stanford, 312-996-1946, Fax: 312-996-1022, E-mail: cmstan60@uic.edu.

College of Education Students: 263 full-time (199 women), 417 part-time (295 women); includes 280 minority (115 Black or African American, non-Hispanic/Latino; 42 Asian, non-Hispanic/Latino; 110 Hispanic/Latino; 13 Two or more races, non-Hispanic/Latino), 28 international. Average age 34. 333 applicants, 54% accepted, 117 enrolled. *Faculty:* 50 full-time (30 women), 16 part-time/adjunct (13 women). *Financial support:* In 2015–16, 118 students received support, including 5 fellowships with full tuition reimbursements available; research assistantships with full tuition reimbursements available, teaching assistantships with full tuition reimbursements available, career-related internships or fieldwork, Federal Work-Study, institutionally sponsored loans, traineeships, tuition waivers (full), and unspecified assistantships also available. Support available to part-time students. Financial award application deadline: 3/1; financial award applicants required to submit FAFSA. In 2015, 197 master's, 25 doctorates awarded. *Degree program information:* Part-time and evening/weekend programs available. Part-time, evening/weekend. Offers curriculum studies (PhD); early childhood education (M Ed); education (M Ed, Ed D, PhD); educational psychology (PhD); elementary education (M Ed); measurement, evaluation, statistics, and assessment (M Ed); policy studies (M Ed); policy studies in urban education (PhD); secondary education (M Ed); special education (M Ed, PhD); urban education leadership (Ed D); youth development (M Ed). *Application deadline:* For fall admission, 1/9 for domestic and international students; for spring admission, 10/1 for domestic and international students. Applications are processed on a rolling basis. *Application fee:* $40 ($50 for international students). Electronic applications accepted. *Application Contact:* Receptionist, 312-413-2550, E-mail: gradcoll@uic.edu. *Interim Dean*, Prof. Alfred Tatum, 312-996-5641, E-mail: atatum1@uic.edu.

College of Engineering Students: 1,336 full-time (358 women), 293 part-time (62 women); includes 175 minority (24 Black or African American, non-Hispanic/Latino; 1 American Indian or Alaska Native, non-Hispanic/Latino; 96 Asian, non-Hispanic/Latino; 49 Hispanic/Latino; 5 Two or more races, non-Hispanic/Latino), 1,200 international. Average age 26. 4,135 applicants, 46% accepted, 625 enrolled. *Faculty:* 132 full-time (28 women), 56 part-time/adjunct (7 women). *Financial support:* In 2015–16, 19 fellowships with full tuition reimbursements were awarded; research assistantships with full tuition reimbursements, teaching assistantships with full tuition reimbursements, career-related internships or fieldwork, Federal Work-Study, scholarships/grants, traineeships, tuition waivers (full), and unspecified assistantships also available. Financial award application deadline: 3/1; financial award applicants required to submit FAFSA. In 2015, 334 master's, 65 doctorates awarded. *Degree program information:* Part-time and evening/weekend programs available. Part-time, evening/weekend. Offers bioengineering (MS, PhD); chemical engineering (MS, PhD); civil and materials engineering (MS, PhD); computer science (MS, PhD); electrical and computer engineering (MS, PhD); energy engineering (MEE); engineering (M Eng, MEE, MS, PhD); fluids engineering (MS, PhD); industrial engineering (MS, PhD); industrial engineering and operations research (PhD); mechanical analysis and design (MS, PhD); mechanical engineering (MS, PhD); thermomechanical and power engineering (MS, PhD). *Application deadline:* For fall admission, 5/15 for domestic students, 1/9 for international students; for spring admission, 11/1 for domestic students. Applications are processed on a rolling basis. *Application fee:* $60. Electronic applications accepted. *Application Contact:* Receptionist, 312-413-2550, E-mail: gradcoll@uic.edu. *Dean*, Prof. Peter C. Nelson, 312-996-2400.

College of Liberal Arts and Sciences Students: 1,055 full-time (517 women), 181 part-time (95 women); includes 235 minority (44 Black or African American, non-Hispanic/Latino; 1 American Indian or Alaska Native, non-Hispanic/Latino; 51 Asian, non-Hispanic/Latino; 113 Hispanic/Latino; 2 Native Hawaiian or other Pacific Islander, non-Hispanic/Latino; 24 Two or more races, non-Hispanic/Latino), 368 international. Average age 30. 2,059 applicants, 23% accepted, 239 enrolled. *Faculty:* 510 full-time (227 women), 122 part-time/adjunct (46 women). *Financial support:* Fellowships with full tuition reimbursements, research assistantships with full tuition reimbursements, teaching assistantships with full tuition reimbursements, career-related internships or fieldwork, Federal Work-Study, institutionally sponsored loans, scholarships/grants, traineeships, tuition waivers (full), and unspecified assistantships available. Support available to part-time students. Financial award application deadline: 3/1; financial award applicants required to submit FAFSA. In 2015, 165 master's, 126 doctorates awarded. *Degree program information:* Part-time and evening/weekend programs available. Part-time, evening/weekend. Offers anthropology (MA, PhD); biological sciences (MS, PhD); chemistry (MS, PhD); communication (MA, PhD); criminology, law, and justice (MA, PhD); earth and environmental sciences (MS, PhD); economics (MA, PhD); English (MA, PhD); environmental and urban geography (MA); history (MA, MAT, PhD); Latin American and Latino studies (MA); liberal arts and sciences (MA, MAT, MS, MST, DA, PhD); mathematics (DA); philosophy (MA, PhD); physics (MS, PhD); political science

(MA, PhD); probability and statistics (PhD); psychology (MA, PhD); secondary school mathematics (MST); sociology (MA, PhD); statistics (MS). *Application deadline:* For fall admission, 5/15 for domestic students, 2/15 for international students; for spring admission, 11/1 for domestic students, 7/15 for international students. Applications are processed on a rolling basis. *Application fee:* $60 ($50 for international students). Electronic applications accepted. *Application Contact:* Receptionist, 312-413-2550, E-mail: gradcoll@uic.edu. *Dean*, Prof. Astrida Orle Tantillo, 312-413-7329, E-mail: tantillo@uic.edu.

School of Literatures, Cultural Studies and Linguistics Students: 96 full-time (63 women), 31 part-time (18 women); includes 30 minority (1 Black or African American, non-Hispanic/Latino; 5 Asian, non-Hispanic/Latino; 22 Hispanic/Latino; 2 Two or more races, non-Hispanic/Latino), 38 international. Average age 31. *Faculty:* 64 full-time (48 women), 80 part-time/adjunct (55 women). *Financial support:* In 2015–16, 2 fellowships with full tuition reimbursements were awarded; research assistantships with full tuition reimbursements, teaching assistantships with full tuition reimbursements, career-related internships or fieldwork, Federal Work-Study, scholarships/grants, traineeships, tuition waivers (full), and unspecified assistantships also available. Financial award application deadline: 3/15; financial award applicants required to submit FAFSA. *Degree program information:* Part-time programs available. Part-time. Offers French and Francophone studies (MA); Germanic studies (MA, PhD); Hispanic and Italian studies (MAT, PhD); Hispanic linguistics (PhD); linguistics (MA); Slavic and Baltic languages and literatures (MA); Slavic and Baltic languages and literatures (PhD); Slavic studies (MA, PhD). *Application deadline:* For fall admission, 1/1 priority date for domestic and international students. Applications are processed on a rolling basis. *Application fee:* $60. Electronic applications accepted. *Director*, Prof. Imke Meyer, 312-413-2137, Fax: 312-413-1044, E-mail: ixmeyer@uic.edu.

College of Medicine Students: 1,382 full-time (655 women), 199 part-time (120 women); includes 763 minority (132 Black or African American, non-Hispanic/Latino; 3 American Indian or Alaska Native, non-Hispanic/Latino; 329 Asian, non-Hispanic/Latino; 245 Hispanic/Latino; 2 Native Hawaiian or other Pacific Islander, non-Hispanic/Latino; 52 Two or more races, non-Hispanic/Latino), 76 international. Average age 27. 1,048 applicants, 74% accepted, 362 enrolled. *Faculty:* 622 full-time (238 women), 350 part-time/adjunct (91 women). *Financial support:* Fellowships, research assistantships, teaching assistantships, career-related internships or fieldwork, institutionally sponsored loans, and tuition waivers (full) available. In 2015, 35 master's, 321 doctorates awarded. *Degree program information:* Part-time programs available. Part-time. Offers anatomy and cell biology (MS); biochemistry and molecular genetics (PhD); medical education (MHPE); medicine (MHPE, MS, MD, PhD); microbiology and immunology (PhD); pharmacology (PhD); physiology and biophysics (MS, PhD); surgery (MS). *Application deadline:* For fall admission, 12/1 for domestic and international students. *Application fee:* $60. *Application Contact:* Jackie Perry, Graduate College Receptionist, 312-413-2550, Fax: 312-413-0185, E-mail: gradcoll@uic.edu. *Head*, Dr. Dimitri T. Azar, 312-996-3500, Fax: 312-996-9006, E-mail: dtazar@uic.edu.

College of Nursing Students: 379 full-time (345 women), 544 part-time (487 women); includes 243 minority (70 Black or African American, non-Hispanic/Latino; 87 Asian, non-Hispanic/Latino; 71 Hispanic/Latino; 1 Native Hawaiian or other Pacific Islander, non-Hispanic/Latino; 14 Two or more races, non-Hispanic/Latino), 39 international. Average age 33. 425 applicants, 53% accepted, 151 enrolled. *Faculty:* 103 full-time (93 women), 88 part-time/adjunct (81 women). *Financial support:* In 2015–16, 3 fellowships with full tuition reimbursements were awarded; research assistantships with full tuition reimbursements, teaching assistantships with full tuition reimbursements, career-related internships or fieldwork, Federal Work-Study, institutionally sponsored loans, scholarships/grants, traineeships, tuition waivers (full and partial), and unspecified assistantships also available. Support available to part-time students. Financial award application deadline: 3/1; financial award applicants required to submit FAFSA. In 2015, 193 master's, 29 doctorates, 4 other advanced degrees awarded. *Degree program information:* Part-time programs available. Part-time. Offers acute care clinical nurse specialist (MS); administrative nursing leadership (Certificate); adult nurse practitioner (MS); adult/geriatric nurse practitioner (MS); advanced community health nurse specialist (MS); family nurse practitioner (MS); geriatric clinical nurse specialist (MS); geriatric nurse practitioner (MS); nurse midwifery (MS); nursing (MS, DNP, PhD, Certificate); nursing practice (DNP); nursing science (PhD); occupational health/advanced community health nurse specialist (MS); occupational health/family nurse practitioner (MS); pediatric nurse practitioner (MS); perinatal clinical nurse specialist (MS); school/advanced community health nurse specialist (MS); school/family nurse practitioner (MS); women's health nurse practitioner (MS). *Application deadline:* For fall admission, 5/15 for domestic students, 2/1 for international students; for spring admission, 10/15 for domestic students. Applications are processed on a rolling basis. *Application fee:* $60 ($50 for international students). Electronic applications accepted. *Application Contact:* Receptionist, 312-413-2550, E-mail: gradcoll@uic.edu. *Dean*, Dr. Terri E. Weaver, 312-996-7808, Fax: 312-996-8066, E-mail: teweaver@uic.edu.

College of Pharmacy Students: 894 full-time (532 women), 22 part-time (11 women); includes 434 minority (51 Black or African American, non-Hispanic/Latino; 1 American Indian or Alaska Native, non-Hispanic/Latino; 307 Asian, non-Hispanic/Latino; 49 Hispanic/Latino; 3 Native Hawaiian or other Pacific Islander, non-Hispanic/Latino; 23 Two or more races, non-Hispanic/Latino), 80 international. Average age 26. 821 applicants, 39% accepted, 226 enrolled. *Faculty:* 241 full-time (146 women), 56 part-time/adjunct (24 women). *Financial support:* Fellowships, research assistantships, teaching assistantships, career-related internships or fieldwork, institutionally sponsored loans, and tuition waivers (full) available. In 2015, 8 master's, 214 doctorates awarded. Offers biopharmaceutical sciences (MS, PhD); forensic science (MS); medicinal chemistry (MS); pharmacognosy (MS, PhD); pharmacy (MS, PhD, Pharm D); pharmacy administration (MS, PhD). *Application fee:* $60. *Application Contact:* Jackie Perry, Graduate College Receptionist, 312-413-2550, Fax: 312-413-0185, E-mail: gradcoll@uic.edu. *Dean*, Dr. Jerry Bauman, 312-996-7240, E-mail: jbauman@uic.edu.

College of Urban Planning and Public Affairs Students: 244 full-time (130 women), 112 part-time (62 women); includes 103 minority (44 Black or African American, non-Hispanic/Latino; 1 American Indian or Alaska Native, non-Hispanic/Latino; 15 Asian, non-Hispanic/Latino; 38 Hispanic/Latino; 5 Two or more races, non-Hispanic/Latino), 90 international. Average age 29. 432 applicants, 79% accepted, 156 enrolled. *Faculty:* 27 full-time (10 women), 14 part-time/adjunct (5 women). *Financial support:* In 2015–16, 1 fellowship with full tuition reimbursement was awarded; research assistantships with full tuition reimbursements, teaching assistantships with full tuition reimbursements, career-related internships or fieldwork, Federal Work-Study, scholarships/grants, traineeships, tuition waivers (full), and unspecified assistantships also available. Financial award application deadline: 3/1; financial award applicants required to submit FAFSA. In 2015, 119 master's, 6 doctorates awarded. *Degree program information:* Part-time and evening/weekend programs available. Part-time, evening/weekend. Offers public administration (MPA, PhD); urban planning and policy (MUPP, PhD); urban planning and public affairs (MPA, MUPP, PhD). *Application deadline:* For fall admission, 1/1 for domestic and international students; for spring admission, 11/1 for domestic students, 7/15 for international students. Applications are processed on a rolling basis. *Application fee:* $60. Electronic applications accepted. *Application Contact:* Receptionist, 312-413-2550, E-mail: gradcoll@uic.edu. *Dean*, Prof. Michael A. Pagano, 312-413-8088, E-mail: mapagano@uic.edu.

Jane Addams College of Social Work Students: 390 full-time (335 women), 85 part-time (65 women); includes 202 minority (72 Black or African American, non-Hispanic/Latino; 1 American Indian or Alaska Native, non-Hispanic/Latino; 22 Asian, non-Hispanic/Latino; 93 Hispanic/Latino; 1 Native Hawaiian or other Pacific Islander, non-Hispanic/Latino; 13 Two or more races, non-Hispanic/Latino), 8 international. Average age 28. 911 applicants, 46% accepted, 231 enrolled. *Faculty:* 25 full-time (16 women), 18 part-time/adjunct (16 women). *Financial support:* Fellowships with full tuition reimbursements, research assistantships with full tuition reimbursements, teaching assistantships with full tuition reimbursements, Federal Work-Study, scholarships/grants, traineeships, tuition waivers (full), and unspecified assistantships available. Financial award applicants required to submit FAFSA. In 2015, 235 master's, 5 doctorates, 12 other advanced degrees awarded. *Degree program information:* Part-time programs available. Part-time. Offers social work (MSW, PhD, Certificate). *Application deadline:* For fall admission, 2/1 priority date for domestic and international students. Applications are processed on a rolling basis. *Application fee:* $60. Electronic applications accepted. *Application Contact:* Dr. Edward Potts, Director of Admissions and Financial Aid, 312-996-3218, E-mail: epotts@uic.edu. *Dean*, Dr. Creasie Finney Hairston, 312-996-3219.

Liautaud Graduate School of Business Students: 594 full-time (268 women), 239 part-time (97 women); includes 124 minority (25 Black or African American, non-Hispanic/Latino; 59 Asian, non-Hispanic/Latino; 37 Hispanic/Latino; 3 Two or more races, non-Hispanic/Latino), 462 international. Average age 28. 1,970 applicants, 44% accepted, 345 enrolled. *Faculty:* 88 full-time (30 women), 29 part-time/adjunct (10 women). *Financial support:* In 2015–16, 8 fellowships with full tuition reimbursements were awarded; research assistantships with full tuition reimbursements, teaching assistantships with full tuition reimbursements, career-related internships or fieldwork, Federal Work-Study, institutionally sponsored loans, traineeships, tuition waivers (full), and unspecified assistantships also available. Support available to part-time students. Financial award application deadline: 3/1; financial award applicants required to submit FAFSA. In 2015, 466 master's, 6 doctorates awarded. *Degree program information:* Part-time and evening/weekend programs available. Part-time, evening/weekend. Offers accounting (MS); business (MA, MBA, MS, PhD); business administration (MBA, PhD); finance (MS); management information systems (PhD); real estate (MA). *Application deadline:* For fall admission, 2/1 for domestic students, 2/15 for international students. *Application fee:* $60. Electronic applications accepted. *Application Contact:* Receptionist, 312-413-2550, E-mail: gradcoll@uic.edu. *Dean*, Prof. Michael Mikhail, 312-996-2671, E-mail: mmikhail@uic.edu.

Program in Learning Sciences Students: 23 full-time (12 women), 3 part-time (2 women); includes 4 minority (1 Black or African American, non-Hispanic/Latino; 1 Asian, non-Hispanic/Latino; 1 Hispanic/Latino; 1 Two or more races, non-Hispanic/Latino), 2 international. Average age 34. 9 applicants, 67% accepted, 2 enrolled. In 2015, 1 doctorate awarded. Offers learning sciences (PhD). *Application fee:* $60. *Application Contact:* Donald Wink, Director of Graduate Studies, 312-413-3901, E-mail: deana@uic.edu. *Graduate Program Chair*, Dr. Susan Goldman, 312-413-3901, E-mail: deana@uic.edu.

Program in Neuroscience Students: 17 full-time (11 women), 1 (woman) part-time; includes 4 minority (1 Asian, non-Hispanic/Latino; 2 Hispanic/Latino; 1 Two or more races, non-Hispanic/Latino), 1 international. Average age 28. 64 applicants, 6% accepted, 2 enrolled. *Faculty:* 1 (woman) full-time, 1 part-time/adjunct (0 women). In 2015, 1 master's, 4 doctorates awarded. Offers cellular and systems neuroscience and cell biology (PhD); neuroscience (MS). *Director of Graduate Studies*, Dr. John Larson, 312-996-7370, Fax: 312-423-3699, E-mail: uicneuroscience@uic.edu.

School of Public Health Students: 421 full-time (298 women), 384 part-time (284 women); includes 344 minority (115 Black or African American, non-Hispanic/Latino; 1 American Indian or Alaska Native, non-Hispanic/Latino; 118 Asian, non-Hispanic/Latino; 86 Hispanic/Latino; 2 Native Hawaiian or other Pacific Islander, non-Hispanic/Latino; 22 Two or more races, non-Hispanic/Latino), 75 international. Average age 32. 1,134 applicants, 53% accepted, 230 enrolled. *Faculty:* 67 full-time (40 women), 65 part-time/adjunct (33 women). *Financial support:* In 2015–16, 4 fellowships with full tuition reimbursements were awarded; research assistantships with full tuition reimbursements, teaching assistantships with full tuition reimbursements, career-related internships or fieldwork, Federal Work-Study, institutionally sponsored loans, scholarships/grants, traineeships, tuition waivers (full), and unspecified assistantships also available. Support available to part-time students. Financial award application deadline: 3/1; financial award applicants required to submit FAFSA. In 2015, 206 master's, 24 doctorates awarded. *Degree program information:* Part-time programs available. Part-time. Offers public health (MHA, MPH, MS, Dr PH, PhD). *Application deadline:* For fall admission, 2/1 for domestic students, 1/1 priority date for international students. Applications are processed on a rolling basis. *Application fee:* $60. Electronic applications accepted. *Application Contact:* Prof. Babette Neuberger, Associate Dean and Director of Graduate Studies, 312-996-5381, Fax: 312-996-1734, E-mail: bjn@uic.edu. *Dean*, Dr. Paul Brandt-Rauf, 312-996-6620.

Division of Community Health Sciences Students: 104 full-time (85 women), 73 part-time (65 women); includes 80 minority (32 Black or African American, non-Hispanic/Latino; 20 Asian, non-Hispanic/Latino; 22 Hispanic/Latino; 1 Native Hawaiian or other Pacific Islander, non-Hispanic/Latino; 5 Two or more races, non-Hispanic/Latino), 6 international. Average age 31. *Faculty:* 19 full-time (14 women), 7 part-time/adjunct (all women). *Financial support:* Fellowships with full tuition reimbursements, research assistantships with full tuition reimbursements, teaching assistantships with full tuition reimbursements, career-related internships or fieldwork, Federal Work-Study, institutionally sponsored loans, scholarships/grants, traineeships, and unspecified assistantships available. Support available to part-time students. Financial award application deadline: 3/1; financial award applicants required to submit FAFSA. *Degree program information:* Part-time programs available. Part-time. Offers community health sciences (MPH, MS, Dr PH, PhD). *Application deadline:* For fall admission, 2/1 for domestic students, 1/1 priority date for international students. Applications are processed on a rolling basis. *Application fee:* $60. Electronic applications accepted. *Application Contact:* David Brand, Academic Coordinator, 312-996-8940, Fax: 312-996-3551, E-mail: dbrand@uic.edu. *Director*, Prof. Jesus Ramirez-Valles, 312-996-6346, E-mail: valles@uic.edu.

Division of Environmental and Occupational Health Sciences Students: 52 full-time (28 women), 10 part-time (8 women); includes 27 minority (12 Black or African American, non-Hispanic/Latino; 4 Asian, non-Hispanic/Latino; 9 Hispanic/Latino; 2 Two or more races, non-Hispanic/Latino), 15 international. Average age 31. *Faculty:*

11 full-time (7 women), 16 part-time/adjunct (6 women). *Financial support:* Fellowships with full tuition reimbursements, research assistantships with full tuition reimbursements, teaching assistantships with full tuition reimbursements, career-related internships or fieldwork, Federal Work-Study, institutionally sponsored loans, scholarships/grants, traineeships, and unspecified assistantships available. Support available to part-time students. Financial award application deadline: 3/1; financial award applicants required to submit FAFSA. *Degree program information:* Part-time programs available. Part-time. Offers environmental and occupational health sciences (MPH, MS, Dr PH, PhD). *Application deadline:* For fall admission, 2/1 for domestic students, 1/1 priority date for international students. *Application fee:* $60. Electronic applications accepted. *Director,* Prof. Linda Forst, 312-355-3826, E-mail: forst-l@uic.edu.

Division of Health Policy and Administration Students: 129 full-time (88 women), 149 part-time (102 women); includes 140 minority (39 Black or African American, non-Hispanic/Latino; 59 Asian, non-Hispanic/Latino; 34 Hispanic/Latino; 1 Native Hawaiian or other Pacific Islander, non-Hispanic/Latino; 7 Two or more races, non-Hispanic/Latino), 18 international. Average age 32. *Faculty:* 16 full-time (9 women), 18 part-time/adjunct (7 women). *Financial support:* In 2015–16, 4 fellowships with full tuition reimbursements were awarded; research assistantships with full tuition reimbursements, teaching assistantships with full tuition reimbursements, career-related internships or fieldwork, Federal Work-Study, institutionally sponsored loans, scholarships/grants, traineeships, and unspecified assistantships also available. Support available to part-time students. Financial award application deadline: 3/1; financial award applicants required to submit FAFSA. *Degree program information:* Part-time programs available. Part-time. Offers clinical and translational science (MS); health policy (PhD); health services research (PhD); healthcare administration (MHA); public health policy management (MPH). *Application deadline:* For fall admission, 2/1 for domestic students, 1/1 priority date for international students. *Application fee:* $60. Electronic applications accepted. *Application Contact:* Aimee Wiebel, Academic Coordinator, 312-996-7816, Fax: 312-996-5356, E-mail: aimee@uic.edu. *Director,* Prof. Jack Zwanziger, 312-996-1062, Fax: 312-996-5356, E-mail: jzwanzig@uic.edu.

Epidemiology and Biostatistics Division Students: 132 full-time (93 women), 58 part-time (43 women); includes 50 minority (12 Black or African American, non-Hispanic/Latino; 26 Asian, non-Hispanic/Latino; 10 Hispanic/Latino; 2 Two or more races, non-Hispanic/Latino), 32 international. Average age 30. *Faculty:* 17 full-time (7 women), 12 part-time/adjunct (5 women). *Financial support:* In 2015–16, 17 students received support. Fellowships with full tuition reimbursements available, research assistantships with full tuition reimbursements available, teaching assistantships with full tuition reimbursements available, career-related internships or fieldwork, Federal Work-Study, institutionally sponsored loans, scholarships/grants, traineeships, tuition waivers (full), and unspecified assistantships available. Support available to part-time students. Financial award application deadline: 3/1; financial award applicants required to submit FAFSA. *Degree program information:* Part-time programs available. Part-time. Offers biostatistics (MPH, MS, PhD); epidemiology (MPH, MS, PhD). *Application deadline:* For fall admission, 2/1 for domestic students, 1/1 priority date for international students. *Application fee:* $60. Electronic applications accepted. *Division Director,* Dr. Ronald Hershow, 312-996-4759, E-mail: rchersho@uic.edu.

UNIVERSITY OF ILLINOIS AT SPRINGFIELD, Springfield, IL 62703-5407

General Information State-supported, coed, comprehensive institution. CGS member. *Enrollment:* 5,402 graduate, professional, and undergraduate students; 1,050 full-time matriculated graduate/professional students (431 women), 1,261 part-time matriculated graduate/professional students (587 women). *Enrollment by degree level:* 2,257 master's, 27 doctoral, 27 other advanced degrees. *Graduate faculty:* 111 full-time (50 women), 39 part-time/adjunct (14 women). Tuition, state resident: part-time $329 per credit hour. Tuition, nonresident: part-time $675 per credit hour. *Graduate housing:* Rooms and/or apartments available on a first-come, first-served basis to single and married students. Housing application deadline: 5/1. *Student services:* Campus employment opportunities, campus safety program, career counseling, child daycare facilities, exercise/wellness program, free psychological counseling, international student services, low-cost health insurance, multicultural affairs office, services for students with disabilities, teacher training, writing training. *Library:* Norris L Brookens Library plus 1 other. *Collection:* Books: 486,917 (physical), 213,380 (digital/electronic); Serial titles: 495 (physical), 68,741 (digital/electronic); Databases: 313. Weekly public service hours: 90; students can reserve study rooms. *Research affiliation:* Interuniversity Consortium for Political and Social Research, Council of Undergraduate Research.

Computer facilities: 550 computers available on campus for general student use. A campuswide network can be accessed from student residence rooms and from off campus. Online class registration is available.
Website: http://www.uis.edu/

General Application Contact: Dr. Cecelia Cornell, Associate Vice Chancellor for Graduate Education, 888-977-4847, Fax: 217-206-7230, E-mail: ccorn1@uis.edu.

GRADUATE UNITS

Graduate Programs Students: 1,050 full-time (431 women), 1,261 part-time (587 women); includes 352 minority (168 Black or African American, non-Hispanic/Latino; 5 American Indian or Alaska Native, non-Hispanic/Latino; 89 Asian, non-Hispanic/Latino; 65 Hispanic/Latino; 25 Two or more races, non-Hispanic/Latino), 881 international. Average age 30. 2,929 applicants, 50% accepted, 746 enrolled. *Faculty:* 111 full-time (50 women), 39 part-time/adjunct (14 women). *Financial support:* In 2015–16, 3 fellowships with full tuition reimbursements (averaging $9,900 per year), 10 research assistantships with full tuition reimbursements (averaging $9,956 per year), 7 teaching assistantships with full tuition reimbursements (averaging $9,956 per year) were awarded; career-related internships or fieldwork, Federal Work-Study, scholarships/grants, health care benefits, and unspecified assistantships also available. Support available to part-time students. Financial award application deadline: 11/15; financial award applicants required to submit FAFSA. In 2015, 776 master's, 1 doctorate, 39 other advanced degrees awarded. *Degree program information:* Part-time and evening/weekend programs available. Part-time, evening/weekend, 100% online, blended/hybrid learning. *Application deadline:* Applications are processed on a rolling basis. *Application fee:* $60 ($75 for international students). Electronic applications accepted. *Application Contact:* Dr. Cecelia Cornell, Associate Vice Chancellor for Graduate Education, 888-977-4847, Fax: 217-206-7230, E-mail: ccorn1@uis.edu. *Office of Graduate Studies,* Dr. Lynn Pardie, 800-252-8533, Fax: 217-206-7623, E-mail: lpard1@uis.edu.

College of Business and Management Students: 424 full-time (154 women), 261 part-time (92 women); includes 87 minority (31 Black or African American, non-Hispanic/Latino; 1 American Indian or Alaska Native, non-Hispanic/Latino; 31 Asian, non-Hispanic/Latino; 18 Hispanic/Latino; 1 Native Hawaiian or other Pacific Islander, non-Hispanic/Latino; 5 Two or more races, non-Hispanic/Latino), 368 international. Average age 29. 986 applicants, 55% accepted, 215 enrolled. *Faculty:* 21 full-time (3 women), 12 part-time/adjunct (4 women). *Financial support:* In 2015–16, fellowships with full tuition reimbursements (averaging $9,900 per year), research assistantships with full tuition reimbursements (averaging $9,956 per year), teaching assistantships with full tuition reimbursements (averaging $9,956 per year) were awarded; career-related internships or fieldwork, Federal Work-Study, scholarships/grants, health care benefits, and unspecified assistantships also available. Support available to part-time students. Financial award application deadline: 11/15; financial award applicants required to submit FAFSA. In 2015, 176 master's awarded. *Degree program information:* Part-time and evening/weekend programs available. Part-time, evening/weekend, 100% online, blended/hybrid learning. Offers accountancy (MA); business administration (MBA); business and management (MA, MBA, MS); management information systems (MS). *Application deadline:* Applications are processed on a rolling basis. *Application fee:* $60 ($75 for international students). Electronic applications accepted. *Application Contact:* Dr. Lynn Pardie, Office of Graduate Studies, 800-252-8533, Fax: 217-206-7623, E-mail: lpard1@uis.edu. *Dean,* Dr. Ronald McNeil, 217-206-6534, Fax: 217-206-7541, E-mail: rmcne1@uis.edu.

College of Education and Human Services Students: 62 full-time (50 women), 223 part-time (167 women); includes 52 minority (36 Black or African American, non-Hispanic/Latino; 1 American Indian or Alaska Native, non-Hispanic/Latino; 1 Asian, non-Hispanic/Latino; 9 Hispanic/Latino; 5 Two or more races, non-Hispanic/Latino), 1 international. Average age 34. 142 applicants, 42% accepted, 47 enrolled. *Faculty:* 16 full-time (10 women), 12 part-time/adjunct (7 women). *Financial support:* In 2015–16, fellowships with full tuition reimbursements (averaging $9,900 per year), research assistantships with full tuition reimbursements (averaging $9,956 per year), teaching assistantships with full tuition reimbursements (averaging $9,956 per year) were awarded; career-related internships or fieldwork, Federal Work-Study, scholarships/grants, health care benefits, and unspecified assistantships also available. Support available to part-time students. Financial award application deadline: 11/15; financial award applicants required to submit FAFSA. In 2015, 118 master's, 8 other advanced degrees awarded. *Degree program information:* Part-time and evening/weekend programs available. Part-time, evening/weekend, 100% online, blended/hybrid learning. Offers alcohol and substance abuse (Graduate Certificate); alcoholism and substance abuse (MA); chief school business official endorsement (CAS); child and family services (MA); education and human services (MA, CAS, Certificate, Graduate Certificate); educational leadership (MA, CAS); English as a second language (Graduate Certificate); gerontology (MA); human development counseling (MA); legal aspects of education (Graduate Certificate); social services administration (MA); superintendent endorsement (CAS); teacher leadership (MA). *Application deadline:* Applications are processed on a rolling basis. *Application fee:* $60 ($75 for international students). Electronic applications accepted. *Application Contact:* Dr. Lynn Pardie, Office of Graduate Studies, 800-252-8533, Fax: 217-206-7623, E-mail: lpard1@uis.edu. *Dean,* Dr. Hanfu Mi, 217-206-6784, Fax: 217-206-6775, E-mail: hmi2@uis.edu.

College of Liberal Arts and Sciences Students: 445 full-time (160 women), 396 part-time (106 women); includes 86 minority (28 Black or African American, non-Hispanic/Latino; 2 American Indian or Alaska Native, non-Hispanic/Latino; 39 Asian, non-Hispanic/Latino; 12 Hispanic/Latino; 5 Two or more races, non-Hispanic/Latino), 477 international. Average age 28. 1,313 applicants, 52% accepted, 352 enrolled. *Faculty:* 40 full-time (20 women), 7 part-time/adjunct (0 women). *Financial support:* In 2015–16, fellowships with full tuition reimbursements (averaging $9,900 per year), research assistantships with full tuition reimbursements (averaging $9,956 per year), teaching assistantships with full tuition reimbursements (averaging $9,956 per year) were awarded; career-related internships or fieldwork, Federal Work-Study, scholarships/grants, health care benefits, and unspecified assistantships also available. Support available to part-time students. Financial award application deadline: 11/15; financial award applicants required to submit FAFSA. In 2015, 320 master's, 1 other advanced degree awarded. *Degree program information:* Part-time and evening/weekend programs available. Part-time, evening/weekend, 100% online, blended/hybrid learning. Offers biology (MS); communication (MA); computer science (MS); English (MA); history (MA); liberal and integrative studies (MA); liberal arts and sciences (MA, MS, Graduate Certificate); teaching English (Graduate Certificate). *Application deadline:* Applications are processed on a rolling basis. *Application fee:* $60 ($75 for international students). Electronic applications accepted. *Application Contact:* Dr. Lynn Pardie, Office of Graduate Studies, 800-252-8533, Fax: 217-206-7623, E-mail: lpard1@uis.edu. *Dean,* Dr. James Ermatinger, 217-206-6512, Fax: 217-206-6217, E-mail: jerma2@uis.edu.

College of Public Affairs and Administration Students: 119 full-time (67 women), 381 part-time (222 women); includes 128 minority (73 Black or African American, non-Hispanic/Latino; 1 American Indian or Alaska Native, non-Hispanic/Latino; 18 Asian, non-Hispanic/Latino; 26 Hispanic/Latino; 10 Two or more races, non-Hispanic/Latino), 35 international. Average age 33. 488 applicants, 36% accepted, 132 enrolled. *Faculty:* 34 full-time (17 women), 7 part-time/adjunct (3 women). *Financial support:* In 2015–16, fellowships with full tuition reimbursements (averaging $9,900 per year), research assistantships with full tuition reimbursements (averaging $9,956 per year), teaching assistantships with full tuition reimbursements (averaging $9,956 per year) were awarded; career-related internships or fieldwork, Federal Work-Study, scholarships/grants, health care benefits, and unspecified assistantships also available. Support available to part-time students. Financial award application deadline: 11/15; financial award applicants required to submit FAFSA. In 2015, 162 master's, 1 doctorate, 30 other advanced degrees awarded. *Degree program information:* Part-time and evening/weekend programs available. Part-time, evening/weekend, 100% online, blended/hybrid learning. Offers community health education (Graduate Certificate); emergency preparedness and homeland security (Graduate Certificate); environmental science (MS); environmental studies (MA); epidemiology (Graduate Certificate); legal studies (MA); management of nonprofit organizations (Graduate Certificate); political science (MA); public administration (MPA, DPA); public affairs and administration (MA, MPA, MPH, MS, DPA, Graduate Certificate); public affairs reporting (MA); public health (MPH). *Application deadline:* Applications are processed on a rolling basis. *Application fee:* $60 ($75 for international students). Electronic applications accepted. *Application Contact:* Dr. Lynn Pardie, Office of Graduate Studies, 800-252-8533, Fax: 217-206-7623, E-mail: lpard1@uis.edu. *Interim Dean,* Dr. James Ermatinger, 217-206-6523, Fax: 217-206-7807, E-mail: cpaa@uis.edu.

UNIVERSITY OF ILLINOIS AT URBANA–CHAMPAIGN, Champaign, IL 61820

General Information State-supported, coed, university. CGS member. *Graduate housing:* Rooms and/or apartments available to single and married students. *Research affiliation:* Midwest Universities Research Association, Sandia National Laboratories, National Center for Atmospheric Research.

GRADUATE UNITS

College of Law Offers law (LL M, MCL, JD, JSD).

College of Veterinary Medicine Offers comparative biosciences (MS, PhD); pathobiology (MS, PhD); veterinary clinical medicine (MS, PhD); veterinary medical science (DVM); veterinary medicine (MS, DVM, PhD).

Graduate College

College of Agricultural, Consumer and Environmental Sciences Offers agricultural and applied economics (MS, PhD); agricultural and biological engineering (MS, PhD); agricultural education (MS); agricultural production (MS); agricultural, consumer and environmental sciences (MS, PSM, PhD); animal sciences (MS, PhD); bioenergy (PSM); bioinformatics: animal sciences (MS); bioinformatics: crop sciences (MS); crop sciences (MS, PhD); food science (MS); food science and human nutrition (MS, PhD); human and community development (MS, PhD); human nutrition (MS); natural resources and environmental science (MS, PhD); nutritional sciences (MS, PhD); technical systems management (MS, PSM).

College of Applied Health Sciences Offers applied health sciences (MA, MPH, MS, MSPH, Au D, PhD); audiology (Au D); community health (MS, MSPH, PhD); kinesiology (MS, PhD); public health (MPH); recreation, sport and tourism (MS, PhD); rehabilitation (MS); speech and hearing science (MA, PhD).

College of Business Online learning. Offers accountancy (MAS, MS, PhD); business (MAS, MBA, MS, PhD); business administration (MS, PhD); finance (MS, PhD); taxation (MS); technology management (MS).

College of Education Degree program information: Part-time programs available. Part-time, online learning. Offers curriculum and instruction (Ed M, MA, MS, Ed D, PhD, CAS); early childhood education (Ed M); education (Ed M, MA, MS, Ed D, PhD, CAS); educational organization and leadership (Ed M, MS, Ed D, PhD, CAS); educational policy studies (Ed M, MA, PhD); educational psychology (Ed M, MA, MS, PhD, CAS); elementary education (Ed M); human resource education (Ed M, MS, Ed D, PhD, CAS); secondary education (Ed M); special education (Ed M, MS, Ed D, PhD, CAS).

College of Engineering Degree program information: Part-time and evening/weekend programs available. Part-time, evening/weekend, online learning. Offers aerospace engineering (MS, PhD); bioengineering (MS, PhD); bioinformatics (MS); civil engineering (MS, PhD); computer science (MCS, MS, PhD); electrical and computer engineering (MS, PhD); energy systems (M Eng); engineering (M Eng, MCS, MS, PhD); environmental engineering in civil engineering (MS, PhD); financial engineering (MS); industrial engineering (MS, PhD); materials science and engineering (M Eng, MS, PhD); mechanical engineering (MS, PhD); nuclear, plasma, and radiological engineering (MS, PhD); physics (MS, PhD); systems and entrepreneurial engineering (MS, PhD); teaching of physics (MS); theoretical and applied mechanics (MS, PhD).

College of Fine and Applied Arts Offers architectural studies (MS); architecture (M Arch, PhD); art and design (MFA); art education (Ed M, MA, PhD); art history (MA, PhD); crafts (MFA); dance (MFA); fine and applied arts (Ed M, M Arch, M Mus, MA, MFA, MLA, MME, MS, MUP, AD, DMA, PhD); graphic design (MFA); industrial design (MFA); landscape architecture (MLA, PhD); metals (MFA); music (M Mus, AD, DMA); music education (MME, PhD); musicology (PhD); painting (MFA); photography (MFA); regional planning (PhD); sculpture (MFA); theatre (MA, MFA, PhD); urban planning (MUP).

College of Liberal Arts and Sciences Online learning. Offers African studies (MA); analytics (MS); animal biology (ecology, ethology and evolution) (MS, PhD); anthropology (MA, PhD); applied mathematics (MS); applied mathematics: actuarial science (MS); applied statistics (MS); astrochemistry (PhD); astronomy (MS, PhD); atmospheric sciences (MS, PhD); biochemistry (MS, PhD); bioinformatics: chemical and biomolecular engineering (MS); biophysics and computational biology (MS, PhD); cell and developmental biology (PhD); chemical engineering (MS, PhD); chemical physics (PhD); chemical sciences (MA, MS, PhD); chemistry (MA, MS, PhD); classical philology (PhD); classics (MA); communication (MA, PhD); comparative literature (MA, PhD); creative writing (MFA); earth, society and environment (MA, MS, PhD); East Asian languages and cultures (PhD); East Asian studies (MA); ecology, evolution and conservation biology (MS, PhD); economics (MS, PhD); English (MA, PhD); entomology (MS, PhD); European Union studies (MA); French (MA, PhD); geography and geographic information science (MA, MS, PhD); geology (MS, PhD); German (MA, PhD); history (MA, PhD); integrative biology (MS, MST, PSM, PhD); Italian (MA, PhD); Latin American studies (MA); liberal arts and sciences (MA, MFA, MS, MST, PSM, PhD); linguistics (MA, PhD); literatures, cultures and linguistics (MA, MS, PhD); mathematics (MS, PhD); microbiology (MS, PhD); molecular and cellular biology (MS, PhD); molecular and integrative physiology (MS, PhD); neuroscience (PhD); philosophy (MA, PhD); plant biology (MS, PhD); plant biotechnology (PSM); policy economics (MS); political science (MA, PhD); Portuguese (MA, PhD); psychology (MA, MS, PhD); religious studies (MA); romance linguistics (PhD); Russian, East European, and Eurasian studies (MA); second language acquisition and teacher education (PhD); Slavic languages and literatures (MA, PhD); sociology (MA, PhD); south Asian and Middle Eastern studies (MA); Spanish (MA, PhD); statistics (MS, PhD); teaching of chemistry (MS); teaching of earth sciences (MS); teaching of English as a second language (MA); teaching of Latin (MA); teaching of mathematics (MS); translation and interpreting (MA).

College of Media Offers advertising (MS); communications and media (PhD); journalism (MS); media (MS, PhD).

Graduate School of Library and Information Science Degree program information: Part-time programs available. Part-time, online learning. Offers bioinformatics (MS); digital libraries (CAS); library and information science (MS, PhD, CAS).

School of Labor and Employment Relations Offers human resources and industrial relations (MHRIR, PhD).

School of Social Work Offers advocacy, leadership, and social change (MSW); children, youth and family services (MSW); health care (MSW); mental health (MSW); school social work (MSW); social work (PhD).

Informatics Institute Offers informatics (PhD).

UNIVERSITY OF INDIANAPOLIS, Indianapolis, IN 46227-3697

General Information Independent-religious, coed, comprehensive institution. CGS member. *Graduate housing:* Rooms and/or apartments available on a first-come, first-served basis to single and married students.

GRADUATE UNITS

Graduate Programs *Degree program information:* Part-time and evening/weekend programs available. Part-time, evening/weekend, online learning.

Center for Aging and Community Degree program information: Part-time and evening/weekend programs available. Part-time, evening/weekend, online learning. Offers gerontology (MS, Certificate).

College of Arts and Sciences Degree program information: Part-time and evening/weekend programs available. Part-time, evening/weekend. Offers anthropology (MS); applied sociology (MA); art (MA); arts and sciences (MA, MS); English (MA); history (MA); human biology (MS); international relations (MA).

College of Health Sciences Offers health sciences (MHS, MOT, MPH, MS, DHS, DPT, OTD); occupational therapy (MOT, DHS, OTD); physical therapy (MHS, DHS, DPT); public health (MPH); sport management (MS).

School of Business Degree program information: Part-time and evening/weekend programs available. Part-time, evening/weekend. Offers business (EMBA, MBA, Graduate Certificate).

School of Education Degree program information: Part-time and evening/weekend programs available. Part-time, evening/weekend. Offers art education (MAT); biology (MAT); chemistry (MAT); curriculum and instruction (MA); earth sciences (MAT); education (MA, MAT); educational leadership (MA); elementary education (MA); English (MAT); French (MAT); math (MAT); physical education (MAT); physics (MAT); secondary education (MA); social studies (MAT); Spanish (MAT).

School of Nursing Offers advanced practice nursing (DNP); family nurse practitioner (MSN); gerontological nurse practitioner (MSN); neonatal nurse practitioner (MSN); nurse-midwifery (MSN); nursing (MSN); nursing and health systems leadership (MSN); nursing education (MSN); women's health nurse practitioner (MSN). Electronic applications accepted.

School of Psychological Sciences Offers clinical psychology (Psy D); clinical psychology/mental health counseling (MA).

THE UNIVERSITY OF IOWA, Iowa City, IA 52242-1316

General Information State-supported, coed, university. CGS member. *Graduate housing:* Rooms and/or apartments available on a first-come, first-served basis to single and married students.

GRADUATE UNITS

College of Dentistry Offers dental public health (MS); dentistry (MS, DDS, PhD, Certificate); endodontics (MS, Certificate); operative dentistry (MS, Certificate); oral and maxillofacial surgery (MS, PhD, Certificate); oral pathology, radiology and medicine (MS, PhD, Certificate); oral science (MS, PhD); orthodontics (MS, Certificate); pediatric dentistry (Certificate); periodontics (MS, Certificate); preventive and community dentistry (MS); prosthodontics (MS, Certificate).

College of Law Students: 395 full-time (165 women), 5 part-time (2 women); includes 78 minority (16 Black or African American, non-Hispanic/Latino; 1 American Indian or Alaska Native, non-Hispanic/Latino; 24 Asian, non-Hispanic/Latino; 24 Hispanic/Latino; 13 Two or more races, non-Hispanic/Latino), 29 international. Average age 25. 1,327 applicants, 44% accepted, 164 enrolled. *Faculty:* 34 full-time (11 women), 14 part-time/adjunct (4 women). *Financial support:* In 2015–16, 332 students received support, including 325 fellowships with partial tuition reimbursements available (averaging $17,907 per year), 94 research assistantships with partial tuition reimbursements available (averaging $2,175 per year); career-related internships or fieldwork, Federal Work-Study, scholarships/grants, and health care benefits also available. Financial award applicants required to submit FAFSA. In 2015, 7 master's, 146 doctorates awarded. Offers law (LL M, MSL, JD, SJD). *Application deadline:* For fall admission, 5/1 priority date for domestic students, 3/1 priority date for international students. Applications are processed on a rolling basis. *Application fee:* $0. Electronic applications accepted. *Application Contact:* Collins Byrd, Assistant Dean of Enrollment Management, 319-335-9095, Fax: 319-335-9646, E-mail: law-admissions@uiowa.edu. *Dean*, Gail Agrawal, 319-335-9034, Fax: 319-335-9019, E-mail: gail-agrawal@uiowa.edu.

College of Pharmacy Offers clinical pharmaceutical sciences (PhD); medicinal and natural products chemistry (PhD); pharmaceutics (PhD); pharmaceutical socioeconomics (PhD); pharmaceutics (MS); pharmacy (Pharm D). Electronic applications accepted.

Graduate College *Degree program information:* Part-time and evening/weekend programs available. Part-time, evening/weekend, online learning. Offers applied mathematical and computational sciences (PhD); bioinformatics (MS, PhD); bioinformatics and computational biology (Certificate); genetics (PhD); geoinformatics (MS, PhD, Certificate); health informatics (MS, PhD, Certificate); human toxicology (MS, PhD); immunology (PhD); information science (MS, PhD, Certificate); molecular and cellular biology (PhD); neuroscience (PhD); translational biomedicine (MS, PhD); urban and regional planning (MA, MS). Electronic applications accepted.

College of Education Offers art education (MA); counseling psychology (PhD); counselor education and supervision (PhD); couple and family therapy (PhD); developmental reading (MA); education (MA, MAT, MM, PhD); educational leadership (MA, PhD, Ed S); educational measurement and statistics (MA, PhD); educational psychology (MA, PhD); elementary education (MA); English education (MA, MAT); foreign and second language education (MAT); foreign language education (MA); foreign language/ESL education (PhD); higher education and student affairs (MA, PhD); language, literacy and culture (PhD); mathematics education (MA, MAT, PhD); music education (MM, PhD); rehabilitation and mental health counseling (MA); rehabilitation counselor education (PhD); school counseling (MA); school psychology (PhD, Ed S); schools, culture, and society (MA, PhD); science education (MA); secondary education (MA); social studies (MA, PhD); special education (MA, PhD). Electronic applications accepted.

College of Engineering Offers biomedical engineering (MS, PhD); chemical and biochemical engineering (MS, PhD); civil and environmental engineering (MS, PhD); electrical and computer engineering (MS, PhD); energy systems (MS, PhD); engineering (MS, PhD); engineering design (MS, PhD); engineering design and manufacturing (MS, PhD); fluid dynamics (MS, PhD); healthcare systems (MS, PhD); human factors (MS, PhD); information and engineering management (MS, PhD); materials and manufacturing (MS, PhD); operations research (MS, PhD); wind energy (MS, PhD). Electronic applications accepted.

College of Liberal Arts and Sciences Degree program information: Part-time programs available. Part-time, online learning. Offers actuarial science (MS); American studies (MA, PhD); anthropology (MA, PhD); art history (MA, PhD); astronomy (MS); athletic training (MS); biology (MS, PhD); cell and developmental biology (MS, PhD); chemistry (PhD); Chinese (MA); classics (MA, PhD); clinical exercise physiology (MS); communication sciences and disorders (MA, Au D, PhD); computer science (MCS, PhD); dance (MFA); earth and environmental science (MS, PhD); English (PhD); evolution (MS, PhD); film and video production (MFA); film studies (MA, PhD); French (MA, PhD); gender, women's and sexuality studies (Certificate); genetics (MS, PhD); geographical and sustainability sciences (MA, PhD,

Certificate); Greek (MA); health and human physiology (PhD); Hindi (MA); history (MA, PhD); interpersonal communication and relationships (MA, PhD); journalism and media communication (MA); Latin (MA); leisure studies (MA, PhD); liberal arts and sciences (MA, MCS, MFA, MS, MSW, Au D, DMA, PhD, Certificate); linguistics (MA, PhD); literary studies (MA); mass communication (PhD); mathematics (MS, PhD); media studies (MA, PhD); music (MA, MFA, DMA, PhD); neurobiology (MS, PhD); nonfiction writing (MFA); philosophy (PhD); physics (MS, PhD); political science (PhD); psychology (MA, PhD); religious studies (MA, PhD); rhetoric and public advocacy (MA, PhD); Sanskrit (MA); second language acquisition (PhD); social work (MSW, PhD); sociology (MA, PhD); South Asian studies (MA); Spanish (MA, PhD); Spanish creative writing (MFA); statistics (MS, PhD); strategic communication (MA); studio art (MA, MFA); theatre arts (MFA). Electronic applications accepted.

College of Nursing Offers nursing (MSN, DNP, PhD). Electronic applications accepted.

College of Public Health Offers agricultural safety and health (MS, PhD); biostatistics (MS, PhD, Certificate); clinical investigation (MS); community and behavioral health (MPH, MS, PhD); epidemiology (MPH, MS, PhD); ergonomics (MPH); health management and policy (MHA, PhD); industrial hygiene (MS, PhD); occupational and environmental health (MPH, MS, PhD, Certificate); public health (MHA, MPH, MS, PhD, Certificate); quantitative methods (MPH). Electronic applications accepted.

School of Library and Information Science Offers library and information science (MA, PhD). Electronic applications accepted.

Henry B. Tippie College of Business *Faculty:* 132 full-time (33 women), 76 part-time/adjunct (17 women). *Financial support:* Applicants required to submit FAFSA. Offers accounting (M Ac, PhD); business (EMBA, M Ac, MBA, MS, PhD); business administration (PhD); business analytics (MS); corporate finance (MBA); economics (PhD); finance (PhD); investment management (MBA); management (MBA); management and organizations (PhD); marketing (MBA). *Application deadline:* Applications are processed on a rolling basis. Electronic applications accepted. *Dean,* Prof. Sarah Fisher Gardial, 319-335-0862, Fax: 319-335-0860, E-mail: sarah-gardial@uiowa.edu.

Roy J. and Lucille A. Carver College of Medicine *Degree program information:* Part-time programs available. Part-time. Offers medicine (MA, MPAS, MS, DPT, MD, PhD). Electronic applications accepted.

Graduate Programs in Medicine Degree program information: Part-time programs available. Part-time. Offers anatomy and cell biology (PhD); biochemistry (MS, PhD); free radical and radiation biology (MS); general microbiology and microbial physiology (MS, PhD); immunology (MS, PhD); medicine (MA, MPAS, MS, DPT, PhD); microbial genetics (MS, PhD); molecular physiology and biophysics (MS, PhD); pathogenic bacteriology (MS, PhD); pathology (MS); pharmacology (MS, PhD); physical rehabilitation science (MA, PhD); physical therapy (DPT); physician assistant studies and services (MPAS); virology (MS, PhD). Electronic applications accepted.

UNIVERSITY OF JAMESTOWN, Jamestown, ND 58405

General Information Independent-religious, coed, comprehensive institution.

GRADUATE UNITS

Program in Education Offers curriculum and instruction (M Ed).

Program in Physical Therapy Offers physical therapy (DPT).

THE UNIVERSITY OF KANSAS, Lawrence, KS 66045

General Information State-supported, coed, university. CGS member. *Enrollment:* 27,259 graduate, professional, and undergraduate students; 5,762 full-time matriculated graduate/professional students (3,078 women), 2,032 part-time matriculated graduate/professional students (1,287 women). *Enrollment by degree level:* 3,311 master's, 4,344 doctoral, 139 other advanced degrees. *Graduate housing:* Rooms and/or apartments available on a first-come, first-served basis to single and married students. Housing application deadline: 3/1. *Student services:* Campus employment opportunities, campus safety program, career counseling, child daycare facilities, exercise/wellness program, free psychological counseling, grant writing training, international student services, low-cost health insurance, multicultural affairs office, services for students with disabilities, teacher training, writing training. *Library:* Watson Library plus 11 others. *Collection:* Books: 4.7 million (physical), 937,567 (digital/electronic). Weekly public service hours: 168; study areas open 24 hours, 5–7 days a week; students can reserve study rooms.

Computer facilities: 1,500 computers available on campus for general student use. A campuswide network can be accessed from student residence rooms and from off campus. Online class registration, online payments are available.
Website: http://www.ku.edu/

General Application Contact: Graduate Studies, 785-864-8040, Fax: 785-864-7209, E-mail: graduate@ku.edu.

GRADUATE UNITS

Graduate Studies Students: 3,498 full-time (1,840 women), 1,584 part-time (928 women); includes 673 minority (178 Black or African American, non-Hispanic/Latino; 49 American Indian or Alaska Native, non-Hispanic/Latino; 141 Asian, non-Hispanic/Latino; 137 Hispanic/Latino; 1 Native Hawaiian or other Pacific Islander, non-Hispanic/Latino; 167 Two or more races, non-Hispanic/Latino), 1,059 international. Average age 30. *Financial support:* Fellowships, research assistantships, teaching assistantships, career-related internships or fieldwork, Federal Work-Study, institutionally sponsored loans, scholarships/grants, traineeships, and unspecified assistantships available. Support available to part-time students. Financial award applicants required to submit FAFSA. *Degree program information:* Part-time and evening/weekend programs available. Part-time, evening/weekend, online learning. *Application fee:* $65 ($85 for international students). Electronic applications accepted. *Application Contact:* Assistant Dean, 785-864-8040, Fax: 785-864-7209, E-mail: graduate@ku.edu.

College of Liberal Arts and Sciences Students: 1,498 full-time (793 women), 224 part-time (111 women); includes 208 minority (47 Black or African American, non-Hispanic/Latino; 21 American Indian or Alaska Native, non-Hispanic/Latino; 39 Asian, non-Hispanic/Latino; 41 Hispanic/Latino; 1 Native Hawaiian or other Pacific Islander, non-Hispanic/Latino; 59 Two or more races, non-Hispanic/Latino), 375 international. Average age 30. 2,344 applicants, 35% accepted, 414 enrolled. *Financial support:* Fellowships, research assistantships with partial tuition reimbursements, teaching assistantships with tuition reimbursements, career-related internships or fieldwork, Federal Work-Study, institutionally sponsored loans, scholarships/grants, traineeships, and unspecified assistantships available. Support available to part-time students. Financial award applicants required to submit FAFSA. In 2015, 335 master's, 187 doctorates, 1 other advanced degree awarded. *Degree program information:* Part-time and evening/weekend programs available. Part-time, evening/weekend. Offers African and African-American studies (MA); African Studies (Graduate Certificate); American studies (MA, PhD); anthropology (MA, PhD); applied behavioral science (MA); art history (MA, PhD); atmospheric science (MS); behavioral psychology (PhD); biochemistry and biophysics (MA, PhD); botany (MA, PhD); Brazilian studies (Graduate Certificate); Central American and Mexican studies (Graduate Certificate); ceramics (MFA); chemistry (MS, PhD); child language (PhD); classics (MA); clinical child psychology (MA, PhD); clinical health and rehabilitation (PhD); cognitive psychology (PhD); communication studies (MA, PhD); computational biology (PhD); computational physics and astronomy (MS); creative writing (MFA); developmental psychology (PhD); drawing and painting (MFA); East Asian languages and cultures (MA); ecology and evolutionary biology (MA, PhD); economics (MA, PhD); English (MA, PhD); entomology (MA, PhD); film and media studies (MA, PhD); foreign area officer (MA); French (MA, PhD); geography (MA, PhD); geology (MS, PhD); German (MA, PhD); gerontology (MA, PhD, Graduate Certificate); global and international studies (MA); history (MA, PhD); indigenous studies (MA, Graduate Certificate); Latin American studies (MA); liberal arts and sciences (MA, MFA, MPA, MS, PhD, Graduate Certificate); linguistics (MA, PhD); mathematics (MA, PhD); metalsmithing/jewelry (MFA); microbiology (MA, PhD); molecular, cellular, and developmental biology (MA, PhD); museum studies (MA, Graduate Certificate); philosophy (MA, PhD); physics (MS, PhD); political science (MA, PhD); printmaking (MFA); public affairs and administration (MPA, PhD); quantitative psychology (PhD); religious studies (MA); Russian, East European and Eurasian studies (MA, Graduate Certificate); sculpture (MFA); Slavic languages and literatures (MA, PhD); social psychology (MA); sociology (MA, PhD); Spanish (MA, PhD); speech-language pathology (MA, PhD); textiles/fibers (MFA); theatre (MA, PhD); theatre design (MFA); visual art education (MA). *Application fee:* $65 ($85 for international students). Electronic applications accepted. *Application Contact:* Kristine Latta, Director of the College Office of Graduate Affairs, 785-864-1784, E-mail: klatta@ku.edu. *Interim Dean,* Don Steeples, 785-864-3661, E-mail: don@ku.edu.

School of Architecture, Design, and Planning Students: 161 full-time (79 women), 36 part-time (16 women); includes 20 minority (8 Black or African American, non-Hispanic/Latino; 1 Asian, non-Hispanic/Latino; 7 Hispanic/Latino; 4 Two or more races, non-Hispanic/Latino), 50 international. Average age 26. 166 applicants, 66% accepted, 39 enrolled. *Financial support:* Fellowships, research assistantships, teaching assistantships, career-related internships or fieldwork, scholarships/grants, health care benefits, and unspecified assistantships available. Financial award application deadline: 2/1; financial award applicants required to submit FAFSA. In 2015, 104 master's, 1 doctorate awarded. *Degree program information:* Part-time programs available. Part-time. Offers architecture (M Arch, MA, PhD); architecture, design, and planning (M Arch, MA, MFA, MUP, PhD, Certificate); design (MA, MFA); design management (MA); facility management (Certificate); interaction design (MA); urban planning (MUP). *Application deadline:* For fall admission, 3/1 priority date for domestic students, 2/1 priority date for international students; for spring admission, 11/1 priority date for domestic and international students. *Application fee:* $65 ($85 for international students). Electronic applications accepted. *Application Contact:* Gera Elliott, Admissions Coordinator, 785-864-3167, E-mail: archku@ku.edu. *Dean,* John C. Gaunt, 785-864-3114, E-mail: jgaunt@ku.edu.

School of Business Students: 292 full-time (96 women), 256 part-time (88 women); includes 78 minority (17 Black or African American, non-Hispanic/Latino; 2 American Indian or Alaska Native, non-Hispanic/Latino; 30 Asian, non-Hispanic/Latino; 14 Hispanic/Latino; 15 Two or more races, non-Hispanic/Latino), 75 international. Average age 30. 594 applicants, 59% accepted, 288 enrolled. *Financial support:* Fellowships, research assistantships, teaching assistantships, career-related internships or fieldwork, Federal Work-Study, and unspecified assistantships available. Financial award application deadline: 1/15; financial award applicants required to submit FAFSA. In 2015, 221 master's, 1 doctorate awarded. *Degree program information:* Part-time and evening/weekend programs available. Part-time, evening/weekend. Offers accounting (M Acc); business (M Acc, MBA, PhD); finance (MBA); human resources management (MBA); information systems (MBA); international business (MBA); management (MBA); marketing (MBA); strategic management (MBA). *Application deadline:* For fall admission, 6/1 for domestic students, 5/1 for international students. *Application fee:* $65 ($85 for international students). Electronic applications accepted. *Application Contact:* Patricia McCaffrey, MBA Coordinator, 785-864-6052, E-mail: pmccaffr@ku.edu. *Dean,* Dr. Neeli Bendapudi, 785-864-7575, E-mail: neeli@ku.edu.

School of Education Students: 530 full-time (337 women), 633 part-time (515 women); includes 181 minority (60 Black or African American, non-Hispanic/Latino; 15 American Indian or Alaska Native, non-Hispanic/Latino; 23 Asian, non-Hispanic/Latino; 37 Hispanic/Latino; 46 Two or more races, non-Hispanic/Latino), 114 international. Average age 33. 904 applicants, 70% accepted, 454 enrolled. *Financial support:* Fellowships, research assistantships, teaching assistantships, career-related internships or fieldwork, scholarships/grants, and unspecified assistantships available. Financial award application deadline: 2/1. In 2015, 210 master's, 73 doctorates, 8 other advanced degrees awarded. *Degree program information:* Part-time programs available. Part-time. Offers counseling psychology (MS, PhD); curriculum and instruction (MA, MS Ed, Ed D, PhD); education (MA, MS, MS Ed, Ed D, PhD, Ed S); education leadership and policy (Ed D, PhD); educational administration (MS Ed, Ed D, PhD); educational psychology and research (MS Ed, PhD); educational technology (MS Ed, PhD); health and physical education (MS Ed, Ed D, PhD); higher education (Ed D, PhD); higher education administration (MS Ed); policy studies (PhD); school psychology (PhD, Ed S); special education (MS Ed, Ed D, PhD). *Application fee:* $65 ($85 for international students). Electronic applications accepted. *Application Contact:* Kim Huggett, Graduate Student Services Manager, 785-864-4510, E-mail: khuggett@ku.edu. *Dean,* Dr. Rick J. Ginsberg, 785-864-3726, E-mail: ginsberg@ku.edu.

School of Engineering Students: 426 full-time (113 women), 265 part-time (67 women); includes 68 minority (15 Black or African American, non-Hispanic/Latino; 2 American Indian or Alaska Native, non-Hispanic/Latino; 26 Asian, non-Hispanic/Latino; 11 Hispanic/Latino; 14 Two or more races, non-Hispanic/Latino), 335 international. Average age 29. 925 applicants, 41% accepted, 147 enrolled. *Financial support:* Fellowships, research assistantships, teaching assistantships, career-related internships or fieldwork, Federal Work-Study, scholarships/grants, and unspecified assistantships available. In 2015, 143 master's, 35 doctorates awarded. *Degree program information:* Part-time and evening/weekend programs available. Part-time, evening/weekend, online learning. Offers aerospace engineering (ME, MS, DE, PhD); architectural engineering (MS); bioengineering (MS, PhD); chemical and petroleum engineering (MS, PhD); chemical engineering (MS); civil engineering (MCE, MS, DE, PhD); computer engineering (MS); computer science (MS, PhD); construction management (MCM); electrical engineering (MS, DE, PhD); engineering (MCE, MCM, ME, MS, DE, PhD); engineering management (MS); environmental engineering (MS, PhD); environmental science (MS, PhD); information technology (MS); mechanical engineering (MS, DE, PhD); petroleum engineering (MS); project management (ME, MS). *Application fee:* $65 ($85 for international students).

Electronic applications accepted. *Application Contact:* Amy Wierman, Assistant to the Dean, 785-864-2930, E-mail: awierman@ku.edu. *Dean,* Dr. Michael S. Branicky, 785-864-2930, E-mail: msb@ku.edu.

School of Journalism and Mass Communications Students: 16 full-time (10 women), 36 part-time (31 women); includes 9 minority (2 Black or African American, non-Hispanic/Latino; 1 American Indian or Alaska Native, non-Hispanic/Latino; 1 Asian, non-Hispanic/Latino; 2 Hispanic/Latino; 3 Two or more races, non-Hispanic/Latino), 6 international. Average age 32. 41 applicants, 54% accepted, 14 enrolled. *Financial support:* Fellowships, research assistantships, teaching assistantships, career-related internships or fieldwork, scholarships/grants, and unspecified assistantships available. Support available to part-time students. Financial award application deadline: 2/1; financial award applicants required to submit FAFSA. In 2015, 23 master's awarded. *Degree program information:* Part-time programs available. Part-time. Offers journalism (MS). *Application deadline:* For fall admission, 2/1 for domestic and international students; for spring admission, 11/1 for domestic and international students. *Application fee:* $65 ($85 for international students). Electronic applications accepted. *Application Contact:* Jammie A. Johnson, Graduate Advisor/Administrative Assistant, 785-864-7649, E-mail: jamjohn@ku.edu. *Associate Dean for Graduate Studies,* Scott Reinardy, 785-864-7691, E-mail: reinardy@ku.edu.

School of Music Students: 173 full-time (89 women), 43 part-time (28 women); includes 19 minority (3 Black or African American, non-Hispanic/Latino; 6 Asian, non-Hispanic/Latino; 4 Hispanic/Latino; 6 Two or more races, non-Hispanic/Latino), 54 international. Average age 30. 257 applicants, 60% accepted, 65 enrolled. *Financial support:* Fellowships, research assistantships, teaching assistantships, scholarships/grants, and unspecified assistantships available. In 2015, 45 master's, 26 doctorates awarded. Offers music (MM, MME, DMA, PhD); music education (MME, PhD); music therapy (MME). *Application fee:* $65 ($85 for international students). Electronic applications accepted. *Application Contact:* Jane Gnojek, Graduate Services Coordinator, 785-864-2862, E-mail: jgnojek@ku.edu. *Dean,* Dr. Robert Walzel, 785-864-3421, E-mail: robert.walzel@ku.edu.

School of Pharmacy Students: 101 full-time (45 women), 22 part-time (13 women); includes 16 minority (1 Black or African American, non-Hispanic/Latino; 9 Asian, non-Hispanic/Latino; 4 Hispanic/Latino; 2 Two or more races, non-Hispanic/Latino), 48 international. Average age 27. 237 applicants, 16% accepted, 27 enrolled. *Financial support:* Fellowships, research assistantships, teaching assistantships, career-related internships or fieldwork, scholarships/grants, traineeships, and unspecified assistantships available. In 2015, 19 master's, 17 doctorates awarded. Offers medicinal chemistry (MS, PhD); neurosciences (MS, PhD); pharmaceutical chemistry (MS, PhD); pharmacology and toxicology (MS, PhD); pharmacy (MS, PhD); pharmacy practice (MS). *Application fee:* $65 ($85 for international students). Electronic applications accepted. *Application Contact:* Gina King, Senior Administrative Associate, 785-864-3592, E-mail: ginaking@ku.edu. *Dean,* Kenneth L. Audus, 785-864-3591, E-mail: audus@ku.edu.

School of Social Welfare Students: 330 full-time (288 women), 69 part-time (59 women); includes 78 minority (25 Black or African American, non-Hispanic/Latino; 8 American Indian or Alaska Native, non-Hispanic/Latino; 7 Asian, non-Hispanic/Latino; 18 Hispanic/Latino; 20 Two or more races, non-Hispanic/Latino), 8 international. Average age 31. 354 applicants, 89% accepted, 212 enrolled. *Financial support:* Fellowships, research assistantships, teaching assistantships, Federal Work-Study, scholarships/grants, and tuition waivers (partial) available. Support available to part-time students. Financial award application deadline: 3/31; financial award applicants required to submit FAFSA. In 2015, 169 master's, 7 doctorates awarded. *Degree program information:* Part-time programs available. Part-time, online learning. Offers social work (MSW, PhD). *Application deadline:* For fall admission, 2/15 for domestic and international students. *Application fee:* $65 ($85 for international students). Electronic applications accepted. *Application Contact:* Becky Hofer, Director of Graduate Admissions, 785-864-8956, E-mail: bhofer@ku.edu. *Interim Dean,* Tom McDonald, 785-864-8959, E-mail: t-mcdonald@ku.edu.

School of Law Students: 362 full-time (158 women), 19 part-time (2 women); includes 53 minority (13 Black or African American, non-Hispanic/Latino; 6 American Indian or Alaska Native, non-Hispanic/Latino; 13 Asian, non-Hispanic/Latino; 21 Hispanic/Latino), 18 international. Average age 25. 663 applicants, 66% accepted, 126 enrolled. *Faculty:* 35 full-time (17 women), 19 part-time/adjunct (7 women). *Financial support:* In 2015–16, 9 fellowships (averaging $1,333 per year), 61 research assistantships (averaging $1,637 per year), 8 teaching assistantships (averaging $2,000 per year) were awarded; career-related internships or fieldwork, Federal Work-Study, institutionally sponsored loans, and scholarships/grants also available. Financial award application deadline: 2/15; financial award applicants required to submit FAFSA. In 2015, 135 doctorates awarded. Offers law (JD). *Application deadline:* For fall admission, 5/1 for domestic and international students. Applications are processed on a rolling basis. *Application fee:* $55. Electronic applications accepted. *Application Contact:* Steven Freedman, Assistant Dean for Admissions, 866-220-3654, E-mail: admitlaw@ku.edu. *Dean,* Stephen W. Mazza, 785-864-4550, Fax: 785-864-5054.

University of Kansas Medical Center Students: 1,519 full-time (835 women), 422 part-time (352 women); includes 370 minority (62 Black or African American, non-Hispanic/Latino; 11 American Indian or Alaska Native, non-Hispanic/Latino; 116 Asian, non-Hispanic/Latino; 91 Hispanic/Latino; 90 Two or more races, non-Hispanic/Latino), 116 international. Average age 29. In 2015, 185 master's, 314 doctorates, 27 other advanced degrees awarded. Offers health informatics (MS, Post Master's Certificate). *Executive Vice Chancellor,* Dr. Doug Girod, 913-588-1440, E-mail: dgirod@kumc.edu.

School of Health Professions Students: 396 full-time (281 women), 52 part-time (47 women); includes 48 minority (9 Black or African American, non-Hispanic/Latino; 3 American Indian or Alaska Native, non-Hispanic/Latino; 7 Asian, non-Hispanic/Latino; 15 Hispanic/Latino; 14 Two or more races, non-Hispanic/Latino), 26 international. Average age 27. *Faculty:* 107. In 2015, 58 master's, 76 doctorates, 21 other advanced degrees awarded. Offers audiology (Au D, PhD); dietetic internship (Graduate Certificate); dietetics and integrative medicine (Graduate Certificate); dietetics and nutrition (MS); health professions (MOT, MS, Au D, DNAP, DPT, OTD, PhD, SLPD, Graduate Certificate); medical nutrition science (PhD); molecular biotechnology (MS); nurse anesthesia education (DNAP); occupational therapy (MOT, OTD); physical therapy (DPT); rehabilitation science (PhD); therapeutic science (PhD). *Dean,* Dr. Abiodun Akinwuntan, 913-588-5235, Fax: 913-588-5254, E-mail: aakinwuntan@kumc.edu.

School of Medicine Students: 1,072 full-time (509 women), 100 part-time (60 women); includes 267 minority (31 Black or African American, non-Hispanic/Latino; 7 American Indian or Alaska Native, non-Hispanic/Latino; 97 Asian, non-Hispanic/Latino; 66 Hispanic/Latino; 66 Two or more races, non-Hispanic/Latino), 84 international. Average age 27. *Faculty:* 1,019. In 2015, 56 master's, 214 doctorates awarded. Offers anatomy and cell biology (MS, PhD); applied statistics and analytics (MS); biochemistry and molecular biology (PhD); biomedical sciences (PhD); biostatistics (MS, PhD, Graduate Certificate); clinical research (MS); environmental health sciences (MPH); epidemiology (MPH); health policy and management (PhD); health services administration (MHSA); medicine (MHSA, MPH, MS, MD, PhD, Graduate Certificate); microbiology, molecular genetics and immunology (MS, PhD); molecular and integrative physiology (PhD); neuroscience (PhD); pathology and laboratory medicine (PhD); pharmacology (PhD); public health management (MPH); social and behavioral health (MPH); statistical applications (Graduate Certificate); toxicology (PhD). *Executive Dean,* Dr. Robert Simari, 913-588-7201, E-mail: rsimari@kumc.edu.

School of Nursing Students: 44 full-time (42 women), 261 part-time (238 women); includes 54 minority (22 Black or African American, non-Hispanic/Latino; 1 American Indian or Alaska Native, non-Hispanic/Latino; 12 Asian, non-Hispanic/Latino; 10 Hispanic/Latino; 9 Two or more races, non-Hispanic/Latino), 1 international. Average age 38. 95 applicants, 97% accepted, 74 enrolled. *Faculty:* 59. *Financial support:* Research assistantships with tuition reimbursements, teaching assistantships with tuition reimbursements, scholarships/grants, and traineeships available. Financial award application deadline: 3/1; financial award applicants required to submit FAFSA. In 2015, 71 master's, 24 doctorates, 6 other advanced degrees awarded. *Degree program information:* Part-time programs available. Part-time, 100% online, blended/hybrid learning. Offers adult/gerontological clinical nurse specialist (PMC); adult/gerontological nurse practitioner (PMC); clinical research management (PMC); health care informatics (PMC); health professions educator (PMC); nurse midwife (PMC); nursing (MS, DNP, PhD); organizational leadership (PMC); psychiatric/mental health nurse practitioner (PMC); public health nursing (PMC). *Application deadline:* For fall admission, 4/1 for domestic and international students; for spring admission, 9/1 for domestic and international students. *Application fee:* $60. Electronic applications accepted. *Application Contact:* Dr. Pamela K. Barnes, Associate Dean, Student Affairs, 913-588-1619, Fax: 913-588-1615, E-mail: pbarnes2@kumc.edu. *Dean,* Dr. Sally Maliski, 913-588-1601, Fax: 913-588-1660, E-mail: smaliski@kumc.edu.

UNIVERSITY OF KENTUCKY, Lexington, KY 40506-0032

General Information State-supported, coed, university. CGS member. *Graduate housing:* Rooms and/or apartments available to single and married students. *Research affiliation:* Continuous Electron Beam Accelerator Facility (high-energy physics), Battelle Pacific Northwest Laboratories (environmental sciences), Oak Ridge National Laboratory (nuclear physics), National Institute of Occupational Health and Safety (environmental health), National Drug Addiction Center (drug abuse and prevention).

GRADUATE UNITS

College of Dentistry Students: 252 full-time (128 women); includes 64 minority (9 Black or African American, non-Hispanic/Latino; 1 American Indian or Alaska Native, non-Hispanic/Latino; 25 Asian, non-Hispanic/Latino; 13 Hispanic/Latino; 16 Two or more races, non-Hispanic/Latino), 3 international. Average age 26. 1,839 applicants, 7% accepted, 65 enrolled. *Faculty:* 63 full-time (22 women), 53 part-time/adjunct (20 women). *Financial support:* In 2015–16, 207 students received support. Fellowships, research assistantships, teaching assistantships, career-related internships or fieldwork, Federal Work-Study, institutionally sponsored loans, and scholarships/grants available. Support available to part-time students. Financial award application deadline: 4/15; financial award applicants required to submit FAFSA. In 2015, 53 doctorates awarded. Offers dentistry (DMD). *Application deadline:* For fall admission, 12/1 priority date for domestic students. Applications are processed on a rolling basis. *Application fee:* $75. Electronic applications accepted. *Application Contact:* Melissa D. Shelton, Admissions Coordinator, 859-323-6071, Fax: 859-257-5550, E-mail: missy.shelton@uky.edu. *Dean,* Dr. Stephanos Kyrkanides, 859-323-1884, Fax: 859-323-1042, E-mail: stephanos@uky.edu.

College of Law Offers law (JD). Electronic applications accepted.

College of Medicine Students: 521 full-time (217 women); includes 105 minority (30 Black or African American, non-Hispanic/Latino; 1 American Indian or Alaska Native, non-Hispanic/Latino; 67 Asian, non-Hispanic/Latino; 7 Hispanic/Latino), 29 international. Average age 24. *Financial support:* Institutionally sponsored loans available. Financial award applicants required to submit FAFSA. Offers medicine (MD). *Application deadline:* For fall admission, 11/1 for domestic students. Applications are processed on a rolling basis. *Application fee:* $50. Electronic applications accepted. *Application Contact:* Kimberly Scott, Assistant Director of Admissions, 859-323-6161, E-mail: kymedap@uky.edu. *Associate Dean for Admissions,* Dr. Carol L. Elam, 859-323-6161.

Graduate School ***Degree program information:*** Part-time and evening/weekend programs available. Part-time, evening/weekend. Offers dentistry (MS); pharmaceutical sciences (MS, PhD); pharmacy (Pharm D). Electronic applications accepted.

College of Agriculture, Food and Environment Degree program information: Part-time programs available. Part-time. Offers agricultural economics (MS, PhD); agriculture, food and environment (MS, MSFOR, PhD); animal and food sciences (MS, PhD); biosystems and agricultural engineering (MS, PhD); entomology (MS, PhD); family studies, human development, and resource management (MS, PhD); forestry (MSFOR); hospitality and dietetics administration (MS); integrated plant and soil sciences (MS, PhD); plant pathology (MS, PhD); veterinary science (MS, PhD). Electronic applications accepted.

College of Arts and Sciences Degree program information: Part-time programs available. Part-time. Offers anthropology (MA, PhD); applied mathematics (MS); arts and sciences (MA, MS, PhD); biology (MS, PhD); chemistry (MS, PhD); English (MA, PhD); geography (MA, PhD); geology (MS, PhD); German (MA); Hispanic studies (MA, PhD); history (MA, PhD); mathematics (MA, MS, PhD); modern and classical languages and literatures (MA); philosophy (MA, PhD); physics and astronomy (MS, PhD); political science (MA, PhD); psychology (MA, PhD); sociology (MA, MS, PhD); statistics (MS, PhD); teaching world languages (MA). Electronic applications accepted.

College of Communication and Information Degree program information: Part-time programs available. Part-time. Offers communication (MA, PhD); communication and information (MA, MSLS, PhD); library and information science (MA, MSLS). Electronic applications accepted.

College of Design Offers architecture (M Arch); design (M Arch, MAIDM, MHP, MSIDM); historic preservation (MHP); interior design (MA). Electronic applications accepted.

College of Education Degree program information: Part-time and evening/weekend programs available. Part-time, evening/weekend. Offers biomechanics (MS); counseling psychology (MS, PhD, Ed S); curriculum and instruction (Ed D, PhD); early childhood (MS Ed); education (M Ed, MA Ed, MRC, MS, MS Ed, Ed D, PhD, Ed S); educational leadership (M Ed, Ed D, PhD, Ed S); educational policy studies and evaluation (Ed D); educational psychology (MS, PhD); educational sciences (PhD); elementary education (MA Ed); exercise physiology (MS, PhD); exercise science (PhD); family resource and youth services (M Ed, Ed S); health promotion (MS, Ed D);

higher education (MS Ed, PhD); instructional system design (MS Ed); literacy (MA Ed); middle school education (MA Ed, MS Ed); physical education training (Ed D); principalship (Ed D, Ed S); rehabilitation counseling (MRC, PhD); school psychology (PhD, Ed S); school technology leadership (M Ed, PhD, Ed S); secondary education (MA Ed, MS Ed); social and philosophical studies (MS Ed); special education (MS Ed, PhD); sport leadership (MS); teacher leadership (M Ed, Ed S); teaching and coaching (MS). Electronic applications accepted.

College of Engineering Degree program information: Part-time programs available. Part-time. Offers biomedical engineering (MSBE, PBME, PhD); chemical engineering (MS, PhD); civil engineering (MSCE, PhD); computer science (MS, PhD); electrical engineering (MSEE, PhD); engineering (M Eng, MCE, MME, MS, MS Ch E, MS Min, MSCE, MSEE, MSEM, MSMAE, MSME, MSMSE, PhD); manufacturing systems engineering (MSMSE); materials science and engineering (MS, PhD); mechanical engineering (MSME, PhD); mining engineering (MME, MS Min, PhD). Electronic applications accepted.

College of Fine Arts Degree program information: Part-time and evening/weekend programs available. Part-time, evening/weekend. Offers art education (MA); art history (MA); art studio (MFA); arts administration (MA); composition (MM, DMA); conducting (MM, DMA); fine arts (MA, MFA, MM, DMA, PhD); music education (MM, PhD); music theory (MA, PhD); music therapy (MM); musicology (MA, PhD); performance (MM, DMA); sacred music (MM). Electronic applications accepted.

College of Health Sciences Degree program information: Part-time programs available. Part-time. Offers athletic training (MS); communication disorders (MS); health administration (MHA); health sciences (MHA, MS, MSCD, MSHP, MSNS, MSPAS, MSPT, MSRMP, DS, PhD); nutritional sciences (MSNS, PhD); physical therapy (DPT); physician assistant studies (MSPAS); rehabilitation sciences (PhD). Electronic applications accepted.

College of Nursing Offers nursing (DNP, PhD). Electronic applications accepted.

College of Public Health Offers clinical research design (MS); epidemiology and biostatistics (PhD); gerontology (PhD, Graduate Certificate); public health (MPH, Dr PH, PhD). Electronic applications accepted.

College of Social Work Offers social work (MSW, PhD). Electronic applications accepted.

Gatton College of Business and Economics Degree program information: Part-time and evening/weekend programs available. Part-time, evening/weekend. Offers accounting (MSACC); business administration (MBA, PhD); business and economics (MBA, MS, MSACC, PhD); economics (MS, PhD). Electronic applications accepted.

Graduate School Programs from the College of Medicine Offers anatomy and neurobiology (PhD); medical science (MS); medicine (MS, PhD); microbiology and immunology (PhD); molecular and biomedical pharmacology (PhD); molecular and cellular biochemistry (PhD); physiology (PhD); radiation sciences (MSRMP); toxicology (MS, PhD). Electronic applications accepted.

Martin School of Public Policy and Administration Offers public administration (MPA); public policy (MPP); public policy and administration (PhD). Electronic applications accepted.

Patterson School of Diplomacy and International Commerce Offers diplomacy and international commerce (MA). Electronic applications accepted.

UNIVERSITY OF KING'S COLLEGE, Halifax, NS B3H 2A1, Canada

General Information Province-supported, coed, comprehensive institution. *Graduate housing:* Room and/or apartments available on a first-come, first-served basis to single students; on-campus housing not available to married students. Housing application deadline: 4/1.

GRADUATE UNITS

Graduate and Advanced Programs Offers creative nonfiction (MFA); journalism (MJ).

UNIVERSITY OF LA VERNE, La Verne, CA 91750-4443

General Information Independent, coed, university. *Enrollment:* 4,883 graduate, professional, and undergraduate students; 1,598 full-time matriculated graduate/professional students (1,031 women), 1,460 part-time matriculated graduate/professional students (979 women). *Enrollment by degree level:* 2,226 master's, 536 doctoral, 296 other advanced degrees. *Graduate faculty:* 150 full-time (80 women), 216 part-time/adjunct (109 women). *Tuition, area resident:* Part-time $795 per credit hour. Tuition and fees vary according to campus/location and program. *Graduate housing:* Room and/or apartments available on a first-come, first-served basis to single students; on-campus housing not available to married students. Typical cost: $9860 per year. Room charges vary according to board plan and housing facility selected. *Student services:* Campus employment opportunities, campus safety program, career counseling, exercise/wellness program, free psychological counseling, international student services, low-cost health insurance, multicultural affairs office, services for students with disabilities, teacher training, writing training. *Library:* Wilson Library. Students can reserve study rooms. *Research affiliation:* Methodist Hospital of Southern California, San Antonio Community Hospital, Riverside Community Hospital, Presbyterian Intercommunity Hospital, Huntington Memorial Hospital (health services management), Southern California Healthcare Systems.

Computer facilities: 520 computers available on campus for general student use. A campuswide network can be accessed from student residence rooms and from off campus. Online class registration, MyLaVerne (online) are available.
Website: http://www.laverne.edu/

General Application Contact: Graduate Admission Office, 877-GO-TO-ULV, Fax: 909-392-2761, E-mail: gradadmission@laverne.edu.

GRADUATE UNITS

College of Arts and Sciences Students: 75 full-time (65 women), 71 part-time (60 women); includes 80 minority (11 Black or African American, non-Hispanic/Latino; 7 Asian, non-Hispanic/Latino; 58 Hispanic/Latino; 4 Two or more races, non-Hispanic/Latino), 1 international. Average age 29. *Faculty:* 11 full-time (5 women), 11 part-time/adjunct (6 women). *Financial support:* Career-related internships or fieldwork, institutionally sponsored loans, and scholarships/grants available. Financial award application deadline: 3/2; financial award applicants required to submit FAFSA. In 2015, 48 master's, 6 doctorates awarded. *Degree program information:* Part-time programs available. Part-time. Offers arts and sciences (MS, Psy D); clinical psychology (Psy D); marriage and family therapy (MS). *Application deadline:* Applications are processed on a rolling basis. *Application Contact:* Christy Ranells, Associate Director of Admission, 909-448-4644, Fax: 909-971-2295, E-mail: cranells@laverne.edu. *Dean, College of Arts and Sciences*, Dr. Lawrence Potter, 909-448-4188, E-mail: lpotter@laverne.edu.

College of Business and Public Management Students: 658 full-time (361 women), 288 part-time (164 women); includes 305 minority (44 Black or African American, non-Hispanic/Latino; 32 Asian, non-Hispanic/Latino; 224 Hispanic/Latino; 1 Native Hawaiian or other Pacific Islander, non-Hispanic/Latino; 4 Two or more races, non-Hispanic/Latino), 466 international. Average age 30. *Faculty:* 35 full-time (19 women), 33 part-time/adjunct (11 women). *Financial support:* Career-related internships or fieldwork, institutionally sponsored loans, and scholarships/grants available. Financial award application deadline: 3/2; financial award applicants required to submit FAFSA. In 2015, 852 master's, 8 doctorates awarded. *Degree program information:* Part-time and evening/weekend programs available. Part-time, evening/weekend, online learning. Offers accounting (MS); business and public management (MBA, MBA-EP, MHA, MPA, MS, DPA, Certificate); executive management (MBA-EP); finance (MBA, MBA-EP, MS); financial management (MHA); geriatric care management (MS); gerontology (Certificate); gerontology administration (MS); health services management (MBA, MS); information technology (MBA, MBA-EP); international business (MBA, MBA-EP); leadership (MBA-EP); leadership and management (MS); managed care (MBA); management (MBA, MBA-EP); management and leadership (MHA); marketing (MBA, MBA-EP); marketing and business development (MHA); non-profit (MPA); nonprofit management (Certificate); organizational leadership (Certificate); policy (MPA); public administration (MPA, DPA); urban management and affairs (MPA). *Application deadline:* Applications are processed on a rolling basis. *Application fee:* $50. *Application Contact:* Rina Lazarian-Chehab, Senior Associate Director of Graduate Admissions, 909-448-4317, Fax: 909-971-2295, E-mail: rlazarian@laverne.edu. *Dean, College of Business and Public Management*, Dr. Abe Helou, 909-448-4455, E-mail: ihelou@laverne.edu.

College of Education and Organizational Leadership Students: 326 full-time (256 women), 487 part-time (382 women); includes 432 minority (49 Black or African American, non-Hispanic/Latino; 5 American Indian or Alaska Native, non-Hispanic/Latino; 20 Asian, non-Hispanic/Latino; 350 Hispanic/Latino; 8 Two or more races, non-Hispanic/Latino), 7 international. Average age 34. *Faculty:* 24 full-time (18 women), 15 part-time/adjunct (13 women). *Financial support:* Federal Work-Study available. Financial award application deadline: 3/2; financial award applicants required to submit FAFSA. In 2015, 267 master's, 35 doctorates, 519 other advanced degrees awarded. *Degree program information:* Part-time and evening/weekend programs available. Part-time, evening/weekend, online learning. Offers advanced teaching skills (M Ed); child development (MS); child life (MS); education (M Ed); education (special emphasis) (M Ed); education and organizational leadership (M Ed, MS, Ed D, Certificate, Credential); educational counseling (MS); educational leadership (M Ed); mild/moderate education specialist (Credential); multiple subject (Credential); organizational leadership (Ed D); pupil personnel services (Credential); reading (M Ed, Certificate); reading and language arts specialist (Credential); school psychology (MS); single subject (Credential); special education studies (MS); teaching (Credential). *Application deadline:* Applications are processed on a rolling basis. *Application fee:* $50. *Application Contact:* Christy Ranells, Admissions Information Specialist, 909-448-4644, Fax: 909-971-2295, E-mail: cranells@laverne.edu. *Interim Dean, College of Education and Organizational Leadership*, Dr. Barbara Poling, 909-448-4380, E-mail: bpoling@laverne.edu.

College of Law ***Degree program information:*** Part-time and evening/weekend programs available. Part-time, evening/weekend. Offers law (JD). Electronic applications accepted.

Regional and Online Campuses Students: 402 full-time (276 women), 560 part-time (345 women); includes 506 minority (66 Black or African American, non-Hispanic/Latino; 7 American Indian or Alaska Native, non-Hispanic/Latino; 65 Asian, non-Hispanic/Latino; 358 Hispanic/Latino; 1 Native Hawaiian or other Pacific Islander, non-Hispanic/Latino; 9 Two or more races, non-Hispanic/Latino), 2 international. Average age 36. *Faculty:* 15 full-time (7 women), 65 part-time/adjunct (31 women). *Financial support:* Application deadline: 3/2; applicants required to submit FAFSA. In 2015, 356 master's, 144 other advanced degrees awarded. *Degree program information:* Part-time and evening/weekend programs available. Part-time, evening/weekend. Offers administration services (preliminary) (Credential); business administration (MBA, MBA-EP); business administration for experienced professionals (MBA, MBA-EP, MS); education (special emphasis) (M Ed); education specialist: mild/moderate (Credential); educational counseling (MS); educational leadership (M Ed); English (Certificate); health administration (MHA); leadership and management (MS); mild/moderate education specialist (Credential); multiple subject (elementary) (Credential); multiple subject teaching (Credential); organizational leadership (Ed D); preliminary administrative services (Credential); pupil personnel services (Credential); pupil personnel services: school counseling (Credential); single subject (secondary) (Credential); single subject teaching (Credential); special education (MS); special education studies (MS); special emphasis (M Ed). *Application deadline:* Applications are processed on a rolling basis. *Application fee:* $50. *Application Contact:* Todd Eckel, Director of Admissions, Regional and Online Campuses, 909-448-4928, E-mail: teckel@laverne.edu. *Dean, Regional and Online Campuses*, David Smith, 909-448-4995, E-mail: dsmith3@laverne.edu.

UNIVERSITY OF LETHBRIDGE, Lethbridge, AB T1K 3M4, Canada

General Information Province-supported, coed, university. CGS member. *Enrollment:* 8,295 graduate, professional, and undergraduate students; 439 full-time matriculated graduate/professional students (243 women), 119 part-time matriculated graduate/professional students (70 women). *Enrollment by degree level:* 474 master's, 84 doctoral. *Graduate faculty:* 358. *Graduate housing:* Rooms and/or apartments available on a first-come, first-served basis to single and married students. Housing application deadline: 4/1. *Student services:* Campus employment opportunities, campus safety program, career counseling, exercise/wellness program, free psychological counseling, grant writing training, international student services, low-cost health insurance, multicultural affairs office, services for students with disabilities, teacher training, writing training. *Library:* The University of Lethbridge Library. Students can reserve study rooms. *Research affiliation:* Plains Midstream Canada ULC, Pacific Forestry Institution.

Computer facilities: Computer purchase and lease plans are available. A campuswide network can be accessed from student residence rooms and from off campus. Online class registration is available.
Website: http://www.uleth.ca/

General Application Contact: School of Graduate Studies, 403-329-5194, E-mail: sgsinquiries@uleth.ca.

GRADUATE UNITS

School of Graduate Studies Students: 448 full-time (249 women), 110 part-time (64 women). Average age 32. 285 applicants, 36% accepted, 96 enrolled. *Financial support:* Fellowships, research assistantships, teaching assistantships, scholarships/grants, health care benefits, and unspecified assistantships available. In 2015, 154 master's, 11 doctorates awarded. *Degree program information:* Part-time and evening/weekend programs available. Part-time, evening/weekend. Offers addictions counseling (M Sc); agricultural biotechnology (M Sc); agricultural studies (M Sc, MA); anthropology (MA); archaeology (M Sc, MA); art (MA, MFA); biochemistry (M Sc); biological sciences (M Sc); biomolecular science (PhD); biosystems and biodiversity (PhD); Canadian studies (MA); chemistry (M Sc); computer science (M Sc); computer science and geographical information science (M Sc); counseling (MC); counseling psychology (M Ed); dramatic arts (MA); earth, space, and physical science (PhD); economics (MA); education (MA, PhD); educational leadership (M Ed); English (MA); environmental science (M Sc); evolution and behavior (PhD); exercise science (M Sc); French (MA); French/German (MA); French/Spanish (MA); general education (M Ed); geography (M Sc, MA); German (MA); health sciences (M Sc); individualized multidisciplinary (M Sc, MA); kinesiology (M Sc, MA); management (M Sc); mathematics (M Sc); music (M Mus, MA); Native American studies (MA); neuroscience (M Sc, PhD); new media (MA, MFA); nursing (M Sc, MN); philosophy (MA); physics (M Sc); political science (MA); psychology (M Sc, MA); religious studies (MA); sociology (MA); theatre and dramatic arts (MFA); theoretical and computational science (PhD); urban and regional studies (MA); women and gender studies (MA). *Application fee:* $100 Canadian dollars ($140 Canadian dollars for international students). Electronic applications accepted. *Application Contact:* School of Graduate Studies, 403-329-5194, E-mail: sgsinquiries@uleth.ca. *Manager, School of Graduate Studies*, Kathleen Schrage, 403-329-2121, E-mail: schrage@uleth.ca.

UNIVERSITY OF LOUISIANA AT LAFAYETTE, Lafayette, LA 70504

General Information State-supported, coed, university. CGS member. *Graduate housing:* Rooms and/or apartments available on a first-come, first-served basis to single and married students. *Research affiliation:* National Wetlands Research Center (biology, wetlands restoration), Louisiana Universities Marine Consortium (marine biology), U.S. Fish and Wildlife Service (ecology), Army Corps of Engineers (wetlands), U.S. Geological Survey (USGS), U.S. Department of Agriculture (USDA).

GRADUATE UNITS

BI Moody III College of Business Administration MBA Program ***Degree program information:*** Part-time and evening/weekend programs available. Part-time, evening/weekend. Offers business administration (MBA).

College of Education ***Degree program information:*** Part-time programs available. Part-time. Offers education (M Ed, Ed D). Electronic applications accepted.

Graduate Studies and Research in Education Offers administration and supervision (M Ed); curriculum and instruction (M Ed); education of the gifted (M Ed); educational leadership (M Ed, Ed D).

College of Engineering ***Degree program information:*** Part-time and evening/weekend programs available. Part-time, evening/weekend. Offers chemical engineering (MSE); civil engineering (MSE); computer engineering (MS, PhD); engineering (MS, MSE, MSET, MSTC, PhD); engineering and technology management (MSET); mechanical engineering (MSE); petroleum engineering (MSE); telecommunications (MSTC). Electronic applications accepted.

Center for Advanced Computer Studies Degree program information: Part-time programs available. Part-time. Offers computer engineering (MS, PhD); computer science (MS, PhD). Electronic applications accepted.

College of Liberal Arts ***Degree program information:*** Part-time programs available. Part-time. Offers British and American literature (MA); communicative disorders (MS, PhD); creative writing (PhD); Francophone studies (PhD); French (MA); history (MA); liberal arts (MA, MS, PhD); literature (PhD); mass communications (MS); psychology (MS); rehabilitation counseling (MS); rhetoric (PhD). Electronic applications accepted.

College of Nursing Offers nursing (MSN). Program offered jointly with Southern Louisiana University, McNeese State University, Southern University and Agricultural and Mechanical College. Electronic applications accepted.

College of Sciences ***Degree program information:*** Part-time programs available. Part-time. Offers biology (MS); environmental and evolutionary biology (PhD); geology (MS); mathematics (MS, PhD); physics (MS); sciences (MS, PhD). Electronic applications accepted.

Institute of Cognitive Science Offers cognitive science (PhD). Electronic applications accepted.

College of the Arts Offers arts (M Arch, MM). Electronic applications accepted.

School of Architecture Offers architecture (M Arch). Electronic applications accepted.

School of Music Offers conducting (MM); pedagogy (MM); vocal and instrumental performance (MM). Electronic applications accepted.

Department of Counselor Education Offers counselor education (MS). Electronic applications accepted.

UNIVERSITY OF LOUISIANA AT MONROE, Monroe, LA 71209-0001

General Information State-supported, coed, university. *Graduate housing:* Room and/or apartments available on a first-come, first-served basis to single students; on-campus housing not available to married students. Housing application deadline: 5/1. *Research affiliation:* Juvenile Diabetes Research Foundation (pharmacology), Philip Morris, Inc. (medicinal chemistry), Harvard Hughes Medical Institute (biology), Xenoport, Inc. (pharmaceutics), U.S. Army Corps of Engineers (toxicology, environmental science), National Center for Toxicological Research (toxicology).

GRADUATE UNITS

Graduate School ***Degree program information:*** Part-time and evening/weekend programs available. Part-time, evening/weekend, online learning. Electronic applications accepted.

College of Arts, Education, and Sciences Degree program information: Part-time and evening/weekend programs available. Part-time, evening/weekend. Offers art education (M Ed); arts, education, and sciences (M Ed, MA, MAT, MS, Ed D); biology (MS); biology education (M Ed); chemistry education (M Ed); communication (MA); curriculum and instruction (M Ed, Ed D); early childhood education (M Ed); earth science education (M Ed); educational leadership (M Ed); elementary education (MAT); elementary education (1-5) (M Ed); English (MA); English as a second language (M Ed); English education (M Ed); family and consumer education (M Ed); French education (M Ed); history (MA); history education (M Ed); math education (M Ed); middle school education (M Ed); music education (M Ed); reading education (K-12) (M Ed); secondary education (MAT); Spanish education (M Ed); special education (MAT); special education - academically gifted (M Ed); special education - early intervention (M Ed); special education - educational diagnostician (M Ed); special education - mild/moderate disabilities (M Ed); speech education (M Ed). Electronic applications accepted.

College of Business and Social Sciences Degree program information: Part-time and evening/weekend programs available. Part-time, evening/weekend, online learning. Offers business and social sciences (MA, MS); criminal justice (MA); forensic psychology (MS); general psychology (MS); psychometrics (MS). Electronic applications accepted.

College of Health and Pharmaceutical Sciences Offers aging studies (MA); applied exercise science (MS); clinical exercise physiology (MS); clinical mental health counseling (MS); gerontology (CGS); health and pharmaceutical sciences (MA, MOT, MS, PhD, CGS); marriage and family therapy (MA, PhD); occupational therapy (MOT); pharmacy (PhD, Pharm D); program administration (MA); school counseling (MS); speech-language pathology (MS); sports, fitness and recreation management (MS); toxicology (PhD). Electronic applications accepted.

UNIVERSITY OF LOUISVILLE, Louisville, KY 40292-0001

General Information State-supported, coed, university. CGS member. *Enrollment:* 21,295 graduate, professional, and undergraduate students; 3,914 full-time matriculated graduate/professional students (2,016 women), 1,477 part-time matriculated graduate/professional students (762 women). *Enrollment by degree level:* 2,759 master's, 2,501 doctoral, 131 other advanced degrees. *Graduate faculty:* 1,734 full-time (701 women), 668 part-time/adjunct (347 women). Tuition, state resident: full-time $11,664; part-time $649 per credit hour. Tuition, nonresident: full-time $24,274; part-time $1350 per credit hour. *Required fees:* $196. Tuition and fees vary according to program and reciprocity agreements. *Graduate housing:* Rooms and/or apartments available on a first-come, first-served basis to single and married students. Typical cost: $7942 per year ($3010 including board) for single students. Room and board charges vary according to board plan and housing facility selected. *Student services:* Campus employment opportunities, campus safety program, career counseling, child daycare facilities, exercise/wellness program, free psychological counseling, grant writing training, international student services, low-cost health insurance, multicultural affairs office, services for students with disabilities, teacher training, writing training. *Library:* William F. Ekstrom Library plus 6 others. *Collection:* Books: 2.2 million (physical), 64,053 (digital/electronic); Serial titles: 2,262 (physical), 90,700 (digital/electronic); Databases: 327. Weekly public service hours: 97; study areas open 24 hours, 5–7 days a week; students can reserve study rooms. *Research affiliation:* Ford Motor Company, General Electric Company (GE), Oak Ridge National Laboratory, Argonne National Laboratory.

Computer facilities: Computer purchase and lease plans are available. 400 computers available on campus for general student use. A campuswide network can be accessed from student residence rooms and from off campus. Online class registration is available.
Website: http://www.louisville.edu/

General Application Contact: Libby Leggett, Executive Director, Graduate Admissions and Recruitment, 502-852-3108, E-mail: gradadm@louisville.edu.

GRADUATE UNITS

Graduate School Students: 3,914 full-time (2,016 women), 1,477 part-time (762 women); includes 990 minority (442 Black or African American, non-Hispanic/Latino; 8 American Indian or Alaska Native, non-Hispanic/Latino; 222 Asian, non-Hispanic/Latino; 183 Hispanic/Latino; 4 Native Hawaiian or other Pacific Islander, non-Hispanic/Latino; 131 Two or more races, non-Hispanic/Latino), 478 international. Average age 29. 7,518 applicants, 31% accepted, 1534 enrolled. *Faculty:* 1,734 full-time (701 women), 668 part-time/adjunct (347 women). *Financial support:* Fellowships with full tuition reimbursements, research assistantships with full tuition reimbursements, teaching assistantships with tuition reimbursements, career-related internships or fieldwork, Federal Work-Study, institutionally sponsored loans, scholarships/grants, traineeships, tuition waivers (partial), and unspecified assistantships available. Financial award applicants required to submit FAFSA. In 2015, 829 master's, 453 doctorates, 89 other advanced degrees awarded. *Degree program information:* Part-time and evening/weekend programs available. Part-time, evening/weekend. *Application deadline:* For fall admission, 5/1 priority date for international students; for spring admission, 11/1 priority date for international students; for summer admission, 4/1 priority date for international students. Applications are processed on a rolling basis. *Application fee:* $60. Electronic applications accepted. *Application Contact:* Libby Leggett, Director, Graduate Admissions, 502-852-3101, Fax: 502-852-6536, E-mail: gradadm@louisville.edu. *Dean*, Dr. Beth A. Boehm, 502-852-6495, Fax: 502-852-2365, E-mail: baboeh01@louisville.edu.

College of Arts and Sciences Students: 608 full-time (319 women), 211 part-time (99 women); includes 144 minority (82 Black or African American, non-Hispanic/Latino; 12 Asian, non-Hispanic/Latino; 30 Hispanic/Latino; 1 Native Hawaiian or other Pacific Islander, non-Hispanic/Latino; 19 Two or more races, non-Hispanic/Latino), 97 international. Average age 31. 729 applicants, 43% accepted, 187 enrolled. *Faculty:* 393 full-time (164 women), 191 part-time/adjunct (105 women). *Financial support:* In 2015–16, 10 research assistantships with full tuition reimbursements (averaging $18,000 per year), 240 teaching assistantships with full tuition reimbursements (averaging $18,000 per year) were awarded; Federal Work-Study, scholarships/grants, health care benefits, and unspecified assistantships also available. In 2015, 128 master's, 19 doctorates, 45 other advanced degrees awarded. *Degree program information:* Part-time programs available. Part-time, 100% online. Offers African and Diaspora studies (MA); African-American studies (MA); analytical chemistry (MS, PhD); anthropology (MA); applied and industrial mathematics (PhD); applied geography (MS); art history (MA, PhD); arts and sciences (MA, MFA, MPA, MS, MUP, PhD, Certificate); biochemistry (MS, PhD); biology (MS); chemical physics (PhD); civic leadership (MA); clinical psychology (PhD); cognition and development (PhD); communication (MA); criminal justice (MS, PhD); culture, criticism, and contemporary thought (PhD); curatorial studies (MA); English (MA); English rhetoric and composition (PhD); environmental biology (PhD); French (MA); history (MA); humanities (MA); inorganic chemistry (MS, PhD); linguistics (MA); mathematics (MA); organic chemistry (MS, PhD); performance (MFA); physical chemistry (MS, PhD); physics (MS, PhD); political science (MA); public administration (MPA); public arts and letters (PhD); public history (Certificate); sociology (MA, PhD); Spanish (MA); studio art (MA, MFA); traditional (MA); urban and public affairs (PhD); urban planning (MUP); vision and hearing (PhD); women's and gender studies (MA, Certificate). *Application deadline:* For fall admission, 5/1 priority date for international students; for spring admission, 11/1 priority date for international students; for summer admission, 4/1 priority date for international students. Applications are processed on a rolling basis. *Application fee:* $60. *Application Contact:* Dr. Janet Woodruff-Borden, Associate Dean for Graduate Education, 502-852-8966, Fax: 502-852-6888, E-mail: j.woodruff-borden@louisville.edu. *Dean*, Dr. Kimberly Kempf-Leonard, 502-852-6490, Fax: 502-852-6888, E-mail: asdean@louisville.edu.

College of Business Students: 246 full-time (81 women), 54 part-time (22 women); includes 33 minority (11 Black or African American, non-Hispanic/Latino; 1 American Indian or Alaska Native, non-Hispanic/Latino; 11 Asian, non-Hispanic/Latino; 8 Hispanic/Latino; 2 Two or more races, non-Hispanic/Latino), 19 international. Average age 31. 344 applicants, 62% accepted, 175 enrolled. *Faculty:* 76 full-time (25 women), 17 part-time/adjunct (4 women). *Financial support:* Fellowships with full tuition reimbursements, research assistantships with full tuition reimbursements, teaching assistantships with full tuition reimbursements, scholarships/grants, health care benefits, and unspecified assistantships available. Financial award application deadline: 3/15; financial award applicants required to submit FAFSA. In 2015, 69 master's awarded. *Degree program information:* Part-time programs available. Part-time. Offers accountancy (MAC); business (MAC, MBA, PhD); entrepreneurship (MBA, PhD); global business (MBA); health sector management (MBA). *Application deadline:* For fall admission, 3/31 for domestic students, 5/1 priority date for international students; for spring admission, 12/1 for domestic students, 11/1 priority date for international students; for summer admission, 4/1 priority date for international students. Applications are processed on a rolling basis. *Application fee:* $60. *Application Contact:* Susan E. Hildebrand, Program Director, 502-852-7257, Fax: 502-852-4901, E-mail: s.hildebrand@louisville.edu. *Dean*, Dr. Rohan Christie-David, 502-852-6443, Fax: 502-852-7557, E-mail: rohan.christiedavid@louisville.edu.

College of Education and Human Development Students: 360 full-time (238 women), 642 part-time (408 women); includes 227 minority (133 Black or African American, non-Hispanic/Latino; 4 American Indian or Alaska Native, non-Hispanic/Latino; 21 Asian, non-Hispanic/Latino; 38 Hispanic/Latino; 2 Native Hawaiian or other Pacific Islander, non-Hispanic/Latino; 29 Two or more races, non-Hispanic/Latino), 18 international. Average age 32. 645 applicants, 62% accepted, 268 enrolled. *Faculty:* 86 full-time (53 women), 101 part-time/adjunct (71 women). *Financial support:* In 2015–16, 4 fellowships with full tuition reimbursements (averaging $32,992 per year), 20 research assistantships with full tuition reimbursements (averaging $32,992 per year), 20 teaching assistantships with full tuition reimbursements (averaging $32,992 per year) were awarded; Federal Work-Study, scholarships/grants, health care benefits, and unspecified assistantships also available. Financial award application deadline: 3/1; financial award applicants required to submit FAFSA. In 2015, 193 master's, 12 doctorates, 20 other advanced degrees awarded. *Degree program information:* Part-time and evening/weekend programs available. Part-time, evening/weekend. Offers art education (MAT); autism and applied behavior analysis (Certificate); community health education (M Ed); counseling and personnel services (M Ed, PhD); curriculum and instruction (PhD); early elementary education (MAT); education and human development (M Ed, MA, MAT, MS, Ed D, PhD, Certificate, Ed S); educational leadership and organizational development (Ed D, PhD); exercise physiology (MS); health and physical education (MAT); health professions education (Certificate); higher education (MA); human resources and organization development (MS); human resources organization development (MS); instructional technology (M Ed); interdisciplinary early childhood education (MAT); middle school education (MAT); music education (MAT); P-12 educational administration (M Ed, Ed S); secondary education (MAT); special education (MAT); sport administration (MS); teacher leadership (M Ed). *Application deadline:* For fall admission, 6/1 priority date for domestic students; for spring admission, 10/1 priority date for domestic students; for summer admission, 3/1 priority date for domestic students. *Application fee:* $60. Electronic applications accepted. *Application Contact:* Betty Hampton, Director, Graduate Student Services, 502-852-0411, Fax: 502-852-1465, E-mail: betty.hampton@louisville.edu. *Interim Dean*, Dr. Elisabeth A. Larson, 502-852-6044, Fax: 502-852-1464, E-mail: ann.larson@louisville.edu.

Raymond A. Kent School of Social Work Students: 371 full-time (318 women), 103 part-time (89 women); includes 128 minority (80 Black or African American, non-Hispanic/Latino; 6 Asian, non-Hispanic/Latino; 23 Hispanic/Latino; 1 Native Hawaiian or other Pacific Islander, non-Hispanic/Latino; 18 Two or more races, non-Hispanic/Latino), 8 international. Average age 32. 461 applicants, 52% accepted, 159 enrolled. *Financial support:* Research assistantships with full tuition reimbursements available, teaching assistantships with full tuition reimbursements available, Federal Work-Study, institutionally sponsored loans, scholarships/grants, health care benefits, and unspecified assistantships available. Support available to part-time students. Financial award application deadline: 5/15; financial award applicants required to submit FAFSA. In 2015, 164 master's, 4 doctorates awarded. *Degree program information:* Part-time and evening/weekend programs available. Part-time, evening/weekend. Offers marriage and family therapy (PMC); social work (MSSW, PhD). *Application deadline:* For fall admission, 7/31 for domestic and international students. Applications are processed on a rolling basis. *Application fee:* $60. Electronic applications accepted. *Application Contact:* Libby Leggett, Director, Graduate Admissions, 502-852-3101, Fax: 502-852-6536, E-mail: gradadm@louisville.edu. *Dean*, Dr. Terry Singer, 502-852-6402, Fax: 502-852-0422, E-mail: terry.singer@louisville.edu.

School of Music Students: 65 full-time (30 women), 3 part-time (0 women); includes 11 minority (5 Black or African American, non-Hispanic/Latino; 3 Hispanic/Latino; 3 Two or more races, non-Hispanic/Latino), 9 international. Average age 26. 83 applicants, 60% accepted, 35 enrolled. *Faculty:* 33 full-time (8 women), 44 part-time/adjunct (22 women). *Financial support:* In 2015–16,1 fellowship with full tuition reimbursement available (averaging $12,000 per year), 12 teaching assistantships with full tuition reimbursements available (averaging $12,000 per year); scholarships/grants, health care benefits, tuition waivers (full), and unspecified assistantships also available. Financial award application deadline: 3/1; financial award applicants required to submit FAFSA. In 2015, 22 degrees awarded. *Degree program information:* Part-time programs available. Part-time. Offers composition (MM); music education (MME); music history and literature (MM); music performance (MM); music theory (MM). *Application deadline:* For fall admission, 3/15 priority date for domestic and international students; for spring admission, 11/15 priority date for domestic and international students. Applications are processed on a rolling basis. *Application fee:* $60. Electronic applications accepted. *Application Contact:* Laura Angermeier, Admissions Counselor/Senior Advising Counselor, 502-852-1623, Fax: 502-852-0520, E-mail: leange01@louisville.edu. *Dean*, Dr. Christopher P. Doane, 502-852-6907, Fax: 502-852-0520, E-mail: c0doan01@louisville.edu.

School of Nursing Students: 110 full-time (99 women), 33 part-time (29 women); includes 17 minority (11 Black or African American, non-Hispanic/Latino; 1 Asian, non-Hispanic/Latino; 2 Hispanic/Latino; 3 Two or more races, non-Hispanic/Latino), 5 international. Average age 34. 62 applicants, 68% accepted, 40 enrolled. *Faculty:* 53 full-time (48 women), 27 part-time/adjunct (23 women). *Financial support:* In 2015–16, 10 research assistantships with full tuition reimbursements available (averaging $20,000 per year), 2 teaching assistantships with full tuition reimbursements available (averaging $15,000 per year); fellowships with full tuition reimbursements available, scholarships/grants, and unspecified assistantships also available. Financial award application deadline: 2/15; financial award applicants required to submit FAFSA. In 2015, 41 master's awarded. *Degree program information:* Part-time programs available. Part-time. Offers adult gerontology nurse practitioner (MSN, DNP); education and administration (MSN); family nurse practitioner (MSN, DNP); neonatal nurse practitioner (MSN, DNP); nursing research (PhD); psychiatric/mental health nurse practitioner (MSN, DNP); women's health nurse practitioner (MSN). *Application deadline:* For fall admission, 3/1 priority date for domestic students, 3/1 for international students. Applications are processed on a rolling basis. *Application fee:* $60. Electronic applications accepted. *Application Contact:* Trish Hart, Assistant Dean for Student Affairs, 502-852-5825, Fax: 502-852-8783, E-mail: trish.hart@louisville.edu. *Dean*, Dr. Marcia J. Hern, 502-852-8300, Fax: 502-852-8783, E-mail: m.hern@louisville.edu.

School of Public Health and Information Sciences Students: 118 full-time (73 women), 53 part-time (35 women); includes 44 minority (18 Black or African American, non-Hispanic/Latino; 17 Asian, non-Hispanic/Latino; 6 Hispanic/Latino; 3 Two or more races, non-Hispanic/Latino), 32 international. Average age 31. 166 applicants, 77% accepted, 70 enrolled. *Faculty:* 39 full-time (13 women), 7 part-time/adjunct (3 women). *Financial support:* Research assistantships with full tuition reimbursements, scholarships/grants, health care benefits, and unspecified assistantships available. Financial award application deadline: 5/1; financial award applicants required to submit FAFSA. In 2015, 48 master's, 7 doctorates awarded. *Degree program information:* Part-time and evening/weekend programs available. Part-time, evening/weekend. Offers biostatistics (MS, PhD); clinical investigation (M Sc); decision science (MS); epidemiology (MPH, MS, PhD); health management and systems sciences (MPH); public health and information sciences (M Sc, MPH, MS, PhD); public health sciences (PhD); public health sciences - health management (PhD). *Application deadline:* For fall admission, 2/1 for domestic and international students. Applications are processed on a rolling basis. *Application fee:* $60. Electronic applications accepted. *Application Contact:* Vicki Lewis, Administrative Assistant, 502-852-1798, Fax: 502-852-3294, E-mail: vicki.lewis@louisville.edu. *Associate Dean for Academic Affairs*, Dr. Craig Blakely, 502-852-3297, Fax: 502-852-3291, E-mail: craig.blakely@louisville.edu.

J. B. Speed School of Engineering Students: 334 full-time (83 women), 310 part-time (51 women); includes 73 minority (23 Black or African American, non-Hispanic/Latino; 19 Asian, non-Hispanic/Latino; 19 Hispanic/Latino; 12 Two or more races, non-Hispanic/Latino), 219 international. Average age 28. 312 applicants, 58% accepted, 75 enrolled. *Faculty:* 98 full-time (18 women), 17 part-time/adjunct (2 women). *Financial support:* In 2015–16, 12 students received support, including 12 fellowships with full tuition reimbursements available (averaging $22,000 per year); research assistantships with full tuition reimbursements available, teaching assistantships with full tuition reimbursements available, and scholarships/grants also available. Financial award application deadline: 2/3. In 2015, 122 master's, 14 doctorates, 3 other advanced degrees awarded. *Degree program information:* Part-time programs available. Part-time, online learning. Offers bioengineering (M Eng); chemical engineering (M Eng, MS, PhD); civil engineering (M Eng, MS, PhD); computer engineering and computer science (M Eng, MS, PhD); data mining (Certificate); electrical and computer engineering (M Eng, MS, PhD); engineering (M Eng, MS, PhD, Certificate, Graduate Certificate); engineering management (M Eng); environmental engineering (Graduate Certificate); industrial engineering (M Eng, MS, PhD); logistics and distribution (Certificate); mechanical engineering (M Eng, MS, PhD); network and information security (Certificate). *Application deadline:* For fall admission, 6/15 for domestic students, 5/1 priority date for international students; for spring admission, 11/22 for domestic students, 11/1 priority date for international students; for summer admission, 3/31 for domestic students, 4/1 priority date for international students. *Application fee:* $60. Electronic applications accepted. *Application Contact:* Dr. Michael Harris, Director of Academic Programs, J. B. Speed School of Engineering, 502-852-6278, Fax: 502-852-7294, E-mail: mharris@louisville.edu. *Dean*, Dr. John S. Usher, 502-852-6281, Fax: 502-852-7033, E-mail: john.usher@louisville.edu.

Louis D. Brandeis School of Law Students: 339 full-time (159 women), 15 part-time (7 women); includes 29 minority (13 Black or African American, non-Hispanic/Latino; 1 American Indian or Alaska Native, non-Hispanic/Latino; 4 Asian, non-Hispanic/Latino; 8 Hispanic/Latino; 3 Two or more races, non-Hispanic/Latino). Average age 26. 608 applicants, 70% accepted, 92 enrolled. *Faculty:* 30 full-time (11 women), 13 part-time/adjunct (4 women). *Financial support:* In 2015–16, 182 students received support, including 15 fellowships (averaging $3,000 per year), 58 research assistantships (averaging $900 per year); teaching assistantships, career-related internships or fieldwork, scholarships/grants, and tuition waivers (partial) also available. Support available to part-time students. Financial award application deadline: 6/1; financial award applicants required to submit FAFSA. In 2015, 128 doctorates awarded. *Degree program information:* Part-time programs available. Part-time. Offers law (JD). *Application deadline:* For fall admission, 4/1 for domestic students, 3/1 for international students. Applications are processed on a rolling basis. *Application fee:* $50. Electronic applications accepted. *Application Contact:* Camilo Ortiz, Assistant Dean for Admission, 502-852-6365, Fax: 502-852-8971, E-mail: lawadmissions@louisville.edu. *Dean*, Susan Hanley Duncan, 502-852-6373, Fax: 502-852-0862, E-mail: susan.duncan@louisville.edu.

School of Dentistry Students: 518 full-time (220 women), 19 part-time (10 women); includes 118 minority (22 Black or African American, non-Hispanic/Latino; 2 American Indian or Alaska Native, non-Hispanic/Latino; 55 Asian, non-Hispanic/Latino; 24 Hispanic/Latino; 15 Two or more races, non-Hispanic/Latino), 26 international. Average age 26. 176 applicants, 93% accepted, 146 enrolled. *Faculty:* 71 full-time (23 women), 81 part-time/adjunct (20 women). *Financial support:* In 2015–16, 1 research assistantship with full tuition reimbursement available (averaging $20,000 per year). Financial award application deadline: 3/15; financial award applicants required to submit FAFSA. In 2015, 2 master's, 115 doctorates awarded. *Degree program information:* Part-time programs available. Part-time. Offers dentistry (DMD); oral biology (MS). *Application deadline:* For fall admission, 1/1 for domestic and international students. Applications are processed on a rolling basis. *Application fee:* $60. Electronic applications accepted. *Application Contact:* Robin Benningfield, Admissions Counselor, 502-852-5081, Fax: 502-852-1210, E-mail: dmdadms@louisville.edu. *Dean*, Dr. John J. Sauk, 502-852-1304, Fax: 502-852-3364, E-mail: jjsauk01@louisville.edu.

School of Interdisciplinary and Graduate Studies Students: 24 full-time (18 women), 10 part-time (3 women); includes 8 minority (1 Asian, non-Hispanic/Latino; 4 Hispanic/Latino; 3 Two or more races, non-Hispanic/Latino), 5 international. Average age 33. 33 applicants, 48% accepted, 13 enrolled. *Financial support:* Fellowships with full tuition reimbursements available, career-related internships or fieldwork, Federal Work-Study, institutionally sponsored loans, scholarships/grants, health care benefits, and tuition waivers (full and partial) available. Financial award application deadline: 2/1; financial award applicants required to submit FAFSA. *Degree program information:* Part-time and evening/weekend programs available. Part-time, evening/weekend. Offers interdisciplinary studies (MA, MS, PhD). *Application deadline:* For fall admission, 5/1 priority date for international students; for spring admission, 11/1 priority date for international students; for summer admission, 4/1 priority date for international students. Applications are processed on a rolling basis. *Application fee:* $60. *Application Contact:* Libby Leggett, Executive Director of Graduate Admissions and Recruitment, 502-852-3108, Fax: 502-852-3111, E-mail: melegg02@louisville.edu. *Dean/Vice Provost*, Dr. Beth A. Boehm, 502-852-6590, Fax: 502-852-6616, E-mail: beth.boehm@louisville.edu.

School of Medicine Students: 879 full-time (420 women), 31 part-time (12 women); includes 167 minority (47 Black or African American, non-Hispanic/Latino; 76 Asian, non-Hispanic/Latino; 21 Hispanic/Latino; 23 Two or more races, non-Hispanic/Latino),

43 international. Average age 26. 4,104 applicants, 10% accepted, 247 enrolled. *Faculty:* 789 full-time (294 women), 111 part-time/adjunct (51 women). *Financial support:* In 2015–16, 165 students received support, including 55 fellowships with full tuition reimbursements available (averaging $23,500 per year), 110 research assistantships with full tuition reimbursements available (averaging $24,000 per year); institutionally sponsored loans, scholarships/grants, traineeships, and unspecified assistantships also available. In 2015, 39 master's, 165 doctorates awarded. Offers anatomical sciences and neurobiology (MS, PhD); audiology (Au D); biochemistry and molecular biology (MS, PhD); communicative disorders (MS); medicine (MS, Au D, MD, PhD); microbiology and immunology (MS, PhD); pharmacology and toxicology (MS, PhD); physiology and biophysics (MS, PhD). *Application deadline:* For fall admission, 10/28 for domestic students, 10/15 for international students. Applications are processed on a rolling basis. *Application fee:* $60. Electronic applications accepted. *Application Contact:* Judy C. Hollkamp, Program Coordinator, 502-852-3805, E-mail: jcholl01@louisville.edu. *Dean*, Dr. Toni M. Ganzel, 502-852-1499, Fax: 502-852-1484, E-mail: toni.ganzel@louisville.edu.

UNIVERSITY OF MAINE, Orono, ME 04469

General Information State-supported, coed, university. CGS member. *Enrollment:* 10,922 graduate, professional, and undergraduate students; 1,056 full-time matriculated graduate/professional students (593 women), 410 part-time matriculated graduate/professional students (275 women). *Enrollment by degree level:* 930 master's, 419 doctoral, 117 other advanced degrees. *Graduate faculty:* 429 full-time (135 women), 266 part-time/adjunct (166 women). *Graduate housing:* Rooms and/or apartments available on a first-come, first-served basis to single and married students. Housing application deadline: 8/1. *Student services:* Campus employment opportunities, campus safety program, career counseling, child daycare facilities, exercise/wellness program, free psychological counseling, grant writing training, international student services, low-cost health insurance, multicultural affairs office, services for students with disabilities, teacher training, writing training. *Library:* Fogler Library. *Collection:* Books: 1.4 million (physical), 557,000 (digital/electronic); Serial titles: 623 (physical), 98,000 (digital/electronic); Databases: 420. Weekly public service hours: 103; students can reserve study rooms. *Research affiliation:* Jackson Laboratory (medical genetics), Bigelow Laboratories for Ocean Sciences (marine science), Mount Desert Island Biological Laboratory (marine molecular biology), Sensor Research Development Corporation (electrical sensors), Maine Medical Center Research Institute (clinical medicine), Maine Institute for Human Genetics (medical genetics).

Computer facilities: Computer purchase and lease plans are available. 600 computers available on campus for general student use. A campuswide network can be accessed from student residence rooms and from off campus. Online class registration, online housing and financial aid information are available.
Website: http://www.umaine.edu/

General Application Contact: Scott G. Delcourt, Assistant Vice President for Graduate Studies and Senior Associate Dean, 207-581-3291, Fax: 207-581-3232, E-mail: graduate@maine.edu.

GRADUATE UNITS

Graduate School Students: 1,056 full-time (593 women), 410 part-time (275 women); includes 79 minority (12 Black or African American, non-Hispanic/Latino; 31 American Indian or Alaska Native, non-Hispanic/Latino; 13 Asian, non-Hispanic/Latino; 18 Hispanic/Latino; 2 Native Hawaiian or other Pacific Islander, non-Hispanic/Latino; 3 Two or more races, non-Hispanic/Latino), 175 international. Average age 33. 1,683 applicants, 46% accepted, 475 enrolled. *Faculty:* 571 full-time (179 women), 390 part-time/adjunct (150 women). *Financial support:* In 2015–16, 1,296 students received support, including 37 fellowships with full tuition reimbursements available (averaging $21,500 per year), 244 research assistantships with full tuition reimbursements available (averaging $18,000 per year), 269 teaching assistantships with full tuition reimbursements available (averaging $14,100 per year); career-related internships or fieldwork, Federal Work-Study, institutionally sponsored loans, scholarships/grants, tuition waivers (full and partial), and unspecified assistantships also available. Support available to part-time students. Financial award application deadline: 3/1; financial award applicants required to submit FAFSA. In 2015, 411 master's, 47 doctorates, 24 other advanced degrees awarded. *Degree program information:* Part-time and evening/weekend programs available. Part-time, evening/weekend, online learning. Offers interdisciplinary studies (MA, PhD). *Application deadline:* For fall admission, 1/15 priority date for domestic and international students; for spring admission, 11/15 priority date for domestic and international students. Applications are processed on a rolling basis. *Application fee:* $65. Electronic applications accepted. *Assistant Vice President for Graduate Studies and Senior Associate Dean*, Scott G. Delcourt, 207-581-3291, Fax: 207-581-3232, E-mail: graduate@maine.edu.

Climate Change Institute Students: 8 full-time (4 women), 1 (woman) part-time; includes 1 minority (American Indian or Alaska Native, non-Hispanic/Latino). Average age 33. 13 applicants, 31% accepted, 2 enrolled. *Faculty:* 41 full-time (11 women). *Financial support:* In 2015–16, 6 students received support, including 4 research assistantships with full tuition reimbursements available (averaging $14,780 per year); unspecified assistantships also available. Financial award application deadline: 3/1. In 2015, 1 master's awarded. *Degree program information:* Part-time programs available. Part-time. Offers climate change (MS, CGS). *Application deadline:* For fall admission, 11/1 priority date for domestic and international students; for spring admission, 2/1 priority date for domestic and international students. Applications are processed on a rolling basis. *Application fee:* $65. Electronic applications accepted. *Application Contact:* Dr. Karl Kreutz, Graduate Coordinator, 207-581-3011, E-mail: karl.kreutz@maine.edu. *Director*, Dr. Paul Mayewski, 207-581-3019, Fax: 207-581-1203, E-mail: paul.mayewski@maine.edu.

College of Education and Human Development Students: 152 full-time (110 women), 191 part-time (153 women); includes 21 minority (8 Black or African American, non-Hispanic/Latino; 3 American Indian or Alaska Native, non-Hispanic/Latino; 6 Hispanic/Latino; 1 Native Hawaiian or other Pacific Islander, non-Hispanic/Latino; 3 Two or more races, non-Hispanic/Latino), 6 international. Average age 36. 301 applicants, 48% accepted, 97 enrolled. *Faculty:* 34 full-time (17 women), 15 part-time/adjunct (8 women). *Financial support:* In 2015–16, 51 students received support, including 1 fellowship (averaging $23,500 per year), 21 teaching assistantships with full tuition reimbursements available (averaging $14,600 per year); career-related internships or fieldwork, Federal Work-Study, institutionally sponsored loans, scholarships/grants, and unspecified assistantships also available. Support available to part-time students. Financial award application deadline: 3/1. In 2015, 85 master's, 4 doctorates, 58 other advanced degrees awarded. *Degree program information:* Part-time and evening/weekend programs available. Part-time, evening/weekend. Offers classroom technology integrationist (CGS); counselor education (M Ed, MA, MS, CAS); early childhood teacher (CGS); education (PhD); education and human development (M Ed, MA, MAT, MS, Ed D, PhD, CAS, CGS); education data specialist (CGS); educational leadership (M Ed, Ed D, CAS); educational technology coordinator (CGS); elementary education (M Ed, CAS); higher education (MA, PhD, CAS); human development (MS); individualized education (M Ed); kinesiology and physical education (M Ed, MS); literacy education (CAS); response to intervention for behavior (CGS); science education (M Ed, MS); secondary education (M Ed, CAS); social studies education (M Ed); special education (M Ed, CAS); STEM education (PhD). *Application deadline:* For fall admission, 1/15 priority date for domestic students. Applications are processed on a rolling basis. *Application fee:* $65. Electronic applications accepted. *Application Contact:* Scott G. Delcourt, Senior Associate Dean of the Graduate School, 207-581-3291, Fax: 207-581-3232, E-mail: graduate@maine.edu. *Interim Dean*, Dr. Ivan Manev, 207-581-2441, Fax: 207-581-2423.

College of Engineering Students: 119 full-time (29 women), 25 part-time (3 women); includes 9 minority (1 American Indian or Alaska Native, non-Hispanic/Latino; 3 Asian, non-Hispanic/Latino; 2 Hispanic/Latino; 3 Two or more races, non-Hispanic/Latino), 62 international. Average age 30. 156 applicants, 56% accepted, 47 enrolled. *Faculty:* 64 full-time (5 women), 52 part-time/adjunct (6 women). *Financial support:* In 2015–16, 89 students received support, including 5 fellowships (averaging $23,100 per year), 41 research assistantships (averaging $14,600 per year), 23 teaching assistantships (averaging $14,600 per year); Federal Work-Study, institutionally sponsored loans, scholarships/grants, tuition waivers (full and partial), and unspecified assistantships also available. Financial award application deadline: 3/1. In 2015, 19 master's, 12 doctorates awarded. *Degree program information:* Part-time programs available. Part-time. Offers chemical engineering (MS, PhD); civil engineering (MS, PhD); computer engineering (MS); electrical engineering (MS, PhD); engineering (ME, MS, PSM, PhD); mechanical engineering (MS, PSM, PhD). *Application deadline:* For fall admission, 2/1 priority date for domestic students. Applications are processed on a rolling basis. *Application fee:* $65. Electronic applications accepted. *Application Contact:* Scott G. Delcourt, Assistant Vice President for Graduate Studies and Senior Associate Dean, 207-581-3291, Fax: 207-581-3232, E-mail: graduate@maine.edu. *Interim Dean*, Dr. Dana Humphrey, 207-581-2217, Fax: 207-581-2220, E-mail: dana.humphrey@umit.maine.edu.

College of Liberal Arts and Sciences Students: 289 full-time (121 women), 51 part-time (32 women); includes 27 minority (2 Black or African American, non-Hispanic/Latino; 9 American Indian or Alaska Native, non-Hispanic/Latino; 5 Asian, non-Hispanic/Latino; 7 Hispanic/Latino; 4 Two or more races, non-Hispanic/Latino), 49 international. Average age 32. 476 applicants, 41% accepted, 102 enrolled. *Faculty:* 159 full-time (43 women), 163 part-time/adjunct (61 women). *Financial support:* In 2015–16, 250 students received support, including 10 fellowships (averaging $19,400 per year), 31 research assistantships (averaging $14,600 per year), 163 teaching assistantships (averaging $14,600 per year); career-related internships or fieldwork, Federal Work-Study, institutionally sponsored loans, scholarships/grants, and tuition waivers (full and partial) also available. Support available to part-time students. Financial award application deadline: 3/1. In 2015, 71 master's, 14 doctorates, 2 other advanced degrees awarded. *Degree program information:* Part-time and evening/weekend programs available. Part-time, evening/weekend. Offers anthropology and environmental policy (PhD); Asian studies (MA); Canadian studies (MA); chemistry (MS, PhD); communication (MA, PhD); composition and pedagogy (MA); computer science (MS, PhD); engineering physics (ME); European studies (MA); gender and literature (MA); geographic information systems (CGS); global policy (MA); information systems (MS); intermedia (MFA); liberal arts and sciences (MA, MAT, ME, MFA, MM, MS, MST, PhD, CGS); mass communication (MA); mathematics and statistics (MA); music performance (MM); North American French (MA); physics (MS, PhD); psychological sciences (PhD); spatial information science and engineering (MS, PhD). *Application deadline:* For fall admission, 2/1 priority date for domestic students. Applications are processed on a rolling basis. *Application fee:* $65. Electronic applications accepted. *Application Contact:* Scott G. Delcourt, Assistant Vice President for Graduate Studies and Senior Associate Dean, 207-581-3291, Fax: 207-581-3232, E-mail: graduate@maine.edu. *Dean*, Dr. Emily Haddad, 207-581-1954, Fax: 207-581-1947, E-mail: emily.haddad@maine.edu.

College of Natural Sciences, Forestry, and Agriculture Students: 471 full-time (295 women), 14 part-time (12 women); includes 30 minority (2 Black or African American, non-Hispanic/Latino; 9 American Indian or Alaska Native, non-Hispanic/Latino; 6 Asian, non-Hispanic/Latino; 6 Hispanic/Latino; 7 Two or more races, non-Hispanic/Latino), 74 international. Average age 30. 746 applicants, 38% accepted, 164 enrolled. *Faculty:* 285 full-time (104 women), 182 part-time/adjunct (50 women). *Financial support:* In 2015–16, 304 students received support, including 4 fellowships (averaging $25,000 per year), 204 research assistantships (averaging $14,600 per year), 77 teaching assistantships (averaging $14,600 per year); career-related internships or fieldwork, Federal Work-Study, institutionally sponsored loans, scholarships/grants, health care benefits, tuition waivers (full and partial), and unspecified assistantships also available. Support available to part-time students. Financial award application deadline: 3/1. In 2015, 129 master's, 27 doctorates, 9 other advanced degrees awarded. *Degree program information:* Part-time and evening/weekend programs available. Part-time, evening/weekend. Offers animal sciences (MPS, MS); biological sciences (PhD); botany and plant pathology (MS); communication sciences and disorders (MA); earth and climate sciences (MS, PhD); ecology and environmental science (MS, PhD); economics (MA); entomology (MS); financial economics (MA); food and human nutrition (PhD); food science and human nutrition (MS); forest resources (MS, PhD); forestry (MF); horticulture (MS); individualized (MS); marine bio-resources (MS, PhD); marine biology (MS, PhD); marine policy (MS); microbiology (PhD); natural sciences, forestry, and agriculture (MA, MF, MPS, MS, MSW, MWC, PSM, PhD, CAS, CGS); nursing education (CGS); oceanography (MS, PhD); plant science (PhD); resource economics and policy (MS); rural health family nurse practitioner (MS, CAS); social work (MSW, CGS); wildlife conservation (MWC); wildlife ecology (MS, PhD); zoology (MS, PhD). *Application deadline:* For fall admission, 2/1 priority date for domestic students. Applications are processed on a rolling basis. *Application fee:* $65. Electronic applications accepted. *Application Contact:* Scott G. Delcourt, Assistant Vice President for Graduate Studies and Senior Associate Dean, 207-581-3291, Fax: 207-581-3232, E-mail: graduate@maine.edu. *Dean*, Dr. Edward Ashworth, 207-581-3206, Fax: 207-581-3207.

Graduate School of Biomedical Science and Engineering Students: 41 full-time (24 women), 2 part-time (both women); includes 2 minority (both Two or more races, non-Hispanic/Latino), 12 international. Average age 31. 69 applicants, 19% accepted, 12 enrolled. *Faculty:* 151 full-time (45 women). *Financial support:* In 2015–16, 28 students received support, including 1 fellowship with full tuition reimbursement available (averaging $20,000 per year), 22 research assistantships with full tuition reimbursements available (averaging $23,000 per year), 5 teaching assistantships (averaging $7,500 per year). Financial award application deadline: 3/1. In 2015, 2 master's, 2 doctorates awarded. Offers bioinformatics (PSM); biomedical engineering (PhD); biomedical science (PhD). *Application deadline:* For fall admission, 12/31 for domestic students. *Application fee:* $65. *Application Contact:* Scott G. Delcourt, Assistant Vice President for Graduate Studies and Senior Associate Dean, 207-581-3291, Fax: 207-581-3232, E-mail: graduate@maine.edu. *Director,* Dr. David Neivandt, 207-581-2803.

The Maine Business School Students: 41 full-time (18 women), 12 part-time (5 women); includes 6 minority (1 Black or African American, non-Hispanic/Latino; 2 American Indian or Alaska Native, non-Hispanic/Latino; 1 Asian, non-Hispanic/Latino; 2 Two or more races, non-Hispanic/Latino), 8 international. Average age 30. 137 applicants, 31% accepted, 23 enrolled. *Faculty:* 20 full-time (7 women), 1 part-time/adjunct (0 women). *Financial support:* In 2015–16, 9 students received support, including 3 teaching assistantships (averaging $14,600 per year); career-related internships or fieldwork, Federal Work-Study, institutionally sponsored loans, scholarships/grants, tuition waivers (full and partial), and unspecified assistantships also available. Financial award application deadline: 3/1. In 2015, 9 master's, 1 other advanced degree awarded. *Degree program information:* Part-time and evening/weekend programs available. Part-time, evening/weekend, online learning. Offers accounting (MBA); business administration (CGS); business and sustainability (MBA); finance (MBA); international business (MBA); management (MBA). *Application deadline:* For fall admission, 7/1 priority date for domestic students, 5/1 priority date for international students; for spring admission, 11/1 priority date for domestic students, 9/1 priority date for international students; for summer admission, 4/1 priority date for domestic students, 2/1 priority date for international students. Applications are processed on a rolling basis. *Application fee:* $65. Electronic applications accepted. *Application Contact:* Scott G. Delcourt, Assistant Vice President for Graduate Studies and Senior Associate Dean, 207-581-3291, Fax: 207-581-3232, E-mail: graduate@maine.edu. *Manager of MBA Programs, Executive Education and Internships,* Richard Borgman, 207-581-1870, Fax: 207-581-1930, E-mail: borgman@maine.edu.

University of Maine School of Law Students: 244 full-time (123 women), 7 part-time (5 women); includes 26 minority (6 Black or African American, non-Hispanic/Latino; 9 American Indian or Alaska Native, non-Hispanic/Latino; 4 Asian, non-Hispanic/Latino; 7 Hispanic/Latino), 2 international. Average age 27. 451 applicants, 69% accepted, 79 enrolled. *Faculty:* 19 full-time (8 women), 19 part-time/adjunct (8 women). *Financial support:* In 2015–16, 149 students received support, including 24 fellowships (averaging $3,000 per year), 6 research assistantships (averaging $2,000 per year); teaching assistantships, Federal Work-Study, and scholarships/grants also available. Financial award application deadline: 2/15; financial award applicants required to submit FAFSA. In 2015, 77 doctorates awarded. *Degree program information:* Part-time programs available. Part-time. Offers law (JD). *Application deadline:* For fall admission, 4/15 for domestic and international students. Applications are processed on a rolling basis. *Application fee:* $0. Electronic applications accepted. *Application Contact:* Caroline Wilshusen, Director of Admissions, 207-780-4341, Fax: 207-780-4239, E-mail: lawadmissions@maine.edu. *Dean,* Danielle Conway, 207-780-4344, Fax: 207-780-4239.

UNIVERSITY OF MAINE AT FARMINGTON, Farmington, ME 04938-1990

General Information State-supported, coed, comprehensive institution. *Enrollment:* 2,016 graduate, professional, and undergraduate students; 73 full-time matriculated graduate/professional students (62 women). *Enrollment by degree level:* 73 master's. *Graduate faculty:* 6 full-time (5 women), 7 part-time/adjunct (5 women). *Student services:* Exercise/wellness program, low-cost health insurance, services for students with disabilities. *Library:* Mantor Library plus 1 other. *Collection:* Books: 63,640 (physical), 159,744 (digital/electronic); Serial titles: 184 (physical), 66,560 (digital/electronic); Databases: 84. Weekly public service hours: 88; students can reserve study rooms.

Computer facilities: Computer purchase and lease plans are available. 220 computers available on campus for general student use. A campuswide network can be accessed from student residence rooms and from off campus. Online class registration is available.
Website: http://www.umf.maine.edu/

General Application Contact: Valerie Soucie, Administrative Specialist, 207-778-7052, Fax: 207-778-8134, E-mail: gradstudies@maine.edu.

GRADUATE UNITS

Graduate Programs in Education Students: 73 full-time (62 women). Average age 35. 60 applicants, 100% accepted, 5 enrolled. *Faculty:* 6 full-time (5 women), 7 part-time/adjunct (5 women). *Financial support:* Applicants required to submit FAFSA. In 2015, 21 master's awarded. *Degree program information:* Part-time and evening/weekend programs available. Part-time-only, evening/weekend, 100% online, blended/hybrid learning. Offers early childhood education (MS Ed); educational leadership (MS Ed). *Application deadline:* For fall admission, 8/10 for domestic students; for spring admission, 1/5 for domestic students; for summer admission, 4/10 for domestic students. Applications are processed on a rolling basis. *Application fee:* $60. Electronic applications accepted. *Application Contact:* Valerie Soucie, Administrative Specialist, 207-778-7502, Fax: 207-778-8134, E-mail: gradstudies@maine.edu. *Director of Graduate Programs in Education,* Dr. Johanna Prince, 207-778-7066, E-mail: gradstudies@maine.edu.

UNIVERSITY OF MANAGEMENT AND TECHNOLOGY, Arlington, VA 22209

General Information Proprietary, coed, comprehensive institution. *Enrollment:* 1,260 graduate, professional, and undergraduate students; 238 full-time matriculated graduate/professional students (64 women), 49 part-time matriculated graduate/professional students (26 women). *Graduate faculty:* 20 full-time (5 women), 100 part-time/adjunct (25 women). *Student services:* Career counseling, international student services. *Collection:* Books: 9,149 (physical), 35 (digital/electronic).

Computer facilities: A campuswide network can be accessed. Online class registration is available.
Website: http://www.umtweb.edu/

General Application Contact: Kenny Hickey, Admissions, 703-516-0035, Fax: 703-516-0985, E-mail: admissions@umtweb.edu.

GRADUATE UNITS

Program in Business Administration ***Degree program information:*** Part-time and evening/weekend programs available. Part-time, evening/weekend, online learning. Offers general management (MBA, DBA); project management (MBA). *Application deadline:* Applications are processed on a rolling basis. *Application fee:* $30. Electronic applications accepted. *Application Contact:* Kenny Hickey, Admissions, 703-516-0035, Fax: 703-516-0985, E-mail: admissions@umtweb.edu. *Academic Dean,* Dr. J. Davidson Frame, 703-516-0035 Ext. 25.

Program in Computer Science ***Degree program information:*** Part-time and evening/weekend programs available. Part-time, evening/weekend, online learning. Offers computer science (MS); information technology (AC); project management (AC); software engineering (MS). *Application deadline:* Applications are processed on a rolling basis. *Application fee:* $30. Electronic applications accepted. *Application Contact:* Kenny Hickey, Admissions, 703-516-0035, Fax: 703-516-0985, E-mail: admissions@umtweb.edu. *Academic Dean,* Dr. J. Davidson Frame, 703-516-0035, Fax: 703-516-0985.

Program in Criminal Justice ***Degree program information:*** Part-time and evening/weekend programs available. Part-time, evening/weekend, online learning. Offers homeland security (MS). *Application Contact:* Kenny Hickey, Admissions, 703-516-0035, Fax: 703-516-0985, E-mail: admissions@umtweb.edu. *Academic Dean,* Dr. J. Davidson Frame, 703-516-0035.

Program in Engineering Management Offers engineering management (MS). *Application Contact:* Kenny Hickey, Admissions, 703-516-0035, Fax: 703-516-0985, E-mail: admissions@umtweb.edu.

Program in Health Administration Offers health administration (MHA). *Application Contact:* Kenny Hickey, Admissions, 703-516-0035, Fax: 703-516-0985, E-mail: admissions@umtweb.edu.

Program in Homeland Security Offers homeland security (MS). *Application Contact:* Kenny Hickey, Admissions, 703-516-0035, Fax: 703-516-0985, E-mail: admissions@umtweb.edu.

Program in Information Technology Offers information technology (MS, Advanced Certificate). *Application Contact:* Kenny Hickey, Admissions, 703-516-0035, Fax: 703-516-0985, E-mail: admissions@umtweb.edu.

Program in Management ***Degree program information:*** Part-time and evening/weekend programs available. Part-time, evening/weekend, online learning. Offers acquisition management (MS, AC); criminal justice administration (MS); general management (MS); project management (MS, AC). *Application deadline:* Applications are processed on a rolling basis. *Application fee:* $30. Electronic applications accepted. *Application Contact:* Kenny Hickey, Admissions, 703-516-0035, Fax: 703-516-0985, E-mail: admissions@umtweb.edu. *Academic Dean,* Dr. J. Davidson Frame, 703-516-0035.

Program in Public Administration Offers public administration (MPA, Advanced Certificate). *Application Contact:* Kenny Hickey, Admissions, 703-516-0035, Fax: 703-516-0985, E-mail: admissions@umtweb.edu.

THE UNIVERSITY OF MANCHESTER, Manchester M13 9PL, United Kingdom

General Information Public, coed, comprehensive institution.

GRADUATE UNITS

Alliance Manchester Business School Students: 1,032 (688 women). 10,759 applicants, 33% accepted, 1032 enrolled. Offers accounting and finance (M Sc); business (M Ent); business analysis and strategic management (M Sc); business analytics: operational research and risk analysis (M Sc); business psychology (M Sc); corporate communications and reputation management (M Sc); finance (M Sc); finance and business economics (M Sc); human resource management and industrial relations (M Sc); innovation management and entrepreneurship (M Sc); international business and management (M Sc); international human resource management and comparative industrial relations (M Sc); management (M Sc); marketing (M Sc); operations, project and supply chain management (M Sc); organizational psychology (M Sc); quantitative finance (M Sc). *Application deadline:* Applications are processed on a rolling basis. Electronic applications accepted. *Application Contact:* Jemma Jamieson, Marketing and Recruitment Assistant, Master's Programs, 44 161 306 1339, E-mail: pg@mbs.ac.uk. *Head of Alliance Manchester Business School,* Fiona Devine.

Faculty of Life Sciences Offers adaptive organismal biology (M Phil, PhD); animal biology (M Phil, PhD); biochemistry (M Phil, PhD); bioinformatics (M Phil, PhD); biomolecular sciences (M Phil, PhD); biotechnology (M Phil, PhD); cell biology (M Phil, PhD); cell matrix research (M Phil, PhD); channels and transporters (M Phil, PhD); developmental biology (M Phil, PhD); Egyptology (M Phil, PhD); environmental biology (M Phil, PhD); evolutionary biology (M Phil, PhD); gene expression (M Phil, PhD); genetics (M Phil, PhD); history of science, technology and medicine (M Phil, PhD); immunology (M Phil, PhD); integrative neurobiology and behavior (M Phil, PhD); membrane trafficking (M Phil, PhD); microbiology (M Phil, PhD); molecular and cellular neuroscience (M Phil, PhD); molecular biology (M Phil, PhD); molecular cancer studies (M Phil, PhD); neuroscience (M Phil, PhD); ophthalmology (M Phil, PhD); optometry (M Phil, PhD); organelle function (M Phil, PhD); pharmacology (M Phil, PhD); physiology (M Phil, PhD); plant sciences (M Phil, PhD); stem cell research (M Phil, PhD); structural biology (M Phil, PhD); systems neuroscience (M Phil, PhD); toxicology (M Phil, PhD).

School of Arts, Histories and Cultures Offers anthropology, media and performance (PhD); applied theatre professional (PhD); archaeology (PhD); art history and visual studies (PhD); arts management and cultural policy (PhD); classics and ancient history (PhD); composition (PhD); creative writing (PhD); drama (PhD); economic and social history (PhD); electroacoustic composition (PhD); English and American studies (PhD); history (PhD); humanitarianism and conflict response (PhD); museology (PhD); music (PhD); musicology (PhD); religions and theology (PhD).

School of Chemical Engineering and Analytical Science Offers biocatalysis (M Phil, PhD); chemical engineering (M Phil, PhD); chemical engineering and analytical science (M Phil, D Eng, PhD); colloids, crystals, interfaces and materials (M Phil, PhD); environment and sustainable technology (M Phil, PhD); instrumentation (M Phil, PhD); multi-scale modeling (M Phil, PhD); process integration (M Phil, PhD); systems biology (M Phil, PhD).

School of Chemistry Offers biological chemistry (PhD); chemistry (M Ent, M Phil, M Sc, D Ent, PhD); inorganic chemistry (PhD); materials chemistry (PhD); nanoscience (PhD); nuclear fission (PhD); organic chemistry (PhD); physical chemistry (PhD); theoretical chemistry (PhD).

School of Computer Science Offers computer science (M Phil, PhD).

School of Dentistry Offers basic dental sciences (cancer studies) (M Phil, PhD); basic dental sciences (molecular genetics) (M Phil, PhD); basic dental sciences (stem cell biology) (M Phil, PhD); biomaterials sciences and dental technology (M Phil, PhD); dental public health/community dentistry (M Phil, PhD); dental science (clinical) (PhD); endodontology (M Phil, PhD); fixed and removable prosthodontics (M Phil, PhD); operative dentistry (M Phil, PhD); oral and maxillofacial surgery (M Phil, PhD); oral radiology (M Phil, PhD); orthodontics (M Phil, PhD); restorative dentistry (M Phil, PhD).

School of Earth, Atmospheric and Environmental Sciences Offers atmospheric sciences (M Phil, M Sc, PhD); basin studies and petroleum geosciences (M Phil, M Sc,

PhD); earth, atmospheric and environmental sciences (M Phil, M Sc, PhD); environmental geochemistry and cosmochemistry (M Phil, M Sc, PhD); isotope geochemistry and cosmochemistry (M Phil, M Sc, PhD); paleontology (M Phil, M Sc, PhD); physics and chemistry of minerals and fluids (M Phil, M Sc, PhD); structural and petrological geosciences (M Phil, M Sc, PhD).

School of Education Offers counseling (D Couns); counseling psychology (D Couns); education (M Phil, Ed D, PhD); educational and child psychology (Ed D); educational psychology (Ed D).

School of Electrical and Electronic Engineering Offers electrical and electronic engineering (M Phil, PhD).

School of Environment and Development Offers architecture (M Phil, PhD); development policy and management (M Phil, PhD); human geography (M Phil, PhD); physical geography (M Phil, PhD); planning and landscape (M Phil, PhD).

School of Languages, Linguistics and Cultures Offers Arab world studies (PhD); Chinese studies (M Phil, PhD); East Asian studies (M Phil, PhD); English language (PhD); French studies (M Phil, PhD); German studies (M Phil, PhD); interpreting studies (PhD); Italian studies (M Phil, PhD); Japanese studies (M Phil, PhD); Latin American cultural studies (M Phil, PhD); linguistics (M Phil, PhD); Middle Eastern studies (M Phil, PhD); Polish studies (M Phil, PhD); Portuguese studies (M Phil, PhD); Russian studies (M Phil, PhD); Spanish studies (M Phil, PhD); translation and intercultural studies (M Phil, PhD).

School of Law Offers bioethics and medical jurisprudence (PhD); criminology (M Phil, PhD); law (M Phil, PhD).

School of Materials Offers advanced aerospace materials engineering (M Sc); advanced metallic systems (PhD); biomedical materials (M Phil, M Sc, PhD); ceramics and glass (M Phil, M Sc, PhD); composite materials (M Sc, PhD); corrosion and protection (M Phil, M Sc, PhD); materials (M Phil, PhD); metallic materials (M Phil, M Sc, PhD); nanostructural materials (M Phil, M Sc, PhD); paper science (M Phil, M Sc, PhD); polymer science and engineering (M Phil, M Sc, PhD); technical textiles (M Sc); textile design, fashion and management (M Phil, M Sc, PhD); textile science and technology (M Phil, M Sc, PhD); textiles (M Phil, PhD); textiles and fashion (M Ent).

School of Mathematics Offers actuarial science (PhD); applied mathematics (M Phil, PhD); applied numerical computing (M Phil, PhD); financial mathematics (M Phil, PhD); mathematical logic (M Phil); probability (M Phil, PhD); pure mathematics (M Phil, PhD); statistics (M Phil, PhD).

School of Mechanical, Aerospace and Civil Engineering Offers advanced manufacturing technology (M Ent); aerospace engineering (M Phil, M Sc, PhD); civil engineering (M Phil, M Sc, PhD); environmental engineering (M Phil, PhD); management of projects (M Phil, M Sc, PhD); mechanical engineering (M Phil, M Sc, PhD); mechanical engineering design (M Ent); nuclear engineering (M Phil, D Eng, PhD).

School of Medicine Offers medicine (M Phil, PhD).

School of Nursing, Midwifery and Social Work Offers nursing (M Phil, PhD); social work (M Phil, PhD).

School of Pharmacy and Pharmaceutical Sciences Offers pharmacy and pharmaceutical sciences (M Phil, PhD).

School of Physics and Astronomy Offers astronomy and astrophysics (M Sc, PhD); biological physics (M Sc, PhD); condensed matter physics (M Sc, PhD); nonlinear and liquid crystals physics (M Sc, PhD); nuclear physics (M Sc, PhD); particle physics (M Sc, PhD); photon physics (M Sc, PhD); physics (M Sc, PhD); theoretical physics (M Sc, PhD).

School of Psychological Sciences Offers audiology (M Phil, PhD); clinical psychology (M Phil, PhD, Psy D); psychology (M Phil, PhD).

School of Social Sciences Offers ethnographic documentary (M Phil); interdisciplinary study of culture (PhD); philosophy (PhD); politics (PhD); social anthropology (PhD); social anthropology with visual media (PhD); social change (PhD); social statistics (PhD); sociology (PhD); visual anthropology (M Phil).

UNIVERSITY OF MANITOBA, Winnipeg, MB R3T 2N2, Canada

General Information Province-supported, coed, university. CGS member. *Graduate housing:* Rooms and/or apartments available to single and married students. *Research affiliation:* Canada Department of Agriculture Research Station, Freshwater Institute, Atomic Energy of Canada, Manitoba Department of Mines, Resources, and Environmental Management, Northern Scientific Training Program (Northern studies), Taiga Biological Research Trust.

GRADUATE UNITS

Faculty of Dentistry Offers dental diagnostic and surgical sciences (M Dent); dentistry (M Dent, M Sc, DMD, PhD); oral and maxillofacial surgery (M Dent); oral biology (M Sc, PhD); orthodontics (M Sc); periodontology (M Dent); preventive dental science (M Sc); restorative dentistry (M Dent).

Faculty of Graduate Studies ***Degree program information:*** Part-time programs available. Part-time.

Asper School of Business Offers business (M Sc, MBA, PhD).

Clayton H. Riddell Faculty of Environment, Earth, and Resources Offers environment (M Env); environment and geography (M Sc); environment, earth, and resources (M Env, M Sc, MA, MNRM, PhD); geography (MA, PhD); geology (M Sc, PhD); geophysics (M Sc, PhD); natural resources and environmental management (PhD); natural resources management (MNRM).

College Universitaire de Saint Boniface Offers Canadian studies (MA); education (M Ed).

Faculty of Agricultural and Food Sciences Offers agribusiness (M Sc, PhD); agricultural and food sciences (M Sc, PhD); agronomy and plant protection (M Sc, PhD); animal science (M Sc, PhD); entomology (M Sc, PhD); food and nutritional sciences (PhD); food science (M Sc); foods and nutrition (M Sc); horticulture (M Sc, PhD); plant breeding and genetics (M Sc, PhD); plant physiology-biochemistry (M Sc, PhD); soil science (M Sc, PhD).

Faculty of Architecture Offers architecture (M Arch, M Land Arch, MCP, MID); city planning (MCP); interior design (MID); landscape architecture (M Land Arch).

Faculty of Arts Offers anthropology (MA, PhD); archival studies (MA); arts (MA, MPA, PhD); classics (MA); clinical psychology (PhD); economics (MA, PhD); English (MA, PhD); French (MA, PhD); German language and literature (MA); history (MA, PhD); Icelandic language and literature (MA); linguistics (MA, PhD); native studies (MA); philosophy (MA); political studies (MA); psychology (MA, PhD); public administration (MPA); religion (MA, PhD); school psychology (MA); Slavic languages and literatures (MA); sociology (MA, PhD).

Faculty of Education Offers adult and post-secondary education (M Ed); education (M Ed, PhD); educational administration (M Ed); guidance and counseling (M Ed); inclusive special education (M Ed); language and literacy (M Ed); second language education (M Ed); social foundations of education (M Ed); studies in curriculum, teaching and learning (M Ed).

Faculty of Engineering Offers biosystems engineering (M Eng, M Sc, PhD); civil engineering (M Eng, M Sc, PhD); electrical and computer engineering (M Eng, M Sc, PhD); engineering (M Eng, M Sc, PhD); mechanical and manufacturing engineering (M Eng, M Sc, PhD).

Faculty of Human Ecology Offers family social sciences (M Sc); human ecology (M Sc); human nutritional sciences (M Sc); textile sciences (M Sc).

Faculty of Kinesiology and Recreation Management Offers kinesiology and recreation (M Sc, MA).

Faculty of Law Offers law (LL M). Electronic applications accepted.

Faculty of Nursing Offers cancer nursing (MN); nursing (MN).

Faculty of Pharmacy Offers pharmacy (M Sc, PhD).

Faculty of Science Offers botany (M Sc, PhD); chemistry (M Sc, PhD); computer science (M Sc, PhD); ecology (M Sc, PhD); mathematical, computational and statistical sciences (MMCSS); mathematics (M Sc, PhD); microbiology (M Sc, PhD); physics and astronomy (M Sc, PhD); science (M Sc, MMCSS, PhD); statistics (M Sc, PhD); zoology (M Sc, PhD).

Faculty of Social Work Offers social work (MSW, PhD).

Interdisciplinary Programs Offers disability studies (M Sc, MA); individual interdisciplinary studies (M Sc, MA, PhD); interdisciplinary studies (M Sc, MA, PhD).

Marcel A. Desautels Faculty of Music Offers music (M Mus).

School of Medical Rehabilitation Offers applied health sciences (PhD); occupational therapy (MOT); physical therapy (MPT); rehabilitation (M Sc).

Faculty of Medicine ***Degree program information:*** Part-time programs available. Part-time. Offers medicine (M Sc, PhD). Electronic applications accepted.

Graduate Programs in Medicine Degree program information: Part-time programs available. Part-time. Offers biochemistry and medical genetics (M Sc, PhD); community health sciences (M Sc, MPH, PhD, G Dip); human anatomy and cell science (M Sc, PhD); immunology (M Sc, PhD); medical microbiology (M Sc, PhD); medicine (M Sc, MPH, PhD, G Dip); pathology (M Sc); pediatrics and child health (M Sc); pharmacology and therapeutics (M Sc, PhD); physiology (M Sc, PhD); psychiatry (M Sc); rehabilitation (M Sc); surgery (M Sc).

UNIVERSITY OF MARY, Bismarck, ND 58504-9652

General Information Independent-religious, coed, comprehensive institution. *Enrollment:* 2,872 graduate, professional, and undergraduate students; 556 full-time matriculated graduate/professional students (361 women), 267 part-time matriculated graduate/professional students (164 women). *Enrollment by degree level:* 647 master's, 109 doctoral. *Graduate faculty:* 46 full-time (37 women), 114 part-time/adjunct (67 women). *Graduate housing:* Room and/or apartments available on a first-come, first-served basis to single students; on-campus housing not available to married students. Housing application deadline: 7/15. *Student services:* Campus employment opportunities, campus safety program, career counseling, exercise/wellness program, free psychological counseling, international student services, services for students with disabilities, teacher training. *Library:* University of Mary Library.

Computer facilities: 130 computers available on campus for general student use. A campuswide network can be accessed from student residence rooms and from off campus. Online class registration is available.
Website: http://www.umary.edu/

General Application Contact: Graduate Admissions Department, 701-355-8128, Fax: 701-255-7687, E-mail: admissions@umary.edu.

GRADUATE UNITS

Gary Tharaldson School of Business ***Financial support:*** Application deadline: 8/1; applicants required to submit FAFSA. *Degree program information:* Part-time and evening/weekend programs available. Part-time, evening/weekend. Offers business administration (MBA); energy management (MBA, MS); executive (MBA, MS); health care (MBA, MS); human resource management (MBA); project management (MBA, MPM); virtuous leadership (MBA, MPM, MS). *Application deadline:* Applications are processed on a rolling basis. *Application fee:* $45. Electronic applications accepted.

Liffrig Family School of Education and Behavioral Sciences Offers curriculum, instruction and assessment (M Ed); education (Ed D); education and behavioral sciences (M Ed, Ed D); elementary administration (M Ed); reading (M Ed); secondary administration (M Ed); special education strategist (M Ed).

School of Health Sciences ***Financial support:*** Application deadline: 8/1; applicants required to submit FAFSA. Offers bioethics (MS); clinical exercise physiology (MS); health sciences (MS, MSN, MSOT, DNP, DPT); kinesiology (MS); occupational therapy (MSOT); physical therapy (DPT); respiratory therapy (MS); sports and physical education administration (MS). *Application deadline:* Applications are processed on a rolling basis. *Application fee:* $45. Electronic applications accepted.

Division of Nursing Financial support: Fellowships with partial tuition reimbursements and teaching assistantships with partial tuition reimbursements available. Financial award application deadline: 8/1; financial award applicants required to submit FAFSA. *Degree program information:* Part-time and evening/weekend programs available. Part-time, evening/weekend, online learning. Offers family nurse practitioner (DNP); nurse administrator (MSN); nursing educator (MSN). *Application deadline:* Applications are processed on a rolling basis. *Application fee:* $40. Electronic applications accepted.

UNIVERSITY OF MARY HARDIN-BAYLOR, Belton, TX 76513

General Information Independent-religious, coed, comprehensive institution. *Enrollment:* 3,898 graduate, professional, and undergraduate students; 414 full-time matriculated graduate/professional students (211 women), 263 part-time matriculated graduate/professional students (113 women). *Enrollment by degree level:* 556 master's, 121 doctoral. *Graduate faculty:* 59 full-time (29 women), 18 part-time/adjunct (8 women). *Tuition, area resident:* Part-time $815 per credit hour. Tuition and fees vary according to course load and degree level. *Graduate housing:* On-campus housing not available. *Student services:* Campus employment opportunities, career counseling, exercise/wellness program, free psychological counseling, international student services, multicultural affairs office, services for students with disabilities, teacher training. *Library:* Townsend Memorial Library. *Collection:* Books: 155,949 (physical), 27,764 (digital/electronic); Serial titles: 697 (physical), 140,385 (digital/electronic); Databases: 115. Weekly public service hours: 99; students can reserve study rooms.

Computer facilities: Computer purchase and lease plans are available. 275 computers available on campus for general student use. A campuswide network can be accessed from student residence rooms and from off campus. Online class registration is available.
Website: http://www.umhb.edu/

General Application Contact: Melissa Williams, Director of Graduate Student Services and Engagement, 254-295-4020, Fax: 254-295-5038, E-mail: mwilliams@umhb.edu.

GRADUATE UNITS

Graduate Studies in Business Administration Students: 14 full-time (10 women), 46 part-time (13 women); includes 17 minority (6 Black or African American, non-Hispanic/Latino; 1 Asian, non-Hispanic/Latino; 8 Hispanic/Latino; 2 Two or more races, non-Hispanic/Latino), 7 international. Average age 29. 140 applicants, 44% accepted, 23 enrolled. *Faculty:* 13 full-time (5 women), 5 part-time/adjunct (1 woman). *Financial support:* Federal Work-Study, unspecified assistantships, and scholarships for some active duty military personnel available. Financial award applicants required to submit FAFSA. In 2015, 35 master's awarded. *Degree program information:* Part-time and evening/weekend programs available. Part-time, evening/weekend. Offers accounting (MBA); information systems management (MBA); international business (MBA); management (MBA). *Application deadline:* For fall admission, 6/1 for domestic students, 4/30 priority date for international students; for spring admission, 11/1 for domestic students, 9/30 priority date for international students. Applications are processed on a rolling basis. *Application fee:* $35 ($135 for international students). Electronic applications accepted. *Application Contact:* Melissa Williams, Director, Graduate Student Services and Engagement, 254-295-4020, Fax: 254-295-5038, E-mail: mwilliams@umhb.edu. *Assistant Professor/Director, Graduate Programs in McLane College of Business*, Dr. Kirk Fischer, 254-295-4655, E-mail: kfischer@umhb.edu.

Graduate Studies in Counseling Students: 51 full-time (41 women), 22 part-time (19 women); includes 28 minority (13 Black or African American, non-Hispanic/Latino; 2 American Indian or Alaska Native, non-Hispanic/Latino; 2 Asian, non-Hispanic/Latino; 10 Hispanic/Latino; 1 Two or more races, non-Hispanic/Latino). Average age 31. 50 applicants, 62% accepted, 24 enrolled. *Faculty:* 5 full-time (3 women), 1 part-time/adjunct (0 women). *Financial support:* Federal Work-Study, unspecified assistantships, and scholarships for some active duty military personnel available. Support available to part-time students. Financial award applicants required to submit FAFSA. In 2015, 30 master's awarded. *Degree program information:* Part-time and evening/weekend programs available. Part-time, evening/weekend. Offers clinical and mental health counseling (MA); marriage, family and child counseling (MA); non-clinical professional studies (MA). *Application deadline:* For fall admission, 6/1 for domestic students, 4/30 priority date for international students; for spring admission, 11/1 for domestic students, 9/30 priority date for international students. Applications are processed on a rolling basis. *Application fee:* $35 ($135 for international students). Electronic applications accepted. *Application Contact:* Melissa Williams, Director, Graduate Student Services and Engagement, 254-295-4020, Fax: 254-295-5038, E-mail: mwilliams@umhb.edu. *Interim Director for Graduate Counseling Program/Associate Professor*, Dr. Ty Leonard, 254-295-5532, E-mail: hleonard@umhb.edu.

Graduate Studies in Education Students: 48 full-time (36 women), 69 part-time (52 women); includes 44 minority (19 Black or African American, non-Hispanic/Latino; 1 American Indian or Alaska Native, non-Hispanic/Latino; 1 Asian, non-Hispanic/Latino; 22 Hispanic/Latino; 1 Two or more races, non-Hispanic/Latino), 4 international. Average age 39. 21 applicants, 81% accepted, 13 enrolled. *Faculty:* 15 full-time (11 women), 4 part-time/adjunct (2 women). *Financial support:* Federal Work-Study and scholarships for some active duty military personnel available. Support available to part-time students. Financial award application deadline: 6/1; financial award applicants required to submit FAFSA. In 2015, 31 master's, 18 doctorates awarded. *Degree program information:* Part-time and evening/weekend programs available. Part-time, evening/weekend. Offers curriculum and instruction (M Ed); educational administration (M Ed, Ed D). *Application deadline:* For fall admission, 6/1 for domestic students, 3/30 priority date for international students; for spring admission, 11/1 for domestic students, 9/30 priority date for international students. Applications are processed on a rolling basis. *Application fee:* $35 ($135 for international students). Electronic applications accepted. *Application Contact:* Melissa Williams, Director, Graduate Student Services and Engagement, 254-295-4020, Fax: 254-295-5038, E-mail: mwilliams@umhb.edu. *Dean, College of Education/Director, Doctor of Education Program*, Dr. Marlene Zipperlen, 254-295-4572, Fax: 254-295-4480, E-mail: mzipperlen@umhb.edu.

Graduate Studies in Exercise Science Students: 9 full-time (8 women), 26 part-time (10 women); includes 14 minority (5 Black or African American, non-Hispanic/Latino; 1 Asian, non-Hispanic/Latino; 7 Hispanic/Latino; 1 Two or more races, non-Hispanic/Latino). Average age 26. 21 applicants, 81% accepted, 13 enrolled. *Faculty:* 7 full-time (2 women). *Financial support:* Federal Work-Study, unspecified assistantships, and scholarships for some active duty military personnel available. Support available to part-time students. Financial award application deadline: 6/1; financial award applicants required to submit FAFSA. In 2015, 18 master's awarded. *Degree program information:* Part-time and evening/weekend programs available. Part-time, evening/weekend. Offers exercise physiology (MS Ed); sport administration (MS Ed). *Application deadline:* For fall admission, 4/30 priority date for international students; for spring admission, 9/30 priority date for international students. *Application fee:* $35 ($135 for international students). *Application Contact:* Melissa Williams, Director, Graduate Student Services and Engagement, 254-295-4020, Fax: 254-295-5038, E-mail: mwilliams@umhb.edu. *Director, Graduate Programs in Exercise and Sport Science/Associate Professor*, Dr. Brian Brabham, 254-295-4194, E-mail: bbrabham@umhb.edu.

Graduate Studies in Information Systems Students: 198 full-time (43 women), 97 part-time (17 women); includes 3 minority (2 Hispanic/Latino; 1 Two or more races, non-Hispanic/Latino), 284 international. Average age 24. 1,071 applicants, 40% accepted, 103 enrolled. *Faculty:* 8 full-time (0 women), 1 (woman) part-time/adjunct. *Financial support:* Federal Work-Study, unspecified assistantships, and scholarships for some active duty military personnel available. Support available to part-time students. Financial award applicants required to submit FAFSA. In 2015, 161 master's awarded. *Degree program information:* Part-time and evening/weekend programs available. Part-time, evening/weekend. Offers information systems (MS). *Application deadline:* For fall admission, 6/1 for domestic students, 4/30 priority date for international students; for spring admission, 11/1 for domestic students, 9/30 priority date for international students. Applications are processed on a rolling basis. *Application fee:* $35 ($135 for international students). Electronic applications accepted. *Application Contact:* Melissa Ford, Director of Graduate Admissions, 254-295-4020, Fax: 254-295-5038, E-mail: mford@umhb.edu. *Assistant Professor/Director, Graduate Programs in McLane College of Business*, Dr. Kirk Fischer, 254-295-4655, E-mail: kfischer@umhb.edu.

Graduate Studies in Nursing Students: 54 full-time (47 women), 2 part-time (1 woman); includes 14 minority (10 Black or African American, non-Hispanic/Latino; 3 Hispanic/Latino; 1 Two or more races, non-Hispanic/Latino), 1 international. Average age 32. 46 applicants, 70% accepted, 26 enrolled. *Faculty:* 6 full-time (all women), 3 part-time/adjunct (2 women). *Financial support:* Applicants required to submit FAFSA. In 2015, 47 master's awarded. *Degree program information:* Part-time and evening/weekend programs available. Part-time, evening/weekend. Offers clinical nurse leader (MSN); family nurse practitioner (MSN, Post-Master's Certificate); nurse educator (Post-Master's Certificate); nursing education (MSN). *Application deadline:* For fall admission, 4/15 for domestic students, 4/30 priority date for international students; for spring admission, 11/1 for domestic students, 9/30 priority date for international students. Applications are processed on a rolling basis. *Application fee:* $35 ($135 for international students). Electronic applications accepted. *Application Contact:* Melissa Williams, Director, Graduate Student Services and Engagement, 254-295-4020, Fax: 254-295-5038, E-mail: mwilliams@umhb.edu. *Associate Professor/Director, Master of Science in Nursing Programs*, Dr. Carrie Johnson, 254-295-4178, E-mail: cjohnson@umhb.edu.

Graduate Studies in Physical Therapy Students: 40 full-time (26 women); includes 8 minority (2 Black or African American, non-Hispanic/Latino; 2 Asian, non-Hispanic/Latino; 4 Hispanic/Latino). Average age 25. 100 applicants, 51% accepted, 40 enrolled. *Faculty:* 10 full-time (7 women), 6 part-time/adjunct (3 women). *Financial support:* Federal Work-Study, unspecified assistantships, and scholarships for some active duty military personnel available. Financial award applicants required to submit FAFSA. Offers physical therapy (DPT). *Application deadline:* For fall admission, 6/1 for domestic students, 4/30 priority date for international students; for spring admission, 11/1 for domestic students, 9/30 priority date for international students. Applications are processed on a rolling basis. *Application fee:* $35 ($135 for international students). Electronic applications accepted. *Application Contact:* Melissa Williams, Director, Graduate Student Services and Engagement, 254-295-4020, Fax: 254-295-5038, E-mail: mwilliams@umhb.edu. *Director*, Dr. Barbara Gresham, 254-295-4921, E-mail: bgresham@umhb.edu.

UNIVERSITY OF MARYLAND, BALTIMORE, Baltimore, MD 21201

General Information State-supported, coed, graduate-only institution. CGS member. *Enrollment by degree level:* 1,879 master's, 3,376 doctoral, 115 other advanced degrees. *Graduate faculty:* 1,845 full-time (856 women), 876 part-time/adjunct (555 women). Tuition and fees vary according to program. *Graduate housing:* Rooms and/or apartments available on a first-come, first-served basis to single and married students. *Student services:* Campus employment opportunities, campus safety program, career counseling, exercise/wellness program, free psychological counseling, grant writing training, international student services, low-cost health insurance, services for students with disabilities, writing training. *Library:* Health Sciences and Human Services Library plus 1 other. *Collection:* Books: 363,204 (physical), 13,000 (digital/electronic); Serial titles: 4,970 (digital/electronic); Databases: 116. Students can reserve study rooms. *Research affiliation:* University of Maryland BioPark (biology), University of Maryland Biotechnology Institute (biology), University of Maryland Medical System (medical research).

Computer facilities: A campuswide network can be accessed from student residence rooms and from off campus. Online class registration is available.
Website: http://www.umaryland.edu/

General Application Contact: Keith T. Brooks, Director, Graduate Enrollment Affairs, 410-706-7131, Fax: 410-706-3473, E-mail: kbrooks@umaryland.edu.

GRADUATE UNITS

Francis King Carey School of Law Students: 563 full-time (296 women), 150 part-time (73 women); includes 255 minority (83 Black or African American, non-Hispanic/Latino; 2 American Indian or Alaska Native, non-Hispanic/Latino; 73 Asian, non-Hispanic/Latino; 67 Hispanic/Latino; 30 Two or more races, non-Hispanic/Latino), 32 international. Average age 27. 2,274 applicants, 47% accepted, 196 enrolled. *Faculty:* 55 full-time (29 women), 62 part-time/adjunct (19 women). *Financial support:* In 2015–16, 485 students received support, including 28 fellowships (averaging $4,000 per year), 90 research assistantships (averaging $1,500 per year); Federal Work-Study, institutionally sponsored loans, and scholarships/grants also available. Support available to part-time students. Financial award application deadline: 3/1; financial award applicants required to submit FAFSA. In 2015, 5 master's, 296 doctorates awarded. *Degree program information:* Part-time and evening/weekend programs available. Part-time, evening/weekend. Offers law (LL M, JD). *Application deadline:* For fall admission, 4/1 priority date for domestic and international students. Applications are processed on a rolling basis. *Application fee:* $70. Electronic applications accepted. *Application Contact:* Susan Krinsky, Associate Dean for Student Affairs, 410-706-3492, Fax: 410-706-1793, E-mail: admissions@law.umaryland.edu. *Dean/Professor*, Donald B. Tobin, 410-706-7214, Fax: 410-706-4045, E-mail: dtobin@law.umaryland.edu.

Graduate School ***Degree program information:*** Part-time and evening/weekend programs available. Part-time, evening/weekend, online learning. Offers biochemistry (MS, PhD); biochemistry and molecular biology (MS, PhD); biomedical sciences (MS, PhD); cancer biology (PhD); cell and molecular physiology (PhD); cellular and molecular biomedical science (MS); clinical research (Postbaccalaureate Certificate); epidemiology (MS, PhD); gerontology (PhD); human genetics and genomic medicine (PhD); marine-estuarine-environmental sciences (MS, PhD); medical and research technology (MS); molecular medicine (MS, PhD); molecular microbiology and immunology (PhD); molecular toxicology and pharmacology (PhD); neuroscience (PhD); oral pathology (PhD); pharmaceutical health service research (MS, PhD); pharmaceutical sciences (PhD); pharmacometrics (MS); pharmacy administration (PhD); physical rehabilitation science (PhD); regulatory science (MS); research ethics (Certificate); thanatology (Certificate); toxicology (MS, PhD). Electronic applications accepted.

School of Nursing Degree program information: Part-time programs available. Part-time. Offers community health nursing (MS); gerontological nursing (MS); maternal-child nursing (MS); medical-surgical nursing (MS); nurse-midwifery education (MS); nursing (MS, DNP, PhD, Postbaccalaureate Certificate); nursing administration (MS); nursing education (MS); nursing health policy (MS); primary care nursing (MS); psychiatric nursing (MS). MS/MBA offered jointly with University of Baltimore. Electronic applications accepted.

School of Social Work Offers social work (MSW, PhD). MSW/MA offered jointly with Baltimore Hebrew University; MBA/MSW with University of Maryland, College Park; MSW/MPH with The Johns Hopkins University. Electronic applications accepted.

Professional and Advanced Education Programs in Dentistry Students: 581 full-time (301 women), 4 part-time (2 women); includes 236 minority (55 Black or African American, non-Hispanic/Latino; 115 Asian, non-Hispanic/Latino; 41 Hispanic/Latino; 1 Native Hawaiian or other Pacific Islander, non-Hispanic/Latino; 24 Two or more races, non-Hispanic/Latino), 32 international. Average age 26. 506 applicants, 89% accepted, 135 enrolled. *Financial support:* Career-related internships or fieldwork, Federal Work-Study, scholarships/grants, and traineeships available. Financial award application deadline: 3/1; financial award applicants required to submit FAFSA. In 2015, 127 doctorates, 27 Certificates awarded. Offers advanced general dentistry (Certificate); dentistry (DDS); endodontics (Certificate); oral-maxillofacial surgery (Certificate); orthodontics (Certificate); pediatric dentistry (Certificate); periodontics (Certificate); prosthodontics (Certificate). *Application deadline:* Applications are processed on a rolling basis. *Application fee:* $85. Electronic applications accepted. *Application Contact:* Dr. Judith A. Porter, Assistant Dean for Admissions and Recruitment, 410-706-7472, Fax: 410-706-0945, E-mail: ddsadmissions@umaryland.edu. *Dean*, Dr. Mark A. Reynolds, 410-706-7461.

Professional Program in Pharmacy Offers pharmacy (Pharm D). Electronic applications accepted.

School of Medicine Students: 1,144 full-time (684 women), 99 part-time (57 women); includes 397 minority (91 Black or African American, non-Hispanic/Latino; 1 American Indian or Alaska Native, non-Hispanic/Latino; 225 Asian, non-Hispanic/Latino; 53 Hispanic/Latino; 27 Two or more races, non-Hispanic/Latino), 58 international. Average age 26. 6,413 applicants, 13% accepted, 366 enrolled. *Financial support:* In 2015–16, research assistantships with partial tuition reimbursements (averaging $25,000 per year) were awarded; fellowships, Federal Work-Study, scholarships/grants, health care benefits, and unspecified assistantships also available. Financial award application deadline: 3/1; financial award applicants required to submit FAFSA. In 2015, 74 master's, 269 doctorates awarded. *Degree program information:* Part-time programs available. Part-time. Offers biostatistics (MS); clinical research (MS); epidemiology and preventive medicine (MPH, MS, PhD); genetic counseling (MGC); gerontology (PhD); human genetics and genomic medicine (MS, PhD); medicine (MGC, MPH, MS, DPT, MD, PhD); molecular epidemiology (MS, PhD); pathologists' assistant (MS); physical rehabilitation science (PhD); physical therapy and rehabilitation science (DPT); toxicology (MS, PhD). Electronic applications accepted. *Application Contact:* 410-706-7478, Fax: 410-706-0467, E-mail: admissions@som.umaryland.edu. *Dean and Vice President for Medical Affairs*, Dr. E. Albert Reece, 410-706-7410, Fax: 410-706-0235, E-mail: deanmed@som.umaryland.edu.

UNIVERSITY OF MARYLAND, BALTIMORE COUNTY, Baltimore, MD 21250

General Information State-supported, coed, university. CGS member. *Enrollment:* 13,839 graduate, professional, and undergraduate students; 1,158 full-time matriculated graduate/professional students (549 women), 1,343 part-time matriculated graduate/professional students (643 women). *Enrollment by degree level:* 1,667 master's, 701 doctoral, 133 other advanced degrees. *Graduate faculty:* 477 full-time, 191 part-time/adjunct. Tuition, state resident: full-time $12,816. Tuition, nonresident: full-time $19,710. *Graduate housing:* Room and/or apartments available on a first-come, first-served basis to single students; on-campus housing not available to married students. Housing application deadline: 6/1. *Student services:* Campus employment opportunities, campus safety program, career counseling, child daycare facilities, exercise/wellness program, free psychological counseling, grant writing training, international student services, low-cost health insurance, multicultural affairs office, services for students with disabilities, teacher training, writing training. *Library:* Albin O. Kuhn Library and Gallery plus 1 other. *Collection:* Books: 685,503 (physical), 153,996 (digital/electronic); Serial titles: 27,432 (physical), 11,100 (digital/electronic); Databases: 384. Weekly public service hours: 94; study areas open 24 hours, 5–7 days a week; students can reserve study rooms. *Research affiliation:* Sciences Applications International Corporation (information systems and technology), Halliburton Energy Services, IBM (computers and information technology), BouMatic (dairy industry), Pfizer, Inc. (pharmaceuticals), Fujitsu Laboratories of America (information technology and communications).

Computer facilities: Computer purchase and lease plans are available. 1,065 computers available on campus for general student use. A campuswide network can be accessed from student residence rooms and from off campus. Online class registration, billing, housing, parking, degree audit and advising are available.
Website: http://www.umbc.edu/

General Application Contact: Kathryn Nee, Coordinator of Domestic Admissions, 410-455-2944, E-mail: nee@umbc.edu.

GRADUATE UNITS

The Graduate School Students: 1,158 full-time (549 women), 1,343 part-time (643 women); includes 649 minority (308 Black or African American, non-Hispanic/Latino; 4 American Indian or Alaska Native, non-Hispanic/Latino; 191 Asian, non-Hispanic/Latino; 104 Hispanic/Latino; 5 Native Hawaiian or other Pacific Islander, non-Hispanic/Latino; 37 Two or more races, non-Hispanic/Latino), 556 international. Average age 32. 2,792 applicants, 50% accepted, 679 enrolled. *Faculty:* 477 full-time, 191 part-time/adjunct. *Financial support:* In 2015–16, 612 students received support, including 28 fellowships with tuition reimbursements available (averaging $18,909 per year), 256 research assistantships with tuition reimbursements available (averaging $18,909 per year), 328 teaching assistantships with tuition reimbursements available (averaging $18,909 per year); career-related internships or fieldwork, Federal Work-Study, scholarships/grants, traineeships, health care benefits, and unspecified assistantships also available. Financial award applicants required to submit FAFSA. In 2015, 694 master's, 100 doctorates, 147 other advanced degrees awarded. *Degree program information:* Part-time and evening/weekend programs available. Part-time, evening/weekend, online learning. Offers engineering management (MS, Postbaccalaureate Certificate); marine-estuarine-environmental sciences (MS, PhD); systems engineering (MS, Postbaccalaureate Certificate). *Application deadline:* For fall admission, 1/1 for international students; for spring admission, 5/1 for international students. Applications are processed on a rolling basis. *Application fee:* $50. Electronic applications accepted. *Application Contact:* Kathryn Nee, Coordinator of Domestic Admissions, 410-455-2944, E-mail: nee@umbc.edu. *Dean and Vice Provost for Graduate Education*, Dr. Janet C. Rutledge, 410-455-2199.

College of Arts, Humanities and Social Sciences Students: 397 full-time (268 women), 623 part-time (413 women); includes 329 minority (131 Black or African American, non-Hispanic/Latino; 2 American Indian or Alaska Native, non-Hispanic/Latino; 71 Asian, non-Hispanic/Latino; 104 Hispanic/Latino; 4 Native Hawaiian or other Pacific Islander, non-Hispanic/Latino; 17 Two or more races, non-Hispanic/Latino), 51 international. Average age 33. 870 applicants, 58% accepted, 284 enrolled. *Faculty:* 248 full-time, 108 part-time/adjunct. *Financial support:* In 2015–16, 11 fellowships (averaging $19,000 per year), 90 research assistantships (averaging $19,000 per year), 104 teaching assistantships (averaging $19,000 per year) were awarded; career-related internships or fieldwork, scholarships/grants, health care benefits, and unspecified assistantships also available. Financial award applicants required to submit FAFSA. In 2015, 279 master's, 39 doctorates, 98 other advanced degrees awarded. *Degree program information:* Part-time and evening/weekend programs available. Part-time, evening/weekend, online learning. Offers administration, planning, and policy (MS); aging policy issues (PhD); American contemporary music (Postbaccalaureate Certificate); applied behavioral analysis (MA); applied developmental psychology (PhD); applied sociology (MA); arts, humanities and social science (MA, MAE, MAE, MAT, MFA, MPP, MPS, MS, PhD, Certificate, Graduate Certificate, Postbaccalaureate Certificate); distance education (Graduate Certificate); early childhood education (MAT); economic policy analysis (MA); education (MS); elementary education (MAT); emergency health services (MS); emergency management (Postbaccalaureate Certificate); English: texts, technologies, and literature (MA); epidemiology of aging (PhD); gender and women's studies (Postbaccalaureate Certificate); geographic information systems (MPS, Certificate); geography and environmental systems (MPS, MS, PhD, Certificate); historical studies (MA); human services psychology (MA, PhD); industrial organizational psychology (MPS); instructional systems development (MA, Graduate Certificate); instructional technology (Graduate Certificate); intercultural communication (MA); intermedia and digital arts (MFA); K-8 mathematics instructional leadership (MAE); K-8 science education (MAE); K-8 STEM education (MAE); language, literacy, and culture (PhD); non-profit sector (Postbaccalaureate Certificate); preventive medicine and epidemiology (MS); public policy (MPP, PhD); secondary mathematics education (MAE); secondary science education (MAE); secondary STEM education (MAE); social, cultural, and behavioral sciences (PhD); teaching (MAT); teaching English to speakers of other languages (MA, Postbaccalaureate Certificate). *Application deadline:* For fall admission, 1/1 for international students; for spring admission, 5/1 for international students. Applications are processed on a rolling basis. *Application fee:* $50. Electronic applications accepted. *Application Contact:* Kathryn Nee, Coordinator of Domestic Admissions, 410-455-2944, E-mail: nee@umbc.edu. *Dean*, Dr. Scot E. Casper, 410-455-2385, Fax: 410-455-1095, E-mail: casper@umbc.edu.

College of Engineering and Information Technology Students: 552 full-time (183 women), 604 part-time (180 women); includes 280 minority (140 Black or African American, non-Hispanic/Latino; 2 American Indian or Alaska Native, non-Hispanic/Latino; 89 Asian, non-Hispanic/Latino; 34 Hispanic/Latino; 1 Native Hawaiian or other Pacific Islander, non-Hispanic/Latino; 14 Two or more races, non-Hispanic/Latino), 434 international. Average age 31. 1,573 applicants, 50% accepted, 326 enrolled. *Faculty:* 117 full-time (36 women), 80 part-time/adjunct (14 women). *Financial support:* In 2015–16, 4 fellowships with full tuition reimbursements (averaging $21,750 per year), 117 research assistantships with full tuition reimbursements (averaging $19,250 per year), 110 teaching assistantships with full tuition reimbursements (averaging $16,750 per year) were awarded; career-related internships or fieldwork, Federal Work-Study, scholarships/grants, health care benefits, tuition waivers (partial), and unspecified assistantships also available. Support available to part-time students. Financial award application deadline: 6/30; financial award applicants required to submit FAFSA. In 2015, 284 master's, 31 doctorates, 98 other advanced degrees awarded. *Degree program information:* Part-time programs available. Part-time. Offers biochemical regulatory engineering (Postbaccalaureate Certificate); chemical and biochemical engineering (MS, PhD); computational thermal fluid dynamics (Postbaccalaureate Certificate); computer engineering (MS, PhD); computer science (MS, PhD); cybersecurity (MPS, Postbaccalaureate Certificate); cybersecurity strategy and policy (Postbaccalaureate Certificate); electrical engineering (MS, PhD); engineering and information technology (MPS, MS, PhD, Postbaccalaureate Certificate); environmental engineering (MS, PhD); health information technology (MPS); human-centered computing (MS, PhD); information systems (MPS, MS, PhD); mechanical engineering (MS, PhD); mechatronics (Postbaccalaureate Certificate). *Application deadline:* For fall admission, 6/1 for domestic students, 1/1 for international students; for spring admission, 11/1 for domestic students, 6/1 for international students. Applications are processed on a rolling basis. *Application fee:* $70. Electronic applications accepted. *Application Contact:* Graduate School, 410-455-2537, E-mail: umbcgrad@umbc.edu. *Dean and Professor*, Dr. Julia M. Ross, 410-455-3270, Fax: 410-455-3559, E-mail: jross@umbc.edu.

College of Natural and Mathematical Sciences Students: 200 full-time (92 women), 57 part-time (27 women); includes 56 minority (17 Black or African American, non-Hispanic/Latino; 28 Asian, non-Hispanic/Latino; 8 Hispanic/Latino; 3 Two or more races, non-Hispanic/Latino), 67 international. Average age 29. 389 applicants, 37% accepted, 59 enrolled. *Faculty:* 111 full-time, 17 part-time/adjunct. *Financial support:* In 2015–16, 164 students received support, including 8 fellowships (averaging $18,909 per year), 57 research assistantships with tuition reimbursements available (averaging $18,909 per year), 99 teaching assistantships with full tuition reimbursements available (averaging $18,909 per year). In 2015, 69 master's, 30 doctorates, 5 other advanced degrees awarded. *Degree program information:* Part-time programs available. Part-time. Offers applied mathematics (MS, PhD); applied molecular biology (MS); atmospheric physics (MS, PhD); biochemistry (PhD); biological sciences (MS, PhD); biostatistics (PhD); biotechnology (MPS); biotechnology (Graduate Certificate); biotechnology management (Graduate Certificate); chemistry (MS, PhD); chemistry and biochemistry (Postbaccalaureate Certificate); environmental statistics (MS); molecular and cell biology (PhD); natural and mathematical sciences (MPS, MS, PhD, Graduate Certificate, Postbaccalaureate Certificate); neuroscience and cognitive sciences (PhD); physics (MS, PhD); statistics (MS, PhD). *Application deadline:* Applications are processed on a rolling basis. *Application fee:* $50. Electronic applications accepted. *Application Contact:* Kathryn Nee, Coordinator of Domestic Admissions, 410-455-2944, E-mail: nee@umbc.edu. *Interim Dean*, Dr. William R. LaCourse, 410-455-5827, Fax: 410-455-5831, E-mail: lacourse@umbc.edu.

Erickson School of Aging Studies Students: 18 full-time (11 women); includes 9 minority (8 Black or African American, non-Hispanic/Latino; 1 Hispanic/Latino). Average age 30. 23 applicants, 91% accepted, 18 enrolled. *Faculty:* 4 full-time (1 woman), 7 part-time/adjunct (1 woman). *Financial support:* In 2015–16, 15 students received support, including 1 teaching assistantship with full tuition reimbursement available (averaging $21,600 per year). Financial award applicants required to submit FAFSA. In 2015, 13 master's awarded. Offers management of aging services (MA). *Application deadline:* Applications are processed on a rolling basis. *Application fee:* $50. Electronic applications accepted. *Application Contact:* Michelle Howell, Administrative Assistant, 443-543-5607, E-mail: mhowell@umbc.edu. *Graduate Program Director*, Bill Holman, 443-543-5603, E-mail: bholman@sagepointcare.org.

UNIVERSITY OF MARYLAND, COLLEGE PARK, College Park, MD 20742

General Information State-supported, coed, university. CGS member. *Graduate housing:* On-campus housing not available. *Research affiliation:* Battelle–Pacific Northwest National Laboratory, Canon US Life Sciences, Inc. - Technology Development & Analysis (technology development and analysis), Bill and Melinda Gates Foundation (international aid and outreach), Lockheed Martin Corporation (science and technology), Lockheed Martin Corporation (science and technology), BAE Systems (science and technology).

GRADUATE UNITS

Academic Affairs ***Degree program information:*** Part-time and evening/weekend programs available. Part-time, evening/weekend, online learning. Offers history, library, and information services. Electronic applications accepted.

A. James Clark School of Engineering Degree program information: Part-time and evening/weekend programs available. Part-time, evening/weekend, online learning. Offers advanced engineering education (M Eng); aerospace engineering (M Eng, MS, PhD); bioengineering (MS, PhD); chemical engineering (M Eng, MS, PhD); civil and environmental engineering (M Eng, MS, PhD); electrical and computer engineering (M Eng, MS, PhD); electrical engineering (MS, PhD); electronic packaging and reliability (MS, PhD); engineering (M Eng, ME, MS, PhD, Certificate); engineering and public policy (MS); fire protection engineering (M Eng, MS); manufacturing and design (MS, PhD); materials science and engineering (MS, PhD); mechanics and materials (MS, PhD); nuclear engineering (ME, MS, PhD); reliability engineering (M Eng, MS, PhD); systems engineering (M Eng, MS); telecommunications (MS); thermal and fluid sciences (MS, PhD).

College of Agriculture and Natural Resources Degree program information: Part-time and evening/weekend programs available. Part-time, evening/weekend. Offers agriculture and natural resources (MS, DVM, PhD); agriculture economics (MS, PhD); animal sciences (MS, PhD); environmental science and technology (MS, PhD); food science (MS, PhD); landscape architecture (MLA); natural resource sciences (MS, PhD); nutrition (MS, PhD); plant science (MS, PhD); resource economics (MS, PhD); veterinary medical sciences (MS, PhD); veterinary medicine (MS, DVM, PhD). Electronic applications accepted.

College of Arts and Humanities Degree program information: Part-time and evening/weekend programs available. Part-time, evening/weekend. Offers American studies (MA, PhD); art (MFA); art history (MA, PhD); arts and humanities (M Ed, MA, MFA, MM, DMA, Ed D, PhD); classics (MA); communication (MA, PhD); comparative literature (MA, PhD); creative writing (MA, MFA, PhD); dance (MFA); English language and literature (MA, PhD); ethnomusicology (MA); French language and literature (MA); Germanic language and literature (MA, PhD); history (MA, PhD); Jewish studies (MA); languages, literatures, and cultures (MA, PhD); linguistics (MA, PhD); modern French studies (PhD); music (M Ed, MA, MM, DMA, Ed D, PhD); performance (MFA); philosophy (MA, PhD); second language instruction (PhD); second language learning (PhD); second language measurement and assessment (PhD); second language use (PhD); Spanish language and literatures (MA, PhD); theatre (MA, MFA, PhD); theatre and performance studies (MA, PhD); theatre design (MFA); women's studies (MA, PhD). Electronic applications accepted.

College of Behavioral and Social Sciences Degree program information: Part-time and evening/weekend programs available. Part-time, evening/weekend. Offers American politics (PhD); applied anthropology (MAA); audiology (MA, PhD); behavioral and social sciences (MA, MAA, MS, Au D, PhD); clinical psychology (PhD); comparative politics (PhD); criminology and criminal justice (MA, PhD); developmental psychology (PhD); economics (MA, PhD); experimental psychology (PhD); geography (MA, PhD); hearing and speech sciences (Au D); industrial psychology (MA, MS, PhD); international relations (PhD); language pathology (MA, PhD); neuroscience (PhD); neurosciences and cognitive sciences (PhD); political economy (PhD); political theory (PhD); social psychology (PhD); sociology (MA, PhD); speech (MA, PhD); survey methodology (MS, PhD). Electronic applications accepted.

College of Computer, Mathematical and Natural Sciences Degree program information: Part-time and evening/weekend programs available. Part-time, evening/weekend, online learning. Offers analytical chemistry (MS, PhD); applied mathematics (MS, PhD); astronomy (MS, PhD); atmospheric and oceanic science (MS, PMS, PhD); behavior, ecology, and systematics (PhD); behavior, ecology, evolution, and systematics (MS, PhD); biochemistry (MS, PhD); biological sciences (PhD); biology (MS, PhD); biophysics (PhD); cell biology and molecular genetics (MS, PhD); chemical physics (MS, PhD); chemistry (MS, PhD); computational biology, bioinformatics, and genomics (PhD); computer science (MS, PhD); computer, mathematical and natural sciences (MA, MLS, MS, PMS, PhD); entomology (MS, PhD); geology (MS, PhD); inorganic chemistry (MS, PhD); life sciences (MLS); marine-estuarine-environmental sciences (MS, PhD); mathematical statistics (MA, PhD); mathematics (MA, PhD); molecular and cellular biology (PhD); organic chemistry (MS, PhD); physical chemistry (MS, PhD); physics (MS, PhD); physiological systems (PhD); plant biology (MS, PhD); sustainable development and conservation biology (MS).

College of Education Degree program information: Part-time and evening/weekend programs available. Part-time, evening/weekend, online learning. Offers college student personnel (M Ed, MA); college student personnel administration (PhD); community counseling (CAGS); community/career counseling (M Ed, MA); counseling and personnel services (M Ed, MA, PhD); counseling psychology (PhD); counselor education (PhD); curriculum and educational communications (M Ed, MA, Ed D, PhD); education (M Ed, MA, Ed D, PhD, AGSC, CAGS); human development and quantitative methodology (MA, Ed D, PhD); reading (M Ed, MA, PhD, CAGS); rehabilitation counseling (M Ed, MA, AGSC); school counseling (M Ed, MA); school psychology (M Ed, MA, PhD); secondary education (M Ed, MA, Ed D, PhD, CAGS); social foundations of education (M Ed, MA, Ed D, PhD, CAGS); teaching English to speakers of other languages (M Ed). Electronic applications accepted.

College of Information Studies Degree program information: Part-time and evening/weekend programs available. Part-time, evening/weekend. Offers information studies (MIM, MLS, PhD). Electronic applications accepted.

Phillip Merrill College of Journalism Degree program information: Part-time and evening/weekend programs available. Part-time, evening/weekend. Offers broadcast journalism (MA); journalism (MA); journalism and media studies (PhD); online news (MA); public affairs reporting (MA). Electronic applications accepted.

Robert H. Smith School of Business Degree program information: Part-time and evening/weekend programs available. Part-time, evening/weekend, online learning. Offers business (EMBA, MBA, MS, PhD); business administration (MBA); business and management (MS, PhD); executive business administration (EMBA). Electronic applications accepted.

School of Architecture, Planning and Preservation Degree program information: Part-time and evening/weekend programs available. Part-time, evening/weekend. Offers architecture (M Arch); architecture, planning and preservation (M Arch, MCP, MHP, MRED, PhD, Certificate); historic preservation (MHP, Certificate); real estate development (MRED); urban and regional planning/design (PhD); urban studies and planning (MCP). Electronic applications accepted.

School of Public Health Degree program information: Part-time and evening/weekend programs available. Part-time, evening/weekend. Offers biostatistics (MPH); community health education (MPH); environmental health sciences (MPH); epidemiology (MPH, PhD); family studies (PhD); health services administration (MHA, PhD); kinesiology (MA, PhD); marriage and family therapy (MS); maternal and child health (PhD); public health (MA, MHA, MPH, MS, PhD); public/community health (PhD). Electronic applications accepted.

School of Public Policy Degree program information: Part-time and evening/weekend programs available. Part-time, evening/weekend, online learning. Offers policy studies (PhD); public management (MPM); public policy (MPM, MPP, PhD). Electronic applications accepted.

UNIVERSITY OF MARYLAND EASTERN SHORE, Princess Anne, MD 21853-1299

General Information State-supported, coed, university. CGS member. *Graduate housing:* On-campus housing not available.

GRADUATE UNITS

Graduate Programs *Degree program information:* Part-time and evening/weekend programs available. Part-time, evening/weekend. Offers applied computer science (MS); career and technology education (M Ed); chemistry (MS); criminal justice (MS); education leadership (Ed D); food and agricultural sciences (MS); food science and technology (PhD); guidance and counseling (M Ed); marine-estuarine-environmental sciences (MS, PhD); organizational leadership (PhD); physical therapy (DPT); quantitative fisheries and resource economics (PMS); rehabilitation counseling (MS); special education (M Ed); teaching (MAT); toxicology (MS, PhD). Electronic applications accepted.

UNIVERSITY OF MARYLAND UNIVERSITY COLLEGE, Adelphi, MD 20783

General Information State-supported, coed, comprehensive institution. *Enrollment:* 50,247 graduate, professional, and undergraduate students; 1,231 full-time matriculated graduate/professional students (705 women), 11,470 part-time matriculated graduate/professional students (6,090 women). *Enrollment by degree level:* 11,906 master's, 141 doctoral, 654 other advanced degrees. *Graduate faculty:* 145 full-time (68 women), 2,666 part-time/adjunct (1,187 women). *Graduate housing:* On-campus housing not available. *Student services:* Campus employment opportunities, career counseling, international student services, services for students with disabilities, writing training. *Library:* Information and Library Services plus 1 other. *Collection:* Books: 1,270 (physical), 108,536 (digital/electronic).

Computer facilities: Computer purchase and lease plans are available. 404 computers available on campus for general student use. A campuswide network can be accessed. Online class registration is available.
Website: http://www.umuc.edu/

General Application Contact: Coordinator, Graduate Admissions, 800-888-UMUC, Fax: 240-684-2151, E-mail: newgrad@umuc.edu.

GRADUATE UNITS

The Graduate School Students: 1,231 full-time (705 women), 11,470 part-time (6,090 women); includes 6,948 minority (4,885 Black or African American, non-Hispanic/Latino; 43 American Indian or Alaska Native, non-Hispanic/Latino; 744 Asian, non-Hispanic/Latino; 845 Hispanic/Latino; 40 Native Hawaiian or other Pacific Islander, non-Hispanic/Latino; 391 Two or more races, non-Hispanic/Latino), 233 international. Average age 34. 4,636 applicants, 100% accepted, 2701 enrolled. *Faculty:* 145 full-time (68 women), 2,666 part-time/adjunct (1,187 women). *Financial support:* Federal Work-Study and scholarships/grants available. Support available to part-time students. Financial award application deadline: 6/1; financial award applicants required to submit FAFSA. In 2015, 3,658 master's, 36 doctorates, 603 other advanced degrees awarded. *Degree program information:* Part-time and evening/weekend programs available. Part-time, evening/weekend, online learning. Offers accounting and financial management (MS, Certificate); accounting and information systems (MS, Certificate); biotechnology (MS, Certificate); business administration (MBA, Certificate); cybersecurity (MS, Certificate); cybersecurity policy (MS, Certificate); data analytics (MS, Certificate); digital forensics and cyber investigation (MS, Postbaccalaureate Certificate); distance education and e-learning (MDE, Certificate); education (M Ed, Certificate); environmental management (MS, Certificate); financial management and information systems (MS, Certificate); health administration informatics (MS, Certificate); health care administration (MS, Certificate); information assurance (MSIT, Certificate); information technology (MS, Certificate); international management (MIM, Certificate); management (MS, DM, Certificate); management and technology (M Ed, MAT, MBA, MDE, MIM, MS, MSIT, DM, Certificate, Postbaccalaureate Certificate); teaching (MAT); technology management (MS, Certificate). *Application deadline:* Applications are processed on a rolling basis. *Application fee:* $50. Electronic applications accepted. *Application Contact:* Coordinator, Graduate Admissions, 800-888-8682, Fax: 240-684-2151, E-mail: newgrad@umuc.edu. *Vice Provost and Dean*, Dr. Aric Krause, 240-684-2400, Fax: 240-684-2401, E-mail: graddean@umuc.edu.

UNIVERSITY OF MARY WASHINGTON, Fredericksburg, VA 22401-5358

General Information State-supported, coed, comprehensive institution. *Enrollment:* 4,647 graduate, professional, and undergraduate students; 128 full-time matriculated graduate/professional students (98 women), 163 part-time matriculated graduate/professional students (98 women). *Enrollment by degree level:* 291 master's. *Graduate faculty:* 27 full-time (12 women), 13 part-time/adjunct (5 women). Tuition, state resident: part-time $510 per credit hour. Tuition, nonresident: part-time $989 per credit hour. *Required fees:* $30 per semester. Tuition and fees vary according to course load and program. *Graduate housing:* Room and/or apartments available on a first-come, first-served basis to single students; on-campus housing not available to married students. *Student services:* Campus employment opportunities, career counseling, free psychological counseling, international student services, multicultural affairs office, services for students with disabilities, teacher training, writing training. *Library:* Simpson Library plus 2 others. *Collection:* Books: 386,960 (physical), 205,133 (digital/electronic); Serial titles: 3,035 (physical), 77,565 (digital/electronic); Databases: 205. Weekly public service hours: 90; students can reserve study rooms.

Computer facilities: Computer purchase and lease plans are available. 900 computers available on campus for general student use. A campuswide network can be accessed from student residence rooms and from off campus. Online class registration is available.
Website: http://www.umw.edu/

General Application Contact: Christy Pack, Director of Graduate Admissions, 540-286-8038, Fax: 540-286-8085, E-mail: dclark@umw.edu.

GRADUATE UNITS

College of Business Students: 19 full-time (7 women), 55 part-time (23 women); includes 19 minority (9 Black or African American, non-Hispanic/Latino; 4 Asian, non-Hispanic/Latino; 4 Hispanic/Latino; 2 Two or more races, non-Hispanic/Latino), 3 international. Average age 34. 61 applicants, 56% accepted, 14 enrolled. *Faculty:* 9 full-time (1 woman), 3 part-time/adjunct (0 women). *Financial support:* In 2015–16, 8 students received support. Available to part-time students. Application deadline: 3/15; applicants required to submit FAFSA. In 2015, 47 master's awarded. *Degree program information:* Part-time and evening/weekend programs available. Part-time, evening/weekend. Offers business (MBA). *Application deadline:* For fall admission, 6/1 priority date for domestic students, 6/1 for international students; for spring admission, 10/1 for domestic and international students. Applications are processed on a rolling basis. *Application fee:* $50. Electronic applications accepted. *Application Contact:* Christy Pack, Director of Graduate Admissions, 540-286-8086, Fax: 540-286-8085, E-mail: dpack@umw.edu. *Dean*, Dr. Lynne D. Richardson, 540-654-2470, Fax: 540-654-2430, E-mail: lynne.richardson@umw.edu.

College of Education Students: 48 full-time (45 women), 212 part-time (178 women); includes 44 minority (16 Black or African American, non-Hispanic/Latino; 1 American Indian or Alaska Native, non-Hispanic/Latino; 4 Asian, non-Hispanic/Latino; 9 Hispanic/Latino; 14 Two or more races, non-Hispanic/Latino). Average age 31. 231 applicants, 59% accepted, 79 enrolled. *Faculty:* 20 full-time (17 women), 6 part-time/adjunct (4 women). *Financial support:* In 2015–16, 29 students received support, including 3 fellowships with partial tuition reimbursements available (averaging $9,000 per year); research assistantships, teaching assistantships, and scholarships/grants also available. Financial award application deadline: 4/25; financial award applicants required to submit FAFSA. In 2015, 78 master's awarded. *Degree program information:* Part-time and evening/weekend programs available. Part-time, evening/weekend. Offers education (M Ed); elementary education (MS). *Application deadline:* For fall admission, 4/15 for domestic and international students; for spring admission, 9/15 for domestic and international students. Applications are processed on a rolling basis. *Application fee:* $50. Electronic applications accepted. *Application Contact:* Deanna C. Pack, Director of Graduate Admissions, 540-286-8030, Fax: 540-286-8085, E-mail: dpack@umw.edu. *Dean*, Dr. Nina Mikhalevsky, 540-654-1290.

UNIVERSITY OF MASSACHUSETTS AMHERST, Amherst, MA 01003

General Information State-supported, coed, university. CGS member. *Graduate housing:* Rooms and/or apartments available on a first-come, first-served basis to single and married students. Housing application deadline: 6/15.

GRADUATE UNITS

Graduate School ***Degree program information:*** Part-time and evening/weekend programs available. Part-time, evening/weekend. Electronic applications accepted.

College of Education Degree program information: Part-time programs available. Part-time, online learning. Offers bilingual, English as a second language, and multicultural education (M Ed, Ed S); child study and early education (M Ed); children, families and schools (Ed D, Ed S); early childhood and elementary teacher education (M Ed); education (M Ed, Ed D, PhD, Ed S); educational leadership (M Ed); educational policy and leadership (Ed D); higher education (M Ed); international education (M Ed); language, literacy and culture (Ed D); learning, media and technology (M Ed, Ed S); mathematics, science, and learning technologies (Ed D); reading and writing (M Ed); research, educational measurement and psychometrics (Ed D); school counselor education (M Ed, Ed S); school psychology (M Ed, PhD, Ed S); science education (Ed S); secondary teacher education (M Ed); social justice education (M Ed, Ed D, Ed S); special education (M Ed, Ed D, Ed S); teacher education and school improvement (Ed D, Ed S). Electronic applications accepted.

College of Engineering Degree program information: Part-time programs available. Part-time. Offers chemical engineering (MSChE, PhD); civil engineering (MSCE, PhD); electrical and computer engineering (MSECE, PhD); engineering (MS, MS Env E, MSCE, MSChE, MSECE, MSEM, MSIE, MSME, PhD); environmental and water resources engineering (MSCE); geotechnical engineering (MSCE); industrial engineering and operations research (MS, PhD); mechanical engineering (MSME, PhD); structural engineering and mechanics (MSCE); transportation engineering (MSCE). Electronic applications accepted.

College of Humanities and Fine Arts Degree program information: Part-time programs available. Part-time. Offers Afro-American studies (MA, PhD); American studies (PhD); architecture (M Arch); art (MA, MFA); Asian languages and literatures (MA); Chinese (MA); collaborative piano (MM); comparative literature (MA, PhD); composition (MM); composition and rhetoric (PhD); conducting (MM); costume design (MFA); creative writing (MFA); design (MS); design in historic preservation (MS); directing (MFA); dramaturgy (MFA); English and American literature (MA, PhD); French (MAT); French and Francophone studies (MA, MAT); German and Scandinavian studies (MA, PhD); Hispanic literatures, cultures and linguistics (MA, PhD); history (MA, PhD); history of art and architecture (MA); humanities and fine arts (M Arch, MA, MAT, MFA, MM, MS, PhD); Italian studies (MAT); Japanese (MA); jazz composition/arranging (MM); Latin and classical humanities (MAT); lighting design (MFA); linguistics (MA, PhD); music education (MM, PhD); music history (MM); music theory (PhD); performance (MM); philosophy (MA, PhD); scenic design (MFA); Spanish and Portuguese studies (MA, MAT, PhD); teaching Spanish (MAT). Electronic applications accepted.

College of Natural Sciences Degree program information: Part-time programs available. Part-time. Offers animal biotechnology and biomedical sciences (MS, PhD); applied mathematics (MS); astronomy (MS, PhD); biochemistry and molecular biology (MS, PhD); building systems (MS, PhD); chemistry (MS, PhD); clinical psychology (MS, PhD); cognitive psychology (MS, PhD); computer science (MS, PhD); developmental science (MS, PhD); environmental policy and human dimensions (MS, PhD); food science (MS, PhD); forest resources (MS, PhD); geography (MS); geosciences (MS, PhD); mathematics (MS, PhD); microbiology (MS, PhD); natural sciences (MS, PhD); physics (MS, PhD); polymer science and engineering (MS, PhD); psychology of peace and violence (MS, PhD); social psychology (MS, PhD); statistics (MS, PhD); sustainability science (MS); water, wetlands and watersheds (MS, PhD); wildlife and fisheries conservation (MS, PhD). Electronic applications accepted.

College of Nursing Degree program information: Part-time programs available. Part-time, online learning. Offers adult gerontology primary care nurse practitioner (DNP); clinical nurse leader (MS); family nurse practitioner (DNP); nursing (PhD); public health nurse leader (DNP). Electronic applications accepted.

College of Social and Behavioral Sciences Degree program information: Part-time programs available. Part-time. Offers anthropology (MA, PhD); communication (MA, PhD); economics (MA, PhD); labor studies (MS); landscape architecture (MLA); political science (MA, PhD); public policy and administration (MPP, MPPA); regional planning (MRP, PhD); resource economics (MS, PhD); social and behavioral sciences (MA, MLA, MPP, MPPA, MRP, MS, PhD); sociology (MA, PhD); union leadership and administration (MS). Electronic applications accepted.

Interdisciplinary Programs Degree program information: Part-time programs available. Part-time. Offers animal behavior and learning (PhD); biochemistry and metabolism (MS, PhD); biological chemistry and molecular biophysics (PhD); biomedicine (PhD); cell biology and physiology (MS, PhD); cellular and developmental biology (PhD); environmental, ecological and integrative biology (MS, PhD); genetics and evolution (MS, PhD); interdisciplinary studies (MS, PhD); marine science and technology (MS, PhD); molecular and cellular neuroscience (PhD); neural and behavioral development (PhD); neuroendocrinology (PhD); neuroscience and behavior (MS); organismic and evolutionary biology (MS, PhD); sensorimotor, cognitive, and computational neuroscience (PhD). Electronic applications accepted.

Isenberg School of Management Degree program information: Part-time and evening/weekend programs available. Part-time, evening/weekend, online learning. Offers accounting (MSA); business administration (MBA); entrepreneurship (MBA); finance (MBA, PhD); healthcare administration (MBA); hospitality and tourism management (PhD); management (MBA, MS, MSA, PhD); management science (PhD); marketing (MBA, PhD); organization studies (PhD); sport management (PhD); strategic management (PhD). Electronic applications accepted.

School of Public Health and Health Sciences Degree program information: Part-time and evening/weekend programs available. Part-time, evening/weekend, online learning. Offers audiology (Au D, PhD); biostatistics (MPH, MS, PhD); clinical audiology (PhD); community health education (MPH, MS, PhD); community nutrition (MS); environmental health sciences (MPH, MS, PhD); epidemiology (MPH, MS, PhD); health policy and management (MPH, MS, PhD); kinesiology (MS, PhD); nutrition (MPH, PhD); nutrition science (MS); public health and health sciences (MA, MPH, MS, Au D, PhD); public health practice (MPH); speech-language pathology (MA, PhD). Electronic applications accepted.

UNIVERSITY OF MASSACHUSETTS BOSTON, Boston, MA 02125-3393

General Information State-supported, coed, university. CGS member. *Enrollment:* 17,030 graduate, professional, and undergraduate students; 1,366 full-time matriculated graduate/professional students (911 women), 2,216 part-time matriculated graduate/professional students (1,534 women). *Enrollment by degree level:* 2,433 master's, 662 doctoral, 487 other advanced degrees. *Graduate faculty:* 699 full-time (359 women), 572 part-time/adjunct (331 women). Tuition, state resident: full-time $2590. Tuition, nonresident: full-time $9758. *Required fees:* $13,525. *Graduate housing:* On-campus housing not available. *Student services:* Campus employment opportunities, campus safety program, career counseling, child daycare facilities, exercise/wellness program, free psychological counseling, international student services, low-cost health insurance, multicultural affairs office, services for students with disabilities, teacher training, writing training. *Library:* Joseph P. Healey Library. *Research affiliation:* New England Aquarium (environmental sciences), Dana Farber/Harvard Cancer Center (biomedical sciences), John F. Kennedy Presidential Library (history).

Computer facilities: 350 computers available on campus for general student use. A campuswide network can be accessed from off campus. Online class registration is available.
Website: http://www.umb.edu/

General Application Contact: Peggy Roldan Patel, Graduate Admissions Coordinator, 617-287-6400, Fax: 617-287-6236, E-mail: gadm@umb.edu.

GRADUATE UNITS

College of Advancing and Professional Studies Online learning. Offers critical and creative thinking (MA, Certificate); instructional design (M Ed, Certificate). *Application Contact:* Peggy Roldan Patel, Graduate Admissions Coordinator, 617-287-6400, Fax: 617-287-6236, E-mail: bos.gadm@dpc.umassp.edu. *Dean*, Dr. Philip DiSalvio, 617-287-5700, Fax: 617-287-5699, E-mail: kristine.alster@umb.edu.

College of Education and Human Development ***Financial support:*** Research assistantships with full tuition reimbursements, teaching assistantships with full tuition reimbursements, career-related internships or fieldwork, Federal Work-Study, and unspecified assistantships available. Support available to part-time students. Financial award application deadline: 3/1; financial award applicants required to submit FAFSA. *Degree program information:* Part-time and evening/weekend programs available. Part-time, evening/weekend. Offers counseling and school psychology (PhD); early childhood (M Ed); education and human development (M Ed, MS, Ed D, PhD); family therapy (MS); general education (M Ed); learning, teaching and educational transformation (M Ed); mental health counseling (MS); middle education (M Ed); school counseling (M Ed); school psychology (M Ed); special education (M Ed). *Application deadline:* For fall admission, 3/1 for domestic students. *Application Contact:* Peggy Roldan Patel, Graduate Admissions Coordinator, 617-287-6400, Fax: 617-287-6236, E-mail: bos.gadm@dpc.umassp.edu. *Interim Dean*, Dr. Peter Langer, 617-287-7600.

College of Liberal Arts ***Financial support:*** Research assistantships with full tuition reimbursements, teaching assistantships with full tuition reimbursements, career-related internships or fieldwork, Federal Work-Study, and unspecified assistantships available. Support available to part-time students. Financial award application deadline: 3/1; financial award applicants required to submit FAFSA. *Degree program information:* Part-time and evening/weekend programs available. Part-time, evening/weekend. Offers American studies (MA); applied economics (MA); applied sociology (MA); archival methods (MA); bilingual education (MA); clinical psychology (PhD); creative writing (MFA); developmental and brain sciences (MA); English (MA); English as a second language (MA); foreign language pedagogy (MA); historical archaeology (MA); history (MA); Latin and classical humanities (MA); liberal arts (MA, MFA, PhD); sociology (PhD). *Application deadline:* For fall admission, 3/1 for domestic students; for spring admission, 1/1 for domestic students. *Application Contact:* Peggy Roldan Patel, Graduate Admissions Coordinator, 617-287-6400, Fax: 617-287-6236, E-mail: bos.gadm@dpc.umassp.edu.

College of Management ***Financial support:*** Research assistantships with full tuition reimbursements, teaching assistantships with full tuition reimbursements, career-related internships or fieldwork, Federal Work-Study, and unspecified assistantships available. Support available to part-time students. Financial award application deadline: 3/1; financial award applicants required to submit FAFSA. *Degree program information:* Part-time and evening/weekend programs available. Part-time, evening/weekend. Offers accounting (MS); business administration (MBA); finance (MS); information technology (MS); international management (MS); management (MBA, MS). *Application deadline:* For fall admission, 3/1 for domestic students; for spring admission, 11/1 for domestic students. *Application Contact:* Peggy Roldan Patel, Graduate Admissions Coordinator, 617-287-6400, Fax: 617-287-6236, E-mail: bos.gadm@dpc.umassp.edu. *Dean*, Dr. Philip Quaglieri, 617-287-7700, E-mail: philip.quaglieri@umb.edu.

College of Nursing and Health Sciences ***Financial support:*** Research assistantships with full tuition reimbursements, teaching assistantships with full tuition reimbursements, career-related internships or fieldwork, Federal Work-Study, and unspecified assistantships available. Support available to part-time students. Financial award application deadline: 3/1; financial award applicants required to submit FAFSA.

Degree program information: Part-time and evening/weekend programs available. Part-time, evening/weekend. Offers exercise and health sciences (MS, PhD); nursing (MS, DNP, PhD). *Application deadline:* For fall admission, 3/1 for domestic students; for spring admission, 11/1 for domestic students. *Application Contact:* Peggy Roldan Patel, Graduate Admissions Coordinator, 617-287-6400, Fax: 617-287-6236, E-mail: bos.gadm@dpc.umassp.edu. *Dean,* Dr. Greer Glazer, 617-287-7500.

College of Public and Community Service ***Financial support:*** Research assistantships with full tuition reimbursements, teaching assistantships with full tuition reimbursements, career-related internships or fieldwork, Federal Work-Study, and unspecified assistantships available. Support available to part-time students. Financial award application deadline: 3/1; financial award applicants required to submit FAFSA. *Degree program information:* Part-time and evening/weekend programs available. Part-time, evening/weekend. Offers human services (MS); public and community service (MS). *Application deadline:* For fall admission, 3/1 for domestic students. Applications are processed on a rolling basis. *Application Contact:* Peggy Roldan Patel, Graduate Admissions Coordinator, 617-287-6400, Fax: 617-287-6236, E-mail: bos.gadm@dpc.umassp.edu. *Dean,* Adenrele Awotona, 617-287-7231, Fax: 617-287-5699.

College of Science and Mathematics ***Financial support:*** Research assistantships with full tuition reimbursements, teaching assistantships with full tuition reimbursements, career-related internships or fieldwork, Federal Work-Study, institutionally sponsored loans, and unspecified assistantships available. Support available to part-time students. Financial award application deadline: 3/1; financial award applicants required to submit FAFSA. *Degree program information:* Part-time and evening/weekend programs available. Part-time, evening/weekend. Offers applied physics (MS); biology (MS, PhD); biomedical engineering and biotechnology (PhD); biotechnology and biomedical sciences (MS); chemistry (MS, PhD); computer science (MS, PhD); environmental sciences (MS, PhD); marine science and technology (MS, PhD); science and mathematics (MS, PhD). *Application deadline:* For fall admission, 3/1 for domestic students; for spring admission, 11/1 for domestic students. Applications are processed on a rolling basis. *Application Contact:* Peggy Roldan Patel, Graduate Admissions Coordinator, 617-287-6400, Fax: 617-287-6236, E-mail: bos.gadm@dpc.umassp.edu. *Interim Dean,* Dr. William Hagar, 617-287-5777.

Graduate School of Global Inclusion and Social Development Offers global inclusion and social development (M Ed, MA, MS, PhD); rehabilitation counseling (MS); vision studies (M Ed). *Application Contact:* Peggy Roldan Patel, Graduate Admissions Coordinator, 617-287-6400, Fax: 617-287-6236, E-mail: bos.gadm@dpc.umassp.edu. *Associate Provost,* Dr. Kristy Alster, 617-287-5700, Fax: 617-287-5699, E-mail: kristine.alster@umb.edu.

John W. McCormack Graduate School of Policy and Global Studies ***Financial support:*** Research assistantships with full tuition reimbursements, teaching assistantships with full tuition reimbursements, career-related internships or fieldwork, Federal Work-Study, and unspecified assistantships available. Support available to part-time students. Financial award application deadline: 3/1; financial award applicants required to submit FAFSA. *Degree program information:* Part-time and evening/weekend programs available. Part-time, evening/weekend. Offers conflict resolution (MA, Certificate); gerontology (MS, PhD, Certificate); gerontology research (MS); global governance and human security (MA); management of aging services (MS); public administration (MPA); public affairs (MS); public policy (PhD). *Application Contact:* Peggy Roldan Patel, Graduate Admissions Coordinator, 617-287-6400, Fax: 617-287-6236, E-mail: bos.gadm@dpc.umassp.edu. *Dean,* Dr. Stephen Crosby, 617-287-5550, E-mail: stephen.crosby@umb.edu.

UNIVERSITY OF MASSACHUSETTS DARTMOUTH, North Dartmouth, MA 02747-2300

General Information State-supported, coed, university. *Enrollment:* 8,916 graduate, professional, and undergraduate students; 638 full-time matriculated graduate/professional students (296 women), 819 part-time matriculated graduate/professional students (470 women). *Enrollment by degree level:* 918 master's, 490 doctoral, 49 other advanced degrees. *Graduate faculty:* 294 full-time (130 women), 129 part-time/adjunct (78 women). Tuition, state resident: full-time $2071; part-time $86.29 per credit. Tuition, nonresident: full-time $8099; part-time $337.46 per credit. *Required fees:* $18,074; $762.08 per credit. Tuition and fees vary according to course load and reciprocity agreements. *Graduate housing:* Room and/or apartments available on a first-come, first-served basis to single students; on-campus housing not available to married students. Typical cost: $7609 per year ($11,622 including board). Room and board charges vary according to board plan and housing facility selected. Housing application deadline: 3/14. *Student services:* Campus employment opportunities, campus safety program, career counseling, exercise/wellness program, free psychological counseling, grant writing training, international student services, low-cost health insurance, multicultural affairs office, services for students with disabilities, teacher training, writing training. *Library:* Claire T. Carney Library plus 1 other. *Collection:* Books: 436,885 (physical), 11,358 (digital/electronic); Serial titles: 7,910 (physical), 1,108 (digital/electronic); Databases: 111. Students can reserve study rooms. *Research affiliation:* Massachusetts Department of Transportation (civil engineering), National Oceanic and Atmospheric Administration (NOAA) (marine sciences), Cape Cod Cranberry Growers Association (agriculture), Woods Hole Oceanographic Institution (marine sciences), Office of Naval Research (ONR) (engineering), L'Oreal USA (chemistry).

Computer facilities: 368 computers available on campus for general student use. A campuswide network can be accessed from student residence rooms and from off campus. Online class registration is available.
Website: http://www.umassd.edu/

General Application Contact: Steven Briggs, Director of Marketing and Recruitment for Graduate Studies, 508-999-8604, Fax: 508-999-8183, E-mail: graduate@umassd.edu.

GRADUATE UNITS

Graduate School Students: 638 full-time (296 women), 819 part-time (470 women); includes 206 minority (62 Black or African American, non-Hispanic/Latino; 2 American Indian or Alaska Native, non-Hispanic/Latino; 33 Asian, non-Hispanic/Latino; 69 Hispanic/Latino; 40 Two or more races, non-Hispanic/Latino), 379 international. Average age 31. 1,903 applicants, 77% accepted, 543 enrolled. *Faculty:* 294 full-time (130 women), 129 part-time/adjunct (78 women). *Financial support:* In 2015–16, 40 fellowships (averaging $17,158 per year), 64 research assistantships (averaging $15,659 per year), 105 teaching assistantships (averaging $11,076 per year) were awarded; career-related internships or fieldwork, scholarships/grants, and unspecified assistantships also available. Financial award application deadline: 3/1; financial award applicants required to submit FAFSA. In 2015, 399 master's, 91 doctorates, 42 other advanced degrees awarded. *Degree program information:* Part-time programs available. Part-time, 100% online. Offers adult health (MS); community health (MS); data science (MS); nursing (PhD); nursing practice (DNP). *Application deadline:* For fall admission, 8/1 for domestic students, 6/1 priority date for international students; for spring admission, 11/15 for domestic students, 10/15 priority date for international students. Applications are processed on a rolling basis. *Application fee:* $60. Electronic applications accepted. *Application Contact:* Steven Briggs, Director of Marketing and Recruitment for Graduate Studies, 508-999-8604, Fax: 508-999-8183, E-mail: graduate@umassd.edu. *Director of Graduate Studies and Admissions,* Scott Webster, 508-999-8202, Fax: 508-999-8183, E-mail: swebster@umassd.edu.

Charlton College of Business Students: 147 full-time (64 women), 183 part-time (98 women); includes 42 minority (12 Black or African American, non-Hispanic/Latino; 1 American Indian or Alaska Native, non-Hispanic/Latino; 12 Asian, non-Hispanic/Latino; 13 Hispanic/Latino; 4 Two or more races, non-Hispanic/Latino), 118 international. Average age 32. 262 applicants, 87% accepted, 136 enrolled. *Faculty:* 40 full-time (14 women), 19 part-time/adjunct (8 women). *Financial support:* Unspecified assistantships available. Financial award application deadline: 3/1; financial award applicants required to submit FAFSA. In 2015, 163 master's, 15 other advanced degrees awarded. *Degree program information:* Part-time programs available. Part-time, 100% online. Offers accounting (MS, Postbaccalaureate Certificate); accounting and finance (MS, Postbaccalaureate Certificate); business administration (MBA, Graduate Certificate, Postbaccalaureate Certificate); business foundations (Graduate Certificate); decision and information sciences (MS); finance (Postbaccalaureate Certificate); healthcare management (MS); international business (Graduate Certificate); marketing (Postbaccalaureate Certificate); organizational leadership (Graduate Certificate); supply chain management and information systems (Postbaccalaureate Certificate); technology management (MS). *Application deadline:* For fall admission, 8/1 priority date for domestic students, 6/1 priority date for international students; for spring admission, 11/15 priority date for domestic students, 10/15 priority date for international students. Applications are processed on a rolling basis. *Application fee:* $60. Electronic applications accepted. *Application Contact:* Steven Briggs, Director of Recruitment and Marketing for Graduate Studies, 508-999-8604, Fax: 508-999-8183, E-mail: graduate@umassd.edu. *Interim Assistant Dean for Graduate Studies,* Donna Sotomayor, 508-999-8543, Fax: 508-999-8776, E-mail: donna.sotomajor@umassd.edu.

College of Arts and Sciences Students: 127 full-time (76 women), 249 part-time (161 women); includes 69 minority (17 Black or African American, non-Hispanic/Latino; 1 American Indian or Alaska Native, non-Hispanic/Latino; 5 Asian, non-Hispanic/Latino; 27 Hispanic/Latino; 19 Two or more races, non-Hispanic/Latino), 29 international. Average age 33. 308 applicants, 78% accepted, 543 enrolled. *Faculty:* 110 full-time (56 women), 39 part-time/adjunct (22 women). *Financial support:* In 2015–16, 24 fellowships (averaging $16,431 per year), 11 research assistantships (averaging $13,109 per year), 30 teaching assistantships (averaging $13,067 per year) were awarded; career-related internships or fieldwork, Federal Work-Study, and unspecified assistantships also available. Support available to part-time students. Financial award application deadline: 3/1; financial award applicants required to submit FAFSA. In 2015, 150 master's, 10 doctorates, 22 other advanced degrees awarded. *Degree program information:* Part-time programs available. Part-time, 100% online. Offers applied behavioral analysis (MA, Post-Master's Certificate); arts and sciences (MA, MAT, MPP, MS, Ed D, PhD, Graduate Certificate, Post-Master's Certificate, Postbaccalaureate Certificate); biology (MS); chemistry (MS, PhD); clinical psychology (MA); educational leadership (Ed D, PhD); educational policy (Graduate Certificate); environmental policy (Graduate Certificate); Luso-Afro Brazilian studies (PhD); marine biology (MS); mathematics education (PhD); middle school education (MAT, Postbaccalaureate Certificate); Portuguese (MA); professional writing (MA, Postbaccalaureate Certificate); public management (Graduate Certificate); public policy (MPP); research psychology (MA); secondary school education (MAT, Postbaccalaureate Certificate); teaching and learning (MAT, Postbaccalaureate Certificate). *Application deadline:* Applications are processed on a rolling basis. *Application fee:* $60. Electronic applications accepted. *Application Contact:* Steven Briggs, Director of Recruitment and Marketing for Graduate Studies, 508-999-8604, Fax: 508-999-8183, E-mail: graduate@umassd.edu. *Dean, College of Arts and Sciences,* Dr. Jeannette Riley, 508-999-8352, Fax: 508-999-9125, E-mail: j1riley@umassd.edu.

College of Engineering Students: 184 full-time (54 women), 125 part-time (21 women); includes 16 minority (3 Black or African American, non-Hispanic/Latino; 8 Asian, non-Hispanic/Latino; 3 Hispanic/Latino; 2 Two or more races, non-Hispanic/Latino), 211 international. Average age 27. 409 applicants, 76% accepted, 95 enrolled. *Faculty:* 38 full-time (6 women), 6 part-time/adjunct (0 women). *Financial support:* In 2015–16, 12 fellowships with tuition reimbursements (averaging $18,831 per year), 29 research assistantships with tuition reimbursements (averaging $13,412 per year), 43 teaching assistantships with tuition reimbursements (averaging $12,320 per year) were awarded; Federal Work-Study and unspecified assistantships also available. Support available to part-time students. Financial award application deadline: 3/1; financial award applicants required to submit FAFSA. In 2015, 54 master's, 6 doctorates, 2 other advanced degrees awarded. *Degree program information:* Part-time programs available. Part-time, online learning. Offers acoustics (Postbaccalaureate Certificate); applied mechanics and materials (PhD); bioengineering (PhD); biology (PhD); biomedical engineering/biotechnology (MS, PhD); chemistry (PhD); civil engineering (MS, PhD); communications (Postbaccalaureate Certificate); computational science and engineering (PhD); computer and information science (PhD); computer engineering (MS, PhD); computer networks and distributed systems (Postbaccalaureate Certificate); computer science (MS, Postbaccalaureate Certificate); computer science and information systems (PhD); computer systems engineering (Postbaccalaureate Certificate); digital signal processing (Postbaccalaureate Certificate); electrical and computer engineering (PhD); electrical engineering (MS, PhD); electrical engineering systems (Postbaccalaureate Certificate); engineering (MS, PhD, Postbaccalaureate Certificate); industrial and systems engineering (MS, PhD); mathematics (PhD); mechanical engineering (MS, PhD); medical laboratory science (MS); physics (MS, PhD); software development and design (Postbaccalaureate Certificate); textile chemistry (MS); textile technology (MS). *Application deadline:* Applications are processed on a rolling basis. *Application fee:* $60. Electronic applications accepted. *Application Contact:* Steven Briggs, Director of Marketing and Recruitment for Graduate Studies, 508-999-8604, Fax: 508-999-8183, E-mail: graduate@umassd.edu. *Dean, College of Engineering,* Dr. Robert Peck, 508-999-8539, Fax: 508-999-9137, E-mail: rpeck@umassd.edu.

College of Visual and Performing Arts Students: 36 full-time (25 women), 28 part-time (22 women); includes 8 minority (2 Black or African American, non-Hispanic/Latino; 1 Asian, non-Hispanic/Latino; 3 Hispanic/Latino; 2 Two or more races, non-Hispanic/Latino), 9 international. Average age 35. 83 applicants, 69% accepted, 22 enrolled. *Faculty:* 20 full-time (17 women), 9 part-time/adjunct (7 women). *Financial support:* In 2015–16, 2 fellowships with full tuition reimbursements (averaging $12,000 per year), 25 teaching assistantships with partial tuition reimbursements (averaging $4,288 per year) were awarded; Federal Work-Study and unspecified assistantships also available. Support available to part-time students. Financial award application deadline: 3/1; financial award applicants required to submit FAFSA. In 2015, 25 master's, 3 other advanced degrees awarded. *Degree program information:* Part-time programs available. Part-time. Offers art education (MAE); ceramics (MFA, Postbaccalaureate Certificate); digital media (MFA); digital multi-media (MFA); drawing (MFA, Postbaccalaureate Certificate); fibers (MFA, Postbaccalaureate Certificate); graphic design (MFA); illustration (MFA); jewelry/metals (MFA, Postbaccalaureate Certificate); painting (MFA, Postbaccalaureate Certificate); photography (MFA); printmaking (MFA, Postbaccalaureate Certificate); sculpture (MFA, Postbaccalaureate Certificate); typography (MFA); visual and performing arts (MAE, MFA, Postbaccalaureate Certificate); Web and interaction design (Postbaccalaureate Certificate); wood/furniture design (MFA, Postbaccalaureate Certificate). *Application deadline:* Applications are processed on a rolling basis. *Application fee:* $60. Electronic applications accepted. *Application Contact:* Steven Briggs, Director of Marketing and Recruitment for Graduate Studies, 508-999-8604, Fax: 508-999-8183, E-mail: graduate@umassd.edu. *Dean, College of Visual and Performing Arts*, Adrian Tio, 508-999-9295, Fax: 508-999-9126, E-mail: atio@umassd.edu.

School for Marine Science and Technology Students: 22 full-time (9 women), 34 part-time (17 women); includes 3 minority (1 Hispanic/Latino; 2 Two or more races, non-Hispanic/Latino), 15 international. Average age 31. 28 applicants, 93% accepted, 11 enrolled. *Faculty:* 13 full-time (1 woman). *Financial support:* In 2015–16, 24 research assistantships with full tuition reimbursements (averaging $17,721 per year), 3 teaching assistantships with full tuition reimbursements (averaging $24,667 per year) were awarded; Federal Work-Study and unspecified assistantships also available. Support available to part-time students. Financial award application deadline: 3/1; financial award applicants required to submit FAFSA. In 2015, 4 master's, 10 doctorates awarded. *Degree program information:* Part-time programs available. Part-time. Offers coastal and ocean administration science and technology (MS). *Application deadline:* For fall admission, 2/15 priority date for domestic students, 1/15 priority date for international students; for spring admission, 11/15 priority date for domestic students, 10/15 priority date for international students. Applications are processed on a rolling basis. *Application fee:* $60. Electronic applications accepted. *Application Contact:* Steven Briggs, Director of Marketing and Recruitment for Graduate Studies, 508-999-8604, Fax: 508-999-8183, E-mail: graduate@umassd.edu. *Graduate Program Director*, Steven Lohrenz, 508-910-6550, Fax: 508-999-8197, E-mail: slohrenz@umassd.edu.

University of Massachusetts School of Law –Dartmouth Students: 126 full-time (59 women), 88 part-time (50 women); includes 53 minority (20 Black or African American, non-Hispanic/Latino; 10 Asian, non-Hispanic/Latino; 15 Hispanic/Latino; 8 Two or more races, non-Hispanic/Latino), 2 international. Average age 31. 627 applicants, 65% accepted, 72 enrolled. *Faculty:* 17 full-time (7 women), 10 part-time/adjunct (5 women). *Financial support:* Scholarships/grants, tuition waivers (full and partial), and summer stipends available. Support available to part-time students. Financial award application deadline: 4/15; financial award applicants required to submit FAFSA. In 2015, 79 doctorates awarded. *Degree program information:* Part-time and evening/weekend programs available. Part-time, evening/weekend. Offers law (JD). *Application deadline:* For fall admission, 6/30 priority date for domestic students, 5/30 priority date for international students. Applications are processed on a rolling basis. *Application fee:* $50. Electronic applications accepted. *Application Contact:* Daniel Fitzpatrick, Interim Associate Dean, 508-985-1109, Fax: 508-985-1104, E-mail: dfitzpatrick@umassd.edu. *Dean, University of Massachusetts School of Law - Dartmouth*, Mary Lu Bilek, 508-985-1149, Fax: 508-985-1104, E-mail: mbilek@umassd.edu.

★ UNIVERSITY OF MASSACHUSETTS LOWELL, Lowell, MA 01854

General Information State-supported, coed, university. CGS member. Tuition, state resident: full-time $14,304. Tuition, nonresident: full-time $25,853. *Required fees:* $375. Full-time tuition and fees vary according to campus/location and reciprocity agreements. *Graduate housing:* Rooms and/or apartments available on a first-come, first-served basis to single students and available to married students. Housing application deadline: 4/1. *Student services:* Campus employment opportunities, campus safety program, career counseling, child daycare facilities, exercise/wellness program, free psychological counseling, grant writing training, international student services, low-cost health insurance, multicultural affairs office, services for students with disabilities, teacher training, writing training. *Library:* O'Leary Library and Learning Commons plus 2 others. *Collection:* Books: 223,491 (physical), 192,502 (digital/electronic); Serial titles: 5,383 (physical), 125,533 (digital/electronic); Databases: 135. Students can reserve study rooms.

Computer facilities: Computer purchase and lease plans are available. 2,145 computers available on campus for general student use. A campuswide network can be accessed from student residence rooms and from off campus. Online class registration is available.
Website: http://www.uml.edu/

General Application Contact: Graduate Admissions Office, 978-934-2390, Fax: 978-934-4058, E-mail: graduate_admissions@uml.edu.

GRADUATE UNITS

College of Fine Arts, Humanities and Social Sciences Offers community social psychology (MA); fine arts, humanities and social sciences (MA, MM, PhD); music education (MM); peace and conflict studies (MA); regional economic and social development (MA, Graduate Certificate).

School of Criminology and Justice Studies Financial support: Research assistantships with full tuition reimbursements, teaching assistantships with full tuition reimbursements, career-related internships or fieldwork, Federal Work-Study, institutionally sponsored loans, scholarships/grants, and traineeships available. Support available to part-time students. Financial award application deadline: 4/1. *Degree program information:* Part-time and evening/weekend programs available. Part-time, evening/weekend. Offers criminal justice (MA). *Application deadline:* For fall admission, 4/1 priority date for domestic students; for spring admission, 10/1 for domestic students. Applications are processed on a rolling basis. *Application fee:* $20 ($35 for international students). Electronic applications accepted.

College of Health Sciences *Financial support:* Fellowships with tuition reimbursements, research assistantships with full tuition reimbursements, teaching assistantships with full tuition reimbursements, career-related internships or fieldwork, Federal Work-Study, institutionally sponsored loans, scholarships/grants, and traineeships available. Support available to part-time students. *Degree program information:* Part-time programs available. Part-time. Offers cleaner production and pollution prevention (Sc D); clinical laboratory sciences (MS); health sciences (MS, DNP, DPT, PhD); physical therapy (DPT). *Application deadline:* Applications are processed on a rolling basis. *Application fee:* $20 ($35 for international students).

School of Nursing Financial support: Fellowships with tuition reimbursements, research assistantships with full tuition reimbursements, teaching assistantships with full tuition reimbursements, career-related internships or fieldwork, Federal Work-Study, institutionally sponsored loans, scholarships/grants, and traineeships available. Support available to part-time students. Financial award application deadline: 4/1. Offers adult/gerontological nursing (MS); family health nursing (MS); nursing (DNP, PhD). *Application deadline:* For fall admission, 4/1 priority date for domestic students; for spring admission, 10/1 for domestic students. Applications are processed on a rolling basis. *Application fee:* $20 ($35 for international students).

College of Sciences *Financial support:* Fellowships with tuition reimbursements, research assistantships with full tuition reimbursements, teaching assistantships with full tuition reimbursements, career-related internships or fieldwork, Federal Work-Study, institutionally sponsored loans, scholarships/grants, and traineeships available. Support available to part-time students. Financial award application deadline: 4/1. *Degree program information:* Part-time and evening/weekend programs available. Part-time, evening/weekend. Offers analytical chemistry (PhD); biochemistry (PhD); biological sciences (MS); chemistry (MS, PhD); computer science (MS, PhD); environmental studies (PhD); green chemistry (PhD); inorganic chemistry (PhD); mathematical sciences (Ed D); organic chemistry (PhD); physics (MS, PhD); polymer science (PhD); radiological sciences and protection (MS, PSM); sciences (MA, MM, MS, Ed D, PhD). *Application deadline:* For fall admission, 4/1 priority date for domestic students; for spring admission, 10/1 for domestic students. Applications are processed on a rolling basis. *Application fee:* $20 ($35 for international students).

Francis College of Engineering *Financial support:* Fellowships with full tuition reimbursements, research assistantships with full tuition reimbursements, teaching assistantships with full tuition reimbursements, career-related internships or fieldwork, Federal Work-Study, and institutionally sponsored loans available. Support available to part-time students. Financial award application deadline: 4/1. *Degree program information:* Part-time and evening/weekend programs available. Part-time, evening/weekend. Offers chemical engineering (MS Eng, PhD); computer engineering (MS Eng, PhD); electrical engineering (MS Eng, PhD); energy engineering (MS Eng, PhD); engineering (MS, MS Eng, PhD); environmental studies (PhD); mechanical engineering (MS Eng, PhD); plastics engineering (MS Eng, PhD). *Application deadline:* For fall admission, 4/1 priority date for domestic students; for spring admission, 10/1 for domestic students. Applications are processed on a rolling basis. *Application fee:* $20 ($35 for international students).

Graduate School of Education *Financial support:* Fellowships with full tuition reimbursements, research assistantships with full tuition reimbursements, teaching assistantships with full tuition reimbursements, career-related internships or fieldwork, Federal Work-Study, institutionally sponsored loans, scholarships/grants, and unspecified assistantships available. Support available to part-time students. Financial award application deadline: 4/1; financial award applicants required to submit FAFSA. *Degree program information:* Part-time and evening/weekend programs available. Part-time, evening/weekend, online learning. Offers curriculum and instruction (M Ed). *Application deadline:* For fall admission, 7/1 priority date for domestic students; for spring admission, 11/1 priority date for domestic students. Applications are processed on a rolling basis. *Application fee:* $20 ($35 for international students). Electronic applications accepted.

Manning School of Business *Financial support:* Fellowships, research assistantships with full tuition reimbursements, teaching assistantships with full tuition reimbursements, career-related internships or fieldwork, Federal Work-Study, institutionally sponsored loans, scholarships/grants, traineeships, and unspecified assistantships available. Support available to part-time students. Financial award application deadline: 4/1. *Degree program information:* Part-time and evening/weekend programs available. Part-time, evening/weekend. Offers business administration (MBA, PhD); healthcare innovation and entrepreneurship (MS). *Application deadline:* For fall admission, 4/1 priority date for domestic students; for spring admission, 10/1 for domestic students. Applications are processed on a rolling basis. *Application fee:* $20 ($35 for international students).

See Display on next page and Close-Up on page 907.

UNIVERSITY OF MASSACHUSETTS MEDICAL SCHOOL, Worcester, MA 01655-0115

General Information State-supported, coed, graduate-only institution. CGS member. *Enrollment by degree level:* 107 master's, 939 doctoral, 2 other advanced degrees. *Graduate faculty:* 1,358 full-time (537 women), 330 part-time/adjunct (213 women). *Graduate housing:* On-campus housing not available. *Student services:* Campus employment opportunities, campus safety program, career counseling, child daycare facilities, exercise/wellness program, free psychological counseling, grant writing training, international student services, low-cost health insurance, multicultural affairs office, services for students with disabilities, teacher training, writing training. *Library:* Lamar Soutter Library. *Collection:* Books: 180,233 (physical), 22,114 (digital/electronic); Serial titles: 10 (physical), 5,360 (digital/electronic); Databases: 468. Weekly public service hours: 87; study areas open 24 hours, 5–7 days a week. *Research affiliation:* Abbott Bioresearch Center (biomedical research and training), Charles River Laboratories (pre-clinical biomedical research).

Computer facilities: 107 computers available on campus for general student use. A campuswide network can be accessed. Online class registration is available.
Website: http://www.umassmed.edu/

General Application Contact: Karen Lawton, Director of Admissions, 508-856-2323, Fax: 508-856-3629, E-mail: admissions@umassmed.edu.

GRADUATE UNITS

Graduate School of Biomedical Sciences Students: 363 full-time (184 women); includes 58 minority (13 Black or African American, non-Hispanic/Latino; 30 Asian, non-Hispanic/Latino; 15 Hispanic/Latino), 141 international. Average age 29. 661 applicants, 26% accepted, 51 enrolled. *Faculty:* 1,339 full-time (521 women), 301 part-time/adjunct (189 women). *Financial support:* In 2015–16, 383 students received support, including research assistantships with full tuition reimbursements available (averaging $30,600 per year); scholarships/grants, health care benefits, tuition waivers (full), and unspecified assistantships also available. Financial award application deadline: 5/16. In 2015, 10 master's, 58 doctorates awarded. Offers biomedical sciences (PhD); biomedical sciences (millennium program) (PhD); clinical and population health research (PhD); clinical investigation (MS). *Application deadline:* For fall admission, 12/15 for domestic and international students; for spring admission, 5/15 for domestic students. *Application fee:* $80. Electronic applications accepted. *Application Contact:* Dr. Kendall Knight, Assistant Vice Provost for Admissions, 508-856-5628, Fax: 508-856-3659, E-mail:

kendall.knight@umassmed.edu. *Dean,* Dr. Anthony Carruthers, 508-856-4135, E-mail: anthony.carruthers@umassmed.edu.

Graduate School of Nursing Students: 143 full-time (119 women), 27 part-time (25 women); includes 28 minority (15 Black or African American, non-Hispanic/Latino; 10 Asian, non-Hispanic/Latino; 3 Hispanic/Latino), 1 international. Average age 34. 129 applicants, 68% accepted, 56 enrolled. *Faculty:* 18 full-time (15 women), 28 part-time/adjunct (22 women). *Financial support:* In 2015–16, 31 students received support. Institutionally sponsored loans, scholarships/grants, traineeships, and tuition waivers (partial) available. Support available to part-time students. Financial award application deadline: 5/16; financial award applicants required to submit FAFSA. In 2015, 43 master's, 10 doctorates, 2 other advanced degrees awarded. Offers adult gerontological acute care nurse practitioner (DNP, Post Master's Certificate); adult gerontological primary care nurse practitioner (DNP, Post Master's Certificate); family nursing practitioner (DNP); nurse administrator (DNP); nurse educator (MS, Post Master's Certificate); nursing (PhD); nursing practitioner (DNP); population health (MS). *Application deadline:* For fall admission, 12/1 priority date for domestic students. Applications are processed on a rolling basis. *Application fee:* $60. Electronic applications accepted. *Application Contact:* Diane Brescia, Admissions Coordinator, 508-856-3488, Fax: 508-856-5851, E-mail: diane.brescia@umassmed.edu. *Dean,* Dr. Joan Vitello-Cicciu, 508-856-5081, Fax: 508-856-6552, E-mail: joan.vitello@umassmed.edu.

School of Medicine Students: 515 full-time (274 women); includes 149 minority (24 Black or African American, non-Hispanic/Latino; 1 American Indian or Alaska Native, non-Hispanic/Latino; 105 Asian, non-Hispanic/Latino; 19 Hispanic/Latino). Average age 27. 1,266 applicants, 17% accepted, 125 enrolled. *Faculty:* 1,339 full-time (521 women), 301 part-time/adjunct (189 women). *Financial support:* In 2015–16, 444 students received support. Institutionally sponsored loans, scholarships/grants, health care benefits, tuition waivers (partial), and unspecified assistantships available. Financial award application deadline: 4/1; financial award applicants required to submit FAFSA. In 2015, 123 doctorates awarded. Offers medicine (MD). *Application deadline:* For fall admission, 12/15 for domestic students. Applications are processed on a rolling basis. *Application fee:* $100. Electronic applications accepted. *Application Contact:* Dr. Mariann M. Manno, Associate Dean for Admissions, 508-856-2323, Fax: 508-856-3629, E-mail: mariann.manno@umassmed.edu. *Dean/Provost/Executive Deputy Chancellor,* Dr. Terence R. Flotte, 508-856-8000, E-mail: terry.flotte@umassmed.edu.

UNIVERSITY OF MEMPHIS, Memphis, TN 38152

General Information State-supported, coed, university. CGS member. *Enrollment:* 20,585 graduate, professional, and undergraduate students; 1,967 full-time matriculated graduate/professional students (1,109 women), 1,979 part-time matriculated graduate/professional students (1,193 women). *Enrollment by degree level:* 3,346 master's. *Graduate faculty:* 533 full-time (189 women), 103 part-time/adjunct (51 women). *Graduate housing:* Rooms and/or apartments available on a first-come, first-served basis to single students and available to married students. Housing application deadline: 7/1. *Student services:* Campus employment opportunities, campus safety program, career counseling, child daycare facilities, exercise/wellness program, free psychological counseling, grant writing training, international student services, low-cost health insurance, multicultural affairs office, services for students with disabilities, teacher training, writing training. *Library:* McWherter Library plus 4 others. *Collection:* Books: 2.3 million (physical), 113,204 (digital/electronic); Serial titles: 288 (physical), 1,098 (digital/electronic); Databases: 739. Weekly public service hours: 83; students can reserve study rooms. *Research affiliation:* Memphis Biotech Foundation, Campbell Clinic Orthopaedics, Federal Express, Oak Ridge National Laboratory, St. Jude Children's Research Hospital, Gulf Coast Research Laboratory.

Computer facilities: 1,600 computers available on campus for general student use. A campuswide network can be accessed from student residence rooms and from off campus. Online class registration is available.
Website: http://www.memphis.edu/

General Application Contact: Dr. Jasbir Dhaliwal, Dean of the Graduate School, 901-678-4653, Fax: 901-678-0378, E-mail: graduateschool@memphis.edu.

GRADUATE UNITS

Cecil C. Humphreys School of Law Students: 312 full-time (125 women), 22 part-time (10 women); includes 82 minority (55 Black or African American, non-Hispanic/Latino; 7 American Indian or Alaska Native, non-Hispanic/Latino; 8 Asian, non-Hispanic/Latino; 12 Hispanic/Latino). Average age 27. 556 applicants, 60% accepted, 97 enrolled. *Faculty:* 22 full-time (9 women), 22 part-time/adjunct (6 women). *Financial support:* In 2015–16, 120 students received support, including 22 fellowships with tuition reimbursements available (averaging $9,023 per year), 17 research assistantships with full tuition reimbursements available (averaging $3,000 per year), 2 teaching assistantships (averaging $3,000 per year); career-related internships or fieldwork, Federal Work-Study, scholarships/grants, and tuition waivers (partial) also available. Support available to part-time students. Financial award application deadline: 5/1; financial award applicants required to submit FAFSA. In 2015, 1 doctorate awarded. Offers law (JD). *Application deadline:* For fall admission, 3/15 priority date for domestic and international students. Applications are processed on a rolling basis. *Application fee:* $0 ($40 for international students). Electronic applications accepted. *Application Contact:* Dr. Sue Ann McClellan, Assistant Dean for Law Admissions, Recruiting and Scholarships, 901-678-5403, Fax: 901-678-0741, E-mail: smcclell@memphis.edu. *Dean,* Peter V. Letsou, 901-678-2421, Fax: 901-678-5210, E-mail: pvletsou@memphis.edu.

Graduate School Students: 1,967 full-time (1,109 women), 1,979 part-time (1,193 women); includes 1,293 minority (911 Black or African American, non-Hispanic/Latino; 6 American Indian or Alaska Native, non-Hispanic/Latino; 154 Asian, non-Hispanic/Latino; 119 Hispanic/Latino; 2 Native Hawaiian or other Pacific Islander, non-Hispanic/Latino; 101 Two or more races, non-Hispanic/Latino), 456 international. Average age 32. 2,964 applicants, 60% accepted, 560 enrolled. *Faculty:* 533 full-time (189 women), 103 part-time/adjunct (51 women). *Financial support:* In 2015–16, 2,179 students received support. Fellowships with full tuition reimbursements available, research assistantships with full tuition reimbursements available, teaching assistantships with full tuition reimbursements available, career-related internships or fieldwork, Federal Work-Study, institutionally sponsored loans, scholarships/grants, and unspecified assistantships available. Support available to part-time students. Financial award application deadline: 2/15; financial award applicants required to submit FAFSA. In 2015, 1,062 master's, 130 doctorates, 112 other advanced degrees awarded. *Degree program information:* Part-time and evening/weekend programs available. Part-time, evening/weekend, online learning. *Application deadline:* For fall admission, 7/1 for domestic students, 5/1 for international students; for spring admission, 12/1 for domestic students, 9/15 for international students. Applications are processed on a rolling basis. *Application fee:* $35 ($60 for international students). Electronic applications accepted. *Application Contact:* Lemmie Griggs, Supervisor of Graduate Admissions, 901-678-5580, Fax: 901-

678-0378, E-mail: lgriggs@memphis.edu. *Interim Vice Provost for Graduate Studies*, Dr. Jasbir Dhaliwal, 901-678-4653, Fax: 901-678-0378, E-mail: gradsch@memphis.edu.

College of Arts and Sciences Students: 617 full-time (332 women), 369 part-time (210 women); includes 293 minority (200 Black or African American, non-Hispanic/Latino; 27 Asian, non-Hispanic/Latino; 39 Hispanic/Latino; 27 Two or more races, non-Hispanic/Latino), 191 international. Average age 32. 830 applicants, 54% accepted, 381 enrolled. *Faculty:* 212 full-time (76 women), 28 part-time/adjunct (14 women). *Financial support:* In 2015–16, 467 students received support. Fellowships with full tuition reimbursements available, research assistantships with full tuition reimbursements available, teaching assistantships with full tuition reimbursements available, career-related internships or fieldwork, Federal Work-Study, institutionally sponsored loans, scholarships/grants, tuition waivers (full and partial), and unspecified assistantships available. Financial award application deadline: 2/15; financial award applicants required to submit FAFSA. In 2015, 241 master's, 50 doctorates, 29 other advanced degrees awarded. *Degree program information:* Part-time and evening/weekend programs available. Part-time, evening/weekend. Offers African-American literature (Graduate Certificate); analytical chemistry (PhD); ancient Egyptian history (MA, PhD); applied linguistics (PhD); applied mathematics (MS); applied statistics (PhD); archaeology (MS); arts and sciences (MA, MCRP, MFA, MPA, MS, PhD, Ed S, Graduate Certificate); bioinformatics (MS); biology (MS, PhD); city and regional planning (MCRP); clinical psychology (MA, PhD); composition studies (PhD); computer science (MS); computer sciences (MS); creative writing (MFA); criminology and criminal justice (MA); earth sciences (PhD); English as a second language (MA); experimental psychology (MA, PhD); French (MA); general psychology (MS); geographic information systems (Graduate Certificate); geography (MA, MS); geology (MS); geophysics (MS); inorganic chemistry (MS); interdisciplinary studies (MA, MS, Graduate Certificate); linguistics (MA); literary and cultural studies (PhD); literature (MA); medical anthropology (MA); philosophy (MA, PhD); physical chemistry (MS); physics (MS); political science (MA); professional writing (MA, PhD); public and nonprofit administration (MPA, Graduate Certificate); school psychology (MA, PhD, Ed S); sociology (MA); statistics (MS); teaching English as a second language (Graduate Certificate); urban anthropology (MA). *Application deadline:* Applications are processed on a rolling basis. *Application fee:* $35 ($60 for international students). Electronic applications accepted. *Associate Dean for Graduate Studies*, Dr. Henry A. Kurtz, 901-678-3067, Fax: 901-678-4831, E-mail: hkurtz@memphis.edu.

College of Communication and Fine Arts Students: 157 full-time (85 women), 93 part-time (48 women); includes 64 minority (31 Black or African American, non-Hispanic/Latino; 9 Asian, non-Hispanic/Latino; 15 Hispanic/Latino; 9 Two or more races, non-Hispanic/Latino), 24 international. Average age 32. 199 applicants, 63% accepted, 56 enrolled. *Faculty:* 90 full-time (26 women), 15 part-time/adjunct (7 women). *Financial support:* In 2015–16, 182 students received support. Research assistantships with full tuition reimbursements available, teaching assistantships with full tuition reimbursements available, career-related internships or fieldwork, Federal Work-Study, institutionally sponsored loans, scholarships/grants, and unspecified assistantships available. Financial award application deadline: 2/15; financial award applicants required to submit FAFSA. In 2015, 58 master's, 13 doctorates, 16 other advanced degrees awarded. *Degree program information:* Part-time programs available. Part-time, online learning. Offers architecture (M Arch); art (Graduate Certificate); art history (MA); ceramics (MFA); communication (MA); communication and fine arts (M Arch, M Mu, MA, MFA, DMA, PhD, Graduate Certificate); communication arts (PhD); conducting (M Mu, DMA); film and video production (MA); graphic design (MFA); historical musicology (PhD); interior design (MFA); journalism (MA); music education (M Mu, DMA); musicology (M Mu); painting (MFA); printmaking/photography (MFA); theatre (MFA). *Application deadline:* For fall admission, 8/1 for domestic students; for spring admission, 12/1 for domestic students. Applications are processed on a rolling basis. *Application fee:* $35 ($60 for international students). Electronic applications accepted. *Application Contact:* Moira J. Logan, Associate Dean/Director of Research and Graduate Studies, 901-678-2350, Fax: 901-678-5118, E-mail: mlogan1@memphis.edu. *Dean*, Dr. Richard R. Ranta, 901-678-2350, Fax: 901-678-5118, E-mail: rranta@memphis.edu.

College of Education Students: 303 full-time (232 women), 516 part-time (370 women); includes 309 minority (256 Black or African American, non-Hispanic/Latino; 2 American Indian or Alaska Native, non-Hispanic/Latino; 12 Asian, non-Hispanic/Latino; 16 Hispanic/Latino; 23 Two or more races, non-Hispanic/Latino), 16 international. Average age 34. 411 applicants, 74% accepted, 86 enrolled. *Faculty:* 60 full-time (34 women), 27 part-time/adjunct (20 women). *Financial support:* In 2015–16, 921 students received support. Research assistantships with full tuition reimbursements available, teaching assistantships with full tuition reimbursements available, career-related internships or fieldwork, Federal Work-Study, scholarships/grants, tuition waivers (partial), and unspecified assistantships available. Financial award application deadline: 2/15; financial award applicants required to submit FAFSA. In 2015, 294 master's, 33 doctorates, 24 other advanced degrees awarded. *Degree program information:* Part-time and evening/weekend programs available. Part-time, evening/weekend. Offers adult education (Ed D); counseling (MS, Ed D); counseling psychology (PhD); early childhood education (MAT, MS, Ed D); education (M Ed, MAT, MS, Ed D, PhD, Graduate Certificate); educational psychology and research (MS, PhD); elementary education (MAT); health and sport sciences (MS); higher education (Ed D); instruction and curriculum (MS, Ed D); instruction design and technology (MS, Ed D); leadership (MS); middle grades education (MAT); policy studies (Ed D); reading (MS, Ed D); secondary education (MAT); special education (MS, Ed D). *Application deadline:* Applications are processed on a rolling basis. *Application fee:* $35 ($60 for international students). *Application Contact:* Dr. Vivian Gunn Morris, Assistant Dean for Faculty and Staff Development and Graduate Programs, 901-678-2352, Fax: 901-678-4778, E-mail: vgmorris@memphis.edu. *Interim Dean*, Dr. Ernest Rakow, 901-678-2363, Fax: 901-678-4778, E-mail: erakow@memphis.edu.

Fogelman College of Business and Economics Students: 218 full-time (93 women), 375 part-time (142 women); includes 177 minority (91 Black or African American, non-Hispanic/Latino; 52 Asian, non-Hispanic/Latino; 16 Hispanic/Latino; 1 Native Hawaiian or other Pacific Islander, non-Hispanic/Latino; 17 Two or more races, non-Hispanic/Latino), 103 international. Average age 32. 380 applicants, 66% accepted, 81 enrolled. *Faculty:* 50 full-time (9 women), 4 part-time/adjunct (0 women). *Financial support:* In 2015–16, 199 students received support. Research assistantships with full tuition reimbursements available, teaching assistantships with full tuition reimbursements available, career-related internships or fieldwork, Federal Work-Study, scholarships/grants, and unspecified assistantships available. Financial award application deadline: 2/15; financial award applicants required to submit FAFSA. In 2015, 318 master's, 9 doctorates awarded. *Degree program information:* Part-time and evening/weekend programs available. Part-time, evening/weekend, online learning. Offers accounting (MBA, MS, PhD); business and economics (IMBA, MA, MBA, MS, PhD); economics (MA, PhD); executive business administration (MBA); finance (PhD); management (PhD); marketing (MS); marketing and supply chain management (PhD); real estate development (MS). *Application deadline:* For fall admission, 7/1 for domestic students, 5/1 for international students; for winter admission, 9/15 for international students; for spring admission, 12/1 for domestic students. *Application fee:* $35 ($60 for international students). *Application Contact:* Dr. Lloyd Brooks, Associate Dean, 901-678-4620, Fax: 901-678-3759, E-mail: lbrooks@memphis.edu. *Dean*, Dr. Rajiv Grover, 901-678-3633, Fax: 901-678-4705, E-mail: rgrover@memphis.edu.

Herff College of Engineering Students: 88 full-time (23 women), 92 part-time (21 women); includes 33 minority (17 Black or African American, non-Hispanic/Latino; 1 American Indian or Alaska Native, non-Hispanic/Latino; 8 Asian, non-Hispanic/Latino; 3 Hispanic/Latino; 4 Two or more races, non-Hispanic/Latino), 100 international. Average age 30. 104 applicants, 77% accepted, 26 enrolled. *Faculty:* 35 full-time (4 women), 2 part-time/adjunct (1 woman). *Financial support:* In 2015–16, 29 students received support. Fellowships with full tuition reimbursements available, research assistantships with full tuition reimbursements available, teaching assistantships with full tuition reimbursements available, career-related internships or fieldwork, Federal Work-Study, scholarships/grants, tuition waivers (full and partial), and unspecified assistantships available. Financial award application deadline: 2/15; financial award applicants required to submit FAFSA. In 2015, 37 master's, 6 doctorates awarded. *Degree program information:* Part-time programs available. Part-time. Offers automatic control systems (MS); biomedical engineering (MS, PhD); biomedical systems (MS); civil engineering (PhD); communications and propagation systems (MS); computer engineering (PhD); computer engineering technology (MS); electrical engineering (PhD); electronics engineering technology (MS); engineering (MS, PhD); engineering computer systems (MS); environmental engineering (MS); foundation engineering (MS); industrial engineering (MS); power systems (MS); structural engineering (MS); transportation engineering (MS); water resources engineering (MS). *Application deadline:* For fall admission, 7/1 for domestic students, 5/1 for international students; for spring admission, 12/1 for domestic students, 9/15 for international students. *Application fee:* $35 ($60 for international students). Electronic applications accepted. *Application Contact:* Dr. Deborah Hochstein, Associate Dean for Academic Affairs and Administration, 901-678-3258, Fax: 901-678-5030, E-mail: dhochstn@memphis.edu. *Dean*, Dr. Richard Joseph Sweigard, 901-678-4306, Fax: 901-678-4180, E-mail: rjswgard@memphis.edu.

School of Communication Sciences and Disorders Students: 86 full-time (83 women), 11 part-time (6 women); includes 8 minority (2 Black or African American, non-Hispanic/Latino; 3 Asian, non-Hispanic/Latino; 3 Two or more races, non-Hispanic/Latino), 9 international. Average age 26. 433 applicants, 23% accepted, 35 enrolled. *Faculty:* 11 full-time (4 women), 2 part-time/adjunct (1 woman). *Financial support:* Research assistantships with full tuition reimbursements, Federal Work-Study, scholarships/grants, and unspecified assistantships available. Financial award application deadline: 2/15; financial award applicants required to submit FAFSA. In 2015, 37 master's, 20 doctorates awarded. *Degree program information:* Part-time programs available. Part-time. Offers communication sciences and disorders (MA, Au D, PhD). *Application deadline:* For fall admission, 2/1 for domestic students. *Application fee:* $35 ($60 for international students). *Application Contact:* Dr. David J. Wark, Coordinator of Graduate Studies, 901-678-5891, E-mail: dwark@memphis.edu. *Dean*, Dr. Maurice Mendel, 901-678-5800, Fax: 901-525-1282, E-mail: dlluna@memphis.edu.

School of Public Health Students: 100 full-time (68 women), 48 part-time (35 women); includes 63 minority (33 Black or African American, non-Hispanic/Latino; 20 Asian, non-Hispanic/Latino; 7 Hispanic/Latino; 3 Two or more races, non-Hispanic/Latino), 17 international. Average age 30. 114 applicants, 83% accepted, 37 enrolled. *Faculty:* 117 full-time (5 women), 5 part-time/adjunct (1 woman). *Financial support:* In 2015–16, 46 students received support. Research assistantships with full tuition reimbursements available, Federal Work-Study, scholarships/grants, and unspecified assistantships available. Financial award application deadline: 2/15; financial award applicants required to submit FAFSA. In 2015, 55 master's awarded. *Degree program information:* Part-time and evening/weekend programs available. Part-time, evening/weekend, online learning. Offers biostatistics (MPH); environmental health (MPH); epidemiology (MPH); health systems management (MPH); public health (MHA); social and behavioral sciences (MPH). *Application deadline:* For fall admission, 4/1 for domestic students; for spring admission, 11/1 for domestic students. *Application fee:* $35 ($60 for international students). Electronic applications accepted. *Application Contact:* Dr. Karen Weddle-West, Information Contact, 901-678-2531, Fax: 901-678-5023, E-mail: gradsch@memphis.edu. *Director*, Dr. Lisa M. Klesges, 901-678-4637, E-mail: lmklsges@memphis.edu.

University College Students: 28 full-time (16 women), 127 part-time (88 women); includes 107 minority (100 Black or African American, non-Hispanic/Latino; 3 Hispanic/Latino; 4 Two or more races, non-Hispanic/Latino), 2 international. Average age 39. 93 applicants, 76% accepted, 10 enrolled. *Faculty:* 2 full-time (1 woman), 1 part-time/adjunct (0 women). *Financial support:* In 2015–16, 123 students received support. Research assistantships with full tuition reimbursements available, teaching assistantships with tuition reimbursements available, Federal Work-Study, scholarships/grants, and unspecified assistantships available. Financial award application deadline: 2/15; financial award applicants required to submit FAFSA. In 2015, 63 master's awarded. *Degree program information:* Part-time and evening/weekend programs available. Part-time, evening/weekend. Offers liberal studies (MALS); merchandising and consumer science (MS); strategic leadership (MPS). *Application deadline:* For fall admission, 7/1 for domestic students, 5/1 for international students; for spring admission, 11/1 for domestic students, 9/15 for international students. Applications are processed on a rolling basis. *Application fee:* $35 ($60 for international students). Electronic applications accepted. *Application Contact:* Dr. Herbert McCree, Coordinator of Graduate Studies, 901-678-4171, Fax: 901-678-3363, E-mail: hmccree@memphis.edu. *Dean*, Dr. Dan Lattimore, 901-678-2991.

Loewenberg College of Nursing Students: 34 full-time (32 women), 220 part-time (196 women); includes 91 minority (80 Black or African American, non-Hispanic/Latino; 8 Asian, non-Hispanic/Latino; 1 Hispanic/Latino; 2 Two or more races, non-Hispanic/Latino). Average age 36. 165 applicants, 48% accepted, 27 enrolled. *Faculty:* 12 full-time (all women), 3 part-time/adjunct (2 women). *Financial support:* In 2015–16, 147 students received support. Federal Work-Study and scholarships/grants available. Financial award application deadline: 2/15; financial award applicants required to submit FAFSA. In 2015, 73 master's, 3 other advanced degrees awarded. *Degree program information:* Part-time and evening/weekend programs available. Part-time, evening/weekend, online learning. Offers executive leadership (MSN); family nurse practitioner (MSN); nursing (Graduate Certificate); nursing administration (MSN);

nursing education (MSN). *Application deadline:* For fall admission, 2/15 for domestic and international students; for spring admission, 10/1 for domestic and international students. *Application fee:* $35 ($60 for international students). *Application Contact:* Dr. Karen Weddle-West, Information Contact, 901-678-2531, Fax: 901-678-5023, E-mail: gradsch@memphis.edu. *Associate Dean*, Dr. Robert Koch, 901-678-3908, Fax: 901-678-4907, E-mail: rakoch@memphis.edu.

UNIVERSITY OF MIAMI, Coral Gables, FL 33124

General Information Independent, coed, university. CGS member. *Graduate housing:* On-campus housing not available. *Research affiliation:* Howard Hughes Medical Institute (biology), The Buoniconti Fund: Miami Project to Cure Paralysis (paralysis research), Organization for Tropical Studies, National Center for Atmospheric Research (atmospheric science).

GRADUATE UNITS

Graduate School ***Degree program information:*** Part-time and evening/weekend programs available. Part-time, evening/weekend, online learning. Offers international administration (MAIA). Electronic applications accepted.

College of Arts and Sciences Degree program information: Part-time and evening/weekend programs available. Part-time, evening/weekend. Offers adult clinical (PhD); art history (MA); arts and sciences (MA, MAIA, MALS, MFA, MPA, MS, PhD); behavioral neuroscience (PhD); biology (MS, PhD); ceramics/glass (MFA); chemistry (MS); child clinical (PhD); computer science (MS, PhD); creative writing (MFA); developmental psychology (PhD); English (MA, PhD); genetics and evolution (MS, PhD); geography (MA); graphic design/multimedia (MFA); health clinical (PhD); history (MA, PhD); inorganic chemistry (PhD); international studies (MA, PhD); Latin American studies (MA); liberal studies (MALS); mathematical finance (MS); mathematics (MA, MS, PhD); organic chemistry (PhD); painting (MFA); philosophy (MA, PhD); photography/digital imaging (MFA); physical chemistry (PhD); physics (MS, PhD); political science (MPA); printmaking (MFA); psychology (MS); romance studies (PhD); sculpture (MFA); sociology (MA, PhD). Electronic applications accepted.

College of Engineering Degree program information: Part-time and evening/weekend programs available. Part-time, evening/weekend. Offers architectural engineering (MSAE); biomedical engineering (MSBE, PhD); civil engineering (MSCE, PhD); electrical and computer engineering (MSECE, PhD); engineering (MS, MSAE, MSBE, MSCE, MSECE, MSIE, MSME, MSOES, PhD); environmental health and safety (MS); ergonomics (PhD); industrial engineering (MSIE, PhD); management of technology (MS); mechanical and aerospace engineering (MSME, PhD); occupational ergonomics and safety (MS, MSOES). Electronic applications accepted.

Frost School of Music Offers accompanying and chamber music (MM, DMA); choral conducting (MM, DMA); composition (MM, DMA); electronic music (MM); instrumental conducting (MM, DMA); instrumental performance (MM, DMA, AD); jazz composition (DMA); jazz pedagogy (MM); jazz performance (MM, DMA); keyboard performance and pedagogy (MM, DMA); media writing and production (MM); multiple woodwinds (MM, DMA); music (MM, MS, DMA, PhD, AD, Spec M); music business and entertainment industries (MM); music education (MM, PhD, Spec M); music engineering (MS); music theory (MM); music therapy (MM); musicology (MM); piano performance (MM, DMA, AD); studio jazz writing (MM); vocal pedagogy (DMA); vocal performance (MM, DMA, AD). Electronic applications accepted.

Miller School of Medicine Offers biochemistry and molecular biology (PhD); cancer biology (PhD); epidemiology (PhD); medicine (MPH, MSPH, DPT, MD, PhD); microbiology and immunology (PhD); molecular and cellular pharmacology (PhD); molecular cell and developmental biology (PhD); neuroscience (PhD); physical therapy (DPT, PhD); physiology and biophysics (PhD); public health (MPH, MSPH). Electronic applications accepted.

Rosenstiel School of Marine and Atmospheric Science Degree program information: Part-time programs available. Part-time. Offers applied marine physics (MS, PhD); marine affairs and policy (MA, MS); marine and atmospheric chemistry (MS, PhD); marine and atmospheric science (MA, MS, PhD); marine biology and fisheries (MA, MS, PhD); marine geology and geophysics (MS, PhD); meteorology (MS, PhD); physical oceanography (MS, PhD). Electronic applications accepted.

School of Architecture Offers architecture (M Arch); suburb and town design (M Arch). Electronic applications accepted.

School of Business Administration Degree program information: Part-time and evening/weekend programs available. Part-time, evening/weekend. Offers business administration (MA, MBA, MP Acc, MS, MS Tax, MSPM, PhD). Electronic applications accepted.

School of Communication Degree program information: Part-time programs available. Part-time. Offers communication (PhD); communication studies (MA); film studies (MA, PhD); motion pictures (MFA); print journalism (MA); public relations (MA); Spanish language journalism (MA); television broadcast journalism (MA). Electronic applications accepted.

School of Education and Human Development Offers advanced professional studies (MS Ed, Ed S); athletic training (MS Ed); community and social change (MS Ed); community well-being (PhD); counseling (MS Ed, Certificate); counseling and research (MS Ed); counseling psychology (PhD); early childhood special education (MS Ed, Ed S); education and human development (MS Ed, Ed D, PhD, Certificate, Ed S); education and social change (MS Ed); enrollment management (MS Ed, Certificate); exercise physiology (MS Ed, PhD); higher education administration (MS Ed, Ed D, Certificate); higher education leadership (Ed D); language and literacy learning in multilingual settings (PhD); Latino mental health (Certificate); marriage and family therapy (MS Ed); mental health counseling (MS Ed); nutrition for health and human performance (MS Ed); research, measurement, and evaluation (MS Ed, PhD); science, technology, engineering and mathematics (PhD); special education (PhD); sport administration (MS Ed); sports medicine (MS Ed); strength and conditioning (MS Ed); student life and development (MS Ed, Certificate); teaching and learning (PhD); women's health (Certificate). Electronic applications accepted.

School of Nursing and Health Studies Degree program information: Part-time programs available. Part-time. Offers acute care (MSN); nursing (PhD); primary care (MSN). Electronic applications accepted.

University of Miami School of Law Students: 976 full-time (482 women), 93 part-time (43 women); includes 359 minority (58 Black or African American, non-Hispanic/Latino; 3 American Indian or Alaska Native, non-Hispanic/Latino; 25 Asian, non-Hispanic/Latino; 252 Hispanic/Latino; 1 Native Hawaiian or other Pacific Islander, non-Hispanic/Latino; 20 Two or more races, non-Hispanic/Latino), 38 international. 2,665 applicants, 54% accepted, 312 enrolled. *Faculty:* 72 full-time (31 women), 90 part-time/adjunct (39 women). *Financial support:* Fellowships, research assistantships, career-related internships or fieldwork, Federal Work-Study, institutionally sponsored loans, scholarships/grants, and unspecified assistantships available. Financial award application deadline: 3/1; financial award applicants required to submit FAFSA. In 2015, 419 doctorates awarded. Offers estate planning (LL M); international arbitration (LL M); international law (LL M); law (JD); ocean and coastal law (LL M); real estate/property development (LL M); taxation (LL M); taxation of cross-border investment (LL M). *Application deadline:* For fall admission, 1/6 priority date for domestic and international students. Applications are processed on a rolling basis. *Application fee:* $60. Electronic applications accepted. *Application Contact:* Therese Lambert, Director of Student Recruitment, 305-284-6746, Fax: 305-284-3084, E-mail: tlambert@law.miami.edu. *Associate Dean of Admissions and Enrollment Management*, Michael Goodnight, 305-284-2527, Fax: 305-284-3084, E-mail: mgoodnig@law.miami.edu.

UNIVERSITY OF MICHIGAN, Ann Arbor, MI 48109

General Information State-supported, coed, university. CGS member. *Enrollment:* 43,651 graduate, professional, and undergraduate students; 13,518 full-time matriculated graduate/professional students (6,240 women), 1,420 part-time matriculated graduate/professional students (558 women). *Enrollment by degree level:* 7,212 master's, 7,655 doctoral, 71 other advanced degrees. *Graduate faculty:* 4,353 full-time (1,656 women), 1,119 part-time/adjunct (603 women). *Graduate housing:* Rooms and/or apartments available on a first-come, first-served basis to single and married students. *Student services:* Campus employment opportunities, campus safety program, career counseling, child daycare facilities, exercise/wellness program, free psychological counseling, grant writing training, international student services, low-cost health insurance, multicultural affairs office, services for students with disabilities, teacher training, writing training. *Library:* Shapiro Undergraduate Library plus 9 others. *Collection:* Books: 9 million (physical), 3.1 million (digital/electronic); Serial titles: 422,079 (physical), 163,947 (digital/electronic); Databases: 9,728. Weekly public service hours: 168; study areas open 24 hours, 5–7 days a week; students can reserve study rooms.

Computer facilities: Computer purchase and lease plans are available. 2,584 computers available on campus for general student use. A campuswide network can be accessed from student residence rooms and from off campus. Online class registration, file storage, personal Web pages, printing are available.
Website: http://www.umich.edu/

General Application Contact: Admissions Office, 734-764-8129, Fax: 734-647-7740, E-mail: rackadmis@umich.edu.

GRADUATE UNITS

College of Engineering Students: 3,005 full-time (710 women), 359 part-time (64 women). 9,696 applicants, 28% accepted, 1116 enrolled. *Faculty:* 378 full-time (77 women). *Financial support:* Fellowships, research assistantships, teaching assistantships, career-related internships or fieldwork, Federal Work-Study, institutionally sponsored loans, scholarships/grants, traineeships, health care benefits, tuition waivers (full and partial), and unspecified assistantships available. Support available to part-time students. Financial award applicants required to submit FAFSA. In 2015, 1,067 master's, 257 doctorates awarded. *Degree program information:* Part-time programs available. Part-time, 100% online. Offers aerospace engineering (M Eng, MS, MSE, PhD); applied climate (M Eng); atmospheric, oceanic and space sciences (MS, PhD); automotive engineering (M Eng); biomedical engineering (MS, MSE, PhD); chemical engineering (MSE, PhD, Ch E); civil engineering (MSE, PhD, CE); computer science and engineering (MS, MSE, PhD); construction engineering and management (M Eng, MSE); design science (MS, PhD); electrical engineering and computer science (MS, MSE, PhD); energy systems engineering (M Eng, MS); engineering (M Eng, MS, MSE, D Eng, PhD, CE, Certificate, Ch E, Mar Eng, Nav Arch, Nuc E); environmental engineering (MSE, PhD); geoscience and remote sensing (PhD); global automotive and manufacturing engineering (M Eng); industrial and operations engineering (MS, MSE, PhD); manufacturing engineering (M Eng, D Eng); materials science and engineering (MS, PhD); mechanical engineering (MSE, PhD); naval architecture and marine engineering (MS, MSE, PhD, Mar Eng, Nav Arch); nuclear engineering (Nuc E); nuclear engineering and radiological sciences (MSE, PhD); nuclear science (MS, PhD); pharmaceutical engineering (M Eng); robotics (MS, PhD); robotics and autonomous vehicles (M Eng); space and planetary sciences (PhD); space engineering (M Eng); structural engineering (M Eng); systems engineering and design (M Eng). *Application deadline:* Applications are processed on a rolling basis. Electronic applications accepted. *Application Contact:* Kim Elliott, Director of Graduate Education, 734-647-7077, Fax: 734-647-7045, E-mail: elliottk@umich.edu. *Dean of Engineering*, Prof. David C. Munson, 734-647-7008, Fax: 734-647-7009, E-mail: munson@umich.edu.

College of Pharmacy Students: 328 full-time (215 women); includes 118 minority (8 Black or African American, non-Hispanic/Latino; 1 American Indian or Alaska Native, non-Hispanic/Latino; 90 Asian, non-Hispanic/Latino; 7 Hispanic/Latino; 12 Two or more races, non-Hispanic/Latino), 6 international. 320 applicants, 43% accepted, 85 enrolled. *Faculty:* 22 full-time (6 women), 7 part-time/adjunct (0 women). Offers clinical pharmacy (PhD); medicinal chemistry (PhD); pharmaceutical sciences (PhD); pharmacy (PhD, Pharm D). *Application deadline:* For fall admission, 12/1 for domestic and international students. Applications are processed on a rolling basis. *Application fee:* $150. Electronic applications accepted. *Application Contact:* Admissions Office, 734-764-8129, Fax: 734-647-7740, E-mail: rackadmis@umich.edu. *Dean*, James T. Dalton, 734-764-7144, Fax: 734-763-2022, E-mail: cop.deansoffice@med.umich.edu.

Gerald R. Ford School of Public Policy Students: 254 full-time (131 women); includes 71 minority (24 Black or African American, non-Hispanic/Latino; 2 American Indian or Alaska Native, non-Hispanic/Latino; 16 Asian, non-Hispanic/Latino; 16 Hispanic/Latino; 13 Two or more races, non-Hispanic/Latino), 44 international. Average age 28. 668 applicants, 63% accepted, 99 enrolled. *Faculty:* 46 full-time (19 women), 30 part-time/adjunct (11 women). *Financial support:* In 2015–16, 186 students received support, including 166 fellowships with tuition reimbursements available, 30 teaching assistantships with tuition reimbursements available; career-related internships or fieldwork, Federal Work-Study, traineeships, and health care benefits also available. Financial award application deadline: 1/15; financial award applicants required to submit FAFSA. In 2015, 116 master's, 6 doctorates awarded. Offers public policy (MPA, MPP, PhD). *Application deadline:* For fall admission, 1/15 priority date for domestic students, 1/15 for international students. *Application fee:* $75 ($90 for international students). Electronic applications accepted. *Application Contact:* Beth Soboleski, Director, Admissions and Recruiting, 734-764-0453, Fax: 734-647-7486, E-mail: fspp-admissions@umich.edu. *Dean*, Dr. Susan M. Collins, 734-764-3490.

Law School Students: 935 full-time (446 women); includes 196 minority (37 Black or African American, non-Hispanic/Latino; 7 American Indian or Alaska Native, non-Hispanic/Latino; 79 Asian, non-Hispanic/Latino; 35 Hispanic/Latino; 38 Two or more races, non-Hispanic/Latino), 51 international. 4,335 applicants, 28% accepted, 267 enrolled. *Faculty:* 97 full-time (36 women), 46 part-time/adjunct (10 women). *Financial support:* In 2015–16, 743 students received support. Career-related internships or fieldwork, Federal Work-Study, institutionally sponsored loans, and scholarships/grants available. Financial award applicants required to submit FAFSA. In 2015, 43 master's, 354 doctorates awarded. Offers comparative law (MCL); international tax (LL M); law (LL M, JD, SJD). *Application deadline:* For fall admission, 2/15 for domestic students. Applications are processed on a rolling basis. *Application fee:* $75. Electronic applications accepted. *Application Contact:* Sarah C. Zearfoss, Assistant Dean and Director of Admissions, 734-764-0537, Fax: 734-647-3218, E-mail: law.jd.admissions@umich.edu. *Dean*, Mark D. West, 734-764-1358.

Medical School Students: 708 full-time (374 women); includes 253 minority (38 Black or African American, non-Hispanic/Latino; 4 American Indian or Alaska Native, non-Hispanic/Latino; 155 Asian, non-Hispanic/Latino; 55 Hispanic/Latino; 1 Native Hawaiian or other Pacific Islander, non-Hispanic/Latino). Average age 27. 5,726 applicants, 7% accepted, 170 enrolled. *Faculty:* 2,315 full-time (831 women), 1,353 part-time/adjunct (676 women). *Financial support:* In 2015–16, 403 students received support. Institutionally sponsored loans and scholarships/grants available. Financial award application deadline: 9/30; financial award applicants required to submit FAFSA. In 2015, 181 doctorates awarded. Offers medicine (MD). *Application deadline:* For fall admission, 9/30 for domestic students. Applications are processed on a rolling basis. Electronic applications accepted. *Application Contact:* Carol Teener, Director of Admissions, 734-764-6317, Fax: 734-936-3510, E-mail: cteener@umich.edu. *Dean*, Dr. Marschall S. Runge, MD, 734-764-8175, E-mail: mrunge@umich.edu.

Rackham Graduate School Students: 7,496 full-time (3,214 women), 862 part-time (459 women); includes 1,447 minority (283 Black or African American, non-Hispanic/Latino; 24 American Indian or Alaska Native, non-Hispanic/Latino; 490 Asian, non-Hispanic/Latino; 458 Hispanic/Latino; 4 Native Hawaiian or other Pacific Islander, non-Hispanic/Latino; 188 Two or more races, non-Hispanic/Latino), 3,114 international. Average age 27. 25,320 applicants, 27% accepted, 2590 enrolled. *Financial support:* Fellowships with tuition reimbursements, research assistantships with tuition reimbursements, teaching assistantships with tuition reimbursements, career-related internships or fieldwork, Federal Work-Study, scholarships/grants, traineeships, health care benefits, and unspecified assistantships available. Support available to part-time students. In 2015, 2,085 master's, 874 doctorates awarded. Offers cancer chemical biology (MS); chemical biology (PhD); data science (MS, PhD); education and psychology (PhD); English and education (PhD); social and psychological (MS, PhD); statistical (MS, PhD); survey methodology (Certificate). *Application deadline:* Applications are processed on a rolling basis. *Application fee:* $75 ($90 for international students). Electronic applications accepted. *Application Contact:* Admissions Office, 734-764-8129, E-mail: rackadmis@umich.edu. *Dean/Vice Provost for Academic Affairs*, Dr. Carol A. Fierke, 734-764-4400.

Center for Middle Eastern and North African Studies Students: 12 full-time (8 women), 1 part-time (0 women); includes 1 minority (Black or African American, non-Hispanic/Latino). Average age 27. 36 applicants, 47% accepted, 5 enrolled. *Faculty:* 78 full-time (24 women), 1 (woman) part-time/adjunct. *Financial support:* In 2015–16, 3 students received support, including 3 fellowships with tuition reimbursements available (averaging $45,000 per year); teaching assistantships, career-related internships or fieldwork, Federal Work-Study, scholarships/grants, health care benefits, and Richard P. Mitchell Memorial Prize also available. Support available to part-time students. Financial award application deadline: 1/15; financial award applicants required to submit FAFSA. In 2015, 4 master's awarded. *Degree program information:* Part-time programs available. Part-time. Offers Middle Eastern and North African studies (AM). *Application deadline:* For fall admission, 12/15 for domestic and international students. *Application fee:* $75 ($90 for international students). Electronic applications accepted. *Application Contact:* Julie E. Burnett, Graduate Academic Services Coordinator, 734-936-1842, Fax: 734-615-9158, E-mail: ii-gradadvising@umich.edu. *Director*, Dr. Juan R. Cole, E-mail: ii-gradadvising@umich.edu.

College of Literature, Science, and the Arts Students: 2,369 full-time (1,143 women). *Financial support:* Fellowships with tuition reimbursements, research assistantships with tuition reimbursements, teaching assistantships with tuition reimbursements, Federal Work-Study, scholarships/grants, traineeships, health care benefits, and unspecified assistantships available. In 2015, 372 master's, 315 doctorates awarded. Offers American culture (AM, PhD); analytical (PhD); ancient Near Eastern studies (AM, PhD); anthropological archaeology (PhD); anthropology and history (PhD); applied and interdisciplinary mathematics (AM, MS, PhD); applied economics (AM); applied physics (PhD); applied statistics (MS); Arabic for professional purposes (AM); Arabic language and literature (AM, PhD); Armenian studies (AM, PhD); Asian languages and cultures (PhD); astronomy and astrophysics (PhD); biological anthropology (PhD); biophysics (PhD); biopsychology (PhD); chemical biology (PhD); Chinese studies (MA, Graduate Certificate); Christianity in late antiquity (AM, PhD); classical art and archaeology (MA, PhD); classical studies (PhD); clinical science (PhD); cognition and cognitive neuroscience (PhD); communication studies (PhD); comparative literature (PhD); creative writing (MFA); developmental psychology (PhD); earth and environmental sciences (MS, PhD); ecology and evolutionary biology (MS, PhD); economics (AM, PhD); Egyptology (AM, PhD); English and education (PhD); English and women's studies (PhD); English language and literature (PhD); French (PhD); German (AM, PhD); Greek and Roman history (PhD, Certificate); Hebrew Bible and ancient Israel (AM, PhD); Hebrew literature (AM, PhD); history (PhD); history and women's studies (PhD); history of art (PhD); inorganic (PhD); Islamic studies (AM, PhD); Italian (PhD); Japanese studies (AM); Jewish cultural studies (AM, PhD); Jewish mysticism (AM, PhD); Judaic studies (MA, Graduate Certificate); LGBTQ studies (Certificate); linguistic anthropology (PhD); linguistics (PhD); literature, science, and the arts (AM, MA, MAT, MFA, MS, PhD, Certificate, Graduate Certificate); materials (PhD); mathematics (AM, MS, PhD); molecular, cellular, and developmental biology (MS, PhD); organic (PhD); Persian and Iranian studies (AM, PhD); personality and social contexts (PhD); philosophy (AM, PhD); physical (PhD); physics (PhD); political science (PhD); political science and public policy (PhD); psychology and women's studies (PhD); public policy and economics (PhD); public policy and sociology (PhD); Rabbinic literature (AM, PhD); Russian, East European, and Eurasian studies (AM, Certificate); screen arts and cultures (PhD, Certificate); Second Temple Judaism (AM, PhD); Slavic languages and literatures (AM, PhD); social psychology (PhD); social work and economics (PhD); social work and political science (PhD); social work and sociology (PhD); sociocultural anthropology (PhD); sociology (PhD); South Asian studies (MA, Certificate); Southeast Asian studies (MA, Graduate Certificate); Spanish (PhD); statistics (AM, PhD); teaching Arabic as a foreign language (AM); teaching Latin (MAT); Turkish studies (AM, PhD); women's studies (Certificate). *Application fee:* $75 ($90 for international students). Electronic applications accepted. *Application Contact:* Rackham Graduate School Admissions Office, 734-764-8129, E-mail: rackadmis@umich.edu. *Dean*, Dr. Andrew D. Martin, 734-764-1817.

Penny W. Stamps School of Art and Design Students: 16 (10 women); includes 1 minority (Asian, non-Hispanic/Latino), 6 international. *Financial support:* Fellowships with tuition reimbursements, research assistantships with tuition reimbursements, teaching assistantships with tuition reimbursements, Federal Work-Study, scholarships/grants, health care benefits, tuition waivers (partial), and unspecified assistantships available. Support available to part-time students. Financial award applicants required to submit FAFSA. In 2015, 10 master's awarded. Offers art and design (MFA); integrative design (M Des). *Application deadline:* For fall admission, 1/1 for domestic and international students. *Application fee:* $75 ($90 for international students). Electronic applications accepted. *Application Contact:* Karina Galvin Moore, Director of Admissions and Enrollment Management, 734-764-0397. *Dean*, Gunalan Nadarajan, E-mail: artdes-dean@umich.edu.

Program in Biomedical Sciences (PIBS) Students: 66 full-time (37 women); includes 18 minority (3 Black or African American, non-Hispanic/Latino; 4 Asian, non-Hispanic/Latino; 9 Hispanic/Latino; 2 Two or more races, non-Hispanic/Latino), 11 international. Average age 25. 754 applicants, 24% accepted, 67 enrolled. *Faculty:* 513 full-time. *Financial support:* In 2015–16, 66 students received support, including 66 fellowships with full tuition reimbursements available (averaging $29,025 per year); scholarships/grants, health care benefits, tuition waivers (full), and unspecified assistantships also available. Financial award application deadline: 12/1. Offers bioinformatics (MS, PhD); biological chemistry (MS, PhD); biomedical sciences (MS, PhD); cancer biology (PhD); cell and developmental biology (PhD); cellular and molecular biology (PhD); genetic counseling (MS); human genetics (MS, PhD); immunology (PhD); microbiology and immunology (MS, PhD); molecular and cellular pathology (PhD); molecular and integrative physiology (MS, PhD); neuroscience (PhD); pharmacology (MS, PhD). *Application deadline:* For fall admission, 12/1 for domestic and international students. *Application fee:* $75 ($90 for international students). Electronic applications accepted. *Application Contact:* Michelle DiMondo, Academic Affairs and Student Success Coordinator, 734-647-5773, Fax: 734-647-7022, E-mail: mdimondo@umich.edu. *Associate Professor, Cell and Developmental Biology/Director of the Program in Biomedical Sciences*, Dr. Scott Barolo, 734-615-7005, Fax: 734-647-7022, E-mail: sbarolo@umich.edu.

School of Information Degree program information: Part-time programs available. Part-time. Offers archives and records management (MSI); health informatics (MS); information (PhD). Electronic applications accepted.

School of Kinesiology Students: 85 full-time (37 women); includes 34 minority (6 Black or African American, non-Hispanic/Latino; 22 Asian, non-Hispanic/Latino; 5 Hispanic/Latino; 1 Two or more races, non-Hispanic/Latino). 169 applicants, 46% accepted, 41 enrolled. *Faculty:* 27 full-time (13 women). *Financial support:* In 2015–16, 12 fellowships, 6 research assistantships, 14 teaching assistantships were awarded; Federal Work-Study, scholarships/grants, health care benefits, and unspecified assistantships also available. Financial award application deadline: 1/15. In 2015, 39 master's, 11 doctorates awarded. Offers movement science (MS, PhD); sport management (MS, PhD). *Application deadline:* For fall admission, 1/15 priority date for domestic students, 1/15 for international students. Applications are processed on a rolling basis. *Application fee:* $75 ($90 for international students). Electronic applications accepted. *Application Contact:* Charlene F. Ruloff, Graduate Program Coordinator, 734-764-1343, Fax: 734-647-2808, E-mail: cruloff@umich.edu. *Associate Dean for Graduate Programs and Faculty Affairs*, Dr. Ketra L. Armstrong, 734-647-3027, Fax: 734-647-2808, E-mail: ketra@umich.edu.

School of Music, Theatre, and Dance Financial support: In 2015–16, 120 students received support. Fellowships, teaching assistantships, career-related internships or fieldwork, Federal Work-Study, institutionally sponsored loans, and scholarships/grants available. Financial award application deadline: 2/1; financial award applicants required to submit FAFSA. Offers composition (MA, MM, A Mus D); composition and theory (PhD); conducting (MM, A Mus D); media arts (MA); modern dance performance and choreography (MFA); music education (MM, PhD, Spec M); music theory (PhD); music, theatre, and dance (MA, MFA, MM, A Mus D, PhD, Spec M); musicology (MA, PhD); performance (MM, A Mus D, Spec M). *Application deadline:* For fall admission, 12/1 for domestic and international students; for winter admission, 9/15 for domestic and international students. Applications are processed on a rolling basis. *Application fee:* $75 ($90 for international students). Electronic applications accepted. *Application Contact:* Laura Hoffman, Assistant Dean for Enrollment Management and Student Services, 734-764-0593, Fax: 734-763-5097, E-mail: lauras@umich.edu. *Dean*, Aaron Dworkin, 734-764-0584, Fax: 734-763-5097, E-mail: aaronpau@umich.edu.

School of Nursing Degree program information: Part-time programs available. Part-time, online learning. Offers acute care pediatric nurse practitioner (MS); nursing (DNP, PhD, Post Master's Certificate). *Application Contact:* E-mail: sn-osams@umich.edu. *Dean*, Dr. Kathleen Potempa, 734-764-7185, Fax: 734-764-7186.

Ross School of Business ***Degree program information:*** Part-time and evening/weekend programs available. Part-time, evening/weekend. Offers accounting (M Acc); business (MBA); business administration (PhD); supply chain management (MSCM). Electronic applications accepted.

School of Dentistry Students: 602 full-time (289 women); includes 153 minority (12 Black or African American, non-Hispanic/Latino; 110 Asian, non-Hispanic/Latino; 19 Hispanic/Latino; 12 Two or more races, non-Hispanic/Latino), 68 international. 2,451 applicants, 10% accepted, 139 enrolled. In 2015, 31 master's, 113 doctorates awarded. Offers dental hygiene (MS); dentistry (MS, DDS, PhD); endodontics (MS); oral health sciences (PhD); orthodontics (MS); pediatric dentistry (MS); periodontics (MS); prosthodontics (MS); restorative dentistry (MS). *Application deadline:* Applications are processed on a rolling basis. *Application fee:* $75 ($90 for international students). Electronic applications accepted. *Application Contact:* Patricia Katcher, Admissions Associate Director, 734-763-3316, Fax: 734-764-1922, E-mail: ddsadmissions@umich.edu. *Dean*, Dr. Laurie McCauley, 734-763-3311, E-mail: mccauley@umich.edu.

School of Education Offers education (MA, MS, PhD). Electronic applications accepted.

School of Natural Resources and Environment Students: 381 full-time (213 women). Average age 26. *Financial support:* Application deadline: 1/6; applicants required to submit FAFSA. Offers behavior, education and communication (MS); conservation ecology (MS); environmental informatics (MS); environmental justice (MS, Certificate); environmental policy and planning (MS); industrial ecology (Certificate); landscape architecture (MLA); natural resources and environment (MS, PhD); spatial analysis (Certificate); sustainability (Certificate); sustainable systems (MS). *Application deadline:* For fall admission, 4/30 for domestic and international students. *Application fee:* $75 ($90 for international students). Electronic applications accepted. *Application Contact:* Sara O'Brien, Director of Academic Programs, 734-764-6453, Fax: 734-936-2195, E-mail: snre.admissions@umich.edu. *Interim Dean*, Dr. Daniel Brown, 734-763-5803, E-mail: danbrown@umich.edu.

School of Public Health Students: 891 full-time (610 women), 28 part-time (18 women); includes 212 minority (44 Black or African American, non-Hispanic/Latino; 116 Asian, non-Hispanic/Latino; 32 Hispanic/Latino; 20 Two or more races, non-

Hispanic/Latino), 179 international. Average age 27. 2,956 applicants, 37% accepted, 441 enrolled. *Faculty:* 136 full-time (62 women), 160 part-time/adjunct (70 women). *Financial support:* Fellowships, research assistantships with tuition reimbursements, teaching assistantships with tuition reimbursements, career-related internships or fieldwork, Federal Work-Study, institutionally sponsored loans, scholarships/grants, traineeships, health care benefits, and unspecified assistantships available. In 2015, 402 master's, 51 doctorates awarded. *Degree program information:* Evening/weekend programs available. Evening/weekend. Offers biostatistics (MPH, MS, PhD); clinical research design and statistical analysis (MS); dietetics (MPH); environmental health sciences (MS, PhD); environmental quality and health (MPH); epidemiological science (PhD); general epidemiology (MPH); global health epidemiology (MPH); health behavior and health education (MPH, PhD); health management and policy (MHSA, MPH); health services organization and policy (PhD); hospital and molecular epidemiology (MPH); industrial hygiene (MPH, MS); nutrition sciences (MPH, MS, PhD); occupational and environmental epidemiology (MPH); public health (MHSA, MPH, MS, PhD); toxicology (MPH, MS, PhD). MS and PhD offered through the Rackham Graduate School. *Application deadline:* For fall admission, 12/15 priority date for domestic students, 1/15 for international students. *Application fee:* $75. Electronic applications accepted. *Application Contact:* Charles Dill, Admissions Coordinator, 734-764-5425, Fax: 734-763-5455, E-mail: sph.inquiries@umich.edu. *Dean*, Martin Philbert, 734-763-4523, Fax: 734-763-5455, E-mail: philbert@umich.edu.

School of Social Work Students: 680 full-time (581 women); includes 198 minority (79 Black or African American, non-Hispanic/Latino; 4 American Indian or Alaska Native, non-Hispanic/Latino; 29 Asian, non-Hispanic/Latino; 60 Hispanic/Latino; 1 Native Hawaiian or other Pacific Islander, non-Hispanic/Latino; 25 Two or more races, non-Hispanic/Latino), 23 international. Average age 25. 1,383 applicants, 61% accepted, 397 enrolled. *Faculty:* 57 full-time (36 women), 72 part-time/adjunct (55 women). *Financial support:* In 2015–16, 530 students received support. Career-related internships or fieldwork, Federal Work-Study, scholarships/grants, traineeships, and unspecified assistantships available. Financial award application deadline: 3/15; financial award applicants required to submit FAFSA. In 2015, 351 master's awarded. Offers social work (MSW, PhD); social work and anthropology (PhD); social work and economics (PhD); social work and political science (PhD); social work and psychology (PhD); social work and sociology (PhD). PhD offered through the Rackham Graduate School. *Application deadline:* For fall admission, 3/1 priority date for domestic students, 2/1 priority date for international students. Applications are processed on a rolling basis. *Application fee:* $75. Electronic applications accepted. *Application Contact:* Timothy Colenback, Assistant Dean for Student Services, 734-936-0961, Fax: 734-936-1961, E-mail: timot@umich.edu. *Dean*, Laura Lein, 734-764-5347, Fax: 734-764-9954, E-mail: leinl@umich.edu.

Taubman College of Architecture and Urban Planning ***Degree program information:*** Part-time programs available. Part-time. Offers architecture (M Arch); architecture and urban planning (M Arch, MS, MUD, MUP, PhD, Graduate Certificate); conservation (MS); design and health (MS); digital technologies (MS); material systems (MS); urban design (MUD); urban planning (MUP, PhD, Graduate Certificate). Electronic applications accepted. *Application Contact:* Lisa Hauser, Assistant Director for Admissions and Recruiting, 734-763-1275, E-mail: taubmancollegestudentservices@umich.edu.

UNIVERSITY OF MICHIGAN–DEARBORN, Dearborn, MI 48128

General Information State-supported, coed, comprehensive institution. *Enrollment:* 9,066 graduate, professional, and undergraduate students; 513 full-time matriculated graduate/professional students (171 women), 1,318 part-time matriculated graduate/professional students (502 women). *Enrollment by degree level:* 1,759 master's, 69 doctoral, 3 other advanced degrees. *Graduate faculty:* 303 full-time (123 women), 269 part-time/adjunct (120 women). *Tuition, area resident:* Full-time $12,600; part-time $2190 per term. Tuition, nonresident: full-time $21,346; part-time $3690 per term. *Required fees:* $826; $626 per unit. $313 per term. Tuition and fees vary according to program. *Student services:* Campus employment opportunities, campus safety program, career counseling, child daycare facilities, exercise/wellness program, free psychological counseling, grant writing training, international student services, low-cost health insurance, multicultural affairs office, services for students with disabilities, teacher training, writing training. *Library:* Mardigian Library.

Computer facilities: Computer purchase and lease plans are available. 975 computers available on campus for general student use. A campuswide network can be accessed. Online class registration, tuition and application payments accepted online are available. Website: http://www.umdearborn.edu/

General Application Contact: Office of Graduate Studies, 313-583-6321, E-mail: umd-graduatestudies@umich.edu.

GRADUATE UNITS

College of Arts, Sciences, and Letters Students: 45 full-time (32 women), 97 part-time (68 women); includes 42 minority (22 Black or African American, non-Hispanic/Latino; 6 Asian, non-Hispanic/Latino; 12 Hispanic/Latino; 2 Two or more races, non-Hispanic/Latino), 8 international. 110 applicants, 65% accepted, 42 enrolled. *Faculty:* 59 full-time (28 women), 11 part-time/adjunct (5 women). *Financial support:* In 2015–16, 45 students received support. Scholarships/grants and non-resident tuition scholarships available. Financial award application deadline: 3/1; financial award applicants required to submit FAFSA. In 2015, 61 master's awarded. *Degree program information:* Part-time and evening/weekend programs available. Part-time, evening/weekend. Offers applied and computational mathematics (MS); arts, sciences, and letters (MPA, MPP, MS); clinical health psychology (MS); environmental science (MS); health psychology (MS); public administration (MPA); public policy (MPP). *Application deadline:* For fall admission, 8/1 priority date for domestic students, 5/1 priority date for international students; for winter admission, 12/1 priority date for domestic students, 9/1 priority date for international students; for spring admission, 4/1 priority date for domestic students, 1/1 priority date for international students. Applications are processed on a rolling basis. *Application fee:* $60. Electronic applications accepted. *Application Contact:* Carol Ligienza, Coordinator, CASL Graduate Programs, 313-593-1183, Fax: 313-583-6700, E-mail: caslgrad@umich.edu. *Dean*, Dr. Martin Hershock, 313-593-5490, Fax: 313-593-5552, E-mail: mhershoc@umich.edu.

College of Business Students: 101 full-time (43 women), 295 part-time (102 women); includes 65 minority (17 Black or African American, non-Hispanic/Latino; 1 American Indian or Alaska Native, non-Hispanic/Latino; 33 Asian, non-Hispanic/Latino; 8 Hispanic/Latino; 6 Two or more races, non-Hispanic/Latino), 90 international. 534 applicants, 37% accepted, 108 enrolled. *Faculty:* 50 full-time (24 women), 26 part-time/adjunct (5 women). *Financial support:* In 2015–16, 110 students received support. Scholarships/grants and non-resident tuition scholarships available. Financial award application deadline: 3/1; financial award applicants required to submit FAFSA. In 2015, 166 master's awarded. *Degree program information:* Part-time and evening/weekend programs available. Part-time, evening/weekend, 100% online. Offers accounting (MS); business (MBA, MS); business administration (MBA); business analytics (MS); finance (MS); information systems (MS); supply chain management (MS). *Application deadline:* For fall admission, 8/1 priority date for domestic students, 5/1 priority date for international students; for winter admission, 12/1 priority date for domestic students, 9/1 priority date for international students; for spring admission, 4/1 priority date for domestic students, 1/1 priority date for international students. Applications are processed on a rolling basis. *Application fee:* $60. Electronic applications accepted. *Application Contact:* Joan Doherty, Academic Advisor/Counselor, 313-593-5460, Fax: 313-271-9838, E-mail: umd-gradbusiness@umich.edu. *Dean*, Dr. Raju Balakrishnan, 313-593-5248, Fax: 313-271-9835, E-mail: rajub@umich.edu.

College of Education, Health, and Human Services Students: 25 full-time (19 women), 245 part-time (200 women); includes 44 minority (27 Black or African American, non-Hispanic/Latino; 4 Asian, non-Hispanic/Latino; 6 Hispanic/Latino; 7 Two or more races, non-Hispanic/Latino), 3 international. 108 applicants, 79% accepted, 63 enrolled. *Faculty:* 24 full-time (18 women), 20 part-time/adjunct (12 women). *Financial support:* In 2015–16, 48 students received support. Career-related internships or fieldwork and scholarships/grants available. Financial award application deadline: 3/1; financial award applicants required to submit FAFSA. In 2015, 70 master's, 4 doctorates, 1 other advanced degree awarded. *Degree program information:* Part-time and evening/weekend programs available. Part-time, evening/weekend, 100% online. Offers curriculum and practice (Ed D, Ed S); early childhood education (MA); education (MA, Ed D, Ed S); education, health, and human services (M Ed, MA, MAT, MS, Ed D, Certificate, Ed S); educational leadership (Ed D, Ed S); educational technology (MA); health information technology (MS); metropolitan education (Ed D, Ed S); science education (MS); special education (M Ed); teaching (MAT). *Application deadline:* For fall admission, 8/1 priority date for domestic students, 5/1 priority date for international students; for winter admission, 12/1 priority date for domestic students, 9/1 priority date for international students; for spring admission, 4/1 priority date for domestic students, 1/1 priority date for international students. Applications are processed on a rolling basis. *Application fee:* $60. Electronic applications accepted. *Application Contact:* Dr. Stein Brunvand, Director, Master's Programs, 313-583-6415, E-mail: sbrunvan@umich.edu. *Dean*, Dr. Janine Janosky, 313-593-5435, E-mail: jjanosky@umich.edu.

College of Engineering and Computer Science Students: 342 full-time (77 women), 681 part-time (132 women); includes 146 minority (33 Black or African American, non-Hispanic/Latino; 1 American Indian or Alaska Native, non-Hispanic/Latino; 69 Asian, non-Hispanic/Latino; 27 Hispanic/Latino; 16 Two or more races, non-Hispanic/Latino), 509 international. 1,324 applicants, 53% accepted, 360 enrolled. *Faculty:* 74 full-time (9 women), 41 part-time/adjunct (5 women). *Financial support:* In 2015–16, 380 students received support, including 49 research assistantships with tuition reimbursements available (averaging $12,597 per year), 6 teaching assistantships (averaging $6,258 per year); career-related internships or fieldwork, scholarships/grants, health care benefits, and non-residential student scholarships also available. Financial award application deadline: 3/1; financial award applicants required to submit FAFSA. In 2015, 296 master's, 3 doctorates awarded. *Degree program information:* Part-time and evening/weekend programs available. Part-time, evening/weekend, 100% online. Offers automotive systems engineering (MSE, PhD); computer and information science (MS); computer engineering (MSE); electrical engineering (MSE); energy systems engineering (MSE); engineering and computer science (MS, MSE, PhD); engineering management (MS); industrial and systems engineering (MSE); information systems and technology (MS); information systems engineering (PhD); manufacturing systems engineering (MSE); mechanical engineering (MSE); program and project management (MS); software engineering (MS). *Application deadline:* For fall admission, 8/1 priority date for domestic students, 5/1 priority date for international students; for winter admission, 12/1 priority date for domestic students, 9/1 priority date for international students; for spring admission, 4/1 priority date for domestic students, 1/1 priority date for international students. Applications are processed on a rolling basis. *Application fee:* $60. Electronic applications accepted. *Application Contact:* Office of Graduate Studies Staff, 313-583-6321, E-mail: umd-graduatestudies@umich.edu. *Dean*, Dr. Anthony England, 313-593-5290, Fax: 313-593-9967, E-mail: england@umich.edu.

UNIVERSITY OF MICHIGAN–FLINT, Flint, MI 48502-1950

General Information State-supported, coed, comprehensive institution. CGS member. *Enrollment:* 8,470 graduate, professional, and undergraduate students; 633 full-time matriculated graduate/professional students (353 women), 969 part-time matriculated graduate/professional students (585 women). *Enrollment by degree level:* 1,076 master's, 504 doctoral, 22 other advanced degrees. *Graduate faculty:* 318 full-time (172 women), 266 part-time/adjunct (173 women). *Graduate housing:* Room and/or apartments available on a first-come, first-served basis to single students; on-campus housing not available to married students. *Student services:* Campus employment opportunities, campus safety program, career counseling, child daycare facilities, exercise/wellness program, free psychological counseling, international student services, services for students with disabilities, teacher training, writing training. *Library:* Frances Willson Thompson Library plus 1 other. *Collection:* Books: 261,362 (physical), 595,284 (digital/electronic); Serial titles: 1,862 (physical), 87,098 (digital/electronic); Databases: 1,120. Weekly public service hours: 96; students can reserve study rooms.

Computer facilities: Computer purchase and lease plans are available. 532 computers available on campus for general student use. A campuswide network can be accessed from student residence rooms and from off campus. Online class registration is available.
Website: http://www.umflint.edu/

General Application Contact: Bradley T. Maki, Director of Graduate Admissions, 810-762-3171, Fax: 810-766-6789, E-mail: bmaki@umflint.edu.

GRADUATE UNITS

College of Arts and Sciences Students: 182 full-time (59 women), 201 part-time (84 women); includes 33 minority (18 Black or African American, non-Hispanic/Latino; 5 Asian, non-Hispanic/Latino; 5 Hispanic/Latino; 5 Two or more races, non-Hispanic/Latino), 244 international. Average age 28. 874 applicants, 32% accepted, 101 enrolled. *Faculty:* 112 full-time (48 women), 36 part-time/adjunct (19 women). *Financial support:* Federal Work-Study, scholarships/grants, and unspecified assistantships available. Support available to part-time students. Financial award application deadline: 3/1; financial award applicants required to submit FAFSA. In 2015, 65 master's awarded. *Degree program information:* Part-time programs available. Part-time. Offers applied communication (MA); arts and sciences (MA, MS); biology (MS); computer science (MS); gender studies (MA); global studies (MA); information systems (MS); literature (MA); mathematics (MA); U.S. history and politics (MA); writing and rhetoric (MA). *Application deadline:* For fall admission, 8/1 for domestic students, 5/1 for international students; for winter admission, 11/15 for domestic students, 9/1 for international students; for spring admission, 3/15 for domestic students, 1/1 for international students; for summer admission, 5/15 for domestic students. Applications are processed on a rolling basis. *Application fee:* $55. Electronic applications accepted. *Application*

Contact: Bradley T. Maki, Director of Graduate Admissions, 810-762-3171, Fax: 810-766-6789, E-mail: bmaki@umflint.edu. *Dean*, Dr. Susan Gano-Phillips, 810-762-3234, Fax: 810-762-3006, E-mail: sganop@umflint.edu.

Graduate Programs Students: 15 full-time (11 women), 137 part-time (92 women); includes 42 minority (30 Black or African American, non-Hispanic/Latino; 2 American Indian or Alaska Native, non-Hispanic/Latino; 1 Asian, non-Hispanic/Latino; 5 Hispanic/Latino; 1 Native Hawaiian or other Pacific Islander, non-Hispanic/Latino; 3 Two or more races, non-Hispanic/Latino), 4 international. Average age 35. 91 applicants, 69% accepted, 39 enrolled. *Faculty:* 8 full-time (5 women), 5 part-time/adjunct (3 women). *Financial support:* Federal Work-Study, scholarships/grants, and unspecified assistantships available. Support available to part-time students. Financial award application deadline: 3/1; financial award applicants required to submit FAFSA. In 2015, 53 master's awarded. *Degree program information:* Part-time and evening/weekend programs available. Part-time, evening/weekend, online learning. Offers administration of non-profit agencies (MPA); arts administration (MA); criminal justice administration (MPA); educational administration (MPA); general public administration (MPA); healthcare administration (MPA); liberal studies (MA). *Application deadline:* For fall admission, 8/1 for domestic students, 5/1 for international students; for winter admission, 11/15 for domestic students, 9/1 for international students; for spring admission, 3/15 for domestic students, 1/1 for international students; for summer admission, 5/15 for domestic students. Applications are processed on a rolling basis. *Application fee:* $55. Electronic applications accepted. *Application Contact:* Bradley T. Maki, Director of Graduate Admissions, 810-762-3171, Fax: 810-766-6789, E-mail: bmaki@umflint.edu. *Dean of Graduate Programs*, Dr. Vahid Lotfi, 810-762-3171, Fax: 810-766-6789.

School of Education and Human Services Students: 29 full-time (16 women), 219 part-time (160 women); includes 57 minority (45 Black or African American, non-Hispanic/Latino; 4 American Indian or Alaska Native, non-Hispanic/Latino; 2 Asian, non-Hispanic/Latino; 4 Hispanic/Latino; 2 Two or more races, non-Hispanic/Latino), 2 international. Average age 39. 153 applicants, 84% accepted, 95 enrolled. *Faculty:* 18 full-time (13 women), 34 part-time/adjunct (22 women). *Financial support:* Federal Work-Study, scholarships/grants, and unspecified assistantships available. Support available to part-time students. Financial award application deadline: 3/1; financial award applicants required to submit FAFSA. In 2015, 70 master's awarded. *Degree program information:* Part-time programs available. Part-time. Offers curriculum and instruction (Ed S); early childhood education (MA); education (Ed D); education and human services (MA, MAC, Ed D, Ed S); educational leadership (Ed S); educational technology (MA); literacy education (MA); secondary education with teacher certification (MAC). *Application deadline:* For fall admission, 8/1 for domestic students, 5/1 for international students; for winter admission, 11/15 for domestic students, 9/1 for international students; for spring admission, 3/15 for domestic students, 1/1 for international students. Applications are processed on a rolling basis. *Application fee:* $55. Electronic applications accepted. *Application Contact:* Bradley T. Maki, Director of Graduate Admissions, 810-762-3171, Fax: 810-766-6789, E-mail: bmaki@umflint.edu. *Interim Dean*, Dr. Bob Barnett, 810-766-6878, Fax: 810-766-6891, E-mail: rbarnett@umflint.edu.

School of Health Professions and Studies Students: 384 full-time (260 women), 225 part-time (175 women); includes 123 minority (56 Black or African American, non-Hispanic/Latino; 5 American Indian or Alaska Native, non-Hispanic/Latino; 29 Asian, non-Hispanic/Latino; 19 Hispanic/Latino; 14 Two or more races, non-Hispanic/Latino), 35 international. Average age 33. 846 applicants, 40% accepted, 184 enrolled. *Faculty:* 58 full-time (48 women), 114 part-time/adjunct (91 women). *Financial support:* Federal Work-Study, scholarships/grants, and unspecified assistantships available. Support available to part-time students. Financial award application deadline: 3/1; financial award applicants required to submit FAFSA. In 2015, 43 master's, 109 doctorates, 1 other advanced degree awarded. *Degree program information:* Part-time programs available. Part-time. Offers adult-gerontology acute care (DNP); adult-gerontology primary care (DNP); anesthesia (MS, DrAP); family nurse practitioner (MSN, DNP); geriatrics (DPT, PhD, Certificate); health administration (MPH); health education (MPH, MS); health professions and studies (MPH, MS, MSN, DNP, DPT, DrAP, PhD, Certificate); neurology (DPT, PhD, Certificate); orthopedics (DPT, PhD, Certificate); pediatrics (DPT, PhD, Certificate); physical therapy (DPT); psychiatric mental health (DNP); psychiatric mental health nurse practitioner (Certificate). *Application deadline:* For fall admission, 8/1 for domestic students, 5/1 for international students; for winter admission, 11/15 for domestic students, 9/1 for international students; for spring admission, 3/15 for domestic students, 1/1 for international students. Applications are processed on a rolling basis. *Application fee:* $55. Electronic applications accepted. *Application Contact:* Bradley T. Maki, Director of Graduate Admissions, 810-762-3171, Fax: 810-766-6789, E-mail: bmaki@umflint.edu. *Dean*, Dr. Donna Fry, 810-237-6503, Fax: 810-237-6532, E-mail: donnafry@umflint.edu.

School of Management Students: 23 full-time (7 women), 187 part-time (74 women); includes 42 minority (16 Black or African American, non-Hispanic/Latino; 3 American Indian or Alaska Native, non-Hispanic/Latino; 15 Asian, non-Hispanic/Latino; 4 Hispanic/Latino; 1 Native Hawaiian or other Pacific Islander, non-Hispanic/Latino; 3 Two or more races, non-Hispanic/Latino), 37 international. Average age 32. 142 applicants, 58% accepted, 48 enrolled. *Faculty:* 4 full-time (1 woman), 6 part-time/adjunct (1 woman). *Financial support:* Federal Work-Study, scholarships/grants, and unspecified assistantships available. Support available to part-time students. Financial award application deadline: 3/1; financial award applicants required to submit FAFSA. In 2015, 93 master's, 1 other advanced degree awarded. *Degree program information:* Part-time and evening/weekend programs available. Part-time, evening/weekend, online learning. Offers accounting (MSA); business (Graduate Certificate); business administration (MBA); business management (MBA); computer information systems (MBA); finance (MBA, Post-Master's Certificate); general business administration (MBA); health care management (MBA); international business (MBA, Post-Master's Certificate); lean manufacturing (MBA); marketing (MBA, Post-Master's Certificate); organizational leadership (MBA). *Application deadline:* For fall admission, 8/1 for domestic students, 5/1 for international students; for winter admission, 11/1 for domestic students, 9/1 for international students. Applications are processed on a rolling basis. *Application fee:* $55. Electronic applications accepted. *Application Contact:* Bradley T. Maki, Director of Graduate Admissions, 810-762-3171, Fax: 810-766-6789, E-mail: bmaki@umflint.edu. *Dean, School of Management*, Dr. Scott Johnson, 810-762-3164, Fax: 810-237-6685, E-mail: scotjohn@umflint.edu.

UNIVERSITY OF MINNESOTA, DULUTH, Duluth, MN 55812-2496

General Information State-supported, coed, comprehensive institution. *Graduate housing:* Room and/or apartments available to single students; on-campus housing not available to married students. Housing application deadline: 3/1. *Research affiliation:* Environmental Protection Agency Environmental Research Laboratory (aquatic biology), Minnesota Geological Survey, Northeastern Minnesota National Historical Center (local history), U.S. Forest Service, Northcentral Forest Experiment Station.

GRADUATE UNITS

Graduate School *Degree program information:* Part-time and evening/weekend programs available. Part-time, evening/weekend, online learning. Offers toxicology (MS, PhD).

College of Education and Human Service Professions Degree program information: Part-time and evening/weekend programs available. Part-time, evening/weekend, online learning. Offers communication sciences and disorders (MA); education (M Ed, Ed D); education and human service professions (M Ed, MA, MSW, Ed D); social work (MSW).

College of Liberal Arts Degree program information: Part-time programs available. Part-time. Offers criminology (MA); English (MA); liberal arts (MA, MLS); liberal studies (MLS).

Labovitz School of Business and Economics Degree program information: Part-time and evening/weekend programs available. Part-time, evening/weekend. Offers business administration (MBA); business and economics (MBA).

School of Fine Arts Degree program information: Part-time programs available. Part-time. Offers fine arts (MFA, MM); graphic design (MFA); music education (MM); performance (MM).

Swenson College of Science and Engineering Degree program information: Part-time and evening/weekend programs available. Part-time, evening/weekend, online learning. Offers applied and computational mathematics (MS); chemistry and biochemistry (MS); computer science (MS); electrical and computer engineering (MSECE); engineering management (MSEM); environmental health and safety (MEHS); geological sciences (MS, PhD); integrated biosciences (MS, PhD); physics (MS); science and engineering (MEHS, MS, MSECE, MSEM, PhD).

Medical School *Degree program information:* Part-time programs available. Part-time. Offers biochemistry, molecular biology and biophysics (MS); biology and biophysics (PhD); medicine (MS, MD, PhD); microbiology, immunology and molecular pathobiology (MS, PhD); pharmacology (MS, PhD); physiology (MS, PhD); social, administrative, and clinical pharmacy (MS, PhD); toxicology (MS, PhD).

UNIVERSITY OF MINNESOTA, TWIN CITIES CAMPUS, Minneapolis, MN 55455-0213

General Information State-supported, coed, comprehensive institution. CGS member. *Graduate housing:* Rooms and/or apartments available on a first-come, first-served basis to single and married students. Housing application deadline: 5/1.

GRADUATE UNITS

Carlson School of Management *Degree program information:* Part-time and evening/weekend programs available. Part-time, evening/weekend. Offers accountancy (M Acc); accounting (PhD); applied economics (MBA); business analytics (MBA); business taxation (MBT); finance (MBA, PhD); human resources and industrial relations (MA); information and decision sciences (PhD); information technology (MBA); management (MBA); marketing (MBA, PhD); medical industry orientation (MBA); operations and management science (PhD); strategic management and entrepreneurship (PhD); supply chain and operations (MBA); work and organizations (PhD). Electronic applications accepted.

College of Pharmacy *Degree program information:* Part-time programs available. Part-time. Offers experimental and clinical pharmacology (MS, PhD); medicinal chemistry (MS, PhD); pharmaceutics (PhD); pharmacy (MS, PhD, Pharm D); social and administrative pharmacy (MS, PhD).

College of Science and Engineering *Degree program information:* Part-time and evening/weekend programs available. Part-time, evening/weekend, online learning. Offers aerospace engineering and mechanics (MS, PhD); biomedical engineering (MS, PhD); chemical engineering (M Ch E, MS Ch E, PhD); chemical physics (MS, PhD); chemistry (MS, PhD); civil engineering (MCE, MS, PhD); computer science (MCS, MS, PhD); data science (MS); earth sciences (MS, PhD); electrical and computer engineering (MSEE, PhD); geological engineering (M Geo E, MS); history of science, technology and medicine (MA, PhD); industrial and systems engineering (MS, PhD); materials science and engineering (M Mat SE, MS Mat SE, PhD); mechanical engineering (MSME, PhD); science and engineering (M Ch E, M Geo E, M Mat SE, MA, MCE, MCS, MFM, MS, MS Ch E, MS Mat SE, MSEE, MSME, MSMOT, MSSE, MSST, PhD, Certificate); scientific computation (MS, PhD); software engineering (MSSE); stream restoration science and engineering (Certificate). Electronic applications accepted.

School of Mathematics Degree program information: Part-time programs available. Part-time. Offers mathematics (MS, PhD); quantitative finance (Certificate). Electronic applications accepted.

School of Physics and Astronomy Degree program information: Part-time programs available. Part-time. Offers astrophysics (MS, PhD); physics (MS, PhD).

Technological Leadership Institute Degree program information: Evening/weekend programs available. Evening/weekend. Offers management of technology (MSMOT); medical device innovation (MS); security technologies (MSST). Electronic applications accepted.

College of Veterinary Medicine *Degree program information:* Part-time programs available. Part-time. Offers comparative and molecular bioscience (MS, PhD); veterinary medicine (MS, PhD). Electronic applications accepted.

Graduate School *Degree program information:* Part-time and evening/weekend programs available. Part-time, evening/weekend, online learning. Offers biophysical sciences and medical physics (MS, PhD); genetic counseling (MS); health informatics (MHI, MS, PhD); history of science, technology and medicine (MA, PhD); integrative biology and physiology (PhD); microbial engineering (MS); microbiology, immunology and cancer biology (PhD); molecular, cellular, developmental biology and genetics (PhD); neuroscience (MS, PhD); stem cell biology (MS). Electronic applications accepted.

College of Biological Sciences Degree program information: Part-time programs available. Part-time. Offers biochemistry, molecular biology and biophysics (PhD); biological science (MBS); biological sciences (MBS, MS, PhD); ecology, evolution, and behavior (MS, PhD); plant biological sciences (MS, PhD). Electronic applications accepted.

College of Design Offers apparel (MA, MS, PhD); architecture (M Arch); design (M Arch, MA, MFA, MLA, MS, PhD, Postbaccalaureate Certificate); design communication (MA, MS, PhD); housing studies (MA, MS, PhD, Postbaccalaureate Certificate); interactive design (MFA); interior design (MA, MS, PhD); landscape architecture (MLA, MS); sustainable design (MS). Electronic applications accepted.

College of Education and Human Development Students: 1,610 full-time (1,178 women), 789 part-time (566 women); includes 474 minority (134 Black or African American, non-Hispanic/Latino; 17 American Indian or Alaska Native, non-Hispanic/Latino; 132 Asian, non-Hispanic/Latino; 115 Hispanic/Latino; 1 Native

Hawaiian or other Pacific Islander, non-Hispanic/Latino; 75 Two or more races, non-Hispanic/Latino), 199 international. Average age 32. 2,196 applicants, 54% accepted, 1061 enrolled. *Faculty:* 178 full-time (95 women). *Financial support:* In 2015–16, 95 fellowships, 286 research assistantships with full tuition reimbursements (averaging $12,090 per year), 231 teaching assistantships with full tuition reimbursements (averaging $10,937 per year) were awarded; scholarships/grants and tuition waivers (partial) also available. Financial award applicants required to submit FAFSA. In 2015, 1,060 master's, 154 doctorates, 273 other advanced degrees awarded. *Degree program information:* Part-time programs available. Part-time. Offers adult education (M Ed, MA, Ed D, PhD, Certificate); agricultural, food and environmental education (M Ed, MA, Ed D, PhD); art education (M Ed, MA, PhD); biomechanics and neuromotor control (PhD); business and industry education (M Ed, MA, Ed D, PhD); business education (M Ed); child psychology (MA, PhD); children's literature (M Ed, MA, PhD); Chinese (M Ed); coaching (Certificate); comparative and international development education (MA, PhD); counseling and student personnel psychology (MA, PhD, Ed S); curriculum and instruction (M Ed, MA, Ed D, PhD, Certificate); developmental adapted physical education (M Ed); disability policy and services (Certificate); early childhood education (M Ed, MA, PhD); earth science (M Ed); education and human development (M Ed, MA, MSW, Ed D, PhD, Certificate, Ed S); educational administration (MA, Ed D, PhD); educational psychology (PhD); elementary education (M Ed, MA, PhD); elementary special education (M Ed); English (M Ed); English as a second language (M Ed); English education (MA, PhD); environmental education (M Ed); evaluation studies (MA, PhD); exercise physiology (PhD); family education (M Ed, MA, Ed D, PhD); French (M Ed); German (M Ed); Hebrew (M Ed); higher education (MA, PhD); human factors and ergonomics (MA, PhD); human resource development (M Ed, MA, Ed D, PhD, Certificate); instructional systems and technology (M Ed, MA, PhD); Japanese (M Ed); kinesiology (M Ed, MA, MS, PhD); language and immersion education (Certificate); language arts (MA, PhD); life sciences (M Ed); literacy education (MA); marketing education (M Ed); marriage and family therapy (MA, PhD); mathematics (M Ed); mathematics education (MA, PhD); middle school science (M Ed); multicultural college teaching and learning (MA); perceptual-motor control and learning (PhD); physical education (M Ed); postsecondary administration (Ed D); program evaluation (Certificate); psychological foundations of education (MA, PhD, Ed S); reading education (MA, PhD); school psychology (MA, PhD, Ed S); school-to-work (Certificate); science (M Ed); science education (MA, PhD); second languages and cultures (M Ed, MA, PhD); social studies (M Ed); social studies education (MA, PhD); social work (MSW, PhD); Spanish (M Ed); special education (M Ed, MA, PhD, Ed S); sport and exercise psychology (PhD); sport and exercise science (M Ed); sport management (M Ed, MA, PhD); sport sociology (PhD); staff development (Certificate); talent development and gifted education (Certificate); teacher leadership (M Ed); teaching (M Ed); technical education (Certificate); technology education (M Ed, MA); technology enhanced learning (Certificate); work and human resource education (M Ed, MA, Ed D, PhD); writing education (M Ed, MA, PhD); youth development leadership (M Ed). *Application fee:* $75 ($95 for international students). *Application Contact:* Dr. Brianne Keeney, Director of Graduate Education Initiatives, 612-626-9145, E-mail: keen0113@umn.edu. *Dean*, Dr. Jean K. Quam, 612-626-9252, Fax: 612-626-7496, E-mail: jquam@umn.edu.

College of Food, Agricultural and Natural Resource Sciences Students: 532 full-time (260 women), 63 part-time (30 women); includes 40 minority (4 Black or African American, non-Hispanic/Latino; 2 American Indian or Alaska Native, non-Hispanic/Latino; 14 Asian, non-Hispanic/Latino; 9 Hispanic/Latino; 1 Native Hawaiian or other Pacific Islander, non-Hispanic/Latino; 10 Two or more races, non-Hispanic/Latino), 183 international. Average age 30. 772 applicants, 40% accepted, 191 enrolled. *Faculty:* 741 full-time (180 women). *Financial support:* In 2015–16, 500 students received support, including 100 fellowships with full tuition reimbursements available (averaging $43,000 per year), 200 research assistantships with tuition reimbursements available (averaging $40,000 per year), 200 teaching assistantships with tuition reimbursements available (averaging $40,000 per year); career-related internships or fieldwork, institutionally sponsored loans, scholarships/grants, health care benefits, tuition waivers (full), and unspecified assistantships also available. Support available to part-time students. Financial award application deadline: 12/15. In 2015, 103 master's, 64 doctorates awarded. *Degree program information:* Part-time programs available. Part-time. Offers animal sciences (MS, PhD); applied economics (MS, PhD); applied plant sciences (MS, PhD); assessment, monitoring, and geospatial analysis (MS, PhD); bioproducts and biosystems science, engineering and management (MS, PhD); conservation biology (MS, PhD); economics, policy, management, and society (MS, PhD); entomology (MS, PhD); food science (MS, PhD); food, agricultural and natural resource sciences (MS, PhD); forest hydrology and watershed management (MS, PhD); forest products (MS, PhD); forests: biology, ecology, conservation, and management (MS, PhD); land and atmospheric science (MS, PhD); natural resources science and management (MS, PhD); nutrition (MS, PhD); paper science and engineering (MS, PhD); plant pathology (MS, PhD); recreation resources, tourism, and environmental education (MS, PhD); water resources science (MS, PhD); wildlife ecology and management (MS, PhD). *Application deadline:* For fall admission, 12/15 priority date for domestic and international students; for spring admission, 10/15 priority date for domestic and international students. Applications are processed on a rolling basis. *Application fee:* $75 ($95 for international students). Electronic applications accepted. *Application Contact:* Lisa Wiley, Coordinator of Graduate Student Services, 612-624-2748, Fax: 612-625-1260, E-mail: lwiley@umn.edu. *Associate Dean for Research and Graduate Programs*, Dr. Gregory J. Cuomo, 612-625-1158, Fax: 612-625-1260, E-mail: cuomogj@umn.edu.

College of Liberal Arts Degree program information: Part-time and evening/weekend programs available. Part-time, evening/weekend. Offers American studies (PhD); ancient and medieval art and archaeology (MA, PhD); anthropology (MA, PhD); art (MFA); art history (MA, PhD); Asian literatures, cultures, and media (PhD); audiology (Au D); biological psychopathology (PhD); classics (MA, PhD); clinical psychology (PhD); cognitive and biological psychology (PhD); communication studies (MA, PhD); comparative literature (PhD); comparative studies in discourse and society (PhD); counseling psychology (PhD); design technology (MFA); economics (MA, PhD); English (MA, PhD); English as a second language (MA); feminist studies (PhD); French (MA, PhD); geographic information science (MGIS); geography, environment and society (MA, PhD); Germanic studies (MA, PhD); Greek (MA, PhD); Hispanic and Lusophone literatures, cultures and linguistics (PhD); Hispanic linguistics (MA); Hispanic literature (MA); history (MA, PhD); industrial/organizational psychology (PhD); Latin (MA, PhD); liberal arts (MA, MFA, MGIS, MM, MS, Au D, DMA, PhD); linguistics (MA, PhD); Lusophone literature (MA); mass communication (MA, PhD); music (MA, MM, DMA, PhD); personality, individual differences, and behavior genetics (PhD); philosophy (MA, PhD); political science (PhD); quantitative/psychometric methods (PhD); religions in antiquity (MA); school psychology (PhD); social psychology (PhD); sociology (MA, PhD); speech-language pathology (MA); speech-language-hearing sciences (PhD); statistics (MS, PhD); strategic communication (professional program) (MA); theatre arts (MA, PhD). Electronic applications accepted.

Hubert H. Humphrey School of Public Affairs Students: 212 (124 women); includes 38 minority (20 Black or African American, non-Hispanic/Latino; 6 American Indian or Alaska Native, non-Hispanic/Latino; 7 Asian, non-Hispanic/Latino; 5 Hispanic/Latino), 29 international. Average age 30. 697 applicants, 60% accepted, 205 enrolled. *Faculty:* 33 full-time (17 women), 27 part-time/adjunct (12 women). *Financial support:* In 2015–16, 239 students received support, including fellowships with tuition reimbursements available (averaging $9,000 per year), research assistantships with tuition reimbursements available (averaging $26,000 per year), teaching assistantships with tuition reimbursements available (averaging $18,000 per year); career-related internships or fieldwork, scholarships/grants, health care benefits, tuition waivers (full and partial), and unspecified assistantships also available. Financial award application deadline: 1/15; financial award applicants required to submit FAFSA. In 2015, 170 master's awarded. *Degree program information:* Part-time and evening/weekend programs available. Part-time, evening/weekend. Offers development practice (MDP); management and governance (PhD); public affairs (MDP, MPA, MPP, MS, MURP, PhD); public policy (PhD); science, technology, and environmental policy (PhD); urban and regional planning (MURP); urban planning (PhD). *Application deadline:* For fall admission, 4/1 for domestic and international students. Applications are processed on a rolling basis. *Application fee:* $75 ($95 for international students). Electronic applications accepted. *Application Contact:* Dan Cheng, Associate Director of Admissions, 612-624-3800, Fax: 612-626-0002, E-mail: chen0609@umn.edu. *Associate Dean*, Laura Bloomberg, 612-625-0608, Fax: 612-626-0002, E-mail: bloom004@umn.edu.

School of Nursing Degree program information: Part-time programs available. Part-time, online learning. Offers adolescent nursing (MS); adult health clinical nurse specialist (MS); advanced clinical specialist in gerontology (MS); children with special health care needs (MS); family nurse practitioner (MS); gerontological nurse practitioner (MS); nurse anesthetist (MS); nurse midwifery (MS); nursing (MN, MS, DNP, PhD); nursing and health care systems administration (MS); pediatric clinical nurse specialist (MS); pediatric nurse practitioner (MS); psychiatric mental health clinical nurse specialist (MS); public health nursing (MS); women's health nurse practitioner (MS).

Law School Students: 632 full-time (273 women), 9 part-time (4 women); includes 119 minority (16 Black or African American, non-Hispanic/Latino; 5 American Indian or Alaska Native, non-Hispanic/Latino; 56 Asian, non-Hispanic/Latino; 10 Hispanic/Latino; 32 Two or more races, non-Hispanic/Latino), 72 international. Average age 25. 1,978 applicants, 44% accepted, 174 enrolled. *Faculty:* 63 full-time (25 women), 103 part-time/adjunct (39 women). *Financial support:* In 2015–16, 542 students received support. Fellowships, research assistantships, career-related internships or fieldwork, Federal Work-Study, institutionally sponsored loans, and scholarships/grants available. Financial award application deadline: 7/15; financial award applicants required to submit FAFSA. In 2015, 60 master's, 244 doctorates awarded. Offers law (LL M, MS, JD, SJD). *Application deadline:* For fall admission, 7/15 for domestic students. Applications are processed on a rolling basis. *Application fee:* $75. Electronic applications accepted. *Application Contact:* Robin Ingli, Interim Director of Admissions, 612-625-0718, Fax: 612-625-2011, E-mail: umnlsadm@umn.edu. *Dean*, David Wippman, 612-625-4841.

Medical School ***Degree program information:*** Part-time and evening/weekend programs available. Part-time, evening/weekend. Offers medicine (MA, MS, DPT, MD, PhD); pharmacology (MS, PhD).

School of Dentistry Offers dentistry (MS, DDS, PhD, Certificate); endodontics (MS, Certificate); oral biology (MS, PhD); oral health services for older adults (geriatrics) (MS, Certificate); orthodontics (MS); pediatric dentistry (MS); periodontology (MS); prosthodontics (MS); temporomandibular joint disorders (MS).

School of Public Health ***Degree program information:*** Part-time programs available. Part-time, online learning. Offers biostatistics (MPH, MS, PhD); clinical research (MS); community health education (MPH); core concepts (Certificate); epidemiology (MPH, PhD); food safety and biosecurity (Certificate); health services research, policy, and administration (MS, PhD); healthcare administration (MHA); maternal and child health (MPH); occupational health and safety (Certificate); preparedness, response and recovery (Certificate); public health (MHA, MPH, MS, PhD, Certificate); public health administration and policy (MPH); public health nutrition (MPH); public health practice (MPH). Electronic applications accepted.

Division of Environmental Health Sciences Degree program information: Part-time programs available. Part-time. Offers environmental and occupational epidemiology (MPH, MS, PhD); environmental chemistry (MS, PhD); environmental health policy (MPH, MS, PhD); environmental infectious diseases (MPH, MS, PhD); environmental toxicology (MPH, MS, PhD); exposure sciences (MS); general environmental health (MPH, MS); global environmental health (MPH, MS, PhD); industrial hygiene (MPH, MS, PhD); occupational health nursing (MPH, MS, PhD); occupational medicine (MPH). Electronic applications accepted.

UNIVERSITY OF MISSISSIPPI, University, MS 38677

General Information State-supported, coed, university. CGS member. *Enrollment:* 23,212 graduate, professional, and undergraduate students; 3,251 full-time matriculated graduate/professional students (1,724 women), 1,093 part-time matriculated graduate/professional students (718 women). *Graduate housing:* Rooms and/or apartments available to single and married students. *Student services:* Campus employment opportunities, campus safety program, career counseling, exercise/wellness program, free psychological counseling, international student services, low-cost health insurance, multicultural affairs office, services for students with disabilities, teacher training, writing training. *Library:* J. D. Williams Library plus 1 other. *Collection:* Books: 3.3 million (physical), 814,143 (digital/electronic); Serial titles: 39,667 (physical), 135,210 (digital/electronic); Databases: 389. Weekly public service hours: 109. *Research affiliation:* Mississippi Geographic Alliance, Mississippi Research Consortium, Mississippi - Alabama Sea Grant Consortium, Oak Ridge Associated Universities, Southeastern Universities Research Association, Mississippi Space Grant Consortium.

Computer facilities: 75 computers available on campus for general student use. A campuswide network can be accessed from student residence rooms and from off campus. Online class registration is available.
Website: http://www.olemiss.edu/

General Application Contact: Dr. Christy M. Wyandt, Associate Dean of Graduate School, 662-915-7474, Fax: 662-915-7577, E-mail: cwyandt@olemiss.edu.

GRADUATE UNITS

Graduate School Students: 2,003 full-time (1,052 women), 740 part-time (413 women); includes 571 minority (366 Black or African American, non-Hispanic/Latino; 7 American Indian or Alaska Native, non-Hispanic/Latino; 72 Asian, non-Hispanic/Latino; 75 Hispanic/Latino; 1 Native Hawaiian or other Pacific Islander, non-Hispanic/Latino; 50 Two or more races, non-Hispanic/Latino), 308 international. *Financial support:* Fellowships, research assistantships, teaching assistantships, career-related internships or fieldwork, Federal Work-Study, institutionally sponsored loans, scholarships/grants, tuition waivers (full), and unspecified assistantships available. Financial award application deadline: 3/1; financial award applicants required to submit FAFSA. *Degree program information:* Part-time programs available. Part-time. *Application deadline:* For fall admission, 4/1 for domestic students; for spring admission, 10/1 for domestic students. Applications are processed on a rolling basis. *Application fee:* $50. Electronic applications accepted. *Application Contact:* Dr. Christy M. Wyandt, Associate Dean, 662-915-7474, Fax: 662-915-7577, E-mail: cwyandt@olemiss.edu. *Dean,* Dr. Johns Z. Kiss, 662-915-7474, Fax: 662-915-7577, E-mail: gschool@olemiss.edu.

College of Liberal Arts Students: 475 full-time (233 women), 79 part-time (37 women); includes 83 minority (42 Black or African American, non-Hispanic/Latino; 9 Asian, non-Hispanic/Latino; 19 Hispanic/Latino; 13 Two or more races, non-Hispanic/Latino), 107 international. *Faculty:* 446 full-time (186 women), 84 part-time/adjunct (36 women). *Financial support:* Fellowships, research assistantships, teaching assistantships, career-related internships or fieldwork, Federal Work-Study, institutionally sponsored loans, scholarships/grants, and unspecified assistantships available. Financial award application deadline: 3/1; financial award applicants required to submit FAFSA. *Degree program information:* Part-time programs available. Part-time. Offers anthropology (MA); biology (MS, PhD); chemistry (MS, PhD); clinical psychology (PhD); economics (MA, PhD); English (MA, MFA, PhD); experimental psychology (PhD); history (MA, PhD); mathematics (MS, PhD); modern languages (MA); music (MM, PhD); philosophy (MA); physics (MA, MS, PhD); political science (MA, PhD); sociology (MA); studio art (MFA). *Application deadline:* For fall admission, 4/1 for domestic students; for spring admission, 10/1 for domestic students. Applications are processed on a rolling basis. *Application fee:* $40. Electronic applications accepted. *Application Contact:* Dr. Christy M. Wyandt, Associate Dean of Graduate School, 662-915-7474, Fax: 662-915-7577, E-mail: cwyandt@olemiss.edu. *Dean,* 662-915-7177, Fax: 662-915-5792, E-mail: libarts@olemiss.edu.

School of Accountancy Students: 117 full-time (44 women), 9 part-time (6 women); includes 17 minority (7 Black or African American, non-Hispanic/Latino; 1 American Indian or Alaska Native, non-Hispanic/Latino; 4 Asian, non-Hispanic/Latino; 3 Hispanic/Latino; 2 Two or more races, non-Hispanic/Latino), 5 international. *Faculty:* 16 full-time (5 women), 4 part-time/adjunct (3 women). *Financial support:* Scholarships/grants available. Financial award application deadline: 3/1; financial award applicants required to submit FAFSA. In 2015, 104 master's, 2 doctorates awarded. Offers accountancy (M Acc, PhD); taxation accounting (M Tax). *Application deadline:* For fall admission, 4/1 for domestic students; for spring admission, 10/1 for domestic students. Applications are processed on a rolling basis. *Application fee:* $40. *Application Contact:* Dr. Christy M. Wyandt, Associate Dean, 662-915-7474, Fax: 662-915-7577, E-mail: cwyandt@olemiss.edu. *Interim Dean,* Dr. Mark Wilder, 662-915-7468, Fax: 662-915-7483, E-mail: umaccy@olemiss.edu.

School of Applied Sciences Students: 192 full-time (148 women), 43 part-time (23 women); includes 47 minority (37 Black or African American, non-Hispanic/Latino; 2 Asian, non-Hispanic/Latino; 7 Hispanic/Latino; 1 Two or more races, non-Hispanic/Latino), 12 international. *Faculty:* 65 full-time (36 women), 32 part-time/adjunct (23 women). *Financial support:* Scholarships/grants available. Financial award application deadline: 3/1; financial award applicants required to submit FAFSA. In 2015, 99 master's, 3 doctorates awarded. Offers communicative disorders (MS); criminal justice (MCJ); exercise science (MS); food and nutrition services (MS); health and kinesiology (PhD); health promotion (MS); park and recreation management (MA); social work (MSW). *Application deadline:* For fall admission, 4/1 for domestic students; for spring admission, 10/1 for domestic students. Applications are processed on a rolling basis. *Application fee:* $40. Electronic applications accepted. *Application Contact:* Dr. Christy M. Wyandt, Associate Dean of Graduate School, 662-915-7474, Fax: 662-915-7577, E-mail: cwyandt@olemiss.edu. *Dean,* Dr. Velmer Stanley Burton, 662-915-1081, Fax: 662-915-5717, E-mail: applsci@olemiss.edu.

School of Business Administration Students: 70 full-time (20 women), 108 part-time (19 women); includes 29 minority (8 Black or African American, non-Hispanic/Latino; 8 Asian, non-Hispanic/Latino; 7 Hispanic/Latino; 6 Two or more races, non-Hispanic/Latino), 22 international. *Faculty:* 58 full-time (18 women), 4 part-time/adjunct (all women). *Financial support:* Fellowships, career-related internships or fieldwork, scholarships/grants, tuition waivers (full), and unspecified assistantships available. Financial award application deadline: 3/1; financial award applicants required to submit FAFSA. In 2015, 83 master's, 6 doctorates awarded. Offers business administration (MBA, PhD); systems management (MS). *Application deadline:* For fall admission, 2/1 for domestic students; for spring admission, 10/1 for domestic students. Applications are processed on a rolling basis. *Application fee:* $40. Electronic applications accepted. *Application Contact:* Dr. Christy M. Wyandt, Associate Dean, 662-915-7474, Fax: 662-915-7577, E-mail: cwyandt@olemiss.edu. *Dean,* Dr. Ken Cyree, 662-915-5820, Fax: 662-915-5821, E-mail: info@bus.olemiss.edu.

School of Education Students: 173 full-time (132 women), 401 part-time (277 women); includes 201 minority (179 Black or African American, non-Hispanic/Latino; 4 Asian, non-Hispanic/Latino; 11 Hispanic/Latino; 7 Two or more races, non-Hispanic/Latino), 6 international. *Faculty:* 40 full-time (29 women), 22 part-time/adjunct (20 women). *Financial support:* Scholarships/grants available. Financial award application deadline: 3/1; financial award applicants required to submit FAFSA. In 2015, 176 master's, 20 doctorates, 37 other advanced degrees awarded. Offers education (M Ed, MA, Ed D, PhD, Ed S, Specialist). *Application deadline:* For fall admission, 4/1 for domestic students; for spring admission, 10/1 for domestic students. Applications are processed on a rolling basis. *Application fee:* $40. Electronic applications accepted. *Application Contact:* Dr. Christy M. Wyandt, Associate Dean, 662-915-7474, Fax: 662-915-7577, E-mail: cwyandt@olemiss.edu. *Interim Dean,* Dr. David Rock, 662-915-7063, Fax: 662-915-7249, E-mail: soe@olemiss.edu.

School of Engineering Students: 132 full-time (30 women), 22 part-time (3 women); includes 15 minority (7 Black or African American, non-Hispanic/Latino; 5 Asian, non-Hispanic/Latino; 2 Hispanic/Latino; 1 Two or more races, non-Hispanic/Latino), 71 international. *Faculty:* 38 full-time (8 women), 3 part-time/adjunct (1 woman). *Financial support:* Scholarships/grants available. Financial award application deadline: 3/1; financial award applicants required to submit FAFSA. In 2015, 28 master's, 12 doctorates awarded. Offers engineering science (MS, PhD). *Application deadline:* For fall admission, 4/1 for domestic students; for spring admission, 10/1 for domestic students. Applications are processed on a rolling basis. *Application fee:* $40. Electronic applications accepted. *Application Contact:* Dr. Christy M. Wyandt, Associate Dean, 662-915-7474, Fax: 662-915-7577, E-mail: cwyandt@olemiss.edu. *Dean,* Dr. Alexander Cheng, 662-915-7407, Fax: 662-915-1287, E-mail: engineer@olemiss.edu.

School of Journalism and New Media Students: 43 full-time (31 women), 10 part-time (2 women); includes 12 minority (8 Black or African American, non-Hispanic/Latino; 2 Hispanic/Latino; 2 Two or more races, non-Hispanic/Latino), 4 international. *Faculty:* 20 full-time (11 women), 8 part-time/adjunct (4 women). In 2015, 11 master's awarded. Offers journalism (MA). *Application fee:* $40. *Application Contact:* Dr. Christy M. Wyandt, Associate Dean, 662-915-7474, Fax: 662-915-7577, E-mail: cwyandt@olemiss.edu. *Dean,* Dr. Will Norton, Jr., 662-915-7146, Fax: 662-915-7765, E-mail: jour@olemiss.edu.

School of Pharmacy Students: 410 full-time (250 women), 12 part-time (4 women); includes 77 minority (26 Black or African American, non-Hispanic/Latino; 3 American Indian or Alaska Native, non-Hispanic/Latino; 37 Asian, non-Hispanic/Latino; 5 Hispanic/Latino; 1 Native Hawaiian or other Pacific Islander, non-Hispanic/Latino; 5 Two or more races, non-Hispanic/Latino), 70 international. *Faculty:* 57 full-time (26 women), 15 part-time/adjunct (6 women). *Financial support:* Fellowships, research assistantships, teaching assistantships, career-related internships or fieldwork, Federal Work-Study, institutionally sponsored loans, scholarships/grants, tuition waivers (full), and unspecified assistantships available. Financial award application deadline: 3/1; financial award applicants required to submit FAFSA. In 2015, 22 master's, 49 doctorates awarded. *Degree program information:* Part-time programs available. Part-time. Offers pharmacy (MS, PhD, Pharm D). *Application deadline:* For fall admission, 4/1 for domestic students; for spring admission, 10/1 for domestic students. Applications are processed on a rolling basis. *Application fee:* $40. Electronic applications accepted. *Dean,* Dr. David D. Allen, II, 662-915-7265, Fax: 662-915-5118, E-mail: sopdean@olemiss.edu.

School of Law Students: 389 full-time (157 women), 5 part-time (1 woman); includes 83 minority (59 Black or African American, non-Hispanic/Latino; 3 American Indian or Alaska Native, non-Hispanic/Latino; 2 Asian, non-Hispanic/Latino; 12 Hispanic/Latino; 7 Two or more races, non-Hispanic/Latino), 1 international. Average age 24. *Financial support:* Fellowships, research assistantships, teaching assistantships, career-related internships or fieldwork, Federal Work-Study, institutionally sponsored loans, and scholarships/grants available. Support available to part-time students. Financial award application deadline: 3/1; financial award applicants required to submit FAFSA. In 2015, 179 doctorates awarded. Offers air and space law (LL M); law (JD). *Application deadline:* For fall admission, 4/1 for domestic students. *Application fee:* $40. *Application Contact:* Cary Lee Cluck, Assistant Dean for Admissions, 662-915-6815, Fax: 662-915-7577, E-mail: clee@olemiss.edu. *Dean,* Dr. Deborah Bell, 662-915-6900, Fax: 662-915-6895, E-mail: igershon@olemiss.edu.

UNIVERSITY OF MISSISSIPPI MEDICAL CENTER, Jackson, MS 39216-4505

General Information State-supported, coed, upper-level institution. *Graduate housing:* On-campus housing not available. *Research affiliation:* NASA-Stennis Space Center (imaging technology), Catfish Genetics Research Unit (immunology), Oak Ridge National Laboratory (physiology, biomedical engineering), Gulf Coast Research Laboratory (microbiology).

GRADUATE UNITS

School of Dentistry Offers craniofacial and dental research (MS, PhD); dentistry (MS, DMD, PhD).

School of Graduate Studies in the Health Sciences ***Degree program information:*** Part-time programs available. Part-time. Offers biochemistry (PhD); biomedical materials science (MS, PhD); biomedical sciences (MS); clinical anatomy (MS, PhD); health sciences (MS, PhD); microbiology (PhD); neuroscience (PhD); pathology (PhD); pharmacology and toxicology (PhD); physiology and biophysics (PhD).

School of Health Related Professions ***Degree program information:*** Part-time programs available. Part-time. Offers health related professions (MOT, MPT); occupational therapy (MOT); physical therapy (MPT).

School of Medicine ***Degree program information:*** Part-time programs available. Part-time. Offers medicine (MD). Electronic applications accepted.

School of Nursing ***Degree program information:*** Part-time and evening/weekend programs available. Part-time, evening/weekend, online learning. Offers nursing (MSN, DNP, PhD). Electronic applications accepted.

UNIVERSITY OF MISSOURI, Columbia, MO 65211

General Information State-supported, coed, university. CGS member. *Graduate housing:* On-campus housing not available.

GRADUATE UNITS

College of Veterinary Medicine ***Financial support:*** Fellowships, research assistantships, teaching assistantships, career-related internships or fieldwork, institutionally sponsored loans, scholarships/grants, traineeships, health care benefits, tuition waivers (full and partial), and unspecified assistantships available. Support available to part-time students. Financial award applicants required to submit FAFSA. Offers veterinary medicine (MS, DVM, PhD). *Application deadline:* For fall admission, 1/5 for domestic and international students; for spring admission, 9/15 for domestic and international students; for summer admission, 1/5 for domestic and international students. *Application fee:* $65 ($90 for international students). Electronic applications accepted.

Graduate Programs in Veterinary Medicine Financial support: Fellowships with full tuition reimbursements, research assistantships with full tuition reimbursements, teaching assistantships with full tuition reimbursements, institutionally sponsored loans, scholarships/grants, traineeships, health care benefits, and unspecified assistantships available. Support available to part-time students. Offers biomedical sciences (MS, PhD); comparative medicine (MS); pathobiology (MS, PhD); veterinary medicine (MS, PhD); veterinary medicine and surgery (MS). *Application fee:* $55 ($75 for international students). Electronic applications accepted.

Office of Research and Graduate Studies ***Financial support:*** Fellowships with tuition reimbursements, research assistantships with tuition reimbursements, teaching assistantships with tuition reimbursements, career-related internships or fieldwork, Federal Work-Study, institutionally sponsored loans, scholarships/grants, traineeships, health care benefits, tuition waivers (full and partial), and unspecified assistantships available. Support available to part-time students. *Degree program information:* Part-time and evening/weekend programs available. Part-time, evening/weekend. Offers dispute resolution (LL M, Certificate, Graduate Certificate); genetics (PhD); global public health (Graduate Certificate); health administration (MHA); health informatics (MS, Certificate); health promotion and policy (MPH); neuroscience (MS, PhD, Graduate Certificate); public health (Graduate Certificate); veterinary public health (MPH).

Application deadline: Applications are processed on a rolling basis. *Application fee:* $55 ($75 for international students).

College of Agriculture, Food and Natural Resources Financial support: Fellowships with tuition reimbursements, research assistantships with tuition reimbursements, teaching assistantships with tuition reimbursements, institutionally sponsored loans, scholarships/grants, traineeships, health care benefits, and unspecified assistantships available. Support available to part-time students. *Degree program information:* Part-time programs available. Part-time. Offers agricultural economics (MS, PhD); agricultural education (MS, PhD); agriculture, food and natural resources (MS, PhD, Certificate, Graduate Certificate); agroforestry (MS, Certificate); animal sciences (MS, PhD); biochemistry (MS, PhD); conservation biology (Certificate, Graduate Certificate); conservation biology (interdisciplinary) (Certificate); crop, soil and pest management (MS, PhD); entomology (MS, PhD); fisheries and wildlife (MS, PhD); fisheries and wildlife sciences (MS, PhD); food science (MS, PhD); forestry (MS, PhD); geographical information science (interdisciplinary) (Certificate); horticulture (MS, PhD); human dimensions of natural resources (MS, PhD); parks, recreation and tourism (MS); plant biology and genetics (MS, PhD); plant stress biology (MS, PhD); rural sociology (MS, PhD); society and ecosystems (interdisciplinary) (Certificate); soil, environmental and atmospheric sciences (PhD); soil,environmental and atmospheric sciences (MS); water resources (MS, PhD). *Application deadline:* Applications are processed on a rolling basis. *Application fee:* $55 ($75 for international students). Electronic applications accepted.

College of Arts and Science Financial support: Fellowships with tuition reimbursements, research assistantships with tuition reimbursements, teaching assistantships with tuition reimbursements, career-related internships or fieldwork, institutionally sponsored loans, scholarships/grants, health care benefits, tuition waivers (full and partial), and unspecified assistantships available. Support available to part-time students. *Degree program information:* Part-time programs available. Part-time. Offers analytical chemistry (MS, PhD); anthropology (MA, PhD); applied mathematics (MS); art (MFA); art history and archaeology (MA, PhD); arts and science (MA, MFA, MM, MS, MST, PhD, Graduate Certificate); classical languages (MA, PhD); classical studies (MA, PhD); communication (MA, PhD); economics (MA, PhD); English (MA, PhD); evolutionary biology and ecology (MA, PhD); French (MA, PhD); geographic information science (Graduate Certificate); geography (MA); geological sciences (MS, PhD); German (MA); history (MA, PhD); literature (MA); mathematics (MA, MST, PhD); music (MA, MM); philosophy (PhD); physics and astronomy (MS, PhD); political science (MA, PhD); psychological sciences (MA, MS, PhD); religious studies (MA); sociology (PhD); Spanish (MA, PhD); statistics (MA, PhD); teaching (MA); theatre (MA, PhD). *Application deadline:* Applications are processed on a rolling basis. *Application fee:* $55 ($75 for international students). Electronic applications accepted.

College of Education Financial support: Fellowships, research assistantships, teaching assistantships, institutionally sponsored loans, scholarships/grants, traineeships, health care benefits, and unspecified assistantships available. Support available to part-time students. *Degree program information:* Part-time and evening/weekend programs available. Part-time, evening/weekend. Offers administration and supervision of special education (PhD); agricultural education (M Ed, PhD, Ed S); art education (M Ed, PhD, Ed S); behavior disorders (M Ed, PhD); business and office education (M Ed, PhD, Ed S); counseling psychology (M Ed, MA, PhD, Ed S); curriculum development of exceptional students (M Ed, PhD); early childhood education (M Ed, PhD, Ed S); early childhood special education (M Ed, PhD); education (M Ed, MA, Ed D, PhD, Certificate, Ed S); education administration (M Ed, MA, Ed D, PhD, Ed S); educational psychology (M Ed, MA, PhD, Ed S); educational technology (M Ed, Ed S); elementary education (M Ed, PhD, Ed S); English education (M Ed, PhD, Ed S); foreign language education (M Ed, PhD, Ed S); general special education (M Ed, MA, PhD); health education and promotion (M Ed, PhD); higher and adult education (M Ed, MA, Ed D, PhD, Ed S); information science and learning technology (PhD, Certificate); learning and instruction (M Ed); learning disabilities (M Ed, PhD); library science (MA); marketing education (M Ed, PhD, Ed S); mathematics education (M Ed, PhD, Ed S); mental retardation (M Ed, PhD); music education (M Ed, PhD, Ed S); reading education (M Ed, PhD, Ed S); school psychology (M Ed, MA, PhD, Ed S); science education (M Ed, PhD, Ed S); social studies education (M Ed, PhD, Ed S); vocational education (M Ed, PhD, Ed S). *Application deadline:* Applications are processed on a rolling basis. *Application fee:* $55 ($75 for international students).

College of Engineering Financial support: Fellowships, research assistantships, teaching assistantships, institutionally sponsored loans, scholarships/grants, traineeships, health care benefits, and unspecified assistantships available. Support available to part-time students. *Degree program information:* Part-time programs available. Part-time. Offers agricultural engineering (MS); biological engineering (MS, PhD); chemical engineering (MS, PhD); civil engineering (MS, PhD); computer science (MS, PhD); electrical and computer engineering (MS, PhD); engineering (M Eng, MS, PhD, Certificate); environmental and regulatory compliance (MS, PhD); environmental engineering (MS, PhD); geotechnical engineering (MS, PhD); industrial and manufacturing systems engineering (M Eng, MS, PhD); mechanical and aerospace engineering (MS, PhD); nuclear engineering (Certificate); structural engineering (MS, PhD); transportation and highway engineering (MS); water resources (MS, PhD). *Application deadline:* Applications are processed on a rolling basis. *Application fee:* $55 ($75 for international students).

College of Human Environmental Sciences Financial support: Fellowships with tuition reimbursements, research assistantships with tuition reimbursements, teaching assistantships with tuition reimbursements, institutionally sponsored loans, scholarships/grants, traineeships, health care benefits, and unspecified assistantships available. Support available to part-time students. *Degree program information:* Part-time programs available. Part-time. Offers architectural studies (M Arch, PhD); exercise physiology (MS); human development and family studies (MA, MS, PhD); human environmental sciences (MA, MS, PhD, Certificate, Graduate Certificate); nutrition sciences (MS); personal financial planning (MS, PhD, Certificate, Graduate Certificate); textile and apparel management (MS, PhD). *Application deadline:* Applications are processed on a rolling basis. *Application fee:* $55 ($75 for international students).

Harry S Truman School of Public Affairs Financial support: Fellowships, research assistantships, teaching assistantships, institutionally sponsored loans, scholarships/grants, traineeships, health care benefits, and unspecified assistantships available. Support available to part-time students. Offers grantsmanship (Graduate Certificate); nonprofit management (Graduate Certificate); organizational change (Graduate Certificate); public affairs (MPA, PhD); public management (Graduate Certificate); science and public policy (Graduate Certificate). *Application deadline:* For fall admission, 2/1 priority date for domestic and international students. Applications are processed on a rolling basis. *Application fee:* $55 ($75 for international students). Electronic applications accepted.

Informatics Institute Financial support: Scholarships/grants, health care benefits, and unspecified assistantships available. Support available to part-time students. Offers informatics (PhD). *Application deadline:* For fall admission, 1/15 priority date for domestic and international students. Applications are processed on a rolling basis. *Application fee:* $55 ($75 for international students). Electronic applications accepted.

Robert J. Trulaske, Sr. College of Business Financial support: Fellowships, research assistantships, teaching assistantships, and institutionally sponsored loans available. *Degree program information:* Part-time programs available. Part-time. Offers accountancy (M Acc, PhD); business (M Acc, MBA, PhD, Certificate); business administration (MBA); executive business administration (MBA); finance (PhD); management (PhD); marketing (PhD); taxation (Certificate). *Application deadline:* Applications are processed on a rolling basis. *Application fee:* $55 ($75 for international students).

School of Journalism Financial support: Fellowships with tuition reimbursements, research assistantships with tuition reimbursements, teaching assistantships with tuition reimbursements, career-related internships or fieldwork, institutionally sponsored loans, scholarships/grants, health care benefits, and unspecified assistantships available. Support available to part-time students. *Degree program information:* Part-time programs available. Part-time. Offers health communications (MA); journalism (PhD). *Application deadline:* For fall admission, 12/15 priority date for domestic and international students; for winter admission, 9/1 priority date for domestic and international students. Applications are processed on a rolling basis. *Application fee:* $55 ($75 for international students). Electronic applications accepted.

School of Social Work Financial support: Fellowships with tuition reimbursements, research assistantships with tuition reimbursements, teaching assistantships with tuition reimbursements, institutionally sponsored loans, scholarships/grants, health care benefits, and unspecified assistantships available. Support available to part-time students. *Degree program information:* Part-time programs available. Part-time. Offers gerontological social work (Certificate); military social work (Certificate); social work (MSW, PhD). *Application deadline:* For fall admission, 1/15 priority date for domestic and international students. Applications are processed on a rolling basis. *Application fee:* $55 ($75 for international students). Electronic applications accepted.

Sinclair School of Nursing Financial support: Fellowships, research assistantships, teaching assistantships, career-related internships or fieldwork, institutionally sponsored loans, scholarships/grants, traineeships, health care benefits, tuition waivers (full), and unspecified assistantships available. Support available to part-time students. *Degree program information:* Part-time programs available. Part-time. Offers adult-gerontology clinical nurse specialist (DNP, Certificate); family nurse practitioner (DNP); family psychiatric and mental health nurse practitioner (DNP); nursing (MS, PhD); nursing leadership and innovations in health care (DNP); pediatric clinical nurse specialist (DNP, Certificate); pediatric nurse practitioner (DNP). *Application deadline:* For fall admission, 2/1 priority date for domestic and international students. Applications are processed on a rolling basis. *Application fee:* $55 ($75 for international students). Electronic applications accepted.

School of Health Professions *Financial support:* Fellowships, research assistantships, teaching assistantships, and institutionally sponsored loans available. Offers communication science and disorders (MHS, PhD); diagnostic medical ultrasound (MHS); health professions (MHS, MOT, DPT, PhD); occupational therapy (MOT); physical therapy (DPT). *Application deadline:* For fall admission, 3/1 priority date for domestic students. Applications are processed on a rolling basis. *Application fee:* $55 ($75 for international students).

School of Law *Financial support:* Fellowships, Federal Work-Study, and institutionally sponsored loans available. Financial award application deadline: 3/1; financial award applicants required to submit FAFSA. Offers dispute resolution (LL M); law (JD). *Application deadline:* For fall admission, 3/1 priority date for domestic students. Applications are processed on a rolling basis.

School of Medicine *Financial support:* Fellowships, research assistantships, teaching assistantships, career-related internships or fieldwork, institutionally sponsored loans, and scholarships/grants available. Support available to part-time students. Financial award applicants required to submit FAFSA. *Degree program information:* Part-time programs available. Part-time. Offers family and community medicine (MS); health administration (MS); medical pharmacology and physiology (MS, PhD); medicine (MS, MD, PhD, Graduate Certificate); molecular microbiology and immunology (PhD); pathology and anatomical sciences (MS); public health (MS, Graduate Certificate). *Application deadline:* Applications are processed on a rolling basis.

UNIVERSITY OF MISSOURI–KANSAS CITY, Kansas City, MO 64110-2499

General Information State-supported, coed, university. CGS member. *Enrollment:* 16,699 graduate, professional, and undergraduate students; 3,369 full-time matriculated graduate/professional students (1,624 women), 1,894 part-time matriculated graduate/professional students (1,065 women). *Enrollment by degree level:* 2,631 master's, 2,565 doctoral, 67 other advanced degrees. *Graduate faculty:* 731 full-time (337 women), 441 part-time/adjunct (211 women). *Graduate housing:* Room and/or apartments available on a first-come, first-served basis to single students; on-campus housing not available to married students. *Student services:* Campus employment opportunities, campus safety program, career counseling, child daycare facilities, exercise/wellness program, free psychological counseling, international student services, multicultural affairs office, services for students with disabilities, teacher training, writing training. *Library:* Miller-Nichols Library plus 3 others. *Research affiliation:* Children's Mercy Hospital (health sciences), Truman Medical Center (health sciences), Veterans Administration Hospital (health sciences), Midwest Research Institute (health sciences), St. Luke's Hospital (health sciences).

Computer facilities: Computer purchase and lease plans are available. 400 computers available on campus for general student use. A campuswide network can be accessed from student residence rooms and from off campus. Online class registration is available.

Website: http://www.umkc.edu/

General Application Contact: Tamera Byland, Director of Admissions, 816-235-1111, Fax: 816-235-5544, E-mail: admit@umkc.edu.

GRADUATE UNITS

College of Arts and Sciences Students: 282 full-time (178 women), 263 part-time (147 women); includes 103 minority (56 Black or African American, non-Hispanic/Latino; 3 American Indian or Alaska Native, non-Hispanic/Latino; 6 Asian, non-Hispanic/Latino; 31 Hispanic/Latino; 7 Two or more races, non-Hispanic/Latino), 68 international. Average age 31. 577 applicants, 42% accepted, 194 enrolled. *Faculty:* 225 full-time (97 women), 140 part-time/adjunct (70 women). *Financial support:* In 2015–16, 72 research assistantships with tuition reimbursements (averaging $12,040 per year), 175 teaching assistantships with tuition reimbursements (averaging $11,227 per year) were awarded; career-related internships or fieldwork, Federal Work-Study, institutionally sponsored loans, scholarships/grants, and tuition waivers (full and partial) also available. Support available to part-time students. Financial award application deadline: 3/1; financial award applicants required to submit FAFSA. In 2015, 228 master's, 3 doctorates awarded. *Degree program information:* Part-time and evening/weekend programs available. Part-time, evening/weekend. Offers acting (MFA); analytical chemistry (MS, PhD); art history (MA, PhD); arts and sciences (MA, MFA, MS, MSW, PhD); clinical psychology (PhD); community psychology (PhD); creative writing and media arts (MFA); criminal justice and criminology (MS); design technology (MFA); economics (MA, PhD); English (MA, PhD); environmental and urban geosciences (MS); geosciences (PhD); health psychology (PhD); history (MA, PhD); inorganic chemistry (MS, PhD); mathematics and statistics (MA, MS, PhD); organic chemistry (MS, PhD); physical chemistry (MS, PhD); physics (MS, PhD); political science (MA); polymer chemistry (MS, PhD); psychology (MA); romance languages and literatures (MA); social work (MSW); sociology (MA); studio art (MA); theatre (MA). *Application deadline:* Applications are processed on a rolling basis. *Application fee:* $45 ($50 for international students). Electronic applications accepted. *Application Contact:* Tamera Byland, Director of Admissions, 816-235-1111, Fax: 816-235-5544, E-mail: admit@umkc.edu. *Dean*, Dr. Wayne Vaught, 816-235-5421, Fax: 816-235-1308.

Conservatory of Music and Dance Students: 166 full-time (67 women), 54 part-time (25 women); includes 23 minority (5 Black or African American, non-Hispanic/Latino; 8 Asian, non-Hispanic/Latino; 8 Hispanic/Latino; 2 Two or more races, non-Hispanic/Latino), 43 international. Average age 29. 347 applicants, 46% accepted, 58 enrolled. *Faculty:* 54 full-time (21 women), 39 part-time/adjunct (14 women). *Financial support:* In 2015–16, 40 teaching assistantships with partial tuition reimbursements (averaging $8,114 per year) were awarded; career-related internships or fieldwork, Federal Work-Study, institutionally sponsored loans, scholarships/grants, tuition waivers (partial), and unspecified assistantships also available. Support available to part-time students. Financial award application deadline: 3/1; financial award applicants required to submit FAFSA. In 2015, 36 master's, 14 doctorates awarded. *Degree program information:* Part-time programs available. Part-time. Offers composition (MM, DMA); conducting (MM, DMA); music (MA); music education (MME, PhD); music history and literature (MM); music theory (MM); music therapy (MA); musicology (MM); performance (MM, DMA). PhD (interdisciplinary) offered through the School of Graduate Studies. *Application deadline:* For fall admission, 1/15 priority date for domestic students, 1/15 for international students. *Application fee:* $45 ($50 for international students). *Application Contact:* William Everett, Associate Dean for Graduate Studies, 816-235-2857, Fax: 816-235-5264, E-mail: everettw@umkc.edu. *Dean*, Peter Witte, 816-235-2731, Fax: 816-235-5265, E-mail: wittep@umkc.edu.

Henry W. Bloch School of Management Students: 240 full-time (108 women), 304 part-time (139 women); includes 72 minority (25 Black or African American, non-Hispanic/Latino; 1 American Indian or Alaska Native, non-Hispanic/Latino; 15 Asian, non-Hispanic/Latino; 21 Hispanic/Latino; 1 Native Hawaiian or other Pacific Islander, non-Hispanic/Latino; 9 Two or more races, non-Hispanic/Latino), 96 international. Average age 30. 386 applicants, 48% accepted, 187 enrolled. *Faculty:* 58 full-time (19 women), 35 part-time/adjunct (8 women). *Financial support:* In 2015–16, 39 research assistantships with partial tuition reimbursements (averaging $10,072 per year), 9 teaching assistantships with partial tuition reimbursements (averaging $16,307 per year) were awarded; career-related internships or fieldwork, Federal Work-Study, institutionally sponsored loans, scholarships/grants, tuition waivers (full and partial), and unspecified assistantships also available. Support available to part-time students. Financial award application deadline: 3/1; financial award applicants required to submit FAFSA. In 2015, 288 master's awarded. *Degree program information:* Part-time and evening/weekend programs available. Part-time, evening/weekend. Offers accounting (MS); business administration (MBA); entrepreneurial real estate (MERE); entrepreneurship and innovation (PhD); finance (MS); public affairs (MPA, PhD). PhD (interdisciplinary) offered through the School of Graduate Studies. *Application deadline:* For fall admission, 5/1 priority date for domestic and international students; for spring admission, 10/1 priority date for domestic and international students. Applications are processed on a rolling basis. *Application fee:* $45 ($50 for international students). Electronic applications accepted. *Application Contact:* 816-235-1111, E-mail: admit@umkc.edu. *Dean*, Dr. David Donnelly, 816-235-1333, Fax: 816-235-2206, E-mail: donnellyd@umkc.edu.

School of Biological Sciences Students: 5 full-time (3 women), 12 part-time (3 women); includes 6 minority (1 Black or African American, non-Hispanic/Latino; 2 Asian, non-Hispanic/Latino; 2 Hispanic/Latino; 1 Two or more races, non-Hispanic/Latino), 1 international. Average age 26. 66 applicants, 26% accepted, 10 enrolled. *Faculty:* 31 full-time (9 women), 3 part-time/adjunct (2 women). *Financial support:* In 2015–16, 11 research assistantships with full tuition reimbursements (averaging $24,189 per year), 17 teaching assistantships with full tuition reimbursements (averaging $15,312 per year) were awarded; Federal Work-Study, institutionally sponsored loans, scholarships/grants, tuition waivers (full and partial), and unspecified assistantships also available. Support available to part-time students. Financial award application deadline: 3/1; financial award applicants required to submit FAFSA. In 2015, 22 master's awarded. *Degree program information:* Part-time and evening/weekend programs available. Part-time, evening/weekend. Offers biology (MA); cell biology and biophysics (PhD); cellular and molecular biology (MS); molecular biology and biochemistry (PhD). PhD (interdisciplinary) offered through the School of Graduate Studies. *Application deadline:* For fall admission, 2/15 priority date for domestic and international students. Applications are processed on a rolling basis. *Application fee:* $45 ($50 for international students). *Application Contact:* Information Contact, 816-235-1330, Fax: 816-235-5158, E-mail: sbsgradrecruit@umkc.edu. *Dean*, Dr. Theodore White, 816-235-2538, Fax: 816-235-5158, E-mail: whitetc@umkc.edu.

School of Computing and Engineering Students: 547 full-time (155 women), 195 part-time (47 women); includes 14 minority (5 Black or African American, non-Hispanic/Latino; 5 Asian, non-Hispanic/Latino; 3 Hispanic/Latino; 1 Two or more races, non-Hispanic/Latino), 663 international. Average age 24. 1,409 applicants, 43% accepted, 256 enrolled. *Faculty:* 44 full-time (6 women), 24 part-time/adjunct (1 woman). *Financial support:* In 2015–16, 28 research assistantships with partial tuition reimbursements (averaging $15,755 per year), 25 teaching assistantships with partial tuition reimbursements (averaging $19,970 per year) were awarded; career-related internships or fieldwork, Federal Work-Study, scholarships/grants, tuition waivers (partial), and unspecified assistantships also available. Support available to part-time students. Financial award application deadline: 3/1; financial award applicants required to submit FAFSA. In 2015, 274 master's, 3 other advanced degrees awarded. *Degree program information:* Part-time programs available. Part-time. Offers civil engineering (MS); computer and electrical engineering (PhD); computer science (MS); computer science and informatics (PhD); computing (PhD); electrical engineering (MS); engineering (PhD); engineering and construction management (Graduate Certificate); mechanical engineering (MS); telecommunications and computer networking (PhD). PhD (interdisciplinary) offered through the School of Graduate Studies. *Application deadline:* For fall admission, 1/15 priority date for domestic students, 1/15 for international students. Applications are processed on a rolling basis. *Application fee:* $45 ($50 for international students). *Application Contact:* 816-235-2399, Fax: 816-235-5159. *Dean*, Dr. Kevin Z. Truman, 816-235-2399, Fax: 816-235-5159.

School of Dentistry Students: 432 full-time (184 women), 54 part-time (26 women); includes 99 minority (12 Black or African American, non-Hispanic/Latino; 3 American Indian or Alaska Native, non-Hispanic/Latino; 46 Asian, non-Hispanic/Latino; 28 Hispanic/Latino; 10 Two or more races, non-Hispanic/Latino), 3 international. Average age 27. 793 applicants, 17% accepted, 129 enrolled. *Faculty:* 84 full-time (38 women), 56 part-time/adjunct (16 women). *Financial support:* In 2015–16, 1 research assistantship (averaging $22,000 per year) was awarded; career-related internships or fieldwork, Federal Work-Study, institutionally sponsored loans, and tuition waivers (full and partial) also available. Support available to part-time students. Financial award application deadline: 3/1; financial award applicants required to submit FAFSA. In 2015, 7 master's, 107 doctorates, 17 other advanced degrees awarded. Offers advanced education in dentistry (Graduate Dental Certificate); dental hygiene education (MS); dentistry (DDS); endodontics (Graduate Dental Certificate); oral and maxillofacial surgery (Graduate Dental Certificate); oral biology (MS, PhD); orthodontics and dentofacial orthopedics (Graduate Dental Certificate); periodontics (Graduate Dental Certificate). PhD (interdisciplinary) offered through the School of Graduate Studies. *Application deadline:* For fall admission, 2/1 for domestic and international students. *Application fee:* $45 ($50 for international students). *Application Contact:* Richard Bigham, Assistant Dean for Student Programs, 816-235-2082, E-mail: bighamr@umkc.edu. *Dean*, Dr. Marsha Pyle, 816-235-2010, E-mail: pylem@umkc.edu.

School of Education Students: 187 full-time (136 women), 379 part-time (281 women); includes 136 minority (85 Black or African American, non-Hispanic/Latino; 5 American Indian or Alaska Native, non-Hispanic/Latino; 10 Asian, non-Hispanic/Latino; 30 Hispanic/Latino; 6 Two or more races, non-Hispanic/Latino), 28 international. Average age 33. 430 applicants, 52% accepted, 220 enrolled. *Faculty:* 35 full-time (26 women), 67 part-time/adjunct (45 women). *Financial support:* In 2015–16, 12 research assistantships with partial tuition reimbursements (averaging $13,509 per year) were awarded; career-related internships or fieldwork, Federal Work-Study, institutionally sponsored loans, and tuition waivers (full and partial) also available. Support available to part-time students. Financial award application deadline: 3/1; financial award applicants required to submit FAFSA. In 2015, 175 master's, 11 doctorates, 30 other advanced degrees awarded. *Degree program information:* Part-time and evening/weekend programs available. Part-time, evening/weekend. Offers administration (Ed D); counseling and guidance (MA, Ed S); counseling psychology (PhD); curriculum and instruction (MA, Ed S); education (PhD); educational administration (MA, Ed S); reading education (MA); special education (MA). PhD in education offered through the School of Graduate Studies. *Application deadline:* For fall admission, 4/1 priority date for domestic and international students; for spring admission, 11/1 priority date for domestic and international students. Applications are processed on a rolling basis. *Application fee:* $45 ($50 for international students). *Application Contact:* Erica Hernandez-Scott, Student Recruiter, 816-235-1295, Fax: 816-235-5270, E-mail: hernandeze@umkc.edu. *Interim Dean*, Chris Brown, 816-235-2234, Fax: 816-235-5270, E-mail: education@umkc.edu.

School of Graduate Studies Students: 73 full-time (22 women), 287 part-time (110 women); includes 41 minority (17 Black or African American, non-Hispanic/Latino; 8 Asian, non-Hispanic/Latino; 13 Hispanic/Latino; 3 Two or more races, non-Hispanic/Latino), 151 international. Average age 35. 238 applicants, 33% accepted, 66 enrolled. *Financial support:* Career-related internships or fieldwork, Federal Work-Study, tuition waivers (partial), and unspecified assistantships available. Support available to part-time students. Financial award application deadline: 3/1; financial award applicants required to submit FAFSA. In 2015, 47 doctorates awarded. Offers interdisciplinary studies (PhD). *Application deadline:* For fall admission, 1/15 priority date for domestic and international students. Applications are processed on a rolling basis. *Application fee:* $45 ($50 for international students). Electronic applications accepted. *Application Contact:* Quincy Bennett Johnson, Coordinator of Admissions and Recruitment, Interdisciplinary PhD Program, 816-235-1559, Fax: 816-235-1310, E-mail: bennettq@umkc.edu. *Dean*, Dr. Denis M. Medeiros, 816-235-1301, Fax: 816-235-1310, E-mail: medeirosd@umkc.edu.

School of Law Students: 445 full-time (197 women), 48 part-time (23 women); includes 82 minority (22 Black or African American, non-Hispanic/Latino; 1 American Indian or Alaska Native, non-Hispanic/Latino; 12 Asian, non-Hispanic/Latino; 41 Hispanic/Latino; 6 Two or more races, non-Hispanic/Latino), 28 international. Average age 27. 556 applicants, 27% accepted, 152 enrolled. *Faculty:* 35 full-time (18 women), 7 part-time/adjunct (1 woman). *Financial support:* In 2015–16, 26 teaching assistantships with partial tuition reimbursements (averaging $2,412 per year) were awarded; career-related internships or fieldwork, Federal Work-Study, institutionally sponsored loans, scholarships/grants, and tuition waivers (full and partial) also available. Support available to part-time students. Financial award application deadline: 3/1; financial award applicants required to submit FAFSA. In 2015, 29 master's, 141 doctorates awarded. *Degree program information:* Part-time programs available. Part-time. Offers law (LL M, JD). *Application deadline:* For fall admission, 3/1 priority date for domestic and international students. Applications are processed on a rolling basis. *Application fee:* $50. Electronic applications accepted. *Application Contact:* Lydia Dagenais, Director of Law School Admissions, 816-235-1677, Fax: 816-235-5276, E-mail: dagenaisl@umkc.edu. *Dean*, Ellen Y. Suni, 816-235-1007, Fax: 816-235-5276, E-mail: sunie@umkc.edu.

School of Medicine Students: 483 full-time (255 women), 39 part-time (25 women); includes 254 minority (34 Black or African American, non-Hispanic/Latino; 3 American Indian or Alaska Native, non-Hispanic/Latino; 172 Asian, non-Hispanic/Latino; 16 Hispanic/Latino; 1 Native Hawaiian or other Pacific Islander, non-Hispanic/Latino; 28 Two or more races, non-Hispanic/Latino), 10 international. Average age 24. 1,004 applicants, 13% accepted, 104 enrolled. *Faculty:* 41 full-time (15 women), 15 part-time/adjunct (7 women). *Financial support:* In 2015–16, 3 fellowships (averaging $38,566 per year), 4 research assistantships (averaging $13,200 per year) were awarded; career-related internships or fieldwork, Federal Work-Study, institutionally sponsored loans, scholarships/grants, and tuition waivers (partial) also available. Financial award application deadline: 3/1; financial award applicants required to submit FAFSA. In 2015, 22 master's, 119 doctorates awarded. Offers anesthesia (MS); bioinformatics (MS); health professions education (MS); medicine (MD); physician assistant (MMS). *Application deadline:* For fall admission, 11/15 for domestic and international students. *Application fee:* $50. *Application Contact:* Janine Kluckhohn, Admissions Coordinator, 816-235-1870, Fax: 816-235-6579, E-mail: kluckhohnj@umkc.edu. *Dean*, Dr. Steven L. Kanter, MD, 816-235-1803, E-mail: kantersl@umkc.edu.

School of Nursing and Health Studies Students: 62 full-time (43 women), 259 part-time (239 women); includes 61 minority (28 Black or African American, non-Hispanic/Latino; 3 American Indian or Alaska Native, non-Hispanic/Latino; 16 Asian, non-Hispanic/Latino; 10 Hispanic/Latino; 4 Two or more races, non-Hispanic/Latino). Average age 35. 102 applicants, 35% accepted, 36 enrolled. *Faculty:* 44 full-time (40 women), 47 part-time/adjunct (45 women). *Financial support:* In 2015–16, 2 teaching assistantships with partial tuition reimbursements (averaging $6,650 per year) were awarded; fellowships, research assistantships, career-related internships or fieldwork, Federal Work-Study, institutionally sponsored loans, and tuition waivers (full and partial) also available. Support available to part-time students. Financial award application deadline: 3/1; financial award applicants required to submit FAFSA. In 2015, 116 master's, 23 doctorates awarded. *Degree program information:* Part-time programs available. Part-time, online learning. Offers adult clinical nurse specialist (MSN); adult clinical nursing practice (DNP); clinical nursing practice (DNP); family nurse practitioner (MSN); neonatal nurse practitioner (MSN); nurse educator (MSN); nurse executive (MSN); nursing (PhD); nursing practice (DNP); pediatric clinical nursing practice (DNP); pediatric nurse practitioner (MSN). *Application deadline:* For fall admission, 2/1 priority date for domestic and international students; for spring admission, 9/1 priority date for domestic and international students. *Application fee:* $45 ($50 for international students). *Application Contact:* Judy Jellison, Coordinator for Admissions and Recruitment, 816-235-1740, Fax: 816-235-1701, E-mail: jellisonj@umkc.edu. *Dean,* Dr. Ann Cary, 816-235-1723, Fax: 816-235-1701, E-mail: caryah@umkc.edu.

School of Pharmacy Students: 447 full-time (276 women); includes 103 minority (24 Black or African American, non-Hispanic/Latino; 1 American Indian or Alaska Native, non-Hispanic/Latino; 53 Asian, non-Hispanic/Latino; 12 Hispanic/Latino; 13 Two or more races, non-Hispanic/Latino), 2 international. Average age 25. 414 applicants, 33% accepted, 133 enrolled. *Faculty:* 49 full-time (26 women), 6 part-time/adjunct (2 women). *Financial support:* In 2015–16, 4 fellowships (averaging $40,082 per year), 14 research assistantships with tuition reimbursements (averaging $13,117 per year), 26 teaching assistantships with full tuition reimbursements (averaging $14,724 per year) were awarded; career-related internships or fieldwork, Federal Work-Study, institutionally sponsored loans, tuition waivers (full and partial), and unspecified assistantships also available. Financial award application deadline: 3/1; financial award applicants required to submit FAFSA. In 2015, 125 doctorates awarded. Online learning. Offers pharmaceutical sciences (PhD); pharmacology and toxicology (PhD); pharmacy (Pharm D). PhD offered through School of Graduate Studies. *Application deadline:* For fall admission, 3/1 for domestic and international students. Applications are processed on a rolling basis. *Application fee:* $45 ($50 for international students). Electronic applications accepted. *Application Contact:* Shelly M. Janasz, Director, Student Services, 816-235-2400, Fax: 816-235-5190, E-mail: janaszs@umkc.edu. *Dean,* Dr. Russell B. Melchert, 816-235-1609, Fax: 816-235-5190, E-mail: melchertr@umkc.edu.

UNIVERSITY OF MISSOURI–ST. LOUIS, St. Louis, MO 63121

General Information State-supported, coed, university. CGS member. *Enrollment:* 16,763 graduate, professional, and undergraduate students; 822 full-time matriculated graduate/professional students (529 women), 2,083 part-time matriculated graduate/professional students (1,378 women). *Enrollment by degree level:* 2,189 master's, 579 doctoral, 137 other advanced degrees. *Graduate faculty:* 377 full-time (173 women), 165 part-time/adjunct (92 women). *Graduate housing:* Rooms and/or apartments available on a first-come, first-served basis to single and married students. Housing application deadline: 7/1. *Student services:* Campus employment opportunities, campus safety program, career counseling, child daycare facilities, exercise/wellness program, free psychological counseling, grant writing training, international student services, low-cost health insurance, multicultural affairs office, services for students with disabilities, teacher training. *Library:* Thomas Jefferson Library plus 1 other. *Collection:* Books: 1.3 million (physical), 205,912 (digital/electronic); Serial titles: 1,105 (physical), 1,205 (digital/electronic); Databases: 204. Weekly public service hours: 82; students can reserve study rooms. *Research affiliation:* Express Scripts (business), St. Louis Zoo (biology), Missouri Botanical Garden (biology), Donald Danforth Plant Science Center (biology).

Computer facilities: Computer purchase and lease plans are available. 1,280 computers available on campus for general student use. A campuswide network can be accessed from student residence rooms and from off campus. Online class registration is available.
Website: http://www.umsl.edu/

General Application Contact: Graduate Admissions, 314-516-5458, Fax: 314-516-6996, E-mail: gradadm@umsl.edu.

GRADUATE UNITS

College of Arts and Sciences Students: 425 full-time (265 women), 361 part-time (196 women); includes 118 minority (66 Black or African American, non-Hispanic/Latino; 1 American Indian or Alaska Native, non-Hispanic/Latino; 22 Asian, non-Hispanic/Latino; 21 Hispanic/Latino; 1 Native Hawaiian or other Pacific Islander, non-Hispanic/Latino; 7 Two or more races, non-Hispanic/Latino), 104 international. Average age 31. 837 applicants, 45% accepted, 226 enrolled. *Faculty:* 202 full-time (78 women), 44 part-time/adjunct (15 women). *Financial support:* Research assistantships with tuition reimbursements, teaching assistantships with tuition reimbursements, career-related internships or fieldwork, Federal Work-Study, health care benefits, and unspecified assistantships available. Support available to part-time students. Financial award applicants required to submit FAFSA. *Degree program information:* Part-time and evening/weekend programs available. Part-time, evening/weekend. Offers American politics (MA); applied physics (MS); arts and sciences (MA, MFA, MS, MSW, PhD, Certificate); astrophysics (MS); behavioral neuroscience (MA, PhD); biochemistry and biotechnology (MS); biology (MS, PhD, Certificate); chemistry (MS, PhD); clinical psychology (PhD); clinical psychology respecialization (Certificate); comparative politics (MA); computer science (MS); creative writing (MFA); criminology and criminal justice (MA, PhD); economics (MA); English (MA); gerontology (MS, Certificate); history (MA); industrial/organizational psychology (MA, PhD); international politics (MA); mathematical and computational sciences (PhD); mathematics (MA); museum studies (MA, Certificate); philosophy (MA); physics (PhD); political process and behavior (MA); political science (PhD); public administration and public policy (MA); public history and cultural heritage (Certificate); trauma studies (Certificate); urban and regional politics (MA). *Application deadline:* For fall admission, 7/1 for domestic and international students; for spring admission, 12/1 for domestic and international students. *Application fee:* $50 ($40 for international students). Electronic applications accepted. *Application Contact:* Graduate Admissions, 314-516-5458, Fax: 314-516-6996, E-mail: gradadm@umsl.edu. *Dean,* Dr. Ronald Yasbin, 314-516-5501.

School of Social Work Students: 109 full-time (96 women), 69 part-time (54 women); includes 40 minority (31 Black or African American, non-Hispanic/Latino; 4 Asian, non-Hispanic/Latino; 3 Hispanic/Latino; 2 Two or more races, non-Hispanic/Latino), 1 international. Average age 32. 139 applicants, 53% accepted, 61 enrolled. *Faculty:* 11 full-time (9 women), 5 part-time/adjunct (4 women). *Financial support:* Research assistantships with tuition reimbursements and teaching assistantships with tuition reimbursements available. Financial award applicants required to submit FAFSA. Offers social work (MSW). *Application deadline:* For fall admission, 3/1 for domestic and international students; for spring admission, 10/15 for domestic and international students. *Application fee:* $50 ($40 for international students). Electronic applications accepted. *Application Contact:* 314-516-5458, Fax: 314-516-6996, E-mail: gradadm@umsl.edu. *Graduate Program Director,* Dr. Baorong Guo, 314-516-6618, Fax: 314-516-5816, E-mail: socialwork@umsl.edu.

College of Business Administration Students: 153 full-time (79 women), 381 part-time (153 women); includes 74 minority (27 Black or African American, non-Hispanic/Latino; 33 Asian, non-Hispanic/Latino; 10 Hispanic/Latino; 2 Native Hawaiian or other Pacific Islander, non-Hispanic/Latino; 2 Two or more races, non-Hispanic/Latino), 77 international. Average age 31. 278 applicants, 85% accepted, 164 enrolled. *Faculty:* 51 full-time (19 women), 19 part-time/adjunct (6 women). *Financial support:* Research assistantships with tuition reimbursements, teaching assistantships with tuition reimbursements, career-related internships or fieldwork, Federal Work-Study, and institutionally sponsored loans available. Support available to part-time students. Financial award application deadline: 4/1; financial award applicants required to submit FAFSA. *Degree program information:* Part-time and evening/weekend programs available. Part-time, evening/weekend. Offers accounting (MBA); business administration (M Acc, MBA, MS, PhD, Certificate); business intelligence (Certificate); cybersecurity (Certificate); digital and social media marketing (Certificate); finance (MBA); human resources management (Certificate); information systems (MBA); international business (MBA); logistics and supply chain management (MBA, PhD, Certificate); management (MBA); marketing (MBA); marketing management (Certificate); operations management (MBA). *Application deadline:* For fall admission, 7/1 priority date for domestic and international students; for spring admission, 12/1 priority date for domestic and international students. Applications are processed on a rolling basis. *Application fee:* $50 ($40 for international students). Electronic applications accepted. *Application Contact:* 314-516-5458, Fax: 314-516-6996, E-mail: gradadm@umsl.edu. *Dean,* Charles E. Hoffman, 314-516-5885, Fax: 314-516-6420.

College of Education Students: 206 full-time (155 women), 1,049 part-time (776 women); includes 357 minority (281 Black or African American, non-Hispanic/Latino; 5 American Indian or Alaska Native, non-Hispanic/Latino; 15 Asian, non-Hispanic/Latino; 36 Hispanic/Latino; 20 Two or more races, non-Hispanic/Latino), 23 international. Average age 34. 438 applicants, 84% accepted, 258 enrolled. *Faculty:* 59 full-time (35 women), 74 part-time/adjunct (53 women). *Financial support:* Research assistantships with tuition reimbursements and teaching assistantships with tuition reimbursements available. Financial award application deadline: 4/1; financial award applicants required to submit FAFSA. *Degree program information:* Part-time and evening/weekend programs available. Part-time, evening/weekend. Offers adult and higher education (M Ed); autism studies (Certificate); clinical mental health counseling (M Ed); community college leadership (Certificate); counseling (PhD); education (M Ed, Ed D, PhD, Certificate, Ed S); educational administration (M Ed, Ed S); educational leadership (Ed D, PhD); educational leadership and policy studies (PhD); educational practice (Ed D); educational psychology (M Ed, PhD); elementary education (M Ed); elementary school counseling (M Ed); program evaluation (Certificate); school psychology (Ed S); secondary education (M Ed); secondary school counseling (M Ed); special education (M Ed); teaching English to speakers of other languages (Certificate); teaching-learning processes (PhD). *Application deadline:* For fall admission, 7/1 priority date for domestic and international students; for spring admission, 12/1 priority date for domestic and international students. Applications are processed on a rolling basis. *Application fee:* $50 ($40 for international students). Electronic applications accepted. *Application Contact:* 314-516-5458, Fax: 314-516-6996, E-mail: gradadm@umsl.edu. *Dean,* Carole G. Basile, 314-516-5109, Fax: 314-516-5227, E-mail: basilec@umsl.edu.

College of Fine Arts and Communication Students: 7 full-time (4 women), 21 part-time (12 women); includes 6 minority (all Black or African American, non-Hispanic/Latino), 3 international. Average age 29. 12 applicants, 67% accepted, 6 enrolled. *Faculty:* 29 full-time (12 women), 9 part-time/adjunct (5 women). *Financial support:* Teaching assistantships available. Offers communication (MA); fine arts and communication (MA, MME); music (MME). *Application deadline:* For fall admission, 7/1 priority date for domestic and international students; for spring admission, 12/1 priority date for domestic and international students. Applications are processed on a rolling basis. *Application fee:* $50 ($40 for international students). Electronic applications accepted. *Application Contact:* 314-516-5458, Fax: 314-516-6996, E-mail: gradadm@umsl.edu. *Dean,* Dr. Jean Miller, 314-516-5911, Fax: 314-516-5910.

College of Nursing Students: 18 full-time (17 women), 227 part-time (215 women); includes 34 minority (22 Black or African American, non-Hispanic/Latino; 8 Asian, non-Hispanic/Latino; 3 Hispanic/Latino; 1 Two or more races, non-Hispanic/Latino), 1 international. Average age 35. 152 applicants, 69% accepted, 83 enrolled. *Faculty:* 21 full-time (19 women), 6 part-time/adjunct (5 women). *Financial support:* Research assistantships with tuition reimbursements available. Financial award application deadline: 4/1; financial award applicants required to submit FAFSA. *Degree program information:* Part-time programs available. Part-time. Offers adult/geriatric nurse practitioner (Post Master's Certificate); family nurse practitioner (Post Master's Certificate); nurse educator (MSN); nurse practitioner (MSN); nursing (DNP, PhD); pediatric nurse practitioner (Post Master's Certificate); psychiatric-mental health nurse practitioner (Post Master's Certificate); women's health nurse practitioner (Post Master's Certificate). *Application deadline:* For fall admission, 2/15 for domestic and international students. *Application fee:* $50 ($40 for international students). Electronic applications accepted. *Application Contact:* 314-516-5458, Fax: 314-516-6996, E-mail: gradadm@umsl.edu. *Director,* Dr. Roberta Lavin, 314-516-6066.

College of Optometry Students: 175 full-time (107 women); includes 21 minority (6 Black or African American, non-Hispanic/Latino; 1 American Indian or Alaska Native, non-Hispanic/Latino; 12 Asian, non-Hispanic/Latino; 2 Hispanic/Latino), 3 international. Average age 23. 403 applicants, 26% accepted, 45 enrolled. *Faculty:* 3 full-time (0 women), 2 part-time/adjunct (0 women). *Financial support:* Fellowships with full tuition reimbursements, research assistantships, Federal Work-Study, institutionally sponsored loans, and scholarships/grants available. Financial award applicants required to submit FAFSA. Offers optometry (OD). *Application deadline:* For fall admission, 2/15 for domestic and international students. Applications are processed on a rolling basis. *Application fee:* $50. Electronic applications accepted. *Application Contact:* Nick Palisch, Director, Student Services, 314-516-6263, Fax: 314-516-6708, E-mail: optstuaff@umsl.edu. *Dean,* Dr. Larry J. Davis, 314-516-5606, Fax: 314-516-6708, E-mail: optometry@umsl.edu.

Graduate School Students: 13 full-time (9 women), 44 part-time (26 women); includes 17 minority (12 Black or African American, non-Hispanic/Latino; 1 American Indian or Alaska Native, non-Hispanic/Latino; 4 Asian, non-Hispanic/Latino). 35 applicants, 80% accepted, 17 enrolled. *Faculty:* 1 (woman) full-time, 4 part-time/adjunct (2 women).

Financial support: Research assistantships with full tuition reimbursements available. Financial award application deadline: 4/1; financial award applicants required to submit FAFSA. *Degree program information:* Part-time and evening/weekend programs available. Part-time, evening/weekend. Offers local government management (MPPA, Certificate); managing human resources and organization (MPPA); nonprofit management and leadership (Certificate); nonprofit organization management and leadership (MPPA); policy and program evaluation (Certificate); policy research and analysis (MPPA). *Application deadline:* For fall admission, 7/1 priority date for domestic and international students; for spring admission, 12/1 priority date for domestic and international students. Applications are processed on a rolling basis. *Application fee:* $50 ($40 for international students). Electronic applications accepted. *Application Contact:* Graduate Admissions, 314-516-5458, Fax: 314-516-6996, E-mail: gradadm@umsl.edu. *Vice Provost for Graduate Studies and Research*, Christopher Spilling, 314-516-5437, Fax: 314-516-7015, E-mail: graduate@umsl.edu.

UNIVERSITY OF MOBILE, Mobile, AL 36613

General Information Independent-religious, coed, comprehensive institution. *Enrollment:* 1,566 graduate, professional, and undergraduate students; 33 full-time matriculated graduate/professional students (30 women), 91 part-time matriculated graduate/professional students (72 women). *Enrollment by degree level:* 124 master's. *Graduate faculty:* 16 full-time (11 women), 3 part-time/adjunct (1 woman). *Tuition, area resident:* Full-time $9036; part-time $6024 per credit hour. *Required fees:* $400. *Graduate housing:* Room and/or apartments available on a first-come, first-served basis to single students; on-campus housing not available to married students. Typical cost: $5200 per year ($9160 including board). Housing application deadline: 8/15. *Student services:* Campus employment opportunities, career counseling, free psychological counseling, international student services, low-cost health insurance. *Library:* J. L. Bedsole Library. *Collection:* Books: 66,089 (physical), 157,420 (digital/electronic).

Computer facilities: A campuswide network can be accessed from student residence rooms and from off campus. Online class registration is available.
Website: http://www.umobile.edu/

General Application Contact: Danielle M. Riley, Administrative Assistant for Graduate Programs, 251-442-2270, Fax: 251-442-2523, E-mail: driley@umobile.edu.

GRADUATE UNITS

Graduate Programs Students: 33 full-time (30 women), 91 part-time (72 women); includes 59 minority (53 Black or African American, non-Hispanic/Latino; 2 American Indian or Alaska Native, non-Hispanic/Latino; 4 Asian, non-Hispanic/Latino). Average age 36. 86 applicants, 81% accepted, 64 enrolled. *Faculty:* 12 full-time (10 women), 3 part-time/adjunct (1 woman). *Financial support:* Application deadline: 8/1; applicants required to submit FAFSA. In 2015, 39 master's awarded. *Degree program information:* Part-time and evening/weekend programs available. Part-time, evening/weekend. Offers business administration (MBA); education (MA); marriage and family counseling (MA); nursing (MSN). *Application deadline:* For fall admission, 8/1 priority date for domestic and international students. Applications are processed on a rolling basis. *Application fee:* $40 ($50 for international students). Electronic applications accepted. *Application Contact:* Danielle M. Riley, Administrative Assistant for Academic Affairs/Graduate Enrollment Counselor, 251-442-2270, Fax: 251-442-2523, E-mail: driley@umobile.edu. *Director*, Daniel B. Chancey, 251-442-2491, Fax: 251-442-2523, E-mail: dbchancey@umobile.edu.

UNIVERSITY OF MONTANA, Missoula, MT 59812-0002

General Information State-supported, coed, university. CGS member. *Graduate housing:* Rooms and/or apartments available on a first-come, first-served basis to single and married students. *Research affiliation:* Arthur Carhart National Wilderness Training Center (environmental research), Nature Center at Ft. Missoula Museum (environmental research), Rocky Mountain National Laboratories (medical research), Community Hospital Medical Center (medical research), Aldo Leopold Wilderness Institute (forestry).

GRADUATE UNITS

Graduate School ***Degree program information:*** Part-time programs available. Part-time. Offers individualized interdisciplinary studies (PhD); interdisciplinary studies (MIS).

College of Forestry and Conservation Offers fish and wildlife biology (PhD); forest and conservation sciences (PhD); forestry (MS); recreation management (MS); resource conservation (MS); systems ecology (MS, PhD); wildlife biology (MS).

College of Health Professions and Biomedical Sciences Offers biomedical and pharmaceutical sciences (MS, PhD); biomedical sciences (PhD); health professions and biomedical sciences (MPH, MS, MSW, DPT, PhD, Pharm D, CPH); medicinal chemistry (MS, PhD); molecular and cellular toxicology (MS, PhD); neuroscience (PhD); pharmaceutical sciences (MS); pharmacy (Pharm D); physical therapy (DPT); public health (MPH, CPH); social work (MSW).

College of Humanities and Sciences Degree program information: Part-time programs available. Part-time. Offers anthropology (MA, PhD); applied anthropology (PhD); applied medical anthropology (MA); cellular and developmental biology (PhD); cellular, molecular and microbial biology (PhD); chemistry (MS, PhD); clinical psychology (PhD); communication studies (MA); community and environmental planning (MA); computer science (MS); creative writing (MFA); criminology (MA); cultural heritage (MA, PhD); economics (MA); environmental studies (MS); experimental psychology (PhD); fiction (MFA); forensic anthropology (MA); French (MA); geography (MA, MS); geosciences (MS, PhD); German (MA); history (MA, PhD); humanities and sciences (MA, MFA, MPA, MS, PhD, Ed S); inequality and social justice (MA); linguistic anthropology (MA); linguistics (MA); literature (MA); mathematics (MA, PhD); mathematics education (MA); microbial evolution and ecology (PhD); microbiology and immunology (PhD); molecular biology and biochemistry (PhD); non-fiction (MFA); organismal biology and ecology (MS, PhD); philosophy (MA); poetry (MFA); political science (MA); public administration (MPA); rural and environmental change (MA); school psychology (MA, PhD, Ed S); sociology (MA); Spanish (MA); systems ecology (MS, PhD); teaching (MA).

College of Visual and Performing Arts Offers design/technology (MFA); digital filmmaking (MFA); fine arts (MA); integrated arts and education (MA); integrated digital media (MFA); performance (MM); photography (MFA); theatre (MA); visual and performing arts (MA, MFA, MM).

Phyllis J. Washington College of Education and Human Sciences Degree program information: Part-time programs available. Part-time. Offers clinical mental health counseling (MA); community health (MS); counseling and supervision (Ed D); counselor education (Ed S); curriculum and instruction (M Ed, Ed D); education and human sciences (M Ed, MA, MS, Ed D, Ed S); educational leadership (M Ed, Ed D, Ed S); exercise science (MS); health and human performance generalist (MS); intercultural youth and family development (MA); school counseling (MA).

School of Business Administration Degree program information: Part-time and evening/weekend programs available. Part-time, evening/weekend, online learning. Offers accounting (M Acct); business administration (M Acct, MBA).

School of Journalism Offers journalism (MA). Electronic applications accepted.

School of Law Offers law (JD).

UNIVERSITY OF MONTEVALLO, Montevallo, AL 35115

General Information State-supported, coed, comprehensive institution. *Enrollment:* 3,033 graduate, professional, and undergraduate students; 185 full-time matriculated graduate/professional students (149 women), 269 part-time matriculated graduate/professional students (182 women). *Enrollment by degree level:* 377 master's, 50 other advanced degrees. Tuition, state resident: full-time $9384. Tuition, nonresident: full-time $19,272. *Required fees:* $670. *Graduate housing:* Room and/or apartments guaranteed to single students; on-campus housing not available to married students. Typical cost: $4300 per year ($6900 including board). *Student services:* Campus employment opportunities, campus safety program, career counseling, free psychological counseling, international student services, low-cost health insurance, services for students with disabilities, writing training. *Library:* Carmichael Library.

Computer facilities: 340 computers available on campus for general student use. A campuswide network can be accessed from student residence rooms and from off campus. Online class registration is available.
Website: http://www.montevallo.edu/

General Application Contact: Kevin Thornthwaite, Director, Graduate Admissions and Records, 205-665-6350, E-mail: graduate@montevallo.edu.

GRADUATE UNITS

College of Arts and Sciences Students: 61 full-time (59 women), 9 part-time (5 women); includes 5 minority (2 Black or African American, non-Hispanic/Latino; 3 Hispanic/Latino). *Financial support:* Federal Work-Study, scholarships/grants, and unspecified assistantships available. In 2015, 24 master's awarded. *Degree program information:* Part-time and evening/weekend programs available. Part-time, evening/weekend. Offers arts and sciences (MA, MS); English literature (MA); speech-language pathology (MS). *Application deadline:* For fall admission, 7/15 for domestic students; for spring admission, 11/15 for domestic students. *Application fee:* $25. *Application Contact:* Kevin Thornthwaite, Director, Graduate Admissions and Records, 205-665-6350, E-mail: graduate@montevallo.edu. *Dean*, Dr. Mary Beth Armstrong, 205-665-6508.

College of Education Students: 107 full-time (80 women), 241 part-time (172 women); includes 73 minority (61 Black or African American, non-Hispanic/Latino; 1 American Indian or Alaska Native, non-Hispanic/Latino; 1 Asian, non-Hispanic/Latino; 7 Hispanic/Latino; 3 Two or more races, non-Hispanic/Latino). *Financial support:* Federal Work-Study, scholarships/grants, and unspecified assistantships available. In 2015, 96 master's, 13 Ed Ss awarded. *Degree program information:* Part-time and evening/weekend programs available. Part-time, evening/weekend. Offers clinical mental health (M Ed); couple, marriage and family (M Ed); education (M Ed, Ed S); educational administration (M Ed, Ed S); elementary education (M Ed); school counseling (M Ed); secondary/high school education (M Ed). *Application deadline:* For fall admission, 7/15 for domestic students; for spring admission, 11/15 for domestic students. *Application fee:* $25. *Application Contact:* Kevin Thornthwaite, Director, Graduate Admissions and Records, 205-665-6350, E-mail: graduate@montevallo.edu. *Dean*, Dr. Anna E. McEwan, 205-665-6360, E-mail: mcewanae@montevallo.edu.

Stephens College of Business Students: 17 full-time (10 women), 19 part-time (5 women); includes 10 minority (6 Black or African American, non-Hispanic/Latino; 2 Asian, non-Hispanic/Latino; 1 Hispanic/Latino; 1 Two or more races, non-Hispanic/Latino), 4 international. In 2015, 20 master's awarded. *Degree program information:* Part-time and evening/weekend programs available. Part-time, evening/weekend. Offers business (MBA). *Application deadline:* For fall admission, 7/15 for domestic students; for spring admission, 11/15 for domestic students. *Application fee:* $25. *Application Contact:* Kevin Thornthwaite, Director, Graduate Admissions and Records, 205-665-6350, E-mail: graduate@montevallo.edu. *Dean*, Dr. Stephen H. Craft, 205-665-6540.

UNIVERSITY OF MOUNT UNION, Alliance, OH 44601-3993

General Information Independent-religious, coed, comprehensive institution. *Enrollment:* 2,191 graduate, professional, and undergraduate students; 97 full-time matriculated graduate/professional students (66 women). *Enrollment by degree level:* 97 master's. *Graduate faculty:* 5 full-time (4 women), 2 part-time/adjunct (1 woman). *Graduate housing:* Room and/or apartments available on a first-come, first-served basis to single students; on-campus housing not available to married students. Typical cost: $6300 per year. *Student services:* Campus safety program, career counseling, exercise/wellness program, international student services, low-cost health insurance, multicultural affairs office, services for students with disabilities, writing training. *Library:* University of Mount Union Library plus 1 other. Study areas open 24 hours, 5–7 days a week; students can reserve study rooms.

Computer facilities: Computer purchase and lease plans are available. 265 computers available on campus for general student use. A campuswide network can be accessed from student residence rooms and from off campus. Online class registration is available.
Website: http://www.mountunion.edu/

General Application Contact: Jessie Canavan, Director of Admissions, 330-823-2579, E-mail: canavajl@mountunion.edu.

GRADUATE UNITS

Program in Educational Leadership Students: 34 full-time (18 women); includes 2 minority (both Hispanic/Latino), 1 international. 45 applicants, 67% accepted, 22 enrolled. *Faculty:* 1 (woman) full-time. *Financial support:* Applicants required to submit FAFSA. In 2015, 14 master's awarded. *Degree program information:* Part-time programs available. Part-time, online learning. Offers educational leadership (MA). *Application deadline:* For fall admission, 8/15 for domestic and international students. Applications are processed on a rolling basis. *Application fee:* $30. Electronic applications accepted. *Application Contact:* Jessie Canavan, Director of Admissions, 330-823-2579, E-mail: canavajl@mountunion.edu. *Director*, Dr. Melissa Askren-Edgehouse, 800-992-6682.

Program in Physician Assistant Studies Students: 63 full-time (48 women); includes 2 minority (both Two or more races, non-Hispanic/Latino). Average age 25. 250 applicants, 20% accepted, 34 enrolled. *Faculty:* 4 full-time (3 women), 2 part-time/adjunct (1 woman). *Financial support:* Applicants required to submit FAFSA. In 2015, 31 master's awarded. Offers physician assistant studies (MS). *Application deadline:* Applications are processed on a rolling basis. Electronic applications accepted. *Application Contact:* Jessie Canavan, Director of Admissions, 330-823-2579, E-mail: canavajl@mountunion.edu. *Director*, Betsey Ekey, 800-992-6682.

UNIVERSITY OF NEBRASKA AT KEARNEY, Kearney, NE 68849-0001

General Information State-supported, coed, comprehensive institution. CGS member. *Enrollment:* 6,747 graduate, professional, and undergraduate students; 181 full-time matriculated graduate/professional students (142 women), 1,044 part-time matriculated graduate/professional students (679 women). *Enrollment by degree level:* 1,163 master's, 62 other advanced degrees. *Graduate faculty:* 232 full-time (94 women). *Tuition, area resident:* Full-time $3965; part-time $220.25 per credit hour. Tuition, nonresident: full-time $8699; part-time $483.25 per credit hour. *Required fees:* $677; $21 per credit hour. $174. Part-time tuition and fees vary according to course load and program. *Graduate housing:* Rooms and/or apartments available on a first-come, first-served basis to single and married students. Typical cost: $4930 per year for single students; $5660 per year for married students. Room charges vary according to board plan and housing facility selected. Housing application deadline: 8/24. *Student services:* Campus employment opportunities, campus safety program, career counseling, child daycare facilities, exercise/wellness program, free psychological counseling, grant writing training, international student services, low-cost health insurance, multicultural affairs office, services for students with disabilities, teacher training, writing training. *Library:* Calvin T. Ryan Library.

Computer facilities: 600 computers available on campus for general student use. A campuswide network can be accessed from student residence rooms and from off campus. Online class registration, online degree audit, online personal information update, online bill viewing and payment, online financial aid awards and acceptance are available.
Website: http://www.unk.edu/

General Application Contact: Linda Johnson, Director, Graduate Admissions and Programs, 800-717-7881, Fax: 308-865-8837, E-mail: gradstudies@unk.edu.

GRADUATE UNITS

Graduate Studies and Research Students: 181 full-time (142 women), 1,044 part-time (679 women); includes 107 minority (22 Black or African American, non-Hispanic/Latino; 3 American Indian or Alaska Native, non-Hispanic/Latino; 7 Asian, non-Hispanic/Latino; 56 Hispanic/Latino; 1 Native Hawaiian or other Pacific Islander, non-Hispanic/Latino; 18 Two or more races, non-Hispanic/Latino), 12 international. 437 applicants, 81% accepted, 270 enrolled. *Faculty:* 214 full-time (76 women). *Financial support:* In 2015–16, 37 research assistantships with full tuition reimbursements (averaging $9,900 per year), 29 teaching assistantships with full tuition reimbursements (averaging $9,900 per year) were awarded; career-related internships or fieldwork, scholarships/grants, health care benefits, and unspecified assistantships also available. Support available to part-time students. Financial award application deadline: 2/28; financial award applicants required to submit FAFSA. In 2015, 392 master's, 20 other advanced degrees awarded. *Degree program information:* Part-time and evening/weekend programs available. Part-time, evening/weekend, 100% online, blended/hybrid learning. *Application deadline:* For fall admission, 6/15 for domestic and international students; for spring admission, 10/15 for domestic and international students; for summer admission, 3/15 for domestic and international students. *Application fee:* $45. Electronic applications accepted. *Application Contact:* Linda Johnson, Director, Graduate Admissions and Programs, 800-717-7881, Fax: 308-865-8837, E-mail: johnsonli@unk.edu. *Dean,* Dr. Kenya Taylor, 800-717-8771, Fax: 308-865-8837, E-mail: taylorks@unk.edu.

College of Business and Technology Students: 5 full-time (4 women), 27 part-time (13 women); includes 3 minority (1 Asian, non-Hispanic/Latino; 2 Hispanic/Latino), 2 international. Average age 31. 24 applicants, 79% accepted, 14 enrolled. *Faculty:* 34 full-time (15 women). *Financial support:* In 2015–16, 2 research assistantships with full tuition reimbursements (averaging $11,500 per year), 2 teaching assistantships with full tuition reimbursements (averaging $11,500 per year) were awarded; career-related internships or fieldwork, scholarships/grants, health care benefits, and unspecified assistantships also available. Support available to part-time students. Financial award application deadline: 2/28; financial award applicants required to submit FAFSA. In 2015, 13 master's awarded. *Degree program information:* Part-time and evening/weekend programs available. Part-time, evening/weekend. Offers accounting (MBA); business and technology (MBA); generalist (MBA); human resources (MBA); human services (MBA); marketing (MBA). *Application deadline:* For fall admission, 6/15 for domestic and international students; for spring admission, 10/15 for domestic and international students; for summer admission, 3/15 for domestic and international students. *Application fee:* $45. Electronic applications accepted. *Application Contact:* Linda Johnson, Director, Graduate Admissions and Programs, 800-717-7881, Fax: 308-865-8837, E-mail: gradstudies@unk.edu. *Graduate Program Chair,* Dr. Sri Seshadri, 308-865-8190, Fax: 308-865-8114, E-mail: seshadris@unk.edu.

College of Education Students: 130 full-time (104 women), 532 part-time (369 women); includes 41 minority (8 Black or African American, non-Hispanic/Latino; 3 Asian, non-Hispanic/Latino; 25 Hispanic/Latino; 5 Two or more races, non-Hispanic/Latino), 5 international. Average age 31. 257 applicants, 75% accepted, 155 enrolled. *Faculty:* 40 full-time (20 women). *Financial support:* In 2015–16, 23 students received support, including 16 research assistantships with full tuition reimbursements available (averaging $11,500 per year), 7 teaching assistantships with full tuition reimbursements available (averaging $11,500 per year); career-related internships or fieldwork, scholarships/grants, health care benefits, and unspecified assistantships also available. Support available to part-time students. Financial award application deadline: 2/28; financial award applicants required to submit FAFSA. In 2015, 174 master's, 15 Ed Ss awarded. *Degree program information:* Part-time and evening/weekend programs available. Part-time, evening/weekend, 100% online. Offers clinical mental health counseling (MS Ed); curriculum and instruction (MA Ed); curriculum supervisor of academic area (MA Ed); education (MA Ed, MS Ed, Ed S); general physical education (MA Ed); instructional technology (MS Ed); physical education exercise science (MA Ed); physical education master teacher (MA Ed); reading PK-12 (MA Ed); school counseling (MS Ed); school principalship 7-12 (MA Ed); school principalship PK-8 (MA Ed); school psychology (Ed S); school superintendent (Ed S); special education (MA Ed); speech/language pathology (MS Ed); student affairs (MS Ed); supervisor of special education (MA Ed). *Application deadline:* For fall admission, 6/15 for domestic and international students; for spring admission, 10/15 for domestic and international students; for summer admission, 3/15 for domestic and international students. *Application fee:* $45. Electronic applications accepted. *Application Contact:* Linda Johnson, Director, Graduate Admissions and Programs, 800-717-7881, Fax: 308-865-8837, E-mail: johnsonli@unk.edu. *Dean,* Dr. Sheryl Feinstein, 308-865-8502.

College of Fine Arts and Humanities Students: 4 full-time (all women), 128 part-time (100 women); includes 15 minority (3 Black or African American, non-Hispanic/Latino; 1 American Indian or Alaska Native, non-Hispanic/Latino; 9 Hispanic/Latino; 2 Two or more races, non-Hispanic/Latino), 3 international. Average age 33. 35 applicants, 86% accepted, 23 enrolled. *Faculty:* 43 full-time (20 women). *Financial support:* In 2015–16, 4 students received support, including 1 research assistantship with full tuition reimbursement available (averaging $11,500 per year), 3 teaching assistantships with full tuition reimbursements available (averaging $11,500 per year); career-related internships or fieldwork, scholarships/grants, health care benefits, and unspecified assistantships also available. Support available to part-time students. Financial award application deadline: 2/28; financial award applicants required to submit FAFSA. In 2015, 35 master's awarded. *Degree program information:* Part-time and evening/weekend programs available. Part-time, evening/weekend, 100% online. Offers art education (MA Ed); children and adolescent literature (MA); creative writing (MA); fine arts and humanities (MA, MA Ed); literature (MA); music education (MA Ed); Spanish education (MA Ed). *Application deadline:* For fall admission, 6/15 for domestic and international students; for spring admission, 10/15 for domestic and international students; for summer admission, 2/15 for domestic students, 3/15 for international students. *Application fee:* $45. Electronic applications accepted. *Application Contact:* Linda Johnson, Director, Graduate Admissions and Programs, 800-717-7881, Fax: 308-865-8837, E-mail: gradstudies@unk.edu. *Dean,* Dr. William Jurma, 308-865-8521, E-mail: jurmaw@unk.edu.

College of Natural and Social Sciences Students: 43 full-time (30 women), 357 part-time (197 women); includes 48 minority (11 Black or African American, non-Hispanic/Latino; 2 American Indian or Alaska Native, non-Hispanic/Latino; 3 Asian, non-Hispanic/Latino; 20 Hispanic/Latino; 1 Native Hawaiian or other Pacific Islander, non-Hispanic/Latino; 11 Two or more races, non-Hispanic/Latino), 2 international. Average age 34. 121 applicants, 93% accepted, 78 enrolled. *Faculty:* 30 full-time (10 women). *Financial support:* Research assistantships, teaching assistantships, career-related internships or fieldwork, scholarships/grants, health care benefits, and unspecified assistantships available. Support available to part-time students. Financial award application deadline: 3/1; financial award applicants required to submit FAFSA. In 2015, 114 master's awarded. *Degree program information:* Part-time and evening/weekend programs available. Part-time, evening/weekend, online learning. Offers biology (MS); history (MA); natural and social sciences (MA, MA Ed, MS); science/math education (MA Ed). *Application deadline:* For fall admission, 6/15 for domestic and international students; for spring admission, 10/15 for domestic and international students; for summer admission, 3/15 for domestic and international students. *Application fee:* $45. Electronic applications accepted. *Application Contact:* Linda Johnson, Graduate Studies and Research Director, 800-717-7881, E-mail: gradstudies@unk.edu. *Dean,* Dr. John LaDuke, 308-865-8518, Fax: 308-865-8880, E-mail: ladukejc@unk.edu.

UNIVERSITY OF NEBRASKA AT OMAHA, Omaha, NE 68182

General Information State-supported, coed, university. CGS member. *Enrollment:* 882 full-time matriculated graduate/professional students (504 women), 1,750 part-time matriculated graduate/professional students (1,020 women). *Enrollment by degree level:* 2,367 master's, 197 doctoral, 68 other advanced degrees. *Graduate faculty:* 229 full-time (113 women). *Graduate housing:* Room and/or apartments available on a first-come, first-served basis to single students; on-campus housing not available to married students. *Student services:* Campus employment opportunities, campus safety program, career counseling, child daycare facilities, exercise/wellness program, free psychological counseling, grant writing training, international student services, low-cost health insurance, multicultural affairs office, services for students with disabilities, teacher training, writing training. *Library:* Criss Library.

Computer facilities: Computer purchase and lease plans are available. 2,450 computers available on campus for general student use. A campuswide network can be accessed from student residence rooms and from off campus. Online class registration is available.
Website: http://www.unomaha.edu/

General Application Contact: Jerilyn Kamm, Director of Graduate Admissions and Academic Services, 402-554-2341, Fax: 402-554-3143, E-mail: graduate@unomaha.edu.

GRADUATE UNITS

Graduate Studies Students: 882 full-time (504 women), 1,750 part-time (1,020 women); includes 328 minority (99 Black or African American, non-Hispanic/Latino; 6 American Indian or Alaska Native, non-Hispanic/Latino; 51 Asian, non-Hispanic/Latino; 107 Hispanic/Latino; 65 Two or more races, non-Hispanic/Latino), 394 international. Average age 31. 2,184 applicants, 48% accepted, 716 enrolled. *Faculty:* 229 full-time (113 women). *Financial support:* In 2015–16, 323 students received support, including 170 research assistantships with tuition reimbursements available, 153 teaching assistantships with tuition reimbursements available; fellowships with tuition reimbursements available, career-related internships or fieldwork, Federal Work-Study, institutionally sponsored loans, health care benefits, tuition waivers (partial), and unspecified assistantships also available. Support available to part-time students. Financial award application deadline: 3/1; financial award applicants required to submit FAFSA. In 2015, 875 master's, 30 doctorates, 64 other advanced degrees awarded. *Degree program information:* Part-time and evening/weekend programs available. Part-time, evening/weekend, online learning. *Application deadline:* Applications are processed on a rolling basis. *Application fee:* $45. Electronic applications accepted. *Dean of Graduate Studies,* Dr. Deborah Smith-Howell, 402-554-2341, E-mail: graduate@unomaha.edu.

College of Arts and Sciences Students: 126 full-time (79 women), 315 part-time (166 women); includes 51 minority (12 Black or African American, non-Hispanic/Latino; 1 American Indian or Alaska Native, non-Hispanic/Latino; 6 Asian, non-Hispanic/Latino; 25 Hispanic/Latino; 7 Two or more races, non-Hispanic/Latino), 21 international. Average age 30. 339 applicants, 47% accepted, 131 enrolled. *Faculty:* 88 full-time (39 women). *Financial support:* In 2015–16, 118 students received support, including 25 research assistantships with tuition reimbursements available, 93 teaching assistantships with tuition reimbursements available; fellowships with tuition reimbursements available, career-related internships or fieldwork, Federal Work-Study, institutionally sponsored loans, scholarships/grants, health care benefits, tuition waivers (partial), and unspecified assistantships also available. Support available to part-time students. Financial award application deadline: 3/1; financial award applicants required to submit FAFSA. In 2015, 136 master's, 6 doctorates, 28 other advanced degrees awarded. *Degree program information:* Part-time and evening/weekend programs available. Part-time, evening/weekend, online learning. Offers advanced writing (Certificate); American government (Certificate); applied behavior analysis (Certificate); arts and sciences (MA, MAT, MS, PhD, Certificate, Ed S); biology (MS); business for bioscientists (Certificate); critical and creative thinking (MA); English (MA); geographic information science (Certificate); geography (MA); global information operations (Certificate); history (MA); human resources and training (Certificate); industrial/organizational psychology (MS); intelligence and national security (Certificate); language teaching (MA); mathematics (MA, MAT, MS);

political science (MS); psychology (MA, PhD); school psychology (MS, Ed S); sociology (MA); teaching English to speakers of other languages (Certificate); technical communication (Certificate). *Application deadline:* Applications are processed on a rolling basis. *Application fee:* $45. Electronic applications accepted. *Dean,* Dr. David Boocker, 402-554-2341, E-mail: graduate@unomaha.edu.

College of Business Administration Students: 105 full-time (42 women), 290 part-time (111 women); includes 44 minority (10 Black or African American, non-Hispanic/Latino; 1 American Indian or Alaska Native, non-Hispanic/Latino; 12 Asian, non-Hispanic/Latino; 9 Hispanic/Latino; 12 Two or more races, non-Hispanic/Latino), 56 international. Average age 30. 234 applicants, 50% accepted, 93 enrolled. *Faculty:* 23 full-time (11 women). *Financial support:* In 2015–16, 27 students received support, including 19 research assistantships with tuition reimbursements available, 8 teaching assistantships with tuition reimbursements available; fellowships, career-related internships or fieldwork, Federal Work-Study, scholarships/grants, health care benefits, tuition waivers (partial), and unspecified assistantships also available. Support available to part-time students. Financial award application deadline: 3/1; financial award applicants required to submit FAFSA. In 2015, 169 master's awarded. *Degree program information:* Part-time and evening/weekend programs available. Part-time, evening/weekend. Offers accounting (M Acc); business administration (MBA); business for bioscientists (Certificate); economics (MA, MS); executive business administration (EMBA); human resources and training (Certificate). *Application deadline:* Applications are processed on a rolling basis. *Application fee:* $45. Electronic applications accepted. *Dean,* Dr. Louis Pol, 402-554-2341, E-mail: graduate@unomaha.edu.

College of Communication, Fine Arts and Media Students: 36 full-time (18 women), 49 part-time (38 women); includes 10 minority (4 Black or African American, non-Hispanic/Latino; 2 Asian, non-Hispanic/Latino; 1 Hispanic/Latino; 3 Two or more races, non-Hispanic/Latino), 4 international. Average age 32. 72 applicants, 71% accepted, 30 enrolled. *Faculty:* 19 full-time (9 women). *Financial support:* In 2015–16, 22 students received support, including 2 research assistantships with tuition reimbursements available, 20 teaching assistantships with tuition reimbursements available; fellowships, career-related internships or fieldwork, Federal Work-Study, institutionally sponsored loans, traineeships, tuition waivers (full), and unspecified assistantships also available. Support available to part-time students. Financial award application deadline: 3/1; financial award applicants required to submit FAFSA. In 2015, 36 master's, 4 other advanced degrees awarded. *Degree program information:* Part-time and evening/weekend programs available. Part-time, evening/weekend. Offers arts (MA); communication (MA); communication, fine arts and media (MA, MFA, MM, Certificate); human resources and training (Certificate); music (MM); technical communication (Certificate); writing (MFA). *Application deadline:* Applications are processed on a rolling basis. *Application fee:* $45. Electronic applications accepted. *Dean,* Dr. Gail Baker, 402-554-2341, E-mail: graduate@unomaha.edu.

College of Education Students: 177 full-time (120 women), 573 part-time (449 women); includes 91 minority (31 Black or African American, non-Hispanic/Latino; 2 American Indian or Alaska Native, non-Hispanic/Latino; 12 Asian, non-Hispanic/Latino; 31 Hispanic/Latino; 15 Two or more races, non-Hispanic/Latino), 23 international. Average age 32. 477 applicants, 39% accepted, 125 enrolled. *Faculty:* 39 full-time (28 women). *Financial support:* In 2015–16, 63 students received support, including 52 research assistantships with tuition reimbursements available, 11 teaching assistantships with tuition reimbursements available; fellowships, career-related internships or fieldwork, Federal Work-Study, institutionally sponsored loans, scholarships/grants, health care benefits, tuition waivers (full), and unspecified assistantships also available. Support available to part-time students. Financial award application deadline: 3/1; financial award applicants required to submit FAFSA. In 2015, 310 master's, 16 doctorates, 2 other advanced degrees awarded. *Degree program information:* Part-time and evening/weekend programs available. Part-time, evening/weekend. Offers athletic training (MA, MS); counseling (MA, MS); education (MA, MS, Ed D, PhD, Certificate, Ed S); educational administration and supervision (Ed D); educational leadership (MS, Ed S); elementary education (MS); exercise science (PhD); health, physical education, and recreation (MA); instruction in urban schools (Certificate); literacy (MS); secondary education (MA, MS, Certificate); special education (MA, MS); speech-language pathology (MA, MS). *Application deadline:* Applications are processed on a rolling basis. *Application fee:* $45. Electronic applications accepted. *Dean,* Dr. Nancy Edick, 402-554-2341, E-mail: graduate@unomaha.edu.

College of Information Science and Technology Students: 246 full-time (92 women), 166 part-time (42 women); includes 35 minority (11 Black or African American, non-Hispanic/Latino; 15 Asian, non-Hispanic/Latino; 3 Hispanic/Latino; 6 Two or more races, non-Hispanic/Latino), 275 international. Average age 28. 649 applicants, 47% accepted, 135 enrolled. *Faculty:* 22 full-time (5 women). *Financial support:* In 2015–16, 41 students received support, including 36 research assistantships with tuition reimbursements available, 5 teaching assistantships with tuition reimbursements available; fellowships, career-related internships or fieldwork, Federal Work-Study, institutionally sponsored loans, scholarships/grants, health care benefits, tuition waivers (full), and unspecified assistantships also available. Financial award application deadline: 3/1; financial award applicants required to submit FAFSA. In 2015, 98 master's, 2 doctorates, 17 other advanced degrees awarded. *Degree program information:* Part-time and evening/weekend programs available. Part-time, evening/weekend. Offers artificial intelligence (Certificate); biomedical informatics (MS, PhD); communication networks (Certificate); computer science (MA, MS); data analytics (Certificate); information assurance (MS); information science and technology (MA, MS, PhD, Certificate); information technology (PhD); management information systems (MS); project management (Certificate); software engineering (Certificate); system and architecture (Certificate); systems analysis and design (Certificate). *Application deadline:* Applications are processed on a rolling basis. *Application fee:* $45. Electronic applications accepted. *Dean,* Dr. Hesham Ali, 402-554-2341, E-mail: graduate@unomaha.edu.

College of Public Affairs and Community Service Students: 195 full-time (155 women), 379 part-time (233 women); includes 101 minority (31 Black or African American, non-Hispanic/Latino; 2 American Indian or Alaska Native, non-Hispanic/Latino; 6 Asian, non-Hispanic/Latino; 40 Hispanic/Latino; 22 Two or more races, non-Hispanic/Latino), 19 international. Average age 31. 431 applicants, 59% accepted, 215 enrolled. *Faculty:* 38 full-time (21 women). *Financial support:* In 2015–16, 52 students received support, including 36 research assistantships with tuition reimbursements available, 16 teaching assistantships with tuition reimbursements available; fellowships, career-related internships or fieldwork, Federal Work-Study, institutionally sponsored loans, scholarships/grants, health care benefits, tuition waivers (partial), and unspecified assistantships also available. Support available to part-time students. Financial award application deadline: 3/1; financial award applicants required to submit FAFSA. In 2015, 126 master's, 6 doctorates, 13 other advanced degrees awarded. *Degree program information:* Part-time and evening/weekend programs available. Part-time, evening/weekend, online learning. Offers criminology and criminal justice (MA, MS, PhD); gerontology (Certificate); managing juvenile and adult populations (Certificate); public administration (MPA, PhD); public affairs and community service (MA, MPA, MS, MSW, PhD, Certificate); public management (Certificate); social gerontology (MA); social work (MSW); urban studies (MS). *Application deadline:* Applications are processed on a rolling basis. *Application fee:* $45. Electronic applications accepted. *Dean,* Dr. John Bartle, 402-554-2341, E-mail: graduate@unomaha.edu.

UNIVERSITY OF NEBRASKA–LINCOLN, Lincoln, NE 68588

General Information State-supported, coed, university. CGS member. *Graduate housing:* Rooms and/or apartments available on a first-come, first-served basis to single and married students. Housing application deadline: 7/1. *Research affiliation:* U.S. Department of Agriculture (USDA), Department of Defense, NASA, National Science Foundation, National Institutes of Health, U.S. Meat Animal Research Center.

GRADUATE UNITS

College of Law Offers law (JD); legal studies (MLS); space and telecommunications law (LL M). Electronic applications accepted.

Graduate College Students: 2,643 full-time (1,251 women), 2,435 part-time (1,417 women); includes 469 minority (114 Black or African American, non-Hispanic/Latino; 15 American Indian or Alaska Native, non-Hispanic/Latino; 84 Asian, non-Hispanic/Latino; 168 Hispanic/Latino; 4 Native Hawaiian or other Pacific Islander, non-Hispanic/Latino; 84 Two or more races, non-Hispanic/Latino), 988 international. Average age 27. 7,716 applicants. *Faculty:* 1,049 full-time (324 women), 10 part-time/adjunct (3 women). *Financial support:* In 2015–16, 1,876 students received support, including 1,051 research assistantships with full tuition reimbursements available (averaging $17,345 per year), 825 teaching assistantships with full tuition reimbursements available (averaging $17,617 per year); fellowships with full tuition reimbursements available, career-related internships or fieldwork, Federal Work-Study, health care benefits, and unspecified assistantships also available. Support available to part-time students. In 2015, 870 master's, 315 doctorates, 17 other advanced degrees awarded. *Degree program information:* Part-time and evening/weekend programs available. Part-time, evening/weekend, online learning. Offers environmental health, occupational health and toxicology (MS, PhD); survey research and methodology (MS, PhD). *Application fee:* $50. Electronic applications accepted. *Application Contact:* Jason Cruise, Associate Director of Admissions, Operations and Technology, 402-472-2875, Fax: 402-472-0589, E-mail: graduate@unl.edu. *Associate Vice Chancellor for Academic Affairs and Dean of Graduate Studies,* Dr. Lance Perez, 402-472-2875, Fax: 402-472-0589, E-mail: graduate@unl.edu.

College of Agricultural Sciences and Natural Resources Offers agribusiness (MBA); agricultural economics (MS, PhD); agricultural sciences and natural resources (M Ag, MA, MBA, MS, PhD); agronomy (MS, PhD); animal science (MS, PhD); biochemistry (MS, PhD); community development (M Ag); entomology (MS, PhD); food science and technology (MS, PhD); geography (PhD); horticulture (MS, PhD); leadership development (MS); leadership education (MS); mechanized systems management (MS); natural resources (MS, PhD); nutrition (MS, PhD); statistics (MS, PhD); teaching and extension education (MS); veterinary science (MS). Electronic applications accepted.

College of Architecture Offers architecture (M Arch, MS, PhD); community and regional planning (MCRP); interior design (MS). Electronic applications accepted.

College of Arts and Sciences Offers analytical chemistry (PhD); anthropology (MA); arts and sciences (M Sc T, MA, MAT, MS, PhD, Graduate Certificate); astronomy (MS, PhD); biochemistry (PhD); bioinformatics (MS, PhD); biological sciences (MA, MS, PhD); biopsychology (PhD); chemistry (MS); classics and religious studies (MA); clinical psychology (PhD); cognitive psychology (PhD); composition and rhetoric (MA, PhD); computer engineering (MS, PhD); computer science (MS, PhD); creative writing (MA, PhD); developmental psychology (PhD); French (MA, PhD); geography (MA, PhD); geosciences (MS, PhD); German (MA, PhD); history (MA, PhD); information technology (PhD); inorganic chemistry (PhD); instructional communication (MA, PhD); interpersonal communication (MA, PhD); literature studies (MA, PhD); marketing, communication studies, and advertising (MA, PhD); materials chemistry (PhD); mathematics (MA, MAT, MS, PhD); mathematics and computer science (PhD); organic chemistry (PhD); organizational communication (MA, PhD); philosophy (MA, PhD); physical chemistry (PhD); physics (MS, PhD); political science (MA, PhD); professional archaeology (MA); psychology (MA); public policy analysis (Graduate Certificate); rhetoric and culture (MA, PhD); social/personality psychology (PhD); sociology (MA, PhD); Spanish (MA, PhD). Electronic applications accepted.

College of Business Administration ***Degree program information:*** Part-time and evening/weekend programs available. Part-time, evening/weekend. Offers accountancy (MPA, PhD); actuarial science (MS); business (MA, MBA, PhD); business administration (MA, MBA, MPA, MS, PhD); economics (MA, PhD); finance (MA, PhD); management (MA, PhD); marketing (MA, PhD). Electronic applications accepted.

College of Education and Human Sciences Offers administration, curriculum and instruction (Ed D, PhD); adult and continuing education (MA); audiology and hearing science (Au D); audiology research (PhD); child development/early childhood education (MS, PhD); child, youth and family studies (MS); clinical audiology (Au D); cognition, learning and development (MA); community nutrition and health promotion (MS); counseling psychology (MA); education and human sciences (M Ed, MA, MS, MST, Au D, Ed D, PhD, Certificate, Ed S); educational administration (M Ed, MA, Ed D, Certificate); educational psychology (MA, Ed S); educational studies (Ed D, PhD); family and consumer sciences education (MS, PhD); family financial planning (MS); family science (MS, PhD); gerontology (PhD); human sciences (PhD); marriage and family therapy (MS); medical family therapy (PhD); merchandising (MS); nutrition (MS, PhD); nutrition and exercise (MS); nutrition and health sciences (MS, PhD); psychological studies in education (PhD); quantitative, qualitative, and psychometric methods (MA); school psychology (MA, Ed S); special education (M Ed, MA, Ed S); speech-language pathology and audiology (MS, Au D); teaching, learning and teacher education (M Ed, MA, MST, Ed D, PhD); textile history/quilt studies (MA); textile science (MS); textile-apparel (MA); textiles, clothing and design (MA, MS); vocational and adult education (M Ed, MA); youth development (MS). Electronic applications accepted.

College of Engineering Offers agricultural and biological systems engineering (MS, PhD); architectural engineering (M Eng, MAE, MS, PhD); biological engineering (PhD); biomedical engineering (PhD); chemical and biomolecular engineering (MS, PhD); civil engineering (MS, PhD); electrical engineering (MS, PhD); engineering (M Eng, MAE, MEE, MS, PhD); engineering management (M Eng); engineering mechanics (MS, PhD); environmental engineering (MS, PhD); industrial and management systems engineering (MS, PhD); manufacturing systems engineering (MS); materials engineering (PhD); mechanical engineering (MS); mechanical engineering and applied mechanics (PhD); mechanized systems management (MS). Electronic applications accepted.

College of Fine and Performing Arts Offers acting (MFA); art history (MA); composition (MM, DMA); conducting (MM, DMA); costume (MFA); directing (MFA); fine and performing arts (MA, MFA, MM, DMA, PhD); music education (MM, PhD); music history (MM); music theory (MM); performance (MM, DMA); piano pedagogy (MM); stage design (MFA); studio art (MFA); woodwind specialties (MM). Electronic applications accepted.

College of Journalism and Mass Communications Online learning. Offers marketing, communication and advertising (MA); professional journalism (MA). Electronic applications accepted.

UNIVERSITY OF NEBRASKA MEDICAL CENTER, Omaha, NE 68198

General Information State-supported, coed, upper-level institution. CGS member. *Enrollment:* 1,996 full-time matriculated graduate/professional students (1,153 women), 387 part-time matriculated graduate/professional students (305 women). *Enrollment by degree level:* 708 master's, 1,520 doctoral, 107 other advanced degrees. *Graduate faculty:* 1,104 full-time (453 women), 200 part-time/adjunct (114 women). Tuition, state resident: full-time $7830; part-time $3915 per credit hour. Tuition, nonresident: full-time $22,410; part-time $11,205 per credit hour. *Required fees:* $521. *Student services:* Campus safety program, child daycare facilities, exercise/wellness program, free psychological counseling, international student services, low-cost health insurance, multicultural affairs office, services for students with disabilities. *Library:* McGoogan Library of Medicine. *Research affiliation:* UNeMed Corporation (biotechnology).

Computer facilities: 120 computers available on campus for general student use. A campuswide network can be accessed from off campus. Online class registration is available.
Website: http://www.unmc.edu/

GRADUATE UNITS

College of Dentistry Offers dentistry (MS, DDS, PhD, Certificate). Electronic applications accepted.

College of Medicine Students: 503 full-time (199 women); includes 72 minority (17 Black or African American, non-Hispanic/Latino; 1 American Indian or Alaska Native, non-Hispanic/Latino; 43 Asian, non-Hispanic/Latino; 11 Hispanic/Latino). Average age 24. 1,838 applicants, 9% accepted, 127 enrolled. *Faculty:* 725 full-time, 146 part-time/adjunct. *Financial support:* Career-related internships or fieldwork, Federal Work-Study, institutionally sponsored loans, and tuition waivers (full and partial) available. Financial award application deadline: 4/1; financial award applicants required to submit FAFSA. In 2015, 121 doctorates awarded. Offers medicine (MD, Certificate). *Application deadline:* For fall admission, 11/1 for domestic students. Applications are processed on a rolling basis. *Application fee:* $70. Electronic applications accepted. *Application Contact:* Gigi R. Rogers, Program Coordinator, 402-559-2259, Fax: 402-559-6840, E-mail: comadmissions@unmc.edu. *Dean*, Dr. Bradley E. Britigan, 402-559-4283, Fax: 402-559-4148, E-mail: bradley.britigan@unmc.edu.

College of Pharmacy Offers pharmacy (Pharm D). Electronic applications accepted.

College of Public Health ***Degree program information:*** Part-time programs available. Part-time, online learning. Offers public health (MPH). Electronic applications accepted.

Department of Biochemistry and Molecular Biology Students: 42 full-time (23 women); includes 3 minority (1 Asian, non-Hispanic/Latino; 1 Hispanic/Latino; 1 Two or more races, non-Hispanic/Latino), 26 international. Average age 28. 18 applicants, 33% accepted, 6 enrolled. *Faculty:* 32 full-time (8 women). *Financial support:* In 2015–16, 13 students received support, including 4 fellowships with full tuition reimbursements available (averaging $23,100 per year), 7 research assistantships with full tuition reimbursements available (averaging $23,100 per year); scholarships/grants, health care benefits, and unspecified assistantships also available. Support available to part-time students. Financial award application deadline: 2/15; financial award applicants required to submit FAFSA. In 2015, 4 doctorates awarded. Offers biochemistry and molecular biology (MS, PhD). *Application deadline:* For fall admission, 3/1 for domestic students, 4/1 for international students; for spring admission, 8/1 for domestic and international students; for summer admission, 1/1 for domestic and international students. *Application fee:* $45. Electronic applications accepted. *Application Contact:* Karen Hankins, Office Associate, 402-559-4417, E-mail: karen.hankins@unmc.edu. *Chairman, Graduate Committee*, Dr. Paul Sorgen, 402-559-7557, Fax: 402-559-6650, E-mail: psorgen@unmc.edu.

Department of Biostatistics Students: 5 full-time (0 women), 3 part-time (2 women); includes 1 minority (Asian, non-Hispanic/Latino), 4 international. Average age 34. 9 applicants, 44% accepted, 4 enrolled. *Faculty:* 8 full-time (5 women). *Financial support:* In 2015–16, research assistantships with full tuition reimbursements (averaging $23,100 per year), teaching assistantships with full tuition reimbursements (averaging $23,100 per year) were awarded. Financial award application deadline: 2/1; financial award applicants required to submit FAFSA. *Degree program information:* Part-time programs available. Part-time, online learning. Offers biostatistics (PhD). *Application deadline:* For fall admission, 4/1 for domestic and international students. *Application fee:* $45. Electronic applications accepted. *Application Contact:* Mary Morris, Coordinator, 402-559-4112, E-mail: mary.morris@unmc.edu. *Professor*, Dr. Gleb Haynatzki, 402-559-3294, E-mail: ghaynatzki@unmc.edu.

Department of Cellular and Integrative Physiology Students: 10 full-time (3 women); includes 2 minority (both Asian, non-Hispanic/Latino), 5 international. Average age 28. 6 applicants, 33% accepted, 2 enrolled. *Faculty:* 17 full-time (4 women). *Financial support:* In 2015–16, fellowships with full tuition reimbursements (averaging $23,100 per year), 7 research assistantships with full tuition reimbursements (averaging $4,620 per year) were awarded; scholarships/grants, health care benefits, unspecified assistantships, and 3 partial assistantships with full tuition reimbursements (for students receiving extramural fellowships) also available. Support available to part-time students. Financial award application deadline: 2/15; financial award applicants required to submit FAFSA. In 2015, 3 doctorates awarded. *Degree program information:* Part-time programs available. Part-time. Offers cellular and integrative physiology (MS, PhD). *Application deadline:* For fall admission, 4/1 for domestic and international students. *Application fee:* $45. Electronic applications accepted. *Application Contact:* Kim Kavan, Office Associate, 402-559-4426, E-mail: kimberly.kavan@unmc.edu. *Vice Chair for Graduate Education, Department of Cellular and Integrative Physiology*, Dr. Pamela K. Carmines, 402-559-9343, Fax: 402-559-4438, E-mail: pcarmines@unmc.edu.

Department of Epidemiology Students: 17 full-time (14 women), 3 part-time (0 women); includes 4 minority (all Asian, non-Hispanic/Latino), 10 international. Average age 31. 21 applicants, 24% accepted, 5 enrolled. *Faculty:* 11 full-time (5 women), 5 part-time/adjunct (2 women). *Financial support:* In 2015–16, 1 teaching assistantship with full tuition reimbursement (averaging $23,100 per year) was awarded; research assistantships with full tuition reimbursements, scholarships/grants, and unspecified assistantships also available. Financial award applicants required to submit FAFSA. *Degree program information:* Part-time programs available. Part-time. Offers epidemiology (PhD). *Application deadline:* For fall admission, 6/1 for domestic students, 3/1 for international students. *Application fee:* $45. Electronic applications accepted. *Application Contact:* Parwin Ibrahim, Coordinator, 402-559-4248, E-mail: parwin.ibrahim@unmc.edu. *Associate Professor*, Dr. Shinobu Watanabe-Galloway, 402-559-5387, E-mail: swatanabe@unmc.edu.

Department of Genetics, Cell Biology and Anatomy Students: 41 full-time (17 women); includes 6 minority (2 Black or African American, non-Hispanic/Latino; 1 American Indian or Alaska Native, non-Hispanic/Latino; 2 Asian, non-Hispanic/Latino; 1 Hispanic/Latino), 9 international. Average age 25. 19 applicants, 32% accepted, 6 enrolled. *Faculty:* 22 full-time (5 women), 1 (woman) part-time/adjunct. *Financial support:* In 2015–16, 1 fellowship with full tuition reimbursement (averaging $23,100 per year), 1 research assistantship with full tuition reimbursement (averaging $24,000 per year) were awarded; scholarships/grants also available. Support available to part-time students. Financial award application deadline: 3/1; financial award applicants required to submit FAFSA. In 2015, 14 master's, 7 doctorates awarded. Offers genetics, cell biology and anatomy (MS, PhD). *Application deadline:* For fall admission, 4/1 priority date for domestic and international students; for spring admission, 8/1 for domestic and international students; for summer admission, 1/1 for domestic and international students. Applications are processed on a rolling basis. *Application fee:* $45. Electronic applications accepted. *Application Contact:* Bryan Katafiasa, Administrative Associate, 402-559-4031, Fax: 402-559-7328, E-mail: bkatafiasz@unmc.edu. *Graduate Committee Chair*, Dr. Karen Gould, 402-559-2456, E-mail: kagould@unmc.edu.

Department of Health Promotion, Social and Behavioral Health Students: 11 full-time (6 women), 2 part-time (both women); includes 2 minority (1 Black or African American, non-Hispanic/Latino; 1 Asian, non-Hispanic/Latino), 2 international. Average age 35. 12 applicants, 33% accepted, 4 enrolled. *Faculty:* 13 full-time (9 women), 1 (woman) part-time/adjunct. *Financial support:* In 2015–16, research assistantships with full tuition reimbursements (averaging $23,100 per year) were awarded; scholarships/grants also available. Support available to part-time students. Financial award application deadline: 2/15; financial award applicants required to submit FAFSA. In 2015, 2 doctorates awarded. *Degree program information:* Part-time programs available. Part-time. Offers health promotion and disease prevention research (PhD). *Application deadline:* For fall admission, 4/1 for domestic and international students. *Application fee:* $45. Electronic applications accepted. *Application Contact:* Kate Kusnerik, Coordinator, 402-559-4325, E-mail: kate.kusnerik@unmc.edu. *Graduate Program Director*, Dr. Ghada Soliman, 402-559-5157, E-mail: ghada.soliman@unmc.edu.

Department of Health Services Research and Administration Students: 13 full-time (10 women), 3 part-time (2 women); includes 1 minority (Two or more races, non-Hispanic/Latino), 10 international. Average age 31. 11 applicants, 36% accepted, 4 enrolled. *Faculty:* 9 full-time (4 women), 1 part-time/adjunct. *Financial support:* In 2015–16, 5 students received support, including 1 research assistantship with full tuition reimbursement available (averaging $23,100 per year); scholarships/grants and unspecified assistantships also available. Financial award application deadline: 2/15; financial award applicants required to submit FAFSA. In 2015, 5 doctorates awarded. Offers health services research, administration, and policy (PhD). *Application deadline:* For fall admission, 6/1 for domestic students, 4/1 for international students. *Application fee:* $45. Electronic applications accepted. *Application Contact:* Denise Howard, Coordinator, 402-559-5260, E-mail: denise.howard@unmc.edu. *Associate Professor*, Dr. Fernando Wilson, 402-552-6948, E-mail: fernando.wilson@unmc.edu.

Department of Pathology and Microbiology Students: 37 full-time (22 women), 2 part-time (1 woman); includes 2 minority (1 Asian, non-Hispanic/Latino; 1 Hispanic/Latino), 22 international. Average age 27. 36 applicants, 17% accepted, 6 enrolled. *Faculty:* 53 full-time (17 women), 4 part-time/adjunct (2 women). *Financial support:* In 2015–16, 7 students received support, including 1 fellowship with full tuition reimbursement available (averaging $23,100 per year), 3 research assistantships with full tuition reimbursements available (averaging $23,100 per year); scholarships/grants also available. Support available to part-time students. Financial award application deadline: 2/15; financial award applicants required to submit FAFSA. In 2015, 4 master's, 10 doctorates awarded. *Degree program information:* Part-time programs available. Part-time. Offers pathology and microbiology (MS, PhD). *Application deadline:* For fall admission, 3/1 for domestic and international students; for spring admission, 10/1 for domestic and international students; for summer admission, 3/1 for domestic and international students. Applications are processed on a rolling basis. *Application fee:* $45. Electronic applications accepted. *Application Contact:* Tuire Cechin, Office Associate, 402-559-4042, Fax: 402-559-5900, E-mail: tcechin@unmc.edu. *Chair, Graduate Committee*, Dr. Rakesh K. Singh, 402-559-9949, Fax: 402-559-5900, E-mail: rsingh@unmc.edu.

Department of Pharmaceutical Sciences Students: 55 full-time (25 women), 1 part-time (0 women), 48 international. Average age 27. 57 applicants, 26% accepted, 15 enrolled. *Faculty:* 20 full-time (3 women), 1 part-time/adjunct (0 women). *Financial support:* In 2015–16, 2 fellowships with full tuition reimbursements (averaging $23,100 per year), 10 research assistantships with full tuition reimbursements (averaging $23,000 per year), teaching assistantships with full tuition reimbursements (averaging $23,000 per year) were awarded; scholarships/grants also available. Support available to part-time students. Financial award application deadline: 3/1; financial award applicants required to submit FAFSA. In 2015, 4 doctorates awarded. Offers pharmaceutical sciences (MS, PhD). *Application deadline:* For fall admission, 4/1 priority date for domestic and international students; for spring admission, 10/1 for domestic students, 8/1 for international students. Applications are processed on a rolling basis. *Application fee:* $45. Electronic applications accepted. *Application Contact:* Katina Winters, Office Associate, 402-559-5320, E-mail: kwinters@unmc.edu. *Chair, Pharmaceutical Sciences Graduate Program Committee*, Dr. David Oupicky, 402-559-9363, E-mail: david.oupicky@unmc.edu.

Department of Pharmacology and Experimental Neuroscience Students: 33 full-time (12 women), 2 part-time (0 women); includes 2 minority (1 Black or African American, non-Hispanic/Latino; 1 Two or more races, non-Hispanic/Latino), 14 international. Average age 27. 22 applicants. *Faculty:* 26 full-time (8 women), 2 part-time/adjunct (0 women). *Financial support:* In 2015–16, 8 students received support, including 2 fellowships with full tuition reimbursements available (averaging $24,000 per year), 3 research assistantships with full tuition reimbursements available (averaging $24,000 per year); scholarships/grants, health care benefits, and unspecified assistantships also available. Financial award application deadline: 2/15. In 2015, 8 doctorates awarded. Offers pharmacology and experimental neuroscience (PhD). *Application deadline:* For fall admission, 4/1 for domestic and international students. Applications are processed on a rolling basis. *Application fee:* $45. Electronic applications accepted. *Application Contact:* Leticia Tran, Office Assistant, 402-559-4044, E-mail: leticia.tran@unmc.edu. *Chair, Graduate Studies*, Dr. Keshore Bidasee, 402-559-9018, Fax: 402-559-7495, E-mail: kbidasee@unmc.edu.

Medical Sciences Interdepartmental Area Students: 49 full-time (28 women), 40 part-time (27 women); includes 10 minority (1 Black or African American, non-Hispanic/Latino; 6 Asian, non-Hispanic/Latino; 3 Hispanic/Latino), 16 international. Average age 32. 46 applicants, 41% accepted, 19 enrolled. *Faculty:* 195 full-time, 20 part-time/adjunct. *Financial support:* In 2015–16, 3 fellowships with full tuition reimbursements (averaging $23,100 per year), 4 research assistantships with full tuition reimbursements (averaging $23,100 per year) were awarded; teaching assistantships and scholarships/grants also available. Support available to part-time students. Financial award application deadline: 2/15; financial award applicants required to submit FAFSA. In 2015, 12 master's, 17 doctorates awarded. *Degree program information:* Part-time programs available. Part-time. Offers genetics, cell biology and anatomy (MS); internal medicine (MS). *Application deadline:* For fall admission, 4/1 for domestic and international students; for spring admission, 8/1 for domestic and international students; for summer admission, 1/1 for domestic and international students. Applications are processed on a rolling basis. *Application fee:* $45. Electronic applications accepted. *Graduate Committee Chair*, Dr. Laura Bilek, 402-559-6923, E-mail: lbilek@unmc.edu.

Program in Biomedical Informatics Students: 3 full-time (1 woman), 4 part-time (0 women), 4 international. Average age 32. 2 applicants. *Financial support:* In 2015–16, fellowships with full tuition reimbursements (averaging $23,100 per year), 2 research assistantships with full tuition reimbursements (averaging $23,100 per year) were awarded; scholarships/grants also available. Support available to part-time students. Financial award application deadline: 2/15; financial award applicants required to submit FAFSA. In 2015, 1 master's, 1 doctorate awarded. *Degree program information:* Part-time programs available. Part-time. Offers biomedical informatics (MS, PhD). *Application deadline:* For fall admission, 6/1 for domestic students, 5/1 for international students; for spring admission, 10/15 for domestic students, 9/15 for international students; for summer admission, 3/1 for domestic students, 2/1 for international students. *Application fee:* $45. Electronic applications accepted. *Director*, Dr. Jim McClay, 402-559-3587, E-mail: jmcclay@unmc.edu.

Program in Cancer Research Students: 31 full-time (19 women), 1 (woman) part-time; includes 4 minority (2 Black or African American, non-Hispanic/Latino; 2 Hispanic/Latino), 7 international. Average age 27. 32 applicants, 19% accepted, 6 enrolled. *Faculty:* 35 full-time (8 women), 3 part-time/adjunct (0 women). *Financial support:* In 2015–16, 41 students received support, including 1 fellowship with full tuition reimbursement available (averaging $23,100 per year), 7 research assistantships with full tuition reimbursements available (averaging $23,100 per year); unspecified assistantships also available. Financial award application deadline: 2/15; financial award applicants required to submit FAFSA. In 2015, 8 doctorates awarded. Offers cancer research (PhD). *Application deadline:* For fall admission, 7/1 for domestic and international students; for spring admission, 11/1 for domestic and international students; for summer admission, 4/1 for domestic and international students. Applications are processed on a rolling basis. *Application fee:* $45. Electronic applications accepted. *Application Contact:* Misty Pocwierz, Education and Project Associate, 402-559-4092, E-mail: misty.pocwierz@unmc.edu. *Graduate Committee Chair*, Dr. Joyce Solheim, 402-559-4539, Fax: 402-559-8270, E-mail: jsolheim@unmc.edu.

Program in Emergency Preparedness Students: 5 full-time (3 women), 6 part-time (5 women); includes 1 minority (Black or African American, non-Hispanic/Latino), 3 international. Average age 34. 4 applicants, 100% accepted, 4 enrolled. *Financial support:* Scholarships/grants available. Support available to part-time students. Financial award application deadline: 2/15; financial award applicants required to submit FAFSA. *Degree program information:* Part-time programs available. Part-time, blended/hybrid learning. Offers emergency preparedness (MS). *Application deadline:* For fall admission, 6/1 for domestic students, 4/1 for international students; for spring admission, 10/1 for domestic students, 8/1 for international students. *Application fee:* $45. Electronic applications accepted. *Application Contact:* Jessica Tschirren, Coordinator, 402-561-7586, Fax: 402-561-7599, E-mail: jtschirren@unmc.edu. *Associate Director, Center for Emergency Preparedness*, Dr. Sharon Medcalf, 402-552-2529, E-mail: smedcalf@unmc.edu.

Program in Environmental Health, Occupational Health and Toxicology Students: 4 full-time (1 woman), 2 part-time (1 woman); includes 1 minority (Asian, non-Hispanic/Latino), 2 international. Average age 40. 7 applicants, 57% accepted, 4 enrolled. *Faculty:* 9 full-time (1 woman). *Financial support:* In 2015–16, fellowships with full tuition reimbursements (averaging $23,100 per year), 1 research assistantship with full tuition reimbursement (averaging $23,100 per year) was awarded; teaching assistantships and scholarships/grants also available. Support available to part-time students. Financial award application deadline: 2/15; financial award applicants required to submit FAFSA. In 2015, 3 doctorates awarded. Offers environmental health, occupational health and toxicology (PhD). *Application deadline:* For fall admission, 4/1 for domestic and international students; for spring admission, 8/1 for domestic and international students; for summer admission, 1/1 for domestic and international students. Applications are processed on a rolling basis. *Application fee:* $45. Electronic applications accepted. *Application Contact:* Sherry Cherek, Coordinator, 402-559-8924, Fax: 402-559-8068, E-mail: scherek@unmc.edu. *Associate Professor*, Dr. Chandran Achutan, 402-559-8599, E-mail: cachutan@unmc.edu.

Program in Nursing Students: 18 full-time (16 women), 7 part-time (all women); includes 4 minority (2 Black or African American, non-Hispanic/Latino; 1 Hispanic/Latino; 1 Two or more races, non-Hispanic/Latino), 2 international. Average age 39. 2 applicants, 100% accepted, 2 enrolled. *Faculty:* 52 full-time (51 women), 8 part-time/adjunct (all women). *Financial support:* In 2015–16, 1 fellowship with full tuition reimbursement (averaging $23,100 per year), 1 research assistantship with full tuition reimbursement (averaging $23,100 per year), teaching assistantships with full tuition reimbursements (averaging $9,000 per year) were awarded; scholarships/grants also available. Support available to part-time students. Financial award application deadline: 2/1; financial award applicants required to submit FAFSA. In 2015, 7 doctorates awarded. *Degree program information:* Part-time programs available. Part-time, online learning. Offers nursing (PhD). *Application deadline:* For fall admission, 4/1 for domestic and international students; for spring admission, 8/1 for domestic and international students. Applications are processed on a rolling basis. *Application fee:* $45. Electronic applications accepted. *Application Contact:* Denise Ott, Office Associate, 402-559-2150, E-mail: denise.ott@unmc.edu. *Professor*, Dr. Kathleen Hanna, 402-559-5468, E-mail: kathy.hanna@unmc.edu.

School of Allied Health Professions Offers allied health professions (MPAS, MPS, DPT, Certificate); cytotechnology (Certificate); dietetic internship (Certificate); distance education perfusion education (MPS); perfusion science (MPS).

Division of Physical Therapy Education Offers physical therapy education (DPT).

Division of Physician Assistant Education Offers physician assistant education (MPAS). Electronic applications accepted.

UNIVERSITY OF NEVADA, LAS VEGAS, Las Vegas, NV 89154

General Information State-supported, coed, university. CGS member. *Graduate housing:* Room and/or apartments available on a first-come, first-served basis to single students; on-campus housing not available to married students. Housing application deadline: 6/1. *Student services:* Campus employment opportunities, campus safety program, career counseling, child daycare facilities, exercise/wellness program, free psychological counseling, grant writing training, international student services, low-cost health insurance, multicultural affairs office, services for students with disabilities, teacher training, writing training. *Library:* Lied Library.

Computer facilities: 1,500 computers available on campus for general student use. A campuswide network can be accessed from student residence rooms and from off campus. Online class registration is available.
Website: http://www.unlv.edu/

General Application Contact: Sebern Coleman, Graduate Recruitment and CRM Specialist, 702-895-3423, Fax: 702-895-4180, E-mail: sebern.coleman@unlv.edu.

GRADUATE UNITS

Graduate College Students: 2,213 full-time (1,281 women), 1,361 part-time (810 women); includes 1,129 minority (254 Black or African American, non-Hispanic/Latino; 16 American Indian or Alaska Native, non-Hispanic/Latino; 217 Asian, non-Hispanic/Latino; 408 Hispanic/Latino; 23 Native Hawaiian or other Pacific Islander, non-Hispanic/Latino; 211 Two or more races, non-Hispanic/Latino), 438 international. Average age 33. 2,381 applicants, 62% accepted, 1026 enrolled. *Faculty:* 457 full-time (163 women), 140 part-time/adjunct (72 women). *Financial support:* In 2015–16, 999 students received support, including 10 fellowships with full tuition reimbursements available (averaging $19,500 per year), 286 research assistantships with partial tuition reimbursements available (averaging $13,759 per year), 703 teaching assistantships with partial tuition reimbursements available (averaging $13,092 per year); institutionally sponsored loans, scholarships/grants, health care benefits, and unspecified assistantships also available. Financial award application deadline: 3/1. In 2015, 1,046 master's, 149 doctorates, 38 other advanced degrees awarded. *Degree program information:* Part-time and evening/weekend programs available. Part-time, evening/weekend, online learning. *Application deadline:* For fall admission, 8/1 for domestic students, 5/1 for international students; for spring admission, 12/1 for domestic students, 10/1 for international students. *Application fee:* $60 ($95 for international students). Electronic applications accepted. *Application Contact:* Graduate College Admissions, 702-895-3367, Fax: 702-895-4180, E-mail: gradadmissions@unlv.edu. *Dean*, Dr. Kathryn Korgan, 702-895-0446, Fax: 702-895-4180, E-mail: kate.korgan@unlv.edu.

College of Education Students: 586 full-time (428 women), 496 part-time (345 women); includes 385 minority (122 Black or African American, non-Hispanic/Latino; 5 American Indian or Alaska Native, non-Hispanic/Latino; 48 Asian, non-Hispanic/Latino; 138 Hispanic/Latino; 4 Native Hawaiian or other Pacific Islander, non-Hispanic/Latino; 68 Two or more races, non-Hispanic/Latino), 58 international. Average age 35. 497 applicants, 85% accepted, 349 enrolled. *Faculty:* 54 full-time (30 women), 39 part-time/adjunct (28 women). *Financial support:* In 2015–16, 107 students received support, including 51 research assistantships with partial tuition reimbursements available (averaging $12,869 per year), 56 teaching assistantships with partial tuition reimbursements available (averaging $13,436 per year); institutionally sponsored loans, scholarships/grants, health care benefits, and unspecified assistantships also available. Financial award application deadline: 3/1. In 2015, 344 master's, 21 doctorates, 5 other advanced degrees awarded. *Degree program information:* Part-time and evening/weekend programs available. Part-time, evening/weekend. Offers addiction studies (Advanced Certificate); chief diversity officer in higher education (Certificate); counselor education (M Ed, MS); early childhood education (M Ed); early childhood special education (Certificate); education (M Ed, MS, Ed D, PhD, Advanced Certificate, Certificate, Ed S); educational psychology (PhD); educational psychology and higher education (M Ed, Ed S); educational psychology and higher learning (MS, Certificate); English language learning (M Ed); higher education (PhD); learning and technology (PhD); mental health counseling (Advanced Certificate); special education (M Ed, PhD); teacher education (PhD); teaching and learning (M Ed, MS, Ed D, PhD, Ed S). *Application deadline:* For fall admission, 3/1 for domestic students, 5/1 for international students; for spring admission, 10/1 for domestic and international students. *Application fee:* $60 ($95 for international students). Electronic applications accepted. *Application Contact:* Graduate College Admissions Evaluator, 702-895-3367, Fax: 702-895-4180, E-mail: gradadmissions@unlv.edu. *Dean*, Dr. Kim Metcalf, 702-895-3375, Fax: 702-895-4068, E-mail: kim.metcalf@unlv.edu.

College of Fine Arts Students: 160 full-time (76 women), 43 part-time (19 women); includes 68 minority (17 Black or African American, non-Hispanic/Latino; 1 American Indian or Alaska Native, non-Hispanic/Latino; 12 Asian, non-Hispanic/Latino; 31 Hispanic/Latino; 2 Native Hawaiian or other Pacific Islander, non-Hispanic/Latino; 5 Two or more races, non-Hispanic/Latino), 29 international. Average age 32. 152 applicants, 63% accepted, 65 enrolled. *Faculty:* 48 full-time (15 women), 25 part-time/adjunct (8 women). *Financial support:* In 2015–16, 99 students received support, including 17 research assistantships with partial tuition reimbursements available (averaging $12,823 per year), 82 teaching assistantships with partial tuition reimbursements available (averaging $12,073 per year); institutionally sponsored loans, scholarships/grants, health care benefits, and unspecified assistantships also available. Financial award application deadline: 3/1. In 2015, 50 master's, 3 doctorates awarded. *Degree program information:* Part-time programs available. Part-time. Offers architecture (M Arch); art (MFA); fine arts (M Arch, MA, MFA, MM, DMA, Certificate); hospitality design (Certificate); K-12 music (Certificate); music (MM, DMA); theatre (MA, MFA); writing for dramatic media (MFA). *Application deadline:* For fall admission, 5/1 for international students; for spring admission, 10/1 for international students. *Application fee:* $60 ($95 for international students). Electronic applications accepted. *Application Contact:* Graduate College Admissions Evaluator, 702-895-3367, Fax: 702-895-4180, E-mail: gradadmissions@unlv.edu. *Interim Dean*, Dr. Helga Watkins, 702-895-5190, Fax: 702-895-4194, E-mail: helga.watkins@unlv.edu.

College of Liberal Arts Students: 230 full-time (125 women), 85 part-time (53 women); includes 65 minority (4 Black or African American, non-Hispanic/Latino; 1 American Indian or Alaska Native, non-Hispanic/Latino; 10 Asian, non-Hispanic/Latino; 34 Hispanic/Latino; 2 Native Hawaiian or other Pacific Islander, non-Hispanic/Latino; 14 Two or more races, non-Hispanic/Latino), 16 international. Average age 33. 428 applicants, 28% accepted, 64 enrolled. *Faculty:* 87 full-time (34 women), 8 part-time/adjunct (4 women). *Financial support:* In 2015–16, 208 students received support, including 6 fellowships with full tuition reimbursements available (averaging

$20,000 per year), 47 research assistantships with partial tuition reimbursements available (averaging $13,240 per year), 155 teaching assistantships with partial tuition reimbursements available (averaging $13,431 per year); institutionally sponsored loans, scholarships/grants, health care benefits, and unspecified assistantships also available. Financial award application deadline: 3/1. In 2015, 68 master's, 31 doctorates awarded. *Degree program information:* Part-time programs available. Part-time. Offers anthropology (MA, PhD); creative writing (MFA); English (MA, PhD); Hispanic studies (MA); history (MA, PhD); liberal arts (MA, MFA, PhD, Certificate); political science (MA, PhD); psychology (MA, PhD, Certificate); sociology (MA, PhD). *Application deadline:* For fall admission, 5/1 for international students; for spring admission, 10/1 for international students. *Application fee:* $60 ($95 for international students). Electronic applications accepted. *Application Contact:* Graduate College Admissions Evaluator, 702-895-3367, Fax: 702-895-4180, E-mail: gradadmissions@unlv.edu. *Dean*, Dr. Chris Heavey, 702-895-3401, Fax: 702-895-4097, E-mail: chris.heavey@unlv.edu.

College of Sciences Students: 189 full-time (67 women), 44 part-time (17 women); includes 45 minority (6 Black or African American, non-Hispanic/Latino; 14 Asian, non-Hispanic/Latino; 17 Hispanic/Latino; 8 Two or more races, non-Hispanic/Latino), 41 international. Average age 30. 190 applicants, 45% accepted, 59 enrolled. *Faculty:* 67 full-time (10 women), 2 part-time/adjunct (1 woman). *Financial support:* In 2015–16, 195 students received support, including 2 fellowships with full tuition reimbursements available (averaging $15,000 per year), 48 research assistantships with partial tuition reimbursements available (averaging $17,663 per year), 145 teaching assistantships with partial tuition reimbursements available (averaging $16,317 per year); institutionally sponsored loans, scholarships/grants, health care benefits, and unspecified assistantships also available. Financial award application deadline: 3/1. In 2015, 30 master's, 20 doctorates awarded. *Degree program information:* Part-time programs available. Part-time. Offers astronomy (MS, PhD); biochemistry (MS); biological sciences (MS, PhD); chemistry (MS, PhD); geoscience (MS, PhD); mathematical sciences (MS, PhD); physics (MS, PhD); radiochemistry (PhD); science (MA); sciences (MA, MS, PhD); water resources management (MS). *Application deadline:* For fall admission, 5/1 for international students; for spring admission, 10/1 for international students. *Application fee:* $60 ($95 for international students). Electronic applications accepted. *Application Contact:* Graduate College Admissions Evaluator, 702-895-3367, Fax: 702-895-4180, E-mail: gradadmissions@unlv.edu. *Dean*, Dr. Timothy Porter, 702-895-2058, Fax: 702-895-4159, E-mail: tim.porter@unlv.edu.

Greenspun College of Urban Affairs Students: 355 full-time (272 women), 209 part-time (126 women); includes 249 minority (79 Black or African American, non-Hispanic/Latino; 4 American Indian or Alaska Native, non-Hispanic/Latino; 25 Asian, non-Hispanic/Latino; 95 Hispanic/Latino; 8 Native Hawaiian or other Pacific Islander, non-Hispanic/Latino; 38 Two or more races, non-Hispanic/Latino), 32 international. Average age 34. 336 applicants, 71% accepted, 182 enrolled. *Faculty:* 45 full-time (26 women), 25 part-time/adjunct (8 women). *Financial support:* In 2015–16, 105 students received support, including 1 fellowship with full tuition reimbursement available (averaging $25,000 per year), 26 research assistantships with partial tuition reimbursements available (averaging $12,222 per year), 78 teaching assistantships with partial tuition reimbursements available (averaging $11,134 per year); institutionally sponsored loans, scholarships/grants, health care benefits, and unspecified assistantships also available. Financial award application deadline: 3/1. In 2015, 184 master's, 6 doctorates, 19 other advanced degrees awarded. *Degree program information:* Part-time and evening/weekend programs available. Part-time, evening/weekend. Offers communication studies (MA); criminal justice (MA, PhD); crisis and emergency management (MS); environmental and public affairs (MPA); environmental science (MS, PhD); journalism and media studies (MA); marriage and family therapy (MS); non-profit management (Certificate); public affairs (PhD); public management (Certificate); social work (MSW); urban affairs (MA, MPA, MS, MSW, PhD, Certificate); urban leadership (MA); workforce development and organizational leadership (PhD). *Application deadline:* For fall admission, 5/1 for international students; for spring admission, 10/1 for international students. *Application fee:* $60 ($95 for international students). Electronic applications accepted. *Application Contact:* Graduate College Admissions Evaluator, 702-895-3367, Fax: 702-895-4180, E-mail: gradadmissions@unlv.edu. *Dean*, Dr. Robert Ulmer, 702-895-0628, E-mail: robert.ulmer@unlv.edu.

Howard R. Hughes College of Engineering Students: 157 full-time (42 women), 78 part-time (23 women); includes 44 minority (5 Black or African American, non-Hispanic/Latino; 1 American Indian or Alaska Native, non-Hispanic/Latino; 12 Asian, non-Hispanic/Latino; 14 Hispanic/Latino; 12 Two or more races, non-Hispanic/Latino), 122 international. Average age 30. 196 applicants, 72% accepted, 60 enrolled. *Faculty:* 55 full-time (8 women), 7 part-time/adjunct (2 women). *Financial support:* In 2015–16, 154 students received support, including 1 fellowship with full tuition reimbursement available (averaging $20,000 per year), 49 research assistantships with partial tuition reimbursements available (averaging $14,113 per year), 104 teaching assistantships with partial tuition reimbursements available (averaging $11,992 per year); institutionally sponsored loans, scholarships/grants, health care benefits, and unspecified assistantships also available. Financial award application deadline: 3/1. In 2015, 44 master's, 15 doctorates, 7 other advanced degrees awarded. *Degree program information:* Part-time programs available. Part-time. Offers aerospace engineering (MS); biomedical engineering (MS); civil and environmental engineering (PhD); computer science (MSCS, PhD); electrical and computer engineering (MS, PhD); engineering (MS, MSCS, PhD, Certificate); materials and nuclear engineering (MS); mechanical engineering (MS, PhD); nuclear criticality safety (Certificate); nuclear safeguards and security (Certificate); solar and renewable energy (Certificate); transportation (MS). *Application deadline:* For fall admission, 5/1 for international students; for spring admission, 10/1 for international students. *Application fee:* $60 ($95 for international students). Electronic applications accepted. *Application Contact:* Graduate College Admissions Evaluator, 702-895-3367, Fax: 702-895-4180, E-mail: gradadmissions@unlv.edu. *Dean*, Dr. Rama Venkat, 702-895-1094, Fax: 702-895-4059, E-mail: venkat@ee.unlv.edu.

Lee Business School Students: 215 full-time (90 women), 166 part-time (62 women); includes 110 minority (8 Black or African American, non-Hispanic/Latino; 1 American Indian or Alaska Native, non-Hispanic/Latino; 36 Asian, non-Hispanic/Latino; 37 Hispanic/Latino; 3 Native Hawaiian or other Pacific Islander, non-Hispanic/Latino; 25 Two or more races, non-Hispanic/Latino), 71 international. Average age 31. 206 applicants, 73% accepted, 103 enrolled. *Faculty:* 31 full-time (7 women), 14 part-time/adjunct (5 women). *Financial support:* In 2015–16, 46 students received support, including 4 research assistantships with partial tuition reimbursements available (averaging $10,889 per year), 42 teaching assistantships with partial tuition reimbursements available (averaging $10,190 per year); institutionally sponsored loans, scholarships/grants, health care benefits, and unspecified assistantships also available. Financial award application deadline: 3/1. In 2015, 170 master's, 4 other advanced degrees awarded. *Degree program information:* Part-time and evening/weekend programs available. Part-time, evening/weekend. Offers accounting (MS, Advanced Certificate, Certificate); business (Exec MBA, MA, MBA, MS, Advanced Certificate, Certificate); business administration (Exec MBA, MBA); economics (MA); management information systems (Certificate); management, entrepreneurship and technology (MS); management, entrepreneurship, and technology (Certificate); new venture management (Certificate). *Application deadline:* For fall admission, 5/1 for domestic and international students; for spring admission, 10/1 for domestic and international students; for summer admission, 2/15 for domestic students. *Application fee:* $60 ($95 for international students). Electronic applications accepted. *Application Contact:* Graduate College Admissions Evaluator, 702-895-3367, Fax: 702-895-4180, E-mail: gradadmissions@unlv.edu. *Dean*, Dr. Brent Hathaway, 702-895-3362, Fax: 702-895-4090, E-mail: brent.hathaway@unlv.edu.

School of Allied Health Sciences Students: 156 full-time (73 women), 19 part-time (4 women); includes 47 minority (2 Black or African American, non-Hispanic/Latino; 16 Asian, non-Hispanic/Latino; 14 Hispanic/Latino; 1 Native Hawaiian or other Pacific Islander, non-Hispanic/Latino; 14 Two or more races, non-Hispanic/Latino), 6 international. Average age 28. 52 applicants, 69% accepted, 21 enrolled. *Faculty:* 22 full-time (7 women), 3 part-time/adjunct (all women). *Financial support:* In 2015–16, 43 students received support, including 21 research assistantships with partial tuition reimbursements available (averaging $12,190 per year), 22 teaching assistantships with partial tuition reimbursements available (averaging $10,909 per year); institutionally sponsored loans, scholarships/grants, health care benefits, and unspecified assistantships also available. Financial award application deadline: 3/1. In 2015, 26 master's, 29 doctorates awarded. *Degree program information:* Part-time programs available. Part-time. Offers allied health sciences (MS, DMP, DPT, PhD, Advanced Certificate); exercise physiology (MS); health physics and diagnostic sciences (MS, DMP, PhD, Advanced Certificate); kinesiology (PhD); physical therapy (DPT). *Application deadline:* For fall admission, 5/1 for international students; for spring admission, 10/1 for international students. *Application fee:* $60 ($95 for international students). Electronic applications accepted. *Application Contact:* Graduate College Admissions Evaluator, 702-895-3367, Fax: 702-895-4180, E-mail: gradadmissions@unlv.edu. *Dean*, Dr. Ronald T. Brown, 702-895-5307, Fax: 702-895-5050.

School of Community Health Sciences Students: 61 full-time (41 women), 69 part-time (51 women); includes 48 minority (7 Black or African American, non-Hispanic/Latino; 3 American Indian or Alaska Native, non-Hispanic/Latino; 11 Asian, non-Hispanic/Latino; 13 Hispanic/Latino; 2 Native Hawaiian or other Pacific Islander, non-Hispanic/Latino; 12 Two or more races, non-Hispanic/Latino), 19 international. Average age 33. 68 applicants, 75% accepted, 35 enrolled. *Faculty:* 18 full-time (6 women), 5 part-time/adjunct (4 women). *Financial support:* In 2015–16, 15 students received support, including 14 research assistantships with partial tuition reimbursements available (averaging $11,879 per year), 1 teaching assistantship (averaging $13,000 per year); institutionally sponsored loans, scholarships/grants, health care benefits, and unspecified assistantships also available. Financial award application deadline: 3/1. In 2015, 40 master's, 6 doctorates awarded. Offers community health sciences (MHA, MPH, PhD); health care administration and policy (MHA); public health (MPH, PhD). *Application deadline:* For fall admission, 4/1 for domestic students, 5/1 for international students; for spring admission, 11/1 for domestic students, 10/1 for international students. *Application fee:* $60 ($95 for international students). Electronic applications accepted. *Application Contact:* Graduate College Admissions Evaluator, 702-895-3367, Fax: 702-895-4180, E-mail: gradadmissions@unlv.edu. *Dean*, Dr. Shawn Gerstenberger, 702-895-1565, Fax: 702-895-5184, E-mail: shawn.gerstenberger@unlv.edu.

School of Nursing Students: 42 full-time (36 women), 87 part-time (77 women); includes 42 minority (2 Black or African American, non-Hispanic/Latino; 21 Asian, non-Hispanic/Latino; 10 Hispanic/Latino; 9 Two or more races, non-Hispanic/Latino), 11 international. Average age 38. 135 applicants, 51% accepted, 53 enrolled. *Faculty:* 10 full-time (all women), 10 part-time/adjunct (9 women). *Financial support:* In 2015–16, 6 students received support, including 6 teaching assistantships with partial tuition reimbursements available (averaging $11,500 per year); institutionally sponsored loans, scholarships/grants, health care benefits, and unspecified assistantships also available. Financial award application deadline: 3/1. In 2015, 26 master's, 14 doctorates, 1 other advanced degree awarded. *Degree program information:* Part-time programs available. Part-time, online learning. Offers family nurse practitioner (Advanced Certificate); nursing (MS, DNP). *Application deadline:* For fall admission, 2/1 for domestic students, 5/1 for international students. *Application fee:* $60 ($95 for international students). Electronic applications accepted. *Application Contact:* Graduate College Admissions Evaluator, 702-895-3367, Fax: 702-895-4180, E-mail: gradadmissions@unlv.edu. *Dean*, Dr. Carolyn Yucha, 702-895-5307, Fax: 702-895-4807, E-mail: carolyn.yucha@unlv.edu.

William F. Harrah College of Hotel Administration Students: 47 full-time (24 women), 65 part-time (33 women); includes 22 minority (2 Black or African American, non-Hispanic/Latino; 8 Asian, non-Hispanic/Latino; 5 Hispanic/Latino; 1 Native Hawaiian or other Pacific Islander, non-Hispanic/Latino; 6 Two or more races, non-Hispanic/Latino), 26 international. Average age 34. 121 applicants, 50% accepted, 35 enrolled. *Faculty:* 17 full-time (8 women), 3 part-time/adjunct (1 woman). *Financial support:* In 2015–16, 21 students received support, including 9 research assistantships with partial tuition reimbursements available (averaging $12,818 per year), 12 teaching assistantships with partial tuition reimbursements available (averaging $12,333 per year); institutionally sponsored loans, scholarships/grants, health care benefits, and unspecified assistantships also available. Financial award application deadline: 3/1. In 2015, 63 master's, 1 doctorate awarded. *Degree program information:* Part-time programs available. Part-time, online learning. Offers hotel administration (MHA, MS, PhD). *Application deadline:* For fall admission, 8/1 for domestic students, 5/1 for international students; for spring admission, 11/15 for domestic students, 10/1 for international students; for summer admission, 4/1 for domestic students. *Application fee:* $60 ($95 for international students). Electronic applications accepted. *Application Contact:* Graduate College Admissions Evaluator, 702-895-3367, Fax: 702-895-4180, E-mail: gradadmissions@unlv.edu. *Dean*, Dr. Stowe Shoemaker, 702-895-3308, E-mail: stowe.shoemaker@unlv.edu.

School of Dental Medicine Students: 97 full-time (43 women); includes 50 minority (1 Black or African American, non-Hispanic/Latino; 1 American Indian or Alaska Native, non-Hispanic/Latino; 39 Asian, non-Hispanic/Latino; 9 Hispanic/Latino), 3 international. Average age 28. 1,930 applicants, 10% accepted, 82 enrolled. *Faculty:* 63 full-time (23 women), 28 part-time/adjunct (6 women). *Financial support:* In 2015–16, 13 students received support. Application deadline: 2/1; applicants required to submit FAFSA. In 2015, 4 master's, 1 doctorate awarded. Offers dental medicine (DMD); oral biology (MS). *Application deadline:* For fall admission, 1/1 for domestic and international students.

Applications are processed on a rolling basis. *Application fee:* $50. *Application Contact:* Dr. Christine Ancajas, Assistant Dean for Admissions and Student Affairs, 702-774-2520, E-mail: christine.ancajas@unlv.edu. *Dean*, Karen West, 702-774-2500, E-mail: karen.west@unlv.edu.

William S. Boyd School of Law Students: 275 full-time (122 women), 103 part-time (53 women); includes 119 minority (22 Black or African American, non-Hispanic/Latino; 1 American Indian or Alaska Native, non-Hispanic/Latino; 26 Asian, non-Hispanic/Latino; 49 Hispanic/Latino; 1 Native Hawaiian or other Pacific Islander, non-Hispanic/Latino; 20 Two or more races, non-Hispanic/Latino), 2 international. Average age 30. 697 applicants, 32% accepted, 104 enrolled. *Faculty:* 41 full-time (24 women), 24 part-time/adjunct (6 women). *Financial support:* In 2015–16, 243 students received support, including 16 fellowships (averaging $11,274 per year), 65 research assistantships (averaging $1,420 per year); career-related internships or fieldwork and scholarships/grants also available. Support available to part-time students. Financial award application deadline: 2/1; financial award applicants required to submit FAFSA. *Degree program information:* Part-time programs available. Part-time. Offers gaming law and regulation (LL M); law (JD). *Application deadline:* For fall admission, 3/15 for domestic and international students. Applications are processed on a rolling basis. *Application fee:* $50. Electronic applications accepted. *Application Contact:* Elizabeth M. Jost, Admissions and Records Assistant III, 702-895-2424, Fax: 702-895-2414, E-mail: elizabeth.jost@unlv.edu. *Dean*, Dr. Daniel Hamilton, 702-895-1875, Fax: 702-895-1095, E-mail: daniel.hamilton@unlv.edu.

UNIVERSITY OF NEVADA, RENO, Reno, NV 89557

General Information State-supported, coed, university. CGS member. *Graduate housing:* Rooms and/or apartments available on a first-come, first-served basis to single and married students. Housing application deadline: 5/16. *Research affiliation:* National Institutes of Health (nursing), Desert Research Institute (natural resource sciences, environmental sciences).

GRADUATE UNITS

Graduate School ***Degree program information:*** Part-time and evening/weekend programs available. Part-time, evening/weekend, online learning. Offers atmospheric sciences (MS, PhD); Basque studies (PhD); biomedical engineering (MS, PhD); cell and molecular biology (MS, PhD); cellular and molecular pharmacology and physiology (PhD); chemical physics (PhD); ecology, evolution, and conservation biology (PhD); environmental sciences and health (MS, PhD); hydrogeology (MS, PhD); hydrology (MS, PhD); social psychology (PhD). Electronic applications accepted.

College of Agriculture, Biotechnology and Natural Resources Offers agriculture, biotechnology and natural resources (MS, PhD); animal science (MS); biochemistry (MS, PhD); biotechnology (MS); natural resources and environmental sciences (MS); nutrition (MS); resource economics (MS, PhD). Electronic applications accepted.

College of Business Administration Degree program information: Part-time programs available. Part-time, online learning. Offers accounting and information systems (M Acc); business administration (M Acc, MA, MBA, MS); economics (MA, MS); finance (MS); information systems (MS). Electronic applications accepted.

College of Education Offers counseling and educational psychology (M Ed, MA, MS, Ed D, PhD, Ed S); curriculum and instruction (PhD); curriculum, teaching and learning (Ed D, PhD); education (M Ed, MA, MS, Ed D, PhD, Ed S); educational leadership (M Ed, MA, MS, Ed D, PhD, Ed S); educational specialties (M Ed, MS, Ed D, PhD); elementary education (M Ed, MA, MS); human development and family studies (MS); literacy studies (M Ed, MA, Ed D, PhD); secondary education (M Ed, MA, MS); special education (M Ed, MA, MS, Ed D, PhD); special education and disability studies (PhD); teaching English to speakers of other languages (MA). Electronic applications accepted.

College of Engineering Offers chemical engineering (MS, PhD); civil and environmental engineering (MS, PhD); computer science and engineering (MS, PhD); electrical engineering (MS, PhD); engineering (MS, PhD); materials science and engineering (MS, PhD); mechanical engineering (MS, PhD). Electronic applications accepted.

College of Liberal Arts Degree program information: Part-time and evening/weekend programs available. Part-time, evening/weekend, online learning. Offers anthropology (MA, PhD); behavior analysis (MA, PhD); clinical psychology (PhD); cognitive brain science (MA, PhD); criminal justice (MA); English (MA, MATE, PhD); fine arts (MFA); French (MA); German (MA); history (MA, PhD); judicial studies (MJS, PhD); justice management (MJM); liberal arts (MA, MATE, MFA, MJM, MJS, MM, MPA, PhD); music (MA, MM); philosophy (MA); political science (MA, PhD); public administration (MPA); public administration and policy (MPA); social research and justice studies (MA, MJM, MJS, PhD); sociology (MA); Spanish (MA); speech communications (MA). Electronic applications accepted.

College of Science Offers biology (MS); chemistry (MS, PhD); earth sciences and engineering (MS, PhD); geochemistry (MS, PhD); geography (MS, PhD); geological engineering (MS, PhD); geology (MS, PhD); geophysics (MS, PhD); land use planning (MS); mathematics (MS); mining engineering (MS); physics (MS, PhD); science (MATM, MS, PhD); teaching mathematics (MATM). Electronic applications accepted.

Division of Health Sciences Offers health sciences (MPH, MS, MSN, MSW, DNP, PhD); nursing (MSN, DNP); public health (MPH, PhD); social work (MSW); speech pathology (PhD); speech pathology and audiology (MS). Electronic applications accepted.

Donald W. Reynolds School of Journalism Offers journalism (MA). Electronic applications accepted.

School of Medicine Offers medicine (MD).

UNIVERSITY OF NEW BRUNSWICK FREDERICTON, Fredericton, NB E3B 5A3, Canada

General Information Province-supported, coed, university. *Enrollment:* 7,667 graduate, professional, and undergraduate students; 1,747 matriculated graduate/professional students (819 women). *Graduate faculty:* 428 full-time (151 women), 219 part-time/adjunct (45 women). *Graduate housing:* Rooms and/or apartments available on a first-come, first-served basis to single and married students. Housing application deadline: 5/31. *Student services:* Campus employment opportunities, campus safety program, career counseling, child daycare facilities, exercise/wellness program, free psychological counseling, grant writing training, international student services, low-cost health insurance, multicultural affairs office, services for students with disabilities, teacher training, writing training. *Library:* Harriet Irving Library plus 4 others. *Research affiliation:* Petroleum Research Atlantic Canada (petroleum), Atlantic Associate for Research in the Mathematical Sciences (mathematical sciences), Atlantic Hydrogen, Inc. (hydrogen), Pulp and Paper Research Institute of Canada (pulp and paper), National Research Council Institute for Information Technology (information technology), Huntsman Marine Science Centre (marine sciences).

Computer facilities: 935 computers available on campus for general student use. A campuswide network can be accessed from student residence rooms and from off campus. Online class registration is available.
Website: http://www.unb.ca/

General Application Contact: Dr. Drew Rendall, Dean of Graduate Studies, 506-458-7154, Fax: 506-453-4817, E-mail: drendall@unb.ca.

GRADUATE UNITS

School of Graduate Studies Students: 1,747 (819 women). *Faculty:* 428 full-time (151 women), 219 part-time/adjunct (45 women). *Financial support:* Fellowships, research assistantships, teaching assistantships, scholarships/grants, and tuition waivers available. Support available to part-time students. In 2015, 487 master's, 111 doctorates awarded. *Degree program information:* Part-time and evening/weekend programs available. Part-time, evening/weekend, online learning. Offers applied health services (MAHSR); citizen engagement/dispute resolution (M Phil); community development (M Phil); interdisciplinary studies (M IDST, PhD); international development (M Phil); leadership (M Phil); sustainability/environmental issues (M Phil); worldviews (M Phil). *Application deadline:* 1/31 for domestic and international students. Applications are processed on a rolling basis. *Application fee:* $50 Canadian dollars. *Dean*, Dr. Drew Rendall, 506-458-7154, Fax: 506-453-4817, E-mail: drendall@unb.ca.

Faculty of Arts Students: 144 full-time (89 women), 41 part-time (19 women). *Faculty:* 91 full-time (41 women), 27 part-time/adjunct (11 women). *Financial support:* Fellowships, research assistantships, and teaching assistantships available. In 2015, 28 master's, 10 doctorates awarded. *Degree program information:* Part-time programs available. Part-time. Offers anthropology (MA); applied economics and finance (M Sc); arts (M Sc, MA, PhD); classics (MA); economics (MA); English (MA, PhD); history (MA, PhD); political science (MA); psychology (MA, PhD); sociology (MA, PhD). *Application deadline:* For fall admission, 1/31 priority date for domestic students; for winter admission, 1/31 priority date for domestic students; for spring admission, 1/31 priority date for domestic students. Applications are processed on a rolling basis. *Application fee:* $50 Canadian dollars. Electronic applications accepted. *Application Contact:* Dr. John Kershaw, Acting Associate Dean of Graduate Studies, 506-447-3065, Fax: 506-453-4817, E-mail: kershaw@unb.ca. *Dean of Arts*, Dr. George MacLean, 506-458-7485, Fax: 506-453-5102, E-mail: george.maclean@unb.ca.

Faculty of Business Administration Students: 33 full-time (13 women), 38 part-time (12 women), 1 international. *Faculty:* 22 full-time (3 women), 4 part-time/adjunct (1 woman). *Financial support:* In 2015–16, 6 fellowships, 3 research assistantships (averaging $4,500 per year), 22 teaching assistantships (averaging $2,250 per year) were awarded. In 2015, 27 master's awarded. *Degree program information:* Part-time programs available. Part-time. Offers business administration (MBA); engineering management (MBA); entrepreneurship (MBA); sports and recreation management (MBA). *Application deadline:* For fall admission, 10/31 priority date for domestic and international students; for spring admission, 3/31 priority date for domestic and international students. *Application fee:* $50 Canadian dollars. Electronic applications accepted. *Application Contact:* Marilyn Davis, Acting Graduate Secretary, 506-453-4766, Fax: 506-453-3561, E-mail: mbacontact@unb.ca. *Director of Graduate Studies*, Dr. Donglei Du, 506-458-7353, Fax: 506-453-3561, E-mail: ddu@unb.ca.

Faculty of Computer Science Students: 120 full-time (27 women), 18 part-time (5 women). *Faculty:* 27 full-time (8 women), 18 part-time/adjunct (1 woman). *Financial support:* In 2015–16, 1 fellowship, 94 research assistantships, 40 teaching assistantships were awarded. In 2015, 40 master's, 4 doctorates awarded. *Degree program information:* Part-time programs available. Part-time. Offers computer science (M Sc CS, PhD). *Application deadline:* For fall admission, 8/31 priority date for domestic students; for winter admission, 2/28 priority date for domestic students. Applications are processed on a rolling basis. *Application fee:* $50 Canadian dollars. Electronic applications accepted. *Application Contact:* Jodi O'Neill, Graduate Secretary, 506-458-7285, Fax: 506-453-3566, E-mail: jodio@unb.ca. *Director of Graduate Studies*, Dr. Patricia Evans, 506-458-7276, Fax: 506-453-3566, E-mail: pevans@unb.ca.

Faculty of Education Students: 75 full-time (58 women), 488 part-time (343 women). *Faculty:* 31 full-time (17 women), 14 part-time/adjunct (9 women). *Financial support:* In 2015–16, 51 research assistantships, 30 teaching assistantships were awarded; fellowships and tuition waivers also available. In 2015, 202 master's, 5 doctorates awarded. *Degree program information:* Part-time programs available. Part-time, online learning. Offers education (M Ed, PhD). *Application deadline:* For fall admission, 8/31 priority date for domestic students, 1/31 priority date for international students; for winter admission, 1/31 priority date for domestic and international students; for spring admission, 1/31 for domestic students, 1/31 priority date for international students. *Application fee:* $50 Canadian dollars. Electronic applications accepted. *Application Contact:* Carol Ann Hatheway, Graduate Secretary, 506-451-6999, Fax: 506-453-3569, E-mail: hatheway@unb.ca. *Associate Dean*, Dr. David Wagner, 506-447-3294, Fax: 506-453-3569, E-mail: dwagner@unb.ca.

Faculty of Engineering Students: 203 full-time (40 women), 51 part-time (13 women). *Faculty:* 63 full-time (9 women), 55 part-time/adjunct (8 women). *Financial support:* In 2015–16, 278 fellowships, 298 research assistantships, 247 teaching assistantships were awarded; career-related internships or fieldwork also available. In 2015, 53 master's, 25 doctorates awarded. *Degree program information:* Part-time programs available. Part-time. Offers applied mechanics (M Eng, M Sc E, PhD); chemical engineering (M Eng, M Sc E, PhD); construction engineering and management (M Eng, M Sc E, PhD); electrical and computer engineering (M Eng, M Sc E, PhD); engineering (M Eng, M Sc E, PhD, Certificate); environmental engineering (M Eng, M Sc E, PhD); environmental studies (M Eng); geodesy and geomatics engineering (M Eng, M Sc E, PhD); geotechnical engineering (M Eng, M Sc E, PhD); groundwater/hydrology (M Eng, M Sc E, PhD); materials (M Eng, M Sc E, PhD); mechanical engineering (M Eng, M Sc E, PhD); pavements (M Eng, M Sc E, PhD); structures (M Eng, M Sc E, PhD); transportation (M Eng, M Sc E, PhD). *Application deadline:* For fall admission, 3/1 priority date for domestic students. Applications are processed on a rolling basis. *Application fee:* $50 Canadian dollars. Electronic applications accepted. *Application Contact:* Dr. John Kershaw, Dean of Graduate Studies, 506-447-3065, Fax: 506-453-4817, E-mail: kershaw@unb.ca. *Dean*, Dr. David Coleman, 506-453-4570, Fax: 506-453-4943, E-mail: dcoleman@unb.ca.

Faculty of Forestry and Environmental Management Students: 58 full-time (21 women), 17 part-time (5 women). *Faculty:* 21 full-time (1 woman), 69 part-time/adjunct (13 women). *Financial support:* In 2015–16, 98 research assistantships, 36 teaching assistantships were awarded; fellowships also available. In 2015, 13 master's, 3 doctorates awarded. *Degree program information:* Part-time programs available. Part-time. Offers ecological foundations of forest management (PhD); environmental management (MEM); forest engineering (M Sc FE, MFE); forest products marketing (MBA); forest resources (M Sc F, MF, PhD). *Application deadline:*

For fall admission, 3/1 for domestic students. Applications are processed on a rolling basis. *Application fee:* $50 Canadian dollars. Electronic applications accepted. *Application Contact:* Faith Sharpe, Graduate Secretary, 506-458-7520, Fax: 506-453-3538, E-mail: fsharpe@unb.ca. *Director of Graduate Studies*, Dr. Marek Krasowski, 506-453-4915, Fax: 506-453-3538, E-mail: marek@unb.ca.

Faculty of Kinesiology Students: 28 full-time (9 women), 4 part-time (3 women). *Faculty:* 13 full-time (8 women), 2 part-time/adjunct (0 women). *Financial support:* In 2015–16, 31 research assistantships, 61 teaching assistantships were awarded; fellowships with tuition reimbursements, career-related internships or fieldwork, and scholarships/grants also available. In 2015, 11 master's awarded. *Degree program information:* Part-time programs available. Part-time. Offers exercise and sport science (M Sc); sport and recreation management (MBA); sport and recreation studies (MA). *Application deadline:* For winter admission, 1/31 for domestic students; for spring admission, 3/31 for domestic students. Applications are processed on a rolling basis. *Application fee:* $50 Canadian dollars. Electronic applications accepted. *Application Contact:* Leslie Harquail, Graduate Secretary, 506-453-4575, Fax: 506-453-3511, E-mail: harquail@unb.ca. *Acting Director of Graduate Studies*, Dr. Usha Kuruganti, 506-447-3101, Fax: 506-453-3511, E-mail: ukurugan@unb.ca.

Faculty of Nursing Students: 14 full-time (13 women), 30 part-time (29 women). *Faculty:* 19 full-time (18 women). *Financial support:* In 2015–16, 7 fellowships, 2 research assistantships were awarded. In 2015, 18 master's awarded. *Degree program information:* Part-time programs available. Part-time, online learning. Offers nurse educator (MN); nurse practitioner (MN); nursing (MN). *Application deadline:* For winter admission, 1/2 priority date for domestic students. *Application fee:* $50 Canadian dollars. Electronic applications accepted. *Application Contact:* Francis Perry, Graduate Secretary, 506-451-6844, Fax: 506-447-3057, E-mail: fperry@unb.ca. *Assistant Dean of Graduate and Advanced RN Studies*, Kathy Wilson, 506-458-7640, Fax: 506-447-3057, E-mail: kewilson@unb.ca.

Faculty of Science Students: 126 full-time (62 women), 16 part-time (11 women). *Faculty:* 77 full-time (10 women), 58 part-time/adjunct (18 women). *Financial support:* Fellowships, research assistantships, and teaching assistantships available. In 2015, 9 master's, 12 doctorates awarded. *Degree program information:* Part-time programs available. Part-time. Offers biology (M Sc, PhD); chemistry (M Sc, PhD); earth sciences (M Sc, PhD); mathematics and statistics (M Sc, PhD); physics (M Sc, PhD); science (M Sc, PhD). *Application deadline:* For fall admission, 3/1 priority date for domestic students. Applications are processed on a rolling basis. *Application fee:* $50 Canadian dollars. Electronic applications accepted. *Application Contact:* Heidi Stewart, Graduate Studies Coordinator, 506-458-7488, E-mail: scigrad@unb.ca. *Dean*, Dr. David Magee, 506-453-4841, Fax: 506-453-3570, E-mail: dmagee@unb.ca.

UNIVERSITY OF NEW BRUNSWICK SAINT JOHN, Saint John, NB E2L 4L5, Canada

General Information Province-supported, coed, comprehensive institution. *Graduate faculty:* 35 full-time (10 women), 34 part-time/adjunct (7 women). *Graduate housing:* Rooms and/or apartments available on a first-come, first-served basis to single and married students. Housing application deadline: 3/31. *Student services:* Campus employment opportunities, campus safety program, career counseling, child daycare facilities, exercise/wellness program, free psychological counseling, grant writing training, international student services, low-cost health insurance, multicultural affairs office, services for students with disabilities, teacher training, writing training. *Library:* Hans W. Klohn Commons. Students can reserve study rooms. *Research affiliation:* Cook Aquaculture (aquaculture), Horizon Health (health research), Dalhousie Medicine New Brunswick (cancer and general health), Fisheries and Oceans Canada (biology/ecology), New Brunswick Community College (health research).

Computer facilities: 100 computers available on campus for general student use. A campuswide network can be accessed from student residence rooms and from off campus. Online class registration is available.
Website: http://www.unb.ca/

General Application Contact: Dr. Lilly Both, Acting Associate Dean of Graduate Studies, 506-648-5620, Fax: 506-648-5769, E-mail: lboth@unb.ca.

GRADUATE UNITS

Department of Biology Students: 41 full-time (24 women), 6 part-time (3 women). *Faculty:* 12 full-time (4 women), 19 part-time/adjunct (4 women). *Financial support:* Fellowships, research assistantships, teaching assistantships, scholarships/grants, and unspecified assistantships available. In 2015, 8 master's, 1 doctorate awarded. *Degree program information:* Part-time programs available. Part-time. Offers biology (M Sc, PhD). *Application deadline:* For fall admission, 2/15 for domestic and international students. Applications are processed on a rolling basis. *Application fee:* $50 Canadian dollars. Electronic applications accepted. *Application Contact:* Kim Banks, Secretary, 506-648-5605, Fax: 506-648-5811, E-mail: kbanks@unb.ca. *Acting Director of Graduate Studies*, Dr. Kate Frego, 506-648-5967, Fax: 506-648-5811, E-mail: jeffhoul@unb.ca.

Department of Psychology Students: 16 full-time (9 women). *Faculty:* 9 full-time (4 women). *Financial support:* In 2015–16, 6 fellowships, 5 research assistantships, 16 teaching assistantships were awarded; unspecified assistantships also available. Support available to part-time students. Financial award application deadline: 2/1. In 2015, 3 master's, 1 doctorate awarded. *Degree program information:* Part-time programs available. Part-time. Offers clinical psychology (PhD); experimental psychology (MA, PhD). *Application deadline:* For fall admission, 1/15 priority date for domestic students. *Application fee:* $50. Electronic applications accepted. *Application Contact:* Laura Galbraith, Secretary, 506-648-5640, Fax: 506-648-5780, E-mail: galbral@unb.ca. *Director of Graduate Studies*, Dr. Enrico Ditommaso, 506-648-5636, Fax: 506-648-5780, E-mail: rico@unb.ca.

Faculty of Business Students: 68 full-time (27 women), 15 part-time (7 women). *Faculty:* 14 full-time (2 women), 15 part-time/adjunct (3 women). *Financial support:* In 2015–16, 4 students received support. Career-related internships or fieldwork and scholarships/grants available. In 2015, 91 master's awarded. *Degree program information:* Part-time programs available. Part-time. Offers administration (MBA); electronic commerce (MBA); international business (MBA); natural resource management (MBA). *Application deadline:* For fall admission, 5/31 for domestic students, 7/15 for international students. *Application fee:* $100. Electronic applications accepted. *Application Contact:* Tammy Morin, Secretary, 506-648-5746, Fax: 506-648-5574, E-mail: tmorin@unbsj.ca. *Director of Graduate Studies*, Dr. Shelley Rinehart, 506-648-5902, Fax: 506-648-5574, E-mail: rinehart@unb.ca.

UNIVERSITY OF NEW ENGLAND, Biddeford, ME 04005-9526

General Information Independent, coed, comprehensive institution. *Enrollment:* 7,795 graduate, professional, and undergraduate students; 3,388 full-time matriculated graduate/professional students (2,370 women), 559 part-time matriculated graduate/professional students (448 women). *Enrollment by degree level:* 2,097 master's, 1,621 doctoral, 229 other advanced degrees. *Graduate faculty:* 157 full-time (81 women), 193 part-time/adjunct (110 women). Tuition and fees vary according to degree level and program. *Graduate housing:* On-campus housing not available. *Student services:* Campus employment opportunities, campus safety program, career counseling, exercise/wellness program, free psychological counseling, international student services, low-cost health insurance, multicultural affairs office, services for students with disabilities, teacher training, writing training. *Library:* Jack S. Ketchum Library plus 1 other. *Collection:* Books: 135,000 (physical), 660,000 (digital/electronic); Serial titles: 95,000 (digital/electronic); Databases: 200. Weekly public service hours: 146; study areas open 24 hours, 5–7 days a week; students can reserve study rooms.

Computer facilities: Computer purchase and lease plans are available. 91 computers available on campus for general student use. A campuswide network can be accessed from student residence rooms and from off campus. Online class registration is available.
Website: http://www.une.edu/

General Application Contact: Scott Steinberg, Dean of University Admission, 207-221-4225, Fax: 207-523-1925, E-mail: ssteinberg@une.edu.

GRADUATE UNITS

College of Arts and Sciences Students: 12 full-time (6 women), 7 part-time (4 women); includes 1 minority (Asian, non-Hispanic/Latino), 1 international. Average age 24. 37 applicants, 30% accepted, 11 enrolled. *Faculty:* 29 full-time (14 women), 5 part-time/adjunct (4 women). *Financial support:* Fellowships, research assistantships, teaching assistantships, career-related internships or fieldwork, scholarships/grants, traineeships, and unspecified assistantships available. Financial award application deadline: 5/1; financial award applicants required to submit FAFSA. In 2015, 5 master's awarded. *Degree program information:* Part-time programs available. Part-time. Offers arts and sciences (MS); biological science (MS); marine sciences (MS). *Application deadline:* Applications are processed on a rolling basis. Electronic applications accepted. *Application Contact:* Scott Steinberg, Dean of University Admissions, 207-221-4225, Fax: 207-523-1925, E-mail: ssteinberg@une.edu. *Dean, College of Arts and Sciences*, Dr. Jeanne A.K. Hey, 207-602-2371, Fax: 207-602-5973, E-mail: jhey@une.edu.

College of Dental Medicine Offers dental medicine (DMD). Electronic applications accepted.

College of Graduate and Professional Studies Students: 872 full-time (646 women), 333 part-time (248 women); includes 271 minority (178 Black or African American, non-Hispanic/Latino; 3 American Indian or Alaska Native, non-Hispanic/Latino; 47 Asian, non-Hispanic/Latino; 23 Hispanic/Latino; 2 Native Hawaiian or other Pacific Islander, non-Hispanic/Latino; 18 Two or more races, non-Hispanic/Latino). Average age 37. 1,036 applicants, 58% accepted, 416 enrolled. *Faculty:* 56 part-time/adjunct (34 women). *Financial support:* Application deadline: 5/1; applicants required to submit FAFSA. In 2015, 217 master's, 1 doctorate, 100 other advanced degrees awarded. *Degree program information:* Part-time and evening/weekend programs available. Part-time, evening/weekend, online learning. Offers advanced educational leadership (CAGS); career and technical education (MS Ed, CAGS); curriculum and instruction strategies (CAGS); curriculum and instruction strategy (MS Ed); educational leadership (MS Ed, CAGS); inclusion education (MS Ed); leadership development in academic medicine (Graduate Certificate); leadership, ethics and change (CAGS); literacy K-12 (MS Ed, CAGS); medical education leadership (MMEL); program development in academic medicine (Graduate Certificate); public health (MPH, Graduate Certificate); reading specialist (MS Ed, CAGS); teaching methodologies (MS Ed). *Application deadline:* Applications are processed on a rolling basis. Electronic applications accepted. *Application Contact:* Scott Steinberg, Dean of University Admissions, 207-221-4225, Fax: 207-523-1925, E-mail: ssteinberg@une.edu. *Associate Provost for Online Worldwide Learning/Dean of the College of Graduate and Professional Studies*, Dr. Martha Wilson, 207-221-4985, E-mail: mwilson13@une.edu.

College of Osteopathic Medicine Students: 640 full-time (315 women), 8 part-time; includes 107 minority (3 Black or African American, non-Hispanic/Latino; 2 American Indian or Alaska Native, non-Hispanic/Latino; 83 Asian, non-Hispanic/Latino; 3 Hispanic/Latino; 16 Two or more races, non-Hispanic/Latino), 22 international. Average age 27. 4,915 applicants, 9% accepted, 177 enrolled. *Faculty:* 30 full-time (13 women), 35 part-time/adjunct (14 women). *Financial support:* Application deadline: 5/1; applicants required to submit FAFSA. In 2015, 114 doctorates awarded. *Degree program information:* Part-time and evening/weekend programs available. Part-time, evening/weekend, online learning. Offers osteopathic medicine (DO). *Application deadline:* For fall admission, 3/1 for domestic students. *Application Contact:* Scott Steinberg, Dean of University Admission, 207-221-4225, Fax: 207-523-1925, E-mail: ssteinberg@une.edu. *Dean, College of Osteopathic Medicine*, Dr. Douglas L. Wood, 207-602-2807, E-mail: deanunecom@une.edu.

College of Pharmacy Students: 393 full-time (238 women); includes 137 minority (34 Black or African American, non-Hispanic/Latino; 3 American Indian or Alaska Native, non-Hispanic/Latino; 80 Asian, non-Hispanic/Latino; 11 Hispanic/Latino; 2 Native Hawaiian or other Pacific Islander, non-Hispanic/Latino; 7 Two or more races, non-Hispanic/Latino), 4 international. Average age 26. 570 applicants, 34% accepted, 99 enrolled. *Faculty:* 28 full-time (9 women), 4 part-time/adjunct (0 women). *Financial support:* Application deadline: 5/1; applicants required to submit FAFSA. In 2015, 90 doctorates awarded. Offers pharmacy (Pharm D). *Application deadline:* For fall admission, 3/1 for domestic students. Applications are processed on a rolling basis. Electronic applications accepted. *Application Contact:* Scott Steinberg, Dean of University Admission, 207-221-4225, Fax: 207-523-1925, E-mail: ssteinberg@une.edu. *Dean, College of Pharmacy*, Dr. Gayle A. Brazeau, 207-221-4500, Fax: 207-523-1927, E-mail: gbrazeau@une.edu.

Westbrook College of Health Professions Students: 1,282 full-time (1,069 women), 229 part-time (206 women); includes 294 minority (188 Black or African American, non-Hispanic/Latino; 8 American Indian or Alaska Native, non-Hispanic/Latino; 43 Asian, non-Hispanic/Latino; 29 Hispanic/Latino; 8 Native Hawaiian or other Pacific Islander, non-Hispanic/Latino; 18 Two or more races, non-Hispanic/Latino), 1 international. Average age 32. 3,678 applicants, 23% accepted, 520 enrolled. *Faculty:* 50 full-time (38 women), 76 part-time/adjunct (55 women). *Financial support:* Application deadline: 5/1; applicants required to submit FAFSA. In 2015, 418 master's, 68 doctorates awarded. *Degree program information:* Part-time programs available. Part-time, online learning. Offers health professions (MS, MSW, DPT, TDPT); nurse anesthesia (MS); occupational therapy (MS); physical therapy (DPT); physician assistant (MS); social work (MSW). *Application deadline:* Applications are processed on a rolling basis. Electronic applications accepted. *Application Contact:* Scott Steinberg, Dean of University Admission, 207-221-4225, Fax: 207-523-1925, E-mail: ssteinberg@une.edu. *Dean, Westbrook College of Health Professions*, Dr. Elizabeth Francis- Connolly, 207-221-4523, E-mail: efrancisconnonlly@une.edu.

UNIVERSITY OF NEW HAMPSHIRE, Durham, NH 03824

General Information State-supported, coed, university. CGS member. *Enrollment:* 15,398 graduate, professional, and undergraduate students; 1,208 full-time matriculated graduate/professional students (714 women), 838 part-time matriculated graduate/professional students (435 women). *Enrollment by degree level:* 1,506 master's, 504 doctoral, 36 other advanced degrees. *Graduate faculty:* 552. Tuition, state resident: full-time $13,840; part-time $770 per credit hour. Tuition, nonresident: full-time $27,130; part-time $1175 per credit hour. *Required fees:* $2080; $1040. Tuition and fees vary according to degree level and program. *Graduate housing:* Rooms and/or apartments available on a first-come, first-served basis to single and married students. Housing application deadline: 7/15. *Student services:* Campus employment opportunities, campus safety program, career counseling, child daycare facilities, exercise/wellness program, free psychological counseling, grant writing training, international student services, low-cost health insurance, multicultural affairs office, services for students with disabilities, teacher training, writing training. *Library:* Dimond Library plus 4 others. *Collection:* Books: 1.6 million (physical), 775,162 (digital/electronic); Serial titles: 37,296 (physical), 90,707 (digital/electronic); Databases: 437. Weekly public service hours: 117; students can reserve study rooms.

Computer facilities: Computer purchase and lease plans are available. 360 computers available on campus for general student use. A campuswide network can be accessed from student residence rooms and from off campus. Online class registration is available.
Website: http://www.unh.edu/

General Application Contact: Dovev L. Levine, Graduate Admissions Officer, 603-862-3000, Fax: 603-862-0275, E-mail: grad.school@unh.edu.

GRADUATE UNITS

Graduate School ***Financial support:*** Fellowships, research assistantships, teaching assistantships, Federal Work-Study, scholarships/grants, health care benefits, tuition waivers, and unspecified assistantships available. Support available to part-time students. Financial award application deadline: 3/1; financial award applicants required to submit FAFSA. *Degree program information:* Part-time and evening/weekend programs available. Part-time, evening/weekend. Offers college teaching (Postbaccalaureate Certificate); earth and environmental sciences (PhD); geospatial science (Postbaccalaureate Certificate); natural resources and earth systems science (PhD); natural resources and environmental studies (PhD). *Application deadline:* For fall admission, 7/1 priority date for domestic students, 4/1 priority date for international students; for spring admission, 2/1 for domestic students. Applications are processed on a rolling basis. *Application fee:* $65. Electronic applications accepted. *Dean*, Dr. Harry J. Richards, 603-862-3005, Fax: 603-862-0275, E-mail: harry.richards@unh.edu.

Carsey School of Public Policy Students: 4 part-time. *Financial support:* Fellowships, research assistantships, teaching assistantships, and scholarships/grants available. Offers community development policy and practice (MA); public policy (MPP). *Application deadline:* For fall admission, 2/15 for domestic students. Applications are processed on a rolling basis. *Application fee:* $65. Electronic applications accepted. *Application Contact:* Robin Husslage, Program Manager, 603-862-2338, E-mail: robin.husslage@unh.edu. *Director*, Michael Ettlinger, 603-862-3201, Fax: 603-862-0275, E-mail: michael.ettlinger@unh.edu.

College of Engineering and Physical Sciences Financial support: Fellowships, research assistantships, teaching assistantships, career-related internships or fieldwork, Federal Work-Study, scholarships/grants, and tuition waivers available. Support available to part-time students. Financial award application deadline: 3/1; financial award applicants required to submit FAFSA. *Degree program information:* Part-time and evening/weekend programs available. Part-time, evening/weekend. Offers applied mathematics (MS); chemical engineering (M Engr, MS, PhD); chemistry (MS, PhD); chemistry education (PhD); civil and environmental engineering (M Engr, MS, PhD); computer science (MS, PhD, Postbaccalaureate Certificate); electrical and computer engineering (MS); electrical engineering (M Engr, PhD); engineering and physical sciences (M Engr, MS, MST, PhD, Postbaccalaureate Certificate); geochemical systems (MS); geology (MS); hydrology (MS); integrated applied mathematics (PhD); materials science (MS, PhD); mathematics (MS, PhD); mathematics education (MST, PhD); mechanical engineering (M Engr, MS, PhD); physics (MS, PhD); statistics (MS, PhD); systems engineering (PhD). *Application deadline:* For fall admission, 7/1 priority date for domestic students, 4/1 for international students; for spring admission, 12/1 priority date for domestic students. Applications are processed on a rolling basis. *Application fee:* $65. Electronic applications accepted. *Application Contact:* Charles Zercher, Interim Dean, 603-862-1781. *Interim Dean*, Charles Zercher, 603-862-1781.

College of Health and Human Services Financial support: Fellowships, research assistantships, teaching assistantships, career-related internships or fieldwork, Federal Work-Study, scholarships/grants, and tuition waivers (full and partial) available. Support available to part-time students. Financial award application deadline: 3/1. *Degree program information:* Part-time and evening/weekend programs available. Part-time, evening/weekend. Offers adapted physical education (Postbaccalaureate Certificate); adolescent development (Postbaccalaureate Certificate); adult neurogenic communication disorders (MS); assistive technology (Postbaccalaureate Certificate); communication sciences and disorders (MS); early childhood communication disorders (MS); exercise science (MS); family practitioner (Postbaccalaureate Certificate); health and human services (MPH, MS, MSW, DNP, Postbaccalaureate Certificate); human development and family studies (MS); kinesiology (MS); language/literacy disorders (MS); marriage and family therapy (MS); nursing (MS, DNP); occupational therapy (MS); outdoor education (MS); public health (MPH, Postbaccalaureate Certificate); recreation administration (MS); social work (MSW, Postbaccalaureate Certificate); sport studies (MS); therapeutic recreation administration (MS). *Application deadline:* For fall admission, 7/1 priority date for domestic students, 4/1 for international students; for spring admission, 12/1 for domestic students. Applications are processed on a rolling basis. *Application fee:* $65. Electronic applications accepted. *Application Contact:* Dr. Michael S. Ferrara, Dean, 603-862-1178. *Dean*, Dr. Michael S. Ferrara, 603-862-1178.

College of Liberal Arts Financial support: Fellowships, research assistantships, teaching assistantships, career-related internships or fieldwork, Federal Work-Study, scholarships/grants, and tuition waivers (full and partial) available. Support available to part-time students. Financial award application deadline: 3/1; financial award applicants required to submit FAFSA. *Degree program information:* Part-time programs available. Part-time. Offers children and youth in communities (PhD); composition (MA, PhD); curriculum and instruction/teacher education (PhD); early childhood education (M Ed); education (PhD); educational administration and supervision (Ed S); educational leadership and policy studies (PhD); educational studies (M Ed); elementary education (M Ed); English education (MST); experiential education/outdoor education (PhD); history (MA, PhD); justice studies (MA); language and linguistics (MA); liberal arts (M Ed, MA, MALS, MAT, MFA, MPA, MST, PhD, Ed S, Postbaccalaureate Certificate); liberal studies (MALS); literature (MA, PhD); museum studies (MA); musicology (MA); painting (MFA); political science (MA, Postbaccalaureate Certificate); psychology (PhD); public administration (MPA); secondary education (MAT); sociology (MA, PhD); Spanish (MA); special education (M Ed); sustainability politics and policy (Postbaccalaureate Certificate); writing (MFA). *Application deadline:* For fall admission, 3/1 for domestic students, 4/1 for international students; for spring admission, 12/1 for domestic students. Applications are processed on a rolling basis. *Application fee:* $65. Electronic applications accepted. *Application Contact:* Heidi Bostic, Dean, 603-862-2062. *Dean*, Heidi Bostic, 603-862-2062.

College of Life Sciences and Agriculture Financial support: Fellowships, research assistantships, teaching assistantships, career-related internships or fieldwork, Federal Work-Study, scholarships/grants, and tuition waivers (full and partial) available. Support available to part-time students. Financial award application deadline: 3/1; financial award applicants required to submit FAFSA. *Degree program information:* Part-time programs available. Part-time. Offers agricultural science (MS, PhD); agricultural sciences (MS, PhD); animal and nutritional sciences (PhD); biochemistry (MS, PhD); environmental conservation (MS); environmental economics (MS); forestry (MS); genetics (MS, PhD); integrative and organismal biology (MS, PhD); life sciences and agriculture (MS, PhD); microbiology (MS, PhD); molecular and evolutionary systems biology (PhD); natural resources (MS); nutritional sciences (MS); resource administration and management (MS); soil and water resource management (MS); wildlife and conservation biology (MS). *Application deadline:* For fall admission, 7/1 for domestic students, 4/1 for international students. Applications are processed on a rolling basis. *Application fee:* $65. Electronic applications accepted. *Application Contact:* Jon Wraith, Dean, 603-862-1453. *Dean*, Jon Wraith, 603-862-1453.

Graduate School Manchester Campus ***Financial support:*** Fellowships, research assistantships, teaching assistantships, Federal Work-Study, scholarships/grants, health care benefits, and unspecified assistantships available. Support available to part-time students. Financial award application deadline: 3/1; financial award applicants required to submit FAFSA. *Degree program information:* Part-time and evening/weekend programs available. Part-time, evening/weekend. Offers business administration (MBA); educational administration and supervision (Ed S); educational studies (M Ed); elementary teacher education (M Ed); information technology (MS); public administration (MPA); public health (MPH, Certificate); secondary teacher education (M Ed, MAT); social work (MSW); substance use disorders (Certificate). *Application deadline:* For fall admission, 6/1 for domestic students, 4/1 for international students; for spring admission, 12/1 for domestic students. Applications are processed on a rolling basis. *Application fee:* $65. Electronic applications accepted. *Application Contact:* Candice Morey, Program Coordinator, 603-641-4313, E-mail: unhm.gradcenter@unh.edu. *Program Coordinator*, Candice Morey, 603-641-4313, E-mail: unhm.gradcenter@unh.edu.

Peter T. Paul College of Business and Economics Financial support: Fellowships, research assistantships, teaching assistantships, career-related internships or fieldwork, Federal Work-Study, scholarships/grants, and tuition waivers (full and partial) available. Support available to part-time students. Financial award application deadline: 2/15. *Degree program information:* Part-time and evening/weekend programs available. Part-time, evening/weekend. Offers accounting (MS); business administration (MBA); business and economics (MA, MBA, MS, PhD); economics (MA, PhD). *Application deadline:* For fall admission, 6/1 for domestic students, 4/1 for international students; for spring admission, 12/1 for domestic students. Applications are processed on a rolling basis. *Application fee:* $65. Electronic applications accepted. *Application Contact:* Deborah Merrill-Sands, Dean, 603-862-1983. *Dean*, Deborah Merrill-Sands, 603-862-1983.

School of Marine Science and Ocean Engineering Financial support: Fellowships, research assistantships, teaching assistantships, Federal Work-Study, scholarships/grants, and tuition waivers (full and partial) available. Support available to part-time students. Financial award application deadline: 2/15. Offers marine biology (MS, PhD); ocean engineering (MS, PhD); ocean mapping (MS, Postbaccalaureate Certificate); oceanography (MS, PhD). *Application deadline:* For fall admission, 4/1 priority date for domestic students; for spring admission, 12/1 for domestic students. Applications are processed on a rolling basis. *Application fee:* $65. Electronic applications accepted. *Application Contact:* Abby Pagan-Allis, Administrative Assistant, 603-862-3433, E-mail: ocean.engineering@unh.edu. *Chairperson*, Dr. Kenneth Baldwin, 603-862-1898.

School of Law Offers intellectual property, commerce and technology (MIP). Diploma awarded as part of Intellectual Property Summer Institute. Electronic applications accepted.

UNIVERSITY OF NEW HAVEN, West Haven, CT 06516-1916

General Information Independent, coed, comprehensive institution. CGS member. *Enrollment:* 6,786 graduate, professional, and undergraduate students; 1,145 full-time matriculated graduate/professional students (533 women), 639 part-time matriculated graduate/professional students (298 women). *Enrollment by degree level:* 1,684 master's, 28 doctoral, 20 other advanced degrees. *Graduate faculty:* 131 full-time (40 women), 101 part-time/adjunct (31 women). *Tuition, area resident:* Full-time $15,282; part-time $849 per credit hour. *Required fees:* $150; $60 per term. Tuition and fees vary according to program. *Graduate housing:* On-campus housing not available. *Student services:* Campus employment opportunities, campus safety program, career counseling, free psychological counseling, international student services, low-cost health insurance, multicultural affairs office, services for students with disabilities, writing training. *Library:* Marvin K. Peterson Library.

Computer facilities: Computer purchase and lease plans are available. 300 computers available on campus for general student use. A campuswide network can be accessed from student residence rooms. Online class registration, computer repair services are available.
Website: http://www.newhaven.edu/

General Application Contact: Michelle Mason, Director of Graduate Enrollment, 203-932-7440, E-mail: gradinfo@newhaven.edu.

GRADUATE UNITS

Graduate School Students: 1,145 full-time (533 women), 639 part-time (298 women); includes 296 minority (152 Black or African American, non-Hispanic/Latino; 7 American Indian or Alaska Native, non-Hispanic/Latino; 43 Asian, non-Hispanic/Latino; 67 Hispanic/Latino; 1 Native Hawaiian or other Pacific Islander, non-Hispanic/Latino; 26 Two or more races, non-Hispanic/Latino), 635 international. Average age 28. 3,101 applicants, 61% accepted, 719 enrolled. *Faculty:* 131 full-time (40 women), 101 part-time/adjunct (31 women). *Financial support:* Research assistantships with partial tuition reimbursements, teaching assistantships with partial tuition reimbursements, career-related internships or fieldwork, Federal Work-Study, scholarships/grants, and unspecified assistantships available. Support available to part-time students. Financial award applicants required to submit FAFSA. In 2015, 814 master's, 137 other advanced degrees awarded. *Degree program information:* Part-time and evening/weekend programs available. Part-time, evening/weekend, 100% online, blended/hybrid learning. *Application deadline:* For fall admission, 5/31 for international students; for winter admission, 10/15 for international students; for spring admission, 1/15 for international students. Applications are processed on a rolling basis. *Application fee:* $75. Electronic applications accepted. *Application Contact:* Michelle Mason, Director of Graduate Admissions, 203-932-7440, E-mail: gradinfo@newhaven.edu.

College of Arts and Sciences Students: 281 full-time (197 women), 116 part-time (79 women); includes 73 minority (34 Black or African American, non-Hispanic/Latino; 1 American Indian or Alaska Native, non-Hispanic/Latino; 12 Asian, non-Hispanic/Latino; 19 Hispanic/Latino; 1 Native Hawaiian or other Pacific Islander, non-Hispanic/Latino; 6 Two or more races, non-Hispanic/Latino), 46 international. 480 applicants, 81% accepted, 203 enrolled. *Faculty:* 33 full-time (17 women), 42 part-time/adjunct (21 women). *Financial support:* Research assistantships with partial tuition reimbursements, teaching assistantships with partial tuition reimbursements, career-related internships or fieldwork, Federal Work-Study, scholarships/grants, and unspecified assistantships available. Support available to part-time students. Financial award application deadline: 5/1; financial award applicants required to submit FAFSA. In 2015, 206 master's, 5 other advanced degrees awarded. *Degree program information:* Part-time and evening/weekend programs available. Part-time, evening/weekend. Offers applications of psychology (Graduate Certificate); arts and sciences (MA, MS, Graduate Certificate); cellular and molecular biology (MS, Graduate Certificate); community clinical services (MA); community psychology (MA); conflict management (MA); environmental ecology (MS); environmental education (MS); environmental geoscience (MS); environmental health and management (MS); environmental science (MS); forensic psychology (MA); geographical information systems (MS, Graduate Certificate); human nutrition (MS); industrial organizational psychology (MA); industrial-human resources psychology (MA); nutritional genomics (MS, Graduate Certificate); organizational development and consultation (MA); program development (MA); psychology of conflict management (Graduate Certificate). *Application deadline:* For fall admission, 5/31 for international students; for winter admission, 10/15 for international students; for spring admission, 1/15 for international students. Applications are processed on a rolling basis. *Application fee:* $75. Electronic applications accepted. *Application Contact:* Eloise Gormley, Director of Graduate Admissions, 203-932-7440, E-mail: gradinfo@newhaven.edu. *Dean of the College of Arts and Sciences*, Dr. Lourdes Alvarez, 203-932-7256, Fax: 203-931-6080, E-mail: lalvarez@newhaven.edu.

College of Business Students: 219 full-time (104 women), 154 part-time (89 women); includes 75 minority (46 Black or African American, non-Hispanic/Latino; 1 American Indian or Alaska Native, non-Hispanic/Latino; 10 Asian, non-Hispanic/Latino; 12 Hispanic/Latino; 6 Two or more races, non-Hispanic/Latino), 96 international. Average age 30. 326 applicants, 84% accepted, 144 enrolled. *Faculty:* 41 full-time (12 women). *Financial support:* Research assistantships with partial tuition reimbursements, teaching assistantships with partial tuition reimbursements, career-related internships or fieldwork, Federal Work-Study, scholarships/grants, and unspecified assistantships available. Support available to part-time students. Financial award application deadline: 5/1; financial award applicants required to submit FAFSA. In 2015, 180 master's, 35 other advanced degrees awarded. *Degree program information:* Part-time and evening/weekend programs available. Part-time, evening/weekend. Offers accounting (Graduate Certificate); business (EMBA, MBA, MS, Graduate Certificate); business administration (EMBA, MBA, Graduate Certificate); business intelligence (MBA); business management (Graduate Certificate); business policy and strategic leadership (MBA); collegiate athletic administration (MS); facility management (MS); finance (MBA); global marketing (MBA); health care administration (MS); health care management (Graduate Certificate); health care marketing (MS); health policy and finance (MS); human resource management in health care (MS); human resources management (MBA, Graduate Certificate); long-term care (MS); long-term health care (Graduate Certificate); managed care (MS); medical group management (MS); sport analytics (MS); sport management (MBA, Graduate Certificate); taxation (MS, Graduate Certificate). *Application deadline:* For fall admission, 5/31 for international students; for winter admission, 10/15 for international students; for spring admission, 1/15 for international students. Applications are processed on a rolling basis. *Application fee:* $75. Electronic applications accepted. *Application Contact:* Michelle Mason, Director of Graduate Enrollment, 203-932-7067, E-mail: mmason@newhaven.edu. *Dean*, Dr. Brian Kench, 203-932-7115, E-mail: bkench@newhaven.edu.

Henry C. Lee College of Criminal Justice and Forensic Sciences Students: 266 full-time (150 women), 182 part-time (96 women); includes 107 minority (58 Black or African American, non-Hispanic/Latino; 7 Asian, non-Hispanic/Latino; 34 Hispanic/Latino; 1 Native Hawaiian or other Pacific Islander, non-Hispanic/Latino; 7 Two or more races, non-Hispanic/Latino), 55 international. Average age 29. 358 applicants, 88% accepted, 174 enrolled. *Financial support:* Research assistantships with partial tuition reimbursements, teaching assistantships with partial tuition reimbursements, career-related internships or fieldwork, Federal Work-Study, scholarships/grants, and unspecified assistantships available. Support available to part-time students. Financial award applicants required to submit FAFSA. In 2015, 177 master's, 52 other advanced degrees awarded. *Degree program information:* Part-time and evening/weekend programs available. Part-time, evening/weekend, online learning. Offers advanced investigation (MS); city management (MPA); community-clinical services (MPA); crime analysis (MS); criminal investigations (MS); criminal justice (MS, PhD); criminal justice and forensic sciences (MPA, MS, PhD, Graduate Certificate); criminal justice management (MS, Graduate Certificate); criminalistics (MS); emergency management (MS, Graduate Certificate); financial crimes investigations (MS); fire administration (MS); fire science (MS); fire science administration (MS); fire/arson investigation (MS, Graduate Certificate); forensic computer investigation (MS, Graduate Certificate); forensic computer investigations (MS); forensic psychology (MS, Graduate Certificate); forensic science (MS); forensic science/fire science (Graduate Certificate); forensic technology (MS); health care management (MPA); information protection and security (MS, Graduate Certificate); long-term health care (MPA); national security (MS, Graduate Certificate); national security administration (Graduate Certificate); personnel and labor relations (MPA); public administration (MPA, Graduate Certificate); public safety management (MS, Graduate Certificate); victim advocacy and services management (Graduate Certificate); victimology (MS). *Application deadline:* For fall admission, 5/31 for international students; for winter admission, 10/15 for international students; for spring admission, 1/15 for international students. Applications are processed on a rolling basis. *Application fee:* $75. Electronic applications accepted. *Application Contact:* Michelle Mason, Director of Graduate Enrollment, 203-932-7067, E-mail: mmason@newhaven.edu. *Dean*, Dr. Mario Gaboury, 203-932-7253, E-mail: mgaboury@newhaven.edu.

Tagliatela College of Engineering Students: 378 full-time (86 women), 192 part-time (38 women); includes 35 minority (9 Black or African American, non-Hispanic/Latino; 3 American Indian or Alaska Native, non-Hispanic/Latino; 14 Asian, non-Hispanic/Latino; 6 Hispanic/Latino; 3 Two or more races, non-Hispanic/Latino), 453 international. Average age 26. 2,038 applicants, 49% accepted, 211 enrolled. *Financial support:* Research assistantships with partial tuition reimbursements, teaching assistantships with partial tuition reimbursements, career-related internships or fieldwork, Federal Work-Study, scholarships/grants, and unspecified assistantships available. Support available to part-time students. Financial award applicants required to submit FAFSA. In 2015, 226 master's, 25 other advanced degrees awarded. *Degree program information:* Part-time and evening/weekend programs available. Part-time, evening/weekend. Offers computer programming (Graduate Certificate); computer science (MS); control systems (MS); cyber systems (MS); data science (MS); digital signal processing and communication (MS); electrical and computer engineering (MS); electrical engineering (MS); engineering (MS, MSIE, Graduate Certificate); engineering and operations management (MS); engineering management (MS); environmental engineering (MS); industrial and hazardous waste (MS); industrial engineering (MSIE); Lean Six Sigma (Graduate Certificate); mechanical engineering (MS); network systems (MS); quality engineering (Graduate Certificate); software development (MS); water and wastewater treatment (MS); water resources (MS). *Application deadline:* For fall admission, 5/30 for international students; for winter admission, 10/15 for international students; for spring admission, 1/15 for international students. Applications are processed on a rolling basis. *Application fee:* $75. Electronic applications accepted. *Application Contact:* Michelle Mason, Director of Graduate Enrollment, 203-932-7440, E-mail: mmason@newhaven.edu. *Dean*, Dr. Ronald Harichandran, 203-932-7167, E-mail: rharichandran@newhaven.edu.

See Display on next page and Close-Up on page 909.

UNIVERSITY OF NEW MEXICO, Albuquerque, NM 87131-2039

General Information State-supported, coed, university. CGS member. *Enrollment:* 27,353 graduate, professional, and undergraduate students; 3,581 full-time matriculated graduate/professional students (1,830 women), 2,405 part-time matriculated graduate/professional students (1,368 women). *Enrollment by degree level:* 2,993 master's, 2,896 doctoral, 97 other advanced degrees. *Graduate faculty:* 824 full-time (359 women), 118 part-time/adjunct (52 women). *Graduate housing:* Rooms and/or apartments available on a first-come, first-served basis to single and married students. Typical cost: $5590 per year for single students; $6390 per year for married students. Room charges vary according to board plan, campus/location and housing facility selected. Housing application deadline: 7/16. *Student services:* Campus employment opportunities, campus safety program, career counseling, child daycare facilities, exercise/wellness program, free psychological counseling, grant writing training, international student services, low-cost health insurance, multicultural affairs office, services for students with disabilities, teacher training, writing training. *Library:* College of University Libraries and Learning Sciences plus 7 others. Students can reserve study rooms. *Research affiliation:* Lovelace Respiratory Research Institute, Phillips Laboratory, Oak Ridge National Laboratories, Sandia National Laboratories, New Mexico Consortium, Los Alamos National Laboratory.

Computer facilities: Computer purchase and lease plans are available. 990 computers available on campus for general student use. A campuswide network can be accessed from student residence rooms and from off campus. Online class registration is available.
Website: http://www.unm.edu/

General Application Contact: Deborah Kieltyka, Associate Director, Admissions, 505-277-3140, Fax: 505-277-6686, E-mail: deborahk@unm.edu.

GRADUATE UNITS

Graduate Studies Students: 2,136 full-time (1,074 women), 2,048 part-time (1,193 women); includes 1,379 minority (79 Black or African American, non-Hispanic/Latino; 158 American Indian or Alaska Native, non-Hispanic/Latino; 96 Asian, non-Hispanic/Latino; 952 Hispanic/Latino; 5 Native Hawaiian or other Pacific Islander, non-Hispanic/Latino; 89 Two or more races, non-Hispanic/Latino), 750 international. Average age 33. 3,498 applicants, 37% accepted, 938 enrolled. *Faculty:* 761 full-time (333 women), 101 part-time/adjunct (44 women). *Financial support:* Fellowships, research assistantships, teaching assistantships, career-related internships or fieldwork, Federal Work-Study, institutionally sponsored loans, scholarships/grants, health care benefits, tuition waivers (full and partial), and project assistantships, residencies available. Support available to part-time students. Financial award application deadline: 3/1; financial award applicants required to submit FAFSA. In 2015, 975 master's, 257 doctorates, 57 other advanced degrees awarded. *Degree program information:* Part-time and evening/weekend programs available. Part-time, evening/weekend, online only, 100% online, blended/hybrid learning. Offers hydroscience (MWR); policy management (MWR). *Application fee:* $50. Electronic applications accepted. *Application Contact:* Deborah Kieltyka, Associate Director, Admissions, 505-277-3140, Fax: 505-277-6686, E-mail: deborahk@unm.edu. *Dean*, Dr. Julie A. Coonrod, 505-277-2711, Fax: 505-277-7405, E-mail: jcoonrod@unm.edu.

College of Arts and Sciences Students: 330 full-time (135 women), 12 part-time (7 women); includes 322 minority (17 Black or African American, non-Hispanic/Latino; 27 American Indian or Alaska Native, non-Hispanic/Latino; 27 Asian, non-Hispanic/Latino; 219 Hispanic/Latino; 1 Native Hawaiian or other Pacific Islander, non-Hispanic/Latino; 31 Two or more races, non-Hispanic/Latino), 262 international. Average age 32. 1,437 applicants, 30% accepted, 286 enrolled. *Faculty:* 330 full-time (135 women), 12 part-time/adjunct (7 women). *Financial support:* Scholarships/grants, health care benefits, tuition waivers (full and partial), and unspecified assistantships available. Financial award application deadline: 3/1; financial award applicants required to submit FAFSA. In 2015, 225 master's, 114 doctorates awarded. *Degree program information:* Part-time programs available. Part-time. Offers American studies (MA, PhD); archaeology (MA, MS, PhD); arts and sciences (MA, MFA, MS, PhD); behavioral neuroscience (PhD); biology (MS, PhD); chemistry (MS, PhD); clinical psychology (PhD); cognitive neuroimaging (PhD); communication (MA, PhD); comparative literature and cultural studies (MA); creative writing (MFA); developmental psychology (PhD); earth and planetary sciences (MS, PhD); econometrics (MA); economic theory (MA); English (MA, PhD); environmental/natural resource economics (MA, PhD); ethnology (MA, MS, PhD); evolution (PhD); evolutionary anthropology (PhD); French (MA); French studies (PhD); geography and environmental studies (MS); German studies (MA); health psychology (PhD); history (MA, PhD); imaging science (MS, PhD); international/development and sustainability economics (MA, PhD); Latin American studies (MA, PhD); linguistics (MA, PhD); mathematics (MS, PhD); optical science and engineering (MS, PhD); philosophy (MA, PhD); photonics (MS, PhD); physics (MS, PhD); political science (MA, PhD); Portuguese (MA); public archaeology (MA, MS, PhD); public economics (MA, PhD); quantitative methodology (PhD); sociology (MA, PhD); Spanish (MA); Spanish and Portuguese (PhD); speech-language pathology (MS); statistics (MS, PhD). *Application fee:* $50. Electronic applications accepted. *Application Contact:* Vicki Hall, Academic Administrator III, 505-277-6131, Fax: 505-277-0351, E-mail: vhall@unm.edu. *Dean,* Dr. Brenda J. Claiborne, 505-277-6131, Fax: 505-277-0351, E-mail: brendac@unm.edu.

College of Education Students: 389 full-time (250 women), 594 part-time (449 women); includes 446 minority (30 Black or African American, non-Hispanic/Latino; 55 American Indian or Alaska Native, non-Hispanic/Latino; 17 Asian, non-Hispanic/Latino; 320 Hispanic/Latino; 1 Native Hawaiian or other Pacific Islander, non-Hispanic/Latino; 23 Two or more races, non-Hispanic/Latino), 79 international. Average age 36. 434 applicants, 59% accepted, 210 enrolled. *Faculty:* 117 full-time (75 women), 22 part-time/adjunct (14 women). *Financial support:* Career-related internships or fieldwork, Federal Work-Study, scholarships/grants, health care benefits, and unspecified assistantships available. Support available to part-time students. Financial award application deadline: 3/1; financial award applicants required to submit FAFSA. In 2015, 288 master's, 33 doctorates, 39 other advanced degrees awarded. *Degree program information:* Part-time and evening/weekend programs available. Part-time, evening/weekend. Offers American Indian education (MA); art education (MA); bilingual education (MA, PhD); community health education (MS); counseling (MA); counselor education (PhD); curriculum and instruction (PhD); education (MA, MS, Ed D, PhD, Ed S, Graduate Certificate); educational leadership (MA, Ed D, Ed S); educational linguistics (PhD); educational psychology (MA, PhD); educational thought and sociocultural studies (MA, PhD); exercise science (PhD); family life education (MA); family relations (MA); family studies (PhD); human development in families (MA); intensive social, language and behavioral needs (Graduate Certificate); learning and behavioral exceptionalities (MA); literacy/language arts (MA, PhD); math, science, and educational technology (MA); mental retardation and severe disabilities (MA); multicultural teacher and childhood education (Ed D, PhD); nutrition (MS); social studies (MA); special education (Ed D, PhD, Ed S); sports administration (PhD); TESOL (MA, PhD). *Application deadline:* For fall admission, 3/1 for international students; for spring admission, 8/1 for international students. *Application fee:* $50. Electronic applications accepted. *Application Contact:* Academic Graduate Coordinator, 505-277-3190, E-mail: coeac@unm.edu. *Dean,* Dr. Richard Howell, 505-277-2231, Fax: 505-277-8427, E-mail: rhowell@unm.edu.

College of Fine Arts Students: 93 full-time (52 women), 73 part-time (50 women); includes 36 minority (4 American Indian or Alaska Native, non-Hispanic/Latino; 3 Asian, non-Hispanic/Latino; 25 Hispanic/Latino; 4 Two or more races, non-Hispanic/Latino), 23 international. Average age 30. 236 applicants, 33% accepted, 47 enrolled. *Faculty:* 73 full-time (33 women), 8 part-time/adjunct (6 women). *Financial support:* Unspecified assistantships available. Financial award application deadline: 3/1; financial award applicants required to submit FAFSA. In 2015, 41 master's awarded. *Degree program information:* Part-time programs available. Part-time. Offers art history (MA); art of the Americas (MA); collaborative piano (M Mu); conducting (M Mu); dance (MFA); dance history (MA); dramatic writing (MFA); fine arts (M Mu, MA, MFA, PhD); history of architecture (PhD); history of graphic arts (PhD); history of photography (PhD); modern Latin American art (PhD); music education (M Mu); music history and literature (M Mu); Native American art (PhD); performance (M Mu); Pre-Columbian art and architecture (PhD); Spanish colonial art (PhD); studio art (MFA); theatre education and outreach (MA); theory and composition (M Mu). *Application fee:* $50. *Application Contact:* Deanna Sanchez-Mulcahy, Associate Director, Admissions, 505-277-4817, Fax: 505-277-0708, E-mail: dmulcahy@unm.edu. *Dean,* Dr. Jim Linnell, 505-277-2112, Fax: 505-277-0708, E-mail: jlinnell@unm.edu.

College of Pharmacy Degree program information: Part-time programs available. Part-time. Offers pharmaceutical sciences (MS, PhD); pharmacy (MS, PhD, Pharm D). Electronic applications accepted.

College of University Libraries and Learning Sciences Students: 27 full-time (15 women), 83 part-time (57 women); includes 49 minority (4 Black or African American, non-Hispanic/Latino; 4 American Indian or Alaska Native, non-Hispanic/Latino; 4 Asian, non-Hispanic/Latino; 35 Hispanic/Latino; 2 Two or more races, non-Hispanic/Latino), 5 international. Average age 44. 26 applicants, 62% accepted, 14 enrolled. *Faculty:* 8 full-time (4 women). *Financial support:* Fellowships, research assistantships, teaching assistantships with tuition reimbursements, and career-related internships or fieldwork available. Financial award application deadline: 3/1; financial award applicants required to submit FAFSA. In 2015, 19 master's, 4 doctorates awarded. *Degree program information:* Part-time and evening/weekend programs available. Part-time, evening/weekend, online learning. Offers organization, information and learning sciences (MA, PhD, Ed S). *Application deadline:* For fall admission, 3/15 for domestic and international students; for spring admission, 10/15 for domestic and international students. *Application fee:* $50. Electronic applications accepted. *Application Contact:* Linda Wood, Program Coordinator, 505-277-4131, Fax: 505-277-1427, E-mail: woodl@unm.edu. *Program Director,* Dr. Charlotte Gunawardens, 505-277-5046, Fax: 505-277-1427, E-mail: lani@unm.edu.

Health Sciences Center Students: 180 full-time (124 women), 88 part-time (61 women); includes 112 minority (7 Black or African American, non-Hispanic/Latino; 7 American Indian or Alaska Native, non-Hispanic/Latino; 12 Asian, non-Hispanic/Latino; 82 Hispanic/Latino; 2 Native Hawaiian or other Pacific Islander, non-Hispanic/Latino; 2 Two or more races, non-Hispanic/Latino), 21 international. Average age 30. Offers biochemistry and molecular biology (MS, PhD); cell biology and physiology (MS, PhD); clinical and translational science (Certificate); community health (MPH); dental hygiene (MS); education (MS); epidemiology (MPH); health sciences (MOT, MPH, MPT, MS, MSN, DNP, DPT, MD, PhD, Pharm D, Certificate); health systems, services and policy (MPH); laboratory management (MS); molecular genetics and microbiology (MS, PhD); neuroscience (MS, PhD); nursing (MSN, DNP, PhD); occupational therapy (MOT); pathology (MS, PhD); physical therapy (DPT); physician assistant studies (MS); research and development (MS); toxicology (MS, PhD). *Application Contact:* Deborah Kieltyka, Associate Director, Admissions, 505-277-3140, Fax: 505-277-6686, E-mail: deborahk@unm.edu. *Interim Vice President,* Dr. R. Philip Eaton.

School of Architecture and Planning Students: 129 full-time (62 women), 55 part-time (28 women); includes 36 minority (7 Black or African American, non-Hispanic/Latino; 15 American Indian or Alaska Native, non-Hispanic/Latino; 6 Asian, non-Hispanic/Latino; 4 Hispanic/Latino; 4 Two or more races, non-Hispanic/Latino), 26 international. Average age 32. 129 applicants, 64% accepted, 57 enrolled. *Faculty:* 25 full-time (7 women), 17 part-time/adjunct (3 women). *Financial support:* Application deadline: 3/1; applicants required to submit FAFSA. In 2015, 73 master's, 11 other advanced degrees awarded. Offers architecture (M Arch); architecture and planning

(M Arch, MCRP, MLA, Graduate Certificate); community and regional planning (MCRP); historic preservation and regionalism (Graduate Certificate); landscape architecture (MLA). *Application deadline:* For fall admission, 2/1 for domestic and international students. *Application fee:* $50. Electronic applications accepted. *Application Contact:* Elizabeth M. Rowe, Senior Academic Adviser, 505-277-1303, Fax: 505-277-0076, E-mail: erowe@unm.edu. *Dean*, Geraldine Forbes Isais, 505-277-2053, E-mail: gforbes@unm.edu.

School of Engineering Students: 430 full-time (89 women), 367 part-time (76 women); includes 147 minority (3 Black or African American, non-Hispanic/Latino; 1 American Indian or Alaska Native, non-Hispanic/Latino; 16 Asian, non-Hispanic/Latino; 112 Hispanic/Latino; 15 Two or more races, non-Hispanic/Latino), 317 international. Average age 30. 867 applicants, 36% accepted, 202 enrolled. *Faculty:* 111 full-time (19 women), 12 part-time/adjunct (2 women). *Financial support:* Federal Work-Study, scholarships/grants, health care benefits, and unspecified assistantships available. Financial award application deadline: 3/1; financial award applicants required to submit FAFSA. In 2015, 142 master's, 53 doctorates awarded. *Degree program information:* Part-time programs available. Part-time. Offers biomedical engineering (MS, PhD); chemical engineering (MS, PhD); civil engineering (M Eng, MSCE); computer engineering (MS, PhD); computer science (MS, PhD); construction management (MCM); electrical and computer engineering (MS, PhD); engineering (M Eng, MCM, MEME, MS, MSCE, PhD); manufacturing engineering (MEME); mechanical engineering (MS, PhD); nanoscience and microsystems engineering (MS, PhD); nuclear engineering (MS, PhD). *Application deadline:* For fall admission, 1/15 priority date for domestic and international students; for spring admission, 7/14 priority date for domestic and international students. Applications are processed on a rolling basis. *Application fee:* $50. Electronic applications accepted. *Application Contact:* Deborah Kieltyka, Associate Director, Admissions, 505-277-3140, Fax: 505-277-6686, E-mail: deborahk@unm.edu. *Dean*, Prof. Gruia-Catalin Roman, 505-277-5522, Fax: 505-277-1422, E-mail: gcroman@unm.edu.

School of Public Administration Students: 63 full-time (40 women), 138 part-time (95 women); includes 118 minority (8 Black or African American, non-Hispanic/Latino; 31 American Indian or Alaska Native, non-Hispanic/Latino; 4 Asian, non-Hispanic/Latino; 71 Hispanic/Latino; 4 Two or more races, non-Hispanic/Latino), 9 international. Average age 37. 73 applicants, 74% accepted, 44 enrolled. *Faculty:* 12 full-time (5 women), 5 part-time/adjunct (0 women). *Financial support:* Fellowships with partial tuition reimbursements, research assistantships with partial tuition reimbursements, career-related internships or fieldwork, scholarships/grants, health care benefits, and unspecified assistantships available. Financial award application deadline: 3/31; financial award applicants required to submit FAFSA. In 2015, 95 master's awarded. *Degree program information:* Part-time and evening/weekend programs available. Part-time, evening/weekend, online learning. Offers health administration (MHA); public administration (MHA, MPA). *Application deadline:* For fall admission, 4/1 for domestic students, 3/1 for international students; for spring admission, 10/1 for domestic students, 8/1 for international students. *Application fee:* $50. Electronic applications accepted. *Application Contact:* Gene V. Henley, Associate Director and Graduate Academic Advisor, 505-277-9196, Fax: 505-277-2529, E-mail: spadvise@unm.edu. *Director*, Dr. Uday Desai, 505-277-1092, Fax: 505-277-2529, E-mail: ucdesai@unm.edu.

Robert O. Anderson Graduate School of Management Students: 272 full-time (121 women), 281 part-time (133 women); includes 247 minority (11 Black or African American, non-Hispanic/Latino; 19 American Indian or Alaska Native, non-Hispanic/Latino; 35 Asian, non-Hispanic/Latino; 166 Hispanic/Latino; 16 Two or more races, non-Hispanic/Latino), 51 international. Average age 31. 337 applicants, 58% accepted, 167 enrolled. *Faculty:* 44 full-time (13 women), 15 part-time/adjunct (7 women). *Financial support:* In 2015–16, 136 students received support, including 30 fellowships (averaging $14,300 per year), 44 research assistantships with partial tuition reimbursements available (averaging $9,099 per year); career-related internships or fieldwork, Federal Work-Study, scholarships/grants, and unspecified assistantships also available. Support available to part-time students. Financial award application deadline: 6/1; financial award applicants required to submit FAFSA. In 2015, 295 master's awarded. *Degree program information:* Part-time and evening/weekend programs available. Part-time, evening/weekend. Offers accounting (MBA); advanced accounting (M Acct); entrepreneurship (MBA); finance (MBA); human resources management (MBA); information assurance (M Acct, MBA); information systems and assurance (MS); international management (MBA); international management in Latin America (MBA); management (EMBA, M Acct, MBA, MS); management information systems (MBA); management of technology (MBA); marketing management (MBA); operations management (MBA); professional accounting (M Acct); strategic management and policy (MBA); tax accounting (M Acct). *Application deadline:* For fall admission, 4/1 priority date for domestic and international students; for spring admission, 10/1 priority date for domestic and international students. Applications are processed on a rolling basis. *Application fee:* $50. Electronic applications accepted. *Application Contact:* Tracy Wilkey, Manager, Academic Advisement, 505-277-3290, Fax: 505-277-8436, E-mail: andersonadvising@unm.edu. *Dean*, Dr. Craig White, 505-277-6471, Fax: 505-277-0344, E-mail: cwhite@unm.edu.

School of Law Offers law (JD). Electronic applications accepted.

School of Medicine Offers medicine (MOT, MPH, MS, DPT, MD, PhD, Certificate); university science teaching (Certificate). Electronic applications accepted.

UNIVERSITY OF NEW ORLEANS, New Orleans, LA 70148

General Information State-supported, coed, university. CGS member. *Graduate housing:* Rooms and/or apartments available on a first-come, first-served basis to single and married students. *Research affiliation:* John C. Stennis Space Center (acoustics, computer science), Northrop Grumman Corporation (engineering), TJ Watson Research Center–IBM (chemistry), Paratek Microwave, Inc. (nanotechnology), Applied Research Lab-Penn State University (engineering), Lockheed Martin Corporation (materials).

GRADUATE UNITS

Graduate School ***Degree program information:*** Part-time and evening/weekend programs available. Part-time, evening/weekend. Electronic applications accepted.

College of Business Administration Degree program information: Part-time and evening/weekend programs available. Part-time, evening/weekend. Offers accounting (MS); business administration (MBA, MS, PhD); economics and finance (MS); financial economics (PhD); health care management (MS); hospitality and tourism management (MS); taxation (MS). Electronic applications accepted.

College of Education and Human Development Degree program information: Part-time programs available. Part-time, online learning. Offers counselor education (M Ed, PhD); curriculum and instruction (M Ed, PhD); education and human development (M Ed, MAT, PhD); educational leadership (M Ed, PhD); special education and habilitative services (M Ed, PhD). Electronic applications accepted.

College of Engineering Degree program information: Part-time programs available. Part-time. Offers engineering (MS, PhD); engineering and applied sciences (PhD); engineering management (MS); mechanical engineering (MS). Electronic applications accepted.

College of Liberal Arts Degree program information: Part-time and evening/weekend programs available. Part-time, evening/weekend. Offers arts administration (MA); design (MFA); English (MA); film production (MFA); fine arts (MFA); foreign languages (MA); geography (MA); history (MA); liberal arts (MA, MFA, MM, MPA, MS, MURP, PhD); music (MM); political science (MA, PhD); public administration (MPA); sociology (MA); theatre performance (MFA); transportation (MS); urban and regional planning (MURP); urban studies (MS, PhD). Electronic applications accepted.

College of Sciences Degree program information: Part-time and evening/weekend programs available. Part-time, evening/weekend. Offers biological sciences (MS, PhD); chemistry (MS, PhD); computer science (MS); earth and environmental sciences (MS); mathematics (MS); physics (MS, PhD); psychology (MS, PhD); sciences (MS, PhD). Electronic applications accepted.

UNIVERSITY OF NORTH ALABAMA, Florence, AL 35632-0001

General Information State-supported, coed, comprehensive institution. *Enrollment:* 7,078 graduate, professional, and undergraduate students; 321 full-time matriculated graduate/professional students (179 women), 643 part-time matriculated graduate/professional students (417 women). *Enrollment by degree level:* 884 master's, 80 other advanced degrees. *Graduate faculty:* 80 full-time (35 women), 18 part-time/adjunct (7 women). Tuition, state resident: full-time $2286; part-time $1524 per semester. Tuition, nonresident: full-time $4572; part-time $3048 per semester. *Required fees:* $801; $579 per semester. Tuition and fees vary according to course load. *Graduate housing:* Rooms and/or apartments available on a first-come, first-served basis to single and married students. Typical cost: $5342 per year for single students; $7704 per year for married students. Room charges vary according to board plan and housing facility selected. *Student services:* Campus employment opportunities, campus safety program, career counseling, child daycare facilities, exercise/wellness program, free psychological counseling, grant writing training, international student services, multicultural affairs office, services for students with disabilities, writing training. *Library:* Collier Library plus 3 others. *Collection:* Books: 364,265 (physical), 446,090 (digital/electronic); Serial titles: 2,756 (physical), 112,907 (digital/electronic); Databases: 166. Weekly public service hours: 98; students can reserve study rooms.

Computer facilities: 925 computers available on campus for general student use. A campuswide network can be accessed. Online class registration is available.
Website: http://www.una.edu/

General Application Contact: Hillary N. Coats, Graduate Admissions Coordinator, 256-765-4447, E-mail: hcoats@una.edu.

GRADUATE UNITS

College of Arts and Sciences Students: 52 full-time (25 women), 86 part-time (53 women); includes 26 minority (20 Black or African American, non-Hispanic/Latino; 1 American Indian or Alaska Native, non-Hispanic/Latino; 2 Asian, non-Hispanic/Latino; 1 Hispanic/Latino; 2 Two or more races, non-Hispanic/Latino), 16 international. Average age 32. 68 applicants, 72% accepted, 42 enrolled. *Faculty:* 25 full-time (12 women), 4 part-time/adjunct (2 women). *Financial support:* In 2015–16, 21 students received support. Career-related internships or fieldwork, scholarships/grants, and unspecified assistantships available. Financial award application deadline: 2/1; financial award applicants required to submit FAFSA. In 2015, 24 master's awarded. *Degree program information:* Part-time programs available. Part-time, 100% online. Offers arts and sciences (MA, MPS, MS, MSCJ); community development (MPS); criminal justice (MSCJ); English (MA); family studies (MS); geospatial science (MS); history (MA); information technology (MPS); public history (MA); security and safety leadership (MPS). *Application deadline:* Applications are processed on a rolling basis. *Application fee:* $50 ($100 for international students). Electronic applications accepted. *Application Contact:* Hillary N. Coats, Graduate Admissions Coordinator, 256-765-4447, E-mail: graduate@una.edu. *Dean*, Dr. Carmen L. Burkhalter, 256-765-4288, Fax: 256-765-4778, E-mail: cburkhalter@una.edu.

College of Business Students: 127 full-time (56 women), 272 part-time (132 women); includes 133 minority (55 Black or African American, non-Hispanic/Latino; 4 American Indian or Alaska Native, non-Hispanic/Latino; 66 Asian, non-Hispanic/Latino; 2 Hispanic/Latino; 4 Native Hawaiian or other Pacific Islander, non-Hispanic/Latino; 2 Two or more races, non-Hispanic/Latino), 33 international. Average age 35. 268 applicants, 76% accepted, 140 enrolled. *Faculty:* 15 full-time (1 woman), 5 part-time/adjunct (1 woman). *Financial support:* In 2015–16, 1 student received support. Scholarships/grants available. Financial award application deadline: 2/1; financial award applicants required to submit FAFSA. In 2015, 133 master's awarded. *Degree program information:* Part-time programs available. Part-time, 100% online, blended/hybrid learning. Offers business administration (MBA). *Application deadline:* Applications are processed on a rolling basis. *Application fee:* $50 ($100 for international students). Electronic applications accepted. *Application Contact:* Hillary N. Coats, Graduate Admissions Coordinator, 256-765-4447, E-mail: graduate@una.edu. *Dean*, Dr. Gregory A. Carnes, 256-765-4261, Fax: 256-765-4170, E-mail: gacarnes@una.edu.

College of Education Students: 95 full-time (54 women), 232 part-time (185 women); includes 39 minority (25 Black or African American, non-Hispanic/Latino; 6 American Indian or Alaska Native, non-Hispanic/Latino; 4 Hispanic/Latino; 4 Two or more races, non-Hispanic/Latino), 3 international. Average age 33. 153 applicants, 73% accepted, 90 enrolled. *Faculty:* 26 full-time (14 women), 12 part-time/adjunct (7 women). *Financial support:* In 2015–16, 14 students received support. Scholarships/grants and unspecified assistantships available. Financial award application deadline: 2/1; financial award applicants required to submit FAFSA. In 2015, 102 master's, 17 other advanced degrees awarded. *Degree program information:* Part-time programs available. Part-time, 100% online, blended/hybrid learning. Offers clinical mental health counseling (MA); collaborative teacher special education (MA Ed); education (MA, MA Ed, MS, Ed S); education leadership (MA Ed, Ed S); elementary education (MA Ed); health and human performance (MS); instructional leadership (MA Ed); school counseling P-12 (MA Ed); secondary education (MA Ed); special education (MA Ed). *Application deadline:* Applications are processed on a rolling basis. *Application fee:* $50 ($100 for international students). Electronic applications accepted. *Application Contact:* Hillary N. Coats, Graduate Admissions Coordinator, 256-765-4447, E-mail: graduate@una.edu. *Dean*, Dr. Donna Lefort, 256-765-4252, Fax: 256-765-4664, E-mail: dpjacobs@una.edu.

College of Nursing and Allied Health Students: 47 full-time (44 women), 53 part-time (47 women); includes 20 minority (18 Black or African American, non-Hispanic/Latino; 1 American Indian or Alaska Native, non-Hispanic/Latino; 1 Asian, non-Hispanic/Latino). Average age 39. 38 applicants, 89% accepted, 26 enrolled. *Faculty:* 4 full-time (all women). *Financial support:* In 2015–16, 4 students received support. Scholarships/grants available. Financial award application deadline: 2/1; financial award applicants required to submit FAFSA. In 2015, 24 master's awarded. 100% online, blended/hybrid learning. Offers nursing and allied health (MSN). *Application deadline:* Applications are processed on a rolling basis. *Application fee:* $50 ($100 for international students). Electronic applications accepted. *Application Contact:* Hillary N. Coats, Graduate Admissions Coordinator, 256-465-4447, E-mail: graduate@una.edu. *Dean*, Dr. Vicky G. Pierce, 256-765-6301, E-mail: vgpierce@una.edu.

UNIVERSITY OF NORTH CAROLINA AT ASHEVILLE, Asheville, NC 28804-3299

General Information State-supported, coed, comprehensive institution. *Enrollment:* 3,891 graduate, professional, and undergraduate students; 3 full-time matriculated graduate/professional students (1 woman), 28 part-time matriculated graduate/professional students (14 women). *Enrollment by degree level:* 31 master's. *Graduate faculty:* 6 full-time (2 women), 4 part-time/adjunct (2 women). Tuition, state resident: full-time $7345. Tuition, nonresident: full-time $22,585. *Required fees:* $2756. Part-time tuition and fees vary according to course load. *Graduate housing:* Room and/or apartments available on a first-come, first-served basis to single students; on-campus housing not available to married students. Typical cost: $4890 per year ($8746 including board). Room and board charges vary according to board plan and housing facility selected. Housing application deadline: 5/1. *Student services:* Campus employment opportunities, career counseling, exercise/wellness program, international student services, low-cost health insurance, multicultural affairs office, services for students with disabilities, writing training. *Library:* D. Hiden Ramsey Library. *Collection:* Books: 306,273 (physical), 487,660 (digital/electronic); Serial titles: 113 (physical), 82,954 (digital/electronic); Databases: 138. Weekly public service hours: 99; students can reserve study rooms.

Computer facilities: Computer purchase and lease plans are available. 477 computers available on campus for general student use. A campuswide network can be accessed from student residence rooms and from off campus. Online class registration is available.
Website: http://www.unca.edu/

General Application Contact: Jordan Dolfi, Program Associate, Graduate Studies, 828-250-2399.

GRADUATE UNITS

Master of Liberal Arts and Sciences Students: 3 full-time (1 woman), 28 part-time (14 women), 1 international. Average age 41. 12 applicants, 92% accepted, 4 enrolled. *Faculty:* 6 full-time (2 women), 4 part-time/adjunct (2 women). *Financial support:* Health care benefits available. Financial award application deadline: 5/1; financial award applicants required to submit FAFSA. In 2015, 9 master's awarded. *Degree program information:* Part-time and evening/weekend programs available. Part-time, evening/weekend. Offers liberal arts and sciences (MLA, Graduate Certificate). *Application deadline:* For fall admission, 4/15 for domestic students; for spring admission, 11/15 for domestic students. *Application fee:* $60. Electronic applications accepted. *Application Contact:* Jordan Dolfi, Program Associate, Master of Liberal Arts and Sciences Program and the Asheville Graduate Center, 828-251-6099, E-mail: jdolfi@unca.edu. *Director, Master of Liberal Arts and Sciences Program and the Asheville Graduate Center*, Gerard Voos, 828-232-5040, E-mail: gvoos@unca.edu.

THE UNIVERSITY OF NORTH CAROLINA AT CHAPEL HILL, Chapel Hill, NC 27599

General Information State-supported, coed, university. CGS member. *Enrollment:* 29,084 graduate, professional, and undergraduate students; 8,473 full-time matriculated graduate/professional students (4,808 women), 1,633 part-time matriculated graduate/professional students (691 women). *Enrollment by degree level:* 4,163 master's, 5,937 doctoral, 6 other advanced degrees. *Graduate faculty:* 3,483 full-time (1,590 women), 292 part-time/adjunct (171 women). *Graduate housing:* Rooms and/or apartments available on a first-come, first-served basis to single and married students. *Student services:* Campus employment opportunities, campus safety program, career counseling, child daycare facilities, exercise/wellness program, free psychological counseling, grant writing training, international student services, low-cost health insurance, multicultural affairs office, services for students with disabilities, teacher training, writing training. *Library:* Davis Library plus 12 others. *Collection:* Books: 6.7 million (physical), 1.5 million (digital/electronic); Serial titles: 147,757 (digital/electronic); Databases: 1,457. Weekly public service hours: 109; study areas open 24 hours, 5–7 days a week; students can reserve study rooms. *Research affiliation:* Research Triangle Institute, Centers for Disease Control (CDC), Triangle Universities Nuclear Laboratory.

Computer facilities: Computer purchase and lease plans are available. 867 computers available on campus for general student use. A campuswide network can be accessed from student residence rooms and from off campus. Online class registration is available.
Website: http://www.unc.edu/

GRADUATE UNITS

Eshelman School of Pharmacy Students: 104 full-time (50 women); includes 30 minority (4 Black or African American, non-Hispanic/Latino; 1 American Indian or Alaska Native, non-Hispanic/Latino; 10 Asian, non-Hispanic/Latino; 4 Hispanic/Latino; 2 Native Hawaiian or other Pacific Islander, non-Hispanic/Latino; 9 Two or more races, non-Hispanic/Latino), 16 international. Average age 26. 268 applicants, 9% accepted, 25 enrolled. *Faculty:* 112 full-time (45 women), 362 part-time/adjunct (188 women). *Financial support:* In 2015–16, 11 students received support, including 18 fellowships with full tuition reimbursements available (averaging $27,500 per year), 56 research assistantships with full tuition reimbursements available (averaging $27,500 per year), teaching assistantships with full tuition reimbursements available (averaging $27,500 per year); career-related internships or fieldwork, Federal Work-Study, institutionally sponsored loans, scholarships/grants, traineeships, health care benefits, tuition waivers (full), and unspecified assistantships also available. Financial award application deadline: 12/15. In 2015, 8 master's, 13 doctorates awarded. Offers health system pharmacy administration (MS); pharmacy (PhD). *Application deadline:* For fall admission, 12/7 priority date for domestic students, 12/15 priority date for international students. Applications are processed on a rolling basis. *Application fee:* $85. Electronic applications accepted. *Application Contact:* Mimi Lewis, Coordinator of Admissions, 919-962-0097, Fax: 919-966-9428, E-mail: mimi_lewis@unc.edu. *Dean*, Dr. Robert A. Blouin, 919-966-1122, Fax: 919-966-6919, E-mail: bob_blouin@unc.edu.

Graduate School Online learning. Electronic applications accepted.

College of Arts and Sciences Degree program information: Part-time programs available. Part-time. Offers acting (MFA); anthropology (MA, PhD); art history (MA, PhD); arts and sciences (MA, MCRP, MFA, MPA, MRP, MS, MSRA, PhD, Certificate); athletic training (MA); behavioral neuroscience psychology (PhD); botany (MA, MS, PhD); cell biology, development, and physiology (MA, MS, PhD); cell motility and cytoskeleton (PhD); chemistry (MA, MS, PhD); city and regional planning (MCRP); classical archaeology (MA, PhD); classics (MA, PhD); clinical psychology (PhD); cognitive psychology (PhD); communication studies (PhD); computer science (MS, PhD); costume production (MFA); developmental psychology (PhD); ecology (MA, MS, PhD); ecology and behavior (MA, MS, PhD); economics (MS, PhD); English (MA, PhD); exercise physiology (MA); folklore (MA); French (MA, PhD); genetics and molecular biology (MA, MS, PhD); geography (MA, PhD); geological sciences (MS, PhD); history (MA, PhD); Italian (MA, PhD); Latin American studies (Certificate); linguistics (MA); literature and linguistics (MA, PhD); marine sciences (MS, PhD); materials science (MS, PhD); mathematics (MA, MS, PhD); morphology, systematics, and evolution (MA, MS, PhD); music (MA, PhD); operations research (MS, PhD); philosophy (MA, PhD); physics (MS, PhD); planning (PhD); Polish literature (PhD); political science (MA, PhD); Portuguese (MA, PhD); public policy (PhD); public policy analysis (PhD); quantitative psychology (PhD); religious studies (MA, PhD); Romance languages (MA, PhD); Romance philology (MA, PhD); Russian and east European studies (MA); Russian literature (MA, PhD); Serbo-Croatian literature (PhD); Slavic linguistics (MA, PhD); social psychology (PhD); sociology (MA, PhD); Spanish (MA, PhD); sport administration (MA); statistics (MS, PhD); studio art (MFA); technical production (MFA); trans-Atlantic studies (MA). Electronic applications accepted.

Gillings School of Global Public Health Students: 1,382 full-time (985 women); includes 441 minority (126 Black or African American, non-Hispanic/Latino; 2 American Indian or Alaska Native, non-Hispanic/Latino; 138 Asian, non-Hispanic/Latino; 82 Hispanic/Latino; 3 Native Hawaiian or other Pacific Islander, non-Hispanic/Latino; 90 Two or more races, non-Hispanic/Latino), 171 international. Average age 31. 1,893 applicants, 40% accepted, 402 enrolled. *Faculty:* 252 full-time (141 women). In 2015, 395 master's, 114 doctorates awarded. *Degree program information:* Part-time programs available. Part-time, 100% online, blended/hybrid learning. Offers air, radiation and industrial hygiene (MPH, MS, MSEE, MSPH, PhD); aquatic and atmospheric sciences (MPH, MS, MSPH, PhD); biostatistics (MPH, MS, Dr PH, PhD); environmental engineering (MPH, MS, MSEE, MSPH, PhD); environmental health sciences (MPH, MS, MSPH, PhD); environmental management and policy (MPH, MS, MSPH, PhD); epidemiology (MPH, MSCR, PhD); global public health (MHA, MPH, MS, MSCR, MSEE, MSPH, Dr PH, PhD); health behavior (MPH, PhD); health care and prevention (MPH); health policy and management (MHA, MPH, MSPH, Dr PH, PhD); leadership (MPH); maternal and child health (MPH, MSPH, Dr PH, PhD); nutrition (MPH, PhD); nutritional biochemistry (MS); occupational health nursing (MPH). *Application deadline:* For fall admission, 12/10 priority date for domestic and international students. Applications are processed on a rolling basis. *Application fee:* $85. Electronic applications accepted. *Application Contact:* Johnston King, Admissions Coordinator, 919-962-6314, Fax: 919-966-6352, E-mail: sph-osa@unc.edu. *Dean*, Dr. Barbara K. Rimer, 919-966-3245, Fax: 919-966-7678.

School of Education Degree program information: Part-time programs available. Part-time. Offers culture, curriculum and change (MA, PhD); early childhood intervention and family support (M Ed); early childhood, intervention and literacy (MA, PhD); education (M Ed, MA, MAT, MSA, Ed D, PhD); education for experienced teachers (K-12) (M Ed); educational leadership (Ed D); educational psychology, measurement and evaluation (MA, PhD); English (Grades 9-12) (MAT); English as a second language (MAT); French (Grades K-12) (MAT); German (Grades K-12) (MAT); Japanese (Grades K-12) (MAT); Latin (Grades 9-12) (MAT); mathematics (Grades 9-12) (MAT); music (Grades K-12) (MAT); school administration (MSA); school counseling (M Ed); school psychology (M Ed, MA, PhD); science (Grades 9-12) (MAT); social studies (Grades 9-12) (MAT); Spanish (Grades K-12) (MAT). Electronic applications accepted.

School of Government Offers government (MPA). Electronic applications accepted.

School of Information and Library Science Students: 164 full-time (118 women), 53 part-time (36 women); includes 46 minority (11 Black or African American, non-Hispanic/Latino; 7 Asian, non-Hispanic/Latino; 8 Hispanic/Latino; 3 Native Hawaiian or other Pacific Islander, non-Hispanic/Latino; 17 Two or more races, non-Hispanic/Latino), 29 international. Average age 28. 291 applicants, 64% accepted, 79 enrolled. *Faculty:* 29 full-time (13 women), 46 part-time/adjunct (23 women). *Financial support:* In 2015–16, 99 fellowships with full tuition reimbursements (averaging $2,565 per year), 68 research assistantships with full tuition reimbursements (averaging $25,120 per year), 10 teaching assistantships with full tuition reimbursements (averaging $11,628 per year) were awarded; career-related internships or fieldwork, Federal Work-Study, scholarships/grants, health care benefits, and unspecified assistantships also available. Financial award application deadline: 12/16. In 2015, 96 master's, 6 doctorates awarded. *Degree program information:* Part-time programs available. Part-time. Offers data curation (PMC); information and library science (PhD); information science (MSIS); library science (MSLS). *Application deadline:* For fall admission, 12/15 priority date for domestic and international students; for spring admission, 10/13 for domestic and international students. Applications are processed on a rolling basis. *Application fee:* $85. Electronic applications accepted. *Application Contact:* Lara Bailey, Student Services Coordinator, 919-962-7601, Fax: 919-962-8071, E-mail: bailey@email.unc.edu. *Dean*, Dr. Gary Marchionini, 919-962-8363, Fax: 919-962-8071, E-mail: gary@ils.unc.edu.

School of Journalism and Mass Communication Degree program information: Part-time programs available. Part-time, online learning. Offers mass communication (MA, PhD); technology and communication (MA). Electronic applications accepted.

School of Social Work Degree program information: Part-time programs available. Part-time. Offers social work (MSW, PhD). Electronic applications accepted.

Kenan-Flagler Business School ***Degree program information:*** Evening/weekend programs available. Evening/weekend, online learning. Offers accounting (MAC); business (MAC, MBA, PhD); business administration (MBA, PhD); finance (PhD); marketing (PhD); operations management (PhD); organizational behavior (PhD); strategy (PhD). Electronic applications accepted.

School of Dentistry Offers dental hygiene (MS); dentistry (MS, DDS, PhD); endodontics (MS); epidemiology (PhD); operative dentistry (MS); oral and maxillofacial pathology (MS); oral and maxillofacial radiology (MS); oral biology (PhD); orthodontics (MS); pediatric dentistry (MS); periodontology (MS); prosthodontics (MS). Electronic applications accepted.

School of Law Offers law (JD). JD/MAPPS offered jointly with Duke University. Electronic applications accepted.

School of Medicine Offers allied health sciences (MPT, MS, Au D, DPT, PhD); audiology (Au D); biochemistry and biophysics (MS, PhD); bioinformatics and computational biology (PhD); biomedical engineering (MS, PhD); cell and developmental biology (PhD); cell and molecular physiology (PhD); experimental pathology (PhD); genetics and molecular biology (PhD); human movement science (PhD); immunology (MS, PhD); medicine (MPT, MS, Au D, DPT, MD, PhD); microbiology (MS, PhD); microbiology and immunology (MS, PhD); neurobiology (PhD); occupational science (MS, PhD); occupational therapy (MS); pathology and laboratory medicine (PhD);

pharmacology (PhD); physical therapy (DPT); physical therapy - off campus (DPT); physical therapy - on campus (DPT); rehabilitation counseling and psychology (MS); speech and hearing sciences (MS, Au D, PhD); toxicology (MS, PhD). Electronic applications accepted.

School of Nursing Students: 208 full-time (186 women), 128 part-time (116 women); includes 109 minority (49 Black or African American, non-Hispanic/Latino; 4 American Indian or Alaska Native, non-Hispanic/Latino; 32 Asian, non-Hispanic/Latino; 7 Hispanic/Latino; 17 Two or more races, non-Hispanic/Latino), 17 international. Average age 33. 624 applicants, 25% accepted, 150 enrolled. *Faculty:* 86 full-time (78 women), 44 part-time/adjunct (40 women). *Financial support:* In 2015–16, 8 fellowships with full tuition reimbursements, 6 research assistantships with partial tuition reimbursements (averaging $8,000 per year), 10 teaching assistantships with partial tuition reimbursements (averaging $8,000 per year) were awarded; scholarships/grants, traineeships, health care benefits, and unspecified assistantships also available. Support available to part-time students. Financial award application deadline: 3/1; financial award applicants required to submit FAFSA. In 2015, 91 master's, 14 doctorates awarded. *Degree program information:* Part-time programs available. Part-time. Offers advanced practice registered nurse (DNP); health care systems (DNP); nursing (MSN, PhD, PMC). *Application deadline:* For fall admission, 12/15 for domestic and international students. *Application fee:* $85. Electronic applications accepted. *Application Contact:* Emily Sayed, Assistant Director, Graduate Admissions, 919-966-4260, Fax: 919-966-3540, E-mail: sayed@unc.edu. *Dean/Professor,* Donna S. Havens, PhD, RN, 919-966-3731, Fax: 919-966-3540, E-mail: dhavens@email.unc.edu.

THE UNIVERSITY OF NORTH CAROLINA AT CHARLOTTE, Charlotte, NC 28223-0001

General Information State-supported, coed, university. CGS member. *Enrollment:* 27,983 graduate, professional, and undergraduate students; 2,419 full-time matriculated graduate/professional students (1,216 women), 2,832 part-time matriculated graduate/professional students (1,696 women). *Enrollment by degree level:* 3,295 master's, 855 doctoral, 1,087 other advanced degrees. *Graduate faculty:* 831 full-time (345 women), 82 part-time/adjunct (47 women). Tuition, state resident: full-time $4128. Tuition, nonresident: full-time $16,799. *Required fees:* $2904. Tuition and fees vary according to course load and program. *Graduate housing:* Room and/or apartments available on a first-come, first-served basis to single students; on-campus housing not available to married students. Typical cost: $5660 per year ($10,220 including board). Room and board charges vary according to board plan and housing facility selected. Housing application deadline: 5/1. *Student services:* Campus employment opportunities, campus safety program, career counseling, exercise/wellness program, free psychological counseling, grant writing training, international student services, low-cost health insurance, multicultural affairs office, services for students with disabilities, writing training. *Library:* J. Murrey Atkins Library plus 1 other. *Collection:* Books: 2.8 million (physical); Serial titles: 86,331 (physical); Databases: 660. Study areas open 24 hours, 5–7 days a week; students can reserve study rooms. *Research affiliation:* McGraw Hill Education (special education and child development), SAS Institute (computer science), SURVICE Engineering Company (physics, optical sciences), Health Resources and Services Administration (HRSA) (public health sciences), National Science Foundation (bioinformatics, genomics), HDR Engineering, Inc. of the Carolinas (civil and environmental engineering).

Computer facilities: 1,600 computers available on campus for general student use. A campuswide network can be accessed from student residence rooms and from off campus. Online class registration is available.
Website: http://www.uncc.edu/

General Application Contact: Kathy B. Giddings, Director of Graduate Admissions, 704-687-5503, Fax: 704-687-1668, E-mail: gradadm@uncc.edu.

GRADUATE UNITS

Belk College of Business Students: 213 full-time (88 women), 372 part-time (118 women); includes 103 minority (43 Black or African American, non-Hispanic/Latino; 28 Asian, non-Hispanic/Latino; 19 Hispanic/Latino; 13 Two or more races, non-Hispanic/Latino), 146 international. Average age 30. 563 applicants, 66% accepted, 213 enrolled. *Faculty:* 82 full-time (26 women), 4 part-time/adjunct (0 women). *Financial support:* In 2015–16, 74 students received support, including 8 research assistantships (averaging $16,250 per year), 66 teaching assistantships (averaging $10,715 per year); career-related internships or fieldwork, institutionally sponsored loans, scholarships/grants, unspecified assistantships, and administrative assistantships also available. Support available to part-time students. Financial award application deadline: 3/1; financial award applicants required to submit FAFSA. In 2015, 284 master's, 4 doctorates, 1 other advanced degree awarded. *Degree program information:* Part-time and evening/weekend programs available. Part-time, evening/weekend. Offers accounting (M Acc); applied econometrics (Graduate Certificate); business (M Acc, MBA, MS, PhD, Graduate Certificate, Post-Master's Certificate); business administration (MBA, PhD); business foundations (Graduate Certificate); economics (MS); management (Post-Master's Certificate); mathematical finance (MS); real estate (MS, Graduate Certificate). *Application fee:* $75. Electronic applications accepted. *Application Contact:* Kathy B. Giddings, Director of Graduate Admissions, 704-687-5503, Fax: 704-687-1668, E-mail: gradadm@uncc.edu. *Dean,* Dr. Steven Ott, 704-687-7577, Fax: 704-687-1393, E-mail: cob-dean@uncc.edu.

College of Arts and Architecture Students: 91 full-time (50 women), 4 part-time (2 women); includes 22 minority (10 Black or African American, non-Hispanic/Latino; 2 Asian, non-Hispanic/Latino; 7 Hispanic/Latino; 3 Two or more races, non-Hispanic/Latino), 14 international. Average age 25. 146 applicants, 76% accepted, 44 enrolled. *Faculty:* 49 full-time (18 women). *Financial support:* In 2015–16, 38 students received support, including 1 fellowship (averaging $50,000 per year), 30 research assistantships (averaging $6,882 per year), 7 teaching assistantships (averaging $5,258 per year); career-related internships or fieldwork, institutionally sponsored loans, scholarships/grants, and unspecified assistantships also available. Support available to part-time students. Financial award application deadline: 3/1; financial award applicants required to submit FAFSA. In 2015, 40 master's awarded. *Degree program information:* Part-time programs available. Part-time. Offers arts and architecture (M Arch I, M Arch II, MUD, Graduate Certificate); violin (Graduate Certificate); vocal pedagogy (Graduate Certificate). *Application fee:* $75. Electronic applications accepted. *Application Contact:* Kathy B. Giddings, Director of Graduate Admissions, 704-687-5503, Fax: 704-687-1668, E-mail: gradadm@uncc.edu. *Dean,* Kenneth A. Lambla, 704-687-0090, E-mail: kalambla@uncc.edu.

School of Architecture Students: 88 full-time (47 women), 4 part-time (2 women); includes 21 minority (9 Black or African American, non-Hispanic/Latino; 2 Asian, non-Hispanic/Latino; 7 Hispanic/Latino; 3 Two or more races, non-Hispanic/Latino), 14 international. Average age 25. 143 applicants, 76% accepted, 41 enrolled. *Faculty:* 19 full-time (6 women). *Financial support:* In 2015–16, 36 students received support, including 1 fellowship (averaging $50,000 per year), 30 research assistantships (averaging $6,882 per year), 5 teaching assistantships (averaging $1,200 per year); institutionally sponsored loans, scholarships/grants, and unspecified assistantships also available. Financial award application deadline: 3/1; financial award applicants required to submit FAFSA. In 2015, 40 master's awarded. Offers architecture (M Arch I, M Arch II); urban design (MUD). *Application deadline:* For fall admission, 1/15 priority date for domestic and international students. *Application fee:* $75. Electronic applications accepted. *Application Contact:* Kathy B. Giddings, Director of Graduate Admissions, 704-687-5503, Fax: 704-687-1668, E-mail: gradadm@uncc.edu. *Dean,* Kenneth A. Lambla, 704-687-0090, E-mail: kalambla@uncc.edu.

College of Computing and Informatics Students: 499 full-time (177 women), 225 part-time (73 women); includes 54 minority (25 Black or African American, non-Hispanic/Latino; 12 Asian, non-Hispanic/Latino; 11 Hispanic/Latino; 1 Native Hawaiian or other Pacific Islander, non-Hispanic/Latino; 5 Two or more races, non-Hispanic/Latino), 565 international. Average age 26. 1,978 applicants, 33% accepted, 226 enrolled. *Faculty:* 62 full-time (21 women), 10 part-time/adjunct (2 women). *Financial support:* In 2015–16, 163 students received support, including 8 fellowships (averaging $49,455 per year), 57 research assistantships (averaging $12,068 per year), 97 teaching assistantships (averaging $8,501 per year); career-related internships or fieldwork, institutionally sponsored loans, scholarships/grants, unspecified assistantships, and administrative assistantships also available. Support available to part-time students. Financial award application deadline: 3/1; financial award applicants required to submit FAFSA. In 2015, 213 master's, 16 doctorates, 26 other advanced degrees awarded. *Degree program information:* Part-time and evening/weekend programs available. Part-time, evening/weekend. Offers advanced databases and knowledge discovery (Graduate Certificate); bioinformatics (PSM); bioinformatics and computational biology (PhD); bioinformatics applications (Graduate Certificate); bioinformatics technology (Graduate Certificate); computer science (MS); computing and informatics (MS, PSM, PhD, Graduate Certificate); computing and information systems (PhD); game design and development (Graduate Certificate); information security and privacy (Graduate Certificate); information technology (MS); management of information technology (Graduate Certificate). *Application fee:* $75. Electronic applications accepted. *Application Contact:* Kathy B. Giddings, Director of Graduate Admissions, 704-687-5503, Fax: 704-687-1668, E-mail: gradadm@uncc.edu. *Dean,* Dr. Yi Deng, 704-687-8450, E-mail: yi.deng@uncc.edu.

College of Education Students: 270 full-time (227 women), 1,140 part-time (896 women); includes 427 minority (328 Black or African American, non-Hispanic/Latino; 22 Asian, non-Hispanic/Latino; 52 Hispanic/Latino; 25 Two or more races, non-Hispanic/Latino), 18 international. Average age 33. 977 applicants, 82% accepted, 627 enrolled. *Faculty:* 113 full-time (70 women), 30 part-time/adjunct (21 women). *Financial support:* In 2015–16, 47 students received support, including 36 research assistantships (averaging $13,939 per year), 7 teaching assistantships (averaging $6,571 per year); career-related internships or fieldwork, institutionally sponsored loans, scholarships/grants, unspecified assistantships, and administrative assistantships also available. Support available to part-time students. Financial award application deadline: 3/1; financial award applicants required to submit FAFSA. In 2015, 230 master's, 42 doctorates, 322 other advanced degrees awarded. *Degree program information:* Part-time and evening/weekend programs available. Part-time, evening/weekend, 100% online, blended/hybrid learning. Offers academically or intellectually gifted (Graduate Certificate); art education (Graduate Certificate); autism spectrum disorders (Graduate Certificate); child and family development: birth through kindergarten (Graduate Certificate); child and family development: early childhood education (MAT); child and family studies: early education (M Ed); counseling (MA, PhD); curriculum and instruction (PhD); curriculum and supervision (M Ed, Post-Master's Certificate); education (M Ed, MA, MAT, MSA, Ed D, PhD, Graduate Certificate, Post-Master's Certificate, Postbaccalaureate Certificate); educational leadership (Ed D); elementary education (M Ed, MAT, Graduate Certificate); elementary mathematics education (Graduate Certificate); foreign language education (MAT); instructional systems technology (M Ed, Graduate Certificate); middle grades and secondary education (M Ed); middle grades education (MAT); play therapy (Postbaccalaureate Certificate); reading education (M Ed); school administration (MSA, Post-Master's Certificate); school counseling (Post-Master's Certificate); secondary education (MAT); special education (M Ed, MAT, PhD, Graduate Certificate); substance abuse counseling (Postbaccalaureate Certificate); teaching (Graduate Certificate); teaching English as a second language (M Ed, MAT, Graduate Certificate); theatre education (Graduate Certificate). *Application fee:* $75. Electronic applications accepted. *Application Contact:* Kathy B. Giddings, Director of Graduate Admissions, 704-687-5503, Fax: 704-687-1668, E-mail: gradadm@uncc.edu. *Dean,* Dr. Ellen McIntyre, 704-687-8722, E-mail: ellen.mcintyre@uncc.edu.

College of Health and Human Services Students: 387 full-time (306 women), 162 part-time (139 women); includes 163 minority (111 Black or African American, non-Hispanic/Latino; 1 American Indian or Alaska Native, non-Hispanic/Latino; 19 Asian, non-Hispanic/Latino; 24 Hispanic/Latino; 8 Two or more races, non-Hispanic/Latino), 23 international. Average age 30. 716 applicants, 51% accepted, 227 enrolled. *Faculty:* 75 full-time (52 women), 23 part-time/adjunct (19 women). *Financial support:* In 2015–16, 75 students received support, including 1 fellowship (averaging $42,000 per year), 47 research assistantships (averaging $5,689 per year), 22 teaching assistantships (averaging $10,992 per year); career-related internships or fieldwork, institutionally sponsored loans, scholarships/grants, traineeships, unspecified assistantships, and administrative assistantships also available. Support available to part-time students. Financial award application deadline: 3/1; financial award applicants required to submit FAFSA. In 2015, 180 master's, 5 doctorates, 11 other advanced degrees awarded. *Degree program information:* Part-time and evening/weekend programs available. Part-time, evening/weekend, 100% online, blended/hybrid learning. Offers community health (Certificate); health administration (MHA); health and human services (MHA, MS, MSN, MSPH, MSW, DNP, PhD, Certificate, Graduate Certificate, Post-Master's Certificate); health services research (PhD); kinesiology (MS); public health (MSPH); public health core concepts (Graduate Certificate); public health sciences (PhD). *Application fee:* $75. Electronic applications accepted. *Application Contact:* Kathy B. Giddings, Director of Graduate Admissions, 704-687-5503, Fax: 704-687-1668, E-mail: gradadm@uncc.edu. *Dean,* Dr. Nancy Fey-Yensan, 704-687-7917, E-mail: fey-yensan@uncc.edu.

School of Nursing Students: 109 full-time (89 women), 112 part-time (107 women); includes 46 minority (37 Black or African American, non-Hispanic/Latino; 3 Asian, non-Hispanic/Latino; 5 Hispanic/Latino; 1 Two or more races, non-Hispanic/Latino). Average age 33. 321 applicants, 34% accepted, 84 enrolled. *Faculty:* 26 full-time (25 women), 4 part-time/adjunct (3 women). *Financial support:* In 2015–16, 9 students received support, including 5 research assistantships (averaging $4,850 per year), 3 teaching assistantships (averaging $2,911 per year); career-related internships or fieldwork, institutionally sponsored loans, scholarships/grants, traineeships, unspecified assistantships, and administrative assistantships also available. Support available to part-time students. Financial award application deadline: 3/1; financial award applicants required to submit FAFSA. In 2015, 76 master's, 4 doctorates, 7 other advanced degrees awarded. *Degree program information:* Part-time programs available. Part-time, blended/hybrid learning. Offers adult-gerontology acute care nurse practitioner (MSN, Post-Master's Certificate); advanced clinical nursing (MSN); community public health nursing (MSN); family nurse practitioner across the lifespan (MSN, Post-Master's Certificate); nurse administrator (MSN, Graduate Certificate); nurse anesthesia (MSN, Post-Master's Certificate); nurse educator (MSN, Graduate Certificate); nursing (DNP); nursing systems/population (MSN). *Application deadline:* For fall admission, 2/1 for domestic and international students; for spring admission, 10/1 priority date for domestic and international students; for summer admission, 4/1 priority date for domestic and international students. Applications are processed on a rolling basis. *Application fee:* $75. Electronic applications accepted. *Application Contact:* Kathy B. Giddings, Director of Graduate Admissions, 704-687-5503, Fax: 704-687-1668, E-mail: gradadm@uncc.edu. *Associate Dean*, Dr. Dee Baldwin, 704-687-7952, Fax: 704-687-6017, E-mail: dbaldwi5@uncc.edu.

School of Social Work Students: 129 full-time (109 women), 6 part-time (5 women); includes 52 minority (35 Black or African American, non-Hispanic/Latino; 4 Asian, non-Hispanic/Latino; 9 Hispanic/Latino; 4 Two or more races, non-Hispanic/Latino). Average age 28. 198 applicants, 59% accepted, 61 enrolled. *Faculty:* 14 full-time (10 women), 11 part-time/adjunct (10 women). *Financial support:* In 2015–16, 14 students received support, including 13 research assistantships (averaging $2,110 per year); career-related internships or fieldwork, Federal Work-Study, institutionally sponsored loans, scholarships/grants, unspecified assistantships, and administrative assistantships also available. Support available to part-time students. Financial award application deadline: 3/1; financial award applicants required to submit FAFSA. In 2015, 45 master's awarded. *Degree program information:* Part-time programs available. Part-time. Offers social work (MSW). *Application deadline:* For fall admission, 2/1 for domestic and international students. *Application fee:* $75. Electronic applications accepted. *Application Contact:* Kathy B. Giddings, Director of Graduate Admissions, 704-687-5503, Fax: 704-687-1668, E-mail: gradadm@uncc.edu. *Interim Director*, Dr. Vivian B. Lord, 704-687-7931, Fax: 704-687-1658, E-mail: vblord@uncc.edu.

College of Liberal Arts and Sciences Students: 417 full-time (237 women), 381 part-time (226 women); includes 167 minority (73 Black or African American, non-Hispanic/Latino; 2 American Indian or Alaska Native, non-Hispanic/Latino; 12 Asian, non-Hispanic/Latino; 58 Hispanic/Latino; 2 Native Hawaiian or other Pacific Islander, non-Hispanic/Latino; 20 Two or more races, non-Hispanic/Latino), 113 international. Average age 29. 736 applicants, 51% accepted, 224 enrolled. *Faculty:* 328 full-time (140 women), 10 part-time/adjunct (2 women). *Financial support:* In 2015–16, 341 students received support, including 11 fellowships (averaging $39,481 per year), 109 research assistantships (averaging $11,194 per year), 221 teaching assistantships (averaging $10,688 per year); career-related internships or fieldwork, institutionally sponsored loans, and scholarships/grants also available. Support available to part-time students. Financial award application deadline: 3/1; financial award applicants required to submit FAFSA. In 2015, 202 master's, 44 doctorates, 43 other advanced degrees awarded. *Degree program information:* Part-time and evening/weekend programs available. Part-time, evening/weekend. Offers Africana studies (Graduate Certificate); anthropology (MA); applied ethics (Graduate Certificate); applied linguistics (Graduate Certificate); applied mathematics (PhD); applied physics (MS); biological sciences (MA, MS, PhD); chemistry (MS); cognitive science (Graduate Certificate); communication studies (MA); criminal justice and criminology (MS); earth sciences (MS); emergency management (Graduate Certificate); English (MA); English education (MA); ethics and applied philosophy (MA); gender, sexuality, and women's studies (Graduate Certificate); geography (MA); geography and urban regional analysis (PhD); gerontology (MA, Graduate Certificate); health psychology (PhD); history (MA); industrial/organizational psychology (MA); Latin American studies (MA); liberal arts and sciences (MA, MPA, MS, PhD, Graduate Certificate); liberal studies (MA); mathematics (MS); mathematics education (MA); nanoscale science (PhD); non-profit management (Graduate Certificate); optical science and engineering (MS, PhD); organizational science (PhD); psychology (MA); public administration (MPA); public budgeting and finance (Graduate Certificate); public policy (PhD); religious studies (MA); sociology (MA); Spanish (MA); technical and professional writing (Graduate Certificate); translating (Graduate Certificate); urban management and policy (Graduate Certificate). *Application fee:* $75. Electronic applications accepted. *Application Contact:* Kathy B. Giddings, Director of Graduate Admissions, 704-687-5503, Fax: 704-687-1668, E-mail: gradadm@uncc.edu. *Dean*, Dr. Nancy A. Gutierrez, 704-687-0081, E-mail: ngutierr@uncc.edu.

The Graduate School Students: 62 full-time (32 women), 85 part-time (44 women); includes 51 minority (28 Black or African American, non-Hispanic/Latino; 14 Asian, non-Hispanic/Latino; 6 Hispanic/Latino; 1 Native Hawaiian or other Pacific Islander, non-Hispanic/Latino; 2 Two or more races, non-Hispanic/Latino), 36 international. Average age 32. 231 applicants, 53% accepted, 69 enrolled. *Faculty:* 1 (woman) full-time, 3 part-time/adjunct (all women). *Financial support:* In 2015–16, 52 students received support, including 26 research assistantships (averaging $12,092 per year), 18 teaching assistantships (averaging $10,144 per year); career-related internships or fieldwork, institutionally sponsored loans, scholarships/grants, traineeships, unspecified assistantships, and administrative assistantships also available. Support available to part-time students. Financial award application deadline: 3/1; financial award applicants required to submit FAFSA. In 2015, 18 master's, 16 Graduate Certificates awarded. *Degree program information:* Part-time and evening/weekend programs available. Part-time, evening/weekend. Offers data science and business analytics (PSM, Graduate Certificate); health informatics (PSM, Graduate Certificate). *Application fee:* $75. Electronic applications accepted. *Application Contact:* Kathy B. Giddings, Director of Graduate Admissions, 704-687-5503, Fax: 704-687-1668, E-mail: gradadm@uncc.edu. *Dean and Associate Provost*, Dr. Thomas L. Reynolds, 704-687-7248, E-mail: gradadm@uncc.edu.

The William States Lee College of Engineering Students: 453 full-time (90 women), 224 part-time (49 women); includes 52 minority (26 Black or African American, non-Hispanic/Latino; 8 Asian, non-Hispanic/Latino; 17 Hispanic/Latino; 1 Two or more races, non-Hispanic/Latino), 446 international. Average age 27. 1,599 applicants, 51% accepted, 211 enrolled. *Faculty:* 120 full-time (17 women), 2 part-time/adjunct (0 women). *Financial support:* In 2015–16, 247 students received support, including 8 fellowships (averaging $33,478 per year), 118 research assistantships (averaging $9,848 per year), 120 teaching assistantships (averaging $6,069 per year); career-related internships or fieldwork, institutionally sponsored loans, scholarships/grants, unspecified assistantships, and administrative assistantships also available. Support available to part-time students. Financial award application deadline: 3/1; financial award applicants required to submit FAFSA. In 2015, 172 master's, 17 doctorates, 9 other advanced degrees awarded. *Degree program information:* Part-time and evening/weekend programs available. Part-time, evening/weekend, blended/hybrid learning. Offers applied energy (Graduate Certificate); applied energy and electromechanical systems (MS); civil engineering (MSCE); construction and facilities management (MS); electrical engineering (MSEE, PhD); energy analytics (Graduate Certificate); engineering (MS, MSCE, MSE, MSEE, MSEM, MSME, PhD, Graduate Certificate); engineering management (MSEM); fire protection and administration (MS); infrastructure and environmental systems (PhD); Lean Six Sigma (Graduate Certificate); logistics and supply chains (Graduate Certificate); mechanical engineering (MSME, PhD); systems analytics (Graduate Certificate). *Application fee:* $75. Electronic applications accepted. *Application Contact:* Kathy B. Giddings, Director of Graduate Admissions, 704-687-5503, Fax: 704-687-1668, E-mail: gradadm@uncc.edu. *Dean*, Dr. Robert E. Johnson, 704-687-8242, E-mail: robejohn@uncc.edu.

THE UNIVERSITY OF NORTH CAROLINA AT GREENSBORO, Greensboro, NC 27412-5001

General Information State-supported, coed, university. CGS member. *Graduate housing:* Room and/or apartments available to single students; on-campus housing not available to married students. Housing application deadline: 5/15. *Research affiliation:* Moses Cone Memorial Hospital, North Carolina Zoological Park, North Carolina Baptist Hospital.

GRADUATE UNITS

Graduate School ***Degree program information:*** Part-time and evening/weekend programs available. Part-time, evening/weekend, online learning. Offers liberal studies (MALS). Electronic applications accepted.

Bryan School of Business and Economics Degree program information: Part-time programs available. Part-time. Offers accounting (MS); applied economics (MA); business administration (MBA, PMC, Postbaccalaureate Certificate); business and economics (MA, MBA, MS, PhD, Certificate, PMC, Postbaccalaureate Certificate); consumer, apparel, and retail studies (MS, PhD); economics (MA, PhD); financial analysis (PMC); financial economics (MA); information systems (PhD); information technology (Certificate); information technology and management (MS); supply chain management (Certificate). Electronic applications accepted.

College of Arts and Sciences Degree program information: Part-time programs available. Part-time. Offers advanced Spanish language and Hispanic cultural studies (Certificate); American literature (PhD); applied geography (MA); arts and sciences (M Ed, MA, MFA, MPA, MS, PhD, Certificate); biochemistry (MS); biology (MS); chemistry (MS); clinical psychology (MA, PhD); cognitive psychology (MA, PhD); communication studies (MA); computer science (MS); creative writing (MFA); criminology (MA); developmental psychology (MA, PhD); English (M Ed, MA, PhD, Certificate); English literature (PhD); film and video production (MFA); French (MA); geographic information science (Certificate); geography (PhD); historic preservation (Certificate); history (MA); interior architecture (MS); Latin (M Ed); mathematics (MA, PhD); museum studies (Certificate); nonprofit management (Certificate); public affairs (MPA); rhetoric and composition (PhD); social psychology (MA, PhD); sociology (MA); Spanish (MA, Certificate); studio arts (MFA); U.S. history (PhD); urban and economic development (Certificate); women's and gender studies (MA, Certificate). Electronic applications accepted.

School of Education Degree program information: Part-time and evening/weekend programs available. Part-time, evening/weekend. Offers advanced school counseling (PMC); college teaching and adult learning (Certificate); counseling and counselor education (PhD); counseling and educational development (MS); couple and family counseling (PMC); cross-categorical special education (M Ed); curriculum and instruction (M Ed); curriculum and teaching (PhD); education (M Ed, MLIS, MS, MSA, Ed D, PhD, Certificate, Ed S, PMC); educational leadership (Ed D, Ed S); educational research, measurement and evaluation (PhD); English as a second language (Certificate); higher education (M Ed, PhD); interdisciplinary studies in special education (M Ed); leadership early care and education (Certificate); library and information studies (MLIS); school administration (MSA); school counseling (PMC); special education (M Ed, PhD); supervision (M Ed); teacher education and development (PhD). Electronic applications accepted.

School of Health and Human Sciences Offers athletic training (MSAT); community health education (MPH, Dr PH); community recreation management (MS); genetic counseling (MS); gerontology (MS, Certificate); health and human sciences (M Ed, MA, MFA, MPH, MS, Dr PH, Ed D, PhD); human development and family studies (M Ed, MS, PhD); kinesiology (MS, Ed D, PhD); nutrition (MS, PhD); peace and conflict studies (MA, Certificate); social work (MSW); speech language pathology (PhD); speech pathology and audiology (MA); therapeutic recreation (MS). Electronic applications accepted.

School of Music, Theatre and Dance Offers acting (MFA); composition (MM); dance (MA, MFA); design (MFA); directing (MFA); education (MM); music education (PhD); performance (MM, DMA); theater education (M Ed); theater for youth (MFA); theatre (M Ed, MFA); theory (MM). Electronic applications accepted.

School of Nursing Offers adult clinical nurse specialist (MSN, PMC); adult/gerontological nurse practitioner (MSN, PMC); nurse anesthesia (MSN, PMC); nursing (PhD); nursing administration (MSN); nursing education (MSN). Electronic applications accepted.

THE UNIVERSITY OF NORTH CAROLINA AT PEMBROKE, Pembroke, NC 28372-1510

General Information State-supported, coed, comprehensive institution. CGS member. *Enrollment:* 6,441 graduate, professional, and undergraduate students; 155 full-time matriculated graduate/professional students (113 women), 599 part-time matriculated graduate/professional students (423 women). *Enrollment by degree level:* 754 master's. *Graduate faculty:* 27 full-time (9 women), 2 part-time/adjunct (1 woman). *Graduate housing:* Room and/or apartments available to single students; on-campus housing not available to married students. Housing application deadline: 4/15. *Student services:* Campus employment opportunities, career counseling, exercise/wellness program, free psychological counseling, international student services, low-cost health insurance, multicultural affairs office, services for students with disabilities. *Library:* Mary Livermore Library. *Collection:* Books: 409,000 (physical), 172,000 (digital/electronic); Serial titles: 53,000 (physical), 53,000 (digital/electronic). Weekly public service hours: 106.

Computer facilities: 501 computers available on campus for general student use. A campuswide network can be accessed from student residence rooms and from off campus. Online class registration, online library, commuter/off campus connection to network, discounted computer software/hardware are available.
Website: http://www.uncp.edu/

General Application Contact: Gary Locklear, Administrative Assistant, 910-521-6271, Fax: 910-521-6751, E-mail: grad@uncp.edu.

GRADUATE UNITS

Graduate School Students: 113 full-time (all women), 599 part-time (423 women); includes 247 minority (121 Black or African American, non-Hispanic/Latino; 107 American Indian or Alaska Native, non-Hispanic/Latino; 5 Asian, non-Hispanic/Latino;

14 Hispanic/Latino). 260 applicants, 95% accepted, 211 enrolled. *Faculty:* 27 full-time (9 women), 2 part-time/adjunct (1 woman). *Financial support:* In 2015–16, 40 research assistantships with partial tuition reimbursements (averaging $8,000 per year) were awarded; career-related internships or fieldwork and unspecified assistantships also available. Support available to part-time students. Financial award application deadline: 4/15; financial award applicants required to submit FAFSA. In 2015, 226 master's awarded. *Degree program information:* Part-time and evening/weekend programs available. Part-time, evening/weekend, 100% online, blended/hybrid learning. Offers art education (MA, MAT); clinical nurse leader (MSN); English education (MA, MAT); mathematics education (MA); nurse educator (MSN); public administration (MPA); rural case manager (MSN); science education (MA, MAT); social studies education (MA, MAT); social work (MSW). *Application deadline:* For fall admission, 3/15 priority date for domestic and international students; for spring admission, 10/15 priority date for domestic and international students. Applications are processed on a rolling basis. *Application fee:* $45 ($60 for international students). Electronic applications accepted. *Application Contact:* Gary Locklear, Executive Assistant, 910-521-6271, Fax: 910-521-6751, E-mail: grad@uncp.edu. *Dean*, Dr. Irene P. Aiken, 910-521-6271, Fax: 910-521-6751, E-mail: grad@uncp.edu.

School of Business Financial support: Research assistantships with full tuition reimbursements and unspecified assistantships available. Support available to part-time students. Financial award application deadline: 4/15; financial award applicants required to submit FAFSA. *Degree program information:* Part-time and evening/weekend programs available. Part-time, evening/weekend. Offers business (MBA). *Application deadline:* For fall admission, 7/15 priority date for domestic and international students; for spring admission, 12/1 priority date for domestic and international students. Applications are processed on a rolling basis. *Application fee:* $45 ($60 for international students). *Application Contact:* Dean of Graduate Studies, 910-521-6271, Fax: 910-521-6751, E-mail: grad@uncp.edu. *Interim Dean*, Dr. W. Stewart Thomas, 910-521-6214, Fax: 910-521-6564.

School of Education Financial support: Research assistantships with full tuition reimbursements, career-related internships or fieldwork, and unspecified assistantships available. Support available to part-time students. Financial award application deadline: 4/15. *Degree program information:* Part-time and evening/weekend programs available. Part-time, evening/weekend. Offers clinical mental health counseling (MA Ed); counseling (MA Ed); elementary education (MA Ed); health and human performance (MA); physical education (MA); professional school counseling (MA Ed); reading education (MA Ed); school administration (MSA). *Application deadline:* For fall admission, 7/15 priority date for domestic and international students; for spring admission, 12/1 priority date for domestic and international students. Applications are processed on a rolling basis. *Application fee:* $45 ($60 for international students). *Application Contact:* Dean of Graduate Studies, 910-521-6271, Fax: 910-521-6751, E-mail: grad@uncp.edu. *Dean*, Dr. Alfred Bryant, Jr., 910-775-4009, Fax: 910-521-6165, E-mail: alfred.bryant@uncp.edu.

UNIVERSITY OF NORTH CAROLINA SCHOOL OF THE ARTS, Winston-Salem, NC 27127-2738

General Information State-supported, coed, comprehensive institution. *Enrollment:* 970 graduate, professional, and undergraduate students; 112 full-time matriculated graduate/professional students (61 women), 2 part-time matriculated graduate/professional students. *Enrollment by degree level:* 114 master's. *Graduate faculty:* 68. Tuition, state resident: full-time $7696; part-time $855 per credit hour. Tuition, nonresident: full-time $20,803; part-time $2311 per credit hour. *Required fees:* $2863. *Graduate housing:* Room and/or apartments available on a first-come, first-served basis to single students. Housing application deadline: 5/1. *Student services:* Campus employment opportunities, campus safety program, career counseling, exercise/wellness program, free psychological counseling, grant writing training, international student services, low-cost health insurance, services for students with disabilities, writing training. *Library:* Semans Library. *Collection:* Books: 124,450 (physical), 44,708 (digital/electronic); Serial titles: 422 (physical), 17,788 (digital/electronic); Databases: 150. Weekly public service hours: 90.

Computer facilities: Computer purchase and lease plans are available. 117 computers available on campus for general student use. A campuswide network can be accessed from student residence rooms and from off campus. Online class registration is available.
Website: http://www.uncsa.edu/

General Application Contact: Sheeler Lawson, Director of Admissions, 336-770-3290, Fax: 336-770-3370, E-mail: admissions@uncsa.edu.

GRADUATE UNITS

School of Design and Production Students: 54 full-time (36 women); includes 7 minority (2 Black or African American, non-Hispanic/Latino; 4 Hispanic/Latino; 1 Two or more races, non-Hispanic/Latino), 3 international. Average age 27. 37 applicants, 62% accepted, 18 enrolled. *Faculty:* 21 full-time (6 women), 4 part-time/adjunct (1 woman). *Financial support:* Career-related internships or fieldwork, Federal Work-Study, and unspecified assistantships available. Support available to part-time students. Financial award application deadline: 3/15; financial award applicants required to submit FAFSA. In 2015, 16 master's awarded. Offers costume design (MFA); costume technology (MFA); performance arts management (MFA); scene design (MFA); scenic art (MFA); sound design (MFA); stage automation (MFA); stage properties (MFA); technical direction (MFA); wig and make-up design (MFA). *Application deadline:* For fall admission, 4/1 priority date for domestic students. Applications are processed on a rolling basis. *Application fee:* $95 ($100 for international students). Electronic applications accepted. *Application Contact:* Sheeler Lawson, Director of Admissions, 336-770-3290, Fax: 336-770-3370, E-mail: admissions@uncsa.edu. *Dean*, Michael J. Kelley, 336-770-3214 Ext. 103, Fax: 336-770-3213, E-mail: kelleym@uncsa.edu.

School of Filmmaking Students: 9 full-time (0 women), 2 part-time (0 women); includes 3 minority (1 Black or African American, non-Hispanic/Latino; 1 Hispanic/Latino; 1 Two or more races, non-Hispanic/Latino), 3 international. Average age 26. 8 applicants, 100% accepted, 6 enrolled. *Faculty:* 5 full-time (1 woman), 1 part-time/adjunct (0 women). *Financial support:* Fellowships, research assistantships, career-related internships or fieldwork, and Federal Work-Study available. Support available to part-time students. Financial award application deadline: 3/15; financial award applicants required to submit FAFSA. In 2015, 4 master's awarded. Offers creative producing (MFA); film music composition (MFA); screenwriting (MFA). *Application deadline:* For fall admission, 4/1 priority date for domestic students. Applications are processed on a rolling basis. *Application fee:* $95 ($100 for international students). Electronic applications accepted. *Application Contact:* Sheeler Lawson, Director of Admissions, 336-770-3290, Fax: 336-770-3370, E-mail: admissions@uncsa.edu. *Dean*, Susan Ruskin, 336-770-1333, Fax: 336-770-1339, E-mail: ruskins@uncsa.edu.

School of Music Students: 47 full-time (23 women), 2 part-time (0 women); includes 10 minority (7 Black or African American, non-Hispanic/Latino; 1 Hispanic/Latino; 2 Two or more races, non-Hispanic/Latino), 5 international. Average age 26. 74 applicants, 88% accepted, 26 enrolled. *Faculty:* 23 full-time (6 women), 14 part-time/adjunct (7 women). *Financial support:* Fellowships with partial tuition reimbursements, teaching assistantships with partial tuition reimbursements, career-related internships or fieldwork, and Federal Work-Study available. Financial award application deadline: 3/15; financial award applicants required to submit FAFSA. In 2015, 17 master's awarded. Offers music (Artist Certificate); music performance (MM). *Application deadline:* For fall admission, 4/1 priority date for domestic students. Applications are processed on a rolling basis. *Application fee:* $95 ($100 for international students). Electronic applications accepted. *Application Contact:* Sheeler Lawson, Director of Admissions, 336-770-3290, Fax: 336-770-3370, E-mail: admissions@uncsa.edu. *Interim Dean*, Karen Beres, 336-631-1226, Fax: 336-770-3248, E-mail: beresk@uncsa.edu.

THE UNIVERSITY OF NORTH CAROLINA WILMINGTON, Wilmington, NC 28403-3297

General Information State-supported, coed, comprehensive institution. CGS member. *Enrollment:* 14,918 graduate, professional, and undergraduate students; 636 full-time matriculated graduate/professional students (425 women), 936 part-time matriculated graduate/professional students (641 women). *Enrollment by degree level:* 1,419 master's, 132 doctoral, 21 other advanced degrees. *Graduate faculty:* 464 full-time (210 women), 1 (woman) part-time/adjunct. Tuition, state resident: full-time $6832. Tuition, nonresident: full-time $18,923. *Required fees:* $2022. Tuition and fees vary according to program. *Graduate housing:* Room and/or apartments available on a first-come, first-served basis to single students; on-campus housing not available to married students. Typical cost: $8246 per year ($11,051 including board). Room and board charges vary according to board plan and housing facility selected. Housing application deadline: 4/30. *Student services:* Campus employment opportunities, campus safety program, career counseling, exercise/wellness program, free psychological counseling, international student services, low-cost health insurance, multicultural affairs office, services for students with disabilities. *Library:* William Madison Randall Library. *Collection:* Books: 930,144 (physical), 74,337 (digital/electronic); Serial titles: 5,253 (physical), 43,781 (digital/electronic); Databases: 191. Weekly public service hours: 132; study areas open 24 hours, 5–7 days a week; students can reserve study rooms.

Computer facilities: Computer purchase and lease plans are available. 1,390 computers available on campus for general student use. A campuswide network can be accessed from student residence rooms and from off campus. Online class registration is available.
Website: http://www.uncw.edu/

General Application Contact: Dr. Ron Vetter, Dean, Graduate School, 910-962-7303, Fax: 910-962-3787, E-mail: vetterr@uncw.edu.

GRADUATE UNITS

Cameron School of Business Students: 73 full-time (33 women), 48 part-time (10 women); includes 15 minority (2 Black or African American, non-Hispanic/Latino; 4 Asian, non-Hispanic/Latino; 7 Hispanic/Latino; 1 Native Hawaiian or other Pacific Islander, non-Hispanic/Latino; 1 Two or more races, non-Hispanic/Latino), 2 international. Average age 30. 174 applicants, 92 enrolled. *Faculty:* 51 full-time (17 women). *Financial support:* Teaching assistantships, scholarships/grants, and unspecified assistantships available. Financial award application deadline: 3/15; financial award applicants required to submit FAFSA. In 2015, 84 master's awarded. *Degree program information:* Part-time programs available. Part-time. Offers assurance (MSA); business (MBA, MSA); business administration (MBA); systems advisory (MSA); tax services (MSA). *Application deadline:* Applications are processed on a rolling basis. *Application fee:* $60. Electronic applications accepted. *Application Contact:* Candace Wilhelm, Graduate Programs Coordinator, 910-962-3903, Fax: 910-962-2184, E-mail: wilhelmc@uncw.edu. *Dean*, Dr. Robert Burrus, 910-962-3226, Fax: 910-962-3815, E-mail: burrusr@uncw.edu.

Center for Marine Science Students: 7 full-time (4 women), 20 part-time (10 women); includes 2 minority (1 Asian, non-Hispanic/Latino; 1 Hispanic/Latino). Average age 27. 16 applicants, 7 enrolled. *Faculty:* 48 full-time (12 women). *Financial support:* Scholarships/grants and unspecified assistantships available. Financial award application deadline: 3/15; financial award applicants required to submit FAFSA. In 2015, 10 master's awarded. *Degree program information:* Part-time programs available. Part-time. Offers marine science (MS). *Application deadline:* For fall admission, 6/15 for domestic students; for spring admission, 11/15 for domestic students. Applications are processed on a rolling basis. *Application fee:* $60. Electronic applications accepted. *Director*, Dr. Stephen Skrabal, 910-962-7160, E-mail: skrabals@uncw.edu.

College of Arts and Sciences Students: 259 full-time (155 women), 362 part-time (202 women); includes 80 minority (31 Black or African American, non-Hispanic/Latino; 3 American Indian or Alaska Native, non-Hispanic/Latino; 9 Asian, non-Hispanic/Latino; 32 Hispanic/Latino; 5 Two or more races, non-Hispanic/Latino), 14 international. Average age 30. 758 applicants, 219 enrolled. *Faculty:* 236 full-time (98 women), 1 (woman) part-time/adjunct. *Financial support:* Research assistantships, teaching assistantships, Federal Work-Study, scholarships/grants, unspecified assistantships, and tuition remission available. Support available to part-time students. Financial award application deadline: 3/15; financial award applicants required to submit FAFSA. In 2015, 228 master's, 1 doctorate awarded. *Degree program information:* Part-time programs available. Part-time. Offers arts and sciences (MA, MFA, MPA, MS, PhD, Graduate Certificate); biology (MS); chemistry (MS); coastal and ocean policy (MS); coastal management (MS); conflict management (Graduate Certificate); conflict management and resolution (MA); creative writing (MFA); English (MA); environmental education and interpretation (MS); environmental management (MS); geoscience (MS); Hispanic studies (Graduate Certificate); history (MA); liberal studies (MA); marine and coastal education (MS); marine biology (MS, PhD); mathematics (MS); psychology (MA); public administration (MPA); sociology and criminology (MA); Spanish (MA); statistics (Graduate Certificate). *Application deadline:* Applications are processed on a rolling basis. *Application fee:* $60. Electronic applications accepted. *Application Contact:* Dr. Ron Vetter, Dean, Graduate School and Research, 910-962-3224, Fax: 910-962-3787, E-mail: vetterr@uncw.edu. *Dean, College of Arts and Sciences*, Dr. Aswani Volety, 910-962-3111, Fax: 910-962-3114, E-mail: voletya@uncw.edu.

Interdisciplinary Program in Computer Science and Information Systems Students: 14 full-time (2 women), 7 part-time (2 women); includes 3 minority (1 Asian, non-Hispanic/Latino; 1 Hispanic/Latino; 1 Two or more races, non-Hispanic/Latino), 3 international. Average age 30. 17 applicants, 4 enrolled. *Faculty:* 13 full-time (3 women). *Financial support:* Scholarships/grants and unspecified assistantships available. Financial award application deadline: 3/15; financial award applicants required to submit FAFSA. In 2015, 7 master's awarded. *Degree program information:* Part-time programs available. Part-time. Offers computer science and information systems (MS). *Application deadline:* For fall admission, 6/1 for domestic students; for spring admission, 11/1 for domestic students. Applications are processed on a rolling basis. *Application fee:* $60. Electronic applications accepted. *Application Contact:* Candace Wilhelm, Graduate Coordinator, 910-962-3903, Fax: 910-962-7457, E-mail: wilhelmc@uncw.edu. *Program Coordinator,* Dr. Clayton Ferner, 910-962-7552, E-mail: cferner@uncw.edu.

School of Health and Applied Human Sciences Students: 5 full-time (all women), 2 part-time (both women); includes 4 minority (all Black or African American, non-Hispanic/Latino). Average age 38. 4 applicants, 4 enrolled. *Faculty:* 16 full-time (11 women). *Financial support:* Scholarships/grants and unspecified assistantships available. Financial award application deadline: 3/15; financial award applicants required to submit FAFSA. In 2015, 3 master's awarded. *Degree program information:* Part-time programs available. Part-time, online learning. Offers applied gerontology (MS); gerontology (Postbaccalaureate Certificate). *Application deadline:* For fall admission, 6/15 for domestic students; for spring admission, 11/15 for domestic students; for summer admission, 3/15 for domestic students. Applications are processed on a rolling basis. *Application fee:* $60. Electronic applications accepted. *Application Contact:* Dr. Anne Glass, Program Coordinator, 910-962-7816, E-mail: glassa@uncw.edu. *Director,* Dr. Chris Lantz, 910-962-2364, Fax: 910-962-7073, E-mail: lantzc@uncw.edu.

School of Nursing Students: 68 full-time (57 women), 84 part-time (73 women); includes 25 minority (15 Black or African American, non-Hispanic/Latino; 5 American Indian or Alaska Native, non-Hispanic/Latino; 2 Hispanic/Latino; 3 Two or more races, non-Hispanic/Latino). Average age 38. 222 applicants, 57 enrolled. *Faculty:* 18 full-time (17 women). *Financial support:* Scholarships/grants available. Financial award application deadline: 3/15; financial award applicants required to submit FAFSA. In 2015, 33 master's awarded. *Degree program information:* Part-time programs available. Part-time, online learning. Offers clinical research and product development (MS); family nurse practitioner (MSN, Post-Master's Certificate). *Application deadline:* For fall admission, 3/1 for domestic students. Applications are processed on a rolling basis. *Application fee:* $60. Electronic applications accepted. *Application Contact:* Dr. Jim Lyon, Graduate Coordinator, 910-962-2936, E-mail: lyonj@uncw.edu. *Director,* Dr. Carol Heinrich, 910-962-7410, Fax: 910-962-3723, E-mail: badzekl@uncw.edu.

School of Social Work Students: 49 full-time (43 women), 36 part-time (34 women); includes 13 minority (4 Black or African American, non-Hispanic/Latino; 7 Hispanic/Latino; 2 Two or more races, non-Hispanic/Latino). Average age 32. 126 applicants, 45 enrolled. *Faculty:* 14 full-time (9 women). *Financial support:* Teaching assistantships, scholarships/grants, and out-of-state tuition remission available. Financial award application deadline: 3/15; financial award applicants required to submit FAFSA. In 2015, 18 master's awarded. *Degree program information:* Part-time programs available. Part-time. Offers social work (MSW). *Application deadline:* For fall admission, 2/1 for domestic students. Applications are processed on a rolling basis. *Application fee:* $60. Electronic applications accepted. *Application Contact:* Dr. Peter Nguyen, Graduate Coordinator, 910-962-7642, Fax: 910-962-7283, E-mail: nguyenp@uncw.edu. *Interim Director,* Dr. Stacey Kolomer, 910-962-2853, Fax: 910-962-7283, E-mail: kolomers@uncw.edu.

Watson College of Education Students: 162 full-time (128 women), 342 part-time (283 women); includes 127 minority (94 Black or African American, non-Hispanic/Latino; 7 American Indian or Alaska Native, non-Hispanic/Latino; 6 Asian, non-Hispanic/Latino; 11 Hispanic/Latino; 1 Native Hawaiian or other Pacific Islander, non-Hispanic/Latino; 8 Two or more races, non-Hispanic/Latino), 2 international. Average age 35. 171 applicants, 139 enrolled. *Faculty:* 62 full-time (39 women). *Financial support:* Scholarships/grants and unspecified assistantships available. Support available to part-time students. Financial award application deadline: 3/15; financial award applicants required to submit FAFSA. In 2015, 146 master's, 11 doctorates awarded. *Degree program information:* Part-time programs available. Part-time. Offers academically and intellectually gifted (M Ed); curriculum, instruction, and supervision (M Ed); education (M Ed, MAT, MS, MSA, Ed D); educational leadership (MSA, Ed D); educational leadership, policy, and advocacy (M Ed); elementary education (M Ed, MAT); English (MAT); English as a second language (M Ed, MAT); higher education (M Ed); history (MAT); instructional technology (MS); language and literacy (M Ed); mathematics (MAT); middle grades education (M Ed, MAT); physical education and health (M Ed); science (MAT). *Application deadline:* For fall admission, 5/15 for domestic students; for spring admission, 10/15 for domestic students. Applications are processed on a rolling basis. *Application fee:* $60. Electronic applications accepted. *Application Contact:* Dr. Ron Vetter, Dean, Graduate School, 910-962-3224, Fax: 910-962-3787, E-mail: vetterr@uncw.edu. *Dean,* Dr. Van Dempsey, 910-962-3354, Fax: 910-962-4081, E-mail: dempseyv@uncw.edu.

UNIVERSITY OF NORTH DAKOTA, Grand Forks, ND 58202

General Information State-supported, coed, university. CGS member. *Graduate housing:* Rooms and/or apartments guaranteed to single students and available on a first-come, first-served basis to married students. *Research affiliation:* North Dakota Geological Survey, U.S. Department of Agriculture (USDA)–Human Nutrition Research Center, Neuropsychiatric Research Institute (neurosciences), Environmental Energy Research Center.

GRADUATE UNITS

Graduate School ***Degree program information:*** Part-time and evening/weekend programs available. Part-time, evening/weekend, online learning. Offers anatomy and cell biology (MS, PhD); biochemistry and molecular biology (MS, PhD); clinical laboratory science (MS); medicine (MOT, MPAS, MPT, MS, DPT, PhD); microbiology and immunology (MS, PhD); occupational therapy (MOT); pharmacology (MS, PhD); physical therapy (MPT, DPT); physician assistant (MPAS); physiology (MS, PhD). Electronic applications accepted.

College of Arts and Sciences Degree program information: Part-time programs available. Part-time, online learning. Offers arts and sciences (M Ed, M Mus, MA, MFA, MS, DA, DMEd, PhD); botany (MS, PhD); chemistry (MS, PhD); clinical psychology (PhD); communication (MA); communication and public discourse (PhD); communication sciences and disorders (PhD); counseling psychology (PhD); criminal justice (PhD); ecology (MS, PhD); English (MA, PhD); entomology (MS, PhD); environmental biology (MS, PhD); experimental psychology (PhD); fisheries/wildlife (MS, PhD); forensic psychology (MA, MS); genetics (MS, PhD); geography (MA, MS); history (MA, DA, PhD); linguistics (MA); mathematics (M Ed, MS); music (M Mus); music education (M Mus, DMEd); physics (MS, PhD); psychology (MA); sociology (MA); speech-language pathology (MS); theatre arts (MA); visual arts (MFA); zoology (MS, PhD). Electronic applications accepted.

College of Business and Public Administration Degree program information: Part-time and evening/weekend programs available. Part-time, evening/weekend, online learning. Offers accountancy (M Acc); applied economics (MSAE); business administration (MBA); business and public administration (M Acc, MBA, MPA, MSAE, MSIT, MST); public administration (MPA); technology (MST). Electronic applications accepted.

College of Education and Human Development Degree program information: Part-time and evening/weekend programs available. Part-time, evening/weekend, online learning. Offers counseling (MA); early childhood education (MS); education and human development (M Ed, MA, MS, MSW, Ed D, PhD, Specialist); education/general studies (MS); educational leadership (M Ed, MS, Ed D, PhD, Specialist); elementary education (M Ed, MS); instructional design and technology (M Ed, MS); kinesiology (MS); measurement and statistics (Ed D, PhD); reading education (M Ed, MS); secondary education (Ed D, PhD); social work (MSW); special education (Ed D, PhD). Electronic applications accepted.

College of Nursing Degree program information: Part-time and evening/weekend programs available. Part-time, evening/weekend, online learning. Offers adult-gerontological nurse practitioner (MSN); advanced public health nurse (MSN); advanced public health nursing (MS); family nurse practitioner (MS, MSN); gerontological nursing (MS); nurse anesthesia (MS, MSN); nurse educator (MSN); nursing (MS, DNP, PhD); nursing education (MS); psychiatric and mental health (MS); psychiatric and mental health nurse practitioner (MSN). Electronic applications accepted.

John D. Odegard School of Aerospace Sciences Degree program information: Part-time and evening/weekend programs available. Part-time, evening/weekend, online learning. Offers aerospace sciences (MEM, MS, PhD); atmospheric sciences (MS, PhD); aviation (MS); computer science (MS, PhD); earth system science and policy (MEM, MS, PhD); space studies (MS). Electronic applications accepted.

School of Engineering and Mines Degree program information: Part-time programs available. Part-time. Offers chemical engineering (M Engr, MS); civil engineering (M Engr); electrical engineering (M Engr, MS); engineering (PhD); engineering and mines (M Engr, MA, MS, PhD); environmental engineering (M Engr, MS); geological engineering (M Engr, MS); geology (MA, MS, PhD); mechanical engineering (M Engr, MS); sanitary engineering (M Engr). Electronic applications accepted.

School of Law Offers law (JD).

School of Medicine and Health Sciences Online learning. Offers medicine (MD); medicine and health sciences (MD).

UNIVERSITY OF NORTHERN BRITISH COLUMBIA, Prince George, BC V2N 4Z9, Canada

General Information Province-supported, coed, university. *Graduate housing:* Room and/or apartments available on a first-come, first-served basis to single students; on-campus housing not available to married students. Housing application deadline: 2/15. *Research affiliation:* Houston Forest Products (forestry–wood debris management), TRC Cedar Ltd. (forestry–cyanolicen growth rate study), Remote Law Online Systems Corporation (computer science), Canadian Natural Oils Ltd. (chemistry–oil fractionation), Stella Jones, Inc. (forestry–Douglas fir cores), Insurance Corporation of British Columbia (moose involved in highway traffic accidents).

GRADUATE UNITS

Office of Graduate Studies ***Degree program information:*** Part-time and evening/weekend programs available. Part-time, evening/weekend, online learning.

UNIVERSITY OF NORTHERN COLORADO, Greeley, CO 80639

General Information State-supported, coed, university. CGS member. *Graduate housing:* Rooms and/or apartments available on a first-come, first-served basis to single and married students. Housing application deadline: 5/30.

GRADUATE UNITS

Graduate School ***Degree program information:*** Part-time and evening/weekend programs available. Part-time, evening/weekend, online learning. Electronic applications accepted.

College of Education and Behavioral Sciences Degree program information: Part-time programs available. Part-time, online learning. Offers applied statistics and research methods (MS, PhD); clinical counseling (MA); counselor education and supervision (PhD); deaf/hard of hearing (MA); early childhood education (MA); early childhood special education (MA); education and behavioral sciences (MA, MAT, MS, Ed D, PhD, Ed S); educational leadership (MA, Ed D, Ed S); educational leadership and policy studies (MA, Ed D, Ed S); educational psychology (MA, PhD); educational studies (MAT, Ed D); educational technology (MA, PhD); gifted and talented (MA); higher education and student affairs leadership (PhD); psychological sciences (MA, PhD); reading (MA); school counseling (MA); school library education (MA); school psychology (PhD, Ed S); special education (MA, Ed D); teacher education (MA, MAT, Ed D); teaching diverse learners (MA); visual impairment (MA).

College of Humanities and Social Sciences Degree program information: Part-time programs available. Part-time. Offers communication (MA); communication studies (MA); criminal justice (MA); English (MA); history (MA); humanities and social sciences (MA); modern languages and cultural studies (MA); sociology (MA); Spanish/teaching (MA). Electronic applications accepted.

College of Natural and Health Sciences Offers audiology (Au D); biology (MS); biology education (PhD); biomedical sciences (MBS); chemical education (MS, PhD); chemistry (MS); clinical nurse specialist in chronic illness (MS); earth sciences (MA); earth sciences and physics (MA); exercise science (MS, PhD); family nurse practitioner (MS); gerontology (MA); human rehabilitation (PhD); human sciences (MA, MPH, Au D, PhD); mathematical teaching (MA); mathematics (MA, PhD); mathematics education (PhD); mathematics: liberal arts (MA); natural and health sciences (MA, MPH, MS, Au D, PhD); nursing education (MS, PhD); public health education (MPH); rehabilitation counseling (MA); speech language pathology (MA); sport administration (MS, PhD); sport pedagogy (MS, PhD). Electronic applications accepted.

College of Performing and Visual Arts Degree program information: Part-time programs available. Part-time. Offers collaborative keyboard (MM); conducting (MM); instrumental performance (MM); jazz studies (MM); music conducting (DA); music education (MM, DA); music history and literature (MM, DA); music performance (DA); music theory and composition (MM, DA); performing and visual arts (MA, MM, DA); visual arts (MA); vocal performance (MM). Electronic applications accepted.

Monfort College of Business Offers accounting (MA).

UNIVERSITY OF NORTHERN IOWA, Cedar Falls, IA 50614

General Information State-supported, coed, comprehensive institution. CGS member. *Enrollment:* 11,981 graduate, professional, and undergraduate students; 523 full-time matriculated graduate/professional students (375 women), 810 part-time matriculated graduate/professional students (525 women). *Enrollment by degree level:* 1,215 master's, 100 doctoral, 18 other advanced degrees. *Graduate faculty:* 503 full-time (220 women), 29 part-time/adjunct (11 women). *Graduate housing:* Rooms and/or apartments available on a first-come, first-served basis to single and married students. *Student services:* Campus employment opportunities, campus safety program, career counseling, child daycare facilities, exercise/wellness program, free psychological counseling, grant writing training, international student services, low-cost health insurance, multicultural affairs office, services for students with disabilities, writing training. *Library:* Rod Library. *Collection:* Books: 780,940 (physical), 211,207 (digital/electronic); Serial titles: 6,391 (physical), 16,652 (digital/electronic); Databases: 936. Weekly public service hours: 99; students can reserve study rooms.

Computer facilities: Computer purchase and lease plans are available. 1,900 computers available on campus for general student use. A campuswide network can be accessed from student residence rooms and from off campus. Online class registration, student account, degree audit, program of study are available.
Website: http://www.uni.edu/

General Application Contact: Laurie S. Russell, Record Analyst, 319-273-2623, Fax: 319-273-2885, E-mail: laurie.russell@uni.edu.

GRADUATE UNITS

Graduate College Students: 523 full-time (375 women), 810 part-time (525 women); includes 106 minority (50 Black or African American, non-Hispanic/Latino; 5 American Indian or Alaska Native, non-Hispanic/Latino; 14 Asian, non-Hispanic/Latino; 20 Hispanic/Latino; 17 Two or more races, non-Hispanic/Latino), 121 international. Average age 31. 1,125 applicants, 43% accepted, 408 enrolled. *Financial support:* In 2015–16, 1,084 students received support. Fellowships, research assistantships, teaching assistantships, career-related internships or fieldwork, Federal Work-Study, institutionally sponsored loans, scholarships/grants, tuition waivers (full and partial), and unspecified assistantships available. Support available to part-time students. Financial award application deadline: 2/1; financial award applicants required to submit FAFSA. In 2015, 438 master's, 14 doctorates, 5 other advanced degrees awarded. *Degree program information:* Part-time and evening/weekend programs available. Part-time, evening/weekend. Offers philanthropy and nonprofit development (MA); women's and gender studies (MA). *Application deadline:* For fall admission, 8/1 for domestic students, 2/1 for international students; for winter admission, 12/1 for domestic students. Applications are processed on a rolling basis. *Application fee:* $50 ($70 for international students). Electronic applications accepted. *Application Contact:* Laurie S. Russell, Record Analyst, 319-273-2623, Fax: 319-273-2885, E-mail: laurie.russell@uni.edu. *Dean,* Dr. Kavita Dhanwada, 319-273-2518, Fax: 319-273-3153, E-mail: kavita.dhanwada@uni.edu.

College of Business Administration Students: 30 full-time (17 women), 39 part-time (11 women); includes 1 minority (Black or African American, non-Hispanic/Latino), 30 international. 73 applicants, 41% accepted, 25 enrolled. *Financial support:* Career-related internships or fieldwork, Federal Work-Study, scholarships/grants, and tuition waivers (full and partial) available. Support available to part-time students. Financial award application deadline: 2/1. In 2015, 61 master's awarded. *Degree program information:* Part-time and evening/weekend programs available. Part-time, evening/weekend. Offers accounting (M Acc); business administration (M Acc, MBA). *Application deadline:* For fall admission, 8/1 priority date for domestic students. Applications are processed on a rolling basis. *Application fee:* $50 ($70 for international students). *Application Contact:* Laurie S. Russell, Record Analyst, 319-273-2623, Fax: 319-273-2885, E-mail: laurie.russell@uni.edu. *Dean,* Dr. Leslie K. Wilson, 319-273-6240, Fax: 319-273-2922, E-mail: leslie.wilson@uni.edu.

College of Education Students: 141 full-time (99 women), 384 part-time (282 women); includes 43 minority (28 Black or African American, non-Hispanic/Latino; 2 Asian, non-Hispanic/Latino; 7 Hispanic/Latino; 6 Two or more races, non-Hispanic/Latino), 43 international. 353 applicants, 57% accepted, 169 enrolled. *Financial support:* Career-related internships or fieldwork, Federal Work-Study, institutionally sponsored loans, scholarships/grants, and tuition waivers (full and partial) available. Support available to part-time students. Financial award application deadline: 2/1. In 2015, 164 master's, 12 doctorates, 5 other advanced degrees awarded. *Degree program information:* Part-time and evening/weekend programs available. Part-time, evening/weekend. Offers allied health, recreation, and community services (Ed D); athletic training (MS); career/vocational programming and transition (MAE); community health education (MA); consultant (MAE); curriculum and instruction (Ed D); early childhood education (MAE); education (MA, MAE, MS, Ed D, Ed S); educational leadership (Ed D); educational psychology: context and techniques of assessment (MAE); educational psychology: context and techniques of assessment (MAE); educational psychology: professional development for teachers (MAE); elementary education (MAE); field specialization (MAE); health education (MA); health promotion/fitness management (MA); instructional technology (MA); kinesiology (MA); leisure, youth and human services (MA); literacy education (MAE); performance and training technology (MA); physical education (MA); postsecondary education: student affairs (MA); principalship (MAE); school health education (MA); school library endorsement (MA); school library studies (MA); school psychology (Ed S); special education (MAE); teaching/coaching (MA). *Application deadline:* For fall admission, 8/1 priority date for domestic students. Applications are processed on a rolling basis. *Application fee:* $50 ($70 for international students). Electronic applications accepted. *Application Contact:* Laurie S. Russell, Record Analyst, 319-273-2623, Fax: 319-273-2885, E-mail: laurie.russell@uni.edu. *Dean,* Gaetane Jean-Marie, 319-273-2717, Fax: 319-273-2607, E-mail: gaetane.jean-marie@uni.edu.

College of Humanities, Arts and Sciences Students: 219 full-time (160 women), 264 part-time (159 women); includes 27 minority (6 Black or African American, non-Hispanic/Latino; 1 American Indian or Alaska Native, non-Hispanic/Latino; 6 Asian, non-Hispanic/Latino; 7 Hispanic/Latino; 7 Two or more races, non-Hispanic/Latino), 37 international. 429 applicants, 35% accepted, 124 enrolled. *Financial support:* Career-related internships or fieldwork, Federal Work-Study, scholarships/grants, and tuition waivers (full and partial) available. Support available to part-time students. Financial award application deadline: 2/1. In 2015, 113 master's, 2 doctorates awarded. *Degree program information:* Part-time and evening/weekend programs available. Part-time, evening/weekend. Offers art education (MA); biology (MS); communication studies (MA); community college teaching (MA); composition (MM); conducting (MM); creative writing (MA); earth science education (MA); English (MA); humanities, arts and sciences (MA, MM, MS, PSM, DIT); industrial mathematics (PSM); industrial technology (DIT); jazz pedagogy (MM); literature (MA); mathematics (MA); mathematics for the middle grades (MA); music (MA, MM); music education (MM); music history (MM); percussion (MM); performance (MM); physics education (MA); piano performance and pedagogy (MM); piano/organ (MM); science education (MA); secondary teaching (MA); Spanish (MA); Spanish teaching (MA); speech-language pathology (MA); strings (MM); teaching English in secondary schools (MA); teaching English to speakers of other languages (MA); technology (MS, DIT); TESOL/Spanish (MA); voice (MM); woodwind (MM). *Application deadline:* For fall admission, 8/1 priority date for domestic students. Applications are processed on a rolling basis. *Application fee:* $50 ($70 for international students). Electronic applications accepted. *Application Contact:* Laurie S. Russell, Record Analyst, 319-273-2623, Fax: 319-273-2885, E-mail: laurie.russell@uni.edu. *Dean,* Dr. John Fritch, 319-273-2725, Fax: 319-273-2731, E-mail: john.fritch@uni.edu.

College of Social and Behavioral Sciences Students: 124 full-time (90 women), 103 part-time (55 women); includes 33 minority (13 Black or African American, non-Hispanic/Latino; 4 American Indian or Alaska Native, non-Hispanic/Latino; 6 Asian, non-Hispanic/Latino; 6 Hispanic/Latino; 4 Two or more races, non-Hispanic/Latino), 10 international. 231 applicants, 34% accepted, 66 enrolled. *Financial support:* Career-related internships or fieldwork, Federal Work-Study, scholarships/grants, and tuition waivers (full and partial) available. Support available to part-time students. Financial award application deadline: 2/1. In 2015, 99 master's awarded. *Degree program information:* Part-time and evening/weekend programs available. Part-time, evening/weekend. Offers counseling (MA); geography (MA); history (MA); mental health counseling (MA); psychology (MA); public history (MA); public policy (MPP); school counseling (MA); social and behavioral sciences (MA, MPP, MSW); social science (MA); social work (MSW). *Application deadline:* For fall admission, 8/1 priority date for domestic students. Applications are processed on a rolling basis. *Application fee:* $50 ($70 for international students). Electronic applications accepted. *Application Contact:* Laurie S. Russell, Record Analyst, 319-273-2623, Fax: 319-273-2885, E-mail: laurie.russell@uni.edu. *Dean,* Dr. Brenda Bass, 319-273-2221, Fax: 319-273-2222, E-mail: brenda.bass@uni.edu.

UNIVERSITY OF NORTH FLORIDA, Jacksonville, FL 32224

General Information State-supported, coed, comprehensive institution. CGS member. *Enrollment:* 15,675 graduate, professional, and undergraduate students; 814 full-time matriculated graduate/professional students (536 women), 991 part-time matriculated graduate/professional students (632 women). *Enrollment by degree level:* 1,454 master's, 351 doctoral. *Graduate faculty:* 403 full-time (196 women), 37 part-time/adjunct (22 women). Tuition, state resident: part-time $408.10 per credit hour. Tuition, nonresident: part-time $932.61 per credit hour. *Required fees:* $111.81 per credit hour. Tuition and fees vary according to course load, campus/location and program. *Graduate housing:* Room and/or apartments available on a first-come, first-served basis to single students; on-campus housing not available to married students. Typical cost: $3715 per year ($9487 including board). Room and board charges vary according to board plan and housing facility selected. Housing application deadline: 7/15. *Student services:* Campus employment opportunities, campus safety program, career counseling, child daycare facilities, exercise/wellness program, free psychological counseling, international student services, low-cost health insurance, multicultural affairs office, services for students with disabilities, teacher training, writing training. *Library:* Thomas G. Carpenter Library. *Collection:* Books: 860,144 (physical), 269,885 (digital/electronic); Serial titles: 898 (physical), 37,138 (digital/electronic); Databases: 269. Weekly public service hours: 137; students can reserve study rooms.

Computer facilities: Computer purchase and lease plans are available. 700 computers available on campus for general student use. A campuswide network can be accessed from student residence rooms and from off campus. Online class registration, reduced prices for students on certain business and design software are available.
Website: http://www.unf.edu/

General Application Contact: Dr. Amanda Pascale, Director, The Graduate School, 904-620-1360, Fax: 904-620-1362, E-mail: graduateschool@unf.edu.

GRADUATE UNITS

Brooks College of Health Students: 378 full-time (273 women), 195 part-time (150 women); includes 153 minority (54 Black or African American, non-Hispanic/Latino; 1 American Indian or Alaska Native, non-Hispanic/Latino; 28 Asian, non-Hispanic/Latino; 45 Hispanic/Latino; 1 Native Hawaiian or other Pacific Islander, non-Hispanic/Latino; 24 Two or more races, non-Hispanic/Latino), 13 international. Average age 32. 304 applicants, 46% accepted, 98 enrolled. *Faculty:* 63 full-time (47 women), 15 part-time/adjunct (10 women). *Financial support:* In 2015–16, 112 students received support, including 24 research assistantships (averaging $1,505 per year), 2 teaching assistantships (averaging $1,939 per year); career-related internships or fieldwork, Federal Work-Study, scholarships/grants, and tuition waivers (partial) also available. Support available to part-time students. Financial award application deadline: 4/1; financial award applicants required to submit FAFSA. In 2015, 137 master's, 36 doctorates awarded. *Degree program information:* Part-time and evening/weekend programs available. Part-time, evening/weekend. Offers aging services (Certificate); community health (MPH); exercise science and chronic disease (MSH); geriatric management (MSH); health (MHA, MPH, MS, MSH, MSN, DNP, DPT, Certificate); health administration (MHA); nutrition and dietetics (MSH); physical therapy (DPT); rehabilitation counseling (MS). *Application deadline:* For fall admission, 7/1 priority date for domestic students, 5/1 for international students; for spring admission, 11/1 priority date for domestic students, 10/1 for international students. Applications are processed on a rolling basis. *Application fee:* $30. Electronic applications accepted. *Application Contact:* Dr. Heather Kenney, Director of Advising, 904-620-2810, Fax: 904-620-1030, E-mail: heather.kenney@unf.edu. *Dean,* Dr. Pamela Chally, 904-620-2810, Fax: 904-620-1030, E-mail: pchally@unf.edu.

School of Nursing Students: 108 full-time (90 women), 117 part-time (93 women); includes 54 minority (17 Black or African American, non-Hispanic/Latino; 1 American Indian or Alaska Native, non-Hispanic/Latino; 13 Asian, non-Hispanic/Latino; 17 Hispanic/Latino; 1 Native Hawaiian or other Pacific Islander, non-Hispanic/Latino; 5 Two or more races, non-Hispanic/Latino), 3 international. Average age 36. 136 applicants, 81% accepted, 74 enrolled. *Faculty:* 23 full-time (17 women), 2 part-time/adjunct (1 woman). *Financial support:* In 2015–16, 35 students received support. Research assistantships available. Financial award application deadline: 4/1; financial award applicants required to submit FAFSA. In 2015, 46 master's, 6 doctorates awarded. *Degree program information:* Part-time programs available. Part-time. Offers clinical nurse leader (MSN); clinical nurse specialist (MSN); family nurse practitioner (Certificate); nurse anesthetist (MSN); nursing practice (DNP); primary care nurse practitioner (MSN). *Application deadline:* For fall admission, 3/15 for domestic students, 4/1 for international students. *Application fee:* $30. Electronic applications accepted. *Application Contact:* Beth Dibble, Assistant Director of Admissions for Nursing and Physical Therapy, 904-620-2684, Fax: 904-620-1832, E-mail: nursingadmissions@unf.edu. *Chair,* Dr. Li Loriz, 904-620-1053, E-mail: lloriz@unf.edu.

Coggin College of Business Students: 126 full-time (64 women), 198 part-time (82 women); includes 57 minority (15 Black or African American, non-Hispanic/Latino; 17 Asian, non-Hispanic/Latino; 18 Hispanic/Latino; 7 Two or more races, non-Hispanic/Latino), 34 international. Average age 28. 268 applicants, 55% accepted, 91 enrolled. *Faculty:* 49 full-time (12 women), 2 part-time/adjunct (0 women). *Financial support:* In 2015–16, 33 students received support, including 3 research assistantships (averaging $2,340 per year); teaching assistantships, career-related internships or fieldwork, Federal Work-Study, scholarships/grants, and tuition waivers (partial) also available. Financial award application deadline: 4/1; financial award applicants required to submit FAFSA. In 2015, 154 master's awarded. *Degree program information:* Part-time and evening/weekend programs available. Part-time, evening/weekend. Offers accountancy (M Acc); accounting (MBA); business (M Acc, MBA); construction management (MBA); e-commerce (MBA); economics (MBA); finance (MBA); human resource management (MBA); international business (MBA); logistics (MBA); management applications (MBA). *Application deadline:* For fall admission, 7/1 priority date for domestic students, 5/1 for international students; for spring admission, 11/1 priority date for domestic students, 10/1 for international students. Applications are processed on a rolling basis. *Application fee:* $30. Electronic applications accepted. *Application Contact:* Paul Schreier, Interim Director of Student Services, 904-620-2575, Fax: 904-620-2832, E-mail: coggin.students@unf.edu. *Dean,* Dr. Ajay Samant, 904-620-2590, Fax: 904-620-2590, E-mail: ajay.samant@unf.edu.

College of Arts and Sciences Students: 154 full-time (83 women), 154 part-time (100 women); includes 76 minority (43 Black or African American, non-Hispanic/Latino; 4 Asian, non-Hispanic/Latino; 22 Hispanic/Latino; 1 Native Hawaiian or other Pacific Islander, non-Hispanic/Latino; 6 Two or more races, non-Hispanic/Latino), 9 international. Average age 30. 300 applicants, 49% accepted, 104 enrolled. *Faculty:* 205 full-time (96 women), 6 part-time/adjunct (4 women). *Financial support:* In 2015–16, 89 students received support, including 4 research assistantships (averaging $2,142 per year), 20 teaching assistantships (averaging $4,590 per year); career-related internships or fieldwork, Federal Work-Study, scholarships/grants, and tuition waivers (partial) also available. Support available to part-time students. Financial award application deadline: 4/1; financial award applicants required to submit FAFSA. In 2015, 96 master's awarded. *Degree program information:* Part-time and evening/weekend programs available. Part-time, evening/weekend. Offers applied ethics (Graduate Certificate); arts and sciences (MA, MAC, MPA, MS, Graduate Certificate); biology (MA, MS); counseling psychology (MAC); criminal justice (MS); English (MA); European history (MA); general psychology (MA); mathematical sciences (MS); nonprofit management (Graduate Certificate); practical philosophy and applied ethics (MA); public administration (MPA); statistics (MS); U.S. history (MA). *Application deadline:* For fall admission, 7/1 priority date for domestic students, 5/1 for international students; for spring admission, 11/1 priority date for domestic students, 10/1 for international students. *Application fee:* $30. Electronic applications accepted. *Application Contact:* Dr. Amanda Pascale, Director, The Graduate School, 904-620-1360, Fax: 904-620-1362, E-mail: graduateschool@unf.edu. *Dean,* Dr. Barbara Hetrick, 904-620-2560, Fax: 904-620-2929, E-mail: barbara.hetrick@unf.edu.

College of Computing, Engineering, and Construction Students: 39 full-time (19 women), 62 part-time (15 women); includes 19 minority (1 Black or African American, non-Hispanic/Latino; 10 Asian, non-Hispanic/Latino; 6 Hispanic/Latino; 2 Two or more races, non-Hispanic/Latino), 33 international. Average age 30. 88 applicants, 42% accepted, 21 enrolled. *Faculty:* 34 full-time (5 women), 1 part-time/adjunct (0 women). *Financial support:* In 2015–16, 33 students received support, including 17 research assistantships (averaging $2,634 per year), 1 teaching assistantship (averaging $2,250 per year); Federal Work-Study, scholarships/grants, tuition waivers (partial), and unspecified assistantships also available. Support available to part-time students. Financial award application deadline: 4/1; financial award applicants required to submit FAFSA. In 2015, 21 master's awarded. *Degree program information:* Part-time programs available. Part-time. Offers computing, engineering, and construction (MS, MSCE, MSEE, MSME). *Application deadline:* For fall admission, 7/1 priority date for domestic students, 5/1 for international students; for spring admission, 11/1 priority date for domestic students, 10/1 for international students. *Application fee:* $30. Electronic applications accepted. *Application Contact:* Dr. Amanda Pascale, Director, The Graduate School, 904-620-1360, Fax: 904-620-1362, E-mail: graduateschool@unf.edu. *Dean,* Dr. Mark Tumeo, 904-620-1350, E-mail: m.tumeo@unf.edu.

School of Computing Students: 24 full-time (14 women), 43 part-time (11 women); includes 10 minority (1 Black or African American, non-Hispanic/Latino; 6 Asian, non-Hispanic/Latino; 2 Hispanic/Latino; 1 Two or more races, non-Hispanic/Latino), 25 international. Average age 31. 47 applicants, 36% accepted, 7 enrolled. *Faculty:* 11 full-time (2 women), 1 part-time/adjunct (0 women). *Financial support:* In 2015–16, 11 students received support, including 10 research assistantships (averaging $1,157 per year), 1 teaching assistantship (averaging $2,250 per year); Federal Work-Study, scholarships/grants, and unspecified assistantships also available. Financial award application deadline: 4/1; financial award applicants required to submit FAFSA. In 2015, 7 master's awarded. *Degree program information:* Part-time programs available. Part-time. Offers computer science (MS); information systems (MS); software engineering (MS). *Application deadline:* For fall admission, 7/1 for domestic students, 5/1 for international students; for spring admission, 11/1 for domestic students, 10/1 for international students. *Application fee:* $30. Electronic applications accepted. *Application Contact:* Dr. Amanda Pascale, Director, The Graduate School, 904-620-1360, Fax: 904-620-1362, E-mail: graduateschool@unf.edu. *Dean,* Dr. Asai Asaithambi, 904-620-2985, E-mail: asai.asaithambi@unf.edu.

School of Engineering Students: 15 full-time (5 women), 19 part-time (4 women); includes 9 minority (4 Asian, non-Hispanic/Latino; 4 Hispanic/Latino; 1 Two or more races, non-Hispanic/Latino), 8 international. Average age 27. 41 applicants, 49% accepted, 14 enrolled. *Faculty:* 18 full-time (2 women). *Financial support:* In 2015–16, 22 students received support, including 7 research assistantships (averaging $3,776 per year); teaching assistantships, Federal Work-Study, scholarships/grants, tuition waivers, and unspecified assistantships also available. Financial award application deadline: 4/1; financial award applicants required to submit FAFSA. In 2015, 14 master's awarded. *Degree program information:* Part-time programs available. Part-time. Offers engineering (MSCE, MSEE, MSME). *Application deadline:* For fall admission, 7/1 for domestic students, 5/1 for international students; for spring admission, 11/1 for domestic students, 10/1 for international students. *Application fee:* $30. *Application Contact:* Dr. Amanda Pascale, Director, The Graduate School, 904-320-1360, Fax: 904-620-1362, E-mail: graduateschool@unf.edu. *Associate Dean,* Dr. Murat Tiryakioglo, 904-620-2504, E-mail: m.tiryakioglo@unf.edu.

College of Education and Human Services Students: 117 full-time (97 women), 382 part-time (285 women); includes 156 minority (93 Black or African American, non-Hispanic/Latino; 1 American Indian or Alaska Native, non-Hispanic/Latino; 19 Asian, non-Hispanic/Latino; 29 Hispanic/Latino; 1 Native Hawaiian or other Pacific Islander, non-Hispanic/Latino; 13 Two or more races, non-Hispanic/Latino), 19 international. Average age 34. 208 applicants, 62% accepted, 92 enrolled. *Faculty:* 53 full-time (36 women), 12 part-time/adjunct (8 women). *Financial support:* In 2015–16, 81 students received support, including 21 research assistantships (averaging $3,549 per year), 1 teaching assistantship (averaging $5,400 per year); career-related internships or fieldwork, Federal Work-Study, scholarships/grants, and tuition waivers (partial) also available. Support available to part-time students. Financial award application deadline: 4/1; financial award applicants required to submit FAFSA. In 2015, 147 master's, 11 doctorates awarded. *Degree program information:* Part-time and evening/weekend programs available. Part-time, evening/weekend. Offers adult learning (M Ed); American Sign Language/English interpreting (M Ed); applied behavior analysis (M Ed); autism (M Ed); counselor education (M Ed); deaf education (M Ed); disability services (M Ed); education and human services (M Ed, Ed D); educational leadership (M Ed, Ed D); exceptional student education (M Ed); literacy (M Ed); professional education (M Ed); TESOL (M Ed). *Application deadline:* For fall admission, 7/1 priority date for domestic students, 5/1 for international students; for spring admission, 11/1 priority date for domestic students, 10/1 for international students. *Application fee:* $30. Electronic applications accepted. *Application Contact:* Dr. John Kemppainen, Director, Office of Student Services, 904-620-2530, Fax: 904-620-1135, E-mail: jkemppai@unf.edu. *Dean,* Dr. Larry Daniel, 904-620-2520, E-mail: ldaniel@unf.edu.

UNIVERSITY OF NORTH GEORGIA, Dahlonega, GA 30597

General Information State-supported, coed, comprehensive institution. *Enrollment:* 17,289 graduate, professional, and undergraduate students; 141 full-time matriculated graduate/professional students (101 women), 419 part-time matriculated graduate/professional students (298 women). *Enrollment by degree level:* 364 master's, 89 doctoral, 107 other advanced degrees. *Graduate faculty:* 65 full-time (35 women), 23 part-time/adjunct (14 women). *International tuition:* $8082 full-time. *Tuition, area resident:* Full-time $2025; part-time $1350 per credit hour. Tuition, state resident: full-time $2025; part-time $1350 per credit hour. Tuition, nonresident: full-time $8082; part-time $5388 per credit hour. *Required fees:* $620.50; $620.50 per semester. Tuition and fees vary according to degree level and program. *Graduate housing:* Room and/or apartments available on a first-come, first-served basis to single students; on-campus housing not available to married students. Housing application deadline: 2/1. *Student services:* Campus employment opportunities, campus safety program, career counseling, exercise/wellness program, free psychological counseling, international student services, low-cost health insurance, multicultural affairs office, services for students with disabilities, teacher training, writing training. *Library:* Library Technology Center plus 4 others. *Collection:* Books: 270,623 (physical), 291,155 (digital/electronic); Databases: 240. Students can reserve study rooms. *Research affiliation:* Northeast Georgia Medical Center, Morehouse School of Medicine, St. Joseph's Hospital, Mettler Electronic Corporation.

Computer facilities: 2,443 computers available on campus for general student use. A campuswide network can be accessed from student residence rooms and from off campus. Online class registration is available.
Website: http://www.ung.edu/

General Application Contact: Melinda Maxwell, Director of Graduate Admissions, 706-864-1543, E-mail: melinda.maxwell@ung.edu.

GRADUATE UNITS

College of Education ***Financial support:*** Teaching assistantships, career-related internships or fieldwork, scholarships/grants, and unspecified assistantships available. Financial award application deadline: 5/1; financial award applicants required to submit CSS PROFILE or FAFSA. *Degree program information:* Part-time and evening/weekend programs available. Part-time, evening/weekend, online learning. Offers art education (MAT); early childhood education (M Ed); English education (MAT); history education (MAT); math education (MAT); middle grades education (M Ed, MAT); physical education (MS); school leadership (Ed S); secondary education (M Ed); teacher education (MAT). *Application deadline:* For fall admission, 8/1 priority date for domestic students, 7/1 priority date for international students; for spring admission, 12/1 priority date for domestic students, 11/1 priority date for international students. Applications are processed on a rolling basis. *Application fee:* $40. Electronic applications accepted.

Department of History, Anthropology and Philosophy ***Financial support:*** Unspecified assistantships available. Financial award applicants required to submit CSS PROFILE or FAFSA. *Degree program information:* Part-time and evening/weekend programs available. Part-time, evening/weekend. Offers history (MA). *Application deadline:* For fall admission, 4/15 priority date for domestic students, 7/1 priority date for international students. Applications are processed on a rolling basis. *Application fee:* $40. Electronic applications accepted.

Department of Nursing ***Financial support:*** Career-related internships or fieldwork and unspecified assistantships available. Financial award application deadline: 5/1; financial award applicants required to submit CSS PROFILE or FAFSA. *Degree program information:* Part-time programs available. Part-time. Offers family nurse practitioner (MS, Post-Master's Certificate). *Application deadline:* For fall admission, 7/1 priority date for domestic students, 6/1 for international students. *Application fee:* $40. Electronic applications accepted.

Department of Performing Arts ***Degree program information:*** Part-time programs available. Part-time. Offers music (MM). Electronic applications accepted.

Department of Physical Therapy ***Financial support:*** Unspecified assistantships available. Financial award application deadline: 5/1; financial award applicants required to submit CSS PROFILE or FAFSA. Offers physical therapy (DPT). *Application deadline:* Applications are processed on a rolling basis. *Application fee:* $50. Electronic applications accepted.

Department of Political Science and International Affairs ***Financial support:*** Career-related internships or fieldwork, scholarships/grants, and unspecified assistantships available. Financial award application deadline: 5/1; financial award applicants required to submit CSS PROFILE or FAFSA. *Degree program information:* Part-time and evening/weekend programs available. Part-time, evening/weekend, online learning. Offers criminal justice (MS); international affairs (MAIA); public administration (MPA). *Application deadline:* For fall admission, 7/1 priority date for domestic and international students; for spring admission, 12/10 priority date for domestic students, 10/1 priority date for international students. Applications are processed on a rolling basis. *Application fee:* $40. Electronic applications accepted.

Department of Psychology and Sociology ***Degree program information:*** Part-time and evening/weekend programs available. Part-time, evening/weekend. Offers clinical mental health counseling (MS). Electronic applications accepted.

Mike Cottrell School of Business ***Financial support:*** Unspecified assistantships available. Financial award applicants required to submit CSS PROFILE or FAFSA. *Degree program information:* Part-time and evening/weekend programs available. Part-time, evening/weekend. Offers business (MBA). *Application deadline:* For fall admission, 4/1 priority date for domestic and international students. *Application fee:* $40. Electronic applications accepted.

UNIVERSITY OF NORTH TEXAS, Denton, TX 76203

General Information State-supported, coed, university. CGS member. *Graduate housing:* Rooms and/or apartments available on a first-come, first-served basis to single and married students. Housing application deadline: 9/1. *Research affiliation:* Semiconductor Research Corporation (materials science), Delta and Pine Land Company (natural science), Semiconductor Research Corporation (materials science),

Tech America (technology transfer), National Business Incubation Association (entrepreneurship), International Economic Development Council (economic growth).

GRADUATE UNITS

Robert B. Toulouse School of Graduate Studies ***Degree program information:*** Part-time and evening/weekend programs available. Part-time, evening/weekend, online learning. Offers accounting (MS); applied anthropology (MA, MS); applied behavior analysis (Certificate); applied geography (MA); applied technology and performance improvement (M Ed, MS); art education (MA); art history (MA); art museum education (Certificate); arts leadership (Certificate); audiology (Au D); behavior analysis (MS); behavioral science (PhD); biochemistry and molecular biology (MS); biology (MA, MS); biomedical engineering (MS); business analysis (MS); chemistry (MS); clinical health psychology (PhD); communication studies (MA, MS); computer engineering (MS); computer science (MS); counseling (M Ed, MS); creative writing (MA); criminal justice (MS); curriculum and instruction (M Ed); decision sciences (MBA); design (MA, MFA); early childhood studies (MS); economics (MS); educational leadership (M Ed, Ed D); educational psychology (MS, PhD); electrical engineering (MS); emergency management (MPA); engineering technology (MS); English (MA); English as a second language (MA); environmental science (MS); finance (MBA, MS); financial management (MPA); French (MA); health services management (MBA); higher education (M Ed, Ed D); history (MA, MS); hospitality management (MS); human resources management (MPA); information science (MS); information systems (PhD); information technologies (MBA); interdisciplinary studies (MA, MS); international studies (MA); international sustainable tourism (MS); jazz studies (MM); journalism (MA, MJ, Graduate Certificate); kinesiology (MS); linguistics (MA); local government management (MPA); logistics (PhD); logistics and supply chain management (MBA); long-term care, senior housing, and aging services (MA); management (PhD); marketing (MBA); mathematics (MA, MS); mechanical and energy engineering (MS, PhD); music (MA); music composition (PhD); music education (MM Ed, PhD); nonprofit management (MPA); operations and supply chain management (MBA); performance (MM, DMA); philosophy (MA); political science (MA); professional and technical communication (MA); radio, television and film (MA, MFA); rehabilitation counseling (Certificate); sociology (MA); Spanish (MA); special education (M Ed); speech-language pathology (MA); strategic management (MBA); studio art (MFA); teaching (M Ed). Electronic applications accepted.

UNIVERSITY OF NORTH TEXAS HEALTH SCIENCE CENTER AT FORT WORTH, Fort Worth, TX 76107-2699

General Information State-supported, coed, graduate-only institution. CGS member. *Graduate housing:* On-campus housing not available. *Research affiliation:* Myogen, Inc. (cardiac research), My-tech, Inc. (cardiovascular research), Novopharm, Inc. (gene control), Ethnobotanical Product Investigation Consortium (natural plant products), Genelink (familial DNA depository), Botanical Research Institutions of Texas.

GRADUATE UNITS

Graduate School of Biomedical Sciences Offers anatomy and cell biology (MS, PhD); biochemistry and molecular biology (MS, PhD); biomedical sciences (MS, PhD); biotechnology (MS); forensic genetics (MS); integrative physiology (MS, PhD); medical science (MS); microbiology and immunology (MS, PhD); pharmacology (MS, PhD); science education (MS).

School of Public Health ***Degree program information:*** Part-time and evening/weekend programs available. Part-time, evening/weekend. Offers biostatistics (MPH); community health (MPH); disease control and prevention (Dr PH); environmental and occupational health sciences (MPH); epidemiology (MPH); health administration (MHA); health policy and management (MPH, Dr PH). MPH offered jointly with University of North Texas; DO/MPH with Texas College of Osteopathic Medicine. Electronic applications accepted.

Texas College of Osteopathic Medicine Offers osteopathic medicine (DO); physician assistant studies (MPAS). DO/MPH offered jointly with University of North Texas. Electronic applications accepted.

School of Health Professions Offers health professions (MPAS).

UNIVERSITY OF NORTHWESTERN–ST. PAUL, St. Paul, MN 55113-1598

General Information Independent-religious, coed, comprehensive institution. *Graduate housing:* Room and/or apartments available to single students. *Library:* Berntsen Library.

Computer facilities: Computer purchase and lease plans are available. 200 computers available on campus for general student use. A campuswide network can be accessed from student residence rooms and from off campus. Online class registration, network file space, personal web site, integrated student portal, b/w and color printing, virtual labs are available.

Website: http://www.unwsp.edu/

General Application Contact: Tami Treder, Graduate Admission Counselor, 651-628-3351, E-mail: tjtreder@unwsp.edu.

GRADUATE UNITS

Master of Arts in Education Program ***Degree program information:*** Part-time and evening/weekend programs available. Part-time, evening/weekend, online learning. Offers education (MA Ed). *Application deadline:* Applications are processed on a rolling basis. Electronic applications accepted.

Master of Arts in Human Services Program ***Degree program information:*** Part-time and evening/weekend programs available. Part-time, evening/weekend, online learning. Offers family studies (MAHS). *Application deadline:* Applications are processed on a rolling basis. Electronic applications accepted.

Master of Arts in Theological Studies Program ***Degree program information:*** Part-time and evening/weekend programs available. Part-time, evening/weekend, online learning. Offers theological studies (MATS). *Application deadline:* Applications are processed on a rolling basis. Electronic applications accepted.

Master of Business Administration Program ***Degree program information:*** Part-time and evening/weekend programs available. Part-time, evening/weekend, online learning. Offers business administration (MBA). *Application deadline:* Applications are processed on a rolling basis. Electronic applications accepted. *Application Contact:* College of Adult and Graduate Studies Admissions, 651-631-5200, E-mail: gradstudies@unwsp.edu.

Master of Divinity Program ***Degree program information:*** Part-time and evening/weekend programs available. Part-time, evening/weekend, online learning. Offers theology and Christian ministry (M Div). *Application deadline:* Applications are processed on a rolling basis. Electronic applications accepted. *Application Contact:* College of Adult and Graduate Studies Admissions, 651-631-5200, E-mail: gradstudies@unwsp.edu.

Master of Organizational Leadership Program ***Degree program information:*** Part-time and evening/weekend programs available. Part-time, evening/weekend, online learning. Offers organizational leadership (MOL). *Application deadline:* Applications are processed on a rolling basis. Electronic applications accepted.

UNIVERSITY OF NOTRE DAME, Notre Dame, IN 46556

General Information Independent-religious, coed, university. CGS member. *Graduate housing:* Rooms and/or apartments available on a first-come, first-served basis to single and married students. Housing application deadline: 5/1. *Research affiliation:* Space Telescope Science Institute, Brookhaven National Laboratory, Fermi National Accelerator Laboratory, Argonne National Laboratory.

GRADUATE UNITS

Graduate School ***Degree program information:*** Part-time programs available. Part-time. Electronic applications accepted.

College of Arts and Letters ***Degree program information:*** Part-time programs available. Part-time. Offers art history (MA); arts and letters (M Div, M Ed, MA, MFA, MMS, MSM, MTS, PhD); cognitive psychology (PhD); counseling psychology (PhD); creative writing (MFA); design (MFA); developmental psychology (PhD); early Christian studies (MA); economics and econometrics (MA, PhD); educational initiatives (M Ed, MA); English (MA, PhD); French and Francophone studies (MA); history (MA, PhD); history and philosophy of science (MA, PhD); humanities (M Div, MA, MFA, MMS, MSM, MTS, PhD); Iberian and Latin American studies (MA); international peace studies (MA, PhD); Italian studies (MA); literature (PhD); medieval studies (MMS, PhD); philosophy (PhD); political science (PhD); quantitative psychology (PhD); Romance literatures (MA); social science (M Ed, MA, PhD); sociology (PhD); studio art (MFA); theology (M Div, MA, MSM, MTS, PhD); theology and science (PhD). Electronic applications accepted.

College of Engineering Offers aerospace and mechanical engineering (M Eng, PhD); aerospace engineering (MS Aero E); bioengineering (MS Bio E); chemical and biomolecular engineering (MS Ch E, PhD); civil engineering (MSCE); civil engineering and geological sciences (PhD); computer science and engineering (MSCSE, PhD); electrical engineering (MSEE, PhD); engineering (M Eng, MEME, MS, MS Aero E, MS Bio E, MS Ch E, MS Env E, MSCE, MSCSE, MSEE, MSME, PhD); environmental engineering (MS Env E); geological sciences (MS); mechanical engineering (MEME, MSME). Electronic applications accepted.

College of Science Offers algebra (PhD); algebraic geometry (PhD); applied and computational mathematics and statistics (PhD); applied mathematics (MSAM); applied statistics (MS); aquatic ecology, evolution and environmental biology (MS, PhD); biochemistry (MS, PhD); cellular and molecular biology (MS, PhD); complex analysis (PhD); computational finance (MS); differential geometry (PhD); genetics (MS, PhD); inorganic chemistry (MS, PhD); logic (PhD); organic chemistry (MS, PhD); partial differential equations (PhD); physical chemistry (MS, PhD); physics (MS, PhD); physiology (MS, PhD); science (MS, MSAM, PhD); topology (PhD); vector biology and parasitology (MS, PhD). Electronic applications accepted.

School of Architecture Offers architectural design and urbanism (M ADU); architecture (M Arch). Electronic applications accepted.

Law School Students: 619 full-time (261 women); includes 147 minority (20 Black or African American, non-Hispanic/Latino; 1 American Indian or Alaska Native, non-Hispanic/Latino; 42 Asian, non-Hispanic/Latino; 64 Hispanic/Latino; 20 Two or more races, non-Hispanic/Latino), 46 international. 2,649 applicants, 36% accepted, 229 enrolled. *Faculty:* 56 full-time (18 women), 55 part-time/adjunct (25 women). *Financial support:* In 2015–16, 425 students received support, including 396 fellowships with tuition reimbursements available (averaging $20,529 per year); research assistantships, teaching assistantships, career-related internships or fieldwork, Federal Work-Study, institutionally sponsored loans, scholarships/grants, health care benefits, unspecified assistantships, and university dormitory rector assistantships also available. Financial award application deadline: 2/28; financial award applicants required to submit FAFSA. In 2015, 25 master's, 179 doctorates awarded. Offers human rights (LL M, JSD); international and comparative law (LL M); law (JD). *Application deadline:* For fall admission, 3/15 for domestic and international students. Applications are processed on a rolling basis. *Application fee:* $75. Electronic applications accepted. *Application Contact:* Jacob Baska, Director of Admissions and Financial Aid, 574-631-6626, Fax: 574-631-5474, E-mail: lawadmit@nd.edu. *Dean,* Nell Jessup Newton, 574-631-6789, Fax: 574-631-8400, E-mail: nell.newton@nd.edu.

Mendoza College of Business Students: 764 full-time (243 women); includes 110 minority (27 Black or African American, non-Hispanic/Latino; 2 American Indian or Alaska Native, non-Hispanic/Latino; 20 Asian, non-Hispanic/Latino; 47 Hispanic/Latino; 14 Two or more races, non-Hispanic/Latino), 122 international. Average age 30. 1,368 applicants, 39% accepted, 294 enrolled. *Faculty:* 83 full-time (14 women), 31 part-time/adjunct (9 women). *Financial support:* In 2015–16, 440 students received support, including 440 fellowships. Financial award applicants required to submit FAFSA. In 2015, 477 degrees awarded. Offers business (MBA, MNA, MSA, MSBA, MSF, MSM); business administration (MBA); business analytics (MSBA); executive business administration (MBA); finance (MSF); financial reporting and assurance services (MSA); management (MSM); nonprofit administration (MNA); tax services (MSA). *Application deadline:* Applications are processed on a rolling basis. Electronic applications accepted. *Dean,* Dr. Roger D. Huang, 574-631-1691, Fax: 574-631-4825, E-mail: roger.huang.31@nd.edu.

UNIVERSITY OF OKLAHOMA, Norman, OK 73019-0390

General Information State-supported, coed, university. CGS member. *Enrollment:* 27,428 graduate, professional, and undergraduate students; 3,008 full-time matriculated graduate/professional students (1,456 women), 3,123 part-time matriculated graduate/professional students (1,593 women). *Enrollment by degree level:* 4,120 master's, 1,980 doctoral, 30 other advanced degrees. *Graduate faculty:* 1,201 full-time (418 women), 66 part-time/adjunct (27 women). Tuition, state resident: full-time $4577; part-time $190.70 per credit hour. Tuition, nonresident: full-time $17,758; part-time $739.90 per credit hour. *Required fees:* $3060; $115.70 per credit hour. $141.50 per semester. *Graduate housing:* Rooms and/or apartments available on a first-come, first-served basis to single and married students. Typical cost: $6750 per year ($11,018 including board) for single students; $6750 per year for married students. Room and board charges vary according to board plan, campus/location and housing facility selected. *Student services:* Campus employment opportunities, campus safety program, career counseling, child daycare facilities, exercise/wellness program, free psychological counseling, grant writing training, international student services, low-cost health insurance, multicultural affairs office, services for students with disabilities, teacher training, writing training. *Library:* Bizzell Memorial Library plus 5 others. *Collection:* Books: 5.4 million (physical), 1.2 million (digital/electronic); Serial titles: 116,374 (physical), 71,040 (digital/electronic); Databases: 310. Students can reserve study rooms. *Research affiliation:* National Oceanic and Atmospheric Administration (NOAA)/National Severe Storms Laboratory (weather), Nanowave Technologies, Inc. (radar), Department of the Interior South Central Region Climate Science Center (climate science), Weathernews International (weather), Sandia National Laboratories (national security), U.S. Department of Transportation Southern Plains Transportation Center (transportation infrastructure).

Computer facilities: Computer purchase and lease plans are available. 4,500 computers available on campus for general student use. A campuswide network can be accessed from student residence rooms and from off campus. Online class registration is available.
Website: http://www.ou.edu/

General Application Contact: Dr. Randall S. Hewes, Interim Dean, 405-325-6765, Fax: 405-325-5346, E-mail: gradinfo@ou.edu.

GRADUATE UNITS

College of Architecture Students: 44 full-time (18 women), 24 part-time (14 women); includes 17 minority (3 Black or African American, non-Hispanic/Latino; 2 Asian, non-Hispanic/Latino; 6 Hispanic/Latino; 6 Two or more races, non-Hispanic/Latino), 18 international. Average age 31. 78 applicants, 64% accepted, 21 enrolled. *Faculty:* 41 full-time (15 women), 2 part-time/adjunct (both women). *Financial support:* In 2015–16, 43 students received support, including 10 research assistantships with partial tuition reimbursements available (averaging $10,372 per year), 4 teaching assistantships with partial tuition reimbursements available (averaging $11,435 per year); scholarships/grants and unspecified assistantships also available. Financial award application deadline: 6/1; financial award applicants required to submit FAFSA. In 2015, 27 master's awarded. *Degree program information:* Part-time and evening/weekend programs available. Part-time, evening/weekend. Offers architecture (M Arch, MLA, MRCP, MS, Graduate Certificate). *Application deadline:* For fall admission, 3/1 for international students. *Application fee:* $50 ($100 for international students). Electronic applications accepted. *Application Contact:* Dr. Charlie Warnken, Associate Dean for Instructional Services, 405-325-2444, Fax: 405-325-7558, E-mail: cwarnken@ou.edu. *Dean of the College of Architecture*, Dr. Charles Graham, 405-325-2444, Fax: 405-325-7558, E-mail: cwgraham@ou.edu.

Division of Architecture Students: 25 full-time (11 women), 11 part-time (2 women); includes 6 minority (1 Black or African American, non-Hispanic/Latino; 1 American Indian or Alaska Native, non-Hispanic/Latino; 1 Asian, non-Hispanic/Latino; 1 Hispanic/Latino; 2 Two or more races, non-Hispanic/Latino), 10 international. Average age 31. 32 applicants, 47% accepted, 7 enrolled. *Faculty:* 41 full-time (16 women), 1 part-time/adjunct (0 women). *Financial support:* In 2015–16, 25 students received support, including 1 research assistantship with partial tuition reimbursement available (averaging $10,372 per year), 2 teaching assistantships with partial tuition reimbursements available (averaging $10,372 per year); fellowships, career-related internships or fieldwork, scholarships/grants, and unspecified assistantships also available. Financial award application deadline: 6/1; financial award applicants required to submit FAFSA. In 2015, 9 master's awarded. Offers architectural urban studies (MS); architecture (M Arch). *Application deadline:* For fall admission, 11/1 for domestic and international students; for spring admission, 3/1 for domestic and international students. *Application fee:* $50 ($100 for international students). Electronic applications accepted. *Application Contact:* Marjorie Callahan, Graduate Liaison, Division of Architecture, 405-325-3866, Fax: 405-325-2444, E-mail: mcallahan@ou.edu. *Interim Director, Division of Architecture*, Dr. Stephanie Pilat, 405-325-9352, Fax: 405-325-2444, E-mail: spilat@ou.edu.

Division of Construction Management Students: 14 full-time (3 women), 1 part-time (0 women); includes 5 minority (2 American Indian or Alaska Native, non-Hispanic/Latino; 3 Hispanic/Latino), 5 international. Average age 30. 21 applicants, 90% accepted, 13 enrolled. *Faculty:* 1 (woman) full-time. *Financial support:* In 2015–16, 12 students received support, including 5 research assistantships with full tuition reimbursements available (averaging $10,997 per year); teaching assistantships with full tuition reimbursements available, scholarships/grants, and unspecified assistantships also available. Financial award application deadline: 6/1; financial award applicants required to submit FAFSA. In 2015, 1 master's awarded. *Degree program information:* Part-time and evening/weekend programs available. Part-time, evening/weekend. Offers construction management (MS). *Application deadline:* Applications are processed on a rolling basis. *Application fee:* $50 ($100 for international students). Electronic applications accepted. *Application Contact:* Lisa Holliday, Graduate Liaison, 405-325-9464, Fax: 405-325-7558, E-mail: lisaholliday@ou.edu. *Interim Director*, Tammy McCuen, 405-325-4131, Fax: 405-325-7558, E-mail: tammymccuen@ou.edu.

Division of Interior Design Students: 2 full-time (both women), both international. Average age 26. 7 applicants, 43% accepted, 2 enrolled. *Financial support:* In 2015–16, 2 students received support, including 2 research assistantships with partial tuition reimbursements available (averaging $10,372 per year), 1 teaching assistantship with partial tuition reimbursement available (averaging $10,372 per year); career-related internships or fieldwork, scholarships/grants, tuition waivers, and unspecified assistantships also available. Financial award application deadline: 6/1; financial award applicants required to submit FAFSA. In 2015, 1 master's awarded. *Degree program information:* Part-time and evening/weekend programs available. Part-time, evening/weekend. Offers interior design (MS); professional applications of interior design (Graduate Certificate). *Application deadline:* For fall admission, 6/1 for domestic and international students. Applications are processed on a rolling basis. *Application fee:* $50 ($100 for international students). Electronic applications accepted. *Application Contact:* Dr. Suchismita Bhattacharjee, Assistant Professor and Graduate Liaison, 405-325-2548, Fax: 405-325-7558, E-mail: suchi@ou.edu. *Academic Director*, Mia Kile, 405-325-1051, Fax: 405-325-7558, E-mail: mkile@ou.edu.

Division of Landscape Architecture Students: 12 full-time (7 women), 2 part-time (1 woman); includes 4 minority (1 Black or African American, non-Hispanic/Latino; 2 Asian, non-Hispanic/Latino; 1 Two or more races, non-Hispanic/Latino), 5 international. Average age 26. 20 applicants, 45% accepted, 7 enrolled. *Financial support:* In 2015–16, 10 students received support, including 7 research assistantships with partial tuition reimbursements available (averaging $10,372 per year), 1 teaching assistantship (averaging $10,372 per year); fellowships, career-related internships or fieldwork, scholarships/grants, health care benefits, and unspecified assistantships also available. Financial award application deadline: 6/1; financial award applicants required to submit FAFSA. In 2015, 2 master's awarded. *Degree program information:* Part-time programs available. Part-time. Offers landscape architecture (MLA). *Application deadline:* For fall admission, 2/15 for domestic and international students; for spring admission, 10/15 for domestic students, 9/15 for international students. Applications are processed on a rolling basis. *Application fee:* $50 ($100 for international students). Electronic applications accepted. *Director and Associate Professor*, Leehu Loon, 405-325-1519, Fax: 405-325-7558, E-mail: lloon@ou.edu.

Division of Regional and City Planning Students: 25 full-time (13 women), 7 part-time (4 women); includes 10 minority (3 Black or African American, non-Hispanic/Latino; 2 American Indian or Alaska Native, non-Hispanic/Latino; 3 Hispanic/Latino; 2 Two or more races, non-Hispanic/Latino), 4 international. Average age 30. 15 applicants, 93% accepted, 12 enrolled. *Financial support:* In 2015–16, 28 students received support, including 2 fellowships (averaging $3,750 per year), 6 research assistantships with tuition reimbursements available (averaging $11,143 per year); scholarships/grants and unspecified assistantships also available. Financial award application deadline: 6/1; financial award applicants required to submit FAFSA. In 2015, 5 master's awarded. *Degree program information:* Part-time programs available. Part-time. Offers regional and city planning (MRCP). *Application deadline:* For fall admission, 8/1 for domestic students, 4/1 for international students; for spring admission, 1/3 for domestic students, 9/1 for international students; for summer admission, 5/1 for domestic students, 2/1 for international students. Applications are processed on a rolling basis. *Application fee:* $50 ($100 for international students). Electronic applications accepted. *Application Contact:* K. Meghan Wieters, Graduate Liaison/Assistant Professor, 405-325-3851, Fax: 405-325-7558, E-mail: kmeghanwieters@ou.edu. *Director*, Dr. Dawn Jourdan, 405-325-3502, Fax: 405-325-7558, E-mail: dawnjourdan@ou.edu.

College of Arts and Sciences Students: 1,171 full-time (716 women), 1,064 part-time (662 women); includes 671 minority (251 Black or African American, non-Hispanic/Latino; 95 American Indian or Alaska Native, non-Hispanic/Latino; 54 Asian, non-Hispanic/Latino; 157 Hispanic/Latino; 9 Native Hawaiian or other Pacific Islander, non-Hispanic/Latino; 105 Two or more races, non-Hispanic/Latino), 212 international. Average age 32. 1,177 applicants, 53% accepted, 493 enrolled. *Faculty:* 537 full-time (206 women), 23 part-time/adjunct (16 women). *Financial support:* In 2015–16, 1,215 students received support, including 51 fellowships with full tuition reimbursements available (averaging $3,898 per year), 195 research assistantships with tuition reimbursements available (averaging $14,897 per year), 591 teaching assistantships with tuition reimbursements available (averaging $15,018 per year); career-related internships or fieldwork, Federal Work-Study, institutionally sponsored loans, scholarships/grants, traineeships, health care benefits, and unspecified assistantships also available. Support available to part-time students. Financial award application deadline: 6/1; financial award applicants required to submit FAFSA. In 2015, 708 master's, 96 doctorates, 96 other advanced degrees awarded. *Degree program information:* Part-time and evening/weekend programs available. Part-time, evening/weekend, online learning. Offers anthropology (MA, PhD); applied economics (MA); applied linguistic anthropology (MA); arts and sciences (MA, MHR, MLIS, MPA, MS, MSW, PhD, Graduate Certificate); bioinformatics (MS, PhD); biology (MS, PhD); cellular and behavioral neurobiology (PhD); chemistry (MS, PhD); communication (MA, PhD); ecology and evolutionary biology (PhD); economics (PhD); English (MA, PhD); exercise physiology (PhD); French (MA, PhD); general (MPA); German (MA); health and exercise science (MS); health promotion (MS, PhD); helping skills in human relations (Graduate Certificate); history (MA, PhD); history of science, technology and medicine (MA, PhD); human relations (MHR); human resource diversity and development (Graduate Certificate); human resource management (MA, Graduate Certificate); individualized intensive study (MPA); industrial organizational psychology (MS, PhD); managerial economics (MA); mathematics (MA, MS, PhD); microbiology (MS, PhD); Native American studies (MA); non-profit management (MPA); organizational communication (MA); organizational dynamics (MA, Graduate Certificate); philosophy (MA, PhD); physics (MS, PhD); plant biology (MS, PhD); political science (MA, MPA, PhD); project management (MA, Graduate Certificate); psychology (MS, PhD); public administration (MPA); sociology (MA, PhD); Spanish (MA, PhD); women's and gender studies (Graduate Certificate). *Application deadline:* For fall admission, 3/1 for international students. *Application fee:* $50 ($100 for international students). Electronic applications accepted. *Application Contact:* Jeff Blahnik, Director of Admissions, 405-325-2252, Fax: 405-325-7124, E-mail: admrec@ou.edu. *Dean*, Kelly Damphousse, 405-325-2077, Fax: 405-325-7709, E-mail: kdamp@ou.edu.

Anne and Henry Zarrow School of Social Work Students: 219 full-time (188 women), 123 part-time (105 women); includes 123 minority (44 Black or African American, non-Hispanic/Latino; 26 American Indian or Alaska Native, non-Hispanic/Latino; 6 Asian, non-Hispanic/Latino; 23 Hispanic/Latino; 2 Native Hawaiian or other Pacific Islander, non-Hispanic/Latino; 22 Two or more races, non-Hispanic/Latino), 1 international. Average age 33. 204 applicants, 69% accepted, 103 enrolled. *Faculty:* 25 full-time (18 women), 13 part-time/adjunct (11 women). *Financial support:* In 2015–16, 142 students received support, including 23 research assistantships with partial tuition reimbursements available (averaging $10,372 per year); career-related internships or fieldwork, scholarships/grants, and unspecified assistantships also available. Support available to part-time students. Financial award application deadline: 6/1; financial award applicants required to submit FAFSA. In 2015, 158 master's awarded. *Degree program information:* Part-time and evening/weekend programs available. Part-time, evening/weekend. Offers social work (MSW). *Application deadline:* For fall admission, 2/1 for domestic and international students. *Application fee:* $50 ($100 for international students). Electronic applications accepted. *Application Contact:* Susan Blossom, Admissions and Recruiting Specialist, 405-325-2821, Fax: 405-325-4683, E-mail: blossom@ou.edu. *Director*, Dr. Julie Miller-Cribbs, 405-325-4704, Fax: 405-325-4683, E-mail: jmcribbs@ou.edu.

School of Library and Information Studies Students: 47 full-time (41 women), 95 part-time (80 women); includes 28 minority (3 Black or African American, non-Hispanic/Latino; 4 American Indian or Alaska Native, non-Hispanic/Latino; 2 Asian, non-Hispanic/Latino; 6 Hispanic/Latino; 1 Native Hawaiian or other Pacific Islander, non-Hispanic/Latino; 12 Two or more races, non-Hispanic/Latino), 1 international. Average age 31. 44 applicants, 91% accepted, 34 enrolled. *Faculty:* 12 full-time (8 women). *Financial support:* In 2015–16, 74 students received support, including 4 research assistantships with partial tuition reimbursements available (averaging $14,552 per year), 6 teaching assistantships with partial tuition reimbursements available (averaging $10,579 per year); scholarships/grants and unspecified assistantships also available. Financial award application deadline: 6/1; financial award applicants required to submit FAFSA. In 2015, 47 master's awarded. *Degree program information:* Part-time and evening/weekend programs available. Part-time, evening/weekend, online learning. Offers library and information studies (MLIS). *Application deadline:* For fall admission, 3/1 priority date for domestic and international students; for spring admission, 10/15 for domestic and international students; for summer admission, 2/15 for domestic and international students. *Application fee:* $50 ($100 for international students). Electronic applications accepted. *Application Contact:* Sarah Connelly, Admissions and Student Services Coordinator, 405-325-3921, Fax: 405-325-7648, E-mail: sarahee@ou.edu. *Director*, Dr. Cecelia Brown, 405-325-3921, Fax: 405-325-7648, E-mail: cbrown@ou.edu.

College of Atmospheric and Geographic Sciences Students: 77 full-time (25 women), 41 part-time (15 women); includes 7 minority (1 American Indian or Alaska

Native, non-Hispanic/Latino; 2 Asian, non-Hispanic/Latino; 2 Hispanic/Latino; 2 Two or more races, non-Hispanic/Latino), 19 international. Average age 28. 77 applicants, 40% accepted, 29 enrolled. *Faculty:* 65 full-time (15 women), 3 part-time/adjunct (1 woman). *Financial support:* In 2015–16, 109 students received support, including 3 fellowships with full tuition reimbursements available (averaging $4,000 per year), 121 research assistantships with full tuition reimbursements available (averaging $18,433 per year), 35 teaching assistantships with full tuition reimbursements available (averaging $17,316 per year); career-related internships or fieldwork, Federal Work-Study, institutionally sponsored loans, scholarships/grants, traineeships, health care benefits, and unspecified assistantships also available. Financial award application deadline: 6/1; financial award applicants required to submit FAFSA. In 2015, 22 master's, 25 doctorates awarded. *Degree program information:* Part-time programs available. Part-time. Offers atmospheric and geographic sciences (MA, MS, PhD); environmental sustainability (MS); geography (MA, PhD). *Application deadline:* For fall admission, 1/15 for domestic and international students; for spring admission, 10/1 for domestic and international students. *Application fee:* $50 ($100 for international students). Electronic applications accepted. *Application Contact:* Mary Anne Hempe, Assistant Dean for Student Services, 405-325-3095, Fax: 405-325-3148, E-mail: mahempe@ou.edu. *Dean,* Dr. Berrien Moore, 405-325-3095, Fax: 405-325-1180, E-mail: berrien@ou.edu.

School of Meteorology Students: 56 full-time (11 women), 23 part-time (6 women); includes 4 minority (1 Asian, non-Hispanic/Latino; 1 Hispanic/Latino; 2 Two or more races, non-Hispanic/Latino), 12 international. Average age 26. 54 applicants, 26% accepted, 14 enrolled. *Faculty:* 44 full-time (9 women), 1 part-time/adjunct (0 women). *Financial support:* In 2015–16, 72 students received support, including 62 research assistantships with full tuition reimbursements available (averaging $18,667 per year), 18 teaching assistantships with full tuition reimbursements available (averaging $18,731 per year); fellowships with full tuition reimbursements available, tuition waivers (full and partial), and unspecified assistantships also available. Financial award application deadline: 6/1; financial award applicants required to submit FAFSA. In 2015, 14 master's, 13 doctorates awarded. Offers meteorology (PhD). *Application deadline:* For fall admission, 2/1 for domestic and international students; for spring admission, 10/1 for domestic and international students. Applications are processed on a rolling basis. *Application fee:* $50 ($100 for international students). Electronic applications accepted. *Application Contact:* Christie Upchurch, Academic Coordinator, 405-325-6571, Fax: 405-325-7689, E-mail: cupchurch@ou.edu. *Director,* Dr. David Parsons, 405-325-6561, Fax: 405-325-7689, E-mail: dparsons@ou.edu.

College of International Studies Students: 26 full-time (10 women), 84 part-time (19 women); includes 27 minority (3 Black or African American, non-Hispanic/Latino; 4 Asian, non-Hispanic/Latino; 8 Hispanic/Latino; 3 Native Hawaiian or other Pacific Islander, non-Hispanic/Latino; 9 Two or more races, non-Hispanic/Latino), 4 international. Average age 31. 40 applicants, 73% accepted, 17 enrolled. *Faculty:* 21 full-time (9 women), 1 part-time/adjunct (0 women). *Financial support:* In 2015–16, 31 students received support, including 1 fellowship with full tuition reimbursement available (averaging $2,000 per year), 5 research assistantships with full tuition reimbursements available (averaging $13,500 per year), 6 teaching assistantships with full tuition reimbursements available (averaging $13,833 per year); career-related internships or fieldwork, scholarships/grants, health care benefits, and unspecified assistantships also available. Financial award application deadline: 6/1; financial award applicants required to submit FAFSA. In 2015, 8 master's awarded. *Degree program information:* Part-time programs available. Part-time, online courses with an 8-10 day study abroad. Offers area studies (MAIS, Graduate Certificate); global studies (MAIS, Graduate Certificate). *Application deadline:* For fall admission, 2/15 for domestic and international students. *Application fee:* $50 ($100 for international students). Electronic applications accepted. *Application Contact:* Katie Watkins, Academic Advisor, 405-325-2337, Fax: 405-325-7738, E-mail: kwatkins@ou.edu. *Professor/Associate Dean for Academic Affairs,* Dr. Mitchell Smith, 405-325-1584, Fax: 405-325-7738, E-mail: mps@ou.edu.

College of Law Students: 495 full-time (220 women), 18 part-time (8 women); includes 140 minority (13 Black or African American, non-Hispanic/Latino; 32 American Indian or Alaska Native, non-Hispanic/Latino; 24 Asian, non-Hispanic/Latino; 24 Hispanic/Latino; 2 Native Hawaiian or other Pacific Islander, non-Hispanic/Latino; 45 Two or more races, non-Hispanic/Latino), 9 international. Average age 25. 956 applicants, 52% accepted, 187 enrolled. *Faculty:* 36 full-time (14 women), 19 part-time/adjunct (7 women). *Financial support:* In 2015–16, 390 students received support. Career-related internships or fieldwork, Federal Work-Study, scholarships/grants, and tuition waivers (full and partial) available. Financial award application deadline: 6/1; financial award applicants required to submit FAFSA. In 2015, 24 master's, 155 doctorates awarded. *Degree program information:* Part-time programs available. Part-time, online learning. Offers law (LL M, JD). *Application deadline:* For fall admission, 3/15 for domestic and international students. Applications are processed on a rolling basis. *Application fee:* $50. Electronic applications accepted. *Application Contact:* Vicki Ferguson, Admissions Coordinator, 405-325-4728, Fax: 405-325-0502, E-mail: admissions@law.ou.edu. *Dean,* Joseph Harroz, Jr., 405-325-4884, Fax: 405-325-7712, E-mail: jharroz@ou.edu.

College of Liberal Studies Students: 65 full-time (38 women), 602 part-time (299 women); includes 184 minority (57 Black or African American, non-Hispanic/Latino; 49 American Indian or Alaska Native, non-Hispanic/Latino; 6 Asian, non-Hispanic/Latino; 39 Hispanic/Latino; 1 Native Hawaiian or other Pacific Islander, non-Hispanic/Latino; 32 Two or more races, non-Hispanic/Latino), 1 international. Average age 35. 205 applicants, 97% accepted, 137 enrolled. *Faculty:* 15 full-time (10 women), 2 part-time/adjunct (0 women). *Financial support:* In 2015–16, 120 students received support. Career-related internships or fieldwork, institutionally sponsored loans, scholarships/grants, health care benefits, and tuition waivers (partial) available. Support available to part-time students. Financial award application deadline: 6/1; financial award applicants required to submit FAFSA. In 2015, 166 master's, 5 other advanced degrees awarded. *Degree program information:* Part-time programs available. Part-time, online only, 100% online, blended/hybrid learning. Offers administrative leadership (MA, Graduate Certificate); corrections management (Graduate Certificate); criminal justice (MS); liberal studies (MA); prevention science (MPS); restorative justice administration (Graduate Certificate). *Application deadline:* For fall admission, 7/1 for domestic and international students; for winter admission, 12/1 for domestic and international students; for spring admission, 5/1 for domestic and international students. Applications are processed on a rolling basis. *Application fee:* $50 ($100 for international students). Electronic applications accepted. *Application Contact:* Michelle Shults, Academic Advisement Services Coordinator, 405-325-2928, Fax: 405-325-7132, E-mail: mshults@ou.edu. *Vice President, University Outreach/Dean, College of Liberal Studies,* Dr. James Pappas, 405-325-6361, E-mail: jpappas@ou.edu.

Gallogly College of Engineering Students: 335 full-time (72 women), 212 part-time (56 women); includes 63 minority (11 Black or African American, non-Hispanic/Latino; 6 American Indian or Alaska Native, non-Hispanic/Latino; 12 Asian, non-Hispanic/Latino; 18 Hispanic/Latino; 16 Two or more races, non-Hispanic/Latino), 319 international. Average age 28. 659 applicants, 29% accepted, 125 enrolled. *Faculty:* 147 full-time (20 women), 2 part-time/adjunct (0 women). *Financial support:* In 2015–16, 423 students received support, including 7 fellowships with full tuition reimbursements available (averaging $4,000 per year), 193 research assistantships with partial tuition reimbursements available (averaging $15,354 per year), 75 teaching assistantships with partial tuition reimbursements available (averaging $12,285 per year); career-related internships or fieldwork, scholarships/grants, health care benefits, tuition waivers (partial), and unspecified assistantships also available. Financial award application deadline: 6/1; financial award applicants required to submit FAFSA. In 2015, 112 master's, 33 doctorates awarded. *Degree program information:* Part-time programs available. Part-time. Offers data science and analytics (MS); engineering (M Env Sc, MS, PhD); engineering physics (MS, PhD); general engineering (MS, PhD). *Application deadline:* For fall admission, 1/15 for domestic and international students; for spring admission, 1/1 for domestic students, 5/15 for international students. *Application fee:* $50 ($100 for international students). Electronic applications accepted. *Application Contact:* Dr. James Sluss, Senior Associate Dean, 405-325-4277, Fax: 405-325-7508, E-mail: sluss@ou.edu. *Dean,* Dr. Thomas Landers, 405-325-2621, Fax: 405-325-7508, E-mail: landers@ou.edu.

School of Aerospace and Mechanical Engineering Students: 26 full-time (4 women), 20 part-time (2 women); includes 6 minority (1 Black or African American, non-Hispanic/Latino; 1 American Indian or Alaska Native, non-Hispanic/Latino; 1 Hispanic/Latino; 3 Two or more races, non-Hispanic/Latino), 21 international. Average age 29. 69 applicants, 20% accepted, 9 enrolled. *Faculty:* 22 full-time (3 women). *Financial support:* In 2015–16, 38 students received support, including 16 research assistantships with full tuition reimbursements available (averaging $13,434 per year), 27 teaching assistantships with full tuition reimbursements available (averaging $11,976 per year); fellowships and scholarships/grants also available. Financial award application deadline: 6/1; financial award applicants required to submit FAFSA. In 2015, 15 master's, 2 doctorates awarded. *Degree program information:* Part-time programs available. Part-time. Offers aerodynamics (MS, PhD); aerospace engineering (MS, PhD); aerospace engineering-general (MS, PhD); combustion (MS, PhD); composites (MS, PhD); controls (MS, PhD); fluid mechanics (MS, PhD); heat transfer (MS, PhD); mechanical engineering (MS, PhD); mechanical engineering-general (MS, PhD); solid mechanics (MS, PhD); structures (MS, PhD). *Application deadline:* For fall admission, 1/15 for domestic and international students; for spring admission, 9/1 for domestic and international students. *Application fee:* $50 ($100 for international students). Electronic applications accepted. *Application Contact:* Kate O'Brien-Hamoush, AME Student Services Coordinator, 405-325-5013, Fax: 405-325-1088, E-mail: ame@ou.edu. *Director,* Dr. M. Cengiz Altan, 405-325-5011, Fax: 405-325-1088, E-mail: altan@ou.edu.

School of Biomedical Engineering Students: 11 full-time (4 women), 4 part-time (1 woman); includes 2 minority (1 Black or African American, non-Hispanic/Latino; 1 Two or more races, non-Hispanic/Latino), 5 international. Average age 28. 18 applicants, 33% accepted, 6 enrolled. *Faculty:* 2 full-time (1 woman). *Financial support:* In 2015–16, 16 students received support, including 8 research assistantships (averaging $13,658 per year), 3 teaching assistantships (averaging $12,953 per year); fellowships with full tuition reimbursements available, scholarships/grants, health care benefits, tuition waivers (partial), and unspecified assistantships also available. Financial award application deadline: 6/1; financial award applicants required to submit FAFSA. In 2015, 1 master's, 3 doctorates awarded. Offers biomedical engineering (MS, PhD). *Application deadline:* For fall admission, 4/1 for domestic students, 3/1 for international students; for spring admission, 11/1 for domestic students, 9/1 for international students. *Application fee:* $50 ($100 for international students). Electronic applications accepted. *Application Contact:* PJ Meek, Assistant to the Director, 405-325-5453, E-mail: pjmeek@ou.edu. *Interim Director,* Dr. Roger Harrison, 405-325-4367, E-mail: rharrison@ou.edu.

School of Chemical, Biological and Materials Engineering Students: 23 full-time (7 women), 19 part-time (7 women); includes 4 minority (1 Black or African American, non-Hispanic/Latino; 1 American Indian or Alaska Native, non-Hispanic/Latino; 1 Hispanic/Latino; 1 Two or more races, non-Hispanic/Latino), 26 international. Average age 26. 85 applicants, 6% accepted, 5 enrolled. *Faculty:* 14 full-time (0 women). *Financial support:* In 2015–16, 40 students received support, including 40 research assistantships with full tuition reimbursements available (averaging $17,398 per year), 1 teaching assistantship (averaging $10,812 per year); assistantships (with tuition waivers and health insurance) also available. Financial award application deadline: 6/1; financial award applicants required to submit FAFSA. In 2015, 12 master's, 8 doctorates awarded. *Degree program information:* Part-time programs available. Part-time. Offers chemical engineering (MS, PhD). *Application deadline:* Applications are processed on a rolling basis. *Application fee:* $50 ($100 for international students). Electronic applications accepted. *Application Contact:* Donna King, Graduate Program Staff Assistant, 405-325-5812, Fax: 405-325-5813, E-mail: donnaking@ou.edu. *Director,* Dr. Brian Grady, 405-325-5814, Fax: 405-325-5813, E-mail: cbme@ou.edu.

School of Civil Engineering and Environmental Science Students: 38 full-time (15 women), 31 part-time (10 women); includes 10 minority (3 Black or African American, non-Hispanic/Latino; 1 Asian, non-Hispanic/Latino; 3 Hispanic/Latino; 3 Two or more races, non-Hispanic/Latino), 30 international. Average age 28. 56 applicants, 41% accepted, 18 enrolled. *Faculty:* 28 full-time (6 women). *Financial support:* In 2015–16, 70 students received support, including 2 fellowships with full tuition reimbursements available (averaging $5,000 per year), 53 research assistantships with partial tuition reimbursements available (averaging $15,302 per year), 1 teaching assistantship with partial tuition reimbursement available (averaging $11,700 per year); scholarships/grants also available. Financial award application deadline: 6/1; financial award applicants required to submit FAFSA. In 2015, 17 master's, 4 doctorates awarded. *Degree program information:* Part-time programs available. Part-time. Offers civil engineering (MS, PhD); environmental engineering (MS, PhD); environmental science (M Env Sc, PhD). *Application deadline:* For fall admission, 1/15 for domestic and international students; for spring admission, 5/15 for domestic and international students. *Application fee:* $50 ($100 for international students). Electronic applications accepted. *Application Contact:* Susan Williams, Graduate Programs Specialist, 405-325-2344, Fax: 405-325-4217, E-mail: srwilliams@ou.edu. *Director,* Dr. Randall Kolar, 405-325-4267, Fax: 405-325-4217, E-mail: kolar@ou.edu.

School of Computer Science Students: 69 full-time (13 women), 23 part-time (7 women); includes 4 minority (2 Asian, non-Hispanic/Latino; 1 Hispanic/Latino; 1 Two or more races, non-Hispanic/Latino), 71 international. Average age 26. 113 applicants, 33% accepted, 22 enrolled. *Faculty:* 17 full-time (3 women). *Financial support:* In 2015–16, 69 students received support, including 1 fellowship (averaging $5,000 per year), 20 research assistantships with full tuition reimbursements available (averaging $15,326 per year), 16 teaching assistantships with full tuition reimbursements available (averaging $12,381 per year); career-related internships or fieldwork, scholarships/grants, and unspecified assistantships also available.

Financial award application deadline: 6/1; financial award applicants required to submit FAFSA. In 2015, 22 master's, 5 doctorates awarded. *Degree program information:* Part-time programs available. Part-time. Offers computer science (MS, PhD). *Application deadline:* For fall admission, 5/1 for domestic students, 3/1 for international students; for spring admission, 10/1 for domestic students, 9/1 for international students. Applications are processed on a rolling basis. *Application fee:* $50 ($100 for international students). Electronic applications accepted. *Application Contact:* Virginie Perez Woods, Academic Programs Coordinator, 405-325-0145, Fax: 405-325-4044, E-mail: virginieperezwoods@ou.edu. *Professor and Director,* Dr. Sridhar Radhakrishnan, 405-325-4042, Fax: 405-325-4044, E-mail: sridhar@ou.edu.

School of Electrical and Computer Engineering Students: 107 full-time (16 women), 57 part-time (14 women); includes 21 minority (2 Black or African American, non-Hispanic/Latino; 1 American Indian or Alaska Native, non-Hispanic/Latino; 6 Asian, non-Hispanic/Latino; 9 Hispanic/Latino; 3 Two or more races, non-Hispanic/Latino), 99 international. Average age 28. 161 applicants, 34% accepted, 31 enrolled. *Faculty:* 45 full-time (2 women), 2 part-time/adjunct (0 women). *Financial support:* In 2015–16, 140 students received support, including 2 fellowships (averaging $2,500 per year), 52 research assistantships with full tuition reimbursements available (averaging $14,759 per year), 18 teaching assistantships with full tuition reimbursements available (averaging $12,198 per year); career-related internships or fieldwork, scholarships/grants, health care benefits, and unspecified assistantships also available. Financial award application deadline: 6/1; financial award applicants required to submit FAFSA. In 2015, 29 master's, 6 doctorates awarded. *Degree program information:* Part-time programs available. Part-time. Offers electrical and computer engineering (MS, PhD); telecommunications engineering (MS). *Application deadline:* For fall admission, 3/1 for international students; for spring admission, 9/1 for international students. Applications are processed on a rolling basis. *Application fee:* $50 ($100 for international students). Electronic applications accepted. *Application Contact:* Lisa Wilkins, Graduate Program Assistant III, 405-325-4285, Fax: 405-325-7066, E-mail: lawilkins@ou.edu. *Director,* Dr. J.R. Cruz, 405-325-8131, Fax: 405-325-7066, E-mail: jcruz@ou.edu.

School of Industrial and Systems Engineering Students: 49 full-time (6 women), 25 part-time (11 women); includes 8 minority (3 Black or African American, non-Hispanic/Latino; 1 American Indian or Alaska Native, non-Hispanic/Latino; 1 Asian, non-Hispanic/Latino; 3 Two or more races, non-Hispanic/Latino), 56 international. Average age 28. 138 applicants, 27% accepted, 22 enrolled. *Faculty:* 16 full-time (3 women). *Financial support:* In 2015–16, 28 students received support, including 3 research assistantships with full tuition reimbursements available (averaging $12,875 per year), 9 teaching assistantships with full tuition reimbursements available (averaging $11,690 per year); scholarships/grants also available. Financial award application deadline: 6/1; financial award applicants required to submit FAFSA. In 2015, 13 master's, 4 doctorates awarded. Offers industrial and systems engineering (MS, PhD). *Application deadline:* For fall admission, 6/1 for domestic students, 4/1 for international students; for spring admission, 11/1 for domestic students, 9/1 for international students. *Application fee:* $50 ($100 for international students). Electronic applications accepted. *Application Contact:* Jenn Covington, Graduate Programs and Student Services Coordinator, 405-325-3721, Fax: 405-325-7555, E-mail: jcovington@ou.edu. *Professor,* Dr. Randa L. Shehab, 405-325-3721, Fax: 405-325-7555, E-mail: rlshehab@ou.edu.

Gaylord College of Journalism and Mass Communication Students: 35 full-time (20 women), 24 part-time (12 women); includes 9 minority (3 Black or African American, non-Hispanic/Latino; 2 American Indian or Alaska Native, non-Hispanic/Latino; 1 Asian, non-Hispanic/Latino; 1 Hispanic/Latino; 2 Two or more races, non-Hispanic/Latino), 19 international. Average age 32. 32 applicants, 66% accepted, 16 enrolled. *Faculty:* 32 full-time (12 women). *Financial support:* In 2015–16, 37 students received support, including 1 fellowship (averaging $5,000 per year), 6 research assistantships with partial tuition reimbursements available (averaging $15,120 per year), 18 teaching assistantships with partial tuition reimbursements available (averaging $14,360 per year); career-related internships or fieldwork, institutionally sponsored loans, scholarships/grants, health care benefits, and unspecified assistantships also available. Support available to part-time students. Financial award application deadline: 6/1; financial award applicants required to submit FAFSA. In 2015, 34 master's, 3 doctorates awarded. *Degree program information:* Part-time programs available. Part-time. Offers journalism and mass communication (MA, MPW, PhD); professional writing (MPW). *Application deadline:* For fall admission, 7/1 for domestic students, 3/1 for international students; for spring admission, 11/1 for domestic students, 9/1 for international students. *Application fee:* $50 ($100 for international students). Electronic applications accepted. *Application Contact:* Larry Laneer, Graduate Advisor, 405-325-2722, Fax: 405-325-7565, E-mail: llaneer@ou.edu. *Director of Graduate Studies,* Dr. Katerina Tsetsura, 405-325-6195, Fax: 405-325-7565, E-mail: tsetsura@ou.edu.

Graduate College Students: 51 full-time (16 women), 309 part-time (86 women); includes 91 minority (23 Black or African American, non-Hispanic/Latino; 5 American Indian or Alaska Native, non-Hispanic/Latino; 13 Asian, non-Hispanic/Latino; 38 Hispanic/Latino; 5 Native Hawaiian or other Pacific Islander, non-Hispanic/Latino; 7 Two or more races, non-Hispanic/Latino), 14 international. Average age 35. 100 applicants, 73% accepted, 32 enrolled. *Faculty:* 31 full-time (15 women), 1 (woman) part-time/adjunct. *Financial support:* In 2015–16, 9 students received support, including 7 research assistantships with partial tuition reimbursements available (averaging $11,227 per year); teaching assistantships, career-related internships or fieldwork, Federal Work-Study, institutionally sponsored loans, scholarships/grants, health care benefits, and unspecified assistantships also available. Support available to part-time students. Financial award application deadline: 6/1; financial award applicants required to submit FAFSA. In 2015, 172 master's, 4 doctorates awarded. *Degree program information:* Part-time and evening/weekend programs available. Part-time, evening/weekend, online learning. Offers interdisciplinary studies (MA, MS, PhD). *Application deadline:* For fall admission, 4/1 for domestic students, 3/1 for international students; for spring admission, 11/1 for domestic students, 9/1 for international students. *Application fee:* $50 ($100 for international students). Electronic applications accepted. *Application Contact:* Amy Shaw, Assistant Director for Graduate Programs, 405-325-6765, Fax: 405-325-5345, E-mail: ashaw@ou.edu. *Dean,* Dr. T.H. Lee Williams, 405-325-3811, Fax: 405-325-5346, E-mail: lwilliams@ou.edu.

Jeannine Rainbolt College of Education Students: 286 full-time (184 women), 497 part-time (359 women); includes 196 minority (72 Black or African American, non-Hispanic/Latino; 38 American Indian or Alaska Native, non-Hispanic/Latino; 10 Asian, non-Hispanic/Latino; 34 Hispanic/Latino; 2 Native Hawaiian or other Pacific Islander, non-Hispanic/Latino; 40 Two or more races, non-Hispanic/Latino), 37 international. Average age 33. 315 applicants, 73% accepted, 180 enrolled. *Faculty:* 70 full-time (46 women), 6 part-time/adjunct (2 women). *Financial support:* In 2015–16, 489 students received support, including 2 fellowships with full tuition reimbursements available (averaging $5,000 per year), 43 research assistantships with partial tuition reimbursements available (averaging $11,915 per year), 11 teaching assistantships with partial tuition reimbursements available (averaging $11,380 per year); career-related internships or fieldwork, Federal Work-Study, scholarships/grants, health care benefits, and unspecified assistantships also available. Support available to part-time students. Financial award application deadline: 6/1; financial award applicants required to submit FAFSA. In 2015, 187 master's, 34 doctorates, 3 other advanced degrees awarded. *Degree program information:* Part-time and evening/weekend programs available. Part-time, evening/weekend. Offers 21st century teaching and learning (M Ed); adult and higher education (M Ed, PhD); applications of educational research and evaluation (Graduate Certificate); college teaching (Graduate Certificate); communication, culture and pedagogy for Hispanic populations in educational settings (Graduate Certificate); counseling psychology (PhD); education (M Ed, Ed D, PhD, Graduate Certificate); educational administration, curriculum and supervision (M Ed, Ed D, PhD); educational psychology (M Ed); educational studies (M Ed, PhD); instructional design and technology (M Ed); instructional leadership and academic curriculum (M Ed, PhD); instructional psychology and technology (M Ed, PhD, Graduate Certificate); integrating technology in teaching (M Ed); professional counseling (M Ed); special education (M Ed, PhD). *Application deadline:* For fall admission, 6/1 for domestic students, 3/1 for international students; for spring admission, 11/1 for domestic students, 9/1 for international students. *Application fee:* $50 ($100 for international students). Electronic applications accepted. *Application Contact:* Dr. Sherry Cox, Assistant Dean, 405-325-2238, Fax: 405-325-7620, E-mail: scox@ou.edu. *Dean,* Dr. Gregg Garn, 405-325-1081, Fax: 405-325-7390, E-mail: garn@ou.edu.

Mewbourne College of Earth and Energy Students: 150 full-time (43 women), 86 part-time (22 women); includes 19 minority (1 Black or African American, non-Hispanic/Latino; 3 American Indian or Alaska Native, non-Hispanic/Latino; 5 Asian, non-Hispanic/Latino; 7 Hispanic/Latino; 3 Two or more races, non-Hispanic/Latino), 161 international. Average age 27. 568 applicants, 12% accepted, 61 enrolled. *Faculty:* 46 full-time (6 women), 2 part-time/adjunct (0 women). *Financial support:* In 2015–16, 193 students received support, including 103 research assistantships with partial tuition reimbursements available (averaging $16,075 per year), 56 teaching assistantships with partial tuition reimbursements available (averaging $15,950 per year); career-related internships or fieldwork, scholarships/grants, and unspecified assistantships also available. Financial award application deadline: 6/1; financial award applicants required to submit FAFSA. In 2015, 61 master's, 13 doctorates awarded. *Degree program information:* Part-time programs available. Part-time. Offers earth and energy (MS, PhD, Graduate Certificate). *Application deadline:* For fall admission, 2/1 for domestic and international students; for spring admission, 9/1 for domestic and international students. *Application fee:* $50 ($100 for international students). Electronic applications accepted. *Dean,* Dr. J. Mike Stice, 405-325-3821, Fax: 405-325-3180, E-mail: mstice@ou.edu.

ConocoPhillips School of Geology and Geophysics Students: 57 full-time (21 women), 44 part-time (18 women); includes 10 minority (1 American Indian or Alaska Native, non-Hispanic/Latino; 2 Asian, non-Hispanic/Latino; 5 Hispanic/Latino; 2 Two or more races, non-Hispanic/Latino), 47 international. Average age 27. 265 applicants, 12% accepted, 30 enrolled. *Faculty:* 26 full-time (4 women). *Financial support:* In 2015–16, 87 students received support, including 37 research assistantships with partial tuition reimbursements available (averaging $19,207 per year), 25 teaching assistantships with partial tuition reimbursements available (averaging $18,448 per year); career-related internships or fieldwork, scholarships/grants, and unspecified assistantships also available. Financial award application deadline: 6/1; financial award applicants required to submit FAFSA. In 2015, 36 master's, 8 doctorates awarded. *Degree program information:* Part-time programs available. Part-time. Offers geology (MS, PhD); geology and geophysics (MS, PhD); geophysics (MS, PhD). *Application deadline:* For fall admission, 1/10 priority date for domestic and international students; for spring admission, 9/1 for domestic and international students. *Application fee:* $50 ($100 for international students). Electronic applications accepted. *Application Contact:* Rebecca Fay, Coordinator of Academic Student Services, 405-325-3253, Fax: 405-325-3140, E-mail: rfay@ou.edu. *Director,* Dr. R. Douglas Elmore, 405-325-3253, Fax: 405-325-3140, E-mail: delmore@ou.edu.

Mewbourne School of Petroleum and Geological Engineering Students: 93 full-time (22 women), 43 part-time (4 women); includes 9 minority (1 Black or African American, non-Hispanic/Latino; 2 American Indian or Alaska Native, non-Hispanic/Latino; 3 Asian, non-Hispanic/Latino; 2 Hispanic/Latino; 1 Two or more races, non-Hispanic/Latino), 115 international. Average age 28. 308 applicants, 12% accepted, 32 enrolled. *Faculty:* 20 full-time (2 women), 2 part-time/adjunct (0 women). *Financial support:* In 2015–16, 106 students received support, including 58 research assistantships with partial tuition reimbursements available (averaging $14,026 per year), 31 teaching assistantships with partial tuition reimbursements available (averaging $13,935 per year); unspecified assistantships also available. Financial award application deadline: 6/1; financial award applicants required to submit FAFSA. In 2015, 25 master's, 5 doctorates awarded. *Degree program information:* Part-time programs available. Part-time. Offers geological engineering (MS, PhD); natural gas engineering and management (MS, Graduate Certificate); natural gas technology (Graduate Certificate); petroleum engineering (MS, PhD). *Application deadline:* For fall admission, 3/1 for domestic and international students; for spring admission, 9/1 for domestic and international students. *Application fee:* $50 ($100 for international students). Electronic applications accepted. *Application Contact:* Dr. Deepak Devegowda, Associate Professor and Graduate Liaison, 405-325-3081, Fax: 405-325-3180, E-mail: deepka.devegowda@ou.edu. *Director/Chair,* Dr. Chandra Rai, 405-325-6866, Fax: 405-325-3180, E-mail: crai@ou.edu.

Price College of Business Students: 175 full-time (45 women), 176 part-time (34 women); includes 61 minority (11 Black or African American, non-Hispanic/Latino; 6 American Indian or Alaska Native, non-Hispanic/Latino; 9 Asian, non-Hispanic/Latino; 17 Hispanic/Latino; 18 Two or more races, non-Hispanic/Latino), 50 international. Average age 30. 348 applicants, 31% accepted, 85 enrolled. *Faculty:* 58 full-time (15 women), 3 part-time/adjunct (0 women). *Financial support:* In 2015–16, 184 students received support, including 10 fellowships with full tuition reimbursements available (averaging $3,295 per year), 47 research assistantships with partial tuition reimbursements available (averaging $13,148 per year), 21 teaching assistantships with partial tuition reimbursements available (averaging $15,722 per year); career-related internships or fieldwork, scholarships/grants, health care benefits, and unspecified assistantships also available. Support available to part-time students. Financial award application deadline: 6/1; financial award applicants required to submit FAFSA. In 2015, 140 master's, 10 doctorates, 7 other advanced degrees awarded. *Degree program information:* Part-time and evening/weekend programs available. Part-time, evening/weekend. Offers accounting (M Acc); business administration (MBA, PhD); business entrepreneurship (Graduate Certificate); management information systems (MS, Graduate Certificate). *Application deadline:* For fall admission, 2/1 for domestic and international students; for spring admission, 11/15 for domestic students, 8/1 for international students. *Application fee:* $50 ($100 for international students). Electronic applications accepted. *Application Contact:* Amber Hasbrook, Academic Counselor, 405-325-5815, Fax: 405-325-7753, E-mail: ahasbrook@ou.edu. *Dean*, Daniel Pullin, JD, 405-325-0100, Fax: 405-325-3421, E-mail: dpullin@ou.edu.

Division of Management Information Systems Students: 24 full-time (8 women), 11 part-time (2 women); includes 6 minority (1 American Indian or Alaska Native, non-Hispanic/Latino; 1 Asian, non-Hispanic/Latino; 1 Hispanic/Latino; 3 Two or more races, non-Hispanic/Latino), 11 international. Average age 29. 36 applicants, 28% accepted, 9 enrolled. *Faculty:* 10 full-time (5 women), 1 part-time/adjunct (0 women). *Financial support:* In 2015–16, 35 students received support, including 10 research assistantships with full tuition reimbursements available (averaging $12,170 per year), 2 teaching assistantships with full tuition reimbursements available (averaging $15,186 per year); career-related internships or fieldwork, scholarships/grants, health care benefits, and unspecified assistantships also available. Support available to part-time students. Financial award application deadline: 6/1; financial award applicants required to submit FAFSA. In 2015, 8 master's, 4 other advanced degrees awarded. *Degree program information:* Part-time and evening/weekend programs available. Part-time, evening/weekend. Offers management information systems (MS, Graduate Certificate). *Application deadline:* For fall admission, 3/15 for domestic students, 3/1 for international students; for spring admission, 11/1 for domestic students, 9/1 for international students. *Application fee:* $50 ($100 for international students). Electronic applications accepted. *Application Contact:* Callen Brehm, Academic Counselor, 405-325-2074, Fax: 405-325-7753, E-mail: cbrehm@ou.edu. *Chair/Director of MIS Division*, Radhika Santhanam, 405-325-0791, E-mail: radhika@ou.edu.

John T. Steed School of Accounting Students: 28 full-time (12 women), 6 part-time (4 women); includes 8 minority (1 American Indian or Alaska Native, non-Hispanic/Latino; 2 Asian, non-Hispanic/Latino; 2 Hispanic/Latino; 3 Two or more races, non-Hispanic/Latino), 5 international. Average age 26. 22 applicants, 41% accepted, 8 enrolled. *Faculty:* 10 full-time (2 women). *Financial support:* In 2015–16, 32 students received support, including 7 research assistantships with partial tuition reimbursements available (averaging $14,451 per year), 6 teaching assistantships with partial tuition reimbursements available (averaging $15,886 per year); career-related internships or fieldwork, scholarships/grants, and unspecified assistantships also available. Support available to part-time students. Financial award application deadline: 6/1; financial award applicants required to submit FAFSA. In 2015, 45 master's awarded. *Degree program information:* Part-time programs available. Part-time. Offers accounting (M Acc, PhD). *Application deadline:* For fall admission, 6/15 for domestic students, 3/1 for international students; for spring admission, 11/15 for domestic students, 8/1 for international students. *Application fee:* $50 ($100 for international students). Electronic applications accepted. *Application Contact:* Amber Hasbrook, Academic Counselor, 405-325-5815, Fax: 405-325-7753, E-mail: ahasbrook@ou.edu. *Director of the School of Accounting/Chair*, Ervin Black, 405-325-2401, Fax: 405-325-7348, E-mail: ervblack@ou.edu.

Weitzenhoffer Family College of Fine Arts Students: 134 full-time (61 women), 85 part-time (47 women); includes 41 minority (6 Black or African American, non-Hispanic/Latino; 9 American Indian or Alaska Native, non-Hispanic/Latino; 8 Asian, non-Hispanic/Latino; 11 Hispanic/Latino; 7 Two or more races, non-Hispanic/Latino), 21 international. Average age 30. 153 applicants, 52% accepted, 69 enrolled. *Faculty:* 102 full-time (34 women), 3 part-time/adjunct (0 women). *Financial support:* In 2015–16, 154 students received support, including 6 fellowships with full tuition reimbursements available (averaging $5,000 per year), 27 research assistantships with tuition reimbursements available (averaging $11,353 per year), 88 teaching assistantships with tuition reimbursements available (averaging $10,626 per year); career-related internships or fieldwork, Federal Work-Study, institutionally sponsored loans, scholarships/grants, health care benefits, tuition waivers (full and partial), and unspecified assistantships also available. Support available to part-time students. Financial award application deadline: 6/1; financial award applicants required to submit FAFSA. In 2015, 57 master's, 11 doctorates awarded. Offers fine arts (M Mus, M Mus Ed, MA, MFA, DMA, PhD, Graduate Certificate). *Application fee:* $50 ($100 for international students). Electronic applications accepted. *Application Contact:* Teri Lodes, Assistant to the Dean, 405-325-7375, Fax: 405-325-1667, E-mail: talodes@ou.edu. *Dean*, Dr. Mary Margaret Holt, 405-325-7370, Fax: 405-325-1667, E-mail: marymholt@ou.edu.

Helmerich School of Drama Students: 2 full-time (1 woman); includes 1 minority (American Indian or Alaska Native, non-Hispanic/Latino). Average age 25. *Faculty:* 8 full-time (3 women), 1 part-time/adjunct (0 women). *Financial support:* In 2015–16, 1 student received support, including 3 teaching assistantships with partial tuition reimbursements available (averaging $12,818 per year); unspecified assistantships also available. Financial award application deadline: 6/1; financial award applicants required to submit FAFSA. In 2015, 5 master's awarded. Offers acting (MFA); design (MFA); directing (MFA). *Application deadline:* For fall admission, 3/15 for domestic and international students; for spring admission, 11/1 for domestic and international students. *Application fee:* $50 ($100 for international students). Electronic applications accepted. *Application Contact:* Dr. Kae Koger, Graduate Liaison, 405-325-4021, Fax: 405-325-0400, E-mail: akoger@ou.edu. *Director*, Dr. Tom Orr, 405-325-4021, Fax: 405-325-0400, E-mail: thorr@ou.edu.

School of Art and Art History Students: 24 full-time (11 women), 12 part-time (9 women); includes 7 minority (4 American Indian or Alaska Native, non-Hispanic/Latino; 3 Two or more races, non-Hispanic/Latino), 2 international. Average age 33. 26 applicants, 38% accepted, 9 enrolled. *Faculty:* 28 full-time (10 women). *Financial support:* In 2015–16, 31 students received support, including 1 fellowship (averaging $5,000 per year), 16 teaching assistantships with partial tuition reimbursements available (averaging $10,689 per year); career-related internships or fieldwork, Federal Work-Study, institutionally sponsored loans, scholarships/grants, tuition waivers (full and partial), and unspecified assistantships also available. Support available to part-time students. Financial award application deadline: 6/1; financial award applicants required to submit FAFSA. In 2015, 7 master's, 1 doctorate awarded. Offers art (MFA); art and technology (MFA); art history (MA, PhD); art of the American West (PhD); ceramics (MFA); film (MFA); Native American art (PhD); painting (MFA); photography (MFA); printmaking (MFA); sculpture (MFA); video (MFA); visual communication (MFA). *Application deadline:* For fall admission, 1/15 for domestic and international students; for spring admission, 10/1 for domestic and international students. *Application fee:* $50 ($100 for international students). Electronic applications accepted. *Director*, Dr. Bette Talvacchia, 405-325-4697, Fax: 405-325-1668.

School of Dance Students: 2 full-time (1 woman), 2 part-time (1 woman). Average age 32. 2 applicants, 50% accepted, 1 enrolled. *Faculty:* 8 full-time (4 women). *Financial support:* In 2015–16, 2 students received support, including 1 fellowship with full tuition reimbursement available (averaging $5,000 per year), 2 research assistantships with partial tuition reimbursements available (averaging $15,311 per year), 1 teaching assistantship with partial tuition reimbursement available (averaging $10,372 per year); health care benefits and unspecified assistantships also available. Support available to part-time students. Financial award application deadline: 6/1; financial award applicants required to submit FAFSA. In 2015, 1 master's awarded. Offers dance (MFA). *Application deadline:* For fall admission, 4/15 for domestic students, 3/1 for international students. *Application fee:* $50 ($100 for international students). Electronic applications accepted. *Application Contact:* Jeremy Lindberg, Associate Professor, 405-325-0567 Ext. 15, Fax: 405-325-7024, E-mail: jlindberg@ou.edu. *Dean/Professor/Director*, Dr. Mary Margaret Holt, 405-325-4051, Fax: 405-325-7024, E-mail: marymholt@ou.edu.

School of Music Students: 106 full-time (48 women), 71 part-time (37 women); includes 33 minority (6 Black or African American, non-Hispanic/Latino; 4 American Indian or Alaska Native, non-Hispanic/Latino; 8 Asian, non-Hispanic/Latino; 11 Hispanic/Latino; 4 Two or more races, non-Hispanic/Latino), 19 international. Average age 29. 125 applicants, 54% accepted, 59 enrolled. *Faculty:* 56 full-time (16 women), 2 part-time/adjunct (0 women). *Financial support:* In 2015–16, 120 students received support, including 4 fellowships with full tuition reimbursements available (averaging $5,000 per year), 25 research assistantships with full tuition reimbursements available (averaging $11,036 per year), 68 teaching assistantships with full tuition reimbursements available (averaging $10,518 per year); Federal Work-Study, scholarships/grants, health care benefits, and unspecified assistantships also available. Financial award application deadline: 6/1; financial award applicants required to submit FAFSA. In 2015, 44 master's, 10 doctorates awarded. Offers choral conducting (M Mus); conducting (M Mus Ed, DMA); general (M Mus Ed); instrumental (M Mus Ed); instrumental conducting (M Mus); music composition (M Mus, DMA); music education (PhD); music performance (Graduate Certificate); music theory (M Mus); musicology (M Mus); organ (M Mus, DMA); piano (M Mus, DMA); piano pedagogy (M Mus Ed); voice (M Mus, DMA); wind/percussion/string (M Mus, DMA). *Application deadline:* For fall admission, 12/1 for domestic and international students; for spring admission, 10/1 for domestic and international students; for summer admission, 12/1 for domestic and international students. Applications are processed on a rolling basis. *Application fee:* $50 ($100 for international students). Electronic applications accepted. *Application Contact:* Jan Russell, Graduate Admissions and Recruiting Advisor, 405-325-5393, Fax: 405-325-7574, E-mail: jrussell@ou.edu. *Director*, Dr. Lawrence R. Mallett, 405-325-2081, Fax: 405-325-7574, E-mail: lmallett@ou.edu.

UNIVERSITY OF OKLAHOMA HEALTH SCIENCES CENTER, Oklahoma City, OK 73190

General Information State-supported, coed, upper-level institution. CGS member. *Graduate housing:* Rooms and/or apartments available on a first-come, first-served basis to single and married students. *Research affiliation:* Oklahoma Medical Research Foundation, Dean A. McGee Eye Institute (ophthalmology), Oklahoma Children's Memorial Hospital (pediatrics), Veterans Administration Medical Center (clinical and applied medicine), University of Oklahoma Medical Center, Peggy and Charles Stephenson Oklahoma Cancer Center (cancer research).

GRADUATE UNITS

College of Dentistry Offers dentistry (MS, DDS, Certificate); general dentistry (Certificate); orthodontics (MS); periodontics (MS). Electronic applications accepted.

College of Medicine Offers biochemistry (MS, PhD); biochemistry and molecular biology (MS, PhD); biological psychology (MS, PhD); cell biology (MS, PhD); genetic counseling (MS); immunology (MS, PhD); medical radiation physics (MS, PhD); medical sciences (MS); medicine (MHS, MS, MD, PhD); microbiology (MS, PhD); microbiology and immunology (MS, PhD); molecular biology (MS, PhD); neuroscience (MS, PhD); pathology (PhD); physician associate (MHS); physiology (MS, PhD); psychiatry and behavioral sciences (MS, PhD); radiological sciences (MS, PhD). Electronic applications accepted.

College of Pharmacy Offers pharmacy (MS, PhD, Pharm D).

Graduate College ***Degree program information:*** Part-time and evening/weekend programs available. Part-time, evening/weekend.

College of Allied Health Degree program information: Part-time programs available. Part-time. Offers allied health (MOT, MPT, MS, Au D, PhD, Certificate); allied health sciences (PhD); audiology (MS, Au D, PhD); communication sciences and disorders (Certificate); education of the deaf (MS); nutritional sciences (MS); occupational therapy (MOT); physical therapy (MPT); rehabilitation sciences (MS); speech-language pathology (MS, PhD).

College of Nursing Degree program information: Part-time programs available. Part-time. Offers nursing (MS). MS/MBA offered jointly with Oklahoma State University and University of Oklahoma.

College of Public Health Degree program information: Part-time programs available. Part-time. Offers biostatistics (MPH, MS, Dr PH, PhD); epidemiology (MPH, MS, Dr PH, PhD); general public health (MPH, Dr PH); health administration and policy (MHA, MPH, MS, Dr PH, PhD); health promotion sciences (MPH, MS, Dr PH, PhD); occupational and environmental health (MPH, MS, Dr PH, PhD); preparedness and terrorism (MPH); public health (MHA, MPH, MS, Dr PH, PhD).

UNIVERSITY OF OREGON, Eugene, OR 97403

General Information State-supported, coed, university. CGS member. *Graduate housing:* Rooms and/or apartments available to single and married students. *Research affiliation:* Oregon Research Institute, Battelle Pacific Northwest Laboratories, National Renewable Energy Laboratory (NREL), Stanford Linear Accelerator Center, Naval Research Laboratories.

GRADUATE UNITS

Graduate School ***Degree program information:*** Part-time and evening/weekend programs available. Part-time, evening/weekend. Offers applied information management (MS).

Charles H. Lundquist College of Business Degree program information: Part-time and evening/weekend programs available. Part-time, evening/weekend. Offers accounting (M Actg, PhD); business (M Actg, MA, MBA, MS, PhD); decision sciences (MA, MS); finance (PhD); management (PhD); management: general business (MBA); marketing (PhD); sports product management (MS).

College of Arts and Sciences Degree program information: Part-time and evening/weekend programs available. Part-time, evening/weekend. Offers anthropology (MA, MS, PhD); arts and sciences (MA, MFA, MS, PhD); Asian studies (MA); biochemistry (MA, MS, PhD); chemistry (MA, MS, PhD); Chinese (MA, PhD); classical civilization (MA); classics (MA); clinical psychology (PhD); cognitive psychology (MA, MS, PhD); comparative literature (MA, PhD); computer and information science (MA, MS, PhD); creative writing (MFA); developmental psychology (MA, MS, PhD); ecology and evolution (MA, MS, PhD); economics (MA, MS, PhD); English (MA, PhD); environmental science, studies, and policy (PhD); environmental studies (MA, MS); French (MA); geography (MA, MS, PhD); geological sciences (MA, MS, PhD); Germanic languages and literatures (MA, PhD); Greek (MA); history (MA, PhD); human physiology (MS, PhD); independent study: folklore (MA, MS); international studies (MA); Italian (MA); Japanese (MA, PhD); Latin (MA); linguistics (MA, PhD); marine biology (MA, MS, PhD); mathematics (MA, MS, PhD); molecular, cellular and genetic biology (PhD); neuroscience and development (PhD); philosophy (MA, PhD); physics (MA, MS, PhD); physiological psychology (MA, MS, PhD); political science (MA, MS, PhD); psychology (MA, MS, PhD); Romance languages (MA, PhD); Russian and East European Studies (MA); social/personality psychology (MA, MS, PhD); sociology (MA, MS, PhD); Spanish (MA); theater arts (MA, MFA, MS, PhD).

College of Education Degree program information: Part-time programs available. Part-time. Offers education (M Ed, MA, MS, D Ed, PhD).

School of Architecture and Allied Arts Degree program information: Part-time and evening/weekend programs available. Part-time, evening/weekend. Offers architecture (M Arch); architecture and allied arts (M Arch, MA, MCRP, MFA, MI Arch, MLA, MPA, MS, PhD); art (MFA); art history (MA, PhD); arts management (MA, MS); community and regional planning (MCRP); historic preservation (MS); interior architecture (MI Arch); landscape architecture (MLA); media management (MA, MS); public policy and management (MA, MPA, MS).

School of Journalism and Communication Degree program information: Part-time programs available. Part-time. Offers journalism (MA, MS); media studies (MA, MS, PhD); multimedia journalism (MA, MS); strategic communication (MA, MS).

School of Music Degree program information: Part-time programs available. Part-time. Offers composition (M Mus, DMA, PhD); conducting (M Mus); dance (MA, MS); jazz studies (M Mus); music (M Mus, MA, MS, DMA, PhD); music education (M Mus, DMA, PhD); music history (PhD); music theory (PhD); performance (M Mus, DMA); piano pedagogy (M Mus).

School of Law Offers law (MA, MS, JD).

UNIVERSITY OF OTTAWA, Ottawa, ON K1N 6N5, Canada

General Information Province-supported, coed, university. CGS member. *Graduate housing:* Rooms and/or apartments available on a first-come, first-served basis to single and married students. Housing application deadline: 3/15. *Research affiliation:* IBM (performance analytics software, supercomputing), General Electric Company (GE) (hardware, imaging, medical devices), Rio Tinto Alcan (aluminum and aluminum products), Pratt Whitney Canada (turbine engines, advanced materials, aerospace), Wright Medical Technology Canada (orthopedic medical devices), Air Products and Chemicals Inc. (industrial gases (hydrogen), performance materials, equipment and technology).

GRADUATE UNITS

Faculty of Graduate and Postdoctoral Studies *Degree program information:* Part-time and evening/weekend programs available. Part-time, evening/weekend. Offers biomedical engineering (MA Sc); e-business technologies (M Sc, MEBT); globalization and international development (MA); population health (PhD); systems science (M Sc, M Sys Sc, Certificate). MCL, MRE, MP Th offered jointly with Saint Paul University. Electronic applications accepted.

Faculty of Arts Degree program information: Part-time and evening/weekend programs available. Part-time, evening/weekend. Offers arts (M Geog, M Mus, M Sc, MA, PhD, Certificate); classical studies (MA); communication (MA); directing for theatre (MA); economics (PhD); English (MA, PhD); geography (M Geog, M Sc, MA, PhD); history (PhD); interpreting (MA); lettres Franlfcaises (MA, PhD); linguistics (MA, PhD); music (M Mus, MA); orchestral studies (Certificate); philosophy (PhD); piano pedagogy research (Certificate); political science (PhD); psychology (PhD); religious studies (PhD); Spanish (MA, PhD); Spanish translation (MA); translation (MA); translation studies (PhD). Electronic applications accepted.

Faculty of Education Online learning. Offers education (M Ed, MA Ed, PhD, Certificate). Electronic applications accepted.

Faculty of Engineering Offers chemical and biological engineering (M Eng, MA Sc, PhD); civil engineering (M Eng, MA Sc, PhD); computer science (MCS, PhD); electrical and computer engineering (M Eng, MA Sc, PhD); engineering (M Eng, MA Sc, MCS, PhD, Certificate); engineering management (M Eng); information technology (Certificate); mechanical and aerospace engineering (M Eng, MA Sc, PhD); project management (Certificate). Electronic applications accepted.

Faculty of Health Sciences Degree program information: Part-time and evening/weekend programs available. Part-time, evening/weekend. Offers audiology (M Sc); health sciences (M Sc, MA, PhD, Certificate); human kinetics (MA); nurse practitioner (Certificate); nursing (M Sc, PhD); nursing/primary health care (M Sc); orthophony (M Sc). Electronic applications accepted.

Faculty of Law Degree program information: Part-time and evening/weekend programs available. Part-time, evening/weekend. Offers law (LL M, LL D). Electronic applications accepted.

Faculty of Medicine Offers biochemistry (M Sc, PhD); cellular and molecular medicine (M Sc, PhD); epidemiology (M Sc); medicine (M Sc, MD, PhD); microbiology and immunology (M Sc, PhD). Electronic applications accepted.

Faculty of Science Degree program information: Part-time and evening/weekend programs available. Part-time, evening/weekend. Offers biology (M Sc, PhD); chemistry (M Sc, PhD); earth sciences (M Sc, PhD); mathematics and statistics (M Sc, PhD); physics (M Sc, PhD); science (M Sc, PhD). Electronic applications accepted.

Faculty of Social Sciences Degree program information: Part-time and evening/weekend programs available. Part-time, evening/weekend. Offers criminology (MA, MCA); economics (MA, PhD); education (MA); English (MA); history (MA); human kinetics (MA); law (LL M); lettres Franlfcaises (MA); nursing (M Sc); pastoral studies (MA); political science (MA); political studies (MA, PhD); psychology (PhD); religious studies (MA); social sciences (LL M, M Sc, MA, MCA, MSS, PhD); social work (MSS); sociology (MA); sociology and anthropology (MA). Electronic applications accepted.

Telfer School of Management Degree program information: Part-time and evening/weekend programs available. Part-time, evening/weekend. Offers business administration (MBA); executive business administration (EMBA); health administration (MHA); management (EMBA, MBA, MHA). Electronic applications accepted.

UNIVERSITY OF PENNSYLVANIA, Philadelphia, PA 19104

General Information Independent, coed, university. CGS member. *Enrollment:* 21,395 graduate, professional, and undergraduate students; 11,066 full-time matriculated graduate/professional students (5,744 women), 1,676 part-time matriculated graduate/professional students (1,131 women). *Enrollment by degree level:* 6,753 master's, 5,803 doctoral, 186 other advanced degrees. *Graduate faculty:* 2,568 full-time (834 women), 2,300 part-time/adjunct (906 women). *Tuition, area resident:* Full-time $31,068; part-time $5762 per course. *Required fees:* $3200; $336 per course. Full-time tuition and fees vary according to degree level, program and student level. Part-time tuition and fees vary according to course load, degree level and program. *Graduate housing:* Rooms and/or apartments available on a first-come, first-served basis to single and married students. *Student services:* Campus employment opportunities, campus safety program, career counseling, child daycare facilities, exercise/wellness program, free psychological counseling, international student services, low-cost health insurance, multicultural affairs office, services for students with disabilities, writing training. *Library:* Van Pelt Library plus 14 others. *Research affiliation:* Children's Hospital of Philadelphia, The Wistar Institute (anatomy and biology), BioAdvance, Regional Nanotechnology Center.

Computer facilities: Computer purchase and lease plans are available. A campuswide network can be accessed from student residence rooms and from off campus. Online class registration, billing information, financial aid application, status, academic records, student services are available.
Website: http://www.upenn.edu/

GRADUATE UNITS

Annenberg School for Communication Students: 86 full-time (51 women), 2 part-time (both women); includes 11 minority (4 Black or African American, non-Hispanic/Latino; 3 Asian, non-Hispanic/Latino; 3 Hispanic/Latino; 1 Two or more races, non-Hispanic/Latino), 31 international. Average age 30. 270 applicants, 6% accepted, 15 enrolled. *Faculty:* 20 full-time (9 women), 5 part-time/adjunct (1 woman). *Financial support:* In 2015–16, 80 students received support. In 2015, 6 doctorates awarded. Offers communication (PhD).

Graduate School of Education Students: 1,216 full-time (870 women), 233 part-time (167 women); includes 469 minority (204 Black or African American, non-Hispanic/Latino; 3 American Indian or Alaska Native, non-Hispanic/Latino; 118 Asian, non-Hispanic/Latino; 95 Hispanic/Latino; 49 Two or more races, non-Hispanic/Latino), 317 international. Average age 31. 2,971 applicants, 49% accepted, 767 enrolled. *Faculty:* 70 full-time (28 women), 44 part-time/adjunct (23 women). In 2015, 521 master's, 79 doctorates awarded. *Degree program information:* Part-time and evening/weekend programs available. Part-time, evening/weekend, online learning. Offers education (M Phil, MS Ed, Ed D, PhD, Certificate); educational leadership (Ed D); learning leadership (Ed D); medical education (MS Ed, Certificate); teaching (MS Ed); urban teaching (MS Ed).

Division of Applied Psychology and Human Development Students: 174 full-time (143 women), 7 part-time (5 women); includes 59 minority (19 Black or African American, non-Hispanic/Latino; 18 Asian, non-Hispanic/Latino; 14 Hispanic/Latino; 8 Two or more races, non-Hispanic/Latino), 54 international. Average age 26. 412 applicants, 57% accepted, 126 enrolled. *Financial support:* In 2015–16, 95 students received support. Fellowships, research assistantships, teaching assistantships, career-related internships or fieldwork, Federal Work-Study, scholarships/grants, health care benefits, and unspecified assistantships available. In 2015, 102 master's, 2 doctorates awarded. *Degree program information:* Part-time and evening/weekend programs available. Part-time-only, evening/weekend. Offers applied psychology and human development (M Phil, MS Ed, PhD); counseling and mental health services (M Phil, MS Ed); human development (MS Ed, PhD); school and mental health counseling (MS Ed). *Application deadline:* For fall admission, 12/8 priority date for domestic and international students. Applications are processed on a rolling basis. *Application fee:* $75. Electronic applications accepted. *Application Contact:* 215-898-6415, Fax: 215-746-6884, E-mail: admissions@gse.upenn.edu. *Program Manager*, Dr. Elizabeth Mackenzie, 215-898-4176, E-mail: emackenz@upenn.edu.

Division of Educational Linguistics Students: 188 full-time (168 women), 12 part-time (10 women); includes 21 minority (5 Black or African American, non-Hispanic/Latino; 12 Asian, non-Hispanic/Latino; 3 Hispanic/Latino; 1 Two or more races, non-Hispanic/Latino), 145 international. Average age 25. 563 applicants, 36% accepted, 90 enrolled. *Financial support:* In 2015–16, 55 students received support. Fellowships, research assistantships, teaching assistantships, Federal Work-Study, scholarships/grants, health care benefits, and unspecified assistantships available. In 2015, 85 master's, 2 doctorates awarded. *Degree program information:* Part-time programs available. Part-time. Offers educational linguistics (MS Ed, PhD); intercultural communication (MS Ed); teaching English to speakers of other languages (MS Ed). *Application deadline:* For fall admission, 12/8 priority date for domestic and international students. Applications are processed on a rolling basis. *Application fee:* $75. Electronic applications accepted. *Program Manager*, Kristina Lewis, 215-898-5212, E-mail: klewi@upenn.edu.

Division of Education, Culture and Society Students: 79 full-time (60 women), 15 part-time (14 women); includes 32 minority (12 Black or African American, non-Hispanic/Latino; 10 Asian, non-Hispanic/Latino; 6 Hispanic/Latino; 4 Two or more races, non-Hispanic/Latino), 28 international. Average age 28. 365 applicants, 43% accepted, 58 enrolled. *Financial support:* In 2015–16, 44 students received support. Fellowships, research assistantships, teaching assistantships, Federal Work-Study, scholarships/grants, and health care benefits available. In 2015, 34 master's, 1 doctorate awarded. *Degree program information:* Part-time programs available. Part-time. Offers education, culture and society (MS Ed, PhD); international educational development (MS Ed). *Application deadline:* For fall admission, 12/8 priority date for domestic and international students. Applications are processed on a rolling basis. *Application fee:* $75. Electronic applications accepted. *Program Manager*, Dr. Alex Posecznick, 215-573-3947, E-mail: alpos@upenn.edu.

Division of Education Policy Students: 35 full-time (25 women), 3 part-time (2 women); includes 13 minority (10 Black or African American, non-Hispanic/Latino; 3 Hispanic/Latino), 8 international. Average age 28. 196 applicants, 51% accepted, 23 enrolled. *Financial support:* In 2015–16, 13 students received support. Fellowships, research assistantships, teaching assistantships, Federal Work-Study, scholarships/grants, and health care benefits available. In 2015, 15 master's, 2 doctorates awarded. *Degree program information:* Part-time programs available. Part-time. Offers education policy (MS Ed, PhD). *Application deadline:* For fall admission, 12/8 priority date for domestic and international students. Applications are processed on a rolling basis. *Application fee:* $75. Electronic applications accepted. *Program Manager*, Krista Featherstone, 215-573-8075, E-mail: kfeat@upenn.edu.

Division of Higher Education Students: 111 full-time (68 women), 33 part-time (23 women); includes 56 minority (30 Black or African American, non-Hispanic/Latino; 8 Asian, non-Hispanic/Latino; 15 Hispanic/Latino; 3 Two or more races, non-Hispanic/Latino), 5 international. Average age 37. 360 applicants, 44% accepted, 74 enrolled. *Financial support:* In 2015–16, 24 students received support. Fellowships, research assistantships, teaching assistantships, Federal Work-Study, scholarships/grants, health care benefits, and unspecified assistantships available. In 2015, 56 master's, 30 doctorates awarded. *Degree program information:* Part-time programs available. Part-time. Offers higher education (MS Ed, Ed D, PhD); higher education management (Ed D). *Application deadline:* For fall admission, 12/8 priority date for domestic and international students. *Application fee:* $75. Electronic applications accepted. *Program Manager,* Dr. Ross Aikins, 215-898-8398, E-mail: raikins@upenn.edu.

Division of Quantitative Methods Students: 38 full-time (31 women), 16 part-time (14 women); includes 6 minority (1 Black or African American, non-Hispanic/Latino; 3 Asian, non-Hispanic/Latino; 2 Two or more races, non-Hispanic/Latino), 35 international. Average age 27. 159 applicants, 38% accepted, 26 enrolled. *Financial support:* In 2015–16, 20 students received support. Fellowships, research assistantships, teaching assistantships, Federal Work-Study, scholarships/grants, health care benefits, and unspecified assistantships available. In 2015, 12 master's, 2 doctorates awarded. *Degree program information:* Part-time programs available. Part-time. Offers quantitative methods (M Phil, MS, MS Ed, PhD); statistics, measurement, assessment, and research technology (MS). *Application deadline:* For fall admission, 12/8 priority date for domestic and international students. Applications are processed on a rolling basis. *Application fee:* $75. Electronic applications accepted. *Program Manager,* Christine Lee, 215-898-0505, E-mail: cplee@upenn.edu.

Division of Reading, Writing, and Literacy Students: 73 full-time (57 women), 27 part-time (23 women); includes 41 minority (20 Black or African American, non-Hispanic/Latino; 10 Asian, non-Hispanic/Latino; 6 Hispanic/Latino; 5 Two or more races, non-Hispanic/Latino), 5 international. Average age 32. 127 applicants, 57% accepted, 40 enrolled. *Financial support:* In 2015–16, 26 students received support. Fellowships, research assistantships, teaching assistantships, Federal Work-Study, scholarships/grants, health care benefits, and unspecified assistantships available. In 2015, 30 master's, 10 doctorates awarded. *Degree program information:* Part-time programs available. Part-time. Offers language and literacy (MS Ed); reading, writing, and literacy (MS Ed, Ed D, PhD); reading/writing/literacy (MS Ed, Ed D, PhD). *Application deadline:* For fall admission, 12/8 priority date for domestic and international students. Applications are processed on a rolling basis. *Application fee:* $75. Electronic applications accepted. *Program Manager,* Penny Creedon, 215-898-3245, E-mail: pennyc@upenn.edu.

Division of Teaching, Learning, and Leadership Students: 214 full-time (128 women), 44 part-time (36 women); includes 71 minority (32 Black or African American, non-Hispanic/Latino; 2 American Indian or Alaska Native, non-Hispanic/Latino; 22 Asian, non-Hispanic/Latino; 8 Hispanic/Latino; 7 Two or more races, non-Hispanic/Latino), 25 international. Average age 32. 542 applicants, 58% accepted, 176 enrolled. *Financial support:* In 2015–16, 13 students received support. Fellowships, research assistantships, teaching assistantships, Federal Work-Study, scholarships/grants, health care benefits, and unspecified assistantships available. In 2015, 94 master's, 10 doctorates awarded. *Degree program information:* Part-time programs available. Part-time. Offers education entrepreneurship (MS Ed); educational leadership (MS Ed); elementary education (MS Ed); learning sciences and technologies (MS Ed); school leadership (MS Ed); secondary education (MS Ed); teaching and learning (MS Ed); teaching, learning, and leadership (MS Ed, Ed D, PhD); teaching, learning, and teacher education (Ed D, PhD). *Application deadline:* For fall admission, 12/8 priority date for domestic and international students. Applications are processed on a rolling basis. *Application fee:* $75. Electronic applications accepted. *Application Contact:* Mercury Meulman, Administrative Coordinator, 215-898-4176, E-mail: mercury@upenn.edu. *Program Manager,* Dr. Veronica Aplenc, 215-898-2566, E-mail: vaplenc@upenn.edu.

Law School Students: 754 full-time (340 women); includes 206 minority (51 Black or African American, non-Hispanic/Latino; 3 American Indian or Alaska Native, non-Hispanic/Latino; 98 Asian, non-Hispanic/Latino; 36 Hispanic/Latino; 18 Two or more races, non-Hispanic/Latino), 38 international. Average age 24. 5,069 applicants, 19% accepted, 238 enrolled. *Faculty:* 75 full-time (27 women), 76 part-time/adjunct (21 women). *Financial support:* In 2015–16, 362 students received support, including 3 fellowships (averaging $1,495 per year), 99 research assistantships (averaging $1,630 per year), 3 teaching assistantships (averaging $2,333 per year); career-related internships or fieldwork, Federal Work-Study, institutionally sponsored loans, and scholarships/grants also available. Financial award application deadline: 3/1; financial award applicants required to submit FAFSA. In 2015, 121 master's, 247 doctorates awarded. Offers law (LL CM, LL M, ML, JD, SJD). JD/LL M offered jointly with Hong Kong University. *Application deadline:* For fall admission, 3/1 for domestic students, 12/15 for international students. Applications are processed on a rolling basis. *Application fee:* $80. Electronic applications accepted. *Application Contact:* Renee Post, Associate Dean of Admissions and Financial Aid, 215-898-7400, Fax: 215-898-9606, E-mail: contactadmissions@law.upenn.edu. *Dean,* Theodore W. Ruger, 215-898-7463, Fax: 215-573-2025.

Perelman School of Medicine Students: 1,760 full-time (898 women), 176 part-time (125 women); includes 720 minority (100 Black or African American, non-Hispanic/Latino; 4 American Indian or Alaska Native, non-Hispanic/Latino; 354 Asian, non-Hispanic/Latino; 177 Hispanic/Latino; 2 Native Hawaiian or other Pacific Islander, non-Hispanic/Latino; 83 Two or more races, non-Hispanic/Latino), 146 international. 7,214 applicants, 11% accepted, 372 enrolled. *Faculty:* 2,924 full-time (1,173 women), 1,197 part-time/adjunct (538 women). *Financial support:* In 2015–16, 1,191 students received support. Applicants required to submit FAFSA. In 2015, 158 master's, 115 doctorates awarded. *Degree program information:* Part-time programs available. Part-time. Offers environmental health (MPH); generalist (MPH); global health (MPH); health policy research (MS); medical ethics and health policy (MBE, MSME); medicine (MBE, MPH, MRA, MS, MSCE, MSME, MTR, MD, PhD).

Biomedical Graduate Studies Students: 800 full-time (417 women), 106 part-time (70 women); includes 275 minority (29 Black or African American, non-Hispanic/Latino; 4 American Indian or Alaska Native, non-Hispanic/Latino; 140 Asian, non-Hispanic/Latino; 66 Hispanic/Latino; 2 Native Hawaiian or other Pacific Islander, non-Hispanic/Latino; 34 Two or more races, non-Hispanic/Latino), 106 international. 1,290 applicants, 20% accepted, 104 enrolled. *Faculty:* 949. *Financial support:* In 2015–16, 740 students received support. In 2015, 81 master's, 115 doctorates awarded. Offers biochemistry and molecular biophysics (PhD); biomedical studies (MS, PhD); biostatistics (MS, PhD); cancer biology (PhD); cell biology, physiology, and metabolism (PhD); developmental stem cell regenerative biology (PhD); epidemiology (PhD); gene therapy and vaccines (PhD); genetics and gene regulation (PhD); genomics and computational biology (PhD); immunology (PhD); microbiology, virology, and parasitology (PhD); neuroscience (PhD); pharmacology (PhD). *Application deadline:* For fall admission, 12/1 priority date for domestic students, 12/1 for international students. Applications are processed on a rolling basis. *Application fee:* $80. Electronic applications accepted. *Application Contact:* Aislinn Wallace, Admissions Coordinator, 215-746-6349, E-mail: aislinnw@mail.med.upenn.edu. *Director,* Dr. Michael Nusbaum, 215-898-1585, E-mail: nusbaum@mail.med.upenn.edu.

Center for Clinical Epidemiology and Biostatistics Students: 94 full-time (63 women), 2 part-time (1 woman); includes 34 minority (6 Black or African American, non-Hispanic/Latino; 17 Asian, non-Hispanic/Latino; 11 Hispanic/Latino). Average age 35. 40 applicants, 95% accepted, 33 enrolled. *Faculty:* 97 full-time (47 women), 90 part-time/adjunct (27 women). *Financial support:* In 2015–16, 60 students received support, including 65 fellowships with tuition reimbursements available (averaging $45,500 per year); career-related internships or fieldwork, scholarships/grants, health care benefits, and unspecified assistantships also available. Financial award application deadline: 12/1. In 2015, 36 master's awarded. *Degree program information:* Part-time programs available. Part-time. Offers clinical epidemiology (MSCE). *Application deadline:* For fall admission, 12/1 priority date for domestic students, 12/1 for international students. *Application fee:* $0. *Application Contact:* Jennifer Kuklinski, Program Coordinator, 215-573-2382, E-mail: jkuklins@mail.med.upenn.edu. *Director,* Dr. Harold I. Feldman, 215-573-0901, E-mail: hfeldman@mail.med.upenn.edu.

Institute for Translational Medicine and Therapeutics Offers translational medicine and therapeutics (MRA, MTR). *Application Contact:* Rachel Bastian, Administrative Director, E-mail: itmated@mail.med.upenn.edu. *Director, Translational Research Programs,* Dr. Emma Meagher, MD, E-mail: itmated@mail.med.upenn.edu.

School of Arts and Sciences Students: 1,625 full-time (771 women), 434 part-time (259 women); includes 338 minority (90 Black or African American, non-Hispanic/Latino; 1 American Indian or Alaska Native, non-Hispanic/Latino; 101 Asian, non-Hispanic/Latino; 86 Hispanic/Latino; 60 Two or more races, non-Hispanic/Latino), 617 international. Average age 30. 6,506 applicants, 18% accepted, 533 enrolled. *Faculty:* 477 full-time (153 women), 14 part-time/adjunct (4 women). In 2015, 480 master's, 204 doctorates, 33 other advanced degrees awarded. *Degree program information:* Part-time and evening/weekend programs available. Part-time, evening/weekend. Offers Africana studies (MA, PhD); ancient history (AM, PhD); anthropology (AM, MS, PhD); applied mathematics and computational science (PhD); art and archaeology of the Mediterranean world (AM, PhD); arts and sciences (AM, MA, MBA, MES, MGA, MGA, MLA, MPA, MS, PhD, Certificate); biology (PhD); chemistry (MS, PhD); classical studies (AM, PhD); comparative literature (AM, PhD); criminology (MA, MS, PhD); demography (AM, PhD); earth and environmental science (MS, PhD); East Asian languages and civilization (AM, PhD); economics (AM, PhD); English (AM, PhD); French (AM, PhD); Germanic languages (AM, PhD); history (AM, PhD); history and sociology of science (AM, PhD); history of art (AM, PhD); international studies (AM); Italian (AM, PhD); linguistics (AM, PhD); literary theory (AM, PhD); mathematics (AM, PhD); medical physics (MS); music (AM, PhD); Near Eastern languages and civilization (AM, PhD); philosophy (AM, PhD); physics (PhD); political science (AM, PhD); psychology (PhD); religious studies (PhD); sociology (AM, PhD); South Asian regional studies (AM, PhD); Spanish (AM, PhD).

College of Liberal and Professional Studies Students: 135 full-time (69 women), 329 part-time (203 women); includes 85 minority (27 Black or African American, non-Hispanic/Latino; 23 Asian, non-Hispanic/Latino; 17 Hispanic/Latino; 18 Two or more races, non-Hispanic/Latino), 61 international. Average age 35. 542 applicants, 52% accepted, 173 enrolled. In 2015, 161 master's awarded. Offers applied geosciences (MSAG); applied positive psychology (MAP); chemical sciences (MCS); environmental studies (MES); individualized study (MLA); liberal arts (M Phil); medical physics (MMP); organization dynamics (M Phil).

Fels Institute of Government Students: 54 full-time (29 women), 78 part-time (44 women); includes 31 minority (19 Black or African American, non-Hispanic/Latino; 1 American Indian or Alaska Native, non-Hispanic/Latino; 5 Asian, non-Hispanic/Latino; 3 Hispanic/Latino; 3 Two or more races, non-Hispanic/Latino), 23 international. Average age 31. 327 applicants, 38% accepted, 61 enrolled. *Financial support:* Application deadline: 1/1. In 2015, 52 master's, 17 other advanced degrees awarded. *Degree program information:* Part-time and evening/weekend programs available. Part-time, evening/weekend. Offers economic development and growth (Certificate); government administration (MGA); nonprofit administration (Certificate); organization dynamics (MS); politics (Certificate); public administration (MPA); public finance (Certificate).

Joseph H. Lauder Institute of Management and International Studies Offers international studies (MA); management and international studies (MBA). Applications must be made concurrently and separately to the Wharton MBA program. Electronic applications accepted.

School of Dental Medicine Offers dental medicine (DMD).

School of Design Students: 692 full-time (402 women), 25 part-time (19 women); includes 100 minority (16 Black or African American, non-Hispanic/Latino; 1 American Indian or Alaska Native, non-Hispanic/Latino; 44 Asian, non-Hispanic/Latino; 27 Hispanic/Latino; 1 Native Hawaiian or other Pacific Islander, non-Hispanic/Latino; 11 Two or more races, non-Hispanic/Latino), 380 international. Average age 26. 1,677 applicants, 50% accepted, 357 enrolled. *Faculty:* 38 full-time (15 women), 18 part-time/adjunct (4 women). *Financial support:* In 2015–16, 29 students received support. In 2015, 259 master's, 9 doctorates, 50 other advanced degrees awarded. *Degree program information:* Part-time programs available. Part-time. Offers architecture (M Arch, PhD); city and regional planning (PhD); city planning (MCP); design (M Arch, MCP, MEBD, MFA, MLA, MS, MUSA, PhD, Advanced Certificate, Certificate); ecological architecture (Certificate); emerging design and research (Certificate); environmental building design (MEBD); fine arts (MFA); GIS and spatial analysis (Certificate); historic preservation (MS, Certificate); land preservation (Certificate); landscape architecture (MLA); landscape studies (Certificate); time-based and interactive media (Certificate); urban design (Certificate); urban redevelopment (Certificate); urban spatial analytics (MUSA).

School of Engineering and Applied Science Students: 1,047 full-time (316 women), 275 part-time (107 women); includes 156 minority (10 Black or African American, non-Hispanic/Latino; 105 Asian, non-Hispanic/Latino; 30 Hispanic/Latino; 11 Two or more races, non-Hispanic/Latino), 832 international. Average age 26. 6,264 applicants, 20% accepted, 714 enrolled. *Faculty:* 115 full-time (18 women), 26 part-time/adjunct (3 women). *Financial support:* In 2015–16, 393 students received support. In 2015, 579 master's, 78 doctorates awarded. *Degree program information:* Part-time and evening/weekend programs available. Part-time, evening/weekend. Offers applied mechanics (MSE, PhD); bioengineering (MSE, PhD); biotechnology (MS); chemical and biomolecular engineering (MSE, PhD); computer and information science (MSE, PhD); computer and information technology (MCIT); computer graphics and game technology (MSE); electrical and systems engineering (MSE, PhD); engineering and applied science (EMBA, MCIT, ME, MIPD, MS, MSE, PhD, AC); integrated product design (ME, MIPD); materials science and engineering (MSE, PhD); mechanical engineering (MSE, PhD); nanotechnology (MSE); robotics (MS, PhD); scientific computing (MSE).

Application deadline: For fall admission, 3/15 priority date for domestic and international students. *Application fee:* $80. Electronic applications accepted. *Application Contact:* William Fenton, Assistant Director of Graduate Admissions, 215-898-4542, Fax: 215-573-5577, E-mail: gradstudies@seas.upenn.edu.

School of Nursing Students: 262 full-time (225 women), 364 part-time (335 women); includes 171 minority (46 Black or African American, non-Hispanic/Latino; 1 American Indian or Alaska Native, non-Hispanic/Latino; 63 Asian, non-Hispanic/Latino; 42 Hispanic/Latino; 19 Two or more races, non-Hispanic/Latino), 15 international. Average age 31. 749 applicants, 62% accepted, 307 enrolled. *Faculty:* 55 full-time (48 women), 34 part-time/adjunct (32 women). In 2015, 294 master's, 13 doctorates awarded. *Degree program information:* Part-time programs available. Part-time, online learning. Offers adult and special populations (MSN); adult gerontology clinical nurse specialist (MSN); adult-gerontology acute care nurse practitioner (MSN); adult-gerontology primary care nurse practitioner (MSN); child and family (MSN); family nurse practitioner (MSN, Certificate); geropsychiatrics (MSN); health leadership (MSN); neonatal clinical nurse specialist (MSN); neonatal nurse practitioner (MSN); nurse anesthesia (MSN); nurse midwifery (MSN); nursing (MSN, PhD, Certificate); nursing and health care administration (MSN, PhD); pediatric acute care nurse practitioner (MSN); pediatric clinical nurse specialist (MSN); pediatric primary care nurse practitioner (MSN); women's health/gender related nurse practitioner (MSN). *Application Contact:* Sylvia English, Enrollment Management Coordinator, 215-898-8439, Fax: 215-573-8439, E-mail: sylviaj@nursing.upenn.edu. *Assistant Dean for Admissions and Academic Affairs*, Dr. Christina Costanzo Clark, 215-898-4271, Fax: 215-573-8439, E-mail: costanzo@nursing.upenn.edu.

School of Social Policy and Practice Students: 425 full-time (346 women), 62 part-time (50 women); includes 133 minority (53 Black or African American, non-Hispanic/Latino; 26 Asian, non-Hispanic/Latino; 7 Hispanic/Latino; 47 Two or more races, non-Hispanic/Latino), 52 international. Average age 27. 895 applicants, 294 enrolled. *Faculty:* 22 full-time (12 women), 67 part-time/adjunct (47 women). *Financial support:* In 2015–16, 291 students received support, including 24 fellowships (averaging $24,378 per year); career-related internships or fieldwork, Federal Work-Study, institutionally sponsored loans, scholarships/grants, tuition waivers (partial), and unspecified assistantships also available. Support available to part-time students. Financial award applicants required to submit FAFSA. In 2015, 182 master's, 17 doctorates awarded. *Degree program information:* Part-time programs available. Part-time, blended/hybrid learning. Offers social policy and practice (MNPL, MSSP, MSW, DSW, PhD); social welfare (PhD); social work (MNPL, MSSP, MSW, DSW). *Application deadline:* For fall admission, 2/1 priority date for domestic and international students. Applications are processed on a rolling basis. *Application fee:* $65. Electronic applications accepted. *Application Contact:* Dr. Mary C. Mazzola, Associate Dean, Enrollment Management, 215-898-5550, Fax: 215-573-2099, E-mail: mmazzola@sp2.upenn.edu. *Dean*, John L. Jackson, Jr., 215-898-5541, Fax: 215-573-2099, E-mail: jjackson@sp2.upenn.edu.

School of Veterinary Medicine Students: 481 full-time (395 women), 9 part-time (6 women); includes 58 minority (7 Black or African American, non-Hispanic/Latino; 29 Asian, non-Hispanic/Latino; 17 Hispanic/Latino; 5 Two or more races, non-Hispanic/Latino), 2 international. Average age 26. 1,190 applicants, 14% accepted, 120 enrolled. *Faculty:* 107 full-time (57 women), 32 part-time/adjunct (13 women). In 2015, 119 doctorates awarded. Offers veterinary medicine (VMD).

Wharton School ***Degree program information:*** Evening/weekend programs available. Evening/weekend. Offers accounting (PhD); applied economics (PhD); business (MBA, PhD); business administration (MBA); business and public policy (MBA, PhD); ethics and legal studies (PhD); finance (PhD); health care management (MBA, PhD); health care management and economics (PhD); insurance and risk management (MBA, PhD); legal studies and business ethics (MBA, PhD); management (PhD); marketing (PhD); operations and information management (PhD); real estate (MBA, PhD); statistics (MBA, PhD). Electronic applications accepted.

The Wharton MBA Program for Executives Degree program information: Evening/weekend programs available. Evening/weekend. Offers executive business administration (MBA).

UNIVERSITY OF PHILOSOPHICAL RESEARCH, Los Angeles, CA 90027

General Information Proprietary, coed, graduate-only institution.

GRADUATE UNITS

Master's in Consciousness Studies Program Offers consciousness studies (MA). Electronic applications accepted.

Master's in Transformational Psychology Program Offers transformational psychology (MA). Electronic applications accepted.

UNIVERSITY OF PHOENIX–ATLANTA CAMPUS, Sandy Springs, GA 30350-4147

General Information Proprietary, coed, comprehensive institution. *Graduate housing:* On-campus housing not available.

GRADUATE UNITS

College of Information Systems and Technology ***Degree program information:*** Evening/weekend programs available. Evening/weekend. Offers information systems (MIS); technology management (MBA). Electronic applications accepted.

College of Nursing ***Degree program information:*** Evening/weekend programs available. Evening/weekend, online learning. Offers health administration (MHA); nursing (MSN); nursing/health care education (MSN). Electronic applications accepted.

School of Business ***Degree program information:*** Evening/weekend programs available. Evening/weekend, online learning. Offers accounting (MBA); business administration (MBA); global management (MBA); human resources management (MBA, MM); management (MM); marketing (MBA); public administration (MM).

UNIVERSITY OF PHOENIX–AUGUSTA CAMPUS, Augusta, GA 30909-4583

General Information Proprietary, coed, comprehensive institution.

GRADUATE UNITS

College of Criminal Justice and Security Offers administration of justice and security (MS).

College of Information Systems and Technology Offers information systems (MIS); technology management (MBA).

College of Nursing Online learning. Offers health administration (MHA); nursing (MSN); nursing/health care education (MSN).

School of Business Online learning. Offers accounting (MBA); business administration (MBA); business and management (MBA, MM); global management (MBA); human resources management (MBA, MM); management (MM); marketing (MBA); public administration (MBA, MM).

UNIVERSITY OF PHOENIX–BAY AREA CAMPUS, San Jose, CA 95134-1805

General Information Proprietary, coed, comprehensive institution. *Graduate housing:* On-campus housing not available.

GRADUATE UNITS

College of Criminal Justice and Security Offers administration of justice and security (MS).

College of Education ***Degree program information:*** Evening/weekend programs available. Evening/weekend, online learning. Offers administration and supervision (MA Ed); adult education and training (MA Ed); early childhood education (MA Ed); education (Ed S); educational leadership (Ed D); elementary teacher education (MA Ed); higher education administration (PhD); secondary teacher education (MA Ed); special education (MA Ed); teacher leadership (MA Ed). Electronic applications accepted.

College of Information Systems and Technology ***Degree program information:*** Evening/weekend programs available. Evening/weekend. Offers information systems (MIS); organizational leadership/information systems and technology (DM). Electronic applications accepted.

College of Nursing ***Degree program information:*** Evening/weekend programs available. Evening/weekend, online learning. Offers education (MHA); gerontology (MHA); health administration (MHA, DHA); informatics (MHA, MSN); nursing (MSN, PhD); nursing/health care education (MSN). Electronic applications accepted.

College of Social Sciences ***Degree program information:*** Evening/weekend programs available. Evening/weekend. Offers marriage, family, and child therapy (MSC).

School of Business ***Degree program information:*** Evening/weekend programs available. Evening/weekend, online learning. Offers accountancy (MS); accounting (MBA); business administration (MBA, DBA); energy management (MBA); global management (MBA); health care management (MBA); human resource management (MBA); human resources management (MM); management (MM); marketing (MBA); organizational leadership (DM); project management (MBA); public administration (MPA); technology management (MBA). Electronic applications accepted.

UNIVERSITY OF PHOENIX–CENTRAL FLORIDA CAMPUS, Orlando, FL 32819

General Information Proprietary, coed, comprehensive institution. *Graduate housing:* On-campus housing not available.

UNIVERSITY OF PHOENIX–CENTRAL VALLEY CAMPUS, Fresno, CA 93720-1552

General Information Proprietary, coed, comprehensive institution.

GRADUATE UNITS

College of Education Offers curriculum and instruction (MA Ed); curriculum and instruction-computer education (MA Ed); elementary teacher education (MA Ed); secondary teacher education (MA Ed).

College of Human Services Offers marriage, family and child therapy (MSC).

College of Information Systems and Technology Offers information systems (MIS); technology management (MBA).

College of Nursing Offers education (MHA); gerontology (MHA); health administration (MHA); nursing (MSN).

School of Business Offers accounting (MBA); business administration (MBA); global management (MBA); human resources management (MBA, MM); management (MM); marketing (MBA); public administration (MBA, MM).

UNIVERSITY OF PHOENIX–CHARLOTTE CAMPUS, Charlotte, NC 28273-3409

General Information Proprietary, coed, comprehensive institution. *Graduate housing:* On-campus housing not available.

GRADUATE UNITS

College of Information Systems and Technology ***Degree program information:*** Evening/weekend programs available. Evening/weekend. Offers information systems (MIS); information systems management (MISM); technology management (MBA). Electronic applications accepted.

College of Nursing ***Degree program information:*** Evening/weekend programs available. Evening/weekend. Offers education (MHA); gerontology (MHA); health administration (MHA); informatics (MHA, MSN); nursing (MSN); nursing/health care education (MSN). Electronic applications accepted.

School of Business ***Degree program information:*** Evening/weekend programs available. Evening/weekend. Offers accounting (MBA); business administration (MBA); global management (MBA). Electronic applications accepted.

UNIVERSITY OF PHOENIX–COLORADO CAMPUS, Lone Tree, CO 80124-5453

General Information Proprietary, coed, comprehensive institution. *Graduate housing:* On-campus housing not available.

GRADUATE UNITS

College of Education ***Degree program information:*** Evening/weekend programs available. Evening/weekend. Offers administration and supervision (MAEd); curriculum instruction (MAEd); elementary teacher education (MAEd); school counseling (MSC); secondary teacher education (MAEd). Electronic applications accepted.

College of Information Systems and Technology ***Degree program information:*** Evening/weekend programs available. Evening/weekend, online learning. Offers e-business (MBA); management (MIS); technology management (MBA). Electronic applications accepted.

College of Nursing ***Degree program information:*** Evening/weekend programs available. Evening/weekend, online learning. Offers health administration (MHA); nursing (MSN). Electronic applications accepted.

School of Business ***Degree program information:*** Evening/weekend programs available. Evening/weekend, online learning. Offers accountancy (MSA); accounting (MBA); business administration (MBA); e-business (MBA); global management (MBA); human resources management (MBA, MM); management (MM); marketing (MBA); public administration (MBA, MM). Electronic applications accepted.

UNIVERSITY OF PHOENIX–COLORADO SPRINGS DOWNTOWN CAMPUS, Colorado Springs, CO 80903

General Information Proprietary, coed, comprehensive institution. *Graduate housing:* On-campus housing not available.

GRADUATE UNITS

College of Education ***Degree program information:*** Evening/weekend programs available. Evening/weekend. Offers administration and supervision (MA Ed); curriculum and instruction (MA Ed); elementary teacher education (MA Ed); principal licensure certification (Certificate); school counseling (MSC); secondary teacher education (MA Ed). Electronic applications accepted.

College of Information Systems and Technology ***Degree program information:*** Evening/weekend programs available. Evening/weekend. Offers technology management (MBA). Electronic applications accepted.

College of Nursing ***Degree program information:*** Evening/weekend programs available. Evening/weekend. Offers education (MHA); gerontology (MHA); health administration (MHA); nursing (MSN). Electronic applications accepted.

School of Business ***Degree program information:*** Evening/weekend programs available. Evening/weekend. Offers accounting (MBA); business administration (MBA); global management (MBA); human resources management (MBA, MM); management (MM); marketing (MBA); public administration (MM). Electronic applications accepted.

UNIVERSITY OF PHOENIX–COLUMBUS GEORGIA CAMPUS, Columbus, GA 31909

General Information Proprietary, coed, comprehensive institution. *Graduate housing:* On-campus housing not available.

GRADUATE UNITS

College of Information Systems and Technology ***Degree program information:*** Evening/weekend programs available. Evening/weekend, online learning. Offers e-business (MBA); information systems (MIS); technology management (MBA). Electronic applications accepted.

College of Nursing Online learning. Offers health administration (MHA); nursing (MSN). Electronic applications accepted.

School of Business ***Degree program information:*** Evening/weekend programs available. Evening/weekend. Offers accounting (MBA); business administration (MBA); global management (MBA); human resources management (MBA, MM); management (MM); marketing (MBA); public administration (MBA). Electronic applications accepted.

UNIVERSITY OF PHOENIX–DALLAS CAMPUS, Dallas, TX 75251

General Information Proprietary, coed, comprehensive institution. *Graduate housing:* On-campus housing not available.

GRADUATE UNITS

College of Criminal Justice and Security Online learning. Offers administration of justice and security (MS). Electronic applications accepted.

College of Education Offers curriculum and instruction (MA Ed).

College of Information Systems and Technology ***Degree program information:*** Evening/weekend programs available. Evening/weekend. Offers e-business (MBA); information systems (MIS); technology management (MBA). Electronic applications accepted.

School of Business ***Degree program information:*** Evening/weekend programs available. Evening/weekend, online learning. Offers accounting (MBA); business administration (MBA); global management (MBA); human resources management (MBA, MM); management (MM); marketing (MBA); public administration (MBA, MM). Electronic applications accepted.

UNIVERSITY OF PHOENIX–HAWAII CAMPUS, Honolulu, HI 96813-3800

General Information Proprietary, coed, comprehensive institution. *Graduate housing:* On-campus housing not available.

GRADUATE UNITS

College of Education ***Degree program information:*** Evening/weekend programs available. Evening/weekend. Offers administration and supervision (MA Ed); curriculum and instruction (MA Ed); elementary education (MA Ed); secondary education (MA Ed); special education (MA Ed); teacher education for elementary licensure (MA Ed). Electronic applications accepted.

College of Information Systems and Technology ***Degree program information:*** Evening/weekend programs available. Evening/weekend. Offers information systems (MIS); technology management (MBA). Electronic applications accepted.

College of Nursing ***Degree program information:*** Evening/weekend programs available. Evening/weekend. Offers education (MHA); family nurse practitioner (MSN); gerontology (MHA); health administration (MHA); nursing (MSN); nursing/health care education (MSN). Electronic applications accepted.

School of Business ***Degree program information:*** Evening/weekend programs available. Evening/weekend. Offers accounting (MBA); business administration (MBA); global management (MBA); human resources management (MBA, MM); management (MM); marketing (MBA); public administration (MBA, MM). Electronic applications accepted.

UNIVERSITY OF PHOENIX–HOUSTON CAMPUS, Houston, TX 77079-2004

General Information Proprietary, coed, comprehensive institution. *Graduate housing:* On-campus housing not available.

GRADUATE UNITS

College of Education Offers curriculum and instruction (MA Ed).

College of Information Systems and Technology ***Degree program information:*** Evening/weekend programs available. Evening/weekend, online learning. Offers e-business (MBA); information systems (MIS); technology management (MBA). Electronic applications accepted.

College of Nursing Online learning. Offers health administration (MHA). Electronic applications accepted.

School of Business ***Degree program information:*** Evening/weekend programs available. Evening/weekend, online learning. Offers accounting (MBA); business administration (MBA); global management (MBA); human resources management (MBA, MM); management (MM); marketing (MBA); public administration (MBA, MM). Electronic applications accepted.

UNIVERSITY OF PHOENIX–JERSEY CITY CAMPUS, Jersey City, NJ 07310

General Information Proprietary, coed, comprehensive institution.

GRADUATE UNITS

College of Criminal Justice and Security Online learning. Offers administration of justice and security (MS).

College of Information Systems and Technology Online learning. Offers information systems (MIS); technology management (MBA).

College of Social Services Online learning. Offers psychology (MS).

School of Business Offers accounting (MBA); business administration (MBA); global management (MBA); human resources management (MBA, MM); management (MM); marketing (MBA); public administration (MBA, MM).

UNIVERSITY OF PHOENIX–LAS VEGAS CAMPUS, Las Vegas, NV 89135

General Information Proprietary, coed, comprehensive institution. *Graduate housing:* On-campus housing not available.

GRADUATE UNITS

College of Education ***Degree program information:*** Evening/weekend programs available. Evening/weekend. Offers administration and supervision (MA Ed); curriculum and instruction (MA Ed); school counseling (MSC); teacher education-elementary licensure (MA Ed). Electronic applications accepted.

College of Human Services Online learning. Offers marriage, family, and child therapy (MSC); mental health counseling (MSC); school counseling (MSC). Electronic applications accepted.

College of Information Systems and Technology ***Degree program information:*** Evening/weekend programs available. Evening/weekend. Offers information systems (MIS); technology management (MBA). Electronic applications accepted.

School of Business ***Degree program information:*** Evening/weekend programs available. Evening/weekend, online learning. Offers accounting (MBA); business administration (MBA); global management (MBA); human resources management (MBA, MM); management (MM); marketing (MBA); public administration (MM). Electronic applications accepted.

UNIVERSITY OF PHOENIX–NEW MEXICO CAMPUS, Albuquerque, NM 87113-1570

General Information Proprietary, coed, comprehensive institution. *Graduate housing:* On-campus housing not available.

GRADUATE UNITS

College of Education ***Degree program information:*** Evening/weekend programs available. Evening/weekend. Offers administration and supervision (MAEd); curriculum and instruction (MAEd); elementary teacher education (MAEd); school counseling (MSC); secondary teacher education (MAEd). Electronic applications accepted.

College of Information Systems and Technology ***Degree program information:*** Evening/weekend programs available. Evening/weekend. Offers e-business (MBA); information systems (MS); technology management (MBA). Electronic applications accepted.

College of Nursing ***Degree program information:*** Evening/weekend programs available. Evening/weekend. Offers health administration (MHA); health care education (MSN); nursing (MSN). Electronic applications accepted.

School of Business ***Degree program information:*** Evening/weekend programs available. Evening/weekend. Offers accounting (MBA); business administration (MBA); global management (MBA); human resources management (MBA, MM); management (MM); marketing (MBA). Electronic applications accepted.

UNIVERSITY OF PHOENIX–NORTH FLORIDA CAMPUS, Jacksonville, FL 32216-0959

General Information Proprietary, coed, comprehensive institution. *Graduate housing:* On-campus housing not available.

GRADUATE UNITS

College of Education ***Degree program information:*** Evening/weekend programs available. Evening/weekend. Offers administration and supervision (MA Ed); curriculum and instruction (MA Ed); early childhood education (MA Ed); elementary teacher education (MA Ed); secondary teacher education (MA Ed). Electronic applications accepted.

College of Information Systems and Technology ***Degree program information:*** Evening/weekend programs available. Evening/weekend. Offers information systems (MIS); management (MIS). Electronic applications accepted.

College of Nursing ***Degree program information:*** Evening/weekend programs available. Evening/weekend. Offers health administration (MHA); health care education (MSN); nursing (MSN). Electronic applications accepted.

School of Business ***Degree program information:*** Evening/weekend programs available. Evening/weekend. Offers accounting (MBA); business administration (MBA); global management (MBA); human resources management (MBA, MM); management (MM); marketing (MBA); public administration (MBA, MM). Electronic applications accepted.

UNIVERSITY OF PHOENIX–ONLINE CAMPUS, Phoenix, AZ 85034-7209

General Information Proprietary, coed, comprehensive institution. *Graduate housing:* On-campus housing not available.

GRADUATE UNITS

College of Education ***Degree program information:*** Evening/weekend programs available. Evening/weekend, online learning. Offers administration and supervision (MAEd, Certificate); adult education and training (MAEd); curriculum and instruction (MAEd); early childhood education (MAEd); educational studies (MAEd); elementary teacher education (MAEd); principal licensure (Certificate); secondary teacher education (MAEd); special education (MAEd, Certificate); teacher education (MAEd); teacher education middle level mathematics (MAEd); teacher education middle level science (MAEd); teacher education secondary mathematics (MAEd); teacher education secondary science (MAEd); teacher leadership (MAEd); teachers of English learners (Certificate); transition to teaching (Certificate). Electronic applications accepted.

College of Health Sciences and Nursing ***Degree program information:*** Evening/weekend programs available. Evening/weekend, online learning. Offers family nurse practitioner (Certificate); health care (Certificate); health care education

(Certificate); health care informatics (Certificate); informatics (MSN); nursing (MSN); nursing and health care education (MSN). Electronic applications accepted.

College of Information Systems and Technology ***Degree program information:*** Evening/weekend programs available. Evening/weekend, online learning. Offers information systems and technology (MIS). Electronic applications accepted.

College of Justice and Security ***Degree program information:*** Evening/weekend programs available. Evening/weekend, online learning. Offers administration of justice and security (MS); public administration (MPA). Electronic applications accepted.

College of Social Science ***Degree program information:*** Evening/weekend programs available. Evening/weekend, online learning. Offers mediation (Certificate); psychology (MS). Electronic applications accepted.

School of Advanced Studies ***Degree program information:*** Evening/weekend programs available. Evening/weekend, online learning. Offers business administration (DBA); education (Ed S); educational leadership (Ed D); health administration (DHA); higher education administration (PhD); industrial/organizational psychology (PhD); nursing (PhD); organizational leadership (DM). Electronic applications accepted.

School of Business ***Degree program information:*** Evening/weekend programs available. Evening/weekend, online learning. Offers accountancy (MS); accounting (MBA, Certificate); business administration (MBA); energy management (MBA); global management (MBA); health care management (MBA); human resource management (MBA, Certificate); human resources management (MM); management (MM); marketing (MBA, Certificate); project management (MBA, Certificate); public administration (MBA, MM); technology management (MBA). Electronic applications accepted.

UNIVERSITY OF PHOENIX–PHOENIX CAMPUS, Tempe, AZ 85282-2371

General Information Proprietary, coed, comprehensive institution. CGS member. *Graduate housing:* On-campus housing not available.

GRADUATE UNITS

College of Criminal Justice and Security ***Degree program information:*** Evening/weekend programs available. Evening/weekend, online learning. Offers administration of justice and security (MS); global and homeland security (MS); law enforcement organizations (MS); public administration (MPA). Electronic applications accepted.

College of Education ***Degree program information:*** Evening/weekend programs available. Evening/weekend, online learning. Offers administration and supervision (MA Ed); adult education and training (MA Ed); curriculum and instruction reading (MA Ed); early childhood education (MA Ed); education studies (MA Ed); elementary teacher education (MA Ed); secondary teacher education (MA Ed); special education (MA Ed); teacher leadership (MA Ed). Electronic applications accepted.

College of Health Sciences and Nursing ***Degree program information:*** Evening/weekend programs available. Evening/weekend, online learning. Offers family nurse practitioner (MSN, Certificate); gerontology health care (Certificate); health care education (MSN, Certificate); health care informatics (Certificate); informatics (MSN); nursing (MSN). Electronic applications accepted.

College of Social Sciences ***Degree program information:*** Evening/weekend programs available. Evening/weekend, online learning. Offers counseling (MS); psychology (MS). Electronic applications accepted.

School of Business ***Degree program information:*** Evening/weekend programs available. Evening/weekend, online learning. Offers accounting (MBA, MS, Certificate); business administration (MBA); energy management (MBA); global management (MBA); health care management (MBA); human resource management (MBA, Certificate); management (MM); marketing (MBA); project management (MBA); technology management (MBA). Electronic applications accepted.

UNIVERSITY OF PHOENIX–SACRAMENTO VALLEY CAMPUS, Sacramento, CA 95833-4334

General Information Proprietary, coed, comprehensive institution. *Graduate housing:* On-campus housing not available.

GRADUATE UNITS

College of Education ***Degree program information:*** Evening/weekend programs available. Evening/weekend. Offers adult education (MA Ed); curriculum instruction (MA Ed); elementary teacher education (MA Ed); secondary teacher education (MA Ed); teacher education (Certificate). Electronic applications accepted.

College of Information Systems and Technology ***Degree program information:*** Evening/weekend programs available. Evening/weekend. Offers management (MIS); technology management (MBA). Electronic applications accepted.

College of Nursing ***Degree program information:*** Evening/weekend programs available. Evening/weekend. Offers family nurse practitioner (MSN); health administration (MHA); health care education (MSN); nursing (MSN). Electronic applications accepted.

School of Business ***Degree program information:*** Evening/weekend programs available. Evening/weekend. Offers accounting (MBA); business administration (MBA); global management (MBA); human resources management (MBA, MM); management (MM); marketing (MBA); public administration (MBA, MM). Electronic applications accepted.

UNIVERSITY OF PHOENIX–SAN ANTONIO CAMPUS, San Antonio, TX 78230

General Information Proprietary, coed, comprehensive institution.

GRADUATE UNITS

College of Criminal Justice and Security Offers administration of justice and security (MS).

College of Education Offers curriculum and instruction (MA Ed).

College of Information Systems and Technology Offers information systems (MIS); technology management (MBA).

College of Nursing Offers health administration (MHA).

School of Business Offers accounting (MBA); business administration (MBA); e-business (MBA); global management (MBA); human resources management (MBA, MM); management (MM); marketing (MBA); public administration (MBA, MM).

UNIVERSITY OF PHOENIX–SAN DIEGO CAMPUS, San Diego, CA 92123

General Information Proprietary, coed, comprehensive institution. *Graduate housing:* On-campus housing not available.

GRADUATE UNITS

College of Education ***Degree program information:*** Evening/weekend programs available. Evening/weekend. Offers curriculum and instruction (MA Ed); elementary teacher education (MA Ed); secondary teacher education (MA Ed). Electronic applications accepted.

College of Information Systems and Technology ***Degree program information:*** Evening/weekend programs available. Evening/weekend. Offers management (MIS); technology management (MBA). Electronic applications accepted.

College of Nursing ***Degree program information:*** Evening/weekend programs available. Evening/weekend. Offers health care education (MSN); nursing (MSN). Electronic applications accepted.

School of Business ***Degree program information:*** Evening/weekend programs available. Evening/weekend. Offers accounting (MBA); business administration (MBA); global management (MBA); human resources management (MBA, MM); management (MM); marketing (MBA); public administration (MBA). Electronic applications accepted.

UNIVERSITY OF PHOENIX–SOUTHERN ARIZONA CAMPUS, Tucson, AZ 85711

General Information Proprietary, coed, comprehensive institution. *Graduate housing:* On-campus housing not available.

GRADUATE UNITS

College of Education ***Degree program information:*** Evening/weekend programs available. Evening/weekend. Offers administration and supervision (MA Ed); adult education and training (MA Ed); curriculum instruction (MA Ed); educational counseling (MA Ed); elementary teacher education (MA Ed); school counseling (MSC); secondary teacher education (MA Ed); special education (MA Ed, Certificate). Electronic applications accepted.

College of Information Systems and Technology ***Degree program information:*** Evening/weekend programs available. Evening/weekend. Offers information systems (MIS); technology management (MBA). Electronic applications accepted.

College of Social Sciences ***Degree program information:*** Evening/weekend programs available. Evening/weekend. Offers psychology (MS). Electronic applications accepted.

School of Business ***Degree program information:*** Evening/weekend programs available. Evening/weekend. Offers accountancy (MS); accounting (MBA); business administration (MBA); global management (MBA); human resources management (MBA); management (MM); marketing (MBA). Electronic applications accepted.

UNIVERSITY OF PHOENIX–SOUTHERN CALIFORNIA CAMPUS, Costa Mesa, CA 92626

General Information Proprietary, coed, comprehensive institution. *Graduate housing:* On-campus housing not available.

GRADUATE UNITS

College of Criminal Justice and Security ***Degree program information:*** Evening/weekend programs available. Evening/weekend, online learning. Offers administration of justice and security (MS); public administration (MPA). Electronic applications accepted.

College of Education ***Degree program information:*** Evening/weekend programs available. Evening/weekend, online learning. Offers administration and supervision (MA Ed, Certificate); adult education and training (MA Ed); educational studies (MA Ed); elementary teacher education (MA Ed); secondary teacher education (MA Ed); teacher leadership (MA Ed); teachers of English learners (Certificate). Electronic applications accepted.

College of Health Sciences and Nursing ***Degree program information:*** Evening/weekend programs available. Evening/weekend, online learning. Offers family nurse practitioner (MSN, Certificate); health care (Certificate); informatics (MSN); nursing (MSN); nursing/health care education (MSN, Certificate). Electronic applications accepted.

College of Social Sciences ***Degree program information:*** Evening/weekend programs available. Evening/weekend, online learning. Offers counseling (MS); psychology (MS). Electronic applications accepted.

School of Business ***Degree program information:*** Evening/weekend programs available. Evening/weekend, online learning. Offers accounting (MBA); business administration (MBA); energy management (MBA); global management (MBA); health care management (MBA); human resource management (MBA); management (MM); marketing (MBA); project management (MBA); technology management (MBA). Electronic applications accepted.

UNIVERSITY OF PHOENIX–SOUTH FLORIDA CAMPUS, Miramar, FL 33027-4145

General Information Proprietary, coed, comprehensive institution. *Graduate housing:* On-campus housing not available.

GRADUATE UNITS

College of Education ***Degree program information:*** Evening/weekend programs available. Evening/weekend. Offers administration and supervision (MA Ed); curriculum and instruction (MA Ed); early childhood education (MA Ed); elementary teacher education (MA Ed); secondary teacher education (MA Ed). Electronic applications accepted.

College of Information Systems and Technology ***Degree program information:*** Evening/weekend programs available. Evening/weekend. Offers management (MIS); technology management (MBA). Electronic applications accepted.

College of Nursing ***Degree program information:*** Evening/weekend programs available. Evening/weekend. Offers health administration (MHA); health care education (MSN); nursing (MSN). Electronic applications accepted.

School of Business ***Degree program information:*** Evening/weekend programs available. Evening/weekend. Offers accounting (MBA); business administration (MBA); global management (MBA); human resource management (MBA); human resources management (MM); management (MM); marketing (MBA); public administration (MBA, MM). Electronic applications accepted.

UNIVERSITY OF PHOENIX–UTAH CAMPUS, Salt Lake City, UT 84123-4642

General Information Proprietary, coed, comprehensive institution. *Graduate housing:* On-campus housing not available.

GRADUATE UNITS

College of Education ***Degree program information:*** Evening/weekend programs available. Evening/weekend. Offers administration and supervision (MA Ed); curriculum and instruction (MA Ed); elementary teacher education (MA Ed); school counseling (MSC); secondary teacher education (MA Ed); special education (MA Ed). Electronic applications accepted.

College of Information Systems and Technology ***Degree program information:*** Evening/weekend programs available. Evening/weekend. Offers information systems and technology (MIS). Electronic applications accepted.

College of Nursing ***Degree program information:*** Evening/weekend programs available. Evening/weekend. Offers health care education (MSN); nursing (MSN). Electronic applications accepted.

School of Business ***Degree program information:*** Evening/weekend programs available. Evening/weekend. Offers accounting (MBA); business administration (MBA); global management (MBA); human resource management (MBA, MM); management (MM); marketing (MBA); technology management (MBA). Electronic applications accepted.

UNIVERSITY OF PHOENIX–WASHINGTON D.C. CAMPUS, Washington, DC 20001

General Information Proprietary, coed, comprehensive institution.

GRADUATE UNITS

College of Criminal Justice and Security Offers administration of justice and security (MS).

College of Education Offers administration and supervision (MA Ed); adult education and training (MA Ed); computer education (MA Ed); curriculum and instruction (MA Ed, Ed D); early childhood education (MA Ed); education (Ed S); educational leadership (Ed D); educational technology (Ed D); elementary teacher education (MA Ed); English and language arts education (MA Ed); English as a second language (MA Ed); higher education administration (PhD); mathematics education (MA Ed); secondary teacher education (MA Ed); special education (MA Ed); teacher leadership (MA Ed).

College of Information Systems and Technology Offers information systems (MIS); organizational leadership/information systems and technology (DM).

College of Nursing Offers education (MHA); gerontology (MHA); health administration (MHA, DHA); informatics (MHA, MSN); nursing (MSN, PhD); nursing/health care education (MSN).

College of Social Sciences Offers industrial/organizational psychology (PhD); psychology (MS).

School of Business Offers accountancy (MS); business administration (MBA, DBA); human resources management (MM); management (MM); organizational leadership (DM); public administration (MPA).

UNIVERSITY OF PHOENIX–WESTERN WASHINGTON CAMPUS, Tukwila, WA 98188

General Information Proprietary, coed, comprehensive institution. *Graduate housing:* On-campus housing not available.

GRADUATE UNITS

College of Criminal Justice and Security ***Degree program information:*** Evening/weekend programs available. Evening/weekend. Offers administration of justice and security (MS). Electronic applications accepted.

School of Business ***Degree program information:*** Evening/weekend programs available. Evening/weekend. Offers business (MBA). Electronic applications accepted.

UNIVERSITY OF PIKEVILLE, Pikeville, KY 41501

General Information Independent-religious, coed, comprehensive institution. *Enrollment:* 2,533 graduate, professional, and undergraduate students; 624 full-time matriculated graduate/professional students (288 women), 3 part-time matriculated graduate/professional students (2 women). *Enrollment by degree level:* 95 master's, 532 doctoral. *Graduate faculty:* 25 full-time (9 women), 48 part-time/adjunct (21 women). *Graduate housing:* Room and/or apartments available on a first-come, first-served basis to single students; on-campus housing not available to married students. Housing application deadline: 5/1. *Student services:* Campus employment opportunities, campus safety program, career counseling, exercise/wellness program, free psychological counseling, international student services, low-cost health insurance, services for students with disabilities. *Library:* Allara Library plus 2 others. *Collection:* Books: 71,763 (physical), 150,829 (digital/electronic); Serial titles: 1,176 (physical), 12,531 (digital/electronic); Databases: 75. Weekly public service hours: 105; students can reserve study rooms.

Computer facilities: 308 computers available on campus for general student use. A campuswide network can be accessed from student residence rooms and from off campus. Website: http://www.upike.edu/

General Application Contact: Teresa Lockhart, Vice President of Enrollment Management, 606-218-5251, Fax: 606-218-5255, E-mail: teresalockhart@upike.edu.

GRADUATE UNITS

Coleman College of Business Students: 45 full-time (18 women), 3 part-time (2 women); includes 5 minority (all Black or African American, non-Hispanic/Latino), 5 international. Average age 29. *Faculty:* 5 part-time/adjunct (1 woman). *Financial support:* Tuition waivers (full) and university employee grants available. Financial award application deadline: 2/15; financial award applicants required to submit FAFSA. In 2015, 11 master's awarded. *Degree program information:* Part-time and evening/weekend programs available. Part-time, evening/weekend. Offers business (MBA). *Application deadline:* For fall admission, 8/15 for domestic students, 7/1 for international students. Applications are processed on a rolling basis. *Application fee:* $50. *Application Contact:* Cathy Maynard, Secretary, Business and Economics, 606-218-5020, Fax: 606-218-5031, E-mail: cathymaynard@upike.edu. *Dean,* Dr. Howard V. Roberts, 606-218-5019, Fax: 606-218-5031, E-mail: howardroberts@upike.edu.

Kentucky College of Osteopathic Medicine Students: 532 full-time (229 women); includes 59 minority (8 Black or African American, non-Hispanic/Latino; 10 American Indian or Alaska Native, non-Hispanic/Latino; 21 Asian, non-Hispanic/Latino; 19 Hispanic/Latino; 1 Native Hawaiian or other Pacific Islander, non-Hispanic/Latino), 2 international. Average age 25. 3,982 applicants, 5% accepted, 135 enrolled. *Faculty:* 25 full-time (9 women), 37 part-time/adjunct (14 women). *Financial support:* In 2015–16, 7 students received support, including 7 fellowships with full tuition reimbursements available (averaging $41,320 per year); scholarships/grants also available. Financial award application deadline: 8/1; financial award applicants required to submit FAFSA. In 2015, 67 doctorates awarded. Offers osteopathic medicine (DO). *Application deadline:* For fall admission, 5/1 for domestic students. Applications are processed on a rolling basis. *Application fee:* $75. *Application Contact:* Dr. Linda Dunatov, Associate Dean for Student Affairs, 606-218-5408, Fax: 606-218-5442, E-mail: lindadunatov@upike.edu. *Dean,* Dr. Boyd Buser, 606-218-5410, Fax: 606-218-8442, E-mail: boydbuser@upike.edu.

Patton College of Education Students: 47 full-time (41 women); includes 1 minority (Black or African American, non-Hispanic/Latino). Average age 34. *Faculty:* 6 part-time/adjunct (5 women). *Degree program information:* Part-time and evening/weekend programs available. Part-time, evening/weekend. Offers teacher leader (MA). *Application deadline:* For fall admission, 8/15 for domestic students. Applications are processed on a rolling basis. *Application fee:* $50. *Application Contact:* Fairy Coleman, Administrative Assistant, 606-218-5314, E-mail: fairycoleman@upike.edu. *Dean,* Dr. David Barnett, 606-218-5318, E-mail: drbarnett@upike.edu.

UNIVERSITY OF PITTSBURGH, Pittsburgh, PA 15260

General Information State-related, coed, university. CGS member. *Enrollment:* 28,649 graduate, professional, and undergraduate students; 7,577 full-time matriculated graduate/professional students (4,106 women), 2,164 part-time matriculated graduate/professional students (1,228 women). *Enrollment by degree level:* 4,492 master's, 4,845 doctoral, 183 other advanced degrees. *Graduate faculty:* 4,143 full-time (1,671 women), 751 part-time/adjunct (360 women). Tuition and fees vary according to program. *Student services:* Campus employment opportunities, campus safety program, career counseling, exercise/wellness program, free psychological counseling, international student services, low-cost health insurance, services for students with disabilities, writing training. *Library:* Hillman Library plus 17 others. *Collection:* Books: 5.9 million (physical), 1.4 million (digital/electronic); Serial titles: 111,137 (physical), 217,449 (digital/electronic); Databases: 565. Weekly public service hours: 145; study areas open 24 hours, 5–7 days a week; students can reserve study rooms. *Research affiliation:* National Institutes of Health, National Science Foundation, National Energy Technology Laboratory, UPMC, Innovation Works, First Energy Services Co.

Computer facilities: Computer purchase and lease plans are available. 2,000 computers available on campus for general student use. A campuswide network can be accessed from student residence rooms and from off campus. Online class registration, online class listings, online tuition payment are available.
Website: http://www.pitt.edu/

General Application Contact: Information Contact, 412-624-4141, E-mail: graduate@pitt.edu.

GRADUATE UNITS

Dietrich School of Arts and Sciences Students: 1,577 full-time (738 women), 25 part-time (19 women); includes 326 minority (49 Black or African American, non-Hispanic/Latino; 6 American Indian or Alaska Native, non-Hispanic/Latino; 197 Asian, non-Hispanic/Latino; 63 Hispanic/Latino; 1 Native Hawaiian or other Pacific Islander, non-Hispanic/Latino; 10 Two or more races, non-Hispanic/Latino), 385 international. Average age 29. 4,154 applicants, 18% accepted, 293 enrolled. *Faculty:* 937 full-time (387 women), 59 part-time/adjunct (23 women). *Financial support:* In 2015–16, 1,403 students received support, including 401 fellowships with full tuition reimbursements available, 405 research assistantships with full tuition reimbursements available, 597 teaching assistantships with full tuition reimbursements available; career-related internships or fieldwork, Federal Work-Study, institutionally sponsored loans, scholarships/grants, traineeships, health care benefits, tuition waivers (full and partial), and unspecified assistantships also available. Support available to part-time students. Financial award applicants required to submit FAFSA. In 2015, 157 master's, 160 doctorates, 16 other advanced degrees awarded. *Degree program information:* Part-time programs available. Part-time. Offers anthropology (MA, PhD); applied linguistics (MA); applied linguistics with TESOL (MA); applied mathematics (MA, MS); applied statistics (MA, MS); arts and sciences (MA, MFA, MS, Pro-MS, PhD, Certificate, Doctoral Certificate, Master's Certificate); biological science (PhD); chemistry (PhD); Chinese (MA); clinical psychology (PhD); communication (MA, PhD); composition (MA); composition and theory (PhD); computer science (MS, PhD); cultural studies (Certificate); ecology and evolution (PhD); economics (MA, PhD); English (MA, PhD); ethnomusicology (PhD); film studies (PhD); French (MA, PhD); gender, sexuality, and women's studies (Doctoral Certificate, Master's Certificate); geographical information systems and remote sensing (Pro-MS); geology and environmental science (MS, PhD); Hispanic languages and literatures (MA, PhD); Hispanic linguistics (MA); history (MA, PhD); history and philosophy of science (MA, PhD); history of art and architecture (MA, PhD); intelligent systems (MS, PhD); Italian (MA); Japanese (MA); jazz (MA); jazz studies (PhD); mathematics (MA, MS, PhD); medieval and Renaissance studies (Certificate); molecular, cellular, and developmental biology (PhD); musicology (PhD); philosophy (PhD); physics and astronomy (MS, PhD); political science (MA, PhD); psychology (PhD); Russian literature and culture (MA, PhD); sociolinguistics (PhD); sociology (MA, PhD); statistics (MA, MS, PhD); teaching English to speakers of other languages (Certificate); TESOL (PhD); theatre arts (MA, MFA, PhD); writing (MFA). *Application deadline:* Applications are processed on a rolling basis. *Application fee:* $50. Electronic applications accepted. *Application Contact:* Lisa Korade, Student Services Assistant, 412-624-6094, Fax: 412-624-6855, E-mail: lmk88@pitt.edu. *Associate Dean, Graduate Studies and Research,* Dr. Kathleen Blee, 412-624-3939, Fax: 412-624-6855.

Center for Bioethics and Health Law Students: 3 full-time (all women), 3 part-time (2 women). Average age 29. 5 applicants, 60% accepted, 2 enrolled. *Faculty:* 11 full-time (3 women), 1 (woman) part-time/adjunct. *Financial support:* Scholarships/grants and tuition waivers (partial) available. Financial award application deadline: 3/1. In 2015, 3 master's awarded. *Degree program information:* Part-time programs available. Part-time. Offers bioethics (MA). *Application deadline:* For fall admission, 3/1 priority date for domestic and international students. Applications are processed on a rolling basis. *Application fee:* $50. Electronic applications accepted. *Application Contact:* Beth Ann Pischke, Administrator, 412-648-7007, Fax: 412-648-2649, E-mail: pischke@pitt.edu. *Director of Graduate Studies,* Lisa S. Parker, 412-648-7007, Fax: 412-648-2649, E-mail: lisap@pitt.edu.

Center for Neuroscience Students: 78 full-time (37 women); includes 13 minority (1 American Indian or Alaska Native, non-Hispanic/Latino; 8 Asian, non-Hispanic/Latino; 4 Hispanic/Latino), 9 international. Average age 25. 182 applicants, 22% accepted, 15 enrolled. *Faculty:* 108 full-time (38 women). *Financial support:* In 2015–16, 69 students received support, including 32 fellowships with full tuition reimbursements available (averaging $27,000 per year), 33 research assistantships with full tuition reimbursements available (averaging $27,000 per year), 5 teaching assistantships with full tuition reimbursements available (averaging $27,000 per year); traineeships, health care benefits, and tuition waivers (full) also available. Financial award application deadline: 12/1. In 2015, 13 doctorates awarded. Offers neurobiology (PhD); neuroscience (PhD). Program held jointly with School of Medicine. *Application deadline:* For fall admission, 12/1 priority date for domestic and international students. *Application fee:* $50. Electronic applications accepted. *Application Contact:* Missy Deasy, Graduate Program Administrator, 412-383-7582, Fax: 412-624-9198, E-mail: deasym@pitt.edu. *Co-Director,* Dr. Alan Sved, 412-624-6996, Fax: 412-624-9198, E-mail: sved@pitt.edu.

Graduate School of Public and International Affairs ***Degree program information:*** Part-time and evening/weekend programs available. Part-time, evening/weekend. Offers energy and environment (MID, MPA); governance and international public management (MID, MPA); human security (MID, MPIA); international affairs (PhD); international development (PhD); international political economy (MPIA); nongovernmental organizations and civil society (MID); policy research and analysis (MPA); public administration (PhD); public and international affairs (MID, MPA, MPIA, MPPM, PhD); public and nonprofit management (MPA); public policy (PhD); public policy and management (MPPM); security and intelligence studies (MPIA); urban affairs and planning (MID, MPA). Electronic applications accepted.

Graduate School of Public Health Students: 387 full-time (261 women), 218 part-time (162 women); includes 119 minority (27 Black or African American, non-Hispanic/Latino; 47 Asian, non-Hispanic/Latino; 27 Hispanic/Latino; 18 Two or more races, non-Hispanic/Latino), 130 international. Average age 28. 1,593 applicants, 49% accepted, 197 enrolled. *Faculty:* 157 full-time (72 women), 131 part-time/adjunct (67 women). *Financial support:* In 2015–16, 152 students received support, including 20 fellowships (averaging $9,838 per year), 124 research assistantships (averaging $20,360 per year), 16 teaching assistantships (averaging $16,339 per year); career-related internships or fieldwork, scholarships/grants, traineeships, health care benefits, and unspecified assistantships also available. Financial award applicants required to submit FAFSA. In 2015, 169 master's, 52 doctorates awarded. *Degree program information:* Part-time programs available. Part-time. Offers applied research and leadership (Dr PH); applied social and behavioral concepts in public health (MPH); biostatistics (MPH, MS, PhD); community-based participatory research (Certificate); decision sciences (MS); environmental and occupational health (MPH, Dr PH); genetic counseling (MS); health equity (Certificate); health policy and economics (MS); health policy and management (MHA, MPH, PhD); human genetics (MS, PhD); infectious disease management, intervention, and community practice (MPH); infectious disease pathogenesis, eradication, and laboratory practice (MPH); infectious diseases and microbiology (MS, PhD); LGBT health and wellness (Certificate); maternal and child health (MPH); program evaluation (Certificate); public health (MHA, MPH, MS, Dr PH, PhD, Certificate); public health genetics (MPH, Certificate); theory and research methods (Dr PH). *Application deadline:* For fall admission, 1/15 for domestic and international students; for spring admission, 10/15 for domestic students, 8/1 for international students; for summer admission, 3/15 for domestic students, 12/1 for international students. Applications are processed on a rolling basis. *Application fee:* $120. Electronic applications accepted. *Application Contact:* Karrie A. Lukin, Admissions Manager, 412-624-3003, Fax: 412-624-3755, E-mail: presutti@pitt.edu. *Dean*, Dr. Donald S. Burke, 412-624-3001, Fax: 412-624-3013, E-mail: bradym1@pitt.edu.

Katz Graduate School of Business Students: 398 full-time (170 women), 476 part-time (161 women); includes 98 minority (27 Black or African American, non-Hispanic/Latino; 41 Asian, non-Hispanic/Latino; 17 Hispanic/Latino; 13 Two or more races, non-Hispanic/Latino), 267 international. Average age 30. 1,907 applicants, 30% accepted, 369 enrolled. *Faculty:* 87 full-time (23 women), 46 part-time/adjunct (10 women). *Financial support:* In 2015–16, 100 students received support. Research assistantships with full tuition reimbursements available, teaching assistantships with full tuition reimbursements available, Federal Work-Study, scholarships/grants, health care benefits, and unspecified assistantships available. Financial award application deadline: 6/1; financial award applicants required to submit FAFSA. In 2015, 368 master's, 10 doctorates awarded. *Degree program information:* Part-time and evening/weekend programs available. Part-time, evening/weekend. Offers accounting (MS); business (EMBA, MBA, MS, MSIS, PhD, Certificate); business administration (EMBA, MBA, PhD); business analytics and operations (PhD); finance (MBA, PhD); information systems (MBA); information systems and technology management (PhD); international business administration (Certificate); marketing (MBA, PhD); operations (MBA); organizational behavior and human resource management (MBA); organizational behavior and human resources management (PhD); strategic management (PhD); strategy, environment and organizations (MBA). *Application deadline:* For fall admission, 4/1 priority date for domestic students, 2/1 priority date for international students; for winter admission, 2/1 for international students. *Application fee:* $50. Electronic applications accepted. *Application Contact:* Thomas Keller, Director of MBA Admissions, 412-648-1700, Fax: 412-648-1659, E-mail: mba@katz.pitt.edu. *Dean*, Dr. Arjang A. Assad, 412-648-1556, Fax: 412-648-1552, E-mail: aassad@katz.pitt.edu.

School of Dental Medicine Offers craniofacial tissue regeneration (PhD); dental anesthesia (Certificate); dental medicine (MDS, MS, DMD, PhD, Advanced Certificate, Certificate); endodontics (MDS, Certificate); general dentistry (Certificate); general practice residency (Certificate); oral and maxillofacial pathology (Advanced Certificate); oral and maxillofacial surgery (Certificate); oral biology (MS, PhD); orthodontics (MDS, Certificate); orthodontics and dentofacial orthopedics (MDS, Certificate); pediatric dentistry (MDS, Certificate); periodontics (MDS, Certificate); prosthodontics (MDS, Certificate). Electronic applications accepted.

School of Education ***Degree program information:*** Part-time and evening/weekend programs available. Part-time, evening/weekend, online learning. Offers applied behavior analysis (M Ed); applied developmental psychology (M Ed, MS, PhD); developmental movement (MS); early childhood education (M Ed); early intervention (M Ed, PhD); education (M Ed, MA, MAT, MS, Ed D, PhD); elementary education (M Ed, MAT); elementary education (MAT); English and communications education (M Ed, MAT); exercise physiology (MS, PhD); foreign language education (M Ed, MAT); general special education (M Ed, Ed D); higher education management (M Ed, Ed D, PhD); language, literacy and culture education (Ed D, PhD); learning sciences and policy (PhD); mathematics education (M Ed, MAT, Ed D, PhD); reading education (PhD); research methodology (M Ed, MA, PhD); school leadership (M Ed, Ed D, PhD); science education (M Ed, MAT, Ed D, PhD); secondary education (M Ed, MAT, Ed D, PhD); social and comparative analysis in education (M Ed, MA, Ed D, PhD); social studies education (M Ed, MAT); special education (M Ed, PhD); special education (Ed D); special education teacher preparation (M Ed); STEM education (Ed D); vision studies (M Ed, PhD). Electronic applications accepted.

School of Health and Rehabilitation Sciences Students: 754 full-time (561 women), 74 part-time (58 women); includes 72 minority (17 Black or African American, non-Hispanic/Latino; 20 Asian, non-Hispanic/Latino; 25 Hispanic/Latino; 10 Two or more races, non-Hispanic/Latino), 110 international. Average age 28. 3,550 applicants, 24% accepted, 377 enrolled. *Faculty:* 132 full-time (78 women), 22 part-time/adjunct (12 women). *Financial support:* Fellowships with full tuition reimbursements, research assistantships with tuition reimbursements, teaching assistantships with full tuition reimbursements, career-related internships or fieldwork, Federal Work-Study, scholarships/grants, traineeships, and unspecified assistantships available. Financial award applicants required to submit FAFSA. In 2015, 257 master's, 95 doctorates awarded. *Degree program information:* Part-time and evening/weekend programs available. Part-time, evening/weekend. Offers communication science and disorders (MA, MS, Au D, CScD, PhD); health and rehabilitation sciences (MS); nutrition and dietetics (MS); occupational therapy (MOT); physical therapy (DPT); physician assistant studies (MS); prosthetics and orthotics (MS); rehabilitation science (PhD). *Application deadline:* For fall admission, 3/1 for international students; for spring admission, 9/1 for international students; for summer admission, 2/1 for international students. Applications are processed on a rolling basis. *Application fee:* $0. Electronic applications accepted. *Application Contact:* Jessica Maguire, Director of Admissions, 412-383-6557, Fax: 412-383-6535, E-mail: maguire@pitt.edu. *Dean*, Dr. Anthony Delitto, 412-383-6560, Fax: 412-383-6535, E-mail: delitto@pitt.edu.

School of Information Sciences Students: 392 full-time (188 women), 112 part-time (62 women); includes 23 minority (5 Black or African American, non-Hispanic/Latino; 10 Asian, non-Hispanic/Latino; 7 Hispanic/Latino; 1 Two or more races, non-Hispanic/Latino), 329 international. Average age 29. 951 applicants, 72% accepted, 222 enrolled. *Faculty:* 28 full-time (9 women), 11 part-time/adjunct (4 women). *Financial support:* Fellowships with tuition reimbursements, research assistantships with tuition reimbursements, teaching assistantships with tuition reimbursements, career-related internships or fieldwork, scholarships/grants, traineeships, health care benefits, and unspecified assistantships available. Support available to part-time students. Financial award application deadline: 1/15; financial award applicants required to submit FAFSA. In 2015, 210 master's, 13 doctorates, 1 other advanced degree awarded. *Degree program information:* Part-time and evening/weekend programs available. Part-time, evening/weekend, 100% online. Offers big data (Post-Master's Certificate, Postbaccalaureate Certificate); information science (MSIS, PhD); information science and technology (Certificate); information sciences (MLIS, MSIS, MST, PhD, Certificate, Post-Master's Certificate, Postbaccalaureate Certificate); library and information science (MLIS, PhD); security assured information systems (Post-Master's Certificate, Postbaccalaureate Certificate); telecommunications and networking (MST, Certificate). *Application deadline:* For fall admission, 1/15 priority date for domestic and international students; for winter admission, 9/15 priority date for domestic students, 6/15 priority date for international students; for spring admission, 9/15 priority date for domestic students, 6/15 priority date for international students; for summer admission, 1/15 priority date for domestic students, 12/15 priority date for international students. Applications are processed on a rolling basis. *Application fee:* $50. Electronic applications accepted. *Application Contact:* Shabana Reza, Enrollment Manager, 412-624-3988, Fax: 412-624-5231, E-mail: sisinq@sis.pitt.edu. *Dean and Professor*, Dr. Ronald L. Larsen, 412-624-5139, Fax: 412-624-5231, E-mail: rlarsen@sis.pitt.edu.

School of Law Students: 503 full-time (218 women), 3 part-time (1 woman); includes 78 minority (34 Black or African American, non-Hispanic/Latino; 1 American Indian or Alaska Native, non-Hispanic/Latino; 15 Asian, non-Hispanic/Latino; 21 Hispanic/Latino; 7 Two or more races, non-Hispanic/Latino), 8 international. Average age 24. 1,401 applicants, 37% accepted, 134 enrolled. *Faculty:* 47 full-time (20 women), 109 part-time/adjunct (26 women). *Financial support:* In 2015–16, 324 students received support. Scholarships/grants available. Financial award application deadline: 3/1; financial award applicants required to submit FAFSA. *Degree program information:* Part-time programs available. Part-time, online learning. Offers American law (LL M); business law (MSL); Constitutional law (MSL); criminal law and justice (MSL); disability law (MSL); disability legal studies (Certificate); education law (MSL); elder and estate planning law (MSL); employment and labor law (MSL); energy law (MSL); environmental and real estate law (MSL); family law (MSL); health law (MSL); intellectual property and technology law (MSL); international and human rights law (MSL); jurisprudence (MSL); law (LL M, MSL, JD, SJD, Certificate); personal injury and civil litigation (MSL); regulatory law (MSL); self-designed (MSL); sports and entertainment law (MSL). *Application deadline:* For fall admission, 4/1 for domestic and international students. Applications are processed on a rolling basis. *Application fee:* $65. Electronic applications accepted. *Application Contact:* Charmaine McCall, Assistant Dean for Admissions and Financial Aid, 412-648-1414, Fax: 412-648-1318, E-mail: admitlaw@pitt.edu. *Dean*, William M. Carter, Jr., 412-648-1401, Fax: 412-648-2647, E-mail: william.carter@law.pitt.edu.

School of Medicine Students: 878 full-time (412 women), 123 part-time (66 women); includes 397 minority (63 Black or African American, non-Hispanic/Latino; 4 American Indian or Alaska Native, non-Hispanic/Latino; 243 Asian, non-Hispanic/Latino; 58 Hispanic/Latino; 29 Two or more races, non-Hispanic/Latino), 58 international. Average age 27. 6,286 applicants, 10% accepted, 265 enrolled. *Faculty:* 2,227 full-time (828 women), 94 part-time/adjunct (54 women). *Financial support:* In 2015–16, 617 students received support, including 113 fellowships with full tuition reimbursements available (averaging $27,000 per year), 165 research assistantships with full tuition reimbursements available (averaging $27,000 per year), 8 teaching assistantships with full tuition reimbursements available (averaging $27,000 per year); institutionally sponsored loans, scholarships/grants, traineeships, and health care benefits also available. Financial award application deadline: 4/15; financial award applicants required to submit FAFSA. In 2015, 34 master's, 209 doctorates, 26 other advanced degrees awarded. *Degree program information:* Part-time programs available. Part-time, blended/hybrid learning. Offers cell biology and molecular physiology (PhD); cellular and molecular pathology (PhD); clinical and translational science (PhD); clinical research (MS, Certificate); computational biology (PhD); immunology (PhD); integrative systems biology (PhD); interdisciplinary biomedical sciences (PhD); medical education (MS, Certificate); medicine (MS, MD, PhD, Certificate); molecular biophysics and structural biology (PhD); molecular genetics and developmental biology (PhD); molecular pharmacology (PhD); molecular virology and microbiology (PhD). *Application deadline:* For fall admission, 10/15 for domestic and international students. Applications are processed on a rolling basis. *Application fee:* $85. Electronic applications accepted. *Application Contact:* Cynthia May Bonetti, Executive Director for Admissions and Financial Aid, 412-648-9891, Fax: 412-648-8768, E-mail: cmb103@pitt.edu. *Associate Dean of Admissions and Financial Aid*, Dr. Beth Piraino, 412-648-9891, Fax: 412-648-8768, E-mail: piraino@pitt.edu.

School of Nursing Students: 221 full-time (179 women), 191 part-time (151 women); includes 39 minority (14 Black or African American, non-Hispanic/Latino; 2 American Indian or Alaska Native, non-Hispanic/Latino; 19 Asian, non-Hispanic/Latino; 4 Hispanic/Latino), 19 international. Average age 31. 324 applicants, 47% accepted, 133 enrolled. *Faculty:* 70 full-time (60 women), 4 part-time/adjunct (all women). *Financial support:* In 2015–16, 44 students received support, including 23 fellowships with tuition reimbursements available (averaging $13,640 per year), 12 research assistantships with tuition reimbursements available (averaging $13,310 per year), 12 teaching assistantships with tuition reimbursements available (averaging $10,732 per year); scholarships/grants, traineeships, health care benefits, and unspecified assistantships also available. Support available to part-time students. In 2015, 73 master's, 39 doctorates awarded. *Degree program information:* Part-time programs available. Part-time. Offers adult-gerontology (DNP); adult-gerontology acute care (DNP); adult-gerontology primary care (DNP); clinical nurse leader (MSN); family (individual across the lifespan) (DNP); neonatal (MSN, DNP); nurse anesthesia (MSN, DNP); nursing (MSN, DNP, PhD); nursing administration (DNP); nursing informatics (MSN); pediatric primary care (DNP); psychiatric mental health (DNP). *Application deadline:* For fall admission, 5/1 priority date for domestic students, 2/15 priority date for international students. *Application fee:* $50. Electronic applications accepted. *Application Contact:* Laurie Lapsley, Administrator of Graduate Student Services, 412-624-9670, Fax: 412-624-2409, E-mail: lapsleyl@pitt.edu. *Dean*, Dr. Jacqueline Dunbar-Jacob, 412-624-7838, Fax: 412-624-2401, E-mail: dunbar@pitt.edu.

School of Pharmacy Students: 521 full-time (324 women), 1 part-time (0 women); includes 100 minority (13 Black or African American, non-Hispanic/Latino; 1 American Indian or Alaska Native, non-Hispanic/Latino; 75 Asian, non-Hispanic/Latino; 5 Hispanic/Latino; 6 Two or more races, non-Hispanic/Latino), 56 international. Average age 23. 647 applicants, 30% accepted, 141 enrolled. *Faculty:* 83 full-time (42 women), 11 part-time/adjunct (3 women). *Financial support:* In 2015–16, 238 students received support, including 1 fellowship with full tuition reimbursement available (averaging $16,885 per year), 15 research assistantships with full tuition reimbursements available (averaging $27,540 per year), 38 teaching assistantships with full tuition reimbursements available (averaging $26,856 per year); Federal Work-Study, institutionally sponsored loans, scholarships/grants, health care benefits, tuition waivers (full), and unspecified assistantships also available. Financial award application deadline: 10/1. In 2015, 29 master's, 116 doctorates awarded. *Degree program information:* Part-time programs available. Part-time. Offers pharmaceutical sciences (MS, PhD); pharmacy (MS, PhD, Pharm D); pharmacy business administration (MS). *Application deadline:* For fall admission, 12/1 for domestic students; for winter admission, 1/5 for domestic students. Applications are processed on a rolling basis. Electronic applications accepted. *Application Contact:* Marcia L. Borrelli, Director of Student Services, 412-383-9000, Fax: 412-383-9996, E-mail: borrelli@pitt.edu. *Dean*, Dr. Patricia D. Kroboth, 412-624-2400, Fax: 412-648-1086, E-mail: pkroboth@pitt.edu.

School of Social Work Students: 449 full-time (380 women), 153 part-time (127 women); includes 136 minority (79 Black or African American, non-Hispanic/Latino; 19 Asian, non-Hispanic/Latino; 23 Hispanic/Latino; 15 Two or more races, non-Hispanic/Latino). Average age 28. 648 applicants, 81% accepted, 244 enrolled. *Faculty:* 34 full-time (21 women), 42 part-time/adjunct (26 women). *Financial support:* In 2015–16, 244 students received support, including 9 teaching assistantships with full tuition reimbursements available (averaging $17,560 per year); fellowships, research assistantships with full tuition reimbursements available, career-related internships or fieldwork, institutionally sponsored loans, scholarships/grants, traineeships, tuition waivers (full), and unspecified assistantships also available. Financial award application deadline: 3/31; financial award applicants required to submit FAFSA. In 2015, 217 master's, 3 doctorates awarded. *Degree program information:* Part-time programs available. Part-time. Offers social work (MSW, PhD, Certificate). *Application deadline:* For fall admission, 12/31 priority date for domestic and international students. Applications are processed on a rolling basis. *Application fee:* $40 ($50 for international students). Electronic applications accepted. *Application Contact:* Philip Mack, Director of Admissions, 412-624-6346, Fax: 412-624-6323, E-mail: psm8@pitt.edu. *Dean*, Dr. Larry E. Davis, 412-624-6304, Fax: 412-624-6323, E-mail: ledavis@pitt.edu.

Swanson School of Engineering ***Degree program information:*** Part-time programs available. Part-time. Offers bioengineering (MSBENG, PhD); civil and environmental engineering (MSCEE, PhD); computer engineering (MS, PhD); electrical engineering (MSEE, PhD); engineering (MS, MS Ch E, MSBENG, MSCEE, MSEE, MSIE, MSME, MSNE, MSPE, PhD); industrial engineering (MSIE, PhD); mechanical engineering and materials science (MSME, MSNE, PhD); petroleum engineering (MSPE). Electronic applications accepted.

University Center for International Studies Students: 215 full-time (119 women), 12 part-time (9 women); includes 99 minority (6 Black or African American, non-Hispanic/Latino; 41 Asian, non-Hispanic/Latino; 50 Hispanic/Latino; 2 Two or more races, non-Hispanic/Latino). Average age 31. *Financial support:* In 2015–16, 23 fellowships with full tuition reimbursements (averaging $17,511 per year) were awarded; scholarships/grants, traineeships, health care benefits, tuition waivers, and unspecified assistantships also available. *Degree program information:* Part-time and evening/weekend programs available. Part-time, evening/weekend, online learning. Offers African studies (Certificate); Asian studies (Certificate); European Union studies (Certificate); global studies (Certificate); Latin American studies (Certificate); Russian and East European studies (Certificate); West European studies (Certificate). *Application deadline:* Applications are processed on a rolling basis. *Director*, Dr. Ariel Armony, 412-648-7374, Fax: 412-624-9298, E-mail: armony@pitt.edu.

UNIVERSITY OF PORTLAND, Portland, OR 97203-5798

General Information Independent-religious, coed, comprehensive institution. *Graduate housing:* On-campus housing not available. *Research affiliation:* Portland Area Nursing Consortium, Kaiser Center Health Resources, Oregon Graduate Institute of Science and Technology (applied engineering, applied physics).

GRADUATE UNITS

Department of Communication Studies ***Degree program information:*** Part-time and evening/weekend programs available. Part-time, evening/weekend. Offers communication (MA); management communication (MS).

Department of Performing and Fine Arts ***Degree program information:*** Part-time and evening/weekend programs available. Part-time, evening/weekend. Offers directing (MFA).

Department of Theology ***Degree program information:*** Part-time programs available. Part-time. Offers pastoral ministry (MA).

Dr. Robert B. Pamplin, Jr. School of Business ***Degree program information:*** Part-time and evening/weekend programs available. Part-time, evening/weekend. Offers entrepreneurship (MBA); finance (MBA, MS); health care management (MBA); marketing (MBA); nonprofit management (EMBA); operations and technology management (MBA, MS); sustainability (MBA).

School of Education ***Degree program information:*** Part-time and evening/weekend programs available. Part-time, evening/weekend. Offers education (MA, MAT); educational leadership (M Ed); English for speakers of other languages (M Ed); initial administrator licensure (M Ed); neuroeducation (M Ed, Ed D); organizational leadership and development (Ed D); reading (M Ed); school leadership and development (Ed D); special education (M Ed). M Ed also available through the Graduate Outreach Program for teachers residing in the Oregon and Washington state areas.

School of Engineering ***Degree program information:*** Part-time and evening/weekend programs available. Part-time, evening/weekend. Offers biomedical engineering (MBME); civil engineering (ME); computer science (ME); electrical engineering (ME); mechanical engineering (ME).

School of Nursing ***Degree program information:*** Part-time and evening/weekend programs available. Part-time, evening/weekend, online learning. Offers clinical nurse leader (MS); family nurse practitioner (DNP); nurse educator (MS).

UNIVERSITY OF PRINCE EDWARD ISLAND, Charlottetown, PE C1A 4P3, Canada

General Information Province-supported, coed, comprehensive institution. *Graduate housing:* Room and/or apartments available on a first-come, first-served basis to single students; on-campus housing not available to married students. *Research affiliation:* National Research Council of Canada Institute for Nutrisciences and Health, PEI Food Technology Centre, Agriculture Canada Research Station, Diagnostic Chemicals, Ltd., Canadian Food Inspection Agency, AquaHealth.

GRADUATE UNITS

Atlantic Veterinary College ***Degree program information:*** Part-time programs available. Part-time. Offers anatomy (M Sc, PhD); bacteriology (M Sc, PhD); clinical pharmacology (M Sc, PhD); clinical sciences (M Sc, PhD); epidemiology (M Sc, PhD); fish health (M Sc, PhD); food animal nutrition (M Sc, PhD); immunology (M Sc, PhD); microanatomy (M Sc, PhD); parasitology (M Sc, PhD); pathology (M Sc, PhD); pharmacology (M Sc, PhD); physiology (M Sc, PhD); toxicology (M Sc, PhD); veterinary medicine (M Sc, M Vet Sc, DVM, PhD); veterinary science (M Vet Sc); virology (M Sc, PhD).

Faculty of Arts ***Degree program information:*** Part-time programs available. Part-time. Offers island studies (MA).

Faculty of Education ***Degree program information:*** Part-time programs available. Part-time. Offers leadership and learning (M Ed).

Faculty of Science Offers biology (M Sc); chemistry (M Sc).

UNIVERSITY OF PUERTO RICO, MAYAGÜEZ CAMPUS, Mayagüez, PR 00681-9000

General Information Commonwealth-supported, coed, university. *Graduate housing:* On-campus housing not available. *Research affiliation:* U.S. Department of Education (DOE) (STEM education), National Endowment for the Humanities, U.S. Department of Education (DOE) (STEM education), Tropical Agriculture Research Station (agriculture), Corporation for the Development and Administration of Marine Resources of Puerto Rico (marine science), National Science Foundation.

GRADUATE UNITS

Graduate Studies ***Degree program information:*** Part-time and evening/weekend programs available. Part-time, evening/weekend. Electronic applications accepted.

College of Agricultural Sciences Degree program information: Part-time programs available. Part-time. Offers agricultural economics (MS); agricultural education (MS); agricultural extension (MS); agricultural sciences (MS); agronomy (MS); animal industries (MS); crop protection (MS); food science and technology (MS); horticulture (MS); soils (MS).

College of Arts and Sciences Degree program information: Part-time programs available. Part-time. Offers applied mathematics (MS); arts and sciences (MA, MS, PhD); biology (MS); chemistry (MS, PhD); English education (MA); geology (MS); Hispanic studies (MA); kinesiology (MA); marine sciences (MS, PhD); physics (MS); pure mathematics (MS); scientific computation (MS); statistics (MS).

College of Business Administration Degree program information: Part-time and evening/weekend programs available. Part-time, evening/weekend. Offers business administration (MBA); finance (MBA); human resources (MBA); industrial management (MBA).

College of Engineering Degree program information: Part-time programs available. Part-time. Offers chemical engineering (ME, MS, PhD); civil engineering (ME, MS, PhD); computer engineering (ME, MS); computing and information sciences and engineering (PhD); electrical engineering (ME, MS); engineering (ME, MS, PhD); industrial engineering (ME, MS); mechanical engineering (ME, MS).

UNIVERSITY OF PUERTO RICO, MEDICAL SCIENCES CAMPUS, San Juan, PR 00936-5067

General Information Commonwealth-supported, coed, primarily women, university. *Graduate housing:* On-campus housing not available.

GRADUATE UNITS

Graduate School of Public Health ***Degree program information:*** Part-time programs available. Part-time. Offers biostatistics (MPH); demography (MS); developmental disabilities-early intervention (Certificate); environmental health (MS, Dr PH); epidemiology (MPH, MS); evaluative research of health systems (MS); gerontology (MPH, Certificate); health services administration (MHSA, MS); industrial hygiene (MS); maternal and child health (MPH); nurse midwifery (MPH, Certificate); nutrition (MS); public health (MHSA, MPH, MPHE, MS, Dr PH, Certificate); public health education (MPHE); school health promotion (Certificate).

School of Dental Medicine Offers dental medicine (DMD, Certificate); dentistry (DMD, Certificate); general dentistry (Certificate); oral and maxillofacial surgery (Certificate); orthodontics (Certificate); pediatric dentistry (Certificate); prosthodontics (Certificate). Electronic applications accepted.

School of Health Professions Offers audiology (Au D); clinical laboratory science (MS); clinical research (MS, Graduate Certificate); cytotechnology (Certificate); dietetics (Certificate); health information administration (MS); health professions (MS, Au D, Certificate); medical technology (Certificate); occupational therapy (MS); physical therapy (MS); speech-language pathology (MS). Electronic applications accepted.

School of Medicine Offers medicine (MS, MD, PhD). Electronic applications accepted.

Biomedical Sciences Graduate Program Offers anatomy (MS, PhD); biochemistry (MS, PhD); biomedical sciences (MS, PhD); microbiology and medical zoology (MS, PhD); pharmacology and toxicology (MS, PhD); physiology (MS, PhD). Electronic applications accepted.

School of Nursing Offers adult and elderly nursing (MSN); child and adolescent nursing (MSN); critical care nursing (MSN); family and community nursing (MSN); family nurse practitioner (MSN); maternity nursing (MSN); mental health and psychiatric nursing (MSN). Electronic applications accepted.

School of Pharmacy ***Degree program information:*** Part-time and evening/weekend programs available. Part-time, evening/weekend. Offers industrial pharmacy (MS); pharmaceutical sciences (MS); pharmacy (Pharm D). Electronic applications accepted.

UNIVERSITY OF PUERTO RICO, RÍO PIEDRAS CAMPUS, San Juan, PR 00931-3300

General Information Commonwealth-supported, coed, university. CGS member. *Graduate housing:* Room and/or apartments available to single students; on-campus housing not available to married students. Housing application deadline: 6/15. *Research affiliation:* U.S. Department of Education (DOE) (social sciences, general studies), U.S. Department of Health and Human Services (social sciences, biology), National Science

Foundation (ecology, biology), Ocean Conservancy (ecology, biology), Ford International (ecology), U.S. Department of Education (DOE) (physics, biology).

GRADUATE UNITS

College of Business Administration ***Degree program information:*** Part-time programs available. Part-time. Offers accounting (MBA); finance (MBA, PhD); general business (MBA); human resources management (MBA); international trade and business (MBA, PhD); marketing (MBA); operations management (MBA); quantitative methods (MBA).

College of Education ***Degree program information:*** Part-time programs available. Part-time. Offers biology education (M Ed); chemistry education (M Ed); curriculum and teaching (Ed D); early child education (M Ed); education (M Ed, MS, Ed D); educational research and evaluation (M Ed); exercise sciences (MS); family ecology and nutrition (M Ed); guidance and counseling (M Ed, Ed D); history education (M Ed); mathematics education (M Ed); physics education (M Ed); school administration and supervision (M Ed, Ed D); Spanish education (M Ed); special and differentiated education (M Ed); teaching English as a second language (M Ed).

College of Humanities ***Degree program information:*** Part-time programs available. Part-time. Offers Caribbean history (PhD); Caribbean linguistics (PhD); Caribbean literature (PhD); comparative literature (MA); English (MA); Hispanic linguistics (PhD); Hispanic studies (MA); history (MA); humanities (MA, PhD, Certificate); Latin American literature (PhD); linguistics (MA); philosophy (MA); Puerto Rican history (PhD); Puerto Rican literature (PhD); Spanish literature (PhD); translation (MA, Certificate).

College of Natural Sciences ***Degree program information:*** Part-time programs available. Part-time. Offers chemical physics (PhD); chemistry (MS, PhD); ecology/systematics (MS, PhD); environmental sciences (MS, PhD); evolution/genetics (MS, PhD); mathematics (MS, PhD); molecular/cellular biology (MS, PhD); natural sciences (MS, PhD); neuroscience (MS, PhD); physics (MS).

College of Social Sciences ***Degree program information:*** Part-time programs available. Part-time. Offers clinical psychology (MA); economics (MA); industrial organizational psychology (MA); investigative academic psychology (MA); psychology (PhD); social sciences (MA, MPA, MRC, MSW, PhD); social-community psychology (MA); sociology (MA).

Graduate School of Rehabilitation Counseling Degree program information: Part-time programs available. Part-time. Offers rehabilitation counseling (MRC).

Graduate School of Social Work Degree program information: Part-time programs available. Part-time. Offers social work (MSW, PhD).

School of Public Administration Degree program information: Part-time programs available. Part-time. Offers public administration (MPA).

Graduate School of Information Sciences and Technologies ***Degree program information:*** Part-time programs available. Part-time. Offers administration of academic libraries (PMC); administration of public libraries (PMC); administration of special libraries (PMC); consultant in information services (PMC); documents and files administration (Post-Graduate Certificate); electronic information resources analyst (Post-Graduate Certificate); information science (MIS); librarianship and information services (MLS); school librarian (Post-Graduate Certificate); school librarian distance education mode (Post-Graduate Certificate); specialist in legal information (PMC).

Graduate School of Planning ***Degree program information:*** Part-time programs available. Part-time. Offers economic planning systems (MP); environmental planning (MP); social policy and planning (MP); urban and territorial planning (MP).

School of Architecture ***Degree program information:*** Part-time programs available. Part-time. Offers architecture (M Arch).

School of Communication ***Degree program information:*** Part-time programs available. Part-time. Offers communication (MA); communication theory and research (MA); journalism (MA).

School of Law ***Degree program information:*** Part-time and evening/weekend programs available. Part-time, evening/weekend. Offers law (LL M, JD).

UNIVERSITY OF PUGET SOUND, Tacoma, WA 98416

General Information Independent, coed, comprehensive institution.

GRADUATE UNITS

School of Education Offers education (M Ed, MAT); elementary education (MAT); learning, teaching, and leadership (M Ed); mental health counseling (M Ed); school counseling (M Ed); secondary education (MAT). Electronic applications accepted.

School of Occupational Therapy Offers occupational therapy (MSOT, Dr OT). Electronic applications accepted.

School of Physical Therapy Offers physical therapy (DPT). Electronic applications accepted.

UNIVERSITY OF REDLANDS, Redlands, CA 92373-0999

General Information Independent, coed, comprehensive institution. *Graduate housing:* Rooms and/or apartments available on a first-come, first-served basis to single students and available to married students. Housing application deadline: 8/19. *Research affiliation:* Environmental Systems Research Institute (geographic information systems).

GRADUATE UNITS

College of Arts and Sciences Offers arts and sciences (MM, MS); communicative disorders (MS); geographic information systems (MS). Electronic applications accepted.

School of Music Degree program information: Part-time programs available. Part-time. Offers music (MM).

School of Business ***Degree program information:*** Evening/weekend programs available. Evening/weekend. Offers business (MBA); information technology (MS); management (MA).

School of Education ***Degree program information:*** Part-time and evening/weekend programs available. Part-time, evening/weekend. Offers education (MA, Ed D, Certificate).

UNIVERSITY OF REGINA, Regina, SK S4S 0A2, Canada

General Information Province-supported, coed, university. CGS member. *Graduate housing:* Room and/or apartments available on a first-come, first-served basis to single students; on-campus housing not available to married students. *Research affiliation:* TR Labs (telecommunications), Regional Centre of Expertise on Education for Sustainable Development in Saskatchewan (sustainable development), Petroleum Technology Research Center (green energy technologies), Saskatchewan Population Health and Evaluation Research Unit (health research), Canadian Plains Research Centre (CPRC) (climate change adaptation), Prairie Adaptation Research Collaborative (climate change and adaptation options).

GRADUATE UNITS

Faculty of Graduate Studies and Research ***Degree program information:*** Part-time and evening/weekend programs available. Part-time, evening/weekend. Electronic applications accepted.

Faculty of Arts Degree program information: Part-time programs available. Part-time. Offers anthropology (MA); applied economics and policy analysis (MA); arts (M Sc, MA, MJ, PhD); Canadian plains studies (MA, PhD); clinical psychology (MA, PhD); creative writing and English (MA); English (MA); experimental and applied psychology (MA, PhD); French (MA); geography (M Sc, MA, PhD); gerontology (M Sc, MA); history (MA); journalism (MJ); justice studies (MA); linguistics (MA); philosophy (MA); police studies (MA); religious studies (MA); social and political thought (MA); social studies (MA); sociology (MA); women's and gender studies (MA). Electronic applications accepted.

Faculty of Education Degree program information: Part-time programs available. Part-time. Offers adult education (MA Ed); curriculum and instruction (M Ed); education (M Ed, MA Ed, MHRD, PhD, Master's Certificate); educational administration (M Ed); educational psychology (M Ed); human resource development (MHRD). Electronic applications accepted.

Faculty of Engineering and Applied Science Degree program information: Part-time programs available. Part-time. Offers electronic systems engineering (M Eng, MA Sc, PhD); engineering and applied science (M Eng, MA Sc, PhD); environmental systems engineering (M Eng, MA Sc, PhD); industrial systems engineering (M Eng, MA Sc, PhD); petroleum systems engineering (M Eng, MA Sc, PhD); process systems engineering (M Eng, MA Sc); software systems engineering (M Eng, MA Sc). Electronic applications accepted.

Faculty of Fine Arts Degree program information: Part-time programs available. Part-time. Offers ceramics (MFA); composition (MMus); conducting (MMus); drawing (MFA); fine arts (MA, MFA, MMus); interdisciplinary studies (MA, MFA); intermedia (MFA); media production (MFA); media studies (MA); music theory (MA); musicology (MA); painting (MFA); performance (MMus); sculpture (MFA). Electronic applications accepted.

Faculty of Kinesiology and Health Studies Offers kinesiology and health studies (M Sc, PhD). Electronic applications accepted.

Faculty of Nursing Offers nursing (MN). Electronic applications accepted.

Faculty of Science Degree program information: Part-time programs available. Part-time. Offers analytical/environmental chemistry (M Sc, PhD); biology (M Sc, PhD); biophysics of biological interfaces (M Sc, PhD); computer science (M Sc, PhD); enzymology/chemical biology (M Sc, PhD); geology (M Sc, PhD); inorganic/organometallic chemistry (M Sc, PhD); mathematics (M Sc, PhD); physics (M Sc, PhD); science (M Sc, PhD); signal transduction and mechanisms of cancer cell regulation (M Sc, PhD); statistics (M Sc, PhD); supramolecular organic photochemistry and photophysics (M Sc, PhD); synthetic organic chemistry (M Sc, PhD); theoretical/computational chemistry (M Sc, PhD). Electronic applications accepted.

Faculty of Social Work Degree program information: Part-time programs available. Part-time. Offers indigenous social work (MISW); social work (MSW, PhD). PhD offered as a special case program. Electronic applications accepted.

Johnson-Shoyama Graduate School of Public Policy Degree program information: Part-time programs available. Part-time. Offers economic analysis for public policy (Master's Certificate); health administration (MHA); health systems management (Master's Certificate); public management (MPA, Master's Certificate); public policy (MPA, MPP, PhD); public policy analysis (Master's Certificate). Electronic applications accepted.

Kenneth Levene Graduate School of Business Degree program information: Part-time and evening/weekend programs available. Part-time, evening/weekend. Offers business (EMBA, M Admin, MBA, MHRM, Master's Certificate, PGD); business foundations (PGD); engineering management (MBA); executive business administration (EMBA); general management (MBA); human resources management (MHRM, Master's Certificate); international business (MBA); leadership (M Admin); organizational leadership (Master's Certificate); project management (Master's Certificate). Electronic applications accepted.

UNIVERSITY OF RHODE ISLAND, Kingston, RI 02881

General Information State-supported, coed, university. CGS member. *Enrollment:* 16,613 graduate, professional, and undergraduate students; 1,910 full-time matriculated graduate/professional students (1,173 women), 929 part-time matriculated graduate/professional students (530 women). *Enrollment by degree level:* 1,221 master's, 1,456 doctoral, 162 other advanced degrees. *Graduate faculty:* 627 full-time (273 women), 57 part-time/adjunct (36 women). Tuition, state resident: full-time $11,796; part-time $655 per credit. Tuition, nonresident: full-time $24,206; part-time $1345 per credit. *Required fees:* $1546; $44 per credit. One-time fee: $155 full-time; $35 part-time. *Graduate housing:* Rooms and/or apartments available on a first-come, first-served basis to single and married students. Housing application deadline: 5/1. *Student services:* Campus employment opportunities, campus safety program, career counseling, free psychological counseling, international student services, low-cost health insurance, multicultural affairs office, services for students with disabilities. *Library:* Robert L. Carothers Library and Learning Commons plus 3 others. *Research affiliation:* Sustainable Coastal Communities and Ecosystems (SUCCESS)-Leader with Associates, Rhode Island Network for Molecular Toxicology, Rhode Island Teacher Education Renewal (RITER), Toward the "First Census of Marine Life"-Education and Outreach Strategies, U.S. Department of Agriculture (USDA) (food stamp nutrition education).

Computer facilities: Computer purchase and lease plans are available. 2,500 computers available on campus for general student use. A campuswide network can be accessed from student residence rooms and from off campus. Online class registration is available.
Website: http://www.uri.edu/

General Application Contact: Shandra Pelagio, Graduate Admission, 401-874-2873, E-mail: shandra@uri.edu.

GRADUATE UNITS

Graduate School Students: 1,910 full-time (1,173 women), 929 part-time (530 women); includes 384 minority (97 Black or African American, non-Hispanic/Latino; 11 American Indian or Alaska Native, non-Hispanic/Latino; 139 Asian, non-Hispanic/Latino; 102 Hispanic/Latino; 1 Native Hawaiian or other Pacific Islander, non-Hispanic/Latino; 34 Two or more races, non-Hispanic/Latino), 291 international. *Faculty:* 627 full-time (273 women), 57 part-time/adjunct (36 women). *Financial support:* In 2015–16, 127 research assistantships with tuition reimbursements (averaging $12,352 per year), 275 teaching assistantships with tuition reimbursements (averaging $12,725 per year) were awarded; tuition waivers (full and partial) also available. Financial award applicants required to submit FAFSA. In 2015, 514 master's, 246 doctorates awarded. *Degree program information:* Part-time and evening/weekend programs available. Part-time, evening/weekend. *Application fee:* $65. Electronic applications accepted. *Application Contact:* Shandra Pelagio, Graduate Admissions, 401-874-2873, E-mail: shandra@uri.edu. *Dean of the Graduate School,* Dr. Nasser H. Zawia, 401-874-5909, Fax: 401-874-5787, E-mail: nzawia@uri.edu.

College of Arts and Sciences Students: 336 full-time (209 women), 272 part-time (157 women); includes 83 minority (35 Black or African American, non-Hispanic/Latino; 3 American Indian or Alaska Native, non-Hispanic/Latino; 15 Asian, non-Hispanic/Latino; 25 Hispanic/Latino; 1 Native Hawaiian or other Pacific Islander, non-Hispanic/Latino; 4 Two or more races, non-Hispanic/Latino), 60 international. *Faculty:* 277 full-time (125 women), 19 part-time/adjunct (15 women). *Financial support:* In 2015–16, 54 research assistantships with tuition reimbursements (averaging $13,716 per year), 112 teaching assistantships with tuition reimbursements (averaging $14,230 per year) were awarded. Financial award applicants required to submit FAFSA. In 2015, 130 master's, 39 doctorates awarded. *Degree program information:* Part-time and evening/weekend programs available. Part-time, evening/weekend. Offers American and British literature and culture (PhD); applied mathematical sciences (MS, PhD); archaeology and anthropology (MA); arts and sciences (MA, MLIS, MM, MPA, MS, PSM, PhD, Graduate Certificate); behavioral science (PhD); chemistry (MS, PhD); clinical psychology (PhD); communication studies (MA); computer science (MS, PhD); creative writing (PhD); cyber security (PSM, Graduate Certificate); digital forensics (Graduate Certificate); English (MA); film (PhD); gender studies (PhD); history (MA); libraries, leadership and transforming communities (MLIS); mathematics (MS, PhD); music education (MM); music performance (MM); organization of digital media (MLIS); physics (MS, PhD); political science (MA); public policy and administration (MPA); school library media (MLIS); school psychology (MS, PhD); Spanish (MA); statistics (MS). *Application fee:* $65. Electronic applications accepted. *Application Contact:* Graduate Admissions, 401-874-2872, E-mail: gradadm@etal.uri.edu. *Dean,* Dr. Winifed E. Brownell, 401-874-4101, Fax: 401-874-2892, E-mail: winnie@uri.edu.

College of Business Administration Students: 87 full-time (35 women), 182 part-time (89 women); includes 43 minority (9 Black or African American, non-Hispanic/Latino; 2 American Indian or Alaska Native, non-Hispanic/Latino; 19 Asian, non-Hispanic/Latino; 7 Hispanic/Latino; 6 Two or more races, non-Hispanic/Latino), 23 international. *Faculty:* 55 full-time (22 women), 7 part-time/adjunct (3 women). *Financial support:* In 2015–16, 3 research assistantships (averaging $15,996 per year), 11 teaching assistantships with tuition reimbursements (averaging $15,414 per year) were awarded. Financial award application deadline: 4/15; financial award applicants required to submit FAFSA. In 2015, 117 master's, 2 doctorates awarded. *Degree program information:* Part-time and evening/weekend programs available. Part-time, evening/weekend. Offers accounting (MS); business administration (PhD); finance (MBA, MS); general business (MBA); health care management (MBA); management (MBA); marketing (MBA); oceanography (MBA); strategic innovation (MBA); supply chain management (MBA). *Application deadline:* For fall admission, 4/15 for domestic students, 2/15 for international students. *Application fee:* $65. Electronic applications accepted. *Application Contact:* Lisa Lancellotta, Coordinator, MBA Programs, 401-874-4241, Fax: 401-874-4312, E-mail: mba@uri.edu. *Dean,* Dr. Maling Ebrahimpour, 401-874-4348, Fax: 401-874-4312, E-mail: mebrahimpour@uri.edu.

College of Engineering Students: 116 full-time (31 women), 105 part-time (13 women); includes 19 minority (4 Black or African American, non-Hispanic/Latino; 5 Asian, non-Hispanic/Latino; 10 Hispanic/Latino), 77 international. *Faculty:* 61 full-time (11 women), 3 part-time/adjunct (0 women). *Financial support:* In 2015–16, 11 research assistantships with tuition reimbursements (averaging $8,743 per year), 24 teaching assistantships with tuition reimbursements (averaging $9,507 per year) were awarded. Financial award applicants required to submit FAFSA. In 2015, 59 master's, 15 doctorates awarded. *Degree program information:* Part-time programs available. Part-time. Offers acoustics (MS, PhD); acoustics and underwater acoustics (MS, PhD); biomedical engineering (MS, PhD); chemical engineering (MS, PhD); circuits and devices (MS, PhD); communication theory (MS, PhD); computer architectures and digital systems (MS, PhD); computer networks (MS, PhD); digital signal processing (MS, PhD); embedded systems and computer applications (MS, PhD); engineering (MS, PhD, Graduate Certificate, Postbaccalaureate Certificate); environmental engineering (MS, PhD); fault-tolerant computing (MS, PhD); geomechanics (MS, PhD); geotechnical engineering (MS, PhD); hydrodynamics (MS, PhD); industrial and systems engineering (MS, PhD); materials and optics (MS, PhD); ocean instrumentation (MS, PhD); offshore energy (MS, PhD); offshore structures (MS, PhD); polymers (Postbaccalaureate Certificate); structural engineering (MS, PhD); systems theory (MS, PhD); transportation engineering (MS, PhD); water wave mechanics (MS, PhD). *Application fee:* $65. Electronic applications accepted. *Application Contact:* Graduate Admission, 401-874-2872, E-mail: gradadm@etal.uri.edu. *Dean,* Dr. Raymond Wright, 401-874-2186, Fax: 401-782-1066, E-mail: dean@egr.uri.edu.

College of Human Science and Services Students: 250 full-time (184 women), 158 part-time (114 women); includes 46 minority (13 Black or African American, non-Hispanic/Latino; 5 American Indian or Alaska Native, non-Hispanic/Latino; 13 Asian, non-Hispanic/Latino; 12 Hispanic/Latino; 3 Two or more races, non-Hispanic/Latino), 13 international. *Faculty:* 63 full-time (41 women), 5 part-time/adjunct (4 women). *Financial support:* In 2015–16, 7 research assistantships with tuition reimbursements (averaging $10,299 per year), 16 teaching assistantships with tuition reimbursements (averaging $8,897 per year) were awarded. Financial award applicants required to submit FAFSA. In 2015, 88 master's, 41 doctorates awarded. *Degree program information:* Part-time and evening/weekend programs available. Part-time, evening/weekend. Offers college student personnel (MS); cultural studies of sport and physical culture (MS); education (PhD); exercise science (MS); fashion merchandise (Certificate); human development and family studies (MS); human science and services (MA, MM, MS, DPT, PhD, Certificate); marriage and family therapy (MS); master seamstress (Certificate); music education (MM); physical therapy (DPT); psychosocial/behavioral aspects of physical activity (MS); reading (MA); special education (MA); speech-language pathology (MS); textiles, fashion merchandising and design (MS). *Application fee:* $65. Electronic applications accepted. *Application Contact:* Graduate Admission, 401-874-2872, E-mail: gradadm@etal.uri.edu. *Interim Dean,* Dr. Lori Ciccomascolo, 401-874-4014, Fax: 401-874-2581, E-mail: lynnm@uri.edu.

College of Nursing Students: 51 full-time (41 women), 77 part-time (70 women); includes 18 minority (11 Black or African American, non-Hispanic/Latino; 2 Asian, non-Hispanic/Latino; 4 Hispanic/Latino; 1 Two or more races, non-Hispanic/Latino), 5 international. *Faculty:* 11 full-time (all women). *Financial support:* In 2015–16, 2 research assistantships (averaging $12,111 per year), 7 teaching assistantships with tuition reimbursements (averaging $13,112 per year) were awarded. Financial award application deadline: 2/15; financial award applicants required to submit FAFSA. In 2015, 19 master's, 7 doctorates awarded. *Degree program information:* Part-time programs available. Part-time. Offers acute care nurse practitioner (MS); adult-gerontological nurse practitioner/clinical nurse specialist (MS); family nurse practitioner (MS); nursing (PhD); nursing education (MS); nursing practice (DNP). *Application deadline:* For fall admission, 2/15 for domestic students, 2/1 for international students; for spring admission, 10/15 for domestic students, 7/15 for international students. *Application fee:* $65. Electronic applications accepted. *Application Contact:* Graduate Admission, 401-874-2872, E-mail: gradadm@etal.uri.edu. *Interim Dean,* Dr. Mary Sullivan, 401-874-5339, Fax: 401-874-2061, E-mail: mcsullivan@uri.edu.

College of Pharmacy Students: 792 full-time (515 women), 12 part-time (4 women); includes 134 minority (12 Black or African American, non-Hispanic/Latino; 68 Asian, non-Hispanic/Latino; 37 Hispanic/Latino; 17 Two or more races, non-Hispanic/Latino), 63 international. *Faculty:* 26 full-time (12 women), 5 part-time/adjunct (3 women). *Financial support:* In 2015–16, 4 research assistantships with tuition reimbursements (averaging $14,828 per year), 18 teaching assistantships with tuition reimbursements (averaging $14,851 per year) were awarded. Financial award applicants required to submit FAFSA. In 2015, 4 master's, 124 doctorates awarded. *Degree program information:* Part-time programs available. Part-time. Offers medicinal chemistry and pharmacognosy (MS, PhD); pharmaceutics and pharmacokinetics (MS, PhD); pharmacoepidemiology and pharmacoeconomics (MS, PhD); pharmacology and toxicology (MS, PhD); pharmacy (MS, PhD, Pharm D); pharmacy practice (Pharm D). *Application fee:* $65. Electronic applications accepted. *Application Contact:* Graduate Admission, 401-874-8272, E-mail: gradadm@etal.uri.edu. *Interim Dean/Professor,* Dr. E. Paul Larrat, 401-874-5003, Fax: 401-874-2181, E-mail: larrat@uri.edu.

College of the Environment and Life Sciences Students: 234 full-time (136 women), 80 part-time (58 women); includes 29 minority (7 Black or African American, non-Hispanic/Latino; 1 American Indian or Alaska Native, non-Hispanic/Latino; 12 Asian, non-Hispanic/Latino; 6 Hispanic/Latino; 3 Two or more races, non-Hispanic/Latino), 42 international. *Faculty:* 86 full-time (31 women), 10 part-time/adjunct (6 women). *Financial support:* In 2015–16, 42 research assistantships with tuition reimbursements (averaging $12,368 per year), 65 teaching assistantships with tuition reimbursements (averaging $12,951 per year) were awarded. Financial award applicants required to submit FAFSA. In 2015, 79 master's, 10 doctorates awarded. *Degree program information:* Part-time programs available. Part-time. Offers animal health and disease (MS); animal science (MS); aquaculture (MS); aquatic pathology (MS); biochemistry (MS, PhD); biological sciences (MS, PhD); clinical laboratory sciences (MS); dietetic internship (MS); environment and life sciences (MA, MESM, MMA, MS, PhD); environmental and natural resource economics (MESM, MS, PhD); environmental science and management (MESM); environmental sciences (MS, PhD); fisheries (MS); marine affairs (MA, MESM, MMA, PhD); microbiology (MS, PhD); molecular genetics (MS, PhD); natural resources science (MESM, MS, PhD); nutrition (MS, PhD). *Application fee:* $65. Electronic applications accepted. *Application Contact:* Graduate Admission, 401-874-2872, E-mail: gradadm@etal.uri.edu. *Dean,* Dr. John Kirby, 401-874-2957, Fax: 401-874-4017, E-mail: jdkirby@uri.edu.

Graduate School of Oceanography Students: 40 full-time (19 women), 23 part-time (11 women); includes 4 minority (all Asian, non-Hispanic/Latino), 8 international. *Faculty:* 27 full-time (9 women), 3 part-time/adjunct (1 woman). *Financial support:* In 2015–16, 5 research assistantships with tuition reimbursements (averaging $10,914 per year), 22 teaching assistantships with tuition reimbursements (averaging $11,011 per year) were awarded. Financial award application deadline: 1/15; financial award applicants required to submit FAFSA. In 2015, 11 master's, 8 doctorates awarded. *Degree program information:* Part-time programs available. Part-time. Offers biological oceanography (MS, PhD); coastal ocean management (MO); general oceanography (MO); marine and atmospheric chemistry (MS, PhD); marine fisheries management (MO); marine geology and geophysics (MS, PhD); ocean technology and data (MO); physical oceanography (MS, PhD). *Application deadline:* For fall admission, 1/15 for domestic and international students; for spring admission, 11/15 for domestic students, 7/15 for international students. *Application fee:* $65. Electronic applications accepted. *Application Contact:* Graduate Admission, 401-874-8272, E-mail: gradadm@etal.uri.edu. *Dean,* Dr. Bruce Corliss, 401-874-6222, Fax: 401-874-6931, E-mail: bruce.corliss@gso.uri.edu.

Schmidt Labor Research Center Students: 4 full-time (3 women), 20 part-time (14 women); includes 8 minority (6 Black or African American, non-Hispanic/Latino; 1 Asian, non-Hispanic/Latino; 1 Hispanic/Latino). *Faculty:* 2 full-time (0 women), 2 part-time/adjunct (1 woman). *Financial support:* In 2015–16, 2 teaching assistantships (averaging $15,844 per year) were awarded; institutionally sponsored loans also available. Financial award application deadline: 2/1; financial award applicants required to submit FAFSA. In 2015, 7 master's awarded. *Degree program information:* Part-time and evening/weekend programs available. Part-time, evening/weekend. Offers human resources (MS, Graduate Certificate); labor relations (MS, Graduate Certificate). *Application deadline:* For fall admission, 7/15 for domestic students, 2/1 for international students; for spring admission, 11/15 for domestic students, 7/15 for international students. *Application fee:* $65. Electronic applications accepted. *Application Contact:* Graduate Admission, 401-874-2872, E-mail: gradadm@etal.uri.edu. *Director,* Dr. Richard Scholl, 401-874-4347, Fax: 401-874-2954, E-mail: rscholl@uri.edu.

UNIVERSITY OF RICHMOND, University of Richmond, VA 23173

General Information Independent, coed, comprehensive institution. *Graduate housing:* On-campus housing not available.

GRADUATE UNITS

Robins School of Business ***Degree program information:*** Part-time and evening/weekend programs available. Part-time, evening/weekend. Offers business (MBA). Electronic applications accepted.

School of Law Offers law (JD). JD/MSW, JD/MHA, JD/MPA offered jointly with Virginia Commonwealth University; JD/MURP with Virginia Commonwealth University; JD/MA with Department of History; JD/MS with Department of Biology. Electronic applications accepted.

UNIVERSITY OF RIO GRANDE, Rio Grande, OH 45674

General Information Independent, coed, comprehensive institution. *Graduate housing:* Room and/or apartments guaranteed to single students; on-campus housing not available to married students.

GRADUATE UNITS

Graduate School ***Degree program information:*** Part-time and evening/weekend programs available. Part-time, evening/weekend. Offers athletic coaching leadership (M Ed); educational leadership (M Ed); entrepreneurship (MBA); integrated arts (M Ed); intervention specialist in early childhood (M Ed); intervention specialist in mild/moderate (M Ed).

UNIVERSITY OF ROCHESTER, Rochester, NY 14627

General Information Independent, coed, university. CGS member. *Enrollment:* 11,105 graduate, professional, and undergraduate students; 3,399 full-time matriculated graduate/professional students (1,583 women), 1,141 part-time matriculated graduate/professional students (697 women). *Enrollment by degree level:* 2,177 master's, 2,206 doctoral, 157 other advanced degrees. *Tuition, area resident:* Full-time $47,450; part-time $1482 per credit hour. *Required fees:* $528. Tuition and fees vary according to program. *Graduate housing:* Rooms and/or apartments available on a first-come, first-served basis to single and married students. *Student services:* Campus employment opportunities, campus safety program, career counseling, exercise/wellness program, free psychological counseling, grant writing training, international student services, low-cost health insurance, multicultural affairs office, services for students with disabilities, teacher training. *Library:* Rush Rhees Library plus 7 others. *Research affiliation:* General Motors (chemical engineering, mechanical engineering, biomedical engineering), American Heart and Lung Associations (biochemistry/biophysics, cardiovascular research, environmental toxicology, oral biology, pulmonary medicine, pathology, pharmacology and physiology), Bausch & Lomb (optics, ophthalmology), Fermilab, Jet Propulsion Laboratory, and Lawrence Livermore National Laboratory (physics and astronomy, laser energetics), Johnson & Johnson (biology, neurosurgery, ophthalmology, psychiatry), IBM (computer science, electrical engineering, computer engineering).

Computer facilities: Computer purchase and lease plans are available. 700 computers available on campus for general student use. A campuswide network can be accessed from student residence rooms and from off campus. Online class registration is available.
Website: http://www.rochester.edu/

General Application Contact: Margaret H. Kearney, PhD, RN, FAAN, Vice Provost and University Dean of Graduate Studies, 585-275-3540.

GRADUATE UNITS

Eastman School of Music ***Degree program information:*** Part-time programs available. Part-time. Offers conducting (MM, DMA); ethnomusicology (MA); jazz studies/contemporary media (MM); music composition (MA, MM, DMA, PhD); music education (MA, MM, DMA, PhD); music theory (PhD); music theory pedagogy (MA); musicology (PhD); performance and literature (MM, DMA); piano accompanying and chamber music (MM, DMA).

Hajim School of Engineering and Applied Sciences Students: 595 full-time (152 women), 36 part-time (9 women); includes 54 minority (7 Black or African American, non-Hispanic/Latino; 1 American Indian or Alaska Native, non-Hispanic/Latino; 22 Asian, non-Hispanic/Latino; 18 Hispanic/Latino; 6 Two or more races, non-Hispanic/Latino), 379 international. 2,152 applicants, 39% accepted, 241 enrolled. *Faculty:* 91 full-time (10 women). *Financial support:* Fellowships, research assistantships, teaching assistantships, and tuition waivers (full and partial) available. Financial award application deadline: 2/1. In 2015, 169 master's, 46 doctorates awarded. *Degree program information:* Part-time programs available. Part-time. Offers alternative energy (MS); biomedical engineering (MS); chemical engineering (MS, PhD); computer science (MS, PhD); electrical and computer engineering (MS); energy and the environment (MS); engineering and applied sciences (MS, PhD); materials science (MS, PhD); mechanical engineering (MS, PhD); optics (MS). *Application deadline:* For fall admission, 1/1 priority date for domestic students. *Application fee:* $60. Electronic applications accepted. *Application Contact:* Dr. Margaret Kearney, Dean of Graduate Studies, 585-275-3540. *Dean*, Dr. Rob Clark, 585-275-4151.

Goergen Institute for Data Science Students: 25 full-time (11 women), 3 part-time (1 woman); includes 4 minority (1 Black or African American, non-Hispanic/Latino; 3 Asian, non-Hispanic/Latino), 9 international. 41 applicants, 73% accepted, 28 enrolled. Offers data science (MS). *Application deadline:* For fall admission, 1/15 for domestic students. *Application fee:* $60. Electronic applications accepted. *Application Contact:* Michelle Vogl, Academic Program Manager, 585-275-5288, E-mail: michelle.vogl@rochester.edu. *Director*, Henry Kautz, 585-520-1200, E-mail: kautz@cs.rochester.edu.

Institute of Optics Students: 116 full-time (26 women), 4 part-time (1 woman); includes 10 minority (1 Black or African American, non-Hispanic/Latino; 5 Asian, non-Hispanic/Latino; 2 Hispanic/Latino; 2 Two or more races, non-Hispanic/Latino), 53 international. 233 applicants, 51% accepted, 44 enrolled. *Faculty:* 16 full-time (1 woman). *Financial support:* Fellowships, research assistantships, teaching assistantships, and tuition waivers (full and partial) available. Financial award application deadline: 2/1. In 2015, 21 master's, 13 doctorates awarded. Offers optics (MS, PhD). *Application deadline:* For fall admission, 2/1 priority date for domestic students. *Application fee:* $60. Electronic applications accepted. *Application Contact:* Betsy Benedict, Graduate Program Coordinator, 585-275-7720. *Interim Director*, Xi-Cheng Zhang, 585-275-0333.

Margaret Warner Graduate School of Education and Human Development ***Degree program information:*** Part-time and evening/weekend programs available. Part-time, evening/weekend. Offers counseling (Ed D); education and human development (MS, Ed D, PhD); educational administration (Ed D); educational policy (MS); educational policy and theory (PhD); higher education (MS, PhD); higher education student affairs (MS); human development (MS); human development in educational context (PhD); school and community counseling (MS); school counseling (MS); school leadership (MS); teaching and curriculum (MS); teaching, curriculum, and change (PhD).

School of Arts and Sciences Students: 647 full-time (283 women), 6 part-time (2 women); includes 71 minority (5 Black or African American, non-Hispanic/Latino; 1 American Indian or Alaska Native, non-Hispanic/Latino; 21 Asian, non-Hispanic/Latino; 32 Hispanic/Latino; 12 Two or more races, non-Hispanic/Latino), 217 international. 1,908 applicants, 23% accepted, 147 enrolled. *Faculty:* 268 full-time (76 women). *Financial support:* Fellowships, research assistantships, teaching assistantships, and tuition waivers (full and partial) available. Financial award application deadline: 1/1. In 2015, 130 master's, 75 doctorates awarded. *Degree program information:* Part-time programs available. Part-time. Offers American history (MA, PhD); arts and sciences (MA, MS, PhD, Graduate Certificate); biology (MS, PhD); brain and cognitive sciences (PhD); chemistry (MS, PhD); clinical psychology (PhD); developmental psychology (PhD); earth and environmental sciences (MS, PhD); economics (MS, PhD); English (MA, PhD); European history (MA, PhD); global history (MA, PhD); linguistics (MA); literary translation studies (MA, Graduate Certificate); mathematics (MS, PhD); philosophy (MA, PhD); photographic preservation and collections management (MA); physics (MA, MS, PhD); physics and astronomy (PhD); political science (PhD); social-personality psychology (PhD); visual and cultural studies (MA, PhD). *Application deadline:* For fall admission, 1/1 priority date for domestic students. *Application fee:* $60. Electronic applications accepted. *Application Contact:* Gretchen Briscoe, Recruiting and Marketing Manager, 585-275-5029, E-mail: graduate.admissions@rochester.edu. *Dean of the School of Arts and Sciences*, Gloria Culver, 585-273-5000.

School of Medicine and Dentistry ***Degree program information:*** Part-time programs available. Part-time. Offers medicine (MD); medicine and dentistry (MA, MPH, MS, MD, PhD, Certificate). Electronic applications accepted.

Graduate Programs in Medicine and Dentistry ***Degree program information:*** Part-time programs available. Part-time. Offers biochemistry (PhD); biochemistry and molecular biology (PhD); biophysics (PhD); biophysics, structural and computational biology (PhD); clinical investigation (MS); clinical translational research (MS); dental science (MS); epidemiology (PhD); genetics, genomics and development (PhD); health services research and policy (PhD); marriage and family therapy (MS); medical microbiology (MS, PhD); medical statistics (MS); medicine and dentistry (MA, MPH, MS, PhD); microbiology and immunology (MS, PhD); neurobiology and anatomy (PhD); neuroscience (PhD); pathology (PhD); pharmacology (MS, PhD); physiology (MS, PhD); public health (MPH, MS); statistics (MA, PhD); toxicology (PhD); translational biomedical science (PhD). Electronic applications accepted.

School of Nursing Students: 21 full-time (20 women), 212 part-time (175 women); includes 35 minority (12 Black or African American, non-Hispanic/Latino; 1 American Indian or Alaska Native, non-Hispanic/Latino; 10 Asian, non-Hispanic/Latino; 7 Hispanic/Latino; 5 Two or more races, non-Hispanic/Latino), 2 international. Average age 35. 111 applicants, 68% accepted, 71 enrolled. *Faculty:* 56 full-time (45 women), 63 part-time/adjunct (55 women). *Financial support:* In 2015–16, 52 students received support, including 2 fellowships with tuition reimbursements available (averaging $30,000 per year); scholarships/grants, traineeships, health care benefits, tuition waivers (full and partial), and unspecified assistantships also available. Support available to part-time students. Financial award application deadline: 6/30. In 2015, 52 master's, 9 doctorates awarded. *Degree program information:* Part-time programs available. Part-time, online learning. Offers adult gerontological acute care nurse practitioner (MS); clinical nurse leader (MS); family nurse practitioner (MS); family psychiatric mental health nurse practitioner (MS); health care organization management and leadership (MS); health practice research (PhD); nursing (DNP); nursing education (MS); pediatric nurse practitioner (MS); pediatric nurse practitioner/neonatal nurse practitioner (MS). *Application deadline:* For fall admission, 4/1 for domestic and international students; for spring admission, 9/1 for domestic and international students; for summer admission, 1/2 for domestic and international students. *Application fee:* $50. Electronic applications accepted. *Application Contact:* Elaine Andolina, Director of Admissions, 585-275-2375, Fax: 585-756-8299, E-mail: elaine_andolina@urmc.rochester.edu. *Dean*, Dr. Kathy H. Rideout, 585-273-8902, Fax: 585-273-1268, E-mail: kathy_rideout@urmc.rochester.edu.

Simon Business School ***Degree program information:*** Part-time and evening/weekend programs available. Part-time, evening/weekend. Offers accountancy (MS); accounting and information systems (MBA); business (MBA, MS, PhD); business administration (MBA, PhD); business environment and public policy (MBA); business systems consulting (MBA); competitive and organizational strategy (MBA); competitive and organizational strategy - pricing (MBA); computers and information systems (MBA); corporate accounting (MBA); electronic commerce (MBA); entrepreneurship (MBA); finance (MS); health sciences management (MBA); international management (MBA); management (MS); manufacturing management (MBA); marketing (MBA); marketing - brand management and pricing (MBA); operations management - manufacturing (MBA); operations management - services (MBA); public accounting (MBA). Electronic applications accepted.

UNIVERSITY OF ST. AUGUSTINE FOR HEALTH SCIENCES, St. Augustine, FL 32086

General Information Proprietary, coed, graduate-only institution. *Graduate housing:* On-campus housing not available.

GRADUATE UNITS

Graduate Programs ***Degree program information:*** Part-time and evening/weekend programs available. Part-time, evening/weekend, online learning. Offers health science (DH Sc); health sciences education (Ed D); occupational therapy (TOTD); physical therapy (TDPT).

UNIVERSITY OF ST. FRANCIS, Joliet, IL 60435-6169

General Information Independent-religious, coed, comprehensive institution. *Enrollment:* 2,555 graduate, professional, and undergraduate students; 350 full-time matriculated graduate/professional students (282 women), 1,112 part-time matriculated graduate/professional students (865 women). *Enrollment by degree level:* 1,240 master's, 177 doctoral, 45 other advanced degrees. *Graduate faculty:* 39 full-time (30 women), 97 part-time/adjunct (56 women). *Tuition, area resident:* Part-time $730 per credit hour. *Required fees:* $125 per semester. Part-time tuition and fees vary according to program. *Student services:* Campus employment opportunities, campus safety program, career counseling, free psychological counseling, international student services, multicultural affairs office, services for students with disabilities, teacher training, writing training. *Library:* Brown Library. *Collection:* Books: 112,226 (physical), 4,125 (digital/electronic); Serial titles: 1,877 (physical), 83 (digital/electronic); Databases: 109. Weekly public service hours: 74; students can reserve study rooms.

Computer facilities: 560 computers available on campus for general student use. A campuswide network can be accessed from student residence rooms and from off campus. Online class registration, billing/payment are available.
Website: http://www.stfrancis.edu/

General Application Contact: Sandra Sloka, Director of Admissions for Graduate and Degree Completion Programs, 800-735-7500, Fax: 815-740-3431, E-mail: ssloka@stfrancis.edu.

GRADUATE UNITS

College of Arts and Sciences Students: 106 full-time (83 women), 24 part-time (21 women); includes 51 minority (16 Black or African American, non-Hispanic/Latino; 1 American Indian or Alaska Native, non-Hispanic/Latino; 11 Asian, non-Hispanic/Latino; 16 Hispanic/Latino; 7 Two or more races, non-Hispanic/Latino), 2 international. Average age 30. 111 applicants, 48% accepted, 28 enrolled. *Faculty:* 9 full-time (8 women). *Financial support:* In 2015–16, 19 students received support. Career-related internships or fieldwork, scholarships/grants, tuition waivers (partial), and unspecified assistantships available. Support available to part-time students. Financial award applicants required to submit FAFSA. In 2015, 47 master's awarded. Offers forensic social work (Post-Master's Certificate); physician assistant practice (MS); social work (MSW). *Application deadline:* Applications are processed on a rolling basis. *Application fee:* $30. Electronic applications accepted. *Application Contact:* Sandra Sloka, Director of Admissions for Graduate and Degree Completion Programs, 800-735-7500, Fax: 815-740-3431, E-mail: ssloka@stfrancis.edu. *Dean*, Dr. Robert Kase, 815-740-3367, Fax: 815-740-6366.

College of Business and Health Administration Students: 135 full-time (104 women), 316 part-time (211 women); includes 117 minority (60 Black or African American, non-Hispanic/Latino; 9 Asian, non-Hispanic/Latino; 40 Hispanic/Latino; 8 Two or more races, non-Hispanic/Latino), 23 international. Average age 39. 267 applicants, 63% accepted, 113 enrolled. *Faculty:* 12 full-time (6 women), 23 part-time/adjunct (11 women). *Financial support:* In 2015–16, 147 students received support. Scholarships/grants, tuition waivers (partial), and unspecified assistantships available. Support available to part-time students. Financial award applicants required to submit FAFSA. In 2015, 172 master's, 1 other advanced degree awarded. *Degree program information:* Part-time and evening/weekend programs available. Part-time, evening/weekend, 100% online, blended/hybrid learning. Offers business and health administration (MBA, MS, MSM, Certificate). *Application deadline:* Applications are processed on a rolling basis. *Application fee:* $30. Electronic applications accepted. *Application Contact:* Sandra Sloka, Director of Admissions for Graduate and Degree Completion Programs, 800-735-7500, Fax: 815-740-3431, E-mail: ssloka@stfrancis.edu. *Dean,* Dr. Orlando Griego, 815-740-3395, Fax: 815-740-3537, E-mail: ogriego@stfrancis.edu.

School of Business Students: 33 full-time (17 women), 146 part-time (80 women); includes 36 minority (18 Black or African American, non-Hispanic/Latino; 3 Asian, non-Hispanic/Latino; 13 Hispanic/Latino; 2 Two or more races, non-Hispanic/Latino), 14 international. Average age 35. 129 applicants, 59% accepted, 48 enrolled. *Faculty:* 7 full-time (4 women), 10 part-time/adjunct (4 women). *Financial support:* In 2015–16, 53 students received support. Career-related internships or fieldwork, scholarships/grants, tuition waivers (partial), and unspecified assistantships available. Support available to part-time students. Financial award applicants required to submit FAFSA. In 2015, 42 master's, 1 other advanced degree awarded. *Degree program information:* Part-time and evening/weekend programs available. Part-time, evening/weekend, 100% online, blended/hybrid learning. Offers accounting (Certificate); business administration (MBA); business analytics (Certificate); finance (Certificate); logistics (Certificate); management (MSM). *Application deadline:* Applications are processed on a rolling basis. *Application fee:* $30. Electronic applications accepted. *Application Contact:* Sandra Sloka, Director of Admissions for Graduate and Degree Completion Programs, 800-735-7500, Fax: 815-740-3431, E-mail: ssloka@stfrancis.edu. *Dean,* Dr. Orlando Griego, 815-740-3395, Fax: 815-740-3537, E-mail: ogriego@stfrancis.edu.

School of Health Administration Students: 97 full-time (82 women), 118 part-time (90 women); includes 62 minority (31 Black or African American, non-Hispanic/Latino; 4 Asian, non-Hispanic/Latino; 22 Hispanic/Latino; 5 Two or more races, non-Hispanic/Latino), 9 international. Average age 41. 104 applicants, 70% accepted, 51 enrolled. *Faculty:* 6 full-time (3 women), 8 part-time/adjunct (4 women). *Financial support:* In 2015–16, 83 students received support. Tuition waivers (partial) and unspecified assistantships available. Support available to part-time students. Financial award applicants required to submit FAFSA. In 2015, 114 master's awarded. *Degree program information:* Part-time and evening/weekend programs available. Part-time, evening/weekend, 100% online. Offers health administration (MS). *Application deadline:* Applications are processed on a rolling basis. *Application fee:* $30. Electronic applications accepted. *Application Contact:* Sandra Sloka, Director of Admissions for Graduate and Degree Completion Programs, 800-735-7500, Fax: 815-740-3431, E-mail: ssloka@stfrancis.edu. *Dean,* Dr. Orlando Griego, 815-740-3395, Fax: 815-740-3537, E-mail: ogriego@stfrancis.edu.

School of Professional Studies Students: 5 full-time (all women), 52 part-time (41 women); includes 19 minority (11 Black or African American, non-Hispanic/Latino; 2 Asian, non-Hispanic/Latino; 5 Hispanic/Latino; 1 Two or more races, non-Hispanic/Latino). Average age 41. 34 applicants, 53% accepted, 14 enrolled. *Faculty:* 1 full-time (0 women), 5 part-time/adjunct (3 women). *Financial support:* In 2015–16, 13 students received support. Tuition waivers (partial) and unspecified assistantships available. Support available to part-time students. Financial award applicants required to submit FAFSA. In 2015, 16 master's awarded. *Degree program information:* Part-time and evening/weekend programs available. Part-time, evening/weekend, 100% online. Offers e-learning (Certificate); management of training and development (Certificate); training and development (MS); training specialist (Certificate). *Application deadline:* Applications are processed on a rolling basis. *Application fee:* $30. Electronic applications accepted. *Application Contact:* Sandra Sloka, Director of Admissions for Graduate and Degree Completion Programs, 800-735-7500, Fax: 815-740-3431, E-mail: ssloka@stfrancis.edu. *Dean,* Dr. Orlando Griego, 815-740-3395, Fax: 815-740-3537, E-mail: ogriego@stfrancis.edu.

College of Education Students: 27 full-time (23 women), 413 part-time (305 women); includes 81 minority (48 Black or African American, non-Hispanic/Latino; 1 Asian, non-Hispanic/Latino; 26 Hispanic/Latino; 6 Two or more races, non-Hispanic/Latino). Average age 36. 235 applicants, 62% accepted, 126 enrolled. *Faculty:* 11 full-time (9 women), 58 part-time/adjunct (32 women). *Financial support:* In 2015–16, 51 students received support. Career-related internships or fieldwork, tuition waivers (partial), and unspecified assistantships available. Support available to part-time students. Financial award applicants required to submit FAFSA. In 2015, 109 master's, 18 doctorates, 8 other advanced degrees awarded. *Degree program information:* Part-time and evening/weekend programs available. Part-time, evening/weekend, 100% online, blended/hybrid learning. Offers educational leadership (MS, Ed D); elementary education (M Ed); higher education (MS); reading (MS); secondary education (M Ed); special education (M Ed); teaching and learning (MS); TESOL (Certificate). *Application deadline:* Applications are processed on a rolling basis. *Application fee:* $30. Electronic applications accepted. *Application Contact:* Sandra Sloka, Director of Admissions for Graduate and Degree Completion Programs, 800-735-7500, Fax: 815-740-3431, E-mail: ssloka@stfrancis.edu. *Dean,* Dr. John Gambro, 815-740-3829, Fax: 815-740-2264, E-mail: jgambro@stfrancis.edu.

Leach College of Nursing Students: 82 full-time (72 women), 356 part-time (325 women); includes 147 minority (62 Black or African American, non-Hispanic/Latino; 1 American Indian or Alaska Native, non-Hispanic/Latino; 27 Asian, non-Hispanic/Latino; 45 Hispanic/Latino; 3 Native Hawaiian or other Pacific Islander, non-Hispanic/Latino; 9 Two or more races, non-Hispanic/Latino). Average age 41. 338 applicants, 42% accepted, 100 enrolled. *Faculty:* 7 full-time (all women), 16 part-time/adjunct (13 women). *Financial support:* In 2015–16, 149 students received support. Career-related internships or fieldwork, scholarships/grants, and tuition waivers (partial) available. Support available to part-time students. Financial award applicants required to submit FAFSA. In 2015, 91 master's, 9 doctorates, 6 other advanced degrees awarded. *Degree program information:* Part-time and evening/weekend programs available. Part-time, evening/weekend, 100% online. Offers family nurse practitioner (MSN, Post-Master's Certificate); family psychology/mental health nurse practitioner (MSN, Post-Master's Certificate); nursing administration (MSN); nursing education (MSN); nursing practice (DNP); teaching in nursing (Certificate). *Application deadline:* Applications are processed on a rolling basis. *Application fee:* $30. Electronic applications accepted. *Application Contact:* Sandra Sloka, Director of Admissions for Graduate and Degree Completion Programs, 800-735-7500, Fax: 815-740-3431, E-mail: ssloka@stfrancis.edu. *Dean,* Dr. Carol Wilson, 815-740-3840, Fax: 815-740-4243, E-mail: cwilson@stfrancis.edu.

UNIVERSITY OF SAINT FRANCIS, Fort Wayne, IN 46808-3994

General Information Independent-religious, coed, comprehensive institution. *Graduate housing:* Rooms and/or apartments available on a first-come, first-served basis to single and married students.

GRADUATE UNITS

Graduate School ***Degree program information:*** Part-time and evening/weekend programs available. Part-time, evening/weekend, online learning. Offers 21st-century interventions (Post Master's Certificate); clinical mental health counseling (MS, Post Master's Certificate); environmental health (MEH); family nurse practitioner (MSN, Post Master's Certificate); pastoral counseling (MS, Post Master's Certificate); physician assistant studies (MS); psychology (MS); rehabilitation counseling (MS, Post Master's Certificate); school counseling (MS Ed); special education (MS Ed); studio art (MA); theology (MA). Electronic applications accepted.

Keith Busse School of Business and Entrepreneurial Leadership Degree program information: Part-time and evening/weekend programs available. Part-time, evening/weekend, online learning. Offers business administration (MBA); environmental health (MEH); healthcare administration (MHA); sustainability (MBA). Electronic applications accepted.

UNIVERSITY OF SAINT JOSEPH, West Hartford, CT 06117-2700

General Information Independent-religious, coed, primarily women, comprehensive institution. *Graduate housing:* On-campus housing not available. *Student services:* Campus safety program, career counseling, exercise/wellness program, free psychological counseling, services for students with disabilities, teacher training. *Library:* Pope Pius XII Library.

Computer facilities: 72 computers available on campus for general student use. A campuswide network can be accessed from student residence rooms and from off campus. Online class registration is available.
Website: http://www.usj.edu/

General Application Contact: Graduate Admissions Office, 860-231-5261, E-mail: graduate@usj.edu.

GRADUATE UNITS

Department of Biology ***Financial support:*** Unspecified assistantships available. Support available to part-time students. Financial award applicants required to submit FAFSA. *Degree program information:* Part-time programs available. Part-time, online learning. Offers biology (MS). *Application deadline:* Applications are processed on a rolling basis. *Application fee:* $50. Electronic applications accepted.

Department of Business Administration ***Financial support:*** Career-related internships or fieldwork and unspecified assistantships available. Support available to part-time students. Financial award applicants required to submit FAFSA. *Degree program information:* Part-time and evening/weekend programs available. Part-time, evening/weekend. Offers management (MS). *Application deadline:* Applications are processed on a rolling basis. *Application fee:* $50. Electronic applications accepted. *Application Contact:* Steven B. Jarett.

Department of Chemistry ***Financial support:*** Career-related internships or fieldwork and unspecified assistantships available. Support available to part-time students. Financial award applicants required to submit FAFSA. *Degree program information:* Part-time and evening/weekend programs available. Part-time, evening/weekend, online learning. Offers biochemistry (MS); chemistry (MS). *Application deadline:* Applications are processed on a rolling basis. *Application fee:* $50. Electronic applications accepted.

Department of Counseling and Applied Behavioral Studies ***Financial support:*** Career-related internships or fieldwork and unspecified assistantships available. Support available to part-time students. Financial award applicants required to submit FAFSA. *Degree program information:* Part-time and evening/weekend programs available. Part-time, evening/weekend. Offers applied behavioral analysis (Graduate Certificate); clinical mental health counseling (MA); school counseling (MA). *Application deadline:* Applications are processed on a rolling basis. *Application fee:* $50. Electronic applications accepted.

Department of Education ***Financial support:*** Career-related internships or fieldwork and unspecified assistantships available. Support available to part-time students. Financial award applicants required to submit FAFSA. *Degree program information:* Part-time and evening/weekend programs available. Part-time, evening/weekend. Offers curriculum and instruction (MA); educational technology (MA); literacy internship (MA); multiple intelligences (MA); reading/language (MA); tesol (MA). *Application deadline:* Applications are processed on a rolling basis. *Application fee:* $50. Electronic applications accepted.

Department of Nursing ***Financial support:*** Career-related internships or fieldwork and unspecified assistantships available. Support available to part-time students. Financial award applicants required to submit FAFSA. *Degree program information:* Part-time and evening/weekend programs available. Part-time, evening/weekend. Offers family nurse practitioner (MS); family psychiatric/mental health nurse practitioner (MS); nurse educator (MS); nursing practice (DNP). *Application deadline:* Applications are processed on a rolling basis. *Application fee:* $50. Electronic applications accepted.

Department of Nutrition and Dietetics ***Financial support:*** Career-related internships or fieldwork and unspecified assistantships available. Support available to part-time students. Financial award applicants required to submit FAFSA. *Degree program information:* Part-time and evening/weekend programs available. Part-time, evening/weekend, online learning. Offers nutrition (MS). *Application deadline:* Applications are processed on a rolling basis. *Application fee:* $50. Electronic applications accepted.

Department of Special Education ***Financial support:*** Career-related internships or fieldwork and unspecified assistantships available. Support available to part-time students. Financial award applicants required to submit FAFSA. *Degree program information:* Part-time and evening/weekend programs available. Part-time, evening/weekend. Offers autism and applied behavior analysis (MS); special education (MA). *Application deadline:* Applications are processed on a rolling basis. *Application fee:* $50. Electronic applications accepted.

Program in Gerontology ***Financial support:*** Career-related internships or fieldwork and unspecified assistantships available. Support available to part-time students. Financial award applicants required to submit FAFSA. *Degree program information:* Part-time and evening/weekend programs available. Part-time, evening/weekend. Offers gerontology (Certificate). *Application deadline:* Applications are processed on a rolling basis. *Application fee:* $50. Electronic applications accepted.

Program in Marriage and Family Therapy ***Financial support:*** Career-related internships or fieldwork and unspecified assistantships available. Support available to part-time students. Financial award applicants required to submit FAFSA. *Degree program information:* Part-time and evening/weekend programs available. Part-time, evening/weekend. Offers marriage and family therapy (MA). *Application deadline:*

Applications are processed on a rolling basis. *Application fee:* $50. Electronic applications accepted.

School of Pharmacy ***Financial support:*** Career-related internships or fieldwork available. Offers pharmacy (Pharm D). *Application deadline:* Applications are processed on a rolling basis. Electronic applications accepted.

UNIVERSITY OF SAINT MARY, Leavenworth, KS 66048-5082

General Information Independent-religious, coed, comprehensive institution. *Enrollment:* 1,427 graduate, professional, and undergraduate students; 445 full-time matriculated graduate/professional students (290 women), 107 part-time matriculated graduate/professional students (75 women). *Enrollment by degree level:* 433 master's, 119 doctoral. *Tuition, area resident:* Full-time $21,420; part-time $595 per credit hour. Tuition and fees vary according to campus/location and program. *Graduate housing:* On-campus housing not available. *Student services:* Career counseling, free psychological counseling. *Library:* De Paul Library plus 1 other. *Collection:* Books: 115,000 (physical), 103,000 (digital/electronic); Serial titles: 25 (physical), 12,000 (digital/electronic); Databases: 59. Weekly public service hours: 68.

Computer facilities: 45 computers available on campus for general student use. A campuswide network can be accessed from student residence rooms. Online class registration is available.
Website: http://www.stmary.edu/

General Application Contact: Dr. Ron Logan, Graduate Dean, 913-345-8288, Fax: 913-345-2802, E-mail: loganr@stmary.edu.

GRADUATE UNITS

Graduate Programs Students: 436 full-time (281 women), 82 part-time (54 women); includes 105 minority (43 Black or African American, non-Hispanic/Latino; 5 American Indian or Alaska Native, non-Hispanic/Latino; 16 Asian, non-Hispanic/Latino; 31 Hispanic/Latino; 1 Native Hawaiian or other Pacific Islander, non-Hispanic/Latino; 9 Two or more races, non-Hispanic/Latino), 6 international. 248 applicants, 68% accepted, 161 enrolled. *Financial support:* Unspecified assistantships available. Financial award applicants required to submit FAFSA. *Degree program information:* Part-time and evening/weekend programs available. Part-time, evening/weekend, online learning. Offers counseling psychology (MA); education (MA); elementary education (MA); enterprise risk management (MBA); general management (MBA); health care management (MBA); human resource management (MBA); marketing and advertising management (MBA); nurse administrator (MSN); nurse educator (MSN); physical therapy (DPT); psychology (MA); special education (MA); teaching (MAT). *Application deadline:* Applications are processed on a rolling basis. *Application fee:* $25. Electronic applications accepted. *Application Contact:* Dr. Ron Logan, Graduate Dean, 913-758-4338, E-mail: loganr@stmary.edu.

UNIVERSITY OF SAINT MARY OF THE LAKE–MUNDELEIN SEMINARY, Mundelein, IL 60060

General Information Independent-religious, men only, graduate-only institution. *Enrollment by degree level:* 221 master's, 19 doctoral, 26 other advanced degrees. *Graduate faculty:* 60 full-time (6 women), 21 part-time/adjunct (9 women). *Tuition, area resident:* Full-time $24,390. *Required fees:* $300. Full-time tuition and fees vary according to program. *Graduate housing:* Room and/or apartments guaranteed to single students; on-campus housing not available to married students. Typical cost: $0 per year ($10,300 including board). Room and board charges vary according to campus/location. Housing application deadline: 8/1. *Student services:* Campus employment opportunities, campus safety program, international student services, low-cost health insurance, multicultural affairs office. *Library:* Feehan Memorial Library and McEssy Theological Resource Center. *Collection:* Books: 180,338 (physical), 512 (digital/electronic); Serial titles: 390 (physical), 98 (digital/electronic); Databases: 15.

Computer facilities: 20 computers available on campus for general student use. A campuswide network can be accessed from student residence rooms and from off campus.
Website: http://www.usml.edu/

General Application Contact: Very Rev. John Kartje, Rector-President, 847-566-6401, Fax: 847-932-3305, E-mail: mulz@usml.edu.

GRADUATE UNITS

Graduate and Professional Programs Students: 266 full-time (8 women); includes 10 minority (2 Black or African American, non-Hispanic/Latino; 3 Asian, non-Hispanic/Latino; 5 Hispanic/Latino), 78 international. 99 applicants, 81% accepted, 80 enrolled. *Faculty:* 42 full-time (7 women), 19 part-time/adjunct (7 women). *Financial support:* Career-related internships or fieldwork available. In 2015, 34 master's awarded. Offers liturgical studies (MA); ministry (D Min); pastoral studies (MA); theology (M Div). *Application deadline:* For fall admission, 8/1 for domestic and international students. Applications are processed on a rolling basis. *Application fee:* $0. Electronic applications accepted. *Application Contact:* Very Rev. John Kartje, Rector-President, 847-566-6401, Fax: 847-932-3305. *Dean of the Seminary and Graduate School*, Very Rev. Thomas A. Baima, 847-566-6401.

UNIVERSITY OF ST. MICHAEL'S COLLEGE, Toronto, ON M5S 1J4, Canada

General Information Independent-religious, coed, graduate-only institution. *Graduate housing:* Rooms and/or apartments available on a first-come, first-served basis to single and married students. Housing application deadline: 8/15.

GRADUATE UNITS

Faculty of Theology ***Degree program information:*** Part-time programs available. Part-time. Offers Catholic leadership (MA); eastern Christian studies (Diploma); religious education (Diploma); theological studies (Diploma); theology (M Div, MA, MRE, MTS, D Min, PhD, Th D); theology and Jewish studies (MA). Th D offered jointly with University of Toronto. Electronic applications accepted.

UNIVERSITY OF ST. THOMAS, St. Paul, MN 55105-1096

General Information Independent-religious, coed, university. *Graduate housing:* On-campus housing not available.

GRADUATE UNITS

Graduate Studies ***Degree program information:*** Part-time and evening/weekend programs available. Part-time, evening/weekend, online learning.

College of Arts and Sciences ***Financial support:*** Fellowships, research assistantships, teaching assistantships, career-related internships or fieldwork, institutionally sponsored loans, and scholarships/grants available. Support available to part-time students. Financial award application deadline: 4/1; financial award applicants required to submit FAFSA. *Degree program information:* Part-time and evening/weekend programs available. Part-time, evening/weekend. Offers art history (MA); arts and sciences (MA); Catholic studies (MA); choral (MA); English (MA); instrumental (MA); Kodaly (MA); Orff Schulwerk (MA); piano pedagogy (MA). *Application deadline:* For fall admission, 4/1 for domestic students, 5/1 priority date for international students; for spring admission, 11/1 for domestic students, 10/1 priority date for international students. *Application fee:* $50. *Dean*, Dr. Terence Langan, 651-962-6001, Fax: 651-962-6004, E-mail: t9langan@stthomas.edu.

Graduate Programs in Software ***Degree program information:*** Part-time and evening/weekend programs available. Part-time, evening/weekend. Offers advanced studies in software engineering (Certificate); big data (Certificate); business analysis (Certificate); computer security (Certificate); information systems (Certificate); information technology (MS); software design and development (Certificate); software engineering (MS); software management (MS); software systems (MSS). Electronic applications accepted.

Graduate School of Professional Psychology Students: 192 (144 women); includes 31 minority (8 Black or African American, non-Hispanic/Latino; 6 Asian, non-Hispanic/Latino; 10 Hispanic/Latino; 7 Two or more races, non-Hispanic/Latino), 5 international. Average age 28. 167 applicants, 63% accepted, 52 enrolled. *Faculty:* 11 full-time, 14 part-time/adjunct. *Financial support:* Fellowships with partial tuition reimbursements, research assistantships, teaching assistantships, institutionally sponsored loans, and scholarships/grants available. Support available to part-time students. Financial award application deadline: 8/1; financial award applicants required to submit FAFSA. In 2015, 49 master's, 13 doctorates awarded. *Degree program information:* Part-time and evening/weekend programs available. Part-time, evening/weekend. Offers counseling psychology (MA, Psy D); family therapy (Certificate). *Application deadline:* For fall admission, 2/5 priority date for domestic students; for winter admission, 1/5 priority date for domestic students; for spring admission, 10/15 priority date for domestic students, 3/1 for international students. Electronic applications accepted. *Application Contact:* Laurie Dupont, Program Coordinator, 651-962-4669, Fax: 651-962-4651, E-mail: ldupont@stthomas.edu. *Chair*, Dr. Christopher S. Vye, 651-962-4666, Fax: 651-962-4666, E-mail: csvye@stthomas.edu.

Opus College of Business Offers accountancy (MS); business (MBA, MBC, MS); business administration (MBA); business communication (MBC); executive business administration (MBA); health care business administration (MBA); real estate (MS).

The Saint Paul Seminary School of Divinity ***Degree program information:*** Part-time and evening/weekend programs available. Part-time, evening/weekend. Offers pastoral ministry (MAPM); religious education (MARE); theology (MA). Electronic applications accepted.

School of Education Students: 145 full-time (101 women), 895 part-time (624 women); includes 173 minority (83 Black or African American, non-Hispanic/Latino; 2 American Indian or Alaska Native, non-Hispanic/Latino; 29 Asian, non-Hispanic/Latino; 32 Hispanic/Latino; 26 Native Hawaiian or other Pacific Islander, non-Hispanic/Latino; 1 Two or more races, non-Hispanic/Latino), 53 international. Average age 31. 391 applicants, 93% accepted, 314 enrolled. *Faculty:* 28 full-time (16 women), 89 part-time/adjunct (60 women). *Financial support:* In 2015–16, 27 students received support. Research assistantships, career-related internships or fieldwork, institutionally sponsored loans, scholarships/grants, and unspecified assistantships available. Support available to part-time students. Financial award application deadline: 8/1; financial award applicants required to submit FAFSA. In 2015, 188 master's, 41 doctorates, 78 other advanced degrees awarded. *Degree program information:* Part-time and evening/weekend programs available. Part-time, evening/weekend, 100% online, blended/hybrid learning. Offers autism spectrum disorders (MA, Certificate); community education administration (MA); curriculum and instruction (K-12) (MA); developmental disabilities (MA); early childhood special education (MA); education (MA, Ed D, Certificate, Ed S); educational leadership (Ed S); educational leadership and administration (MA); elementary education (MA); emotional behavioral disorders (MA); English as a second language (MA); human resources and change leadership (MA); international leadership (MA, Certificate); leadership (Ed D); leadership in student affairs (MA, Certificate); learning disabilities (MA); math education (Certificate); multicultural education (Certificate); organization development (Ed D); public policy and leadership (MA, Certificate); public safety and law enforcement leadership (MA); reading (Certificate); reading (K-12) (MA); special education (MA). *Application deadline:* For fall admission, 7/15 priority date for domestic students, 7/15 for international students; for spring admission, 12/9 priority date for domestic students, 12/9 for international students; for summer admission, 4/3 for domestic and international students. Applications are processed on a rolling basis. Electronic applications accepted. *Dean*, Dr. Mark Salisbury, 651-962-4435, Fax: 651-962-4169, E-mail: marksalisbury@stthomas.edu.

School of Engineering Offers electrical engineering (MS); manufacturing engineering and operations (MS); manufacturing systems (Certificate); mechanical engineering (MS); medical device development (Certificate); regulatory science (MS); software engineering (MS); software management (MS); systems engineering (MS); technology leadership (Certificate); technology management (MS). Electronic applications accepted.

School of Law Offers law (JD); organizational ethics and compliance (LL M, MSL); U.S. law (LL M). Electronic applications accepted.

School of Social Work Students: 86 full-time (79 women), 259 part-time (233 women); includes 43 minority (18 Black or African American, non-Hispanic/Latino; 6 American Indian or Alaska Native, non-Hispanic/Latino; 9 Asian, non-Hispanic/Latino; 10 Two or more races, non-Hispanic/Latino). Average age 32. 228 applicants, 91% accepted, 126 enrolled. *Faculty:* 25 full-time (20 women), 21 part-time/adjunct (15 women). *Financial support:* In 2015–16, 15 research assistantships (averaging $1,375 per year) were awarded; fellowships, career-related internships or fieldwork, Federal Work-Study, institutionally sponsored loans, scholarships/grants, and unspecified assistantships also available. Support available to part-time students. Financial award application deadline: 7/1; financial award applicants required to submit FAFSA. In 2015, 134 master's awarded. *Degree program information:* Part-time and evening/weekend programs available. Part-time, evening/weekend, blended/hybrid learning. Offers social work (MSW). *Application deadline:* For fall admission, 1/10 for domestic students. *Application fee:* $35. Electronic applications accepted. *Application Contact:* Mary Palin, Graduate Admissions Counselor, 651-690-6185, Fax: 651-690-6549, E-mail: mbpalin@stkate.edu. *Dean and Professor*, Dr. Barbara W. Shank, 651-962-5801, Fax: 651-962-5819, E-mail: bwshank@stthomas.edu.

UNIVERSITY OF ST. THOMAS, Houston, TX 77006-4696

General Information Independent-religious, coed, comprehensive institution. *Enrollment:* 3,411 graduate, professional, and undergraduate students; 315 full-time matriculated graduate/professional students (140 women), 1,267 part-time matriculated graduate/professional students (973 women). *Enrollment by degree level:* 1,522 master's, 25 doctoral, 35 other advanced degrees. *Graduate faculty:* 118 full-time (57 women), 56 part-time/adjunct (31 women). *Tuition, area resident:* Full-time $20,124; part-time $1118 per credit hour. *Required fees:* $83 per semester. One-time fee: $100. Part-time tuition and fees vary according to course level, course load, campus/location and program. *Graduate housing:* Room and/or apartments available on a first-come, first-served basis to single students; on-campus housing not available to married students. *Student services:* Campus employment opportunities, campus safety program, career counseling, free psychological counseling, international student services, services for students with disabilities. *Library:* Doherty Library. *Collection:* Books: 262,422 (physical), 2,491 (digital/electronic); Serial titles: 78,316 (physical), 78,316 (digital/electronic); Databases: 265. Weekly public service hours: 100.

Computer facilities: Computer purchase and lease plans are available. 390 computers available on campus for general student use. A campuswide network can be accessed from student residence rooms. Online class registration is available.
Website: http://www.stthom.edu/

General Application Contact: Dr. Ravi Srinivas, Associate Vice President for Academic Affairs, 713-525-3804, Fax: 713-525-6924, E-mail: srinivas@stthom.edu.

GRADUATE UNITS

Cameron School of Business Students: 169 full-time (81 women), 238 part-time (136 women); includes 170 minority (43 Black or African American, non-Hispanic/Latino; 29 Asian, non-Hispanic/Latino; 94 Hispanic/Latino; 4 Two or more races, non-Hispanic/Latino), 132 international. Average age 31. 168 applicants, 90% accepted, 100 enrolled. *Faculty:* 27 full-time (12 women), 5 part-time/adjunct (1 woman). *Financial support:* In 2015–16, 38 students received support, including research assistantships with partial tuition reimbursements available (averaging $3,000 per year); Federal Work-Study, scholarships/grants, unspecified assistantships, and state work-study, institutional employment also available. Support available to part-time students. Financial award application deadline: 4/15; financial award applicants required to submit FAFSA. In 2015, 167 master's awarded. *Degree program information:* Part-time and evening/weekend programs available. Part-time, evening/weekend. Offers business (MBA, MCTM, MIB, MSA, MSF). *Application deadline:* For fall admission, 7/15 for domestic and international students; for winter admission, 7/15 for domestic and international students; for spring admission, 11/15 for domestic students, 10/15 for international students. Applications are processed on a rolling basis. *Application fee:* $35. Electronic applications accepted. *Application Contact:* Fran Wilson Mayes, Academic Coordinator, 713-525-2100, Fax: 713-525-2110, E-mail: cameron@stthom.edu. *Dean,* Dr. Beena George, 713-525-2100, Fax: 713-525-2110, E-mail: cameron@stthom.edu.

Center for Faith and Culture Students: 1 (woman) full-time, 20 part-time (13 women); includes 6 minority (3 Black or African American, non-Hispanic/Latino; 1 Asian, non-Hispanic/Latino; 2 Hispanic/Latino). Average age 47. 4 applicants, 75% accepted, 3 enrolled. *Faculty:* 6 full-time (1 woman), 1 part-time/adjunct (0 women). *Financial support:* In 2015–16, 16 students received support. Federal Work-Study, scholarships/grants, and state work-study, institutional employment available. Support available to part-time students. Financial award application deadline: 4/15; financial award applicants required to submit FAFSA. In 2015, 5 master's awarded. *Degree program information:* Part-time programs available. Part-time. Offers faith and culture (MA). *Application deadline:* For fall admission, 7/1 for domestic students, 6/1 for international students; for spring admission, 11/1 for domestic students, 10/1 for international students. Applications are processed on a rolling basis. *Application fee:* $35. Electronic applications accepted. *Application Contact:* Dr. Adam Martinez, Program Director, 713-942-5066, E-mail: cfc@stthom.edu. *Director,* Fr. Donald S. Nesti, 713-942-5066, E-mail: cfc@stthom.edu.

Center for Thomistic Studies Students: 10 full-time (3 women), 21 part-time (1 woman); includes 5 minority (1 Asian, non-Hispanic/Latino; 4 Hispanic/Latino), 1 international. Average age 33. 11 applicants, 64% accepted, 6 enrolled. *Faculty:* 6 full-time (1 woman). *Financial support:* In 2015–16, 9 students received support. Fellowships with tuition reimbursements available, teaching assistantships, Federal Work-Study, scholarships/grants, unspecified assistantships, and state work-study, institutional employment available. Support available to part-time students. Financial award application deadline: 2/1; financial award applicants required to submit FAFSA. In 2015, 1 master's, 2 doctorates awarded. *Degree program information:* Part-time programs available. Part-time. Offers philosophy (MA, PhD). *Application deadline:* For fall admission, 2/1 priority date for domestic and international students. Applications are processed on a rolling basis. *Application fee:* $35. Electronic applications accepted. *Application Contact:* Valerie Hall, Administrative Assistant II, 713-525-3591, Fax: 713-942-3464, E-mail: hallvl@stthom.edu. *Director,* Dr. Thomas Osborne, 713-942-3483, Fax: 713-942-3464, E-mail: osborntm@stthom.edu.

Program in Liberal Arts Students: 12 full-time (9 women), 68 part-time (56 women); includes 40 minority (12 Black or African American, non-Hispanic/Latino; 1 Asian, non-Hispanic/Latino; 23 Hispanic/Latino; 4 Two or more races, non-Hispanic/Latino), 6 international. Average age 36. 11 applicants, 64% accepted, 6 enrolled. *Faculty:* 31 full-time (12 women), 10 part-time/adjunct (7 women). *Financial support:* In 2015–16, 16 students received support. Federal Work-Study, scholarships/grants, and state work-study, institutional employment available. Support available to part-time students. Financial award application deadline: 4/15; financial award applicants required to submit FAFSA. In 2015, 33 master's awarded. *Degree program information:* Part-time and evening/weekend programs available. Part-time, evening/weekend. Offers liberal arts (MLA). *Application deadline:* Applications are processed on a rolling basis. *Application fee:* $35. Electronic applications accepted. *Application Contact:* Kate Henderson, Program Coordinator, 713-525-3556, Fax: 713-525-6924, E-mail: mla@stthom.edu. *Associate Vice President for Academic Affairs/Dean of Extended Programs/MLA Director,* Dr. Ravi Srinivas, 713-525-3804, Fax: 713-525-6924, E-mail: mla@stthom.edu.

School of Arts and Sciences Students: 4 full-time (0 women), 11 part-time (4 women); includes 10 minority (5 Black or African American, non-Hispanic/Latino; 5 Hispanic/Latino). Average age 36. 14 applicants, 100% accepted, 7 enrolled. *Faculty:* 6 full-time (0 women), 3 part-time/adjunct (2 women). *Financial support:* In 2015–16, 3 students received support. Federal Work-Study, scholarships/grants, and state work-study, institutional employment available. Support available to part-time students. Financial award application deadline: 4/15; financial award applicants required to submit FAFSA. In 2015, 3 master's awarded. *Degree program information:* Part-time programs available. Part-time. Offers public policy administration (MPPA); sacred music (MSM). *Application deadline:* For fall admission, 7/15 priority date for domestic and international students; for spring admission, 12/1 priority date for domestic and international students; for summer admission, 5/1 priority date for domestic and international students. Applications are processed on a rolling basis. Electronic applications accepted. *Application Contact:* Todd Boutte, Director of Graduate Admissions, 713-942-3403, E-mail: bouttet@stthom.edu. *Interim Dean, School of Arts and Sciences,* Dr. John W. Starner, Jr., 713-525-3527, E-mail: starner@stthom.edu.

School of Education and Human Services Students: 48 full-time (42 women), 800 part-time (704 women); includes 558 minority (172 Black or African American, non-Hispanic/Latino; 24 Asian, non-Hispanic/Latino; 350 Hispanic/Latino; 12 Two or more races, non-Hispanic/Latino), 22 international. Average age 36. 314 applicants, 90% accepted, 218 enrolled. *Faculty:* 45 full-time (30 women), 33 part-time/adjunct (22 women). *Financial support:* In 2015–16, 59 students received support. Federal Work-Study, scholarships/grants, and state work-study, institutional employment available. Support available to part-time students. Financial award application deadline: 4/15; financial award applicants required to submit FAFSA. In 2015, 440 master's awarded. *Degree program information:* Part-time and evening/weekend programs available. Part-time, evening/weekend, online learning. Offers all level education (M Ed); bilingual/dual language (M Ed); Catholic school teaching (M Ed); Catholic/private school leadership (M Ed); counselor education (M Ed); curriculum and instruction (M Ed); educational leadership (M Ed); elementary teaching (M Ed); English as a second language (M Ed); exceptionality/educational diagnostician (M Ed); exceptionality/special education (M Ed); generalist (M Ed); reading (M Ed); secondary teaching (M Ed); teaching (MAT). *Application deadline:* Applications are processed on a rolling basis. *Application fee:* $35. Electronic applications accepted. *Application Contact:* Rita Paredes, Administrative Assistant, 713-525-3442, Fax: 713-525-3871, E-mail: rparede@stthom.edu. *Dean,* Dr. Robert LeBlanc, 713-525-3540, Fax: 713-525-3871, E-mail: education@stthom.edu.

School of Theology Students: 71 full-time (4 women), 74 part-time (28 women); includes 170 minority (43 Black or African American, non-Hispanic/Latino; 29 Asian, non-Hispanic/Latino; 94 Hispanic/Latino; 4 Two or more races, non-Hispanic/Latino), 132 international. Average age 38. 31 applicants, 100% accepted, 26 enrolled. *Faculty:* 27 full-time (12 women), 5 part-time/adjunct (1 woman). *Financial support:* In 2015–16, 11 students received support. Scholarships/grants available. Support available to part-time students. Financial award application deadline: 4/15; financial award applicants required to submit FAFSA. In 2015, 74 master's awarded. *Degree program information:* Part-time programs available. Part-time. Offers divinity (M Div); pastoral studies (MAPS); theological studies (MA). *Application deadline:* Applications are processed on a rolling basis. *Application fee:* $10. Electronic applications accepted. *Application Contact:* Connie M. Henry, Office Manager, 713-686-4345 Ext. 231, Fax: 713-683-8673, E-mail: sms@stthom.edu. *Dean,* Dr. Sandra C. Magie, 713-686-4345 Ext. 242, Fax: 713-683-8673, E-mail: smagie@stthom.edu.

UNIVERSITY OF SAN DIEGO, San Diego, CA 92110-2492

General Information Independent-religious, coed, university. *Enrollment:* 8,251 graduate, professional, and undergraduate students; 1,433 full-time matriculated graduate/professional students (843 women), 988 part-time matriculated graduate/professional students (591 women). *Enrollment by degree level:* 1,470 master's, 950 doctoral, 1 other advanced degree. *Graduate faculty:* 154 full-time (70 women), 208 part-time/adjunct (115 women). *Graduate housing:* Rooms and/or apartments available on a first-come, first-served basis to single and married students. Housing application deadline: 5/1. *Student services:* Campus employment opportunities, career counseling, child daycare facilities, exercise/wellness program, free psychological counseling, international student services, low-cost health insurance, multicultural affairs office, services for students with disabilities, teacher training. *Library:* Helen K. and James S. Copley Library plus 1 other. *Collection:* Books: 659,562 (physical), 662,972 (digital/electronic); Serial titles: 17,232 (physical), 427 (digital/electronic); Databases: 260. Weekly public service hours: 116; students can reserve study rooms. *Research affiliation:* Leon R. Hubbard Hatchery (marine science), Southwest Fisheries Science Center (marine science), Hubbs Seaworld Research Institute (marine science), Tijuana River National Estuarine Research Reserve. (marine science), Old Globe Theater (dramatic arts).

Computer facilities: Computer purchase and lease plans are available. 951 computers available on campus for general student use. A campuswide network can be accessed from student residence rooms and from off campus. Online class registration is available.
Website: http://www.sandiego.edu/

General Application Contact: Monica Mahon, Associate Director of Graduate Admissions, 619-260-4524, Fax: 619-260-4158, E-mail: grads@sandiego.edu.

GRADUATE UNITS

College of Arts and Sciences Students: 39 full-time (20 women), 35 part-time (18 women); includes 21 minority (6 Black or African American, non-Hispanic/Latino; 1 American Indian or Alaska Native, non-Hispanic/Latino; 5 Asian, non-Hispanic/Latino; 8 Hispanic/Latino; 1 Two or more races, non-Hispanic/Latino), 2 international. Average age 29. *Faculty:* 14 full-time (5 women), 4 part-time/adjunct (1 woman). *Financial support:* In 2015–16, 55 students received support, including 13 fellowships; career-related internships or fieldwork, Federal Work-Study, institutionally sponsored loans, scholarships/grants, and unspecified assistantships also available. Support available to part-time students. Financial award application deadline: 4/1; financial award applicants required to submit FAFSA. In 2015, 29 master's awarded. *Degree program information:* Part-time and evening/weekend programs available. Part-time, evening/weekend. Offers acting (MFA); arts and sciences (MA, MFA, MS); international relations (MA); marine science (MS). *Application deadline:* Applications are processed on a rolling basis. *Application fee:* $45. Electronic applications accepted. *Application Contact:* Monica Mahon, Associate Director of Graduate Admissions, 619-260-4524, Fax: 619-260-4158, E-mail: grads@sandiego.edu. *Dean,* Dr. Noelle Norton, 619-260-4545.

Division of Professional and Continuing Education Students: 92 part-time (22 women); includes 39 minority (3 Black or African American, non-Hispanic/Latino; 3 Asian, non-Hispanic/Latino; 31 Hispanic/Latino; 1 Native Hawaiian or other Pacific Islander, non-Hispanic/Latino; 1 Two or more races, non-Hispanic/Latino). Average age 36. 110 applicants, 93% accepted, 92 enrolled. *Faculty:* 2 part-time/adjunct (1 woman). *Financial support:* Application deadline: 4/1; applicants required to submit FAFSA. *Degree program information:* Part-time and evening/weekend programs available. Part-time-only, evening/weekend, 100% online. Offers law enforcement and public safety leadership (MS). *Application deadline:* For fall admission, 8/2 for domestic students; for spring admission, 11/7 for domestic students; for summer admission, 4/11 for domestic students. Applications are processed on a rolling basis. *Application fee:* $45. Electronic applications accepted. *Application Contact:* Monica Mahon, Associate Director of Graduate Admissions, 619-260-4524, Fax: 619-260-4158, E-mail: grads@sandiego.edu. *Dean,* Dr. Jason Lemon, 619-260-4585, E-mail: jasonlemon@sandiego.edu.

Hahn School of Nursing and Health Science Students: 178 full-time (151 women), 157 part-time (131 women); includes 143 minority (25 Black or African American, non-Hispanic/Latino; 2 American Indian or Alaska Native, non-Hispanic/Latino; 53 Asian, non-Hispanic/Latino; 49 Hispanic/Latino; 4 Native Hawaiian or other Pacific Islander, non-Hispanic/Latino; 10 Two or more races, non-Hispanic/Latino), 5 international. Average age 36. *Faculty:* 27 full-time (23 women), 46 part-time/adjunct (41 women). *Financial support:* In 2015–16, 217 students received support. Scholarships/grants and traineeships available. Support available to part-time students. Financial award application deadline: 4/1; financial award applicants required to submit FAFSA. In 2015, 122 master's, 43 doctorates awarded. *Degree program information:* Part-time and evening/weekend programs available. Part-time, evening/weekend. Offers adult-gerontology clinical nurse specialist (MSN); adult-gerontology nurse practitioner/family nurse practitioner (MSN); executive nurse leader (MSN); family nurse practitioner (MSN); family/lifespan psychiatric-mental health nurse practitioner (MSN); healthcare informatics (MS, MSN); nursing (PhD); nursing practice (DNP). *Application deadline:* Applications are processed on a rolling basis. *Application fee:* $45. Electronic applications accepted. *Application Contact:* Monica Mahon, Associate Director of Graduate Admissions, 619-260-4524, Fax: 619-260-4158, E-mail: grads@sandiego.edu. *Dean,* Dr. Sally Hardin, 619-260-4550, Fax: 619-260-6814.

Joan B. Kroc School of Peace Studies Students: 33 full-time (22 women); includes 8 minority (1 Black or African American, non-Hispanic/Latino; 2 Asian, non-Hispanic/Latino; 4 Hispanic/Latino; 1 Two or more races, non-Hispanic/Latino), 7 international. Average age 28. *Faculty:* 5 full-time (2 women), 2 part-time/adjunct (1 woman). *Financial support:* In 2015–16, 31 students received support. Career-related internships or fieldwork, Federal Work-Study, institutionally sponsored loans, scholarships/grants, and unspecified assistantships available. Support available to part-time students. Financial award application deadline: 4/1; financial award applicants required to submit FAFSA. In 2015, 25 master's awarded. Offers peace and justice (MA); peacebuilding (MA). *Application deadline:* For fall admission, 1/15 for domestic and international students. *Application fee:* $45. Electronic applications accepted. *Application Contact:* Monica Mahon, Associate Director of Graduate Admissions, 619-260-4524, Fax: 619-260-4158, E-mail: grads@sandiego.edu. *Dean,* Dr. Patricia Marquez, 619-260-7919.

School of Business Students: 216 full-time (77 women), 191 part-time (70 women); includes 102 minority (17 Black or African American, non-Hispanic/Latino; 26 Asian, non-Hispanic/Latino; 48 Hispanic/Latino; 2 Native Hawaiian or other Pacific Islander, non-Hispanic/Latino; 9 Two or more races, non-Hispanic/Latino), 79 international. Average age 32. *Faculty:* 33 full-time (9 women), 21 part-time/adjunct (7 women). *Financial support:* In 2015–16, 200 students received support. Career-related internships or fieldwork, Federal Work-Study, institutionally sponsored loans, and scholarships/grants available. Support available to part-time students. Financial award application deadline: 4/1; financial award applicants required to submit FAFSA. In 2015, 261 master's awarded. *Degree program information:* Part-time and evening/weekend programs available. Part-time, evening/weekend. Offers accountancy (MS); business (IMBA, MBA, MS, MSF, Certificate); business administration (MBA); executive leadership (MS); finance (MSF); global leadership (MS); real estate (MS); supply chain management (MS, Certificate); taxation (MS). *Application fee:* $80. Electronic applications accepted. *Application Contact:* Monica Mahon, Associate Director of Graduate Admissions, 619-260-4524, Fax: 619-260-4158, E-mail: grads@sandiego.edu. *Dean,* Dr. Jaime Alonso Gmez, 619-260-4886, E-mail: sbadean@sandiego.edu.

School of Law Students: 680 full-time (340 women), 132 part-time (52 women); includes 251 minority (22 Black or African American, non-Hispanic/Latino; 9 American Indian or Alaska Native, non-Hispanic/Latino; 115 Asian, non-Hispanic/Latino; 97 Hispanic/Latino; 2 Native Hawaiian or other Pacific Islander, non-Hispanic/Latino; 6 Two or more races, non-Hispanic/Latino), 26 international. Average age 27. 3,286 applicants, 262 enrolled. *Faculty:* 46 full-time (15 women), 55 part-time/adjunct (17 women). *Financial support:* In 2015–16, 565 students received support. Career-related internships or fieldwork, Federal Work-Study, institutionally sponsored loans, and scholarships/grants available. Support available to part-time students. Financial award application deadline: 3/1; financial award applicants required to submit FAFSA. In 2015, 60 master's, 248 doctorates awarded. *Degree program information:* Part-time and evening/weekend programs available. Part-time, evening/weekend. Offers business and corporate law (LL M); comparative law (LL M); general studies (LL M); international law (LL M); law (JD); taxation (LL M, Diploma). *Application deadline:* For fall admission, 2/1 priority date for domestic students. Applications are processed on a rolling basis. Electronic applications accepted. *Application Contact:* Jorge Garcia, Assistant Dean, JD Admissions, 619-260-4528, Fax: 619-260-2218, E-mail: jdinfo@sandiego.edu. *Dean,* Dr. Stephen C. Ferruolo, 619-260-4527, E-mail: lawdean@sandiego.edu.

School of Leadership and Education Sciences Students: 287 full-time (233 women), 381 part-time (298 women); includes 266 minority (42 Black or African American, non-Hispanic/Latino; 1 American Indian or Alaska Native, non-Hispanic/Latino; 42 Asian, non-Hispanic/Latino; 144 Hispanic/Latino; 2 Native Hawaiian or other Pacific Islander, non-Hispanic/Latino; 35 Two or more races, non-Hispanic/Latino), 25 international. Average age 32. *Faculty:* 29 full-time (16 women), 78 part-time/adjunct (47 women). *Financial support:* In 2015–16, 375 students received support. Career-related internships or fieldwork, Federal Work-Study, institutionally sponsored loans, unspecified assistantships, and stipends available. Support available to part-time students. Financial award application deadline: 4/1; financial award applicants required to submit FAFSA. In 2015, 216 master's, 10 doctorates awarded. *Degree program information:* Part-time and evening/weekend programs available. Part-time, evening/weekend. Offers clinical mental health counseling (MA); higher education leadership (MA); leadership and education sciences (M Ed, MA, MAT, PhD, Certificate); leadership studies (MA, PhD, Certificate); marital and family therapy (MA); nonprofit leadership and management (MA); special education with deaf and hard of hearing (M Ed); teaching (MAT); TESOL, literacy and culture (M Ed). *Application fee:* $45. *Application Contact:* Monica Mahon, Associate Director of Graduate Admissions, 619-260-4524, Fax: 619-260-4158, E-mail: grads@sandiego.edu. *Dean,* Dr. Nicholas Ladany, 619-260-4540, Fax: 619-260-6835, E-mail: nladany@sandiego.edu.

UNIVERSITY OF SAN FRANCISCO, San Francisco, CA 94117-1080

General Information Independent-religious, coed, university. *Enrollment:* 10,828 graduate, professional, and undergraduate students; 3,298 full-time matriculated graduate/professional students (2,088 women), 690 part-time matriculated graduate/professional students (495 women). *Enrollment by degree level:* 3,046 master's, 942 doctoral. *Graduate faculty:* 206 full-time (106 women), 302 part-time/adjunct (171 women). *Tuition, area resident:* Full-time $22,410; part-time $1245 per credit. Tuition and fees vary according to course load, degree level and campus/location. *Graduate housing:* Room and/or apartments available on a first-come, first-served basis to single students; on-campus housing not available to married students. Typical cost: $11,010 per year ($15,490 including board). Room and board charges vary according to board plan, campus/location and housing facility selected. *Student services:* Campus employment opportunities, career counseling, exercise/wellness program, free psychological counseling, international student services, low-cost health insurance, multicultural affairs office, services for students with disabilities, teacher training, writing training. *Library:* Gleeson Library plus 2 others. *Collection:* Books: 738,947 (physical), 407,670 (digital/electronic); Serial titles: 924 (physical), 144,845 (digital/electronic); Databases: 240. Study areas open 24 hours, 5–7 days a week; students can reserve study rooms. *Research affiliation:* NASA-Ames Research Center.

Computer facilities: Computer purchase and lease plans are available. 265 computers available on campus for general student use. A campuswide network can be accessed from student residence rooms and from off campus. Online class registration is available.
Website: http://www.usfca.edu/

General Application Contact: Information Contact, 415-422-4723, Fax: 415-422-2217, E-mail: graduate@usfca.edu.

GRADUATE UNITS

College of Arts and Sciences Students: 748 full-time (377 women), 95 part-time (56 women); includes 279 minority (44 Black or African American, non-Hispanic/Latino; 71 Asian, non-Hispanic/Latino; 126 Hispanic/Latino; 4 Native Hawaiian or other Pacific Islander, non-Hispanic/Latino; 34 Two or more races, non-Hispanic/Latino), 187 international. Average age 27. 1,816 applicants, 51% accepted, 397 enrolled. *Faculty:* 59 full-time (25 women), 60 part-time/adjunct (25 women). *Financial support:* In 2015–16, 324 students received support. Fellowships, research assistantships, teaching assistantships, career-related internships or fieldwork, Federal Work-Study, institutionally sponsored loans, scholarships/grants, and tuition waivers (partial) available. Support available to part-time students. Financial award application deadline: 8/1; financial award applicants required to submit FAFSA. In 2015, 379 master's awarded. *Degree program information:* Part-time and evening/weekend programs available. Part-time, evening/weekend. Offers analytics (MS); arts and sciences (MA, MCA, MFA, MMS, MPA, MS, PSM); Asia Pacific studies (MA); biology (MS); biotechnology (PSM); chemistry (MS); collegiate athletics (MCA); computer science (MS); economics (MA, MS); energy systems management (MS); environmental management (MS); international and development economics (MA); international studies (MA); migration studies (MMS); museum studies (MA); professional communication (MA); public affairs (MPA); sport management (MA); urban affairs (MA); writing (MFA). *Application fee:* $55. Electronic applications accepted. *Application Contact:* Mark Landerghini, Information Contact, 415-422-5101, Fax: 415-422-5134, E-mail: asgraduate@usfca.edu. *Dean,* Dr. Marcelo Camperi, 415-422-6373.

School of Education Students: 814 full-time (617 women), 241 part-time (186 women); includes 489 minority (86 Black or African American, non-Hispanic/Latino; 126 Asian, non-Hispanic/Latino; 220 Hispanic/Latino; 10 Native Hawaiian or other Pacific Islander, non-Hispanic/Latino; 47 Two or more races, non-Hispanic/Latino), 75 international. Average age 32. 1,203 applicants, 78% accepted, 496 enrolled. *Faculty:* 36 full-time (23 women), 122 part-time/adjunct (83 women). *Financial support:* In 2015–16, 137 students received support. Fellowships, research assistantships, and teaching assistantships available. Financial award application deadline: 3/2; financial award applicants required to submit FAFSA. In 2015, 394 master's, 21 doctorates awarded. *Degree program information:* Part-time and evening/weekend programs available. Part-time, evening/weekend. Offers Catholic school leadership (MA, Ed D); Catholic school teaching (MA); counseling (MA); digital media and learning (MA); digital technologies for teaching and learning (MA); education (MA, Ed D); human rights education (MA); international and multicultural education (MA, Ed D); learning and instruction (MA, Ed D); multicultural literature for children and young adults (MA); organization and leadership (MA, Ed D); special education (MA, Ed D); teaching (MA); teaching English to speakers of other languages (MA); teaching reading (MA); teaching urban education and social justice (MA). *Application deadline:* For fall admission, 5/1 priority date for domestic and international students; for spring admission, 10/1 priority date for domestic and international students. Applications are processed on a rolling basis. *Application fee:* $55 ($65 for international students). Electronic applications accepted. *Application Contact:* Peter Cole, Admission Coordinator, 415-422-5467, E-mail: schoolofeducation@usfca.edu. *Dean,* Dr. Kevin Kumashiro, 415-422-6525.

School of Law Students: 454 full-time (244 women), 144 part-time (79 women); includes 301 minority (41 Black or African American, non-Hispanic/Latino; 101 Asian, non-Hispanic/Latino; 116 Hispanic/Latino; 2 Native Hawaiian or other Pacific Islander, non-Hispanic/Latino; 41 Two or more races, non-Hispanic/Latino), 18 international. Average age 28. 2,321 applicants, 63% accepted, 255 enrolled. *Faculty:* 34 full-time (17 women), 32 part-time/adjunct (4 women). *Financial support:* In 2015–16, 274 students received support. Career-related internships or fieldwork, Federal Work-Study, and institutionally sponsored loans available. Support available to part-time students. Financial award application deadline: 3/2; financial award applicants required to submit FAFSA. In 2015, 17 master's, 164 doctorates awarded. *Degree program information:* Part-time and evening/weekend programs available. Part-time, evening/weekend. Offers intellectual property and technology law (LL M); international transactions and comparative law (LL M); law (LL M, JD). *Application deadline:* For fall admission, 4/1 for domestic students. Applications are processed on a rolling basis. Electronic applications accepted. *Application Contact:* Alan P. Guerrero, Director of Admissions, 415-422-2975, E-mail: lawadmissions@usfca.edu. *Dean,* John Trasvina, 415-422-6304.

School of Management Students: 706 full-time (379 women), 26 part-time (18 women); includes 275 minority (48 Black or African American, non-Hispanic/Latino; 100 Asian, non-Hispanic/Latino; 96 Hispanic/Latino; 8 Native Hawaiian or other Pacific Islander, non-Hispanic/Latino; 23 Two or more races, non-Hispanic/Latino), 189 international. Average age 31. 1,031 applicants, 72% accepted, 340 enrolled. *Faculty:* 45 full-time (12 women), 29 part-time/adjunct (9 women). *Financial support:* In 2015–16, 179 students received support. Scholarships/grants available. Support available to part-time students. Financial award application deadline: 3/2; financial award applicants required to submit FAFSA. In 2015, 341 master's awarded. *Degree program information:* Part-time and evening/weekend programs available. Part-time, evening/weekend, online learning. Offers entrepreneurship and innovation (MBA); executive business administration (MBA); finance (MBA); financial analysis (MSFA); global entrepreneurial management (MGEM); health services administration (MPA); information systems (MS); international business (MBA); management (MBA, MGEM, MNA, MPA, MS, MSFA, MSOD, MSRM); marketing (MBA); nonprofit administration (MNA); organization development (MBA); public administration (MPA). *Application fee:* $55. Electronic applications accepted. *Application Contact:* Elisabeth Merkel, 415-422-2221, Fax: 415-422-6315, E-mail: management@usfca.edu. *Dean,* Dr. Elizabeth Davis, 415-422-2221, E-mail: management@usfca.edu.

School of Nursing and Health Professions Students: 576 full-time (471 women), 184 part-time (156 women); includes 419 minority (70 Black or African American, non-Hispanic/Latino; 1 American Indian or Alaska Native, non-Hispanic/Latino; 196 Asian, non-Hispanic/Latino; 99 Hispanic/Latino; 17 Native Hawaiian or other Pacific Islander, non-Hispanic/Latino; 36 Two or more races, non-Hispanic/Latino), 25 international. Average age 35. 663 applicants, 63% accepted, 260 enrolled. *Faculty:* 43 full-time (33 women), 59 part-time/adjunct (50 women). *Financial support:* In 2015–16, 108 students received support. Institutionally sponsored loans available. Financial award application deadline: 3/2. In 2015, 201 master's, 31 doctorates awarded. *Degree program information:* Part-time programs available. Part-time, 100% online, blended/hybrid learning. Offers behavioral health (MSBH); clinical nurse leader (MS); executive leadership (DNP); family nurse practitioner (DNP); healthcare systems leadership (DNP); nursing and health professions

(MPH, MSBH, MSN, DNP, Psy D); psychiatric mental health nurse practitioner (DNP); public health (MPH). *Application deadline:* Applications are processed on a rolling basis. Electronic applications accepted. *Application Contact:* Ingrid McVanner, Information Contact, 415-422-2746, Fax: 415-422-2217. *Dean,* Dr. Judith Karshmer, 415-422-6681, Fax: 415-422-6877, E-mail: nursing@usfca.edu.

UNIVERSITY OF SASKATCHEWAN, Saskatoon, SK S7N 5A2, Canada

General Information Province-supported, coed, university. *Graduate housing:* Rooms and/or apartments available on a first-come, first-served basis to single and married students. *Research affiliation:* Canada Agriculture (agriculture research), Saskatchewan Research Council, University Hospital (cancer research), Innovation Place, Vaccine and Infectious Disease Organization/InterVac Laboratory (vaccinology and immunotherapeutics), Canadian Light Source.

GRADUATE UNITS

College of Dentistry Offers dentistry (DMD). Electronic applications accepted.

College of Graduate Studies and Research ***Degree program information:*** Part-time programs available. Part-time. Electronic applications accepted.

College of Agriculture Degree program information: Part-time programs available. Part-time. Offers agricultural economics (M Ag, M Sc, MA, PhD, PGD); agriculture (M Ag, M Sc, MA, PhD, Diploma, PGD); animal and poultry science (M Ag, M Sc, PhD); applied microbiology and food science (M Ag, M Sc, PhD); plant sciences (M Sc, PhD); soil science (M Ag, M Sc, PhD, Diploma).

College of Arts and Science Degree program information: Part-time programs available. Part-time. Offers archaeology (MA, PhD); art and art history (MFA); arts and science (M Math, M Mus, M Sc, MA, MFA, PhD, Diploma); biology (M Sc, PhD); chemistry (M Sc, PhD); computer science (M Sc, PhD); drama (MA); economics (MA, Diploma); English (MA, PhD); geography (M Sc, MA, PhD); geological sciences (M Sc, PhD, Diploma); history (MA, PhD); languages and linguistics (MA); mathematics and statistics (M Math, MA, PhD); music (M Mus, MA); native studies (MA, PhD); philosophy (MA); physics and engineering physics (M Sc, PhD); political studies (MA); psychology (MA, PhD); religion and culture (MA); sociology (MA, PhD); women's and gender studies (MA, PhD). Electronic applications accepted.

College of Education Degree program information: Part-time programs available. Part-time. Offers curriculum studies (M Ed, PhD, Diploma); education (M Ed, MC Ed, PhD, Diploma); educational administration (M Ed, PhD, Diploma); educational foundations (M Ed, MC Ed, PhD, Diploma); educational psychology and special education (M Ed, PhD, Diploma). Electronic applications accepted.

College of Engineering Degree program information: Part-time programs available. Part-time. Offers biological engineering (M Eng, M Sc, PhD); biomedical engineering (M Eng, M Sc, PhD); chemical engineering (M Eng, M Sc, PhD); civil and geological engineering (M Eng, M Sc, PhD); electrical engineering (M Eng, M Sc, PhD, PGD); engineering (M Eng, M Sc, PhD, PGD); mechanical engineering (M Eng, M Sc, PhD). Electronic applications accepted.

College of Kinesiology Offers kinesiology (M Sc, PhD, Diploma).

College of Law Degree program information: Part-time programs available. Part-time. Offers law (LL M, JD).

College of Nursing Degree program information: Part-time programs available. Part-time. Offers nursing (MN).

College of Pharmacy and Nutrition Offers pharmacy and nutrition (M Sc, PhD).

Edwards School of Business Degree program information: Part-time programs available. Part-time. Offers accounting (M Sc, MP Acc); agribusiness management (MBA); biotechnology management (MBA); business (M Sc, MBA, MP Acc); finance (M Sc); health services management (MBA); indigenous management (MBA); international business management (MBA); marketing (M Sc).

School of Environment and Sustainability Offers environment and sustainability (MES).

School of Public Policy Offers public policy (MIT, MPA, MPP, PhD).

Toxicology Centre Offers toxicology (M Sc, PhD, Diploma).

College of Medicine Offers anatomy and cell biology (M Sc, PhD); biochemistry (M Sc, PhD); community health and epidemiology (M Sc, PhD); medicine (M Sc, DPT, MD, PhD); microbiology and immunology (M Sc, PhD); obstetrics, gynecology and reproductive services (M Sc, PhD); pathology (M Sc, PhD); pharmacology (M Sc, PhD); physiology (M Sc, PhD); psychiatry (M Sc, PhD); surgery (M Sc).

Western College of Veterinary Medicine Offers large animal clinical sciences (M Sc, M Vet Sc, PhD); small animal clinical sciences (M Sc, M Vet Sc, PhD); veterinary anatomy (M Sc); veterinary anesthesiology, radiology and surgery (M Vet Sc); veterinary biomedical sciences (M Sc, M Vet Sc, PhD); veterinary internal medicine (M Vet Sc); veterinary medicine (M Sc, M Vet Sc, DVM, PhD); veterinary microbiology (M Sc, M Vet Sc, PhD); veterinary pathology (M Sc, M Vet Sc, PhD); veterinary physiological sciences (M Sc, PhD).

THE UNIVERSITY OF SCRANTON, Scranton, PA 18510

General Information Independent-religious, coed, comprehensive institution. CGS member. *Enrollment:* 5,422 graduate, professional, and undergraduate students; 502 full-time matriculated graduate/professional students (299 women), 929 part-time matriculated graduate/professional students (531 women). *Enrollment by degree level:* 1,290 master's, 128 doctoral, 5 other advanced degrees. *Graduate faculty:* 94 full-time (40 women), 59 part-time/adjunct (32 women). *Graduate housing:* Room and/or apartments available on a first-come, first-served basis to single students; on-campus housing not available to married students. Typical cost: $8100 per year. Room charges vary according to board plan and housing facility selected. *Student services:* Campus employment opportunities, campus safety program, career counseling, exercise/wellness program, free psychological counseling, international student services, multicultural affairs office, services for students with disabilities, writing training. *Library:* Harry and Jeanette Weinberg Memorial Library. *Collection:* Books: 329,019 (physical), 174,291 (digital/electronic); Serial titles: 2,704 (physical), 51,182 (digital/electronic); Databases: 118. Weekly public service hours: 95; study areas open 24 hours, 5–7 days a week; students can reserve study rooms. *Research affiliation:* Allied Services (rehabilitation), Lackawanna River Corridor Association (environment), Universidad Iberoamericana (counseling and human services), Wyoming Valley Health Care System (nursing), Community Medical Center (health services), National Health Management Center (health care management).

Computer facilities: Computer purchase and lease plans are available. 883 computers available on campus for general student use. A campuswide network can be accessed from student residence rooms and from off campus. Online class registration is available.
Website: http://www.scranton.edu/

General Application Contact: Caitlyn Hollingshead, Director of Graduate, Transfer and International Admissions, 570-941-6202, Fax: 570-941-5995, E-mail: caitlyn.hollingshead@scranton.edu.

GRADUATE UNITS

College of Arts and Sciences Students: 15 full-time (3 women), 22 part-time (6 women); includes 6 minority (1 Asian, non-Hispanic/Latino; 3 Hispanic/Latino; 2 Two or more races, non-Hispanic/Latino), 2 international. Average age 24. 105 applicants, 37% accepted, 27 enrolled. *Financial support:* Application deadline: 3/1; applicants required to submit FAFSA. *Degree program information:* Part-time and evening/weekend programs available. Part-time, evening/weekend, 100% online. Offers arts and sciences (MA, MS); biochemistry (MS); chemistry (MS); clinical chemistry (MS); theology (MA). *Application deadline:* For fall admission, 6/1 for international students; for spring admission, 11/1 for international students; for summer admission, 3/1 for international students. Applications are processed on a rolling basis. *Application fee:* $0. Electronic applications accepted. *Application Contact:* Caitlyn Hollingshead, Director of Graduate, Transfer and International Admissions, 570-941-6202, Fax: 570-941-5995, E-mail: caitlyn.hollingshead@scranton.edu. *Dean,* Dr. Brian P. Conniff, 570-941-7560, E-mail: brian.conniff@scranton.edu.

Kania School of Management Students: 107 full-time (27 women), 398 part-time (172 women); includes 89 minority (41 Black or African American, non-Hispanic/Latino; 1 American Indian or Alaska Native, non-Hispanic/Latino; 24 Asian, non-Hispanic/Latino; 17 Hispanic/Latino; 6 Two or more races, non-Hispanic/Latino), 64 international. Average age 34. Offers accountancy (M Acc); accounting (MBA); finance (MBA); general business administration (MBA); health care management (MBA); international business (MBA); management (M Acc, MBA, MS); management information systems (MBA); marketing (MBA); operations management (MBA); software engineering (MS). *Application Contact:* Caitlyn Hollingshead, Director of Graduate, Transfer and International Admissions, 570-941-6202, Fax: 570-941-5995, E-mail: caitlyn.hollingshead@scranton.edu. *Dean,* Dr. Michael O. Mensah, 570-941-4049, E-mail: mensahm2@scranton.edu.

Panuska College of Professional Studies Students: 380 full-time (269 women), 509 part-time (353 women); includes 112 minority (46 Black or African American, non-Hispanic/Latino; 23 Asian, non-Hispanic/Latino; 38 Hispanic/Latino; 5 Two or more races, non-Hispanic/Latino), 14 international. Average age 30. Offers clinical mental health counseling (MS); curriculum and instruction (MS); educational administration (MS); family nurse practitioner (MSN, PMC); health administration (MHA); human resources (MS); nurse anesthesia (MSN, PMC); nursing leadership (DNP); occupational therapy (MS); physical therapy (DPT); professional counseling (CAGS); reading education (MS); rehabilitation counseling (MS); school counseling (MS); secondary education (MS); special education (MS). *Application Contact:* Caitlyn Hollingshead, Director of Graduate, Transfer and International Admissions, 570-941-6202, Fax: 570-941-5995, E-mail: caitlyn.hollingshead@scranton.edu. *Dean,* Dr. Debra A. Pellegrino, 570-941-6305, E-mail: pellegrinod2@scranton.edu.

UNIVERSITY OF SIOUX FALLS, Sioux Falls, SD 57105-1699

General Information Independent-religious, coed, comprehensive institution. *Graduate housing:* Rooms and/or apartments available on a first-come, first-served basis to single and married students.

GRADUATE UNITS

Fredrikson School of Education ***Degree program information:*** Part-time and evening/weekend programs available. Part-time, evening/weekend. Offers educational administration (Ed S); leadership in reading (M Ed); leadership in schools (M Ed); leadership in technology (M Ed); teaching (M Ed). Admission in summer only.

Vucurevich School of Business ***Degree program information:*** Part-time and evening/weekend programs available. Part-time, evening/weekend. Offers entrepreneurial leadership (MBA); general management (MBA); health care management (MBA); marketing (MBA).

UNIVERSITY OF SOUTH AFRICA, Pretoria 0003, South Africa

General Information Private, coed, university.

GRADUATE UNITS

College of Agriculture and Environmental Sciences Offers agriculture (MS); consumer science (MCS); environmental management (MA, MS, PhD); environmental science (MA, MS, PhD); geography (MA, MS, PhD); horticulture (M Tech); human ecology (MHE); life sciences (MS); nature conservation (M Tech).

College of Economic and Management Sciences Offers accounting (D Admin, D Com); accounting science (DA); auditing (D Admin, D Com); business administration (M Tech); business economics (D Admin); business leadership (DBL); business management (D Admin, D Com); economic management analysis (M Tech); economics (D Admin, D Com, PhD); human resource development (M Tech); industrial psychology (D Admin, D Com, PhD); logistics (D Com); marketing (M Tech); public administration (D Admin, D Com, DPA, PhD); public management (M Tech); quantitative management (D Admin, D Com); real estate (M Tech); statistics (D Admin, PhD); tourism management (D Admin, D Com); transport economics (D Admin, D Com).

College of Human Sciences Offers adult education (M Ed); African languages (MA, PhD); African politics (MA, PhD); Afrikaans (MA, PhD); ancient history (MA, PhD); ancient Near Eastern studies (MA, PhD); anthropology (MA, PhD); applied linguistics (MA); Arabic (MA, PhD); archaeology (MA); art history (MA); Biblical archaeology (MA); Biblical studies (M Th, D Th, PhD); Christian spirituality (M Th, D Th); church history (M Th, D Th); classical studies (MA, PhD); clinical psychology (MA); communication (MA, PhD); comparative education (M Ed, Ed D); consulting psychology (D Admin, D Com, PhD); curriculum studies (M Ed, Ed D); development studies (M Admin, MA, D Admin, PhD); didactics (M Ed, Ed D); education (M Tech); education management (M Ed, Ed D); educational psychology (M Ed); English (MA); environmental education (M Ed); French (MA, PhD); German (MA, PhD); Greek (MA); guidance and counseling (M Ed); health studies (MA, PhD); history (MA, PhD); history of education (Ed D); inclusive education (M Ed, Ed D); information and communications technology policy and regulation (MA); information science (MA, MIS, PhD); international politics (MA, PhD); Islamic studies (MA, PhD); Italian (MA, PhD); Judaica (MA, PhD); linguistics (MA, PhD); mathematical education (M Ed); mathematics education (MA); missiology (M Th, D Th); modern Hebrew (MA, PhD); musicology (MA, MMus, D Mus, PhD); natural science education (M Ed); New Testament (M Th, D Th); Old Testament (D Th); pastoral therapy (M Th, D Th); philosophy (MA); philosophy of education (M Ed, Ed D); politics (MA, PhD); Portuguese (MA, PhD); practical theology (M Th, D Th); psychology (MA, MS, PhD); psychology of education (M Ed, Ed D); public health (MA); religious studies (MA, D Th, PhD); Romance languages (MA); Russian (MA, PhD); Semitic languages (MA, PhD); social behavior studies in HIV/AIDS (MA); social science (mental health) (MA); social science in development studies (MA); social science in psychology (MA); social science in social work (MA); social science in sociology (MA); social work (MSW,

DSW, PhD); socio-education (M Ed, Ed D); sociolinguistics (MA); sociology (MA, PhD); Spanish (MA, PhD); systematic theology (M Th, D Th); TESOL (teaching English to speakers of other languages) (MA); theological ethics (M Th, D Th); theory of literature (MA, PhD); urban ministries (D Th); urban ministry (M Th).

College of Law Offers correctional services management (M Tech); criminology (MA, PhD); law (LL M, LL D); penology (MA, PhD); police science (MA, PhD); policing (M Tech); security risk management (M Tech); social science in criminology (MA).

College of Science, Engineering and Technology Offers chemical engineering (M Tech); information technology (M Tech).

Graduate School of Business Leadership Offers business leadership (MBA, MBL, DBL).

Institute for Science and Technology Education Offers mathematics, science and technology education (M Sc, PhD).

UNIVERSITY OF SOUTH ALABAMA, Mobile, AL 36688-0002

General Information State-supported, coed, university. CGS member. *Enrollment:* 16,211 graduate, professional, and undergraduate students; 4,101 full-time matriculated graduate/professional students (3,050 women), 586 part-time matriculated graduate/professional students (462 women). *Enrollment by degree level:* 3,583 master's, 952 doctoral, 152 other advanced degrees. *Graduate faculty:* 304 full-time (141 women), 129 part-time/adjunct (108 women). Tuition, state resident: full-time $9480; part-time $395 per credit hour. Tuition, nonresident: full-time $18,960; part-time $790 per credit hour. *Graduate housing:* Room and/or apartments available on a first-come, first-served basis to single students; on-campus housing not available to married students. Typical cost: $3850 per year ($7250 including board). Room and board charges vary according to board plan and housing facility selected. Housing application deadline: 5/1. *Student services:* Campus employment opportunities, career counseling, exercise/wellness program, free psychological counseling, grant writing training, international student services, low-cost health insurance, multicultural affairs office, services for students with disabilities, writing training. *Library:* Marx Library plus 5 others. *Collection:* Books: 65,647 (physical), 290,596 (digital/electronic); Serial titles: 3,190 (physical); Databases: 31. *Research affiliation:* Dauphin Island Marine Laboratory (marine sciences), Mobile County Health Department (health), Morehouse School of Medicine (medicine), National Institute on Minority Health and Health Disparities (health), Oak Ridge National Laboratories (physics), Jackson State University (health).

Computer facilities: A campuswide network can be accessed from student residence rooms and from off campus. Online class registration is available.
Website: http://www.southalabama.edu/

General Application Contact: Dr. B. Keith Harrison, Dean, Graduate School, 251-460-6310, Fax: 251-461-1513, E-mail: kharrison@southalabama.edu.

GRADUATE UNITS

College of Arts and Sciences Students: 126 full-time (76 women), 50 part-time (30 women); includes 35 minority (25 Black or African American, non-Hispanic/Latino; 1 American Indian or Alaska Native, non-Hispanic/Latino; 5 Asian, non-Hispanic/Latino; 1 Native Hawaiian or other Pacific Islander, non-Hispanic/Latino; 3 Two or more races, non-Hispanic/Latino), 5 international. Average age 29. 187 applicants, 40% accepted, 57 enrolled. *Faculty:* 87 full-time (25 women), 5 part-time/adjunct (2 women). *Financial support:* Research assistantships, teaching assistantships, career-related internships or fieldwork, Federal Work-Study, institutionally sponsored loans, scholarships/grants, and unspecified assistantships available. Support available to part-time students. Financial award application deadline: 4/1. In 2015, 56 master's, 2 doctorates awarded. *Degree program information:* Part-time and evening/weekend programs available. Part-time, evening/weekend. Offers arts and sciences (MA, MM, MPA, MS, PhD); biological sciences (MS); collaborative keyboard (MM); communication (MA); English (MA); history (MA); marine sciences (MS, PhD); mathematics (MS); music education (MM); performance-piano (MM); performance-voice (MM); psychology (MS); public administration (MPA); sociology (MA). *Application deadline:* For fall admission, 7/15 priority date for domestic students, 6/15 priority date for international students; for spring admission, 12/1 priority date for domestic students, 11/1 priority date for international students. Applications are processed on a rolling basis. *Application fee:* $35. Electronic applications accepted. *Application Contact:* Dr. Eric Loomis, Associate Dean, College of Arts and Sciences, 251-460-7811, Fax: 251-461-1744, E-mail: ejloomis@southalabama.edu. *Dean, College of Arts and Sciences,* Dr. Andrzej Wierzbicki, 251-460-6280, Fax: 251-460-7928, E-mail: awierzbicki@southalabama.edu.

College of Education Students: 313 full-time (238 women), 130 part-time (106 women); includes 112 minority (85 Black or African American, non-Hispanic/Latino; 4 American Indian or Alaska Native, non-Hispanic/Latino; 6 Asian, non-Hispanic/Latino; 9 Hispanic/Latino; 2 Native Hawaiian or other Pacific Islander, non-Hispanic/Latino; 6 Two or more races, non-Hispanic/Latino), 2 international. Average age 34. 228 applicants, 43% accepted, 83 enrolled. *Faculty:* 35 full-time (19 women), 13 part-time/adjunct (10 women). *Financial support:* Fellowships, research assistantships, teaching assistantships, career-related internships or fieldwork, Federal Work-Study, institutionally sponsored loans, scholarships/grants, and unspecified assistantships available. Support available to part-time students. Financial award application deadline: 5/31; financial award applicants required to submit FAFSA. In 2015, 123 master's, 4 doctorates, 5 other advanced degrees awarded. *Degree program information:* Part-time programs available. Part-time, online learning. Offers clinical mental health counseling (MS); early childhood education (M Ed); education (M Ed, MS, Ed D, PhD, Ed S); education leadership (Ed S); educational leadership (M Ed, Ed D); educational media (M Ed); elementary education (M Ed); exercise science (MS); health education (M Ed); instructional design and development (M Ed, PhD); physical education (M Ed); reading education (M Ed); school counseling (M Ed); science education (M Ed); secondary education (M Ed); special education (M Ed, Ed S); teacher leader (Ed S). *Application deadline:* For fall admission, 7/15 priority date for domestic students, 6/15 priority date for international students; for spring admission, 11/1 priority date for domestic and international students; for summer admission, 4/15 priority date for domestic students. Applications are processed on a rolling basis. *Application fee:* $35. Electronic applications accepted. *Application Contact:* Dr. Susan Santoli, Director of Graduate Studies, 251-380-2738, Fax: 251-380-2758, E-mail: ssantoli@southalabama.edu. *Dean, College of Education,* Dr. Andrea M. Kent, 251-380-2738, E-mail: akent@southalabama.edu.

College of Engineering Students: 180 full-time (33 women), 23 part-time (4 women); includes 12 minority (6 Black or African American, non-Hispanic/Latino; 1 Asian, non-Hispanic/Latino; 4 Hispanic/Latino; 1 Two or more races, non-Hispanic/Latino), 155 international. Average age 24. 524 applicants, 43% accepted, 55 enrolled. *Faculty:* 27 full-time (2 women), 2 part-time/adjunct (0 women). *Financial support:* Fellowships, research assistantships, teaching assistantships, career-related internships or fieldwork, Federal Work-Study, institutionally sponsored loans, scholarships/grants, and unspecified assistantships available. Support available to part-time students. Financial award application deadline: 5/31; financial award applicants required to submit FAFSA. In 2015, 55 master's awarded. *Degree program information:* Part-time programs available. Part-time. Offers chemical engineering (MS Ch E); civil engineering (MSCE); computer engineering (MSEE); electrical engineering (MSEE); engineering (MS Ch E, MSCE, MSEE, MSME, D Sc); mechanical engineering (MSME); systems engineering (D Sc). *Application deadline:* For fall admission, 7/1 priority date for domestic students, 6/15 priority date for international students; for spring admission, 12/1 priority date for domestic students, 11/1 priority date for international students; for summer admission, 5/1 priority date for domestic students, 4/1 priority date for international students. Applications are processed on a rolling basis. *Application fee:* $35. Electronic applications accepted. *Application Contact:* Brenda Poole, Academic Records Specialist, 251-460-6140, Fax: 251-460-6343, E-mail: engineering@southalabama.edu. *Dean, College of Engineering,* Dr. John Steadman, 251-460-6140, Fax: 251-460-6343, E-mail: engineering@southalabama.edu.

College of Medicine Students: 341 full-time (142 women), 6 part-time (3 women); includes 76 minority (30 Black or African American, non-Hispanic/Latino; 1 American Indian or Alaska Native, non-Hispanic/Latino; 37 Asian, non-Hispanic/Latino; 3 Hispanic/Latino; 1 Native Hawaiian or other Pacific Islander, non-Hispanic/Latino; 4 Two or more races, non-Hispanic/Latino), 6 international. Average age 26. *Faculty:* 193 full-time (57 women), 17 part-time/adjunct (6 women). *Financial support:* Fellowships, research assistantships, teaching assistantships, career-related internships or fieldwork, Federal Work-Study, institutionally sponsored loans, scholarships/grants, and unspecified assistantships available. Support available to part-time students. Financial award application deadline: 5/31; financial award applicants required to submit FAFSA. In 2015, 79 doctorates awarded. Offers basic medical sciences (PhD); medicine (MD). *Application deadline:* For fall admission, 11/15 for domestic and international students. *Application fee:* $75. Electronic applications accepted. *Application Contact:* Mark Scott, Director, Medical Admissions, 251-460-7176, Fax: 251-460-6278, E-mail: mscott@southalabama.edu. *Dean,* Dr. Samuel Strada, 251-460-6041, Fax: 251-460-6073, E-mail: sstrada@southalabama.edu.

College of Nursing Students: 2,489 full-time (2,179 women), 341 part-time (297 women); includes 789 minority (520 Black or African American, non-Hispanic/Latino; 26 American Indian or Alaska Native, non-Hispanic/Latino; 118 Asian, non-Hispanic/Latino; 82 Hispanic/Latino; 9 Native Hawaiian or other Pacific Islander, non-Hispanic/Latino; 34 Two or more races, non-Hispanic/Latino), 7 international. Average age 35. 1,923 applicants, 51% accepted, 722 enrolled. *Faculty:* 69 full-time (63 women), 97 part-time/adjunct (89 women). *Financial support:* Fellowships, research assistantships, teaching assistantships, career-related internships or fieldwork, Federal Work-Study, institutionally sponsored loans, scholarships/grants, and unspecified assistantships available. Support available to part-time students. Financial award application deadline: 5/31; financial award applicants required to submit FAFSA. In 2015, 572 master's, 90 doctorates, 79 other advanced degrees awarded. *Degree program information:* Part-time programs available. Part-time, online learning. Offers nursing (MSN, DNP); nursing administration (Certificate); nursing education (MAIA); nursing practice (Certificate). *Application deadline:* For fall admission, 3/15 for domestic students; for spring admission, 7/15 priority date for domestic students; for summer admission, 1/15 priority date for domestic students. Applications are processed on a rolling basis. *Application fee:* $85. Electronic applications accepted. *Application Contact:* Gail Soles, Academic Records Specialist, 251-445-9400, Fax: 251-445-9416, E-mail: gsoles@southalabama.edu. *Dean, College of Nursing,* Dr. Debra Davis, 251-445-9400, Fax: 251-445-9416, E-mail: ddavis@southalabama.edu.

Graduate School Students: 28 full-time (22 women), 14 part-time (10 women); includes 8 minority (5 Black or African American, non-Hispanic/Latino; 1 American Indian or Alaska Native, non-Hispanic/Latino; 1 Hispanic/Latino; 1 Two or more races, non-Hispanic/Latino). Average age 28. 132 applicants, 14% accepted, 14 enrolled. *Faculty:* 8 full-time (3 women). *Financial support:* Fellowships, research assistantships, teaching assistantships, career-related internships or fieldwork, Federal Work-Study, institutionally sponsored loans, scholarships/grants, and unspecified assistantships available. Support available to part-time students. Financial award application deadline: 5/31; financial award applicants required to submit FAFSA. In 2015, 5 master's, 4 doctorates awarded. *Degree program information:* Part-time and evening/weekend programs available. Part-time, evening/weekend. Offers clinical and counseling psychology (PhD); environmental toxicology (MS). *Application deadline:* For fall admission, 7/15 priority date for domestic students, 6/15 priority date for international students; for spring admission, 12/1 priority date for domestic students, 11/1 priority date for international students. Applications are processed on a rolling basis. *Application fee:* $35. Electronic applications accepted. *Dean and Associate Vice President for Academic Affairs,* Dr. B. Keith Harrison, 251-460-6310, E-mail: gradschool@southalabama.edu.

Mitchell College of Business Students: 86 full-time (32 women), 8 part-time (6 women); includes 16 minority (7 Black or African American, non-Hispanic/Latino; 1 American Indian or Alaska Native, non-Hispanic/Latino; 4 Asian, non-Hispanic/Latino; 3 Hispanic/Latino; 1 Two or more races, non-Hispanic/Latino), 6 international. Average age 32. 88 applicants, 51% accepted, 36 enrolled. *Faculty:* 11 full-time (3 women), 2 part-time/adjunct (0 women). *Financial support:* Fellowships, research assistantships, teaching assistantships, career-related internships or fieldwork, Federal Work-Study, institutionally sponsored loans, scholarships/grants, and unspecified assistantships available. Support available to part-time students. Financial award application deadline: 5/31; financial award applicants required to submit FAFSA. In 2015, 32 master's awarded. *Degree program information:* Part-time and evening/weekend programs available. Part-time, evening/weekend. Offers accounting (M Acc); business administration (MBA, DBA); business management (MBA, DBA). *Application deadline:* For fall admission, 7/15 for domestic students, 6/15 for international students; for spring admission, 12/1 for domestic students, 11/1 for international students; for summer admission, 10/15 for domestic students. *Application fee:* $35. Electronic applications accepted. *Application Contact:* Dr. Alex Sharland, Interim Assistant Dean of Business, 251-460-6412, Fax: 251-460-6529, E-mail: mcobgraduate@southalabama.edu. *Dean, Business,* Dr. Bob Wood, 251-460-7167, Fax: 251-460-6529, E-mail: bgwood@southalabama.edu.

Pat Capps Covey College of Allied Health Professions Students: 365 full-time (283 women), 2 part-time (both women); includes 19 minority (9 Black or African American, non-Hispanic/Latino; 2 American Indian or Alaska Native, non-Hispanic/Latino; 4 Asian, non-Hispanic/Latino; 3 Hispanic/Latino; 1 Native Hawaiian or other Pacific Islander, non-Hispanic/Latino), 1 international. Average age 25. 653 applicants, 40% accepted, 94 enrolled. *Faculty:* 31 full-time (22 women), 10 part-time/adjunct (7 women). *Financial support:* Fellowships, research assistantships, teaching assistantships, career-related internships or fieldwork, Federal Work-Study, institutionally sponsored loans, scholarships/grants, and unspecified assistantships available. Support available to part-time students. Financial award application deadline: 5/31; financial award applicants required to submit FAFSA. In 2015, 88 master's, 43 doctorates awarded. Offers allied health professions (MHS, MS, Au D, DPT, PhD); audiology (Au D); communication sciences and disorders (PhD); occupational therapy (MS); physical therapy (DPT); physician assistant studies (MHS); speech-language pathology (MS). *Application deadline:* For fall admission, 7/15 priority date for domestic students, 6/15 priority date for international students; for spring admission, 12/1 priority date for domestic students, 11/1 priority date for international students. Applications are processed on a rolling basis. *Application fee:* $35. Electronic applications accepted. *Application Contact:* Dr. Susan Gordon-Hickey, Associate Dean, College of Allied Health, 251-445-9250, Fax: 251-445-9259, E-mail: gordonhickey@southalabama.edu. *Dean, College of Allied Health,* Dr. Gregory Frazer, 251-445-9250, Fax: 251-445-9259, E-mail: gfrazer@southalabama.edu.

School of Computing Students: 173 full-time (45 women), 14 part-time (4 women); includes 14 minority (6 Black or African American, non-Hispanic/Latino; 3 Asian, non-Hispanic/Latino; 3 Hispanic/Latino; 1 Native Hawaiian or other Pacific Islander, non-Hispanic/Latino; 1 Two or more races, non-Hispanic/Latino), 122 international. Average age 26. 435 applicants, 51% accepted, 77 enrolled. *Faculty:* 15 full-time (2 women), 2 part-time/adjunct (0 women). *Financial support:* Fellowships, research assistantships, teaching assistantships, Federal Work-Study, institutionally sponsored loans, scholarships/grants, and unspecified assistantships available. Support available to part-time students. Financial award application deadline: 5/31; financial award applicants required to submit FAFSA. In 2015, 51 master's awarded. *Degree program information:* Part-time and evening/weekend programs available. Part-time, evening/weekend. Offers computer science (MS); information systems (MS). *Application deadline:* For fall admission, 7/15 priority date for domestic students, 6/15 priority date for international students; for spring admission, 12/1 priority date for domestic students, 11/1 priority date for international students; for summer admission, 5/1 priority date for domestic students, 4/1 priority date for international students. Applications are processed on a rolling basis. *Application fee:* $35. Electronic applications accepted. *Application Contact:* Dr. Harold Pardue, Director of School of Computing Graduate Studies, 251-460-1600, Fax: 251-460-7274, E-mail: hpardue@southalabama.edu. *Dean, School of Computing,* Dr. Alec Yasinsac, 251-460-6390, Fax: 251-460-7274, E-mail: yasinsac@southalabama.edu.

UNIVERSITY OF SOUTH CAROLINA, Columbia, SC 29208

General Information State-supported, coed, university. CGS member. *Graduate housing:* Rooms and/or apartments available to single and married students. *Research affiliation:* E.I. du Pont de Nemours and Company (engineering, chemical engineering), Westinghouse/Savannah River Corporation (environmental restoration, hazardous waste remediation), Motorola Corporation–Energy Production Division (electrochemical engineering), Glaxo-Wellcome (pharmaceuticals), NCR Corporation (electrical and computer engineering).

GRADUATE UNITS

The Graduate School ***Degree program information:*** Part-time and evening/weekend programs available. Part-time, evening/weekend, online learning. Offers gerontology (Certificate). Electronic applications accepted.

Arnold School of Public Health Degree program information: Part-time programs available. Part-time, online learning. Offers biostatistics (MPH, MSPH, Dr PH, PhD); communication sciences and disorders (MCD, MSP, PhD); environmental health science (MS); environmental quality (MPH, MS, MSPH, PhD); epidemiology (MPH, MSPH, Dr PH, PhD); exercise science (MS, DPT, PhD); general public health (MPH); hazardous materials management (MPH, MSPH, PhD); health education (MAT); health promotion, education, and behavior (MPH, MS, MSPH, Dr PH, PhD); health services policy and management (MHA, MPH, Dr PH, PhD); industrial hygiene (MPH, MSPH, PhD); physical activity and public health (MPH); public health (MAT, MCD, MHA, MPH, MS, MSP, MSPH, DPT, Dr PH, PhD, Certificate); school health education (Certificate). Electronic applications accepted.

College of Arts and Sciences Degree program information: Part-time and evening/weekend programs available. Part-time, evening/weekend. Offers anthropology (MA, PhD); applied statistics (CAS); archive management (MA); art education (IMA, MA, MAT); art history (MA); art studio (MA); arts and sciences (IMA, M Math, MA, MAT, MFA, MIS, MMA, MPA, MS, PSM, PhD, CAS, Certificate); biology (MS, PhD); biology education (IMA, MAT); chemistry and biochemistry (IMA, MAT, MS, PhD); clinical/community psychology (MA, PhD); comparative literature (MA, PhD); creative writing (MFA); criminology and criminal justice (MA, PhD); ecology, evolution and organismal biology (MS, PhD); English (MA, PhD); English education (MAT); experimental psychology (MA, PhD); foreign languages (MAT); French (MA); general psychology (MA); geography (MA, MS, PhD); geography education (IMA); geological sciences (MS, PhD); German (MA); historic preservation (MA); history (MA, PhD); industrial statistics (MIS); international studies (MA, PhD); linguistics (MA, PhD); marine science (MS, PhD); mathematics (MA, MS, PhD); mathematics education (M Math, MAT); media arts (MMA); molecular, cellular, and developmental biology (MS, PhD); museum administration (MA); museum management (Certificate); philosophy (MA, PhD); physics and astronomy (IMA, MAT, MS, PSM, PhD); political science (MA, MPA, PhD); public administration (MPA); public history (MA, Certificate); religious studies (MA); school psychology (PhD); sociology (MA, PhD); Spanish (MA); statistics (MS, PhD); studio art (MFA); teaching English to speakers of other languages (Certificate); theatre (MA, MAT, MFA); women's studies (Certificate). Electronic applications accepted.

College of Education Degree program information: Part-time and evening/weekend programs available. Part-time, evening/weekend, online learning. Offers art education (IMA, MAT); business education (IMA, MAT); counseling education (PhD, Ed S); curriculum and instruction (Ed D); early childhood education (M Ed, Ed D, PhD); education (IMA, M Ed, MAT, MS, MT, Ed D, PhD, Certificate, Ed S); educational administration (M Ed, PhD, Ed S); educational psychology, research (M Ed, PhD); educational technology (M Ed); elementary education (MAT, Ed D, PhD); English (MAT); foreign language (MAT); foundations in education (PhD); health education (MAT); higher education and student affairs (M Ed); higher education leadership (Certificate); language and literacy (M Ed, PhD); mathematics (MAT); physical education (IMA, MAT, MS, PhD); science (IMA, MAT); secondary (Ed D); secondary education (IMA, MAT, MT, Ed D, PhD); social studies (MAT); special education (M Ed, MAT, PhD); teaching (M Ed, Ed S); theatre and speech (MAT). Electronic applications accepted.

College of Engineering and Computing Degree program information: Part-time and evening/weekend programs available. Part-time, evening/weekend, online learning. Offers chemical engineering (ME, MS, PhD); civil engineering (ME, MS, PhD); computer science and engineering (ME, MS, PhD); electrical engineering (ME, MS, PhD); engineering and computing (ME, MS, PhD); mechanical engineering (ME, MS, PhD); nuclear engineering (ME, MS, PhD); software engineering (MS). Electronic applications accepted.

College of Hospitality, Retail, and Sport Management Degree program information: Part-time programs available. Part-time, online learning. Offers hospitality, retail, and sport management (MIHTM, MR, MS); hotel, restaurant and tourism management (MIHTM); live sport and entertainment events (MS); public assembly facilities management (MS); retailing (MR). Electronic applications accepted.

College of Mass Communications and Information Studies Offers journalism and mass communications (MA, MMC, PhD); library and information science (MLIS, PhD, Certificate, Specialist); mass communications and information studies (MA, MLIS, MMC, PhD, Certificate, Specialist).

College of Nursing Degree program information: Part-time programs available. Part-time, online learning. Offers acute care clinical specialist (MSN); acute care nurse practitioner (MSN, Certificate); adult nurse practitioner (MSN); advanced practice clinical nursing (MSN, Certificate); advanced practice nursing in primary care (MSN, Certificate); advanced practice nursing in psychiatric mental health (MSN, Certificate); clinical nursing (MSN); community mental health and psychiatric health nursing (MSN); community/public health clinical nurse specialist (MSN); family nurse practitioner (MSN); health nursing (MSN); nursing administration (MSN); nursing practice (DNP); nursing science (PhD); pediatric nurse practitioner (MSN); psychiatric/mental health nurse practitioner (MSN); psychiatric/mental health specialist (MSN); women's health nurse practitioner (MSN). Electronic applications accepted.

College of Social Work Degree program information: Part-time programs available. Part-time. Offers social work (MSW, PhD). Electronic applications accepted.

Darla Moore School of Business Degree program information: Part-time and evening/weekend programs available. Part-time, evening/weekend, online learning. Offers accountancy (M Acc); business administration (MBA, PhD); business measurement and assurance (M Acc); economics (MA, PhD); human resources (MHR); international business administration (IMBA). Electronic applications accepted.

School of Music Degree program information: Part-time programs available. Part-time. Offers composition (MM, DMA); conducting (MM, DMA); jazz studies (MM); music education (MM Ed, PhD); music history (MM); music performance (Certificate); music theory (MM); opera theater (MM); performance (MM, DMA); piano pedagogy (MM, DMA). Electronic applications accepted.

School of the Environment Degree program information: Part-time programs available. Part-time, online learning. Offers earth and environmental resources management (MEERM); environment (MEERM). Electronic applications accepted.

School of Law Offers law (JD).

School of Medicine Offers biomedical science (MBS, PhD); genetic counseling (MS); medicine (MBS, MNA, MRC, MS, MD, PhD, Certificate); nurse anesthesia (MNA); psychiatric rehabilitation (Certificate); rehabilitation counseling (MRC, Certificate). Electronic applications accepted.

South Carolina College of Pharmacy ***Degree program information:*** Part-time programs available. Part-time. Offers pharmaceutical sciences (MS, PhD); pharmacy (MS, PhD, Pharm D). Electronic applications accepted.

UNIVERSITY OF SOUTH CAROLINA AIKEN, Aiken, SC 29801

General Information State-supported, coed, comprehensive institution. *Enrollment:* 3,448 graduate, professional, and undergraduate students; 20 full-time matriculated graduate/professional students (14 women), 26 part-time matriculated graduate/professional students (17 women). *Enrollment by degree level:* 46 master's. *Graduate faculty:* 14 full-time (9 women). Tuition, state resident: full-time $12,384; part-time $516 per credit hour. Tuition, nonresident: full-time $26,532; part-time $1105.50 per credit hour. *Required fees:* $9 per credit hour. $25 per semester. Full-time tuition and fees vary according to course load. *Graduate housing:* Room and/or apartments available on a first-come, first-served basis to single students; on-campus housing not available to married students. Typical cost: $4740 per year ($7290 including board). Room and board charges vary according to board plan. Housing application deadline: 6/1. *Student services:* Campus employment opportunities, campus safety program, career counseling, child daycare facilities, exercise/wellness program, free psychological counseling, grant writing training, international student services, multicultural affairs office, services for students with disabilities, teacher training, writing training. *Library:* Gregg-Graniteville Library. *Collection:* Books: 172,423 (physical), 357,807 (digital/electronic); Serial titles: 113 (physical), 30,447 (digital/electronic); Databases: 232. Weekly public service hours: 78; students can reserve study rooms. *Research affiliation:* VA Boston Healthcare System (Post Traumatic Stress Disorder), Dwight D. Eisenhower Army Medical Center (neuroscience), University of South Florida (psychology), Baruch College (psychology), Illinois Institute of Technology (psychology), University of Rochester (psychology).

Computer facilities: 550 computers available on campus for general student use. A campuswide network can be accessed from student residence rooms and from off campus. Online class registration is available.
Website: http://www.usca.edu/

General Application Contact: Dan Robb, Associate Vice Chancellor for Enrollment Management, 803-641-3487, Fax: 803-641-3727, E-mail: danr@usca.edu.

GRADUATE UNITS

Program in Applied Clinical Psychology Students: 20 full-time (14 women), 11 part-time (8 women); includes 3 minority (2 Black or African American, non-Hispanic/Latino; 1 Two or more races, non-Hispanic/Latino). Average age 26. 53 applicants, 34% accepted, 11 enrolled. *Faculty:* 9 full-time (7 women). *Financial support:* In 2015–16, 24 students received support, including 17 research assistantships with partial tuition reimbursements available (averaging $4,044 per year), 3 teaching assistantships with partial tuition reimbursements available (averaging $3,333 per year); career-related internships or fieldwork, Federal Work-Study, scholarships/grants, tuition waivers (partial), and unspecified assistantships also available. Financial award application deadline: 3/15; financial award applicants required to submit FAFSA. In 2015, 9 master's awarded. *Degree program information:* Part-time programs available. Part-time. Offers applied clinical psychology (MS). *Application deadline:* For fall admission, 5/1 priority date for domestic and international students. Applications are processed on a rolling basis. *Application fee:* $45. Electronic applications accepted. *Application Contact:* Dan Robb, Associate Vice Chancellor for Enrollment Management, 803-641-3487, Fax: 803-641-3727, E-mail: danr@usca.edu. *Director,* Dr. Jane Stafford, 803-641-3358, Fax: 803-641-3720, E-mail: jstafford@usca.edu.

Program in Business Administration for STEM and Liberal Arts Students: 9 part-time (5 women). Average age 32. 12 applicants, 100% accepted, 9 enrolled. *Faculty:* 2 full-time (both women). *Financial support:* In 2015–16, 1 student received support. Scholarships/grants and tuition waivers (partial) available. Support available to part-time students. Financial award application deadline: 3/15; financial award applicants required to submit FAFSA. *Degree program information:* Part-time and evening/weekend programs available. Part-time-only, evening/weekend. Offers business administration (MBA). *Application deadline:* For fall admission, 8/1 for domestic and international students; for spring admission, 12/3 for domestic and international students. Applications are processed on a rolling basis. *Application fee:* $45. Electronic applications accepted. *Application Contact:* Dan Robb, Associate Vice Chancellor for Enrollment Management, 803-641-3487, Fax: 803-641-3727, E-mail: danr@usca.edu. *Dean for School of Business Administration*, Dr. Michael J. Fekula, 803-641-3340, E-mail: mickf@usca.edu.

Program in Educational Technology Students: 6 part-time (4 women); includes 1 minority (Black or African American, non-Hispanic/Latino). Average age 30. 4 applicants, 75% accepted, 2 enrolled. *Faculty:* 3 full-time (0 women). *Financial support:* In 2015–16, 2 students received support. Fellowships with partial tuition reimbursements available, career-related internships or fieldwork, Federal Work-Study, scholarships/grants, tuition waivers (partial), and unspecified assistantships available. Support available to part-time students. Financial award application deadline: 3/15; financial award applicants required to submit FAFSA. In 2015, 9 master's awarded. *Degree program information:* Part-time and evening/weekend programs available. Part-time, evening/weekend, online only, 100% online. Offers educational technology (M Ed). *Application deadline:* Applications are processed on a rolling basis. *Application fee:* $45. Electronic applications accepted. *Application Contact:* Dan Robb, Associate Vice Chancellor for Enrollment Management, 803-641-3487, Fax: 803-641-3727, E-mail: danr@usca.edu. *Education Technology Program Coordinator*, Dr. Tom Smyth, 803-641-3527, E-mail: smyth@usca.edu.

UNIVERSITY OF SOUTH CAROLINA UPSTATE, Spartanburg, SC 29303-4999

General Information State-supported, coed, comprehensive institution. *Graduate housing:* On-campus housing not available.

GRADUATE UNITS

Graduate Programs ***Degree program information:*** Part-time and evening/weekend programs available. Part-time, evening/weekend. Offers early childhood education (M Ed); elementary education (M Ed); informatics (MS); special education: visual impairment (M Ed).

THE UNIVERSITY OF SOUTH DAKOTA, Vermillion, SD 57069-2390

General Information State-supported, coed, university. CGS member. *Enrollment:* 732 full-time matriculated graduate/professional students (453 women), 1,241 part-time matriculated graduate/professional students (711 women). *Enrollment by degree level:* 1,144 master's, 569 doctoral, 260 other advanced degrees. *Graduate faculty:* 364 full-time (163 women), 54 part-time/adjunct (31 women). *Graduate housing:* Rooms and/or apartments available on a first-come, first-served basis to single and married students. Housing application deadline: 5/1. *Student services:* Campus employment opportunities, campus safety program, career counseling, child daycare facilities, exercise/wellness program, free psychological counseling, grant writing training, international student services, low-cost health insurance, multicultural affairs office, services for students with disabilities, teacher training, writing training. *Library:* I. D. Weeks Library plus 2 others.

Computer facilities: 975 computers available on campus for general student use. A campuswide network can be accessed from student residence rooms and from off campus. Online class registration is available.
Website: http://www.usd.edu/

General Application Contact: Brandy Durham, Graduate School Recruitment Coordinator, 605-658-6138, Fax: 605-677-6118, E-mail: grad@usd.edu.

GRADUATE UNITS

Graduate School Students: 732 full-time (453 women), 1,241 part-time (711 women); includes 240 minority (42 Black or African American, non-Hispanic/Latino; 53 American Indian or Alaska Native, non-Hispanic/Latino; 47 Asian, non-Hispanic/Latino; 47 Hispanic/Latino; 3 Native Hawaiian or other Pacific Islander, non-Hispanic/Latino; 48 Two or more races, non-Hispanic/Latino), 137 international. 1,844 applicants, 40% accepted, 515 enrolled. *Faculty:* 364 full-time (163 women), 51 part-time/adjunct (30 women). *Financial support:* In 2015–16, 565 students received support. Research assistantships with partial tuition reimbursements available, teaching assistantships with partial tuition reimbursements available, career-related internships or fieldwork, Federal Work-Study, scholarships/grants, unspecified assistantships, and clinical assistantships available. Support available to part-time students. Financial award applicants required to submit FAFSA. In 2015, 570 master's, 219 doctorates, 88 other advanced degrees awarded. *Degree program information:* Part-time and evening/weekend programs available. Part-time, evening/weekend, 100% online, blended/hybrid learning. Offers interdisciplinary studies (MA). *Application deadline:* For fall admission, 7/20 for international students; for spring admission, 12/10 for international students. Applications are processed on a rolling basis. *Application fee:* $35. Electronic applications accepted. *Application Contact:* Brandy Durham, Director of Recruitment and Marketing, 605-658-6138, Fax: 605-677-6118, E-mail: grad@usd.edu. *Graduate Advising Coordinator*, Brittany Wagner, 605-658-6140, Fax: 605-677-6118, E-mail: grad@usd.edu.

Beacom School of Business Financial support: Research assistantships with partial tuition reimbursements, teaching assistantships with partial tuition reimbursements, career-related internships or fieldwork, Federal Work-Study, and unspecified assistantships available. Support available to part-time students. Financial award applicants required to submit FAFSA. *Degree program information:* Part-time and evening/weekend programs available. Part-time, evening/weekend, online learning. Offers business (MBA, MP Acc); business administration (MBA); business analytics (MBA); health services administration (MBA); professional accountancy (MP Acc). *Application deadline:* For fall admission, 6/1 priority date for domestic students, 5/1 priority date for international students; for spring admission, 10/1 priority date for domestic students, 9/1 priority date for international students. Applications are processed on a rolling basis. *Application fee:* $35. Electronic applications accepted. *Application Contact:* Graduate School, 605-658-6140, Fax: 605-677-6118, E-mail: cde@usd.edu. *Dean*, Venky Venkatachalam, 605-677-5455, E-mail: venky.venkatachalam@usd.edu.

College of Arts and Sciences Financial support: Research assistantships with partial tuition reimbursements, teaching assistantships with partial tuition reimbursements, career-related internships or fieldwork, Federal Work-Study, scholarships/grants, unspecified assistantships, and clinical assistantships available. Support available to part-time students. Financial award applicants required to submit FAFSA. *Degree program information:* Part-time programs available. Part-time, online learning. Offers alcohol and drug studies (MSA); American political institutions (PhD); American politics and public policy (MA); arts and sciences (EMPA, MA, MNS, MPA, MS, MSA, Au D, PhD); audiology (Au D); biology (MA, MS, PhD); chemistry (MS, PhD); clinical psychology (MA, PhD); communication studies (MA); computer science (MS); criminal justice (MSA); English (MA, PhD); health services administration (MSA); history (MA); human factors (MA, PhD); human resource management (MSA); interdisciplinary (MSA); long term care administration (MSA); mathematics (MA, MS); organizational leadership (MSA); physics (MS, PhD); political science (EMPA, MA); public administration (MPA, PhD); public policy (PhD); speech-language pathology (MA). *Application deadline:* Applications are processed on a rolling basis. *Application fee:* $35. Electronic applications accepted. *Application Contact:* John Dudley, Associate Dean for Academics, 605-677-5221, Fax: 605-677-6409, E-mail: john.dudley@usd.edu. *Dean*, Dr. Matthew C. Moen, 605-677-5221, Fax: 605-677-6409, E-mail: matthew.moen@usd.edu.

College of Fine Arts Financial support: Research assistantships with partial tuition reimbursements, teaching assistantships with partial tuition reimbursements, Federal Work-Study, and unspecified assistantships available. Financial award applicants required to submit FAFSA. Offers art education (MFA); ceramics (MFA); collaborative piano (MM); conducting (MM); design/technology (MFA); directing (MFA); fine arts (MA, MFA, MM); graphic design (MFA); history of musical instruments (MM); music education (MM); music history (MM); music performance (MM); painting (MFA); photography (MFA); printmaking (MFA); sculpture (MFA); theatre (MA). *Application deadline:* Applications are processed on a rolling basis. *Application fee:* $35. Electronic applications accepted. *Application Contact:* Graduate School, 605-658-6140, Fax: 605-677-6118, E-mail: cde@usd.edu. *Dean*, Dr. Larry Schou, 605-677-5713, E-mail: larry.schou@usd.edu.

Sanford School of Medicine Average age 25. *Financial support:* In 2015–16, 197 students received support. Fellowships with partial tuition reimbursements available, research assistantships with partial tuition reimbursements available, teaching assistantships with partial tuition reimbursements available, career-related internships or fieldwork, institutionally sponsored loans, scholarships/grants, traineeships, tuition waivers (partial), and unspecified assistantships available. Financial award application deadline: 5/1; financial award applicants required to submit FAFSA. *Degree program information:* Part-time programs available. Part-time. Offers cardiovascular research (MS, PhD); cellular and molecular biology (MS, PhD); medicine (MS, MD, PhD); molecular microbiology and immunology (MS, PhD); neuroscience (MS, PhD); physiology and pharmacology (MS, PhD). *Application deadline:* For fall admission, 4/15 for international students. Applications are processed on a rolling basis. *Application fee:* $35.

School of Education Financial support: Research assistantships with partial tuition reimbursements, teaching assistantships with partial tuition reimbursements, career-related internships or fieldwork, Federal Work-Study, and unspecified assistantships available. Support available to part-time students. Financial award applicants required to submit FAFSA. *Degree program information:* Part-time and evening/weekend programs available. Part-time, evening/weekend, online learning. Offers counseling (MA, PhD, Ed S); curriculum and instruction (Ed D, Ed S); education (MA, MS, Ed D, PhD, Ed S); educational administration (MA, Ed D, Ed S); elementary education (MA); human development and educational psychology (MA, PhD, Ed S); kinesiology and sport management (MA); school psychology (PhD, Ed S); secondary education (MA); secondary education plus certification (MA); special education (MA); technology for education and training (MS). *Application deadline:* Applications are processed on a rolling basis. *Application fee:* $35. Electronic applications accepted. *Dean*, Dr. Donald Easton-Brooks, 605-677-5437, E-mail: donald.eastonbrooks@usd.edu.

School of Health Sciences Financial support: Research assistantships, teaching assistantships, career-related internships or fieldwork, Federal Work-Study, scholarships/grants, traineeships, and unspecified assistantships available. *Degree program information:* Part-time programs available. Part-time. Offers health sciences (MA, MPH, MS, MSW, DPT, OTD, PhD, TDPT, Graduate Certificate); occupational therapy (MS, OTD); physical therapy (DPT, TDPT); physician assistant studies (MS); post-professional occupational therapy (OTD). *Application fee:* $35. *Application Contact:* Graduate School, 605-658-6140, E-mail: cde@usd.edu. *Dean*, Dr. Michael Lawler, 605-677-5000, E-mail: michael.lawler@usd.edu.

School of Law Financial support: Research assistantships with partial tuition reimbursements, career-related internships or fieldwork, Federal Work-Study, scholarships/grants, and unspecified assistantships available. Financial award application deadline: 4/1; financial award applicants required to submit FAFSA. *Degree program information:* Part-time programs available. Part-time. Offers law (JD). *Application deadline:* For fall admission, 3/1 priority date for domestic students. Applications are processed on a rolling basis. *Application fee:* $35. Electronic applications accepted. *Application Contact:* Jean Henriques, Admissions Officer/Registrar, 605-677-5444, E-mail: jean.henriques@usd.edu. *Interim Dean*, Thomas E. Geu, 605-677-6362, E-mail: thomas.geu@usd.edu.

UNIVERSITY OF SOUTHERN CALIFORNIA, Los Angeles, CA 90089

General Information Independent, coed, university. CGS member. *Graduate housing:* Rooms and/or apartments available on a first-come, first-served basis to single and married students. *Research affiliation:* SETI Institute (astronomy/astrobiology), Rancho Los Amigos Medical Center (medicine), Children's Hospital Los Angeles (medicine), Doheny Eye Institute (medicine), House Ear Institute (medicine), Jet Propulsion Laboratory (engineering and technology).

GRADUATE UNITS

Graduate School Electronic applications accepted.

Annenberg School for Communication and Journalism Degree program information: Part-time and evening/weekend programs available. Part-time, evening/weekend, online learning. Offers communication (MA, MCM, MPD, MS, PhD); communication and journalism (MA, MCM, MPD, MS, PhD); communication management (MCM); culture and community (PhD); digital social media (MS); global and transnational communication (PhD); groups, organizations and networks (PhD); health communication and social dynamics (PhD); information, political economy and entertainment (PhD); journalism (MA, MS); new media and technology (PhD); public diplomacy (MPD); rhetoric, politics and public media (PhD); specialized journalism (MA); specialized journalism (the arts) (MA); strategic public relations (MA). Electronic applications accepted.

Dana and David Dornsife College of Letters, Arts and Sciences Offers American studies and ethnicity (PhD); applied mathematics (MA, MS, PhD); art history (MA, PhD); biology (MS); brain and cognitive science (PhD); chemistry (PhD); classical Chinese literature (MA, PhD); classical Japanese literature (MA, PhD); classics (MA, PhD); clinical science (PhD); comparative literature (PhD); comparative media and culture (PhD); computational biology and bioinformatics (PhD); computational molecular biology (MS); developmental psychology (PhD); earth sciences (MS, PhD); East Asian linguistics (PhD); East Asian studies (MA); economic development programming (MA, PhD); English (MA, PhD); geographic information science and technology (MS, Graduate Certificate); Hispanic linguistics (PhD); history (PhD); human behavior (MHB); integrative and evolutionary biology (PhD); letters, arts and sciences (MA, MHB, MMM, MPW, MS, PhD, Graduate Certificate); linguistics (MA, PhD); literature and creative writing (PhD); marine and environmental biology (MS);

marine biology and biological oceanography (MS, PhD); mathematical finance (MS); mathematics (MA, PhD); modern Chinese literature (MA, PhD); modern Japanese literature (MA, PhD); modern Korean literature (MA, PhD); molecular and computational biology (PhD); molecular biology (PhD); neurobiology (PhD); neuroscience (MS, PhD); ocean sciences (MS, PhD); philosophy (MA, PhD); physical chemistry (PhD); physics (MA, MS, PhD); political science and international relations (PhD); professional writing (MPW); quantitative methods (PhD); Slavic languages and literatures (MA, PhD); Slavic linguistics (PhD); social psychology (PhD); sociology (PhD); Spanish and Latin American studies (PhD); statistics (MS); visual studies (Graduate Certificate). Electronic applications accepted.

Davis School of Gerontology Degree program information: Part-time programs available. Part-time, online learning. Offers aging services management (MASM); biology of aging (PhD); gerontology (MA, MS, PhD, Graduate Certificate); long term care administration (MLTCA). PhD in biology of aging offered jointly with Buck Institute for Research on Aging. Electronic applications accepted.

Gould School of Law Offers comparative law for foreign attorneys (MCL); law (JD); law for foreign-educated attorneys (LL M).

Herman Ostrow School of Dentistry Offers biokinesiology (MS, PhD); craniofacial biology (MS, PhD, Graduate Certificate); dentistry (MA, MS, DDS, DPT, OTD, PhD, Graduate Certificate); occupational science (PhD); occupational therapy (MA, OTD); physical therapy (DPT). Electronic applications accepted.

Marshall School of Business Offers accounting (M Acc); business (M Acc, MBA, MBT, MBV, MMM, MS, PhD); business administration (MBA, MMM, MS, PhD); business taxation (MBT); entrepreneurship and innovation (MS). Electronic applications accepted.

Roski School of Fine Arts Offers art and curatorial practices in the public sphere (MA); fine arts (MA, MFA); new genres (MFA); painting/drawing (MFA); photography (MFA); sculpture (MFA). Electronic applications accepted.

Rossier School of Education Offers education (MAT, ME, MMFT, Ed D, PhD); educational counseling (ME); educational psychology (Ed D, PhD); higher education administration (Ed D); higher education administration and policy (PhD); K-12 leadership in urban school settings (Ed D); K-12 policy and practice (PhD); marriage, family and child counseling (MMFT); postsecondary administration and student affairs [PASA] (ME); school counseling (ME); teacher education in multicultural societies (Ed D); teaching (online) (MAT); teaching and teaching credential (MAT); teaching English to speakers of other languages (MAT). Electronic applications accepted.

School of Architecture Offers architecture (M Arch, MBS, MHP, MLA, PhD). Electronic applications accepted.

School of Cinematic Arts Offers animation and digital arts (MFA); cinema-television (MA); cinema-television (critical studies) (PhD); cinematic arts (MA, MFA, PhD); film and television production (MFA); interactive media (MFA); media arts and practice (PhD); motion picture producing (MFA); writing for screen and television (MFA). Electronic applications accepted.

School of Pharmacy Offers clinical and experimental therapeutics (PhD); clinical research design and management (Graduate Certificate); food safety (Graduate Certificate); healthcare decision analysis (MS); patient and product safety (Graduate Certificate); pharmaceutical economics and policy (MS, PhD); pharmacology and pharmaceutical sciences (MS, PhD); pharmacy (MS, DRSc, PhD, Pharm D, Graduate Certificate); preclinical drug development (Graduate Certificate); regulatory and clinical affairs (Graduate Certificate); regulatory science (MS, DRSc).

School of Policy, Planning, and Development Offers ambulatory care (Graduate Certificate); health administration (EMHA, MHA, Graduate Certificate); homeland security and public policy (Graduate Certificate); international public policy and management (MPPM); leadership (EML); long-term care (Graduate Certificate); nonprofit management and policy (Graduate Certificate); policy, planning, and development (EMHA, EML, M Pl, MHA, MPA, MPP, MPPM, MRED, DPPD, PhD, Graduate Certificate); political management (Graduate Certificate); public administration (MPA); public management (Graduate Certificate); public policy (MPP, Graduate Certificate); public policy and management (PhD); real estate development (MRED); sustainable cities (Graduate Certificate); transportation systems (Graduate Certificate); urban planning (M Pl); urban planning and development (PhD). Electronic applications accepted.

School of Social Work Offers community organization, planning and administration (MSW); families and children (MSW); health (MSW); mental health (MSW); military social work and veterans services (MSW); older adults (MSW); public child welfare (MSW); school settings (MSW); social work (MSW, PhD); systems of mental illness recovery (MSW); work and life (MSW). Electronic applications accepted.

School of Theatre Offers acting (MFA); applied theatre arts (MA); dramatic writing (MFA). Electronic applications accepted.

Thornton School of Music Degree program information: Part-time and evening/weekend programs available. Part-time, evening/weekend. Offers brass performance (MM, DMA, Graduate Certificate); choral and sacred music (MM, DMA); classical guitar (MM, DMA, Graduate Certificate); composition (MM, DMA); early music (MA, DMA); harp performance (MM, DMA, Graduate Certificate); historical musicology (PhD); jazz studies (MM, DMA, Graduate Certificate); keyboard collaborative arts (MM, DMA, Graduate Certificate); music education (MM, DMA); organ performance (MM, DMA, Graduate Certificate); percussion performance (MM, DMA, Graduate Certificate); piano performance (MM, DMA, Graduate Certificate); scoring for motion pictures and television (Graduate Certificate); strings performance (MM, DMA, Graduate Certificate); studio jazz guitar (MM, DMA, Graduate Certificate); teaching music (MA); vocal arts (classical voice/opera) (MM, DMA, Graduate Certificate); woodwind performance (MM, DMA, Graduate Certificate). Electronic applications accepted.

Viterbi School of Engineering Degree program information: Part-time programs available. Part-time, online learning. Offers aerospace and mechanical engineering: computational fluid and solid mechanics (MS); aerospace and mechanical engineering: dynamics and control (MS); aerospace engineering (MS, PhD, Engr); applied mechanics (MS); astronautical engineering (MS, PhD, Engr, Graduate Certificate); biomedical engineering (PhD); chemical engineering (MS, PhD, Engr); civil engineering (MS, PhD); computer engineering (MS, PhD); computer networks (MS); computer science (MS, PhD); computer security (MS); computer-aided engineering (ME, Graduate Certificate); construction management (MCM); digital supply chain management (MS); electric power (MS); electrical engineering (MS, PhD, Engr); engineering (MCM, ME, MS, PhD, Engr, Graduate Certificate); engineering management (MS); engineering technology commercialization (Graduate Certificate); engineering technology communication (Graduate Certificate); environmental engineering (MS, PhD); environmental quality management (ME); game development (MS); geoscience technologies (MS); green technologies (MS); health systems operations (Graduate Certificate); high performance computing and simulations (MS); human language technology (MS); industrial and systems engineering (MS, PhD, Engr); intelligent robotics (MS); manufacturing engineering (MS); materials engineering (MS); materials science (MS, PhD, Engr); mechanical engineering (MS, PhD, Engr); medical device and diagnostic engineering (MS); medical imaging and imaging informatics (MS); multimedia and creative technologies (MS); operations research engineering (MS); optimization and supply chain management (Graduate Certificate); petroleum engineering (MS, PhD, Engr); product development engineering (MS); safety systems and security (MS); smart oilfield technologies (MS, Graduate Certificate); software engineering (MS); structural design (ME); sustainable cities (Graduate Certificate); systems architecting and engineering (MS, Graduate Certificate); systems safety and security (Graduate Certificate); telecommunications (MS); transportation systems (MS, Graduate Certificate); VLSI design (MS); water and waste management (MS); wireless health technology (MS). Electronic applications accepted.

Keck School of Medicine Students: 1,577 full-time (913 women), 44 part-time (27 women); includes 787 minority (89 Black or African American, non-Hispanic/Latino; 4 American Indian or Alaska Native, non-Hispanic/Latino; 511 Asian, non-Hispanic/Latino; 171 Hispanic/Latino; 6 Native Hawaiian or other Pacific Islander, non-Hispanic/Latino; 6 Two or more races, non-Hispanic/Latino), 205 international. Average age 25. 10,155 applicants, 10% accepted, 552 enrolled. *Faculty:* 420 full-time (128 women), 20 part-time/adjunct (9 women). *Financial support:* In 2015–16, 28 fellowships with tuition reimbursements (averaging $32,000 per year), 98 research assistantships with tuition reimbursements (averaging $29,750 per year), 43 teaching assistantships with tuition reimbursements (averaging $32,000 per year) were awarded; career-related internships or fieldwork, Federal Work-Study, institutionally sponsored loans, scholarships/grants, traineeships, health care benefits, and unspecified assistantships also available. Support available to part-time students. Financial award applicants required to submit CSS PROFILE or FAFSA. In 2015, 311 master's, 183 doctorates awarded. Offers cancer biology and genomics (PhD); development, stem cells and regenerative medicine (PhD); medical biology (PhD); medicine (MPAP, MPH, MS, MD, PhD, Certificate); molecular structure and signaling (PhD). *Application deadline:* Applications are processed on a rolling basis. Electronic applications accepted. *Application Contact:* Marisela Zuniga, Administrative Coordinator, Graduate Affairs, 323-442-1607, Fax: 323-442-1199, E-mail: mzuniga@usc.edu. *Dean,* Dr. Carmen A. Puliafito, 323-442-1900.

Graduate Programs in Medicine Students: 841 full-time (560 women), 44 part-time (27 women); includes 393 minority (46 Black or African American, non-Hispanic/Latino; 2 American Indian or Alaska Native, non-Hispanic/Latino; 226 Asian, non-Hispanic/Latino; 108 Hispanic/Latino; 5 Native Hawaiian or other Pacific Islander, non-Hispanic/Latino; 6 Two or more races, non-Hispanic/Latino), 204 international. Average age 25. 1,966 applicants, 29% accepted, 366 enrolled. *Faculty:* 420 full-time (128 women), 20 part-time/adjunct (9 women). *Financial support:* In 2015–16, 28 fellowships with tuition reimbursements (averaging $32,000 per year), 82 research assistantships with tuition reimbursements (averaging $32,000 per year), 43 teaching assistantships with tuition reimbursements (averaging $32,000 per year) were awarded; career-related internships or fieldwork, Federal Work-Study, institutionally sponsored loans, scholarships/grants, traineeships, health care benefits, and unspecified assistantships also available. Support available to part-time students. Financial award application deadline: 5/4; financial award applicants required to submit CSS PROFILE or FAFSA. In 2015, 311 master's, 15 doctorates awarded. Offers applied biostatistics and epidemiology (MS); biochemistry and molecular biology (MS); biomedical and biological sciences (PhD); biostatistics (MS, PhD); biostatistics and epidemiology (MPH); child and family health (MPH); environmental health (MPH); epidemiology (PhD); experimental and molecular pathology (MS); global health leadership (MPH); global medicine (MS, Certificate); health behavior research (PhD); health communication (MPH); health education and promotion (MPH); medicine (MPAP, MPH, MS, PhD, Certificate); molecular epidemiology (MS); molecular microbiology and immunology (MS); physiology and biophysics (MS); primary care physician assistant (MPAP); public health (MPH); public health policy (MPH); stem cell biology and regenerative medicine (MS). *Application deadline:* Applications are processed on a rolling basis. *Application fee:* $85. Electronic applications accepted. *Application Contact:* Marisela Zuniga, Administrative Coordinator, 323-442-1607, Fax: 323-442-1199, E-mail: mzuniga@usc.edu. *Associate Dean for Graduate Affairs,* Dr. Peggy Farnham, 323-442-8015, Fax: 323-442-7739, E-mail: pfarnham@usc.edu.

UNIVERSITY OF SOUTHERN INDIANA, Evansville, IN 47712-3590

General Information State-supported, coed, comprehensive institution. CGS member. *Enrollment:* 9,029 graduate, professional, and undergraduate students; 156 full-time matriculated graduate/professional students (124 women), 743 part-time matriculated graduate/professional students (581 women). *Enrollment by degree level:* 803 master's, 42 doctoral. *Graduate faculty:* 126 full-time (62 women), 16 part-time/adjunct (7 women). Tuition, state resident: full-time $8110. Tuition, nonresident: full-time $15,989. *Required fees:* $340; $115 per semester. Tuition and fees vary according to program. *Graduate housing:* Room and/or apartments available on a first-come, first-served basis to single students; on-campus housing not available to married students. Typical cost: $9656 per year ($13,568 including board). Room and board charges vary according to board plan. Housing application deadline: 3/1. *Student services:* Campus employment opportunities, campus safety program, career counseling, child daycare facilities, exercise/wellness program, free psychological counseling, international student services, low-cost health insurance, multicultural affairs office, services for students with disabilities. *Library:* David L. Rice Library. *Collection:* Books: 257,442 (physical), 206,203 (digital/electronic); Serial titles: 1,986 (physical), 66,592 (digital/electronic); Databases: 122. Weekly public service hours: 114.

Computer facilities: 579 computers available on campus for general student use. A campuswide network can be accessed from student residence rooms and from off campus. Online class registration is available. Website: http://www.usi.edu/

General Application Contact: Dr. Mayola Rowser, Director, Graduate Studies, 812-465-7016, Fax: 812-464-1956, E-mail: mrowser@usi.edu.

GRADUATE UNITS

Graduate Studies Students: 149 full-time (122 women), 751 part-time (585 women); includes 71 minority (37 Black or African American, non-Hispanic/Latino; 3 American Indian or Alaska Native, non-Hispanic/Latino; 9 Asian, non-Hispanic/Latino; 10 Hispanic/Latino; 1 Native Hawaiian or other Pacific Islander, non-Hispanic/Latino; 11 Two or more races, non-Hispanic/Latino), 25 international. Average age 33. 847 applicants, 43% accepted, 294 enrolled. *Faculty:* 126 full-time (62 women), 16 part-time/adjunct (7 women). *Financial support:* Federal Work-Study, scholarships/grants, tuition waivers (full and partial), and unspecified assistantships available. Financial award application deadline: 3/1; financial award applicants required to submit FAFSA. In 2015, 284 master's, 16 doctorates awarded. *Degree program information:* Part-time and evening/weekend programs available. Part-time, evening/weekend. *Application deadline:*

Applications are processed on a rolling basis. *Application fee:* $40. Electronic applications accepted. *Director*, Dr. Mayola Rowser, 812-465-7016, Fax: 812-464-1956, E-mail: mrowser@usi.edu.

College of Liberal Arts Students: 59 full-time (48 women), 96 part-time (71 women); includes 17 minority (9 Black or African American, non-Hispanic/Latino; 1 American Indian or Alaska Native, non-Hispanic/Latino; 2 Hispanic/Latino; 5 Two or more races, non-Hispanic/Latino), 3 international. Average age 30. *Faculty:* 67 full-time (37 women), 8 part-time/adjunct (3 women). *Financial support:* Federal Work-Study, scholarships/grants, tuition waivers (full and partial), and unspecified assistantships available. Financial award application deadline: 3/1; financial award applicants required to submit FAFSA. In 2015, 75 master's awarded. *Degree program information:* Part-time and evening/weekend programs available. Part-time, evening/weekend. Offers communication (MA); English (MA); liberal studies (MA); public administration (MPA); social work (MSW). *Application deadline:* Applications are processed on a rolling basis. *Application fee:* $40. Electronic applications accepted. *Application Contact:* Dr. Mayola Rowser, Director, Graduate Studies, 812-465-7016, E-mail: mrowser@usi.edu. *Dean*, Dr. James M. Beeby, 812-464-1853, E-mail: jmbeeby@usi.edu.

College of Nursing and Health Professions Students: 61 full-time (52 women), 487 part-time (426 women); includes 45 minority (20 Black or African American, non-Hispanic/Latino; 3 American Indian or Alaska Native, non-Hispanic/Latino; 5 Asian, non-Hispanic/Latino; 14 Hispanic/Latino; 3 Two or more races, non-Hispanic/Latino), 3 international. Average age 35. *Faculty:* 13 full-time (10 women), 3 part-time/adjunct (2 women). *Financial support:* Federal Work-Study, scholarships/grants, tuition waivers (full and partial), and unspecified assistantships available. Financial award application deadline: 3/1; financial award applicants required to submit FAFSA. In 2015, 151 master's, 17 doctorates awarded. *Degree program information:* Part-time programs available. Part-time, blended/hybrid learning. Offers health administration (MHA); nursing (MSN, DNP); nursing and health professions (MHA, MSN, MSOT, DNP); occupational therapy (MSOT). *Application deadline:* For fall admission, 2/1 for domestic and international students. Applications are processed on a rolling basis. *Application fee:* $40. Electronic applications accepted. *Application Contact:* Dr. Mayola Rowser, Director, Graduate Studies, 812-465-7016, Fax: 812-464-1956, E-mail: mrowser@usi.edu. *Dean*, Dr. Ann White, 812-465-1151, E-mail: awhite@usi.edu.

Pott College of Science, Engineering, and Education Students: 6 full-time (5 women), 39 part-time (24 women); includes 2 minority (1 Black or African American, non-Hispanic/Latino; 1 Two or more races, non-Hispanic/Latino), 6 international. Average age 32. *Faculty:* 23 full-time (11 women), 2 part-time/adjunct (both women). *Financial support:* In 2015–16, 12 students received support. Federal Work-Study, scholarships/grants, tuition waivers (full and partial), and unspecified assistantships available. Financial award application deadline: 3/1; financial award applicants required to submit FAFSA. In 2015, 24 master's awarded. *Degree program information:* Part-time and evening/weekend programs available. Part-time, evening/weekend. Offers elementary education (MSE); industrial management (MS); kinesiology, health and sport (MSE); mathematics teaching (MSE); science, engineering, and education (MS, MSE); secondary education (MSE). *Application deadline:* For fall admission, 8/15 priority date for domestic students, 3/1 priority date for international students. Applications are processed on a rolling basis. *Application fee:* $40. Electronic applications accepted. *Application Contact:* Dr. Mayola Rowser, Director, Graduate Studies, 812-465-7016, Fax: 812-464-1956, E-mail: mrowser@usi.edu. *Dean*, Dr. Scott A. Gordon, 812-465-7137, E-mail: sgordon@usi.edu.

Romain College of Business Students: 8 full-time (3 women), 99 part-time (38 women); includes 6 minority (1 Black or African American, non-Hispanic/Latino; 1 Asian, non-Hispanic/Latino; 2 Hispanic/Latino; 1 Native Hawaiian or other Pacific Islander, non-Hispanic/Latino; 1 Two or more races, non-Hispanic/Latino), 6 international. Average age 29. *Faculty:* 23 full-time (4 women), 3 part-time/adjunct (0 women). *Financial support:* Career-related internships or fieldwork, Federal Work-Study, scholarships/grants, tuition waivers (full and partial), and unspecified assistantships available. Financial award application deadline: 3/1; financial award applicants required to submit FAFSA. In 2015, 34 master's awarded. *Degree program information:* Part-time and evening/weekend programs available. Part-time, evening/weekend. Offers business (MBA); business administration (MBA). *Application deadline:* For fall admission, 8/1 for domestic students, 3/1 priority date for international students. Applications are processed on a rolling basis. *Application fee:* $40. Electronic applications accepted. *Application Contact:* Dr. Ernest Hall, Jr., MBA Director, 812-465-7038, Fax: 812-464-1956, E-mail: ehall@usi.edu. *Dean*, Dr. Mohammed F. Khayum, 812-465-1681, E-mail: mkhayum@usi.edu.

UNIVERSITY OF SOUTHERN MAINE, Portland, ME 04103

General Information State-supported, coed, comprehensive institution. *Enrollment:* 7,739 graduate, professional, and undergraduate students; 707 full-time matriculated graduate/professional students (480 women), 710 part-time matriculated graduate/professional students (504 women). *Enrollment by degree level:* 1,058 master's, 267 doctoral, 91 other advanced degrees. *Graduate faculty:* 99 full-time (57 women), 56 part-time/adjunct (35 women). *Tuition, area resident:* Full-time $6840; part-time $380 per credit hour. Tuition, state resident: full-time $10,260; part-time $570 per credit hour. Tuition, nonresident: full-time $18,468; part-time $1026 per credit hour. *Required fees:* $830; $83 per credit hour. Tuition and fees vary according to course load and program. *Graduate housing:* Rooms and/or apartments available on a first-come, first-served basis to single and married students. Typical cost: $9150 (including board) for single students. Room and board charges vary according to board plan and housing facility selected. Housing application deadline: 5/1. *Student services:* Campus employment opportunities, campus safety program, career counseling, child daycare facilities, exercise/wellness program, free psychological counseling, international student services, low-cost health insurance, multicultural affairs office, services for students with disabilities, teacher training. *Library:* Glickman Library plus 3 others.

Computer facilities: Computer purchase and lease plans are available. 219 computers available on campus for general student use. A campuswide network can be accessed from student residence rooms and from off campus. Online class registration is available. Website: http://www.usm.maine.edu/

General Application Contact: Mary Sloan, Assistant Dean of Graduate Studies, 207-780-4812, Fax: 207-780-4969, E-mail: gradstudies@usm.maine.edu.

GRADUATE UNITS

College of Arts, Humanities, and Social Sciences ***Degree program information:*** Part-time and evening/weekend programs available. Part-time, evening/weekend, online learning. Offers American and New England studies (MA, CGS); arts, humanities, and social sciences (MA, MFA, MM, CGS); creative writing (MFA). Electronic applications accepted.

School of Music Offers composition (MM); conducting (MM); jazz studies (MM); music education (MM); performance (MM).

College of Management and Human Service Offers management and human service (MBA, MCPD, MPH, MPPM, MS, MS Ed, MSW, Psy D, CAS, CGS).

Muskie School of Public Service Degree program information: Part-time and evening/weekend programs available. Part-time, evening/weekend, online learning. Offers community planning and development (MCPD, CGS); health policy and management (MPH, CGS); public policy and management (MPPM). Electronic applications accepted.

School of Business Degree program information: Part-time and evening/weekend programs available. Part-time, evening/weekend. Offers accounting (MBA); business administration (MBA); finance (MBA); health management and policy (MBA); sustainability (MBA). Electronic applications accepted.

School of Education and Human Development Degree program information: Part-time and evening/weekend programs available. Part-time, evening/weekend, online learning. Offers adult and higher education (MS); adult learning (CAS); applied behavior analysis (MS, CGS); applied literacy (MS Ed); assistant principal (CGS); clinical mental health counseling (MS); counseling (CAS); culturally responsive practices in education and human development (CGS); education and human development (MS, MS Ed, Psy D, CAS, CGS); educational leadership (MS Ed, CAS); English as a second language (MS Ed, CAS, CGS); gifted and talented education (CGS); literacy education (MS Ed, CAS, CGS); mental health rehabilitation technician/community (CGS); professional educator (MS Ed); professional teacher (MS Ed); rehabilitation counseling (MS); school counseling (MS); school psychology (MS, Psy D); special education (MS); substance abuse counseling (CGS); teaching all students (CGS); teaching and learning (MS Ed); youth with moderate to severe disabilities (CGS). Electronic applications accepted.

School of Social Work Degree program information: Part-time and evening/weekend programs available. Part-time, evening/weekend. Offers social work (MSW). Electronic applications accepted.

College of Science, Technology, and Health ***Degree program information:*** Part-time and evening/weekend programs available. Part-time, evening/weekend. Offers applied medical sciences (MS); biology (MS); computer science (MS); science, technology, and health (MS, DNP, CAS, CGS, PMC); software systems (CGS); statistics (MS, CGS). Electronic applications accepted.

School of Nursing Degree program information: Part-time programs available. Part-time. Offers adult-gerontology primary care nurse practitioner (MS, PMC); education (MS); family nurse practitioner (MS, PMC); family psychiatric/mental health nurse practitioner (MS); management (MS); nursing (CAS, CGS); psychiatric-mental health nurse practitioner (PMC). Electronic applications accepted.

Lewiston-Auburn College Offers creative leadership/global strategies (CGS); leadership studies (MA); occupational therapy (MOT).

UNIVERSITY OF SOUTHERN MISSISSIPPI, Hattiesburg, MS 39406-0001

General Information State-supported, coed, university. CGS member. *Graduate housing:* Room and/or apartments available on a first-come, first-served basis to single students; on-campus housing not available to married students. Housing application deadline: 6/15. *Research affiliation:* Oak Ridge Associated Universities.

GRADUATE UNITS

Graduate School ***Degree program information:*** Part-time and evening/weekend programs available. Part-time, evening/weekend. Electronic applications accepted.

College of Arts and Letters Degree program information: Part-time and evening/weekend programs available. Part-time, evening/weekend, online learning. Offers anthropology (MA); arts and letters (MA, MATL, MFA, MM, MME, MS, DMA, PhD); communication studies (MA, MS, PhD); conducting (DMA); directing (MFA); French (MATL); history (MA, MS, PhD); history and literature (MM); literature (MA); mass communication and journalism (MA, MS, PhD); music education (MME, PhD); performance (MFA, MM); performance and pedagogy (DMA); political science (MS); Spanish (MATL); teaching English to speakers of other languages (TESOL) (MATL); theory (MM); woodwind performance and pedagogy (MM). Electronic applications accepted.

College of Business Degree program information: Part-time and evening/weekend programs available. Part-time, evening/weekend. Offers accountancy (MPA); business (MBA, MPA, MS); business administration (MBA); economic development (MS). Electronic applications accepted.

College of Education and Psychology Degree program information: Part-time programs available. Part-time. Offers child and family studies (MS); clinical psychology (PhD); counseling psychology (MS, PhD); education and psychology (M Ed, MA, MLIS, MS, Ed D, PhD, Ed S, Graduate Certificate); education: social justice (MS); educational administration (P-12) (Ed D, PhD, Ed S); educational administration and supervision (P-12) (M Ed); educational studies and research (MS); elementary education (M Ed, PhD, Ed S); experimental psychology (PhD); higher education administration (PhD); higher education: student affairs administration (M Ed); instructional technology (MS); instructional technology and design (PhD); library and information science (MLIS, Graduate Certificate); marriage and family therapy (MS); research, evaluation, statistics, and assessment (PhD); school psychology (PhD); special education (M Ed, PhD, Ed S). Electronic applications accepted.

College of Health Degree program information: Part-time and evening/weekend programs available. Part-time, evening/weekend. Offers audiology (Au D); epidemiology and biostatistics (MPH); health (MA, MLS, MPH, MS, MSW, Au D, PhD); health education (MPH); health policy and administration (MPH); medical laboratory science (MLS); nutrition (MS, PhD); social work (MSW); speech language pathology (MA, MS); sport management (MS). Electronic applications accepted.

College of Nursing Degree program information: Part-time and evening/weekend programs available. Part-time, evening/weekend. Offers family nurse practitioner (MSN, Graduate Certificate); family psychiatric-mental health nurse practitioner (Graduate Certificate); nursing (DNP, PhD); psychiatric-mental health nurse practitioner (Graduate Certificate). Electronic applications accepted.

College of Science and Technology Degree program information: Part-time and evening/weekend programs available. Part-time, evening/weekend. Offers coastal sciences (MS, PhD); computational science (MS, PhD); computer science (MS); construction (MS); environmental biology (MS); forensic science (MS); geography and geology (MS, PhD); hydrographic science (MS); inorganic chemistry (MS); marine biology (MS); marine science (MS, PhD); mathematics (MS); microbiology (MS, PhD); molecular biology (MS, PhD); organic chemistry (MS); physical chemistry (MS); physics (MS); polymer science (MS); polymer science and engineering (PhD); science and mathematics education (MS, PhD); science and technology (MA, MS, PhD).

UNIVERSITY OF SOUTH FLORIDA, Tampa, FL 33620-9951

General Information State-supported, coed, university. CGS member. *Enrollment:* 42,067 graduate, professional, and undergraduate students; 4,988 full-time matriculated graduate/professional students (2,797 women), 4,914 part-time matriculated graduate/professional students (3,076 women). *Enrollment by degree level:* 6,300 master's, 3,602 doctoral. *Graduate faculty:* 993 full-time (403 women), 38 part-time/adjunct (16 women). *Graduate housing:* Rooms and/or apartments available on a first-come, first-served basis to single students and available to married students. Housing application deadline: 7/1. *Student services:* Campus employment opportunities, campus safety program, career counseling, child daycare facilities, exercise/wellness program, free psychological counseling, grant writing training, international student services, low-cost health insurance, multicultural affairs office, services for students with disabilities, teacher training, writing training. *Library:* Tampa Campus Library plus 5 others. *Collection:* Books: 1.8 million (physical), 652,513 (digital/electronic); Serial titles: 537 (physical), 58,975 (digital/electronic); Databases: 930. Weekly public service hours: 116; study areas open 24 hours, 5–7 days a week; students can reserve study rooms. *Research affiliation:* Veterans Administration Medical Center, All Children's Hospital, Harris Corporation (electronics), Tampa General Hospital, Shriners Hospitals, H.L. Moffitt Cancer Center (cancer biology, oncology).

Computer facilities: 825 computers available on campus for general student use. A campuswide network can be accessed from student residence rooms and from off campus. Online class registration is available.
Website: http://www.usf.edu/

General Application Contact: Dr. Dwayne Smith, Senior Vice Provost and Dean, Office of Graduate Studies, 813-974-2846, Fax: 813-974-5762, E-mail: mdsmith3@usf.edu.

GRADUATE UNITS

College of Arts and Sciences Students: 1,149 full-time (622 women), 526 part-time (308 women); includes 329 minority (80 Black or African American, non-Hispanic/Latino; 2 American Indian or Alaska Native, non-Hispanic/Latino; 51 Asian, non-Hispanic/Latino; 160 Hispanic/Latino; 3 Native Hawaiian or other Pacific Islander, non-Hispanic/Latino; 33 Two or more races, non-Hispanic/Latino), 271 international. Average age 32. 1,942 applicants, 38% accepted, 425 enrolled. *Faculty:* 365 full-time (132 women), 2 part-time/adjunct (0 women). *Financial support:* In 2015–16, 2 students received support, including 2 research assistantships with tuition reimbursements available (averaging $13,650 per year); career-related internships or fieldwork, Federal Work-Study, institutionally sponsored loans, scholarships/grants, tuition waivers (full and partial), and unspecified assistantships also available. Support available to part-time students. Financial award applicants required to submit FAFSA. In 2015, 376 master's, 125 doctorates awarded. *Degree program information:* Part-time and evening/weekend programs available. Part-time, evening/weekend, online learning. Offers applied anthropology (MA, PhD); applied linguistics: English as a second language (MA); applied physics (PhD); arts and sciences (MA, MFA, MPA, MS, MURP, PhD, Graduate Certificate); biology (MS); cancer biology (PhD); cell and molecular biology (PhD); chemistry (MA, MS, PhD); communication (MA, PhD); creative writing (MFA); economics (MA, PhD); English (MA, PhD); French (MA); government (PhD); history (MA, PhD); integrative biology (PhD); liberal arts (MA); mathematics (MA, PhD); medical anthropology (Graduate Certificate); microbiology (MS); philosophy (MA, PhD); physics (MS); political science (MA); psychology (PhD); religious studies (MA); sociology (MA, PhD); Spanish (MA); statistics (MA, PhD); women's and gender studies (MA). *Application deadline:* For fall admission, 2/15 priority date for domestic students, 1/2 priority date for international students; for spring admission, 10/15 priority date for domestic students, 6/1 priority date for international students. *Application fee:* $30. *Application Contact:* Susan Hall, Executive Assistant to the Dean, 813-974-0853, Fax: 813-974-5911, E-mail: hall@usf.edu. *Dean*, Dr. Eric Eisenberg, 813-974-2804, Fax: 813-974-5911, E-mail: eisenberg@usf.edu.

School of Geosciences Students: 87 full-time (41 women), 45 part-time (19 women); includes 18 minority (7 Black or African American, non-Hispanic/Latino; 3 Asian, non-Hispanic/Latino; 7 Hispanic/Latino; 1 Two or more races, non-Hispanic/Latino), 29 international. Average age 34. 39 applicants, 62% accepted, 9 enrolled. *Faculty:* 32 full-time (7 women). *Financial support:* In 2015–16, 26 students received support, including 3 research assistantships (averaging $12,345 per year), 25 teaching assistantships with tuition reimbursements available (averaging $12,807 per year); unspecified assistantships also available. Financial award application deadline: 3/1. In 2015, 10 master's awarded. *Degree program information:* Part-time and evening/weekend programs available. Part-time, evening/weekend. Offers environmental science and policy (MS, PhD); geography (MA, PhD); geology (MS, PhD); urban and regional planning (MURP). *Application deadline:* For fall admission, 2/15 for domestic students, 1/2 for international students; for spring admission, 10/15 for domestic students, 6/1 for international students. *Application fee:* $30. *Application Contact:* Dr. Jennifer Collins, Associate Professor and Graduate Program Coordinator, 813-974-4242, Fax: 813-974-5911, E-mail: collinsjm@usf.edu. *Professor and Chair, Geography Division*, Dr. Jayajit Chakraborty, 813-974-8188, Fax: 813-974-5911, E-mail: jchakrab@usf.edu.

School of Information Students: 71 full-time (53 women), 129 part-time (101 women); includes 59 minority (16 Black or African American, non-Hispanic/Latino; 7 Asian, non-Hispanic/Latino; 26 Hispanic/Latino; 1 Native Hawaiian or other Pacific Islander, non-Hispanic/Latino; 9 Two or more races, non-Hispanic/Latino), 2 international. Average age 33. 127 applicants, 75% accepted, 61 enrolled. *Financial support:* Unspecified assistantships available. Financial award application deadline: 6/30. In 2015, 87 master's awarded. *Degree program information:* Part-time and evening/weekend programs available. Part-time, evening/weekend, online learning. Offers intelligence studies (MS); library and information science (MA). *Application deadline:* For fall admission, 6/1 for domestic students, 1/2 for international students; for spring admission, 10/15 for domestic students, 6/1 for international students. Applications are processed on a rolling basis. *Application fee:* $30. Electronic applications accepted. *Application Contact:* Dr. Diane Austin, Assistant Director, 813-974-6364, Fax: 813-974-6840, E-mail: dianeaustin@usf.edu. *Director and Associate Professor*, Dr. Jim Andrews, 813-974-2108, Fax: 813-974-6840, E-mail: jimandrews@usf.edu.

School of Mass Communications Students: 26 full-time (19 women), 16 part-time (9 women); includes 4 minority (2 Black or African American, non-Hispanic/Latino; 1 Hispanic/Latino; 1 Native Hawaiian or other Pacific Islander, non-Hispanic/Latino), 18 international. Average age 28. 37 applicants, 70% accepted, 16 enrolled. *Faculty:* 11 full-time (7 women). *Financial support:* In 2015–16, 9 students received support, including 9 teaching assistantships with tuition reimbursements available (averaging $10,513 per year); unspecified assistantships also available. Financial award application deadline: 2/28. In 2015, 8 master's awarded. *Degree program information:* Part-time and evening/weekend programs available. Part-time, evening/weekend. Offers mass communications (MA). *Application deadline:* For fall admission, 2/15 for domestic students, 1/2 for international students; for spring admission, 10/15 for domestic students, 6/1 for international students. *Application fee:* $30. Electronic applications accepted. *Application Contact:* Dr. Michael Mitrook, Assistant Professor, 813-974-8890, Fax: 813-974-2592, E-mail: mmitrook@usf.edu. *Interim Director and Associate Professor*, Dr. Jim Andrews, 813-974-2108, Fax: 813-974-2592, E-mail: jimandrews@usf.edu.

College of Behavioral and Community Sciences Students: 478 full-time (407 women), 263 part-time (216 women); includes 216 minority (66 Black or African American, non-Hispanic/Latino; 2 American Indian or Alaska Native, non-Hispanic/Latino; 20 Asian, non-Hispanic/Latino; 109 Hispanic/Latino; 19 Two or more races, non-Hispanic/Latino), 13 international. Average age 29. 1,278 applicants, 30% accepted, 254 enrolled. *Faculty:* 93 full-time (61 women), 3 part-time/adjunct (2 women). In 2015, 239 master's, 25 doctorates awarded. Offers applied behavior analysis (MA, PhD); audiology (Au D); behavioral and community sciences (MA, MS, MSW, Au D, PhD, Graduate Certificate); child and adolescent behavioral health (MS); communication sciences and disorders (PhD); criminal justice administration (MA); criminology (MA, PhD); rehabilitation and mental health counseling (MA); speech-language pathology (MS). *Application Contact:* Francisco Vera, Assistant Director for Graduate Admissions, 813-974-2829, E-mail: fvera@usf.edu. *Dean*, Dr. Julianne Serovich, 813-974-1990, Fax: 813-974-2365, E-mail: jserovich@usf.edu.

School of Aging Studies Students: 25 full-time (21 women), 8 part-time (5 women); includes 13 minority (3 Black or African American, non-Hispanic/Latino; 1 Asian, non-Hispanic/Latino; 6 Hispanic/Latino; 3 Two or more races, non-Hispanic/Latino). Average age 31. 36 applicants, 39% accepted, 9 enrolled. *Faculty:* 11 full-time (7 women). *Financial support:* In 2015–16, 15 students received support, including 2 research assistantships with tuition reimbursements available (averaging $15,690 per year), 13 teaching assistantships with tuition reimbursements available (averaging $13,503 per year). Financial award application deadline: 2/3. In 2015, 12 master's, 3 doctorates awarded. *Degree program information:* Part-time and evening/weekend programs available. Part-time, evening/weekend. Offers aging studies (PhD); gerontology (MA). *Application deadline:* For fall admission, 1/15 priority date for domestic and international students. *Application fee:* $30. Electronic applications accepted. *Application Contact:* Brent Small, Professor, 813-974-9746, Fax: 813-974-9754, E-mail: bsmall@usf.edu. *Director and Professor*, Dr. Cathy L. McEvoy, 813-974-1940, Fax: 813-974-9754, E-mail: cmcevoy@usf.edu.

School of Social Work Students: 109 full-time (92 women), 59 part-time (53 women); includes 60 minority (26 Black or African American, non-Hispanic/Latino; 1 American Indian or Alaska Native, non-Hispanic/Latino; 3 Asian, non-Hispanic/Latino; 24 Hispanic/Latino; 6 Two or more races, non-Hispanic/Latino), 1 international. Average age 30. 185 applicants, 39% accepted, 38 enrolled. *Faculty:* 9 full-time (all women). *Financial support:* In 2015–16, 1 student received support, including 1 research assistantship with tuition reimbursement available (averaging $9,001 per year); unspecified assistantships also available. Financial award application deadline: 3/15; financial award applicants required to submit FAFSA. In 2015, 63 master's, 3 doctorates awarded. *Degree program information:* Part-time and evening/weekend programs available. Part-time, evening/weekend. Offers social work (MSW, PhD). *Application deadline:* For fall admission, 2/15 priority date for domestic students, 1/2 for international students. Applications are processed on a rolling basis. *Application fee:* $30. Electronic applications accepted. *Application Contact:* Dr. Marion Becker, Master of Social Work Chair/Professor, 813-974-7188, Fax: 813-974-4675, E-mail: mbecker2@usf.edu. *PhD Program Chair/Assistant Professor*, Dr. Nan Sook Park, 813-974-4194, Fax: 813-974-4675, E-mail: nanpark@usf.edu.

College of Education *Degree program information:* Part-time and evening/weekend programs available. Part-time, evening/weekend, online learning. Offers adult education (MA, Ed D, PhD, Ed S); autism spectrum disorders and severe intellectual disabilities (MA); behavior disorders (MA); career and technical education (MA); career and workforce education (PhD); college student affairs (M Ed); counselor education (MA, PhD, Ed S); early childhood education (M Ed, MA, PhD); education (M Ed, MA, MAT, Ed D, PhD, Ed S); educational leadership (M Ed, Ed D, Ed S); elementary education (MA, MAT, PhD); English education (M Ed, MA, MAT, PhD); exceptional student education (MA, MAT); foreign language education/ESOL (M Ed, MA, MAT); gifted education (MA); higher education/community college teaching (MA, Ed D, PhD); instructional technology (M Ed, PhD, Ed S); interdisciplinary (PhD, Ed S); mathematics education (M Ed, MA, MAT, PhD, Ed S); measurement and evaluation (M Ed, PhD, Ed S); mental retardation (MA); reading/language arts (MA, PhD, Ed S); school psychology (PhD, Ed S); science education (M Ed, MA, MAT, PhD); second language acquisition/instructional technology (PhD); secondary education (M Ed, PhD); secondary education/TESOL (M Ed); social science education (M Ed, MA, MAT); special education (PhD); specific learning disabilities (MA); teaching and learning in the content area (PhD); vocational education (Ed S). Electronic applications accepted.

School of Physical Education and Exercise Science *Degree program information:* Part-time and evening/weekend programs available. Part-time, evening/weekend, online learning. Offers exercise science (MA); physical education teacher preparation (MA). Electronic applications accepted.

College of Engineering Students: 773 full-time (171 women), 302 part-time (71 women); includes 155 minority (38 Black or African American, non-Hispanic/Latino; 1 American Indian or Alaska Native, non-Hispanic/Latino; 26 Asian, non-Hispanic/Latino; 75 Hispanic/Latino; 15 Two or more races, non-Hispanic/Latino), 667 international. Average age 29. 1,941 applicants, 49% accepted, 353 enrolled. *Faculty:* 115 full-time (20 women), 2 part-time/adjunct (0 women). *Financial support:* Career-related internships or fieldwork, Federal Work-Study, scholarships/grants, health care benefits, and unspecified assistantships available. Financial award application deadline: 3/1. In 2015, 337 master's, 57 doctorates awarded. *Degree program information:* Part-time and evening/weekend programs available. Part-time, evening/weekend. Offers biomedical engineering (MSBE, PhD); chemical engineering (M Ch E, PhD); civil engineering (MCE, MSCE, PhD); computer engineering (MSCP); computer science (MSCS); computer science and engineering (PhD); electrical engineering (MSEE, PhD); engineering (M Ch E, MCE, MEVE, MME, MSBE, MSCE, MSCH, MSCP, MSCS, MSEE, MSEM, MSES, MSEV, MSIE, MSIT, MSME, MSMSE, PhD, Graduate Certificate); engineering management (MSEM); engineering science (MSES, PhD); environmental engineering (MEVE, MSEV, PhD); industrial engineering (MSIE, PhD); information technology (MSIT); materials science and engineering (MSMSE); mechanical engineering (MME, MSME, PhD). *Application deadline:* For fall admission, 2/15 for domestic students, 1/2 priority date for international students; for spring admission, 10/15 for domestic students, 6/1 priority date for international students. Applications are processed on a rolling basis. *Application fee:* $30. Electronic applications accepted. *Application Contact:* Dr. Rafael Perez, Associate Dean for Academic Affairs, 813-974-3934, Fax: 813-974-5094, E-mail: perez@usf.edu. *Dean*, Dr. Robert Bishop, 813-974-3864, Fax: 813-974-5094, E-mail: robertbishop@usf.edu.

College of Global Sustainability Students: 46 full-time (28 women), 47 part-time (27 women); includes 33 minority (3 Black or African American, non-Hispanic/Latino; 3 Asian, non-Hispanic/Latino; 24 Hispanic/Latino; 3 Two or more races, non-Hispanic/Latino), 13 international. Average age 29. 118 applicants, 68% accepted, 61 enrolled. *Faculty:* 4 full-time (0 women). In 2015, 43 master's awarded. Offers energy, global, water and sustainable tourism (Graduate Certificate); global sustainability (MA). *Application deadline:* For fall admission, 2/15 for domestic students, 1/2 for international students. *Interim Dean*, Dr. Rafael Perez, 813-974-9694, E-mail: perez@usf.edu.

College of Marine Science Students: 77 full-time (52 women), 21 part-time (10 women); includes 16 minority (1 Black or African American, non-Hispanic/Latino; 1 Asian, non-Hispanic/Latino; 11 Hispanic/Latino; 3 Two or more races, non-Hispanic/Latino), 10 international. Average age 31. 87 applicants, 32% accepted, 21 enrolled. *Faculty:* 25 full-time (7 women). *Financial support:* In 2015–16, 55 students received support, including 45 research assistantships with partial tuition reimbursements available (averaging $14,199 per year), 10 teaching assistantships with partial tuition reimbursements available (averaging $14,196 per year); health care benefits and unspecified assistantships also available. Financial award application deadline: 1/15. In 2015, 12 master's, 8 doctorates awarded. *Degree program information:* Part-time programs available. Part-time. Offers marine science (MS, PhD). *Application deadline:* For fall admission, 1/10 for domestic students, 1/2 for international students; for spring admission, 10/1 for domestic students, 6/1 for international students. Applications are processed on a rolling basis. *Application fee:* $30. *Application Contact:* Dr. David F. Naar, Associate Professor and Director of Academic Affairs, 727-553-1637, Fax: 727-553-1189, E-mail: naar@usf.edu. *Dean*, Dr. Jacqueline E. Dixon, 727-553-3369, Fax: 727-553-1189, E-mail: jdixon@usf.edu.

College of Nursing Students: 159 full-time (135 women), 721 part-time (625 women); includes 292 minority (119 Black or African American, non-Hispanic/Latino; 2 American Indian or Alaska Native, non-Hispanic/Latino; 60 Asian, non-Hispanic/Latino; 90 Hispanic/Latino; 1 Native Hawaiian or other Pacific Islander, non-Hispanic/Latino; 20 Two or more races, non-Hispanic/Latino), 12 international. Average age 35. 636 applicants, 44% accepted, 215 enrolled. *Faculty:* 43 full-time (38 women), 7 part-time/adjunct (4 women). *Financial support:* In 2015–16, 36 students received support, including 7 research assistantships with tuition reimbursements available (averaging $18,935 per year), 29 teaching assistantships with tuition reimbursements available (averaging $30,814 per year); tuition waivers (partial) and unspecified assistantships also available. Financial award application deadline: 2/1; financial award applicants required to submit FAFSA. In 2015, 333 master's, 18 doctorates awarded. *Degree program information:* Part-time programs available. Part-time. Offers advanced pain management (Graduate Certificate); nursing (MS, DNP); nursing education (Post Master's Certificate); nursing science (PhD). *Application deadline:* For fall admission, 2/15 for domestic students, 1/2 for international students; for spring admission, 10/1 for domestic students, 6/1 for international students. *Application fee:* $30. Electronic applications accepted. *Application Contact:* Dr. Brian Graves, Assistant Professor/Assistant Dean, 813-974-8054, Fax: 813-974-5418, E-mail: bgraves1@health.usf.edu. *Dean and Professor, College of Nursing*, Dr. Dianne C. Morrison-Beedy, 813-974-9091, Fax: 813-974-5418, E-mail: dmbeedy@health.usf.edu.

College of Pharmacy Students: 344 full-time (191 women); includes 146 minority (30 Black or African American, non-Hispanic/Latino; 53 Asian, non-Hispanic/Latino; 54 Hispanic/Latino; 3 Native Hawaiian or other Pacific Islander, non-Hispanic/Latino; 6 Two or more races, non-Hispanic/Latino). Average age 26. 678 applicants, 25% accepted, 92 enrolled. *Faculty:* 4 full-time (0 women). In 2015, 49 doctorates awarded. Offers pharmaceutical nanotechnology (MS); pharmacy (Pharm D). *Application Contact:* Dr. Amy Schwartz, Associate Dean, 813-974-2251, E-mail: aschwar1@health.usf.edu. *Dean*, Dr. Kevin Sneed, 813-974-5699, E-mail: ksneed@health.usf.edu.

College of Public Health *Degree program information:* Part-time and evening/weekend programs available. Part-time, evening/weekend, online learning. Offers community and family health (MPH, MSPH, Dr PH, PhD); environmental and occupational health (MPH, MSPH, PhD); epidemiology and biostatistics (MPH, MSPH, PhD); global health (MPH, MSPH, Dr PH, PhD); health policy and management (MHA, MPH, MSPH, PhD); public health (MHA, MPH, MSPH, Dr PH, PhD); public health practice (MPH). Electronic applications accepted.

College of The Arts Students: 195 full-time (87 women), 44 part-time (18 women); includes 68 minority (8 Black or African American, non-Hispanic/Latino; 1 American Indian or Alaska Native, non-Hispanic/Latino; 9 Asian, non-Hispanic/Latino; 45 Hispanic/Latino; 1 Native Hawaiian or other Pacific Islander, non-Hispanic/Latino; 4 Two or more races, non-Hispanic/Latino), 34 international. Average age 29. *Faculty:* 57 full-time (18 women), 1 part-time/adjunct (0 women). *Financial support:* Unspecified assistantships available. In 2015, 93 master's, 3 doctorates awarded. *Degree program information:* Part-time and evening/weekend programs available. Part-time, evening/weekend. Offers the arts (M Arch, MA, MFA, MM, MUCD, PhD). *Application deadline:* For fall admission, 1/15 for domestic students, 1/2 for international students. *Application fee:* $30. *Application Contact:* Prof. Barton Lee, Senior Associate Dean, 813-974-2301, Fax: 813-974-2091, E-mail: blee@usf.edu. *Dean*, Dr. James S. Moy, 813-974-7380, Fax: 813-974-2091, E-mail: moy@usf.edu.

School of Architecture and Community Design Students: 91 full-time (35 women), 27 part-time (12 women); includes 47 minority (4 Black or African American, non-Hispanic/Latino; 1 American Indian or Alaska Native, non-Hispanic/Latino; 7 Asian, non-Hispanic/Latino; 32 Hispanic/Latino; 1 Native Hawaiian or other Pacific Islander, non-Hispanic/Latino; 2 Two or more races, non-Hispanic/Latino), 10 international. Average age 26. 63 applicants, 48% accepted, 19 enrolled. *Faculty:* 10 full-time (1 woman). *Financial support:* In 2015–16, 3 students received support, including 3 teaching assistantships with tuition reimbursements available (averaging $9,360 per year); Federal Work-Study, scholarships/grants, and unspecified assistantships also available. In 2015, 49 master's awarded. Offers architecture (M Arch); urban and community design (MUCD). *Application deadline:* For fall admission, 2/1 priority date for domestic students, 1/2 for international students. Applications are processed on a rolling basis. *Application fee:* $30. Electronic applications accepted. *Application Contact:* Mildred Abreu, Academic Advisor, 813-974-1216, Fax: 813-974-2557, E-mail: abreu@arch.usf.edu. *Director and Professor, School of Architecture and Community Design*, Dr. Robert MacLeod, 813-974-6015, Fax: 813-974-2557, E-mail: rmacleod@arch.usf.edu.

School of Art and Art History Students: 41 full-time (23 women), 1 part-time (0 women); includes 8 minority (1 Black or African American, non-Hispanic/Latino; 6 Hispanic/Latino; 1 Two or more races, non-Hispanic/Latino), 4 international. Average age 29. 68 applicants, 18% accepted, 12 enrolled. *Faculty:* 19 full-time (10 women). *Financial support:* In 2015–16, 37 students received support, including 37 teaching assistantships with partial tuition reimbursements available (averaging $9,440 per year); scholarships/grants, health care benefits, and unspecified assistantships also available. Support available to part-time students. Financial award application deadline: 2/15; financial award applicants required to submit FAFSA. In 2015, 15 master's awarded. *Degree program information:* Part-time programs available. Part-time. Offers art (MFA); art history (MA). *Application deadline:* For fall admission, 1/15 for domestic students, 1/2 for international students. *Application fee:* $30. *Application Contact:* Prof. Neil Bender, Associate Professor and Graduate Program Director, 813-974-2360, Fax: 813-974-9226, E-mail: nb2@usf.edu. *Director*, Prof. Wallace Wilson, 813-974-2360, Fax: 813-974-9226, E-mail: wwilson2@usf.edu.

School of Music Students: 63 full-time (29 women), 16 part-time (6 women); includes 13 minority (3 Black or African American, non-Hispanic/Latino; 2 Asian, non-Hispanic/Latino; 7 Hispanic/Latino; 1 Two or more races, non-Hispanic/Latino), 20 international. Average age 31. 79 applicants, 59% accepted, 25 enrolled. *Faculty:* 27 full-time (7 women), 1 part-time/adjunct (0 women). *Financial support:* In 2015–16, 47 students received support, including 1 research assistantship with tuition reimbursement available (averaging $15,724 per year), 46 teaching assistantships with tuition reimbursements available (averaging $10,099 per year); unspecified assistantships also available. Financial award application deadline: 2/15. In 2015, 29 master's, 3 doctorates awarded. *Degree program information:* Part-time and evening/weekend programs available. Part-time, evening/weekend. Offers music (MM, PhD); music education (MA). *Application deadline:* For fall admission, 2/15 priority date for domestic students, 2/1 for international students; for spring admission, 10/15 for domestic students, 9/15 for international students; for summer admission, 2/15 for domestic students, 1/15 for international students. *Application fee:* $30. *Application Contact:* Dr. William Hayden, Associate Professor and Graduate Program Director, 813-974-1753, Fax: 813-974-8721, E-mail: wphayden@usf.edu. *Director*, Dr. Karen Bryan, 813-974-2311, Fax: 813-974-8721, E-mail: kmbryan@usf.edu.

Innovative Education Offers adult, career and higher education (Graduate Certificate); Africana studies (Graduate Certificate); aging studies (Graduate Certificate); art research (Graduate Certificate); business foundations (Graduate Certificate); chemical and biomedical engineering (Graduate Certificate); child and family studies (Graduate Certificate); civil and industrial engineering (Graduate Certificate); community and family health (Graduate Certificate); criminology (Graduate Certificate); educational measurement and research (Graduate Certificate); English (Graduate Certificate); entrepreneurship (Graduate Certificate); environmental health (Graduate Certificate); epidemiology and biostatistics (Graduate Certificate); geography, environment and planning (Graduate Certificate); geology (Graduate Certificate); global health (Graduate Certificate); government and international affairs (Graduate Certificate); health policy and management (Graduate Certificate); hearing specialist: early intervention (Graduate Certificate); industrial and management systems engineering (Graduate Certificate); information studies (Graduate Certificate); information systems/decision sciences (Graduate Certificate); instructional technology (Graduate Certificate); internal medicine, bioethics and medical humanities (Graduate Certificate); Latin American and Caribbean studies (Graduate Certificate); mass communications (Graduate Certificate); mathematics and statistics (Graduate Certificate); medicine (Graduate Certificate); national and competitive intelligence (Graduate Certificate); psychological and social foundations (Graduate Certificate); public affairs (Graduate Certificate); public health (Graduate Certificate); public health practices (Graduate Certificate); rehabilitation and mental health counseling (Graduate Certificate); secondary education (Graduate Certificate); social work (Graduate Certificate); special education (Graduate Certificate); world languages (Graduate Certificate). *Application Contact:* Karen Tylinski, Metro Initiatives, 813-974-9943, Fax: 813-974-7061, E-mail: ktylinsk@usf.edu. *Interdisciplinary Programs Coordinator*, Kathy Barnes, 813-974-8031, Fax: 813-974-7061, E-mail: barnesk@usf.edu.

Morsani College of Medicine Students: 652 full-time (357 women), 1,011 part-time (508 women); includes 672 minority (144 Black or African American, non-Hispanic/Latino; 10 American Indian or Alaska Native, non-Hispanic/Latino; 287 Asian, non-Hispanic/Latino; 200 Hispanic/Latino; 1 Native Hawaiian or other Pacific Islander, non-Hispanic/Latino; 30 Two or more races, non-Hispanic/Latino), 52 international. Average age 28. 8,060 applicants, 14% accepted, 703 enrolled. *Faculty:* 94 full-time (31 women), 15 part-time/adjunct (5 women). In 2015, 330 master's, 241 doctorates awarded. *Degree program information:* Part-time programs available. Part-time. Offers advanced athletic training (MS); athletic training (MS); bioinformatics and computational biology (MSBCB); biotechnology (MSB); health informatics (MSHI); medical sciences (MSMS, PhD); medicine (MS, MSB, MSBCB, MSHI, MSMS, DPT, MD, PhD). *Application deadline:* For fall admission, 2/15 for domestic students, 1/2 for international students. *Application fee:* $30. Electronic applications accepted. *Application Contact:* Dr. Michael Barber, Associate Dean/Professor, 813-974-9702, Fax: 813-974-4990, E-mail: mbarber@health.usf.edu. *Dean*, Dr. Charles J. Lockwood, 813-974-0533, Fax: 813-974-4990, E-mail: cjlockwood@health.usf.edu.

School of Physical Therapy Students: 134 full-time (91 women), 1 part-time (0 women); includes 29 minority (6 Black or African American, non-Hispanic/Latino; 1 American Indian or Alaska Native, non-Hispanic/Latino; 9 Asian, non-Hispanic/Latino; 13 Hispanic/Latino). Average age 25. 1,300 applicants, 8% accepted, 48 enrolled. In 2015, 95 doctorates awarded. Offers physical therapy (DPT); rehabilitation sciences (PhD). *Application deadline:* For fall admission, 9/1 for domestic students, 2/1 for international students. *Application fee:* $30. *Application Contact:* Dr. Gina Maria Musolino, Associate Professor and Coordinator for Clinical Education, 813-974-2254, Fax: 813-974-8915, E-mail: gmusolin@health.usf.edu. *Director*, Dr. William S. Quillen, 813-974-9863, Fax: 813-974-8915, E-mail: wquillen@health.usf.edu.

Muma College of Business Students: 672 full-time (241 women), 328 part-time (116 women); includes 171 minority (43 Black or African American, non-Hispanic/Latino; 2 American Indian or Alaska Native, non-Hispanic/Latino; 45 Asian, non-Hispanic/Latino; 72 Hispanic/Latino; 9 Two or more races, non-Hispanic/Latino), 430 international. Average age 29. 2,173 applicants, 40% accepted, 363 enrolled. *Faculty:* 68 full-time (19 women). *Financial support:* Career-related internships or fieldwork, scholarships/grants, health care benefits, and unspecified assistantships available. Financial award applicants required to submit FAFSA. In 2015, 499 master's, 11 doctorates awarded. *Degree program information:* Part-time and evening/weekend programs available. Part-time, evening/weekend. Offers business (EMBA, M Acc, MBA, MS, MSM, MSRE, DBA, PhD); business administration (MBA, PhD); business analytics (MS); executive business administration (EMBA); finance (MS); management (MS); marketing (MSM); real estate (MSRE). *Application deadline:* For fall admission, 6/1 for domestic students, 1/2 for international students; for spring admission, 10/15 for domestic students, 6/1 for international students. *Application fee:* $30. *Application Contact:* Dr. Jacqueline Reck, Professor/Interim Associate Dean, 813-974-6721, Fax: 813-974-6528, E-mail: jreck@usf.edu. *Dean*, Dr. Moez Limayem, 813-974-4281, Fax: 813-974-3030, E-mail: mlimayem@usf.edu.

Center for Entrepreneurship Students: 66 full-time (32 women), 32 part-time (12 women); includes 20 minority (3 Black or African American, non-Hispanic/Latino; 4 Asian, non-Hispanic/Latino; 11 Hispanic/Latino; 2 Two or more races, non-Hispanic/Latino), 46 international. Average age 29. 84 applicants, 64% accepted, 43 enrolled. *Faculty:* 4 full-time (2 women). In 2015, 41 master's awarded. *Degree* *program information:* Part-time and evening/weekend programs available. Part-time, evening/weekend. Offers entrepreneurship and applied technologies (MS). *Application deadline:* For fall admission, 2/15 for domestic students, 1/2 for international students; for spring admission, 10/15 for domestic students, 6/1 for international students. Applications are processed on a rolling basis. *Application fee:* $30. Electronic applications accepted. *Application Contact:* Dr. Tapas Das, Assistant Director/Professor, 813-974-5585, Fax: 813-974-5953, E-mail: das@usf.edu. *Director, Center for Entrepreneurship*, Dr. Michael W. Fountain, 813-974-7825, Fax: 813-974-6175, E-mail: fountain@usf.edu.

Lynn Pippenger School of Accountancy Students: 58 full-time (27 women), 42 part-time (21 women); includes 28 minority (7 Black or African American, non-Hispanic/Latino; 6 Asian, non-Hispanic/Latino; 14 Hispanic/Latino; 1 Two or more races, non-Hispanic/Latino), 5 international. Average age 27. 91 applicants, 59% accepted, 39 enrolled. *Faculty:* 9 full-time (4 women). *Financial support:* In 2015–16, 18 students received support, including 18 teaching assistantships with tuition reimbursements available (averaging $12,273 per year); scholarships/grants, health care benefits, and unspecified assistantships also available. Financial award applicants required to submit FAFSA. In 2015, 53 master's, 1 doctorate awarded. *Degree program information:* Part-time and evening/weekend programs available. Part-time, evening/weekend. Offers accountancy (M Acc); business administration (PhD). *Application deadline:* For fall admission, 6/1 for domestic students, 1/2 for international students; for spring admission, 10/15 for domestic students, 6/1 for international students. *Application fee:* $30. Electronic applications accepted. *Application Contact:* Christy Ward, Advisor and Graduation Specialist, 813-974-4290, Fax: 813-974-2797, E-mail: cward@usf.edu. *Interim Director, School of Accountancy*, Dr. Uday Murthy, 813-974-6516, Fax: 813-974-6528, E-mail: umurthy@usf.edu.

UNIVERSITY OF SOUTH FLORIDA, ST. PETERSBURG, St. Petersburg, FL 33701

General Information State-supported, coed, comprehensive institution. *Graduate housing:* Rooms and/or apartments available on a first-come, first-served basis to single and married students.

GRADUATE UNITS

College of Arts and Sciences ***Degree program information:*** Part-time programs available. Part-time, online learning. Offers digital journalism and design (MA); environmental science and policy (MA, MS); Florida studies (MLA); journalism and media studies (MA); liberal studies (MLA); psychology (MA). Electronic applications accepted.

College of Business ***Degree program information:*** Part-time programs available. Part-time. Offers business (MBA). Electronic applications accepted.

College of Education ***Degree program information:*** Part-time programs available. Part-time. Offers educational leadership development (M Ed); elementary education (MA); English education (MA); middle grades STEM education (MS); reading education (MA). Electronic applications accepted.

UNIVERSITY OF SOUTH FLORIDA SARASOTA-MANATEE, Sarasota, FL 34243

General Information State-supported, coed, comprehensive institution. *Enrollment:* 2,041 graduate, professional, and undergraduate students; 39 full-time matriculated graduate/professional students (28 women), 136 part-time matriculated graduate/professional students (85 women). *Enrollment by degree level:* 175 master's. *Graduate faculty:* 29 full-time (18 women), 5 part-time/adjunct (all women). Tuition, state resident: full-time $8350; part-time $348 per credit hour. Tuition, nonresident: full-time $19,047; part-time $793.65 per credit hour. *Required fees:* $1689; $70 per credit hour. $5. Tuition and fees vary according to program. *Student services:* Campus employment opportunities, campus safety program, career counseling, exercise/wellness program, free psychological counseling, international student services, low-cost health insurance, services for students with disabilities, teacher training, writing training. *Library:* USF Libraries. *Collection:* Books: 1,279 (physical), 297,253 (digital/electronic); Serial titles: 139 (physical), 43,142 (digital/electronic); Databases: 930. Weekly public service hours: 96; students can reserve study rooms.

Computer facilities: Computer purchase and lease plans are available. 18 computers available on campus for general student use. A campuswide network can be accessed. Online class registration is available.
Website: http://www.usfsm.edu/

General Application Contact: Andy Telatovich, Director, Admissions, 941-359-4330, E-mail: atelatovich@sar.usf.edu.

GRADUATE UNITS

College of Arts and Sciences Students: 20 part-time (13 women); includes 7 minority (1 Black or African American, non-Hispanic/Latino; 1 American Indian or Alaska Native, non-Hispanic/Latino; 5 Hispanic/Latino). Average age 33. 17 applicants, 47% accepted, 7 enrolled. *Faculty:* 5 full-time (3 women), 1 (woman) part-time/adjunct. *Financial support:* Career-related internships or fieldwork, institutionally sponsored loans, scholarships/grants, health care benefits, and unspecified assistantships available. Support available to part-time students. Financial award application deadline: 3/1; financial award applicants required to submit FAFSA. In 2015, 3 master's awarded. *Degree program information:* Part-time programs available. Part-time, blended/hybrid learning. Offers criminal justice administration (MA). *Application deadline:* For fall admission, 3/1 priority date for domestic students, 3/1 for international students; for spring admission, 10/1 priority date for domestic students, 10/1 for international students. Applications are processed on a rolling basis. *Application fee:* $30. Electronic applications accepted. *Application Contact:* Andy Telatovich, Director, Admissions, 941-359-4330, Fax: 941-359-4585, E-mail: atelatovich@sar.usf.edu. *Dean*, Dr. Jane Rose, 941-359-4469, Fax: 941-359-4489, E-mail: jane.rose@sar.usf.edu.

College of Business Students: 5 full-time (3 women), 64 part-time (34 women); includes 20 minority (6 Black or African American, non-Hispanic/Latino; 1 American Indian or Alaska Native, non-Hispanic/Latino; 6 Asian, non-Hispanic/Latino; 7 Hispanic/Latino). Average age 32. 68 applicants, 41% accepted, 26 enrolled. *Faculty:* 8 full-time (1 woman). *Financial support:* In 2015–16, 1 student received support. Federal Work-Study, scholarships/grants, health care benefits, and unspecified assistantships available. Support available to part-time students. Financial award application deadline: 3/1; financial award applicants required to submit FAFSA. In 2015, 16 master's awarded. *Degree program information:* Part-time and evening/weekend programs available. Part-time, evening/weekend. Offers business (MBA). *Application deadline:* For fall admission, 3/1 priority date for domestic students, 3/1 for international students; for spring admission, 10/1 priority date for domestic students, 10/1 for international students. Applications are processed on a rolling basis. *Application fee:* $30. Electronic applications accepted. *Application Contact:* Andy Telatovich, Director, Admissions, 941-359-4330, E-mail: atelatovich@sar.usf.edu. *Dean*, Dr. James M. Curran, 941-359-4605, Fax: 941-359-4367, E-mail: jmcurran@sar.usf.edu.

College of Education Students: 10 full-time (6 women), 45 part-time (35 women); includes 9 minority (3 Black or African American, non-Hispanic/Latino; 1 American Indian or Alaska Native, non-Hispanic/Latino; 2 Asian, non-Hispanic/Latino; 3 Hispanic/Latino). Average age 38. 42 applicants, 45% accepted, 16 enrolled. *Faculty:* 8 full-time (7 women), 5 part-time/adjunct (all women). *Financial support:* In 2015–16, 14 students received support. Career-related internships or fieldwork, institutionally sponsored loans, scholarships/grants, health care benefits, and unspecified assistantships available. Support available to part-time students. Financial award application deadline: 3/1; financial award applicants required to submit FAFSA. In 2015, 19 master's awarded. *Degree program information:* Part-time programs available. Part-time, 100% online. Offers education (MA); educational leadership (M Ed); elementary education (MAT); English education (MA). *Application deadline:* For fall admission, 3/1 priority date for domestic students, 3/1 for international students; for spring admission, 10/1 priority date for domestic students, 10/1 for international students. Applications are processed on a rolling basis. *Application fee:* $30. Electronic applications accepted. *Application Contact:* Andy Telatovich, Director, Admissions, 941-359-4330, Fax: 941-359-4585, E-mail: atelatovich@sar.usf.edu. *Interim Dean*, Dr. Georgia Pat Wilson, 941-359-4531, Fax: 941-359-4778, E-mail: gpwilson@sar.usf.edu.

College of Hospitality and Technology Leadership Students: 24 full-time (19 women), 7 part-time (3 women); includes 3 minority (1 Asian, non-Hispanic/Latino; 1 Hispanic/Latino; 1 Two or more races, non-Hispanic/Latino), 14 international. Average age 33. 30 applicants, 60% accepted, 15 enrolled. *Faculty:* 3 full-time (2 women). *Financial support:* In 2015–16, 1 student received support, including 7 research assistantships with tuition reimbursements available (averaging $7,904 per year); teaching assistantships with tuition reimbursements available, career-related internships or fieldwork, institutionally sponsored loans, health care benefits, and unspecified assistantships also available. Support available to part-time students. Financial award application deadline: 3/1; financial award applicants required to submit FAFSA. In 2015, 12 master's awarded. *Degree program information:* Part-time programs available. Part-time. Offers hospitality management (MS). *Application deadline:* For fall admission, 3/1 priority date for domestic students, 3/1 for international students; for spring admission, 10/1 priority date for domestic students, 10/1 for international students. Applications are processed on a rolling basis. *Application fee:* $30. Electronic applications accepted. *Application Contact:* Andy Telatovich, Director, Admissions, 941-359-4330, E-mail: atelatovich@sar.usf.edu. *Interim Dean*, Dr. James M. Curran, 941-359-4605, E-mail: jmcurran@sar.usf.edu.

★ THE UNIVERSITY OF TAMPA, Tampa, FL 33606-1490

General Information Independent, coed, comprehensive institution. *Enrollment:* 7,959 graduate, professional, and undergraduate students; 386 full-time matriculated graduate/professional students (146 women), 494 part-time matriculated graduate/professional students (304 women). *Enrollment by degree level:* 880 master's. *Graduate faculty:* 73 full-time (33 women), 11 part-time/adjunct (5 women). *Tuition, area resident:* Full-time $7056; part-time $588 per credit. *Required fees:* $80; $40 per term. Tuition and fees vary according to program. *Graduate housing:* Rooms and/or apartments available on a first-come, first-served basis to single and married students. Typical cost: $4157 per year for single students; $4157 per year for married students. Room charges vary according to board plan and housing facility selected. Housing application deadline: 5/1. *Student services:* Campus employment opportunities, campus safety program, career counseling, international student services, services for students with disabilities. *Library:* Macdonald Kelce Library. *Collection:* Books: 204,709 (physical), 115,020 (digital/electronic); Serial titles: 1,214 (physical), 138,927 (digital/electronic); Databases: 159. Weekly public service hours: 107; students can reserve study rooms. *Research affiliation:* Tampa General Hospital (nursing).

Computer facilities: Computer purchase and lease plans are available. 795 computers available on campus for general student use. A campuswide network can be accessed from student residence rooms and from off campus. Online class registration is available.
Website: http://www.ut.edu/

General Application Contact: Dr. Joshua Stagner, Director of Graduate and Continuing Studies, 813-257-3016, Fax: 813-258-7451, E-mail: jstagner@ut.edu.

GRADUATE UNITS

Program in Creative Writing Students: 63 full-time (40 women); includes 16 minority (4 Black or African American, non-Hispanic/Latino; 1 Asian, non-Hispanic/Latino; 8 Hispanic/Latino; 3 Two or more races, non-Hispanic/Latino), 1 international. Average age 39. 46 applicants, 59% accepted, 14 enrolled. *Faculty:* 12 full-time (4 women). *Financial support:* In 2015–16, 18 students received support. Career-related internships or fieldwork, scholarships/grants, and unspecified assistantships available. Financial award applicants required to submit FAFSA. In 2015, 30 master's awarded. *Degree program information:* Part-time programs available. Part-time. Offers creative writing (MFA). *Application deadline:* Applications are processed on a rolling basis. *Application fee:* $40. Electronic applications accepted. *Application Contact:* Chanelle Cox, Staff Assistant, Graduate and Continuing Studies, 813-253-6249, E-mail: ccox@ut.edu. *Director*, Dr. Erica Dawson, 813-257-6311, E-mail: edawson@ut.edu.

Program in Exercise and Nutrition Science Students: 47 full-time (17 women), 5 part-time (2 women); includes 2 minority (both Black or African American, non-Hispanic/Latino), 3 international. Average age 25. 185 applicants, 40% accepted, 42 enrolled. *Faculty:* 6 full-time (3 women). *Financial support:* In 2015–16, 5 students received support. Career-related internships or fieldwork, scholarships/grants, and unspecified assistantships available. Financial award applicants required to submit FAFSA. *Degree program information:* Part-time and evening/weekend programs available. Part-time, evening/weekend. Offers exercise and nutrition science (MS). *Application deadline:* Applications are processed on a rolling basis. *Application fee:* $40. Electronic applications accepted. *Application Contact:* Chanelle Cox, Staff Assistant, Admissions for Graduate and Continuing Studies, 813-253-6249, E-mail: ccox@ut.edu.

Program in Nursing Students: 1 (woman) full-time, 152 part-time (130 women); includes 27 minority (9 Black or African American, non-Hispanic/Latino; 1 American Indian or Alaska Native, non-Hispanic/Latino; 9 Asian, non-Hispanic/Latino; 8 Two or more races, non-Hispanic/Latino). Average age 33. 112 applicants, 54% accepted, 32 enrolled. *Faculty:* 15 full-time (13 women), 4 part-time/adjunct (3 women). *Financial support:* In 2015–16, 5 students received support. Career-related internships or fieldwork, scholarships/grants, and unspecified assistantships available. Financial award applicants required to submit FAFSA. In 2015, 33 master's awarded. *Degree program information:* Part-time and evening/weekend programs available. Part-time, evening/weekend. Offers adult nursing practitioner (MSN); family nursing practitioner (MSN); nursing (MS). *Application deadline:* Applications are processed on a rolling basis. *Application fee:* $40. Electronic applications accepted. *Application Contact:* Chanelle Cox, Staff Assistant, Admissions for Graduate and Continuing Studies, 813-

253-6249, E-mail: ccox@ut.edu. *Director*, Dr. Cathy Kessenich, 813-257-3160, Fax: 813-258-7214, E-mail: ckessenich@ut.edu.

Programs in Education Students: 15 full-time (11 women), 41 part-time (34 women); includes 4 minority (3 Black or African American, non-Hispanic/Latino; 1 Asian, non-Hispanic/Latino), 8 international. Average age 30. 113 applicants, 50% accepted, 22 enrolled. *Faculty:* 16 full-time (12 women). *Financial support:* In 2015–16, 28 students received support. Career-related internships or fieldwork, scholarships/grants, and unspecified assistantships available. Financial award applicants required to submit FAFSA. In 2015, 26 master's awarded. *Degree program information:* Part-time and evening/weekend programs available. Part-time, evening/weekend. Offers curriculum and instruction (M Ed); instructional design and technology (MS). *Application deadline:* Applications are processed on a rolling basis. *Application fee:* $40. Electronic applications accepted. *Application Contact:* Chanelle Cox, Staff Assistant I, Admissions for Graduate and Continuing Studies, 813-253-6249, E-mail: ccox@ut.edu. *Chair*, Dr. Antony Erben, 813-257-3414, E-mail: terben@ut.edu.

Sykes College of Business Students: 323 full-time (117 women), 292 part-time (137 women); includes 38 minority (17 Black or African American, non-Hispanic/Latino; 1 American Indian or Alaska Native, non-Hispanic/Latino; 14 Asian, non-Hispanic/Latino; 1 Native Hawaiian or other Pacific Islander, non-Hispanic/Latino; 5 Two or more races, non-Hispanic/Latino), 233 international. Average age 28. 1,588 applicants, 34% accepted, 226 enrolled. *Faculty:* 54 full-time (20 women), 7 part-time/adjunct (2 women). *Financial support:* In 2015–16, 117 students received support. Career-related internships or fieldwork, scholarships/grants, and unspecified assistantships available. Financial award applicants required to submit FAFSA. In 2015, 220 master's awarded. *Degree program information:* Part-time and evening/weekend programs available. Part-time, evening/weekend. Offers accounting (MS); entrepreneurship (MBA); finance (MBA, MS); information systems management (MBA); innovation management (MBA); international business (MBA); marketing (MBA, MS); nonprofit management (MBA). *Application deadline:* Applications are processed on a rolling basis. *Application fee:* $40. Electronic applications accepted. *Application Contact:* Chanelle Cox, Staff Assistant I, Admissions for Graduate and Continuing Studies, 813-253-6249, E-mail: ccox@ut.edu. *Associate Dean*, Dr. Stephanie Thomason, 813-253-6289, E-mail: sthomason@ut.edu.

See Display below and Close-Up on page 911.

THE UNIVERSITY OF TENNESSEE, Knoxville, TN 37996

General Information State-supported, coed, university. CGS member. *Graduate housing:* Room and/or apartments available on a first-come, first-served basis to single students; on-campus housing not available to married students. Housing application deadline: 2/1. *Research affiliation:* Intel Corporation (computational science), Boeing (mechanical and aerospace engineering), Eastman Chemical (chemical engineering, chemistry), Mars (materials science and engineering, polymer science, food science), DuPont (biofuels), Goodyear (chemical engineering; materials science and engineering; polymer science).

GRADUATE UNITS

College of Law Students: 385 full-time (175 women); includes 75 minority (38 Black or African American, non-Hispanic/Latino; 1 American Indian or Alaska Native, non-Hispanic/Latino; 10 Asian, non-Hispanic/Latino; 12 Hispanic/Latino; 14 Two or more races, non-Hispanic/Latino), 2 international. Average age 23. 1,004 applicants, 37% accepted, 116 enrolled. *Faculty:* 42 full-time (22 women), 38 part-time/adjunct (14 women). *Financial support:* In 2015–16, 233 students received support, including 12 research assistantships with full tuition reimbursements available (averaging $32,388 per year); career-related internships or fieldwork, Federal Work-Study, institutionally sponsored loans, scholarships/grants, and unspecified assistantships also available. Support available to part-time students. Financial award application deadline: 3/1; financial award applicants required to submit FAFSA. In 2015, 127 doctorates awarded. Offers business transactions (JD); law (JD); trial advocacy and dispute resolution (JD). *Application deadline:* For fall admission, 3/1 priority date for domestic and international students. Applications are processed on a rolling basis. *Application fee:* $15. Electronic applications accepted. *Application Contact:* Janet S. Hatcher, Interim Director of Admissions and Financial Aid, 865-974-4131, Fax: 865-974-1572, E-mail: hatcher@utk.edu. *Interim Director of Admissions and Financial Aid*, Janet S. Hatcher, 865-974-4131, Fax: 865-974-1572, E-mail: lawadmit@utk.edu.

Graduate School *Degree program information:* Part-time and evening/weekend programs available. Part-time, evening/weekend, online learning. Offers aviation systems (MS); comparative and experimental medicine (MS, PhD). Electronic applications accepted.

College of Agricultural Sciences and Natural Resources ***Degree program information:*** Part-time programs available. Part-time, online learning. Offers agricultural education (MS); agricultural extension education (MS); agricultural sciences and natural resources (MS, PhD); animal anatomy (PhD); biosystems engineering (MS, PhD); biosystems engineering technology (MS); breeding (MS, PhD); entomology (MS, PhD); floriculture (MS); food science and technology (MS, PhD); forestry (MS); integrated pest management and bioactive natural products (PhD); landscape design (MS); management (MS, PhD); nutrition (MS, PhD); physiology (MS, PhD); plant pathology (MS, PhD); public horticulture (MS); turfgrass (MS); wildlife and fisheries science (MS); woody ornamentals (MS). Electronic applications accepted.

College of Architecture and Design Offers architecture (professional) (M Arch); architecture (research) (M Arch); architecture and design (M Arch, MA, MLA, MS); landscape architecture (MLA); landscape architecture (research) (MA, MS). Electronic applications accepted.

College of Arts and Sciences ***Degree program information:*** Part-time and evening/weekend programs available. Part-time, evening/weekend. Offers accompanying (MM); American history (PhD); analytical chemistry (MS, PhD); applied linguistics (PhD); applied mathematics (MS); archaeology (MA, PhD); arts and sciences (M Math, MA, MFA, MM, MPA, MS, PhD); audiology (MA); behavior (MS, PhD); biochemistry, cellular and molecular biology (MS, PhD); biological anthropology (MA, PhD); ceramics (MFA); chemical physics (PhD); choral conducting (MM); clinical psychology (PhD); composition (MM); computer science (MS, PhD); costume design (MFA); criminology (MA, PhD); cultural anthropology (MA, PhD); drawing (MFA); ecology (MS, PhD); energy, environment, and resource policy (MA, PhD); English (MA, PhD); environmental chemistry (MS, PhD); European history (PhD); evolutionary biology (MS, PhD); experimental psychology (MA, PhD); French (MA, PhD); genome science and technology (MS, PhD); geography (MS, PhD); geology (MS, PhD); German (MA); graphic design (MFA); hearing science (PhD); history (MA); inorganic chemistry (MS, PhD); instrumental conducting (MM); inter-area studies (MFA); Italian (PhD); jazz (MM); lighting design (MFA); mathematical ecology (PhD); mathematics (M Math, MS, PhD); media arts (MFA); medical ethics (MA, PhD); microbiology (MS, PhD); modern foreign languages (PhD); music education (MM); music theory (MM); musicology (MM); organic chemistry (MS, PhD);

painting (MFA); performance (MFA, MM); philosophy (MA, PhD); physical chemistry (MS, PhD); physics (MS, PhD); piano pedagogy and literature (MM); plant physiology and genetics (MS, PhD); political economy (MA, PhD); political science (MA, MPA, PhD); polymer chemistry (MS, PhD); Portuguese (PhD); printmaking (MFA); psychology (MA); public administration (MPA); religious studies (MA); Russian (PhD); scene design (MFA); sculpture (MFA); Spanish (MA); speech and hearing science (PhD); speech and language pathology (PhD); speech and language science (PhD); speech pathology (MA); theatre technology (MFA); theoretical chemistry (PhD); watercolor (MFA); zoo-archaeology (MA, PhD). Electronic applications accepted.

College of Business Administration Degree program information: Part-time programs available. Part-time, online learning. Offers accounting (M Acc, PhD); business administration (M Acc, MA, MBA, MS, PhD); economics (MA, PhD); finance (MBA, PhD); industrial and organizational psychology (PhD); industrial statistics (MS); logistics and transportation (MBA, PhD); management (PhD); management science (MS, PhD); marketing (MBA, PhD); operations management (MBA); professional business administration (MBA); statistics (MS, PhD); systems (M Acc); taxation (M Acc); teacher licensure (MS); training and development (MS). Electronic applications accepted.

College of Communication and Information Degree program information: Part-time and evening/weekend programs available. Part-time, evening/weekend, online learning. Offers advertising (MS, PhD); broadcasting (MS, PhD); communications (MS, PhD); information sciences (MS, PhD); journalism (MS, PhD); public relations (MS, PhD); speech communication (MS, PhD). Electronic applications accepted.

College of Education, Health and Human Sciences Degree program information: Part-time and evening/weekend programs available. Part-time, evening/weekend, online learning. Offers adult education (MS); applied educational psychology (MS); art education (MS); biomechanics/sports medicine (MS, PhD); child and family studies (MS, PhD); collaborative learning (Ed D); college student personnel (MS); community health (PhD); community health education (MPH); consumer services management (MS); counseling education (PhD); cultural studies in education (PhD); curriculum (MS, Ed S); curriculum, educational research and evaluation (Ed D, PhD); early childhood education (MS, PhD); early childhood special education (MS); education of deaf and hard of hearing (MS); education, health and human sciences (MPH, MS, Ed D, PhD, Ed S); educational administration and policy studies (Ed D, PhD); educational administration and supervision (MS, Ed S); educational psychology (Ed D, PhD); elementary education (MS, Ed S); elementary teaching (MS); English education (MS, Ed S); exercise physiology (MS, PhD); exercise science (MS, PhD); foreign language/ESL education (MS, Ed S); gerontology (MPH); health planning/administration (MPH); health promotion and health education (MS); hospitality management (MS); hotel, restaurant, and tourism management (MS); instructional technology (MS, Ed D, PhD, Ed S); literacy, language and ESL education (PhD); literacy, language education, and ESL education (Ed D); mathematics education (MS, Ed S); mental health counseling (MS); modified and comprehensive special education (MS); nutrition (MS); nutrition science (PhD); reading education (MS, Ed S); recreation and leisure studies (MS); rehabilitation counseling (MS); retail and consumer sciences (MS); retailing and consumer sciences (PhD); safety (MS); school counseling (MS, Ed S); school psychology (PhD, Ed S); science education (MS, Ed S); secondary teaching (MS); social foundations (MS); social science education (MS, Ed S); socio-cultural foundations of sports and education (PhD); special education (Ed S); sport management (MS); sport studies (MS, PhD); teacher education (Ed D, PhD); textile science (MS, PhD); therapeutic recreation (MS); tourism (MS). Electronic applications accepted.

College of Engineering Students: 751 full-time (158 women), 239 part-time (41 women); includes 88 minority (20 Black or African American, non-Hispanic/Latino; 4 American Indian or Alaska Native, non-Hispanic/Latino; 29 Asian, non-Hispanic/Latino; 26 Hispanic/Latino; 9 Two or more races, non-Hispanic/Latino), 382 international. Average age 30. 1,349 applicants, 32% accepted, 230 enrolled. *Faculty:* 262 full-time (39 women), 56 part-time/adjunct (8 women). *Financial support:* In 2015–16, 617 students received support, including 95 fellowships with full tuition reimbursements available (averaging $27,207 per year), 456 research assistantships with full tuition reimbursements available (averaging $22,413 per year), 199 teaching assistantships with full tuition reimbursements available (averaging $19,617 per year); career-related internships or fieldwork, Federal Work-Study, institutionally sponsored loans, health care benefits, and unspecified assistantships also available. Financial award application deadline: 2/1; financial award applicants required to submit FAFSA. In 2015, 152 master's, 85 doctorates awarded. *Degree program information:* Part-time programs available. Part-time, online learning. Offers aerospace engineering (MS, PhD); biomedical engineering (MS, PhD); chemical engineering (MS, PhD); civil engineering (MS, PhD); computer engineering (MS, PhD); computer science (MS, PhD); electrical engineering (MS, PhD); energy science and engineering (PhD); engineering (MS, PhD); engineering management (MS); engineering science (MS, PhD); environmental engineering (MS); industrial engineering (MS, PhD); materials science and engineering (MS, PhD); mechanical engineering (MS, PhD); nuclear engineering (MS, PhD); polymer engineering (MS, PhD); reliability and maintainability engineering (MS). *Application deadline:* For fall admission, 2/1 priority date for domestic and international students; for spring admission, 6/15 for domestic and international students. Applications are processed on a rolling basis. *Application fee:* $35. Electronic applications accepted. *Application Contact:* Dr. Masood Parang, Associate Dean of Student Affairs, 865-974-2454, Fax: 865-974-9871, E-mail: mparang@utk.edu. *Dean*, Dr. Wayne T. Davis, 865-974-5321, Fax: 865-974-8890, E-mail: wtdavis@utk.edu.

College of Nursing Degree program information: Part-time programs available. Part-time. Offers nursing (MSN, PhD). Electronic applications accepted.

College of Social Work Degree program information: Part-time programs available. Part-time, online learning. Offers clinical practice and leadership (DSW); evidenced-based interpersonal practice (MSSW); management leadership and community practice (MSSW); social work (MSSW, DSW, PhD). Electronic applications accepted.

College of Veterinary Medicine Offers veterinary medicine (DVM).

The University of Tennessee Space Institute Students: 32 full-time (7 women), 71 part-time (10 women); includes 10 minority (5 Black or African American, non-Hispanic/Latino; 1 American Indian or Alaska Native, non-Hispanic/Latino; 3 Asian, non-Hispanic/Latino; 1 Hispanic/Latino), 11 international. *Faculty:* 27 full-time (1 woman), 12 part-time/adjunct (1 woman). *Financial support:* In 2015–16, 2 fellowships with full tuition reimbursements (averaging $2,496 per year), 24 research assistantships with full tuition reimbursements (averaging $22,872 per year) were awarded; career-related internships or fieldwork, Federal Work-Study, institutionally sponsored loans, health care benefits, and unspecified assistantships also available. In 2015, 26 master's, 2 doctorates awarded. *Degree program information:* Part-time programs available. Part-time, blended/hybrid learning. Offers aerospace engineering (MS, PhD); biomedical engineering (MS, PhD); engineering science (MS, PhD); industrial and systems engineering/engineering management (MS, PhD); mechanical engineering (MS, PhD); physics (MS, PhD). *Application deadline:* For fall admission, 2/1 for international students; for spring admission, 6/15 for international students. Applications are processed on a rolling basis. *Application fee:* $60. Electronic applications accepted. *Application Contact:* Dee Merriman, Director, 931-393-7213, Fax: 931-393-7211, E-mail: dmerrima@utsi.edu. *Associate Executive Director*, Dr. James Simonton, 931-393-7319, Fax: 931-393-7211, E-mail: jsimonto@utsi.edu.

THE UNIVERSITY OF TENNESSEE AT CHATTANOOGA, Chattanooga, TN 37403-2598

General Information State-supported, coed, comprehensive institution. CGS member. *Enrollment:* 11,388 graduate, professional, and undergraduate students; 601 full-time matriculated graduate/professional students (354 women), 667 part-time matriculated graduate/professional students (336 women). *Enrollment by degree level:* 961 master's, 272 doctoral, 35 other advanced degrees. *Graduate faculty:* 155 full-time (58 women), 22 part-time/adjunct (10 women). Tuition, state resident: full-time $7938; part-time $441 per credit hour. Tuition, nonresident: full-time $24,056; part-time $1336 per credit hour. *Required fees:* $1732; $253 per credit hour. *Graduate housing:* Room and/or apartments available on a first-come, first-served basis to single students; on-campus housing not available to married students. Typical cost: $5068 per year ($8388 including board). Room and board charges vary according to board plan and housing facility selected. Housing application deadline: 6/1. *Student services:* Campus employment opportunities, campus safety program, career counseling, exercise/wellness program, free psychological counseling, grant writing training, international student services, low-cost health insurance, multicultural affairs office, services for students with disabilities, teacher training, writing training. *Library:* UTC Library plus 1 other. *Collection:* Books: 602,870 (physical); Databases: 158. Study areas open 24 hours, 5–7 days a week; students can reserve study rooms. *Research affiliation:* Law Enforcement Innovation Center (criminal justice), Highland Biological Field Station (biology and environmental science), Tennessee Valley Authority, Gulf Coast Research Laboratory (biology and environmental science), Tennessee Coalition against Domestic and Sexual Violence (criminal justice).

Computer facilities: A campuswide network can be accessed from student residence rooms and from off campus. Online class registration is available.
Website: http://www.utc.edu/

General Application Contact: Dr. J. Randy Walker, Interim Dean of Graduate Studies, 423-425-4478, Fax: 423-425-5223, E-mail: randy-walker@utc.edu.

GRADUATE UNITS

Department of Health and Human Performance Students: 9 full-time (3 women), 1 (woman) part-time; includes 2 minority (both Black or African American, non-Hispanic/Latino). Average age 24. 17 applicants, 35% accepted, 4 enrolled. *Faculty:* 5 full-time (3 women). *Financial support:* In 2015–16, 6 research assistantships with tuition reimbursements (averaging $5,320 per year), 2 teaching assistantships with tuition reimbursements (averaging $3,432 per year) were awarded; career-related internships or fieldwork, scholarships/grants, and unspecified assistantships also available. Support available to part-time students. Financial award applicants required to submit FAFSA. In 2015, 22 master's awarded. Offers athletic training (MSAT); health and human performance (MS). *Application deadline:* For fall admission, 6/13 priority date for domestic students, 6/1 for international students; for spring admission, 10/15 priority date for domestic students, 10/1 for international students. Applications are processed on a rolling basis. *Application fee:* $30 ($35 for international students). Electronic applications accepted. *Application Contact:* Dr. J. Randy Walker, Interim Dean of Graduate Studies, 423-425-4478, Fax: 423-425-5223, E-mail: randy-walker@utc.edu. *Department Head*, Dr. Gary Liguori, 423-425-4196, Fax: 423-425-4457, E-mail: gary-liguori@utc.edu.

Department of Political Science Students: 13 full-time (6 women), 18 part-time (12 women); includes 4 minority (3 Black or African American, non-Hispanic/Latino; 1 Hispanic/Latino). Average age 29. 16 applicants, 88% accepted, 11 enrolled. *Faculty:* 3 full-time (0 women). *Financial support:* In 2015–16, 3 research assistantships with tuition reimbursements (averaging $6,860 per year) were awarded; career-related internships or fieldwork, scholarships/grants, and unspecified assistantships also available. Support available to part-time students. Financial award applicants required to submit FAFSA. In 2015, 12 master's awarded. *Degree program information:* Part-time and evening/weekend programs available. Part-time, evening/weekend. Offers local government management (MPA); non profit management (MPA); public administration (MPA); public administration and non-profit management (Postbaccalaureate Certificate). *Application deadline:* For fall admission, 6/13 priority date for domestic students, 6/1 for international students; for spring admission, 10/15 priority date for domestic students, 10/1 for international students. Applications are processed on a rolling basis. *Application fee:* $30 ($35 for international students). Electronic applications accepted. *Application Contact:* Dr. J. Randy Walker, Interim Dean of Graduate Studies, 423-425-4478, Fax: 423-425-5223, E-mail: randy-walker@utc.edu. *Department Head*, Dr. Michelle D. Deardorf, 423-425-4231, Fax: 423-425-2373, E-mail: michelle-deardorff@utc.edu.

Engineering Management and Technology Program Students: 19 full-time (7 women), 55 part-time (9 women); includes 17 minority (8 Black or African American, non-Hispanic/Latino; 4 Asian, non-Hispanic/Latino; 3 Hispanic/Latino; 2 Two or more races, non-Hispanic/Latino), 20 international. Average age 31. 31 applicants, 45% accepted, 16 enrolled. *Faculty:* 5 full-time (1 woman). *Financial support:* In 2015–16, 5 research assistantships (averaging $6,528 per year), 3 teaching assistantships (averaging $6,781 per year) were awarded; career-related internships or fieldwork, scholarships/grants, and unspecified assistantships also available. Support available to part-time students. Financial award applicants required to submit FAFSA. In 2015, 31 master's, 17 other advanced degrees awarded. 100% online, blended/hybrid learning. Offers engineering management (MS); fundamentals of engineering management (Graduate Certificate); leadership and ethics (Graduate Certificate); logistics and supply chain management (Graduate Certificate); nuclear engineering (Graduate Certificate); power system protection (Graduate Certificate); power systems management (Graduate Certificate); project and technology management (Graduate Certificate); quality management (Graduate Certificate); sustainable electric energy (Graduate Certificate). *Application deadline:* For fall admission, 6/13 priority date for domestic students, 6/1 for international students; for spring admission, 10/15 priority date for domestic students, 10/1 for international students. Applications are processed on a rolling basis. *Application fee:* $30 ($35 for international students). Electronic applications accepted. *Application Contact:* Dr. J. Randy Walker, Interim Dean of Graduate Studies, 423-425-4478, Fax: 423-425-5223, E-mail: randy-walker@utc.edu. *Department Head*, Dr. Neslihan Alp, 423-425-4032, Fax: 423-425-5229, E-mail: neslihan-alp@utc.edu.

Program in Accountancy Students: 9 full-time (6 women), 13 part-time (7 women); includes 4 minority (1 Black or African American, non-Hispanic/Latino; 2 Asian, non-Hispanic/Latino; 1 Two or more races, non-Hispanic/Latino), 2 international. Average

age 28. 43 applicants, 33% accepted, 5 enrolled. *Faculty:* 5 full-time (2 women). *Financial support:* Research assistantships, teaching assistantships, career-related internships or fieldwork, scholarships/grants, and unspecified assistantships available. Support available to part-time students. Financial award applicants required to submit FAFSA. In 2015, 25 master's awarded. *Degree program information:* Part-time and evening/weekend programs available. Part-time, evening/weekend. Offers accountancy (M Acc). *Application deadline:* For fall admission, 6/13 priority date for domestic students, 6/1 for international students; for spring admission, 10/15 priority date for domestic students, 10/1 for international students. Applications are processed on a rolling basis. *Application fee:* $30 ($35 for international students). Electronic applications accepted. *Application Contact:* Dr. J. Randy Walker, Interim Dean of Graduate Studies, 423-425-4478, Fax: 423-425-5223, E-mail: randy-walker@utc.edu. *Department Head*, Dr. Dan Hollingsworth, 423-425-4664, Fax: 423-425-5255, E-mail: dan-hollingsworth@utc.edu.

Program in Business Administration Students: 65 full-time (27 women), 222 part-time (95 women); includes 43 minority (11 Black or African American, non-Hispanic/Latino; 11 Asian, non-Hispanic/Latino; 8 Hispanic/Latino; 1 Native Hawaiian or other Pacific Islander, non-Hispanic/Latino; 12 Two or more races, non-Hispanic/Latino), 6 international. Average age 31. 97 applicants, 71% accepted, 48 enrolled. *Faculty:* 15 full-time (1 woman), 3 part-time/adjunct (2 women). *Financial support:* Research assistantships, teaching assistantships, career-related internships or fieldwork, scholarships/grants, health care benefits, tuition waivers (partial), and unspecified assistantships available. Support available to part-time students. In 2015, 98 master's awarded. *Degree program information:* Part-time and evening/weekend programs available. Part-time, evening/weekend. Offers business administration (EMBA, MBA, PMBA). *Application deadline:* For fall admission, 6/13 priority date for domestic students, 6/1 for international students; for spring admission, 10/15 priority date for domestic students, 10/1 for international students. Applications are processed on a rolling basis. *Application fee:* $30 ($35 for international students). Electronic applications accepted. *Application Contact:* Dr. J. Randy Walker, Interim Dean of Graduate Studies, 423-425-4478, Fax: 423-425-5223, E-mail: randy-walker@utc.edu. *Director of Graduate Programs*, Elizabeth Bell, 423-425-2326, Fax: 423-425-5255, E-mail: elizabeth-bell@utc.edu.

Program in Computational Science Students: 4 full-time (2 women), 18 part-time (3 women); includes 2 minority (1 Black or African American, non-Hispanic/Latino; 1 Two or more races, non-Hispanic/Latino), 14 international. Average age 31. *Faculty:* 7 full-time (0 women). *Financial support:* Research assistantships, career-related internships or fieldwork, scholarships/grants, and unspecified assistantships available. Support available to part-time students. In 2015, 2 doctorates awarded. Offers computational science (PhD). *Application deadline:* For fall admission, 6/13 priority date for domestic students, 6/1 for international students; for spring admission, 10/15 priority date for domestic students, 10/1 for international students. Applications are processed on a rolling basis. *Application fee:* $30 ($35 for international students). Electronic applications accepted. *Application Contact:* Dr. J. Randy Walker, Interim Dean of Graduate Studies, 423-425-4478, Fax: 423-425-5223, E-mail: randy-walker@utc.edu. *Dean*, Dr. Tim W. Swafford, 423-425-5507, Fax: 423-425-5517, E-mail: tim-swafford@utc.edu.

Program in Computer Science Students: 20 full-time (6 women), 28 part-time (8 women); includes 13 minority (4 Black or African American, non-Hispanic/Latino; 4 Asian, non-Hispanic/Latino; 2 Hispanic/Latino; 3 Two or more races, non-Hispanic/Latino), 14 international. Average age 31. *Faculty:* 5 full-time (2 women). *Financial support:* Research assistantships, teaching assistantships, career-related internships or fieldwork, scholarships/grants, health care benefits, and unspecified assistantships available. Support available to part-time students. In 2015, 8 master's awarded. *Degree program information:* Part-time programs available. Part-time. Offers computer science (MS). *Application deadline:* For fall admission, 6/13 priority date for domestic students, 6/1 for international students; for spring admission, 10/15 priority date for domestic students, 10/1 for international students. Applications are processed on a rolling basis. *Application fee:* $30 ($35 for international students). Electronic applications accepted. *Application Contact:* Dr. J. Randy Walker, Interim Dean of Graduate Studies, 423-425-4478, Fax: 423-425-5223, E-mail: randy-walker@utc.edu. *Department Head*, Dr. Joseph Kizza, 423-425-4349, Fax: 423-425-5442, E-mail: joseph-kizza@utc.edu.

Program in Criminal Justice Students: 16 full-time (8 women), 16 part-time (9 women); includes 12 minority (9 Black or African American, non-Hispanic/Latino; 2 Hispanic/Latino; 1 Two or more races, non-Hispanic/Latino). Average age 30. *Faculty:* 5 full-time (2 women). *Financial support:* Research assistantships, teaching assistantships, career-related internships or fieldwork, scholarships/grants, and unspecified assistantships available. Support available to part-time students. Financial award applicants required to submit FAFSA. In 2015, 12 master's awarded. *Degree program information:* Part-time programs available. Part-time. Offers criminal justice (MSCJ). *Application deadline:* For fall admission, 6/13 priority date for domestic students, 6/1 for international students; for spring admission, 10/15 priority date for domestic students, 10/1 for international students. Applications are processed on a rolling basis. *Application fee:* $30 ($35 for international students). Electronic applications accepted. *Application Contact:* Dr. J. Randy Walker, Interim Dean of Graduate Studies, 423-425-4478, Fax: 423-425-5223, E-mail: randy-walker@utc.edu. *Acting Department Head*, Dr. Tammy Garland, 423-425-5245, Fax: 423-425-2228, E-mail: tammy-garland@utc.edu.

Program in Engineering Students: 36 full-time (13 women), 39 part-time (6 women); includes 8 minority (3 Black or African American, non-Hispanic/Latino; 4 Asian, non-Hispanic/Latino; 1 Hispanic/Latino), 32 international. Average age 29. *Faculty:* 20 full-time (3 women), 3 part-time/adjunct (0 women). *Financial support:* Research assistantships, teaching assistantships, career-related internships or fieldwork, scholarships/grants, health care benefits, and unspecified assistantships available. Support available to part-time students. In 2015, 29 master's awarded. *Degree program information:* Part-time programs available. Part-time. Offers automotive systems (MS Engr); chemical engineering (MS Engr); civil engineering (MS Engr); computational engineering (MS Engr); electrical engineering (MS Engr); industrial engineering (MS Engr); mechanical engineering (MS Engr). *Application deadline:* For fall admission, 6/13 priority date for domestic students, 6/1 for international students; for spring admission, 10/15 priority date for domestic students, 10/1 for international students. Applications are processed on a rolling basis. *Application fee:* $30 ($35 for international students). Electronic applications accepted. *Application Contact:* Dr. J. Randy Walker, Interim Dean of Graduate Studies, 423-425-4478, Fax: 423-425-5223, E-mail: randy-walker@utc.edu. *Dean*, Dr. Daniel Pack, 423-425-2256, Fax: 423-425-5311, E-mail: daniel-pack@utc.edu.

Program in English Students: 12 full-time (11 women), 13 part-time (8 women); includes 2 minority (1 Hispanic/Latino; 1 Two or more races, non-Hispanic/Latino). Average age 31. *Faculty:* 13 full-time (7 women). *Financial support:* Research assistantships, teaching assistantships, career-related internships or fieldwork, scholarships/grants, health care benefits, and unspecified assistantships available. Support available to part-time students. Financial award applicants required to submit FAFSA. In 2015, 17 master's awarded. *Degree program information:* Part-time programs available. Part-time. Offers creative writing (MA); literary study (MA); rhetoric and writing (MA, Graduate Certificate). *Application deadline:* For fall admission, 6/13 priority date for domestic students, 6/1 for international students; for spring admission, 10/15 priority date for domestic students, 10/1 for international students. Applications are processed on a rolling basis. *Application fee:* $30 ($35 for international students). Electronic applications accepted. *Application Contact:* Dr. J. Randy Walker, Interim Dean of Graduate Studies, 423-425-4478, Fax: 423-425-5223, E-mail: randy-walker@utc.edu. *Department Head*, Dr. Christopher Stuart, 423-425-2140, Fax: 423-425-2282, E-mail: joe-wilferth@utc.edu.

Program in Environmental Science Students: 18 full-time (12 women), 14 part-time (8 women); includes 5 minority (2 Black or African American, non-Hispanic/Latino; 1 Asian, non-Hispanic/Latino; 1 Hispanic/Latino; 1 Two or more races, non-Hispanic/Latino), 1 international. Average age 28. *Faculty:* 9 full-time (2 women), 1 (woman) part-time/adjunct. *Financial support:* Research assistantships, teaching assistantships, career-related internships or fieldwork, scholarships/grants, and unspecified assistantships available. Support available to part-time students. Financial award applicants required to submit FAFSA. In 2015, 8 master's awarded. *Degree program information:* Part-time programs available. Part-time. Offers environmental science (MS). *Application deadline:* For fall admission, 6/13 priority date for domestic students, 6/1 for international students; for spring admission, 10/15 priority date for domestic students, 10/1 for international students. Applications are processed on a rolling basis. *Application fee:* $30 ($35 for international students). Electronic applications accepted. *Application Contact:* Dr. J. Randy Walker, Interim Dean of Graduate Studies, 423-425-4478, Fax: 423-425-5223, E-mail: randy-walker@utc.edu. *Department Head*, Dr. John Tucker, 423-425-4341, Fax: 423-425-2285, E-mail: john-tucker@utc.edu.

Program in Mathematics Students: 14 full-time (4 women), 3 part-time (2 women); includes 4 minority (1 Asian, non-Hispanic/Latino; 2 Hispanic/Latino; 1 Two or more races, non-Hispanic/Latino), 1 international. Average age 27. *Faculty:* 8 full-time (1 woman). *Financial support:* Research assistantships available. Financial award applicants required to submit FAFSA. In 2015, 7 master's awarded. *Degree program information:* Part-time programs available. Part-time. Offers applied mathematics (MS); applied statistics (MS); mathematics education (MS); pre-professional mathematics (MS). *Application deadline:* For fall admission, 6/13 for domestic students, 6/1 for international students; for spring admission, 10/15 for domestic students, 10/1 for international students. Applications are processed on a rolling basis. *Application fee:* $30 ($35 for international students). Electronic applications accepted. *Application Contact:* Dr. J. Randy Walker, Interim Dean of Graduate Studies, 423-425-4478, Fax: 423-425-5223, E-mail: randy-walker@utc.edu. *Graduate Program Coordinator*, Dr. Francesco Barioli, 423-425-2198, E-mail: francesco-barioli@utc.edu.

Program in Music Students: 6 full-time (5 women), 7 part-time (3 women); includes 2 minority (both Black or African American, non-Hispanic/Latino). Average age 30. *Faculty:* 9 full-time (2 women), 1 part-time/adjunct (0 women). *Financial support:* Research assistantships, Federal Work-Study, scholarships/grants, and unspecified assistantships available. Financial award applicants required to submit FAFSA. In 2015, 7 master's awarded. Offers music education (MM); performance (MM). *Application deadline:* For fall admission, 6/13 priority date for domestic students, 6/1 for international students; for spring admission, 10/15 priority date for domestic students, 10/1 for international students. Applications are processed on a rolling basis. *Application fee:* $30 ($35 for international students). Electronic applications accepted. *Application Contact:* Dr. J. Randy Walker, Interim Dean of Graduate Studies, 423-425-4478, Fax: 423-425-5223, E-mail: randy-walker@utc.edu. *Department Head*, Dr. Lee Harris, 423-425-4601, Fax: 423-425-4603, E-mail: lee-harris@utc.edu.

Program in Physical Therapy Students: 100 full-time (64 women); includes 16 minority (3 Hispanic/Latino; 13 Two or more races, non-Hispanic/Latino). Average age 24. *Faculty:* 8 full-time (5 women), 5 part-time/adjunct (3 women). *Financial support:* Research assistantships, teaching assistantships, career-related internships or fieldwork, scholarships/grants, and unspecified assistantships available. Support available to part-time students. In 2015, 36 doctorates awarded. Offers physical therapy (DPT). *Application deadline:* For fall admission, 6/13 priority date for domestic students, 6/1 for international students; for spring admission, 10/15 priority date for domestic students, 10/1 for international students. Applications are processed on a rolling basis. *Application fee:* $30 ($35 for international students). Electronic applications accepted. *Application Contact:* Dr. J. Randy Walker, Dean of Graduate Studies, 423-425-4478, Fax: 423-425-5223, E-mail: randy-walker@utc.edu. *Interim Department Head*, Dr. Debbie Ingram, 423-425-4767, Fax: 423-425-2215, E-mail: debbie-ingram@utc.edu.

Program in Psychology Students: 46 full-time (26 women), 5 part-time (4 women); includes 8 minority (1 Black or African American, non-Hispanic/Latino; 1 Asian, non-Hispanic/Latino; 3 Hispanic/Latino; 1 Native Hawaiian or other Pacific Islander, non-Hispanic/Latino; 2 Two or more races, non-Hispanic/Latino). Average age 27. *Faculty:* 10 full-time (4 women), 1 part-time/adjunct (0 women). *Financial support:* Research assistantships, teaching assistantships, career-related internships or fieldwork, scholarships/grants, and unspecified assistantships available. Support available to part-time students. Financial award applicants required to submit FAFSA. In 2015, 18 master's awarded. *Degree program information:* Part-time programs available. Part-time. Offers industrial/organizational psychology (MS); research psychology (MS). *Application deadline:* For fall admission, 6/13 priority date for domestic students, 6/1 for international students; for spring admission, 10/15 priority date for domestic students, 10/1 for international students. Applications are processed on a rolling basis. *Application fee:* $30 ($35 for international students). Electronic applications accepted. *Application Contact:* Dr. J. Randy Walker, Interim Dean of Graduate Studies, 423-425-4478, Fax: 423-425-5223, E-mail: randy-walker@utc.edu. *Department Head*, Dr. Brian O'Leary, 423-425-4283, Fax: 423-425-4284, E-mail: brian-o'leary@utc.edu.

School of Education Students: 100 full-time (78 women), 171 part-time (115 women); includes 52 minority (35 Black or African American, non-Hispanic/Latino; 5 Asian, non-Hispanic/Latino; 4 Hispanic/Latino; 8 Two or more races, non-Hispanic/Latino), 1 international. Average age 34. *Faculty:* 24 full-time (17 women), 6 part-time/adjunct (4 women). *Financial support:* Research assistantships, teaching assistantships, career-related internships or fieldwork, institutionally sponsored loans, scholarships/grants, and unspecified assistantships available. Support available to part-time students. Financial award applicants required to submit FAFSA. In 2015, 110 master's, 14 doctorates, 5 other advanced degrees awarded. *Degree program information:* Part-time programs available. Part-time. Offers counseling (M Ed); education (M Ed, Post-Master's Certificate); educational specialist (Ed S); learning and leadership (Ed D). *Application deadline:* For fall admission, 6/13 for domestic students, 6/1 for international students; for spring admission, 10/15 for domestic students, 10/1 for international students. Applications are processed on a rolling basis. *Application fee:* $30 ($35 for international students). Electronic applications accepted. *Application Contact:* Dr. J. Randy Walker, Interim Dean of Graduate Studies, 423-425-4478, Fax: 423-425-5223, E-mail: randy-walker@utc.edu. *Director,* Dr. Linda Johnston, 423-425-4122, Fax: 423-425-5380, E-mail: linda-johnston@utc.edu.

School of Nursing Students: 50 full-time (25 women), 43 part-time (37 women); includes 14 minority (7 Black or African American, non-Hispanic/Latino; 1 American Indian or Alaska Native, non-Hispanic/Latino; 4 Asian, non-Hispanic/Latino; 2 Two or more races, non-Hispanic/Latino). Average age 34. *Faculty:* 9 full-time (7 women), 2 part-time/adjunct (1 woman). *Financial support:* Career-related internships or fieldwork and scholarships/grants available. Support available to part-time students. In 2015, 40 master's, 12 doctorates, 1 other advanced degree awarded. Offers administration (MSN); certified nurse anesthetist (Post-Master's Certificate); education (MSN); family nurse practitioner (MSN, Post-Master's Certificate); health care informatics (Post-Master's Certificate); nurse anesthesia (MSN); nurse education (Post-Master's Certificate); nursing (DNP). *Application deadline:* For fall admission, 6/13 priority date for domestic students, 6/1 for international students; for spring admission, 10/15 priority date for domestic students, 10/1 for international students. Applications are processed on a rolling basis. *Application fee:* $30 ($35 for international students). Electronic applications accepted. *Application Contact:* Dr. J. Randy Walker, Interim Dean of Graduate Studies, 423-425-4478, Fax: 423-425-5223, E-mail: randy-walker@utc.edu. *Interim Director,* Dr. Chris Smith, 423-425-1741, Fax: 423-425-4668, E-mail: chris-smith@utc.edu.

THE UNIVERSITY OF TENNESSEE AT MARTIN, Martin, TN 38238

General Information State-supported, coed, comprehensive institution. *Enrollment:* 6,827 graduate, professional, and undergraduate students; 14 full-time matriculated graduate/professional students (3 women), 331 part-time matriculated graduate/professional students (231 women). *Enrollment by degree level:* 345 master's. *Graduate faculty:* 140. Tuition, state resident: full-time $8254; part-time $459 per credit hour. Tuition, nonresident: full-time $22,198; part-time $1234 per credit hour. *Required fees:* $79 per credit hour. Part-time tuition and fees vary according to course load and campus/location. *Graduate housing:* Rooms and/or apartments available on a first-come, first-served basis to single and married students. Typical cost: $2780 per year ($5896 including board) for single students; $5460 per year for married students. Room and board charges vary according to board plan and housing facility selected. Housing application deadline: 3/1. *Student services:* Campus employment opportunities, campus safety program, career counseling, child daycare facilities, exercise/wellness program, free psychological counseling, international student services, low-cost health insurance, multicultural affairs office, services for students with disabilities, teacher training, writing training. *Library:* Paul Meek Library. *Collection:* Books: 347,063 (physical), 152,527 (digital/electronic); Serial titles: 731 (physical), 230,498 (digital/electronic); Databases: 71. Weekly public service hours: 92; study areas open 24 hours, 5–7 days a week. *Research affiliation:* Department of Education (academic extensions), National Writing Project (humanities), Health and Human Services (infant health), U.S. Department of Justice (criminal justice), The University of Tennessee Research Foundation (science and technology), Oak Ridge National Laboratories (science, technology, engineering, and math (STEM)).

Computer facilities: 948 computers available on campus for general student use. A campuswide network can be accessed from student residence rooms and from off campus. Online class registration, online fee payments, degree progress, financial aid data, housing applications, transcripts are available.
Website: http://www.utm.edu/

General Application Contact: Jolene L. Cunningham, Student Services Specialist, 731-881-7012, Fax: 731-881-7499, E-mail: jcunningham@utm.edu.

GRADUATE UNITS

Graduate Programs Students: 345 (234 women); includes 45 minority (39 Black or African American, non-Hispanic/Latino; 4 Hispanic/Latino; 2 Two or more races, non-Hispanic/Latino), 6 international. Average age 32. 272 applicants, 60% accepted, 112 enrolled. *Faculty:* 140. *Financial support:* In 2015–16, 33 students received support, including 6 research assistantships with full tuition reimbursements available (averaging $7,917 per year), 23 teaching assistantships with full tuition reimbursements available (averaging $8,229 per year); scholarships/grants and unspecified assistantships also available. Financial award application deadline: 2/1; financial award applicants required to submit FAFSA. In 2015, 92 master's awarded. *Degree program information:* Part-time programs available. Part-time, 100% online, blended/hybrid learning. *Application deadline:* For fall admission, 7/27 priority date for domestic and international students; for spring admission, 12/17 priority date for domestic and international students; for summer admission, 5/10 priority date for domestic and international students. Applications are processed on a rolling basis. *Application fee:* $30 ($130 for international students). Electronic applications accepted. *Application Contact:* Jolene L. Cunningham, Student Services Specialist, 731-881-7012, Fax: 731-881-7499, E-mail: jcunningham@utm.edu. *Associate Vice Chancellor and Dean of Graduate Studies,* Dr. Victoria S. Seng, 731-881-7012, Fax: 731-881-7499, E-mail: vseng@utm.edu.

College of Agriculture and Applied Sciences Students: 7 full-time (3 women), 68 part-time (46 women); includes 13 minority (9 Black or African American, non-Hispanic/Latino; 3 Hispanic/Latino; 1 Two or more races, non-Hispanic/Latino). Average age 30. 88 applicants, 73% accepted, 31 enrolled. *Faculty:* 29. *Financial support:* In 2015–16, 9 students received support, including 2 research assistantships with full tuition reimbursements available (averaging $8,671 per year), 6 teaching assistantships (averaging $7,518 per year); scholarships/grants and unspecified assistantships also available. Financial award application deadline: 2/1; financial award applicants required to submit FAFSA. In 2015, 21 master's awarded. *Degree program information:* Part-time programs available. Part-time, 100% online, blended/hybrid learning. Offers agricultural and natural resources management (MSANR); agriculture and applied sciences (MSANR, MSFCS); dietetics (MSFCS); general family and consumer sciences (MSFCS). *Application deadline:* For fall admission, 7/27 priority date for domestic and international students; for spring admission, 12/17 priority date for domestic and international students; for summer admission, 5/10 priority date for domestic and international students. Applications are processed on a rolling basis. *Application fee:* $30 ($130 for international students). Electronic applications accepted. *Application Contact:* Jolene L. Cunningham, Student Services Specialist, 731-881-7012, Fax: 731-881-7499, E-mail: jcunningham@utm.edu. *Dean,* Dr. Todd Winters, 731-881-7250, E-mail: winters@utm.edu.

College of Business and Global Affairs Students: 12 full-time (6 women), 70 part-time (23 women); includes 7 minority (5 Black or African American, non-Hispanic/Latino; 1 Asian, non-Hispanic/Latino; 1 Hispanic/Latino). Average age 33. 62 applicants, 47% accepted, 25 enrolled. *Faculty:* 30. *Financial support:* In 2015–16, 8 students received support, including 2 research assistantships with full tuition reimbursements available (averaging $7,540 per year), 6 teaching assistantships with full tuition reimbursements available (averaging $8,193 per year); scholarships/grants and unspecified assistantships also available. Financial award application deadline: 2/1; financial award applicants required to submit FAFSA. In 2015, 12 master's awarded. *Degree program information:* Part-time programs available. Part-time, 100% online, blended/hybrid learning. Offers agricultural business (MBA); business (MBA); financial services (MBA); general business (MBA). *Application deadline:* For fall admission, 7/27 priority date for domestic and international students; for spring admission, 12/17 priority date for domestic and international students; for summer admission, 5/10 priority date for domestic and international students. Applications are processed on a rolling basis. *Application fee:* $30 ($130 for international students). Electronic applications accepted. *Application Contact:* Jolene L. Cunningham, Student Services Specialist, 731-881-7012, Fax: 731-881-7499, E-mail: jcunningham@utm.edu. *Dean,* Dr. Ross Dickens, 731-881-7227, Fax: 731-881-7241, E-mail: rdicken2@utm.edu.

College of Education, Health and Behavioral Sciences Students: 30 full-time (29 women), 154 part-time (124 women); includes 31 minority (25 Black or African American, non-Hispanic/Latino; 5 Hispanic/Latino; 1 Two or more races, non-Hispanic/Latino). Average age 33. 119 applicants, 57% accepted, 53 enrolled. *Faculty:* 45. *Financial support:* In 2015–16, 16 students received support, including 2 research assistantships with full tuition reimbursements available (averaging $7,540 per year), 11 teaching assistantships with full tuition reimbursements available (averaging $8,637 per year); scholarships/grants and unspecified assistantships also available. Financial award application deadline: 2/1; financial award applicants required to submit FAFSA. In 2015, 59 master's awarded. *Degree program information:* Part-time programs available. Part-time, online only, 100% online. Offers addictions counseling (MS Ed); community counseling (MS Ed); curriculum and instruction (MS Ed); education, health and behavioral sciences (MS Ed); educational leadership (MS Ed); initial licensure (MS Ed); initial licensure K-12 (MS Ed); interdisciplinary (MS Ed); school counseling (MS Ed); student affairs and college counseling (MS Ed). *Application deadline:* For fall admission, 7/27 priority date for domestic and international students; for spring admission, 12/17 priority date for domestic and international students; for summer admission, 5/10 priority date for domestic and international students. Applications are processed on a rolling basis. *Application fee:* $30 ($130 for international students). Electronic applications accepted. *Application Contact:* Jolene L. Cunningham, Student Services Specialist, 731-881-7012, Fax: 731-881-7499, E-mail: jcunningham@utm.edu. *Dean,* Cynthia West, 731-881-7127, Fax: 731-881-7975, E-mail: cwest@utm.edu.

College of Humanities and Fine Arts Students: 4 full-time (3 women). Average age 28. 4 applicants, 100% accepted, 4 enrolled. *Faculty:* 21 full-time (7 women). *Financial support:* Research assistantships, teaching assistantships, scholarships/grants, and unspecified assistantships available. Financial award application deadline: 2/1; financial award applicants required to submit FAFSA. *Degree program information:* Part-time programs available. Part-time, blended/hybrid learning. Offers strategic communication (MASC). *Application deadline:* For fall admission, 7/27 priority date for domestic and international students; for spring admission, 12/15 priority date for domestic and international students; for summer admission, 5/10 priority date for domestic and international students. Applications are processed on a rolling basis. *Application fee:* $30 ($130 for international students). Electronic applications accepted. *Application Contact:* Jolene L. Cunningham, Student Services Specialist, 731-881-7012, Fax: 731-881-7499, E-mail: jcunningham@utm.edu. *Dean,* Dr. Lynn Alexander, 731-881-7490, Fax: 731-881-7276, E-mail: lalexand@utm.edu.

THE UNIVERSITY OF TENNESSEE HEALTH SCIENCE CENTER, Memphis, TN 38163-0002

General Information State-supported, coed, upper-level institution. CGS member. *Graduate housing:* Room and/or apartments available on a first-come, first-served basis to single students; on-campus housing not available to married students. Housing application deadline: 2/28. *Research affiliation:* Saint Jude's Children's Research Hospital, Veterans Administration Medical Center, LePasses Rehabilitation Center, LeBonheur Children's Medical Center.

GRADUATE UNITS

College of Dentistry Offers dentistry (DDS). Electronic applications accepted.

College of Graduate Health Sciences Offers biomedical engineering (MS, PhD); biomedical sciences (PhD); dental sciences (MDS); epidemiology (MS); health outcomes and policy research (PhD); laboratory research and management (MS); nursing science (PhD); pharmaceutical sciences (PhD); pharmacology (MS); speech and hearing science (PhD). Electronic applications accepted.

College of Health Professions ***Degree program information:*** Part-time and evening/weekend programs available. Part-time, evening/weekend, online learning. Offers audiology (MS, Au D); clinical laboratory science (MSCLS); cytopathology practice (MCP); health informatics and information management (MHIIM); occupational therapy (MOT); physical therapy (DPT, ScDPT); physician assistant (MMS); speech-language pathology (MS). Electronic applications accepted.

College of Medicine Offers medicine (MD). Electronic applications accepted.

College of Nursing ***Degree program information:*** Part-time programs available. Part-time, online learning. Offers adult-gerontology acute care nurse practitioner (Certificate); advanced practice nursing (DNP); clinical nurse leader (MSN). Electronic applications accepted.

College of Pharmacy Offers pharmacy (MS, PhD, Pharm D). Electronic applications accepted.

THE UNIVERSITY OF TENNESSEE–OAK RIDGE NATIONAL LABORATORY, Oak Ridge, TN 37830-8026

General Information State-supported, coed, graduate-only institution. *Research affiliation:* Oak Ridge National Laboratory.

GRADUATE UNITS

Graduate Program in Genome Science and Technology Offers life sciences (MS, PhD). Electronic applications accepted.

THE UNIVERSITY OF TEXAS AT ARLINGTON, Arlington, TX 76019

General Information State-supported, coed, university. CGS member. *Graduate housing:* Rooms and/or apartments available on a first-come, first-served basis to single and married students. *Research affiliation:* Texas Health Resources (medical technologies), Center for Innovation (technology development and commercialization), Facebook (energy efficient electronic systems), Department of Energy (bioengineering), National Science Foundation (materials science and engineering), Texas Instruments (medical technologies).

GRADUATE UNITS

Graduate School ***Degree program information:*** Part-time and evening/weekend programs available. Part-time, evening/weekend, online learning. Offers curriculum and instruction (M Ed); teaching (with certification) (M Ed T).

College of Business Degree program information: Part-time and evening/weekend programs available. Part-time, evening/weekend, online learning. Offers accounting (MP Acc, MS, PhD); business (MA, MBA, MP Acc, MS, MSHRM, PhD); business statistics (PhD); economics (MA); finance (MBA, PhD); health care administration (MS); human resources (MSHRM); information systems (MBA, MS, PhD); management (MBA, PhD); marketing (MBA, PhD); marketing research (MS); operations management (MBA, PhD); quantitative finance (MS); real estate (MBA, MS); taxation (MS). Electronic applications accepted.

College of Education and Health Professions Offers dual language (M Ed); education and health professions (M Ed, MS, PhD); education leadership and policy studies (PhD); exercise science (MS); higher education (M Ed); principal certification (M Ed).

College of Engineering Degree program information: Part-time and evening/weekend programs available. Part-time, evening/weekend, online learning. Offers aerospace engineering (M Engr, MS, PhD); bioengineering (MS, PhD); civil engineering (M Engr, MS, PhD); computer engineering (MS, PhD); computer science (MS, PhD); construction management (MCM); electrical engineering (M Engr, MS, PhD); engineering (M Engr, MCM, MS, PhD); engineering management (MS); industrial engineering (MS, PhD); logistics (MS); materials science and engineering (M Engr, MS, PhD); mathematical sciences, computer science (PhD); mechanical engineering (M Engr, MS, PhD); software engineering (MS); systems engineering (MS).

College of Liberal Arts Degree program information: Part-time and evening/weekend programs available. Part-time, evening/weekend. Offers anthropology (MA); communication (MA); criminology and criminal justice (MA); education (MM); English (MA); film and video (MFA); French (MA); glass (MFA); history (MA); intermedia (MFA); liberal arts (MA, MFA, MM, PhD); linguistics (MA, PhD); literature (PhD); performance (MM); political science (MA); sociology (MA); Spanish (MA); teaching English to speakers of other languages (MA); transatlantic history (PhD); visual communication (MFA).

College of Nursing Degree program information: Part-time and evening/weekend programs available. Part-time, evening/weekend, online learning. Offers nurse practitioner (MSN); nursing administration (MSN); nursing education (MSN); nursing practice (DNP); nursing science (PhD).

College of Science Degree program information: Part-time and evening/weekend programs available. Part-time, evening/weekend. Offers applied math (MS); biology (MS); chemistry (MS, PhD); environmental and earth sciences (MS, PhD); environmental science (MS, PhD); experimental psychology (PhD); geology (MS, PhD); health psychology (PhD); industrial organizational psychology (MS); mathematics (PhD); mathematics education (MA); physics (MS); physics and applied physics (PhD); psychology (MS); quantitative biology (PhD); science (MA, MS, PhD).

School of Architecture Degree program information: Part-time programs available. Part-time. Offers architecture (M Arch, MLA); landscape architecture (MLA). Electronic applications accepted.

School of Social Work Degree program information: Part-time and evening/weekend programs available. Part-time, evening/weekend, online learning. Offers social work (MSSW, PhD). Electronic applications accepted.

School of Urban and Public Affairs Degree program information: Part-time and evening/weekend programs available. Part-time, evening/weekend, online learning. Offers city and regional planning (MCRP); public administration (MPA); public and urban administration (MA); sustainability (MA); urban affairs (MA); urban and public affairs (MA, MCRP, MPA, PhD); urban planning and public policy (PhD). Electronic applications accepted.

THE UNIVERSITY OF TEXAS AT AUSTIN, Austin, TX 78712-1111

General Information State-supported, coed, university. CGS member. *Graduate housing:* Rooms and/or apartments available to single students and available on a first-come, first-served basis to married students.

GRADUATE UNITS

Graduate School ***Degree program information:*** Part-time and evening/weekend programs available. Part-time, evening/weekend. Offers computational science, engineering, and mathematics (MS, PhD). Electronic applications accepted.

Cockrell School of Engineering Degree program information: Part-time and evening/weekend programs available. Part-time, evening/weekend. Offers aerospace engineering (MSE, PhD); architectural engineering (MSE); biomedical engineering (MS, PhD); chemical engineering (MSE, PhD); civil engineering (MS, PhD); electrical and computer engineering (MS, PhD); energy and earth resources (MA); engineering (MA, MS, MSE, PhD); engineering mechanics (MS, PhD); environmental and water resources engineering (MS, PhD); materials science and engineering (MS, PhD); mechanical engineering (MS, PhD); operations research and industrial engineering (MS, PhD); petroleum engineering (MS, PhD). Electronic applications accepted.

College of Communication Degree program information: Part-time programs available. Part-time. Offers advertising (MA, PhD); audiology (Au D); communication (MA, MFA, Au D, PhD); communication sciences and disorders (PhD); communication studies (MA, PhD); film and media production (MFA); journalism (MA, PhD); media studies (MA, PhD); screenwriting (MFA); speech language pathology (MA). Electronic applications accepted.

College of Education Degree program information: Part-time programs available. Part-time. Offers academic educational psychology (M Ed, MA); autism and developmental disabilities (Ed D, PhD); autism and developmental disability (M Ed, MA); behavioral health (PhD); bilingual/bicultural education (M Ed, MA, PhD); counseling psychology (PhD); counselor education (M Ed); cultural studies in education (M Ed, MA, PhD); early childhood education (M Ed, MA, PhD); early childhood special education (M Ed, MA, Ed D, PhD); education (M Ed, MA, MS, Ed D, PhD); educational administration (M Ed, Ed D, PhD); exercise and sport psychology (M Ed, MA); exercise science (M Ed, MS, PhD); health education (M Ed, MS, Ed D, PhD); human development, culture and learning sciences (PhD); language and literacy studies (M Ed, PhD); learning disabilities (Ed D, PhD); learning disabilities/behavior disorders (M Ed, MA); learning technologies (M Ed, MA, PhD); multicultural special education (M Ed, MA, Ed D, PhD); physical education (M Ed, MA, PhD); program evaluation (MA); quantitative methods (M Ed, MA, PhD); rehabilitation counselor (M Ed); rehabilitation counselor education (Ed D, PhD); school psychology (MA, PhD); special education administration (Ed D, PhD). Electronic applications accepted.

College of Fine Arts Degree program information: Part-time programs available. Part-time. Offers acting (MFA); art education (MA); art history (MA, PhD); band and wind conducting (M Music, DMA); brass/woodwind/percussion (MM, DMA); chamber music (MM); choral conducting (MM, DMA); collaborative piano (MM, DMA); composition (MM, DMA); dance (MFA); design (MFA); directing (MFA); drama and theatre for youth (MFA); ethnomusicology (MM, PhD); fine arts (M Music, MA, MFA, MM, DMA, PhD); literature and pedagogy (MM); music and human learning (MM, PhD); music and human learning (DMA); musicology (MM, PhD); opera performance (MM, DMA); orchestral conducting (MM, DMA); organ (MM); organ performance (MM, DMA); performance (MM); performance (DMA); performance as public practice (MA, MFA, PhD); piano (DMA); piano literature and pedagogy (MM); piano performance (MM, DMA); playwriting (MFA); string performance (MM, DMA); studio art (MFA); theatre technology (MFA); theatrical design (MFA); theory (MM, PhD); vocal performance (MM, DMA); voice (DMA); voice performance pedagogy (DMA); woodwind, brass, percussion performance (MM). Electronic applications accepted.

College of Liberal Arts Degree program information: Part-time programs available. Part-time. Offers African Diaspora studies (MA, PhD); American studies (MA, PhD); applied linguistics/pedagogy (PhD); archaeology (MA, PhD); Asian cultures and languages (MA, PhD); Asian studies (MA); behavioral neuroscience (PhD); classics (MA, PhD); clinical psychology (PhD); cognitive systems (PhD); comparative literature (MA, PhD); creative writing (MFA); cultural forms (MA, PhD); cultural politics of Afro-Latin and indigenous peoples (MA); development studies (MA); developmental psychology (PhD); economics (MA, MS Econ, PhD); English (MA, PhD); environmental studies (MA); French linguistics (MA, PhD); French studies (MA, PhD); geography and the environment (MA, PhD); Germanic studies (MA, PhD); government (MA, PhD); Hispanic linguistics (MA, PhD); Hispanic literature (MA, PhD); history (MA, PhD); human dimensions of organizations (MA); human rights (MA); Ibero-romance philology and linguistics (PhD); individual differences and evolutionary psychology (PhD); Italian studies (MA, PhD); Latin American and international law (LL M); liberal arts (LL M, MA, MFA, MS Econ, PhD); linguistic anthropology (MA, PhD); linguistics (MA, PhD); literature and culture (PhD); Luso-Brazilian literature (MA, PhD); Mexican American studies (MA); Middle Eastern languages and cultures (MA, PhD); Middle Eastern studies (MA); perceptual systems (PhD); philosophy (PhD); physical anthropology (MA, PhD); Romance linguistics (PhD); Russian, East European, and Eurasian studies (MA); Slavic languages (MA); Slavic linguistics (PhD); social anthropology (MA, PhD); social psychology (PhD); sociology (MA, PhD). Electronic applications accepted.

College of Natural Sciences Degree program information: Part-time programs available. Part-time. Offers analytical chemistry (PhD); astronomy (MA, PhD); biochemistry (PhD); computer sciences (MSCS, PhD); ecology, evolution and behavior (PhD); human development and family sciences (MA, PhD); inorganic chemistry (PhD); marine science (MS, PhD); mathematics (MA, PhD); microbiology (PhD); natural sciences (MA, MS, MSCS, PhD); nutrition (MA); nutritional sciences (MA, PhD); organic chemistry (PhD); physical chemistry (PhD); physics (MA, MS, PhD); plant biology (MA, PhD); statistics (MS, PhD); textile and apparel technology (MS). Electronic applications accepted.

College of Pharmacy Offers health outcomes and pharmacy practice (PhD); health outcomes and pharmacy practice (MS); medicinal chemistry (PhD); pharmaceutics (PhD); pharmacology and toxicology (PhD); pharmacotherapy (MS, PhD); pharmacy (MS, PhD, Pharm D); translational science (PhD). Electronic applications accepted.

Institute for Cellular and Molecular Biology Offers cellular and molecular biology (PhD).

The Institute for Neuroscience Offers neuroscience (PhD). Electronic applications accepted.

Jackson School of Geosciences Degree program information: Part-time programs available. Part-time. Offers geosciences (MA, MS, PhD). Electronic applications accepted.

Lyndon B. Johnson School of Public Affairs Degree program information: Part-time programs available. Part-time. Offers global policy studies (MGPS); public affairs (MP Aff); public leadership (EMPL); public policy (PhD). Electronic applications accepted.

McCombs School of Business Offers accounting (MPA, PhD); business (MBA, MPA, MS, MSF, PhD); business administration (MBA); executive business administration (MBA); finance (MSF, PhD); information management (MBA); information systems (PhD); management (PhD); marketing (MBA, PhD); risk analysis and decision making (PhD); risk management (MBA); supply chain and operations management (MBA, PhD); technology commercialization (MS). Electronic applications accepted.

Michener Center for Writers Offers fiction (MFA); playwriting (MFA); poetry (MFA); screenwriting (MFA). Electronic applications accepted.

School of Architecture Offers architectural history (MA, PhD); architecture (M Arch, M Arch I, M Arch II, MA, MID, MLA, MS, MSAS, MSCRP, MSSD, MSUD, PhD); community and regional planning (MSCRP, PhD); historic preservation (M Arch, MS, MSCRP); interior design (MID); landscape architecture (MLA); sustainable design (M Arch I, M Arch II, MSSD); urban design (M Arch, MSUD). Electronic applications accepted.

School of Information Degree program information: Part-time programs available. Part-time. Offers identity management and security (MSIMS); information (PhD); information studies (MSIS). MSIMS program offered in conjunction with the Center for Identity. Electronic applications accepted.

School of Nursing Degree program information: Part-time programs available. Part-time. Offers adult - gerontology clinical nurse specialist (MSN); child health (MSN); family nurse practitioner (MSN); family psychiatric/mental health nurse practitioner (MSN); holistic adult health (MSN); maternity (MSN); nursing (PhD); nursing administration and healthcare systems management (MSN); nursing practice (DNP); pediatric nurse practitioner (MSN); public health nursing (MSN). Electronic applications accepted.

School of Social Work Degree program information: Part-time programs available. Part-time. Offers social work (MSSW, PhD).

School of Law Students: 956 full-time (416 women); includes 307 minority (53 Black or African American, non-Hispanic/Latino; 2 American Indian or Alaska Native, non-Hispanic/Latino; 68 Asian, non-Hispanic/Latino; 138 Hispanic/Latino; 46 Two or more races, non-Hispanic/Latino), 19 international. Average age 24. 4,303 applicants, 22% accepted, 265 enrolled. *Faculty:* 80 full-time (33 women), 73 part-time/adjunct (24 women). *Financial support:* In 2015–16, 891 students received support, including 4 fellowships (averaging $54,584 per year), 175 research assistantships (averaging $4,020 per year), 30 teaching assistantships with partial tuition reimbursements available (averaging $3,000 per year); career-related internships or fieldwork, scholarships/grants, and tuition waivers (full) also available. Financial award application deadline: 3/15; financial award applicants required to submit FAFSA. In 2015, 60 master's, 358 doctorates awarded. Offers law (LL M, JD). *Application deadline:* For fall admission, 11/1 for domestic students; for spring admission, 3/1 for domestic students.

Application fee: $70. Electronic applications accepted. *Application Contact:* School of Law Admissions, 512-232-1200, Fax: 512-471-2765, E-mail: admissions@law.utexas.edu. *Dean*, Ward Farnsworth, 512-232-1120, Fax: 512-471-6987, E-mail: wfarnsworth@law.utexas.edu.

THE UNIVERSITY OF TEXAS AT DALLAS, Richardson, TX 75080

General Information State-supported, coed, university. CGS member. *Enrollment:* 24,554 graduate, professional, and undergraduate students; 6,089 full-time matriculated graduate/professional students (2,657 women), 2,592 part-time matriculated graduate/professional students (1,056 women). *Enrollment by degree level:* 7,733 master's, 948 doctoral. *Graduate faculty:* 553 full-time (126 women), 130 part-time/adjunct (43 women). Tuition, state resident: full-time $11,940; part-time $663 per semester hour. Tuition, nonresident: full-time $22,786; part-time $1266 per semester hour. Tuition and fees vary according to course load. *Graduate housing:* Rooms and/or apartments available on a first-come, first-served basis to single and married students. Typical cost: $9944 (including board) for single students; $9944 (including board) for married students. Room and board charges vary according to board plan and housing facility selected. Housing application deadline: 5/31. *Student services:* Campus employment opportunities, campus safety program, career counseling, child daycare facilities, exercise/wellness program, free psychological counseling, grant writing training, international student services, low-cost health insurance, multicultural affairs office, services for students with disabilities, teacher training, writing training. *Library:* Eugene McDermott Library plus 1 other. *Collection:* Books: 559,827 (physical), 1.1 million (digital/electronic); Serial titles: 43,779 (physical), 124,415 (digital/electronic); Databases: 1,171. Weekly public service hours: 152; study areas open 24 hours, 5–7 days a week.

Computer facilities: Computer purchase and lease plans are available. 170 computers available on campus for general student use. A campuswide network can be accessed from student residence rooms and from off campus. Online class registration is available.
Website: http://www.utdallas.edu/

General Application Contact: Dr. Marion Underwood, Dean of Graduate Studies, 972-883-2234, Fax: 972-883-4308, E-mail: undrwd@utdallas.edu.

GRADUATE UNITS

Erik Jonsson School of Engineering and Computer Science Students: 1,915 full-time (535 women), 682 part-time (182 women); includes 185 minority (25 Black or African American, non-Hispanic/Latino; 2 American Indian or Alaska Native, non-Hispanic/Latino; 95 Asian, non-Hispanic/Latino; 50 Hispanic/Latino; 13 Two or more races, non-Hispanic/Latino), 2,186 international. Average age 27. 6,717 applicants, 31% accepted, 752 enrolled. *Faculty:* 149 full-time (21 women), 20 part-time/adjunct (2 women). *Financial support:* In 2015–16, 769 students received support, including 29 fellowships with partial tuition reimbursements available (averaging $6,103 per year), 325 research assistantships with partial tuition reimbursements available (averaging $23,737 per year), 196 teaching assistantships with partial tuition reimbursements available (averaging $17,146 per year); career-related internships or fieldwork, Federal Work-Study, institutionally sponsored loans, scholarships/grants, and unspecified assistantships also available. Support available to part-time students. Financial award application deadline: 4/30; financial award applicants required to submit FAFSA. In 2015, 800 master's, 64 doctorates awarded. *Degree program information:* Part-time and evening/weekend programs available. Part-time, evening/weekend. Offers biomedical engineering (MS, PhD); computer engineering (MS, PhD); computer science (MS, PhD); electrical engineering (MSEE, PhD); engineering and computer science (MS, MSEE, MSME, MSTE, PhD); materials science and engineering (MS, PhD); mechanical engineering (MSME, PhD); software engineering (MS, PhD); systems engineering and management (MS); telecommunications engineering (MSTE, PhD). *Application deadline:* For fall admission, 7/15 for domestic students, 5/1 priority date for international students; for spring admission, 11/15 for domestic students, 9/1 priority date for international students. Applications are processed on a rolling basis. *Application fee:* $50 ($100 for international students). Electronic applications accepted. *Application Contact:* Leiane Davis, Administrative Associate, 972-883-6851, Fax: 972-883-2813, E-mail: leiane.davis@utdallas.edu. *Dean*, Dr. Mark W. Spong, 972-883-2974, Fax: 972-883-2813, E-mail: ecsdean@utdallas.edu.

Naveen Jindal School of Management Students: 2,729 full-time (1,255 women), 1,413 part-time (593 women); includes 697 minority (115 Black or African American, non-Hispanic/Latino; 3 American Indian or Alaska Native, non-Hispanic/Latino; 389 Asian, non-Hispanic/Latino; 127 Hispanic/Latino; 1 Native Hawaiian or other Pacific Islander, non-Hispanic/Latino; 62 Two or more races, non-Hispanic/Latino), 2,588 international. Average age 29. 5,945 applicants, 56% accepted, 1527 enrolled. *Faculty:* 102 full-time (19 women), 74 part-time/adjunct (23 women). *Financial support:* In 2015–16, 1,142 students received support, including 28 research assistantships with partial tuition reimbursements available (averaging $22,529 per year), 153 teaching assistantships with partial tuition reimbursements available (averaging $14,684 per year); career-related internships or fieldwork, Federal Work-Study, institutionally sponsored loans, scholarships/grants, and unspecified assistantships also available. Support available to part-time students. Financial award application deadline: 4/30; financial award applicants required to submit FAFSA. In 2015, 1,802 master's, 16 doctorates awarded. *Degree program information:* Part-time and evening/weekend programs available. Part-time, evening/weekend, online learning. Offers accounting (MS); business administration (MBA); business analytics (MS); energy risk management (MS); executive business administration (EMBA); finance (PhD); financial analyst (MS); financial risk management (MS); global leadership (EMBA); healthcare management (MS); healthcare management for physicians (EMBA); information systems (PhD); information technology and management (MS); innovation and entrepreneurship (MS); international management studies (MS, PhD); investment management (MS); management (EMBA, MBA, MS, PhD); management and administrative sciences (MS); marketing (MS, PhD); operations management (PhD); professional sales (MS); project management (EMBA, MS); supply chain management (MS); systems engineering and management (MS). *Application deadline:* For fall admission, 7/15 for domestic students, 5/1 priority date for international students; for spring admission, 11/15 for domestic students, 9/1 priority date for international students. Applications are processed on a rolling basis. *Application fee:* $50 ($100 for international students). Electronic applications accepted. *Application Contact:* David B. Ritchey, Director of Advising, 972-883-2750, Fax: 972-883-6425, E-mail: davidr@utdallas.edu. *Dean*, Dr. Hasan Pirkul, 972-883-2705, Fax: 972-883-2799, E-mail: hpirkul@utdallas.edu.

School of Arts and Humanities Students: 122 full-time (76 women), 120 part-time (76 women); includes 69 minority (18 Black or African American, non-Hispanic/Latino; 3 American Indian or Alaska Native, non-Hispanic/Latino; 15 Asian, non-Hispanic/Latino; 25 Hispanic/Latino; 8 Two or more races, non-Hispanic/Latino), 19 international. Average age 41. 98 applicants, 56% accepted, 37 enrolled. *Faculty:* 44 full-time (15 women), 3 part-time/adjunct (0 women). *Financial support:* In 2015–16, 163 students received support, including 13 research assistantships with partial tuition reimbursements available (averaging $22,159 per year), 66 teaching assistantships with partial tuition reimbursements available (averaging $10,350 per year); fellowships, Federal Work-Study, institutionally sponsored loans, scholarships/grants, and unspecified assistantships also available. Support available to part-time students. Financial award application deadline: 4/30; financial award applicants required to submit FAFSA. In 2015, 53 master's, 16 doctorates awarded. *Degree program information:* Part-time and evening/weekend programs available. Part-time, evening/weekend. Offers history (MA); humanities (MA, PhD); humanities (MA, PhD); Latin American studies (MA). *Application deadline:* For fall admission, 7/15 for domestic students, 5/1 priority date for international students; for spring admission, 11/15 for domestic students, 9/1 priority date for international students. Applications are processed on a rolling basis. *Application fee:* $50 ($100 for international students). Electronic applications accepted. *Application Contact:* Dr. Michael Wilson, III, Associate Dean of Graduate Studies, 972-883-2756, Fax: 972-883-2989, E-mail: john.gooch@utdallas.edu. *Dean*, Dr. Dennis M. Kratz, 972-883-2984, Fax: 972-883-2989, E-mail: dkratz@utdallas.edu.

School of Arts, Technology, and Emerging Communication Students: 98 full-time (43 women), 50 part-time (21 women); includes 44 minority (14 Black or African American, non-Hispanic/Latino; 11 Asian, non-Hispanic/Latino; 17 Hispanic/Latino; 2 Two or more races, non-Hispanic/Latino), 20 international. Average age 34. 103 applicants, 41% accepted, 27 enrolled. *Faculty:* 24 full-time (10 women), 4 part-time/adjunct (1 woman). *Financial support:* In 2015–16, 103 students received support, including 5 research assistantships with partial tuition reimbursements available (averaging $22,760 per year), 25 teaching assistantships with partial tuition reimbursements available (averaging $10,350 per year); career-related internships or fieldwork, Federal Work-Study, institutionally sponsored loans, scholarships/grants, and unspecified assistantships also available. Support available to part-time students. Financial award application deadline: 4/30; financial award applicants required to submit FAFSA. In 2015, 72 master's, 1 doctorate awarded. Offers arts and technology (MA, MFA, PhD); emerging media and communication (MA). *Application deadline:* For fall admission, 7/15 for domestic students, 5/1 priority date for international students; for spring admission, 11/15 for domestic students, 9/1 priority date for international students. Applications are processed on a rolling basis. *Application fee:* $50 ($100 for international students). Electronic applications accepted. *Application Contact:* Ellen Curtis, Graduate Advisor, 972-883-7533, E-mail: ecurtis@utdallas.edu. *Interim Dean*, Dr. Todd Fechter, 972-883-2796, E-mail: todd.fechter@utdallas.edu.

School of Behavioral and Brain Sciences Students: 506 full-time (403 women), 63 part-time (54 women); includes 160 minority (18 Black or African American, non-Hispanic/Latino; 1 American Indian or Alaska Native, non-Hispanic/Latino; 52 Asian, non-Hispanic/Latino; 69 Hispanic/Latino; 20 Two or more races, non-Hispanic/Latino), 52 international. Average age 27. 988 applicants, 20% accepted, 155 enrolled. *Faculty:* 55 full-time (27 women), 18 part-time/adjunct (15 women). *Financial support:* In 2015–16, 441 students received support, including 1 fellowship (averaging $5,000 per year), 36 research assistantships with partial tuition reimbursements available (averaging $25,788 per year), 79 teaching assistantships with partial tuition reimbursements available (averaging $17,590 per year); career-related internships or fieldwork, Federal Work-Study, institutionally sponsored loans, scholarships/grants, and unspecified assistantships also available. Support available to part-time students. Financial award application deadline: 4/30; financial award applicants required to submit FAFSA. In 2015, 215 master's, 19 doctorates awarded. *Degree program information:* Part-time and evening/weekend programs available. Part-time, evening/weekend. Offers applied cognition and neuroscience (MS); audiology (Au D); behavioral and brain sciences (MS, Au D, PhD); cognition and neuroscience (PhD); communication disorders (MS); communication science and disorders (PhD); early childhood disorders (MS); psychological sciences (MS, PhD). *Application deadline:* For fall admission, 7/15 for domestic students, 5/1 priority date for international students; for spring admission, 11/15 for domestic students, 9/1 priority date for international students. Applications are processed on a rolling basis. *Application fee:* $50 ($100 for international students). Electronic applications accepted. *Application Contact:* Dr. Robert D. Stillman, Associate Dean of Graduate Programs, 214-905-3106, Fax: 972-883-2491, E-mail: stillman@utdallas.edu. *Interim Dean*, Dr. James Bartlett, 972-883-2355, Fax: 972-883-2491, E-mail: jbartlet@utdallas.edu.

School of Economic, Political and Policy Sciences Students: 246 full-time (124 women), 171 part-time (88 women); includes 121 minority (47 Black or African American, non-Hispanic/Latino; 1 American Indian or Alaska Native, non-Hispanic/Latino; 21 Asian, non-Hispanic/Latino; 46 Hispanic/Latino; 6 Two or more races, non-Hispanic/Latino), 116 international. Average age 34. 359 applicants, 52% accepted, 116 enrolled. *Faculty:* 63 full-time (16 women), 9 part-time/adjunct (2 women). *Financial support:* In 2015–16, 269 students received support, including 20 research assistantships with partial tuition reimbursements available (averaging $18,539 per year), 82 teaching assistantships with partial tuition reimbursements available (averaging $12,079 per year); fellowships, career-related internships or fieldwork, Federal Work-Study, institutionally sponsored loans, scholarships/grants, and unspecified assistantships also available. Support available to part-time students. Financial award application deadline: 4/30; financial award applicants required to submit FAFSA. In 2015, 102 master's, 57 doctorates awarded. *Degree program information:* Part-time and evening/weekend programs available. Part-time, evening/weekend. Offers applied sociology (MS); Constitutional law (MA); criminology (MS, PhD); economic, political and policy sciences (MA, MPA, MPP, MS, PhD); economics (MS, PhD); geospatial information sciences (MS, PhD); international political economy (MS); justice administration and leadership (MS); legislative studies (MA); political science (MA, PhD); public affairs (MPA, PhD); public policy (MPP); public policy and political economy (PhD). *Application deadline:* For fall admission, 7/15 for domestic students, 5/1 priority date for international students; for spring admission, 11/15 for domestic students, 9/1 priority date for international students. Applications are processed on a rolling basis. *Application fee:* $50 ($100 for international students). Electronic applications accepted. *Application Contact:* Dr. Alex Piquero, Associate Dean for Graduate Education, 972-883-2482, Fax: 972-883-6297, E-mail: apiquero@utdallas.edu. *Dean*, Dr. Denis Dean, 972-883-6852, Fax: 972-883-6297, E-mail: denis.dean@utdallas.edu.

School of Interdisciplinary Studies Students: 8 full-time (all women), 9 part-time (5 women); includes 10 minority (4 Black or African American, non-Hispanic/Latino; 1 Asian, non-Hispanic/Latino; 2 Hispanic/Latino; 3 Two or more races, non-Hispanic/Latino), 1 international. Average age 34. 15 applicants, 67% accepted, 9 enrolled. *Faculty:* 3 full-time (2 women). *Financial support:* In 2015–16, 14 students received support. Research assistantships with partial tuition reimbursements available, teaching assistantships with partial tuition reimbursements available, career-related internships or fieldwork, Federal Work-Study, institutionally sponsored loans, and scholarships/grants available. Support available to part-time students. Financial award application deadline: 4/30; financial award applicants required to submit FAFSA. In 2015, 8 master's awarded. *Degree program information:* Part-time and evening/weekend programs available. Part-time, evening/weekend. Offers interdisciplinary studies (MA). *Application deadline:* For fall admission, 7/15 for domestic students, 5/1 priority date for international students; for spring admission, 11/15 for domestic students, 9/1 priority date for international students. Applications are processed on a rolling basis. *Application fee:* $50 ($100 for international students). Electronic applications accepted. *Application Contact:* Rebecca Wiser, Academic Support Coordinator, 972-883-2354, Fax: 972-883-2440, E-mail: rwiser@utdallas.edu. *Dean,* Dr. George Fair, 972-883-2350, Fax: 972-883-2440, E-mail: gwfair@utdallas.edu.

School of Natural Sciences and Mathematics Students: 465 full-time (213 women), 84 part-time (37 women); includes 96 minority (14 Black or African American, non-Hispanic/Latino; 44 Asian, non-Hispanic/Latino; 30 Hispanic/Latino; 8 Two or more races, non-Hispanic/Latino), 301 international. Average age 29. 889 applicants, 32% accepted, 161 enrolled. *Faculty:* 113 full-time (16 women), 2 part-time/adjunct (0 women). *Financial support:* In 2015–16, 386 students received support, including 3 fellowships with partial tuition reimbursements available (averaging $350 per year), 93 research assistantships with partial tuition reimbursements available (averaging $23,174 per year), 227 teaching assistantships with partial tuition reimbursements available (averaging $17,171 per year); career-related internships or fieldwork, Federal Work-Study, institutionally sponsored loans, scholarships/grants, and unspecified assistantships also available. Support available to part-time students. Financial award application deadline: 4/30. In 2015, 92 master's, 32 doctorates awarded. *Degree program information:* Part-time and evening/weekend programs available. Part-time, evening/weekend. Offers actuarial science (MS); bioinformatics and computational biology (MS); biotechnology (MS); chemistry (MS, PhD); geochemistry (MS, PhD); geophysics (MS, PhD); geospatial information sciences (MS, PhD); hydrogeology (MS, PhD); mathematics (MS); mathematics (MS, PhD); mathematics education (MAT); molecular and cell biology (MS, PhD); natural sciences and mathematics (MAT, MS, PhD); physics (MS, PhD); science education (MAT); sedimentology, stratigraphy, and paleontology (MS, PhD); statistics (MS, PhD); structural geology and tectonics (MS, PhD). *Application deadline:* For fall admission, 7/15 for domestic students, 5/1 priority date for international students; for spring admission, 11/15 for domestic students, 9/1 priority date for international students. Applications are processed on a rolling basis. *Application fee:* $50 ($100 for international students). Electronic applications accepted. *Application Contact:* Dr. Juan E. Gonzalez, Associate Dean for Graduate Studies, 972-883-2526, Fax: 972-883-6371, E-mail: jgonzal@utdallas.edu. *Dean,* Dr. Bruce Novak, 972-883-2416, Fax: 972-883-6371, E-mail: bruce.novak@utdallas.edu.

THE UNIVERSITY OF TEXAS AT EL PASO, El Paso, TX 79968-0001

General Information State-supported, coed, university. CGS member. *Graduate housing:* Room and/or apartments available on a first-come, first-served basis to single students; on-campus housing not available to married students.

GRADUATE UNITS

Graduate School ***Degree program information:*** Part-time and evening/weekend programs available. Part-time, evening/weekend, online learning. Offers environmental science and engineering (PhD); materials science and engineering (PhD). Electronic applications accepted.

College of Business Administration Degree program information: Part-time and evening/weekend programs available. Part-time, evening/weekend, online learning. Offers accounting (M Acc); business administration (M Acc, MBA, MS, PhD, Certificate); economics (MS); international business (PhD). Electronic applications accepted.

College of Education Degree program information: Part-time and evening/weekend programs available. Part-time, evening/weekend, online learning. Offers education (M Ed, MA, Ed D, PhD); educational administration (M Ed); educational diagnostics (M Ed); educational leadership and administration (Ed D); guidance and counseling (M Ed); instruction (M Ed); reading education (M Ed); special education (M Ed); teaching, learning, and culture (PhD). Electronic applications accepted.

College of Engineering Degree program information: Part-time and evening/weekend programs available. Part-time, evening/weekend. Offers biomedical engineering (PhD); civil engineering (MEENE, MS, MSENE, PhD, Certificate); computer engineering (MS); computer science (MS, MSIT, PhD); construction management (MS, Certificate); education engineering (M Eng); electrical and computer engineering (MS, PhD); electrical engineering (MS); environmental engineering (MEENE, MSENE); environmental science and engineering (PhD); industrial engineering (MS, Certificate); information technology (MSIT); manufacturing engineering (MS); materials science and engineering (PhD); mechanical engineering (MS, PhD); metallurgical and materials engineering (MS, PhD); software engineering (M Eng); systems engineering (MS, Certificate). Electronic applications accepted.

College of Health Sciences Degree program information: Part-time and evening/weekend programs available. Part-time, evening/weekend, online learning. Offers health sciences (MOT, MRC, MS, MSN, MSW, DPT, PhD); interdisciplinary health sciences (PhD); kinesiology (MS); occupational therapy (MOT); physical therapy (DPT); rehabilitation counseling (MRC); social work in the border region (MSW); speech-language pathology (MS). Electronic applications accepted.

College of Liberal Arts Degree program information: Part-time and evening/weekend programs available. Part-time, evening/weekend, online learning. Offers applied anthropology (Certificate); applied social sciences (Certificate); art education (MA); bilingual professional writing (Certificate); border history (MA); borderlands history (PhD); clinical psychology (MA); communication (MA); creative writing (MFA); creative writing of the Americas (MFA); English and American literature (MA); experimental psychology (MA); history (MA); interdisciplinary studies (MAIS); liberal arts (MA, MAIS, MAT, MFA, MM, PhD, Certificate); linguistics (MA); music education (MM); music performance (MM); philosophy (MA); political science (MA); psychology (PhD); rhetoric and composition (PhD); rhetoric and writing studies (MA); sociology (MA); Spanish (MA); studio art (MA); teaching English (MAT); teaching English to speakers of other languages (Certificate). Electronic applications accepted.

College of Science Degree program information: Part-time and evening/weekend programs available. Part-time, evening/weekend. Offers bioinformatics (MS); biological sciences (MS, PhD); chemistry (MS, PhD); computational science (MS, PMS, PhD); environmental science (MS); geological sciences (MS, PhD); geophysics (MS); mathematical sciences (MS); mathematics (teaching) (MAT); physics (MS); science (MAT, MS, PMS, PhD); statistics (MS); teaching science (MAT). Electronic applications accepted.

School of Nursing Online learning. Offers family nurse practitioner (MSN); health care leadership and management (Certificate); interdisciplinary health sciences (PhD); nursing (DNP); nursing education (MSN, Certificate); nursing systems management (MSN). Electronic applications accepted.

THE UNIVERSITY OF TEXAS AT SAN ANTONIO, San Antonio, TX 78249-0617

General Information State-supported, coed, university. CGS member. *Enrollment:* 28,787 graduate, professional, and undergraduate students; 1,843 full-time matriculated graduate/professional students (921 women), 2,203 part-time matriculated graduate/professional students (1,276 women). *Enrollment by degree level:* 3,264 master's, 782 doctoral. *Graduate faculty:* 522 full-time (177 women), 84 part-time/adjunct (27 women). *Graduate housing:* Room and/or apartments available on a first-come, first-served basis to single students; on-campus housing not available to married students. *Student services:* Campus employment opportunities, campus safety program, career counseling, child daycare facilities, exercise/wellness program, free psychological counseling, grant writing training, international student services, low-cost health insurance, multicultural affairs office, services for students with disabilities, teacher training, writing training. *Library:* John Peace Library plus 3 others. *Research affiliation:* CPS Energy (engineering), Air Force Research Laboratory (information assurance and security), Carnegie Mellon University/National Security Agency (computer security), National Science Foundation (virtual reality, computer architecture, real-time systems), Cancer Prevention and Research Institute of Texas (chemistry), Army Research Laboratory (computer science, management science and statistics, electrical engineering).

Computer facilities: A campuswide network can be accessed from student residence rooms and from off campus. Online class registration is available.
Website: http://www.utsa.edu/

General Application Contact: Monica Rodriguez, Director of Graduate Admissions, 210-458-4331, Fax: 210-458-4332, E-mail: graduateadmissions@utsa.edu.

GRADUATE UNITS

College of Architecture Students: 75 full-time (37 women), 40 part-time (20 women); includes 59 minority (2 Black or African American, non-Hispanic/Latino; 3 Asian, non-Hispanic/Latino; 53 Hispanic/Latino; 1 Two or more races, non-Hispanic/Latino), 17 international. Average age 30. 75 applicants, 71% accepted, 35 enrolled. *Faculty:* 25 full-time (8 women), 3 part-time/adjunct (0 women). In 2015, 41 master's awarded. *Degree program information:* Part-time programs available. Part-time. Offers architecture (M Arch, MS, MS Arch); urban and regional planning (MS). *Application deadline:* For fall admission, 7/1 for domestic students, 4/1 for international students; for spring admission, 11/1 for domestic students, 9/1 for international students. Applications are processed on a rolling basis. *Application fee:* $45 ($80 for international students). Electronic applications accepted. *Application Contact:* Monica Rodriguez, Director of Graduate Admissions, 210-458-4331, Fax: 210-458-3016, E-mail: graduatestudies@utsa.edu. *Dean, Architecture,* Dr. John Murphy, 210-458-3090, Fax: 210-458-3091, E-mail: john.murphy@utsa.edu.

College of Business Students: 361 full-time (132 women), 289 part-time (82 women); includes 218 minority (18 Black or African American, non-Hispanic/Latino; 3 American Indian or Alaska Native, non-Hispanic/Latino; 37 Asian, non-Hispanic/Latino; 150 Hispanic/Latino; 2 Native Hawaiian or other Pacific Islander, non-Hispanic/Latino; 8 Two or more races, non-Hispanic/Latino), 109 international. Average age 31. 662 applicants, 39% accepted, 180 enrolled. *Faculty:* 69 full-time (13 women), 11 part-time/adjunct (2 women). In 2015, 209 master's, 11 doctorates, 6 other advanced degrees awarded. *Degree program information:* Part-time and evening/weekend programs available. Part-time, evening/weekend. Offers accounting (M Acy, PhD); applied statistics (MS, PhD); business (M Acy, MA, MBA, MS, MSIT, PhD, Certificate); business economics (MBA); cyber security (MSIT); economics (MA); finance (MBA, MS, PhD); information technology (MS, PhD); management and organization studies (PhD); management of technology (MBA); management science (MBA); marketing (PhD); marketing management (MBA); technology entrepreneurship and management (Certificate); tourism destination development (MBA). *Application deadline:* For fall admission, 7/1 for domestic students, 4/1 for international students; for spring admission, 11/1 for domestic students, 9/1 for international students. Applications are processed on a rolling basis. *Application fee:* $45 ($80 for international students). Electronic applications accepted. *Application Contact:* Katherine Pope, Director, Graduate Student Services, 210-458-4641, Fax: 210-458-4641, E-mail: mbainfo@utsa.edu. *Dean,* Dr. William Gerard Sanders, 210-458-4313, Fax: 210-458-4308, E-mail: gerry.sanders@utsa.edu.

College of Education and Human Development Students: 488 full-time (369 women), 936 part-time (716 women); includes 859 minority (106 Black or African American, non-Hispanic/Latino; 5 American Indian or Alaska Native, non-Hispanic/Latino; 28 Asian, non-Hispanic/Latino; 695 Hispanic/Latino; 2 Native Hawaiian or other Pacific Islander, non-Hispanic/Latino; 23 Two or more races, non-Hispanic/Latino), 24 international. Average age 33. 576 applicants, 78% accepted, 341 enrolled. *Faculty:* 98 full-time (56 women), 31 part-time/adjunct (18 women). *Financial support:* Federal Work-Study, scholarships/grants, health care benefits, and unspecified assistantships available. Support available to part-time students. In 2015, 381 master's, 34 doctorates, 18 other advanced degrees awarded. *Degree program information:* Part-time and evening/weekend programs available. Part-time, evening/weekend, online learning. Offers applied behavioral analysis (Certificate); bicultural and bilingual studies (MA); counselor education and supervision (PhD); culture, literacy, and language (PhD); digital learning design (Certificate); education (MA); education and human development (M Ed, MA, MS, Ed D, PhD, Certificate); educational leadership (Ed D); educational leadership and policy studies (M Ed); health and kinesiology (MS); interdisciplinary learning and teaching (PhD); language acquisition and bilingual psychoeducational assessment (Certificate); school counseling (M Ed); school psychology (MA); teaching English as a second language (MA). *Application deadline:* For fall admission, 7/1 for domestic students, 4/1 for international students; for spring admission, 11/1 for domestic students, 9/1 for international students. *Application fee:* $45 ($80 for international students). Electronic applications accepted. *Application Contact:* Monica Rodriguez, Director of Graduate Admissions, 210-458-4723, Fax: 210-458-4332, E-mail: monica.rodriguez@utsa.edu. *Dean,* Dr. Betty M. Merchant, 210-458-4370, Fax: 210-458-4487, E-mail: betty.merchant@utsa.edu.

College of Engineering Students: 333 full-time (81 women), 220 part-time (48 women); includes 126 minority (17 Black or African American, non-Hispanic/Latino; 29 Asian, non-Hispanic/Latino; 68 Hispanic/Latino; 12 Two or more races, non-Hispanic/Latino), 323 international. Average age 28. 557 applicants, 60% accepted, 138 enrolled. *Faculty:* 59 full-time (6 women), 9 part-time/adjunct (0 women). *Financial support:* In 2015–16, 120 students received support. Career-related internships or fieldwork, Federal Work-Study, institutionally sponsored loans, scholarships/grants, health care benefits, unspecified assistantships, and Valero Research Scholar awards available. Financial award application deadline: 9/15. In 2015, 130 master's, 25 doctorates awarded. *Degree program information:* Part-time and evening/weekend programs available. Part-time, evening/weekend. Offers advanced manufacturing and enterprise engineering (MS); advanced materials engineering (MS); biomedical engineering (MS, PhD); civil engineering (MCE, MSCE); computer engineering (MS); electrical engineering (MSEE,

PhD); engineering (MCE, MS, MSCE, MSEE, PhD); environmental science and engineering (PhD); mechanical engineering (MS, PhD). *Application deadline:* For fall admission, 7/1 for domestic students, 4/1 for international students; for spring admission, 11/1 for domestic students, 9/1 for international students. *Application fee:* $45 ($80 for international students). *Application Contact:* Monica Rodriguez, Director of Graduate Admissions, 210-458-4331, Fax: 210-458-4332, E-mail: graduateadmissions@utsa.edu. *Dean of Engineering*, Dr. JoAnn Browning, 210-458-5526, Fax: 210-458-5515, E-mail: joann.browning@utsa.edu.

College of Liberal and Fine Arts Students: 155 full-time (95 women), 239 part-time (151 women); includes 186 minority (11 Black or African American, non-Hispanic/Latino; 5 Asian, non-Hispanic/Latino; 150 Hispanic/Latino; 2 Native Hawaiian or other Pacific Islander, non-Hispanic/Latino; 18 Two or more races, non-Hispanic/Latino), 12 international. Average age 31. 234 applicants, 68% accepted, 104 enrolled. *Faculty:* 123 full-time (57 women), 9 part-time/adjunct (4 women). *Financial support:* In 2015–16, 92 students received support, including 21 fellowships with full tuition reimbursements available (averaging $23,810 per year), 24 research assistantships (averaging $8,105 per year), 47 teaching assistantships (averaging $9,078 per year); Federal Work-Study, scholarships/grants, and unspecified assistantships also available. Financial award applicants required to submit FAFSA. In 2015, 109 master's, 8 doctorates awarded. Offers anthropology (MA, PhD); art (MFA); art history (MA); communication (MA); English (MA, PhD); history (MA); liberal and fine arts (MA, MFA, MM, MS, PhD); music (MM); philosophy and classics (MA); political science (MA); psychology (MS, PhD); sociology (MS); Spanish (MA). *Application deadline:* For fall admission, 7/1 for domestic students, 4/1 for international students; for spring admission, 11/1 for domestic students, 9/1 for international students. *Application fee:* $45 ($80 for international students). Electronic applications accepted. *Application Contact:* Monica Rodriguez, Director of Graduate Admissions, 210-458-4331, Fax: 210-458-4332, E-mail: graduatestudies@utsa.edu. *Dean*, Dr. Daniel J. Gelo, 210-458-4359, Fax: 210-458-4347, E-mail: daniel.gelo@utsa.edu.

College of Public Policy Students: 156 full-time (108 women), 268 part-time (187 women); includes 272 minority (52 Black or African American, non-Hispanic/Latino; 2 American Indian or Alaska Native, non-Hispanic/Latino; 10 Asian, non-Hispanic/Latino; 192 Hispanic/Latino; 1 Native Hawaiian or other Pacific Islander, non-Hispanic/Latino; 15 Two or more races, non-Hispanic/Latino), 10 international. Average age 32. 172 applicants, 82% accepted, 109 enrolled. *Faculty:* 34 full-time (19 women), 13 part-time/adjunct (5 women). *Financial support:* In 2015–16, 12 fellowships with partial tuition reimbursements (averaging $22,500 per year), 27 research assistantships (averaging $8,445 per year), 4 teaching assistantships (averaging $8,418 per year) were awarded; scholarships/grants and unspecified assistantships also available. Financial award applicants required to submit FAFSA. In 2015, 151 master's, 4 doctorates awarded. *Degree program information:* Part-time and evening/weekend programs available. Part-time, evening/weekend. Offers applied demography (PhD); criminology (MS); public administration (MPA); public policy (MPA, MS, MSW, PhD); social work (MSW). *Application deadline:* For fall admission, 7/1 for domestic students, 4/1 for international students; for spring admission, 11/1 for domestic students, 9/1 for international students. *Application fee:* $45 ($80 for international students). *Application Contact:* Monica Rodriguez, Director of Graduate Admissions, 210-458-4331, Fax: 210-458-4332, E-mail: graduateadmissions@utsa.edu. *Dean*, Dr. Rogelio Saenz, 210-458-2715, E-mail: rogelio.saenz@utsa.edu.

College of Sciences Students: 327 full-time (125 women), 174 part-time (65 women); includes 166 minority (14 Black or African American, non-Hispanic/Latino; 2 American Indian or Alaska Native, non-Hispanic/Latino; 28 Asian, non-Hispanic/Latino; 104 Hispanic/Latino; 1 Native Hawaiian or other Pacific Islander, non-Hispanic/Latino; 17 Two or more races, non-Hispanic/Latino), 161 international. Average age 29. 563 applicants, 47% accepted, 126 enrolled. *Faculty:* 106 full-time (20 women), 16 part-time/adjunct (0 women). *Financial support:* Teaching assistantships available. Financial award applicants required to submit FAFSA. In 2015, 118 master's, 36 doctorates awarded. Offers applied mathematics (MS); biology (MS); biotechnology (MS); cell and molecular biology (PhD); chemistry (MS, PhD); computer science (MS, PhD); geological sciences (MS); mathematics (MS); mathematics education (MS); neurobiology (PhD); physics (MS, PhD); sciences (MS, PhD). *Application deadline:* For fall admission, 7/1 for domestic students, 4/1 for international students; for spring admission, 11/1 for domestic students, 9/1 for international students. *Application fee:* $45 ($80 for international students). Electronic applications accepted. *Application Contact:* Monica Rodriguez, Director of Graduate Admissions, 210-458-4331, Fax: 210-458-4332, E-mail: graduateadmissions@utsa.edu. *Dean*, Dr. George Perry, 210-458-4450, Fax: 210-458-4445, E-mail: george.perry@utsa.edu.

Joint PhD Program in Translational Science ***Financial support:*** In 2015–16, 1 student received support, including 3 research assistantships (averaging $26,000 per year), 3 teaching assistantships (averaging $34,000 per year); scholarships/grants and unspecified assistantships also available. *Degree program information:* Part-time programs available. Part-time. Offers translational science (PhD). Program offered in partnership with The University of Texas Health Science Center at San Antonio, The University of Texas at Austin, and The University of Texas Health Science Center at Houston. *Application deadline:* For fall admission, 11/1 for domestic and international students. *Application fee:* $45 ($80 for international students). Electronic applications accepted. *Application Contact:* Susan Stappenbeck, Senior Project Coordinator, 210-567-4304, Fax: 210-567-4301, E-mail: stappenbeck@uthscsa.edu. *Program Director*, Dr. Michael J. Lichtenstein, 210-567-4304, Fax: 210-564-4301, E-mail: lichtenstei@uthscsa.edu.

THE UNIVERSITY OF TEXAS AT TYLER, Tyler, TX 75799-0001

General Information State-supported, coed, comprehensive institution. *Graduate housing:* Rooms and/or apartments available on a first-come, first-served basis to single and married students. *Research affiliation:* Embassy of Arab Republic of Egypt Cultural and Education Bureau (electrical engineering), TransAtlantic Lines, Inc. (civil engineering), American Society of Civil Engineers (civil engineering), McGraw-Hill Company (civil engineering), Renaissance Society of America (art history), American Lung Association of the Central States (biology).

GRADUATE UNITS

College of Arts and Sciences ***Degree program information:*** Part-time and evening/weekend programs available. Part-time, evening/weekend, online learning. Offers art history (MA); arts and sciences (MA, MAIS, MAT, MFA, MPA, MS, MSIS); biology (MS); communication (MA); criminal justice (MS); English (MA); history (MA); interdisciplinary (MAIS); interdisciplinary studies (MAIS, MSIS); mathematics (MS, MSIS); political science (MA); public administration (MPA); sociology (MS); studio art (MFA). Electronic applications accepted.

College of Business and Technology ***Degree program information:*** Part-time and evening/weekend programs available. Part-time, evening/weekend, online learning. Offers business and technology (MBA, MS, PhD). Electronic applications accepted.

School of Business Administration Degree program information: Part-time programs available. Part-time, online learning. Offers business administration (MBA); general management (MBA); health care (MBA).

School of Human Resource Development and Technology Degree program information: Part-time and evening/weekend programs available. Part-time, evening/weekend, online learning. Offers human resource development (MS, PhD); industrial management (MS). Electronic applications accepted.

College of Education and Psychology ***Degree program information:*** Part-time and evening/weekend programs available. Part-time, evening/weekend. Offers clinical psychology (MS); counseling psychology (MA); education and psychology (M Ed, MA, MS, MSIS); educational leadership (M Ed); interdisciplinary studies (MSIS); school counseling (MA).

School of Education Degree program information: Part-time and evening/weekend programs available. Part-time, evening/weekend. Offers early childhood education (M Ed, MA); reading (M Ed, MA); special education (M Ed, MA). Electronic applications accepted.

College of Engineering and Computer Science ***Degree program information:*** Part-time programs available. Part-time. Offers computer science (MS); electrical engineering (MS); engineering and computer science (MS, MSIS); environmental engineering (MS); industrial safety (MS); interdisciplinary studies (MSIS); mechanical engineering (MS); structural engineering (MS); transportation engineering (MS); water resources engineering (MS). Electronic applications accepted.

College of Nursing and Health Sciences ***Degree program information:*** Part-time and evening/weekend programs available. Part-time, evening/weekend, online learning. Offers health and kinesiology (M Ed, MA); health sciences (MS); kinesiology (MS); nurse practitioner (MSN); nursing (PhD); nursing administration (MSN); nursing and health sciences (M Ed, MA, MS, MSN, PhD); nursing education (MSN). Electronic applications accepted.

THE UNIVERSITY OF TEXAS HEALTH SCIENCE CENTER AT HOUSTON, Houston, TX 77225-0036

General Information State-supported, coed, upper-level institution. CGS member. *Graduate housing:* On-campus housing not available.

GRADUATE UNITS

Graduate School of Biomedical Sciences Offers biochemistry and molecular biology (MS, PhD); biomathematics and biostatistics (MS, PhD); biomedical sciences (MS, PhD); cancer biology (MS, PhD); cell and regulatory biology (MS, PhD); genes and development (MS, PhD); genetic counseling (MS); human and molecular genetics (MS, PhD); immunology (MS, PhD); medical physics (MS, PhD); microbiology and molecular genetics (MS, PhD); molecular carcinogenesis (MS, PhD); molecular pathology (MS, PhD); neuroscience (MS, PhD); virology and gene therapy (MS, PhD). Electronic applications accepted.

School of Health Information Sciences ***Degree program information:*** Part-time programs available. Part-time, online learning. Offers health informatics (MS, PhD, Certificate). Electronic applications accepted.

School of Nursing ***Degree program information:*** Part-time programs available. Part-time. Offers nursing (MSN, DNP, PhD). Electronic applications accepted.

University of Texas Medical School at Houston Offers medicine (MD). Electronic applications accepted.

The University of Texas School of Dentistry at Houston Students: 399 full-time (214 women); includes 191 minority (18 Black or African American, non-Hispanic/Latino; 2 American Indian or Alaska Native, non-Hispanic/Latino; 80 Asian, non-Hispanic/Latino; 86 Hispanic/Latino; 5 Two or more races, non-Hispanic/Latino). Average age 25. 1,379 applicants, 10% accepted, 101 enrolled. *Faculty:* 118 full-time (48 women), 105 part-time/adjunct (47 women). *Financial support:* In 2015–16, 318 students received support. Institutionally sponsored loans and scholarships/grants available. Financial award application deadline: 3/1; financial award applicants required to submit FAFSA. In 2015, 86 doctorates awarded. Offers dentistry (MS, DDS). *Application deadline:* For fall admission, 9/30 for domestic students. Applications are processed on a rolling basis. *Application fee:* $150. Electronic applications accepted. *Application Contact:* Dr. H. Philip Pierpont, Associate Dean for Student and Alumni Affairs, 713-486-4151, Fax: 713-486-4425. *Dean*, Dr. John A. Valenza, 713-486-4021, Fax: 713-486-4089.

The University of Texas School of Public Health ***Degree program information:*** Part-time programs available. Part-time. Offers public health (MPH, MS, Dr PH, PhD, Certificate). Applications to dual degree programs are handled independently between the collaborating institutions. Electronic applications accepted.

THE UNIVERSITY OF TEXAS HEALTH SCIENCE CENTER AT SAN ANTONIO, San Antonio, TX 78229-3900

General Information State-supported, coed, upper-level institution. CGS member. *Research affiliation:* University Hospital, Southwest Research Institute, Southwest Foundation for Biomedical Research, Veterans Administration Hospital.

GRADUATE UNITS

Graduate School of Biomedical Sciences Offers biochemistry (MS, PhD); biomedical engineering (MS, PhD); biomedical sciences (MS, PhD); cellular and structural biology (MS, PhD); clinical investigation (MS); dental science (MS); integrated biomedical sciences (PhD); microbiology and immunology (MS, PhD); molecular medicine (MS, PhD); neuroscience (PhD); nursing science (PhD); radiological sciences (PhD); toxicology (MS); translational science (PhD).

School of Dentistry Students: 497 full-time (244 women), 41 part-time (20 women); includes 228 minority (16 Black or African American, non-Hispanic/Latino; 100 Asian, non-Hispanic/Latino; 99 Hispanic/Latino; 1 Native Hawaiian or other Pacific Islander, non-Hispanic/Latino; 12 Two or more races, non-Hispanic/Latino), 35 international. Average age 26. 1,462 applicants, 21% accepted, 190 enrolled. *Faculty:* 100 full-time (37 women), 97 part-time/adjunct (22 women). *Financial support:* In 2015–16, 121 students received support, including 7 research assistantships (averaging $3,080 per year), 83 teaching assistantships (averaging $14,550 per year); Federal Work-Study and institutionally sponsored loans also available. Financial award application deadline: 3/1; financial award applicants required to submit FAFSA. In 2015, 25 master's, 104 doctorates, 46 other advanced degrees awarded. Offers dentistry (MS, DDS, Certificate). *Application deadline:* For fall admission, 10/1 for domestic students, 10/31 for international students. Applications are processed on a rolling basis. *Application fee:* $150. Electronic applications accepted. *Application Contact:* E-mail: dsadmissions@uthscsa.edu. *Associate Dean for Student Affairs*, Dr. Adriana Segura, 210-567-3180, Fax: 210-567-4776, E-mail: seguraa@uthscsa.edu.

School of Health Professions Offers occupational therapy (MOT); physical therapy (DPT); physician assistant studies (MS).

School of Medicine Offers deaf education and hearing (MS); medicine (MD). Electronic applications accepted.

School of Nursing ***Degree program information:*** Part-time programs available. Part-time. Offers administrative management (MSN); adult-gerontology acute care nurse practitioner (PGC); advanced practice leadership (DNP); clinical nurse leader (MSN); executive administrative management (DNP); family nurse practitioner (MSN, PGC); nursing (MSN, PhD); nursing education (MSN, PGC); pediatric nurse practitioner primary care (PGC); psychiatric mental health nurse practitioner (PGC); public health nurse leader (DNP).

THE UNIVERSITY OF TEXAS MD ANDERSON CANCER CENTER, Houston, TX 77030

General Information State-supported, coed, upper-level institution.

GRADUATE UNITS

School of Health Professions Offers diagnostic genetics (MS).

THE UNIVERSITY OF TEXAS MEDICAL BRANCH, Galveston, TX 77555

General Information State-supported, coed, comprehensive institution. CGS member. *Graduate housing:* Rooms and/or apartments available on a first-come, first-served basis to single and married students. *Research affiliation:* Shriners Hospitals (burns and wound healing).

GRADUATE UNITS

Graduate School of Biomedical Sciences Offers biochemistry (PhD); bioinformatics (PhD); biomedical sciences (MA, MMS, MPH, MS, PhD); biophysics (PhD); cell biology (PhD); cellular physiology and molecular biophysics (MS, PhD); clinical science (MS, PhD); computational biology (PhD); emerging and tropical infectious diseases (PhD); experimental pathology (PhD); medical humanities (MA, PhD); medical science (MMS); microbiology and immunology (MS, PhD); neuroscience (PhD); nursing (PhD); pharmacology (MS); pharmacology and toxicology (PhD); population health sciences (MS, PhD); public health (MPH); rehabilitation sciences (PhD); structural biology (PhD). Electronic applications accepted.

School of Health Professions Offers health professions (MOT, MPAS, MPT, DPT); occupational therapy (MOT); physical therapy (MPT, DPT); physician assistant studies (MPAS). Electronic applications accepted.

School of Medicine Offers medicine (MD).

School of Nursing ***Degree program information:*** Part-time programs available. Part-time, online learning. Offers nursing (MSN, PhD). Electronic applications accepted.

THE UNIVERSITY OF TEXAS OF THE PERMIAN BASIN, Odessa, TX 79762-0001

General Information State-supported, coed, comprehensive institution. *Graduate housing:* Rooms and/or apartments available on a first-come, first-served basis to single and married students. Housing application deadline: 6/15.

GRADUATE UNITS

Office of Graduate Studies ***Degree program information:*** Part-time and evening/weekend programs available. Part-time, evening/weekend.

College of Arts and Sciences Degree program information: Part-time and evening/weekend programs available. Part-time, evening/weekend. Offers applied research psychology (MA); arts and sciences (MA, MS); biology (MS); clinical psychology (MA); computer science (MS); criminal justice administration (MS); English (MA); geology (MS); history (MA); kinesiology (MS); political science (MPA); Spanish (MA).

School of Business Degree program information: Part-time and evening/weekend programs available. Part-time, evening/weekend. Offers accountancy (MPA); business (MBA, MPA); management (MBA).

School of Education Offers bilingual/English as a second language education (MA); counseling (MA); early childhood education (MA); education (MA); educational leadership (MA); professional education (MA); reading (MA); special education (MA).

THE UNIVERSITY OF TEXAS RIO GRANDE VALLEY, Edinburg, TX 78539

General Information State-supported, coed, comprehensive institution. CGS member. *Enrollment:* 28,584 graduate, professional, and undergraduate students; 1,173 full-time matriculated graduate/professional students (690 women), 2,474 part-time matriculated graduate/professional students (1,556 women). *Enrollment by degree level:* 3,404 master's, 243 doctoral. *Graduate faculty:* 371 full-time (140 women), 27 part-time/adjunct (15 women). Tuition and fees vary according to course load and program. *Graduate housing:* Rooms and/or apartments available on a first-come, first-served basis to single and married students. Housing application deadline: 7/1. *Student services:* Campus employment opportunities, campus safety program, career counseling, child daycare facilities, exercise/wellness program, free psychological counseling, grant writing training, international student services, low-cost health insurance, services for students with disabilities, teacher training, writing training. *Library:* University Library. Students can reserve study rooms. *Research affiliation:* Robert Wood Johnson (health science), Lockheed Martin Corporation (manufacturing engineering), Texas Instruments (curriculum and instruction), Pfizer, Inc. (health disparities), Howard Hughes Medical Institute (medical science), Boeing Company (engineering).

Computer facilities: A campuswide network can be accessed from student residence rooms and from off campus. Online class registration is available.
Website: http://www.utrgv.edu/

General Application Contact: Stephanie Ozuna, Graduate Student Recruiter, 956-665-3558, E-mail: stephanie.ozuna@utrgv.edu.

GRADUATE UNITS

College of Business and Entrepreneurship ***Degree program information:*** Part-time and evening/weekend programs available. Part-time, evening/weekend. Offers accounting (M Acc, MS); business administration (MBA); business and entrepreneurship (M Acc, MBA, MS, PhD); finance (PhD); management (PhD); marketing (PhD).

College of Education and P-16 Integration ***Degree program information:*** Part-time and evening/weekend programs available. Part-time, evening/weekend. Offers bilingual education (M Ed); early childhood education (M Ed); education and P-16 integration (M Ed, MA, MS, Ed D, PhD); educational diagnostician (M Ed); educational leadership (M Ed, Ed D); elementary education (M Ed); gifted education (M Ed); guidance and counseling (M Ed); reading (M Ed); school psychology (MA); secondary education (M Ed); special education (M Ed). Ed D offered jointly with The University of Texas at Austin.

College of Engineering and Computer Science ***Degree program information:*** Part-time and evening/weekend programs available. Part-time, evening/weekend. Offers computer science (MS); electrical engineering (MS); engineering and computer science (MS); engineering management (MS); information technology (MS); manufacturing engineering (MS); mechanical engineering (MS); systems engineering (MS).

College of Fine Arts Offers creative writing (MFA); fine arts (M Mus, MAIS, MFA).

School of Art Students: 16 full-time (11 women), 12 part-time (8 women); includes 20 minority (all Hispanic/Latino), 1 international. Average age 40. *Faculty:* 4 full-time (1 woman). *Financial support:* Unspecified assistantships available. *Degree program information:* Part-time and evening/weekend programs available. Part-time, evening/weekend, online learning. Offers art (MFA). *Application deadline:* Applications are processed on a rolling basis. *Application Contact:* Stephanie Ozuna, Graduate Student Recruiter, 956-665-3558, E-mail: stephanie.ozuna@utrgv.edu. *Director,* Dr. Susan Fitzsimmons, E-mail: susan.fitzsimmons@utrgv.edu.

School of Music Degree program information: Part-time programs available. Part-time. Offers ethnomusicology (M Mus); interdisciplinary studies (MAIS); music education (M Mus); performance (M Mus).

College of Health Affairs ***Degree program information:*** Part-time and evening/weekend programs available. Part-time, evening/weekend. Offers communication sciences and disorders (MS); exercise sceince (MS); health affairs (MS, MSN, MSSW, PhD); kinesiology (MS); occupational therapy (MS); social work (MSSW).

School of Nursing Degree program information: Part-time and evening/weekend programs available. Part-time, evening/weekend. Offers adult health nursing (MSN); family nurse practitioner (MSN). Electronic applications accepted.

School of Rehabilitation Services and Counseling Degree program information: Part-time and evening/weekend programs available. Part-time, evening/weekend. Offers rehabilitation services and counseling (MS, PhD).

College of Liberal Arts ***Degree program information:*** Part-time and evening/weekend programs available. Part-time, evening/weekend. Offers communication (MA); communication training and consulting (Graduate Certificate); criminal justice (MS); English (MA, MAIS); English as a second language (MA); English: rhetoric, composition and literacy studies (MA); global security studies and leadership (MPA); history (MA, MAIS); interdisciplinary studies (MAIS, MSIS); liberal arts (M Mus, MA, MAIS, MFA, MS, MSIS, PhD, Graduate Certificate); psychology (MA); public administration (MPA); public policy and management (MPA); sociology and anthropology (MS); Spanish (MA); strategic communication and media relations (Graduate Certificate); theatre (MA).

College of Sciences ***Degree program information:*** Part-time and evening/weekend programs available. Part-time, evening/weekend. Offers biology (MS); chemistry (MS, MSIS); physics (MS); sciences (MS, MSIS). Electronic applications accepted.

School of Mathematical and Statistical Science Students: 27 full-time (10 women), 36 part-time (17 women); includes 37 minority (1 Black or African American, non-Hispanic/Latino; 5 Asian, non-Hispanic/Latino; 31 Hispanic/Latino), 9 international. Average age 33. 23 applicants, 96% accepted, 17 enrolled. *Faculty:* 16 full-time (1 woman). *Financial support:* Teaching assistantships, institutionally sponsored loans, and unspecified assistantships available. *Degree program information:* Part-time and evening/weekend programs available. Part-time, evening/weekend, online learning. Offers mathematical sciences (MS); mathematics (MS). *Application deadline:* Applications are processed on a rolling basis. *Application fee:* $50 ($100 for international students). Electronic applications accepted. *Application Contact:* Dr. Tim Huber, Graduate Program Coordinator, 956-665-2173, E-mail: timothy.huber@utrgv.edu.

School of Medicine ***Degree program information:*** Part-time and evening/weekend programs available. Part-time, evening/weekend, online learning. Offers medicine (MD).

THE UNIVERSITY OF TEXAS SOUTHWESTERN MEDICAL CENTER, Dallas, TX 75390

General Information State-supported, coed, graduate-only institution. *Graduate housing:* Rooms and/or apartments available on a first-come, first-served basis to single and married students.

GRADUATE UNITS

Southwestern Graduate School of Biomedical Sciences Offers biomedical sciences (MCS, MS, MSCS, PhD); clinical psychology (PhD); clinical science (MCS, MSCS); medical scientist training (PhD). Electronic applications accepted.

Division of Basic Science Offers biological chemistry (PhD); biomedical engineering (MS, PhD); cancer biology (PhD); cell regulation (PhD); genetics and development (PhD); immunology (PhD); integrative biology (PhD); molecular biophysics (PhD); molecular microbiology (PhD); neuroscience (PhD). Electronic applications accepted.

Southwestern Medical School Offers medicine (MD). Electronic applications accepted.

Southwestern School of Health Professions Offers clinical nutrition (MCN); health professions (MCN, MPAS, MPO, MRC, DPT); physical therapy (DPT); physician assistant studies (MPAS); prosthetics - orthotics (MPO); rehabilitation counseling psychology (MRC).

THE UNIVERSITY OF THE ARTS, Philadelphia, PA 19102-4944

General Information Independent, coed, comprehensive institution. *Graduate housing:* Room and/or apartments available to single students; on-campus housing not available to married students. Housing application deadline: 6/1. *Research affiliation:* The Franklin Institute (general science education), Philadelphia Museum of Art (arts and culture), School District of Philadelphia (education), Ben Franklin Technology Partners (high tech department and creative/cultural production in Philadelphia).

GRADUATE UNITS

College of Art, Media and Design ***Degree program information:*** Part-time programs available. Part-time. Offers art education (MA); art, media and design (MA, MAT, MFA, MID); book arts/printmaking (MFA); industrial design (MID); museum communication (MA); museum education (MA); museum exhibition planning and design (MFA); studio art (MFA); visual arts (MAT). Electronic applications accepted.

College of Performing Arts ***Degree program information:*** Part-time programs available. Part-time. Offers performing arts (MAT, MM).

School of Music Degree program information: Part-time programs available. Part-time. Offers jazz studies (MM); music education (MAT, MM). Electronic applications accepted.

UNIVERSITY OF THE CUMBERLANDS, Williamsburg, KY 40769-1372

General Information Independent-religious, coed, university. *Graduate housing:* Room and/or apartments available on a first-come, first-served basis to single students; on-campus housing not available to married students.

GRADUATE UNITS

Graduate Programs in Education ***Degree program information:*** Part-time and evening/weekend programs available. Part-time, evening/weekend, online learning. Offers all grades (P-12) (M Ed); business and marketing (MA Ed, MAT); counselor education and supervision (Ed D); director of pupil personnel (Certificate); director of special education (Certificate); educational administration and supervision (Ed S); educational leadership (Ed D); elementary education (MA Ed, MAT); instructional leadership - principalship (MA Ed); instructional leadership - school principal (Certificate); middle school education (MA Ed, MAT); reading and writing (MA Ed); school counseling (MA Ed); school superintendent (Certificate); secondary education (MA Ed, MAT); special education (MAT); supervisor of instruction (Certificate); teacher leader (MA Ed). Electronic applications accepted.

Hutton School of Business ***Degree program information:*** Part-time programs available. Part-time, online learning. Offers accounting (MBA); business (MBA). Electronic applications accepted.

Program in Christian Studies ***Degree program information:*** Part-time and evening/weekend programs available. Part-time, evening/weekend, online learning. Offers Christian studies (MA). Electronic applications accepted.

Program in Clinical Psychology ***Degree program information:*** Part-time and evening/weekend programs available. Part-time, evening/weekend, online learning. Offers clinical psychology (PhD).

Program in Physician Assistant Studies Offers physician assistant studies (MPAS). Electronic applications accepted.

Program in Professional Counseling ***Degree program information:*** Part-time and evening/weekend programs available. Part-time, evening/weekend, online learning. Offers professional counseling (MA). Program also offered in San Francisco. Electronic applications accepted.

UNIVERSITY OF THE DISTRICT OF COLUMBIA, Washington, DC 20008-1175

General Information District-supported, coed, comprehensive institution. CGS member.

GRADUATE UNITS

College of Agriculture, Urban Sustainability and Environmental Sciences Offers agriculture, urban sustainability and environmental sciences (M Arch, M Arch II, MS, PSM); architecture (M Arch, M Arch II); nutrition and dietetics (MS); water resources management (PSM). *Application Contact:* Saundra Carter, Associate Director for Graduate Recruitment and Operations, 202-274-7075. *Dean,* Sabine O'Hara, 202-274-7124.

College of Arts and Sciences ***Financial support:*** Fellowships, research assistantships, teaching assistantships, career-related internships or fieldwork, and Federal Work-Study available. *Degree program information:* Part-time and evening/weekend programs available. Part-time, evening/weekend. Offers adult education (Graduate Certificate); arts and sciences (MA, MAT, MS, Graduate Certificate); cancer biology, prevention and control (MS); counseling (MS); early childhood education (MA); elementary education (MAT); homeland security (MS); middle school mathematics (MAT); rehabilitation counseling (MA); secondary English language arts (MAT); secondary social studies (MAT); speech-language pathology (MS). *Application deadline:* For fall admission, 6/15 priority date for domestic students; for spring admission, 11/1 for domestic students. Applications are processed on a rolling basis. *Application fee:* $75 ($100 for international students).

David A. Clarke School of Law ***Degree program information:*** Part-time and evening/weekend programs available. Part-time, evening/weekend. Offers clinical teaching and social justice (LL M); law (JD). Electronic applications accepted.

School of Business and Public Administration ***Financial support:*** Career-related internships or fieldwork and Federal Work-Study available. *Degree program information:* Part-time and evening/weekend programs available. Part-time, evening/weekend. Offers business administration (MBA); business and public administration (MBA, MPA); public administration (MPA). *Application deadline:* For fall admission, 6/15 priority date for domestic students; for spring admission, 11/1 for domestic students. Applications are processed on a rolling basis. *Application fee:* $75 ($100 for international students).

School of Engineering and Applied Sciences Offers computer science (MS, MSCS); electrical engineering (MSEE); engineering and applied sciences (MSCS, MSEE).

UNIVERSITY OF THE FRASER VALLEY, Abbotsford, BC V2S 7M8, Canada

General Information Province-supported, coed, comprehensive institution. *Enrollment:* 8,423 graduate, professional, and undergraduate students; 36 full-time matriculated graduate/professional students (21 women), 2 part-time matriculated graduate/professional students (both women). *Enrollment by degree level:* 38 master's. *Graduate faculty:* 23 full-time (13 women). *Tuition, area resident:* Part-time $562 Canadian dollars per credit. One-time fee: $215 Canadian dollars full-time. *Graduate housing:* Room and/or apartments available on a first-come, first-served basis to single students; on-campus housing not available to married students. Housing application deadline: 5/15. *Student services:* Campus employment opportunities, campus safety program, career counseling, exercise/wellness program, free psychological counseling, grant writing training, international student services, low-cost health insurance, services for students with disabilities, writing training. *Library:* Peter Jones Library plus 3 others.
Website: http://www.ufv.ca/

General Application Contact: Educational Advisors, 604-854-4528, Fax: 604-855-7614, E-mail: advising@ufv.ca.

GRADUATE UNITS

Graduate Studies Students: 36 full-time (21 women), 2 part-time (both women). Average age 41. 41 applicants, 39% accepted, 16 enrolled. *Faculty:* 23 full-time (13 women). *Financial support:* Research assistantships, scholarships/grants, health care benefits, and bursaries available. Financial award application deadline: 5/10. In 2015, 18 master's awarded. *Degree program information:* Evening/weekend programs available. Evening/weekend. Offers criminal justice (MA); social work (MSW). *Application deadline:* For fall admission, 1/31 priority date for domestic students, 4/1 priority date for international students; for winter admission, 9/30 priority date for domestic students, 10/1 priority date for international students; for spring admission, 12/31 priority date for domestic students, 2/1 priority date for international students. *Application fee:* $45 ($150 for international students). Electronic applications accepted. *Application Contact:* Educational Advisors, 604-854-4528, Fax: 604-855-7614, E-mail: advising@ufv.ca. *Associate Vice President for Research, Engagement and Graduate Studies,* Dr. Adrienne Chan, 604-504-4074, Fax: 778-880-0356, E-mail: adrienne.chan@ufv.ca.

UNIVERSITY OF THE INCARNATE WORD, San Antonio, TX 78209-6397

General Information Independent-religious, coed, comprehensive institution. *Enrollment:* 8,666 graduate, professional, and undergraduate students; 1,064 full-time matriculated graduate/professional students (624 women), 1,142 part-time matriculated graduate/professional students (667 women). *Enrollment by degree level:* 1,159 master's, 1,047 doctoral. *Graduate faculty:* 104 full-time (59 women), 36 part-time/adjunct (19 women). *Tuition, area resident:* Part-time $885 per credit hour. *Required fees:* $40 per credit hour. Tuition and fees vary according to course load, degree level, campus/location, program and student level. *Graduate housing:* Room and/or apartments available on a first-come, first-served basis to single students; on-campus housing not available to married students. Typical cost: $6600 per year. Room charges vary according to board plan and housing facility selected. Housing application deadline: 5/1. *Student services:* Campus employment opportunities, campus safety program, career counseling, exercise/wellness program, free psychological counseling, grant writing training, international student services, low-cost health insurance, services for students with disabilities, teacher training, writing training. *Library:* J. E. and M. E. Mabee Library plus 1 other. *Collection:* Books: 270,398 (physical), 31,458 (digital/electronic); Serial titles: 103 (physical), 224 (digital/electronic); Databases: 167. Weekly public service hours: 105.

Computer facilities: Computer purchase and lease plans are available. 185 computers available on campus for general student use. A campuswide network can be accessed from student residence rooms and from off campus. Online class registration, Ports available in general use area and other locations. Also dedicated computers for graduate/doctoral students are available.
Website: http://www.uiw.edu/

General Application Contact: Johnny Garcia, Assistant Director of Graduate Admissions, 210-805-3554, Fax: 210-829-3921, E-mail: jsgarcia@uiwtx.edu.

GRADUATE UNITS

Extended Academic Programs Students: 5 full-time (2 women), 577 part-time (293 women); includes 365 minority (86 Black or African American, non-Hispanic/Latino; 15 Asian, non-Hispanic/Latino; 260 Hispanic/Latino; 4 Two or more races, non-Hispanic/Latino), 1 international. Average age 36. 270 applicants, 99% accepted, 185 enrolled. *Faculty:* 1 full-time (0 women), 17 part-time/adjunct (7 women). *Financial support:* Scholarships/grants and unspecified assistantships available. Financial award applicants required to submit FAFSA. In 2015, 267 master's awarded. *Degree program information:* Part-time and evening/weekend programs available. Part-time, evening/weekend, 100% online, blended/hybrid learning. Offers applied administration (MAA); asset management (MBA); business administration (MS); data analytics (MBA); educational psychology (MS); human resources (MBA); industrial and organizational psychology (MS); organizational development (MAA); organizational development and leadership (MS); teacher leadership (MA). *Application deadline:* Applications are processed on a rolling basis. Electronic applications accepted. *Application Contact:* Julie Weber, Director of Marketing and Recruitment, 210-318-1876, Fax: 210-829-2756, E-mail: eapadmission@uiwtx.edu. *Vice President,* Dr. Cyndi Porter, 877-603-1130, E-mail: porter@uiwtx.edu.

Feik School of Pharmacy Students: 370 full-time (244 women), 14 part-time (11 women); includes 248 minority (23 Black or African American, non-Hispanic/Latino; 77 Asian, non-Hispanic/Latino; 137 Hispanic/Latino; 1 Native Hawaiian or other Pacific Islander, non-Hispanic/Latino; 10 Two or more races, non-Hispanic/Latino), 6 international. Average age 26. *Faculty:* 27 full-time (17 women), 1 (woman) part-time/adjunct. *Financial support:* Research assistantships, Federal Work-Study, scholarships/grants, and unspecified assistantships available. Financial award applicants required to submit FAFSA. In 2015, 95 doctorates awarded. Offers pharmacy (Pharm D). *Application deadline:* For fall admission, 12/1 for domestic and international students. *Application fee:* $50. Electronic applications accepted. *Application Contact:* Dr. Amy Diepenbrock, Assistant Dean, Student Affairs, 210-883-1060, Fax: 210-822-1521, E-mail: diepenbr@uiwtx.edu. *Founding Dean,* Dr. Arcelia Johnson-Fannin, 210-883-1015, Fax: 210-822-1516, E-mail: johnsonf@uiwtx.edu.

Rosenberg School of Optometry Students: 261 full-time (157 women); includes 136 minority (8 Black or African American, non-Hispanic/Latino; 1 American Indian or Alaska Native, non-Hispanic/Latino; 82 Asian, non-Hispanic/Latino; 42 Hispanic/Latino; 1 Native Hawaiian or other Pacific Islander, non-Hispanic/Latino; 2 Two or more races, non-Hispanic/Latino), 8 international. Average age 25. *Faculty:* 15 full-time (5 women), 2 part-time/adjunct (both women). *Financial support:* In 2015–16, 5 fellowships (averaging $4,000 per year) were awarded; Federal Work-Study and scholarships/grants also available. Financial award applicants required to submit FAFSA. In 2015, 58 doctorates awarded. Offers optometry (OD). *Application deadline:* For fall admission, 5/1 for domestic students. *Application fee:* $50. Electronic applications accepted. *Application Contact:* Kristine Benne, Assistant Dean of Student Affairs, 210-883-1190, Fax: 210-883-1191, E-mail: benne@uiwtx.edu. *Dean,* Dr. Timothy Wingert, 210-883-1195, Fax: 210-283-6890, E-mail: twingert@uiwtx.edu.

School of Graduate Studies and Research Students: 330 full-time (173 women), 473 part-time (311 women); includes 462 minority (56 Black or African American, non-Hispanic/Latino; 4 American Indian or Alaska Native, non-Hispanic/Latino; 15 Asian, non-Hispanic/Latino; 373 Hispanic/Latino; 2 Native Hawaiian or other Pacific Islander, non-Hispanic/Latino; 12 Two or more races, non-Hispanic/Latino), 129 international. Average age 28. 430 applicants, 92% accepted, 248 enrolled. *Faculty:* 49 full-time (26 women), 20 part-time/adjunct (9 women). *Financial support:* In 2015–16, 25 research assistantships (averaging $3,600 per year) were awarded; Federal Work-Study, scholarships/grants, and tuition waivers (partial) also available. Financial award applicants required to submit FAFSA. In 2015, 297 master's, 15 doctorates awarded. *Degree program information:* Part-time and evening/weekend programs available. Part-time, evening/weekend. *Application deadline:* Applications are processed on a rolling basis. *Application fee:* $20. Electronic applications accepted. *Application Contact:* Johnny Garcia, Associate Director of Graduate Recruitment, 210-805-3554, Fax: 210-829-3921, E-mail: jsgarcia@uiwtx.edu. *Dean,* Dr. Osman Ozturgut, 210-805-5885, Fax: 210-805-3559, E-mail: ozturgut@uiwtx.edu.

College of Humanities, Arts, and Social Sciences Students: 3 full-time (0 women), 10 part-time (4 women); includes 4 minority (all Hispanic/Latino), 1 international. Average age 45. 5 applicants, 100% accepted, 1 enrolled. *Faculty:* 3 full-time (2 women). *Financial support:* Research assistantships, scholarships/grants, tuition waivers, and unspecified assistantships available. Financial award applicants required to submit FAFSA. In 2015, 8 master's awarded. *Degree program information:* Part-time and evening/weekend programs available. Part-time, evening/weekend. Offers humanities, arts, and social sciences (MA); religious studies (MA). *Application deadline:* Applications are processed on a rolling basis. *Application fee:* $20. Electronic applications accepted. *Application Contact:* Johnny Garcia, Graduate Admissions

Counselor, 210-829-6005, Fax: 210-829-3921, E-mail: admis@uiwtx.edu. *Dean,* Dr. Kevin Vichcales, 210-829-2759, Fax: 210-829-3830, E-mail: healy@uiwtx.edu.

Dreeben School of Education Students: 33 full-time (25 women), 194 part-time (130 women); includes 132 minority (23 Black or African American, non-Hispanic/Latino; 2 Asian, non-Hispanic/Latino; 106 Hispanic/Latino; 1 Two or more races, non-Hispanic/Latino), 38 international. Average age 39. 90 applicants, 96% accepted, 40 enrolled. *Faculty:* 11 full-time (5 women), 3 part-time/adjunct (all women). *Financial support:* In 2015–16, 4 research assistantships were awarded; Federal Work-Study, scholarships/grants, tuition waivers (partial), and unspecified assistantships also available. Financial award applicants required to submit FAFSA. In 2015, 42 master's, 15 doctorates awarded. *Degree program information:* Part-time and evening/weekend programs available. Part-time, evening/weekend, online learning. Offers adult education (M Ed, MA); all-level teaching (MAT); education (M Ed, MA, MAT, PhD); elementary teaching (MAT); general education (M Ed, MA); higher education (PhD); international education and entrepreneurship (PhD); kinesiology (M Ed, MA); multidisciplinary studies (MA); online teaching and training (M Ed, MA); organizational leadership (PhD); program evaluation (M Ed, MA); secondary teaching (MAT); student services in higher education (M Ed, MA). *Application deadline:* Applications are processed on a rolling basis. *Application fee:* $20. Electronic applications accepted. *Application Contact:* Johnny Garcia, Graduate Admissions Counselor, 210-805-3554, Fax: 210-829-3921, E-mail: admis@uiwtx.edu. *Dean,* Dr. Denise Staudt, 210-829-2761, Fax: 210-829-2765, E-mail: staudt@uiwtx.edu.

H-E-B School of Business and Administration Students: 225 full-time (109 women), 123 part-time (65 women); includes 194 minority (17 Black or African American, non-Hispanic/Latino; 2 American Indian or Alaska Native, non-Hispanic/Latino; 7 Asian, non-Hispanic/Latino; 158 Hispanic/Latino; 2 Native Hawaiian or other Pacific Islander, non-Hispanic/Latino; 8 Two or more races, non-Hispanic/Latino), 67 international. Average age 30. 229 applicants, 93% accepted, 143 enrolled. *Faculty:* 13 full-time (5 women), 14 part-time/adjunct (5 women). *Financial support:* In 2015–16, 4 research assistantships were awarded; Federal Work-Study, scholarships/grants, tuition waivers (partial), and unspecified assistantships also available. Financial award applicants required to submit FAFSA. In 2015, 193 master's awarded. *Degree program information:* Part-time and evening/weekend programs available. Part-time, evening/weekend, online learning. Offers accounting (MS); adult education (MAA); business administration (MBA, DBA); business and administration (MAA, MBA, MHA, MS, DBA); communication arts (MAA); finance (MBA); health administration (MHA); international business (MBA); marketing (MBA); nutrition (MAA); organizational development (MAA); sports management (MAA, MBA). *Application deadline:* Applications are processed on a rolling basis. *Application fee:* $20. Electronic applications accepted. *Application Contact:* Johnny Garcia, Assistant Director of Graduate Admissions, 210-805-3554, Fax: 210-829-3921, E-mail: jsgarcia@uiwtx.edu. *Dean,* Dr. Forrest Aven, 210-805-5884, Fax: 210-805-3564, E-mail: aven@uiwtx.edu.

School of Mathematics, Science, and Engineering Students: 21 full-time (19 women), 45 part-time (38 women); includes 40 minority (3 Asian, non-Hispanic/Latino; 37 Hispanic/Latino), 11 international. Average age 29. 57 applicants, 84% accepted, 23 enrolled. *Faculty:* 8 full-time (4 women), 1 (woman) part-time/adjunct. *Financial support:* In 2015–16, 1 research assistantship (averaging $5,000 per year) was awarded; Federal Work-Study, scholarships/grants, tuition waivers (partial), and unspecified assistantships also available. Financial award applicants required to submit FAFSA. In 2015, 16 master's awarded. *Degree program information:* Part-time and evening/weekend programs available. Part-time, evening/weekend. Offers administration (MS); biology (MA, MS); mathematics teaching (MA); mathematics, science, and engineering (MA, MS); multidisciplinary sciences (MA); nutrition education and health promotion (MS); research statistics (MS). *Application deadline:* Applications are processed on a rolling basis. *Application fee:* $20. Electronic applications accepted. *Application Contact:* Johnny Garcia, Graduate Admissions Counselor, 210-805-3554, Fax: 210-829-3921, E-mail: admis@uiwtx.edu. *Dean,* Dr. Carlos A. Garcia, 210-829-2717, Fax: 210-829-3153, E-mail: cagarci9@uiwtx.edu.

School of Media and Design Students: 19 full-time (14 women), 13 part-time (9 women); includes 18 minority (2 Black or African American, non-Hispanic/Latino; 16 Hispanic/Latino), 6 international. Average age 27. 21 applicants, 100% accepted, 16 enrolled. *Faculty:* 3 full-time (2 women). *Financial support:* Federal Work-Study, scholarships/grants, tuition waivers (partial), and unspecified assistantships available. Financial award applicants required to submit FAFSA. In 2015, 18 master's awarded. *Degree program information:* Part-time and evening/weekend programs available. Part-time, evening/weekend. Offers communication arts (MA); fashion design (MA). *Application deadline:* Applications are processed on a rolling basis. *Application fee:* $20. Electronic applications accepted. *Application Contact:* Johnny Garcia, Graduate Admissions Counselor, 210-805-3554, Fax: 210-829-3921, E-mail: admis@uiwtx.edu. *Dean,* Dr. Sharon Welkey, 210-829-6091, Fax: 210-829-3196, E-mail: welkey@uiwtx.edu.

School of Nursing and Health Professions Students: 31 full-time (9 women), 89 part-time (66 women); includes 75 minority (14 Black or African American, non-Hispanic/Latino; 2 American Indian or Alaska Native, non-Hispanic/Latino; 3 Asian, non-Hispanic/Latino; 53 Hispanic/Latino; 3 Two or more races, non-Hispanic/Latino), 9 international. Average age 34. 32 applicants, 91% accepted, 25 enrolled. *Faculty:* 10 full-time (7 women), 1 (woman) part-time/adjunct. *Financial support:* Research assistantships, Federal Work-Study, scholarships/grants, tuition waivers (partial), and unspecified assistantships available. Financial award applicants required to submit FAFSA. In 2015, 26 master's awarded. *Degree program information:* Part-time and evening/weekend programs available. Part-time, evening/weekend. Offers clinical nursing leader (MSN); clinical nursing specialist (MSN); kinesiology (MS); nursing (DNP); nursing and health professions (MS, MSN, DNP); sports management (MS). *Application deadline:* Applications are processed on a rolling basis. *Application fee:* $20. Electronic applications accepted. *Application Contact:* Johnny Garcia, Graduate Admissions Counselor, 210-805-3554, Fax: 210-829-3921, E-mail: admis@uiwtx.edu. *Dean,* Dr. Mary Hoke, 210-829-3982, Fax: 210-829-3174, E-mail: mhoke@uiwtx.edu.

UNIVERSITY OF THE PACIFIC, Stockton, CA 95211-0197

General Information Independent, coed, university. CGS member. *Enrollment:* 6,281 graduate, professional, and undergraduate students; 1,898 full-time matriculated graduate/professional students (1,111 women), 575 part-time matriculated graduate/professional students (334 women). *Enrollment by degree level:* 596 master's, 1,877 doctoral. *Graduate housing:* Rooms and/or apartments available on a first-come, first-served basis to single and married students. Housing application deadline: 7/1. *Student services:* Campus employment opportunities, campus safety program, career counseling, free psychological counseling, international student services, low-cost health insurance, multicultural affairs office, services for students with disabilities, teacher training. *Library:* University of the Pacific Library plus 1 other. *Research affiliation:* Lawrence Hall of Science.

Computer facilities: A campuswide network can be accessed from student residence rooms and from off campus. Online class registration is available.
Website: http://www.pacific.edu/

General Application Contact: Office of Graduate Admissions, 209-946-2011.

GRADUATE UNITS

Arthur A. Dugoni School of Dentistry Offers dentistry (MSD, DDS, Certificate). Electronic applications accepted.

College of the Pacific Offers biological sciences (MS); communication (MA); health, exercise and sport science (MA); psychology (MA).

Conservatory of Music Offers music education (MM); music therapy (MA).

Eberhardt School of Business ***Degree program information:*** Part-time programs available. Part-time. Offers business (M Acc, MBA).

Gladys L. Benerd School of Education Offers curriculum and instruction (MA); education (M Ed, MA, Ed D, Ed S); educational administration (MA, Ed D); educational psychology (MA, Ed D); school psychology (Ed S); special education (MA).

McGeorge School of Law ***Degree program information:*** Part-time and evening/weekend programs available. Part-time, evening/weekend. Offers advocacy (JD); international water resources law (JSD); public policy and law (LL M). Electronic applications accepted.

School of Engineering and Computer Science Offers engineering science (MS). Electronic applications accepted.

Thomas J. Long School of Pharmacy and Health Sciences Offers pharmaceutical and chemical sciences (MS, PhD); pharmacy (Pharm D); pharmacy and health sciences (MS, DPT, PhD, Pharm D); physical therapy (MS, DPT); speech-language pathology (MS).

UNIVERSITY OF THE POTOMAC, Washington, DC 20005

General Information Proprietary, coed, comprehensive institution.

GRADUATE UNITS

Program in Business Administration Online learning. Offers business administration (MBA). Program also offered at Vienna, VA campus.

UNIVERSITY OF THE ROCKIES, Colorado Springs, CO 80903

General Information Independent, coed, graduate-only institution.

GRADUATE UNITS

Graduate Programs Offers psychology (MA, Psy D).

UNIVERSITY OF THE SACRED HEART, San Juan, PR 00914-0383

General Information Independent-religious, coed, comprehensive institution. *Graduate housing:* Room and/or apartments available on a first-come, first-served basis to single students; on-campus housing not available to married students. Housing application deadline: 5/31.

GRADUATE UNITS

Graduate Programs ***Degree program information:*** Part-time and evening/weekend programs available. Part-time, evening/weekend. Offers contemporary culture and media (MA); creative writing (MFA, Certificate); digital journalism (MA, Certificate); early childhood education (M Ed); editing for media (MA, Certificate); human resource management (MBA); human rights and anti-discriminatory processes (MASJ); information systems auditing (MS); information systems management (MBA); information technology (Certificate); information technology and multimedia (Certificate); instruction systems and education technology (M Ed); international marketing (MBA); management information systems (MBA); mediation and transformation of conflicts (MASJ); nonprofit organization administration (MBA); occupational health and safety (MS); occupational nursing (MSN); production and marketing of special events (Certificate); public relations (MA, Certificate); publicity (MA, Certificate); scriptwriting (MA, Certificate); taxation (MBA).

UNIVERSITY OF THE SCIENCES, Philadelphia, PA 19104-4495

General Information Independent, coed, university. CGS member. *Graduate housing:* On-campus housing not available. *Research affiliation:* Progenra (molecular biology), Biotech, Pharma & Device (drug delivery), Encapsulation Systems (analytical chemistry), Johnson & Johnson (cell biology), Ortho-McNeil Pharmaceuticals, Inc. (pharmacy), Polymedix (computational chemistry).

GRADUATE UNITS

Doctor of Physical Therapy Program ***Degree program information:*** Part-time and evening/weekend programs available. Part-time, evening/weekend, online learning. Offers physical therapy (DPT). *Application deadline:* For spring admission, 11/1 for domestic students. *Application fee:* $0. *Application Contact:* Lorraine Cella, Assistant to Dean of Graduate Studies, 215-596-8926, E-mail: l.cella@usp.edu. *Director,* Dr. Susan Wainwright, 215-596-8849, Fax: 215-596-3121, E-mail: s.wainwr@usp.edu.

Philadelphia College of Pharmacy ***Financial support:*** Fellowships, research assistantships, teaching assistantships, and career-related internships or fieldwork available. Support available to part-time students. Financial award application deadline: 4/15; financial award applicants required to submit FAFSA. Offers pharmacy (Pharm D). *Application deadline:* For fall admission, 4/15 for domestic students; for spring admission, 10/24 for domestic students. *Application fee:* $50.

Program in Bioinformatics ***Financial support:*** Tuition waivers (partial) available. *Degree program information:* Part-time and evening/weekend programs available. Part-time, evening/weekend. Offers bioinformatics (MS). *Application deadline:* For fall admission, 5/1 for international students; for winter admission, 10/1 for international students; for spring admission, 3/1 for international students. Applications are processed on a rolling basis. *Application fee:* $50. *Application Contact:* Dr. Randy J. Zauhar, Program Director, 215-596-8691, E-mail: r.zauhar@usciences.edu. *Program Director,* Dr. Randy J. Zauhar, 215-596-8691, E-mail: r.zauhar@usciences.edu.

Program in Biomedical Writing ***Financial support:*** Tuition waivers (partial) available. Support available to part-time students. Financial award application deadline: 5/1. *Degree program information:* Part-time and evening/weekend programs available. Part-time, evening/weekend, online learning. Offers biomedical writing (MS); medical marketing writing (Certificate); regulatory affairs writing (Certificate). *Application deadline:* For fall admission, 5/1 for international students; for winter admission, 10/1 for international students; for spring admission, 3/1 for international students. Applications are processed on a rolling basis. *Application fee:* $50. *Application Contact:* Dr. Danny A. Benau, Director, 215-596-7509, E-mail: d.benau@usciences.edu. *Director,* Dr. Danny A. Benau, 215-596-7509, E-mail: d.benau@usciences.edu.

Program in Cell Biology and Biotechnology ***Financial support:*** Teaching assistantships with full tuition reimbursements, scholarships/grants, and tuition waivers (partial) available. Financial award application deadline: 5/1. *Degree program information:* Part-time and evening/weekend programs available. Part-time, evening/weekend. Offers cell biology and biotechnology (MS). *Application deadline:* For fall admission, 5/1 for international students; for winter admission, 10/1 for international students; for spring admission, 3/1 for international students. Applications are processed on a rolling basis. *Application fee:* $50. *Application Contact:* Dr. James R. McKee, Director, 215-596-8847, E-mail: j.mckee@usciences.edu. *Director,* Dr. James R. McKee, 215-596-8847, E-mail: j.mckee@usciences.edu.

Program in Chemistry, Biochemistry and Pharmacognosy ***Financial support:*** Fellowships with full tuition reimbursements, research assistantships with full tuition reimbursements, teaching assistantships with full tuition reimbursements, institutionally sponsored loans, scholarships/grants, and tuition waivers (full) available. Financial award application deadline: 5/1. *Degree program information:* Part-time programs available. Part-time. Offers biochemistry (MS, PhD); chemistry (MS, PhD); pharmacognosy (MS, PhD). *Application deadline:* For fall admission, 5/1 for international students; for winter admission, 10/1 for international students; for spring admission, 3/1 for international students. Applications are processed on a rolling basis. *Application fee:* $50. *Application Contact:* Dr. James R. McKee, Director, 215-596-8847, E-mail: j.mckee@usciences.edu. *Director,* Dr. James R. McKee, 215-596-8847, E-mail: j.mckee@usciences.edu.

Program in Health Policy ***Financial support:*** Tuition waivers (partial) and unspecified assistantships available. Support available to part-time students. Financial award application deadline: 5/1. *Degree program information:* Part-time and evening/weekend programs available. Part-time, evening/weekend, online learning. Offers health policy (MS, PhD). *Application deadline:* For fall admission, 6/1 for domestic students, 5/1 for international students; for winter admission, 12/1 for domestic students, 10/1 for international students; for spring admission, 3/1 for international students. Applications are processed on a rolling basis. *Application fee:* $50. *Application Contact:* Dr. Stephen Metraux, Interim Director, 215-596-7614, E-mail: s.metrau@usciences.edu. *Interim Director,* Dr. Stephen Metraux, 215-596-7614, E-mail: s.metrau@usciences.edu.

Program in Health Psychology ***Financial support:*** Research assistantships and tuition waivers (partial) available. Financial award application deadline: 5/1. Offers health psychology (MS). *Application deadline:* For fall admission, 5/1 for international students; for winter admission, 10/1 for international students; for spring admission, 3/1 for international students. Applications are processed on a rolling basis. *Application fee:* $50. *Application Contact:* Christopher Miciek, Associate Director, Graduate Admissions, 215-596-8597, E-mail: c.miciek@usciences.edu. *Director,* Dr. E. Amy Janke, 215-596-8517, E-mail: e.janke@usciences.edu.

Program in Occupational Therapy Online learning. Offers occupational therapy (MOT, Dr OT). Electronic applications accepted.

Program in Pharmaceutical and Healthcare Business ***Financial support:*** Tuition waivers (partial) available. *Degree program information:* Part-time and evening/weekend programs available. Part-time, evening/weekend, online learning. Offers pharmaceutical and healthcare business (MBA). *Application deadline:* For fall admission, 5/1 for international students; for winter admission, 10/1 for international students; for spring admission, 3/1 for international students. Applications are processed on a rolling basis. *Application fee:* $50. *Application Contact:* Robert Mueller, Director, 215-596-8879, E-mail: r.mueller@usciences.edu. *Director,* Robert Mueller, 215-596-8879, E-mail: r.mueller@usciences.edu.

Program in Pharmaceutics ***Financial support:*** Fellowships with full tuition reimbursements, research assistantships with full tuition reimbursements, teaching assistantships with full tuition reimbursements, institutionally sponsored loans, and tuition waivers (full and partial) available. Financial award application deadline: 3/1. *Degree program information:* Part-time programs available. Part-time. Offers pharmaceutics (MS, PhD). *Application deadline:* For fall admission, 5/1 for international students; for winter admission, 10/1 for international students; for spring admission, 3/1 for international students. Applications are processed on a rolling basis. *Application fee:* $50. *Application Contact:* Dr. Steven Neau, Director, 215-596-8825, E-mail: s.neau@usciences.edu. *Director,* Dr. Steven Neau, 215-596-8825, E-mail: s.neau@usciences.edu.

Program in Pharmacology and Toxicology ***Financial support:*** Teaching assistantships with tuition reimbursements, institutionally sponsored loans, and tuition waivers (partial) available. Financial award application deadline: 5/1. Offers pharmacology (MS, PhD); toxicology (MS, PhD). *Application deadline:* For fall admission, 5/1 for international students; for winter admission, 10/1 for international students; for spring admission, 3/1 for international students. Applications are processed on a rolling basis. *Application fee:* $50. *Application Contact:* Dr. Bin Chen, Director, 215-596-7481, E-mail: b.chen@usciences.edu. *Director,* Dr. Bin Chen, 215-596-7481, E-mail: b.chen@usciences.edu.

Program in Pharmacy Administration ***Financial support:*** Research assistantships with full tuition reimbursements, teaching assistantships, institutionally sponsored loans, traineeships, tuition waivers (partial), and unspecified assistantships available. Financial award application deadline: 5/1. *Degree program information:* Part-time programs available. Part-time. Offers pharmacy administration (MS). *Application deadline:* For fall admission, 5/1 for international students; for winter admission, 10/1 for international students; for spring admission, 3/1 for international students. Applications are processed on a rolling basis. *Application fee:* $50. *Application Contact:* Dr. William F. McGhan, Director, 215-596-8852, E-mail: w.mcghan@usciences.edu. *Director,* Dr. William F. McGhan, 215-596-8852, E-mail: w.mcghan@usciences.edu.

Program in Physician Assistant Studies Offers physician assistant studies (MSPAS).

Program in Public Health ***Degree program information:*** Part-time and evening/weekend programs available. Part-time, evening/weekend, online learning. Offers public health (MPH). *Application Contact:* Dr. Amalia M. Issa, Chair/Director, 267-295-7033, E-mail: a.issa@usciences.edu. *Chair/Director,* Dr. Amalia M. Issa, 267-295-7033, E-mail: a.issa@usciences.edu.

UNIVERSITY OF THE SOUTHWEST, Hobbs, NM 88240-9129

General Information Independent-religious, coed, comprehensive institution. *Graduate housing:* On-campus housing not available.

GRADUATE UNITS

Graduate Programs ***Degree program information:*** Part-time and evening/weekend programs available. Part-time, evening/weekend, online learning. Offers business administration (MBA); curriculum and instruction (MSE); curriculum and instruction: bilingual (MSE); curriculum and instruction: TESOL (MSE); early childhood education (MSE); educational administration (MSE); mental health counseling (MSE); school counseling (MSE); special education (MSE); sports management (MBA). Electronic applications accepted.

UNIVERSITY OF THE VIRGIN ISLANDS, Saint Thomas, VI 00802-9990

General Information Territory-supported, coed, comprehensive institution. *Graduate housing:* On-campus housing not available.

GRADUATE UNITS

Graduate Programs ***Degree program information:*** Part-time and evening/weekend programs available. Part-time, evening/weekend.

Division of Business Administration Degree program information: Part-time and evening/weekend programs available. Part-time, evening/weekend. Offers business administration (MBA).

Division of Education Degree program information: Part-time and evening/weekend programs available. Part-time, evening/weekend. Offers education (MAE).

Division of Humanities and Social Sciences Degree program information: Part-time and evening/weekend programs available. Part-time, evening/weekend. Offers humanities and social sciences (MPA).

Division of Science and Mathematics Degree program information: Part-time programs available. Part-time, online learning. Offers environmental and marine science (MS); mathematics for secondary teachers (MA); science and mathematics (MA, MS).

UNIVERSITY OF THE WEST, Rosemead, CA 91770

General Information Independent, coed, comprehensive institution. *Graduate housing:* Rooms and/or apartments guaranteed to single students and available on a first-come, first-served basis to married students. Housing application deadline: 9/22.

GRADUATE UNITS

Department of Business Administration ***Degree program information:*** Part-time and evening/weekend programs available. Part-time, evening/weekend. Offers business administration (EMBA); computer information systems (MBA); finance (MBA); international business (MBA); nonprofit organization management (MBA).

Department of Psychology ***Degree program information:*** Part-time and evening/weekend programs available. Part-time, evening/weekend. Offers Buddhist psychology (MA); multicultural counseling (MA).

Department of Religious Studies ***Degree program information:*** Part-time and evening/weekend programs available. Part-time, evening/weekend. Offers Buddhism (PhD); Buddhist studies (MA); comparative religions (PhD); comparative religious studies (MA); religious studies (PhD).

Program in Buddhist Chaplaincy Offers Buddhist chaplaincy (M Div).

THE UNIVERSITY OF TOLEDO, Toledo, OH 43606-3390

General Information State-supported, coed, university. CGS member. *Graduate housing:* Room and/or apartments available to single students; on-campus housing not available to married students. *Research affiliation:* Merck & Company, Inc. (pharmaceutical research), Midwest Astronomical Data Reduction and Analysis Facility (astronomy), Edison Industrial Systems Center (systems integration, quality control, mathematical modeling), Ohio Aerospace Institute (aerospace research), National Renewable Energy Laboratory (NREL) (thin films, photovoltaics), NASA–Glen Research Center at Lewis Field (aerospace engineering).

GRADUATE UNITS

College of Graduate Studies ***Degree program information:*** Part-time and evening/weekend programs available. Part-time, evening/weekend, online learning. Electronic applications accepted.

College of Business and Innovation Degree program information: Part-time and evening/weekend programs available. Part-time, evening/weekend. Offers accounting (MBA, MSA); business administration-general (MBA); business and innovation (EMBA, MBA, MSA, DME, PhD, Certificate); finance (MBA); information operations and technology management (MBA, DME, PhD, Certificate); management (MBA); marketing and international business (MBA). Electronic applications accepted.

College of Communication and the Arts Offers communication (Certificate); communication and the arts (ME, MME, MMP, Certificate); music (Certificate); music performance (MMP). Electronic applications accepted.

College of Engineering Degree program information: Part-time and evening/weekend programs available. Part-time, evening/weekend, online learning. Offers bioengineering (MS, PhD); biomedical engineering (PhD); chemical engineering (MS, PhD); civil engineering (MS, PhD); computer science (MS, PhD); electrical engineering (MS, PhD); engineering (MS, PhD); general engineering (MS); industrial engineering (MS, PhD); mechanical engineering (MS, PhD). Electronic applications accepted.

College of Health Sciences Offers exercise science (MSES, PhD); health education (PhD); health sciences (MA, ME, MSES, DPT, OTD, PhD, Certificate, Ed S); occupational therapy (OTD); physical therapy (DPT); recreation and leisure studies (MA); speech-language pathology (MA). Electronic applications accepted.

College of Languages, Literature and Social Sciences Degree program information: Part-time programs available. Part-time. Offers applied econometric specialization (MA); clinical psychology (MA, PhD); economics (MA); English as a second language (MA); experimental psychology (MA, PhD); French (MA); geographic information science and applied geographics (Certificate); geography and planning (MA); German (MA); health care policy and administration (Certificate); history (MA, PhD); languages, literature and social sciences (MA, MLS, MPA, PhD, Certificate); liberal studies (MLS); management of non-profit organizations (Certificate); municipal administration (Certificate); philosophy (MA); political science (MA); public administration (MPA); sociology (MA); Spanish (MA); spatially-integrated social science (PhD); teaching of writing (Certificate); women's and gender studies (Certificate). Electronic applications accepted.

College of Medicine and Life Sciences Degree program information: Part-time and evening/weekend programs available. Part-time, evening/weekend. Offers bioinformatics and proteomics/genomics (MSBS); biomarkers and bioinformatics (Certificate); biomarkers and diagnostics (PSM); biostatistics and epidemiology (Certificate); cancer biology (MSBS, PhD); cardiovascular and metabolic diseases (MSBS, PhD); contemporary gerontological practice (Certificate); environmental and occupational health and safety (MPH); epidemiology (Certificate); global public health (Certificate); health promotion and education (MPH); human donation sciences (MSBS); industrial hygiene (MSOH); infection, immunity, and transplantation (MSBS, PhD); medical and health science teaching and learning (Certificate); medical physics (MSBS); medical sciences (MSBS); medicine and life sciences (MPH, MS, MSBS, MSOH, PhD, Certificate); neurosciences (MSBS, PhD); occupational health (Certificate); oral biology (MSBS); orthopedic surgery (MSBS); pathology (Certificate); pathology assistant (MSBS); physician assistant studies (MSBS); public health administration (MPH); public health and emergency response (Certificate);

public health epidemiology (MPH); public health nutrition (MPH). Electronic applications accepted.

College of Natural Sciences and Mathematics Degree program information: Part-time programs available. Part-time. Offers analytical chemistry (MS, PhD); applied mathematics (MS, PhD); biological chemistry (MS, PhD); biology (MS, PhD); geology (MS); inorganic chemistry (MS, PhD); natural sciences and mathematics (MS, PSM, PhD); organic chemistry (MS, PhD); photovoltaics (PSM); physical chemistry (MS, PhD); physics (MS, PhD); statistics (MS, PhD). Electronic applications accepted.

College of Nursing Degree program information: Part-time programs available. Part-time, online learning. Offers clinical nurse leader (MSN); family nurse practitioner (MSN, Certificate); health promotions, outcomes, systems, and policy (MSN, DNP); nurse educator (MSN, Certificate); nursing (MSN, DNP, Certificate); pediatric nurse practitioner (MSN, Certificate). Electronic applications accepted.

College of Pharmacy and Pharmaceutical Sciences Offers administrative pharmacy (MSPS); experimental therapeutics (PhD); industrial pharmacy (MSPS); medicinal and biological chemistry (MS, PhD); pharmacology toxicology (MSPS); pharmacy and pharmaceutical sciences (MS, MSPS, PhD). Electronic applications accepted.

College of Social Justice and Human Service Offers child advocacy (Certificate); counselor education (MA, PhD); criminal justice (MA); elder law (Certificate); higher education (ME, PhD, Certificate); juvenile justice (Certificate); patient advocacy (Certificate); school psychology (MA, Ed S); social justice and human service (MA, ME, MSW, PhD, Certificate, Ed S); social work (MSW).

Judith Herb College of Education Degree program information: Part-time and evening/weekend programs available. Part-time, evening/weekend. Offers art education (ME); career and technical education (ME, Ed S); curriculum and instruction (ME, PhD, Ed S); early childhood education (ME, Ed S); education (MAE, ME, MES, MME, DE, PhD, Certificate, Ed S); education and anthropology (MAE); education and biology (MES); education and chemistry (MES); education and classics (MAE); education and economics (MAE); education and English (MAE); education and French (MAE); education and geology (MES); education and German (MAE); education and history (MAE); education and mathematics (MAE, MES); education and physics (MES); education and political science (MAE); education and sociology (MAE); education and Spanish (MAE); educational administration and supervision (ME, DE, Ed S); educational media (PhD); educational psychology (ME, PhD); educational research and measurement (ME, PhD); educational sociology (PhD); educational technology (ME); educational technology: virtual educator (Certificate); educational theory and social foundations (ME); elementary education (PhD); English as a second language (MAE); foundations of education (DE, PhD); gifted and talented education (PhD); history of education (PhD); middle childhood education (ME); philosophy of education (PhD); physical education (ME); secondary education (ME, PhD); special education (ME, PhD). Electronic applications accepted.

College of Law Students: 197 full-time (86 women), 67 part-time (38 women); includes 45 minority (25 Black or African American, non-Hispanic/Latino; 7 Asian, non-Hispanic/Latino; 9 Hispanic/Latino; 4 Two or more races, non-Hispanic/Latino). Average age 29. 351 applicants, 70% accepted, 80 enrolled. *Faculty:* 29 full-time (14 women), 15 part-time/adjunct (2 women). *Financial support:* In 2015–16, 204 students received support, including 17 research assistantships, 12 teaching assistantships; career-related internships or fieldwork, Federal Work-Study, and scholarships/grants also available. Support available to part-time students. Financial award application deadline: 8/1; financial award applicants required to submit FAFSA. In 2015, 1 master's, 106 doctorates awarded. *Degree program information:* Part-time and evening/weekend programs available. Part-time-only, evening/weekend. Offers law (MLW, JD). *Application deadline:* For fall admission, 7/31 priority date for domestic students, 7/31 for international students; for winter admission, 11/15 for domestic students; for summer admission, 4/15 for domestic students. Applications are processed on a rolling basis. *Application fee:* $0. Electronic applications accepted. *Application Contact:* Jessica Mehl, Assistant Dean of Law Admissions, 419-530-4131, Fax: 419-530-4345, E-mail: law.admissions@utoledo.edu. *Dean,* D. Benjamin Barros, 419-530-2379, Fax: 419-530-4526, E-mail: ben.barros@utoledo.edu.

UNIVERSITY OF TORONTO, Toronto, ON M5S 1A1, Canada

General Information Province-supported, coed, university. CGS member. *Graduate housing:* Rooms and/or apartments available on a first-come, first-served basis to single students and available to married students. *Research affiliation:* Fields Institute for Research in Mathematical Sciences, Canadian Institute for Theoretical Astrophysics, Royal Ontario Museum, Pontifical Institute of Medieval Studies, Hospital for Sick Children, Center for Addiction and Mental Health.

GRADUATE UNITS

Faculty of Medicine Offers biochemistry (M Sc, PhD); genetic counseling (M Sc); immunology (M Sc, PhD); laboratory medicine and pathobiology (M Sc, PhD); management of innovation (MMI); medical biophysics (M Sc, PhD); medicine (M Sc, M Sc BMC, M Sc OT, M Sc PT, MH Sc, MD, PhD); molecular genetics (M Sc, PhD); nutritional sciences (M Sc, PhD); occupational therapy (M Sc OT); pharmacology (M Sc, PhD); physical therapy (M Sc PT); physiology (M Sc, PhD); rehabilitation science (M Sc, PhD); speech-language pathology (M Sc, MH Sc, PhD). Electronic applications accepted.

Institute of Health Policy, Management and Evaluation Offers health administration (MH Sc); health informatics (MHI); health policy, management and evaluation (PhD). Electronic applications accepted.

Institute of Medical Science Offers bioethics (MH Sc); biomedical communications (M Sc BMC); medical radiation science (MH Sc); medical science (PhD). Electronic applications accepted.

School of Graduate Studies ***Degree program information:*** Part-time and evening/weekend programs available. Part-time, evening/weekend. Offers biotechnology (MBiotech); environmental science (M Env Sc, PhD). Electronic applications accepted.

Advanced Design and Manufacturing Institute Degree program information: Part-time programs available. Part-time. Offers design and manufacturing (M Eng). Program offered jointly with McMaster University, Queen's University, and The University of Western Ontario; available only to Canadian citizens and permanent residents of Canada. Electronic applications accepted.

Department of Nursing Science Degree program information: Part-time programs available. Part-time. Offers nursing (MN, PhD). Electronic applications accepted.

Department of Public Health Sciences Degree program information: Part-time programs available. Part-time. Offers biostatistics (M Sc, PhD); community health (M Sc); community nutrition (MPH); epidemiology (MPH, PhD); family and community medicine (MPH); occupational and environmental health (MPH); social and behavioral health science (PhD); social and behavioral health sciences (MPH). Electronic applications accepted.

Faculty of Applied Science and Engineering Degree program information: Part-time programs available. Part-time. Offers aerospace studies (M Eng, MA Sc, PhD); applied science and engineering (M Eng, MA Sc, MH Sc, PhD); biomedical engineering (MA Sc, PhD); chemical engineering and applied chemistry (M Eng, MA Sc, PhD); civil engineering (M Eng, MA Sc, PhD); clinical engineering (MH Sc, PhD); electrical and computer engineering (M Eng, MA Sc, PhD); materials science and engineering (M Eng, MA Sc, PhD); mechanical and industrial engineering (M Eng, MA Sc, PhD).

Faculty of Arts and Science Degree program information: Part-time programs available. Part-time. Offers anthropology (M Sc, MA, PhD); applied computing (M Sc AC); art history (MA, PhD); arts and science (M Sc, M Sc AC, M Sc Pl, MA, MA Sc, MFE, MIRHR, MMF, MUD, MUDS, MVS, PhD); astronomy and astrophysics (M Sc, PhD); cell and systems biology (M Sc, PhD); chemistry (M Sc, PhD); cinema studies (MA, PhD); classics (MA, PhD); comparative literature (MA, PhD); computer science (M Sc, PhD); creative writing (MA); criminology and sociolegal studies (MA, PhD); drama, theatre and performance studies (MA, PhD); earth sciences (M Sc, MA Sc, PhD); East Asian studies (MA, PhD); ecology and evolutionary biology (M Sc, PhD); economics (MA, PhD); English (MA, PhD); financial economics (MFE); French language and literature (MA, PhD); geography (M Sc, MA, PhD); German (MA, PhD); history (MA, PhD); history and philosophy of science and technology (MA, PhD); industrial relations and human resources (MIRHR, PhD); Italian studies (MA, PhD); linguistics (MA, PhD); mathematical finance (MMF); mathematics (M Sc, PhD); medieval studies (MA, PhD); Near and Middle Eastern civilizations (MA, PhD); philosophy (MA, PhD); physics (M Sc, PhD); planning (M Sc Pl, MUDS, PhD); political science (MA, PhD); psychology (MA, PhD); religion (MA, PhD); Slavic languages and literatures (MA, PhD); sociology (MA, PhD); Spanish and Portuguese (MA, PhD); statistical sciences (M Sc, PhD); urban design (MUD); women and gender studies (MA, PhD). Electronic applications accepted.

Faculty of Dentistry Offers dental public health (M Sc); dentistry (M Sc, DDS, PhD); endodontics (M Sc); oral and maxillofacial radiology (M Sc); oral and maxillofacial surgery (M Sc); oral medicine (M Sc); orthodontics and dentofacial orthopedics (M Sc); pediatric dentistry (M Sc); periodontology (M Sc). Electronic applications accepted.

Faculty of Forestry Offers forestry (M Sc F, MFC, PhD). Electronic applications accepted.

Faculty of Information Studies Degree program information: Part-time programs available. Part-time. Offers information (MI, PhD); museum studies (MM St). Electronic applications accepted.

Faculty of Kinesiology and Physical Education Offers kinesiology and physical education (M Sc, PhD). Electronic applications accepted.

Faculty of Law Degree program information: Part-time programs available. Part-time. Offers law (LL M, MSL, JD, SJD). Electronic applications accepted.

Faculty of Management Degree program information: Part-time and evening/weekend programs available. Part-time, evening/weekend. Offers management (MBA, MF, PhD).

Faculty of Music Degree program information: Part-time programs available. Part-time. Offers composition (M Mus, DMA); ethnomusicology (MA, PhD); jazz (M Mus); music education (MA, PhD); musicology/theory (MA, PhD); opera (M Mus); performance (M Mus, DMA). Electronic applications accepted.

Faculty of Social Work Degree program information: Part-time programs available. Part-time. Offers social work (MSW, PhD). Electronic applications accepted.

John H. Daniels Faculty of Architecture, Landscape, and Design Offers architecture, landscape, and design (M Arch, MLA, MUD, MVS). Electronic applications accepted.

Leslie Dan Faculty of Pharmacy Degree program information: Part-time programs available. Part-time. Offers pharmacy (M Sc, PhD, Pharm D). Electronic applications accepted.

Munk School of Global Affairs Offers European, Russian and Eurasian studies (MA); global affairs (MGA). Electronic applications accepted.

Ontario Institute for Studies in Education Degree program information: Part-time and evening/weekend programs available. Part-time, evening/weekend. Offers education (M Ed, MA, MT, Ed D, PhD).

THE UNIVERSITY OF TULSA, Tulsa, OK 74104-3189

General Information Independent, coed, university. CGS member. *Enrollment:* 4,671 graduate, professional, and undergraduate students; 475 full-time matriculated graduate/professional students (194 women), 307 part-time matriculated graduate/professional students (94 women). *Enrollment by degree level:* 545 master's, 237 doctoral. *Graduate faculty:* 194 full-time (54 women), 11 part-time/adjunct (5 women). *Tuition, area resident:* Full-time $22,230; part-time $1176 per credit hour. *Required fees:* $590 per semester. Tuition and fees vary according to course load. *Graduate housing:* Rooms and/or apartments available on a first-come, first-served basis to single and married students. Typical cost: $6394 per year ($11,116 including board) for single students; $9394 per year ($14,116 including board) for married students. Room and board charges vary according to board plan, campus/location and housing facility selected. Housing application deadline: 2/1. *Student services:* Campus employment opportunities, campus safety program, career counseling, child daycare facilities, exercise/wellness program, free psychological counseling, international student services, low-cost health insurance, multicultural affairs office, services for students with disabilities, teacher training, writing training. *Library:* McFarlin Library plus 1 other. *Collection:* Books: 1.2 million (physical), 460,240 (digital/electronic); Serial titles: 59,171 (digital/electronic); Databases: 289. Weekly public service hours: 94; study areas open 24 hours, 5–7 days a week; students can reserve study rooms. *Research affiliation:* Network of Excellence in Training (NEXT) (petrophysics), Chevron Texaco (petroleum engineering).

Computer facilities: Computer purchase and lease plans are available. 728 computers available on campus for general student use. A campuswide network can be accessed from student residence rooms and from off campus. Online class registration is available.
Website: http://www.utulsa.edu/

General Application Contact: Dr. Janet A. Haggerty, Vice Provost for Research/Dean of the Graduate School, 918-631-2336, Fax: 918-631-2156, E-mail: grad@utulsa.edu.

GRADUATE UNITS

College of Law Students: 238 full-time (120 women), 24 part-time (11 women); includes 65 minority (8 Black or African American, non-Hispanic/Latino; 11 American Indian or Alaska Native, non-Hispanic/Latino; 1 Asian, non-Hispanic/Latino; 14 Hispanic/Latino; 31 Two or more races, non-Hispanic/Latino), 4 international. Average age 26. 659 applicants, 37% accepted, 86 enrolled. *Faculty:* 29 full-time (16 women), 14 part-time/adjunct (5 women). *Financial support:* In 2015–16, 255 students received support.

Scholarships/grants available. Support available to part-time students. Financial award application deadline: 8/1; financial award applicants required to submit FAFSA. In 2015, 5 master's, 1 doctorate awarded. *Degree program information:* Part-time programs available. Part-time, 100% online. Offers American Indian and indigenous law (LL M); American law for foreign lawyers (LL M); energy and natural resources law (LL M); energy law (MJ); health law (Certificate); Indian law (MJ); law (JD); Native American law (Certificate); natural resources, energy, and environmental law (Certificate). *Application deadline:* For fall admission, 7/31 priority date for domestic and international students; for spring admission, 12/5 priority date for domestic students, 12/5 for international students; for summer admission, 4/13 for domestic and international students. Applications are processed on a rolling basis. *Application fee:* $30. Electronic applications accepted. *Application Contact:* April M. Fox, Associate Dean of Admissions and Financial Aid, 918-631-2406, Fax: 918-631-3630, E-mail: april-fox@utulsa.edu. *Dean,* Lyn Suzanne Entzeroth, 918-631-2400, Fax: 918-631-3126, E-mail: lyn-entzeroth@utulsa.edu.

Graduate School Students: 503 full-time (232 women), 305 part-time (93 women); includes 107 minority (15 Black or African American, non-Hispanic/Latino; 36 American Indian or Alaska Native, non-Hispanic/Latino; 17 Asian, non-Hispanic/Latino; 23 Hispanic/Latino; 1 Native Hawaiian or other Pacific Islander, non-Hispanic/Latino; 15 Two or more races, non-Hispanic/Latino), 253 international. Average age 28. 1,443 applicants, 31% accepted, 237 enrolled. *Faculty:* 194 full-time (54 women), 11 part-time/adjunct (5 women). *Financial support:* In 2015–16, 352 students received support, including 104 fellowships with full tuition reimbursements available (averaging $9,381 per year), 194 research assistantships with full tuition reimbursements available (averaging $12,208 per year), 271 teaching assistantships with full tuition reimbursements available (averaging $11,585 per year); career-related internships or fieldwork, Federal Work-Study, institutionally sponsored loans, scholarships/grants, traineeships, health care benefits, tuition waivers (partial), and unspecified assistantships also available. Support available to part-time students. Financial award application deadline: 2/1; financial award applicants required to submit FAFSA. In 2015, 217 master's, 30 doctorates awarded. *Degree program information:* Part-time and evening/weekend programs available. Part-time, evening/weekend. Offers museum science and management (MA). *Application deadline:* Applications are processed on a rolling basis. *Application fee:* $55. Electronic applications accepted. *Application Contact:* Graduate School, 918-631-2336, Fax: 918-631-2156, E-mail: grad@utulsa.edu. *Vice Provost for Research/Dean of the Graduate School,* Dr. Janet A. Haggerty, 918-631-2336, Fax: 918-631-2156, E-mail: grad@utulsa.edu.

College of Engineering and Natural Sciences Students: 258 full-time (68 women), 87 part-time (28 women); includes 25 minority (3 Black or African American, non-Hispanic/Latino; 9 American Indian or Alaska Native, non-Hispanic/Latino; 3 Asian, non-Hispanic/Latino; 6 Hispanic/Latino; 1 Native Hawaiian or other Pacific Islander, non-Hispanic/Latino; 3 Two or more races, non-Hispanic/Latino), 207 international. Average age 28. 766 applicants, 26% accepted, 99 enrolled. *Faculty:* 102 full-time (11 women), 2 part-time/adjunct (1 woman). *Financial support:* In 2015–16, 189 students received support, including 69 fellowships with full tuition reimbursements available (averaging $4,354 per year), 161 research assistantships with full tuition reimbursements available (averaging $12,350 per year), 97 teaching assistantships with full tuition reimbursements available (averaging $11,696 per year); career-related internships or fieldwork, Federal Work-Study, scholarships/grants, health care benefits, tuition waivers (full and partial), and unspecified assistantships also available. Support available to part-time students. Financial award application deadline: 2/1; financial award applicants required to submit FAFSA. In 2015, 63 master's, 24 doctorates awarded. *Degree program information:* Part-time programs available. Part-time. Offers biochemistry (MS); biological science (MS, MTA, PhD); chemical engineering (ME, MSE, PhD); chemistry (MS, PhD); computer engineering (ME, MSE, PhD); computer science (MS, PhD); electrical engineering (ME, MSE); engineering and natural sciences (ME, MS, MSE, MTA, PhD); engineering physics (MS); geophysics (MS); geosciences (MS, PhD); mathematics (MS, MTA, PhD); mechanical engineering (ME, MSE, PhD); petroleum engineering (ME, MSE, PhD); physics (MS, PhD). *Application deadline:* Applications are processed on a rolling basis. *Application fee:* $55. Electronic applications accepted. *Application Contact:* Graduate School, 918-631-2336, Fax: 918-631-2156, E-mail: grad@utulsa.edu. *Dean,* Dr. James Sorem, 918-631-2288, E-mail: james-sorem@utulsa.edu.

Collins College of Business Students: 84 full-time (37 women), 178 part-time (45 women); includes 37 minority (7 Black or African American, non-Hispanic/Latino; 7 American Indian or Alaska Native, non-Hispanic/Latino; 8 Asian, non-Hispanic/Latino; 8 Hispanic/Latino; 7 Two or more races, non-Hispanic/Latino), 31 international. Average age 28. 294 applicants, 40% accepted, 74 enrolled. *Faculty:* 42 full-time (27 women), 2 part-time/adjunct (0 women). *Financial support:* In 2015–16, 50 students received support, including 1 research assistantship with full tuition reimbursement available (averaging $5,400 per year), 51 teaching assistantships with full tuition reimbursements available (averaging $11,297 per year); fellowships with tuition reimbursements available, career-related internships or fieldwork, Federal Work-Study, institutionally sponsored loans, scholarships/grants, health care benefits, tuition waivers (full and partial), and unspecified assistantships also available. Support available to part-time students. Financial award application deadline: 2/1; financial award applicants required to submit FAFSA. In 2015, 92 master's awarded. *Degree program information:* Part-time and evening/weekend programs available. Part-time, evening/weekend, 100% online. Offers accounting (M Acc); business (M Acc, MBA, MEB, MS); business administration (MBA); corporate finance (MS); energy business (MEB); investments and portfolio management (MS); risk management (MS). *Application deadline:* Applications are processed on a rolling basis. *Application fee:* $55. Electronic applications accepted. *Application Contact:* Information Contact, 918-631-2242, E-mail: graduate-business@utulsa.edu. *Dean,* Dr. W. Gale Sullenburger, 918-631-2213, E-mail: gale-sullenberger@utulsa.edu.

Kendall College of Arts and Sciences Students: 115 full-time (82 women), 39 part-time (20 women); includes 35 minority (5 Black or African American, non-Hispanic/Latino; 11 American Indian or Alaska Native, non-Hispanic/Latino; 6 Asian, non-Hispanic/Latino; 8 Hispanic/Latino; 5 Two or more races, non-Hispanic/Latino), 13 international. Average age 31. 258 applicants, 32% accepted, 39 enrolled. *Faculty:* 65 full-time (30 women), 9 part-time/adjunct (5 women). *Financial support:* In 2015–16, 134 students received support, including 31 fellowships with full tuition reimbursements available (averaging $9,243 per year), 29 research assistantships with full tuition reimbursements available (averaging $16,215 per year), 104 teaching assistantships with full tuition reimbursements available (averaging $13,178 per year); career-related internships or fieldwork, Federal Work-Study, scholarships/grants, traineeships, health care benefits, tuition waivers (full and partial), and unspecified assistantships also available. Support available to part-time students. Financial award application deadline: 2/1; financial award applicants required to submit FAFSA. In 2015, 35 master's, 6 doctorates awarded. *Degree program information:* Part-time and evening/weekend programs available. Part-time, evening/weekend. Offers anthropology (MA, PhD); art (MTA); arts and sciences (M Ed, MA, MFA, MS, MSMSE, MTA, PhD); biology (MTA); clinical psychology (MA, PhD); education (M Ed); educational studies (MA); elementary certification (M Ed); English (MTA); English language and literature (MA, MTA, PhD); history (MA, MTA); industrial/organizational psychology (MA, PhD); mathematics (MTA); mathematics and science education (MSMSE); secondary certification (M Ed); speech-language pathology (MS); teaching arts (MTA). *Application deadline:* Applications are processed on a rolling basis. *Application fee:* $55. Electronic applications accepted. *Application Contact:* Graduate School, 918-631-2336, Fax: 918-631-2156, E-mail: grad@utulsa.edu. *Dean,* Dr. Kalpana Misra, 918-631-2222, Fax: 918-631-3721, E-mail: kalpana-misra@utulsa.edu.

UNIVERSITY OF UTAH, Salt Lake City, UT 84112-1107

General Information State-supported, coed, university. CGS member. *Enrollment:* 31,551 graduate, professional, and undergraduate students; 6,011 full-time matriculated graduate/professional students (2,639 women), 1,753 part-time matriculated graduate/professional students (787 women). *Enrollment by degree level:* 3,896 master's, 3,768 doctoral. *Graduate faculty:* 1,421 full-time (469 women), 1,887 part-time/adjunct (789 women). *Graduate housing:* Rooms and/or apartments available on a first-come, first-served basis to single and married students. Housing application deadline: 4/1. *Student services:* Campus employment opportunities, campus safety program, career counseling, child daycare facilities, exercise/wellness program, free psychological counseling, grant writing training, international student services, low-cost health insurance, multicultural affairs office, services for students with disabilities, teacher training, writing training. *Library:* J. Willard Marriott Library plus 3 others. *Collection:* Books: 3.2 million (physical), 460,258 (digital/electronic); Databases: 230. Weekly public service hours: 111; students can reserve study rooms. *Research affiliation:* Watson Laboratory (pharmaceutical research), Myriad Genetics (pharmaceutical research/manufacturing), Neuropsychiatric Institute (brain research, mental health and substance abuse treatment), ARUP Laboratories (medical research), John A. Moran Eye Center (vision treatment and research).

Computer facilities: 1,099 computers available on campus for general student use. A campuswide network can be accessed from student residence rooms and from off campus. Online class registration, online classes are available.
Website: http://www.utah.edu/

General Application Contact: Office of Admissions, 801-581-7283, Fax: 801-585-7864, E-mail: graduate@sa.utah.edu.

GRADUATE UNITS

Graduate School Students: 4,792 full-time (2,096 women), 1,579 part-time (700 women); includes 825 minority (64 Black or African American, non-Hispanic/Latino; 19 American Indian or Alaska Native, non-Hispanic/Latino; 256 Asian, non-Hispanic/Latino; 343 Hispanic/Latino; 15 Native Hawaiian or other Pacific Islander, non-Hispanic/Latino; 128 Two or more races, non-Hispanic/Latino), 1,120 international. Average age 30. 9,370 applicants, 38% accepted, 2511 enrolled. *Faculty:* 937 full-time (334 women), 783 part-time/adjunct (361 women). *Financial support:* Fellowships with tuition reimbursements, research assistantships with tuition reimbursements, teaching assistantships with tuition reimbursements, career-related internships or fieldwork, Federal Work-Study, institutionally sponsored loans, scholarships/grants, traineeships, health care benefits, tuition waivers (full and partial), and unspecified assistantships available. Support available to part-time students. Financial award application deadline: 2/1; financial award applicants required to submit FAFSA. In 2015, 1,948 master's, 767 doctorates awarded. *Degree program information:* Part-time and evening/weekend programs available. Part-time, evening/weekend, online learning. Offers biostatistics (M Stat); biotechnology (PSM); computational science (PSM); econometrics (M Stat); educational psychology (M Stat); environmental science (PSM); mathematics (M Stat); science instrumentation (PSM); sociology (M Stat). *Application deadline:* For fall admission, 4/1 for domestic and international students; for spring admission, 11/1 for domestic and international students. *Application fee:* $55 ($65 for international students). Electronic applications accepted. *Application Contact:* Admissions Office, 801-581-7283, Fax: 801-585-7864, E-mail: graduate@sa.utah.edu. *Dean,* Dr. David Kieda, 801-581-6926, Fax: 801-585-7864, E-mail: dave.kieda@utah.edu.

College of Architecture and Planning Students: 117 full-time (44 women), 18 part-time (6 women); includes 14 minority (3 Black or African American, non-Hispanic/Latino; 4 Asian, non-Hispanic/Latino; 4 Hispanic/Latino; 3 Two or more races, non-Hispanic/Latino), 19 international. Average age 29. 126 applicants, 83% accepted, 49 enrolled. *Faculty:* 19 full-time (10 women), 23 part-time/adjunct (7 women). *Financial support:* Fellowships with tuition reimbursements, research assistantships with tuition reimbursements, teaching assistantships with partial tuition reimbursements, career-related internships or fieldwork, Federal Work-Study, institutionally sponsored loans, scholarships/grants, and unspecified assistantships available. Financial award application deadline: 1/1; financial award applicants required to submit FAFSA. In 2015, 35 master's awarded. *Degree program information:* Part-time programs available. Part-time. Offers architectural studies (MS); architecture (M Arch); architecture and planning (M Arch, MCMP, MS, PhD); city and metropolitan planning (MCMP); metropolitan planning, policy and design (PhD). *Application deadline:* For fall admission, 1/1 for domestic students, 12/1 for international students. *Application fee:* $55 ($65 for international students). Electronic applications accepted. *Application Contact:* Saolo Manumaleuga Utu, Recruitment and Admissions, 801-585-2361, Fax: 801-581-8217, E-mail: recruitment@arch.utah.edu. *Dean,* Dr. Keith Diaz Moore, 801-585-1766, Fax: 801-581-8217, E-mail: diazmoore@arch.utah.edu.

College of Education Students: 263 full-time (170 women), 261 part-time (183 women); includes 134 minority (15 Black or African American, non-Hispanic/Latino; 3 American Indian or Alaska Native, non-Hispanic/Latino; 21 Asian, non-Hispanic/Latino; 75 Hispanic/Latino; 2 Native Hawaiian or other Pacific Islander, non-Hispanic/Latino; 18 Two or more races, non-Hispanic/Latino), 14 international. Average age 34. 448 applicants, 60% accepted, 203 enrolled. *Faculty:* 52 full-time (30 women), 29 part-time/adjunct (23 women). *Financial support:* Fellowships with tuition reimbursements, research assistantships with tuition reimbursements, teaching assistantships with tuition reimbursements, career-related internships or fieldwork, Federal Work-Study, institutionally sponsored loans, scholarships/grants, health care benefits, tuition waivers (full), and unspecified assistantships available. Support available to part-time students. Financial award application deadline: 2/1; financial award applicants required to submit FAFSA. In 2015, 139 master's, 22 doctorates awarded. Offers clinical mental health counseling (M Ed); counseling psychology (PhD); deaf and hard of hearing (M Ed); deaf/blind (M Ed, MS); early childhood deaf and hard of hearing (MS); early childhood special education (M Ed, MS, PhD); early childhood vision impairments (M Ed); education (M Ed, M Stat, MA, MS, Ed D, PhD); education, culture, and society (M Ed, MA, MS, PhD); educational leadership and policy (Ed D, PhD); elementary education (M Ed); instructional design and educational technology (M Ed); instructional design and technology (MS); K-12 school administration (M Ed); K-12 teacher instructional leadership (M Ed); learning and cognition (MS, PhD); mild/moderate disabilities (M Ed, MS, PhD); reading and literacy (M Ed, PhD); school counseling (M Ed); school psychology (M Ed, PhD); severe disabilities (M Ed, MS, PhD); statistics (M Stat); student affairs (M Ed); visual impairment (M Ed, MS). *Application deadline:* For fall admission, 2/15 for domestic and international students; for spring admission, 11/1 for domestic and international students. *Application fee:* $55 ($65 for international students). Electronic applications accepted. *Dean*, Maria E. Franquiz, 801-581-8221, E-mail: maria.franquiz@utah.edu.

College of Engineering Students: 878 full-time (193 women), 270 part-time (46 women); includes 96 minority (6 Black or African American, non-Hispanic/Latino; 1 American Indian or Alaska Native, non-Hispanic/Latino; 51 Asian, non-Hispanic/Latino; 21 Hispanic/Latino; 1 Native Hawaiian or other Pacific Islander, non-Hispanic/Latino; 16 Two or more races, non-Hispanic/Latino), 540 international. Average age 28. 2,286 applicants, 33% accepted, 377 enrolled. *Faculty:* 146 full-time (22 women), 73 part-time/adjunct (10 women). *Financial support:* Fellowships with full tuition reimbursements, research assistantships with tuition reimbursements, teaching assistantships with tuition reimbursements, career-related internships or fieldwork, Federal Work-Study, institutionally sponsored loans, scholarships/grants, traineeships, health care benefits, tuition waivers (full and partial), and unspecified assistantships available. Support available to part-time students. Financial award applicants required to submit FAFSA. In 2015, 311 master's, 88 doctorates awarded. *Degree program information:* Part-time and evening/weekend programs available. Part-time, evening/weekend. Offers bioengineering (MS, PhD); chemical engineering (MS, PhD); civil and environmental engineering (MS, PhD); computational engineering and science (MS); computer science (MS, PhD); computing (MS, PhD); electrical and computer engineering (MS, PhD); electrical engineering (ME); engineering (ME, MEAE, MS, PhD); environmental engineering (PhD); game art (MEAE); game engineering (MEAE); game production (MEAE); materials science and engineering (MS, PhD); mechanical engineering (MS, PhD); nuclear engineering (MS, PhD); petroleum engineering (MS); technical art (MEAE). *Application fee:* $55 ($65 for international students). Electronic applications accepted. *Application Contact:* Megan Shannahan, Direct Admission and Graduate Coordinator, 801-581-8954, Fax: 801-581-8692, E-mail: megan.shannahan@utah.edu. *Dean*, Dr. Richard B. Brown, 801-585-7498, E-mail: brown@utah.edu.

College of Fine Arts Students: 127 full-time (70 women), 25 part-time (13 women); includes 21 minority (1 Black or African American, non-Hispanic/Latino; 1 American Indian or Alaska Native, non-Hispanic/Latino; 4 Asian, non-Hispanic/Latino; 11 Hispanic/Latino; 4 Two or more races, non-Hispanic/Latino), 26 international. Average age 31. 174 applicants, 52% accepted, 57 enrolled. *Faculty:* 75 full-time (35 women), 132 part-time/adjunct (61 women). *Financial support:* Fellowships with tuition reimbursements, research assistantships with tuition reimbursements, teaching assistantships with tuition reimbursements, career-related internships or fieldwork, Federal Work-Study, institutionally sponsored loans, scholarships/grants, health care benefits, tuition waivers (partial), and unspecified assistantships available. Financial award applicants required to submit FAFSA. In 2015, 46 master's, 16 doctorates awarded. Offers art history (MA); ceramics (MFA); choral conducting (M Mus, DMA); collaborative piano (M Mus); community-based art education (MFA); composition (M Mus, PhD); dance (MFA); drawing (MFA); film and media arts (MFA); fine arts (M Mus, MA, MFA, DMA, PhD); graphic design (MFA); instrumental conducting (M Mus); instrumental performance (M Mus, DMA); jazz studies (M Mus); music education (M Mus, PhD); music history and literature (M Mus); musicology (MA); organ performance (M Mus); painting (MFA); photography/digital imaging (MFA); piano performance (M Mus, DMA); printmaking (MFA); sculpture/intermedia (MFA); string performance and pedagogy (M Mus); theory (M Mus); vocal performance (DMA). *Application fee:* $55 ($65 for international students). *Application Contact:* Sarah Projansky, Associate Dean for Faculty and Academic Affairs, 801-581-6764, E-mail: sarah.projansky@utah.edu. *Dean and Associate Vice-President for the Arts*, Dr. Raymond Tymas Jones, 801-581-3887, Fax: 801-581-3066, E-mail: r.tymasjones@utah.edu.

College of Health Students: 561 full-time (372 women), 76 part-time (57 women); includes 67 minority (4 Black or African American, non-Hispanic/Latino; 3 American Indian or Alaska Native, non-Hispanic/Latino; 13 Asian, non-Hispanic/Latino; 28 Hispanic/Latino; 4 Native Hawaiian or other Pacific Islander, non-Hispanic/Latino; 15 Two or more races, non-Hispanic/Latino), 26 international. Average age 28. 107 applicants, 332% accepted, 258 enrolled. *Faculty:* 39 full-time (19 women), 72 part-time/adjunct (50 women). *Financial support:* Fellowships with tuition reimbursements, research assistantships with tuition reimbursements, teaching assistantships with tuition reimbursements, career-related internships or fieldwork, Federal Work-Study, institutionally sponsored loans, scholarships/grants, traineeships, health care benefits, tuition waivers (partial), and unspecified assistantships available. Financial award applicants required to submit FAFSA. In 2015, 141 master's, 76 doctorates awarded. Offers audiology (Au D, PhD); exercise and sport science (MS, PhD); health (M Phil, MA, MOT, MS, Au D, DPT, Ed D, OTD, PhD); health promotion and education (M Phil, MS, Ed D, PhD); nutrition and integrative physiology (MS, PhD); occupational therapy (MOT, OTD); parks, recreation, and tourism (M Phil, MS, PhD); physical therapy (DPT); rehabilitation science (PhD); speech-language pathology (MA, MS, PhD). *Application fee:* $55 ($65 for international students). *Application Contact:* Dr. Shari Lindsey, Assistant Dean of Students, Academic Affairs, 801-585-5764, Fax: 801-581-5580, E-mail: shari.lindsey@health.utah.edu. *Dean*, Dr. David H. Perrin, 801-581-8537, Fax: 801-581-5580, E-mail: david.perrin@health.utah.edu.

College of Humanities Students: 181 full-time (84 women), 95 part-time (59 women); includes 36 minority (2 Black or African American, non-Hispanic/Latino; 3 American Indian or Alaska Native, non-Hispanic/Latino; 9 Asian, non-Hispanic/Latino; 16 Hispanic/Latino; 1 Native Hawaiian or other Pacific Islander, non-Hispanic/Latino; 5 Two or more races, non-Hispanic/Latino), 24 international. Average age 33. 483 applicants, 23% accepted, 73 enrolled. *Faculty:* 7,538 full-time (67 women), 56 part-time/adjunct (21 women). *Financial support:* In 2015–16, 144 students received support. Fellowships with full tuition reimbursements available, teaching assistantships with tuition reimbursements available, health care benefits, and unspecified assistantships available. Financial award application deadline: 2/1. In 2015, 63 master's, 34 doctorates awarded. Offers American studies (MA, PhD); Arabic (MA, PhD); Asian studies (MA); British and American literature (MA, PhD); communication (MA, MS, PhD); comparative literary and cultural studies (MA, PhD); creative writing (MFA, PhD); environmental humanities (MA, MS); French (MA); Hebrew (MA); history (MA, PhD); humanities (MA, MALP, MFA, MS, PhD); Latin American studies (MA); linguistics (MA, PhD); Persian (MA, PhD); philosophy (MA, MS, PhD); political science (MA, PhD); rhetoric and composition (MA, PhD); Spanish (MA, MALP, PhD); world languages (MA). *Application deadline:* For fall admission, 4/1 for domestic and international students; for spring admission, 11/1 for domestic and international students. *Application fee:* $55 ($65 for international students). Electronic applications accepted. *Application Contact:* Dr. Stuart Culver, Associate Dean, 801-581-6214, E-mail: stuart.culver@utah.edu. *Dean*, Dr. Dianne Harris, 801-581-8816, E-mail: dianne.harris@utah.edu.

College of Mines and Earth Sciences Students: 158 full-time (47 women), 28 part-time (10 women); includes 15 minority (2 Black or African American, non-Hispanic/Latino; 1 American Indian or Alaska Native, non-Hispanic/Latino; 3 Asian, non-Hispanic/Latino; 8 Hispanic/Latino; 1 Two or more races, non-Hispanic/Latino), 67 international. Average age 27. 389 applicants, 21% accepted, 49 enrolled. *Faculty:* 47 full-time (7 women), 29 part-time/adjunct (5 women). *Financial support:* Fellowships with full tuition reimbursements, research assistantships with full tuition reimbursements, teaching assistantships with full tuition reimbursements, career-related internships or fieldwork, institutionally sponsored loans, scholarships/grants, and unspecified assistantships available. Support available to part-time students. Financial award application deadline: 2/15; financial award applicants required to submit FAFSA. In 2015, 45 master's, 23 doctorates awarded. *Degree program information:* Part-time programs available. Part-time. Offers atmospheric sciences (MS, PhD); environmental engineering (ME, MS, PhD); geological engineering (ME, MS, PhD); geology (MS, PhD); geophysics (MS, PhD); metallurgical engineering (ME, MS, PhD); mines and earth sciences (ME, MS, PhD); mining engineering (ME, MS, PhD). *Application deadline:* For fall admission, 4/1 for domestic and international students; for spring admission, 11/1 for domestic and international students. *Application fee:* $55 ($65 for international students). Electronic applications accepted. *Application Contact:* Anita Austin Tromp, Executive Assistant to the Dean, 801-581-8767, Fax: 801-581-5560, E-mail: anita.austin@utah.edu. *Dean*, Dr. Francis H. Brown, 801-581-8767, Fax: 801-581-5560, E-mail: frank.brown@utah.edu.

College of Nursing Students: 284 full-time (219 women), 63 part-time (49 women); includes 42 minority (8 Black or African American, non-Hispanic/Latino; 1 American Indian or Alaska Native, non-Hispanic/Latino; 10 Asian, non-Hispanic/Latino; 17 Hispanic/Latino; 6 Two or more races, non-Hispanic/Latino), 9 international. Average age 36. 238 applicants, 62% accepted, 120 enrolled. *Faculty:* 25 full-time (23 women), 84 part-time/adjunct (74 women). *Financial support:* In 2015–16, 77 students received support, including 77 fellowships with tuition reimbursements available, 4 research assistantships with tuition reimbursements available, 9 teaching assistantships with partial tuition reimbursements available; scholarships/grants, traineeships, health care benefits, and unspecified assistantships also available. Support available to part-time students. Financial award application deadline: 1/15; financial award applicants required to submit FAFSA. In 2015, 29 master's, 79 doctorates awarded. *Degree program information:* Part-time programs available. Part-time, online learning. Offers gerontology (MS, Certificate); nursing (MS, DNP, PhD, Certificate). *Application deadline:* For fall admission, 1/15 for domestic and international students; for spring admission, 11/1 for domestic and international students. *Application fee:* $55 ($65 for international students). Electronic applications accepted. *Application Contact:* Carrie Radmall, Associate Director of Student Services, 801-581-8798, Fax: 801-585-9705, E-mail: carrie.radmall@nurs.utah.edu. *Dean*, Patricia Morton, RN, PhD, 801-581-8262, Fax: 801-585-9705, E-mail: trish.morton@nurs.utah.edu.

College of Pharmacy Students: 274 full-time (124 women), 10 part-time (6 women); includes 78 minority (2 Black or African American, non-Hispanic/Latino; 54 Asian, non-Hispanic/Latino; 13 Hispanic/Latino; 1 Native Hawaiian or other Pacific Islander, non-Hispanic/Latino; 8 Two or more races, non-Hispanic/Latino), 28 international. Average age 27. 208 applicants, 34% accepted, 63 enrolled. *Faculty:* 30 full-time (9 women), 42 part-time/adjunct (25 women). *Financial support:* In 2015–16, fellowships with full tuition reimbursements (averaging $25,000 per year), research assistantships with full tuition reimbursements (averaging $25,000 per year), teaching assistantships (averaging $1,500 per year) were awarded; scholarships/grants, health care benefits, tuition waivers (full), and unspecified assistantships also available. In 2015, 3 master's, 72 doctorates awarded. Offers health system pharmacy administration (MS); medicinal chemistry (MS, PhD); outcomes research and health policy (PhD); pharmaceutics and pharmaceutical chemistry (PhD); pharmacology and toxicology (PhD); pharmacy (MS, PhD, Pharm D). *Application deadline:* For fall admission, 12/1 for domestic and international students. *Application fee:* $55 ($65 for international students). *Application Contact:* Dr. Madeline Marshall, Academic Advisor, 801-581-6731, Fax: 801-581-3716, E-mail: pharmd.admissions@pharm.utah.edu. *Interim Dean*, Dr. Kristen A. Keefe, 801-581-6731, Fax: 801-581-3716.

College of Science Students: 400 full-time (145 women), 122 part-time (50 women); includes 38 minority (4 Black or African American, non-Hispanic/Latino; 1 American Indian or Alaska Native, non-Hispanic/Latino; 13 Asian, non-Hispanic/Latino; 15 Hispanic/Latino; 5 Two or more races, non-Hispanic/Latino), 163 international. Average age 28. 858 applicants, 18% accepted, 126 enrolled. *Faculty:* 151 full-time (27 women), 88 part-time/adjunct (26 women). *Financial support:* Fellowships with full tuition reimbursements, research assistantships with full tuition reimbursements, teaching assistantships with full tuition reimbursements, career-related internships or fieldwork, Federal Work-Study, institutionally sponsored loans, scholarships/grants, traineeships, health care benefits, tuition waivers (full), and unspecified assistantships available. Financial award application deadline: 2/15; financial award applicants required to submit FAFSA. In 2015, 63 master's, 55 doctorates awarded. *Degree program information:* Part-time programs available. Part-time. Offers biology (MS, PhD); chemical physics (PhD); chemistry (MS, PhD); mathematics (MA, MS, PhD); mathematics teaching (MS); medical physics (MS, PhD); physics (MA, MS, PhD); physics teaching (PhD); science (M Stat, MA, MS, PhD); science teacher education (MS); statistics (M Stat). *Application deadline:* For fall admission, 4/1 for domestic and international students; for spring admission, 11/1 for domestic and international students. *Application fee:* $55 ($65 for international students). Electronic applications accepted. *Application Contact:* Lisa Batchelder, Administrative Program Coordinator, 801-581-3374, E-mail: office@science.utah.edu. *Dean*, Dr. Henry S. White, 801-581-6958, Fax: 801-585-3169, E-mail: white@chem.utah.edu.

College of Social and Behavioral Science Students: 311 full-time (165 women), 240 part-time (110 women); includes 75 minority (8 Black or African American, non-Hispanic/Latino; 20 Asian, non-Hispanic/Latino; 32 Hispanic/Latino; 2 Native Hawaiian or other Pacific Islander, non-Hispanic/Latino; 13 Two or more races, non-Hispanic/Latino), 66 international. Average age 32. 772 applicants, 33% accepted, 161 enrolled. *Faculty:* 133 full-time (53 women), 66 part-time/adjunct (23 women). *Financial support:* Fellowships with tuition reimbursements, research assistantships with tuition reimbursements, teaching assistantships with tuition reimbursements, career-related internships or fieldwork, Federal Work-Study, scholarships/grants, health care benefits, and unspecified assistantships available. Financial award application deadline: 2/1; financial award applicants required to submit FAFSA. In 2015, 174 master's, 33 doctorates awarded. Offers American politics (MA, MS, PhD);

anthropology (M Phil, MA, MS, PhD); clinical psychology (PhD); comparative politics (MA, MS, PhD); econometrics (M Stat); economics (M Phil, MA, MS, PhD); geographic information science (MS); geography (MS, PhD); human development and social policy (MS); international affairs and global enterprise (MS); international relations (MA, MS, PhD); political science (MA, MS, PhD); political theory (MA, MS, PhD); psychology (PhD); public administration (Exec MPA, MPA); public policy (MPP); social and behavioral science (Exec MPA, M Phil, M Stat, MA, MPA, MPP, MS, PhD); sociology (M Stat, MA, MS, PhD). *Application fee:* $55 ($65 for international students). *Application Contact:* Richard Foster, Interim Associate Dean, 801-581-8620, Fax: 801-585-5081, E-mail: rick.forster@csbs.utah.edu. *Interim Dean*, Cynthia Berg, 801-581-8620, Fax: 801-585-5081, E-mail: cynthia.berg@csbs.utah.edu.

College of Social Work Students: 311 full-time (221 women), 42 part-time (30 women); includes 68 minority (2 Black or African American, non-Hispanic/Latino; 4 American Indian or Alaska Native, non-Hispanic/Latino; 6 Asian, non-Hispanic/Latino; 42 Hispanic/Latino; 3 Native Hawaiian or other Pacific Islander, non-Hispanic/Latino; 11 Two or more races, non-Hispanic/Latino), 5 international. Average age 33. 254 applicants, 71% accepted, 135 enrolled. *Faculty:* 18 full-time (10 women), 38 part-time/adjunct (26 women). *Financial support:* In 2015–16, 55 students received support, including 19 fellowships with tuition reimbursements available (averaging $8,505 per year), 14 research assistantships with tuition reimbursements available (averaging $14,250 per year), 8 teaching assistantships with partial tuition reimbursements available (averaging $3,250 per year); career-related internships or fieldwork, scholarships/grants, and unspecified assistantships also available. Financial award application deadline: 3/15; financial award applicants required to submit FAFSA. In 2015, 179 master's, 8 doctorates awarded. *Degree program information:* Part-time and evening/weekend programs available. Part-time, evening/weekend. Offers social work (MSW, PhD). *Application deadline:* For fall admission, 11/1 for domestic and international students. *Application fee:* $55 ($65 for international students). Electronic applications accepted. *Application Contact:* Dr. Mary Jane Taylor, Associate Dean, 801-581-6192, Fax: 801-585-3219, E-mail: hank.liese@socwk.utah.edu. *Interim Dean*, Dr. Hank Liese, 801-581-6192, Fax: 801-585-3219, E-mail: hank.liese@socwk.utah.edu.

David Eccles School of Business Students: 900 full-time (230 women), 298 part-time (70 women); includes 138 minority (7 Black or African American, non-Hispanic/Latino; 1 American Indian or Alaska Native, non-Hispanic/Latino; 46 Asian, non-Hispanic/Latino; 61 Hispanic/Latino; 1 Native Hawaiian or other Pacific Islander, non-Hispanic/Latino; 22 Two or more races, non-Hispanic/Latino), 130 international. Average age 30. 1,255 applicants, 61% accepted, 588 enrolled. *Faculty:* 64 full-time (22 women), 45 part-time/adjunct (10 women). *Financial support:* Fellowships with partial tuition reimbursements, research assistantships with partial tuition reimbursements, teaching assistantships with tuition reimbursements, scholarships/grants, tuition waivers (full and partial), and unspecified assistantships available. Financial award applicants required to submit FAFSA. In 2015, 571 master's, 13 doctorates awarded. *Degree program information:* Part-time and evening/weekend programs available. Part-time, evening/weekend. Offers accounting (PhD); business (EMBA, M Acc, MBA, MHA, MRED, MS, PMBA, PhD, Graduate Certificate); business administration (EMBA, MBA, PMBA); finance (MS); healthcare administration (MHA); information systems (MS, PhD, Graduate Certificate); marketing (PhD); operations management (PhD); organizational behavior (PhD); real estate (MRED); strategic management (PhD). *Application fee:* $55 ($65 for international students). Electronic applications accepted. *Application Contact:* Andrea Miller, Director of Graduate Admissions, 801-585-7366, E-mail: andrea.miller@business.utah.edu. *Dean*, Dr. Taylor Randall, 801-581-3074, E-mail: dean@business.utah.edu.

School of Dentistry Students: 71 full-time (22 women); includes 13 minority (1 Asian, non-Hispanic/Latino; 10 Hispanic/Latino; 2 Two or more races, non-Hispanic/Latino). Average age 26. 775 applicants, 3% accepted, 20 enrolled. *Faculty:* 3 full-time (2 women), 30 part-time/adjunct (4 women). *Financial support:* Application deadline: 4/1; applicants required to submit FAFSA. Offers dentistry (DDS). *Application deadline:* For fall admission, 12/31 priority date for domestic students, 12/31 for international students. *Application fee:* $75. Electronic applications accepted. *Application Contact:* Gary W. Lowder, DDS, Office of Admissions, 801-581-8951, Fax: 801-585-6485, E-mail: dental.admissions@hsc.utah.edu. *Interim Dean*, Glen R. Hanson, PhD, 801-581-3174, Fax: 801-585-6485, E-mail: glen.hanson@hsc.utah.edu.

School of Medicine Offers biochemistry (MS, PhD); biostatistics (M Stat); experimental pathology (PhD); human genetics (MS, PhD); laboratory medicine and biomedical science (MS); medical informatics (MS, PhD, Certificate); medicine (M Phil, M Stat, MPAS, MPH, MS, MSPH, MD, PhD, Certificate); molecular biology (PhD); neurobiology and anatomy (PhD); neuroscience (PhD); oncological sciences (M Phil, MS, PhD); physician assistant (MPAS); physiology (PhD); public health (MPH, MSPH, PhD).

S. J. Quinney College of Law Students: 322 full-time (132 women), 14 part-time (6 women); includes 43 minority (2 Black or African American, non-Hispanic/Latino; 1 American Indian or Alaska Native, non-Hispanic/Latino; 12 Asian, non-Hispanic/Latino; 26 Hispanic/Latino; 2 Native Hawaiian or other Pacific Islander, non-Hispanic/Latino), 2 international. Average age 27. 630 applicants, 47% accepted, 92 enrolled. *Faculty:* 35 full-time (14 women), 36 part-time/adjunct (14 women). *Financial support:* In 2015–16, 213 students received support, including 159 fellowships with partial tuition reimbursements available (averaging $5,383 per year), 35 research assistantships with partial tuition reimbursements available (averaging $7,043 per year); career-related internships or fieldwork, Federal Work-Study, institutionally sponsored loans, and scholarships/grants also available. Financial award application deadline: 4/1; financial award applicants required to submit FAFSA. In 2015, 125 doctorates awarded. Offers law (LL M, JD). *Application deadline:* For fall admission, 2/15 for domestic and international students. Applications are processed on a rolling basis. *Application fee:* $60. Electronic applications accepted. *Application Contact:* Susan Baca, Operations Manager for Admissions and Financial Aid, 801-581-7479, Fax: 801-581-6897, E-mail: susan.baca@law.utah.edu. *Associate Dean of Admissions and Financial Aid*, Reyes Aguilar, Jr., 801-581-6833, Fax: 801-581-6897, E-mail: reyes.aguilar@utah.edu.

UNIVERSITY OF VALLEY FORGE, Phoenixville, PA 19460

General Information Independent-religious, coed, comprehensive institution.

GRADUATE UNITS

Program in Christian Leadership Offers Christian leadership (MA).

Program in Music Technology Online learning. Offers music technology (MM).

Program in Theology Offers theology (MA).

Program in Worship Studies Offers worship studies (MA).

UNIVERSITY OF VERMONT, Burlington, VT 05405

General Information State-supported, coed, university. CGS member. *Graduate housing:* Rooms and/or apartments available on a first-come, first-served basis to single and married students. *Student services:* Career counseling, free psychological counseling, low-cost health insurance. *Library:* Bailey-Howe Library plus 2 others. Weekly public service hours: 104; students can reserve study rooms. *Research affiliation:* Miner Institute (animal sciences).

Computer facilities: Computer purchase and lease plans are available. 850 computers available on campus for general student use. A campuswide network can be accessed from student residence rooms and from off campus. Online class registration, Web pages, online course support are available.
Website: http://www.uvm.edu/

General Application Contact: Sydnee Viray, Director of Admissions and Enrollment Management, 802-656-2699, Fax: 802-656-0519, E-mail: graduate.admissions@uvm.edu.

GRADUATE UNITS

College of Medicine ***Financial support:*** Fellowships, research assistantships, teaching assistantships, and Federal Work-Study available. Offers medicine (MS, MD, PhD, Certificate). *Application deadline:* Applications are processed on a rolling basis.

Graduate Programs in Medicine Financial support: Fellowships, research assistantships, teaching assistantships, traineeships, and analytical assistantships available. Financial award application deadline: 3/1. Offers clinical and translational science (MS, PhD, Certificate); medicine (MS, PhD, Certificate); neuroscience (PhD); pathology (MS); pharmacology (MS, PhD). *Application deadline:* For fall admission, 4/1 priority date for domestic students, 4/1 for international students. Applications are processed on a rolling basis. *Application fee:* $65. Electronic applications accepted.

Graduate College ***Financial support:*** Fellowships, research assistantships, teaching assistantships, career-related internships or fieldwork, Federal Work-Study, traineeships, tuition waivers (full and partial), and analytical assistantships available. Support available to part-time students. *Degree program information:* Part-time programs available. Part-time. Offers cellular, molecular and biomedical sciences (PhD). *Application deadline:* For fall admission, 4/1 priority date for domestic and international students; for spring admission, 11/15 priority date for domestic and international students. Applications are processed on a rolling basis. *Application fee:* $65. Electronic applications accepted.

College of Agriculture and Life Sciences Financial support: Fellowships, research assistantships, teaching assistantships, career-related internships or fieldwork, Federal Work-Study, and tuition waivers (full and partial) available. Financial award application deadline: 3/1. *Degree program information:* Part-time programs available. Part-time. Offers agriculture and life sciences (MPA, MS, MSD, PhD); animal sciences (MS); animal, nutrition and food sciences (PhD); community development and applied economics (MS); dietetics (MSD); field naturalist (MS); food systems (MS, PhD); nutritional sciences (MS); plant and soil science (MS, PhD); plant biology (MS, PhD); public administration (MPA). *Application fee:* $65. Electronic applications accepted. *Application Contact:* Ralph Swenson, Director of Graduate Admissions, 802-656-2699, Fax: 802-656-0519, E-mail: graduate.admissions@uvm.edu. *Dean*, Dr. Thomas C. Vogelmann, 802-656-0321.

College of Arts and Sciences Financial support: Fellowships, research assistantships, teaching assistantships, career-related internships or fieldwork, and Federal Work-Study available. *Degree program information:* Part-time programs available. Part-time. Offers arts and sciences (MA, MS, MST, PhD); biology (MS, PhD); biology education (MST); chemistry (MS, PhD); clinical psychology (PhD); English (MA); geology (MS); German (MA); historic preservation (MS); history (MA); physics (MS); psychology (PhD). *Application fee:* $65. Electronic applications accepted.

College of Education and Social Services Financial support: Fellowships, research assistantships, teaching assistantships, career-related internships or fieldwork, and Federal Work-Study available. *Degree program information:* Part-time programs available. Part-time. Offers counseling (MS); curriculum and instruction (MAT); education and social services (M Ed, MAT, MS, MSW, Ed D, PhD); educational leadership (M Ed); educational leadership and policy studies (Ed D, PhD); higher education and student affairs administration (M Ed); social work (MSW); special education (M Ed). *Application fee:* $65. Electronic applications accepted.

College of Engineering and Mathematics Financial support: Fellowships, research assistantships, teaching assistantships, and Federal Work-Study available. Financial award application deadline: 3/1. *Degree program information:* Part-time programs available. Part-time. Offers bioengineering (PhD); biostatistics (MS); civil and environmental engineering (MS, PhD); computer science (MS, PhD); electrical engineering (MS, PhD); engineering and mathematics (MS, MST, PhD); materials science (MS, PhD); mathematics (MS); mathematics education (MST); mechanical engineering (MS, PhD); statistics (MS). *Application deadline:* For fall admission, 4/1 priority date for domestic students. Applications are processed on a rolling basis. *Application fee:* $65. Electronic applications accepted.

College of Nursing and Health Sciences Financial support: Fellowships, research assistantships, teaching assistantships, and Federal Work-Study available. Financial award application deadline: 3/1. Offers communication sciences and disorders (MS); nursing (MS, DNP); nursing and health sciences (MS, DNP, DPT); physical therapy (DPT). *Application deadline:* For fall admission, 4/1 priority date for domestic students. Applications are processed on a rolling basis. *Application fee:* $65. Electronic applications accepted.

The Rubenstein School of Environment and Natural Resources Financial support: Fellowships, research assistantships, teaching assistantships, and Federal Work-Study available. Financial award application deadline: 3/1. *Degree program information:* Part-time programs available. Part-time. Offers environment and natural resources (MS, PhD); natural resources (MS, PhD). *Application deadline:* For fall admission, 2/1 priority date for domestic students, 2/1 for international students; for spring admission, 11/1 for domestic and international students. Applications are processed on a rolling basis. *Application fee:* $65. Electronic applications accepted. *Application Contact:* Dr. Kimberly Wallin, Coordinator, 802-656-2511.

School of Business Administration Financial support: Fellowships, teaching assistantships, and Federal Work-Study available. Financial award application deadline: 3/1. *Degree program information:* Part-time programs available. Part-time. Offers accounting (M Acc); business administration (M Acc, MBA). *Application deadline:* For fall admission, 1/15 for domestic and international students. Applications are processed on a rolling basis. *Application fee:* $65. Electronic applications accepted. *Application Contact:* Prof. William Cats-Baril, Coordinator, 802-656-4119. *Dean*, Dr. Sanjay Sharma, 802-656-4119.

UNIVERSITY OF VICTORIA, Victoria, BC V8W 2Y2, Canada

General Information Province-supported, coed, university. CGS member. *Graduate housing:* Rooms and/or apartments available on a first-come, first-served basis to single and married students. Housing application deadline: 2/1. *Research affiliation:* Dominion

Astrophysical Observatory, Bamfield Marine Research Station (marine biology), Tri-University Meson Facility, Canada/France/Hawaii Telescope Observatory, Institute of Ocean Sciences (geography, oceanography).

GRADUATE UNITS

Faculty of Graduate Studies ***Degree program information:*** Part-time programs available. Part-time, online learning. Electronic applications accepted.

Faculty of Business ***Degree program information:*** Part-time programs available. Part-time. Offers business (MBA). Electronic applications accepted.

Faculty of Education Offers aboriginal communities counseling (M Ed); art education (M Ed, PhD); coaching studies (co-operative education) (M Ed); counseling (M Ed, MA); curriculum studies (M Ed, MA, PhD); early childhood education (M Ed, PhD); education (M Ed, M Sc, MA, PhD); educational psychology (M Ed, MA, PhD); educational studies (PhD); kinesiology (M Sc, MA); language and literacy (M Ed, MA, PhD); leadership studies (M Ed, MA); leisure service administration (MA); mathematics (M Ed, MA, PhD); music education (M Ed, MA, PhD); physical education (MA); science (M Ed, MA, PhD); social studies (M Ed, MA); social, cultural and foundational studies (MA, PhD); technology and environmental education (PhD).

Faculty of Engineering Offers computer science (M Sc, PhD); electrical and computer engineering (M Eng, MA Sc, PhD); engineering (M Eng, M Sc, MA Sc, PhD); mechanical engineering (M Eng, MA Sc, PhD).

Faculty of Fine Arts Offers composition (M Mus); design (MFA); digital multimedia (MFA); directing (MFA); drawing (MFA); fine arts (M Mus, MA, MFA, PhD); history in art (MA, PhD); musicology (MA, PhD); musicology with performance (MA); painting (MFA); performance (M Mus); photography (MFA); sculpture (MFA); theatre history (MA); video (MFA); writing (MFA).

Faculty of Human and Social Development Offers advanced nursing practice (advanced practice leadership option) (MN); advanced nursing practice (nurse educator option) (MN); advanced nursing practice (nurse practitioner option) (MN); child and youth care (MA, PhD); dispute resolution (MADR); health information science (M Sc); human and social development (M Sc, MA, MADR, MN, MPA, MSW, PhD); indigenous governance (MA); nursing (PhD); public administration (MPA, PhD); social work (MSW); studies in policy and practice (MA).

Faculty of Humanities Offers applied linguistics (MA); English (MA, PhD); German studies (MA); Greek and Roman studies (MA, PhD); Hispanic and Italian studies (MA); Hispanic studies (MA); history (MA, PhD); humanities (MA, PhD); linguistics (MA, PhD); literature (MA); Pacific and Asian studies (MA); philosophy (MA); teaching emphasis (MA).

Faculty of Science Offers astronomy and astrophysics (M Sc, PhD); biochemistry (M Sc, PhD); biology (M Sc, PhD); chemistry (M Sc, PhD); condensed matter physics (M Sc, PhD); earth and ocean sciences (M Sc, PhD); experimental particle physics (M Sc, PhD); mathematics and statistics (M Sc, MA, PhD); medical physics (M Sc, PhD); microbiology (M Sc, PhD); ocean physics (M Sc, PhD); science (M Sc, MA, PhD); theoretical physics (M Sc, PhD). Electronic applications accepted.

Faculty of Social Sciences Offers anthropology (MA); clinical psychology (PhD); clinical psychology (neuropsychology) (M Sc); cognition and brain science (M Sc, PhD); economics (MA, PhD); experimental neuropsychology (M Sc, PhD); geography (M Sc, MA, PhD); individualized study (M Sc, PhD); life span development psychology (PhD); life span developmental psychology (M Sc); political science (MA, PhD); social psychology (M Sc, PhD); social sciences (M Sc, MA, PhD); sociology (MA, PhD).

Faculty of Law ***Degree program information:*** Part-time programs available. Part-time. Offers law (LL M, JD, PhD). Electronic applications accepted.

UNIVERSITY OF VIRGINIA, Charlottesville, VA 22903

General Information State-supported, coed, university. CGS member. *Graduate housing:* Rooms and/or apartments available on a first-come, first-served basis to single and married students. Housing application deadline: 6/1. *Research affiliation:* Federal Executive Institute, National Radio Astronomy Observatory, The Judge Advocate General's School, U. S. Army.

GRADUATE UNITS

College and Graduate School of Arts and Sciences ***Degree program information:*** Part-time programs available. Part-time. Offers anthropology (MA, PhD); art and architectural history (MA, PhD); arts and sciences (MA, MAPE, MFA, MS, PhD); astronomy (MS, PhD); biology (MA, MS, PhD); chemistry (MA, MS, PhD); classics (MA, PhD); creative writing (MFA); drama (MFA); East Asian studies (MA); economics (MA, PhD); English (MA, PhD); environmental sciences (MA, MS, PhD); foreign affairs (MA, PhD); French (MA, PhD); German (MA, PhD); government (MA, PhD); history (MA, PhD); Italian (MA); linguistics (MA); math education (MA); mathematics (MA, MS, PhD); Middle Eastern and South Asian studies (MA); music (MA, PhD); philosophy (MA, PhD); physics (MA, MS, PhD); physics education (MAPE); psychology (MA, PhD); religion, politics and global society (MA); religious studies (MA, PhD); Slavic languages and literatures (MA, PhD); sociology (MA, PhD); Spanish (MA, PhD); statistics (MS, PhD). Electronic applications accepted.

Curry School of Education Offers administration and supervision (M Ed, Ed D, PhD, Ed S); applied developmental science (M Ed, PhD); clinical and school psychology (PhD); communication disorders (M Ed); counselor education (M Ed, Ed S); curriculum and instruction (M Ed, Ed D, PhD, Ed S); early childhood special education (MT); education (M Ed, MT, Ed D, PhD, Ed S); education evaluation (PhD); educational evaluation (M Ed); educational policy studies (M Ed, PhD); educational psychology (M Ed, Ed D, PhD, Ed S); educational research (Ed D, PhD); elementary education (M Ed, MT, Ed D); English education (M Ed, MT, Ed D, PhD); foreign language education (M Ed, MT); gifted education (M Ed); higher education (M Ed, Ed D, PhD, Ed S); instructional technology (M Ed, PhD, Ed S); kinesiology (M Ed, PhD); math education (PhD); mathematics education (M Ed, Ed D); reading education (PhD); research statistics and evaluation (Ed D); research, statistics and evaluation (PhD); school psychology (Ed D, PhD); science education (Ed D, PhD); social studies education (M Ed, MT, PhD); special education (M Ed, Ed D, Ed S); student affairs practice (M Ed); world languages education (MT). Electronic applications accepted.

Darden School of Business Offers business (MBA, PhD). Electronic applications accepted.

Data Science Institute Offers data science (MS).

Frank Batten Sr. School of Leadership and Public Policy Offers leadership and public policy (MPP). Electronic applications accepted.

McIntire School of Commerce ***Degree program information:*** Evening/weekend programs available. Evening/weekend. Offers accounting (MS); business analytics (MSC); commerce (MS, MSC, Certificate); finance (MSC); global commerce (MS); global strategic management (MS); international management (Certificate); management of information technology (MS); marketing and management (MSC). Electronic applications accepted.

School of Architecture Offers architectural history (M Arch H, PhD); architecture (M Arch, M Arch H, M Land Arch, MUEP, PhD); landscape architecture (M Land Arch); the constructed environment (PhD); urban and environmental planning (MUEP). Electronic applications accepted.

School of Engineering and Applied Science ***Degree program information:*** Part-time programs available. Part-time, online learning. Offers biomedical engineering (ME, MS, PhD); chemical engineering (ME, MS, PhD); civil and environmental engineering (ME, MS, PhD); computer engineering (ME, MS, PhD); computer science (MCS, MS, PhD); electrical engineering (ME, MS, PhD); engineering and applied science (MCS, ME, MEP, MMSE, MS, PhD); engineering physics (MEP, MS, PhD); materials science (MMSE, MS, PhD); mechanical and aerospace engineering (ME, MS, PhD); systems and information engineering (ME, MS, PhD). Electronic applications accepted.

School of Law Offers law (LL M, JD, SJD). JD/MA in international relations offered jointly with The Johns Hopkins University. Electronic applications accepted.

School of Medicine Offers biochemistry (PhD); biological and physical sciences (MS); biophysics (PhD); cell biology (PhD); clinical investigation and patient-oriented research (MS); clinical research (MS); experimental pathology (PhD); informatics in medicine (MS); medicine (MPH, MS, MD, PhD); microbiology, immunology, and cancer biology (PhD); neuroscience (PhD); pharmacology (PhD); physiology (PhD); public health (MPH). Electronic applications accepted.

School of Nursing ***Degree program information:*** Part-time programs available. Part-time. Offers acute and specialty care (MSN); acute care nurse practitioner (MSN); clinical nurse leadership (MSN); community-public health leadership (MSN); nursing (DNP, PhD); psychiatric mental health counseling (MSN). Electronic applications accepted.

UNIVERSITY OF WASHINGTON, Seattle, WA 98195

General Information State-supported, coed, university. CGS member. *Graduate housing:* Rooms and/or apartments available on a first-come, first-served basis to single and married students. Housing application deadline: 5/1. *Research affiliation:* Fred Hutchinson Cancer Research Center, Children's Hospital and Regional Medical Center (pediatric research).

GRADUATE UNITS

Graduate School ***Degree program information:*** Part-time and evening/weekend programs available. Part-time, evening/weekend, online learning. Offers biology for teachers (MS); global trade, transportation and logistics studies (Certificate); museology (MA); Near and Middle Eastern studies (PhD); quantitative ecology and resource management (MS, PhD). Electronic applications accepted.

College of Arts and Sciences ***Degree program information:*** Part-time and evening/weekend programs available. Part-time, evening/weekend. Offers acting (MFA); animal behavior (PhD); anthropology (MA, PhD); applied mathematics (MS, PhD); art (MFA); art history (MA, PhD); arts and sciences (MA, MAIS, MAT, MC, MFA, MM, MS, Au D, DMA, PhD); astronomy (MS, PhD); audiology (Au D); biology (PhD); Buddhist studies (MA, PhD); Central Asian studies (MAIS); chemistry (MS, PhD); child psychology (PhD); China studies (MAIS); Chinese language and literature (MA, PhD); choral conducting (MM, DMA); classics (MA, PhD); classics and philosophy (PhD); clinical psychology (PhD); cognition and perception (PhD); communication (MA, MC, PhD); comparative literature (MA, PhD); comparative religion (MAIS); computational linguistics (MA); costume design (MFA); creative writing (MFA); dance (MFA); design (MFA); developmental psychology (PhD); directing (MFA); dramatic theory (PhD); East European studies (MAIS); economics (PhD); English as a second language (MAT); English literature and language (MA, MAT, PhD); ethnomusicology (MA); French (MA, PhD); gender, women and sexuality studies (PhD); geography (MA, PhD); Germanics (MA, PhD); global studies (MAIS); Hispanic literary and cultural studies (MA); history (MA, PhD); industrial design (MFA); international studies (MAIS, PhD); Italian (MA); Japan studies (MAIS); Japanese language and literature (MA, PhD); Korea studies (MAIS); Korean language and literature (MA, PhD); lighting design (MFA); linguistics (MA, PhD); mathematics (MA, MS, PhD); Middle East studies (MAIS); music (MA, MM, DMA, PhD); music education (MA, PhD); music history (MA, PhD); Near Eastern languages and civilization (MA); numerical analysis (MS); optimization (MS); painting and drawing (MFA); philosophy (MA, PhD); photography (MFA); physics (MS, PhD); political science (MA, PhD); quantitative psychology (PhD); Romance linguistics (MA, PhD); Russian literature (MA, PhD); Russian studies (MAIS); Russian, East European and Central Asian studies (MAIS); Scandinavian studies (MA, PhD); scenic design (MFA); Slavic linguistics (MA, PhD); social psychology and personality (PhD); sociology (MA, PhD); South Asian language and literature (MA, PhD); South Asian studies (MAIS); Southeast Asian studies (MAIS); speech and hearing sciences (PhD); speech-language pathology (MS); statistics (MS, PhD); theatre and performance history (PhD); visual communication design (MFA). Electronic applications accepted.

College of Built Environments ***Degree program information:*** Part-time and evening/weekend programs available. Part-time, evening/weekend. Offers architecture (M Arch, MS); built environment (PhD); built environments (M Arch, MLA, MS, MSCM, MUP, PhD, Certificate); construction management (MSCM); design computing (Certificate); design firm leadership and management (Certificate); historic preservation (Certificate); landscape architecture (MLA); lighting (Certificate); urban design (Certificate); urban design and planning (PhD); urban planning (MUP). Electronic applications accepted.

College of Education ***Degree program information:*** Part-time and evening/weekend programs available. Part-time, evening/weekend. Offers curriculum and instruction (M Ed, Ed D, PhD); early childhood special education (M Ed); educational leadership and policy studies (M Ed, Ed D, PhD); educational psychology (M Ed, PhD); emotional and behavioral disabilities (M Ed); human development and cognition (M Ed); instructional leadership (M Ed); intercollegiate athletic leadership (M Ed); learning disabilities (M Ed); learning sciences (M Ed, PhD); low-incidence disabilities (M Ed); measurement, statistics and research design (M Ed, PhD); school psychology (M Ed); severe disabilities (M Ed); special education (M Ed, Ed D, PhD); teacher education (MIT). Electronic applications accepted.

College of Engineering Students: 1,532 full-time (464 women), 801 part-time (199 women); includes 497 minority (27 Black or African American, non-Hispanic/Latino; 2 American Indian or Alaska Native, non-Hispanic/Latino; 298 Asian, non-Hispanic/Latino; 109 Hispanic/Latino; 2 Native Hawaiian or other Pacific Islander, non-Hispanic/Latino; 59 Two or more races, non-Hispanic/Latino), 767 international. Average age 28. 6,790 applicants, 29% accepted, 837 enrolled. *Faculty:* 257 full-time (57 women). *Financial support:* In 2015–16, 1,039 students received support, including 168 fellowships with full tuition reimbursements available, 651 research assistantships with full tuition reimbursements available, 220 teaching assistantships with full tuition reimbursements available; career-related internships or fieldwork, Federal Work-Study, institutionally sponsored loans, scholarships/grants, traineeships, health care benefits, tuition waivers (full), unspecified assistantships, and stipend supplements also available. Financial award application deadline: 2/28; financial award applicants required to submit FAFSA. In 2015, 562 master's, 131 doctorates awarded. *Degree program information:* Part-time programs available. Part-time, online learning. Offers aeronautics and astronautics (MAE, MSAA, PhD); applied bioengineering (MAB); applied materials science and engineering (MS); bioengineering (MS, PhD); bioengineering and nanotechnology (PhD); chemical engineering (MS, PhD); chemical engineering and nanotechnology (PhD); computer science and engineering (MS, PhD); construction engineering (MSCE, PhD); electrical engineering (MS, PhD); electrical engineering and nanotechnology (PhD); engineering (MAB, MAE, MISE, MS, MSAA, MSCE, MSE, MSME, PhD, Certificate); environmental engineering (MSCE, PhD); geotechnical engineering (MSCE, PhD); human centered design and engineering (MS, PhD); hydrology and hydrodynamics (MSCE, PhD); industrial and systems engineering (MISE, MS, PhD); materials science and engineering (MS, PhD); mechanical engineering (MSE, MSME, PhD); pharmaceutical bioengineering (MS); structural engineering and mechanics (MSCE, PhD); transportation engineering (MSCE, PhD); user centered design (Certificate). *Application deadline:* For fall admission, 12/1 for domestic and international students. *Application fee:* $85. Electronic applications accepted. *Application Contact:* Scott Winter, Director, Academic Affairs, 206-685-4074, Fax: 206-685-0666, E-mail: swinter@uw.edu. *Dean of Engineering,* Dr. Michael B. Bragg, 206-543-0340, Fax: 206-685-0666, E-mail: mbragg@uw.edu.

College of the Environment Offers aquatic and fishery sciences (MS, PhD); atmospheric sciences (MS, PhD); biological oceanography (MS, PhD); bioresource science and engineering (MS, PhD); chemical oceanography (MS, PhD); environment (MEH, MFR, MMA, MS, PhD, Graduate Certificate); environmental horticulture (MEH); forest ecology (MS, PhD); forest management (MFR); forest soils (MS, PhD); geology (MS, PhD); geophysics (MS, PhD); marine and environmental affairs (MMA, Graduate Certificate); marine geology and geophysics (MS, PhD); physical oceanography (MS, PhD); restoration ecology (MS, PhD); restoration ecology and environmental horticulture (MS, PhD); social sciences (MS, PhD); sustainable resource management (MS, PhD); wildlife science (MS, PhD). Electronic applications accepted.

Evans School of Public Affairs Degree program information: Part-time and evening/weekend programs available. Part-time, evening/weekend. Offers public administration (MPA); public policy and management (PhD). Electronic applications accepted.

The Information School Students: 375 full-time (236 women), 242 part-time (180 women); includes 132 minority (22 Black or African American, non-Hispanic/Latino; 5 American Indian or Alaska Native, non-Hispanic/Latino; 56 Asian, non-Hispanic/Latino; 45 Hispanic/Latino; 4 Native Hawaiian or other Pacific Islander, non-Hispanic/Latino), 149 international. Average age 32. 1,486 applicants, 33% accepted, 268 enrolled. *Faculty:* 35 full-time (19 women), 22 part-time/adjunct (12 women). *Financial support:* In 2015–16, 56 students received support, including 1 fellowship with full tuition reimbursement available (averaging $6,651 per year), 27 research assistantships with full tuition reimbursements available (averaging $19,418 per year), 27 teaching assistantships with full tuition reimbursements available (averaging $19,521 per year); Federal Work-Study, institutionally sponsored loans, scholarships/grants, health care benefits, tuition waivers (full and partial), and unspecified assistantships also available. Support available to part-time students. Financial award application deadline: 1/15; financial award applicants required to submit FAFSA. In 2015, 225 master's, 5 doctorates awarded. *Degree program information:* Part-time and evening/weekend programs available. Part-time, evening/weekend, 100% online coursework with required attendance at on-campus orientation at start of program. Offers information management (MSIM); information science (PhD); library and information science (MLIS). *Application deadline:* For fall admission, 12/1 priority date for domestic and international students. *Application fee:* $85. Electronic applications accepted. *Application Contact:* Kari Brothers, Admissions Counselor, 206-616-5541, Fax: 206-616-3152, E-mail: kari683@uw.edu. *Dean,* Dr. Harry Bruce, 206-616-0985, E-mail: harryb@uw.edu.

Michael G. Foster School of Business Students: 469 full-time (173 women), 638 part-time (216 women); includes 314 minority (15 Black or African American, non-Hispanic/Latino; 6 American Indian or Alaska Native, non-Hispanic/Latino; 246 Asian, non-Hispanic/Latino; 28 Hispanic/Latino; 5 Native Hawaiian or other Pacific Islander, non-Hispanic/Latino; 14 Two or more races, non-Hispanic/Latino), 125 international. Average age 32. 3,544 applicants, 25% accepted, 524 enrolled. *Faculty:* 104 full-time (29 women), 57 part-time/adjunct (26 women). *Financial support:* Fellowships with partial tuition reimbursements, research assistantships with partial tuition reimbursements, teaching assistantships with partial tuition reimbursements, Federal Work-Study, institutionally sponsored loans, and scholarships/grants available. Financial award application deadline: 2/28; financial award applicants required to submit FAFSA. In 2015, 497 master's, 10 doctorates awarded. *Degree program information:* Part-time and evening/weekend programs available. Part-time, evening/weekend. Offers auditing and assurance (MP Acc); business administration (MBA, PhD); entrepreneurship (MS); executive business administration (MBA); global executive business administration (MBA); information systems (MSIS); supply chain management (MSSCM); taxation (MP Acc); technology management (MBA). *Application deadline:* For fall admission, 3/15 for domestic students, 1/15 for international students. *Application fee:* $85. Electronic applications accepted. *Application Contact:* Erin Town, Director of Admissions, 206-543-4661, Fax: 206-616-7351, E-mail: mba@uw.edu. *Dean,* Dr. James Jiambalvo, 206-543-4750.

School of Dentistry Offers dental surgery (DDS); dentistry (MS, MSD, DDS, PhD, Certificate); endodontics (MSD, Certificate); oral biology (MS, MSD, PhD); oral medicine (MSD); orthodontics (MSD, Certificate); pediatric dentistry (MSD, Certificate); periodontics (MSD, PhD, Certificate); prosthodontics (MSD, Certificate).

School of Law Offers Asian law (LL M, PhD); intellectual property law and policy (LL M); law (JD); law of sustainable international development (LL M); taxation (LL M).

School of Medicine Degree program information: Part-time programs available. Part-time. Offers biochemistry (PhD); bioethics (MA); biological structure (PhD); biomedical and health informatics (MS, PhD); comparative medicine (MS); experimental and molecular pathology (PhD); genome sciences (PhD); immunology (PhD); laboratory medicine (MS); medicine (MA, MOT, MPO, MS, DPT, MD, PhD); microbiology (PhD); molecular and cellular biology (PhD); neurobiology and behavior (PhD); occupational therapy (MOT); pharmacology (PhD); physical therapy (DPT); physiology and biophysics (PhD); prosthetics and orthotics (MPO); rehabilitation science (PhD). Electronic applications accepted.

School of Nursing Degree program information: Part-time programs available. Part-time. Offers nursing (MN, MS, DNP, PhD, Graduate Certificate).

School of Public Health Degree program information: Part-time and evening/weekend programs available. Part-time, evening/weekend, online learning. Offers biostatistics (MPH, MS, PhD); clinical research (MS); community-oriented public health practice (MPH); environmental and occupational health (MPH); environmental and occupational hygiene (PhD); environmental health (MS); epidemiology (MPH, MS, PhD); evaluative sciences and statistics (PhD); genetic epidemiology (MS); global health (MPH); global health metrics and implementation science (PhD); health behavior and social determinants of health (PhD); health economics (PhD); health informatics and health information management (MHIHIM); health metrics and evaluation (MPH); health services (MS, PhD); health services administration (EMHA, MHA); health systems and policy (MPH); health systems research (PhD); leadership, policy and management (MPH); maternal and child health (MPH); maternal/child health (MPH); nutritional sciences (MPH, MS, PhD); occupational and environmental exposure sciences (MS); occupational and environmental medicine (MPH); pathobiology (PhD); public health (EMHA, MHA, MHIHIM, MPH, MS, PhD); public health genetics (MPH, PhD); social and behavioral sciences (MPH); statistical genetics (PhD); toxicology (MS, PhD). Electronic applications accepted.

School of Social Work Degree program information: Evening/weekend programs available. Evening/weekend, online learning. Offers social work (MSW, PhD).

School of Pharmacy Offers biomedical regulatory affairs (MS); medicinal chemistry (PhD); pharmaceutics (MS, PhD); pharmacy (MS, PhD).

UNIVERSITY OF WASHINGTON, BOTHELL, Bothell, WA 98011-8246

General Information State-supported, coed, comprehensive institution. *Graduate housing:* Room and/or apartments available on a first-come, first-served basis to single students; on-campus housing not available to married students. Housing application deadline: 5/1. *Research affiliation:* Bill and Melinda Gates Foundation (improving health and reducing poverty in developing countries, providing opportunities to succeed in school and life in the U.S.), Carnegie Corporation of New York (doing real and permanent good in this world by creating ladders on which the aspiring can rise), American Institutes for Research (labor market success), Michael and Susan Dell Foundation (portfolio network scale-up project), William and Flora Hewlett Foundation (planning for the state education agency of the future), Walton Family Foundation (student-based allocation systems).

GRADUATE UNITS

Master of Arts in Cultural Studies Program ***Degree program information:*** Evening/weekend programs available. Evening/weekend. Offers cultural studies (MA). Electronic applications accepted.

Master of Arts in Policy Studies Program ***Degree program information:*** Evening/weekend programs available. Evening/weekend. Offers policy studies (MA). Electronic applications accepted.

Program in Computing and Software Systems ***Degree program information:*** Part-time and evening/weekend programs available. Part-time, evening/weekend. Offers computing and software systems (MS). Electronic applications accepted.

Program in Creative Writing and Poetics Offers creative writing and poetics (MFA).

Program in Education ***Degree program information:*** Part-time and evening/weekend programs available. Part-time, evening/weekend. Offers education (M Ed); leadership development for educators (M Ed); secondary/middle level endorsement (M Ed). Electronic applications accepted.

Program in Nursing ***Degree program information:*** Part-time programs available. Part-time. Offers nursing (MN). Electronic applications accepted.

School of Business ***Degree program information:*** Part-time and evening/weekend programs available. Part-time, evening/weekend. Offers leadership (MBA); technology (MBA). Electronic applications accepted.

UNIVERSITY OF WASHINGTON, TACOMA, Tacoma, WA 98402-3100

General Information State-supported, coed, comprehensive institution. *Graduate housing:* Room and/or apartments available on a first-come, first-served basis to single students; on-campus housing not available to married students. Housing application deadline: 5/14. *Research affiliation:* City of Tacoma/Port of Tacoma (water quality and sustainability studies), South Sound Public and Private Schools (internships and educational research).

GRADUATE UNITS

Graduate Programs ***Degree program information:*** Part-time and evening/weekend programs available. Part-time, evening/weekend. Offers accounting (MBA); advanced integrative practice (MSW); business administration (MBA); certified financial analyst (MBA); communities, populations and health (MN); computing and software systems (MS); education (M Ed); educational administration (principal or program administrator certification) (M Ed); elementary education teacher certification (M Ed); elementary education/special education teacher certification (M Ed); interdisciplinary studies (MA); leadership in healthcare (MN); nurse educator (MN); secondary science or math teacher certification (M Ed); social work (MSW). Electronic applications accepted.

UNIVERSITY OF WATERLOO, Waterloo, ON N2L 3G1, Canada

General Information Province-supported, coed, university. CGS member. *Enrollment:* 35,464 graduate, professional, and undergraduate students; 4,204 full-time matriculated graduate/professional students, 1,230 part-time matriculated graduate/professional students. *Enrollment by degree level:* 3,429 master's, 2,005 doctoral. *Graduate housing:* Rooms and/or apartments available on a first-come, first-served basis to single and married students. *Student services:* Campus employment opportunities, campus safety program, career counseling, child daycare facilities, exercise/wellness program, free psychological counseling, international student services, low-cost health insurance, services for students with disabilities, teacher training, writing training. *Library:* Dana Porter Library plus 11 others. Students can reserve study rooms. *Research affiliation:* Waterloo Maple, Inc. (symbolic computation research), Bell Canada, GM Canada, IBM, Com Dev International (telecommunications), Nortel (telecommunications).

Computer facilities: 6,000 computers available on campus for general student use. A campuswide network can be accessed from student residence rooms and from off campus. Online class registration is available.
Website: http://www.uwaterloo.ca/

General Application Contact: Graduate Studies Office, 519-888-4567 Ext. 35209, Fax: 519-746-3051, E-mail: gsoffice@uwaterloo.ca.

GRADUATE UNITS

Graduate Studies Students: 4,204 full-time, 1,230 part-time. *Financial support:* Fellowships with partial tuition reimbursements, research assistantships with partial tuition reimbursements, teaching assistantships with partial tuition reimbursements, career-related internships or fieldwork, Federal Work-Study, institutionally sponsored loans, scholarships/grants, and tuition waivers (partial) available. Support available to part-time students. In 2015, 1,698 master's, 303 doctorates awarded. *Degree program information:* Part-time and evening/weekend programs available. Part-time, evening/weekend, online learning. *Application deadline:* Applications are processed on a rolling basis. *Application fee:* $100 Canadian dollars. Electronic applications accepted. *Application Contact:* Graduate Studies, 519-888-4567 Ext. 35209, Fax: 519-746-3051, E-mail: gsoffice@uwaterloo.ca.

Faculty of Applied Health Sciences Financial support: Research assistantships, teaching assistantships, career-related internships or fieldwork, Federal Work-Study, institutionally sponsored loans, scholarships/grants, and university-sponsored bursaries available. *Degree program information:* Part-time programs available. Part-time. Offers applied health sciences (M Sc, MA, MHE, MHI, MPH, PhD); health evaluation (MHE); health informatics (MHI); health studies and gerontology (M Sc, PhD); kinesiology (M Sc, PhD); public health (MPH); recreation and leisure studies (MA, PhD). *Application deadline:* For fall admission, 2/1 for domestic and international students. *Application fee:* $100 Canadian dollars. Electronic applications accepted. *Application Contact:* Tracy Taves, Graduate Studies Coordinator, 519-888-4567 Ext. 36149, Fax: 519-746-6776, E-mail: tltaves@uwaterloo.ca. *Associate Dean,* Dr. Rhona Hanning, 519-888-4567 Ext. 36585, Fax: 519-746-6776, E-mail: rhanning@uwaterloo.ca.

Faculty of Arts Financial support: Fellowships, research assistantships, teaching assistantships, career-related internships or fieldwork, and scholarships/grants available. *Degree program information:* Part-time and evening/weekend programs available. Part-time, evening/weekend. Offers accounting (M Acc, PhD); ancient Mediterranean cultures (MA); anthropology (MA); arts (M Acc, M Tax, MA, MA Sc, MFA, MPS, PhD); economics (MA, PhD); English language and literature (PhD); finance (M Acc); French (MA, PhD); German (MA, PhD); global governance (MA, PhD); history (MA, PhD); literary studies (MA); philosophy (MA, PhD); psychology (MA, MA Sc, PhD); public issues (MA); religious diversity in North America (PhD); rhetoric and communication design (MA); Russian (MA); sociology (MA, PhD); studio art (MFA); taxation (M Tax). *Application deadline:* Applications are processed on a rolling basis. *Application fee:* $100 Canadian dollars. Electronic applications accepted.

Faculty of Engineering Financial support: Fellowships, research assistantships, teaching assistantships, career-related internships or fieldwork, Federal Work-Study, and institutionally sponsored loans available. *Degree program information:* Part-time and evening/weekend programs available. Part-time, evening/weekend, online learning. Offers applied operations research (MA Sc, MMS, PhD); architecture (M Arch); business, entrepreneurship and technology (MBET); chemical engineering (M Eng, MA Sc, PhD); civil and environmental engineering (M Eng, MA Sc, PhD); electrical and computer engineering (M Eng, MA Sc, PhD); engineering (M Arch, M Eng, MA Sc, MBET, MMS, PhD); information systems (MA Sc, MMS, PhD); management of technology (MA Sc, MMS, PhD); mechanical engineering (M Eng, MA Sc, PhD); mechanical engineering design and manufacturing (M Eng); systems design engineering (M Eng, MA Sc, PhD). *Application deadline:* Applications are processed on a rolling basis. *Application fee:* $100 Canadian dollars. Electronic applications accepted.

Faculty of Environment Financial support: Fellowships, research assistantships, teaching assistantships, career-related internships or fieldwork, institutionally sponsored loans, and scholarships/grants available. Support available to part-time students. *Degree program information:* Part-time programs available. Part-time. Offers environment (M Plan, MA, MAES, MES, PhD); environment, resources and sustainability (MES, PhD); geography and environmental management (MA, PhD); local economic development (MAES); planning (M Plan, MA, MAES, MES, PhD). *Application fee:* $100 Canadian dollars. Electronic applications accepted.

Faculty of Mathematics Financial support: Research assistantships, teaching assistantships, career-related internships or fieldwork, and scholarships/grants available. Offers actuarial science (M Math, MAS, PhD); applied mathematics (M Math, PhD); biostatistics (PhD); combinatorics and optimization (M Math, PhD); computer science (M Math, PhD); mathematics (M Math, MAS, MMT, PhD); pure mathematics (M Math, PhD); software engineering (M Math); statistics (M Math, PhD); statistics and computing (M Math); statistics-biostatistics (M Math); statistics-computing (M Math); statistics-finance (M Math). *Application deadline:* For fall admission, 2/1 for domestic and international students. *Application fee:* $100 Canadian dollars. Electronic applications accepted.

Faculty of Science Financial support: Fellowships, research assistantships, teaching assistantships, career-related internships or fieldwork, and institutionally sponsored loans available. *Degree program information:* Part-time programs available. Part-time. Offers biology (M Sc, PhD); chemistry and biochemistry (M Sc, PhD); earth and environmental sciences (M Sc, PhD); optometry (OD); physics (M Sc, PhD); science (M Sc, OD, PhD); vision science (M Sc, PhD). *Application deadline:* Applications are processed on a rolling basis. Electronic applications accepted.

THE UNIVERSITY OF WEST ALABAMA, Livingston, AL 35470

General Information State-supported, coed, comprehensive institution. *Enrollment:* 4,032 graduate, professional, and undergraduate students; 1,952 full-time matriculated graduate/professional students (1,628 women), 165 part-time matriculated graduate/professional students (127 women). *Enrollment by degree level:* 1,800 master's, 317 other advanced degrees. *Graduate faculty:* 55 full-time (27 women), 71 part-time/adjunct (45 women). Tuition, state resident: part-time $334 per credit hour. Tuition, nonresident: part-time $668 per credit hour. *Required fees:* $380; $130 per semester. *Graduate housing:* Room and/or apartments available on a first-come, first-served basis to single students; on-campus housing not available to married students. Typical cost: $3920 per year ($6460 including board). Room and board charges vary according to board plan and housing facility selected. Housing application deadline: 5/1. *Student services:* Campus employment opportunities, campus safety program, career counseling, exercise/wellness program, free psychological counseling, international student services, services for students with disabilities. *Library:* Julia Tutwiler Library plus 1 other. *Collection:* Books: 160,137 (physical), 1,789 (digital/electronic); Serial titles: 43 (physical); Databases: 96,027. Students can reserve study rooms.

Computer facilities: 400 computers available on campus for general student use. A campuswide network can be accessed from student residence rooms. Online class registration, Wireless intranet is available campuswide for all students are available. Website: http://www.uwa.edu/

General Application Contact: Dr. B. J. Kimbrough, Dean of Graduate Studies, 205-652-3647, Fax: 205-652-3670, E-mail: bkimbrough@uwa.edu.

GRADUATE UNITS

School of Graduate Studies Students: 1,952 full-time (1,628 women), 165 part-time (127 women); includes 907 minority (847 Black or African American, non-Hispanic/Latino; 15 American Indian or Alaska Native, non-Hispanic/Latino; 3 Asian, non-Hispanic/Latino; 11 Hispanic/Latino; 1 Native Hawaiian or other Pacific Islander, non-Hispanic/Latino; 30 Two or more races, non-Hispanic/Latino), 40 international. Average age 34. 773 applicants, 87% accepted, 486 enrolled. *Faculty:* 55 full-time (27 women), 71 part-time/adjunct (45 women). *Financial support:* In 2015–16, 22 teaching assistantships (averaging $7,462 per year) were awarded; career-related internships or fieldwork, Federal Work-Study, scholarships/grants, and unspecified assistantships also available. Support available to part-time students. Financial award application deadline: 3/1; financial award applicants required to submit FAFSA. In 2015, 569 master's, 126 other advanced degrees awarded. *Degree program information:* Part-time and evening/weekend programs available. Part-time, evening/weekend, online learning. *Application deadline:* Applications are processed on a rolling basis. *Application fee:* $40. Electronic applications accepted. *Dean of Graduate Studies,* Dr. B. J. Kimbrough, 205-652-3647, Fax: 205-652-3670, E-mail: bkimbrough@uwa.edu.

College of Business Students: 39 (23 women); includes 20 minority (17 Black or African American, non-Hispanic/Latino; 2 Asian, non-Hispanic/Latino; 1 Two or more races, non-Hispanic/Latino). Average age 30. 21 applicants, 81% accepted, 14 enrolled. *Faculty:* 8 full-time (3 women), 3 part-time/adjunct (0 women). *Financial support:* Application deadline: 3/1; applicants required to submit FAFSA. In 2015, 3 master's awarded. *Degree program information:* Part-time and evening/weekend programs available. Part-time, evening/weekend, online learning. Offers finance (MBA); general business (MBA). *Application deadline:* Applications are processed on a rolling basis. *Application fee:* $40. Electronic applications accepted. *Dean,* Dr. Wayne Bedford, 205-652-3687, Fax: 205-652-3776, E-mail: dbedford@uwa.edu.

College of Education Students: 2,083 (1,738 women); includes 896 minority (835 Black or African American, non-Hispanic/Latino; 15 American Indian or Alaska Native, non-Hispanic/Latino; 5 Asian, non-Hispanic/Latino; 11 Hispanic/Latino; 1 Native Hawaiian or other Pacific Islander, non-Hispanic/Latino; 29 Two or more races, non-Hispanic/Latino). Average age 34. 710 applicants, 87% accepted, 461 enrolled. *Faculty:* 47 full-time (24 women), 68 part-time/adjunct (45 women). *Financial support:* In 2015–16, 22 teaching assistantships (averaging $7,462 per year) were awarded; career-related internships or fieldwork, Federal Work-Study, scholarships/grants, and unspecified assistantships also available. Support available to part-time students. Financial award application deadline: 3/1; financial award applicants required to submit FAFSA. In 2015, 566 master's, 126 other advanced degrees awarded. *Degree program information:* Part-time and evening/weekend programs available. Part-time, evening/weekend, 100% online. Offers biology (MAT); collaborative special education 6-12 (Ed S); collaborative special education K-6 (Ed S); continuing education (MSCE); counseling and psychology (MSCE); early childhood development (M Ed); early childhood education (M Ed, Ed S); early childhood education P-3 (M Ed); education (M Ed, MAT, MSCE, Ed S); elementary education (M Ed, Ed S); elementary education K-6 (M Ed); English language arts (MAT); family counseling (MSCE); general (MSCE); guidance and counseling (MSCE); high school 6-12 (M Ed); history (MAT); instructional leadership (M Ed, Ed S); library media (M Ed, Ed S); mathematics (MAT); physical education (M Ed, MAT); school counseling (M Ed, Ed S); science (MAT); secondary education (M Ed, MAT); social science (MAT); special education (M Ed, Ed S); special education collaborative teacher 6-12 (M Ed); special education collaborative teacher K-6 (M Ed); student affairs in higher education (MSCE); teacher leader (Ed S). *Application deadline:* Applications are processed on a rolling basis. *Application fee:* $40. Electronic applications accepted. *Dean of Graduate Studies,* Dr. B. J. Kimbrough, 205-652-3647, Fax: 205-652-3706, E-mail: bkimbrough@uwa.edu.

College of Liberal Arts Students: 2 (1 woman). Average age 25. 4 applicants, 50% accepted, 1 enrolled. *Faculty:* 3 full-time (0 women), 7 part-time/adjunct (5 women). *Financial support:* Teaching assistantships, career-related internships or fieldwork, Federal Work-Study, scholarships/grants, and unspecified assistantships available. Support available to part-time students. Financial award application deadline: 3/1; financial award applicants required to submit FAFSA. *Degree program information:* Part-time and evening/weekend programs available. Part-time, evening/weekend, 100% online. Offers experimental psychology (MS). *Application deadline:* Applications are processed on a rolling basis. *Application fee:* $40. Electronic applications accepted. *Dean,* Dr. Mark Davis, 205-652-3570, Fax: 205-652-3717, E-mail: mdavis@uwa.edu.

THE UNIVERSITY OF WESTERN ONTARIO, London, ON N6A 5B8, Canada

General Information Province-supported, coed, university. CGS member. *Graduate housing:* Rooms and/or apartments available on a first-come, first-served basis to single and married students.

GRADUATE UNITS

Faculty of Graduate Studies ***Degree program information:*** Part-time and evening/weekend programs available. Part-time, evening/weekend, online learning. Electronic applications accepted.

Biosciences Division Degree program information: Part-time programs available. Part-time, online learning. Offers anatomy and cell biology (M Sc, PhD); biochemistry (M Sc, PhD); biology (M Sc, PhD); biosciences (M Cl Sc, M Sc, MA, MPT, PhD, CAS); clinical anatomy (M Sc); clinical neurological sciences (M Sc, PhD); epidemiology and biostatistics (M Sc, PhD); family medicine (M Cl Sc); manipulative therapy (CAS); medical biophysics (M Sc, PhD); microbiology and immunology (M Sc, PhD); pathology (M Sc, PhD); physical therapy (MPT); physiology (M Sc, PhD); psychology (MA, PhD); wound healing (CAS).

Center for the Study of Theory and Criticism Offers theory and criticism (MA, PhD).

Don Wright Faculty of Music Degree program information: Part-time programs available. Part-time. Offers music (M Mus, PhD); popular music and culture (MA).

Faculty of Arts and Humanities Degree program information: Part-time programs available. Part-time. Offers arts and humanities (M Mus, MA, PhD); Canadian literature (MA); classical studies (MA); comparative literature (MA, PhD); English (PhD); English literature (MA); French studies (MA, PhD); Hispanic studies (MA, PhD); philosophy (MA, PhD).

Faculty of Information and Media Studies Offers journalism (MA); library and information science (MLIS, PhD); media studies (MA, PhD).

Health Sciences Division Offers audiology (M Cl Sc, M Sc); health sciences (M Cl Sc, M Sc, M Sc N, MA, MCTS, MN NP, PhD); kinesiology (M Sc, MA, PhD); nurse practitioner (MN NP); nursing (M Sc N, MN NP, PhD); occupational therapy (M Sc); speech-language pathology (M Cl Sc, M Sc).

Physical Sciences Division Degree program information: Part-time programs available. Part-time. Offers applied mathematics (M Sc, PhD); astronomy (M Sc, PhD); chemical and biochemical engineering (ME Sc, PhD); chemistry (M Sc, PhD); civil and environmental engineering (M Eng, ME Sc, PhD); computer science (M Sc, PhD); electrical and computer engineering (M Eng, ME Sc, PhD); environment and sustainability (MES); geology (M Sc, PhD); geology and environmental science (M Sc, PhD); geophysics (M Sc, PhD); geophysics and environmental science (M Sc, PhD); mathematics (M Sc, PhD); mechanical and materials engineering (M Eng, ME Sc, PhD); physical sciences (M Eng, M Sc, ME Sc, MES, PhD); physics (M Sc, PhD); statistical and actuarial sciences (M Sc, PhD); theoretical physics (PhD). Electronic applications accepted.

Social Sciences Division Degree program information: Part-time and evening/weekend programs available. Part-time, evening/weekend. Offers anthropology (MA, PhD); counseling psychology (M Ed); curriculum studies (M Ed); economics (MA, PhD); education (M Ed); educational policy studies (M Ed); educational psychology/special education (M Ed); geography (M Sc, MA, PhD); history (MA, PhD); political science (MA, MPA, PhD); social sciences (M Ed, M Sc, MA, MPA, PhD); sociology (MA, PhD).

Faculty of Law Offers law (LL M, MLS, JD, Diploma).

Richard Ivey School of Business Offers business (EMBA, PhD); corporate strategy and leadership elective (MBA); entrepreneurship elective (MBA); finance elective (MBA); health sector stream (MBA); international management elective (MBA); marketing elective (MBA). Electronic applications accepted.

Schulich School of Medicine and Dentistry Offers dentistry (M Cl D, DDS); medicine (MD); medicine and dentistry (M Cl D, M Cl Sc, M Sc, MA, DDS, MD, PhD); orthodontics (M Cl D).

UNIVERSITY OF WESTERN STATES, Portland, OR 97230-3099

General Information Independent, coed, graduate-only institution. *Graduate housing:* On-campus housing not available. *Research affiliation:* Oregon Center for Complimentary and Alternative Medicine in Craniofacial Disorders (complimentary and alternative medicine), Consortial Center for Chiropractic Research (Palmer College of Chiropractic) (chiropractic).

GRADUATE UNITS

Professional Program Offers chiropractic (DC).

UNIVERSITY OF WEST FLORIDA, Pensacola, FL 32514-5750

General Information State-supported, coed, comprehensive institution. CGS member. *Graduate housing:* Room and/or apartments available on a first-come, first-served basis to single students; on-campus housing not available to married students. *Research affiliation:* Pensacola Bay Area Convention and Visitors Bureau (Pensacola tourism study), Software Engineering Research Consortium (Motorola, Northrup Grumman through Ball State University) (software engineering), University of Southern Mississippi Consortium on Coastal Estuarine Research (microbial biofilms and coastal estuarine research).

GRADUATE UNITS

College of Arts, Social Sciences, and Humanities *Degree program information:* Part-time and evening/weekend programs available. Part-time, evening/weekend. Offers arts, social sciences, and humanities (MA); communication arts (MA); counseling (MA); counseling-licensed mental health counselor (MA); creative writing (MA); general psychology (MA); history (MA); industrial-organizational (MA); literature (MA); military history (MA); political science (MA); public history (MA).

Division of Anthropology and Archaeology Offers anthropology (MA); historical archaeology (MA).

College of Business *Degree program information:* Part-time and evening/weekend programs available. Part-time, evening/weekend. Offers accounting (M Acc); business (M Acc, MBA); business administration (MBA).

College of Education and Professional Studies *Degree program information:* Part-time and evening/weekend programs available. Part-time, evening/weekend. Offers acquisition and contract administration (MSA); aging studies (MS); career and technical education (M Ed); college personnel administration (M Ed); college student personnel administration (M Ed); community health education (MS); curriculum and instruction (M Ed, Ed S); curriculum and instruction: instructional technology (Ed D); database administration (MSA); education and professional studies (M Ed, MA, MS, MSA, MSW, Ed D, Ed S); education and training management (M Ed); educational leadership (M Ed); exercise science (MS); guidance and counseling (M Ed); health care administration (MSA); health promotion and worksite wellness (MS); health, leisure, and exercise science (MS); human performance technology (MSA); instructional technology (M Ed); leadership (MSA); middle and secondary level education and ESOL (M Ed); physical education (MS); psychosocial (MS); public administration (MSA); software engineering administration (MSA).

Ed D Programs Degree program information: Part-time and evening/weekend programs available. Part-time, evening/weekend. Offers curriculum and instruction: administrative studies (Ed D); curriculum and instruction: curriculum and diversity studies (Ed D); curriculum and instruction: instructional technology (Ed D); curriculum and instruction: physical education and health (Ed D); curriculum and instruction: science and social sciences (Ed D); curriculum and instruction: teacher education (Ed D); education (Ed D).

School of Education Degree program information: Part-time and evening/weekend programs available. Part-time, evening/weekend. Offers clinical teaching (MA); curriculum and instruction: special education (M Ed); education (M Ed, MA, Ed D, Ed S); educational leadership (M Ed); educational leadership specialist (Ed S); elementary education (M Ed); habilitative science (MA); primary education (M Ed); reading education (M Ed).

School of Justice Studies and Social Work Degree program information: Part-time and evening/weekend programs available. Part-time, evening/weekend. Offers criminal justice (MS); justice studies and social work (MS, MSW); social work (MSW). Electronic applications accepted.

College of Science and Engineering *Degree program information:* Part-time and evening/weekend programs available. Part-time, evening/weekend. Offers applied statistics (MS); computer science (MS); database systems (MS); earth and environmental sciences (MS); mathematical sciences (MS); science and engineering (MPH, MS, MSN, MST); software engineering (MS).

School of Allied Health and Life Sciences Degree program information: Part-time programs available. Part-time. Offers allied health and life sciences (MPH, MS, MSN, MST); biological chemistry (MS); biology (MS); biology education (MST); biotechnology (MS); coastal zone studies (MS); environmental biology (MS); nursing (MSN); public health (MPH).

UNIVERSITY OF WEST GEORGIA, Carrollton, GA 30118

General Information State-supported, coed, comprehensive institution. CGS member. *Enrollment:* 12,834 graduate, professional, and undergraduate students; 615 full-time matriculated graduate/professional students (448 women), 1,332 part-time matriculated graduate/professional students (967 women). *Enrollment by degree level:* 1,391 master's, 173 doctoral, 383 other advanced degrees. *Graduate faculty:* 268 full-time (130 women). Tuition, state resident: full-time $5316; part-time $222 per semester hour. Tuition, nonresident: full-time $20,658; part-time $861 per semester hour. *Required fees:* $1962. Tuition and fees vary according to course load, degree level and program. *Graduate housing:* Rooms and/or apartments available on a first-come, first-served basis to single and married students. Housing application deadline: 6/1. *Student services:* Campus employment opportunities, campus safety program, career counseling, exercise/wellness program, free psychological counseling, international student services, multicultural affairs office, services for students with disabilities, teacher training, writing training. *Library:* Irvine Sullivan Ingram Library plus 1 other. Weekly public service hours: 137; study areas open 24 hours, 5–7 days a week; students can reserve study rooms.

Computer facilities: 1,200 computers available on campus for general student use. A campuswide network can be accessed from student residence rooms and from off campus. Online class registration is available.
Website: http://www.westga.edu/

General Application Contact: Dr. Toby Ziglar, Director for Graduate Studies and International Admissions, 678-839-1394, Fax: 648-839-1395, E-mail: graduate@westga.edu.

GRADUATE UNITS

College of Arts and Humanities Students: 21 full-time (12 women), 62 part-time (38 women); includes 13 minority (10 Black or African American, non-Hispanic/Latino; 3 Hispanic/Latino). Average age 33. 22 applicants, 91% accepted, 18 enrolled. *Faculty:* 72 full-time (39 women). *Financial support:* Fellowships, research assistantships, teaching assistantships, career-related internships or fieldwork, Federal Work-Study, institutionally sponsored loans, scholarships/grants, and unspecified assistantships available. Support available to part-time students. Financial award application deadline: 4/1; financial award applicants required to submit FAFSA. In 2015, 18 master's, 6 other advanced degrees awarded. *Degree program information:* Part-time and evening/weekend programs available. Part-time, evening/weekend, 100% online. Offers English (MA); history (MA); museum studies (Postbaccalaureate Certificate); music teacher education (M Mus); performance (M Mus); public history (Postbaccalaureate Certificate). *Application deadline:* For fall admission, 8/1 for domestic students, 6/1 for international students; for spring admission, 11/15 for domestic students, 10/15 for international students; for summer admission, 5/15 for domestic students, 3/30 for international students. Applications are processed on a rolling basis. *Application fee:* $40. Electronic applications accepted. *Application Contact:* Dr. Toby Ziglar, Director of Graduate Studies and International Admissions, 678-839-1394, Fax: 678-839-1395, E-mail: graduate@westga.edu. *Interim Dean*, Dr. Pauline D. Gagnon, 678-839-5450, Fax: 678-839-5451, E-mail: pgagnon@westga.edu.

College of Education Students: 352 full-time (280 women), 910 part-time (734 women); includes 444 minority (395 Black or African American, non-Hispanic/Latino; 1 American Indian or Alaska Native, non-Hispanic/Latino; 10 Asian, non-Hispanic/Latino; 29 Hispanic/Latino; 9 Two or more races, non-Hispanic/Latino), 11 international. Average age 34. 586 applicants, 81% accepted, 377 enrolled. *Faculty:* 41 full-time (27 women). *Financial support:* Fellowships, research assistantships, teaching assistantships, career-related internships or fieldwork, Federal Work-Study, institutionally sponsored loans, scholarships/grants, and unspecified assistantships available. Support available to part-time students. Financial award application deadline: 4/1; financial award applicants required to submit FAFSA. In 2015, 271 master's, 31 doctorates, 161 other advanced degrees awarded. *Degree program information:* Part-time and evening/weekend programs available. Part-time, evening/weekend, 100% online. Offers business education (M Ed); early childhood education (M Ed, Ed S); educational leadership (M Ed, Ed S); media (M Ed, Ed S); professional counseling (M Ed, Ed S); professional counseling and supervision (Ed D); reading instruction (M Ed); school improvement (Ed D); secondary education (M Ed); special education (M Ed, Ed S); speech language pathology (M Ed); teaching (MAT). *Application deadline:* For fall admission, 7/21 for domestic students, 6/1 for international students; for spring admission, 11/30 for domestic students, 10/15 for international students; for summer admission, 4/15 for domestic students, 3/30 for international students. Applications are processed on a rolling basis. *Application fee:* $40. Electronic applications accepted. *Application Contact:* Dr. Toby Ziglar, Director of Graduate Studies and International Admissions, 678-839-1394, Fax: 678-839-1395, E-mail: graduate@westga.edu. *Dean*, Dr. Diane Hoff, 678-839-6570, Fax: 678-839-6098, E-mail: dhoff@westga.edu.

College of Science and Mathematics Students: 20 full-time (8 women), 69 part-time (18 women); includes 15 minority (10 Black or African American, non-Hispanic/Latino; 2 Asian, non-Hispanic/Latino; 1 Hispanic/Latino; 1 Native Hawaiian or other Pacific Islander, non-Hispanic/Latino; 1 Two or more races, non-Hispanic/Latino), 9 international. Average age 35. 75 applicants, 88% accepted, 53 enrolled. *Faculty:* 54 full-time (19 women). *Financial support:* Fellowships, research assistantships, teaching assistantships, career-related internships or fieldwork, Federal Work-Study, institutionally sponsored loans, scholarships/grants, and unspecified assistantships available. Support available to part-time students. Financial award application deadline: 4/1; financial award applicants required to submit FAFSA. In 2015, 21 master's, 4 other advanced degrees awarded. *Degree program information:* Part-time and evening/weekend programs available. Part-time, evening/weekend, 100% online. Offers biology (MS); computer science (MS); geographic information systems (Postbaccalaureate Certificate); mathematics (MS). *Application deadline:* For fall admission, 6/1 for domestic and international students; for spring admission, 11/15 for domestic students, 10/15 for international students; for summer admission, 4/1 for domestic students, 3/30 for international students. Applications are processed on a rolling basis. *Application fee:* $40. Electronic applications accepted. *Application Contact:* Dr. Toby Ziglar, Director of Graduate Studies and International Admissions, 678-839-1394, Fax: 678-839-1395, E-mail: graduate@westga.edu. *Interim Dean*, Dr. Scott Gordon, 678-839-5190, Fax: 678-839-5191, E-mail: sgordon@westga.edu.

College of Social Sciences Students: 110 full-time (68 women), 65 part-time (36 women); includes 50 minority (38 Black or African American, non-Hispanic/Latino; 6 Asian, non-Hispanic/Latino; 4 Hispanic/Latino; 2 Two or more races, non-Hispanic/Latino), 5 international. Average age 32. 92 applicants, 78% accepted, 52 enrolled. *Faculty:* 49 full-time (19 women). *Financial support:* Fellowships, research assistantships, teaching assistantships, career-related internships or fieldwork, Federal Work-Study, institutionally sponsored loans, scholarships/grants, and unspecified assistantships available. Support available to part-time students. Financial award application deadline: 4/1; financial award applicants required to submit FAFSA. In 2015, 49 master's, 5 doctorates, 2 other advanced degrees awarded. *Degree program information:* Part-time and evening/weekend programs available. Part-time, evening/weekend, 100% online, blended/hybrid learning. Offers criminology (MA); data analysis and evaluation methods (Postbaccalaureate Certificate); European Union studies (Postbaccalaureate Certificate); integrative health systems (Postbaccalaureate Certificate); nonprofit management and community development (Postbaccalaureate

Certificate); psychology (MA, PhD); public administration (MPA); public management (Postbaccalaureate Certificate); sociology (MA). *Application deadline:* For fall admission, 7/15 for domestic students, 6/1 for international students; for spring admission, 11/30 for domestic students, 10/15 for international students; for summer admission, 5/15 for domestic students, 3/30 for international students. Applications are processed on a rolling basis. *Application fee:* $40. Electronic applications accepted. *Application Contact:* Dr. Toby Ziglar, Director of Graduate Studies and International Admissions, 678-839-1394, Fax: 678-839-1395, E-mail: graduate@westga.edu. *Dean*, Dr. N. Jane McCandless, 678-839-5170, Fax: 678-839-5171, E-mail: jmccandl@westga.edu.

Richards College of Business Students: 54 full-time (29 women), 157 part-time (80 women); includes 88 minority (61 Black or African American, non-Hispanic/Latino; 2 American Indian or Alaska Native, non-Hispanic/Latino; 10 Asian, non-Hispanic/Latino; 13 Hispanic/Latino; 2 Two or more races, non-Hispanic/Latino), 13 international. Average age 31. 123 applicants, 91% accepted, 87 enrolled. *Faculty:* 39 full-time (13 women). *Financial support:* Fellowships, research assistantships, teaching assistantships, career-related internships or fieldwork, Federal Work-Study, institutionally sponsored loans, scholarships/grants, and unspecified assistantships available. Support available to part-time students. Financial award application deadline: 4/1; financial award applicants required to submit FAFSA. In 2015, 87 master's awarded. *Degree program information:* Part-time and evening/weekend programs available. Part-time, evening/weekend, 100% online. Offers accounting (MP Acc); business administration (MBA). *Application deadline:* For fall admission, 7/15 for domestic students, 6/1 for international students; for spring admission, 11/15 for domestic students, 10/15 for international students; for summer admission, 5/15 for domestic students, 3/30 for international students. Applications are processed on a rolling basis. *Application fee:* $40. Electronic applications accepted. *Application Contact:* Dr. Toby Ziglar, Director of Graduate Studies and International Admissions, 678-839-1394, Fax: 678-839-1395, E-mail: graduate@westga.edu. *Dean*, Dr. Faye S. McIntyre, 678-839-6467, Fax: 678-839-5040, E-mail: fmcintyr@westga.edu.

Tanner Health System School of Nursing Students: 58 full-time (51 women), 69 part-time (61 women); includes 33 minority (29 Black or African American, non-Hispanic/Latino; 1 Asian, non-Hispanic/Latino; 3 Hispanic/Latino). Average age 42. 78 applicants, 90% accepted, 58 enrolled. *Faculty:* 13 full-time (all women). *Financial support:* Fellowships, research assistantships, teaching assistantships, career-related internships or fieldwork, Federal Work-Study, institutionally sponsored loans, scholarships/grants, and unspecified assistantships available. Support available to part-time students. Financial award application deadline: 4/1; financial award applicants required to submit FAFSA. In 2015, 32 master's, 1 other advanced degree awarded. *Degree program information:* Part-time and evening/weekend programs available. Part-time, evening/weekend, 100% online. Offers health systems leadership (Post-Master's Certificate); nursing (MSN); nursing education (Ed D, Post-Master's Certificate). *Application deadline:* For fall admission, 2/1 priority date for domestic and international students. Applications are processed on a rolling basis. *Application fee:* $40. Electronic applications accepted. *Application Contact:* Dr. Toby Ziglar, Director of Graduate and International Admissions, 678-839-1390, Fax: 678-839-1395, E-mail: graduate@westga.edu. *Dean*, Dr. Jennifer Schuessler, 678-839-5640, Fax: 678-839-6553, E-mail: jschuess@westga.edu.

UNIVERSITY OF WINDSOR, Windsor, ON N9B 3P4, Canada

General Information Province-supported, coed, university. *Graduate housing:* Rooms and/or apartments available on a first-come, first-served basis to single and married students. Housing application deadline: 6/7. *Research affiliation:* Daimler/Chrysler Automotive Research and Development Centre.

GRADUATE UNITS

Faculty of Graduate Studies ***Degree program information:*** Part-time and evening/weekend programs available. Part-time, evening/weekend. Electronic applications accepted.

Faculty of Arts and Social Sciences Degree program information: Part-time programs available. Part-time. Offers adult clinical (MA, PhD); applied social psychology (MA, PhD); arts and social sciences (MA, MFA, MSW, PhD); child clinical (MA, PhD); clinical neuropsychology (MA, PhD); communication and social justice (MA); criminology (MA); English: creative writing and language and literature (MA); English: language and literature (MA); history (MA); philosophy (MA); political science (MA); social work (MSW); sociology (MA); sociology-social justice (PhD); visual arts (MFA). Electronic applications accepted.

Faculty of Education Degree program information: Part-time and evening/weekend programs available. Part-time, evening/weekend. Offers education (M Ed); educational studies (PhD). Electronic applications accepted.

Faculty of Engineering Degree program information: Part-time programs available. Part-time. Offers civil engineering (M Eng, MA Sc, PhD); electrical engineering (M Eng, MA Sc, PhD); engineering (M Eng, MA Sc, PhD); engineering materials (M Eng, MA Sc, PhD); environmental engineering (M Eng, MA Sc, PhD); industrial engineering (M Eng, MA Sc); manufacturing systems engineering (PhD); mechanical engineering (M Eng, MA Sc, PhD). Electronic applications accepted.

Faculty of Human Kinetics Degree program information: Part-time programs available. Part-time. Offers human kinetics (MHK). Electronic applications accepted.

Faculty of Nursing Offers nursing (M Sc, MN). Electronic applications accepted.

Faculty of Science Degree program information: Part-time programs available. Part-time. Offers biological sciences (M Sc, PhD); chemistry and biochemistry (M Sc, PhD); computer science (M Sc, PhD); earth sciences (M Sc, PhD); economics (MA); mathematics (M Sc); physics (M Sc, PhD); science (M Sc, MA, PhD); statistics (M Sc, PhD). Electronic applications accepted.

GLIER-Great Lakes Institute for Environmental Research Offers environmental science (M Sc, PhD). Electronic applications accepted.

Odette School of Business Degree program information: Evening/weekend programs available. Evening/weekend. Offers business (MBA, MM). Electronic applications accepted.

THE UNIVERSITY OF WINNIPEG, Winnipeg, MB R3B 2E9, Canada

General Information Province-supported, coed, comprehensive institution. *Graduate housing:* On-campus housing not available.

GRADUATE UNITS

Faculty of Theology ***Degree program information:*** Part-time programs available. Part-time. Offers marriage and family therapy (MMFT, Certificate); sacred theology (STM); theology (M Div).

Graduate Studies ***Degree program information:*** Part-time and evening/weekend programs available. Part-time, evening/weekend. Offers history (MA); public administration (MPA); religious studies (MA).

UNIVERSITY OF WISCONSIN–EAU CLAIRE, Eau Claire, WI 54702-4004

General Information State-supported, coed, comprehensive institution. CGS member. *Graduate housing:* Room and/or apartments available on a first-come, first-served basis to single students; on-campus housing not available to married students. Housing application deadline: 5/1. *Research affiliation:* Geological Survey of Canada (geology), Chevron Phillips Chemical Company (chemistry), Excel Energy (geography), American Chemical Society Petroleum Research Fund (chemistry, geology), ASIANetwork (anthropology, biology, geography), Research Corporation (chemistry).

GRADUATE UNITS

College of Arts and Sciences Offers arts and sciences (MA, MSE, Ed S); literature and textual interpretation (MA); public history (MA); school psychology (MSE, Ed S); writing (MA). Electronic applications accepted.

College of Business Offers business (MBA); business administration (MBA). Electronic applications accepted.

College of Education and Human Sciences Offers communication sciences and disorders (MS); education and human sciences (ME-PD, MS, MSE, MST); professional development (ME-PD); reading (MST); special education (MSE). Electronic applications accepted.

College of Nursing and Health Sciences Offers adult-gerontological administration (DNP); adult-gerontological clinical nurse specialist (DNP); adult-gerontological education (MSN); adult-gerontological primary care nurse practitioner (DNP); family health administration (DNP); family health in education (MSN); family health nurse practitioner (DNP); nursing (MSN); nursing and health sciences (MSN, DNP); nursing practice (DNP). Electronic applications accepted.

UNIVERSITY OF WISCONSIN–GREEN BAY, Green Bay, WI 54311-7001

General Information State-supported, coed, comprehensive institution. *Enrollment:* 6,779 graduate, professional, and undergraduate students; 58 full-time matriculated graduate/professional students (41 women), 160 part-time matriculated graduate/professional students (112 women). *Enrollment by degree level:* 218 master's. *Graduate faculty:* 31 full-time (14 women), 7 part-time/adjunct (4 women). Tuition, state resident: full-time $7640; part-time $424 per credit hour. Tuition, nonresident: full-time $16,771; part-time $932 per credit hour. *Required fees:* $1526; $85 per credit hour. $85 per semester. Tuition and fees vary according to program and reciprocity agreements. *Graduate housing:* Room and/or apartments available on a first-come, first-served basis to single students; on-campus housing not available to married students. Typical cost: $4138 per year ($7270 including board). Room and board charges vary according to housing facility selected. Housing application deadline: 5/1. *Student services:* Campus employment opportunities, campus safety program, career counseling, free psychological counseling, international student services, low-cost health insurance, multicultural affairs office, services for students with disabilities, teacher training. *Library:* Cofrin Library. *Collection:* Books: 353,331 (physical); Serial titles: 7,592 (physical); Databases: 179. Weekly public service hours: 100; students can reserve study rooms. *Research affiliation:* Wisconsin Space Grant Consortium (space and aerospace science), UW Sea Grant Institute (Great Lakes and ocean sustainability and stewardship), UW System Applied Research Program (biogas generation), UW Extension Solid and Hazardous Waste Education Center (sustainable use of natural resources), Abbott Laboratories (anaerobic digestion systems).

Computer facilities: Computer purchase and lease plans are available. 550 computers available on campus for general student use. A campuswide network can be accessed from student residence rooms and from off campus. Online class registration, online degree progress, online financial records and bill paying are available.
Website: http://www.uwgb.edu/

General Application Contact: Mary Valitchka, Coordinator of Graduate Programs, 920-465-2123, Fax: 920-465-2043, E-mail: valitchm@uwgb.edu.

GRADUATE UNITS

Graduate Studies Students: 58 full-time (41 women), 160 part-time (112 women); includes 33 minority (4 Black or African American, non-Hispanic/Latino; 7 American Indian or Alaska Native, non-Hispanic/Latino; 9 Asian, non-Hispanic/Latino; 5 Hispanic/Latino; 8 Two or more races, non-Hispanic/Latino), 5 international. Average age 33. 213 applicants, 89% accepted, 140 enrolled. *Faculty:* 31 full-time (14 women), 7 part-time/adjunct (4 women). *Financial support:* In 2015–16, 21 students received support. Research assistantships, career-related internships or fieldwork, scholarships/grants, unspecified assistantships, and aid for veterans and their family members available. Support available to part-time students. Financial award application deadline: 7/15; financial award applicants required to submit FAFSA. In 2015, 59 master's awarded. *Degree program information:* Part-time and evening/weekend programs available. Part-time, evening/weekend, 100% online. Offers applied leadership for teaching and learning (MS Ed); environmental science and policy (MS); management (MS); nursing leadership and management in health systems (MSN); social work (MSW); sustainable management (MS). *Application deadline:* For fall admission, 8/1 for domestic students; for spring admission, 11/1 for domestic students. Applications are processed on a rolling basis. *Application fee:* $56. Electronic applications accepted. *Application Contact:* Mary Valitchka, Graduate Studies Coordinator, 920-465-2123, Fax: 920-465-5043, E-mail: valitchm@uwgb.edu. *Director of Graduate Studies*, Dr. Matthew Dornbush, 920-465-2033, Fax: 920-465-2043, E-mail: dornbusm@uwgb.edu.

UNIVERSITY OF WISCONSIN–LA CROSSE, La Crosse, WI 54601-3742

General Information State-supported, coed, comprehensive institution. CGS member. *Enrollment:* 10,387 graduate, professional, and undergraduate students; 446 full-time matriculated graduate/professional students (301 women), 285 part-time matriculated graduate/professional students (169 women). *Enrollment by degree level:* 598 master's, 133 doctoral. *Graduate housing:* Room and/or apartments available on a first-come, first-served basis to single students; on-campus housing not available to married students. Housing application deadline: 5/1. *Student services:* Campus employment opportunities, campus safety program, career counseling, child daycare facilities, exercise/wellness program, free psychological counseling, grant writing training, international student services, low-cost health insurance, multicultural affairs office, services for students with disabilities, teacher training, writing training. *Library:* Murphy Library plus 6 others. Weekly public service hours: 55; students can reserve study rooms.

Computer facilities: 200 computers available on campus for general student use. A campuswide network can be accessed from student residence rooms and from off campus. Online class registration is available.
Website: http://www.uwlax.edu/

General Application Contact: Brandon Schaller, Senior Graduate Student Status Examiner, 608-785-8941, E-mail: admissions@uwlax.edu.

GRADUATE UNITS

College of Business Administration Students: 12 full-time (5 women), 27 part-time (9 women); includes 1 minority (Asian, non-Hispanic/Latino), 8 international. Average age 30. 21 applicants, 95% accepted, 14 enrolled. *Financial support:* Research assistantships with partial tuition reimbursements, Federal Work-Study, scholarships/grants, health care benefits, and tuition waivers (partial) available. Support available to part-time students. Financial award application deadline: 3/15; financial award applicants required to submit FAFSA. In 2015, 29 master's awarded. *Degree program information:* Part-time and evening/weekend programs available. Part-time, evening/weekend. Offers business administration (MBA). *Application deadline:* For fall admission, 6/15 priority date for domestic and international students; for spring admission, 11/15 priority date for domestic and international students. Applications are processed on a rolling basis. Electronic applications accepted. *Application Contact:* Brandon Schaller, Senior Graduate Student Status Examiner, 608-785-8941, Fax: 608-785-6700, E-mail: mskobic@uwlax.edu. *Dean*, Dr. Bruce May, 608-785-8095, Fax: 608-785-6700, E-mail: may.bruce@uwlax.edu.

College of Liberal Studies Students: 73 full-time (59 women), 46 part-time (35 women); includes 20 minority (2 Black or African American, non-Hispanic/Latino; 2 American Indian or Alaska Native, non-Hispanic/Latino; 5 Asian, non-Hispanic/Latino; 7 Hispanic/Latino; 4 Two or more races, non-Hispanic/Latino). Average age 25. *Financial support:* Research assistantships with partial tuition reimbursements, Federal Work-Study, scholarships/grants, health care benefits, and tuition waivers (partial) available. Support available to part-time students. Financial award applicants required to submit FAFSA. Offers liberal studies (MS Ed, Ed D, Ed S); school psychology (MS Ed, Ed S); student affairs administration (MS Ed, Ed D). *Application fee:* $56. Electronic applications accepted. *Application Contact:* Brandon Schaller, Senior Graduate Student Status Examiner, 608-785-8941, E-mail: admissions@uwlax.edu. *Dean*, Dr. Julia Johnson, 608-785-8113, Fax: 608-785-8119, E-mail: jjohnson2@uwlax.edu.

College of Science and Health Students: 351 full-time (241 women), 161 part-time (94 women); includes 31 minority (3 Black or African American, non-Hispanic/Latino; 15 Asian, non-Hispanic/Latino; 7 Hispanic/Latino; 6 Two or more races, non-Hispanic/Latino), 31 international. Average age 26. *Financial support:* Research assistantships with tuition reimbursements, Federal Work-Study, scholarships/grants, health care benefits, and tuition waivers (partial) available. Support available to part-time students. Financial award applicants required to submit CSS PROFILE or FAFSA. Offers adapted physical education (MS); adventure education (MS); applied sport science (MS); aquatic sciences (MS); biology (MS); cellular and molecular biology (MS); clinical exercise physiology (MS); clinical microbiology (MS); community health education (MPH, MS); data science (MS); human performance (MS); medical dosimetry (MS); microbiology (MS); nurse anesthesia (MS); occupational therapy (MS); physical education teaching (MS); physical therapy (DPT); physician assistant studies (MS); physiology (MS); recreation management (MS); school health education (MS); science and health (MPH, MS, MSE, DPT); software engineering (MSE); strength and conditioning (MS); therapeutic recreation (MS). *Application fee:* $56. Electronic applications accepted. *Application Contact:* Brandon Schaller, Senior Graduate Student Status Examiner, 608-785-8941, E-mail: admissions@uwlax.edu. *Dean*, Dr. Bruce Riley, 608-785-8218, Fax: 608-785-8221, E-mail: riley.bruc@uwlax.edu.

School of Education Students: 74 part-time (61 women), 1 international. Average age 34. 37 applicants, 100% accepted, 26 enrolled. *Financial support:* Research assistantships, Federal Work-Study, scholarships/grants, health care benefits, and tuition waivers (partial) available. Support available to part-time students. Financial award application deadline: 3/15; financial award applicants required to submit FAFSA. In 2015, 39 master's awarded. *Degree program information:* Part-time and evening/weekend programs available. Part-time, evening/weekend. Offers professional development (ME-PD); reading (MS Ed); special education (MS Ed). *Application deadline:* Applications are processed on a rolling basis. Electronic applications accepted. *Application Contact:* Brandon Schaller, Senior Graduate Student Status Examiner, 608-785-8941, E-mail: admissions@uwlax.edu. *Dean, School of Education*, Marcie Wycoff-Horn, 608-785-6786, E-mail: mwycoff-horn@uwlax.edu.

UNIVERSITY OF WISCONSIN–MADISON, Madison, WI 53706-1380

General Information State-supported, coed, university. CGS member. *Enrollment:* 43,389 graduate, professional, and undergraduate students; 10,221 full-time matriculated graduate/professional students (5,055 women), 1,502 part-time matriculated graduate/professional students (838 women). *Enrollment by degree level:* 3,861 master's, 7,856 doctoral, 6 other advanced degrees. *Graduate faculty:* 3,749 full-time (1,236 women), 22 part-time/adjunct (6 women). Tuition, state resident: full-time $5364. Tuition, nonresident: full-time $12,027. *Required fees:* $571. Tuition and fees vary according to campus/location, program and reciprocity agreements. *Graduate housing:* Rooms and/or apartments available on a first-come, first-served basis to single and married students. Typical cost: $7920 per year ($11,420 including board) for single students. Room and board charges vary according to board plan and housing facility selected. *Student services:* Campus employment opportunities, campus safety program, career counseling, child daycare facilities, exercise/wellness program, free psychological counseling, grant writing training, international student services, low-cost health insurance, multicultural affairs office, services for students with disabilities, teacher training, writing training. *Library:* Memorial Library plus 40 others. Study areas open 24 hours, 5–7 days a week; students can reserve study rooms. *Research affiliation:* Morgridge Institute for Research (life sciences: biological sciences), WiCell Research Institute (life sciences: biological sciences), University of Wisconsin Hospitals and Clinics (life sciences: health and medical sciences), William S. Middleton Memorial Veterans Hospital (life sciences: health and medical sciences), Universities Research Association, Inc. (physical and earth sciences: physics and astronomy), U.S. Department of Agriculture (USDA), Dairy Forage Center (life sciences: agriculture).

Computer facilities: 1,000 computers available on campus for general student use. A campuswide network can be accessed from student residence rooms and from off campus. Online class registration is available.
Website: http://www.wisc.edu/

General Application Contact: Information Contact, 608-262-2433, Fax: 608-265-6742, E-mail: gradadmiss@grad.wisc.edu.

GRADUATE UNITS

Graduate School Students: 7,824 full-time (3,674 women), 1,413 part-time (782 women); includes 1,228 minority (226 Black or African American, non-Hispanic/Latino; 26 American Indian or Alaska Native, non-Hispanic/Latino; 345 Asian, non-Hispanic/Latino; 450 Hispanic/Latino; 5 Native Hawaiian or other Pacific Islander, non-Hispanic/Latino; 176 Two or more races, non-Hispanic/Latino), 2,655 international. Average age 29. 18,200 applicants, 28% accepted, 2208 enrolled. *Faculty:* 3,749 full-time (1,236 women), 22 part-time/adjunct (6 women). *Financial support:* In 2015–16, 5,867 students received support, including 288 fellowships with full tuition reimbursements available (averaging $19,710 per year), 2,108 research assistantships with full tuition reimbursements available (averaging $21,648 per year), 2,007 teaching assistantships with full tuition reimbursements available (averaging $15,342 per year); career-related internships or fieldwork, Federal Work-Study, institutionally sponsored loans, scholarships/grants, traineeships, health care benefits, and unspecified assistantships also available. Support available to part-time students. Financial award applicants required to submit FAFSA. In 2015, 1,986 master's, 876 doctorates awarded. *Degree program information:* Part-time and evening/weekend programs available. Part-time, evening/weekend, 100% online, blended/hybrid learning. Offers biophysics (PhD); cellular and molecular biology (PhD). *Application deadline:* Applications are processed on a rolling basis. *Application fee:* $56 ($62 for international students). Electronic applications accepted. *Application Contact:* Graduate School Reception, 608-262-2433, Fax: 608-265-6742, E-mail: gradadmiss@grad.wisc.edu. *Dean, Graduate School*, Dr. William Karpus, 608-262-2433, Fax: 608-265-6742, E-mail: gsdean@grad.wisc.edu.

College of Agricultural and Life Sciences Degree program information: Part-time programs available. Part-time. Offers agricultural and applied economics (MA, MS, PhD); agricultural and life sciences (MA, MPS, MS, PhD); agroecology (MS); agronomy (MS, PhD); animal sciences (MS, PhD); bacteriology (MS); biochemistry (PhD); biological systems engineering (MS, PhD); dairy science (MS, PhD); entomology (MS, PhD); food science (MS, PhD); forestry (MS, PhD); genetic counseling (MS); genetics (PhD); horticulture (MS, PhD); landscape architecture (MA, MS); life sciences communication (MPS, MS); mass communications (PhD); nutritional sciences (MS, PhD); plant breeding and plant genetics (MS, PhD); plant pathology (MS, PhD); soil science (MS, PhD); wildlife ecology (MS, PhD). Electronic applications accepted.

College of Engineering Students: 1,136 full-time (265 women), 339 part-time (48 women); includes 165 minority (22 Black or African American, non-Hispanic/Latino; 5 American Indian or Alaska Native, non-Hispanic/Latino; 50 Asian, non-Hispanic/Latino; 70 Hispanic/Latino; 1 Native Hawaiian or other Pacific Islander, non-Hispanic/Latino; 17 Two or more races, non-Hispanic/Latino), 680 international. Average age 27. 4,489 applicants, 18% accepted, 280 enrolled. *Faculty:* 192 full-time (36 women). *Financial support:* In 2015–16, 964 students received support, including 52 fellowships with full tuition reimbursements available (averaging $27,325 per year), 679 research assistantships with full tuition reimbursements available (averaging $22,035 per year), 168 teaching assistantships with full tuition reimbursements available (averaging $12,343 per year); career-related internships or fieldwork, Federal Work-Study, institutionally sponsored loans, scholarships/grants, and unspecified assistantships also available. Support available to part-time students. In 2015, 441 master's, 160 doctorates awarded. *Degree program information:* Part-time programs available. Part-time, online learning. Offers biomedical engineering (MS, PhD); chemical engineering (MS, PhD); civil and environmental engineering (MS, PhD); electrical engineering (MS, PhD); engineering (ME, MS, PhD); engineering mechanics (MS, PhD); environmental chemistry and technology (MS, PhD); geological engineering (MS, PhD); industrial and systems engineering (MS, PhD); manufacturing systems engineering (MS); materials science and engineering (MS, PhD); mechanical engineering (MS, PhD); nuclear engineering and engineering physics (MS, PhD); polymers (ME). *Application deadline:* Applications are processed on a rolling basis. *Application fee:* $56 ($62 for international students). Electronic applications accepted. *Application Contact:* Information Contact, 608-262-2433, Fax: 608-265-9505, E-mail: gradadmiss@grad.wisc.edu. *Dean*, Paul S. Peercy, 608-262-3482, Fax: 608-262-6400, E-mail: engr-dean_engr@wisc.edu.

College of Letters and Science Degree program information: Part-time and evening/weekend programs available. Part-time, evening/weekend, online learning. Offers African history (MA, PhD); African languages and literature (MA, PhD); Afro-American studies (MA); applied English linguistics (MA); archaeology (PhD); area studies (MA); art history (MA, PhD); astronomy (PhD); atmospheric and oceanic sciences (MS, PhD); biological anthropology (PhD); biology of brain and behavior (PhD); biometry (MS); botany (MS, PhD); cartography and geographic information systems (MS); Central Asian history (MA, PhD); chemistry (MS, PhD); Chinese literature (MA, PhD); Chinese thought (MA, PhD); choral (MM, DMA); civilizations and cultures (PhD); classics (MA, PhD); clinical psychology (PhD); cognitive neurosciences (PhD); communication science (MA, PhD); comparative literature (MA, PhD); comparative world history (MA, PhD); composition (MM, DMA); composition and rhetoric (PhD); computer sciences (MS, PhD); creative writing (MFA); cultural anthropology (PhD); curriculum and instruction (MS, PhD); developmental psychology (PhD); East Asian history (MA, PhD); economics (PhD); English language and linguistics (PhD); ethnomusicology (MA, PhD); European history (MA, PhD); family and consumer journalism (PhD); film (MA, PhD); folklore (PhD); French (MA, PhD); French studies (MFS, Certificate); gender and women's history (MA, PhD); geographic information systems (Certificate); geography (MS, PhD); geology (MS, PhD); geophysics (MS, PhD); German (MA, PhD); Greek (MA); Hebrew and Semitic studies (MA, PhD); historical musicology (PhD); history of medicine (MA); history of science (MA, PhD); instrumental (MM, DMA); Italian (MA, PhD); Japanese linguistics (MA, PhD); Japanese literature (MA, PhD); journalism and mass communication (MA); languages and cultures of Asia (MA); languages and literatures (PhD); Latin (MA); Latin American and Caribbean history (MA, PhD); Latin American, Caribbean and Iberian studies (MA); letters and science (MA, MFA, MFS, MIPA, MM, MPA, MS, MSW, DMA, PhD, Certificate); library and information studies (MA, PhD); linguistics (MA, PhD); literary studies (MA, PhD); literature (MA, PhD); mass communication (PhD); mathematics (PhD); media and cultural studies (MA, PhD); Middle Eastern history (MA, PhD); music (MA, MM, DMA, PhD); music education (MM); music history (MA); music performance (MM, DMA); music theory (MA, PhD); normal aspects of speech, language and hearing (MS, PhD); orchestral (MM, DMA); perception (PhD); philology (PhD); philosophy (MA, PhD); physics (MA, MS, PhD); political science (PhD); Portuguese (MA, PhD); psychology (PhD); public policy and administration (MIPA, MPA); religions of Asia (PhD); rhetoric (MA, PhD); rural sociology (MS); Slavic languages and literature (MA, PhD); social and personality psychology (PhD); social welfare (PhD); social work (MSW); sociology (MS, PhD); South Asian history (MA, PhD); Southeast Asian history (MA, PhD); Southeast Asian studies (MA); Spanish (MA, PhD); speech-language pathology (MS, PhD); statistics (MS, PhD); theatre and drama (MA, MFA, PhD); United States history (MA, PhD); urban and regional planning (MS, PhD); zoology (MA, MS, PhD). Electronic applications accepted.

Gaylord Nelson Institute for Environmental Studies Degree program information: Part-time programs available. Part-time. Offers environment and resources (MS, PhD); environmental conservation (MS); environmental studies (MS, PhD); water resources management (MS). Electronic applications accepted.

School of Education Offers administration (Certificate); art (MA, MFA); art education (MA); counseling (MS); counseling psychology (MS, PhD); curriculum and instruction

(MS, PhD); education (MA, MFA, MS, PhD, Certificate); education and mathematics (MA); educational policy (MS, PhD); educational policy studies (MA, PhD); educational psychology (MS, PhD); French education (MA); German education (MA); global higher education (MS); kinesiology (MS, PhD); music education (MS); occupational therapy (MS, PhD); rehabilitation psychology (MA, MS, PhD); science education (MS); Spanish education (MA); special education (MA, MS, PhD).

School of Human Ecology Offers consumer behavior and family economics (MS, PhD); design studies (MFA, MS, PhD); human development and family studies (MS, PhD). Electronic applications accepted.

Wisconsin School of Business Students: 458 full-time (185 women), 165 part-time (52 women); includes 90 minority (22 Black or African American, non-Hispanic/Latino; 1 American Indian or Alaska Native, non-Hispanic/Latino; 41 Asian, non-Hispanic/Latino; 24 Hispanic/Latino; 1 Native Hawaiian or other Pacific Islander, non-Hispanic/Latino; 1 Two or more races, non-Hispanic/Latino), 131 international. Average age 30. 1,414 applicants, 30% accepted, 320 enrolled. *Faculty:* 68 full-time (12 women), 47 part-time/adjunct (21 women). *Financial support:* Fellowships with full tuition reimbursements, research assistantships with full tuition reimbursements, teaching assistantships with full tuition reimbursements, career-related internships or fieldwork, Federal Work-Study, institutionally sponsored loans, scholarships/grants, health care benefits, and unspecified assistantships available. Support available to part-time students. Financial award application deadline: 7/1; financial award applicants required to submit FAFSA. In 2015, 219 master's, 8 doctorates awarded. *Degree program information:* Part-time and evening/weekend programs available. Part-time, evening/weekend. Offers accountancy (M Acc); accounting and information systems (PhD); actuarial science, risk management and insurance (PhD); applied security analysis (MBA); arts administration (MBA); brand and product management (MBA); business (M Acc, MBA, PhD); corporate finance and investment banking (MBA); finance, investment and banking (PhD); general management (MBA); information systems (PhD); management and human resources (PhD); marketing (PhD); marketing research (MBA); operations and technology management (MBA); operations management (PhD); real estate (MBA); real estate and urban land economics (PhD); risk management and insurance (MBA); strategic human resource management (MBA); supply chain management (MBA); taxation (M Acc). *Application deadline:* Applications are processed on a rolling basis. *Application fee:* $56 ($62 for international students). Electronic applications accepted. *Application Contact:* Betsy Kacizak, Director of MBA Admissions and Recruitment, 608-262-4000, Fax: 608-265-9505, E-mail: gradadmiss@grad.wisc.edu. *Senior Associate Dean for Academic Programs,* Elizabeth W. Odders-White, 608-263-1254, Fax: 608-265-4192, E-mail: elizabeth.odderswhite@wisc.edu.

Law School Students: 585 full-time (291 women), 27 part-time (11 women); includes 117 minority (32 Black or African American, non-Hispanic/Latino; 1 American Indian or Alaska Native, non-Hispanic/Latino; 16 Asian, non-Hispanic/Latino; 47 Hispanic/Latino; 21 Two or more races, non-Hispanic/Latino), 85 international. Average age 24. 1,412 applicants, 52% accepted, 225 enrolled. *Faculty:* 62 full-time (35 women), 40 part-time/adjunct (13 women). *Financial support:* In 2015–16, 470 students received support. Fellowships with partial tuition reimbursements available, research assistantships with full tuition reimbursements available, career-related internships or fieldwork, Federal Work-Study, institutionally sponsored loans, scholarships/grants, health care benefits, tuition waivers (partial), and unspecified assistantships available. Support available to part-time students. Financial award application deadline: 4/1; financial award applicants required to submit FAFSA. In 2015, 43 master's, 223 doctorates awarded. *Degree program information:* Part-time programs available. Part-time. Offers law (LL M, JD, SJD). *Application deadline:* For fall admission, 4/1 for domestic students, 3/1 for international students. Applications are processed on a rolling basis. *Application fee:* $56. Electronic applications accepted. *Application Contact:* Rebecca L. Scheller, Assistant Dean for Admissions and Financial Aid, 608-262-5914, Fax: 608-263-3190, E-mail: admissions@law.wisc.edu. *Dean,* Margaret Raymond, 608-262-0618, Fax: 608-262-5485.

School of Medicine and Public Health ***Degree program information:*** Part-time programs available. Part-time, online learning. Offers biochemistry (MS, PhD); biomedical informatics (MS); cancer biology (PhD); cellular and molecular pathology (PhD); clinical investigation (MS, PhD); endocrinology-reproductive physiology (MS, PhD); epidemiology (MS, PhD); genetic counselor studies (MGCS); health physics (MS); medical physics (MS, PhD); medicine (MD); medicine and public health (MGCS, MPA, MPH, MS, DPT, MD, PhD); microbiology (PhD); molecular and cellular pharmacology (PhD); molecular and environmental toxicology (MS, PhD); neuroscience (PhD); physical therapy (DPT); physician assistant (MPA); physiology (PhD); population health (MS, PhD); public health (MPH). Electronic applications accepted. *Dean,* Dr. Robert N. Golden.

School of Nursing ***Degree program information:*** Part-time programs available. Part-time. Offers adult/gerontology (DNP); nursing (PhD); pediatrics (DNP); psychiatric mental health (DNP). Electronic applications accepted.

School of Pharmacy Offers pharmaceutical sciences (PhD); pharmacy (MS, PhD, Pharm D); social and administrative sciences in pharmacy (MS, PhD). Electronic applications accepted.

School of Veterinary Medicine Offers veterinary medicine (MS, DVM, PhD).

UNIVERSITY OF WISCONSIN–MILWAUKEE, Milwaukee, WI 53201-0413

General Information State-supported, coed, university. CGS member. *Enrollment:* 27,109 graduate, professional, and undergraduate students; 2,659 full-time matriculated graduate/professional students (1,538 women), 1,898 part-time matriculated graduate/professional students (1,149 women). *Enrollment by degree level:* 3,026 master's, 1,414 doctoral, 117 other advanced degrees. *Graduate housing:* Rooms and/or apartments available on a first-come, first-served basis to single and married students. Typical cost: $6200 (including board) for single students. Housing application deadline: 5/1. *Student services:* Campus employment opportunities, campus safety program, career counseling, child daycare facilities, exercise/wellness program, free psychological counseling, grant writing training, international student services, low-cost health insurance, multicultural affairs office, services for students with disabilities, writing training. *Library:* Golda Meir Library. *Collection:* Books: 2.5 million (physical), 178,268 (digital/electronic); Serial titles: 112,752 (physical). Students can reserve study rooms. *Research affiliation:* Rockwell Automation (informatics, sensors and devices, materials), Johnson Controls (environment, advanced automation), GE Healthcare (informatics, biomedical imaging), Veolia Water S. A. (water research), We Energies (environment, wind turbine technology).

Computer facilities: Computer purchase and lease plans are available. 500 computers available on campus for general student use. A campuswide network can be accessed from student residence rooms and from off campus. Online class registration is available.
Website: http://www.uwm.edu/

General Application Contact: General Information Contact, 414-229-4982, Fax: 414-229-6967, E-mail: gradschool@uwm.edu.

GRADUATE UNITS

Graduate School Students: 2,626 full-time (1,517 women), 1,889 part-time (1,129 women); includes 670 minority (215 Black or African American, non-Hispanic/Latino; 9 American Indian or Alaska Native, non-Hispanic/Latino; 157 Asian, non-Hispanic/Latino; 47 Hispanic/Latino; 3 Native Hawaiian or other Pacific Islander, non-Hispanic/Latino; 239 Two or more races, non-Hispanic/Latino), 720 international. Average age 31. 4,653 applicants, 46% accepted, 1300 enrolled. *Financial support:* Fellowships with partial tuition reimbursements, research assistantships with full tuition reimbursements, teaching assistantships with full tuition reimbursements, career-related internships or fieldwork, Federal Work-Study, scholarships/grants, health care benefits, tuition waivers (partial), and unspecified assistantships available. Support available to part-time students. Financial award application deadline: 6/30; financial award applicants required to submit FAFSA. In 2015, 1,229 master's, 215 doctorates, 53 other advanced degrees awarded. *Degree program information:* Part-time and evening/weekend programs available. Part-time, evening/weekend. *Application deadline:* For fall admission, 1/1 for domestic students, 3/1 for international students; for spring admission, 9/1 for domestic students, 8/1 for international students. Applications are processed on a rolling basis. *Application fee:* $56 ($96 for international students). Electronic applications accepted. *Application Contact:* General Information Contact, 414-229-6569, Fax: 414-229-6967, E-mail: gradschool@uwm.edu. *Dean,* Marija Gajdardziska-Josifovska, 414-229-5220, E-mail: mgj@uwm.edu.

College of Engineering and Applied Science Students: 241 full-time (61 women), 195 part-time (52 women); includes 11 minority (2 Black or African American, non-Hispanic/Latino; 5 Asian, non-Hispanic/Latino; 1 Hispanic/Latino; 3 Two or more races, non-Hispanic/Latino), 187 international. Average age 30. 546 applicants, 54% accepted, 112 enrolled. *Financial support:* In 2015–16, 31 research assistantships, 82 teaching assistantships were awarded; fellowships, career-related internships or fieldwork, Federal Work-Study, and unspecified assistantships also available. Support available to part-time students. Financial award application deadline: 4/15. In 2015, 87 master's, 18 doctorates, 3 other advanced degrees awarded. *Degree program information:* Part-time programs available. Part-time. Offers advanced computational imaging (Graduate Certificate); biomedical and health informatics (PhD); civil engineering (MS); computer science (MS); electrical and computer engineering (MS); energy engineering (Certificate); engineering (PhD); engineering and applied science (MS, PhD, Certificate, Graduate Certificate); engineering management (MS); engineering mechanics (MS); ergonomics (Certificate); industrial and management engineering (MS); manufacturing engineering (MS); materials engineering (MS); mechanical engineering (MS). *Application deadline:* For fall admission, 1/1 for domestic students; for spring admission, 9/1 for domestic students. Applications are processed on a rolling basis. *Application fee:* $56 ($96 for international students). Electronic applications accepted. *Application Contact:* Betty Warras, General Information Contact, 414-229-6169, Fax: 414-229-6958, E-mail: ceas-graduate@uwm.edu. *Dean,* Dr. Brett Peters, 414-229-4126, E-mail: ceas-deans-office@uwm.edu.

College of Health Sciences Students: 265 full-time (201 women), 44 part-time (26 women); includes 27 minority (2 Black or African American, non-Hispanic/Latino; 13 Asian, non-Hispanic/Latino; 1 Native Hawaiian or other Pacific Islander, non-Hispanic/Latino; 11 Two or more races, non-Hispanic/Latino), 26 international. Average age 28. 244 applicants, 40% accepted, 82 enrolled. *Financial support:* Research assistantships, teaching assistantships, career-related internships or fieldwork, Federal Work-Study, and unspecified assistantships available. Support available to part-time students. Financial award application deadline: 3/30. In 2015, 85 master's, 24 doctorates, 5 other advanced degrees awarded. *Degree program information:* Part-time programs available. Part-time. Offers assistive technology and accessible design (Graduate Certificate); cancer (MS); communication sciences and disorders (MS); health sciences (PhD); healthcare informatics (MS); immunology (MS); kinesiology (MS, PhD); microbiology (MS); neurodegenerative disease (MS); occupational therapy (MS); pharmacology and toxicology (MS); photobiomodulation (MS); physical therapy (DPT); therapeutic recreation (Graduate Certificate). *Application deadline:* For fall admission, 1/1 priority date for domestic students; for spring admission, 9/1 for domestic students. Applications are processed on a rolling basis. *Application fee:* $56 ($96 for international students). *Application Contact:* Roger O. Smith, General Information Contact, 414-229-6697, Fax: 414-229-6697, E-mail: smithro@uwm.edu. *Interim Dean,* Paula M. Rhyner, PhD, 414-229-4878, E-mail: prhyner@uwm.edu.

College of Letters and Science Students: 725 full-time (362 women), 388 part-time (221 women); includes 132 minority (42 Black or African American, non-Hispanic/Latino; 27 Asian, non-Hispanic/Latino; 12 Hispanic/Latino; 51 Two or more races, non-Hispanic/Latino), 226 international. Average age 32. 1,650 applicants, 30% accepted, 254 enrolled. *Financial support:* Fellowships, research assistantships, teaching assistantships, career-related internships or fieldwork, Federal Work-Study, unspecified assistantships, and project assistantships available. Support available to part-time students. Financial award application deadline: 4/15. In 2015, 212 master's, 95 doctorates, 16 other advanced degrees awarded. *Degree program information:* Part-time programs available. Part-time. Offers Africology (PhD); American Indian studies (MLS); anthropology (PhD); archaeology (MS); art history (MA); art museum studies (Certificate); biological anthropology (MS); biological sciences (MS, PhD); chemistry (MS, PhD); classic Greek (MA); classics (MA); clinical psychology (MS, PhD); communication (MA, PhD); comparative literature (MA); creative writing (PhD); development (PhD); econometrics (PhD); economics (MA); English (MA); ethnic studies (MLS); foreign language and literature (MA); French (MA); geography (MA, MS, PhD); geological sciences (MS, PhD); German (MA); global history (PhD); history (MA); industrial organization (PhD); international economics (PhD); international technical communication (Certificate); labor economics (PhD); Latin (MA); letters and science (MA, MAFLL, MHRLR, MLS, MPA, MS, PhD, Certificate, Graduate Certificate); linguistics (MA, PhD); mathematics (MS, PhD); media studies (MA); mediation and negotiation (Certificate); modern studies (PhD); monetary theory and policy (PhD); museum studies (Certificate); organizational administration (MLS); philosophy (MA); physics (MS, PhD); political science (MA, PhD); professional writing (PhD); professional writing and communication (Certificate); psychology (MS, PhD); rhetoric and composition (PhD); rhetorical leadership (Certificate); sociology (MA, PhD); Spanish (MA); TESOL (Graduate Certificate); translation (MA, Certificate); urban history (PhD); urban studies (MS, PhD); women's studies (MA, Certificate). *Application deadline:* For fall admission, 1/1 priority date for domestic students; for spring admission, 9/1 for domestic students. Applications are processed on a rolling basis. *Application fee:* $56 ($96 for international students). *Application Contact:* General Information Contact, 414-229-4982, Fax: 414-229-6967, E-mail: gradschool@uwm.edu. *Dean,* Rodney A. Swain, 414-229-5895, E-mail: rswain@uwm.edu.

College of Nursing Students: 168 full-time (144 women), 126 part-time (115 women); includes 47 minority (16 Black or African American, non-Hispanic/Latino; 16 Asian, non-Hispanic/Latino; 3 Hispanic/Latino; 12 Two or more races, non-Hispanic/Latino), 12 international. Average age 36. 146 applicants, 64% accepted, 59 enrolled. *Financial support:* Fellowships, research assistantships, teaching assistantships, career-related internships or fieldwork, Federal Work-Study, health care benefits, unspecified assistantships, and project assistantships available. Support available to part-time students. Financial award application deadline: 4/15; financial award applicants required to submit FAFSA. In 2015, 22 master's, 28 doctorates, 15 other advanced degrees awarded. *Degree program information:* Part-time programs available. Part-time. Offers clinical nurse specialist (Certificate); family nurse practitioner (Certificate); nursing (MN, MS, PhD); nursing practice (DNP). *Application deadline:* For fall admission, 1/1 priority date for domestic students; for spring admission, 9/1 for domestic students. Applications are processed on a rolling basis. *Application fee:* $56 ($96 for international students). Electronic applications accepted. *Application Contact:* Kim Litwack, Representative, 414-229-5098. *Dean,* Dr. Sally Lundeen, 414-229-4189, E-mail: slundeen@uwm.edu.

Peck School of the Arts Students: 100 full-time (51 women), 15 part-time (11 women); includes 11 minority (3 Black or African American, non-Hispanic/Latino; 1 American Indian or Alaska Native, non-Hispanic/Latino; 1 Asian, non-Hispanic/Latino; 6 Two or more races, non-Hispanic/Latino), 16 international. Average age 31. 147 applicants, 38% accepted, 36 enrolled. *Financial support:* Teaching assistantships, career-related internships or fieldwork, Federal Work-Study, health care benefits, unspecified assistantships, and project assistantships available. Support available to part-time students. Financial award application deadline: 4/15; financial award applicants required to submit FAFSA. In 2015, 66 master's awarded. *Degree program information:* Part-time programs available. Part-time. Offers arts (MA, MFA, MM, MS, Certificate). *Application deadline:* For fall admission, 1/1 priority date for domestic students; for spring admission, 9/1 for domestic students. Applications are processed on a rolling basis. *Application fee:* $56 ($96 for international students). Electronic applications accepted. *Application Contact:* General Information Contact, 414-229-4982, Fax: 414-229-6967, E-mail: gradschool@uwm.edu. *Dean,* Scott Emmons, 414-229-4762, E-mail: semm@uwm.edu.

School of Architecture and Urban Planning Students: 164 full-time (66 women), 20 part-time (4 women); includes 26 minority (5 Black or African American, non-Hispanic/Latino; 1 American Indian or Alaska Native, non-Hispanic/Latino; 5 Asian, non-Hispanic/Latino; 5 Hispanic/Latino; 10 Two or more races, non-Hispanic/Latino), 27 international. Average age 29. 175 applicants, 67% accepted, 62 enrolled. *Financial support:* Fellowships, research assistantships, teaching assistantships, career-related internships or fieldwork, Federal Work-Study, health care benefits, unspecified assistantships, and project assistantships available. Support available to part-time students. Financial award application deadline: 4/15; financial award applicants required to submit FAFSA. In 2015, 76 master's, 3 doctorates, 13 other advanced degrees awarded. *Degree program information:* Part-time programs available. Part-time. Offers architecture (PhD); architecture and urban planning (M Arch, MUP, PhD, Certificate); geographic information systems (Certificate); preservation studies (Certificate); real estate development (Certificate); urban planning (MUP). *Application deadline:* For fall admission, 1/1 priority date for domestic students; for spring admission, 9/1 for domestic students. Applications are processed on a rolling basis. *Application fee:* $56 ($96 for international students). Electronic applications accepted. *Application Contact:* Joan Simuncak, Senior Administrative Program Specialist, 414-229-4015, Fax: 414-229-6967, E-mail: joanarch@uwm.edu. *Dean,* Robert Greenstreet, 414-229-4016, E-mail: bobg@uwm.edu.

School of Education Students: 266 full-time (196 women), 388 part-time (287 women); includes 182 minority (67 Black or African American, non-Hispanic/Latino; 5 American Indian or Alaska Native, non-Hispanic/Latino; 18 Asian, non-Hispanic/Latino; 18 Hispanic/Latino; 74 Two or more races, non-Hispanic/Latino), 20 international. Average age 34. 425 applicants, 55% accepted, 152 enrolled. *Financial support:* Fellowships, teaching assistantships, career-related internships or fieldwork, Federal Work-Study, health care benefits, unspecified assistantships, and project assistantships available. Support available to part-time students. Financial award application deadline: 4/15; financial award applicants required to submit FAFSA. In 2015, 166 master's, 18 doctorates, 34 other advanced degrees awarded. *Degree program information:* Part-time programs available. Part-time. Offers administrative leadership and supervision in education (MS); adult, continuing and higher education leadership (PhD); assistive technology and accessible design (Certificate); counseling psychology (PhD); cultural foundations of education (MS); curriculum and instruction (PhD); curriculum planning and instruction improvement (MS); early childhood education (MS); education (MS, PhD, Certificate, Ed S); educational administration (PhD); educational statistics and measurement (MS, PhD); elementary education (MS); exceptional education (MS, PhD); junior high/middle school education (MS); learning and development (MS, PhD); multicultural studies (PhD); reading education (MS); school and community counseling (MS); school psychology (PhD, Ed S); secondary education (MS); social foundations of education (PhD); specialist in administrative leadership (Certificate); teaching and learning in higher education (Certificate); teaching in an urban setting (MS). *Application deadline:* For fall admission, 1/1 priority date for domestic students; for spring admission, 9/1 for domestic students. Applications are processed on a rolling basis. *Application fee:* $56 ($96 for international students). Electronic applications accepted. *Application Contact:* General Information Contact, 414-229-4982, Fax: 414-229-6967, E-mail: gradschool@uwm.edu. *Dean,* Carol Colbeck, 414-229-4181, E-mail: colbeck@uwm.edu.

School of Freshwater Sciences Students: 29 full-time (11 women), 22 part-time (6 women); includes 1 minority (Asian, non-Hispanic/Latino), 2 international. Average age 30. 35 applicants, 57% accepted, 8 enrolled. *Financial support:* Fellowships, research assistantships, teaching assistantships, and unspecified assistantships available. Financial award applicants required to submit FAFSA. In 2015, 8 master's, 2 doctorates awarded. Offers freshwater sciences (PhD); freshwater sciences and technology (MS). *Application fee:* $56 ($96 for international students). *Application Contact:* General Information Contact, 414-229-4982, Fax: 414-229-6967, E-mail: gradschool@uwm.edu. *Founding Dean,* David Garman, 414-382-1700, E-mail: garmand@uwm.edu.

School of Information Studies Students: 122 full-time (86 women), 270 part-time (224 women); includes 61 minority (17 Black or African American, non-Hispanic/Latino; 1 American Indian or Alaska Native, non-Hispanic/Latino; 16 Asian, non-Hispanic/Latino; 2 Hispanic/Latino; 25 Two or more races, non-Hispanic/Latino), 23 international. Average age 34. 266 applicants, 59% accepted, 109 enrolled. *Financial support:* In 2015–16, 4 teaching assistantships were awarded; fellowships, research assistantships, career-related internships or fieldwork, Federal Work-Study, health care benefits, unspecified assistantships, and project assistantships also available. Support available to part-time students. Financial award application deadline: 4/15; financial award applicants required to submit FAFSA. In 2015, 148 master's, 4 doctorates, 7 other advanced degrees awarded. *Degree program information:* Part-time programs available. Part-time. Offers advanced studies in library and information science (CAS); archives and records administration (CAS); digital libraries (Certificate); information studies (MLIS, PhD). *Application deadline:* For fall admission, 1/1 priority date for domestic students; for spring admission, 9/1 for domestic students. Applications are processed on a rolling basis. *Application fee:* $56 ($96 for international students). Electronic applications accepted. *Application Contact:* Hur-Li Lee, Representative, 414-229-6838, E-mail: hurli@uwm.edu. *Interim Dean/Associate Professor,* Wooseob Jeong, 414-229-6167, E-mail: wjj8612@uwm.edu.

School of Social Welfare Students: 244 full-time (204 women), 97 part-time (78 women); includes 81 minority (39 Black or African American, non-Hispanic/Latino; 1 American Indian or Alaska Native, non-Hispanic/Latino; 8 Asian, non-Hispanic/Latino; 1 Hispanic/Latino; 32 Two or more races, non-Hispanic/Latino), 2 international. Average age 30. 421 applicants, 58% accepted, 151 enrolled. *Financial support:* Fellowships with full tuition reimbursements, research assistantships with full tuition reimbursements, teaching assistantships with full tuition reimbursements, career-related internships or fieldwork, Federal Work-Study, health care benefits, unspecified assistantships, and project assistantships available. Support available to part-time students. Financial award application deadline: 4/15; financial award applicants required to submit FAFSA. In 2015, 134 master's, 1 other advanced degree awarded. *Degree program information:* Part-time programs available. Part-time. Offers administration (MS); applied gerontology (Certificate); corrections (MS); law enforcement (MS); marriage and family therapy (Certificate); non-profit management (Certificate); social welfare (MS, MSW, PhD, Certificate); social work (MSW, PhD). *Application deadline:* For fall admission, 1/1 priority date for domestic students; for spring admission, 9/1 for domestic students. Applications are processed on a rolling basis. *Application fee:* $56 ($96 for international students). Electronic applications accepted. *Application Contact:* Deborah Padgett, General Information Contact, 414-229-4851, Fax: 414-229-6967, E-mail: dpadgett@uwm.edu. *Dean,* Stan Stojkovic, 414-229-4400, E-mail: stojkovi@uwm.edu.

Sheldon B. Lubar School of Business Students: 280 full-time (115 women), 308 part-time (107 women); includes 87 minority (28 Black or African American, non-Hispanic/Latino; 2 American Indian or Alaska Native, non-Hispanic/Latino; 28 Asian, non-Hispanic/Latino; 7 Hispanic/Latino; 22 Two or more races, non-Hispanic/Latino), 95 international. Average age 32. 452 applicants, 52% accepted, 167 enrolled. *Financial support:* Fellowships with full tuition reimbursements, research assistantships with full tuition reimbursements, teaching assistantships with full tuition reimbursements, career-related internships or fieldwork, Federal Work-Study, health care benefits, unspecified assistantships, and project assistantships available. Support available to part-time students. Financial award application deadline: 4/15; financial award applicants required to submit FAFSA. In 2015, 249 master's, 10 doctorates, 24 other advanced degrees awarded. *Degree program information:* Part-time and evening/weekend programs available. Part-time, evening/weekend. Offers business administration (MBA); enterprise resource planning (Certificate); executive business administration (Exec MBA); investment management (Certificate); management science (MS, PhD); nonprofit management and leadership (MS, Certificate); state and local taxation (Certificate). *Application deadline:* For fall admission, 1/1 priority date for domestic students; for spring admission, 9/1 for domestic students. Applications are processed on a rolling basis. *Application fee:* $56 ($96 for international students). Electronic applications accepted. *Application Contact:* Matthew Jensen, Administrative Program Manager III, 414-229-5403, E-mail: mba-ms@uwm.edu. *Dean,* Timothy L. Smunt, 414-229-6256, Fax: 414-229-2372, E-mail: tsmunt@uwm.edu.

Zilber School of Public Health Students: 59 full-time (41 women), 18 part-time (14 women); includes 17 minority (6 Black or African American, non-Hispanic/Latino; 6 Asian, non-Hispanic/Latino; 5 Two or more races, non-Hispanic/Latino), 4 international. Average age 31. 120 applicants, 56% accepted, 35 enrolled. In 2015, 10 master's, 3 doctorates awarded. Offers community and behavioral health promotion (PhD); environmental and occupational health (PhD); public health (MPH, PhD, Graduate Certificate). *Application Contact:* Darcie K. G. Warren, Graduate Program Manager, 414-229-5633, E-mail: darcie@uwm.edu. *Founding Dean,* Magda G. Peck, 414-229-5319, E-mail: mpeck@uwm.edu.

UNIVERSITY OF WISCONSIN–OSHKOSH, Oshkosh, WI 54901

General Information State-supported, coed, comprehensive institution. *Graduate housing:* Room and/or apartments available on a first-come, first-served basis to single students; on-campus housing not available to married students.

GRADUATE UNITS

Graduate Studies ***Degree program information:*** Part-time and evening/weekend programs available. Part-time, evening/weekend. Offers social work (MSW). Electronic applications accepted.

College of Business Degree program information: Part-time programs available. Part-time. Offers business (GMBA, MBA); business administration (MBA); global business administration (GMBA). Electronic applications accepted.

College of Education and Human Services Degree program information: Part-time and evening/weekend programs available. Part-time, evening/weekend. Offers counseling (MSE); cross-categorical (MSE); curriculum and instruction (MSE); early childhood: exceptional education needs (MSE); education and human services (MS, MSE); educational leadership (MS); non-licensure (MSE); reading education (MSE). Electronic applications accepted.

College of Letters and Science Degree program information: Part-time and evening/weekend programs available. Part-time, evening/weekend. Offers biology (MS); English (MA); experimental psychology (MS); general agency (MPA); health care (MPA); industrial/organizational psychology (MS); letters and science (MA, MPA, MS, MSW); mathematics education (MS). Electronic applications accepted.

College of Nursing Degree program information: Part-time programs available. Part-time. Offers adult health and illness (MSN); family nurse practitioner (MSN). Electronic applications accepted.

UNIVERSITY OF WISCONSIN–PARKSIDE, Kenosha, WI 53141-2000

General Information State-supported, coed, comprehensive institution. *Graduate housing:* Room and/or apartments available on a first-come, first-served basis to single students; on-campus housing not available to married students.

GRADUATE UNITS

College of Natural and Health Sciences ***Degree program information:*** Part-time programs available. Part-time. Offers applied molecular biology (MSBS); natural and health sciences (MSBS). Electronic applications accepted.

School of Business and Technology ***Degree program information:*** Part-time and evening/weekend programs available. Part-time, evening/weekend. Offers business administration (MBA); business and technology (MBA, MSCIS); computer and information systems (MSCIS). Electronic applications accepted.

UNIVERSITY OF WISCONSIN–PLATTEVILLE, Platteville, WI 53818-3099

General Information State-supported, coed, comprehensive institution. *Enrollment:* 8,945 graduate, professional, and undergraduate students; 366 full-time matriculated graduate/professional students (202 women), 425 part-time matriculated graduate/professional students (143 women). *Enrollment by degree level:* 791 master's. *Graduate faculty:* 5 full-time (2 women), 90 part-time/adjunct (16 women). *Graduate housing:* On-campus housing not available. *Student services:* Campus employment opportunities, campus safety program, career counseling, child daycare facilities, exercise/wellness program, free psychological counseling, grant writing training, international student services, low-cost health insurance, multicultural affairs office, services for students with disabilities, teacher training, writing training. *Library:* Karrmann Library plus 1 other.

Computer facilities: A campuswide network can be accessed from student residence rooms and from off campus. Online class registration is available.
Website: http://www.uwplatt.edu/

General Application Contact: Dee Dunbar, School of Graduate Studies, 608-342-1322, Fax: 608-342-1389, E-mail: dunbard@uwplatt.edu.

GRADUATE UNITS

School of Graduate Studies Students: 366 full-time (202 women), 425 part-time (143 women); includes 120 minority (67 Black or African American, non-Hispanic/Latino; 5 American Indian or Alaska Native, non-Hispanic/Latino; 18 Asian, non-Hispanic/Latino; 26 Hispanic/Latino; 4 Native Hawaiian or other Pacific Islander, non-Hispanic/Latino), 63 international. 257 applicants, 80% accepted, 127 enrolled. *Financial support:* Research assistantships with partial tuition reimbursements, career-related internships or fieldwork, Federal Work-Study, institutionally sponsored loans, scholarships/grants, and unspecified assistantships available. Support available to part-time students. Financial award applicants required to submit FAFSA. In 2015, 154 master's awarded. *Degree program information:* Part-time and evening/weekend programs available. Part-time, evening/weekend, online learning. *Application deadline:* For fall admission, 7/1 priority date for domestic students; for spring admission, 11/1 for domestic students. Applications are processed on a rolling basis. *Application fee:* $56. Electronic applications accepted. *Application Contact:* Dee Dunbar, School of Graduate Studies, 608-342-1322, Fax: 608-342-1389, E-mail: dunbard@uwplatt.edu. *Dean*, Dr. Dominic P. Barraclough, 608-342-1262, Fax: 608-342-1270, E-mail: barracld@uwplatt.edu.

College of Engineering, Mathematics and Science Students: 3 full-time (0 women), all international. 10 applicants, 20% accepted. *Financial support:* Research assistantships with partial tuition reimbursements available. In 2015, 1 master's awarded. *Degree program information:* Part-time programs available. Part-time. Offers computer science (MS); engineering, mathematics and science (MS). *Application deadline:* For fall admission, 7/1 priority date for domestic students; for spring admission, 11/1 for domestic students. *Application fee:* $56. *Application Contact:* Dee Dunbar, School of Graduate Studies, 608-342-1322, Fax: 608-342-1389, E-mail: dunbard@uwplatt.edu. *Dean*, Molly Gribb, 608-342-1561, Fax: 608-342-1566, E-mail: ems@uwplatt.edu.

College of Liberal Arts and Education Students: 120 full-time (85 women), 31 part-time (17 women); includes 19 minority (17 Black or African American, non-Hispanic/Latino; 1 Asian, non-Hispanic/Latino; 1 Hispanic/Latino), 51 international. 26 applicants, 77% accepted, 17 enrolled. *Faculty:* 10 full-time (5 women), 13 part-time/adjunct (7 women). *Financial support:* Research assistantships with partial tuition reimbursements, career-related internships or fieldwork, Federal Work-Study, institutionally sponsored loans, scholarships/grants, and unspecified assistantships available. Support available to part-time students. Financial award applicants required to submit FAFSA. In 2015, 48 master's awarded. *Degree program information:* Part-time programs available. Part-time. Offers adult education (MSE); counselor education (MSE); elementary education (MSE); English education (MSE); liberal arts and education (MSE); middle school education (MSE); secondary education (MSE). *Application deadline:* For fall admission, 7/1 priority date for domestic students; for spring admission, 11/1 for domestic students. Applications are processed on a rolling basis. *Application fee:* $56. Electronic applications accepted. *Application Contact:* Dee Dunbar, School of Graduate Studies, 608-342-1322, Fax: 608-342-1389, E-mail: dunbard@uwplatt.edu. *Dean*, Elizabeth Throop, 608-342-1151, Fax: 608-342-1409.

Distance Learning Center Students: 243 full-time (117 women), 394 part-time (126 women); includes 101 minority (50 Black or African American, non-Hispanic/Latino; 5 American Indian or Alaska Native, non-Hispanic/Latino; 17 Asian, non-Hispanic/Latino; 25 Hispanic/Latino; 4 Native Hawaiian or other Pacific Islander, non-Hispanic/Latino), 9 international. 221 applicants, 83% accepted, 110 enrolled. *Financial support:* Scholarships/grants available. Support available to part-time students. In 2015, 105 master's awarded. *Degree program information:* Part-time and evening/weekend programs available. Part-time, evening/weekend, online learning. Offers criminal justice (MS); engineering (MS); integrated supply chain management (MS); organizational change leadership (MS); project management (MS). *Application deadline:* For fall admission, 7/1 priority date for domestic students; for spring admission, 11/1 priority date for domestic students. Applications are processed on a rolling basis. *Application fee:* $56. Electronic applications accepted. *Application Contact:* Karen Adams, Marketing Director, 800-362-5460, Fax: 608-342-1071, E-mail: adamskar@uwplatt.edu. *Executive Director*, Dawn Drake, 800-362-5460, Fax: 608-342-1071, E-mail: disted@uwplatt.edu.

UNIVERSITY OF WISCONSIN–RIVER FALLS, River Falls, WI 54022

General Information State-supported, coed, comprehensive institution. *Graduate housing:* Room and/or apartments available on a first-come, first-served basis to single students; on-campus housing not available to married students.

GRADUATE UNITS

Outreach and Graduate Studies ***Degree program information:*** Part-time programs available. Part-time. Electronic applications accepted.

College of Agriculture, Food, and Environmental Sciences Degree program information: Part-time programs available. Part-time. Offers agricultural education (MS); agriculture, food, and environmental sciences (MS). Electronic applications accepted.

College of Arts and Science Degree program information: Part-time programs available. Part-time. Offers arts and science (MA, MSE); fine arts (MSE); mathematics education (MSE); science education (MSE); social science education (MSE); teaching English to speakers of other languages (MA). Electronic applications accepted.

College of Business and Economics Offers business and economics (MBA, MM). Electronic applications accepted.

College of Education and Professional Studies Degree program information: Part-time programs available. Part-time. Offers communicative disorders (MS); counseling (MSE); education and professional studies (MS, MSE, Ed S); elementary education (MSE); professional development shared inquiry communities (MSE); reading (MSE); school psychology (MSE, Ed S); secondary education-communicative disorders (MSE).

UNIVERSITY OF WISCONSIN–STEVENS POINT, Stevens Point, WI 54481-3897

General Information State-supported, coed, comprehensive institution. *Graduate housing:* Room and/or apartments available on a first-come, first-served basis to single students; on-campus housing not available to married students.

GRADUATE UNITS

College of Fine Arts and Communication ***Degree program information:*** Part-time programs available. Part-time. Offers elementary/secondary (MM Ed); fine arts and communication (MA, MM Ed); studio pedagogy (MM Ed); Suzuki talent education (MM Ed).

Division of Communication Degree program information: Part-time programs available. Part-time. Offers interpersonal communication (MA); media studies (MA); organizational communication (MA); public relations (MA).

College of Letters and Science Offers biology (MST); English (MST); history (MST); letters and science (MBA, MST).

Division of Business and Economics Offers business and economics (MBA). Program offered jointly with University of Wisconsin–Oshkosh.

College of Natural Resources ***Degree program information:*** Part-time programs available. Part-time. Offers natural resources (MS).

College of Professional Studies ***Degree program information:*** Part-time programs available. Part-time.

School of Communicative Disorders Offers audiology (Au D); speech-language pathology (MS).

School of Education Degree program information: Part-time programs available. Part-time. Offers education—general/reading (MSE); education—general/special (MSE); educational administration (MSE); elementary education (MSE); guidance and counseling (MSE).

School of Health Promotion and Human Development Degree program information: Part-time programs available. Part-time. Offers human and community resources (MS); nutritional sciences (MS).

UNIVERSITY OF WISCONSIN–STOUT, Menomonie, WI 54751

General Information State-supported, coed, comprehensive institution. *Graduate housing:* Room and/or apartments available on a first-come, first-served basis to single students; on-campus housing not available to married students.

GRADUATE UNITS

Graduate School ***Degree program information:*** Part-time programs available. Part-time, online learning. Electronic applications accepted.

College of Arts, Humanities and Social Sciences Offers design (MFA); technical and professional communication (MS).

College of Education, Health and Human Sciences Degree program information: Part-time programs available. Part-time, online learning. Offers applied psychology (MS); career and technical education (MS, Ed D, Ed S); clinical mental health counseling (MS); education (MS, MS Ed, Ed D, Ed S); education, health and human sciences (MS, Ed S); food and nutritional sciences (MS); marriage and family therapy (MS); school counseling (MS); school psychology (MS Ed, Ed S); vocational rehabilitation (MS). Electronic applications accepted.

College of Management Offers management (MS); operations management (MS); project management (MS); quality management (MS); risk control (MS); supply chain management (MS); sustainable management (MS); training and human resource development (MS).

College of Science, Technology, Engineering and Mathematics Degree program information: Part-time programs available. Part-time, online learning. Offers conservation biology (PSM); construction management (MS); industrial and applied mathematics (PSM); information and communication technologies (MS); manufacturing engineering (MS); science, technology, engineering and mathematics (MS). Electronic applications accepted.

UNIVERSITY OF WISCONSIN–SUPERIOR, Superior, WI 54880-4500

General Information State-supported, coed, comprehensive institution. *Graduate housing:* Rooms and/or apartments available on a first-come, first-served basis to single students and available to married students. Housing application deadline: 7/1. *Research affiliation:* Great Lakes Indian Fish and Wildlife Commission, Wisconsin Department of Natural Resources (biology), Environmental Protection Agency (biology), The Mexican National Institute for Ecology (biology), The Mexican Marine National Park Service (biology), Coastal Zone Management Institute and Authority of Belize (biology), Fisheries Department, Government of Belize (biology).

GRADUATE UNITS

Graduate Division ***Degree program information:*** Part-time and evening/weekend programs available. Part-time, evening/weekend, online learning. Offers art education (MA); art history (MA); art therapy (MA); community counseling (MSE); educational administration (MSE, Ed S); emotional/behavior disabilities (MSE); human relations (MSE); instruction (MSE); learning disabilities (MSE); mass communication (MA); school counseling (MSE); special education (MSE); speech communication (MA); studio arts (MA); sustainable management (MS); teaching reading (MSE); theater (MA). Electronic applications accepted.

UNIVERSITY OF WISCONSIN–WHITEWATER, Whitewater, WI 53190-1790

General Information State-supported, coed, comprehensive institution. Tuition, state resident: full-time $9008. Tuition, nonresident: full-time $18,600. *Graduate housing:* Rooms and/or apartments available on a first-come, first-served basis to single students and available to married students. Typical cost: $8004 (including board) for single students; $8004 (including board) for married students. Housing application deadline:

9/1. *Student services:* Campus employment opportunities, campus safety program, career counseling, child daycare facilities, exercise/wellness program, free psychological counseling, grant writing training, international student services, low-cost health insurance, multicultural affairs office, services for students with disabilities. *Library:* Andersen Library. Students can reserve study rooms. *Research affiliation:* Generac Power Systems (manufacturing), American Ag-Tec International (international marketing), American Family Insurance (insurance), R.A. Smith and Associates (civil engineering), Sho-Deen (property management and development), Webco Industries, Inc. (lightning radioactive transfer).

Computer facilities: Computer purchase and lease plans are available. A campuswide network can be accessed from student residence rooms and from off campus. Online class registration is available.
Website: http://www.uww.edu/

General Application Contact: Sally A. Lange, School of Graduate Studies, 262-472-1006, Fax: 262-472-5027, E-mail: gradschl@uww.edu.

GRADUATE UNITS

School of Graduate Studies ***Financial support:*** Research assistantships, career-related internships or fieldwork, Federal Work-Study, unspecified assistantships, and out-of-state fee waivers available. Support available to part-time students. Financial award application deadline: 3/15; financial award applicants required to submit FAFSA. *Degree program information:* Part-time and evening/weekend programs available. Part-time, evening/weekend, online learning. *Application deadline:* For fall admission, 2/1 priority date for domestic and international students. Applications are processed on a rolling basis. *Application fee:* $56. Electronic applications accepted. *Application Contact:* Sally A. Lange, School of Graduate Studies, 262-472-1006, Fax: 262-472-5027, E-mail: gradschl@uww.edu. *Interim Dean*, Seth Meisel, 262-472-1006, Fax: 262-472-5027, E-mail: gradschl@uww.edu.

College of Arts and Communications Financial support: Research assistantships, Federal Work-Study, unspecified assistantships, and out-of-state fee waivers available. Support available to part-time students. Financial award application deadline: 3/15; financial award applicants required to submit FAFSA. *Degree program information:* Part-time and evening/weekend programs available. Part-time, evening/weekend, online learning. Offers arts and communications (MS); corporate communication (MS); mass communication (MS). *Application deadline:* For fall admission, 7/15 priority date for domestic students, 7/15 for international students; for spring admission, 12/1 priority date for domestic students, 12/1 for international students. Applications are processed on a rolling basis. *Application fee:* $56. Electronic applications accepted.

College of Business and Economics Financial support: Research assistantships, career-related internships or fieldwork, Federal Work-Study, unspecified assistantships, and out-of-state fee waivers available. Support available to part-time students. Financial award application deadline: 3/15; financial award applicants required to submit FAFSA. *Degree program information:* Part-time and evening/weekend programs available. Part-time, evening/weekend, online learning. Offers accounting (MPA); business and economics (MBA, MPA, MS, MSE); business and marketing education (MS); finance (MBA); school business management (MSE). *Application deadline:* For fall admission, 7/15 priority date for domestic students, 7/15 for international students; for spring admission, 12/1 priority date for domestic students, 12/1 for international students. Applications are processed on a rolling basis. *Application fee:* $56. Electronic applications accepted.

College of Education and Professional Studies Financial support: Research assistantships, career-related internships or fieldwork, Federal Work-Study, unspecified assistantships, and out-of-state fee waivers available. Support available to part-time students. Financial award application deadline: 3/15; financial award applicants required to submit FAFSA. *Degree program information:* Part-time and evening/weekend programs available. Part-time, evening/weekend, online learning. Offers communication sciences and disorders (MS); cross categorical licensure (MSE); education and professional studies (MS, MSE, Postbaccalaureate Certificate); professional development (MSE); safety (MS); special education (Postbaccalaureate Certificate). *Application deadline:* For fall admission, 7/15 priority date for domestic students; for spring admission, 12/1 priority date for domestic students. Applications are processed on a rolling basis. *Application fee:* $56. Electronic applications accepted.

College of Letters and Sciences Financial support: Research assistantships with partial tuition reimbursements, Federal Work-Study, unspecified assistantships, and out-of-state fee waivers available. Support available to part-time students. Financial award application deadline: 3/15; financial award applicants required to submit FAFSA. *Degree program information:* Part-time and evening/weekend programs available. Part-time, evening/weekend. Offers letters and sciences (MSE, Ed S); school psychology (MSE, Ed S). *Application deadline:* For fall admission, 2/1 for domestic students, 1/15 for international students. Applications are processed on a rolling basis. *Application fee:* $56. Electronic applications accepted. *Application Contact:* Sally A. Lange, School of Graduate Studies, 262-472-1006, Fax: 262-472-5027, E-mail: gradschl@uww.edu. *Dean*, David Travis, 262-472-1710, Fax: 262-472-5238, E-mail: travisd@uww.edu.

UNIVERSITY OF WYOMING, Laramie, WY 82071

General Information State-supported, coed, university. CGS member. *Graduate housing:* Rooms and/or apartments available on a first-come, first-served basis to single and married students.

GRADUATE UNITS

College of Agriculture and Natural Resources ***Degree program information:*** Part-time programs available. Part-time. Offers agricultural and applied economics (MS); agriculture and natural resources (MA, MS, PhD); agroecology (MS); agronomy (MS, PhD); animal sciences (MS, PhD); early childhood development (MS); entomology (MS, PhD); entomology/water resources (MS, PhD); family and consumer sciences (MS); food science and human nutrition (MS); molecular biology (MA, MS, PhD); pathobiology (MS); rangeland ecology and watershed management (MS, PhD); rangeland ecology and watershed management/water resources (MS, PhD); reproductive biology (MS, PhD); soil science (MS); soil science/water resources (PhD). Electronic applications accepted.

College of Arts and Sciences ***Degree program information:*** Part-time programs available. Part-time. Offers American studies (MA); anthropology (MA, PhD); arts and sciences (MA, MAT, MFA, MM, MME, MP, MPA, MS, MST, PhD); botany (MS, PhD); botany/water resources (MS); chemistry (MS, PhD); communication (MA); community and regional planning and natural resources (MP); creative writing (MFA); English (MA); French (MA); geography (MA, MP, MST); geography/water resources (MA); geology (MS, PhD); geophysics (MS, PhD); German (MA); history (MA, MAT); international peace corps (MA); international studies (MA); mathematics (MA, MAT, MS, MST, PhD); mathematics/computer science (PhD); music education (MME); performance (MM); philosophy (MA); political science (MA, MPA); psychology (MA, MS, PhD); public administration (MPA); rural planning and natural resources (MP); sociology (MA); Spanish (MA); statistics (MS, PhD); zoology and physiology (MS, PhD). Electronic applications accepted.

College of Business ***Degree program information:*** Part-time and evening/weekend programs available. Part-time, evening/weekend, online learning. Offers accounting (MS); business (MBA, MS, PhD); business administration (MBA); economics (MS, PhD); economics and finance (MS); finance (MS).

College of Education Online learning. Offers community mental health (MS); counselor education and supervision (PhD); curriculum and instruction (MA, Ed D, PhD); education (MA, MS, MST, Ed D, PhD, Certificate, Ed S); educational leadership (MA, Ed D, Certificate); instructional technology (MS, Ed D, PhD); school counseling (MS); special education (MA, PhD, Ed S); student affairs (MS). Electronic applications accepted.

Science and Mathematics Teaching Center Offers science and mathematics teaching (MS, MST). Electronic applications accepted.

College of Engineering and Applied Sciences ***Degree program information:*** Part-time programs available. Part-time. Offers atmospheric science (MS, PhD); chemical engineering (MS, PhD); civil engineering (MS, PhD); computer science (MS, PhD); electrical engineering (MS, PhD); engineering and applied sciences (MS, PhD); environmental engineering (MS); mechanical engineering (MS, PhD); petroleum engineering (MS, PhD). Electronic applications accepted.

College of Health Sciences ***Degree program information:*** Part-time programs available. Part-time, online learning. Offers health sciences (MS, MSW, Pharm D). Electronic applications accepted.

Division of Communication Disorders Degree program information: Part-time programs available. Part-time, online learning. Offers speech-language pathology (MS). Electronic applications accepted.

Division of Kinesiology and Health Degree program information: Part-time programs available. Part-time, online learning. Offers kinesiology and health (MS). Electronic applications accepted.

Division of Social Work Offers social work (MSW).

Fay W. Whitney School of Nursing Degree program information: Part-time programs available. Part-time, online learning. Offers nursing (MS).

School of Pharmacy Online learning. Offers health services administration (MS); pharmacy (Pharm D).

College of Law Offers law (JD). Electronic applications accepted.

Graduate Program in Molecular and Cellular Life Sciences Offers molecular and cellular life sciences (PhD).

Program in Ecology Offers ecology (MS, PhD).

UPPER IOWA UNIVERSITY, Fayette, IA 52142-1857

General Information Independent, coed, comprehensive institution. *Enrollment:* 723 full-time matriculated graduate/professional students (442 women). *Enrollment by degree level:* 723 master's. *Graduate faculty:* 3 full-time (0 women), 66 part-time/adjunct (27 women). *Tuition, area resident:* Part-time $1323 per course. Part-time tuition and fees vary according to program. *Graduate housing:* Room and/or apartments available to single students. *Student services:* Career counseling, international student services, services for students with disabilities, writing training. *Library:* Henderson Wilder Library.

Computer facilities: Computer purchase and lease plans are available. 630 computers available on campus for general student use. A campuswide network can be accessed from student residence rooms and from off campus. Online class registration is available.
Website: http://www.uiu.edu/

General Application Contact: Colene Sassmann, Admissions Advisor, 800-553-4150, Fax: 563-425-5287, E-mail: info@uiu.edu.

GRADUATE UNITS

Master of Education Program Offers early childhood (M Ed); English as a second language (M Ed); higher education (M Ed); instructional strategist (M Ed); reading (M Ed); teacher leadership (M Ed). *Application fee:* $25. *Application Contact:* Tiffany Phillips, Admissions Counselor, 800-553-4150, E-mail: phillipst@uiu.edu. *Dean of the Andres School of Education*, Dr. Gail Moorman Behrens, 563-425-5211, E-mail: behrensg@uiu.edu.

Online Master's Programs Students: 723 full-time (442 women). *Faculty:* 3 full-time (0 women), 66 part-time/adjunct (27 women). *Financial support:* Available to part-time students. Applicants required to submit FAFSA. *Degree program information:* Part-time programs available. Part-time, online learning. Offers accounting (MBA); corporate financial management (MBA); emergency management and homeland security (MPA); general management (MBA); general studies (MPA); government administration (MPA); health and human services (MPA); human resources management (MBA); nonprofit organizational management (MPA); organizational development (MBA); public management (MPA); sport administration (MSA). MBA also available at Madison, WI campus. *Application deadline:* Applications are processed on a rolling basis. *Application fee:* $50. Electronic applications accepted. *Application Contact:* David Hannum, Admissions Advisor, 800-603-3756, E-mail: hannumd@uiu.edu.

URBANA UNIVERSITY, Urbana, OH 43078-2091

General Information Independent, coed, comprehensive institution. *Graduate housing:* Room and/or apartments available on a first-come, first-served basis to single students; on-campus housing not available to married students.

GRADUATE UNITS

College of Education and Sports Studies ***Degree program information:*** Part-time and evening/weekend programs available. Part-time, evening/weekend. Offers classroom education (M Ed).

College of Nursing and Allied Health Offers nursing (MSN).

College of Social and Behavioral Sciences Offers criminal justice administration (MA).

Division of Business Administration ***Degree program information:*** Part-time and evening/weekend programs available. Part-time, evening/weekend. Offers business administration (MBA).

URSHAN GRADUATE SCHOOL OF THEOLOGY, Florissant, MO 63031

General Information Independent-religious, coed, graduate-only institution.

GRADUATE UNITS

Graduate Programs Online learning. Offers theology (M Div, MACM, MTS).

URSULINE COLLEGE, Pepper Pike, OH 44124-4398

General Information Independent-religious, coed, primarily women, comprehensive institution. *Enrollment:* 1,236 graduate, professional, and undergraduate students; 83 full-time matriculated graduate/professional students (75 women), 435 part-time matriculated graduate/professional students (392 women). *Enrollment by degree level:* 456 master's, 13 doctoral, 49 other advanced degrees. *Graduate faculty:* 26 full-time (22 women), 44 part-time/adjunct (30 women). *Tuition, area resident:* Full-time $18,036; part-time $6012 per semester. *Required fees:* $290; $210 per credit. $105 per semester. Tuition and fees vary according to program. *Graduate housing:* Room and/or apartments available on a first-come, first-served basis to single students; on-campus housing not available to married students. Housing application deadline: 8/20. *Student services:* Campus employment opportunities, career counseling, exercise/wellness program, free psychological counseling, multicultural affairs office, services for students with disabilities, teacher training. *Library:* Ralph M. Besse Library. *Collection:* Books: 134,397 (physical), 110,963 (digital/electronic); Serial titles: 880 (physical), 49,163 (digital/electronic); Databases: 161. Weekly public service hours: 91; students can reserve study rooms.

Computer facilities: 72 computers available on campus for general student use. A campuswide network can be accessed from student residence rooms. Online class registration is available.
Website: http://www.ursuline.edu/

General Application Contact: Melanie Steele, Director, Graduate Admission, 440-646-8119, Fax: 440-684-6138, E-mail: graduateadmissions@ursuline.edu.

GRADUATE UNITS

School of Graduate Studies Students: 237 full-time (211 women), 174 part-time (147 women); includes 123 minority (102 Black or African American, non-Hispanic/Latino; 9 Asian, non-Hispanic/Latino; 7 Hispanic/Latino; 5 Two or more races, non-Hispanic/Latino), 7 international. Average age 35. 205 applicants, 88% accepted, 140 enrolled. *Faculty:* 14 full-time (12 women), 37 part-time/adjunct (29 women). *Financial support:* In 2015–16, 69 students received support. Federal Work-Study available. Financial award application deadline: 3/1; financial award applicants required to submit FAFSA. In 2015, 213 master's, 3 doctorates awarded. *Degree program information:* Part-time programs available. Part-time, online learning. Offers adult nurse practitioner (MSN); adult-gerontology clinical nurse specialist (MSN); art education (MA); business administration (MBA); counseling and art therapy (MA); early childhood education (MA); educational administration (MA); family nurse practitioner (MSN); historic preservation (MA); language arts education (MA); liberal studies (MALS); life science education (MA); math education (MA); middle childhood education (MA); ministry (MA); nursing (DNP); nursing education (MSN); palliative care (MSN); reading specialist (MA); social studies education (MA); special education (MA). *Application deadline:* For fall admission, 8/1 priority date for domestic students. Applications are processed on a rolling basis. *Application fee:* $25. Electronic applications accepted. *Application Contact:* Stephanie Pratt McRoberts, Graduate Admission Coordinator, 440-646-8119, Fax: 440-684-6138, E-mail: graduateadmissions@ursuline.edu. *Interim Dean*, Joseph LaGuardia, 440-646-8120, Fax: 440-684-6088, E-mail: jlaguardia@ursuline.edu.

UTAH STATE UNIVERSITY, Logan, UT 84322

General Information State-supported, coed, university. CGS member. *Graduate housing:* Rooms and/or apartments available on a first-come, first-served basis to single and married students. *Research affiliation:* Boeing Aerospace and Engineering (science and engineering), Duke Energy Corporation (engineering), Kennecott Copper Corporation (natural resources), Kraft Foods, Inc. (agriculture), National Endowment for Financial Education (education).

GRADUATE UNITS

School of Graduate Studies ***Degree program information:*** Part-time and evening/weekend programs available. Part-time, evening/weekend, online learning.

College of Agriculture Degree program information: Part-time programs available. Part-time, online learning. Offers agricultural systems technology (MS); agriculture (MDA, MS, PhD); animal science (MS, PhD); biometeorology (MS, PhD); bioveterinary science (MS, PhD); dairy science (MS); dietetic administration (MDA); ecology (MS, PhD); family and consumer sciences education (MS); nutrition and food sciences (MS, PhD); plant science (MS, PhD); soil science (MS, PhD); toxicology (MS, PhD).

College of Business Degree program information: Part-time and evening/weekend programs available. Part-time, evening/weekend, online learning. Offers accountancy (M Acc); applied economics (MS); business (M Acc, MA, MBA, MS, Ed D, PhD); business administration (MBA); business education (MS); business information systems (MS); business information systems and education (Ed D); economics (MA, MS, PhD); education (PhD); human resource management (MS).

College of Engineering Degree program information: Part-time and evening/weekend programs available. Part-time, evening/weekend. Offers aerospace engineering (MS, PhD); biological and agricultural engineering (MS, PhD); civil and environmental engineering (ME, MS, PhD, CE); electrical engineering (ME, MS, PhD); engineering (ME, MS, PhD, CE); industrial technology (MS); irrigation engineering (MS, PhD); mechanical engineering (ME, MS, PhD). Electronic applications accepted.

College of Humanities, Arts and Social Sciences Degree program information: Part-time and evening/weekend programs available. Part-time, evening/weekend, online learning. Offers advanced technical practice (MFA); American studies (MA, MS); art (MA, MFA); bioregional planning (MS); design (MFA); English (MA, MS); folklore (MA, MS); history (MA, MS); humanities, arts and social sciences (MA, MFA, MLA, MS, MSLT, MSS, PhD); interior design (MS); journalism and communication (MA, MS); landscape architecture (MLA); political science (MA, MS); second language teaching (MSLT); sociology (MA, MS, MSS, PhD); theatre arts (MA, MFA); western American literature and culture (MA, MS).

College of Natural Resources Degree program information: Part-time programs available. Part-time. Offers bioregional planning (MS); ecology (MS, PhD); fisheries biology (MS, PhD); forestry (MS, PhD); geography (MA, MS); human dimensions of ecosystem science and management (MS, PhD); natural resources (MA, MNR, MS, PhD); range science (MS, PhD); recreation resource management (MS, PhD); watershed science (MS, PhD); wildlife biology (MS, PhD).

College of Science Degree program information: Part-time and evening/weekend programs available. Part-time, evening/weekend. Offers biochemistry (MS, PhD); biology (MS, PhD); chemistry (MS, PhD); computer science (MCS, MS, PhD); ecology (MS, PhD); geology (MS); industrial mathematics (MS); mathematical sciences (PhD); mathematics (M Math, MS); physics (MS, PhD); science (M Math, MCS, MS, PhD); statistics (MS).

Emma Eccles Jones College of Education and Human Services Degree program information: Part-time and evening/weekend programs available. Part-time, evening/weekend, online learning. Offers audiology (Au D, Ed S); business information systems (Ed D, PhD); clinical/counseling/school psychology (PhD); communication disorders and deaf education (M Ed); communicative disorders and deaf education (MA, MS); curriculum and instruction (Ed D, PhD); disability disciplines (PhD); education and human services (M Ed, MA, MFHD, MRC, MS, Au D, Ed D, PhD, Ed S); elementary education (M Ed, MA, MS); family and human development (MFHD); family, consumer, and human development (MS, PhD); health, physical education and recreation (M Ed, MS); instructional technology and learning sciences (M Ed, MS, PhD, Ed S); rehabilitation counselor education (MRC); research and evaluation (PhD); research and evaluation methodology (PhD); school counseling (MS); school psychology (MS); secondary education (M Ed, MA, MS); special education (M Ed, MS, Ed S).

UTAH VALLEY UNIVERSITY, Orem, UT 84058-5999

General Information State-supported, coed, comprehensive institution. *Enrollment:* 33,211 graduate, professional, and undergraduate students. *Student services:* Campus employment opportunities, campus safety program, career counseling, child daycare facilities, exercise/wellness program, free psychological counseling, grant writing training, international student services, low-cost health insurance, multicultural affairs office, services for students with disabilities, teacher training. *Library:* Utah Valley University Library plus 1 other.

Computer facilities: 1,000 computers available on campus for general student use. A campuswide network can be accessed. Online class registration is available.
Website: http://www.uvu.edu/

General Application Contact: Shauna Reher, Administrative Assistant, 801-863-7348, E-mail: graduate_studies@uvu.edu.

GRADUATE UNITS

MBA Program Students: 39 full-time (10 women), 96 part-time (18 women); includes 15 minority (1 Black or African American, non-Hispanic/Latino; 1 American Indian or Alaska Native, non-Hispanic/Latino; 4 Asian, non-Hispanic/Latino; 5 Hispanic/Latino; 1 Native Hawaiian or other Pacific Islander, non-Hispanic/Latino; 3 Two or more races, non-Hispanic/Latino), 1 international. Average age 32. 114 applicants, 73% accepted, 74 enrolled. *Financial support:* Applicants required to submit FAFSA. In 2015, 39 master's awarded. *Degree program information:* Part-time and evening/weekend programs available. Part-time, evening/weekend. Offers accounting (MBA); management (MBA). *Application deadline:* For fall admission, 2/1 priority date for domestic and international students. Applications are processed on a rolling basis. *Application fee:* $45. Electronic applications accepted. *Application Contact:* Matthew Moon, Admissions and Marketing Coordinator, E-mail: mmoon@uvu.edu. *Director*, Bill Neal, E-mail: william.neal@uvu.edu.

Program in Education Students: 43 part-time (28 women); includes 8 minority (1 American Indian or Alaska Native, non-Hispanic/Latino; 2 Asian, non-Hispanic/Latino; 5 Hispanic/Latino). Average age 34. *Financial support:* Scholarships/grants available. Financial award application deadline: 5/1; financial award applicants required to submit FAFSA. In 2015, 17 master's awarded. *Degree program information:* Part-time programs available. Part-time. Offers educational technology (M Ed); elementary mathematics (M Ed); elementary STEM (M Ed); English as a second language (M Ed); reading (M Ed); teachers as leaders (M Ed). *Application deadline:* For fall admission, 3/31 for domestic and international students. Applications are processed on a rolling basis. *Application fee:* $45. Electronic applications accepted. *Application Contact:* Mary Sowder, Coordinator of Graduate Studies, 801-863-6723. *Dean, School of Education*, Parker Fawson, 801-863-8006.

Program in Nursing ***Financial support:*** Application deadline: 5/1; applicants required to submit FAFSA. *Degree program information:* Part-time programs available. Part-time, online learning. Offers nursing (MSN). *Application deadline:* For fall admission, 4/1 for domestic and international students. *Application fee:* $45 ($100 for international students). Electronic applications accepted. *Application Contact:* Diane Evans, Administrative Assistant, 801-863-8199, E-mail: dianee@uvu.edu. *Department Chair*, Dale Maughan, 801-863-7411, E-mail: dale.maughan@uvu.edu.

UTICA COLLEGE, Utica, NY 13502-4892

General Information Independent, coed, comprehensive institution. *Enrollment:* 4,463 graduate, professional, and undergraduate students; 228 full-time matriculated graduate/professional students (164 women), 1,137 part-time matriculated graduate/professional students (628 women). *Enrollment by degree level:* 894 master's, 470 doctoral, 1 other advanced degree. *Graduate faculty:* 65 full-time (28 women). Tuition and fees vary according to course load, degree level, campus/location and program. *Graduate housing:* Room and/or apartments available on a first-come, first-served basis to single students; on-campus housing not available to married students. Housing application deadline: 3/1. *Student services:* Campus employment opportunities, campus safety program, career counseling, international student services, low-cost health insurance, services for students with disabilities. *Library:* Frank E. Gannett Memorial Library. *Collection:* Books: 307,523 (physical); Serial titles: 267,023 (physical). Students can reserve study rooms.

Computer facilities: 430 computers available on campus for general student use. A campuswide network can be accessed from student residence rooms. Online class registration is available.
Website: http://www.utica.edu/

General Application Contact: John D. Rowe, Director of Graduate Admissions, 315-792-3824, Fax: 315-792-3003, E-mail: jrowe@utica.edu.

GRADUATE UNITS

Department of Physical Therapy Students: 81 full-time (52 women), 389 part-time (251 women); includes 293 minority (23 Black or African American, non-Hispanic/Latino; 1 American Indian or Alaska Native, non-Hispanic/Latino; 253 Asian, non-Hispanic/Latino; 13 Hispanic/Latino; 2 Native Hawaiian or other Pacific Islander, non-Hispanic/Latino; 1 Two or more races, non-Hispanic/Latino). Average age 37. 256 applicants, 97% accepted, 216 enrolled. *Faculty:* 10 full-time (4 women). *Financial support:* Career-related internships or fieldwork, scholarships/grants, tuition waivers (partial), and unspecified assistantships available. Support available to part-time students. Financial award application deadline: 3/15; financial award applicants required to submit FAFSA. In 2015, 263 doctorates awarded. *Degree program information:* Part-time and evening/weekend programs available. Part-time, evening/weekend, online learning. Offers physical therapy (DPT, TDPT). *Application deadline:* Applications are processed on a rolling basis. *Application fee:* $50. Electronic applications accepted. *Application Contact:* John D. Rowe, Director of Graduate Admissions, 315-792-3824, Fax: 315-792-3003, E-mail: jrowe@utica.edu. *Director*, Dr. Shauna Malta, 315-792-3313, E-mail: smalta@utica.edu.

Liberal Studies Program Students: 1 (woman) full-time, 20 part-time (14 women); includes 5 minority (1 Black or African American, non-Hispanic/Latino; 1 American Indian or Alaska Native, non-Hispanic/Latino; 1 Asian, non-Hispanic/Latino; 1

Hispanic/Latino; 1 Two or more races, non-Hispanic/Latino). Average age 34. 6 applicants, 67% accepted, 2 enrolled. *Faculty:* 19 full-time (8 women). *Financial support:* Career-related internships or fieldwork, scholarships/grants, tuition waivers (partial), and unspecified assistantships available. Support available to part-time students. Financial award application deadline: 3/15; financial award applicants required to submit FAFSA. In 2015, 4 master's awarded. *Degree program information:* Part-time and evening/weekend programs available. Part-time, evening/weekend, online only. Offers liberal studies (MS). *Application deadline:* Applications are processed on a rolling basis. *Application fee:* $50. Electronic applications accepted. *Application Contact:* John D. Rowe, Director of Graduate Admissions, 315-792-3824, Fax: 315-792-3003, E-mail: jrowe@utica.edu. *Director*, Prof. Polly Smith, 315-792-3221, E-mail: mhutchinson@utica.edu.

Program in Accountancy Students: 13 full-time (6 women), 16 part-time (13 women); includes 3 minority (1 Black or African American, non-Hispanic/Latino; 1 Hispanic/Latino; 1 Two or more races, non-Hispanic/Latino). Average age 35. 29 applicants, 62% accepted, 10 enrolled. *Faculty:* 3 full-time (1 woman). *Financial support:* Career-related internships or fieldwork, scholarships/grants, tuition waivers (partial), and unspecified assistantships available. Support available to part-time students. Financial award application deadline: 3/15; financial award applicants required to submit FAFSA. In 2015, 11 master's awarded. *Degree program information:* Part-time and evening/weekend programs available. Part-time, evening/weekend. Offers accountancy (MBA). *Application deadline:* Applications are processed on a rolling basis. *Application fee:* $50. Electronic applications accepted. *Application Contact:* John D. Rowe, Director of Graduate Admissions, 315-792-3824, Fax: 315-792-3003, E-mail: jrowe@utica.edu. *MBA Director*, Dr. Zhaodan Huang, 315-792-3247, E-mail: zhuang@utica.edu.

Program in Cybersecurity Students: 2 full-time (0 women), 340 part-time (103 women); includes 102 minority (51 Black or African American, non-Hispanic/Latino; 4 American Indian or Alaska Native, non-Hispanic/Latino; 13 Asian, non-Hispanic/Latino; 26 Hispanic/Latino; 8 Two or more races, non-Hispanic/Latino). Average age 35. 182 applicants, 98% accepted, 152 enrolled. *Faculty:* 5 full-time (0 women), 8 part-time/adjunct (0 women). *Financial support:* Application deadline: 3/15; applicants required to submit FAFSA. In 2015, 89 master's awarded. *Degree program information:* Part-time and evening/weekend programs available. Part-time, evening/weekend, 100% online. Offers cybersecurity (MS). *Application deadline:* Applications are processed on a rolling basis. Electronic applications accepted. *Application Contact:* John D. Rowe, Director of Graduate Admissions, 315-792-3824, Fax: 315-792-3003, E-mail: jrowe@utica.edu. *Chair*, Joseph Giordano, 315-792-2521.

Program in Economic Crime and Fraud Management Students: 8 full-time (5 women), 109 part-time (61 women); includes 36 minority (24 Black or African American, non-Hispanic/Latino; 3 Asian, non-Hispanic/Latino; 9 Hispanic/Latino). Average age 34. 47 applicants, 94% accepted, 36 enrolled. *Faculty:* 7 full-time (0 women). *Financial support:* Career-related internships or fieldwork, scholarships/grants, tuition waivers (partial), and unspecified assistantships available. Support available to part-time students. Financial award application deadline: 3/15; financial award applicants required to submit FAFSA. In 2015, 72 master's awarded. *Degree program information:* Part-time and evening/weekend programs available. Part-time, evening/weekend, 100% online. Offers economic crime and fraud management (MS). *Application deadline:* Applications are processed on a rolling basis. *Application fee:* $50. Electronic applications accepted. *Application Contact:* John D. Rowe, Director of Graduate Admissions, 315-792-3824, Fax: 315-792-3003, E-mail: jrowe@utica.edu. *Director of Economic Crime Graduate Programs*, Dr. R. Bruce McBride, 315-792-3808, E-mail: rmcbride@utica.edu.

Program in Economic Crime Management Students: 1 full-time (0 women), 52 part-time (28 women); includes 17 minority (11 Black or African American, non-Hispanic/Latino; 1 Asian, non-Hispanic/Latino; 4 Hispanic/Latino; 1 Two or more races, non-Hispanic/Latino). Average age 39. 5 applicants, 100% accepted, 5 enrolled. *Faculty:* 4 full-time (0 women). *Financial support:* Career-related internships or fieldwork, scholarships/grants, tuition waivers (partial), and unspecified assistantships available. Support available to part-time students. Financial award application deadline: 3/15; financial award applicants required to submit FAFSA. *Degree program information:* Part-time and evening/weekend programs available. Part-time, evening/weekend, online learning. Offers economic crime management (MS). *Application deadline:* Applications are processed on a rolling basis. *Application fee:* $50. Electronic applications accepted. *Application Contact:* John D. Rowe, Director of Graduate Admissions, 315-792-3824, Fax: 315-792-3003, E-mail: jrowe@utica.edu. *Director of Economic Crime Graduate Programs*, Dr. R. Bruce McBride, 315-792-3808, E-mail: rmcbride@utica.edu.

Program in Health Care Administration Students: 4 full-time (all women), 158 part-time (130 women); includes 35 minority (20 Black or African American, non-Hispanic/Latino; 7 Asian, non-Hispanic/Latino; 6 Hispanic/Latino; 2 Two or more races, non-Hispanic/Latino). Average age 34. 82 applicants, 95% accepted, 67 enrolled. *Financial support:* Application deadline: 3/15; applicants required to submit FAFSA. In 2015, 70 master's awarded. *Degree program information:* Part-time and evening/weekend programs available. Part-time, evening/weekend, online learning. Offers health care administration (MS). *Application deadline:* Applications are processed on a rolling basis. *Application fee:* $50. Electronic applications accepted. *Application Contact:* John D. Rowe, Director of Graduate Admissions, 315-792-3824, Fax: 315-792-3003, E-mail: jrowe@utica.edu. *Head*, Dr. Dana Hart, 315-792-3375, E-mail: dhart@utica.edu.

Program in Occupational Therapy Students: 94 full-time (78 women); includes 6 minority (1 Black or African American, non-Hispanic/Latino; 2 Asian, non-Hispanic/Latino; 2 Hispanic/Latino; 1 Two or more races, non-Hispanic/Latino), 1 international. Average age 26. 69 applicants, 100% accepted, 63 enrolled. *Faculty:* 7 full-time (all women). *Financial support:* Career-related internships or fieldwork, scholarships/grants, tuition waivers (partial), and unspecified assistantships available. Support available to part-time students. Financial award application deadline: 3/15; financial award applicants required to submit FAFSA. In 2015, 62 master's awarded. *Degree program information:* Part-time and evening/weekend programs available. Part-time, evening/weekend. Offers occupational therapy (MS). *Application deadline:* Applications are processed on a rolling basis. *Application fee:* $50. Electronic applications accepted. *Application Contact:* John D. Rowe, Director of Graduate Admissions, 315-792-3824, Fax: 315-792-3003, E-mail: jrowe@utica.edu. *Director*, Cora Bruns, 315-792-3125, E-mail: cbruns@utica.edu.

Teacher Education Programs Students: 23 full-time (17 women), 26 part-time (15 women); includes 3 minority (1 Hispanic/Latino; 2 Two or more races, non-Hispanic/Latino), 1 international. Average age 28. 33 applicants, 73% accepted, 11 enrolled. *Faculty:* 10 full-time (7 women). *Financial support:* Career-related internships or fieldwork, scholarships/grants, tuition waivers (partial), and unspecified assistantships available. Support available to part-time students. Financial award application deadline: 3/15; financial award applicants required to submit FAFSA. In 2015, 26 master's awarded. Offers teacher education (MS, MS Ed, CAS). *Application deadline:* Applications are processed on a rolling basis. *Application fee:* $50. Electronic applications accepted. *Application Contact:* John D. Rowe, Director of Graduate Admissions, 315-792-3824, Fax: 315-792-3003, E-mail: jrowe@utica.edu. *Director, Institute for Excellence in Education*, Dr. Patrice Hallock, 315-792-3162, E-mail: phallock@utica.edu.

VALDOSTA STATE UNIVERSITY, Valdosta, GA 31698

General Information State-supported, coed, university. CGS member. *Enrollment:* 11,302 graduate, professional, and undergraduate students; 790 full-time matriculated graduate/professional students (589 women), 1,716 part-time matriculated graduate/professional students (1,226 women). *Enrollment by degree level:* 1,998 master's, 508 doctoral. *Graduate faculty:* 206 full-time (71 women). *Tuition, area resident:* Part-time $243 per credit hour. Tuition and fees vary according to course load and campus/location. *Graduate housing:* Rooms and/or apartments available on a first-come, first-served basis to single and married students. Housing application deadline: 7/1. *Student services:* Campus employment opportunities, campus safety program, career counseling, exercise/wellness program, free psychological counseling, grant writing training, international student services, low-cost health insurance, multicultural affairs office, services for students with disabilities, teacher training, writing training. *Library:* Odum Library. *Collection:* Books: 567,133 (physical), 48,600 (digital/electronic); Serial titles: 11,702 (physical), 48,348 (digital/electronic); Databases: 210. Students can reserve study rooms.

Computer facilities: Computer purchase and lease plans are available. 1,652 computers available on campus for general student use. A campuswide network can be accessed from student residence rooms and from off campus. Online class registration is available.
Website: http://www.valdosta.edu/

General Application Contact: Rebecca Petrella, Graduate Admissions Coordinator, 229-333-5694, Fax: 229-245-3853, E-mail: rlwaters@valdosta.edu.

GRADUATE UNITS

Department of Early Childhood and Special Education Students: 41 full-time (40 women), 47 part-time (46 women); includes 18 minority (all Black or African American, non-Hispanic/Latino), 2 international. Average age 24. 33 applicants, 94% accepted, 25 enrolled. *Faculty:* 11 full-time (10 women), 2 part-time/adjunct (both women). *Financial support:* In 2015–16, 4 students received support, including 4 research assistantships with full tuition reimbursements available (averaging $3,252 per year); institutionally sponsored loans, scholarships/grants, and unspecified assistantships also available. Support available to part-time students. Financial award application deadline: 7/1; financial award applicants required to submit FAFSA. In 2015, 15 master's awarded. *Degree program information:* Part-time and evening/weekend programs available. Part-time, evening/weekend, blended/hybrid learning. Offers early childhood (M Ed); special education (M Ed, MAT, Ed S). *Application deadline:* For fall and spring admission, 7/1 for domestic and international students. Applications are processed on a rolling basis. *Application fee:* $35. Electronic applications accepted. *Application Contact:* Rebecca Petrella, Graduate Admissions Coordinator, 229-333-5694, Fax: 229-245-3853, E-mail: rlwaters@valdosta.edu. *Interim Head*, Dr. Lynn Minor, 229-333-5929.

Department of English Students: 7 full-time (6 women), 23 part-time (18 women); includes 2 minority (1 Hispanic/Latino; 1 Two or more races, non-Hispanic/Latino). Average age 25. 7 applicants, 86% accepted, 6 enrolled. *Faculty:* 14 full-time (11 women). *Financial support:* In 2015–16, 11 students received support, including 4 research assistantships with full tuition reimbursements available (averaging $4,000 per year), 3 teaching assistantships with full tuition reimbursements available (averaging $8,000 per year); institutionally sponsored loans, scholarships/grants, and unspecified assistantships also available. Support available to part-time students. Financial award application deadline: 7/1; financial award applicants required to submit FAFSA. *Degree program information:* Part-time programs available. Part-time, 100% online, blended/hybrid learning. Offers literature (MA); rhetoric and composition (MA); studies for language arts teachers (MA). *Application deadline:* For fall admission, 7/1 for domestic and international students; for spring admission, 11/1 for domestic and international students. Applications are processed on a rolling basis. *Application fee:* $35. Electronic applications accepted. *Application Contact:* Jessica Powers, Admissions Specialist, 229-333-5694, Fax: 229-245-3853, E-mail: jldevane@valdosta.edu. *Program Coordinator*, Dr. Maren Clegg Hyer, 229-333-5946, E-mail: mclegghyer@valdosta.edu.

Department of Psychology, Counseling, and Family Therapy Students: 7 full-time (all women), 8 part-time (7 women); includes 5 minority (all Black or African American, non-Hispanic/Latino). Average age 24. 3 applicants, 100% accepted, 2 enrolled. *Faculty:* 13 full-time (8 women), 3 part-time/adjunct (2 women). *Financial support:* In 2015–16, 5 students received support, including 2 research assistantships with full tuition reimbursements available (averaging $3,652 per year); institutionally sponsored loans and unspecified assistantships also available. Support available to part-time students. Financial award application deadline: 7/1; financial award applicants required to submit FAFSA. In 2015, 10 master's awarded. *Degree program information:* Part-time and evening/weekend programs available. Part-time, evening/weekend, 100% online, blended/hybrid learning. Offers school counseling (M Ed, Ed S). *Application deadline:* For fall admission, 7/1 for domestic and international students; for spring admission, 11/15 for domestic and international students. Applications are processed on a rolling basis. *Application fee:* $35. Electronic applications accepted. *Application Contact:* Jessica Powers, Admissions Specialist, 229-333-5694, Fax: 229-245-3853, E-mail: jldevane@valdosta.edu. *Chair*, Dr. Kate Warner, 229-333-5930, Fax: 229-259-5576, E-mail: kwarner@valdosta.edu.

Department of Social Work Students: 98 full-time (84 women), 21 part-time (19 women); includes 33 minority (23 Black or African American, non-Hispanic/Latino; 8 Hispanic/Latino; 2 Two or more races, non-Hispanic/Latino), 1 international. Average age 24. 67 applicants, 78% accepted, 47 enrolled. *Faculty:* 19 full-time (13 women). *Financial support:* In 2015–16, 4 students received support, including 2 research assistantships with full tuition reimbursements available (averaging $3,652 per year); career-related internships or fieldwork, institutionally sponsored loans, scholarships/grants, and unspecified assistantships also available. Financial award application deadline: 7/1; financial award applicants required to submit FAFSA. In 2015, 47 master's awarded. *Degree program information:* Part-time and evening/weekend programs available. Part-time, evening/weekend, online learning. Offers social work (MSW). *Application deadline:* For fall admission, 3/15 for domestic and international students. Applications are processed on a rolling basis. *Application fee:* $35. *Application Contact:* Rebecca Powers, Admissions Specialist, 229-333-5694, Fax: 229-245-3853, E-mail: rlwaters@valdosta.edu. *Head*, Dr. Mizanur Miah, 229-249-4864, Fax: 229-245-4341, E-mail: mrmiah@valdosta.edu.

Masters of Business Administration Program Students: 18 full-time (12 women), 53 part-time (29 women); includes 21 minority (18 Black or African American, non-Hispanic/Latino; 3 Two or more races, non-Hispanic/Latino), 8 international. Average age 24. 38 applicants, 79% accepted, 25 enrolled. *Faculty:* 7 full-time (0 women). *Financial support:* In 2015–16, 5 students received support, including 4 research assistantships with full tuition reimbursements available (averaging $3,652 per year); institutionally sponsored loans and scholarships/grants also available. Support available to part-time students. Financial award application deadline: 7/1; financial award applicants required to submit FAFSA. In 2015, 32 master's awarded. *Degree program information:* Part-time and evening/weekend programs available. Part-time, evening/weekend, 100% online, blended/hybrid learning. Offers business administration (MBA); healthcare administration (MBA). Program is a member of the Georgia WebMBA. *Application deadline:* For fall admission, 7/1 for domestic and international students; for spring admission, 11/1 for domestic and international students. Applications are processed on a rolling basis. *Application fee:* $35. Electronic applications accepted. *Application Contact:* Jessica Powers, Admissions Specialist, 229-333-5694, Fax: 229-245-3853, E-mail: jldevane@valdosta.edu. *Director,* Dr. Mel Schnake, 229-245-2233, Fax: 229-245-2795, E-mail: mschnake@valdosta.edu.

Program in Educational Leadership Students: 30 full-time (14 women), 9 part-time (7 women); includes 16 minority (12 Black or African American, non-Hispanic/Latino; 1 Hispanic/Latino; 3 Two or more races, non-Hispanic/Latino), 2 international. Average age 25. 32 applicants, 75% accepted, 22 enrolled. *Faculty:* 18 full-time (7 women). *Financial support:* In 2015–16, 3 students received support, including 3 research assistantships with full tuition reimbursements available (averaging $3,652 per year); institutionally sponsored loans, scholarships/grants, and unspecified assistantships also available. Support available to part-time students. Financial award application deadline: 7/1; financial award applicants required to submit FAFSA. In 2015, 24 master's awarded. 100% online, blended/hybrid learning. Offers educational leadership (M Ed). *Application deadline:* For fall admission, 7/1 for domestic and international students; for spring admission, 11/15 for domestic and international students. Applications are processed on a rolling basis. *Application fee:* $35. Electronic applications accepted. *Application Contact:* Rebecca Petrella, Coordinator of Graduate Programs, 229-333-5694, Fax: 229-245-3853, E-mail: rlwaters@valdosta.edu. *Department Head,* Dr. Leon Pate, 229-333-5633, E-mail: jlpate@valdosta.edu.

Program in Library and Information Science Students: 15 full-time (7 women), 207 part-time (168 women); includes 42 minority (18 Black or African American, non-Hispanic/Latino; 4 American Indian or Alaska Native, non-Hispanic/Latino; 2 Asian, non-Hispanic/Latino; 10 Hispanic/Latino; 1 Native Hawaiian or other Pacific Islander, non-Hispanic/Latino; 7 Two or more races, non-Hispanic/Latino), 3 international. Average age 25. 101 applicants, 54% accepted, 54 enrolled. *Faculty:* 5 full-time (3 women), 6 part-time/adjunct (4 women). *Financial support:* In 2015–16, 4 students received support, including 3 research assistantships with full tuition reimbursements available (averaging $3,652 per year); institutionally sponsored loans, scholarships/grants, and unspecified assistantships also available. Support available to part-time students. Financial award application deadline: 7/1; financial award applicants required to submit FAFSA. In 2015, 35 master's awarded. 100% online. Offers library and information science (MLIS). *Application deadline:* For fall admission, 4/15 for domestic and international students. *Application fee:* $35. *Application Contact:* Jessica Powers, Admissions Specialist, 229-333-5694, Fax: 229-245-3853, E-mail: jldevane@valdosta.edu. *Director,* Dr. Linda Most, 229-245-3732, Fax: 229-333-5862, E-mail: lrmost@valdosta.edu.

VALLEY CITY STATE UNIVERSITY, Valley City, ND 58072

General Information State-supported, coed, comprehensive institution. *Enrollment:* 1,422 graduate, professional, and undergraduate students; 5 full-time matriculated graduate/professional students (4 women), 139 part-time matriculated graduate/professional students (101 women). *Enrollment by degree level:* 144 master's. *Graduate faculty:* 20 full-time (14 women), 12 part-time/adjunct (8 women). *Student services:* Career counseling, free psychological counseling, multicultural affairs office, services for students with disabilities, writing training. *Library:* Allen Memorial Library.

Computer facilities: Computer purchase and lease plans are available. 995 computers available on campus for general student use. A campuswide network can be accessed from student residence rooms and from off campus. Online class registration is available.
Website: http://www.vcsu.edu/

General Application Contact: Misty Lindgren, Administrative Assistant for Office of Graduate Studies and Research, 701-845-7303, Fax: 701-845-7190, E-mail: misty.lindgren@vcsu.edu.

GRADUATE UNITS

Online Master of Education Program Students: 5 full-time (4 women), 139 part-time (101 women); includes 6 minority (3 Hispanic/Latino; 1 Native Hawaiian or other Pacific Islander, non-Hispanic/Latino; 2 Two or more races, non-Hispanic/Latino), 2 international. Average age 36. 25 applicants, 96% accepted, 19 enrolled. *Faculty:* 20 full-time (14 women), 12 part-time/adjunct (8 women). *Financial support:* In 2015–16, 33 students received support. Scholarships/grants, tuition waivers (full and partial), and unspecified assistantships available. Financial award application deadline: 6/15; financial award applicants required to submit FAFSA. In 2015, 59 master's awarded. *Degree program information:* Part-time and evening/weekend programs available. Part-time, evening/weekend, 100% online. Offers elementary education (M Ed); English education (M Ed); library and information technologies (M Ed); teaching and technology (M Ed); teaching English language learners (M Ed); technology education (M Ed). *Application deadline:* For fall admission, 7/22 priority date for domestic and international students; for spring admission, 12/9 priority date for domestic and international students; for summer admission, 5/6 priority date for domestic and international students. Applications are processed on a rolling basis. *Application fee:* $35. Electronic applications accepted. *Application Contact:* Misty Lindgren, Graduate Studies, 701-845-7303, Fax: 701-845-7190, E-mail: misty.lindgren@vcsu.edu. *Dean,* Dr. Gary Thompson, 701-845-7197, E-mail: gary.thompson@vcsu.edu.

VALPARAISO UNIVERSITY, Valparaiso, IN 46383

General Information Independent-religious, coed, university. *Enrollment:* 4,540 graduate, professional, and undergraduate students; 951 full-time matriculated graduate/professional students (439 women), 388 part-time matriculated graduate/professional students (203 women). *Enrollment by degree level:* 814 master's, 484 doctoral, 41 other advanced degrees. *Graduate faculty:* 39 full-time (18 women), 131 part-time/adjunct (65 women). *Graduate housing:* Room and/or apartments available on a first-come, first-served basis to single students; on-campus housing not available to married students. *Student services:* Campus employment opportunities, campus safety program, career counseling, exercise/wellness program, free psychological counseling, international student services, low-cost health insurance, multicultural affairs office, services for students with disabilities, teacher training, writing training. *Library:* Christopher Center for Library and Information Resources plus 1 other. *Collection:* Books: 429,201 (physical), 455,854 (digital/electronic); Serial titles: 3,524 (physical), 81,601 (digital/electronic); Databases: 1,136. Weekly public service hours: 112.

Computer facilities: 500 computers available on campus for general student use. A campuswide network can be accessed from student residence rooms and from off campus. Online class registration, Web academic information, degree audit, online course evaluations are available.
Website: http://www.valpo.edu/

General Application Contact: Dr. Jennifer A. Ziegler, Dean, Graduate School and Continuing Education, 219-464-5313, Fax: 219-464-5381, E-mail: jennifer.ziegler@valpo.edu.

GRADUATE UNITS

Graduate School Students: 539 full-time (231 women), 355 part-time (188 women); includes 75 minority (38 Black or African American, non-Hispanic/Latino; 16 Asian, non-Hispanic/Latino; 15 Hispanic/Latino; 6 Two or more races, non-Hispanic/Latino), 472 international. Average age 29. *Faculty:* 119 part-time/adjunct (59 women). *Financial support:* Career-related internships or fieldwork, scholarships/grants, traineeships, health care benefits, and unspecified assistantships available. Support available to part-time students. Financial award applicants required to submit FAFSA. In 2015, 357 master's, 16 doctorates, 27 other advanced degrees awarded. *Degree program information:* Part-time and evening/weekend programs available. Part-time, evening/weekend, online learning. Offers analytics and modeling (MS); arts and entertainment administration (MA); Chinese studies (MA); clinical mental health counseling (MA); cyber security (MS); digital media (MS); English (MALS, Post-Master's Certificate); English studies and communication (MA); ethics and values (MALS, Post-Master's Certificate); health administration (MHA, MS); history (MALS, Post-Master's Certificate); human behavior and society (MALS, Post-Master's Certificate); humane education (M Ed, MA, MALS, Graduate Certificate); individualized liberal studies (MALS); information technology and management (MS); initial licensure (M Ed); instructional leadership (M Ed); international commerce and policy (MS); international economics and finance (MS); legal studies and principles (Certificate); liberal studies (MALS, Post-Master's Certificate); ministry leadership and administration (MMA); sports administration (MS); sports media (MS, Certificate); teaching English to speakers of other languages (TESOL) (MA, Certificate); theology (MALS, Post-Master's Certificate); theology and ministry (MALS, Post-Master's Certificate). *Application deadline:* Applications are processed on a rolling basis. *Application fee:* $30 ($50 for international students). Electronic applications accepted. *Application Contact:* Jessica Choquette, Graduate Admissions Specialist, 219-464-6510, Fax: 219-464-5381, E-mail: jessica.choquette@valpo.edu. *Dean, Graduate School and Continuing Education,* Dr. Jennifer A. Ziegler, 219-464-5313, Fax: 219-464-5381, E-mail: jennifer.ziegler@valpo.edu.

College of Business Students: 15 full-time (9 women), 40 part-time (18 women); includes 4 minority (2 Black or African American, non-Hispanic/Latino; 2 Asian, non-Hispanic/Latino), 4 international. Average age 32. *Faculty:* 6 part-time/adjunct (2 women). *Financial support:* Available to part-time students. Applicants required to submit FAFSA. In 2015, 35 master's awarded. *Degree program information:* Part-time and evening/weekend programs available. Part-time, evening/weekend, online learning. Offers business administration (MBA); business intelligence (Certificate); engineering management (Certificate); entrepreneurship (Certificate); finance (Certificate); general business (Certificate); management (Certificate); marketing (Certificate); sustainability (Certificate). *Application deadline:* Applications are processed on a rolling basis. *Application fee:* $30 ($50 for international students). Electronic applications accepted. *Application Contact:* Cindy Scanlan, Director of Graduate Programs in Management, 219-465-7952, Fax: 219-464-5789, E-mail: cindy.scanlan@valpo.edu. *Director of Graduate Programs in Management,* Cindy Scanlan, 219-465-7952, Fax: 219-464-5789, E-mail: cindy.scanlan@valpo.edu.

College of Nursing and Health Professions Students: 52 full-time (43 women), 33 part-time (30 women); includes 9 minority (4 Black or African American, non-Hispanic/Latino; 1 Asian, non-Hispanic/Latino; 4 Hispanic/Latino), 22 international. Average age 33. *Faculty:* 13 part-time/adjunct (all women). *Financial support:* Available to part-time students. Applicants required to submit FAFSA. In 2015, 9 master's, 16 doctorates awarded. *Degree program information:* Part-time and evening/weekend programs available. Part-time, evening/weekend, online learning. Offers nursing (DNP); nursing education (MSN, Certificate); public health (MPH). *Application deadline:* Applications are processed on a rolling basis. *Application fee:* $30 ($50 for international students). Electronic applications accepted. *Application Contact:* Jessica Choquette, Graduate Admissions Specialist, 219-464-6510, Fax: 219-464-5381, E-mail: jessica.choquette@valpo.edu. *Dean,* Dr. Janet Brown, 219-464-5289, Fax: 219-464-5425, E-mail: janet.brown@valpo.edu.

School of Law Students: 407 full-time (207 women), 26 part-time (14 women); includes 166 minority (79 Black or African American, non-Hispanic/Latino; 4 American Indian or Alaska Native, non-Hispanic/Latino; 10 Asian, non-Hispanic/Latino; 64 Hispanic/Latino; 1 Native Hawaiian or other Pacific Islander, non-Hispanic/Latino; 8 Two or more races, non-Hispanic/Latino), 2 international. 928 applicants, 66% accepted, 130 enrolled. *Faculty:* 42 full-time (20 women), 20 part-time/adjunct (8 women). *Financial support:* In 2015–16, 281 students received support, including 19 fellowships, 13 research assistantships, 42 teaching assistantships; career-related internships or fieldwork, Federal Work-Study, institutionally sponsored loans, scholarships/grants, and tuition waivers (partial) also available. Support available to part-time students. Financial award application deadline: 3/1; financial award applicants required to submit FAFSA. In 2015, 130 doctorates awarded. *Degree program information:* Part-time programs available. Part-time. Offers law (LL M, JD). *Application deadline:* For fall admission, 7/15 priority date for domestic students. Applications are processed on a rolling basis. *Application fee:* $0. Electronic applications accepted. *Application Contact:* Kelly Anthony, Associate Director of Admissions, 219-465-7821, Fax: 219-465-7975, E-mail: law.admissions@valpo.edu. *Dean and Professor of Law,* Andrea D. Lyon, 219-465-7834, Fax: 219-465-7872, E-mail: andrea.lyon@valpo.edu.

VAN ANDEL INSTITUTE GRADUATE SCHOOL, Grand Rapids, MI 49503

General Information Private, coed, graduate-only institution. *Enrollment by degree level:* 22 doctoral. *Graduate faculty:* 33 full-time (24 women). *Tuition, area resident:* Full-time $25,000; part-time $835 per credit. *Student services:* Career counseling, exercise/wellness program, free psychological counseling, grant writing training, international student services, low-cost health insurance, services for students with disabilities, writing training. *Library:* Van Andel Institute Library. Study areas open 24 hours, 5–7 days a week.

Computer facilities: 4 computers available on campus for general student use. A campuswide network can be accessed from off campus.
Website: http://www.vaei.vai.org/grad-school/

General Application Contact: Christy Mayo, Enrollment and Records Administrator, 616-234-5722, Fax: 616-234-5709, E-mail: christy.mayo@vai.org.

GRADUATE UNITS

PhD Program Students: 22 full-time (13 women); includes 3 minority (1 Black or African American, non-Hispanic/Latino; 2 Asian, non-Hispanic/Latino). Average age 24. 38 applicants, 24% accepted, 7 enrolled. *Faculty:* 33 full-time (9 women). *Financial support:* In 2015–16, 22 students received support, including 22 fellowships; health care benefits also available. In 2015, 3 degrees awarded. Offers cell and molecular genetics (PhD). *Application deadline:* For fall admission, 1/5 for domestic and international students. Applications are processed on a rolling basis. *Application fee:* $0. Electronic applications accepted. *President and Dean,* Steve Triezeberg, 616-234-5708, Fax: 616-234-5709, E-mail: steve.triezenberg@vai.org.

VANCOUVER ISLAND UNIVERSITY, Nanaimo, BC V9R 5S5, Canada

General Information Province-supported, coed, comprehensive institution. *Graduate housing:* Room and/or apartments available on a first-come, first-served basis to single students; on-campus housing not available to married students. Housing application deadline: 3/5.

GRADUATE UNITS

Master of Business Administration Program ***Degree program information:*** Part-time programs available. Part-time. Offers international business (MBA). Program offered jointly with University of Hertfordshire. Electronic applications accepted.

VANCOUVER SCHOOL OF THEOLOGY, Vancouver, BC V6T 1L4, Canada

General Information Independent-religious, coed, graduate-only institution. *Graduate housing:* Rooms and/or apartments guaranteed to single students and available to married students. Housing application deadline: 4/7.

GRADUATE UNITS

Graduate and Professional Programs ***Degree program information:*** Part-time programs available. Part-time, online learning. Offers indigenous and inter-religious studies (MA, Th M); theological studies (MATS, Diploma); theology (M Div, Th M). Electronic applications accepted.

VANDERBILT UNIVERSITY, Nashville, TN 37240-1001

General Information Independent, coed, university. CGS member. *Enrollment:* 12,567 graduate, professional, and undergraduate students; 5,023 full-time matriculated graduate/professional students (2,776 women), 699 part-time matriculated graduate/professional students (540 women). *Enrollment by degree level:* 2,565 master's, 3,132 doctoral, 25 other advanced degrees. *Graduate faculty:* 1,007 full-time (290 women), 61 part-time/adjunct (17 women). *Graduate housing:* On-campus housing not available. *Student services:* Campus employment opportunities, campus safety program, career counseling, child daycare facilities, exercise/wellness program, free psychological counseling, grant writing training, international student services, low-cost health insurance, multicultural affairs office, services for students with disabilities, teacher training, writing training. *Library:* Jean and Alexander Heard Library plus 7 others. *Research affiliation:* Celgene Corporation (biopharmaceuticals), Medtronic, Incorporated (medical research), Sandhill Scientific, Inc. (medical research), Westat, Inc. (research and evaluation), Amgen (medicine), Boston Scientific Corporation (health science and technology).

Computer facilities: A campuswide network can be accessed from student residence rooms and from off campus. Online class registration, productivity and educational software are available.
Website: http://www.vanderbilt.edu/

General Application Contact: Walter B. Bieschke, Program Coordinator for Graduate Admissions, 615-322-0236, Fax: 615-343-9936, E-mail: vandygrad@vanderbilt.edu.

GRADUATE UNITS

Center for Medicine, Health, and Society Students: 6 full-time (3 women); all minorities (4 Black or African American, non-Hispanic/Latino; 1 Asian, non-Hispanic/Latino; 1 Two or more races, non-Hispanic/Latino). Average age 23. 16 applicants, 69% accepted, 10 enrolled. *Faculty:* 4 full-time (2 women). *Financial support:* Federal Work-Study, scholarships/grants, and health care benefits available. Financial award application deadline: 1/15; financial award applicants required to submit CSS PROFILE or FAFSA. In 2015, 10 master's awarded. Offers medicine, health, and society (MA). *Application deadline:* For fall admission, 1/15 for domestic and international students. Electronic applications accepted. *Application Contact:* Elisabeth Sandberg, Assistant Director, 615-343-0916, Fax: 615-322-2731, E-mail: elisabeth.sandberg@vanderbilt.edu. *Director,* Dr. Jonathan Metzl, 615-343-0916, Fax: 615-343-8889, E-mail: jonathan.metzl@vanderbilt.edu.

Department of Anthropology Students: 28 full-time (19 women); includes 6 minority (all Hispanic/Latino), 8 international. Average age 32. 55 applicants, 11% accepted, 3 enrolled. *Faculty:* 12 full-time (3 women). *Financial support:* Fellowships with tuition reimbursements, research assistantships with full tuition reimbursements, teaching assistantships with full tuition reimbursements, career-related internships or fieldwork, Federal Work-Study, institutionally sponsored loans, scholarships/grants, and health care benefits available. Financial award application deadline: 1/15; financial award applicants required to submit CSS PROFILE or FAFSA. In 2015, 4 master's, 6 doctorates awarded. Offers anthropology (MA, PhD). *Application deadline:* For fall admission, 1/15 for domestic and international students. *Application fee:* $0. Electronic applications accepted. *Director of Graduate Studies,* Dr. Tiffiny Tung, 615-343-6120, Fax: 615-343-0230, E-mail: t.tung@vanderbilt.edu.

Department of Biological Sciences Students: 49 full-time (27 women); includes 9 minority (2 Black or African American, non-Hispanic/Latino; 4 Asian, non-Hispanic/Latino; 2 Hispanic/Latino; 1 Two or more races, non-Hispanic/Latino), 13 international. Average age 26. 133 applicants, 6% accepted, 5 enrolled. *Faculty:* 20 full-time (3 women), 1 part-time/adjunct. *Financial support:* Fellowships with tuition reimbursements, research assistantships with full tuition reimbursements, teaching assistantships with full tuition reimbursements, Federal Work-Study, institutionally sponsored loans, scholarships/grants, traineeships, and health care benefits available. Financial award application deadline: 1/15; financial award applicants required to submit CSS PROFILE or FAFSA. In 2015, 1 master's, 11 doctorates awarded. Offers biological sciences (MS, PhD). *Application deadline:* For fall admission, 1/15 for domestic and international students. Electronic applications accepted. *Application Contact:* Leslie L. Maxwell, Program Coordinator, 615-343-3076, Fax: 615-343-6707, E-mail: leslie.l.maxwell@vanderbilt.edu. *Director of Graduate Studies,* Dr. Katherine Friedman, 615-322-2008, Fax: 615-343-6707, E-mail: donna.webb@vanderbilt.edu.

Department of Biomedical Informatics Students: 26 full-time (10 women), 3 part-time (1 woman); includes 8 minority (2 Black or African American, non-Hispanic/Latino; 5 Asian, non-Hispanic/Latino; 1 Hispanic/Latino), 1 international. Average age 31. 54 applicants, 11% accepted, 4 enrolled. *Faculty:* 16 full-time (3 women). *Financial support:* Fellowships with tuition reimbursements, research assistantships with tuition reimbursements, teaching assistantships with tuition reimbursements, Federal Work-Study, institutionally sponsored loans, scholarships/grants, traineeships, and health care benefits available. Financial award application deadline: 1/15; financial award applicants required to submit CSS PROFILE or FAFSA. In 2015, 5 master's, 1 doctorate awarded. *Degree program information:* Part-time programs available. Part-time. Offers biomedical informatics (MS, PhD). *Application deadline:* For fall admission, 1/15 for domestic and international students. Electronic applications accepted. *Application Contact:* Rischelle Jenkins, Administrative Assistant, 615-936-1068, Fax: 615-936-1427, E-mail: rischelle.jenkins@vanderbilt.edu. *Director of Graduate Studies,* Dr. Cindy Gadd, 615-936-1423, Fax: 615-936-1427, E-mail: cindy.gadd@vanderbilt.edu.

Department of Cancer Biology Students: 31 full-time (22 women); includes 10 minority (4 Black or African American, non-Hispanic/Latino; 3 Asian, non-Hispanic/Latino; 2 Hispanic/Latino; 1 Two or more races, non-Hispanic/Latino), 2 international. Average age 27. *Faculty:* 11 full-time (6 women). *Financial support:* Fellowships with tuition reimbursements, research assistantships with tuition reimbursements, Federal Work-Study, institutionally sponsored loans, scholarships/grants, traineeships, and health care benefits available. Financial award application deadline: 1/15; financial award applicants required to submit CSS PROFILE or FAFSA. In 2015, 1 master's, 10 doctorates awarded. Offers cancer biology (MS, PhD). *Application deadline:* For fall admission, 1/15 for domestic and international students. *Application fee:* $0. Electronic applications accepted. *Application Contact:* Tracy Tveit, Graduate Program Coordinator, 615-936-2910, Fax: 615-936-2911, E-mail: tracy.s.tveit@vanderbilt.edu. *Director of Graduate Studies,* Dr. Jin Chen, 615-322-0375, Fax: 615-936-2911, E-mail: jin.chen@vanderbilt.edu.

Department of Chemistry Students: 114 full-time (41 women); includes 19 minority (5 Black or African American, non-Hispanic/Latino; 3 Asian, non-Hispanic/Latino; 7 Hispanic/Latino; 4 Two or more races, non-Hispanic/Latino), 8 international. Average age 26. 339 applicants, 17% accepted, 19 enrolled. *Faculty:* 19 full-time (3 women). *Financial support:* Fellowships with tuition reimbursements, research assistantships with full tuition reimbursements, teaching assistantships with full tuition reimbursements, Federal Work-Study, institutionally sponsored loans, scholarships/grants, traineeships, and health care benefits available. Financial award application deadline: 1/15; financial award applicants required to submit CSS PROFILE or FAFSA. In 2015, 11 master's, 13 doctorates awarded. Offers analytical chemistry (MAT, MS, PhD); inorganic chemistry (MAT, MS, PhD); organic chemistry (MAT, MS, PhD); physical chemistry (MAT, MS, PhD); theoretical chemistry (MAT, MS). *Application deadline:* For fall admission, 1/15 for domestic and international students. *Application fee:* $0. Electronic applications accepted. *Application Contact:* Sandra Ford, Administrative Assistant, 615-322-8695, Fax: 615-322-4936, E-mail: sandra.e.ford@vanderbilt.edu. *Director of Graduate Studies,* Dr. Carmello Rizzo, 615-322-2861, Fax: 615-322-4936, E-mail: c.rizzo@vanderbilt.edu.

Department of Classical Studies Average age 24. *Faculty:* 4 full-time (2 women). *Financial support:* Fellowships with tuition reimbursements, teaching assistantships with tuition reimbursements, Federal Work-Study, institutionally sponsored loans, scholarships/grants, and health care benefits available. Financial award application deadline: 1/15; financial award applicants required to submit CSS PROFILE or FAFSA. In 2015, 1 master's awarded. Offers classics (MA). *Application deadline:* For fall admission, 1/15 for domestic and international students. Electronic applications accepted. *Application Contact:* Walter B. Bieschke, Program Coordinator for Graduate Admissions, 615-322-0236, Fax: 615-343-9936, E-mail: vandygrad@vanderbilt.edu. *Director of Graduate Studies,* Dr. Barbara Tsakirgis, 615-322-2516, Fax: 615-343-7261, E-mail: barbara.tsakirgis@vanderbilt.edu.

Department of Earth and Environmental Sciences Students: 7 full-time (4 women), 4 part-time (3 women); includes 1 minority (Black or African American, non-Hispanic/Latino). Average age 23. 54 applicants, 15% accepted, 5 enrolled. *Faculty:* 10 full-time (2 women). *Financial support:* Fellowships with tuition reimbursements, research assistantships with tuition reimbursements, teaching assistantships with full tuition reimbursements, career-related internships or fieldwork, Federal Work-Study, institutionally sponsored loans, and health care benefits available. Financial award application deadline: 1/15; financial award applicants required to submit CSS PROFILE or FAFSA. In 2015, 8 master's awarded. Offers earth and environmental sciences (MAT, MS). *Application deadline:* For fall admission, 1/15 for domestic and international students. *Application fee:* $0. Electronic applications accepted. *Application Contact:* Teri Pugh, Office Assistant, 615-322-2976, E-mail: teri.pugh@vanderbilt.edu. *Director of Graduate Studies,* Dr. Guil Gualda, 615-322-2976, E-mail: g.gualda@vanderbilt.edu.

Department of Economics Students: 118 full-time (48 women), 1 part-time; includes 10 minority (1 Black or African American, non-Hispanic/Latino; 2 Asian, non-Hispanic/Latino; 5 Hispanic/Latino; 2 Two or more races, non-Hispanic/Latino), 80 international. Average age 26. 589 applicants, 29% accepted, 44 enrolled. *Faculty:* 32 full-time (5 women). *Financial support:* Fellowships with tuition reimbursements, teaching assistantships with tuition reimbursements, career-related internships or fieldwork, Federal Work-Study, institutionally sponsored loans, scholarships/grants, and health care benefits available. Financial award application deadline: 1/15; financial award applicants required to submit CSS PROFILE or FAFSA. In 2015, 43 master's, 2 doctorates awarded. Offers economic development (MA); economics (PhD). *Application deadline:* For fall admission, 1/15 for domestic and international students; for spring admission, 11/1 for domestic students. Applications are processed on a rolling basis. Electronic applications accepted. *Application Contact:* Kathleen Finn, Assistant to the Director of Graduate Studies, 615-322-3419, Fax: 615-343-8495, E-mail: kathleen.finn@vanderbilt.edu. *Director of Graduate Studies,* Dr. Jennifer Reinganum, 615-322-2871, Fax: 615-343-8495, E-mail: jennifer.f.reinganum@vanderbilt.edu.

Department of English Students: 40 full-time (30 women); includes 16 minority (9 Black or African American, non-Hispanic/Latino; 3 Asian, non-Hispanic/Latino; 4 Hispanic/Latino), 3 international. Average age 28. 296 applicants, 6% accepted, 8 enrolled. *Faculty:* 32 full-time (20 women). *Financial support:* Fellowships with tuition reimbursements, research assistantships with tuition reimbursements, teaching assistantships with full tuition reimbursements, Federal Work-Study, institutionally sponsored loans, scholarships/grants, and health care benefits available. Financial award application deadline: 1/15; financial award applicants required to submit CSS PROFILE or FAFSA. In 2015, 7 master's, 4 doctorates awarded. Offers English (MA, MAT, PhD). *Application deadline:* For fall admission, 1/15 for domestic and international students. Electronic applications accepted. *Application Contact:* Donna Caplan, Administrative Assistant, 615-322-2541, Fax: 615-343-8028, E-mail: donna.caplan@vanderbilt.edu. *Director of Graduate Studies,* Dr. Mark Wollaeger, 615-322-2541, Fax: 615-343-8028, E-mail: mark.wollaeger@vanderbilt.edu.

Department of French and Italian Students: 8 full-time (7 women), 3 international. Average age 28. 24 applicants, 13% accepted, 3 enrolled. *Faculty:* 10 full-time (5 women). *Financial support:* Fellowships with tuition reimbursements, teaching assistantships with tuition reimbursements, career-related internships or fieldwork, Federal Work-Study, institutionally sponsored loans, scholarships/grants, and health care benefits available. Financial award application deadline: 1/15; financial award applicants required to submit CSS PROFILE or FAFSA. In 2015, 1 master's, 3 doctorates awarded. Offers French (MA, MAT, PhD). *Application deadline:* For fall admission, 1/15 for domestic and international students. Electronic applications accepted. *Application Contact:* Laura Dossett, Coordinator, 615-343-0426, Fax: 615-343-6909, E-mail: laura.dossett@vanderbilt.edu. *Director of Graduate Studies,* Dr. Nathalie Debrauwere-Miller, 615-322-6900, Fax: 615-343-6909, E-mail: n.debrau@vanderbilt.edu.

Department of Germanic and Slavic Languages Students: 25 full-time (18 women); includes 4 minority (1 Black or African American, non-Hispanic/Latino; 2 Hispanic/Latino; 1 Two or more races, non-Hispanic/Latino), 7 international. Average age 32. 11 applicants, 55% accepted, 4 enrolled. *Faculty:* 5 full-time (2 women). *Financial support:* Fellowships with tuition reimbursements, teaching assistantships with tuition reimbursements, career-related internships or fieldwork, Federal Work-Study, institutionally sponsored loans, scholarships/grants, and health care benefits available. Financial award application deadline: 1/15; financial award applicants required to submit CSS PROFILE or FAFSA. In 2015, 1 master's, 1 doctorate awarded. Offers German (MA, MAT, PhD). *Application deadline:* For fall admission, 1/15 for domestic and international students. Electronic applications accepted. *Application Contact:* Amber Miller, Coordinator, 615-322-2611, Fax: 615-343-7258, E-mail: amber.miller@vanderbilt.edu. *Director of Graduate Studies,* Dr. Christoph Zeller, 615-875-9065, Fax: 615-343-7258, E-mail: christoph.zeller@vanderbilt.edu.

Department of History Students: 58 full-time (31 women); includes 12 minority (4 Black or African American, non-Hispanic/Latino; 1 Asian, non-Hispanic/Latino; 5 Hispanic/Latino; 2 Two or more races, non-Hispanic/Latino), 9 international. Average age 30. 169 applicants, 14% accepted, 9 enrolled. *Faculty:* 34 full-time (10 women). *Financial support:* Fellowships with full tuition reimbursements, teaching assistantships with full tuition reimbursements, Federal Work-Study, institutionally sponsored loans, scholarships/grants, and health care benefits available. Financial award application deadline: 1/15; financial award applicants required to submit CSS PROFILE or FAFSA. In 2015, 10 master's, 8 doctorates awarded. Offers history (MA, MAT, PhD). *Application deadline:* For fall admission, 1/15 for domestic and international students. *Application fee:* $0. Electronic applications accepted. *Application Contact:* Susan Hilderbrand, Program Coordinator, 615-322-2575, Fax: 615-343-6002, E-mail: susan.hilderbrand@vanderbilt.edu. *Acting Director of Graduate Studies,* Dr. Celia Applegate, 615-322-2575, Fax: 615-343-6002, E-mail: celia.applegate@vanderbilt.edu.

Department of Mathematics Students: 32 full-time (1 woman); includes 2 minority (1 Black or African American, non-Hispanic/Latino; 1 Asian, non-Hispanic/Latino), 21 international. Average age 25. 93 applicants, 30% accepted, 4 enrolled. *Faculty:* 31 full-time (1 woman). *Financial support:* Fellowships with tuition reimbursements, research assistantships with full tuition reimbursements, teaching assistantships with full tuition reimbursements, Federal Work-Study, institutionally sponsored loans, scholarships/grants, and health care benefits available. Financial award application deadline: 1/15; financial award applicants required to submit CSS PROFILE or FAFSA. In 2015, 11 master's, 5 doctorates awarded. Offers mathematics (MA, MAT, MS, PhD). *Application deadline:* For fall admission, 1/15 for domestic and international students. *Application fee:* $0. Electronic applications accepted. *Application Contact:* Laura Rongione, Office Assistant, 615-322-6672, Fax: 315-343-0215, E-mail: laura.rongione@vanderbilt.edu. *Director of Graduate Studies,* Dr. Denis Osin, 615-322-6672, Fax: 615-343-0215, E-mail: denis.v.osin@vanderbilt.edu.

Department of Philosophy Students: 29 full-time (17 women); includes 6 minority (1 Asian, non-Hispanic/Latino; 4 Hispanic/Latino; 1 Two or more races, non-Hispanic/Latino), 2 international. Average age 31. 192 applicants, 5% accepted, 5 enrolled. *Faculty:* 15 full-time (4 women). *Financial support:* Fellowships with full tuition reimbursements, teaching assistantships with full tuition reimbursements, Federal Work-Study, institutionally sponsored loans, scholarships/grants, and health care benefits available. Financial award application deadline: 1/15; financial award applicants required to submit CSS PROFILE or FAFSA. In 2015, 2 master's, 13 doctorates awarded. Offers philosophy (MA, PhD). *Application deadline:* For fall admission, 1/15 for domestic and international students. Electronic applications accepted. *Application Contact:* Rebecca Davenport, Administrative Assistant, 615-322-2637, Fax: 615-343-7259, E-mail: rebecca.davenport@vanderbilt.edu. *Director of Graduate Studies,* Dr. Julian Wuerth, 615-322-2637, Fax: 615-343-7259, E-mail: julian.wuerth@vanderbilt.edu.

Department of Physics and Astronomy Students: 55 full-time (9 women); includes 10 minority (2 Black or African American, non-Hispanic/Latino; 1 Asian, non-Hispanic/Latino; 6 Hispanic/Latino; 1 Two or more races, non-Hispanic/Latino), 18 international. Average age 27. 169 applicants, 19% accepted, 7 enrolled. *Faculty:* 26 full-time (3 women). *Financial support:* Fellowships with tuition reimbursements, research assistantships with full tuition reimbursements, teaching assistantships with full tuition reimbursements, career-related internships or fieldwork, Federal Work-Study, and institutionally sponsored loans available. Financial award application deadline: 1/15; financial award applicants required to submit CSS PROFILE or FAFSA. In 2015, 4 master's, 12 doctorates awarded. Offers astronomy (MS); health physics (MA); physics (MAT, MS, PhD). *Application deadline:* For fall admission, 1/15 for domestic and international students. Electronic applications accepted. *Application Contact:* Donald Pickert, Administrative Assistant, 615-343-1026, Fax: 615-343-7263, E-mail: donald.pickert@vanderbilt.edu. *Director of Graduate Studies,* Dr. Julia Velkovska, 615-322-2828, Fax: 615-343-7263, E-mail: julia.velkovska@vanderbilt.edu.

Department of Political Science Students: 39 full-time (16 women); includes 4 minority (1 Black or African American, non-Hispanic/Latino; 1 Asian, non-Hispanic/Latino; 1 Hispanic/Latino; 1 Two or more races, non-Hispanic/Latino), 10 international. Average age 28. 159 applicants, 12% accepted, 7 enrolled. *Faculty:* 24 full-time (10 women). *Financial support:* Fellowships with full tuition reimbursements, research assistantships with full tuition reimbursements, teaching assistantships with full tuition reimbursements, Federal Work-Study, institutionally sponsored loans, scholarships/grants, and health care benefits available. Financial award application deadline: 1/15; financial award applicants required to submit CSS PROFILE or FAFSA. In 2015, 1 master's, 3 doctorates awarded. Offers political science (MA, MAT, PhD). *Application deadline:* For fall admission, 1/15 for domestic and international students. Electronic applications accepted. *Application Contact:* Darlene Davidson, Administrative Assistant, 615-322-6781, Fax: 615-343-6003, E-mail: darlene.l.davidson@vanderbilt.edu. *Director of Graduate Studies,* Dr. Jon Hiskey, 615-322-6222, Fax: 615-343-6003, E-mail: j.hiskey@vanderbilt.edu.

Department of Religion Students: 74 full-time (32 women); includes 18 minority (13 Black or African American, non-Hispanic/Latino; 2 Asian, non-Hispanic/Latino; 2 Hispanic/Latino; 1 Two or more races, non-Hispanic/Latino), 8 international. Average age 33. 149 applicants, 13% accepted, 11 enrolled. *Faculty:* 8 full-time (4 women). *Financial support:* Fellowships with tuition reimbursements, teaching assistantships with tuition reimbursements, Federal Work-Study, institutionally sponsored loans, health care benefits, and tuition waivers (full and partial) available. Support available to part-time students. Financial award application deadline: 1/15; financial award applicants required to submit CSS PROFILE or FAFSA. In 2015, 15 master's, 13 doctorates awarded. Offers religion (MA, PhD). *Application deadline:* For fall admission, 1/15 for domestic and international students. Electronic applications accepted. *Application Contact:* Marie McEntire, Administrative Assistant, 615-322-2776, Fax: 615-343-9957, E-mail: marie.mcentire@vanderbilt.edu. *Director of Graduate Studies,* Dr. James Byrd, Jr., 615-343-9977, Fax: 615-343-9957, E-mail: james.p.byrd@vanderbilt.edu.

Department of Sociology Students: 36 full-time (28 women); includes 10 minority (5 Black or African American, non-Hispanic/Latino; 2 Asian, non-Hispanic/Latino; 3 Hispanic/Latino), 3 international. Average age 28. 136 applicants, 18% accepted, 12 enrolled. *Faculty:* 19 full-time (7 women). *Financial support:* Fellowships with full tuition reimbursements, research assistantships, teaching assistantships with full tuition reimbursements, Federal Work-Study, institutionally sponsored loans, scholarships/grants, and health care benefits available. Financial award application deadline: 1/15; financial award applicants required to submit CSS PROFILE or FAFSA. In 2015, 8 master's, 7 doctorates awarded. Offers sociology (MA, PhD). *Application deadline:* For fall admission, 1/15 for domestic and international students. Electronic applications accepted. *Application Contact:* Anne Wall, Coordinator, 615-322-7500, Fax: 615-322-7505, E-mail: anne.wall@vanderbilt.edu. *Director of Graduate Studies,* Dr. Mariano Sana, 615-322-7626, Fax: 615-322-7505, E-mail: mariano.sana@vanderbilt.edu.

Department of Spanish and Portuguese Students: 21 full-time (9 women), 1 (woman) part-time; includes 4 minority (1 Black or African American, non-Hispanic/Latino; 3 Hispanic/Latino), 8 international. Average age 31. 59 applicants, 17% accepted, 7 enrolled. *Faculty:* 14 full-time (6 women). *Financial support:* Fellowships with tuition reimbursements, teaching assistantships with full tuition reimbursements, Federal Work-Study, institutionally sponsored loans, and health care benefits available. Financial award application deadline: 1/15; financial award applicants required to submit CSS PROFILE or FAFSA. In 2015, 3 master's, 4 doctorates awarded. Offers Portuguese (MA); Spanish (MA, MAT, PhD); Spanish and Portuguese (PhD). *Application deadline:* For fall admission, 1/15 for domestic and international students. Electronic applications accepted. *Application Contact:* Cindy Martinez, Administrative Assistant, 615-322-6930, Fax: 615-343-7260, E-mail: cindy.m.martinez@vanderbilt.edu. *Director of Graduate Studies,* Dr. Christina Kargeorgou-Bastea, 615-322-6858, Fax: 615-343-7260, E-mail: christina.karageorgou@vanderbilt.edu.

Divinity School Students: 216. Average age 29. *Faculty:* 38 full-time (13 women), 3 part-time/adjunct (1 woman). *Financial support:* In 2015–16, 214 students received support. Federal Work-Study and scholarships/grants available. Support available to part-time students. Financial award application deadline: 4/1. In 2015, 64 master's awarded. *Degree program information:* Part-time programs available. Part-time. Offers divinity (M Div, MTS). *Application deadline:* For winter admission, 1/15 priority date for domestic and international students; for spring admission, 4/1 for domestic and international students. Applications are processed on a rolling basis. *Application fee:* $0. Electronic applications accepted. *Application Contact:* Rev. Katherine H. Smith, Assistant Dean for Admissions, Vocation, and Stewardship, 615-343-3963, Fax: 615-322-0691, E-mail: katherine.smith@vanderbilt.edu. *Dean,* Dr. Emilie M Townes, 615-322-2776, Fax: 615-343-9957, E-mail: emilie.m.townes@vanderbilt.edu.

Peabody College Students: 518 full-time (434 women), 184 part-time (120 women); includes 107 minority (44 Black or African American, non-Hispanic/Latino; 20 Asian, non-Hispanic/Latino; 28 Hispanic/Latino; 15 Two or more races, non-Hispanic/Latino), 76 international. Average age 27. 1,411 applicants, 61% accepted, 352 enrolled. *Faculty:* 146 full-time (93 women), 71 part-time/adjunct (43 women). *Financial support:* In 2015–16, 418 students received support, including 5 fellowships with partial tuition reimbursements available, 142 research assistantships with partial tuition reimbursements available, 80 teaching assistantships with partial tuition reimbursements available; career-related internships or fieldwork, Federal Work-Study, institutionally sponsored loans, scholarships/grants, traineeships, tuition waivers (partial), and unspecified assistantships also available. Support available to part-time students. Financial award application deadline: 1/15; financial award applicants required to submit FAFSA. In 2015, 321 master's, 16 doctorates awarded. *Degree program information:* Part-time programs available. Part-time. Offers child studies (M Ed); clinical psychological assessment (M Ed); community development and action (M Ed); community research and action (PhD); education and human development (M Ed, MPP, Ed D, PhD); education policy (MPP); educational leadership and policy (Ed D); elementary education (M Ed); English language learners (M Ed); higher education (M Ed); higher education leadership and policy (Ed D, PhD); human development counseling (M Ed); independent school leadership (M Ed); international education policy and management (M Ed); K-12 educational leadership and policy (PhD); leadership and organizational performance (M Ed); leadership and policy studies (PhD); learning and design (M Ed); learning, diversity, and urban studies (M Ed); learning, teaching and diversity (PhD); psychological sciences (PhD); quantitative methods (M Ed); reading education (M Ed); secondary education (M Ed); special education (M Ed, PhD). *Application deadline:* For fall admission, 12/31 priority date for domestic and international students; for spring admission, 11/1 priority date for domestic and international students. Applications are processed on a rolling basis. *Application fee:* $0. Electronic applications accepted. *Application Contact:* Kimberly Brazil, Director of Graduate and Professional Admissions, 615-332-8410, Fax: 615-343-3474, E-mail: kim.brazil@vanderbilt.edu. *Dean,* Dr. Camilla P. Benbow, 615-322-8407, Fax: 615-322-8501, E-mail: camilla.benbow@vanderbilt.edu.

Program in Creative Writing Students: 15 full-time (7 women); includes 3 minority (1 Asian, non-Hispanic/Latino; 2 Two or more races, non-Hispanic/Latino). Average age 27. 561 applicants, 1% accepted, 6 enrolled. *Faculty:* 32 full-time (20 women). *Financial support:* Fellowships with tuition reimbursements, teaching assistantships with tuition reimbursements, Federal Work-Study, institutionally sponsored loans, and health care benefits available. Financial award application deadline: 1/15; financial award applicants required to submit CSS PROFILE or FAFSA. In 2015, 5 master's awarded. Offers creative writing (MFA). *Application deadline:* For fall admission, 1/15 for domestic and international students. Electronic applications accepted. *Application Contact:* Walter B. Bieschke, Program Coordinator for Graduate Admissions, 615-342-0236, E-mail: vandygrad@vanderbilt.edu. *Director,* Dr. Mark Jarman, 615-322-2618, E-mail: mark.jarman@vanderbilt.edu.

Program in Human Genetics Students: 13 full-time (7 women); includes 2 minority (1 American Indian or Alaska Native, non-Hispanic/Latino; 1 Hispanic/Latino). Average age 29. *Faculty:* 27 full-time (5 women). *Financial support:* Fellowships with tuition reimbursements, research assistantships with tuition reimbursements, Federal Work-Study, institutionally sponsored loans, traineeships, and health care benefits available. Financial award application deadline: 1/15; financial award applicants required to submit CSS PROFILE or FAFSA. In 2015, 7 doctorates awarded. Offers human genetics (PhD). *Application deadline:* For fall admission, 1/15 for domestic and international students. *Application fee:* $0. Electronic applications accepted. *Application Contact:* Walter B.

Bieschke, Program Coordinator for Graduate Admissions, 615-342-0236, E-mail: vandygrad@vanderbilt.edu. *Director of Graduate Studies*, Dr. David Samuels, 615-343-8555, Fax: 615-322-1453, E-mail: david.c.samuels@vanderbilt.edu.

Program in Latin American Studies Students: 11 full-time (8 women), 1 part-time (0 women); includes 3 minority (1 Black or African American, non-Hispanic/Latino; 2 Hispanic/Latino), 1 international. Average age 25. 12 applicants, 67% accepted, 6 enrolled. *Faculty:* 1 (woman) full-time. *Financial support:* Teaching assistantships with full tuition reimbursements, Federal Work-Study, institutionally sponsored loans, and health care benefits available. Financial award application deadline: 1/15; financial award applicants required to submit CSS PROFILE or FAFSA. In 2015, 5 master's awarded. Offers Latin American studies (MA). *Application deadline:* For fall admission, 1/15 for domestic and international students. *Application fee:* $0. Electronic applications accepted. *Application Contact:* Alma Paz-Sanmiguel, Coordinator, 615-322-2527, Fax: 615-343-6002, E-mail: alma.paz-sanmiguel@vanderbilt.edu. *Associate Director of Center for Latin American Studies*, Dr. W. Frank Robinson, 615-322-2527, Fax: 615-343-6002, E-mail: william.f.robinson@vanderbilt.edu.

Program in Liberal Arts and Science Students: 1 (woman) full-time, 33 part-time (21 women); includes 9 minority (4 Black or African American, non-Hispanic/Latino; 1 American Indian or Alaska Native, non-Hispanic/Latino; 1 Hispanic/Latino; 3 Two or more races, non-Hispanic/Latino). Average age 41. 14 applicants, 57% accepted, 7 enrolled. *Financial support:* Institutionally sponsored loans and tuition waivers (partial) available. In 2015, 6 master's awarded. *Degree program information:* Part-time programs available. Part-time. Offers liberal arts and science (MLAS). *Application deadline:* For fall admission, 1/15 priority date for domestic students, 1/15 for international students; for spring admission, 11/15 for domestic and international students. Applications are processed on a rolling basis. *Application Contact:* Lisa Poynter, Coordinator, 615-343-3140, Fax: 615-343-8702, E-mail: lisa.poynter@vanderbilt.edu. *Associate Dean and Director of Graduate Studies*, Dr. Martin Rapisarda, 615-343-3140, Fax: 615-343-8702, E-mail: martin.rapisarda@vanderbilt.edu.

Program in Nursing Science Students: 26 full-time (20 women), 5 part-time (4 women); includes 3 minority (1 Black or African American, non-Hispanic/Latino; 1 Hispanic/Latino; 1 Native Hawaiian or other Pacific Islander, non-Hispanic/Latino). Average age 39. 39 applicants, 18% accepted, 6 enrolled. *Faculty:* 20 full-time (16 women), 1 part-time/adjunct (0 women). *Financial support:* Fellowships with full tuition reimbursements, research assistantships with full tuition reimbursements, teaching assistantships with full tuition reimbursements, career-related internships or fieldwork, Federal Work-Study, institutionally sponsored loans, scholarships/grants, health care benefits, and tuition waivers (full and partial) available. Financial award application deadline: 1/15; financial award applicants required to submit CSS PROFILE or FAFSA. In 2015, 3 doctorates awarded. Offers nursing science (PhD). *Application deadline:* For fall admission, 1/15 for domestic and international students. Electronic applications accepted. *Application Contact:* Irene McKirgan, Administrative Manager, 615-322-7410, E-mail: irene.mckirgan@vanderbilt.edu. *Director of Graduate Studies*, Sheila Ridner, 615-322-3800, Fax: 615-343-5898, E-mail: sheila.ridner@vanderbilt.edu.

School of Engineering ***Degree program information:*** Part-time programs available. Part-time. Offers biomedical engineering (M Eng, MS, PhD); chemical and biomolecular engineering (M Eng, MS, PhD); civil engineering (M Eng, MS, PhD); computer science (M Eng, MS, PhD); electrical engineering (M Eng, MS, PhD); engineering (M Eng, MS, PhD); environmental engineering (M Eng, MS, PhD); environmental management (MS, PhD); materials science (M Eng, MS, PhD); mechanical engineering (M Eng, MS, PhD). MS and PhD offered through the Graduate School. Electronic applications accepted.

School of Medicine Average age 20. *Financial support:* Institutionally sponsored loans and scholarships/grants available. Financial award application deadline: 3/1; financial award applicants required to submit FAFSA. Offers audiology (Au D, PhD); biochemistry (MS, PhD); cell and developmental biology (MS, PhD); chemical and physical biology (PhD); clinical investigation (MS); deaf education (MED); medicine (MDE, MMP, MS, MSCI, Au D, DMP, MD, PhD); microbiology and immunology (MS, PhD); molecular physiology and biophysics (MS, PhD); pathology (PhD); pharmacology (PhD); speech-language pathology (MS). *Application deadline:* For fall admission, 11/15 for domestic and international students. *Application fee:* $50. *Dean, School of Medicine*, Dr. Jeffrey R. Balser, 615-936-3030, E-mail: jeffrey.balser@vanderbilt.edu.

Vanderbilt Law School Offers law (LL M, JD); law and economics (PhD). Electronic applications accepted.

Vanderbilt University Owen Graduate School of Management Students: 343 full-time (95 women); includes 37 minority (11 Black or African American, non-Hispanic/Latino; 9 Asian, non-Hispanic/Latino; 7 Hispanic/Latino; 10 Two or more races, non-Hispanic/Latino), 68 international. Average age 28. *Faculty:* 47 full-time (9 women). *Financial support:* In 2015–16, 324 students received support. Scholarships/grants and tuition waivers (full and partial) available. Financial award application deadline: 5/1. In 2015, 331 master's awarded. *Degree program information:* Evening/weekend programs available. Evening/weekend. Offers accountancy (M Acc); accounting (MBA); business administration (EMBA, MBA); finance (MBA, MS); general management (MBA); health care (MBA); healthcare (MM); human and organizational performance (MBA); management (EMBA, M Acc, M Mark, MBA, MM, MS); marketing (M Mark); operations (MBA); strategy (MBA); valuation (M Acc). *Application deadline:* For fall admission, 11/28 for domestic and international students; for winter admission, 1/16 for domestic and international students; for spring admission, 3/5 for domestic and international students. *Dean*, Eric Johnson, 615-343-1673, E-mail: officeofdean@owen.vanderbilt.edu.

Vanderbilt University School of Nursing Students: 478 full-time (424 women), 342 part-time (317 women); includes 140 minority (36 Black or African American, non-Hispanic/Latino; 3 American Indian or Alaska Native, non-Hispanic/Latino; 24 Asian, non-Hispanic/Latino; 43 Hispanic/Latino; 3 Native Hawaiian or other Pacific Islander, non-Hispanic/Latino; 31 Two or more races, non-Hispanic/Latino), 11 international. Average age 31. 1,268 applicants, 49% accepted, 477 enrolled. *Faculty:* 258 full-time (232 women), 363 part-time/adjunct (271 women). *Financial support:* In 2015–16, 585 students received support. Scholarships/grants available. Financial award application deadline: 3/15; financial award applicants required to submit FAFSA. In 2015, 343 master's, 55 doctorates awarded. *Degree program information:* Part-time programs available. Part-time, 100% online, blended/hybrid learning. Offers adult-gerontology acute care nurse practitioner (MSN); adult-gerontology primary care nurse practitioner (MSN); emergency nurse practitioner (MSN); family nurse practitioner (MSN); healthcare leadership (MSN); neonatal nurse practitioner (MSN); nurse midwifery (MSN); nurse midwifery/family nurse practitioner (MSN); nursing (Post-Master's Certificate); nursing informatics (MSN); nursing practice (DNP); nursing science (PhD); pediatric acute care nurse practitioner (MSN); pediatric primary care nurse practitioner (MSN); psychiatric-mental health nurse practitioner (MSN); women's health nurse practitioner (MSN); women's health nurse practitioner/adult gerontology primary care nurse practitioner (MSN). *Application deadline:* For fall admission, 11/1 priority date for domestic and international students. Applications are processed on a rolling basis. *Application fee:* $50. Electronic applications accepted. *Application Contact:* Patricia Peerman, Assistant Dean for Enrollment Management, 615-322-3800, Fax: 615-343-0333, E-mail: vusn-admissions@vanderbilt.edu. *Dean*, Dr. Linda Norman, 615-343-8876, Fax: 615-343-7711, E-mail: linda.norman@vanderbilt.edu.

VANDERCOOK COLLEGE OF MUSIC, Chicago, IL 60616-3731

General Information Independent, coed, comprehensive institution. *Enrollment:* 298 graduate, professional, and undergraduate students; 115 full-time matriculated graduate/professional students (57 women), 25 part-time matriculated graduate/professional students (12 women). *Enrollment by degree level:* 140 master's. *Graduate faculty:* 11 full-time (6 women), 66 part-time/adjunct (17 women). *Tuition, area resident:* Full-time $6120; part-time $510 per credit hour. One-time fee: $625. *Graduate housing:* Rooms and/or apartments available on a first-come, first-served basis to single and married students. Typical cost: $2790 per year for single students; $2160 per year for married students. Room charges vary according to board plan and housing facility selected. Housing application deadline: 6/1. *Student services:* Career counseling. *Library:* Harry Ruppel Memorial Library plus 1 other. *Collection:* Books: 16,576 (physical); Serial titles: 5,681 (physical). Weekly public service hours: 72; study areas open 24 hours, 5–7 days a week.

Computer facilities: 21 computers available on campus for general student use. A campuswide network can be accessed from student residence rooms and from off campus.
Website: http://www.vandercook.edu/

General Application Contact: LeeAnn Meyer, Director of Admissions and Retention, 312-788-1120, Fax: 312-225-5211, E-mail: admissions@vandercook.edu.

GRADUATE UNITS

Master of Music Education Program Students: 115 full-time (57 women), 25 part-time (12 women); includes 17 minority (10 Black or African American, non-Hispanic/Latino; 4 Asian, non-Hispanic/Latino; 1 Hispanic/Latino; 2 Two or more races, non-Hispanic/Latino). Average age 30. *Faculty:* 11 full-time (6 women), 66 part-time/adjunct (17 women). *Financial support:* Federal Work-Study, scholarships/grants, and unspecified assistantships available. Financial award application deadline: 5/1; financial award applicants required to submit FAFSA. *Degree program information:* Part-time programs available. Part-time. Offers music education (MM Ed). *Application deadline:* For fall admission, 4/1 for domestic and international students; for spring admission, 11/1 for domestic and international students. Applications are processed on a rolling basis. *Application fee:* $50. *Application Contact:* LeeAnn Meyer, Director of Admissions and Retention, 312-788-1120, Fax: 312-225-5211, E-mail: admissions@vandercook.edu. *Interim Dean of Graduate Studies*, Dr. Robert L. Sinclair, 312-788-1144, Fax: 312-225-5211, E-mail: rsinclair@vandercook.edu.

VANGUARD UNIVERSITY OF SOUTHERN CALIFORNIA, Costa Mesa, CA 92626-9601

General Information Independent-religious, coed, comprehensive institution.

GRADUATE UNITS

Graduate Program in Clinical Psychology ***Degree program information:*** Part-time and evening/weekend programs available. Part-time, evening/weekend. Offers clinical psychology (MS). Electronic applications accepted.

Graduate Program in Nursing ***Degree program information:*** Part-time and evening/weekend programs available. Part-time, evening/weekend. Offers nursing (MS).

Graduate Programs in Education ***Degree program information:*** Evening/weekend programs available. Evening/weekend. Offers education (MA). Electronic applications accepted.

Graduate Programs in Religion ***Degree program information:*** Part-time and evening/weekend programs available. Part-time, evening/weekend. Offers leadership studies (MA); theological studies (MTS). Electronic applications accepted.

VAUGHN COLLEGE OF AERONAUTICS AND TECHNOLOGY, Flushing, NY 11369

General Information Independent, coed, primarily men, comprehensive institution.

GRADUATE UNITS

Graduate Programs Offers airport management (MS).

VERMONT COLLEGE OF FINE ARTS, Montpelier, VT 05602

General Information Independent, coed, graduate-only institution. *Enrollment by degree level:* 366 master's. *Graduate faculty:* 112 part-time/adjunct (58 women). *Tuition, area resident:* Full-time $22,894; part-time $779 per credit hour. *Required fees:* $618; $618 per unit. $309 per semester. Full-time tuition and fees vary according to program. *Graduate housing:* Room and/or apartments available on a first-come, first-served basis to single students; on-campus housing not available to married students. Typical cost: $2000 (including board). Room and board charges vary according to board plan. *Student services:* Campus safety program, international student services, services for students with disabilities. *Library:* The Gary Library. *Collection:* Books: 60,000 (physical), 110,000 (digital/electronic); Serial titles: 250 (physical), 250 (digital/electronic); Databases: 10. Weekly public service hours: 40.

Computer facilities: 26 computers available on campus for general student use. A campuswide network can be accessed from student residence rooms and from off campus.
Website: http://www.vcfa.edu/

General Application Contact: David Markow, Director of Enrollment Management, 802-828-8535, E-mail: admissions@vcfa.edu.

GRADUATE UNITS

Graduate Studies in Art and Design Education Students: 7 full-time (6 women), 1 part-time; includes 1 minority (Two or more races, non-Hispanic/Latino). Average age 28. *Faculty:* 4 full-time (3 women). Offers art and design education (MA, MAT). *Application Contact:* David Markow, Director of Enrollment Management, 802-828-8535, E-mail: admissions@vcfa.edu. *Director*, Marni Leiken.

MFA in Film Program Students: 32 full-time (10 women); includes 7 minority (3 Black or African American, non-Hispanic/Latino; 2 Hispanic/Latino; 1 Native Hawaiian or other Pacific Islander, non-Hispanic/Latino; 1 Two or more races, non-Hispanic/Latino). Average age 43. *Faculty:* 7 part-time/adjunct (3 women). *Financial support:* Application deadline: 6/15. Offers film (MFA). *Application deadline:* For fall admission, 8/15 for domestic students; for spring admission, 2/15 for domestic students. Applications are processed on a rolling basis. *Application fee:* $75. Electronic applications accepted. *Application Contact:* Sharon Trautwein, Assistant Director of Admissions, 802-828-8829, E-mail: sharon.trautwein@vcfa.edu. *Director*, Stephen Pite, 802-828-8529, E-mail: stephen.pite@vcfa.edu.

MFA in Graphic Design Program Students: 31 full-time (17 women); includes 9 minority (4 Black or African American, non-Hispanic/Latino; 5 Hispanic/Latino). Average age 40. 31 applicants, 74% accepted, 14 enrolled. *Faculty:* 10 part-time/adjunct (5 women). *Financial support:* Scholarships/grants available. Financial award applicants required to submit FAFSA. In 2015, 18 master's awarded. Offers graphic design (MFA). *Application deadline:* For fall admission, 7/13 priority date for domestic and international students; for spring admission, 1/15 priority date for domestic and international students. Applications are processed on a rolling basis. *Application fee:* $75. Electronic applications accepted. *Program Director,* Jennifer Renko, 866-934-8232 Ext. 8896, E-mail: jennifer.renko@vcfa.edu.

MFA in Music Composition Program Students: 35 full-time (4 women); includes 5 minority (3 Black or African American, non-Hispanic/Latino; 1 Hispanic/Latino; 1 Two or more races, non-Hispanic/Latino), 2 international. Average age 39. 13 applicants, 77% accepted, 6 enrolled. *Faculty:* 10 part-time/adjunct (1 woman). *Financial support:* Scholarships/grants available. Financial award applicants required to submit FAFSA. In 2015, 11 master's awarded. Offers music composition (MFA). *Application deadline:* For fall admission, 6/15 for domestic and international students; for spring admission, 12/15 for domestic and international students. Applications are processed on a rolling basis. *Application fee:* $75. *Application Contact:* Sarah Madru, Assistant Program Director, 802-828-8534, E-mail: sarah.madru@vcfa.edu. *Program Director,* Carol Beatty, 866-934-8232 Ext. 8610, E-mail: carol.beatty@vcfa.edu.

MFA in Visual Art Program Students: 41 full-time (31 women), 1 (woman) part-time; includes 3 minority (1 Black or African American, non-Hispanic/Latino; 1 Hispanic/Latino; 1 Native Hawaiian or other Pacific Islander, non-Hispanic/Latino), 3 international. Average age 44. 45 applicants, 58% accepted, 16 enrolled. *Faculty:* 12 part-time/adjunct (6 women). *Financial support:* Scholarships/grants available. Financial award applicants required to submit FAFSA. In 2015, 30 master's awarded. Offers visual art (MFA). *Application deadline:* For fall admission, 2/15 priority date for domestic students, 2/15 for international students; for spring admission, 9/15 priority date for domestic students, 9/15 for international students. Applications are processed on a rolling basis. *Application fee:* $75. Electronic applications accepted. *Application Contact:* Renee Lauzon, Assistant Director of Admissions, 802-828-8636, E-mail: renee.lauzon@vcfa.edu. *Program Director,* Danielle Dahline, 802-828-8703, E-mail: danielle.dahline@vcfa.edu.

MFA in Writing and Publishing Program Students: 7 full-time (6 women). Average age 29. *Faculty:* 5 full-time (3 women). *Financial support:* Fellowships and scholarships/grants available. Offers writing and publishing (MFA). *Application Contact:* David Markow, Director of Enrollment Management, 802-828-8535, E-mail: admissions@vcfa.edu. *Director,* Miciah Gault.

MFA in Writing for Children and Young Adults Program Students: 93 full-time (82 women); includes 9 minority (2 Black or African American, non-Hispanic/Latino; 1 Asian, non-Hispanic/Latino; 4 Hispanic/Latino; 2 Two or more races, non-Hispanic/Latino), 3 international. Average age 43. 47 applicants, 68% accepted, 28 enrolled. *Faculty:* 25 part-time/adjunct (18 women). *Financial support:* Scholarships/grants available. Financial award applicants required to submit FAFSA. In 2015, 44 master's awarded. Offers writing for children and young adults (MFA). *Application deadline:* For fall admission, 3/1 for domestic and international students; for spring admission, 9/1 for domestic and international students. Applications are processed on a rolling basis. *Application fee:* $75. Electronic applications accepted. *Application Contact:* Ann Cardinal, Director of Student and Alumni Recruitment, 802-828-8589, E-mail: ann.cardinal@vcfa.edu. *Program Director,* Melissa Fisher, 802-828-8696, E-mail: melissa.fisher@vcfa.edu.

MFA in Writing Program Students: 118 full-time (92 women); includes 9 minority (1 Black or African American, non-Hispanic/Latino; 4 Asian, non-Hispanic/Latino; 3 Hispanic/Latino; 1 Two or more races, non-Hispanic/Latino), 1 international. Average age 43. 123 applicants, 63% accepted, 36 enrolled. *Faculty:* 36 part-time/adjunct (17 women). *Financial support:* Scholarships/grants available. Financial award applicants required to submit FAFSA. In 2015, 50 master's awarded. Offers writing (MFA). *Application deadline:* For fall admission, 3/20 for domestic and international students; for spring admission, 8/15 for domestic and international students. *Application fee:* $75. *Program Director,* Louise Crowley, 802-828-8840, E-mail: louise.crowley@vcfa.edu.

VERMONT LAW SCHOOL, South Royalton, VT 05068-0096

General Information Independent, coed, graduate-only institution. *Graduate housing:* On-campus housing not available.

GRADUATE UNITS

Graduate and Professional Programs ***Degree program information:*** Part-time programs available. Part-time. Offers law (LL M, MELP, MERL, MFALP, JD). Electronic applications accepted.

Master's Programs Degree program information: Part-time programs available. Part-time, online learning. Offers energy law (LL M); energy regulation and law (MERL); environmental law (LL M); environmental law and policy (MELP); food and agriculture law (LL M); food and agriculture law and policy (MFALP).

VICTORIA UNIVERSITY, Toronto, ON M5S 1K7, Canada

General Information Independent-religious, coed, graduate-only institution. *Graduate housing:* Rooms and/or apartments available on a first-come, first-served basis to single and married students. Housing application deadline: 6/30.

GRADUATE UNITS

Emmanuel College Offers theology (M Div, MA, MPS, MRE, MSMus, MTS, Th M, D Min, PhD, Th D, Certificate, Diploma, L Th). M Div, MRE, Th M, Th D, M Div/MA, M Div/MRE, M Div/MPS offered jointly with University of Toronto; MA, PhD with University of St. Michael's College. Electronic applications accepted.

VILLANOVA UNIVERSITY, Villanova, PA 19085-1699

General Information Independent-religious, coed, comprehensive institution. CGS member. *Enrollment:* 10,925 graduate, professional, and undergraduate students; 2,641 full-time matriculated graduate/professional students (1,373 women), 1,155 part-time matriculated graduate/professional students (554 women). *Enrollment by degree level:* 3,051 master's, 697 doctoral, 48 other advanced degrees. *Graduate faculty:* 395. *Graduate housing:* On-campus housing not available. *Student services:* Campus employment opportunities, campus safety program, career counseling, exercise/wellness program, free psychological counseling, international student services, low-cost health insurance, multicultural affairs office, services for students with disabilities. *Library:* Falvey Memorial Library plus 1 other.

Computer facilities: Computer purchase and lease plans are available. 700 computers available on campus for general student use. A campuswide network can be accessed from student residence rooms and from off campus. Online class registration, learning management system with anti-plagiarism software, testing software, online faculty hours, videoconferencing, electronic portfolios, data vaulting/backup service, software are available.
Website: http://www.villanova.edu/

GRADUATE UNITS

College of Engineering ***Degree program information:*** Part-time and evening/weekend programs available. Part-time, evening/weekend, online learning. Offers biochemical engineering (Certificate); chemical engineering (MSChE); civil engineering (MSCE); computer architectures (Certificate); computer engineering (MSCPE, Certificate); electric power systems (Certificate); electrical engineering (MSEE, Certificate); electro mechanical systems (Certificate); electro-mechanical systems (Certificate); engineering (MSCPE, MSChE, MSEE, MSME, MSWREE, PhD, Certificate); environmental protection in the chemical process industries (Certificate); high frequency systems (Certificate); intelligent control systems (Certificate); machinery dynamics (Certificate); mechanical engineering (MSME); nonlinear dynamics and control (Certificate); thermofluid systems (Certificate); urban water resources design (Certificate); water resources and environmental engineering (MSWREE, Certificate); wireless and digital communications (Certificate). Electronic applications accepted.

College of Nursing Students: 219 full-time (198 women), 108 part-time (96 women); includes 36 minority (25 Black or African American, non-Hispanic/Latino; 9 Asian, non-Hispanic/Latino; 2 Hispanic/Latino), 16 international. Average age 31. 147 applicants, 78% accepted, 106 enrolled. *Faculty:* 16 full-time (15 women), 9 part-time/adjunct (7 women). *Financial support:* In 2015–16, 22 students received support, including 5 teaching assistantships with full tuition reimbursements available (averaging $15,475 per year); institutionally sponsored loans, scholarships/grants, traineeships, tuition waivers (full), and unspecified assistantships also available. Financial award application deadline: 7/1; financial award applicants required to submit FAFSA. In 2015, 64 master's, 8 doctorates, 9 other advanced degrees awarded. *Degree program information:* Part-time programs available. Part-time, online learning. Offers adult nurse practitioner (MSN, Post Master's Certificate); family nurse practitioner (MSN, Post Master's Certificate); nurse anesthetist (MSN, Post Master's Certificate); nursing (PhD); nursing education (MSN, Post Master's Certificate); nursing practice (DNP); pediatric nurse practitioner (MSN, Post Master's Certificate). *Application deadline:* For fall admission, 7/1 priority date for domestic students, 7/1 for international students; for spring admission, 11/1 priority date for domestic students, 11/1 for international students; for summer admission, 4/1 priority date for domestic students, 3/1 for international students. Applications are processed on a rolling basis. *Application fee:* $50. Electronic applications accepted. *Application Contact:* Rebecca Harold, Administrative Assistant, 610-519-4934, Fax: 610-519-7650, E-mail: rebecca.harold@villanova.edu. *Assistant Dean/Director, Graduate Programs,* Dr. Marguerite K. Schlag, 610-519-4907, Fax: 610-519-7650, E-mail: marguerite.schlag@villanova.edu.

Graduate School of Liberal Arts and Sciences Students: 1,027 full-time (623 women), 453 part-time (277 women); includes 297 minority (127 Black or African American, non-Hispanic/Latino; 3 American Indian or Alaska Native, non-Hispanic/Latino; 48 Asian, non-Hispanic/Latino; 90 Hispanic/Latino; 5 Native Hawaiian or other Pacific Islander, non-Hispanic/Latino; 24 Two or more races, non-Hispanic/Latino), 156 international. Average age 32. 870 applicants, 66% accepted, 349 enrolled. *Faculty:* 191. *Financial support:* Research assistantships, teaching assistantships, career-related internships or fieldwork, scholarships/grants, and unspecified assistantships available. Financial award applicants required to submit FAFSA. In 2015, 557 master's, 6 doctorates awarded. *Degree program information:* Part-time and evening/weekend programs available. Part-time, evening/weekend, online learning. Offers applied statistics (MS); biology (MA, MS); chemistry (MS); classical studies (MA); clinical mental health counseling (MS); communication (MA); computer science (MS); education plus teacher certification (MA); elementary school counseling (MS); English (MA); graduate education (MA); Hispanic studies (MA); history (MA); human resource development (MS); liberal arts and sciences (MA, MPA, MS, PhD); mathematical sciences (MA, MS); philosophy (PhD); political science (MA); psychology (MS); public administration (MPA); secondary school counseling (MS); software engineering (MS); teacher leadership (MA); theatre (MA); theology (MA). *Application deadline:* For fall admission, 3/1 for domestic students, 5/1 for international students; for spring admission, 11/15 for domestic students, 10/15 for international students; for summer admission, 5/1 for domestic students. Applications are processed on a rolling basis. *Application fee:* $50. Electronic applications accepted. *Dean,* Dr. Christine Palus, 610-519-7090, Fax: 610-519-7096.

School of Law Students: 538 full-time (265 women), 54 part-time (27 women); includes 97 minority (25 Black or African American, non-Hispanic/Latino; 2 American Indian or Alaska Native, non-Hispanic/Latino; 23 Asian, non-Hispanic/Latino; 31 Hispanic/Latino; 1 Native Hawaiian or other Pacific Islander, non-Hispanic/Latino; 15 Two or more races, non-Hispanic/Latino), 3 international. Average age 29. 1,373 applicants, 52% accepted, 169 enrolled. *Faculty:* 46 full-time (21 women), 65 part-time/adjunct (15 women). *Financial support:* In 2015–16, 381 students received support, including 33 research assistantships, 10 teaching assistantships; career-related internships or fieldwork, Federal Work-Study, scholarships/grants, and unspecified assistantships also available. Support available to part-time students. Financial award application deadline: 3/15; financial award applicants required to submit FAFSA. In 2015, 24 master's, 212 doctorates awarded. *Degree program information:* Part-time and evening/weekend programs available. Part-time, evening/weekend. Offers law (LL M, JD); tax (LL M). *Application deadline:* For fall admission, 4/1 for domestic and international students. Applications are processed on a rolling basis. *Application fee:* $0. Electronic applications accepted. *Application Contact:* Bayrex Marti, Executive Director, Admissions and Financial Aid, 610-519-7010, Fax: 610-519-6291, E-mail: admissions@law.villanova.edu. *Dean/Professor of Law,* John Y. Gotanda, 610-519-7007, Fax: 610-519-6472, E-mail: gotanda@law.villanova.edu.

Villanova School of Business Students: 33 full-time (6 women), 893 part-time (312 women); includes 153 minority (50 Black or African American, non-Hispanic/Latino; 1 American Indian or Alaska Native, non-Hispanic/Latino; 60 Asian, non-Hispanic/Latino; 34 Hispanic/Latino; 8 Two or more races, non-Hispanic/Latino), 27 international. Average age 31. *Faculty:* 101 full-time (33 women), 27 part-time/adjunct (6 women). *Financial support:* In 2015–16, 17 research assistantships with tuition reimbursements (averaging $13,100 per year) were awarded; scholarships/grants and unspecified assistantships also available. Support available to part-time students. Financial award application deadline: 6/30; financial award applicants required to submit FAFSA. In 2015, 262 master's awarded. 100% online, blended/hybrid learning. Offers accountancy (MAC); analytics (MSA); business (EMBA, MAC, MBA, MSA, MSCM, MSF); business administration (MBA); church management (MSCM); executive business administration (EMBA); finance (MSF); health care management (MBA); international business (MBA);

management information systems (MBA); marketing (MBA); real estate (MBA); strategic management (MBA). *Application deadline:* For fall admission, 6/30 for domestic and international students; for winter admission, 11/15 for domestic and international students; for spring admission, 11/15 for domestic and international students; for summer admission, 3/31 for domestic and international students. Applications are processed on a rolling basis. *Application fee:* $50. Electronic applications accepted. *Application Contact:* Claire Bruno, Director of Recruitment and Enrollment Management, 610-519-4336, Fax: 610-519-6273, E-mail: claire.bruno@villanova.edu. *Associate Dean of Graduate and Executive Business Programs,* Michael L. Capella, 610-519-4336, Fax: 610-519-6273, E-mail: michael.l.capella@villanova.edu.

VIRGINIA BEACH THEOLOGICAL SEMINARY, Virginia Beach, VA 23464

General Information Independent-religious, coed, graduate-only institution.

GRADUATE UNITS

Graduate Programs Offers biblical studies (M Div, MBS, Th M). Electronic applications accepted.

VIRGINIA COLLEGE IN BIRMINGHAM, Birmingham, AL 35209

General Information Proprietary, coed, comprehensive institution.

GRADUATE UNITS

Program in Business Administration ***Degree program information:*** Part-time and evening/weekend programs available. Part-time, evening/weekend, online learning. Offers healthcare (MBA); management (MBA).

Virginia College Online ***Degree program information:*** Part-time and evening/weekend programs available. Part-time, evening/weekend, online learning. Offers business administration (MBA); criminal justice (MCJ); cybersecurity (MC).

VIRGINIA COMMONWEALTH UNIVERSITY, Richmond, VA 23284-9005

General Information State-supported, coed, university. CGS member. *Graduate housing:* Room and/or apartments available on a first-come, first-served basis to single students; on-campus housing not available to married students. *Research affiliation:* Virginia Biotechnology Research Park (biotechnology), Virginia Biotechnology Research Park.

GRADUATE UNITS

Graduate School ***Degree program information:*** Part-time and evening/weekend programs available. Part-time, evening/weekend. Offers interdisciplinary studies (MIS). Electronic applications accepted.

College of Humanities and Sciences ***Degree program information:*** Part-time and evening/weekend programs available. Part-time, evening/weekend. Offers analytical chemistry (MS, PhD); applied mathematics (MS); applied social research (CASR); art direction (MS); behavioral medicine (PhD); biology (MS); biopsychology (PhD); chemical physics (PhD); clinical child psychology (PhD); clinical psychology (PhD); communication strategy (MS); copywriting (MS); counseling psychology (PhD); creative brand management (MS); creative media planning (MS); creative writing (MFA); criminal justice (MS, CCJA); developmental psychology (PhD); English (MA); fiction (MFA); fictional poetry (MFA); forensic biology (MS); forensic chemistry/drugs and toxicology (MS); forensic chemistry/trace (MS); forensic physical evidence (MS); general psychology (PhD); geographic information systems (Certificate); government and public affairs (MA, MPA, MS, MURP, PhD, CASR, CCJA, CPM, CURP, Certificate, Graduate Certificate); health psychology (PhD); historic preservation planning (Certificate); history (MA); homeland security and emergency preparedness (MA, Graduate Certificate); humanities and sciences (MA, MFA, MPA, MS, MURP, PhD, CASR, CCJA, CPM, CURP, Certificate, Graduate Certificate); inorganic chemistry (MS, PhD); literature (MA); mass communications (MS, PhD); mathematics (MS); media, art, and text (PhD); medical physics (MS, PhD); multimedia journalism (MS); nanoscience and nanotechnology (PhD); nanosciences (PhD); nonprofit management (CPM); operations research (MS); organic chemistry (MS, PhD); physical chemistry (MS, PhD); physics and applied physics (MS); poetry (MFA); public administration (MPA); public management (CPM); public policy and administration (PhD); social psychology (PhD); sociology (MS); statistics (MS); strategic public relations (MS); systems modeling and analysis (PhD); urban and regional planning (MURP, Certificate); urban revitalization (Certificate); writing and rhetoric (MA). Electronic applications accepted.

da Vinci Center for Innovation ***Degree program information:*** Part-time programs available. Part-time. Offers product innovation (MPI).

School of Allied Health Professions ***Degree program information:*** Part-time programs available. Part-time. Offers advanced physical therapy (DPT); aging studies (CAS); allied health professions (MHA, MS, MSHA, MSNA, MSOT, DNAP, DPT, OTD, PhD, CAS, CPC); clinical laboratory sciences (PhD); entry-level physical therapy (DPT); gerontology (MS, PhD); health administration (MHA, MSHA, PhD); health related sciences (PhD); health services organization and research (PhD); nurse anesthesia (PhD); occupational therapy (MS, MSOT, OTD); patient counseling (MS, CPC); physical therapy (PhD); physiology/physical therapy (PhD); radiation sciences (PhD); rehabilitation counseling (MS, CPC); rehabilitation leadership (PhD). Electronic applications accepted.

School of Business ***Degree program information:*** Part-time and evening/weekend programs available. Part-time, evening/weekend. Offers accounting (M Acc, MBA, PhD); business (M Acc, MA, MBA, MS, PhD, Certificate, Postbaccalaureate Certificate); business administration (MBA, Postbaccalaureate Certificate); decision sciences and business analytics (MBA, MS); economics (MA); finance, insurance, and real estate (MS); information systems (MS, PhD); management (Certificate); marketing and business law (MS); real estate and urban land development (Certificate). Electronic applications accepted.

School of Education ***Degree program information:*** Part-time programs available. Part-time. Offers adult literacy (M Ed); athletic training (MSAT); autism spectrum disorders (Certificate); college student development and counseling (M Ed); disability leadership (Certificate); early and elementary education (MT); early childhood (M Ed); education (M Ed, MS, MSAT, MT, Ed D, PhD, Certificate); educational leadership (PhD); educational psychology (PhD); general education (M Ed); health and movement sciences (MS); health and physical education (MT); human resource development (M Ed); instructional leadership (PhD); leadership (Ed D); reading (M Ed); reading specialist (Certificate); rehabilitation and movement science (PhD); research and evaluation (PhD); school counseling (M Ed); secondary 6-12 education (MT); secondary education (Certificate); severe disabilities (M Ed); special education and disability leadership (PhD); sport leadership (MS); teaching and learning with technology (M Ed); urban services leadership (PhD). Electronic applications accepted.

School of Engineering Offers biomedical engineering (MS, PhD); chemical and life science engineering (MS, PhD); computer science (MS, PhD); electrical engineering (MS, PhD); engineering (MS, PhD); mechanical and nuclear engineering (MS, PhD). Electronic applications accepted.

School of Life Sciences Offers bioinformatics (MS); environmental studies (M Env Sc, MS); integrative life sciences (PhD); life sciences (M Env Sc, MB, MS, PhD). Electronic applications accepted.

School of Nursing ***Degree program information:*** Part-time and evening/weekend programs available. Part-time, evening/weekend, online learning. Offers adult health acute nursing (MS); adult health primary nursing (MS); biobehavioral clinical research (PhD); child health nursing (MS); clinical nurse leader (MS); family health nursing (MS); nurse educator (MS); nurse practitioner (MS); nursing (Certificate); nursing administration (MS); psychiatric-mental health nursing (MS); quality and safety in health care (DNP); women's health nursing (MS). Electronic applications accepted.

School of Social Work Offers social work (MSW, PhD). Electronic applications accepted.

School of the Arts ***Degree program information:*** Part-time programs available. Part-time. Offers architectural history (MA); art education (MAE); art history (MA, PhD); ceramics (MFA); costume design (MFA); design/visual communications (MFA); education (MM); fibers (MFA); furniture design (MFA); glassworking (MFA); graphic design (MFA); historical studies (MA); interior environment (MFA); jewelry/metalworking (MFA); kinetic imaging (MFA); museum studies (MA); music (MM); painting (MFA); pedagogy (MFA); printmaking (MFA); scene design/technical theater (MFA); sculpture (MFA); theatre (MFA). Electronic applications accepted.

Medical College of Virginia-Professional Programs ***Degree program information:*** Part-time programs available. Part-time. Offers medicine (MPH, MS, DDS, MD, PhD, Pharm D). Electronic applications accepted.

School of Dentistry Offers dentistry (MS, DDS). Electronic applications accepted.

School of Medicine Offers anatomy (MS); anatomy and neurobiology (PhD); biochemistry (MS, PhD); biostatistics (MS, PhD); epidemiology (MPH, PhD); genetic counseling (MS); healthcare policy and research (PhD); human genetics (PhD); medicine (MPH, MS, MD, PhD, Certificate); microbiology and immunology (MS, PhD); molecular biology (MS, PhD); molecular biology and genetics (MS, PhD); neurobiology (MS); neuroscience (MS, PhD); pathology (PhD); pharmacology (Certificate); pharmacology and toxicology (MS, PhD); physical therapy (PhD); physiology (MS, PhD); public health practice (MPH); social and behavioral science (MPH). Electronic applications accepted.

School of Pharmacy ***Degree program information:*** Part-time programs available. Part-time. Offers medicinal chemistry (MS); pharmaceutical sciences (PhD); pharmaceutics (MS); pharmacotherapy and pharmacy administration (MS); pharmacy (MS, PhD, Pharm D). Electronic applications accepted.

Program in Pre-Medical Basic Health Sciences Offers anatomy (CBHS); biochemistry (CBHS); human genetics (CBHS); microbiology (CBHS); pharmacology (CBHS); physiology (CBHS). Electronic applications accepted.

VIRGINIA INTERNATIONAL UNIVERSITY, Fairfax, VA 22030

General Information Proprietary, coed, comprehensive institution. *Research affiliation:* Apple Federal Credit Union (financial management).

GRADUATE UNITS

School of Business ***Degree program information:*** Part-time programs available. Part-time, online learning. Offers accounting (MBA, MS); entrepreneurship (MBA); executive management (Graduate Certificate); global logistics (MBA); health care management (MBA); hospitality and tourism management (MBA); human resources management (MBA); international business management (MBA); international finance (MBA); marketing management (MBA); mass media and public relations (MBA); project management (MBA, MS). Electronic applications accepted.

School of Computer Information Systems ***Degree program information:*** Part-time programs available. Part-time, online learning. Offers business intelligence (Graduate Certificate); business intelligence and data analytics (MIS); computer science (MS); cybersecurity (MIS); data management (MIS); enterprise project management (MIS); health informatics (MIS); information assurance (MIS); information systems (Graduate Certificate); information systems management (MS, Graduate Certificate); information technology (MS); information technology audit and compliance (Graduate Certificate); knowledge management (MIS); software engineering (MS). Electronic applications accepted.

School of Education ***Degree program information:*** Part-time programs available. Part-time, online learning. Offers applied linguistics (MS); education (M Ed); teaching English to speakers of other languages (MA). Electronic applications accepted.

School of Public and International Affairs Offers international relations (MS); public administration (MPA).

VIRGINIA POLYTECHNIC INSTITUTE AND STATE UNIVERSITY, Blacksburg, VA 24061

General Information State-supported, coed, university. CGS member. *Graduate housing:* Room and/or apartments available on a first-come, first-served basis to single students; on-campus housing not available to married students. *Research affiliation:* CRDF Global (software technology), Virginia's Center for Innovative Technology, Wellcome Trust Centre for Neuroimaging (health research), Virginia Biosciences Health Research Corporation (health research), Transport Canada (transportation), Elanco Animal Health (agriculture).

GRADUATE UNITS

Graduate School

College of Agriculture and Life Sciences Offers agricultural and applied economics (MS); agricultural and life sciences (MS); animal and poultry science (MS, PhD); crop and soil environmental sciences (MS, PhD); dairy science (MS); entomology (PhD); horticulture (MS, PhD); human nutrition, foods and exercise (MS, PhD); life sciences (MS, PhD); plant pathology, physiology and weed science (PhD). Electronic applications accepted.

College of Architecture and Urban Studies Offers architecture (MS Arch); architecture and design research (PhD); building/construction science and management (MS); creative technologies (MFA); environmental design and planning (PhD); landscape architecture (MLA); planning, governance, and globalization (PhD); public administration (MPA); public administration/public affairs (PhD, Certificate); public and international affairs (MPIA); urban and regional planning (MURP). Electronic applications accepted.

College of Engineering Offers aerospace engineering (ME, MS, PhD); biological systems engineering (ME, MS, PhD); biomedical engineering (MS, PhD); chemical engineering (ME, MS, PhD); civil engineering (ME, MS, PhD); computer engineering

(ME, MS, PhD); computer science (MS, PhD); electrical engineering (ME, PhD); engineering education (PhD); engineering mechanics (ME, MS, PhD); environmental engineering (MS); environmental science and engineering (MS); industrial and systems engineering (ME, MS, PhD); materials science and engineering (ME, MS, PhD); mechanical engineering (ME, MS, PhD); mining and minerals engineering (PhD); mining engineering (ME, MS); nuclear engineering (MS, PhD); ocean engineering (MS); systems engineering (ME, MS). Electronic applications accepted.

College of Liberal Arts and Human Sciences Offers career and technical education (MS Ed, Ed D, PhD, Ed S); communication (MA); counselor education (MA Ed, Ed D, PhD, Ed S); creative writing (MFA); curriculum and instruction (MA Ed, Ed D, PhD, Ed S); educational leadership and policy studies (MA Ed, Ed D, PhD, Ed S); educational research and evaluation (PhD); English (MA); foreign languages, cultures, and literatures (MA); higher education and student affairs (MA Ed); history (MA); human development (MS, PhD); material culture and public humanities (MA); philosophy (MA); political science (MA); rhetoric and writing (PhD); science and technology studies (MS, PhD); social, political, ethical, and cultural thought (PhD); sociology (MS, PhD); theater arts (MFA). Electronic applications accepted.

College of Natural Resources and Environment Offers fisheries and wildlife (MS, PhD); forestry and forest products (MF, MS, PhD); geography (MS); geospatial and environmental analysis (PhD); natural resources (MNR). Electronic applications accepted.

College of Science Offers biological sciences (MS, PhD); biomedical technology development and management (MS); chemistry (MS, PhD); economics (MA, PhD); geosciences (MS, PhD); mathematics (MS, PhD); physics (MS, PhD); psychology (MS, PhD); statistics (MS, PhD). Electronic applications accepted.

Intercollege Offers genetics, bioinformatics and computational biology (PhD); information technology (MIT); macromolecular science and engineering (MS, PhD). Electronic applications accepted.

Pamplin College of Business Offers accounting and information systems (MACIS); business (PhD); business administration (MBA, MS); hospitality and tourism management (MS, PhD). Electronic applications accepted.

Virginia-Maryland Regional College of Veterinary Medicine Offers biomedical and veterinary sciences (MS, PhD); public health (MPH); research in translational medicine (Certificate); veterinary medicine (DVM). Electronic applications accepted.

VT Online Offers advanced transportation systems (Certificate); aerospace engineering (MS); agricultural and life sciences (MSLFS); business information systems (Graduate Certificate); career and technical education (MS); civil engineering (MS); computer engineering (M Eng, MS); decision support systems (Graduate Certificate); eLearning leadership (MA); electrical engineering (M Eng, MS); engineering administration (MEA); environmental engineering (Certificate); environmental politics and policy (Graduate Certificate); environmental sciences and engineering (MS); foundations of political analysis (Graduate Certificate); health product risk management (Graduate Certificate); industrial and systems engineering (MS); information policy and society (Graduate Certificate); information security (Graduate Certificate); information technology (MIT); instructional technology (MA); integrative STEM education (MA Ed); liberal arts (Graduate Certificate); life sciences: health product risk management (MS); natural resources (MNR, Graduate Certificate); networking (Graduate Certificate); nonprofit and nongovernmental organization management (Graduate Certificate); ocean engineering (MS); political science (MA); security studies (Graduate Certificate); software development (Graduate Certificate).

VIRGINIA STATE UNIVERSITY, Petersburg, VA 23806-0001

General Information State-supported, coed, comprehensive institution. *Graduate housing:* Room and/or apartments available on a first-come, first-served basis to single students; on-campus housing not available to married students. Housing application deadline: 5/1. *Research affiliation:* Medical College of Virginia/Virginia Commonwealth University (biology), The College of William and Mary (biology), University of Massachusetts (biology), Rolls Royce USA (engineering), C-CAM Technologies (engineering).

GRADUATE UNITS

College of Graduate Studies *Financial support:* Fellowships with tuition reimbursements and unspecified assistantships available. Financial award application deadline: 5/1; financial award applicants required to submit FAFSA. *Degree program information:* Part-time and evening/weekend programs available. Part-time, evening/weekend. Offers interdisciplinary studies (MIS). *Application deadline:* For fall admission, 5/1 priority date for domestic students, 5/1 for international students; for spring admission, 11/1 for domestic students, 9/1 for international students. Applications are processed on a rolling basis. *Application fee:* $25.

College of Education Offers administration and supervision (M Ed); education (M Ed, MS, Ed D); educational administration and supervision (Ed D); school and community counseling (M Ed, MS).

College of Engineering and Technology Financial support: Fellowships and career-related internships or fieldwork available. Financial award application deadline: 5/1. Offers computer science (MS); engineering and technology (M Ed, MS); mathematics (MS); mathematics education (MS). *Application deadline:* For fall admission, 5/1 priority date for domestic students. Applications are processed on a rolling basis. *Application fee:* $25. *Application Contact:* Dr. Wayne F. Virag, Dean, Graduate Studies, Research, and Outreach, 804-524-5985, Fax: 804-524-5104, E-mail: wvirag@vsu.edu.

College of Humanities and Social Sciences Financial support: Fellowships and Federal Work-Study available. Financial award application deadline: 5/1. *Degree program information:* Part-time and evening/weekend programs available. Part-time, evening/weekend. Offers criminal justice (MS); economics (MA); humanities and social sciences (M Ed, MA, MS); media management (MA). *Application deadline:* For fall admission, 5/1 priority date for domestic students. Applications are processed on a rolling basis. *Application fee:* $25.

College of Natural and Health Sciences Offers behavioral and community health sciences (PhD); biology (MS); clinical health psychology (PhD); clinical psychology (MS); general psychology (MS); natural and health sciences (MS, PhD).

VIRGINIA THEOLOGICAL SEMINARY, Alexandria, VA 22304

General Information Independent-religious, coed, graduate-only institution. *Graduate faculty:* 26 full-time (11 women), 29 part-time/adjunct (11 women). *Tuition, area resident:* Full-time $13,600; part-time $630 per credit hour. *Graduate housing:* Room and/or apartments available on a first-come, first-served basis to single students; on-campus housing not available to married students. Typical cost: $4000 per year ($5600 including board). Housing application deadline: 5/1. *Student services:* Campus employment opportunities, child daycare facilities, exercise/wellness program, international student services, low-cost health insurance, services for students with disabilities, writing training. *Library:* Bishop Payne Library plus 1 other.

Computer facilities: 20 computers available on campus for general student use. Website: http://www.vts.edu/

General Application Contact: Jan Sienkiewicz, Director of Admissions, 703-370-6600.

GRADUATE UNITS

Graduate and Professional Programs *Financial support:* Career-related internships or fieldwork, Federal Work-Study, and institutionally sponsored loans available. *Degree program information:* Part-time programs available. Part-time. Offers Christian spirituality (D Min); educational leadership (D Min); ministry development (D Min); theology (M Div, MA). *Application deadline:* For fall admission, 5/1 for domestic students. *Application fee:* $0. *Application Contact:* Jan Sienkiewicz, Director of Admissions, 703-461-1706.

VIRGINIA UNION UNIVERSITY, Richmond, VA 23220-1170

General Information Independent-religious, coed, comprehensive institution. *Graduate housing:* Room and/or apartments available on a first-come, first-served basis to single students; on-campus housing not available to married students.

GRADUATE UNITS

Evelyn R. Syphax School of Education, Psychology and Interdisciplinary Studies Offers curriculum and instruction (MA).

Samuel DeWitt Proctor School of Theology *Degree program information:* Part-time and evening/weekend programs available. Part-time, evening/weekend. Offers theology (M Div, D Min).

VIRGINIA UNIVERSITY OF LYNCHBURG, Lynchburg, VA 24501-6417

General Information Independent-religious, coed, comprehensive institution.

GRADUATE UNITS

Graduate Programs

VITERBO UNIVERSITY, La Crosse, WI 54601-4797

General Information Independent-religious, coed, comprehensive institution. *Enrollment:* 2,756 graduate, professional, and undergraduate students; 402 full-time matriculated graduate/professional students (290 women), 484 part-time matriculated graduate/professional students (374 women). *Enrollment by degree level:* 349 master's, 42 doctoral. *Graduate faculty:* 20 full-time (14 women), 93 part-time/adjunct (68 women). Tuition and fees vary according to program. *Graduate housing:* Room and/or apartments available on a first-come, first-served basis to single students; on-campus housing not available to married students. Typical cost: $3650 per year. Room charges vary according to board plan. Housing application deadline: 4/2. *Student services:* Campus safety program, career counseling, exercise/wellness program, free psychological counseling, international student services, multicultural affairs office, services for students with disabilities, writing training. *Library:* Todd Wehr Memorial Library. *Collection:* Books: 67,808 (physical), 202 (digital/electronic); Serial titles: 96 (physical), 81 (digital/electronic); Databases: 37. Weekly public service hours: 97; study areas open 24 hours, 5–7 days a week; students can reserve study rooms.

Computer facilities: 400 computers available on campus for general student use. A campuswide network can be accessed from student residence rooms and from off campus. Online class registration, Blackboard courses are available. Website: http://www.viterbo.edu/

General Application Contact: Paula Baus, Administrative Assistant, 608-796-3370, Fax: 608-796-3372, E-mail: pjbaus@viterbo.edu.

GRADUATE UNITS

Graduate Program in Nursing Students: 26 full-time (23 women), 24 part-time (all women); includes 6 minority (3 Black or African American, non-Hispanic/Latino; 1 American Indian or Alaska Native, non-Hispanic/Latino; 1 Asian, non-Hispanic/Latino; 1 Hispanic/Latino). Average age 35. 25 applicants, 96% accepted, 19 enrolled. *Faculty:* 4 full-time (all women), 15 part-time/adjunct (14 women). *Financial support:* In 2015–16, 7 students received support. Institutionally sponsored loans, scholarships/grants, and tuition remission available. Financial award application deadline: 3/1; financial award applicants required to submit FAFSA. *Degree program information:* Part-time programs available. Part-time. Offers nursing (DNP). *Application deadline:* For spring admission, 1/15 priority date for domestic students. Applications are processed on a rolling basis. *Application fee:* $0. Electronic applications accepted. *Application Contact:* Bobbi Hundt, Graduate Nursing Program Administrative Assistant, 608-796-3671, Fax: 608-796-3668, E-mail: bmhundt@viterbo.edu. *Graduate Nursing Program Director,* Dr. Mary E. Stolder, 608-796-3625, Fax: 608-796-3668, E-mail: mestolder@viterbo.edu.

Graduate Programs in Education Students: 73 full-time (46 women), 92 part-time (73 women); includes 2 minority (1 Hispanic/Latino; 1 Two or more races, non-Hispanic/Latino). Average age 34. *Faculty:* 6 full-time (4 women), 71 part-time/adjunct (48 women). In 2015, 111 master's, 147 other advanced degrees awarded. *Degree program information:* Part-time and evening/weekend programs available. Part-time, evening/weekend. Offers cross-categorical special education (Certificate); director of instruction (Certificate); director of special education and pupil services (Certificate); early childhood (Certificate); education (MAE); literacy coaching (Certificate); PreK-12 principal/supervisor of special education (Certificate); principal (Certificate); reading specialist endorsement (Certificate); reading teacher (Certificate); reading teacher 5-12 endorsement (Certificate); reading teacher K-8 endorsement (Certificate); superintendent (Certificate); talented and gifted endorsement (Certificate); Wisconsin school business administrator (Certificate). Weekend courses available in summer. *Application fee:* $50. Electronic applications accepted. *Application Contact:* Susan Hughes, Program Specialist/Graduate Student Advisor, 608-796-3394, E-mail: srhughes@viterbo.edu. *Director of Graduate Programs in Education,* Jeannette Armstrong, 608-796-3395, E-mail: jearmstrong@viterbo.edu.

Master of Arts in Servant Leadership Program Students: 18 full-time (7 women), 38 part-time (27 women); includes 3 minority (2 Black or African American, non-Hispanic/Latino; 1 Hispanic/Latino), 1 international. Average age 44. *Faculty:* 2 full-time (0 women), 2 part-time/adjunct (1 woman). *Financial support:* In 2015–16, 12 students received support. Scholarships/grants available. Financial award application deadline: 2/1; financial award applicants required to submit FAFSA. In 2015, 17 master's, 1 other advanced degree awarded. *Degree program information:* Part-time and evening/weekend programs available. Part-time, evening/weekend. Offers ethical leadership in organizations (Certificate); servant leadership (MA). *Application deadline:* For fall admission, 8/1 for domestic students; for spring admission, 12/1 for domestic students; for summer admission, 5/1 for domestic students. Applications are processed on a rolling basis. Electronic applications accepted. *Application Contact:* Maureen Cooney, Administrative Assistant, 608-796-3082, E-mail: mjcooney@viterbo.edu. *Director,* Tom Thibodeau, 608-796-3705, E-mail: tathibodeau@viterbo.edu.

Master of Business Administration Program Students: 101 full-time (58 women), 14 part-time (11 women); includes 6 minority (1 Black or African American, non-Hispanic/Latino; 1 Asian, non-Hispanic/Latino; 3 Hispanic/Latino; 1 Two or more races, non-Hispanic/Latino), 9 international. Average age 33. *Faculty:* 6 full-time (2 women), 2 part-time/adjunct (1 woman). *Financial support:* Applicants required to submit FAFSA. In 2015, 47 master's awarded. *Degree program information:* Part-time and evening/weekend programs available. Part-time, evening/weekend. Offers general business administration (MBA); health care management (MBA); international business (MBA); leadership (MBA); project management (MBA). *Application deadline:* Applications are processed on a rolling basis. Electronic applications accepted. *Application Contact:* Tiffany Morey, MBA Coordinator, 608-796-3379, E-mail: tlmorey@viterbo.edu. *MBA Director*, Sara Cook, 608-796-3374, E-mail: slcook@viterbo.edu.

Master of Science in Mental Health Counseling Program Students: 49 full-time (42 women), 7 part-time (all women); includes 4 minority (1 Black or African American, non-Hispanic/Latino; 1 Hispanic/Latino; 2 Two or more races, non-Hispanic/Latino), 2 international. Average age 30. *Faculty:* 3 full-time (1 woman), 6 part-time/adjunct (3 women). *Financial support:* Applicants required to submit FAFSA. In 2015, 25 master's awarded. *Degree program information:* Part-time and evening/weekend programs available. Part-time, evening/weekend. Offers addiction counseling (MS); child and adolescent counseling (MS); complementary health and wellness counseling (MS). *Application deadline:* For fall admission, 3/15 priority date for domestic students, 7/31 priority date for international students. Applications are processed on a rolling basis. *Application fee:* $50. Electronic applications accepted. *Application Contact:* Dr. Debra A. Murray, Program Director, 608-796-3720, E-mail: damurray@viterbo.edu. *Program Director*, Dr. Debra A. Murray, 608-796-3720, E-mail: damurray@viterbo.edu.

WAGNER COLLEGE, Staten Island, NY 10301-4495

General Information Independent, coed, comprehensive institution. CGS member. *Enrollment:* 2,202 graduate, professional, and undergraduate students; 193 full-time matriculated graduate/professional students (105 women), 249 part-time matriculated graduate/professional students (191 women). *Enrollment by degree level:* 420 master's, 22 doctoral. *Graduate faculty:* 33 full-time (18 women), 31 part-time/adjunct (18 women). *Graduate housing:* Room and/or apartments available on a first-come, first-served basis to single students; on-campus housing not available to married students. Typical cost: $13,000 (including board). Housing application deadline: 4/1. *Student services:* Campus employment opportunities, campus safety program, career counseling, child daycare facilities, exercise/wellness program, free psychological counseling, international student services, multicultural affairs office, services for students with disabilities, teacher training, writing training. *Library:* August Horrmann Library. *Collection:* Books: 70,465 (physical), 180,000 (digital/electronic); Serial titles: 79,532 (physical); Databases: 61. Weekly public service hours: 120; students can reserve study rooms. *Research affiliation:* Staten Island University Hospital.

Computer facilities: 230 computers available on campus for general student use. A campuswide network can be accessed from student residence rooms and from off campus. Online class registration is available.
Website: http://www.wagner.edu/

General Application Contact: Robert Herr, Dean of Enrollment, 718-420-4242, Fax: 718-390-3105, E-mail: robert.herr@wagner.edu.

GRADUATE UNITS

Division of Graduate Studies ***Degree program information:*** Part-time and evening/weekend programs available. Part-time, evening/weekend. Offers accounting (MS); business administration (MBA); childhood education/students with disabilities (MS Ed); early childhood education/students with disabilities (birth-grade 2) (MS Ed); educational leadership (MS Ed, Certificate); finance (MBA); health care administration (MBA); international business (MBA); literacy (B-6) (MS Ed); management (Exec MBA); marketing (MBA); microbiology (MS); school district leadership (MS Ed, Certificate); secondary education 7-12 (MS Ed); secondary education/students with disabilities (MS Ed).

WAKE FOREST UNIVERSITY, Winston-Salem, NC 27109

General Information Independent, coed, university. CGS member. *Graduate housing:* On-campus housing not available.

GRADUATE UNITS

Graduate School of Arts and Sciences ***Degree program information:*** Part-time programs available. Part-time. Offers accountancy (MSA); analytical chemistry (MS, PhD); arts and sciences (MA, MA Ed, MALS, MS, MSA, PhD); biology (MS, PhD); computer science (MS); counseling (MA); English (MA); health and exercise science (MS); inorganic chemistry (MS, PhD); liberal studies (MALS); mathematics (MA); organic chemistry (MS, PhD); physical chemistry (MS, PhD); physics (MS, PhD); psychology (MA); religion (MA); secondary education (MA Ed); speech communication (MA). Electronic applications accepted.

School of Business ***Degree program information:*** Evening/weekend programs available. Evening/weekend. Offers assurance services (MSA); business (MA, MBA, MSA); business administration (MBA); management (MA); tax consulting (MSA); transaction services (MSA). Electronic applications accepted.

School of Law Students: 492 full-time (247 women), 14 part-time; includes 112 minority (48 Black or African American, non-Hispanic/Latino; 5 American Indian or Alaska Native, non-Hispanic/Latino; 9 Asian, non-Hispanic/Latino; 37 Hispanic/Latino; 13 Two or more races, non-Hispanic/Latino), 11 international. Average age 25. 1,989 applicants, 56% accepted, 140 enrolled. *Faculty:* 38 full-time (17 women), 23 part-time/adjunct (6 women). *Financial support:* In 2015–16, 428 students received support. Fellowships, research assistantships, teaching assistantships, career-related internships or fieldwork, Federal Work-Study, institutionally sponsored loans, and scholarships/grants available. Support available to part-time students. Financial award application deadline: 4/30; financial award applicants required to submit FAFSA. In 2015, 11 master's, 184 doctorates awarded. Offers law (LL M, MSL, JD, SJD). LL M program is designed for foreign law graduates in American law. *Application deadline:* For fall admission, 3/15 for domestic students, 6/15 for international students. Applications are processed on a rolling basis. *Application fee:* $75. Electronic applications accepted. *Application Contact:* R. Jay Shively, Assistant Dean for Admissions and Financial Aid, 336-758-5437, Fax: 336-758-3930, E-mail: admissions@law.wfu.edu. *Dean*, Suzanne Reynolds, 336-758-5435, Fax: 336-758-4632.

School of Medicine Offers medicine (MS, MD, PhD). Electronic applications accepted.

Graduate Programs in Medicine Offers biochemistry (PhD); cancer biology (PhD); comparative medicine (MS); health sciences research (MS); medicine (MS, PhD); microbiology and immunology (PhD); molecular and cellular pathobiology (MS, PhD); molecular genetics and genomics (PhD); molecular medicine (MS, PhD); neurobiology and anatomy (PhD); neuroscience (PhD); pharmacology (PhD); physiology (PhD). Electronic applications accepted.

Virginia Tech-Wake Forest University School of Biomedical Engineering and Sciences Offers biomedical engineering (MS, PhD). Electronic applications accepted.

WALDEN UNIVERSITY, Minneapolis, MN 55401

General Information Proprietary, coed, university. CGS member. *Enrollment:* 52,799 graduate, professional, and undergraduate students; 26,637 full-time matriculated graduate/professional students (20,513 women), 16,525 part-time matriculated graduate/professional students (12,623 women). *Enrollment by degree level:* 25,711 master's, 16,276 doctoral, 1,175 other advanced degrees. *Graduate faculty:* 195 full-time (131 women), 2,368 part-time/adjunct (1,562 women). *Student services:* Campus employment opportunities, career counseling, free psychological counseling, services for students with disabilities, writing training. *Library:* Walden University Library. *Collection:* Books: 206,177 (digital/electronic); Serial titles: 69,602 (digital/electronic); Databases: 106. Weekly public service hours: 69.

Computer facilities: Online class registration is available.
Website: http://www.waldenu.edu/

General Application Contact: Meghan Thomas, Vice President of Enrollment Management, 866-492-5336, E-mail: info@waldenu.edu.

GRADUATE UNITS

Graduate Programs Students: 18,857 full-time (14,220 women), 25,579 part-time (19,642 women); includes 21,534 minority (16,822 Black or African American, non-Hispanic/Latino; 226 American Indian or Alaska Native, non-Hispanic/Latino; 1,248 Asian, non-Hispanic/Latino; 2,102 Hispanic/Latino; 114 Native Hawaiian or other Pacific Islander, non-Hispanic/Latino; 1,022 Two or more races, non-Hispanic/Latino), 533 international. Average age 40. 10,931 applicants, 99% accepted, 4126 enrolled. *Faculty:* 195 full-time (131 women), 2,368 part-time/adjunct (1,562 women). *Financial support:* Fellowships, Federal Work-Study, scholarships/grants, unspecified assistantships, and family tuition reduction, active duty/veteran tuition reduction, group tuition reduction, interest-free payment plans, employee tuition reduction available. Support available to part-time students. Financial award applicants required to submit FAFSA. In 2015, 8,018 master's, 964 doctorates, 774 other advanced degrees awarded. *Degree program information:* Part-time and evening/weekend programs available. Part-time, evening/weekend, online only, 100% online. *Application deadline:* Applications are processed on a rolling basis. *Application fee:* $0. Electronic applications accepted. *Application Contact:* Meghan Thomas, Vice President of Enrollment Management, 866-492-5336, E-mail: info@waldenu.edu. *President*, Jonathan A. Kaplan.

Richard W. Riley College of Education and Leadership Students: 7,043 full-time (5,895 women), 2,362 part-time (1,884 women); includes 4,077 minority (3,273 Black or African American, non-Hispanic/Latino; 40 American Indian or Alaska Native, non-Hispanic/Latino; 131 Asian, non-Hispanic/Latino; 421 Hispanic/Latino; 32 Native Hawaiian or other Pacific Islander, non-Hispanic/Latino; 180 Two or more races, non-Hispanic/Latino), 61 international. Average age 40. 2,210 applicants, 100% accepted, 1739 enrolled. *Faculty:* 25 full-time (17 women), 652 part-time/adjunct (443 women). *Financial support:* Fellowships, Federal Work-Study, scholarships/grants, unspecified assistantships, and family tuition reduction, active duty/veteran tuition reduction, group tuition reduction, interest-free payment plans, employee tuition reduction available. Support available to part-time students. Financial award applicants required to submit FAFSA. In 2015, 1,843 master's, 317 doctorates, 484 other advanced degrees awarded. *Degree program information:* Part-time and evening/weekend programs available. Part-time, evening/weekend, online only, 100% online. Offers adult education (Post-Master's Certificate); adult learning (Graduate Certificate); college teaching and learning (Graduate Certificate); community college leadership (Ed D); curriculum, instruction and assessment (Ed D, Ed S, Graduate Certificate); developmental education (Graduate Certificate); early childhood administration, management, and leadership (Graduate Certificate); early childhood education (Ed D, Ed S); early childhood public policy and advocacy (Graduate Certificate); early childhood studies (MS); education (MS, PhD); educational administration and leadership (Ed D); educational leadership and administration (principal preparation) (Ed S); educational technology (Ed D, Ed S, Post Master's Certificate); elementary reading and literacy (Graduate Certificate); engaging culturally diverse learners (Graduate Certificate); enrollment management and institutional marketing (Graduate Certificate); higher education (MS); higher education and adult learning (Ed D); higher education leadership and management (Ed D); higher education leadership for student success (Graduate Certificate); instructional design and technology (MS, Postbaccalaureate Certificate); integrating technology in the classroom (Graduate Certificate); mathematics 5-8 (Graduate Certificate); mathematics K-6 (Graduate Certificate); online teaching for adult educators (Graduate Certificate); reading, literacy, and assessment (Ed D, Ed S); science K-8 (Graduate Certificate); special education (Ed D, Ed S, Graduate Certificate); special education (K-age 21) (MAT); teacher leadership (Graduate Certificate); teaching adults English as a second language (Graduate Certificate); teaching adults in the early childhood field (Graduate Certificate); teaching and diversity in early childhood education (Graduate Certificate); teaching English language learners (grades K-12) (Graduate Certificate); teaching K-12 students online (Graduate Certificate). *Application deadline:* Applications are processed on a rolling basis. *Application fee:* $0. Electronic applications accepted. *Application Contact:* Meghan Thomas, Vice President of Enrollment Management, 866-492-5336, E-mail: info@waldenu.edu. *Dean*, Dr. Kate Steffens, 866-492-5336.

School of Counseling Students: 1,827 full-time (1,569 women), 1,352 part-time (1,158 women); includes 1,484 minority (1,110 Black or African American, non-Hispanic/Latino; 19 American Indian or Alaska Native, non-Hispanic/Latino; 38 Asian, non-Hispanic/Latino; 189 Hispanic/Latino; 128 Two or more races, non-Hispanic/Latino), 21 international. Average age 38. 711 applicants, 94% accepted, 513 enrolled. *Faculty:* 76 full-time (60 women), 155 part-time/adjunct (115 women). *Financial support:* Federal Work-Study, scholarships/grants, unspecified assistantships, and family tuition reduction, active duty/veteran tuition reduction, group tuition reduction, interest-free payment plans, employee tuition reduction available. Support available to part-time students. Financial award applicants required to submit FAFSA. In 2015, 531 master's, 14 doctorates awarded. *Degree program information:* Part-time and evening/weekend programs available. Part-time, evening/weekend, online only, 100% online. Offers addiction counseling (MS); clinical mental health counseling (MS); counselor education and supervision (PhD); marriage, couple, and family counseling (MS); school counseling (MS). *Application deadline:* Applications are processed on a rolling basis. *Application fee:* $0. Electronic applications accepted. *Application Contact:* Meghan Thomas, Vice President of Enrollment Management, 866-492-5336, E-mail: info@waldenu.edu. *Dean*, Dr. Savitri Dixon-Saxon, 866-492-5336.

School of Health Sciences Students: 2,487 full-time (1,804 women), 2,282 part-time (1,540 women); includes 2,763 minority (2,129 Black or African American, non-Hispanic/Latino; 30 American Indian or Alaska Native, non-Hispanic/Latino; 237 Asian, non-Hispanic/Latino; 268 Hispanic/Latino; 13 Native Hawaiian or other Pacific

Islander, non-Hispanic/Latino; 86 Two or more races, non-Hispanic/Latino), 87 international. Average age 39. 1,205 applicants, 98% accepted, 820 enrolled. *Faculty:* 14 full-time (8 women), 222 part-time/adjunct (121 women). *Financial support:* Fellowships, Federal Work-Study, scholarships/grants, unspecified assistantships, and family tuition reduction, active duty/veteran tuition reduction, group tuition reduction, interest-free payment plans, employee tuition reduction available. Support available to part-time students. Financial award applicants required to submit FAFSA. In 2015, 641 master's, 147 doctorates, 18 other advanced degrees awarded. *Degree program information:* Part-time and evening/weekend programs available. Part-time, evening/weekend, online only, 100% online. Offers clinical research administration (MS, Graduate Certificate); health education and promotion (MS, PhD); health informatics (MS); health services (PhD); healthcare administration (MHA); leadership and organizational development (MHA); public health (MPH, Dr PH, PhD, Graduate Certificate); systems policy (MHA). *Application deadline:* Applications are processed on a rolling basis. *Application fee:* $0. Electronic applications accepted. *Application Contact:* Meghan Thomas, Vice President of Enrollment Management, 866-492-5336, E-mail: info@waldenu.edu. *Dean*, Dr. Jorg Westermann, 866-492-5336.

School of Information Systems and Technology Students: 449 full-time (140 women), 284 part-time (81 women); includes 351 minority (284 Black or African American, non-Hispanic/Latino; 25 Asian, non-Hispanic/Latino; 24 Hispanic/Latino; 18 Two or more races, non-Hispanic/Latino), 12 international. Average age 39. 326 applicants, 100% accepted, 247 enrolled. *Faculty:* 4 full-time (0 women), 27 part-time/adjunct (8 women). *Financial support:* Fellowships, Federal Work-Study, scholarships/grants, unspecified assistantships, and family tuition reduction, active duty/veteran tuition reduction, group tuition reduction, interest-free payment plans, employee tuition reduction available. Support available to part-time students. Financial award applicants required to submit FAFSA. In 2015, 61 master's, 46 other advanced degrees awarded. *Degree program information:* Part-time and evening/weekend programs available. Part-time, evening/weekend, online only, 100% online. Offers information systems (Graduate Certificate); information systems management (MISM); information technology (MS, DIT). *Application deadline:* Applications are processed on a rolling basis. *Application fee:* $0. Electronic applications accepted. *Application Contact:* Meghan Thomas, Vice President of Enrollment Management, 866-492-5336, E-mail: info@waldenu.edu. *Dean*, Dr. Karlyn A. Barilovits, 866-492-5336.

School of Management Students: 4,351 full-time (2,480 women), 2,750 part-time (1,591 women); includes 4,010 minority (3,368 Black or African American, non-Hispanic/Latino; 31 American Indian or Alaska Native, non-Hispanic/Latino; 159 Asian, non-Hispanic/Latino; 265 Hispanic/Latino; 14 Native Hawaiian or other Pacific Islander, non-Hispanic/Latino; 173 Two or more races, non-Hispanic/Latino), 69 international. Average age 41. 2,163 applicants, 100% accepted, 1643 enrolled. *Faculty:* 22 full-time (8 women), 292 part-time/adjunct (115 women). *Financial support:* Fellowships, Federal Work-Study, scholarships/grants, unspecified assistantships, and family tuition reduction, active duty/veteran tuition reduction, group tuition reduction, interest-free payment plans, employee tuition reduction available. Support available to part-time students. Financial award applicants required to submit FAFSA. In 2015, 862 master's, 149 doctorates, 138 other advanced degrees awarded. *Degree program information:* Part-time and evening/weekend programs available. Part-time, evening/weekend, online only, 100% online. Offers accounting (MBA, MS, DBA); advanced project management (Graduate Certificate); applied project management (Graduate Certificate); auditing (Graduate Certificate); bridge to business administration (Post-Doctoral Certificate); bridge to management (Post-Doctoral Certificate); business management (Graduate Certificate); communication (MBA); corporate finance (MBA); digital marketing (Graduate Certificate); entrepreneurship (DBA); entrepreneurship and small business (MBA); finance (MS, DBA); global supply chain management (DBA); healthcare management (MBA, DBA); human resource management (MBA, MS, Graduate Certificate); human resources management (DBA); information systems management (DBA); international business (MBA, DBA); leadership (MBA, MS, DBA, Graduate Certificate); management (MS, PhD); managerial accounting (Graduate Certificate); marketing (MBA, MS, DBA); project management (MBA, MS, DBA); self-designed (MBA, DBA); social impact management (DBA); technology entrepreneurship (DBA). *Application deadline:* Applications are processed on a rolling basis. *Application fee:* $0. Electronic applications accepted. *Application Contact:* Meghan Thomas, Vice President of Enrollment Management, 866-492-5336, E-mail: info@waldenu.edu. *Dean*, Dr. Freda Turner, 866-492-5336.

School of Nursing Students: 4,320 full-time (3,773 women), 5,250 part-time (4,740 women); includes 3,550 minority (2,360 Black or African American, non-Hispanic/Latino; 29 American Indian or Alaska Native, non-Hispanic/Latino; 523 Asian, non-Hispanic/Latino; 421 Hispanic/Latino; 25 Native Hawaiian or other Pacific Islander, non-Hispanic/Latino; 192 Two or more races, non-Hispanic/Latino), 221 international. Average age 40. 2,057 applicants, 100% accepted, 1507 enrolled. *Faculty:* 22 full-time (18 women), 540 part-time/adjunct (487 women). *Financial support:* Fellowships, Federal Work-Study, scholarships/grants, unspecified assistantships, and family tuition reduction, active duty/veteran tuition reduction, group tuition reduction, interest-free payment plans, employee tuition reduction available. Support available to part-time students. Financial award applicants required to submit FAFSA. In 2015, 3,022 master's, 86 doctorates, 34 other advanced degrees awarded. *Degree program information:* Part-time and evening/weekend programs available. Part-time, evening/weekend, online only, 100% online. Offers adult-gerontology acute care nurse practitioner (MSN); adult-gerontology nurse practitioner (MSN); education (MSN); family nurse practitioner (MSN); informatics (MSN); leadership and management (MSN); nursing (PhD, Post-Master's Certificate); nursing practice (DNP); psychiatric mental health (MSN). *Application deadline:* Applications are processed on a rolling basis. *Application fee:* $0. Electronic applications accepted. *Application Contact:* Meghan Thomas, Vice President of Enrollment Management, 866-492-5336, E-mail: info@waldenu.edu. *Dean*, Dr. Andrea Lindell, 866-492-5336.

School of Psychology Students: 2,498 full-time (1,986 women), 1,613 part-time (1,250 women); includes 1,810 minority (1,319 Black or African American, non-Hispanic/Latino; 41 American Indian or Alaska Native, non-Hispanic/Latino; 73 Asian, non-Hispanic/Latino; 260 Hispanic/Latino; 8 Native Hawaiian or other Pacific Islander, non-Hispanic/Latino; 109 Two or more races, non-Hispanic/Latino), 25 international. Average age 41. 867 applicants, 95% accepted, 597 enrolled. *Faculty:* 18 full-time (13 women), 235 part-time/adjunct (131 women). *Financial support:* Fellowships, Federal Work-Study, scholarships/grants, unspecified assistantships, and family tuition reduction, active duty/veteran tuition reduction, group tuition reduction, interest-free payment plans, employee tuition reduction available. Support available to part-time students. Financial award applicants required to submit FAFSA. In 2015, 595 master's, 160 doctorates, 22 other advanced degrees awarded. *Degree program information:* Part-time and evening/weekend programs available. Part-time, evening/weekend, online only, 100% online. Offers clinical psychology (MS); forensic psychology (MS); industrial organizational (MS, PhD); online teaching in psychology (Post-Master's Certificate); organizational psychology and development (Postbaccalaureate Certificate); psychology (MS, PhD); psychology respecialization (Post-Doctoral Certificate). *Application deadline:* Applications are processed on a rolling basis. *Application fee:* $0. Electronic applications accepted. *Application Contact:* Meghan Thomas, Vice President of Enrollment Management, 866-492-5336, E-mail: info@waldenu.edu. *Dean*, Dr. Marilyn Powell, 866-492-5366.

School of Public Policy and Administration Students: 1,025 full-time (619 women), 1,788 part-time (983 women); includes 1,640 minority (1,375 Black or African American, non-Hispanic/Latino; 18 American Indian or Alaska Native, non-Hispanic/Latino; 42 Asian, non-Hispanic/Latino; 130 Hispanic/Latino; 10 Native Hawaiian or other Pacific Islander, non-Hispanic/Latino; 65 Two or more races, non-Hispanic/Latino), 23 international. Average age 43. 637 applicants, 100% accepted, 478 enrolled. *Faculty:* 7 full-time (2 women), 107 part-time/adjunct (46 women). *Financial support:* Fellowships, Federal Work-Study, scholarships/grants, unspecified assistantships, and family tuition reduction, active duty/veteran tuition reduction, group tuition reduction, interest-free payment plans, employee tuition reduction available. Support available to part-time students. Financial award applicants required to submit FAFSA. In 2015, 298 master's, 79 doctorates, 32 other advanced degrees awarded. *Degree program information:* Part-time and evening/weekend programs available. Part-time, evening/weekend, online only, 100% online. Offers criminal justice (MPA, MPP, MS, Graduate Certificate); criminal justice and executive management (MS); criminal justice leadership and executive management (MS); emergency management (MPA, MPP, MS); general program (MPA, MPP); global leadership (MPA, MPP); government management (Graduate Certificate); health policy (MPA, MPP); homeland security (Graduate Certificate); homeland security and policy coordination (MPA, MPP); international nongovernmental organizations (MPA, MPP); law and public policy (MPA, MPP); local government management for sustainable communities (MPA, MPP); nonprofit management (Graduate Certificate); nonprofit management and leadership (MPA, MPP, MS); online teaching in higher education (Post-Master's Certificate); policy analysis (MPA); public management and leadership (MPA, MPP, Graduate Certificate); public policy (Graduate Certificate); public policy and administration (PhD); strategic planning and public policy (Graduate Certificate); terrorism, mediation, and peace (MPA, MPP). *Application deadline:* Applications are processed on a rolling basis. *Application fee:* $0. Electronic applications accepted. *Application Contact:* Meghan Thomas, Vice President of Enrollment Management, 866-492-5336, E-mail: info@waldenu.edu. *Dean*, Dr. Shana Garrett, 866-492-5336.

School of Social Work and Human Services Students: 1,579 full-time (1,387 women), 1,176 part-time (991 women); includes 1,840 minority (1,604 Black or African American, non-Hispanic/Latino; 16 American Indian or Alaska Native, non-Hispanic/Latino; 20 Asian, non-Hispanic/Latino; 124 Hispanic/Latino; 5 Native Hawaiian or other Pacific Islander, non-Hispanic/Latino; 71 Two or more races, non-Hispanic/Latino), 14 international. Average age 40. 761 applicants, 96% accepted, 567 enrolled. *Faculty:* 7 full-time (5 women), 138 part-time/adjunct (96 women). *Financial support:* Fellowships, Federal Work-Study, scholarships/grants, unspecified assistantships, and family tuition reduction, active duty/veteran tuition reduction, group tuition reduction, interest-free payment plans, employee tuition reduction available. Support available to part-time students. Financial award applicants required to submit FAFSA. In 2015, 165 master's, 12 doctorates awarded. *Degree program information:* Part-time and evening/weekend programs available. Part-time, evening/weekend, online only, 100% online. Offers addictions and social work (DSW); advanced clinical practice (MSW); clinical expertise (DSW); criminal justice (DSW); disaster, crisis, and intervention (DSW); family studies and interventions (DSW); human and social services (PhD); medical social work (DSW); military social work (MSW); policy practice (DSW); social work (PhD); social work administration (DSW); social work in healthcare (MSW); social work with children and families (MSW). *Application deadline:* Applications are processed on a rolling basis. *Application fee:* $0. Electronic applications accepted. *Application Contact:* Meghan Thomas, Vice President of Enrollment Management, 866-492-5336, E-mail: info@waldenu.edu. *Dean*, Dr. Savitri Dixon-Saxon, 866-492-5336.

WALDORF COLLEGE, Forest City, IA 50436-1713

General Information Independent-religious, coed, comprehensive institution.

GRADUATE UNITS

Program in Organizational Leadership Offers criminal justice leadership (MA); emergency management leadership (MA); fire/rescue executive leadership (MA); human resource development (MA); public administration (MA); sport management (MA); teacher leader (MA).

WALLA WALLA UNIVERSITY, College Place, WA 99324-1198

General Information Independent-religious, coed, comprehensive institution. *Graduate housing:* Rooms and/or apartments available on a first-come, first-served basis to single and married students.

GRADUATE UNITS

Graduate School ***Degree program information:*** Part-time and evening/weekend programs available. Part-time, evening/weekend. Offers biology (MS). Electronic applications accepted.

School of Education and Psychology Degree program information: Part-time programs available. Part-time. Offers counseling psychology (MA); curriculum and instruction (M Ed, MA, MAT); educational leadership (M Ed, MA, MAT); literacy instruction (M Ed, MA, MAT); students at risk (M Ed, MA, MAT); teaching (MAT). Electronic applications accepted.

Wilma Hepker School of Social Work and Sociology Degree program information: Part-time programs available. Part-time. Offers social work (MSW). Electronic applications accepted.

WALSH COLLEGE OF ACCOUNTANCY AND BUSINESS ADMINISTRATION, Troy, MI 48007-7006

General Information Independent, coed, upper-level institution. *Enrollment:* 2,549 graduate, professional, and undergraduate students; 38 full-time matriculated graduate/professional students (17 women), 1,544 part-time matriculated graduate/professional students (781 women). *Enrollment by degree level:* 1,582 master's. *Graduate faculty:* 21 full-time (11 women), 63 part-time/adjunct (26 women). *International tuition:* $13,980 full-time. *Tuition, area resident:* Full-time $19,545; part-time $13,155 per semester. *Graduate housing:* On-campus housing not available. *Student services:* Campus employment opportunities, career counseling, international student services, services for students with disabilities, writing training. *Library:* Vollbrecht

Library plus 1 other. *Collection:* Books: 23,586 (physical), 2,695 (digital/electronic); Serial titles: 515 (physical), 23,818 (digital/electronic); Databases: 72. Weekly public service hours: 113.

Computer facilities: Computer purchase and lease plans are available. 350 computers available on campus for general student use. A campuswide network can be accessed. Online class registration is available.
Website: http://www.walshcollege.edu/

General Application Contact: Heather Rigby, Director of Admissions and Academic Advising, 248-823-1610, Fax: 248-689-0938, E-mail: hrigby@walshcollege.edu.

GRADUATE UNITS

Graduate Programs Students: 1,425 (701 women); includes 350 minority (180 Black or African American, non-Hispanic/Latino; 3 American Indian or Alaska Native, non-Hispanic/Latino; 108 Asian, non-Hispanic/Latino; 40 Hispanic/Latino; 19 Two or more races, non-Hispanic/Latino), 43 international. Average age 34. 639 applicants, 86% accepted, 438 enrolled. *Faculty:* 30 full-time (15 women), 63 part-time/adjunct (20 women). *Financial support:* Scholarships/grants available. Support available to part-time students. Financial award application deadline: 6/30; financial award applicants required to submit FAFSA. *Degree program information:* Part-time and evening/weekend programs available. Part-time, evening/weekend. Offers accountancy (MAC); business administration (MBA); chief information officer (MS); chief security officer (MS); financial management (MSF); financial services (MSF); human resource management (MS); information technology (MSBIT); international business (MS); marketing (MS); program management office (MS); strategic management (MS); taxation (MST). *Application deadline:* For fall admission, 8/24 priority date for domestic students; for winter admission, 1/1 priority date for domestic students; for spring admission, 4/1 priority date for domestic students. Applications are processed on a rolling basis. *Application fee:* $25. Electronic applications accepted. *Application Contact:* Heather Rigby, Director of Admissions and Academic Advising, 248-823-1610, Fax: 248-689-0938, E-mail: hrigby@walshcollege.edu. *Chief Academic Officer/Executive Vice President*, Dr. Paul Shields, 248-823-1269, Fax: 248-689-0920, E-mail: pshields@walshcollege.edu.

WALSH UNIVERSITY, North Canton, OH 44720-3396

General Information Independent-religious, coed, comprehensive institution. CGS member. *Enrollment:* 2,859 graduate, professional, and undergraduate students; 225 full-time matriculated graduate/professional students (144 women), 256 part-time matriculated graduate/professional students (187 women). *Enrollment by degree level:* 382 master's, 96 doctoral, 3 other advanced degrees. *Graduate faculty:* 35 full-time (22 women), 46 part-time/adjunct (21 women). *Tuition, area resident:* Full-time $11,610; part-time $7740 per credit hour. Full-time tuition and fees vary according to program. *Graduate housing:* Room and/or apartments available on a first-come, first-served basis to single students; on-campus housing not available to married students. Typical cost: $5260 per year ($9920 including board). Room and board charges vary according to board plan and housing facility selected. Housing application deadline: 7/15. *Student services:* Campus employment opportunities, campus safety program, career counseling, exercise/wellness program, free psychological counseling, international student services, low-cost health insurance, multicultural affairs office, services for students with disabilities, teacher training, writing training. *Library:* Brother Edmond Drouin Library. *Collection:* Books: 132,214 (physical), 239,180 (digital/electronic); Serial titles: 135 (physical), 25,078 (digital/electronic); Databases: 125. Weekly public service hours: 79. *Research affiliation:* North Canton Public Schools (Straight A grants (student development)), Research Foundation of the Carolinas (surgery), Akron General Health System (patient satisfaction), Mercy Medical Center (orthopedics, nursing, physical therapy), Akron Children's Hospital (orthopedics).

Computer facilities: 336 computers available on campus for general student use. A campuswide network can be accessed from student residence rooms and from off campus. Online class registration is available.
Website: http://www.walsh.edu/

General Application Contact: Audra Dice, Director of Graduate Admissions, 330-490-7181, Fax: 330-490-7165, E-mail: adice@walsh.edu.

GRADUATE UNITS

Graduate Studies Students: 217 full-time (138 women), 251 part-time (185 women); includes 31 minority (19 Black or African American, non-Hispanic/Latino; 1 American Indian or Alaska Native, non-Hispanic/Latino; 3 Asian, non-Hispanic/Latino; 7 Hispanic/Latino; 1 Two or more races, non-Hispanic/Latino), 13 international. Average age 32. 584 applicants, 37% accepted, 166 enrolled. *Faculty:* 39 full-time (24 women), 42 part-time/adjunct (19 women). *Financial support:* In 2015–16, 28 students received support, including 28 research assistantships (averaging $8,164 per year). Financial award application deadline: 12/31. In 2015, 128 master's, 33 doctorates awarded. *Degree program information:* Part-time and evening/weekend programs available. Part-time, evening/weekend, online learning. Offers 21st century technologies (MA Ed); clinical mental health counseling (MA); healthcare management (Graduate Certificate); leadership with principal license (MA Ed); management (MBA); marketing (MBA); parish administration (MA); pastoral ministry (MA); physical therapy (DPT); reading literacy (MA Ed); religious education (MA); school counseling (MA); student affairs in higher education (MA). *Application deadline:* Applications are processed on a rolling basis. *Application fee:* $25. Electronic applications accepted. *Application Contact:* Audra Dice, Director of Graduate Admissions, 330-490-7181, Fax: 330-244-4680, E-mail: adice@walsh.edu. *Director of Graduate Studies*, Dr. Linda Barclay, 330-490-7264, Fax: 330-490-7371, E-mail: lbarclay@walsh.edu.

Gary and Linda Byers School of Nursing Students: 25 full-time (20 women), 38 part-time (34 women); includes 2 minority (1 Black or African American, non-Hispanic/Latino; 1 Hispanic/Latino). Average age 36. 45 applicants, 71% accepted, 22 enrolled. *Faculty:* 6 full-time (all women), 6 part-time/adjunct (4 women). *Financial support:* In 2015–16, 1 student received support, including 1 research assistantship (averaging $3,870 per year). Financial award application deadline: 12/31; financial award applicants required to submit FAFSA. In 2015, 9 master's, 5 doctorates awarded. *Degree program information:* Part-time and evening/weekend programs available. Part-time, evening/weekend, online only, 100% online. Offers academic nurse educator (MSN); clinical nurse leader (MSN); nursing practice (DNP). *Application deadline:* Applications are processed on a rolling basis. *Application fee:* $25. Electronic applications accepted. *Application Contact:* Audra Dice, Graduate and Transfer Admissions Counselor, 330-490-7181, Fax: 330-244-4680, E-mail: adice@walsh.edu. *Director of Graduate Nursing Programs*, Dr. Maris Pappas-Rogich, 330-490-7283, Fax: 330-490-7371, E-mail: mpappas@walsh.edu.

WARNER PACIFIC COLLEGE, Portland, OR 97215-4099

General Information Independent-religious, coed, comprehensive institution. *Enrollment:* 554 graduate, professional, and undergraduate students; 57 full-time matriculated graduate/professional students (26 women), 4 part-time matriculated graduate/professional students (2 women). *Enrollment by degree level:* 61 master's. *Graduate faculty:* 20 part-time/adjunct (6 women). *Tuition, area resident:* Full-time $3990; part-time $665 per credit. *Required fees:* $55. *Graduate housing:* On-campus housing not available. *Student services:* Campus employment opportunities, campus safety program, career counseling, child daycare facilities, exercise/wellness program, free psychological counseling, multicultural affairs office, teacher training. *Library:* Otto F. Linn Library.

Computer facilities: 90 computers available on campus for general student use. A campuswide network can be accessed from student residence rooms and from off campus. Online class registration is available.
Website: http://www.warnerpacific.edu/

General Application Contact: 503-517-1020, E-mail: admissions@warnerpacific.edu.

GRADUATE UNITS

Graduate Programs ***Financial support:*** Application deadline: 7/1; applicants required to submit FAFSA. *Degree program information:* Part-time and evening/weekend programs available. Part-time, evening/weekend. Offers human services (MA); not-for-profit leadership (MS); organizational leadership (MS); teaching (MAT). *Application deadline:* Applications are processed on a rolling basis. *President*, Dr. Andrea P. Cook, 503-517-1045, Fax: 503-517-1350.

WARNER UNIVERSITY, Lake Wales, FL 33859

General Information Independent-religious, coed, comprehensive institution. *Graduate housing:* Room and/or apartments available on a first-come, first-served basis to single students; on-campus housing not available to married students.

GRADUATE UNITS

School of Business ***Degree program information:*** Part-time and evening/weekend programs available. Part-time, evening/weekend, online learning. Offers business (MBA). Electronic applications accepted.

School of Education ***Degree program information:*** Part-time and evening/weekend programs available. Part-time, evening/weekend. Offers education (MAEd). Electronic applications accepted.

WARREN WILSON COLLEGE, Asheville, NC 28815-9000

General Information Independent-religious, coed, comprehensive institution. *Enrollment:* 812 graduate, professional, and undergraduate students; 87 full-time matriculated graduate/professional students (60 women). *Enrollment by degree level:* 87 master's. *Graduate faculty:* 25 full-time (10 women). *Graduate housing:* Room and/or apartments guaranteed to single students; on-campus housing not available to married students. *Library:* Pew Learning Center and Ellison Library.

Computer facilities: A campuswide network can be accessed from student residence rooms and from off campus. Online class registration, home directory and public html for each user, word processing, GIS, Statistical Analysis are available.
Website: http://www.warren-wilson.edu/

General Application Contact: Elana Roseberry, MFA Program Manager, 828-771-3717, Fax: 828-771-7005.

GRADUATE UNITS

MFA Program for Writers Students: 87 full-time (60 women); includes 18 minority (2 Black or African American, non-Hispanic/Latino; 1 American Indian or Alaska Native, non-Hispanic/Latino; 9 Asian, non-Hispanic/Latino; 4 Hispanic/Latino; 2 Two or more races, non-Hispanic/Latino). Average age 38. 132 applicants, 13% accepted, 17 enrolled. *Faculty:* 25 full-time (10 women). *Financial support:* In 2015–16, 32 students received support, including 2 fellowships (averaging $18,400 per year); scholarships/grants also available. Financial award application deadline: 3/1; financial award applicants required to submit FAFSA. In 2015, 28 master's awarded. Online learning. Offers creative writing (MFA). *Application deadline:* For fall admission, 9/1 for domestic and international students; for spring admission, 3/1 for domestic and international students. *Application fee:* $75. Electronic applications accepted. *Application Contact:* Elana Roseberry, MFA Project Manager, 828-771-3717, Fax: 828-771-7005, E-mail: eroseberry@warren-wilson.edu. *Director*, Prof. Debra Allbery, 828-771-3716, Fax: 828-771-7005, E-mail: dallbery@warren-wilson.edu.

WARTBURG THEOLOGICAL SEMINARY, Dubuque, IA 52004-5004

General Information Independent-religious, coed, graduate-only institution. *Graduate housing:* Rooms and/or apartments available on a first-come, first-served basis to single and married students. Housing application deadline: 4/30. *Research affiliation:* Menighetsfakultet, Augustana Theologische Hochschule.

GRADUATE UNITS

Graduate and Professional Programs Online learning. Offers diaconal ministry (MA); ministry (M Div); theology (MA). Electronic applications accepted.

WASHBURN UNIVERSITY, Topeka, KS 66621

General Information City-supported, coed, comprehensive institution. *Enrollment:* 6,615 graduate, professional, and undergraduate students; 485 full-time matriculated graduate/professional students (244 women), 337 part-time matriculated graduate/professional students (237 women). *Enrollment by degree level:* 485 master's, 337 doctoral. Tuition, state resident: full-time $6426; part-time $357 per credit hour. Tuition, nonresident: full-time $13,086; part-time $727 per credit hour. *Required fees:* $110; $55 per semester. Tuition and fees vary according to degree level and program. *Graduate housing:* Room and/or apartments available on a first-come, first-served basis to single students; on-campus housing not available to married students. Typical cost: $3890 per year ($6830 including board). Room and board charges vary according to board plan and housing facility selected. *Student services:* Campus employment opportunities, campus safety program, career counseling, exercise/wellness program, free psychological counseling, international student services, low-cost health insurance, multicultural affairs office, services for students with disabilities, teacher training, writing training. *Library:* Mabee Library plus 1 other. *Collection:* Books: 441,448 (physical), 292,840 (digital/electronic); Serial titles: 93,914 (physical). Weekly public service hours: 104; students can reserve study rooms.

Computer facilities: 542 computers available on campus for general student use. A campuswide network can be accessed from student residence rooms and from off campus. Online class registration is available.
Website: http://www.washburn.edu/

General Application Contact: Kris Klima, Director of Admissions, 785-670-1030, Fax: 785-670-1113, E-mail: admissions@washburn.edu.

GRADUATE UNITS

College of Arts and Sciences Students: 25 full-time (19 women), 32 part-time (19 women). Average age 31. *Financial support:* Research assistantships, career-related internships or fieldwork, Federal Work-Study, institutionally sponsored loans, and scholarships/grants available. Support available to part-time students. Financial award applicants required to submit FAFSA. In 2015, 22 master's awarded. *Degree program information:* Part-time and evening/weekend programs available. Part-time, evening/weekend. Offers arts and sciences (M Ed, MA, MLS); clinical psychology (MA); curriculum and instruction (M Ed); educational leadership (M Ed); liberal studies (MLS); reading (M Ed); special education (M Ed). *Application deadline:* For fall admission, 3/1 for domestic students; for spring admission, 10/1 for domestic students. *Application fee:* $40. Electronic applications accepted. *Application Contact:* Kris Klima, Director of Admissions, 785-670-1030, Fax: 785-670-1113, E-mail: admissions@washburn.edu. *Dean,* Dr. Laura Stephenson, 785-670-1561, Fax: 785-670-1297, E-mail: laura.stephenson@washburn.edu.

School of Applied Studies Students: 97 full-time (78 women), 88 part-time (67 women). Average age 36. *Financial support:* Career-related internships or fieldwork, Federal Work-Study, institutionally sponsored loans, and scholarships/grants available. Support available to part-time students. Financial award applicants required to submit FAFSA. In 2015, 61 master's awarded. *Degree program information:* Part-time and evening/weekend programs available. Part-time, evening/weekend, online learning. Offers addiction counseling (MA); applied studies (MA, MCJ, MHS, MSW); clinical social work (MSW); criminal justice and legal studies (MCJ); health care education (MHS). *Application fee:* $40. *Application Contact:* Kris Klima, Director of Admissions, 785-670-1030, Fax: 785-670-1113, E-mail: admissions@washburn.edu. *Dean,* Dr. Pat Munzer, 785-670-2111, Fax: 785-670-1027, E-mail: pat.munzer@washburn.edu.

School of Business ***Degree program information:*** Part-time and evening/weekend programs available. Part-time, evening/weekend. Offers accountancy (M Acc). Electronic applications accepted.

School of Law Offers global legal studies (LL M); law (MSL, JD). Electronic applications accepted.

School of Nursing Students: 17 full-time (15 women), 110 part-time (96 women). Average age 37. *Financial support:* Application deadline: 2/15; applicants required to submit FAFSA. In 2015, 43 master's, 1 doctorate, 11 other advanced degrees awarded. *Degree program information:* Part-time programs available. Part-time. Offers clinical nurse leader (MSN); nursing (DNP); psychiatric mental health nurse practitioner (Post-Graduate Certificate). *Application deadline:* For fall admission, 3/15 for domestic and international students. *Application fee:* $40. *Application Contact:* Mary V. Allen, Director of Student Services, 785-670-1533, E-mail: mary.allen@washburn.edu. *Dean,* Dr. Monica S. Scheibmeir, 785-670-1526, E-mail: monica.scheibmeir@washburn.edu.

WASHINGTON ADVENTIST UNIVERSITY, Takoma Park, MD 20912

General Information Independent-religious, coed, comprehensive institution. *Graduate housing:* Rooms and/or apartments available to single and married students.

GRADUATE UNITS

MBA Program ***Degree program information:*** Part-time and evening/weekend programs available. Part-time, evening/weekend, online learning. Offers business administration (MBA).

Program in Counseling Psychology ***Degree program information:*** Part-time programs available. Part-time. Offers counseling psychology (MA).

Program in Health Care Administration ***Degree program information:*** Part-time programs available. Part-time. Offers health care administration (MA).

Program in Nursing - Business Leadership ***Degree program information:*** Part-time programs available. Part-time. Offers nursing - business leadership (MSN).

Program in Nursing - Education ***Degree program information:*** Part-time programs available. Part-time. Offers nursing - education (MS).

Program in Professional Counseling Psychology ***Degree program information:*** Part-time programs available. Part-time. Offers professional counseling psychology (MA).

Program in Public Administration ***Degree program information:*** Part-time programs available. Part-time. Offers public administration (MPA).

Program in Religion ***Degree program information:*** Part-time programs available. Part-time. Offers religion (MAR).

WASHINGTON AND LEE UNIVERSITY, Lexington, VA 24450-0303

General Information Independent, coed, comprehensive institution. *Research affiliation:* Future of Privacy Forum (data privacy, data security, and related fields).

GRADUATE UNITS

School of Law Offers law (JD); U.S. law (LL M). Electronic applications accepted.

WASHINGTON STATE UNIVERSITY, Pullman, WA 99164

General Information State-supported, coed, university. CGS member. *Graduate housing:* Rooms and/or apartments available on a first-come, first-served basis to single and married students. Housing application deadline: 3/1. *Research affiliation:* Battelle Pacific Northwest Laboratories (biochemistry, engineering).

GRADUATE UNITS

Carson College of Business Online learning. Offers accounting (M Acc); business (M Acc, MBA, PhD). Programs also offered at the Tri-Cities, Vancouver, and Global (online) campuses.

College of Agricultural, Human, and Natural Resource Sciences ***Degree program information:*** Part-time programs available. Part-time, online learning. Offers agricultural, human, and natural resource sciences (MA, MS, PhD, Graduate Certificate); animal sciences (MS, PhD); apparel, merchandising, design, and textiles (MA); biological and agricultural engineering (MS, PhD); crop sciences (MS, PhD); entomology (MS, PhD); horticulture (MS, PhD); interior design and landscape architecture (MA, MS); plant pathology (MS, PhD); prevention science (PhD); soil sciences (MS, PhD). Programs also offered at the Global (online) campuses. Electronic applications accepted.

School of Economic Sciences Offers agricultural economics (PhD); economics (PhD). Programs offered at the Pullman campus. Electronic applications accepted.

School of Food Science Degree program information: Part-time programs available. Part-time. Offers food science (MS, PhD). Programs offered at the Pullman campus. Electronic applications accepted.

School of the Environment Offers environmental and natural resource sciences (PhD); natural resource sciences (MS). Program applications must be made through the Pullman campus.

College of Arts and Sciences Offers American studies (MA, PhD); applied mathematics (MS, PhD); archaeology (MA, PhD); arts and sciences (MA, MFA, MPA, MS, PhD, Graduate Certificate); chemistry (MS, PhD); clinical psychology (PhD); criminal justice and criminology (MA, PhD); cultural anthropology (PhD); English (MA, PhD); evolutionary anthropology (MA, PhD); experimental psychology (PhD); fine arts (MFA); foreign languages and cultures (MA); history (MA, PhD); mathematics (MS, PhD); mathematics teaching (MS, PhD); physics and astronomy (MS, PhD); sociology (MA, PhD). Electronic applications accepted.

School of Biological Sciences Offers biological sciences (MS, PhD). Programs are offered at the Pullman campus.

School of Music Degree program information: Part-time programs available. Part-time. Offers music (MA). Electronic applications accepted.

School of Politics, Philosophy and Public Affairs Online learning. Offers bioethics (Graduate Certificate); political science (MA, PhD); public affairs (MPA). MPA, MA, and PhD programs also offered at the Vancouver campus; Graduate Certificate offered through Global (online) campus. Electronic applications accepted.

School of the Environment Offers environmental and natural resource sciences (PhD); environmental science (MS); geology (MS, PhD); natural resource science (MS).

College of Education Offers counseling psychology (PhD); cultural studies and social thought in education (PhD); curriculum and instruction (Ed M, MA); education (Ed M, MA, MIT, Ed D, PhD); educational leadership (Ed M, MA, Ed D, PhD); educational psychology (MA, PhD); English language learners (Ed M, MA); language, literacy and technology (PhD); literacy education (Ed M, MA); mathematics education (PhD); special education (Ed M, MA, PhD); sport management (MA); teacher leadership (Ed D); teaching (MIT). Electronic applications accepted.

College of Medicine Offers medicine (MS); speech and hearing sciences (MS).

College of Nursing Offers advanced population health (MN, DNP); family nurse practitioner (MN, DNP); nursing (PhD); psychiatric/mental health nurse practitioner (DNP); psychiatric/mental health practitioner (MN). Programs offered at the Spokane, Tri-Cities, and Vancouver campuses.

College of Pharmacy Offers health policy and administration (MHPA); nutrition and exercise physiology (MS); pharmacy (Pharm D). Programs offered at the Spokane campus.

College of Veterinary Medicine Students: 516 full-time (386 women); includes 53 minority (1 Black or African American, non-Hispanic/Latino; 4 American Indian or Alaska Native, non-Hispanic/Latino; 7 Asian, non-Hispanic/Latino; 10 Hispanic/Latino; 1 Native Hawaiian or other Pacific Islander, non-Hispanic/Latino; 30 Two or more races, non-Hispanic/Latino), 1 international. Average age 24. 1,236 applicants, 19% accepted, 137 enrolled. *Faculty:* 37 full-time (8 women), 43 part-time/adjunct (10 women). *Financial support:* In 2015–16, 446 students received support, including 28 fellowships with full tuition reimbursements available, 87 research assistantships with full tuition reimbursements available (averaging $23,000 per year), 34 teaching assistantships with full tuition reimbursements available (averaging $22,000 per year); career-related internships or fieldwork, Federal Work-Study, institutionally sponsored loans, scholarships/grants, traineeships, health care benefits, and unspecified assistantships also available. Support available to part-time students. Financial award application deadline: 2/15; financial award applicants required to submit FAFSA. In 2015, 18 master's, 99 doctorates awarded. Offers molecular biology (PhD); molecular biosciences (PSM, PhD); neuroscience (MS, PhD); veterinary clinical sciences (MS, PhD); veterinary medicine (MS, PSM, DVM, PhD); veterinary science (MS, PhD). *Application deadline:* For fall admission, 9/15 for domestic and international students; for spring admission, 8/1 for international students. *Application fee:* $60. Electronic applications accepted. *Application Contact:* Barbara Hodson, Program Coordinator, 509-335-9515, E-mail: bhodson@vetmed.wsu.edu. *Dean,* Dr. Bryan Slinker, 509-335-9515, Fax: 509-335-0160, E-mail: vetmed-dean@vetmed.wsu.edu.

Paul G. Allen School for Global Animal Health Students: 20 full-time (9 women); includes 2 minority (1 Black or African American, non-Hispanic/Latino; 1 Native Hawaiian or other Pacific Islander, non-Hispanic/Latino). Average age 30. 2 applicants, 100% accepted, 2 enrolled. *Faculty:* 14 full-time (4 women), 13 part-time/adjunct (6 women). *Financial support:* In 2015–16, 13 students received support, including 2 fellowships with full tuition reimbursements available (averaging $7,000 per year), 10 research assistantships with full tuition reimbursements available (averaging $23,544 per year), 1 teaching assistantship (averaging $21,738 per year); scholarships/grants and health care benefits also available. Financial award application deadline: 1/1; financial award applicants required to submit FAFSA. In 2015, 1 doctorate awarded. *Degree program information:* Part-time programs available. Part-time. Offers immunology and infectious diseases (MS, PhD). *Application deadline:* For fall admission, 1/10 priority date for domestic and international students; for spring admission, 7/1 priority date for domestic and international students. *Application fee:* $75. Electronic applications accepted. *Application Contact:* Jill Griffin, Administrative Manager, 509-335-5861, Fax: 509-335-6328, E-mail: griffinj@vetmed.wsu.edu. *Director, Paul G. Allen School for Global Animal Health,* Dr. Guy H. Palmer, 509-335-5861, Fax: 509-335-6328, E-mail: gpalmer@vetmed.wsu.edu.

The Edward R. Murrow College of Communication Offers communication (MA, PhD); strategic communication (MA). MA in strategic communication offered at the Global (online) campus. Electronic applications accepted.

Voiland College of Engineering and Architecture Offers architecture (M Arch); civil engineering (MS, PhD); engineering and architecture (M Arch, METM, MS, PhD, Certificate); engineering and computer science (MS); engineering and technology management (METM, Certificate); environmental engineering (MS).

The Gene and Linda Voiland School of Chemical Engineering and Bioengineering Offers chemical engineering and bioengineering (MS, PhD).

School of Electrical Engineering and Computer Science Degree program information: Part-time programs available. Part-time. Offers computer engineering (MS); computer science (MS); electrical engineering (MS); electrical engineering and computer science (PhD); electrical power engineering (MS). MS programs in computer engineering, computer science and electrical engineering also offered at Tri-Cities campus; MS in electrical power engineering offered at the Global (online) campus.

School of Mechanical and Materials Engineering Degree program information: Part-time programs available. Part-time. Offers materials science and engineering (MS, PhD); mechanical engineering (MS, PhD). MS programs also offered at Tri-Cities campus. Electronic applications accepted.

★ WASHINGTON UNIVERSITY IN ST. LOUIS, St. Louis, MO 63130-4899

General Information Independent, coed, university. CGS member. *Graduate housing:* Rooms and/or apartments available on a first-come, first-served basis to single and married students.

GRADUATE UNITS

Brown School Students: 303 full-time (256 women); includes 125 minority (42 Black or African American, non-Hispanic/Latino; 16 American Indian or Alaska Native, non-Hispanic/Latino; 47 Asian, non-Hispanic/Latino; 9 Hispanic/Latino; 11 Two or more races, non-Hispanic/Latino), 71 international. Average age 26. 923 applicants, 322 enrolled. *Faculty:* 54 full-time (31 women), 87 part-time/adjunct (61 women). *Financial support:* In 2015–16, 267 students received support. Fellowships, research assistantships, Federal Work-Study, institutionally sponsored loans, scholarships/grants, health care benefits, tuition waivers (partial), and unspecified assistantships available. Support available to part-time students. Financial award application deadline: 3/1; financial award applicants required to submit FAFSA. In 2015, 239 master's, 5 doctorates awarded. Offers affordable housing and mixed-income community management (Certificate); American Indian and Alaska native (MSW); children, youth and families (MSW); health (MSW); individualized (MSW); mental health (MSW); older adults and aging societies (MSW); public health (MPH); public health sciences (PhD); social and economic development (MSW); social work (MSW, PhD); violence and injury prevention (MSW, Certificate). MSW/M Div and MSW/MAPS offered in partnership with Eden Theological Seminary. *Application deadline:* For fall admission, 12/15 priority date for domestic and international students; for winter admission, 3/1 priority date for domestic and international students. Applications are processed on a rolling basis. *Application fee:* $50. Electronic applications accepted. *Application Contact:* Office of Admissions and Recruitment, 314-935-6676, Fax: 314-935-4859, E-mail: brownadmissions@wustl.ed. *Director of Admissions and Recruitment*, Jamie L. Adkisson, 314-935-3524, Fax: 314-935-4859, E-mail: jadkisson@wustl.edu.

Graduate School of Arts and Sciences Students: 1,788 full-time (797 women), 26 part-time (13 women); includes 285 minority (61 Black or African American, non-Hispanic/Latino; 15 American Indian or Alaska Native, non-Hispanic/Latino; 131 Asian, non-Hispanic/Latino; 24 Hispanic/Latino; 54 Two or more races, non-Hispanic/Latino), 680 international. 3,758 applicants, 20% accepted, 307 enrolled. *Financial support:* Fellowships, research assistantships, teaching assistantships, career-related internships or fieldwork, scholarships/grants, traineeships, health care benefits, tuition waivers (full and partial), and unspecified assistantships available. In 2015, 139 master's, 286 doctorates awarded. Offers aging and development (PhD); anthropology (PhD); art history and archaeology (AM, PhD); arts and sciences (AM, MA, MA Ed, MAT, MFA, PhD); chemistry (PhD); Chinese (MA); Chinese and comparative literature (PhD); Chinese language and literature (PhD); classics (MA, PhD); comparative literature (PhD); dance (MFA); earth and planetary sciences (PhD); East Asian studies (MA); economics (PhD); educational research (PhD); elementary education (MA Ed); English and American literature (PhD); French (PhD); French and comparative literature (PhD); French language and literature (PhD); Germanic languages and literatures (PhD); Hispanic languages and literatures (PhD); history (PhD); Islamic and Near Eastern studies (MA); Japanese (MA); Japanese and comparative literature (PhD); Japanese language and literature (PhD); Jewish studies (MA); mathematics (MA, PhD); music (MA, PhD); philosophy (PhD); philosophy-neuroscience-psychology (PhD); physics (PhD); political science (PhD); secondary education (MAT); Spanish (PhD); Spanish and comparative literature (PhD); statistics (MA, PhD); theater and performance studies (MA); writing (MFA). *Application deadline:* For fall admission, 1/15 for domestic students. Applications are processed on a rolling basis. *Application fee:* $45. Electronic applications accepted. *Application Contact:* Bridget Coleman, Director of Admissions, 314-935-6880, Fax: 314-935-4887. *Dean/Vice Chancellor for Graduate Education*, Dr. William Tate, 314-935-6843, Fax: 314-935-4887.

Division of Biology and Biomedical Sciences Students: 542 full-time (246 women); includes 106 minority (27 Black or African American, non-Hispanic/Latino; 5 American Indian or Alaska Native, non-Hispanic/Latino; 60 Asian, non-Hispanic/Latino; 11 Hispanic/Latino; 3 Two or more races, non-Hispanic/Latino), 115 international. 1,085 applicants, 21% accepted, 77 enrolled. *Financial support:* Fellowships, research assistantships, and tuition waivers (full) available. Financial award application deadline: 1/15. In 2015, 87 doctorates awarded. Offers biochemistry (PhD); computational and molecular biophysics (PhD); computational and systems biology (PhD); developmental, regenerative, and stem cell biology (PhD); ecology (PhD); evolution, ecology and population biology (PhD); human and statistical genetics (PhD); immunology (PhD); molecular cell biology (PhD); molecular genetics and genomics (PhD); molecular microbiology and microbial pathogenesis (PhD); neurosciences (PhD); plant and microbial biosciences (PhD). *Application deadline:* For fall admission, 12/1 for domestic students. *Application fee:* $0. Electronic applications accepted. *Application Contact:* Rebecca Riney, 314-474-4648, E-mail: dbbsphdadmissions@wusm.wustl.edu. *Associate Dean*, Dr. John Russell, 314-747-0840.

Olin Business School Students: 661 full-time (286 women), 610 part-time (189 women); includes 273 minority (54 Black or African American, non-Hispanic/Latino; 1 American Indian or Alaska Native, non-Hispanic/Latino; 166 Asian, non-Hispanic/Latino; 17 Hispanic/Latino; 1 Native Hawaiian or other Pacific Islander, non-Hispanic/Latino; 34 Two or more races, non-Hispanic/Latino), 405 international. *Faculty:* 93 full-time (22 women), 46 part-time/adjunct (10 women). Offers accounting (MS); business (EMBA, M Acc, MBA, MS, DBA, PhD); business administration (EMBA, MBA, PhD); corporate finance and investments (MS); customer analytics (MS); finance (MS, DBA); leadership (MS); quantitative finance (MS); supply chain management (MS). Electronic applications accepted. *Application Contact:* Information Contact, 314-935-6880, Fax: 314-935-4887, E-mail: graduateschool@artsci.wustl.edu. *Dean*, Dr. Mahendra Gupta, 314-935-6344.

Sam Fox School of Design and Visual Arts Offers architecture (M Arch, MLA); design and visual arts (M Arch, MFA, MLA, MUD); urban design (MUD).

Graduate School of Art Offers visual art (MFA). Electronic applications accepted.

School of Engineering and Applied Science ***Degree program information:*** Part-time and evening/weekend programs available. Part-time, evening/weekend. Offers aerospace engineering (MS, PhD); biomedical engineering (MS, D Sc, PhD); chemical engineering (MS, D Sc); computer engineering (MS, PhD); computer science (MS, PhD); computer science and engineering (M Eng); engineering and applied science (M Eng, MCE, MCM, MEM, MIM, MPM, MS, MSEE, MSEE, MSI, D Sc, PhD); environmental engineering (MS, D Sc); materials science (MS); mechanical engineering (M Eng, MS, PhD). Electronic applications accepted.

School of Law Offers law (LL M, MJS, JD, JSD). Electronic applications accepted.

School of Medicine Offers audiology (Au D); clinical epidemiology (MPHS); clinical investigation (MS); deaf education (MS); health behavior planning and evaluation (Graduate Certificate); health behavior research (MS); health education, program planning and evaluation (MS); health services (MPHS); medicine (MPHS, MS, MSOT, Au D, DPT, MD, OTD, PPDPT, PhD, Certificate, Graduate Certificate); movement science (PhD); occupational therapy (MSOT, OTD); physical therapy (DPT); psychiatric and behavioral health sciences (MPHS); quantitative methods (MPHS); rehabilitation and participation science (PhD); speech and hearing sciences (PhD).

Division of Biostatistics ***Degree program information:*** Part-time programs available. Part-time. Offers biostatistics (MS); genetic epidemiology (Certificate). Electronic applications accepted.

See Close-Up on page 913.

WAYLAND BAPTIST UNIVERSITY, Plainview, TX 79072-6998

General Information Independent-religious, coed, comprehensive institution. *Enrollment:* 5,223 graduate, professional, and undergraduate students; 81 full-time matriculated graduate/professional students (46 women), 1,440 part-time matriculated graduate/professional students (777 women). *Enrollment by degree level:* 1,521 master's. *Graduate faculty:* 121 full-time (41 women), 102 part-time/adjunct (37 women). *Graduate housing:* Rooms and/or apartments available on a first-come, first-served basis to single and married students. *Student services:* Campus employment opportunities, campus safety program, career counseling, free psychological counseling, international student services, services for students with disabilities, teacher training, writing training. *Library:* J.E. and L.E. Mabee Learning Resource Center. *Collection:* Books: 129,396 (physical), 48,643 (digital/electronic); Serial titles: 3,139 (digital/electronic); Databases: 132.

Computer facilities: Computer purchase and lease plans are available. 840 computers available on campus for general student use. A campuswide network can be accessed from student residence rooms and from off campus. Online class registration is available.
Website: http://www.wbu.edu/

General Application Contact: Amanda Stanton, Coordinator of Graduate Studies, 806-291-3423, Fax: 806-291-1953, E-mail: stanton@wbu.edu.

GRADUATE UNITS

Graduate Programs Students: 75 full-time (42 women), 1,300 part-time (691 women); includes 656 minority (265 Black or African American, non-Hispanic/Latino; 11 American Indian or Alaska Native, non-Hispanic/Latino; 41 Asian, non-Hispanic/Latino; 274 Hispanic/Latino; 13 Native Hawaiian or other Pacific Islander, non-Hispanic/Latino; 52 Two or more races, non-Hispanic/Latino), 5 international. Average age 40. 255 applicants, 94% accepted, 107 enrolled. *Faculty:* 121 full-time (41 women), 102 part-time/adjunct (37 women). *Financial support:* Federal Work-Study, institutionally sponsored loans, and scholarships/grants available. Support available to part-time students. Financial award application deadline: 5/1; financial award applicants required to submit FAFSA. In 2015, 597 master's awarded. *Degree program information:* Part-time and evening/weekend programs available. Part-time, evening/weekend, online learning. Offers accounting (MBA); Christian ministry (MCM); counseling (MA); criminal justice (MACJ); divinity (M Div); education administration (M Ed); education diagnostics (M Ed); education literacy (M Ed); elementary certification (M Ed); English (M Ed); English as a second language (M Ed); general business (MBA); government administration (MPA); health care administration (MAM, MBA); higher education administration (M Ed); history (MA); homeland security (MPA); human resource management (MAM, MBA); human resources (M Ed); humanities (MAH); instructional leadership (M Ed); instructional technology (M Ed); international management (MBA); justice administration (MPA); leadership training and development (M Ed); management (MBA, D Mgt); management information systems (MBA); multidisciplinary science (MS); organization management (MAM); project management (MBA); religion (MA); science education (M Ed); secondary certification (M Ed); social studies (M Ed); special education (M Ed); sports administration and management (M Ed). *Application deadline:* Applications are processed on a rolling basis. *Application fee:* $50. Electronic applications accepted. *Application Contact:* Amanda Stanton, Coordinator of Graduate Studies, 806-291-3423, Fax: 806-291-1950, E-mail: stanton@wbu.edu. *Executive Vice President and Provost*, Dr. Bobby Hall, 806-291-3410, Fax: 806-291-1953, E-mail: hallb@wbu.edu.

WAYNESBURG UNIVERSITY, Waynesburg, PA 15370-1222

General Information Independent-religious, coed, comprehensive institution. *Graduate housing:* Room and/or apartments available on a first-come, first-served basis to single students; on-campus housing not available to married students. Housing application deadline: 8/1.

GRADUATE UNITS

Graduate and Professional Studies ***Degree program information:*** Part-time and evening/weekend programs available. Part-time, evening/weekend. Offers business (MBA); counseling (MA); counselor education and supervision (PhD); criminal investigation (MA); education (M Ed); nursing (MSN); nursing practice (DNP); special education (M Ed); technology (M Ed). Electronic applications accepted.

WAYNE STATE COLLEGE, Wayne, NE 68787

General Information State-supported, coed, comprehensive institution. CGS member. *Graduate housing:* Room and/or apartments available on a first-come, first-served basis to single students; on-campus housing not available to married students. *Research affiliation:* Nebraska Business Development Center, Social Sciences Research Center.

GRADUATE UNITS

Department of Health, Human Performance and Sport ***Degree program information:*** Part-time and evening/weekend programs available. Part-time, evening/weekend. Offers exercise science (MSE); organizational management (MS). Electronic applications accepted.

School of Business and Technology ***Degree program information:*** Part-time and evening/weekend programs available. Part-time, evening/weekend, online learning. Offers business and technology (MBA).

School of Education and Counseling ***Degree program information:*** Part-time and evening/weekend programs available. Part-time, evening/weekend. Offers alternative education (MSE); business and information technology education (MSE); communication arts education (MSE); counseling (MSE); counselor education (MSE); curriculum and instruction (MSE); early childhood education (MSE); education and counseling (MSE, Ed S); educational administration (MSE, Ed S); elementary administration (MSE); elementary and secondary administration (MSE); elementary education (MSE); English as a second language (MSE); English education (MSE); family and consumer sciences education (MSE); guidance and counseling (MSE); industrial technology and vocational education (MSE); learning communities (MSE); mathematics education (MSE); music education (MSE); school counseling (MSE); science education (MSE); secondary administration (MSE); social science education (MSE); special education (MSE).

WAYNE STATE UNIVERSITY, Detroit, MI 48202

General Information State-supported, coed, university. CGS member. *Enrollment:* 27,222 graduate, professional, and undergraduate students; 6,053 full-time matriculated graduate/professional students (3,121 women), 3,404 part-time matriculated graduate/professional students (2,062 women). *Enrollment by degree level:* 5,380 master's, 3,806 doctoral, 271 other advanced degrees. *Graduate faculty:* 869. Tuition, state resident: full-time $14,165; part-time $590.20 per credit hour. Tuition, nonresident: full-time $30,682; part-time $1278.40 per credit hour. *Required fees:* $1688; $47.45 per credit hour. $274.60 per semester. Tuition and fees vary according to course load and program. *Graduate housing:* Rooms and/or apartments available on a first-come, first-served basis to single and married students. Typical cost: $5901 per year ($10,061 including board) for single students. Room and board charges vary according to board plan and housing facility selected. *Student services:* Campus employment opportunities, campus safety program, career counseling, child daycare facilities, exercise/wellness program, free psychological counseling, grant writing training, international student services, multicultural affairs office, services for students with disabilities, teacher training, writing training. *Library:* David Adamany Undergraduate Library plus 5 others. *Collection:* Books: 2 million (physical), 1 million (digital/electronic); Serial titles: 63,572 (physical), 105,564 (digital/electronic); Databases: 750. Weekly public service hours: 138; study areas open 24 hours, 5–7 days a week. *Research affiliation:* Michigan State University, Children's Hospital of Michigan, University of Michigan, Henry Ford Health System, Health Resources and Services Administration, Karmanos Cancer Institute.

Computer facilities: A campuswide network can be accessed from student residence rooms. Online class registration is available.
Website: http://www.wayne.edu/

General Application Contact: Deirdre S. Baker, Office of Graduate Admissions, 313-577-4723, Fax: 313-577-0131, E-mail: gradadmissions@wayne.edu.

GRADUATE UNITS

College of Education Students: 518 full-time (395 women), 948 part-time (708 women); includes 554 minority (417 Black or African American, non-Hispanic/Latino; 5 American Indian or Alaska Native, non-Hispanic/Latino; 34 Asian, non-Hispanic/Latino; 56 Hispanic/Latino; 1 Native Hawaiian or other Pacific Islander, non-Hispanic/Latino; 41 Two or more races, non-Hispanic/Latino), 67 international. Average age 35. 859 applicants, 40% accepted, 222 enrolled. *Faculty:* 61. *Financial support:* In 2015–16, 416 students received support, including 8 fellowships with tuition reimbursements available (averaging $14,458 per year), 12 research assistantships (averaging $16,901 per year); teaching assistantships with tuition reimbursements available, Federal Work-Study, scholarships/grants, health care benefits, and unspecified assistantships also available. Support available to part-time students. Financial award application deadline: 3/31; financial award applicants required to submit FAFSA. In 2015, 371 master's, 39 doctorates, 64 other advanced degrees awarded. *Degree program information:* Part-time and evening/weekend programs available. Part-time, evening/weekend, 100% online. Offers education (M Ed, MA, MAT, Ed D, PhD, Certificate, Ed S); health education (M Ed); kinesiology (M Ed, PhD); sports administration (MA). *Application deadline:* For fall admission, 6/1 priority date for domestic students, 5/1 for international students; for winter admission, 10/1 priority date for domestic students, 9/1 priority date for international students; for spring admission, 2/1 priority date for domestic students, 1/1 priority date for international students. Applications are processed on a rolling basis. *Application fee:* $0. Electronic applications accepted. *Application Contact:* Janice Green, Assistant Dean, 313-577-1620, E-mail: jwgreen@wayne.edu. *Dean,* Dr. R. Douglass Whitman, 313-577-1620, E-mail: dwhitman@wayne.edu.

Division of Administrative and Organizational Studies Students: 99 full-time (64 women), 223 part-time (152 women); includes 155 minority (123 Black or African American, non-Hispanic/Latino; 1 American Indian or Alaska Native, non-Hispanic/Latino; 9 Asian, non-Hispanic/Latino; 14 Hispanic/Latino; 8 Two or more races, non-Hispanic/Latino), 19 international. Average age 39. 139 applicants, 41% accepted, 31 enrolled. *Financial support:* In 2015–16, 102 students received support, including 5 research assistantships with tuition reimbursements available (averaging $17,427 per year); fellowships with tuition reimbursements available, scholarships/grants, and unspecified assistantships also available. Support available to part-time students. Financial award application deadline: 3/31; financial award applicants required to submit FAFSA. In 2015, 33 master's, 10 doctorates, 32 other advanced degrees awarded. *Degree program information:* Part-time programs available. Part-time, online learning. Offers college and university teaching (Certificate); educational administration and supervision (Ed S); educational leadership (M Ed); educational leadership and policy studies (Ed D, PhD); educational technology (Certificate); instructional technology (M Ed, Ed D, PhD, Ed S); online teaching (Certificate). *Application deadline:* For fall admission, 6/1 priority date for domestic students, 5/1 priority date for international students; for winter admission, 10/1 priority date for domestic students, 9/1 priority date for international students; for spring admission, 2/1 priority date for domestic students, 1/1 priority date for international students. Applications are processed on a rolling basis. *Application fee:* $0. Electronic applications accepted. *Application Contact:* Janice Green, Assistant Dean, 313-577-1605, E-mail: jwgreen@wayne.edu. *Assistant Dean,* Dr. William Hill, 313-577-9316, E-mail: william_e_hill@wayne.edu.

Division of Teacher Education Students: 138 full-time (106 women), 389 part-time (309 women); includes 175 minority (119 Black or African American, non-Hispanic/Latino; 1 American Indian or Alaska Native, non-Hispanic/Latino; 12 Asian, non-Hispanic/Latino; 28 Hispanic/Latino; 1 Native Hawaiian or other Pacific Islander, non-Hispanic/Latino; 14 Two or more races, non-Hispanic/Latino), 10 international. Average age 37. 283 applicants, 35% accepted, 60 enrolled. *Financial support:* In 2015–16, 158 students received support, including 2 fellowships (averaging $13,857 per year); research assistantships with tuition reimbursements available, Federal Work-Study, scholarships/grants, and unspecified assistantships also available. Support available to part-time students. Financial award application deadline: 3/31; financial award applicants required to submit FAFSA. In 2015, 208 master's, 13 doctorates, 20 other advanced degrees awarded. *Degree program information:* Part-time programs available. Part-time, online learning. Offers art education (M Ed); bilingual/bicultural education (M Ed, Certificate); career and technical education (M Ed); curriculum and instruction (Ed D, PhD, Ed S); early childhood education (M Ed); elementary education (M Ed, MAT); English as a second language (Certificate); English education (M Ed); foreign language education (M Ed); mathematics education (M Ed); reading (M Ed, Ed S); reading, language and literature (Ed D); science education (M Ed); secondary education (MAT); social studies education (M Ed); special education (M Ed, MAT, Ed D, PhD, Ed S). *Application deadline:* For fall admission, 6/1 priority date for domestic students, 5/1 priority date for international students; for winter admission, 10/1 priority date for domestic students, 9/1 priority date for international students; for spring admission, 2/1 priority date for domestic students, 1/1 priority date for international students. Applications are processed on a rolling basis. *Application fee:* $0. Electronic applications accepted. *Application Contact:* Janice Green, Assistant Dean, 313-577-1605, E-mail: jwgreen@wayne.edu. *Assistant Dean,* Dr. Kathleen Crawford-McKinney, 313-577-0122.

Division of Theoretical and Behavioral Foundations Students: 203 full-time (179 women), 238 part-time (199 women); includes 160 minority (120 Black or African American, non-Hispanic/Latino; 1 American Indian or Alaska Native, non-Hispanic/Latino; 12 Asian, non-Hispanic/Latino; 12 Hispanic/Latino; 15 Two or more races, non-Hispanic/Latino), 26 international. Average age 32. 279 applicants, 33% accepted, 62 enrolled. *Financial support:* In 2015–16, 135 students received support, including 1 fellowship with tuition reimbursement available (averaging $10,418 per year), 3 research assistantships with tuition reimbursements available (averaging $17,427 per year); teaching assistantships with tuition reimbursements available, Federal Work-Study, scholarships/grants, health care benefits, and unspecified assistantships also available. Support available to part-time students. Financial award application deadline: 3/31; financial award applicants required to submit FAFSA. In 2015, 88 master's, 15 doctorates, 12 other advanced degrees awarded. *Degree program information:* Evening/weekend programs available. Evening/weekend. Offers applied behavior analysis (Certificate); counseling (M Ed, MA, Ed D, PhD, Ed S); counseling psychology (MA); education evaluation and research (M Ed, Ed D, PhD); educational psychology (M Ed, PhD); rehabilitation counseling and community inclusion (MA); school and community psychology (MA); school psychology (Certificate). *Application deadline:* For fall admission, 6/1 priority date for domestic students, 5/1 priority date for international students; for winter admission, 10/1 priority date for domestic students, 9/1 priority date for international students; for spring admission, 2/1 priority date for domestic students, 1/1 priority date for international students. Applications are processed on a rolling basis. *Application fee:* $0. Electronic applications accepted. *Application Contact:* Janice Green, Assistant Dean, 313-577-1605, E-mail: jwgreen@wayne.edu. *Interim Assistant Dean,* Dr. Joanne Holbert, 313-577-1691, E-mail: jholbert@wayne.edu.

College of Engineering Students: 1,055 full-time (195 women), 376 part-time (84 women); includes 132 minority (37 Black or African American, non-Hispanic/Latino; 1 American Indian or Alaska Native, non-Hispanic/Latino; 70 Asian, non-Hispanic/Latino; 12 Hispanic/Latino; 12 Two or more races, non-Hispanic/Latino), 1,037 international. Average age 27. 4,057 applicants, 43% accepted, 483 enrolled. *Faculty:* 103 full-time (11 women). *Financial support:* In 2015–16, 451 students received support, including 22 fellowships with tuition reimbursements available (averaging $15,454 per year), 78 research assistantships with tuition reimbursements available (averaging $19,119 per year), 101 teaching assistantships with tuition reimbursements available (averaging $19,233 per year); Federal Work-Study, scholarships/grants, tuition waivers (full and partial), and unspecified assistantships also available. Support available to part-time students. Financial award application deadline: 3/31; financial award applicants required to submit FAFSA. In 2015, 359 master's, 46 doctorates, 1 other advanced degree awarded. *Degree program information:* Part-time and evening/weekend programs available. Part-time, evening/weekend. Offers alternative energy technology (MS, Graduate Certificate); biomedical engineering (MS, PhD); chemical engineering (MS, PhD); civil engineering (MS); computer engineering (MS, PhD); computer science (MS, PhD); electric-drive vehicle engineering (MS, Graduate Certificate); electrical engineering (MS, PhD); engineering (MS, MSET, PhD, Certificate, Graduate Certificate, Postbaccalaureate Certificate); engineering management (MS, Certificate); industrial engineering (MS, PhD); injury biomechanics (Graduate Certificate); manufacturing engineering (MS); materials science and engineering (MS, PhD, Graduate Certificate); mechanical engineering (MS, PhD); polymer engineering (Graduate Certificate); scientific computing (Graduate Certificate); systems engineering (Certificate). *Application deadline:* For fall admission, 6/1 priority date for domestic students, 5/1 priority date for international students; for winter admission, 10/1 priority date for domestic students, 9/1 priority date for international students; for spring admission, 2/1 priority date for domestic students, 1/1 priority date for international students. Applications are processed on a rolling basis. *Application fee:* $0. Electronic applications accepted. *Application Contact:* Deirdre S. Baker, Director, Office of Graduate Admissions, 313-577-8141, E-mail: gradadmissions@wayne.edu. *Dean,* Dr. Farshad Fotouhi, 313-577-3776, E-mail: fotouhi@wayne.edu.

Division of Engineering Technology Students: 6 full-time (1 woman), 8 part-time (0 women); includes 3 minority (all Black or African American, non-Hispanic/Latino), 3 international. Average age 42. 25 applicants, 80% accepted, 1 enrolled. *Financial support:* Career-related internships or fieldwork and scholarships/grants available. Financial award application deadline: 3/31; financial award applicants required to submit FAFSA. In 2015, 1 master's awarded. Offers engineering technology (MSET). *Application deadline:* For fall admission, 6/1 priority date for domestic students, 5/1 priority date for international students; for winter admission, 10/1 priority date for domestic students, 9/1 priority date for international students; for spring admission, 2/1 priority date for domestic students, 1/1 priority date for international students. Applications are processed on a rolling basis. *Application fee:* $0. Electronic applications accepted. *Department Chair,* Dr. Chih Ping Yeh, 313-577-0800, E-mail: yeh@eng.wayne.edu.

College of Fine, Performing and Communication Arts Students: 128 full-time (70 women), 118 part-time (79 women); includes 83 minority (67 Black or African American, non-Hispanic/Latino; 1 American Indian or Alaska Native, non-Hispanic/Latino; 8 Hispanic/Latino; 7 Two or more races, non-Hispanic/Latino), 15 international. Average age 33. 415 applicants, 28% accepted, 81 enrolled. *Faculty:* 36. *Financial support:* In 2015–16, 141 students received support, including 34 research assistantships with tuition reimbursements available (averaging $17,482 per year), 26 teaching assistantships with tuition reimbursements available (averaging $17,520 per year); career-related internships or fieldwork, scholarships/grants, health care benefits, and unspecified assistantships also available. Financial award application deadline: 3/31; financial award applicants required to submit FAFSA. In 2015, 55 master's, 7 doctorates, 6 other advanced degrees awarded. Online learning. Offers art (MA, MFA); art history (MA); ceramics (MA, MFA); communication (PhD); communication and new media (Graduate Certificate); communication studies (MA); composition/theory (MM); conducting (MM); dispute resolution (MADR, Graduate Certificate); drawing (MA, MFA); fibers (MA, MFA); fine, performing and communication arts (MA, MADR, MFA, MM, PhD, Graduate Certificate); graphic design (MA, MFA); health communication (Graduate Certificate); industrial design (MA); interior design (MA); jazz performance (MM); journalism (MA); media arts (MA); media studies (MA); metalsmithing (MA, MFA); music (MA); music education (MM); orchestral studies (Certificate); painting (MA, MFA); performance (MM); photography (MA, MFA); printmaking (MA, MFA); public relations and organizational communication (MA); sculpture (MA, MFA); teaching and artistry (MA); theatre (MFA). *Application deadline:* For fall admission, 6/1 priority date for domestic students, 5/1 priority date for international students; for winter admission, 10/1 priority date for domestic students, 9/1 priority date for international students; for spring admission, 2/1 priority date for domestic students, 1/1 priority date for international students. Applications are processed on a rolling basis. *Application fee:* $0. Electronic applications accepted. *Application Contact:* Deirdre S. Baker, Director, Office of Graduate Admissions, 313-577-8141, E-mail: gd2267@wayne.edu. *Dean,* Dr. Matthew Seeger, 313-577-5342, Fax: 313-577-5342, E-mail: matthew.seeger@wayne.edu.

College of Liberal Arts and Sciences Students: 901 full-time (494 women), 394 part-time (227 women); includes 230 minority (116 Black or African American, non-Hispanic/Latino; 1 American Indian or Alaska Native, non-Hispanic/Latino; 32 Asian, non-Hispanic/Latino; 43 Hispanic/Latino; 38 Two or more races, non-Hispanic/Latino), 307 international. Average age 31. 2,380 applicants, 24% accepted, 289 enrolled.

Faculty: 318. *Financial support:* In 2015–16, 730 students received support, including 68 fellowships with tuition reimbursements available (averaging $16,661 per year), 104 research assistantships with tuition reimbursements available (averaging $20,277 per year), 332 teaching assistantships with tuition reimbursements available (averaging $18,870 per year); scholarships/grants, health care benefits, and unspecified assistantships also available. Support available to part-time students. Financial award application deadline: 3/31; financial award applicants required to submit FAFSA. In 2015, 248 master's, 110 doctorates, 4 other advanced degrees awarded. *Degree program information:* Part-time and evening/weekend programs available. Part-time, evening/weekend, online learning. Offers advanced macroeconomics (PhD); Africa (PhD); America (PhD); analytical chemistry (PhD); anthropology (MA, PhD); applied mathematics (MA, PhD); applied sociology and urban studies (MA); Arabic (MA, MALL); archival administration (Graduate Certificate); Asia (PhD); audiology (Au D); behavioral and cognitive neuroscience (PhD); biochemistry (PhD); biological sciences (MA, MS); cell development and neurobiology (PhD); chemistry (MA, MS); classics (MA, MALL); clinical psychology (PhD); cognitive, developmental and social psychology (PhD); communication disorders and science (PhD); creative writing (MA); criminal justice (MS); dietetics (Postbaccalaureate Certificate); econometrics (MA); economic development (Graduate Certificate); employment and labor relations (MA); English (MA); Europe (PhD); evolution and organismal biology (PhD); film and media studies (MA, PhD); food science (PhD); French (MA, MALL, PhD); gender (PhD); geology (MS); German (MA, MALL, PhD); health economics (MA, PhD); Hebrew (MA); history (MA); industrial organization (MA, PhD); industrial/organizational psychology (MA, PhD); inorganic chemistry (PhD); international economics (MA, PhD); Italian (MA, MALL); labor (PhD); labor and human resources (MA); labor economics (PhD); language learning (MALL); liberal arts and sciences (MA, MALL, MPA, MS, MUP, Au D, PhD, Graduate Certificate, Postbaccalaureate Certificate); linguistics (MA); literary and cultural studies (PhD); macroeconomics (MA); mathematical statistics (MA, PhD); mathematics (MA, MS); microeconomics (MA); modern languages (PhD); molecular biology and biotechnology (PhD); molecular biotechnology (MS); Near Eastern languages (MA); nutrition (PhD); nutrition and food science (MA, MS); organic chemistry (PhD); philosophy (MA, PhD); physical chemistry (PhD); physics (MA, MS, PhD); political science (MA, PhD); public administration (MPA); pure mathematics (PhD); rhetoric and composition (MA); rhetoric and composition studies (PhD); Romance languages (MA); science and technology (PhD); social psychology (PhD); sociology (MA, PhD); Spanish (MA, MALL, PhD); speech-language pathology (MA); urban studies and planning (MUP); world history (PhD, Graduate Certificate). *Application deadline:* For fall admission, 6/1 priority date for domestic students, 5/1 priority date for international students; for winter admission, 10/1 priority date for domestic students, 9/1 priority date for international students; for spring admission, 2/1 priority date for domestic students, 1/1 priority date for international students. Applications are processed on a rolling basis. *Application fee:* $0. Electronic applications accepted. *Application Contact:* Deirdre Baker, Director, Graduate Admissions, 313-577-8141, E-mail: gradadmissions@wayne.edu. *Dean,* Wayne Raskind, 313-577-2519, E-mail: raskind@wayne.edu.

Center for Peace and Conflict Studies Students: 2 full-time (0 women), 1 part-time (0 women). Average age 27. 5 applicants, 60% accepted. *Faculty:* 13. *Financial support:* Scholarships/grants available. Financial award application deadline: 3/31; financial award applicants required to submit FAFSA. In 2015, 2 Graduate Certificates awarded. Offers peace and security studies (Graduate Certificate). *Application deadline:* For fall admission, 6/1 priority date for domestic students, 5/1 priority date for international students; for winter admission, 10/1 priority date for domestic students, 9/1 priority date for international students; for spring admission, 2/1 priority date for domestic students, 1/1 priority date for international students; for summer admission, 2/1 priority date for domestic students, 1/1 priority date for international students. Applications are processed on a rolling basis. *Application fee:* $0. Electronic applications accepted. *Professor and Program Director,* Dr. Fred Pearson, 313-577-3453, E-mail: ab3440@wayne.edu.

College of Nursing Students: 127 full-time (119 women), 139 part-time (127 women); includes 72 minority (41 Black or African American, non-Hispanic/Latino; 15 Asian, non-Hispanic/Latino; 7 Hispanic/Latino; 9 Two or more races, non-Hispanic/Latino), 18 international. Average age 35. 244 applicants, 27% accepted, 45 enrolled. *Faculty:* 37. *Financial support:* In 2015–16, 74 students received support, including 28 fellowships with tuition reimbursements available (averaging $16,534 per year), 5 teaching assistantships with tuition reimbursements available (averaging $25,904 per year); scholarships/grants and unspecified assistantships also available. Support available to part-time students. Financial award application deadline: 3/31; financial award applicants required to submit FAFSA. In 2015, 108 master's, 20 doctorates, 11 other advanced degrees awarded. *Degree program information:* Part-time programs available. Part-time. Offers acute care nurse practitioner (Graduate Certificate); adult gerontology nurse practitioner - acute care (DNP); adult gerontology nurse practitioner - primary care (DNP); advanced practice nursing with women, neonates and children (MSN, DNP); family nurse practitioner (DNP); infant mental health (DNP); neonatal nurse practitioner (DNP); nurse midwifery (DNP, Graduate Certificate); nurse-midwifery (MSN); nursing (MSN, DNP, PhD, Graduate Certificate); nursing education (Graduate Certificate); nursing practice (DNP); pediatric nurse practitioner - acute care (DNP, Graduate Certificate); pediatric nurse practitioner - primary care (DNP, Graduate Certificate); pediatric nurse practitioner acute care (MSN); psychiatric mental health nurse practitioner (MSN, DNP, Graduate Certificate). Doctoral programs admit for fall only. *Application fee:* $0. Electronic applications accepted. *Application Contact:* Dr. Eric Brown, Associate Professor/Interim Dean, Office of Student Affairs in College of Nursing, 313-577-4082, Fax: 313-577-6949, E-mail: nursinginfo@wayne.edu. *Dean, College of Nursing,* Dr. Laurie Lauzon Clabo, 313-577-4082, E-mail: laurie.lauzon.clabo@wayne.edu.

Eugene Applebaum College of Pharmacy and Health Sciences Students: 686 full-time (432 women), 38 part-time (25 women); includes 94 minority (14 Black or African American, non-Hispanic/Latino; 2 American Indian or Alaska Native, non-Hispanic/Latino; 58 Asian, non-Hispanic/Latino; 8 Hispanic/Latino; 12 Two or more races, non-Hispanic/Latino), 55 international. Average age 26. 801 applicants, 26% accepted, 146 enrolled. *Faculty:* 25. *Financial support:* In 2015–16, 212 students received support, including 2 fellowships with tuition reimbursements available (averaging $24,179 per year), 10 research assistantships with tuition reimbursements available (averaging $24,595 per year); teaching assistantships with tuition reimbursements available, scholarships/grants, health care benefits, and unspecified assistantships also available. Financial award application deadline: 3/31; financial award applicants required to submit FAFSA. In 2015, 102 master's, 134 doctorates, 1 other advanced degree awarded. *Degree program information:* Part-time and evening/weekend programs available. Part-time, evening/weekend. Offers anesthesia (MS); medicinal chemistry (MS, PhD); nurse anesthesia (MS, Certificate); occupational therapy (MOT); pediatric anesthesia (Certificate); pharmaceutics (MS, PhD); pharmacology/toxicology (MS, PhD); pharmacy (Pharm D); pharmacy and health sciences (MOT, MS, DPT, PhD, Pharm D, Certificate); physical therapy (DPT); physician assistant studies (MS). Electronic applications accepted. *Application Contact:* Dr. Mary K. Clark, Assistant Dean, Office of Student and Alumni Affairs, 313-577-1716, Fax: 313-577-5589, E-mail: cphsinfo@wayne.edu. *Dean,* Dr. Serrine S. Lau, 313-577-1574, E-mail: serrine.lau@wayne.edu.

Law School Students: 384 full-time (162 women), 52 part-time (23 women); includes 61 minority (29 Black or African American, non-Hispanic/Latino; 3 American Indian or Alaska Native, non-Hispanic/Latino; 11 Asian, non-Hispanic/Latino; 6 Hispanic/Latino; 12 Two or more races, non-Hispanic/Latino), 19 international. Average age 27. 702 applicants, 51% accepted, 131 enrolled. *Faculty:* 41 full-time (17 women), 28 part-time/adjunct (7 women). *Financial support:* In 2015–16, 302 students received support. Federal Work-Study and scholarships/grants available. Support available to part-time students. Financial award application deadline: 3/31; financial award applicants required to submit FAFSA. In 2015, 7 master's, 163 doctorates awarded. *Degree program information:* Part-time and evening/weekend programs available. Part-time, evening/weekend. Offers corporate and finance law (LL M); labor and employment law (LL M); law (JD); taxation (LL M); United States law (LL M). *Application deadline:* For fall admission, 7/1 for domestic students, 5/1 priority date for international students. *Application fee:* $0. Electronic applications accepted. *Application Contact:* Kathy Fox, Assistant Dean of Admissions, 313-577-3937, Fax: 313-577-8129, E-mail: lawinquire@wayne.edu. *Dean,* Jocelyn Benson, 313-577-3933, E-mail: jbenson@wayne.edu.

Mike Ilitch School of Business Students: 167 full-time (74 women), 681 part-time (293 women); includes 228 minority (117 Black or African American, non-Hispanic/Latino; 1 American Indian or Alaska Native, non-Hispanic/Latino; 60 Asian, non-Hispanic/Latino; 28 Hispanic/Latino; 22 Two or more races, non-Hispanic/Latino), 83 international. Average age 30. 1,015 applicants, 51% accepted, 325 enrolled. *Faculty:* 29. *Financial support:* In 2015–16, 173 students received support, including 1 fellowship with tuition reimbursement available (averaging $18,000 per year), 4 teaching assistantships with tuition reimbursements available (averaging $18,000 per year); scholarships/grants, health care benefits, and unspecified assistantships also available. Support available to part-time students. Financial award application deadline: 3/31; financial award applicants required to submit FAFSA. In 2015, 213 master's, 2 doctorates, 4 other advanced degrees awarded. *Degree program information:* Part-time and evening/weekend programs available. Part-time, evening/weekend. Offers accounting (MS, Postbaccalaureate Certificate); business (Graduate Certificate); business administration (MBA, PhD); information systems management (Postbaccalaureate Certificate); taxation (MST). Application deadline for PhD is February 15. *Application deadline:* For fall admission, 7/1 for domestic students, 5/1 priority date for international students; for winter admission, 11/1 for domestic students, 9/1 priority date for international students; for spring admission, 3/1 for domestic students, 1/1 priority date for international students. Applications are processed on a rolling basis. *Application fee:* $0. Electronic applications accepted. *Application Contact:* Kiantee N. Rupert-Jones, Director, 313-577-4511, Fax: 313-577-9442, E-mail: gradbusiness@wayne.edu. *Dean, School of Business Administration,* Dr. Robert Forsythe, 313-577-4501, E-mail: robert.forsythe@wayne.edu.

School of Library and Information Science Students: 77 full-time (63 women), 360 part-time (293 women); includes 67 minority (36 Black or African American, non-Hispanic/Latino; 1 American Indian or Alaska Native, non-Hispanic/Latino; 2 Asian, non-Hispanic/Latino; 17 Hispanic/Latino; 11 Two or more races, non-Hispanic/Latino), 1 international. Average age 33. 247 applicants, 70% accepted, 98 enrolled. *Faculty:* 11 full-time (8 women), 23 part-time/adjunct (18 women). *Financial support:* In 2015–16, 109 students received support. Fellowships with tuition reimbursements available, scholarships/grants, health care benefits, and unspecified assistantships available. Support available to part-time students. Financial award application deadline: 3/31; financial award applicants required to submit FAFSA. In 2015, 187 master's, 48 other advanced degrees awarded. *Degree program information:* Part-time and evening/weekend programs available. Part-time, evening/weekend, online learning. Offers archival administration (Graduate Certificate); information management (Graduate Certificate); library and information science (MLIS, Spec); public library services to children and young adults (Graduate Certificate). *Application deadline:* For fall admission, 7/1 for domestic students, 5/1 priority date for international students; for winter admission, 10/1 for domestic students, 9/1 priority date for international students; for spring admission, 3/15 for domestic students, 1/1 priority date for international students. Applications are processed on a rolling basis. *Application fee:* $0. Electronic applications accepted. *Application Contact:* Academic Services Officer II, 313-577-1825, E-mail: asklis@wayne.edu. *Dean,* Dr. Sandra Yee, 313-577-4059, E-mail: aj0533@wayne.edu.

School of Medicine Students: 1,472 full-time (656 women), 147 part-time (75 women); includes 419 minority (58 Black or African American, non-Hispanic/Latino; 2 American Indian or Alaska Native, non-Hispanic/Latino; 305 Asian, non-Hispanic/Latino; 32 Hispanic/Latino; 22 Two or more races, non-Hispanic/Latino), 161 international. Average age 26. 5,754 applicants, 13% accepted, 471 enrolled. *Faculty:* 228. *Financial support:* In 2015–16, 1,058 students received support, including 64 fellowships with tuition reimbursements available (averaging $25,445 per year), 103 research assistantships with tuition reimbursements available (averaging $26,275 per year); teaching assistantships, Federal Work-Study, scholarships/grants, health care benefits, and unspecified assistantships also available. Support available to part-time students. Financial award application deadline: 3/31; financial award applicants required to submit FAFSA. In 2015, 69 master's, 309 doctorates, 13 other advanced degrees awarded. Offers anatomy (PhD); anatomy and cell biology (PhD); basic medical science (MS); basic medical sciences (MS); biochemistry and molecular biology (MS, PhD); cancer biology (PhD); clinical and translational science (Graduate Certificate); family medicine and public health sciences (MPH, Graduate Certificate); genetic counseling (MS); immunology and microbiology (MS, PhD); medical physics (MS, PhD); medical research (MS); medicine (MPH, MS, MD, PhD, Graduate Certificate); molecular genetics and genomics (MS, PhD); molecular medicine and genomics (MS, PhD); pathology (PhD); pharmacology (MS, PhD); physiology (MS, PhD); psychiatry and behavioral neurosciences (PhD); public health practice (MPH, Graduate Certificate); reproductive sciences (PhD); translational neuroscience (PhD). Electronic applications accepted. *Application Contact:* Dr. Kevin Sprague, Interim Associate Dean of Admissions, 313-577-1466, Fax: 313-577-9420, E-mail: admissions@med.wayne.edu. *Dean,* Dr. Jack Sobel, 313-577-1335, Fax: 313-577-8777, E-mail: ad6283@wayne.edu.

School of Social Work Students: 524 full-time (454 women), 149 part-time (126 women); includes 242 minority (191 Black or African American, non-Hispanic/Latino; 3 American Indian or Alaska Native, non-Hispanic/Latino; 11 Asian, non-Hispanic/Latino; 24 Hispanic/Latino; 13 Two or more races, non-Hispanic/Latino), 22 international. Average age 32. 885 applicants, 35% accepted, 190 enrolled. *Faculty:* 24. *Financial support:* In 2015–16, 115 students received support, including 7 fellowships with tuition reimbursements available (averaging $17,714 per year), 4 research assistantships with tuition reimbursements available (averaging $17,070 per year); scholarships/grants and unspecified assistantships also available. Financial award application deadline: 3/31;

financial award applicants required to submit FAFSA. In 2015, 327 master's, 3 doctorates, 16 other advanced degrees awarded. *Degree program information:* Part-time and evening/weekend programs available. Part-time, evening/weekend. Offers alcohol and drug abuse studies (Certificate); clinical social work theory and practice (Certificate); disabilities (Certificate); gerontology (Certificate); social welfare research and evaluation (Certificate); social work (MSW, PhD); social work and anthropology (PhD); social work and gerontology (PhD); social work and infant mental health (MSW, PhD); social work practice with families and couples (Certificate). Application deadlines: April 1 for MSW, December 19 for PhD. *Application fee:* $0. Electronic applications accepted. *Application Contact:* Julie Alter-Kay, Director, Office of Admissions and Student Services, 313-577-4409, E-mail: ae8440@wayne.edu. *Dean and Professor,* Dr. Cheryl E. Waites, 313-577-4400, E-mail: dv7029@wayne.edu.

WEBBER INTERNATIONAL UNIVERSITY, Babson Park, FL 33827-0096

General Information Independent, coed, comprehensive institution.

GRADUATE UNITS

Graduate School of Business ***Degree program information:*** Part-time and evening/weekend programs available. Part-time, evening/weekend. Offers accounting (MBA); criminal justice management (MBA); management (MBA); sports management (MBA).

WEBER STATE UNIVERSITY, Ogden, UT 84408-1001

General Information State-supported, coed, comprehensive institution. *Enrollment:* 25,955 graduate, professional, and undergraduate students; 285 full-time matriculated graduate/professional students (133 women), 352 part-time matriculated graduate/professional students (163 women). *Enrollment by degree level:* 637 master's. *Graduate faculty:* 89 full-time (42 women), 9 part-time/adjunct (5 women). Tuition, state resident: full-time $6520; part-time $1252 per credit hour. Tuition, nonresident: full-time $15,003; part-time $2998 per credit hour. *Required fees:* $380; $180 per credit hour. $8.50 per term. Tuition and fees vary according to course level and program. *Graduate housing:* Room and/or apartments available on a first-come, first-served basis to single students; on-campus housing not available to married students. Typical cost: $3278 per year ($4566 including board). Room and board charges vary according to board plan, campus/location and housing facility selected. *Student services:* Campus employment opportunities, campus safety program, career counseling, child daycare facilities, exercise/wellness program, free psychological counseling, grant writing training, international student services, low-cost health insurance, multicultural affairs office, services for students with disabilities, teacher training, writing training. *Library:* Stewart Library. *Collection:* Books: 534,760 (physical); Serial titles: 450 (physical). *Research affiliation:* Raytheon Training Corporation (education).

Computer facilities: Computer purchase and lease plans are available. 1,000 computers available on campus for general student use. A campuswide network can be accessed from student residence rooms and from off campus. Online class registration is available.
Website: http://www.weber.edu/

General Application Contact: Scott Teichert, Director of Admissions, 801-626-7670, Fax: 801-626-6045, E-mail: scottteichert@weber.edu.

GRADUATE UNITS

College of Health Professions Students: 134 full-time (72 women), 18 part-time (4 women); includes 6 minority (1 Black or African American, non-Hispanic/Latino; 5 Hispanic/Latino), 2 international. Average age 34. *Faculty:* 12 full-time (8 women), 3 part-time/adjunct (2 women). *Financial support:* In 2015–16, 24 students received support. Scholarships/grants available. Financial award application deadline: 4/1; financial award applicants required to submit FAFSA. In 2015, 51 master's awarded. *Degree program information:* Part-time and evening/weekend programs available. Part-time, evening/weekend. Offers health administration (MHA); health professions (MHA, MSN, MSRS); radiologic sciences (MSRS). *Application deadline:* For fall admission, 3/15 for domestic students, 2/20 for international students. Applications are processed on a rolling basis. *Application fee:* $60 ($90 for international students). Electronic applications accepted. *Application Contact:* Ann Gessel, Office Manager, 801-626-7127, Fax: 801-626-7683, E-mail: anngessel@weber.edu. *Dean,* Dr. Yasmin Simonian, 801-626-7117, Fax: 801-626-7683, E-mail: ysimonian@weber.edu.

School of Nursing Students: 45 full-time (37 women), 3 part-time (1 woman); includes 10 minority (all Asian, non-Hispanic/Latino). Average age 35. *Faculty:* 4 full-time (all women), 2 part-time/adjunct (both women). *Financial support:* Scholarships/grants available. Financial award application deadline: 4/1; financial award applicants required to submit FAFSA. In 2015, 27 master's awarded. Offers nursing (MSN). *Application deadline:* For fall admission, 4/1 priority date for domestic students. *Application fee:* $60 ($90 for international students). Electronic applications accepted. *Application Contact:* Robert Holt, Director of Enrollment, 801-626-7774, Fax: 801-626-6397, E-mail: rholt@weber.edu. *MSN Program Director,* Dr. Melissa Neville, 801-626-6204, Fax: 801-626-6397, E-mail: mneville@weber.edu.

College of Social and Behavioral Sciences Students: 5 full-time (1 woman), 27 part-time (7 women); includes 6 minority (2 Black or African American, non-Hispanic/Latino; 1 Asian, non-Hispanic/Latino; 2 Hispanic/Latino; 1 Two or more races, non-Hispanic/Latino). Average age 35. *Faculty:* 5 full-time (1 woman). *Financial support:* In 2015–16, 6 students received support. Scholarships/grants available. Financial award application deadline: 4/1; financial award applicants required to submit FAFSA. In 2015, 1 master's awarded. *Degree program information:* Part-time and evening/weekend programs available. Part-time, evening/weekend, online learning. Offers criminal justice (MCJ); social and behavioral sciences (MCJ). *Application deadline:* For fall admission, 7/29 for domestic students; for spring admission, 12/11 for domestic students; for summer admission, 4/1 for domestic students. Applications are processed on a rolling basis. *Application fee:* $60 ($90 for international students). *Application Contact:* Faye Medd, Enrollment Director, 801-626-6146, Fax: 801-626-6145, E-mail: fmedd@weber.edu. *Dean,* Dr. Francis Harrold, 801-626-6232, Fax: 801-626-7130, E-mail: francisharrold@weber.edu.

Jerry and Vickie Moyes College of Education Students: 50 full-time (32 women), 108 part-time (73 women); includes 10 minority (1 American Indian or Alaska Native, non-Hispanic/Latino; 4 Asian, non-Hispanic/Latino; 4 Hispanic/Latino; 1 Two or more races, non-Hispanic/Latino), 2 international. Average age 34. *Faculty:* 27 full-time (16 women), 1 (woman) part-time/adjunct. *Financial support:* In 2015–16, 31 students received support. Institutionally sponsored loans, scholarships/grants, tuition waivers (full and partial), and unspecified assistantships available. Support available to part-time students. Financial award application deadline: 4/1; financial award applicants required to submit FAFSA. In 2015, 77 master's awarded. *Degree program information:* Part-time and evening/weekend programs available. Part-time, evening/weekend. Offers athletic training (MSAT); curriculum and instruction (M Ed); education (M Ed, MSAT). *Application deadline:* For fall admission, 5/15 for domestic students; for spring admission, 9/15 for domestic students; for summer admission, 1/15 for domestic students. Applications are processed on a rolling basis. *Application fee:* $60 ($90 for international students). *Application Contact:* Nathan Alexander, College of Education Recruiter, 801-626-8124, Fax: 801-626-7427, E-mail: nathanalexander@weber.edu. *Dean,* Dr. Jack Rasmussen, 801-626-6273, Fax: 801-626-7427, E-mail: jrasmussen@weber.edu.

John B. Goddard School of Business and Economics Students: 83 full-time (19 women), 133 part-time (32 women); includes 9 minority (1 Black or African American, non-Hispanic/Latino; 4 Asian, non-Hispanic/Latino; 3 Hispanic/Latino; 1 Two or more races, non-Hispanic/Latino), 7 international. Average age 34. *Faculty:* 20 full-time (3 women), 3 part-time/adjunct (0 women). *Financial support:* In 2015–16, 43 students received support. Scholarships/grants available. Financial award application deadline: 4/1; financial award applicants required to submit FAFSA. In 2015, 84 master's awarded. *Degree program information:* Part-time and evening/weekend programs available. Part-time, evening/weekend. Offers business administration (MBA); business and economics (M Acc, M Tax, MBA). *Application deadline:* For fall admission, 5/1 for domestic students; for spring admission, 9/1 for domestic students. *Application fee:* $60 ($90 for international students). Electronic applications accepted. *Application Contact:* Mara Sikkink, Coordinator of Academic Advisement, 801-626-6534, Fax: 801-626-6747, E-mail: marasikkink@weber.edu. *Dean,* Dr. Jeffery W. Steagall, 801-626-7253, Fax: 801-626-6687, E-mail: jeffsteagall@weber.edu.

School of Accountancy Students: 38 full-time (12 women), 19 part-time (8 women); includes 5 minority (2 Asian, non-Hispanic/Latino; 2 Hispanic/Latino; 1 Two or more races, non-Hispanic/Latino), 4 international. Average age 31. *Faculty:* 7 full-time (1 woman). *Financial support:* In 2015–16, 26 students received support. Scholarships/grants available. Financial award application deadline: 4/1; financial award applicants required to submit FAFSA. In 2015, 36 master's awarded. *Degree program information:* Part-time and evening/weekend programs available. Part-time, evening/weekend. Offers accounting (M Acc); taxation (M Tax). *Application deadline:* For fall admission, 8/1 for domestic students; for spring admission, 12/1 for domestic students; for summer admission, 4/1 for domestic students. *Application fee:* $60 ($90 for international students). Electronic applications accepted. *Application Contact:* Dr. Larry A. Deppe, Graduate Coordinator, 801-626-7838, Fax: 801-626-7423, E-mail: ldeppe1@weber.edu. *Program Director,* Dr. Ryan Pace, 801-626-7562, Fax: 801-626-7423, E-mail: rpace@weber.edu.

Telitha E. Lindquist College of Arts and Humanities Students: 13 full-time (9 women), 65 part-time (46 women); includes 6 minority (1 Asian, non-Hispanic/Latino; 5 Hispanic/Latino), 1 international. Average age 32. *Faculty:* 26 full-time (14 women), 2 part-time/adjunct (both women). *Financial support:* In 2015–16, 29 students received support. Scholarships/grants and tuition waivers (full and partial) available. Financial award application deadline: 4/1. In 2015, 47 master's awarded. *Degree program information:* Part-time and evening/weekend programs available. Part-time, evening/weekend. Offers arts and humanities (MA, MPC); communication (MPC); English (MA). *Application deadline:* For fall admission, 4/1 for domestic students. Applications are processed on a rolling basis. *Application fee:* $60 ($90 for international students). Electronic applications accepted. *Application Contact:* Scott Teichert, Director of Admissions, 801-626-7670, Fax: 801-626-6045, E-mail: scottteichert@weber.edu. *Interim Dean, College of Arts and Humanities,* Dr. Catherine Zublin, 801-626-6424, Fax: 801-626-7422, E-mail: arts_humanities@weber.edu.

WEBSTER UNIVERSITY, St. Louis, MO 63119-3194

General Information Independent, coed, comprehensive institution. *Enrollment:* 2,901 full-time matriculated graduate/professional students (1,525 women), 9,768 part-time matriculated graduate/professional students (5,572 women). *Enrollment by degree level:* 12,404 master's, 40 doctoral, 225 other advanced degrees. *Graduate faculty:* 200 full-time (95 women), 932 part-time/adjunct (341 women). *Tuition, area resident:* Full-time $20,550; part-time $685 per credit hour. Tuition and fees vary according to campus/location and program. *Graduate housing:* Room and/or apartments available on a first-come, first-served basis to single students; on-campus housing not available to married students. Typical cost: $7240 per year. Room charges vary according to housing facility selected. Housing application deadline: 4/1. *Student services:* Campus employment opportunities, campus safety program, career counseling, exercise/wellness program, free psychological counseling, international student services, multicultural affairs office, services for students with disabilities, teacher training, writing training. *Library:* Emerson Library. *Collection:* Books: 260,133 (physical), 70,612 (digital/electronic); Serial titles: 1,167 (physical), 180 (digital/electronic); Databases: 165. Weekly public service hours: 91; study areas open 24 hours, 5–7 days a week; students can reserve study rooms. *Research affiliation:* Literacy Investment for Tomorrow.

Computer facilities: Computer purchase and lease plans are available. 714 computers available on campus for general student use. A campuswide network can be accessed from student residence rooms and from off campus. Online class registration is available.
Website: http://www.webster.edu/

General Application Contact: John Massena, Interim Director of Graduate Admissions, 314-968-7114, E-mail: johnmassena24@webster.edu.

GRADUATE UNITS

College of Arts and Sciences ***Degree program information:*** Part-time and evening/weekend programs available. Part-time, evening/weekend, online learning. Offers arts and sciences (MA, MS, MSN); counseling (MA); counseling psychology (MS); environmental management (MS); gerontology (MS); human services (MA); international relations (MA); legal studies (MA); nurse anesthesia (MS); nurse educator (MSN); nurse leader (MSN); science management and leadership (MS); U.S. patent practice (MS).

Institute for Human Rights and Humanitarian Studies Offers international human rights (MA).

George Herbert Walker School of Business and Technology ***Degree program information:*** Part-time and evening/weekend programs available. Part-time, evening/weekend, online learning. Offers business and organizational security management (MA, MBA); business and technology (MA, MBA, MHA, MHA, MPA, MS, DM); computer science/distributed systems (MS); decision support systems (MBA); environmental management (MBA); finance (MBA, MS); forensic accounting (MS); gerontology (MBA); health administration (MHA); health care management (MA); health services management (MA); human resources development (MA, MBA); human resources management (MA, MBA); information technology management (MBA, MS); international business (MA, MBA); international relations (MBA); management and leadership (MA, MBA); marketing (MA, MBA); media communications (MBA); nonprofit leadership (MA); procurement and acquisitions management (MA, MBA); public administration (MPA); space systems operations management (MS); Web services (MBA).

Leigh Gerdine College of Fine Arts ***Degree program information:*** Part-time and evening/weekend programs available. Part-time, evening/weekend. Offers art history and criticism (MA); church music (MM); composition (MM); fine arts (MA, MM); jazz studies (MM); music (MA); music education (MM); organ (MM); performance (MM); piano (MM); studio art (MA); voice (MM).

School of Communications ***Degree program information:*** Part-time and evening/weekend programs available. Part-time, evening/weekend, online learning. Offers advertising and marketing communications (MA); communications (MA); communications management (MA); media communications (MA); media literacy (MA); new media production (MA); public relations (MA).

School of Education ***Degree program information:*** Part-time programs available. Part-time, online learning. Offers applied educational psychology (MA, Ed S); communication arts (MAT); education (MA, MAT, Ed S); educational technology (MAT); mathematics (MA); multidisciplinary studies (MAT, Ed S); reading (MA); social science (MAT); special education (MA).

WEILL CORNELL MEDICINE, New York, NY 10065

General Information Independent, coed, graduate-only institution. *Graduate housing:* Rooms and/or apartments guaranteed to single students and available on a first-come, first-served basis to married students. Housing application deadline: 4/30. *Research affiliation:* Memorial Sloan-Kettering Cancer Center (cancer), Houston Methodist Hospital (general medicine and surgery), The Rockefeller University (biomedical research), New York Methodist (general medicine and surgery), Hospital For Special Surgery (orthopedics), Burke Medical Research Institute (neurology).

GRADUATE UNITS

Weill Cornell Graduate School of Medical Sciences Offers biochemistry, cell and molecular biology (MS, PhD); chemical biology (PhD); clinical epidemiology and health services research (MS); computational biology and medicine (PhD); health informatics (MS); health sciences (MS); immunology (MS, PhD); medical sciences (MS, PhD); neuroscience (MS, PhD); pharmacology (MS, PhD); physiology, biophysics and systems biology (MS, PhD). Electronic applications accepted.

Weill Cornell/Rockefeller/Sloan-Kettering Tri-Institutional MD-PhD Program Offered jointly with The Rockefeller University and Sloan-Kettering Institute. Electronic applications accepted.

WENTWORTH INSTITUTE OF TECHNOLOGY, Boston, MA 02115-5998

General Information Independent, coed, comprehensive institution. *Enrollment:* 4,576 graduate, professional, and undergraduate students; 91 full-time matriculated graduate/professional students (35 women), 151 part-time matriculated graduate/professional students (27 women). *Enrollment by degree level:* 242 master's. *Graduate faculty:* 56 full-time (23 women), 64 part-time/adjunct (20 women). *Tuition, area resident:* Full-time $35,100; part-time $1100 per credit hour. *Required fees:* $1740. *Graduate housing:* Room and/or apartments available on a first-come, first-served basis to single students; on-campus housing not available to married students. Typical cost: $13,013 (including board). Housing application deadline: 5/1. *Student services:* Campus employment opportunities, campus safety program, career counseling, exercise/wellness program, international student services, low-cost health insurance, multicultural affairs office, services for students with disabilities. *Library:* Wentworth Alumni Library plus 1 other. *Collection:* Books: 55,923 (physical), 301,141 (digital/electronic); Serial titles: 209 (physical), 36,310 (digital/electronic); Databases: 83. Weekly public service hours: 95.

Computer facilities: Computer purchase and lease plans are available. 320 computers available on campus for general student use. A campuswide network can be accessed from student residence rooms and from off campus. Online class registration is available.
Website: http://www.wit.edu/

General Application Contact: Martha Sheehan, Director of Admissions and Marketing, 617-989-4661, Fax: 617-989-4399, E-mail: sheehanm@wit.edu.

GRADUATE UNITS

Department of Architecture Students: 89 full-time (34 women), 2 part-time (0 women); includes 11 minority (1 Black or African American, non-Hispanic/Latino; 2 Asian, non-Hispanic/Latino; 3 Hispanic/Latino; 5 Two or more races, non-Hispanic/Latino), 4 international. Average age 24. 129 applicants, 90% accepted, 87 enrolled. *Faculty:* 21 full-time (8 women), 22 part-time/adjunct (8 women). *Financial support:* In 2015–16, 88 students received support, including 87 fellowships (averaging $6,100 per year), 37 teaching assistantships (averaging $2,700 per year). Financial award application deadline: 5/1; financial award applicants required to submit FAFSA. In 2015, 82 master's awarded. Offers architecture (M Arch). *Application deadline:* For fall admission, 1/15 priority date for domestic and international students. Applications are processed on a rolling basis. *Application fee:* $50. Electronic applications accepted. *Application Contact:* Kelly Hutzell, Director of Graduate Programs, 617-989-4494, E-mail: hutzelk@wit.edu. *Architecture Department Chair,* Michael Macphail, 617-989-4455, E-mail: macphailm@wit.edu.

Master of Engineering in Civil Engineering Program Students: 13 part-time (4 women); includes 4 minority (1 Black or African American, non-Hispanic/Latino; 2 Hispanic/Latino; 1 Two or more races, non-Hispanic/Latino), 1 international. Average age 27. 20 applicants, 65% accepted, 12 enrolled. *Faculty:* 8 full-time (2 women), 2 part-time/adjunct (1 woman). *Financial support:* Scholarships/grants available. Support available to part-time students. Financial award application deadline: 8/1; financial award applicants required to submit FAFSA. *Degree program information:* Part-time and evening/weekend programs available. Part-time-only, evening/weekend. Offers construction engineering (M Eng); infrastructure engineering (M Eng). *Application deadline:* For fall admission, 8/1 for domestic and international students. Applications are processed on a rolling basis. *Application fee:* $50. Electronic applications accepted. *Application Contact:* Martha Sheehan, Director of Admissions and Marketing, 617-989-4661, Fax: 617-989-4399, E-mail: sheehanm@wit.edu. *Director of Graduate Programs,* Philip Hammond, 617-989-4594, Fax: 617-989-4399, E-mail: hammondp1@wit.edu.

Master of Science in Construction Management Program Students: 2 full-time (1 woman), 71 part-time (14 women); includes 20 minority (7 Black or African American, non-Hispanic/Latino; 3 Asian, non-Hispanic/Latino; 2 Hispanic/Latino; 8 Two or more races, non-Hispanic/Latino). Average age 32. 43 applicants, 70% accepted, 21 enrolled. *Faculty:* 8 full-time (3 women), 9 part-time/adjunct (3 women). *Financial support:* Scholarships/grants available. Support available to part-time students. Financial award application deadline: 8/1; financial award applicants required to submit FAFSA. In 2015, 27 master's awarded. *Degree program information:* Part-time and evening/weekend programs available. Part-time-only, evening/weekend, 100% online, blended/hybrid learning. Offers construction management (MS). *Application deadline:* For fall admission, 8/1 for domestic and international students; for spring admission, 12/20 for domestic and international students. Applications are processed on a rolling basis. *Application fee:* $50. Electronic applications accepted. *Application Contact:* Martha Sheehan, Director of Admissions and Marketing, 617-989-4661, Fax: 617-989-4399, E-mail: sheehanm@wit.edu. *Director of Graduate Programs,* Philip Hammond, 617-989-4594, Fax: 617-989-4399, E-mail: hammondp1@wit.edu.

Master of Science in Facility Management Program Students: 30 part-time (12 women); includes 4 minority (1 Asian, non-Hispanic/Latino; 3 Hispanic/Latino). Average age 36. 18 applicants, 61% accepted, 11 enrolled. *Faculty:* 5 full-time (3 women), 7 part-time/adjunct (1 woman). *Financial support:* Scholarships/grants available. Support available to part-time students. Financial award application deadline: 8/1; financial award applicants required to submit FAFSA. In 2015, 6 master's awarded. *Degree program information:* Part-time and evening/weekend programs available. Part-time, evening/weekend, online only, 100% online, blended/hybrid learning. Offers facility management (MS). *Application deadline:* For fall admission, 8/1 for domestic and international students. Applications are processed on a rolling basis. *Application fee:* $50. Electronic applications accepted. *Application Contact:* Martha Sheehan, Director of Admissions and Marketing, 617-989-4661, Fax: 617-989-4399, E-mail: sheehanm@wit.edu. *Director of Graduate Programs,* Philip Hammond, 617-989-4594, Fax: 617-989-4399, E-mail: hammondp1@wit.edu.

Online Master of Science in Technology Management Program Students: 45 part-time (8 women); includes 11 minority (4 Black or African American, non-Hispanic/Latino; 5 Asian, non-Hispanic/Latino; 1 Hispanic/Latino; 1 Two or more races, non-Hispanic/Latino). Average age 32. 18 applicants, 94% accepted, 17 enrolled. *Faculty:* 3 full-time (2 women), 16 part-time/adjunct (7 women). *Financial support:* Scholarships/grants available. Support available to part-time students. Financial award application deadline: 8/1; financial award applicants required to submit FAFSA. *Degree program information:* Part-time and evening/weekend programs available. Part-time-only, evening/weekend, online only, 100% online. Offers technology management (MS). *Application deadline:* For fall admission, 8/1 for domestic and international students; for spring admission, 12/20 for domestic and international students. Applications are processed on a rolling basis. *Application fee:* $50. Electronic applications accepted. *Application Contact:* Martha Sheehan, Director of Admissions and Marketing, 617-989-4661, Fax: 617-989-4399, E-mail: sheehanm@wit.edu. *Director of Graduate Programs,* Philip Hammond, 617-989-4594, Fax: 617-989-4399, E-mail: hammondp1@wit.edu.

WESLEYAN COLLEGE, Macon, GA 31210-4462

General Information Independent-religious, Undergraduate: women only; graduate: coed, comprehensive institution. *Graduate housing:* Room and/or apartments available on a first-come, first-served basis to single students; on-campus housing not available to married students. Housing application deadline: 5/1.

GRADUATE UNITS

Department of Business and Economics Offers business administration (EMBA); business and economics (EMBA).

Department of Education ***Degree program information:*** Part-time programs available. Part-time. Offers early childhood education (MA).

WESLEYAN UNIVERSITY, Middletown, CT 06459

General Information Independent, coed, university. CGS member. *Enrollment:* 3,138 graduate, professional, and undergraduate students; 232 full-time matriculated graduate/professional students (106 women), 2 part-time matriculated graduate/professional students. *Graduate faculty:* 146 full-time (38 women), 8 part-time/adjunct (3 women). *Graduate housing:* Rooms and/or apartments available on a first-come, first-served basis to single and married students. Housing application deadline: 7/15. *Student services:* Campus employment opportunities, campus safety program, career counseling, child daycare facilities, exercise/wellness program, free psychological counseling, international student services, low-cost health insurance, multicultural affairs office, writing training. *Library:* Olin Memorial Library plus 1 other. *Collection:* Books: 1.6 million (physical), 489,183 (digital/electronic); Serial titles: 1,094 (physical), 74,616 (digital/electronic); Databases: 216. Weekly public service hours: 113. *Research affiliation:* Woods Hole Oceanographic Institution, Cold Spring Harbor Laboratory.

Computer facilities: Computer purchase and lease plans are available. 1,600 computers available on campus for general student use. A campuswide network can be accessed from student residence rooms and from off campus. Online class registration, Electronic Portfolio, Online Course Drop/Add, Moodle, Lynda.com are available.
Website: http://www.wesleyan.edu/

General Application Contact: Cheryl-Ann Hagner, Director, Graduate Student Services, 860-685-2223, Fax: 860-685-2439, E-mail: chagner@wesleyan.edu.

GRADUATE UNITS

Graduate Liberal Studies Program ***Financial support:*** Scholarships/grants available. Support available to part-time students. *Degree program information:* Part-time and evening/weekend programs available. Part-time, evening/weekend. Offers liberal studies (M Phil, MALS). *Application deadline:* For fall admission, 7/15 for domestic students; for spring admission, 11/1 for domestic students; for summer admission, 4/15 for domestic students. Applications are processed on a rolling basis. *Application fee:* $100. *Application Contact:* Sarah-Jane Ripa, Associate Director, Student Services and Outreach, 860-685-3345, Fax: 860-685-2901, E-mail: sripa@wesleyan.edu. *Director,* Jennifer Curran, 860-685-3338, Fax: 860-685-2901, E-mail: jcurran@wesleyan.edu.

Graduate Studies Students: 138 full-time (66 women); includes 57 minority (5 Black or African American, non-Hispanic/Latino; 1 American Indian or Alaska Native, non-Hispanic/Latino; 37 Asian, non-Hispanic/Latino; 13 Hispanic/Latino; 1 Native Hawaiian or other Pacific Islander, non-Hispanic/Latino). Average age 27. 343 applicants, 13% accepted, 24 enrolled. *Faculty:* 77 full-time (20 women). *Financial support:* In 2015–16, 74 students received support, including 29 research assistantships (averaging $29,118 per year), 74 teaching assistantships (averaging $29,118 per year); institutionally sponsored loans, health care benefits, tuition waivers (full), and unspecified assistantships also available. Financial award application deadline: 4/15. In 2015, 29 master's, 16 doctorates awarded. Offers astronomy (MA); biochemistry (PhD); cell and developmental biology (PhD); chemical physics (PhD); composition (MA); computer science (MA); earth and environmental sciences (MA); ethnomusicology (MA, PhD); evolution and ecology (PhD); genetics and genomics (PhD); inorganic chemistry (PhD); mathematics (MA, PhD); molecular biology (PhD); molecular biophysics (PhD); molecular genetics (PhD); neurobiology and behavior (PhD); organic chemistry (PhD); physical chemistry (PhD); physics (PhD); theoretical chemistry (PhD). *Application fee:* $0. Electronic applications accepted. *Application Contact:* Cheryl-Ann Hagner, Director of Graduate Student Services, 860-685-2223, Fax: 860-685-2439, E-mail: chagner@

wesleyan.edu. *Director of Graduate Studies*, Dr. Ann C. Burke, 860-685-3518, E-mail: acburke@wesleyan.edu.

WESLEY BIBLICAL SEMINARY, Jackson, MS 39206

General Information Independent-religious, coed, graduate-only institution.

GRADUATE UNITS

Graduate Programs ***Degree program information:*** Part-time programs available. Part-time. Offers apologetics (MA); Biblical languages (M Div); Biblical literature (MA); Christian studies (MA); context and mission (M Div); honors research (M Div); interpretation (M Div); ministry (M Div); spiritual formation (M Div); teaching (M Div); theology (MA). Electronic applications accepted.

WESLEY COLLEGE, Dover, DE 19901-3875

General Information Independent-religious, coed, comprehensive institution. *Graduate housing:* On-campus housing not available.

GRADUATE UNITS

Business Program ***Degree program information:*** Part-time and evening/weekend programs available. Part-time, evening/weekend. Offers environmental management (MBA); executive leadership (MBA); management (MBA). Executive leadership concentration also offered at New Castle, DE location.

Education Program ***Degree program information:*** Part-time and evening/weekend programs available. Part-time, evening/weekend. Offers education (M Ed, MA Ed, MAT).

Environmental Studies Program ***Degree program information:*** Part-time and evening/weekend programs available. Part-time, evening/weekend. Offers environmental studies (MS).

Nursing Program ***Degree program information:*** Part-time and evening/weekend programs available. Part-time, evening/weekend. Offers nursing (MSN). Electronic applications accepted.

WESLEY THEOLOGICAL SEMINARY, Washington, DC 20016-5690

General Information Independent-religious, coed, graduate-only institution. *Graduate housing:* Rooms and/or apartments available to single and married students. Housing application deadline: 7/1.

GRADUATE UNITS

Graduate and Professional Programs ***Degree program information:*** Part-time programs available. Part-time. Offers theology (M Div, MA, MTS, D Min).

WEST CHESTER UNIVERSITY OF PENNSYLVANIA, West Chester, PA 19383

General Information State-supported, coed, comprehensive institution. CGS member. *Enrollment:* 16,606 graduate, professional, and undergraduate students; 853 full-time matriculated graduate/professional students (629 women), 1,402 part-time matriculated graduate/professional students (998 women). *Enrollment by degree level:* 1,973 master's, 78 doctoral, 204 other advanced degrees. *Graduate faculty:* 247 full-time (138 women), 53 part-time/adjunct (37 women). Tuition, state resident: full-time $8460; part-time $470 per credit. Tuition, nonresident: full-time $12,690; part-time $705 per credit. *Required fees:* $2312; $126.75 per credit. Tuition and fees vary according to campus/location and program. *Graduate housing:* Room and/or apartments available on a first-come, first-served basis to single students; on-campus housing not available to married students. Typical cost: $5148 per year ($8427 including board). Room and board charges vary according to board plan and housing facility selected. Housing application deadline: 5/1. *Student services:* Campus employment opportunities, campus safety program, career counseling, exercise/wellness program, free psychological counseling, international student services, multicultural affairs office, services for students with disabilities, teacher training, writing training. *Library:* Francis Harvey Green Library plus 1 other. *Collection:* Databases: 289. Weekly public service hours: 107. *Research affiliation:* Pennsylvania Equine Toxicology and Research Laboratory (chemistry), Temple University Collaborative on Community Inclusion of Individuals with Psychiatric Disabilities (social work), University of Pennsylvania (social work), University of Connecticut Human Rights Institute Research Program on Economic and Social Rights (social work), The Soldier's Project (social work), Independent Blue Cross (IBC) (nursing).

Computer facilities: Computer purchase and lease plans are available. 2,300 computers available on campus for general student use. A campuswide network can be accessed from student residence rooms and from off campus. Online class registration is available.
Website: http://www.wcupa.edu/

General Application Contact: Office of Graduate Studies, 610-436-2943, Fax: 610-436-2763, E-mail: gradstudy@wcupa.edu.

GRADUATE UNITS

College of Arts and Sciences Students: 180 full-time (116 women), 322 part-time (182 women); includes 75 minority (34 Black or African American, non-Hispanic/Latino; 21 Asian, non-Hispanic/Latino; 15 Hispanic/Latino; 5 Two or more races, non-Hispanic/Latino), 40 international. Average age 30. 403 applicants, 82% accepted, 191 enrolled. *Faculty:* 93 full-time (46 women), 11 part-time/adjunct (7 women). *Financial support:* Scholarships/grants and unspecified assistantships available. Financial award application deadline: 2/15; financial award applicants required to submit FAFSA. In 2015, 172 master's, 12 other advanced degrees awarded. *Degree program information:* Part-time and evening/weekend programs available. Part-time, evening/weekend. Offers applied and computational mathematics (MS); applied statistics (MS, Certificate); arts and sciences (M Ed, MA, MS, Certificate, Teaching Certificate); biology (MS, Teaching Certificate); business ethics (Certificate); chemistry (Teaching Certificate); clinical psychology (MA); communication studies (MA); computer science (MS); computer security (Certificate); English (MA, Teaching Certificate); French (Teaching Certificate); general psychology (MA); geoscience (MA); German (Teaching Certificate); health care ethics (Certificate); history (M Ed, MA); Holocaust and genocide studies (MA, Certificate); industrial psychology (MA); information systems (Certificate); languages and cultures (MA); mathematics (MA, Teaching Certificate); mathematics education (MA); philosophy (MA); philosophy: applied ethics (MA); physics (Teaching Certificate); publishing (Certificate); Spanish (Teaching Certificate); TESL (MA, Certificate); Web technology (Certificate). *Application deadline:* For fall admission, 5/15 for international students; for spring admission, 10/15 for international students. Applications are processed on a rolling basis. *Application fee:* $50. Electronic applications accepted. *Application Contact:* Office of Graduate Studies and Extended Education, 610-436-2943, Fax: 610-436-2763, E-mail: gradstudy@wcupa.edu. *Dean of the College of Arts and Sciences*, Dr. Lori A. Vermeulen, 610-436-3521, Fax: 610-436-3150, E-mail: lvermeulen@wcupa.edu.

College of Business and Public Affairs Students: 289 full-time (214 women), 342 part-time (193 women); includes 231 minority (172 Black or African American, non-Hispanic/Latino; 2 American Indian or Alaska Native, non-Hispanic/Latino; 14 Asian, non-Hispanic/Latino; 27 Hispanic/Latino; 16 Two or more races, non-Hispanic/Latino), 6 international. Average age 31. 502 applicants, 79% accepted, 248 enrolled. *Faculty:* 40 full-time (24 women), 19 part-time/adjunct (13 women). *Financial support:* Scholarships/grants and unspecified assistantships available. Financial award application deadline: 2/15; financial award applicants required to submit FAFSA. In 2015, 200 master's, 32 other advanced degrees awarded. *Degree program information:* Part-time and evening/weekend programs available. Part-time, evening/weekend, 100% online. Offers business and public affairs (MA, MBA, MPA, MS, MSA, MSW, Certificate, DPA); criminal justice (MS); general public administration (MPA); geographic information systems (Certificate); geography (MA); human resource management (MPA, Certificate); human resources management (DPA); non profit administration (Certificate); nonprofit administration (MPA); public administration (Certificate); social work (MSW); urban and regional planning (MPA, Certificate). *Application deadline:* For fall admission, 5/15 for international students; for spring admission, 10/15 for international students. Applications are processed on a rolling basis. *Application fee:* $50. Electronic applications accepted. *Application Contact:* Office of Graduate Studies and Extended Education, 610-436-2943, Fax: 610-436-2763, E-mail: gradstudy@wcupa.edu. *Dean*, Dr. Michelle L. Patrick, 610-436-2930, Fax: 610-436-3170, E-mail: mpatrick@wcupa.edu.

The School of Business Students: 11 full-time (2 women), 119 part-time (47 women); includes 20 minority (3 Black or African American, non-Hispanic/Latino; 11 Asian, non-Hispanic/Latino; 5 Hispanic/Latino; 1 Two or more races, non-Hispanic/Latino). Average age 31. 60 applicants, 93% accepted, 34 enrolled. *Faculty:* 9 full-time (4 women). *Financial support:* Scholarships/grants and unspecified assistantships available. Financial award application deadline: 2/15; financial award applicants required to submit FAFSA. In 2015, 40 master's, 12 other advanced degrees awarded. *Degree program information:* Part-time and evening/weekend programs available. Part-time, evening/weekend, 100% online. Offers business education (MBA); entrepreneurship (Certificate). *Application deadline:* For fall admission, 5/15 for international students; for spring admission, 10/15 for international students. Applications are processed on a rolling basis. *Application fee:* $50. Electronic applications accepted. *Application Contact:* Office of Graduate Studies and Extended Education, 610-436-2943, Fax: 610-436-2763, E-mail: gradstudy@wcupa.edu. *MBA Director/Graduate Coordinator*, Dr. Brian Halsey, 610-425-5000, E-mail: mba@wcupa.edu.

College of Education Students: 150 full-time (120 women), 494 part-time (436 women); includes 74 minority (37 Black or African American, non-Hispanic/Latino; 5 Asian, non-Hispanic/Latino; 22 Hispanic/Latino; 10 Two or more races, non-Hispanic/Latino), 3 international. Average age 29. 310 applicants, 92% accepted, 184 enrolled. *Faculty:* 41 full-time (27 women), 13 part-time/adjunct (9 women). *Financial support:* Scholarships/grants and unspecified assistantships available. Financial award application deadline: 2/15; financial award applicants required to submit FAFSA. In 2015, 143 master's, 61 other advanced degrees awarded. *Degree program information:* Part-time and evening/weekend programs available. Part-time, evening/weekend, 100% online, blended/hybrid learning. Offers applied studies in teaching and learning (M Ed); autism (Certificate); clinical mental health counseling (MS); early childhood education (M Ed); education (M Ed, MS, Certificate, Teaching Certificate); education for sustainability (Certificate); educational technology (Certificate); entrepreneurial education (Certificate); grades 4-8 (Teaching Certificate); grades preK-4 (Teaching Certificate); higher education counseling/student affairs (MS, Certificate); literacy (Certificate); literacy coaching (Certificate); reading (M Ed, Teaching Certificate); school counseling (M Ed, Certificate); secondary education (M Ed); special education (Teaching Certificate); special education (M Ed); universal design for learning and assistive technology (Certificate). *Application deadline:* For fall admission, 5/15 for international students; for spring admission, 10/15 for international students. Applications are processed on a rolling basis. *Application fee:* $50. Electronic applications accepted. *Application Contact:* Office of Graduate Studies and Extended Education, 610-436-2943, Fax: 610-436-2763, E-mail: gradstudy@wcupa.edu. *Dean*, Dr. Kenneth D. Witmer, Jr., 610-436-2321, Fax: 610-436-3102, E-mail: kcrouse@wcupa.edu.

College of Health Sciences Students: 210 full-time (166 women), 205 part-time (164 women); includes 93 minority (69 Black or African American, non-Hispanic/Latino; 12 Asian, non-Hispanic/Latino; 7 Hispanic/Latino; 5 Two or more races, non-Hispanic/Latino), 27 international. Average age 32. 576 applicants, 52% accepted, 151 enrolled. *Faculty:* 42 full-time (32 women), 7 part-time/adjunct (6 women). *Financial support:* Scholarships/grants and unspecified assistantships available. Financial award application deadline: 2/15; financial award applicants required to submit FAFSA. In 2015, 141 master's, 26 other advanced degrees awarded. *Degree program information:* Part-time and evening/weekend programs available. Part-time, evening/weekend. Offers adapted physical education (Certificate); adult-gerontology clinical nurse specialist (MSN); communicative disorders (MA); community health (MPH); community nutrition (MS); emergency preparedness (Certificate); environmental health (MPH); exercise and sport physiology (MS); general physical education (MS); gerontology (Certificate); health care management (MPH, Certificate); health sciences (M Ed, MA, MPA, MPH, MS, MSN, DNP, Certificate, Teaching Certificate); integrative health (Certificate); nursing (DNP); nursing education (MSN); school health (M Ed); school nurse (Certificate); sport management and athletics (MPA). *Application deadline:* For fall admission, 5/15 for international students; for spring admission, 10/15 for international students. Applications are processed on a rolling basis. *Application fee:* $50. Electronic applications accepted. *Application Contact:* Office of Graduate Studies, 610-436-2943, Fax: 610-436-2763, E-mail: gradstudy@wcupa.edu. *Dean*, Dr. Linda Adams, 610-436-2825, Fax: 610-436-2860, E-mail: ladams@wcupa.edu.

College of Visual and Performing Arts Students: 24 full-time (13 women), 39 part-time (23 women); includes 3 minority (1 Black or African American, non-Hispanic/Latino; 1 Asian, non-Hispanic/Latino; 1 Two or more races, non-Hispanic/Latino), 8 international. Average age 29. 38 applicants, 82% accepted, 20 enrolled. *Faculty:* 31 full-time (9 women), 3 part-time/adjunct (2 women). *Financial support:* Scholarships/grants and unspecified assistantships available. Financial award application deadline: 2/15; financial award applicants required to submit FAFSA. In 2015, 39 master's, 4 other advanced degrees awarded. *Degree program information:* Part-time and evening/weekend programs available. Part-time, evening/weekend. Offers Kodaly methodology (Certificate); music (MM); music education (Teaching Certificate); music history (MA); music technology (MM, Certificate); music theory/composition (MM); Orff-Schulwerk (Certificate); performance (MM); piano pedagogy (MM, Certificate); visual and performing arts (MA, MM, Certificate, Teaching Certificate). *Application deadline:* For fall admission, 5/15 for international students; for spring admission, 10/15 for international students. Applications are processed on a rolling basis. *Application fee:* $50. Electronic applications accepted. *Application Contact:* Dr. M. Gregory Martin,

Graduate Coordinator, 610-436-2646, E-mail: mmartin@wcupa.edu. *Dean*, Dr. Timothy Blair, 610-436-2739, Fax: 610-436-2873, E-mail: tblair@wcupa.edu.

WEST COAST UNIVERSITY, North Hollywood, CA 91606

General Information Proprietary, coed, comprehensive institution.

GRADUATE UNITS

Graduate Programs

WESTERN CAROLINA UNIVERSITY, Cullowhee, NC 28723

General Information State-supported, coed, comprehensive institution. CGS member. *Enrollment:* 630 full-time matriculated graduate/professional students (421 women), 934 part-time matriculated graduate/professional students (628 women). *Enrollment by degree level:* 1,432 master's, 68 doctoral, 64 other advanced degrees. *Graduate faculty:* 233 full-time (110 women), 36 part-time/adjunct (17 women). *Graduate housing:* Rooms and/or apartments available to single students and guaranteed to married students. *Student services:* Campus employment opportunities, campus safety program, career counseling, child daycare facilities, exercise/wellness program, free psychological counseling, international student services, low-cost health insurance, multicultural affairs office, services for students with disabilities, teacher training, writing training. *Library:* Hunter Library. *Research affiliation:* North Carolina Center for the Advancement of Teaching.

Computer facilities: Computer purchase and lease plans are available. A campuswide network can be accessed from student residence rooms and from off campus. Online class registration is available.
Website: http://www.wcu.edu/

General Application Contact: Admissions Specialist, 828-227-7398, Fax: 828-227-7480, E-mail: gradsch@email.wcu.edu.

GRADUATE UNITS

Graduate School ***Financial support:*** Fellowships, research assistantships with tuition reimbursements, teaching assistantships with tuition reimbursements, career-related internships or fieldwork, institutionally sponsored loans, scholarships/grants, and unspecified assistantships available. Financial award application deadline: 3/31; financial award applicants required to submit FAFSA. *Degree program information:* Part-time and evening/weekend programs available. Part-time, evening/weekend, online learning. *Application deadline:* For fall admission, 5/1 priority date for domestic students, 4/1 for international students; for spring admission, 9/1 priority date for domestic students, 9/1 for international students. Applications are processed on a rolling basis. *Application fee:* $50. *Application Contact:* Admissions Specialist, 828-227-7398, Fax: 828-227-7480, E-mail: gradsch@email.wcu.edu. *Dean*, Dr. Brian Kloeppel, 828-227-3174, Fax: 828-227-7480, E-mail: bkloeppel@wcu.edu.

College of Arts and Sciences Financial support: Fellowships, research assistantships with tuition reimbursements, teaching assistantships with tuition reimbursements, career-related internships or fieldwork, institutionally sponsored loans, scholarships/grants, and unspecified assistantships available. Financial award application deadline: 3/31; financial award applicants required to submit FAFSA. *Degree program information:* Part-time and evening/weekend programs available. Part-time, evening/weekend. Offers arts and sciences (MA, MPA, MS, Graduate Certificate); biology (MS); chemistry (MS); history (MA); political science and public affairs (MPA); teaching English as a second language or foreign language (MA). *Application deadline:* For fall admission, 5/1 priority date for domestic students; for spring admission, 9/1 priority date for domestic students. Applications are processed on a rolling basis. *Application fee:* $50.

College of Business Financial support: Fellowships, research assistantships with tuition reimbursements, teaching assistantships with tuition reimbursements, career-related internships or fieldwork, institutionally sponsored loans, scholarships/grants, and unspecified assistantships available. Financial award application deadline: 3/31; financial award applicants required to submit FAFSA. *Degree program information:* Part-time and evening/weekend programs available. Part-time, evening/weekend, online learning. Offers accountancy (M Ac); business administration (MBA); entrepreneurship (ME); project management (MPM). *Application deadline:* For fall admission, 5/1 priority date for domestic students; for spring admission, 9/1 priority date for domestic students. Applications are processed on a rolling basis. *Application fee:* $50.

College of Education and Allied Professions Financial support: In 2015–16, 102 students received support. Fellowships, research assistantships with tuition reimbursements available, teaching assistantships with tuition reimbursements available, career-related internships or fieldwork, institutionally sponsored loans, scholarships/grants, and unspecified assistantships available. Financial award application deadline: 3/31; financial award applicants required to submit FAFSA. *Degree program information:* Part-time and evening/weekend programs available. Part-time, evening/weekend, online learning. Offers education and allied professions (MA); general psychology (MA). *Application deadline:* For fall admission, 2/1 for domestic students; for spring admission, 9/1 priority date for domestic students. Applications are processed on a rolling basis. *Application fee:* $50.

College of Fine and Performing Arts Financial support: Fellowships, research assistantships with tuition reimbursements, teaching assistantships with tuition reimbursements, career-related internships or fieldwork, institutionally sponsored loans, scholarships/grants, and unspecified assistantships available. Financial award application deadline: 3/31; financial award applicants required to submit FAFSA. *Degree program information:* Part-time programs available. Part-time. Offers art and design (MFA); fine and performing arts (MFA). *Application deadline:* For fall admission, 3/1 for domestic students. Applications are processed on a rolling basis. *Application fee:* $50.

College of Health and Human Sciences Degree program information: Part-time and evening/weekend programs available. Part-time, evening/weekend. Offers communication sciences and disorders (MS); health and human sciences (MHS, MS, MSW, DNP, DPT, Post-Master's Certificate, Postbaccalaureate Certificate); health sciences (MHS); nursing (MS, DNP, Post-Master's Certificate, Postbaccalaureate Certificate); physical therapy (DPT); social work (MSW).

Kimmel School of Construction Management and Technology Financial support: Fellowships, research assistantships with tuition reimbursements, teaching assistantships with tuition reimbursements, career-related internships or fieldwork, institutionally sponsored loans, scholarships/grants, and unspecified assistantships available. Financial award application deadline: 3/31; financial award applicants required to submit FAFSA. *Degree program information:* Part-time and evening/weekend programs available. Part-time, evening/weekend, online learning. Offers construction management (MCM); construction management and technology (MCM). *Application deadline:* For fall admission, 5/1 priority date for domestic students. Applications are processed on a rolling basis. *Application fee:* $50.

WESTERN CONNECTICUT STATE UNIVERSITY, Danbury, CT 06810-6885

General Information State-supported, coed, comprehensive institution. *Enrollment:* 5,826 graduate, professional, and undergraduate students. *Enrollment by degree level:* 358 master's, 68 doctoral, 11 other advanced degrees. Tuition, state resident: full-time $6188; part-time $343 per credit hour. Tuition, nonresident: full-time $17,240; part-time $350 per credit hour. *Required fees:* $4399; $173 per credit hour. One-time fee: $60 part-time. Tuition and fees vary according to degree level and program. *Graduate housing:* Rooms and/or apartments available on a first-come, first-served basis to single and married students. Housing application deadline: 4/1. *Student services:* Campus employment opportunities, career counseling, child daycare facilities, free psychological counseling, international student services, low-cost health insurance, multicultural affairs office, services for students with disabilities, teacher training. *Library:* Ruth Haas Library plus 2 others. *Collection:* Books: 187,746 (physical), 140,027 (digital/electronic); Serial titles: 320 (physical), 45,000 (digital/electronic); Databases: 102. Weekly public service hours: 144; students can reserve study rooms. *Research affiliation:* Smithsonian Institution Affiliations Program, The Jane Goodall Institute, Center for Financial Forensics and Informational Security, New England Educational Assessment Network, American Society for Microbiology.

Computer facilities: 666 computers available on campus for general student use. A campuswide network can be accessed from student residence rooms and from off campus. Online class registration, online payment are available.
Website: http://www.wcsu.edu/

General Application Contact: Chris Shankle, Associate Director of Graduate Studies, 203-837-9005, Fax: 203-837-8326, E-mail: shanklec@wcsu.edu.

GRADUATE UNITS

Division of Graduate Studies ***Degree program information:*** Part-time programs available. Part-time.

Ancell School of Business Degree program information: Part-time programs available. Part-time. Offers accounting (MBA); business (MBA, MHA, MS); business administration (MBA); health administration (MHA); justice administration (MS).

Maricostas School of Arts and Sciences Degree program information: Part-time programs available. Part-time. Offers arts and sciences (MA, MAT, MFA); biological and environmental sciences (MAT); creative and professional writing (MFA); earth and planetary sciences (MA); history and non-Western cultures (MA); literature (MA); mathematics (MA).

School of Professional Studies Degree program information: Part-time programs available. Part-time. Offers adult gerontology clinical nurse specialist (MSN); adult gerontology nurse practitioner (MSN); clinical mental health counseling (MS); curriculum (MS); instructional leadership (Ed D); instructional technology (MS); nursing education (Ed D); reading (MS); school counseling (MS); special education (MS).

School of Visual and Performing Arts Degree program information: Part-time programs available. Part-time. Offers illustration (MFA); music education (MS); painting (MFA); visual and performing arts (MFA, MS).

WESTERN GOVERNORS UNIVERSITY, Salt Lake City, UT 84107

General Information Independent, coed, comprehensive institution.

GRADUATE UNITS

College of Business ***Degree program information:*** Evening/weekend programs available. Evening/weekend. Offers information technology management (MBA); management and strategy (MBA); strategic leadership (MBA). Electronic applications accepted.

College of Health Professions ***Degree program information:*** Evening/weekend programs available. Evening/weekend. Offers healthcare management (MBA); leadership and management (MSN); nursing education (MSN). Electronic applications accepted.

College of Information Technology Online learning. Offers information security and assurance (MS); information technology (MS).

Teachers College ***Degree program information:*** Evening/weekend programs available. Evening/weekend, online learning. Offers curriculum and instruction (MS); educational leadership (MS); educational studies (MA); educational studies (5-12) (MA); elementary education (K-8) (MAT, Postbaccalaureate Certificate); elementary education (PreK-8) (MAT); English language learning (K-12) (MA); instructional design (MAT); learning and technology (M Ed, MA); management and innovation (M Ed); mathematics (5-12) (MAT, Postbaccalaureate Certificate); mathematics (5-9) (MAT, Postbaccalaureate Certificate); mathematics education (5-12) (MA); mathematics education (5-9) (MA); mathematics education (K-6) (MA); measurement and evaluation (M Ed); science (5-12) (Postbaccalaureate Certificate); science (5-9) (MAT, Postbaccalaureate Certificate); science education (5-12) (MA); science education (5-9) (MA); social science (5-12) (MAT, Postbaccalaureate Certificate); special education (MAT, MS). Electronic applications accepted.

WESTERN ILLINOIS UNIVERSITY, Macomb, IL 61455-1390

General Information State-supported, coed, comprehensive institution. CGS member. *Enrollment:* 11,094 graduate, professional, and undergraduate students; 838 full-time matriculated graduate/professional students (465 women), 975 part-time matriculated graduate/professional students (627 women). *Enrollment by degree level:* 1,479 master's, 37 doctoral, 67 other advanced degrees. *Graduate housing:* Rooms and/or apartments available on a first-come, first-served basis to single and married students. *Student services:* Campus employment opportunities, campus safety program, career counseling, exercise/wellness program, free psychological counseling, international student services, low-cost health insurance, multicultural affairs office, services for students with disabilities, teacher training, writing training. *Library:* Leslie Malpass Library plus 4 others. *Collection:* Books: 1 million (physical), 44,230 (digital/electronic); Databases: 126. *Research affiliation:* National Council of Teachers of English (English and journalism), Petroleum Research Fund (chemistry), Bayer Crop Services (agriculture), McDonald's Corporation (education), The Ceres Trust (agriculture), Quad Cities Manufacturing Lab (engineering).

Computer facilities: A campuswide network can be accessed from student residence rooms and from off campus. Online class registration is available.
Website: http://www.wiu.edu/

General Application Contact: Dr. Nancy Parsons, Associate Provost and Director of Graduate Studies, 309-298-1806, Fax: 309-298-2345, E-mail: grad-office@wiu.edu.

GRADUATE UNITS

School of Graduate Studies Students: 858 full-time (457 women), 824 part-time (522 women); includes 212 minority (102 Black or African American, non-Hispanic/Latino; 2

American Indian or Alaska Native, non-Hispanic/Latino; 17 Asian, non-Hispanic/Latino; 63 Hispanic/Latino; 28 Two or more races, non-Hispanic/Latino), 318 international. Average age 31. 1,332 applicants, 70% accepted, 518 enrolled. *Financial support:* In 2015–16, 29 research assistantships with full tuition reimbursements (averaging $7,544 per year), 59 teaching assistantships with full tuition reimbursements (averaging $8,688 per year) were awarded; unspecified assistantships also available. Financial award applicants required to submit FAFSA. In 2015, 545 master's, 7 doctorates, 74 other advanced degrees awarded. *Degree program information:* Part-time programs available. Part-time, online learning. *Application fee:* $30. Electronic applications accepted. *Associate Provost and Director of Graduate Studies*, Dr. Nancy Parsons, 309-298-1806, Fax: 309-298-2345, E-mail: grad-office@wiu.edu.

College of Arts and Sciences Students: 245 full-time (133 women), 139 part-time (81 women); includes 51 minority (26 Black or African American, non-Hispanic/Latino; 1 American Indian or Alaska Native, non-Hispanic/Latino; 3 Asian, non-Hispanic/Latino; 11 Hispanic/Latino; 10 Two or more races, non-Hispanic/Latino), 99 international. Average age 31. 304 applicants, 67% accepted, 115 enrolled. *Financial support:* In 2015–16, 17 research assistantships with full tuition reimbursements (averaging $7,544 per year), 37 teaching assistantships with full tuition reimbursements (averaging $8,688 per year) were awarded; unspecified assistantships also available. Financial award applicants required to submit FAFSA. In 2015, 112 master's, 30 other advanced degrees awarded. *Degree program information:* Part-time programs available. Part-time. Offers applied math (Certificate); arts and sciences (MA, MLAS, MS, PhD, Certificate, SSP); biological sciences (MS); chemistry (MS); clinical/community mental health (MS); community development and planning (Certificate); English (MA); environmental geographic information systems (Certificate); environmental science: large river ecosystems (PhD); general experimental psychology (MS); geography (MA); GIS analysis (Certificate); history (MA); liberal arts and sciences (MLAS); literary studies (Certificate); mathematics (MS); physics (MS); political science (MA); professional writing (Certificate); school psychology (SSP); sociology (MA); teaching writing (Certificate); zoo and aquarium studies (Certificate). *Application deadline:* Applications are processed on a rolling basis. *Application fee:* $30. Electronic applications accepted. *Application Contact:* Dr. Nancy Parsons, Associate Provost and Director of Graduate Studies, 309-298-1806, Fax: 309-298-2345, E-mail: grad-office@wiu.edu. *Dean*, Dr. Susan Martinelli-Fernandez, 309-298-1828.

College of Business and Technology Students: 239 full-time (93 women), 102 part-time (45 women); includes 23 minority (14 Black or African American, non-Hispanic/Latino; 6 Asian, non-Hispanic/Latino; 3 Hispanic/Latino), 183 international. Average age 28. 317 applicants, 79% accepted, 124 enrolled. *Financial support:* In 2015–16, 3 research assistantships, 7 teaching assistantships with full tuition reimbursements (averaging $8,688 per year) were awarded; unspecified assistantships also available. Financial award applicants required to submit FAFSA. In 2015, 107 master's awarded. *Degree program information:* Part-time programs available. Part-time. Offers accountancy (M Acct); business administration (MBA, Certificate); business analytics (Certificate); business and technology (M Acct, MA, MBA, MS, Certificate); community development (Certificate); computer science (MS); economics (MA); engineering technology leadership (MS); supply chain management (Certificate). *Application deadline:* Applications are processed on a rolling basis. *Application fee:* $30. Electronic applications accepted. *Application Contact:* Dr. Nancy Parsons, Associate Provost and Director of Graduate Studies, 309-298-1806, Fax: 309-298-2345, E-mail: grad-office@wiu.edu. *Interim Dean*, Dr. William Bailey, 309-298-2442.

College of Education and Human Services Students: 405 full-time (237 women), 937 part-time (644 women); includes 193 minority (76 Black or African American, non-Hispanic/Latino; 11 Asian, non-Hispanic/Latino; 77 Hispanic/Latino; 29 Two or more races, non-Hispanic/Latino), 33 international. Average age 36. 778 applicants, 75% accepted, 355 enrolled. *Financial support:* In 2015–16, 164 students received support, including 8 research assistantships with full tuition reimbursements available (averaging $7,544 per year), 6 teaching assistantships with full tuition reimbursements available (averaging $8,688 per year); unspecified assistantships also available. Financial award applicants required to submit FAFSA. In 2015, 234 master's, 14 doctorates, 62 other advanced degrees awarded. *Degree program information:* Part-time and evening/weekend programs available. Part-time, evening/weekend, online learning. Offers college student personnel (MS); counseling (MS Ed); distance learning (Certificate); education and human services (MA, MS, MS Ed, Ed D, Certificate, Ed S); educational and interdisciplinary studies (MS Ed, Certificate); educational leadership (MS Ed, Ed D, Ed S); educational technology specialist (Certificate); elementary education (MS Ed); graphic applications (Certificate); health sciences (MS); health services administration (Certificate); instructional design and technology (MS); kinesiology (MS); law enforcement and justice administration (MA); multimedia (Certificate); police executive administration (Certificate); reading (MS Ed); recreation, park, and tourism administration (MS); special education (MS Ed); sport management (MS); teaching English to speakers of other languages (Certificate); technology integration in education (Certificate); training development (Certificate). *Application deadline:* Applications are processed on a rolling basis. *Application fee:* $30. Electronic applications accepted. *Application Contact:* Dr. Nancy Parsons, Associate Provost and Director of Graduate Studies, 309-298-1806, Fax: 309-298-2345, E-mail: grad-office@wiu.edu. *Dean*, Dr. Erskine Smith, 309-298-1690.

College of Fine Arts and Communication Students: 113 full-time (72 women), 25 part-time (18 women); includes 13 minority (9 Black or African American, non-Hispanic/Latino; 3 Hispanic/Latino; 1 Two or more races, non-Hispanic/Latino), 10 international. Average age 29. 236 applicants, 50% accepted, 60 enrolled. *Financial support:* In 2015–16, 2 research assistantships with full tuition reimbursements (averaging $7,544 per year), 10 teaching assistantships with full tuition reimbursements (averaging $8,688 per year) were awarded; unspecified assistantships also available. Financial award applicants required to submit FAFSA. In 2015, 60 master's awarded. *Degree program information:* Part-time programs available. Part-time. Offers communication (MA); communication sciences and disorders (MS); fine arts and communication (MA, MFA, MM, MS, Certificate); museum studies (MA, Certificate); music (MM); theatre (MFA). *Application deadline:* Applications are processed on a rolling basis. *Application fee:* $30. Electronic applications accepted. *Application Contact:* Dr. Nancy Parsons, Associate Provost and Director of Graduate Studies, 309-298-1806, Fax: 309-298-2345, E-mail: grad-office@wiu.edu. *Dean*, Billy Clow, 309-298-1552.

WESTERN INTERNATIONAL UNIVERSITY, Phoenix, AZ 85021-2718

General Information Proprietary, coed, comprehensive institution. *Graduate housing:* On-campus housing not available.

GRADUATE UNITS

Graduate Programs in Business ***Degree program information:*** Evening/weekend programs available. Evening/weekend, online learning. Offers business (MA, MBA, MPA, MS); business administration (MBA); finance (MBA); human dynamics (MA); information system engineering (MS); information technology (MBA); innovative leadership (MA); international business (MBA); management (MBA); marketing (MBA); organization development (MBA); public administration (MPA).

WESTERN KENTUCKY UNIVERSITY, Bowling Green, KY 42101

General Information State-supported, coed, comprehensive institution. CGS member. *Graduate housing:* Room and/or apartments guaranteed to single students; on-campus housing not available to married students. Housing application deadline: 4/1. *Research affiliation:* Bowling Green Field Station for Animal Studies (U.S. Fish and Wildlife Service), Roybal Center (gerontology).

GRADUATE UNITS

Graduate Studies ***Degree program information:*** Part-time and evening/weekend programs available. Part-time, evening/weekend, online learning.

College of Education and Behavioral Sciences Degree program information: Part-time and evening/weekend programs available. Part-time, evening/weekend, online learning. Offers adult education (MAE); clinical psychology (MA); counseling (MA Ed); education and behavioral sciences (MA, MAE, MS, Ed D, Ed S); educational leadership (Ed D); elementary education (MAE, Ed S); exceptional education: learning and behavioral disorders (MAE); exceptional education: moderate and severe disabilities (MAE); experimental psychology (MA); general psychology (MA); industrial/organizational psychology (MA); instructional design (MS); interdisciplinary early childhood education (MAE); library media education (MS); literacy education (MAE); middle grades education (MAE); school administration (Ed S); school counseling (P-12) (MA Ed); school principal (MAE); school psychology (Ed S); secondary education (MAE, Ed S); student affairs in higher education (MA Ed).

College of Health and Human Services Degree program information: Part-time and evening/weekend programs available. Part-time, evening/weekend. Offers athletic administration and coaching (MS); communication disorders (MS); health and human services (MHA, MPH, MS, MSN, MSW, DPT); healthcare administration (MHA); nursing (MSN); physical education (MS); physical therapy (DPT); public health (MPH); recreation and sport administration (MS); social work (MSW).

Gordon Ford College of Business Degree program information: Part-time and evening/weekend programs available. Part-time, evening/weekend. Offers applied economics (MA); business (MA, MBA); business administration (MBA).

Ogden College of Science and Engineering Degree program information: Part-time and evening/weekend programs available. Part-time, evening/weekend. Offers agriculture (MA Ed, MS); biology (MS); chemistry (MA Ed, MS); computational mathematics (MS); computer science (MS); geoscience (MS); homeland security sciences (MS); mathematics (MA, MS); physics (MA Ed); science and engineering (MA Ed, MS); technology management (MS).

Potter College of Arts and Letters Degree program information: Part-time and evening/weekend programs available. Part-time, evening/weekend, online learning. Offers art education (MA Ed); arts and letters (MA, MA Ed, MPA); communication (MA); criminology (MA); education (MA); English (MA Ed); folk studies (MA); French (MA Ed); German (MA Ed); history (MA, MA Ed); literature (MA); music (MA Ed); organizational communication (Graduate Certificate); political science (MPA); sociology (MA); Spanish (MA Ed); teaching English as a second language (MA); writing (MA).

WESTERN MICHIGAN UNIVERSITY, Kalamazoo, MI 49008

General Information State-supported, coed, university. CGS member. *Graduate housing:* Rooms and/or apartments available on a first-come, first-served basis to single and married students. Housing application deadline: 7/1. *Library:* Waldo Library plus 4 others. *Collection:* Books: 2.1 million (physical), 607,238 (digital/electronic); Serial titles: 867 (physical), 137,688 (digital/electronic); Databases: 490. Weekly public service hours: 106; students can reserve study rooms. *Research affiliation:* Argonne National Laboratory (particle physics), Central States Universities, Inc., Ames Research Center (manufacturing education), Copper Development Association, Inc. (plastics extrusion), Pharmacia and Upjohn Company (electron microscopy), Flowserve Corporation (mechanical pumps and seals).

Computer facilities: Computer purchase and lease plans are available. 2,438 computers available on campus for general student use. A campuswide network can be accessed from student residence rooms and from off campus. Online class registration is available.
Website: http://www.wmich.edu/

General Application Contact: Admissions, 269-387-2000, Fax: 269-387-2096, E-mail: ask-wmu@wmich.edu.

GRADUATE UNITS

Graduate College ***Degree program information:*** Part-time and evening/weekend programs available. Part-time, evening/weekend.

College of Arts and Sciences Degree program information: Part-time programs available. Part-time. Offers anthropology (MA); applied and computational mathematics (MS); applied economics (MA, PhD); arts and sciences (MA, MFA, MIDA, MPA, MS, PhD, Graduate Certificate); behavior analysis (MA, PhD); biological sciences (MS, PhD); chemistry (MS, PhD); clinical psychology (PhD); communication (MA); comparative religion (MA, Graduate Certificate); creative writing (MFA, PhD); earth science (MA); English (MA, PhD); English teaching (MA); geographic information science (Graduate Certificate); geography (MA); geosciences (MS, PhD); health care administration (MPA, Graduate Certificate); history (MA, PhD); industrial/organizational behavior management (MA); international development administration (MIDA); mathematics education (MA, PhD); nonprofit leadership and administration (Graduate Certificate); philosophy (MA); physics (MA, PhD); political science (MA, PhD); public administration (PhD); science education (MA, PhD); sociology (MA, PhD); Spanish (MA, PhD); statistics (MS, PhD, Graduate Certificate).

College of Education and Human Development Degree program information: Part-time programs available. Part-time. Offers athletic training (MS); career and technical education (MA); counseling psychology (MA, PhD); counselor education (MA, PhD); education and human development (MA, MS, Ed D, PhD, Ed S, Graduate Certificate); educational leadership (MA, PhD, Ed S); educational technology (MA, Graduate Certificate); evaluation, measurement and research (MA, PhD); family and consumer sciences (MA); interdisciplinary education (PhD); literacy studies (MA); organizational learning and performance (MA); practice of teaching (MA); socio-cultural studies of education (MA); special education (MA, Ed D); sport management (MA); teaching children with visual impairments (MA).

College of Engineering and Applied Sciences Degree program information: Part-time programs available. Part-time. Offers chemical and paper engineering (MS, MSE, PhD); civil and construction engineering (MSE); computer engineering (MSE); computer science (MS, PhD); electrical and computer engineering (PhD); electrical engineering (MSE); engineering and applied sciences (MS, MSE, PhD); engineering design, manufacturing, and management systems (MS); engineering management (MS); industrial engineering (MSE, PhD); mechanical engineering (MSE, PhD).

College of Fine Arts Degree program information: Part-time programs available. Part-time. Offers art education (MA); fine arts (MA, MM, Graduate Certificate); music (MA); music composition (MM); music conducting (MM); music education (MM); music performance (MM); music therapy (MM).

College of Health and Human Services Degree program information: Part-time programs available. Part-time. Offers audiology (Au D); health and human services (MA, MS, MSM, MSN, MSW, Au D, PhD, Graduate Certificate); interdisciplinary health services (PhD); nursing (MSN); occupational therapy (MS); orientation and mobility (MA); orientation and mobility of children (MA); physician assistant (MSM); social work (MSW); speech pathology and audiology (MA); vision rehabilitation therapy (MA).

Haworth College of Business Degree program information: Part-time programs available. Part-time. Offers accountancy (MSA); business (MBA, MSA); business administration (MBA).

WESTERN MICHIGAN UNIVERSITY THOMAS M. COOLEY LAW SCHOOL, Lansing, MI 48901-3038

General Information Independent, coed, graduate-only institution. *Enrollment by degree level:* 102 master's, 1,342 doctoral. *Graduate faculty:* 55 full-time (25 women), 115 part-time/adjunct (41 women). *Tuition, area resident:* Full-time $47,850; part-time $28,050 per year. *Required fees:* $40; $40 per unit. Tuition and fees vary according to student level. *Graduate housing:* On-campus housing not available. *Student services:* Campus employment opportunities, campus safety program, career counseling, international student services, services for students with disabilities, writing training. *Library:* WMU-Cooley Law Libraries plus 3 others. *Collection:* Books: 67,797 (physical), 22,135 (digital/electronic); Serial titles: 7,214 (physical), 11,129 (digital/electronic); Databases: 164. Weekly public service hours: 106; study areas open 24 hours, 5–7 days a week; students can reserve study rooms.

Computer facilities: 132 computers available on campus for general student use. A campuswide network can be accessed from off campus. Online class registration is available.
Website: http://www.cooley.edu/

General Application Contact: Dr. Paul Zelenski, Associate Dean of Enrollment and Student Services, 517-371-5140 Ext. 2224, Fax: 517-334-5718, E-mail: admissions@cooley.edu.

GRADUATE UNITS

Graduate Programs ***Financial support:*** Research assistantships, teaching assistantships, career-related internships or fieldwork, Federal Work-Study, scholarships/grants, and unspecified assistantships available. Support available to part-time students. Financial award application deadline: 9/1; financial award applicants required to submit FAFSA. *Degree program information:* Part-time and evening/weekend programs available. Part-time, evening/weekend, 100% online, blended/hybrid learning. Offers administrative law (public law) (JD); business transactions (JD); Canadian law practice (JD); constitutional law/civil rights (public law) (JD); corporate law and finance (LL M); environmental law (public law) (JD); general practice (JD); homeland and national security law (LL M); insurance law (LL M); intellectual property (JD); intellectual property law (LL M); international law (JD); litigation (JD); self-directed (LL M, JD); tax law (LL M); taxation (JD); U.S. legal studies for foreign attorneys (LL M). *Application deadline:* For fall admission, 9/1 for domestic and international students; for winter admission, 1/1 for domestic and international students; for spring admission, 5/1 for domestic and international students. Applications are processed on a rolling basis. *Application fee:* $0. Electronic applications accepted. *Application Contact:* Catherine McCollum, Director of Graduate and Extended Programs, 517-371-5140 Ext. 2703, Fax: 517-334-5788, E-mail: mccolluc@cooley.edu. *Associate Dean of Library and Instructional Support/Professor,* Duane Strojny, 517-371-5140 Ext. 3400, E-mail: strojnyd@cooley.edu.

WESTERN NEW ENGLAND UNIVERSITY, Springfield, MA 01119

General Information Independent, coed, comprehensive institution. *Enrollment:* 3,954 graduate, professional, and undergraduate students; 509 full-time matriculated graduate/professional students (297 women), 670 part-time matriculated graduate/professional students (370 women). *Enrollment by degree level:* 498 master's, 673 doctoral, 8 other advanced degrees. *Graduate faculty:* 229 full-time (96 women), 40 part-time/adjunct (12 women). Tuition and fees vary according to program. *Graduate housing:* Rooms and/or apartments available to single and married students. Typical cost: $12,894 (including board) for single students. Room and board charges vary according to board plan and housing facility selected. Housing application deadline: 3/9. *Student services:* Campus employment opportunities, campus safety program, career counseling, exercise/wellness program, free psychological counseling, international student services, services for students with disabilities, teacher training, writing training. *Library:* D'Amour Library plus 1 other. *Collection:* Books: 121,677 (physical), 24,358 (digital/electronic); Serial titles: 46 (physical), 36,665 (digital/electronic); Databases: 124. Weekly public service hours: 100; study areas open 24 hours, 5–7 days a week. *Research affiliation:* New England Center for Children (applied behavior analysis).

Computer facilities: 530 computers available on campus for general student use. A campuswide network can be accessed from student residence rooms and from off campus. Online class registration is available.
Website: http://www.wne.edu/

General Application Contact: Matthew Fox, Director of Admissions for Graduate Students and Adult Learners, 413-782-1517, Fax: 413-782-1777, E-mail: study@wne.edu.

GRADUATE UNITS

College of Arts and Sciences Students: 244 part-time (186 women); includes 29 minority (10 Black or African American, non-Hispanic/Latino; 7 Asian, non-Hispanic/Latino; 11 Hispanic/Latino; 1 Two or more races, non-Hispanic/Latino), 11 international. Average age 30. *Faculty:* 112 full-time (55 women). *Financial support:* Fellowships with tuition reimbursements available. Support available to part-time students. Financial award application deadline: 4/15; financial award applicants required to submit FAFSA. In 2015, 48 master's, 7 doctorates awarded. *Degree program information:* Part-time and evening/weekend programs available. Part-time-only, evening/weekend, online learning. Offers applied behavior analysis (MS); arts and sciences (M Ed, MA, MAET, MAMT, MFA, MS, PhD); behavior analysis (PhD); creative writing (MFA); curriculum and instruction (M Ed); elementary education (M Ed); English for teachers (MAET); mathematics for teachers (MAMT); public relations (MA). *Application fee:* $30. Electronic applications accepted. *Application Contact:* Matthew Fox, Director of Admissions for Graduate Students and Adult Learners, 413-782-1517, Fax: 413-782-1777, E-mail: study@wne.edu. *Dean,* Dr. Saeed Ghahramani, 413-782-1218, Fax: 413-796-2118, E-mail: sghahram@wne.edu.

College of Business Students: 159 part-time (70 women); includes 13 minority (8 Black or African American, non-Hispanic/Latino; 3 Asian, non-Hispanic/Latino; 2 Hispanic/Latino), 5 international. Average age 31. *Faculty:* 34 full-time (11 women). *Financial support:* Application deadline: 4/15; applicants required to submit FAFSA. In 2015, 74 master's awarded. *Degree program information:* Part-time and evening/weekend programs available. Part-time, evening/weekend, online learning. Offers accounting (MSA); business (MBA, MS, MSA); general business (MBA); organizational leadership (MS); sport management (MBA). *Application deadline:* Applications are processed on a rolling basis. *Application fee:* $30. Electronic applications accepted. *Application Contact:* Matthew Fox, Director of Admissions for Graduate Students and Adult Learners, 413-782-1517, Fax: 413-782-1777, E-mail: study@wne.edu. *Dean,* Dr. Julie Siciliano, 413-782-1224, E-mail: julie.siciliano@wne.edu.

College of Engineering Students: 113 part-time (22 women); includes 13 minority (1 Black or African American, non-Hispanic/Latino; 1 American Indian or Alaska Native, non-Hispanic/Latino; 2 Asian, non-Hispanic/Latino; 5 Hispanic/Latino; 4 Two or more races, non-Hispanic/Latino), 28 international. Average age 29. *Faculty:* 34 full-time (5 women). *Financial support:* In 2015–16, 6 fellowships with tuition reimbursements were awarded. Financial award application deadline: 4/15; financial award applicants required to submit FAFSA. In 2015, 30 master's awarded. *Degree program information:* Part-time and evening/weekend programs available. Part-time, evening/weekend, online learning. Offers business and engineering information systems (MSEM); electrical engineering (MSEE); engineering (MSEE, MSEM, MSME, PhD); engineering management (MSEM, PhD); general engineering management (MSEM); mechanical engineering (MSME); production and manufacturing systems (MSEM); quality engineering (MSEM). *Application deadline:* For fall admission, 1/15 priority date for domestic students. Applications are processed on a rolling basis. *Application fee:* $30. Electronic applications accepted. *Application Contact:* Matthew Fox, Director of Admissions for Graduate Students and Adult Learners, 413-782-1517, Fax: 413-782-1777, E-mail: study@wne.edu. *Dean,* Dr. S. Hossein Cheraghi, 413-782-1285, E-mail: cheraghi@wne.edu.

College of Pharmacy Students: 297 full-time (178 women); includes 41 minority (8 Black or African American, non-Hispanic/Latino; 26 Asian, non-Hispanic/Latino; 7 Hispanic/Latino), 3 international. Average age 24. 397 applicants, 34% accepted, 75 enrolled. *Faculty:* 29 full-time (13 women), 2 part-time/adjunct (both women). *Financial support:* Scholarships/grants available. Financial award application deadline: 4/15; financial award applicants required to submit FAFSA. In 2015, 68 doctorates awarded. Offers pharmacy (Pharm D). *Application deadline:* For fall admission, 3/1 for domestic students. Applications are processed on a rolling basis. *Application fee:* $150. Electronic applications accepted. *Application Contact:* Bonnie Mannix, Director of Pharmacy Admissions and Recruitment, 413-796-2300, Fax: 413-796-2266, E-mail: rxadmissions@wne.edu. *Dean,* Dr. Evan T. Robinson, 413-796-2323, E-mail: erobinson@wne.edu.

School of Law Students: 212 full-time (119 women), 146 part-time (88 women); includes 96 minority (51 Black or African American, non-Hispanic/Latino; 2 American Indian or Alaska Native, non-Hispanic/Latino; 16 Asian, non-Hispanic/Latino; 27 Hispanic/Latino), 1 international. Average age 30. 624 applicants, 69% accepted, 88 enrolled. *Faculty:* 20 full-time (12 women), 23 part-time/adjunct (6 women). *Financial support:* Career-related internships or fieldwork, Federal Work-Study, and scholarships/grants available. Support available to part-time students. Financial award application deadline: 4/15; financial award applicants required to submit FAFSA. In 2015, 21 master's, 89 doctorates awarded. *Degree program information:* Part-time and evening/weekend programs available. Part-time, evening/weekend. Offers estate planning and elder law (LL M); law (JD). *Application deadline:* For fall admission, 3/15 priority date for domestic students. Applications are processed on a rolling basis. *Application fee:* $0. Electronic applications accepted. *Application Contact:* Amy Mangione, Assistant Dean of Law/Director of Law Admissions, 413-782-1406, Fax: 413-796-2067, E-mail: admissions@law.wne.edu. *Dean/Professor,* Eric Gouvin, 413-796-2031, E-mail: eric.gouvin@law.wne.edu.

See Display on next page and Close-Up on page 915.

WESTERN NEW MEXICO UNIVERSITY, Silver City, NM 88062-0680

General Information State-supported, coed, comprehensive institution. *Graduate housing:* Rooms and/or apartments available on a first-come, first-served basis to single and married students. Housing application deadline: 6/30.

GRADUATE UNITS

Graduate Division ***Degree program information:*** Part-time and evening/weekend programs available. Part-time, evening/weekend, online learning. Offers interdisciplinary studies (MA); occupational therapy (MOT); social work (MSW). Electronic applications accepted.

School of Business Degree program information: Part-time programs available. Part-time, online learning. Offers business administration (MBA). Electronic applications accepted.

School of Education Degree program information: Part-time programs available. Part-time, online learning. Offers bilingual education (MAT); educational leadership (MA); elementary education (MAT); reading (MAT); secondary education (MAT); special education (MAT); TESOL (teaching English to speakers of other languages) (MAT). Electronic applications accepted.

WESTERN OREGON UNIVERSITY, Monmouth, OR 97361-1394

General Information State-supported, coed, comprehensive institution. *Graduate housing:* Room and/or apartments available on a first-come, first-served basis to single students; on-campus housing not available to married students. *Research affiliation:* Teaching Research Institute (education).

GRADUATE UNITS

Graduate Programs ***Degree program information:*** Part-time and evening/weekend programs available. Part-time, evening/weekend, online learning.

College of Education Degree program information: Part-time and evening/weekend programs available. Part-time, evening/weekend, online learning. Offers bilingual education (MS Ed); deaf education (MS Ed); early childhood special education (MS Ed); education (MAT, MS, MS Ed); health (MS Ed); humanities (MAT, MS Ed); information technology (MS Ed); initial licensure (MAT); mathematics (MAT, MS Ed); rehabilitation counseling (MS); science (MAT, MS Ed); secondary education (MAT, MS Ed); social science (MAT, MS Ed); special education (MS, MS Ed).

College of Liberal Arts and Sciences Degree program information: Part-time and evening/weekend programs available. Part-time, evening/weekend. Offers contemporary music (MM); criminal justice (MA, MS); liberal arts and sciences (MA, MM, MS).

WESTERN SEMINARY, Portland, OR 97215-3367

General Information Independent-religious, coed, graduate-only institution. *Graduate housing:* On-campus housing not available.

GRADUATE UNITS

Graduate Programs ***Degree program information:*** Part-time and evening/weekend programs available. Part-time, evening/weekend, online learning. Offers biblical and theological studies (MA, G Dip); biblical studies (Certificate); chaplaincy (MA); coaching (MA); counseling (MA, Certificate); divinity (M Div); intercultural studies (MA, D Miss, Certificate, G Dip); Jewish ministry (MA); pastoral care to women (MA); pastoral counseling (M Div); theology (Th M); youth ministry (MA).

WESTERN SEMINARY–SACRAMENTO CAMPUS, Sacramento, CA 95821

General Information Independent-religious, coed, graduate-only institution.

GRADUATE UNITS

Graduate Certificate Programs Online learning. Offers Bible (Graduate Certificate); coaching (Graduate Certificate); pastoral care to women (Graduate Certificate); theology (Graduate Certificate); youth and family (Graduate Certificate).

Graduate Diploma Programs Offers Bible and theology (Graduate Diploma); ministry (Graduate Diploma); pastoral care to women (Graduate Diploma).

Master of Divinity Program Offers divinity (M Div).

Program in Biblical and Theological Studies Offers biblical and theological studies (MA).

Program in Marital and Family Therapy Offers marital and family therapy (MA).

Program in Ministry and Leadership Offers ministry and leadership (MA).

WESTERN SEMINARY–SAN JOSE CAMPUS, Los Gatos, CA 95032-4520

General Information Independent-religious, coed, graduate-only institution. *Graduate housing:* On-campus housing not available.

GRADUATE UNITS

Graduate Programs ***Degree program information:*** Part-time and evening/weekend programs available. Part-time, evening/weekend, online learning. Offers Bible and theology (Graduate Diploma); Bible, camp and conference ministry (CGS); Biblical and theological studies (MA); coaching (CGS); expositional ministry (M Div); marital and family therapy (MA); ministry (Graduate Diploma); ministry and leadership (MA); pastoral care to women (CGS, Graduate Diploma); pastoral ministry (M Div); theology (CGS); youth and family (CGS). Electronic applications accepted.

WESTERN STATE COLLEGE OF LAW AT ARGOSY UNIVERSITY, Irvine, CA 92618-3601

General Information Proprietary, coed, graduate-only institution. *Enrollment by degree level:* 339 doctoral. *Graduate faculty:* 26 full-time (14 women), 30 part-time/adjunct (9 women). *Tuition, area resident:* Full-time $42,860; part-time $35,825 per unit. *Required fees:* $490; $590 per year. *Graduate housing:* On-campus housing not available. *Student services:* Campus employment opportunities, career counseling, free psychological counseling, international student services, low-cost health insurance, services for students with disabilities. *Library:* Western State College of Law Library. *Collection:* Books: 51,828 (physical); Serial titles: 1,011 (physical); Databases: 12. Weekly public service hours: 133; students can reserve study rooms.

Computer facilities: 12 computers available on campus for general student use. A campuswide network can be accessed. Online class registration is available. Website: http://www.wsulaw.edu/

General Application Contact: Rhonda Cohen, Assistant Director of Admission, 714-459-1101, Fax: 714-441-1748, E-mail: adm@wsulaw.edu.

GRADUATE UNITS

Professional Program Students: 223 full-time (121 women), 116 part-time (66 women); includes 198 minority (25 Black or African American, non-Hispanic/Latino; 2 American Indian or Alaska Native, non-Hispanic/Latino; 62 Asian, non-Hispanic/Latino; 108 Hispanic/Latino; 1 Two or more races, non-Hispanic/Latino), 2 international. Average age 29. 663 applicants, 63% accepted, 120 enrolled. *Faculty:* 26 full-time (14 women), 30 part-time/adjunct (9 women). *Financial support:* In 2015–16, 263 students received support, including 13 fellowships (averaging $5,732 per year); career-related internships or fieldwork, Federal Work-Study, scholarships/grants, and health care benefits also available. Support available to part-time students. Financial award application deadline: 9/15; financial award applicants required to submit FAFSA. In 2015, 151 doctorates awarded. *Degree program information:* Part-time and evening/weekend programs available. Part-time, evening/weekend. Offers law (JD). *Application deadline:* For fall admission, 7/1 for domestic students, 6/1 for international students; for spring admission, 12/1 for domestic students, 11/1 for international students. Applications are processed on a rolling basis. *Application fee:* $60. Electronic applications accepted. *Application Contact:* Rhonda Cohen, Assistant Director of Admission, 714-459-1101, Fax: 714-441-1748, E-mail: adm@wsulaw.edu. *Interim Assistant Dean of Admission,* James Cheydleur, 714-459-1101, E-mail: adm@wsulaw.edu.

WESTERN STATE COLORADO UNIVERSITY, Gunnison, CO 81231

General Information State-supported, coed, comprehensive institution.

GRADUATE UNITS

Graduate Programs in Education Online learning. Offers education administrator leadership (MA); reading leadership (MA); teacher leadership (MA).

Program in Creative Writing Online learning. Offers mainstream genre fiction (MFA); poetry (MFA); screenwriting (MFA).

Program in Environmental Management Online learning. Offers integrative land management (MEM); sustainable and resilient communities (MEM).

WESTERN THEOLOGICAL SEMINARY, Holland, MI 49423-3622

General Information Independent-religious, coed, graduate-only institution. *Enrollment by degree level:* 248 master's, 31 doctoral. *Graduate faculty:* 17 full-time (4 women), 18 part-time/adjunct (4 women). *Tuition, area resident:* Full-time $13,376; part-time $6688 per credit hour. *Required fees:* $60; $60 per unit. *Graduate housing:* Rooms and/or apartments available on a first-come, first-served basis to single and married students. Housing application deadline: 5/1. *Student services:* Campus employment opportunities, free psychological counseling, services for students with disabilities, writing training.

Library: Beardslee Library plus 1 other. *Collection:* Books: 86,079 (physical); Serial titles: 185 (physical). Students can reserve study rooms.

Computer facilities: 16 computers available on campus for general student use. A campuswide network can be accessed. Online class registration is available.
Website: http://www.westernsem.edu/

General Application Contact: Mark Poppen, Director of Admissions, 616-392-8555, Fax: 616-392-7717, E-mail: mark@westernsem.edu.

GRADUATE UNITS

Graduate and Professional Programs Students: 189 full-time (66 women), 95 part-time (38 women); includes 38 minority (12 Black or African American, non-Hispanic/Latino; 11 Asian, non-Hispanic/Latino; 13 Hispanic/Latino; 2 Two or more races, non-Hispanic/Latino), 4 international. 113 applicants, 92% accepted, 82 enrolled. *Faculty:* 17 full-time (4 women), 21 part-time/adjunct (4 women). *Financial support:* Career-related internships or fieldwork, institutionally sponsored loans, and scholarships/grants available. Support available to part-time students. Financial award application deadline: 4/15; financial award applicants required to submit FAFSA. In 2015, 53 master's, 6 doctorates awarded. *Degree program information:* Part-time programs available. Part-time, 100% online, blended/hybrid learning. Offers divinity (M Div); ministry (D Min); theology (M Th, MA); urban pastoral ministry (Graduate Certificate). *Application deadline:* For fall admission, 4/1 priority date for domestic students, 3/15 priority date for international students; for spring admission, 12/1 for domestic students. Applications are processed on a rolling basis. *Application fee:* $50. Electronic applications accepted. *Application Contact:* Mark Poppen, Director of Admissions, 616-392-8555, Fax: 616-392-7717, E-mail: mark@westernsem.edu. *President*, Dr. Timothy Brown, 616-392-8555 Ext. 137, Fax: 616-392-7717, E-mail: tim.brown@westernsem.edu.

WESTERN UNIVERSITY OF HEALTH SCIENCES, Pomona, CA 91766-1854

General Information Independent, coed, graduate-only institution. *Enrollment by degree level:* 589 master's, 3,274 doctoral. *Graduate faculty:* 290 full-time (144 women), 72 part-time/adjunct (30 women). Tuition and fees vary according to course level, course load, degree level, program and student level. *Graduate housing:* Rooms and/or apartments available on a first-come, first-served basis to single and married students. *Student services:* Campus employment opportunities, campus safety program, career counseling, exercise/wellness program, free psychological counseling, grant writing training, international student services, low-cost health insurance, services for students with disabilities, teacher training. *Library:* Pumerantz Library plus 1 other. *Collection:* Books: 24,500 (physical), 2,623 (digital/electronic); Serial titles: 205 (physical), 26,597 (digital/electronic); Databases: 80. Weekly public service hours: 91; students can reserve study rooms. *Research affiliation:* Healthnet, CalOptima, Inland Empire United Way (optometry), Boehringer Ingelheim (veterinary medicine), Ohio University, Thomas Jefferson University Hospitals, Inc./TJU Physicians (pharmacy).

Computer facilities: 56 computers available on campus for general student use. Online class registration is available.
Website: http://www.westernu.edu/

General Application Contact: Admissions Office, 909-469-5335, Fax: 909-469-5570, E-mail: admissions@westernu.edu.

GRADUATE UNITS

College of Allied Health Professions Students: 366 full-time (231 women), 52 part-time (35 women); includes 194 minority (17 Black or African American, non-Hispanic/Latino; 93 Asian, non-Hispanic/Latino; 61 Hispanic/Latino; 1 Native Hawaiian or other Pacific Islander, non-Hispanic/Latino; 22 Two or more races, non-Hispanic/Latino), 4 international. Average age 28. 3,580 applicants, 7% accepted, 180 enrolled. *Faculty:* 25 full-time (18 women), 4 part-time/adjunct (2 women). *Financial support:* Scholarships/grants available. Financial award application deadline: 3/2; financial award applicants required to submit FAFSA. In 2015, 108 master's, 79 doctorates awarded. Offers allied health professions (MS, DPT); health sciences (MS); physical therapy (DPT); physician assistant studies (MS). Electronic applications accepted. *Application Contact:* Karen Hutton-Lopez, Director of Admissions, 909-469-5335, Fax: 909-469-5570, E-mail: admissions@westernu.edu. *Dean*, Dr. Stephanie Bowlin, 909-469-5390, Fax: 909-469-5438, E-mail: sbowlin@westernu.edu.

College of Dental Medicine Students: 273 full-time (133 women); includes 166 minority (2 Black or African American, non-Hispanic/Latino; 3 American Indian or Alaska Native, non-Hispanic/Latino; 104 Asian, non-Hispanic/Latino; 33 Hispanic/Latino; 1 Native Hawaiian or other Pacific Islander, non-Hispanic/Latino; 23 Two or more races, non-Hispanic/Latino), 7 international. Average age 28. 2,576 applicants, 7% accepted, 68 enrolled. *Faculty:* 35 full-time (15 women), 21 part-time/adjunct (8 women). *Financial support:* Scholarships/grants available. Financial award application deadline: 3/2; financial award applicants required to submit FAFSA. In 2015, 74 doctorates awarded. Offers dental medicine (DMD). *Application deadline:* For fall admission, 12/1 for domestic and international students. *Application fee:* $60. Electronic applications accepted. *Application Contact:* Marie Anderson, Director of Admissions, 909-469-5335, Fax: 909-469-5570, E-mail: admissions@westernu.edu. *Dean*, Dr. Steven Friedrichsen, 909-706-3911, E-mail: sfriedrichsen@westernu.edu.

College of Graduate Nursing Students: 320 full-time (274 women), 30 part-time (23 women); includes 206 minority (9 Black or African American, non-Hispanic/Latino; 108 Asian, non-Hispanic/Latino; 66 Hispanic/Latino; 23 Two or more races, non-Hispanic/Latino), 1 international. Average age 33. 555 applicants, 42% accepted, 144 enrolled. *Faculty:* 18 full-time (17 women), 18 part-time/adjunct (10 women). *Financial support:* Fellowships, research assistantships, teaching assistantships, and scholarships/grants available. Support available to part-time students. Financial award application deadline: 3/2; financial award applicants required to submit FAFSA. In 2015, 97 master's, 23 doctorates awarded. *Degree program information:* Part-time and evening/weekend programs available. Part-time, evening/weekend, blended/hybrid learning. Offers administrative nurse leader (MSN); ambulatory care (MSN); clinical nurse leader (MSN); family nurse practitioner (MSN); nursing (MSN); nursing practice (DNP). *Application fee:* $60. Electronic applications accepted. *Application Contact:* Kathryn Ford, Director of Admissions/International Student Advisor, 909-469-5335, Fax: 909-469-5570, E-mail: admissions@westernu.edu. *Dean*, Dr. Karen J. Hanford, 909-469-5523, Fax: 909-469-5521, E-mail: khanford@westernu.edu.

College of Optometry Students: 337 full-time (240 women); includes 218 minority (13 Black or African American, non-Hispanic/Latino; 1 American Indian or Alaska Native, non-Hispanic/Latino; 129 Asian, non-Hispanic/Latino; 40 Hispanic/Latino; 35 Two or more races, non-Hispanic/Latino), 21 international. Average age 27. 855 applicants, 25% accepted, 85 enrolled. *Faculty:* 31 full-time (14 women), 4 part-time/adjunct (3 women). *Financial support:* Career-related internships or fieldwork, scholarships/grants, and traineeships available. Financial award application deadline: 3/2; financial award applicants required to submit FAFSA. In 2015, 80 doctorates awarded. Offers optometry (OD). *Application deadline:* For fall admission, 5/1 for domestic and international students. *Application fee:* $65. Electronic applications accepted. *Application Contact:* Marie Anderson, Director of Admissions, 909-469-5335, Fax: 909-469-5570, E-mail: admissions@westernu.edu. *Dean*, Dr. Elizabeth Hoppe, 909-706-3497, E-mail: ehoppe@westernu.edu.

College of Osteopathic Medicine of the Pacific Students: 1,333 full-time (614 women); includes 574 minority (18 Black or African American, non-Hispanic/Latino; 1 American Indian or Alaska Native, non-Hispanic/Latino; 391 Asian, non-Hispanic/Latino; 73 Hispanic/Latino; 3 Native Hawaiian or other Pacific Islander, non-Hispanic/Latino; 88 Two or more races, non-Hispanic/Latino), 18 international. Average age 27. 10,315 applicants, 7% accepted, 325 enrolled. *Faculty:* 64 full-time (29 women), 26 part-time/adjunct (7 women). *Financial support:* Scholarships/grants and unspecified assistantships available. Financial award application deadline: 3/2; financial award applicants required to submit FAFSA. In 2015, 322 doctorates awarded. Offers osteopathic medicine (DO). *Application deadline:* For fall admission, 2/1 for domestic and international students. Applications are processed on a rolling basis. *Application fee:* $65. Electronic applications accepted. *Application Contact:* Susan Hanson, Director of Admissions, 909-469-5335, Fax: 909-469-5570, E-mail: admissions@westernu.edu. *Dean*, Dr. Paula Crone, 541-259-0206, Fax: 541-259-0201, E-mail: pcrone@westernu.edu.

College of Pharmacy Students: 524 full-time (355 women), 6 part-time (2 women); includes 359 minority (16 Black or African American, non-Hispanic/Latino; 1 American Indian or Alaska Native, non-Hispanic/Latino; 285 Asian, non-Hispanic/Latino; 33 Hispanic/Latino; 24 Two or more races, non-Hispanic/Latino), 18 international. Average age 28. 1,243 applicants, 28% accepted, 133 enrolled. *Faculty:* 38 full-time (16 women). *Financial support:* Scholarships/grants available. Financial award application deadline: 3/2; financial award applicants required to submit FAFSA. In 2015, 6 master's, 137 doctorates awarded. Offers pharmaceutical sciences (MS); pharmacy (MS, Pharm D). Electronic applications accepted. *Application Contact:* Kathryn Ford, Director of Admissions, 909-469-5335, Fax: 909-469-5570, E-mail: admissions@westernu.edu. *Dean*, Dr. Daniel Robinson, 909-469-5533, Fax: 909-469-5539, E-mail: drobinson@westernu.edu.

College of Podiatric Medicine Students: 159 full-time (59 women); includes 86 minority (7 Black or African American, non-Hispanic/Latino; 1 American Indian or Alaska Native, non-Hispanic/Latino; 49 Asian, non-Hispanic/Latino; 16 Hispanic/Latino; 13 Two or more races, non-Hispanic/Latino), 2 international. Average age 27. 519 applicants, 21% accepted, 46 enrolled. *Faculty:* 11 full-time (5 women), 4 part-time/adjunct (1 woman). *Financial support:* Scholarships/grants available. Financial award application deadline: 3/2; financial award applicants required to submit FAFSA. In 2015, 30 doctorates awarded. Offers podiatric medicine (DPM). *Application deadline:* For fall admission, 6/30 for domestic and international students. *Application fee:* $0. Electronic applications accepted. *Application Contact:* Marie Anderson, Director of Admissions, 909-469-5335, Fax: 909-469-5570, E-mail: admissions@westernu.edu. *Dean*, Dr. Lawrence B. Harkless, 909-706-3498, E-mail: lharkless@westernu.edu.

College of Veterinary Medicine Students: 423 full-time (334 women); includes 165 minority (13 Black or African American, non-Hispanic/Latino; 1 American Indian or Alaska Native, non-Hispanic/Latino; 60 Asian, non-Hispanic/Latino; 70 Hispanic/Latino; 1 Native Hawaiian or other Pacific Islander, non-Hispanic/Latino; 20 Two or more races, non-Hispanic/Latino), 6 international. Average age 27. 800 applicants, 30% accepted, 102 enrolled. *Faculty:* 53 full-time (25 women), 7 part-time/adjunct (2 women). *Financial support:* Institutionally sponsored loans, scholarships/grants, and veterans' educational benefits available. Financial award application deadline: 3/2; financial award applicants required to submit FAFSA. In 2015, 109 doctorates awarded. Offers veterinary medicine (DVM). *Application deadline:* For fall admission, 11/1 for domestic and international students. *Application fee:* $50. Electronic applications accepted. *Application Contact:* Karen Hutton-Lopez, Director of Admissions, 909-469-5335, Fax: 909-469-5570, E-mail: admissions@westernu.edu. *Dean*, Dr. Phil Nelson, 909-469-5661, Fax: 909-469-5635, E-mail: pnelson@westernu.edu.

Graduate College of Biomedical Sciences Students: 40 full-time (26 women); includes 34 minority (2 Black or African American, non-Hispanic/Latino; 18 Asian, non-Hispanic/Latino; 12 Hispanic/Latino; 2 Two or more races, non-Hispanic/Latino). Average age 26. 302 applicants, 16% accepted, 35 enrolled. *Faculty:* 6 full-time (1 woman), 5 part-time/adjunct (2 women). *Financial support:* Scholarships/grants available. Financial award application deadline: 3/2; financial award applicants required to submit FAFSA. In 2015, 38 master's awarded. Offers biomedical sciences (MS); medical sciences (MS). *Application fee:* $50. Electronic applications accepted. *Application Contact:* Kathryn Ford, Director of Admissions/International Student Advisor, 909-469-5335, Fax: 909-469-5570, E-mail: kford@westernu.edu. *Dean*, Dr. Michel Baudry, 909-469-8271, E-mail: mbaudry@westernu.edu.

WESTERN WASHINGTON UNIVERSITY, Bellingham, WA 98225-5996

General Information State-supported, coed, comprehensive institution. CGS member. *Graduate housing:* Rooms and/or apartments available on a first-come, first-served basis to single and married students. Housing application deadline: 5/1. *Research affiliation:* Golden Associates, American Metals Technology, Teck Cominco Ltd., Research Corporation, Dreyfus Foundation, NARSAD (mental health).

GRADUATE UNITS

Graduate School ***Degree program information:*** Part-time programs available. Part-time. Electronic applications accepted.

College of Business and Economics Degree program information: Part-time and evening/weekend programs available. Part-time, evening/weekend. Offers business and economics (MBA, MP Acc). Electronic applications accepted.

College of Fine and Performing Arts Degree program information: Part-time programs available. Part-time. Offers fine and performing arts (M Mus, MA); music (M Mus). Electronic applications accepted.

College of Humanities and Social Sciences Degree program information: Part-time programs available. Part-time. Offers anthropology (MA); communication sciences and disorders (MA); English (MA); exercise science (MS); experimental psychology (MS); history (MA); humanities and social sciences (M Ed, MA, MS); mental health counseling (MS); political science (MA); school counseling (M Ed); sport psychology (MS). Electronic applications accepted.

College of Sciences and Technology Offers biology (MS); chemistry (MS); computer science (MS); geology (MS); mathematics (MS); natural science/science education (M Ed); sciences and technology (M Ed, MS). Electronic applications accepted.

Huxley College of the Environment Degree program information: Part-time programs available. Part-time. Offers environment (M Ed, MS); environmental education (M Ed); environmental science (MS); geography (MS); marine and estuarine science (MS). Electronic applications accepted.

Woodring College of Education Degree program information: Part-time programs available. Part-time, online learning. Offers continuing and college education (M Ed); education (M Ed, MA, MIT); educational administration (M Ed); elementary education (M Ed); rehabilitation counseling (MA); secondary education (MIT); special education (M Ed); student affairs administration (M Ed). Electronic applications accepted.

WESTFIELD STATE UNIVERSITY, Westfield, MA 01086

General Information State-supported, coed, comprehensive institution. *Graduate housing:* On-campus housing not available.

GRADUATE UNITS

Division of Graduate and Continuing Education ***Degree program information:*** Part-time and evening/weekend programs available. Part-time, evening/weekend. Offers applied behavior analysis (MA); criminal justice (MS); early childhood education (M Ed); elementary education (M Ed); English (MA); history (M Ed); mental health counseling (MA); occupational education (M Ed, CAGS); physical education (M Ed); reading (M Ed); school administration (M Ed, CAGS); school guidance (MA); secondary education (M Ed); special education (M Ed); technology for educators (M Ed).

WEST LIBERTY UNIVERSITY, West Liberty, WV 26074

General Information State-supported, coed, comprehensive institution. *Enrollment:* 2,340 graduate, professional, and undergraduate students; 90 full-time matriculated graduate/professional students (60 women), 84 part-time matriculated graduate/professional students (60 women). *Enrollment by degree level:* 174 master's. *Graduate faculty:* 6 full-time (3 women). Tuition, state resident: full-time $7074; part-time $393 per credit. Tuition, nonresident: full-time $11,124; part-time $618 per credit. *Library:* Paul N. Elbin Library.

Computer facilities: Computer purchase and lease plans are available. A campuswide network can be accessed from student residence rooms and from off campus. Online class registration is available.
Website: http://www.westliberty.edu/

GRADUATE UNITS

College of Education Offers education (MA Ed). Electronic applications accepted. *Dean,* Dr. Keely Camden, 304-336-8247, E-mail: kcamden@westliberty.edu.

School of Professional Studies Offers justice leadership (MPS); organizational leadership (MPS). *Dean,* Dr. Thomas Michaud, 304-217-2800, E-mail: tmichaud@westliberty.edu.

WESTMINSTER COLLEGE, New Wilmington, PA 16172-0001

General Information Independent-religious, coed, comprehensive institution. *Graduate housing:* On-campus housing not available.

GRADUATE UNITS

Programs in Education ***Degree program information:*** Part-time and evening/weekend programs available. Part-time, evening/weekend. Offers administration (M Ed, Certificate); reading (M Ed, Certificate); school counseling (M Ed, Certificate).

WESTMINSTER COLLEGE, Salt Lake City, UT 84105-3697

General Information Independent, coed, comprehensive institution. *Enrollment:* 2,821 graduate, professional, and undergraduate students; 490 full-time matriculated graduate/professional students (269 women), 258 part-time matriculated graduate/professional students (140 women). *Enrollment by degree level:* 747 master's, 1 other advanced degree. *Graduate faculty:* 72 full-time (38 women), 38 part-time/adjunct (24 women). *Graduate housing:* Room and/or apartments available on a first-come, first-served basis to single students; on-campus housing not available to married students. Typical cost: $7340 (including board). *Student services:* Campus employment opportunities, campus safety program, career counseling, exercise/wellness program, free psychological counseling, grant writing training, international student services, low-cost health insurance, multicultural affairs office, services for students with disabilities, teacher training, writing training. *Library:* Giovale Library plus 1 other. *Collection:* Books: 103,618 (physical), 169,048 (digital/electronic); Serial titles: 488 (physical), 305,622 (digital/electronic); Databases: 108. Weekly public service hours: 94; students can reserve study rooms. *Research affiliation:* Key Bank (entrepreneurship), Zions Bank (entrepreneurship), International Psychotherapy (clinical training).

Computer facilities: 200 computers available on campus for general student use. A campuswide network can be accessed from student residence rooms and from off campus. Online class registration is available.
Website: http://www.westminstercollege.edu/

General Application Contact: Dr. John Baworowsky, Vice President for Enrollment Management and Student Success, 801-832-2200, Fax: 801-832-3101, E-mail: admission@westminstercollege.edu.

GRADUATE UNITS

The Bill and Vieve Gore School of Business Students: 138 full-time (50 women), 131 part-time (39 women); includes 49 minority (9 Black or African American, non-Hispanic/Latino; 1 American Indian or Alaska Native, non-Hispanic/Latino; 16 Asian, non-Hispanic/Latino; 20 Hispanic/Latino; 1 Native Hawaiian or other Pacific Islander, non-Hispanic/Latino; 2 Two or more races, non-Hispanic/Latino), 13 international. Average age 34. 120 applicants, 74% accepted, 71 enrolled. *Faculty:* 23 full-time (8 women), 14 part-time/adjunct (4 women). *Financial support:* In 2015–16, 109 students received support. Career-related internships or fieldwork, scholarships/grants, unspecified assistantships, and tuition reimbursements, tuition remission available. Financial award applicants required to submit FAFSA. In 2015, 182 master's, 15 other advanced degrees awarded. *Degree program information:* Part-time and evening/weekend programs available. Part-time, evening/weekend, 100% online. Offers accountancy (M Acc); business administration (MBA, Certificate); technology commercialization (MBA). *Application deadline:* For fall admission, 5/20 priority date for domestic and international students; for spring admission, 10/7 priority date for domestic and international students; for summer admission, 2/5 priority date for domestic and international students. Applications are processed on a rolling basis. *Application fee:* $50. Electronic applications accepted. *Application Contact:* Dr. John Baworowsky, Vice President of Enrollment Management, 801-832-2200, Fax: 801-832-3101, E-mail: admission@westminstercollege.edu. *Interim Dean, Bill and Vieve Gore School of Business,* Melissa Koerner, 801-832-2600, Fax: 801-832-3106, E-mail: mkoerner@westminstercollege.edu.

Master of Science in Mental Health Counseling Program Students: 25 full-time (21 women), 16 part-time (13 women); includes 6 minority (5 Hispanic/Latino; 1 Two or more races, non-Hispanic/Latino). Average age 31. 40 applicants, 48% accepted, 11 enrolled. *Faculty:* 4 full-time (all women), 3 part-time/adjunct (1 woman). *Financial support:* In 2015–16, 2 students received support. Career-related internships or fieldwork, scholarships/grants, unspecified assistantships, and tuition reimbursements, tuition remission available. Support available to part-time students. Financial award applicants required to submit FAFSA. In 2015, 12 master's awarded. *Degree program information:* Part-time and evening/weekend programs available. Part-time, evening/weekend. Offers mental health counseling (MSMHC). *Application deadline:* For fall admission, 2/1 priority date for domestic and international students. Applications are processed on a rolling basis. *Application fee:* $50. Electronic applications accepted. *Application Contact:* Dr. John Baworowsky, Vice President of Enrollment Management, 801-832-2200, Fax: 801-832-3101, E-mail: admission@westminstercollege.edu. *Director,* Colleen Sandor Bennett-Murphy, 801-832-2422, E-mail: lbennett-murphy@westminstercollege.edu.

Program in Professional Communication Students: 29 full-time (15 women), 15 part-time (10 women); includes 12 minority (3 American Indian or Alaska Native, non-Hispanic/Latino; 3 Asian, non-Hispanic/Latino; 4 Hispanic/Latino; 1 Native Hawaiian or other Pacific Islander, non-Hispanic/Latino; 1 Two or more races, non-Hispanic/Latino), 3 international. Average age 34. 7 applicants, 71% accepted, 4 enrolled. *Faculty:* 9 full-time (5 women), 4 part-time/adjunct (2 women). *Financial support:* In 2015–16, 12 students received support. Career-related internships or fieldwork, scholarships/grants, unspecified assistantships, and tuition reimbursements, tuition remission available. Support available to part-time students. Financial award applicants required to submit FAFSA. In 2015, 35 master's awarded. *Degree program information:* Part-time and evening/weekend programs available. Part-time, evening/weekend. Offers professional communication (MPC, MSC). *Application deadline:* For fall admission, 4/1 priority date for domestic and international students; for spring admission, 10/16 priority date for domestic and international students. Applications are processed on a rolling basis. *Application fee:* $50. Electronic applications accepted. *Application Contact:* Dr. John Baworowsky, Vice President of Enrollment Management, 801-832-2200, Fax: 801-832-3101, E-mail: admission@westminstercollege.edu. *Director,* Dr. Helen Hodgson, 801-832-2821, Fax: 801-832-3102, E-mail: hhodgson@westminstercollege.edu.

School of Education Students: 72 full-time (58 women), 69 part-time (55 women); includes 31 minority (5 Black or African American, non-Hispanic/Latino; 3 Asian, non-Hispanic/Latino; 16 Hispanic/Latino; 1 Native Hawaiian or other Pacific Islander, non-Hispanic/Latino; 6 Two or more races, non-Hispanic/Latino), 4 international. Average age 33. 53 applicants, 87% accepted, 39 enrolled. *Faculty:* 16 full-time (10 women), 18 part-time/adjunct (14 women). *Financial support:* In 2015–16, 21 students received support. Career-related internships or fieldwork, scholarships/grants, unspecified assistantships, and tuition reimbursements, tuition remission available. Support available to part-time students. Financial award applicants required to submit FAFSA. In 2015, 89 master's awarded. *Degree program information:* Part-time and evening/weekend programs available. Part-time, evening/weekend. Offers community leadership (MACL); education (M Ed); teaching (MAT). *Application deadline:* For fall admission, 6/3 priority date for domestic and international students; for spring admission, 10/16 priority date for domestic and international students; for summer admission, 1/22 priority date for domestic and international students. Applications are processed on a rolling basis. *Application fee:* $50. Electronic applications accepted. *Application Contact:* Dr. John Baworowsky, Vice President of Enrollment Management, 801-832-2200, Fax: 801-832-3101, E-mail: admission@westminstercollege.edu. *Interim Dean, School of Education,* Peter Ingle, 801-832-2470, Fax: 801-832-3105.

School of Nursing and Health Sciences Students: 120 full-time (79 women), 3 part-time (all women); includes 18 minority (1 Black or African American, non-Hispanic/Latino; 3 Asian, non-Hispanic/Latino; 10 Hispanic/Latino; 4 Two or more races, non-Hispanic/Latino), 3 international. Average age 32. 157 applicants, 40% accepted, 45 enrolled. *Faculty:* 15 full-time (9 women), 7 part-time/adjunct (2 women). *Financial support:* In 2015–16, 8 students received support. Career-related internships or fieldwork, unspecified assistantships, and tuition reimbursements, tuition remission available. Support available to part-time students. Financial award applicants required to submit FAFSA. In 2015, 56 master's awarded. Offers family nurse practitioner (MSN); nurse anesthesia (MSNA); nurse education (MSNED); public health (MPH). *Application fee:* $50. Electronic applications accepted. *Application Contact:* Dr. John Baworowsky, Vice President of Enrollment Management, 801-832-2200, Fax: 801-832-3101, E-mail: admission@westminstercollege.edu. *Dean,* Dr. Sheryl Steadman, 801-832-2164, Fax: 801-832-3110, E-mail: ssteadman@westminstercollege.edu.

WESTMINSTER SEMINARY CALIFORNIA, Escondido, CA 92027-4128

General Information Independent-religious, coed, primarily men, graduate-only institution. *Graduate housing:* On-campus housing not available.

GRADUATE UNITS

Programs in Theology ***Degree program information:*** Part-time and evening/weekend programs available. Part-time, evening/weekend. Offers Biblical studies (MA); historical theology (MA); theological studies (M Div, MA).

WESTMINSTER THEOLOGICAL SEMINARY, Philadelphia, PA 19118

General Information Independent-religious, coed, primarily men, graduate-only institution. *Graduate housing:* Room and/or apartments available on a first-come, first-served basis to single students; on-campus housing not available to married students.

GRADUATE UNITS

Graduate and Professional Programs ***Degree program information:*** Part-time programs available. Part-time. Offers apologetics (Th M); Biblical and urban studies (Certificate); Biblical counseling (MA); biblical studies (MAR); Christian studies (Certificate); church history (Th M); counseling (M Div); general studies (M Div, MAR); hermeneutics and Bible interpretations (PhD); historical and theological studies (PhD); historical theology (Th M); New Testament (Th M); Old Testament (Th M); pastoral counseling (D Min); pastoral ministry (M Div, D Min); systematic theology (Th M); theological studies (MAR); urban missions (M Div, MA, MAR, D Min).

WEST TEXAS A&M UNIVERSITY, Canyon, TX 79016-0001

General Information State-supported, coed, comprehensive institution. CGS member. *Graduate housing:* Room and/or apartments available on a first-come, first-served basis to single students; on-campus housing not available to married students. *Research affiliation:* Owens Corning (sports exercise), Pantex (chemistry), Agriculture Experiment Station (agriculture), Engineering Experiment Station (math, science).

GRADUATE UNITS

College of Agriculture, Science and Engineering ***Degree program information:*** Part-time programs available. Part-time. Offers agricultural business and economics (MS); agriculture (MS, PhD); agriculture, science and engineering (MS, PhD); animal science (MS); biology (MS); chemistry (MS); engineering technology (MS); environmental science (MS); mathematics (MS); plant, soil and environmental science (MS). Electronic applications accepted.

School of Engineering and Computer Science Degree program information: Part-time programs available. Part-time. Offers engineering technology (MS). Electronic applications accepted.

College of Business ***Degree program information:*** Part-time and evening/weekend programs available. Part-time, evening/weekend, online learning. Offers accounting (MP Acc); accounting/business administration (MPA); business (MBA, MPA, MS); business administration (MBA); finance and economics (MS); professional accounting (MPA). Electronic applications accepted.

College of Education and Social Sciences ***Degree program information:*** Part-time and evening/weekend programs available. Part-time, evening/weekend, online learning. Offers clinical mental health (MA); criminal justice (MA); curriculum and instruction (M Ed); education and social sciences (M Ed, MA, MS); educational diagnostician (M Ed); educational leadership (M Ed); instructional design and technology (M Ed); psychology (MA); reading education (M Ed); school counseling (M Ed); social work (MS); special education (M Ed); teaching (MAT). Electronic applications accepted.

College of Fine Arts and Humanities ***Degree program information:*** Part-time and evening/weekend programs available. Part-time, evening/weekend. Offers art (MA); communication (MA); English (MA); fine arts and humanities (MA, MFA, MM); history (MA); studio art (MFA). Electronic applications accepted.

School of Music Degree program information: Part-time programs available. Part-time. Offers music (MA); performance (MM). Electronic applications accepted.

College of Nursing and Health Sciences ***Degree program information:*** Part-time and evening/weekend programs available. Part-time, evening/weekend. Offers communication disorders (MS); family nurse practitioner (MSN); nursing (MSN); nursing and health sciences (MS, MSN); sport management (MS); sports and exercise sciences (MS). Electronic applications accepted.

Program in Interdisciplinary Studies ***Degree program information:*** Part-time and evening/weekend programs available. Part-time, evening/weekend. Offers interdisciplinary studies (MA, MS). Electronic applications accepted.

WEST VIRGINIA SCHOOL OF OSTEOPATHIC MEDICINE, Lewisburg, WV 24901-1196

General Information State-supported, coed, graduate-only institution. *Graduate housing:* On-campus housing not available.

GRADUATE UNITS

Professional Program Offers osteopathic medicine (DO). Electronic applications accepted.

WEST VIRGINIA STATE UNIVERSITY, Institute, WV 25112-1000

General Information State-supported, coed, comprehensive institution. *Graduate housing:* Rooms and/or apartments available on a first-come, first-served basis to single and married students. Housing application deadline: 9/1.

GRADUATE UNITS

Biotechnology Graduate Program Offers biotechnology (MA, MS). Electronic applications accepted.

Master of Science Program in Law Enforcement and Administration Offers law enforcement and administration (MS). Electronic applications accepted.

Media Studies Graduate Program Offers media studies (MA). Electronic applications accepted.

WEST VIRGINIA UNIVERSITY, Morgantown, WV 26506

General Information State-supported, coed, university. CGS member. *Enrollment:* 29,175 graduate, professional, and undergraduate students; 4,634 full-time matriculated graduate/professional students (2,426 women), 1,644 part-time matriculated graduate/professional students (1,078 women). *Enrollment by degree level:* 3,324 master's, 2,954 doctoral. *Graduate faculty:* 872 full-time (355 women), 119 part-time/adjunct (53 women). Tuition, state resident: full-time $8568. Tuition, nonresident: full-time $22,140. Tuition and fees vary according to program. *Graduate housing:* Rooms and/or apartments available on a first-come, first-served basis to single and married students. Housing application deadline: 1/22. *Student services:* Campus employment opportunities, campus safety program, career counseling, child daycare facilities, exercise/wellness program, free psychological counseling, grant writing training, international student services, low-cost health insurance, multicultural affairs office, services for students with disabilities, teacher training, writing training. *Library:* Downtown Library Complex plus 5 others. *Collection:* Books: 2.4 million (physical); Serial titles: 89,824 (physical); Databases: 390,341. Study areas open 24 hours, 5–7 days a week; students can reserve study rooms. *Research affiliation:* Federal Bureau of Investigation (FBI) (biometrics research), NASA IV and V Center (software verification/validation), Research Partnership for an Energy Secure America (energy research), Florida Agricultural and Mechanical University (plasma physics), University of Pittsburgh, Carnegie Mellon University (energy research), National Energy Technology Laboratory (fossil energy and environmental research).

Computer facilities: Computer purchase and lease plans are available. 1,800 computers available on campus for general student use. A campuswide network can be accessed from student residence rooms and from off campus. Online class registration is available.
Website: http://www.wvu.edu/

General Application Contact: Dr. Tracey L. Sheetz, Director, Graduate Admissions, 304-293-7173, Fax: 304-293-8657, E-mail: graded@mail.wvu.edu.

GRADUATE UNITS

College of Business and Economics Students: 364 full-time (133 women), 46 part-time (16 women); includes 44 minority (9 Black or African American, non-Hispanic/Latino; 13 Asian, non-Hispanic/Latino; 13 Hispanic/Latino; 9 Two or more races, non-Hispanic/Latino), 70 international. Average age 30. *Faculty:* 53 full-time (13 women), 5 part-time/adjunct (1 woman). *Financial support:* Fellowships, research assistantships, teaching assistantships, career-related internships or fieldwork, Federal Work-Study, institutionally sponsored loans, scholarships/grants, health care benefits, tuition waivers (full and partial), unspecified assistantships, and administrative assistantships available. Financial award application deadline: 2/1; financial award applicants required to submit FAFSA. In 2015, 208 master's, 4 doctorates awarded. *Degree program information:* Part-time programs available. Part-time, online learning. Offers business administration (MBA); business and economics (MA, MBA, MPA, MS, MSIR, PhD, Certificate); industrial relations (MSIR). *Application deadline:* For fall admission, 10/15 priority date for domestic and international students; for spring admission, 3/1 priority date for domestic and international students. Applications are processed on a rolling basis. *Application fee:* $60. Electronic applications accepted. *Application Contact:* Dr. Gerald Blakely, Professor and Director for Graduate Programs, 304-293-5505, Fax: 304-293-7188, E-mail: gerald.blakely@mail.wvu.edu. *Interim Dean,* Dr. Nancy H. McIntyre, 304-293-7800, Fax: 304-293-4056, E-mail: nancy.mcintyre@mail.wvu.edu.

Division of Accounting Degree program information: Part-time and evening/weekend programs available. Part-time, evening/weekend. Offers accounting (MPA). Electronic applications accepted.

Division of Economics and Finance Offers business analysis (MA); developmental financial economics (PhD); environmental and resource economics (PhD); international economics (PhD); mathematical economics (MA); monetary economics (PhD); public finance (PhD); public policy (MA); regional and urban economics (PhD); statistics and economics (MA). Electronic applications accepted.

College of Creative Arts Students: 100 full-time (54 women), 34 part-time (22 women); includes 19 minority (5 Black or African American, non-Hispanic/Latino; 5 Asian, non-Hispanic/Latino; 5 Hispanic/Latino; 4 Two or more races, non-Hispanic/Latino), 37 international. Average age 32. *Faculty:* 60 full-time (23 women), 7 part-time/adjunct (4 women). *Financial support:* Research assistantships, teaching assistantships, career-related internships or fieldwork, Federal Work-Study, institutionally sponsored loans, scholarships/grants, health care benefits, tuition waivers (partial), and administrative assistantships available. Financial award applicants required to submit FAFSA. In 2015, 30 master's, 7 doctorates awarded. *Degree program information:* Part-time programs available. Part-time. Offers creative arts (MA, MFA, MM, DMA, PhD). *Application deadline:* For fall admission, 3/1 priority date for domestic students, 2/15 for international students; for spring admission, 11/1 for domestic students, 9/15 for international students. Applications are processed on a rolling basis. *Application fee:* $60. Electronic applications accepted. *Application Contact:* Records Officer, 304-293-4841, Fax: 304-293-2533, E-mail: rachel.hanks@mail.wvu.edu. *Dean,* Dr. Paul Kreider, 304-293-4841 Ext. 3109, Fax: 304-293-6896, E-mail: paul.kreider@mail.wvu.edu.

School of Art and Design Offers art education (MA); art history (MA); ceramics (MFA); graphic design (MFA); painting (MFA); printmaking (MFA); sculpture (MFA); studio art (MA).

School of Music Offers music composition (MM, DMA); music education (MM, PhD); music history (MM); music industry (MA); music performance (MM, DMA); music theory (MM).

School of Theatre and Dance Degree program information: Part-time programs available. Part-time. Offers acting (MFA); theatre design/technology (MFA).

College of Education and Human Services Students: 476 full-time (380 women), 489 part-time (405 women); includes 72 minority (24 Black or African American, non-Hispanic/Latino; 7 Asian, non-Hispanic/Latino; 24 Hispanic/Latino; 17 Two or more races, non-Hispanic/Latino), 16 international. Average age 31. *Faculty:* 77 full-time (49 women), 2 part-time/adjunct (0 women). *Financial support:* Fellowships, research assistantships, teaching assistantships, career-related internships or fieldwork, Federal Work-Study, institutionally sponsored loans, health care benefits, tuition waivers (full and partial), and administrative assistantships available. Financial award applicants required to submit FAFSA. In 2015, 383 master's, 29 doctorates awarded. *Degree program information:* Part-time and evening/weekend programs available. Part-time, evening/weekend, online learning. Offers audiology (Au D); autism spectrum disorder (5-adult) (MA); autism spectrum disorder (K-6) (MA); child development and family studies (MA); counseling (MA); counseling psychology (PhD); curriculum and instruction (Ed D); early intervention/early childhood special education (MA); education and human services (MA, MS, Au D, Ed D, PhD); educational leadership (Ed D); educational psychology (MA); elementary education (MA); gifted education (1-12) (MA); higher education administration (MA); higher education curriculum and teaching (MA); instructional design and technology (MA, Ed D); low vision (PreK-adult) (MA); multicategorical special education (5-adult) (MA); multicategorical special education (K-6) (MA); public school administration (MA); reading (MA); rehabilitation counseling (MS); secondary education (MA); severe/multiple disabilities (K-adult) (MA); special education (MA, Ed D); speech-language pathology (MS); vision impairments (PreK-adult) (MA). *Application deadline:* For fall admission, 8/1 for domestic students; for spring admission, 1/1 for domestic students; for summer admission, 5/1 for domestic students. *Application fee:* $60. Electronic applications accepted. *Application Contact:* Dr. M. Cecil Smith, Associate Dean for Research and Graduate Education, 304-293-2174, Fax: 304-293-3802, E-mail: mcecil.smith@mail.wvu.edu. *Dean,* Dr. Gypsy Denzine, 304-293-5703, Fax: 304-293-7565, E-mail: gypsy.denzine@mail.wvu.edu.

College of Law Students: 330 full-time (136 women), 3 part-time (2 women); includes 36 minority (8 Black or African American, non-Hispanic/Latino; 9 Asian, non-Hispanic/Latino; 7 Hispanic/Latino; 12 Two or more races, non-Hispanic/Latino). Average age 26. *Faculty:* 41 full-time (15 women), 14 part-time/adjunct (4 women). *Financial support:* Fellowships, research assistantships, teaching assistantships, career-related internships or fieldwork, Federal Work-Study, institutionally sponsored loans, scholarships/grants, health care benefits, tuition waivers (full), unspecified assistantships, and administrative assistantships, resident assistantships available. Support available to part-time students. Financial award application deadline: 3/1; financial award applicants required to submit FAFSA. In 2015, 126 doctorates awarded. *Degree program information:* Part-time programs available. Part-time. Offers law (LL M, JD). *Application deadline:* For fall admission, 2/1 for domestic and international students. Applications are processed on a rolling basis. *Application fee:* $60. Electronic applications accepted. *Application Contact:* Janet Long Armistead, Assistant Dean for Admissions and Student Affairs, 304-293-5304, Fax: 304-293-6891, E-mail: janet.armistead@mail.wvu.edu. *Dean,* Gregory W. Bowman, 304-293-4712, Fax: 304-293-6891, E-mail: gregory.bowman@mail.wvu.edu.

College of Physical Activity and Sport Sciences Students: 124 full-time (61 women), 76 part-time (27 women); includes 25 minority (16 Black or African American, non-Hispanic/Latino; 1 Asian, non-Hispanic/Latino; 3 Hispanic/Latino; 5 Two or more races, non-Hispanic/Latino), 16 international. Average age 28. *Faculty:* 24 full-time (9 women), 8 part-time/adjunct (2 women). *Financial support:* Research assistantships, teaching assistantships, career-related internships or fieldwork, Federal Work-Study, institutionally sponsored loans, health care benefits, tuition waivers (full and partial), and administrative assistantships available. Support available to part-time students. Financial award application deadline: 2/1; financial award applicants required to submit FAFSA. In 2015, 77 master's, 9 doctorates awarded. Offers athletic training (MS); coaching and sport education (MS); coaching and teaching studies (Ed D); physical education/teacher education (MS, PhD); sport and exercise psychology (MS, PhD); sport coaching (MS); sport management (MS). *Application deadline:* For fall admission, 12/15 for domestic students, 10/1 for international students. *Application fee:* $60. Electronic applications accepted. *Application Contact:* Greg Goodwin, Student Services Specialist, 304-293-9979, Fax: 304-293-4641, E-mail: greg.goodwin@mail.wvu.edu. *Dean,* Dr. Dana D. Brooks, 304-293-3295 Ext. 5285, Fax: 304-293-4641, E-mail: dana.brooks@mail.wvu.edu.

Davis College of Agriculture, Forestry and Consumer Sciences Students: 212 full-time (117 women), 53 part-time (29 women); includes 28 minority (10 Black or African American, non-Hispanic/Latino; 4 Asian, non-Hispanic/Latino; 7 Hispanic/Latino; 7 Two or more races, non-Hispanic/Latino), 65 international. Average age 29. *Faculty:* 72 full-time (15 women). *Financial support:* Fellowships, research assistantships, teaching assistantships, career-related internships or fieldwork, Federal Work-Study, institutionally sponsored loans, tuition waivers (full and partial), and unspecified assistantships available. Financial award application deadline: 2/1; financial award applicants required to submit FAFSA. In 2015, 65 master's, 20 doctorates awarded. *Degree program information:* Part-time programs available. Part-time. Offers agriculture, forestry and consumer sciences (M Agr, MLA, MS, MSF, PhD); animal breeding (MS, PhD); biochemical and molecular genetics (MS, PhD); cytogenetics (MS, PhD); descriptive embryology (MS, PhD); developmental genetics (MS); experimental morphogenesis/teratology (MS); human genetics (MS, PhD); immunogenetics (MS, PhD); life cycles of animals and plants (MS, PhD); molecular aspects of development (MS, PhD); mutagenesis (MS, PhD); oncology (MS, PhD); plant genetics (MS, PhD); population and quantitative genetics (MS, PhD); regeneration (MS, PhD); reproductive physiology (MS, PhD); teratology (PhD); toxicology (MS, PhD). *Application deadline:* For fall admission, 6/1 priority date for domestic students, 6/1 for international students; for spring admission, 1/5 for domestic and international students. Applications are processed on a rolling basis. *Application fee:* $60. Electronic applications accepted. *Application Contact:* Dr. Dennis K. Smith, Associate Dean, 304-293-2275, Fax: 304-293-3740, E-mail: denny.smith@mail.wvu.edu. *Dean,* Dr. Dan J. Robison, 304-293-2395, Fax: 304-293-3740, E-mail: dan.robison@mail.wvu.edu.

Division of Animal and Nutritional Sciences Degree program information: Part-time programs available. Part-time. Offers animal and nutritional sciences (MS); breeding (MS); food sciences (MS); nutrition (MS); physiology (MS); production management (MS); reproduction (MS).

Division of Forestry Degree program information: Part-time programs available. Part-time. Offers forest resource science (PhD); forestry (MSF); recreation, parks and tourism resources (MS); wildlife and fisheries resources (MS).

Division of Plant and Soil Sciences Offers agricultural sciences (PhD); agronomy (MS); animal and food sciences (PhD); entomology (MS); environmental microbiology (MS); horticulture (MS); plant and soil sciences (PhD); plant pathology (MS).

Division of Resource Management and Sustainable Development Degree program information: Part-time programs available. Part-time. Offers agricultural and extension education (MS, PhD); agricultural and resource economics (MS); human and community development (PhD); natural resource economics (PhD); resource management (PhD); resource management and sustainable development (PhD); teaching vocational-agriculture (MS).

Eberly College of Arts and Sciences *Degree program information:* Part-time and evening/weekend programs available. Part-time, evening/weekend, online learning. Offers African history (MA, PhD); African-American history (MA, PhD); American history (MA, PhD); American public policy and politics (MA); analytical chemistry (MS, PhD); Appalachian/regional history (MA, PhD); applied mathematics (MS, PhD); applied physics (MS, PhD); arts and sciences (MA, MALS, MFA, MLS, MPA, MS, MSW, PhD); astrophysics (MS, PhD); behavior analysis (PhD); cell and molecular biology (MS, PhD); chemical physics (MS, PhD); clinical psychology (MA, PhD); communication in instruction (MA); communication studies (PhD); communication theory and research (MA); condensed matter physics (MS, PhD); corporate and organizational communication (MA); creative writing (MFA); development psychology (PhD); discrete mathematics (PhD); East Asian history (MA, PhD); elementary particle physics (MS, PhD); energy and environmental resources (MA); English (MA, PhD); environmental and evolutionary biology (MS, PhD); European history (MA, PhD); forensic biology (MS, PhD); French (MA); genomic biology (MS, PhD); geographic information systems (PhD); geography (MA, PhD); geography-regional development (PhD); geology (MS, PhD); geomorphology (MS, PhD); geophysics (MS, PhD); GIS/cartographic analysis (MA); history of science and technology (MA, PhD); hydrogeology (MS, PhD); inorganic chemistry (MS, PhD); interdisciplinary mathematics (MS); international and comparative public policy and politics (MA); Latin American history (MA); liberal studies (MALS); linguistics (MA); literary/cultural studies (MA, PhD); materials physics (MS, PhD); mathematics for secondary education (MS); neurobiology (MS, PhD); organic chemistry (MS, PhD); paleontology (MS, PhD); petroleum geology (PhD); petrology (MS, PhD); physical chemistry (MS, PhD); plasma physics (MS, PhD); political science (PhD); psychology (MS); public policy analysis (PhD); pure mathematics (MS); regional development (MA); solid state physics (MS, PhD); Spanish (MA); statistical physics (MS, PhD); statistics (MS); stratigraphy (MS, PhD); structure (MS, PhD); teaching English to speakers of other languages (MA); theoretical chemistry (MS, PhD); theoretical physics (MS, PhD); writing (MA). Electronic applications accepted.

School of Applied Social Sciences Degree program information: Part-time programs available. Part-time. Offers aging and health care (MSW); applied social research (MA); applied social sciences (MA, MLS, MPA, MSW); children and families (MSW); community mental health (MSW); community organization and social administration (MSW); direct (clinical) social work practice (MSW); legal studies (MLS); public administration (MPA).

Reed College of Media Students: 147 full-time (103 women), 259 part-time (194 women); includes 90 minority (59 Black or African American, non-Hispanic/Latino; 6 Asian, non-Hispanic/Latino; 13 Hispanic/Latino; 1 Native Hawaiian or other Pacific Islander, non-Hispanic/Latino; 11 Two or more races, non-Hispanic/Latino), 5 international. Average age 32. *Faculty:* 12 full-time (6 women), 26 part-time/adjunct (13 women). *Financial support:* In 2015–16, 118 students received support. Research assistantships, teaching assistantships, career-related internships or fieldwork, Federal Work-Study, institutionally sponsored loans, health care benefits, tuition waivers (full and partial), and administrative assistantships available. Financial award application deadline: 2/1; financial award applicants required to submit FAFSA. In 2015, 159 degrees awarded. *Degree program information:* Part-time programs available. Part-time, online learning. Offers digital marketing communications (Graduate Certificate); integrated marketing communications (MS, Graduate Certificate); journalism (MSJ). *Application deadline:* For fall admission, 3/1 priority date for domestic students, 3/1 for international students. *Application fee:* $60. Electronic applications accepted. *Application Contact:* Dr. Steve Urbanski, Director of Graduate Studies/Associate Professor, 304-293-6797, Fax: 304-293-3072, E-mail: steve.urbanski@mail.wvu.edu. *Dean,* Dr. Maryann Reed, 304-293-3505 Ext. 5409, Fax: 304-293-3072, E-mail: maryann.reed@mail.wvu.edu.

School of Dentistry Students: 239 full-time (119 women), 1 part-time (0 women); includes 38 minority (2 Black or African American, non-Hispanic/Latino; 25 Asian, non-Hispanic/Latino; 4 Hispanic/Latino; 7 Two or more races, non-Hispanic/Latino), 11 international. Average age 30. *Faculty:* 9 full-time (2 women), 1 part-time/adjunct (0 women). *Financial support:* Research assistantships, teaching assistantships, Federal Work-Study, institutionally sponsored loans, scholarships/grants, health care benefits, and tuition waivers (partial) available. Financial award application deadline: 3/1; financial award applicants required to submit FAFSA. In 2015, 10 master's, 48 doctorates awarded. Offers dentistry (MS, DDS); endodontics (MS); orthodontics (MS); prosthodontics (MS). *Application deadline:* For fall admission, 11/1 for domestic and international students. Applications are processed on a rolling basis. *Application fee:* $60. Electronic applications accepted. *Application Contact:* Dr. Sheila Price, Associate Dean for Admissions, Recruitment, and Access, 304-293-1980, E-mail: sprice@hsc.wvu.edu. *Dean,* Dr. Tom Borgia, 304-293-2521, E-mail: aborgia@hsc.wvu.edu.

Division of Dental Hygiene Degree program information: Part-time programs available. Part-time. Offers dental hygiene (MS).

School of Medicine Students: 748 full-time (401 women), 16 part-time (9 women); includes 111 minority (11 Black or African American, non-Hispanic/Latino; 52 Asian, non-Hispanic/Latino; 28 Hispanic/Latino; 2 Native Hawaiian or other Pacific Islander, non-Hispanic/Latino; 18 Two or more races, non-Hispanic/Latino), 18 international. Average age 26. *Faculty:* 72 full-time (34 women), 4 part-time/adjunct (0 women). *Financial support:* Fellowships, research assistantships, teaching assistantships, career-related internships or fieldwork, Federal Work-Study, institutionally sponsored loans, health care benefits, tuition waivers (full and partial), and administrative assistantships available. Financial award applicants required to submit FAFSA. In 2015, 70 master's, 9 doctorates, 140 other advanced degrees awarded. *Degree program information:* Part-time and evening/weekend programs available. Part-time, evening/weekend. Offers medicine (MHS, MOT, MS, DPT, MD, PhD, Graduate Certificate); occupational therapy (MOT); physical therapy (DPT); public health (MPH); public health sciences (PhD). *Application deadline:* Applications are processed on a rolling basis. *Application fee:* $60. Electronic applications accepted. *Application Contact:* Lisa M. Salati, Assistant Vice President, Graduate Education, 304-293-7759, Fax: 304-293-3080, E-mail: lsalati@hsc.wvu.edu. *Executive Dean,* Dr. Clay Marsh, 304-293-6607, Fax: 304-293-6627, E-mail: clay.marsh@hsc.wvu.edu.

Graduate Programs at the Health Sciences Center Degree program information: Part-time and evening/weekend programs available. Part-time, evening/weekend, online learning. Offers biochemistry and molecular biology (MS, PhD); cancer cell biology (PhD); cellular and integrative physiology (MS, PhD); exercise physiology (MS, PhD); health sciences (MS, PhD); immunology and microbial pathogenesis (MS, PhD); neuroscience (PhD); pharmaceutical and pharmacological sciences (MS, PhD).

School of Nursing Students: 53 full-time (48 women), 96 part-time (88 women); includes 9 minority (2 Black or African American, non-Hispanic/Latino; 1 Hispanic/Latino; 6 Two or more races, non-Hispanic/Latino). Average age 36. *Faculty:* 20 full-time (all women), 9 part-time/adjunct (all women). *Financial support:* Teaching assistantships, Federal Work-Study, institutionally sponsored loans, health care benefits, tuition waivers (partial), and administrative assistantships available. Financial award application deadline: 2/1; financial award applicants required to submit FAFSA. In 2015, 44 master's, 10 doctorates awarded. *Degree program information:* Part-time programs available. Part-time, online learning. Offers nurse practitioner (Certificate); nursing (MSN, DNP, PhD). *Application deadline:* For fall admission, 6/1 for domestic students. *Application fee:* $60. Electronic applications accepted. *Application Contact:* Brandy Sue Toothman, Program Assistant III, 304-293-4298, Fax: 304-293-2546, E-mail: btoothman@hsc.wvu.edu. *Dean,* Dr. Tara Hulsey, 304-293-6521, Fax: 304-293-6826, E-mail: tmhulsey@hsc.wvu.edu.

School of Pharmacy Students: 367 full-time (229 women), 4 part-time (1 woman); includes 38 minority (9 Black or African American, non-Hispanic/Latino; 1 American Indian or Alaska Native, non-Hispanic/Latino; 12 Asian, non-Hispanic/Latino; 10 Hispanic/Latino; 6 Two or more races, non-Hispanic/Latino), 22 international. Average age 26. *Faculty:* 36 full-time (17 women), 1 (woman) part-time/adjunct. *Financial support:* Research assistantships, teaching assistantships, career-related internships or fieldwork, Federal Work-Study, institutionally sponsored loans, health care benefits, tuition waivers (full and partial), and unspecified assistantships available. Financial award application deadline: 3/1; financial award applicants required to submit FAFSA. In 2015, 96 doctorates awarded. Offers administrative pharmacy (PhD); behavioral pharmacy (MS, PhD); biopharmaceutics/pharmacokinetics (MS, PhD); clinical pharmacy (Pharm D); industrial pharmacy (MS); medicinal chemistry (MS, PhD); pharmaceutical chemistry (MS, PhD); pharmaceutics (MS, PhD); pharmacology and toxicology (MS); pharmacy (MS); pharmacy administration (MS). *Application deadline:* For fall admission, 3/1 priority date for domestic and international students. *Application fee:* $60. Electronic applications accepted. *Application Contact:* Dr. Mary L. Euler, Associate Dean for Student Services, 304-293-7806, Fax: 304-293-5483, E-mail: mleuler@hsc.wvu.edu. *Interim Dean,* Dr. Mary K. Stamatakis, 304-293-5101, Fax: 304-293-5483, E-mail: mkstamatakis@hsc.wvu.edu.

School of Public Health Students: 85 full-time (55 women), 52 part-time (34 women); includes 28 minority (8 Black or African American, non-Hispanic/Latino; 1 American Indian or Alaska Native, non-Hispanic/Latino; 13 Asian, non-Hispanic/Latino; 3 Hispanic/Latino; 3 Two or more races, non-Hispanic/Latino), 10 international. Average age 31. *Faculty:* 37 full-time (17 women), 3 part-time/adjunct (2 women). *Financial support:* Research assistantships, teaching assistantships, scholarships/grants, and health care benefits available. Financial award application deadline: 2/1; financial award applicants required to submit FAFSA. In 2015, 11 doctorates awarded. *Degree program information:* Part-time programs available. Part-time, online learning. Offers biostatistics (MS); community health/preventative medicine (MPH); public health sciences (PhD); school health education (MS). *Application deadline:* For fall admission, 4/15 priority date for domestic students; for spring admission, 12/1 for domestic students. Applications are processed on a rolling basis. *Application fee:* $60. *Application Contact:* Sherry Kuhl, Director, Office of Student Services, 304-293-1795, Fax: 304-293-6685, E-mail: skuhl@hsc.wvu.edu. *Dean, School of Public Health,* Dr. Gregory A. Hand, 304-293-2502, Fax: 304-293-6685, E-mail: gahand@hsc.wvu.edu.

Statler College of Engineering and Mineral Resources Students: 528 full-time (136 women), 175 part-time (33 women); includes 42 minority (13 Black or African American, non-Hispanic/Latino; 1 American Indian or Alaska Native, non-Hispanic/Latino; 12 Asian, non-Hispanic/Latino; 8 Hispanic/Latino; 8 Two or more races, non-Hispanic/Latino), 383 international. Average age 28. *Faculty:* 88 full-time (11 women), 8 part-time/adjunct (0 women). *Financial support:* Fellowships, research assistantships, teaching assistantships, career-related internships or fieldwork, Federal Work-Study, institutionally sponsored loans, health care benefits, tuition waivers (full and partial), unspecified assistantships, and administrative assistantships available. Financial award application deadline: 2/1; financial award applicants required to submit FAFSA. In 2015, 174 master's, 44 doctorates awarded. *Degree program information:* Part-time programs available. Part-time. Offers aerospace engineering (MSAE, PhD); chemical engineering (MS Ch E, PhD); civil engineering (MSCE, MSE, PhD); computer engineering (PhD); computer science (MSCS, PhD); electrical engineering (MSEE, PhD); engineering (MSE); industrial engineering (MSE, MSIE, PhD); industrial hygiene (MS); interactive technologies and serious gaming (Graduate Certificate); material science and engineering (MSMSE); mechanical engineering (MSME, PhD); mining engineering (MS Min E, PhD); occupational safety and health (PhD); petroleum and natural gas engineering (MSPNGE, PhD); safety management (MS); software engineering (MSSE). *Application deadline:* For fall admission, 4/1 for international students; for winter admission, 4/1 for international students; for spring admission, 10/1 for international students. Applications are processed on a rolling basis. *Application fee:* $60. Electronic applications accepted. *Application Contact:* Dr. David A. Wyrick, Associate Dean, Academic Affairs, 304-293-4334, Fax: 304-293-5024, E-mail: david.wyrick@mail.wvu.edu. *Dean*, Dr. Eugene V. Cilento, 304-293-4821 Ext. 2237, Fax: 304-293-2037, E-mail: gene.cilento@mail.wvu.edu.

WEST VIRGINIA WESLEYAN COLLEGE, Buckhannon, WV 26201

General Information Independent-religious, coed, comprehensive institution. *Graduate housing:* Room and/or apartments available to single students; on-campus housing not available to married students.

GRADUATE UNITS

Department of Education Offers education (M Ed).

Department of Exercise Science Offers athletic training (MS).

Department of Nursing Offers family nurse practitioner (Post Master's Certificate); family nurse practitoner (MS); nurse administrator (MS); nurse educator (MS); nurse-midwifery (MS); nursing administration (Post Master's Certificate); nursing education (Post Master's Certificate); psychiatric mental health nurse practitioner (MS).

MBA Program ***Degree program information:*** Part-time and evening/weekend programs available. Part-time, evening/weekend. Offers business administration (MBA).

Program in Creative Writing Offers creative writing (MFA).

WHEATON COLLEGE, Wheaton, IL 60187-5593

General Information Independent-religious, coed, comprehensive institution. CGS member. *Enrollment:* 2,929 graduate, professional, and undergraduate students; 268 full-time matriculated graduate/professional students (157 women), 127 part-time matriculated graduate/professional students (66 women). *Enrollment by degree level:* 309 master's, 86 doctoral. *Graduate faculty:* 31 full-time (11 women), 19 part-time/adjunct (8 women). *Tuition, area resident:* Full-time $18,720; part-time $780 per credit hour. Tuition and fees vary according to degree level. *Graduate housing:* Rooms and/or apartments available on a first-come, first-served basis to single and married students. Housing application deadline: 4/1. *Student services:* Campus employment opportunities, campus safety program, career counseling, exercise/wellness program, free psychological counseling, grant writing training, international student services, multicultural affairs office, services for students with disabilities, writing training. *Library:* Buswell Memorial Library. *Collection:* Books: 458,369 (physical), 155,328 (digital/electronic); Serial titles: 6,599 (physical); Databases: 130. Weekly public service hours: 94; students can reserve study rooms.

Computer facilities: 325 computers available on campus for general student use. A campuswide network can be accessed from student residence rooms and from off campus. Online class registration, financial information, degree requirements evaluation are available.
Website: http://www.wheaton.edu/

General Application Contact: Dusty Di Santo, Director of Graduate Admissions, 630-752-5195, Fax: 630-752-7047, E-mail: graduate.admissions@wheaton.edu.

GRADUATE UNITS

Graduate School Students: 248 full-time (148 women), 153 part-time (75 women); includes 67 minority (20 Black or African American, non-Hispanic/Latino; 2 American Indian or Alaska Native, non-Hispanic/Latino; 27 Asian, non-Hispanic/Latino; 5 Hispanic/Latino; 13 Two or more races, non-Hispanic/Latino), 50 international. Average age 30. 409 applicants, 81% accepted, 214 enrolled. *Faculty:* 30 full-time (10 women), 8 part-time/adjunct (5 women). *Financial support:* Career-related internships or fieldwork, Federal Work-Study, scholarships/grants, and unspecified assistantships available. Financial award application deadline: 3/1; financial award applicants required to submit FAFSA. In 2015, 150 master's, 27 doctorates awarded. *Degree program information:* Part-time programs available. Part-time. Offers Biblical and theological studies (PhD); Biblical archaeology (MA); Biblical exegesis (MA); Biblical studies (MA); Christian formation and ministry (MA); clinical mental health counseling (MA); clinical psychology (Psy D); counseling ministries (MA); elementary education (MAT); evangelism and leadership (MA); general theological studies (MA); historical and systematic theology (MA); history of Christianity (MA); intercultural studies (MA); intercultural studies/teaching English as a second language (MA); marriage and family therapy (MA); missional church movements (MA); missions (MA); secondary education (MAT); teaching English as a second language (Certificate). *Application deadline:* For fall admission, 1/1 priority date for domestic students, 1/1 for international students; for spring admission, 11/1 for domestic students. Applications are processed on a rolling basis. *Application fee:* $30. *Application Contact:* Dusty Di Santo, Director of Graduate Admissions, 630-752-5195, Fax: 630-752-7047, E-mail: graduate.admissions@wheaton.edu. *Dean*, Dr. Nicholas Perrin, 630-752-5933.

WHEELING JESUIT UNIVERSITY, Wheeling, WV 26003-6295

General Information Independent-religious, coed, comprehensive institution. *Graduate housing:* Rooms and/or apartments available on a first-come, first-served basis to single and married students.

GRADUATE UNITS

Department of Business ***Degree program information:*** Part-time and evening/weekend programs available. Part-time, evening/weekend. Offers accounting (MSA); business administration (MBA). Electronic applications accepted.

Department of Education ***Degree program information:*** Part-time and evening/weekend programs available. Part-time, evening/weekend, online learning. Offers education (MEL). Electronic applications accepted.

Department of Nursing ***Degree program information:*** Part-time and evening/weekend programs available. Part-time, evening/weekend, online learning. Offers nursing (MSN). Electronic applications accepted.

Department of Physical Therapy Offers physical therapy (DPT). Electronic applications accepted.

Department of Social Sciences ***Degree program information:*** Part-time and evening/weekend programs available. Part-time, evening/weekend. Offers social sciences (MSOL). Electronic applications accepted.

WHEELOCK COLLEGE, Boston, MA 02215-4176

General Information Independent, coed, primarily women, comprehensive institution. *Graduate housing:* Room and/or apartments available on a first-come, first-served basis to single students; on-campus housing not available to married students. Housing application deadline: 5/1.

GRADUATE UNITS

Graduate Programs ***Degree program information:*** Part-time and evening/weekend programs available. Part-time, evening/weekend, online learning. Offers education (MS, MSW).

Division of Arts and Sciences Offers human development (MS). Electronic applications accepted.

Division of Child and Family Studies Degree program information: Part-time programs available. Part-time, online learning. Offers family studies (MS); family support and parent education (MS); family, culture, and society (MS). Electronic applications accepted.

Division of Education Online learning. Offers early childhood education (MS); education leadership (MS); elementary education (MS); language, literacy, and reading (MS); teaching students with moderate disabilities (MS). Electronic applications accepted.

Division of Social Work Offers social work (MSW). Electronic applications accepted.

WHITTIER COLLEGE, Whittier, CA 90608-0634

General Information Independent, coed, comprehensive institution. *Graduate housing:* On-campus housing not available.

GRADUATE UNITS

Graduate Programs ***Degree program information:*** Part-time and evening/weekend programs available. Part-time, evening/weekend. Offers educational administration (MA Ed); elementary education (MA Ed); secondary education (MA Ed).

Whittier Law School Students: 326 full-time (189 women), 130 part-time (79 women); includes 229 minority (28 Black or African American, non-Hispanic/Latino; 3 American Indian or Alaska Native, non-Hispanic/Latino; 52 Asian, non-Hispanic/Latino; 131 Hispanic/Latino; 4 Native Hawaiian or other Pacific Islander, non-Hispanic/Latino; 11 Two or more races, non-Hispanic/Latino), 3 international. Average age 26. 1,140 applicants, 62% accepted, 146 enrolled. *Faculty:* 35 full-time (19 women), 14 part-time/adjunct (3 women). *Financial support:* In 2015–16, 258 students received support, including 64 fellowships (averaging $5,341 per year); Federal Work-Study, scholarships/grants, and unspecified assistantships also available. Financial award application deadline: 5/1; financial award applicants required to submit FAFSA. In 2015, 140 doctorates awarded. *Degree program information:* Part-time programs available. Part-time. Offers business law (JD); child and family law (JD); criminal law (JD); environmental law (JD); intellectual property law (JD); international and comparative law (JD); law (JD); trial and appellate practice (JD). *Application deadline:* For fall admission, 4/1 priority date for domestic students, 3/15 priority date for international students. Applications are processed on a rolling basis. *Application fee:* $60. Electronic applications accepted. *Application Contact:* Tom McColl, Associate Dean of Enrollment Management and Administration, 714-444-4141 Ext. 123, Fax: 714-444-0250. *Interim Dean*, John Fitzgerald, 714-444-4141 Ext. 109, Fax: 714-444-0855.

WHITWORTH UNIVERSITY, Spokane, WA 99251-0001

General Information Independent-religious, coed, comprehensive institution. *Enrollment:* 2,650 graduate, professional, and undergraduate students; 95 full-time matriculated graduate/professional students (64 women), 222 part-time matriculated graduate/professional students (136 women). *Enrollment by degree level:* 298 master's, 19 other advanced degrees. *Graduate faculty:* 16 full-time (7 women), 40 part-time/adjunct (21 women). *Tuition, area resident:* Full-time $10,710; part-time $5355 per semester. Tuition and fees vary according to program. *Graduate housing:* Room and/or apartments available on a first-come, first-served basis to single students; on-campus housing not available to married students. Typical cost: $10,714 (including board). Room and board charges vary according to board plan and campus/location. Housing application deadline: 5/1. *Student services:* Campus employment opportunities, career counseling, exercise/wellness program, free psychological counseling, grant writing training, international student services, low-cost health insurance, multicultural affairs office, services for students with disabilities, teacher training, writing training. *Library:* Harriet Cheney Cowles Library. *Collection:* Books: 164,385 (physical), 127,866 (digital/electronic); Serial titles: 330 (physical), 1,200 (digital/electronic); Databases: 153. Weekly public service hours: 96; students can reserve study rooms.

Computer facilities: 280 computers available on campus for general student use. A campuswide network can be accessed from student residence rooms and from off campus. Online class registration is available.
Website: http://www.whitworth.edu/

General Application Contact: Office of Admissions, 509-777-3222, E-mail: graduateandcsadmissions@whitworth.edu.

GRADUATE UNITS

Master of Arts in Theology Program ***Degree program information:*** Part-time and evening/weekend programs available. Part-time, evening/weekend. Offers theology (MA).

School of Business ***Degree program information:*** Part-time and evening/weekend programs available. Part-time, evening/weekend. Offers business (MBA). Electronic applications accepted.

School of Education ***Degree program information:*** Part-time and evening/weekend programs available. Part-time, evening/weekend, online learning. Offers administration (M Ed); counseling (M Ed); education (M Ed, MAT, MIT); elementary education (M Ed); gifted and talented (MAT); school counselors (M Ed); secondary education (M Ed); social agency/church setting (M Ed); special education (MAT); teaching (MIT).

WICHITA STATE UNIVERSITY, Wichita, KS 67260

General Information State-supported, coed, university. CGS member. *Enrollment:* 14,495 graduate, professional, and undergraduate students; 1,520 full-time matriculated graduate/professional students (725 women), 1,504 part-time matriculated graduate/professional students (814 women). *Enrollment by degree level:* 2,185 master's, 483 doctoral, 356 other advanced degrees. *Graduate faculty:* 394 full-time (146 women), 26 part-time/adjunct (17 women). *Graduate housing:* Rooms and/or apartments available on a first-come, first-served basis to single and married students. *Student services:* Campus employment opportunities, campus safety program, career counseling, child daycare facilities, exercise/wellness program, free psychological counseling, grant writing training, international student services, low-cost health insurance, multicultural affairs office, services for students with disabilities, teacher training, writing training. *Library:* Ablah Library plus 2 others. *Collection:* Books: 1.9 million (physical), 428,856 (digital/electronic); Serial titles: 281 (physical), 76,462 (digital/electronic); Databases: 250. Weekly public service hours: 92; study areas open 24 hours, 5–7 days a week; students can reserve study rooms. *Research affiliation:* Spirit Aerosystems (aerospace engineering), General Atomics (aerospace engineering), Wesley Medical Center (industrial and manufacturing engineering), NASA (aerospace engineering), Cisco Systems (computer engineering), NetApp (computer engineering).

Computer facilities: 1,500 computers available on campus for general student use. A campuswide network can be accessed from student residence rooms and from off campus. Online class registration, online Blackboard are available.
Website: http://www.wichita.edu/

General Application Contact: Jordan Oleson, Admissions Coordinator, 316-978-3095, Fax: 316-978-3253, E-mail: jordan.oleson@wichita.edu.

GRADUATE UNITS

Graduate School Students: 1,427 full-time (723 women), 1,377 part-time (729 women); includes 452 minority (118 Black or African American, non-Hispanic/Latino; 14 American Indian or Alaska Native, non-Hispanic/Latino; 110 Asian, non-Hispanic/Latino; 148 Hispanic/Latino; 2 Native Hawaiian or other Pacific Islander, non-Hispanic/Latino; 60 Two or more races, non-Hispanic/Latino), 721 international. Average age 31. 2,618 applicants, 57% accepted, 728 enrolled. *Faculty:* 418 full-time (163 women), 26 part-time/adjunct (15 women). *Financial support:* In 2015–16, 494 research assistantships with partial tuition reimbursements (averaging $10,496 per year), 380 teaching assistantships with partial tuition reimbursements (averaging $9,000 per year) were awarded; fellowships, career-related internships or fieldwork, Federal Work-Study, institutionally sponsored loans, scholarships/grants, traineeships, health care benefits, and unspecified assistantships also available. Support available to part-time students. Financial award application deadline: 4/1; financial award applicants required to submit FAFSA. In 2015, 795 master's, 100 doctorates, 1 other advanced degree awarded. *Degree program information:* Part-time and evening/weekend programs available. Part-time, evening/weekend, 100% online, blended/hybrid learning. *Application deadline:* For fall admission, 7/15 priority date for domestic students, 4/1 for international students; for spring admission, 12/1 priority date for domestic students, 8/1 for international students. Applications are processed on a rolling basis. *Application fee:* $50 ($65 for international students). Electronic applications accepted. *Application Contact:* Jordan Oleson, Admissions Coordinator, 316-978-3095, Fax: 316-978-3253, E-mail: jordan.oleson@wichita.edu. *Dean of the Graduate School/Associate Vice President of Research and Technology Transfer*, Dr. Dennis R. Livesay, 316-978-3095, Fax: 316-978-3253, E-mail: dennis.livesay@wichita.edu.

College of Education Degree program information: Part-time and evening/weekend programs available. Part-time, evening/weekend. Offers counseling (M Ed); education (M Ed, MAT, Ed D, Ed S); educational leadership (M Ed, Ed D); educational psychology (M Ed); exercise science (M Ed); learning and instructional design (M Ed); school psychology (Ed S); special education (M Ed); sport management (M Ed); teaching (MAT). *Application Contact:* Jordan Oleson, Admissions Coordinator, 316-978-3095, Fax: 316-978-3253, E-mail: jordan.oleson@wichita.edu. *Dean*, Dr. Shirley Lefever, 316-978-3301, Fax: 316-978-3302, E-mail: shirley.lefever-davis@wichita.edu.

College of Engineering Degree program information: Part-time and evening/weekend programs available. Part-time, evening/weekend. Offers aerospace engineering (MS, PhD); computer networking (MS); computer science (MS); electrical engineering (MS); electrical engineering and computer science (PhD); engineering (MEM, MS, PhD); engineering management (MEM); industrial engineering (MS, PhD); mechanical engineering (MS, PhD). *Application Contact:* Jordan Oleson, Admissions Coordinator, 316-978-3095, Fax: 316-978-3253, E-mail: jordan.oleson@wichita.edu. *Dean*, Dr. Royce O. Bowden, 316-978-3400, Fax: 316-978-3853, E-mail: royce.bowden@wichita.edu.

College of Fine Arts Degree program information: Part-time programs available. Part-time. Offers fine arts (MFA, MM, MME); music (MM); music education (MME); studio arts (MFA). *Application Contact:* Jordan Oleson, Admissions Coordinator, 316-978-3095, Fax: 316-978-3253, E-mail: jordan.oleson@wichita.edu. *Dean*, Dr. Rodney E. Miller, 316-978-3389, Fax: 316-978-3951, E-mail: rodney.miller@wichita.edu.

College of Health Professions Degree program information: Part-time programs available. Part-time. Offers aging studies (MA); communication sciences and disorders (MA, Au D, PhD); health professions (MA, MPA, MSN, Au D, DNP, DPT, PhD); nursing (MSN); nursing practice (DNP); physical therapy (DPT); physician assistant (MPA). *Application Contact:* Jordan Oleson, Admissions Coordinator, 316-978-3095, Fax: 316-978-3253, E-mail: jordan.oleson@wichita.edu. *Dean*, Dr. Sandra C. Bibb, 316-978-3600, Fax: 316-978-3025, E-mail: sandra.bibb@wichita.edu.

Fairmount College of Liberal Arts and Sciences Degree program information: Part-time and evening/weekend programs available. Part-time, evening/weekend. Offers anthropology (MA); applied mathematics (PhD); biological sciences (MS); chemistry (MS, PhD); clinical (PhD); communication (MA); community (PhD); creative writing (MFA); criminal justice (MA); earth, environmental, and physical sciences (MS); English (MA); history (MA); human factors (PhD); liberal arts and sciences (MA, MFA, MPA, MS, MSW, PhD); liberal studies (MA); mathematics (MS); physics (MS); public administration (MPA); social work (MSW); sociology (MA); Spanish (MA). *Application Contact:* Jordan Oleson, Admissions Coordinator, 316-978-3095, Fax: 316-978-3253, E-mail: jordan.oleson@wichita.edu. *Dean*, Dr. Ronald Matson, 316-978-3100, Fax: 316-978-3234, E-mail: ron.matson@wichita.edu.

Institute for Interdisciplinary Creativity Offers innovation design (MID). *Application Contact:* Jordan Oleson, Admissions Coordinator, 316-978-3095, Fax: 316-978-3253, E-mail: jordan.oleson@wichita.edu. *Interim Coordinator*, Dr. Richard Muma, 316-978-3010, E-mail: richard.muma@wichita.edu.

W. Frank Barton School of Business Degree program information: Part-time and evening/weekend programs available. Part-time, evening/weekend. Offers accounting information systems (M Acc); business (EMBA, M Acc, MA, MBA); economic analysis (MA); financial economics (MA); international economics (MA); taxation (M Acc). *Application Contact:* Jordan Oleson, Admissions Coordinator, 316-978-3095, Fax: 316-978-3253, E-mail: jordan.oleson@wichita.edu. *Dean*, Dr. Anand Desai, 316-978-3200, Fax: 316-978-3845, E-mail: anand.desai@wichita.edu.

WIDENER UNIVERSITY, Chester, PA 19013-5792

General Information Independent, coed, comprehensive institution. CGS member. *Enrollment:* 6,218 graduate, professional, and undergraduate students; 1,428 full-time matriculated graduate/professional students (885 women), 1,165 part-time matriculated graduate/professional students (892 women). *Enrollment by degree level:* 1,203 master's, 1,362 doctoral, 28 other advanced degrees. *Graduate faculty:* 167 full-time (97 women), 177 part-time/adjunct (92 women). Tuition and fees vary according to degree level and program. *Graduate housing:* Rooms and/or apartments available on a first-come, first-served basis to single students and available to married students. Housing application deadline: 5/30. *Student services:* Campus employment opportunities, career counseling, child daycare facilities, exercise/wellness program, free psychological counseling, international student services, multicultural affairs office, services for students with disabilities, teacher training, writing training. *Library:* Wolfgram Memorial Library. *Research affiliation:* Small Business Administration, Riverfront Development Corporation (engineering, management), Advanced Technology Center (engineering).

Computer facilities: 710 computers available on campus for general student use. A campuswide network can be accessed from student residence rooms and from off campus. Online class registration is available.
Website: http://www.widener.edu/

General Application Contact: Dr. Roberta Nolan, Assistant to Associate Provost for Graduate Studies, 610-499-4125, Fax: 610-499-4676, E-mail: gradmc@mail.widener.edu.

GRADUATE UNITS

College of Arts and Sciences Students: 2 full-time (0 women), 27 part-time (16 women); includes 13 minority (9 Black or African American, non-Hispanic/Latino; 2 Asian, non-Hispanic/Latino; 1 Hispanic/Latino; 1 Two or more races, non-Hispanic/Latino). Average age 31. 30 applicants, 50% accepted, 6 enrolled. *Faculty:* 9 full-time (2 women), 8 part-time/adjunct (1 woman). *Financial support:* Career-related internships or fieldwork and institutionally sponsored loans available. Support available to part-time students. Financial award application deadline: 4/1. In 2015, 13 master's awarded. *Degree program information:* Part-time and evening/weekend programs available. Part-time, evening/weekend. Offers arts and sciences (MA, MPA); criminal justice (MA); liberal studies (MA); public administration (MPA). *Application deadline:* Applications are processed on a rolling basis. *Application fee:* $25 ($300 for international students). *Application Contact:* Dr. Roberta Nolan, Assistant to Associate Provost for Graduate Studies, 610-499-4125, Fax: 610-499-4676, E-mail: gradmc@mail.widener.edu. *Dean*, Dr. Sharon Meaghar, 610-499-4007, E-mail: smmeagher@widener.edu.

Commonwealth Law School Students: 196 full-time (91 women), 8 part-time (5 women); includes 35 minority (15 Black or African American, non-Hispanic/Latino; 3 American Indian or Alaska Native, non-Hispanic/Latino; 5 Asian, non-Hispanic/Latino; 9 Hispanic/Latino; 3 Two or more races, non-Hispanic/Latino). Average age 25. 506 applicants, 67% accepted, 66 enrolled. *Faculty:* 17 full-time (8 women), 18 part-time/adjunct (6 women). *Financial support:* Fellowships, research assistantships, career-related internships or fieldwork, Federal Work-Study, institutionally sponsored loans, and scholarships/grants available. Support available to part-time students. Financial award application deadline: 2/15; financial award applicants required to submit FAFSA. *Degree program information:* Part-time programs available. Part-time. Offers law (JD). *Application deadline:* For fall admission, 5/15 for domestic students. Applications are processed on a rolling basis. *Application fee:* $60. Electronic applications accepted. *Application Contact:* John Benfield, Associate Dean for Admissions and Administration, 302-477-2210, Fax: 302-477-2224, E-mail: jsbenfield@widener.edu. *Dean*, Christian Johnson, 302-477-2100, Fax: 302-477-2282, E-mail: cajohnson2@widener.edu.

Delaware Law School Students: 521 full-time (269 women), 40 part-time (24 women); includes 150 minority (86 Black or African American, non-Hispanic/Latino; 11 American Indian or Alaska Native, non-Hispanic/Latino; 15 Asian, non-Hispanic/Latino; 33 Hispanic/Latino; 5 Two or more races, non-Hispanic/Latino), 15 international. Average age 26. 735 applicants, 80% accepted, 126 enrolled. *Faculty:* 37 full-time (21 women), 42 part-time/adjunct (15 women). *Financial support:* Career-related internships or fieldwork, Federal Work-Study, institutionally sponsored loans, and scholarships/grants available. Support available to part-time students. Financial award application deadline: 2/15; financial award applicants required to submit FAFSA. *Degree program information:* Part-time programs available. Part-time, 100% online. Offers corporate law and finance (LL M); health law (LL M, MJ, D Law); juridical science (SJD); law (JD). *Application deadline:* For fall admission, 5/15 for domestic students; for spring admission, 12/1 for domestic students. Applications are processed on a rolling basis. *Application fee:* $60. *Application Contact:* Barbara L. Ayars, Assistant Dean of Admissions, 302-477-2210, Fax: 302-477-2224, E-mail: barbara.l.ayars@law.widener.edu. *Dean*, Rod Smolla, 302-477-2100, Fax: 302-477-2282, E-mail: rasmolla@widener.edu.

Graduate Programs in Engineering Students: 15 full-time (2 women), 16 part-time (2 women); includes 3 minority (2 Asian, non-Hispanic/Latino; 1 Hispanic/Latino), 10 international. Average age 29. 75 applicants, 19% accepted, 8 enrolled. *Faculty:* 18 full-time (2 women), 7 part-time/adjunct (0 women). *Financial support:* In 2015–16, 5 teaching assistantships with partial tuition reimbursements (averaging $8,000 per year) were awarded; research assistantships and unspecified assistantships also available. Financial award application deadline: 3/15. In 2015, 12 master's awarded. *Degree program information:* Part-time and evening/weekend programs available. Part-time, evening/weekend. Offers biomedical engineering (M Eng); chemical engineering (M Eng); civil engineering (M Eng); electrical engineering (M Eng); engineering (M Eng); engineering management (M Eng); mechanical engineering (M Eng). *Application deadline:* For fall admission, 8/1 priority date for domestic students, 4/1 priority date for international students; for winter admission, 2/1 priority date for international students; for spring admission, 12/1 priority date for domestic students, 9/1 priority date for international students. Applications are processed on a rolling basis. *Application fee:* $0. Electronic applications accepted. *Assistant Dean/Director of Graduate Programs*, Rudolph Treichel, 610-499-1294, Fax: 610-499-4059, E-mail: rjtreichel@widener.edu.

School of Business Administration Students: 48 full-time (18 women), 124 part-time (59 women); includes 34 minority (24 Black or African American, non-Hispanic/Latino; 5 Asian, non-Hispanic/Latino; 5 Hispanic/Latino), 38 international. Average age 34. 154 applicants, 49% accepted, 43 enrolled. *Faculty:* 14 full-time (6 women), 6 part-time/adjunct (2 women). *Financial support:* In 2015–16, 11 research assistantships with full tuition reimbursements were awarded; career-related internships or fieldwork, Federal Work-Study, and traineeships also available. Support available to part-time students. Financial award application deadline: 5/1. In 2015, 45 master's awarded. *Degree program information:* Part-time and evening/weekend programs available. Part-time, evening/weekend, 100% online, blended/hybrid learning. Offers business administration (MBA, MHA, MS); health and medical services administration (MBA, MHA); taxation (MS). *Application deadline:* For fall admission, 8/1 priority date for domestic students; for spring admission, 12/1 for domestic students. Applications are processed on a rolling basis. *Application fee:* $25 ($300 for international students). Electronic applications accepted. *Application Contact:* Ann Seltzer, Graduate Enrollment Administrator, 610-499-4305, E-mail: apseltzer@widener.edu. *Interim Dean*, Dr. Catherine Morgan, 610-499-4300, Fax: 610-499-4615.

School of Human Service Professions Students: 530 full-time (412 women), 563 part-time (495 women); includes 397 minority (276 Black or African American, non-Hispanic/Latino; 6 American Indian or Alaska Native, non-Hispanic/Latino; 29 Asian, non-Hispanic/Latino; 65 Hispanic/Latino; 1 Native Hawaiian or other Pacific Islander, non-Hispanic/Latino; 20 Two or more races, non-Hispanic/Latino), 13 international. Average age 34. 1,251 applicants, 34% accepted, 271 enrolled. *Faculty:* 64 full-time (39 women), 70 part-time/adjunct (34 women). *Financial support:* Fellowships, research assistantships, teaching assistantships, career-related internships or fieldwork, Federal Work-Study, institutionally sponsored loans, tuition waivers (partial), unspecified assistantships, and stipends available. Support available to part-time students. Financial award applicants required to submit FAFSA. In 2015, 232 master's, 96 doctorates awarded. *Degree program information:* Part-time and evening/weekend programs available. Part-time, evening/weekend, 100% online, blended/hybrid learning. Offers human service professions (M Ed, MS, MSW, DPT, Ed D, PhD, Psy D). *Application Contact:* 610-499-4372, E-mail: gradmc@mail.widener.edu. *Dean*, Dr. Paula T. Silver, 610-499-4351, Fax: 610-499-4277, E-mail: ptsilver@widener.edu.

Center for Social Work Education Students: 75 full-time (62 women), 453 part-time (402 women); includes 268 minority (216 Black or African American, non-Hispanic/Latino; 2 American Indian or Alaska Native, non-Hispanic/Latino; 8 Asian, non-Hispanic/Latino; 32 Hispanic/Latino; 10 Two or more races, non-Hispanic/Latino), 1 international. Average age 33. 307 applicants, 60% accepted, 156 enrolled. *Faculty:* 15 full-time (9 women), 16 part-time/adjunct (9 women). *Financial support:* In 2015–16, 11 students received support, including 6 fellowships; career-related internships or fieldwork, Federal Work-Study, institutionally sponsored loans, and unspecified assistantships also available. Support available to part-time students. Financial award applicants required to submit FAFSA. In 2015, 138 master's, 7 doctorates awarded. *Degree program information:* Part-time programs available. Part-time, 100% online, blended/hybrid learning. Offers social work education (MSW, PhD). *Application deadline:* For fall admission, 3/1 for domestic students. Applications are processed on a rolling basis. *Application fee:* $25 ($300 for international students). Electronic applications accepted. *Application Contact:* Jill L. Brinker, Secretary, 610-499-1513, Fax: 610-499-4617, E-mail: socialwork@widener.edu. *Associate Dean and Director*, Dr. Paula T. Silver, 610-499-1150, Fax: 610-499-4617, E-mail: socialwork@widener.edu.

Institute for Graduate Clinical Psychology Offers clinical psychology (Psy D). Electronic applications accepted.

Institute for Physical Therapy Education Offers physical therapy education (MS, DPT).

School of Education, Hospitality, and Continuing Studies Students: 64 full-time (44 women), 209 part-time (146 women); includes 49 minority (39 Black or African American, non-Hispanic/Latino; 1 American Indian or Alaska Native, non-Hispanic/Latino; 4 Asian, non-Hispanic/Latino; 4 Hispanic/Latino; 1 Two or more races, non-Hispanic/Latino), 8 international. Average age 39. 139 applicants, 88% accepted. *Faculty:* 34 full-time (22 women), 37 part-time/adjunct (14 women). *Financial support:* Career-related internships or fieldwork, tuition waivers (full and partial), and unspecified assistantships available. Support available to part-time students. Financial award application deadline: 5/1. In 2015, 45 master's, 21 doctorates awarded. *Degree program information:* Part-time and evening/weekend programs available. Part-time, evening/weekend. Offers adult education (M Ed); counseling in higher education (M Ed); counselor education (M Ed); early childhood education (M Ed); educational foundations (M Ed); educational leadership (M Ed); educational psychology (M Ed); elementary education (M Ed); English and language arts (M Ed); health education (M Ed); higher education leadership (Ed D); home and school visitor (M Ed); human sexuality (M Ed, PhD); mathematics education (M Ed); middle school education (M Ed); principalship (M Ed); reading and language arts (Ed D); reading education (M Ed); school administration (Ed D); science education (M Ed); social studies education (M Ed); special education (M Ed); technology education (M Ed). *Application deadline:* Applications are processed on a rolling basis. *Application fee:* $25 ($300 for international students). Electronic applications accepted. *Application Contact:* Dr. Roberta Nolan, Director of Graduate Admissions, 610-499-4125, E-mail: rdnolan@widener.edu. *Dean*, Dr. Shawn Fitzgerald, 610-499-4294, Fax: 610-499-4623, E-mail: smfitzgerald@widener.edu.

School of Nursing Students: 43 full-time (42 women), 157 part-time (141 women); includes 65 minority (46 Black or African American, non-Hispanic/Latino; 13 Asian, non-Hispanic/Latino; 3 Hispanic/Latino; 3 Two or more races, non-Hispanic/Latino), 6 international. Average age 33. 64 applicants, 47% accepted, 25 enrolled. *Faculty:* 12 full-time (all women), 4 part-time/adjunct (3 women). *Financial support:* Career-related internships or fieldwork, Federal Work-Study, and traineeships available. Support available to part-time students. Financial award application deadline: 4/1. In 2015, 64 master's, 12 doctorates awarded. *Degree program information:* Part-time and evening/weekend programs available. Part-time, evening/weekend. Offers nursing (MSN, DN Sc, PhD, PMC). *Application deadline:* For fall admission, 7/1 for domestic students; for winter admission, 3/1 for domestic students; for spring admission, 11/1 for domestic students. Applications are processed on a rolling basis. *Application fee:* $25 ($300 for international students). Electronic applications accepted. *Dean*, Dr. Laura Dzurec, 610-499-4214, E-mail: lcdzurec@widener.edu.

WILBERFORCE UNIVERSITY, Wilberforce, OH 45384

General Information Independent-religious, coed, comprehensive institution.

GRADUATE UNITS

Program in Rehabilitation Counseling Offers rehabilitation counseling (MS).

WILFRID LAURIER UNIVERSITY, Waterloo, ON N2L 3C5, Canada

General Information Province-supported, coed, comprehensive institution.

GRADUATE UNITS

Faculty of Graduate and Postdoctoral Studies *Degree program information:* Part-time and evening/weekend programs available. Part-time, evening/weekend. Electronic applications accepted.

Faculty of Arts Degree program information: Part-time programs available. Part-time. Offers agency (MA); arts (M Sc, MA, MES, MIPP, PhD); body politics (MA); Canadian political studies (MA); community (MA); comparative politics/international relations (MA); cultural representation and social theory (MA); English (MA); English and film (PhD); environmental and resource management (MA, MES, PhD); environmental science (M Sc, MES, PhD); gender, sexuality and embodiment (MA); geomatics (M Sc, MES, PhD); globalization, identity and social movements (MA); health, family and well-being (MA); history (MA, PhD); human geography (MES, PhD); internationalization, migration and human rights (MA); media, technology and culture (MA); religion and culture (MA); religious diversity of North America (PhD); self (MA); visual communication and culture (MA). Electronic applications accepted.

Faculty of Music Offers music (MMT). Electronic applications accepted.

Faculty of Science Offers behavioral neuroscience (M Sc, PhD); chemistry (M Sc); cognitive neuroscience (M Sc, PhD); community psychology (MA, PhD); integrative biology (M Sc); mathematics for science and finance (M Sc); physical activity and health (M Sc); science (M Sc, MA, PhD); social and developmental psychology (MA, PhD). Electronic applications accepted.

Lyle S. Hallman Faculty of Social Work Degree program information: Part-time programs available. Part-time. Offers Aboriginal studies (MSW); community, policy, planning and organizations (MSW); critical social policy and organizational studies (PhD); individuals, families and groups (MSW); social work practice (individuals, families, groups and communities) (PhD); social work practice: individuals, families, groups and communities (PhD). Electronic applications accepted.

School of Business and Economics Degree program information: Part-time and evening/weekend programs available. Part-time, evening/weekend. Offers accounting (PhD); business and economics (EMTM, M Fin, M Sc, MA, MBA, PhD); co-op (MBA); economics (MA); finance (M Fin); financial economics (PhD); full-time (MBA); marketing (PhD); operations and supply chain management (PhD); organizational behavior and human resource management (M Sc); organizational behaviour and human resource management (PhD); part-time (MBA); supply chain management (M Sc); technology management (EMTM). Electronic applications accepted.

School of International Policy and Governance Offers conflict and security (PhD); global environment (PhD); global governance (MIPP); global justice and human rights (PhD); global political economy (PhD); global social governance (PhD); human security (MIPP); international economic relations (MIPP); international environmental policy (MIPP); international policy and governance (MIPP, PhD); multilateral institutions and diplomacy (PhD).

Laurier Brantford Offers criminology (MA). Electronic applications accepted.

Waterloo Lutheran Seminary *Degree program information:* Part-time programs available. Part-time. Offers divinity (M Div); multifaith spiritual care and counseling (Diploma); pastoral leadership (D Min); spiritual care and counseling (D Min); theology (M Th, MTS). Electronic applications accepted.

WILKES UNIVERSITY, Wilkes-Barre, PA 18766-0002

General Information Independent, coed, comprehensive institution. *Enrollment:* 5,053 graduate, professional, and undergraduate students; 482 full-time matriculated graduate/professional students (278 women), 2,150 part-time matriculated graduate/professional students (1,651 women). *Enrollment by degree level:* 2,178 master's, 454 doctoral. *Graduate housing:* On-campus housing not available. *Student services:* Campus employment opportunities, career counseling, free psychological counseling, international student services, low-cost health insurance, multicultural affairs office, services for students with disabilities. *Library:* Eugene S. Farley Library. Students can reserve study rooms.

Computer facilities: Computer purchase and lease plans are available. 809 computers available on campus for general student use. A campuswide network can be accessed from student residence rooms and from off campus. Online class registration is available.

Website: http://www.wilkes.edu/

General Application Contact: Joanne Thomas, Director of Graduate Education, 570-408-4234, Fax: 570-408-7846, E-mail: joanne.thomas1@wilkes.edu.

GRADUATE UNITS

College of Graduate and Professional Studies Students: 482 full-time (278 women), 2,150 part-time (1,651 women); includes 266 minority (108 Black or African American, non-Hispanic/Latino; 3 American Indian or Alaska Native, non-Hispanic/Latino; 35 Asian, non-Hispanic/Latino; 67 Hispanic/Latino; 6 Native Hawaiian or other Pacific Islander, non-Hispanic/Latino; 47 Two or more races, non-Hispanic/Latino), 39 international. Average age 34. *Financial support:* Unspecified assistantships available. Financial award application deadline: 3/1; financial award applicants required to submit FAFSA. In 2015, 802 master's, 103 doctorates awarded. *Degree program information:* Part-time and evening/weekend programs available. Part-time, evening/weekend, 100% online, blended/hybrid learning. Offers creative writing (MA, MFA). *Application deadline:* Applications are processed on a rolling basis. *Application fee:* $45 ($65 for international students). Electronic applications accepted. *Application Contact:* Joanne Thomas, Director of Graduate Enrollment, 570-408-4234, Fax: 570-408-7846, E-mail: joanne.thomas1@wilkes.edu.

College of Science and Engineering Students: 41 full-time (9 women), 20 part-time (4 women); includes 7 minority (1 Black or African American, non-Hispanic/Latino; 2 Asian, non-Hispanic/Latino; 3 Hispanic/Latino; 1 Two or more races, non-Hispanic/Latino), 20 international. Average age 28. *Financial support:* Unspecified assistantships available. Financial award application deadline: 3/1; financial award applicants required to submit FAFSA. In 2015, 25 master's awarded. *Degree program information:* Part-time programs available. Part-time. Offers bioengineering (MS); electrical engineering (MSEE); engineering management (MS); mathematics (MS); mechanical engineering (MS); science and engineering (MS, MSEE). *Application deadline:* Applications are processed on a rolling basis. *Application fee:* $45 ($65 for international students). Electronic applications accepted. *Application Contact:* Joanne Thomas, Director of Graduate Enrollment, 570-408-4234, Fax: 570-408-7846, E-mail: joanne.thomas1@wilkes.edu. *Dean*, Dr. William Hudson, 570-408-4600, Fax: 570-408-7860, E-mail: william.hudson@wilkes.edu.

Jay S. Sidhu School of Business and Leadership Students: 46 full-time (19 women), 122 part-time (59 women); includes 15 minority (5 Black or African American, non-Hispanic/Latino; 2 Asian, non-Hispanic/Latino; 5 Hispanic/Latino; 3 Two or more races, non-Hispanic/Latino), 18 international. Average age 30. *Financial support:* Unspecified assistantships available. Financial award application deadline: 3/1; financial award applicants required to submit FAFSA. In 2015, 59 master's awarded. *Degree program information:* Part-time and evening/weekend programs available. Part-time, evening/weekend. Offers accounting (MBA); entrepreneurship (MBA); finance (MBA); health care administration (MBA); human resource management (MBA); international business (MBA); marketing (MBA); operations management (MBA); organizational leadership and development (MBA). *Application deadline:* Applications are processed on a rolling basis. *Application fee:* $45 ($65 for international students). Electronic applications accepted. *Application Contact:* Joanne Thomas, Director of Graduate Enrollment, 570-408-4234, Fax: 570-408-7846, E-mail: joanne.thomas1@wilkes.edu. *Interim Dean*, Dr. Jennifer Edmonds, 570-408-4725, Fax: 570-408-7846, E-mail: jennifer.edmonds@wilkes.edu.

Nesbitt School of Pharmacy Students: 284 full-time (179 women), 1 part-time (0 women); includes 25 minority (4 Black or African American, non-Hispanic/Latino; 7 Asian, non-Hispanic/Latino; 6 Hispanic/Latino; 8 Two or more races, non-Hispanic/Latino), 1 international. Average age 23. *Financial support:* Federal Work-Study and unspecified assistantships available. Financial award application deadline: 3/1; financial award applicants required to submit FAFSA. In 2015, 71 doctorates awarded. *Degree program information:* Part-time and evening/weekend programs available. Part-time, evening/weekend. Offers pharmacy (Pharm D). *Application deadline:* Applications are processed on a rolling basis. *Application Contact:* Joanne Thomas, Director of Graduate Enrollment, 570-408-4234, Fax: 570-408-7846, E-mail: joanne.thomas1@wilkes.edu. *Dean*, Dr. Bernard Graham, 570-408-4280, Fax: 570-408-7828, E-mail: bernard.graham@wilkes.edu.

Passan School of Nursing Students: 11 full-time (9 women), 545 part-time (494 women); includes 136 minority (81 Black or African American, non-Hispanic/Latino; 2 American Indian or Alaska Native, non-Hispanic/Latino; 13 Asian, non-Hispanic/Latino; 29 Hispanic/Latino; 5 Native Hawaiian or other Pacific Islander, non-Hispanic/Latino; 6 Two or more races, non-Hispanic/Latino). Average age 43.

Financial support: Unspecified assistantships available. Financial award application deadline: 3/1; financial award applicants required to submit FAFSA. In 2015, 16 master's, 21 doctorates awarded. *Degree program information:* Part-time and evening/weekend programs available. Part-time, evening/weekend, 100% online. Offers nursing (MSN, DNP). *Application deadline:* Applications are processed on a rolling basis. *Application fee:* $45. Electronic applications accepted. *Application Contact:* Joanne Thomas, Director of Graduate Enrollment, 570-408-4234, Fax: 570-408-7846, E-mail: joanne.thomas1@wilkes.edu. *Dean*, Dr. Deborah Zbegner, 570-408-4086, Fax: 570-408-7807, E-mail: deborah.zbegner@wilkes.edu.

School of Education Students: 49 full-time (36 women), 1,370 part-time (1,021 women); includes 70 minority (12 Black or African American, non-Hispanic/Latino; 1 American Indian or Alaska Native, non-Hispanic/Latino; 11 Asian, non-Hispanic/Latino; 21 Hispanic/Latino; 1 Native Hawaiian or other Pacific Islander, non-Hispanic/Latino; 24 Two or more races, non-Hispanic/Latino). Average age 33. *Financial support:* Unspecified assistantships available. Financial award application deadline: 3/1; financial award applicants required to submit FAFSA. In 2015, 652 master's, 11 doctorates awarded. *Degree program information:* Part-time and evening/weekend programs available. Part-time, evening/weekend, 100% online, blended/hybrid learning. Offers art and science of teaching (MS Ed); classroom technology (MS Ed); early childhood literacy (MS Ed); educational development and strategies (MS Ed); educational leadership (MS Ed); educational technology (Ed D); higher education administration (Ed D); instructional media (MS Ed); instructional technology (MS Ed); international school leadership (MS Ed); K-12 administration (Ed D); middle level education (MS Ed); online teaching (MS Ed); reading (MS Ed); school business leadership (MS Ed); secondary education (MS Ed); special education (MS Ed); teaching English as a second language (MS Ed); twenty-first century teaching and learning (MS Ed). *Application deadline:* Applications are processed on a rolling basis. *Application fee:* $45. Electronic applications accepted. *Application Contact:* Joanne Thomas, Director of Graduate Enrollment, 570-408-4234, Fax: 570-408-7846, E-mail: joanne.thomas1@wilkes.edu. *Dean*, Dr. Rhonda Rabbitt, 570-408-4680, Fax: 570-408-7872, E-mail: rhonda.rabbitt@wilkes.edu.

WILLAMETTE UNIVERSITY, Salem, OR 97301-3931

General Information Independent-religious, coed, comprehensive institution. *Graduate housing:* Room and/or apartments available on a first-come, first-served basis to single students; on-campus housing not available to married students. Housing application deadline: 6/1.

GRADUATE UNITS

Atkinson Graduate School of Management Students: 189 full-time (83 women), 114 part-time (57 women); includes 47 minority (7 Black or African American, non-Hispanic/Latino; 3 American Indian or Alaska Native, non-Hispanic/Latino; 18 Asian, non-Hispanic/Latino; 15 Hispanic/Latino; 3 Native Hawaiian or other Pacific Islander, non-Hispanic/Latino; 1 Two or more races, non-Hispanic/Latino), 82 international. Average age 29. 336 applicants, 76% accepted, 147 enrolled. *Faculty:* 18 full-time (3 women), 19 part-time/adjunct (8 women). *Financial support:* In 2015–16, 209 students received support. Career-related internships or fieldwork, Federal Work-Study, scholarships/grants, and unspecified assistantships available. Financial award application deadline: 5/1; financial award applicants required to submit FAFSA. In 2015, 114 master's awarded. *Degree program information:* Part-time and evening/weekend programs available. Part-time, evening/weekend. Offers management (MBA). *Application deadline:* 5/1 priority date for domestic and international students. Applications are processed on a rolling basis. *Application fee:* $100. Electronic applications accepted. *Application Contact:* Aimee Akimoff, Director of Recruitment, 503-370-6167, Fax: 503-370-3011, E-mail: aakimoff@willamette.edu. *Dean and Professor of Free Enterprise*, Dr. Debra J. Ringold, 503-370-6790, Fax: 503-370-3011, E-mail: dringold@willamette.edu.

College of Law ***Degree program information:*** Part-time programs available. Part-time. Offers dispute resolution (LL M); law (MLS, JD); transnational law (LL M). Electronic applications accepted.

WILLIAM CAREY UNIVERSITY, Hattiesburg, MS 39401-5499

General Information Independent-religious, coed, comprehensive institution. *Graduate housing:* Room and/or apartments available on a first-come, first-served basis to single students; on-campus housing not available to married students. Housing application deadline: 8/15.

GRADUATE UNITS

School of Business ***Degree program information:*** Part-time programs available. Part-time. Offers business (MBA).

School of Education ***Degree program information:*** Part-time programs available. Part-time. Offers art education (M Ed); art of teaching (M Ed); elementary education (M Ed, Ed S); English education (M Ed); gifted education (M Ed); history and social science (M Ed); mild/moderate disabilities (M Ed); secondary education (M Ed).

School of Nursing ***Degree program information:*** Part-time programs available. Part-time. Offers nursing (MSN).

School of Psychology and Counseling ***Degree program information:*** Part-time programs available. Part-time. Offers counseling psychology (MS).

WILLIAM JAMES COLLEGE, Newton, MA 02459

General Information Independent, coed, primarily women, graduate-only institution. *Graduate housing:* On-campus housing not available.

GRADUATE UNITS

Graduate Programs Offers applied psychology in higher education student personnel administration (MA); clinical psychology (Psy D); counseling psychology (MA); counseling psychology and community mental health (MA); counseling psychology and global mental health (MA); executive coaching (Graduate Certificate); forensic and counseling psychology (MA); leadership psychology (Psy D); organizational psychology (MA); primary care psychology (MA); respecialization in clinical psychology (Certificate); school psychology (Psy D). Electronic applications accepted.

WILLIAM JESSUP UNIVERSITY, Rocklin, CA 95765

General Information Independent-religious, coed, comprehensive institution.

GRADUATE UNITS

Program in Teaching ***Degree program information:*** Evening/weekend programs available. Evening/weekend. Offers single subject English (MAT); single subject math (MAT).

WILLIAM JEWELL COLLEGE, Liberty, MO 64068-1843

General Information Independent, coed, comprehensive institution.

GRADUATE UNITS

Department of Education Offers differentiated instruction (MS Ed).

WILLIAM PATERSON UNIVERSITY OF NEW JERSEY, Wayne, NJ 07470-8420

General Information State-supported, coed, comprehensive institution. CGS member. *Enrollment:* 10,862 graduate, professional, and undergraduate students; 296 full-time matriculated graduate/professional students (185 women), 1,037 part-time matriculated graduate/professional students (809 women). *Enrollment by degree level:* 923 master's, 24 doctoral, 386 other advanced degrees. *Graduate faculty:* 130 full-time (58 women), 67 part-time/adjunct (25 women). Tuition, state resident: full-time $11,544; part-time $577.21 per credit. Tuition, nonresident: full-time $19,024; part-time $951.21 per credit. *Required fees:* $1916; $95.79 per credit. $62.50 per semester. Tuition and fees vary according to course load and degree level. *Graduate housing:* Room and/or apartments available on a first-come, first-served basis to single students; on-campus housing not available to married students. Typical cost: $8834 per year. Room charges vary according to board plan and housing facility selected. Housing application deadline: 5/1. *Student services:* Campus employment opportunities, campus safety program, career counseling, exercise/wellness program, free psychological counseling, international student services, multicultural affairs office, services for students with disabilities, teacher training, writing training. *Library:* David and Lorraine Cheng Library. *Collection:* Books: 369,216 (physical), 116,597 (digital/electronic); Serial titles: 3,772 (physical), 164,249 (digital/electronic); Databases: 126. Weekly public service hours: 102; students can reserve study rooms. *Research affiliation:* Sun Chemical (chemistry), Arysta Life Sciences (biology).

Computer facilities: Computer purchase and lease plans are available. 1,271 computers available on campus for general student use. A campuswide network can be accessed from student residence rooms and from off campus. Online class registration is available.
Website: http://www.wpunj.edu/

General Application Contact: Augustus Kubeyinje, Director of Graduate Admissions and Enrollment Services, 973-720-3641, Fax: 973-720-2035, E-mail: kubeyinjea@wpunj.edu.

GRADUATE UNITS

College of Education Students: 94 full-time (67 women), 591 part-time (480 women); includes 195 minority (53 Black or African American, non-Hispanic/Latino; 23 Asian, non-Hispanic/Latino; 109 Hispanic/Latino; 10 Two or more races, non-Hispanic/Latino), 2 international. Average age 36. 416 applicants, 80% accepted, 265 enrolled. *Faculty:* 36 full-time (9 women), 36 part-time/adjunct (10 women). *Financial support:* Research assistantships with full tuition reimbursements, career-related internships or fieldwork, Federal Work-Study, scholarships/grants, and unspecified assistantships available. Support available to part-time students. Financial award application deadline: 4/1; financial award applicants required to submit FAFSA. In 2015, 126 master's awarded. *Degree program information:* Part-time and evening/weekend programs available. Part-time, evening/weekend, 100% online. Offers curriculum and learning (M Ed); educational leadership (M Ed); elementary education (MAT); literacy (M Ed); professional counseling (M Ed); secondary education (MAT); special education (M Ed). *Application deadline:* For fall admission, 6/1 for domestic students, 3/1 for international students; for spring admission, 11/1 for domestic students, 10/1 for international students. Applications are processed on a rolling basis. *Application fee:* $50. Electronic applications accepted. *Application Contact:* Liana Fornarotto, Director of Education Enrollment and Certification, 973-720-2206, Fax: 973-720-2989, E-mail: fornarottol@wpunj.edu. *Dean*, Dr. Candace Burns, 973-720-2137, Fax: 973-720-3467, E-mail: burnsc@wpunj.edu.

College of Humanities and Social Sciences Students: 50 full-time (28 women), 108 part-time (78 women); includes 53 minority (8 Black or African American, non-Hispanic/Latino; 6 Asian, non-Hispanic/Latino; 36 Hispanic/Latino; 3 Two or more races, non-Hispanic/Latino), 1 international. Average age 33. 142 applicants, 63% accepted, 61 enrolled. *Faculty:* 35 full-time (12 women), 4 part-time/adjunct (2 women). *Financial support:* Research assistantships with full tuition reimbursements, Federal Work-Study, scholarships/grants, and unspecified assistantships available. Support available to part-time students. Financial award application deadline: 4/1; financial award applicants required to submit FAFSA. In 2015, 23 master's awarded. *Degree program information:* Part-time and evening/weekend programs available. Part-time, evening/weekend. Offers applied sociology (MA); clinical and counseling psychology (MA); clinical psychology (Psy D); creative and professional writing (MFA); English (MA); history (MA); public policy and international affairs (MA). *Application deadline:* For fall admission, 6/1 for domestic students, 3/1 for international students; for spring admission, 11/1 for domestic students, 10/1 for international students. Applications are processed on a rolling basis. *Application fee:* $50. Electronic applications accepted. *Application Contact:* Tinu Adeniran, Associate Director, Graduate Admissions, 973-720-2764, Fax: 973-720-2035, E-mail: adenirant@wpunj.edu. *Dean*, Dr. Kara Rabbitt, 973-720-2180, Fax: 973-720-2955, E-mail: rabbittk@wpunj.edu.

College of Science and Health Students: 73 full-time (58 women), 208 part-time (183 women); includes 111 minority (18 Black or African American, non-Hispanic/Latino; 40 Asian, non-Hispanic/Latino; 50 Hispanic/Latino; 3 Two or more races, non-Hispanic/Latino), 5 international. Average age 34. 495 applicants, 27% accepted, 74 enrolled. *Faculty:* 25 full-time (11 women), 13 part-time/adjunct (4 women). *Financial support:* Research assistantships with full tuition reimbursements, career-related internships or fieldwork, Federal Work-Study, scholarships/grants, and unspecified assistantships available. Support available to part-time students. Financial award application deadline: 4/1; financial award applicants required to submit FAFSA. In 2015, 63 master's, 10 doctorates awarded. *Degree program information:* Part-time and evening/weekend programs available. Part-time, evening/weekend. Offers biology (MS); biotechnology (MS); communication disorders (MS); exercise and sports studies (MS); nursing (MSN); nursing practice (DNP). *Application deadline:* For fall admission, 6/1 for domestic students, 3/1 for international students; for spring admission, 11/1 for domestic students, 10/1 for international students. Applications are processed on a rolling basis. *Application fee:* $50. Electronic applications accepted. *Application Contact:* Christina Aiello, Assistant Director, Graduate Admissions, 973-720-2506, Fax: 973-720-2035, E-mail: aielloc@wpunj.edu. *Dean*, Dr. Kenneth Wolf, 973-720-2194, Fax: 973-720-3414, E-mail: wolfk@wpunj.edu.

College of the Arts and Communication Students: 33 full-time (10 women), 18 part-time (14 women); includes 15 minority (5 Black or African American, non-Hispanic/Latino; 3 Asian, non-Hispanic/Latino; 7 Hispanic/Latino), 3 international. Average age 32. 63 applicants, 56% accepted, 17 enrolled. *Faculty:* 19 full-time (13 women), 13 part-time/adjunct (8 women). *Financial support:* Research assistantships with full tuition reimbursements, career-related internships or fieldwork, Federal Work-Study, scholarships/grants, and unspecified assistantships available. Support available to part-time students. Financial award application deadline: 4/1; financial award applicants required to submit FAFSA. In 2015, 17 master's awarded. *Degree program information:* Part-time and evening/weekend programs available. Part-time, evening/weekend. Offers art (MFA); music (MM); professional communication (MA). *Application deadline:* For fall admission, 6/1 for domestic students, 3/1 for international students; for spring admission, 11/5 for domestic students, 10/15 for international students. Applications are processed on a rolling basis. *Application fee:* $50. Electronic applications accepted. *Application Contact:* Christina Aiello, Assistant Director, Graduate Admissions, 973-720-2506, Fax: 973-720-2035, E-mail: aielloc@wpunj.edu. *Dean*, Daryl Moore, 973-720-2232, E-mail: moored@wpunj.edu.

Cotsakos College of Business Students: 46 full-time (22 women), 112 part-time (54 women); includes 58 minority (18 Black or African American, non-Hispanic/Latino; 13 Asian, non-Hispanic/Latino; 23 Hispanic/Latino; 4 Two or more races, non-Hispanic/Latino), 11 international. Average age 32. 103 applicants, 79% accepted, 60 enrolled. *Faculty:* 15 full-time (13 women), 1 (woman) part-time/adjunct. *Financial support:* Research assistantships with full tuition reimbursements, Federal Work-Study, scholarships/grants, and unspecified assistantships available. Support available to part-time students. Financial award application deadline: 4/1; financial award applicants required to submit FAFSA. In 2015, 40 master's awarded. *Degree program information:* Part-time and evening/weekend programs available. Part-time, evening/weekend. Offers business administration (MBA). *Application deadline:* For fall admission, 6/1 for domestic students, 3/1 for international students; for spring admission, 11/1 for domestic students, 10/1 for international students. Applications are processed on a rolling basis. *Application fee:* $50. Electronic applications accepted. *Application Contact:* Tinu Adeniran, Assistant Director, Graduate Admissions, 973-720-2764, Fax: 973-720-2035, E-mail: adenirant@wpunj.edu. *Dean*, Dr. Siamack Shojai, 973-720-2964, Fax: 973-720-2809, E-mail: shojais@wpunj.edu.

WILLIAM PENN UNIVERSITY, Oskaloosa, IA 52577-1799

General Information Independent-religious, coed, comprehensive institution.

GRADUATE UNITS

College for Working Adults Online learning.

WILLIAMS COLLEGE, Williamstown, MA 01267

General Information Independent, coed, comprehensive institution. *Enrollment:* 2,153 graduate, professional, and undergraduate students; 23 full-time matriculated graduate/professional students (12 women). *Enrollment by degree level:* 23 master's. *Graduate faculty:* 24. *Tuition, area resident:* Full-time $49,780. *Graduate housing:* Room and/or apartments available on a first-come, first-served basis to single students; on-campus housing not available to married students. Typical cost: $6930 per year. *Student services:* Campus employment opportunities, campus safety program, career counseling, exercise/wellness program, free psychological counseling, international student services, low-cost health insurance, multicultural affairs office, services for students with disabilities, writing training. *Library:* Sawyer Library plus 2 others. *Collection:* Books: 970,281 (physical), 140,954 (digital/electronic); Serial titles: 12,900 (physical), 94,410 (digital/electronic); Databases: 1,435. Weekly public service hours: 118; study areas open 24 hours, 5–7 days a week; students can reserve study rooms. *Research affiliation:* Clark Art Institute.

Computer facilities: 252 computers available on campus for general student use. A campuswide network can be accessed from student residence rooms and from off campus. Online class registration is available.
Website: http://www.williams.edu/

General Application Contact: Karen E. Kowitz, Program Administrator, 413-458-0596, Fax: 413-458-2317, E-mail: karen.kowitz@williams.edu.

GRADUATE UNITS

Graduate Program in the History of Art Students: 23 full-time (12 women); includes 3 minority (1 Black or African American, non-Hispanic/Latino; 2 Hispanic/Latino). 94 applicants, 26% accepted, 12 enrolled. *Faculty:* 24. *Financial support:* In 2015–16, 16 students received support. Fellowships with tuition reimbursements available and tuition waivers (full and partial) available. Financial award application deadline: 4/1; financial award applicants required to submit FAFSA. In 2015, 12 master's awarded. Offers development economics (MA); history of art (MA). MA in history of art offered jointly with Sterling and Francine Clark Art Institute. *Application deadline:* For fall admission, 1/6 for domestic and international students. *Application fee:* $70. Electronic applications accepted. *Application Contact:* Karen E. Kowitz, Program Administrator, 413-458-0596, Fax: 413-458-2317, E-mail: karen.kowitz@williams.edu.

WILLIAMSON COLLEGE, Franklin, TN 37067

General Information Independent-religious, coed, comprehensive institution.

GRADUATE UNITS

Program in Organizational Leadership *Degree program information:* Evening/weekend programs available. Evening/weekend. Offers organizational leadership (MA).

WILLIAM WOODS UNIVERSITY, Fulton, MO 65251-1098

General Information Independent-religious, coed, comprehensive institution. *Graduate housing:* On-campus housing not available.

GRADUATE UNITS

Graduate and Adult Studies *Degree program information:* Part-time and evening/weekend programs available. Part-time, evening/weekend. Offers administration (M Ed, Ed S); athletic/activities administration (M Ed); curriculum and instruction (M Ed, Ed S); educational leadership (Ed D); equestrian education (M Ed); health management (MBA); human resources (MBA); leadership (MBA); marketing, advertising, and public relations (MBA); teaching and technology (M Ed). Electronic applications accepted.

WILMINGTON COLLEGE, Wilmington, OH 45177

General Information Independent-religious, coed, comprehensive institution. *Graduate housing:* On-campus housing not available.

GRADUATE UNITS

Department of Education *Degree program information:* Part-time programs available. Part-time. Offers reading (M Ed); special education (M Ed).

WILMINGTON UNIVERSITY, New Castle, DE 19720-6491

General Information Independent, coed, university. *Graduate housing:* On-campus housing not available.

GRADUATE UNITS

College of Business *Degree program information:* Part-time and evening/weekend programs available. Part-time, evening/weekend. Offers accounting (MBA, MS); business administration (MBA, DBA); environmental stewardship (MBA); finance (MBA); health care administration (MBA, MSM); homeland security (MBA, MSM); human resource management (MSM); management information systems (MBA, MSN); marketing (MSM); marketing management (MBA); military leadership (MSM); organizational leadership (MBA, MSM); public administration (MSM). Electronic applications accepted.

College of Education *Degree program information:* Part-time and evening/weekend programs available. Part-time, evening/weekend. Offers applied technology in education (M Ed); career and technical education (M Ed); educational leadership (Ed D); elementary and secondary school counseling (M Ed); elementary studies (M Ed); ESOL literacy (M Ed); higher education leadership (Ed D); instruction: gifted and talented (M Ed); instruction: teacher of reading (M Ed); instruction: teaching and learning (M Ed); organizational leadership (Ed D); school leadership (M Ed); secondary education (MAT); special education (M Ed). Electronic applications accepted.

College of Health Professions *Degree program information:* Part-time programs available. Part-time. Offers adult nurse practitioner (MSN); family nurse practitioner (MSN); gerontology nurse practitioner (MSN); nursing (MSN); nursing leadership (MSN); nursing practice (DNP). Electronic applications accepted.

College of Social and Behavioral Sciences *Degree program information:* Part-time and evening/weekend programs available. Part-time, evening/weekend. Offers administration of human services (MS); administration of justice (MS); clinical mental health counseling (MS); homeland security (MS). Electronic applications accepted.

College of Technology *Degree program information:* Part-time and evening/weekend programs available. Part-time, evening/weekend. Offers geographic information systems (MS); information assurance (MS); information systems technologies (MS); Internet/Web design (MS); management and management information systems (MS). Electronic applications accepted.

WILSON COLLEGE, Chambersburg, PA 17201-1285

General Information Independent-religious, coed, primarily women, comprehensive institution.

GRADUATE UNITS

Graduate Programs *Degree program information:* Evening/weekend programs available. Evening/weekend. Offers accounting (M Acc); choreography and visual art (MFA); education (M Ed); healthcare management for sustainability (MHM); humanities (MA); nursing (MSN). Electronic applications accepted.

WINEBRENNER THEOLOGICAL SEMINARY, Findlay, OH 45840

General Information Independent-religious, coed, graduate-only institution. *Enrollment by degree level:* 64 master's, 10 doctoral. *Graduate faculty:* 6 full-time (1 woman), 13 part-time/adjunct (4 women). *Tuition, area resident:* Full-time $13,230; part-time $490 per credit hour. *Required fees:* $426; $142 per trimester. $142 per trimester. Tuition and fees vary according to degree level. *Graduate housing:* On-campus housing not available. *Student services:* Campus safety program, career counseling, free psychological counseling, international student services, multicultural affairs office, services for students with disabilities. *Library:* Shafer Library plus 1 other. *Collection:* Books: 43,848 (physical), 29 (digital/electronic); Serial titles: 3 (physical), 4 (digital/electronic). Weekly public service hours: 94; study areas open 24 hours, 5–7 days a week.

Computer facilities: 224 computers available on campus for general student use. A campuswide network can be accessed from student residence rooms and from off campus. Online class registration is available.
Website: http://www.winebrenner.edu/

General Application Contact: Jim Smarkel, Director of Enrollment Management, 419-434-4220, Fax: 419-434-4267, E-mail: admissions@winebrenner.edu.

GRADUATE UNITS

Graduate Programs Students: 35 full-time (16 women), 39 part-time (23 women); includes 13 minority (9 Black or African American, non-Hispanic/Latino; 3 Asian, non-Hispanic/Latino; 1 Two or more races, non-Hispanic/Latino), 1 international. Average age 42. 37 applicants, 100% accepted, 25 enrolled. *Faculty:* 6 full-time (1 woman), 13 part-time/adjunct (4 women). *Financial support:* In 2015–16, 51 students received support, including 3 teaching assistantships with partial tuition reimbursements available (averaging $1,470 per year); research assistantships, institutionally sponsored loans, scholarships/grants, unspecified assistantships, and denominational discounts, spousal discounts also available. Financial award applicants required to submit FAFSA. In 2015, 16 master's, 4 doctorates awarded. *Degree program information:* Part-time programs available. Part-time, 100% online, blended/hybrid learning. Offers clinical counseling (MA); family ministry (MA); practical theology (MA); theological and ministerial studies (M Div, D Min); theological studies (MA). *Application deadline:* For fall admission, 8/15 priority date for domestic students, 7/15 priority date for international students; for winter admission, 12/15 priority date for domestic students, 11/15 priority date for international students; for spring admission, 4/15 priority date for domestic students, 3/15 priority date for international students. Applications are processed on a rolling basis. *Application fee:* $30. Electronic applications accepted. *Application Contact:* Jim Smarkel, Director of Enrollment Management, 419-434-4220, Fax: 419-434-4267, E-mail: admissions@winebrenner.edu. *Academic Dean*, Dr. Joel W. Cocklin, 419-434-4250, Fax: 419-434-4267, E-mail: jcocklin@winebrenner.edu.

WINGATE UNIVERSITY, Wingate, NC 28174

General Information Independent-religious, coed, comprehensive institution. *Graduate housing:* Rooms and/or apartments available on a first-come, first-served basis to single and married students. Housing application deadline: 8/15.

GRADUATE UNITS

Byrum School of Business *Degree program information:* Part-time and evening/weekend programs available. Part-time, evening/weekend. Offers business (MAC, MBA). Electronic applications accepted.

School of Pharmacy Offers pharmacy (Pharm D). Electronic applications accepted.

Thayer School of Education *Degree program information:* Part-time and evening/weekend programs available. Part-time, evening/weekend. Offers community college leadership (Ed D); educational leadership (MA Ed, Ed D); elementary education (MA Ed, MAT); health and physical education (MA Ed); sport administration (MA Ed).

WINONA STATE UNIVERSITY, Winona, MN 55987

General Information State-supported, coed, comprehensive institution. *Graduate housing:* Room and/or apartments available to single students; on-campus housing not available to married students. Housing application deadline: 3/2.

GRADUATE UNITS

College of Education *Degree program information:* Part-time and evening/weekend programs available. Part-time, evening/weekend. Offers community counseling (MS); education (MS, Ed S); educational leadership (Ed S); general school leadership (MS); K-12 principalship (MS); outdoor education/adventure-based leadership (MS); professional development (MS); school counseling (MS); special education (MS); sports management (MS); teacher leadership (MS).

College of Liberal Arts ***Degree program information:*** Part-time programs available. Part-time. Offers English (MA, MS); liberal arts (MA, MS).

College of Nursing and Health Sciences ***Degree program information:*** Part-time programs available. Part-time, online learning. Offers adult nurse practitioner (MS, Post Master's Certificate); clinical nurse specialist (MS, Post Master's Certificate); family nurse practitioner (MS, Post Master's Certificate); nurse administrator (MS); nurse educator (MS, Post Master's Certificate); nursing (DNP).

WINSTON-SALEM STATE UNIVERSITY, Winston-Salem, NC 27110-0003

General Information State-supported, coed, comprehensive institution. *Graduate housing:* On-campus housing not available.

GRADUATE UNITS

Department of Occupational Therapy Offers occupational therapy (MS). Electronic applications accepted.

Department of Physical Therapy Offers physical therapy (DPT). Electronic applications accepted.

MAT Program ***Degree program information:*** Part-time and evening/weekend programs available. Part-time, evening/weekend, online learning. Offers middle grades education (MAT); special education (MAT). Electronic applications accepted.

Program in Business Administration ***Degree program information:*** Part-time and evening/weekend programs available. Part-time, evening/weekend, online learning. Offers business administration (MBA). Electronic applications accepted.

Program in Computer Science and Information Technology ***Degree program information:*** Part-time programs available. Part-time. Offers computer science and information technology (MS). Electronic applications accepted.

Program in Health Administration Offers health administration (MHA).

Program in Nursing ***Degree program information:*** Part-time and evening/weekend programs available. Part-time, evening/weekend, online learning. Offers advanced nurse educator (MSN); family nurse practitioner (MSN); nursing (DNP). Electronic applications accepted.

Program in Rehabilitation Counseling ***Degree program information:*** Part-time programs available. Part-time, online learning. Offers rehabilitation counseling (MRC). Electronic applications accepted.

WINTHROP UNIVERSITY, Rock Hill, SC 29733

General Information State-supported, coed, comprehensive institution. CGS member. *Enrollment:* 6,031 graduate, professional, and undergraduate students; 466 full-time matriculated graduate/professional students (359 women), 492 part-time matriculated graduate/professional students (370 women). *Enrollment by degree level:* 756 master's, 202 other advanced degrees. *Graduate faculty:* 282 full-time (151 women), 273 part-time/adjunct (180 women). *Tuition, area resident:* Part-time $579 per credit hour. Tuition, state resident: full-time $13,828. Tuition, nonresident: full-time $26,638; part-time $1114 per credit hour. *Graduate housing:* Rooms and/or apartments available on a first-come, first-served basis to single and married students. Typical cost: $5140 per year ($8320 including board) for single students; $5140 per year ($8320 including board) for married students. Room and board charges vary according to board plan and housing facility selected. Housing application deadline: 3/1. *Student services:* Campus employment opportunities, campus safety program, career counseling, exercise/wellness program, free psychological counseling, international student services, low-cost health insurance, multicultural affairs office, services for students with disabilities. *Library:* Dacus Library plus 1 other. *Collection:* Books: 438,816 (physical), 15,746 (digital/electronic); Serial titles: 12,205 (physical), 15,873 (digital/electronic); Databases: 127. Weekly public service hours: 49; study areas open 24 hours, 5–7 days a week; students can reserve study rooms.

Computer facilities: Computer purchase and lease plans are available. 620 computers available on campus for general student use. A campuswide network can be accessed from student residence rooms and from off campus. Online class registration, the majority of university services are available online are available.
Website: http://www.winthrop.edu/

General Application Contact: The Graduate School, 800-411-7041, Fax: 803-323-2204, E-mail: gradschool@winthrop.edu.

GRADUATE UNITS

College of Arts and Sciences Students: 202 full-time (173 women), 132 part-time (101 women); includes 86 minority (70 Black or African American, non-Hispanic/Latino; 1 Asian, non-Hispanic/Latino; 9 Hispanic/Latino; 6 Two or more races, non-Hispanic/Latino), 4 international. Average age 34. *Faculty:* 30 full-time, 9 part-time/adjunct. *Financial support:* Research assistantships with full tuition reimbursements, career-related internships or fieldwork, Federal Work-Study, scholarships/grants, and unspecified assistantships available. Support available to part-time students. Financial award application deadline: 2/1; financial award applicants required to submit FAFSA. In 2015, 329 master's, 24 other advanced degrees awarded. *Degree program information:* Part-time programs available. Part-time. Offers arts and sciences (MA, MLA, MS, MSW, Certificate, SSP); biology (MS); dietics (Certificate); English (MA); history (MA); human nutrition (MS); liberal arts (MLA); psychology (MS, SSP); social work (MSW). *Application deadline:* Applications are processed on a rolling basis. *Application fee:* $50. Electronic applications accepted. *Application Contact:* 800-411-7041, Fax: 803-323-2292, E-mail: gradschool@winthrop.edu. *Dean,* Karen M. Kedrowski, 803-323-2160, E-mail: kedrowskik@winthrop.edu.

College of Business Administration Students: 462 full-time (355 women), 496 part-time (374 women); includes 229 minority (189 Black or African American, non-Hispanic/Latino; 1 American Indian or Alaska Native, non-Hispanic/Latino; 7 Asian, non-Hispanic/Latino; 21 Hispanic/Latino; 11 Two or more races, non-Hispanic/Latino), 41 international. Average age 23. *Faculty:* 10 full-time, 8 part-time/adjunct. *Financial support:* Research assistantships with full tuition reimbursements, Federal Work-Study, scholarships/grants, and unspecified assistantships available. Support available to part-time students. Financial award application deadline: 2/1; financial award applicants required to submit FAFSA. In 2015, 87 master's awarded. *Degree program information:* Part-time and evening/weekend programs available. Part-time, evening/weekend, online learning. Offers business administration (MBA). *Application deadline:* For fall admission, 7/15 priority date for domestic students; for spring admission, 12/1 for domestic students. Applications are processed on a rolling basis. *Application fee:* $50. Electronic applications accepted. *Application Contact:* 800-411-7041, Fax: 803-323-2292, E-mail: gradschool@winthrop.edu. *Dean,* Dr. Roger Weikle, 803-323-2186, Fax: 803-323-3960, E-mail: weikler@winthrop.edu.

College of Education Students: 186 full-time (138 women), 219 part-time (180 women); includes 92 minority (77 Black or African American, non-Hispanic/Latino; 4 Asian, non-Hispanic/Latino; 8 Hispanic/Latino; 3 Two or more races, non-Hispanic/Latino), 8 international. Average age 31. *Faculty:* 21 full-time. *Financial support:* Research assistantships with full tuition reimbursements, career-related internships or fieldwork, Federal Work-Study, scholarships/grants, and unspecified assistantships available. Support available to part-time students. Financial award application deadline: 2/1; financial award applicants required to submit FAFSA. In 2015, 136 master's awarded. *Degree program information:* Part-time programs available. Part-time. Offers agency counseling (M Ed); education (M Ed, MAT); educational leadership (M Ed); physical education (MAT); school counseling (M Ed); secondary education (M Ed); special education (M Ed). *Application deadline:* For fall admission, 7/15 priority date for domestic students; for spring admission, 12/1 for domestic students. Applications are processed on a rolling basis. *Application fee:* $50. Electronic applications accepted. *Application Contact:* 800-411-7041, Fax: 803-323-2292, E-mail: gradschool@winthrop.edu. *Dean,* Dr. Jeannie Rakestraw, 803-323-2151, Fax: 803-323-4369, E-mail: rakestrawj@winthrop.edu.

College of Visual and Performing Arts Students: 18 full-time (7 women), 36 part-time (28 women); includes 13 minority (8 Black or African American, non-Hispanic/Latino; 1 American Indian or Alaska Native, non-Hispanic/Latino; 1 Asian, non-Hispanic/Latino; 2 Hispanic/Latino; 1 Two or more races, non-Hispanic/Latino), 1 international. Average age 34. *Faculty:* 16 full-time, 10 part-time/adjunct. *Financial support:* Research assistantships with full tuition reimbursements, Federal Work-Study, scholarships/grants, and unspecified assistantships available. Support available to part-time students. Financial award application deadline: 2/1; financial award applicants required to submit FAFSA. In 2015, 13 master's awarded. *Degree program information:* Part-time programs available. Part-time. Offers art (MFA); art administration (MA); art education (MA); conducting (MM); music education (MME); performance (MM); visual and performing arts (MA, MFA, MM, MME). *Application deadline:* Applications are processed on a rolling basis. *Application fee:* $50. Electronic applications accepted. *Application Contact:* 800-411-7041, Fax: 803-323-2292, E-mail: gradschool@winthrop.edu. *Dean,* Dr. David Wohl, 803-323-2323, Fax: 803-323-2333, E-mail: wohld@winthrop.edu.

WISCONSIN LUTHERAN COLLEGE, Milwaukee, WI 53226-9942

General Information Independent-religious, coed, comprehensive institution.

GRADUATE UNITS

College of Adult and Graduate Studies

WISCONSIN SCHOOL OF PROFESSIONAL PSYCHOLOGY, Milwaukee, WI 53225-4960

General Information Independent, coed, graduate-only institution. *Graduate housing:* On-campus housing not available.

GRADUATE UNITS

Program in Clinical Psychology ***Degree program information:*** Part-time and evening/weekend programs available. Part-time, evening/weekend. Offers clinical psychology (MA, Psy D).

WITTENBERG UNIVERSITY, Springfield, OH 45501-0720

General Information Independent-religious, coed, comprehensive institution.

GRADUATE UNITS

Graduate Program

WON INSTITUTE OF GRADUATE STUDIES, Glenside, PA 19038

General Information Proprietary, coed, graduate-only institution. *Enrollment by degree level:* 71 master's, 10 other advanced degrees. *Graduate faculty:* 9 full-time (5 women), 21 part-time/adjunct (16 women). *Student services:* Career counseling, writing training. *Library:* Won Institute Library plus 1 other. *Collection:* Books: 4,912 (physical), 5 (digital/electronic); Databases: 3. Study areas open 24 hours, 5–7 days a week; students can reserve study rooms.

Computer facilities: 4 computers available on campus for general student use. A campuswide network can be accessed from off campus. Online class registration is available.
Website: http://www.woninstitute.edu/

General Application Contact: Jennifer Cake, Enrollment Management Counselor, 215-884-8942 Ext. 219, Fax: 215-884-9002, E-mail: jennifer.cake@woninstitute.edu.

GRADUATE UNITS

Acupuncture Studies Program Offers acupuncture studies (M Ac). Electronic applications accepted.

Applied Meditation Studies Program ***Degree program information:*** Part-time and evening/weekend programs available. Part-time, evening/weekend. Offers applied meditation studies (MAMS, Certificate).

Program in Chinese Herbal Medicine Offers Chinese herbal medicine (Certificate). Electronic applications accepted.

Won Buddhist Studies Program ***Degree program information:*** Part-time programs available. Part-time. Offers Won Buddhist studies (MA).

WOODBURY UNIVERSITY, Burbank, CA 91504-1099

General Information Independent, coed, comprehensive institution. *Graduate housing:* Room and/or apartments available on a first-come, first-served basis to single students; on-campus housing not available to married students.

GRADUATE UNITS

School of Architecture Offers architecture (M Arch, MIA, MS Arch).

School of Business and Management ***Degree program information:*** Part-time and evening/weekend programs available. Part-time, evening/weekend. Offers business administration (MBA); organizational leadership (MA).

WOODS HOLE OCEANOGRAPHIC INSTITUTION, Woods Hole, MA 02543-1541

General Information Independent, coed, graduate-only institution. CGS member. *Graduate housing:* Rooms and/or apartments guaranteed to single students and available on a first-come, first-served basis to married students.

GRADUATE UNITS

MIT/WHOI Joint Program in Oceanography/Applied Ocean Science and Engineering Offers applied ocean science and engineering (PhD); biological oceanography (PhD); chemical oceanography (PhD); marine geology and geophysics (PhD); physical oceanography (PhD). Program offered jointly with Massachusetts Institute of Technology. Electronic applications accepted.

WORCESTER POLYTECHNIC INSTITUTE, Worcester, MA 01609-2280

General Information Independent, coed, university. CGS member. *Enrollment:* 6,573 graduate, professional, and undergraduate students; 1,148 full-time matriculated graduate/professional students (383 women), 814 part-time matriculated graduate/professional students (188 women). *Enrollment by degree level:* 1,560 master's, 340 doctoral, 62 other advanced degrees. *Graduate faculty:* 171 full-time (37 women), 92 part-time/adjunct (16 women). *Graduate housing:* Rooms and/or apartments available on a first-come, first-served basis to single and married students. *Student services:* Campus employment opportunities, campus safety program, career counseling, exercise/wellness program, free psychological counseling, grant writing training, international student services, low-cost health insurance, multicultural affairs office, services for students with disabilities, teacher training, writing training. *Library:* George C. Gordon Library. *Collection:* Books: 242,660 (physical), 941,222 (digital/electronic); Serial titles: 5,556 (physical), 70,140 (digital/electronic); Databases: 322. Weekly public service hours: 107; students can reserve study rooms. *Research affiliation:* Children's Hospital, Boston (3D MRI-based modeling), Burroughs Wellcome Co. (neural circuit dynamics and behavior using microtechnology), SRI International (educational software), ArcelorMittal USA (catalyst design, heat transfer, and reaction), Massachusetts Eye and Ear Infirmary (medical devices), University of Massachusetts Medical School at Worcester (basic transitional and clinical medical research).

Computer facilities: Computer purchase and lease plans are available. 860 computers available on campus for general student use. A campuswide network can be accessed from student residence rooms and from off campus. Online class registration, online course content are available.
Website: http://www.wpi.edu/

General Application Contact: Lynne Dougherty, Administrative Assistant, 508-831-5301, Fax: 508-831-5717, E-mail: grad@wpi.edu.

GRADUATE UNITS

Graduate Studies and Research Students: 1,148 full-time (383 women), 814 part-time (188 women); includes 238 minority (40 Black or African American, non-Hispanic/Latino; 2 American Indian or Alaska Native, non-Hispanic/Latino; 93 Asian, non-Hispanic/Latino; 73 Hispanic/Latino; 1 Native Hawaiian or other Pacific Islander, non-Hispanic/Latino; 29 Two or more races, non-Hispanic/Latino), 819 international. 3,711 applicants, 51% accepted, 720 enrolled. *Faculty:* 171 full-time (37 women), 92 part-time/adjunct (16 women). *Financial support:* Research assistantships, teaching assistantships, career-related internships or fieldwork, institutionally sponsored loans, scholarships/grants, health care benefits, tuition waivers, and unspecified assistantships available. Financial award application deadline: 1/1; financial award applicants required to submit FAFSA. In 2015, 681 master's, 42 doctorates awarded. *Degree program information:* Part-time and evening/weekend programs available. Part-time, evening/weekend, 100% online, blended/hybrid learning. Offers aerospace engineering (MS, PhD); applied mathematics (MS); applied statistics (MS); biochemistry (MS, PhD); bioinformatics and computational biology (MS, PhD); biology and biotechnology (MS); biomedical engineering (M Eng, MS, PhD, Graduate Certificate); bioscience administration (MS); biotechnology (PhD); chemical engineering (MS, PhD); chemistry (MS, PhD); civil and environmental engineering (Advanced Certificate, Graduate Certificate); civil engineering (ME, MS, PhD); computer and communications networks (MS); computer science (MS, PhD, Advanced Certificate, Graduate Certificate); construction project management (MS); data science (MS, Graduate Certificate); electrical and computer engineering (Advanced Certificate, Graduate Certificate); electrical engineering (M Eng, MS, PhD); environmental engineering (M Eng, MS); financial mathematics (MS); fire protection engineering (MS, PhD, Advanced Certificate, Graduate Certificate); impact engineering (MS); industrial mathematics (MS); interactive media and game development (MS); interdisciplinary social science (PhD); learning sciences and technologies (MS, PhD); manufacturing engineering (MS, PhD); manufacturing engineering management (MS); master builder (M Eng); materials process engineering (MS); materials science and engineering (MS, PhD); mathematical sciences (PhD, Graduate Certificate); mathematics (MME); mechanical engineering (MS, PhD, Graduate Certificate); physics (MS, PhD); physics for educators (MS); power systems management (MS); robotics engineering (MS, PhD); social science (PhD); system dynamics (MS, Graduate Certificate); systems engineering (MS, Graduate Certificate); systems modeling (MS). *Application deadline:* For fall admission, 1/1 priority date for domestic and international students; for spring admission, 10/1 priority date for domestic and international students. Applications are processed on a rolling basis. *Application fee:* $70. Electronic applications accepted. *Application Contact:* Lynne Dougherty, Administrative Assistant, 508-831-5301, Fax: 508-831-5717, E-mail: grad@wpi.edu. *Dean*, Dr. Terri Camesano, 508-831-5380, E-mail: grad@wpi.edu.

School of Business Students: 211 full-time (126 women), 221 part-time (72 women); includes 42 minority (5 Black or African American, non-Hispanic/Latino; 21 Asian, non-Hispanic/Latino; 14 Hispanic/Latino; 2 Two or more races, non-Hispanic/Latino), 200 international. 665 applicants, 62% accepted, 142 enrolled. *Faculty:* 15 full-time (9 women), 23 part-time/adjunct (4 women). *Financial support:* Career-related internships or fieldwork, institutionally sponsored loans, scholarships/grants, and unspecified assistantships available. Financial award application deadline: 6/1; financial award applicants required to submit FAFSA. In 2015, 150 master's awarded. *Degree program information:* Part-time and evening/weekend programs available. Part-time, evening/weekend, 100% online, blended/hybrid learning. Offers information technology (MS); management (Graduate Certificate); marketing and technological innovation (MS); operations design and leadership (MS); technology (MBA, MS). *Application deadline:* For fall admission, 6/1 priority date for domestic and international students; for spring admission, 11/1 priority date for domestic students, 10/1 priority date for international students. Applications are processed on a rolling basis. *Application fee:* $70. Electronic applications accepted. *Application Contact:* Eileen Dagostino, Recruiting Operations Coordinator, 508-831-4665, Fax: 508-831-5720, E-mail: edag@wpi.edu. *Graduate Coordinator*, Dr. Paul Mack, 508-831-4665, E-mail: binwilkins@wpi.edu.

WORCESTER STATE UNIVERSITY, Worcester, MA 01602-2597

General Information State-supported, coed, comprehensive institution. *Enrollment:* 6,306 graduate, professional, and undergraduate students; 170 full-time matriculated graduate/professional students (145 women), 389 part-time matriculated graduate/professional students (290 women). *Enrollment by degree level:* 496 master's, 63 other advanced degrees. *Graduate faculty:* 55 full-time (38 women), 30 part-time/adjunct (17 women). Tuition, state resident: part-time $150 per credit. Tuition, nonresident: part-time $150 per credit. *Graduate housing:* On-campus housing not available. *Student services:* Campus employment opportunities, campus safety program, career counseling, free psychological counseling, international student services, low-cost health insurance, multicultural affairs office, services for students with disabilities, teacher training, writing training. *Library:* Worcester State University Library. *Collection:* Books: 144,910 (physical), 140,521 (digital/electronic); Serial titles: 129 (physical), 56,397 (digital/electronic); Databases: 133. Weekly public service hours: 100.

Computer facilities: Computer purchase and lease plans are available. 500 computers available on campus for general student use. A campuswide network can be accessed from student residence rooms and from off campus. Online class registration is available.
Website: http://www.worcester.edu/

General Application Contact: Sara Grady, Associate Dean of Graduate and Continuing Education, 508-929-8130, Fax: 508-929-8100, E-mail: sara.grady@worcester.edu.

GRADUATE UNITS

Graduate Studies Students: 170 full-time (145 women), 389 part-time (290 women); includes 60 minority (19 Black or African American, non-Hispanic/Latino; 3 American Indian or Alaska Native, non-Hispanic/Latino; 8 Asian, non-Hispanic/Latino; 22 Hispanic/Latino; 8 Two or more races, non-Hispanic/Latino), 13 international. Average age 34. 724 applicants, 54% accepted, 182 enrolled. *Faculty:* 55 full-time (38 women), 30 part-time/adjunct (17 women). *Financial support:* Career-related internships or fieldwork, scholarships/grants, and unspecified assistantships available. Financial award application deadline: 3/1; financial award applicants required to submit FAFSA. In 2015, 192 master's, 119 other advanced degrees awarded. *Degree program information:* Part-time and evening/weekend programs available. Part-time, evening/weekend. Offers accounting (MS); biotechnology (MS); community and public health nursing (MSN); early childhood education (M Ed); education (M Ed, CAGS, Postbaccalaureate Certificate); elementary education (M Ed); English (MA); English as a second language (M Ed, Postbaccalaureate Certificate); health care administration (MS); health education (M Ed); history (MA); leadership and administration (M Ed, CAGS); managerial leadership (MS); middle school education (M Ed, Postbaccalaureate Certificate); moderate disabilities (M Ed, Postbaccalaureate Certificate); non-profit management (MS); nurse educator (MSN); occupational therapy (MOT); reading (M Ed, CAGS, Postbaccalaureate Certificate); school psychology (CAGS); secondary education (M Ed, CAGS); Spanish (MA); speech-language pathology (MS). *Application deadline:* For fall admission, 6/15 for domestic and international students; for spring admission, 11/1 for domestic and international students; for summer admission, 4/1 for domestic and international students. Applications are processed on a rolling basis. *Application fee:* $50. Electronic applications accepted. *Application Contact:* Sara Grady, Associate Dean of Graduate and Continuing Education, 508-929-8787, Fax: 508-929-8100, E-mail: sara.grady@worcester.edu. *Associate Vice President for Continuing Education/Dean of the Graduate Studies*, Dr. Roberta Kyle, 508-929-8111, Fax: 508-929-8100, E-mail: rkyle@worcester.edu.

WORLD MEDICINE INSTITUTE, Honolulu, HI 96821

General Information Independent, coed, graduate-only institution. *Graduate housing:* On-campus housing not available.

GRADUATE UNITS

Program in Acupuncture and Oriental Medicine ***Degree program information:*** Part-time and evening/weekend programs available. Part-time, evening/weekend. Offers acupuncture and Oriental medicine (M Ac OM).

WRIGHT INSTITUTE, Berkeley, CA 94704-1796

General Information Independent, coed, graduate-only institution. *Graduate housing:* On-campus housing not available.

GRADUATE UNITS

Doctoral Program in Clinical Psychology Offers clinical psychology (Psy D). Electronic applications accepted.

Program in Counseling Psychology ***Degree program information:*** Part-time and evening/weekend programs available. Part-time, evening/weekend. Offers counseling psychology (MA). Electronic applications accepted.

WRIGHT STATE UNIVERSITY, Dayton, OH 45435

General Information State-supported, coed, university. CGS member. *Graduate housing:* Rooms and/or apartments available on a first-come, first-served basis to single students and available to married students. *Research affiliation:* Wright-Patterson Air Force Base (research and development, systems and logistics), Wright-Patterson Air Force Base Medical Center, Veterans Administration Medical Center, Scott-Kettering Magnetic Resonance Research Laboratory (medical science), Edison Biotechnology Center, Edison Materials Technology Center (processing).

GRADUATE UNITS

School of Graduate Studies ***Degree program information:*** Part-time and evening/weekend programs available. Part-time, evening/weekend. Offers interdisciplinary studies (MA, MS). Electronic applications accepted.

College of Education and Human Services Degree program information: Part-time and evening/weekend programs available. Part-time, evening/weekend. Offers adolescent young adult (M Ed, MA); advanced curriculum and instruction (Ed S); advanced educational leadership (Ed S); career, technology and vocational education (M Ed, MA); chemical dependency (MRC); classroom teacher education (M Ed, MA); computer/technology education (M Ed, MA); counseling (M Ed, MA, MS); curriculum and instruction: teacher leader (MA); early childhood education (M Ed, MA); education and human services (M Ed, MA, MRC, MS, MST, Ed S); educational administrative specialist: teacher leader (M Ed); educational administrative specialist: vocational education administration (M Ed, MA); educational leadership (M Ed, MA); gifted educational needs (M Ed, MA); health, physical education, and recreation (M Ed, MA); higher education-adult education (Ed S); intervention specialist (M Ed, MA); library/media (M Ed, MA); middle childhood education (M Ed, MA); mild to moderate educational needs (M Ed, MA); moderate to intensive educational needs (M Ed, MA); multi-age (M Ed, MA); pupil personnel services (M Ed, MA); rehabilitation counseling (MRC); severe disabilities (MRC); student affairs in higher education-administration (M Ed, MA); superintendent (Ed S); vocational education (M Ed, MA); workforce education (M Ed, MA).

College of Engineering and Computer Science Degree program information: Part-time and evening/weekend programs available. Part-time, evening/weekend. Offers biomedical and human factors engineering (MSE); biomedical engineering (MSE); computer engineering (MSCE); computer science (MS); computer science and engineering (PhD); electrical engineering (MSE); engineering (MSE, PhD); engineering and computer science (MS, MSCE, MSE, PhD); human factors engineering (MSE); materials science and engineering (MSE); mechanical and materials engineering (MSE); mechanical engineering (MSE).

College of Liberal Arts Degree program information: Part-time programs available. Part-time. Offers composition and rhetoric (MA); criminal justice and social problems (MA); English (MA); history (MA); humanities (M Hum); international and comparative politics (MA); liberal arts (M Hum, M Mus, MA, MPA); literature (MA); music education (M Mus); performance (M Mus); public administration (MPA); teaching English to speakers of other languages (MA).

College of Nursing and Health Degree program information: Part-time and evening/weekend programs available. Part-time, evening/weekend. Offers acute care nurse practitioner (MS); administration of nursing and health care systems (MS); adult health (MS); child and adolescent health (MS); community health (MS); family nurse practitioner (MS); nurse practitioner (MS); nursing and health (MS); school nurse (MS).

College of Science and Mathematics Degree program information: Part-time and evening/weekend programs available. Part-time, evening/weekend. Offers anatomy (MS); applied mathematics (MS); applied statistics (MS); biochemistry and molecular biology (MS); biological sciences (MS); biomedical sciences (PhD); chemistry (MS); earth science education (MST); environmental sciences (PhD); geological sciences (MS); geophysics (MS); human factors and industrial/organizational psychology (MS, PhD); mathematics (MS); medical physics (MS); microbiology and immunology (MS); physics (MS); physics education (MST); physiology and biophysics (MS); science and mathematics (MS, MST, PhD).

Raj Soin College of Business Degree program information: Part-time and evening/weekend programs available. Part-time, evening/weekend. Offers accountancy (M Acc); accounting (MBA); business (M Acc, MBA, MIS, MS); business administration (MBA); business economics (MBA); finance (MBA); flexible business (MBA); health care management (MBA); information systems (MIS); international business (MBA); logistics and supply chain management (MS); management information technology (MBA); management, innovation and change (MBA); marketing (MBA); project management (MBA); social and applied economics (MS); supply chain management (MBA).

School of Medicine Offers aerospace medicine (MS); health promotion and education (MPH); medicine (MPH, MS, MD, PhD); pharmacology and toxicology (MS); public health management (MPH); public health nursing (MPH).

School of Professional Psychology Offers clinical psychology (Psy D).

WYCLIFFE COLLEGE, Toronto, ON M5S 1H7, Canada

General Information Independent-religious, coed, graduate-only institution. *Graduate housing:* Rooms and/or apartments guaranteed to single students and available on a first-come, first-served basis to married students. Housing application deadline: 5/1.

GRADUATE UNITS

Division of Advanced Degree Studies ***Degree program information:*** Part-time programs available. Part-time. Offers theology (MA, Th M, D Min, PhD, Th D). PhD, D Min, MA offered jointly with Toronto School of Theology; Th D, Th M with University of Toronto.

Division of Basic Degree Studies ***Degree program information:*** Part-time programs available. Part-time. Offers Christian Studies (Diploma); theology (M Div, M Rel, MTS). M Div, M Rel, MTS offered jointly with University of Toronto.

XAVIER UNIVERSITY, Cincinnati, OH 45207

General Information Independent-religious, coed, university. *Graduate housing:* On-campus housing not available.

GRADUATE UNITS

College of Arts and Sciences ***Degree program information:*** Part-time programs available. Part-time. Offers arts and sciences (MA); English (MA); health care mission integration (MA); theology (MA); urban sustainability and resilience (MA). Electronic applications accepted.

College of Social Sciences, Health and Education Offers clinical psychology (Psy D); coaching education and athlete development (M Ed); criminal justice (MS); health services administration (MHSA); industrial-organizational psychology (MA); occupational therapy (MOT); social sciences, health and education (M Ed, MA, MHSA, MOT, MS, MSN, DNP, Ed D, Psy D, PMC); sport administration (M Ed).

School of Education Offers children's multicultural literature (M Ed); clinical mental health counseling (MA); education (M Ed, MA, MS, Ed D); educational administration (M Ed); elementary education (M Ed); human resource development (MS); Montessori education (M Ed); reading (M Ed); school counseling (MA); secondary education (M Ed); special education (M Ed). Electronic applications accepted.

School of Nursing Degree program information: Part-time and evening/weekend programs available. Part-time, evening/weekend. Offers nursing (MSN, DNP, PMC). Electronic applications accepted.

Williams College of Business ***Degree program information:*** Part-time and evening/weekend programs available. Part-time, evening/weekend. Offers accountancy (MS); business (Exec MBA, MBA, MS); business administration (Exec MBA, MBA); business intelligence (MBA); finance (MBA); health industry (MBA); international business (MBA); marketing (MBA); values-based leadership (MBA). Electronic applications accepted.

XAVIER UNIVERSITY OF LOUISIANA, New Orleans, LA 70125-1098

General Information Independent-religious, coed, comprehensive institution. *Graduate housing:* On-campus housing not available.

GRADUATE UNITS

College of Pharmacy Offers pharmacy (Pharm D). Electronic applications accepted.

Graduate School ***Degree program information:*** Part-time and evening/weekend programs available. Part-time, evening/weekend. Offers counseling (MA); curriculum and instruction (MA); educational leadership (MA).

Institute for Black Catholic Studies Degree program information: Part-time programs available. Part-time. Offers pastoral theology (Th M).

YALE UNIVERSITY, New Haven, CT 06520

General Information Independent, coed, university. CGS member. *Graduate housing:* Rooms and/or apartments available on a first-come, first-served basis to single and married students. Housing application deadline: 6/1. *Research affiliation:* Howard Hughes Medical Institute, J.B. Pierce Foundation (environmental physiology), Haskins Laboratories (speech, hearing, reading).

GRADUATE UNITS

Divinity School ***Degree program information:*** Part-time programs available. Part-time. Offers divinity (M Div, MAR, STM). Electronic applications accepted.

Graduate School of Arts and Sciences ***Degree program information:*** Part-time programs available. Part-time. Offers African studies (MA); African-American studies (PhD); American studies (PhD); anthropology (M Phil, MA, PhD); applied mathematics (M Phil, MS, PhD); Arabic and Islamic studies (MA, PhD); archaeological studies (MA); archaeology of the ancient Near East (MA, PhD); arts and sciences (M Phil, MA, MS, PhD); Assyriology (MA, PhD); astronomy (PhD); behavioral neuroscience (PhD); biochemistry, molecular biology and chemical biology (PhD); biogeochemistry (PhD); biophysical chemistry (PhD); cell biology (PhD); cellular and developmental biology (PhD); cellular and molecular physiology (PhD); classics (M Phil, MA, PhD); climate dynamics (PhD); clinical psychology (PhD); cognitive psychology (PhD); comparative and historical sociology (PhD); comparative literature (PhD); computer science (MS, PhD); cultural sociology and social theory (PhD); developmental psychology (PhD); East Asian languages and literatures (PhD); East Asian languages and literatures and film studies (PhD); East Asian studies (MA); ecology and evolutionary biology (PhD); economics (PhD); Egyptology (MA, PhD); English language and literature (MA, PhD); environmental sciences (PhD); experimental pathology (MS, PhD); film studies (PhD); forestry (PhD); French (M Phil, MA, PhD); genetics (PhD); geochemistry (PhD); geophysics (PhD); German (PhD); global affairs (MA); Graeco-Arabic studies (MA, PhD); history (M Phil, MA, PhD); history of art (PhD); history of science and medicine (MS, PhD); immunobiology (PhD); inorganic chemistry (PhD); international and development economics (MA); Italian language and literature (PhD); Latin American literature (PhD); linguistics (PhD); Luso-Brazilian and Spanish/Spanish American literatures (PhD); mathematics (M Phil, MS, PhD); medieval Slavic literature and philology (PhD); medieval studies (M Phil, PhD); meteorology (PhD); molecular biophysics and biochemistry (PhD); music history (MA); music theory (MA); neurobiology (PhD); neuroscience (PhD); Northwest Semitic, Bible, comparative Semitics (MA, PhD); oceanography (PhD); organic chemistry (PhD); paleontology (PhD); paleooceanography (PhD); petrology (PhD); philosophy (PhD); physical and theoretical chemistry (PhD); physics (PhD); plant sciences (PhD); Polish literature (PhD); political science (PhD); religious studies (PhD); Renaissance studies (PhD); Russian and East European studies (MA); Russian literature (PhD); Slavic languages and literatures and film studies (PhD); social stratification and the life course (PhD); social/personality psychology (PhD); solar and terrestrial physics (PhD); Spanish peninsular literature (PhD); statistics (MA, PhD); tectonics (PhD).

School of Engineering and Applied Science Degree program information: Part-time programs available. Part-time. Offers applied physics (MS, PhD); biomedical engineering (MS, PhD); chemical engineering (MS, PhD); electrical engineering (MS, PhD); engineering and applied science (MS, PhD); environmental engineering (MS, PhD); mechanical engineering (MS, PhD).

School of Architecture Students: 199 full-time (92 women); includes 41 minority (2 Black or African American, non-Hispanic/Latino; 23 Asian, non-Hispanic/Latino; 10 Hispanic/Latino; 6 Two or more races, non-Hispanic/Latino), 61 international. 923 applicants, 15% accepted, 75 enrolled. *Faculty:* 18 full-time (4 women), 80 part-time/adjunct (22 women). *Financial support:* In 2015–16, 157 students received support. Fellowships, teaching assistantships, Federal Work-Study, and institutionally sponsored loans available. Financial award application deadline: 2/1; financial award applicants required to submit FAFSA. In 2015, 68 master's awarded. Offers architecture (M Arch, M Env Des, MEM, PhD). *Application deadline:* For fall admission, 1/2 for domestic and international students. *Application fee:* $85. Electronic applications accepted. *Application Contact:* Marilyn Weiss, Registrar, 203-432-2288, Fax: 203-432-6576, E-mail: gradarch.admissions@yale.edu. *Dean*, Robert A. M. Stern, 203-432-2279, Fax: 203-432-7175.

School of Art Offers graphic design (MFA); painting/printmaking (MFA); photography (MFA); sculpture (MFA). Electronic applications accepted.

School of Drama Offers acting (MFA, Certificate); design (MFA, Certificate); directing (MFA, Certificate); dramaturgy and dramatic criticism (MFA, DFA); playwriting (MFA, Certificate); sound design (MFA, Certificate); stage management (MFA, Certificate); technical design and production (MFA, Certificate); theater management (MFA). Electronic applications accepted.

School of Forestry and Environmental Studies Students: 300 full-time. Average age 27. 600 applicants, 150 enrolled. *Faculty:* 32 full-time, 50 part-time/adjunct. *Financial support:* In 2015–16, 240 students received support. Fellowships, research assistantships, teaching assistantships, career-related internships or fieldwork, Federal Work-Study, institutionally sponsored loans, scholarships/grants, and health care benefits available. Support available to part-time students. Financial award application deadline: 2/15; financial award applicants required to submit FAFSA. In 2015, 152 master's, 15 doctorates awarded. *Degree program information:* Part-time programs available. Part-time. Offers environmental management (MEM); environmental science (MES); forest science (MFS); forestry (MF); forestry and environmental studies (PhD). *Application deadline:* For fall admission, 12/15 priority date for domestic and international students. *Application fee:* $80. Electronic applications accepted. *Application Contact:* Rebecca DeSalvo, Director of Enrollment Management and Diversity Initiatives, 800-825-0330, Fax: 203-432-5528, E-mail: fesinfo@yale.edu. *Dean, School of Forestry and Environmental Studies*, Peter Crane, 203-432-5109, Fax: 203-432-3051.

School of Medicine ***Degree program information:*** Part-time programs available. Part-time. Offers biological and biomedical sciences (PhD); computational biology and bioinformatics (PhD); immunology (PhD); medicine (APMPH, MM Sc, MPH, MS, MD, PhD); microbiology (PhD); molecular biophysics and biochemistry (PhD); molecular cell biology, genetics, and development (PhD); neurobiology (PhD); neuroscience (PhD); pharmacological sciences and molecular medicine (PhD); pharmacology (PhD); physician associate (MM Sc); physiology and integrative medical biology (PhD). Electronic applications accepted.

Yale School of Public Health Degree program information: Part-time programs available. Part-time. Offers applied biostatistics and epidemiology (APMPH); biostatistics (MPH, MS, PhD); chronic disease epidemiology (MPH, PhD); environmental health sciences (MPH, PhD); epidemiology of microbial diseases (MPH, PhD); global health (APMPH); health management (MPH); health policy (MPH); health policy and administration (APMPH, PhD); occupational and environmental medicine (APMPH); preventive medicine (APMPH); social and behavioral sciences (APMPH, MPH). MS and PhD offered through the Graduate School. Electronic applications accepted.

School of Music Students: 218 full-time (88 women); includes 29 minority (3 Black or African American, non-Hispanic/Latino; 1 American Indian or Alaska Native, non-Hispanic/Latino; 15 Asian, non-Hispanic/Latino; 1 Native Hawaiian or other Pacific Islander, non-Hispanic/Latino; 9 Two or more races, non-Hispanic/Latino), 85 international. Average age 23. 1,479 applicants, 10% accepted, 109 enrolled. *Faculty:* 29 full-time (9 women), 29 part-time/adjunct (6 women). *Financial support:* In 2015–16, 211 students received support, including 218 fellowships (averaging $34,000 per year); Federal Work-Study and scholarships/grants also available. Financial award application deadline: 5/30; financial award applicants required to submit FAFSA. In 2015, 79 master's, 3 doctorates, 25 ADs awarded. Offers music (MM, MMA, DMA, AD, Certificate). *Application deadline:* For fall admission, 12/1 for domestic and international students. *Application fee:* $125. Electronic applications accepted. *Application Contact:* Suzanne M. Stringer, Director of Student Services, 203-432-1962, Fax: 203-432-7448, E-mail: suzanne.stringer@yale.edu. *Dean*, Robert Blocker, 203-432-4160, Fax: 203-432-7542.

School of Nursing ***Degree program information:*** Part-time programs available. Part-time, online learning. Offers nursing (MSN, DNP, PhD, Post Master's Certificate). Electronic applications accepted.

Yale Law School Students: 614 full-time (285 women). Average age 25. 2,809 applicants, 8% accepted, 200 enrolled. *Faculty:* 71 full-time, 82 part-time/adjunct. *Financial support:* Application deadline: 3/15; applicants required to submit FAFSA. Offers law (LL M, MSL, JD, JSD, PhD). *Application deadline:* For fall admission, 2/28 for domestic students. Applications are processed on a rolling basis. *Application fee:* $60. Electronic applications accepted. *Application Contact:* Asha Rangappa, Associate Dean, 203-432-4995, E-mail: admissions.law@yale.edu. *Dean,* Robert Post, 203-432-1660.

Yale School of Management Offers accounting (PhD); business administration (MBA); financial economics (PhD); management (MBA, PhD); marketing (PhD); organizations and management (PhD).

YESHIVA BETH MOSHE, Scranton, PA 18505-2124

General Information Independent-religious, men only, comprehensive institution.

GRADUATE UNITS

Graduate Programs

YESHIVA DERECH CHAIM, Brooklyn, NY 11218

General Information Independent-religious, men only, comprehensive institution.

GRADUATE UNITS

Graduate Program Offers Talmudic studies (PhD).

YESHIVA KARLIN STOLIN RABBINICAL INSTITUTE, Brooklyn, NY 11204

General Information Independent-religious, men only, comprehensive institution. *Graduate housing:* On-campus housing not available.

GRADUATE UNITS

Graduate Programs

YESHIVA OF NITRA RABBINICAL COLLEGE, Mount Kisco, NY 10549

General Information Independent-religious, men only, comprehensive institution.

GRADUATE UNITS

Graduate Programs

YESHIVA SHAAR HATORAH TALMUDIC RESEARCH INSTITUTE, Kew Gardens, NY 11418-1469

General Information Independent-religious, men only, comprehensive institution.

GRADUATE UNITS

Graduate Programs

YESHIVATH VIZNITZ, Monsey, NY 10952

General Information Independent-religious, men only, comprehensive institution.

GRADUATE UNITS

Graduate Programs

YESHIVATH ZICHRON MOSHE, South Fallsburg, NY 12779

General Information Independent-religious, men only, comprehensive institution.

GRADUATE UNITS

Graduate Programs ***Degree program information:*** Part-time programs available. Part-time.

YESHIVA TORAS CHAIM TALMUDICAL SEMINARY, Denver, CO 80204-1415

General Information Independent-religious, men only, comprehensive institution.

GRADUATE UNITS

Graduate Programs

YESHIVA UNIVERSITY, New York, NY 10033-3201

General Information Independent, coed, university. *Graduate housing:* On-campus housing not available.

GRADUATE UNITS

Azrieli Graduate School of Jewish Education and Administration ***Degree program information:*** Part-time and evening/weekend programs available. Part-time, evening/weekend. Offers Jewish education and administration (MS, Ed D, Specialist).

Benjamin N. Cardozo School of Law Offers comparative legal thought (LL M); dispute resolution and advocacy (LL M); general studies (LL M); intellectual property law (LL M); law (JD). Electronic applications accepted.

Bernard Revel Graduate School of Jewish Studies ***Degree program information:*** Part-time programs available. Part-time. Offers Jewish studies (MA, PhD).

Ferkauf Graduate School of Psychology ***Degree program information:*** Part-time programs available. Part-time. Offers clinical health psychology (PhD); clinical psychology (Psy D); mental health counseling psychology (MA); psychology (MA, PhD, Psy D); school/clinical-child psychology (Psy D).

Graduate Programs in Arts and Sciences Offers mathematical sciences (PhD); mathematics (MA); quantitative economics (MS); speech-language pathology (MS).

Sy Syms School of Business ***Degree program information:*** Part-time programs available. Part-time. Offers accounting (MS).

Wurzweiler School of Social Work ***Degree program information:*** Part-time and evening/weekend programs available. Part-time, evening/weekend. Offers social work (MSW, PhD).

YORK COLLEGE OF PENNSYLVANIA, York, PA 17405-7199

General Information Independent, coed, comprehensive institution. *Enrollment:* 4,739 graduate, professional, and undergraduate students; 40 full-time matriculated graduate/professional students (26 women), 161 part-time matriculated graduate/professional students (100 women). *Enrollment by degree level:* 194 master's, 7 doctoral. *Graduate faculty:* 21 full-time (16 women), 14 part-time/adjunct (6 women). *Tuition, area resident:* Full-time $13,770. *Required fees:* $1750; $380. Tuition and fees vary according to degree level. *Graduate housing:* On-campus housing not available. *Student services:* Campus employment opportunities, campus safety program, career counseling, free psychological counseling, international student services, low-cost health insurance, multicultural affairs office, services for students with disabilities. *Library:* Schmidt Library.

Computer facilities: A campuswide network can be accessed from student residence rooms and from off campus. Online class registration is available.
Website: http://www.ycp.edu/

General Application Contact: David Adams, Director of Admissions, 717-815-1600, Fax: 717-849-1607, E-mail: admissions@ycp.edu.

GRADUATE UNITS

Department of Education Students: 28 part-time (22 women). Average age 32. 19 applicants, 32% accepted, 4 enrolled. *Faculty:* 1 (woman) full-time, 4 part-time/adjunct (3 women). In 2015, 12 master's awarded. *Degree program information:* Part-time and evening/weekend programs available. Part-time, evening/weekend. Offers educational leadership (M Ed); educational technology (M Ed); reading specialist (M Ed). *Application deadline:* For fall admission, 7/15 priority date for domestic students; for spring admission, 11/15 priority date for domestic students; for summer admission, 4/15 priority date for domestic students. Applications are processed on a rolling basis. *Application fee:* $0. Electronic applications accepted. *Application Contact:* Dr. Philip Monteith, Interim Director, 717-815-1762, Fax: 717-849-1629, E-mail: med@ycp.edu. *Interim Director,* Dr. Philip Monteith, 717-815-1762, E-mail: med@ycp.edu.

Department of Nursing Students: 36 full-time (26 women), 55 part-time (47 women); includes 14 minority (4 Black or African American, non-Hispanic/Latino; 2 American Indian or Alaska Native, non-Hispanic/Latino; 5 Asian, non-Hispanic/Latino; 2 Hispanic/Latino; 1 Two or more races, non-Hispanic/Latino), 1 international. Average age 33. 115 applicants, 28% accepted, 28 enrolled. *Faculty:* 9 full-time (all women), 5 part-time/adjunct (2 women). *Financial support:* Federal Work-Study available. In 2015, 24 master's, 4 doctorates awarded. *Degree program information:* Part-time and evening/weekend programs available. Part-time, evening/weekend. Offers adult gerontology clinical nurse specialist (MS); adult gerontology nurse practitioner (MS); nurse anesthetist (MS); nurse educator (MS); nursing practice (DNP). *Application deadline:* Applications are processed on a rolling basis. *Application fee:* $0. Electronic applications accepted. *Application Contact:* Allison Malachosky, Administrative Assistant, 717-815-1243, E-mail: amalacho@ycp.edu. *Graduate Program Director,* Dr. Kimberly Fenstermacher, 717-815-1383, E-mail: kfenster@ycp.edu.

Graham School of Business Students: 4 full-time (0 women), 79 part-time (31 women); includes 7 minority (2 Black or African American, non-Hispanic/Latino; 2 Asian, non-Hispanic/Latino; 3 Two or more races, non-Hispanic/Latino). Average age 32. 44 applicants, 66% accepted, 8 enrolled. *Faculty:* 8 full-time (2 women), 3 part-time/adjunct (0 women). *Financial support:* Scholarships/grants available. Financial award application deadline: 4/15; financial award applicants required to submit FAFSA. In 2015, 22 master's awarded. *Degree program information:* Part-time and evening/weekend programs available. Part-time, evening/weekend. Offers continuous improvement (MBA); financial management (MBA); health care management (MBA); management (MBA); marketing (MBA); self-designed (MBA). *Application deadline:* For fall admission, 7/15 priority date for domestic students; for spring admission, 11/15 priority date for domestic students; for summer admission, 4/15 priority date for domestic students. Applications are processed on a rolling basis. *Application fee:* $0. Electronic applications accepted. *Application Contact:* MBA Office, 717-815-1491, Fax: 717-600-3999, E-mail: mba@ycp.edu. *MBA Director,* Nicole Cornell Sadowski, 717-815-1491, Fax: 717-600-3999, E-mail: ncornell@ycp.edu.

YORK UNIVERSITY, Toronto, ON M3J 1P3, Canada

General Information Province-supported, coed, university. CGS member. *Graduate housing:* Rooms and/or apartments available on a first-come, first-served basis to single and married students. *Research affiliation:* Imperial Oil Limited, National Palace Museum, Unicorn Children's Foundation (developmental and learning disorders), Smithsonian Institution (astronomy, physics, space), Beijing Municipality (management training), German Academic Exchange (German studies).

GRADUATE UNITS

Faculty of Graduate Studies ***Degree program information:*** Part-time and evening/weekend programs available. Part-time, evening/weekend. Offers communication and culture (MA, PhD); environmental studies (MES, PhD); interdisciplinary studies (MA); social and political thought (MA, PhD). Electronic applications accepted.

Faculty of Education ***Degree program information:*** Part-time programs available. Part-time. Offers education (M Ed, PhD). Electronic applications accepted.

Faculty of Fine Arts ***Degree program information:*** Part-time programs available. Part-time. Offers art history (MA, PhD); composition (MA); dance (MA, MFA, PhD); design (M Des); film (MA, MFA, PhD); fine arts (M Des, MA, MFA, PhD); music (PhD); musicology and ethnomusicology (MA); theatre (MFA); theatre and performance studies (MA, PhD); visual arts (MFA, PhD). Electronic applications accepted.

Faculty of Health Offers critical disability studies (MA, PhD); health (M Sc, M Sc N, MA, PhD); kinesiology and health science (M Sc, MA, PhD); nursing (M Sc N); psychology (MA, PhD).

Faculty of Liberal Arts and Professional Studies Offers disaster and emergency management (MA); economics (MA, PhD); English (MA, PhD); gender, feminist and women's studies (MA, PhD); geography (M Sc, MA, PhD); history (MA, PhD); human resources management (MHRM, PhD); humanities (MA, PhD); liberal arts and professional studies (M Sc, MA, MHRM, MPPAL, MSW, PhD); linguistics and applied linguistics (MA, PhD); philosophy (MA, PhD); political science (MA, PhD); public policy, administration and law (MPPAL); social anthropology (MA, PhD); social work (MSW, PhD); sociology (MA, PhD).

Faculty of Science ***Degree program information:*** Part-time and evening/weekend programs available. Part-time, evening/weekend. Offers biology (M Sc, PhD); chemistry (M Sc, PhD); industrial and applied mathematics (M Sc); mathematics and statistics (MA, PhD); physics and astronomy (M Sc, PhD); science (M Sc, MA, PhD).

Glendon Campus Offers French studies (MA, PhD); public and international affairs (MA); translation (MA).

Lassonde School of Engineering Offers computer science (M Sc, PhD); earth and space science (M Sc, PhD); engineering (M Sc, PhD).

Osgoode Hall Law School ***Degree program information:*** Part-time and evening/weekend programs available. Part-time, evening/weekend. Offers law (LL M, JD, PhD). Electronic applications accepted.

Schulich School of Business ***Degree program information:*** Part-time and evening/weekend programs available. Part-time, evening/weekend. Offers accounting (M Acc); administration (PhD); business (MBA); business analytics (MBA); finance (MF); international business (IMBA). Electronic applications accepted.

YO SAN UNIVERSITY OF TRADITIONAL CHINESE MEDICINE, Los Angeles, CA 90066

General Information Private, coed, graduate-only institution. *Graduate housing:* On-campus housing not available.

GRADUATE UNITS

Program in Acupuncture and Traditional Chinese Medicine ***Degree program information:*** Part-time programs available. Part-time, online learning. Offers acupuncture and traditional Chinese medicine (MATCM).

YOUNGSTOWN STATE UNIVERSITY, Youngstown, OH 44555-0001

General Information State-supported, coed, comprehensive institution. CGS member. *Graduate housing:* Room and/or apartments available on a first-come, first-served basis to single students; on-campus housing not available to married students. *Research affiliation:* Ohio Supercomputer Center (computational chemistry and physics), Northeast Ohio Medical University (medicine), Parker-Hannifin Corporation (engineering technology), Ohio Mass Spectrometry Consortium (chemistry and biology), BioRemedial Technologies Inc. (environmental bioremediation).

GRADUATE UNITS

Graduate School ***Degree program information:*** Part-time and evening/weekend programs available. Part-time, evening/weekend.

Beeghly College of Education Degree program information: Part-time and evening/weekend programs available. Part-time, evening/weekend. Offers adolescent/young adult education (MS Ed); community counseling (MS Ed); content area concentration (MS Ed); early childhood education (MS Ed); education (MS Ed, Ed D); educational administration (MS Ed); educational leadership (Ed D); educational technology (MS Ed); gifted and talented education (MS Ed); literacy (MS Ed); middle childhood education (MS Ed); school counseling (MS Ed); special education (MS Ed).

Bitonte College of Health and Human Services Degree program information: Part-time and evening/weekend programs available. Part-time, evening/weekend. Offers criminal justice (MS); health and human services (MHHS, MPH, MS, MSN, DPT); nursing (MSN); physical therapy (DPT); public health (MPH).

College of Fine and Performing Arts Degree program information: Part-time and evening/weekend programs available. Part-time, evening/weekend. Offers fine and performing arts (MM); jazz studies (MM); music education (MM); music history and literature (MM); music theory and composition (MM); performance (MM).

College of Liberal Arts and Social Sciences Degree program information: Part-time programs available. Part-time. Offers applied behavior analysis (MS); economics (MA); English (MA); environmental studies (MS); financial economics (MA); gerontology (MA); history (MA); industrial/institutional management (Certificate); liberal arts and social sciences (MA, MS, Certificate); risk management (Certificate).

College of Science, Technology, Engineering and Mathematics Degree program information: Part-time and evening/weekend programs available. Part-time, evening/weekend. Offers analytical chemistry (MS); applied mathematics (MS); biochemistry (MS); chemistry education (MS); civil and environmental engineering (MSE); computer engineering (MSE); computer science (MS); computing and information systems (MCIS); electrical engineering (MSE); environmental biology (MS); industrial and systems engineering (MSE); inorganic chemistry (MS); mechanical engineering (MSE); molecular biology, microbiology, and genetic (MS); organic chemistry (MS); physical chemistry (MS); physiology and anatomy (MS); science, technology, engineering and mathematics (MCIS, MSE); secondary mathematics (MS); statistics (MS).

Williamson College of Business Administration Degree program information: Part-time and evening/weekend programs available. Part-time, evening/weekend. Offers accounting (MBA); business administration (MBA, Certificate); enterprise resource planning (Certificate); marketing (MBA).

CLOSE-UPS OF INSTITUTIONS OFFERING GRADUATE AND PROFESSIONAL WORK

ACADEMY OF ART UNIVERSITY

Graduate Programs

ACADEMY *of* ART UNIVERSITY®
FOUNDED IN SAN FRANCISCO 1929
BY ARTISTS FOR ARTISTS

Programs of Study

Academy of Art University offers Master of Arts (M.A.), Master of Fine Arts (M.F.A.), Master of Architecture (M.Arch.), and Master of Arts in Teaching (M.A.T.) degrees as well as an Art Teaching Credential. Courses are available online and in San Francisco in the following areas of study: Acting (speech, improv, physical acting), Advertising (creative strategy, art direction, copywriting), Animation & Visual Effects (background painting/layout design, character development, storyboard art, 3-D modeling, VFX/compositing), Architecture (structures, materials and methods of construction, design process, structural and environmental systems), Art Education (learning to teach in museums, developmental psychology, teaching art in the community and in the California K–12 classroom), Art History (Renaissance art, American art history, ancient art history, looking at art, philosophy), Art Teaching Credential (learning to teach both children and adults), Fashion (design, knitwear, merchandising, textiles, product design, costume design), Fashion Costume Design (2-D concept design, 3-D production for film, research for costume needs, story and character costume design), Fashion Journalism (fashion writing, editorials for magazines, newspaper writing, fashion news), Fine Art (painting, printmaking, sculpture), Game Development (game engines, prototyping, level design, game art, 3-D modeling), Graphic Design (corporate and brand identity, package design, print and collateral), illustration (traditional and comic book), Industrial Design (furniture design, product design, toy design), Interior Architecture & Design (commercial and residential design), Jewelry & Metal Arts (fashion jewelry design, enameling, stone setting, casting, welded and fabricated sculpture), Landscape Architecture (plant design, elements in landscape, grading and drainage, urban open spaces), Motion Pictures & Television (cinematography, directing, editing, producing, production design, screenwriting), Multimedia Communications (journalism, editing, short-form documentary), Music Production & Sound Design for Visual Media (harmony, arranging, orchestration, music production techniques, scoring for film, sound design), Photography (architecture, advertising, digital documentary, editorial, fashion, fine art, landscape, photojournalism, portraiture), Visual Development (concept art for animation, film and games, digital painting, character design, cinematic storytelling, maquettes, environment creation), Web Design & New Media (user experience design, interactive design, new media, web design), and Writing for Film, Television & Digital Media (writing, pitching, and the business side of being a professional writer).

Academy of Art University graduate candidates engage in a unique interdisciplinary approach to master's degree preparation. Comprised of studio work and academic investigation, the programs prepare students for the rigors of the industry. Attainment of the various master's degrees requires the graduate candidate to successfully complete studio courses, directed study, academic study, and electives. Total units required to graduate varies depending on the degree.

Academy of Art University also offers revolutionary online graduate degree programs that provide the same exceptional education offered on campus, but with greater flexibility. Studying online allows students to balance course work with career, family, and other responsibilities. The Academy's accreditation assures the highest standard of education, instruction, and effectiveness. Online classes teach students the skills and techniques used by professional artists and designers, skills which can help students make the most of their creative abilities.

Facilities

Academy of Art University's state-of-the-art facilities offer students the tools they need to prepare for professional careers in art and design. The Academy invests in top-notch equipment to ensure it remains on the cutting edge of technology. Learning on industry-standard equipment, students gain hands-on experience.

Academy of Art University students have access to an array of digital tools. The School of Game Development and the School of Animation & Visual Effects provide the latest equipment, as well as a video and Cintiq lab, green screen studio, and sound booth. The School of Web Design & New Media houses a usability lab with the most current software, while the School of Music Production & Sound Design for Visual Media offers the latest sound design and video editing tools.

The School of Advertising is designed to look, feel, and function like an ad agency. Located in the heart of San Francisco's Financial District, the School of Graphic Design has the latest industry tools that enable students to have a seamless transition into post-graduation work. The School of Illustration is housed in a unique historic building in San Francisco's Union Square District. The original libraries, meeting rooms, theater, and a ballroom have been transformed into drawing/painting studios and classrooms.

Both undergraduate and graduate students in Architecture and Interior Architecture & Design share an 800-square-foot materials library and plotting room, as well as a model shop. The School of Industrial Design offers multiple shop facilities and a 3-D computer lab. The School of Landscape Architecture benefits from being located in San Francisco, the hub of urban landscape design.

Fashion students have access to studio facilities for women's, men's, and children's wear, as well as textile design, knitwear design, fashion merchandising, and marketing. In 2005, the Academy's School of Fashion was the first school to premiere collections of recent graduates at Mercedes-Benz Fashion Week at Bryant Park and continues with this tradition today. Surrounded by world-renowned museums and galleries, the School of Fine Art and the School of Art History facilities include thousands of square feet of studio space with everything students need to bring their individual visions to life.

The School of Motion Pictures & Television and the School of Acting facilities include a postproduction facility, green screen studio, screenwriting lab, custom-built voiceover room, and several soundstage studios. Students of the School of Multimedia Communications have access to a cutting-edge radio studio and television studio, complete with robotic cameras, anchor desks and interview sets, teleprompters, and green screens. The School of Photography facilities are equipped with both traditional and digital photographic technology.

The library provides state-of-the-art digital tools, making it possible for students to access extensive art and design image resources and information on demand. The Academy Resource Center offers all students free learning support services that include study hall tutoring, academic coaching, English as a second language support programs, a writing lab, and a multimedia language lab.

Financial Aid

Academy of Art University offers financial aid packages consisting of loans, interest-free payment plans, and work-study to eligible students. As financial aid programs, procedures, and eligibility requirements change frequently, applicants should contact the Financial Aid office at 79 New Montgomery Street, 4th Floor, San Francisco, California 94105, or by telephone at 800-544-2787 (U.S. only) or 415-274-2222 to check current requirements.

Cost of Study

For 2016–17, tuition is $982 per credit unit for graduate study. There is a $50 application fee and a $95 enrollment fee. Course fees average $400 per semester, depending on the class and area of study. Tuition and fees are subject to change at any time. Through the Academy, students already have access to most of the expensive technical equipment necessary for their area of study. Estimated graduate expenses for a full-time student are $26,452 per academic year.

Student Group

The master's programs accommodate approximately 5,000 students. Of those, 61 percent are women and 47 percent are international. Approximately 38 percent of the students receive financial aid.

Student Outcomes

Academy of Art University guides students to professional creative futures. Firms hiring Academy of Art University graduates include Pixar, NBC, Apple, Nike, Publicis/Hal Riney, Louis Vuitton, Williams-Sonoma Inc., Mazda, Electronic Arts, Architecture Planning Interiors, Carnal Comics, Hang Art Gallery, Architecture International, Blizzard, BMW, Tesla Motors, DreamWorks, and many others.

Location

Strategically located in the heart of San Francisco, Academy of Art University's campus is ideal for emerging artists and designers. Academy students benefit from the location which is centered within the creative industry, near Silicon Valley, Pixar Animation Studios, LucasArts, and more. Beautiful San Francisco is more than an inspiring backdrop for creative students. From its museums and theaters to its diverse population, the city is renowned as a center for technology, design, arts, and culture.

Academy of Art University has created a vibrant community of artists and designers, providing students with the opportunity to collaborate among disciplines to bring their dreams to life. This community enables students to grow as artists and designers, and develop a solid network of colleagues within their field.

The University

In 1929, Academy of Art University founder Richard S. Stephens—the advertising Creative Director of *Sunset* magazine—acted on his belief that "aspiring artists and designers, given proper instruction, hard work, and dedication, can learn the skills needed to become successful professionals." His new school of advertising art consisted of 46 students meeting in one room on San Francisco's Kearny Street.

The instructors, who were professional artists, brought real-world problems, situations, solutions, and practical experience to the students. Based on this idea, the school's philosophy was formulated: hire established professionals to teach the art and design professionals of tomorrow. At that time, advertising consisted primarily of illustrations, photos, and copy. Consequently, it became necessary to teach beginning students the fundamentals of drawing, painting, color, light, and photography, as well as layout and typography.

When Richard A. Stephens succeeded his father as President in 1951, the Foundations Department was added, ensuring all students mastered the principles of traditional art and design. Illustration soon expanded to include fine arts (drawing, painting, sculpture, and printmaking), and advertising design led to the School of Graphic Design. Fashion (design, textiles, and merchandising) and an Interior Design School were also added. In 1966, the Academy officially became a college, and a decade later began to offer the Master of Fine Arts degree. By 1992, there were more than 2,500 students.

The leadership of the Academy was then turned over to the third generation. Dr. Elisa Stephens, granddaughter of the founder, quickly determined that the small School of Web Design & New Media had enormous potential to prepare students for multimedia careers with companies such as Pixar, Adobe, and Disney.

Today, Academy of Art University is the largest accredited private art and design university in the nation with an enrollment of over 16,000. More than one fifth of the student body is made up of international students. The Academy has over 40 facilities that house classrooms, studios, galleries, and residence halls. The students, who are admitted through an open-enrollment policy, aspire to earn A.A., B.A., B.S., B.F.A., B.Arch., M.A., M.F.A., M.A.T., or M.Arch. degrees or an Art Teaching Credential. Students can study in San Francisco or through the Academy's flexible online programs.

The Academy maintains a system of courtesy shuttles to connect the different points of the campus, all of which are located within the city limits of San Francisco. The instructors, who are working art and design professionals, are drawn from all around the world to the Academy and the creative and intellectual center that is the Bay Area. Extensive senior-year internship programs allow students to gain valuable experience and develop strong portfolios in their chosen field before graduation.

Academy of Art University is an accredited member of the Western Association of Schools and Colleges (WSCUC), National Association of Schools of Art and Design (NASAD), Council for Interior Design Accreditation (CIDA) for BFA-IAD and MFA-IAD, National Architectural Accrediting Board (NAAB) for B.Arch. and M.Arch., and California Commission on Teacher Credentialing (CTC).

What Sets the Academy Apart

The Academy is one of the few art and design schools that believes in nurturing the whole artist; this includes developing athletic ability along with artistic talent. Students can participate in intercollegiate, intramural, and club sports, and with Pacific West honors and national championships, the University offers basketball, baseball, softball, cross country, track and field, soccer, golf, volleyball, and tennis for its students to partake. Furthermore, the Academy is proud to be the only higher arts education institution in the U.S. to have an NCAA athletics program.

Faculty

Academy of Art University has assembled a faculty of top creative professionals. These award-winning industry leaders have a passion for inspiring the next generation of artists and designers. With a focus on hands-on experience, instructors guide students to achieve their full creative potential. Specific information about faculty members can be found on the University's website at www.academyart.edu.

Applying

Admission to the master's programs requires official transcripts indicating at least the completion of a bachelor's degree, submission of a portfolio of work (portfolio requirements vary by discipline), a statement of intent outlining graduate study goals, and a resume. Admission to the program is permitted at the beginning of each semester. Additional materials may be required. Students should contact the Graduate Admissions Office for further details.

Correspondence and Information

Academy of Art University Graduate Admissions
P.O. Box 193844
San Francisco, California 94119
United States
Phone: 415-274-2222
800-544-2787 (toll-free in the U.S. only)
Fax: 415-618-6287
E-mail: info@academyart.edu
Website: http://www.academyart.edu

Academy of Art University, Downtown San Francisco Campus.

BINGHAMTON UNIVERSITY, STATE UNIVERSITY OF NEW YORK

The Graduate School

BINGHAMTON UNIVERSITY
STATE UNIVERSITY OF NEW YORK

Programs of Study

Binghamton University–State University of New York (SUNY) offers more than 60 master's, 30 doctoral, and 50 accelerated (combined bachelor's/master's) degrees, plus 15 certificates and non-degree coursework through seven schools: the College of Community and Public Affairs, the Decker School of Nursing, the Graduate School of Education, the Harpur College of Arts and Sciences, the School of Management, the School of Pharmacy and Pharmaceutical Sciences, and the Thomas J. Watson School of Engineering and Applied Science.

GRADUATE DEGREE PROGRAMS

College of Community and Public Affairs
Community and Public Affairs
Public Administration
Social Work
Student Affairs Administration
Sustainable Communities

Decker School of Nursing
Adult-Gerontological Nursing
Community Health Nursing
Family Nursing
Family Psychiatric Mental Health Nursing
Nursing

Graduate School of Education
Adolescence Education
Childhood and Early Childhood Education
Educational Studies
Educational Theory and Practice
Literacy Education
Special Education
Teaching English to Speakers of Other Languages

Harpur College of Arts and Sciences
Anthropology
Anthropology—Biomedical
Applied Statistics
Art History
Asian and Asian American Studies
Biological Sciences
Chemistry
Comparative Literature
Economics
English
French
Geography
Geological Sciences
History
Italian
Materials Science and Engineering
Mathematical Sciences
Music
Philosophy—Social, Political, Ethical and Legal
Physics
Political Science
Psychology, Behavioral Neuroscience
Psychology, Clinical Science
Psychology, Cognitive and Brain Sciences
Sociology
Spanish
Sustainable Communities
Theatre
Translation Studies

School of Management
Accounting
Business Administration
Management

School of Pharmacy and Pharmaceutical Sciences
Pharmacy

Thomas J. Watson School of Engineering and Applied Science
Biomedical Engineering
Computer Science
Electrical and Computer Engineering
Health Systems
Industrial and Systems Engineering
Industrial Engineering
Materials Science and Engineering
Mechanical Engineering
Systems Engineering
Systems Science

CERTIFICATE PROGRAMS

Asian and Asian American Studies
Clinically Rich Intensive Teacher Institute in English as a Second Language (CRITI ESL)
Complex Systems Science and Engineering
Disaster Management
Educational Leadership (CAS)
Evolutionary Studies
Forensic Health
Geriatric and Gerontological Social Work
German Cultural Studies
Local Government Management
Medieval and Renaissance Studies
Non-Profit Administration
Nursing Education
Nurse Practitioner Post-Master's
Professional Science Management
Professional Science Master's
- Biomedical Anthropology
- Geography
- Materials Science and Engineering

Social Work in Health Care
Teaching, College/University
Teaching, Community College
Translation Studies
Watershed Studies and Management

The University

Established in 1946, Binghamton University is a mid-sized public institution and one of four research university centers in the State University of New York (SUNY) system. The University has a reputation as a world-class institution that combines a broadly interdisciplinary, international education with one of the most vibrant research programs in the nation.

Each year, Binghamton enrolls nearly 17,000 students, including almost 3,300 graduate students, in programs leading to bachelor's, master's, and doctoral degrees. Students come from 115 countries and 53 U.S. states/territories.

The academic culture at Binghamton rivals a first-rate private university—rigorous, collaborative, and innovative—while the campus culture exemplifies the best kind of public university experience, with richly diverse students, active social life, and deep engagement with the community.

Binghamton has received many honors and accolades. *U.S. News & World Report* recognized Binghamton as having more than ten programs ranked in the top 100 Best Grad Schools (2016). *American City Business Journal* ranked Binghamton the best public college in New York and 18th in the nation (2015), while *U.S. News & World Report* ranked Binghamton one of the nation's top 40 public universities (2016). *Fiske Guide to Colleges* rated Binghamton a best buy and one of the premier public universities in the Northeast (2014) and *Kiplinger's Personal Finance* consistently places Binghamton among its top schools, ranking the University as a best value (2014).

Location

The University's main campus is spread over 930 acres in the town of Vestal, New York, one mile west of the city of Binghamton. Greater Binghamton is a friendly, affordable, and safe community only hours from major metropolitan areas such as New York City, Boston, Philadelphia, and Washington, D.C.

The resources on the main campus include extensive libraries, a five-building science complex with a multi-climate teaching greenhouse, a 190-acre forest and wetland area (the Nature Preserve), a performing arts center and art museum, a fitness center, and extensive athletic facilities. The University's Innovative Technologies Complex, located next to the main campus, is home to the Bioengineering Building, Engineering and Science Building, and a New York State Center of Excellence in the Small Scale Systems Integration and Packaging Center. A fourth building, the Smart Energy Research and Development Facility, is under construction and expected to be completed in 2017.

The University's College of Community and Public Affairs makes its home at the University Downtown Center in downtown Binghamton. This location offers faculty, staff, and students the opportunity to collaborate easily and regularly with community groups and organizations.

Research

Advanced research is conducted across every discipline and every school at Binghamton. This research leads to new insights, new technologies, and new jobs. From developing biofilm technology and community schools to studying human trafficking and brain prints, Binghamton graduate students collaborate with faculty experts and thrive in a diverse community that promotes the vigorous exchange of innovative ideas. More than thirty specialized research centers and institutes—including the Institute for Multigenerational Studies, the Center for Energy-Smart Electronic Systems, the Public Archaeology Facility, and the Institute for Evolutionary Studies—unite University researchers across the disciplines.

The University's Transdisciplinary Areas of Excellence (TAEs) explore critical social, scientific, technological, economic, cultural, and policy issues, aiming to develop solutions to today's complex and consequential problems. Graduate students have the opportunity to work with faculty researchers in these TAEs, which focus inquiry and innovation in five distinct areas: citizenship, rights, and cultural belonging; health sciences; material and visual worlds; smart energy; and sustainable communities. Multidisciplinary collaborations and partnerships with industry also help to ensure that ideas developed on Binghamton's campus have an impact far beyond the state and the nation.

Faculty

Binghamton University faculty members are top scholars and groundbreaking researchers; most (93 percent) hold the highest degree offered in their field. Binghamton professors have received many honors, including the Fulbright, Ford, and Guggenheim fellowships; National Science Foundation and National Book awards; and grants from the National Institutes of Health and the U.S. Departments of Energy, Defense, Commerce, and Education.

Student Outcomes

There are more than 120,000 Binghamton alumni around the globe, and graduates have gone on to become technology innovators, best-selling authors, trailblazing researchers, business leaders, respected educators, and more. Alumni often credit Binghamton with providing them with the foundation of their success. Many support current students by offering internships, serving as mentors, and participating in networking initiatives.

Funding and Financial Aid

Aside from maintaining reasonable tuition rates, Binghamton University offers numerous funding options. Many students receive fellowships and scholarships or hold graduate, research project, or teaching assistantships. From loans and fellowships to student employment and travel funding, Binghamton University works to help students find the resources they need to make education attainable and to enhance their future careers.

Cost of Study

For full-time matriculated graduate students, 2016–17 tuition and fees are approximately $10,870 annually for New York State residents and $22,210 annually for nonresidents. Rates differ for M.B.A., nursing D.N.P., M.S.W., and Pharm.D. programs.

Living and Housing Costs

Most graduate students live off campus. The affordability and availability of off-campus housing, coupled with free bus service, make it easy to live in the surrounding area.

The Off-Campus College (OCC) is a resource for all students who live off campus: the office maintains lists of housing options, provides a forum to facilitate connections with other students looking for housemates, and runs a legal clinic that can assist with lease reviews. The OCC also hosts a variety of community events and educational programs, helping students to become part of the greater Binghamton community.

Applying

Binghamton University welcomes applications from students who have earned (or are earning) bachelor's degrees from accredited colleges or universities. Typically, applicants must submit an online graduate degree application, transcript(s), a personal statement, a résumé or curriculum vitae (CV), letters of recommendation, and official GRE or GMAT scores, as well as any program-specific application materials, such as writing or work samples, licenses or certifications, and test scores. Application deadlines vary by semester and program. Complete application instructions can be found online at http://www.binghamton.edu/grad-school/apply.

Correspondence and Information

The Graduate School
Binghamton University–SUNY
P.O. Box 6000
Binghamton, New York 13902-6000
United States
Phone: 607-777-2151
Fax: 607-777-2501
E-mail: gradadmission@binghamton.edu
Website: http://www.binghamton.edu/grad-school/

Students on the Peace Quad, surrounded by beautiful upstate New York fall foliage.

Omowunmi Sadik, professor of chemistry in the Harpur College of Arts and Sciences, and Seokheun Choi, assistant professor of electrical and computer engineering in the Thomas J. Watson School of Engineering and Applied Science, collaborating on their research.

COLLEGE OF MOUNT SAINT VINCENT

School of Professional and Graduate School

★ **For more information, visit http://petersons.to/collegeofmountsaintvincent-grad**

Programs of Study

The College of Mount Saint Vincent (CMSV) offers graduate students in-demand academic programs as well as the flexibility to work at their own pace. Its graduate programs allow a diverse range of students, from new graduates to working adults, to complete their education and advance their careers.

These affordable programs are nationally accredited and meet the highest academic standards. Their curricula integrate liberal arts education with real-world learning through service, research, and internships.

To enhance academic achievement, students receive close mentoring, comprehensive resources, and convenient class scheduling. Students receive guidance about applying to programs, transferring credits, and registering for classes. Many classes are scheduled during the day and in the evenings, which allows students to fit classes into their schedules more easily.

Master of Business Administration: The Master of Business Administration (MBA) program equips students with the business know-how and leadership skills to succeed in both the private and nonprofit sectors. The program is accredited by the Accreditation Council for Business Schools and Programs (ACBSP).

The MBA Program curriculum consists of 60 credits of courses (up to 24 of these credits can be waived). The Business Core/Common Professional component consists of 30 credits; Capstone Courses total 12 credits; and the Concentration/Advanced Study component includes 18 credits in one of the following concentrations:

- Health Care Management
- International Business
- Management and Organizational Behavior
- Comprehensive Track (six 600-level courses)
- Comprehensive Track for students in the master's program in International Development and Service

The College also offers an MBA for International Students, which is delivered on the Riverdale campus. It provides the same rigorous curriculum as the general MBA program, and it includes accommodations and meals.

Master of Science in Adolescent Education & Special Education: This uniquely designed and highly experiential Master of Science program is geared for career-changers or recent college graduates who wish to receive a New York State teaching license. Successful completion of the program and required licensure exams leads to a master's degree plus two teaching licenses covering grades 7–12: one is in a content area such as biology, chemistry, English, history, or mathematics, and the other is in special education.

This accelerated 14-month program consists of 45 credits and blends vital academic content with practical classroom teaching experience through a Teaching Fellows residency program, where participants serve as Teaching Fellows and are paired with a classroom mentor-teacher. Teaching Fellows work alongside their mentors in a grade-appropriate classroom, attend school-based staff meetings and professional development seminars, and assume instructional responsibilities as assigned. Before starting classroom-based activities in the fall, all Teaching Fellows attend a CMSV summer institute designed to provide the professional knowledge and skills upon which to build a successful career in education.

Special features of this accelerated master's degree program include the CMSV Summer Educare Institute; placement and mentoring in a school residency program as a Teaching Fellow; and two certifications: special education licensure and adolescent (grades 7–12) licensure in a content area.

There are also special scholarship opportunities associated with this program. All applicants are encouraged to apply for one of all of the following: $10,000 CMSV Commitment to Teaching Scholarship, $23,000 CMSV Teaching Fellows Scholarship, and $12,000 Teaching Assistantship.

Master of Science in Teaching English to Speakers of Other Languages: The M.S. in Teaching English to Speakers of Other Languages (TESOL) prepares individuals to teach English language learners from pre-kindergarten through grade 12. It also prepares them for state certification in TESOL.

Its 30-credit curriculum consists of professional and skills-based, clinically-oriented courses in pedagogical core courses (18 credits), pedagogical knowledge courses (6 credits), and field experience (6 credits). There is also a comprehensive examination that demonstrates students' knowledge of the curriculum.

Master of Science in Nursing: The M.S. in Nursing prepares in-service nurses for career advancement. Its curriculum—which integrates theory, research, and experience—provides specialization in three areas: nursing education (36 credits), nursing administration (36 credits), and family nurse practitioner (42 credits).

The nursing program also provides advanced certificate programs in family nurse practitioner (27 credits) and nurse educator (12 credits). These programs are designed for nurses who have already earned a master's degree in nursing.

Master of Science in International Development and Service: The M.S. in International Development and Service program was created to meet the demand for leaders who can promote partnerships in diverse communities throughout the world. Its 36-credit, interdisciplinary curriculum encompasses topics such as global health, multicultural education, social policy and development, and other important areas. It also integrates classroom learning with volunteer service in Asia, Europe, South America, and the United States.

Concurrent Master of Science in International Development and Service and MBA: The joint M.S. in International Development and Service and MBA programs can be completed with as little as 18 additional credits. This unique dual-degree program equips individuals with the skills to effectively manage nonprofit organizations from multiple angles. It also enables students to develop a valuable set of competencies including budgeting, policy implementation, regulatory compliance, and strategic planning at the organizational level.

Research Facilities

CMSV offers students state-of-the-art science laboratories, a new sports medicine suite, and fully wireless academic buildings.

The Elizabeth Seton Library provides traditional and innovative resources to the College community. The library offers books, ebooks, journals, databases, videos, and more. Students can also utilize computer access, printing, study space, and expert research help via the library.

Financial Aid

An important component of graduate education is managing and financing the cost. The College is committed to guiding students through the process with the help of its knowledgeable and dedicated staff. A variety of federal loans, private loans, and scholarships are available to graduate students.

Several payment plans are available to help make costs more manageable; the College's Tuition Management Services can arrange a semester-based plan.

Cost of Study

Graduate tuition and fees vary depending on the course of study. The most current and specific cost information can be found at https://mountsaintvincent.edu/campus-life/campus-services/student-accounts/tuition-and-fees/graduate-tuition-and-fees.

The Faculty

The College of Mount Saint Vincent has highly skilled and experienced faculty members who care about their students.

Professor of Management Nina Aversano, Ph.D. is an accomplished teacher, executive, and administrator who is devoted to both her community and profession. Her areas of interest include executive management, international business management, and management organizational behavior. Dr. Aversano's distinguished career includes a position at AT&T as vice president of global operations.

Professor of Teacher Education Mary Ellen Sullivan, Ph.D. is also a talented practitioner. She has been an elementary school teacher, a high school English teacher, and an educational consultant. She is the cofounder of Charter High School for Law and Social Justice and the principal investigator for the Robert Noyce Teacher Scholarship Program. Her areas of interest include adolescent education, English language learners, literacy development, and urban education.

Location

The College of Mount Saint Vincent is located in Riverdale, New York, in the northeastern region of the United States. Its 70-acre campus, with rolling lawns and wooded hills, overlooks the Hudson River. The College's location, just 12 miles from midtown Manhattan in New York City, provides many cultural, educational, and employment opportunities.

The College

Established in 1847, the College of Mount Saint Vincent offers programs of exceptional quality in the Catholic and ecumenical tradition. It offers programs in the arts, sciences, and humanities; mathematics; and social sciences as well as professional programs in accounting, business, communication, education, and nursing. Its friendly and supportive community includes more than 1,800 undergraduate and graduate students who represent 28 states and nine countries.

Admissions Requirements and Applying

The application process, requirements, and deadlines vary depending on the course of study; specific details are available on the graduate program application website at https://mountsaintvincent.edu/admission/graduate-studies/apply-for-graduate-programs. But in general, applicants need to submit a completed application, official transcripts from all post-secondary institutions attended, letters of recommendation, a resume, test scores, and other materials as required by each program. International applicants must also meet CMSV's language criteria with sufficient scores on the TOEFL, IELTS, and GMAT.

Applications are reviewed on a rolling admission basis. All required documents should be submitted four to six weeks prior to the beginning of the semester for which the applicant intends to enroll.

Correspondence and Information

Office of Admission
School of Professional and Graduate Studies
Founders Hall 105
College of Mount Saint Vincent
6301 Riverdale Avenue
Riverdale, New York 10471
United States
Phone: 718-405-3320
E-mail: spgs@mountsaintvincent.edu
Website: https://mountsaintvincent.edu/academics/school-of-professional-graduate-studies/graduate-programs/

THE COLLEGE OF NEW JERSEY

Graduate Programs

★ For more information, visit http://petersons.to/collegeofnewjerseygrad

Programs of Study

The College of New Jersey (TCNJ) offers the following advanced degrees: Master of Arts (M.A.) in counselor education (areas include school counseling; clinical mental health counseling; and marriage, couple, and family counseling and therapy) or English (literature); Master of Arts in Teaching (M.A.T.) in early childhood education, elementary education, secondary education (social studies, English, iSTEM math, iSTEM science, and iSTEM technology education), special education/elementary; five-year programs (for TCNJ undergraduate students only) in education of the deaf and hard of hearing/elementary education, special education, urban education, and English; Master of Education (M.Ed.) in educational leadership–principal certification, educational leadership: instruction (a collaborative program in conjunction with the Regional Training Center), elementary and secondary education (off-site Global Program only), reading K–12, special education, special education/teacher of the blind or visually impaired, Integrative Science, Technology, Engineering, and Math (iSTEM), or teaching English as a second language; Master of Science in Nursing (M.S.N.) in adult/gerontological primary care nurse practitioner studies, clinical nurse leader studies, family nurse practitioner studies, neonatal nurse practitioner studies, or school nurse certification (instructional and non-instructional options); and Educational Specialist (Ed.S.) in marriage, couple, and family therapy.

Graduate certificate programs and/or post-master's programs are offered in adult/gerontological primary care nurse practitioner studies, family nurse practitioner studies, school nurse certification (instructional and non-instructional options), bilingual education (main campus and off-site Global Program), educational leadership–principal certification, instructional licensure-teacher of preschool–grade 3, learning disabilities teacher/consultant studies, teacher of students with blindness and visual impairments studies, reading specialist studies, student assistance coordinator studies, teacher certification for international schools (off-site Global Program only), teacher of students with disabilities, teaching English as a second language, or gender studies.

Global opportunities in education are also available for graduate students. Graduate global programs at TCNJ have been in existence for over thirty-five years and provide course work leading toward master's-level degrees in education and certification in teaching, administration, and substance abuse counseling. Courses are taught by TCNJ faculty members and other internationally recognized professors. Courses are offered June through July at TCNJ sites in Mallorca, Spain; Bangkok, Thailand; Lisbon, Portugal; and Johannesburg, South Africa. During the academic year, courses are available in Cairo, Egypt; Hsinchu, Taiwan; and Ho Chi Minh City, Vietnam.

For the convenience of the majority of graduate students who pursue degrees while employed full-time, graduate courses held on the Ewing campus are offered during the day and in the evening.

Research Facilities

TCNJ offers a state-of-the-art library that serves as an exciting intellectual, cultural, and social center for the College community. The five-story, 135,000-square-foot facility will provide cutting-edge services to the TCNJ community well into the twenty-first century. In addition to housing traditional library collections and services in an atmosphere that is both friendly and elegant, a key feature of the recently built library is its wide array of carefully considered and thoughtful amenities, which make using the facility both a pleasure and a convenience. The library provides twenty-four group-study rooms (one reserved for graduate students), ample and comfortable seating, tables and carrels, and both WiFi and LAN Internet access throughout, with power connections available at every carrel and study table. Special design features include a café, a secure, late night/24-hour study area, and a 105-seat multipurpose auditorium. The library also houses the Instructional Technology Services facility, creating ideal one-stop shopping for students working on projects.

Library collections include more than 560,000 volumes and 200,000 microforms as well as subscriptions to more than 1,400 periodicals. The library also subscribes to more than seventy-five electronic indexes covering more than 14,000 scholarly journals, including full-text resources. A media facility offers viewing and listening equipment as well as sound recordings, videos, and interactive computer software. PCs are available for public access to electronic resources. Collections are constantly augmented by new acquisitions, and interlibrary loan and document delivery services are available to students. The library is also an active participant in a number of library networks and maintains cooperative arrangements with many regional academic libraries, from which students may borrow directly. TCNJ librarians are an important resource in and of themselves. In addition to advanced studies in library and information science, each subject librarian has additional graduate degrees in one of the major academic areas, and students are encouraged to consult them in person and online.

In addition to providing new library facilities for the College community, TCNJ has met the challenge of the computer field's phenomenal growth with installations of computer facilities in each of its seven schools.

Financial Aid

The College of New Jersey offers financial aid to qualified matriculated students through a combination of loans, assistantships, and/or student employment opportunities. To be considered for all financial aid programs, students must submit the Free Application for Federal Student Aid (FAFSA) to the College Financial Assistance Office. Graduate assistantships are available to qualified full-time students on a competitive basis. Prospective students must apply through the Office of Graduate Studies by April 15 to be considered for a graduate assistantship.

Cost of Study

Tuition for graduate courses for the 2016–17 academic year is $895.61 per semester hour of credit for New Jersey residents and $1,305.77 per semester hour of credit for out-of-state residents. Additional fees include ID, student center, computer access and service fees, and health insurance (for full-time students). Tuition and fees are subject to change by action of the New Jersey State Legislature.

Living and Housing Costs

As the majority of TCNJ's graduate students attend classes part-time in the evenings, the College does not offer on-campus housing for graduate students. Graduate students who seek housing in the area may obtain assistance from the Office of Residence Life.

Student Group

The College of New Jersey has an enrollment of approximately 6,500 undergraduate students and 1,000 graduate students.

Student Outcomes

The College of New Jersey's excellent reputation has afforded graduates outstanding opportunities when entering their professional fields. Many TCNJ graduates receive job placements through various on-campus recruitment programs sponsored by the Office of Career Services.

Location

The College of New Jersey is located on 289 tree-lined acres in suburban Ewing, New Jersey, 7 miles from the state capital in Trenton. Woodlands and two lakes surround the academic and residential buildings. More than thirty-five buildings make up the physical plant, most of which are built in the classic Georgian Colonial architecture. The campus is 30 miles from Philadelphia and 60 miles from New York's theaters, museums, and other attractions. The nearby towns of Princeton and New Hope offer additional cultural activities.

The College

Founded in 1855, the College has grown from its early years as a teachers' college to a multipurpose institution comprising seven schools: Arts and Communication; Business; Education; Engineering; Humanities and Social Sciences; Nursing, Health, and Exercise Science; and Science. Graduate study is available in the Schools of Education, Humanities and Social Sciences, and Nursing, Health, and Exercise Science.

TCNJ introduced its first advanced degree program, a Master of Science in elementary education, in 1947. Over the years, the number of graduate programs has steadily increased. At present, there are more than fifty specialized graduate degree and certificate programs.

TCNJ's academic programs are accredited by the Middle States Association of Colleges and Schools, the National Council for Accreditation of Teacher Education (NCATE)/Council for the Accreditation of Educator Preparation (CAEP), the Council for the Accreditation of Counseling and Related Educational Programs (CACREP), Commission on Collegiate Nursing Education (CCNE), and other appropriate professional associations.

Applying

Students of proven ability with undergraduate degrees in appropriate fields are eligible to apply for graduate study. Applications should be submitted online (http://graduate.tcnj.edu/apply) along with a $75 nonrefundable application fee. Transcripts of all previous college or university work and other supporting documentation, as noted on the website, should be forwarded to the Office of Graduate Studies. Acceptable scores on the appropriate national standardized tests are required for most degree and initial teacher certificate programs.

Application deadlines for matriculation and non-matriculation for the various graduate programs are located on the Graduate Studies website (http://graduate.tcnj.edu/apply).

Correspondence and Information

Office of Graduate and Advancing Education
Paul Loser Hall, Room 109
The College of New Jersey
P.O. Box 7718
2000 Pennington Road
Ewing, New Jersey 08628
United States
Phone: 609-771-2300
Fax: 609-637-5105
E-mail: graduate@tcnj.edu
Website: http://graduate.tcnj.edu

DEANS AND PROGRAM COORDINATORS

SCHOOL OF HUMANITIES AND SOCIAL SCIENCES

Jane Wong, Dean; Ph.D.

Graduate Program Coordinator

English: Jo Carney, Ph.D., Iowa.

SCHOOL OF EDUCATION

Jeff Passe, Dean; Ph.D., Florida.

Graduate Program Coordinators

Counselor Education: Mark Woodford, Ph.D., Virginia. Marion Cavallaro, Ph.D., Ohio State. Atsuko Seto, Ph.D., Wyoming. Stuart Roe, Ph.D., Penn State.
Deaf and Hard of Hearing/Elementary Education Five-Year Program: Barbara Strassman, Ed.D., Columbia Teachers College.
Early Childhood Education (P–3 Certificate): Jody Eberly, Ph.D., Rutgers.
Educational Leadership–Instruction: Alan Amtzis, Ph.D., Boston College.
Educational Leadership–Principal: Donald Leake, Ph.D., Ohio State.
Elementary and Early Childhood Education (M.A.T.): Arti Joshi, Ph.D., Syracuse.
Instructional Licensure–Teacher of Preschool–Grade 3: Jody Eberly, Ph.D., Rutgers.
Reading K–12: Matthew Hall, Ph.D., NYU.
Secondary Education: Donald Leake, Ph.D., Ohio State.
Special Education: Amy Dell, Ph.D., Rochester.
TESOL/Bilingual Education: Yiqiang Wu, Ph.D., Texas A&M.

SCHOOL OF NURSING, HEALTH, AND EXERCISE SCIENCE

Carole Kenner, Dean; Ph.D., Indiana.

Graduate Program Coordinators

Nursing: Connie Kartoz, Ph.D., Pennsylvania.
Health and Exercise Science: Anne Farrell, Ph.D., New Mexico.

MAJOR RESEARCH PROJECTS, AWARDS, GRANTS, AND INITIATIVES

School of Education

Intoxicated Drivers' Resource Center (IDRC); Dr. Cassandra Gibson and the TCNJ Clinic, School of Education.
Community Reinforcement and Family Training (CRAFT); Dr. Cassandra Gibson and Dr. Mark Woodford, School of Education.
Collegiate Recovery Support and Environmental Change (CRC); Dr. Cassandra Gibson, School of Education.
Trenton Violence Reduction Strategy (TVRS); Dr. Cassandra Gibson, School of Education.
LifeChoices; Dr. Cassandra Gibson and Dr. Stuart Roe, School of Education.
Creating a team of highly qualified professionals for English language learners (CTHQP) grant; Dr. Yiqiang Wu, School of Education.
Adaptive Technology Center grant; Dr. Amy G. Dell, School of Education.
Preparing special and elementary educators to use inquiry and design-based learning; Dr. Amy Dell, School of Education.
Provisional Teacher Program; Dr. Anthony Evangelisto, School of Education.
TECH-NJ (Technology, Educators, and Children with Disabilities–New Jersey); Dr. Amy G. Dell, School of Education.
Deaf/Blind Family and Community Educational Support; Dr. Jerry Petroff, School of Education.
Conversation analysis of native/non-native speakers; Dr. Jean Wong, School of Education.
Facilitating transition from school to employment for individuals with challenging behavior; Dr. Shridevi Rao, School of Education.
Issues of literacy and teaching elementary students of color; Dr. Deborah Thompson, School of Education.
Fulbright Scholar Award to teach at the University of Bahrain, Bahrain Teachers College; Dr. Lynnette Mawhinney, School of Education

School of Nursing, Health and Exercise Science

Advanced education nursing traineeship program; Dr. Claire Lindberg, School of Nursing
HIV symptom distress project; Dr. Claire Lindberg, School of Nursing.

School of Humanities and Social Sciences

The reception of Dante and Chaucer within the work of their literary successors; Dr. Glenn Steinberg, School of Culture and Society.
Book-length research project in family memoir based on research and interviews: "The Seven: A Family Holocaust Story"; Ellen Friedman, School of Humanities and Social Sciences.
Research in Early Modern Grammars and Spelling Books; Felicia Steele, School of Humanities and Social Sciences.
"'Universal Mixing' and Interpenetrating Standing: Disability and Community in Melville's Moby-Dick"; Harriet Hustis, School of Humanities and Social Sciences.
Executive Director of the Thornton Wilder Society, which is headquartered at TCNJ, and co-founder and officer of the Edward Albee Society; Lincoln Konkle, School of Humanities and Social Sciences.
Thornton Wilder: New Perspectives; Lincoln Konkle, School of Humanities and Social Sciences.
Thornton Wilder and The Puritan Narrative Tradition; Lincoln Konkle, School of Humanities and Social Sciences.
National Endowment for the Humanities Fellowship; Michael Robertson, School of Humanities and Social Sciences.
Worshipping Walt: The Whitman Disciples; Michael Robertson, School of Humanities and Social Sciences.
Walt Whitman, Where the Future Becomes Present; David Blake and Michael Robertson, School of Humanities and Social Sciences.

The clock tower above Green Hall, the main administrative building on campus, is a well-known symbol of TCNJ tradition.

TCNJ offers a state-of-the-art library that serves as an exciting intellectual, cultural, and social center for the College community.

COLLEGE OF STATEN ISLAND OF THE CITY UNIVERSITY OF NEW YORK

Graduate Degree Programs

THE CITY UNIVERSITY OF NEW YORK
College of Staten Island

Programs of Study

The College of Staten Island (CSI) offers master's degrees in Accounting (M.S.); Biology (M.S.); Business Management (M.S.); Cinema and Media Studies (M.A.); Clinical Mental Health Counseling (M.A.); Computer Science (M.S.); Education: Childhood (elementary) Education (M.S.Ed.), Adolescence (secondary) Education (M.S.Ed.), Special Education (grades 1–6) (M.S.Ed.), Special Education (grades 7–12) (M.S.Ed.), Teaching of English to Speakers of other Languages (M.S.Ed.); English (M.A.); Environmental Science (M.S.); History (M.A.); Liberal Studies (M.A.); Neuroscience and Developmental Disabilities (M.S.); Nursing: Adult-Gerontological Health Nursing (M.S.); and Social Work (M.S.W.).

Post-master's degrees are awarded in Education: School District Leader, School Building Leader and School District Leader (dual certificate) and in Nursing: Adult-Gerontological Health Nursing. Advanced certificates are offered in Autism Spectrum Disorders, Business Analytics of Large-Scale Data, Cultural Competence, and Teaching of English to Speakers of other Languages. The College of Staten Island offers an Adult-Gerontological Health Nursing (D.N.P.) program and a Clinical Doctorate in Physical Therapy (D.P.T.).

In addition, the College offers the following doctoral programs jointly with the Graduate Center of the City University of New York (CUNY): Biochemistry (Ph.D.), Biology (Ph.D.), Computer Science (Ph.D.), Nursing (Ph.D.), Physics (Ph.D.), and Polymer Chemistry (Ph.D.).

Research Facilities

The Center for Developmental Neuroscience and Developmental Disabilities is supported jointly with the New York State Institute for Basic Research (IBR). The center conducts, promotes, and sponsors research, education, and training in the developmental neurosciences, with special emphasis on research and educational programs in the specific field of developmental disabilities. The center provides for collaborative efforts between the College and IBR in offering the master's degree in Neuroscience and Developmental Disabilities, as well as with the University's doctoral programs in biology (subprogram in neuroscience), and in psychology (subprogram in learning processes). The center provides advanced research training for graduate students.

The Center for Environmental Science provides support for research and policy recommendations concerning environmental problems. One of the major purposes of the center is to define and solve environmental problems on Staten Island and its environs through research that includes studies of respiratory diseases, toxic and carcinogenic chemicals in the air, and the population at risk for lung cancer.

The Center for the Study of Staten Island: Staten Island Project (SIP) is designed to integrate the work of the College with the public affairs concerns of the people of Staten Island. To that end, it mediates and facilitates the collaboration of the College's faculty, students, and staff with government, civic organizations, and businesses in order to identify and assist in finding solutions to the borough's pressing public issues. The center serves as an information and consultation resource to prepare citizens and leaders to make better-informed decisions about public life; it fosters the development of faculty research and graduate education through engagement with the community; and it builds bridges to other public affairs institutes and local communities as a spur to innovations in public life on Staten Island.

The Center for Interdisciplinary Applied Mathematics and Computational Sciences brings together a diverse group of research faculty members and students with interests in interdisciplinary applications of mathematics and computational science. The center's activities include the use of the campus supercomputer, faculty collaboration, grant writing, student mentoring and research, and sponsored lectures.

The CUNY High-Performance Computing Center (HPCC) is located on the CSI campus. Goals of the HPCC are to: support the scientific computing needs of university faculty, student, staff, and their public and private sector partners; create opportunities for the CUNY research community to develop new partnerships with the government and private sectors; and leverage the center's capabilities to acquire additional research resources for its faculty and graduate students in existing and major new programs.

Financial Aid

The Office of Student Financial Aid administers federal and state grant, loan, and work-study programs to assist students with financial need to attend the College of Staten Island. Students should contact the Office of Student Financial Aid early in the admission process to discuss eligibility requirements and responsibilities. Graduate assistant positions are available for full-time graduate students in some departments. Information about these positions may be obtained from the individual program departments.

Cost of Study

For the 2016–17 academic year, tuition for master's programs for New York State residents is $425 per credit, or $5,065 per semester for 12 or more credits. Tuition for non-state residents is $780 per credit. Tuition for the Master in Social Work program is $560 per credit, or $6,685 per semester for New York State residents. Tuition for non-state residents is $910 per credit. Tuition for the Clinical Doctorate in Physical Therapy program for New York State residents is $625 per credit, or $5,460 per semester. Tuition for non-state residents is $985 per credit. Tuition for the Doctorate in Nursing Practice program for New York State residents is $560 per credit, or $6,685 per semester. Tuition for non-state residents is $910 per credit.

Living and Housing Costs

For the 2016–17 academic year, students living with parents budgeted a minimum of $1,364 for books and supplies, $1,054 for local transportation, $2,948 for meals and personal expenses, and $4,270 for housing. Students living away from parents budgeted the same amounts for books, supplies, and transportation, plus $17,961 for food, housing, and personal expenses for a nine-month academic year. The College of Staten Island's first on-campus student housing is now open. Floor plans and rates are available online at www.csi.cuny.edu/housing.

Student Group

Nearly 1,000 graduate students enrolled at the College of Staten Island in the 2015 fall semester. The graduate population reflects a wide range of ethnicity, social and economic backgrounds, educational and professional experiences, and aspirations.

Location

The College of Staten Island is located in New York City in the Borough of Staten Island. Completed in 1994, the 204-acre campus of the College of Staten Island is the largest one for a college in New York City. Set in a park-like landscape, the campus is centrally located on Staten Island and is accessible by automobile and public transportation.

The College

The College of Staten Island is a college of the City University of New York that offers exceptional opportunities to all its students. Programs in the liberal arts and sciences and professional studies lead to bachelor's and associate degrees, in addition to the graduate programs previously listed.

Graduate Program Faculty Heads

A full listing of graduate program directors, contact information, and office hours is available at the College website. Please visit http://www.csi.cuny.edu/graduatestudies and click on "Graduate Programs and Requirements."

Applying

Requirements for admission and application deadlines vary by program and department. Students should contact the Graduate Admissions' Office for additional information or to arrange an admissions interview or campus tour.

Correspondence and Information

Sasha Spence, Associate Director for Graduate Admissions
Office of Recruitment and Admissions
North Administration Building (2A), Room 103
College of Staten Island
2800 Victory Boulevard
Staten Island, New York 10314
Phone: 718-982-2019
Fax: 718-982-2500
E-mail: masterit@csi.cuny.edu
Website: http://www.csi.cuny.edu/graduatestudies

Graduate students at the College of Staten Island are provided with the tools and opportunities they need to make positive contributions to society. CSI students perform research with faculty from every academic discipline on campus, using the College's state-of-the-art equipment and facilities.

Instructors at the College of Staten Island are committed to each graduate student's success. Whether offering guidance on a rigorous course of study, engaging students in stimulating research, or sharing their professional experiences, CSI faculty members help students shape and achieve their goals.

COLORADO SCHOOL OF MINES

Graduate School

★ For more information, visit http://petersons.to/coloradoschoolofminesgrad

MINES™

Programs of Studies

Specialized and focused, Colorado School of Mines (Mines) is a unique research university with an extensive array of resource-related programs. The need for Mines' rare mix of expertise has never been greater. The availability and sustainable use of natural resources is one of the world's greatest challenges, and Mines' graduates and faculty members are creating solutions.

Those interested in pursuing a graduate degree find significant academic and research opportunities in globally significant growth areas:

- Engineering—mechanical, electrical, civil and environmental, chemical and biological, nuclear
- Environment—environmental engineering science, chemistry, hydrology
- Geotechnics—geology, petroleum, mining, geophysics, underground construction and tunneling
- Business—mineral and energy economics, engineering and technology management

Graduate degree options range from Master of Engineering, Master of Science (thesis and non-thesis options), and Ph.D.'s.

Research

Mines is a global leader in research and the advancement of technology. Led by world-class faculty, the research conducted at Mines enhances the educational experience of its graduates. Students have the opportunity to actively participate in research at every level of their education.

With an annual research budget of more than $55 million and a faculty that has pioneered numerous advances in a wide range of technical fields, opportunities to conduct innovative research is virtually unlimited. Graduate students are able to work hand-in-hand with researchers at Mines and from around the world on both applied and academic research problems. Proximity to a number of governmental research facilities such as the U.S. Geological Survey, the National Renewable Energy Laboratory, the U.S. Bureau of Reclamation, and the National Institute of Standards and Technology provides unparalleled access to a wide variety of scholars, facilities, and research opportunities.

Research spans many highly relevant areas, with a specific focus on energy and environmental stewardship. Mines' first-rate facilities and partnerships with industry, national laboratories, other universities, funding agencies, and international institutions help maintain its cutting-edge research and have a significant impact on real-world problems. Research is a cooperative effort in the Mines community; more information can be found at http://www.minesnewsroom.com/.

Financial Aid

At Mines, the awarding policy gives priority to the neediest students, as determined by the FAFSA. In the last academic year, more than $27.9 million of financial assistance was awarded. Typically more than 85 percent of the student body receives some form of aid, which includes scholarships, grants, loans, or work-study employment.

Cost of Study

For the 2016–17 academic year, full-time (9–15 credits) tuition per semester is $7,845 for residents and $17,010 for nonresidents. Mandatory fees are $1,076. The estimated cost of books and supplies is $750 per semester. More information on tuition and fees is available online at www.mines.edu/Costs_GS.

Living and Housing Costs

The Apartments at Mines Park house undergraduate and graduate degree seeking students. Single student housing is available in 1, 2, and 3 bedroom apartments. Family housing is available in 1 and 2 bedroom apartments. Additional information on Mines Park is available from the Department of Residence Life or online at http://residencelife.mines.edu/Apartments-at-Mines-Park.

In addition, Golden and the surrounding communities—Lakewood, Arvada, Denver, Boulder, and Littleton—offer other affordable housing options (http://residencelife.mines.edu/Off-Campus-Housing-Resources).

Student Group and Outcomes

The Graduate School at Mines draws together nearly 1,300 graduate students from the United States and over sixty other countries, and encourages problem investigation from diverse, real-world perspectives. Together, faculty and staff members and undergraduate and graduate students build a strong community of shared interests. The Mines community understands the challenges that can arise in leaving a home community to attend graduate school and works collectively to help maintain those community ties while building and growing new ones.

A graduate student at Colorado School of Mines becomes an important member of a community that is dedicated to generating new knowledge and educating students and professionals in fields related to the:

- discovery and recovery of the Earth's resources, their conversion to materials and energy, and their utilization in advanced processes and products
- economic and social systems necessary to ensure the prudent and provident use of Earth's resources in a sustainable global society
- preservation and stewardship of the Earth's environment

Mines' renowned reputation, attained through the tremendous work of its students, faculty and staff; its high admission standards; and its alumni network combine to give students an edge in the job market. Mines' strong master's and professional degrees are extremely valuable and more than just precursors to a doctoral degree. More than 96 percent of the recipients of Mines' master's and professional degrees find employment by graduation. More than 70 percent of these graduates are employed in industry, with the remainder employed by governmental agencies or matriculating into doctoral degree programs.

Location

Mines is located in Golden, Colorado, in the foothills of the Rocky Mountains, 15 miles west of Denver's downtown business district. Golden, a thriving community of 17,000, offers outdoor adventure with small-town atmosphere and convenient access to big-city attractions. With more than 300 days of sunshine each year, Golden is a great place to visit or live in during any season. Founded during the Gold Rush of 1859, Golden is one of Colorado's oldest communities and served as the Capital of Colorado Territory from 1862 to 1867. Golden retains its small-town character and remains the seat of Jefferson County. Historic buildings and homes have been preserved and blend with new construction throughout the downtown area, which offers many shops and restaurants.

The school has some big-name neighbors in Golden, including the National Renewable Energy Laboratory, a frequent research partner, and Coors Brewing Company.

Outdoor enthusiasts will find the proximity of the Mines campus to Colorado's Rocky Mountains an exciting prospect. Colorado offers a legendary abundance of activity in its nearby mountains, open spaces, and parks including alpine skiing, snowboarding, cross-country skiing, snowshoeing, mountain climbing, river rafting, hiking, biking, camping, exploring and fishing—to name a few.

The Mines campus features beautifully renovated historical architecture, as well as award-winning, new, state-of-the-art buildings.

The School

Colorado School of Mines is a public research university devoted to engineering and applied science. Founded in 1874, Mines' role and mission has remained constant and is written in the Colorado statute as:

"The Colorado School of Mines shall be a specialized baccalaureate and graduate research institution with high admission standards. The Colorado School of Mines shall have a unique mission in energy, mineral, and materials science and engineering and associated engineering and science fields. The school shall be the primary institution of higher education offering energy, mineral and materials science and mineral engineering degrees at both the graduate and undergraduate levels." *(Colorado Revised Statutes, Section 23-41-105)*

Mines offers all the advantages of a world-class research institution with a size that allows for personal attention. Innovative ideas have the chance to flourish and with a strong work ethic, students have the opportunity to help drive positive change locally, nationally, and globally.

Applying

The Graduate School at Mines is open to graduates from four-year baccalaureate programs at recognized colleges and universities. Admission to all graduate programs is competitive, based on an evaluation of academic performance (undergraduate or graduate), test scores, and references. Each department evaluates applications separately and admissions decisions are based on distinct admission criteria.

All application materials are submitted to the Office of Graduate Studies. Once an application file is complete, it is forwarded to the academic department review committee. Prospective students should consult the Graduate Admissions website at www.mines.edu/gradutate_admissions for more information.

Correspondence and Information

Graduate School
Colorado School of Mines
1500 Illinois Street
Golden, Colorado 80401
United States
Phone: 303-273-3247
800-446-9488 Ext. 3247
E-mail: grad-app@mines.edu
Website: http://www.mines.edu

Finding innovative solutions to global challenges.

Focused on responsible stewardship of the earth and its resources.

DARTMOUTH COLLEGE

School of Graduate and Advanced Studies

★ For more information, visit http://petersons.to/dartmouthcollege-grad

Programs of Study

Since 1885, graduate and advanced studies at Dartmouth has combined world-class research facilities with an outstanding faculty. Dartmouth's graduate programs facilitate innovation, support collaboration, and deliver a unique blend of research opportunities and individualized education.

The School of Graduate and Advanced studies at Dartmouth offers masters and doctoral degrees across a broad range of programs, including several interdisciplinary programs and doctoral programs connected to the professional schools at Dartmouth. There are 16 programs leading to the Ph.D., 12 on the master's track, and 7 cross-disciplinary programs.

Master's degrees are offered in chemistry, comparative literature, computer science, digital music, engineering, earth sciences, liberal studies, health care delivery, health policy and clinical practice, physics and astronomy, and quantitative biomedical sciences.

Doctoral programs are offered in biochemistry, biology, chemistry, cognitive neuroscience, computer science, earth sciences, ecology evolution ecosystems and society, engineering, experimental and molecular medicine, genetics, health policy and clinical practice, mathematics, microbiology and immunology, physics and astronomy, psychological and brain sciences, and quantitative biomedical science.

Special interdisciplinary training programs include environmental sciences, Master of Engineering Management, medical physics, M.D./M.S. program in biomedical engineering, Ph.D. engineering innovation program, M.D./Ph.D. program, and Ph.D./MBA program.

The School supports over 1,000 students from 62 countries, including the United States. The graduate alumni network connects more than 4,000 graduates.

The School of Graduate and Advance Studies has fused the liberal arts tradition with research and believes that intense collaboration among brilliant people and strong departments accelerates discovery. It seeks to develop scholars who can approach problems from multiple perspectives and who can work across fields of study.

Research Facilities

Graduate and postdoctoral education at Dartmouth is more intimate than at the big research universities it is often compared to. Faculty members lead small, intense, research teams and students enjoy unparalleled access to leaders in their fields. There are over 75 centers and institutes, and sponsored research attracted $209 million in fiscal year 2014.

Dartmouth boasts world-class research and teaching facilities designed to promote cross-disciplinary intellectual exchange. A physical sciences center and chemistry building house science programs, libraries, computer labs, and service shops, encouraging students and faculty from different fields to interact. The medical complex offers state-of-the-art research facilities created to provide training in life sciences programs.

Financial Aid

Dartmouth offers full financial support to all students in doctoral programs. Financial support includes a paid yearly stipend or fellowship. Financial aid at the master's level varies by program.

Cost of Study

Dartmouth operates on a quarterly schedule. Students normally enroll for three quarters per year. Tuition and fees vary depending on the program in which the student is enrolled. The most current and complete list of charges is available online at http://www.dartmouth.edu/~control/docs/studentfin/charges1617.pdf.

Living and Housing

Many graduate students choose to live on campus. Reserved for first-year graduate students, North Park is a short walk to campus, as well as shopping and restaurants in downtown Hanover. Students with families may apply for apartments in Sachem Village, the student college housing complex located two miles south of campus.

There are several options off campus; information is available through the Dartmouth Real Estate Office (https://realestate.dartmouth.edu) and Craigslist. There will be housing information on the graduate studies' electronic bulletin board. The classified advertisement section of the Valley News (local newspaper) is another source.

Student Life

Roughly 1,050 graduate students attend Dartmouth, enjoying a coeducational college community built for them and the 4,276 undergraduates. Campus cultural life centers around the Hopkins Center for the Performing Arts, which sponsors an active film society, two full concert series, and a very active drama program. Facilities are available for students interested in joining a musical group or participating in arts workshops including sculpture, painting, and design. Graduate students also have access to the extensive facilities of the Dartmouth College Athletic Council, and can participate in a variety of clubs, including the Dartmouth Graduate Outing Club.

Dartmouth's Entrepreneurial Network helps students learn valuable entrepreneurial skills, and offers strategic advice and mentoring to prepare students to leverage their knowledge and abilities.

The Dartmouth Career Network is a professional network of thousands of alumni who are willing to advise students and fellow alumni on their career path.

The Faculty

Dartmouth faculty members are experts in their fields, renowned for their scholarship in their respective disciplines and for their teaching ability. The faculty is accessible and available for consultation with students. The small program sizes ensure close collaborative relationships between faculty and students.

Students across the disciplines also interact with faculty at the professional schools including the Tuck School of Business, Thayer

School of Engineering, and Geisel School of Medicine ensuring breadth of knowledge while pursuing their specific graduate program. A complete listing of the Dartmouth faculty and their areas of expertise and research is available at http://dartmouth.edu/research/faculty-experts.

Location

Dartmouth is located in Hanover, New Hampshire on the western side of the state in the scenic Upper Connecticut River Valley. The river forms the border between Vermont and New Hampshire. Its location provides a gateway to nature in all seasons both on land and water, and is a 2–3 hour drive from Boston. The Dartmouth Coach travels daily to Boston and to New York City. Montreal, Canada is also just a few hours away.

Dartmouth College has 160 buildings across its 269-acre campus. It is the ninth-oldest college in the United States and home to the original Winter Carnival programs.

The University

Founded in 1769, Dartmouth is a member of the Ivy League and consistently ranks among the world's greatest academic institutions. Dartmouth has forged a singular identity for combining its deep commitment to outstanding undergraduate liberal arts and graduate education with distinguished research and scholarship in the arts and sciences.

Professional and graduate programs across Dartmouth's schools—Geisel School of Medicine, the School of Graduate and Advanced Studies, Thayer School of Engineering, and the Tuck School of Business—have a distinguished history of training practitioners and scholars whose discoveries and expertise change the world.

Application and Admissions Information

The School of Graduate and Advanced Studies admits the most highly qualified applicants whose academic backgrounds and personal and professional experiences have prepared them for achievement and excellence in graduate studies.

Applications generally include a completed application form, undergraduate transcripts, three letters of recommendation, and scores from the General Test of the Graduate Record Examinations (GRE).

Application requirements vary by program; exact requirements can be obtained from each department. The complete list of programs online (http://dartmouth.edu/education/departments-programs-arts-sciences) includes links to department websites.

Dartmouth is committed to the principle of equal opportunity for all its students, faculty, employees, and applicants for admission and employment. Please see our non-discrimination policy and information for students with disabilities.

Correspondence and Information

Ruth Friend, Admissions Coordinator
School of Graduate and Advanced Studies
Suite 6062, Room 437
Dartmouth College
37 Dewey Field Road
Hanover, New Hampshire 03755-1419
Phone: 603-646-8193
E-mail: Ruth.E.Friend@Dartmouth.edu
Website: http://dartmouth.edu/education/graduate-schools

FLORIDA INTERNATIONAL UNIVERSITY

Graduate Programs

FIU
FLORIDA INTERNATIONAL UNIVERSITY

★ For more information, visit http://petersons.to/floridainternationalgrad

Programs of Study

Florida International University (FIU) offers more than 120 graduate degrees and certificates across eight colleges and schools: College of Communication, Architecture + the Arts, College of Arts and Sciences and Education, Chapman Graduate School of Business, College of Engineering and Computing, Nicole Wertheim College of Nursing and Health Sciences, Steven J. Green School of International and Public Affairs, Robert Stempel College of Public Health and Social Work, and Chaplin School of Hospitality and Tourism Management.

Programs regularly cited among the best in the nation include international relations, Latin American and Caribbean studies, hospitality management, music, political science, creative writing, public administration, and business administration. The university places emphasis on interdisciplinary research, allowing students to collaborate across fields to explore ethical challenges in business, create plans for better schools and urban centers, discover new applications for nanotechnology, bring life to architectural landscapes, and advance the field of biomedicine.

Graduate students at FIU will have the opportunity to collaborate with top scholars and researchers. Students will study in Miami, a city of remarkable resources located at the crossroads of two continents. With access to the latest technologies and facilities, students will gain a competitive edge in their fields. Most importantly, students will earn degrees from a university that has garnered international respect. The value of an FIU degree can be seen in what graduates do every day: serve the community, spearhead groundbreaking initiatives, and take the lead in crafting solutions to some of society's greatest challenges. By advancing to the highest levels in their chosen fields, graduates lead and contribute across a wide range of enterprises throughout the world.

Research Facilities

With annual research expenditures exceeding $163 million, FIU is committed to the advancement of innovative and groundbreaking research. Faculty members look for students whose ideas and insights will contribute to the university's proactive research mission, ensuring that FIU remains a model of progress. FIU offers world-class research resources from a modern computing facility, to a stand-alone engineering campus, to state-of-the-art laboratories such as the world's only operating undersea research laboratory, Aquarius.

The libraries at the Modesto Maidique and Biscayne Bay campuses house more than one million volumes along with tens-of-thousands of periodicals, maps, microfilms, institutional archives, curriculum materials and government documents. The Green Library is FIU's main library, and is the largest building on-campus, and one of the largest libraries in the Southeastern United States. In addition, there is access to more than 10,000 journals and serials and a wide range of on-line resources.

More than 50 special centers and institutes at FIU add to the multidisciplinary nature of the university environment. Some of these centers include the Biomedical Engineering Institute, the High-Performance Database Research Center, the International Hurricane Research Center, the Latin American and Caribbean Center, the Center for Tourism and Technology, the Eugenio Pino and Family Global Entrepreneurship Center, and the International Forensic Research Institute.

Financial Aid

Students at FIU are highly successful in obtaining grants, fellowships, and other funding sources to support their graduate studies and research. Many assistantships allow graduate students to gain valuable experience as instructors while covering the cost of tuition. In addition, unique fellowships are available to advance research at the highest levels. These include the McKnight Doctoral Fellowship Program, the Ronald E. McNair Post Baccalaureate Achievement Program, and FIU's Presidential Fellowship Program. The University Graduate School provides information about such opportunities and supports students in the application process.

Cost of Study

Tuition for the 2016–17 academic year is $455.64 per credit for Florida residents and $1,001.69 per credit for out-of-state students. Rates are subject to change.

Living and Housing Costs

Graduate students at FIU must find off-campus housing. Florida International University's Off-Campus Housing Service (https://classifieds.fiu.edu) is designed to help students find housing that meets their needs and budgets.

Student Group

A research university that takes diversity seriously, FIU attracts students from all 50 states and more than 130 nations. FIU's graduate student community includes more than 8,000 students. All graduate programs offer different levels of flexibility to better serve the needs and schedules of the students, providing the option to complete programs either as full-time or part-time students.

The University

As Miami's only public research university, Florida International University leads the way in its commitment to vibrant learning, research, entrepreneurship, innovation, and creativity. Renowned scholars from prestigious universities around the world come to Florida International University to engage in world-class scholarship within a world-class city. This international community of scholars and researchers collaborates with students to push the frontiers of knowledge and discovery to solve 21st–century global challenges. Both the university and its remarkable setting represent the future.

Graduate students interact with faculty members whose innovative and timely scholarship places FIU among the ranks of America's leading research universities. The Carnegie Foundation for the Advancement of Teaching ranks FIU in R1: Doctoral Universities–Highest Research Activity category of its prestigious classification system; FIU has reached this level only a few decades since its founding.

Applying

General requirements for application to FIU's graduate programs include the online application ($30 fee), GRE or GMAT scores (depends on chosen major), official university or college transcripts from all institutions previously attended, TOEFL or IELTS scores, and official translations of university or college transcripts if they are in a language other than English. International students must also submit proof of degree/diploma (translated if necessary), bank and sponsor letter, declaration and certification of finances, and F-1 transfer form if currently in the U.S. There may also be additional requirements, such as letter of intent, letters of recommendation, resume, and a departmental application depending upon the chosen major.

Applications for the master's, specialist, and graduate certificate programs are due June 1 for the fall term, October 1 for the spring term, and March 1 for the summer term; for international applicants the due dates are February 15 for fall term, August 1 for spring term, and December 1 for summer term. Doctoral program applications for both domestic and international students are due February 15 for the fall term, August 1 for the spring term, and December 1 for the summer term.

Correspondence and Information

Office of Graduate and International Admissions and Recruitment Services
Florida International University
11200 S.W. 8th Street
Miami, Florida 33199
Phone: 305-348-7442
Fax: 305-348-7441
Website: http://gradschool.fiu.edu
Facebook: https://www.facebook.com/UGSGradschool

GODDARD COLLEGE

Graduate Programs

Goddard College

★ For more information, visit http://petersons.to/goddardcollegegrad

Programs of Study

Individualized Master of Arts: Students seeking an Individualized M.A. at Goddard pursue a question, project, or career interest that is interdisciplinary, trans-disciplinary, and personally absorbing. The program requires students to complete 48 hours of credit over four semesters. The program is available at the Plainfield, Vermont campus.

Master of Arts in Education: The M.A. in Education program offers professional concentrations and licensure curriculum. Students can choose an individualized non-licensure focus in community education or dual-language studies, or complete a traditional M.A. in Education or School Counseling degree program ending in professional licensure.

All tracks are offered at the Plainfield location, while the non-licensure individual focus track is also available at the college's Seattle, Washington campus.

Master of Arts in Health Arts and Sciences: The M.A. in Health Arts degree program teaches students how to foster health and healing practices. Students can focus on body and movement therapies, botanical medicine and ethnobotany, community and environmental health, men's health, nutritional health, expressive arts, integrative health systems, integrative nursing, mind-body studies, ecopsychology, women's health and midwifery, and cross-cultural healing. The M.A. in Health Arts degree program is offered at the Plainfield campus.

Master of Arts in Psychology and Counseling: Goddard awards M.A. degrees in both psychology and clinical mental health counseling according to Council of Applied Master's Programs in Psychology specifications. Coursework is completed over four or five semesters of low-residency learning at the Plainfield campus.

Goddard also offers a sexual orientation concentration to both psychology and counseling students, as well as to non-licensure track students and as a continuing education option for professionals.

Master of Fine Arts (M.F.A.) in Creative Writing: Students in Goddard's M.F.A. program each graduate with a completed novel, a collection of stories or poems, a screenplay, a collection of plays, a memoir, or a graphic novel script. Each student's study plan is individually tailored to meet their ambitions and interests. Paired with a faculty member, the student receives a series of packets containing criticism, highlights of particularly excellent work, and reading assignments.

A unique feature of the M.F.A. program is the requirement for a teaching practicum, which can occur at grade schools, community centers, colleges, or any level in between, whether the student aspires to teach after finishing the degree or not.

Master of Fine Arts (M.F.A.) in Interdisciplinary Arts: One of the only graduate programs in the world committed to art as a transformational practice, Goddard's M.F.A. in Interdisciplinary Arts program is designed to support artists with diverse life experiences and goals ranging from the social or political, to the aesthetic, spiritual, or autobiographical. Goddard's learning community supports the development of a robust, lifelong art practice. The program envisions making art as a form of critical thinking that integrates research and interdisciplinary problem-solving and engages ethically in public contexts.

Students can enroll in the M.F.A. in Interdisciplinary Arts at two locations: Plainfield, Vermont—Goddard's historic main campus—or Port Townsend, Washington—a vibrant arts community on the Pacific Coast.

Financial Aid

While Goddard's admissions process is need-blind (meaning income has no bearing on whether a student is admitted), the College commits to offer as much aid as possible to every eligible admitted student. Approximately 90 percent of the students who apply to Goddard's graduate and undergraduate programs are independent, working adults.

The College participates in the Federal Student Aid program. Students receive aid in the form of subsidized and unsubsidized federal loans, and the College awards more than $450,000 in institutional scholarships and grants. Applicants are encouraged to complete the Free Application for Federal Student Aid as soon as they start the application process.

Cost of Study

Tuition in Goddard's graduate programs varies by degree. Specific details on tuition and fees can be found online at www.goddard.edu/tuition.

Living and Housing Costs

Room and board costs are assessed for the period of the 8-day residency that starts the semester. Current room and board costs are available online at goddard.edu/tuition.

Student Group

Students have the opportunity to experience the pleasures and challenges of editing with the student-run literary journal, *Pitkin Review.* Publishing workshops are offered at every residency of the M.F.A. in Creative Writing program, and faculty members are available to address questions about publishing.

Location

The Plainfield, Vermont campus, located just outside Montpelier, is a sprawling former farm with a manor garden, woods, and Victorian-period architecture. The buildings were added to the National Register of Historic Places in 1996. The Port Townsend, Washington campus is located at Fort Worden, a former Victorian-era Army base with beaches, trails, and a seaside town within walking distance.

The M.A. in Education degree program is available at Goddard's new Columbia City campus, in one of Seattle's most ethnically and racially diverse neighborhoods.

The Faculty

Faculty members at Goddard give students personalized feedback every three weeks during the semester, helping students organize their work, understand their subject matter, and find their way in the world. One such faculty member is Professor Kyle Bass. A member of the Drama Guild of America, Professor Bass has been a finalist for both the Princess Grace Award and the Pushcart Prize. His works have appeared onstage in New York City, Syracuse, and foreign venues. In addition to his teaching duties, Professor Bass serves as drama editor of the acclaimed journal *Stone Canoe* where he has edited works by such noted authors as Kenneth Lin, Rogelio Martinez, and Chiori Miyagawa.

Professor Deborah Brevoort is a two-time winner of the Frederick Loewe Award for American Musical Theater. Her play, *Signs of Life*, won the Jane Chambers Award and was a Pinter Review Prize for Drama Gold Medalist. Her interests as a writer have always had an international focus, and her works have often featured theatrical conventions and forms from around the world to explore contemporary American subjects, such as her use of Japanese Noh drama to highlight the utter American-ness of Elvis in her *Blue Moon over Hawaii.*

Professor Sharon Cronin is coauthor of *Soy Bilingüe: Language, Culture, and Young Latino Children.* Dr. Cronin has over 25 years of experience in bilingual education and is a lead researcher in the Teaching Umoja Participatory Action Research 15-Year Commitment, which examines the ethnic identity, bicultural, cross-cultural, and tri-literacy development of children of color in Port Royal and Moore Town, Jamaica.

The College

The mission of Goddard College is to advance cultures of rigorous inquiry, collaboration, and lifelong learning, where individuals take imaginative and responsible action in the world.

Students at Goddard work with faculty to direct their studies according to their personal and professional interests, goals, gifts, and desires. Students develop the capacity to understand their lives in an ever-changing social context, and thereby to take meaningful action in the world. They are encouraged to question received knowledge and the status quo and to create new understandings of the world and of human experience. As a collaborative interdependent learning community, Goddard respects, includes, and appreciates differing perspectives. The College community challenges themselves and each other to embrace uncertainty, experiment, and imagine unexpected outcomes. Goddard's faculty and students recognize their interconnectedness with others and with the earth, and hold their scholarship and actions to the highest standards of integrity, authenticity, and compassion.

Goddard recognizes that teaching and learning are fully realized when they include a wide range of people, cultures, experiences, abilities, and fields of knowledge. Understanding that access to resources and social and political power are not equally distributed, the College offers the means to explore and articulate a wide range of personal and cultural understandings of well-being and justice, and to take action to create a more-just world. In addition to keeping education affordable, Goddard seeks to create academic and campus environments that all learning community members can use. The College also recognizes the increasing impact of human activity on the planet's limited resources. In educational and institutional practices, Goddard is committed to thoughtful and sustainable action that increases individual and social capacity for environmental stewardship and an improved future.

Goddard College has embodied this educational philosophy and these values for nearly 150 years. Initially chartered as a Universalist seminary in 1863, Green Mountain Central Institute, later renamed Goddard Seminary, exemplified the inclusive, socially engaged values of its community. Goddard College's founder, Royce "Tim" Pitkin, was a graduate of Goddard Seminary and a student of John Dewey. Alarmed by the rise of fascism in Europe, Pitkin founded Goddard College in 1938 to unite the liberal values of the seminary with Dewey's belief that interactive, self-directed education could help build civil, democratic societies. An experimenting college, Goddard has continually offered new educational models in response to societal needs. It was one of the first colleges to include adult learning in its charter, the first to develop a low-residency model for higher education, and the first to offer residential programs for single parents receiving public assistance. The College continues to grow and change along with its students, who come to Goddard to transform themselves, their communities, and their world.

Applying

Prospective students need to apply online. There is a $65 application fee. The GRE is not required. Applicants must submit an application essay, three letters of recommendation, and official transcripts. Applicants should visit http://www.goddard.edu/admissions and click through to "Graduate Admissions" in the right-hand menu for specific instructions on applying.

Correspondence and Information

Goddard College
123 Pitkin Road
Plainfield, Vermont 05667
United States
Phone: 800-906-8312 (toll-free)
Fax: 802-454-1029
E-mail: admissions@goddard.edu
Website: http://www.goddard.edu/admissions

INDIANA STATE UNIVERSITY

College of Graduate and Professional Studies

Indiana State University

★ For more information, visit http://petersons.to/indianastategrad

Programs of Study

Indiana State University (ISU) offers more than 75 graduate programs ranging from a graduate certificate or a master's, education specialist, or doctoral degree in the Colleges of Arts and Sciences; Business; Education; Nursing, Health, and Human Services; and Technology.

The College of Arts and Sciences offers the Psy.D. in clinical psychology and the Ph.D. in biology and spatial and earth sciences. The Department of Art offers the M.F.A. The Department of Music offers the M.M. degree. The Department of Political Science offers the M.P.A. Both the M.A. and the M.S. are available in communication disorders, criminology and criminal justice, history, mathematics, political science, psychology, and special education. The M.A. degree is offered in art, communication, English, geography, and linguistics/TESL/cross linguistics. The M.S. degree is offered in biology, clinical mental health counseling, computer science, earth and quaternary sciences, educational technology, electronics and computer technology, human resource development for higher education, industrial technology, occupational therapy, science education, student affairs and higher education career, technical education, and a Master of Social Work (M.S.W.).

The College of Business offers the M.B.A. degree. The College of Education offers the Ph.D. in guidance and psychological services, educational administration, and curriculum and instruction. The Ed.S. degree is offered in school administration and school psychology. The M.Ed. is offered in curriculum and instruction, elementary education, school administration and supervision, school counseling, and school psychology.

The College of Nursing, Health, and Human Services offers the M.A. and M.S. in health and safety, as well as physical education. The M.S. is offered in athletic training, nursing, physician assistant studies, and recreation and sport management. The College of Nursing, Health, and Human Services also offers courses of study leading to the Doctor Nursing Practice, the Doctor of Physical Therapy, and the Doctor of Athletic Training degrees.

The College of Technology offers a Ph.D. in technology management.

Research Facilities

Indiana State University Cunningham Memorial Library houses more than 2.5 million items, subscribes to more than 5,000 periodicals, and provides access to more than 20,000 full-text electronic periodicals. These can be accessed through an online system that also connects with other college libraries in Terre Haute and Indiana. The ISU library provides collaborative workstations to facilitate group and collaborative research. All students enrolled at ISU have access to a wireless network that allows them to access the Internet from most locations on the campus. Several departments offer specialized research facilities. The Instructional and Research Technology Services offers services (at no cost to students) that include statistical design consultation, research design consultation, design and analysis of sample research surveys, and presentation of statistical graphs and tables.

Financial Aid

Eligible graduate students may apply for institutional graduate assistantships through the respective academic departments. ISU graduate assistantships include a stipend and a tuition fee waiver. The tuition fee waivers are exclusive of building and student services fees, for up to 18 hours per academic year. For policies regarding graduate assistantships and fee waivers, students should visit the College of Graduate and Professional Studies website.

The Office of Student Financial Aid assists ISU graduate students in obtaining further educational funding opportunities through the Federal Perkins Loan (National Direct Student Loans) and Federal Stafford Student Loan programs, PLUS loans, or the College Work-Study Program. The office can be contacted at 812-237-2215 or at ISU-finaid@mail.indstate.edu.

Cost of Study

Tuition and fees for the 2016–17 academic year are $396 per semester hour for in-state students, $499 per semester hour for out-of-state students, and $770 per semester hour for international students.

Living and Housing Costs

Indiana State University offers furnished and unfurnished apartment-style housing for graduate students at its University Apartments at reasonable and competitive rental rates. Each apartment is self-contained with its own bedroom(s), bathroom, living/dining area, and kitchen with an electric range, refrigerator, and garbage disposal. Utilities and free local telephone service are also included. Furnished apartments range from $659 to $737 per month. Unfurnished apartments range from $547 to $824 per month. Low-cost housing is also available in the surrounding community.

Student Group

Since 1927, ISU's graduate programs have prepared students for careers in a wide range of teaching, research, and service professions. The campus has the highest diversity of students among four-year institutions in Indiana. Approximately 15 percent of the graduate students are international, 33 percent are out-of-state students, 15.7 percent are members of minority groups, and 58 percent are women. The average graduate student age is 33.

Location

The campus is located adjacent to the central business district of Terre Haute, Indiana, which is an industrial and commercial city of approximately 61,000 located in west-central Indiana. Cultural activities include amateur and professional theatrical productions, symphonies, and art exhibits. Excellent county and state parks are within easy driving distance. The city is convenient to the four major metropolitan areas of Indianapolis, St. Louis, Chicago, and Cincinnati.

The University and The School

Indiana State University is listed as one of the nation's best-value colleges by the Princeton Review in its 2008 edition of *America's Best Value Colleges*. Indiana State University has grown during its 140-year history from Indiana State Normal School to Indiana State Teachers College and Indiana State College to full university status. With a graduate student population of approximately 2,000, students can be assured of a close mentoring experience and significant research opportunities within their academic program.

Applying

Applications to the College of Graduate and Professional Studies can be submitted online, by mail, or in person.

Prospective applicants should visit the College of Graduate and Professional Studies website at http://indstate.edu/graduate and check with their respective departments for specific deadlines and additional required admissions materials. Students generally receive a response acknowledging receipt of the application and other communication within one to two weeks. Once admitted, students receive instructions regarding academic advisement and registration.

International students must submit a TOEFL score of 550 or better and an Affidavit of Financial Support. For additional requirements and documentation, prospective students should visit the Graduate School website or the International Programs and Services at http://www.indstate.edu/IPS.

Correspondence and Information

Dr. Lynn M. Maurer, Dean and Chief Research Officer
College of Graduate and Professional Studies
Indiana State University
Terre Haute, Indiana 47809-1904
United States
Phone: 812-237-3005
800-444-GRAD (4723) (toll-free)
Fax: 812-237-8060
E-mail: ISU-GradStudy@mail.indstate.edu
Website: http://indstate.edu/graduate

For U.S. applicants, mail to:
Graduate Admissions
Indiana State University
Welcome Center 318 North Sixth Street
Terre Haute, Indiana 47809-1904
Phone: 812-237-3005
800-444-GRAD (4723) (toll-free)
Fax: 812-237-8060
E-mail: ISU-GradInfo@mail.indstate.edu

For international applicants, mail to:
Graduate Admissions
Indiana State University
Welcome Center 318 North Sixth Street
Terre Haute, Indiana 47809-1904
United States
Phone: 812-237-3005
800-444-GRAD (4723) toll-free)
Fax: 812-237-8060
E-mail: ISU-GradInfo@mail.indstate.edu
Website: http://indstate.edu/graduate

THE FACULTY

Deans

Lynn M. Maurer, Ph.D.; Dean and Chief Research Officer, College of Graduate and Professional Studies.
John D. Murray, Ph.D.; Dean, College of Arts and Sciences.
Brien N. Smith, Ph.D.; Dean, Scott College of Business.
Kandi Hill-Clarke, Ph.D.; Dean, Bayh College of Education.
Eliezer Bermudez, Ph.D.; Dean, College of Nursing, Health, and Human Services.
Robert English, Ph.D.; Dean, College of Technology.

Directors of Graduate Degree Programs

Art: Nancy Nichols-Pethick, M.F.A., Assistant Professor.
Athletic Training: Lindsey Eberman, Ph.D., Assistant Professor.
Biology: Rusty Gonser, Ph.D., Professor.
Business Administration: Jeff Harper, Ph.D., Professor.
Center for Science Education: Carolyn S. Wallace, Ph.D., Associate Professor and Director.
Clinical Psychology: Liz O'Laughlin, Ph.D., Professor.
Communication: Mary Kahl, Ph.D., Professor and Chairperson.
Communication Disorders and School Counseling, School, and Educational Psychology: Vicki Hammen, Ph.D., Associate Professor.
Counseling Psychology: Tonya Balch, Ph.D., Assistant Professor.
Criminology and Criminal Justice: DeVere Woods, Ph.D., Associate Professor and Chairperson.
Curriculum, Instruction, and Media Technology: Susan Kiger, Ph.D., Associate Professor and Chairperson.
Educational and School Psychology: Carrie Ball, Ph.D., Assistant Professor.
Educational Leadership, Administration, and Foundations: Steve Gruenert, Ph.D., Professor and Chairperson.
Electronics, Computer, and Mechanical Engineering Technology: Joe Ashby, Ph.D., Assistant Professor.
Elementary, Early, and Special Education: Karen Liu, Ph.D., Professor.
English: Kit Kincade, Ph.D., Associate Professor.
Earth and Environmental Systems: C. Russell Stafford, Ph.D., Professor and Chairperson.
Health, Safety, and Environmental Health Sciences: Eliezer Bermudez, Ph.D., Associate Professor and Chairperson.
History: Richard Schneirov, Ph.D., Professor.
Human Resource Development: Tad Foster, Ph.D., Professor.
Industrial Technology: Michael Hayden, Ph.D., Professor.
Languages, Literatures, and Linguistics: Leslie Barratt, Ph.D., Professor and Chairperson.
Mathematics and Computer Science: Ralph Oberste-Vorth, Ph.D., Professor and Chairperson.
Mental Health Counseling: Catherine Tucker, Ph.D., Assistant Professor.
Music: Paul Bro, Ph.D., Professor and Chairperson.
Nursing: Susan Eley, Ph.D., Associate Professor and Chairperson.
Physical Education: Jolynn Kuhlman, Ph.D., Associate Professor.
Political Science: Michael Chambers, Ph.D., Professor and Chairperson.
Psychology: Veanne Anderson, Ph.D., Associate Professor.
Public Administration: Stan Buchanan, Ph.D., Associate Professor.
Recreation and Sport Management: Athanassios Strigas, Associate Professor.
School Administration and Supervision: Steve Gruenert, Ph.D., Professor and Chairperson.
School Counseling, M.Ed., and Licensure Programs: Tonya Balch, Ph.D., Assistant Professor.
School Psychology: Carrie Ball, Ph.D., Assistant Professor.
Student Affairs and Higher Education: William, Barratt, Ph.D., Associate Professor.
Technology Education: Kara Harris, Ed.D., Assistant Professor.
Technology Management: Ali Mehran Shahhosseini, D.Eng., Associate Professor.

Dede Plaza is home to Indiana State University's iconic fountain. The fountain is surrounded by seating for students to congregate with friends or study in the warmth of the sun.

ISU sits in the heart of downtown Terre Haute. The aerial view highlights the Vigo County Courthouse, Sycamore Towers, and in the distance, a view of the Wabash River.

JAMES MADISON UNIVERSITY

Graduate Programs

★ For more information, visit http://petersons.to/jmu-grad

Programs of Study

James Madison University (JMU) graduate programs help develop the professional knowledge and skills that enable students to pursue careers that impact society. JMU ignites students' professional and scholarly passions through individual mentorship by outstanding and supportive faculty members, world-class facilities and a 125,000-member alumni and professional network. As a result, 75 percent of May 2016 graduates were either employed or accepted into a doctoral program within one month of graduation.

The JMU Graduate School has a 61-year history and offers a wide range of programs at the master's, educational specialist, and doctoral levels. Programs are available in each of the following domains:

Art and Music graduate programs provide a stimulating environment in which students create, perform, interpret, research, teach, and think critically about the arts.

Business programs include three distinct MBA concentrations, as well as excellent programs in Accounting, Sport and Recreation Leadership, and a unique Ph.D. program in Strategic Leadership.

Communication, Humanities, and Social Sciences programs include Communication and Advocacy; English; History; Political Science; Public Administration; and Writing, Rhetoric, and Technical Communication. A European Union Policy Studies program in Political Science is offered in Florence, Italy.

Education programs prepare students to become a licensed teacher of children, adolescents, or adults; for specialist or leadership roles; or help develop the skills necessary to assume nonteaching roles in an educational context. A Spanish Language and Culture program is available that includes a summer program in Salamanca.

Health, Wellness, Psychology, and Counseling programs include Assessment and Measurement, Audiology, Clinical Psychology, School Psychology, College Student Personnel Administration (Student Affairs), Communication Sciences and Disorders, Counseling, Health Sciences, Kinesiology, Nursing, Occupational Therapy, Physician Assistant, and Speech-Language Pathology.

Science, Technology, and Mathematics programs include Biology, Computer Science, Mathematics, and Psychological Sciences. An Integrated Science and Technology program that focuses on environmental sustainability is offered in Malta.

Financial Aid

Nearly half of all full-time graduate students on campus receive full or partial financial support; most of these students earn this support by serving as a graduate assistant, teaching assistant, or doctoral assistant. Tuition for students with assistantships is reduced and often completely covered. These students work for a university department 20 hours per week and earn a stipend.

Graduate Assistantships provide students with both tuition support and a stipend associated with an expectation that the student work for an academic department, typically 20 hours per week. Students can apply for an assistantship through the JMU graduate program to which they applied, or through JMU's JobLink at http://joblink.jmu.edu.

Concurrent employment is another possibility. Many programs offer coursework during evenings, weekends or online to allow students to continue their current position or find full or part-time employment during graduate school.

Students can also take advantage of scholarship programs. JMU offers a limited number of need-based scholarships to graduate students. Veterans may be able to utilize special programs available to people who are, or have been, in the military and their families. More information is available online at http://www.jmu.edu/grad/prospective/veterans.shtml.

Loans may not be necessary, but they should be considered. Given the future earning potential of someone with a graduate degree, a small loan balance may be quite reasonable. JMU's Office of Financial Aid is available to assist with loan applications and manage other financial aid. More information can be found at http://www.jmu.edu/financialaid/finaid-grad.shtml.

Cost of Study

For most people, graduate school will increase their lifetime earning potential, but students are advised to complete their graduate education without accumulating more debt than they are likely able to afford. Tuition at JMU is competitive, and general activity fees are included, not extra. Substantial tuition discounts are available to Virginia residents. Program costs depend on the number of credit hours required for the student's chosen program of study; some programs have fees for laboratory expenses, study abroad, etc. The latest information regarding tuition amounts is online at http://www.jmu.edu/ubo.

Living and Housing Costs

JMU does not have an on-campus housing option for graduate students, so they must live off-campus. Living expenses will vary depending on the number of semesters required to complete the student's program of study (full- or part-time) and whether the student chooses to live individually, share housing with others, or live with family. More information about housing is available online at http://info.jmu.edu/ocl.

Student Outcomes

James Madison University is proud of the diverse accomplishments of its graduate students. Many work collaboratively with their faculty, and sometimes with teams of undergraduate students. Many students benefit from well-supervised and highly engaging internships, clinical practica, and teaching opportunities on campus and throughout the local community. The University encourages and supports scholarly and creative activities by students. The graduate school offers travel grants that provide financial support to students so that they can present their work at professional meetings. Examples of recent graduate student accomplishments can be seen at www.jmu.edu/grad/about/graduate-student-accomplishments-2015-16.shtml.

Location

JMU is in a small city, situated in the beautiful Shenandoah Valley of Virginia, 2 hours south of Washington, D.C. The campus offers two libraries, an enormous recreation center, and a center for performing arts. Harrisonburg is a diverse community with a wide range of ethnic groceries, many churches, a Jewish synagogue, and a Muslim mosque, great schools and after-school activities for children, a historic downtown with a vibrant arts community, and many dining and shopping opportunities. Nearby national parks, the Appalachian Trail, rivers, caverns, golf courses, wineries, and ski resorts make this an ideal location for students seeking outdoor activities.

The University and The Graduate School

JMU is a diverse, rapidly growing university consisting of preprofessional, professional, and research-intensive programs spread across seven colleges within the university, including Arts and Letters, Business, Education, Health and Behavioral Studies, Integrated Science and Engineering, Science and Mathematics, and Visual and Performing Arts.

The Graduate School emphasizes the university's commitment to addressing complex, real-world problems and contemporary issues. Graduate students at JMU have the opportunity to take classes that are taught by engaged faculty members who place a priority on teaching.

Graduate education at JMU serves the public good by providing graduate students with high-quality academic experiences and professional development through its diverse, collaborative, and engaged community.

Admissions Requirements and Application Information

Anyone who has or will obtain a bachelor's degree from a regionally accredited institution in the U.S. or a comparable degree from an officially recognized college or university outside the U.S. may apply for graduate admission. All programs make admission decisions based on transcripts from all schools attended. Grades that predict graduate school success are expected. Individual graduate programs have additional admission requirements that are posted on their websites. Additional requirements may include: test scores on the Graduate Record Exam (GRE), Graduate Management Admission Test (GMAT) or Miller Analogy Test (MAT); letters of recommendation; portfolios, resumes, auditions, personal statements, and/or writing samples; and personal interviews.

International applicants must also demonstrate English language proficiency based on satisfactory scores on the TOEFL or IELTS, completion of a bachelor's degree at an institution where the primary language of instruction is English, or a certificate of completion of an acceptable English Language program. Submission of a Financial Declaration form indicating sufficient resources to cover all costs is also required. If the international applicant did not complete their bachelor's degree in the United States, a credential evaluation may be needed.

Correspondence and Information

Tracie Esmaili,
Graduate Enrollment and International Student Coordinator
The Graduate School
James Madison University
MSC 6702, 17 West Grace Street
Harrisonburg, Virginia 22807
United States
Phone: 540-568-6131
Fax: 540-568-7860
E-mail: grad@jmu.edu
Website: www.jmu.edu/grad

THE FACULTY—PROGRAM DIRECTORS

Art and Music

Art Education (M.A.): Karin Tollefson-Hall, tollefkl@jmu.edu.
Art/Studio Art (M.A. and M.F.A.): Cole Welter, welterch@jmu.edu.
Music (M.M. and D.M.A.): Mary Jean Speare, spearemj@jmu.edu.

Business

Accounting (M.S.): Nancy Nichols, nicholnb@jmu.edu.
Business Administration-Information Security (MBA): Tisha McCoy-Ntiamoah, mccoynta@jmu.edu.
Business Administration (MBA): Tisha McCoy-Ntiamoah, mccoynta@jmu.edu.
Kinesiology (Sports and Recreation Leadership) (M.S.): Ben Carr, carrbh@jmu.edu.
Strategic Leadership (Ph.D.): Karen Ford, fordka@jmu.edu.

Communication, Humanities, and Social Sciences

Communication and Advocacy (M.A.): Pete Bsumek, bsumekpk@jmu.edu.
English (M.A.): Brooks Hefner, hefnerbe@jmu.edu.
History (M.A.): David Dillard, dillarpd@jmu.edu.
Political Science-European Union Policy Studies (M.A.): John Scherpereel, scherpja@jmu.edu.
Public Administration (M.P.A.): Fred Mayhew, mayhewfd@jmu.edu.
Strategic Leadership (Ph.D.): Karen Ford, fordka@jmu.edu.
Writing, Rhetoric, and Technical Communication (M.A. or M.S.): Michael Klein, kleinmj@jmu.edu.

Education

Early Childhood Education (M.A.T.): Holly McCartney, mccarthb@jmu.edu.
Educational Leadership (M.Ed.): Robin Crowder, crowderg@jmu.edu.
Educational Technology (M.Ed.): Michele Estes, estesmd@jmu.edu.
Elementary Education (M.A.T.): Michelle Hughes, hughesma@jmu.edu.
Equity and Cultural Diversity (M.Ed.): Stephanie Wasta, wastasa@jmu.edu.
Inclusive Early Childhood Education, 5th year (M.A.T.): Mira Williams, willi9mc@jmu.edu.
Mathematics Specialist (M.Ed.): Ann Wallace, wallacah@jmu.edu.
Middle Education (M.A.T.): Kyle Schultz, schultkt@jmu.edu.
Reading (M.Ed.): Joy Myers, myersjk@jmu.edu.
Secondary Education (M.A.T.): Kyle Schultz, schultkt@jmu.edu.
Spanish Language and Culture for Educators (M.Ed.): Diane Wilcox, wilcoxdm@jmu.edu.
Special Education (M.A.T. and M.Ed.): Dani Bronaugh, bronauda@jmu.edu.
TESOL (M.A.T.): Stephanie Wasta, wastasa@jmu.edu.

Health and Behavioral Studies

Communication Sciences and Disorders (M.S. and Ph.D.): Rory DePaolis, depaolra@jmu.edu.
Communication Sciences and Disorders–Speech Pathology (M.S.): Carol Dudding, duddincc@jmu.edu.
Communication Sciences and Disorders–Speech Pathology DLVE (M.S.): Erin Clinard, clinares @jmu.edu.
Communication Sciences and Disorders–Clinical Audiology (Au.D.): Ayasakanta Rout, routax@jmu.edu.
Health Sciences (M.S.): Jeremy Akers, akersjd@jmu.edu.
Kinesiology–Physical and Health Education (M.S. and M.A.T.): Nick Luden, ludennd@jmu.edu.
Nursing (M.S.N.): Melody Eaton, eatonmk@jmu.edu.
Nursing (Ph.D.): Linda Hulton, hultonlj@jmu.edu.
Occupational Therapy (M.O.T.): Twylla Kirchen, kirchetm@jmu.edu.
Physicians Assistant Studies (M.P.A.S.): Gerald Weniger, paprogram@jmu.edu.
PSYC/Combined–Integrated Clinical and School Psychology (Psy.D.): Gregg Henriques, henriqgx@jmu.edu.
PSYC/Clinical Mental Health Counseling (M.A./Ed.S.): Debbie Sturm, sturmdc@jmu.edu.
PSYC/College Student Personnel Administration (M.Ed.): Donna Harper or Josh Bacon, harperdl@jmu.edu or baconjj@jmu.edu.
PSYC/Counseling and Supervision (Ph.D.): Debbie Sturm, sturmdc@jmu.edu.
PSYC/Psychological Sciences (M.A.): Jeff Dyche, dychejs@jmu.edu.
PSYC/School Counseling (M.Ed.): Debbie Sturm, sturmdc@jmu.edu.
PSYC/School Psychology (M.A./Ed.S.): Tammy Gilligan, gilligtd@jmu.edu.

Science, Technology, and Mathematics

Biology (M.S.): Janet Daniel, danie2jc@jmu.edu.
Computer Science–Digital Forensics (M.S.): Florian Buchholz, buchhofp@jmu.edu.
Computer Science–Information Security (M.S.): Hossain Heydari, heydarmh@jmu.edu.
Integrated Science and Technology (M.S.): Maria Papadakis, papadamc@jmu.edu.
Integrated Science and Technology–MALTA (M.S.): Maria Papadakis, papadamc@jmu.edu.
Mathematics (M.Ed.): Anthony Tongen, tongenal@jmu.edu.

James Madison University graduate students impact society through their activities as they develop into professionals and scholars. This transformation happens through mentorship from outstanding and supportive faculty members, world-class facilities, and a 125,000-member alumni and professional network.

KANSAS STATE UNIVERSITY

Graduate School

KANSAS STATE UNIVERSITY | Graduate School

Programs of Study

The Graduate School at Kansas State University offers preparation for a variety of scholarly and research careers and a wide range of professional positions through advanced study in more than 39 doctoral, 73 master's, 4 educational doctoral programs, and 43 certificate programs. Opportunities for research and scholarly activities exist in the areas of agriculture, architecture and design, business administration, education, engineering, food science, genetics, human ecology, humanities and fine arts, natural sciences, security studies, social sciences, veterinary medicine, and many others. Most programs are offered at the main Manhattan campus. A limited number of programs are offered at the K-State Salina and K-State Olathe campuses and via distance education through the K-State Global Campus.

A minimum of 30 semester hours of graduate credit is required for a master's degree, with some academic programs requiring more. The Graduate School recognizes the following plans for a master's degree as part of the degree program: thesis option (students complete a thesis for 6–8 hours credit); report option (students complete a written report on research or a problem in the major field for 2 hours credit); and course work option (the degree program consists of course work only, but includes evidence of advanced work such as term papers, objects of art, music, or designs). Not all programs offer all three options.

Doctoral programs require 90 semester hours and educational doctoral programs require 94 semester hours beyond the bachelor's degree. Both degrees require original research and a dissertation. Students with a master's degree may transfer up to 30 hours of that degree toward a doctoral degree upon approval from the supervisory committee.

Research Facilities

K-State respects and admires the enthusiastic scholarship graduate students bring to the university. A vast library network houses more than 2 million books and provides online access to thousands of journals, databases, and books. Students receive dynamic training as they perform research alongside faculty in leading facilities. The Sensory and Consumer Research Center provides students with the opportunity to perform qualitative and quantitative consumer research. Atomic, molecular, and optical physics students work with ultrafast intense lasers in the James R. Macdonald Lab. K-State was selected as the location of the National Bio and Agro-Defense Facility in 2008. More than 85 additional specialized research centers unite researchers across disciplines and drive innovative research and discoveries at K-State. A complete list of research facilities and centers is available online at http://www.k-state.edu/directories/research-facilities.html.

Financial Aid

Many forms of financial assistance are available to graduate students, including graduate teaching or research assistantships, fellowships, scholarships, and loans. The Office of Student Financial Assistance administers federal assistance programs and a work-study program. Teaching and research assistantships are awarded on a competitive basis by individual departments. Research assistants qualify to pay tuition at resident rates if appointed to at least a 0.4 assistantship. Up to 10 hours of tuition is paid for fall and spring semesters for students who have a 0.5 teaching assistantship.

Cost of Study

Tuition in 2015–16 was $380.80 per credit hour for Kansas residents and $859.40 per credit hour for nonresidents. Some colleges have additional tuition surcharges and equipment fees. Graduate students are considered full-time if enrolled in at least 6 credit hours and employed on an assistantship. In addition to tuition, campus privilege fees range from $97.30 to $416.30 per semester.

Living and Housing Costs

The Jardine Apartment Complex features more than 700 on-campus apartments for students and families. One- to four-bedroom units are available and prices start at $475 per month. Residence hall meal plans are also available to Jardine residents. Numerous other off-campus apartments and housing options are also available. Monthly rates for off-campus apartments in Manhattan start around $550 for a one-bedroom and $800 for a two-bedroom.

Student Group

Over 4,200 graduate students from more than 92 countries around the world attend K-State. More than half of all graduate students at K-State are full-time students. Approximately 56 percent of all graduate students are female.

Student Outcomes

Students with advanced degrees from K-State are highly sought by employers. Students often receive multiple job offers and many find employment well before graduation. K-State graduates are leaders within all levels of public, private, and business sectors and government agencies.

Frequent employers of K-State graduates include: the National Institutes of Health, Argonne and Sandia National Labs, Nintendo, Merck, Pfizer, Cargill, Kellogg's, Hershey Foods, Anheuser-Busch, Motorola, Texas Instruments, Rockwell International, and Sprint.

Location

K-State's main campus is located on 668 acres in Manhattan, Kansas, approximately 125 miles west of Kansas City. With a population of more than 56,000, Manhattan has many urban amenities but still retains the best qualities of a small town. Manhattan features a regional airport, public and private schools, and a variety of shopping, entertainment, arts, and recreational activities.

Two additional campus locations in Kansas—Salina and Olathe—complement the main campus in Manhattan.

The University

Founded in 1863 as America's first land-grant university, K-State is an internationally recognized comprehensive research institution with academic programs offered in a lively intellectual and cultural atmosphere. In 1996, the university was one of only ten universities selected to receive the National Science Foundation's Recognition Award for the Integration of Research and Education. The university has since launched an ambitious planning initiative with a goal of being recognized as a top 50 public research university by 2025. One of the plan's main goals is to improve the scholarly experience for graduate students and advance a culture of excellence that attracts highly talented, diverse graduate students and produces graduates who are recognized as outstanding in their respective professions.

Applying

Applicants should complete the online application via the Graduate School website at www.k-state.edu/grad.

Applications for U.S. citizens and permanent residents are accepted year round. International residents must apply by January 8 for fall enrollment, August 1 for spring enrollment, and December 1 for summer enrollment. Application materials and deadlines for individual degree programs may vary. Contact each department for specific requirements and information.

Correspondence and Information

Graduate School
Kansas State University
103 Fairchild Hall
Manhattan, Kansas 66506-1103
Phone: 785-532-6191
800-651-1816 (toll-free in the U.S.)
Fax: 785-532-2983
E-mail: grad@k-state.edu
Website: http://www.k-state.edu/grad

GRADUATE PROGRAMS

For more information about the degrees offered within each department and contact information, prospective students should visit http://catalog.k-state.edu/content.php?catoid=2&navoid=634.

COLLEGE OF AGRICULTURE

Agricultural Economics
Agronomy
Animal Sciences and Industry
Communications and Agricultural Education
Entomology
Grain Science and Industry
Horticulture, Forestry, and Recreation Resources
Plant Pathology

COLLEGE OF ARCHITECTURE, PLANNING, AND DESIGN
Architecture
Environmental Design and Planning
Interior Architecture and Product Design
Landscape Architecture/Regional and Community Planning

COLLEGE OF ARTS AND SCIENCES
American Ethnic Studies
Art
Biology
Chemistry
Communication Studies
Economics
English
Gender, Women, and Sexuality Studies
Geography
Geology
History
Journalism and Mass Communications
Mathematics
Modern Languages
Music, Theatre, and Dance
Physics
Political Science
Psychological Sciences
Security Studies
Sociology, Anthropology, and Social Work
Statistics

COLLEGE OF BUSINESS ADMINISTRATION
Accounting
Finance
Management
Marketing

COLLEGE OF EDUCATION
Curriculum and Instruction
Educational Leadership
Special Education, Counseling, and Student Affairs

COLLEGE OF ENGINEERING
Architectural Engineering and Construction Science
Biological and Agricultural Engineering
Chemical Engineering
Civil Engineering
Computer Science
Electrical and Computer Engineering
Industrial and Manufacturing Systems Engineering
Mechanical and Nuclear Engineering

COLLEGE OF HUMAN ECOLOGY
Apparel, Textiles, and Interior Design
Family Studies and Human Services
Food, Nutrition, Dietetics, and Health
Gerontology
Hospitality Management
Kinesiology

COLLEGE OF VETERINARY MEDICINE
Anatomy and Physiology
Clinical Sciences
Pathobiology

INTERDISCIPLINARY PROGRAMS
Biochemistry and Molecular Biophysics
Food Science
Genetics
Public Health

KANSAS STATE POLYTECHNIC
Technology

A graduate student explains her research during one of the many research forums held on campus each year. Graduate Student Council also provides travel funding for graduate students to present their research at national and international conferences.

Part of the Manhattan campus. Fairchild Hall, home of the Graduate School, is one of the oldest remaining buildings on campus.

MASSACHUSETTS COLLEGE OF ART AND DESIGN

Graduate Programs

★ For more information, visit http://petersons.to/mcad-grad

MASSART
MASSACHUSETTS COLLEGE OF ART AND DESIGN

Programs of Study

Founded in 1873, Massachusetts College of Art and Design (MassArt) is the nation's first and only freestanding, publicly supported college of art and design, and the first to grant a degree. The college offers a variety of disciplines including architecture, industrial design, fine arts, and art education, with graduate and undergraduate programs that prepare students to participate in the creative economy as designers, fine artists, and art educators.

The opportunity to work and create in a diverse community of innovative, hard-working artists, designers, and educators fosters a learning environment that encourages multidisciplinary practice and dialogue, a central value of the graduate programs.

MassArt awards the Master of Fine Arts (M.F.A.) degree in five separate fine arts disciplines: 2D Fine Arts, 3D Fine Arts, Design, Media Arts: Film/Video, and Media Arts: Photography. Admission to the M.F.A. program is highly competitive and attracts a global pool of applicants with professional portfolios who are interested in pursuing intensive study in the fine arts.

The full-residency M.F.A. program requires a full-time commitment over two years. The Low-Residency Fine Arts Program spans three years, and is highlighted by annual, six-week intensive summer residencies in Boston that allow artists who work across disciplines to develop a self-directed course of study.

MassArt also awards the following additional graduate degree programs: Master of Architecture (M.Arch.), Master of Arts: Teaching/Art Education (M.A.T.), and Master of Design Innovation (M.Des.).

M.F.A. in 2D Fine Arts: This program combines painting, drawing, and printmaking practices and techniques, with the emphasis on each student's evolution as an artist. Students have individual studios distributed throughout the FA2D undergraduate department, allowing for interaction between students that becomes dynamic when graduates participate in lectures, open houses, exhibitions, field trips, social media, and teaching assistantships.

The primary form of graduate studio instruction is critique. Three critiques are scheduled throughout the semester. During the third, called Review Board, students present their semester's work for critical review by their peers, resident faculty, an outside critic, and other invited guests. The capstone is the M.F.A. Thesis Exhibit, where students select and install their work in MassArt's Bakalar & Paine Galleries.

M.F.A. in 3D Fine Arts: This program focuses on creating the artistic object in one of five media: ceramics, fibers, glass, metals (jewelry and metalsmithing), and sculpture. Students study structure, form-making, idea development, tool handling, and studio safety, then advance to classes that develop and refine their aesthetic vision and build their technical, conceptual, and critical skills in their chosen medium.

M.F.A. in Film/Video: This program provides a personalized, intense environment where students acquire advanced skills in production and develop an informed perspective on film/video that is individual, political, conceptual, abstract, visceral, and visionary. The curriculum is enriched by the weekly screenings of The MassArt Film Society, drawing on a wide range of films and videos and often including a live discussion with the artist. Students have access to state-of-the-art facilities and resources, including advanced high-definition digital film and video production equipment, and more.

M.F.A. in Media Arts: Photography: This program teaches photography as fine art with an emphasis on personal vision, experimentation, and an understanding of the history of photography and the body of criticism that impacts it. The curriculum covers both analog and digital production, and offers a variety of elective courses providing a strong foundation for critical thinking, collaboration, and a career in photographic arts. The 11,000-square-foot photography facility offers three-studio digital capability with large-format printers, Flextight scanners, and 40 workstations. Analog black and white developing and printing areas are central to the curriculum, with two large-gang darkrooms, individual darkrooms, and a non-silver darkroom.

M.F.A.: Fine Arts (Low-Residency in Boston): This program is ideal for artists who work across disciplines in that it allows self-directed students to develop a course of study that might involve a combination of media, technologies, and techniques. The six-week summer residencies in Boston foster an intense studio environment and establish creative collaborations.

Students live on campus in the Artists' Residence or in off-campus housing of their choosing. Between residencies, students work under the guidance of artist/mentors through monthly studio visits and critiques, returning to campus in January for midterm reviews.

M.F.A. in Design: The Dynamic Media Institute (DMI) at MassArt offers an M.F.A. program for anyone passionate about the future of dynamic media in communication design. Students are fine artists, designers, architects, engineers, programmers, educators, and others who pursue a unique thesis vision through a rigorous practice of research, prototyping, and writing. Students emerge with a rich body of original work, empowered to become leading educators, practitioners, and entrepreneurs.

Master of Design Innovation (M.Des.): This program integrates deep expertise in design practice with business discipline in a broad-based curriculum that uses market challenges and social initiatives as the context for learning. The full-time, two-year interdisciplinary curriculum is intended for students who want to lead the design and planning of new products, services, environments, systems, and organizations.

Master of Architecture (M.Arch.): This full-residency program offers two tracks. Track I is designed for students who hold a bachelor's degree in fields other than architecture. Track II is intended for students with a bachelor's degree in architecture and professional portfolios. Accredited by the National Architecture Accrediting Board, the M.Arch. program combines professional requirements with hands-on design, and builds experience focused on community-based teaching and working spaces. Visiting architects, engineers, and related professionals enrich discussions in design critique.

Master of Arts: Teaching/Art Education (M.A.T.): This program provides artists with substantive, graduate-level education in teaching. The curriculum was developed for students with strong backgrounds in studio work who want to teach in schools, museums, social service agencies, or community agencies. The program leads to the Initial

Teacher License in Massachusetts while also providing the course work requirements for a Professional Teacher License.

Art Galleries

There are galleries located all across MassArt's campus, from the Arnheim and Brant galleries in South Hall, to the Student Life Gallery in the Kennedy Building, and the Godine Family Gallery in North Hall. Curated and managed by students and faculty, these galleries enrich the campus and curriculum through the presentation of departmental exhibitions (http://www.massart.edu/Galleries/Campus_Galleries.html).

As the largest free, contemporary art venue in New England, MassArt's Bakalar & Paine Galleries showcase some of the most exciting and influential artists from the world. Curated exhibitions feature both rising talents and well-known artists in exhibitions that are a public resource for the college, Boston, and beyond. (http://www.massart.edu/Galleries/Bakalar_and_Paine_Galleries.html).

The President's Gallery features exhibitions celebrating innovation in all artistic disciplines, the work of artists being honored and celebrated by the college, and the outstanding achievements of MassArt's alumni, staff, and students.

Faculty and Visiting Artists

The core faculty at MassArt comprises a diverse group of accomplished artists, artisans, designers, architects, programmers, engineers, filmmakers, photographers, and educators. Many have received prestigious fellowships, and exhibit and publish worldwide. Students are also exposed to working designers and artists through the Visiting Artist Program, which features lectures, seminars, workshops, and classroom interaction.

Financial Assistance

More than 80 percent of MassArt graduate students receive financial assistance in some form, including federal loans, scholarships, and assistantships.

Cost of Study

Graduate tuition for summer 2016 to spring 2017 is $780 per credit. Graduate students pay on a per-credit basis. The tuition fee per credit varies with the program, but does not vary based on the residency status of the student.

Living and Housing Costs

MassArt's Artists' Residence offers a few co-ed apartments to graduate students. For a double room, the total cost is $5,775 per semester. For a single room, the total cost is $6,315 per semester. The estimated cost for off-campus living expenses is about $18,281 for nine months and $24,376 for twelve months.

Student Group

MassArt's graduate students come from 12 countries. A full 25 percent of MassArt's students are international, including 4 Fulbright Scholars.

Location

The MassArt campus in downtown Boston encompasses more than a million square feet of studios, workshops, and galleries within walking distance of three world-class museums.

Applying

Applicants to Massachusetts College of Art and Design are evaluated according to standards that gauge abilities and talent in the arts along with potential, motivation, and desire. There is no one formula that determines an applicant's potential for success. In evaluating an applicant, the admissions committee tries to be flexible, sensitive, and personal.

Admission to degree programs at Massachusetts College of Art and Design is extremely competitive. Each year the number of applicants for admission far exceeds the number of spaces available. This is true at all levels of admission, although the competition for admission to specific programs may vary from year to year.

Required items include the online application, a $75 application fee (paid online), statement of purpose, resume, official post-secondary/college transcripts, two letters of reference, and a portfolio. Students applying to the M.Arch. program must submit additional items with their application; specific details are available at http://www.massart.edu/Admissions/Graduate_Programs/Master_of_Architecture.html.

International applicants must meet the graduate application requirements as well as the additional requirements specific to international applicants, including official transcript translation and evaluation and scores on the TOEFL/IELTS (for non-native English speakers). Additional information can be found at http://www.massart.edu/Admissions/Graduate_Programs/International_Graduate_Students.html.

For a tour of MassArt's facilities, prospective graduate students should contact gradadmissions@massart.edu or 617-879-7203.

Correspondence and Information

Graduate Admissions
Massachusetts College of Art and Design
621 Huntington Avenue
Boston, Massachusetts 02115
United States
Phone: 617-879-7222
E-mail: gradadmissions@massart.edu
Website: http://www.massart.edu/Admissions/Graduate_Programs.html

The Tower Building on the campus of MassArt.

MILWAUKEE SCHOOL OF ENGINEERING

Graduate Programs

Programs of Study

Milwaukee School of Engineering (MSOE) offers eleven master's degree programs in engineering, business, and nursing.

The MSOE M.B.A. is an innovative program designed for future leaders in organizations. The program utilizes an integrated curriculum designed to develop leadership competencies with a combination of core content and field projects. It features strategic M.B.A. content with analyses of leading edge business cases and requires learners to apply their new skills to solve real problems in their workplace. The MSOE M.B.A. offers learners the option to complete courses 100 percent online or in a blended format.

MSOE's new M.B.A. in Education Leadership is an innovative program that prepares a new breed of school leader. The program seeks to provide the business knowledge and leadership development that is missing from traditional Master's in Education programs and prepare leaders who can become outstanding principals and bring American schools up to world-class levels of performance. Throughout the program, students hold positions in their schools or districts, with clinical practicum field projects completed as part of their work assignments.

MSOE's M.B.A. in STEM Leadership is a groundbreaking program that prepares PK–12 teachers and college instructors to advance STEM initiatives in their classrooms, schools, and communities. It blends Project Lead the Way (PLTW) and Center for BioMolecular Modeling (CBM) teacher education with the MSOE M.B.A. program core. Program graduates earn the MSOE M.B.A. through the completion of a 33-quarter-credit core. In addition, graduates learn to effectively assimilate new teaching techniques into their schools and communities.

The Master of Science in Engineering (M.S.E.) is an interdisciplinary engineering program with primary emphases in the areas of electrical engineering (EE) and mechanical engineering (ME). A key benefit of the M.S.E. program is the breadth of engineering skills and knowledge that graduates attain in areas of systems engineering, EE, and ME.

The Master of Science in Engineering Management (M.S.E.M.) program is best described as a master's degree in general management with a technological orientation. The M.S.E.M. program is based on the philosophy that, in order for American companies to grow and compete domestically and internationally, their technical personnel must have the tools to effectively manage and participate in the decision-making process. This program is offered in blended and 100 percent online formats.

The Master of Science in Marketing and Export Management degree program (M.S.X.M.) is a technology-oriented leadership program designed to meet the needs of engineers, business managers, and other professional and technical persons. The program offers a portal to successful export practices.

The Master of Science in New Product Management (M.S.N.P.) degree program provides students a framework to enhance an organization's ability to effectively identify, develop, and deploy new products and services. Students will learn how to apply the tools and knowledge needed to find the products and/or services that are aligned with the unique strengths and position of an organization.

The Master of Science in Architectural Engineering (M.S.A.E.) program allows specialization in the analysis and design of building structural systems or in building mechanical, electrical, and plumbing systems (MEP). Attainment of degree requirements enables architectural engineers to apply advanced knowledge and skill sets to design structural or MEP systems for modern buildings. This program is offered in a face-to-face format.

The Master of Science in Civil Engineering (M.S.C.V.E.) program is designed to equip students with the advanced knowledge and skills necessary for professional practice. Students are able to specialize in one of the following three areas: (1) construction management, (2) environmental and water resources engineering, and (3) structural engineering. This program is offered in a face-to-face format.

A Master of Science in Nursing (M.S.N.) in Health Care Systems Management from MSOE, with its unique blend of nursing, business, and engineering concepts, will equip graduates with the knowledge and skills necessary to function effectively in the health-care environment.

The Master of Science in Perfusion (M.S.P.) prepares graduates to utilize their competencies in a hospital operating room. This profession requires the application of invasive surgical techniques, particularly in open-heart surgery. The M.S.P. is for full-time students only. Students start in September of each year and attend for six consecutive quarters. Upon completion of the M.S.P. program, students are eligible to sit for the Certified Clinical Perfusionist examination. The application deadline is December 15 each year for the following September's class. Applications will be considered until the class is full, after which applicants will have the option of being considered for the waiting list as well as carrying over their application for the following year.

Research Facilities

The Applied Technology Center™ (ATC) is the research arm of MSOE. It conducts applied (strategic) research in conjunction with the University's various academic programs, utilizing faculty and student expertise as well as industrial-size laboratories to solve technological problems confronting business and industry. The close association between MSOE and the business and industrial community has long been one of the University's strengths. The ATC is heavily involved in transferring new technologies into real business practice through the Rapid Prototyping Center, the Fluid Power Institute™, the Photonics and Applied Optics Center, the Construction Science and Engineering Center, the NanoEngineering Laboratory, and the Center for BioMolecular Modeling. MSOE is the only university in the world to possess five leading rapid prototyping technologies, and America's first fluid power research facility university. The ATC deals in research operations that include: advanced manufacturing technologies, motion control and ultrafast videography, engineering and manufacturing consultation, and environmental areas. Both graduate and undergraduate students pursue research opportunities in the ATC.

Financial Aid

Most graduate students receive some type of tuition reimbursement from their employers. For those students who do not have this benefit, several loan options may be available. Nonimmigrant alien graduate students are not eligible for federal or state financial assistance or MSOE loan money. MSOE offers a limited number of graduate research assistantships.

Cost of Study

The 2016–17 tuition for all graduate programs is $760 per credit hour.

Living and Housing Costs

MSOE operates three on-campus residence halls. Although undergraduate students compose the largest segment of the resident population, the residence halls offer an on-campus option to the graduate student. The Housing Department can provide more information on what is available and how personal needs might be accommodated. Alternative off-campus housing is available from the many independently-owned rental units near the University.

Student Group

In fall 2015, MSOE had 2,349 full- and part-time students. Of these, 227 were graduate students. The majority of graduate students at MSOE have prior professional experience in their field.

Location

MSOE is located just a few blocks from Lake Michigan on the east side of downtown Milwaukee, which is approximately 90 miles north of Chicago. MSOE is in a vibrant downtown neighborhood in Milwaukee called East Town. There are countless activities within walking distance from campus including shopping, theaters, restaurants, professional sporting venues, and more.

The University

Milwaukee School of Engineering is an independent, nonprofit university with about 2,800 students that was founded in 1903. MSOE offers bachelor's and master's degrees in engineering, business, mathematics, and nursing. The University has a national academic reputation, longstanding ties to business and industry, dedicated professors with real-world experience, a 96 percent undergraduate placement rate, and the highest ROI and average starting and midcareer salaries of any Wisconsin university according to PayScale Inc. MSOE graduates are well-rounded, technologically experienced, and highly productive professionals and leaders.

Applying

Applicants can submit an application online for no cost at http://msoe.edu/apply.

General application requirements include an official transcript of all undergraduate and graduate course work, two or three letters of recommendation (depending on the program), and GMAT/GRE test scores, depending upon the program and/or undergraduate cumulative grade point average.

International students are required to submit additional documentation. Some programs may have additional requirements; program-specific details are available on MSOE's website.

Correspondence and Information

Graduate and Professional Education
Milwaukee School of Engineering
1025 North Broadway
Milwaukee, Wisconsin 53202-3109
United States
Phone: 800-321-6763 (toll-free)
E-mail: gpe@msoe.edu
Website: http://www.msoe.edu/graduate
http://facebook.com/msoegpe (Facebook)
http://twitter.com/msoegpe (Twitter)

THE FACULTY AND THEIR RESEARCH

MSOE's faculty focus is on teaching, both in the classroom and in its world-class research facilities. Unlike many educational institutions, MSOE does not utilize teaching assistants. MSOE has more than 200 full- and part-time faculty members. Small classes, a low 12:1 student-faculty ratio for undergraduate courses, and a 7:1 student-faculty ratio for graduate courses ensures that students receive personal attention.

The Applied Technology Center™ (ATC) is the research arm of the University. It serves as a technology transfer catalyst among academia, business and industry, and governmental agencies. The close association between MSOE and the business and industrial community has long been one of the University's strengths; applied research serves as a renewable resource in this linkage. The ATC undertakes more than 250 company-sponsored projects per year that involve faculty, staff members, and students. Interdisciplinary capabilities provide a major advantage and can span fields such as engineering, science, health care, business, computers, and technical communication. Modes of interaction include applied research and consulting by faculty members with industrial experience, often with graduate and undergraduate research assistants; projects in engineering and business disciplines, which are coordinated by company and faculty advisers; and referrals, which serve as an initial contact point for networking with others to optimize expertise and facilities for technology transfer.

The ATC is organized into several areas:

The Rapid Prototyping Center (RPC) is a joint effort of industry, government, and MSOE that is dedicated to the application of proven technologies to novel challenges. MSOE is the only university that has a laboratory devoted to all five commercially available rapid prototyping systems—stereolithography (SLA), laminated object manufacturing (LOM), selective laser sintering (SLS), fused deposition modeling (FDM), and Z-Corp processing. A rapid scanning system has recently been acquired, which allows the automatic preparation of 3-D databases from laser scanning of any object, thereby making it possible to reproduce the object using rapid prototyping systems. Rapid prototyping historically has been a tool for reducing product development cycle times. The RPC continues to advance the state-of-the-art in this area, using computer-based manufacturing techniques and complementary processes to reduce the time and cost of industrial products ranging from functional models to full-scale production.

Established in 1991, the Rapid Prototyping Consortium continues MSOE's tradition of building strong ties to business and industry. The consortium includes industrial companies and educational institutions that cooperate in understanding the consortium's vitality and success in a high level of industrial parts design and fabrication activity. Companies that take advantage of the facilities and expertise within the consortium become stronger and more competitive.

The RPC also is extending the use of rapid prototyping through research projects as diverse as biomolecular and biomedical modeling, architectural modeling, and manufacturing tooling. Rapid prototyping research is involved in several biomolecular technology development programs, including nanomagnetics, liquid crystals, and digital manufacturing. There is significant activity in novel internally structured solid objects and advanced high-resolution metal casting processes.

The Center for BioMolecular Modeling (CBMM) is established within MSOE's RPC. The center creates unique physical models of molecular structures using rapid prototyping technologies and works with research scientists to create custom models of the proteins whose structures they are investigating. The center also works closely with educators at both the secondary and postsecondary levels to create innovative products that make the molecular world real for students. The center is unique in the world, bringing together the disciplines of engineering, structural biology, and computer visualization.

The Fluid Power Institute™ (FPI) was established in 1962 as one of the first research facilities of its kind in the country and has remained a pioneer in motion control and fluid power education. Through its state-of-the-art facilities, it conducts a variety of performance, endurance, and environmental evaluations of components and systems. FPI also performs component and system design, modeling and simulation, contamination, and various education programs. A $5-million endowment from the estate of Otto J. Maha provides resources to ensure continued advancement of fluid power education. FPI uses an interdisciplinary workforce comprised of faculty and staff members from various academic departments and undergraduate and graduate students to conduct fluid power, motion control, and related industry projects. FPI's approach uses mechanical, electrical, computer, and software engineering along with MSOE's Rapid Prototyping Center. MSOE is a member of the National Fluid Power Association and supports the activities of the Fluid Power Society and the Fluid Power Educational Foundation. It has expanded into electrohydraulic interface studies and currently has active programs in fluid power systems design, applications of fluid power to manufacturing, computerized fluid dynamics (CFD), electromagnetic actuators and sensors, component evaluation, and filtration and contamination testing.

The NanoEngineering Laboratory allows research and education at the nanoscale, which is becoming more critical each year as research and development focuses on nanoscale phenomena, ultrafine structures, and interfaces between matters. Atomic Force Microscopy (AFM) allows the force between a small tip and a chosen sample surface to be measured with atomic-scale resolution. Initially, lateral forces between the tip and the sample can also be measured to better understand the origins of friction at the molecular scale. Other types of AFM surface measurement models include plastic deformations, electrical conductivity, and thermal conductivity. All these capabilities make the AFM an indispensable tool for characterization and manipulation in all areas of the emerging field of technology called nanotechnology. Leveraging the state-of-the-art AFM capabilities, research is conducted in the areas of wear reduction and surface enhancement. Other areas include Solid Freeform Fabrication (SFF) of metal matrix composites and numerous projects for biological and industrial applications (e.g., MEMS).

The High-Speed Video Analysis system has the ability to digitally capture—and immediately play back—events in the 1,000 to 12,000 frames per second range. Powerful motion analysis software is used to track and graph up to nine points in the visual field.

The Photonics and Applied Optics Center features state-of-the-art optical sensor, laser, fiber-optic, and other photonic instrumentation. The center includes six 4 by 8-foot optical tables and a collection of optical instruments and apparatus that includes picowatt optical power meters, computer-controlled monochromators, and a broad array of optical sources, including an optical time-domain reflectometer. The center focuses on sensing, holography, spectral analysis, and communication applied research.

The Construction Science and Engineering Center promotes innovation in the building design and construction industries by conducting applied research in structural materials and systems as well as construction methods. The lab has multiple computerized data acquisition capabilities and an extensive array of transducers for measuring force, displacement, and strain.

MSOE's new Grohmann Tower apartments,
which opened in the fall of 2014.

MISSOURI STATE UNIVERSITY

Graduate College

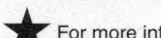

★ For more information, visit http://petersons.to/missouristateu-grad

Missouri State UNIVERSITY

Programs of Study

The Graduate College at Missouri State University (www.graduate.missouristate.edu) offers outstanding academic programs that prepare students for lifelong success. The college has over 100 graduate programs including master's degrees, specialist degrees, clinical doctoral degrees, cooperative degree programs, and certificate programs. In addition, it offers full- and part-time options, evening programs, online courses and programs, and blended formats, all of which enable students to earn their degrees while managing their personal and professional lives.

Missouri State University offers 43 **graduate certificate programs** (generally 12 credits) in special areas. Many of these can be expanded into a master's degree, or earned in conjunction with a master's degree in a related area.

Missouri State University has **Master of Arts (M.A.)** degree programs in several disciplines including Communication, English, History, Religious Studies, Teaching, and Writing. In addition there is a Teaching and Learning (M.A.T.L.) program available to cohorts in the Southwest Missouri area K–12 school districts. These programs give students opportunities to build upon previous study and professional experience to acquire the knowledge and skills needed to advance their careers or pursue doctoral study.

Students who are interested in earning **Master of Science (M.S.)** degrees can choose from more than 20 programs at Missouri State University including Administrative Studies (M.S.A.S.), Applied Anthropology, Applied Behavior Analysis, Athletic Training, Biology, Cell and Molecular Biology, Chemistry, Child Life Studies, Communication Sciences and Disorders, Counseling, Criminology and Criminal Justice, Cybersecurity, Defense and Strategic Studies, Early Childhood and Family Development, Geospatial Sciences in Geography, Geology and Planning, Health Promotion and Wellness Management, Materials Science, Mathematics, Physician Assistant Studies, Plant Science, Project Management, Psychology, and Student Affairs in Higher Education.

Individuals who are interested in earning advanced degrees in education, training, or instruction can choose from several **Master of Science in Education (M.S.Ed.)** programs including Educational Administration, Educational Technology, Elementary Education, Literacy, Secondary Education, and Special Education.

Missouri State also offers several **other master's degree programs**, such as: Accountancy (MAcc.), Applied Second Language Acquisition (M.A.S.L.A.), Business Administration (MBA), Global Studies (M.G.S.), Health Administration (M.H.A.), Health Administration and Public Health dual-degree program, Interdisciplinary Studies (M.S.I.S.), Music (M.M.), Natural and Applied Science (M.N.A.S.), Nursing–Nurse Educator (M.S.N.), Occupational Therapy (M.O.T.), Public Administration (M.P.A.), Public Health (M.P.H.), Social Work (M.S.W.), and Visual Studies (M.F.A.).

MSU offers two **Specialist (Ed.S.)** programs: Educational Administration, and Counseling and Assessment. There is also a Specialist in Education, Teacher Leadership (SETL) program available to cohorts in the Southwest Missouri area K–12 school districts.

Individuals who are interested in **professional doctoral programs** will find Missouri State to be a great fit. Offerings include: Audiology (Au.D.); Educational Leadership (Ed.D.)—a cooperative program with the University of Missouri; Nurse Anesthesia (D.N.A.P.); Nursing (D.N.P.); Pharmacy (Pharm.D.)—a cooperative program with the University of Missouri Kansas City; and Physical Therapy (D.P.T.).

All students are assigned an academic adviser in their graduate program, and work closely with that adviser throughout the pursuit of their degree/certificate. Most of the Missouri State University master's programs provide for either a thesis, seminar/degree paper option, or internship option as the research component to be completed in partial fulfillment of the degree

Financial Aid

Missouri State proudly offers approximately 500 graduate assistantships each year to qualified grad students. These assistantships are offered in teaching, research, and/or administrative areas. In exchange for working the required 20 hours per week on campus, students receive a tuition fee waiver which covers up to 15 credit hours in the fall or spring semesters, and a stipend. The 2016–17 stipend amount is $8,772 (for the 9-month academic year). More information about graduate assistantships is available online at http://graduate.missouristate.edu/currentstudents/FeeWaiver.htm.

There are also a limited number of scholarships available to qualified graduate students. The most popular scholarships are the MOGO, Need-Based, and Midwest Student Exchange Program. A complete list of scholarships and qualifying requirements can be found at http://www.missouristate.edu/FinancialAid/scholarships/Graduate.htm.

Cost of Study

Base tuition for graduate students for 2016–17 is $258 per credit hour for Missouri residents and $518 per credit hour for nonresidents. Base tuition for online courses is $285 per credit hour for Missouri and Non-Missouri residents. (Note: Some graduate programs charge more than the base tuition.)

Student services fees are assessed in addition to tuition and are based on the total credit hours for which a student enrolls. (Note: Intersession courses, iCourses, Internet/online courses, courses taught in a location other than the Springfield campus, and courses scheduled to meet on the Springfield campus fewer than four times are excluded from student services fees.) Additional details regarding tuition and fees are available at http://www.missouristate.edu/registrar/costs.htm.

Location

Missouri State University's main campus is located in Springfield, Missouri, in the Midwestern region of the United States. The city of Springfield, Missouri, and the surrounding Ozarks provide numerous services and activities to meet the needs of its citizens. Missouri's third largest city is within a 500-mile radius of nearly 50 percent of the U.S. population. Springfield has the feel of a big city with the convenience of a small town, including friendly people, an affordable cost of living, and healthcare options that are among the best in the country. The city offers an array of options in terms of entertainment, the arts, sports, recreation, and entertainment. Downtown Springfield is less than a mile from the MSU campus.

The University

Founded in 1905, and now with a strong public affairs mission, Missouri State University serves more than 23,000 traditional and non-traditional students from over 70 countries and 46 states, offering nearly 200 undergraduate degrees and graduate programs. The University is committed to providing graduate programs that meet the needs of a changing workforce and positively impact the region, state, nation, and world.

MSU seeks to be the university of choice to develop successful students who excel academically and in ethical leadership, cultural competence and community engagement.

Applying

Prospective students should review the Graduate Catalog to review the admission requirements for the Graduate College and their program of interest. Some programs require additional materials such as letters of recommendation, a resume, and a departmental or program application. Applicants should check with the program and the test requirements section of the Graduate Catalog for any standardized tests requirements. MSU's GRE school code is 6665. Students are required to submit official transcripts showing their bachelor's degree course work and any graduate-level work. Electronic transcripts should be sent to GraduateAdmissions@missouristate.edu through a clearinghouse or university's Registrar.

Interested students are encouraged to apply online. The online system allows applicants to apply and pay the fee, return to complete a saved application, check the status of an application, and change or add a graduate program.

After the Graduate College receives the application materials, they will be evaluated against the admission requirements. Applications will then be forwarded to their program for a program admission decision. Competitive programs cannot accept all students who meet the minimum requirements. The program's decision will be submitted to the Graduate College admission's office, which will notify the student via e-mail and/or mail.

International students need to complete an International Student Application, fulfill the academic requirements for admission, provide documentation of financial support, and submit an official TOEFL score if English is not the student's primary language. The minimum TOEFL score requirement is 79 or more for graduate applicants. Complete admission requirements for international students are available on the University's website at http://international.missouristate.edu/services/70306.htm.

Correspondence and Information

Dr. Julie Masterson, Graduate College Dean
Dr. Tom Tomasi, Graduate College Associate Dean
Michael Edwards, Admissions Coordinator
Misty Stewart, Recruitment Coordinator
Graduate College
Missouri State University
901 South National Avenue
Springfield, Missouri 65897
United States
Phone: 417-836-5335 (Main Office)
417-836-5331 (Admissions)
E-mail: GraduateAdmissions@missouristate.edu
Website: www.graduate.missouristate.edu

Missouri State University campus and downtown Springfield, Missouri.

Missouri State University's main entrance, Bear Boulevard and National Avenue.

MISSOURI WESTERN STATE UNIVERSITY

Graduate Programs

★ **For more information, visit http://petersons.to/mwsu-grad**

Programs of Study

Missouri Western State University (MWSU) offers a variety of graduate degree and certificate programs through the Craig School of Business, Graduate School, School of Fine Arts, College of Liberal Arts and Sciences, and College of Professional Studies.

Missouri Western State University offers students at every life stage graduate programs that help them increase their potential and advance their careers. For example, the Master of Applied Science programs integrate advanced training in science and technology with business and professional skills. Similarly, the Master of Applied Arts programs focus on the skills in writing and the arts that are in high demand by employers. Most graduate programs are designed to be completed in two years, and graduate certificates can usually be completed within one year. Classes are offered primarily in the late afternoon and evenings to help accommodate working professionals.

Starting in fall 2017, MWSU will be offering a **Master of Business Administration (MBA)** degree program.

Master of Science (M.S.) in Information Technology Assurance Administration: This 36-credit program provides practical understanding about computer forensics, data protection, and network security. It also introduces students to policy, legal, and ethical issues regarding information security.

Master's in Information Management: This program, with a concentration in enterprise resource planning (ERP), trains students to apply ERP methods in a variety of business settings. Its 30-credit curriculum focuses on SAP software and provides in-depth understanding of all business areas.

Missouri Western State University offers five **Master of Applied Science (M.A.S.)** programs, including Chemistry, Industrial Life Science, Engineering Technology Management, Human Factors and Usability Testing, and Sport and Fitness Management.

M.A.S. in Chemistry: This 35-credit program provides advanced training in industry-focused chemistry with cross-training in business and communications.

M.A.S. in Industrial Life Science: This 35-credit program integrates biology and chemistry with skills-based course work in business fundamentals, intellectual property, project management, and laboratory management.

M.A.S. in Engineering and Technology Management: This 33-credit program focuses on applied research and hands-on experience to prepare students for a variety of positions including assembly line supervisor, plant manager, and secondary or post-secondary teacher.

M.A.S. in Human Factors and Usability Testing: This 36-credit program trains students to evaluate human-computer interfaces and interaction, conduct research, make analyses, and provide recommendations to design products, increase productivity, improve work settings, and reduce human error.

M.A.S. in Sport and Fitness Management: This 33- to 36-credit program prepares graduates to manage and lead in areas such as intercollegiate and professional sports, and sport and fitness facilities.

The online **Master of Applied Science in Assessment** includes three options: Autism Spectrum Disorders, Teaching English to Speakers of Other Languages (TESOL), and Writing.

Autism Spectrum Disorders: This 33-credit option trains students to teach learners with autism disorders in inclusive Pre-K through 12th grade classrooms.

Teaching English to Speakers of Other Languages (TESOL): This 33-credit option provides students with the specific skill set and knowledge to teach English language learners and advocate for TESOL educational programs.

Writing: This 33-credit option helps teachers improve their abilities to teach writing. Focus areas include applying innovative methods to writing, evaluating writing, developing writing assignments, and integrating writing into curricula.

Master of Applied Arts in Digital Media: This program trains students for the digital arts workplace. Students strengthen their creative thinking skills and obtain hands-on and team-based experience. The 38-credit program allows students to successfully address the challenges that businesses, digital artists, and media professionals face in the 21st-century business environment.

The interdisciplinary, 33-credit **Master of Applied Arts in Written Communication** has two options: Technical Communication and Writing Studies.

Technical Communication: This option is ideal for individuals who want to advance their careers in business, government, and industry. It helps them improve their writing, supervisory, training, and technical communication skills.

Writing Studies: This option is designed for educators who want to strengthen their writing as a content area and individuals interested in teaching at the post-secondary level. Students will improve their knowledge base in pedagogy and theory and their ability to use technology as a teaching tool.

Master of Science in Nursing (M.S.N.): This program prepares students for leadership roles in nursing practice. Its 32-credit curriculum has two tracks: Health Care Leadership and Nurse Educator. Both programs help graduates emerge as advocates for excellence and leaders in nursing, and nursing education and training.

Master of Applied Science (M.A.S.) in Forensic Investigations: This 36-credit program provides broad-based knowledge of the field and strengthens students' professional expertise in law enforcement investigation. It includes 18 credits of core and 18 credits of elective courses taught by forensic scientists and law enforcement professionals.

Graduate Certificates: Missouri Western State University offers six graduate certificate programs, most associated with full master's-level programs: Autism Spectrum Disorders, Digital Media, Forensic Investigations, Nurse Educator, Professional Skills, Teaching of Writing, and Teachers of English to Speakers of Other Languages (TESOL).

Research Facilities

The MWSU Library maintains over 228,000 volumes and holds more than 1,150 journal titles. It is also a State Government Documents Depository. Microfilm, company annual reports, CD-ROM products, pamphlet files, newspapers, and Internet resources provide additional unique information for users. Through its computer-based catalog and circulation system, students can gain quick access to the Library's collection. The TOWERS online catalog and 75 plus online databases are also available via the Web. Professionally trained librarians provide individual assistance to students and other users. Reference Chat, Book-a-Librarian, any My Librarian are additional specialized services to help the student or faculty researcher. The Library has access to a national data base of over 120 million items, assuring that clients can usually obtain the specific item needed. Group information instruction is enhanced by the availability of a specially equipped computer classroom within the library.

Financial Aid

Degree-seeking graduate students are generally eligible for scholarships and loans. Qualified educators may be eligible for Teacher Education Assistance for College and Higher Education (TEACH) grants. A limited number of graduate assistantships are available, and these are offered by individual graduate programs when available. Assistantships may include a stipend and in-state tuition for up to 18 credits per academic year (not including summers). More information on assistantships and scholarships is available on the Graduate School website. International students who are fully admitted may be eligible for International Excellence Scholarships.

Cost of Study

Tuition for the 2016–17 academic year is $327 per credit hour for in-state students and $592 per credit hour for out-of-state and international students. Beginning in the fall semester of 2017, students accepted to the Graduate School who are U.S. citizens from Arkansas, Illinois, Iowa, Kansas, Kentucky, Nebraska, Oklahoma, and Tennessee will be admitted to Missouri Western State University under the **Griffon Rate** and be eligible to pay the equivalent of in-state tuition.

Housing

On-campus housing is available for graduate students primarily in Griffon Hall's apartments. Each apartment consists of four single bedrooms, two bathrooms, a shared living space, and a full kitchen. Each bedroom has built-in closets and a desk. For added convenience only two people share a bathroom. Other housing options are available. More information can be found on the Residential Life website (www.missouriwestern.edu/reslife).

Location

The University's main campus is located on more than 700 wooded acres in historic St. Joseph, Missouri. This bustling city of approximately 76,000 residents offers many amenities including arts and culture, entertainment and nightlife, restaurants and shopping, and sports and recreation. St. Joseph is 35 minutes north of the Kansas City International Airport, providing convenient access to the university and an easy commute from the Kansas City metro area.

The University

Missouri Western State University offers high-quality, student-centered education that emphasizes applied learning and community service. It provides 83 degree programs, 119 majors, and 61 minors.

The university also has many co-curricular and recreational options including nearly 80 clubs and organizations, cultural events, and NCAA Division II athletics. In addition, it provides extensive support services including the Center for Academic Support, Counseling Center, Disability Services, Center for Multicultural Education, Student Health Center, Career Development Center, and International Student Services.

Applying

Applications can be submitted directly through the Graduate School website (http://www.missouriwestern.edu/graduate). A bachelor's or master's degree from an accredited college or university with a minimum GPA of 2.75 (on a 4.0 scale) is required for graduate admission. Many programs require a 3.0 GPA or additional admission materials (GRE, GMAT, examples of representative work, letters of recommendation). International students must earn a TOEFL score of 79 or better (use code 6625 for automatic score submission) or an IELTS score of 6.0 or better for full admission. All international transcripts must be evaluated for U.S. equivalencies.

The application deadline for fall admission is July 15; for spring admission, November 1; and for summer admission, April 29. Certain programs may have earlier deadlines; applicants should consult the department offering their desired degree program for more information.

Applications are submitted online, and required documents may be uploaded directly. Applicants should check individual graduate program requirements for any additional documents or materials that may be required for admission. Once all application materials have been submitted, applications are forwarded to the specified graduate program for evaluation and final admission decision. Competitive programs may not be able to accept all applicants who meet the minimum requirements. Final program admission decisions are communicated to the Graduate School which will then notify students by mail or e-mail.

Correspondence and Information

Dr. Benjamin D. Caldwell, Dean of Graduate Studies
Tina Washburn, Admissions Coordinator
Missouri Western State University Graduate School
4525 Downs Drive
St. Joseph, Missouri 64507
United States
Phone: 816-271-4394
E-mail: graduate@missouriwestern.edu
Website: http://www.missouriwestern.edu/graduate

The Glenn Marion Memorial Clock Tower has been an icon at the center of the Missouri Western State University campus since 1997. The beautiful clock tower fills the campus with music throughout the day.

The Griffon Plaza greets visitors on the east side of the Missouri Western State University campus. The mythical Griffon has been the mascot and symbol of the University since 1918 and was chosen because it is a guardian of education. Its wings are spread in the shape of the state of Missouri to signify the union of the university with the state.

QUINNIPIAC UNIVERSITY

Graduate Studies

Quinnipiac university

Programs of Study

Quinnipiac University is a lively, challenging, and supportive academic community, offering more than 25 world-class graduate programs that give students a solid foundation for their careers with both rigorous academic preparation and in-depth practical experience.

The School of Health Sciences and School of Nursing offer a range of programs for students interested in the health professions, including the Master of Health Science (M.H.S.) with specializations in cardiovascular perfusion, medical laboratory sciences, pathologists' assistant, physician assistant, and radiologist assistant; the Master of Social Work (M.S.W.); the Doctor of Nursing Practice (D.N.P.), with tracks including adult-gerontology, family nurse practitioner, nurse anesthesia, care of populations, and nursing leadership; and the Master of Science in Nursing Operational Leadership. Also offered are the Doctor of Physical Therapy (D.P.T.) (freshman entry only), the Doctor of Occupational Therapy (D.O.T.), and the Master of Science (M.S.) in Molecular and Cell Biology (College of Arts & Sciences). The Frank H. Netter M.D. School of Medicine offers the Doctor of Medicine (M.D.) and the Anesthesiologist Assistant programs.

The School of Business offers the Master of Business Administration (M.B.A.). Students can choose the general M.B.A. or from among the following tracks: chartered financial analyst®, health care management, and supply chain management. Other degree programs include the Master of Science (M.S.) in Business Analytics and the M.S. in Organizational Leadership. Graduate certificates are available in Long Term Care Administration and Health Care Compliance.

The School of Communications offers the M.S. programs in Journalism and Sports Journalism; the M.S. in Public Relations; and the M.S. in Interactive Media.

The School of Education offers the Master of Arts in Teaching (M.A.T.), elementary and secondary; the Sixth-Year Diploma in Educational Leadership; the M.S. in Instructional Design; the M.S. in Teacher Leadership; the M.S. in Special Education; and the Certificate of Completion in Special Education.

The School of Law offers the Juris Doctor (J.D.), J.D./M.B.A., J.D./ Master of Environmental Law and Policy (with Vermont Law School), and the Master of Laws (L.L.M.) in Health Law.

Most graduate programs range in length from one to three years. Both full- and part-time study are available in most programs, and a number of programs and tracks are offered online. All graduate programs at Quinnipiac University share three key foundations: instruction is provided by faculty members with the highest available academic credentials and practicing professionals; every graduate student has the opportunity to earn practical experience through residencies, internships, thesis research, special projects, clinical rotations, consulting practicums, or small laboratory classes; and study builds upon both undergraduate education and professional experience.

Research Facilities

The university features facilities on both academic campuses with state-of-the-art equipment for research and professional preparation across disciplines. The Mount Carmel Campus features biology laboratories for candidates in the master's programs in Molecular and Cell Biology and Medical Laboratory Sciences. M.B.A. and other business students practice analytical finance methods, conduct trading simulations, develop financial models, analyze economic databases, and study stocks, bonds, currency, and interest rates at the Terry W. Goodwin '67 Financial Technology Center, with real-time financial data from markets all over the world. For students in the School of Communications, the Ed McMahon Mass Communications Center offers a fully digital high-definition television studio, multimedia lab, audio production studio, master edit room, video editing lab, a media innovation classroom and lab modeled after a working newsroom, and an equipment loan room with a full complement of remote audio and video production gear.

The North Haven Campus is home to the cutting-edge Center for Medicine, Nursing and Health Sciences, with learning labs including a professional SimMan suite of life-size patient simulators, a pediatric and neonatal lab, magnetic resonance simulators and 3-D workstations, an orthopedics lab, a rehabilitative sciences lab, a clinical skills lab, an intensive care unit, a health assessment lab, a physical diagnostics lab, a motion analysis lab, an operating room suite with two additional high fidelity simulation rooms, and 48 prosection stations.

At the School of Law, the Center for Health Law and Policy and the Center on Dispute Resolution offer legal research opportunities. Other university institutes and centers include the Alternative Investments Institute, the National Institute for Community Health Education, the Center for Women and Business, the Center for Interprofessional Healthcare Education, the Bristol-Myers Squibb Center for Science Teaching and Learning, the Bioanthropology Research Institute, and the Albert Schweitzer Institute. In addition, the university's new Frank H. Netter M.D. School of Medicine has plans to develop the Institute for Primary Care, the Institute for Rehabilitation Medicine, and the Institute for Global Public Health.

Financial Aid

Graduate students are eligible to apply for several options to fund their education. Both full- and part-time students can apply for federal fixed-rate student loans.

The university offers institutional funds through a select number of merit-based scholarships to qualified full-time incoming (non-online) graduate students within certain disciplines: M.B.A., cardiovascular perfusion, journalism, medical laboratory sciences, molecular and cell biology, nursing, pathologists' assistant, physician assistant, public relations, radiologist assistant, and social work.

All full-time, on-ground domestic graduate students are also eligible to apply for the institutional need-based grant.

The university also offers two types of work programs. Eligible graduate students with financial need have the opportunity to work on campus through the Federal Work Study Program (not available in all academic programs). Graduate assistantships are available on a limited basis to both full- and part-time students.

Students in the Master of Arts in Teaching (M.A.T.) program also receive reduced tuition rates while they are participating in the internship semesters of the program.

Students applying to programs in law, medicine, or through QU Online, should consult the website for financial aid information.

Cost of Study

Tuition in 2016–17 is $985 per credit hour for most on-campus graduate programs. Student fees are $40 per credit (not to exceed $360 per semester), and there is a $25 summer registration fee.

Living and Housing Costs

Hamden, North Haven, and surrounding communities in greater New Haven offer a wide array of housing options for graduate students in a range of prices, including apartment complexes, rentals within multi-unit homes, and single family houses for rent. There is also a limited amount of on-campus housing available for graduate students. The university's Office of Residential Life maintains a listing of off-campus housing and can provide information about on-campus housing. In addition, the Quinnipiac Offices of Graduate Admissions and Graduate Student Affairs can provide information about the locales and communities within commuting distance of the campuses.

Student Group

Quinnipiac University enrolls approximately 6,500 undergraduates and 2,500 graduate students. Of the university's graduate student population, approximately 54 percent are enrolled in full-time programs, and 46 percent are enrolled in part-time programs. Many graduate students come from the Northeast region and northern mid-Atlantic region. Certain programs also attract graduate students from across the United States and internationally.

Location

The university's graduate programs are located on two beautiful, state-of-the-art campuses in Hamden and North Haven, Connecticut, located just outside of New Haven, approximately 90 minutes from New York City and two hours from Boston. The Mount Carmel Campus in Hamden is home to graduate programs in business, communications, and molecular and cell biology. The North Haven Campus is home to graduate programs in health sciences, nursing, education, law, and medicine. A third campus, York Hill, features the TD Bank Sports Center, home to Quinnipiac's Division I hockey and basketball teams, and the Rocky Top Student Center, featuring stunning views of Long Island Sound and a fitness facility, open to graduate students.

The University

Quinnipiac University is nationally recognized as a dynamic center for higher learning in the Northeast and is consistently ranked among the best master's-level universities in the North in *U.S. News & World Report*'s Guide to America's Best Colleges and its Best Online Graduate Business Programs. The Princeton Review has included Quinnipiac among its Best Business Schools and Best Law Schools.

Applying

Applicants should check the requirements on the university website for the specific program to which they plan to apply. Applications should be submitted online and by sending required materials to the Office of Graduate Admissions. International students should visit the website for application information; students from non–English-speaking countries must supply a notarized translation of their transcripts as well as Test of English as a Foreign Language (TOEFL) or International English Language Testing System (IELTS) scores.

Correspondence and Information:

Office of Graduate Admissions
Quinnipiac University
275 Mount Carmel Avenue
Hamden, Connecticut 06518-1940
United States
Phone: 203-582-8672
800-462-1944 (toll-free)
E-mail: graduate@quinnipiac.edu
Website: www.qu.edu

THE FACULTY

Quinnipiac faculty members demonstrate a high level of commitment to their fields, and notable faculty members work in each of the graduate areas of study. The following are key members of the Quinnipiac University faculty.

Matthew L. O'Connor, Ph.D., Dean of the School of Business and Professor of Finance, has published extensively in peer-reviewed journals and is an active participant at professional conferences. Recipient of the 2005 Excellence in Teaching Award by the university's Center for Excellence in Teaching and Service to Students, Dean O'Connor currently teaches courses in applied portfolio management.

Kevin G. Basmadjian, Ph.D., Dean of the School of Education and Associate Professor of Education, is a former public school teacher whose research looks at the role of technology in education and English teacher preparation for diverse learning communities. Dr. Basmadjian teaches several subjects in the M.A.T. program.

Jennifer Gerarda Brown, J.D., is the Dean of the School of Law. Her research looks at LGBT rights, dispute resolution, and the professional responsibilities of lawyers.

Lee Kamlet, B.A., Dean of the School of Communications, is an Emmy Award-winning television news producer whose credits include Dateline NBC, and ABC's World News with Peter Jennings.

Bruce M. Koeppen, M.D., Dean of the School of Medicine and Vice President of Health Affairs, has directed and published research on kidney function, has earned numerous awards for teaching, and has more than three decades of experience as a medical school professor and administrator.

William C. Kohlhepp, D.H.S., is Dean of the School of Health Sciences and teaches medical microbiology and infectious diseases. His professional experience includes clinical practice as a physician assistant, administrative directorship of an area occupational health center, and service as an officer or board member of several national physician assistant organizations.

Jean W. Lange, Ph.D., Dean of the School of Nursing, teaches clinical scholarship in addition to her administrative role. Her clinical experience encompasses cardiology, critical care, and neurology, and her academic work focuses on senior and Hispanic health issues. Dr. Lange is a Fellow of the American Academy of Nursing.

Allan Smits, Ph.D., is the Associate Dean of Sciences and Graduate Programs in the College of Arts and Sciences, which includes the M.S. in Molecular and Cell Biology program. He has been named an outstanding professor by the university's Center for Excellence in Teaching and Service to Students.

Students at Quinnipiac join a welcoming community that is supportive and collaborative.

Quinnipiac's campuses provide state-of-the-art resources in a dynamic and architecturally distinctive setting.

SALISBURY UNIVERSITY

Graduate Studies and Research

Salisbury UNIVERSITY

Programs of Study

Graduate study at Salisbury University (SU) provides baccalaureate degree holders from the United States and abroad with opportunities for professional advancement and personal enrichment. The graduate curriculum is designed to assist students in attaining greater mastery of their fields of specialization, improving skills in pursuing independent study, and increasing professional knowledge and ability through the study of new findings in areas of special interest.

Master's degree programs available at SU include the following: applied biology (M.S.), applied health physiology (M.S.), athletic training (M.S.A.T.), business administration (M.B.A.), conflict analysis and dispute resolution (M.A.), education (M.Ed.: curriculum and instruction; educational leadership; post-secondary education track; reading specialist), English (M.A.), geographic information systems management (M.S.), history (M.A.), mathematics education (M.S.M.E.), nursing (M.S.: clinical nurse educator; health care leadership), social work (M.S.W.), and teaching (M.A.T.).

Doctoral programs are available in education (Ed.D.: contemporary curriculum theory and instruction in literacy) and nursing (D.N.P.: post-B.S.; post-masters).

A graduate certificate program is offered in Teaching English to Speakers of Other Languages (TESOL).

Research Facilities

Salisbury University is home to Henson Science Hall, a $42 million science education and research building, and the new $117 million Patricia R. Guerrieri Academic Commons, the largest academic building in University history. An epicenter for learning, research, and creativity, it houses SU Libraries, the Nabb Research Center for Delmarva History and Culture, a Graduate Student Commons, and numerous academic centers and services.

Financial Aid

A limited amount of financial aid in the form of graduate assistantships from the University and scholarships from the Maryland State Scholarship Administration (Maryland residents only) are available each year to selected graduate students. Students applying for aid must complete the Free Application for Federal Student Aid (FAFSA) and indicate Salisbury University (title IV code of 002091). Students may also apply online at www.fafsa.ed.gov. For more information about financial assistance, prospective students should contact the Financial Aid Office at 410-543-6165 or finaid@salisbury.edu, or visit www.salisbury.edu/admissions/finaid/graduate.html.

Graduate assistants are eligible to receive a stipend and tuition waiver of up to 18 credits per fiscal year. To be eligible for the waiver, students must enroll for a minimum of 6 credits in both the fall and spring terms. Tuition is waived only for graduate courses applicable toward master's degree requirements. The tuition waiver does not include waiver of fees. A full-time assistantship requires a time commitment of approximately 20 hours per week, and a half-time assistantship requires 10 hours per week. For details, prospective students should visit www.salisbury.edu/gsr/gradstudies/grad_assistantships.html or consult the Graduate Assistantship section of the Graduate Student Handbook.

Enrolled graduate students are eligible for competitive research and funding opportunities within their academic schools and for Research and Presentation Grants providing up to $500 to support scholarly projects and presentations.

Cost of Study

All graduate tuition rates are charged on a per credit-hour basis; there is no full-time tuition rate. Prospective students should visit www.salisbury.edu/cashiers for information and an updated listing of tuition, fees, special course fees, and other related expenses. Tuition and fees for each semester may be changed and new ones established at any time by action of the Board of Regents of the University System of Maryland.

Living and Housing Costs

Salisbury University does not offer on-campus housing for graduate students; however, there are numerous off-campus housing options nearby. Prospective students should visit SU's Commuter and Connections' website at www.salisbury.edu/commuters.

Student Group

The Graduate Student Council (GSC) at SU provides opportunities for intellectual, professional, personal, and social development through grants, advocacy, public presentation of research, graduate community events, and campus service. The GSC is part of the campus' Governance Consortium.

Student Outcomes

SU offers a network of over 47,000 alumni nationwide.

Location

With a regional population of roughly 99,000, Salisbury is the cultural and economic hub of Delmarva (containing portions of Delaware, Maryland, and Virginia), a historically and ecologically rich peninsula located between the Atlantic Ocean and Chesapeake Bay. The city is 30 minutes west of the beaches of Assateague and Ocean City, Maryland; about 2 hours from Baltimore, Maryland; Wilmington, Delaware; Norfolk, Virginia; and Washington, D.C.; and 4½ hours from New York City.

The University

A member of the University System of Maryland, SU is a regionally accredited four-year comprehensive institution offering 59 distinct graduate and undergraduate programs.

Applying

To be considered for admission, the Salisbury University application, all transcripts and supporting documents, and $65 nonrefundable application fee must be submitted. For questions regarding the application process, prospective students should call the Office of Graduate Studies at 410-548-3546. For more information about specific program admission requirements, including priority application deadlines, applicants should contact the appropriate graduate program director. Additional information can be found online at www.salisbury.edu/gsr/gradstudies/admissions.html.

Correspondence and Information

Office of Graduate Studies
Holloway Hall 262
Salisbury University
1101 Camden Avenue
Salisbury, Maryland 21801
Phone: 410-548-3546
Fax: 410-677-0052
E-mail: graduateadmissions@salisbury.edu
Website: http://www.salisbury.edu/gsr/gradstudies/

GRADUATE PROGRAMS AND THEIR DIRECTORS

Applied Biology (M.S.)
Dana Price, Ph.D., Graduate Program Director:
410-543-6498, dlprice@salisbury.edu.
http://www.salisbury.edu/gsr/gradstudies/MSBIOpage.html

Applied Health Physiology (M.S.)
Carlton Insley, Ph.D., RRT-NPS, RPFT, ACSM-CES; Graduate Program Director:
410-677-0145, rcinsley@salisbury.edu.
http://www.salisbury.edu/gsr/gradstudies/MSAHPHpage.html

Athletic Training (M.S.A.T.)
Jenny Toonstra, Ph.D., Graduate Program Director:
410-677-5493, jltoonstra@salisbury.edu.
http://www.salisbury.edu/hss/atgrad/default.html

Business Administration (M.B.A.)
Yvonne Downie, Graduate Program Director:
410-548-3983, yxdownie@salisbury.edu.
http://www.salisbury.edu/gsr/gradstudies/MBApage.html

Conflict Analysis and Dispute Resolution (M.A.)
Vitus Ozoke, Ph.D., Graduate Program Director:
410-677-0276, vaozoke@salisbury.edu.
http://www.salisbury.edu/gsr/gradstudies/CADRpage.html

Education (Ed.D., M.Ed)
Ed.D.: Judith Franzak, Ph.D., Graduate Program Director:
410-677-0238, jkfranzak@salisbury.edu.
http://www.salisbury.edu/gsr/gradstudies/EDDpage.html
M.Ed. Curriculum and Instruction: Diana Wagner, Ph.D., Graduate Program Director:
410-677-5490, dmwagner@salisbury.edu.
http://www.salisbury.edu/gsr/gradstudies/MEDpage.html.
M.Ed. Education Leadership: Doug DeWitt, Ph.D., Graduate Program Director:
410-543-6286, dmdewitt@salisbury.edu.
http://www.salisbury.edu/gsr/gradstudies/MEDpage.html.
M.Ed. Reading Specialist: Joyce Wiencek, Ph.D., Graduate Program Director:
410-543-6288, bjwiencek@salisbury.edu.
http://www.salisbury.edu/gsr/gradstudies/MEDpage.html

English (M.A.)
T. Ross Leasure, Ph.D., Graduate Program Director:
410-677-5009, trleasure@salisbury.edu.
http://www.salisbury.edu/gsr/gradstudies/ENGpage.html

Geographic Information Systems Management (M.S.)
Stuart Hamilton, Ph.D., Graduate Program Director:
410-548-3518, sehamilton@salisbury.edu.
http://www.salisbury.edu/gsr/gradstudies/GISpage.html

History (M.A.)
Celine Carayon, Ph.D., Graduate Program Director:
410-677-3251, cxcarayon@salisbury.edu.
http://www.salisbury.edu/gsr/gradstudies/HISTpage.html

Mathematics Education (M.S.M.E.)
Jennifer Bergner, Ph.D., Graduate Program Director:
410-677-5429, jabergner@salisbury.edu.
http://www.salisbury.edu/gsr/gradstudies/MSMEpage.html

Nursing
D.N.P.: Erica Alessandrini, Ph.D., RN, Graduate Program Director:
410-548-1497, eaalessandrini@salisbury.edu.
http://www.salisbury.edu/gsr/gradstudies/DNPpage.html
M.S.: Erica Alessandrini, Ph.D., RN, Graduate Program Director:
410-548-1497, eaalessandrini@salisbury.edu.
http://www.salisbury.edu/gsr/gradstudies/MSNpage.html

Social Work (M.S.W.)
Vicki Root, Ph.D., Graduate Program Director:
410-677-3948, vbroot@salisbury.edu.
http://www.salisbury.edu/gsr/gradstudies/MSWpage.html

Teaching (M.A.T.)
Regina Royer, Ed.D., Graduate Program Director:
410-548-3949, rdroyer@salisbury.edu.
http://www.salisbury.edu/gsr/gradstudies/MATpage.html

Teaching English to Speakers of Other Languages (TESOL)
http://www.salisbury.edu/english/grad/tesolD.html#tesol

SU's Patricia R. Guerrieri Academic Commons, opened fall 2016, houses SU Libraries, the Nabb Research Center, and a Graduate Student Commons.

Conway Hall has been cited as one of the nation's best designed higher education buildings.

SPRINGFIELD COLLEGE

Graduate Programs

Programs of Study

Education at Springfield College is all about taking action. Graduate students at Springfield College put their classroom education to practice through fieldwork and service learning. It's a learning advantage based on the College's historic mission, the Humanics philosophy, which calls for educating students in spirit, mind, and body for leadership in service to others. Humanics is at the base of everything the College does—in academics, athletics, and student life.

With an international reputation for educating tomorrow's leaders in some of the most vital career fields, Springfield College provides students with a competitive edge—top-quality academic preparation, research opportunities in state-of-the-art facilities, and real-world experience before graduating.

Springfield's graduate programs provide students with the employable skills and knowledge needed to advance their education and increase their job prospects and are taught by faculty members who are passionate about their disciplines. The programs integrate experiential learning opportunities, including fieldwork, internships, practicum, and research. Graduate courses at Springfield College challenge students to gain knowledge from the classroom, experience in the field, and think outside the box. Students leave Springfield College with a degree and real, applicable expertise in their fields.

Springfield offers more than 25 master's degree programs including: art therapy/counseling, business administration, education (concentrations: in special education initial [preK–8, 5–12], elementary initial, secondary initial), exercise science and sport studies (concentrations: athletic training, clinical exercise physiology, exercise physiology, sport and exercise psychology, strength and conditioning), human services, occupational therapy, physical education (concentrations: adapted physical education, advanced-level coaching, athletic administration, health promotion and disease prevention, physical education teacher licensure, physical education teacher–professional licensure, certificate of advanced graduate study), physician assistant, psychology and counseling (concentrations: athletic counseling, clinical mental health counseling, industrial/organizational psychology, school guidance counseling, student personnel administration in higher education), rehabilitation counseling and services (concentrations: alcohol and substance abuse counseling, counseling and case management, pediatric and developmental disability, special services, substance abuse and psychiatric rehabilitation counseling), social work (concentrations: M.S.W. weekday program, M.S.W. weekend program in Worcester and Springfield, advanced standing program, post-master's certificate program in trauma-informed practice), and sport management and recreation (concentrations: recreation management, therapeutic recreation management). Doctoral degree programs are also available: Ph.D. in Physical Education with specializations in sport and exercise psychology, exercise physiology, and teaching and administration; Doctor of Physical Therapy (D.P.T.); and Doctor of Psychology (Psy.D.) in counseling psychology.

Research Facilities

The campus is home to numerous research facilities, including a medical simulation lab, featuring high-fidelity 3G adult and baby patient simulator mannequins that respond to treatment as human patients would. The exercise physiology/biomechanics lab is where many graduate students conduct their own research, as well as working closely with faculty advisers on exciting new endeavors.

Financial Aid

Eight-five percent of traditional graduate students receive some form of financial assistance. Springfield College offers fellowships and professional development opportunities that assist in paying for tuition. During the 2015–16 academic year, the Office of Academic Affairs administered a total of $2.7 million in fellowship funding to graduate students. Assistantships, which pay students an hourly wage, also are available. For some graduate students, AmeriCorps positions provide additional funding and professional opportunity that supplement their education. Federal financial aid, in the form of loans, is also available to those who qualify.

Cost of Study

The price per credit hour for graduate courses at Springfield College is $988. There is a graduate student fee of $97.50, which only applies to students taking nine or more credits.

Living and Housing Costs

Springfield College offers on-campus and off-campus housing options for graduate students. Housing costs range from $9,800 to $13,250 per academic year. Meal plans vary and there are many options from which to choose.

Student Group

Springfield College has 3,408 undergraduate students and 1,500 graduate students on the main campus and at eight regional campuses across the country. Students come from 29 states and eight other countries, mostly from the northeastern corridor of the United States. The majority of undergraduate and graduate students reside on campus.

Student Outcomes

Springfield's graduate students are motivated, innovative, and focused on success, all while working to improve the world around them. According to a recent post-graduation survey, 97 percent of 2014–15 master's and doctoral graduates are employed or seeking advanced education.

Location

Located on the shores of Lake Massasoit, Springfield College is home to beautiful landscaping and top-notch facilities that combine function with artistry, while maintaining the historic beauty of the campus. Students have the best of both worlds—a campus located within a city with a classic New England charm.

The College

Springfield College provides a caring and inclusive environment, geared toward sharing ideas and research while collaborating with faculty members and other students. Ninety-two percent of the 2014–15 master's and doctoral students report that their academic experience at Springfield met or exceeded their expectations and 90 percent of those students would choose Springfield again if they had the opportunity.

Faculty

The College's classrooms provide an environment where discussions are welcomed and faculty members will always know students by name. Class sizes are small, with an approximate 13:1 student-to-faculty ratio. Approximately 84 percent of full-time faculty members have earned the highest degrees attainable in their areas of expertise, and 70 percent hold doctorates.

Applying

Each graduate program has its own admissions requirements. Specific details about the requirements, as well as the graduate admissions process, are available online at springfield.edu/grad.

Correspondence and Information

Office of Graduate Admissions
Springfield College
263 Alden Street
Springfield, Massachusetts 01109
United States
Phone: 413-748-3225
TTY: 413-748-3383
E-mail: graduate@springfieldcollege.edu
Website: springfield.edu/grad

STEVENS INSTITUTE OF TECHNOLOGY

Graduate Programs

Programs of Study

Stevens Institute of Technology's graduate programs are intended to enable professionals to advance in industries increasingly influenced by technology and to enable scholars to explore the frontiers of their disciplines. Concentrations tailored to the specific needs of the graduate student are available within almost all Stevens' master's degree programs; interdisciplinary degree programs can also be fashioned to meet specific needs. Stevens places a strong emphasis on examining real-world problems and applying knowledge from across disciplines. Research opportunities are available for all major fields of study.

Stevens' technology orientation, combined with its business, science, and engineering offerings, enable students to make an impact on society. Stevens also offers many programs of study designated by the Department of Homeland Security as eligible for the 17-month extension of Optional Practical Training for F-1 students.

Graduate degrees include the Master of Science (M.S.), the Master of Engineering (M.Eng.), the Master of Business Administration (MBA), and the Ph.D. and are offered through three schools and one college: the Charles V. Schaefer, Jr. School of Engineering and Science, the School of Business, the School of Systems and Enterprises, and the College of Arts and Letters.

Arts and Letters Degree Programs:

- Policy and Innovation, M.A.

Business Degree Programs:

- Business Intelligence and Analytics, M.S.
- Enterprise Project Management, M.S.
- Finance, M.S.
- Information Systems, M.S.
- Management, M.S.
- Master of Business Administration, MBA
- Technology Management, M.S.
- Network and Communication Management and Services, M.S.

Engineering and Science Degree Programs:

- Applied Mathematics, M.S.
- Biomedical Engineering, M.Eng., M.S.
- Chemical Biology, M.S.
- Chemical Engineering, M.Eng.
- Chemistry, M.S.
- Civil Engineering, M.Eng.
- Computer Engineering, M.Eng.
- Computer Science, M.S.
- Construction Management, M.S.
- Cybersecurity, M.S.
- Electrical Engineering, M.Eng.
- Engineering Physics, M.Eng.
- Enterprise and Cloud Computing, M.S.
- Environmental Engineering, M.Eng.
- Information and Data Engineering, M.Eng.
- Integrated Product Development, M.Eng. (interdisciplinary)
- Maritime Systems, M.S.
- Materials Science and Engineering, M.Eng.
- Mathematics, M.S.
- Mechanical Engineering, M.Eng.
- Media and Broadcast Engineering, M.S. (interdisciplinary)
- Ocean Engineering, M.Eng.
- Pharmaceutical Manufacturing, M.Eng., M.S.
- Physics, M.S.
- Product-Architecture and Engineering, M.Eng. (interdisciplinary)
- Service-Oriented Computing, M.S.
- Stochastic Systems, M.S.

Ph.D. Programs:

- Biomedical Engineering
- Business Administration
- Chemistry and Chemical Biology
- Chemical Engineering
- Civil Engineering
- Computer Engineering
- Computer Science
- Electrical Engineering
- Engineering Management
- Environmental Engineering
- Financial Engineering
- Materials Science and Engineering
- Mathematics
- Mechanical Engineering
- Ocean Engineering
- Physics
- Socio-Technical Systems
- Systems Engineering

Systems and Enterprises Degree Programs:

- Engineering Management, M.Eng.
- Financial Engineering, M.S.
- Software Engineering, M.S.
- Socio-Technical Systems, M.S.
- Space Systems Engineering, M.Eng.
- Systems Analytics, M.S.
- Systems Engineering, M.Eng.
- Systems Security Engineering, M.S.

Several online graduate programs are also available. Online education offers many advantages for busy students, professionals, and lifelong learners. Stevens strives to enhance teaching and learning with technology through a variety of applications. There are 17 master's degree programs available in business, computer science, engineering, and the sciences.

A broad range of graduate certificate programs are also available online and on the Stevens campus. These self-contained and highly-focused classes are designed to provide students with a foundation of strategic knowledge and practical skills to enhance their careers. Most graduate certificate programs consist of 4 courses. Credits earned for graduate certificates may be applied toward the corresponding master's degree.

Research Facilities

Stevens supports leading-edge research: in collaboration with faculty, Stevens graduate students frequently publish and co-publish original research in leading journals of engineering, physics, chemistry, biology, materials, nanotechnology, and business.

Stevens provides a technology-focused environment. Classroom buildings feature the latest learning and teaching technologies. Students also learn and conduct research in state-of-the-art laboratories. Resources include smart classrooms, computer-aided design and manufacturing labs, an Immersion Lab for visualizing complex data, robotic labs, a media arts center, a sound synthesis lab, a computer-aided education lab, a hydrodynamics tank and lab for craft design, and a motion-capture lab. The Hanlon Financial Systems Lab deploys the latest analytics software and real-time market data to enable research in high-frequency trading, quantitative methods, big data analytics, market performance and more.

Stevens also houses three National Centers of Excellence—advanced research facilities selected by the U.S. government to lead national research, development, and educational efforts to address critical global needs in areas such as cybersecurity, defense, and port security.

Financial Aid

Stevens offers a range of options to help make a graduate degree as affordable as possible: scholarships, fellowships, and assistantships are designed to support graduate students. Applicants are strongly encouraged to apply for financial aid. Even if an exceptional financial need is not demonstrated, other forms of assistance are available.

Graduate students may be eligible for a number of assistantships and fellowships. These highly competitive funding opportunities are limited in number and awarded to exceptional candidates on a merit basis by individual academic departments.

There are also scholarships, federal financial aid, and special resources for international graduate students. Alternative financial options are available to help with costs not covered by financial aid.

Cost of Study

Full-time graduate tuition for 2016–17 is $16,664 per semester. Part-time students pay $1,501 per credit. Full-time students also pay a general services fee of $438 per semester and an activity fee of $155 per semester. Part-time students pay a general services fee of $283 per semester.

Faculty

Stevens' graduate faculty are drawn from leading industry firms in finance, technology, engineering and management. The faculty numbered 268 in 2014–15, 90 of whom were tenured. Stevens' faculty members have won nine National Science Foundation CAREER Awards in the last nine years.

Student Body

Stevens is home to a diverse community of students from across the globe. Students come from 45 states and close to 70 countries. Services for international students include English language assistance.

Enrollment is approximately 6,800. There are roughly 3,300 graduate students. Stevens has 40,000 alumni worldwide, many of whom hold prominent positions in a variety of fields. Students have access to exceptional opportunities for project-based learning and state-of-the-art research facilities.

Student Outcomes

Stevens was ranked 13th for "Best Career Services" by the Princeton Review in the 2013 edition of "The Best 377 Colleges." Stevens offers career exploration programs, experiential education opportunities, and individual guidance, as well as comprehensive internships programming and an award-winning cooperative education program. Corporate, government, and nonprofit employers regularly recruit on campus.

The Institute

Stevens Institute of Technology is a premier private research university in Hoboken, New Jersey. Stevens inspires students to become leaders in the sciences, engineering, and business by applying technology and cross-disciplinary insights to complex, real-world problems. The university draws upon a distinguished history as a leader in technology and innovation to offer powerful classroom experiences and research opportunities that often lead to breakthrough solutions.

Founded in 1870, Stevens has grown from a pioneering engineering college into an institution that educates inventors, entrepreneurs, and business leaders who are highly sought after by corporations, research institutions, and government agencies. Stevens consistently ranks among the nation's top universities for total return on investment and mid-career salaries of graduates.

Located near the heart of one of the world's premiere centers of finance, technology, and culture, Stevens' broad offerings include unique degrees such as cybersecurity and quantitative finance.

Location

Stevens is located in Hoboken, New Jersey, a youthful, bustling city dotted with quaint homes, a thriving restaurant scene, and numerous shops. The 55-acre campus offers dramatic views of New York City. Stevens is just a 10-minute ride from the excitement and opportunity offered by the nation's largest city.

Admissions

Stevens is highly competitive. Admission is on a rolling basis. Graduate applicants must submit college transcripts from all institutions attended and two letters of recommendation. GRE scores are required for all applying to full-time graduate programs in the Schaefer School of Engineering and Sciences or the School of Systems and Enterprises. In the School of Business, the GRE/GMAT is required of all applicants applying to full-time graduate programs. Students wishing to attend on a part-time basis should refer to individual program pages for admission requirements.

Every international applicant must demonstrate English language proficiency by submitting the results of a TOEFL or an IELTS test.

Correspondence and Information

Office of Graduate Admissions
Stevens Institute of Technology
1 Castle Point Terrace
Hoboken, New Jersey 07030
United States
Phone: 201-216-5000
888-STEVENS (toll-free)
E-mail: graduate@stevens.edu
Website: https://www.stevens.edu/admissions/graduate-admissions

TEMPLE UNIVERSITY

Graduate School

★ For more information, visit http://petersons.to/templeugrad

TEMPLE UNIVERSITY
Graduate School

Programs of Study

Doctor of Philosophy programs are offered in Africology and African American studies, anthropology, art history, bioengineering, biology, biomedical sciences (cancer biology and genetics, infectious disease and immunity, molecular and cellular biosciences, neuroscience, organ systems and translational medicine), business administration (accounting, finance, human resource management and organizational behavior, interdisciplinary study, international business administration, management information systems, marketing, risk management and insurance, strategic management, tourism and sport), chemistry, civil engineering, communication sciences and disorders, computer and information science, criminal justice, dance, decision neuroscience, economics, education (applied linguistics, educational psychology, literacy and learners, math and science education, special education, urban education), electrical engineering, engineering, English, environmental engineering, epidemiology, geography and urban studies, geoscience, health policy, history, kinesiology (athletic training, integrative exercise physiology, psychology of movement), mathematics, mechanical engineering, media and communication, music (composition, music studies, music theory, musicology), music education, music therapy, neuromotor science, pharmaceutical sciences (medicinal chemistry, pharmaceutics, pharmacodynamics), philosophy, physics, political science, psychology (brain and cognitive sciences, clinical psychology, developmental psychology, social psychology), religion, school psychology, social and behavioral health sciences, sociology, Spanish, and statistics.

The Doctor of Musical Arts is offered in music performance (bassoon, cello, clarinet, double bass, flute, French horn, harp, historical keyboard, oboe, percussion, piano, trombone, trumpet, tuba, viola, violin, voice). The Doctor of Education degree is offered in educational leadership (higher education, K–12). Other specialized doctoral degrees include the Doctor of Athletic Training, Doctor of Nursing Practice (adult-gerontology primary care, family-individual across the lifespan), Clinical Doctorate in Occupational Therapy, Doctor of Physical Therapy, and executive D.B.A.

Master's degree programs are available in accomplished teaching; accountancy; accounting; actuarial science; adult and organizational development; Africology and African American studies; applied behavior analysis; architecture; art education; art history; athletic training; bioengineering; biology; biomedical sciences (cancer biology and genetics, general biomedical sciences, infectious disease and immunity, molecular and cellular biosciences, neuroscience, organ systems and translational medicine); business administration (business analytics, business management, enterprise risk management, entrepreneurship, financial management, health sector management, human resource management, information technology management, innovation management, marketing management, strategic management); business analytics; career and technical education (business, computer and information technology; industrial education; marketing education); chemistry; choral conducting; city and regional planning; civil engineering; clinical research and translational medicine; collaborative piano and chamber music; collaborative piano and opera coaching; communication management; computational data science; computer science; corporate compliance and ethics; counseling psychology; criminal justice; dance; digital innovation in marketing; early childhood education; early childhood education and special education; economics; educational psychology; electrical engineering; engineering management; engineering technology management (civil engineering, electrical engineering, mechanical engineering); English; environmental engineering; epidemiology; financial analysis and risk management; financial engineering; geography and urban studies; geology; global clinical and pharmacovigilance regulations; globalization and development communication; health administration; health informatics; higher education (access and success, institutional effectiveness, student affairs leadership); history; human resource management; information science and technology; information technology auditing and cybersecurity; innovation management and entrepreneurship (entrepreneurship, innovative strategy, technology and innovation management); instrumental conducting: wind-band emphasis; investment management; jazz studies; journalism; kinesiology (athletic training, curriculum and instruction, integrative exercise physiology, psychology of movement); landscape architecture; liberal arts; marketing; mathematics; mechanical engineering; media studies and production; mediaXarts: cinema for new technologies and environments; middle grades education (language arts, mathematics, mathematics and language arts, mathematics and science, science, science and language arts, social studies); music; music composition; music education; music history; music performance (bassoon, cello, clarinet, classical guitar, double bass, flute, French horn, harp, harpsichord, oboe, percussion, piano, saxophone, trombone, trumpet, tuba, viola, violin, voice); music theory; music therapy; musical theater studies; neuromotor science; neuroscience: systems, behavior and plasticity; occupational therapy; opera; oral biology; pharmaceutical sciences (medicinal chemistry, pharmaceutics, pharmacodynamics); philosophy; physician assistant; physics; piano pedagogy; political science; psychological research; public policy; recreation therapy; regulatory affairs and quality assurance; religion; risk management and insurance; school leadership (curriculum supervision, principal leadership, reform and change leadership); secondary education (English, mathematics, science, social studies, world/foreign languages); secondary education and special education (English, mathematics, science, social studies, world/foreign languages); social work; sociology; Spanish; special education (autism spectrum disorders, mild disabilities, severe disabilities); speech, language and hearing science; sport business (athletics administration, recreation and event management, sport analytics, sport marketing and promotions); statistics; string pedagogy; taxation; teacher leadership; teaching English to speakers of other languages; tourism and hospitality management (hospitality operations management, tourism and hospitality marketing); urban bioethics; urban education; urban school leadership; and vocal arts. Also offered are an executive M.B.A. and an Ed.S. in school psychology.

Master of Fine Arts degree programs are available in ceramics/glass, creative writing, dance, fibers and materials studies, film and media arts, graphic and interactive design, metals/jewelry/CAD-CAM, painting, photography, printmaking, sculpture, and theater (acting, design, directing, playwriting). Master of Public Health degrees are offered in applied biostatistics, environmental health, epidemiology, health policy and management, and social and behavioral sciences. The Professional Science Master's (P.S.M.) degree is offered in bioinformatics, bioinnovation, biotechnology, computer and systems security, cyber defense and information assurance, forensic chemistry, geographic information systems, and high-performance computing for scientific applications.

Rounding out the offerings are 93 graduate, post-master's, and specialty certificates in a range of disciplines.

Research Facilities

The world-class Science Education and Research Center (SERC) opened in fall 2014 with leading-edge laboratories to fully support moving scientific breakthroughs from the lab to the real world. To promote scientific collaboration, SERC offers breakout rooms and offices, storage and support areas, and seminar and conference rooms in addition to classroom space. The Materials Research Facility houses three X-ray diffractometers; a transmission electron microscope; and an accurate-mass quadrupole time-of-flight mass spectrometer, which offers superior sensitivity and data quality for profiling, identifying, characterizing, and quantifying compounds. The Research and Instructional Support Facility is home to glass-blowing design services and a computer numerical-control milling machine that enables the design and manufacture of an array of tools, prototypes, and products essential for advanced research. Less than 2 miles north of the main academic campus, on the Health Sciences Center campus at Broad and Ontario Streets, excellent and varied facilities for research are accessible. Finally, the University libraries contain more than 4 million bound volumes and are custodians of thousands of special collections of rare books and primary archival sources.

Financial Aid

Graduate students are eligible for financial assistance from private, University, state, and federal sources. The Office of Student Financial Services (http://sfs.temple.edu/) administers loans, grants, work-study, and other forms of financial aid. Students can contact the SFS office directly at 215-204-2244 for additional information.

Cost of Study

Resident tuition for the 2016–17 academic year ranges from $684 per credit for the Physician Assistant M.M.S. in the Lewis Katz School of Medicine to $2,300 per credit for the Fox School of Business and Management's executive D.B.A. Nonresident tuition ranges from $718 per credit for the Physician Assistant M.M.S. to $2,300 per credit for Fox School's executive D.B.A. A breakdown of tuition by school/college or program, in some cases, is available at http://bulletin.temple.edu/graduate/tuition-fees/.

Living and Housing Costs

On-campus housing is limited. For information on availability, students can contact the Office of University Housing and Residential Life at 215-204-7184 or visit http://housing.temple.edu/graduate.

Student Group

With a student body of more than 39,000 students, Temple University is among the fifty largest universities in the country. Since becoming a part of the Commonwealth System of Higher Education, it has increasingly emphasized upper-division and graduate work. Although the institution historically served the greater metropolitan area of southeastern Pennsylvania, Temple University now consistently attracts a significant and growing portion of the student body worldwide.

Location

With a population of more than 1.5 million, Philadelphia is the fifth-largest city in the country. It offers a variety of cultural attractions, including a world-renowned symphony orchestra, professional repertory theater, historic shrines, parks, and sports facilities. The climate is temperate, with an average temperature in winter of 38 degrees and 75 degrees in summer.

The University

With a rich heritage of populist tradition, Temple University provides students with an opportunity for education of high quality without regard to race, creed, or station in life. Affiliation with the Commonwealth System of Higher Education undergirds Temple's character as a public institution. Temple's academic programs are conducted on six campuses in central and north Philadelphia and its nearby suburbs.

Applying

Departmental deadlines for admissions and financial aid vary. Applicants should consult a particular program's page in the Graduate Bulletin (http://bulletin.temple.edu/graduate/) and the program's website, which is identified on its Contacts tab in the Graduate Bulletin. Notification regarding admission and financial aid is made following the screening of the application.

Correspondence and Information

Zebulon V. Kendrick, Ph.D.
Vice Provost for Graduate Education
Temple University
501 Carnell Hall
1803 North Broad Street
Philadelphia, Pennsylvania 19122-6104
United States
Phone: 215-204-1380
Fax: 215-204-8781
E-mail: grad@temple.edu
Website: http://www.temple.edu/grad

FACULTY HEADS

Graduate School: Zebulon V. Kendrick, Ph.D., Vice Provost.
Beasley School of Law: Gregory N. Mandel, J.D., Interim Dean.
Center for the Performing and Cinematic Arts, including Boyer College of Music and Dance and the School of Theater, Film and Media Arts: Robert T. Stroker, Ph.D., Dean.
College of Education: Gregory M. Anderson, Ph.D., Dean.
College of Engineering: Keyanoush Sadeghipour, Ph.D., Dean.
College of Liberal Arts: Richard Deeg, Ph.D., Dean.
College of Public Health: Laura A. Siminoff, Ph.D., Dean.
College of Science and Technology: Michael L. Klein, Ph.D., Dean.
Fox School of Business and Management: M. Moshe Porat, Ph.D., Dean.
Kornberg School of Dentistry: Amid I. Ismail, Dr.P.H., Dean.
Lewis Katz School of Medicine: Larry R. Kaiser, M.D., Dean.
School of Media and Communication: David Boardman, M.A., Dean.
School of Pharmacy: Peter H. Doukas, Ph.D., Dean.
School of Podiatric Medicine: John A. Mattiacci, D.P.M., Dean.
School of Sport, Tourism and Hospitality Management: M. Moshe Porat, Ph.D., Dean.
Tyler School of Art: Hester Stinnett, M.F.A., Interim Dean.

Two-story lobby of the Science Education and Research Center (SERC) on Temple University's main campus. This LEED Gold Registered structure has 247,000 square feet of space across 7 floors.

TUFTS UNIVERSITY

Graduate School of Arts and Sciences

★ For more information, visit http://petersons.to/tuftsuniv-arts-sciences

Tufts UNIVERSITY | Graduate School of Arts and Sciences

Programs of Study

The Graduate School of Arts and Sciences at Tufts University offers master's, certificate, and doctoral programs in the natural sciences, social sciences, and the arts and humanities.

The Doctor of Philosophy (Ph.D.) degree is offered in biology, chemistry, chemistry/biotechnology, child study and human development, cognitive science, drama, economic policy, education, English, history, human developmental economics, mathematics, physics, and psychology. A highly selective interdisciplinary doctorate is available in other areas. Tufts also offers a Doctor of Occupational Therapy.

The Master of Arts degree may be earned in art history, art history and museum studies, child study and human development, classical archaeology, classics, digital tools for premodern studies, education, English, French, German, history, history and museum studies, museum education, music, philosophy, school psychology, and urban and environmental policy and planning. The Master of Science is offered in biology, chemistry, chemistry/biotechnology, economics, education, mathematics, occupational therapy, and physics. The Master of Arts in Teaching is available in education with concentrations in art, early childhood education, secondary education, and child study and human development. The Master of Fine Arts degree is awarded through the School of the Museum of Fine Arts (SMFA) at Tufts. Tufts also offers the Master of Public Policy degree. Certificate programs are available in community environmental studies, early childhood technology, environmental management, interdisciplinary studio art, management of community organizations, museum studies, occupational therapy, program evaluation, science education, and urban justice and sustainability.

Full-time students can take one course per semester, for both a grade and credit, through cross-registration agreements with Boston College, Boston University, and Brandeis University.

Research Facilities

The Tufts University library system includes the Tisch Library, the Lilly Music Library, the Edward Ginn Library of The Fletcher School, and the W. Van Alan Clark, Jr. Library at the SMFA. Through Tufts' membership in the Boston Library Consortium, graduate students also have library privileges at the Massachusetts State Library, the Woods Hole Oceanographic Institute, the Boston Public Library, and the libraries of Amherst College, Boston College, Boston University, Brandeis University, the Massachusetts Institute of Technology, Northeastern University, the University of Connecticut, the University of Massachusetts, the University of New Hampshire, Wellesley College, and Williams College. Drama students have access to the Harvard Theatre Collection.

Special research facilities for science and engineering students include the campus-based Science and Technology Center, housing selected areas of research in physics and electrical and chemical engineering as well as laboratory facilities in biology, chemistry, psychology, and electrical and civil engineering, and the Collaborative Learning and Innovation Complex (CLIC), housing the departments of physics and astronomy, occupational therapy, community health, child study and human development and faculty working in human-centered engineering. Students are encouraged to pursue collaborative research at off-site facilities, which have included Fermilab, the Woods Hole Oceanographic Institute, and Brookhaven Laboratories. Many student and faculty researchers carry out collaborative research with colleagues at nearby Boston universities.

Financial Aid

In 2016–17, the Graduate School of Arts and Sciences awarded more than $17 million in tuition scholarships. Teaching and research assistantships are available, as are some fellowships. Tufts also awards need-based financial aid through the Federal Perkins Loan, Federal Work-Study, and Federal Direct Student Loan programs.

Cost of Study

Tuition for most master's programs for 2016–17 is $49,892, and is only charged in the student's first year. The 2016–17 tuition for the occupational therapy Master of Science program is $49,892 charged for two years; for the school psychology Master of Arts and educational specialist program is $42,408 charged for two years; for the urban and environmental policy and planning Master of Arts program is $34,932 charged for two years; and for the Master of Fine Arts program is $43,696 charged for one year. Part-time tuition in 2016–17 is $4,990 per course. The 2016–17 tuition for doctoral programs is $29,936, and is charged for five years. The 2016-17 tuition for Doctor of Occupational Therapy students is $49,892, and is charged for one year. Other charges include student health insurance, a health service fee, and a student activity fee.

Living and Housing Costs

Living expenses are estimated at about $1,200 a month, including food, housing, utilities, transportation, and textbook costs. There is limited on-campus housing for graduate students. Rents for one-bedroom apartments in Medford and Somerville begin at approximately $1,200 per month. The cost of sharing an apartment averages about $750 per person, and over 90 percent of students share apartments with at least one other individual. A public transportation system serves the greater Boston area and provides easy access to and from the campus, while a free, local shuttle runs throughout the academic year, providing easy access between campus, the subway, and Boston.

Student Group

In 2015–16, 1,029 students were enrolled in the Graduate School of Arts and Sciences. Of these, 68 percent were women and 18 percent were international students.

Location

The main campus, which spans the Medford-Somerville city line, is 7 miles from downtown Boston, a city where the arts (music, drama, and dance), museums, and sporting events abound. Cape Cod beaches and the mountains and forests of Maine, New Hampshire, and Vermont can be easily reached.

The University

Chartered as a liberal arts college in 1852, today Tufts is a small, selective, private university offering opportunities for undergraduate, graduate, and professional education to more than 7,500 students. The Graduate School of Arts and Sciences, the School of Engineering, The Fletcher School of Law and Diplomacy, The Friedman School of Nutrition Science and Policy, The Sackler School of Graduate

Biomedical Sciences, The Cummings School of Veterinary Medicine, The School of Dental Medicine, and The School of Medicine offer graduate and/or professional education. The university is accredited by the New England Association of Schools and Colleges.

Applying

Deadlines for applications vary by program. Applicants applying to a degree program are required to submit three letters of recommendation, a resume, official transcripts from all colleges and universities attended, and a personal statement. Most departments also require the results of the Graduate Record Examinations (GRE). Students whose native language is not English must submit official results of the Test of English as a Foreign Language (TOEFL).

Correspondence and Information

Office of Graduate Admissions
Tufts University
Bendetson Hall
Medford, Massachusetts 02155
United States
Phone: 617-627-3395
E-mail: gradadmissions@tufts.edu
Website: http://asegrad.tufts.edu

FIELDS OF STUDY AND FACULTY ADVISERS

Art and Art History: Karen Overbey
Biology: Catherine Freudenreich
Chemistry: Samuel Thomas
Child Study and Human Development: Martha Pott (M.A. program); Ellen Pinderhughes (Ph.D. program)
Classics: Marie-Claire Beaulieu
Drama: Noe Montez
Economics: Jeffrey Zabel
Education: Susan Barahal (Art Education); Sabina Vaught (Educational Studies); Brian Gravel (Elemetary Education); Cynthia Robinson (Museum Education); Steven Luz-Alterman and Laura Rogers (School Psychology); David Hammer (STEM Education); Linda Beardsley (Teacher Education)
English: Elizabeth Ammons
French: Gerard Gasarian
German: Markus Wilczek
History: Steven Marrone
Interdisciplinary Doctorate: Susan Ernst
Mathematics: Kim Ruane
Music: Stephan Pennington
Museum Studies: Cynthia Robinson
Occupational Therapy: Sharan Schwartzberg and Janet Curran Brooks
Philosophy: Patrick Forber
Physics: Danilo Marchesini
Psychology: Ayanna Thomas
Studio Art: Lisa Bynoe
Urban and Environmental Policy and Planning: Barbara Parmenter

UNIVERSITY OF MASSACHUSETTS LOWELL

Graduate School

★ For more information, visit http://petersons.to/umasslowellgrad

Programs of Study

The University of Massachusetts (UMass) Lowell offers more than 100 areas of graduate study in thirty-six doctoral degrees, thirty-nine master's degrees, and more than sixty graduate certificate programs, which are regionally and nationally accredited. The Doctor of Philosophy (Ph.D.) is offered in applied psychology and prevention science, biomedical engineering and biotechnology (intercampus), business administration, chemistry, computer science, criminal justice, global studies, marine sciences and technology, nursing, pharmaceutical sciences, physics (with an option in radiological sciences), polymer science, pharmaceutical science, and engineering (chemical engineering, civil and environmental engineering, computer engineering, electrical engineering, energy engineering [with options in nuclear or renewable/solar], mechanical engineering, and plastics engineering. In addition to two Ph.D.s, the College of Health Sciences offers a Doctor of Science (Sc.D.) in work environment, a Doctor of Pharmacy (beginning September 2017), a Doctor of Physical Therapy (D.P.T.), and post-master's Doctorate in Nursing Practice (D.N.P.). The Ph.D. in Education offers specializations in literacy, leadership, and research and evaluation in education, and the Doctor of Education (Ed.D.) is available in leadership in schooling, and mathematics and science education. The Education Specialist (Ed.S.) is offered in curriculum and instruction; educational planning and policy; and reading and language.

The Master of Arts (M.A.) is offered in community social psychology, criminal justice, history, peace and conflict studies, and security studies.

The Master of Science (M.S.) is available in accounting, autism studies, biological sciences, biomedical engineering and biotechnology, business analytics, chemistry, clinical laboratory sciences, computer science, environmental studies (with options in atmospheric science, finance, geoscience and environmental engineering sciences), health informatics and management, information technology, innovation and technological entrepreneurship, marine sciences and technology (intercampus), mathematics, nursing, pharmaceutical sciences, physics, public health, radiological science and protection, security studies, and work environment. Professional Science Master's options are available in many health and science disciplines.

The Master of Science in Engineering (M.S.Eng.) is offered in chemical engineering, civil engineering, computer engineering, electrical engineering, energy engineering (nuclear and renewable options), mechanical engineering, and plastics engineering. The Master of Education (M.Ed.) is offered in curriculum and instruction (a science education option is available online), educational administration, and reading and language. The Master of Music (M.M.) is available in music education (teaching) and sound recording technology. In addition to an accredited Master of Business Administration (M.B.A.), which is available on-campus, online, or blended, UMass Lowell offers of Master of Public Administration (M.P.A.) and a Master of Public Health (M.P.H.).

For a full list of options and concentrations within each degree program and graduate certificates available, visit the specific department's website or visit www.uml.edu/grad.

UMass Lowell is among the national leaders in graduate certificate education. A number of these programs are available online.

Research Facilities

UMass Lowell is a nationally ranked research university with more than $70 million in funded research being conducted in academic departments, through thirty-seven interdisciplinary research groups, by graduate and undergraduate students, and with corporate sponsorship and leading national research institutes. The Emerging Technologies and Innovation Center (ETIC) is an 84,000-square-foot facility which provides core facilities for use in fundamental and translational research. It houses Class 100, Class 1,000, and Class 10,000 clean room spaces, wet lab and engineering lab space, and a plastics processing high bay. This research and academic facility is one of several new buildings on campus.

In addition to departmental lab facilities, the University has hundreds of workstations, PCs, and terminals connected to multiple servers via a state-of-the-art network infrastructure. Multimedia labs and distance learning classrooms are available throughout the campus. UMass Lowell's electronic library includes more than 300 databases, more than 28,000 journals, and computer workstations and wireless systems. The library has consortium arrangements with other major libraries, and remote computer access is available.

Financial Aid

Over 500 teaching and research assistantships (TAs/RAs) carrying stipends, tuition and operating fee waivers (full or partial), and partial health insurance waivers were awarded to qualified graduate students across all disciplines in 2015–16. Students interested in an assistantship should contact the graduate coordinator or chair of the department to which they are applying. The Office of Financial Aid assists students through the Federal Direct, Perkins, and Stafford Student Loan programs. Low-interest student loans are also available for citizens of Massachusetts and Canada through the Massachusetts Educational Financing Authority (MEFA).

Cost of Study

In 2016–17, approximate tuition and fees for a 3-credit graduate course are $2,440 for Massachusetts residents and $4,370 for out-of-state students. Updated graduate tuition and fees information is available online at http://uml.edu/tuition-fees/graduate/. New England Regional Tuition is available for some programs of study, in which qualified out-of-state students pay 150 percent of the Massachusetts resident tuition charges. All graduate students are billed based on the total number of credit hours for which they are registered.

Living and Housing Costs

Graduate students can find reasonably priced furnished and unfurnished rooms and apartments in the greater Lowell area. The cost of living varies with the type of accommodations desired and the needs and resources of the individual. Apartments commonly require one month's security deposit.

Student Group

The fall 2015 total enrollment was 17,450, of which 4,184 were graduate students and 13,266 were undergraduates. Of the graduate students enrolled 44.1 percent were women and 22.7 percent were international students. Lowell's internationally renowned research faculty members take a strong personal interest in the professional development of their students.

Student Outcomes

UMass Lowell awards a significant percentage of its total degrees at the graduate level. Response from both graduate student alumni and industry employers reveals high satisfaction with education received and level of preparedness and professional perspective. Graduate students are highly sought by major corporations, both as interns during the course of their studies and as full-time employees upon graduation.

Location

Lowell, Massachusetts is 25 miles from Boston and home to the first urban national park in the U.S. The Merrimack River runs through this city of 105,000, which hosts professional baseball adjacent to the campus. Access to Boston is easy via car or commuter train. New Hampshire, Vermont, Maine, and the shores and beaches of the Atlantic Ocean and Cape Cod are short driving distances away.

The University

UMass Lowell is a comprehensive public institution with a national reputation which is committed to educating students for lifelong success in a diverse world and to conduct research and outreach activities that sustain economic, environmental, and social health. The University offers students more than 100 undergraduate, thirty-nine master's, and thirty-six doctoral degree choices through programs in the colleges of Fine Arts, Humanities, and Social Sciences; intercampus programs; Sciences; Engineering; Management; Health Sciences; the Graduate School of Education, and intercampus programs. Graduate students have access to selected courses at other campuses through the UMass Graduate Studies Consortium.

Applying

Master's degree applications can be submitted at any time; however, early applications ensure that all materials are processed on time and that due consideration is given to those seeking scholarships and financial aid. Applications for doctoral program are typically due in February, but applicants should check each program's website for specific dates. Doctoral candidates seeking teaching and research assistantships and fellowship awards should apply well before the deadline for their program of study. Scores from the GRE General Test, GMAT (for the M.B.A.), MTEL (for the Graduate School of Education), and TOEFL or IELTS (for all international students); official transcripts; a statement of purpose; a nonrefundable application fee; resume; and three letters of reference are required. Some departments have additional requirements. Prospective students should check with individual departments of study for specific deadlines. Online applications are recommended and are available on the Graduate Admissions website.

Correspondence and Information

Linda Southworth, Director, Graduate Admissions Office
University of Massachusetts Lowell
One University Avenue
Cumnock Hall, Suite 110
Lowell, Massachusetts 01854-5130
Phone: 978-934-2390
800-656-GRAD (toll-free)
Fax: 978-934-4058
E-mail: graduate_admissions@uml.edu
Website: http://www.uml.edu/grad

THE FACULTY

COLLEGES AND PROGRAM CONTACTS

E-mail format for faculty members is first name_last name@uml.edu unless otherwise noted.

Biomedical Engineering and Biotechnology (intercampus)
Dr. Stephen McCarthy, Director; Ball 207; 978-934-3417.

Manning School of Business
Dr. Sandra Richtermeyer, Dean; Pasteur 305; 978-934-2580.

Accounting
Dr. Stefanie Tate, Coordinator; Pasteur 214; 978-934-2815.
Dr. Khondkar Karim. Chair; Pasteur 218; 978-934-2831.

Business Analytics
Dr. Thomas Sloan, Coordinator; Pasteur, 3rd floor; 978-934-2857.

Business Management
Leticia Porter, Director (M.B.A.); Pasteur 305; 978-934-2853.
Lauren Hildreth, Coordinator, Pasteur 303; 978-934-2848.
Dr. Yi Yang, Coordinator (Ph.D.); Falmouth 207A; 978-934-2813.

Finance
ChunWung Kim, Coordinator; Pasteur, 2nd floor; 978-934-2516.

Innovation and Technological Entrepreneurship
Ashwin Mehta, Coordinator; Falmouth 202C; 978-934-2728.

Fine Arts, Humanities, and Social Sciences
Dr. Luis Falcon, Dean; 820 Broadway Street; 978-934-4191.

School of Criminology and Justice Studies
Dr. Kareen Jordan, Coordinator; Health and Human Sciences Building; 413; 978-934-4139.
Dr. April Pativina, Chair; Health and Human Sciences Building, 4th floor; 978-934-3956.

Global Studies
Dr. Jenifer Whitten-Woodring, Director; Dugan Hall, 2nd floor; 978-934-4242.

Music
Dr. Gena Greher, Coordinator (music education); Durgin 326; 978-934-3893.
Dr. Alex Case, Coordinator (sound recording technology) and Acting Music Department Chair; Durgin 323; 978-934-3878.

Peace and Conflict Studies
Dr. David Turcotte, Director, Mahoney 212E; 978-934-4682.

Psychology
Dr. Richard Serna, Coordinator (autism studies); Health and Human Sciences Building 353; 978-934-4385.
Dr. Meg Bond and Dr. Michelle Haynes, Coordinators (community social psychology); Health and Human Sciences Building 383; 978-934-3925; csp@uml.edu.
Dr. Allyssa McCabe, Coordinator (Ph.D.); Health and Human Sciences Building, 3rd floor; 978-934-3968.
Dr. Richard Siegel, Chair; Health and Human Sciences Building 315; 978-934-3961.

Public Administration
Dr. Thomas Pineros Shields, Coordinator; Dugan Hall, 2nd floor; 978-934-2169.

Security Studies
Dr. James Forrest, Director, Health and Sciences Building 437; 978-934-4773.

Graduate School of Education
Dr. Anita Greenwood, Dean; O'Leary 510; 978-934-4601.
Dr. James Nehring, Coordinator (doctoral, master's [nonlicensure], and Ed.S.); O'Leary 520; 978-934-4619.
Dr. Patricia Fontaine, Coordinator (M.Ed. for curriculum and instruction and all add-on licensure programs); O'Leary 532; 978-934-4622.
Dr. Charmaine Hickey, Coordinator (M.Ed. for curriculum and instruction and Higher Education Administration); O'Leary 522; 978-934-4658.
Dr. Michaela Wyman-Colombo, Chair; O'Leary 522; 978-934-4610.

Engineering
Dr. Joseph Hartman, Dean; Kitson Hall 311; 978-934-2570.

Chemical Engineering
Dr. Zhiyong Gu, Coordinator; Perry 222; 978-934-3540.
Dr. Alfred Donatelli, Chair; Perry 104; 978-934-3156.

Civil and Environmental Engineering
Dr. Chronis Stamatiadis, Coordinator; Pasteur 113; 978-934-2283.
Dr. Pradeep Kurup, Chair; Falmouth 108A; 978-934-2278.

Electrical and Computer Engineering
Dr. Xuejun Lu, Coordinator (master's); Ball, 3rd floor; 978-934-3359.
Dr. Alkim Akyurtlu, Coordinator (doctoral); Ball 417; 978-934-3336.
Dr. Martin Margala, Chair; Ball 301; 978-934-2986.

Energy Engineering (M.E.)
Dr. Walter Thomas, Coordinator (alternative/solar); Perry, 3rd floor; 978-934-5276.
Dr. Sukesh Aghara, Coordinator (nuclear); Perry, 3rd floor; 978-934-3115.

Environmental Studies
Dr. Xiaoqi Zhang, Coordinator (environmental engineering sciences); Pasteur 107; 978-934-2287.
Dr. Clifford Bruell, Chair; Perry 105; 978-934-2284.

Mechanical Engineering
Dr. Emmanuelle Reynaud, Coordinator; Perry 326; 978-934-2961.
Dr. Christopher Niezrecki, Chair; Engineering 218; 978-934-2963.

Plastics Engineering
Dr. Bridgette Budhall, Coordinator (master's program); Ball 203B; 978-934-3414.
Dr. Jan-Chan Huang, Coordinator (doctoral programs); Ball 213; 978-934-3428.
Dr. Robert Malloy, Chair; Ball 204; 978-934-3435.

College of Health Sciences
Dr. Shortie McKinney, Dean; Weed Hall; 978-934-4460.

Clinical Laboratory and Nutritional Sciences
Dr. Nancy Goodyear, Coordinator; Weed, 1st floor; 978-934-4427.
Dr. Garry Handelman, Chair; Weed, 1st floor; 978-934-4503.

Health Informatics and Management
Dr. Robert Holmes, Coordinator; Southwick, 3rd floor; 978-934-4515.
Dr. Nicole Champagne, Chair; Southwick, 3rd floor; 978-934-4132.

School of Nursing
Dr. Barbara Mawn, Coordinator (Ph.D. and D.N.P.); Health and Human Sciences Building 204; 978-934-4415.
Dr. Valerie King, Coordinator (M.S., FNP); Health and Human Sciences Building 291; 978-934-4454.
Dr. Lisa Abdallah, Chair; Health and Human Sciences Building 213; 978-934-4432.
Dr. Karen Devereaux Melillo, Interim Dean, School of Nursing; Health and Human Sciences Building; 978-934-4417.

Pharmaceutical Sciences
Dr. Brenda Geiger, Coordinator; Weed 222C; 978-934-3872.

Physical Therapy
Dr. Keith Hallbourg, Coordinator; Weed 322B; 978-934-4402.
Dr. Erika Lewis, Chair; Weed 202; 978-934-4405.

Public Health
Dr. Lee Ackerson, Coordinator; Southwick, 3rd floor; 978-934-3128.

Work Environment
Dr. David Kriebel, Coordinator; Kitson 204B; 978-934-3270.
Dr. Bryan Buchholz, Chair; Kitson 204D; 978-934-3241.

Intercampus Graduate School of Marine Sciences and Technology
Dr. David Ryan, Director, Olney 318A; 978-934-3698.

Sciences
Dr. Noureddine Melikechi, Dean; Olney 524; 978-934-3839.

Biological Sciences
Dr. Rick Hochberg, Coordinator; Olsen 609; 978-934-2884.
Dr. Matthew Nugent, Chair; Olsen 414A; 978-934-2888.

Chemistry/Polymer Science
Dr. Matthew Gage, Coordinator; Olney, 1st floor; 978-934-3750.
Dr. David Ryan, Chair; Olney 318A; 978-934-3698.

Computer Science
Dr. Cindy Chen, Coordinator; Olsen 205; 978-934-1968.
Dr. Haim Levkowitz, Chair; Olsen, 3rd floor; 978-934-3654.

Environmental Studies and Earth, Environmental, and Atmospheric Sciences
Dr. Kate Swanger, Coordinator (atmospheric and geo sciences); Olney 302; 978-934-3069.
Dr. Nelson Eby, Chair (atmospheric and geo sciences); Olney 302B; 978-934-3097.

Information Technology
Dr. William Moloney, Coordinator; Olson 222; 978-934-3640.

Mathematical Sciences
Dr. Ravi Montenegro, Coordinator; Olney 428M; 978-934-2442.
Dr. Daniel Klain, Chair; Olney, 4th floor; 978-934-4474.

Physics
Dr. Partha Chowdhury, Coordinator; Olney 133; 978-934-3730.
Dr. Robert Giles, Chair; Olney 122; 978-934-3780.

Radiological Sciences (Physics)
Dr. Mark Tries, Coordinator; Olney, 1st floor; 978-934-3353.

UNIVERSITY OF NEW HAVEN

Graduate Studies

University *of* New Haven

Programs of Study

Recognized as a national leader in experiential education, the University of New Haven is a private, comprehensive university where more than 1,700 graduate students from across the country, and the globe, benefit from small class sizes, personalized attention, and state-of-the-art facilities on the University's main campus in West Haven, Connecticut. Founded in 1969, the Graduate School at the University of New Haven offers more than 40 graduate degree and certificate programs to prepare students for successful careers in the arts and sciences, business, engineering, public safety, and more.

In the College of Arts and Sciences, master's degree programs include Cellular and Molecular Biology, Community Psychology, Environmental Science, Industrial/Organizational Psychology, and Human Nutrition.

The AACSB-accredited College of Business offers M.S. degrees in Healthcare Administration, Sport Management, Finance, and Taxation. Also available are a Master of Business Administration (M.B.A.), an Executive M.B.A. and a dual M.B.A./M.P.A. degree that is offered in conjunction with the Henry C. Lee College of Criminal Justice and Forensic Sciences.

Tagliatela College of Engineering programs include M.S. offerings in Biomedical Engineering, Computer Science, Electrical Engineering, Engineering and Operations Management, Environmental Engineering, Industrial Engineering, Mechanical Engineering, Cyber Systems, and the M.B.A./M.S.I.E. dual-degree program, offered in conjunction with the College of Business.

Students in the Henry C. Lee College of Criminal Justice and Forensic Sciences, named for world-famous forensic scientist and University of New Haven professor emeritus Dr. Henry C. Lee, can choose from master's programs in Criminal Justice, Emergency Management, Investigations, Fire Science, Forensic Science, Forensic Technology, National Security, Labor Relations, and a Master of Public Administration (M.P.A.), as well as a Ph.D. program in Criminal Justice.

The University of New Haven's graduate programs are available in full- or part-time study options, with a variety of convenient evening, weekend, online, and community-based classes. Small, personalized classes are designed to maximize student-faculty interaction. The University offers graduate students numerous professional internships and research opportunities and more than 160 recognized student organizations.

The University's Career Services Center offers employment-related services to graduate students. Among these are career counseling, advising, on-campus employment interviewing, and extensive information about job opportunities. The office can also assist with resume writing, interviewing skills, and cover and thank-you letters—all the tools necessary to perform an effective job search.

Experiential Education

The University of New Haven's philosophy can be summed up by a single word: DO. The University has flipped the model of most universities, so students aren't learning how to eventually do it—they're doing it now to learn it. The University believes education is maximized when students gain knowledge from a core academic foundation and immediately apply it with real feet-on-the-pavement, hands-on-the-controls experience. This hands-on approach is more than a belief—experiential learning is extremely effective in preparing students for careers. As a nationally-recognized leader in this movement, the University of New Haven also trains other universities in experiential learning.

Financial Aid

The University of New Haven offers its highest achieving incoming graduate students the opportunity to participate in the Experiential Graduate Assistantship Program (EGAP). Students offered a graduate assistantship (GA) position in this highly competitive program work 15–20 hours a week for an academic or administrative department within the university, and in return, receive an experiential learning and work opportunity for the entirety of their graduate program, a 75 percent tuition discount, and an hourly wage.

The University has a number of other financing options available to graduate students. Roughly 80 percent of the University's graduate students utilize student loans at some point in their graduate school career. There are also tuition reimbursement and tuition waivers for those that qualify; grants, scholarships, and fellowships are available as well.

Cost of Study

Tuition for master's degree students for the 2016–17 academic year is $870 per graduate credit or $2,610 per course for most graduate courses. The Graduate and technology fees are $140 each term. All charges and fees are subject to change.

Living and Housing Costs

There is no on-campus housing for graduate students, but the Office of Residential Life maintains an off-campus housing website with listings of apartments, local maps, and information on local services.

Student Group

The graduate student body of 1,784 includes 1,145 full-time students and 639 part-time students, 831 females and 953 males, 75 military veterans, and 635 international students.

Faculty

The faculty members who teach in the Graduate School represent a combination of full-time academics that hold doctoral degrees in their specialties, and part-time faculty members employed in business, industry, and other professions. In addition to their academic credentials, they bring a wealth of experience and practical insight to their classrooms. They enjoy outstanding professional reputations in their fields through accomplishments in research and writing, and as visiting lecturers in business, industry, public sector, and academic venues. Faculty members take an active role with students and act as advisers in discussions about career options and plans for personal and professional growth and development.

Location

The University of New Haven is located on the beautiful Connecticut shoreline. Only 75 miles northeast of New York City, this location offers an array of cultural, social, and recreational opportunities along the coastline and throughout the Greater New Haven region. Although the campus is located in West Haven, it is less than three miles from downtown New Haven, which is home to several major colleges and universities, and offers an abundance of nightlife, restaurants, museums, and more. New Haven has rail, bus, and air service, and its location at the junction of two major interstate highways places the school within easy driving distance of New York, Boston, and Providence. The University also operates a campus in Orange, Connecticut, for graduate business programs.

The University

The University of New Haven was founded in 1920 and is accredited by the New England Association of Schools and Colleges. Most graduate classes are held on the main campus, while a number of cohort program options are delivered in New London, Connecticut. Many business courses are offered at the brand-new Graduate Business Campus in Orange, Connecticut. Most graduate classes are held in the early evening to accommodate both part-time and full-time students.

Applying

Applicants must hold a baccalaureate degree from an accredited college or university and must submit the following items before the initial registration: a formal online or paper application; two letters of recommendation; final official transcripts from all previous college work; a personal statement; and standardized test scores (if applicable).

In addition, a satisfactory TOEFL score (except for students whose native language is English) and certified financial support forms are required for all international students. All correspondence and requests for materials should be directed to the Graduate Enrollment Office. Descriptions of programs and procedures are available in the Graduate Catalog and additional information available on the University's website at http://www.newhaven.edu/grad.

Correspondence and Information

Graduate Enrollment Office
University of New Haven
Echlin Hall
300 Boston Post Road
West Haven, Connecticut 06516
United States
Phone: 203-932-7440
800-DIAL-UNH (toll-free)
Fax: 203-932-7137
E-mail: gradinfo@newhaven.edu
Website: http://www.newhaven.edu/grad

Maxcy Hall on the main campus of the University of New Haven.

The Executive M.B.A., M.B.A., and Sport Management classes in the College of Business are being offered exclusively at the Orange Campus.

THE UNIVERSITY OF TAMPA

Graduate Programs

★ For more information, visit http://petersons.to/utampagrad

Programs of Study

The University of Tampa (UT) is a private nonprofit institution located on the west coast of Florida that offers graduate programs in business, nursing, education, creative writing, and exercise and nutrition science. *U.S. News & World Report* ranks UT among the Best Business Schools (with a Best Part-Time M.B.A. program) and Best Nursing Schools, as well as among the Top 25 Regional Universities in the South. UT has also been included in the *Forbes* annual ranking of America's Best Colleges every year since 2008. Likewise, The Princeton Review includes UT in its lists of Best Southeastern Colleges and Best 380 Colleges.

Graduate Business Programs for Full-Time and Working Students: The University of Tampa offers five graduate degree programs in business including an M.B.A., Professional M.B.A., and Executive M.B.A. and four specialized master's programs. The Master of Business Administration gives students eight concentration options:

- Business analytics
- Entrepreneurship
- Finance
- Information systems management
- Innovation management
- International business
- Marketing
- Nonprofit management

M.B.A. students may choose to enroll in the full-time/day program or part-time/evening program. Full-time business students typically complete the program in as few as twelve months. This schedule also applies to UT's M.S. in Accounting, M.S. in Entrepreneurship, M.S. in Finance, and M.S. in Marketing programs.

Working professionals who want to earn their M.B.A. may choose to apply for UT's part-time Professional M.B.A. (P.M.B.A.) or the unique Executive M.B.A. (E.M.B.A.), which is designed for professionals with seven or more years of work experience. E.M.B.A. classes are held on alternate Saturdays and focus on the most current problem-solving and decision-making practices. The program takes two years to complete and includes a ten-day study abroad trip during the second year.

The Sykes College of Business is AACSB (Association to Advance Collegiate Schools of Business) accredited.

Graduate Programs in Education and Instructional Design: UT's Master of Education (M.Ed.) in Curriculum and Instruction program enjoys a solid, long-established relationship with Tampa Bay area school districts and administrators. The program helps develop and extend the teaching and leadership skills of certified teachers. The M.Ed. in Educational Leadership prepares educators for administrative roles and covers topics such as instructional leadership, school budgeting and finance, and community relations. Education classes are offered in the evenings, on weekends, and during summers, allowing students to complete either M.Ed. program in as little as a year.

The M.S. in Instructional Design and Technology program addresses a growing field in learning and human performance, providing an interdisciplinary approach to its study. It emphasizes theories of learning and cognition, multimedia development, systematic instructional design, technology, and open learning environments. The hybrid classroom-online curriculum allows students to complete the program within two years.

Master of Science in Exercise and Nutrition Science: This internationally recognized program focuses on the relationship between exercise physiology and nutrition, with the goal of optimizing athletic performance. During a one-year course of study, students undertake numerous hands-on experiences in UT's Human Performance Research Lab, combined with rigorous classroom learning. Students may begin the program in the summer, fall, or spring semester.

Master of Science in Nursing: The M.S.N. program at UT offers graduate-level study with adult/gerontology and family nurse practitioner concentrations, all in a part-time format. Students benefit from UT's numerous clinical affiliations, and are well equipped to serve as primary care providers in a variety of settings. Admission to the program is competitive.

Master of Fine Arts in Creative Writing: UT's Master of Fine Arts in Creative Writing is a low-residency program intended to develop the skills of poets, fiction, and creative nonfiction writers through supportive critique and mentoring. Students attend four ten-day working residencies on campus, followed by semester-long faculty mentorships designed to support an individualized plan of study. The program takes approximately two years to complete.

Research Opportunities for Graduate Students

UT faculty members conduct and coordinate research in numerous fields across the disciplines. The Naimoli Institute for Business Strategy connects groups of students with more than 600 Tampa Bay area enterprises to conduct strategic evaluations and make performance improvement recommendations.

Research done by students in UT's renowned Human Performance Research Lab has been presented at the National Strength and Conditioning Conference.

Financial Aid and Scholarship Opportunities

The University of Tampa prides itself on its competitive graduate tuition rates. UT offers a limited number of merit-based scholarships for graduate students. Each program also offers graduate assistantship positions, which provide a tuition waiver for up to 12 credit hours per semester, plus a stipend. Reimbursement and stipend amounts vary by program. Graduate assistants are expected to work 20 hours per week for an academic or administrative office and to carry a full course load. Part-time employment is also available on campus.

Cost of Study

For the 2016–17 academic year, tuition for most graduate programs is $588 per credit hour. The cost for the Executive M.B.A. program is $46,302 for the entire two-year program. The M.F.A. in Creative Writing program is $7,917 per semester.

Living and Housing Costs

Most UT graduate students choose to live off campus. However, on-campus housing is also available, primarily in Urso or Straz halls. Costs for on-campus housing range from $3,633 to $4,975 per semester, depending on the room chosen. Students living on campus are also required to purchase a meal plan, with costs ranging from $1,336 to $2,478 per semester.

Student Life

UT's graduate student body reflects the global nature of the city and the school. For example, about 40 percent of the University's graduate business students come from outside the United States. UT enrolls students from more than 140 countries and all 50 states, providing opportunities for diverse cultural and educational exchange.

Location

The University's 105-acre campus is located in downtown Tampa, just north of Hillsborough Bay and a short drive from Gulf Coast beaches. The city is a cultural crossroads where national and global corporations offer opportunities for internships, networking, and job recruitment.

The University

Known for academic excellence, personal attention, and real-world experience in its undergraduate and graduate programs, UT offers more than 200 programs of study, including 13 master's degree programs and numerous study-abroad opportunities. Boasting a $235 million annual budget and an $850 million estimated annual economic impact, UT serves approximately 8,300 undergraduate and graduate students.

Applying

The University of Tampa has rolling admissions. Applicants are advised to submit applications and supporting documents by June 1 for the fall semester, which begins in August. The deadline for the spring semester is November 1.

In general, applicants should submit a complete online application, the application fee, completed bachelor's degree official transcripts, two recommendation letters, and a personal statement and resume. For graduate business applicants, a GMAT or GRE score is required; TOEFL or IELTS scores are required for international applicants.

Contact Information

Joshua Stagner, Ed.D.
Director of Graduate and Continuing Studies
The University of Tampa
401 West Kennedy Boulevard
Tampa, Florida 33606-1490
United States
Phone: 813-257-3016
E-mail: jstagner@ut.edu
Website: www.ut.edu/graduate

WASHINGTON UNIVERSITY IN ST. LOUIS

Graduate School

Washington University in St. Louis
GRADUATE SCHOOL OF ARTS & SCIENCES

★ For more information, visit http://petersons.to/washingtonustlouisgrad

Programs of Study

The Graduate School offers more than thirty programs leading to the doctorate (Ph.D.) and to the Master of Arts (A.M.). In addition, programs are offered leading to the Master of Arts in Education (M.A.Ed.), Master of Arts in Teaching (M.A.T.), and Master of Fine Arts in Writing (M.F.A.W.).

Opportunities for combining a degree available through the Graduate School with a degree from one of the University's professional schools (business, law, medicine) are also available.

Research Facilities

The Washington University community is served by a network of libraries designed to meet the instructional and research needs of faculty members, students, and staff members. Washington University libraries contain the largest collection of any private academic library system between the Mississippi River and California. John M. Olin Library, the central University library, and twelve school and departmental libraries house many important and unique collections and provide state-of-the-art computerized information retrieval. The combined holdings include more than 3 million books and bound periodicals, 18,000 current serial subscriptions, and access to thousands of electronic journals and databases. For more information, students can visit http://library.wustl.edu.

More than thirty centers and institutes provide a spectrum of research opportunities. They include the Center for Air Pollution Impact and Trend Analysis; Center for the Study of American Business; Center for American Indian Studies; Business, Law, and Economics Center; Arts and Sciences Computing Center; Institutes for Biomedical Computing; McDonnell Center for Cellular and Molecular Neurobiology; Construction Management Center; Carolyne Roehm Electronic Media Center; Center for Engineering Computing; Center for Genetics in Medicine; McDonnell Center for Studies of Higher Brain Function; Center for the History of Freedom; Office of International Studies; International Writers Center; Center for the Study of Islamic Societies and Civilizations; Management Center; Fred Gasche Laboratory for Microstructured Materials Technologies; Markey Center for Research in Molecular Biology of Human Disease; Center for Optimization and Semantic Control; Center for Plant Science and Biotechnology; Center for the Study of Public Affairs; Center for Robotics and Automation; Social Work Research Development Center; McDonnell Center for Space Sciences; Center for the Application of Information Technology; and Urban Research and Design Center.

Financial Aid

The majority of full-time students receive financial support. Financial assistance in the form of scholarships, fellowships, and traineeships is offered annually on a competitive basis through the Graduate School from government, private, or endowed sources. Also available are scholarships, teaching assistantships, research assistantships, and, in applied social sciences, clinical internships; grants and fellowships in national competition; and loans. Specific information may be obtained from the departmental or administrative unit to which the student intends to apply.

Cost of Study

Tuition for the 2016–17 academic year for the Graduate School is $48,950. The cost per credit unit is $2,040.

Living and Housing Costs

Many graduate students live in University-owned apartments, some with data connections and shuttle bus service. Listing information for these units as well as non-University housing is available through the University's Apartment Referral Service (http://offcampushousing.wustl.edu/). Average rent ranges from $450 to $950 per month.

Student Group

Of the more than 14,000 people attending Washington University, more than 5,000 are graduate students; approximately 2,000 of them are enrolled in the Graduate School. Students come to Washington University from all fifty states and more than eighty international locations.

Location

Washington University has two campuses that lie at opposite ends of Forest Park (one of the largest municipal parks in the nation). The campuses are approximately 5 miles west of downtown St. Louis. The Danforth campus is the location of the Graduate School of Arts and Sciences and all other schools of the University except Medicine. The latter is located on the east, or medical campus. The Division of Biology and Biomedical Sciences is also located on the medical campus. Free shuttle buses run between the campuses on a regular schedule.

The St. Louis area has nearly 2.4 million residents. The cost of living is affordable. The University's central location provides easy access to the zoo, museums, Science Center, Missouri Botanical Gardens, St. Louis Symphony, Opera Theatre, St. Louis Repertory Theatre, Black Repertory Theatre, Blues hockey, Rams football, and Cardinals baseball. Outdoor adventure beyond the city can be found in the Ozark Mountains and on the rivers of Missouri. Camping, hiking, floating, rock climbing, and spelunking are among the many possibilities within a few hours' drive of St. Louis.

The Graduate School

The Graduate School is a charter member of both the Association of Graduate Schools and the Council of Graduate Schools. The School provides a physical and academic environment in which inquiry, intellectual growth, and discovery can thrive and flourish.

Applying

Prospective students may apply online. Applicants should check with the department or program to which they are applying, as application deadlines vary. Most programs require GRE scores. For international students whose native language is not English, most programs require an official copy of a TOEFL score.

Correspondence and Information

Graduate School
Campus Box 1187
Washington University in St. Louis
One Brookings Drive
St. Louis, Missouri 63130-4899
United States
Phone: 314-935-6880
Fax: 314-935-4887
E-mail: GraduateSchool@wustl.edu
Website: http://graduateschool.wustl.edu

FACULTY HEADS, DEGREES OFFERED, AND DEPARTMENTAL INTERESTS

Anthropology (Ph.D.): T. R. Kidder (trkidder@wustl.edu). Sociocultural anthropology (including medical anthropology), archaeology, physical anthropology (including primate studies, paleontology and human biology).

Art History and Archaeology (A.M., Ph.D.): Liz Childs (ecchilds@wustl.edu). Ancient, medieval, Renaissance, early modern, European, modern and contemporary European and American, and Asian art history; classical archaeology.

Division of Biology and Biomedical Sciences (Ph.D.): John Russell (800-852-9074, toll-free); e-mail: DBBSPhDAdmissions@wustl.edu).

Biochemistry: Peter Burgers (DBBSPhDAdmissions@wustl.edu). Metabolic regulation, signal transduction, receptors, membrane channels and transporters, membrane structure and dynamics, membrane trafficking, cholesterol and lipid metabolism, nucleic acid-protein structure interactions and function, DNA replication and repair, recombination, transcription, translation, enzyme kinetics, cancer biology, cell cycle regulation, apoptosis, cell motility, cytoskeleton, cell division, extracellular matrix, vascular biology, aging, senescence, telomere biology, heat-shock proteins, prion proteins, gene expression, RNA editing and binding proteins, microbial pathogenesis, parasitology, virology, drug design and metabolism, plant natural products, photosynthesis and plant energy production, molecular imaging in cells and tissues, carbohydrate metabolism, proteases.

Computational and Molecular Biophysics: Daved Fremont (DBBSPhDAdmissions@wustl.edu). Structural biology, protein and nucleic acid kinetics and thermodynamics, single-molecule enzymology, protein design, nanoscience, ion channels and lipid membranes, computational biophysics.

Computational and Systems Biology: Barak Cohen (DBBSPhDAdmissions@wustl.edu). Systems biology, genomics, sequence analysis, regulatory networks, synthetic biology, metagenomics, metabolomics, proteomics, single cell dynamics, high-throughput technology development, applied math and mathematical models of biological processes, computational biology, comparative genomics, personalized medicine, next generation sequencing and its applications, bioinformatics.

Developmental, Regenerative, and Stem Cell Biology: Kerry Kornfeld and James Skeath (DBBSPhDAdmissions@wustl.edu). Development, stem cell biology, regenerative biology, cell biology, genetics, cell signaling, the biology of cancer, epigenetics, circadian rhythms, systems biology.

Evolution, Ecology, and Population Biology: David Queller (DBBSPhDAdmissions@wustl.edu). Population ecology, community ecology, plant and animal evolution, microbial evolution, evolution of behavior, phylogenetics, systematics, theoretical and experimental population genetics.

Human and Statistical Genetics: Patrick Jay and John Rice (DBBSPhDAdmissions@wustl.edu). Human genetics, statistical genetics, functional genomics, molecular genetics, Mendelian disease, complex disease, Mammalian genetics, systems biology.

Immunology: Paul Allen (DBBSPhDAdmissions@wustl.edu). Cellular immunology; molecular immunology; lineage development; autoimmunity; cancer immunotherapy; transcription factors; epigenomics; mucosal immunity; innate immunity; bacterial, viral, and parasite immunity; immune evasion; antigen processing and presentation; dendritic cells; T cell signaling; antigen receptor diversification.

Molecular Cell Biology: Heather True-Krob and Jason Weber (DBBSPhDAdmissions@wustl.edu). Cell adhesion, protein trafficking and organelle biogenesis, cell cycle, receptors, signal transduction, gene expression, metabolism, cytoskeleton and motility, membrane excitability, molecular basis of diseases.

Molecular Genetics and Genomics: Tim Schedl and James Skeath (DBBSPhDAdmissions@wustl.edu). Genetics, genetic basis of disease, genomics, epigenetics, genetic engineering, genome editing, model organism genetics, development, cell biology, molecular biology, complex traits, bioinformatics, systems biology.

Molecular Microbiology and Microbial Pathogenesis: David Sibley (DBBSPhDAdmissions@wustl.edu). Host-pathogen interactions, cellular microbiology, comparative genomics, molecular microbiology, microbial pathogenesis, pathogen discovery, emerging infectious diseases, microbial physiology, microbial ecology and engergetics, virology, bacteriology, mycology, parasitology.

Neurosciences: Lawrence Snyder and Erik Herzog (DBBSPhDAdmissions@wustl.edu). Neurobiology, neurology, functional imaging, behavior, cognition, computational neuroscience, electrophysiology, sensory systems, motor systems, neuroglia, neuronal development, learning, memory, language, synaptic plasticity, mind, consciousness, neurodegeneration, diseases of the nervous system, neuronal injury, clinical neuroscience, motor control, biological rhythms, connectivity mapping.

Plant and Microbial Bioscience: Joseph Jez and Petra Levin (DBBSPhDAdmissions@wustl.edu). Cell biology, development, physiology, signaling, development, metabolic regulation, photosynthesis, bioenergy, protein structure-function, synthetic biology, biogeochemistry, environmental microbiology, ecology, population genetics, molecular evolution.

Business (Ph.D.): Anjan Thakor (phdinfo@olin.wustl.edu). Accounting, business economics, finance, marketing, organizational behavior, strategy, operations and manufacturing management.

Chemistry (Ph.D.): Bill Buhro (chemistry-admissions@wustl.edu). Bioinorganic, biological, bioorganic, biophysical, materials, nuclear, organic, organometallic, physical, polymer, radiochemistry, spectroscopy, theoretical.

Classics (A.M., Ph.D.): Timothy Moore (classics@wustl.edu). Greek and Latin language and literature, ancient performance, philosophy, history, and material culture.

Comparative Literature (Ph.D.): Lynne Tatlock (ltatlock@wustl.edu). World literature; literary theory; translation studies; global and multicultural theory; comparative drama; comparative arts; studies in literature, politics, and society; narrative theory; media ecologies, histories, and poetics.

Earth and Planetary Sciences (Ph.D.): Viatcheslav Solomatov (mwysession@wustl.edu). Planetary sciences, geology, geobiology, geochemistry, geodynamics.

East Asian Languages and Cultures (A.M., J.D./A.M., Ph.D.): Rebecca Copeland (ealc@wustl.edu). Chinese; Japanese; Chinese fiction, theater, poetry, modern literature; Japanese modern and classical fiction; translation theory; East Asian studies.

Economics (Ph.D.): John Nachbar (nachbar@wustl.edu). Economic theory, industrial organization, political economy, public economics, macroeconomics, public finance, development economics.

Education (M.A.Ed., M.A.T., Ph.D.): Kit Wellmon (kwellman@wustl.edu). Teacher education, educational studies, urban education, policy studies, science and math education, second language research.

English and American Literature (Ph.D.): Wolfram Schmidgen (wschmidg@wustl.edu). Medieval, early modern, early American, eighteenth-century British, nineteenth-century British, nineteenth-century American, twentieth-century British, twentieth-century American, African-American literature and culture, Irish literature, Anglophone postcolonial literature, gender and sexuality studies, modernism, poetry and poetics, theory.

Film and Media Studies (A.M.): Gaylyn Studlar (gstudlar@wustl.edu). Criticism, history, and theories of film and electronic media; all moving image forms of visual culture.

Germanic Languages and Literatures (Ph.D.): Matt Erlin (merlin@wustl.edu). German literature and culture from the Middle Ages through the twenty-first century, intellectual history, film and media studies, gender studies, Holocaust studies, history of the book, digital humanities.

History (Ph.D.): Peter Kastor (pjkastor@wustl.edu). Seventeenth- through nineteenth-century America, twentieth-century America, African history, central Europe, early modern Europe, East Asian history, history of American political culture, international urban history, Middle East, religion in the medieval Mediterranean world.

Institute of Materials Science and Engineering (Ph.D.): Kathy Flores (floresk@wustl.edu). Materials structure, properties, processing, and performance, particularly as related to materials for energy harvesting and storage; materials for environmental remediation and sustainability; materials for regenerative medicine; metallic glasses and other structurally complex materials; plasmonics, photonics, and materials for sensors and imaging; and computational materials science.

Jewish, Islamic, and Near Eastern Languages and Cultures (A.M.): Nancy Berg (nberg@wustl.edu). Islamic and Near Eastern studies (Islamic history, Arabic language and literature, modern Middle East history), Jewish studies (Hebrew Bible, Rabbinic literature, Jewish history, modern Hebrew literature).

Mathematics (A.M., Ph.D.): John McCarthy (mccarthy@wustl.edu). Algebra, algebraic geometry, real and complex analysis, differential geometry, topology, mathematical statistics, survival analysis, modeling, statistical computing for massive data, Bayesian regularization, bioinformatics, longitudinal and functional data analysis, statistical computation, application of statistics to medicine.

Movement Science (Ph.D.): Gammon Earhart (earhartg@wustl.edu). Philosophy of human movement function and dysfunction, with special emphasis on bioenergetics, biomechanics, and biocontrol.

Music (A.M., M.M., Ph.D.): Todd Decker (tdecker@wustl.edu). Musicology, ethnomusicology, theory, piano performance and pedagogy.

Performing Arts (A.M.): Mark Rollins (mark@wustl.edu). Theater studies, performance studies, dance.

Philosophy (Ph.D.): Ron Mallon (rmallon@wustl.edu). Ethics, social and political philosophy, history of philosophy, philosophy of law, philosophy of science, philosophy of mind, philosophy of language, theory of knowledge, aesthetics.

Philosophy/Neuroscience/Psychology (Ph.D.): Ron Mallon (pnp@wustl.edu). Philosophy of mind and language, with a special emphasis on the philosophical dimensions of psychology, neuroscience, and linguistics.

Physics (Ph.D.): Mark Alford (alford@wustl.edu). Experimental: astrophysics and space sciences, condensed matter and material physics, applications in biology and medicine, nuclear physics. Theoretical: astrophysics, biophysics, condensed matter and materials physics, elementary particles, many-body theory.

Political Science (Ph.D.): Jim Spriggs (jspriggs@wustl.edu). American politics, comparative politics, formal theory, international politics, law and courts, normative theory, political methodology.

Psychological & Brain Sciences (Ph.D.): Deanna Barch (dbarch@wustl.edu). Behavior/brain/cognition, clinical, development and aging, social/personality.

Rehabilitation and Participation Science (Ph.D.): Carolyn Baum (baumc@wustl.edu). Science of rehabilitation and participation with special emphasis placed on neurorehabilitation, performance, and community participation.

Romance Languages and Literatures (Ph.D.): Michael Sherberg (sherberg@wustl.edu). French language and literature, Latin American and Iberian literature and languages, Spanish and comparative literature.

Social Work (Ph.D.): Renee Cunningham Williams (williamsr@wustl.edu). Mental health, disparities, social and economic development, addictions, aging, child welfare, civic service, disabilities, health, poverty and social policy. Social determinants of health, health disparities, health promotion and disease prevention, health policy, dissemination and implementation, epidemiology, global health.

Speech and Hearing Sciences (Ph.D.): William Clark (elliottb@wustl.edu). Speech and hearing sciences, clinical audiology, deaf education, speech and language, sensory neuroscience.

The Writing Program (M.F.A.W.): David Schuman (dschuman@wustl.edu). Fiction, creative nonfiction, poetry-writing workshops and academic courses.

Programs of Study

A better job, financial security, and personal satisfaction are just some of the end goals for students seeking to earn an advanced degree through graduate study at Western New England University. From business to communication, creative writing to behavior analysis, and programs for teachers and engineers, students gain essential skills and expertise for success in their careers.

Programs in Communication and Curriculum and Instruction are offered entirely online and were developed specifically for that delivery model. Business programs and most of the engineering master's programs follow a blended model, allowing students to study completely online or attend select live sessions on campus. This flexibility enables working professionals to learn at their own pace. Education programs are offered in late afternoon and early evening to accommodate the schedules of working teachers. The low-residency M.F.A. in Creative Writing program includes four short-term residencies with author mentors.

The University is regionally accredited by the New England Association of Schools and Colleges.

The **College of Arts and Sciences** offers the following graduate programs:

- Master of Arts in Communication with a public relations concentration
- Master of Arts in English for Teachers
- Master of Arts in Mathematics for Teachers
- Master of Education in Curriculum and Instruction
- Master of Fine Arts in Creative Writing
- Master of Science in Applied Behavior Analysis
- Ph.D. in Behavior Analysis

The **College of Business** offers the following graduate programs:

- Master of Business Administration (M.B.A.)
- Master of Science in Accounting (M.S.A.)
- M.S.A. with Forensic Accounting and Fraud Investigation concentration
- Master of Science in Organizational Leadership (M.S.O.L.)
- J.D./M.B.A. combined degree program
- J.D./M.S.A. combined degree program
- J.D./M.S.O.L. combined degree program
- Pharm.D./M.B.A. combined degree program
- Pharm.D./M.S.O.L. combined degree program

The **College of Engineering** offers these graduate programs:

- Master of Science in Civil Engineering (M.S.C.E.)
- Master of Science in Electrical Engineering (M.S.E.E.)
- M.S.E.E. with Mechatronics concentration
- Master of Science in Engineering Management (M.S.E.M.)
- Master of Science in Industrial Engineering (M.S.I.E.)
- Master of Science in Mechanical Engineering (M.S.M.E.)
- M.S.M.E. with Mechatronics concentration
- M.S.E.M./M.B.A. combined degree program
- Ph.D. in Engineering Management
- J.D./M.S.E.M. combined degree program

The University also offers programs though the College of Pharmacy and the Law School.

Financial Aid

To be considered for financial aid, a student must have final approval into a degree program and be enrolled in a minimum of 3 credits per term. Financial need-based resources, including grants and low-interest federal loans, may be available for eligible students.

Cost of Study

Western New England University is committed to keeping a high-quality private education affordable for its students. Western New England's graduate tuition rates are some of the most affordable in the region. Tuition for graduate programs is as follows:

College of Arts and Sciences:

- Online M.Ed.: $646 per credit
- M.A.E.T., M.A.M.T., and M.E.E.E.: $350 per credit
- M.A. in Communication: $750 per credit
- M.F.A. in Creative Writing: $600 per credit
- M.S. in Applied Behavior Analysis: $1,025 per credit
- Ph.D. in Behavior Analysis: $1,280 per credit

College of Business:

- M.B.A., M.S.A., M.S.O.L.: $804 per credit

College of Engineering:

- M.S.C.E., M.S.E.E., M.S.E.M., M.S.I.E., and M.S.M.E.: $1,074 per credit
- Ph.D. in Engineering Management: $1,280 per credit

Living and Housing Costs

Graduate students have the option of living on campus. Housing costs range between $7,844 and $12,187, depending upon the apartment type and duration (10 to 12 months).

Career Development

The Career Development Center assists students and alumni with career planning, occupational exploration, and job search strategies. The center's staff members implement the University's strong commitment to the development of a student's career decision-making by providing individual career advising and assistance in identifying career options.

The Career Development Center staff brings students in contact with employers through dynamic on-campus recruiting, employer information sessions, and career fairs. In addition, students are assisted with resources for part-time and summer employment. A weekly newsletter is published online at www.wne.edu/careercenter and serves as one tool for alerting students to employment opportunities, internships, recruiting schedules, and career-related workshops and activities.

Location

Western New England University's beautiful 215-acre suburban campus is located in Springfield, Massachusetts, the cultural urban center of the western part of the state. Perhaps best known as the birthplace of basketball and home of the Naismith Memorial Basketball Hall of Fame, Springfield is midway between New York and Boston and on the road between New York and Canada. Springfield is ideally located for travel in all directions, and there is convenient access from the University to both the Mass Pike and Interstate 91.

Faculty

With an average class size of 20, students work closely with the University's full-time faculty members who bring outstanding professional and academic credentials to the classroom. On average, 85 percent of graduate courses are taught by full-time faculty members. Ninety percent of the faculty hold terminal degrees in their field.

Additional details about the faculty for specific departments/programs can be found at wne.edu.

The University

Originally established in 1919 to serve working adults, Western New England University is renowned for its innovative programs, culture of collaboration, and faculty members who are focused on student success. Today that commitment continues through the University's graduate programs on campus and online.

Accredited by AACSB International, the College of Business is widely respected throughout the region for the caliber of its flagship M.B.A. program, sought-after M.S.A. degree, and dynamic new offering in organizational leadership. The College of Arts and Sciences offers high-quality master's programs for teachers at an affordable tuition rate and an immersive M.F.A. in Creative Writing program. The College's master's and doctoral programs in Behavior Analysis have positioned the University as a global leader in research and education in that discipline. Recently accredited by the Association of Behavior Analysis International (ABAI), the Ph.D. in Behavior Analysis program has been cited by the ABAI as ranking third in total scholarly publications out of 74 programs. The thriving College of Engineering is recognized as an educational leader by major corporations in the northeast who seek out graduates of the University's master's and combined engineering/business and law degree programs.

Applying

Western New England University has a rolling admissions policy for most programs, not a set admission deadline. Admission decisions are typically released within two to three weeks of an application being complete. The University urges prospective students to apply as early as possible in relation to the anticipated start date. Most of the graduate programs offer multiple entry points annually. Graduate students can apply online at www.wne.edu/gradapp.

Correspondence and Information

Office of Graduate Admissions
Western New England University
1215 Wilbraham Road
Springfield, Massachusetts 01119
United States
Phone: 413-782-1517
800-325-1122, Ext. 1517 (toll-free)
E-mail: study@wne.edu
Website: wne.edu/grad

APPENDIXES

Institutional Changes Since the 2016 Edition

Following is an alphabetical listing of institutions that have recently closed, merged with other institutions, or changed their names or status. In the case of a name change, the former name appears first, followed by the new name.

American Baptist College of American Baptist Theological Seminary (Nashville, TN): *no longer offers graduate degrees*

American College of Traditional Chinese Medicine (San Francisco, CA): *merged with California Institute of Integral Studies (San Francisco, CA)*

Augustana College (Sioux Falls, SD): *name changed to Augustana University*

Bainbridge Graduate Institute (Bainbridge Island, WA): *name changed to Pinchot University*

Benedictine University at Springfield (Springfield, IL): *degree programs now offered through Benedictine University's National Moser Center for Adult Learning*

The Boston Conservatory (Boston, MA): *merged with Berklee College of Music (Boston, MA)*

Burlington College (Burlington, VT): *closed*

Cabrini College (Radnor, PA): *name changed to Cabrini University*

Carolina Evangelical Divinity School (High Point, NC): *name changed to Carolina Graduate School of Divinity*

Castleton State College (Castleton, VT): *name changed to Castleton University*

Charles Drew University of Medicine and Science (Los Angeles, CA): *name changed to Charles R. Drew University of Medicine and Science*

The Chicago School of Professional Psychology at Westwood (Los Angeles, CA): *closed*

Concordia University (Irvine, CA): *name changed to Concordia University Irvine*

Concordia University College of Alberta (Edmonton, AB, Canada): *name changed to Concordia University of Edmonton*

The Criswell College (Dallas, TX): *name changed to Criswell College*

DeVry University (Louisville, KY): *closed*

DeVry University (Bethesda, MD): *closed*

DeVry University (Sandy, UT): *closed*

Doane College (Crete, NE): *name changed to Doane University*

Dowling College (Oakdale, NY): *closed*

Emmanuel Christian Seminary (Johnson City, TN): *merged with Milligan College (Milligan College, TN)*

Everest University (Jacksonville, FL): *closed*

Everest University (Melbourne, FL): *closed*

Everest University (Orlando, FL): *closed*

Everest University (Pompano Beach, FL): *closed*

Felician College (Lodi, NJ): *name changed to Felician University*

Five Branches University: Graduate School of Traditional Chinese Medicine (Santa Cruz, CA): *name changed to Five Branches University*

Georgia Regents University (Augusta, GA): *name changed to Augusta University*

Golden Gate Baptist Theological Seminary (Mill Valley, CA): *name changed to Gateway Seminary*

Gooding Institute of Nurse Anesthesia (Panama City, FL): *closed*

Hawaii College of Oriental Medicine (Kamuela, HI): *closed*

Institut Franco-Européen de Chiropratique (94200 Ivry-sur-Seine, France): *name changed to Institut Franco-Européen de Chiropraxie*

King's University (Southlake, TX): *name changed to The King's University*

Lakeland College (Plymouth, WI): *name changed to Lakeland University*

Laurel University (High Point, NC): *name changed to John Wesley University*

Lutheran Theological Southern Seminary (Columbia, SC): *merged with Lenoir-Rhyne University (Hickory, NC)*

Massachusetts School of Professional Psychology (Boston, MA): *name changed to William James College*

Middlebury Institute of International Studies (Monterey, CA): *name changed to Middlebury Institute of International Studies at Monterey*

Midway College (Midway, KY): *name changed to Midway University*

Nashotah House (Nashotah, WI): *name changed to Nashotah House Theological Seminary*

The New England College of Optometry (Boston, MA): *name changed to New England College of Optometry*

New England School of Acupuncture (Newton, MA): *merged with MCPHS University (Boston, MA)*

Northern Baptist Theological Seminary (Lombard, IL): *name changed to Northern Seminary*

Northwest Institute of Literary Arts (Freeland, WA): *closed*

Our Lady of Holy Cross College (New Orleans, LA): *name changed to University of Holy Cross*

Penn State Dickinson School of Law (University Park, PA): *name changed to Penn State University–Dickinson Law*

Purdue University Calumet (Hammond, IN): *name changed to Purdue University Northwest*

Purdue University North Central (Westville, IN): *name changed to Purdue University Northwest*

Rutgers, The State University of New Jersey, Camden (Camden, NJ): *name changed to Rutgers University–Camden*

Rutgers, The State University of New Jersey, Newark (Newark, NJ): *name changed to Rutgers University–Newark*

Rutgers, The State University of New Jersey, New Brunswick (Piscataway, NJ): *name changed to Rutgers University–New Brunswick*

St. Catharine College (St. Catharine, KY): *closed*

Samra University of Oriental Medicine (Los Angeles, CA): *closed*

The School of Professional Psychology at Forest Institute (Springfield, MO): *closed*

Skidmore College (Saratoga Springs, NY): *no longer offers graduate degrees*

Southern Baptist Theological Seminary (Louisville, KY): *name changed to The Southern Baptist Theological Seminary*

Southern Polytechnic State University (Marietta, GA): *merged with Kennesaw State University (Kennesaw, GA)*

South Texas College of Law (Houston, TX): *name changed to Houston College of Law*

Stevens-Henager College–Salt Lake City/Murray (Salt Lake City, UT): *name changed to Stevens-Henager College*

Taft Law School (Santa Ana, CA): *merged into a single entry for Taft University System (Denver, CO)*

Temple Baptist Seminary (Chattanooga, TN): *merged with Piedmont International University (Winston-Salem, NC)*

Texas A&M Health Science Center (College Station, TX): *merged into a single entry for Texas A&M University (College Station, TX)*

Thomas Edison State College (Trenton, NJ): *name changed to Thomas Edison State University*

Thunderbird School of Global Management (Glendale, AZ): *merged with Arizona State University at the Tempe campus (Tempe, AZ)*

Touro University (Vallejo, CA): *name changed to Touro University California*

Toyota Technological Institute of Chicago (Chicago, IL): *name changed to Toyota Technological Institute at Chicago*

Trinity International University, South Florida Campus (Davie, FL): *name changed to Trinity International University Florida*

Union Graduate College (Schenectady, NY): *merged with Clarkson University (Potsdam, NY)*

United States International University (Nairobi, Kenya): *name changed to United States International University–Africa*

United States University (Cypress, CA): *closed*

University of Massachusetts Worcester (Worcester, MA): *name changed to University of Massachusetts Medical School*

The University of Montana (Missoula, MT): *name changed to University of Montana*

University of Phoenix–Austin Campus (Austin, TX): *closed*

University of Phoenix–Birmingham Campus (Birmingham, AL): *closed*

University of Phoenix–Boston Campus (Braintree, MA): *closed*

University of Phoenix–Chicago Campus (Schaumburg, IL): *closed*

University of Phoenix–Cleveland Campus (Beachwood, OH): *closed*

University of Phoenix–Columbia Campus (Columbia, SC): *closed*

University of Phoenix–Des Moines Campus (Des Moines, IA): *closed*

University of Phoenix–Idaho Campus (Meridian, ID): *closed*

University of Phoenix–Indianapolis Campus (Indianapolis, IN): *closed*

University of Phoenix–Kansas City Campus (Kansas City, MO): *closed*

University of Phoenix–Little Rock Campus (Little Rock, AR): *closed*

University of Phoenix–Louisville Campus (Louisville, KY): *closed*

University of Phoenix–Maryland Campus (Columbia, MD): *closed*

University of Phoenix–Memphis Campus (Cordova, TN): *closed*

University of Phoenix–Milwaukee Campus (Milwaukee, WI): *closed*

University of Phoenix–Minneapolis/St. Paul Campus (St. Louis Park, MN): *closed*

University of Phoenix–Nashville Campus (Nashville, TN): *closed*

University of Phoenix–Oklahoma City Campus (Oklahoma City, OK): *closed*

University of Phoenix–Oregon Campus (Tigard, OR): *closed*

University of Phoenix–Philadelphia Campus (Wayne, PA): *closed*

University of Phoenix–Puerto Rico Campus (Guaynabo, PR): *closed*

University of Phoenix–Richmond-Virginia Beach Campus (Glen Allen, VA): *closed*

University of Phoenix–St. Louis Campus (St. Louis, MO): *closed*

University of Phoenix–Savannah Campus (Savannah, GA): *closed*

University of Southernmost Florida (Jacksonville, FL): *closed*

The University of Texas at Brownsville (Brownsville, TX): *merged with The University of Texas–Pan American to become The University of Texas Rio Grande Valley (Edinburg, TX)*

The University of Texas–Pan American (Edinburg, TX): *merged with The University of Texas at Brownsville to become The University of Texas Rio Grande Valley (Edinburg, TX)*

Washington College (Chestertown, MD): *no longer offers graduate degrees*

Weill Cornell Medical College (New York, NY): *name changed to Weill Cornell Medicine*

Western Michigan University Cooley Law School (Lansing, MI): *name changed to Western Michigan University Thomas M. Cooley Law School*

William Howard Taft University (Santa Ana, CA): *merged into a single entry for Taft University System (Denver, CO)*

William Mitchell College of Law (St. Paul, MN): *merged with Hamline University School of Law, a unit of Hamline University (St. Paul, MN)*

Abbreviations Used in the Guides

The following list includes abbreviations of degree names used in the profiles in the 2016 edition of the guides. Because some degrees (e.g., Doctor of Education) can be abbreviated in more than one way (e.g., D.Ed. or Ed.D.), and because the abbreviations used in the guides reflect the preferences of the individual colleges and universities, the list may include two or more abbreviations for a single degree.

DEGREES

A Mus D	Doctor of Musical Arts
AC	Advanced Certificate
AD	Artist's Diploma
	Doctor of Arts
ADP	Artist's Diploma
Adv C	Advanced Certificate
AGC	Advanced Graduate Certificate
AGSC	Advanced Graduate Specialist Certificate
ALM	Master of Liberal Arts
AM	Master of Arts
AMBA	Accelerated Master of Business Administration
AMRS	Master of Arts in Religious Studies
APC	Advanced Professional Certificate
APMPH	Advanced Professional Master of Public Health
App Sc	Applied Scientist
App Sc D	Doctor of Applied Science
AstE	Astronautical Engineer
ATC	Advanced Training Certificate
Au D	Doctor of Audiology
B Th	Bachelor of Theology
BN	Bachelor of Naturopathy
CAES	Certificate of Advanced Educational Specialization
CAGS	Certificate of Advanced Graduate Studies
CAL	Certificate in Applied Linguistics
CAPS	Certificate of Advanced Professional Studies
CAS	Certificate of Advanced Studies
CASPA	Certificate of Advanced Study in Public Administration
CASR	Certificate in Advanced Social Research
CATS	Certificate of Achievement in Theological Studies
CBHS	Certificate in Basic Health Sciences
CCJA	Certificate in Criminal Justice Administration
CCTS	Certificate in Clinical and Translational Science
CE	Civil Engineer
CEM	Certificate of Environmental Management
CET	Certificate in Educational Technologies
CGS	Certificate of Graduate Studies
Ch E	Chemical Engineer
Clin Sc D	Doctor of Clinical Science
CM	Certificate in Management
CMH	Certificate in Medical Humanities
CMM	Master of Church Ministries
CMS	Certificate in Ministerial Studies
CNM	Certificate in Nonprofit Management
CPASF	Certificate Program for Advanced Study in Finance
CPC	Certificate in Professional Counseling
	Certificate in Publication and Communication
CPH	Certificate in Public Health
CPM	Certificate in Public Management
CPS	Certificate of Professional Studies
CScD	Doctor of Clinical Science
CSD	Certificate in Spiritual Direction
CSS	Certificate of Special Studies
CTS	Certificate of Theological Studies
CURP	Certificate in Urban and Regional Planning
D Admin	Doctor of Administration
D Arch	Doctor of Architecture
D Be	Doctor in Bioethics
D Com	Doctor of Commerce
D Couns	Doctor of Counseling
D Des	Doctorate of Design
D Div	Doctor of Divinity
D Ed	Doctor of Education
D Ed Min	Doctor of Educational Ministry
D Eng	Doctor of Engineering
D Engr	Doctor of Engineering
D Ent	Doctor of Enterprise
D Env	Doctor of Environment
D Law	Doctor of Law
D Litt	Doctor of Letters
D Med Sc	Doctor of Medical Science
D Min	Doctor of Ministry
D Miss	Doctor of Missiology
D Mus	Doctor of Music
D Mus A	Doctor of Musical Arts
D Phil	Doctor of Philosophy
D Prof	Doctor of Professional Studies
D Ps	Doctor of Psychology
D Sc	Doctor of Science
D Sc D	Doctor of Science in Dentistry
D Sc IS	Doctor of Science in Information Systems
D Sc PA	Doctor of Science in Physician Assistant Studies
D Th	Doctor of Theology
D Th P	Doctor of Practical Theology
DA	Doctor of Accounting
	Doctor of Arts
DAH	Doctor of Arts in Humanities
DAOM	Doctorate in Acupuncture and Oriental Medicine
DAT	Doctorate of Athletic Training
	Professional Doctor of Art Therapy
DBA	Doctor of Business Administration
DBH	Doctor of Behavioral Health
DBL	Doctor of Business Leadership
DC	Doctor of Chiropractic
DCC	Doctor of Computer Science
DCD	Doctor of Communications Design
DCL	Doctor of Civil Law
	Doctor of Comparative Law
DCM	Doctor of Church Music
DCN	Doctor of Clinical Nutrition
DCS	Doctor of Computer Science
DDN	Diplôme du Droit Notarial
DDS	Doctor of Dental Surgery
DE	Doctor of Education
	Doctor of Engineering
DED	Doctor of Economic Development
DEIT	Doctor of Educational Innovation and Technology
DEL	Doctor of Executive Leadership
DEM	Doctor of Educational Ministry
DEPD	Diplôme Études Spécialisées
DES	Doctor of Engineering Science
DESS	Diplôme Études Supérieures Spécialisées
DET	Doctor of Educational Technology
DFA	Doctor of Fine Arts
DGP	Diploma in Graduate and Professional Studies
DH Ed	Doctor of Health Education
DH Sc	Doctor of Health Sciences
DHA	Doctor of Health Administration
DHCE	Doctor of Health Care Ethics
DHL	Doctor of Hebrew Letters
DHPE	Doctorate of Health Professionals Education
DHS	Doctor of Health Science
DHSc	Doctor of Health Science
Dip CS	Diploma in Christian Studies
DIT	Doctor of Industrial Technology
	Doctor of Information Technology
DJS	Doctor of Jewish Studies

DLS	Doctor of Liberal Studies
DM	Doctor of Management
	Doctor of Music
DMA	Doctor of Musical Arts
DMD	Doctor of Dental Medicine
DME	Doctor of Manufacturing Management
	Doctor of Music Education
DMEd	Doctor of Music Education
DMFT	Doctor of Marital and Family Therapy
DMH	Doctor of Medical Humanities
DML	Doctor of Modern Languages
DMP	Doctorate in Medical Physics
DMPNA	Doctor of Management Practice in Nurse Anesthesia
DN Sc	Doctor of Nursing Science
DNAP	Doctor of Nurse Anesthesia Practice
DNP	Doctor of Nursing Practice
DNP-A	Doctor of Nursing Practice - Anesthesia
DNS	Doctor of Nursing Science
DO	Doctor of Osteopathy
DOT	Doctor of Occupational Therapy
DPA	Doctor of Public Administration
DPDS	Doctor of Planning and Development Studies
DPH	Doctor of Public Health
DPM	Doctor of Plant Medicine
	Doctor of Podiatric Medicine
DPPD	Doctor of Policy, Planning, and Development
DPS	Doctor of Professional Studies
DPT	Doctor of Physical Therapy
DPTSc	Doctor of Physical Therapy Science
Dr DES	Doctor of Design
Dr NP	Doctor of Nursing Practice
Dr OT	Doctor of Occupational Therapy
Dr PH	Doctor of Public Health
Dr Sc PT	Doctor of Science in Physical Therapy
DrAP	Doctor of Anesthesia Practice
DRSc	Doctor of Regulatory Science
DS	Doctor of Science
DS Sc	Doctor of Social Science
DSJS	Doctor of Science in Jewish Studies
DSL	Doctor of Strategic Leadership
DSS	Doctor of Strategic Security
DSW	Doctor of Social Work
DTL	Doctor of Talmudic Law
	Doctor of Transformational Leadership
DV Sc	Doctor of Veterinary Science
DVM	Doctor of Veterinary Medicine
DWS	Doctor of Worship Studies
EAA	Engineer in Aeronautics and Astronautics
EASPh D	Engineering and Applied Science Doctor of Philosophy
ECS	Engineer in Computer Science
Ed D	Doctor of Education
Ed DCT	Doctor of Education in College Teaching
Ed L D	Doctor of Education Leadership
Ed M	Master of Education
Ed S	Specialist in Education
Ed Sp	Specialist in Education
EDB	Executive Doctorate in Business
EDBA	Executive Doctor of Business Administration
EDM	Executive Doctorate in Management
EE	Electrical Engineer
EJD	Executive Juris Doctor
EMBA	Executive Master of Business Administration
EMFA	Executive Master of Forensic Accounting
EMHA	Executive Master of Health Administration
EMIB	Executive Master of International Business
EML	Executive Master of Leadership
EMPA	Executive Master of Public Administration
EMPL	Executive Master in Public Leadership
EMS	Executive Master of Science
EMTM	Executive Master of Technology Management
Eng	Engineer
Eng Sc D	Doctor of Engineering Science
Engr	Engineer
Exec M Tax	Executive Master of Taxation
Exec MAC	Executive Master of Accounting
Exec Ed D	Executive Doctor of Education
Exec MBA	Executive Master of Business Administration
Exec MPA	Executive Master of Public Administration
Exec MPH	Executive Master of Public Health
Exec MS	Executive Master of Science
Executive Fellows MBA	Executive Fellows Master of Business Administration
G Dip	Graduate Diploma
GBC	Graduate Business Certificate
GDM	Graduate Diploma in Management
GDPA	Graduate Diploma in Public Administration
GDRE	Graduate Diploma in Religious Education
GEMBA	Global Executive Master of Business Administration
GMBA	Global Master of Business Administration
GP LL M	Global Professional Master of Laws
GPD	Graduate Performance Diploma
GSS	Graduate Special Certificate for Students in Special Situations
IEMBA	International Executive Master of Business Administration
IMA	Interdisciplinary Master of Arts
IMBA	International Master of Business Administration
IMES	International Master's in Environmental Studies
Ingeniero	Engineer
JCD	Doctor of Canon Law
JCL	Licentiate in Canon Law
JD	Juris Doctor
JM	Juris Master
JSD	Doctor of Juridical Science
	Doctor of Jurisprudence
	Doctor of the Science of Law
JSM	Master of the Science of Law
L Th	Licenciate in Theology
LL B	Bachelor of Laws
LL CM	Master of Comparative Law
LL D	Doctor of Laws
LL M	Master of Laws
LL M in Tax	Master of Laws in Taxation
LL M CL	Master of Laws in Common Law
M Ac	Master of Accountancy
	Master of Accounting
	Master of Acupuncture
M Ac OM	Master of Acupuncture and Oriental Medicine
M Acc	Master of Accountancy
	Master of Accounting
M Acct	Master of Accountancy
	Master of Accounting
M Accy	Master of Accountancy
M Actg	Master of Accounting
M Acy	Master of Accountancy
M Ad	Master of Administration
M Ad Ed	Master of Adult Education
M Adm	Master of Administration
M Adm Mgt	Master of Administrative Management
M Admin	Master of Administration
M ADU	Master of Architectural Design and Urbanism
M Adv	Master of Advertising
M AEST	Master of Applied Environmental Science and Technology
M Ag	Master of Agriculture
M Ag Ed	Master of Agricultural Education
M Agr	Master of Agriculture
M Anesth Ed	Master of Anesthesiology Education
M App Comp Sc	Master of Applied Computer Science
M App St	Master of Applied Statistics
M Appl Stat	Master of Applied Statistics
M Aq	Master of Aquaculture
M Arc	Master of Architecture
M Arch	Master of Architecture
M Arch I	Master of Architecture I
M Arch II	Master of Architecture II
M Arch E	Master of Architectural Engineering
M Arch H	Master of Architectural History
M Bioethics	Master in Bioethics
M Biomath	Master of Biomathematics
M Ch E	Master of Chemical Engineering

M Chem	Master of Chemistry
M Cl D	Master of Clinical Dentistry
M Cl Sc	Master of Clinical Science
M Comp	Master of Computing
M Comp Sc	Master of Computer Science
M Coun	Master of Counseling
M Dent	Master of Dentistry
M Dent Sc	Master of Dental Sciences
M Des	Master of Design
M Des S	Master of Design Studies
M Div	Master of Divinity
M E Sci	Master of Earth Science
M Ec	Master of Economics
M Econ	Master of Economics
M Ed	Master of Education
M Ed T	Master of Education in Teaching
M En	Master of Engineering
M En S	Master of Environmental Sciences
M Eng	Master of Engineering
M Eng Mgt	Master of Engineering Management
M Engr	Master of Engineering
M Ent	Master of Enterprise
M Env	Master of Environment
M Env Des	Master of Environmental Design
M Env E	Master of Environmental Engineering
M Env Sc	Master of Environmental Science
M Fin	Master of Finance
M FSc	Master of Fisheries Science
M Geo E	Master of Geological Engineering
M Geoenv E	Master of Geoenvironmental Engineering
M Geog	Master of Geography
M Hum	Master of Humanities
M IDST	Master's in Interdisciplinary Studies
M Kin	Master of Kinesiology
M Land Arch	Master of Landscape Architecture
M Litt	Master of Letters
M Mat SE	Master of Material Science and Engineering
M Math	Master of Mathematics
M Mech E	Master of Mechanical Engineering
M Med Sc	Master of Medical Science
M Mgmt	Master of Management
M Mgt	Master of Management
M Min	Master of Ministries
M Mtl E	Master of Materials Engineering
M Mu	Master of Music
M Mus	Master of Music
M Mus Ed	Master of Music Education
M Music	Master of Music
M Nat Sci	Master of Natural Science
M Pet E	Master of Petroleum Engineering
M Pharm	Master of Pharmacy
M Phil	Master of Philosophy
M Phil F	Master of Philosophical Foundations
M Pl	Master of Planning
M Plan	Master of Planning
M Pol	Master of Political Science
M Pr Met	Master of Professional Meteorology
M Prob S	Master of Probability and Statistics
M Psych	Master of Psychology
M Pub	Master of Publishing
M Rel	Master of Religion
M Sc	Master of Science
M Sc A	Master of Science (Applied)
M Sc AC	Master of Science in Applied Computing
M Sc AHN	Master of Science in Applied Human Nutrition
M Sc BMC	Master of Science in Biomedical Communications
M Sc CS	Master of Science in Computer Science
M Sc E	Master of Science in Engineering
M Sc Eng	Master of Science in Engineering
M Sc Engr	Master of Science in Engineering
M Sc F	Master of Science in Forestry
M Sc FE	Master of Science in Forest Engineering
M Sc Geogr	Master of Science in Geography
M Sc N	Master of Science in Nursing
M Sc OT	Master of Science in Occupational Therapy
M Sc P	Master of Science in Planning
M Sc Pl	Master of Science in Planning
M Sc PT	Master of Science in Physical Therapy
M Sc T	Master of Science in Teaching
M SEM	Master of Sustainable Environmental Management
M Serv Soc	Master of Social Service
M Soc	Master of Sociology
M Sp Ed	Master of Special Education
M St	Master of Studies
M Stat	Master of Statistics
M Sys E	Master of Systems Engineering
M Sys Sc	Master of Systems Science
M Tax	Master of Taxation
M Tech	Master of Technology
M Th	Master of Theology
M Tox	Master of Toxicology
M Trans E	Master of Transportation Engineering
M U Ed	Master of Urban Education
M Urb	Master of Urban Planning
M Vet Sc	Master of Veterinary Science
MA	Master of Accounting
	Master of Administration
	Master of Arts
MA Comm	Master of Arts in Communication
MA Ed	Master of Arts in Education
MA Ed/HD	Master of Arts in Education and Human Development
MA Ext	Master of Agricultural Extension
MA Min	Master of Arts in Ministry
MA Past St	Master of Arts in Pastoral Studies
MA Ph	Master of Arts in Philosophy
MA Psych	Master of Arts in Psychology
MA Sc	Master of Applied Science
MA Sp	Master of Arts (Spirituality)
MA Th	Master of Arts in Theology
MA-R	Master of Arts (Research)
MAA	Master of Administrative Arts
	Master of Applied Anthropology
	Master of Applied Arts
	Master of Arts in Administration
MAAA	Master of Arts in Arts Administration
MAAAP	Master of Arts Administration and Policy
MAAD	Master of Advanced Architectural Design
MAAE	Master of Arts in Art Education
MAAPPS	Master of Arts in Asia Pacific Policy Studies
MAAS	Master of Arts in Aging and Spirituality
MAASJ	Master of Arts in Applied Social Justice
MAAT	Master of Arts in Applied Theology
	Master of Arts in Art Therapy
MAB	Master of Agribusiness
MABC	Master of Arts in Biblical Counseling
MABE	Master of Arts in Bible Exposition
MABL	Master of Arts in Biblical Languages
MABM	Master of Agribusiness Management
MABS	Master of Arts in Biblical Studies
MABT	Master of Arts in Bible Teaching
MAC	Master of Accountancy
	Master of Accounting
	Master of Arts in Communication
	Master of Arts in Counseling
MACC	Master of Arts in Christian Counseling
	Master of Arts in Clinical Counseling
MACCT	Master of Accounting
MACD	Master of Arts in Christian Doctrine
MACE	Master of Arts in Christian Education
MACH	Master of Arts in Church History
MACI	Master of Arts in Curriculum and Instruction
MACIS	Master of Accounting and Information Systems
MACJ	Master of Arts in Criminal Justice
MACL	Master of Arts in Christian Leadership
	Master of Arts in Community Leadership
MACM	Master of Arts in Christian Ministries
	Master of Arts in Christian Ministry
	Master of Arts in Church Music
	Master of Arts in Counseling Ministries
MACN	Master of Arts in Counseling
MACO	Master of Arts in Counseling
MAcOM	Master of Acupuncture and Oriental Medicine

MACP	Master of Arts in Christian Practice
	Master of Arts in Church Planting
	Master of Arts in Counseling Psychology
MACS	Master of Applied Computer Science
	Master of Arts in Catholic Studies
	Master of Arts in Christian Studies
MACSE	Master of Arts in Christian School Education
MACT	Master of Arts in Communications and Technology
MAD	Master in Educational Institution Administration
	Master of Art and Design
MADR	Master of Arts in Dispute Resolution
MADS	Master of Animal and Dairy Science
	Master of Applied Disability Studies
MAE	Master of Aerospace Engineering
	Master of Agricultural Economics
	Master of Agricultural Education
	Master of Applied Economics
	Master of Architectural Engineering
	Master of Art Education
	Master of Arts in Education
	Master of Arts in English
MAEd	Master of Arts Education
MAEL	Master of Arts in Educational Leadership
MAEM	Master of Arts in Educational Ministries
MAEP	Master of Arts in Economic Policy
	Master of Arts in Educational Psychology
MAES	Master of Arts in Environmental Sciences
MAET	Master of Arts in English Teaching
MAF	Master of Arts in Finance
MAFE	Master of Arts in Financial Economics
MAFLL	Master of Arts in Foreign Language and Literature
MAFM	Master of Accounting and Financial Management
MAFS	Master of Arts in Family Studies
MAG	Master of Applied Geography
MAGS	Master of Arts in Global Service
MAGU	Master of Urban Analysis and Management
MAH	Master of Arts in Humanities
MAHA	Master of Arts in Humanitarian Assistance
MAHCM	Master of Arts in Health Care Mission
MAHG	Master of American History and Government
MAHL	Master of Arts in Hebrew Letters
MAHN	Master of Applied Human Nutrition
MAHR	Master of Applied Historical Research
MAHS	Master of Arts in Human Services
MAHSR	Master in Applied Health Services Research
MAIA	Master of Arts in International Administration
	Master of Arts in International Affairs
MAIDM	Master of Arts in Interior Design and Merchandising
MAIH	Master of Arts in Interdisciplinary Humanities
MAIOP	Master of Applied Industrial/Organizational Psychology
MAIPCR	Master of Arts in International Peace and Conflict Management
MAIS	Master of Arts in Intercultural Studies
	Master of Arts in Interdisciplinary Studies
	Master of Arts in International Studies
MAIT	Master of Administration in Information Technology
MAJ	Master of Arts in Journalism
MAJ Ed	Master of Arts in Jewish Education
MAJCS	Master of Arts in Jewish Communal Service
MAJE	Master of Arts in Jewish Education
MAJPS	Master of Arts in Jewish Professional Studies
MAJS	Master of Arts in Jewish Studies
MAL	Master in Agricultural Leadership
MALA	Master of Arts in Liberal Arts
MALD	Master of Arts in Law and Diplomacy
MALER	Master of Arts in Labor and Employment Relations
MALL	Master of Arts in Language Learning
MALP	Master of Arts in Language Pedagogy
MALS	Master of Arts in Liberal Studies
MAM	Master of Acquisition Management
	Master of Agriculture and Management
	Master of Applied Mathematics
	Master of Arts in Management
	Master of Arts in Ministry
	Master of Arts Management
	Master of Avian Medicine
MAMB	Master of Applied Molecular Biology
MAMC	Master of Arts in Mass Communication
	Master of Arts in Ministry and Culture
	Master of Arts in Ministry for a Multicultural Church
	Master of Arts in Missional Christianity
MAME	Master of Arts in Missions/Evangelism
MAMFC	Master of Arts in Marriage and Family Counseling
MAMFT	Master of Arts in Marriage and Family Therapy
MAMHC	Master of Arts in Mental Health Counseling
MAMS	Master of Applied Mathematical Sciences
	Master of Applied Meditation Studies
	Master of Arts in Ministerial Studies
	Master of Arts in Ministry and Spirituality
MAMT	Master of Arts in Mathematics Teaching
MAN	Master of Applied Nutrition
MANT	Master of Arts in New Testament
MAOL	Master of Arts in Organizational Leadership
MAOM	Master of Acupuncture and Oriental Medicine
MAOT	Master of Arts in Old Testament
MAP	Master of Applied Politics
	Master of Applied Psychology
	Master of Arts in Planning
	Master of Psychology
	Master of Public Administration
MAP Min	Master of Arts in Pastoral Ministry
MAPA	Master of Arts in Public Administration
MAPC	Master of Arts in Pastoral Counseling
MAPE	Master of Arts in Physics Education
	Master of Arts in Political Economy
MAPM	Master of Arts in Pastoral Ministry
	Master of Arts in Pastoral Music
	Master of Arts in Practical Ministry
MAPP	Master of Arts in Public Policy
MAPS	Master of Arts in Pastoral Studies
	Master of Arts in Public Service
MAPT	Master of Practical Theology
MAPW	Master of Arts in Professional Writing
MAR	Master of Arts in Reading
	Master of Arts in Religion
Mar Eng	Marine Engineer
MARC	Master of Arts in Rehabilitation Counseling
MARE	Master of Arts in Religious Education
MARL	Master of Arts in Religious Leadership
MARS	Master of Arts in Religious Studies
MAS	Master of Accounting Science
	Master of Actuarial Science
	Master of Administrative Science
	Master of Advanced Study
	Master of Aeronautical Science
	Master of American Studies
	Master of Animal Science
	Master of Applied Science
	Master of Applied Statistics
	Master of Archival Studies
MASA	Master of Advanced Studies in Architecture
MASD	Master of Arts in Spiritual Direction
MASE	Master of Arts in Special Education
MASF	Master of Arts in Spiritual Formation
MASJ	Master of Arts in Systems of Justice
MASLA	Master of Advanced Studies in Landscape Architecture
MASM	Master of Aging Services Management
	Master of Arts in Specialized Ministries
MASP	Master of Applied Social Psychology
	Master of Arts in School Psychology
MASPAA	Master of Arts in Sports and Athletic Administration
MASS	Master of Applied Social Science
	Master of Arts in Social Science
MAST	Master of Arts in Science Teaching

MAT	Master of Arts in Teaching
	Master of Arts in Theology
	Master of Athletic Training
	Master's in Administration of Telecommunications
Mat E	Materials Engineer
MATCM	Master of Acupuncture and Traditional Chinese Medicine
MATDE	Master of Arts in Theology, Development, and Evangelism
MATDR	Master of Territorial Management and Regional Development
MATE	Master of Arts for the Teaching of English
MATESL	Master of Arts in Teaching English as a Second Language
MATESOL	Master of Arts in Teaching English to Speakers of Other Languages
MATF	Master of Arts in Teaching English as a Foreign Language/Intercultural Studies
MATFL	Master of Arts in Teaching Foreign Language
MATH	Master of Arts in Therapy
MATI	Master of Administration of Information Technology
MATL	Master of Arts in Teacher Leadership
	Master of Arts in Teaching of Languages
	Master of Arts in Transformational Leadership
MATM	Master of Arts in Teaching of Mathematics
MATS	Master of Arts in Theological Studies
	Master of Arts in Transforming Spirituality
MATSL	Master of Arts in Teaching a Second Language
MAUA	Master of Arts in Urban Affairs
MAUD	Master of Arts in Urban Design
MAURP	Master of Arts in Urban and Regional Planning
MAW	Master of Arts in Worship
MAWSHP	Master of Arts in Worship
MAYM	Master of Arts in Youth Ministry
MB	Master of Bioinformatics
MBA	Master of Business Administration
MBA-AM	Master of Business Administration in Aviation Management
MBA-EP	Master of Business Administration–Experienced Professionals
MBAA	Master of Business Administration in Aviation
MBAE	Master of Biological and Agricultural Engineering
	Master of Biosystems and Agricultural Engineering
MBAH	Master of Business Administration in Health
MBAi	Master of Business Administration–International
MBAICT	Master of Business Administration in Information and Communication Technology
MBATM	Master of Business Administration in Technology Management
MBC	Master of Building Construction
MBE	Master of Bilingual Education
	Master of Bioengineering
	Master of Bioethics
	Master of Biomedical Engineering
	Master of Business Economics
	Master of Business Education
MBEE	Master in Biotechnology Enterprise and Entrepreneurship
MBET	Master of Business, Entrepreneurship and Technology
MBID	Master of Biomedical Innovation and Development
MBIOT	Master of Biotechnology
MBiotech	Master of Biotechnology
MBL	Master of Business Law
	Master of Business Leadership
MBLE	Master in Business Logistics Engineering
MBME	Master's in Biomedical Engineering
MBMSE	Master of Business Management and Software Engineering
MBOE	Master of Business Operational Excellence
MBS	Master of Biblical Studies
	Master of Biological Science
	Master of Biomedical Sciences
	Master of Bioscience
	Master of Building Science
	Master of Business and Science
MBST	Master of Biostatistics
MBT	Master of Biomedical Technology
	Master of Biotechnology
	Master of Business Taxation
MBV	Master of Business for Veterans
MC	Master of Communication
	Master of Counseling
	Master of Cybersecurity
MC Ed	Master of Continuing Education
MC Sc	Master of Computer Science
MCA	Master in Collegiate Athletics
	Master of Commercial Aviation
	Master of Criminology (Applied)
MCAM	Master of Computational and Applied Mathematics
MCC	Master of Computer Science
MCD	Master of Communications Disorders
	Master of Community Development
MCE	Master in Electronic Commerce
	Master of Christian Education
	Master of Civil Engineering
	Master of Control Engineering
MCEM	Master of Construction Engineering Management
MCHE	Master of Chemical Engineering
MCIS	Master of Communication and Information Studies
	Master of Computer and Information Science
	Master of Computer Information Systems
MCIT	Master of Computer and Information Technology
MCJ	Master of Criminal Justice
MCL	Master in Communication Leadership
	Master of Canon Law
	Master of Comparative Law
MCM	Master of Christian Ministry
	Master of Church Music
	Master of City Management
	Master of Communication Management
	Master of Community Medicine
	Master of Construction Management
	Master of Contract Management
MCMin	Master of Christian Ministry
MCMP	Master of City and Metropolitan Planning
MCMS	Master of Clinical Medical Science
MCN	Master of Clinical Nutrition
MCOL	Master of Arts in Community and Organizational Leadership
MCP	Master of City Planning
	Master of Community Planning
	Master of Counseling Psychology
	Master of Cytopathology Practice
	Master of Science in Quality Systems and Productivity
MCPC	Master of Arts in Chaplaincy and Pastoral Care
MCPD	Master of Community Planning and Development
MCR	Master in Clinical Research
MCRP	Master of City and Regional Planning
	Master of Community and Regional Planning
MCRS	Master of City and Regional Studies
MCS	Master of Chemical Sciences
	Master of Christian Studies
	Master of Clinical Science
	Master of Combined Sciences
	Master of Communication Studies
	Master of Computer Science
	Master of Consumer Science
MCSE	Master of Computer Science and Engineering
MCSL	Master of Catholic School Leadership
MCSM	Master of Construction Science and Management
MCTM	Master of Clinical Translation Management
MCTP	Master of Communication Technology and Policy
MCTS	Master of Clinical and Translational Science

MCVS	Master of Cardiovascular Science
MD	Doctor of Medicine
MDA	Master of Dietetic Administration
MDB	Master of Design-Build
MDE	Master of Developmental Economics
	Master of Distance Education
	Master of the Education of the Deaf
MDH	Master of Dental Hygiene
MDM	Master of Design Methods
	Master of Digital Media
MDP	Master in Sustainable Development Practice
	Master of Development Practice
MDR	Master of Dispute Resolution
MDS	Master of Dental Surgery
	Master of Design Studies
	Master of Digital Sciences
ME	Master of Education
	Master of Engineering
	Master of Entrepreneurship
ME Sc	Master of Engineering Science
ME-PD	Master of Education–Professional Development
MEA	Master of Educational Administration
	Master of Engineering Administration
MEAE	Master of Entertainment Arts and Engineering
MEAP	Master of Environmental Administration and Planning
MEB	Master of Energy Business
MEBD	Master in Environmental Building Design
MEBT	Master in Electronic Business Technologies
MEC	Master of Electronic Commerce
Mech E	Mechanical Engineer
MED	Master of Education of the Deaf
MEDS	Master of Environmental Design Studies
MEE	Master in Education
	Master of Electrical Engineering
	Master of Energy Engineering
	Master of Environmental Engineering
MEEM	Master of Environmental Engineering and Management
MEENE	Master of Engineering in Environmental Engineering
MEEP	Master of Environmental and Energy Policy
MEERM	Master of Earth and Environmental Resource Management
MEH	Master in Humanistic Studies
	Master of Environmental Health
	Master of Environmental Horticulture
MEHS	Master of Environmental Health and Safety
MEIM	Master of Entertainment Industry Management
	Master of Equine Industry Management
MEL	Master of Educational Leadership
	Master of English Literature
MELP	Master of Environmental Law and Policy
MEM	Master of Engineering Management
	Master of Environmental Management
	Master of Marketing
MEME	Master of Engineering in Manufacturing Engineering
	Master of Engineering in Mechanical Engineering
MENR	Master of Environment and Natural Resources
MENVEGR	Master of Environmental Engineering
MEP	Master of Engineering Physics
MEPC	Master of Environmental Pollution Control
MEPD	Master of Environmental Planning and Design
MER	Master of Employment Relations
MERE	Master of Entrepreneurial Real Estate
MERL	Master of Energy Regulation and Law
MES	Master of Education and Science
	Master of Engineering Science
	Master of Environment and Sustainability
	Master of Environmental Science
	Master of Environmental Studies
	Master of Environmental Systems
	Master of Special Education
MESM	Master of Environmental Science and Management
MET	Master of Educational Technology
	Master of Engineering Technology
	Master of Entertainment Technology
	Master of Environmental Toxicology
METM	Master of Engineering and Technology Management
MEVE	Master of Environmental Engineering
MF	Master of Finance
	Master of Forestry
MFA	Master of Fine Arts
MFALP	Master of Food and Agriculture Law and Policy
MFAM	Master's of Food Animal Medicine
MFAS	Master of Fisheries and Aquatic Science
MFAW	Master of Fine Arts in Writing
MFC	Master of Forest Conservation
MFCS	Master of Family and Consumer Sciences
MFE	Master of Financial Economics
	Master of Financial Engineering
	Master of Forest Engineering
MFES	Master of Fire and Emergency Services
MFG	Master of Functional Genomics
MFHD	Master of Family and Human Development
MFM	Master of Financial Management
	Master of Financial Mathematics
MFPE	Master of Food Process Engineering
MFR	Master of Forest Resources
MFRC	Master of Forest Resources and Conservation
MFRE	Master of Food and Resource Economics
MFS	Master of Food Science
	Master of Forensic Sciences
	Master of Forest Science
	Master of Forest Studies
	Master of French Studies
MFST	Master of Food Safety and Technology
MFT	Master of Family Therapy
	Master of Food Technology
MFWB	Master of Fishery and Wildlife Biology
MFWCB	Master of Fish, Wildlife and Conservation Biology
MFWS	Master of Fisheries and Wildlife Sciences
MFYCS	Master of Family, Youth and Community Sciences
MG	Master of Genetics
MGA	Master of Global Affairs
	Master of Government Administration
	Master of Governmental Administration
MGC	Master of Genetic Counseling
MGD	Master of Graphic Design
MGE	Master of Geotechnical Engineering
MGEM	Master of Global Entrepreneurship and Management
MGIS	Master of Geographic Information Science
	Master of Geographic Information Systems
MGM	Master of Global Management
MGP	Master of Gestion de Projet
MGPS	Master of Global Policy Studies
MGREM	Master of Global Real Estate Management
MGS	Master of Gerontological Studies
	Master of Global Studies
MGsc	Master of Geoscience
MH	Master of Humanities
MH Sc	Master of Health Sciences
MHA	Master of Health Administration
	Master of Healthcare Administration
	Master of Hospital Administration
	Master of Hospitality Administration
MHB	Master of Human Behavior
MHC	Master of Mental Health Counseling
MHCA	Master of Health Care Administration
MHCD	Master of Health Care Design
MHCI	Master of Human-Computer Interaction
MHCL	Master of Health Care Leadership
MHE	Master of Health Education
	Master of Human Ecology
MHE Ed	Master of Home Economics Education
MHEA	Master of Higher Education Administration
MHHS	Master of Health and Human Services
MHI	Master of Health Informatics
	Master of Healthcare Innovation

MHIHIM	Master of Health Informatics and Health Information Management
MHIIM	Master of Health Informatics and Information Management
MHIS	Master of Health Information Systems
MHK	Master of Human Kinetics
MHM	Master of Healthcare Management
MHMS	Master of Health Management Systems
MHP	Master of Health Physics
	Master of Heritage Preservation
	Master of Historic Preservation
MHPA	Master of Heath Policy and Administration
MHPE	Master of Health Professions Education
MHR	Master of Human Resources
MHRD	Master in Human Resource Development
MHRIR	Master of Human Resources and Industrial Relations
MHRLR	Master of Human Resources and Labor Relations
MHRM	Master of Human Resources Management
MHS	Master of Health Science
	Master of Health Sciences
	Master of Health Studies
	Master of Hispanic Studies
	Master of Human Services
	Master of Humanistic Studies
MHSA	Master of Health Services Administration
MHSE	Master of Health Science Education
MHSM	Master of Health Systems Management
MI	Master of Information
	Master of Instruction
MI Arch	Master of Interior Architecture
MIA	Master of Interior Architecture
	Master of International Affairs
MIAA	Master of International Affairs and Administration
MIAM	Master of International Agribusiness Management
MIAPD	Master of Interior Architecture and Product Design
MIB	Master of International Business
MIBA	Master of International Business Administration
MICM	Master of International Construction Management
MID	Master of Industrial Design
	Master of Industrial Distribution
	Master of Interior Design
	Master of International Development
MIDA	Master of International Development Administration
MIDC	Master of Integrated Design and Construction
MIDP	Master of International Development Policy
MIE	Master of Industrial Engineering
MIHTM	Master of International Hospitality and Tourism Management
MIJ	Master of International Journalism
MILR	Master of Industrial and Labor Relations
MIM	Master in Ministry
	Master of Information Management
	Master of International Management
MIMLAE	Master of International Management for Latin American Executives
MIMS	Master of Information Management and Systems
	Master of Integrated Manufacturing Systems
MIP	Master of Infrastructure Planning
	Master of Intellectual Property
	Master of International Policy
MIPA	Master of International Public Affairs
MIPD	Master of Integrated Product Design
MIPM	Master of International Policy Management
MIPP	Master of International Policy and Practice
	Master of International Public Policy
MIPS	Master of International Planning Studies
MIR	Master of Industrial Relations
	Master of International Relations
MIRHR	Master of Industrial Relations and Human Resources
MIS	Master of Imaging Science
	Master of Industrial Statistics
	Master of Information Science
	Master of Information Systems
	Master of Integrated Science
	Master of Interdisciplinary Studies
	Master of International Service
	Master of International Studies
MISE	Master of Industrial and Systems Engineering
MISKM	Master of Information Sciences and Knowledge Management
MISM	Master of Information Systems Management
MISW	Master of Indigenous Social Work
MIT	Master in Teaching
	Master of Industrial Technology
	Master of Information Technology
	Master of Initial Teaching
	Master of International Trade
	Master of Internet Technology
MITA	Master of Information Technology Administration
MITM	Master of Information Technology and Management
MJ	Master of Journalism
	Master of Jurisprudence
MJ Ed	Master of Jewish Education
MJA	Master of Justice Administration
MJM	Master of Justice Management
MJS	Master of Judicial Studies
	Master of Juridical Studies
MK	Master of Kinesiology
MKM	Master of Knowledge Management
ML	Master of Latin
ML Arch	Master of Landscape Architecture
MLA	Master of Landscape Architecture
	Master of Liberal Arts
MLAS	Master of Laboratory Animal Science
	Master of Liberal Arts and Sciences
MLAUD	Master of Landscape Architecture in Urban Development
MLD	Master of Leadership Development
	Master of Leadership Studies
MLE	Master of Applied Linguistics and Exegesis
MLER	Master of Labor and Employment Relations
MLI Sc	Master of Library and Information Science
MLIS	Master of Library and Information Science
	Master of Library and Information Studies
MLM	Master of Leadership in Ministry
MLPD	Master of Land and Property Development
MLRHR	Master of Labor Relations and Human Resources
MLS	Master of Leadership Studies
	Master of Legal Studies
	Master of Liberal Studies
	Master of Library Science
	Master of Life Sciences
MLSCM	Master of Logistics and Supply Chain Management
MLSP	Master of Law and Social Policy
MLT	Master of Language Technologies
MLTCA	Master of Long Term Care Administration
MLW	Master of Studies in Law
MLWS	Master of Land and Water Systems
MM	Master of Management
	Master of Ministry
	Master of Missiology
	Master of Music
MM Ed	Master of Music Education
MM Sc	Master of Medical Science
MM St	Master of Museum Studies
MMA	Master of Marine Affairs
	Master of Media Arts
	Master of Ministry Administration
	Master of Musical Arts
MMAL	Master of Maritime Administration and Logistics
MMAS	Master of Military Art and Science
MMB	Master of Microbial Biotechnology

MMC	Master of Manufacturing Competitiveness
	Master of Mass Communications
	Master of Music Conducting
MMCM	Master of Music in Church Music
MMCSS	Master of Mathematical Computational and Statistical Sciences
MME	Master of Manufacturing Engineering
	Master of Mathematics Education
	Master of Mathematics for Educators
	Master of Mechanical Engineering
	Master of Mining Engineering
	Master of Music Education
MMF	Master of Mathematical Finance
MMFT	Master of Marriage and Family Therapy
MMH	Master of Management in Hospitality
	Master of Medical Humanities
MMI	Master of Management of Innovation
MMIS	Master of Management Information Systems
MML	Master of Managerial Logistics
MMM	Master of Manufacturing Management
	Master of Marine Management
	Master of Medical Management
MMP	Master of Management Practice
	Master of Marine Policy
	Master of Medical Physics
	Master of Music Performance
MMPA	Master of Management and Professional Accounting
MMQM	Master of Manufacturing Quality Management
MMR	Master of Marketing Research
MMRM	Master of Marine Resources Management
MMS	Master of Management Science
	Master of Management Studies
	Master of Manufacturing Systems
	Master of Marine Studies
	Master of Materials Science
	Master of Mathematical Sciences
	Master of Medical Science
	Master of Medieval Studies
MMSE	Master of Manufacturing Systems Engineering
MMSM	Master of Music in Sacred Music
MMT	Master in Marketing
	Master of Music Teaching
	Master of Music Therapy
	Master's in Marketing Technology
MMus	Master of Music
MN	Master of Nursing
	Master of Nutrition
MN NP	Master of Nursing in Nurse Practitioner
MNA	Master of Nonprofit Administration
	Master of Nurse Anesthesia
MNAL	Master of Nonprofit Administration and Leadership
MNAS	Master of Natural and Applied Science
MNCM	Master of Network and Communications Management
MNE	Master of Nuclear Engineering
MNL	Master in International Business for Latin America
MNM	Master of Nonprofit Management
MNO	Master of Nonprofit Organization
MNPL	Master of Not-for-Profit Leadership
MNpS	Master of Nonprofit Studies
MNR	Master of Natural Resources
MNRD	Master of Natural Resources Development
MNRES	Master of Natural Resources and Environmental Studies
MNRM	Master of Natural Resource Management
MNRMG	Master of Natural Resource Management and Geography
MNRS	Master of Natural Resource Stewardship
MNS	Master of Natural Science
MO	Master of Oceanography
MOD	Master of Organizational Development
MOGS	Master of Oil and Gas Studies
MOL	Master of Organizational Leadership
MOM	Master of Organizational Management
	Master of Oriental Medicine
MOR	Master of Operations Research
MOT	Master of Occupational Therapy
MP	Master of Physiology
	Master of Planning
MP Ac	Master of Professional Accountancy
MP Acc	Master of Professional Accountancy
	Master of Professional Accounting
	Master of Public Accounting
MP Aff	Master of Public Affairs
MP Th	Master of Pastoral Theology
MPA	Master of Performing Arts
	Master of Physician Assistant
	Master of Professional Accountancy
	Master of Professional Accounting
	Master of Public Administration
	Master of Public Affairs
MPAC	Master of Professional Accounting
MPAID	Master of Public Administration and International Development
MPAP	Master of Physician Assistant Practice
	Master of Public Administration and Policy
	Master of Public Affairs and Politics
MPAS	Master of Physician Assistant Science
	Master of Physician Assistant Studies
MPC	Master of Professional Communication
	Master of Professional Counseling
MPD	Master of Product Development
	Master of Public Diplomacy
MPDS	Master of Planning and Development Studies
MPE	Master of Physical Education
MPEM	Master of Project Engineering and Management
MPH	Master of Public Health
MPHE	Master of Public Health Education
MPHM	Master in Plant Health Management
MPHS	Master of Population Health Sciences
MPHTM	Master of Public Health and Tropical Medicine
MPI	Master of Product Innovation
MPIA	Master of Public and International Affairs
MPM	Master of Pastoral Ministry
	Master of Pest Management
	Master of Policy Management
	Master of Practical Ministries
	Master of Project Management
	Master of Public Management
MPNA	Master of Public and Nonprofit Administration
MPNL	Master of Philanthropy and Nonprofit Leadership
MPO	Master of Prosthetics and Orthotics
MPOD	Master of Positive Organizational Development
MPP	Master of Public Policy
MPPA	Master of Public Policy Administration
	Master of Public Policy and Administration
MPPAL	Master of Public Policy, Administration and Law
MPPM	Master of Public and Private Management
	Master of Public Policy and Management
MPPPM	Master of Plant Protection and Pest Management
MPRTM	Master of Parks, Recreation, and Tourism Management
MPS	Master of Pastoral Studies
	Master of Perfusion Science
	Master of Planning Studies
	Master of Political Science
	Master of Preservation Studies
	Master of Prevention Science
	Master of Professional Studies
	Master of Public Service
MPSA	Master of Public Service Administration
MPSG	Master of Population and Social Gerontology
MPSIA	Master of Political Science and International Affairs
MPSL	Master of Public Safety Leadership
MPSRE	Master of Professional Studies in Real Estate
MPT	Master of Pastoral Theology
	Master of Physical Therapy
	Master of Practical Theology
MPVM	Master of Preventive Veterinary Medicine

MPW	Master of Professional Writing
	Master of Public Works
MQM	Master of Quality Management
MQS	Master of Quality Systems
MR	Master of Recreation
	Master of Retailing
MRA	Master in Research Administration
MRC	Master of Rehabilitation Counseling
MRCP	Master of Regional and City Planning
	Master of Regional and Community Planning
MRD	Master of Rural Development
MRE	Master of Real Estate
	Master of Religious Education
MRED	Master of Real Estate Development
MREM	Master of Resource and Environmental Management
MRLS	Master of Resources Law Studies
MRM	Master of Resources Management
MRP	Master of Regional Planning
MRRD	Master in Recreation Resource Development
MRS	Master of Religious Studies
MRSc	Master of Rehabilitation Science
MRTP	Master of Rural and Town Planning
MS	Master of Science
MS Cmp E	Master of Science in Computer Engineering
MS Kin	Master of Science in Kinesiology
MS Acct	Master of Science in Accounting
MS Accy	Master of Science in Accountancy
MS Aero E	Master of Science in Aerospace Engineering
MS Ag	Master of Science in Agriculture
MS Arch	Master of Science in Architecture
MS Arch St	Master of Science in Architectural Studies
MS Bio E	Master of Science in Bioengineering
MS Bm E	Master of Science in Biomedical Engineering
MS Ch E	Master of Science in Chemical Engineering
MS Cp E	Master of Science in Computer Engineering
MS Eco	Master of Science in Economics
MS Econ	Master of Science in Economics
MS Ed	Master of Science in Education
MS El	Master of Science in Educational Leadership and Administration
MS En E	Master of Science in Environmental Engineering
MS Eng	Master of Science in Engineering
MS Engr	Master of Science in Engineering
MS Env E	Master of Science in Environmental Engineering
MS Exp Surg	Master of Science in Experimental Surgery
MS Mat E	Master of Science in Materials Engineering
MS Mat SE	Master of Science in Material Science and Engineering
MS Met E	Master of Science in Metallurgical Engineering
MS Mgt	Master of Science in Management
MS Min	Master of Science in Mining
MS Min E	Master of Science in Mining Engineering
MS Mt E	Master of Science in Materials Engineering
MS Otol	Master of Science in Otolaryngology
MS Pet E	Master of Science in Petroleum Engineering
MS Sc	Master of Social Science
MS Sp Ed	Master of Science in Special Education
MS Stat	Master of Science in Statistics
MS Surg	Master of Science in Surgery
MS Tax	Master of Science in Taxation
MS Tc E	Master of Science in Telecommunications Engineering
MS-R	Master of Science (Research)
MSA	Master of School Administration
	Master of Science in Accountancy
	Master of Science in Accounting
	Master of Science in Administration
	Master of Science in Aeronautics
	Master of Science in Agriculture
	Master of Science in Analytics
	Master of Science in Anesthesia
	Master of Science in Architecture
	Master of Science in Aviation
	Master of Sports Administration
	Master of Surgical Assisting
MSAA	Master of Science in Astronautics and Aeronautics
MSAAE	Master of Science in Aeronautical and Astronautical Engineering
MSABE	Master of Science in Agricultural and Biological Engineering
MSAC	Master of Science in Acupuncture
MSACC	Master of Science in Accounting
MSACS	Master of Science in Applied Computer Science
MSAE	Master of Science in Aeronautical Engineering
	Master of Science in Aerospace Engineering
	Master of Science in Applied Economics
	Master of Science in Applied Engineering
	Master of Science in Architectural Engineering
MSAEM	Master of Science in Aerospace Engineering and Mechanics
MSAF	Master of Science in Aviation Finance
MSAG	Master of Science in Applied Geosciences
MSAH	Master of Science in Allied Health
MSAL	Master of Sport Administration and Leadership
MSAM	Master of Science in Applied Mathematics
MSANR	Master of Science in Agriculture and Natural Resources
MSAPM	Master of Security Analysis and Portfolio Management
MSAS	Master of Science in Applied Statistics
	Master of Science in Architectural Studies
MSAT	Master of Science in Accounting and Taxation
	Master of Science in Advanced Technology
	Master of Science in Athletic Training
MSB	Master of Science in Biotechnology
	Master of Sustainable Business
MSBA	Master of Science in Business Administration
	Master of Science in Business Analysis
MSBAE	Master of Science in Biological and Agricultural Engineering
	Master of Science in Biosystems and Agricultural Engineering
MSBC	Master of Science in Building Construction
	Master of Science in Business Communication
MSBCB	Master's in Bioinformatics and Computational Biology
MSBE	Master of Science in Biological Engineering
	Master of Science in Biomedical Engineering
MSBENG	Master of Science in Bioengineering
MSBH	Master of Science in Behavioral Health
MSBIT	Master of Science in Business Information Technology
MSBM	Master of Sport Business Management
MSBME	Master of Science in Biomedical Engineering
MSBMS	Master of Science in Basic Medical Science
MSBS	Master of Science in Biomedical Sciences
MSBTM	Master of Science in Biotechnology and Management
MSC	Master of Science in Commerce
	Master of Science in Communication
	Master of Science in Computers
	Master of Science in Counseling
	Master of Science in Criminology
	Master of Strategic Communication
MSCC	Master of Science in Community Counseling
MSCD	Master of Science in Communication Disorders
	Master of Science in Community Development
MSCE	Master of Science in Civil Engineering
	Master of Science in Clinical Epidemiology
	Master of Science in Computer Engineering
	Master of Science in Continuing Education
MSCEE	Master of Science in Civil and Environmental Engineering
MSCF	Master of Science in Computational Finance
MSCH	Master of Science in Chemical Engineering
MSChE	Master of Science in Chemical Engineering
MSCI	Master of Science in Clinical Investigation
MSCIS	Master of Science in Computer and Information Science
	Master of Science in Computer and Information Systems
	Master of Science in Computer Information Science

	Master of Science in Computer Information Systems
MSCIT	Master of Science in Computer Information Technology
MSCJ	Master of Science in Criminal Justice
MSCJA	Master of Science in Criminal Justice Administration
MSCJS	Master of Science in Crime and Justice Studies
MSCLS	Master of Science in Clinical Laboratory Studies
MSCM	Master of Science in Church Management
	Master of Science in Conflict Management
	Master of Science in Construction Management
	Master of Supply Chain Management
MSCNU	Master of Science in Clinical Nutrition
MSCP	Master of Science in Clinical Psychology
	Master of Science in Community Psychology
	Master of Science in Computer Engineering
	Master of Science in Counseling Psychology
MSCPE	Master of Science in Computer Engineering
MSCPharm	Master of Science in Pharmacy
MSCR	Master of Science in Clinical Research
MSCRP	Master of Science in City and Regional Planning
	Master of Science in Community and Regional Planning
MSCS	Master of Science in Clinical Science
	Master of Science in Computer Science
	Master of Science in Cyber Security
MSCSD	Master of Science in Communication Sciences and Disorders
MSCSE	Master of Science in Computer Science and Engineering
MSCTE	Master of Science in Career and Technical Education
MSD	Master of Science in Dentistry
	Master of Science in Design
	Master of Science in Dietetics
MSE	Master of Science Education
	Master of Science in Economics
	Master of Science in Education
	Master of Science in Engineering
	Master of Science in Engineering Management
	Master of Software Engineering
	Master of Special Education
	Master of Structural Engineering
MSECE	Master of Science in Electrical and Computer Engineering
MSED	Master of Sustainable Economic Development
MSEE	Master of Science in Electrical Engineering
	Master of Science in Environmental Engineering
MSEH	Master of Science in Environmental Health
MSEL	Master of Science in Educational Leadership
MSEM	Master of Science in Engineering Management
	Master of Science in Engineering Mechanics
	Master of Science in Environmental Management
MSENE	Master of Science in Environmental Engineering
MSEO	Master of Science in Electro-Optics
MSEP	Master of Science in Economic Policy
MSES	Master of Science in Embedded Software Engineering
	Master of Science in Engineering Science
	Master of Science in Environmental Science
	Master of Science in Environmental Studies
	Master of Science in Exercise Science
MSET	Master of Science in Educational Technology
	Master of Science in Engineering Technology
MSEV	Master of Science in Environmental Engineering
MSF	Master of Science in Finance
	Master of Science in Forestry
	Master of Spiritual Formation
MSFA	Master of Science in Financial Analysis
MSFCS	Master of Science in Family and Consumer Science
MSFE	Master of Science in Financial Engineering
MSFM	Master of Sustainable Forest Management
MSFOR	Master of Science in Forestry
MSFP	Master of Science in Financial Planning
MSFS	Master of Science in Financial Sciences
	Master of Science in Forensic Science
MSFSB	Master of Science in Financial Services and Banking
MSFT	Master of Science in Family Therapy
MSGC	Master of Science in Genetic Counseling
MSH	Master of Science in Health
	Master of Science in Hospice
MSHA	Master of Science in Health Administration
MSHCA	Master of Science in Health Care Administration
MSHCI	Master of Science in Human Computer Interaction
MSHCPM	Master of Science in Health Care Policy and Management
MSHE	Master of Science in Health Education
MSHES	Master of Science in Human Environmental Sciences
MSHFID	Master of Science in Human Factors in Information Design
MSHFS	Master of Science in Human Factors and Systems
MSHI	Master of Science in Health Informatics
MSHP	Master of Science in Health Professions
	Master of Science in Health Promotion
MSHR	Master of Science in Human Resources
MSHRL	Master of Science in Human Resource Leadership
MSHRM	Master of Science in Human Resource Management
MSHROD	Master of Science in Human Resources and Organizational Development
MSHS	Master of Science in Health Science
	Master of Science in Health Services
	Master of Science in Homeland Security
MSI	Master of Science in Information
	Master of Science in Instruction
	Master of System Integration
MSIA	Master of Science in Industrial Administration
	Master of Science in Information Assurance
MSIB	Master of Science in International Business
MSIDM	Master of Science in Interior Design and Merchandising
MSIE	Master of Science in Industrial Engineering
	Master of Science in International Economics
MSIEM	Master of Science in Information Engineering and Management
MSIID	Master of Science in Information and Instructional Design
MSIM	Master of Science in Information Management
	Master of Science in International Management
MSIMC	Master of Science in Integrated Marketing Communications
MSIR	Master of Science in Industrial Relations
MSIS	Master of Science in Information Science
	Master of Science in Information Studies
	Master of Science in Information Systems
	Master of Science in Interdisciplinary Studies
MSISE	Master of Science in Infrastructure Systems Engineering
MSISM	Master of Science in Information Systems Management
MSISPM	Master of Science in Information Security Policy and Management
MSIST	Master of Science in Information Systems Technology
MSIT	Master of Science in Industrial Technology
	Master of Science in Information Technology
	Master of Science in Instructional Technology
MSITM	Master of Science in Information Technology Management
MSJ	Master of Science in Journalism
	Master of Science in Jurisprudence
MSJC	Master of Social Justice and Criminology
MSJE	Master of Science in Jewish Education
MSJFP	Master of Science in Juvenile Forensic Psychology
MSJJ	Master of Science in Juvenile Justice

MSJPS	Master of Science in Justice and Public Safety
MSJS	Master of Science in Jewish Studies
MSL	Master of School Leadership
	Master of Science in Leadership
	Master of Science in Limnology
	Master of Strategic Leadership
	Master of Studies in Law
MSLA	Master of Science in Legal Administration
MSLFS	Master of Science in Life Sciences
MSLP	Master of Speech-Language Pathology
MSLS	Master of Science in Library Science
MSLSCM	Master of Science in Logistics and Supply Chain Management
MSLT	Master of Second Language Teaching
MSM	Master of Sacred Ministry
	Master of Sacred Music
	Master of School Mathematics
	Master of Science in Management
	Master of Science in Medicine
	Master of Science in Organization Management
	Master of Security Management
MSMA	Master of Science in Marketing Analysis
MSMAE	Master of Science in Materials Engineering
MSMC	Master of Science in Mass Communications
MSME	Master of Science in Mathematics Education
	Master of Science in Mechanical Engineering
MSMFT	Master of Science in Marriage and Family Therapy
MSMHC	Master of Science in Mental Health Counseling
MSMIS	Master of Science in Management Information Systems
MSMIT	Master of Science in Management and Information Technology
MSMLS	Master of Science in Medical Laboratory Science
MSMOT	Master of Science in Management of Technology
MSMP	Master of Science in Medical Physics
MSMS	Master of Science in Management Science
	Master of Science in Marine Science
	Master of Science in Medical Sciences
MSMSE	Master of Science in Manufacturing Systems Engineering
	Master of Science in Material Science and Engineering
	Master of Science in Mathematics and Science Education
MSMT	Master of Science in Management and Technology
MSMus	Master of Sacred Music
MSN	Master of Science in Nursing
MSNA	Master of Science in Nurse Anesthesia
MSNE	Master of Science in Nuclear Engineering
MSNED	Master of Science in Nurse Education
MSNM	Master of Science in Nonprofit Management
MSNS	Master of Science in Natural Science
	Master of Science in Nutritional Science
MSOD	Master of Science in Organization Development
	Master of Science in Organizational Development
MSOEE	Master of Science in Outdoor and Environmental Education
MSOES	Master of Science in Occupational Ergonomics and Safety
MSOH	Master of Science in Occupational Health
MSOL	Master of Science in Organizational Leadership
MSOM	Master of Science in Operations Management
	Master of Science in Oriental Medicine
MSOR	Master of Science in Operations Research
MSOT	Master of Science in Occupational Technology
	Master of Science in Occupational Therapy
MSP	Master of Science in Pharmacy
	Master of Science in Planning
	Master of Speech Pathology
MSPA	Master of Science in Physician Assistant
	Master of Science in Professional Accountancy
MSPAS	Master of Science in Physician Assistant Studies
MSPC	Master of Science in Professional Communications
MSPE	Master of Science in Petroleum Engineering
MSPH	Master of Science in Public Health
MSPHR	Master of Science in Pharmacy
MSPM	Master of Science in Professional Management
	Master of Science in Project Management
MSPNGE	Master of Science in Petroleum and Natural Gas Engineering
MSPO	Master of Science in Prosthetics and Orthotics
MSPPM	Master of Science in Public Policy and Management
MSPS	Master of Science in Pharmaceutical Science
	Master of Science in Political Science
	Master of Science in Psychological Services
MSPT	Master of Science in Physical Therapy
MSpVM	Master of Specialized Veterinary Medicine
MSR	Master of Science in Radiology
	Master of Science in Reading
MSRA	Master of Science in Recreation Administration
MSRE	Master of Science in Real Estate
	Master of Science in Religious Education
MSRED	Master of Science in Real Estate Development
	Master of Sustainable Real Estate Development
MSRLS	Master of Science in Recreation and Leisure Studies
MSRM	Master of Science in Risk Management
MSRMP	Master of Science in Radiological Medical Physics
MSRS	Master of Science in Radiological Sciences
	Master of Science in Rehabilitation Science
MSS	Master of Security Studies
	Master of Social Science
	Master of Social Services
	Master of Software Systems
	Master of Sports Science
	Master of Strategic Studies
	Master's in Statistical Science
MSSA	Master of Science in Social Administration
MSSCM	Master of Science in Supply Chain Management
MSSD	Master of Arts in Software Driven Systems Design
	Master of Science in Sustainable Design
MSSE	Master of Science in Software Engineering
	Master of Science in Special Education
MSSEM	Master of Science in Systems and Engineering Management
MSSI	Master of Science in Security Informatics
	Master of Science in Strategic Intelligence
MSSL	Master of Science in School Leadership
	Master of Science in Strategic Leadership
MSSLP	Master of Science in Speech-Language Pathology
MSSM	Master of Science in Sports Medicine
MSSP	Master of Science in Social Policy
MSSPA	Master of Science in Student Personnel Administration
MSSS	Master of Science in Safety Science
	Master of Science in Systems Science
MSST	Master of Science in Security Technologies
MSSW	Master of Science in Social Work
MSSWE	Master of Science in Software Engineering
MST	Master of Science and Technology
	Master of Science in Taxation
	Master of Science in Teaching
	Master of Science in Technology
	Master of Science in Telecommunications
	Master of Science Teaching
MSTC	Master of Science in Technical Communication
	Master of Science in Telecommunications
MSTCM	Master of Science in Traditional Chinese Medicine
MSTE	Master of Science in Telecommunications Engineering
	Master of Science in Transportation Engineering
MSTL	Master of Science in Teacher Leadership
MSTM	Master of Science in Technology Management
	Master of Science in Transfusion Medicine

MSTOM	Master of Science in Traditional Oriental Medicine
MSUASE	Master of Science in Unmanned and Autonomous Systems Engineering
MSUD	Master of Science in Urban Design
MSUS	Master of Science in Urban Studies
MSW	Master of Social Work
MSWE	Master of Software Engineering
MSWREE	Master of Science in Water Resources and Environmental Engineering
MT	Master of Taxation
	Master of Teaching
	Master of Technology
	Master of Textiles
MTA	Master of Tax Accounting
	Master of Teaching Arts
	Master of Tourism Administration
MTCM	Master of Traditional Chinese Medicine
MTD	Master of Training and Development
MTE	Master in Educational Technology
MTESOL	Master in Teaching English to Speakers of Other Languages
MTHM	Master of Tourism and Hospitality Management
MTI	Master of Information Technology
MTID	Master of Tangible Interaction Design
MTL	Master of Talmudic Law
MTM	Master of Technology Management
	Master of Telecommunications Management
	Master of the Teaching of Mathematics
MTMH	Master of Tropical Medicine and Hygiene
MTMS	Master in Teaching Mathematics and Science
MTOM	Master of Traditional Oriental Medicine
MTPC	Master of Technical and Professional Communication
MTR	Master of Translational Research
MTS	Master of Theatre Studies
	Master of Theological Studies
MTWM	Master of Trust and Wealth Management
MTX	Master of Taxation
MUA	Master of Urban Affairs
MUCD	Master of Urban and Community Design
MUD	Master of Urban Design
MUDS	Master of Urban Design Studies
MUEP	Master of Urban and Environmental Planning
MUP	Master of Urban Planning
MUPDD	Master of Urban Planning, Design, and Development
MUPP	Master of Urban Planning and Policy
MUPRED	Master of Urban Planning and Real Estate Development
MURP	Master of Urban and Regional Planning
	Master of Urban and Rural Planning
MUS	Master of Urban Studies
MUSA	Master of Urban Spatial Analytics
MVP	Master of Voice Pedagogy
MVPH	Master of Veterinary Public Health
MVS	Master of Visual Studies
MWC	Master of Wildlife Conservation
MWM	Master of Water Management
MWPS	Master of Wood and Paper Science
MWR	Master of Water Resources
MWS	Master of Women's Studies
	Master of Worship Studies
MWSc	Master of Wildlife Science
MZS	Master of Zoological Science
Nav Arch	Naval Architecture
Naval E	Naval Engineer
ND	Doctor of Naturopathic Medicine
NE	Nuclear Engineer
Nuc E	Nuclear Engineer
OD	Doctor of Optometry
OTD	Doctor of Occupational Therapy
PBME	Professional Master of Biomedical Engineering
PC	Performer's Certificate
PD	Professional Diploma
PGC	Post-Graduate Certificate
PGD	Postgraduate Diploma
Ph L	Licentiate of Philosophy
Pharm D	Doctor of Pharmacy
PhD	Doctor of Philosophy
PhD Otol	Doctor of Philosophy in Otolaryngology
PhD Surg	Doctor of Philosophy in Surgery
PhDEE	Doctor of Philosophy in Electrical Engineering
PMBA	Professional Master of Business Administration
PMC	Post Master Certificate
PMD	Post-Master's Diploma
PMS	Professional Master of Science
	Professional Master's
Post-Doctoral MS	Post-Doctoral Master of Science
Post-MSN Certificate	Post-Master of Science in Nursing Certificate
PPDPT	Postprofessional Doctor of Physical Therapy
Pro-MS	Professional Science Master's
Professional MA	Professional Master of Arts
Professional MBA	Professional Master of Business Administration
Professional MS	Professional Master of Science
PSM	Professional Master of Science
	Professional Science Master's
Psy D	Doctor of Psychology
Psy M	Master of Psychology
Psy S	Specialist in Psychology
Psya D	Doctor of Psychoanalysis
S Psy S	Specialist in Psychological Services
Sc D	Doctor of Science
Sc M	Master of Science
SCCT	Specialist in Community College Teaching
ScDPT	Doctor of Physical Therapy Science
SD	Doctor of Science
	Specialist Degree
SJD	Doctor of Juridical Sciences
SLPD	Doctor of Speech-Language Pathology
SM	Master of Science
SM Arch S	Master of Science in Architectural Studies
SMACT	Master of Science in Art, Culture and Technology
SMBT	Master of Science in Building Technology
SP	Specialist Degree
Sp Ed	Specialist in Education
Sp LIS	Specialist in Library and Information Science
SPA	Specialist in Arts
Spec	Specialist's Certificate
Spec M	Specialist in Music
Spt	Specialist Degree
SSP	Specialist in School Psychology
STB	Bachelor of Sacred Theology
STD	Doctor of Sacred Theology
STL	Licentiate of Sacred Theology
STM	Master of Sacred Theology
TDPT	Transitional Doctor of Physical Therapy
Th D	Doctor of Theology
Th M	Master of Theology
TOTD	Transitional Doctor of Occupational Therapy
VMD	Doctor of Veterinary Medicine
WEMBA	Weekend Executive Master of Business Administration
XMA	Executive Master of Arts

INDEXES

Profiles, Displays, and Close-Ups

Page numbers appear in regular type for an institution's profile, in *italics* for a display ad, and in **bold** for a two-page Close-Up description.

Directories and Subject Areas

Following is an alphabetical listing of directories and subject areas. Also listed are cross-references for subject area names not used in the directory structure of the guides, for example, "City and Regional Planning (*see* Urban and Regional Planning)."

Graduate Programs in the Humanities, Arts & Social Sciences

Addictions/Substance Abuse Counseling
Administration (*see* Arts Administration; Public Administration)
African-American Studies
African Languages and Literatures (*see* African Studies)
African Studies
Agribusiness (*see* Agricultural Economics and Agribusiness)
Agricultural Economics and Agribusiness
Alcohol Abuse Counseling (*see* Addictions/Substance Abuse Counseling)
American Indian/Native American Studies
American Studies
Anthropology
Applied Arts and Design—General
Applied Behavior Analysis
Applied Economics
Applied History (*see* Public History)
Applied Psychology
Applied Social Research
Arabic (*see* Near and Middle Eastern Languages)
Arab Studies (*see* Near and Middle Eastern Studies)
Archaeology
Architectural History
Architecture
Archives Administration (*see* Public History)
Area and Cultural Studies (*see* African-American Studies; African Studies; American Indian/Native American Studies; American Studies; Asian-American Studies; Asian Studies; Canadian Studies; Cultural Studies; East European and Russian Studies; Ethnic Studies; Folklore; Gender Studies; Hispanic Studies; Holocaust Studies; Jewish Studies; Latin American Studies; Near and Middle Eastern Studies; Northern Studies; Pacific Area/Pacific Rim Studies; Western European Studies; Women's Studies)
Art/Fine Arts
Art History
Arts Administration
Arts Journalism
Art Therapy
Asian-American Studies
Asian Languages
Asian Studies
Behavioral Sciences (*see* Psychology)
Bible Studies (*see* Religion; Theology)
Biological Anthropology
Black Studies (*see* African-American Studies)
Broadcasting (*see* Communication; Film, Television, and Video Production)
Broadcast Journalism
Building Science
Canadian Studies
Celtic Languages
Ceramics (*see* Art/Fine Arts)
Child and Family Studies
Child Development
Chinese
Chinese Studies (*see* Asian Languages; Asian Studies)
Christian Studies (*see* Missions and Missiology; Religion; Theology)
Cinema (*see* Film, Television, and Video Production)
City and Regional Planning (*see* Urban and Regional Planning)
Classical Languages and Literatures (*see* Classics)
Classics
Clinical Psychology
Clothing and Textiles
Cognitive Psychology (*see* Psychology—General; Cognitive Sciences)
Cognitive Sciences
Communication—General
Community Affairs (*see* Urban and Regional Planning; Urban Studies)
Community Planning (*see* Architecture; Environmental Design; Urban and Regional Planning; Urban Design; Urban Studies)
Community Psychology (*see* Social Psychology)
Comparative and Interdisciplinary Arts
Comparative Literature
Composition (*see* Music)
Computer Art and Design
Conflict Resolution and Mediation/Peace Studies
Consumer Economics
Corporate and Organizational Communication
Corrections (*see* Criminal Justice and Criminology)
Counseling (*see* Counseling Psychology; Pastoral Ministry and Counseling)
Counseling Psychology
Crafts (*see* Art/Fine Arts)
Creative Arts Therapies (*see* Art Therapy; Therapies—Dance, Drama, and Music)
Criminal Justice and Criminology
Cultural Anthropology
Cultural Studies
Dance
Decorative Arts
Demography and Population Studies
Design (*see* Applied Arts and Design; Architecture; Art/Fine Arts; Environmental Design; Graphic Design; Industrial Design; Interior Design; Textile Design; Urban Design)
Developmental Psychology
Diplomacy (*see* International Affairs)
Disability Studies
Drama Therapy (*see* Therapies—Dance, Drama, and Music)
Dramatic Arts (*see* Theater)
Drawing (*see* Art/Fine Arts)
Drug Abuse Counseling (*see* Addictions/Substance Abuse Counseling)
Drug and Alcohol Abuse Counseling (*see* Addictions/Substance Abuse Counseling)
East Asian Studies (*see* Asian Studies)
East European and Russian Studies
Economic Development
Economics
Educational Theater (*see* Theater; Therapies—Dance, Drama, and Music)
Emergency Management
English
Environmental Design
Ethics
Ethnic Studies
Ethnomusicology (*see* Music)
Experimental Psychology
Family and Consumer Sciences—General
Family Studies (*see* Child and Family Studies)
Family Therapy (*see* Child and Family Studies; Clinical Psychology; Counseling Psychology; Marriage and Family Therapy)
Filmmaking (*see* Film, Television, and Video Production)
Film Studies (*see* Film, Television, and Video Production)
Film, Television, and Video Production
Film, Television, and Video Theory and Criticism
Fine Arts (*see* Art/Fine Arts)
Folklore

Technical Communication
Technical Writing
Telecommunications (*see* Film, Television, and Video Production)
Television (*see* Film, Television, and Video Production)
Textile Design
Textiles (*see* Clothing and Textiles; Textile Design)
Thanatology
Theater
Theater Arts (*see* Theater)
Theology
Therapies—Dance, Drama, and Music
Translation and Interpretation
Transpersonal and Humanistic Psychology
Urban and Regional Planning
Urban Design
Urban Planning (*see* Architecture; Urban and Regional Planning; Urban Design; Urban Studies)
Urban Studies
Video (*see* Film, Television, and Video Production)
Visual Arts (*see* Applied Arts and Design; Art/Fine Arts; Film, Television, and Video Production; Graphic Design; Illustration; Photography)
Western European Studies
Women's Studies
World Wide Web (*see* Internet and Interactive Multimedia)
Writing

Graduate Programs in the Biological/ Biomedical Sciences & Health-Related Medical Professions

Acupuncture and Oriental Medicine
Acute Care/Critical Care Nursing Administration (*see* Health Services Management and Hospital Administration; Nursing and Healthcare Administration; Pharmaceutical Administration)
Adult Nursing
Advanced Practice Nursing (*see* Family Nurse Practitioner Studies)
Allied Health—General
Allied Health Professions (*see* Clinical Laboratory Sciences/Medical Technology; Clinical Research; Communication Disorders; Dental Hygiene; Emergency Medical Services; Occupational Therapy; Physical Therapy; Physician Assistant Studies; Rehabilitation Sciences)
Allopathic Medicine
Anatomy
Anesthesiologist Assistant Studies
Animal Behavior
Bacteriology
Behavioral Sciences (*see* Biopsychology; Neuroscience; Zoology)
Biochemistry
Bioethics
Biological and Biomedical Sciences—General Biological Chemistry (*see* Biochemistry)
Biological Oceanography (*see* Marine Biology)
Biophysics
Biopsychology
Botany
Breeding (*see* Botany; Plant Biology; Genetics)
Cancer Biology/Oncology
Cardiovascular Sciences
Cell Biology
Cellular Physiology (*see* Cell Biology; Physiology)
Child-Care Nursing (*see* Maternal and Child/Neonatal Nursing)
Chiropractic
Clinical Laboratory Sciences/Medical Technology
Clinical Research
Community Health
Community Health Nursing
Computational Biology
Conservation (*see* Conservation Biology; Environmental Biology)
Conservation Biology
Crop Sciences (*see* Botany; Plant Biology)
Cytology (*see* Cell Biology)
Dental and Oral Surgery (*see* Oral and Dental Sciences)
Dental Assistant Studies (*see* Dental Hygiene)
Dental Hygiene
Dental Services (*see* Dental Hygiene)
Dentistry
Developmental Biology Dietetics (*see* Nutrition)
Ecology
Embryology (*see* Developmental Biology)
Emergency Medical Services
Endocrinology (*see* Physiology)
Entomology
Environmental Biology
Environmental and Occupational Health
Epidemiology
Evolutionary Biology
Family Nurse Practitioner Studies
Foods (*see* Nutrition)
Forensic Nursing
Genetics
Genomic Sciences
Gerontological Nursing
Health Physics/Radiological Health
Health Promotion
Health-Related Professions (*see* individual allied health professions)
Health Services Management and Hospital Administration
Health Services Research
Histology (*see* Anatomy; Cell Biology)
HIV/AIDS Nursing
Hospice Nursing
Hospital Administration (*see* Health Services Management and Hospital Administration)
Human Genetics
Immunology
Industrial Hygiene
Infectious Diseases
International Health
Laboratory Medicine (*see* Clinical Laboratory Sciences/Medical Technology; Immunology; Microbiology; Pathology)
Life Sciences (*see* Biological and Biomedical Sciences)
Marine Biology
Maternal and Child Health
Maternal and Child/Neonatal Nursing
Medical Imaging
Medical Microbiology
Medical Nursing (*see* Medical/Surgical Nursing)
Medical Physics
Medical/Surgical Nursing
Medical Technology (*see* Clinical Laboratory Sciences/Medical Technology)
Medical Sciences (*see* Biological and Biomedical Sciences)
Medical Science Training Programs (*see* Biological and Biomedical Sciences)
Medicinal and Pharmaceutical Chemistry
Medicinal Chemistry (*see* Medicinal and Pharmaceutical Chemistry)
Medicine (*see* Allopathic Medicine; Naturopathic Medicine; Osteopathic Medicine; Podiatric Medicine)
Microbiology
Midwifery (*see* Nurse Midwifery)
Molecular Biology
Molecular Biophysics
Molecular Genetics
Molecular Medicine
Molecular Pathogenesis
Molecular Pathology
Molecular Pharmacology
Molecular Physiology
Molecular Toxicology
Naturopathic Medicine
Neural Sciences (*see* Biopsychology; Neurobiology; Neuroscience)
Neurobiology

Graduate Programs in the Physical Sciences, Mathematics, Agricultural Sciences, the Environment & Natural Resources

Hydrology
Inorganic Chemistry
Limnology
Marine Affairs
Marine Geology
Marine Sciences
Marine Studies (*see* Marine Affairs; Marine Geology; Marine Sciences; Oceanography)
Mathematical and Computational Finance
Mathematical Physics
Mathematical Statistics (*see* Applied Statistics; Statistics)
Mathematics
Meteorology
Mineralogy
Natural Resource Management (*see* Environmental Management and Policy; Natural Resources)
Natural Resources
Nuclear Physics (*see* Physics)
Ocean Engineering (*see* Marine Affairs; Marine Geology; Marine Sciences; Oceanography)
Oceanography
Optical Sciences
Optical Technologies (*see* Optical Sciences)
Optics (*see* Applied Physics; Optical Sciences; Physics)
Organic Chemistry
Paleontology
Paper Chemistry (*see* Chemistry)
Photonics
Physical Chemistry
Physics
Planetary and Space Sciences
Plant Sciences
Plasma Physics
Poultry Science (*see* Animal Sciences)
Radiological Physics (*see* Physics)
Range Management (*see* Range Science)
Range Science
Resource Management (*see* Environmental Management and Policy; Natural Resources)
Solid-Earth Sciences (*see* Geosciences)
Space Sciences (*see* Planetary and Space Sciences)
Statistics
Theoretical Chemistry
Theoretical Physics
Viticulture and Enology
Water Resources

Graduate Programs in Engineering & Applied Sciences

Aeronautical Engineering (*see* Aerospace/Aeronautical Engineering)
Aerospace/Aeronautical Engineering
Aerospace Studies (*see* Aerospace/Aeronautical Engineering)
Agricultural Engineering
Applied Mechanics (*see* Mechanics)
Applied Science and Technology
Architectural Engineering
Artificial Intelligence/Robotics
Astronautical Engineering (*see* Aerospace/Aeronautical Engineering)
Automotive Engineering
Aviation
Biochemical Engineering
Bioengineering
Bioinformatics
Biological Engineering (*see* Bioengineering)
Biomedical Engineering
Biosystems Engineering
Biotechnology
Ceramic Engineering (*see* Ceramic Sciences and Engineering)
Ceramic Sciences and Engineering
Ceramics (*see* Ceramic Sciences and Engineering)
Chemical Engineering
Civil Engineering
Computer and Information Systems Security
Computer Engineering
Computer Science
Computing Technology (*see* Computer Science)
Construction Engineering
Construction Management
Database Systems
Electrical Engineering
Electronic Materials
Electronics Engineering (*see* Electrical Engineering)
Energy and Power Engineering
Energy Management and Policy
Engineering and Applied Sciences
Engineering and Public Affairs (*see* Technology and Public Policy)
Engineering and Public Policy (*see* Energy Management and Policy; Technology and Public Policy)
Engineering Design
Engineering Management
Engineering Mechanics (*see* Mechanics)
Engineering Metallurgy (*see* Metallurgical Engineering and Metallurgy)
Engineering Physics
Environmental Design (*see* Environmental Engineering)
Environmental Engineering
Ergonomics and Human Factors
Financial Engineering
Fire Protection Engineering
Food Engineering (*see* Agricultural Engineering)
Game Design and Development
Gas Engineering (*see* Petroleum Engineering)
Geological Engineering
Geophysics Engineering (*see* Geological Engineering)
Geotechnical Engineering
Hazardous Materials Management
Health Informatics
Health Systems (*see* Safety Engineering; Systems Engineering)
Highway Engineering (*see* Transportation and Highway Engineering)
Human-Computer Interaction
Human Factors (*see* Ergonomics and Human Factors)
Hydraulics
Hydrology (*see* Water Resources Engineering)
Industrial Engineering (*see* Industrial/Management Engineering)
Industrial/Management Engineering
Information Science
Internet Engineering
Macromolecular Science (*see* Polymer Science and Engineering)
Management Engineering (*see* Engineering Management; Industrial/Management Engineering)
Management of Technology
Manufacturing Engineering
Marine Engineering (*see* Civil Engineering)
Materials Engineering
Materials Sciences
Mechanical Engineering
Mechanics
Medical Informatics
Metallurgical Engineering and Metallurgy
Metallurgy (*see* Metallurgical Engineering and Metallurgy)
Mineral/Mining Engineering
Modeling and Simulation
Nanotechnology
Nuclear Engineering
Ocean Engineering
Operations Research
Paper and Pulp Engineering
Petroleum Engineering
Pharmaceutical Engineering
Plastics Engineering (*see* Polymer Science and Engineering)
Polymer Science and Engineering
Public Policy (*see* Energy Management and Policy; Technology and Public Policy)
Reliability Engineering

Robotics (*see* Artificial Intelligence/Robotics)
Safety Engineering
Software Engineering
Solid-State Sciences (*see* Materials Sciences)
Structural Engineering
Surveying Science and Engineering
Systems Analysis (*see* Systems Engineering)
Systems Engineering
Systems Science
Technology and Public Policy
Telecommunications
Telecommunications Management
Textile Sciences and Engineering
Textiles (*see* Textile Sciences and Engineering)
Transportation and Highway Engineering
Urban Systems Engineering (*see* Systems Engineering)
Waste Management (*see* Hazardous Materials Management)
Water Resources Engineering

Graduate Programs in Business, Education, Information Studies, Law & Social Work

Accounting
Actuarial Science
Adult Education
Advertising and Public Relations
Agricultural Education
Alcohol Abuse Counseling (*see* Counselor Education)
Archival Management and Studies
Art Education
Athletics Administration (*see* Kinesiology and Movement Studies)
Athletic Training and Sports Medicine
Audiology (*see* Communication Disorders)
Aviation Management
Banking (*see* Finance and Banking)
Business Administration and Management—General
Business Education
Communication Disorders
Community College Education
Computer Education
Continuing Education (*see* Adult Education)
Counseling (*see* Counselor Education)
Counselor Education
Curriculum and Instruction
Developmental Education
Distance Education Development
Drug Abuse Counseling (*see* Counselor Education)
Early Childhood Education
Educational Leadership and Administration
Educational Measurement and Evaluation
Educational Media/Instructional Technology
Educational Policy
Educational Psychology
ducation—General
ucation of the Blind (*see* Special Education)
ucation of the Deaf (*see* Special Education)
cation of the Gifted
cation of the Hearing Impaired (*see* Special Education)
cation of the Learning Disabled (*see* Special Education)
cation of the Mentally Retarded (*see* Special Education)
cation of the Physically Handicapped (*see* Special Education)
ation of Students with Severe/Multiple Disabilities
ation of the Visually Handicapped (*see* Special Education)
onic Commerce
ntary Education
as a Second Language
Education
ment Management
neurship

Environmental Education
Environmental Law
Exercise and Sports Science
Exercise Physiology (*see* Kinesiology and Movement Studies)
Facilities and Entertainment Management
Finance and Banking
Food Services Management (*see* Hospitality Management)
Foreign Languages Education
Foundations and Philosophy of Education
Guidance and Counseling (*see* Counselor Education)
Health Education
Health Law
Hearing Sciences (*see* Communication Disorders)
Higher Education
Home Economics Education
Hospitality Management
Hotel Management (*see* Travel and Tourism)
Human Resources Development
Human Resources Management
Human Services
Industrial Administration (*see* Industrial and Manufacturing Management)
Industrial and Manufacturing Management
Industrial Education (*see* Vocational and Technical Education)
Information Studies
Instructional Technology (*see* Educational Media/Instructional Technology)
Insurance
Intellectual Property Law
International and Comparative Education
International Business
International Commerce (*see* International Business)
International Economics (*see* International Business)
International Trade (*see* International Business)
Investment and Securities (*see* Business Administration and Management; Finance and Banking; Investment Management)
Investment Management
Junior College Education (*see* Community College Education)
Kinesiology and Movement Studies
Law
Legal and Justice Studies
Leisure Services (*see* Recreation and Park Management)
Leisure Studies
Library Science
Logistics
Management (*see* Business Administration and Management)
Management Information Systems
Management Strategy and Policy
Marketing
Marketing Research
Mathematics Education
Middle School Education
Movement Studies (*see* Kinesiology and Movement Studies)
Multilingual and Multicultural Education
Museum Education
Music Education
Nonprofit Management
Nursery School Education (*see* Early Childhood Education)
Occupational Education (*see* Vocational and Technical Education)
Organizational Behavior
Organizational Management
Parks Administration (*see* Recreation and Park Management)
Personnel (*see* Human Resources Development; Human Resources Management; Organizational Behavior; Organizational Management; Student Affairs)
Philosophy of Education (*see* Foundations and Philosophy of Education)
Physical Education
Project Management
Public Relations (*see* Advertising and Public Relations)
Quality Management
Quantitative Analysis
Reading Education

Real Estate
Recreation and Park Management
Recreation Therapy (*see* Recreation and Park Management)
Religious Education
Remedial Education (*see* Special Education)
Restaurant Administration (*see* Hospitality Management)
Science Education
Secondary Education
Social Sciences Education
Social Studies Education (*see* Social Sciences Education)
Social Work
Special Education
Speech-Language Pathology and Audiology (*see* Communication Disorders)
Sports Management
Sports Medicine (*see* Athletic Training and Sports Medicine)
Sports Psychology and Sociology (*see* Kinesiology and Movement Studies)
Student Affairs
Substance Abuse Counseling (*see* Counselor Education)
Supply Chain Management
Sustainability Management
Systems Management (*see* Management Information Systems)
Taxation
Teacher Education (*see* specific subject areas)
Teaching English as a Second Language (*see* English as a Second Language)
Technical Education (*see* Vocational and Technical Education)
Transportation Management
Travel and Tourism
Urban Education
Vocational and Technical Education
Vocational Counseling (*see* Counselor Education)